CHILTON'S
TRUCK, VAN & SUV
SERVICE MANUAL
2001

C.E.O.
Rick Van Dalen

President
Dean F. Morgantini, S.A.E.

Vice President—Sales
Glenn D. Potere

Vice President—Finance
Barry L. Beck

Vice President—Electronic Product Sales
Charles J. McGroarty

Executive Editor
Kevin M. G. Maher, A.S.E.

Manager—Professional Service Information
Richard J. Rivele

Manager—Consumer Service Information
Richard Schwartz, A.S.E.

Manager—Marine/Recreation
James R. Marotta, A.S.E.

Project Managers
Thomas A. Mellon, A.S.E., S.A.E., Eric Michael Mihalyi, A.S.E., S.T.S, S.A.E.,
Christine Sheeky, S.A.E., Richard T. Smith, Ron Webb

Editors—Professional Service Information
Tim Crain, A.S.E., Michael Magliano, Richard E. Rathman

Editorial Staff
David R. Back, A.S.E., Paul DeSanto, A.S.E., Jim Keating, Robert McAnally,
Norman D. Norville, A.S.E., Joe Pellicciotti, Keith Reynolds

Production Specialists
Brian Hollingsworth, Melinda Possinger

Schematics Editors
Christopher G. Ritchie, A.S.E., S.A.E., S.T.S., Stephanie Spunt

CHILTON *AUTOMOTIVE INFORMATION*

PUBLISHED BY **W. G. NICHOLS, INC.**

Manufactured in USA, © 2000 W. G. Nichols, Inc., 1025 Andrew Drive, West Chester, PA 19380
ISBN 0-8019-9308-3
Library of Congress Catalog Card No. 00-132202
0123456789 9876543210

Table of Contents

Table of Contents

Model Index

HOW TO USE THIS MANUAL

Specifications

Specifications charts for all models covered in this book are located in Chapter 1. They include: Vehicle and Engine Identification, General Engine Specifications, Engine Tune-Up Specifications, Capacities, Valve Specifications, Crankshaft & Connecting Rod Specifications, Piston & Ring Specifications, Engine Fastener Torque Specifications, Brake Specifications, Maintenance Interval Specifications, Ball Joint Specifications and Wheel & Tire Specifications.

Unit Repair Sections

The Unit Repair Sections (URS's) are written to cover all applicable 1997-01 models for the specific URS system or component, unless specifically noted otherwise. The procedures covered in the URS's are not repeated in the model specific sections; therefore, refer to the URS's for the service procedures for the applicable systems or components. Refer to the Table of Contents for URS coverage.

Model Specific Sections

The model specific sections are grouped by manufacturer and arranged in alphabetical order. The text and illustrations that comprise the service procedures in each model specific section are arranged in the following order of systems and components: Engine Repair (Gasoline, then Diesel if applicable), Fuel System (Gasoline, then Diesel if applicable), Drive Train, Steering and Suspension.

All illustrations are located as close as possible to the applicable procedure. Procedures are for all models in the particular section unless specifically noted otherwise.

Locating Information

The Table of Contents, located at the front of the book, lists each Unit Repair Section (URS) and model specific section in this manual.

To find where a particular model specific section is located in the book, you need only look in the Table of Contents. Once you have found the proper section, you may wish to find where specific procedures located in that section. Turn to the Index at the front of the model specific section. At the upper left-hand side is a listing of the main topics within that section and the page number on which they may be found. Following the main topics is an alphabetical listing of all of the procedures within the section and their page numbers.

The Model Index, located just after the Table of Contents in the beginning of this manual, may also be used to locate the specific section for any vehicle model covered in this manual.

Safety Notice

Proper service and repair procedures are vital to the safe, reliable operation of all motor vehicles, as well as the personal safety of those performing the repairs. This manual outlines procedures for servicing and repairing vehicles using safe effective methods. The procedures contain many NOTES, WARNINGS and CAUTIONS which should be followed along with standard safety procedures to eliminate the possibility of personal injury or improper service which could damage the vehicle or compromise its safety.

It is important to note that repair procedures and techniques, tools and parts for servicing vehicles, as well as the skill and experience of the individual performing the work vary widely. It is not possible to anticipate all of the conceivable ways or conditions under which vehicles may be serviced, or to provide cautions as to all of the possible hazards that may result. Standard and accepted safety precautions and equipment should be used when handling toxic or flammable fluids, and safety goggles or other protection should be used during cutting, grinding, chiseling, prying, or any other process that can cause material removal or projectiles.

Some procedures require the use of tools specially designed for a specific purpose. Before substituting another tool or procedure, you must be completely satisfied that neither your personal safety, nor the performance of the vehicle will be endangered.

Although information in this manual is based on industry sources and is as complete as possible at the time of publication, the possibility exists that some vehicle manufacturers made later changes which could not be included here. Information on very late models may not be available in some circumstances. While striving for total accuracy, Nichols Publishing cannot assume responsibility for any errors, changes, or omissions that may occur in the compilation of this data.

Part Numbers

Part numbers listed in this book are not recommendations by Nichols Publishing for any product by brand name. They are references that can be used with interchanges manuals and aftermarket supplier catalogs to locate each brand supplier's discrete part number.

Special Tools

Special tools are recommended by the vehicle manufacturer to perform their specific job. Use has been kept to a minimum, but where absolutely necessary, they are referred to in the text by the part number of the tool manufacturer. These tools may be purchased, under the appropriate part number, from your local dealer or regional distributor, or an equivalent tool can be purchased locally from a tool supplier or parts outlet. Before substituting any tool for the one recommended, read the previous Safety Notice.

Acknowledgements

This publication contains material that is reproduced and distributed under a license from Ford Motor Company. No further reproduction or distribution of the Ford Motor Company material is allowed without the expressed written permission from Ford Motor Company.

Portions of the material contained herein have been reprinted with permission of General Motors Corporation, Service Technology Group.

Nichols Publishing would like to express thanks to all of the fine companies who participate in the production of our books:
- Hand tools supplied by Craftsman are used during all phases of our vehicle teardown and photography.
- Many of the fine specialty tools used in our procedures were provided courtesy of Lisle Corporation.
- Lincoln Automotive Products (1 Lincoln Way, St. Louis, MO 63120) has provided their industrial shop equipment, including jacks (engine, transmission and floor), engine stands, fluid and lubrication tools, as well as shop presses.
- Rotary Lifts (1-800-640-5438 or www.Rotary-Lift.com), the largest automobile lift manufacturer in the world, offering the biggest variety of surface and in-ground lifts available, has fulfilled our shop's lift needs.
- Much of our shop's electronic testing equipment was supplied by Universal Enterprises Inc. (UEI).
- Safety-Kleen Systems Inc. has provided parts cleaning stations and assistance with environmentally sound disposal of residual wastes.
- United Gilsonite Laboratories (UGL), manufacturer of Drylok® concrete floor paint, has provided materials and expertise for the coating and protection of our shop floor.

SPECIFICATIONS

1

ACURA
SLX

ENGINE AND VEHICLE IDENTIFICATION

			Engine					Model Year	
Code	Liters (cc)	Cu. In.	Cyl.	Fuel Sys.	Engine Type	Eng. Mfg.		Code ①	Year
V	3.2 (3165)	193	6	SMFI	SOHC	Isuzu		V	1997
X	3.5 (3494)	213	6	SMFI	DOHC	Isuzu		W	1998
								X	1999
								Y	2000
								1	2001

SMFI: Sequential Multi-port Fuel Injection

DOHC :Double Overhead Camshaft

SOHC: Single Overhead Camshaft

① 10th position of VIN

93081C01

GENERAL ENGINE SPECIFICATIONS

Year	Model	Engine Displacement Liters (cc)	Engine Series (ID/VIN)	Fuel System	Net Horsepower @ rpm	Net Torque @ rpm (ft. lbs.)	Bore x Stroke (in.)	Compression Ratio	Oil Pressure @ rpm
1997	SLX	3.2 (3165)	6VD1/V	SMFI	190@5600	188@4000	3.68x3.03	9.1:1	57-80@3000
1998	SLX	3.5 (3494)	6VE1/X	SMFI	215@5400	230@3000	3.68x3.35	9.1:1	60-80@3000
1999	SLX	3.5 (3494)	6VE1/X	SMFI	215@5400	230@3000	3.68x3.35	9.1:1	60-80@3000
2000-01	SLX	3.5 (3494)	6VE1/X	SMFI	215@5400	230@3000	3.68x3.35	9.1:1	60-80@3000

SMFI: Sequential Multi-port Fuel Injection

93081C02

ENGINE TUNE-UP SPECIFICATIONS

Year	Engine Displacement Liters (cc)	Engine ID/VIN	Spark Plug Gap (in.)	Ignition Timing (deg.) ① MT	Ignition Timing (deg.) ① AT	Fuel Pump (psi)	Idle Speed (rpm) ① MT	Idle Speed (rpm) ① AT	Valve Clearance ② In.	Valve Clearance ② Ex.
1997	3.2 (3165)	6VD1/V	0.040-0.043	—	5B	41-46	—	750	HYD	HYD
1998	3.5 (3494)	6VE1/X	0.040-0.043	—	20B	48-55	—	750	0.009-0.013	0.010-0.014
1999	3.5 (3494)	6VE1/X	0.040-0.043	—	20B	48-55	—	750	0.009-0.013	0.010-0.014
2000-01	3.5 (3494)	6VE1/X	0.040-0.043	—	20B	48-55	—	750	0.009-0.013	0.010-0.014

NOTE: The Vehicle Emission Control Information label reflects production specification changes and must be used if different from this chart.

B: Before top dead center

HYD: Hydraulic

93081C03

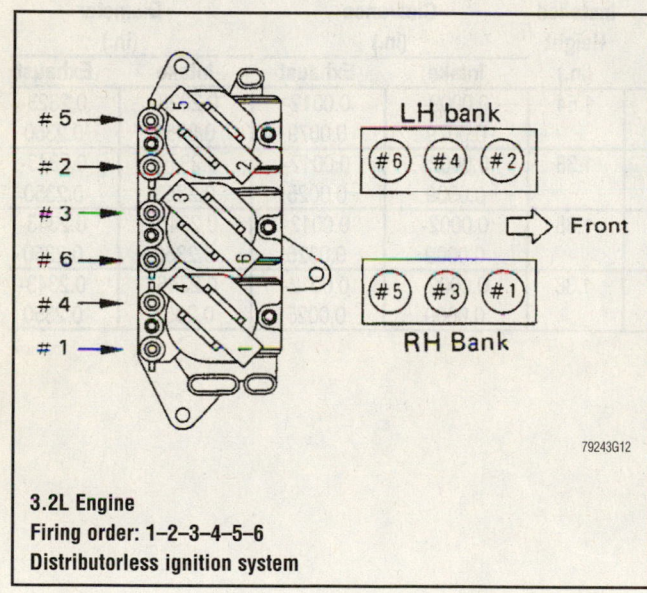

3.2L Engine
Firing order: 1–2–3–4–5–6
Distributorless ignition system

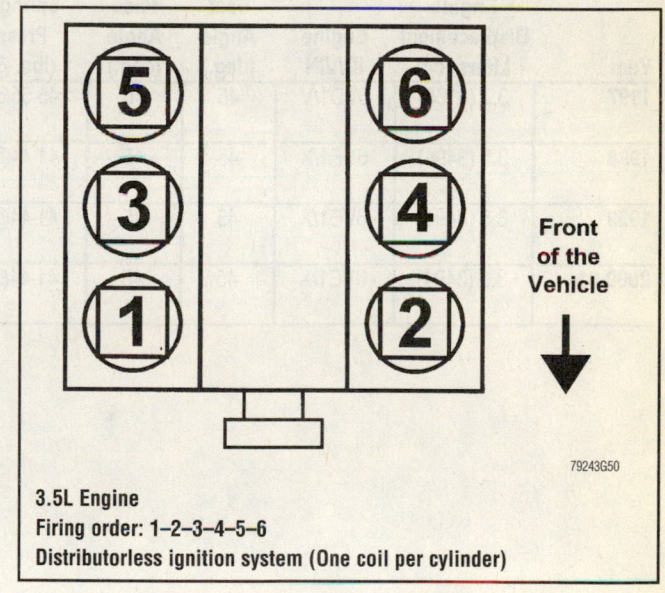

3.5L Engine
Firing order: 1–2–3–4–5–6
Distributorless ignition system (One coil per cylinder)

CAPACITIES

Year	Model	Engine Displacement Liters (cc)	Engine ID/VIN	Engine Oil with Filter (qts.)	Trans-mission (pts.)	Transfer Case (pts.)	Drive Axle Front (pts.)	Drive Axle Rear (pts.)	Fuel Tank (gal.)	Cooling System (qts.)
1997	SLX	3.2 (3165)	6VD1/V	5.7	18.2	3.0	3.2	3.8	22.5	9.0
1998	SLX	3.5 (3494)	6VE1/X	5.0	18.2	3.0 ①	3.0	6.4	22.5	7.4
1999	SLX	3.5 (3494)	6VE1/X	5.0	18.2	3.0 ①	3.0	6.4	22.5	7.4
2000-01	SLX	3.5 (3494)	6VE1/X	5.0	18.2	3.0 ①	3.0	6.4	22.5	7.4

NOTE: All capacities are approximate. Add fluid gradually and check to ensure a proper level has been reached.

① 4.0 pts. if equipped with Torque On Demand (TOD)

93081C04

VALVE SPECIFICATIONS

Year	Engine Displacement Liters (cc)	Engine ID/VIN	Seat Angle (deg.)	Face Angle (deg.)	Spring Test Pressure (lbs. @ in.)	Spring Installed Height (in.)	Stem-to-Guide Clearance (in.) Intake	Stem-to-Guide Clearance (in.) Exhaust	Stem Diameter (in.) Intake	Stem Diameter (in.) Exhaust
1997	3.2 (3165)	6VD1/V	45	45	45-55@1.54	1.54	0.0009-0.0079	0.0012-0.0079	0.2323-0.2353	0.2323-0.2350
1998	3.5 (3494)	6VE1/X	45	45	41-44@1.38	1.38	0.0002-0.0009	0.0012-0.0025	0.2346-0.2353	0.2343-0.2350
1999	3.5 (3494)	6VE1/X	45	45	41-44@1.38	1.38	0.0002-0.0009	0.0012-0.0025	0.2346-0.2353	0.2343-0.2350
2000-01	3.5 (3494)	6VE1/X	45	45	41-44@1.38	1.38	0.0002-0.0009	0.0012-0.0025	0.2346-0.2353	0.2343-0.2350

93081C05

CRANKSHAFT AND CONNECTING ROD SPECIFICATIONS

All measurements are given in inches.

Year	Engine Displacement Liters (cc)	Engine ID/VIN	Crankshaft				Connecting Rod		
			Main Brg. Journal Dia.	Main Brg. Oil Clearance	Shaft End-play	Thrust on No.	Journal Diameter	Oil Clearance	Side Clearance
1997	3.2 (3165)	6VD1/V	2.5165-2.5170	0.0007-0.0017	0.0024-0.0094	3	2.1229-2.1235	0.0010-0.0023	0.0063-0.0138
1998	3.5 (3494)	6VE1/X	2.5165-2.5170	0.0007-0.0017	0.0024-0.0094	3	2.1229-2.1235	0.0010-0.0023	0.0050-0.0150
1999	3.5 (3494)	6VE1/X	2.5165-2.5170	0.0007-0.0017	0.0024-0.0094	3	2.1229-2.1235	0.0010-0.0023	0.0050-0.0150
2000-01	3.5 (3494)	6VE1/X	2.5165-2.5170	0.0007-0.0017	0.0024-0.0094	3	2.1229-2.1235	0.0010-0.0023	0.0050-0.0150

93081C06

PISTON AND RING SPECIFICATIONS

All measurements are given in inches.

Year	Engine Displacement Liters (cc)	Engine ID/VIN	Piston Clearance	Ring Gap			Ring Side Clearance		
				Top Compression	Bottom Compression	Oil Control	Top Compression	Bottom Compression	Oil Control
1997	3.2 (3165)	6VD1/V	0.0009-0.0022	0.0138-0.0185	0.0177-0.0236	0.0059-0.0177	0.0006-0.0015	0.0006-0.0015	NA
1998	3.5 (3494)	6VE1/X	0.0012-0.0020	0.0118-0.0157	0.0177-0.0236	0.0059-0.0177	0.0006-0.0015	0.0006-0.0015	NA
1999	3.5 (3494)	6VE1/X	0.0012-0.0020	0.0118-0.0157	0.0177-0.0236	0.0059-0.0177	0.0006-0.0015	0.0006-0.0015	NA
2000-01	3.5 (3494)	6VE1/X	0.0012-0.0020	0.0118-0.0157	0.0177-0.0236	0.0059-0.0177	0.0006-0.0015	0.0006-0.0015	NA

NA: Not Available

93081C07

Timing chain and gear service is covered in the model specific sections of this manual

TORQUE SPECIFICATIONS
All readings in ft. lbs.

Year	Engine Displacement Liters (cc)	Engine ID/VIN	Cylinder Head Bolts	Main Bearing Bolts	Rod Bearing Bolts	Crankshaft Damper Bolts	Flywheel Bolts	Manifold		Spark Plugs	Lug Nuts
								Intake	Exhaust		
1997	3.2 (3165)	6VD1/V	①	②	40	123	40	17	42	13	87
1998	3.5 (3494)	6VE1/X	③	②	40	123	40	18	38	13	87
1999	3.5 (3494)	6VE1/X	③	②	40	123	40	18	38	13	87
2000-01	3.5 (3494)	6VE1/X	③	②	40	123	40	18	38	13	87

① 8 x 1.25 bolts: 15 ft. lbs.
   11 x 1.5 bolts: 47 ft. lbs.

② Main bearing cap bolts: 29 ft. lbs.
   Oil gallery bolts: 21 ft. lbs. plus 55-65 degree turn
   Buttress bolts: 29 ft. lbs.

③ Step 1: 21 ft. lbs.
   Step 2: 47 ft. lbs.

93081C08

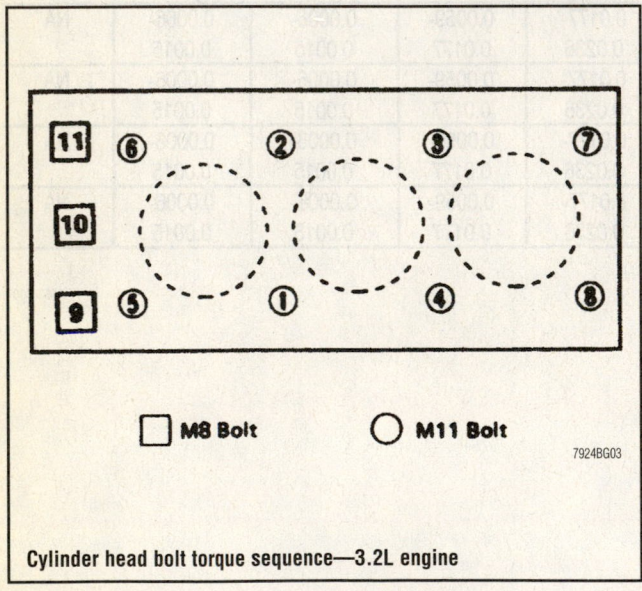

M8 Bolt   **M11 Bolt**

7924BG03

Cylinder head bolt torque sequence—3.2L engine

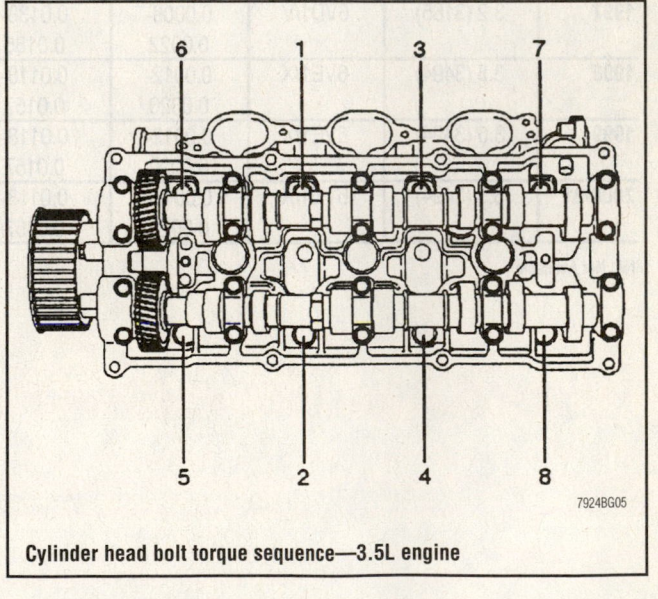

7924BG05

Cylinder head bolt torque sequence—3.5L engine

BRAKE SPECIFICATIONS
All measurements in inches unless noted

Year	Model		Brake Disc				Brake Drum Diameter			Minimum Lining Thickness		Brake Caliper	
			Original Thickness	Machine Thickness	Discard Thickness	Maximum Runout	Original Inside Diameter	Max. Wear Limit	Maximum Machine Diameter	Front	Rear	Bracket Bolts (ft. lbs.)	Mounting Bolts (ft. lbs.)
1997	SLX	F	1.024	0.983	0.969	0.005	—	—	—	0.039	—	115	54
		R	0.710	0.668	0.654	0.005	8.27	8.32	8.32	—	0.039	76	32
1998	SLX	F	1.020	0.983	0.969	0.005	—	—	—	0.039	—	115	54
		R	0.710	0.668	0.654	0.005	8.27	8.32	8.32	—	0.039	76	32
1999	SLX	F	1.020	0.983	0.969	0.005	—	—	—	0.039	—	115	54
		R	0.710	0.668	0.654	0.005	8.27	8.32	8.32	—	0.039	76	32
2000-01	SLX	F	1.020	0.983	0.969	0.005	—	—	—	0.039	—	115	54
		R	0.710	0.668	0.654	0.005	8.27	8.32	8.32	—	0.039	76	32

NA: Not Available

① Specification is for discard.
 Minimum machine thickness: 0.983 in.

② Specification is for discard.
 Minimum machine thickness: 0.668 in.

93081C09

Ignition system service is covered in the model specific sections of this manual

SCHEDULED MAINTENANCE INTERVALS
(ACURA SLX)

TO BE SERVICED	TYPE OF SERVICE	VEHICLE MILEAGE INTERVAL (x1000)															
		7.5	15	22.5	30	37.5	45	52.5	60	67.5	75	82.5	90	97.5	105	112.5	120
Accelerator linkage ①	L	✓	✓	✓	✓	✓	✓	✓	✓	✓	✓	✓	✓	✓	✓	✓	✓
Accessory drive belts ②	S/I				✓				✓				✓				✓
Air cleaner filter	R				✓				✓				✓				✓
Auto cruise control linkage & hose ③	S/I		✓		✓		✓		✓		✓		✓		✓		✓
Automatic transmission fluid level ③	S/I	✓		✓		✓		✓		✓		✓		✓		✓	
Battery fluid level ③	S/I	✓	✓	✓	✓	✓	✓	✓	✓	✓	✓	✓	✓	✓	✓	✓	✓
Body and chassis ①	L	✓	✓	✓	✓	✓	✓	✓	✓	✓	✓	✓	✓	✓	✓	✓	✓
Brake fluid level ③	S/I	✓	✓	✓	✓	✓	✓	✓	✓	✓	✓	✓	✓	✓	✓	✓	✓
Brake lines & hoses ③	S/I	✓	✓	✓	✓	✓	✓	✓	✓	✓	✓	✓	✓	✓	✓	✓	✓
Brake pedal play ③	S/I		✓		✓		✓		✓		✓		✓		✓		✓
Clutch fluid level ③	S/I	✓	✓	✓	✓	✓	✓	✓	✓	✓	✓	✓	✓	✓	✓	✓	✓
Clutch lines & hose ③	S/I				✓				✓				✓				✓
Clutch pedal free-play ③	S/I		✓		✓		✓		✓		✓		✓		✓		✓
Clutch pedal spring, bushing and clevis pin ①	S/I		✓		✓		✓		✓		✓		✓		✓		✓
Cooling and heating system hoses ③	S/I		✓		✓		✓		✓		✓		✓		✓		✓
Driveshaft flange torque ③	S/I	✓		✓		✓		✓		✓		✓		✓		✓	
Drum and disc brakes ③	S/I		✓		✓		✓		✓		✓		✓		✓		✓
Engine coolant	R				✓				✓				✓				✓
Engine coolant level ③	S/I	✓	✓	✓	✓	✓	✓	✓	✓	✓	✓	✓	✓	✓	✓	✓	✓
Engine oil & filter ③	R	✓	✓	✓	✓	✓	✓	✓	✓	✓	✓	✓	✓	✓	✓	✓	✓
Exhaust system ③	S/I	✓	✓	✓	✓	✓	✓	✓	✓	✓	✓	✓	✓	✓	✓	✓	✓
Front and rear axle lubricant	R		✓		✓				✓				✓				✓
Front and rear driveshafts ①	S/I	✓	✓	✓	✓	✓	✓	✓	✓	✓	✓	✓	✓	✓	✓	✓	✓
Front wheel bearings	S/I & L				✓				✓				✓				✓
Fuel lines & tank cap ③	S/I								✓								✓
Inspect for fluid leaks ③	S/I	✓	✓	✓	✓	✓	✓	✓	✓	✓	✓	✓	✓	✓	✓	✓	✓
Key lock cylinder ③	L		✓		✓		✓		✓		✓		✓		✓		✓
Manual transmission and transfer case fluid	R		✓		✓				✓				✓				✓
Parking brake system ③	S/I		✓		✓		✓		✓		✓		✓		✓		✓

93081C10

SCHEDULED MAINTENANCE INTERVALS
(ACURA SLX) (Cont.)

TO BE SERVICED	TYPE OF SERVICE	VEHICLE MILEAGE INTERVAL (x1000)															
		7.5	15	22.5	30	37.5	45	52.5	60	67.5	75	82.5	90	97.5	105	112.5	120
Power steering fluid	R				✓				✓				✓				✓
Radiator core and A/C condenser	S/I & C								✓								✓
Rotate tires	S/I	✓	✓	✓	✓	✓	✓	✓	✓	✓	✓	✓	✓	✓	✓	✓	✓
Shift-on-the-fly system gear fluid ③	S/I		✓		✓		✓		✓		✓		✓		✓		✓
Spark plugs	R	Every 100,000 miles.															
Starter safety switch ③	S/I	✓	✓	✓	✓	✓	✓	✓	✓	✓	✓	✓	✓	✓	✓	✓	✓
Steering operation ③	S/I	✓	✓	✓	✓	✓	✓	✓	✓	✓	✓	✓	✓	✓	✓	✓	✓
Suspension & steering ③	S/I	✓	✓	✓	✓	✓	✓	✓	✓	✓	✓	✓	✓	✓	✓	✓	✓
Throttle linkage ③	S/I		✓		✓		✓		✓		✓		✓		✓		✓
Timing belt	R										✓						
Tires and wheels ③	S/I	✓	✓	✓	✓	✓	✓	✓	✓	✓	✓	✓	✓	✓	✓	✓	✓
Valve clearance	A									✓							✓

R: Replace   S/I: Service or Inspect   L: Lubricate   A: Adjust   C: Clean

① Perform this at the mileage indicated or every 6 months, whichever occurs first.

② Perform this at the mileage indicated or every 24 months, whichever occurs first.

③ Perform this at the mileage indicated or every 12 months, whichever occurs first.

FREQUENT OPERATION MAINTENANCE (SEVERE SERVICE)

If a vehicle is operated under any of the following conditions it is considered severe service:

- Towing a trailer or using a camper or car-top carrier.

- Repeated short trips of less than 5 miles in temperatures below freezing, or trips of less than 10 miles in any temperature.

- Extensive idling or low-speed driving for long distances as in heavy commercial use, such as delivery, taxi or police cars.

- Operating on rough, muddy or salt-covered roads.

- Operating on unpaved or dusty roads.

- Frequent operation in temperatures above 90°F.

Air cleaner element: replace every 15,000 miles

Engine oil and filter: replace every 3000 miles or 3 months, whichever occurs first.

Automatic transmission fluid: replace every 20,000 miles.

Rear axle lubricant: replace every 15,000 miles.

93081C11

SCHEDULED MAINTENANCE INTERVALS
ACURA
SLX

The following should be used as a guide when determining the amount of work required for a particular service.
In estimating how long a particular Scheduled Maintenance Service should take, please observe the following:

● Labor Time is time based on field research and data supplied by the vehicle manufacturer.
● Labor time operations are given in hours and tenths of an hour.
● All labor operations are to be used as a guide.

Mechanic Skill Level Codes:
(A) PRECISION: Highly skilled with multiple certification.
(B) GENERAL: Normally skilled with certification.
(C) MAINTENANCE: Semi-skilled working on certification.

	LABOR TIME
7500 Mile Service (C)	
1997	2.1
1998-01	2.7
15000 Mile Service (B)	
1997	4.1
1998-01	4.4
22500 Mile Service (C)	
1997	2.1
1998-01	2.7
30000 Mile Service (B)	
1997	7.9
1998-01	8.4
37500 Mile Service (C)	
1997	2.1
1998-01	2.7
45000 Mile Service (B)	
1997	3.3

	LABOR TIME
1998-01	3.8
52500 Mile Service (C)	
1997	2.1
1998-01	2.7
60000 Mile Service (B)	
1997	12.7
1998-01	11.0
67500 Mile Service (C)	
1997	2.1
1998-01	2.7
75000 Mile Service (B)	
1997	3.2
1998-01	7.2
82500 Mile Service (C)	
1997	2.1
1998-01	2.7

	LABOR TIME
90000 Mile Service (B)	
1997	7.9
1998-01	8.4
97500 Mile Service (C)	
1997	2.1
1998-01	2.7
100000 Mile Service (C)	
1998-01	
Replace spark plugs	.9
105000 Mile Service (C)	
1998-01	3.8
112500 Mile Service (C)	
1998-01	2.7
120000 Mile Service (B)	
1998-01	11.0

93081C12

TIRE, WHEEL AND BALL JOINT SPECIFICATIONS
Acura Truck

Year	Model	OEM Tires		Tire Pressures (psi)		Wheel Size	Ball Joint Inspection
		Standard	Optional	Front	Rear		
1997	SLX	245/70R16	None	29	29	7-JJ	U: 4-28 ① L: 4-55
1998	SLX	245/70R16	None	29	29	7-JJ	U: 4-28 ① L: 4-55
1999	SLX	245/70R16	None	29	29	7-JJ	U: 4-28 ① L: 4-55

OEM: Original Equipment Manufacturer

PSI: Pounds Per Square Inch

STD: Standard

OPT: Optional

L: Lower

U: Upper

① Torque required in inch lbs. to rotate ball joint when removed from the knuckle

93081C13

Refer to the model specific sections for engine mechanical service procedures

BMW
X5

ENGINE AND VEHICLE IDENTIFICATION

		Engine							Model Year	
Code ①	Liters (cc)	Cu. In.	Cyl.	Fuel Sys.	Engine Type	Eng. Mfg.		Code ②		Year
M54	3.0 (2979)	182	6	SMPI	DOHC	BMW		1		2001
M62	4.4 (4398)	268	8	SMPI	DOHC	BMW				

DOHC: Double Overhead Camshaft

① 8th position of VIN

② 10th position of VIN

93081C14

GENERAL ENGINE SPECIFICATIONS

Year	Model	Engine Displacement Liters (cc)	Engine Series (ID/VIN)	Fuel System	Net Horsepower @ rpm	Net Torque @ rpm (ft. lbs.)	Bore x Stroke (in.)	Com- pression Ratio	Oil Pressure @ rpm
2001	X5	3.0 (2979)	M54	SMPI	225@5900	214@3500	3.31x3.53	10.2:1	7.4@700
	X5	4.4 (4398)	M62	SMPI	282@6400	324@3600	3.62x3.26	10.0:1	7.4@580

SMPI: Sequential Multi-port Fuel Injection

93081C15

CAPACITIES

Year	Model	Engine Displacement Liters (cc)	Engine ID/VIN	Engine Oil with Filter (qts.)	Automatic Transaxle (qts.)	Manual Transaxle (qts.)	Rear Drive Axle (pts.)	Fuel Tank (gal.)	Cooling System (qts.)
2001	X5	3.0 (2979)	M54	7.0	7.0	3.2	3.4	24.6	11.1
	X5	4.4 (4398)	M62	7.9	11.7	—	3.4	24.6	13.3

NOTE: All capacities are approximate. Add fluid gradually and check to be sure a proper fluid level is obtained.

93081C17

ENGINE TUNE-UP SPECIFICATIONS

Year	Engine Displacement Liters (cc)	Engine ID/VIN	Spark Plug Gap (in.)	Ignition Timing (deg.)	Fuel Pump (psi)	Idle Speed (rpm)	Valve Clearance In.	Ex.
2001	3.0 (2979)	M54	0.024-0.028	①	48-54	②	HYD	HYD
	4.4 (4398)	M62	0.024-0.028	①	48-54	②	HYD	HYD

NOTE: The Vehicle Emission Control Information label often reflects specification changes made during production. The label figures must be used if they differ from those in this chart.

HYD: Hydraulic

① Ignition timing is regulated by the Electronic Control Module (ECM), and cannot be adjusted.

② Idle speed is controled by the Electronic Control Module (ECM), and cannot be adjusted.

93081C16

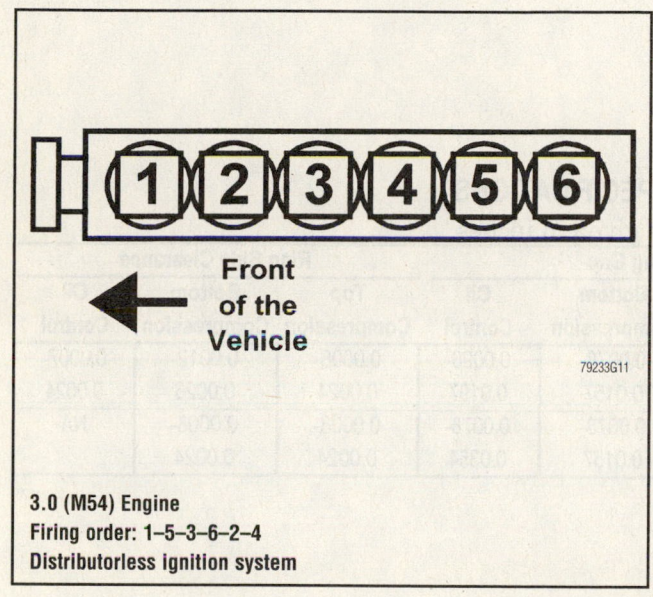

Front of the Vehicle

79233G11

3.0 (M54) Engine
Firing order: 1–5–3–6–2–4
Distributorless ignition system

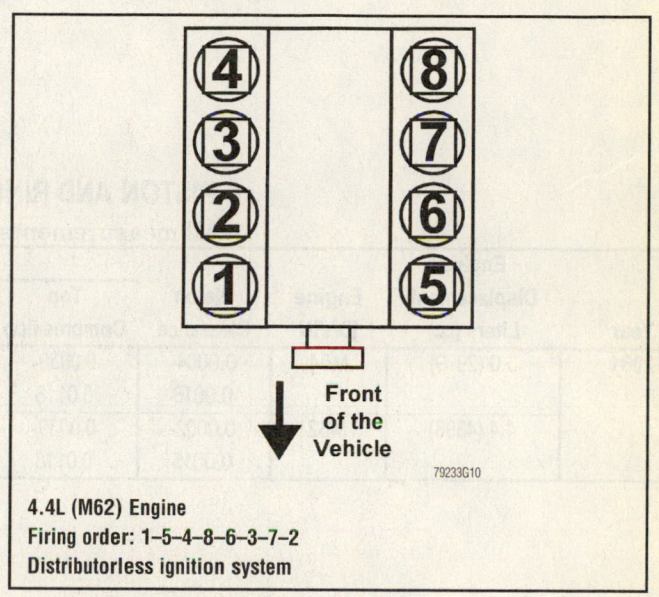

Front of the Vehicle

79233G10

4.4L (M62) Engine
Firing order: 1–5–4–8–6–3–7–2
Distributorless ignition system

VALVE SPECIFICATIONS

Year	Engine Displacement Liters (cc)	Engine ID/VIN	Seat Angle (deg.)	Face Angle (deg.)	Spring Test Pressure (lbs. @ in.)	Spring Installed Height (in.)	Stem-to-Guide Clearance (in.) Intake	Exhaust	Stem Diameter (in.) Intake	Exhaust
2001	3.0 (2979)	M54	45	45	NA	NA	0.0197	0.0197	0.2372-0.2340	0.2378 0.2384
	4.4 (4398)	M62	45	45	NA	NA	0.0018-	0.0197	0.2156-0.2159	0.2146 0.2150

NA: Not Available

93081C18

Refer to the model specific sections for fuel system service procedures

CRANKSHAFT AND CONNECTING ROD SPECIFICATIONS

All measurements are given in inches.

Year	Engine Displacement Liters (cc)	Engine ID/VIN	Crankshaft				Connecting Rod		
			Main Brg. Journal Dia.	Main Brg. Oil Clearance	Shaft End-play	Thrust on No.	Journal Diameter	Oil Clearance	Side Clearance
2001	3.0 (2979)	M54	①	0.0007-0.0029	0.0031-7 0.0064	5	1.7720-1.7706	0.0007-0.0022	0.0060-0.0160
	4.4 (4398)	M62	①	0.0007-0.0018	0.0033-0.0101	3	1.8901-1.8887	0.0007-0.0022	0.0060-0.0196

① Standard yellow: 2.3615-2.3618 inches

  Standard green: 2.3613-2.3615 inches

  Standard white: 2.3611-2.3613 inches

93081C19

PISTON AND RING SPECIFICATIONS

All measurements are given in inches.

Year	Engine Displacement Liters (cc)	Engine ID/VIN	Piston Clearance	Ring Gap			Ring Side Clearance		
				Top Compression	Bottom Compression	Oil Control	Top Compression	Bottom Compression	Oil Control
2001	3.0 (2979)	M54	0.0004-0.0016	0.0039-0.0118	0.0078-0.0157	0.0098-0.0197	0.0008-0.0024	0.0012-0.0026	0.0007-0.0024
	4.4 (4398)	M62	0.0002-0.0015	0.0039-0.0118	0.0078-0.0157	0.0078-0.0354	0.0008-0.0024	0.0008-0.0024	NA

93081C20

BRAKE SPECIFICATIONS

All measurements in inches unless noted

Year	Model		Brake Disc			Brake Drum Diameter			Min. Lining Thickness	Caliper Guide Pin Bolts (ft. lbs.)
			Original Thickness	Minimum Thickness	Maximum Run-out	Original Inside Diameter	Max. Wear Limit	Maximum Machine Diameter		
2001	M54	F	0.803	①	0.005	—	—	—	0.118	25
		R	②	①	0.005	8.63-8.65	NA	NA	①	25
	M62	F	1.118	①	0.007	—	—	—	118.000	25
		R	0.409	①	0.007	8.63-8.65	NA	NA	①	25

NA: Not Available

F: Front

R: Rear

① Minimum thickness is stamped in the brake disc shell

② Solid brake rotor: 0.409 inches

93081C22

TORQUE SPECIFICATIONS
All readings in ft. lbs.

Year	Engine Displacement Liters (cc)	Engine ID/VIN	Cylinder Head Bolts	Main Bearing Bolts	Rod Bearing Bolts	Crankshaft Damper Bolts	Flywheel Bolts	Manifold		Spark Plugs	Lug Nuts
								Intake	Exhaust		
2001	3.0 (2979)	M54	15	8	15	100	88	17	15	15	95
	4.4 (4398)	M62	22	8	15	100	NA	17	15	15	95

93081C21

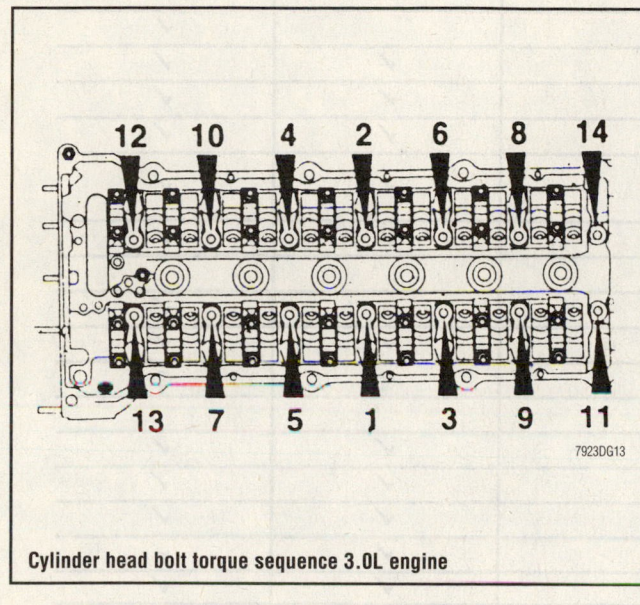

Cylinder head bolt torque sequence 3.0L engine

7923DG13

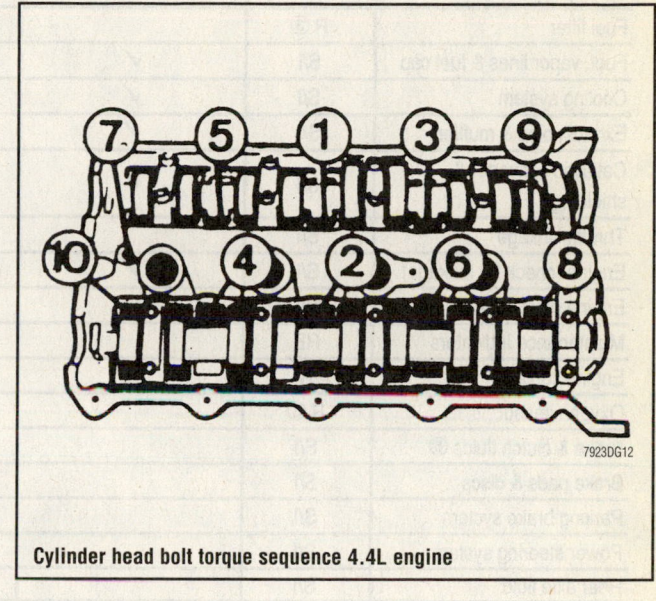

Cylinder head bolt torque sequence 4.4L engine

7923DG12

Refer to the model specific sections for engine electrical system service procedures

SCHEDULED MAINTENANCE INTERVALS
(BMW X5 Series)

TO BE SERVICED	TYPE OF SERVICE	SERVICE INTERVALS			
		INITIAL 1200 MILES	OIL SERVICE	INSPECTION I	INSPECTION II
Oil level	S/I	✓			
Engine oil	R	✓			
Engine oil & filter	R①		✓	✓	✓
Engine air cleaner element	R②				✓
Spark plugs	R				✓
Fuel filter	R③				✓
Fuel, vapor lines & fuel cap	S/I	✓		✓	✓
Cooling system	S/I	✓		✓	✓
Exhaust pipe & muffler	S/I	✓		✓	✓
Catalytic converter & shielding	S/I	✓		✓	✓
Throttle linkage	S/I			✓	✓
Engine (check for leakage)	S/I	✓			
Engine drive belts	S/I				✓
Maintenance Indicators	RE		④	✓	✓
Engine coolant	R			⑤	⑤
Oxygen sensor	R⑥				
Brake & clutch fluids ⑥	S/I			✓	✓
Brake pads & discs	S/I			✓	✓
Parking brake system	S/I			✓	✓
Power steering system	S/I			✓	✓
Rear axle fluid	S/I			✓	✓
Steering play, suspension track rods, front axle joints, steering linkage & joint disc	S/I			✓	✓
Transmission fluid/oil	S/I			✓	✓
Wheel centering hubs	S/I			✓	✓
Rear axle fluid	R		✓		✓
OBD system for codes	S/I	✓		✓	✓

R: Replace   S/I: Service or Inspect   RE: Reset

Note: BMW does not rely solely on vehicle mileage to determine service intervals. An on-oboard diagnostic center, monitors engine operating conditions, along with mileage, to determine the most effective maintenance intervals. The information is then conveyed to the driver through the service indicator lights, located in the center of the instrument panel.

Note: Maintenance and most wear items are covered by the manufacturer. Refer to the operator's manual for additional information.

① On vehicles operated less than 6200 miles per year, more frequent service may be required.

② Replace more frequently if vehicle is operated in dusty conditions.

③ Recommended service for California models, required for all other models.

④ Reset the oil service indicator lights only.

⑤ Replace every 2 years with inspection service.

⑥ Replace every 100,000 miles on all models.

FREQUENT OPERATION MAINTENANCE (SEVERE SERVICE)

If a vehicle is operated under any of the following conditions it is considered severe service

- Extremely dusty areas.

- 50% or more of the vehicle operation is in 32°C (90°F) or higher temperatures, or constant operation in temperatures below 0°C (32°F).

- Prolonged idling (vehicle operation in stop and go traffic).

- Frequent short running periods (engine does not warm to normal operating temperatures).

- Police, taxi, delivery usage or trailer towing usage.

93061CBC

TIRE, WHEEL AND BALL JOINT SPECIFICATIONS
BMW X5

| Year | Model | OEM Tires | | Tire Pressures (psi) | | Wheel Size | Ball Joint Inspection |
		Standard	Optional	Front	Rear		
2000-01	X5	P255/55HR18	NA	NA	NA	NA	NA

OEM: Original Equipment Manufacturer

PSI: Pounds Per Square Inch

STD: Standard

OPT: Optional

NA: Not Available

93081CAW

For accessory drive belt replacement procedures see the model specific sections of this manual

CHRYSLER CORP.
Chrysler Town & Country • Dodge Caravan • Plymouth Voyager

ENGINE AND VEHICLE IDENTIFICATION

Engine							Model Year		
Code ①	Liters (cc)	Cu. In.	Cyl.	Fuel Sys.	Engine Type	Eng. Mfg.	Code ②		Year
3	3.0 (2972)	181	6	SMFI	SOHC	Mitsubishi	V		1997
B	2.4 (2429)	148	4	SMFI	DOHC	Chrysler	W		1998
L	3.8 (3785)	231	6	SMFI	OHV	Chrysler	X		1999
R	3.3 (3300)	201	6	SMFI	OHV	Chrysler	Y		2000
							1		2001

SMFI: Sequential Multi-port Fuel Injection

DOHC: Double Overhead Camshaft

SOHC: Single Overhead Camshaft

OHV: Overhead Valve

① 8th position of VIN

② 10th position of VIN

93081C25

GENERAL ENGINE SPECIFICATIONS

Year	Model	Engine Displacement Liters (cc)	Engine Series (ID/VIN)	Fuel System	Net Horsepower @ rpm	Net Torque @ rpm (ft. lbs.)	Bore x Stroke (in.)	Compression Ratio	Oil Pressure @ rpm
1997	Caravan	2.4 (2429)	B	SMFI	150@5200	167@4000	3.44x3.98	9.4:1	25-80@3000
		3.0 (2972)	3	SMFI	150@5000	176@2800	3.59x2.99	8.9:1	30-80@3000
		3.3 (3300)	R	SMFI	158@4800	203@3600	3.66x3.19	8.9:1	30-80@3000
		3.8 (3785)	L	SMFI	180@4400	240@3300	3.78x3.43	9.0:1	30-80@3000
	Town & Country	3.3 (3300)	R	SMFI	158@4800	203@3600	3.66x3.19	8.9:1	30-80@3000
		3.8 (3785)	L	SMFI	180@4400	240@3300	3.78x3.43	9.0:1	30-80@3000
	Voyager	2.4 (2429)	B	SMFI	150@5200	167@4000	3.44x3.98	9.4:1	25-80@3000
		3.0 (2972)	3	SMFI	150@5000	176@2800	3.59x2.99	8.9:1	30-80@3000
		3.3 (3300)	R	SMFI	158@4800	203@3600	3.66x3.19	8.9:1	30-80@3000
		3.8 (3785)	L	SMFI	180@4400	240@3300	3.78x3.43	9.0:1	30-80@3000
1998	Caravan	2.4 (2429)	B	SMFI	150@5200	167@4000	3.44x3.98	9.4:1	25-80@3000
		3.0 (2972)	3	SMFI	150@5000	176@2800	3.59x2.99	8.9:1	30-80@3000
		3.3 (3300)	R	SMFI	158@4800	203@3600	3.66x3.19	8.9:1	30-80@3000
		3.8 (3785)	L	SMFI	180@4400	240@3300	3.78x3.43	9.0:1	30-80@3000
	Town & Country	3.3 (3300)	R	SMFI	158@4800	203@3600	3.66x3.19	8.9:1	30-80@3000
		3.8 (3785)	L	SMFI	180@4400	240@3300	3.78x3.43	9.0:1	30-80@3000
	Voyager	2.4 (2429)	B	SMFI	150@5200	167@4000	3.44x3.98	9.4:1	25-80@3000
		3.0 (2972)	3	SMFI	150@5000	176@2800	3.59x2.99	8.9:1	30-80@3000
		3.3 (3300)	R	SMFI	158@4800	203@3600	3.66x3.19	8.9:1	30-80@3000
		3.8 (3785)	L	SMFI	180@4400	240@3300	3.78x3.43	9.0:1	30-80@3000
1999	Caravan	2.4 (2429)	B	SMFI	150@5200	167@4000	3.44x3.98	9.4:1	25-80@3000
		3.0 (2972)	3	SMFI	150@5000	176@2800	3.59x2.99	8.9:1	30-80@3000
		3.3 (3300)	R	SMFI	158@4800	203@3600	3.66x3.19	8.9:1	30-80@3000
		3.8 (3785)	L	SMFI	180@4400	240@3300	3.78x3.43	9.0:1	30-80@3000
	Town & Country	3.3 (3300)	R	SMFI	158@4800	203@3600	3.66x3.19	8.9:1	30-80@3000
		3.8 (3785)	L	SMFI	180@4400	240@3300	3.78x3.43	9.0:1	30-80@3000
	Voyager	2.4 (2429)	B	SMFI	150@5200	167@4000	3.44x3.98	9.4:1	25-80@3000
		3.0 (2972)	3	SMFI	150@5000	176@2800	3.59x2.99	8.9:1	30-80@3000
		3.3 (3300)	R	SMFI	158@4800	203@3600	3.66x3.19	8.9:1	30-80@3000
		3.8 (3785)	L	SMFI	180@4400	240@3300	3.78x3.43	9.0:1	30-80@3000
2000-01	Caravan	2.4 (2429)	B	SMFI	150@5200	167@4000	3.44x3.98	9.4:1	25-80@3000
		3.0 (2972)	3	SMFI	150@5000	176@2800	3.59x2.99	8.9:1	30-80@3000
		3.3 (3300)	R	SMFI	158@4800	203@3600	3.66x3.19	8.9:1	30-80@3000
		3.8 (3785)	L	SMFI	180@4400	240@3300	3.78x3.43	9.0:1	30-80@3000
	Town & Country	3.3 (3300)	R	SMFI	158@4800	203@3600	3.66x3.19	8.9:1	30-80@3000
		3.8 (3785)	L	SMFI	180@4400	240@3300	3.78x3.43	9.0:1	30-80@3000
	Voyager	2.4 (2429)	B	SMFI	150@5200	167@4000	3.44x3.98	9.4:1	25-80@3000
		3.0 (2972)	3	SMFI	150@5000	176@2800	3.59x2.99	8.9:1	30-80@3000
		3.3 (3300)	R	SMFI	158@4800	203@3600	3.66x3.19	8.9:1	30-80@3000
		3.8 (3785)	L	SMFI	180@4400	240@3300	3.78x3.43	9.0:1	30-80@3000

SMFI: Sequential Multi-port Fuel Injection

93081C26

For brake related suspension and axle service, refer to the model specific sections of this manual

ENGINE TUNE-UP SPECIFICATIONS

Year	Engine Displacement Liters (cc)	Engine ID/VIN	Spark Plug Gap (in.)	Ignition Timing (deg.)	Fuel Pump (psi)	Idle Speed (rpm)	Valve Clearance In.	Valve Clearance Ex.
1997	2.4 (2429)	B	0.050	①	49	②	HYD	HYD
	3.0 (2972)	3	0.035	①	48	②	HYD	HYD
	3.3 (3300)	R	0.050	①	49	②	HYD	HYD
	3.8 (3785)	L	0.050	①	49	②	HYD	HYD
1998	2.4 (2429)	B	0.048-0.053	①	49	②	HYD	HYD
	3.0 (2972)	3	0.039-0.044	①	48	②	HYD	HYD
	3.3 (3300)	R	0.048-0.053	①	49	②	HYD	HYD
	3.8 (3785)	L	0.048-0.053	①	49	②	HYD	HYD
1999	2.4 (2429)	B	0.048-0.053	①	49	②	HYD	HYD
	3.0 (2972)	3	0.039-0.044	①	48	②	HYD	HYD
	3.3 (3300)	R	0.048-0.053	①	55	②	HYD	HYD
	3.8 (3785)	L	0.048-0.053	①	49	②	HYD	HYD
2000-01	2.4 (2429)	B	0.048-0.053	①	49	②	HYD	HYD
	3.0 (2972)	3	0.039-0.044	①	48	②	HYD	HYD
	3.3 (3300)	R	0.048-0.053	①	55	②	HYD	HYD
	3.8 (3785)	L	0.048-0.053	①	49	②	HYD	HYD

NOTE: The Vehicle Emission Control Information label often reflects specification changes made during production. The label figures must be used if they differ from those in this chart.

HYD: Hydraulic

① Ignition timing is regulated by the Powertrain Control Module (PCM), and cannot be adjusted.

② Idle speed is controled by the Powertrain Control Module (PCM), and cannot be adjusted.

93081C27

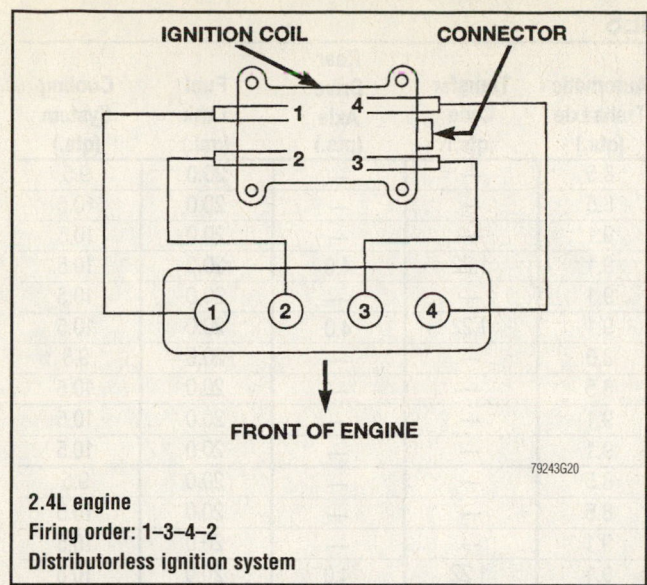

2.4L engine
Firing order: 1–3–4–2
Distributorless ignition system

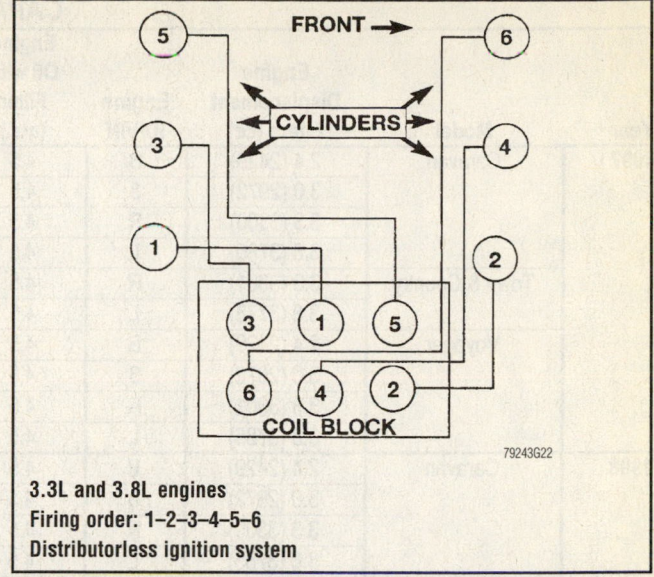

3.3L and 3.8L engines
Firing order: 1–2–3–4–5–6
Distributorless ignition system

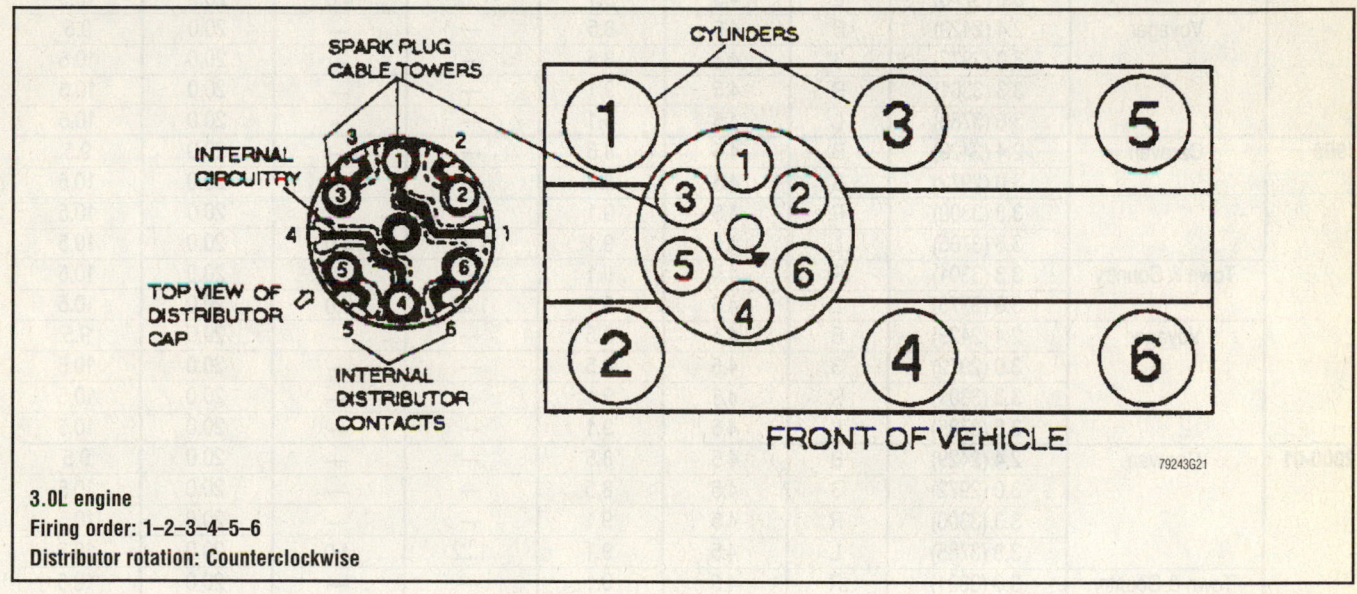

3.0L engine
Firing order: 1–2–3–4–5–6
Distributor rotation: Counterclockwise

Refer to the model specific sections for driveline service procedures

CAPACITIES

Year	Model	Engine Displacement Liters (cc)	Engine ID/VIN	Engine Oil with Filter (qts.)	Automatic Transaxle (qts.)	Transfer Case (qts.)	Rear Drive Axle (pts.)	Fuel Tank (gal.)	Cooling System (qts.)
1997	Caravan	2.4 (2429)	B	4.5	8.5	—	—	20.0	9.5
		3.0 (2972)	3	4.5	8.5	—	—	20.0	10.5
		3.3 (3300)	R	4.5	9.1	—	—	20.0	10.5
		3.8 (3785)	L	4.5	9.1	1.22	4.0	20.0	10.5
	Town & Country	3.3 (3301)	R	4.5	9.1	—	—	20.0	10.5
		3.8 (3778)	L	4.5	9.1	1.22	4.0	20.0	10.5
	Voyager	2.4 (2429)	B	4.5	8.5	—	—	20.0	9.5
		3.0 (2972)	3	4.5	8.5	—	—	20.0	10.5
		3.3 (3301)	R	4.5	9.1	—	—	20.0	10.5
		3.8 (3785)	L	4.5	9.1	—	—	20.0	10.5
1998	Caravan	2.4 (2429)	B	4.5	8.5	—	—	20.0	9.5
		3.0 (2972)	3	4.5	8.5	—	—	20.0	10.5
		3.3 (3300)	R	4.5	9.1	—	—	20.0	10.5
		3.8 (3785)	L	4.5	9.1	1.22	4.0	20.0	10.5
	Town & Country	3.3 (3301)	R	4.5	9.1	—	—	20.0	10.5
		3.8 (3778)	L	4.5	9.1	1.22	4.0	20.0	10.5
	Voyager	2.4 (2429)	B	4.5	8.5	—	—	20.0	9.5
		3.0 (2972)	3	4.5	8.5	—	—	20.0	10.5
		3.3 (3301)	R	4.5	9.1	—	—	20.0	10.5
		3.8 (3785)	L	4.5	9.1	—	—	20.0	10.5
1999	Caravan	2.4 (2429)	B	4.5	8.5	—	—	20.0	9.5
		3.0 (2972)	3	4.5	8.5	—	—	20.0	10.5
		3.3 (3300)	R	4.5	9.1	—	—	20.0	10.5
		3.8 (3785)	L	4.5	9.1	1.22	4.0	20.0	10.5
	Town & Country	3.3 (3301)	R	4.5	9.1	—	—	20.0	10.5
		3.8 (3778)	L	4.5	9.1	1.22	4.0	20.0	10.5
	Voyager	2.4 (2429)	B	4.5	8.5	—	—	20.0	9.5
		3.0 (2972)	3	4.5	8.5	—	—	20.0	10.5
		3.3 (3301)	R	4.5	9.1	—	—	20.0	10.5
		3.8 (3785)	L	4.5	9.1	—	—	20.0	10.5
2000-01	Caravan	2.4 (2429)	B	4.5	8.5	—	—	20.0	9.5
		3.0 (2972)	3	4.5	8.5	—	—	20.0	10.5
		3.3 (3300)	R	4.5	9.1	—	—	20.0	10.5
		3.8 (3785)	L	4.5	9.1	1.22	4.0	20.0	10.5
	Town & Country	3.3 (3301)	R	4.5	9.1	—	—	20.0	10.5
		3.8 (3778)	L	4.5	9.1	1.22	4.0	20.0	10.5
	Voyager	2.4 (2429)	B	4.5	8.5	—	—	20.0	9.5
		3.0 (2972)	3	4.5	8.5	—	—	20.0	10.5
		3.3 (3301)	R	4.5	9.1	—	—	20.0	10.5
		3.8 (3785)	L	4.5	9.1	—	—	20.0	10.5

NOTE: All capacities are approximate. Add fluid gradually and check to be sure a proper fluid level is obtained.

93081C28

TORQUE SPECIFICATIONS
All readings in ft. lbs.

Year	Engine Displacement Liters (cc)	Engine ID/VIN	Cylinder Head Bolts	Main Bearing Bolts	Rod Bearing Bolts	Crankshaft Damper Bolts	Flywheel Bolts	Manifold Intake	Manifold Exhaust	Spark Plugs	Lug Nuts
1997	2.4 (2429)	B	①	②	③	100	70	20	17	20	95
	3.0 (2972)	3	80	②	③	112	70	20	17	20	95
	3.3 (3300)	R	④	⑤	⑥	40	70	17	17	20	95
	3.8 (3785)	L	④	⑤	⑥	40	70	17	17	20	95
1998	2.4 (2429)	B	①	②	③	100	70	20	17	20	85-115
	3.0 (2972)	3	80	②	③	100	70	20	17	20	85-115
	3.3 (3300)	R	④	⑤	⑥	40	70	17	17	20	85-115
	3.8 (3785)	L	④	⑤	⑥	40	70	17	17	20	85-115
1999	2.4 (2429)	B	①	②	③	100	70	20	17	20	85-115
	3.0 (2972)	3	80	②	③	100	70	20	17	20	85-115
	3.3 (3300)	R	④	⑤	⑥	40	70	17	17	20	85-115
	3.8 (3785)	L	④	⑤	⑥	40	70	17	17	20	85-115
2000-01	2.4 (2429)	B	①	②	③	100	70	20	17	20	85-115
	3.0 (2972)	3	80	②	③	100	70	20	17	20	85-115
	3.3 (3300)	R	④	⑤	⑥	40	70	17	17	20	85-115
	3.8 (3785)	L	④	⑤	⑥	40	70	17	17	20	85-115

① Step 1: 25 ft. lbs.
Step 2: 50 ft. lbs.
Step 3: 50 ft. lbs.
Step 4: Plus 1/4 turn

② M8 bolts: 21 ft. lbs.
M11 bolts: 30 ft. lbs. plus 90 degrees

③ Step 1: 20 ft. lbs.
Step 2: Plus 90 degrees

④ Step 1: 45 ft. lbs.
Step 2: 65 ft. lbs.
Step 3: 65 ft. lbs.
Step 4: Plus 90 degrees

⑤ Step 1: 30 ft. lbs.
Step 2: Plus 90 degrees

⑥ Step 1: 40 ft. lbs.
Step 2: Plus 90 degrees

93081C32

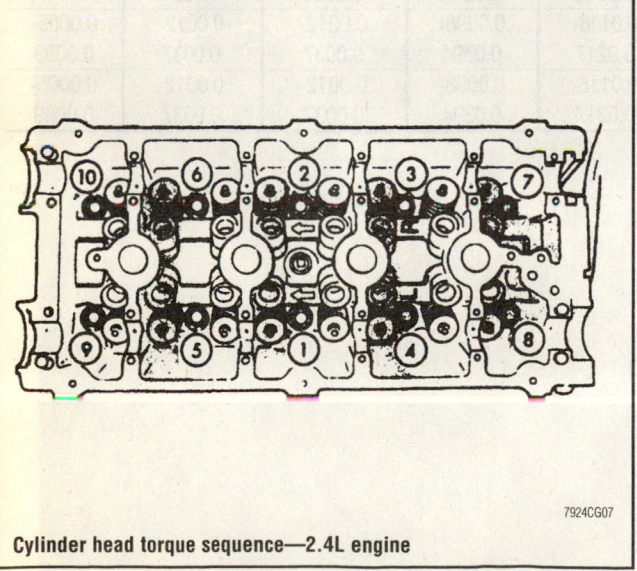

Cylinder head torque sequence—2.4L engine

7924CG07

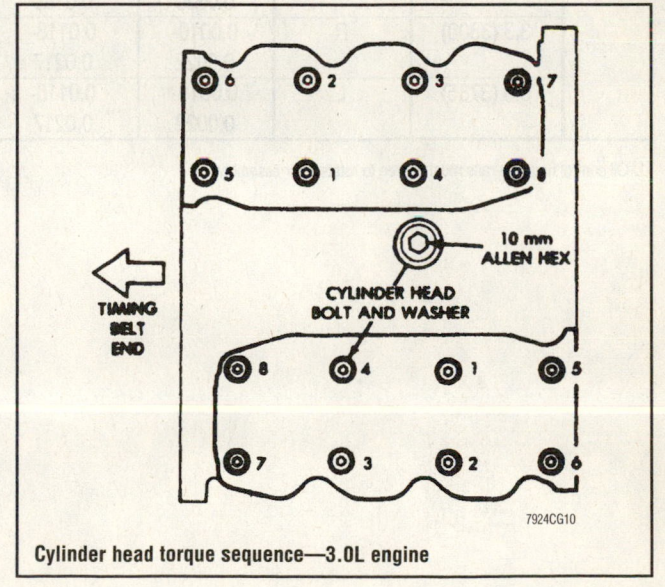

Cylinder head torque sequence—3.0L engine

7924CG10

VALVE SPECIFICATIONS

Year	Engine Displacement Liters (cc)	Engine ID/VIN	Seat Angle (deg.)	Face Angle (deg.)	Spring Test Pressure (lbs. @ in.)	Spring Installed Height (in.)	Stem-to-Guide Clearance (in.) Intake	Stem-to-Guide Clearance (in.) Exhaust	Stem Diameter (in.) Intake	Stem Diameter (in.) Exhaust
1997	2.4 (2429)	B	45	44.5-45.0	129-143@1.17	1.50	0.0018-0.0025	0.0029-0.0037	0.2340	0.2330
	3.0 (2972)	3	44.5	45.5	73@1.59	1.59	0.0010-0.0020	0.0020-0.0030	0.3130-0.3140	0.3120-0.3130
	3.3 (3300)	R	45	44.5	207-229@1.17	1.62-1.68	0.0010-0.0030	0.0020-0.0060	0.3120-0.3130	0.3110-0.3120
	3.8 (3785)	L	45	44.5	207-229@1.17	1.62-1.68	0.0010-0.0030	0.0020-0.0060	0.3120-0.3130	0.3110-0.3120
1998	2.4 (2429)	B	45	44.5-45.0	129-143@1.17	1.50	0.0018-0.0025	0.0029-0.0037	0.2340	0.2330
	3.0 (2972)	3	44.0-44.3	45.0-45.3	73@1.59	1.59	0.0010-0.0040	0.0020-0.0060	0.3130-0.3140	0.3120-0.3125
	3.3 (3300)	R	45.0-45.5	①	207-229@1.169	1.62-1.68	0.0010-0.0030	0.0020-0.0060	0.3120-0.3130	0.3112-0.3119
	3.8 (3785)	L	45.0-45.5	①	207-229@1.169	1.62-1.68	0.0010-0.0030	0.0020-0.0060	0.3120-0.3130	0.3112-0.3119
1999	2.4 (2429)	B	45	44.5-45.0	129-143@1.17	1.50	0.0018-0.0025	0.0029-0.0037	0.2340	0.2330
	3.0 (2972)	3	44.0-44.3	45.0-45.3	73@1.59	1.59	0.0010-0.0040	0.0020-0.0060	0.3130-0.3140	0.3120-0.3125
	3.3 (3300)	R	45.0-45.5	①	207-229@1.169	1.62-1.68	0.0010-0.0030	0.0020-0.0060	0.3120-0.3130	0.3112-0.3119
	3.8 (3785)	L	45.0-45.5	①	207-229@1.169	1.62-1.68	0.0010-0.0030	0.0020-0.0060	0.3120-0.3130	0.3112-0.3119
2000-01	2.4 (2429)	B	45	44.5-45.0	129-143@1.17	1.50	0.0018-0.0025	0.0029-0.0037	0.2340	0.2330
	3.0 (2972)	3	44.0-44.3	45.0-45.3	73@1.59	1.59	0.0010-0.0040	0.0020-0.0060	0.3130-0.3140	0.3120-0.3125
	3.3 (3300)	R	45.0-45.5	①	207-229@1.169	1.62-1.68	0.0010-0.0030	0.0020-0.0060	0.3120-0.3130	0.3112-0.3119
	3.8 (3785)	L	45.0-45.5	①	207-229@1.169	1.62-1.68	0.0010-0.0030	0.0020-0.0060	0.3120-0.3130	0.3112-0.3119

① Intake valve: 44.5 degrees
Exhaust valve: 45 degrees

93081C29

For exhaust manifold replacement procedures, see the model specific sections of this manual

CRANKSHAFT AND CONNECTING ROD SPECIFICATIONS
All measurements are given in inches.

| Year | Engine Displacement Liters (cc) | Engine ID/VIN | Crankshaft | | | | Connecting Rod | | |
			Main Brg. Journal Dia.	Main Brg. Oil Clearance	Shaft End-play	Thrust on No.	Journal Diameter	Oil Clearance	Side Clearance
1997	2.4 (2429)	B	2.3610-2.3625	0.0007-0.0023	0.0035-0.0094	2	1.9670-1.9685	0.0009-0.0027	0.0051-0.0150
	3.0 (2972)	3	2.3610-2.3620	0.0007-0.0014	0.0020-0.0100	2	1.9680-1.9690	0.0007-0.0014	0.0040-0.0100
	3.3 (3300)	R	2.5202-2.5195	0.0023-0.0043	0.0036-0.0095	2	2.1240-2.1250	0.0008-0.0026	0.0050-0.0150
	3.8 (3785)	L	2.5202-2.5195	0.0023-0.0043	0.0036-0.0095	2	2.1240-2.1250	0.0008-0.0026	0.0050-0.0150
1998	2.4 (2429)	B	2.3610-2.3625	0.0007-0.0023	0.0035-0.0094	2	1.9670-1.9685	0.0009-0.0027	0.0051-0.0150
	3.0 (2972)	3	2.3610-2.3620	0.0007-0.0014	0.0020-0.0100	2	1.9680-1.9690	0.0007-0.0014	0.0040-0.0100
	3.3 (3300)	R	2.5202-2.5195	0.0023-0.0043	0.0036-0.0095	2	2.1240-2.1250	0.0008-0.0026	0.0050-0.0150
	3.8 (3785)	L	2.5202-2.5195	0.0023-0.0043	0.0036-0.0095	2	2.1240-2.1250	0.0008-0.0026	0.0050-0.0150
1999	2.4 (2429)	B	2.3610-2.3625	0.0007-0.0023	0.0035-0.0094	2	1.9670-1.9685	0.0009-0.0027	0.0051-0.0150
	3.0 (2972)	3	2.3610-2.3620	0.0007-0.0014	0.0020-0.0100	2	1.9680-1.9690	0.0007-0.0014	0.0040-0.0100
	3.3 (3300)	R	2.5202-2.5195	0.0023-0.0043	0.0036-0.0095	2	2.1240-2.1250	0.0008-0.0026	0.0050-0.0150
	3.8 (3785)	L	2.5202-2.5195	0.0023-0.0043	0.0036-0.0095	2	2.1240-2.1250	0.0008-0.0026	0.0050-0.0150
2000-01	2.4 (2429)	B	2.3610-2.3625	0.0007-0.0023	0.0035-0.0094	2	1.9670-1.9685	0.0009-0.0027	0.0051-0.0150
	3.0 (2972)	3	2.3610-2.3620	0.0007-0.0014	0.0020-0.0100	2	1.9680-1.9690	0.0007-0.0014	0.0040-0.0100
	3.3 (3300)	R	2.5202-2.5195	0.0023-0.0043	0.0036-0.0095	2	2.1240-2.1250	0.0008-0.0026	0.0050-0.0150
	3.8 (3785)	L	2.5202-2.5195	0.0023-0.0043	0.0036-0.0095	2	2.1240-2.1250	0.0008-0.0026	0.0050-0.0150

93081C30

PISTON AND RING SPECIFICATIONS
All measurements are given in inches.

| Year | Engine Displacement Liters (cc) | Engine ID/VIN | Piston Clearance | Ring Gap | | | Ring Side Clearance | | |
				Top Compression	Bottom Compression	Oil Control	Top Compression	Bottom Compression	Oil Control
1997	2.4 (2429)	B	0.0009-0.0022	0.0098-0.0200	0.0090-0.0180	0.0098-0.0250	0.0011-0.0031	0.0011-0.0031	0.0004-0.0070
	3.0 (2972)	3	0.0012-0.0020	0.0120-0.0180	0.0180-0.0240	0.0080-0.0240	0.0012-0.0028	0.0008-0.0024	①
	3.3 (3300)	R	0.0010-0.0022	0.0118-0.0217	0.0118-0.0217	0.0098-0.0394	0.0012-0.0037	0.0012-0.0037	0.0005-0.0089
	3.8 (3785)	L	0.0010-0.0022	0.0118-0.0217	0.0118-0.0217	0.0098-0.0394	0.0012-0.0037	0.0012-0.0037	0.0005-0.0089
1998	2.4 (2429)	B	0.0009-0.0022	0.0098-0.0200	0.0090-0.0180	0.0098-0.0250	0.0011-0.0031	0.0011-0.0031	0.0004-0.0070
	3.0 (2972)	3	0.0012-0.0020	0.0120-0.0180	0.0180-0.0240	0.0080-0.0240	0.0012-0.0028	0.0008-0.0024	①
	3.3 (3300)	R	0.0010-0.0022	0.0118-0.0217	0.0118-0.0217	0.0098-0.0394	0.0012-0.0037	0.0012-0.0037	0.0005-0.0089
	3.8 (3785)	L	0.0010-0.0022	0.0118-0.0217	0.0118-0.0217	0.0098-0.0394	0.0012-0.0037	0.0012-0.0037	0.0005-0.0089
1999	2.4 (2429)	B	0.0009-0.0022	0.0098-0.0200	0.0090-0.0180	0.0098-0.0250	0.0011-0.0031	0.0011-0.0031	0.0004-0.0070
	3.0 (2972)	3	0.0012-0.0020	0.0120-0.0180	0.0180-0.0240	0.0080-0.0240	0.0012-0.0028	0.0008-0.0024	①
	3.3 (3300)	R	0.0010-0.0022	0.0118-0.0217	0.0118-0.0217	0.0098-0.0394	0.0012-0.0037	0.0012-0.0037	0.0005-0.0089
	3.8 (3785)	L	0.0010-0.0022	0.0118-0.0217	0.0118-0.0217	0.0098-0.0394	0.0012-0.0037	0.0012-0.0037	0.0005-0.0089
2000-01	2.4 (2429)	B	0.0009-0.0022	0.0098-0.0200	0.0090-0.0180	0.0098-0.0250	0.0011-0.0031	0.0011-0.0031	0.0004-0.0070
	3.0 (2972)	3	0.0012-0.0020	0.0120-0.0180	0.0180-0.0240	0.0080-0.0240	0.0012-0.0028	0.0008-0.0024	①
	3.3 (3300)	R	0.0010-0.0022	0.0118-0.0217	0.0118-0.0217	0.0098-0.0394	0.0012-0.0037	0.0012-0.0037	0.0005-0.0089
	3.8 (3785)	L	0.0010-0.0022	0.0118-0.0217	0.0118-0.0217	0.0098-0.0394	0.0012-0.0037	0.0012-0.0037	0.0005-0.0089

① Oil control ring side rails must be free to rotate after assembly

9308

Refer to the model specific sections for cooling system service procedures

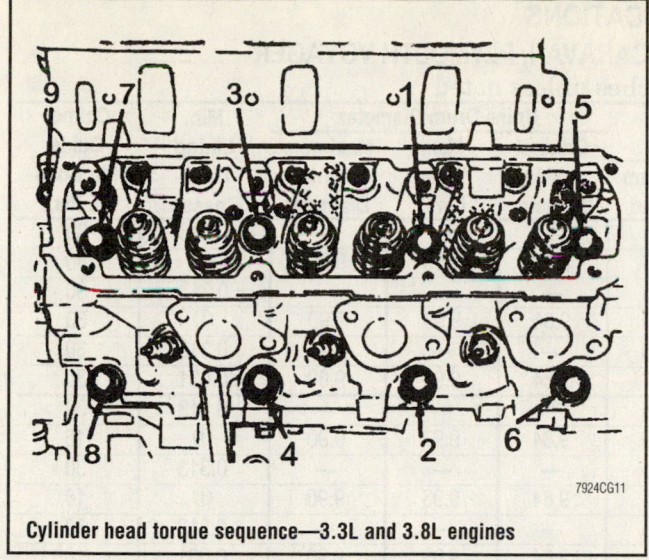

Cylinder head torque sequence—3.3L and 3.8L engines

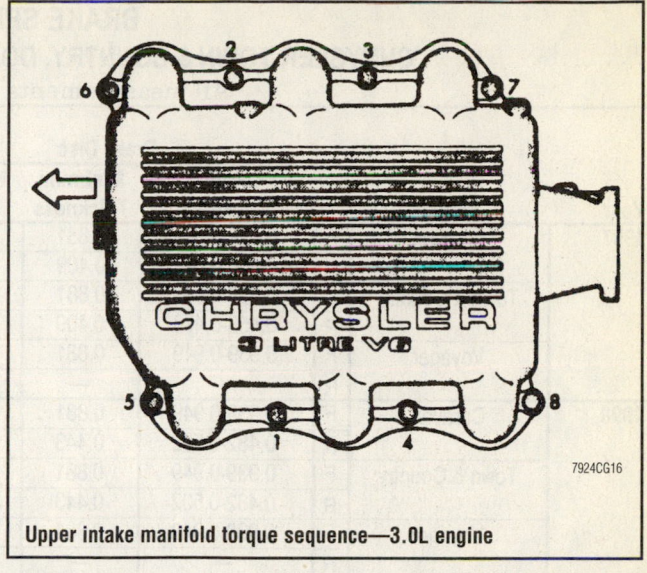

Upper intake manifold torque sequence—3.0L engine

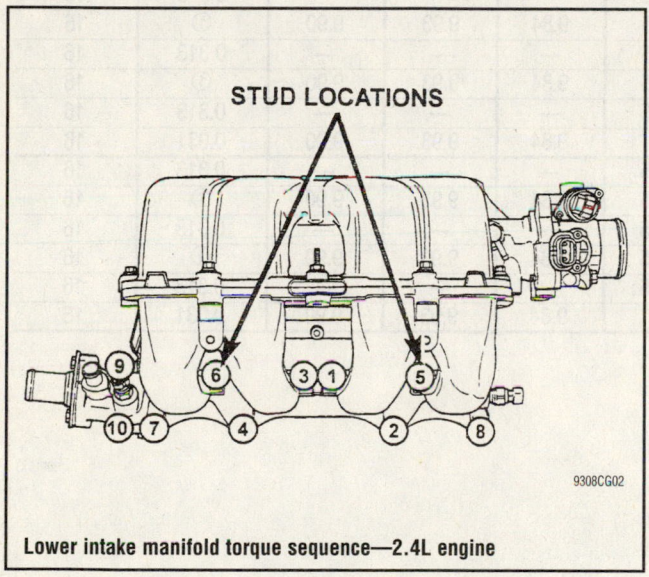

Lower intake manifold torque sequence—2.4L engine

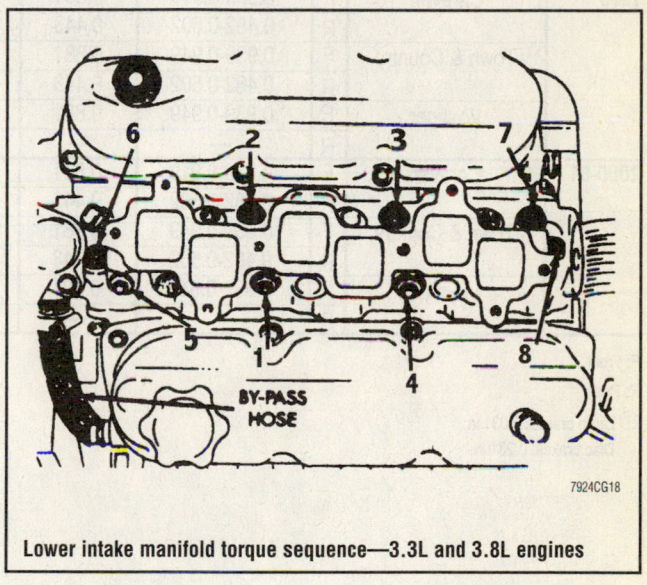

Lower intake manifold torque sequence—3.3L and 3.8L engines

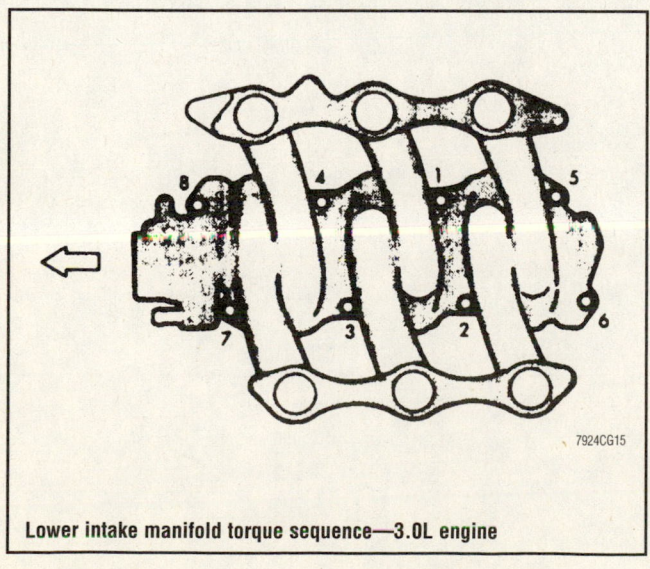

Lower intake manifold torque sequence—3.0L engine

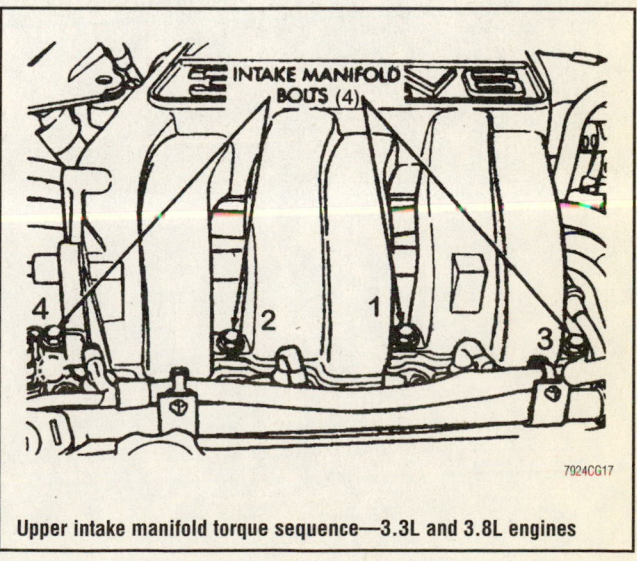

Upper intake manifold torque sequence—3.3L and 3.8L engines

BRAKE SPECIFICATIONS
CHRYSLER TOWN & COUNTRY, DODGE CARAVAN, PLYMOUTH VOYAGER
All measurements in inches unless noted

Year	Model		Brake Disc Original Thickness	Brake Disc Minimum Thickness	Brake Disc Maximum Run-out	Brake Drum Diameter Original Inside Diameter	Brake Drum Diameter Max. Wear Limit	Brake Drum Diameter Maximum Machine Diameter	Min. Lining Thickness	Caliper Guide Pin Bolts (ft. lbs.)
1997	Caravan	F	0.939-0.949	0.881	0.005	—	—	—	0.313	30
		R	0.458-0.478	0.409	0.005	9.84	9.93	9.90	①	30
	Town & Country	F	0.939-0.949	0.881	0.005	—	—	—	0.313	30
		R	0.458-0.478	0.409	0.005	9.84	9.93	9.90	①	30
	Voyager	F	0.939-0.949	0.881	0.005	—	—	—	0.313	30
		R	—	—	—	9.84	9.93	9.90	0.031	30
1998	Caravan	F	0.939-0.949	0.881	0.005	—	—	—	0.313	30
		R	0.482-0.502	0.443	0.005	9.84	9.93	9.90	①	16
	Town & Country	F	0.939-0.949	0.881	0.005	—	—	—	0.313	30
		R	0.482-0.502	0.443	0.005	9.84	9.93	9.90	①	16
	Voyager	F	0.939-0.949	0.881	0.005	—	—	—	0.313	30
		R	—	—	—	9.84	9.93	9.90	0.031	16
1999	Caravan	F	0.939-0.949	0.881	0.005	—	—	—	0.313	16
		R	0.482-0.502	0.443	0.005	9.84	9.93	9.90	①	16
	Town & Country	F	0.939-0.949	0.881	0.005	—	—	—	0.313	16
		R	0.482-0.502	0.443	0.005	9.84	9.93	9.90	①	16
	Voyager	F	0.939-0.949	0.881	0.005	—	—	—	0.313	16
		R	—	—	—	9.84	9.93	9.90	0.031	16
2000-01	Caravan	F	0.939-0.949	0.881	0.005	—	—	—	0.313	16
		R	0.482-0.502	0.443	0.005	9.84	9.93	9.90	①	16
	Town & Country	F	0.939-0.949	0.881	0.005	—	—	—	0.313	16
		R	0.482-0.502	0.443	0.005	9.84	9.93	9.90	①	16
	Voyager	F	0.939-0.949	0.881	0.005	—	—	—	0.313	16
		R	—	—	—	9.84	9.93	9.90	0.031	16

F: Front

R: Rear

① Drum brakes: 0.031 in
   Disc brakes: 0.281 in.

93081C33

SCHEDULED MAINTENANCE INTERVALS
(CHRYSLER CARAVAN, TOWN & COUNTRY & VOYAGER)

TO BE SERVICED	TYPE OF SERVICE	VEHICLE MILEAGE INTERVAL (x1000)												
		7.5	15	22.5	30	37.5	45	52.5	60	67.5	75	82.5	90	97.5
Engine oil & filter	R	✓	✓	✓	✓	✓	✓	✓	✓	✓	✓	✓	✓	✓
Driveshaft boots	S/I	✓	✓	✓	✓	✓	✓	✓	✓	✓	✓	✓	✓	✓
Exhaust system	S/I	✓	✓	✓	✓	✓	✓	✓	✓	✓	✓	✓	✓	✓
Engine coolant level, hoses & clamps	S/I	✓	✓	✓	✓	✓	✓	✓	✓	✓	✓	✓	✓	✓
Rotate tires	S/I	✓	✓	✓	✓	✓	✓	✓	✓	✓	✓	✓	✓	✓
Drive belts	S/I		✓		✓		✓		✓		✓		✓		
Brake hoses & linings	S/I			✓			✓			✓			✓		
Automatic transaxle fluid & filter	R				✓				✓				✓		
Air filter	R				✓				✓				✓		
Spark plugs ①	R				✓				✓				✓		
Serpentine belts (3.0L & 3.3L)	S/I								✓		✓		✓		
Lubricate tie rod ends	S/I				✓				✓				✓		
PCV valve	S/I				✓				✓				✓		
Engine coolant	R								✓			✓			
Timing belt (3.0L)	R								✓						
Distributor cap & rotor	R							✓							
Ignition cables (3.0L)	R								✓						
Ignition timing	S/I								✓						

R: Replace   S/I: Service or Inspect

① Platinum tip spark plugs & ignition cables (3.3L & 3.8L): replace every 100,000 miles.

FREQUENT OPERATION MAINTENANCE (SEVERE SERVICE)

If a vehicle is operated under any of the following conditions it is considered severe service:

- Extremely dusty areas.

- 50% or more of the vehicle operation is in 32°C (90°F) or higher temperatures, or constant operation in temperatures below 0°C (32°F).

- Prolonged idling (vehicle operation in stop and go traffic.

- Frequent short running periods (engine does not warm to normal operating temperatures).

- Police, taxi, delivery usage or trailer towing usage.

Oil & oil filter change: change every 3000 miles.

Automatic transaxle fluid & filter: change every 15,000 miles.

Brake hoses & linings: check every 9000 miles.

CV-joints & front suspension ball joints: check every 3000 miles.

Tie rod ends & steering linkage: check every 15,000 miles.

Air filter: change every 15,000 miles.

93081C34

Timing chain and gear service is covered in the model specific sections of this manual

SCHEDULED MAINTENANCE INTERVALS
DAIMLERCHRYSLER CORPORATION
CHRYSLER CARAVAN,
TOWN & COUNTRY, VOYAGER

The following should be used as a guide when determining the amount of work required for a particular service.
In estimating how long a particular Scheduled Maintenance Service should take, please observe the following:

- Labor Time is time based on field research and data supplied by the vehicle manufacturer.
- Labor time operations are given in hours and tenths of an hour.
- All labor operations are to be used as a guide.

Mechanic Skill Level Codes:
(A) PRECISION: Highly skilled with multiple certification.
(B) GENERAL: Normally skilled with certification.
(C) MAINTENANCE: Semi-skilled working on certification.

	LABOR TIME			LABOR TIME			LABOR TIME
7500 Mile Service (C)			**45000 Mile Service (C)**			**75000 Mile Service (C)**	
All Models	1.2		All Models	1.5		All Models	
15000 Mile Service (C)			**52500 Mile Service (C)**			2.5L	1.3
All Models	1.3		All Models	1.7		3.0L, 3.3L, 3.8L	1.4
22500 Mile Service (C)			*Replace dist. cap & rotor add*	.4		**82500 Mile Service (C)**	
All Models	1.4		**60000 Mile Service (B)**			All Models	1.7
30000 Mile Service (B)			All Models			**90000 Mile Service (B)**	
All Models	2.4		2.5L	2.7		All Models	
Replace spark plugs (2.4L, 3.0L) add	1.1		3.0L	8.5		2.5L	6.0
			3.3L, 3.8L	2.8		3.0L	7.5
37500 Mile Service (C)			**67500 Mile Service (C)**			3.3L, 3.8L	2.8
All Models	1.2		All Models	1.4		**97500 Mile Service (C)**	
						All Models	1.2

93081C35

CHRYSLER CORP.
Dodge Dakota, Durango • RAM Trucks • RAM Vans

ENGINE AND VEHICLE IDENTIFICATION

Engine								Model Year	
Code ①	Liters (cc)	Cu. In.	Cyl.	Fuel Sys.	Engine Type	Eng. Mfg.		Code ②	Year
5	5.9 (5899)	360	8	SMFI	OHV	Chrysler		V	1997
6	5.9 (5882)	359	6	DSL-24V	OHV	Cummins		W	1998
D	5.9 (5882)	359	6	DSL-12V	OHV	Cummins		X	1999
N	4.7 (4701)	287	6	SMFI	SOHC	Chrysler		Y	2000
P	2.5 (2507)	153	4	SMFI	OHV	Chrysler		1	2001
W	8.0 (7994)	488	10	SMFI	OHV	Chrysler			
X	3.9 (3916)	238	6	SMFI	OHV	Chrysler			
Y	5.2 (5208)	318	8	SMFI	OHV	Chrysler			
Z	5.9 (5899)	360	8	SMFI	OHV	Chrysler			

OHV: Overhead Valve

DSL-12V: Diesel with 12-valve cylinder head

DSL-24V: Diesel with 24-valve cylinder head

SMFI: Sequential Multi-port Fuel Injection

① 8th position of VIN

② 10th position of VIN

93081C36

Ignition system service is covered in the model specific sections of this manual

GENERAL ENGINE SPECIFICATIONS

Year	Model	Engine Displacement Liters (cc)	Engine Series (ID/VIN)	Fuel System	Net Horsepower @ rpm	Net Torque @ rpm (ft. lbs.)	Bore x Stroke (in.)	Compression Ratio	Oil Pressure @ rpm
1997	Dakota	2.5 (2458)	P	SMFI	120@5200	145@3400	3.88x3.19	9.2:1	25-80@3000
		3.9 (3916)	X	SMFI	175@4800	220@3200	3.91x3.31	9.1:1	30-80@3000
		5.2 (5211)	Y	SMFI	220@4400	300@3200	3.91x3.31	9.1:1	30-80@3000
	Ram Truck 1500	3.9 (3916)	X	SMFI	175@4800	220@3200	3.91x3.31	9.1:1	30-80@3000
		5.2 (5211)	Y	SMFI	220@4400	300@3200	3.91x3.31	9.1:1	30-80@3000
		5.9 (5899)	Z	SMFI	230@4000	330@3250	4.00x3.58	9.1:1	30-80@3000
	Ram Truck 2500	5.2 (5211)	Y	SMFI	220@4400	300@3200	3.91x3.31	9.1:1	30-80@3000
		5.9 (5882)	D	DSL	160@2500	400@1600	4.02x4.72	17.5:1	30@2500
		5.9 (5899)	Z	SMFI	230@4000	330@3250	4.00x3.58	9.1:1	30-80@3000
		8.0 (7997)	W	SMFI	300@4000	450@2400	4.00x3.58	8.4:1	50-60@3000
	Ram Truck 3500	5.9 (5882)	D	DSL	160@2500	400@1600	4.02x4.72	17.5:1	30@2500
		5.9 (5899)	5	SMFI	230@4000	330@2800	4.00x3.58	8.9:1	30-80@3000
		8.0 (7997)	W	SMFI	300@4000	450@2400	4.00x3.58	8.4:1	50-60@3000
	Ram Van 1500	3.9 (3916)	X	SMFI	175@4800	220@3200	3.91x3.31	9.1:1	30-80@3000
		5.2 (5211)	Y	SMFI	220@4400	300@3200	3.91x3.31	9.1:1	30-80@3000
	Ram Van 2500	3.9 (3916)	X	SMFI	175@4800	220@3200	3.91x3.31	9.1:1	30-80@3000
		5.2 (5211)	Y	SMFI	220@4400	300@3200	3.91x3.31	9.1:1	30-80@3000
		5.9 (5899)	Z	SMFI	230@4000	330@3250	4.00x3.58	9.1:1	30-80@3000
	Ram Van 3500	5.2 (5211)	Y	SMFI	220@4400	300@3200	3.91x3.31	9.1:1	30-80@3000
		5.9 (5899)	Z	SMFI	230@4000	330@3250	4.00x3.58	9.1:1	30-80@3000
1998	Dakota	2.5 (2464)	P	SMFI	120@5200	145@3400	3.88x3.19	9.2:1	25-80@3000
		3.9 (3906)	X	SMFI	175@4800	220@3200	3.91x3.31	9.1:1	30-80@3000
		5.2 (5208)	Y	SMFI	220@4400	300@3200	3.91x3.31	9.1:1	30-80@3000
		5.9 (5899)	Z	SMFI	230@4000	330@3250	4.00x3.58	9.1:1	30-80@3000
	Durango	3.9 (3906)	X	SMFI	175@4800	220@3200	3.91x3.31	9.1:1	30-80@3000
		5.2 (5208)	Y	SMFI	220@4400	300@3200	3.91x3.31	9.1:1	30-80@3000
		5.9 (5899)	Z	SMFI	230@4000	330@3250	4.00x3.58	9.1:1	30-80@3000
	Ram Truck 1500	3.9 (3906)	X	SMFI	175@4800	220@3200	3.91x3.31	9.1:1	30-80@3000
		5.2 (5208)	Y	SMFI	220@4400	300@3200	3.91x3.31	9.1:1	30-80@3000
		5.9 (5899)	Z	SMFI	230@4000	330@3250	4.00x3.58	9.1:1	30-80@3000
	Ram Truck 2500	5.9 (5882)	D	DSL-12V	160@2500	400@1600	4.02x4.72	17.5:1	30@2500
		5.9 (5899)	Z	SMFI	230@4000	330@3250	4.00x3.58	9.1:1	30-80@3000
		8.0 (7994)	W	SMFI	300@4000	450@2400	4.00x3.58	8.4:1	50-60@3000
	Ram Truck 3500	5.9 (5882)	D	DSL-12V	160@2500	400@1600	4.02x4.72	17.5:1	30@2500
		5.9 (5899)	5	SMFI	230@4000	330@2800	4.00x3.58	8.9:1	30-80@3000
		8.0 (7994)	W	SMFI	300@4000	450@2400	4.00x3.58	8.4:1	50-60@3000
	Ram Van 1500	3.9 (3916)	X	SMFI	175@4800	220@3200	3.91x3.31	9.1:1	30-80@3000
		5.2 (5208)	Y	SMFI	220@4400	300@3200	3.91x3.31	9.1:1	30-80@3000
	Ram Van 2500	3.9 (3916)	X	SMFI	175@4800	220@3200	3.91x3.31	9.1:1	30-80@3000
		5.2 (5208)	Y	SMFI	220@4400	300@3200	3.91x3.31	9.1:1	30-80@3000
		5.9 (5899)	Z	SMFI	230@4000	330@3250	4.00x3.58	9.1:1	30-80@3000
	Ram Van 3500	5.2 (5208)	Y	SMFI	220@4400	300@3200	3.91x3.31	9.1:1	30-80@3000
		5.9 (5899)	Z	SMFI	230@4000	330@3250	4.00x3.58	9.1:1	30-80@3000
1999	Dakota	2.5 (2464)	P	SMFI	120@5200	145@3400	3.88x3.19	9.2:1	25-80@3000
		3.9 (3906)	X	SMFI	175@4800	220@3200	3.91x3.31	9.1:1	30-80@3000
		5.2 (5208)	Y	SMFI	220@4400	300@3200	3.91x3.31	9.1:1	30-80@3000
		5.9 (5899)	Z	SMFI	230@4000	330@3250	4.00x3.58	9.1:1	30-80@3000
	Durango	3.9 (3906)	X	SMFI	175@4800	220@3200	3.91x3.31	9.1:1	30-80@3000
		5.2 (5208)	Y	SMFI	220@4400	300@3200	3.91x3.31	9.1:1	30-80@3000
		5.9 (5899)	Z	SMFI	230@4000	330@3250	4.00x3.58	9.1:1	30-80@3000

93081C37

GENERAL ENGINE SPECIFICATIONS

Year	Model	Engine Displacement Liters (cc)	Engine Series (ID/VIN)	Fuel System	Net Horsepower @ rpm	Net Torque @ rpm (ft. lbs.)	Bore x Stroke (in.)	Compression Ratio	Oil Pressure @ rpm
1999 (cont.)	Ram Truck 1500	3.9 (3906)	X	SMFI	175@4800	220@3200	3.91x3.31	9.1:1	30-80@3000
		5.2 (5208)	Y	SMFI	220@4400	300@3200	3.91x3.31	9.1:1	30-80@3000
		5.9 (5899)	Z	SMFI	230@4000	330@3250	4.00x3.58	9.1:1	30-80@3000
	Ram Truck 2500	5.9 (5882)	6	DSL-24V	①	②	4.02x4.72	16.5	30@2500
		5.9 (5899)	Z	SMFI	230@4000	330@3250	4.00x3.58	9.1:1	30-80@3000
		8.0 (7994)	W	SMFI	300@4000	450@2400	4.00x3.58	8.4:1	50-60@3000
	Ram Truck 3500	5.9 (5882)	6	DSL-24V	①	②	4.02x4.72	16.5	30@2500
		5.9 (5899)	5	SMFI	230@4000	330@2800	4.00x3.58	8.9:1	30-80@3000
		8.0 (7994)	W	SMFI	300@4000	450@2400	4.00x3.58	8.4:1	50-60@3000
	Ram Van 1500	3.9 (3916)	X	SMFI	175@4800	220@3200	3.91x3.31	9.1:1	30-80@3000
		5.2 (5208)	Y	SMFI	220@4400	300@3200	3.91x3.31	9.1:1	30-80@3000
	Ram Van 2500	3.9 (3916)	X	SMFI	175@4800	220@3200	3.91x3.31	9.1:1	30-80@3000
		5.2 (5208)	Y	SMFI	220@4400	300@3200	3.91x3.31	9.1:1	30-80@3000
		5.9 (5899)	Z	SMFI	230@4000	330@3250	4.00x3.58	9.1:1	30-80@3000
	Ram Van 3500	5.2 (5208)	Y	SMFI	220@4400	300@3200	3.91x3.31	9.1:1	30-80@3000
		5.9 (5899)	Z	SMFI	230@4000	330@3250	4.00x3.58	9.1:1	30-80@3000
2000-01	Dakota	2.5 (2464)	P	SMFI	120@5200	145@3400	3.88x3.19	9.2:1	25-80@3000
		3.9 (3906)	X	SMFI	175@4800	220@3200	3.91x3.31	9.1:1	30-80@3000
		5.2 (5208)	Y	SMFI	220@4400	300@3200	3.91x3.31	9.1:1	30-80@3000
		5.9 (5899)	Z	SMFI	230@4000	330@3250	4.00x3.58	9.1:1	30-80@3000
	Durango	4.7 (4701)	N	SMFI	235@4800	295@3200	3.66x3.40	9.3:1	25@3000
		5.2 (5208)	Y	SMFI	220@4400	300@3200	3.91x3.31	9.1:1	30-80@3000
		5.9 (5899)	Z	SMFI	230@4000	330@3250	4.00x3.58	9.1:1	30-80@3000
	Ram Truck 1500	3.9 (3906)	X	SMFI	175@4800	220@3200	3.91x3.31	9.1:1	30-80@3000
		5.2 (5208)	Y	SMFI	220@4400	300@3200	3.91x3.31	9.1:1	30-80@3000
		5.9 (5899)	Z	SMFI	230@4000	330@3250	4.00x3.58	9.1:1	30-80@3000
	Ram Truck 2500	5.9 (5882)	6	DSL-24V	①	②	4.02x4.72	16.5	30@2500
		5.9 (5899)	Z	SMFI	230@4000	330@3250	4.00x3.58	9.1:1	30-80@3000
		8.0 (7994)	W	SMFI	300@4000	450@2400	4.00x3.58	8.4:1	50-60@3000
	Ram Truck 3500	5.9 (5882)	6	DSL-24V	①	②	4.02x4.72	16.5	30@2500
		5.9 (5899)	5	SMFI	230@4000	330@2800	4.00x3.58	8.9:1	30-80@3000
		8.0 (7994)	W	SMFI	300@4000	450@2400	4.00x3.58	8.4:1	50-60@3000
	Ram Van 1500	3.9 (3916)	X	SMFI	175@4800	220@3200	3.91x3.31	9.1:1	30-80@3000
		5.2 (5208)	Y	SMFI	220@4400	300@3200	3.91x3.31	9.1:1	30-80@3000
	Ram Van 2500	3.9 (3916)	X	SMFI	175@4800	220@3200	3.91x3.31	9.1:1	30-80@3000
		5.2 (5208)	Y	SMFI	220@4400	300@3200	3.91x3.31	9.1:1	30-80@3000
		5.9 (5899)	Z	SMFI	230@4000	330@3250	4.00x3.58	9.1:1	30-80@3000
	Ram Van 3500	5.2 (5208)	Y	SMFI	220@4400	300@3200	3.91x3.31	9.1:1	30-80@3000
		5.9 (5899)	Z	SMFI	230@4000	330@3250	4.00x3.58	9.1:1	30-80@3000

DSL-12V: Diesel engine with 12 valve cylinder head
DSL-24V: Diesel engine with 24 valve cylinder head
SMFI: Sequential Multi-port Fuel Injection

① AT: 215@2700rpm
   MT: 235@2700rpm
② AT: 420@1600rpm
   MT: 460@1600rpm

93081C38

Please visit our web site at www.chiltononline.com

GASOLINE ENGINE TUNE-UP SPECIFICATIONS

Year	Engine Displacement Liters (cc)	Engine ID/VIN	Spark Plug Gap (in.)	Ignition Timing (deg.)	Fuel Pump (psi)	Idle Speed (rpm)	Valve Clearance Intake	Valve Clearance Exhaust
1997	2.5 (2458)	P	0.035	①	49.2	②	HYD	HYD
	3.9 (3916)	X	0.035	①	49.2	②	HYD	HYD
	5.2 (5211)	Y	0.035	①	49.2	②	HYD	HYD
	5.9 (5899)	5	0.035	①	49.2	②	HYD	HYD
	5.9 (5899)	Z	0.035	①	49.2	②	HYD	HYD
	8.0 (7997)	W	0.045	①	49.2	②	HYD	HYD
1998	2.5 (2464)	P	0.035	①	44.2 - 54.2	②	HYD	HYD
	3.9 (3916)	X	0.040	①	44.2 - 54.2	②	HYD	HYD
	5.2 (5208)	Y	0.040	①	44.2 - 54.2	②	HYD	HYD
	5.9 (5899)	5	0.040	①	44.2 - 54.2	②	HYD	HYD
	5.9 (5899)	Z	0.040	①	44.2 - 54.2	②	HYD	HYD
	8.0 (7994)	W	0.045	①	44.2 - 54.2	②	HYD	HYD
1999	2.5 (2464)	P	0.035	①	44.2 - 54.2	②	HYD	HYD
	3.9 (3916)	X	0.040	①	44.2 - 54.2	②	HYD	HYD
	5.2 (5208)	Y	0.040	①	44.2 - 54.2	②	HYD	HYD
	5.9 (5899)	5	0.040	①	44.2 - 54.2	②	HYD	HYD
	5.9 (5899)	Z	0.040	①	44.2 - 54.2	②	HYD	HYD
	8.0 (7994)	W	0.045	①	44.2 - 54.2	②	HYD	HYD
2000-01	2.5 (2464)	P	0.035	①	44.2 - 54.2	②	HYD	HYD
	3.9 (3916)	X	0.040	①	44.2 - 54.2	②	HYD	HYD
	4.7 (4701)	N	0.040	①	47-51	②	HYD	HYD
	5.2 (5208)	Y	0.040	①	44.2 - 54.2	②	HYD	HYD
	5.9 (5899)	5	0.040	①	44.2 - 54.2	②	HYD	HYD
	5.9 (5899)	Z	0.040	①	44.2 - 54.2	②	HYD	HYD
	8.0 (7994)	W	0.045	①	44.2 - 54.2	②	HYD	HYD

NOTE: The Vehicle Emission Control Information (VECI) label often reflects specification changes made during production.
The label figures must be used if they differ from those in this chart.

HYD: Hydraulic

① Ignition timing is controlled by the PCM and is not adjustable.

② Idle speed is controlled by the PCM and is not adjustable

93081C39

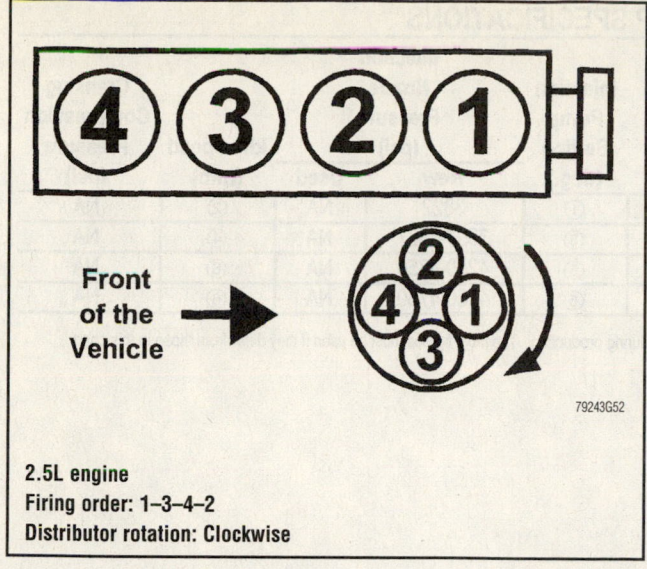

2.5L engine
Firing order: 1–3–4–2
Distributor rotation: Clockwise

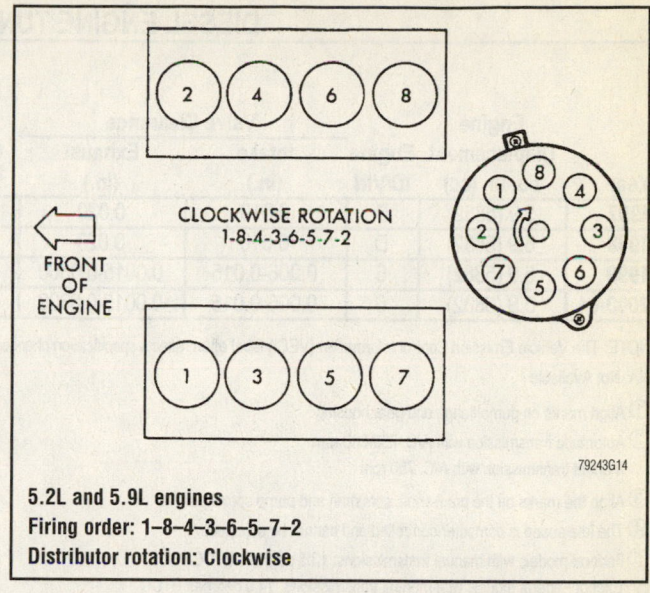

5.2L and 5.9L engines
Firing order: 1–8–4–3–6–5–7–2
Distributor rotation: Clockwise

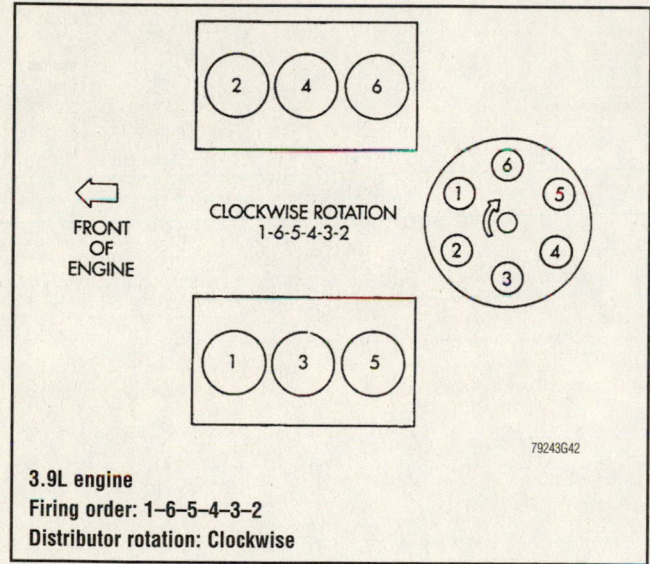

3.9L engine
Firing order: 1–6–5–4–3–2
Distributor rotation: Clockwise

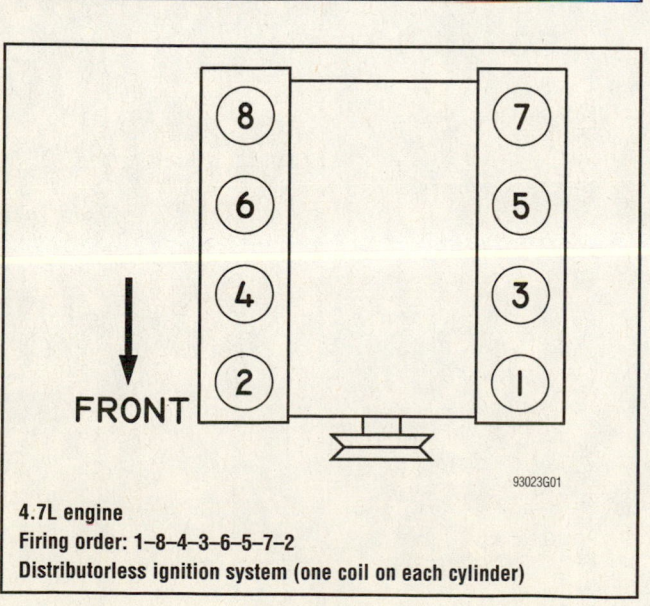

4.7L engine
Firing order: 1–8–4–3–6–5–7–2
Distributorless ignition system (one coil on each cylinder)

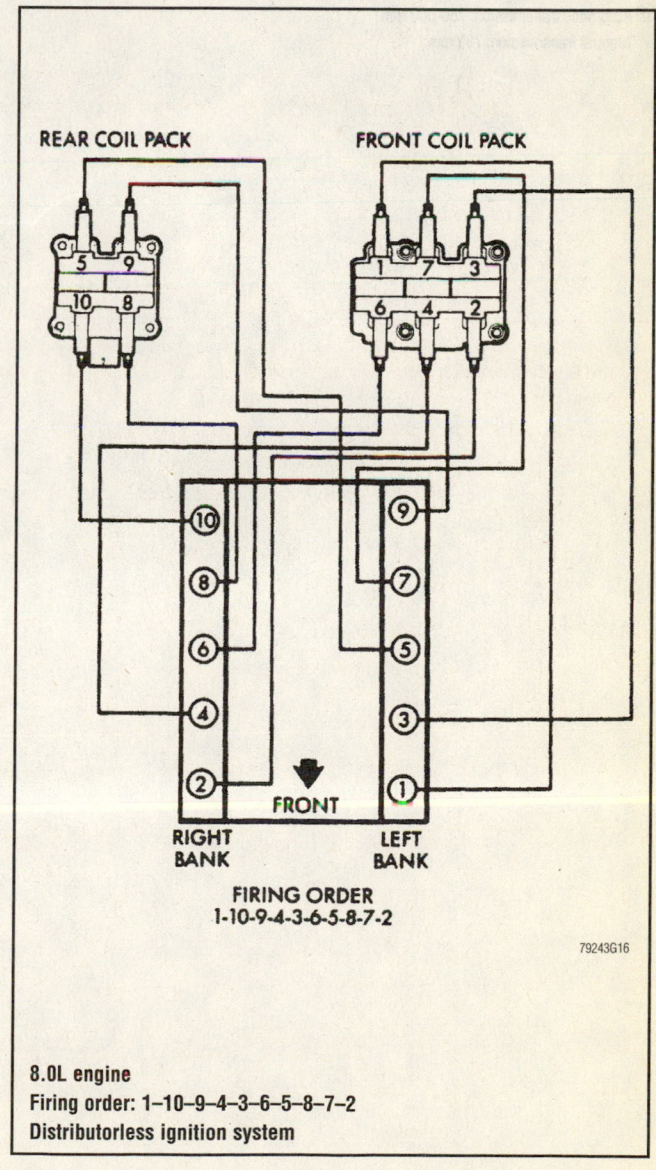

8.0L engine
Firing order: 1–10–9–4–3–6–5–8–7–2
Distributorless ignition system

Refer to the model specific sections for engine mechanical service procedures

DIESEL ENGINE TUNE-UP SPECIFICATIONS

Year	Engine Displacement cu. in. (cc)	Engine ID/VIN	Valve Clearance		Intake Valve Opens (deg.)	Injection Pump Setting (deg.)	Injection Nozzle Pressure (psi)		Idle Speed (rpm)	Cranking Compression Pressure (psi)
			Intake (in.)	Exhaust (in.)			New	Used		
1997	5.9 (5882)	D	0.010	0.020	NA	①	3822	NA	②	NA
1998	5.9 (5882)	D	0.010	0.020	NA	③	3394-3887	NA	④	NA
1999	5.9 (5882)	6	0.006-0.015	0.0015-0.0300	NA	⑤	4250-4750	NA	⑥	NA
2000-01	5.9 (5882)	6	0.006-0.015	0.0015-0.0300	NA	⑤	4250-4750	NA	⑥	NA

NOTE: The Vehicle Emission Control Information (VECI) label often reflects specification changes made during production. The label figures must be used if they differ from those in this chart

NA: Not Available

① Align marks on pump flange and gear housing

② Automatic transmission with A/C: 750-800 rpm

Manual transmission with A/C: 780 rpm

③ Align the marks on the crankshaft, camshaft and pump sprockets.

④ The idle speed is computer-controlled and cannot be adjusted.

⑤ Federal models with manual transmissions: 13.5 degrees BTDC

Except Federal models with manual transmissions: 14.0 degrees BTDC

⑥ Automatic transmission: 750-800 rpm

Manual transmission: 780 rpm

93081C40

CAPACITIES

Year	Model	Engine Displacement Liters (cc)	Engine ID/VIN	Oil with Filter (qts.)	Transmission (pts.) Manual	Transmission (pts.) Auto.	Transfer Case (pts.)	Drive Axle Front (pts.)	Drive Axle Rear (pts.)	Fuel Tank (gal.)	Cooling System (qts.)
1997	Dakota	2.5 (2458)	P	4.5	[1]	[2]	—	—	[3]	[4]	9.8
		3.9 (3916)	X	4.5	[1]	[2]	2.5	3.0	[3]	[4]	14.0
		5.2 (5211)	Y	5.0	[1]	[2]	2.5	3.0	[3]	[4]	14.3
	Ram Truck 1500	3.9 (3916)	X	4.0	[1]	[2]	—	—	[5]	26.0[6]	20.0
		5.2 (5211)	Y	5.0	[1]	[2]	[7]	[8]	[5]	26.0[6]	20.0
		5.9 (5899)	Z	5.0	[1]	[2]	[7]	[8]	[5]	26.0[6]	20.0
	Ram Truck 2500	5.2 (5211)	Y	5.0	[1]	[2]	[7]	[8]	[5]	26.0[6]	20.0
		5.9 (5882)	D	11.0	[1]	[2]	[7]	[8]	[5]	26.0[6]	26.0
		5.9 (5899)	Z	5.0	[1]	[2]	[7]	[8]	[5]	26.0[6]	20.0
		8.0 (7997)	W	7.0	[1]	[2]	[7]	[8]	[5]	26.0[6]	24.0
	Ram Truck 3500	5.9 (5882)	D	11.0	[1]	[2]	[7]	[8]	[5]	26.0[6]	26.0
		5.9 (5899)	5	5.0	[1]	[2]	[7]	[8]	[5]	26.0[6]	20.0
	Ram Truck 3500	8.0 (7997)	W	7.0	[1]	[2]	[7]	[8]	[5]	26.0[6]	24.0
	Ram Van 1500	3.9 (3916)	X	4.0	—	[2]	—	—	[9]	22.0[6]	14.6
		5.2 (5211)	Y	5.0	—	[2]	—	—	[9]	22.0[6]	16.5
	Ram Van 2500	3.9 (3916)	X	4.0	—	[2]	—	—	[9]	22.0[6]	14.6
		5.2 (5211)	Y	5.0	—	[2]	—	—	[9]	22.0[6]	16.5
		5.9 (5899)	Z	5.0	—	[2]	—	—	[9]	35.0	15.0[10]
	Ram Van 3500	5.2 (5211)	Y	5.0	—	[2]	—	—	[9]	22.0	16.5
		5.9 (5899)	Z	5.0	—	[2]	—	—	[9]	35.0	15.0[10]
1998	Dakota	2.5 (2458)	P	4.5	[11]	[12]	—	—	[13]	[4]	9.8
		3.9 (3916)	X	4.0	[11]	[12]	2.5	3.0	[13]	[4]	14.0
		5.2 (5211)	Y	5.0	[11]	[12]	2.5	3.0	[13]	[4]	14.3
		5.9 (5899)	Z	5.0	[11]	[12]	2.5	3.0	[13]	[4]	14.3
	Durango	3.9 (3916)	X	4.0	—	[12]	[14]	3.0	[13]	25.0	14.0
		5.2 (5211)	Y	5.0	—	[12]	[14]	3.0	[13]	25.0	14.3
		5.9 (5899)	Z	5.0	—	[12]	[14]	3.0	[13]	25.0	14.3
	Ram Truck 1500	3.9 (3916)	X	4.0	4.2	3.0[15]	2.5	[16]	[17]	[18]	20.0
		5.2 (5211)	Y	5.0	4.2	3.0[15]	2.5	[16]	[17]	[18]	20.0
		5.9 (5899)	Z	5.0	—	3.0[15]	2.5	[16]	[17]	[18]	20.0
	Ram Truck 2500	5.9 (5882)	D	11.0	8.0	3.0[15]	[19]	[16]	[17]	[18]	26.0
		5.9 (5899)	Z	5.0	8.0	3.0[15]	[19]	[16]	[17]	[18]	20.0
		8.0 (7997)	W	7.0	8.0	3.0[15]	[19]	[16]	[17]	[18]	24.0
	Ram Truck 3500	5.9 (5882)	D	11.0	8.0	3.0[15]	[19]	[16]	[17]	[18]	26.0
		5.9 (5899)	5	5.0	8.0	3.0[15]	[19]	[16]	[17]	[18]	20.0
		8.0 (7997)	W	7.0	8.0	3.0[15]	[19]	[16]	[17]	[18]	24.0
	Ram Van	3.9 (3916)	X	4.0	4.2	3.0[15]	2.5	[16]	[17]	[18]	20.0
		5.2 (5211)	Y	5.0	4.2	3.0[15]	2.5	[16]	[17]	[18]	20.0
		5.9 (5899)	Z	5.0	—	3.0[15]	2.5	[16]	[17]	[18]	20.0
1999	Dakota	2.5 (2458)	P	4.5	[11]	—	—	—	[13]	[4]	9.8
		3.9 (3916)	X	4.0	[11]	[12]	2.5	3.0	[13]	[4]	14.0
		5.2 (5211)	Y	5.0	[11]	[12]	2.5	3.0	[13]	[4]	14.3
		5.9 (5899)	Z	5.0	—	[12]	2.5	3.0	[13]	[4]	14.3
	Durango	3.9 (3916)	X	4.0	—	[12]	[14]	3.0	[13]	25.0	14.0
		5.2 (5211)	Y	5.0	—	[12]	[14]	3.0	[13]	25.0	14.3
		5.9 (5899)	Z	5.0	—	[12]	[14]	3.0	[13]	25.0	14.3
	Ram Truck 1500	3.9 (3916)	X	4.0	4.2	3.0[15]	2.5	[16]	[17]	[18]	20.0
		5.2 (5211)	Y	5.0	4.2	3.0[15]	2.5	[16]	[17]	[18]	20.0
		5.9 (5899)	Z	5.0	—	3.0[15]	2.5	[16]	[17]	[18]	20.0

93081C41

Refer to the model specific sections for fuel system service procedures

CAPACITIES

Year	Model	Engine Displacement Liters (cc)	Engine ID/VIN	Oil with Filter (qts.)	Engine Transmission (pts.)		Transfer Case (pts.)	Drive Axle		Fuel Tank (gal.)	Cooling System (qts.)
					Manual	Auto.		Front (pts.)	Rear (pts.)		
1999 (cont.)	Ram Truck 2500	5.9 (5882)	6	11.0	8.0	3.0⑮	⑲	⑯	⑰	⑱	26.0
		5.9 (5899)	Z	5.0	8.0	3.0⑮	⑲	⑯	⑰	⑱	20.0
		8.0 (7997)	W	7.0	8.0	3.0⑮	⑲	⑯	⑰	⑱	24.0
	Ram Truck 3500	5.9 (5882)	6	11.0	8.0	3.0⑮	⑲	⑯	⑰	⑱	26.0
		5.9 (5899)	5	5.0	8.0	3.0⑮	⑲	⑯	⑰	⑱	20.0
		8.0 (7997)	W	7.0	8.0	3.0⑮	⑲	⑯	⑰	⑱	24.0
	Ram Van	3.9 (3916)	X	4.0	4.2	3.0⑮	2.5	⑯	⑰	⑱	20.0
		5.2 (5211)	Y	5.0	4.2	3.0⑮	2.5	⑯	⑰	⑱	20.0
		5.9 (5899)	Z	5.0	—	3.0⑮	2.5	⑯	⑰	⑱	20.0
2000-01	Dakota	2.5 (2458)	P	4.5	⑪	—	—	—	⑬	④	9.8
		3.9 (3916)	X	4.0	⑪	⑫	2.5	3.0	⑬	④	14.0
		5.2 (5211)	Y	5.0	⑪	⑫	2.5	3.0	⑬	④	14.3
		5.9 (5899)	Z	5.0	—	⑫	2.5	3.0	⑬	④	14.3
	Durango	4.7 (4701)	N	6.0	—	⑫	⑭	3.0	⑬	25.0	14.3
		5.2 (5211)	Y	5.0	—	⑫	⑭	3.0	⑬	25.0	14.3
		5.9 (5899)	Z	5.0	—	⑫	⑭	3.0	⑬	25.0	14.3
	Ram Truck 1500	3.9 (3916)	X	4.0	4.2	3.0⑮	2.5	⑯	⑰	⑱	20.0
		5.2 (5211)	Y	5.0	4.2	3.0⑮	2.5	⑯	⑰	⑱	20.0
		5.9 (5899)	Z	5.0	—	3.0⑮	2.5	⑯	⑰	⑱	20.0
	Ram Truck 2500	5.9 (5882)	6	11.0	8.0	3.0⑮	⑲	⑯	⑰	⑱	26.0
		5.9 (5899)	Z	5.0	8.0	3.0⑮	⑲	⑯	⑰	⑱	20.0
		8.0 (7997)	W	7.0	8.0	3.0⑮	⑲	⑯	⑰	⑱	24.0
	Ram Truck 3500	5.9 (5882)	6	11.0	8.0	3.0⑮	⑲	⑯	⑰	⑱	26.0
		5.9 (5899)	5	5.0	8.0	3.0⑮	⑲	⑯	⑰	⑱	20.0
		8.0 (7997)	W	7.0	8.0	3.0⑮	⑲	⑯	⑰	⑱	24.0
	Ram Van	3.9 (3916)	X	4.0	4.2	3.0⑮	2.5	⑯	⑰	⑱	20.0
		5.2 (5211)	Y	5.0	4.2	3.0⑮	2.5	⑯	⑰	⑱	20.0
		5.9 (5899)	Z	5.0	—	3.0⑮	2.5	⑯	⑰	⑱	20.0

NOTE: All capacities are approximate. Add fluid gradually and check to be sure a proper fluid level is obtained.

① NV3500: 4.2 pts.
NV4500: 8.0 pts.
AX15: 6.6 pts.
Getrag: 7.0 pts.

② 32RH: 17.0 pts.
36RH: 16.6 pts.
42RH: 20.2 pts.
32RH: 17.0 pts.
36RH: 16.6 pts.
42RH: 20.2 pts.

③ 7.25 in.: 2.9 pts.
8.25 in.: 4.4 pts.

④ Standard fuel tank: 15 gal.
Optional fuel tank: 22 gal.

⑤ Chrysler 7.25 in.: 3 pts.
Chrysler 8.25 in. and 9.25 in.
4.8 pts Spicer and Dana 60
6.0 pts.]Dana 70 and 80: 7.0 pts.

⑥ Optional fuel tank: 35 gals.

⑦ NP231HD: 2.5 pts.
NP241: 4.7 pts.
NP241HD: 6.5 pts.

⑧ 7.25 in.: 3 pts.
Dana 44: 5.6 pts.
Dana 60: 6.5 pts.

⑨ Chrysler 8.25 in.: 4.4 pts.
Chrysler 9.25 in.: 4.8 pts.
Dana 60: 6.3 pts.

⑩ With rear heater: 16.0 qts.

⑪ AX15 Transmission: 6.6 pts.
NV3500 Transmission: 4.2 pts.

⑫ Fluid drain/filter service: 8.0 pts.
Overhaul dry fill: 20-23 pts.

⑬ The following values include 0.25 pt. of friction modifier for LSD axles.
8.25 axle: 4.4 pts.
9.25 axle: 4.9 pts.

⑭ NV231: 2.5 pts.
NV231-HD: 2.5 pts.
NV242: 3.0 pts.

⑮ For fluid drain and filter replacement only.
For complete overhaul, or dry fill-
42 RE: 17-22 pts.
46 RE: 19-23 pts.
47 RE: 29-33 pts.

⑯ 216-FBI front axle: 4.8
248-FBI front axle: 7.6

⑰ 9.25 in. axle: 4.9; includes 0.25 pts. of friction modifier for LSD axles.
248-RBI axle: 6.3; includes 0.25 pts. of friction modifier for LSD axles.
267-RBI axle: 7.0; includes 0.25 pts. of friction modifier for LSD axles.
286-RBI (2WD): 6.8; includes 0.25 pts. of friction modifier for LSD axles.
286-RBI (4WD): 10.1; includes 0.4 pts. of friction modifier for LSD axles.

⑱ 119 in. wheel base models: 26 gal.
135 in. wheel base models: 26 gal.
All other models: 35 gal.

⑲ NV241: 5.0
NV241 HD: 6.5
NV241 HD w/PTO: 9.0

93081C42

DIESEL ENGINE TUNE-UP SPECIFICATIONS

| Year | Engine Displacement cu. in. (cc) | Engine ID/VIN | Valve Clearance | | Intake Valve Opens (deg.) | Injection Pump Setting (deg.) | Injection Nozzle Pressure (psi) | | Idle Speed (rpm) | Cranking Compression Pressure (psi) |
			Intake (in.)	Exhaust (in.)			New	Used		
1997	5.9 (5882)	D	0.010	0.020	NA	①	3822	NA	②	NA
1998	5.9 (5882)	D	0.010	0.020	NA	③	3394-3887	NA	④	NA
1999	5.9 (5882)	6	0.006-0.015	0.0015-0.0300	NA	⑤	4250-4750	NA	⑥	NA
2000-01	5.9 (5882)	6	0.006-0.015	0.0015-0.0300	NA	⑤	4250-4750	NA	⑥	NA

NOTE: The Vehicle Emission Control Information (VECI) label often reflects specification changes made during production. The label figures must be used if they differ from those in this chart

NA: Not Available

① Align marks on pump flange and gear housing

② Automatic transmission with A/C: 750-800 rpm
Manual transmission with A/C: 780 rpm

③ Align the marks on the crankshaft, camshaft and pump sprockets.

④ The idle speed is computer-controlled and cannot be adjusted.

⑤ Federal models with manual transmissions: 13.5 degrees BTDC
Except Federal models with manual transmissions: 14.0 degrees BTDC

⑥ Automatic transmission: 750-800 rpm
Manual transmission: 780 rpm

93081C40

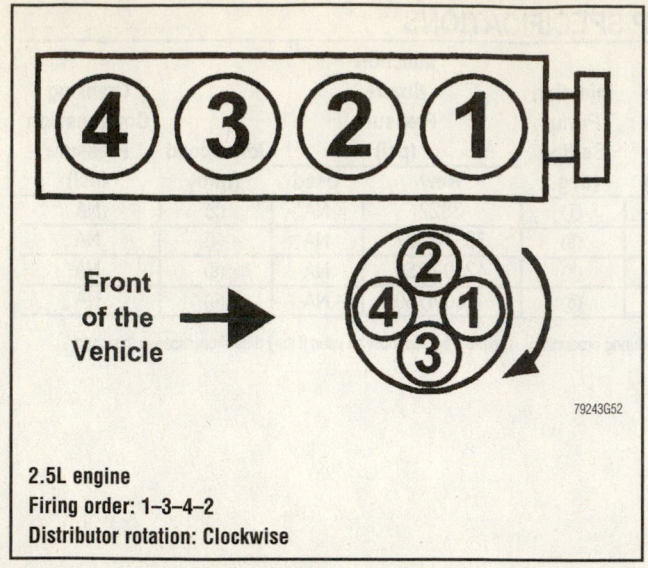

2.5L engine
Firing order: 1–3–4–2
Distributor rotation: Clockwise

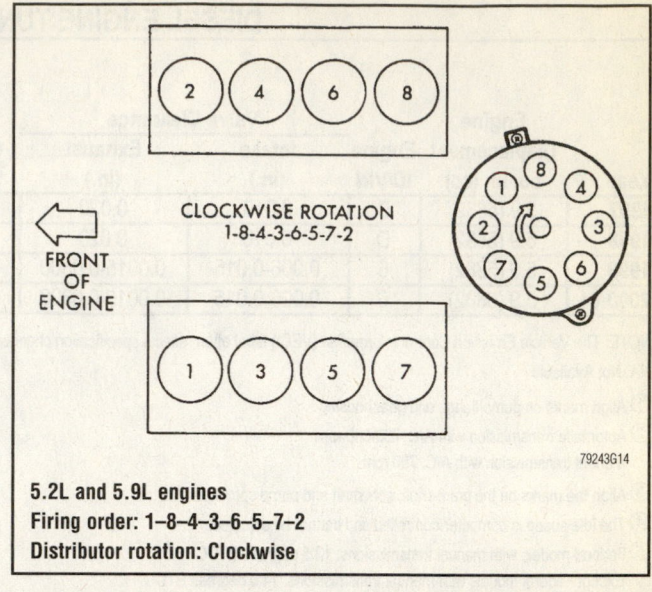

5.2L and 5.9L engines
Firing order: 1–8–4–3–6–5–7–2
Distributor rotation: Clockwise

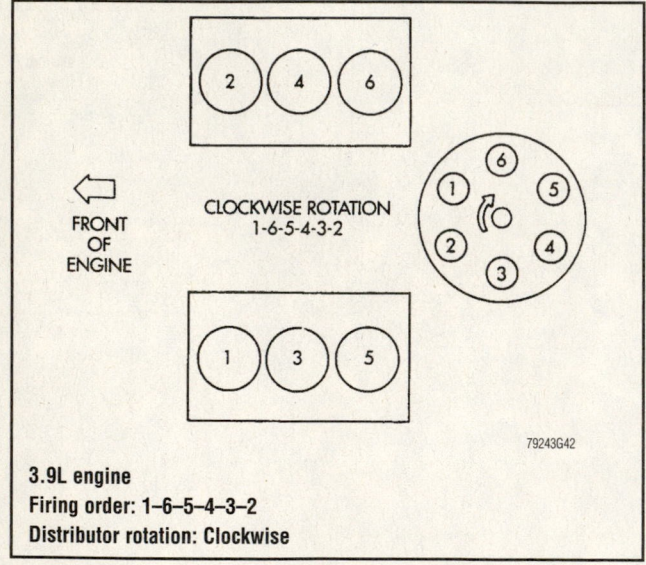

3.9L engine
Firing order: 1–6–5–4–3–2
Distributor rotation: Clockwise

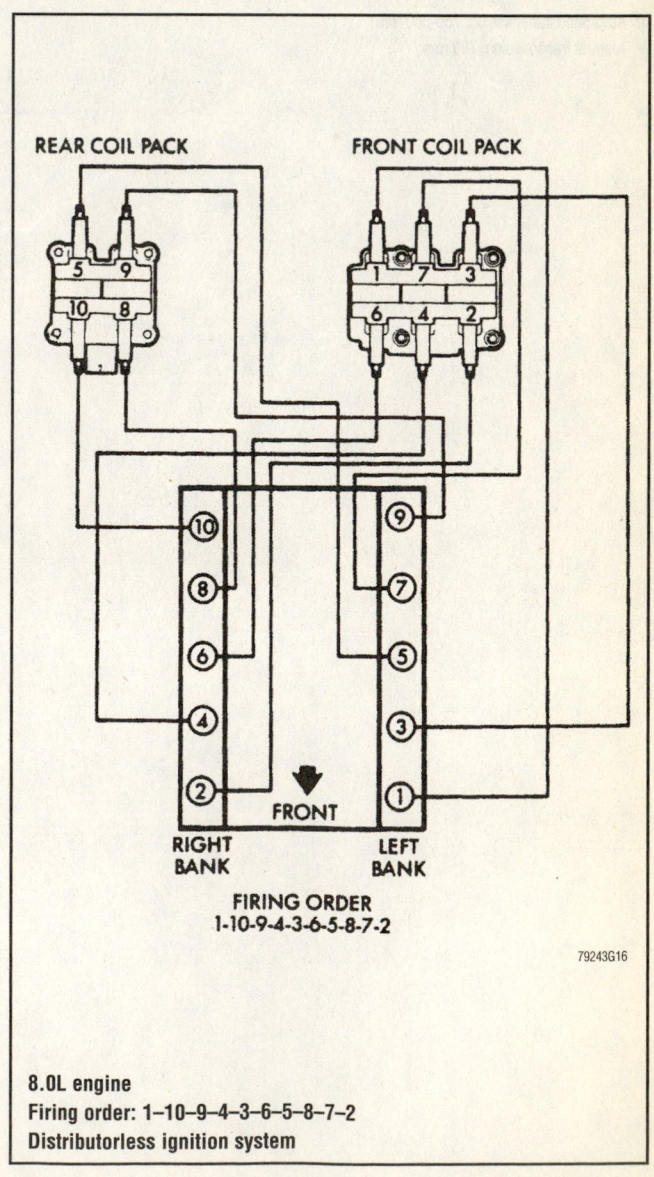

8.0L engine
Firing order: 1–10–9–4–3–6–5–8–7–2
Distributorless ignition system

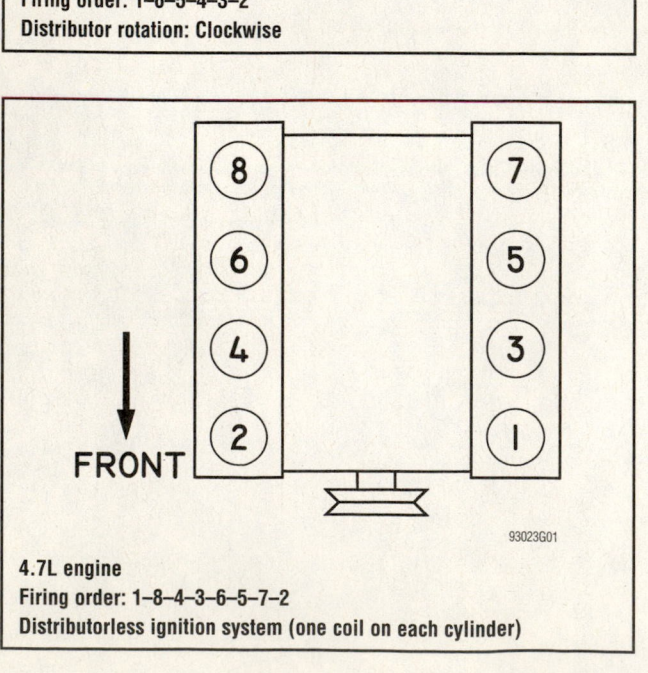

4.7L engine
Firing order: 1–8–4–3–6–5–7–2
Distributorless ignition system (one coil on each cylinder)

Refer to the model specific sections for engine mechanical service procedures

GASOLINE ENGINE TUNE-UP SPECIFICATIONS

Year	Engine Displacement Liters (cc)	Engine ID/VIN	Spark Plug Gap (in.)	Ignition Timing (deg.)	Fuel Pump (psi)	Idle Speed (rpm)	Valve Clearance Intake	Valve Clearance Exhaust
1997	2.5 (2458)	P	0.035	①	49.2	②	HYD	HYD
	3.9 (3916)	X	0.035	①	49.2	②	HYD	HYD
	5.2 (5211)	Y	0.035	①	49.2	②	HYD	HYD
	5.9 (5899)	5	0.035	①	49.2	②	HYD	HYD
	5.9 (5899)	Z	0.035	①	49.2	②	HYD	HYD
	8.0 (7997)	W	0.045	①	49.2	②	HYD	HYD
1998	2.5 (2464)	P	0.035	①	44.2 - 54.2	②	HYD	HYD
	3.9 (3916)	X	0.040	①	44.2 - 54.2	②	HYD	HYD
	5.2 (5208)	Y	0.040	①	44.2 - 54.2	②	HYD	HYD
	5.9 (5899)	5	0.040	①	44.2 - 54.2	②	HYD	HYD
	5.9 (5899)	Z	0.040	①	44.2 - 54.2	②	HYD	HYD
	8.0 (7994)	W	0.045	①	44.2 - 54.2	②	HYD	HYD
1999	2.5 (2464)	P	0.035	①	44.2 - 54.2	②	HYD	HYD
	3.9 (3916)	X	0.040	①	44.2 - 54.2	②	HYD	HYD
	5.2 (5208)	Y	0.040	①	44.2 - 54.2	②	HYD	HYD
	5.9 (5899)	5	0.040	①	44.2 - 54.2	②	HYD	HYD
	5.9 (5899)	Z	0.040	①	44.2 - 54.2	②	HYD	HYD
	8.0 (7994)	W	0.045	①	44.2 - 54.2	②	HYD	HYD
2000-01	2.5 (2464)	P	0.035	①	44.2 - 54.2	②	HYD	HYD
	3.9 (3916)	X	0.040	①	44.2 - 54.2	②	HYD	HYD
	4.7 (4701)	N	0.040	①	47-51	②	HYD	HYD
	5.2 (5208)	Y	0.040	①	44.2 - 54.2	②	HYD	HYD
	5.9 (5899)	5	0.040	①	44.2 - 54.2	②	HYD	HYD
	5.9 (5899)	Z	0.040	①	44.2 - 54.2	②	HYD	HYD
	8.0 (7994)	W	0.045	①	44.2 - 54.2	②	HYD	HYD

NOTE: The Vehicle Emission Control Information (VECI) label often reflects specification changes made during production.
The label figures must be used if they differ from those in this chart.

HYD: Hydraulic

① Ignition timing is controlled by the PCM and is not adjustable.

② Idle speed is controlled by the PCM and is not adjustable

93081C39

GENERAL ENGINE SPECIFICATIONS

Year	Model	Engine Displacement Liters (cc)	Engine Series (ID/VIN)	Fuel System	Net Horsepower @ rpm	Net Torque @ rpm (ft. lbs.)	Bore x Stroke (in.)	Compression Ratio	Oil Pressure @ rpm
1999 (cont.)	Ram Truck 1500	3.9 (3906)	X	SMFI	175@4800	220@3200	3.91x3.31	9.1:1	30-80@3000
		5.2 (5208)	Y	SMFI	220@4400	300@3200	3.91x3.31	9.1:1	30-80@3000
		5.9 (5899)	Z	SMFI	230@4000	330@3250	4.00x3.58	9.1:1	30-80@3000
	Ram Truck 2500	5.9 (5882)	6	DSL-24V	①	②	4.02x4.72	16.5	30@2500
		5.9 (5899)	Z	SMFI	230@4000	330@3250	4.00x3.58	9.1:1	30-80@3000
		8.0 (7994)	W	SMFI	300@4000	450@2400	4.00x3.58	8.4:1	50-60@3000
	Ram Truck 3500	5.9 (5882)	6	DSL-24V	①	②	4.02x4.72	16.5	30@2500
		5.9 (5899)	5	SMFI	230@4000	330@2800	4.00x3.58	8.9:1	30-80@3000
		8.0 (7994)	W	SMFI	300@4000	450@2400	4.00x3.58	8.4:1	50-60@3000
	Ram Van 1500	3.9 (3916)	X	SMFI	175@4800	220@3200	3.91x3.31	9.1:1	30-80@3000
		5.2 (5208)	Y	SMFI	220@4400	300@3200	3.91x3.31	9.1:1	30-80@3000
	Ram Van 2500	3.9 (3916)	X	SMFI	175@4800	220@3200	3.91x3.31	9.1:1	30-80@3000
		5.2 (5208)	Y	SMFI	220@4400	300@3200	3.91x3.31	9.1:1	30-80@3000
		5.9 (5899)	Z	SMFI	230@4000	330@3250	4.00x3.58	9.1:1	30-80@3000
	Ram Van 3500	5.2 (5208)	Y	SMFI	220@4400	300@3200	3.91x3.31	9.1:1	30-80@3000
		5.9 (5899)	Z	SMFI	230@4000	330@3250	4.00x3.58	9.1:1	30-80@3000
2000-01	Dakota	2.5 (2464)	P	SMFI	120@5200	145@3400	3.88x3.19	9.2:1	25-80@3000
		3.9 (3906)	X	SMFI	175@4800	220@3200	3.91x3.31	9.1:1	30-80@3000
		5.2 (5208)	Y	SMFI	220@4400	300@3200	3.91x3.31	9.1:1	30-80@3000
		5.9 (5899)	Z	SMFI	230@4000	330@3250	4.00x3.58	9.1:1	30-80@3000
	Durango	4.7 (4701)	N	SMFI	235@4800	295@3200	3.66x3.40	9.3:1	25@3000
		5.2 (5208)	Y	SMFI	220@4400	300@3200	3.91x3.31	9.1:1	30-80@3000
		5.9 (5899)	Z	SMFI	230@4000	330@3250	4.00x3.58	9.1:1	30-80@3000
	Ram Truck 1500	3.9 (3906)	X	SMFI	175@4800	220@3200	3.91x3.31	9.1:1	30-80@3000
		5.2 (5208)	Y	SMFI	220@4400	300@3200	3.91x3.31	9.1:1	30-80@3000
		5.9 (5899)	Z	SMFI	230@4000	330@3250	4.00x3.58	9.1:1	30-80@3000
	Ram Truck 2500	5.9 (5882)	6	DSL-24V	①	②	4.02x4.72	16.5	30@2500
		5.9 (5899)	Z	SMFI	230@4000	330@3250	4.00x3.58	9.1:1	30-80@3000
		8.0 (7994)	W	SMFI	300@4000	450@2400	4.00x3.58	8.4:1	50-60@3000
	Ram Truck 3500	5.9 (5882)	6	DSL-24V	①	②	4.02x4.72	16.5	30@2500
		5.9 (5899)	5	SMFI	230@4000	330@2800	4.00x3.58	8.9:1	30-80@3000
		8.0 (7994)	W	SMFI	300@4000	450@2400	4.00x3.58	8.4:1	50-60@3000
	Ram Van 1500	3.9 (3916)	X	SMFI	175@4800	220@3200	3.91x3.31	9.1:1	30-80@3000
		5.2 (5208)	Y	SMFI	220@4400	300@3200	3.91x3.31	9.1:1	30-80@3000
	Ram Van 2500	3.9 (3916)	X	SMFI	175@4800	220@3200	3.91x3.31	9.1:1	30-80@3000
		5.2 (5208)	Y	SMFI	220@4400	300@3200	3.91x3.31	9.1:1	30-80@3000
		5.9 (5899)	Z	SMFI	230@4000	330@3250	4.00x3.58	9.1:1	30-80@3000
	Ram Van 3500	5.2 (5208)	Y	SMFI	220@4400	300@3200	3.91x3.31	9.1:1	30-80@3000
		5.9 (5899)	Z	SMFI	230@4000	330@3250	4.00x3.58	9.1:1	30-80@3000

DSL-12V: Diesel engine with 12 valve cylinder head

DSL-24V: Diesel engine with 24 valve cylinder head

SMFI: Sequential Multi-port Fuel Injection

① AT: 215@2700rpm
   MT: 235@2700rpm

② AT: 420@1600rpm
   MT: 460@1600rpm

93081C38

GENERAL ENGINE SPECIFICATIONS

Year	Model	Engine Displacement Liters (cc)	Engine Series (ID/VIN)	Fuel System	Net Horsepower @ rpm	Net Torque @ rpm (ft. lbs.)	Bore x Stroke (in.)	Compression Ratio	Oil Pressure @ rpm
1997	Dakota	2.5 (2458)	P	SMFI	120@5200	145@3400	3.88x3.19	9.2:1	25-80@3000
		3.9 (3916)	X	SMFI	175@4800	220@3200	3.91x3.31	9.1:1	30-80@3000
		5.2 (5211)	Y	SMFI	220@4400	300@3200	3.91x3.31	9.1:1	30-80@3000
	Ram Truck 1500	3.9 (3916)	X	SMFI	175@4800	220@3200	3.91x3.31	9.1:1	30-80@3000
		5.2 (5211)	Y	SMFI	220@4400	300@3200	3.91x3.31	9.1:1	30-80@3000
		5.9 (5899)	Z	SMFI	230@4000	330@3250	4.00x3.58	9.1:1	30-80@3000
	Ram Truck 2500	5.2 (5211)	Y	SMFI	220@4400	300@3200	3.91x3.31	9.1:1	30-80@3000
		5.9 (5882)	D	DSL	160@2500	400@1600	4.02x4.72	17.5:1	30@2500
		5.9 (5899)	Z	SMFI	230@4000	330@3250	4.00x3.58	9.1:1	30-80@3000
		8.0 (7997)	W	SMFI	300@4000	450@2400	4.00x3.58	8.4:1	50-60@3000
	Ram Truck 3500	5.9 (5882)	D	DSL	160@2500	400@1600	4.02x4.72	17.5:1	30@2500
		5.9 (5899)	5	SMFI	230@4000	330@2800	4.00x3.58	8.9:1	30-80@3000
		8.0 (7997)	W	SMFI	300@4000	450@2400	4.00x3.58	8.4:1	50-60@3000
	Ram Van 1500	3.9 (3916)	X	SMFI	175@4800	220@3200	3.91x3.31	9.1:1	30-80@3000
		5.2 (5211)	Y	SMFI	220@4400	300@3200	3.91x3.31	9.1:1	30-80@3000
	Ram Van 2500	3.9 (3916)	X	SMFI	175@4800	220@3200	3.91x3.31	9.1:1	30-80@3000
		5.2 (5211)	Y	SMFI	220@4400	300@3200	3.91x3.31	9.1:1	30-80@3000
		5.9 (5899)	Z	SMFI	230@4000	330@3250	4.00x3.58	9.1:1	30-80@3000
	Ram Van 3500	5.2 (5211)	Y	SMFI	220@4400	300@3200	3.91x3.31	9.1:1	30-80@3000
		5.9 (5899)	Z	SMFI	230@4000	330@3250	4.00x3.58	9.1:1	30-80@3000
1998	Dakota	2.5 (2464)	P	SMFI	120@5200	145@3400	3.88x3.19	9.2:1	25-80@3000
		3.9 (3906)	X	SMFI	175@4800	220@3200	3.91x3.31	9.1:1	30-80@3000
		5.2 (5208)	Y	SMFI	220@4400	300@3200	3.91x3.31	9.1:1	30-80@3000
		5.9 (5899)	Z	SMFI	230@4000	330@3250	4.00x3.58	9.1:1	30-80@3000
	Durango	3.9 (3906)	X	SMFI	175@4800	220@3200	3.91x3.31	9.1:1	30-80@3000
		5.2 (5208)	Y	SMFI	220@4400	300@3200	3.91x3.31	9.1:1	30-80@3000
		5.9 (5899)	Z	SMFI	230@4000	330@3250	4.00x3.58	9.1:1	30-80@3000
	Ram Truck 1500	3.9 (3906)	X	SMFI	175@4800	220@3200	3.91x3.31	9.1:1	30-80@3000
		5.2 (5208)	Y	SMFI	220@4400	300@3200	3.91x3.31	9.1:1	30-80@3000
		5.9 (5899)	Z	SMFI	230@4000	330@3250	4.00x3.58	9.1:1	30-80@3000
	Ram Truck 2500	5.9 (5882)	D	DSL-12V	160@2500	400@1600	4.02x4.72	17.5:1	30@2500
		5.9 (5899)	Z	SMFI	230@4000	330@3250	4.00x3.58	9.1:1	30-80@3000
		8.0 (7994)	W	SMFI	300@4000	450@2400	4.00x3.58	8.4:1	50-60@3000
	Ram Truck 3500	5.9 (5882)	D	DSL-12V	160@2500	400@1600	4.02x4.72	17.5:1	30@2500
		5.9 (5899)	5	SMFI	230@4000	330@2800	4.00x3.58	8.9:1	30-80@3000
		8.0 (7994)	W	SMFI	300@4000	450@2400	4.00x3.58	8.4:1	50-60@3000
	Ram Van 1500	3.9 (3916)	X	SMFI	175@4800	220@3200	3.91x3.31	9.1:1	30-80@3000
		5.2 (5208)	Y	SMFI	220@4400	300@3200	3.91x3.31	9.1:1	30-80@3000
	Ram Van 2500	3.9 (3916)	X	SMFI	175@4800	220@3200	3.91x3.31	9.1:1	30-80@3000
		5.2 (5208)	Y	SMFI	220@4400	300@3200	3.91x3.31	9.1:1	30-80@3000
		5.9 (5899)	Z	SMFI	230@4000	330@3250	4.00x3.58	9.1:1	30-80@3000
	Ram Van 3500	5.2 (5208)	Y	SMFI	220@4400	300@3200	3.91x3.31	9.1:1	30-80@3000
		5.9 (5899)	Z	SMFI	230@4000	330@3250	4.00x3.58	9.1:1	30-80@3000
1999	Dakota	2.5 (2464)	P	SMFI	120@5200	145@3400	3.88x3.19	9.2:1	25-80@3000
		3.9 (3906)	X	SMFI	175@4800	220@3200	3.91x3.31	9.1:1	30-80@3000
		5.2 (5208)	Y	SMFI	220@4400	300@3200	3.91x3.31	9.1:1	30-80@3000
		5.9 (5899)	Z	SMFI	230@4000	330@3250	4.00x3.58	9.1:1	30-80@3000
	Durango	3.9 (3906)	X	SMFI	175@4800	220@3200	3.91x3.31	9.1:1	30-80@3000
		5.2 (5208)	Y	SMFI	220@4400	300@3200	3.91x3.31	9.1:1	30-80@3000
		5.9 (5899)	Z	SMFI	230@4000	330@3250	4.00x3.58	9.1:1	30-80@3000

93081C37

CHRYSLER CORP.
Dodge Dakota, Durango • RAM Trucks • RAM Vans

ENGINE AND VEHICLE IDENTIFICATION

Code ①	Liters (cc)	Cu. In.	Cyl.	Fuel Sys.	Engine Type	Eng. Mfg.
5	5.9 (5899)	360	8	SMFI	OHV	Chrysler
6	5.9 (5882)	359	6	DSL-24V	OHV	Cummins
D	5.9 (5882)	359	6	DSL-12V	OHV	Cummins
N	4.7 (4701)	287	6	SMFI	SOHC	Chrysler
P	2.5 (2507)	153	4	SMFI	OHV	Chrysler
W	8.0 (7994)	488	10	SMFI	OHV	Chrysler
X	3.9 (3916)	238	6	SMFI	OHV	Chrysler
Y	5.2 (5208)	318	8	SMFI	OHV	Chrysler
Z	5.9 (5899)	360	8	SMFI	OHV	Chrysler

Model Year	
Code ②	Year
V	1997
W	1998
X	1999
Y	2000
1	2001

OHV: Overhead Valve
DSL-12V: Diesel with 12-valve cylinder head
DSL-24V: Diesel with 24-valve cylinder head
SMFI: Sequential Multi-port Fuel Injection

① 8th position of VIN
② 10th position of VIN

93081C36

Ignition system service is covered in the model specific sections of this manual

SCHEDULED MAINTENANCE INTERVALS
DAIMLERCHRYSLER CORPORATION
CHRYSLER CARAVAN,
TOWN & COUNTRY, VOYAGER

The following should be used as a guide when determining the amount of work required for a particular service.
In estimating how long a particular Scheduled Maintenance Service should take, please observe the following:

- Labor Time is time based on field research and data supplied by the vehicle manufacturer.
- Labor time operations are given in hours and tenths of an hour.
- All labor operations are to be used as a guide.

Mechanic Skill Level Codes:
(A) PRECISION: Highly skilled with multiple certification.
(B) GENERAL: Normally skilled with certification.
(C) MAINTENANCE: Semi-skilled working on certification.

	LABOR TIME		LABOR TIME		LABOR TIME
7500 Mile Service (C)		**45000 Mile Service (C)**		**75000 Mile Service (C)**	
All Models	1.2	All Models	1.5	All Models	
				2.5L	1.3
15000 Mile Service (C)		**52500 Mile Service (C)**		3.0L, 3.3L, 3.8L	1.4
All Models	1.3	All Models	1.7		
		Replace dist. cap & rotor		**82500 Mile Service (C)**	
22500 Mile Service (C)		*add*	.4	All Models	1.7
All Models	1.4	**60000 Mile Service (B)**		**90000 Mile Service (B)**	
30000 Mile Service (B)		All Models		All Models	
All Models	2.4	2.5L	2.7	2.5L	6.0
Replace spark plugs (2.4L, 3.0L)		3.0L	8.5	3.0L	7.5
add	1.1	3.3L, 3.8L	2.8	3.3L, 3.8L	2.8
37500 Mile Service (C)		**67500 Mile Service (C)**		**97500 Mile Service (C)**	
All Models	1.2	All Models	1.4	All Models	1.2

93081C35

SCHEDULED MAINTENANCE INTERVALS
(CHRYSLER CARAVAN, TOWN & COUNTRY & VOYAGER)

TO BE SERVICED	TYPE OF SERVICE	VEHICLE MILEAGE INTERVAL (x1000)												
		7.5	15	22.5	30	37.5	45	52.5	60	67.5	75	82.5	90	97.5
Engine oil & filter	R	✓	✓	✓	✓	✓	✓	✓	✓	✓	✓	✓	✓	✓
Driveshaft boots	S/I	✓	✓	✓	✓	✓	✓	✓	✓	✓	✓	✓	✓	✓
Exhaust system	S/I	✓	✓	✓	✓	✓	✓	✓	✓	✓	✓	✓	✓	✓
Engine coolant level, hoses & clamps	S/I	✓	✓	✓	✓	✓	✓	✓	✓	✓	✓	✓	✓	✓
Rotate tires	S/I	✓	✓	✓	✓	✓	✓	✓	✓	✓	✓	✓	✓	✓
Drive belts	S/I		✓		✓		✓		✓		✓		✓	
Brake hoses & linings	S/I			✓			✓			✓			✓	
Automatic transaxle fluid & filter	R				✓				✓				✓	
Air filter	R				✓				✓				✓	
Spark plugs ①	R				✓				✓				✓	
Serpentine belts (3.0L & 3.3L)	S/I								✓		✓		✓	
Lubricate tie rod ends	S/I				✓				✓				✓	
PCV valve	S/I				✓				✓				✓	
Engine coolant	R								✓			✓		
Timing belt (3.0L)	R								✓					
Distributor cap & rotor	R							✓						
Ignition cables (3.0L)	R								✓					
Ignition timing	S/I								✓					

R: Replace   S/I: Service or Inspect

① Platinum tip spark plugs & ignition cables (3.3L & 3.8L): replace every 100,000 miles.

FREQUENT OPERATION MAINTENANCE (SEVERE SERVICE)

If a vehicle is operated under any of the following conditions it is considered severe service:

- Extremely dusty areas.

- 50% or more of the vehicle operation is in 32°C (90°F) or higher temperatures, or constant operation in temperatures below 0°C (32°F).

- Prolonged idling (vehicle operation in stop and go traffic.

- Frequent short running periods (engine does not warm to normal operating temperatures).

- Police, taxi, delivery usage or trailer towing usage.

Oil & oil filter change: change every 3000 miles.

Automatic transaxle fluid & filter: change every 15,000 miles.

Brake hoses & linings: check every 9000 miles.

CV-joints & front suspension ball joints: check every 3000 miles.

Tie rod ends & steering linkage: check every 15,000 miles.

Air filter: change every 15,000 miles.

93081C34

Timing chain and gear service is covered in the model specific sections of this manual

BRAKE SPECIFICATIONS
CHRYSLER TOWN & COUNTRY, DODGE CARAVAN, PLYMOUTH VOYAGER
All measurements in inches unless noted

Year	Model		Brake Disc			Brake Drum Diameter			Min. Lining Thickness	Caliper Guide Pin Bolts (ft. lbs.)
			Original Thickness	Minimum Thickness	Maximum Run-out	Original Inside Diameter	Max. Wear Limit	Maximum Machine Diameter		
1997	Caravan	F	0.939-0.949	0.881	0.005	—	—	—	0.313	30
		R	0.458-0.478	0.409	0.005	9.84	9.93	9.90	①	30
	Town & Country	F	0.939-0.949	0.881	0.005	—	—	—	0.313	30
		R	0.458-0.478	0.409	0.005	9.84	9.93	9.90	①	30
	Voyager	F	0.939-0.949	0.881	0.005	—	—	—	0.313	30
		R	—	—	—	9.84	9.93	9.90	0.031	30
1998	Caravan	F	0.939-0.949	0.881	0.005	—	—	—	0.313	30
		R	0.482-0.502	0.443	0.005	9.84	9.93	9.90	①	16
	Town & Country	F	0.939-0.949	0.881	0.005	—	—	—	0.313	30
		R	0.482-0.502	0.443	0.005	9.84	9.93	9.90	①	16
	Voyager	F	0.939-0.949	0.881	0.005	—	—	—	0.313	30
		R	—	—	—	9.84	9.93	9.90	0.031	16
1999	Caravan	F	0.939-0.949	0.881	0.005	—	—	—	0.313	16
		R	0.482-0.502	0.443	0.005	9.84	9.93	9.90	①	16
	Town & Country	F	0.939-0.949	0.881	0.005	—	—	—	0.313	16
		R	0.482-0.502	0.443	0.005	9.84	9.93	9.90	①	16
	Voyager	F	0.939-0.949	0.881	0.005	—	—	—	0.313	16
		R	—	—	—	9.84	9.93	9.90	0.031	16
2000-01	Caravan	F	0.939-0.949	0.881	0.005	—	—	—	0.313	16
		R	0.482-0.502	0.443	0.005	9.84	9.93	9.90	①	16
	Town & Country	F	0.939-0.949	0.881	0.005	—	—	—	0.313	16
		R	0.482-0.502	0.443	0.005	9.84	9.93	9.90	①	16
	Voyager	F	0.939-0.949	0.881	0.005	—	—	—	0.313	16
		R	—	—	—	9.84	9.93	9.90	0.031	16

F: Front

R: Rear

① Drum brakes: 0.031 in
   Disc brakes: 0.281 in.

93081C33

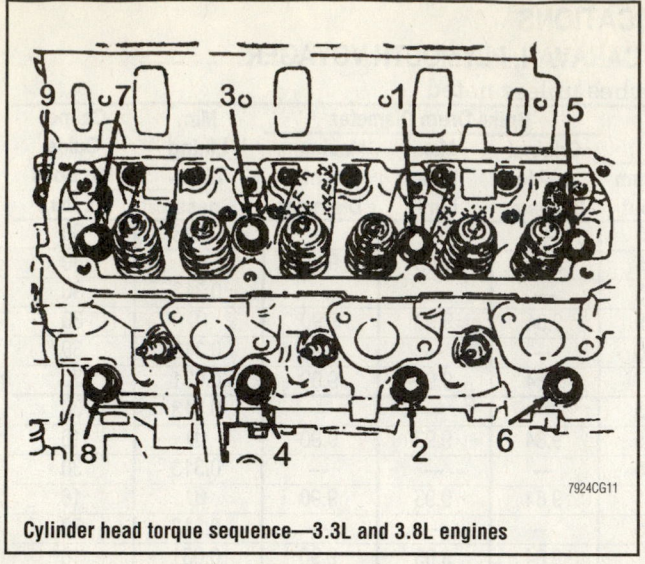

Cylinder head torque sequence—3.3L and 3.8L engines

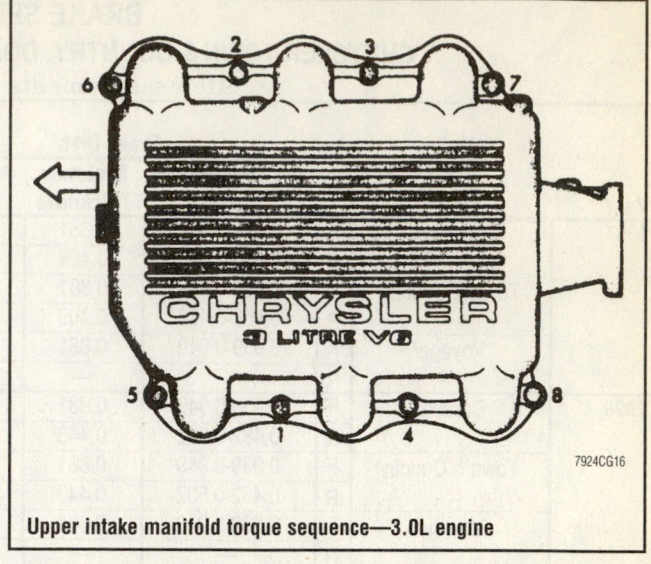

Upper intake manifold torque sequence—3.0L engine

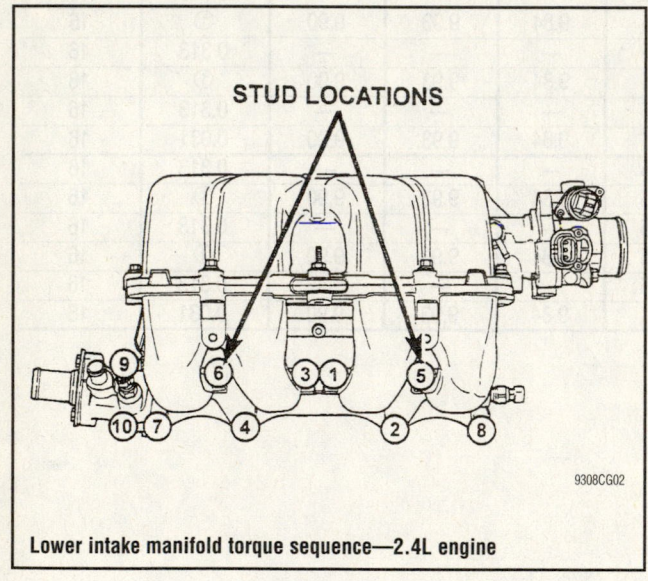

Lower intake manifold torque sequence—2.4L engine

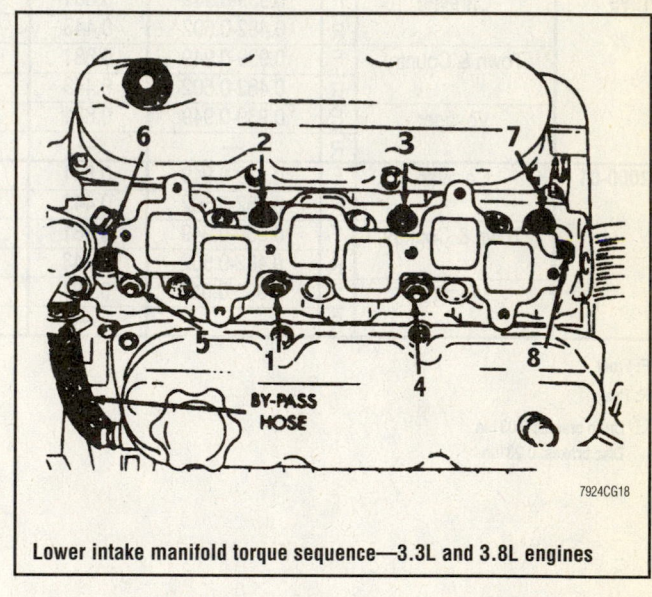

Lower intake manifold torque sequence—3.3L and 3.8L engines

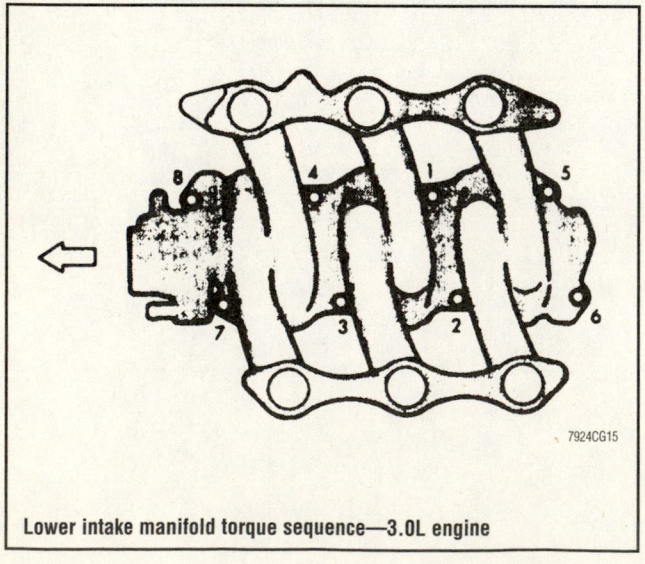

Lower intake manifold torque sequence—3.0L engine

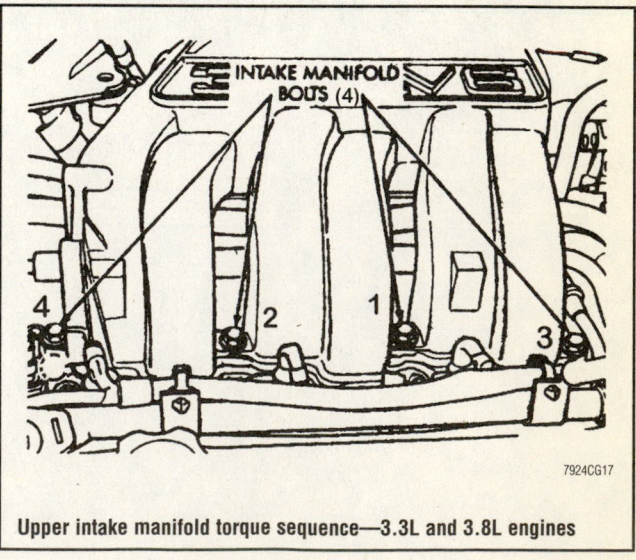

Upper intake manifold torque sequence—3.3L and 3.8L engines

VALVE SPECIFICATIONS

Year	Engine Displacement Liters (cc)	Engine ID/VIN	Seat Angle (deg.)	Face Angle (deg.)	Spring Test Pressure (lbs. @ in.)	Spring Installed Height (in.)	Stem-to-Guide Clearance (in.)		Stem Diameter (in.)	
							Intake	Exhaust	Intake	Exhaust
1997	2.4 (2429)	B	45	44.5-45.0	129-143@1.17	1.50	0.0018-0.0025	0.0029-0.0037	0.2340	0.2330
	3.0 (2972)	3	44.5	45.5	73@1.59	1.59	0.0010-0.0020	0.0020-0.0030	0.3130-0.3140	0.3120-0.3130
	3.3 (3300)	R	45	44.5	207-229@1.17	1.62-1.68	0.0010-0.0030	0.0020-0.0060	0.3120-0.3130	0.3110-0.3120
	3.8 (3785)	L	45	44.5	207-229@1.17	1.62-1.68	0.0010-0.0030	0.0020-0.0060	0.3120-0.3130	0.3110-0.3120
1998	2.4 (2429)	B	45	44.5-45.0	129-143@1.17	1.50	0.0018-0.0025	0.0029-0.0037	0.2340	0.2330
	3.0 (2972)	3	44.0-44.3	45.0-45.3	73@1.59	1.59	0.0010-0.0040	0.0020-0.0060	0.3130-0.3140	0.3120-0.3125
	3.3 (3300)	R	45.0-45.5	①	207-229@1.169	1.62-1.68	0.0010-0.0030	0.0020-0.0060	0.3120-0.3130	0.3112-0.3119
	3.8 (3785)	L	45.0-45.5	①	207-229@1.169	1.62-1.68	0.0010-0.0030	0.0020-0.0060	0.3120-0.3130	0.3112-0.3119
1999	2.4 (2429)	B	45	44.5-45.0	129-143@1.17	1.50	0.0018-0.0025	0.0029-0.0037	0.2340	0.2330
	3.0 (2972)	3	44.0-44.3	45.0-45.3	73@1.59	1.59	0.0010-0.0040	0.0020-0.0060	0.3130-0.3140	0.3120-0.3125
	3.3 (3300)	R	45.0-45.5	①	207-229@1.169	1.62-1.68	0.0010-0.0030	0.0020-0.0060	0.3120-0.3130	0.3112-0.3119
	3.8 (3785)	L	45.0-45.5	①	207-229@1.169	1.62-1.68	0.0010-0.0030	0.0020-0.0060	0.3120-0.3130	0.3112-0.3119
2000-01	2.4 (2429)	B	45	44.5-45.0	129-143@1.17	1.50	0.0018-0.0025	0.0029-0.0037	0.2340	0.2330
	3.0 (2972)	3	44.0-44.3	45.0-45.3	73@1.59	1.59	0.0010-0.0040	0.0020-0.0060	0.3130-0.3140	0.3120-0.3125
	3.3 (3300)	R	45.0-45.5	①	207-229@1.169	1.62-1.68	0.0010-0.0030	0.0020-0.0060	0.3120-0.3130	0.3112-0.3119
	3.8 (3785)	L	45.0-45.5	①	207-229@1.169	1.62-1.68	0.0010-0.0030	0.0020-0.0060	0.3120-0.3130	0.3112-0.3119

① Intake valve: 44.5 degrees
Exhaust valve: 45 degrees

93081C29

For exhaust manifold replacement procedures, see the model specific sections of this manual

CRANKSHAFT AND CONNECTING ROD SPECIFICATIONS

All measurements are given in inches.

Year	Engine Displacement Liters (cc)	Engine ID/VIN	Crankshaft				Connecting Rod		
			Main Brg. Journal Dia.	Main Brg. Oil Clearance	Shaft End-play	Thrust on No.	Journal Diameter	Oil Clearance	Side Clearance
1997	2.4 (2429)	B	2.3610-2.3625	0.0007-0.0023	0.0035-0.0094	2	1.9670-1.9685	0.0009-0.0027	0.0051-0.0150
	3.0 (2972)	3	2.3610-2.3620	0.0007-0.0014	0.0020-0.0100	2	1.9680-1.9690	0.0007-0.0014	0.0040-0.0100
	3.3 (3300)	R	2.5202-2.5195	0.0023-0.0043	0.0036-0.0095	2	2.1240-2.1250	0.0008-0.0026	0.0050-0.0150
	3.8 (3785)	L	2.5202-2.5195	0.0023-0.0043	0.0036-0.0095	2	2.1240-2.1250	0.0008-0.0026	0.0050-0.0150
1998	2.4 (2429)	B	2.3610-2.3625	0.0007-0.0023	0.0035-0.0094	2	1.9670-1.9685	0.0009-0.0027	0.0051-0.0150
	3.0 (2972)	3	2.3610-2.3620	0.0007-0.0014	0.0020-0.0100	2	1.9680-1.9690	0.0007-0.0014	0.0040-0.0100
	3.3 (3300)	R	2.5202-2.5195	0.0023-0.0043	0.0036-0.0095	2	2.1240-2.1250	0.0008-0.0026	0.0050-0.0150
	3.8 (3785)	L	2.5202-2.5195	0.0023-0.0043	0.0036-0.0095	2	2.1240-2.1250	0.0008-0.0026	0.0050-0.0150
1999	2.4 (2429)	B	2.3610-2.3625	0.0007-0.0023	0.0035-0.0094	2	1.9670-1.9685	0.0009-0.0027	0.0051-0.0150
	3.0 (2972)	3	2.3610-2.3620	0.0007-0.0014	0.0020-0.0100	2	1.9680-1.9690	0.0007-0.0014	0.0040-0.0100
	3.3 (3300)	R	2.5202-2.5195	0.0023-0.0043	0.0036-0.0095	2	2.1240-2.1250	0.0008-0.0026	0.0050-0.0150
	3.8 (3785)	L	2.5202-2.5195	0.0023-0.0043	0.0036-0.0095	2	2.1240-2.1250	0.0008-0.0026	0.0050-0.0150
2000-01	2.4 (2429)	B	2.3610-2.3625	0.0007-0.0023	0.0035-0.0094	2	1.9670-1.9685	0.0009-0.0027	0.0051-0.0150
	3.0 (2972)	3	2.3610-2.3620	0.0007-0.0014	0.0020-0.0100	2	1.9680-1.9690	0.0007-0.0014	0.0040-0.0100
	3.3 (3300)	R	2.5202-2.5195	0.0023-0.0043	0.0036-0.0095	2	2.1240-2.1250	0.0008-0.0026	0.0050-0.0150
	3.8 (3785)	L	2.5202-2.5195	0.0023-0.0043	0.0036-0.0095	2	2.1240-2.1250	0.0008-0.0026	0.0050-0.0150

93081C30

PISTON AND RING SPECIFICATIONS
All measurements are given in inches.

Year	Engine Displacement Liters (cc)	Engine ID/VIN	Piston Clearance	Ring Gap			Ring Side Clearance		
				Top Compression	Bottom Compression	Oil Control	Top Compression	Bottom Compression	Oil Control
1997	2.4 (2429)	B	0.0009-0.0022	0.0098-0.0200	0.0090-0.0180	0.0098-0.0250	0.0011-0.0031	0.0011-0.0031	0.0004-0.0070
	3.0 (2972)	3	0.0012-0.0020	0.0120-0.0180	0.0180-0.0240	0.0080-0.0240	0.0012-0.0028	0.0008-0.0024	①
	3.3 (3300)	R	0.0010-0.0022	0.0118-0.0217	0.0118-0.0217	0.0098-0.0394	0.0012-0.0037	0.0012-0.0037	0.0005-0.0089
	3.8 (3785)	L	0.0010-0.0022	0.0118-0.0217	0.0118-0.0217	0.0098-0.0394	0.0012-0.0037	0.0012-0.0037	0.0005-0.0089
1998	2.4 (2429)	B	0.0009-0.0022	0.0098-0.0200	0.0090-0.0180	0.0098-0.0250	0.0011-0.0031	0.0011-0.0031	0.0004-0.0070
	3.0 (2972)	3	0.0012-0.0020	0.0120-0.0180	0.0180-0.0240	0.0080-0.0240	0.0012-0.0028	0.0008-0.0024	①
	3.3 (3300)	R	0.0010-0.0022	0.0118-0.0217	0.0118-0.0217	0.0098-0.0394	0.0012-0.0037	0.0012-0.0037	0.0005-0.0089
	3.8 (3785)	L	0.0010-0.0022	0.0118-0.0217	0.0118-0.0217	0.0098-0.0394	0.0012-0.0037	0.0012-0.0037	0.0005-0.0089
1999	2.4 (2429)	B	0.0009-0.0022	0.0098-0.0200	0.0090-0.0180	0.0098-0.0250	0.0011-0.0031	0.0011-0.0031	0.0004-0.0070
	3.0 (2972)	3	0.0012-0.0020	0.0120-0.0180	0.0180-0.0240	0.0080-0.0240	0.0012-0.0028	0.0008-0.0024	①
	3.3 (3300)	R	0.0010-0.0022	0.0118-0.0217	0.0118-0.0217	0.0098-0.0394	0.0012-0.0037	0.0012-0.0037	0.0005-0.0089
	3.8 (3785)	L	0.0010-0.0022	0.0118-0.0217	0.0118-0.0217	0.0098-0.0394	0.0012-0.0037	0.0012-0.0037	0.0005-0.0089
2000-01	2.4 (2429)	B	0.0009-0.0022	0.0098-0.0200	0.0090-0.0180	0.0098-0.0250	0.0011-0.0031	0.0011-0.0031	0.0004-0.0070
	3.0 (2972)	3	0.0012-0.0020	0.0120-0.0180	0.0180-0.0240	0.0080-0.0240	0.0012-0.0028	0.0008-0.0024	①
	3.3 (3300)	R	0.0010-0.0022	0.0118-0.0217	0.0118-0.0217	0.0098-0.0394	0.0012-0.0037	0.0012-0.0037	0.0005-0.0089
	3.8 (3785)	L	0.0010-0.0022	0.0118-0.0217	0.0118-0.0217	0.0098-0.0394	0.0012-0.0037	0.0012-0.0037	0.0005-0.0089

① Oil control ring side rails must be free to rotate after assembly

93081C31

Refer to the model specific sections for cooling system service procedures

TORQUE SPECIFICATIONS
All readings in ft. lbs.

Year	Engine Displacement Liters (cc)	Engine ID/VIN	Cylinder Head Bolts	Main Bearing Bolts	Rod Bearing Bolts	Crankshaft Damper Bolts	Flywheel Bolts	Manifold		Spark Plugs	Lug Nuts
								Intake	Exhaust		
1997	2.4 (2429)	B	①	②	③	100	70	20	17	20	95
	3.0 (2972)	3	80	②	③	112	70	20	17	20	95
	3.3 (3300)	R	④	⑤	⑥	40	70	17	17	20	95
	3.8 (3785)	L	④	⑤	⑥	40	70	17	17	20	95
1998	2.4 (2429)	B	①	②	③	100	70	20	17	20	85-115
	3.0 (2972)	3	80	②	③	100	70	20	17	20	85-115
	3.3 (3300)	R	④	⑤	⑥	40	70	17	17	20	85-115
	3.8 (3785)	L	④	⑤	⑥	40	70	17	17	20	85-115
1999	2.4 (2429)	B	①	②	③	100	70	20	17	20	85-115
	3.0 (2972)	3	80	②	③	100	70	20	17	20	85-115
	3.3 (3300)	R	④	⑤	⑥	40	70	17	17	20	85-115
	3.8 (3785)	L	④	⑤	⑥	40	70	17	17	20	85-115
2000-01	2.4 (2429)	B	①	②	③	100	70	20	17	20	85-115
	3.0 (2972)	3	80	②	③	100	70	20	17	20	85-115
	3.3 (3300)	R	④	⑤	⑥	40	70	17	17	20	85-115
	3.8 (3785)	L	④	⑤	⑥	40	70	17	17	20	85-115

① Step 1: 25 ft. lbs.
  Step 2: 50 ft. lbs.
  Step 3: 50 ft. lbs.
  Step 4: Plus 1/4 turn

② M8 bolts: 21 ft. lbs.
  M11 bolts: 30 ft. lbs. plus 90 degrees

③ Step 1: 20 ft. lbs.
  Step 2: Plus 90 degrees

④ Step 1: 45 ft. lbs.
  Step 2: 65 ft. lbs.
  Step 3: 65 ft. lbs.
  Step 4: Plus 90 degrees

⑤ Step 1: 30 ft. lbs.
  Step 2: Plus 90 degrees

⑥ Step 1: 40 ft. lbs.
  Step 2: Plus 90 degrees

93081C32

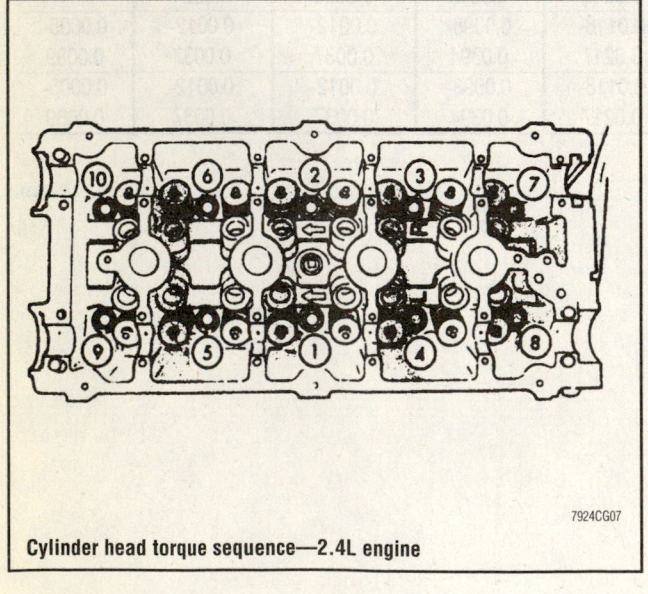

Cylinder head torque sequence—2.4L engine

7924CG07

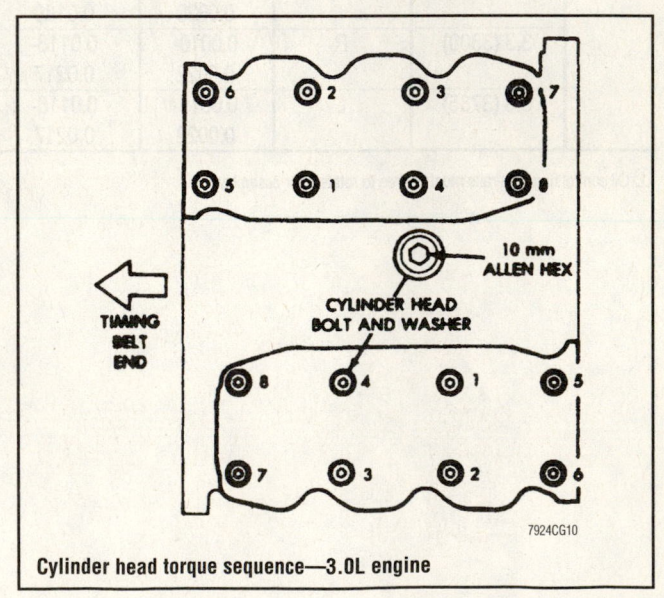

10 mm ALLEN HEX

CYLINDER HEAD BOLT AND WASHER

TIMING BELT END

Cylinder head torque sequence—3.0L engine

7924CG10

VALVE SPECIFICATIONS

Year	Engine Displacement Liters (cc)	Engine ID/VIN	Seat Angle (deg.)	Face Angle (deg.)	Spring Test Pressure (lbs. @ in.)	Spring Installed Height (in.)	Stem-to-Guide Clearance (in.)		Stem Diameter (in.)	
							Intake	Exhaust	Intake	Exhaust
1997	2.5 (2507)	P	45.0	45.0	184-196@ 1.22	1.65	0.001- 0.003	0.001- 0.003	0.311- 0.312	0.311- 0.312
	3.9 (3916)	X	44.25- 44.75	43.25- 43.75	200@1.21	1.64	0.001- 0.003	0.001- 0.003	0.311- 0.312	0.311- 0.312
	5.2 (5211)	Y	44.25- 44.75	43.25- 43.75	200@1.21	1.64	0.001- 0.003	0.001- 0.003	0.311- 0.312	0.311- 0.312
	5.9 (5882)	D	①	①	81@1.94	2.36	0.002- 0.006	0.002- 0.006	0.313- 0.314	0.313- 0.314
	5.9 (5899)	5	44.25- 44.75	43.25- 43.75	200@1.21	1.64	0.001- 0.003	0.002- 0.004	0.372- 0.373	0.371- 0.372
	5.9 (5899)	Z	44.25- 44.75	43.25- 43.75	200@1.21	1.64	0.001- 0.003	0.002- 0.004	0.372- 0.373	0.371- 0.372
	8.0 (7997)	W	44.5	45.0	190-210@ 1.22	1.64	0.001- 0.003	0.001- 0.003	0.311- 0.312	0.311- 0.312
1998	2.5 (2458)	P	44.5	45.0	184-196@ 1.216	1.64	0.001- 0.003	0.001- 0.003	0.311- 0.312	0.311- 0.312
	3.9 (3916)	X	44.25- 44.75	43.25- 43.75	200@1.21	1.64	0.001- 0.003	0.001- 0.003	0.311- 0.312	0.311- 0.312
	5.2 (5208)	Y	44.25- 44.75	43.25- 43.75	200@1.21	1.64	0.001- 0.003	0.001- 0.003	0.311- 0.312	0.311- 0.312
	5.9 (5899)	Z	44.25- 44.75	43.25- 43.75	200@1.21	1.64	0.001- 0.003	0.002- 0.004	0.372- 0.373	0.371- 0.372
	5.9 (5825)	D	①	①	81@1.94	1.94	0.003- 0.005	0.003- 0.005	0.313- 0.313	0.313- 0.313
	5.9 (5825)	6	①	①	76.4@1.39	1.39	0.002	0.002	0.275- 0.276	0.275- 0.276
	8.0 (7994)	W	44.5	45.0	200@1.212	1.64	0.001- 0.003	0.001- 0.003	0.311- 0.312	0.311- 0.312
	5.9 (5899)	5	44.25- 44.75	43.25- 43.75	200@1.21	1.64	0.001- 0.003	0.002- 0.004	0.372- 0.373	0.371- 0.372
1999	2.5 (2458)	P	44.5	45.0	184-196@ 1.216	1.64	0.001- 0.003	0.001- 0.003	0.311- 0.312	0.311- 0.312
	3.9 (3916)	X	44.25- 44.75	43.25- 43.75	200@1.21	1.64	0.001- 0.003	0.001- 0.003	0.311- 0.312	0.311- 0.312
	5.2 (5208)	Y	44.25- 44.75	43.25- 43.75	200@1.21	1.64	0.001- 0.003	0.001- 0.003	0.311- 0.312	0.311- 0.312
	5.9 (5899)	Z	44.25- 44.75	43.25- 43.75	200@1.21	1.64	0.001- 0.003	0.002- 0.004	0.372- 0.373	0.371- 0.372
	5.9 (5825)	6	①	①	76.4@1.39	1.39	0.002	0.002	0.275- 0.276	0.275- 0.276
	8.0 (7994)	W	44.5	45.0	200@1.212	1.64	0.001- 0.003	0.001- 0.003	0.311- 0.312	0.311- 0.312
	5.9 (5899)	5	44.25- 44.75	43.25- 43.75	200@1.21	1.64	0.001- 0.003	0.002- 0.004	0.372- 0.373	0.371- 0.372

93081C43

Refer to the model specific sections for engine electrical system service procedures

VALVE SPECIFICATIONS

Year	Engine Displacement Liters (cc)	Engine ID/VIN	Seat Angle (deg.)	Face Angle (deg.)	Spring Test Pressure (lbs. @ in.)	Spring Installed Height (in.)	Stem-to-Guide Clearance (in.)		Stem Diameter (in.)	
							Intake	Exhaust	Intake	Exhaust
2000-01	2.5 (2458)	P	44.5	45.0	184-196@ 1.216	1.64	0.001-0.003	0.001-0.003	0.311-0.312	0.311-0.312
	3.9 (3916)	X	44.25-44.75	43.25-43.75	200@1.21	1.64	0.001-0.003	0.001-0.003	0.311-0.312	0.311-0.312
	4.7 (4701)	N	44.5-45	45-45.5	176.2-192.4 @1.1532	1.602	0.0011-0.0017	0.0029	0.2728-0.2739	0.2717-0.2728
	5.2 (5208)	Y	44.25-44.75	43.25-43.75	200@1.21	1.64	0.001-0.003	0.001-0.003	0.311-0.312	0.311-0.312
	5.9 (5899)	Z	44.25-44.75	43.25-43.75	200@1.21	1.64	0.001-0.003	0.002-0.004	0.372-0.373	0.371-0.372
	5.9 (5825)	6	①	①	76.4@1.39	1.39	0.002	0.002	0.275-0.276	0.275-0.276
	8.0 (7994)	W	44.5	45.0	200@1.212	1.64	0.001-0.003	0.001-0.003	0.311-0.312	0.311-0.312
	5.9 (5899)	5	44.25-44.75	43.25-43.75	200@1.21	1.64	0.001-0.003	0.002-0.004	0.372-0.373	0.371-0.372

① Intake: 30 degrees
　Exhaust: 45 degrees

93081C44

CRANKSHAFT AND CONNECTING ROD SPECIFICATIONS
All measurements are given in inches.

Year	Engine Displacement Liters (cc)	Engine ID/VIN	Crankshaft Main Brg. Journal Dia.	Crankshaft Main Brg. Oil Clearance	Crankshaft Shaft End-play	Crankshaft Thrust on No.	Connecting Rod Journal Diameter	Connecting Rod Oil Clearance	Connecting Rod Side Clearance
1997	2.5 (2507)	P	2.4996-2.5001	0.0010-0.0025	0.0015-0.0065	2	2.2080-2.2085	0.0015-0.0020	0.0100-0.0190
	3.9 (3916)	X	2.4995-2.5005	0.0005-0.0015	0.0020-0.0070	2	2.1240-2.1250	0.0005-0.0022	0.0060-0.0140
	5.2 (5211)	Y	2.4995-2.5005	0.0005-0.0015	0.0020-0.0070	2	2.1240-2.1250	0.0005-0.0022	0.0060-0.0140
	5.9 (5882)	D	3.2662	0.0047	0.0040-0.0017	2	2.7150	0.0035	0.0040-0.0120
	5.9 (5899)	5	2.8095-2.8105	0.0005-0.0015	0.0020-0.0070	2	2.1240-2.1250	0.0005-0.0022	0.0060-0.0140
	5.9 (5899)	Z	2.8095-2.8105	0.0005-0.0015	0.0020-0.0070	2	2.1240-2.1250	0.0005-0.0022	0.0060-0.0140
	8.0 (7997)	W	2.9995-3.0005	0.0002-0.0023	0.0030-0.0120	2	2.1240-2.1250	0.0002-0.0029	0.0100-0.0180
1998	2.5 (2507)	P	2.4996-2.5001	0.0010-0.0025	0.0015-0.0065	2	2.2080-2.2085	0.0015-0.0020	0.0100-0.0190
	3.9 (3916)	X	2.4995-2.5005	0.0005-0.0015	0.0020-0.0070	2	2.1240-2.1250	0.0005-0.0022	0.0060-0.0140
	5.2 (5211)	Y	2.4995-2.5005	0.0005-0.0015	0.0020-0.0070	2	2.1240-2.1250	0.0005-0.0022	0.0060-0.0140
	5.9 (5882)	D	3.2662	0.0047	0.0040-0.0017	2	2.7150	0.0035	0.0040-0.0120
	5.9 (5899)	5	2.8095-2.8105	0.0005-0.0015	0.0020-0.0070	2	2.1240-2.1250	0.0005-0.0022	0.0060-0.0140
	5.9 (5899)	Z	2.8095-2.8105	0.0005-0.0015	0.0020-0.0070	2	2.1240-2.1250	0.0005-0.0022	0.0060-0.0140
	8.0 (7997)	W	2.9995-3.0005	0.0002-0.0023	0.0030-0.0120	2	2.1240-2.1250	0.0002-0.0029	0.0100-0.0180
1999	2.5 (2507)	P	2.4996-2.5001	0.0010-0.0025	0.0015-0.0065	2	2.2080-2.2085	0.0015-0.0020	0.010-0.0190
	3.9 (3916)	X	2.4995-2.5005	0.0005-0.0015	0.0020-0.0070	2	2.1240-2.1250	0.0005-0.0022	0.0060-0.0140
	5.2 (5211)	Y	2.4995-2.5005	0.0005-0.0015	0.0020-0.0070	2	2.1240-2.1250	0.0005-0.0022	0.0060-0.0140
	5.9 (5882)	6	3.2662	0.0047	0.0040-0.0017	2	2.7150	0.0035	0.0040-0.0120
	5.9 (5899)	5	2.8095-2.8105	0.0005-0.0015	0.0020-0.0070	2	2.1240-2.1250	0.0005-0.0022	0.0060-0.0140
	5.9 (5899)	Z	2.8095-2.8105	0.0005-0.0015	0.0020-0.0070	2	2.1240-2.1250	0.0005-0.0022	0.0060-0.0140
	8.0 (7997)	W	2.9995-3.0005	0.0002-0.0023	0.0030-0.0120	2	2.1240-2.1250	0.0002-0.0029	0.0100-0.0180

93081C45

For accessory drive belt replacement procedures see the model specific sections of this manual

CRANKSHAFT AND CONNECTING ROD SPECIFICATIONS

All measurements are given in inches.

Year	Engine Displacement Liters (cc)	Engine ID/VIN	Crankshaft Main Brg. Journal Dia.	Crankshaft Main Brg. Oil Clearance	Crankshaft Shaft End-play	Crankshaft Thrust on No.	Connecting Rod Journal Diameter	Connecting Rod Oil Clearance	Connecting Rod Side Clearance
2000-01	2.5 (2507)	P	2.4996-2.5001	0.0010-0.0025	0.0015-0.0065	2	2.2080-2.2085	0.0015-0.0020	0.010-0.0190
	3.9 (3916)	X	2.4995-2.5005	0.0005-0.0015	0.0020-0.0070	2	2.1240-2.1250	0.0005-0.0022	0.0060-0.0140
	4.7 (4701)	N	2.4996-2.5005	0.0002-0.0013	0.0021-0.0112	2	2.0076-2.0082	0.0004-0.0019	0.0040-0.0138
	5.2 (5211)	Y	2.4995-2.5005	0.0005-0.0015	0.0020-0.0070	2	2.1240-2.1250	0.0005-0.0022	0.0060-0.0140
	5.9 (5882)	6	3.2662	0.0047	0.0040-0.0017	2	2.7150	0.0035	0.0040-0.0120
	5.9 (5899)	5	2.8095-2.8105	0.0005-0.0015	0.0020-0.0070	2	2.1240-2.1250	0.0005-0.0022	0.0060-0.0140
	5.9 (5899)	Z	2.8095-2.8105	0.0005-0.0015	0.0020-0.0070	2	2.1240-2.1250	0.0005-0.0022	0.0060-0.0140
	8.0 (7997)	W	2.9995-3.0005	0.0002-0.0023	0.0030-0.0120	2	2.1240-2.1250	0.0002-0.0029	0.0100-0.0180

93081C46

PISTON AND RING SPECIFICATIONS
All measurements are given in inches.

Year	Engine Displacement Liters (cc)	Engine ID/VIN	Piston Clearance	Ring Gap			Ring Side Clearance		
				Top Compression	Bottom Compression	Oil Control	Top Compression	Bottom Compression	Oil Control
1997	2.5 (2507)	P	0.0013-0.0021	0.0090-0.0240	0.0190-0.0380	0.0100-0.0600	0.0017-0.0033	0.0017-0.0033	0.0024-0.0083
	3.9 (3916)	X	0.0005-0.0015	0.0100-0.0200	0.0100-0.0200	0.0020-0.0080	0.0015-0.0030	0.0015-0.0030	0.1515-0.1565
	5.2 (5211)	Y	0.0005-0.0015	0.0100-0.0200	0.0100-0.0200	0.0100-0.0500	0.0015-0.0030	0.0015-0.0030	0.0020-0.0080
	5.9 (5882)	D	NA	0.0160-0.0275	0.0100-0.0215	0.0100-0.0215	0.0037	0.0037	0.0033
	5.9 (5899)	5	0.0005-0.0015	0.0120-0.0220	0.0220-0.0310	0.0150-0.0550	0.0016-0.0033	0.0016-0.0033	0.0020-0.0080
	5.9 (5899)	Z	0.0005-0.0015	0.0120-0.0220	0.0220-0.0310	0.0150-0.0550	0.0016-0.0033	0.0016-0.0033	0.0020-0.0080
	8.0 (7997)	W	0.0005-0.0015	0.0100-0.0200	0.0100-0.0200	0.0150-0.0550	0.0029-0.0038	0.0029-0.0038	0.0073-0.0097
1998	2.5 (2507)	P	0.0013-0.0021	0.0090-0.0240	0.0190-0.0380	0.0100-0.0600	0.0017-0.0033	0.0017-0.0033	0.0024-0.0083
	3.9 (3916)	X	0.0005-0.0015	0.0100-0.0200	0.0100-0.0200	0.0020-0.0080	0.0015-0.0030	0.0015-0.0030	0.1515-0.1565
	5.2 (5211)	Y	0.0005-0.0015	0.0100-0.0200	0.0100-0.0200	0.0100-0.0500	0.0015-0.0030	0.0015-0.0030	0.0020-0.0080
	5.9 (5882)	D	NA	0.0160-0.0275	0.0100-0.0215	0.0100-0.0215	0.0037	0.0037	0.0033
	5.9 (5899)	5	0.0005-0.0015	0.0120-0.0220	0.0220-0.0310	0.0150-0.0550	0.0016-0.0033	0.0016-0.0033	0.0020-0.0080
	5.9 (5899)	Z	0.0005-0.0015	0.0120-0.0220	0.0220-0.0310	0.0150-0.0550	0.0016-0.0033	0.0016-0.0033	0.0020-0.0080
	8.0 (7997)	W	0.0005-0.0015	0.0100-0.0200	0.0100-0.0200	0.0150-0.0550	0.0029-0.0038	0.0029-0.0038	0.0073-0.0097
1999	2.5 (2507)	P	0.0013-0.0021	0.0090-0.0240	0.0190-0.0380	0.0100-0.0600	0.0017-0.0033	0.0017-0.0033	0.0024-0.0083
	3.9 (3916)	X	0.0005-0.0015	0.0100-0.0200	0.0100-0.0200	0.0020-0.0080	0.0015-0.0030	0.0015-0.0030	0.1515-0.1565
	5.2 (5211)	Y	0.0005-0.0015	0.0100-0.0200	0.0100-0.0200	0.0100-0.0500	0.0015-0.0030	0.0015-0.0030	0.0020-0.0080
	5.9 (5882)	6	NA	0.0160-0.0275	0.0100-0.0215	0.0100-0.0215	0.0037	0.0037	0.0033
	5.9 (5899)	5	0.0005-0.0015	0.0120-0.0220	0.0220-0.0310	0.0150-0.0550	0.0016-0.0033	0.0016-0.0033	0.0020-0.0080
	5.9 (5899)	Z	0.0005-0.0015	0.0120-0.0220	0.0220-0.0310	0.0150-0.0550	0.0016-0.0033	0.0016-0.0033	0.0020-0.0080
	8.0 (7997)	W	0.0005-0.0015	0.0100-0.0200	0.0100-0.0200	0.0150-0.0550	0.0029-0.0038	0.0029-0.0038	0.0073-0.0097

93081C47

PISTON AND RING SPECIFICATIONS

All measurements are given in inches.

Year	Engine Displacement Liters (cc)	Engine ID/VIN	Piston Clearance	Ring Gap			Ring Side Clearance		
				Top Compression	Bottom Compression	Oil Control	Top Compression	Bottom Compression	Oil Control
2000-01	2.5 (2507)	P	0.0013-0.0021	0.0090-0.0240	0.0190-0.0380	0.0100-0.0600	0.0017-0.0033	0.0017-0.0033	0.0024-0.0083
	3.9 (3916)	X	0.0005-0.0015	0.0100-0.0200	0.0100-0.0200	0.0020-0.0080	0.0015-0.0030	0.0015-0.0030	0.1515-0.1565
	4.7 (4701)	N	0.0008-0.0020	0.0146-0.0249	0.0146-0.0249	0.0100-0.0500	0.0020-0.0041	0.0016-0.0032	0.0007-0.0091
	5.2 (5211)	Y	0.0005-0.0015	0.0100-0.0200	0.0100-0.0200	0.0100-0.0500	0.0015-0.0030	0.0015-0.0030	0.0020-0.0080
	5.9 (5882)	6	NA	0.0160-0.0275	0.0100-0.0215	0.0100-0.0215	0.0037	0.0037	0.0033
	5.9 (5899)	5	0.0005-0.0015	0.0120-0.0220	0.0220-0.0310	0.0150-0.0550	0.0016-0.0033	0.0016-0.0033	0.0020-0.0080
	5.9 (5899)	Z	0.0005-0.0015	0.0120-0.0220	0.0220-0.0310	0.0150-0.0550	0.0016-0.0033	0.0016-0.0033	0.0020-0.0080
	8.0 (7997)	W	0.0005-0.0015	0.0100-0.0200	0.0100-0.0200	0.0150-0.0550	0.0029-0.0038	0.0029-0.0038	0.0073-0.0097

NA: Not Available

93081C48

TORQUE SPECIFICATIONS
All readings in ft. lbs.

Year	Engine Displacement Liters (cc)	Engine ID/VIN	Cylinder Head Bolts	Main Bearing Bolts	Rod Bearing Bolts	Crankshaft Damper Bolts	Flywheel Bolts	Manifold Intake	Manifold Exhaust	Spark Plugs	Lug Nuts
1997	2.5 (2507)	P	①	80	33	80	105	17	17	27	②
	3.9 (3916)	X	③	85	45	135	55	④	25	30	②
	5.2 (5211)	Y	③	85	45	135	55	⑤	25	30	②
	5.9 (5882)	D	⑥	⑦	⑧	92	101	⑨	32	—	②
	5.9 (5899)	5	③	85	45	135	55	⑤	25	30	②
	5.9 (5899)	Z	③	85	45	135	55	⑤	25	30	②
	8.0 (7997)	W	③	85	45	135	55	⑩	16	30	②
1998	2.5 (2458)	P	①	80	33	80	105	⑪	⑪	27	②
	3.9 (3916)	X	①	85	45	18	23	⑫	25	30	②
	5.2 (5211)	Y	①	85	45	18	55	⑫	25	30	②
	5.9 (5825)	D	⑬	⑭	⑮	92	⑯	18	32	—	②
	5.9 (5899)	5	①	85	45	18	55	⑫	25	30	②
	5.9 (5899)	Z	①	85	45	18	55	⑫	25	30	②
	8.0 (7994)	W	⑰	⑱	45	135	55	40	16	30	②
1999	2.5 (2458)	P	①	80	33	80	105	⑪	⑪	27	②
	3.9 (3916)	X	①	85	45	18	23	⑫	25	30	②
	5.2 (5211)	Y	①	85	45	18	55	⑫	25	30	②
	5.9 (5825)	D	⑬	⑭	⑮	92	⑯	18	32	—	②
	5.9 (5899)	5	①	85	45	18	55	⑫	25	30	②
	5.9 (5899)	Z	①	85	45	18	55	⑫	25	30	②
	8.0 (7994)	W	⑰	⑱	45	135	55	40	16	30	②
2000-01	2.5 (2458)	P	①	80	33	80	105	⑪	⑪	27	②
	3.9 (3916)	X	①	85	45	18	23	⑫	25	30	②
	5.2 (5211)	Y	①	85	45	18	55	⑫	25	30	②
	4.7 (4701)	N	⑲	⑳	15 ㉑	130	45	9	18	27	②
	5.9 (5825)	D	⑬	⑭	⑮	92	⑯	18	32	—	②
	5.9 (5899)	5	①	85	45	18	55	⑫	25	30	②
	5.9 (5899)	Z	①	85	45	18	55	⑫	25	30	②
	8.0 (7994)	W	⑰	⑱	45	135	55	40	16	30	②

① 1-6 and 8-10: 110 ft. lbs.
  Bolt 7: 100 ft. lbs.

② 5 stud wheel: 95 ft. lbs.
  8 stud wheel: 135 ft. lbs.
  8 stud dual wheel: 145 ft. lbs.

③ Step 1: 50 ft. lbs.
  Step 2: 105 ft. lbs.

④ Step 1: Bolts 1-2: 72 inch lbs. in sequence and in 12 inch lbs. steps.
  Step 2: Bolts 3-12: 72 inch lbs.
  Step 3: Check that all bolts are tightened to 72 inch lbs.
  Step 4: Tighten all bolts in sequence to 12 ft. lbs.
  Step 5: Check that all bolts are tightened to 12 ft. lbs.

⑤ Step 1: Bolts 1-4: 72 inch lbs. in sequence and in 12 inch lbs. steps.
  Step 2: Bolts 5-12: 72 inch lbs.
  Step 3: Check that all bolts are tightened to 72 inch lbs.
  Step 4: Tighten all bolts in sequence to 12 ft. lbs.
  Step 5: Check that all bolts are tightened to 12 ft. lbs.

⑥ All bolts: 66 ft. lbs.
  Long bolts: 89 ft. lbs.
  All bolts and additional 1/4 turn

⑦ Step 1: 45 ft. lbs.
  Step 2: 88 ft. lbs.
  Step 3: 129 ft. lbs.

⑧ Step 1: 26 ft. lbs.
  Step 2: 51 ft. lbs.

⑨ Intake manifold cover bolts: 18 ft. lbs.

⑩ Lower intake manifold: 40 ft. lbs.
  Upper intake manifold: 16 ft. lbs.

⑪ Exhaust manifold bolt 1: 30 ft. lbs.
  Intake/exhaust manifold bolts 2-5: 23 ft. lbs.
  Exhaust manifold nuts 6 & 7: 23 ft. lbs.

⑫ Step 1: 24 inch lbs.
  Step 2: 48 inch lbs.
  Step 3: 84 inch lbs.

⑬ Step 1: 66 ft. lbs.
  Step 2: Recheck at 66 ft. lbs.
  Step 3: 90 ft. lbs. (long bolts only)
  Step 4: Recheck at 90 ft. lbs. (long bolts only)
  Step 5: All bolts an additional 1/4 turn (90 degrees)

⑭ Step 1: 45 ft. lbs.
  Step 2: 60 ft. lbs.
  Step 3: additional 1/4 turn (90 degrees)

⑮ Step 1: 26 ft. lbs.
  Step 2: 51 ft. lbs.
  Step 3: 73 ft. lbs.

⑯ Manual transmission: 101 ft. lbs.
  Automatic transmission: 32 ft. lbs.

⑰ Step 1: 43 ft. lbs.
  Step 2: 105 ft. lbs.

⑱ Step 1: 20 ft. lbs.
  Step 2: 85 ft. lbs.

⑲ M11 bolts: 60 ft. lbs.
  M8 bolts: 250 inch lbs.

⑳ Step 1: Bolts 1-10 to 25 inch lbs.
  Step 2: Bolts 1-10 plus 90 degrees
  Step 3: Bolts A-K to 40 ft. lbs.
  Step 4: Bolts A1-A5 to 20 ft. lbs.

㉑ Plus 110 degrees

93081C49

Refer to the model specific sections for driveline service procedures

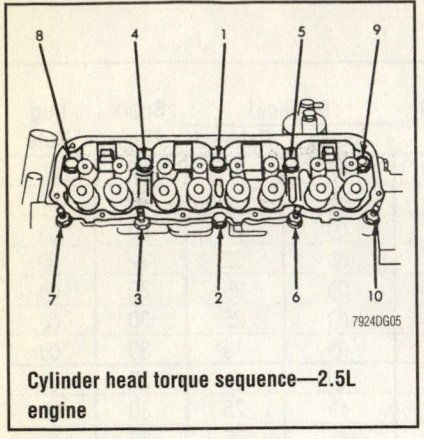

Cylinder head torque sequence—2.5L engine

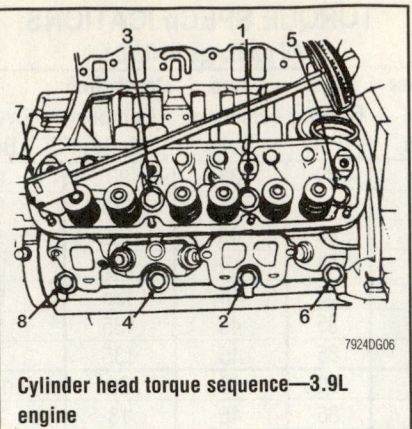

Cylinder head torque sequence—3.9L engine

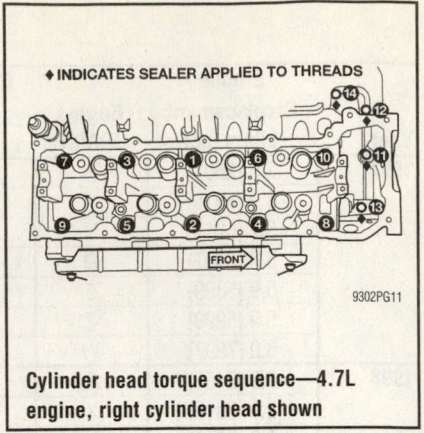

Cylinder head torque sequence—4.7L engine, right cylinder head shown

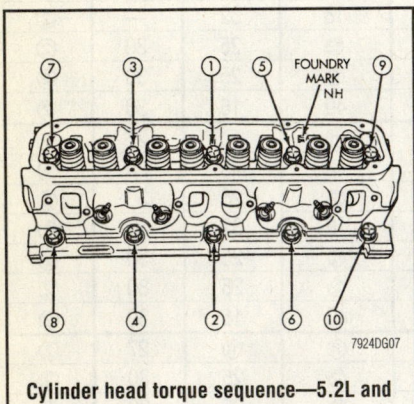

Cylinder head torque sequence—5.2L and 5.9L engines

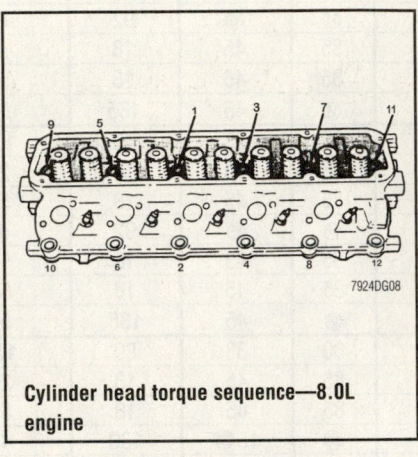

Cylinder head torque sequence—8.0L engine

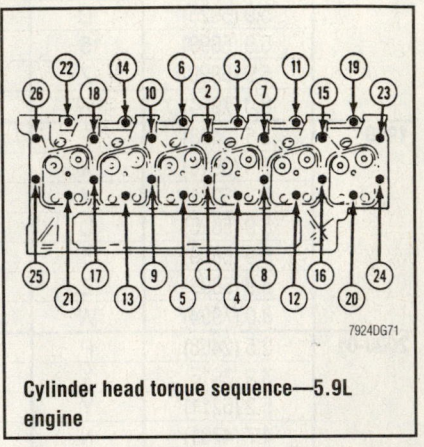

Cylinder head torque sequence—5.9L engine

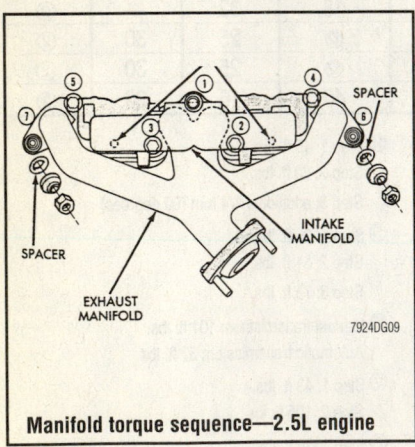

Manifold torque sequence—2.5L engine

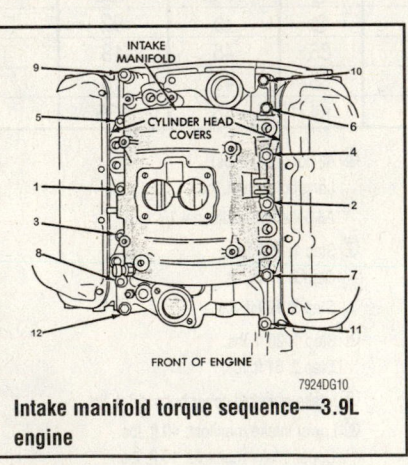

Intake manifold torque sequence—3.9L engine

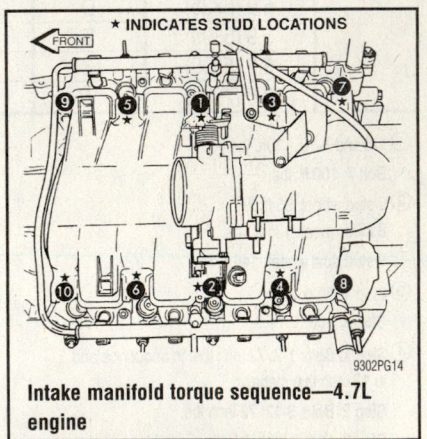

Intake manifold torque sequence—4.7L engine

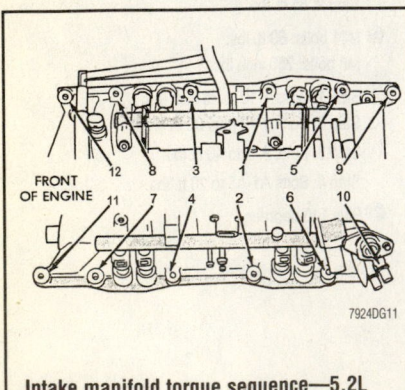

Intake manifold torque sequence—5.2L and 5.9L engines

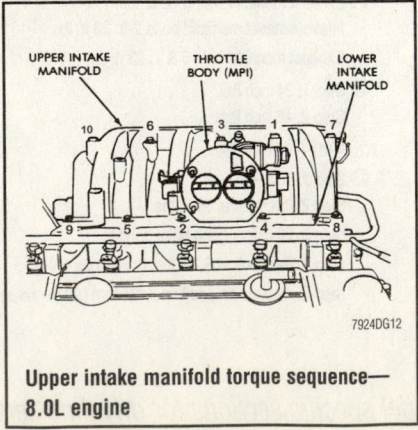

Upper intake manifold torque sequence—8.0L engine

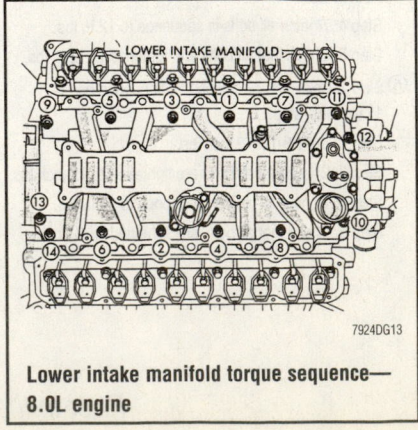

Lower intake manifold torque sequence—8.0L engine

BRAKE SPECIFICATIONS
DODGE DAKOTA, DURANGO, RAM TRUCKS, RAM VANS
All measurements in inches unless noted

Year	Model	Brake Disc			Brake Drum			Minimum Lining Thickness		Brake Caliper	
		Original Thickness	Minimum Thickness	Maximum Run-out	Original Inside Diameter	Max. Wear Limit	Maximum Machine Diameter	Front	Rear	Bracket Bolts (ft. lbs.)	Mounting Bolts (ft. lbs.)
1997	Dakota①	0.861	0.810	0.004	9.00	9.09	9.06	0.060	②	47	22
	Dakota③	0.861	0.810	0.004	10.00	10.09	10.06	0.060	②	47	22
	B1500 Van	NA	④	0.004	11.00	11.09	11.06	0.125	②	110	15
	B2500 Van	NA	④	0.004	11.00	11.09	11.06	0.125	②	110	15
	B3500 Van	NA	④	0.004	12.00	12.09	12.06	0.125	②	110	15
	Ram 1500 Pick-up	1.260	④	0.004	11.00	11.09	11.06	0.062	②	—	38
	Ram 2500 Pick-up	1.500	④	0.005	13.00	13.09	13.06	0.062	②	—	38
	Ram 3500 Pick-up	1.500	④	0.005	13.00	13.09	13.06	0.062	②	—	38
1998	Dakota①	0.944	0.890	0.004	9.00	⑤	⑤	⑥	⑦	47	22
	Dakota③	0.944	0.890	0.004	10.00	⑤	⑤	⑥	⑦	47	22
	B1500 Van	1.26	1.181	0.004	11.03	⑤	⑤	⑥	⑦	110	15
	B2500 Van	1.26	1.181	0.004	11.03	⑤	⑤	⑥	⑦	110	15
	B3500 Van	1.26	1.181	0.004	12.125	⑤	⑤	⑥	⑦	110	15
	Durango	0.900	0.890	0.004	11.00	⑤	⑤	⑥	⑦	47	22
	Ram 1500 Pick-up	⑧	⑨	0.005	11.00	11.09	11.06	⑥	⑦	—	38
	Ram 2500 Pick-up	⑩	⑪	0.005	11.00	11.09	11.06	⑥	⑦	—	38
	Ram 3500 Pick-up	⑫	⑬	0.005	12.00	12.09	12.06	⑥	⑦	—	38
1999	Dakota①	0.944	0.890	0.004	9.00	⑤	⑤	⑥	⑦	47	22
	Dakota③	0.944	0.890	0.004	10.00	⑤	⑤	⑥	⑦	47	22
	B1500 Van	1.26	1.181	0.004	11.03	⑤	⑤	⑥	⑦	110	15
	B2500 Van	1.26	1.181	0.004	11.03	⑤	⑤	⑥	⑦	110	15
	B3500 Van	1.26	1.181	0.004	12.125	⑤	⑤	⑥	⑦	110	15
	Durango	0.900	0.890	0.004	11.00	⑤	⑤	⑥	⑦	47	22
	Ram 1500 Pick-up	⑧	⑨	0.005	11.00	11.09	11.06	⑥	⑦	—	38
	Ram 2500 Pick-up	⑩	⑪	0.005	11.00	11.09	11.06	⑥	⑦	—	38
	Ram 3500 Pick-up	⑫	⑬	0.005	12.00	12.09	12.06	⑥	⑦	—	38
2000-01	Dakota①	0.944	0.890	0.004	9.00	⑤	⑤	⑥	⑦	47	22
	Dakota③	0.944	0.890	0.004	10.00	⑤	⑤	⑥	⑦	47	22
	B1500 Van	1.26	1.181	0.004	11.03	⑤	⑤	⑥	⑦	110	15
	B2500 Van	1.26	1.181	0.004	11.03	⑤	⑤	⑥	⑦	110	15
	B3500 Van	1.26	1.181	0.004	12.125	⑤	⑤	⑥	⑦	110	15
	Durango	0.900	0.890	0.004	11.00	⑤	⑤	⑥	⑦	47	22
	Ram 1500 Pick-up	⑧	⑨	0.005	11.00	11.09	11.06	⑥	⑦	—	38
	Ram 2500 Pick-up	⑩	⑪	0.005	11.00	11.09	11.06	⑥	⑦	—	38
	Ram 3500 Pick-up	⑫	⑬	0.005	12.00	12.09	12.06	⑥	⑦	—	38

NA: Not Available

① With 9 inch rear brakes

② Riveted brake shoes: 0.031 in.
Bonded brake shoes: 0.0620 in.

③ With 10 inch rear brakes

④ Minimum thickness indicated on rotor hub

⑤ Maximum allowable drum diameter, either from wear or machining, is stamped on the drum.

⑥ Riveted brake pads: 0.0625 in.
Bonded brake pads: 0.1875 in.

⑦ Riveted brake shoes: 0.031 in.
Bonded brake shoes: 0.0625 in.

⑧ 2WD: 1.26 in.
4WD: 1.5 in.

⑨ 2WD: 1.215 in.
4WD: 1.269 in.

⑩ 2WD: 1.5 in.
4WD LD: 1.5 in.
4WD HD: 1.75 in.

⑪ 2WD: 1.269 in.
4WD LD: 1.269 in.
4WD HD: 1.521

⑫ 2WD: 1.75 in.
4WD: 1.75 in.

⑬ 2WD: 1.518 in.
4WD: 1.521 in.

93081C50

For exhaust manifold replacement procedures, see the model specific sections of this manual

SCHEDULED MAINTENANCE INTERVALS
(DODGE RAM VAN, DAKOTA, DURANGO & RAM TRUCK — LIGHT DUTY)

TO BE SERVICED	TYPE OF SERVICE	7.5	15	22.5	30	37.5	45	52.5	60	67.5	75	82.5	90	97.5
		VEHICLE MILEAGE INTERVAL (x1000)												
Engine oil & filter	R	✓	✓	✓	✓	✓	✓	✓	✓	✓	✓	✓	✓	✓
Exhaust system	S/I	✓	✓	✓	✓	✓	✓	✓	✓	✓	✓	✓	✓	✓
Engine coolant level, hoses & clamps	S/I	✓	✓	✓	✓	✓	✓	✓	✓	✓	✓	✓	✓	✓
Rotate tires	S/I	✓		✓		✓		✓		✓		✓		✓
Drive belts	S/I		✓		✓		✓		✓		✓		✓	
Brake booster bellcrank pivot	S/I		✓		✓		✓		✓		✓		✓	
Steering linkage	S/I		✓		✓		✓		✓		✓		✓	
Brake hoses & linings	S/I			✓		✓				✓			✓	
Front suspension ball joints	S/I			✓		✓				✓			✓	
Front wheel bearings	S/I			✓		✓				✓			✓	
Steering linkage	S/I			✓		✓				✓			✓	
Spark plugs	R					✓			✓				✓	
Engine air cleaner element	R					✓			✓				✓	
Automatic transmission fluid, filter & adjust bands	S/I					✓					✓			
Manual transmission fluid	R					✓					✓			
Transfer case fluid	R					✓					✓			
Engine coolant	R						✓				✓			
PCV valve ①	S/I								✓					
Fuel filter	R								✓					
Ignition cables, distributor cap & rotor	R								✓					
Timing belt (2.5L)	R								✓					

R: Replace   S/I: Service or Inspect

① Inspect and replace if necessary.

FREQUENT OPERATION MAINTENANCE (SEVERE SERVICE)

If a vehicle is operated under any of the following conditions it is considered severe service:

- Extremely dusty areas.

- 50% or more of the vehicle operation is in 32°C (90°F) or higher temperatures, or constant operation in temperatures below 0°C (32°F).

- Prolonged idling (vehicle operation in stop and go traffic.

- Frequent short running periods (engine does not warm to normal operating temperatures).

- Police, taxi, delivery usage or trailer towing usage.

Oil & oil filter change: change every 3000 miles.

Air filter/air pump air filter: change every 24,000 miles.

Engine coolant level, hoses & clamps: check every 6,000 miles.

Exhaust system: check every 6000 miles.

Drive belts: check every 18,000 miles; replace every 24,000 miles.

Crankcase inlet air filter (6 & 8 cyl.): clean every 24,000 miles.

Oxygen sensor: replace every 82,500 miles.

Automatic transmission fluid, filter & bands: change & adjust every 12,000 miles.

Steering linkage: lubricate every 6000 miles.

Rear axle fluid: change every 12,000 miles.

93081C51

SCHEDULED MAINTENANCE INTERVALS
(DODGE RAM TRUCK—GASOLINE MEDIUM & HEAVY DUTY)

TO BE SERVICED	TYPE OF SERVICE	6	12	18	24	30	36	42	48	54	60	66	72	78
		VEHICLE MILEAGE INTERVAL (x1000)												
Engine oil & filter	R	✓	✓	✓	✓	✓	✓	✓	✓	✓	✓	✓	✓	✓
Exhaust system	S/I	✓	✓	✓	✓	✓	✓	✓	✓	✓	✓	✓	✓	✓
Engine coolant level, hoses & clamps	S/I	✓	✓	✓	✓	✓	✓	✓	✓	✓	✓	✓	✓	✓
Rotate tires	S/I	✓		✓		✓		✓		✓		✓		✓
Drive belts	S/I		✓		✓		✓		✓		✓		✓	
Brake hoses & linings	S/I			✓			✓			✓			✓	
Engine air cleaner element & air pump filter (heavy duty)	R				✓				✓				✓	
Automatic transmission fluid, filter & adjust bands	S/I				✓				✓				✓	
Crankcase inlet air filter (5.9L) (heavy duty)	S/I				✓				✓				✓	
Front wheel bearings (4x2)	S/I				✓				✓				✓	
Engine air cleaner element & air pump filter (medium duty)	R					✓					✓			
Engine coolant	R						✓					✓		
Spark plugs	R					✓					✓			
Transfer case fluid	R						✓						✓	
Distributor cap & rotor (5.9L) (heavy duty)	R										✓			
EGR valve (5.9L) (heavy duty)	R										✓			
Ignition cables	R										✓			

93081C52

Refer to the model specific sections for cooling system service procedures

SCHEDULED MAINTENANCE INTERVALS
(DODGE RAM TRUCK—GASOLINE MEDIUM & HEAVY DUTY) (Cont.)

TO BE SERVICED	TYPE OF SERVICE	VEHICLE MILEAGE INTERVAL (x1000)												
		6	12	18	24	30	36	42	48	54	60	66	72	78
Oxygen sensor (5.9L) (heavy duty)	R										✓			
PCV valve (5.9L) (heavy duty)	R										✓			
EGR passages (5.9L) (heavy duty)	S/I										✓			

R: Replace   S/I: Service or Inspect

FREQUENT OPERATION MAINTENANCE (SEVERE SERVICE)

If a vehicle is operated under any of the following conditions it is considered severe service:

- Extremely dusty areas.

- 50% or more of the vehicle operation is in 32°C (90°F) or higher temperatures, or constant operation in temperatures below 0°C (32°F).

- Prolonged idling (vehicle operation in stop and go traffic.

- Frequent short running periods (engine does not warm to normal operating temperatures).

- Police, taxi, delivery usage or trailer towing usage.

Oil & oil filter change: change every 3000 miles.

Automatic transmission fluid, filter & bands: change & adjust every 12,000 miles.

Rear axle fluid: change every 12,000 miles.

Brake hoses & linings: check every 12,000 miles.

Front axle fluid (4x4): change every 24,000 miles.

Engine air cleaner element & air pump filter: change every 24,000 miles.

Crankcase inlet air filter (5.9L) (heavy duty): clean and relubricate every 12,000 miles.

PCV valve (5.9L) (heavy duty): check every 30,000 miles.

93081C53

SCHEDULED MAINTENANCE INTERVALS
(DODGE RAM TRUCK—DIESEL)

TO BE SERVICED	TYPE OF SERVICE	VEHICLE MILEAGE INTERVAL (x1000)												
		6	12	18	24	30	36	42	48	54	60	66	72	78
Engine oil & filter	R	✓	✓	✓	✓	✓	✓	✓	✓	✓	✓	✓	✓	✓
Brake hoses	S/I	✓	✓	✓	✓	✓	✓	✓	✓	✓	✓	✓	✓	✓
Exhaust system	S/I	✓	✓	✓	✓	✓	✓	✓	✓	✓	✓	✓	✓	✓
Engine coolant level, hoses & clamps	S/I	✓	✓	✓	✓	✓	✓	✓	✓	✓	✓	✓	✓	✓
Rotate tires	S/I	✓		✓		✓		✓		✓		✓		✓
Fuel filter	R		✓		✓		✓		✓		✓		✓	
Water pump weep hole	S/I		✓		✓		✓		✓		✓		✓	
Drive belts	S/I			✓			✓			✓			✓	
Brake linings	S/I			✓			✓			✓			✓	
Automatic transmission fluid, filter & adjust bands	S/I				✓				✓				✓	
Damper	S/I				✓				✓				✓	
Fan hub	S/I				✓				✓				✓	
Front wheel bearings	S/I				✓				✓				✓	
Valve lash clearance	S/I				✓				✓				✓	
Air filter	R					✓					✓			
Engine coolant	R						✓					✓		
Transfer case fluid	R						✓						✓	

R: Replace   S/I: Service or Inspect

FREQUENT OPERATION MAINTENANCE (SEVERE SERVICE)

If a vehicle is operated under any of the following conditions it is considered severe service:

- Extremely dusty areas.

- 50% or more of the vehicle operation is in 32°C (90°F) or higher temperatures, or constant operation in temperatures below 0°C (32°F).

- Prolonged idling (vehicle operation in stop and go traffic.

- Frequent short running periods (engine does not warm to normal operating temperatures).

- Police, taxi, delivery usage or trailer towing usage.

Oil & oil filter change: change every 3000 miles.

Automatic transmission fluid, filter & bands: change & adjust every 12,000 miles.

Rear axle fluid: change every 12,000 miles.

Brake linings: check every 12,000 miles.

Front axle fluid (4x4): change every 24,000 miles.

93081C54

SCHEDULED MAINTENANCE INTERVALS
DAMILERCHRYSLER CORPORATION
DODGE RAM VAN, DAKOTA,
DURANGO, RAM TRUCK (LIGHT DUTY)

The following should be used as a guide when determining the amount of work required for a particular service.
In estimating how long a particular Scheduled Maintenance Service should take, please observe the following:

- Labor Time is time based on field research and data supplied by the vehicle manufacturer.
- Labor time operations are given in hours and tenths of an hour.
- All labor operations are to be used as a guide.

Mechanic Skill Level Codes:
(A) PRECISION: Highly skilled with multiple certification.
(B) GENERAL: Normally skilled with certification.
(C) MAINTENANCE: Semi-skilled working on certification.

	LABOR TIME		LABOR TIME		LABOR TIME
7500 Mile Service (C)		**45000 Mile Service (C)**		**75000 Mile Service (B)**	
All Models	1.1	All Models	1.7	All Models	4.0
15000 Mile Service (C)		**52500 Mile Service (C)**		**82500 Mile Service (C)**	
All Models	.9	All Models	1.1	All Models	1.1
22500 Mile Service (C)		**60000 Mile Service (B)**		**90000 Mile Service (B)**	
All Models	1.5	All Models	6.5	All Models	2.9
30000 Mile Service (B)		**67500 Mile Service (C)**		**97500 Mile Service (C)**	
All Models	2.2	All Models	1.5	All Models	1.1
37500 Mile Service (B)					
All Models	3.7				

93081C55

SCHEDULED MAINTENANCE INTERVALS
DAIMLERCHRYSLER CORPORATION
DODGE RAM TRUCK
GASOLINE MEDIUM & HEAVY DUTY, DIESEL

The following should be used as a guide when determining the amount of work required for a particular service.
In estimating how long a particular Scheduled Maintenance Service should take, please observe the following:

- Labor Time is time based on field research and data supplied by the vehicle manufacturer.
- Labor time operations are given in hours and tenths of an hour.
- All labor operations are to be used as a guide.

Mechanic Skill Level Codes:
(A) PRECISION: Highly skilled with multiple certification.
(B) GENERAL: Normally skilled with certification.
(C) MAINTENANCE: Semi-skilled working on certification.

	LABOR TIME
6000 Mile Service (C)	
All Models	
Gasoline	1.1
Diesel	1.3
7500 Mile Service (C)	
All Models	1.1
12000 Mile Service (C)	
All Models	
Gasoline	.7
Diesel	1.2
15000 Mile Service (C)	
All Models	.9
18000 Mile Service (C)	
All Models	
Gasoline	1.3
Diesel	1.6
22500 Mile Service (C)	
All Models	1.6
24000 Mile Service (B)	
All Models	
Gasoline	
medium duty	3.1
heavy duty	3.2
Diesel	3.5
Inspect wheel bearings 2WD	
add	.2

	LABOR TIME
30000 Mile Service (B)	
All Models	
Gasoline	
light duty	2.2
medium/heavy duty	2.4
Diesel	1.6
36000 Mile Service (C)	
All Models	
Gasoline	1.6
Diesel	2.3
37500 Mile Service (B)	
All Models	3.7
42000 Mile Service (C)	
All Models	
Gasoline	1.1
Diesel	1.3
45000 Mile Service (C)	
All Models	1.7
48000 Mile Service (B)	
All Models	
Gasoline	
medium duty	3.1
heavy duty	3.2
Diesel	3.5
Inspect wheel bearings 2WD	
add	.2
52500 Mile Service (C)	
All Models	1.1
54000 Mile Service (C)	
All Models	
Gasoline	1.3
Diesel	1.6

	LABOR TIME
60000 Mile Service (B)	
All Models	
Gasoline	
light duty	4.9
medium duty	3.1
heavy duty	5.0
Diesel	1.4
66000 Mile Service (C)	
All Models	
Gasoline	1.0
Diesel	1.7
67500 Mile Service (C)	
All Models	1.5
72000 Mile Service (B)	
All Models	
Gasoline	
medium duty	3.6
heavy duty	3.7
Diesel	4.0
Inspect wheel bearings 2WD	
add	.2
75000 Mile Service (B)	
All Models	3.9
78000 Mile Service (C)	
All Models	
Gasoline	1.0
Diesel	1.2

93081C56

Timing chain and gear service is covered in the model specific sections of this manual

TIRE, WHEEL AND BALL JOINT SPECIFICATIONS
Dodge/Plymouth

Year	Model	OEM Tires		Tire Pressures (psi)		Wheel Size	Ball Joint Inspection
		Standard	Optional	Front	Rear		
1997	Caravan/Voyager, base	P205/75SR14	None	35	35	6-J	0.030 in. ①
	Caravan/Voyager SE, LE	P215/65SR15	P215/65R16	35	35	6.5-J	0.030 in. ①
	Caravan/Voyager ES	P215/65R16	None	35	35	6.5-J	0.030 in. ①
	Dakota, 2wd	P215/75R15	P235/75R15	35	35	6.5-JJ	0.060 in. ①
	Dakota, 4wd	P215/75R15	P235/75R15	35	35	6.5-JJ	0.060 in. ①
			31x10.5R15LT	35	35	8-J	
	1500 PU 2wd	P225/75R16	P245/75R16C	35	35	7-J	0.030 in. ①
			LT265/75R16C	35	35	7-J	
	1500 PU 4wd	LT225/75R16C	LT245/75R16C	Std: 35	Std: 35	7-J	0.030 in. ①
			LT265/75R16C	Opt: 40	Opt: 40	7-J	0.030 in. ①
	2500 PU 2wd	LT225/75R16D	LT245/75R16E	40	40	7-J	0.030 in. ①
	2500 PU 4wd	LT225/75R16D	LT245/75R16E	40	40	7-J	0.030 in. ①
	3500 PU	LT225/75R16E	None	55	80	6.5-J	0.030 in. ①
	1500 Van	P235/75R15	None	35	40	6.5-J	0.030 in. ①
	2500 Van	LT225/75R16	None	50	65	6.5-J	0.030 in. ①
	3500 Van	LT225/75R16E	None	55	80	6.5-J	0.030 in. ①
1998	Caravan/Voyager, base	P205/75SR14	None	35	35	6-J	0.030 in. ①
	Caravan/Voyager SE, LE	P215/65SR15	P215/65R16	35	35	6.5-J	0.030 in. ①
	Caravan/Voyager ES	P215/65R16	None	35	35	6.5-J	0.030 in. ①
	Dakota, 2wd	P215/75R15	P235/75R15	35	35	6.5-JJ	0.060 in. ①
	Dakota, 4wd	P215/75R15	P235/75R15	35	35	6.5-JJ	0.060 in. ①
			31x10.5R15LT	35	35	8-J	
	Durango	P235/75R15XL	31x10.5R15LT	35	35	6.5-JJ	0.060 in. ①
	1500 PU 2wd	P225/75R16	P245/75R16C	35	35	7-J	0.030 in. ①
			P275/60R17			9-J	
	2500 PU 2wd, w/6400 GVW	P225/75R16	P245/75R16C	35	35	7-J	0.030 in. ①
			P275/60R17			9-J	
	2500 PU 2wd, w/8800 GVW	LT245/75R16E	None	40	40	6.5-J	0.030 in. ①
	1500 PU 4wd	P245/75R16	P265/75R16	40	35	7-J	0.030 in. ①
	2500 PU 4wd, w/6400 GVW	P245/75R16	P265/75R16	40	35	7-J	0.030 in. ①
	2500 PU 4wd/8800 GVW	P245/75R16E	None	40	40	6.5-J	0.030 in. ①
	1500 Van	P235/75R15	None	35	40	6.5-J	0.030 in. ①
	2500 Van	LT225/75R16	None	50	65	6.5-J	0.030 in. ①
	3500 Van	LT225/75R16E	None	55	80	6.5-J	0.030 in. ①
1999	Caravan/Voyager, base	P205/75SR14	None	35	35	6-J	0.030 in. ①
	Caravan/Voyager SE, LE	P215/65SR15	P215/65R16	35	35	6.5-J	0.030 in. ①
	Caravan/Voyager ES	P215/65R16	None	35	35	6.5-J	0.030 in. ①
	Dakota, 2wd	P215/75R15	P235/75R15	35	35	6.5-JJ	0.060 in. ①
	Dakota, 4wd	P215/75R15	P235/75R15	35	35	6.5-JJ	0.060 in. ①
			31x10.5R15LT	35	35	8-J	
	Durango	P235/75R15XL	31x10.5R15LT	35	35	6.5-JJ	0.060 in. ①
	1500 PU 2wd	P225/75R16	P245/75R16C	35	35	7-J	0.030 in. ①
			P275/60R17			9-J	
	2500 PU 2wd, w/6400 GVW	P225/75R16	P245/75R16C	35	35	7-J	0.030 in. ①
			P275/60R17			9-J	
	2500 PU 2wd, w/8800 GVW	LT245/75R16E	None	40	40	6.5-J	0.030 in. ①
				w/V10: 45	40		
				w/Diesel: 50	65		
				w/Club Cab: 45	80		

93081C57

TIRE, WHEEL AND BALL JOINT SPECIFICATIONS
Dodge/Plymouth

Year	Model	OEM Tires		Tire Pressures (psi)		Wheel Size	Ball Joint Inspection
		Standard	Optional	Front	Rear		
1999 (cont.)	1500 PU 4wd	P245/75R16	P265/75R16	35	35	7-J	0.030 in. ①
	2500 PU 4wd, w/6400 GVW	P245/75R16	P265/75R16	35	35	7-J	0.030 in. ①
	2500 PU 4wd w/8800 GVW	P245/75R16E	None	40	40	6.5-J	0.030 in. ①
				w/V10: 45	40		
				w/Diesel: 50	65		
				w/Club Cab: 45	80		
	1500 Van	P235/75R15	None	35	40	6.5-J	0.030 in. ①
	2500 Van	LT225/75R16	None	50	65	6.5-J	0.030 in. ①
	3500 Van	LT225/75R16E	None	55	80	6.5-J	0.030 in. ①
2000-01	Caravan/Voyager, base	P205/75SR14	None	35	35	6-J	0.030 in. ①
	Caravan/Voyager SE, LE	P215/65SR15	P215/65R16	35	35	6.5-J	0.030 in. ①
	Caravan/Voyager ES	P215/65R16	None	35	35	6.5-J	0.030 in. ①
	Dakota, 2wd	P215/75R15	P235/75R15	35	35	6.5-JJ	0.060 in. ①
	Dakota, 4wd	P215/75R15	P235/75R15	35	35	6.5-JJ	0.060 in. ①
			31x10.5R15LT	35	35	8-J	
	Durango	P235/75R15XL	31x10.5R15LT	35	35	6.5-JJ	0.060 in. ①
	1500 PU 2wd	P225/75R16	P245/75R16C	35	35	7-J	0.030 in. ①
			P275/60R17			9-J	
	2500 PU 2wd, w/6400 GVW	P225/75R16	P245/75R16C	35	35	7-J	0.030 in. ①
			P275/60R17			9-J	
	2500 PU 2wd, w/8800 GVW	LT245/75R16E	None	40	40	6.5-J	0.030 in. ①
				w/V10: 45	40		
				w/Diesel: 50	65		
				w/Club Cab: 45	80		
	1500 PU 4wd	P245/75R16	P265/75R16	35	35	7-J	0.030 in. ①
	2500 PU 4wd, w/6400 GVW	P245/75R16	P265/75R16	35	35	7-J	0.030 in. ①
	2500 PU 4wd w/8800 GVW	P245/75R16E	None	40	40	6.5-J	0.030 in. ①
				w/V10: 45	40		
				w/Diesel: 50	65		
				w/Club Cab: 45	80		
	1500 Van	P235/75R15	None	35	40	6.5-J	0.030 in. ①
	2500 Van	LT225/75R16	None	50	65	6.5-J	0.030 in. ①
	3500 Van	LT225/75R16E	None	55	80	6.5-J	0.030 in. ①

OEM: Original Equipment Manufacturer

PSI: Pounds Per Square Inch

STD: Standard

OPT: Optional

① Both upper and lower

93081C58

Ignition system service is covered in the model specific sections of this manual

CHRYSLER CORP.
Jeep Cherokee • Grand Cherokee • Wrangler

ENGINE AND VEHICLE IDENTIFICATION

	Engine							Model Year	
Code ①	Liters (cc)	Cu. In.	Cyl.	Fuel Sys.	Engine Type	Eng. Mfg.	Code ②		Year
N	4.7 (4701)	287	8	MFI	SOHC	Chrysler	V		1997
P	2.5 (2458)	150	4	MFI	OHV	Chrysler	W		1998
S	4.0 (3966)	242	6	MFI	OHV	Chrysler	X		1999
Y	5.2 (5211)	318	8	MFI	OHV	Chrysler	Y		2000
Z	5.9 (5899)	360	8	MFI	OHV	Chrysler	1		2001

MFI: Multi-port Fuel Injection

OHV: Over Head Valve

SOHC: Single Overhead Camshaft

① 8th position of VIN

② 10th position of VIN

93081C59

GENERAL ENGINE SPECIFICATIONS

Year	Model	Engine Displacement Liters (cc)	Engine Series (ID/VIN)	Fuel System	Net Horsepower @ rpm	Net Torque @ rpm (ft. lbs.)	Bore x Stroke (in.)	Com-pression Ratio	Oil Pressure @ rpm
1997	Cherokee	2.5 (2458)	P	MFI	125@5400	149@3250	3.88x3.19	9.1:1	37@1600
		4.0 (3966)	S	MFI	190@4750	225@4000	3.88x3.44	8.8:1	37@1600
	Grand Cherokee	4.0 (3966)	S	MFI	190@4750	225@4000	3.88x3.44	8.8:1	37@1600
		5.2 (5211)	Y	MFI	220@4400	285@3600	3.91x3.31	9.1:1	30@3000
	Wrangler	2.5 (2464)	P	MFI	120@5400	139@3500	3.88x3.19	9.1:1	37@1600
		4.0 (3958)	S	MFI	181@4600	222@2800	3.88x3.44	8.8:1	37@1600
1998	Cherokee	2.5 (2458)	P	MFI	125@5400	149@3250	3.88x3.19	9.1:1	37@1600
		4.0 (3966)	S	MFI	190@4750	225@4000	3.88x3.44	8.8:1	37@1600
	Grand Cherokee	4.0 (3966)	S	MFI	190@4750	225@4000	3.88x3.44	8.8:1	37@1600
		5.2 (5211)	Y	MFI	220@4400	285@3600	3.91x3.31	9.1:1	30@3000
		5.9 (5899)	Z	MFI	245@4000	345@3200	4.00x3.58	9.1:1	30@3000
	Wrangler	2.5 (2464)	P	MFI	120@5400	139@3500	3.88x3.19	9.1:1	37@1600
		4.0 (3958)	S	MFI	181@4600	222@2800	3.88x3.44	8.8:1	37@1600
1999	Cherokee	2.5 (2458)	P	MFI	125@5400	149@3250	3.88x3.19	9.1:1	37@1600
		4.0 (3966)	S	MFI	190@4750	225@4000	3.88x3.44	8.8:1	37@1600
	Grand Cherokee	4.0 (3966)	S	MFI	195@4600	230@3000	3.88x3.44	8.8:1	37@1600
		4.7 (4701)	N	MFI	235@4800	295@3200	3.66x3.40	9.3:1	25@3000
	Wrangler	2.5 (2464)	P	MFI	120@5400	139@3500	3.88x3.19	9.1:1	37@1600
		4.0 (3958)	S	MFI	181@4600	222@2800	3.88x3.44	8.8:1	37@1600
2000-01	Cherokee	2.5 (2458)	P	MFI	125@5400	149@3250	3.88x3.19	9.1:1	37@1600
		4.0 (3966)	S	MFI	190@4750	225@4000	3.88x3.44	8.8:1	37@1600
	Grand Cherokee	4.0 (3966)	S	MFI	195@4600	230@3000	3.88x3.44	8.8:1	37@1600
		4.7 (4701)	N	MFI	235@4800	295@3200	3.66x3.40	9.3:1	25@3000
	Wrangler	2.5 (2464)	P	MFI	120@5400	139@3500	3.88x3.19	9.1:1	37@1600
		4.0 (3958)	S	MFI	181@4600	222@2800	3.88x3.44	8.8:1	37@1600

MFI: Multi Port Fuel Injection

93081C60

ENGINE TUNE-UP SPECIFICATIONS

Year	Engine Displacement Liters (cc)	Engine ID/VIN	Spark Plug Gap (in.)	Ignition Timing (deg.)	Fuel Pump (psi)	Idle Speed (rpm)	Valve Clearance	
							Intake	Exhaust
1997	2.5 (2458)	P	0.035	①	47-51	①	HYD	HYD
	4.0 (3966)	S	0.035	①	47-51	①	HYD	HYD
	5.2 (5211)	Y	0.035	①	47-51	①	HYD	HYD
1998	2.5 (2458)	P	0.035	①	47-51	①	HYD	HYD
	4.0 (3966)	S	0.035	①	47-51	①	HYD	HYD
	5.2 (5211)	Y	0.040	①	47-51	①	HYD	HYD
	5.9 (5899)	Z	0.040	①	47-51	①	HYD	HYD
1999	2.5 (2458)	P	0.035	①	47-51	①	HYD	HYD
	4.0 (3966)	S	0.035	①	47-51	①	HYD	HYD
	4.7 (4701)	N	0.040	①	47-51	①	HYD	HYD
2000-01	2.5 (2458)	P	0.035	①	47-51	①	HYD	HYD
	4.0 (3966)	S	0.035	①	47-51	①	HYD	HYD
	4.7 (4701)	N	0.040	①	47-51	①	HYD	HYD

NOTE: The Vehicle Emission Control Information label often reflects specification changes made during production. The label figures must be used if they differ from those in this chart.

HYD: Hydraulic

① Ignition timing and idle speed are controlled by the PCM. No adjustment is necessary.

93081C61

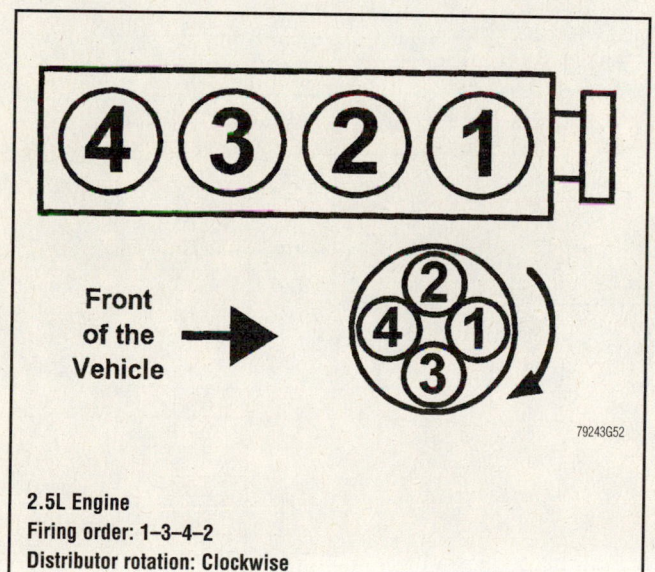

2.5L Engine
Firing order: 1-3-4-2
Distributor rotation: Clockwise

79243G52

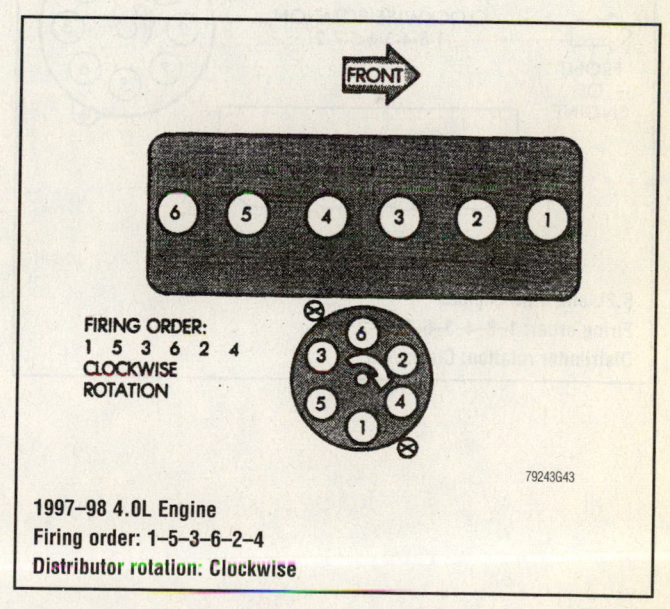

1997-98 4.0L Engine
Firing order: 1-5-3-6-2-4
Distributor rotation: Clockwise

79243G43

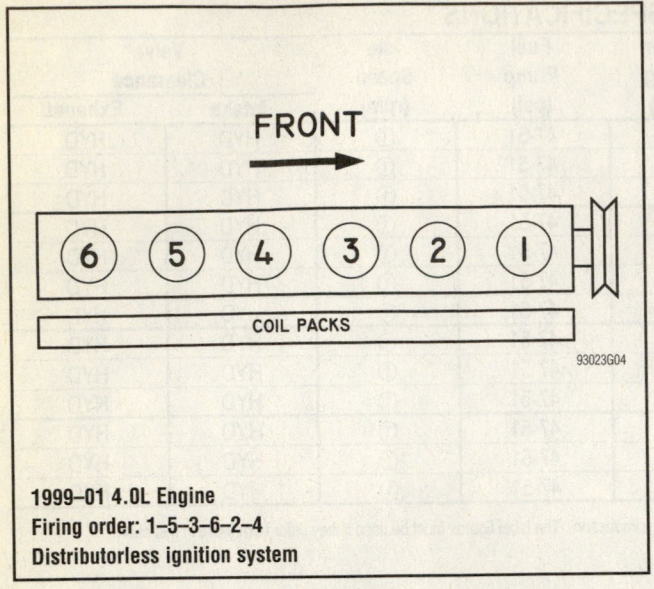

FRONT →

COIL PACKS

93023G04

1999–01 4.0L Engine
Firing order: 1–5–3–6–2–4
Distributorless ignition system

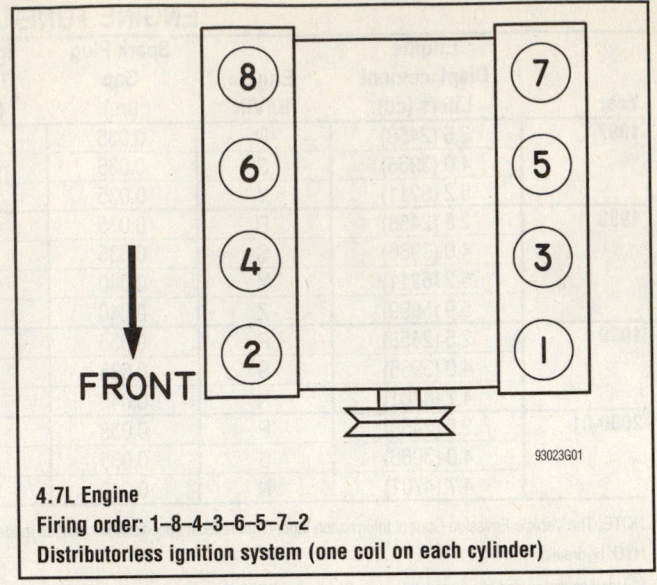

FRONT ↓

93023G01

4.7L Engine
Firing order: 1–8–4–3–6–5–7–2
Distributorless ignition system (one coil on each cylinder)

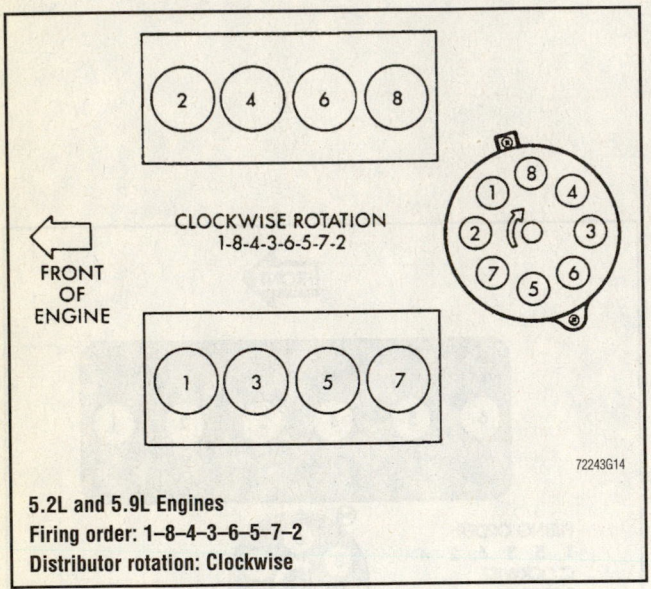

CLOCKWISE ROTATION
1-8-4-3-6-5-7-2

FRONT
OF
ENGINE

72243G14

5.2L and 5.9L Engines
Firing order: 1–8–4–3–6–5–7–2
Distributor rotation: Clockwise

CAPACITIES

Year	Model	Engine Displacement Liters (cc)	Engine ID/VIN	Engine Oil with Filter	Transmission (pts.) Man.	Transmission (pts.) Auto.	Transfer Case (pts.)	Drive Axle Front (pts.)	Drive Axle Rear (pts.)	Fuel Tank (gal.)	Cooling System (qts.)
1997	Cherokee	2.5 (2468)	P	4.0	6.6①	17.0	3.0②	3.1	3.5③	20.2	10.0
		4.0 (3966)	S	6.0	6.6	17.0	3.0②	3.1	3.5③	20.2	12.0
	Grand Cherokee	4.0 (3966)	S	6.0	6.5	17.0	3.2④	3.1	3.4	23.0	12.0
		5.2 (5211)	Y	5.0	6.5	19.5	3.2④	3.1	3.4	23.0	14.9
	Wrangler	2.5 (2464)	P	4.0	6.6	17.5	⑤	3.7	3.5	⑥	9.0
		4.0 (3958)	S	6.0	6.6	17.5	⑤	3.7	3.5	⑥	10.5
1998	Cherokee	2.5 (2468)	P	4.0	6.6①	17.0	3.0②	3.1	3.5③	20.2	10.0
		4.0 (3966)	S	6.0	6.6	17.0	3.0②	3.1	3.5③	20.2	12.0
	Grand Cherokee	4.0 (3966)	S	6.0	—	⑦	⑧	3.1	⑨	23.0	12.0
		5.2 (5211)	Y	5.0	—	⑦	⑧	3.1	⑨	23.0	14.9
		5.9 (5899)	Z	5.0	—	⑦	⑧	2.5	⑨	23.0	14.9
	Wrangler	2.5 (2464)	P	4.0	6.6	17.5	⑤	3.7	3.5	⑥	9.0
		4.0 (3958)	S	6.0	6.6	17.5	⑤	3.7	3.5	⑥	10.5
1999	Cherokee	2.5 (2468)	P	4.0	6.6①	17.0	3.0②	3.1	3.5 E	20.2	10.0
		4.0 (3966)	S	6.0	6.6	17.0	3.0②	3.1	3.5 E	20.2	12.0
	Grand Cherokee	4.0 (3966)	S	6.0	—	⑦	⑧	3.1	⑨	20.5	12.0
		4.7 (4701)	N	6.0	—	⑦	⑧	2.5	⑨	20.5	13.0
	Wrangler	2.5 (2464)	P	4.0	6.6	17.5	⑧	3.7	3.5	⑥	9.0
		4.0 (3958)	S	6.0	6.6	17.5	⑤	3.7	3.5	⑥	10.5
2000-01	Cherokee	2.5 (2468)	P	4.0	6.6①	17.0	3.0②	3.1	3.5 E	20.2	10.0
		4.0 (3966)	S	6.0	6.6	17.0	3.0②	3.1	3.5 E	20.2	12.0
	Grand Cherokee	4.0 (3966)	S	6.0	—	⑦	⑧	3.1	⑨	20.5	12.0
		4.7 (4701)	N	6.0	—	⑦	⑧	2.5	⑨	20.5	13.0
	Wrangler	2.5 (2464)	P	4.0	6.6	17.5	⑧	3.7	3.5	⑥	9.0
		4.0 (3958)	S	6.0	6.6	17.5	⑤	3.7	3.5	⑥	10.5

① 2WD: 7.0 pts.

② Command-Trac - 2.2 pts.

③ 8 1/4 axle: 4.4 pts.

④ NP242: 2.9 pts.
NP249: 2.5 pts.

⑤ Command-Trac:
Automatic: 2.2 pts.
Manual: 3.3 pts.

⑥ Standard: 15.0 gals.
Optional: 19.6 gals.

⑦ 42RE: 19-22 pts.
44RE: 19-22 pts.
45RFE: 28.0 pts.
46RE: 19.5-28.0 pts.

⑧ 242 NVG: 3.0 pts.
247 NVG: 2.5 pts.
249 NVG: 2.5 pts.

⑨ 194 RBI: 3.5 pts.
198 RBI: 3.75 pts.
216 RBA: 4.75 pts.
226 RBA: 4.75 pts.

93081C62

Refer to the model specific sections for engine mechanical service procedures

VALVE SPECIFICATIONS

Year	Engine Displacement Liters (cc)	Engine ID/VIN	Seat Angle (deg.)	Face Angle (deg.)	Spring Test Pressure (lbs. @ in.)	Spring Installed Height (in.)	Stem-to-Guide Clearance (in.)		Stem Diameter (in.)	
							Intake	Exhaust	Intake	Exhaust
1997	2.5 (2458)	P	44.5	45	184-196@1.216	1.640	0.0010-0.0030	0.0010-0.0030	0.3110-0.3120	0.3110-0.3120
	4.0 (3966)	S	44.5	45	184-196@1.216	1.640	0.0010-0.0030	0.0010-0.0030	0.3110-0.3120	0.3110-0.3120
	5.2 (5211)	Y	44.25-44.75	43.25-43.75	200@1.212	1.640	0.0010-0.0030	0.0010-0.0030	0.3110-0.3120	0.3110-0.3120
1998	2.5 (2458)	P	44.5	45	184-196@1.216	1.640	0.0010-0.0030	0.0010-0.0030	0.3110-0.3120	0.3110-0.3120
	4.0 (3966)	S	44.5	45	184-196@1.216	1.640	0.0010-0.0030	0.0010-0.0030	0.3110-0.3120	0.3110-0.3120
	5.2 (5211)	Y	44.25-44.75	43.25-43.75	200@1.212	1.640	0.0010-0.0030	0.0010-0.0030	0.3110-0.3120	0.3110-0.3120
	5.9 (5899)	Z	44.25-44.75	43.25-43.75	200@1.212	1.640	0.0010-0.0030	0.0020-0.0040	0.3720-0.3730	0.3710-0.3720
1999	2.5 (2458)	P	44.5	45	184-196@1.216	1.640	0.0010-0.0030	0.0010-0.0030	0.3110-0.3120	0.3110-0.3120
	4.0 (3966)	S	44.5	45	184-196@1.216	1.640	0.0010-0.0030	0.0010-0.0030	0.3110-0.3120	0.3110-0.3120
	4.7 (4701)	N	44.5-45	45-45.5	176.2-192.4@1.1532	1.602	0.0011-0.0017	0.0029	0.2728-0.2739	0.2717-0.2728
2000-01	2.5 (2458)	P	44.5	45	184-196@1.216	1.640	0.0010-0.0030	0.0010-0.0030	0.3110-0.3120	0.3110-0.3120
	4.0 (3966)	S	44.5	45	184-196@1.216	1.640	0.0010-0.0030	0.0010-0.0030	0.3110-0.3120	0.3110-0.3120
	4.7 (4701)	N	44.5-45	45-45.5	176.2-192.4@1.1532	1.602	0.0011-0.0017	0.0029	0.2728-0.2739	0.2717-0.2728

93081C63

CRANKSHAFT AND CONNECTING ROD SPECIFICATIONS

All measurements are given in inches.

Year	Engine Displacement Liters (cc)	Engine ID/VIN	Crankshaft				Connecting Rod		
			Main Brg. Journal Dia.	Main Brg. Oil Clearance	Shaft End-play	Thrust on No.	Journal Diameter	Oil Clearance	Side Clearance
1997	2.5 (2507)	P	2.4996-2.5001	0.0010-0.0025	0.0015-0.0065	2	2.2080-2.2085	0.0015-0.0020	0.0100-0.0190
	4.0 (3966)	S	2.4996-2.5001 ①	0.0010-0.0025	0.0015-0.0065	2	2.0934-2.0955	0.0015-0.0020	0.0100-0.0190
	5.2 (5211)	Y	2.4995-2.5005	0.0005-0.0015	0.0020-0.0070	2	2.1240-2.1250	0.0005-0.0022	0.0060-0.0140
1998	2.5 (2507)	P	2.4996-2.5001	0.0010-0.0025	0.0015-0.0065	2	2.2080-2.2085	0.0015-0.0020	0.0100-0.0190
	4.0 (3966)	S	2.4996-2.5001 ①	0.0010-0.0025	0.0015-0.0065	2	2.0934-2.0955	0.0015-0.0020	0.0100-0.0190
	5.2 (5211)	Y	2.4995-2.5005	0.0005-0.0015	0.0020-0.0070	2	2.1240-2.1250	0.0005-0.0022	0.0060-0.0140
	5.9 (5899)	Z	2.8095-2.8105	0.0005-0.0015	0.0020-0.0070	2	2.1240-2.1250	0.0005-0.0022	0.0060-0.0140
1999	2.5 (2507)	P	2.4996-2.5001	0.0010-0.0025	0.0015-0.0065	2	2.2080-2.2085	0.0015-0.0020	0.0100-0.0190
	4.0 (3966)	S	2.4996-2.5001 ①	0.0010-0.0025	0.0015-0.0065	2	2.0934-2.0955	0.0015-0.0020	0.0100-0.0190
	4.7 (4701)	N	2.4996-2.5005	0.0002-0.0013	0.0021-0.0112	2	2.0076-2.0082	0.0004-0.0019	0.0040-0.0138
2000-01	2.5 (2507)	P	2.4996-2.5001	0.0010-0.0025	0.0015-0.0065	2	2.2080-2.2085	0.0015-0.0020	0.0100-0.0190
	4.0 (3966)	S	2.4996-2.5001 ①	0.0010-0.0025	0.0015-0.0065	2	2.0934-2.0955	0.0015-0.0020	0.0100-0.0190
	4.7 (4701)	N	2.4996-2.5005	0.0002-0.0013	0.0021-0.0112	2	2.0076-2.0082	0.0004-0.0019	0.0040-0.0138

① No 7: 2.4980-2.4995

93081C64

Refer to the model specific sections for fuel system service procedures

PISTON AND RING SPECIFICATIONS
All measurements are given in inches.

Year	Engine Displacement Liters (cc)	Engine ID/VIN	Piston Clearance	Ring Gap			Ring Side Clearance		
				Top Compression	Bottom Compression	Oil Control	Top Compression	Bottom Compression	Oil Control
1997	2.5 (2507)	P	0.0013-0.0021	0.0090-0.0240	0.0190-0.0380	0.0100-0.0600	0.0017-0.0033	0.0017-0.0033	0.0024-0.0083
	4.0 (3966)	S	0.0008-0.0015	0.0090-0.0240	0.0190-0.0380	0.0100-0.0600	0.0017-0.0033	0.0017-0.0033	0.0024-0.0083
	5.2 (5211)	Y	0.0005-0.0015	0.0100-0.0200	0.0100-0.0200	0.0100-0.0500	0.0015-0.0030	0.0015-0.0030	0.0020-0.0080
1998	2.5 (2507)	P	0.0013-0.0021	0.0090-0.0240	0.0190-0.0380	0.0100-0.0600	0.0017-0.0033	0.0017-0.0033	0.0024-0.0083
	4.0 (3966)	S	0.0008-0.0015	0.0090-0.0240	0.0190-0.0380	0.0100-0.0600	0.0017-0.0033	0.0017-0.0033	0.0024-0.0083
	5.2 (5211)	Y	0.0005-0.0015	0.0100-0.0200	0.0100-0.0200	0.0100-0.0500	0.0015-0.0030	0.0015-0.0030	0.0020-0.0080
	5.9 (5899)	Z	0.0005-0.0015	0.0120-0.0220	0.0220-0.0310	0.0150-0.0550	0.0016-0.0033	0.0016-0.0033	0.0020-0.0080
1999	2.5 (2507)	P	0.0013-0.0021	0.0090-0.0240	0.0190-0.0380	0.0100-0.0600	0.0017-0.0033	0.0017-0.0033	0.0024-0.0083
	4.0 (3966)	S	0.0008-0.0015	0.0090-0.0240	0.0190-0.0380	0.0100-0.0600	0.0017-0.0033	0.0017-0.0033	0.0024-0.0083
	4.7 (4701)	N	0.0008-0.0020	0.0146-0.0249	0.0146-0.0249	0.0100-0.0500	0.0020-0.0041	0.0016-0.0032	0.0007-0.0091
2000-01	2.5 (2507)	P	0.0013-0.0021	0.0090-0.0240	0.0190-0.0380	0.0100-0.0600	0.0017-0.0033	0.0017-0.0033	0.0024-0.0083
	4.0 (3966)	S	0.0008-0.0015	0.0090-0.0240	0.0190-0.0380	0.0100-0.0600	0.0017-0.0033	0.0017-0.0033	0.0024-0.0083
	4.7 (4701)	N	0.0008-0.0020	0.0146-0.0249	0.0146-0.0249	0.0100-0.0500	0.0020-0.0041	0.0016-0.0032	0.0007-0.0091

93081C65

TORQUE SPECIFICATIONS
All readings in ft. lbs.

Year	Engine Displacement Liters (cc)	Engine ID/VIN	Cylinder Head Bolts	Main Bearing Bolts	Rod Bearing Bolts	Crankshaft Damper Bolts	Flywheel Bolts	Manifold Intake	Manifold Exhaust	Spark Plugs	Lug Nuts
1997	2.5 (2458)	P	①	80	33	80	105	②	②	27	80-110
	4.0 (3966)	S	③	80	33	80	105	④	④	27	80-110
	5.2 (5211)	Y	⑤	85	45	135	105	⑥	20	30	80-110
1998	2.5 (2458)	P	①	80	33	80	105	②	②	27	85-115
	4.0 (3966)	S	③	80	33	80	105	④	④	27	85-115
	5.2 (5211)	Y	⑤	85	45	135	105	⑥	20	30	85-115
	5.9 (5899)	Z	⑤	85	45	135	55	⑥	20	30	85-115
1999	2.5 (2458)	P	①	80	33	80	105	②	②	27	85-115
	4.0 (3966)	S	③	80	33	80	105	④	④	27	85-115
	4.7 (4701)	N	⑦	⑧	15 ⑨	130	45	9	18	27	85-115
2000-01	2.5 (2458)	P	①	80	33	80	105	②	②	27	85-115
	4.0 (3966)	S	③	80	33	80	105	④	④	27	85-115
	4.7 (4701)	N	⑦	⑧	15 ⑨	130	45	9	18	27	85-115

① Step 1: 22 ft. lbs.
Step 2: 45 ft. lbs.
Step 3: Bolts 1-6 to 110 ft. lbs.
Step 4: Bolt 7 to 100 ft. lbs.
Step 5: Bolts 8-10 to 110 ft. lbs.

② Bolt 1: 30 ft. lbs.
Bolts 2-7: 23 ft. lbs.

③ Step 1: 22 ft. lbs.
Step 2: 45 ft. lbs.
Step 3: Bolts 1-10 to 110 ft. lbs.
Step 4: Bolt 11 to 100 ft. lbs.
Step 5: Bolts 12-14 to 110 ft. lbs.

④ Bolts 1-5 and 8-11: 24 ft. lbs.
Bolts 6-7: 23 ft. lbs.

⑤ Step 1: 50 ft. lbs.
Step 2: 105 ft. lbs.

⑥ Step 1: Bolts 1-4 to 72 inch lbs. in 12 inch lb. increments
Step 2: Bolts 5-12 to 72 inch lbs.
Step 3: All bolts to 72 inch lbs.
Step 4: All bolts to 12 ft. lbs.
Step 5: All bolts to 12 ft. lbs.

⑦ M11 bolts: 60 ft. lbs.
M8 bolts: 250 inch lbs.

⑧ Step 1: Bolts 1-10 to 25 inch lbs.
Step 2: Bolts 1-10 plus 90 degrees
Step 3: Bolts A-K to 40 ft. lbs.
Step 4: Bolts A1-A5 to 20 ft. lbs.

⑨ Plus 110 degrees

93081C66

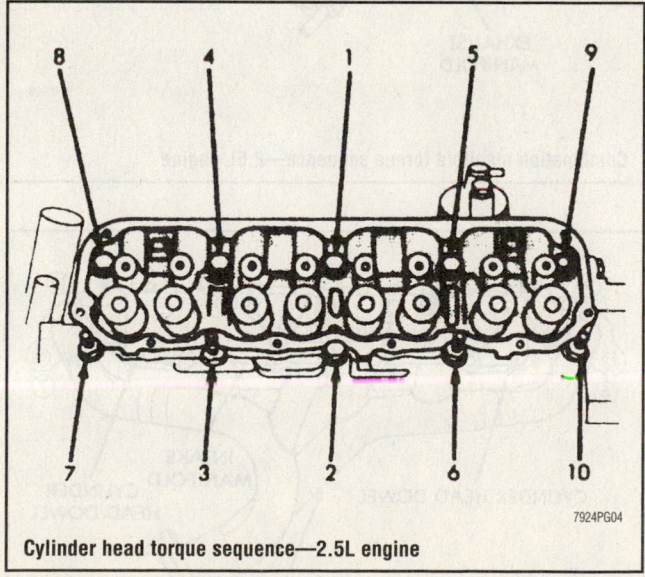

Cylinder head torque sequence—2.5L engine

7924PG04

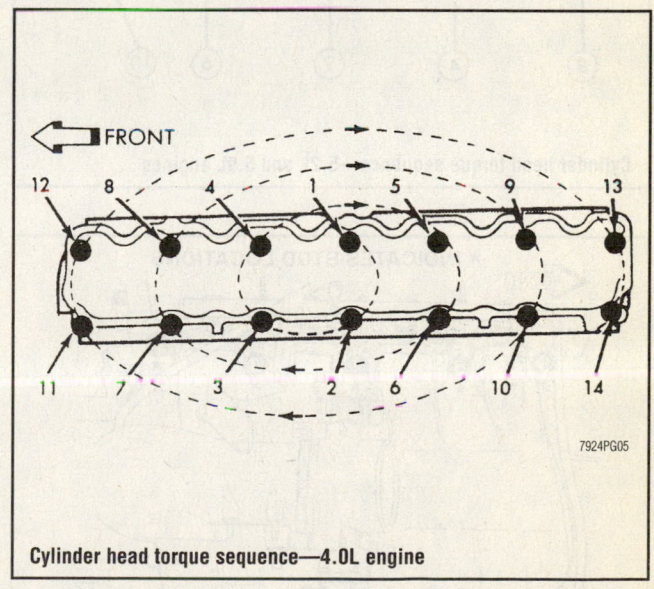

Cylinder head torque sequence—4.0L engine

7924PG05

Refer to the model specific sections for engine electrical system service procedures

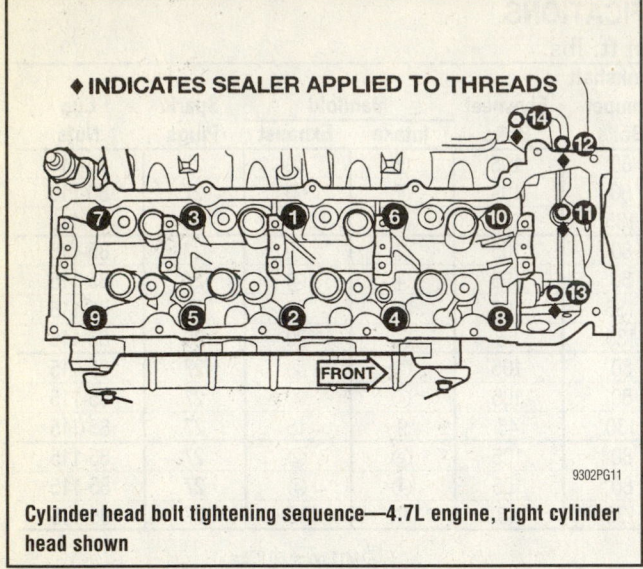

◆ INDICATES SEALER APPLIED TO THREADS

Cylinder head bolt tightening sequence—4.7L engine, right cylinder head shown

9302PG11

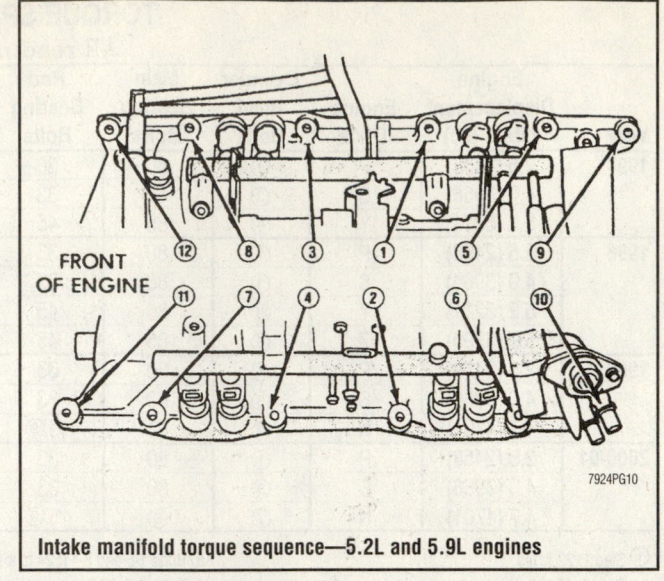

FRONT OF ENGINE

Intake manifold torque sequence—5.2L and 5.9L engines

7924PG10

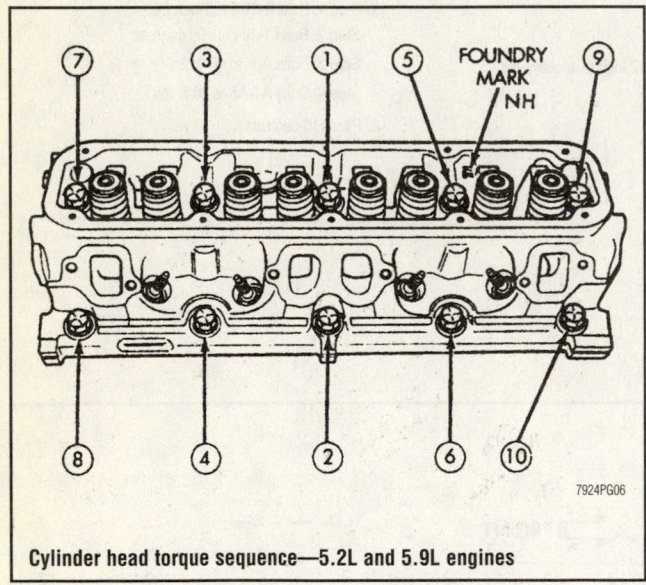

FOUNDRY MARK NH

Cylinder head torque sequence—5.2L and 5.9L engines

7924PG06

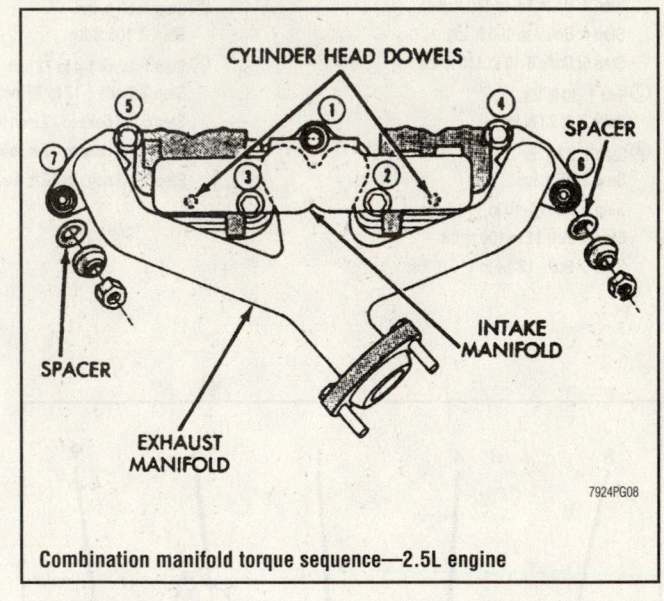

CYLINDER HEAD DOWELS

SPACER

INTAKE MANIFOLD

SPACER

EXHAUST MANIFOLD

Combination manifold torque sequence—2.5L engine

7924PG08

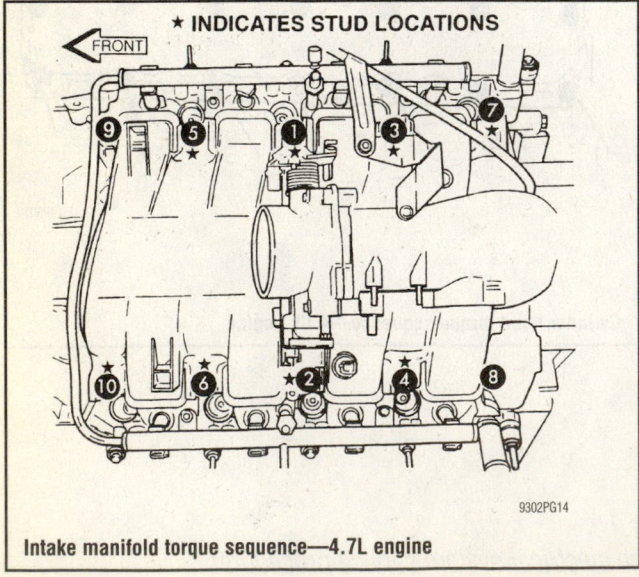

★ INDICATES STUD LOCATIONS

FRONT

Intake manifold torque sequence—4.7L engine

9302PG14

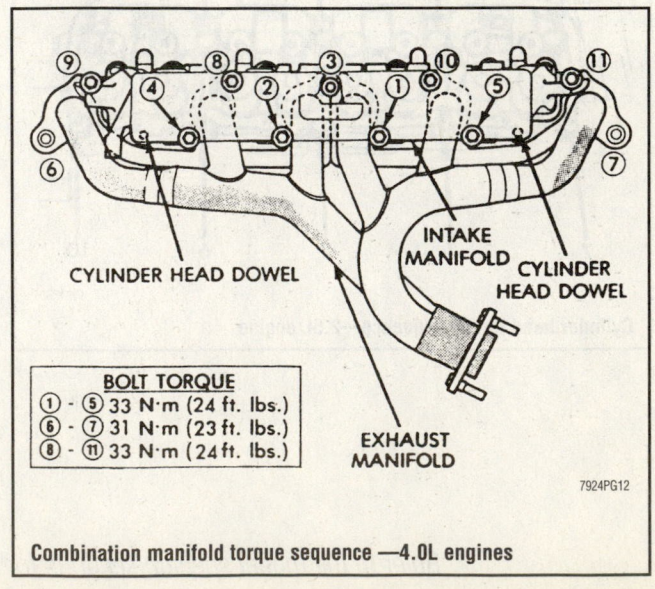

CYLINDER HEAD DOWEL

INTAKE MANIFOLD

CYLINDER HEAD DOWEL

EXHAUST MANIFOLD

BOLT TORQUE
① - ⑤ 33 N·m (24 ft. lbs.)
⑥ - ⑦ 31 N·m (23 ft. lbs.)
⑧ - ⑪ 33 N·m (24 ft. lbs.)

Combination manifold torque sequence —4.0L engines

7924PG12

BRAKE SPECIFICATIONS
JEEP CHEROKEE, GRAND CHEROKEE, WRANGLER
All measurements in inches unless noted

Year	Model	Brake Disc			Brake Drum			Minimum Lining Thickness		Brake Caliper Mounting Bolts (ft. lbs.)
		Original Thickness	Minimum Thickness	Maximum Run-out	Original Inside Diameter	Max. Wear Limit	Maximum Machine Diameter	Front	Rear	
1997	Cherokee	0.94	0.89	- 0.005	9.00	①	9.06	0.030	0.030	11
	Grand Cherokee	②	③	0.005	—	—	—	0.030	0.030	7-15
	Wrangler	0.94	0.89	0.005	9.00	①	9.06	0.030	0.030	11
1998	Cherokee	0.94	0.89	0.005	9.00	①	9.06	0.030	④	11
	Grand Cherokee	②	③	0.005	—	—	—	0.030	0.030	7-15
	Wrangler	0.94	0.89	0.005	9.00	①	9.06	0.030	④	11
1999	Cherokee	0.94	0.89	0.005	⑤	①	⑥	0.030	④	11
	Grand Cherokee	—	⑦	0.003	—	—	—	0.030	0.030	⑧
	Wrangler	0.94	0.89	0.005	9.00	①	9.06	0.030	④	11
2000-01	Cherokee	0.94	0.89	0.005	⑤	①	⑥	0.030	④	11
	Grand Cherokee	—	⑦	0.003	—	—	—	0.030	0.030	⑧
	Wrangler	0.94	0.89	0.005	9.00	①	9.06	0.030	④	11

① Maximum diameter is listed on outside of drum
② Front: 0.94 in.
　Rear: 0.440 in.
③ Front: 0.89 in.
　Rear: 0.37 in.
④ Riveted brake shoes: 0.030 in.
　Bonded brake shoes: 0.060 in.

⑤ Standard: 9.00 in.
　Optional 10.00 in.
⑥ Standard: 9.06 in.
　Optional 10.06 in.
⑦ Front: 0.965 in.
　Rear: 0.335 in.
⑧ Slide pin bolts: 21-30 ft. lbs.
　Anchor bolts: 66-85 ft. lbs.

93081C67

For accessory drive belt replacement procedures see the model specific sections of this manual

SCHEDULED MAINTENANCE INTERVALS
(JEEP CHEROKEE, GRAND CHEROKEE & WRANGLER)

TO BE SERVICED	TYPE OF SERVICE	VEHICLE MILEAGE INTERVAL (x1000)												
		7.5	15	22.5	30	37.5	45	52.5	60	67.5	75	82.5	90	97.5
Engine oil & filter	R	✓	✓	✓	✓	✓	✓	✓	✓	✓	✓	✓	✓	✓
Brake hoses & linings	S/I	✓	✓	✓	✓	✓	✓	✓	✓	✓	✓	✓	✓	✓
Engine coolant level, hoses & clamps	S/I	✓	✓	✓	✓	✓	✓	✓	✓	✓	✓	✓	✓	✓
Exhaust system	S/I	✓	✓	✓	✓	✓	✓	✓	✓	✓	✓	✓	✓	✓
Lubricate steering linkage (4x2)	S/I	✓	✓	✓	✓	✓	✓	✓	✓	✓	✓	✓	✓	✓
Lubricate steering linkage (4x4)	S/I	✓		✓		✓		✓		✓		✓		✓
Air filter	R				✓				✓				✓	
Automatic transmission fluid & filter	R				✓				✓				✓	
Spark plugs	R				✓				✓				✓	
Transfer case fluid	R				✓				✓				✓	
Drive belts	S/I				✓				✓				✓	
Front & rear axle oil	R				✓				✓				✓	
Prop shaft universal joints	S/I				✓				✓				✓	
Rotate tires	S/I				✓				✓				✓	
Engine coolant	R						✓				✓			
Manual transmission fluid	R					✓					✓			
Distributor cap & rotor	R								✓					
Fuel filter	R								✓					
Ignition cables	R								✓					

R: Replace   S/I: Service or Inspect

FREQUENT OPERATION MAINTENANCE (SEVERE SERVICE)

If a vehicle is operated under any of the following conditions it is considered severe service:

- Extremely dusty areas.

- 50% or more of the vehicle operation is in 32°C (90°F) or higher temperatures, or constant operation in temperatures below 0°C (32°F).

- Prolonged idling (vehicle operation in stop and go traffic).

- Frequent short running periods (engine does not warm to normal operating temperatures).

- Police, taxi, delivery usage or trailer towing usage.

Oil & oil filter change: change every 3000 miles.

Automatic transmission fluid, filter & bands: change & adjust every 12,000 miles.

Brake hoses & linings: check every 12,000 miles.

Liubricate steering linkage: check every 3000 miles.

Manual transmission fluid: change every 18,000 miles.

Prop shaft universal joints: lubricate every 3000 miles.

Front & rear axle oil: change every 12,000 miles.

93081C68

SCHEDULED MAINTENANCE INTERVALS
DAIMLERCHRYSLER CORPORATION
JEEP CHEROKEE, GRAND CHEROKEE, WRANGLER

The following should be used as a guide when determining the amount of work required for a particular service. In estimating how long a particular Scheduled Maintenance Service should take, please observe the following:

- Labor Time is time based on field research and data supplied by the vehicle manufacturer.
- Labor time operations are given in hours and tenths of an hour.
- All labor operations are to be used as a guide.

Mechanic Skill Level Codes:
(A) PRECISION: Highly skilled with multiple certification.
(B) GENERAL: Normally skilled with certification.
(C) MAINTENANCE: Semi-skilled working on certification.

	LABOR TIME		LABOR TIME		LABOR TIME
7500 Mile Service (C)		**45000 Mile Service (B)**		**75000 Mile Service (B)**	
All Models	.9	All Models	1.8	All Models	2.0
w/4WD add	.1				
15000 Mile Service (C)		**52500 Mile Service (C)**		**82500 Mile Service (C)**	
All Models	.9	All Models	.9	All Models	.9
		w/4WD add	.1	w/4WD add	.1
22500 Mile Service (C)		**60000 Mile Service (B)**		**90000 Mile Service (B)**	
All Models	.9	All Models	4.5	All Models	3.1
w/4WD add	.1	w/AT add	.5	w/AT add	.5
30000 Mile Service (B)		w/4WD add	.5	w/4WD add	.5
All Models	3.0	**67500 Mile Service (C)**		**97500 Mile Service (C)**	
w/AT add	.5	All Models	.9	All Models	.9
w/4WD add	.5	w/4WD add	.1	w/4WD add	.1
37500 Mile Service (B)					
All Models	1.4				
w/4WD add	.1				

93081C69

For brake related suspension and axle service, refer to the model specific sections of this manual

TIRE, WHEEL AND BALL JOINT SPECIFICATIONS
Jeep

Year	Model	OEM Tires Standard	OEM Tires Optional	Tire Pressures (psi) Front	Tire Pressures (psi) Rear	Wheel Size	Ball Joint Inspection
1997	Cherokee	P215/75R15	P225/75R15 P225/70R15	33	33	7-J	①
	Grand Cherokee	P215/75R15	P225/75R15 P235/75R15 P245/70R15 P225/70R16	36	36	7-J	①
	Wrangler	P205/75R15	P215/75R15 P225/75R15 29x9.5R15LT	30	Std: 30 Opt: LT: 30 Opt: P225: 35	7-JJ	①
1998	Cherokee	P215/75R15	P225/75R15 P225/70R15	33	33	7-J	①
	Grand Cherokee	P215/75R15	P225/75R15 P235/75R15 P245/70R15 P225/70R16	36	36	7-J	①
	Wrangler	P205/75R15	P215/75R15 P225/75R15 30x9.5R15LT	33	33	7-JJ	①
1999	Cherokee	P215/75R15	P225/75R15 P225/70R15	33	33	7-J	①
	Grand Cherokee	P215/75R15	P225/75R15 P235/75R15 P245/70R15 P225/70R16	36	36	7-J	①
	Wrangler	P205/75R15	P215/75R15 P225/75R15 30x9.5R15LT	33	33	7-JJ	①
2000-01	Cherokee	P215/75R15	P225/75R15 P225/70R15	33	33	7-J	①
	Grand Cherokee	P215/75R15	P225/75R15 P235/75R15 P245/70R15 P225/70R16	36	36	7-J	①
	Wrangler	P205/75R15	P215/75R15 P225/75R15 30x9.5R15LT	33	33	7-JJ	①

OEM: Original Equipment Manufacturer

PSI: Pounds Per Square Inch

STD: Standard

OPT: Optional

① Replace if any measurable movement is found.

93081C70

FORD MOTOR CO.
Ford Escape

ENGINE AND VEHICLE IDENTIFICATION

Engine							Model Year	
Code ①	Liters (cc)	Cu. In.	Cyl.	Fuel Sys.	Engine Type	Eng. Mfg.	Code ②	Year
B	2.0 (1998)	121	4	SFI	DOHC	Ford	1	2001
1	3.0 (3049)	182	6	SFI	DOHC	Ford		

SFI: Multi-port Fuel Injection

DOHC: Double Overhead Camshafts

① 8th digit of VIN

② 10th digit of VIN

93081C71

GENERAL ENGINE SPECIFICATIONS

Year	Model	Engine Displacement Liters (cc)	Engine ID/VIN	Fuel System Type	Net Horsepower @ rpm	Net Torque @ rpm (ft. lbs.)	Bore x Stroke (in.)	Compression Ratio	Oil Pressure @ rpm
2001	Escape	2.0 (1998)	B	SFI	135@5500	135@4500	3.34x3.46	9.6:1	54-80 ①
	Escape	3.0 (3049)	1	SFI	200@5500	200@4500	3.39x3.39	10.0:1	45 ①

SFI: Multi-port Fuel Injection

① The manufacturer does not provide an engine speed specification for oil pump pressure.

93081C72

Refer to the model specific sections for driveline service procedures

ENGINE TUNE-UP SPECIFICATIONS

Year	Engine Displacement Liters (cc)	Engine ID/VIN	Spark Plug Gap (in.)	Ignition Timing (deg.)		Fuel Pump (psi)	Idle Speed (rpm)		Valve Clearance	
				MT	AT		MT	AT	Intake	Exhaust
2001	2.0 (1998)	B	0.039-0.043	10 BTDC	—	65	①	—	HYD.	HYD.
	3.0 (3049)	1	0.052-0.056	10 BTDC	10 BTDC	65	①	①	HYD.	HYD.

BTDC: Before Top Dead Center

HYD: Hydraulic lash adjusters

① Refer to Vehicle Emission Control Information Label

93081C73

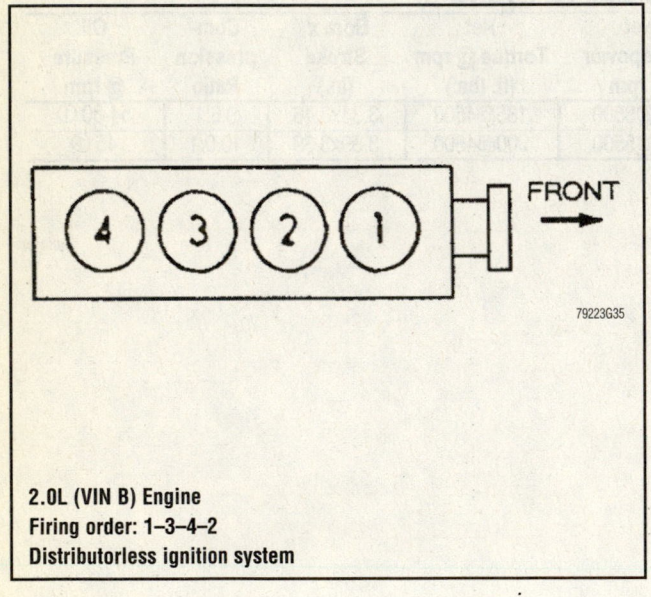

2.0L (VIN B) Engine
Firing order: 1–3–4–2
Distributorless ignition system

79223G35

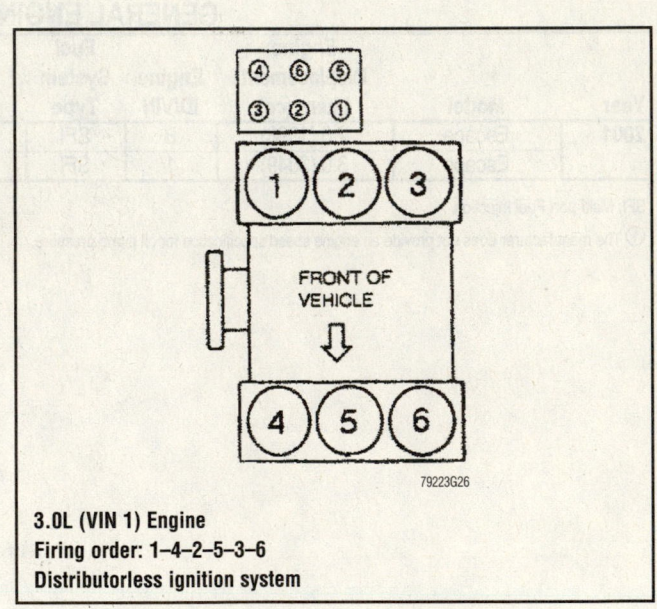

3.0L (VIN 1) Engine
Firing order: 1–4–2–5–3–6
Distributorless ignition system

79223G26

CAPACITIES

Year	Model	Engine Displacement Liters (cc)	Engine ID/VIN	Engine Oil with Filter (qts.)	Transmission (pts.)		Transfer Case (pts.)	Drive Axle		Fuel Tank (gal.)	Cooling System (qts.)
					Manual	Auto.		Front (pts.)	Rear (pts.)		
2001	Escape	2.0 (1998)	B	4.5	5.7	—	3.0	2.6	3.0	15.0	7.0
	Escape	3.0 (3049)	1	5.8	5.7	2.5	3.0	2.6	3.0	16.0	10.5

NOTE: All capacities are approximate. Add fluid gradually and check to be sure a proper fluid level is obtained.

93081C74

VALVE SPECIFICATIONS

Year	Engine Displacement Liters (cc)	Engine ID/VIN	Seat Angle (deg.)	Face Angle (deg.)	Spring Test Pressure (lbs. @ in.)	Spring Installed Height (in.)	Stem-to-Guide Clearance (in.)		Stem Diameter (in.)	
							Intake	Exhaust	Intake	Exhaust
2001	2.0 (1998)	B	45	45	82.1@ 0.988	1.420-1.54	0.0007-0.0027	0.0017-0.0037	0.2374	0.2374
	3.0 (3049)	1	44.75	45	153@ 1.18	1.57	0.0010-0.0024	0.0012-0.0026	0.2350-0.2358	0.2343-0.2358

93081C75

CRANKSHAFT AND CONNECTING ROD SPECIFICATIONS
All measurements are given in inches.

Year	Engine Displacement Liters (cc)	Engine ID/VIN	Crankshaft				Connecting Rod		
			Main Brg. Journal Dia.	Main Brg. Oil Clearance	Shaft End-play	Thrust on No.	Journal Diameter	Oil Clearance	Side Clearance
2001	2.0 (1998)	B	2.282-2.284	①	0.0035-0.0102	3	1.7279-1.7287	0.0080-0.0026	0.0040-0.0110
	3.0 (3049)	1	2.467-2.479	①	0.0009-0.0019	3	1.9670-1.9680	0.0010-0.0025	0.0039-0.0118

① Journals 1, 2 and 4: 0.0010 - 0.0017 in.
Journal 3: 0.0012 - 0.0019 in.

93081C76

For exhaust manifold replacement procedures, see the model specific sections of this manual

PISTON AND RING SPECIFICATIONS
All measurements are given in inches.

Year	Engine Displacement Liters (cc)	Engine ID/VIN	Piston Clearance	Ring Gap			Ring Side Clearance		
				Top Compression	Bottom Compression	Oil Control	Top Compression	Bottom Compression	Oil Control
2001	2.0 (1998)	B	0.0004- 0.0012	0.010- 0.030	0.010- 0.030	0.016- 0.066	0.0015- 0.0032	0.0015- 0.0035	—
	3.0 (3049)	1	0.0005- 0.0009	0.004- 0.016	0.008- 0.014	0.008- 0.028	0.0018- 0.0031	0.0012- 0.0028	—

93081C77

TORQUE SPECIFICATIONS
All readings in ft. lbs.

Year	Engine Displacement Liters (cc)	Engine ID/VIN	Cylinder Head Bolts	Main Bearing Bolts	Rod Bearing Bolts	Crankshaft Damper Bolts	Flywheel Bolts	Manifold		Spark Plugs	Lug Nuts
								Intake	Exhaust		
2001	2.0 (1998)	B	①	66-79	26-30	80-87	83	13	8	11	98
	3.0 (3049)	1	②	63	50	11	83	8	15	11	98

① Step 1: 15 ft. lbs. (20 Nm).
   Step 2: 30 ft. lbs. (40 Nm).
   Step 3: Plus an additional 90 degrees.

② Step 1: 30 ft. lbs. (40 Nm).
   Step 2: Tighten the bolts 90 degrees.
   Step 3: Loosen the bolts one full turn.
   Step 4: 30 ft. lbs. (40 Nm).
   Step 5: Tighten the bolts 90 degrees.
   Step 6: Tighten the bolts 90 degrees.

93081C78

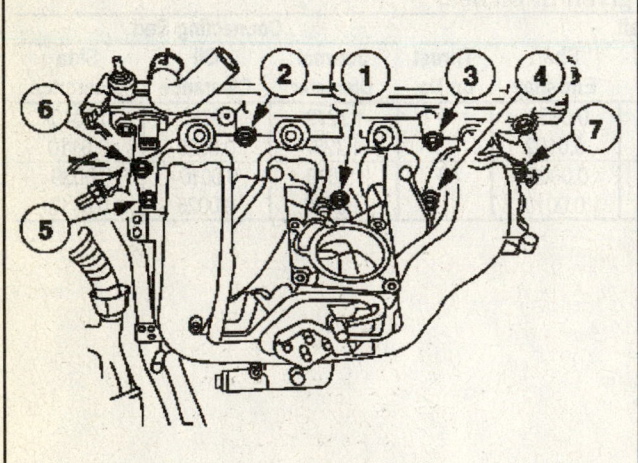

Tighten the intake manifold bolts in the sequence shown—2.0L engine

9308TG01

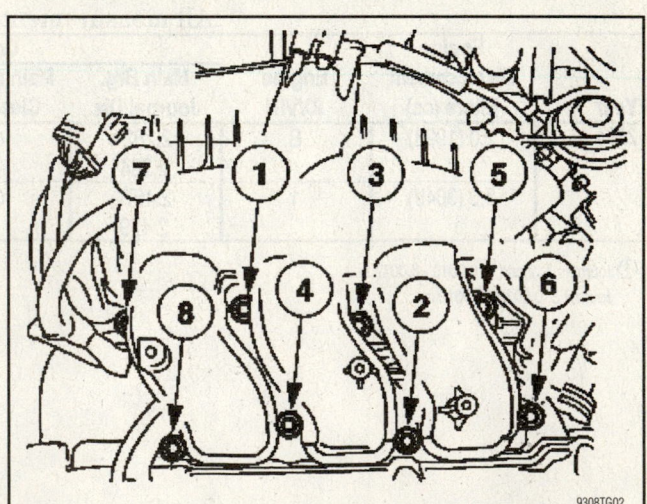

Tighten the upper intake manifold bolts in the sequence shown—3.0L engine

9308TG02

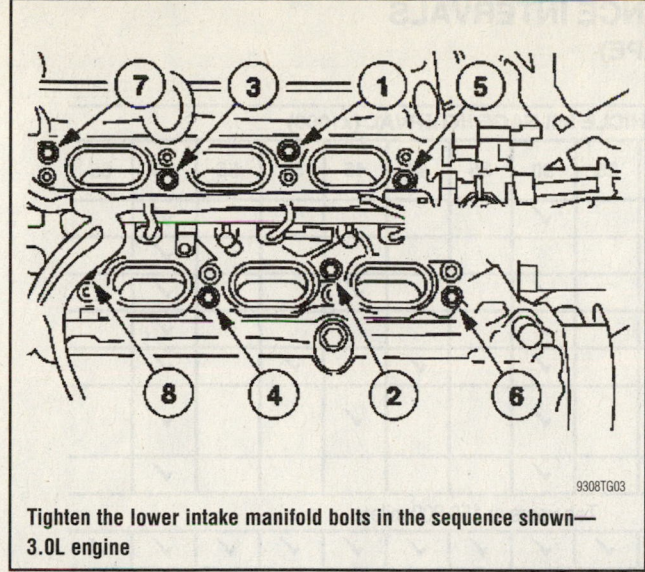

Tighten the lower intake manifold bolts in the sequence shown—
3.0L engine

9308TG03

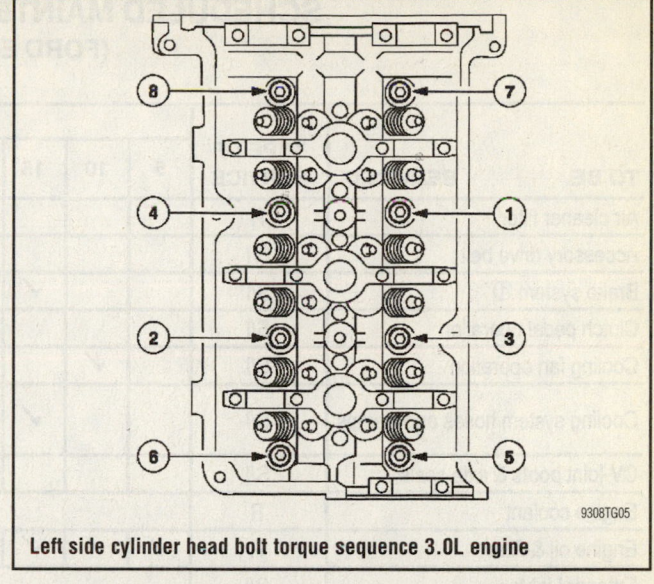

Left side cylinder head bolt torque sequence 3.0L engine

9308TG05

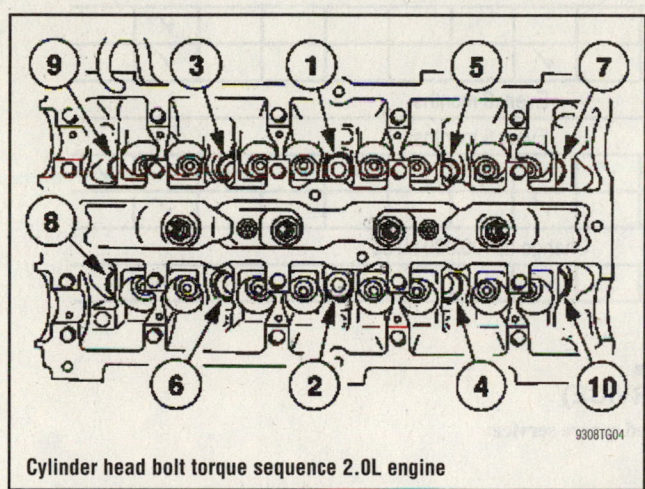

Cylinder head bolt torque sequence 2.0L engine

9308TG04

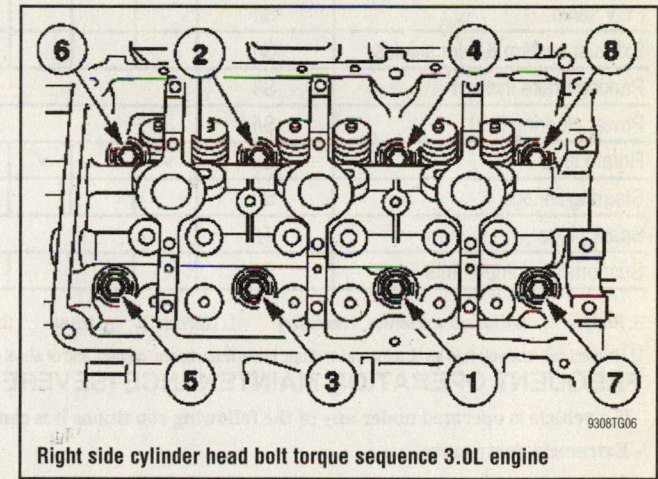

Right side cylinder head bolt torque sequence 3.0L engine

9308TG06

FORD ESCAPE
All measurements in inches unless noted

Year	Model		Brake Disc Original Thickness	Brake Disc Minimum Thickness	Brake Disc Maximum Run-out	Brake Drum Original Inside Diameter	Brake Drum Max. Wear Limit	Brake Drum Maximum Machine Diameter	Minimum Lining Thickness	Brake Caliper Bracket Bolts (ft. lbs.)	Brake Caliper Mounting Bolts (ft. lbs.)
2001	Escape	F	0.94	0.86	0.002	—	—	—	0.039	111	26
		R	0.550	0.500	0.004	9.06	0.06	8.92	0.039	87	25

93081C79

Refer to the model specific sections for cooling system service procedures

SCHEDULED MAINTENANCE INTERVALS
(FORD ESCAPE)

TO BE SERVICED	TYPE OF SERVICE	VEHICLE MILEAGE INTERVAL (x1000)												
		5	10	15	20	25	30	35	40	45	50	55	60	65
Air cleaner filter	R						✓						✓	
Accessory drive belt	S/I												✓	
Brake system ①	S/I			✓			✓			✓			✓	
Clutch pedal operation	S/I						✓						✓	
Cooling fan operation	S/I		✓		✓		✓		✓		✓		✓	
Cooling system hoses and clamps	S/I			✓			✓			✓			✓	
CV-joint boots & axle seals	S/I						✓						✓	
Engine coolant	R	Ten years or 150,000 miles												
Engine oil & filter	R	✓	✓	✓	✓	✓	✓	✓	✓	✓	✓	✓	✓	✓
Exterior Lights	S/I	Check monthly												
PCV valve	S/I												✓	
Exhaust system & heat shields	S/I						✓						✓	
Parking brake system	S/I	Every 6 months												
Power steering fluid	S/I	Every 6 months												
Rotate tires	S/I	✓		✓		✓		✓		✓		✓		✓
Steering linkage	S/I						✓						✓	
Spark plugs	R	Change at 100,000 miles												
Suspension components	S/I						✓						✓	

R: Replace   S/I: Inspect and service, if necessary   L: Lubricate   A: Adjust   C: Clean

① Inspect the reservoir fluid level, rotor and or drum, brake lines, hoses, calipers and or wheel cylinders

FREQUENT OPERATION MAINTENANCE (SEVERE SERVICE)

If a vehicle is operated under any of the following conditions it is considered severe service:

- Extremely dusty areas.

- 50% or more of the vehicle operation is in 32°C (90°F) or higher temperatures, or constant operation in temperatures below 0°C (32°F).

- Prolonged idling (vehicle operation in stop and go traffic).

- Frequent short running periods (engine does not warm to normal operating temperatures).

- Police, taxi, delivery usage or trailer towing usage.

Oil & oil filter change: change every 3000 miles.

Air filter element: change every 15,000 miles.

93081C80

SCHEDULED MAINTENANCE INTERVALS
FORD MOTOR COMPANY
ESCAPE

The following should be used as a guide when determining the amount of work required for a particular service. In estimating how long a particular Scheduled Maintenance Service should take, please observe the following:

● Labor Time is time based on field research and data supplied by the vehicle manufacturer.
● Labor time operations are given in hours and tenths of an hour.
● All labor operations are to be used as a guide.

Mechanic Skill Level Codes:
(A) PRECISION: Highly skilled with multiple certification.
(B) GENERAL: Normally skilled with certification.
(C) MAINTENANCE: Semi-skilled working on certification.

	LABOR TIME		LABOR TIME		LABOR TIME
5000 Mile Service (C)		**25000 Mile Service (C)**		**50000 Mile Service (C)**	
All Models	.9	All Models	.9	All Models	.7
10000 Mile Service (C)		**30000 Mile Service (B)**		**55000 Mile Service (C)**	
All Models	.5	All Models	1.9	All Models	.9
15000 Mile Service (C)		**35000 Mile Service (C)**		**60000 Mile Service (B)**	
All Models	1.6	All Models	.9	All Models	1.9
20000 Mile Service (C)		**40000 Mile Service (C)**		**65000 Mile Service (C)**	
All Models	.5	All Models	.5	All Models	.9
		45000 Mile Service (C)			
		All Models	1.6		

93081C81

TIRE, WHEEL AND BALL JOINT SPECIFICATIONS
Ford Escape

		OEM Tires		Tire Pressures (psi)		Wheel	Ball Joint
Year	Model	Standard	Optional	Front	Rear	Size	Inspection
2001	Escape	P225/70SR15	P235/70R16	NA	NA	NA	0.030 in.

OEM: Original Equipment Manufacturer

PSI: Pounds Per Square Inch

STD: Standard

OPT: Optional

NA: Not Available

93081CAX

FORD MOTOR CO.

Ford F-Series • E-Series • Aerostar • Club Wagon • Excursion • Expedition • Explorer • Ranger • Super Duty • Lincoln Navigator • Mercury Mountaineer

ENGINE AND VEHICLE IDENTIFICATION

Engine								Model Year	
Code ①	Liters (cc)	Cu. In.	Cyl.	Fuel Sys.	Type	Eng. Mfg.		Code ②	Year
2	4.2 (4195)	256	6	MFI	OHV	Ford		V	1997
3	5.4 (5409)	330	8	SFI	SOHC	Ford		W	1998
5	6.8 (6802)	415	10	MFI	SOHC	Ford		X	1999
6	4.6 (4588)	280	8	MFI	SOHC	Ford		Y	2000
A	2.3 (2294)	140	4	MFI	SOHC	Ford		1	2001
A	5.4 (5409)	330	8	EFI	DOHC	Ford			
C	2.5 (2500)	152	4	MFI	SOHC	Ford			
E	4.0 (4000)	244	6	MFI	SOHC	Ford			
F	7.3 (7292)	445	8	DI	OHV	Navistar			
G	7.5 (7538)	460	8	MFI	OHV	Ford			
H	5.8 (5752)	351	8	MFI	OHV	Ford			
L	5.4 (5409)	330	8	EFI	SOHC	Ford			
M	5.4 (5409)	330	8	EFI ③	SOHC	Ford			
N	5.0 (4949)	302	8	MFI	OHV	Ford			
P	5.0 (4949)	302	8	MFI	OHV	Ford			
U	3.0 (2999)	183	6	MFI	OHV	Ford			
W	4.6 (4588)	280	8	MFI	SOHC	Ford			
X	4.0 (3998)	244	6	MFI	OHV	Ford			
Y	4.9 (4916)	300	6	MFI	OHV	Ford			
Z	5.4 (5409)	330	8	EFI ④	SOHC	Ford			

MFI: Multi-port Fuel Injection

DI: Direct Injection Turbo-Diesel

EFI: Electronic Fuel Injection

SFI: Sequential Fuel Injection

OHV: Overhead Valve

SOHC: Single Overhead Camshaft

① 8th digit of the Vehicle Identification Number (VIN)

② 10th digit of the Vehicle Identification Number (VIN)

③ Natural Gas Vehicle (NGV)

④ Bi-fuel Vehicle (Natural Gas/Propane)

93081C82

GENERAL ENGINE SPECIFICATIONS

Year	Model	Engine Displacement Liters (cc)	Engine Series (ID/VIN)	Fuel System Type	Net Horsepower @ rpm	Net Torque @ rpm (ft. lbs.)	Bore x Stroke (in.)	Compression Ratio	Oil Pressure @ rpm
1997	Aerostar	3.0 (2982)	U	MFI	147@5000	162@3250	3.50x3.14	9.3:1	40-60@2500
	Aerostar	4.0 (3950)	X	MFI	160@4000	225@2500	3.81x3.39	9.0:1	40-60@2000
	E-150	4.9 (4916)	Y	MFI	145@3400	265@2000	4.00x3.98	8.8:1	40-60@2000
	E-150	5.0 (4949)	N	MFI	199@4200	270@2400	4.00x3.00	9.0:1	40-60@2000
	E-150	5.8 (5752)	H	MFI	210@3600	325@2800	4.00x3.50	8.8:1	40-65@2000
	E-250	4.9 (4916)	Y	MFI	145@3400	265@2000	4.00x3.98	8.8:1	40-60@2000
	E-250	5.0 (4949)	N	MFI	199@4200	270@2400	4.00x3.00	9.0:1	40-60@2000
	E-250	5.8 (5752)	H	MFI	210@3600	325@2800	4.00x3.50	8.8:1	40-65@2000
	E-350	4.9 (4916)	Y	MFI	145@3400	265@2000	4.00x3.98	8.8:1	40-60@2000
	E-350	5.8 (5752)	H	MFI	210@3600	325@2800	4.00x3.50	8.8:1	40-65@2000
	E-350	7.3 (7292)	F	DI	210@3000	425@2000	4.11x4.18	17.5:1	40-70@3000
	E-350	7.5 (7538)	G	MFI	245@4000	400@2200	4.36x3.85	8.5:1	40-88@2000
	Explorer	4.0 (3950)	X	MFI	160@4000	225@2500	3.81x3.39	9.0:1	40-60@2000
	Explorer	5.0 (4949)	P	MFI	210@4500	280@3500	4.00x3.00	9.0:1	40-60@2500
	F-150	4.9 (4916)	Y	MFI	145@3400	265@2000	4.00x3.98	8.8:1	40-60@2000
	F-150	5.0 (4949)	N	MFI	199@4200	270@2400	4.00x3.00	9.0:1	40-60@2000
	F-150	5.8 (5752)	H	MFI	210@3600	325@2800	4.00x3.50	8.8:1	40-65@2000
	F-250	4.9 (4916)	Y	MFI	145@3400	265@2000	4.00x3.98	8.8:1	40-60@2000
	F-250	5.0 (4949)	N	MFI	199@4200	270@2400	4.00x3.00	9.0:1	40-60@2000
	F-250	5.8 (5752)	H	MFI	210@3600	325@2800	4.00x3.50	8.8:1	40-65@2000
	F-250	7.3 (7292)	F	DI	210@3000	425@2000	4.11x4.18	17.5:1	40-70@3000
	F-250	7.5 (7538)	G	MFI	245@4000	400@2200	4.36x3.85	8.5:1	40-88@2000
	F-350	4.9 (4916)	Y	MFI	145@3400	265@2000	4.00x3.98	8.8:1	40-60@2000
	F-350	5.8 (5752)	H	MFI	210@3600	325@2800	4.00x3.50	8.8:1	40-65@2000
	F-350	7.3 (7292)	F	DI	210@3000	425@2000	4.11x4.18	17.5:1	40-70@3000
	F-350	7.5 (7538)	G	MFI	245@4000	400@2200	4.36x3.85	8.5:1	40-88@2000
	F-Super Duty	7.3 (7292)	F	DI	210@3000	425@2000	4.11x4.18	17.5:1	40-70@3000
	F-Super Duty	7.5 (7538)	G	MFI	245@4000	400@2200	4.36x3.85	8.5:1	40-88@2000
	Mountaineer	5.0 (4949)	P	MFI	210@4500	280@3500	4.00x3.00	9.0:1	40-60@2500
	Ranger	2.3 (2300)	A	MFI	112@4800	135@2400	3.78x3.13	9.4:1	40-60@2000
	Ranger	3.0 (2982)	U	MFI	147@5000	162@3250	3.50x3.14	9.3:1	40-60@2500
	Ranger	4.0 (3950)	X	MFI	160@4000	225@2500	3.81x3.39	9.0:1	40-60@2000
1998	E-150	4.2 (4195)	2	MFI	205@4400	255@3000	3.81x3.74	9.3:1	50@2000
	E-150	4.6 (4588)	6/W	MFI	210@4400	290@3250	3.55x3.54	9.0:1	20-45@1500
	E-150	5.4 (5409)	L	MFI	235@4250	330@3000	3.55X4.17	9.0:1	40-70@1500
	E-250	4.2 (4195)	2	MFI	205@4400	255@3000	3.81x3.74	9.3:1	50@2000
	E-250	5.4 (5409)	L	MFI	235@4250	330@3000	3.55X4.17	9.0:1	40-70@1500
	E-350	5.4 (5409)	L	MFI	235@4250	330@3000	3.55X4.17	9.0:1	40-70@1500
	E-350	6.8 (6802)	5	MFI	265@4250	410@2750	4.09X4.17	9.0:1	40-70@1500
	E-350	7.3 (7292)	F	DI	210@3000	425@2000	4.11x4.18	17.5:1	40-70@3000
	Expedition	4.6 (4588)	6	MFI	210@4400	290@3250	3.55x3.54	9.0:1	20-45@1500
	Expedition	5.4 (5409)	L	MFI	235@4250	330@3000	3.55X4.17	9.0:1	40-70@1500
	Explorer	4.0 (4000)	X	MFI	160@4000	225@2500	3.81x3.39	9.0:1	40-60@2000
	Explorer	5.0 (4949)	P	MFI	210@4500	280@3500	4.00x3.00	9.0:1	40-60@2500
	F-150	4.2 (4195)	2	MFI	205@4400	255@3000	3.81x3.74	9.3:1	50@2000
	F-150	4.6 (4588)	W	MFI	210@4400	290@3250	3.55x3.54	9.0:1	20-45@1500
	F-150	4.6 (4588)	6	MFI	210@4400	290@3250	3.55x3.54	9.0:1	20-45@1500
	F-150	5.4 (5409)	L	MFI	235@4250	330@3000	3.55X4.17	9.0:1	40-70@1500
	F-250	5.8 (5752)	H	MFI	210@3600	325@2800	4.00x3.50	8.8:1	40-65@2000
	F-250	7.3 (7292)	F	DI	210@3000	425@2000	4.11x4.18	17.5:1	40-70@3000
	F-250	7.5 (7538)	G	MFI	245@4000	400@2200	4.36x3.85	8.5:1	40-88@2000
	F-250HD	5.8 (5752)	H	EFI	210@3600	325@2800	4.00x3.50	8.8:1	40-65@2000

93081C83

Timing chain and gear service is covered in the model specific sections of this manual

GENERAL ENGINE SPECIFICATIONS

Year	Model	Engine Displacement Liters (cc)	Engine Series (ID/VIN)	Fuel System Type	Net Horsepower @ rpm	Net Torque @ rpm (ft. lbs.)	Bore x Stroke (in.)	Com- pression Ratio	Oil Pressure @ rpm
1998 (cont.)	F-250HD	7.3 (7292)	F	DIT	210@3000	425@2000	4.11x4.18	17.5:1	40-70@3000
	F-250HD	7.5 (7538)	G	EFI	245@4000	400@2200	4.36x3.85	8.5:1	40-88@2000
	F-350	5.8 (5752)	H	MFI	210@3600	325@2800	4.00x3.50	8.8:1	40-65@2000
	F-350	7.3 (7292)	F	DI	210@3000	425@2000	4.11x4.18	17.5:1	40-70@3000
	F-350	7.5 (7538)	G	MFI	245@4000	400@2200	4.36x3.85	8.5:1	40-88@2000
	F-Super Duty	5.8 (5752)	H	MFI	210@3600	325@2800	4.00x3.50	8.8:1	40-65@2000
	F-Super Duty	7.3 (7292)	F	DI	210@3000	425@2000	4.11x4.18	17.5:1	40-70@3000
	F-Super Duty	7.5 (7538)	G	MFI	245@4000	400@2200	4.36x3.85	8.5:1	40-88@2000
	Mountaineer	5.0 (4949)	P	MFI	210@4500	280@3500	4.00x3.00	9.0:1	40-60@2500
	Ranger	2.5 (2500)	C	MFI	119@5000	146@3000	3.78X3.90	9.1:1	40-60@2000
	Ranger	3.0 (2982)	U	MFI	147@5000	162@3250	3.50x3.14	9.3:1	40-60@2500
	Ranger	4.0 (3950)	X	MFI	160@4000	225@2500	3.81x3.39	9.0:1	40-60@2000
1999	E-150	4.2 (4195)	2	MFI	205@4400	255@3000	3.81x3.74	9.3:1	50@2000
	E-150	4.6 (4588)	6/W	MFI	210@4400	290@3250	3.55x3.54	9.0:1	20-45@1500
	E-150	5.4 (5409)	L	MFI	235@4250	330@3000	3.55X4.17	9.0:1	40-70@1500
	E-250	4.2 (4195)	2	MFI	205@4400	255@3000	3.81x3.74	9.3:1	50@2000
	E-250	5.4 (5409)	L	MFI	235@4250	330@3000	3.55X4.17	9.0:1	40-70@1500
	E-350	5.4 (5409)	L	MFI	235@4250	330@3000	3.55X4.17	9.0:1	40-70@1500
	E-350	6.8 (6802)	5	MFI	265@4250	410@2750	4.09X4.17	9.0:1	40-70@1500
	E-350	7.3 (7292)	F	DI	210@3000	425@2000	4.11x4.18	17.5:1	40-70@3000
	Expedition	4.6 (4588)	6/W	MFI	210@4400	290@3250	3.55x3.54	9.0:1	20-45@1500
	Expedition	5.4 (5409)	L	MFI	235@4250	330@3000	3.55X4.17	9.0:1	40-70@1500
	Explorer	4.0 (4000)	X	MFI	160@4000	225@2500	3.81x3.39	9.0:1	40-60@2000
	Explorer	5.0 (4949)	P	MFI	210@4500	280@3500	4.00x3.00	9.0:1	40-60@2500
	F-150	4.2 (4195)	2	MFI	205@4400	255@3000	3.81x3.74	9.3:1	50@2000
	F-150	4.6 (4588)	6/W	MFI	210@4400	290@3250	3.55x3.54	9.0:1	20-45@1500
	F-150	5.4 (5409)	L	MFI	235@4250	330@3000	3.55X4.17	9.0:1	40-70@1500
	F-250	4.6 (4588)	6/W	MFI	210@4400	290@3250	3.55x3.54	9.0:1	20-45@1500
	F-250	5.4 (5409)	L	MFI	235@4250	330@3000	3.55X4.17	9.0:1	40-70@1500
	F-350	5.4 (5409)	L	MFI	235@4250	330@3000	3.55X4.17	9.0:1	40-70@1500
	F-350	5.8 (5752)	H	MFI	210@3600	325@2800	4.00x3.50	8.8:1	40-65@2000
	F-350	6.8 (6802)	5	MFI	265@4250	410@2750	4.09X4.17	9.0:1	40-70@1500
	F-350	7.3 (7292)	F	DI	210@3000	425@2000	4.11x4.18	17.5:1	40-70@3000
	F-350	7.5 (7538)	G	MFI	245@4000	400@2200	4.36x3.85	8.5:1	40-88@2000
	F-Super Duty	5.4 (5409)	L	MFI	235@4250	330@3000	3.55X4.17	9.0:1	40-70@1500
	F-Super Duty	5.8 (5752)	H	MFI	210@3600	325@2800	4.00x3.50	8.8:1	40-65@2000
	F-Super Duty	6.8 (6802)	5	MFI	265@4250	410@2750	4.09X4.17	9.0:1	40-70@1500
	F-Super Duty	7.3 (7292)	F	DI	210@3000	425@2000	4.11x4.18	17.5:1	40-70@3000
	F-Super Duty	7.5 (7538)	G	MFI	245@4000	400@2200	4.36x3.85	8.5:1	40-88@2000
	Mountaineer	5.0 (4949)	P	MFI	210@4500	280@3500	4.00x3.00	9.0:1	40-60@2500
	Navigator	5.4 (5409)	L	MFI	235@4250	330@3000	3.55X4.17	9.0:1	40-70@1500
	Ranger	2.5 (2500)	C	MFI	119@5000	146@3000	3.78X3.90	9.1:1	40-60@2000
	Ranger	3.0 (2982)	U	MFI	147@5000	162@3250	3.50x3.14	9.3:1	40-60@2000
	Ranger	4.0 (3950)	X	MFI	160@4000	225@2500	3.81x3.39	9.0:1	40-60@2000
2000-01	E-150	4.2 (4195)	2	MFI	205@4400	255@3000	3.81x3.74	9.3:1	50@2000
	E-150	4.6 (4588)	6/W	MFI	210@4400	290@3250	3.55x3.54	9.0:1	20-45@1500
	E-150	5.4 (5409)	L	MFI	235@4250	330@3000	3.55X4.17	9.0:1	40-70@1500
	E-250	4.2 (4195)	2	MFI	205@4400	255@3000	3.81x3.74	9.3:1	50@2000
	E-250	5.4 (5409)	L	MFI	235@4250	330@3000	3.55X4.17	9.0:1	40-70@1500
	E-350	5.4 (5409)	L	MFI	235@4250	330@3000	3.55X4.17	9.0:1	40-70@1500
	E-350	6.8 (6802)	5	MFI	265@4250	410@2750	4.09X4.17	9.0:1	40-70@1500
	E-350	7.3 (7292)	F	DI	210@3000	425@2000	4.11x4.18	17.5:1	40-70@3000
	Excursion	5.4 (5409)	L	MFI	235@4250	330@3000	3.55X4.17	9.0:1	40-70@1500
	Excursion	6.8 (6802)	5	MFI	265@4250	410@2750	4.09X4.17	9.0:1	40-70@1500

93081C84

GENERAL ENGINE SPECIFICATIONS

Year	Model	Engine Displacement Liters (cc)	Engine Series (ID/VIN)	Fuel System Type	Net Horsepower @ rpm	Net Torque @ rpm (ft. lbs.)	Bore x Stroke (in.)	Compression Ratio	Oil Pressure @ rpm
2000-01 (cont.)	Excursion	7.3 (7292)	F	DI	210@3000	425@2000	4.11x4.18	17.5:1	40-70@3000
	Expedition	4.6 (4588)	6/W	MFI	210@4400	290@3250	3.55x3.54	9.0:1	20-45@1500
	Expedition	5.4 (5409)	L	MFI	235@4250	330@3000	3.55X4.17	9.0:1	40-70@1500
	Explorer	4.0 (4000)	X	MFI	160@4000	225@2500	3.81x3.39	9.0:1	40-60@2000
	Explorer	5.0 (4949)	P	MFI	210@4500	280@3500	4.00x3.00	9.0:1	40-60@2500
	F-150	4.2 (4195)	2	MFI	205@4400	255@3000	3.81x3.74	9.3:1	50@2000
	F-150	4.6 (4588)	6/W	MFI	210@4400	290@3250	3.55x3.54	9.0:1	20-45@1500
	F-150	5.4 (5409)	L	MFI	235@4250	330@3000	3.55X4.17	9.0:1	40-70@1500
	F-250	4.6 (4588)	6/W	MFI	210@4400	290@3250	3.55x3.54	9.0:1	20-45@1500
	F-250	5.4 (5409)	L	MFI	235@4250	330@3000	3.55X4.17	9.0:1	40-70@1500
	F-350	5.4 (5409)	L	MFI	235@4250	330@3000	3.55X4.17	9.0:1	40-70@1500
	F-350	5.8 (5752)	H	MFI	210@3600	325@2800	4.00x3.50	8.8:1	40-65@2000
	F-350	6.8 (6802)	5	MFI	265@4250	410@2750	4.09x4.17	9.0:1	40-70@1500
	F-350	7.3 (7292)	F	DI	210@3000	425@2000	4.11x4.18	17.5:1	40-70@3000
	F-350	7.5 (7538)	G	MFI	245@4000	400@2200	4.36x3.85	8.5:1	40-88@2000
	F-Super Duty	5.4 (5409)	L	MFI	235@4250	330@3000	3.55X4.17	9.0:1	40-70@1500
	F-Super Duty	5.8 (5752)	H	MFI	210@3600	325@2800	4.00x3.50	8.8:1	40-65@2000
	F-Super Duty	6.8 (6802)	5	MFI	265@4250	410@2750	4.09x4.17	9.0:1	40-70@1500
	F-Super Duty	7.3 (7292)	F	DI	210@3000	425@2000	4.11x4.18	17.5:1	40-70@3000
	F-Super Duty	7.5 (7538)	G	MFI	245@4000	400@2200	4.36x3.85	8.5:1	40-88@2000
	Mountaineer	5.0 (4949)	P	MFI	210@4500	280@3500	4.00x3.00	9.0:1	40-60@2500
	Navigator	5.4 (5409)	L	MFI	260@4250	330@3000	3.55X4.17	9.0:1	40-70@1500
	Ranger	2.5 (2500)	C	MFI	119@5000	146@3000	3.78x3.90	9.1:1	40-60@2000
	Ranger	3.0 (2982)	U	MFI	147@5000	162@3250	3.50x3.14	9.3:1	40-60@2500
	Ranger	4.0 (3950)	X	MFI	160@4000	225@2500	3.81x3.39	9.0:1	40-60@2000

MFI: Multi-port Fuel Injection
EFI: Electronic Fuel Injection
DI: Direct Injection Turbo-Diesel

93081C85

Ignition system service is covered in the model specific sections of this manual

GASOLINE ENGINE TUNE-UP SPECIFICATIONS

Year	Engine Displacement Liters (cc)	Engine ID/VIN	Spark Plug Gap (in.)	Ignition Timing (deg.) MT	AT	Fuel Pump (psi)	Idle Speed (rpm) MT	AT	Valve Clearance In.	Ex.
1997	2.3 (2300)	A	0.044	10B	10B	35-45	725	675	HYD	HYD
	3.0 (2982)	U	0.044	10B	10B	35-45	①	①	HYD	HYD
	4.0 (3950)	X	0.054	10B	10B	35-45	①	①	HYD	HYD
	4.9 (4916)	Y	0.044	10B	10B	50-60	700	575	HYD	HYD
	5.0 (4949)	N	0.044	10B	10B	35-45	775	675	HYD	HYD
	5.0 (4949)	P	0.044	—	10B	35-45	—	①	HYD	HYD
	5.8 (5752)	H	0.044	10B	10B	35-45	775	675	HYD	HYD
	7.5 (7538)	G	0.044	10B	10B	35-45	775	675	HYD	HYD
1998	2.5 (2500)	C	0.044	10B ②	10B ②	56-72	①	①	HYD	HYD
	3.0 (2982)	U	0.044	10B	10B	35-45	①	①	HYD	HYD
	4.0 (3950)	X	0.054	10B	10B	35-45	①	①	HYD	HYD
	4.2 (4195)	2	0.052-0.056	10B ②	10B ②	30-45 ③	NA	NA	HYD	HYD
	4.6 (4588)	6	0.052-0.056	8-12B ②	8-12B ②	30-45 ③	NA	NA	HYD	HYD
	4.6 (4588)	W	0.052-0.056	8-12B ②	8-12B ②	30-45 ③	NA	NA	HYD	HYD
	5.4 (5409)	L	0.052-0.056	10B ②	10B ②	28-45	①	①	HYD	HYD
	5.0 (4949)	N	0.044	10B	10B	35-45	775	675	HYD	HYD
	5.0 (4949)	P	0.044	—	10B	35-45	—	①	HYD	HYD
	5.8 (5752)	H	0.044	10B	10B	35-45	775	675	HYD	HYD
	6.8 (6802)	5	0.052-0.055	10B ②	10B ②	28-45	①	①	HYD	HYD
	7.5 (7538)	G	0.044	10B	10B	35-45	775	675	HYD	HYD
1999	2.5 (2500)	C	0.044	10B ②	10B ②	56-72	①	①	HYD	HYD
	3.0 (2982)	U	0.044	10B	10B	35-45	①	①	HYD	HYD
	4.0 (3950)	X	0.054	10B	10B	35-45	①	①	HYD	HYD
	4.2 (4195)	2	0.052-0.056	10B ②	10B ②	30-45 ③	NA	NA	HYD	HYD
	4.6 (4588)	6/W	0.052-0.056	8-12B ②	8-12B ②	30-45 ③	NA	NA	HYD	HYD
	5.0 (4949)	P	0.044	—	10B	35-45	—	①	HYD	HYD
	5.4 (5409)	L	0.052-0.056	10B ②	10B ②	28-45	①	①	HYD	HYD
	5.8 (5752)	H	0.044	10B	10B	35-45	775	675	HYD	HYD
	6.8 (6802)	5	0.052-0.055	10B ②	10B ②	28-45	①	①	HYD	HYD
	7.5 (7538)	G	0.044	10B	10B	35-45	775	675	HYD	HYD
2000-01	2.5 (2500)	C	0.044	10B ②	10B ②	56-72	①	①	HYD	HYD
	3.0 (2982)	U	0.044	10B	10B	35-45	①	①	HYD	HYD
	4.0 (3950)	E	0.052-0.056	10B ②	10B ②	35-45	①	①	HYD	HYD
	4.0 (3950)	X	0.054	10B	10B	35-45	①	①	HYD	HYD
	4.2 (4195)	2	0.052-0.056	10B ②	10B ②	30-45 ③	NA	NA	HYD	HYD
	4.6 (4588)	6/W	0.052-0.056	8-12B ②	8-12B ②	30-45 ③	NA	NA	HYD	HYD
	5.0 (4949)	P	0.044	—	10B	35-45	—	①	HYD	HYD
	5.4 (5409)	L/M/Z/A	0.052-0.056	10B ②	10B ②	28-45	①	①	HYD	HYD
	5.4 (5409)	3	0.052-0.056	10B ②	10B ②	28-45	①	①	HYD	HYD
	5.8 (5752)	H	0.044	10B	10B	35-45	775	675	HYD	HYD
	6.8 (6802)	5	0.052-0.055	10B ②	10B ②	28-45	①	①	HYD	HYD
	7.5 (7538)	G	0.044	10B	10B	35-45	775	675	HYD	HYD

NOTE: The Vehicle Emission Control Information label often reflects specification changes changes made during production. The label figures must be used if they differ from those in this chart.

B: Before top dead center

HYD: Hydraulic

NA: Not Available

① Idle speed is electronically controlled and cannot be adjusted

② Ignition timing is preset and cannot be adjusted

③ With engine running

93081C86

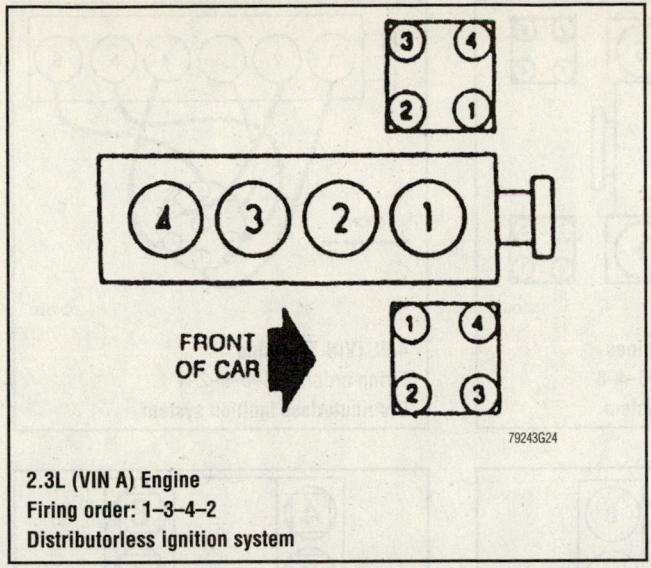

2.3L (VIN A) Engine
Firing order: 1–3–4–2
Distributorless ignition system

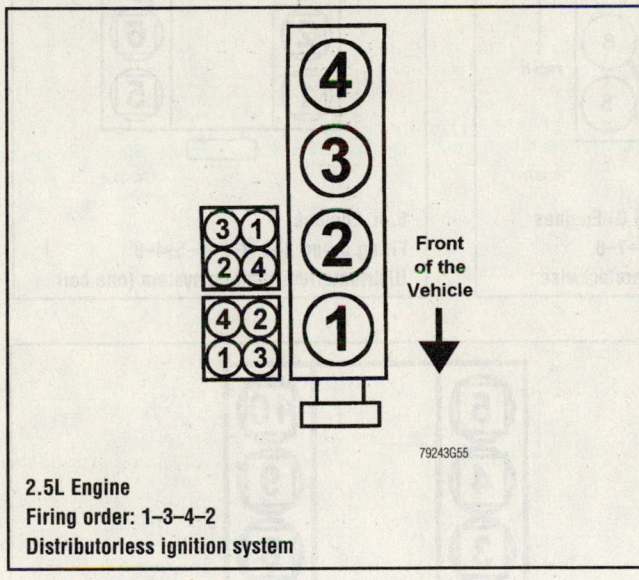

2.5L Engine
Firing order: 1–3–4–2
Distributorless ignition system

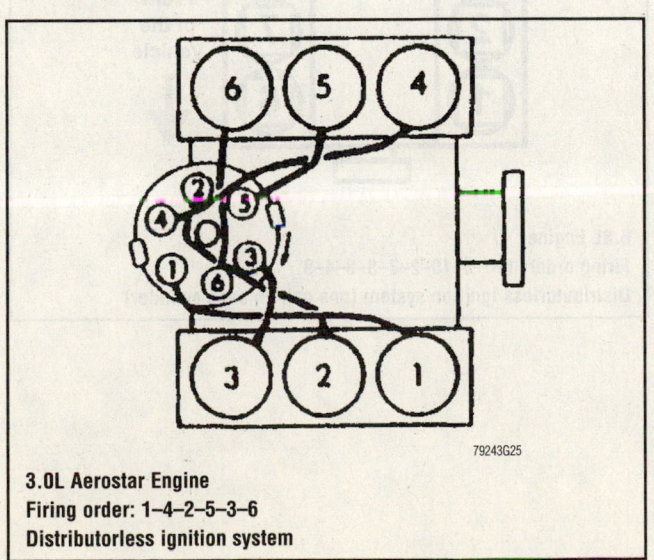

3.0L Aerostar Engine
Firing order: 1–4–2–5–3–6
Distributorless ignition system

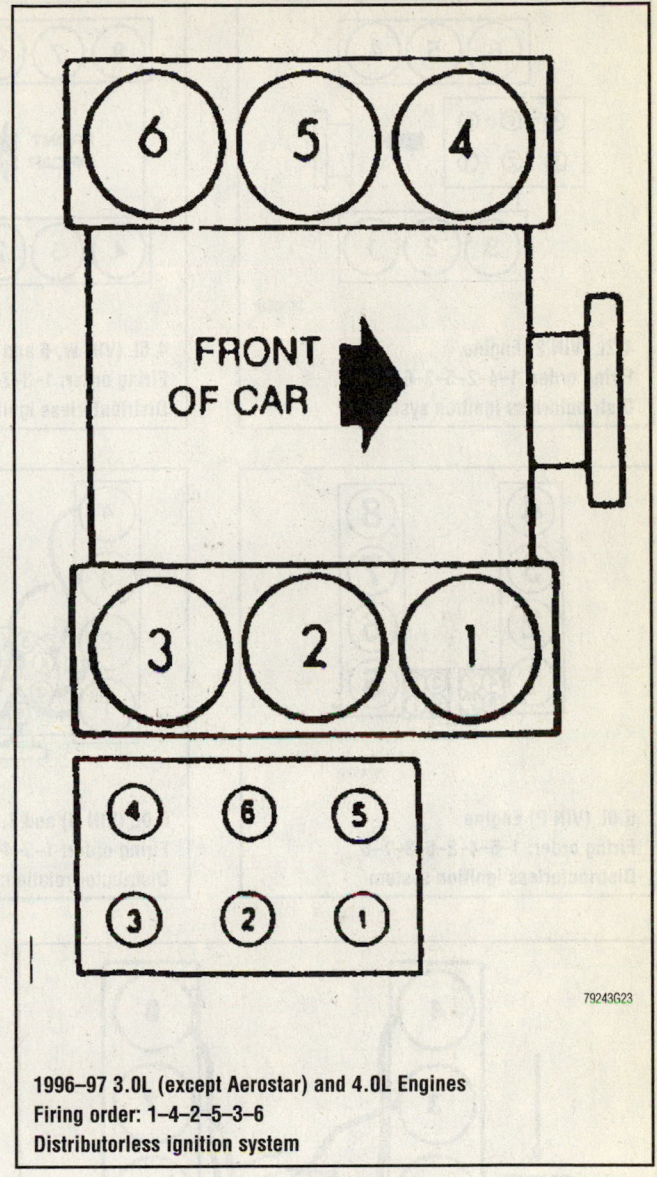

1996–97 3.0L (except Aerostar) and 4.0L Engines
Firing order: 1–4–2–5–3–6
Distributorless ignition system

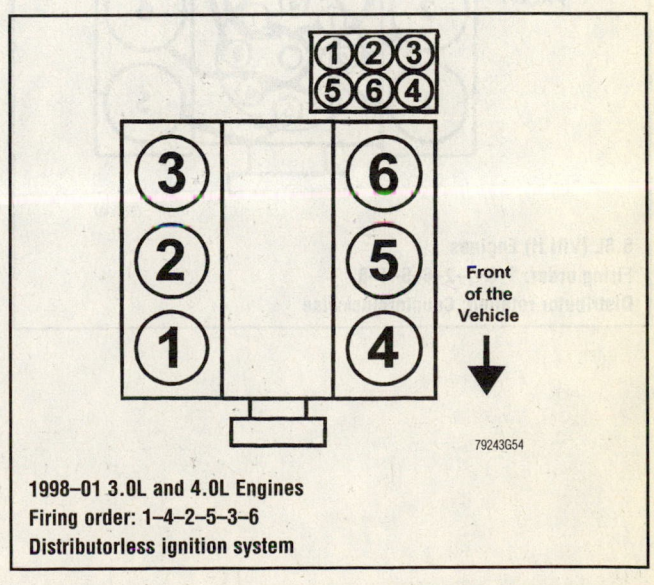

1998–01 3.0L and 4.0L Engines
Firing order: 1–4–2–5–3–6
Distributorless ignition system

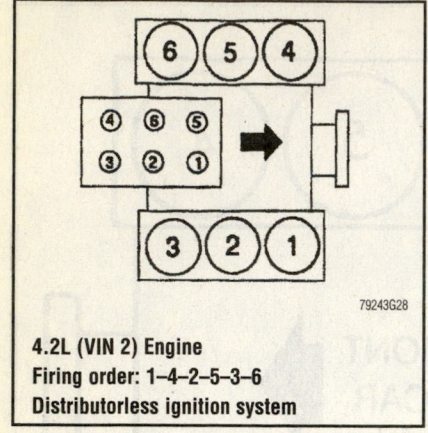

4.2L (VIN 2) Engine
Firing order: 1–4–2–5–3–6
Distributorless ignition system

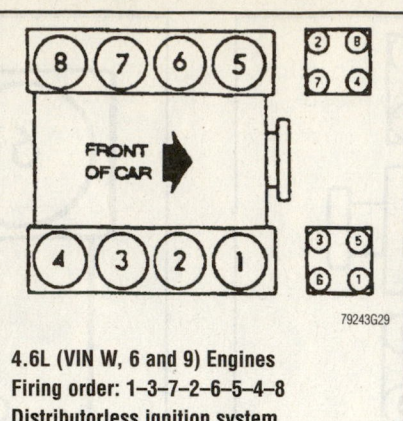

4.6L (VIN W, 6 and 9) Engines
Firing order: 1–3–7–2–6–5–4–8
Distributorless ignition system

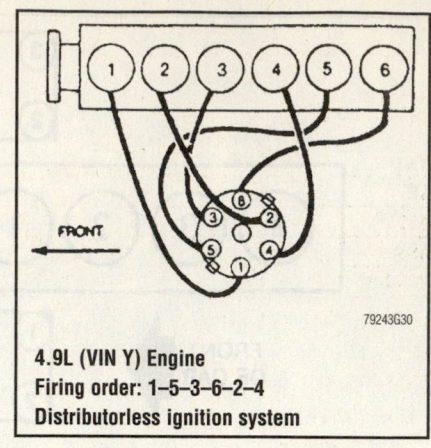

4.9L (VIN Y) Engine
Firing order: 1–5–3–6–2–4
Distributorless ignition system

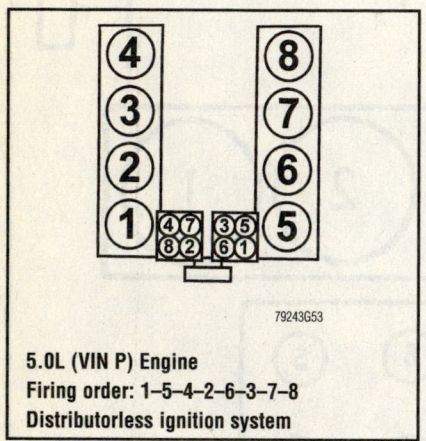

5.0L (VIN P) Engine
Firing order: 1–5–4–2–6–3–7–8
Distributorless ignition system

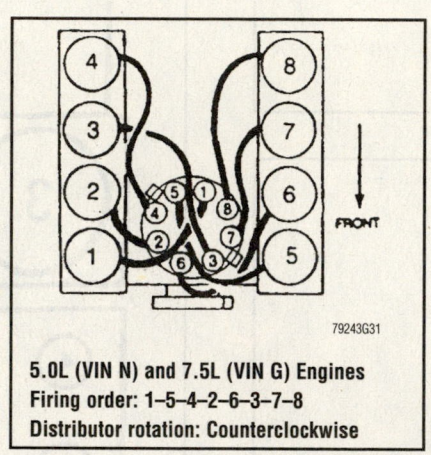

5.0L (VIN N) and 7.5L (VIN G) Engines
Firing order: 1–5–4–2–6–3–7–8
Distributor rotation: Counterclockwise

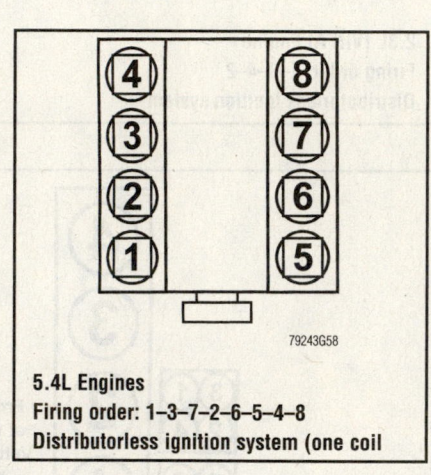

5.4L Engines
Firing order: 1–3–7–2–6–5–4–8
Distributorless ignition system (one coil

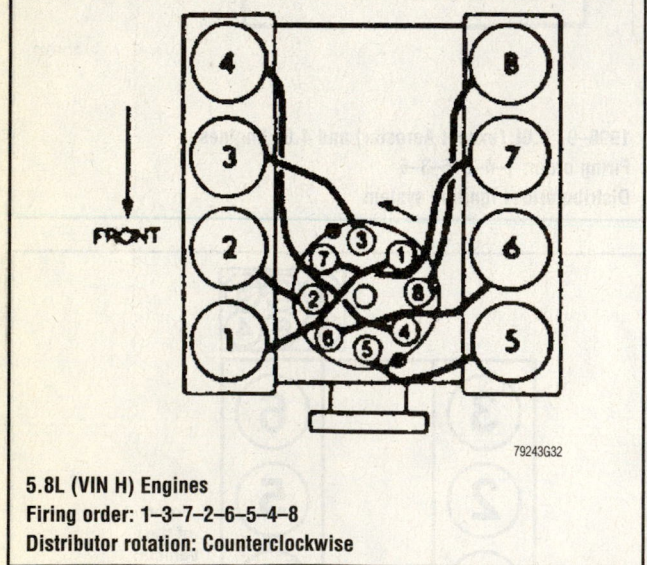

5.8L (VIN H) Engines
Firing order: 1–3–7–2–6–5–4–8
Distributor rotation: Counterclockwise

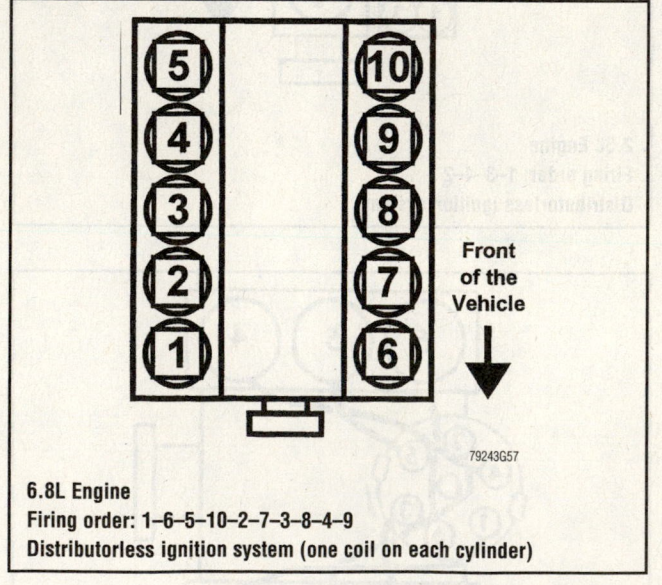

6.8L Engine
Firing order: 1–6–5–10–2–7–3–8–4–9
Distributorless ignition system (one coil on each cylinder)

DIESEL ENGINE TUNE-UP SPECIFICATIONS

Year	Engine ID/VIN	Engine Displacement cu. in. (cc)	Valve Clearance Intake (in.)	Valve Clearance Exhaust (in.)	Intake Valve Opens (deg.)	Injection Pump Setting (deg.)	Injection Nozzle Pressure (psi) New	Injection Nozzle Pressure (psi) Used	Idle Speed (rpm)	Cranking Compression Pressure (psi)
1997	F	7.3 (7292)	HYD	HYD	—	①	1875	1425	②	③
1998	F	7.3 (7292)	HYD	HYD	—	①	1875	1425	②	③
1999	F	7.3 (7292)	HYD	HYD	—	①	1875	1425	②	③
2000-01	F	7.3 (7292)	HYD	HYD	—	①	1875	1425	②	③

NOTE: The Vehicle Emission Control Information label often reflects specification changes made during production. The label figures must be used if they differ from those in this chart

HYD: Hydraulic

B: Before top dead center

NA: Not Available

① PCM controlled

② See underhood emission label

③ Compression pressure in the lowest cylinder must be at least 75% of the highest cylinder

    Minimum pressure: 195 psi

    Maximum pressure: 440 psi

93081C87

Refer to the model specific sections for engine mechanical service procedures

CAPACITIES

Year	Model	Engine Displacement Liters (cc)	Engine ID/VIN	Engine Oil with Filter (qts.)	Transmission (pts.) 5-Spd	Transmission (pts.) Auto.	Transfer Case (pts.)	Drive Axle Front (pts.)	Drive Axle Rear (pts.)	Fuel Tank (gal.)	Cooling System (qts.)
1997	Aerostar	3.0 (2982)	U	5.0	5.6	19.0	2.5	3.0	①	21.0	11.8
	Aerostar	4.0 (3950)	X	5.0	5.6	19.0	2.5	3.0	①	21.0	12.6
	E-150	4.9 (4916)	Y	6.0	7.6	24.0 ③	—	—	6.0 ④	⑤	14.0
	E-150	5.0 (4949)	N	6.0	7.6	24.0 ③	—	—	6.0 ④	⑤	15.0
	E-150	5.8 (5752)	H	6.0	7.6	24.0 ③	—	—	6.0 ④	⑤	14.0
	E-250	4.9 (4916)	Y	6.0	7.6	24.0 ③	—	—	6.0 ④	⑤	14.0
	E-250	5.0 (4949)	N	6.0	7.6	24.0 ③	—	—	6.0 ④	⑤	15.0
	E-250	5.8 (5752)	H	6.0	7.6	24.0 ③	—	—	6.0 ④	⑤	15.0
	E-250	7.5 (7538)	L	6.0	7.6	24.0 ③	—	—	6.0 ④	⑤	10.9
	E-350	4.9 (4916)	Y	6.0	7.6	24.0 ③	—	—	6.0 ④	⑤	17.5
	E-350	5.8 (5752)	H	6.0	7.6	24.0 ③	—	—	6.0 ④	⑤	15.0
	E-350	7.3 (7292)	F	14.0	7.6	24.0 ③	—	—	6.0 ④	⑤	23.0
	E-350	7.5 (7538)	L	6.0	7.6	24.0 ③	—	—	6.0 ④	⑤	19.8
	Explorer	4.0 (3950)	X	5.0	5.6	⑥	3.0	①	①	19.3	8.6
	Explorer	5.0 (4949)	P	5.0	—	13.9	—	—	5.5	19.0	12.8
	F-150	4.2 (4195)	2	6.0	7.6	26.0	4.0	3.7	5.5	24.5 ⑧	15.7 ⑨
	F-150	4.6 (4588)	6	6.0	7.6	26.0	4.0	3.7	5.5	24.5 ⑧	17.9
	F-150	4.6 (4588)	9	6.0	7.6	26.0	4.0	3.7	5.5	24.5 ⑧	17.9
	F-150	4.6 (4588)	W	6.0	7.6	26.0	4.0	3.7	5.5	24.5 ⑧	17.9
	F-150	4.9 (4916)	Y	6.0	7.6	24.0 ③	②	6.0	6.0 ④	⑩	⑪
	F-150	5.0 (4949)	N	6.0	7.6	24.0 ③	②	6.0	6.0 ④	⑩	⑫
	F-150	5.8 (5752)	H	6.0	7.6	24.0 ③	②	6.0	6.0 ④	⑩	⑬
	F-250	4.9 (4916)	Y	6.0	7.6	24.0 ③	②	6.0	6.0 ④	⑩	⑪
	F-250	5.0 (4949)	N	6.0	7.6	24.0 ③	②	6.0	6.0 ④	⑩	⑫
	F-250	5.8 (5752)	H	6.0	7.6	24.0 ③	②	6.0	6.0 ④	⑩	⑬
	F-250	7.3 (7292)	F	14.0	7.6	24.0 ③	②	6.0	6.0 ④	⑩	23.0
	F-250	7.5 (7538)	L	6.0	7.6	24.0 ③	②	6.0	6.0 ④	⑩	19.8
	F-350	4.9 (4916)	Y	6.0	7.6	24.0 ③	②	6.0	6.0 ④	⑩	⑩
	F-350	5.8 (5752)	H	6.0	7.6	24.0 ③	②	6.0	6.0 ④	⑩	⑬
	F-350	7.3 (7292)	F	14.0	7.6	24.0 ③	②	6.0	6.0 ④	⑩	23.0
	F-350	7.5 (7538)	L	6.0	7.6	24.0 ③	②	6.0	6.0 ④	⑩	19.8
	F-Super Duty	7.3 (7292)	F	14.0	7.6	24.0 ③	②	6.0	6.0 ④	⑩	23.0
	F-Super Duty	7.5 (7538)	L	6.0	7.6	24.0 ③	②	6.0	6.0 ④	⑩	19.8
	Mountaineer	5.0 (4949)	P	5.0	—	13.9	—	—	5.5	⑳	12.8
	Ranger	2.3 (2300)	A	5.0	⑭	⑥	3.0	①	5.5	⑮	⑯
	Ranger	3.0 (2982)	U	4.5	3.0	⑥	⑰	⑦	⑦	⑮	⑲
	Ranger	4.0 (3950)	X	5.0	3.0	⑥	⑰	⑦	⑦	⑮	⑱
1998	E-150	4.2 (4195)	2	6.0	—	③	—	—	6.0	35.0	15.7
	E-150	4.6 (4588)	6/W	6.0	—	③	—	—	6.0	35.0	17.9
	E-150	5.4 (5409)	L	7.0	—	③	—	—	6.0	35.0	19.8
	E-250	4.2 (4195)	2	6.0	—	③	—	—	6.0 ④	35.0	15.7
	E-250	5.4 (5409)	L	7.0	—	③	—	—	6.0 ④	35.0	19.8
	E-350	5.4 (5409)	L	7.0	—	③	—	—	6.0 ④	35.0	19.8
	E-350	6.8 (6802)	5	7.0	—	③	—	—	6.0 ④	35.0	23.0
	E-350	7.3 (7292)	F	14.0	—	③	—	—	6.0 ④	35.0	23.0
	Expedition	4.6 (4588)	6/W	6.0	—	③	4.0	3.7	5.5	24.5 ⑧	17.9
	Expedition	5.4 (5409)	L	7.0	—	③	4.0	3.7	5.5	24.5 ⑧	20.8
	Explorer	4.0 (3950)	X	5.0	5.6	⑥	3.0	①	①	19.3	⑦
	Explorer	4.0 (4000)	E	7.0	—	③	—	—	6.0 ④	⑮	23.0
	Explorer	5.0 (4949)	P	5.0	—	13.9	—	—	5.5	19.0	12.8
	F-150	4.2 (4195)	2	6.0	7.6	26.0	4.0	3.7	5.5	24.5 ⑧	15.7 ⑨
	F-150	4.6 (4588)	6	6.0	7.6	26.0	4.0	3.7	5.5	24.5 ⑧	17.9
	F-150	4.6 (4588)	W	6.0	7.6	26.0	4.0	3.7	5.5	24.5 ⑧	17.9
	F-150	5.4 (5409)	L	7.0	7.6	③	4.2	6.0	6.0	30.0	19.8

93081C88

CAPACITIES

Year	Model	Engine Displacement Liters (cc)	Engine ID/VIN	Engine Oil with Filter (qts.)	Transmission (pts.) 5-Spd	Transmission (pts.) Auto.	Transfer Case (pts.)	Drive Axle Front (pts.)	Drive Axle Rear (pts.)	Fuel Tank (gal.)	Cooling System (qts.)
1998 (cont.)	F-250	5.8 (5752)	H	6.0	7.6	24.0 [3]	[2]	6.0	6.0 [4]	[10]	[13]
	F-250	7.3 (7292)	F	14.0	7.6	24.0 [3]	[2]	6.0	6.0 [4]	[10]	23.0
	F-250	7.5 (7538)	L	6.0	7.6	24.0 [3]	[2]	6.0	6.0 [4]	[10]	19.8
	F-350	5.8 (5752)	H	6.0	7.6	24.0 [3]	[2]	6.0	6.0 [4]	[10]	[13]
	F-350	7.3 (7292)	F	14.0	7.6	24.0 [3]	[2]	6.0	6.0 [4]	[10]	23.0
	F-350	7.5 (7538)	L	6.0	7.6	24.0 [3]	[2]	6.0	6.0 [4]	[10]	19.8
	F-Super Duty	5.8 (5758)	R	7.0	7.0	24.0	[2]	6.0 [4]	6.0 [4]	35.0	23.0
	F-Super Duty	7.3 (7292)	F	14.0	7.6	24.0 [3]	[2]	6.0	6.0 [4]	[10]	23.0
	Mountaineer	5.0 (4949)	P	5.0	—	13.9	—	—	5.5	[16]	12.8
	Ranger	2.3 (2300)	A	5.0	[14]	[6]	3.0	[1]	5.5	[16]	[17]
	Ranger	3.0 (2982)	U	4.5	3.0	[6]	[20]	[7]	[7]	[16]	[19]
	Ranger	4.0 (3950)	X	5.0	3.0	[6]	[20]	[7]	[7]	[16]	[18]
1999	E-150	4.2 (4195)	2	6.0	—	[3]	—	—	6.0	35.0	15.7
	E-150	4.6 (4588)	6/W	6.0	—	[3]	—	—	6.0	35.0	17.9
	E-150	5.4 (5409)	L	7.0	—	[3]	—	—	6.0	35.0	19.8
	E-250	4.2 (4195)	2	6.0	—	[3]	—	—	6.0 [4]	35.0	15.7
	E-250	5.4 (5409)	L	7.0	—	[3]	—	—	6.0 [4]	35.0	19.8
	E-350	5.4 (5409)	L	7.0	—	[3]	—	—	6.0 [4]	35.0	19.8
	E-350	6.8 (6802)	5	7.0	—	[3]	—	—	6.0 [4]	35.0	23.0
	E-350	7.3 (7292)	F	14.0	—	[3]	—	—	6.0 [4]	35.0	23.0
	Expedition	4.6 (4588)	6/W	6.0	—	[3]	4.0	3.7	5.5	24.5 [21]	17.9
	Expedition	5.4 (5409)	L	7.0	—	[3]	4.0	3.7	5.5	24.5 [21]	20.8
	Explorer	4.0 (3950)	X	5.0	5.6	[3]	3.0	[1]	[1]	[20]	[18]
	Explorer	4.0 (4000)	E	7.0	—	[3]	—	—	6.0 [4]	[20]	23.0
	Explorer	5.0 (4949)	P	5.0	—	13.9	—	—	5.5	[20]	12.8
	F-150	4.2 (4195)	2	6.0	7.6	26.0	4.0	3.7	5.5	24.5 [8]	15.7 [9]
	F-150	4.6 (4588)	6/W	6.0	7.6	26.0	4.0	3.7	5.5	24.5 [8]	17.9
	F-150	5.4 (5409)	L	7.0	7.6	[3]	4.2	6.0	6.0	30.0	19.8
	F-250	4.6 (4588)	6/W	6.0	7.6	26.0	4.0	3.7	5.5	24.5 [8]	17.9
	F-250	5.4 (5409)	L	7.0	7.6	[3]	4.2	6.0	6.0	30.0	19.8
	F-350	5.4 (5409)	L	7.0	7.6	[3]	4.2	6.0	6.0	30.0	19.8
	F-350	5.8 (5758)	R	7.0	7.0	24.0	[21]	6.0 [4]	6.0 [4]	35.0	23.0
	F-350	6.8 (6802)	5	7.0	7.6	[3]	4.2	6.0 [4]	6.0 [4]	35.0	23.0
	F-350	7.3 (7292)	F	14.0	7.6	[3]	4.2	6.0 [4]	6.0 [4]	35.0	23.0
	F-350	7.5 (7538)	G	7.0	7.6	[3]	4.2	6.0 [4]	6.0 [4]	35.0	23.0
	F-Super Duty	5.4 (5409)	L	7.0	7.6	[3]	4.2	6.0	6.0	30.0	19.8
	F-Super Duty	5.8 (5758)	R	7.0	7.0	24.0	[21]	6.0 [4]	6.0 [4]	35.0	23.0
	F-Super Duty	6.8 (6802)	5	7.0	7.6	[3]	4.2	6.0 [4]	6.0 [4]	35.0	23.0
	F-Super Duty	7.3 (7292)	F	14.0	7.6	[3]	4.2	6.0 [4]	6.0 [4]	35.0	23.0
	F-Super Duty	7.5 (7538)	G	7.0	7.6	Auto. [3]	4.2	6.0 [4]	6.0 [4]	35.0	23.0
	Mountaineer	5.0 (4949)	P	5.0	—	13.9	—	—	5.5	[20]	12.8
	Navigator	5.4 (5409)	L	7.0	—	[3]	4.0	3.7	5.5	24.5 [21]	20.8
	Ranger	2.5 (2500)	C	5.0	[14]	[6]	3.0	[1]	5.5	[15]	[16]
	Ranger	3.0 (2982)	U	4.5	3.0	[6]	[21]	[7]	[7]	[15]	[10]
	Ranger	4.0 (3950)	X	5.0	3.0	[6]	[21]	[7]	[7]	[15]	[18]
2000-01	E-150	4.2 (4195)	2	6.0	—	[3]	—	—	6.0	35.0	15.7
	E-150	4.6 (4588)	6/W	6.0	—	[3]	—	—	6.0	35.0	17.9
	E-150	5.4 (5409)	L	7.0	—	[3]	—	—	6.0	35.0	19.8
	E-250	4.2 (4195)	2	6.0	—	[3]	—	—	6.0 [4]	35.0	15.7
	E-250	5.4 (5409)	L	7.0	—	[3]	—	—	6.0 [4]	35.0	19.8
	E-350	5.4 (5409)	L	7.0	—	[3]	—	—	6.0 [4]	35.0	19.8
	E-350	6.8 (6802)	5	7.0	—	[3]	—	—	6.0 [4]	35.0	23.0
	E-350	7.3 (7292)	F	14.0	—	[3]	—	—	6.0 [4]	35.0	23.0

93081C89

Refer to the model specific sections for fuel system service procedures

CAPACITIES

Year	Model	Engine Displacement Liters (cc)	Engine ID/VIN	Engine Oil with Filter (qts.)	Transmission (pts.) 5-Spd	Auto.	Transfer Case (pts.)	Drive Axle Front (pts.)	Rear (pts.)	Fuel Tank (gal.)	Cooling System (qts.)
2000-01 (Cont.)	Excursion	5.4 (5409)	L	7.0	—	③	4.2	6.0	6.0	44.0	19.8
	Excursion	6.8 (6802)	5	7.0	—	③	4.2	6.0 ④	6.0 ④	44.0	23.0
	Excursion	7.3 (7292)	F	14.0	—	③	4.2	6.0 ④	6.0 ④	44.0	23.0
	Expedition	4.6 (4588)	6/W	6.0	—	③	4.0	3.7	5.5	24.5 ㉑	17.9
	Expedition	5.4 (5409)	L	7.0	—	③	4.0	3.7	5.5	24.5 ㉑	20.8
	Explorer	4.0 (3950)	X	5.0	5.6	⑥	3.0	①	①	⑳	⑱
	Explorer	4.0 (4000)	E	7.0	—	③	—	—	6.0 ④	⑳	23.0
	Explorer	5.0 (4949)	P	5.0	—	13.9	—	—	5.5	⑳	12.8
	F-150	4.2 (4195)	2	6.0	7.6	26.0	4.0	3.7	5.5	24.5 ⑧	15.7 ⑨
	F-150	4.6 (4588)	6/W	6.0	7.6	26.0	4.0	3.7	5.5	24.5 ⑧	17.9
	F-150	5.4 (5409)	L	7.0	7.6	③	4.2	6.0	6.0	30.0	19.8
	F-250	4.6 (4588)	6/W	6.0	7.6	26.0	4.0	3.7	5.5	24.5 ⑧	17.9
	F-250	5.4 (5409)	L	7.0	7.6	③	4.2	6.0	6.0	30.0	19.8
	F-350	5.4 (5409)	L	7.0	7.6	③	4.2	6.0	6.0	30.0	19.8
	F-350	5.8 (5758)	R	7.0	7.0	24.0	㉑	6.0 ④	6.0 ④	35.0	23.0
	F-350	6.8 (6802)	5	7.0	7.6	③	4.2	6.0 ④	6.0 ④	35.0	23.0
	F-350	7.3 (7292)	F	14.0	7.6	③	4.2	6.0 ④	6.0 ④	35.0	23.0
	F-350	7.5 (7538)	G	7.0	7.6	③	4.2	6.0 ④	6.0 ④	35.0	23.0
	F-Super Duty	5.4 (5409)	L	7.0	7.6	③	4.2	6.0	6.0	30.0	19.8
	F-Super Duty	5.8 (5758)	R	7.0	7.0	24.0	㉑	6.0 ④	6.0 ④	35.0	23.0
	F-Super Duty	6.8 (6802)	5	7.0	7.6	③	4.2	6.0 ④	6.0 ④	35.0	23.0
	F-Super Duty	7.3 (7292)	F	14.0	7.6	③	4.2	6.0 ④	6.0 ④	35.0	23.0
	F-Super Duty	7.5 (7538)	G	7.0	7.6	③	4.2	6.0 ④	6.0 ④	35.0	23.0
	Mountaineer	5.0 (4949)	P	5.0	—	13.9	—	—	5.5	⑳	12.8
	Navigator	5.4 (5409)	L	7.0	—	③	4.0	3.7	5.5	24.5 ㉑	20.8
	Ranger	2.5 (2500)	C	5.0	⑭	⑥	3.0	①	5.5	⑮	⑯
	Ranger	3.0 (2982)	U	4.5	3.0	⑥	㉑	⑦	⑦	⑮	⑲
	Ranger	4.0 (3950)	X	5.0	3.0	⑥	㉑	⑦	⑦	⑮	

NOTE: All capacities are approximate. Add fluid gradually and check to be sure a proper fluid level is obtained.

① Front axle Dana 28: 1.1 pts.
Front axle Dana 35: 3.5 pts.
Rear axle: 5.5 pts.

② Without PTO: 4.2 pts.
With PTO: 12.0 pts.

③ With 4R70W: 28 pts.
With E40D: 32.0 pts.

④ Heavy duty: 7.5 pts.

⑤ 124 inch Wheelbase: 18 gal.
138, 158 or 176 inch Wheelbase with front tank: 22 gal.
138, 158 or 176 inch Wheelbase with rear tank: 16 gal.

⑥ 2WD: 19.4 pts.
4WD: 20.0 pts.

⑦ 6.75 inch ring gear: 3 pts.
7.50 inch ring gear: 5 pts.

⑧ Also available with a 30 gallon tank with 8 ft. box

⑨ Includes recovery reservoir

⑩ 35.0 gal.

⑪ 4.9L without AC: 13.0 qts.
4.9L with AC or supercooling: 14.0 qts.
4.9L with AC and supercooling: 15.6 qts.

⑫ 5.0L with manual trans. and standard cooling system: 15.7 qts.
5.0L with automatic trans. and standard cooling: 16.5 qts.
5.0L with manual/automatic trans. and AC: 16.4 qts.
5.0L with manual/automatic trans. with supercooling/AC: 18.3 qts.

⑬ Manual trans. with standard cooling: 15.7 qts.
Automatic trans. with standard cooling: 16.4 qts.
Manual/automatic trans. with AC: 16.4 qts.
Manual/automatic trans. with supercooling and AC: 18.0 qts.

⑭ Mazda trans.: 3 pts.
Mitsubishi trans.: 4.8 pts.

⑮ 2-door: 17.5 gal.
4-door: 21.0 gal.

⑯ Short wheelbase: 16.3 gal.
Long wheelbase: 19.6 gal.
Ranger Supercab: 19.6 gal.

⑰ 2.3L without AC: 6.5 qts.
2.3L with AC: 7.2 qts.

⑱ BW 13-50 manual shift: 3.0 pts.
BW 13-50 electric shift: 6.5 pts.
BW 13-54 mechanical shift: 3.0 pts.
BW 13-50 contains no lubricant and none should be added

⑲ 3.0L without AC: 9.5 qts.
3.0L with AC: 10.2 qts.

⑳ 4.6L: 26.0 gal.
5.4L: 30.0 gal.

㉑ New Process: 9 pts. Dexron II
BW 1345: 6.5 pts. Dexron II
BW 1356: 4 pts. Mercon

93081C90

VALVE SPECIFICATIONS

Year	Engine Displacement Liters (cc)	Engine ID/VIN	Seat Angle (deg.)	Face Angle (deg.)	Spring Test Pressure (lbs. @ in.)	Spring Installed Height (in.)	Stem-to-Guide Clearance (in.)		Stem Diameter (in.)	
							Intake	Exhaust	Intake	Exhaust
1997	2.3 (2300)	A	45	44	126-142@ 1.12	1.530- 1.590	0.0010- 0.0027	0.0015- 0.0032	0.3416- 0.3423	0.3411- 0.3418
	3.0 (2982)	U	45	44	185@1.16	1.580- 1.610	0.0010- 0.0027	0.0015- 0.0032	0.3126- 0.3134	0.3121- 0.3129
	4.0 (3950)	X	45	44	138@1.22	1.580- 1.610	0.0008- 0.0025	0.0018- 0.0035	0.3159- 0.3167	0.3149- 0.3156
	4.9 (4916)	Y	45	44	⑥	①	0.0010- 0.0027	0.0010- 0.0027	0.3415- 0.3423	0.3415- 0.3423
	5.0 (4949)	N	45	44	200@1.20	⑤	0.0010- 0.0027	0.0015- 0.0032	0.3415- 0.3423	0.3415- 0.3423
	5.0 (4949)	P	45	44	200@1.20	⑤	0.0010- 0.0027	0.0015- 0.0032	0.3415- 0.3423	0.3410- 0.3418
	5.8 (5752)	H	45	44	200@1.20	②	0.0010- 0.0027	0.0010- 0.0027	0.3415- 0.3420	0.3415- 0.3420
	7.3 (7292)	F	③	③	200@1.38	④	0.0055	0.0055	0.3119- 0.3126	0.3119- 0.3126
	7.5 (7538)	G	45	44	220@1.33	1.830	0.0010- 0.0027	0.0010- 0.0027	0.3415- 0.3423	0.3415- 0.3423
1998	2.5 (2500)	C	45	44	57-63@ 1.56	1.540- 1.580	0.0008- 0.0025	0.0018- 0.0037	0.2746- 0.2754	0.2736- 0.2744
	3.0 (2982)	U	45	44	185@1.16	1.580- 1.610	0.0010- 0.0027	0.0015- 0.0032	0.3126- 0.3134	0.3121- 0.3129
	4.0 (3950)	X	45	44	138@1.22	1.580- 1.610	0.0008- 0.0025	0.0018- 0.0035	0.3159- 0.3167	0.3149- 0.3156
	4.0 (4000)	E	45	45	202-225@ 1.413-1.445	1.569- 1.601	0.0010- 0.0020	0.0010- 0.0020	0.274- 0.2748	0.273- 0.2740
	4.2 (4195)	2	44.75	NA	NA	1.566- 1.637	0.0008- 0.0027	0.0018- 0.0037	0.3423- 0.3415	0.3418- 0.3410
	4.6 (4588)	W	45	45.5	132@1.100	1.570	0.0008- 0.0027	0.0018- 0.0037	0.2750- 0.2746	0.2740- 0.2736
	4.6 (4588)	6	45	45.5	132@1.100	1.570	0.0008- 0.0027	0.0018- 0.0037	0.2750- 0.2746	0.2740- 0.2736
	5.0 (4949)	N	45	44	200@1.20	⑤	0.0010- 0.0027	0.0015- 0.0032	0.3415- 0.3423	0.3415- 0.3423
	5.0 (4949)	P	45	44	200@1.20	⑤	0.0010- 0.0027	0.0015- 0.0032	0.3415- 0.3423	0.3410- 0.3418
	5.4 (5409)	L	45	45.5	150@1.10	1.570	0.0008- 0.0027	0.0018- 0.0037	0.275- 0.2746	0.274- 0.2736
	5.8 (5752)	H	45	44	200@1.20	②	0.0010- 0.0027	0.0010- 0.0027	0.3415- 0.3420	0.3415- 0.3420
	6.8 (6802)	5	44.50- 45.25	45.25- 45.75	150@1.10	1.570	0.0008- 0.0027	0.0018- 0.0037	0.275- 0.2746	0.274- 0.2735
	7.3 (7292)	F	③	③	200@1.38	④	0.0055	0.0055	0.3119- 0.3126	0.3119- 0.3126
	7.5 (7538)	G	45	44	220@1.33	1.830	0.0010- 0.0027	0.0010- 0.0027	0.3415- 0.3423	0.3415- 0.3423

93081C91

Refer to the model specific sections for engine electrical system service procedures

VALVE SPECIFICATIONS

Year	Engine Displacement Liters (cc)	Engine ID/VIN	Seat Angle (deg.)	Face Angle (deg.)	Spring Test Pressure (lbs. @ in.)	Spring Installed Height (in.)	Stem-to-Guide Clearance (in.) Intake	Stem-to-Guide Clearance (in.) Exhaust	Stem Diameter (in.) Intake	Stem Diameter (in.) Exhaust
1999	2.5 (2500)	C	45	44	57-63@ 1.56	1.540- 1.580	0.0008- 0.0025	0.0018- 0.0037	0.2746- 0.2754	0.2736- 0.2744
	3.0 (2982)	U	45	44	185@1.16	1.580- 1.610	0.0010- 0.0027	0.0015- 0.0032	0.3126- 0.3134	0.3121- 0.3129
	4.0 (3950)	X	45	44	138@1.22	1.580- 1.610	0.0008- 0.0025	0.0018- 0.0035	0.3159- 0.3167	0.3149- 0.3156
	4.0 (4000)	E	45	45	202-225@ 1.413-1.445	1.569- 1.601	0.0010- 0.0020	0.0010- 0.0020	0.274- 0.2748	0.273- 0.2740
	4.2 (4195)	2	44.75	NA	NA	1.566- 1.637	0.0008- 0.0027	0.0018- 0.0037	0.3423- 0.3415	0.3418- 0.3410
	4.6 (4588)	6/W	45	45.5	132@1.100	1.570	0.0008- 0.0027	0.0018- 0.0037	0.2750- 0.2746	0.2740- 0.2736
	5.4 (5409)	L	45	45.5	150@1.10	1.570	0.0008- 0.0027	0.0018- 0.0037	0.275- 0.2746	0.274- 0.2736
	5.8 (5752)	H	45	44	200@1.20	②	0.0010- 0.0027	0.0010- 0.0027	0.3415- 0.3420	0.3415- 0.3420
	6.8 (6802)	5	44.50- 45.25	45.25- 45.75	150@1.10	1.570	0.0008- 0.0027	0.0018- 0.0037	0.275- 0.2746	0.274- 0.2735
	7.3 (7292)	F	③	③	200@1.38	④	0.0055	0.0055	0.3119- 0.3126	0.3119- 0.3126
	7.5 (7538)	G	45	44	220@1.33	1.830	0.0010- 0.0027	0.0010- 0.0027	0.3415- 0.3423	0.3415- 0.3423
2000-01	2.5 (2500)	C	45	44	57-63@ 1.56	1.540- 1.580	0.0008- 0.0025	0.0018- 0.0037	0.2746- 0.2754	0.2736- 0.2744
	3.0 (2982)	U	45	44	185@1.16	1.580- 1.610	0.0010- 0.0027	0.0015- 0.0032	0.3126- 0.3134	0.3121- 0.3129
	4.0 (3950)	X	45	44	138@1.22	1.580- 1.610	0.0008- 0.0025	0.0018- 0.0035	0.3159- 0.3167	0.3149- 0.3156
	4.0 (4000)	E	45	45	202-225@ 1.413-1.445	1.569- 1.601	0.0010- 0.0020	0.0010- 0.0020	0.274- 0.2748	0.273- 0.2740
	4.2 (4195)	2	44.75	NA	NA	1.566- 1.637	0.0008- 0.0027	0.0018- 0.0037	0.3423- 0.3415	0.3418- 0.3410
	4.6 (4588)	6/W	45	45.5	132@1.100	1.570	0.0008- 0.0027	0.0018- 0.0037	0.2750- 0.2746	0.2740- 0.2736
	5.4 (5409)	L	45	45.5	150@1.10	1.570	0.0008- 0.0027	0.0018- 0.0037	0.275- 0.2746	0.274- 0.2736
	5.8 (5752)	H	45	44	200@1.20	②	0.0010- 0.0027	0.0010- 0.0027	0.3415- 0.3420	0.3415- 0.3420
	6.8 (6802)	5	44.50- 45.25	45.25- 45.75	150@1.10	1.570	0.0008- 0.0027	0.0018- 0.0037	0.275- 0.2746	0.274- 0.2735
	7.3 (7292)	F	③	③	200@1.38	④	0.0055	0.0055	0.3119- 0.3126	0.3119- 0.3126
	7.5 (7538)	G	45	44	220@1.33	1.830	0.0010- 0.0027	0.0010- 0.0027	0.3415- 0.3423	0.3415- 0.3423

① Intake: 1.64 in.
Exhaust: 1.47 in.

② Intake: 1.78 in.
Exhaust: 1.59 in.

③ Intake: 30 degrees
Exhaust: 37.5 degrees

④ Intake: 1.767 in.
Exhaust: 1.833 in.

⑤ Intake: 1.75-1.81 in.
Exhaust: 1.59 in.

⑥ Intake: 166-184 lbs. @1.240 in.
Exhaust: 166-184 lbs. @ 1.070 in.

93081C92

CRANKSHAFT AND CONNECTING ROD SPECIFICATIONS
All measurements are given in inches.

Year	Engine Displacement Liters (cc)	Engine ID/VIN	Crankshaft				Connecting Rod		
			Main Brg. Journal Dia.	Main Brg. Oil Clearance	Shaft End-play	Thrust on No.	Journal Diameter	Oil Clearance	Side Clearance
1997	2.3 (2300)	A	2.2059-2.2051	0.0008-0.0015	0.0040-0.0080	3	2.0462-2.0472	0.0008-0.0015	0.0035-0.0115
	3.0 (2982)	U	2.5190-2.5198	0.0010-0.0014	0.0040-0.0080	3	2.1253-2.1261	0.0010-0.0014	0.0060-0.0140
	4.0 (3950)	X	2.2433-2.2441	0.0008-0.0015	0.0020-0.0120	3	2.1252-2.1260	0.0003-0.0024	0.0060-0.0140
	4.9 (4916)	Y	2.3982-2.3390	0.0008-0.0015	0.0040-0.0080	5	2.1228-2.1236	0.0008-0.0015	0.0060-0.0140
	5.0 (4949)	N	2.2482-2.2490	0.0005-0.0015	0.0040-0.0080	3	2.1228-2.1236	0.0008-0.0015	0.0010-0.0020
	5.0 (4949)	P	2.2482-2.2490	0.0008-0.0015	0.0040-0.0080	3	2.1228-2.1236	0.0008-0.0015	0.0010-0.0020
	5.8 (5752)	H	2.5190-2.5200	0.0008-0.0015	0.0040-0.0080	3	2.3103-2.3111	0.0008-0.0015	0.0010-0.0020
	7.3 (7292)	F	3.1228-3.1236	0.0018-0.0036	0.0025-0.0085	4	2.4980-2.4990	0.0015-0.0045	0.0120-0.0240
	7.5 (7538)	G	2.9994-3.0002	①	0.0040-0.0080	3	2.4992-2.5000	0.0008-0.0025	0.0010-0.0020
1998	2.5 (2500)	C	2.2051-2.2059	0.0008-0.0015	0.0040-0.0080	3	2.0464-2.0472	0.0008-0.0015	0.0035-0.0115
	3.0 (2982)	U	2.5190-2.5198	0.0010-0.0014	0.0040-0.0080	3	2.1253-2.1261	0.0010-0.0014	0.0060-0.0140
	4.0 (3950)	X	2.2433-2.2441	0.0008-0.0015	0.0020-0.0120	3	2.1252-2.1260	0.0003-0.0024	0.0060-0.0140
	4.0 (4000)	E	2.2430-2.2440	0.0008-0.0015	0.0020-0.0125	3	2.7252-2.7260	0.0003-0.0024	0.0036-0.0106
	4.2 (4195)	2	2.5190-2.5198	0.0008-0.0015	0.0000-0.0079	3	2.3103-2.3111	0.0003-0.0024	0.0047-0.0193
	4.6 (4588)	6	2.6500-2.6570	0.0011-0.0026	0.0051-0.0120	5	2.0870-2.8670	0.0011-0.0026	0.0006-0.0177
	4.6 (4588)	W	2.6500-2.6570	0.0011-0.0026	0.0051-0.0120	5	2.0870-2.8670	0.0011-0.0026	0.0006-0.0177
	5.0 (4949)	N	2.2482-2.2490	0.0005-0.0015	0.0040-0.0080	3	2.1228-2.1236	0.0008-0.0015	0.0010-0.0020
	5.0 (4949)	P	2.2482-2.2490	0.0008-0.0015	0.0040-0.0080	3	2.1228-2.1236	0.0008-0.0015	0.0010-0.0020
	5.4 (5409)	L	2.6568-2.6576	0.0009-0.0019	0.0015-0.0030	5	2.0859-2.0867	0.0010-0.0025	0.0006-0.0177
	5.8 (5752)	H	2.5190-2.5200	0.0008-0.0015	0.0040-0.0080	3	2.3103-2.3111	0.0008-0.0015	0.0010-0.0020
	6.8 (6802)	5	2.6568-2.6576	0.0009-0.0019	0.0015-0.0030	5	2.0859-2.0867	0.0010-0.0025	0.0006-0.0177
	7.3 (7292)	F	3.1228-3.1236	0.0018-0.0036	0.0025-0.0085	4	2.4980-2.4990	0.0015-0.0045	0.0120-0.0240
	7.5 (7538)	G	2.9994-3.0002	①	0.0040-0.0080	3	2.4992-2.5000	0.0008-0.0025	0.0010-0.0020

93081C93

For accessory drive belt replacement procedures see the model specific sections of this manual

CRANKSHAFT AND CONNECTING ROD SPECIFICATIONS
All measurements are given in inches.

Year	Engine Displacement Liters (cc)	Engine ID/VIN	Crankshaft				Connecting Rod		
			Main Brg. Journal Dia.	Main Brg. Oil Clearance	Shaft End-play	Thrust on No.	Journal Diameter	Oil Clearance	Side Clearance
1999	2.5 (2500)	C	2.2051-2.2059	0.0008-0.0015	0.0040-0.0080	3	2.0464-2.0472	0.0008-0.0015	0.0035-0.0115
	3.0 (2982)	U	2.5190-2.5198	0.0010-0.0014	0.0040-0.0080	3	2.1253-2.1261	0.0010-0.0014	0.0060-0.0140
	4.0 (3950)	X	2.2433-2.2441	0.0008-0.0015	0.0020-0.0120	3	2.1252-2.1260	0.0003-0.0024	0.0002-0.0025
	4.0 (4000)	E	2.2430-2.2440	0.0008-0.0015	0.0020-0.0125	3	2.7252-2.7260	0.0003-0.0024	0.0036-0.0106
	4.2 (4195)	2	2.5190-2.5198	0.0008-0.0015	0.0000-0.0079	3	2.3103-2.3111	0.0003-0.0024	0.0047-0.0193
	4.6 (4588)	6/W	2.6500-2.6570	0.0011-0.0026	0.0051-0.0120	5	2.0870-2.8670	0.0011-0.0026	0.0006-0.0177
	5.0 (4949)	P	2.2482-2.2490	0.0008-0.0015	0.0040-0.0080	3	2.1228-2.1236	0.0008-0.0015	0.0010-0.0020
	5.4 (5409)	L	2.6568-2.6576	0.0009-0.0019	0.0015-0.0030	5	2.0859-2.0867	0.0010-0.0025	0.0006-0.0177
	5.8 (5752)	H	2.5190-2.5200	0.0008-0.0015	0.0040-0.0080	3	2.3103-2.3111	0.0008-0.0015	0.0010-0.0020
	6.8 (6802)	5	2.6568-2.6576	0.0009-0.0019	0.0015-0.0030	5	2.0859-2.0867	0.0010-0.0025	0.0006-0.0177
	7.3 (7292)	F	3.1228-3.1236	0.0018-0.0036	0.0025-0.0085	4	2.4980-2.4990	0.0015-0.0045	0.0120-0.0240
	7.5 (7538)	G	2.9994-3.0002	①	0.0040-0.0080	3	2.4992-2.5000	0.0008-0.0025	0.0010-0.0020
2000-01	2.5 (2500)	C	2.2051-2.2059	0.0008-0.0015	0.0040-0.0080	3	2.0464-2.0472	0.0008-0.0015	0.0035-0.0115
	3.0 (2982)	U	2.5190-2.5198	0.0010-0.0014	0.0040-0.0080	3	2.1253-2.1261	0.0010-0.0014	0.0060-0.0140
	4.0 (3950)	X	2.2433-2.2441	0.0008-0.0015	0.0020-0.0120	3	2.1252-2.1260	0.0003-0.0024	0.0002-0.0025
	4.0 (4000)	E	2.2430-2.2440	0.0008-0.0015	0.0020-0.0125	3	2.7252-2.7260	0.0003-0.0024	0.0036-0.0106
	4.2 (4195)	2	2.5190-2.5198	0.0008-0.0015	0.0000-0.0079	3	2.3103-2.3111	0.0003-0.0024	0.0047-0.0193
	4.6 (4588)	6/W	2.6500-2.6570	0.0011-0.0026	0.0051-0.0120	5	2.0870-2.8670	0.0011-0.0026	0.0006-0.0177
	5.0 (4949)	P	2.2482-2.2490	0.0008-0.0015	0.0040-0.0080	3	2.1228-2.1236	0.0008-0.0015	0.0010-0.0020
	5.4 (5409)	L	2.6568-2.6576	0.0009-0.0019	0.0015-0.0030	5	2.0859-2.0867	0.0010-0.0025	0.0006-0.0177
	5.8 (5752)	H	2.5190-2.5200	0.0008-0.0015	0.0040-0.0080	3	2.3103-2.3111	0.0008-0.0015	0.0010-0.0020
	6.8 (6802)	5	2.6568-2.6576	0.0009-0.0019	0.0015-0.0030	5	2.0859-2.0867	0.0010-0.0025	0.0006-0.0177
	7.3 (7292)	F	3.1228-3.1236	0.0018-0.0036	0.0025-0.0085	4	2.4980-2.4990	0.0015-0.0045	0.0120-0.0240
	7.5 (7538)	G	2.9994-3.0002	①	0.0040-0.0080	3	2.4992-2.5000	0.0008-0.0025	0.0010-0.0020

① Journal 1: 0.0004 - 0.0022 inches
Journals 2, 3, 4 and 5: 0.0009 - 0.0027 inches

93081C94

PISTON AND RING SPECIFICATIONS
All measurements are given in inches.

Year	Engine Displacement Liters (cc)	Engine ID/VIN	Piston Clearance	Ring Gap			Ring Side Clearance		
				Top Compression	Bottom Compression	Oil Control	Top Compression	Bottom Compression	Oil Control
1997	2.3 (2300)	A	0.0100-0.0200	0.008-0.016	0.013-0.019	0.010-0.030	0.0016-0.0033	0.0016-0.0033	SNUG
	3.0 (2982)	U	0.0012-0.0023	0.010-0.020	0.010-0.020	0.010-0.049	0.0602-0.0612	0.0602-0.0612	SNUG
	4.0 (3950)	X	0.0008-0.0019	0.015-0.023	0.015-0.023	0.015-0.055	0.0020-0.0033	0.0020-0.0033	SNUG
	4.9 (4916)	Y	0.0010-0.0018	0.010-0.020	0.010-0.020	0.015-0.055	0.0019-0.0036	0.0019-0.0036	SNUG
	5.0 (4949)	N	0.0014-0.0022	0.010-0.020	0.010-0.020	0.015-0.055	0.0013-0.0033	0.0013-0.0033	SNUG
	5.0 (4949)	P	0.0012-0.0020	0.010-0.020	0.018-0.028	0.010-0.040	0.0013-0.0033	0.0013-0.0033	SNUG
	5.8 (5752)	H	0.0015-0.0023	0.010-0.020	0.018-0.028	0.010-0.040	0.0013-0.0033	0.0013-0.0033	SNUG
	7.3 (7292)	F	0.0044-0.0057	0.014-0.024	0.062-0.072	0.012-0.024	0.0013-0.0033	0.0013-0.0033	SNUG
	7.5 (7538)	G	0.0014-0.0022	0.010-0.015	0.011-0.021	0.010-0.030	0.0012-0.0022	0.0012-0.0022	SNUG
1998	2.5 (2500)	C	0.0010-0.0020	0.008-0.018	0.013-0.023	0.010-0.035	0.0014-0.0030	0.0014-0.0030	SNUG
	3.0 (2982)	U	0.0012-0.0023	0.010-0.020	0.010-0.020	0.010-0.049	0.0602-0.0612	0.0602-0.0612	SNUG
	4.0 (3950)	X	0.0008-0.0019	0.015-0.023	0.015-0.023	0.015-0.055	0.0020-0.0033	0.0020-0.0033	SNUG
	4.0 (4000)	E	0.0008-0.0019	0.015-0.023	0.015-0.023	0.015-0.055	0.0010-0.0030	0.0010-0.0030	SNUG
	4.2 (4195)	2	0.0007-0.0018	0.001-0.002	0.001-0.002	0.006-0.007	0.0012-0.0031	0.0012-0.0031	SNUG
	4.6 (4588)	6	0.0005-0.0010	0.010-0.020	0.010-0.020	0.006-0.026	0.0016-0.0031	0.0012-0.0031	SNUG
	4.6 (4588)	W	0.0005-0.0010	0.010-0.020	0.010-0.020	0.006-0.026	0.0016-0.0031	0.0012-0.0031	SNUG
	5.0 (4949)	N	0.0014-0.0022	0.010-0.020	0.010-0.020	0.015-0.055	0.0013-0.0033	0.0013-0.0033	SNUG
	5.0 (4949)	P	0.0012-0.0020	0.010-0.020	0.018-0.028	0.010-0.040	0.0013-0.0033	0.0013-0.0033	SNUG
	5.4 (5409)	L	0.0000-0.0010	0.005-0.011	0.010-0.016	0.006-0.026	0.0012-0.0037	0.0012-0.0037	SNUG
	5.8 (5752)	H	0.0015-0.0023	0.010-0.020	0.018-0.028	0.010-0.040	0.0013-0.0033	0.0013-0.0033	SNUG
	6.8 (6802)	5	0.0000-0.0010	0.005-0.011	0.010-0.016	0.006-0.026	0.0012-0.0037	0.0012-0.0037	SNUG
	7.3 (7292)	F	0.0044-0.0057	0.014-0.024	0.062-0.072	0.012-0.024	0.0013-0.0033	0.0013-0.0033	SNUG
	7.5 (7538)	G	0.0014-0.0022	0.010-0.015	0.011-0.021	0.010-0.030	0.0012-0.0022	0.0012-0.0022	SNUG

93081C95

For brake related suspension and axle service, refer to the model specific sections of this manual

PISTON AND RING SPECIFICATIONS
All measurements are given in inches.

Year	Engine Displacement Liters (cc)	Engine ID/VIN	Piston Clearance	Ring Gap			Ring Side Clearance		
				Top Compression	Bottom Compression	Oil Control	Top Compression	Bottom Compression	Oil Control
1999	2.5 (2500)	C	0.0010-0.0020	0.008-0.018	0.013-0.023	0.010-0.035	0.0014-0.0030	0.0014-0.0030	SNUG
	3.0 (2982)	U	0.0012-0.0023	0.010-0.020	0.010-0.020	0.010-0.049	0.0602-0.0612	0.0602-0.0612	SNUG
	4.0 (3950)	X	0.0008-0.0019	0.015-0.023	0.015-0.023	0.015-0.055	0.0020-0.0033	0.0020-0.0033	SNUG
	4.0 (4000)	E	0.0008-0.0019	0.015-0.023	0.015-0.023	0.015-0.055	0.0010-0.0030	0.0010-0.0030	SNUG
	4.2 (4195)	2	0.0007-0.0018	0.001-0.002	0.001-0.002	0.006-0.007	0.0012-0.0031	0.0012-0.0031	SNUG
	4.6 (4588)	6/W	0.0005-0.0010	0.010-0.020	0.010-0.020	0.006-0.026	0.0016-0.0031	0.0012-0.0031	SNUG
	5.0 (4949)	P	0.0012-0.0020	0.010-0.020	0.018-0.028	0.010-0.040	0.0013-0.0033	0.0013-0.0033	SNUG
	5.4 (5409)	L	0.0000-0.0010	0.005-0.011	0.010-0.016	0.006-0.026	0.0012-0.0037	0.0012-0.0037	SNUG
	5.8 (5752)	H	0.0015-0.0023	0.010-0.020	0.018-0.028	0.010-0.040	0.0013-0.0033	0.0013-0.0033	SNUG
	6.8 (6802)	5	0.0000-0.0010	0.005-0.011	0.010-0.016	0.006-0.026	0.0012-0.0037	0.0012-0.0037	SNUG
	7.3 (7292)	F	0.0044-0.0057	0.014-0.024	0.062-0.072	0.012-0.024	0.0013-0.0033	0.0013-0.0033	SNUG
	7.5 (7538)	G	0.0014-0.0022	0.010-0.015	0.011-0.021	0.010-0.030	0.0012-0.0022	0.0012-0.0022	SNUG
2000-01	2.5 (2500)	C	0.0010-0.0020	0.008-0.018	0.013-0.023	0.010-0.035	0.0014-0.0030	0.0014-0.0030	SNUG
	3.0 (2982)	U	0.0012-0.0023	0.010-0.020	0.010-0.020	0.010-0.049	0.0602-0.0612	0.0602-0.0612	SNUG
	4.0 (3950)	X	0.0008-0.0019	0.015-0.023	0.015-0.023	0.015-0.055	0.0020-0.0033	0.0020-0.0033	SNUG
	4.0 (4000)	E	0.0008-0.0019	0.015-0.023	0.015-0.023	0.015-0.055	0.0010-0.0030	0.0010-0.0030	SNUG
	4.2 (4195)	2	0.0007-0.0018	0.001-0.002	0.001-0.002	0.006-0.007	0.0012-0.0031	0.0012-0.0031	SNUG
	4.6 (4588)	6/W	0.0005-0.0010	0.010-0.020	0.010-0.020	0.006-0.026	0.0016-0.0031	0.0012-0.0031	SNUG
	5.0 (4949)	P	0.0012-0.0020	0.010-0.020	0.018-0.028	0.010-0.040	0.0013-0.0033	0.0013-0.0033	SNUG
	5.4 (5409)	L	0.0000-0.0010	0.005-0.011	0.010-0.016	0.006-0.026	0.0012-0.0037	0.0012-0.0037	SNUG
	5.8 (5752)	H	0.0015-0.0023	0.010-0.020	0.018-0.028	0.010-0.040	0.0013-0.0033	0.0013-0.0033	SNUG
	6.8 (6802)	5	0.0000-0.0010	0.005-0.011	0.010-0.016	0.006-0.026	0.0012-0.0037	0.0012-0.0037	SNUG
	7.3 (7292)	F	0.0044-0.0057	0.014-0.024	0.062-0.072	0.012-0.024	0.0013-0.0033	0.0013-0.0033	SNUG
	7.5 (7538)	G	0.0014-0.0022	0.010-0.015	0.011-0.021	0.010-0.030	0.0012-0.0022	0.0012-0.0022	SNUG

93081C96

TORQUE SPECIFICATIONS
All readings in ft. lbs.

Year	Engine Displacement Liters (cc)	Engine ID/VIN	Cylinder Head Bolts	Main Bearing Bolts	Rod Bearing Bolts	Crankshaft Damper Bolts	Flywheel Bolts	Manifold Intake *	Manifold Exhaust	Spark Plugs	Lug Nut
1997	2.3 (2300)	A	51	75-85	30-36	103-133	54-64	19-28	14-21	5-10	100
	3.0 (2982)	U	(1)	60	26	107	54-64	24	25	8-10	100
	4.0 (3950)	X	(2)	66-77	19-24	(3)	59	(4)	19	10-15	100
	4.9 (4916)	Y	(13)	60-70	40-45	130-150	75-85	22-32	22-32	10-15	(14)
	5.0 (4949)	N	(15)	60-70	19-24	70-90	75-85	23-25	18-24	10-15	(14)
	5.0 (4949)	P	(15)	60-70	19-24	110-130	75-85	12-18	26-32	7-15	100
	5.8 (5752)	H	(16)	95-105	40-45	70-90	75-90	23-25	20-24	10-15	(14)
	7.3 (7292)	F	(17)	95	70	90	89	18	45	—	(14)
	7.5 (7538)	G	(18)	95-105	40-45	70-90	75-85	22-32	28-33	5-10	(14)
1998	2.5 (2500)	C	51	75-85	30-36	103-133	54-64	19-28	14-21	5-10	100
	3.0 (2982)	U	(1)	60	26	107	54-64	24	25	8-10	100
	4.0 (3950)	X	(2)	66-77	19-24	(3)	59	(4)	19	10-15	100
	4.0 (4000)	E	(19)	67-74	19-24	(20)	54-64	9-10	15-18	7-14	100
	4.2 (4195)	2	(5)	81-88	(6)	103-117	54-63	(7)	15-22	8-14	83-113
	4.6 (4588)	6	(12)	(9)	29-33	(10)	54-64	(11)	15	7-14	83-113
	4.6 (4588)	W	(12)	(8)	29-33	(10)	54-64	(11)	15	7-14	83-113
	5.0 (4949)	N	(15)	60-70	19-24	70-90	75-85	23-25	18-24	10-15	(14)
	5.0 (4949)	P	(15)	60-70	19-24	110-130	75-85	12-18	26-32	7-15	100
	5.4 (5409)	L	(21)	(22)	(23)	(10)	54-64	(24)	17-19	9-20	100
	5.8 (5752)	H	(16)	95-105	40-45	70-90	75-90	23-25	20-24	10-15	(14)
	6.8 (6802)	5	(21)	(22)	(23)	(10)	54-64	(24)	17-20	7-14	140
	7.3 (7292)	F	(17)	95	70	90	89	18	45	—	(14)
	7.5 (7538)	G	(18)	95-105	40-45	70-90	75-85	22-32	28-33	5-10	(14)
1999	2.5 (2500)	C	51	75-85	30-36	103-133	54-64	19-28	14-21	5-10	100
	3.0 (2982)	U	(1)	60	26	107	54-64	24	25	8-10	100
	4.0 (3950)	X	(2)	66-77	19-24	(3)	59	(4)	19	10-15	100
	4.0 (4000)	E	(19)	67-74	19-24	(20)	54-64	9-10	15-18	7-14	100
	4.2 (4195)	2	(5)	81-88	(6)	103-117	54-63	(7)	15-22	8-14	83-113
	4.6 (4588)	6/W	(12)	(9)	29-33	(10)	54-64	(11)	15	7-14	83-113
	5.0 (4949)	P	(15)	60-70	19-24	110-130	75-85	12-18	26-32	7-15	100
	5.4 (5409)	L	(21)	(22)	(23)	(10)	54-64	(24)	17-19	9-20	100
	5.8 (5752)	H	(16)	95-105	40-45	70-90	75-90	23-25	20-24	10-15	(14)
	6.8 (6802)	5	(21)	(22)	(23)	(10)	54-64	(24)	17-20	7-14	140
	7.3 (7292)	F	(17)	95	70	90	89	18	45	—	(14)
	7.5 (7538)	G	(18)	95-105	40-45	70-90	75-85	22-32	28-33	5-10	(14)
2000-01	2.5 (2500)	C	51	75-85	30-36	103-133	54-64	19-28	14-21	5-10	100
	3.0 (2982)	U	(1)	60	26	107	54-64	24	25	8-10	100
	4.0 (3950)	X	(2)	66-77	19-24	(3)	59	(4)	19	10-15	100
	4.0 (4000)	E	(19)	67-74	19-24	(20)	54-64	9-10	15-18	7-14	100
	4.2 (4195)	2	(5)	81-88	(6)	103-117	54-63	(7)	15-22	8-14	83-113
	4.6 (4588)	0/W	(12)	(9)	29-33	(10)	54-64	(11)	15	7-14	83-113
	5.0 (4949)	P	(15)	60-70	19-24	110-130	75-85	12-18	26-32	7-15	100
	5.4 (5409)	L	(21)	(22)	(23)	(10)	54-64	(24)	17-19	9-20	100

93081C97

Refer to the model specific sections for driveline service procedures

TORQUE SPECIFICATIONS
All readings in ft. lbs.

Engine Displacement Liters (cc)	Engine ID/VIN	Cylinder Head Bolts	Main Bearing Bolts	Rod Bearing Bolts	Crankshaft Damper Bolts	Flywheel Bolts	Manifold		Spark Plugs	Lug Nut
							Intake *	Exhaust		
2000-01 (cont.) 5.8 (5752)	H	⑯	95-105	40-45	70-90	75-90	23-25	20-24	10-15	⑭
6.8 (6802)	5	㉑	㉒	㉓	⑩	54-64	㉔	17-20	7-14	140
7.3 (7292)	F	⑰	95	70	90	89	18	45	—	⑭
7.5 (7538)	G	⑱	95-105	40-45	70-90	75-85	22-32	28-33	5-10	⑭

* NOTE: Applies to Lower Manifold only.

① Step 1: 37 ft. lbs.
  Step 2: 68 ft. lbs.

② Step 1: 44 ft. lbs.
  Step 2: 59 ft. lbs.
  Step 3: Plus 85 degrees

③ Step 1: 30-37 ft. lbs.
  Step 2: Turn 90 degrees

④ Step 1: 3-6 ft. lbs.
  Step 2: 6-11 ft. lbs.
  Step 3: 11-15 ft. lbs.
  Step 4: 15-18 ft. lbs.

⑤ Step 1: 29 ft. lbs.
  Step 2: 36 ft. lbs.
  Step 3: Loosen, and torque one at a time
  Short bolts to 32 ft. lbs.
  Long bolts to 36 ft. lbs.
  Step 4: Turn each bolt 135 degrees

⑥ Step 1: 29 ft. lbs.
  Step 2: Plus 90 degrees

⑦ Tighten bolts to 71-101 inch lbs.

⑧ Main bearing jack screws:
  Step 1: 45 inch lbs.
  Step 2: 98 inch lbs.
  Cross-mounted cap bolts:
  Step 1: 89 inch lbs.
  Step 2: 17 ft. lbs.

⑨ Jack screws:
  Step 1: 45 inch lbs.
  Step 2: 98 inch lbs.
  Cross-mounted cap bolts:
  Step 1: 24 ft. lbs.
  Step 2: Plus 90 degrees

⑩ Step 1: 88 ft. lbs.
  Step 2: Loosen bolt
  Step 3: 39 ft. lbs.
  Step 4: Plus 90 degrees

⑪ Step 1: 18 inch lbs.
  Step 2: 96 inch lbs.

⑫ Step 1: 31 ft. lbs.
  Step 2: Plus 90 degrees
  Step 3: Plus 90 degrees

⑬ Step 1: 55 ft. lbs.
  Step 2: 65 ft. lbs.
  Step 3: 85 ft. lbs.

⑭ E-F100, 150, 250: 90 ft. lbs.
  E-F350: Single rear wheels: 135 ft. lbs.
  F350: Dual rear wheels: 210 ft. lbs.

⑮ With flanged head bolts:
  Step 1: 25-35 ft. lbs.
  Step 2: 45-55 ft. lbs.
  Step 3: Plus 90 degrees
  With hex head bolts:
  Step 1: 55-65 ft. lbs.
  Step 2: 65-72 ft. lbs.

⑯ Step 1: 95-105 ft. lbs.
  Step 2: 105-112 ft. lbs.

⑰ Step 1: 65 ft. lbs.
  Step 2: 85 ft. lbs.
  Step 3: 105 ft. lbs.

⑱ Step 1: 70-80 ft. lbs.
  Step 2: 100-110 ft. lbs.
  Step 3: 130-140 ft. lbs.

⑲ Step 1: 28 ft. lbs.
  Step 2: Plus 90 degrees
  Step 3: Plus 90 degrees

⑳ Step 1: 20-28 ft. lbs.
  Step 2: Loosen two turns
  Step 3: 20-25 ft. lbs.

㉑ Step 1: 27-32 inch lbs.
  Step 2: Plus 90 degrees
  Step 3: Plus 90 degrees

㉒ Step 1: 27-32 inch lbs.
  Step 2: Plus 90 degrees

㉓ Step 1: 30-33 ft. lbs.
  Step 2: 90-120 degrees

㉔ Step 1: 18 inch lbs.
  Step 2: 71-106 inch lbs.

93081C98

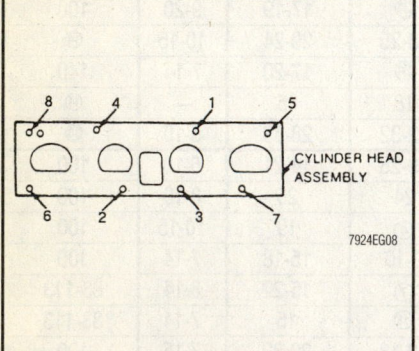

Tighten the lower manifold bolts in the sequence shown—2.3L engine

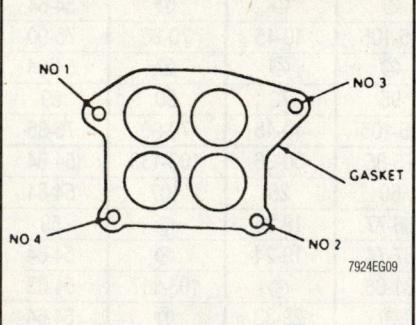

Tighten the upper manifold bolts in the sequence shown—2.3L engine

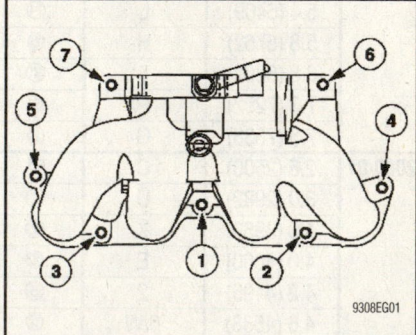

Tighten the lower manifold bolts in the sequence shown—2.5L engine

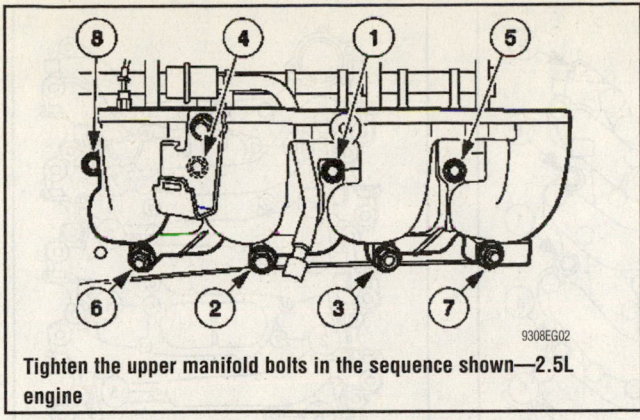

Tighten the upper manifold bolts in the sequence shown—2.5L engine

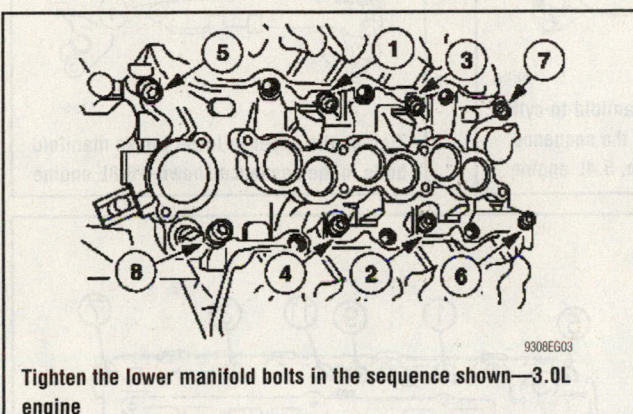

Tighten the lower manifold bolts in the sequence shown—3.0L engine

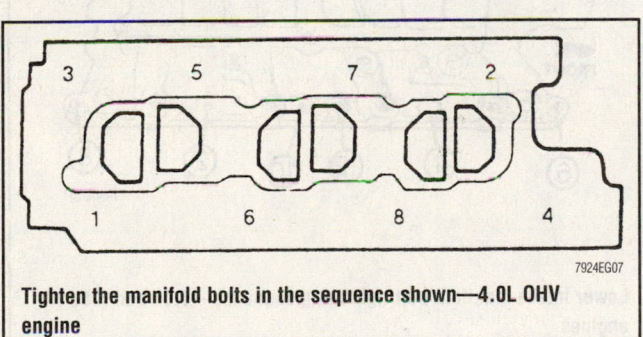

Tighten the manifold bolts in the sequence shown—4.0L OHV engine

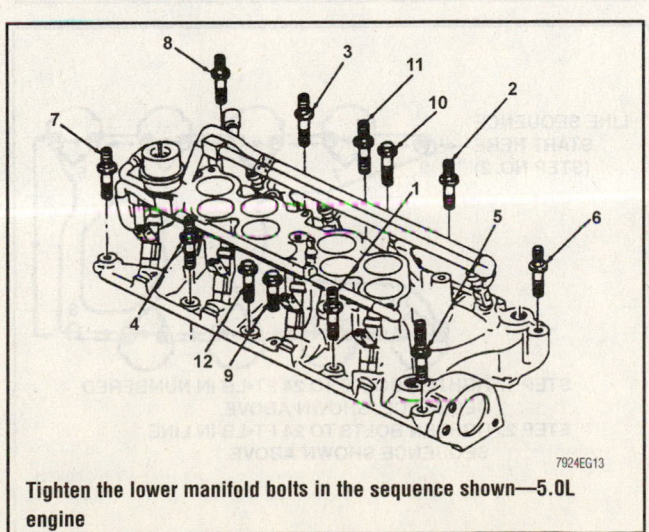

Tighten the lower manifold bolts in the sequence shown—5.0L engine

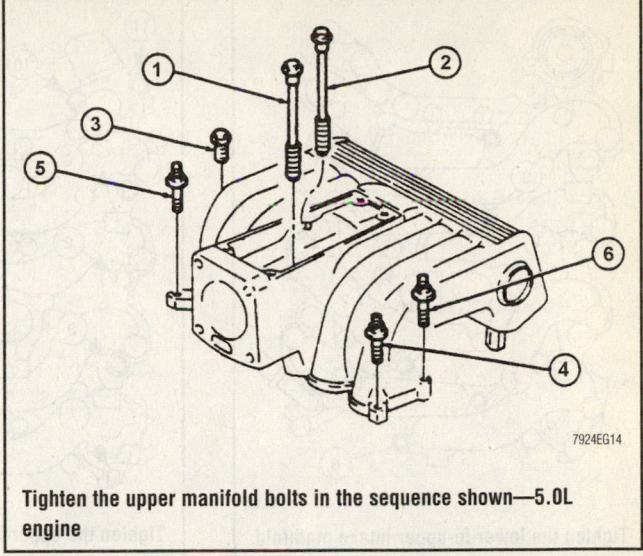

Tighten the upper manifold bolts in the sequence shown—5.0L engine

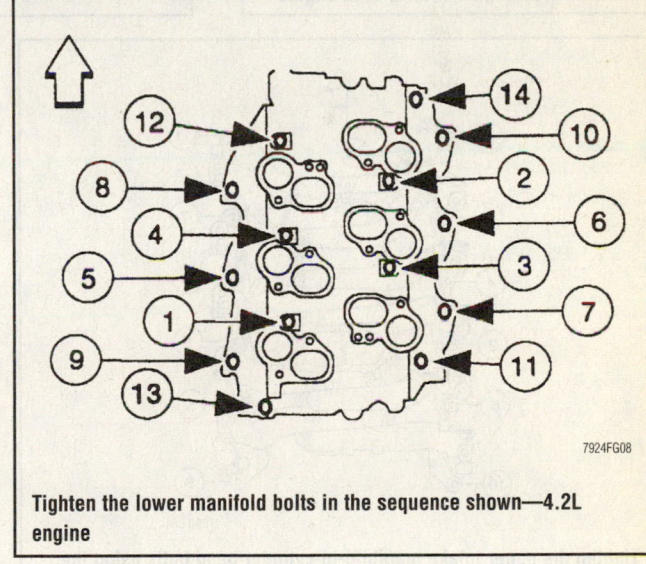

Tighten the lower manifold bolts in the sequence shown—4.2L engine

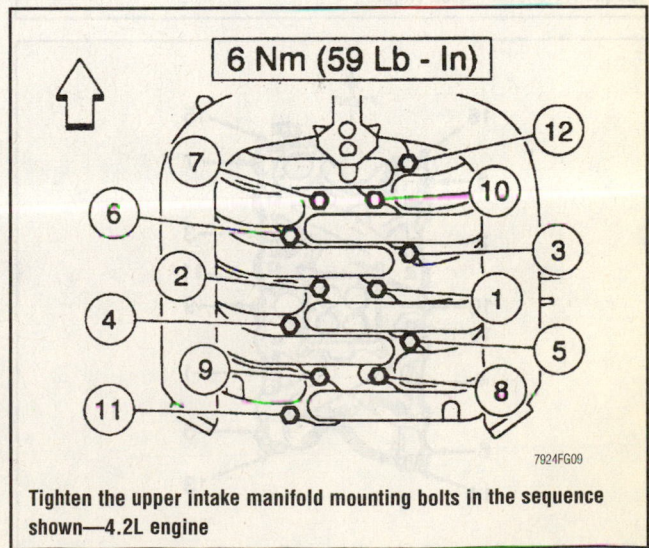

Tighten the upper intake manifold mounting bolts in the sequence shown—4.2L engine

For exhaust manifold replacement procedures, see the model specific sections of this manual

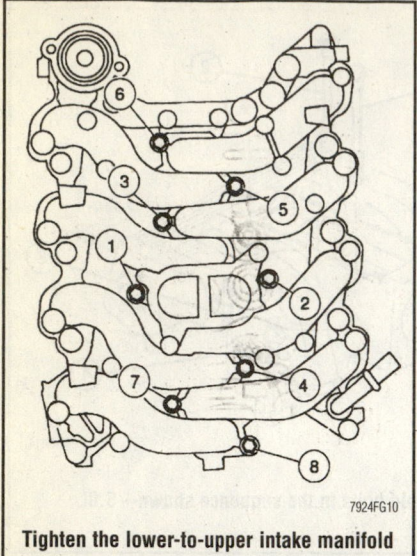

Tighten the lower-to-upper intake manifold bolts in 2 steps following the sequence shown—4.6L engine shown, 5.4L engine

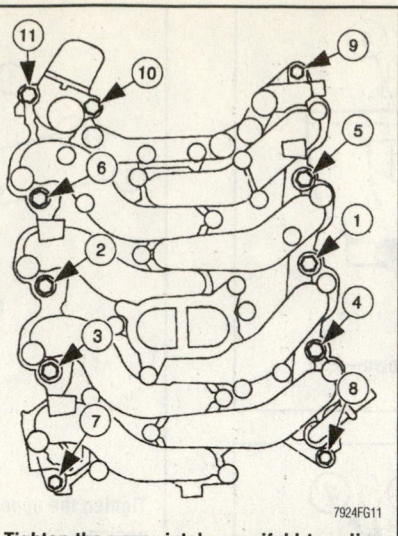

Tighten the upper intake manifold-to-cylinder head mounting bolts in the sequence shown—4.6L engine shown, 5.4L engine

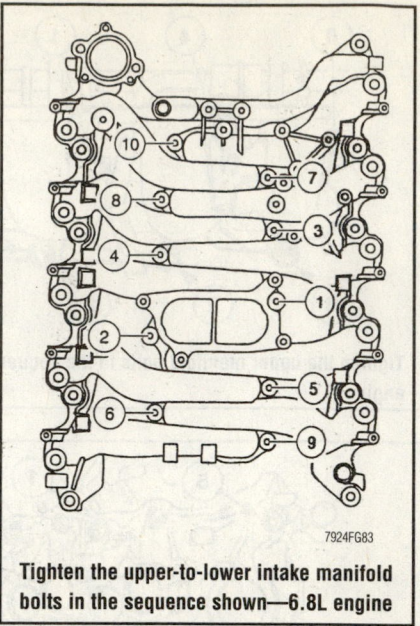

Tighten the upper-to-lower intake manifold bolts in the sequence shown—6.8L engine

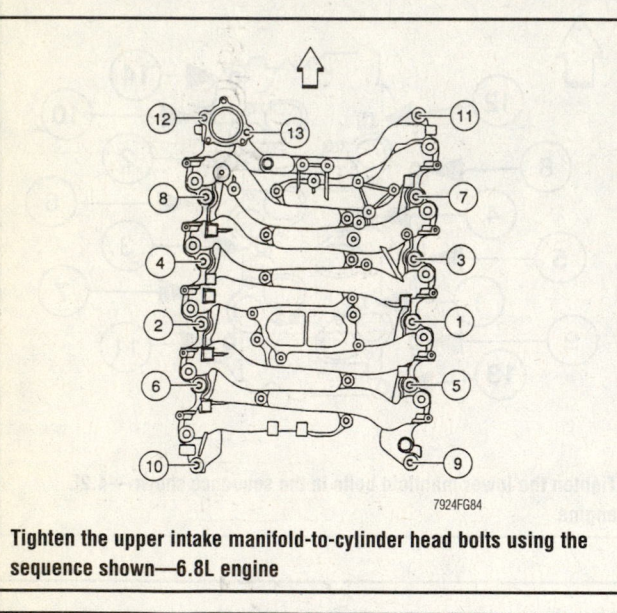

Tighten the upper intake manifold-to-cylinder head bolts using the sequence shown—6.8L engine

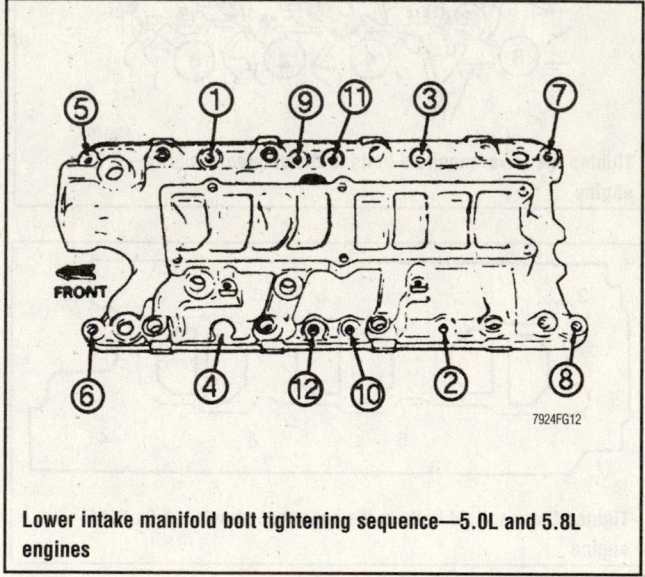

Lower intake manifold bolt tightening sequence—5.0L and 5.8L engines

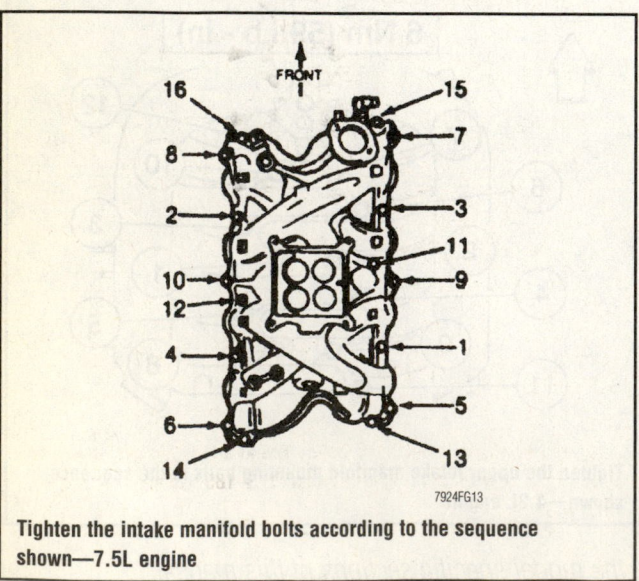

Tighten the intake manifold bolts according to the sequence shown—7.5L engine

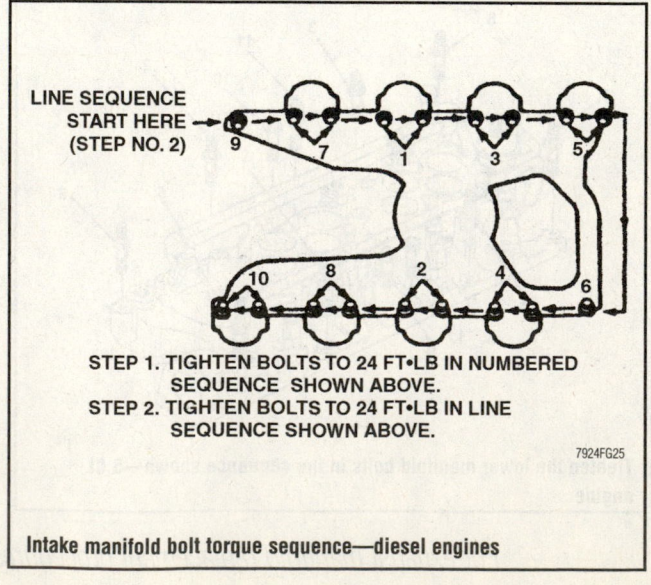

LINE SEQUENCE START HERE (STEP NO. 2)

STEP 1. TIGHTEN BOLTS TO 24 FT•LB IN NUMBERED SEQUENCE SHOWN ABOVE.
STEP 2. TIGHTEN BOLTS TO 24 FT•LB IN LINE SEQUENCE SHOWN ABOVE.

Intake manifold bolt torque sequence—diesel engines

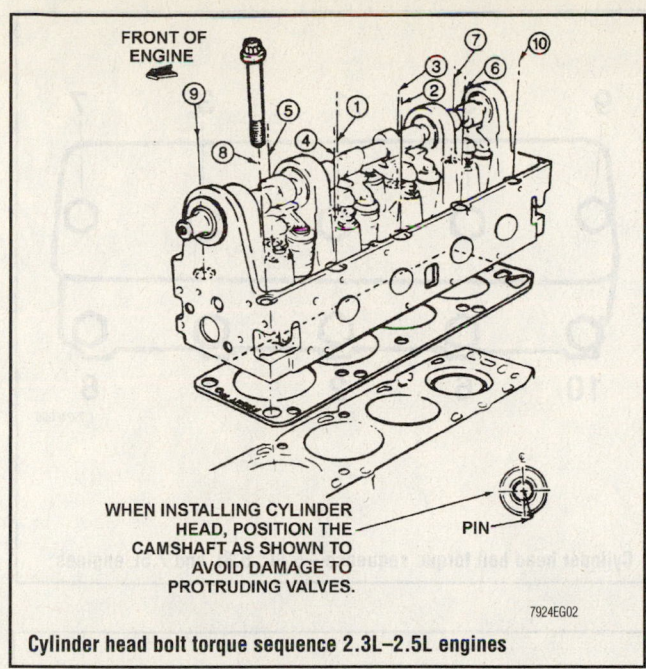

WHEN INSTALLING CYLINDER HEAD, POSITION THE CAMSHAFT AS SHOWN TO AVOID DAMAGE TO PROTRUDING VALVES.

Cylinder head bolt torque sequence 2.3L–2.5L engines

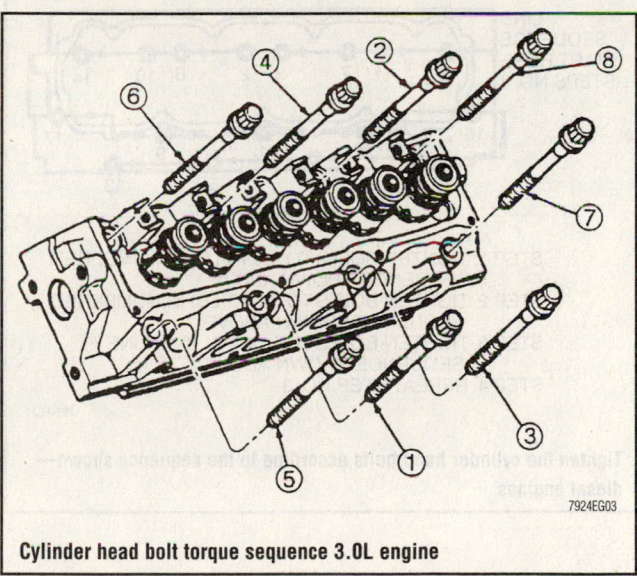

Cylinder head bolt torque sequence 3.0L engine

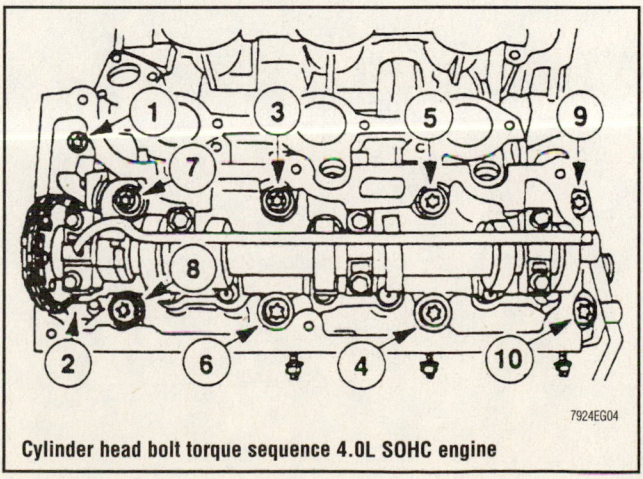

Cylinder head bolt torque sequence 4.0L SOHC engine

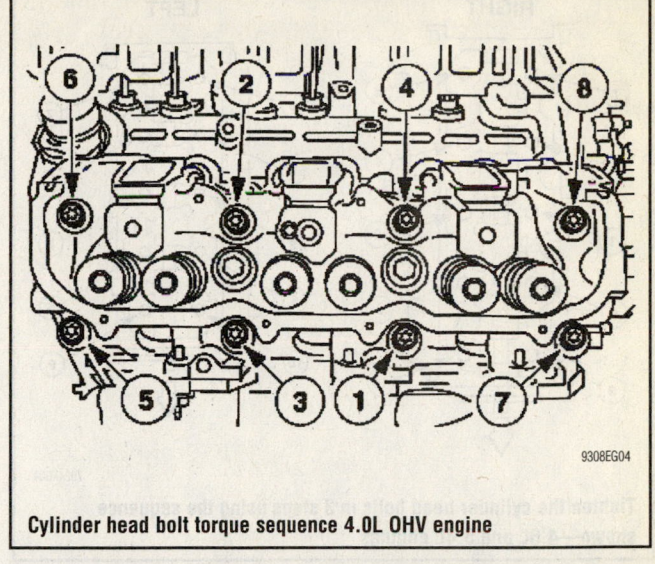

Cylinder head bolt torque sequence 4.0L OHV engine

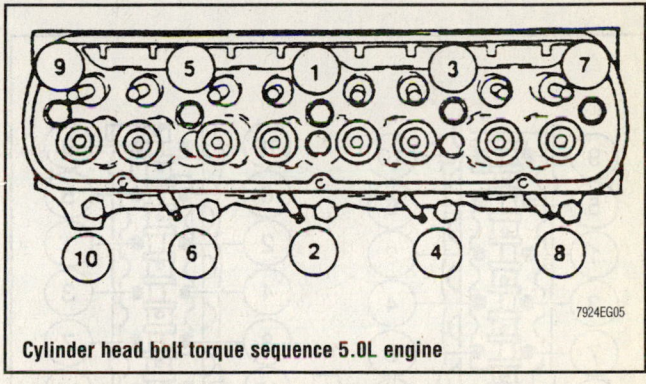

Cylinder head bolt torque sequence 5.0L engine

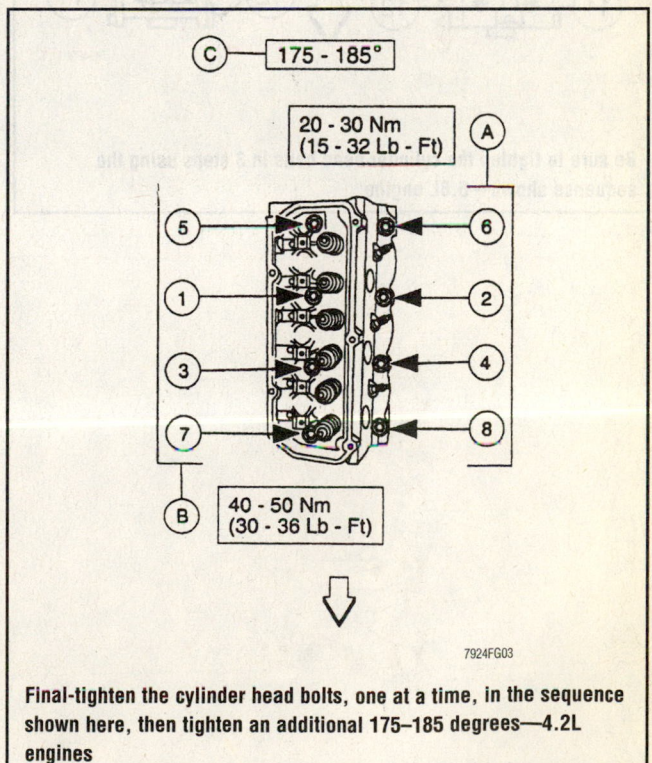

Final-tighten the cylinder head bolts, one at a time, in the sequence shown here, then tighten an additional 175–185 degrees—4.2L engines

Refer to the model specific sections for cooling system service procedures

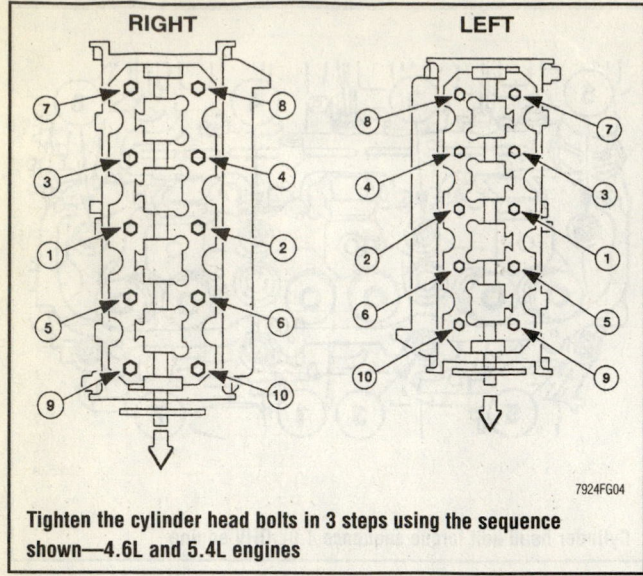

Tighten the cylinder head bolts in 3 steps using the sequence shown—4.6L and 5.4L engines

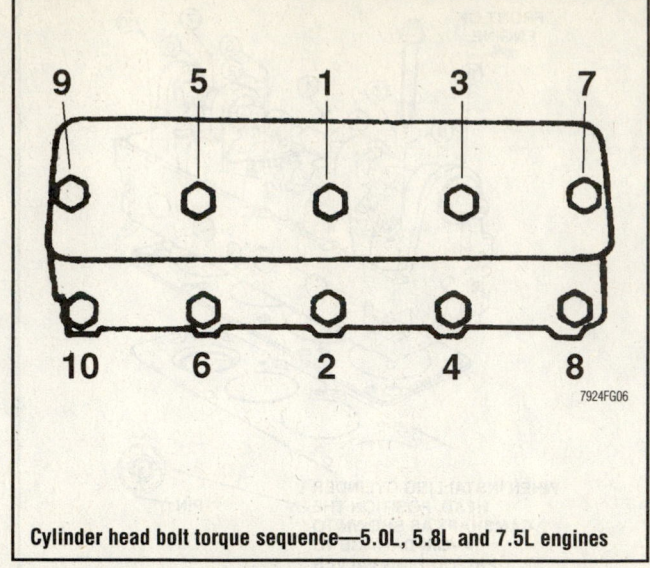

Cylinder head bolt torque sequence—5.0L, 5.8L and 7.5L engines

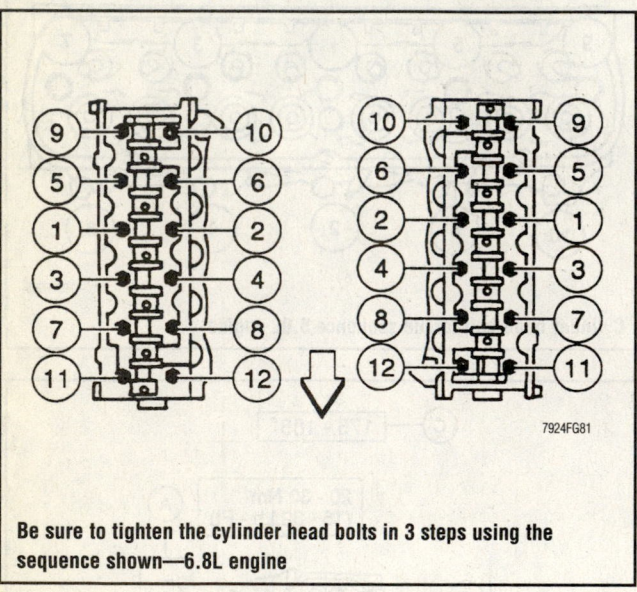

Be sure to tighten the cylinder head bolts in 3 steps using the sequence shown—6.8L engine

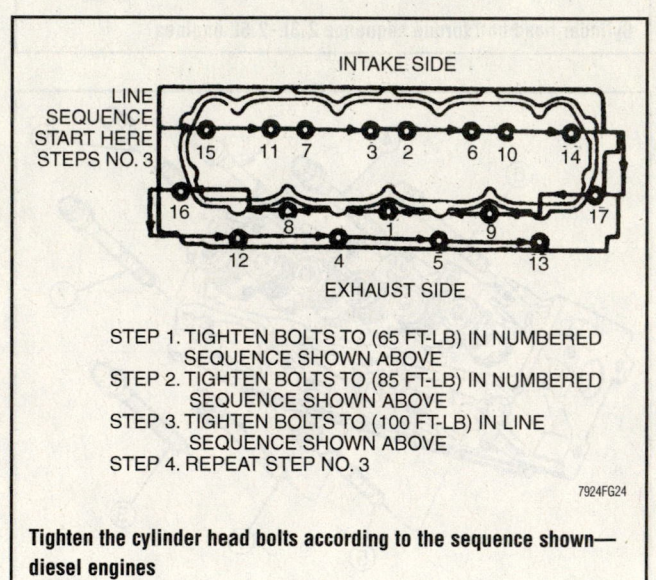

STEP 1. TIGHTEN BOLTS TO (65 FT-LB) IN NUMBERED SEQUENCE SHOWN ABOVE
STEP 2. TIGHTEN BOLTS TO (85 FT-LB) IN NUMBERED SEQUENCE SHOWN ABOVE
STEP 3. TIGHTEN BOLTS TO (100 FT-LB) IN LINE SEQUENCE SHOWN ABOVE
STEP 4. REPEAT STEP NO. 3

Tighten the cylinder head bolts according to the sequence shown—diesel engines

BRAKE SPECIFICATIONS
FORD AEROSTAR, E-SERIES, EXCURSION, EXPEDITION, EXPLORER, F-SERIES, RANGER
LINCOLN NAVIGATOR, MERCURY MOUNTAINEER
All measurements in inches unless noted

Year	Model		Master Cyl. Bore	Brake Disc Original Thickness	Minimum Thickness	Maximum Runout	Brake Drum Diameter Original Inside Diameter	Max. Wear Limit	Maximum Machine Diameter	Minimum Lining Thickness	Brake Caliper Bracket Bolts (ft. lbs.)	Mounting Bolts (ft. lbs.)
1997	Aerostar	①	0.938	0.850	0.810	0.0030	9.00	9.09	9.06	0.030	72-97	21-26
		②	0.938	0.850	0.810	0.0030	10.00	10.09	10.06	0.030	72-97	21-26
	E-150		1.000	1.160	1.120	0.0030	11.03	11.09	11.06	0.030	141-191	22-36
	E-250	③		1.220	1.180	0.0030	12.00	12.09	12.06	0.030	141-191	22-36
	E-350		NA	1.220	1.180	0.0030	12.00	12.09	12.06	0.030	141-191	22-36
	Explorer	①	0.938	0.850	0.810	0.0030	9.00	9.09	9.06	0.030	72-97	21-26
		④	0.938	0.850	0.810	0.0030	10.00	10.09	10.06	0.030	72-97	21-26
		⑤	0.938	0.850	0.810	0.0030	10.00	10.09	10.06	0.030	72-97	21-26
	F-150	⑥	1.062	NA	0.972	NA	11.03	11.12	NA	0.156	125-169	21-26
	F-150		1.000	1.160	0.960	0.0030	11.03	11.09	11.06	0.030	125-169	21-26
	F-250	③		1.220	⑦	0.0030	12.00	12.09	12.06	0.030	125-169	21-26
	F-350		1.125	1.220	⑦	⑧	12.00	12.09	12.06	0.030	125-169	21-26
	Mountaineer	①	0.938	0.850	0.810	0.0030	9.00	9.09	9.06	0.030	72-97	21-26
		④	0.938	0.850	0.810	0.0030	10.00	10.09	10.06	0.030	72-97	21-26
		⑤	0.938	0.850	0.810	0.0030	10.00	10.09	10.06	0.030	72-97	21-26
	Ranger	①	0.938	0.850	0.810	0.0030	9.00	9.09	9.06	0.030	72-97	21-26
		④	0.938	0.850	0.810	0.0030	10.00	10.09	10.06	0.030	72-97	21-26
		⑤	0.938	0.850	0.810	0.0030	10.00	10.09	10.06	0.030	72-97	21-26
	F-Super Duty	F	NA	1.220	1.180	0.0080	—	—	—	0.030	166	42
		R	—	NA	1.430	0.0080	—	—	—	—	—	—
1998	E-150		1.000	1.160	1.120	0.0030	11.03	11.09	11.06	0.030	141-191	22-36
	E-250	③		1.220	1.180	0.0030	12.00	12.09	12.06	0.030	141-191	22-36
	E-350		NA	1.220	1.180	0.0030	12.00	12.09	12.06	0.030	141-191	22-36
	Explorer	①	0.938	0.850	0.810	0.0030	9.00	9.09	9.06	0.030	72-97	21-26
		④	0.938	0.850	0.810	0.0030	10.00	10.09	10.06	0.030	72-97	21-26
		⑤	0.938	0.850	0.810	0.0030	10.00	10.09	10.06	0.030	72-97	21-26
	F-150	⑥	1.062	NA	0.972	NA	11.03	11.12	NA	0.156	125-169	21-26
	F-150		1.000	1.160	0.960	0.0030	11.03	11.09	11.06	0.030	125-169	21-26
	F-250	③		1.220	⑦	0.0030	12.00	12.09	12.06	0.030	125-169	21-26
	F-350		1.125	1.220	⑦	⑧	12.00	12.09	12.06	0.030	125-169	21-26
	Mountaineer	①	0.938	0.850	0.810	0.0030	9.00	9.09	9.06	0.030	72-97	21-26
		④	0.938	0.850	0.810	0.0030	10.00	10.09	10.06	0.030	72-97	21-26
		⑤	0.938	0.850	0.810	0.0030	10.00	10.09	10.06	0.030	72-97	21-26
	Ranger	①	0.938	0.850	0.810	0.0030	9.00	9.09	9.06	0.030	72-97	21-26
		④	0.938	0.850	0.810	0.0030	10.00	10.09	10.06	0.030	72-97	21-26
		⑤	0.938	0.850	0.810	0.0030	10.00	10.09	10.06	0.030	72-97	21-26
	F-Super Duty	F	NA	1.220	1.180	0.0080	—	—	—	0.030	166	42
		R	—	NA	1.430	0.0080	—	—	—	—	—	—
	Expedition	F	1.000	1.023	0.964	0.0025	—	—	—	0.030	125-168	21-26
		R	—	0.700	0.657	0.0250	—	—	—	0.030	120	20
1999	E-150		0.938	1.160	0.960	0.0025	11.03	11.09	11.06	0.030	141-191	22-26
	E-250		1.000	1.300	1.100	0.0003	12.00	12.09	12.06	0.030	141-191	22-26
	E-350		1.125	1.300	1.100	0.0003	12.00	12.09	12.06	0.030	141-191	22-26
	F-150		1.000	⑨	⑩	0.0025	11.03	11.09	11.06	0.030	125-169	21-26
	F-250		1.062	⑨	⑩	0.0025	12.00	12.09	12.06	0.030	125-169	21-26
	F-350		1.125	⑨	⑩	0.0025	12.00	12.09	12.06	0.030	125-169	21-26

93081C99

For complete service labor times order Nichols' Chilton Labor Guide Manual

BRAKE SPECIFICATIONS
FORD AEROSTAR, E-SERIES, EXCURSION, EXPEDITION, EXPLORER, F-SERIES, RANGER
LINCOLN NAVIGATOR, MERCURY MOUNTAINEER
All measurements in inches unless noted

Year	Model		Master Cyl. Bore	Brake Disc Original Thickness	Brake Disc Minimum Thickness	Brake Disc Maximum Runout	Brake Drum Diameter Original Inside Diameter	Brake Drum Diameter Max. Wear Limit	Brake Drum Diameter Maximum Machine Diameter	Minimum Lining Thickness	Brake Caliper Bracket Bolts (ft. lbs.)	Brake Caliper Mounting Bolts (ft. lbs.)
1999 (cont.)	F-Super Duty		1.125	1.220	1.180	0.0025	12.00	12.09	12.06	0.030	166	42
	Expedition	F	1.000	1.023	0.964	0.0025	—	—	—	0.030	125-168	21-26
		R	—	0.700	0.657	0.0250	—	—	—	0.030	120	20
	Navigator	F	1.000	1.023	0.964	0.0025	—	—	—	0.030	125-168	21-26
		R	—	0.700	0.657	0.0250	—	—	—	0.030	120	20
	Explorer	①	0.938	0.850	0.810	0.0030	9.00	9.09	9.06	0.030	72-97	21-26
		④	0.938	0.850	0.810	0.0030	10.00	10.09	10.06	0.030	72-97	21-26
		⑤	0.938	0.850	0.810	0.0030	10.00	10.09	10.06	0.030	72-97	21-26
	Mountaineer	①	0.938	0.850	0.810	0.0030	9.00	9.09	9.06	0.030	72-97	21-26
		④	0.938	0.850	0.810	0.0030	10.00	10.09	10.06	0.030	72-97	21-26
		⑤	0.938	0.850	0.810	0.0030	10.00	10.09	10.06	0.030	72-97	21-26
	Ranger	①	0.938	0.850	0.810	0.0030	9.00	9.09	9.06	0.030	72-97	21-26
		④	0.938	0.850	0.810	0.0030	10.00	10.09	10.06	0.030	72-97	21-26
		⑤	0.938	0.850	0.810	0.0030	10.00	10.09	10.06	0.030	72-97	21-26
2000-01	E-150		0.938	1.160	0.960	0.0025	11.03	11.09	11.06	0.030	141-191	22-26
	E-250		1.000	1.300	1.100	0.0003	12.00	12.09	12.06	0.030	141-191	22-26
	E-350		1.125	1.300	1.100	0.0003	12.00	12.09	12.06	0.030	141-191	22-26
	F-150		1.000	⑨	⑩	0.0025	11.03	11.09	11.06	0.030	125-169	21-26
	F-250		1.062	⑨	⑩	0.0025	12.00	12.09	12.06	0.030	125-169	21-26
	F-350		1.125	⑨	⑩	0.0025	12.00	12.09	12.06	0.030	125-169	21-26
	Excursion		1.125	1.220	1.180	0.0025	12.00	12.09	12.06	0.030	166	42
	F-Super Duty		1.125	1.220	1.180	0.0025	12.00	12.09	12.06	0.030	166	42
	Expedition	F	1.000	1.023	0.964	0.0025	—	—	—	0.030	125-168	21-26
		R	—	0.700	0.657	0.0250	—	—	—	0.030	120	20
	Navigator	F	1.000	1.023	0.964	0.0025	—	—	—	0.030	125-168	21-26
		R	—	0.700	0.657	0.0250	—	—	—	0.030	120	20
	Explorer	①	0.938	0.850	0.810	0.0030	9.00	9.09	9.06	0.030	72-97	21-26
		④	0.938	0.850	0.810	0.0030	10.00	10.09	10.06	0.030	72-97	21-26
		⑤	0.938	0.850	0.810	0.0030	10.00	10.09	10.06	0.030	72-97	21-26
	Mountaineer	①	0.938	0.850	0.810	0.0030	9.00	9.09	9.06	0.030	72-97	21-26
		④	0.938	0.850	0.810	0.0030	10.00	10.09	10.06	0.030	72-97	21-26
		⑤	0.938	0.850	0.810	0.0030	10.00	10.09	10.06	0.030	72-97	21-26
	Ranger	①	0.938	0.850	0.810	0.0030	9.00	9.09	9.06	0.030	72-97	21-26
		④	0.938	0.850	0.810	0.0030	10.00	10.09	10.06	0.030	72-97	21-26
		⑤	0.938	0.850	0.810	0.0030	10.00	10.09	10.06	0.030	72-97	21-26

NOTE: Due to changes made during production, refer to manufacturer's specifications if they differ from those in this chart

NA: Not Available

F: Front

R: Rear

① With 9 inch brakes

② With 10 inch brakes

③ Under 6900 GVW: 1.062 inches
   Over 6900 GVW: 1.125 inches

④ 4x2 with 10 inch brakes

⑤ 4x4 with 10 inch brakes

⑥ 1997 only

⑦ 4x2: 1.100 inches
   4x4: 1.120 inches

⑧ Except F-350 4x2 dual rear wheel and 2-piece rotor/hub: 0.003 inches
   F-350 4x2 dual rear wheel and 2-piece rotor/hub: 0.010 inches

⑨ 1.020 inches for 4x2
   1.220 inches for 4x4

⑩ 0.972 inches for 4x2
   1.090 inches for 4x4

93081CA1

SCHEDULED MAINTENANCE INTERVALS
(FORD AEROSTAR, RANGER, EXPLORER & MOUNTAINEER)

TO BE SERVICED	TYPE OF SERVICE	VEHICLE MILEAGE INTERVAL (x1000)												
		5	10	15	20	25	30	35	40	45	50	55	60	65
Engine oil & filter	R	✓	✓	✓	✓	✓	✓	✓	✓	✓	✓	✓	✓	✓
Automatic transmission shift linkage (Bell crank system)	S/I	✓	✓	✓	✓	✓	✓	✓	✓	✓	✓	✓	✓	✓
Exhaust system & heat shields	S/I	✓		✓		✓		✓		✓		✓		✓
Rotate tires	S/I	✓		✓		✓		✓		✓		✓		✓
Steering linkage & driveshaft U-joint (if equipped without fitting)	S/I	✓		✓		✓		✓		✓		✓		✓
Clutch reservoir fluid level (Ranger, Explorer & Mountaineer)	S/I	✓		✓		✓		✓		✓		✓		✓
Rear driveshaft double cardan joint centering ball (Ranger, Explorer & Mountaineer SWB 4x4)	S/I	✓		✓		✓		✓		✓		✓		✓
Disc brake system & caliper slide rails	S/I			✓			✓			✓			✓	
Drum brake systems, hoses & lines	S/I			✓			✓			✓			✓	
Engine coolant strength hoses & clamps	S/I			✓			✓			✓			✓	
Transfer case shift lever pivot bolt & control rod connecting pins (Ranger, Explorer & Mountaineer 4x4)	S/I			✓			✓			✓			✓	
Air cleaner filter	R						✓						✓	
Automatic transmission fluid & filter	R						✓						✓	
Engine coolant ①	R						✓						✓	
Fuel filter	R						✓						✓	
Front axle RH axle shaft slip yoke (Ranger, Explorer & Mountaineer 4x4)	S/I												✓	
Front suspension ball joints, bushings, arms, springs & rear jounce bumpers (Aerostar)	S/I						✓						✓	

93081CA2

Timing chain and gear service is covered in the model specific sections of this manual

SCHEDULED MAINTENANCE INTERVALS
(FORD AEROSTAR, RANGER, EXPLORER & MOUNTAINEER) (Cont.)

TO BE SERVICED	TYPE OF SERVICE	VEHICLE MILEAGE INTERVAL (x1000)												
		5	10	15	20	25	30	35	40	45	50	55	60	65
Front wheel bearings (4x2)	S/I						✓						✓	
Hub lock (Ranger, Explorer & Mountaineer 4x4)	S/I						✓						✓	
Parking brake system	S/I						✓						✓	
Spindle needle bearing (Ranger, Explorer & Mountaineer 4x4)	S/I						✓						✓	
Throttle or TV lever ball studs	S/I						✓						✓	
Front axle & transfer case oil (E-4WD)	R												✓	
Manual transmission fluid	R												✓	
PCV valve	R												✓	
Spark plugs ②	R												✓	
Transfer case oil (Ranger, Explorer & Mountaineer 4x4)	R												✓	
Drive belts	S/I						✓						✓	

R: Replace   S/I: Service or Inspect

① Engine coolant: change initially at 50,000 miles and every 30,000 miles thereafter.

② Spark plugs (3.0L & 4.0L): replace every 100,000 miles.

FREQUENT OPERATION MAINTENANCE (SEVERE SERVICE)

If a vehicle is operated under any of the following conditions it is considered severe service:

- Towing a trailer or using a camper or car-top carrier.

- Repeated short trips of less than 5 miles in temperatures below freezing, or trips of less than 10 miles in any temperature.

- Extensive idling or low-speed driving for long distance as in heavy commercial use, such as delivery, taxi or police cars.

- Operating on rough, muddy or salt-covered roads.

- Operating on unpaved or dusty roads.

- Driving in extremely hot (over 90°) conditions.

Engine oil & filter: replace every 3000 miles.

Air cleaner filter: service or inspect every 6000 miles.

Exhaust system: check every 6000 miles.

Rotate tires every 9000 miles. (City delivery vehicles & other unique applications that require constant turning may need frequent tire rotation.)

Automatic transmission fluid & filter: change every 21,000 miles.

93081CA3

SCHEDULED MAINTENANCE INTERVALS
(FORD F-150, LIGHT-DUTY F-250, EXPEDITION & NAVIGATOR)

TO BE SERVICED	TYPE OF SERVICE	VEHICLE MILEAGE INTERVAL (x1000)																							
		5	10	15	20	25	30	35	40	45	50	55	60	65	70	75	80	85	90	95	100	105	110	115	120
Accessory drive belt	S/I												✓												✓
Air cleaner filter ①	R						✓						✓						✓			✓			✓
Automatic transmission fluid	R						✓						✓						✓			✓			✓
Automatic transmission shift linkage	S/I & L	✓	✓	✓	✓	✓	✓	✓	✓	✓	✓	✓	✓	✓	✓	✓	✓	✓	✓	✓	✓	✓	✓	✓	✓
Brake caliper, slide rails	L		✓				✓			✓			✓			✓			✓			✓			✓
Brake system, hoses & lines	S/I			✓			✓			✓			✓			✓			✓			✓			✓
Clutch reservoir fluid level	S/I	✓	✓	✓	✓	✓	✓	✓	✓	✓	✓	✓	✓	✓	✓	✓	✓	✓	✓	✓	✓	✓	✓	✓	✓
Engine coolant ②	R										✓				✓							✓			
Engine cooling system hoses, clamps & coolant	S/I			✓			✓			✓			✓			✓			✓			✓			✓
Engine oil & filter	R	✓	✓	✓	✓	✓	✓	✓	✓	✓	✓	✓	✓	✓	✓	✓	✓	✓	✓	✓	✓	✓	✓	✓	✓
Exhaust system	S/I	✓	✓	✓	✓	✓	✓	✓	✓	✓	✓	✓	✓	✓	✓	✓	✓	✓	✓	✓	✓	✓	✓	✓	✓
Front wheel bearings	S/I & L						✓						✓						✓						✓
Front/rear axle driveshaft slip yoke	L						✓						✓						✓						✓
Front/rear axle fluid ③	R																				✓				
Fuel filter	R			✓			✓			✓			✓			✓			✓			✓			✓
Manual transmission fluid	R												✓												✓
Parking brake system	S/I						✓						✓						✓						✓
PCV valve	R												✓												✓

93081CA4

Ignition system service is covered in the model specific sections of this manual

SCHEDULED MAINTENANCE INTERVALS
(FORD F-150, LIGHT-DUTY F-250, EXPEDITION & NAVIGATOR) (Cont.)

TO BE SERVICED	TYPE OF SERVICE	VEHICLE MILEAGE INTERVAL (x1000)																							
		5	10	15	20	25	30	35	40	45	50	55	60	65	70	75	80	85	90	95	100	105	110	115	120
Rotate tires	S/I	✓	✓	✓	✓	✓	✓	✓	✓	✓	✓	✓	✓	✓	✓	✓	✓	✓	✓	✓	✓	✓	✓	✓	✓
Spark plugs	R																				✓				
Steering linkage, suspension, driveshaft U joints	S/I & L	✓	✓	✓	✓	✓	✓	✓	✓	✓	✓	✓	✓	✓	✓	✓	✓	✓	✓	✓	✓	✓	✓	✓	✓

R: Replace   S/I: Service or Inspect

① Perform this at the mileage shown or every 30 months, whichever occurs first.

② Drain, flush and refill the cooling system initially at 50,000 miles or 48 months, whichever occurs first, then every 30,000 miles or 30 months thereafter.

③ The axle lubricant must be replaced every 100,000 miles or if the axle has been submerged under water. Otherwise the lube should not be checked or changed unless a repair is required.

FREQUENT OPERATION MAINTENANCE (SEVERE SERVICE)

If a vehicle is operated under any of the following conditions it is considered severe service:

- Towing a trailer or using a camper or car-top carrier.
- Repeated short trips of less than 5 miles in temperatures below freezing, or trips of less than 10 miles in any temperature.
- Extensive idling or low-speed driving for long distance as in heavy commercial use, such as delivery, taxi or police cars.
- Operating on rough, muddy or salt-covered roads.
- Operating on unpaved or dusty roads.
- Driving in extremely hot (over 90°) conditions.

Engine oil & filter: replace every 3000 miles.

Tires: rotate and inspect every 6000 miles.

Clutch reservoir fluid level: inspect every 6000 miles.

Automatic transmission shift linkage: lubricate every 6000 miles.

Steering linkage: suspension, U-joints: lubricate every 6000 miles.

Exhaust system: inspect for leaks of damage every 6000 miles.

Fuel filter: replace every 15,000 miles.

Automatic transmission fluid: change every 21,000 miles.

Crankcase emission air filter: replace every 60,000 miles.

PCV valve: replace every 60,000 miles.

Accessory drive belt: inspect every 60,000 miles.

Spark plugs: replace every 99,000 miles.

93081CA5

SCHEDULED MAINTENANCE INTERVALS
(FORD ECONOLINE, CLUB WAGON, EXCURSION, HEAVY-DUTY F-250 & F-350)

TO BE SERVICED	TYPE OF SERVICE	VEHICLE MILEAGE INTERVAL (x1000)																			
		5	10	15	20	25	30	35	40	45	50	55	60	65	70	75	80	85	90	95	100
Accessory drive belt	S/I																				✓
Air cleaner filter ①②	R						✓						✓						✓		
Automatic transmission fluid ③	R						✓						✓						✓		
Engine coolant ④⑤	R										✓						✓				
Engine cooling system hoses, clamps & coolant ⑥	S/I			✓			✓			✓			✓			✓			✓		
Engine oil & filter	R	✓	✓	✓	✓	✓	✓	✓	✓	✓	✓	✓	✓	✓	✓	✓	✓	✓	✓	✓	✓
Exhaust system	S/I			✓			✓			✓			✓			✓			✓		
Front wheel bearings	S/I & L																		✓		
Front/rear axle lubricant ⑦	R																				✓
Fuel filter ⑧	R						✓						✓						✓		
PCV valve	R	Every 120,000 miles																			
Rotate tires	S/I	✓	✓	✓	✓	✓	✓	✓	✓	✓	✓	✓	✓	✓	✓	✓	✓	✓	✓	✓	✓
Spark plugs	R																				✓
Steering linkage, suspension, driveshaft U joints	S/I & L	✓	✓	✓	✓	✓	✓	✓	✓	✓	✓	✓	✓	✓	✓	✓	✓	✓	✓	✓	✓

R: Replace   S/I: Service or Inspect

① Perform this at the mileage shown or every 30 months, whichever occurs first.

② 7.3L DIT Diesel engine: the air filter should be replaced when the restriction gauge is in the red zone.

③ Except the E40D transmission.

④ Drain, flush and refill the cooling system initially at 50,000 miles or 48 months, whichever occurs first, then every 30,000 miles or 30 months thereafter.

⑤ 7.3L DIT Diesel engine: add 4 pints of FW-15 each time the coolant is replaced.

⑥ 7.3L DIT Diesel engine: add 8-10 oz. of FW-15 to the engine coolant every 15,000 miles.

⑦ The axle lubricant must be replaced every 100,000 miles of if the axle has been submerged under water. Otherwise the lube should not be checked or changed unless a repair is required.

⑧ 7.3L DIT Diesel engine: the fuel filter should be replaced when the restriction lamp is illuminated.

FREQUENT OPERATION MAINTENANCE (SEVERE SERVICE)

If a vehicle is operated under any of the following conditions it is considered severe service:

- Towing a trailer or using a camper or car-top carrier.
- Repeated short trips of less than 5 miles in temperatures below freezing, or trips of less than 10 miles in any temperature.
- Extensive idling or low-speed driving for long distances as in heavy commercial use, such as delivery, taxi or police cars.
- Operating on rough, muddy or salt-covered roads.
- Operating on unpaved or dusty roads.

Engine oil & filter: replace every 3000 miles.
Tires: rotate and inspect every 6000 miles.
Steering linkage, suspension, U-joints: lubricate every 6000 miles.
Exhaust system: inspect for leaks or damage every 12,000 miles.
Fuel filter: replace every 15,000 miles.
Automatic transmission fluid: change ever 21,000 miles.
Front wheel bearings (2WD): inspect and repack every 30,000 miles.
Rear axle lubricant (E-Super Duty only): replace every 30,000 miles.
Spark plugs (except 4.2L engine): replace every 60,000 miles.
PCV valve: replace every 60,000 miles.
Accessory drive belt: inspect every 60,000 miles.
Spark plugs: replace every 99,000 miles.

93081CA6

SCHEDULED MAINTENANCE INTERVALS
FORD MOTOR COMPANY
FORD AEROSTAR, RANGER,
EXPLORER, MOUNTAINEER

The following should be used as a guide when determining the amount of work required for a particular service. In estimating how long a particular Scheduled Maintenance Service should take, please observe the following:

- Labor Time is time based on field research and data supplied by the vehicle manufacturer.
- Labor time operations are given in hours and tenths of an hour.
- All labor operations are to be used as a guide.

Mechanic Skill Level Codes:
(A) PRECISION: Highly skilled with multiple certification.
(B) GENERAL: Normally skilled with certification.
(C) MAINTENANCE: Semi-skilled working on certification.

	LABOR TIME		LABOR TIME		LABOR TIME
5000 Mile Service (B)		**30000 Mile Service (B)**		**50000 Mile Service (B)**	
All models	1.5	All models	3.0	All models	.4
w/AT add	.1	w/AT add	.7	w/AT add	.1
w/4WD add	.2	w/4WD add	.5	**55000 Mile Service (B)**	
10000 Mile Service (B)		**35000 Mile Service (B)**		All models	1.5
All models	.4	All models	1.5	w/AT add	.1
w/AT add	.1	w/AT add	.1	w/4WD add	.1
15000 Mile Service (B)		w/4WD add	.1	**60000 Mile Service (B)**	
All models	2.1	**40000 Mile Service (B)**		All models	3.0
w/AT add	.1	All models	.4	w/AT add	.7
w/4WD add	.2	w/AT add	.1	w/4WD add	.7
20000 Mile Service (B)		**45000 Mile Service (B)**		**65000 Mile Service (B)**	
All models	.4	All models	1.1	All models	1.5
w/AT add	.1	w/AT add	.1	w/AT add	.1
25000 Mile Service (B)		w/4WD add	.2	w/4WD add	.1
All models	1.5				
w/AT add	.1				
w/4WD add	.1				

93081CA7

SCHEDULED MAINTENANCE INTERVALS
FORD MOTOR COMPANY
FORD F-150, LIGHT DUTY F-250,
EXPEDITION & NAVIGATOR

The following should be used as a guide when determining the amount of work required for a particular service.
In estimating how long a particular Scheduled Maintenance Service should take, please observe the following:

- Labor Time is time based on field research and data supplied by the vehicle manufacturer.
- Labor time operations are given in hours and tenths of an hour.
- All labor operations are to be used as a guide.

Mechanic Skill Level Codes:
(A) PRECISION: Highly skilled with multiple certification.
(B) GENERAL: Normally skilled with certification.
(C) MAINTENANCE: Semi-skilled working on certification.

	LABOR TIME			LABOR TIME			LABOR TIME
5000 Mile Service (C)			**45000 Mile Service (B)**			**85000 Mile Service (B)**	
All Models	1.1		All Models	1.5		All Models	1.1
7500 Mile Service (C)			w/Diesel add	.1		**90000 Mile Service (B)**	
Diesel	1.8		**50000 Mile Service (B)**			All Models	2.4
10000 Mile Service (C)			All Models	1.1		**95000 Mile Service (B)**	
All Models	.9		w/Diesel add	.1		All Models	1.0
15000 Mile Service (B)			**55000 Mile Service (C)**			**100000 Mile Service (B)**	
All Models	1.6		All Models	1.1		All Models	1.6
w/Diesel add	.6		**60000 Mile Service (B)**			w/5.4L add	1.3
20000 Mile Service (C)			All Models	2.4		**105000 Mile Service (B)**	
All Models	1.1		w/AT add	.3		All Models	1.6
25000 Mile Service (C)			**65000 Mile Service (C)**			**110000 Mile Service (B)**	
All Models	1.0		All Models	1.1		All Models	1.1
30000 Mile Service (B)			**70000 Mile Service (C)**			**115000 Mile Service (C)**	
All Models	2.4		All Models	.5		All Models	1.1
w/AT add	.6		**75000 Mile Service (B)**			**120000 Mile Service (B)**	
35000 Mile Service (C)			All Models	1.8		All Models	2.4
All Models	1.1		**80000 Mile Service (B)**			w/AT add	.3
40000 Mile Service (B)			All Models	1.1			
All Models	1.1						

93081CA8

Refer to the model specific sections for engine mechanical service procedures

SCHEDULED MAINTENANCE INTERVALS
FORD MOTOR COMPANY
FORD ECONOLINE, CLUB WAGON
HEAVY DUTY F-250 & F-350

The following should be used as a guide when determining the amount of work required for a particular service.
In estimating how long a particular Scheduled Maintenance Service should take, please observe the following:

- Labor Time is time based on field research and data supplied by the vehicle manufacturer.
- Labor time operations are given in hours and tenths of an hour.
- All labor operations are to be used as a guide.

Mechanic Skill Level Codes:
(A) PRECISION: Highly skilled with multiple certification.
(B) GENERAL: Normally skilled with certification.
(C) MAINTENANCE: Semi-skilled working on certification.

	LABOR TIME		LABOR TIME		LABOR TIME
5000 Mile Service (C)		**35000 Mile Service (C)**		**70000 Mile Service (C)**	
All Models	.7	All Models	.7	All Models	8
Rotate tires add	.7	*Rotate tires add*	.7	*Rotate tires add*	.7
10000 Mile Service (C)		**40000 Mile Service (C)**		**75000 Mile Service (B)**	
All Models	.7	All Models	.7	All Models	1.8
Rotate tires add	.7	*Rotate tires add*	.7	*Rotate tires add*	.7
15000 Mile Service (B)		**45000 Mile Service (B)**		**80000 Mile Service (B)**	
All Models	1.7	All Models	1.6	All Models	1.6
Rotate tires add	.7	*Rotate tires add*	.7	*Rotate tires add*	.7
20000 Mile Service (C)		**50000 Mile Service (B)**		**90000 Mile Service (B)**	
All Models	.7	All Models	1.5	All Models	2.4
Rotate tires add	.7	*Rotate tires add*	.7	*Rotate tires add*	.7
25000 Mile Service (C)		**55000 Mile Service (C)**		**95000 Mile Service (C)**	
All Models	.7	All Models	8	All Models	8
Rotate tires add	.7	*Rotate tires add*	.7	*Rotate tires add*	.7
30000 Mile Service (B)		**60000 Mile Service (B)**		**100000 Mile Service (B)**	
All Models	2.3	All Models	2.5	All Models	1.5
Rotate tires add	.7	*Rotate tires add*	.7	*Rotate tires add*	.7
		65000 Mile Service (C)			
		All Models	8		
		Rotate tires add	.7		

93081CA9

FORD MOTOR CO.
Ford Windstar

VEHICLE AND ENGINE IDENTIFICATION CHART

			Engine Code					Model Year	
Code	Liters (cc)	Cu. In.	Cyl.	Fuel Sys.	Engine Type	Eng. Mfg.		Code	Year
U	3.0 (2982)	181	6	SEFI	OHV	Ford		V	1997
4	3.8 (3802)	231	6	SEFI	OHV	Ford		W	1998
								X	1999
								Y	2000
								1	2001

SEFI: Sequential Multi-port Fuel Injection

93081CA0

GENERAL ENGINE SPECIFICATIONS

Year	Engine Displacement Liters (cc)	Engine VIN	Fuel System Type	Net Horsepower @ rpm	Net Torque @ rpm (ft. lbs.)	Bore x Stroke (in.)	Com-pression Ratio	Oil Pressure @ rpm
1997	3.0 (2982)	U	SEFI	147@5000	162@3250	3.50x3.14	9.3:1	40-60@2500
	3.8 (3802)	4	SEFI	200@5000	230@3000	3.81x3.39	9.3:1	40-60@2500
1998	3.0 (2986)	U	SEFI	150@5000	172@3300	3.50x3.14	9.3:1	40-60@2500
	3.8 (3802)	4	SEFI	200@5000	225@3000	3.81x3.39	9.3:1	40-60@2500
1999	3.0 (2986)	U	SEFI	150@5000	172@3300	3.50x3.14	9.3:1	40-60@2500
	3.8 (3802)	4	SEFI	200@5000	225@3000	3.81x3.39	9.3:1	40-60@2500
2000-01 ①	3.0 (2986)	U	SEFI	150@5000	172@3300	3.50x3.14	9.3:1	40-60@2500
	3.8 (3802)	4	SEFI	200@5000	225@3000	3.81x3.39	9.3:1	40-60@2500

① The 3.8L VIN 4 is the only engine available in 2001. The 3.0L VIN U engine was not used after 2000.

93081CB1

Refer to the model specific sections for fuel system service procedures

GASOLINE ENGINE TUNE-UP SPECIFICATIONS

Year	Engine Displacement Liters (cc)	Engine VIN	Spark Plugs Gap (in.)	Ignition Timing (deg.) MT	Ignition Timing (deg.) AT	Fuel Pump (psi)	Idle Speed (rpm) MT	Idle Speed (rpm) AT	Valve Clearance In.	Valve Clearance Ex.
1997	3.0 (2982)	U	0.042–0.046	—	10B	35–45	—	①	HYD	HYD
	3.8 (3802)	4	0.052–0.056	—	10B	30–45	—	①	HYD	HYD
1998	3.0 (2986)	U	0.042–0.046	—	①	②	—	①	HYD	HYD
	3.8 (3800)	4	0.052–0.056	—	①	②	—	①	HYD	HYD
1999	3.0 (2986)	U	0.042–0.046	—	①	②	—	①	HYD	HYD
	3.8 (3800)	4	0.052–0.056	—	①	②	—	①	HYD	HYD
2000-01 ③	3.0 (2986)	U	0.042–0.046	—	①	②	—	①	HYD	HYD
	3.8 (3800)	4	0.052–0.056	—	①	②	—	①	HYD	HYD

NOTE: The Vehicle Emission Control Information label often reflects specification changes changes made during production. The label figures must be used if they differ from those in this chart.

B: Before top dead center

HYD: Hydraulic

① Controlled by the Powertrain Control Module (PCM) and cannot be manually adjusted.

② Engine running: 28-45 psi

Key On, Engine Off (KOEO): 35-45 psi

③ The 3.8L VIN 4 is the only engine available in 2001. The 3.0L VIN U engine was not used after 2000.

93081CB2

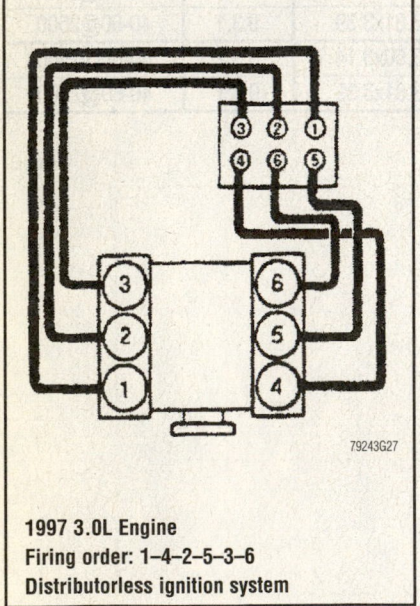

1997 3.0L Engine
Firing order: 1–4–2–5–3–6
Distributorless ignition system

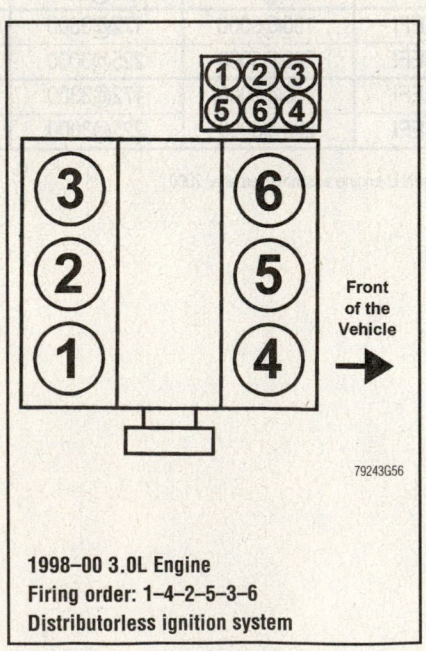

1998–00 3.0L Engine
Firing order: 1–4–2–5–3–6
Distributorless ignition system

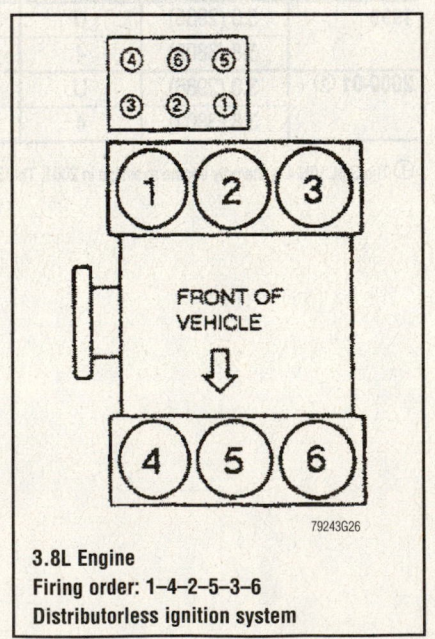

3.8L Engine
Firing order: 1–4–2–5–3–6
Distributorless ignition system

CAPACITIES

Year	Model	Engine Displacement Liters (cc)	Engine ID/VIN	Engine Oil with Filter (qts.)	Transmission (pts.) 4-Spd	Transmission (pts.) 5-Spd	Transmission (pts.) Auto.	Drive Axle Front (pts.)	Drive Axle Rear (pts.)	Fuel Tank (gal.)	Cooling System (qts.)
1997	Windstar	3.0 (2982)	U	4.2	—	—	16.5	①	—	②	③
		3.8 (3802)	4	4.5	—	—	24.5	①	—	②	12.1
1998	Windstar	3.0 (2982)	U	4.5	—	—	24.5	①	—	②	12.1
		3.8 (3802)	4	4.5	—	—	24.5	①	—	②	12.1
1999	Windstar	3.0 (2982)	U	4.5	—	—	24.5	①	—	②	12.1
		3.8 (3802)	4	4.5	—	—	24.5	①	—	②	12.1
2000-01 ④	Windstar	3.0 (2982)	U	4.5	—	—	24.5	①	—	26	12.1
		3.8 (3802)	4	4.5	—	—	24.5	①	—	26	12.1

NOTE: All capacities are approximate. Add fluid gradually and check to be sure a proper fluid level is obtained.

① Included in transaxle capacity

② Standard: 20; Optional: 26 gals.

③ With coolant recovery reservoir: 7.9

Without coolant recovery reservoir: 5.8

④ The 3.8L VIN 4 is the only engine available in 2001. The 3.0L VIN U engine was not used after 2000.

93081CB3

VALVE SPECIFICATIONS

Year	Engine VIN	Engine Displacement Liters (cc)	Seat Angle (deg.)	Face Angle (deg.)	Spring Test Pressure (lbs. @ in.)	Spring Installed Height (in.)	Stem-to-Guide Clearance (in.) Intake	Stem-to-Guide Clearance (in.) Exhaust	Stem Diameter (in.) Intake	Stem Diameter (in.) Exhaust
1997	U	3.0 (2982)	45	44	185@1.16	1.580-1.610	0.0010-0.0027	0.0015-0.0032	0.3126-0.3134	0.3121-0.3129
	4	3.8 (3802)	44.75	45.8	198-220@1.18	1.970	0.0010-0.0028	0.0015-0.0033	0.3423-0.3415	0.3410-0.3418
1998	U	3.0 (2986)	45	44	180@1.16	1.650-1.736	0.0010-0.0027	0.0015-0.0032	0.3126-0.3134	0.3121-0.3129
	4	3.8 (3800)	44.75	45.8	198-220@1.18	1.970	0.0010-0.0028	0.0015-0.0033	0.3415-0.3423	0.3410-0.3418
1999	U	3.0 (2986)	45	44	180@1.16	1.650-1.736	0.0010-0.0027	0.0015-0.0032	0.3126-0.3134	0.3121-0.3129
	4	3.8 (3800)	44.75	45.8	198-220@1.18	1.970	0.0010-0.0028	0.0015-0.0033	0.3415-0.3423	0.3410-0.3418
2000-01 ①	U	3.0 (2986)	45	44	180@1.16	1.650-1.736	0.0010-0.0027	0.0015-0.0032	0.3126-0.3134	0.3121-0.3129
	4	3.8 (3800)	44.75	45.8	198-220@1.18	1.970	0.0010-0.0028	0.0015-0.0033	0.3415-0.3423	0.3410-0.3418

① The 3.8L VIN 4 is the only engine available in 2001. The 3.0L VIN U engine was not used after 2000.

93081CB4

Refer to the model specific sections for engine electrical system service procedures

CRANKSHAFT AND CONNECTING ROD SPECIFICATIONS

All measurements are given in inches.

Year	Engine Displacement Liters (cc)	Engine VIN	Crankshaft				Connecting Rod		
			Main Brg. Journal Dia.	Main Brg. Oil Clearance	Shaft End-play	Thrust on No.	Journal Diameter	Oil Clearance	Side Clearance
1997	3.0 (2982)	U	2.5190-2.5198	0.0010-0.0014	0.0040-0.0080	3	2.1253-1.1261	0.0010-0.0015	0.0060-0.0140
	3.8 (3802)	4	2.5190-2.5198	0.0010-0.0014	0.0040-0.0080	3	2.3103-2.3111	0.0010-0.0015	0.0043-0.0192
1998	3.0 (2982)	U	2.5190-2.5198	0.0010-0.0014	0.0040-0.0080	3	2.1253-1.1261	0.0010-0.0015	0.0060-0.0140
	3.8 (3802)	4	2.5190-2.5198	0.0010-0.0014	0.0040-0.0080	3	2.3103-2.3111	0.0010-0.0015	0.0043-0.0192
1999	3.0 (2982)	U	2.5190-2.5198	0.0010-0.0014	0.0040-0.0080	3	2.1253-1.1261	0.0010-0.0015	0.0060-0.0140
	3.8 (3802)	4	2.5190-2.5198	0.0010-0.0014	0.0040-0.0080	3	2.3103-2.3111	0.0010-0.0015	0.0043-0.0192
2000-01 ①	3.0 (2982)	U	2.5190-2.5198	0.0010-0.0014	0.0040-0.0080	3	2.1253-1.1261	0.0010-0.0015	0.0060-0.0140
	3.8 (3802)	4	2.5190-2.5198	0.0010-0.0014	0.0040-0.0080	3	2.3103-2.3111	0.0010-0.0015	0.0043-0.0192

① The 3.8L VIN 4 is the only engine available in 2001. The 3.0L VIN U engine was not used after 2000.

93081CB5

PISTON AND RING SPECIFICATIONS

All measurements are given in inches.

Year	Engine Displacement Liters (cc)	Engine VIN	Piston Clearance	Ring Gap			Ring Side Clearance		
				Top Compression	Bottom Compression	Oil Control	Top Compression	Bottom Compression	Oil Control
1997	3.0 (2982)	U	0.0012-0.0022	0.0100-0.0200	0.0100-0.0200	0.0100-0.0490	0.0016-0.0037	0.0016-0.0037	Snug
	3.8 (3802)	4	0.0007-0.0017	0.0098-0.0161	0.0150-0.0252	0.0059-0.0650	0.0012-0.0031	0.0012-0.0031	Snug
1998	3.0 (2982)	U	0.0012-0.0022	0.0100-0.0200	0.0100-0.0200	0.0100-0.0490	0.0016-0.0037	0.0016-0.0037	Snug
	3.8 (3802)	4	0.0007-0.0017	0.0098-0.0161	0.0150-0.0252	0.0059-0.0650	0.0012-0.0031	0.0012-0.0031	Snug
1999	3.0 (2982)	U	0.0012-0.0022	0.0100-0.0200	0.0100-0.0200	0.0100-0.0490	0.0016-0.0037	0.0016-0.0037	Snug
	3.8 (3802)	4	0.0007-0.0017	0.0098-0.0161	0.0150-0.0252	0.0059-0.0650	0.0012-0.0031	0.0012-0.0031	Snug
2000-01 ①	3.0 (2982)	U	0.0012-0.0022	0.0100-0.0200	0.0100-0.0200	0.0100-0.0490	0.0016-0.0037	0.0016-0.0037	Snug
	3.8 (3802)	4	0.0007-0.0017	0.0098-0.0161	0.0150-0.0252	0.0059-0.0650	0.0012-0.0031	0.0012-0.0031	Snug

① The 3.8L VIN 4 is the only engine available in 2001. The 3.0L VIN U engine was not used after 2000.

93081CB6

TORQUE SPECIFICATIONS
All readings in ft. lbs.

Year	Engine VIN	Engine Displacement Liters (cc)	Cylinder Head Bolts	Main Bearing Bolts	Rod Bearing Bolts	Crankshaft Damper Bolts	Flywheel Bolts	Manifold Intake	Manifold Exhaust	Spark Plugs	Lug Nut
1997	U	3.0 (2982)	①	60	26	107	54-64	24	25	8-10	100
	4	3.8 (3802)	②	65-81	31-36	103-132	54-64	③	19	8-10	100
1998	U	3.0 (2982)	④	56-62	23-28	93-121	54-64	⑤	15-22	7-14	100
	4	3.8 (3802)	⑥	82-88	⑦	104-132	54-64	71-106	15-22	7-15	100
1999	U	3.0 (2982)	⑦	56-62	23-28	93-121	54-64	④	15-22	7-14	100
	4	3.8 (3802)	⑥	82-88	⑦	104-132	54-64	71-106	15-22	7-15	100
2000-01 ⑧	U	3.0 (2982)	⑦	56-62	23-28	93-121	54-64	④	15-22	7-14	100
	4	3.8 (3802)	⑥	82-88	⑦	104-132	54-64	71-106	15-22	7-15	100

① Step 1: 37 ft. lbs.
   Step 2: 68 ft. lbs.

② Step 1: 15 ft. lbs.
   Step 2: 29 ft. lbs.
   Step 3: 37 ft. lbs.
   Step 4: Loosen each bolt one at a time
   Step 5: Long bolts to 11-19 ft. lbs. plus 1/4 turn
   Step 6: Short bolts to 7-15 ft. lbs. plus 1/4 turn

③ Lower intake manifold:
   Step 1: 13 ft. lbs.
   Step 2: 16 ft. lbs.
   Upper intake manifold:
   Step 1: 8 ft. lbs.
   Step 2: 15 ft. lbs.
   Step 3: 24 ft. lbs.

④ Step 1: 59 ft. lbs.
   Step 2: Loosen all bolts 360 degrees
   Step 3: 36 ft. lbs.
   Step 4: 67 ft. lbs.

⑤ Step 1: 15-22 ft. lbs.
   Step 2: 20-23 ft. lbs.

⑥ Step 1: 15 ft. lbs.
   Step 2: 29 ft. lbs.
   Step 3: 37 ft. lbs.
   Step 4: Loosen all bolts in sequence
   Step 5: Long bolts to 30-36 ft. lbs. plus 1/2 turn

⑦ Step 1: 30-34 ft. lbs.
   Step 2: Tighten an additional 90-120 degrees

⑧ The 3.8L VIN 4 is the only engine available in 2001.
   The 3.0L VIN U engine was not used after 2000.

93081CB7

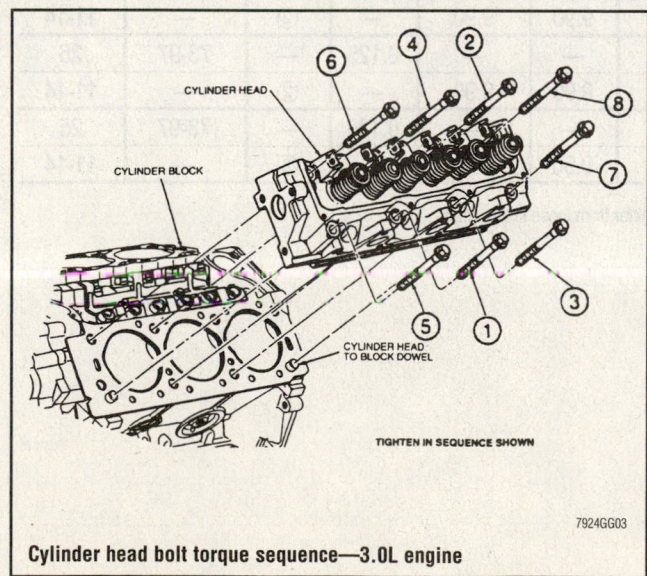

Cylinder head bolt torque sequence—3.0L engine

7924GG03

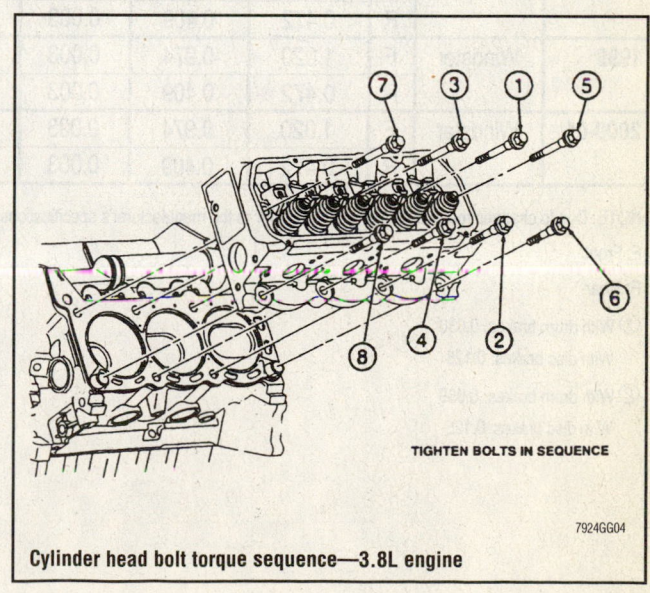

Cylinder head bolt torque sequence—3.8L engine

7924GG04

For accessory drive belt replacement procedures see the model specific sections of this manual

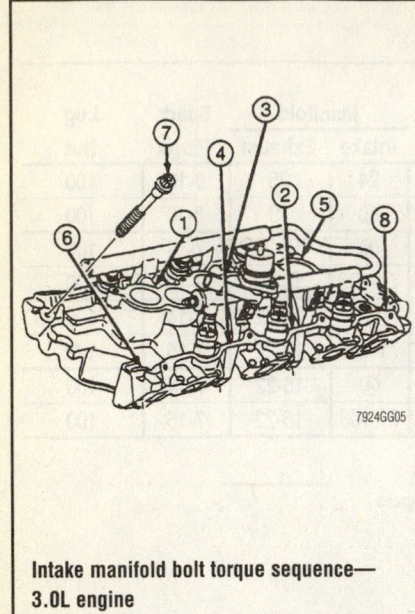

Intake manifold bolt torque sequence—
3.0L engine

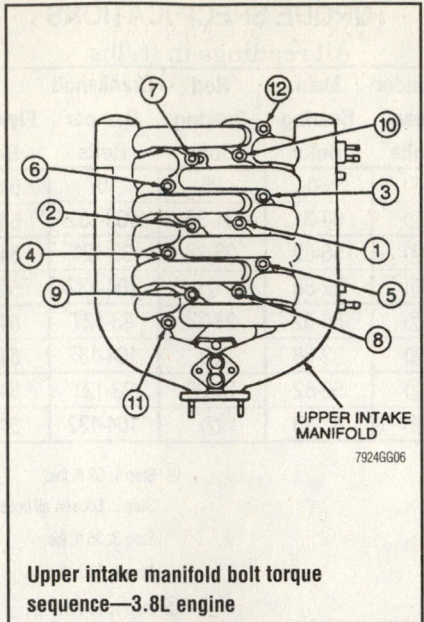

Upper intake manifold bolt torque
sequence—3.8L engine

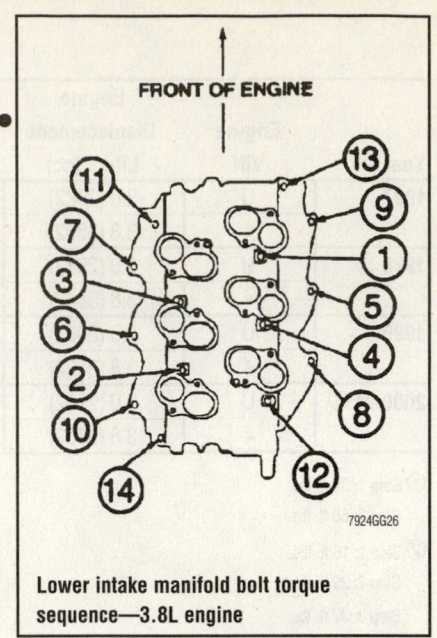

Lower intake manifold bolt torque
sequence—3.8L engine

BRAKE SPECIFICATIONS
FORD WINDSTAR
All measurements in inches unless noted

Year	Model		Brake Disc Original Thickness	Brake Disc Minimum Thickness	Brake Disc Maximum Runout	Brake Drum Diameter Original Inside Diameter	Brake Drum Diameter Max, Wear Limit	Brake Drum Diameter Maximum Machine Diameter	Minimum Lining Thickness Front	Minimum Lining Thickness Rear	Brake Caliper Bracket-to-Hub Bolt (ft. lbs.)	Brake Caliper Mounting Pin or Bolt (ft. lbs.)
1997	Windstar	F	1.020	0.907	0.003	—	—	—	0.125	—	73-97	25
		R	0.472	0.409	0.003	9.84	9.90	9.90	—	①	—	11-14
1998	Windstar	F	1.020	0.974	0.003	—	—	—	0.125	—	73-97	25
		R	0.472	0.409	0.003	9.84	9.90	9.90	—	②	—	11-14
1999	Windstar	F	1.020	0.974	0.003	—	—	—	0.125	—	73-97	25
		R	0.472	0.409	0.003	9.84	9.90	9.90	—	②	—	11-14
2000-01	Windstar	F	1.020	0.974	0.003	—	—	—	0.125	—	73-97	25
		R	0.472	0.409	0.003	9.84	9.90	9.90	—	②	—	11-14

NOTE: Due to changes made during production, refer to the manufacturer's specifications if they differ from those in this chart

F: Front

R: Rear

① With drum brakes: 0.030
  With disc brakes: 0.125

② With drum brakes: 0.059
  With disc brakes: 0.125

93081CB8

FORD MOTOR CO.
Mercury Villager

VEHICLE AND ENGINE IDENTIFICATION CHART

	Engine Code							Model Year	
Code	Liters (cc)	Cu. In.	Cyl.	Fuel Sys.	Engine Type	Eng. Mfg.		Code	Year
W	3.0 (2960)	181	6	MFI	SOHC	Nissan		V	1997
1	3.0 (2960)	181	6	SEFI	SOHC	Nissan		W	1998
T	3.3 (3275)	200	6	SEFI	SOHC	Nissan		X	1999
								Y	2000
								1	2001

MFI: Multi-port Fuel Injection

SEFI: Sequential Multi-port Fuel Injection

93081CB9

GENERAL ENGINE SPECIFICATIONS

Year	Engine Displacement Liters (cc)	Engine VIN	Fuel System Type	Net Horsepower @ rpm	Net Torque @ rpm (ft. lbs.)	Bore x Stroke (in.)	Compression Ratio	Oil Pressure @ rpm
1997	3.0 (2960)	W	MFI	151@4800	174@4400	3.43x3.27	9.0:1	40-60@2500
1998	3.0 (2960)	1	SEFI	151@4800	174@4400	3.43x3.27	9.0:1	40-60@2500
1999	3.3 (3275)	T	SEFI	195@4500	190@3800	3.60x3.27	8.9:1	40-60@2500
2000-01	3.3 (3275)	T	SEFI	195@4500	190@3800	3.60x3.27	8.9:1	40-60@2500

MFI: Multiport fuel injection

SEFI: Sequential Multi-port Fuel Injection

93081CB0

For brake related suspension and axle service, refer to the model specific sections of this manual

ENGINE TUNE-UP SPECIFICATIONS

Year	Engine Displacement Liters (cc)	Engine ID/VIN	Spark Plug Gap (in.)	Ignition Timing (deg.) MT	AT	Fuel Pump (psi) ①	Idle Speed (rpm) MT	AT ②	Valve Clearance In.	Ex.
1997	3.0 (2960)	W	0.033	—	15B	34	—	700	HYD	HYD
1998	3.0 (2960)	1	0.033	—	15B	34	—	700-800	HYD	HYD
1999	3.3 (3277)	T	0.041	—	15B	34	—	700-800	HYD	HYD
2000-01	3.3 (3277)	T	0.041	—	15B	34	—	700-800	HYD	HYD

NOTE: The Vehicle Emission Control Information label must be used if they differ from those in this chart.

B: Before top dead center

HYD: Hydraulic

① System pressure at idle with vacuum hose connected should increase to 43 psi when disconnected

② Transmission in Neutral

93081CC1

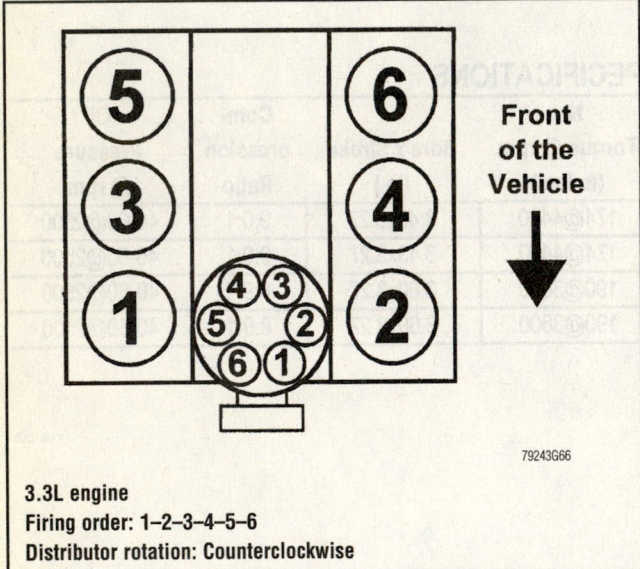

3.3L engine
Firing order: 1–2–3–4–5–6
Distributor rotation: Counterclockwise

79243G66

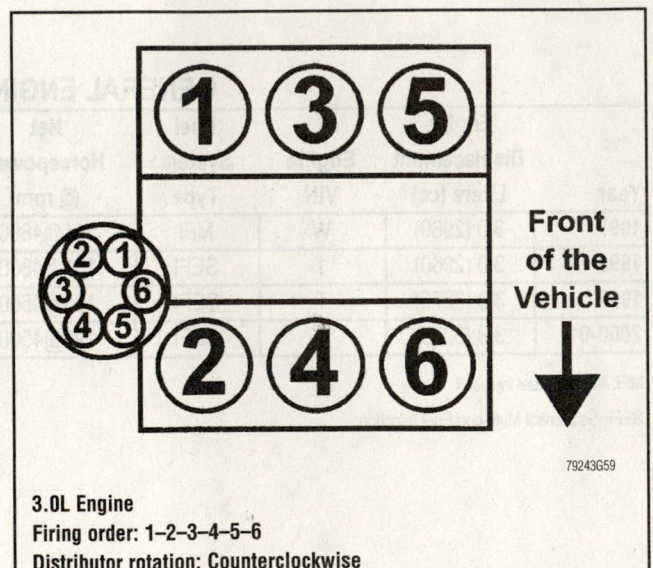

3.0L Engine
Firing order: 1–2–3–4–5–6
Distributor rotation: Counterclockwise

79243G59

CAPACITIES

Year	Model	Engine Displacement Liters (cc)	Engine VIN	Engine Oil with Filter (qts.)	Transmission (pts.) 4-Spd	Transmission (pts.) 5-Spd	Transmission (pts.) Auto.	Drive Axle Front (pts.)	Drive Axle Rear (pts.)	Fuel Tank (gal.)	Cooling System (qts.)
1997	Villager	3.0 (2960)	W	4.2	—	—	16.5	①	—	20	②
1998	Villager	3.0 (2960)	1	4.2	—	—	17.4	①	—	20	②
1999	Villager	3.3 (3275)	T	4.0	—	—	20.0	①	—	20	11.25
2000-01	Villager	3.3 (3275)	T	4.0	—	—	20.0	①	—	20	11.25

NOTE: All capacities are approximate. Add fluid gradually and check to be sure a proper fluid level is obtained.

① Included in transaxle capacity

② With rear heater: 12.7

   Without rear heater: 11.4

93081CC2

CRANKSHAFT AND CONNECTING ROD SPECIFICATIONS
All measurements are given in inches.

Year	Engine Displacement Liters (cc)	Engine VIN	Crankshaft Main Brg. Journal Dia.	Crankshaft Main Brg. Oil Clearance	Crankshaft Shaft End-play	Crankshaft Thrust on No.	Connecting Rod Journal Diameter	Connecting Rod Oil Clearance	Connecting Rod Side Clearance
1997	3.0 (2960)	W	2.4790-2.4793	0.0011-0.0022	0.0020-0.0067	3	1.9667-1.9675	0.0006-0.0021	0.0079-0.0138
1998	3.0 (2960)	1	2.4790-2.4793	0.0011-0.0022	0.0020-0.0067	3	1.9667-1.9675	0.0006-0.0021	0.0079-0.0138
1999	3.3 (3275)	T	2.4790-2.4793	0.0011-0.0022	0.0020-0.0067	3	1.9667-1.9675	0.0006-0.0021	0.0079-0.0138
2000-01	3.3 (3275)	T	2.4790-2.4793	0.0011-0.0022	0.0020-0.0067	3	1.9667-1.9675	0.0006-0.0021	0.0079-0.0138

93081CC3

PISTON AND RING SPECIFICATIONS
All measurements are given in inches.

Year	Engine Displacement Liters (cc)	Engine VIN	Piston Clearance	Ring Gap			Ring Side Clearance		
				Top Compression	Bottom Compression	Oil Control	Top Compression	Bottom Compression	Oil Control
1997	3.0 (2960)	W	0.0010-0.0018	0.0083-0.0173	0.0071-0.0173	0.0079-0.0299	0.0016-0.0029	0.0012-0.0025	0.0006-0.0075
1998	3.0 (2960)	1	0.0010-0.0018	0.0083-0.0173	0.0071-0.0173	0.0079-0.0299	0.0016-0.0029	0.0012-0.0025	0.0006-0.0075
1999	3.3 (3275)	T	①	0.0083-0.0157	0.0197-0.0272	0.0079-0.0272	0.0009-0.0030	0.0012-0.0028	0.0006-0.0073
2000	3.3 (3275)	T	①	0.0083-0.0157	0.0197-0.0272	0.0079-0.0272	0.0009-0.0030	0.0012-0.0028	0.0006-0.0073
2001	3.3 (3275)	T	①	0.0083-0.0157	0.0197-0.0272	0.0079-0.0272	0.0009-0.0030	0.0012-0.0028	0.0006-0.0073

① Journals 1, 5 and 6: 0.0010 - 0.0018 in.
Journals 3 and 4: 0.0006 - 0.0010 in.

93081CC4

VALVE SPECIFICATIONS

Year	Engine VIN	Engine Displacement Liters (cc)	Seat Angle (deg.)	Face Angle (deg.)	Spring Test Pressure (lbs. @ in.)	Spring Installed Height (in.)	Stem-to-Guide Clearance (in.)		Stem Diameter (in.)	
							Intake	Exhaust	Intake	Exhaust
1997	W	3.0 (2966)	45	45	①	②	0.0008-0.0021	0.0016-0.0029	0.2742-0.2748	0.3136-0.3138
1998	1	3.0 (2960)	45	45	③	②	④	⑤	0.2742-0.2748	0.3136-0.3138
1999	T	3.3 (3275)	45.5	45	③	②	0.0008-0.0021	0.0012-0.0019	0.2742-0.2748	0.3136-0.3138
2000	T	3.0 (2960)	45.5	45	③	②	0.0008-0.0021	0.0012-0.0019	0.2742-0.2748	0.3136-0.3138
2001	T	3.0 (2960)	45.5	45	③	②	0.0008-0.0021	0.0012-0.0019	0.2742-0.2748	0.3136-0.3138

① Outer spring: 118@1.81
Inner spring: 57.3@0.984

② Spring height measured unloaded
Minimum length. outer spring: 2.016
Minimum length. inner spring: 1.736

③ Outer spring: 118@1.81
Inner spring: 57.3@0.984

④ Nominal: 0.0008-0.0021
Maximum: 0.0039

⑤ Nominal: 0.0016-0.0029
Maximum: 0.0039

93081CC5

TORQUE SPECIFICATIONS
All readings in ft. lbs.

Year	Engine VIN	Engine Displacement Liters (cc)	Cylinder Head Bolts	Main Bearing Bolts	Rod Bearing Bolts	Crankshaft Damper Bolts	Flywheel Bolts	Manifold		Spark Plugs	Lug Nut
								Intake	Exhaust		
1997	W	3.0 (2966)	①	67-74	②	141-156	61-69	③	13-16	14-22	80
1998	1	3.0 (2960)	④	⑤	②	141-156	61-69	⑥	13-16	14-22	80
1999	T	3.3 (3275)	⑦	⑤	②	141-156	61-69	⑦	13-16	14-22	80
2000-01	T	3.3 (3275)	⑦	⑤	②	141-156	61-69	⑦	13-16	14-22	80

① Step 1: 22 ft. lbs.
Step 2: 43 ft. lbs.
Step 3: Loosen bolts one turn
Step 4: 22 ft. lbs.
Step 5: Rotate 60-65 degrees or 40-47 ft. lbs.
Step 6: Small cylinder head bolt outside of valve cover: 72 inch lbs.

② Step 1: 10-12 ft. lbs.
Step 2: 28-33 ft. lbs.

③ Step 1: Nuts and bolts: 36 inch lbs.
Step 2: Nuts: 17-20 ft. lbs., Bolts: 12-14 ft. lbs.
Step 3: Repeat Step 2

④ Step 1: 22 ft. lbs.
Step 2: 43 ft. lbs.
Step 3: Loosen all bolts completely
Step 4: 22 ft. lbs.
Step 5: Tighten an additional 60-65 degrees or to 40-47 ft. lbs.
Step 6: Head bolt A to 80-104 inch lbs.

⑤ Step 1: 34-37 ft. lbs.
Step 2: 67-74 ft. lbs.

⑥ Step 1: 26-44 inch lbs.
Step 2: bolts to 9-12 ft. lbs.; nuts to 17-20 ft. lbs.
Step 3: Repeat Step 2

⑦ Intake manifold and cylinder heads are installed at the same time.
Step 1: cylinder head bolts to 22 ft. lbs.
Step 2: cylinder head bolts to 43 ft. lbs.
Step 3: Loosen all bolts completely
Step 4: cylinder head bolts to 84 inch lbs.
Step 5: Intake manifold bolts to 36 inch lbs.
Step 6: Intake manifold bolts to 12 ft. lbs.
Step 7: Intake manifold bolts to 14 ft. lbs.
Step 8: Loosen all maifold bolts completely
Step 9: Cylinder head bolts to 26 inch lbs.
Step 10: cylinder head bolts to 47 ft. lbs. Or, an additional 65 degrees
Step 11: cylinder head sub-bolts to 104 inch lbs.
Step 12: Intake manifold bolts to 36 inch lbs.
Step 13: Intake manifold bolts to 78 inch lbs.
Step 14: Intake manifold bolts to 84 inch lbs.

93081CC6

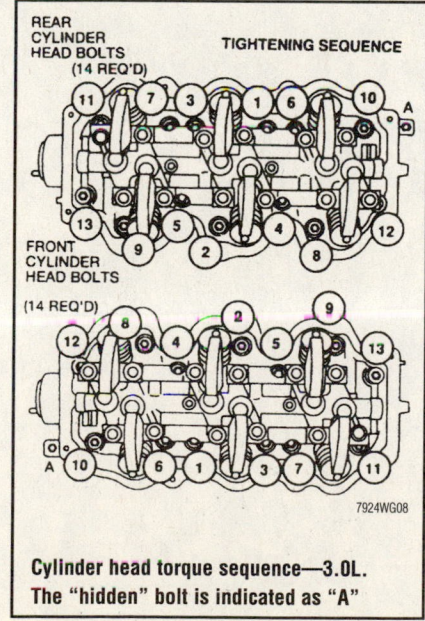

Cylinder head torque sequence—3.0L.
The "hidden" bolt is indicated as "A"
7924WG08

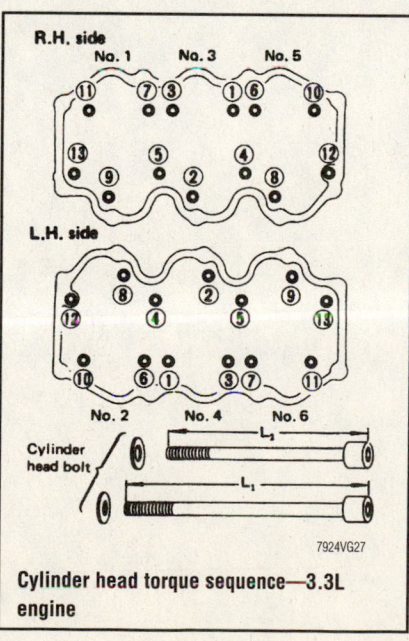

Cylinder head torque sequence—3.3L engine
7924VG27

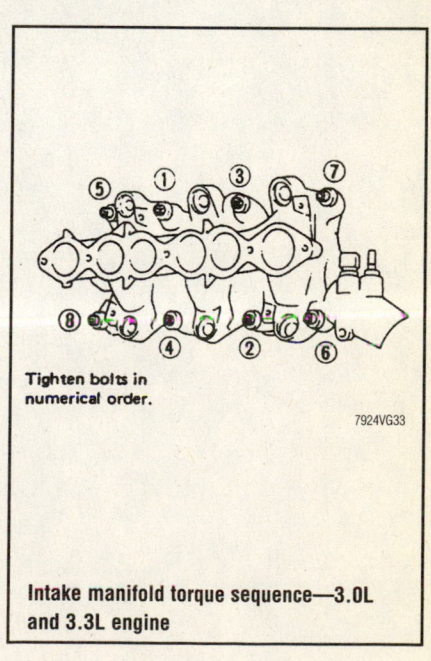

Intake manifold torque sequence—3.0L and 3.3L engine
7924VG33

For exhaust manifold replacement procedures, see the model specific sections of this manual

BRAKE SPECIFICATIONS
MERCURY VILLAGER
All measurements in inches unless noted

Year	Model		Brake Disc Original Thickness	Brake Disc Minimum Thickness	Brake Disc Maximum Runout	Brake Drum Diameter Original Inside Diameter	Brake Drum Diameter Max, Wear Limit	Brake Drum Diameter Maximum Machine Diameter	Minimum Lining Thickness Front	Minimum Lining Thickness Rear	Brake Caliper Bracket-to-Hub Bolt (ft. lbs.)	Brake Caliper Mounting Pin or Bolt (ft. lbs.)
1997	Villager	F	1.005	0.945	0.0028	—	—	—	0.079	—	—	18-25
		R	—	—	—	9.84	9.90	9.86	—	0.059	—	—
1998	Villager	F	1.005	0.945	0.0028	—	—	—	0.079	—	—	18-25
		R	—	—	—	9.84	9.90	9.86	—	0.059	—	—
1999	Villager	F	1.005	0.945	0.0028	—	—	—	0.079	—	—	18-25
		R	—	—	—	9.84	9.90	9.86	—	0.059	—	—
2000-01	Villager	F	1.005	0.945	0.0028	—	—	—	0.079	—	—	18-25
		R	—	—	—	9.84	9.90	9.86	—	0.059	—	—

NOTE: Due to changes made during production, refer to the manufacturer's specifications if they differ from those in this chart

F: Front

R: Rear

93081CC7

SCHEDULED MAINTENANCE INTERVALS
(FORD WINDSTAR & MERCURY VILLAGER)

TO BE SERVICED	TYPE OF SERVICE	VEHICLE MILEAGE INTERVAL (x1000)												
		5	10	15	20	25	30	35	40	45	50	55	60	65
Engine oil & filter	R	✓	✓	✓	✓	✓	✓	✓	✓	✓	✓	✓	✓	✓
Rotate tires	S/I	✓		✓		✓		✓		✓		✓		✓
Engine coolant strength hoses & clamps	S/I			✓			✓			✓			✓	
Air cleaner filter	R						✓						✓	
Automatic transmission fluid & filter	R						✓						✓	
Engine coolant ①	R						✓						✓	
PCV valve	R												✓	
Spark plugs ②	R						✓						✓	
Drive belts	S/I						✓						✓	
Exhaust system & heat shields	S/I						✓						✓	
Front & rear brakes	S/I						✓						✓	

R: Replace   S/I: Service or Inspect

① Engine coolant: change initially at 50,000 miles and every 30,000 miles thereafter.

② Spark plugs (Windstar): replace every 100,000 miles.

FREQUENT OPERATION MAINTENANCE (SEVERE SERVICE)

If a vehicle is operated under any of the following conditions it is considered severe service:

- Extremely dusty areas.

- 50% or more of the vehicle operation is in 32°C (90°F) or higher temperatures, or constant operation in temperatures below 0°C (32°F).

- Prolonged idling (vehicle operation in stop and go traffic.

- Frequent short running periods (engine does not warm to normal operating temperatures).

- Police, taxi, delivery usage or trailer towing usage.

Engine oil & filter: replace every 3000 miles.

Rotate tires initially at 6000 miles and every 9000 miles thereafter.

Air cleaner filter: change every 15,000 miles.

Engine coolant strength, hoses & clamps: check every 15,000 miles.

Exhaust system: check every 15,000 miles.

Automatic transmission fluid & filter: change every 21,000 miles.

93081CC8

Refer to the model specific sections for cooling system service procedures

SCHEDULED MAINTENANCE INTERVALS
FORD MOTOR COMPANY
FORD WINDSTAR, MERCURY VILLAGER

The following should be used as a guide when determining the amount of work required for a particular service.
In estimating how long a particular Scheduled Maintenance Service should take, please observe the following:

- Labor Time is time based on field research and data supplied by the vehicle manufacturer.
- Labor time operations are given in hours and tenths of an hour.
- All labor operations are to be used as a guide.

Mechanic Skill Level Codes:
(A) PRECISION: Highly skilled with multiple certification.
(B) GENERAL: Normally skilled with certification.
(C) MAINTENANCE: Semi-skilled working on certification.

	LABOR TIME		LABOR TIME		LABOR TIME
5000 Mile Service (C)		**25000 Mile Service (C)**		**50000 Mile Service (C)**	
All Models	.9	All Models	.9	All Models	.5
10000 Mile Service (C)		**30000 Mile Service (B)**		**55000 Mile Service (C)**	
All Models	.5	All Models	3.5	All Models	.9
15000 Mile Service (C)		**35000 Mile Service (C)**		**60000 Mile Service (B)**	
All Models	1.0	All Models	.9	All Models	3.6
20000 Mile Service (C)		**40000 Mile Service (C)**		**65000 Mile Service (C)**	
All Models	.5	All Models	.5	All Models	.9
		45000 Mile Service (B)			
		All Models	1.0		

93081CC9

TIRE, WHEEL AND BALL JOINT SPECIFICATIONS
Ford Truck

Year	Model	OEM Tires		Tire Pressures (psi)		Wheel Size	Ball Joint Inspection
		Standard	Optional	Front	Rear		
1997	Aerostar	P215/70R14	P215/75R14	32	35	6-JJ	0.030 in. ①
	E150, 5500 GVW	P215/75R15S	P225/75R15S	35	35	6-JJ	0.030 in. ①
	E-150, 6500-6700 GVW	P235/75R15XL	none	41	41	7-J	0.030 in. ①
	E-250 LD	LT225/75R16D	LT225/75R16E	50	55	7-J, K	0.030 in. ①
	E-250 HD	LT225/75R16D	LT225/75R16E	50	55	7-J, K	0.030 in. ①
	E-350	LT245/75R16E	none	35	35	7-J, K	0.030 in. ①
	Club Wagon, base	P235/75R15XL	LT225/75R16E	35	35	7-J, K	0.030 in. ①
	Club Wagon HD	LT225/75R16E	LT245/75R16E	35	35	7-J, K	0.030 in. ①
	Club Wagon Super Duty	LT245/75R16E	none	35	35	7-J, K	0.030 in. ①
	Expedition	P255/70R16	P265/70R17	35	35	7-J, K	0.030 in. ①
	F-150	P235/70R16	P255/70R16 P265/70R17	35	35	7-J	0.030 in. ①
	F-250	LT245/75R16	P255/70R16	35	35	7-J	0.030 in. ①
	F-350	P235/85R16	none	35	35	7-J	0.030 in. ①
	F-Super Duty	P235/85R16	none	35	35	7-J	0.030 in. ①
	Explorer	P225/70R15	P235/75R15SL	30	35	7-JJ	0.030 in. ①
			P255/70R16	26	26	7-JJ	
	Ranger 2wd	P195/70R14SL	P215/70R14SL	35	35	6-JJ	0.030 in. ①
			P225/70R14SL				0.030 in. ①
	Ranger 4wd	P215/75R15SL	P235/75R15SL P265/75R15SL	35	35	Std: 6-J Opt: 7-J	0.030 in. ①
	Windstar	P215/70R15	P205/70R15	35	35	6-JJ	0.030 in. ①
1998	E-150	P225/75R15SL	P235/75R15XL LT225/75R16E	35	35	7-J	0.030 in. ①
	E-250	LT225/75R16D	LT225/75R16E	35	35	7-J, K	0.030 in. ①
	E-350	LT245/75R16E	none	35	35	7-J, K	0.030 in. ①
	Club Wagon, base	P235/75R15XL	LT225/75R16E	35	35	7-J, K	0.030 in. ①
	Club Wagon HD	LT225/75R16E	LT245/75R16E	35	35	7-J, K	0.030 in. ①
	Club Wagon Super Duty	LT245/75R16E	none	35	35	7-J, K	0.030 in. ①
	Expedition	P255/70R16	P265/70R17	35	35	7-J, K	0.030 in. ①
	F-150	P235/70R16	P255/70R16 P265/70R17	35	35	7-J	0.030 in. ①
	F-250	LT245/75R16	P255/70R16	35	35	7-J	0.030 in. ①
	F-350	P235/85R16	none	35	35	7-J	0.030 in. ①
	F-Super Duty	P235/85R16	none	35	35	7-J	0.030 in. ①
	Explorer	P225/70R15	P235/75R15SL	30	35	7-JJ	0.030 in. ①
			P255/70R16	26	26	7-JJ	
	Ranger 2wd, XL	P205/75R14SL	P225/70R14SL	35	35	6-JJ	0.030 in. ①
	Ranger 2wd XLT	P205/75R14SL	P225/70R14SL	35	35	6-JJ	0.030 in. ①
	Ranger Splash, 2wd	P235/60R15SL	P235/75R15SL	35	35	7-J, K	0.030 in. ①
	Ranger 4wd, XL	P215/75R15SL	P235/75R15SL	35	35	7-J, K	0.030 in. ①
	Ranger 4wd, XLT	P215/75R15SL	P235/75R15SL P235/70R16SL P265/75R15SL	35	35	7-J	0.030 in. ①
	Ranger Splash 4wd	P235/75R15SL		35	35	7-J	0.030 in. ①
	Windstar	P215/70R15	P205/70R15	35	35	6-JJ	0.030 in. ①

93081CC0

For complete service labor times order Nichols' Chilton Labor Guide Manual

TIRE, WHEEL AND BALL JOINT SPECIFICATIONS
Ford Truck

| Year | Model | OEM Tires | | Tire Pressures (psi) | | Wheel Size | Ball Joint Inspection |
		Standard	Optional	Front	Rear		
1999	E-150 Club Wagon	P235/75R15XL	none	35	35	6-JJ	0.030 in. ①
	E-150 Van	P225/75R15SL	none	35	35	7-J	0.030 in. ①
	E-250	LT225/75RX16	none	35	35	7-K	0.030 in. ①
	E-350	LT225/75RX16	none	35	35	7-K	0.030 in. ①
	E-350 Super Duty	LT245/75RX16E	none	35	35	7-K	0.030 in. ①
	Expedition	P255/70R16	P265/70R17	35	35	7-JJ	0.030 in. ①
	F-150	P235/70R16	P255/70R16	35	35	7-J	0.030 in. ①
			P265/70R17				
	F-250	LT245/75R16	P255/70R16	35	35	7-J	0.030 in. ①
	F-350	P235/85R16	none	35	35	7-JJ	0.030 in. ①
	F-Super Duty	P235/85R16	none	35	35	7-JJ	0.030 in. ①
	Explorer	P225/70R15	P235/75R15SL	30	35	7-JJ	0.030 in. ①
			P255/70R16	26	26	7-JJ	
	Ranger 2wd, XL	P205/75R14SL	P225/70R14SL	35	35	6-JJ	0.030 in. ①
	Ranger 2wd XLT	P205/75R14SL	P225/70R14SL	35	35	6-JJ	0.030 in. ①
	Ranger Splash, 2wd	P235/60R15SL	none	35	35	6-JJ	0.030 in. ①
	Ranger 4wd, XL	P215/75R15SL	P235/75R15SL	35	35	7-JJ	0.030 in. ①
	Ranger 4wd, XLT	P215/75R15SL	P235/75R15SL	35	35	7-JJ	0.030 in. ①
			P235/70R16SL				
			P265/75R15SL				
	Ranger Splash 4wd	P235/75R15SL	P235/75R15SL	35	35	7-J	0.030 in. ①
	Windstar	P215/70R15	P205/70R15	35	35	6-JJ	0.030 in. ①
2000-01	E-150 Club Wagon	P235/75R15XL	none	35	35	6-JJ	0.030 in. ①
	E-150 Van	P225/75R15SL	none	35	35	7-J	0.030 in. ①
	E-250	LT225/75RX16	none	35	35	7-K	0.030 in. ①
	E-350	LT225/75RX16	none	35	35	7-K	0.030 in. ①
	E-350 Super Duty	LT245/75RX16E	none	35	35	7-K	0.030 in. ①
	Expedition	P255/70R16	P265/70R17	35	35	7-JJ	0.030 in. ①
	F-150	P235/70R16	P255/70R16	35	35	7-J	0.030 in. ①
			P265/70R17				
	F-250	LT245/75R16	P255/70R16	35	35	7-J	0.030 in. ①
	F-350	P235/85R16	none	35	35	7-J	0.030 in. ①
	F-Super Duty	P235/85R16	none	35	35	7-J	0.030 in. ①
	Explorer	P225/70R15	P235/75R15SL	30	35	7-JJ	0.030 in. ①
			P255/70R16	26	26	7-JJ	
	Ranger 2wd, XL	P205/75R14SL	P225/70R14SL	35	35	6-JJ	0.030 in. ①
	Ranger 2wd XLT	P205/75R14SL	P225/70R14SL	35	35	6-JJ	0.030 in. ①
	Ranger Splash, 2wd	P235/60R15SL	P235/75R15SL	35	35	6-JJ	0.030 in. ①
	Ranger 4wd, XL	P215/75R15SL	P235/75R15SL	35	35	6-JJ	0.030 in. ①
	Ranger 4wd, XLT	P215/75R15SL	P235/75R15SL	35	35	7-JJ	0.030 in. ①
			P235/70R16SL				
			P265/75R15SL				
	Ranger Splash 4wd	P235/75R15SL	P235/75R15SL	35	35	7-JJ	0.030 in. ①
	Windstar	P215/70R15	P205/70R15	35	35	6-JJ	0.030 in. ①

OEM: Original Equipment Manufacturer

PSI: Pounds Per Square Inch

TIRE, WHEEL AND BALL JOINT SPECIFICATIONS
Lincoln

| Year | Model | OEM Tires | | Tire Pressures (psi) | | Wheel Size | Ball Joint Inspection |
		Standard	Optional	Front	Rear		
1997	Navigator	P255/70R16	P265/70R17	30	35	7.5	0.030 in. ①
1998	Navigator	P255/70R16	P265/70R17	30	35	7.5	0.030 in. ①
1999	Navigator	P245/75R16	P255/75R17	30	35	7.5	0.030 in. ①
2000-01	Navigator	P245/75R16	P255/75R17	30	35	7.5	0.030 in. ①

OEM: Original Equipment Manufacturer

PSI: Pounds Per Square Inch

STD: Standard

OPT: Optional

① Both upper and lower

93081CD2

TIRE, WHEEL AND BALL JOINT SPECIFICATIONS
Mercury Truck

| Year | Model | OEM Tires | | Tire Pressures (psi) | | Wheel Size | Ball Joint Inspection |
		Standard	Optional	Front	Rear		
1997	Mountaineer	P225/70R15	P235/75R15SL	30	35	7-JJ	0.030 in. ①
			P255/70R16	26	26	7-JJ	
1998	Mountaineer	P225/70R15	P235/75R15SL	30	35	7-JJ	0.030 in. ①
			P255/70R16	26	26	7-JJ	
1999	Mountaineer	P225/70R15	P235/75R15SL	30	35	7-JJ	0.030 in. ①
			P255/70R16	26	26	7-JJ	
2000-01	Mountaineer	P225/70R15	P235/75R15SL	30	35	7-JJ	0.030 in. ①
			P255/70R16	26	26	7-JJ	

OEM: Original Equipment Manufacturer

PSI: Pounds Per Square Inch

STD: Standard

OPT: Optional

① Both upper and lower

93081CD3

Timing chain and gear service is covered in the model specific sections of this manual

GENERAL MOTORS
Cadillac Escalade • Chevrolet C/K Pickups • G/P Van • Suburban • Tahoe • GMC C/K Pickups • Denali • Envoy • G/P Vans • Sierra • Silverado • Yukon

ENGINE AND VEHICLE IDENTIFICATION

Engine							Model Year	
Code ①	Liters (cc)	Cu. In.	Cyl.	Fuel Sys.	Engine Type	Eng. Mfg.	Code ②	Year
F	6.5 (6473)	395	8	DSL	OHV	CPC	V	1997
J	7.4 (7440)	454	8	MFI	OHV	CPC	W	1998
M	5.0 (4999)	305	8	MFI	OHV	CPC	X	1999
P	6.5 (6473)	395	8	DSL	OHV	CPC	Y	2000
R	5.7 (5735)	350	8	MFI	OHV	CPC	1	2001
S	6.5 (6473)	395	8	DSL	OHV	CPC		
T	5.3 (5327)	325	8	MFI	OHV	CPC		
W	4.3 (4293)	263	6	MFI	OHV	CPC		
X	4.3 (4293)	263	6	MFI	OHV	CPC		
Y	6.5 (6473)	395	8	DSL	OHV	CPC		
U	6.0 (5966)	364	8	MFI	OHV	CPC		
V	4.8 (4802)	293	8	MFI	OHV	CPC		
Z	4.3 (4293)	263	6	MFI	OHV	CPC		

CPC: Chevrolet/Pontiac/Canada

DSL: Diesel

MFI: Multi-port Fuel Injection

① 8th position of VIN

② 10th position of VIN

93081CD4

GENERAL ENGINE SPECIFICATIONS

All measurements are given in inches.

Year	Model	Engine Displacement Liters (cc)	Engine Series (ID/VIN)	Fuel System	Net Horsepower @ rpm	Net Torque @ rpm (ft. lbs.)	Bore x Stroke (in.)	Com-pression Ratio	Oil Pressure @ rpm
1997	C1500	4.3 (4293)	W	MFI	①	②	4.00x3.48	9.2:1	18@2000
	C1500	5.0 (4999)	M	MFI	①	②	3.74x3.48	9.4:1	18@2000
	C1500	5.7 (5735)	R	MFI	250@4600	335@2800	4.00x3.48	9.4:1	18@2000
	C2500	4.3 (4293)	W	MFI	①	②	4.00x3.48	9.2:1	18@2000
	C2500	5.0 (4999)	M	MFI	①	②	3.74x3.48	9.4:1	18@2000
	C2500	5.7 (5735)	R	MFI	250@4600	335@2800	4.00x3.48	9.4:1	18@2000
	C2500	6.5 (6374)	F	DSL	③	④	4.05x3.80	21.5:1	40-45@2000
	C3500	6.5 (6374)	F	DSL	③	④	4.05x3.80	21.5:1	40-45@2000
	C3500	7.4 (7440)	J	MFI	290@4200	410@3200	4.25x4.00	9.0:1	40@2000
	G/P1500	4.3 (4293)	W	MFI	①	②	4.00x3.48	9.2:1	18@2000
	G/P1500	5.0 (4999)	M	MFI	220@4600	285@2800	3.74x3.48	9.4:1	18@2000
	G/P1500	5.7 (5735)	R	MFI	250@4600	335@2800	4.00x3.48	9.4:1	18@2000
	G/P2500	5.0 (4999)	M	MFI	220@4600	285@2800	3.74x3.48	9.4:1	18@2000
	G/P2500	5.7 (5735)	R	MFI	250@4600	335@2800	4.00x3.48	9.4:1	18@2000
	G/P3500	6.5 (6374)	F	DSL	③	④	4.05x3.80	21.5:1	40-45@2000
	G/P3500	7.4 (7440)	J	MFI	290@4200	410@3200	4.25x4.00	9.0:1	40@2000
	K1500	4.3 (4293)	W	MFI	①	②	4.00x3.48	9.2:1	18@2000
	K1500	5.0 (4999)	M	MFI	220@4600	285@2800	3.74x3.48	9.4:1	18@2000
	K1500	5.7 (5735)	R	MFI	250@4600	335@2800	4.00x3.48	9.4:1	18@2000
	K1500	6.5 (6374)	F	DSL	③	④	4.05x3.80	21.5:1	40-45@2000
	K2500	5.0 (4999)	M	MFI	220@4600	285@2800	3.74x3.48	9.4:1	18@2000
	K2500	5.7 (5735)	R	MFI	250@4600	335@2800	4.00x3.48	9.4:1	18@2000
	K2500	6.5 (6374)	F	DSL	③	④	4.05x3.80	21.5:1	40-45@2000
	K3500	5.7 (5735)	R	MFI	250@4600	335@2800	4.00x3.48	9.4:1	18@2000
	K3500	6.5 (6374)	F	DSL	③	④	4.05x3.80	21.5:1	40-45@2000
	K3500	7.4 (7440)	J	MFI	290@4200	410@3200	4.25x4.00	9.0:1	40@2000
	Suburban	5.7 (5735)	R	MFI	250@4600	335@2800	4.00x3.48	9.4:1	18@2000
	Suburban	7.4 (7440)	J	MFI	290@4200	410@3200	4.25x4.00	9.0:1	40@2000
	Tahoe/Yukon	6.5 (6374)	S	DSL	180@3400	360@1700	4.06x3.82	21.5:1	40-45@2000
	Tahoe/Yukon	5.7 (5735)	R	MFI	250@4600	335@2800	4.00x3.48	9.4:1	18@2000
1998	C1500	4.3 (4293)	W	MFI	230@4600	285@2800	3.74x3.48	9.4:1	18@2000
	C1500	5.0 (4999)	M	MFI	230@4600	285@2800	3.74x3.48	9.4:1	18@2000
	C1500	5.7 (5735)	R	MFI	255@4600	335@2800	4.00x3.48	9.4:1	18@2000
	C2500	4.3 (4293)	W	MFI	230@4600	285@2800	3.74x3.48	9.4:1	18@2000
	C2500	5.0 (4999)	M	MFI	230@4600	285@2800	3.74x3.48	9.4:1	18@2000
	C2500	5.7 (5735)	R	MFI	255@4600	335@2800	4.00x3.48	9.4:1	18@2000
	C2500	6.5 (6374)	F	DSL	195@3400	430@1800	4.05x3.80	21.5:1	30-43@2000
	C3500	6.5 (6374)	F	DSL	195@3400	430@1800	4.05x3.80	21.5:1	30-43@2000
	C3500	7.4 (7440)	J	MFI	290@4200	410@3200	4.25x4.00	9.0:1	40@2000
	Denali	5.7 (5735)	R	MFI	255@4600	335@2800	4.00x3.48	9.4:1	18@2000
	Denali	6.5 (6374)	S	DSL	180@3400	360@1700	4.06x3.82	21.5:1	30-43@2000
	Escalade	5.7 (5735)	R	MFI	255@4600	335@2800	4.00x3.48	9.4:1	18@2000
	Escalade	6.5 (6374)	S	DSL	180@3400	360@1700	4.06x3.82	21.5:1	30-43@2000
	G/P1500	4.3 (4293)	W	MFI	230@4600	285@2800	3.74x3.48	9.4:1	18@2000
	G/P1500	5.0 (4999)	M	MFI	230@4600	285@2800	3.74x3.48	9.4:1	18@2000
	G/P1500	5.7 (5735)	R	MFI	255@4600	335@2800	4.00x3.48	9.4:1	18@2000

93081CD5

Ignition system service is covered In the model specific sections of this manual

GENERAL ENGINE SPECIFICATIONS

All measurements are given in inches.

Year	Model	Engine Displacement Liters (cc)	Engine Series (ID/VIN)	Fuel System	Net Horsepower @ rpm	Net Torque @ rpm (ft. lbs.)	Bore x Stroke (in.)	Compression Ratio	Oil Pressure @ rpm
1998 (Cont.)	G/P2500	5.0 (4999)	M	MFI	230@4600	285@2800	3.74x3.48	9.4:1	18@2000
	G/P2500	5.7 (5735)	R	MFI	255@4600	335@2800	4.00x3.48	9.4:1	18@2000
	G/P3500	6.5 (6374)	F	DSL	195@3400	430@1800	4.05x3.80	21.5:1	30-43@2000
	G/P3500	7.4 (7440)	J	MFI	290@4200	410@3200	4.25x4.00	9.0:1	40@2000
	K1500	4.3 (4293)	W	MFI	230@4600	285@2800	3.74x3.48	9.4:1	18@2000
	K1500	5.0 (4999)	M	MFI	230@4600	285@2800	3.74x3.48	9.4:1	18@2000
	K1500	5.7 (5735)	R	MFI	255@4600	335@2800	4.00x3.48	9.4:1	18@2000
	K1500	6.5 (6374)	F	DSL	195@3400	430@1800	4.05x3.80	21.5:1	30-43@2000
	K2500	5.0 (4999)	M	MFI	230@4600	285@2800	3.74x3.48	9.4:1	18@2000
	K2500	5.7 (5735)	R	MFI	255@4600	335@2800	4.00x3.48	9.4:1	18@2000
	K2500	6.5 (6374)	F	DSL	195@3400	430@1800	4.05x3.80	21.5:1	30-43@2000
	K3500	5.7 (5735)	R	MFI	255@4600	335@2800	4.00x3.48	9.4:1	18@2000
	K3500	6.5 (6374)	F	DSL	195@3400	430@1800	4.05x3.80	21.5:1	30-43@2000
	K3500	7.4 (7440)	J	MFI	290@4200	410@3200	4.25x4.00	9.0:1	40@2000
	Suburban	5.7 (5735)	R	MFI	255@4600	335@2800	4.00x3.48	9.4:1	18@2000
	Suburban	7.4 (7440)	J	MFI	290@4200	410@3200	4.25x4.00	9.0:1	40@2000
	Suburban	6.5 (6374)	S	DSL	180@3400	360@1700	4.06x3.82	21.5:1	30-43@2000
	Tahoe/Yukon	5.7 (5735)	R	MFI	255@4600	335@2800	4.00x3.48	9.4:1	18@2000
1999	C1500	4.3 (4293)	W	MFI	230@4600	285@2800	3.74x3.48	9.4:1	18@2000
	C1500	5.0 (4999)	M	MFI	230@4600	285@2800	3.74x3.48	9.4:1	18@2000
	C1500	5.7 (5735)	R	MFI	255@4600	335@2800	4.00x3.48	9.4:1	18@2000
	C2500	4.3 (4293)	W	MFI	230@4600	285@2800	3.74x3.48	9.4:1	18@2000
	C2500	5.0 (4999)	M	MFI	230@4600	285@2800	3.74x3.48	9.4:1	18@2000
	C2500	5.7 (5735)	R	MFI	255@4600	335@2800	4.00x3.48	9.4:1	18@2000
	C2500	6.5 (6374)	F	DSL	195@3400	430@1800	4.05x3.80	21.5:1	30-43@2000
	C3500	6.5 (6374)	F	DSL	195@3400	430@1800	4.05x3.80	21.5:1	30-43@2000
	C3500	7.4 (7440)	J	MFI	290@4200	410@3200	4.25x4.00	9.0:1	40@2000
	Denali	5.7 (5735)	R	MFI	255@4600	335@2800	4.00x3.48	9.4:1	18@2000
	Denali	6.5 (6374)	S	DSL	180@3400	360@1700	4.06x3.82	21.5:1	30-43@2000
	Escalade	5.7 (5735)	R	MFI	255@4600	335@2800	4.00x3.48	9.4:1	18@2000
	Escalade	6.5 (6374)	S	DSL	180@3400	360@1700	4.06x3.82	21.5:1	30-43@2000
	G/P1500	4.3 (4293)	W	MFI	230@4600	285@2800	3.74x3.48	9.4:1	18@2000
	G/P1500	5.0 (4999)	M	MFI	230@4600	285@2800	3.74x3.48	9.4:1	18@2000
	G/P1500	5.7 (5735)	R	MFI	255@4600	335@2800	4.00x3.48	9.4:1	18@2000
	G/P2500	5.0 (4999)	M	MFI	230@4600	285@2800	3.74x3.48	9.4:1	18@2000
	G/P2500	5.7 (5735)	R	MFI	255@4600	335@2800	4.00x3.48	9.4:1	18@2000
	G/P3500	6.5 (6374)	F	DSL	195@3400	430@1800	4.05x3.80	21.5:1	30-43@2000
	G/P3500	7.4 (7440)	J	MFI	290@4200	410@3200	4.25x4.00	9.0:1	40@2000
	K1500	4.3 (4293)	W	MFI	230@4600	285@2800	3.74x3.48	9.4:1	18@2000
	K1500	5.0 (4999)	M	MFI	230@4600	285@2800	3.74x3.48	9.4:1	18@2000
	K1500	5.7 (5735)	R	MFI	255@4600	335@2800	4.00x3.48	9.4:1	18@2000
	K1500	6.5 (6374)	F	DSL	195@3400	430@1800	4.05x3.80	21.5:1	30-43@2000
	K2500	5.0 (4999)	M	MFI	230@4600	285@2800	3.74x3.48	9.4:1	18@2000
	K2500	5.7 (5735)	R	MFI	255@4600	335@2800	4.00x3.48	9.4:1	18@2000
	K2500	6.5 (6374)	F	DSL	195@3400	430@1800	4.05x3.80	21.5:1	30-43@2000
	K3500	5.7 (5735)	R	MFI	255@4600	335@2800	4.00x3.48	9.4:1	18@2000

93081CD6

GENERAL ENGINE SPECIFICATIONS
All measurements are given in inches.

Year	Model	Engine Displacement Liters (cc)	Engine Series (ID/VIN)	Fuel System	Net Horsepower @ rpm	Net Torque @ rpm (ft. lbs.)	Bore x Stroke (in.)	Compression Ratio	Oil Pressure @ rpm
1999 (Cont.)	K3500	6.5 (6374)	F	DSL	195@3400	430@1800	4.05x3.80	20:01	30-43@2000
	K3500	7.4 (7440)	J	MFI	290@4200	410@3200	4.25x4.00	9.0:1	40@2000
	Sierra	4.3 (4293)	W	MFI	200@4600	260@2800	4.00x3.48	9.2:1	18@2000
	Sierra	4.8 (4802)	V	MFI	255@5200	285@4000	3.78x3.27	9.5:1	18@2000
	Sierra	5.3 (5327)	T	MFI	270@5000	315@4000	3.78x6.62	9.5:1	18@2000
	Sierra	6.0 (5966)	U	MFI	300@4800	355@4000	4.00x3.62	9.4:1	18@2000
	Sierra	6.5 (6374)	F	DSL	195@3400	430@1800	4.05x3.80	20:01	30-43@2000
	Silverado	4.3 (4293)	W	MFI	200@4600	260@2800	4.00x3.48	9.2:1	18@2000
	Silverado	4.8 (4802)	V	MFI	255@5200	285@4000	3.78x3.27	9.5:1	18@2000
	Silverado	5.3 (5327)	T	MFI	270@5000	315@4000	3.78x6.62	9.5:1	18@2000
	Silverado	6.0 (5966)	U	MFI	300@4800	355@4000	4.00x3.62	9.4:1	18@2000
	Silverado	6.5 (6374)	F	DSL	195@3400	430@1800	4.05x3.80	20:01	30-43@2000
	Suburban	5.7 (5735)	R	MFI	255@4600	335@2800	4.00x3.48	9.4:1	18@2000
	Suburban	7.4 (7440)	J	MFI	290@4200	410@3200	4.25x4.00	9.0:1	40@2000
	Suburban	6.5 (6374)	S	DSL	180@3400	360@1700	4.06x3.82	21.5:1	30-43@2000
	Tahoe/Yukon	5.7 (5735)	R	MFI	255@4600	335@2800	4.00x3.48	9.4:1	18@2000
2000-01	C1500	4.3 (4293)	W	MFI	230@4600	285@2800	3.74x3.48	9.4:1	18@2000
	C1500	5.0 (4999)	M	MFI	230@4600	285@2800	3.74x3.48	9.4:1	18@2000
	C1500	5.7 (5735)	R	MFI	255@4600	335@2800	4.00x3.48	9.4:1	18@2000
	C2500	4.3 (4293)	W	MFI	230@4600	285@2800	3.74x3.48	9.4:1	18@2000
	C2500	5.0 (4999)	M	MFI	230@4600	285@2800	3.74x3.48	9.4:1	18@2000
	C2500	5.7 (5735)	R	MFI	255@4600	335@2800	4.00x3.48	9.4:1	18@2000
	C2500	6.5 (6374)	F	DSL	195@3400	430@1800	4.05x3.80	21.5:1	30-43@2000
	C3500	6.5 (6374)	F	DSL	195@3400	430@1800	4.05x3.80	21.5:1	30-43@2000
	C3500	7.4 (7440)	J	MFI	290@4200	410@3200	4.25x4.00	9.0:1	40@2000
	Denali	5.7 (5735)	R	MFI	255@4600	335@2800	4.00x3.48	9.4:1	18@2000
	Denali	6.5 (6374)	S	DSL	180@3400	360@1700	4.06x3.82	21.5:1	30-43@2000
	Escalade	5.7 (5735)	R	MFI	255@4600	335@2800	4.00x3.48	9.4:1	18@2000
	Escalade	6.5 (6374)	S	DSL	180@3400	360@1700	4.06x3.82	21.5:1	30-43@2000
	G/P1500	4.3 (4293)	W	MFI	230@4600	285@2800	3.74x3.48	9.4:1	18@2000
	G/P1500	5.0 (4999)	M	MFI	230@4600	285@2800	3.74x3.48	9.4:1	18@2000
	G/P1500	5.7 (5735)	R	MFI	255@4600	335@2800	4.00x3.48	9.4:1	18@2000
	G/P2500	5.0 (4999)	M	MFI	230@4600	285@2800	3.74x3.48	9.4:1	18@2000
	G/P2500	5.7 (5735)	R	MFI	255@4600	335@2800	4.00x3.48	9.4:1	18@2000
	G/P3500	6.5 (6374)	F	DSL	195@3400	430@1800	4.05x3.80	21.5:1	30-43@2000
	G/P3500	7.4 (7440)	J	MFI	290@4200	410@3200	4.25x4.00	9.0:1	40@2000
	K1500	4.3 (4293)	W	MFI	230@4600	285@2800	3.74x3.48	9.4:1	18@2000
	K1500	5.0 (4999)	M	MFI	230@4600	285@2800	3.74x3.48	9.4:1	18@2000
	K1500	5.7 (5735)	R	MFI	255@4600	335@2800	4.00x3.48	9.4:1	18@2000
	K1500	6.5 (6374)	F	DSL	195@3400	430@1800	4.05x3.80	21.5:1	30-43@2000
	K2500	5.0 (4999)	M	MFI	230@4600	285@2800	3.74x3.48	9.4:1	18@2000
	K2500	5.7 (5735)	R	MFI	255@4600	335@2800	4.00x3.48	9.4:1	18@2000
	K2500	6.5 (6374)	F	DSL	195@3400	430@1800	4.05x3.80	21.5:1	30-43@2000
	K3500	5.7 (5735)	R	MFI	255@4600	335@2800	4.00x3.48	9.4:1	18@2000
	K3500	6.5 (6374)	F	DSL	195@3400	430@1800	4.05x3.80	20:01	30-43@2000

93081CD7

GENERAL ENGINE SPECIFICATIONS

All measurements are given in inches.

Year	Model	Engine Displacement Liters (cc)	Engine Series (ID/VIN)	Fuel System	Net Horsepower @ rpm	Net Torque @ rpm (ft. lbs.)	Bore x Stroke (in.)	Com-pression Ratio	Oil Pressure @ rpm
2000-01 (Cont.)	K3500	7.4 (7440)	J	MFI	290@4200	410@3200	4.25x4.00	9.0:1	40@2000
	Sierra	4.3 (4293)	W	MFI	200@4600	260@2800	4.00x3.48	9.2:1	18@2000
	Sierra	4.8 (4802)	V	MFI	255@5200	285@4000	3.78x3.27	9.5:1	18@2000
	Sierra	5.3 (5327)	T	MFI	270@5000	315@4000	3.78x6.62	9.5:1	18@2000
	Sierra	6.0 (5966)	U	MFI	300@4800	355@4000	4.00x3.62	9.4:1	18@2000
	Sierra	6.5 (6374)	F	DSL	195@3400	430@1800	4.05x3.80	20:01	30-43@2000
	Silverado	4.3 (4293)	W	MFI	200@4600	260@2800	4.00x3.48	9.2:1	18@2000
	Silverado	4.8 (4802)	V	MFI	255@5200	285@4000	3.78x3.27	9.5:1	18@2000
	Silverado	5.3 (5327)	T	MFI	270@5000	315@4000	3.78x6.62	9.5:1	18@2000
	Silverado	6.0 (5966)	U	MFI	300@4800	355@4000	4.00x3.62	9.4:1	18@2000
	Silverado	6.5 (6374)	F	DSL	195@3400	430@1800	4.05x3.80	20:01	30-43@2000
	Suburban	5.7 (5735)	R	MFI	255@4600	335@2800	4.00x3.48	9.4:1	18@2000
	Suburban	7.4 (7440)	J	MFI	290@4200	410@3200	4.25x4.00	9.0:1	40@2000
	Suburban	6.5 (6374)	S	DSL	180@3400	360@1700	4.06x3.82	21.5:1	30-43@2000
	Tahoe/Yukon	5.7 (5735)	R	MFI	255@4600	335@2800	4.00x3.48	9.4:1	18@2000

DSL: Diesel

MFI: Multi-port Fuel Injection

① Below 15,000 GVWR: 180@3400
   Above 15,000 GVWR: 190@3400

② 2WD: 180@4400
   4WD: 190@4400

③ 2WD: 235@2800
   4WD: 240@2800

④ Below 8500 GVWR: 275@1700
   Above 8500 GVWR: 290@1700

93081CD8

GASOLINE ENGINE TUNE-UP SPECIFICATIONS

Year	Engine Displacement Liters (cc)	Engine ID/VIN	Spark Plugs Gap (in.)	Ignition Timing (deg.) MT	Ignition Timing (deg.) AT	Fuel Pump (psi)	Idle Speed (rpm) MT	Idle Speed (rpm) AT	Valve Clearance In.	Valve Clearance Ex.
1997	4.3 (4293)	W	0.060	①	①	58-64 ②	600	625	HYD	HYD
	4.3 (4293)	X	0.045	③	③	41-47	④	④	HYD	HYD
	5.0 (4999)	M	0.060	①	①	60-66 ②	650 ⑤	550	HYD	HYD
	5.7 (5735)	R	0.060	①	①	60-66 ②	660 ⑥	525	HYD	HYD
	7.4 (7440)	J	0.060	①	①	60-66 ②	750 ⑥	675 ⑥	HYD	HYD
1998	4.3 (4293)	W	0.060	①	①	58-64 ②	600	625	HYD	HYD
	4.3 (4293)	X	0.045	③	③	41-47	④	④	HYD	HYD
	5.0 (4999)	M	0.060	①	①	60-66 ②	650 ⑤	550	HYD	HYD
	5.7 (5735)	R	0.060	①	①	60-66 ②	660 ⑥	525	HYD	HYD
	7.4 (7440)	J	0.060	①	①	60-66 ②	750 ⑥	675 ⑥	HYD	HYD
1999	4.3 (4293)	W	0.060	①	①	58-64 ②	600	625	HYD	HYD
	4.3 (4293)	X	0.045	③	③	41-47	④	④	HYD	HYD
	4.8 (4802)	V	0.060	①	①	55-62 ②	④	④	HYD	HYD
	5.0 (4999)	M	0.060	①	①	60-66 ②	650 ⑤	550	HYD	HYD
	5.3 (5327)	T	0.060	①	①	55-62 ②	④	④	HYD	HYD
	5.7 (5735)	R	0.060	①	①	60-66 ②	660 ⑥	525	HYD	HYD
	6.0 (5966)	U	0.060	①	①	55-62 ②	④	④	HYD	HYD
	7.4 (7440)	J	0.060	①	①	60-66 ②	750 ⑥	675 ⑥	HYD	HYD
2000-01	4.3 (4293)	W	0.060	①	①	58-64 ②	600	625	HYD	HYD
	4.3 (4293)	X	0.045	③	③	41-47	④	④	HYD	HYD
	4.8 (4802)	V	0.060	①	①	55-62 ②	④	④	HYD	HYD
	5.0 (4999)	M	0.060	①	①	60-66 ②	650 ⑤	550	HYD	HYD
	5.3 (5327)	T	0.060	①	①	55-62 ②	④	④	HYD	HYD
	5.7 (5735)	R	0.060	①	①	60-66 ②	660 ⑥	525	HYD	HYD
	6.0 (5966)	U	0.060	①	①	55-62 ②	④	④	HYD	HYD
	7.4 (7440)	J	0.060	①	①	60-66 ②	750 ⑥	675 ⑥	HYD	HYD

NOTE: The Vehicle Emission Control Information label often reflects specification changes made during production. The label figures must be used if they differ from those in this chart.

HYD: Hydraulic

① Ignition timing is preset and cannot be adjusted

② With key ON and engine OFF

③ Distributorless ignition, cannot be adjusted

④ Idle speed is maintained by the Powertrain Control Module (PCM)

⑤ Under 8500 GVW

⑥ Over 8500 GVW

93081CD9

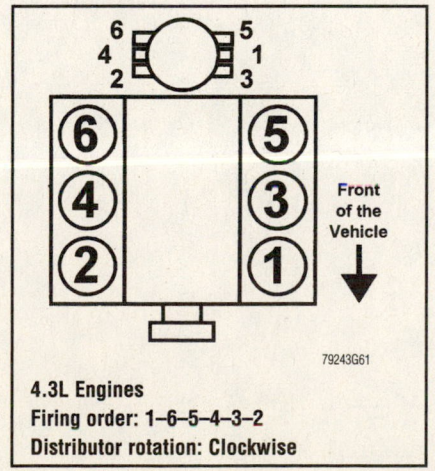

4.3L Engines
Firing order: 1-6-5-4-3-2
Distributor rotation: Clockwise

79243G61

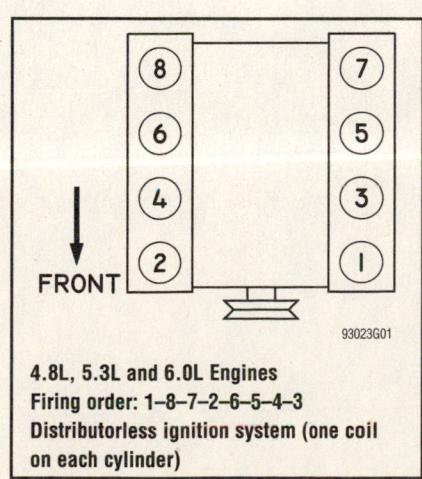

FRONT

4.8L, 5.3L and 6.0L Engines
Firing order: 1-8-7-2-6-5-4-3
Distributorless ignition system (one coil on each cylinder)

93023G01

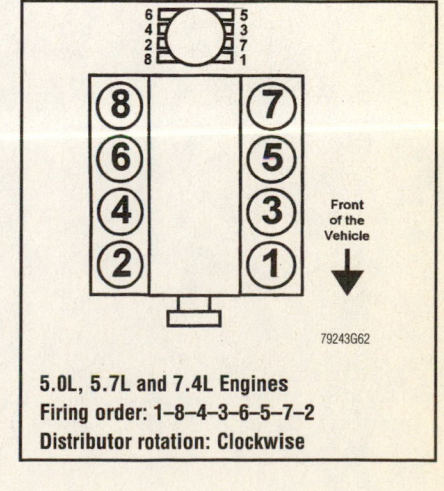

5.0L, 5.7L and 7.4L Engines
Firing order: 1-8-4-3-6-5-7-2
Distributor rotation: Clockwise

79243G62

Refer to the model specific sections for engine mechanical service procedures

DIESEL ENGINE TUNE-UP SPECIFICATIONS

Year	Engine Displacement cu. in. (cc)	Engine ID/VIN	Valve Clearance		Intake Valve Opens (deg.)	Injection Pump Setting (deg.)	Injection Nozzle Pressure (psi)		Idle Speed (rpm)	Cranking Compression Pressure (psi)
			Intake (in.)	Exhaust (in.)			New	Used		
1997	6.5 (6473)	F	HYD	HYD	①	①	1800	1700	①	380-400
	6.5 (6473)	S	HYD	HYD	①	①	1800	1700	①	380-400
1998	6.5 (6473)	F	HYD	HYD	①	①	1800	1700	①	380-400
	6.5 (6473)	S	HYD	HYD	①	①	1800	1700	①	380-400
1999	6.5 (6473)	F	HYD	HYD	①	①	1800	1700	①	380-400
	6.5 (6473)	S	HYD	HYD	①	①	1800	1700	①	380-400
2000-01	6.5 (6473)	F	HYD	HYD	①	①	1800	1700	①	380-400
	6.5 (6473)	S	HYD	HYD	①	①	1800	1700	①	380-400

NOTE: The Vehicle Emission Control Information label often reflects specification changes made during production. The label figures must be used if they differ from those in this chart.

HYD: Hydraulic

NA: Not Available

① Refer to Vehicle Emission Control Information label

93081CD0

CAPACITIES

Year	Model	Engine Displacement Liters (cc)	Engine ID/VIN	Engine Oil with Filter (qts.)	Transmission (pts.) 5-Spd	Transmission (pts.) Auto.	Transfer Case (pts.)	Drive Axle Front (pts.)	Drive Axle Rear (pts.)	Fuel Tank (gal.)	Cooling System (qts.)
1997	C1500	4.3 (4293)	W	5.0	①	②	—	—	③	④	13.0
	C1500	5.0 (4999)	M	5.0	①	②	—	—	③	④	18.0
	C1500	5.7 (5735)	R	5.0	①	②	—	—	③	④	18.0
	C2500	4.3 (4293)	W	5.0	①	②	—	—	③	④	13.0
	C2500	5.0 (4999)	M	5.0	①	②	—	—	③	④	18.0
	C2500	5.7 (5735)	R	5.0	①	②	—	—	③	④	18.0
	C2500	6.5 (6473)	F	7.0	①	②	—	—	③	④	27.5
	C2500	6.5 (6473)	S	7.0	①	②	—	—	③	④	27.5
	C3500	6.5 (6473)	F	7.0	①	②	—	—	③	④	27.5
	C3500	7.4 (7440)	J	6.0	①	②	—	—	③	④	25.0 ⑤
	G/P1500	4.3 (4293)	W	5.0	①	②	—	—	③	22.0 ⑥	13.0 ⑦
	G/P1500	5.0 (4999)	M	5.0	①	②	—	—	③	22.0 ⑥	17.0 ⑦
	G/P1500	5.7 (5735)	R	5.0	①	②	—	—	③	⑥	18.0 ⑦
	G/P2500	5.0 (4999)	M	5.0	①	②	—	—	③	22.0 ⑥	17.0 ⑦
	G/P2500	5.7 (5735)	R	5.0	①	②	—	—	③	⑥	18.0 ⑦
	G/P3500	6.5 (6473)	F	7.0	①	②	—	—	③	22.0 ⑥	27.5 ⑦
	G/P3500	7.4 (7440)	J	6.0	①	②	—	—	③	⑧	24.5 ⑦
	K1500	4.3 (4293)	W	5.0	①	②	⑨	⑩	③	④	11.0
	K1500	5.0 (4999)	M	5.0	①	②	⑨	⑩	③	④	18.0
	K1500	5.7 (5735)	R	5.0	①	②	⑨	⑩	③	④	18.0
	K1500	6.5 (6473)	F	7.0	①	②	⑨	⑩	③	④	27.5
	K2500	5.0 (4999)	M	5.0	①	②	⑨	⑩	③	④	18.0
	K2500	5.7 (5735)	R	5.0	①	②	⑨	⑩	③	④	18.0
	K2500	6.5 (6473)	F	7.0	①	②	⑨	⑩	③	④	27.5
	K3500	6.5 (6473)	F	7.0	①	②	⑨	⑩	③	④	27.5
	K3500	7.4 (7440)	J	6.0	①	②	⑨	⑩	③	④	25.0
	Suburban	5.7 (5735)	R	5.0	—	②	—	—	③	⑥	18.0
	Suburban	7.4 (7440)	F	6.0	—	②	⑨	⑩	③	25.0 ⑥	24.5
	Tahoe	5.7 (5735)	R	5.0	—	②	⑨	⑩	③	④	18.0
	Tahoe	6.5 (6473)	S	7.0	—	②	—	⑩	③	④	23.8
	Yukon	5.7 (5735)	R	5.0	—	②	⑨	⑩	③	④	18.0
	Yukon	6.5 (6473)	S	7.0	—	②	—	—	③	④	23.8
1998	C1500	5.0 (4999)	M	5.0	①	②	—	—	③	④	18.0
	C1500	5.7 (5735)	R	5.0	①	②	—	—	③	④	18.0
	C1500	4.3 (4293)	W	5.0	①	②	—	—	③	④	13.0
	C2500	6.5 (6473)	F	7.0	①	②	—	—	③	④	27.5
	C2500	5.0 (4999)	M	5.0	①	②	—	—	③	④	18.0
	C2500	5.7 (5735)	R	5.0	①	②	—	—	③	④	18.0
	C2500	6.5 (6473)	S	7.0	①	②	—	—	③	④	27.5
	C2500	4.3 (4293)	W	5.0	①	②	—	—	③	④	13.0
	C3500	6.5 (6473)	F	7.0	①	②	—	—	③	④	27.5
	C3500	7.4 (7440)	J	6.0	①	②	—	—	③	④	25.0 ⑤
	Denali	5.7 (5735)	R	5.0	—	②	⑨	⑩	③	④	18.0
	Denali	6.5 (6473)	S	7.0	—	②	—	—	③	④	23.8
	Escalade	5.7 (5735)	R	5.0	—	②	⑨	⑩	③	④	18.0
	Escalade	6.5 (6473)	S	7.0	—	②	—	—	③	④	23.8
	G/P1500	5.0 (4999)	M	5.0	①	②	—	—	③	22.0 ⑥	17.0 ⑦
	G/P1500	5.7 (5735)	R	5.0	①	②	—	—	③	⑥	18.0 ⑦

93081CE1

Refer to the model specific sections for fuel system service procedures

CAPACITIES

Year	Model	Engine Displacement Liters (cc)	Engine ID/VIN	Engine Oil with Filter (qts.)	Transmission (pts.) 5-Spd	Transmission (pts.) Auto.	Transfer Case (pts.)	Drive Axle Front (pts.)	Drive Axle Rear (pts.)	Fuel Tank (gal.)	Cooling System (qts.)
1998 (Cont.)	G/P1500	4.3 (4293)	W	5.0	①	②	—	—	③	22 ⑥	13.0 ⑦
	G/P2500	5.0 (4999)	M	5.0	①	②	—	—	③	22.0 ⑥	17.0 ⑦
	G/P2500	5.7 (5735)	R	5.0	①	②	—	—	③	⑥	18.0 ⑦
	G/P3500	6.5 (6473)	F	7.0	①	②	—	—	③	22.0 ⑥	27.5 ⑦
	G/P3500	7.4 (7440)	J	6.0	①	②	—	—	③	⑧	24.5 ⑦
	K1500	6.5 (6473)	F	7.0	①	②	⑨	⑩	③	④	27.5
	K1500	5.0 (4999)	M	5.0	①	②	⑨	⑩	③	④	18.0
	K1500	5.7 (5735)	R	5.0	①	②	⑨	⑩	③	④	18.0
	K1500	4.3 (4293)	W	5.0	①	②	⑨	⑩	③	④	11.0
	K2500	6.5 (6473)	F	7.0	①	②	⑨	⑩	③	④	27.5
	K2500	5.0 (4999)	M	5.0	①	②	⑨	⑩	③	④	18.0
	K2500	5.7 (5735)	R	5.0	①	②	⑨	⑩	③	④	18.0
	K3500	6.5 (6473)	F	7.0	①	②	⑨	⑩	③	④	27.5
	K3500	7.4 (7440)	J	6.0	①	②	⑨	⑩	③	④	25.0
	Suburban	7.4 (7440)	F	6.0	—	②	⑨	⑩	③	25.0 ⑥	24.5
	Suburban	5.7 (5735)	R	5.0	—	②	—	—	③	④	18.0
	Tahoe	5.7 (5735)	R	5.0	—	②	⑨	⑩	③	④	18.0
	Tahoe	6.5 (6473)	S	7.0	—	②	—	—	③	④	23.8
	Yukon	5.7 (5735)	R	5.0	—	②	⑨	⑩	③	④	18.0
	Yukon	6.5 (6473)	S	7.0	—	②	—	—	③	④	23.8
1999	C1500	5.0 (4999)	M	5.0	①	②	—	—	③	④	18.0
	C1500	5.7 (5735)	R	5.0	①	②	—	—	③	④	18.0
	C1500	4.3 (4293)	W	5.0	①	②	—	—	③	④	13.0
	C2500	6.5 (6473)	F	7.0	①	②	—	—	③	④	27.5
	C2500	5.0 (4999)	M	5.0	①	②	—	—	③	④	18.0
	C2500	5.7 (5735)	R	5.0	①	②	—	—	③	④	18.0
	C2500	6.5 (6473)	S	7.0	①	②	—	—	③	④	27.5
	C2500	4.3 (4293)	W	5.0	①	②	—	—	③	④	13.0
	C3500	6.5 (6473)	F	7.0	①	②	—	—	③	④	27.5
	C3500	7.4 (7440)	J	6.0	①	②	—	—	③	④	25.0 ⑤
	Denali	5.7 (5735)	R	5.0	—	②	⑨	⑩	③	④	18.0
	Denali	6.5 (6473)	S	7.0	—	②	—	—	③	④	23.8
	Escalade	5.7 (5735)	R	5.0	—	②	⑨	⑩	③	④	18.0
	Escalade	6.5 (6473)	S	7.0	—	②	—	—	③	④	23.8
	G/P1500	5.0 (4999)	M	5.0	①	②	—	—	③	22.0 ⑥	17.0 ⑦
	G/P1500	5.7 (5735)	R	5.0	①	②	—	—	③	⑥	18.0 ⑦
	G/P1500	4.3 (4293)	W	5.0	①	②	—	—	③	22.0 ⑥	13.0 ⑦
	G/P2500	5.0 (4999)	M	5.0	①	②	—	—	③	22.0 ⑥	17.0 ⑦
	G/P2500	5.7 (5735)	R	5.0	①	②	—	—	③	⑥	18.0 ⑦
	G/P3500	6.5 (6473)	F	7.0	①	②	—	—	③	22.0 ⑥	27.5 ⑦
	G/P3500	7.4 (7440)	J	6.0	①	②	—	—	③	⑧	24.5 ⑦
	K1500	6.5 (6473)	F	7.0	①	②	⑨	⑩	③	④	27.5
	K1500	5.0 (4999)	M	5.0	①	②	⑨	⑩	③	④	18.0
	K1500	5.7 (5735)	R	5.0	①	②	⑨	⑩	③	④	18.0
	K1500	4.3 (4293)	W	5.0	①	②	⑨	⑩	③	④	11.0
	K2500	6.5 (6473)	F	7.0	①	②	⑨	⑩	③	④	27.5
	K2500	5.0 (4999)	M	5.0	①	②	⑨	⑩	③	④	18.0
	K2500	5.7 (5735)	R	5.0	①	②	⑨	⑩	③	④	18.0

93081CE2

CAPACITIES

Year	Model	Engine Displacement Liters (cc)	Engine ID/VIN	Engine Oil with Filter (qts.)	Transmission (pts.) 5-Spd	Transmission (pts.) Auto.	Transfer Case (pts.)	Drive Axle Front (pts.)	Drive Axle Rear (pts.)	Fuel Tank (gal.)	Cooling System (qts.)
1999 (Cont.)	K3500	6.5 (6473)	F	7.0	①	②	⑨	⑩	③	④	27.5
	K3500	7.4 (7440)	J	6.0	①	②	⑨	⑩	③	④	25.0
	Sierra	4.3 (4293)	W	5.0	8.0	10.0	4.8	3.5	③	⑪	14.5
	Sierra	4.8 (4802)	V	6.0	8.0	10.0	4.8	3.5	③	⑪	14.5
	Sierra	5.3 (5327)	T	6.0	8.0	10.0	4.8	3.5	③	⑪	14.5
	Sierra	6.0 (5966)	U	6.0	8.0	10.0	4.8	3.5	③	⑪	14.5
	Sierra	6.5 (6374)	F	6.0	8.0	10.0	4.8	3.5	③	⑪	14.5
	Silverado	4.3 (4293)	W	5.0	8.0	10.0	4.8	3.5	③	⑪	14.5
	Silverado	4.8 (4802)	V	6.0	8.0	10.0	4.8	3.5	③	⑪	14.5
	Silverado	5.3 (5327)	T	6.0	8.0	10.0	4.8	3.5	③	⑪	14.5
	Silverado	6.0 (5966)	U	6.0	8.0	10.0	4.8	3.5	③	⑪	14.5
	Silverado	6.5 (6374)	F	6.0	8.0	10.0	4.8	3.5	③	⑪	14.5
	Suburban	7.4 (7440)	J	6.0	—	②	⑨	⑩	③	25.0 ⑥	24.5
	Suburban	5.7 (5735)	R	5.0	—	②	—	—	③	④	18.0
	Tahoe	5.7 (5735)	R	5.0	—	②	⑨	⑩	③	④	18.0
	Tahoe	6.5 (6473)	S	7.0	—	②	—	—	③	④	23.8
	Yukon	5.7 (5735)	R	5.0	—	②	⑨	⑩	③	④	18.0
	Yukon	6.5 (6473)	S	7.0	—	②	—	—	③	④	23.8
2000-01	C1500	5.0 (4999)	M	5.0	①	②	—	—	③	④	18.0
	C1500	5.7 (5735)	R	5.0	①	②	—	—	③	④	18.0
	C1500	4.3 (4293)	W	5.0	①	②	—	—	③	④	13.0
	C2500	6.5 (6473)	F	7.0	①	②	—	—	③	④	27.5
	C2500	5.0 (4999)	M	5.0	①	②	—	—	③	④	18.0
	C2500	5.7 (5735)	R	5.0	①	②	—	—	③	④	18.0
	C2500	6.5 (6473)	S	7.0	①	②	—	—	③	④	27.5
	C2500	4.3 (4293)	W	5.0	①	②	—	—	③	④	13.0
	C3500	6.5 (6473)	F	7.0	①	②	—	—	③	④	27.5
	C3500	7.4 (7440)	J	6.0	①	②	—	—	③	④	25.0 ⑤
	Denali	5.7 (5735)	R	5.0	—	②	⑨	⑩	③	④	18.0
	Denali	6.5 (6473)	S	7.0	—	②	—	—	③	④	23.8
	Escalade	5.7 (5735)	R	5.0	—	②	⑨	⑩	③	④	18.0
	Escalade	6.5 (6473)	S	7.0	—	②	—	—	③	④	23.8
	G/P1500	5.0 (4999)	M	5.0	①	②	—	—	③	22.0 ⑥	17.0 ⑦
	G/P1500	5.7 (5735)	R	5.0	①	②	—	—	③	⑥	18.0 ⑦
	G/P1500	4.3 (4293)	W	5.0	①	②	—	—	③	22.0 ⑥	13.0 ⑦
	G/P2500	5.0 (4999)	M	5.0	①	②	—	—	③	22.0 ⑥	17.0 ⑦
	G/P2500	5.7 (5735)	R	5.0	①	②	—	—	③	⑥	18.0 ⑦
	G/P3500	6.5 (6473)	F	7.0	①	②	—	—	③	22.0 ⑥	27.5 ⑦
	G/P3500	7.4 (7440)	J	6.0	①	②	—	—	⑧		24.5 ⑦
	K1500	6.5 (6473)	F	7.0	①	②	⑨	⑩	③	④	27.5
	K1500	5.0 (4999)	M	5.0	①	②	⑨	⑩	③	④	18.0
	K1500	5.7 (5735)	R	5.0	①	②	⑨	⑩	③	④	18.0
	K1500	4.3 (4293)	W	5.0	①	②	⑨	⑩	③	④	11.0
	K2500	6.5 (6473)	F	7.0	①	②	⑨	⑩	③	④	27.5
	K2500	5.0 (4999)	M	5.0	①	②	⑨	⑩	③	④	18.0
	K2500	5.7 (5735)	R	5.0	①	②	⑨	⑩	③	④	18.0
	K3500	6.5 (6473)	F	7.0	①	②	⑨	⑩	③	④	27.5
	K3500	7.4 (7440)	J	6.0	①	②	⑨	⑩	③	④	25.0

93081CE3

Refer to the model specific sections for engine electrical system service procedures

CAPACITIES

Year	Model	Engine Displacement Liters (cc)	Engine ID/VIN	Engine Oil with Filter (qts.)	Transmission (pts.)		Transfer Case (pts.)	Drive Axle		Fuel Tank (gal.)	Cooling System (qts.)
					5-Spd	Auto.		Front (pts.)	Rear (pts.)		
2000-01 (Cont.)	Sierra	4.3 (4293)	W	5.0	8.0	10.0	4.8	3.5	③	⑪	14.5
	Sierra	4.8 (4802)	V	6.0	8.0	10.0	4.8	3.5	③	⑪	14.5
	Sierra	5.3 (5327)	T	6.0	8.0	10.0	4.8	3.5	③	⑪	14.5
	Sierra	6.0 (5966)	U	6.0	8.0	10.0	4.8	3.5	③	⑪	14.5
	Sierra	6.5 (6374)	F	6.0	8.0	10.0	4.8	3.5	③	⑪	14.5
	Silverado	4.3 (4293)	W	5.0	8.0	10.0	4.8	3.5	③	⑪	14.5
	Silverado	4.8 (4802)	V	6.0	8.0	10.0	4.8	3.5	③	⑪	14.5
	Silverado	5.3 (5327)	T	6.0	8.0	10.0	4.8	3.5	③	⑪	14.5
	Silverado	6.0 (5966)	U	6.0	8.0	10.0	4.8	3.5	③	⑪	14.5
	Silverado	6.5 (6374)	F	6.0	8.0	10.0	4.8	3.5	③	⑪	14.5
	Suburban	7.4 (7440)	J	6.0	—	②	⑨	⑩	③	25.0 ⑥	24.5
	Suburban	5.7 (5735)	R	5.0	—	②	—	—	③	④	18.0
	Tahoe	5.7 (5735)	R	5.0	—	②	⑨	⑩	③	④	18.0
	Tahoe	6.5 (6473)	S	7.0	—	②	—	—	③	④	23.8
	Yukon	5.7 (5735)	R	5.0	—	②	⑨	⑩	③	④	18.0
	Yukon	6.5 (6473)	S	7.0	—	②	—	—	③	④	23.8

NOTE: All capacities are approximate. Add fluid gradually and check to be sure a proper fluid level is obtained.

① New Venture gear 4500: 8.0 pts.
  New Venture gear 5LM60: 4.4 pts.

② 4L60E trans.: 10.0 pts.
  4L80E trans.: 14.5 pts.

③ 8.5 in. ring gear: 4.2 pts.
  9.5 in. ring gear: 6.5 pts.
  9.75 in. ring gear: 6.0 pts.
  10.5 in. ring gear: 6.5 pts.

④ Std. available with 25 and 34 gallon tanks
  Chassis cab available with 22, 30 and 34 gallon tanks

⑤ 3500HD: 28.5 qts. capacity

⑥ Optional 31 and 40 gallon tanks

⑦ Add three qts. with rear heater

⑧ Available with a variety of fuel tanks

⑨ NV241 and NV243: 4.5 pts.
  4401 and 4470: 6.6 pts.

⑩ K2 models: 1.75 qts.
  K3 models: 2.25 qts.

⑪ Short bed: 26 gals.
  Long bed: 34 gals.

93081CE4

VALVE SPECIFICATIONS

Year	Engine Displacement Liters (cc)	Engine ID/VIN	Seat Angle (deg.)	Face Angle (deg.)	Spring Test Pressure (lbs. @ in.)	Spring Installed Height (in.)	Stem-to-Guide Clearance (in.)		Stem Diameter (in.)	
							Intake	Exhaust	Intake	Exhaust
1997	4.3 (4293)	W	46	45	187-203@1.27	1.69-1.71	0.0010	0.0020	NA	NA
	4.3 (4293)	X	46	45	187-203@1.27	1.69-1.71	0.0010	0.0020	NA	NA
	5.0 (4999)	M	46	45	187-203@1.27	1.69-1.71	0.0010-0.0027	0.0010-0.0027	NA	NA
	5.7 (5735)	R	46	45	187-203@1.27	1.69-1.71	0.0010-0.0027	0.0010-0.0027	NA	NA
	6.5 (6473)	F	46	45	230@1.40	1.80	0.0010-0.0027	0.0010-0.0027	NA	NA
	6.5 (6473)	S	46	45	230@1.40	1.80	0.0010-0.0027	0.0010-0.0027	NA	NA
	7.4 (7440)	J	46	45	238-262@1.34	1.83	0.0010-0.0029 ①	0.0012-0.0031 ①	NA	NA
1998	4.3 (4293)	W	46	45	187-203@1.27	1.69-1.71	0.0010	0.0020	NA	NA
	4.3 (4293)	X	46	45	187-203@1.27	1.69-1.71	0.0010	0.0020	NA	NA
	5.0 (4999)	M	46	45	187-203@1.27	1.69-1.71	0.0010-0.0027	0.0010-0.0027	NA	NA
	5.7 (5735)	R	46	45	187-203@1.27	1.69-1.71	0.0010-0.0027	0.0010-0.0027	NA	NA
	6.5 (6473)	F	46	45	230@1.40	1.80	0.0010-0.0027	0.0010-0.0027	NA	NA
	6.5 (6473)	S	46	45	230@1.40	1.80	0.0010-0.0027	0.0010-0.0027	NA	NA
	7.4 (7440)	J	46	45	238-262@1.34	1.83	0.0010-0.0029 ①	0.0012-0.0031 ①	NA	NA
1999	4.3 (4293)	W	46	45	187-203@1.27	1.69-1.71	0.0010	0.0020	NA	NA
	4.3 (4293)	X	46	45	187-203@1.27	1.69-1.71	0.0010	0.0020	NA	NA
	4.8 (4802)	V	46	45	220@1.32	1.80	0.0010-0.0037	0.0010-0.0037	0.3132-0.3110	0.3132-0.3110
	5.0 (4999)	M	46	45	187-203@1.27	1.69-1.71	0.0010-0.0027	0.0010-0.0027	NA	NA
	5.3 (5327)	T	46	45	220@1.32	1.80	0.0010-0.0037	0.0010-0.0037	0.3132-0.3110	0.3132-0.3110
	5.7 (5735)	R	46	45	187-203@1.27	1.69-1.71	0.0010-0.0027	0.0010-0.0027	NA	NA
	6.0 (5966)	U	46	45	220@1.32	1.80	0.0010-0.0037	0.0010-0.0037	0.3132-0.3110	0.3132-0.3110
	6.5 (6473)	F	46	45	230@1.40	1.80	0.0010-0.0027	0.0010-0.0027	NA	NA
	6.5 (6473)	S	46	45	230@1.40	1.80	0.0010-0.0027	0.0010-0.0027	NA	NA
	7.4 (7440)	J	46	45	238-262@1.34	1.83	0.0010-0.0029 ①	0.0012-0.0031 ①	NA	NA

93081CE5

For accessory drive belt replacement procedures see the model specific sections of this manual

VALVE SPECIFICATIONS

Year	Engine Displacement Liters (cc)	Engine ID/VIN	Seat Angle (deg.)	Face Angle (deg.)	Spring Test Pressure (lbs. @ in.)	Spring Installed Height (in.)	Stem-to-Guide Clearance (in.)		Stem Diameter (in.)	
							Intake	Exhaust	Intake	Exhaust
2000-01	4.3 (4293)	W	46	45	187-203@1.27	1.69-1.71	0.0010	0.0020	NA	NA
	4.3 (4293)	X	46	45	187-203@1.27	1.69-1.71	0.0010	0.0020	NA	NA
	4.8 (4802)	V	46	45	220@1.32	1.80	0.0010-0.0037	0.0010-0.0037	0.3132-0.3110	0.3132-0.3110
	5.0 (4999)	M	46	45	187-203@1.27	1.69-1.71	0.0010-0.0027	0.0010-0.0027	NA	NA
	5.3 (5327)	T	46	45	220@1.32	1.80	0.0010-0.0037	0.0010-0.0037	0.3132-0.3110	0.3132-0.3110
	5.7 (5735)	R	46	45	187-203@1.27	1.69-1.71	0.0010-0.0027	0.0010-0.0027	NA	NA
	6.0 (5966)	U	46	45	220@1.32	1.80	0.0010-0.0037	0.0010-0.0037	0.3132-0.3110	0.3132-0.3110
	6.5 (6473)	F	46	45	230@1.40	1.80	0.0010-0.0027	0.0010-0.0027	NA	NA
	6.5 (6473)	S	46	45	230@1.40	1.80	0.0010-0.0027	0.0010-0.0027	NA	NA
	7.4 (7440)	J	46	45	238-262@1.34	1.83	0.0010-0.0029 ①	0.0012-0.0031 ①	NA	NA

NA: Not Available

① Service limit:
Intake: 0.0037 MAX
Exhaust: 0.0049 MAX

93081CE6

CRANKSHAFT AND CONNECTING ROD SPECIFICATIONS
All measurements are given in inches.

Year	Engine Displacement Liters (cc)	Engine ID/VIN	Crankshaft Main Brg. Journal Dia.	Crankshaft Main Brg. Oil Clearance	Crankshaft Shaft End-play	Crankshaft Thrust on No.	Connecting Rod Journal Diameter	Connecting Rod Oil Clearance	Connecting Rod Side Clearance
1997	4.3 (4293)	W	①	②	0.0020-0.0070	4	2.2487-2.2497	0.0013-0.0035	0.0060-0.0140
	4.3 (4293)	X	③	②	0.0020-0.0060	4	2.2487-2.2497	0.0013-0.0035	0.0060-0.0140
	5.0 (4999)	M	④	⑤	0.0020-0.0080	5	2.0978-2.0998	0.0013-0.0035	0.0060-0.0140
	5.7 (5735)	R	④	⑤	0.0020-0.0080	5	2.0978-2.0998	0.0013-0.0035	0.0060-0.0140
	6.5 (6473)	F	⑥	⑦	0.0039-0.0100	3	⑧	0.0018-0.0039	0.0067-0.0248
	6.5 (6473)	S	⑥	⑦	0.0039-0.0100	3	⑧	0.0018-0.0039	0.0067-0.0248
	7.4 (7440)	J	2.7482-2.7489	⑨	0.0050-0.0110	5	2.1990-2.1996	0.0011-0.0029	0.0013-0.0230
1998	4.3 (4293)	W	①	②	0.0020-0.0070	4	2.2487-2.2497	0.0013-0.0035	0.0060-0.0140
	4.3 (4293)	X	③	②	0.0020-0.0060	4	2.2487-2.2497	0.0013-0.0035	0.0060-0.0140
	5.0 (4999)	M	④	⑤	0.0020-0.0080	5	2.0978-2.0998	0.0013-0.0035	0.0060-0.0140
	5.7 (5735)	R	④	⑤	0.0020-0.0080	5	2.0978-2.0998	0.0013-0.0035	0.0060-0.0140
	6.5 (6473)	F	⑥	⑦	0.0039-0.0100	3	⑧	0.0018-0.0039	0.0067-0.0248
	6.5 (6473)	S	⑥	⑦	0.0039-0.0100	3	⑧	0.0018-0.0039	0.0067-0.0248
	7.4 (7440)	J	2.7482-2.7489	⑨	0.0050-0.0110	5	2.1990-2.1996	0.0011-0.0029	0.0013-0.0230
1999	4.3 (4293)	W	①	②	0.0020-0.0070	4	2.2487-2.2497	0.0013-0.0035	0.0060-0.0140
	4.3 (4293)	X	③	②	0.0020-0.0060	4	2.2487-2.2497	0.0013-0.0035	0.0060-0.0140
	5.0 (4999)	M	④	⑤	0.0020-0.0080	5	2.0978-2.0998	0.0013-0.0035	0.0060-0.0140
	5.7 (5735)	R	④	⑤	0.0020-0.0080	5	2.0978-2.0998	0.0013-0.0035	0.0060-0.0140
	6.5 (6473)	F	⑥	⑦	0.0039-0.0100	3	⑧	0.0018-0.0039	0.0067-0.0248
	6.5 (6473)	S	⑥	⑦	0.0039-0.0100	3	⑧	0.0018-0.0039	0.0067-0.0248
	7.4 (7440)	J	2.7482-2.7489	⑨	0.0050-0.0110	5	2.1990-2.1996	0.0011-0.0029	0.0013-0.0230

93081CE7

For brake related suspension and axle service, refer to the model specific sections of this manual

CRANKSHAFT AND CONNECTING ROD SPECIFICATIONS
All measurements are given in inches.

Year	Engine Displacement Liters (cc)	Engine ID/VIN	Crankshaft				Connecting Rod		
			Main Brg. Journal Dia.	Main Brg. Oil Clearance	Shaft End-play	Thrust on No.	Journal Diameter	Oil Clearance	Side Clearance
2000-01	4.3 (4293)	W	①	②	0.0020-0.0070	4	2.2487-2.2497	0.0013-0.0035	0.0060-0.0140
	4.3 (4293)	X	③	②	0.0020-0.0060	4	2.2487-2.2497	0.0013-0.0035	0.0060-0.0140
	4.8 (4802)	V	2.5580-2.5593	0.0007-0.0021	0.0015-0.0078	5	2.0990-2.1000	0.0006-0.0030	0.0043-0.0200
	5.0 (4999)	M	④	⑤	0.0020-0.0080	5	2.0978-2.0998	0.0013-0.0035	0.0060-0.0140
	5.3 (5327)	T	2.5580-2.5593	0.0007-0.0021	0.0015-0.0078	5	2.0990-2.1000	0.0006-0.0030	0.0043-0.0200
	5.7 (5735)	R	④	⑤	0.0020-0.0080	5	2.0978-2.0998	0.0013-0.0035	0.0060-0.0140
	6.0 (5966)	U	2.5580-2.5593	0.0007-0.0021	0.0015-0.0078	5	2.0990-2.1000	0.0006-0.0030	0.0043-0.0200
	6.5 (6473)	F	⑥	⑦	0.0039-0.0100	3	⑧	0.0018-0.0039	0.0067-0.0248
	6.5 (6473)	S	⑥	⑦	0.0039-0.0100	3	⑧	0.0018-0.0039	0.0067-0.0248
	7.4 (7440)	J	2.7482-2.7489	⑨	0.0050-0.0110	5	2.1990-2.1996	0.0011-0.0029	0.0013-0.0230

① No. 1: 2.4488 in.-2.4495 in.
  Nos. 2, 3: 2.4485 in.-2.4494 in.
  No. 4: 2.4480 in.-2.4489 in.

② No. 1: 0.0008 in.-0.0020 in.
  Nos. 2, 3: 0.0011 in.-0.0023 in.
  No. 4: 0.0017 in.-0.0032 in.

③ No. 1: 2.4484 in.-2.4493 in.
  Nos. 2, 3: 2.4481 in.-2.4490 in.
  No. 4: 2.4479 in.-2.4488 in.

④ No. 1: 2.4484 in.-2.4493 in.
  Nos. 2, 3, 4: 2.4481 in.-2.4490 in.
  No. 5: 2.4479 in.-2.4488 in.

⑤ No. 1: 0.0007 in.-0.0021 in.
  Nos. 2, 3, 4: 0.0009 in.-0.0024 in.
  No. 5: 0.0010 in.-0.0027 in.

⑥ No. 1, 2, 3, 4: 2.9517 in.-2.9520 in. (Blue)
  2.9520 in.-2.9524 in. (Orange/Red)
  2.9524 in.-2.9527 in. (White)
  No. 5: 2.9515 in.-2.9518 in. (Blue)
  2.9518 in.-2.9522 in. (Orange/Red)
  2.9522 in.-2.9525 in. (White)

⑦ No. 1, 2, 3, 4: 0.0018 in.-0.0033 in.
  No. 5: 0.0022 in.-0.0037 in.

⑧ 2.399 in.-2.400 in. (Green)
  2.400 in.-2.401 in. (Yellow)

⑨ No. 1: 0.0017 in.-0.0030 in.
  No. 2, 3, 4: 0.0011 in.-0.0024 in.
  No. 5: 0.0025 in.-0.0038 in.

93081CE8

PISTON AND RING SPECIFICATIONS

All measurements are given in inches.

Year	Engine Displacement Liters (cc)	Engine ID/VIN	Piston Clearance	Ring Gap			Ring Side Clearance		
				Top Compression	Bottom Compression	Oil Control	Top Compression	Bottom Compression	Oil Control
1997	4.3 (4293)	W	0.0007-0.0017	0.010-0.030	0.018-0.026	0.065 Max.	0.0042 Max.	0.0042 Max.	0.0020-0.0070
	4.3 (4293)	X	0.0007-0.0017	0.010-0.030	0.018-0.026	0.065 Max.	0.0042 Max.	0.0042 Max.	0.0020-0.0070
	5.0 (4999)	M	0.0007-0.0021	0.010-0.020	0.018-0.026	0.010-0.030	0.0012-0.0032	0.0012-0.0032	0.0020-0.0070
	5.7 (5735)	R	0.0007-0.0021	0.010-0.020	0.018-0.026	0.010-0.030	0.0012-0.0032	0.0012-0.0032	0.0020-0.0070
	6.5 (6473)	F	①	0.010-0.020	0.030-0.039	0.010-0.020	0.0015-0.0031	0.0015-0.0031	0.0016-0.0035
	6.5 (6473)	S	①	0.010-0.020	0.030-0.039	0.010-0.020	0.0015-0.0031	0.0015-0.0031	0.0016-0.0035
	7.4 (7440)	J	0.0018-0.0030	0.010-0.0180	0.016-0.0240	0.010-0.030	0.0012-0.0029	0.0012-0.0029	0.0050-0.0065
1998	4.3 (4293)	W	0.0007-0.0017	0.010-0.030	0.018-0.026	0.065 Max.	0.0042 Max.	0.0042 Max.	0.0020-0.0070
	4.3 (4293)	X	0.0007-0.0017	0.010-0.030	0.018-0.026	0.065 Max.	0.0042 Max.	0.0042 Max.	0.0020-0.0070
	5.0 (4999)	M	0.0007-0.0021	0.010-0.020	0.018-0.026	0.010-0.030	0.0012-0.0032	0.0012-0.0032	0.0020-0.0070
	5.7 (5735)	R	0.0007-0.0021	0.010-0.020	0.018-0.026	0.010-0.030	0.0012-0.0032	0.0012-0.0032	0.0020-0.0070
	6.5 (6473)	F	①	0.010-0.020	0.030-0.039	0.010-0.020	0.0015-0.0031	0.0015-0.0031	0.0016-0.0035
	6.5 (6473)	S	①	0.010-0.020	0.030-0.039	0.010-0.020	0.0015-0.0031	0.0015-0.0031	0.0016-0.0035
	7.4 (7440)	J	0.0018-0.0030	0.010-0.0180	0.016-0.0240	0.010-0.030	0.0012-0.0029	0.0012-0.0029	0.0050-0.0065
1999	4.3 (4293)	W	0.0007-0.0017	0.010-0.030	0.018-0.026	0.065 Max.	0.0042 Max.	0.0042 Max.	0.0020-0.0070
	4.3 (4293)	X	0.0007-0.0017	0.010-0.030	0.018-0.026	0.065 Max.	0.0042 Max.	0.0042 Max.	0.0020-0.0070
	4.8 (4802)	V	0.0010-0.0024	0.009-0.015	0.017-0.025	0.007-0.027	0.0016-0.0033	0.0016-0.0031	0.0004-0.0087
	5.0 (4999)	M	0.0007-0.0021	0.010-0.020	0.018-0.026	0.010-0.030	0.0012-0.0032	0.0012-0.0032	0.0020-0.0070
	5.3 (5327)	T	0.0010-0.0024	0.009-0.015	0.017-0.025	0.007-0.027	0.0016-0.0033	0.0016-0.0031	0.0004-0.0087
	5.7 (5735)	R	0.0007-0.0021	0.010-0.020	0.018-0.026	0.010-0.030	0.0012-0.0032	0.0012-0.0032	0.0020-0.0070
	6.0 (5966)	U	0.0010-0.0024	0.009-0.015	0.017-0.025	0.007-0.027	0.0016-0.0033	0.0016-0.0031	0.0004-0.0087
	6.5 (6473)	F	①	0.010-0.020	0.030-0.039	0.010-0.020	0.0015-0.0031	0.0015-0.0031	0.0016-0.0035
	6.5 (6473)	S	①	0.010-0.020	0.030-0.039	0.010-0.020	0.0015-0.0031	0.0015-0.0031	0.0016-0.0035
	7.4 (7440)	J	0.0018-0.0030	0.010-0.0180	0.016-0.0240	0.010-0.030	0.0012-0.0029	0.0012-0.0029	0.0050-0.0065

93081CE9

Refer to the model specific sections for driveline service procedures

PISTON AND RING SPECIFICATIONS

All measurements are given in inches.

Year	Engine Displacement Liters (cc)	Engine ID/VIN	Piston Clearance	Ring Gap			Ring Side Clearance		
				Top Compression	Bottom Compression	Oil Control	Top Compression	Bottom Compression	Oil Control
2000-01	4.3 (4293)	W	0.0007-0.0017	0.010-0.030	0.018-0.026	0.065 Max.	0.0042 Max.	0.0042 Max.	0.0020-0.0070
	4.3 (4293)	X	0.0007-0.0017	0.010-0.030	0.018-0.026	0.065 Max.	0.0042 Max.	0.0042 Max.	0.0020-0.0070
	4.8 (4802)	V	0.0010-0.0024	0.009-0.015	0.017-0.025	0.007-0.027	0.0016-0.0033	0.0016-0.0031	0.0004-0.0087
	5.0 (4999)	M	0.0007-0.0021	0.010-0.020	0.018-0.026	0.010-0.030	0.0012-0.0032	0.0012-0.0032	0.0020-0.0070
	5.3 (5327)	T	0.0010-0.0024	0.009-0.015	0.017-0.025	0.007-0.027	0.0016-0.0033	0.0016-0.0031	0.0004-0.0087
	5.7 (5735)	R	0.0007-0.0021	0.010-0.020	0.018-0.026	0.010-0.030	0.0012-0.0032	0.0012-0.0032	0.0020-0.0070
	6.0 (5966)	U	0.0010-0.0024	0.009-0.015	0.017-0.025	0.007-0.027	0.0016-0.0033	0.0016-0.0031	0.0004-0.0087
	6.5 (6473)	F	①	0.010-0.020	0.030-0.039	0.010-0.020	0.0015-0.0031	0.0015-0.0031	0.0016-0.0035
	6.5 (6473)	S	①	0.010-0.020	0.030-0.039	0.010-0.020	0.0015-0.0031	0.0015-0.0031	0.0016-0.0035
	7.4 (7440)	J	0.0018-0.0030	0.010-0.0180	0.016-0.0240	0.010-0.030	0.0012-0.0029	0.0012-0.0029	0.0050-0.0065

① 1-6: 0.0037-0.0047 in.
  7-8: 0.0042-0.0052 in.

93081CE0

TORQUE SPECIFICATIONS
All readings in ft. lbs.

Year	Engine Displacement Liters (cc)	Engine ID/VIN	Cylinder Head Bolts	Main Bearing Bolts	Rod Bearing Bolts	Crankshaft Damper Bolts	Flywheel Bolts	Manifold Intake *	Manifold Exhaust	Spark Plugs	Lug Nut
1997	4.3 (4293)	W	①	77	②	74	74	③	④	11	90
	4.3 (4293)	X	①	77	②	74	74	③	④	11	90
	5.0 (4999)	M	⑤	⑥	⑦	74	74	③	④	15	⑧
	5.7 (5735)	R	⑤	⑥	⑦	74	74	③	④	15	⑧
	6.5 (6473)	F	⑨	⑩	48	200	65	31	26	—	⑧
	6.5 (6473)	S	⑨	⑩	48	200	65	31	26	—	⑧
	7.4 (7440)	J	85	100	45	110	67	30	22	15	⑧
1998	4.3 (4293)	W	①	77	②	74	74	③	④	11	90
	4.3 (4293)	X	①	77	②	74	74	③	④	11	90
	5.0 (4999)	M	⑥	⑥	⑦	74	74	③	④	15	⑧
	5.7 (5735)	R	⑨	⑥	⑦	74	74	③	④	15	⑧
	6.5 (6473)	F	⑨	⑩	48	200	65	31	26	—	⑧
	6.5 (6473)	S	⑨	⑩	48	200	65	31	26	—	⑧
	7.4 (7440)	J	85	100	45	110	67	30	22	15	⑧
1999	4.3 (4293)	W	①	77	②	74	74	③	④	11	90
	4.3 (4293)	X	①	77	②	74	74	③	④	11	90
	4.8 (4802)	V	⑪	⑫	⑬	⑭	⑮	⑯	⑰	12	140
	5.0 (4999)	M	⑨	⑥	⑦	74	74	③	④	15	⑧
	5.3 (5327)	T	⑪	⑫	⑬	⑭	⑮	⑯	⑰	12	140
	5.7 (5735)	R	⑪	⑧	⑨	74	74	⑤	④	15	⑧
	6.0 (5966)	U	⑪	⑫	⑬	⑭	⑮	⑯	⑰	12	140
	6.5 (6473)	F	⑨	⑩	48	200	65	31	26	—	⑧
	6.5 (6473)	S	⑨	⑩	48	200	65	31	26	—	⑧
	7.4 (7440)	J	85	100	45	110	67	30	22	15	⑧
2000-01	4.3 (4293)	W	①	77	②	74	74	③	④	11	90
	4.3 (4293)	X	①	77	②	74	74	③	④	11	90
	4.8 (4802)	V	⑪	⑫	⑬	⑭	⑮	⑯	⑰	12	140
	5.0 (4999)	M	⑪	⑧	⑨	74	74	⑤	④	15	⑧
	5.3 (5327)	T	⑪	⑫	⑬	⑭	⑮	⑯	⑰	12	140
	5.7 (5735)	R	⑨	⑥	⑦	74	74	⑤	④	15	⑧
	6.0 (5966)	U	⑪	⑫	⑬	⑭	⑮	⑯	⑰	12	140
	6.5 (6473)	F	⑨	⑩	48	200	65	31	26	—	⑧
	6.5 (6473)	S	⑨	⑩	48	200	65	31	26	—	⑧
	7.4 (7440)	J	85	100	45	110	67	30	22	15	⑧

* NOTE: Applies to Lower Manifold only.

① 1st pass: 22 ft. lbs.
2nd pass:
Short bolt: Plus 55 degrees
Medium bolt: Plus 65 degrees
Long bolt: Plus 75 degrees

② 20 ft. lbs. plus 70 degrees

③ Lower intake manifold:
1st pass: 27 in. lbs.
2nd pass: 106 in. lbs.
Final pass: 11 ft. lbs.
Upper manifold bolts:
1st pass: 44 in. lbs.
2nd pass: 88 in. lbs.

④ Tighten bolts to 12 ft. lbs.
Retorque to 22 ft. lbs.

⑤ Step 1: 22 ft. lbs.
Step 2:
Short bolt: Plus 55 degrees
Medium bolt: Plus 65 degrees
Long bolt: Plus 75 degrees

⑥ Outer bolts on caps 2-4: 67 ft. lbs.
All others: 74 ft. lbs.

⑦ Tighten all bolts to 20 ft. lbs.
Retorque to 50 ft. lbs.

⑧ All 5 & 6 stud single rear wheels: 110 ft. lbs.
All 8 stud single rear wheels: 120 ft. lbs.
All 8 stud dual rear wheels: 140 ft. lbs.
All 10 stud dual wheels: 175 ft. lbs.

⑨ Step 1: 20 ft. lbs.
Step 2: 50 ft. lbs.
Step 3: 50 ft. lbs.
Step 4: Plus 90-100 degrees

⑩ Outer bolts: 100 ft. lbs.
Inner bolts: 111 ft. lbs.

⑪ Step 1: 22 ft. lbs.
Step 2: 90 degrees
Step 3: 90 degrees,
(except medium length bolts at front and rear)
Step 4: Tighten medium length bolts,
at front and rear an additional 50 degrees

⑫ Inner bolts;
Step 1: 15 ft. lbs.
Step 2: 80 degrees
Side bolts: 18 ft. lbs.
Outer studs:
Step 1: 15 ft. lbs.
Step 2: 51 degrees

⑬ Step 1: 15 ft. lbs.
Step 2: 60 degrees

⑭ Use a new bolt
Step 1: 37 ft. lbs.
Step 2: 140 degrees

⑮ Step 1: 15 ft. lbs.
Step 2: 37 ft. lbs.
Step 3: 74 ft. lbs.

⑯ Step 1: 44 in. lbs.
Step 2: 89 in. lbs.

⑰ Nuts: 39 ft. lbs.
Stud: 16 ft. lbs.

93081CF1

For exhaust manifold replacement procedures, see the model specific sections of this manual

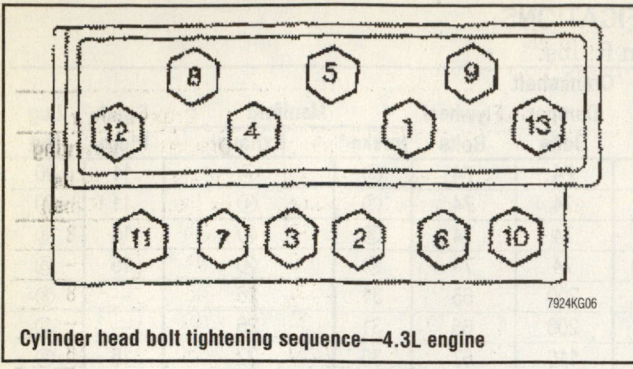

Cylinder head bolt tightening sequence—4.3L engine

7924KG06

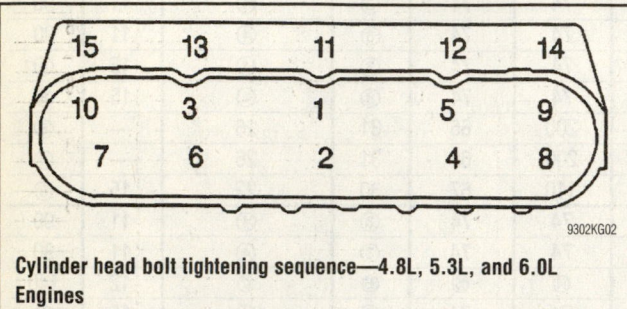

Cylinder head bolt tightening sequence—4.8L, 5.3L, and 6.0L Engines

9302KG02

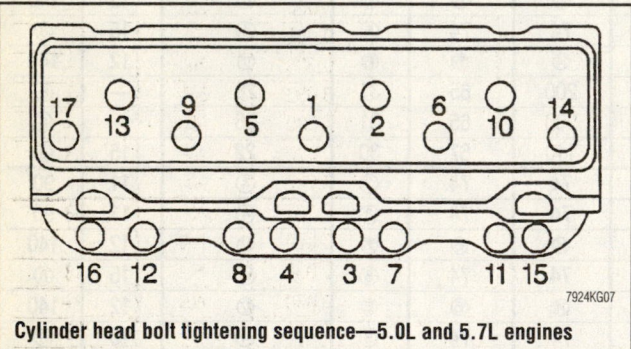

Cylinder head bolt tightening sequence—5.0L and 5.7L engines

7924KG07

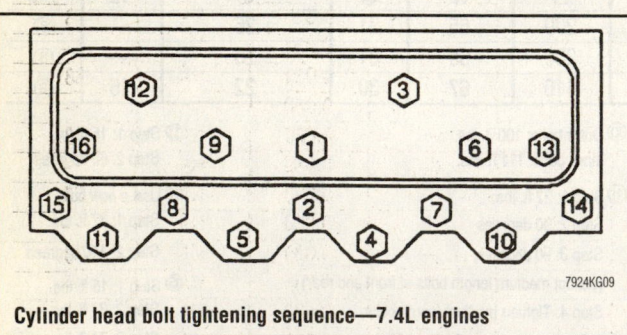

Cylinder head bolt tightening sequence—7.4L engines

7924KG09

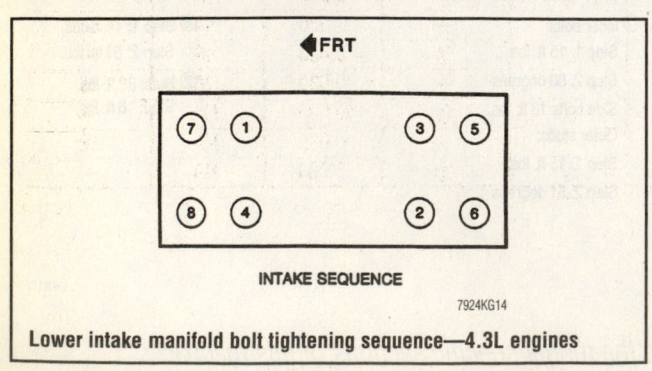

Lower intake manifold bolt tightening sequence—4.3L engines

7924KG14

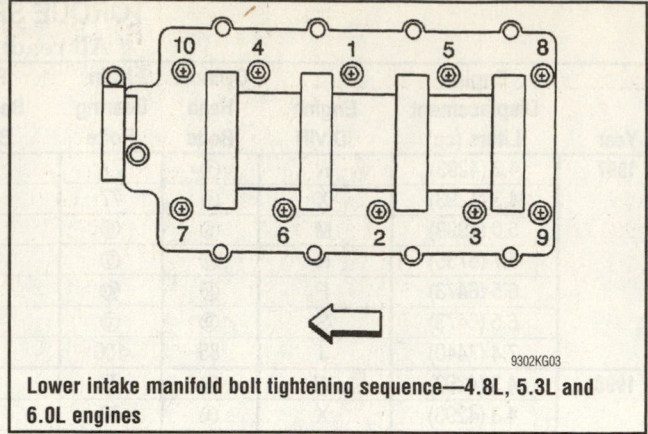

Lower intake manifold bolt tightening sequence—4.8L, 5.3L and 6.0L engines

9302KG03

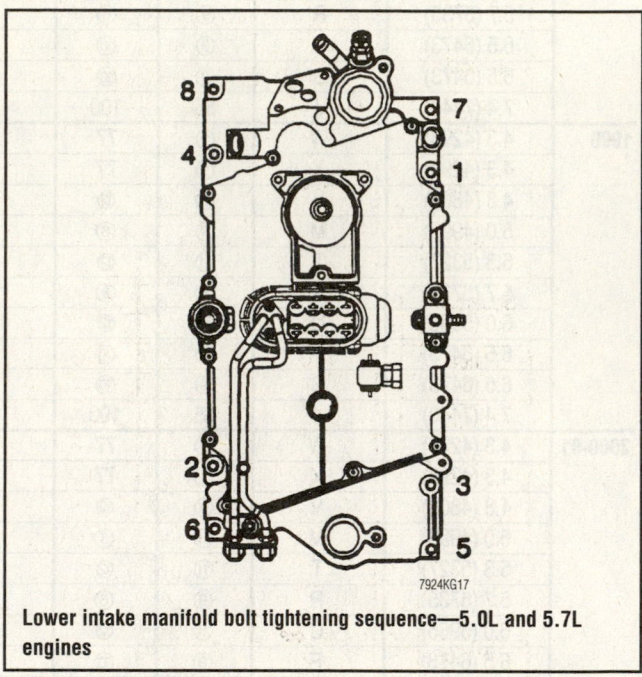

Lower intake manifold bolt tightening sequence—5.0L and 5.7L engines

7924KG17

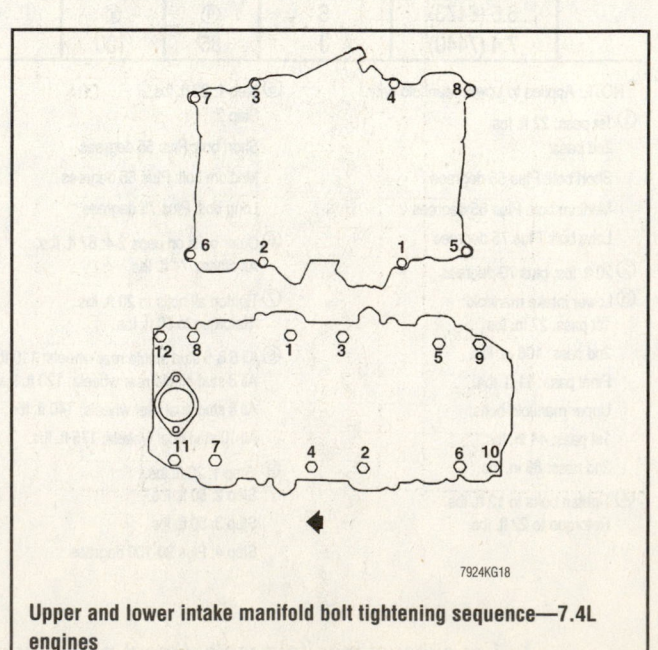

Upper and lower intake manifold bolt tightening sequence—7.4L engines

7924KG18

BRAKE SPECIFICATIONS
All measurements in inches unless noted

Year	Model		Brake Disc Original Thickness	Brake Disc Minimum Thickness	Brake Disc Maximum Runout	Brake Drum Diameter Original Inside Diameter	Brake Drum Diameter Max. Wear Limit	Brake Drum Diameter Maximum Machine Diameter	Minimum Lining Thickness	Brake Caliper Bracket Bolts (ft. lbs.)	Brake Caliper Mounting Bolts (ft. lbs.)
1997	C1500	F	1.250	1.230	0.004	—	—	—	0.030	NA	38
		R	—	—	—	①	②	③	0.030	NA	—
	C2500	F	1.500	1.480	0.004	—	—	—	0.030	NA	38
		R	—	—	—	①	②	③	0.030	NA	—
	C3500	F	1.500	1.480	0.004	—	—	—	0.030	NA	38
		R	—	—	—	①	②	③	0.030	NA	—
	G/P1500	F	④	⑤	0.004	—	—	—	0.030	NA	38
		R	—	—	—	①	②	③	0.030	NA	—
	G/P2500	F	④	⑤	0.004	—	—	—	0.030	NA	38
		R	—	—	—	①	②	③	0.030	NA	—
	G/P3500	F	④	⑤	0.004	—	—	—	0.030	NA	38
		R	—	—	—	①	②	③	0.030	NA	—
	K1500	F	1.500	1.480	0.004	—	—	—	0.030	NA	38
		R	—	—	—	①	②	③	0.030	NA	—
	K2500	F	1.500	1.480	0.004	—	—	—	0.030	NA	38
		R	—	—	—	①	②	③	0.030	NA	—
	K3500	F	1.500	1.480	0.004	—	—	—	0.030	NA	38
		R	—	—	—	③	②	③	0.030	NA	—
	Suburban	F	1.500	1.480	0.004	—	—	—	0.030	NA	38
		R	—	—	—	①	②	③	0.030	NA	—
	Tahoe	F	1.500	1.480	0.004	—	—	—	0.030	NA	38
		R	—	—	—	①	②	③	0.030	NA	—
	Yukon	F	1.500	1.480	0.004	—	—	—	0.030	NA	38
		R	—	—	—	①	②	③	0.030	NA	—
1998	C1500	F	1.250	1.230	0.004	—	—	—	0.030	NA	38
		R	—	—	—	①	②	③	0.030	NA	—
	C2500	F	1.500	1.480	0.004	—	—	—	0.030	NA	38
		R	—	—	—	①	②	③	0.030	NA	—
	C3500	F	1.500	1.480	0.004	—	—	—	0.030	NA	38
		R	—	—	—	①	②	③	0.030	NA	—
	G/P1500	F	④	⑤	0.004	—	—	—	0.030	NA	38
		R	—	—	—	①	②	③	0.030	NA	—
	G/P2500	F	④	⑤	0.004	—	—	—	0.030	NA	38
		R	—	—	—	①	②	③	0.030	NA	—
	G/P3500	F	④	⑤	0.004	—	—	—	0.030	NA	38
		R	—	—	—	①	②	③	0.030	NA	—
	K1500	F	1.500	1.480	0.004	—	—	—	0.030	NA	38
		R	—	—	—	①	②	③	0.030	NA	—
	K2500	F	1.500	1.480	Runout	—	—	—	0.030	NA	38
		R	—	—	—	①	②	③	0.030	NA	—
	K3500	F	1.500	1.480	0.004	—	—	—	0.030	NA	38
		R	—	—	—	①	②	③	0.030	NA	—
	Suburban	F	1.500	1.480	0.004	—	—	—	0.030	NA	38
		R	—	—	—	①	②	③	0.030	NA	—
	Tahoe	F	1.500	1.480	0.004	—	—	—	0.030	NA	38
		R	—	—	—	①	②	③	0.030	NA	—
	Yukon	F	1.500	1.480	0.004	—	—	—	0.030	NA	38
		R	—	—	—	①	②	③	0.030	NA	—

93081CF2

Refer to the model specific sections for cooling system service procedures

BRAKE SPECIFICATIONS
All measurements in inches unless noted

Year	Model		Brake Disc			Brake Drum Diameter			Minimum Lining Thickness	Brake Caliper	
			Original Thickness	Minimum Thickness	Maximum Runout	Original Inside Diameter	Max. Wear Limit	Maximum Machine Diameter		Bracket Bolts (ft. lbs.)	Mounting Bolts (ft. lbs.)
1999	C1500	F	1.250	1.230	0.004	—	—	—	0.030	NA	38
		R	—	—	—	①	②	③	0.030	NA	—
	C2500	F	1.500	1.480	0.004	—	—	—	0.030	NA	38
		R	—	—	—	①	②	③	0.030	NA	—
	C3500	F	1.500	1.480	0.004	—	—	—	0.030	NA	38
		R	—	—	—	①	②	③	0.030	NA	—
	Denali	F	1.500	1.480	0.004	—	—	—	0.030	NA	38
		R	—	—	—	①	②	③	0.030	NA	—
	Envoy	F	1.030	0.965	0.003	—	—	—	0.030	52	⑥
		R	0.787	0.728	0.004	9.50	9.59	9.56	0.030	NA	—
	Escalade	F	1.500	1.480	0.004	—	—	—	0.030	NA	38
		R	—	—	—	①	②	③	0.030	NA	—
	G/P1500	F	④	⑤	0.004	—	—	—	0.030	NA	38
		R	—	—	—	①	②	③	0.030	NA	—
	G/P2500	F	④	⑤	0.004	—	—	—	0.030	NA	38
		R	—	—	—	①	②	③	0.030	NA	—
	G/P3500	F	④	⑤	0.004	—	—	—	0.030	NA	38
		R	—	—	—	①	②	③	0.030	NA	—
	K1500	F	1.500	1.480	0.004	—	—	—	0.030	NA	38
		R	—	—	—	①	②	③	0.030	NA	—
	K2500	F	1.500	1.480	0.004	—	—	—	0.030	NA	38
		R	—	—	—	①	②	③	0.030	NA	—
	K3500	F	1.500	1.480	0.004	—	—	—	0.030	NA	38
		R	—	—	—	①	②	③	0.030	NA	—
	Sierra	F	⑦	⑧	0.005	—	—	—	0.030	NA	80
		R	⑨	⑩	0.005	—	—	—	0.030	NA	⑪
	Silverado	F	⑦	⑧	0.005	—	—	—	0.030	NA	80
		R	⑨	⑩	0.005	—	—	—	0.030	NA	⑪
	Suburban	F	1.500	1.480	0.004	—	—	—	0.030	NA	38
		R	—	—	—	①	②	③	0.030	NA	—
	Tahoe	F	1.500	1.480	0.004	—	—	—	0.030	NA	38
		R	—	—	—	①	②	③	0.030	NA	—
	Yukon	F	1.500	1.480	0.004	—	—	—	0.030	NA	38
		R	—	—	—	①	②	③	0.030	NA	—
2000-01	C1500	F	1.250	1.230	0.004	—	—	—	0.030	NA	38
		R	—	—	—	①	②	③	0.030	NA	—
	C2500	F	1.500	1.480	0.004	—	—	—	0.030	NA	38
		R	—	—	—	①	②	③	0.030	NA	—
	C3500	F	1.500	1.480	0.004	—	—	—	0.030	NA	38
		R	—	—	—	①	②	③	0.030	NA	—
	Denali	F	1.500	1.480	0.004	—	—	—	0.030	NA	38
		R	—	—	—	①	②	③	0.030	NA	—
	Envoy	F	1.030	0.965	0.003	—	—	—	0.030	52	⑥
		R	0.787	0.728	0.004	9.50	9.59	9.56	0.030	NA	—
	Escalade	F	1.500	1.480	0.004	—	—	—	0.030	NA	38
		R	—	—	—	①	②	③	0.030	NA	—
	G/P1500	F	④	⑤	0.004	—	—	—	0.030	NA	38
		R	—	—	—	①	②	③	0.030	NA	—
	G/P2500	F	④	⑤	0.004	—	—	—	0.030	NA	38
		R	—	—	—	①	②	③	0.030	NA	—

93081CF3

BRAKE SPECIFICATIONS
All measurements in inches unless noted

Year	Model		Brake Disc			Brake Drum Diameter				Brake Caliper	
			Original Thickness	Minimum Thickness	Maximum Runout	Original Inside Diameter	Max. Wear Limit	Maximum Machine Diameter	Minimum Lining Thickness	Bracket Bolts (ft. lbs.)	Mounting Bolts (ft. lbs.)
2000-01 Cont,	G/P3500	F	④	⑤	0.004	—	—	—	0.030	NA	38
		R	—	—	—	①	②	③	0.030	NA	—
	K1500	F	1.500	1.480	0.004	—	—	—	0.030	NA	38
		R	—	—	—	①	②	③	0.030	NA	—
	K2500	F	1.500	1.480	0.004	—	—	—	0.030	NA	38
		R	—	—	—	①	②	③	0.030	NA	—
	K3500	F	1.500	1.480	0.004	—	—	—	0.030	NA	38
		R	—	—	—	①	②	③	0.030	NA	—
	Sierra	F	⑦	⑧	0.005	—	—	—	0.030	NA	80
		R	⑨	⑩	0.005	—	—	—	0.030	NA	⑪
	Silverado	F	⑦	⑧	0.005	—	—	—	0.030	NA	80
		R	⑨	⑩	0.005	—	—	—	0.030	NA	⑪
	Suburban	F	1.500	1.480	0.004	—	—	—	0.030	NA	38
		R	—	—	—	①	②	③	0.030	NA	—
	Tahoe	F	1.500	1.480	0.004	—	—	—	0.030	NA	38
		R	—	—	—	①	②	③	0.030	NA	—
	Yukon	F	1.500	1.480	0.004	—	—	—	0.030	NA	38
		R	—	—	—	①	②	③	0.030	NA	—

NA: Not Available

① Available with 1 in., 11.15 in. and 13 in. drums
② 10 in. drum: 10.05
  11.15 in. drum: 11.24
  1 in. drum: 13.09
③ 1 in. drum: 10.09
  11.15 in. drum: 11.21
  1 in. drum: 13.06
④ Available with 1.280 in. and 1.540 in. discs
⑤ 1.2 in. disc: 1.230
  1.5 in. disc: 1.480

⑥ 2WD: 38 ft. lbs.
  4WD: 77 ft. lbs.
⑦ Vacuum: 1.1 in.
  Hydraulic: 1.5 in.
⑧ Vacuum: 1.08 in.
  Hydraulic: 1.44 in.
⑨ Vacuum: 0.787 in.
  Hydraulic: 1.14 in.
⑩ Vacuum: 0.728 in.
  Hydraulic: 1.08 in.

⑪ 15 series: 31 ft. lbs.
  25 series: 80 ft. lbs.

93081CF4

SCHEDULED MAINTENANCE INTERVALS
(GENERAL MOTORS C/K SERIES PICK-UP, DENALI, ESCALADE, SIERRA, SUBURBAN, TAHOE & YUKON—GASOLINE)

TO BE SERVICED	TYPE OF SERVICE	VEHICLE MILEAGE INTERVAL (x1000)															
		7.5	15	22.5	30	37.5	45	52.5	60	67.5	75	82.5	90	97.5	105	112.5	120
Accessory drive belt	S/I								✓								✓
Automatic transmission fluid ①	R	Every 50,000 miles															
Brake system	S/I	✓	✓	✓	✓	✓	✓	✓	✓	✓	✓	✓	✓	✓	✓	✓	✓
Chassis & suspension grease points	L	✓	✓	✓	✓	✓	✓	✓	✓	✓	✓	✓	✓	✓	✓	✓	✓
Cooling fan operation	S/I		✓		✓		✓		✓		✓		✓		✓		✓
CV-joint boots & axle seals	S/I	✓	✓	✓	✓	✓	✓	✓	✓	✓	✓	✓	✓	✓	✓	✓	✓
EGR system	S/I								✓								✓
Engine coolant	R	Every 150,000 miles															
Engine oil & filter	R	✓	✓	✓	✓	✓	✓	✓	✓	✓	✓	✓	✓	✓	✓	✓	✓
EVAP system	S/I								✓								✓
Front wheel bearings ②	S/I & L				✓				✓				✓				✓
Fuel filter	R								✓								✓
Fuel system	S/I								✓								✓
Rear/front axle fluid level	S/I	✓	✓	✓	✓	✓	✓	✓	✓	✓	✓	✓	✓	✓	✓	✓	✓
Rotate tires	S/I	✓	✓	✓	✓	✓	✓	✓	✓	✓	✓	✓	✓	✓	✓	✓	✓
Shields & underhood insulation ①	S/I		✓		✓		✓		✓		✓		✓		✓		✓
Spark plugs	R	Every 100,000 miles															
Spark plug wires	S/I	Every 100,000 miles															

R: Replace   S/I: Inspect and service, if necessary   L: Lubricate

① Vehicles with a GVWR or 8500 lbs. or more only.

② 2-wheel drive models only.

FREQUENT OPERATION MAINTENANCE (SEVERE SERVICE)

If a vehicle is operated under any of the following conditions it is considered severe service:

- Towing a trailer or using a camper or car-top carrier.
- Repeated short trips of less than 5 miles in temperatures below freezing, or trips of less than 10 miles in any temperature.
- Extensive idling or low-speed driving for long distances as in heavy commercial use, such as delivery, taxi or police cars.
- Operating on rough, muddy or salt-covered roads.
- Operating on unpaved or dusty roads.
- Driving in extremely hot (over 90°) conditions.

Engine oil & filter: replace every 3000 miles or 3 months, whichever occurs first.

Chassis and suspension grease points: lubricate every 3000 miles.

Rear/front axle fluid level: inspect every 3000 miles.

Rotate the tires ever 6000 miles.

Brake system components: inspect ever 6000 miles.

Front wheel bearings (2-wheel drive only): clean, inspect and repack every 15,000 miles.

Shields & underhood insulation (vehicles w/GVWR over 8500 lbs. only): inspect every 15,000 miles.

Cooling fan system hoses & connections: inspect every 15,000 miles.

Fuel filter: replace every 30,000 miles.

Air cleaner filter: inspect every 45,000 miles.

Automatic transmission fluid & filter: replace every 50,000 miles.

Accessory drive belt: inspect every 60,000 miles.

Fuel system tank, cap and lines: inspect every 60,000 miles.

EVAP system: inspect every 60,000 miles.

EGR system: inspect every 60,000 miles.

PCV system: inspect every 100,000 miles.

Engine cooling system components: inspect and clean every 150,000 miles.

93081CF5

SCHEDULED MAINTENANCE INTERVALS
(GENERAL MOTORS G/P SERIES VAN, EXPRESS & SAVANA—GASOLINE)

TO BE SERVICED	TYPE OF SERVICE	7.5	15	22.5	30	37.5	45	52.5	60	67.5	75	82.5	90	97.5	105	112.5	120
Accessory drive belt	S/I								✓								✓
Air cleaner filter	R				✓				✓				✓				✓
Automatic transmission fluid ①	R	Every 50,000 miles															
Chassis & suspension grease points	L	✓	✓	✓	✓	✓	✓	✓	✓	✓	✓	✓	✓	✓	✓	✓	✓
CV-joint boots & axle seals	S/I	✓	✓	✓	✓	✓	✓	✓	✓	✓	✓	✓	✓	✓	✓	✓	✓
EGR system	S/I								✓								✓
Engine coolant	R	Every 150,000 miles															
Engine oil & filter	R	✓	✓	✓	✓	✓	✓	✓	✓	✓	✓	✓	✓	✓	✓	✓	✓
EVAP system	S/I								✓								
Front wheel bearings	S/I & L				✓				✓				✓				✓
Fuel filter	R				✓				✓				✓				✓
Fuel system	S/I								✓								✓
PCV system	S/I	Every 100,000 miles															
Rear axle fluid level	S/I	✓	✓	✓	✓	✓	✓	✓	✓	✓	✓	✓	✓	✓	✓	✓	✓
Rotate tires	S/I	✓	✓	✓	✓	✓	✓	✓	✓	✓	✓	✓	✓	✓	✓	✓	✓
Shields & underhood insulation ①	S/I		✓		✓		✓		✓		✓		✓		✓		✓
Spark plugs	R	Every 100,000 miles															
Spark plug wires	S/I	Every 100,000 miles															

R: Replace   S/I: Inspect and service, if necessary   L: Lubricate
① Vehicles with a GVWR or 8500 lbs. or more only.

FREQUENT OPERATION MAINTENANCE (SEVERE SERVICE)
If a vehicle is operated under any of the following conditions it is considered severe service:
- Towing a trailer or using a camper or car-top carrier.
- Repeated short trips of less than 5 miles in temperatures below freezing, or trips of less than 10 miles in any temperature.
- Extensive idling or low-speed driving for long distances as in heavy commercial use, such as delivery, taxi or police cars.
- Operating on rough, muddy or salt-covered roads.
- Operating on unpaved or dusty roads.
- Driving in extremely hot (over 90°) conditions.

Engine oil & filter: replace every 3000 miles or 3 months, whichever occurs first.
Chassis and suspension grease points: lubricate every 3000 miles.
Rear/front axle fluid level: inspect every 3000 miles.
Rotate the tires ever 6000 miles.
Brake system components: inspect ever 6000 miles.
Front wheel bearings (2-wheel drive only): clean, inspect and repack every 15,000 miles.
Shields & underhood insulation (vehicles w/GVWR over 8500 lbs. Only): inspect every 15,000 miles
Cooling fan system hoses & connections: inspect every 15,000 miles.
Fuel filter: replace every 30,000 miles.
Air cleaner filter: inspect every 45,000 miles.
Automatic transmission fluid & filter: replace every 50,000 miles.
Accessory drive belt: inspect every 60,000 miles.
Fuel system tank, cap and lines: inspect every 60,000 miles.
EVAP system: inspect every 60,000 miles.
EGR system: inspect every 60,000 miles.
PCV system: inspect every 100,000 miles.
Engine cooling system components: inspect and clean every 150,000 miles.

93081CF6

Timing chain and gear service is covered in the model specific sections of this manual

SCHEDULED MAINTENANCE INTERVALS
(GENERAL MOTORS G/P SERIES VAN, EXPRESS & SAVANA—DIESEL)

TO BE SERVICED	TYPE OF SERVICE	5	10	15	20	25	30	35	40	45	50	55	60	65	70	75	80	85	90	95	100	105	110	115	120
Air cleaner filter	R						✓						✓						✓						✓
Air intake system	S/I		✓		✓		✓		✓		✓		✓		✓		✓		✓		✓		✓		✓
Automatic transmission fluid ①	R										✓										✓				
Chassis & suspension grease points	L	✓	✓	✓	✓	✓	✓	✓	✓	✓	✓	✓	✓	✓	✓	✓	✓	✓	✓	✓	✓	✓	✓	✓	✓
Cooling fan, ducts & hoses	S/I												✓												✓
Crankcase depression regulator valve system hoses	S/I												✓												✓
CV-joint boots & axle seals	S/I	✓	✓	✓	✓	✓	✓	✓	✓	✓	✓	✓	✓	✓	✓	✓	✓	✓	✓	✓	✓	✓	✓	✓	✓
EGR system ②	S/I												✓												
Engine coolant	R	Every 100,000 miles																							
Engine cooling system hoses & radiator	S/I & C	Initially at 100,000 miles, then every 50,000 miles																							
Engine oil & filter ③	R	✓	✓	✓	✓	✓	✓	✓	✓	✓	✓	✓	✓	✓	✓	✓	✓	✓	✓	✓	✓	✓	✓	✓	✓
Front wheel bearings	S/I & L						✓						✓						✓						✓
Fuel filter	R												✓												✓
Rear axle fluid level	S/I	✓	✓	✓	✓	✓	✓	✓	✓	✓	✓	✓	✓	✓	✓	✓	✓	✓	✓	✓	✓	✓	✓	✓	✓
Rotate tires	S/I	✓	✓	✓	✓	✓	✓	✓	✓	✓	✓	✓	✓	✓	✓	✓	✓	✓	✓	✓	✓	✓	✓	✓	✓
Shields & underhood insulation	S/I						✓						✓						✓						✓

R: Replace   S/I: Inspect and service, if necessary   L: Lubricate   C: Clean

① For vehicles with a GVWR of 8500 lbs. or more.

② If equipped.

③ Perform at the mileage specified or every 3 months, whichever occurs first.

FREQUENT OPERATION MAINTENANCE (SEVERE SERVICE)

If a vehicle is operated under any of the following conditions it is considered severe service:

- Towing a trailer or using a camper or car-top carrier.
- Repeated short trips of less than 5 miles in temperatures below freezing, or trips of less than 10 miles in any temperature.
- Extensive idling or low-speed driving for long distances as in heavy commercial use, such as delivery, taxi or police cars.
- Operating on rough, muddy or salt-covered roads.
- Operating on unpaved or dusty roads.
- Driving in extremely hot (over 90°) conditions.

Engine oil & filter: replace every 2500 miles.

Chassis and suspension grease points: lubricate every 2500 miles.

Rear axle fluid level: inspect every 2500 miles.

CV-joint boots and axle seals: inspect for leakage every 2500 miles.

Rotate tires: every 7500 miles.

Air cleaner filter: inspect every 15,000 miles.

Front wheel bearings (2-wheel drive only): clean, inspect and repack every 15,000 miles.

Automatic transmission fluid & filter: replace every 50,000 miles.

SCHEDULED MAINTENANCE INTERVALS
GENERAL MOTORS CORPORATION
C/K SERIES PICK-UP, DENALI, ESCLADE, SIERRA, SUBURBAN, TAHOE & YUKON

The following should be used as a guide when determining the amount of work required for a particular service. In estimating how long a particular Scheduled Maintenance Service should take, please observe the following:

- Labor Time is time based on field research and data supplied by the vehicle manufacturer.
- Labor time operations are given in hours and tenths of an hour.
- All labor operations are to be used as a guide.

Mechanic Skill Level Codes:
(A) PRECISION: Highly skilled with multiple certification.
(B) GENERAL: Normally skilled with certification.
(C) MAINTENANCE: Semi-skilled working on certification.

	LABOR TIME
5000 Mile Service (B)	
All Models	2.2
w/4WD add	.1
7500 Mile Service (B)	
All Models	1.9
w/4WD add	.1
10000 Mile Service (B)	
All Models	2.1
w/4WD add	.1
12000 Mile Service (B)	
All Models	1.6
15000 Mile Service (B)	
Gasoline	1.6
Diesel	2.3
w/4WD add	.1
20000 Mile Service (B)	
All Models	2.3
w/4WD add	.1
22500 Mile Service (B)	
All Models	1.9
w/4WD add	.1
25000 Mile Service (B)	
All Models	1.9
w/4WD add	.1
30000 Mile Service (B)	
Gasoline	4.1
Diesel	3.0
w/AT add	.5
w/4WD add	.1

	LABOR TIME
35000 Mile Service (B)	
All Models	1.9
w/4WD add	.1
37500 Mile Service (B)	
All Models	2.1
w/4WD add	.1
40000 Mile Service (B)	
All Models	2.3
w/4WD add	.1
45000 Mile Service (B)	
Gasoline	1.7
Diesel	1.9
w/4WD add	.1
50000 Mile Service (B)	
All Models	2.5
w/4WD add	.1
52500 Mile Service (B)	
All Models	2.0
w/4WD add	.1
55000 Mile Service (B)	
All Models	2.1
w/4WD add	.1
60000 Mile Service (B)	
Gasoline	4.5
Diesel	3.5
w/AT add	.5
w/4WD add	.1
65000 Mile Service (B)	
All Models	2.0
w/4WD add	.1

	LABOR TIME
67500 Mile Service (B)	
All Models	2.0
w/4WD add	.1
75000 Mile Service (B)	
All Models	1.5
w/4WD add	.1
82500 Mile Service (B)	
All Models	2.0
w/4WD add	.1
90000 Mile Service (B)	
All Models	4.3
w/AT add	.5
w/4WD add	.1
97500 Mile Service (B)	
All Models	1.9
w/4WD add	.1
105000 Mile Service (B)	
Gasoline	1.7
Diesel	1.9
w/4WD add	.1
112500 Mile Service (B)	
All Models	2.0
w/4WD add	.1
120000 Mile Service (B)	
Gasoline	4.5
Diesel	3.5
w/AT add	.5
w/4WD add	.1

93081CF8

Ignition system service is covered in the model specific sections of this manual

SCHEDULED MAINTENANCE INTERVALS
GENERAL MOTORS CORPORATION
G/P VAN, EXPRESS & SAVANA

The following should be used as a guide when determining the amount of work required for a particular service. In estimating how long a particular Scheduled Maintenance Service should take, please observe the following:

- Labor Time is time based on field research and data supplied by the vehicle manufacturer.
- Labor time operations are given in hours and tenths of an hour.
- All labor operations are to be used as a guide.

Mechanic Skill Level Codes:
(A) PRECISION: Highly skilled with multiple certification.
(B) GENERAL: Normally skilled with certification.
(C) MAINTENANCE: Semi-skilled working on certification.

	LABOR TIME
5000 Mile Service (B)	
All Models	2.3
7500 Mile Service (B)	
All Models	2.1
10000 Mile Service (B)	
All Models	2.1
15000 Mile Service (B)	
All Models	
Gasoline	1.6
Diesel	2.3
20000 Mile Service (B)	
All Models	2.3
22500 Mile Service (B)	
All Models	1.9
25000 Mile Service (B)	
All Models	2.1
30000 Mile Service (B)	
All Models	
Gasoline	4.2
Diesel	2.8
w/AT add	.5

	LABOR TIME
35000 Mile Service (B)	
All Models	1.9
37500 Mile Service (B)	
All Models	2.1
40000 Mile Service (B)	
All Models	2.5
45000 Mile Service (B)	
All Models	
Gasoline	1.5
Diesel	1.9
50000 Mile Service (B)	
All Models	2.3
52500 Mile Service (B)	
All Models	2.1
55000 Mile Service (B)	
All Models	2.0
60000 Mile Service (B)	
All Models	
Gasoline	4.6
Diesel	3.6
w/AT add	.5
65000 Mile Service (B)	
All Models	2.0

	LABOR TIME
67500 Mile Service (B)	
All Models	1.9
75000 Mile Service (B)	
All Models	1.6
82500 Mile Service (B)	
All Models	2.0
90000 Mile Service (B)	
All Models	4.2
w/AT add	.5
97500 Mile Service (B)	
All Models	2.1
105000 Mile Service (B)	
All Models	
Gasoline	1.5
Diesel	1.9
112500 Mile Service (B)	
All Models	2.1
120000 Mile Service (B)	
All Models	
Gasoline	4.6
Diesel	3.6
w/AT add	.5

93081CF9

SCHEDULED MAINTENANCE INTERVALS
(1999-01 Chevrolet Silverado, GMC Sierra)
(GASOLINE LIGHT DUTY EMISSIONS)

TO BE SERVICED	TYPE OF SERVICE	VEHICLE MILEAGE INTERVAL (x1000)														
		7.5	15	22.5	30	37.5	45	52.5	60	67.5	75	82.5	90	97.5	100	150
Engine oil & filter	R	✓	✓	✓	✓	✓	✓	✓	✓	✓	✓	✓	✓	✓		
Chassis lubrication	S/I	✓	✓	✓	✓	✓	✓	✓	✓	✓	✓	✓	✓	✓		
Oil Life Monitor	S/I	✓	✓	✓	✓	✓	✓	✓	✓	✓	✓	✓	✓	✓		
Front/Rear Axle Fluid	S/I ①	✓	✓	✓	✓	✓	✓	✓	✓	✓	✓	✓	✓	✓		
CV joints & axle seals	S/I	✓	✓	✓	✓	✓	✓	✓	✓	✓	✓	✓	✓	✓		
Rotate tires	S/I	✓	✓	✓	✓	✓	✓	✓	✓	✓	✓	✓	✓	✓		
Passenger Compartment Air Filter	R		✓		✓		✓		✓		✓		✓			
Underhood Sound Shield	S/I	✓		✓		✓		✓		✓		✓		✓		
Fuel filter	R				✓				✓				✓			
Automatic transmission fluid & filter	R ②														✓	
Engine accessory drive belt	S/I							✓								
Fuel Tank, cap and lines	S/I								✓							
EGR System	S/I								✓							
EVAP System	S/I								✓							
Spark plugs	R														✓	
Spark Plug Wires	S/I														✓	
PCV Valve	S/I														✓	
Coolant	R															✓
Air cleaner filter	R				✓				✓				✓			

R: Replace   S/I: Service or Inspect

① If the vehicle is used for continuous trailer towing, change the fluid in the rear axle after the first 500 miles, then, every 7,500 miles

② Vehicles over 8,600 lbs. GVWR: every 50,000 miles

FREQUENT OPERATION MAINTENANCE (SEVERE SERVICE)

If a vehicle is operated under any of the following conditions it is considered severe service:

- Extremely dusty areas.
- 50% or more of the vehicle operation is in 32°C (90°F) or higher temperatures, or constant operation in temperatures below 0°C (32°F).
- Prolonged idling (vehicle operation in stop and go traffic.
- Frequent short running periods (engine does not warm to normal operating temperatures).
- Police, taxi, delivery usage or trailer towing usage.

Oil & oil filter change: change every 3000 miles

Lubricate chassis every 3000 miles

Drive axle: check every 3000 miles

Rotate tires every 6000 miles

Air cleaner filter: change every 24,000 miles

93081CXY

SCHEDULED MAINTENANCE INTERVALS
GENERAL MOTORS CORPORATION
1999-01 CHEVROLET SILVERADO
1999-01 GMC SIERRA

The following should be used as a guide when determining the amount of work required for a particular service.
In estimating how long a particular Scheduled Maintenance Service should take, please observe the following:

- Labor Time is time based on field research and data supplied by the vehicle manufacturer.
- Labor time operations are given in hours and tenths of an hour.
- All labor operations are to be used as a guide.

Mechanic Skill Level Codes:
(A) PRECISION: Highly skilled with multiple certification.
(B) GENERAL: Normally skilled with certification.
(C) MAINTENANCE: Semi-skilled working on certification.

	LABOR TIME		LABOR TIME		LABOR TIME
7500 Mile Service (B)		**45000 Mile Service (B)**		**82500 Mile Service (B)**	
All Models	1.9	All Models	1.5	All Models	1.9
w/4WD add	.1	w/4WD add	.1	w/4WD add	.1
15000 Mile Service (B)		**52500 Mile Service (B)**		**90000 Mile Service (B)**	
Gasoline	1.6	All Models	1.9	All Models	2.6
w/4WD add	.1	w/4WD add	.1	w/4WD add	.1
22500 Mile Service (B)		**60000 Mile Service (B)**		**97500 Mile Service (B)**	
All Models	1.9	All Models	3.5	All Models	1.9
w/4WD add	.1	w/4WD add	.1	w/4WD add	.1
30000 Mile Service (B)		**67500 Mile Service (B)**		**100000 Mile Service (B)**	
All Models	2.6	All Models	1.9	All Models	2.9
w/4WD add	.1	w/4WD add	.1	w/4WD add	.1
37500 Mile Service (B)		**75000 Mile Service (B)**		**150000 Mile Service (B)**	
All Models	1.9	All Models	1.5	All Models	1.2
w/4WD add	.1	w/4WD add	.1		

93081CXZ

GENERAL MOTORS
Chevrolet Astro • Blazer • S-10 Pick-up GMC • Envoy • Jimmy • Safari • Sonoma Oldsmobile Bravada

ENGINE AND VEHICLE IDENTIFICATION

Code ①	Liters (cc)	Cu. In.	Cyl.	Fuel Sys.	Engine Type	Eng. Mfg.
4	2.2 (2189)	134	4	MFI	OHV	CPC
W	4.3 (4293)	262	6	MFI	OHV	CPC
X	4.3 (4293)	262	6	MFI	OHV	CPC

Code ②	Year
V	1997
W	1998
X	1999
Y	2000
1	2001

CPC: Chevrolet/Pontiac/Canada

MFI: Multiport Fuel Injection

OHV: Overhead Valve

① 8th position of VIN

② 10th position of VIN

93081CF0

GENERAL ENGINE SPECIFICATIONS

Year	Model	Engine Displacement Liters (cc)	Engine Series (ID/VIN)	Fuel System	Net Horsepower @ rpm	Net Torque @ rpm (ft. lbs.)	Bore x Stroke (in.)	Compression Ratio	Oil Pressure @ rpm
1997	Astro/Safari	4.3 (4293)	W	MFI	191@4500	260@3600	4.00x3.48	9.2:1	18@2000
	Blazer/Jimmy/Bravada	4.3 (4293)	W	MFI	190@4400	250@2800	4.00x3.48	9.2:1	18@2000
	S10 Pick-up/Sonoma	2.2 (2189)	4	MFI	118@5200	130@2800	3.50x3.46	9.0:1	56@3000
	S10 Pick-up/Sonoma	4.3 (4293)	W	MFI	①	②	4.00x3.48	9.2:1	18@2000
	S10 Pick-up/Sonoma	4.3 (4293)	X	MFI	③	④	4.00x3.48	9.2:1	18@2000
1998	Astro/Safari	4.3 (4293)	W	MFI	190@4400	250@2800	4.00x3.48	9.2:1	18@2000
	Blazer/Jimmy/Bravada/Envoy	4.3 (4293)	W	MFI	190@4400	250@2800	4.00x3.48	9.2:1	18@2000
	S10 Pick-up/Sonoma	2.2 (2189)	4	MFI	118@5200	130@2800	3.50x3.46	9.0:1	56@3000
	S10 Pick-up/Sonoma	4.3 (4293)	W	MFI	①	②	4.00x3.48	9.2:1	18@2000
	S10 Pick-up/Sonoma	4.3 (4293)	X	MFI	③	④	4.00x3.48	9.2:1	18@2000
1999	Astro/Safari	4.3 (4293)	W	MFI	190@4400	250@2800	4.00x3.48	9.2:1	18@2000
	Blazer/Jimmy/Bravada/Envoy	4.3 (4293)	W	MFI	190@4400	250@2800	4.00x3.48	9.2:1	18@2000
	S10 Pick-up/Sonoma	2.2 (2189)	4	MFI	120@5000	140@3600	3.50x3.46	9.0:1	56@3000
	S10 Pick-up/Sonoma	4.3 (4293)	W	MFI	①	②	4.00x3.48	9.2:1	18@2000
	S10 Pick-up/Sonoma	4.3 (4293)	X	MFI	③	④	4.00x3.48	9.2:1	18@2000
2000-01	Astro/Safari	4.3 (4293)	W	MFI	190@4400	250@2800	4.00x3.48	9.2:1	18@2000
	S10 Pick-up/Sonoma	4.3 (4293)	W	MFI	190@4400	250@2800	4.00x3.48	9.2:1	18@2000
	S10 Pick-up/Sonoma	2.2 (2189)	4	MFI	120@5000	140@3600	3.50x3.46	9.0:1	56@3000
	S10 Pick-up/Sonoma	4.3 (4293)	W	MFI	①	②	4.00x3.48	9.2:1	18@2000

MFI - Multi-port Fuel Injection

① 2WD: 180@4400   4WD: 190@4400

② 2WD: 245@2800   4WD: 250@2800

③ 2WD: 175@4400   4WD: 180@4400

④ 2WD: 240@2800   4WD: 245@2800

93081CG1

Refer to the model specific sections for engine mechanical service procedures

ENGINE TUNE-UP SPECIFICATIONS

Year	Engine Displacement Liters (cc)	Engine ID/VIN	Spark Plug Gap (in.)	Ignition Timing (deg.) MT	Ignition Timing (deg.) AT	Fuel Pump (psi)	Idle Speed (rpm) MT	Idle Speed (rpm) AT	Valve Clearance Intake	Valve Clearance Exhaust
1997	2.2 (2189)	4	0.060	①	①	41-47	④	④	HYD	HYD
	4.3 (4293)	W	0.060	③	③	58-64 ④	600	625	HYD	HYD
	4.3 (4293)	X	0.060	③	③	41-47	④	④	HYD	HYD
1998	2.2 (2189)	4	0.060	①	①	41-47	④	④	HYD	HYD
	4.3 (4293)	W	0.060	③	③	58-64 ④	600	625	HYD	HYD
	4.3 (4293)	X	0.060	③	③	41-47	④	④	HYD	HYD
1999	2.2 (2189)	4	0.060	①	①	41-47	④	④	HYD	HYD
	4.3 (4293)	W	0.060	③	③	58-64 ④	600	625	HYD	HYD
	4.3 (4293)	X	0.060	③	③	41-47	④	④	HYD	HYD
2000-01	2.2 (2189)	4	0.060	①	①	41-47	④	④	HYD	HYD
	4.3 (4293)	W	0.060	③	③	58-64 ④	600	625	HYD	HYD
	4.3 (4293)	X	0.060	③	③	41-47	④	④	HYD	HYD

NOTE: The Vehicle Emission Control Information label often reflects specification changes made during production. The label figures must be used if they differ from those in this chart.

Hyd.: Hydraulic

① Distributorless ignition, cannot be adjusted

② Idle speed is maintained by the PCM

③ Refer to underfood label for exact setting. On most models, periodic ignition timing adjustments are not necessary.

④ With key on and engine off.

93081CG2

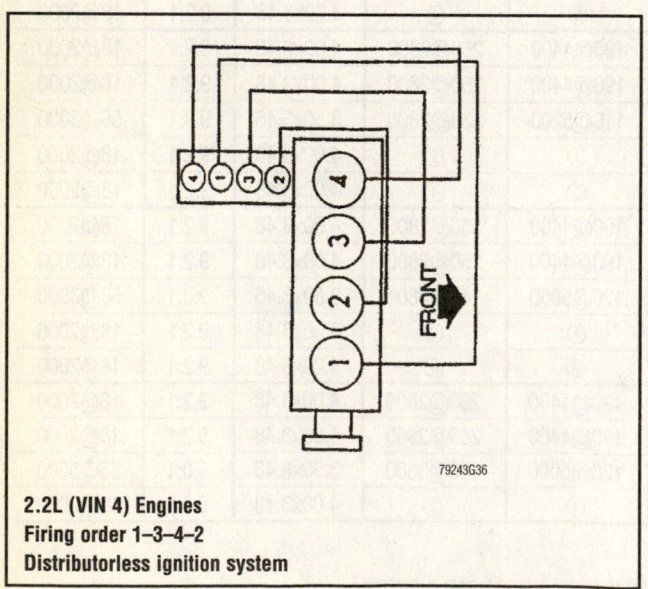

2.2L (VIN 4) Engines
Firing order 1–3–4–2
Distributorless ignition system

79243G36

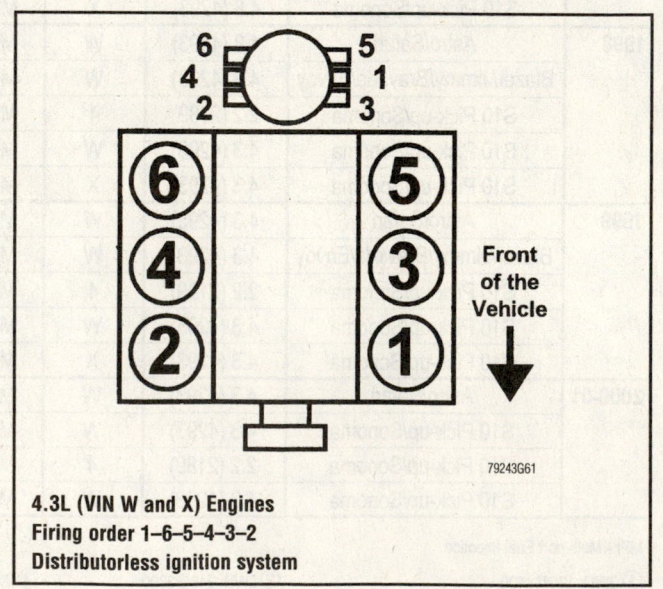

4.3L (VIN W and X) Engines
Firing order 1–6–5–4–3–2
Distributorless ignition system

79243G61

CAPACITIES

Year	Model	Engine Displacement Liters (cc)	Engine ID/VIN	Engine Oil with Filter (qts.)	Transmission (pts.) 5-Spd	Transmission (pts.) Auto. ①	Transfer Case (pts.)	Drive Axle Front (pts.)	Drive Axle Rear (pts.)	Fuel Tank (gal.)	Cooling System (qts.)
1997	Astro/Safari	4.3 (4293)	W	5.0	—	10.0	3.0	2.6	3.8	27.0	14.3 ②
	Blazer/Jimmy/Bravada	4.3 (4293)	W	5.0	4.4	10.0	2.6	2.6	3.9	18.0 ③	11.9
	S10 Pick-up/Sonoma	2.2 (2189)	4	4.0	4.4	10.0	—	—	3.9	19.0	11.5
	S10 Pick-up/Sonoma	4.3 (4293)	W	5.0	4.4	10.0	2.6	2.6	3.9	19.0	11.9
	S10 Pick-up/Sonoma	4.3 (4293)	X	5.0	4.4	10.0	2.6	2.6	3.9	19.0	11.9
1998	Astro/Safari	4.3 (4293)	W	5.0	—	10.0	3.0	2.6	3.8	27.0	14.3 ②
	Blazer/Jimmy/Bravada/Envoy	4.3 (4293)	W	5.0	4.4	11.0	④	3.0	3.9	⑤	12.1
	S10 Pick-up/Sonoma	2.2 (2189)	4	4.0	4.4	11.0	—	—	3.9	⑤	11.5
	S10 Pick-up/Sonoma	4.3 (4293)	W	5.0	4.4	11.0	④	3.0	3.9	⑤	12.1
	S10 Pick-up/Sonoma	4.3 (4293)	X	5.0	4.4	11.0	④	3.0	3.9	⑤	12.1
1999	Astro/Safari	4.3 (4293)	W	5.0	—	10.0	3.0	2.6	3.8	27.0	14.3 ②
	Blazer/Jimmy/Bravada/Envoy	4.3 (4293)	W	5.0	4.4	11.0	④	3.0	3.9	⑤	12.1
	S10 Pick-up/Sonoma	2.2 (2189)	4	4.0	4.4	11.0	—	—	3.9	⑤	11.5
	S10 Pick-up/Sonoma	4.3 (4293)	W	5.0	4.4	11.0	④	3.0	3.9	⑤	12.1
	S10 Pick-up/Sonoma	4.3 (4293)	X	5.0	4.4	11.0	④	3.0	3.9	⑤	12.1
2000-01	Astro/Safari	4.3 (4293)	W	5.0	—	10.0	3.0	2.6	3.8	27.0	14.3 ②
	S10 Pick-up/Sonoma	4.3 (4293)	W	5.0	4.4	11.0	④	3.0	3.9	⑤	12.1
	S10 Pick-up/Sonoma	2.2 (2189)	4	4.0	4.4	11.0	—	—	3.9	⑤	11.5
	S10 Pick-up/Sonoma	4.3 (4293)	W	5.0	4.4	11.0	④	3.0	3.9	⑤	12.1

Note: All capacities are approximate. Add fluid gradually and check to be sure a proper fluid level is obtained.

① Specifications are for pan removal, complete overhaul is usually double.

② 16.5 quarts w/ rear heater

③ Spec is for 4-door utility, 2-door is 19.0 gallons

④ Capacity varies w/ Transfer Case:

New Venture Gear 136: 4.86 pint

New Venture Gear 233: 2.5 pints

New Venture Gear 236: 4.6 pints

⑤ Steel tank: 19.0 gallons

Plastic tank: 18.0 gallons

93081CG3

Refer to the model specific sections for fuel system service procedures

VALVE SPECIFICATIONS

Year	Engine Displacement Liters (cc)	Engine ID/VIN	Seat Angle (deg.)	Face Angle (deg.)	Spring Test Pressure (lbs. @ in.)	Spring Installed Height (in.)	Stem-to-Guide Clearance (in.)		Stem Diameter (in.)	
							Intake	Exhaust	Intake	Exhaust
1997	2.2 (2189)	4	46	45	228@1.28	1.71	0.0010-0.0020	0.0010-0.0030	NA	NA
	4.3 (4293)	W	46	45	187-203@1.27	1.69-1.71	0.0010	0.0020	NA	NA
	4.3 (4293)	X	46	45	187-203@1.27	1.69-1.71	0.0010	0.0020	NA	NA
1998	2.2 (2189)	4	46	45	228@1.28	1.71	0.0010-0.0020	0.0010-0.0030	NA	NA
	4.3 (4293)	W	46	45	187-203@1.27	1.69-1.71	0.0010	0.0020	NA	NA
	4.3 (4293)	X	46	45	187-203@1.27	1.69-1.71	0.0010	0.0020	NA	NA
1999	2.2 (2189)	4	46	45	228@1.28	1.71	0.0010-0.0020	0.0010-0.0030	NA	NA
	4.3 (4293)	W	46	45	187-203@1.27	1.69-1.71	0.0010	0.0020	NA	NA
	4.3 (4293)	X	46	45	187-203@1.27	1.69-1.71	0.0010	0.0020	NA	NA
2000-01	2.2 (2189)	4	46	45	228@1.28	1.71	0.0010-0.0020	0.0010-0.0030	NA	NA
	4.3 (4293)	W	46	45	187-203@1.27	1.69-1.71	0.0010	0.0020	NA	NA
	4.3 (4293)	X	46	45	187-203@1.27	1.69-1.71	0.0010	0.0020	NA	NA

NA: Not Available

93081CG4

CRANKSHAFT AND CONNECTING ROD SPECIFICATIONS

All measurements are given in inches.

Year	Engine Displacement Liters (cc)	Engine ID/VIN	Crankshaft				Connecting Rod		
			Main Brg. Journal Dia.	Main Brg. Oil Clearance	Shaft End-play	Thrust on No.	Journal Diameter	Oil Clearance	Side Clearance
1997	2.2 (2189)	4	2.4945-2.4954	0.0006-0.0019	0.0020-0.0070	4	1.9983-1.9994	0.0010-0.0031	0.0039-0.0149
	4.3 (4293)	W	①	②	0.0020-0.0070	4	2.2487-2.2497	0.0013-0.0035	0.0060-0.0140
	4.3 (4293)	X	③	②	0.0020-0.0060	4	2.2487-2.2497	0.0013-0.0035	0.0060-0.0140
1998	2.2 (2189)	4	2.4945-2.4954	0.0006-0.0019	0.0020-0.0070	4	1.9983-1.9994	0.0010-0.0031	0.0039-0.0149
	4.3 (4293)	W	①	②	0.0020-0.0070	4	2.2487-2.2497	0.0013-0.0035	0.0060-0.0140
	4.3 (4293)	X	③	②	0.0020-0.0060	4	2.2487-2.2497	0.0013-0.0035	0.0060-0.0140
1999	2.2 (2189)	4	2.4945-2.4954	0.0006-0.0019	0.0020-0.0070	4	1.9983-1.9994	0.0010-0.0031	0.0039-0.0149
	4.3 (4293)	W	①	②	0.0020-0.0070	4	2.2487-2.2497	0.0013-0.0035	0.0060-0.0140
	4.3 (4293)	X	③	②	0.0020-0.0060	4	2.2487-2.2497	0.0013-0.0035	0.0060-0.0140
2000-01	2.2 (2189)	4	2.4945-2.4954	0.0006-0.0019	0.0020-0.0070	4	1.9983-1.9994	0.0010-0.0031	0.0039-0.0149
	4.3 (4293)	W	①	②	0.0020-0.0070	4	2.2487-2.2497	0.0013-0.0035	0.0060-0.0140
	4.3 (4293)	X	③	②	0.0020-0.0060	4	2.2487-2.2497	0.0013-0.0035	0.0060-0.0140

① No. 1: 2.4488-2.4495
Nos. 2, 3: 2.4485-2.4494
No. 4: 2.4480-2.4489

② No. 1: 0.0008-0.0020
Nos. 2, 3: 0.0011-0.0023
No. 4: 0.0017-0.0032

③ No. 1: 2.4484-2.4493
Nos. 2, 3: 2.4481-2.4490
No. 4: 2.4479-2.4488

93081CG5

Refer to the model specific sections for engine electrical system service procedures

PISTON AND RING SPECIFICATIONS
All measurements are given in inches.

Year	Engine Displacement Liters (cc)	Engine ID/VIN	Piston Clearance	Ring Gap			Ring Side Clearance		
				Top Compression	Bottom Compression	Oil Control	Top Compression	Bottom Compression	Oil Control
1997	2.2 (2189)	4	0.0007-0.0017	0.010-0.020	0.010-0.020	0.010-0.03	0.0019-0.0027	0.0019-0.0027	0.0019-0.0082
	4.3 (4293)	W	0.0007-0.0017	0.010-0.030	0.018-0.026	0.065 Max.	0.0042 Max.	0.0042 Max.	0.0020-0.0070
	4.3 (4293)	X	0.0007-0.0017	0.010-0.030	0.018-0.026	0.065 Max.	0.0042 Max.	0.0042 Max.	0.0020-0.0070
1998	2.2 (2189)	4	0.0007-0.0017	0.010-0.020	0.010-0.020	0.010-0.03	0.0019-0.0027	0.0019-0.0027	0.0019-0.0082
	4.3 (4293)	W	0.0007-0.0017	0.010-0.030	0.018-0.026	0.065 Max.	0.0042 Max.	0.0042 Max.	0.0020-0.0070
	4.3 (4293)	X	0.0007-0.0017	0.010-0.030	0.018-0.026	0.065 Max.	0.0042 Max.	0.0042 Max.	0.0020-0.0070
1999	2.2 (2189)	4	0.0007-0.0017	0.010-0.020	0.010-0.020	0.010-0.03	0.0019-0.0027	0.0019-0.0027	0.0019-0.0082
	4.3 (4293)	W	0.0007-0.0017	0.010-0.030	0.018-0.026	0.065 Max.	0.0042 Max.	0.0042 Max.	0.0020-0.0070
	4.3 (4293)	X	0.0007-0.0017	0.010-0.030	0.018-0.026	0.065 Max.	0.0042 Max.	0.0042 Max.	0.0020-0.0070
2000-01	2.2 (2189)	4	0.0007-0.0017	0.010-0.020	0.010-0.020	0.010-0.03	0.0019-0.0027	0.0019-0.0027	0.0019-0.0082
	4.3 (4293)	W	0.0007-0.0017	0.010-0.030	0.018-0.026	0.065 Max.	0.0042 Max.	0.0042 Max.	0.0020-0.0070
	4.3 (4293)	X	0.0007-0.0017	0.010-0.030	0.018-0.026	0.065 Max.	0.0042 Max.	0.0042 Max.	0.0020-0.0070

93081CG6

TORQUE SPECIFICATIONS

All readings in ft. lbs.

Year	Engine Displacement Liters (cc)	Engine ID/VIN	Cylinder Head Bolts	Main Bearing Bolts	Rod Bearing Bolts	Crankshaft Damper Bolts	Flywheel Bolts	Manifold Intake *	Manifold Exhaust	Spark Plugs	Lug Nut
1997	2.2 (2189)	4	①	70	38	77	55	②	10	11	100
	4.3 (4293)	W	③	77	④	74	74	⑤	⑥	11	90
	4.3 (4293)	X	③	77	④	74	74	⑤	⑥	11	90
1998	2.2 (2189)	4	①	70	38	77	55	②	10	11	100
	4.3 (4293)	W	③	77	④	74	74	⑤	⑥	11	90
	4.3 (4293)	X	③	77	④	74	74	⑤	⑥	11	90
1999	2.2 (2189)	4	①	70	38	77	55	②	10	11	100
	4.3 (4293)	W	③	77	④	74	74	⑤	⑥	11	90
	4.3 (4293)	X	③	77	④	74	74	⑤	⑥	11	90
2000-01	2.2 (2189)	4	①	70	38	77	55	②	10	11	100
	4.3 (4293)	W	③	77	④	74	74	⑤	⑥	11	90
	4.3 (4293)	X	③	77	④	74	74	⑤	⑥	11	90

* NOTE: Applies to Lower Manifold only.

① Short bolts: 43 ft. lbs. plus 90 degrees
   Long bolts: 46 ft. lbs. plus 90 degrees

② Lower intake manifold nuts: 24 ft. lbs.
   Lower intake manifold studs: 22 ft. lbs.
   Upper intake manifold bolts: 22 ft. lbs.

③ 1st pass: 22 ft. lbs.
   2nd pass:
   Short bolt: Plus 55 degrees
   Medium bolt: Plus 65 degrees
   Long bolt: Plus 75 degrees

④ 20 ft. lbs. plus 70 degrees

⑤ Lower intake manifold:
   1st pass: 27 inch lbs.
   2nd pass: 106 inch lbs.
   Final pass: 11 ft. lbs.
   Upper manifold bolts:
   1st pass: 44 inch lbs.
   2nd pass: 88 inch lbs.

⑥ Tighten bolts to 12 ft. lbs.
   Retorque to 22 ft. lbs.

93081CG7

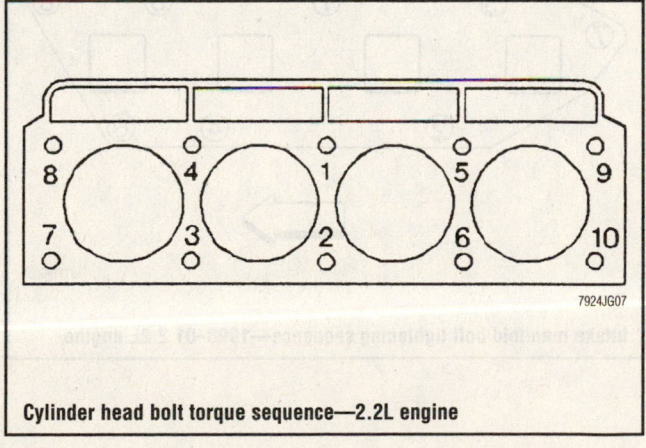

Cylinder head bolt torque sequence—2.2L engine

7924JG07

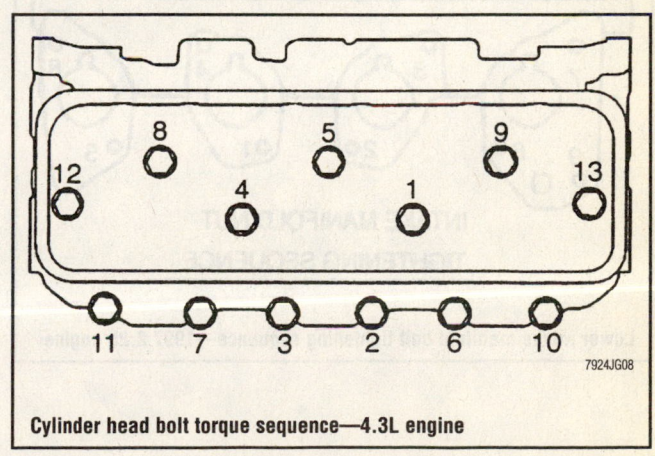

Cylinder head bolt torque sequence—4.3L engine

7924JG08

For accessory drive belt replacement procedures see the model specific sections of this manual

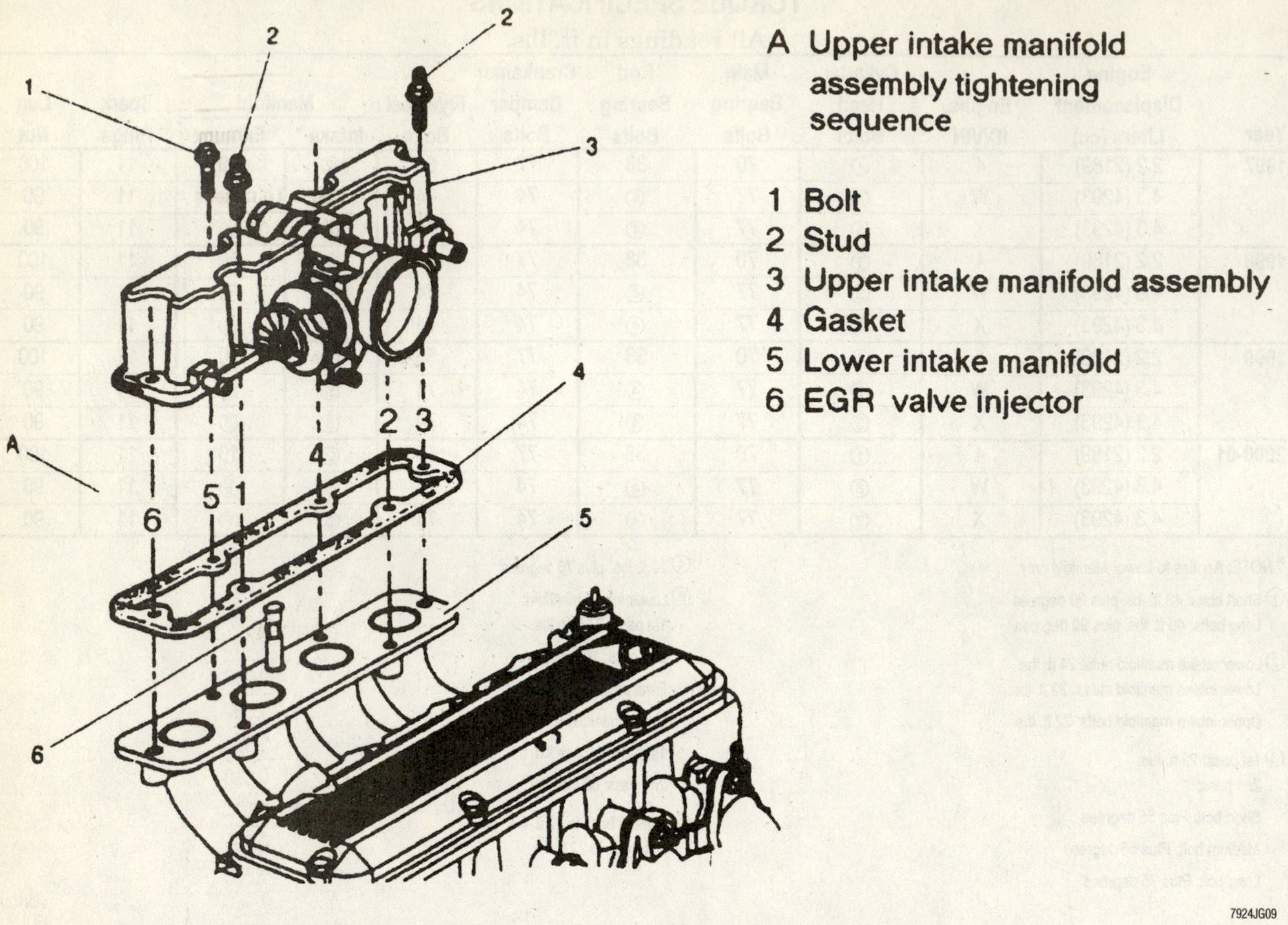

A Upper intake manifold assembly tightening sequence

1 Bolt
2 Stud
3 Upper intake manifold assembly
4 Gasket
5 Lower intake manifold
6 EGR valve injector

7924JG09

Exploded view of the upper intake manifold mounting showing the torque sequence—1997 2.2L engine

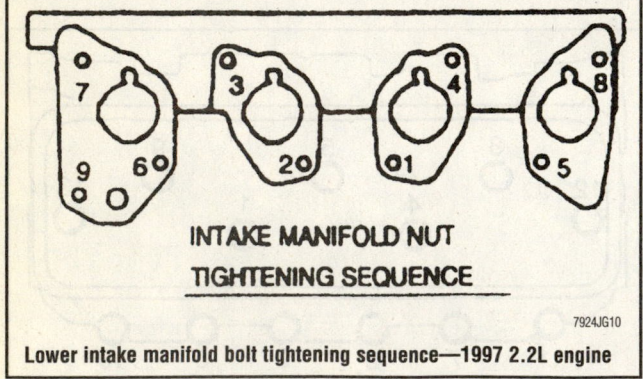

INTAKE MANIFOLD NUT
TIGHTENING SEQUENCE

7924JG10

Lower intake manifold bolt tightening sequence—1997 2.2L engine

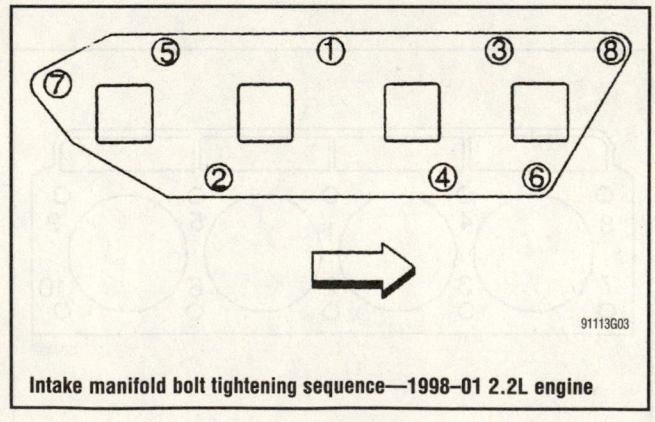

91113G03

Intake manifold bolt tightening sequence—1998–01 2.2L engine

BRAKE SPECIFICATIONS
All measurements in inches unless noted

Year	Model			Brake Disc			Brake Drum Diameter				Brake Caliper	
			Original Thickness	Minimum Thickness	Maximum Runout	Original Inside Diameter	Max. Wear Limit	Maximum Machine Diameter	Minimum Lining Thickness	Bracket Bolts (ft. lbs.)	Mounting Bolts (ft. lbs.)
1997	Astro/Safari	F	①	②	0.004	—	—	—	0.030	NA	38
		R	—	—	—	9.50	9.59	9.56	0.030	NA	—
	Blazer/Jimmy/Bravada	F	1.030	0.965	0.003	—	—	—	0.030	52	③
		R	0.787	0.728	0.004	9.50	9.59	9.56	0.030	NA	23
	S10 Pick-Up/Sonoma	F	1.030	0.965	0.003	—	—	—	0.030	52	③
		R	0.787	0.728	0.004	9.50	9.59	9.56	0.030	NA	23
1998	Astro/Safari	F	①	②	0.004	—	—	—	0.030	NA	38
		R	—	—	—	9.50	9.59	9.56	0.030	NA	—
	Blazer/Jimmy/Bravada/Envoy	F	1.030	0.965	0.003	—	—	—	0.030	52	③
		R	0.787	0.728	0.004	9.50	9.59	9.56	0.030	NA	23
	S10 Pick-Up/Sonoma	F	1.030	0.965	0.003	—	—	—	0.030	52	③
		R	0.787	0.728	0.004	9.50	9.59	9.56	0.030	NA	23
1999	Astro/Safari	F	①	②	0.004	—	—	—	0.030	NA	38
		R	—	—	—	9.50	9.59	9.56	0.030	NA	—
	Blazer/Jimmy/Bravada/Envoy	F	1.030	0.965	0.003	—	—	—	0.030	52	③
		R	0.787	0.728	0.004	9.50	9.59	9.56	0.030	NA	23
	S10 Pick-Up/Sonoma	F	1.030	0.965	0.003	—	—	—	0.030	52	③
		R	0.787	0.728	0.004	9.50	9.59	9.56	0.030	NA	23
2000-01	Astro/Safari	F	①	②	0.004	—	—	—	0.030	NA	38
		R	—	—	—	9.50	9.59	9.56	0.030	NA	—
	Blazer/Jimmy/Bravada/Envoy	F	1.030	0.965	0.003	—	—	—	0.030	52	③
		R	0.787	0.728	0.004	9.50	9.59	9.56	0.030	NA	23
	S10 Pick-Up/Sonoma	F	1.030	0.965	0.003	—	—	—	0.030	52	③
		R	0.787	0.728	0.004	9.50	9.59	9.56	0.030	NA	23

NA: Not Available

① Available with 1.040 and 1.250 in. rotors

② 1.040 in. rotors: 0.980
   1.250 in. rotors: 1.230

③ 2-Wheel Disc only: 38 ft. lbs.
   4-Wheel Disc Vehicles: 77 ft. lbs.

93081CG8

For brake related suspension and axle service, refer to the model specific sections of this manual

SCHEDULED MAINTENANCE INTERVALS
(GENERAL MOTORS S/T SERIES ASTRO, BLAZER, BRAVADA, ENVOY, PICK-UP, JIMMY, SAFARI & SONOMA)

TO BE SERVICED	TYPE OF SERVICE	VEHICLE MILEAGE INTERVAL (x1000)															
		7.5	15	22.5	30	37.5	45	52.5	60	67.5	75	82.5	90	97.5	105	112.5	120
Accessory drive belt	S/I								✓								✓
Air cleaner filter	R				✓				✓				✓				✓
Automatic transmission fluid	R	Every 50,000 miles															
Brake system ①	S/I	✓	✓	✓	✓	✓	✓	✓	✓	✓	✓	✓	✓	✓	✓	✓	✓
Chassis & suspension grease points	L	✓	✓	✓	✓	✓	✓	✓	✓	✓	✓	✓	✓	✓	✓	✓	✓
CV-joint boots & axle seals	S/I	✓	✓	✓	✓	✓	✓	✓	✓	✓	✓	✓	✓	✓	✓	✓	✓
Engine coolant system ②	S/I	Every 150,000 miles															
Engine oil & filter	R	✓	✓	✓	✓	✓	✓	✓	✓	✓	✓	✓	✓	✓	✓	✓	✓
Front wheel bearings ③	S/I & L				✓				✓				✓				✓
Fuel filter	R				✓				✓				✓				✓
Fuel tank, cap & lines	S/I								✓								✓
PCV valve	S/I	Every 100,000 miles															
Rear/front axle fluid level	S/I	✓	✓	✓	✓	✓	✓	✓	✓	✓	✓	✓	✓	✓	✓	✓	✓
Rotate tires	S/I	✓	✓	✓	✓	✓	✓	✓	✓	✓	✓	✓	✓	✓	✓	✓	✓
Spark plug wires	S/I	Every 100,000 miles															
Spark plugs	R	Every 100,000 miles															

R: Replace   S/I: Inspect and service, if necessary   L: Lubricate

① This should be performed when the tires are removed for rotation.

② Drain, flush and refill the cooling system, inspect the system hoses, and clean the radiator and condenser.

③ 2-wheel drive models only.

FREQUENT OPERATION MAINTENANCE (SEVERE SERVICE)

If a vehicle is operated under any of the following conditions it is considered severe service:

- Towing a trailer or using a camper or car-top carrier.

- Repeated short trips of less than 5 miles in temperatures below freezing, or trips of less than 10 miles in any temperature.

- Extensive idling or low-speed driving for long distances as in heavy commercial use, such as delivery, taxi or police cars.

- Operating on rough, muddy or salt-covered roads.

- Operating on unpaved or dusty roads.

- Driving in extremely hot (over 90°) conditions.

Engine oil & filter: replace every 3000 miles or 3 months, whichever occurs first.

Chassis and suspension grease points: lubricate every 3000 miles.

Rear/front axle fluid level: inspect every 3000 miles.

Rotate the tires ever 6000 miles.

Brake system components: inspect ever 6000 miles.

Front wheel bearings (2-wheel drive only): clean, inspect and repack every 15,000 miles.

Air cleaner filter: inspect every 15,000 miles.

Automatic transmission fluid & filter: replace every 15,000 miles.

93081CG8A

SCHEDULED MAINTENANCE INTERVALS
GENERAL MOTORS CORPORATION
S/T SERIES, ASTRO, BLAZER, BRAVADA, ENVOY,
PICK-UP, JIMMY, SAFARI & SONOMA

The following should be used as a guide when determining the amount of work required for a particular service. In estimating how long a particular Scheduled Maintenance Service should take, please observe the following:

- Labor Time is time based on field research and data supplied by the vehicle manufacturer.
- Labor time operations are given in hours and tenths of an hour.
- All labor operations are to be used as a guide.

Mechanic Skill Level Codes:
(A) PRECISION: Highly skilled with multiple certification.
(B) GENERAL: Normally skilled with certification.
(C) MAINTENANCE: Semi-skilled working on certification.

	LABOR TIME
7500 Mile Service (B)	
All models	1.6
w/4WD add	.2
15000 Mile Service (B)	
All models	.7
w/4WD add	.2
22500 Mile Service (B)	
All models	1.6
w/4WD add	.2
30000 Mile Service (B)	
All models	3.6
w/AT add	.5
w/4WD add	.2
37500 Mile Service (B)	
All models	1.6
w/4WD add	.2
45000 Mile Service (B)	
All models	.7
w/4WD add	.2

	LABOR TIME
52500 Mile Service (B)	
All models	1.6
w/4WD add	.2
60000 Mile Service (B)	
All models	4.0
w/AT add	.5
w/4WD add	.2
67500 Mile Service (B)	
All models	1.6
w/4WD add	.2
75000 Mile Service (B)	
All models	.7
w/4WD add	.2
82500 Mile Service (B)	
All models	1.6
w/4WD add	.2

	LABOR TIME
90000 Mile Service (B)	
All models	3.8
w/AT add	.5
w/4WD add	.2
97500 Mile Service (B)	
All models	1.6
w/4WD add	.2
105000 Mile Service (B)	
All models	1.6
w/4WD add	.2
112500 Mile Service (B)	
All models	1.6
w/4WD add	.2
120000 Mile Service (B)	
All models	4.0
w/AT add	.5
w/4WD add	.2

93081CG9

Refer to the model specific sections for driveline service procedures

GENERAL MOTORS
Chevrolet Venture • Oldsmobile Silhouette •
Pontiac Trans Sport • Montana

ENGINE AND VEHICLE IDENTIFICATION

			Engine				Model Year	
Code ①	Liters (cc)	Cu. In.	Cyl.	Fuel Sys.	Engine Type	Eng. Mfg.	Code ②	Year
E	3.4 (3350)	207	6	MFI/SFI	OHV	CPC	V	1997
							W	1998
							X	1999
							Y	2000
							1	2001

MFI : Multi-port Fuel Injection

OHV: Overhead Valves

SFI : Sequential Fuel Injection

CPC: Chevrolet/Pontiac/Canada

① 8th position of VIN

② 10th position of VIN

93081CG0

GENERAL ENGINE SPECIFICATIONS
All measurements are given in inches.

Year	Model	Engine Displacement Liters (cc)	Engine Series (ID/VIN)	Fuel System	Net Horsepower @ rpm	Net Torque @ rpm (ft. lbs.)	Bore x Stroke (in.)	Compression Ratio	Oil Pressure @ rpm
1997	Silhouette	3.4 (3350)	E	MFI	180@5200	205@4000	3.62x3.31	9.5:1	15@1100
	Trans Sport	3.4 (3350)	E	MFI	180@5200	205@4000	3.62x3.31	9.5:1	15@1100
	Venture	3.4 (3350)	E	MFI	180@5200	205@4000	3.62x3.31	9.5:1	15@1100
1998	Silhouette	3.4 (3350)	E	SFI	180@5200	205@4000	3.62x3.31	9.5:1	15@1100
	Montana	3.4 (3350)	E	SFI	180@5200	205@4000	3.62x3.31	9.5:1	15@1100
	Trans Sport	3.4 (3350)	E	SFI	180@5200	205@4000	3.62x3.31	9.5:1	15@1100
	Venture	3.4 (3350)	E	SFI	180@5200	205@4000	3.62x3.31	9.5:1	15@1100
1999	Premier	3.4 (3350)	E	SFI	185@5200	210@4000	3.62x3.31	9.5:1	15@1100
	Silhouette	3.4 (3350)	E	SFI	180@5200	205@4000	3.62x3.31	9.5:1	15@1100
	Montana	3.4 (3350)	E	SFI	180@5200	205@4000	3.62x3.31	9.5:1	15@1100
	Trans Sport	3.4 (3350)	E	SFI	180@5200	205@4000	3.62x3.31	9.5:1	15@1100
	Venture	3.4 (3350)	E	SFI	180@5200	205@4000	3.62x3.31	9.5:1	15@1100
2000-01	Premier	3.4 (3350)	E	SFI	185@5200	210@4000	3.62x3.31	9.5:1	15@1100
	Silhouette	3.4 (3350)	E	SFI	180@5200	205@4000	3.62x3.31	9.5:1	15@1100
	Montana	3.4 (3350)	E	SFI	180@5200	205@4000	3.62x3.31	9.5:1	15@1100
	Trans Sport	3.4 (3350)	E	SFI	180@5200	205@4000	3.62x3.31	9.5:1	15@1100
	Venture	3.4 (3350)	E	SFI	180@5200	205@4000	3.62x3.31	9.5:1	15@1100

MFI: Multi-port Fuel Injection

SFI: Sequential Fuel Injection

93081CH1

ENGINE TUNE-UP SPECIFICATIONS

Year	Engine Displacement Liters (cc)	Engine ID/VIN	Spark Plug Gap (in.)	Ignition Timing (deg.)	Fuel Pump (psi)	Idle Speed (rpm)	Valve Clearance	
							Intake	Exhaust
1997	3.4 (3350)	E	0.060	①	41-47	②	HYD	HYD
1998	3.4 (3350)	E	0.060	①	41-47	②	HYD	HYD
1999	3.4 (3350)	E	0.060	①	41-47	②	HYD	HYD
2000-01	3.4 (3350)	E	0.060	①	41-47	②	HYD	HYD

NOTE: The Vehicle Emissions Control Information label often reflects specification changes made during production. The label figures must be used if they differ from those in this chart.

HYD: Hydraulic

① Refer to underhood label for exact setting.

② Idle speed is maintained by the PCM.

93081CH2

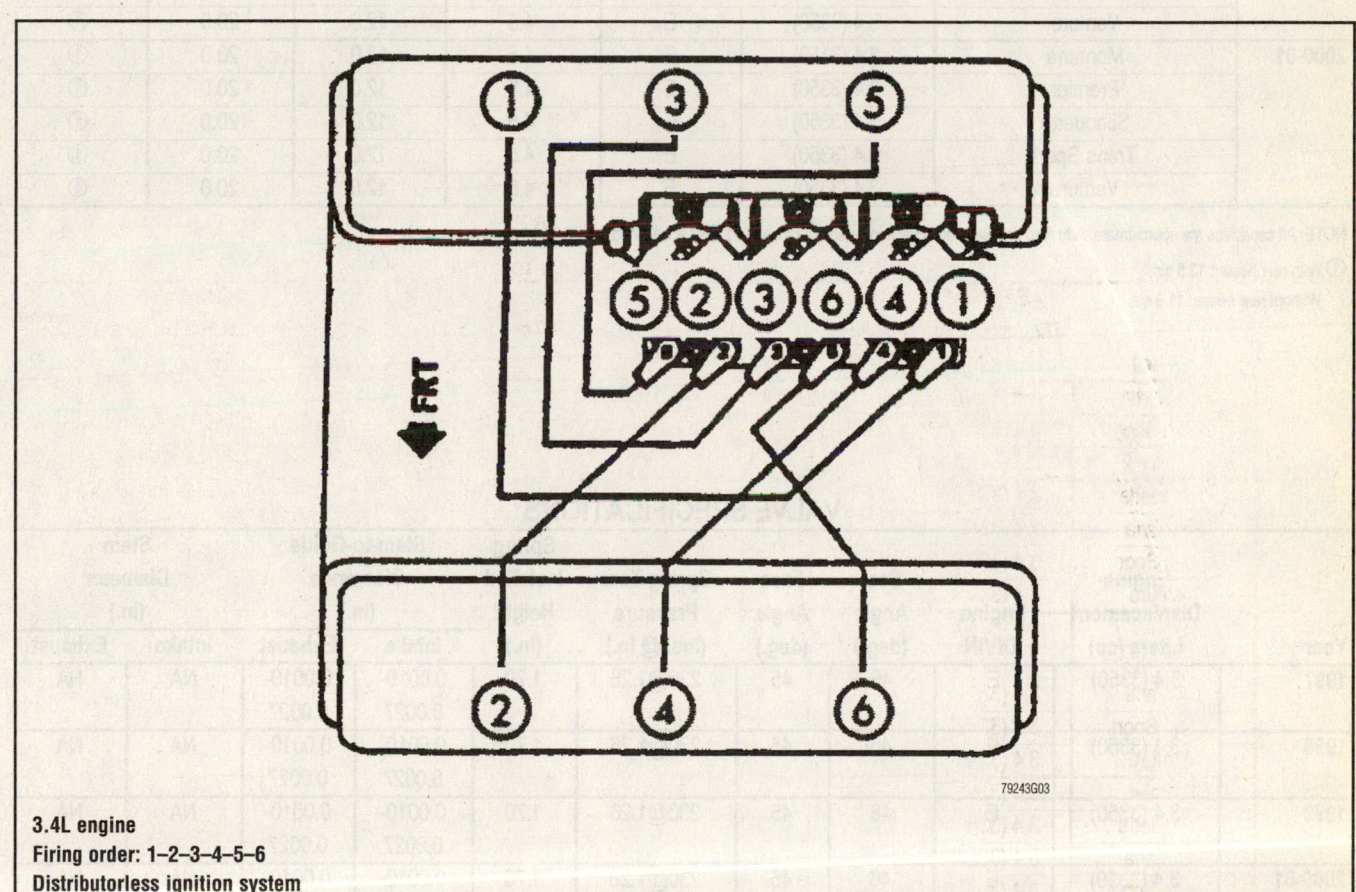

FRT

3.4L engine
Firing order: 1–2–3–4–5–6
Distributorless ignition system

79243G03

For exhaust manifold replacement procedures, see the model specific sections of this manual

CAPACITIES

Year	Model	Engine Displacement Liters (cc)	Engine ID/VIN	Engine Oil with Filter (qts.)	Transmission (pts.)	Fuel Tank (gal.)	Cooling System (qts.)
1997	Venture	3.4 (3350)	E	4.5	12.0	20.0	①
	Silhouette	3.4 (3350)	E	4.5	12.0	20.0	①
	Trans Sport	3.4 (3350)	E	4.5	12.0	20.0	①
1998	Montana	3.4 (3350)	E	4.5	12.0	20.0	①
	Silhouette	3.4 (3350)	E	4.5	12.0	20.0	①
	Trans Sport	3.4 (3350)	E	4.5	12.0	20.0	①
	Venture	3.4 (3350)	E	4.5	12.0	20.0	①
1999	Montana	3.4 (3350)	E	4.5	12.0	20.0	①
	Silhouette	3.4 (3350)	E	4.5	12.0	20.0	①
	Premier	3.4 (3350)	E	4.5	12.0	20.0	①
	Trans Sport	3.4 (3350)	E	4.5	12.0	20.0	①
	Venture	3.4 (3350)	E	4.5	12.0	20.0	①
2000-01	Montana	3.4 (3350)	E	4.5	12.0	20.0	①
	Premier	3.4 (3350)	E	4.5	12.0	20.0	①
	Silhouette	3.4 (3350)	E	4.5	12.0	20.0	①
	Trans Sport	3.4 (3350)	E	4.5	12.0	20.0	①
	Venture	3.4 (3350)	E	4.5	12.0	20.0	①

NOTE: All capacities are approximate. Add fluid gradually and check to be sure a proper fluid level is obtained.

① With rear heater: 13.5 qts.

Without rear heater: 11.8 qts.

93081CH3

VALVE SPECIFICATIONS

Year	Engine Displacement Liters (cc)	Engine ID/VIN	Seat Angle (deg.)	Face Angle (deg.)	Spring Test Pressure (lbs. @ in.)	Spring Installed Height (in.)	Stem-to-Guide Clearance (in.) Intake	Stem-to-Guide Clearance (in.) Exhaust	Stem Diameter (in.) Intake	Stem Diameter (in.) Exhaust
1997	3.4 (3350)	E	46	45	230@1.26	1.70	0.0010-0.0027	0.0010-0.0027	NA	NA
1998	3.4 (3350)	E	46	45	230@1.26	1.70	0.0010-0.0027	0.0010-0.0027	NA	NA
1999	3.4 (3350)	E	46	45	230@1.26	1.70	0.0010-0.0027	0.0010-0.0027	NA	NA
2000-01	3.4 (3350)	E	46	45	230@1.26	1.70	0.0010-0.0027	0.0010-0.0027	NA	NA

NA: Not Available

93081CH4

CRANKSHAFT AND CONNECTING ROD SPECIFICATIONS

All measurements are given in inches.

| Year | Engine Displacement Liters (cc) | Engine ID/VIN | Crankshaft | | | | Connecting Rod | | |
			Main Brg. Journal Dia.	Main Brg. Oil Clearance	Shaft End-play	Thrust on No.	Journal Diameter	Oil Clearance	Side Clearance
1997	3.4 (3350)	E	2.6473-2.6483	0.0008-0.0023	0.0024-0.0083	3	1.9987-1.9994	0.0007-0.0024	0.007-0.017
1998	3.4 (3350)	E	2.6473-2.6483	0.0008-0.0023	0.0024-0.0083	3	1.9987-1.9994	0.0007-0.0024	0.007-0.017
1999	3.4 (3350)	E	2.6473-2.6483	0.0008-0.0023	0.0024-0.0083	3	1.9987-1.9994	0.0007-0.0024	0.007-0.017
2000-01	3.4 (3350)	E	2.6473-2.6483	0.0008-0.0023	0.0024-0.0083	3	1.9987-1.9994	0.0007-0.0024	0.007-0.017

93081CH5

PISTON AND RING SPECIFICATIONS

All measurements are given in inches.

| Year | Engine Displacement Liters (cc) | Engine ID/VIN | Piston Clearance | Ring Gap | | | Ring Side Clearance | | |
				Top Compression	Bottom Compression	Oil Control	Top Compression	Bottom Compression	Oil Control
1997	3.4 (3350)	E	0.0013-0.0027	0.006-0.014	0.020-0.028	NA	0.0020-0.0033	0.0020-0.0035	NA
1998	3.4 (3350)	E	0.0013-0.0027	0.006-0.014	0.020-0.028	NA	0.0020-0.0033	0.0020-0.0035	NA
1999	3.4 (3350)	E	0.0013-0.0027	0.006-0.014	0.020-0.028	NA	0.0020-0.0033	0.0020-0.0035	NA
2000-01	3.4 (3350)	E	0.0013-0.0027	0.006-0.014	0.020-0.028	NA	0.0020-0.0033	0.0020-0.0035	NA

NA: Not available

93081CH6

Refer to the model specific sections for cooling system service procedures

TORQUE SPECIFICATIONS
All readings in ft. lbs.

Year	Engine Displacement Liters (cc)	Engine ID/VIN	Cylinder Head Bolts	Main Bearing Bolts	Rod Bearing Bolts	Crankshaft Damper Bolts	Flywheel Bolts	Manifold Intake	Exhaust	Spark Plugs	Lug Nuts
1997	3.4 (3350)	E	①	②	③	76	61	④	12	11	100
1998	3.4 (3350)	E	①	②	③	76	61	④	12	11	100
1999	3.4 (3350)	E	①	②	③	76	61	④	12	11	100
2000-01	3.4 (3350)	E	①	②	③	76	61	④	12	11	100

① Coat threads with sealer
  Tighten all bolts to 33 ft. lbs.
  Tighten all an additional 90 degrees (1/4 turn)
② 37 ft. lbs. plus 77 degrees

③ Step 1: 15 ft. lbs.
  Step 2: Plus 75 degrees
④ Lower manifold: 10 ft. lbs.
  Upper manifold: 18 ft. lbs.

93081CH7

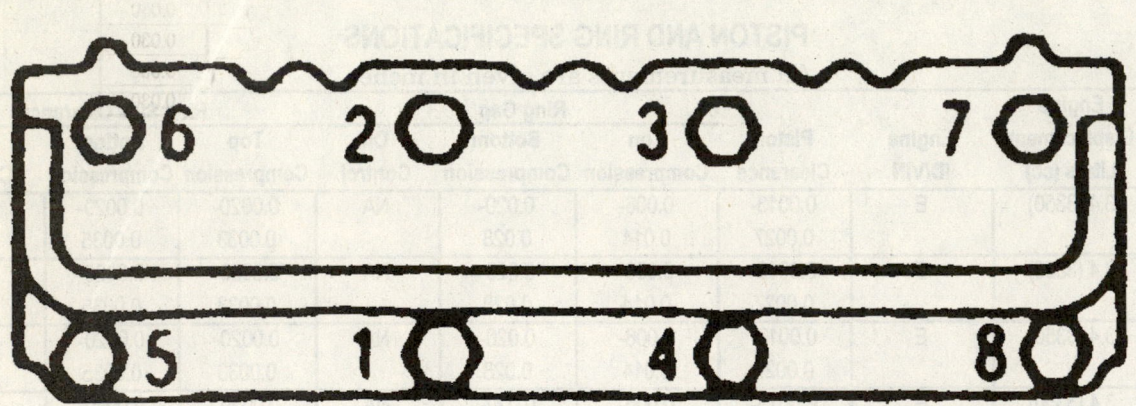

7924LG03

Cylinder head bolt torque sequence—3.4L engine

BRAKE SPECIFICATIONS
CHEVROLET VENTURE, OLDSMOBILE PREMIER, SILHOUETTE, PONTIAC MONTANA, TRANS SPORT

All measurements in inches unless noted

Year	Model	Brake Disc			Brake Drum Diameter			Minimum Lining Thickness		Brake Caliper	
		Original Thickness	Minimum Thickness	Maximum Runout	Original Inside Diameter	Max. Wear Limit	Maximum Machine Diameter	Front	Rear	Bracket Bolts (ft. lbs.)	Mounting Bolts (ft. lbs.)
1997	Venture	1.260	1.209	0.002	8.86	8.92	8.90	0.030	0.030	—	38
	Silhouette	1.260	1.209	0.002	8.86	8.92	8.91	0.030	0.030	—	38
	Trans Sport	1.260	1.209	0.002	8.86	8.92	8.92	0.030	0.030	—	38
1998	Silhouette	1.260	1.209	0.002	8.86	8.92	8.91	0.030	0.030	137	63
	Montana	1.260	1.209	0.002	8.86	8.92	8.92	0.030	0.030	NA	NA
	Trans Sport	1.260	1.209	0.002	8.86	8.92	8.92	0.030	0.030	137	63
	Venture	1.260	1.209	0.002	8.86	8.92	8.90	0.030	0.030	137	63
1999	Silhouette	1.260	1.209	0.002	8.86	8.92	8.91	0.030	0.030	NA	NA
	Premier	1.260	1.209	0.002	8.86	8.92	8.92	0.030	0.030	NA	NA
	Montana	1.260	1.209	0.002	8.86	8.92	8.92	0.030	0.030	NA	NA
	Trans Sport	1.260	1.209	0.002	8.86	8.92	8.92	0.030	0.030	NA	NA
	Venture	1.260	1.209	0.002	8.86	8.92	8.90	0.030	0.030	NA	NA
2000-01	Silhouette	1.260	1.209	0.002	8.86	8.92	8.91	0.030	0.030	NA	NA
	Premier	1.260	1.209	0.002	8.86	8.92	8.92	0.030	0.030	NA	NA
	Montana	1.260	1.209	0.002	8.86	8.92	8.92	0.030	0.030	NA	NA
	Trans Sport	1.260	1.209	0.002	8.86	8.92	8.92	0.030	0.030	NA	NA
	Venture	1.260	1.209	0.002	8.86	8.92	8.90	0.030	0.030	NA	NA

NA: Not Available

93081CH8

SCHEDULED MAINTENANCE INTERVALS
(GENERAL MOTORS CHEVROLET VENTURE, OLDSMOBILE PREMIER, SILHOUETTE, PONTIAC MONTANA & TRANS SPORT)

TO BE SERVICED	TYPE OF SERVICE	VEHICLE MILEAGE INTERVAL (x1000)														
		7.5	15	22.5	30	37.5	45	52.5	60	67.5	75	82.5	90	97.5	105	112.5	120
Accessory drive belt	I								✓								✓
Air cleaner filter	R								✓								✓
Air distributor air filter	R		✓		✓		✓		✓		✓		✓		✓		✓
Brake system	I	✓	✓	✓	✓	✓	✓	✓	✓	✓	✓	✓	✓	✓	✓	✓	✓
Engine coolant	R	Every 150,000 miles															
Engine oil & filter ①	S/I	✓	✓	✓	✓	✓	✓	✓	✓	✓	✓	✓	✓	✓	✓	✓	✓
Fuel system tank, cap & lines	I								✓								✓
Rotate tires	S/I	✓	✓	✓	✓	✓	✓	✓	✓	✓	✓	✓	✓	✓	✓	✓	✓
Spark plug wires	S/I	Every 100,000 miles															
Spark plugs	R	Every 100,000 miles															

R: Replace I: Inspect S: Service

① Perform this at the mileage indicated or every 12 months, whichever occurs first.

FREQUENT OPERATION MAINTENANCE (SEVERE SERVICE)

If a vehicle is operated under any of the following conditions it is considered severe service:

- Towing a trailer or using a camper or car-top carrier.

- Repeated short trips of less than 5 miles in temperatures below freezing, or trips of less than 10 miles in any temperature.

- Extensive idling or low-speed driving for long distances as in heavy commercial use, such as delivery, taxi or police cars.

- Operating on rough, muddy or salt-covered roads.

- Operating on unpaved or dusty roads.

- Driving in extremely hot (over 90°) conditions.

Automatic transaxle fluid and filter: replace every 50,000 miles.

Tires: rotate every 6000 miles.

Brake system: inspect every 6000 miles.

Air distributor air filter: replace every 12,000 miles.

93081CH9

SCHEDULED MAINTENANCE INTERVALS
GENERAL MOTORS CORPORATION
CHEVROLET VENTURE, OLDSMOBILE SILHOUTTE,
PONTIAC MONTANA & TRANS SPORT

The following should be used as a guide when determining the amount of work required for a particular service. In estimating how long a particular Scheduled Maintenance Service should take, please observe the following:

- Labor Time is time based on field research and data supplied by the vehicle manufacturer.
- Labor time operations are given in hours and tenths of an hour.
- All labor operations are to be used as a guide.

Mechanic Skill Level Codes:
(A) PRECISION: Highly skilled with multiple certification.
(B) GENERAL: Normally skilled with certification.
(C) MAINTENANCE: Semi-skilled working on certification.

	LABOR TIME		LABOR TIME		LABOR TIME
7500 Mile Service (B)		**45000 Mile Service (B)**		**90000 Mile Service (B)**	
All Models	1.7	All Models	.5	All Models	3.4
w/AT add	.1	w/AT add	.1	w/AT add	.1
15000 Mile Service (B)		**52500 Mile Service (B)**		**97500 Mile Service (B)**	
All Models	.5	All Models	1.4	All Models	1.6
w/AT add	.1	w/AT add	.1	w/AT add	.1
22500 Mile Service (B)		**60000 Mile Service (B)**		**105000 Mile Service (B)**	
All Models	1.5	All Models	3.5	All Models	.5
w/AT add	.1	w/AT add	.1	w/AT add	.1
30000 Mile Service (B)		**67500 Mile Service (B)**		**112500 Mile Service (B)**	
All Models	3.4	All Models	1.5	All Models	1.7
w/AT add	.1	w/AT add	.1	w/AT add	.1
37500 Mile Service (B)		**75000 Mile Service (B)**		**60000 Mile Service (B)**	
All Models	1.5	All Models	.5	All Models	3.5
w/AT add	.1	w/AT add	.1	w/AT add	.1
		82500 Mile Service (B)			
		All Models	1.4		
		w/AT add	.1		

93081CH0

Timing chain and gear service is covered in the model specific sections of this manual

TIRE, WHEEL AND BALL JOINT SPECIFICATIONS
Chevrolet/GMC

| Year | Model | OEM Tires | | Tire Pressures (psi) | | Wheel Size | Ball Joint Inspection |
		Standard	Optional	Front	Rear		
1997	Astro/Safari	P215/75R15	None	36	36	6-JJ	U: 0.125 in. L ①
	Tahoe/Yukon, 2wd	P235/75R15	None	36	36	6.5-JJ	U ② L: 0.090 in.
	Tahoe/Yukon, 4wd	P245/75R16	P265/75R16	36	36	7-JJ	③
	Venture	P205/70R15	P215/70R15	36	36	6-JJ	U ② L: 0.090 in.
	1500 PU 2wd	P235/75R15	None	36	36	6-JJ	L ①
	1500 PU 4wd	P245/75R16	None	36	36	7-JJ	L ①
	2500 PU	LT225/75R16D	LT245/75R16C LT245/75R16E	36	36	7-JJ	L ①
	3500 PU SRW	LT245/75R16E	None	36	36	7-JJ	0.125 in.④
	3500 PU DRW	LT225/75R16D	LT215/85R16D	36	36		0.125 in.④
	1500 Suburban 2wd	P235/75R15XL	LT245/75R16E	36	36	7-JJ	L ①
	1500 Suburban 4wd	P245/75R16C	LT245/75R16E	36	36	6.5-JJ	L ①
	2500 Suburban	LT245/75R16E	None	36	36	6.5-JJ	L ①
	Blazer/Jimmy	P205/70R15	P235/70R15 P235/75R15	36	36	6-JJ	U: 0.125 in. L ①
	S Pickup, 2wd, base	P205/70R15	P235/70R15	36	36	6-JJ	U: 0.125 in. L ①
	S Pickup, 2wd, Sport	P215/65R15	None	36	36	6-JJ	U: 0.125 in. L ①
	S Pickup, 4wd, Reg. Cab, w/117.9 WB	P235/75R15	P235/75R15	36	36	6-JJ	U: 0.125 in. L ①
	S Pickup, 4wd, all others	P235/75R15	None	36	36	6-JJ	U: 0.125 in. L ①
1998	Denali	P265/70R16	None	36	36	7-JJ	U ② L: 0.090 in.
	Astro/Safari	P215/75R15	None	36	36	6-JJ	U: 0.125 in. L ①
	Tahoe/Yukon, 2wd	P235/75R15	None	36	36	6.5-JJ	U ② L: 0.090 in.
	Tahoe/Yukon, 4wd	P245/75R16	P265/75R16	36	36	7-JJ	③
	Venture	P205/70R15	P215/70R15	36	36	6-JJ	U ② L: 0.090 in.
	1500 PU 2wd	P235/75R15	None	36	36	6-JJ	L ①
	1500 PU 4wd	P245/75R16	None	36	36	7-JJ	L ①
	2500 PU	LT225/75R16D	LT245/75R16C LT245/75R16E	36	36	7-JJ	L ①
	3500 PU SRW	LT245/75R16E	None	36	36	7-JJ	0.125 in.④
	3500 PU DRW	LT225/75R16D	LT215/85R16D	36	36	7-JJ	0.125 in.④
	1500 Suburban 2wd	P235/75R15XL	LT245/75R16E	36	36	7-JJ	L ①
	1500 Suburban 4wd	P245/75R16C	LT245/75R16E	36	36	6.5-JJ	L ①
	2500 Suburban	LT245/75R16E	None	36	36	6.5-JJ	L ①
	Blazer/Jimmy	P205/70R15	P235/70R15 P235/75R15	36	36	6-JJ	U: 0.125 in. L ①
	S Pickup, 2wd, base	P205/70R15	P235/70R15	36	36	6-JJ	U: 0.125 in. L ①

93081CI1

TIRE, WHEEL AND BALL JOINT SPECIFICATIONS
Chevrolet/GMC

Year	Model	OEM Tires		Tire Pressures (psi)		Wheel Size	Ball Joint Inspection
		Standard	Optional	Front	Rear		
1998 (Cont.)	S Pickup, 2wd, Sport	P215/65R15	None	36	36	6-JJ	U: 0.125 in. L ①
	S Pickup, 4wd, Reg. Cab, w/117.9 WB	P235/70R15	P235/75R15	36	36	6-JJ	U: 0.125 in. L ①
	S Pickup, 4wd, all others	P235/75R15	None	36	36	6-JJ	U: 0.125 in. L ①
1999	Denali	P265/70R16	None	36	36	7-JJ	U ② L: 0.090 in.
	Astro/Safari	P215/75R15	None	36	36	6-JJ	U: 0.125 in. L ①
	Tahoe/Yukon, 2wd	P235/75R15	None	36	36	6.5-JJ	U ② L: 0.090 in.
	Tahoe/Yukon, 4wd	P245/75R16	P265/75R16	36	36	7-JJ	③
	Venture	P205/70R15	P215/70R15	36	36	6-JJ	U ② L: 0.090 in.
	1500 PU 2wd	P235/75R15	None	36	36	6-JJ	L ①
	1500 PU 4wd	P245/75R16	None	36	36	7-JJ	L ①
	2500 PU	LT225/75R16D	LT245/75R16C LT245/75R16E	36	36	7-JJ	L ①
	3500 PU SRW	LT245/75R16E	None	36	36	7-JJ	0.125 in.④
	3500 PU DRW	LT225/75R16D	LT215/85R16D	36	36	7-JJ	0.125 in.④
	1500 Suburban 2wd	P235/75R15XL	LT245/75R16E	36	36	7-JJ	L ①
	1500 Suburban 4wd	P245/75R16C	LT245/75R16E	36	36	6.5-JJ	L ①
	2500 Suburban	LT245/75R16E	None	36	36	6.5-JJ	L ①
	Blazer/Jimmy	P205/70R15	P235/70R15 P235/75R15	36	36	6-JJ	U: 0.125 in. L ①
	S Pickup, 2wd, base	P205/70R15	P235/70R15	36	36	6-JJ	U: 0.125 in. L ①
	S Pickup, 2wd, Sport	P215/65R15	None	36	36	6-JJ	U: 0.125 in. L ①
	S Pickup, 4wd, Reg. Cab, w/117.9 WB	P235/70R15	P235/75R15	36	36	6-JJ	U: 0.125 in. L ①
	S Pickup, 4wd, all others	P235/75R15	None	36	36	6-JJ	U: 0.125 in. L ①
2000-01	Denali	P265/70R16	None	36	36	7-JJ	U ③ L: 0.090 in.
	Astro/Safari	P215/75R15	None	36	36	6-JJ	U: 0.125 in. L ①
	Tahoe/Yukon, 2wd	P235/75R15	None	36	36	6.5-JJ	U ② L: 0.090 in.
	Tahoe/Yukon, 4wd	P245/75R16	P265/75R16	36	36	7-JJ	③
	1500 PU 2wd	P235/75R15	None	36	36	6-JJ	L ①
	1500 PU 4wd	P245/75R16	None	36	36	7-JJ	L ①
	2500 PU	LT225/75R16D	LT245/75R16C LT245/75R16E	36 36	36 36	7-JJ	L ①
	3500 PU SRW	LT245/75R16E	None	36	36	7-JJ	0.125 in.④
	3500 PU DRW	LT225/75R16D	LT215/85R16D	36	36	7-JJ	0.125 in.④
	1500 Suburban 2wd	P235/75R15XL	LT245/75R16E	36	36	7-JJ	① L
	1500 Suburban 4wd	P245/75R16C	LT245/75R16E	36	36	6.5-JJ	① L

93081CI2

Ignition system service is covered in the model specific sections of this manual

TIRE, WHEEL AND BALL JOINT SPECIFICATIONS
Chevrolet/GMC

| Year | Model | OEM Tires | | Tire Pressures (psi) | | Wheel Size | Ball Joint Inspection |
		Standard	Optional	Front	Rear		
2000-01 (Cont.)	2500 Suburban	LT245/75R16E	None	36	36	6.5-JJ	U: 0.125 in. L ①
	Blazer/Jimmy	P205/70R15	P235/70R15 P235/75R15	36	36	6-JJ	L ①
	S Pickup, 2wd, base	P205/70R15	P235/70R15	36	36	6-JJ	U: 0.125 in. L ①
	S Pickup, 2wd, Sport	P215/65R15	None	36	36	6-JJ	U: 0.125 in. L ①
	S Pickup, 4wd, Reg. Cab, w/117.9 WB	P235/70R15	P235/75R15	36	36	6-JJ	U: 0.125 in. L ①
	S Pickup, 4wd, all others	P235/75R15	None	36	36	6-JJ	U: 0.125 in. L ①

OEM: Original Equipment Manufacturer

PSI: Pounds Per Square Inch

STD: Standard

OPT: Optional

L: Lower

U: Upper

① Do not lift truck. Inspect the boss into which the grease fitting is threaded. Replace if the boss is flush or receded below the surface of the ball joint

② Replace if any movement is noted or if stud can be moved by hand

③ Ball joint is adjustable, refer to manual for procedure

④ Applies to both upper and lower

93081CI3

TIRE, WHEEL AND BALL JOINT SPECIFICATIONS
Oldsmobile Truck

Year	Model	OEM Tires		Tire Pressures (psi)		Wheel Size	Ball Joint Inspection
		Standard	Optional	Front	Rear		
1997	Silhouette	P205/70R15	P215/70R15	33	35	7-JJ	①
	Bravada	P235/70R15	None	33	35	7-JJ	①
1998	Silhouette	P205/70R15	P215/70R15	33	35	7-JJ	①
	Bravada	P235/70R15	None	33	35	7-JJ	①
1999	Silhouette	P205/70R15	P215/70R15	33	35	7-JJ	①
	Bravada	P235/70R15	None	33	35	7-JJ	①
2000-01	Silhouette	P205/70R15	P215/70R15	33	35	7-JJ	①
	Bravada	P235/70R15	None	33	35	7-JJ	①

OEM: Original Equipment Manufacturer

PSI: Pounds Per Square Inch

STD: Standard

OPT: Optional

① Replace if any measurable movement is found.

93081CI4

TIRE, WHEEL AND BALL JOINT SPECIFICATIONS
Pontiac Truck

Year	Model	OEM Tires		Tire Pressures (psi)		Wheel Size	Ball Joint Inspection
		Standard	Optional	Front	Rear		
1997	Trans Sport	P205/70R15	215/70R15	35	35	6-J	①
1998	Trans Sport	P205/70R15	215/70R15	35	35	6-J	①
1999	Trans Sport	P205/70R15	215/70R15	35	35	6-J	①

OEM: Original Equipment Manufacturer

PSI: Pounds Per Square Inch

STD: Standard

OPT: Optional

① Replace if any measurable movement is found.

93081CI5

GEO CHEVROLET
Tracker

ENGINE AND VEHICLE IDENTIFICATION CHART

		Engine						Model Year	
Code ①	Liters	Cu. In. (cc)	Cyl.	Fuel Sys.	Engine Type	Eng. Mfg.		Code ②	Year
6	1.6	98 (1590)	4	MFI	SOHC	Suzuki		V	1997
C	2.0	122 (1997)	4	MFI	DOHC	Suzuki		W	1998
								X	1999
								Y	2000
								1	2001

MFI: Multi-port Fuel Injection
DOHC: Dual Overhead Cam
SOHC: Single Overhead Cam
① 8th digit of the VIN
② 10th digit of the VIN

93081CI6

GENERAL ENGINE SPECIFICATIONS

Year	Model	Engine Displacement Liters (cc)	Engine ID/VIN	Fuel System Type	Net Horsepower @ rpm	Net Torque @ rpm (ft. lbs.)	Bore x Stroke (in.)	Compression Ratio	Oil Pressure @ rpm
1997	Tracker	1.6 (1590)	6	MFI	95@5600	98@4000	2.95x3.54	9.5:1	47-61@4000
1998	Tracker	1.6 (1590)	6	MFI	95@5600	98@4000	2.95x3.54	9.5:1	47-61@4000
1999	Tracker	1.6 (1590)	6	MFI	95@5600	98@4000	2.95x3.54	9.5:1	47-61@4000
		2.0 (1997)	C	MFI	127@6000	134@3000	3.31x3.54	NA	55-67@4000
2000-01	Tracker	1.6 (1590)	6	MFI	95@5600	98@4000	2.95x3.54	9.5:1	47-61@4000
		2.0 (1997)	C	MFI	127@6000	134@3000	3.31x3.54	NA	55-67@4000

MFI: Multiport Fuel Injection
NA: Not Available

93081CI7

ENGINE TUNE-UP SPECIFICATIONS

Year	Engine Displacement Liters (cc)	Engine ID/VIN	Spark Plugs Gap (in.)	Ignition Timing (deg.)		Fuel Pump (psi)	Idle Speed (rpm)		Valve Clearance	
				MT	AT		MT	AT	In.	Ex.
1997	1.6 (1590)	6	0.030	5B	5B	30-37	800-850	800-850	0.0050-0.0070	0.0050-0.0070
1998	1.6 (1590)	6	0.030	5B	5B	30-37	800-850	800-850	0.0050-0.0070	0.0050-0.0070
1999	1.6 (1590)	6	0.030	5B	5B	30-37	800-850	800-850	0.0050-0.0070	0.0050-0.0070
	2.0 (1997)	C	0.041	5B	5B	35-43	700-800	700-800	HYD	HYD
2000-01	1.6 (1590)	6	0.030	5B	5B	30-37	800-850	800-850	0.0050-0.0070	0.0050-0.0070
	2.0 (1997)	C	0.041	5B	5B	35-43	700-800	700-800	HYD	HYD

NOTE: The Vehicle Emission Control Information label often reflects specification changes made during production. The label figures must be used if they differ from those in this chart.

B: Before top dead center

HYD: Hydraulic

93081CI8

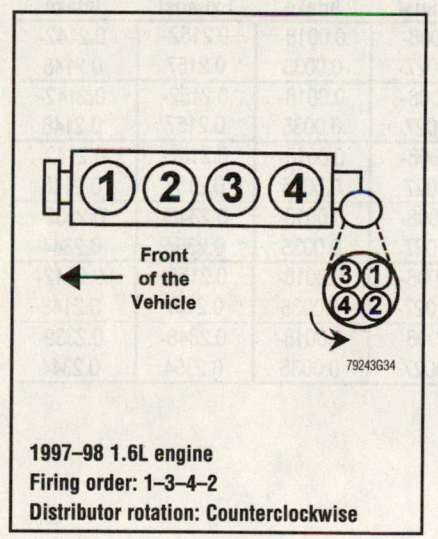

1997–98 1.6L engine
Firing order: 1–3–4–2
Distributor rotation: Counterclockwise

79243G34

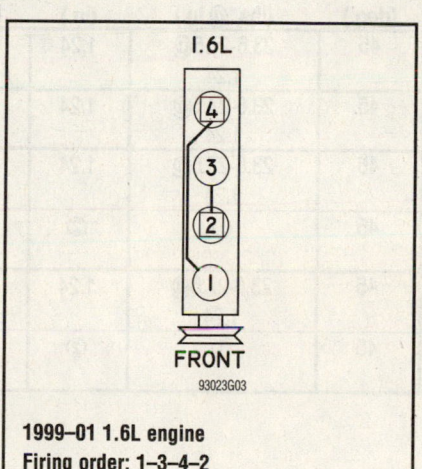

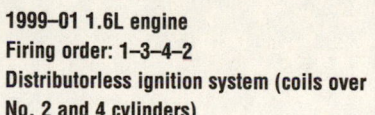

93023G03

1999–01 1.6L engine
Firing order: 1–3–4–2
Distributorless ignition system (coils over No. 2 and 4 cylinders)

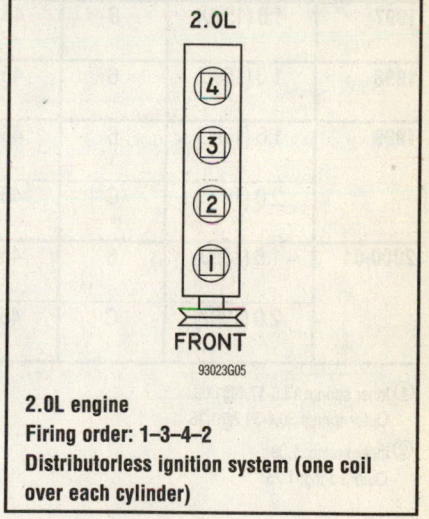

93023G05

2.0L engine
Firing order: 1–3–4–2
Distributorless ignition system (one coil over each cylinder)

Refer to the model specific sections for engine mechanical service procedures

CAPACITIES

Year	Model	Engine Displacement Liters (cc)	Engine VIN	Engine Oil with Filter (qts.)	Transmission (pts.)		Transfer Case (pts.)	Drive Axle		Fuel Tank (gal.)	Cooling System (qts.)
					5-Spd	Auto.		Front (pts.)	Rear (pts.)		
1997	Tracker	1.6 (1590)	6	4.75	3.2	10.6	3.6	2.4	4.6	11.0	5.5
1998	Tracker	1.6 (1590)	6	4.75	3.2	10.6	3.6	2.4	4.6	11.0	5.5
1999	Tracker	1.6 (1590)	6	4.75	3.2	10.6	3.6	2.4	4.6	11.0	5.5
	Tracker	2.0 (1997)	C	5.90	3.2	10.6	3.6	2.4	4.6	11.0	6.5
2000-01	Tracker	1.6 (1590)	6	4.75	3.2	10.6	3.6	2.4	4.6	11.0	5.5
	Tracker	2.0 (1997)	C	5.90	3.2	10.6	3.6	2.4	4.6	11.0	6.5

NOTE: All capacities are approximate. Add fluid gradually and check to be sure a proper fluid level is obtained.

93081CI9

VALVE SPECIFICATIONS

Year	Engine Displacement Liters (cc)	Engine ID/VIN	Seat Angle (deg.)	Face MFI (deg.)	Spring Test Pressure (lbs. @ in.)	Spring Installed Height (in.)	Stem-to-Guide Clearance (in.)		Stem Diameter (in.)	
							Exhaust	Intake	Exhaust	Intake
1997	1.6 (1590)	6	45	45	23.6-27.5@ 1.24	1.24	0.0008-0.0027	0.0018-0.0035	0.2152-0.2157	0.2142-0.2148
1998	1.6 (1590)	6	45	45	23.6-27.5@ 1.24	1.24	0.0008-0.0027	0.0018-0.0035	0.2152-0.2157	0.2142-0.2148
1999	1.6 (1590)	6	45	45	23.6-27.5@ 1.24	1.24	0.0008-0.0027	0.0018-0.0035	0.2152-0.2157	0.2142-0.2148
	2.0 (1997)	C	45	45	①	②	0.0008-0.0027	0.0018-0.0035	0.2348-0.2354	0.2339-0.2344
2000-01	1.6 (1590)	6	45	45	23.6-27.5@ 1.24	1.24	0.0008-0.0027	0.0018-0.0035	0.2152-0.2157	0.2142-0.2148
	2.0 (1997)	C	45	45	①	②	0.0008-0.0027	0.0018-0.0035	0.2348-0.2354	0.2339-0.2344

① Inner spring: 13.6-17.4@1.08
  Outer spring: 30.4-39.2@1.25

② Inner spring: 1.08
  Outer spring: 1.25

93081CI0

CRANKSHAFT AND CONNECTING ROD SPECIFICATIONS
All measurements are given in inches.

Year	Engine Displacement Liters (cc)	Engine ID/VIN	Crankshaft				Connecting Rod		
			Main Brg. Journal Dia.	Main Brg. Oil Clearance	Shaft End-play	Thrust on No.	Journal Diameter	Oil Clearance	Side Clearance
1997	1.6 (1590)	6	2.0465-2.0472	0.0006-0.0023	0.0044-0.0149	3	1.7316-1.7322	0.0008-0.0031	NA
1998	1.6 (1590)	6	2.0465-2.0472	0.0006-0.0023	0.0044-0.0149	3	1.7316-1.7322	0.0008-0.0031	NA
1999	1.6 (1590)	6	2.0465-2.0472	0.0006-0.0023	0.0044-0.0149	3	1.7316-1.7322	0.0008-0.0031	NA
	2.0 (1997)	C	2.2828-2.2834	0.0008-0.0023	0.0039-0.0165	3	1.9678-1.9685	0.0016-0.0031	NA
2000-01	1.6 (1590)	6	2.0465-2.0472	0.0006-0.0023	0.0044-0.0149	3	1.7316-1.7322	0.0008-0.0031	NA
	2.0 (1997)	C	2.2828-2.2834	0.0008-0.0023	0.0039-0.0165	3	1.9678-1.9685	0.0016-0.0031	NA

NA: Not Available

93081CJ1

PISTON AND RING SPECIFICATIONS
All measurements are given in inches.

Year	Engine Displacement Liters (cc)	Engine ID/VIN	Piston Clearance	Ring Gap			Ring Side Clearance		
				Top Compression	Bottom Compression	Oil Control	Top Compression	Bottom Compression	Oil Control
1997	1.6 (1590)	6	0.0008-0.0015	0.0079-0.0275	0.0138-0.0275	0.0039-0.0669	0.0012-0.0027	0.0008-0.0023	NA
1998	1.6 (1590)	6	0.0008-0.0015	0.0079-0.0275	0.0138-0.0275	0.0039-0.0669	0.0012-0.0027	0.0008-0.0023	NA
1999	1.6 (1590)	6	0.0008-0.0015	0.0079-0.0275	0.0138-0.0275	0.0039-0.0669	0.0012-0.0027	0.0008-0.0023	NA
	2.0 (1997)	C	0.0008-0.0015	0.0079-0.0276	0.0138-0.0276	0.0079-0.0709	0.0012-0.0027	0.0008-0.0023	NA
2000-01	1.6 (1590)	6	0.0008-0.0015	0.0079-0.0275	0.0138-0.0275	0.0039-0.0669	0.0012-0.0027	0.0008-0.0023	NA
	2.0 (1997)	C	0.0008-0.0015	0.0079-0.0276	0.0138-0.0276	0.0079-0.0709	0.0012-0.0027	0.0008-0.0023	NA

NA: Not Available

93081CJ2

TORQUE SPECIFICATIONS
All readings in ft. lbs.

Year	Engine Displacement Liters (cc)	Engine ID/VIN	Cylinder Head Bolts	Main Bearing Bolts	Rod Bearing Bolts	Crankshaft Damper Bolts	Flywheel Bolts	Manifold Intake	Manifold Exhaust	Spark Plugs	Lug Nut
1997	1.6 (1590)	6	①	39②	25.5	94③	58	17	17	21	70
1998	1.6 (1590)	6	①	39②	25.5	94③	58	17	17	21	70
1999	1.6 (1590)	6	④	39②	25.5	94③	58	17	17	21	70
	2.0 (1997)	C	⑤	⑥	33	109	51	17	17	18	70
2000-01	1.6 (1590)	6	④	39②	25.5	94③	58	17	17	21	70
	2.0 (1997)	C	⑤	⑥	33	109	51	17	17	18	70

① Step 1: 26 ft. lbs.
  Step 2: 41 ft. lbs.
  Step 3: 52 ft. lbs.

② Use multiple passes to arrive at final torque.

③ Value shown is for crankshaft timing belt sprocket

④ Step 1: 26 ft. lbs.
  Step 2: 41 ft. lbs.
  Step 3: Loosen in reverse order to 0 ft. lbs.
  Step 4: 26 ft. lbs.
  Step 5: 52 ft. lbs.

⑤ Step 1: 38.5 ft. lbs.
  Step 2: 61 ft. lbs.
  Step 3: Loosen in reverse order to 0 ft. lbs.
  Step 4: 38.5 ft. lbs.
  Step 5: 76 ft. lbs.
  Step 6: Tighten 6mm bolt to 8 ft. lbs.

⑥ 10mm: 43.5 ft. lbs.
  8mm: 19.5 ft. lbs.

93081CJ3

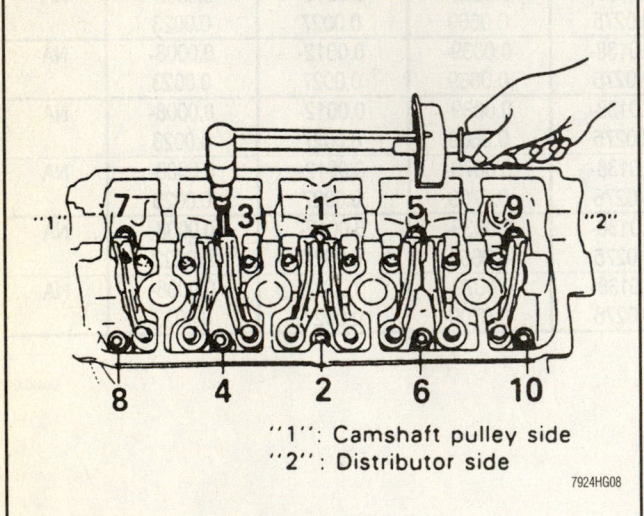

"1": Camshaft pulley side
"2": Distributor side

7924HG08

Cylinder head torque sequence—1.6L engine

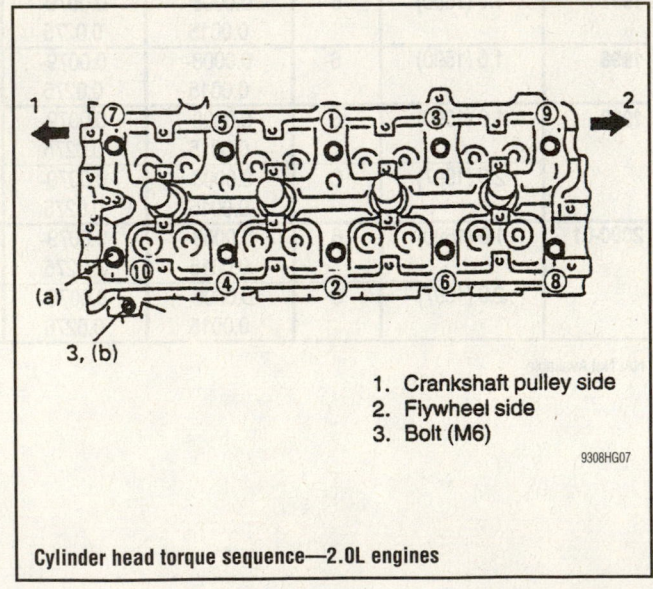

1. Crankshaft pulley side
2. Flywheel side
3. Bolt (M6)

9308HG07

Cylinder head torque sequence—2.0L engines

BRAKE SPECIFICATIONS
CHEVROLET TRACKER, GEO TRACKER
All measurements in inches unless noted

| Year | Model | Brake Disc | | | Brake Drum Diameter | | | Minimum Lining Thickness ① | | Brake Caliper | |
		Original Thickness	Minimum Thickness	Maximum Runout	Original Inside Diameter	Max. Wear Limit	Maximum Machine Diameter	Front	Rear	Bracket Bolts (ft. lbs.)	Mounting Bolts (ft. lbs.)
1997	Tracker ②	0.394	0.315	0.006	8.66	8.74	8.74	0.236	0.210	51-72	19-21
	Tracker ③	0.670	0.590	0.006	10.00	10.07	10.07	0.236	0.210	51-72	19-21
1998	Tracker ②	0.394	0.315	0.006	8.66	8.74	8.74	0.236	0.210	51-72	19-21
	Tracker ③	0.670	0.590	0.006	10.00	10.07	10.07	0.236	0.210	51-72	19-21
1999	Tracker ②	0.394	0.315	0.006	8.66	8.74	8.74	0.236	0.210	51-72	19-21
	Tracker ③	0.670	0.590	0.006	10.00	10.07	10.07	0.236	0.210	51-72	19-21
2000-01	Tracker ②	0.394	0.315	0.006	8.66	8.74	8.74	0.236	0.210	51-72	19-21
	Tracker ③	0.670	0.590	0.006	10.00	10.07	10.07	0.236	0.210	51-72	19-21

NA: Not Available

① Minimum lining thickness includes pad/shoe backing
② 2-door model
③ 4-door model

93081CJ4

SCHEDULED MAINTENANCE INTERVALS
(GEO TRACKER)

TO BE SERVICED	TYPE OF SERVICE	VEHICLE MILEAGE INTERVAL (x1000)												
		7.5	15	22.5	30	37.5	45	52.5	60	67.5	75	82.5	90	97.5
Engine oil & filter	R	✓	✓	✓	✓	✓	✓	✓	✓	✓	✓	✓	✓	✓
Automatic transmission fluid ①	S/I	✓	✓	✓	✓	✓	✓	✓	✓	✓	✓	✓	✓	✓
Disc brake pads, rotors, drum brake linings, drums, wheel cylinders & parking brake	S/I	✓	✓	✓	✓	✓	✓	✓	✓	✓	✓	✓	✓	✓
Exhaust system	S/I	✓	✓	✓	✓	✓	✓	✓	✓	✓	✓	✓	✓	✓
Free-wheeling hubs	S/I	✓	✓	✓	✓	✓	✓	✓	✓	✓	✓	✓	✓	✓
Locking front hubs	S/I	✓	✓	✓	✓	✓	✓	✓	✓	✓	✓	✓	✓	✓
Manual transmission/transfer case fluids ②	S/I	✓	✓	✓	✓	✓	✓	✓	✓	✓	✓	✓	✓	✓
Rotate tires	S/I	✓	✓	✓	✓	✓	✓	✓	✓	✓	✓	✓	✓	✓
Steering & suspension	S/I	✓	✓	✓	✓	✓	✓	✓	✓	✓	✓	✓	✓	✓
Throttle linkage	S/I	✓	✓	✓	✓	✓	✓	✓	✓	✓	✓	✓	✓	✓
Adjust valve lash	S/I		✓		✓		✓		✓		✓		✓	
Engine idle speed	S/I		✓		✓		✓		✓		✓		✓	
Propeller shafts & U-joints	S/I		✓		✓		✓		✓		✓		✓	
Air cleaner filter	R					✓			✓				✓	
Camshaft timing belt	R								✓					
Fuel filter	R				✓				✓				✓	
Spark plugs	R				✓				✓				✓	
Engine coolant	R				✓				✓				✓	
Engine accessory drive belt ③	S/I				✓				✓				✓	
Front wheel bearings	S/I				✓				✓				✓	
Fuel tank, cap & lines	S/I				✓				✓				✓	
Brake fluid	R								✓					
Fuel tank cap gasket	R								✓					
Ignition wires	R								✓					
Emission system hoses	S/I								✓					
Engine timing	S/I								✓					

93081CJ5

SCHEDULED MAINTENANCE INTERVALS
(GEO TRACKER) (Cont.)

TO BE SERVICED	TYPE OF SERVICE	VEHICLE MILEAGE INTERVAL (x1000)												
		7.5	15	22.5	30	37.5	45	52.5	60	67.5	75	82.5	90	97.5
EVAP canister ①	R													
PCV valve ④	R													
Fuel injectors ⑤	S/I													

R: Replace   S/I: Service or Inspect

① Replace every 100,000 miles.
② Replace every 30,000 miles.
③ Replace every 60,000 miles.
④ Replace every 50,000 miles.
⑤ Service or inspect every 100,000 miles.

FREQUENT OPERATION MAINTENANCE (SEVERE SERVICE)

If a vehicle is operated under any of the following conditions it is considered severe service:

- Extremely dusty areas.

- 50% or more of the vehicle operation is in 32°C (90°F) or higher temperatures, or constant operation in temperatures below 0°C (32°F).

- Prolonged idling (vehicle operation in stop and go traffic.

- Frequent short running periods (engine does not warm to normal operating temperatures).

- Police, taxi, delivery usage or trailer towing usage.

Oil filter change: change every 5000 miles.

Free-wheeling hubs: service or inspect every 3000 miles.

Rotate tires every 6000 miles.

Air cleaner filter: service or inspect every 15,000 miles.

Repack front wheel bearings every 15,000 miles.

Manual transmission fluid: change every 15,000 miles.

Engine idle speed: check every 15,000 miles.

Propeller shafts & U-joints: service or inspect every 15,000 miles.

Automatic transmission fluid & filter: change every 50,000 miles.

93081CJ6

For accessory drive belt replacement procedures see the model specific sections of this manual

SCHEDULED MAINTENANCE INTERVALS
GENERAL MOTORS CORPORATION
CHEVROLET/GEO TRACKER

The following should be used as a guide when determining the amount of work required for a particular service. In estimating how long a particular Scheduled Maintenance Service should take, please observe the following:

● Labor Time is time based on field research and data supplied by the vehicle manufacturer.
● Labor time operations are given in hours and tenths of an hour.
● All labor operations are to be used as a guide.

Mechanic Skill Level Codes:
(A) PRECISION: Highly skilled with multiple certification.
(B) GENERAL: Normally skilled with certification.
(C) MAINTENANCE: Semi-skilled working on certification.

	LABOR TIME		LABOR TIME		LABOR TIME
7500 Mile Service (B)		**37500 Mile Service (B)**		**75000 Mile Service (B)**	
All models	1.7	All models	1.9	All models	2.1
w/AT add	.1	w/AT add	.1	w/AT add	.1
w/4WD add	.2	w/4WD add	.2	w/4WD add	.2
15000 Mile Service (B)		**45000 Mile Service (B)**		**82500 Mile Service (B)**	
All models	2.2	All models	2.1	All models	1.7
w/AT add	.1	w/AT add	.1	w/AT add	.1
w/4WD add	.2	w/4WD add	.2	w/4WD add	.2
22500 Mile Service (B)		**52500 Mile Service (B)**		**90000 Mile Service (B)**	
All models	1.7	All models	1.7	All models	4.0
w/AT add	.1	w/AT add	.1	w/AT add	.1
w/4WD add	.2	w/4WD add	.2	w/4WD add	.2
30000 Mile Service (B)		**60000 Mile Service (B)**		**97500 Mile Service (B)**	
All models	4.1	All models	7.3	All models	1.8
w/AT add	.1	w/AT add	.1	w/AT add	.1
w/4WD add	.2	w/4WD add	.2	w/4WD add	.2
		67500 Mile Service (B)			
		All models	1.8		
		w/AT add	.1		
		w/4WD add	.2		

93081CJ7

TIRE, WHEEL AND BALL JOINT SPECIFICATIONS
Tracker

| Year | Model | OEM Tires | | Tire Pressures (psi) | | Wheel Size | Ball Joint Inspection |
		Standard	Optional	Front	Rear		
1997	2wd	P195/75R15	None	23	23	5.5-JJ	①
	4wd	P205/75R15	None	23	23	5.5-JJ	①
1998	2wd	P195/75R15	None	23	23	5.5-JJ	①
	4wd	P205/75R15	None	23	23	5.5-JJ	①
1999	2wd	P195/75R15	None	23	23	5.5-JJ	①
	4wd	P205/75R15	None	23	23	5.5-JJ	①
2000	2wd	P195/75R15	None	23	23	5.5-JJ	①
	4wd	P205/75R15	None	23	23	5.5-JJ	①

OEM: Original Equipment Manufacturer

PSI: Pounds Per Square Inch

STD: Standard

OPT: Optional

① Replace if any measurable movement is found.

93081CJ8

For brake related suspension and axle service, refer to the model specific sections of this manual

HONDA
CR-V • Odyssey • Passport

ENGINE AND VEHICLE IDENTIFICATION CHART

			Engine Code					Model Year	
Code	Liters (cc)	Cu. In.	Cyl.	Fuel Sys.	Engine Type	Eng. Mfg.	Code ①		Year
B20B4	2.0 (1973)	120	4	SMFI	DOHC	Honda	V		1997
B20Z2	2.0 (1973)	120	4	SMFI	DOHC	Honda	W		1998
F22B6	2.2 (2156)	132	4	SMFI	SOHC	Honda	X		1999
F23A7	2.3 (2254)	137	4	SMFI	SOHC	Honda	Y		2000
6VD1/V	3.2 (3165)	193	6	SMFI	SOHC	Isuzu	1		2001
6VD1/W	3.2 (3165)	193	6	SMFI	DOHC	Isuzu			
J35A1	3.5 (3471)	212	6	SMFI	SOHC	Honda			

DOHC: Double Overhead Cam

SOHC: Single Overhead Cam

SMFI: Sequential Multi-port Fuel Injection

① 10th position of VIN

93081CJ9

GENERAL ENGINE SPECIFICATIONS

Year	Model	Engine Displacement Liters (cc)	Engine ID/VIN	Fuel System Type	Net Horsepower @ rpm	Net Torque @ rpm (ft. lbs.)	Bore x Stroke (in.)	Com-pression Ratio	Oil Pressure @ rpm
1997	CR-V	2.0 (1973)	B20B4	SMFI	126@5400	133@4300	3.31x3.50	9.2:1	50@3000
	Odyssey	2.2 (2156)	F22B6	SMFI	140@5600	145@4600	3.35x3.74	8.8:1	50@3000
	Passport	3.2 (3165)	6VD1 (V)	SMFI	190@5600	188@4000	3.68x3.03	9.0:1	57-80@3000
1998	CR-V	2.0 (1973)	B20B4	SMFI	126@5400	133@4300	3.31x3.50	9.2:1	50@3000
	Odyssey	2.3 (2254)	F23A7	SMFI	150@5600	152@4700	3.39x3.82	9.3:1	50@3000
	Passport	3.2 (3165)	6VD1 (W)	SMFI	205@5400	214@3000	3.68x3.03	9.1:1	57-80@3000
1999	CR-V	2.0 (1973)	B20Z2	SMFI	146@6200	133@4500	3.31x3.50	9.6:1	50@3000
	Odyssey	3.5 (3471)	J35A1	SMFI	210@5200	229@4300	3.50x3.66	9.4:1	71@3000
	Passport	3.2 (3165)	6VD1 (W)	SMFI	205@5400	214@3000	3.68x3.03	9.1:1	57-80@3000
2000-01	CR-V	2.0 (1973)	B20Z2	SMFI	146@6200	133@4500	3.31x3.50	9.6:1	50@3000
	Odyssey	3.5 (3471)	J35A1	SMFI	210@5200	229@4300	3.50x3.66	9.4:1	71@3000
	Passport	3.2 (3165)	6VD1 (W)	SMFI	205@5400	214@3000	3.68x3.03	9.1:1	57-80@3000

SMFI: Sequential Multi-port Fuel Injection

93081CJ0

ENGINE TUNE-UP SPECIFICATIONS

Year	Engine Displacement Liters (cc)	Engine ID/VIN	Spark Plug Gap (in.)	Ignition Timing (deg.) MT	Ignition Timing (deg.) AT	Fuel Pump (psi)	Idle Speed (rpm) MT	Idle Speed (rpm) AT	Valve Clearance (in.) In.	Valve Clearance (in.) Ex.
1997	2.0 (1973)	B20B4	0.039-0.043	—	14-18B	38-46	—	700-800	0.003-0.005	0.006-0.008
	2.2 (2156)	F22B6	0.039-0.043	—	13-17B	30-37	—	650-750	0.009-0.011	0.011-0.013
	3.2 (3156)	6VD1 (V)	0.040-0.043	5B	5B	41-46	750	750	HYD	HYD
1998	2.0 (1973)	B20B4	0.039-0.043	14-18B	14-18B	38-46	700-800	700-800	0.003-0.005	0.006-0.008
	2.3 (2254)	F23A7	0.039-0.043	—	10-14B	38-46	—	650-750	0.009-0.011	0.011-0.013
	3.2 (3165)	6VD1 (W)	0.040-0.043	16B	16B	48-55	750	750	0.009-0.013	0.010-0.014
1999	2.0 (1973)	B20Z2	0.039-0.043	14-18B	14-18B	38-46	700-800	700-800	0.003-0.005	0.006-0.008
	3.2 (3165)	6VD1 (W)	0.040-0.043	16B	16B	48-55	750	750	0.009-0.011	0.010-0.013
	3.5 (3471)	J35A1	0.039-0.043	—	8-12B	32-40	—	680-780	0.008-0.009	0.011-0.013
2000-01	2.0 (1973)	B20Z2	0.039-0.043	14-18B	14-18B	38-46	700-800	700-800	0.003-0.005	0.006-0.008
	3.2 (3165)	6VD1 (W)	0.040-0.043	16B	16B	48-55	750	750	0.009-0.011	0.010-0.013
	3.5 (3471)	J35A1	0.039-0.043	—	8-12B	32-40	—	680-780	0.008-0.009	0.011-0.013

NOTE: The Vehicle Emission Control Information label often reflects changes made during production and must be used if they differ from this chart.

NOTE: The fuel pressure readings are given with the vacuum hose connected to the regulator and the engine running

B: Before top dead center

HYD: Hydraulic

93081CK1

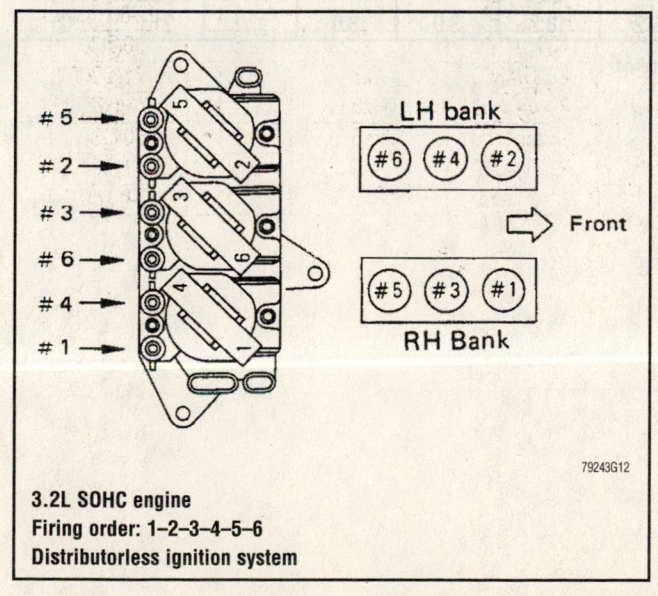

3.2L SOHC engine
Firing order: 1-2-3-4-5-6
Distributorless ignition system

79243G12

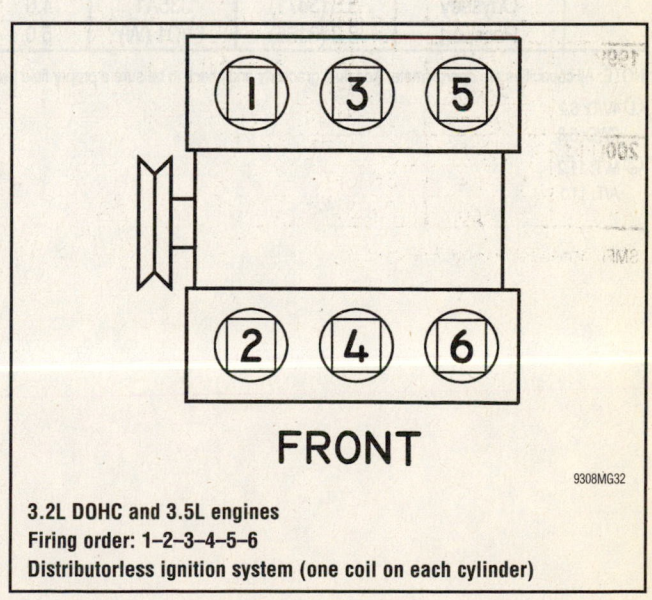

FRONT

9308MG32

3.2L DOHC and 3.5L engines
Firing order: 1-2-3-4-5-6
Distributorless ignition system (one coil on each cylinder)

Refer to the model specific sections for driveline service procedures

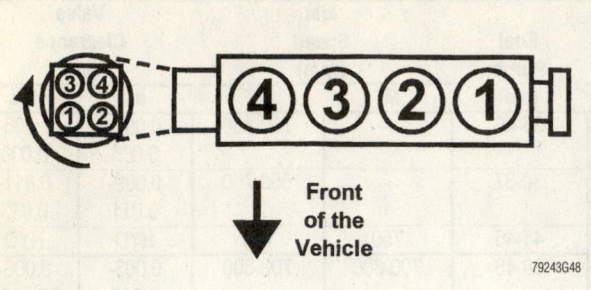

2.0L engine
Firing order: 1–3–4–2
Distributor rotation: Clockwise

79243G48

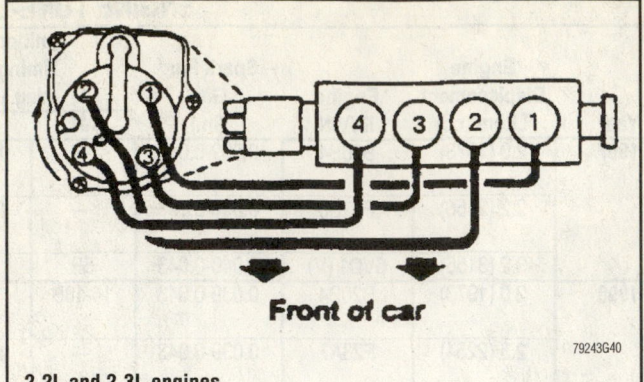

Front of car

2.2L and 2.3L engines
Firing order: 1–3–4–2
Distributor rotation: Clockwise

79243G40

CAPACITIES

Year	Model	Engine Displacement Liters (cc)	Engine ID/VIN	Engine Oil with Filter (qts.)	Transmission (pts.)		Transfer Case (pts.)	Drive Axle		Fuel Tank (gal.)	Cooling System (qts.)
					5-Spd	Auto.		Front (pts.)	Rear (pts.)		
1997	CR-V	2.0 (1973)	B20B4	4.0	—	①	—	—	2.2	15.3	4.1
	Odyssey	2.2 (2156)	F22B6	4.0	—	5.0	—	—	—	17.2	6.7
	Passport	3.2 (3165)	6VD1 (V)	5.0	6.2	18.2	3.0	3.0	3.74	21.1	②
1998	CR-V	2.0 (1973)	B20B4	4.0	3.6	①	—	—	2.2	15.3	4.1
	Odyssey	2.3 (2254)	F23A7	4.5	—	5.8	—	—	—	17.2	6.7
	Passport	3.2 (3165)	6VD1 (W)	5.0	6.2	18.2	3.0	3.0	3.74	21.1	②
1999	CR-V	2.0 (1973)	B20Z2	4.0	3.6	①	—	—	2.2	15.3	4.1
	Odyssey	3.5 (3471)	J35A1	4.6	—	6.2	—	—	—	20.0	7.0
	Passport	3.2 (3165)	6VD1 (W)	5.0	6.2	18.2	3.0	3.0	3.74	21.1	②
2000-01	CR-V	2.0 (1973)	B20Z2	4.0	3.6	①	—	—	2.2	15.3	4.1
	Odyssey	3.5 (3471)	J35A1	4.6	—	6.2	—	—	—	20.0	7.0
	Passport	3.2 (3165)	6VD1 (W)	5.0	6.2	18.2	3.0	3.0	3.74	21.1	②

NOTE: All capacities are approximate. Add fluid gradually and check to be sure a proper fluid level is obtained.

① 4WD: 6.2
  2WD: 5.8

② M/T: 11.2
  A/T: 11.1

93081CK2

VALVE SPECIFICATIONS

Year	Engine Displacement Liters (cc)	Engine ID/VIN	Seat Angle (deg.)	Face Angle (deg.)	Spring Test Pressure (lbs. @ in.)	Spring Installed Height (in.)	Stem-to-Guide Clearance (in.)		Stem Diameter (in.)	
							Intake	Exhaust	Intake	Exhaust
1997	2.2 (2156)	F22B6	45	45	NA	①	0.0008-0.0018	0.0022-0.0031	0.2159-0.2163	0.2146-0.2150
	2.0 (1973)	B20B4	45	45	NA	②	0.0010-0.0020	0.0020-0.0030	0.2591-0.2594	0.2579-0.2583
	3.2 (3165)	6VD1 (V)	45	45	45-55@1.54	1.540	0.0009-0.0079	0.0012-0.0079	0.2323-0.2353	0.2323-0.2350
1998	2.0 (1973)	B20B4	45	45	NA	②	0.0010-0.0020	0.0020-0.0030	0.2591-0.2594	0.2579-0.2583
	2.3 (2254)	F23A7	45	45	NA	③	0.00080-0.0018	0.0022-0.0031	0.2159-0.2163	0.2146-0.2150
	3.2 (3165)	6VD1 (W)	45	45	44@1.38	1.380	0.0009-0.0079	0.0012-0.0079	0.2323-0.2353	0.2323-0.2350
1999	2.0 (1973)	B20Z2	45	45	NA	①	0.0010-0.0020	0.0020-0.0030	0.2591-0.2594	0.2579-0.2583
	3.2 (3165)	6VD1 (W)	45	45	44@1.38	1.380	0.0009-0.0079	0.0012-0.0079	0.2323-0.2353	0.2323-0.2350
	3.5 (3471)	J35A1	45	45	NA	④	0.0008-0.0018	0.0022-0.0031	0.2159-0.2163	0.2146-0.2150
2000-01	2.0 (1973)	B20Z2	45	45	NA	①	0.0010-0.0020	0.0020-0.0030	0.2591-0.2594	0.2579-0.2583
	3.2 (3165)	6VD1 (W)	45	45	44@1.38	1.380	0.0009-0.0079	0.0012-0.0079	0.2323-0.2353	0.2323-0.2350
	3.5 (3471)	J35A1	45	45	NA	④	0.0008-0.0018	0.0022-0.0031	0.2159-0.2163	0.2146-0.2150

NA: Not Available

① Valve spring free length:
Intake: 2.103 in.
Exhaust: 2.152 in.

② Valve spring free length:
Intake: 1.668 in.
Exhaust: 1.745 in.

③ Valve spring free length:
Intake: 2.011 in.
Exhaust: 2.188 in.

④ Valve spring free length:
Intake: 1.9713 in.
Exhaust: 2.1060 in.

93081CK3

For exhaust manifold replacement procedures, see the model specific sections of this manual

CRANKSHAFT AND CONNECTING ROD SPECIFICATIONS

All measurements are given in inches

Year	Engine Displacement Liters (cc)	Engine ID/VIN	Crankshaft				Connecting Rod		
			Main Brg. Journal Dia.	Main Brg. Oil Clearance	Shaft End-play	Thrust on No.	Journal Diameter	Oil Clearance	Side Clearance
1997	2.0 (1973)	B20B4	①	②	0.0040-0.0140	4	1.7707-1.7717	0.0008-0.0015	0.0060-0.0120
	2.2 (2156)	F22B6	③	④	0.0040-0.0180	4	1.8888-1.8898	0.0008-0.0024	0.0060-0.0160
	3.2 (3156)	6VD1 (V)	2.5165-2.5170	0.0007-0.0031	0.0024-0.0094	3	2.1229-2.1235	0.0010-0.0023	0.0063-0.0138
1998	2.0 (1973)	B20B4	①	②	0.0040-0.0140	4	1.7707-1.7717	0.0008-0.0015	0.0060-0.0120
	2.3 (2254)	F23A7	⑤	⑥	0.0040-0.0180	4	1.7708-1.7717	0.0008-0.0019	0.0060-0.0120
	3.2 (3165)	6VD1 (W)	2.5165-2.5170	0.0007-0.0031	0.0024-0.0094	3	2.1229-2.1235	0.0010-0.0023	0.0063-0.0138
1999	2.0 (1973)	B20Z2	①	②	0.0040-0.0140	4	1.7707-1.7717	0.0008-0.0015	0.0060-0.0120
	3.2 (3165)	6VD1 (W)	2.5165-2.5170	0.0007-0.0031	0.0024-0.0094	3	2.1229-2.1235	0.0010-0.0023	0.0063-0.0138
	3.5 (3471)	J35A1	2.8337-2.8346	0.0008-0.0017	0.0040-0.0140	3	2.1644-2.1654	0.0008-0.0017	0.0060-0.0140
2000-01	2.0 (1973)	B20Z2	①	②	0.0040-0.0140	4	1.7707-1.7717	0.0008-0.0015	0.0060-0.0120
	3.2 (3165)	6VD1 (W)	2.5165-2.5170	0.0007-0.0031	0.0024-0.0094	3	2.1229-2.1235	0.0010-0.0023	0.0063-0.0138
	3.5 (3471)	J35A1	2.8337-2.8346	0.0008-0.0017	0.0040-0.0140	3	2.1644-2.1654	0.0008-0.0017	0.0060-0.0140

① Nos. 1, 2, 4 and 5: 2.1644-2.1654
No. 3: 2.1642-2.1651

② Nos. 1, 2, 4 and 5: 0.0009-0.0017
No. 3: 0.0012-0.0019

③ Nos. 1 and 4: 1.9679-1.9688
No. 2: 1.9676-1.9685
No. 3: 1.9674-1.9683
No. 5: 1.9680-1.9690

④ Nos. 1 and 4: 0.0005-0.0020
No. 2: 0.0008-0.002
No. 3: 0.0010-0.0022
No. 5: 0.0004-0.0016

⑤ Nos. 1, 2 and 4: 2.1646-2.1655
No. 3: 2.1644-2.1654
No. 5: 2.1650-2.1660

⑥ Nos. 1, 2 and 4: 0.0008-0.0020
No. 3: 0.0010-0.0022
No. 5: 0.0004-0.0016

93081CK4

PISTON AND RING SPECIFICATIONS
All measurements are given in inches

Year	Engine Displacement Liters (cc)	Engine ID/VIN	Piston Clearance	Ring Gap			Ring Side Clearance		
				Top Compression	Bottom Compression	Oil Control	Top Compression	Bottom Compression	Oil Control
1997	2.0 (1973)	B20B4	0.0004-0.0016	0.0080-0.0120	0.0160-0.0220	0.0080-0.0200	0.0022-0.0031	0.0014-0.0024	NA
	2.2 (2156)	F22B6	0.0080-0.0020	0.0080-0.0140	0.0160-0.0220	0.0080-0.0280	0.0014-0.0024	0.0012-0.0022	NA
	3.2 (3156)	6VD1 (V)	0.0016-0.0020	0.0118-0.0394	0.0177-0.0472	0.0059-0.0413	0.0006-0.0059	0.0006-0.0059	NA
1998	2.0 (1973)	B20B4	0.0004-0.0016	0.0080-0.0120	0.0160-0.0220	0.0080-0.0200	0.0022-0.0031	0.0014-0.0024	NA
	2.3 (2254)	F23A7	0.0008-0.0020	0.0080-0.0140	0.0160-0.0220	0.0080-0.0280	0.0014-0.0024	0.0012-0.0022	NA
	3.2 (3165)	6VD1 (W)	0.0016-0.0020	0.0118-0.0394	0.0177-0.0472	0.0059-0.0413	0.0006-0.0059	0.0006-0.0059	NA
1999	2.0 (1973)	B20Z2	0.0004-0.0016	0.0080-0.0120	0.0160-0.0220	0.0080-0.0200	0.0022-0.0031	0.0014-0.0024	NA
	3.2 (3165)	6VD1 (W)	0.0016-0.0020	0.0118-0.0394	0.0177-0.0472	0.0059-0.0413	0.0006-0.0059	0.0006-0.0059	NA
	3.5 (3471)	J35A1	0.0006-0.0016	0.0080-0.0140	0.0160-0.0220	0.0080-0.0280	0.0014-0.0024	0.0012-0.0022	NA
2000-01	2.0 (1973)	B20Z2	0.0004-0.0016	0.0080-0.0120	0.0160-0.0220	0.0080-0.0200	0.0022-0.0031	0.0014-0.0024	NA
	3.2 (3165)	6VD1 (W)	0.0016-0.0020	0.0118-0.0394	0.0177-0.0472	0.0059-0.0413	0.0006-0.0059	0.0006-0.0059	NA
	3.5 (3471)	J35A1	0.0006-0.0016	0.0080-0.0140	0.0160-0.0220	0.0080-0.0280	0.0014-0.0024	0.0012-0.0022	NA

NA: Not Applicable

93081CK5

Refer to the model specific sections for cooling system service procedures

TORQUE SPECIFICATIONS
All readings in ft. lbs.

Year	Engine Displacement Liters (cc)	Engine ID/VIN	Cylinder Head Bolts	Main Bearing Bolts	Rod Bearing Bolts	Crankshaft Damper Bolts	Flywheel Bolts	Manifold Intake	Manifold Exhaust	Spark Plugs	Lug Nut
1997	2.0 (1973)	B20B4	①	②	23	130	54	17	23	13	80
	2.2 (2156)	F22B6	③	④	34	181	54	16	23	13	80
	3.2 (3165)	6VD1/V	⑤	⑥	40	123	40	17	42	13	87
1998	2.0 (1973)	B20B4	①	②	23	130	54	17	23	13	80
	2.3 (2254)	F23A7	⑦	51	14	181	54	16	23	13	80
	3.2 (3165)	6VD1/W	⑧	29	40	123	40	17	42	13	87
1999	2.0 (1973)	B20Z2	①	②	23	130	54	17	23	13	80
	3.2 (3165)	6VD1/W	⑧	29	40	123	40	17	42	13	87
	3.5 (3471)	J35A1	③	⑨	⑩	181	54	16	23	13	80
2000-01	2.0 (1973)	B20Z2	①	②	23	130	54	17	23	13	80
	3.2 (3165)	6VD1/W	⑧	29	40	123	40	17	42	13	87
	3.5 (3471)	J35A1	③	⑨	⑩	181	54	16	23	13	80

NOTE: Dip main bearing bolts and crankshaft damper bolt in clean engine oil prior to tightening.

① Step 1: 22 ft. lbs.
Step 2: 63 ft. lbs.

② Step 1: 18 ft. lbs.
Step 2: 56 ft. lbs.

③ Step 1: 29 ft. lbs.
Step 2: 51 ft. lbs.
Step 3: 72 ft. lbs.

④ Step 1: 22 ft. lbs.
Step 2: 54 ft. lbs.

⑤ 8mm bolts: 15 ft. lbs.
11mm bolts: 47 ft. lbs.

⑥ Main bearing cap bolts: 29 ft. lbs.
Oil gallery bolts: 29 ft. lbs. plus 55-65 degrees
Buttress bolts: 29 ft. lbs.

⑦ Step 1: 22 ft. lbs.
Step 2: 90 degrees
Step 3: 90 degrees
Step 4: New bolts 90 degrees

⑧ Step 1: 21 ft. lbs.
Step 2: 47 ft. lbs.

⑨ 11mm bolt 56 ft. lbs.
10mm bolt 36 ft. lbs.

⑩ Step 1: 14 ft. lbs.
Step 2: 90 degrees

93081CK6

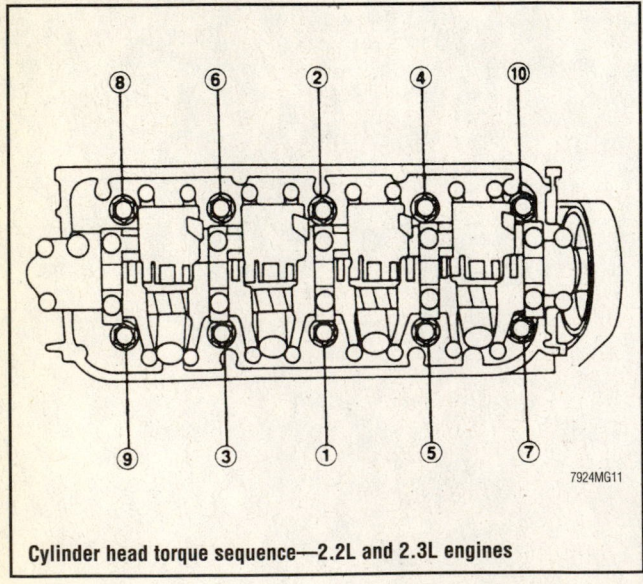

Cylinder head torque sequence—2.2L and 2.3L engines

7924MG11

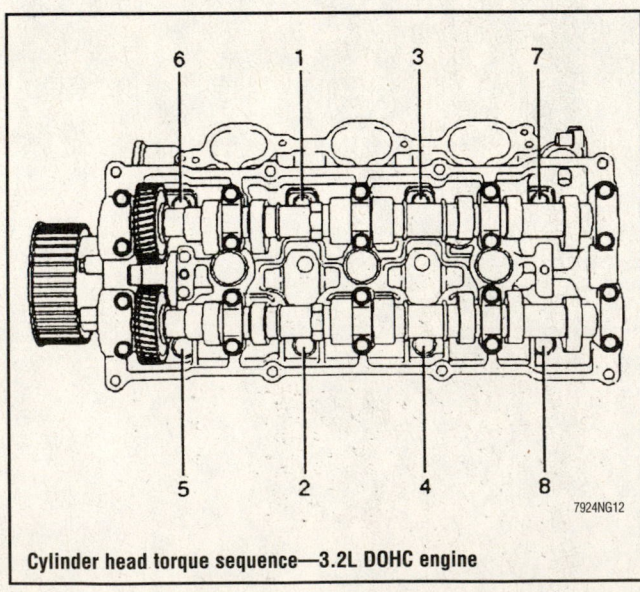

Cylinder head torque sequence—3.2L DOHC engine

7924NG12

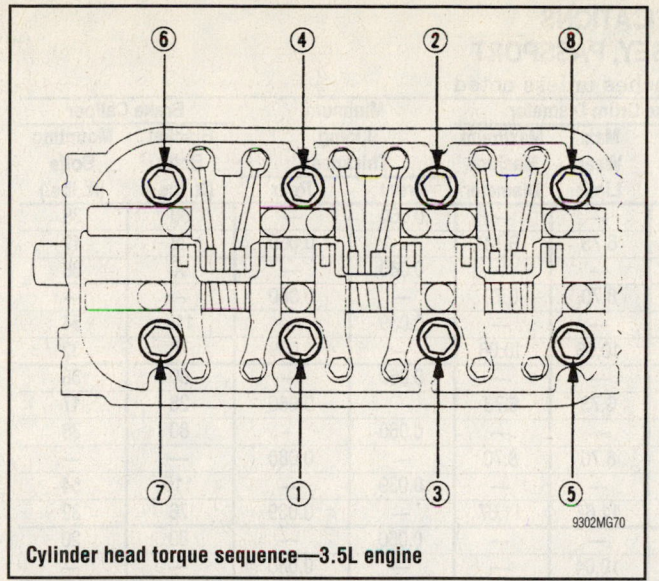

Cylinder head torque sequence—3.5L engine

9302MG70

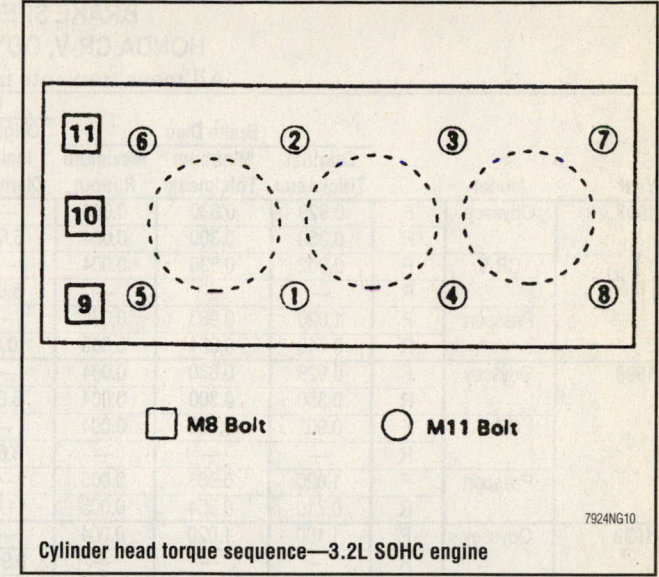

☐ **M8 Bolt**   ◯ **M11 Bolt**

Cylinder head torque sequence—3.2L SOHC engine

7924NG10

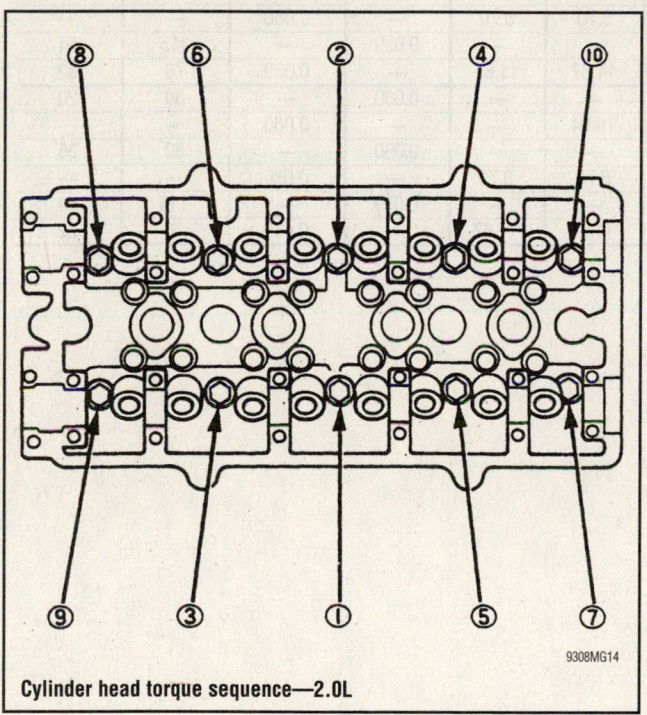

Cylinder head torque sequence—2.0L

9308MG14

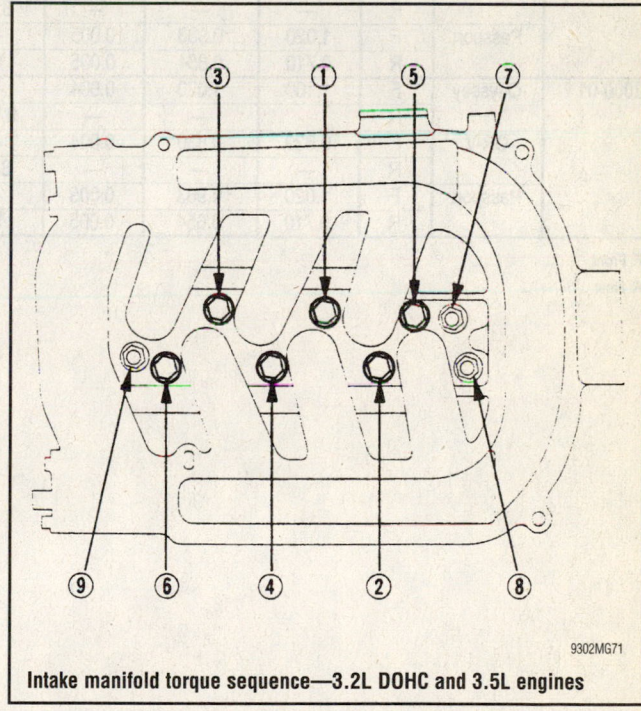

Intake manifold torque sequence—3.2L DOHC and 3.5L engines

9302MG71

BRAKE SPECIFICATIONS
HONDA CR-V, ODYSSEY, PASSPORT
All measurements in inches unless noted

Year	Model		Brake Disc Original Thickness	Brake Disc Minimum Thickness	Brake Disc Maximum Runout	Brake Drum Diameter Original Inside Diameter	Brake Drum Diameter Max. Wear Limit	Brake Drum Diameter Maximum Machine Diameter	Minimum Lining Thickness Front	Minimum Lining Thickness Rear	Brake Caliper Bracket Bolts (ft. lbs.)	Brake Caliper Mounting Bolts (ft. lbs.)
1997	Odyssey	F	0.929	0.830	0.004	—	—	—	0.060	—	80	36
		R	0.350	0.300	0.004	6.69	6.73	6.73	—	0.060	28	17
	CR-V	F	0.902	0.830	0.004	—	—	—	0.060	—	80	36
		R	—	—	—	8.66	8.70	8.70	—	0.080	—	—
	Passport	F	1.020	0.983	0.005	—	—	—	0.039	—	115	54
		R	0.710	0.654	0.005	10.00	10.06	10.06	—	0.039	76	32
1998	Odyssey	F	0.929	0.830	0.004	—	—	—	0.060	—	80	36
		R	0.350	0.300	0.004	6.69	6.73	6.73	—	0.060	28	17
	CR-V	F	0.902	0.830	0.004	—	—	—	0.060	—	80	36
		R	—	—	—	8.66	8.70	8.70	—	0.080	—	—
	Passport	F	1.020	0.983	0.005	—	—	—	0.039	—	115	54
		R	0.710	0.654	0.005	11.60	11.67	11.67	—	0.039	76	32
1999	Odyssey	F	1.100	1.020	0.004	—	—	—	0.060	—	80	20
		R	—	—	—	9.996	10.04	—	—	0.080	—	—
	CR-V	F	0.929	0.830	0.004	—	—	—	0.060	—	80	36
		R	—	—	—	8.66	8.70	8.70	—	0.080	—	—
	Passport	F	1.020	0.983	0.005	—	—	—	0.039	—	115	54
		R	0.710	0.654	0.005	11.60	11.67	11.67	—	0.039	76	32
2000-01	Odyssey	F	1.100	1.020	0.004	—	—	—	0.060	—	80	20
		R	—	—	—	9.996	10.04	—	—	0.080	—	—
	CR-V	F	0.929	0.830	0.004	—	—	—	0.060	—	80	36
		R	—	—	—	8.66	8.70	8.70	—	0.080	—	—
	Passport	F	1.020	0.983	0.005	—	—	—	0.039	—	115	54
		R	0.710	0.654	0.005	11.60	11.67	11.67	—	0.039	76	32

F: Front
R: Rear

93081CK7

SCHEDULED MAINTENANCE INTERVALS
(HONDA PASSPORT)

TO BE SERVICED	TYPE OF SERVICE	7.5	15	22.5	30	37.5	45	52.5	60	67.5	75	82.5	90	97.5	105	112.5	120
Accelerator linkage ①	L	✓	✓	✓	✓	✓	✓	✓	✓	✓	✓	✓	✓	✓	✓	✓	✓
Accessory drive belts ②	S/I			✓					✓				✓				✓
Air cleaner filter	R			✓					✓				✓				✓
Auto cruise control linkage & hose ③	S/I		✓		✓		✓		✓		✓		✓		✓		✓
Automatic transmission fluid level ③	S/I	✓		✓		✓		✓		✓		✓		✓		✓	
Battery fluid level ③	S/I	✓	✓	✓	✓	✓	✓	✓	✓	✓	✓	✓	✓	✓	✓	✓	✓
Body and chassis ①	L	✓	✓	✓	✓	✓	✓	✓	✓	✓	✓	✓	✓	✓	✓	✓	✓
Brake fluid level ③	S/I	✓	✓	✓	✓	✓	✓	✓	✓	✓	✓	✓	✓	✓	✓	✓	✓
Brake lines & hoses ③	S/I	✓	✓	✓	✓	✓	✓	✓	✓	✓	✓	✓	✓	✓	✓	✓	✓
Brake pedal play ③	S/I		✓		✓		✓		✓		✓		✓		✓		✓
Clutch fluid level ③	S/I	✓	✓	✓	✓	✓	✓	✓	✓	✓	✓	✓	✓	✓	✓	✓	✓
Clutch lines & hose ③	S/I				✓				✓				✓				✓
Clutch pedal free-play ③	S/I		✓		✓		✓		✓		✓		✓		✓		✓
Clutch pedal spring, bushing and clevis pin ①	S/I		✓		✓		✓		✓		✓		✓		✓		✓
Cooling and heating system hoses ③	S/I		✓		✓		✓		✓		✓		✓		✓		✓
Driveshaft flange torque ③	S/I	✓		✓		✓		✓		✓		✓		✓		✓	
Drum and disc brakes ③	S/I		✓		✓		✓		✓		✓		✓		✓		✓
Engine coolant	R				✓				✓				✓				✓
Engine coolant level ③	S/I	✓	✓	✓	✓	✓	✓	✓	✓	✓	✓	✓	✓	✓	✓	✓	✓
Engine oil & filter ③	R	✓	✓	✓	✓	✓	✓	✓	✓	✓	✓	✓	✓	✓	✓	✓	✓
Exhaust system ③	S/I	✓	✓	✓	✓	✓	✓	✓	✓	✓	✓	✓	✓	✓	✓	✓	✓
Front and rear axle lubricant	R		✓		✓				✓				✓				✓
Front and rear driveshafts ①	S/I	✓	✓	✓	✓	✓	✓	✓	✓	✓	✓	✓	✓	✓	✓	✓	✓
Front wheel bearings	S/I & L				✓				✓				✓				✓
Fuel lines & tank cap ③	S/I								✓								✓
Inspect for fluid leaks ③	S/I	✓	✓	✓	✓	✓	✓	✓	✓	✓	✓	✓	✓	✓	✓	✓	✓
Key lock cylinder ③	L		✓		✓		✓		✓		✓		✓		✓		✓
Manual transmission and transfer case fluid ④	R		✓		✓				✓				✓				✓
Parking brake system ③	S/I		✓		✓		✓		✓		✓		✓		✓		✓

93081CK8

Timing chain and gear service is covered in the model specific sections of this manual

SCHEDULED MAINTENANCE INTERVALS
(HONDA PASSPORT) (Cont.)

TO BE SERVICED	TYPE OF SERVICE	VEHICLE MILEAGE INTERVAL (x1000)															
		7.5	15	22.5	30	37.5	45	52.5	60	67.5	75	82.5	90	97.5	105	112.5	120
Power steering fluid	R				✓				✓				✓				✓
Radiator core and A/C condenser	S/I & C								✓								✓
Rotate tires	S/I	✓	✓	✓	✓	✓	✓	✓	✓	✓	✓	✓	✓	✓	✓	✓	✓
Shift-on-the-fly system gear fluid ③	S/I		✓		✓			✓	✓		✓		✓		✓		✓
Spark plugs ⑤	R				✓				✓				✓				✓
Starter safety switch ③	S/I	✓	✓	✓	✓	✓	✓	✓	✓	✓	✓	✓	✓	✓	✓	✓	✓
Steering operation ③	S/I	✓	✓	✓	✓	✓	✓	✓	✓	✓	✓	✓	✓	✓	✓	✓	✓
Suspension & steering ③	S/I	✓	✓	✓	✓	✓	✓	✓	✓	✓	✓	✓	✓	✓	✓	✓	✓
Throttle linkage ③	S/I		✓		✓		✓		✓		✓		✓		✓		✓
Timing belt	R								✓								✓
Tires and wheels ③	S/I	✓	✓	✓	✓	✓	✓	✓	✓	✓	✓	✓	✓	✓	✓	✓	✓
Valve clearance ⑤	A		✓		✓		✓		✓		✓		✓		✓		✓

R: Replace   S/I: Service or Inspect   L: Lubricate   A: Adjust   C: Clean

① Perform this at the mileage indicated or every 6 months, whichever occurs first.

② Perform this at the mileage indicated or every 24 months, whichever occurs first.

③ Perform this at the mileage indicated or every 12 months, whichever occurs first.

④ 3.2L V6 engine.

⑤ 2.6L I4 engine.

FREQUENT OPERATION MAINTENANCE (SEVERE SERVICE)

If a vehicle is operated under any of the following conditions it is considered severe service:

- Towing a trailer or using a camper or car-top carrier.

- Repeated short trips of less than 5 miles in temperatures below freezing.

- Extensive idling or low-speed driving for long distances as in heavy commercial use, such as delivery, taxi or police cars.

- Operating on rough, muddy or salt-covered roads.

- Operating on unpaved or dusty roads.

Air cleaner element: replace every 15,000 miles

Engine oil and filter: replace every 3000 miles or 3 months, whichever occurs first.

Automatic transmission fluid: replace every 20,000 miles.

Rear axle lubricant: replace every 15,000 miles.

93081CK9

SCHEDULED MAINTENANCE INTERVALS
(HONDA CR-V & ODYSSEY)

TO BE SERVICED	TYPE OF SERVICE	VEHICLE MILEAGE INTERVAL (x1000)															
		7.5	15	22.5	30	37.5	45	52.5	60	67.5	75	82.5	90	97.5	105	112.5	120
Accessory drive belts	I & A				✓				✓				✓				✓
Air cleaner element	R				✓				✓				✓				✓
Air conditioning filter	R				✓				✓				✓				✓
Brake fluid	R						✓										
Brake hoses & lines (including ABS)	I		✓		✓		✓		✓		✓		✓		✓		✓
Cooling system hoses & connections	I		✓		✓		✓		✓		✓		✓		✓		✓
Engine coolant	R						✓						✓				
Engine oil	R	✓	✓	✓	✓	✓	✓	✓	✓	✓	✓	✓	✓	✓	✓	✓	✓
Engine oil and coolant levels	I	Inspect at each fuel stop															
Engine oil filter	R		✓		✓		✓		✓		✓		✓		✓		✓
Exhaust system	I		✓		✓		✓		✓		✓		✓		✓		✓
Fluid levels and condition	I		✓		✓		✓		✓		✓		✓		✓		✓
Front and rear brakes	I		✓		✓		✓		✓		✓		✓		✓		✓
Fuel lines & connection	I		✓		✓		✓		✓		✓		✓		✓		✓
Halfshaft boots	I		✓		✓		✓		✓		✓		✓		✓		✓
Idle speed	I & A													✓			
Parking brake system	I & A		✓		✓		✓		✓		✓		✓		✓		✓
Rear differential fluid	R												✓				
Rotate and inspect tires	I	✓	✓	✓	✓	✓	✓	✓	✓	✓	✓	✓	✓	✓	✓	✓	✓
Spark plugs	R				✓				✓				✓				✓
Supplemental Restrain system (SRS)	I	Inspect the SRS 10 years after production															
Suspension components	I		✓		✓		✓		✓		✓		✓		✓		✓
Tie rod ends, steering gear box & boots	I		✓		✓		✓		✓		✓		✓		✓		✓
Timing balancer belt ①	R														✓		
Timing belt	R														✓		
Transmission fluid ②	R												✓				
Transmission fluid ①	R						✓				✓				✓		
Valve clearance ②	I	Adjust if valves are noisy															
Valve clearance ①	I				✓				✓				✓				✓

93081CK0

Ignition system service is covered in the model specific sections of this manual

SCHEDULED MAINTENANCE INTERVALS
(HONDA CR-V & ODYSSEY) (Cont.)

TO BE SERVICED	TYPE OF SERVICE	VEHICLE MILEAGE INTERVAL (x1000)														
		7.5	15	22.5	30	37.5	45	52.5	60	67.5	75	82.5	90	97.5	105	112.5	120
Water pump	S/I														✓		

R: Replace   I: Inspect   A: Adjust

① Odyssey

② CR-V

FREQUENT OPERATION MAINTENANCE (SEVERE SERVICE)

If a vehicle is operated under any of the following conditions it is considered severe service:

- Towing a trailer or using a camper or car-top carrier.
- Repeated short trips of less than 5 miles in temperatures below freezing, or trips of less than 10 miles in any temperature.
- Extensive idling or low-speed driving for long distances as in heavy commercial use, such as delivery, taxi or police cars.
- Operating on rough, muddy or salt-covered roads.
- Operating on unpaved or dusty roads.
- Driving in extremely hot (over 90°) conditions.

Air cleaner element: replace every 15,000 miles

Engine oil and filter: replace every 3750 miles or 6 months, whichever occurs first.

Timing belt: replace every 60,000 miles if the vehicle is regularly driven in temperatures above 110°F or below -20°F.

Transmission fluid: replace every 30,000 miles.

Rear differential fluid: replace every 60,000 miles.

Front and rear brakes: inspect every 7500 miles or 6 months, whichever occurs first.

Locks and hinges: lubricate every 15,000 miles.

Tie rods, steering gear box, boots: inspect every 7500 miles or 6 months, whichever occurs first.

Suspension components: inspect every 7500 miles or 6 months, whichever occurs first.

Halfshaft boots: inspect every 7500 miles or 6 months, whichever occurs first.

93081CL1

SCHEDULED MAINTENANCE INTERVALS
HONDA
PASSPORT, CR-V, ODYSSEY

The following should be used as a guide when determining the amount of work required for a particular service.
In estimating how long a particular Scheduled Maintenance Service should take, please observe the following:

- Labor Time is time based on field research and data supplied by the vehicle manufacturer.
- Labor time operations are given in hours and tenths of an hour.
- All labor operations are to be used as a guide.

Mechanic Skill Level Codes:
(A) PRECISION: Highly skilled with multiple certification.
(B) GENERAL: Normally skilled with certification.
(C) MAINTENANCE: Semi-skilled working on certification.

	LABOR TIME			LABOR TIME			LABOR TIME
7500 Mile Service (C)			**52500 Mile Service (C)**			**90000 Mile Service (B)**	
Passport	1.8		Passport	1.8		Passport	
Odyssey, CR-V	1.3		Odyssey, CR-V	1.3		2.6L	7.3
15000 Mile Service (B)			**60000 Mile Service (B)**			3.2L	6.6
Passport			Passport			Odyssey, CR-V	6.9
2.6L	4.7		2.6L	8.8		**97500 Mile Service (C)**	
3.2L	3.6		3.2L	8.1		Passport	1.8
Odyssey, CR-V	1.4		Odyssey, CR-V	3.9		Odyssey, CR-V	1.3
22500 Mile Service (C)			**67500 Mile Service (C)**			**105000 Mile Service (B)**	
Passport	1.8		Passport	1.8		Passport	4.1
Odyssey, CR-V	1.3		Odyssey, CR-V	1.3		Odyssey, CR-V	1.8
30000 Mile Service (B)			**75000 Mile Service (B)**			*Replace timing belt add*	2.4
Passport			Passport			**112500 Mile Service (C)**	
2.6L	7.3		2.6L	2.8		Passport	1.8
3.2L	3.6		3.2L	1.9		Odyssey, CR-V	1.4
Odyssey, CR-V	4.0		Odyssey, CR-V	1.8		**120000 Mile Service (B)**	
37500 Mile Service (C)			**82500 Mile Service (C)**			Passport	
Passport	1.8		Passport	1.8		2.6L	7.4
Odyssey, CR-V	1.3		Odyssey, CR-V	1.3		3.2L	6.7
45000 Mile Service (B)						Odyssey, CR-V	4.0
Passport	4.1						
2.6L	2.8						
3.2L	1.9						
Odyssey, CR-V	1.8						

93081CL2

TIRE, WHEEL AND BALL JOINT SPECIFICATIONS
Honda Truck

Year	Model	OEM Tires		Tire Pressures (psi)		Wheel Size	Ball Joint Inspection
		Standard	Optional	Front	Rear		
1997	Passport, 2wd	P225/75R16	None	29	32	6-JJ	NS
	Passport, 4wd	P245/70R16	None	26	26	7-JJ	NS
1998	Passport 2wd	P215/75R15	None	29	29	6.5-JJ	NS
	Passport LX 4wd	P235/75R15	P245/70R16	Std: 29 Opt: 26	Std: 29 Opt: 26	Std: 6.5-JJ Opt: 7-JJ	NS
	Passport EX 4wd	P245/70R16	None	26	26	7-JJ	NS
1999	Passport 2wd	P235/75R15	None	29	29	6.5-JJ	NS
	Passport 4wd 4-cyl.	P235/75R15	P245/70R16	Std: 29 Opt: 26	Std: 29 Opt: 26	6.5-JJ 7-JJ	NS
	Passport 4wd 6-cyl.	P245/70R16	None	26	26	7-JJ	NS
2000-01	Passport 2wd	P235/75R15	None	29	29	6.5-JJ	NS
	Passport 4wd 4-cyl.	P235/75R15	P245/70R16	Std: 29 Opt: 26	Std: 29 Opt: 26	6.5-JJ 7-JJ	NS
	Passport 4wd 6-cyl.	P245/70R16	None	26	26	7-JJ	NS

OEM: Original Equipment Manufacturer

PSI: Pounds Per Square Inch

STD: Standard

OPT: Optional

NS: Not specified by manufacturer

93081CL3

INFINITI
QX4

ENGINE AND VEHICLE IDENTIFICATION

			Engine					Model Year	
Code ①	Liters (cc)	Cu. In.	Cyl.	Fuel Sys.	Engine Type	Eng. Mfg.		Code ②	Year
VG33E	3.3 (3277)	199	6	MFI	SOHC	Nissan		V	1997
								W	1998
								X	1999
								Y	2000
								1	2001

MFI: Multi-port Fuel Injection

SOHC: Single Overhead Camshaft

① Located on the timing belt cover

② 10th digit of the Vehicle Identification Number (VIN)

93081CL4

GENERAL ENGINE SPECIFICATIONS

Year	Model	Engine Displacement Liters (cc)	Engine ID/VIN	Fuel System Type	Net Horsepower @ rpm	Net Torque @ rpm (ft. lbs.)	Bore x Stroke (in.)	Com-pression Ratio	Oil Pressure @ rpm
1997	QX4	3.3 (3277)	VG33E	MFI	170@4800	200@2800	3.60x3.27	8.9:1	53@3200
1998	QX4	3.3 (3277)	VG33E	MFI	170@4800	200@2800	3.60x3.27	8.9:1	60-65@2000
1999	QX4	3.3 (3277)	VG33E	MFI	170@4800	200@2800	3.60x3.27	8.9:1	60-65@2000
2000-01	QX4	3.3 (3277)	VG33E	MFI	170@4800	200@2800	3.60x3.27	8.9:1	60-65@2000

MFI: Multi-port Fuel Injection

93081CL5

Refer to the model specific sections for engine mechanical service procedures

ENGINE TUNE-UP SPECIFICATIONS

Year	Engine Displacement Liters (cc)	Engine ID/VIN	Spark Plug Gap (in.)	Ignition Timing (deg.)		Fuel Pump (psi) ①	Idle Speed (rpm)		Valve Clearance	
				MT	AT		MT	AT ②	Intake	Exhaust
1997	3.3 (3277)	VG33E	0.041	15B	15B	34	750	750	HYD	HYD
1998	3.3 (3277)	VG33E	0.039-0.043	13-17B	13-17B	34	700-800	700-800	HYD	HYD
1999	3.3 (3277)	VG33E	0.039-0.043	13-17B	13-17B	34	700-800	700-800	HYD	HYD
2000-01	3.3 (3277)	VG33E	0.039-0.043	13-17B	13-17B	34	700-800	700-800	HYD	HYD

NOTE: The Vehicle Emission Control Information label often reflects specification changes made during production. The label figures must be used if they differ from those in this chart.

B: Before top dead center

HYD: Hydraulic

① System pressure at idle with vacuum hose connected
   Should increase to 43 psi when disconnected

② Automatic transmission in Neutral

93081CL6

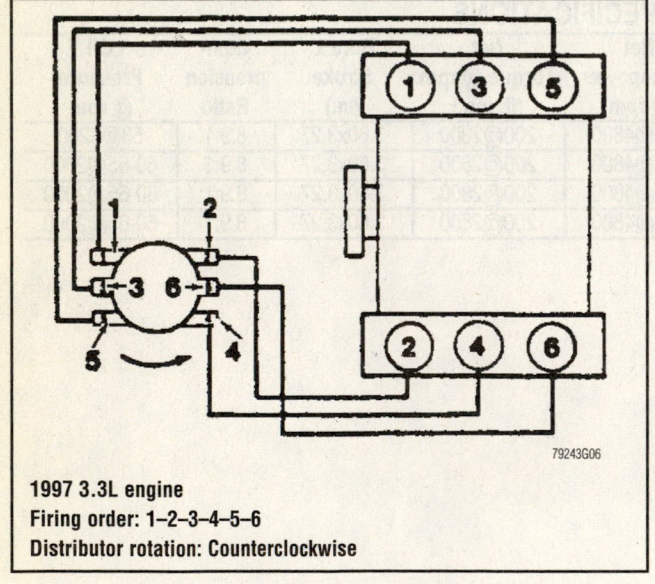

1997 3.3L engine
Firing order: 1–2–3–4–5–6
Distributor rotation: Counterclockwise

79243G06

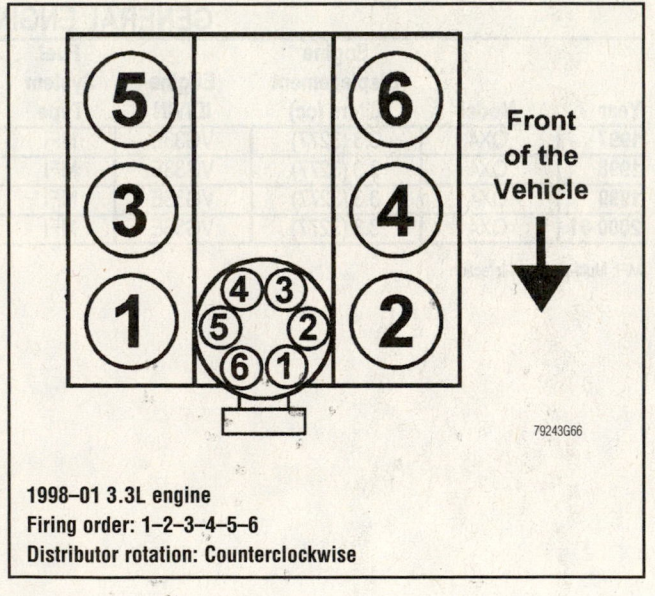

1998–01 3.3L engine
Firing order: 1–2–3–4–5–6
Distributor rotation: Counterclockwise

79243G66

Front of the Vehicle

CAPACITIES

Year	Model	Engine Displacement Liters (cc)	Engine ID/VIN	Engine Oil with Filter (qts.)	Transmission (pts.) Auto.	Transfer Case (pts.)	Drive Axle Front (pts.)	Rear (pts.)	Fuel Tank (gal.)	Cooling System (qts.)
1997	QX4	3.3 (3277)	VG33E	3.8	18	5.3	4.4	5.9	21.1	11.25
1998	QX4	3.3 (3277)	VG33E	3.8	18	5.3	4.4	5.9	21.1	11.25
1999	QX4	3.3 (3277)	VG33E	3.8	18	5.3	4.4	5.9	21.1	11.25
2000-01	QX4	3.3 (3277)	VG33E	3.8	18	5.3	4.4	5.9	21.1	11.25

NOTE: All capacities are approximate. Add fluid gradually and check to be sure a proper fluid level is obtained.

93081CL7

VALVE SPECIFICATIONS

Year	Engine Displacement Liters (cc)	Engine ID/VIN	Seat Angle (deg.)	Face Angle (deg.)	Spring Test Pressure (lbs. @ in.)	Spring Installed Height (in.)	Stem-to-Guide Clearance (in.) Intake	Exhaust	Stem Diameter (in.) Intake	Exhaust
1997	3.3 (3277)	VG33E	45	45.25-46.75	①	NA	0.0008-0.0021	0.0016-0.0029	0.2742-0.2748	0.3136-0.3138
1998	3.3 (3277)	VG33E	45	45.25-46.75	①	NA	0.0008-0.0021	0.0016-0.0029	0.2742-0.2748	0.3135-0.3138
1999	3.3 (3277)	VG33E	45	45.25-46.75	①	NA	0.0008-0.0021	0.0016-0.0029	0.2742-0.2748	0.3135-0.3138
2000-01	3.3 (3277)	VG33E	45	45.25-46.75	①	NA	0.0008-0.0021	0.0016-0.0029	0.2742-0.2748	0.3135-0.3138

NA: Not Available

① Inner: 57.3 @ 0.984
   Outer: 117.7 @ 1.181

93081CL8

Refer to the model specific sections for fuel system service procedures

CAPACITIES

Year	Model	Engine Displacement Liters (cc)	Engine VIN	Engine Oil with Filter (qts.)	Transmission (pts.) 5-Spd	Transmission (pts.) Auto.	Transfer Case (pts.)	Drive Axle Front (pts.)	Drive Axle Rear (pts.)	Fuel Tank (gal.)	Cooling System (qts.)
1997	Tracker	1.6 (1590)	6	4.75	3.2	10.6	3.6	2.4	4.6	11.0	5.5
1998	Tracker	1.6 (1590)	6	4.75	3.2	10.6	3.6	2.4	4.6	11.0	5.5
1999	Tracker	1.6 (1590)	6	4.75	3.2	10.6	3.6	2.4	4.6	11.0	5.5
	Tracker	2.0 (1997)	C	5.90	3.2	10.6	3.6	2.4	4.6	11.0	6.5
2000-01	Tracker	1.6 (1590)	6	4.75	3.2	10.6	3.6	2.4	4.6	11.0	5.5
	Tracker	2.0 (1997)	C	5.90	3.2	10.6	3.6	2.4	4.6	11.0	6.5

NOTE: All capacities are approximate. Add fluid gradually and check to be sure a proper fluid level is obtained.

93081CL9

PISTON AND RING SPECIFICATIONS
All measurements are given in inches.

Year	Engine Displacement Liters (cc)	Engine ID/VIN	Piston Clearance	Ring Gap Top Compression	Ring Gap Bottom Compression	Ring Gap Oil Control	Ring Side Clearance Top Compression	Ring Side Clearance Bottom Compression	Ring Side Clearance Oil Control
1997	3.3 (3277)	VG33E	①	0.0083-0.0157	0.0197-0.0272	0.0079-0.0272	0.0009-0.0030	0.0012-0.0028	0.0006-0.0073
1998	3.3 (3277)	VG33E	①	0.0083-0.0157	0.0197-0.0272	0.0079-0.0272	0.0009-0.0030	0.0012-0.0028	0.0006-0.0073
1999	3.3 (3277)	VG33E	①	0.0083-0.0157	0.0197-0.0272	0.0079-0.0272	0.0009-0.0030	0.0012-0.0028	0.0006-0.0073
2000-01	3.3 (3277)	VG33E	①	0.0083-0.0157	0.0197-0.0272	0.0079-0.0272	0.0009-0.0030	0.0012-0.0028	0.0006-0.0073

① Except cylinders 3 and 4: 0.0010 - 0.0018 in.
   Cylinders 3 and 4: 0.0006 - 0.0010 in.

93081CL0

TORQUE SPECIFICATIONS
All readings in ft. lbs.

Year	Engine Displacement Liters (cc)	Engine ID/VIN	Cylinder Head Bolts	Main Bearing Bolts	Rod Bearing Bolts	Crankshaft Damper Bolts	Flywheel Bolts	Manifold		Spark Plugs	Lug Nuts
								Intake	Exhaust		
1997	3.3 (3277)	VG33E	①	67-74	②	141-156	61-69	③	21-25	18	87-108
1998	3.3 (3277)	VG33E	④	67-74	②	141-156	61-69	③	21-25	14-22	87-108
1999	3.3 (3277)	VG33E	④	67-74	②	141-156	61-69	③	21-25	14-22	87-108
2000-01	3.3 (3277)	VG33E	④	67-74	②	141-156	61-69	③	21-25	14-22	87-108

① Step 1: 22 ft. lbs.
Step 2: 43 ft. lbs.
Step 3: Loosen completely then retorque to 22 ft. lbs.
Step 4: 40-47 ft. lbs. or an additional 60-65 degrees

② 10-12 ft. lbs. plus 60-65 degrees or 28-33 ft. lbs.

③ Step 1: Tighten nuts and bolts to 3 ft. lbs.
Step 2: Tighten bolts to 12-14 ft. lbs.; nuts to 17-20 ft. lbs.
Step 3: Repeat Step 2

④ The cylinder heads and the lower intake manifold are installed together
Step 1: Tighten the cylinder head bolts to 22 ft. lbs.
Step 2: Tighten the cylinder head bolts to 43 ft. lbs.
Step 3: Loosen the cylinder head bolts completely
Step 4: Tighten the cylinder head bolts to 84 inch lbs.
Step 5: Tighten the intake manifold fasteners to 35 inch lbs.
Step 6: Tighten the intake manifold fasteners to 13 ft. lbs.
Step 7: Tighten the intake manifold fasteners to 12-14 ft. lbs.
Step 8: Loosen all intake manifold fasteners completely
Step 9: Tighten the cylinder head bolts to 22 ft. lbs.
Step 10: Tighten the cylinder head bolts 60-65 degrees
Step 11: Tighten the cylinder head sub-bolts to 80-105 inch lbs.
Step 12: Tighten the intake manifold fasteners to 35 inch lbs.
Step 13: Tighten the intake manifold fasteners to 78 inch lbs.
Step 14: Tighten the intake manifold fasteners to 70-84 inch lbs.

93081CM1

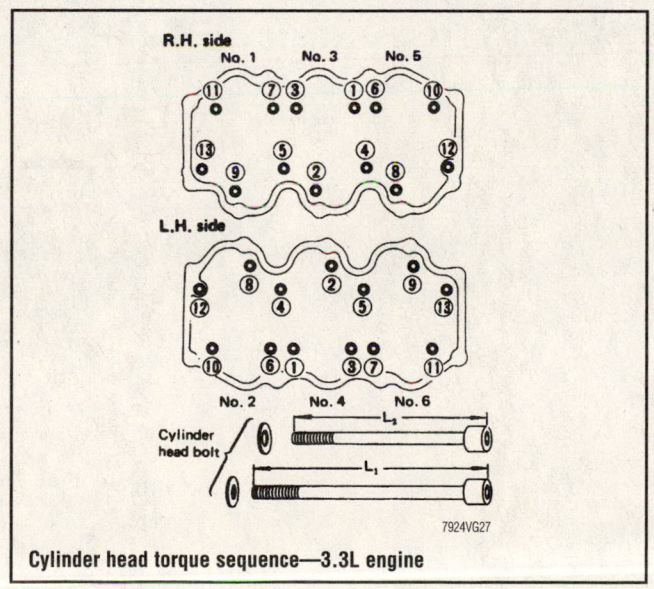

Cylinder head torque sequence—3.3L engine

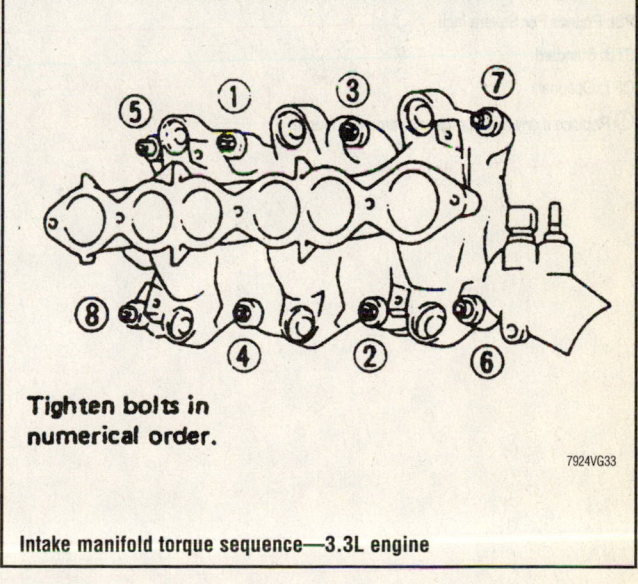

Tighten bolts in numerical order.

Intake manifold torque sequence—3.3L engine

Refer to the model specific sections for engine electrical system service procedures

BRAKE SPECIFICATIONS
INFINITI QX4
All measurements in inches unless noted

| Year | Model | Brake Disc | | | Brake Drum Diameter | | | Minimum Lining Thickness | | Brake Caliper | |
		Original Thickness	Minimum Thickness	Maximum Runout	Original Inside Diameter	Max. Wear Limit	Maximum Machine Diameter	Front	Rear	Bracket Bolts (ft. lbs.)	Mounting Bolts (ft. lbs.)
1997	QX4	1.100	1.024	0.004	11.60	NA	11.67	0.079	0.059	53-72	24-31
1998	QX4	1.100	1.024	0.004	11.60	NA	11.67	0.079	0.059	53-72	24-31
1999	QX4	1.100	1.024	0.004	11.60	NA	11.67	0.079	0.059	53-72	24-31
2000-01	QX4	1.100	1.024	0.004	11.60	NA	11.67	0.079	0.059	53-72	24-31

NA: Not Available

93081CM2

TIRE, WHEEL AND BALL JOINT SPECIFICATIONS
Infiniti Truck

| Year | Model | OEM Tires | | Tire Pressures (psi) | | Wheel Size | Ball Joint Inspection |
		Standard	Optional	Front	Rear		
1997	QX4	P245/70R16	None	35	35	7-JJ	①
1998	QX4	P245/70R16	None	35	35	7-JJ	①
1999	QX4	P245/70R16	None	35	35	7-JJ	①
2000-01	QX4	P245/70R16	None	35	35	7-JJ	①

OEM: Original Equipment Manufacturer

PSI: Pounds Per Square Inch

STD: Standard

OPT: Optional

① Replace if any measurable movement is found.

93081CM3

SCHEDULED MAINTENANCE INTERVALS
(INFINTI QX4)

TO BE SERVICED	TYPE OF SERVICE	VEHICLE MILEAGE INTERVAL (x1000)												
		7.5	15	22.5	30	37.5	45	52.5	60	67.5	75	82.5	90	97.5
Engine oil & filter	R	✓	✓	✓	✓	✓	✓	✓	✓	✓	✓	✓	✓	✓
Brake lines & cables	S/I		✓		✓		✓		✓		✓		✓	
Brake pads, discs, drums & linings	S/I		✓		✓		✓		✓		✓		✓	
Driveshaft boots & propeller shaft (1997 models)	S/I		✓		✓		✓		✓		✓		✓	
Driveshaft boots & propeller shaft (1998-01 models)	S/I				✓				✓				✓	
Front wheel bearings (4x2 models)	S/I				✓				✓				✓	
Automatic & manual transmission, transfer & differential gear oil ①	S/I		✓		✓		✓		✓		✓		✓	
Front wheel bearings (1997 4x4 models)	S/I		✓		✓		✓		✓		✓		✓	
Front wheel bearings (1998-01 4x4 models)	S/I				✓				✓				✓	
Propeller shaft (1997 models)	S/I		✓		✓		✓		✓		✓		✓	
Propeller shaft (1998-01 models)	S/I	✓		✓		✓		✓		✓		✓		✓
Air cleaner filter	R				✓				✓				✓	
Engine coolant	R				✓				✓				✓	
PCV filter	R				✓				✓				✓	
Spark plugs	R				✓				✓				✓	
Drive belt(s)	S/I				✓				✓				✓	
Exhaust system	S/I				✓				✓				✓	

93081CM4

For accessory drive belt replacement procedures see the model specific sections of this manual

SCHEDULED MAINTENANCE INTERVALS
(INFINITI QX4) (Cont.)

TO BE SERVICED	TYPE OF SERVICE	VEHICLE MILEAGE INTERVAL (x1000)												
		7.5	15	22.5	30	37.5	45	52.5	60	67.5	75	82.5	90	97.5
Fuel lines	S/I				✓				✓				✓	
Steering gear (box) & linkage, (steering dumper-4x4), axle & suspension parts	S/I				✓				✓				✓	
Vapor lines	S/I				✓				✓				✓	
Steering linkage ball joints & front suspension ball joints	S/I								✓					
Timing belt ②	R													

R: Replace   S/I: Service or Inspect

① Differential (w/limited-slip differential) oil: replace oil every 30,000 miles.

② Timing belt: replace at 105,000 miles.

FREQUENT OPERATION MAINTENANCE (SEVERE SERVICE)

If a vehicle is operated under any of the following conditions it is considered severe service:

- Extremely dusty areas.

- 50% or more of the vehicle operation is in 32°C (90°F) or higher temperatures, or constant operation in temperatures below 0°C (32°F).

- Prolonged idling (vehicle operation in stop and go traffic).

- Frequent short running periods (engine does not warm to normal operating temperatures).

- Police, taxi, delivery usage or trailer towing usage.

Oil & oil filter: replace every 3750 miles.

Brake pads, discs, drums & linings: service or inspect every 7500 miles.

Driveshaft boots (Quest): service or inspect every 7500 miles.

Driveshaft boots & propeller shaft (Pathfinder): service or inspect every 7500 miles.

Exhaust system: service or inspect every 7500 miles.

Propeller shaft (Pathfinder): service or inspect every 7500 miles. (If immersed in water, grease daily.)

Steering gear (box) & linkage, (steering damper-4x4), axle & suspension parts (Pathfinder): service or inspect every 7500 miles.

Steering gear linkage, axle & suspension parts (Quest): service or inspect every 7500 miles.

Steering linkage ball joints & front suspension ball joints: service or inspect every 7500 miles.

93081CM5

SCHEDULED MAINTENANCE INTERVALS
INFINITI
QX4

The following should be used as a guide when determining the amount of work required for a particular service.
In estimating how long a particular Scheduled Maintenance Service should take, please observe the following:

- Labor Time is time based on field research and data supplied by the vehicle manufacturer.
- Labor time operations are given in hours and tenths of an hour.
- All labor operations are to be used as a guide.

Mechanic Skill Level Codes:
(A) PRECISION: Highly skilled with multiple certification.
(B) GENERAL: Normally skilled with certification.
(C) MAINTENANCE: Semi-skilled working on certification.

	LABOR TIME		LABOR TIME		LABOR TIME
7500 Mile Service (C)		**37500 Mile Service (C)**		**75000 Mile Service (B)**	
All Models	.6	1994-99	.6	All Models	2.1
15000 Mile Service (B)		**45000 Mile Service (B)**		**82500 Mile Service (C)**	
All Models	2.1	All Models	2.1	All Models	.6
22500 Mile Service (C)		**52500 Mile Service (C)**		**90000 Mile Service (B)**	
All Models	.6	All Models	.6	All Models	6.1
30000 Mile Service (B)		**60000 Mile Service (B)**		**97500 Mile Service (C)**	
All Models	5.1	All Models	6.1	All Models	.6
		67500 Mile Service (C)			
		All Models	.6		

93081CM6

For brake related suspension and axle service, refer to the model specific sections of this manual

ISUZU
Amigo • Hombre • Rodeo • Trooper • Oasis

ENGINE AND VEHICLE IDENTIFICATION

Engine							Model Year	
Code	Liters (cc)	Cu. In.	Cyl.	Fuel Sys.	Engine Type	Eng. Mfg.	Code ①	Year
4	2.2 (2189)	134	4	MFI	OHV	GM	V	1997
D	2.2 (2198)	134	4	MFI	DOHC	Isuzu	W	1998
E	2.6 (2559)	156	4	MFI	SOHC	Isuzu	X	1999
F22B6	2.2 (2156)	134	4	MFI	SOHC	Honda	Y	2000
F23A7	2.3 (2253)	138	4	MFI	SOHC	Honda	1	2001
V	3.2 (3165)	193	6	MFI	SOHC	Isuzu		
W	3.2 (3165)	193	6	MFI	DOHC	Isuzu		
W	4.3 (4293)	263	6	MFI	OHV	GM		
X	3.5 (3494)	213	6	MFI	DOHC	Isuzu		
X	4.3 (4300)	262	6	CPI	OHV	GM		

MFI: Multi-port Fuel Injection
CPI: Central Port Injection
DOHC: Double Overhead Camshaft
OHV: Overhead Valve
SOHC: Single Overhead Camshaft
① 10th position of VIN

93081CM7

GENERAL ENGINE SPECIFICATIONS

Year	Model	Engine Displacement Liters (cc)	Engine Series (ID/VIN)	Fuel System	Net Horsepower @ rpm	Net Torque @ rpm (ft. lbs.)	Bore x Stroke (in.)	Com-pression Ratio	Oil Pressure @ rpm
1997	Hombre	2.2 (2189)	4	MFI	118@5200	130@2800	3.50x3.46	9.0:1	56@3000
		4.3 (4300)	X	CPI	180@4400	240@2800	4.00x3.48	9.2:1	24@4000
	Oasis	2.2 (2156)	F22B6	MFI	140@5600	145@4500	3.35x3.74	8.8:1	50@3000
	Rodeo	2.6 (2559)	E	MFI	120@4600	150@2600	3.65x3.74	8.6:1	57-80@3000
		3.2 (3165)	V	MFI	190@5600	188@4000	3.68x3.03	9.1:1	57-80@3000
	Trooper	3.2 (3165)	V	MFI	190@5600	188@4000	3.68x3.03	9.1:1	57-80@3000
1998	Amigo	2.2 (2198)	D	MFI	130@5200	144@4000	3.39x3.72	9.6:1	22@800
		3.2 (3165)	W	MFI	205@5400	214@3000	3.68x3.03	9.1:1	60-80@3000
	Hombre	2.2 (2189)	4	MFI	118@5200	130@2800	3.50x3.46	9.0:1	56@3000
		4.3 (4293)	W	MFI	200@4600	260@2800	4.00x3.48	9.2:1	18@2000
		4.3 (4293)	X	CPI	180@4400	240@2800	4.00x3.48	9.2:1	24@4000
	Oasis	2.3 (2253)	F23A7	MFI	150@5600	152@4700	3.39x3.82	9.3:1	50@3000
	Rodeo	2.2 (2198)	D	MFI	130@5200	144@4000	3.39x3.72	9.6:1	22@800
		3.2 (3165)	W	MFI	205@5400	214@3000	3.68x3.03	9.1:1	60-80@3000
	Trooper	3.5 (3494)	X	MFI	215@5400	230@3000	3.68x3.35	9.1:1	60-80@3000
1999	Amigo	2.2 (2198)	D	MFI	130@5200	144@4000	3.39x3.72	9.6:1	22@800
		3.2 (3165)	W	MFI	205@5400	214@3000	3.68x3.03	9.1:1	60-80@3000
	Hombre	2.2 (2189)	4	MFI	118@5200	130@2800	3.50x3.46	9.0:1	56@3000
		4.3 (4293)	W	MFI	205@5400	214@3000	4.00x3.48	9.1:1	60-80@3000
		4.3 (4293)	X	CPI	180@4400	240@2800	4.00x3.48	9.2:1	24@4000
	Oasis	2.3 (2253)	F23A7	MFI	150@5600	152@4700	3.39x3.82	9.3:1	50@3000
	Rodeo	2.2 (2198)	D	MFI	130@5200	144@4000	3.39x3.72	9.6:1	22@800
		3.2 (3165)	W	MFI	205@5400	214@3000	3.68x3.03	9.1:1	60-80@3000
	Trooper	3.5 (3494)	X	MFI	215@5400	230@3000	3.68x3.35	9.1:1	60-80@3000
2000-01	Amigo	2.2 (2198)	D	MFI	130@5200	144@4000	3.39x3.72	9.6:1	22@800
		3.2 (3165)	W	MFI	205@5400	214@3000	3.68x3.03	9.1:1	60-80@3000
	Hombre	2.2 (2189)	4	MFI	118@5200	130@2800	3.50x3.46	9.0:1	56@3000
		4.3 (4293)	W	MFI	205@5400	214@3000	4.00x3.48	9.1:1	60-80@3000
		4.3 (4293)	X	CPI	180@4400	240@2800	4.00x3.48	9.2:1	24@4000
	Rodeo	2.2 (2198)	D	MFI	130@5200	144@4000	3.39x3.72	9.6:1	22@800
		3.2 (3165)	W	MFI	205@5400	214@3000	3.68x3.03	9.1:1	60-80@3000
	Trooper	3.5 (3494)	X	MFI	215@5400	230@3000	3.68x3.35	9.1:1	60-80@3000

CPI: Central Port Injection

MFI: Multiport fuel injection

93081CM8

Refer to the model specific sections for driveline service procedures

ENGINE TUNE-UP SPECIFICATIONS

Year	Engine Displacement Liters (cc)	Engine ID/VIN	Spark Plug Gap (in.)	Ignition Timing (deg.) MT	Ignition Timing (deg.) AT	Fuel Pump (psi)	Idle Speed (rpm) MT	Idle Speed (rpm) AT	Valve Clearance In.	Valve Clearance Ex.
1997	2.2 (2189)	4	0.060	①	①	41-47	①	①	HYD	HYD
	2.6 (2559)	E	0.040	12B	12B	35	900	900	0.006	0.010
	2.2 (2156)	F22B6	0.039-0.043	—	15B	38-46	—	650-750	0.009-0.011	0.011-0.013
	3.2 (3165)	V	0.040	5B	5B	41-46	750	750	HYD	HYD
	4.3 (4300)	X	0.060	①	①	60-66	①	①	HYD	HYD
1998	2.2 (2189)	4	0.060	①	①	41-47	①	①	HYD	HYD
	2.2 (2198)	D	0.040	①	①	41-55	800	800	HYD	HYD
	2.3 (2253)	F23A7	0.039-0.043	—	10-14B	47-54	—	650-750	0.009-0.011	0.011-0.013
	3.2 (3165)	W	0.040	①	①	48-55	750	750	0.009-0.013	0.010-0.014
	3.5 (3494)	X	0.040	①	①	48-55	750	750	0.009-0.013	0.010-0.014
	4.3 (4293)	W	0.060	①	①	60-66	①	①	HYD	HYD
	4.3 (4293)	X	0.060	①	①	60-66	①	①	HYD	HYD
1999	2.2 (2189)	4	0.060	①	①	41-47	①	①	HYD	HYD
	2.2 (2198)	D	0.040	①	①	41-55	800	800	HYD	HYD
	2.3 (2253)	F23A7	0.039-0.043	—	10-14B	47-54	—	650-750	0.009-0.011	0.011-0.013
	3.2 (3165)	W	0.040	①	①	48-55	750	750	0.009-0.013	0.010-0.014
	3.5 (3494)	X	0.040	①	①	48-55	750	750	0.009-0.013	0.010-0.014
	4.3 (4293)	W	0.060	①	①	60-66	①	①	HYD	HYD
	4.3 (4293)	X	0.060	①	①	60-66	①	①	HYD	HYD
2000-01	2.2 (2189)	4	0.060	①	①	41-47	①	①	HYD	HYD
	2.2 (2198)	D	0.040	①	①	41-55	800	800	HYD	HYD
	3.2 (3165)	W	0.040	①	①	48-55	750	750	0.009-0.013	0.010-0.014
	3.5 (3494)	X	0.040	①	①	48-55	750	750	0.009-0.013	0.010-0.014
	4.3 (4293)	W	0.060	①	①	60-66	①	①	HYD	HYD
	4.3 (4293)	X	0.060	①	①	60-66	①	①	HYD	HYD

NOTE: The Vehicle Emission Control Information label often reflects specification changes made during production. The label figures must be used if they differ from those in this chart.

B: Before top dead center

HYD: Hydraulic

① Controlled by the PCM

93081CM9

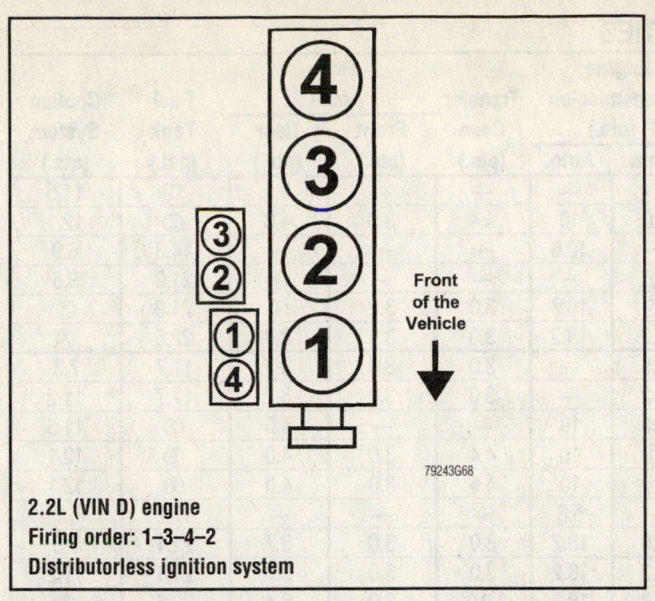

2.2L (VIN D) engine
Firing order: 1–3–4–2
Distributorless ignition system

79243G68

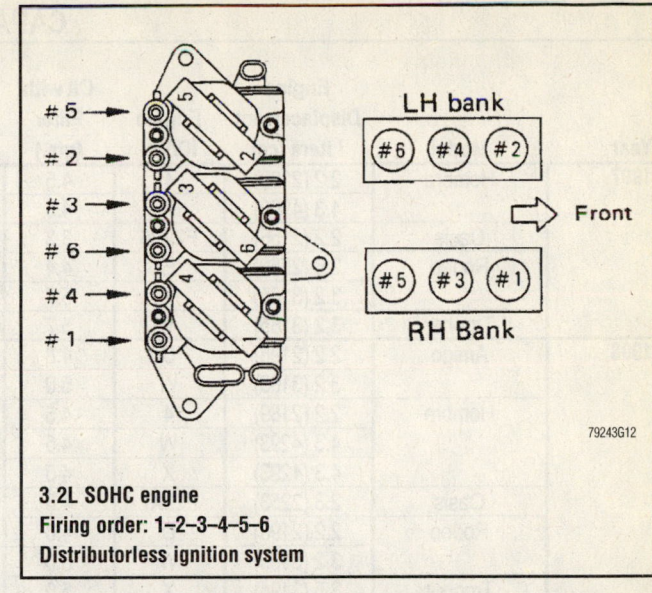

3.2L SOHC engine
Firing order: 1–2–3–4–5–6
Distributorless ignition system

79243G12

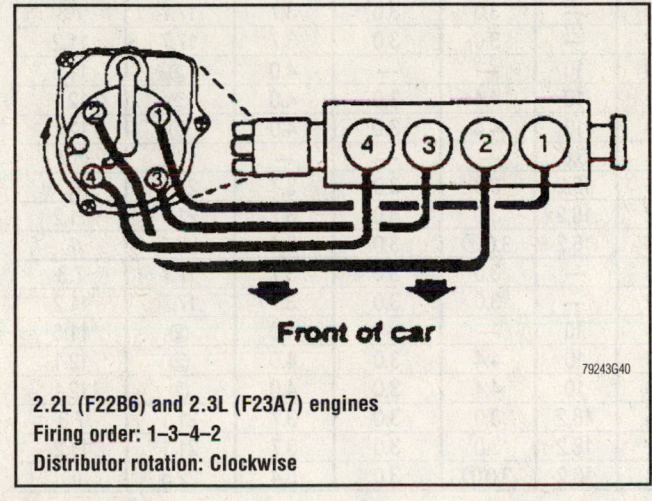

2.2L (F22B6) and 2.3L (F23A7) engines
Firing order: 1–3–4–2
Distributor rotation: Clockwise

79243G40

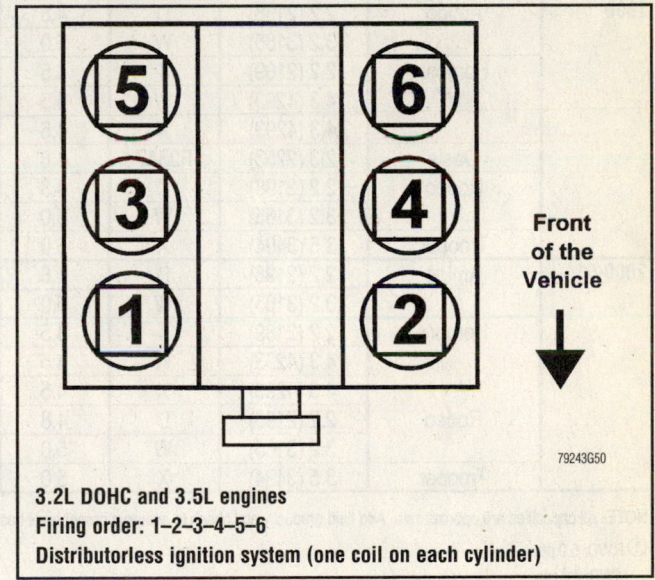

3.2L DOHC and 3.5L engines
Firing order: 1–2–3–4–5–6
Distributorless ignition system (one coil on each cylinder)

79243G50

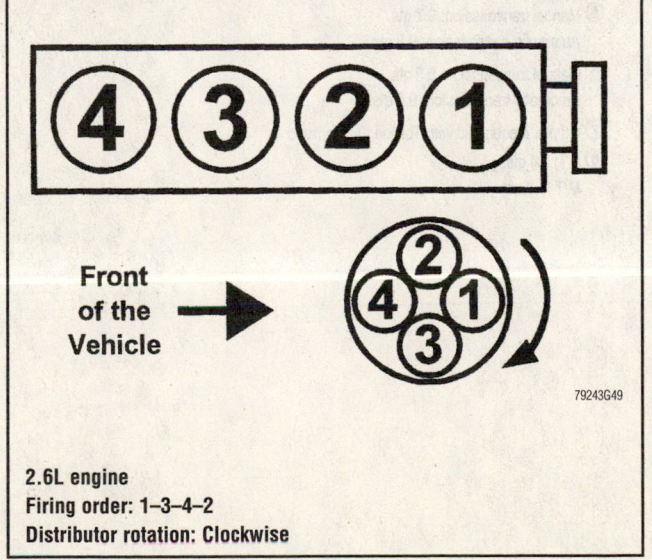

2.6L engine
Firing order: 1–3–4–2
Distributor rotation: Clockwise

79243G49

For exhaust manifold replacement procedures, see the model specific sections of this manual

CAPACITIES

Year	Model	Engine Displacement Liters (cc)	Engine ID/VIN	Oil with Filter (qts.)	Engine Transmission (pts.) Man.	Engine Transmission (pts.) Auto.	Transfer Case (pts.)	Drive Axle Front (pts.)	Drive Axle Rear (pts.)	Fuel Tank (gal.)	Cooling System (qts.)
1997	Hombre	2.2 (2189)	4	4.5	4.4	—	—	—	3.9	19	11.5
		4.3 (4300)	X	4.5	①	10	4.4	3.0	4.0	②	12.1
	Oasis	2.2 (2156)	F22B6	3.3	—	10.6	—	—	—	14.3	6.9
	Rodeo	2.6 (2559)	E	4.4	③	—	—	—	④	21.9	9.5
		3.2 (3165)	V	5.7	③	18.2	3.0	3.2	④	21.9	⑤
	Trooper	3.2 (3165)	V	5.7	6.2	18.2	3.0	3.2	3.8	22.5	⑥
1998	Amigo	2.2 (2198)	D	4.8	4.5	—	3.0	3.0	3.7	17.7	7.3
		3.2 (3165)	W	5.0	6.2	—	3.0	3.0	3.7	17.7	11.2
	Hombre	2.2 (2189)	4	4.5	5.8	10	—	—	4.0	②	11.5
		4.3 (4293)	W	4.5	①	10	4.4	3.0	4.0	②	12.1
		4.3 (4293)	X	4.5	①	10	4.4	3.0	4.0	②	12.1
	Oasis	2.3 (2253)	F23A7	4.8	—	5.8	—	—	—	17.2	6.7
	Rodeo	2.2 (2198)	D	4.8	4.5	18.2	3.0	3.0	3.7	21.1	7.3
		3.2 (3165)	W	5.0	6.2	18.2	3.0	3.0	3.7	21.1	11.2
	Trooper	3.5 (3494)	X	5.0	5.8	18.2	3.0⑦	3.0	6.4	22.5	⑧
1999	Amigo	2.2 (2198)	D	4.8	4.5	—	3.0	3.0	3.7	17.7	7.3
		3.2 (3165)	W	5.0	6.2	—	3.0	3.0	3.7	17.7	11.2
	Hombre	2.2 (2189)	4	4.5	5.8	10	—	—	4.0	②	11.5
		4.3 (4293)	W	4.5	①	10	4.4	3.0	4.0	②	12.1
		4.3 (4293)	X	4.5	①	10	4.4	3.0	4.0	②	12.1
	Oasis	2.3 (2253)	F23A7	4.8	—	5.8	—	—	—	17.2	6.7
	Rodeo	2.2 (2198)	D	4.8	4.5	18.2	3.0	3.0	3.7	21.1	7.3
		3.2 (3165)	W	5.0	6.2	18.2	3.0	3.0	3.7	21.1	11.2
	Trooper	3.5 (3494)	X	5.0	5.8	18.2	3.0⑦	3.0	6.4	22.5	⑧
2000-01	Amigo	2.2 (2198)	D	4.8	4.5	—	3.0	3.0	3.7	17.7	7.3
		3.2 (3165)	W	5.0	6.2	—	3.0	3.0	3.7	17.7	11.2
	Hombre	2.2 (2189)	4	4.5	5.8	10	—	—	4.0	②	11.5
		4.3 (4293)	W	4.5	①	10	4.4	3.0	4.0	②	12.1
		4.3 (4293)	X	4.5	①	10	4.4	3.0	4.0	②	12.1
	Rodeo	2.2 (2198)	D	4.8	4.5	18.2	3.0	3.0	3.7	21.1	7.3
		3.2 (3165)	W	5.0	6.2	18.2	3.0	3.0	3.7	21.1	11.2
	Trooper	3.5 (3494)	X	5.0	5.8	18.2	3.0⑦	3.0	6.4	22.5	⑧

NOTE: All capacities are approximate. Add fluid gradually and check to ensure a proper level has been reached.

① RWD: 5.0 pts.
  4WD: 4.4 pts.

② Steel tank: 19.0 gal.
  Plastic tank: 18.0 gal.

③ MUA transmission: 6.2 pts.
  Borg-Warner transmission: 4.8 pts.

④ Saginaw: 4.0 pts.
  Dana: 3.8 pts.

⑤ Manual transmission: 9.7 qts.
  Automatic transmission: 9.3 qts.

⑥ Manual transmission: 9.3 qts.
  Automatic transmission: 9.0 qts.

⑦ 4.0 pts. if equipped with Torque On Demand

⑧ A/T: 7.4 qts.
  M/T: 7.0 qts.

93081CM0

VALVE SPECIFICATIONS

Year	Engine Displacement Liters (cc)	Engine ID/VIN	Seat Angle (deg.)	Face Angle (deg.)	Spring Test Pressure (lbs. @ in.)	Spring Installed Height (in.)	Stem-to-Guide Clearance (in.)		Stem Diameter (in.)	
							Intake	Exhaust	Intake	Exhaust
1997	2.2 (2189)	4	45	45	75-81@ 1.71	1.71	0.0010- 0.0027	0.0014- 0.0031	NA	NA
	2.6 (2559)	E	45	45	45-55@ 1.61	1.61	0.0009- 0.0079	0.0015- 0.0098	0.3102- 0.3134	0.3091- 0.3124
	2.2 (2156)	F22B6	45	45	NA	NA	0.0008- 0.0018	0.0022- 0.0031	0.2159- 0.2163	0.2146- 0.2150
	3.2 (3165)	V	45	45	45-55@ 1.54	1.54	0.0009- 0.0079	0.0012- 0.0079	0.2323- 0.2353	0.2323- 0.2350
	4.3 (4293)	X	46	45	187-203@ 1.27	①	0.0011- 0.0027	0.0011- 0.0027	NA	NA
1998	2.2 (2189)	4	45	45	201-215@ 1.175	②	0.0007- 0.0020	0.0014- 0.0029	NA	NA
	2.2 (2198)	D	NA	NA	NA	NA	0.0012- 0.0022	0.0016- 0.0026	NA	NA
	2.3 (2253)	F23A7	45	45	NA	③	0.0008- 0.0018	0.0022- 0.0031	0.2159- 0.2163	0.2146- 0.2150
	3.2 (3165)	W	45	45	41-44@ 1.38	1.38	0.0002- 0.0009	0.0012- 0.0025	0.2346- 0.2353	0.2343- 0.2350
	3.5 (3494)	X	45	45	41-44@ 1.38	1.38	0.0002- 0.0009	0.0012- 0.0025	0.2346- 0.2353	0.2343- 0.2350
	4.3 (4293)	W	46	45	187-203@ 1.27	1.69- 1.71	0.0010	0.0020	NA	NA
	4.3 (4293)	X	46	45	187-203@ 1.27	①	0.0011- 0.0027	0.0011- 0.0027	NA	NA
1999	2.2 (2189)	4	45	45	201-215@ 1.175	②	0.0007- 0.0020	0.0014- 0.0029	NA	NA
	2.2 (2198)	D	NA	NA	NA	NA	0.0012- 0.0022	0.0016- 0.0026	NA	NA
	2.3 (2253)	F23A7	45	45	NA	③	0.0008- 0.0018	0.0022- 0.0031	0.2159- 0.2163	0.2146- 0.2150
	3.2 (3165)	W	45	45	41-44@ 1.38	1.38	0.0002- 0.0009	0.0012- 0.0025	0.2346- 0.2353	0.2343- 0.2350
	3.5 (3494)	X	45	45	41-44@ 1.38	1.38	0.0002- 0.0009	0.0012- 0.0025	0.2346- 0.2353	0.2343- 0.2350
	4.3 (4293)	W	46	45	187-203@ 1.27	1.69- 1.71	0.0010	0.0020	NA	NA
	4.3 (4293)	X	46	45	187-203@ 1.27	①	0.0011- 0.0027	0.0011- 0.0027	NA	NA

93081CN1

Refer to the model specific sections for cooling system service procedures

VALVE SPECIFICATIONS

Year	Engine Displacement Liters (cc)	Engine ID/VIN	Seat Angle (deg.)	Face Angle (deg.)	Spring Test Pressure (lbs. @ in.)	Spring Installed Height (in.)	Stem-to-Guide Clearance (in.)		Stem Diameter (in.)	
							Intake	Exhaust	Intake	Exhaust
2000-01	2.2 (2189)	4	45	45	201-215@ 1.175	②	0.0007- 0.0020	0.0014- 0.0029	NA	NA
	2.2 (2198)	D	NA	NA	NA	NA	0.0012- 0.0022	0.0016- 0.0026	NA	NA
	3.2 (3165)	W	45	45	41-44@ 1.38	1.38	0.0002- 0.0009	0.0012- 0.0025	0.2346- 0.2353	0.2343- 0.2350
	3.5 (3494)	X	45	45	41-44@ 1.38	1.38	0.0002- 0.0009	0.0012- 0.0025	0.2346- 0.2353	0.2343- 0.2350
	4.3 (4293)	W	46	45	187-203@ 1.27	1.69- 1.71	0.0010	0.0020	NA	NA
	4.3 (4293)	X	46	45	187-203@ 1.27	①	0.0011- 0.0027	0.0011- 0.0027	NA	NA

NA: Not Available

① Intake: 1.78 in.
  Exhaust: 1.69-1.71 in.

② Free length: 1.91 in.

③ Free length
  Intake: 2.011 in.
  Exhaust: 2.188 in.

93081CN2

CRANKSHAFT AND CONNECTING ROD SPECIFICATIONS
All measurements are given in inches.

| Year | Engine Displacement Liters (cc) | Engine ID/VIN | Crankshaft | | | | Connecting Rod | | |
			Main Brg. Journal Dia.	Main Brg. Oil Clearance	Shaft End-play	Thrust on No.	Journal Diameter	Oil Clearance	Side Clearance
1997	2.2 (2156)	F22B6	①	②	0.0040-0.0140	3	1.8888-1.8898	0.0008-0.0019	0.0060-0.0120
	2.2 (2189)	4	2.4945-2.4954	0.0006-0.0019	0.0020-0.0070	4	1.9983-1.9994	0.0010-0.0031	0.0039-0.0149
	2.6 (2559)	E	2.2016-2.2022	0.0009-0.0020	0.0024-0.0098	3	1.9262-1.9268	0.0012-0.0024	0.0079-0.0130
	3.2 (3165)	V	2.5165-2.5170	0.0007-0.0017	0.0024-0.0094	3	2.1229-2.1235	0.0010-0.0023	0.0063-0.0138
	4.3 (4293)	X	③	④	0.0020-0.0060	4	2.2487-2.2497	0.0013-0.0035	0.0060-0.0140
1998	2.2 (2189)	4	2.4945-2.4954	0.0006-0.0019	0.0020-0.0070	4	1.9983-1.9994	0.0010-0.0031	0.0039-0.0149
	2.2 (2198)	D	2.2590-2.2610	0.0007-0.0016	0.0004-0.0008	2	1.9090-1.9100	0.0002-0.0012	0.0050-0.0150
	2.3 (2253)	F23A7	⑤	⑥	0.0040-0.0140	3	1.7707-1.7717	0.0008-0.0019	0.0060-0.0120
	3.2 (3165)	W	2.5165-2.5170	0.0007-0.0017	0.0024-0.0094	3	2.1229-2.1235	0.0010-0.0023	0.0050-0.0150
	3.5 (3494)	X	2.5165-2.5170	0.0007-0.0017	0.0024-0.0094	3	2.1229-2.1235	0.0010-0.0023	0.0050-0.0150
	4.3 (4293)	W	③	④	0.0020-0.0060	4	2.2487-2.2497	0.0013-0.0035	0.0060-0.0140
	4.3 (4293)	X	③	④	0.0020-0.0060	4	2.2487-2.2497	0.0013-0.0035	0.0060-0.0140
1999	2.2 (2189)	4	2.5190	0.0004-0.0022	0.0040-0.0090	2	2.2830	0.0008-0.0026	0.0050-0.0150
	2.2 (2198)	D	2.2590-2.2610	0.0007-0.0016	0.0004-0.0008	2	1.9090-1.9100	0.0002-0.0012	0.0050-0.0150
	2.3 (2253)	F23A7	⑤	⑥	0.0040-0.0140	3	1.7707-1.7717	0.0008-0.0019	0.0060-0.0120
	3.2 (3165)	W	2.5165-2.5170	0.0007-0.0017	0.0024-0.0094	3	2.1229-2.1235	0.0010-0.0023	0.0050-0.0150
	3.5 (3494)	X	2.5165-2.5170	0.0007-0.0017	0.0024-0.0094	3	2.1229-2.1235	0.0010-0.0023	0.0050-0.0150
	4.3 (4293)	W	⑦	④	0.0020-0.0070	4	2.2487-2.2497	0.0013-0.0035	0.0060-0.0140
	4.3 (4293)	X	③	④	0.0020-0.0070	4	2.2487-2.2497	0.0013-0.0035	0.0060-0.0140

93081CN3

CRANKSHAFT AND CONNECTING ROD SPECIFICATIONS
All measurements are given in inches.

Year	Engine Displacement Liters (cc)	Engine ID/VIN	Crankshaft				Connecting Rod		
			Main Brg. Journal Dia.	Main Brg. Oil Clearance	Shaft End-play	Thrust on No.	Journal Diameter	Oil Clearance	Side Clearance
2000-01	2.2 (2189)	4	2.5190	0.0004-0.0022	0.0040-0.0090	2	2.2830	0.0008-0.0026	0.0050-0.0150
	2.2 (2198)	D	2.2590-2.2610	0.0007-0.0016	0.0004-0.0008	2	1.9090-1.9100	0.0002-0.0012	0.0050-0.0150
	3.2 (3165)	W	2.5165-2.5170	0.0007-0.0017	0.0024-0.0094	3	2.1229-2.1235	0.0010-0.0023	0.0050-0.0150
	3.5 (3494)	X	2.5165-2.5170	0.0007-0.0017	0.0024-0.0094	3	2.1229-2.1235	0.0010-0.0023	0.0050-0.0150
	4.3 (4293)	W	⑦	④	0.0020-0.0070	4	2.2487-2.2497	0.0013-0.0035	0.0060-0.0140
	4.3 (4293)	X	③	④	0.0020-0.0070	4	2.2487-2.2497	0.0013-0.0035	0.0060-0.0140

① Nos. 1 and 4: 1.9679-1.9688
No. 2: 1.9676-1.9688
No. 3: 1.9674-1.9683
No. 5: 1.9680-1.9690

② Nos. 1 and 4: 0.0005-0.0015
No. 2: 0.0008-0.0018
No. 3: 0.0010-0.0019
No. 5: 0.0004-0.0013

③ No. 1: 2.4484-2.4493
Nos. 2 and 3: 2.4481-2.4490
No. 4: 2.4479-2.4488

④ No. 1: 0.0008-0.0020
Nos. 2 and 3: 0.0011-0.0023
No. 4: 0.0017-0.0032

⑤ Nos. 1, 2 and 4: 2.1646-2.1655
No. 3: 2.1644-2.1654
No. 5: 2.1650-2.1660

⑥ Nos. 1, 2 and 4: 0.0008-0.0018
No. 3: 0.0010-0.0019
No. 5: 0.0004-0.0013

⑦ No. 1: 2.4488-2.4495
Nos. 2 and 3: 2.4485-2.4494
No. 4: 2.4480-2.4489

93081CN4

PISTON AND RING SPECIFICATIONS
All measurements are given in inches.

Year	Engine Displacement Liters (cc)	Engine ID/VIN	Piston Clearance	Ring Gap			Ring Side Clearance		
				Top Compression	Bottom Compression	Oil Control	Top Compression	Bottom Compression	Oil Control
1997	2.2 (2156)	F22B6	0.0008-0.0016	0.0080-0.0140	0.0160-0.0220	0.008-0.028	0.0014-0.0024	0.0012-0.0022	NA
	2.2 (2189)	4	0.0007-0.0017	0.0100-0.0200	0.0100-0.0200	0.010-0.040	0.0019-0.0027	0.0019-0.0027	0.0019-0.0082
	2.6 (2559)	E	NA	0.0118-0.0177	0.0236-0.0283	0.008-0.028	0.0010-0.0024	0.0008-0.0022	NA
	3.2 (3165)	V	NA	0.0138-0.0185	0.0177-0.0236	0.006-0.018	0.0006-0.0015	0.0006-0.0015	NA
	4.3 (4293)	X	0.0007-0.0017	0.0100-0.0300	0.0180-0.0260	0.065 Max.	0.0042 Max.	0.0042 Max.	0.0020-0.0070
1998	2.2 (2189)	4	0.0007-0.0017	0.0100-0.0200	0.0100-0.0200	0.010-0.040	0.0019-0.0027	0.0019-0.0027	0.0019-0.0082
	2.2 (2198)	D	NA	0.0118-0.0195	0.0118-0.0195	0.016-0.055	0.0008-0.0546	0.0008-0.0546	NA
	2.3 (2253)	F23A7	0.0008-0.0016	0.0080-0.0140	0.0160-0.0220	0.008-0.028	0.0014-0.0024	0.0012-0.0022	NA
	3.2 (3165)	W	NA	0.0118-0.0157	0.0177-0.0236	0.006-0.018	0.0006-0.0015	0.0006-0.0015	NA
	3.5 (3494)	X	NA	0.0118-0.0157	0.0177-0.0236	0.006-0.018	0.0006-0.0015	0.0006-0.0015	NA
	4.3 (4293)	W	0.0007-0.0017	0.0100-0.0300	0.0180-0.0260	0.065 Max.	0.0042 Max.	0.0042 Max.	0.0020-0.0070
	4.3 (4293)	X	0.0007-0.0017	0.0100-0.0300	0.0180-0.0260	0.065 Max.	0.0042 Max.	0.0042 Max.	0.0020-0.0070
1999	2.2 (2189)	4	0.0007-0.0017	0.0100-0.0200	0.0100-0.0200	0.010-0.040	0.0019-0.0027	0.0019-0.0027	0.0019-0.0082
	2.2 (2198)	D	NA	0.0118-0.0195	0.0118-0.0195	0.016-0.055	0.0008-0.0546	0.0008-0.0546	NA
	2.3 (2253)	F23A7	0.0008-0.0016	0.0080-0.0140	0.0160-0.0220	0.008-0.028	0.0014-0.0024	0.0012-0.0022	NA
	3.2 (3165)	W	NA	0.0118-0.0157	0.0177-0.0236	0.006-0.018	0.0006-0.0015	0.0006-0.0015	NA
	3.5 (3494)	X	NA	0.0118-0.0157	0.0177-0.0236	0.006-0.016	0.0006-0.0015	0.0006-0.0015	NA
	4.3 (4293)	W	0.0007-0.0017	0.0100-0.0300	0.0180-0.0260	0.065 Max.	0.0042 Max.	0.0042 Max.	0.0020-0.0070
	4.3 (4293)	X	0.0007-0.0017	0.0100-0.0300	0.0180-0.0260	0.065 Max.	0.0042 Max.	0.0042 Max.	0.0020-0.0070

93081CN5

Timing chain and gear service is covered in the model specific sections of this manual

PISTON AND RING SPECIFICATIONS
All measurements are given in inches.

Year	Engine Displacement Liters (cc)	Engine ID/VIN	Piston Clearance	Ring Gap			Ring Side Clearance		
				Top Compression	Bottom Compression	Oil Control	Top Compression	Bottom Compression	Oil Control
2000-01	2.2 (2189)	4	0.0007-0.0017	0.0100-0.0200	0.0100-0.0200	0.010-0.040	0.0019-0.0027	0.0019-0.0027	0.0019-0.0082
	2.2 (2198)	D	NA	0.0118-0.0195	0.0118-0.0195	0.016-0.055	0.0008-0.0546	0.0008-0.0546	NA
	3.2 (3165)	W	NA	0.0118-0.0157	0.0177-0.0236	0.0060-0.018	0.0006-0.002	0.0006-0.0015	NA
	3.5 (3494)	X	NA	0.0118-0.0157	0.0177-0.0236	0.006-0.018	0.0006-0.0015	0.0006-0.0015	NA
	4.3 (4293)	W	0.0007-0.0017	0.0100-0.0300	0.0180-0.0260	0.065 Max.	0.0042 Max.	0.0042 Max.	0.0020-0.0070
	4.3 (4293)	X	0.0007-0.0017	0.0100-0.0300	0.0180-0.0260	0.065 Max.	0.0042 Max.	0.0042 Max.	0.0020-0.0070

NA: Not Available

93081CN6

TORQUE SPECIFICATIONS
All readings in ft. lbs.

Year	Engine Displacement Liters (cc)	Engine ID/VIN	Cylinder Head Bolts	Main Bearing Bolts	Rod Bearing Bolts	Crankshaft Damper Bolts	Flywheel Bolts	Manifold Intake	Manifold Exhaust	Spark Plugs	Lug Nuts
1997	2.2 (2156)	F22B6	①	54	34	181	54	16	23	13	80
	2.2 (2189)	4	②	70	38	77	55	22	10	13	95
	2.6 (2559)	E	③	72	43	87	40	16	33	14	④
	3.2 (3165)	V	47 ⑤	⑥	40	123	40	17	42	13	87
	4.3 (4293)	X	⑦	⑧	⑨	74	74	⑩	⑪	15 ⑫	95
1998	2.2 (2189)	4	②	70	38	77	55	⑪	10	13	95
	2.2 (2198)	D	⑬	⑭	⑮	⑯	⑰	16	⑱	18	87
	2.3 (2253)	F23A7	⑲	⑳	㉑	181	54	16	23	13	80
	3.2 (3165)	W	㉒	29	40	123	40	18	42	13	87
	3.5 (3494)	X	㉒	㉓	40	123	40	18	38	13	87
	4.3 (4293)	W	⑦	⑧	⑨	74	74	⑩	⑪	15 ⑫	95
	4.3 (4293)	X	⑦	⑧	⑨	74	74	⑩	⑪	15 ⑫	95
1999	2.2 (2189)	4	②	70	38	77	55	⑪	10	13	95
	2.2 (2198)	D	⑬	⑭	⑮	⑯	⑰	16	⑱	18	87
	2.3 (2253)	F23A7	⑲	⑳	㉑	181	54	16	23	13	80
	3.2 (3165)	W	㉒	29	40	123	40	18	42	13	87
	3.5 (3494)	X	㉒	㉓	40	123	40	18	38	13	87
	4.3 (4293)	W	⑦	⑧	⑨	74	74	⑩	⑪	15 ⑫	95
	4.3 (4293)	X	⑦	⑧	⑨	74	74	⑩	⑪	15 ⑫	95
2000-01	2.2 (2189)	4	②	70	38	77	55	⑪	10	13	95
	2.2 (2198)	D	⑬	⑭	⑮	⑯	⑰	16	⑱	18	87
	3.2 (3165)	W	㉒	29	40	123	40	18	42	13	87
	3.5 (3494)	X	㉒	㉓	40	123	40	18	38	13	87
	4.3 (4293)	W	⑦	⑧	⑨	74	74	⑩	⑪	15 ⑫	95
	4.3 (4293)	X	⑦	⑧	⑨	74	74	⑩	⑪	15 ⑫	95

① Step 1: 29 ft. lbs.
Step 2: 51 ft. lbs.
Step 3: 72 ft. lbs.

② Step 1:
Long bolts: 46 ft. lbs.
Short bolts: 43 ft. lbs.
Step 2:
All bolts: Plus 90 degrees

③ Step 1: 58 ft. lbs.
Step 2: 72 ft. lbs.

④ Steel wheels: 58-72 ft. lbs.
Aluminum wheels: 80-94 ft. lbs.

⑤ 8mm bolts: 15 ft. lbs.

⑥ Main bearing cap bolts: 29 ft. lbs.
Oil gallery bolts: 29 ft. lbs. plus 55-65 degrees
Buttress bolts: 29 ft. lbs.

⑦ Step 1: 22 ft. lbs.
Step 2: Plus 75 degrees for long bolts
Plus 65 degrees for medium bolts
Plus 55 degrees for short bolts

⑧ Step 1: 15 ft. lbs.
Step 2: Plus 73 degrees

⑨ Step 1: 20 ft. lbs.
Step 2: Plus 70 degrees

⑩ Lower intake manifold:
Step 1: 27 inch lbs.
Step 2: 106 inch lbs.
Step 3: 11 ft. lbs.
Upper intake manifold:
Step 1: 44 inch lbs.
Step 2: 88 inch lbs.

⑪ Step 1: 11 ft. lbs.
Step 2: 22 ft. lbs.

⑫ New cylinder head first installation: 22 ft. lbs.

⑬ Step 1: 18 ft. lbs.
Step 2: Plus 90 degrees
Step 3: Plus 90 degrees
Step 4: Plus 90 degrees

⑭ Step 1: 37 ft. lbs.
Step 2: Plus 45 degrees
Step 3: Plus 15 degrees

⑮ Step 1: 25 ft. lbs.
Step 2: Plus 45 degrees
Step 3: Plus 15 degrees

⑯ Crankshaft sprocket:
Step 1: 94 ft. lbs.
Step 2: Plus 45 degrees
Crankshaft balancer:
Step 1: 14 ft. lbs.
Step 2: Plus 45 degrees

⑰ Step 1: 48 ft. lbs.
Step 2: Plus 30 degrees
Step 3: Plus 15 degrees

⑱ Step 1: 112 inch lbs.
Step 2: 14 ft. lbs.
Step 3: 14 ft. lbs.

⑲ Step 1: 22 ft. lbs.
Step 2: Plus 180 degrees
Step 3: For new bolts, tighten an additional 90 degrees

⑳ 11 mm bolts:
Step 1: 22 ft. lbs.
Step 2: 58 ft. lbs.
6 mm bolts: 8.7 ft. lbs.

㉑ Step 1: 14 ft. lbs.
Step 2: Plus 90 degrees

㉒ Step 1: 21 ft. lbs.
Step 2: 47 ft. lbs.

㉓ Step 1: 22 ft. lbs.
Step 2: Plus 55-65 degrees
Step 3: Crankcase side bolts to 29 ft. lbs.

93081CN7

Ignition system service is covered in the model specific sections of this manual

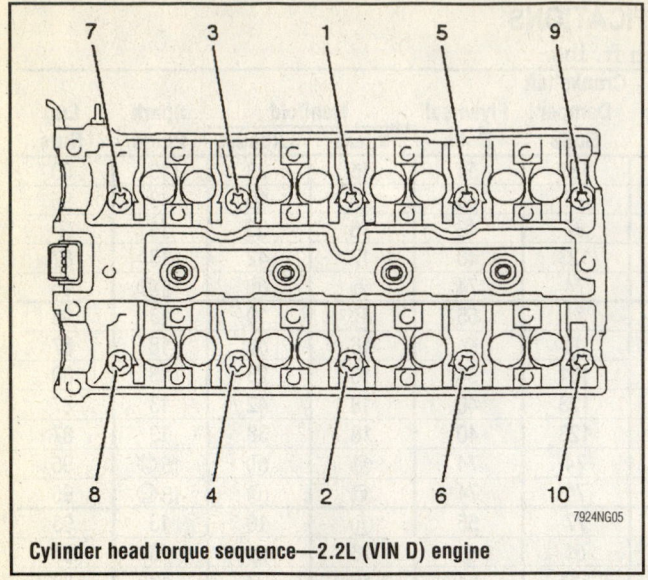

Cylinder head torque sequence—2.2L (VIN D) engine

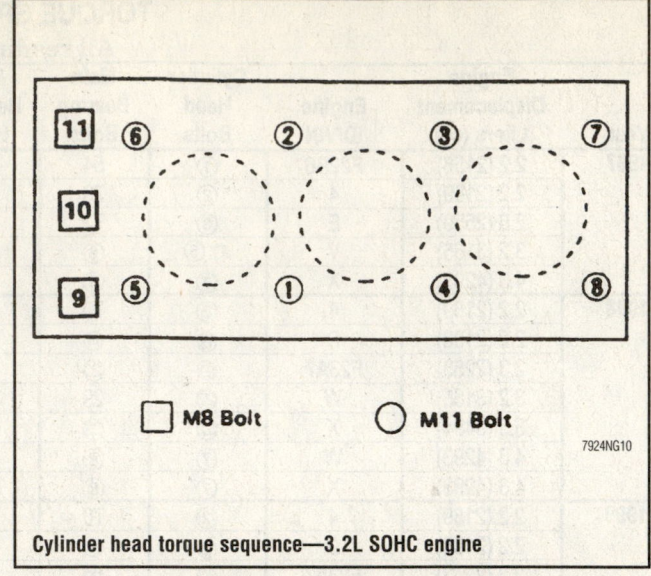

M8 Bolt   M11 Bolt

Cylinder head torque sequence—3.2L SOHC engine

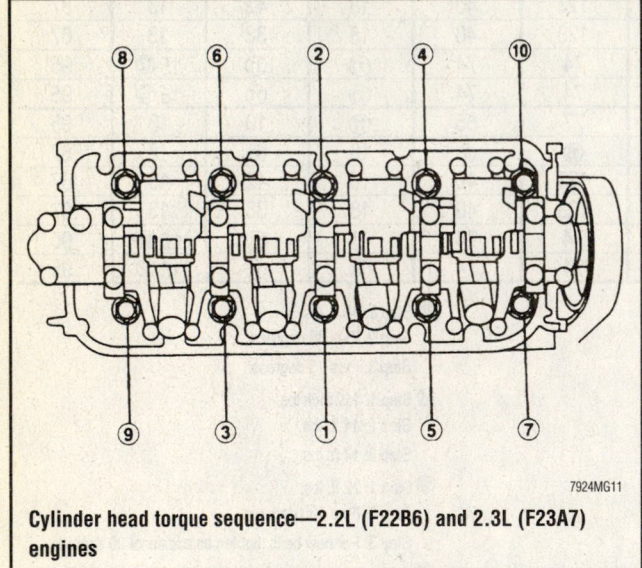

Cylinder head torque sequence—2.2L (F22B6) and 2.3L (F23A7) engines

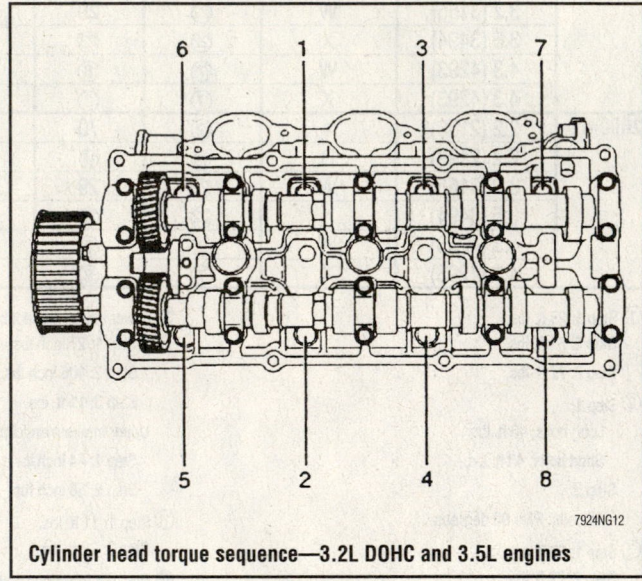

Cylinder head torque sequence—3.2L DOHC and 3.5L engines

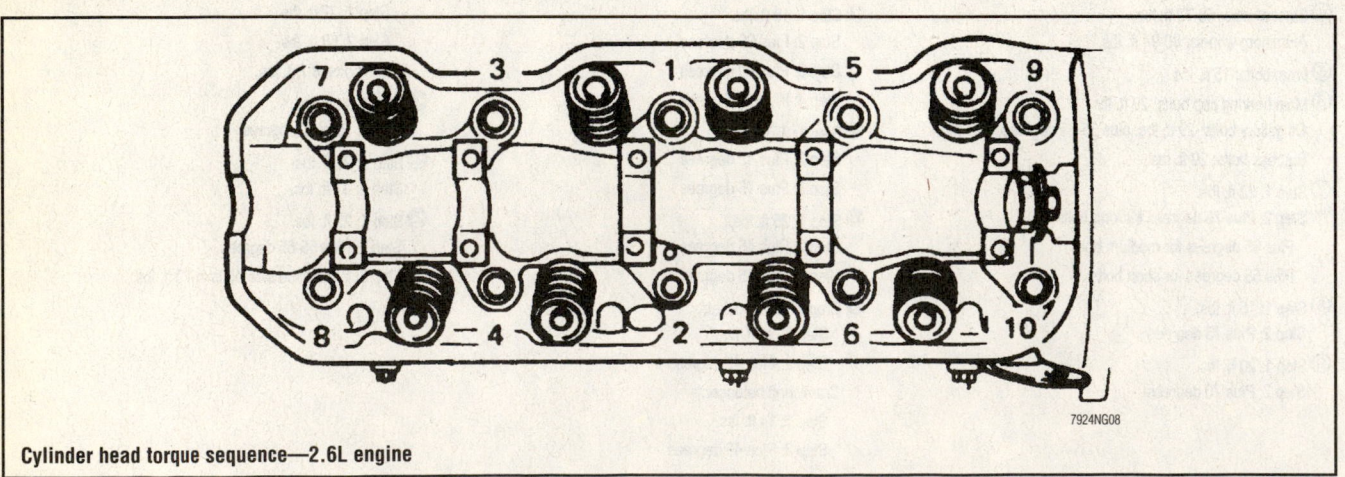

Cylinder head torque sequence—2.6L engine

BRAKE SPECIFICATIONS
ISUZU AMIGO, HOMBRE, OASIS, RODEO, TROOPER
All measurements in inches unless noted

Year	Model		Original Thickness	Brake Disc Machine Thickness	Brake Disc Minimum Thickness	Maximum Runout	Brake Drum Diameter Original Inside Diameter	Max. Wear Limit	Maximum Machine Diameter	Minimum Lining Thickness Front	Minimum Lining Thickness Rear	Brake Caliper Bracket Bolts (ft. lbs.)	Brake Caliper Mounting Bolts (ft. lbs.)
1997	Hombre	F	1.027①	0.980②	0.965③	0.004	—	—	—	0.030	—	—	38
		R	0.787	0.735	0.728	0.004	9.50	9.59	9.56	—	0.030	52	23
	Oasis	F	0.930	—	0.830	0.004	—	—	—	0.060	—	—	36
		R	0.350	—	0.300	0.004	6.69	6.73	6.73	—	0.040	—	17
	Rodeo	F	1.020	0.983	0.969	0.005	—	—	—	0.039	—	115	54
		R	0.710	0.668	0.654	0.005	10.00	10.06	10.06	—	0.039	76	32
	Trooper	F	1.024	0.983	0.969	0.005	—	—	—	0.039	—	115	54
		R	0.710	0.668	0.654	0.005	8.27	8.32	8.32	—	0.039	76	32
1998	Amigo	F	1.020	0.983	0.969	0.005	—	—	—	0.039	—	115	54
		R	0.710	0.668	0.654	0.005	11.6	11.67	NA	—	0.039	76	32
	Hombre	F	1.027①	0.980②	0.965③	0.004	—	—	—	0.030	—	—	38
		R	0.787	0.735	0.728	0.004	9.50	9.59	9.56	—	0.030	52	23
	Oasis	F	0.930	—	0.830	0.004	—	—	—	0.060	—	—	36
		R	0.350	—	0.300	0.004	6.69	6.73	NA	—	0.060	—	17
	Rodeo	F	1.020	0.983	0.969	0.005	—	—	—	0.039	—	115	54
		R	0.710	0.668	0.654	0.005	11.6	11.67	NA	—	0.039	76	32
	Trooper	F	1.024	0.983	0.969	0.005	—	—	—	0.039	—	115	54
		R	0.710	0.668	0.654	0.005	8.27	8.32	NA	—	0.039	76	32
1999	Amigo	F	1.020	0.983	0.969	0.005	—	—	—	0.039	—	115	54
		R	0.710	0.668	0.654	0.005	11.6	11.67	NA	—	0.039	76	32
	Hombre	F	1.027①	0.980②	0.965③	0.004	—	—	—	0.030	—	—	38
		R	0.787	0.735	0.728	0.004	9.50	9.59	9.56	—	0.030	52	23
	Oasis	F	0.930	—	0.830	0.004	—	—	—	0.060	—	—	36
		R	0.350	—	0.300	0.004	6.69	6.73	NA	—	0.060	—	17
	Rodeo	F	1.020	0.983	0.969	0.005	—	—	—	0.039	—	115	54
		R	0.710	0.668	0.654	0.005	11.6	11.67	NA	—	0.039	76	32
	Trooper	F	1.024	0.983	0.969	0.005	—	—	—	0.039	—	115	54
		R	0.710	0.668	0.654	0.005	8.27	8.32	NA	—	0.039	76	32
2000-01	Amigo	F	1.020	0.983	0.969	0.005	—	—	—	0.039	—	115	54
		R	0.710	0.668	0.654	0.005	11.6	11.67	NA	—	0.039	76	32
	Hombre	F	1.027①	0.980②	0.965③	0.004	—	—	—	0.030	—	—	38
		R	0.787	0.735	0.728	0.004	9.50	9.59	9.56	—	0.030	52	23
	Rodeo	F	1.020	0.983	0.969	0.005	—	—	—	0.039	—	115	54
		R	0.710	0.668	0.654	0.005	11.6	11.67	NA	—	0.039	76	32
	Trooper	F	1.024	0.983	0.969	0.005	—	—	—	0.039	—	115	54
		R	0.710	0.668	0.654	0.005	8.27	8.32	NA	—	0.039	76	32

NA: Not Available

① Heavy duty models: 1.140 in.
② Heavy duty models: 1.100 in.
③ Heavy duty models: 1.080 in.

93081CN8

1997 SCHEDULED MAINTENANCE INTERVALS
(ISUZU HOMBRE, OASIS, RODEO & TROOPER)

TO BE SERVICED	TYPE OF SERVICE	VEHICLE MILEAGE INTERVAL (x1000)												
		7.5	15	22.5	30	37.5	45	52.5	60	67.5	75	82.5	90	97.5
Engine oil & filter	R	✓	✓	✓	✓	✓	✓	✓	✓	✓	✓	✓	✓	✓
Automatic transmission fluid	S/I	✓	✓	✓	✓	✓	✓	✓	✓	✓	✓	✓	✓	✓
Battery fluid level	S/I	✓	✓	✓	✓	✓	✓	✓	✓	✓	✓	✓	✓	✓
Body & chassis lubrication	S/I	✓	✓	✓	✓	✓	✓	✓	✓	✓	✓	✓	✓	✓
Brake & clutch fluid level	S/I	✓	✓	✓	✓	✓	✓	✓	✓	✓	✓	✓	✓	✓
Brake lines & hoses	S/I	✓	✓	✓	✓	✓	✓	✓	✓	✓	✓	✓	✓	✓
Check & rotate tires	S/I	✓	✓	✓	✓	✓	✓	✓	✓	✓	✓	✓	✓	✓
Engine coolant strength, hoses & clamps	S/I	✓	✓	✓	✓	✓	✓	✓	✓	✓	✓	✓	✓	✓
Exhaust system	S/I	✓	✓	✓	✓	✓	✓	✓	✓	✓	✓	✓	✓	✓
Front suspension, ball joints, steering linkage, parking brake cable guides, propeller shaft splines, universal joints, brake & clutch pedal springs (Hombre)	S/I	✓	✓	✓	✓	✓	✓	✓	✓	✓	✓	✓	✓	✓
Lubricate accelerator linkage (except Rodeo)	S/I	✓	✓	✓	✓	✓	✓	✓	✓	✓	✓	✓	✓	✓
Rear axle seals (Hombre)	S/I	✓	✓	✓	✓	✓	✓	✓	✓	✓	✓	✓	✓	✓
Starter safety switch	S/I	✓	✓	✓	✓	✓	✓	✓	✓	✓	✓	✓	✓	✓
Suspension & steering (Rodeo)	S/I	✓	✓	✓	✓	✓	✓	✓	✓	✓	✓	✓	✓	✓
Suspension & steering (Trooper)	S/I		✓		✓		✓		✓		✓		✓	
Lubricate front & rear propeller shaft	S/I	✓		✓		✓		✓		✓		✓		✓
Propeller shaft flange torque 46 lb. ft. (63 Nm)	S/I	✓		✓		✓		✓		✓		✓		✓
Auto cruise control linkage & hose	S/I		✓		✓		✓		✓		✓		✓	
Brake & clutch pedal play	S/I		✓		✓		✓		✓		✓		✓	
Cooling & heater hoses	S/I		✓		✓		✓		✓		✓		✓	
Disc brakes (Trooper)	S/I		✓		✓		✓		✓		✓		✓	
Disc & drum brakes (Rodeo)	S/I		✓		✓		✓		✓		✓		✓	
Lubricate clutch pedal spring, bushing & clevis pin	S/I		✓		✓		✓		✓		✓		✓	
Lubricate key lock cylinder	S/I		✓		✓		✓		✓		✓		✓	
Parking brake	S/I		✓		✓		✓		✓		✓		✓	

93081CN9

1997 SCHEDULED MAINTENANCE INTERVALS
(ISUZU HOMBRE, OASIS, RODEO & TROOPER) (Cont.)

TO BE SERVICED	TYPE OF SERVICE	VEHICLE MILEAGE INTERVAL (x1000)												
		7.5	15	22.5	30	37.5	45	52.5	60	67.5	75	82.5	90	97.5
Shift-on-the-fly system gear fluid (Rodeo)	S/I		✔		✔		✔		✔		✔		✔	
Throttle linkage (Rodeo)	S/I		✔		✔		✔		✔		✔		✔	
Valve clearance (Rodeo 2.6L)	S/I		✔		✔		✔		✔		✔		✔	
Manual transmission & transfer case oil	R		✔		✔				✔				✔	
Front & rear axle oil (Trooper)	R		✔		✔				✔				✔	
Air cleaner filter	R				✔				✔				✔	
Automatic transmission fluid & filter (Oasis)	R				✔				✔				✔	
Brake fluid (include ABS) (Oasis)	R				✔				✔				✔	
Engine coolant (Trooper)	R				✔				✔				✔	
Engine coolant (Rodeo)	R				✔								✔	
Front & rear axle oil	R		✔		✔				✔					
Fuel filter (Hombre)	R				✔				✔				✔	
Power steering fluid	R				✔				✔				✔	
Spark plugs (Rodeo 2.6L) ①	R				✔				✔				✔	
Spark plugs (Rodeo 3.2L & Trooper) ①	R								✔					
Clutch lines & hose	S/I			✔					✔				✔	
Engine drive belts	S/I			✔					✔				✔	
Engine idle speed (Rodeo 2.6L)	S/I	✔							✔				✔	
Front wheel bearings & free wheeling hubs	S/I				✔				✔				✔	
Clean radiator core & A/C condenser	S/I				✔				✔				✔	
Ignition wires (Hombre & Rodeo 2.6L)	S/I								✔				✔	
Timing belt (Oasis)	R												✔	
Timing belt (Rodeo 2.6L)	R								✔					

93081CN0

Refer to the model specific sections for engine mechanical service procedures

1997 SCHEDULED MAINTENANCE INTERVALS
(ISUZU HOMBRE, OASIS, RODEO & TROOPER) (Cont.)

TO BE SERVICED	TYPE OF SERVICE	VEHICLE MILEAGE INTERVAL (x1000)												
		7.5	15	22.5	30	37.5	45	52.5	60	67.5	75	82.5	90	97.5
Engine timing (Hombre)	S/I								✓					
Fuel tank, cap & lines	S/I								✓					
PCV valve (Oasis)	S/I								✓					

R: Replace   S/I: Service or Inspect

① Spark plugs (Hombre): replace every 100,000 miles.

FREQUENT OPERATION MAINTENANCE (SEVERE SERVICE)

If a vehicle is operated under any of the following conditions it is considered severe service:

- Extremely dusty areas.

- 50% or more of the vehicle operation is in 32°C (90°F) or higher temperatures, or constant operation in temperatures below 0°C (32°F).

- Prolonged idling (vehicle operation in stop and go traffic.

- Frequent short running periods (engine does not warm to normal operating temperatures).

- Police, taxi, delivery usage or trailer towing usage.

Oil & oil filter change, body & chassis lubrication: every 3000 miles.

Rotate tires every 6000 miles.

Front & rear axle oil: change every 15,000 miles.

Automatic transmission fluid & filter: change every 20,000 miles.

93081C01

1998-01 SCHEDULED MAINTENANCE INTERVALS
(ISUZU AMIGO, HOMBRE, OASIS, RODEO & TROOPER)

TO BE SERVICED	TYPE OF SERVICE	VEHICLE MILEAGE INTERVAL (x1000)														
		7.5	15	22.5	30	37.5	45	52.5	60	67.5	75	82.5	90	97.5	105	112.5	120
Accelerator linkage ①	L	✓	✓	✓	✓	✓	✓	✓	✓	✓	✓	✓	✓	✓	✓	✓	✓
Accessory drive belts ②	S/I				✓				✓				✓				✓
Air cleaner filter	R				✓				✓				✓				✓
Auto cruise control linkage & hose ③	S/I		✓		✓		✓		✓		✓		✓		✓		✓
Automatic transmission fluid level ③	S/I	✓		✓		✓		✓		✓		✓		✓		✓	
Battery fluid level ③	S/I	✓	✓	✓	✓	✓	✓	✓	✓	✓	✓	✓	✓	✓	✓	✓	✓
Body and chassis ①	L	✓	✓	✓	✓	✓	✓	✓	✓	✓	✓	✓	✓	✓	✓	✓	✓
Brake fluid level ③	S/I	✓	✓	✓	✓	✓	✓	✓	✓	✓	✓	✓	✓	✓	✓	✓	✓
Brake lines & hoses ③	S/I	✓	✓	✓	✓	✓	✓	✓	✓	✓	✓	✓	✓	✓	✓	✓	✓
Brake pedal play ③	S/I			✓		✓		✓		✓		✓		✓		✓	✓
Clutch fluid level ③	S/I	✓	✓	✓	✓	✓	✓	✓	✓	✓	✓	✓	✓	✓	✓	✓	✓
Clutch lines & hose ③	S/I				✓				✓				✓				✓
Clutch pedal free-play ③	S/I		✓		✓		✓		✓		✓		✓		✓		✓
Clutch pedal spring, bushing and clevis pin ①	S/I		✓		✓		✓		✓		✓		✓		✓		✓
Cooling and heating system hoses ③	S/I		✓		✓		✓		✓		✓		✓		✓		✓
Driveshaft flange torque ③	S/I	✓		✓		✓		✓		✓		✓		✓		✓	
Drum and disc brakes ③	S/I		✓		✓		✓		✓		✓		✓		✓		✓
Engine coolant	R				✓				✓				✓				✓
Engine coolant level ③	S/I	✓	✓	✓	✓	✓	✓	✓	✓	✓	✓	✓	✓	✓	✓	✓	✓
Engine oil & filter ③	R	✓	✓	✓	✓	✓	✓	✓	✓	✓	✓	✓	✓	✓	✓	✓	✓
Exhaust system ③	S/I	✓	✓	✓	✓	✓	✓	✓	✓	✓	✓	✓	✓	✓	✓	✓	✓
Front and rear axle lubricant	R		✓		✓				✓				✓				✓
Front and rear driveshafts ①	S/I	✓	✓	✓	✓	✓	✓	✓	✓	✓	✓	✓	✓	✓	✓	✓	✓
Front wheel bearings	S/I & L				✓				✓				✓				✓
Fuel lines & tank cap ③	S/I								✓								✓
Inspect for fluid leaks ③	S/I	✓	✓	✓	✓	✓	✓	✓	✓	✓	✓	✓	✓	✓	✓	✓	✓
Key lock cylinder ③	L		✓		✓				✓		✓		✓		✓		✓

93081C02

1998-01 SCHEDULED MAINTENANCE INTERVALS
(ISUZU AMIGO, HOMBRE, OASIS, RODEO & TROOPER) (Cont.)

TO BE SERVICED	TYPE OF SERVICE	VEHICLE MILEAGE INTERVAL (x1000)															
		7.5	15	22.5	30	37.5	45	52.5	60	67.5	75	82.5	90	97.5	105	112.5	120
Manual transmission and transfer case fluid ④	R		✓		✓				✓				✓				✓
Parking brake system ③	S/I		✓		✓		✓		✓		✓		✓		✓		✓
Power steering fluid	R				✓				✓				✓				✓
Radiator core and A/C condenser	S/I & C								✓								✓
Rotate tires	S/I	✓	✓	✓	✓	✓	✓	✓	✓	✓	✓	✓	✓	✓	✓	✓	✓
Shift-on-the-fly system gear fluid ③	S/I		✓		✓		✓		✓		✓		✓				✓
Spark plug wires ⑤	S/I								✓								✓
Spark plugs	R						Every 100,000 miles										
Starter safety switch ③	S/I	✓	✓	✓	✓	✓	✓	✓	✓	✓	✓	✓	✓	✓	✓	✓	✓
Steering operation ③	S/I	✓	✓	✓	✓	✓	✓	✓	✓	✓	✓	✓	✓	✓	✓	✓	✓
Suspension & steering ③	S/I	✓	✓	✓	✓	✓	✓	✓	✓	✓	✓	✓	✓	✓	✓	✓	✓
Throttle linkage ③	S/I		✓		✓		✓		✓		✓		✓		✓		✓
Timing belt	R										✓						
Tires and wheels ③	S/I	✓	✓	✓	✓	✓	✓	✓	✓	✓	✓	✓	✓	✓	✓	✓	✓
Valve clearance ④	A								✓								✓

R: Replace   S/I: Service or Inspect   L: Lubricate   A: Adjust   C: Clean

① Perform this at the mileage indicated or every 6 months, whichever occurs first.

② Perform this at the mileage indicated or every 24 months, whichever occurs first.

③ Perform this at the mileage indicated or every 12 months, whichever occurs first.

④ 3.2L V6 engine.

⑤ 2.6L 4 cyl. engine.

FREQUENT OPERATION MAINTENANCE (SEVERE SERVICE)

 If a vehicle is operated under any of the following conditions it is considered severe service:

- Towing a trailer or using a camper or car-top carrier.

- Repeated short trips of less than 5 miles in temperatures below freezing.

- Extensive idling or low-speed driving for long distances as in heavy commercial use, such as delivery, taxi or police cars.

- Operating on rough, muddy or salt-covered roads.

- Operating on unpaved or dusty roads.

Air cleaner element: replace every 15,000 miles

Engine oil and filter: replace every 3000 miles or 3 months, whichever occurs first.

Automatic transmission fluid: replace every 20,000 miles.

Rear axle lubricant: replace every 15,000 miles.

93081C03

SCHEDULED MAINTENANCE INTERVALS
ISUZU
AMIGO, HOMBRE, OASIS, RODEO, TROOPER

The following should be used as a guide when determining the amount of work required for a particular service. In estimating how long a particular Scheduled Maintenance Service should take, please observe the following:

- Labor Time is time based on field research and data supplied by the vehicle manufacturer.
- Labor time operations are given in hours and tenths of an hour.
- All labor operations are to be used as a guide.

Mechanic Skill Level Codes:
(A) PRECISION: Highly skilled with multiple certification.
(B) GENERAL: Normally skilled with certification.
(C) MAINTENANCE: Semi-skilled working on certification.

	LABOR TIME
7500 Mile Service (C)	
Amigo	2.8
Hombre	2.1
Oasis	2.1
Rodeo	1.8
Trooper	2.8
15000 Mile Service (B)	
Amigo	5.1
Hombre	4.8
Oasis	5.1
Rodeo	5.5
Trooper	5.1
22500 Mile Service (C)	
Amigo	2.8
Hombre	3.1
Oasis	3.1
Rodeo	2.8
Trooper	2.8
30000 Mile Service (B)	
Amigo	9.8
Hombre	7.1
Oasis	7.3
Rodeo	7.2
Trooper	9.8
37500 Mile Service (C)	
Amigo	2.8
Hombre	3.1
Oasis	3.1
Rodeo	2.1
Trooper	2.8

	LABOR TIME
45000 Mile Service (B)	
Amigo	5.5
Hombre	5.1
Oasis	5.1
Rodeo	4.5
Trooper	5.5
52500 Mile Service (C)	
Amigo	3.1
Hombre	3.1
Oasis	3.3
Rodeo	3.1
Trooper	3.1
60000 Mile Service (B)	
Amigo	11.1
Hombre	10.7
Oasis	10.8
Rodeo	10.8
Trooper	11.1
67500 Mile Service (C)	
Amigo	2.1
Hombre	1.8
Oasis	2.1
Rodeo	2.1
Trooper	2.8
75000 Mile Service (B)	
Amigo	5.1
Hombre	4.8
Oasis	5.1
Rodeo	4.5
Trooper	5.1
Replace timing belt add	2.7
82500 Mile Service (C)	
Amigo	2.8
Hombre	1.8
Oasis	2.1
Rodeo	2.1
Trooper	2.8

	LABOR TIME
90000 Mile Service (B)	
Amigo	11.1
Hombre	10.7
Oasis	10.8
Rodeo	7.2
Trooper	11.1
Replace timing belt add	2.5
97500 Mile Service (C)	
Amigo	2.8
Hombre	1.8
Oasis	2.1
Rodeo	2.1
Trooper	2.8
105000 Mile Service (B)	
Amigo	5.5
Hombre	4.8
Oasis	5.1
Rodeo	4.5
Trooper	5.5
112500 Mile Service (C)	
Amigo	3.1
Hombre	3.1
Oasis	3.3
Rodeo	3.1
Trooper	3.1
120000 Mile Service (B)	
Amigo	11.1
Hombre	10.7
Oasis	10.8
Rodeo	10.8
Trooper	11.1

93081C04

Refer to the model specific sections for fuel system service procedures

TIRE, WHEEL AND BALL JOINT SPECIFICATIONS
Isuzu Truck

Year	Model	OEM Tires		Tire Pressures (psi)		Wheel Size	Ball Joint Inspection
		Standard	Optional	Front	Rear		
1997	Hombre	P205/75R15	none	30	30	6-JJ	U: 4-28 ① L: 4-55
	Rodeo 2wd	P225/75R16	none	29	32	6-JJ	U: 4-28 ① L: 4-55
	Rodeo 4wd	P245/70R16	none	29	32	6-JJ	U: 4-28 ① L: 4-55
	Oasis	P205/65R15	none	32	32	6-JJ	U: 4-28 ① L: 4-55
	Trooper	P245/70R16	none	30	35	7-JJ	U: 4-28 ① L: 4-55
1998	Hombre 2wd	P205/75R15	none	35	35	6-JJ	U: 4-28 ① L: 4-55
	Hombre 4wd	P235/75R15	31x10.5R15LT	35	35	6-JJ	U: 4-28 ① L: 4-55
	Amigo	P235/75R15	P245/70R16	26	29	6.5-JJ	U: 4-28 ① L: 4-55
	Rodeo 2wd	P215/75R15	P235/75R15	29	29	6.5-JJ	U: 4-28 ① L: 4-55
	Rodeo 4wd	P235/75R15	P245/70R16	26	29	7-JJ	U: 4-28 ① L: 4-55
	Hombre 4wd	P235/75R15	31x10.5R15LT	35	35	6-JJ	U: 4-28 ① L: 4-55
	Amigo	P235/75R15	P245/70R16	26	29	6.5-JJ	U: 4-28 ① L: 4-55
	Rodeo 2wd	P215/75R15	P235/75R15	29	29	6.5-JJ	U: 4-28 ① L: 4-55
	Rodeo 4wd	P235/75R15	P245/70R16	26	29	7-JJ	U: 4-28 ① L: 4-55
	Trooper	P245/70R15	none	26	26	7-JJ	U: 4-28 ① L: 4-55
1999	Hombre 2wd	P205/75R15	none	35	35	6-JJ	U: 4-28 ① L: 4-55
	Hombre 4wd	P235/75R15	31x10.5R15LT	35	35	6-JJ	U: 4-28 ① L: 4-55
	Amigo	P235/75R15	P245/70R16	26	29	6.5-JJ	U: 4-28 ① L: 4-55
	Rodeo 2wd	P215/75R15	P235/75R15	29	29	6.5-JJ	U: 4-28 ① L: 4-55
	Rodeo 4wd	P235/75R15	P245/70R16	26	29	7-JJ	U: 4-28 ① L: 4-55
	Trooper	P245/70R15	none	26	26	7-JJ	U: 4-28 ① L: 4-55
2000-01	Hombre 2wd	P205/75R15	none	35	35	6-JJ	U: 4-28 ① L: 4-55
	Hombre 4wd	P235/75R15	31x10.5R15LT	35	35	6-JJ	U: 4-28 ① L: 4-55
	Amigo	P235/75R15	P245/70R16	26	29	6.5-JJ	U: 4-28 ① L: 4-55

93081C05

TIRE, WHEEL AND BALL JOINT SPECIFICATIONS
Isuzu Truck

Year	Model	OEM Tires		Tire Pressures (psi)		Wheel Size	Ball Joint Inspection
		Standard	Optional	Front	Rear		
2000-01 (Cont.)	Rodeo 2wd	P215/75R15	P235/75R15	29	29	6.5-JJ	U: 4-28 ① L: 4-55
	Rodeo 4wd	P235/75R15	P245/70R16	26	29	7-JJ	U: 4-28 ① L: 4-55
	Trooper	P245/70R15	none	26	26	7-JJ	U: 4-28 ① L: 4-55
	VehiCROSS	P245/70R15	none	26	26	7-JJ	NS

OEM: Original Equipment Manufacturer

PSI: Pounds Per Square Inch

STD: Standard

OPT: Optional

L: Lower

U: Upper

NS: Not specified by manufacturer

① Torque required in inch lbs. to rotate ball joint when removed from the knuckle

93081C06

Refer to thc model specific sections for engine electrical system service procedures

KIA
Sportage

ENGINE AND VEHICLE IDENTIFICATION

Engine							Model Year	
Code ①	Liters (cc)	Cu. In.	Cyl.	Fuel Sys.	Engine Type	Eng. Mfg.	Code ②	Year
3	2.0 (1998)	122	4	MFI	DOHC	KIA	V	1997
							W	1998
MFI: Multi-port Fuel Injection							X	1999
DOHC: Double Overhead Camshafts							Y	2000
① 8th digit of VIN							1	2001
② 10th digit of VIN								

93081C07

GENERAL ENGINE SPECIFICATIONS

Year	Model	Engine Displacement Liters (cc)	Engine ID/VIN	Fuel System Type	Net Horsepower @ rpm	Net Torque @ rpm (ft. lbs.)	Bore x Stroke (in.)	Com-pression Ratio	Oil Pressure @ rpm
1997	Sportage	2.0 (1998)	3	MFI	130@5500	127@4000	3.39x3.39	9.2:1	43-57 ①
1998	Sportage	2.0 (1998)	3	MFI	130@5500	127@4000	3.39x3.39	9.2:1	43-57 ①
1999	Sportage	2.0 (1998)	3	MFI	130@5500	127@4000	3.39x3.39	9.2:1	43-57 ①
2000-01	Sportage	2.0 (1998)	3	MFI	130@5500	127@4000	3.39x3.39	9.2:1	43-57 ①

MFI: Multi-port Fuel Injection

① The manufacturer does not provide an engine speed specification for oil pump pressure.

93081C08

ENGINE TUNE-UP SPECIFICATIONS

Year	Engine Displacement Liters (cc)	Engine ID/VIN	Spark Plug Gap (in.)	Ignition Timing (deg.)		Fuel Pump (psi)	Idle Speed (rpm)		Valve Clearance	
				MT	AT		MT	AT	Intake	Exhaust
1997	2.0 (1998)	3	0.039-0.043	4° BTDC	4° BTDC	50	750-850	750-850	HYD.	HYD.
1998	2.0 (1998)	3	0.039-0.043	4° BTDC	4° BTDC	50	750-850	750-850	HYD.	HYD.
1999	2.0 (1998)	3	0.039-0.043	4° BTDC	4° BTDC	38	750-850	750-850	HYD.	HYD.
2000-01	2.0 (1998)	3	0.039-0.043	4° BTDC	4° BTDC	38	750-850	750-850	HYD.	HYD.

BTDC: Before Top Dead Center
HYD: Hydraulic lash adjusters

93081C09

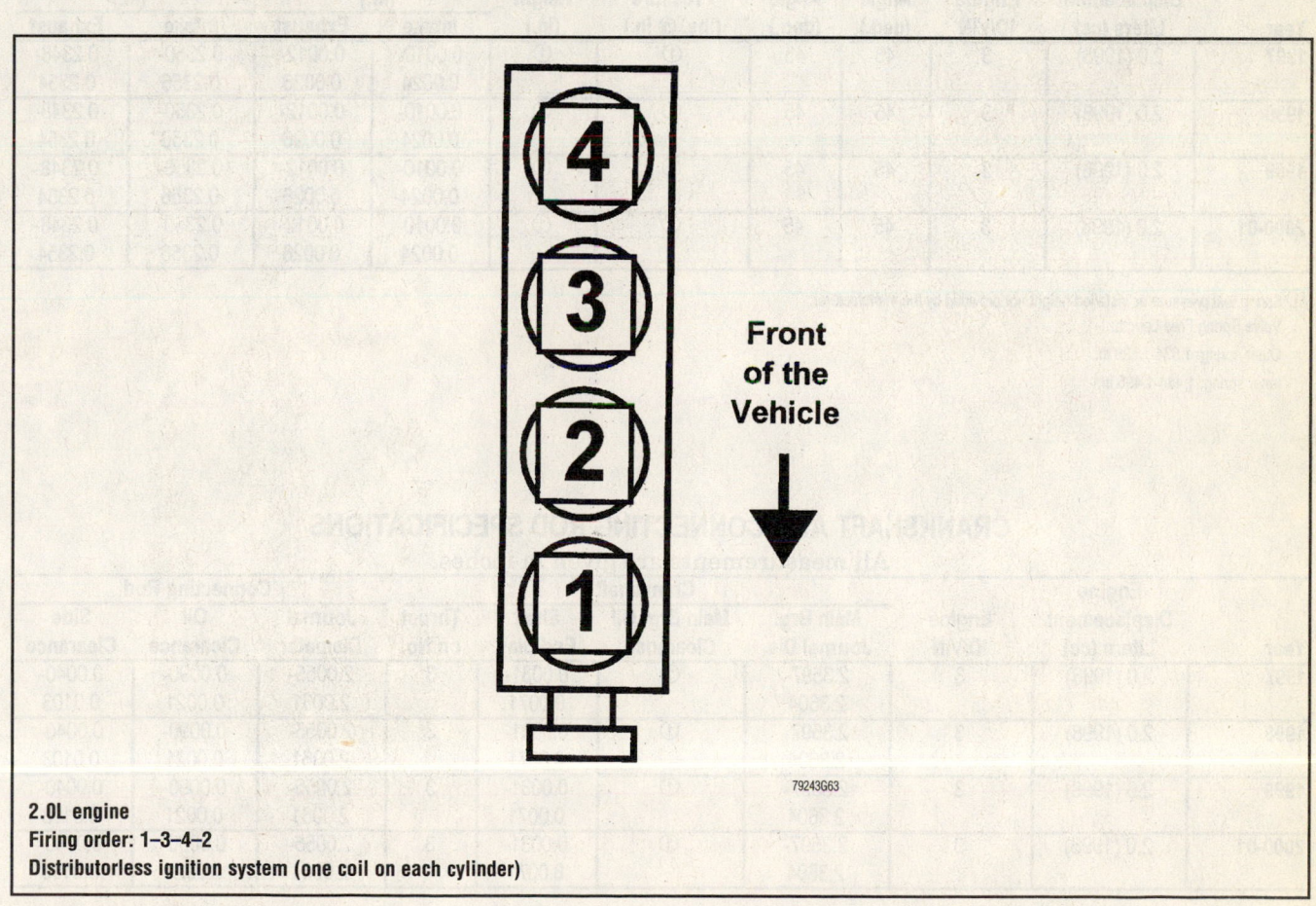

79243G63

2.0L engine
Firing order: 1–3–4–2
Distributorless ignition system (one coil on each cylinder)

For accessory drive belt replacement procedures see the model specific sections of this manual

CAPACITIES

Year	Model	Engine Displacement Liters (cc)	Engine ID/VIN	Engine Oil with Filter (qts.)	Transmission (pts.)		Transfer Case (pts.)	Drive Axle		Fuel Tank (gal.)	Cooling System (qts.)
					Manual	Auto.		Front (pts.)	Rear (pts.)		
1997	Sportage	2.0 (1998)	3	4.4	2.6	5.4	2.8	2.6	2.6	15.8	7.9
1998	Sportage	2.0 (1998)	3	4.4	2.6	5.4	2.8	2.6	2.6	15.8	7.9
1999	Sportage	2.0 (1998)	3	4.4	2.6	5.4	2.8	2.6	2.6	15.8	7.9
2000-01	Sportage	2.0 (1998)	3	4.4	2.6	5.4	2.8	2.6	2.6	15.8	7.9

NOTE: All capacities are approximate. Add fluid gradually and check to be sure a proper fluid level is obtained.

93081C00

VALVE SPECIFICATIONS

Year	Engine Displacement Liters (cc)	Engine ID/VIN	Seat Angle (deg.)	Face Angle (deg.)	Spring Test Pressure (lbs. @ in.)	Spring Installed Height (in.)	Stem-to-Guide Clearance (in.)		Stem Diameter (in.)	
							Intake	Exhaust	Intake	Exhaust
1997	2.0 (1998)	3	45	45	①	①	0.0010-0.0024	0.0012-0.0026	0.2350-0.2356	0.2348-0.2354
1998	2.0 (1998)	3	45	45	①	①	0.0010-0.0024	0.0012-0.0026	0.2350-0.2356	0.2348-0.2354
1999	2.0 (1998)	3	45	45	①	①	0.0010-0.0024	0.0012-0.0026	0.2350-0.2356	0.2348-0.2354
2000-01	2.0 (1998)	3	45	45	①	①	0.0010-0.0024	0.0012-0.0026	0.2350-0.2356	0.2348-0.2354

① Spring test pressure or installed height not provided by the manufacturer.

Valve Spring Free Length:

Outer spring: 1.524-1.539 in.

Inner spring: 1.484-1.496 in.

93081CP1

CRANKSHAFT AND CONNECTING ROD SPECIFICATIONS

All measurements are given in inches.

Year	Engine Displacement Liters (cc)	Engine ID/VIN	Crankshaft				Connecting Rod		
			Main Brg. Journal Dia.	Main Brg. Oil Clearance	Shaft End-play	Thrust on No.	Journal Diameter	Oil Clearance	Side Clearance
1997	2.0 (1998)	3	2.3597-2.3604	①	0.0031-0.0071	3	2.0055-2.0061	0.0090-0.0021	0.0040-0.0103
1998	2.0 (1998)	3	2.3597-2.3604	①	0.0031-0.0071	3	2.0055-2.0061	0.0090-0.0021	0.0040-0.0103
1999	2.0 (1998)	3	2.3597-2.3604	①	0.0031-0.0071	3	2.0055-2.0061	0.0090-0.0021	0.0040-0.0103
2000-01	2.0 (1998)	3	2.3597-2.3604	①	0.0031-0.0071	3	2.0055-2.0061	0.0090-0.0021	0.0040-0.0103

① Journals 1, 2 and 4: 0.0010 - 0.0017 in.

Journal 3: 0.0012 - 0.0019 in.

93081CP2

PISTON AND RING SPECIFICATIONS
All measurements are given in inches.

| Year | Engine Displacement Liters (cc) | Engine ID/VIN | Piston Clearance | Ring Gap | | | Ring Side Clearance | | |
				Top Compression	Bottom Compression	Oil Control	Top Compression	Bottom Compression	Oil Control
1997	2.0 (1998)	3	0.0019-0.0024	0.006-0.012	0.008-0.014	0.008-0.028	0.001-0.003	0.001-0.003	SNUG
1998	2.0 (1998)	3	0.0019-0.0024	0.006-0.012	0.008-0.014	0.008-0.028	0.001-0.003	0.001-0.003	SNUG
1999	2.0 (1998)	3	0.0019-0.0024	0.006-0.012	0.008-0.014	0.008-0.028	0.001-0.003	0.001-0.003	SNUG
2000-01	2.0 (1998)	3	0.0019-0.0024	0.006-0.012	0.008-0.014	0.008-0.028	0.001-0.003	0.001-0.003	SNUG

93081CP3

TORQUE SPECIFICATIONS
All readings in ft. lbs.

| Year | Engine Displacement Liters (cc) | Engine ID/VIN | Cylinder Head Bolts | Main Bearing Bolts | Rod Bearing Bolts | Crankshaft Damper Bolts | Flywheel Bolts | Manifold | | Spark Plugs | Lug Nuts |
								Intake	Exhaust		
1997	2.0 (1998)	3	62	63	50	11	73	16	31	11-17	73
1998	2.0 (1998)	3	62	63	50	11	73	16	31	11-17	73
1999	2.0 (1998)	3	62	63	50	11	73	16	31	11-17	73
2000-01	2.0 (1998)	3	62	63	50	11	73	16	31	11-17	73

93081CP4

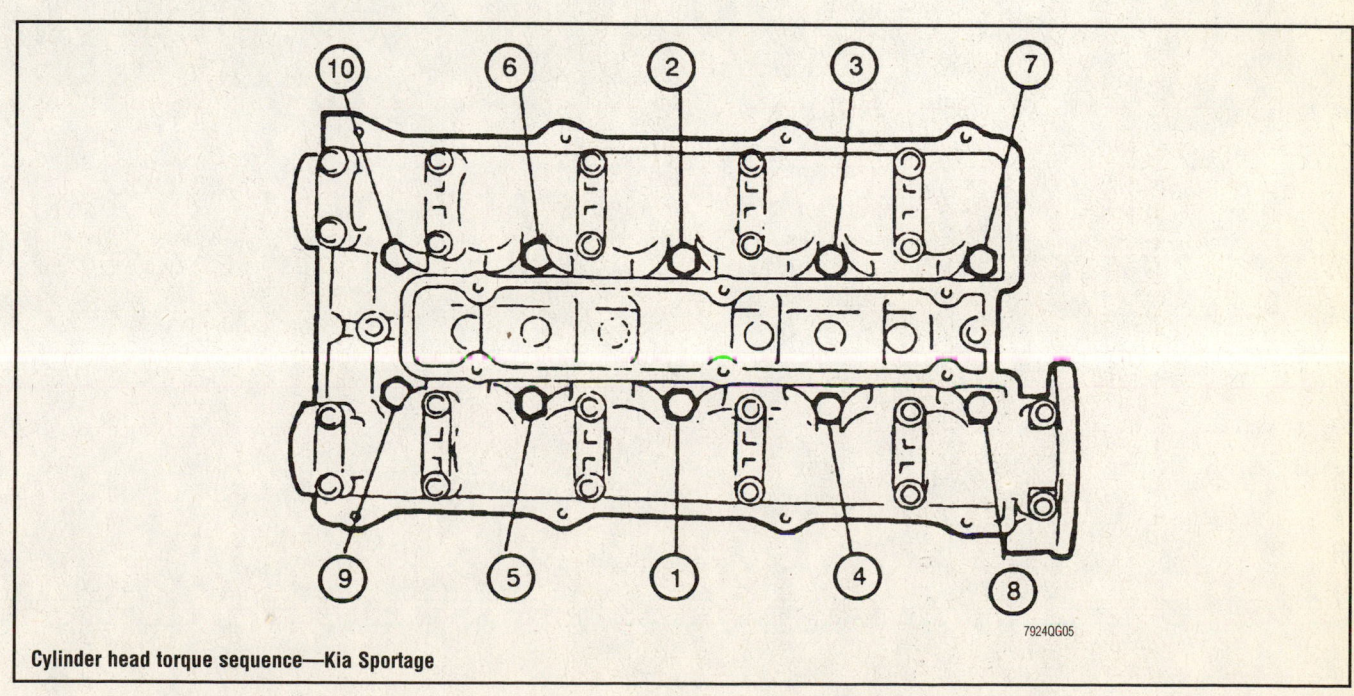

Cylinder head torque sequence—Kia Sportage

7924QG05

For brake related suspension and axle service, refer to the model specific sections of this manual

BRAKE SPECIFICATIONS
KIA SPORTAGE
All measurements in inches unless noted

| Year | Model | Brake Disc | | | Brake Drum | | | Minimum Lining Thickness | | Brake Caliper Mounting Bolts (ft. lbs.) |
		Original Thickness	Minimum Thickness	Maximum Run-out	Original Inside Diameter	Max. Wear Limit	Maximum Machine Diameter	Front	Rear	
1997	Sportage	0.940	0.880	0.004	NA	9.89	NA	0.080	0.060	72
1998	Sportage	0.940	0.880	0.004	NA	9.89	NA	0.080	0.060	72
1999	Sportage	0.940	0.880	0.004	NA	9.89	NA	0.080	0.060	72
2000-01	Sportage	0.940	0.880	0.004	NA	9.89	NA	0.080	0.060	72

NA: Not Available

93081CP5

SCHEDULED MAINTENANCE INTERVALS
(KIA SPORTAGE)

TO BE SERVICED	TYPE OF SERVICE	VEHICLE MILEAGE INTERVAL (x1000)															
		7.5	15	22.5	30	37.5	45	52.5	60	67.5	75	82.5	90	97.5	105	112.5	120
Accessory drive belt	S/I				✓				✓				✓				✓
Air cleaner filter	R				✓				✓				✓				✓
Automatic transmission fluid	R				✓		✓		✓		✓		✓		✓		✓
Ball joints	S/I				✓				✓				✓				✓
Brake lines & connections	S/I				✓				✓				✓				✓
Chassis/body fasteners	S/I				✓				✓				✓				✓
Cooling system	S/I				✓				✓				✓				✓
CV-joint boots	S/I		✓		✓		✓		✓		✓		✓		✓		✓
Disc brakes	S/I		✓		✓		✓		✓		✓		✓		✓		✓
Driveshaft U-joints	L		✓		✓		✓		✓		✓		✓		✓		✓
Drum brakes	S/I				✓				✓				✓				✓
Emission hoses & tubes	S/I								✓								✓
Emission hoses & tubes (California)	R															✓	
Engine coolant	R				✓				✓				✓				✓
Engine oil & filter	R	✓	✓	✓	✓	✓	✓	✓	✓	✓	✓	✓	✓	✓	✓	✓	✓
Exhaust system heat shields	S/I				✓				✓				✓				✓
Front differential fluid ①	R				✓				✓				✓				✓
	S/I	✓	✓	✓	✓	✓	✓	✓	✓	✓	✓	✓	✓	✓	✓	✓	✓
Fuel filter	R				✓				✓				✓				✓
Fuel lines & hoses	S/I				✓				✓				✓				✓
Idle speed	S/I				✓				✓				✓				✓
Locks & hinges	L	✓	✓	✓	✓	✓	✓	✓	✓	✓	✓	✓	✓	✓	✓	✓	✓
Manual transmission fluid	R				✓				✓				✓				✓
PCV valve	S/I								✓								✓
Rear differential fluid	R				✓				✓				✓				✓
	S/I	✓	✓	✓	✓	✓	✓	✓	✓	✓	✓	✓	✓	✓	✓	✓	✓
Spark plug wires	S/I								✓								✓
Spark plugs	R				✓				✓				✓				✓
Steering operation & linkage	S/I				✓				✓				✓				✓

93081CP6

Refer to the model specific sections for driveline service procedures

SCHEDULED MAINTENANCE INTERVALS
(KIA SPORTAGE) (cont.)

TO BE SERVICED	TYPE OF SERVICE	VEHICLE MILEAGE INTERVAL (x1000)															
		7.5	15	22.5	30	37.5	45	52.5	60	67.5	75	82.5	90	97.5	105	112.5	120
Timing belt	R														✓		
	S/I								✓				✓				
Timing belt (non-California)	R								✓								✓
Transfer case fluid ①	R				✓				✓				✓				✓
Transfer case fluid ①	S/I		✓		✓		✓		✓		✓		✓		✓		✓
Transmission fluid	S/I	✓	✓	✓	✓	✓	✓	✓	✓	✓	✓	✓	✓	✓	✓	✓	✓

R: Replace   S/I: Inspect and service, if needed   L: Lubricate

① If equipped.

FREQUENT OPERATION MAINTENANCE (SEVERE SERVICE)

If a vehicle is operated under any of the following conditions it is considered severe service:

- Towing a trailer or using a camper or car-top carrier.
- Repeated short trips of less than 5 miles in temperatures below freezing, or trips of less than 10 miles in any temperature.
- Extensive idling or low-speed driving for long distances as in heavy commercial use, such as delivery, taxi or police cars.
- Operating on rough, muddy or salt-covered roads.
- Operating on unpaved or dusty roads.
- Driving in extremely hot (over 90°) conditions.

Engine oil & filter: replace every 5000 miles or 5 months, whichever occurs first.

Air cleaner filter: inspect and replace if necessary, every 15,000 miles or 15 months, whichever occurs first.

Transfer case fluid: inspect the level every 5000 miles or 5 months, and replace every 15,000 miles or 15 months, whichever occurs first.

Transmission fluid: inspect the level every 5000 miles or 5 months, and replace every 15,000 miles or 15 months, whichever occurs first.

Front differential fluid: inspect the level every 5000 miles or 5 months, and replace every 15,000 miles or 15 months, whichever occurs first.

Rear differential fluid: inspect the level every 5000 miles or 5 months, and replace every 15,000 miles or 15 months, whichever occurs first.

93081CP7

SCHEDULED MAINTENANCE INTERVALS
KIA
SPORTAGE

The following should be used as a guide when determining the amount of work required for a particular service.
In estimating how long a particular Scheduled Maintenance Service should take, please observe the following:

● Labor Time is time based on field research and data supplied by the vehicle manufacturer.
● Labor time operations are given in hours and tenths of an hour.
● All labor operations are to be used as a guide.

Mechanic Skill Level Codes:
(A) PRECISION: Highly skilled with multiple certification.
(B) GENERAL: Normally skilled with certification.
(C) MAINTENANCE: Semi-skilled working on certification.

	LABOR TIME		LABOR TIME		LABOR TIME
7500 Mile Service (C)		**45000 Mile Service (C)**		**90000 Mile Service (B)**	
All models	.6	All models	1.1	All models	5.3
15000 Mile Service (C)		**52500 Mile Service (C)**		**97500 Mile Service (C)**	
All models	1.1	All models	.6	All models	.6
22500 Mile Service (C)		**60000 Mile Service (B)**		**105000 Mile Service (C)**	
All models	.6	All models	5.3	All models	1.1
30000 Mile Service (B)		**67500 Mile Service (C)**		**112500 Mile Service (C)**	
All models	3.1	All models	.6	All models	.6
37500 Mile Service (C)		**75000 Mile Service (C)**		**120000 Mile Service (B)**	
All models	.6	All models	1.1	All models	5.3
		82500 Mile Service (C)			
		All models	.6		

93081CP8

TIRE, WHEEL AND BALL JOINT SPECIFICATIONS
Kia Sportage

Year	Model	OEM Tires		Tire Pressures (psi)		Wheel Size	Ball Joint Inspection
		Standard	Optional	Front	Rear		
1997	Sportage	P205/75R15	none	26	26	6-JJ	①
1998	Sportage	P205/75R15	none	26	26	6-JJ	①
1999	Sportage	P205/75R15	none	26	26	6-JJ	①
2000-01	Sportage	P205/75R15	none	26	26	6-JJ	①

OEM: Original Equipment Manufacturer

PSI: Pounds Per Square Inch

STD: Standard

OPT: Optional

① Replace if any measurable movement is found.

93081CAY

For exhaust manifold replacement procedures, see the model specific sections of this manual

LAND ROVER
Defender 90 • Discovery • Discovery Series II • Range Rover

ENGINE AND VEHICLE IDENTIFICATION

		Engine						Model Year	
Code ①	Liters (cc)	Cu. In.	Cyl.	Fuel Sys.	Engine Type	Eng. Mfg.		Code ②	Year
2	4.0 (3950)	241	8	MFI	OHV	Land Rover		V	1997
J	4.6 (4554)	278	8	MFI	OHV	Land Rover		W	1998
V	4.0 (3950)	241	8	MFI	OHV	Land Rover		X	1999
								Y	2000
								1	2001

MFI: Multi-port Fuel Injection

OHV: Over Head Valve

① 8th digit of the Vehicle Identification Number (VIN)

② 10th digit of the Vehicle Identification Number (VIN)

93081CP9

GENERAL ENGINE SPECIFICATIONS

Year	Model	Engine Displacement Liters (cc)	Engine ID/VIN	Fuel System Type	Net Horsepower @ rpm	Net Torque @ rpm (ft. lbs.)	Bore x Stroke (in.)	Compression Ratio	Oil Pressure @ rpm
1997	Defender 90	4.0 (3950)	2	MFI	190@4750	236@3000	3.7x2.8	9.34:1	35@2400
	Discovery	4.0 (3950)	2	MFI	182@4750	233@3000	3.7x2.8	9.34:1	35@2400
	Range Rover	4.0 (3950)	V	MFI	190@4750	236@3000	3.7x2.8	9.34:1	35@2400
		4.6 (4554)	J	MFI	225@4750	280@3000	3.7x3.2	9.34:1	35@2400
1998	Discovery	4.0 (3950)	2	MFI	182@4750	233@3000	3.7x2.8	9.34:1	35@2400
	Range Rover	4.0 (3950)	V	MFI	190@4750	236@3000	3.7x2.8	9.34:1	35@2400
		4.6 (4554)	J	MFI	225@4750	280@3000	3.7x3.2	9.34:1	35@2400
1999	Discovery	4.0 (3950)	2	MFI	182@4750	233@3000	3.7x2.8	9.34:1	35@2400
	Range Rover	4.0 (3950)	V	MFI	190@4750	236@3000	3.7x2.8	9.34:1	35@2400
		4.6 (4554)	J	MFI	225@4750	280@3000	3.7x3.2	9.34:1	35@2400
2000-01	Discovery Series II	4.0 (3950)	2	MFI	182@4750	233@3000	3.7x2.8	9.34:1	35@2400
	Range Rover	4.0 (3950)	V	MFI	190@4750	236@3000	3.7x2.8	9.34:1	35@2400
		4.6 (4554)	J	MFI	225@4750	280@3000	3.7x3.2	9.34:1	35@2400

MFI: Multi-port Fuel Injection

93081CP0

GASOLINE ENGINE TUNE-UP SPECIFICATIONS

Year	Engine Displacement Liters (cc)	Engine ID/VIN	Spark Plug Gap (in.)	Ignition Timing (deg.) MT	Ignition Timing (deg.) AT	Fuel Pump (psi)	Idle Speed (rpm) MT	Idle Speed (rpm) AT	Valve Clearance Intake	Valve Clearance Exhaust
1997	4.0 (3950)	2	0.032-0.039	①	①	34-37	675-725	675-725	HYD	HYD
	4.0 (3950)	V	0.035-0.040	①	①	34-37	675-725	675-725	HYD	HYD
	4.6 (4554)	J	0.035-0.040	①	①	34-37	680-720	680-720	HYD	HYD
1998	4.0 (3950)	2	0.032-0.039	①	①	34-37	675-725	675-725	HYD	HYD
	4.0 (3950)	V	0.035-0.040	①	①	34-37	675-725	675-725	HYD	HYD
	4.6 (4554)	J	0.035-0.040	①	①	34-37	680-720	680-720	HYD	HYD
1999	4.0 (3950)	2	0.032-0.039	—	①	34-37	675-725	675-725	HYD	HYD
	4.0 (3950)	V	0.035-0.040	—	①	34-37	675-725	675-725	HYD	HYD
	4.6 (4554)	J	0.035-0.040	—	①	34-37	680-720	680-720	HYD	HYD
2000-01	4.0 (3950)	2	0.032-0.039	—	①	34-37	675-725	675-725	HYD	HYD
	4.0 (3950)	V	0.035-0.040	—	①	34-37	675-725	675-725	HYD	HYD
	4.6 (4554)	J	0.035-0.040	—	①	34-37	680-720	680-720	HYD	HYD

HYD: Hydraulic

① Automatically controlled by the Powertrain Control Module (PCM).

93081CQ1

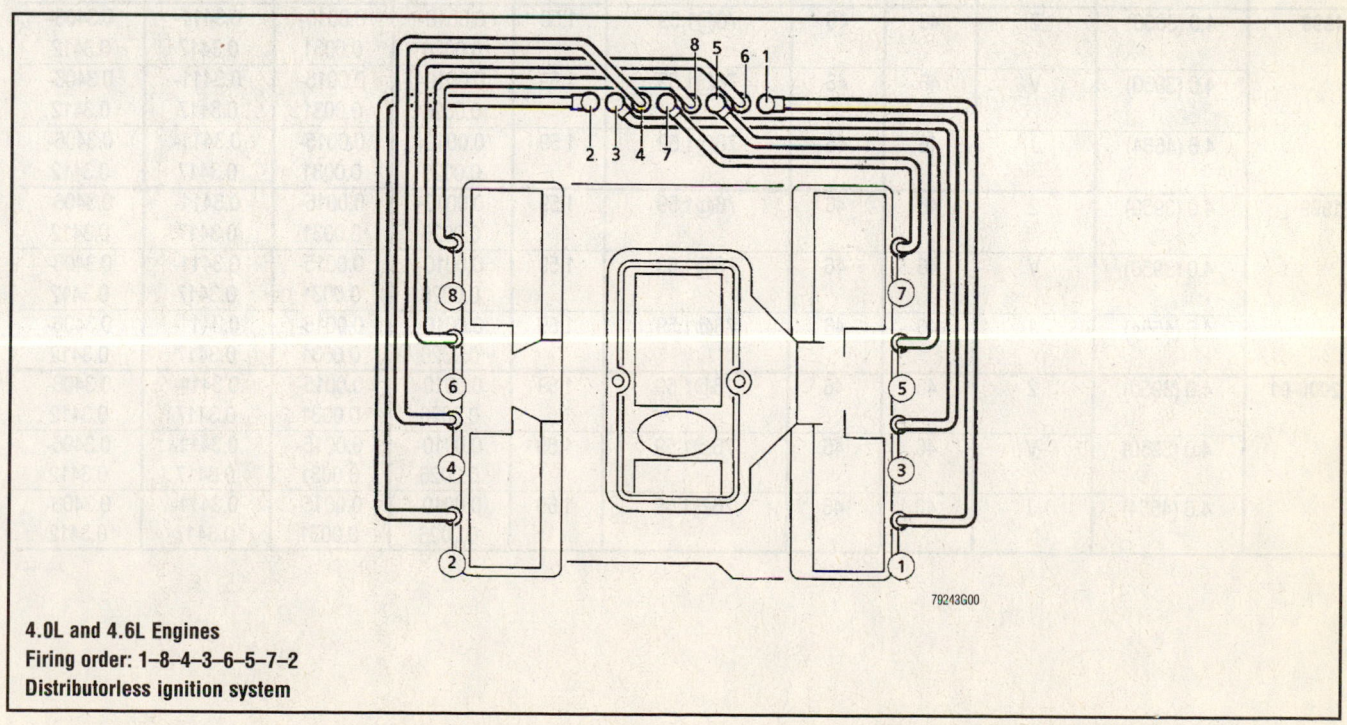

79243G00

4.0L and 4.6L Engines
Firing order: 1-8-4-3-6-5-7-2
Distributorless ignition system

Refer to the model specific sections for cooling system service procedures

CAPACITIES

Year	Model	Engine Displacement Liters (cc)	Engine ID/VIN	Engine Oil with Filter (qts.)	Transmission (pts.) 5-Spd	Auto.	Transfer Case (pts.)	Drive Axle Front (pts.)	Rear (pts.)	Fuel Tank (gal.)	Cooling System (qts.)
1997	Defender 90	4.0 (3950)	V	5.6	—	19.2	4.8	3.6	4.8	15.6	13.5
	Discovery	4.0 (3950)	V	5.6	5.7	19.2	4.9	3.6	3.6	23	24
	Range Rover	4.0 (3950)	2	7	5.7	20.5	5.0	3.6	3.6	26.4	24
		4.6 (4554)	J	7	5.7	23.2	5.0	3.6	3.6	26.4	24
1998	Discovery	4.0 (3950)	V	5.6	5.7	19.2	4.9	3.6	3.6	23	24
	Range Rover	4.0 (3950)	2	7	5.7	20.5	5.0	3.6	3.6	26.4	24
		4.6 (4554)	J	7	5.7	23.2	5.0	3.6	3.6	26.4	24
1999	Discovery	4.0 (3950)	V	5.6	—	19.2	4.9	3.6	3.6	23	24
	Range Rover	4.0 (3950)	2	7	—	20.5	5.0	3.6	3.6	26.4	24
		4.6 (4554)	J	7	—	23.2	5.0	3.6	3.6	26.4	24
2000-01	Discovery Series II	4.0 (3950)	V	5.6	—	19.2	4.9	3.6	3.6	24.6	24
	Range Rover	4.0 (3950)	2	7	—	20.5	5.0	3.6	3.6	24.6	24
		4.6 (4554)	J	7	—	23.2	5.0	3.6	3.6	24.6	24

NOTE: All capacities are approximate. Add fluid gradually and check to be sure a proper fluid level is obtained.

93081CQ2

VALVE SPECIFICATIONS

Year	Engine Displacement Liters (cc)	Engine ID/VIN	Seat Angle (deg.)	Face Angle (deg.)	Spring Test Pressure (lbs. @ in.)	Spring Installed Height (in.)	Stem-to-Guide Clearance (in.) Intake	Exhaust	Stem Diameter (in.) Intake	Exhaust
1997	4.0 (3950)	2	46	46	65@1.59	1.59	0.0010-0.0026	0.0015-0.0031	0.3411-0.3417	0.3406-0.3412
	4.0 (3950)	V	46	46	65@1.59	1.59	0.0010-0.0026	0.0015-0.0031	0.3411-0.3417	0.3406-0.3412
	4.6 (4554)	J	46	46	65@1.59	1.59	0.0010-0.0026	0.0015-0.0031	0.3411-0.3417	0.3406-0.3412
1998	4.0 (3950)	2	46	46	76@1.59	1.59	0.0010-0.0026	0.0015-0.0031	0.3411-0.3417	0.3406-0.3412
	4.0 (3950)	V	46	46	76@1.59	1.59	0.0010-0.0026	0.0015-0.0031	0.3411-0.3417	0.3406-0.3412
	4.6 (4554)	J	46	46	76@1.59	1.59	0.0010-0.0026	0.0015-0.0031	0.3411-0.3417	0.3406-0.3412
1999	4.0 (3950)	2	46	46	76@1.59	1.59	0.0010-0.0026	0.0015-0.0031	0.3411-0.3417	0.3406-0.3412
	4.0 (3950)	V	46	46	76@1.59	1.59	0.0010-0.0026	0.0015-0.0031	0.3411-0.3417	0.3406-0.3412
	4.6 (4554)	J	46	46	76@1.59	1.59	0.0010-0.0026	0.0015-0.0031	0.3411-0.3417	0.3406-0.3412
2000-01	4.0 (3950)	2	46	46	76@1.59	1.59	0.0010-0.0026	0.0015-0.0031	0.3411-0.3417	0.3406-0.3412
	4.0 (3950)	V	46	46	76@1.59	1.59	0.0010-0.0026	0.0015-0.0031	0.3411-0.3417	0.3406-0.3412
	4.6 (4554)	J	46	46	76@1.59	1.59	0.0010-0.0026	0.0015-0.0031	0.3411-0.3417	0.3406-0.3412

93081CQ3

CRANKSHAFT AND CONNECTING ROD SPECIFICATIONS
All measurements are given in inches.

Year	Engine Displacement Liters (cc)	Engine ID/VIN	Crankshaft				Connecting Rod		
			Main Brg. Journal Dia.	Main Brg. Oil Clearance	Shaft End-play	Thrust on No.	Journal Diameter	Oil Clearance	Side Clearance
1997	4.0 (3950)	2	2.4995-2.5000	0.0004-0.0019	0.004-0.008	3	2.1850-2.1856	0.0006-0.0022	0.006-0.014
	4.0 (3950)	V	2.4995-2.5000	0.0004-0.0019	0.004-0.008	3	2.1850-2.1856	0.0006-0.0022	0.006-0.014
	4.6 (4554)	J	2.4995-2.5000	0.0004-0.0019	0.004-0.008	3	2.1850-2.1856	0.0006-0.0022	0.006-0.014
1998	4.0 (3950)	2	2.4995-2.5000	0.0004-0.0019	0.004-0.008	3	2.1850-2.1856	0.0006-0.0022	0.006-0.014
	4.0 (3950)	V	2.4995-2.5000	0.0004-0.0019	0.004-0.008	3	2.1850-2.1856	0.0006-0.0022	0.006-0.014
	4.6 (4554)	J	2.4995-2.5000	0.0004-0.0019	0.004-0.008	3	2.1850-2.1856	0.0006-0.0022	0.006-0.014
1999	4.0 (3950)	2	2.4995-2.5000	0.0004-0.0019	0.004-0.008	3	2.1850-2.1856	0.0006-0.0022	0.006-0.014
	4.0 (3950)	V	2.4995-2.5000	0.0004-0.0019	0.004-0.008	3	2.1850-2.1856	0.0006-0.0022	0.006-0.014
	4.6 (4554)	J	2.4995-2.5000	0.0004-0.0019	0.004-0.008	3	2.1850-2.1856	0.0006-0.0022	0.006-0.014
2000-01	4.0 (3950)	2	2.4995-2.5000	0.0004-0.0019	0.004-0.008	3	2.1850-2.1856	0.0006-0.0022	0.006-0.014
	4.0 (3950)	V	2.4995-2.5000	0.0004-0.0019	0.004-0.008	3	2.1850-2.1856	0.0006-0.0022	0.006-0.014
	4.6 (4554)	J	2.4995-2.5000	0.0004-0.0019	0.004-0.008	3	2.1850-2.1856	0.0006-0.0022	0.006-0.014

93081CQ4

PISTON AND RING SPECIFICATIONS

All measurements are given in inches.

Year	Engine Displacement Liters (cc)	Engine ID/VIN	Piston Clearance	Ring Gap			Ring Side Clearance		
				Top Compression	Bottom Compression	Oil Control	Top Compression	Bottom Compression	Oil Control
1997	4.0 (3950)	2	0.0010-0.0020	0.010-0.020	0.016-0.030	0.014-0.050	0.0020-0.0040	0.0020-0.0040	SNUG
	4.0 (3950)	V	0.0010-0.0020	0.010-0.020	0.016-0.030	0.014-0.050	0.0020-0.0040	0.0020-0.0040	SNUG
	4.6 (4554)	J	0.0010-0.0020	0.010-0.020	0.016-0.030	0.014-0.050	0.0020-0.0040	0.0020-0.0040	SNUG
1998	4.0 (3950)	2	0.0010-0.0020	0.010-0.020	0.016-0.030	0.014-0.050	0.0020-0.0040	0.0020-0.0040	SNUG
	4.0 (3950)	V	0.0010-0.0020	0.010-0.020	0.016-0.030	0.014-0.050	0.0020-0.0040	0.0020-0.0040	SNUG
	4.6 (4554)	J	0.0010-0.0020	0.010-0.020	0.016-0.030	0.014-0.050	0.0020-0.0040	0.0020-0.0040	SNUG
1999	4.0 (3950)	2	0.0010-0.0020	0.010-0.020	0.016-0.030	0.014-0.050	0.0020-0.0040	0.0020-0.0040	SNUG
	4.0 (3950)	V	0.0010-0.0020	0.010-0.020	0.016-0.030	0.014-0.050	0.0020-0.0040	0.0020-0.0040	SNUG
	4.6 (4554)	J	0.0010-0.0020	0.010-0.020	0.016-0.030	0.014-0.050	0.0020-0.0040	0.0020-0.0040	SNUG
2000-01	4.0 (3950)	2	0.0010-0.0020	0.010-0.020	0.016-0.030	0.014-0.050	0.0020-0.0040	0.0020-0.0040	SNUG
	4.0 (3950)	V	0.0010-0.0020	0.010-0.020	0.016-0.030	0.014-0.050	0.0020-0.0040	0.0020-0.0040	SNUG
	4.6 (4554)	J	0.0010-0.0020	0.010-0.020	0.016-0.030	0.014-0.050	0.0020-0.0040	0.0020-0.0040	SNUG

93081CQ5

TORQUE SPECIFICATIONS
All readings in ft. lbs.

Year	Engine Displacement Liters (cc)	Engine ID/VIN	Cylinder Head Bolts	Main Bearing Bolts	Rod Bearing Bolts	Crankshaft Damper Bolts	Flywheel Bolts	Manifold Intake	Manifold Exhaust	Spark Plugs	Lug Nuts
1997	4.0 (3950)	2	①	52	37	200	58	②	40	12	103
	4.0 (3950)	V	①	52	37	200	58	②	40	12	103
	4.6 (4554)	J	③	52	37	200	58	②	40	14	103
1998	4.0 (3950)	2	③	④	⑤	200	58	②	40	15	103
	4.0 (3950)	V	③	④	⑤	200	58	②	40	15	103
	4.6 (4554)	J	③	④	⑤	200	58	②	40	15	103
1999	4.0 (3950)	2	③	④	⑤	200	58	②	40	15	103
	4.0 (3950)	V	③	④	⑤	200	58	②	40	15	103
	4.6 (4554)	J	③	④	⑤	200	58	②	40	15	103
2000-01	4.0 (3950)	2	③	④	⑤	200	58	②	40	15	103
	4.0 (3950)	V	③	④	⑤	200	58	②	40	15	103
	4.6 (4554)	J	④	④	⑤	200	58	②	40	15	103

① Step 1: Outer row - 44 ft. lbs.
  Step 2: Center row - 67 ft. lbs.
  Step 3: Inner row - 67 ft. lbs.

② Step 1: 84 inch lbs.
  Step 2: 38 ft. lbs.

③ Step 1: 15 ft. lbs.
  Step 2: additional 90 degrees
  Step 3: additional 90 degrees

④ Bolts 1-8
  Step 1: 10 ft. lbs.
  Step 2: 53 ft. lbs.
  Bolts 9 & 10
  Step 1: 10 ft. lbs.
  Step 2: 68 ft. lbs.
  Bolts 11-20
  Step 1: 10 ft. lbs.
  Step 2: 33 ft. lbs.

⑤ Step 1: 15 ft. lbs.
  Step 2: additional 80 degrees

93081CQ6

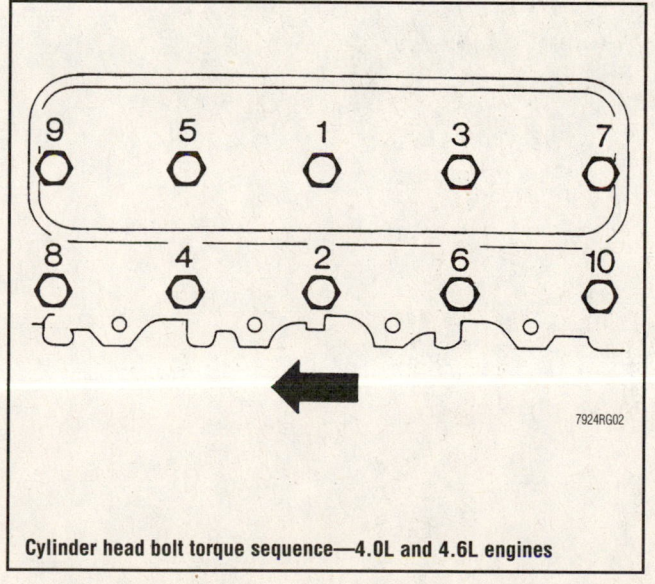

Cylinder head bolt torque sequence—4.0L and 4.6L engines

7924RG02

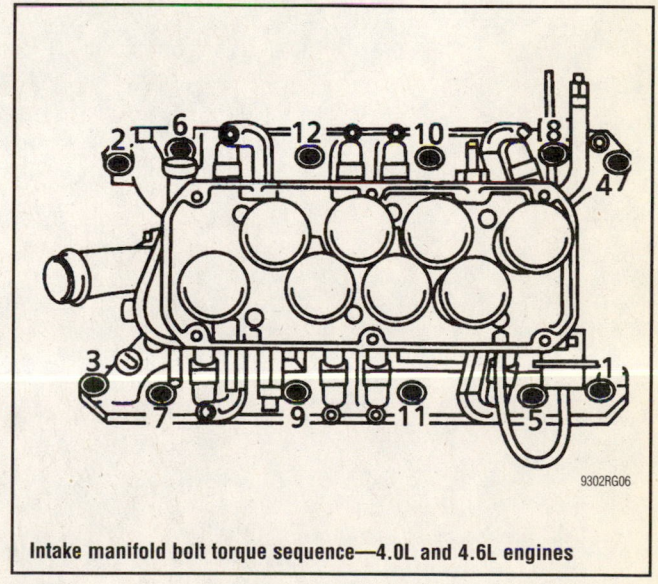

Intake manifold bolt torque sequence—4.0L and 4.6L engines

9302RG06

Timing chain and gear service is covered in the model specific sections of this manual

BRAKE SPECIFICATIONS
LAND ROVER DEFENDER 90, DISCOVERY, RANGE ROVER
All measurements in inches unless noted

Year	Model	Front Brake Disc			Rear Brake Disc			Minimum Lining Thickness		Brake Caliper Bracket Bolts (ft. lbs.)	Brake Caliper Mounting Bolts (ft.-lbs.)
		Original Thickness	Minimum Thickness	Maximum Run-out	Original Thickness	Minimum Thickness	Maximum Run-out	Front	Rear		
1997	Defender 90	0.945	0.080	0.006	0.490	0.030	0.006	0.120	0.120	—	①
	Discovery	1.000	0.870	0.006	0.500	0.460	0.006	0.080	0.080	—	①
	Range Rover	1.000	0.870	0.006	0.500	0.460	0.006	0.080	0.080	②	③
1998	Discovery	1.000	0.870	0.006	0.500	0.460	0.006	0.080	0.080	—	①
	Range Rover	1.000	0.870	0.006	0.500	0.460	0.006	0.080	0.080	②	③
1999	Discovery	0.984	0.866	0.006	0.500	0.461	0.006	0.079	0.079	④	⑤
	Range Rover	1.000	0.870	0.006	0.500	0.460	0.006	0.080	0.080	②	③
2000	Discovery	0.984	0.866	0.006	0.500	0.461	0.006	0.079	0.079	④	⑤
	Range Rover	1.000	0.870	0.006	0.500	0.460	0.006	0.080	0.080	②	③
2001	Discovery	0.984	0.866	0.006	0.500	0.461	0.006	0.079	0.079	④	⑤
	Range Rover	1.000	0.870	0.006	0.500	0.460	0.006	0.080	0.080	②	③

① Both front and rear calipers: 60 ft. lbs.
② Front: 122 ft. lbs.
  Rear: 74 ft. lbs.
③ Front: 19 ft. lbs.
  Rear: 26 ft. lbs.
④ Front: 129 ft. lbs.
  Rear: 70 ft. lbs.
⑤ Both front and rear calipers: 22 ft. lbs.

93081CQ7

SCHEDULED MAINTENANCE INTERVALS
(LAND ROVER DISCOVERY, DEFENDER 90 & RANGE ROVER)

TO BE SERVICED	TYPE OF SERVICE	VEHICLE MILEAGE INTERVAL (x1000)															
		7.5	15	22.5	30	37.5	45	52.5	60	67.5	75	82.5	90	97.5	105	112.5	120
Air cleaner filter	R				✓				✓				✓				✓
Battery fluid level	R				✓				✓				✓				✓
Brake fluid level	S/I		✓				✓				✓				✓		
Brake lines	S/I	✓	✓	✓	✓	✓	✓	✓	✓	✓	✓	✓	✓	✓	✓	✓	✓
Brake pads, calipers & rotors	S/I	✓	✓	✓	✓	✓	✓	✓	✓	✓	✓	✓	✓	✓	✓	✓	✓
Coolant hoses	S/I	✓	✓	✓	✓	✓	✓	✓	✓	✓	✓	✓	✓	✓	✓	✓	✓
Door locks & hinges	L		✓		✓		✓		✓		✓		✓		✓		✓
Driveshafts & U-joints	L		✓		✓		✓		✓		✓		✓		✓		✓
Engine & transmission mounts	S/I							✓					✓				
Engine coolant	R				✓				✓				✓				✓
Engine oil & filter	R	✓	✓	✓	✓	✓	✓	✓	✓	✓	✓	✓	✓	✓	✓	✓	✓
Exhaust system & heat shields	S/I	✓	✓	✓	✓	✓	✓	✓	✓	✓	✓	✓	✓	✓	✓	✓	✓
Front and rear axle oil	R				✓				✓				✓				✓
Fuel filter	R								✓								✓
Fuel lines	S/I		✓		✓		✓		✓		✓		✓		✓		✓
Hood latch, safety catch & fuel door hinges	L		✓		✓		✓		✓		✓		✓		✓		✓
Oxygen sensors	R											✓					
Parking brake	S/I		✓		✓		✓		✓		✓		✓		✓		✓
Power steering fluid	S/I		✓		✓		✓		✓		✓		✓		✓		✓
Radiator core and A/C condenser	S/I		✓		✓		✓		✓		✓		✓		✓		✓
Seat belts	S/I		✓		✓		✓		✓		✓		✓		✓		✓
Serpentine drive belt	R										✓						
Serpentine drive belt	S/I				✓				✓				✓				✓
Shock absorbers	S/I		✓		✓		✓		✓		✓		✓		✓		✓
Spark plugs	R				✓				✓				✓				✓
Steering box	S/I & A						✓						✓				
Steering rods, joints & dust covers	S/I		✓		✓		✓		✓		✓		✓		✓		✓
Supplemental Restraint System (SRS)	S/I	Every 10 years															

93081CQ8

Ignition system service is covered in the model specific sections of this manual

SCHEDULED MAINTENANCE INTERVALS
(LAND ROVER DISCOVERY, DEFENDER 90 & RANGE ROVER) (Cont.)

TO BE SERVICED	TYPE OF SERVICE	VEHICLE MILEAGE INTERVAL (x1000)															
		7.5	15	22.5	30	37.5	45	52.5	60	67.5	75	82.5	90	97.5	105	112.5	120
Suspension links & mountings	S/I		✓		✓		✓		✓		✓		✓		✓		✓
Tires	S/I	✓	✓	✓	✓	✓	✓	✓	✓	✓	✓	✓	✓	✓	✓	✓	✓
Transfer gearbox oil	R				✓				✓				✓				✓
Transmission fluid	R				✓				✓				✓				✓
Transmission fluid filter	R				✓								✓				
Wheel speed sensor wiring	S/I		✓		✓		✓		✓		✓		✓		✓		✓
Wiper blades	S/I	✓	✓	✓	✓	✓	✓	✓	✓	✓	✓	✓	✓	✓	✓	✓	✓

R: Replace   S/I: Service or Inspect   L: Lubricate   A: Adjust

FREQUENT OPERATION MAINTENANCE (SEVERE SERVICE)

If a vehicle is operated under any of the following conditions it is considered severe service:

- Towing a trailer or using a camper or car-top carrier.
- Repeated short trips of less than 5 miles in temperatures below freezing, or trips of less than 10 miles in any temperature.
- Extensive idling or low-speed driving for long distances as in heavy commercial use, such as delivery, taxi or police cars.
- Operating on rough, muddy or salt-covered roads.
- Operating on unpaved or dusty roads.
- Frequent operation in temperatures above 90°F.

Air cleaner element: replace every 15,000 miles

Brake fluid: replace every 15,000 miles

Brake fluid level: inspect initially at 7,500 miles, then every 15,000 miles

Brake pads, calipers & rotors: inspect every 3,750 miles

Driveshafts & U-joints: lubricate every 7,500 miles

Engine & transmission mounts: inspect every 22,500 miles

Engine coolant: replace every 15,000 miles

Engine oil & filter: replace every 3,750 miles.

Front & rear axle oil: replace every 15,000 miles.

Fuel filter: replace every 30,000 miles.

Power steering fluid level: inspect every 7,500 miles.

Serpentine drive belt: inspect every 15,000 miles and replace every 30,000 miles.

Shock absorbers: inspect every 7,500 miles.

Spark plugs: replace every 15,000 miles.

Steering rods, joints & dust covers: inspect every 7,500 miles.

Suspension links & mountings: inspect every 7,500 miles.

Tires: inspect every 3,750 miles.

Transfer gearbox oil: replace every 15,000 miles.

Transmission fluid & filter: replace every 15,000 miles.

93081CQ9

SCHEDULED MAINTENANCE INTERVALS
LAND ROVER
DISCOVERY, DEFENDER 90
RANGE ROVER

The following should be used as a guide when determining the amount of work required for a particular service.
In estimating how long a particular Scheduled Maintenance Service should take, please observe the following:

- Labor Time is time based on field research and data supplied by the vehicle manufacturer.
- Labor time operations are given in hours and tenths of an hour.
- All labor operations are to be used as a guide.

Mechanic Skill Level Codes:
(A) PRECISION: Highly skilled with multiple certification.
(B) GENERAL: Normally skilled with certification.
(C) MAINTENANCE: Semi-skilled working on certification.

	LABOR TIME		LABOR TIME		LABOR TIME
7500 Mile Service (C)		**45000 Mile Service (C)**		**90000 Mile Service (B)**	
All Models	2.4	All Models	1.1	All Models	6.0
15000 Mile Service (B)		**52500 Mile Service (C)**		**97500 Mile Service (C)**	
All Models	5.0	All Models	2.7	All Models	2.4
22500 Mile Service (C)		**60000 Mile Service (B)**		**105000 Mile Service (B)**	
All Models	3.0	All Models	5.9	All Models	5.2
30000 Mile Service (B)		**67500 Mile Service (C)**		**112500 Mile Service (C)**	
All Models	5.9	All Models	2.6	All Models	2.6
37500 Mile Service (C)		**75000 Mile Service (B)**		**120000 Mile Service (B)**	
All Models	2.4	All Models	5.2	All Models	5.9
		82500 Mile Service (C)			
		All Models	2.4		

93081CQ0

TIRE, WHEEL AND BALL JOINT SPECIFICATIONS
Land Rover

| Year | Model | OEM Tires | | Tire Pressures (psi) | | Wheel Size | Ball Joint Inspection |
		Standard	Optional	Front	Rear		
1997	Discovery	235/70HR16	None	28	36	7-J	①
	Range Rover	255/65HR16	None	28	36	8-J	①
1998	Discovery	235/70HR16	None	28	36	7-J	①
	Range Rover	255/65HR16	None	28	36	8-J	①
1999	Discovery	235/70HR16	None	28	36	7-J	①
	Range Rover	255/65HR16	None	28	36	8-J	①
2000-01	Discovery	235/70HR16	None	28	36	7-J	①
	Range Rover	255/65HR16	None	28	36	8-J	①

OEM: Original Equipment Manufacturer

PSI: Pounds Per Square Inch

STD: Standard

OPT: Optional

① Replace if any measurable movement is found.

93081CR1

LEXUS
LX450 • LX470 • RX300

ENGINE AND VEHICLE IDENTIFICATION

	Engine							Model Year	
Code ①	Liters (cc)	Cu. In.	Cyl.	Fuel Sys.	EngineType	Eng. Mfg.		Code ②	Year
1FZ-FE	4.5 (4477)	273	6	SFI	DOHC	Toyota		V	1997
1MZ-FE	3.0 (2995)	183	6	SFI	DOHC	Toyota		W	1998
2UZ-FE	4.7 (4665)	285	8	SFI	DOHC	Toyota		X	1999
								Y	2000
								1	2001

SFI: Sequential Fuel Injection

DOHC: Double Overhead Camshaft

① Located on the timing belt cover.

② 10th digit of the VIN

93081CR2

GENERAL ENGINE SPECIFICATIONS

Year	Model	Engine Displacement Liters (cc)	Engine ID/VIN	Fuel System Type	Net Horsepower @ rpm	Net Torque @ rpm (ft. lbs.)	Bore x Stroke (in.)	Com-pression Ratio	Oil Pressure @ rpm
1997	LX450	4.5 (4477)	1FZ-FE	SFI	212@4600	275@3200	3.94x3.74	9.0:1	36-71@3000
1998	LX470	4.7 (4665)	2UZ-FE	SFI	230@4800	320@3400	3.70x3.31	9.6:1	43-85@3000
	RX300	3.0 (2995)	1MZ-FE	SFI	194@5200	209@4400	3.44x3.27	10.5:1	43-78@3000
1999	LX470	4.7 (4665)	2UZ-FE	SFI	230@4800	320@3400	3.70x3.31	9.6:1	43-85@3000
	RX300	3.0 (2995)	1MZ-FE	SFI	220@5800	222@4400	3.44x3.27	10.5:1	43-78@3000
2000-01	LX470	4.7 (4665)	2UZ-FE	SFI	230@4800	320@3400	3.70x3.31	9.6:1	43-85@3000
	RX300	3.0 (2995)	1MZ-FE	SFI	220@5800	222@4400	3.44x3.27	10.5:1	43-78@3000

SFI: Sequential Fuel Injection

93081CR3

Refer to the model specific sections for engine mechanical service procedures

ENGINE TUNE-UP SPECIFICATIONS

Year	Engine Displacement Liters (cc)	Engine ID/VIN	Spark Plug Gap (in.)	Ignition Timing (deg.)	Fuel Pump (psi)	Idle Speed (rpm)	Valve Clearance	
							Intake	Exhaust
1997	4.5 (4477)	1FZ-FE	0.031	3B	38-44	600-700	0.006-0.010	0.010-0.014
1998	3.0 (2995)	1MZ-FE	0.043	8-12B	44-50	650-750	0.006-0.010	0.010-0.014
	4.7 (4665)	2UZ-FE	0.047	5-15B	38-44	650-750	0.006-0.010	0.010-0.014
1999	3.0 (2995)	1MZ-FE	0.043	8-12B	44-50	650-750	0.006-0.010	0.010-0.014
	4.7 (4665)	2UZ-FE	0.047	5-15B	38-44	650-750	0.006-0.010	0.010-0.014
2000-01	3.0 (2995)	1MZ-FE	0.043	8-12B	44-50	650-750	0.006-0.010	0.010-0.014
	4.7 (4665)	2UZ-FE	0.047	5-15B	38-44	650-750	0.006-0.010	0.010-0.014

NOTE: The Vehicle Emission Control Information label often reflects specification changes made during production. The label figures must be used if they differ from those in this chart.

B: Before top dead center

93081CR4

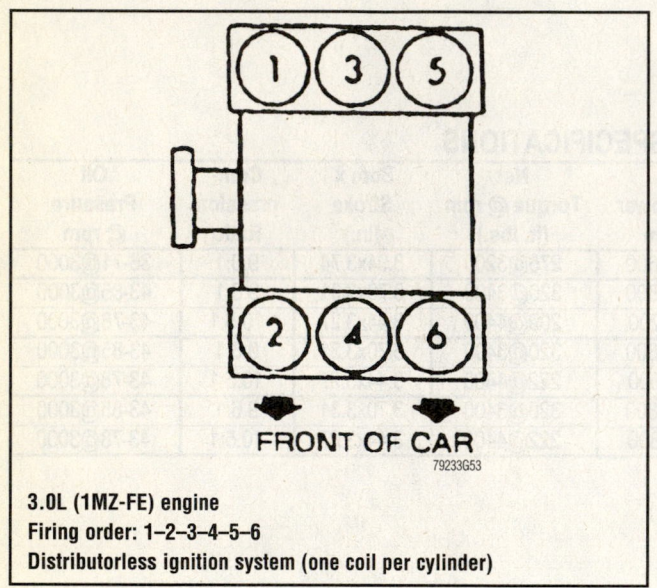

3.0L (1MZ-FE) engine
Firing order: 1–2–3–4–5–6
Distributorless ignition system (one coil per cylinder)

79233G53

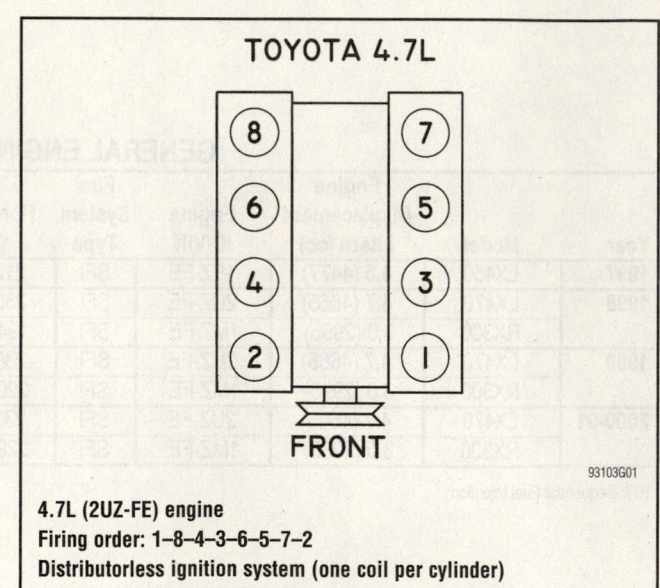

4.7L (2UZ-FE) engine
Firing order: 1–8–4–3–6–5–7–2
Distributorless ignition system (one coil per cylinder)

93103G01

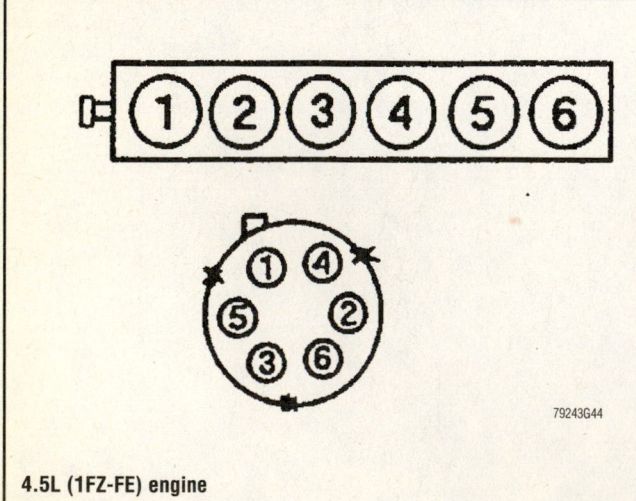

4.5L (1FZ-FE) engine
Firing order: 1–5–3–6–2–4
Distributor rotation: Counterclockwise

79243G44

CAPACITIES

Year	Model	Engine Displacement Liters (cc)	Engine ID/VIN	Engine Oil with Filter (qts.)	Transmission (pts.)	Transfer Case (pts.)	Drive Axle Front (pts.)	Drive Axle Rear (pts.)	Fuel Tank (gal.)	Cooling System (qts.)
1997	LX450	4.5 (4477)	1FZ-FE	7.8	4.0	3.6	①	6.8	25.1	②
1998	LX470	4.7 (4665)	2UZ-FE	7.2	4.0	2.8	3.6	③	25.4	④
	RX300	3.0 (2995)	1MZ-FE	5	⑤	—	1.9	1.9	17.2	9.5
1999	LX470	4.7 (4665)	2UZ-FE	7.2	4.0	2.8	3.6	③	25.1	④
	RX300	3.0 (2995)	1MZ-FE	5	⑤	—	1.9	1.9	17.2	9.5
2000-01	LX470	4.7 (4665)	2UZ-FE	7.2	4.0	2.8	3.6	③	25.1	④
	RX300	3.0 (2995)	1MZ-FE	5	⑤	—	1.9	1.9	17.2	9.5

NOTE: All capacities are approximate. Add fluid gradually and check to be sure a proper fluid level is obtained.

① With differential lock: 5.6
   Without differential lock: 5.8

② With rear heater: 14.2
   Without rear heater: 13.2

③ With differential lock: 6.8 pts.
   Without differential lock: 7.0 pts.

④ With rear heater: 16.2
   Without rear heater: 15.6

⑤ U140E Transaxle:
   Dry Fill: 17.44 pts.
   Drain and Refill: 7.4 pts.
   U140F Transaxle:
   Dry Fill: 19.34 pts.
   Drain and Refill: 8.6 pts.

93081CR5

VALVE SPECIFICATIONS

Year	Engine Displacement Liters (cc)	Engine ID/VIN	Seat Angle (deg.)	Face Angle (deg.)	Spring Test Pressure (lbs. @ in.)	Spring Installed Height (in.)	Stem-to-Guide Clearance (in.) Intake	Stem-to-Guide Clearance (in.) Exhaust	Stem Diameter (in.) Intake	Stem Diameter (in.) Exhaust
1997	4.5 (4477)	1FZ-FE	45	44.5	48.1-53.4@ 1.437	1.437	0.0010- 0.0024	0.0012- 0.0026	0.2744- 0.2750	0.2742- 0.2748
1998	3.0 (2995)	1MZ-FE	45	40.5	41.9-46.3@ 1.437	1.331	0.0010- 0.0024	0.0012- 0.0026	0.2154- 0.2159	0.2152- 0.2156
	4.7 (4665)	2UZ-FE	45	44.5	45.9-50.7@ 1.378	1.378	0.0010- 0.0024	0.0012- 0.0026	0.2154- 0.2159	0.2152- 0.2157
1999	3.0 (2995)	1MZ-FE	45	40.5	41.9-46.3@ 1.437	1.331	0.0010- 0.0024	0.0012- 0.0026	0.2154- 0.2159	0.2152- 0.2156
	4.7 (4665)	2UZ-FE	45	44.5	45.9-50.7@ 1.378	1.378	0.0010- 0.0024	0.0012- 0.0026	0.2154- 0.2159	0.2152- 0.2157
2000-01	3.0 (2995)	1MZ-FE	45	40.5	41.9-46.3@ 1.437	1.331	0.0010- 0.0024	0.0012- 0.0026	0.2154- 0.2159	0.2152- 0.2156
	4.7 (4665)	2UZ-FE	45	44.5	45.9-50.7@ 1.378	1.378	0.0010- 0.0024	0.0012- 0.0026	0.2154- 0.2159	0.2152- 0.2157

93081CR6

Refer to the model specific sections for fuel system service procedures

CRANKSHAFT AND CONNECTING ROD SPECIFICATIONS
All measurements are given in inches.

Year	Engine Displacement Liters (cc)	Engine ID/VIN	Crankshaft				Connecting Rod		
			Main Brg. Journal Dia.	Main Brg. Oil Clearance	Shaft End-play	Thrust on No.	Journal Diameter	Oil Clearance	Side Clearance
1997	4.5 (4477)	1FZ-FE	2.7158-2.7165	0.0017-0.0024	0.0008-0.0087	4	2.2434-2.2441	0.0013-0.0020	0.0063-0.0103
1998	3.0 (2995)	1MZ-FE	2.4011-2.4016	①	0.0016-0.0095	2	2.0863-2.0866	0.0015-0.0025	0.0059-0.0188
	4.7 (4665)	2UZ-FE	2.6373-2.6378	0.0016-0.0023	0.0008-0.0087	3	2.0465-2.0472	0.0011-0.0021	0.0063-0.0138
1999	3.0 (2995)	1MZ-FE	2.4011-2.4016	①	0.0016-0.0095	2	2.0863-2.0866	0.0015-0.0025	0.0059-0.0188
	4.7 (4665)	2UZ-FE	2.6373-2.6378	0.0016-0.0023	0.0008-0.0087	3	2.0465-2.0472	0.0011-0.0021	0.0063-0.0138
2000-01	3.0 (2995)	1MZ-FE	2.4011-2.4016	①	0.0016-0.0095	2	2.0863-2.0866	0.0015-0.0025	0.0059-0.0188
	4.7 (4665)	2UZ-FE	2.6373-2.6378	0.0016-0.0023	0.0008-0.0087	3	2.0465-2.0472	0.0011-0.0021	0.0063-0.0138

① Journals 1 and 4: 0.0006 - 0.0013 in.
Journals 2 and 3: 0.0010 - 0.0018 in.

93081CR7

PISTON AND RING SPECIFICATIONS
All measurements are given in inches.

Year	Engine Displacement Liters (cc)	Engine ID/VIN	Piston Clearance	Ring Gap			Ring Side Clearance		
				Top Compression	Bottom Compression	Oil Control	Top Compression	Bottom Compression	Oil Control
1997	4.5 (4477)	1FZ-FE	0.0016-0.0024	0.0118-0.0205	0.0177-0.0264	0.0059-0.0205	0.0016-0.0031	0.0012-0.0028	SNUG
1998	3.0 (2995)	1MZ-FE	0.0033-0.0042	0.0098-0.0138	0.0138-0.0177	0.0059-0.0157	0.0008-0.0028	0.0008-0.0024	SNUG
	4.7 (4665)	2UZ-FE	0.0035-0.0044	0.0118-0.0197	0.0157-0.0256	0.0051-0.0189	0.0012-0.0031	0.0012-0.0028	SNUG
1999	3.0 (2995)	1MZ-FE	0.0033-0.0042	0.0098-0.0138	0.0138-0.0177	0.0059-0.0157	0.0008-0.0028	0.0008-0.0024	SNUG
	4.7 (4665)	2UZ-FE	0.0035-0.0044	0.0118-0.0197	0.0157-0.0256	0.0051-0.0189	0.0012-0.0031	0.0012-0.0028	SNUG
2000-01	3.0 (2995)	1MZ-FE	0.0033-0.0042	0.0098-0.0138	0.0138-0.0177	0.0059-0.0157	0.0008-0.0028	0.0008-0.0024	SNUG
	4.7 (4665)	2UZ-FE	0.0035-0.0044	0.0118-0.0197	0.0157-0.0256	0.0051-0.0189	0.0012-0.0031	0.0012-0.0028	SNUG

93081CR8

TORQUE SPECIFICATIONS
All readings in ft. lbs.

Year	Engine Displacement Liters (cc)	Engine ID/VIN	Cylinder Head Bolts	Main Bearing Bolts	Rod Bearing Bolts	Crankshaft Damper Bolts	Flywheel Bolts	Manifold		Spark Plugs	Lug Nuts
								Intake	Exhaust		
1997	4.5 (4477)	1FZ-FE	①	②	③	304	74	15	29	14	④
1998	3.0 (2995)	1MZ-FE	⑤	⑥	⑦	159	61	32	36	13	70
	4.7 (4665)	2UZ-FE	⑧	⑨	⑦	181	③	13	33	13	97
1999	3.0 (2995)	1MZ-FE	⑤	⑥	⑦	159	61	32	36	13	70
	4.7 (4665)	2UZ-FE	⑧	⑨	⑦	181	③	15	29	14	97
2000-01	3.0 (2995)	1MZ-FE	⑤	⑥	⑦	159	61	32	36	13	70
	4.7 (4665)	2UZ-FE	⑧	⑨	⑦	181	③	15	29	14	97

① Step 1: 29 ft. lbs.
   Step 2: Plus 90 degrees
   Step 3: Plus 90 degrees
② Step 1: 54 ft. lbs.
   Step 2: Plus 90 degrees
③ Step 1: 35 ft. lbs.
   Step 2: Plus 90 degrees
④ Steel wheels: 109 ft. lbs.
   Aluminum wheels: 76 ft. lbs.
⑤ Step 1: 12 point bolts to 40 ft. lbs.
   Step 2: 12 point bolts plus 90 degrees
   Step 3: Hex head recessed bolt to 13 ft. lbs.
⑥ Step 1: 12 point cap bolts to 16 ft. lbs.
   Step 2: 12 point cap bolts plus 90 degrees
   Step 3: Hex head side bolts to 20 ft. lbs.
⑦ Step 1: 18 ft. lbs.
   Step 2: Plus 90 degrees
⑧ Step 1: 24 ft. lbs.
   Step 2: Plus 180 degrees
⑨ Step 1: 20 ft. lbs.
   Step 2: Plus 90 degrees

93081CR9

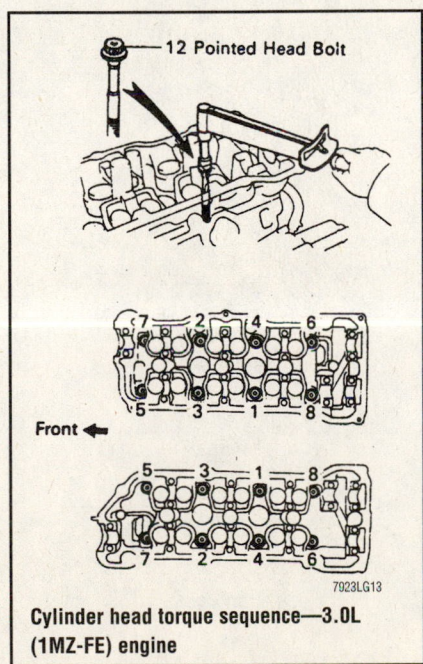

Cylinder head torque sequence—3.0L (1MZ-FE) engine

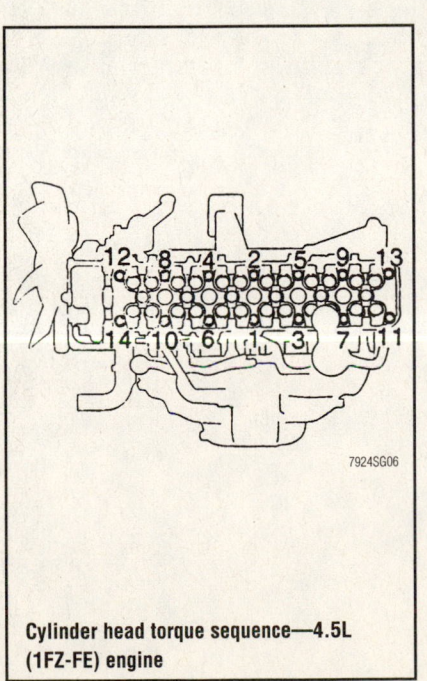

Cylinder head torque sequence—4.5L (1FZ-FE) engine

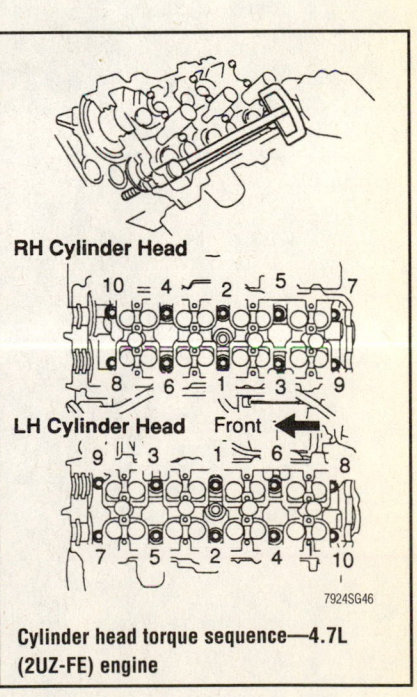

Cylinder head torque sequence—4.7L (2UZ-FE) engine

Refer to the model specific sections for engine electrical system service procedures

BRAKE SPECIFICATIONS
LEXUS LX450, LX470 and RX300
All measurements in inches unless noted

| Year | Model | Front Brake Disc | | | Rear Brake Disc | | | Minimum Lining Thickness | Brake Caliper | |
		Original Thickness	Minimum Thickness	Maximum Run-out	Original Thickness	Minimum Thickness	Maximum Run-out		Bracket Bolts (ft. lbs.)	Mounting Bolts (ft. lbs.)
1997	LX450	1.260	1.181	0.0059	0.709	0.630	0.0059	0.039	76	①
1998	LX470	1.260	1.181	0.0028	0.709	0.611	0.0040	0.039	76	①
	RX300	1.020	1.024	0.0020	0.394	0.354	0.0059	0.039	②	③
1999	LX470	1.260	1.181	0.0028	0.709	0.611	0.0040	0.039	76	①
	RX300	1.020	1.024	0.0020	0.394	0.354	0.0059	0.039	②	③
2000-01	LX470	1.260	1.181	0.0028	0.709	0.611	0.0040	0.039	76	①
	RX300	1.020	1.024	0.0020	0.394	0.354	0.0059	0.039	②	③

① Front: 90 ft. lbs.
  Rear: 65 ft. lbs.

② Front: 79 ft. lbs.
  Rear: 34 ft. lbs.

③ Front: 25 ft. lbs.
  Rear: 14 ft. lbs.

93081CR0

SCHEDULED MAINTENANCE INTERVALS
(LEXUS LX450, LX470 & RX300)

TO BE SERVICED	TYPE OF SERVICE	VEHICLE MILEAGE INTERVAL (x1000)												
		7.5	15	22.5	30	37.5	45	52.5	60	67.5	75	82.5	90	97.5
Engine oil & filter	R	✓	✓	✓	✓	✓	✓	✓	✓	✓	✓	✓	✓	✓
Automatic transmission fluid & filter	S/I		✓		✓		✓		✓		✓		✓	
Ball joints & dust covers	S/I		✓		✓		✓		✓		✓		✓	
Bolts & nuts on chassis & body	S/I		✓		✓		✓		✓		✓		✓	
Brake linings & drums	S/I		✓		✓		✓		✓		✓		✓	
Brake line pipes & hoses	S/I		✓		✓		✓		✓		✓		✓	
Brake pads & discs (front & rear)	S/I		✓		✓		✓		✓		✓		✓	
Propeller shaft grease	S/I		✓		✓		✓		✓		✓		✓	
Steering knuckle & chassis grease	S/I		✓		✓		✓		✓		✓		✓	
Steering linkage	S/I		✓		✓		✓		✓		✓		✓	
Transfer, differential & steering gear box oil	S/I		✓		✓		✓		✓		✓		✓	
Air cleaner filter	R				✓				✓				✓	
Front wheel bearing & thrust bush grease	R				✓				✓				✓	
Spark plugs	R				✓				✓				✓	
Drive belts	S/I				✓				✓				✓	
Exhaust pipes & mountings	S/I				✓				✓				✓	
Fuel lines & connections	S/I				✓				✓				✓	
Engine coolant	R						✓				✓			
Charcoal canister	R								✓					

93081CS1

For accessory drive belt replacement procedures see the model specific sections of this manual

SCHEDULED MAINTENANCE INTERVALS
(LEXUS LX450, LX470 & RX300) (Cont.)

TO BE SERVICED	TYPE OF SERVICE	VEHICLE MILEAGE INTERVAL (x1000)												
		7.5	15	22.5	30	37.5	45	52.5	60	67.5	75	82.5	90	97.5
Fuel tank cap gasket	R								✓					
Heated oxygen sensors (except Calif.)①	R													

R: Replace   S/I: Service or Inspect

① Heated oxygen sensors (except Calif.): replace every 80,000 miles.

FREQUENT OPERATION MAINTENANCE (SEVERE SERVICE)

If a vehicle is operated under any of the following conditions it is considered severe service:

- Extremely dusty areas.

- 50% or more of the vehicle operation is in 32°C (90°F) or higher temperatures, or constant operation in temperatures below 0°C (32°F).

- Prolonged idling (vehicle operation in stop and go traffic).

- Frequent short running periods (engine does not warm to normal operating temperatures).

- Police, taxi, delivery usage or trailer towing usage.

Air cleaner filter: service or inspect every 3750 miles.

Engine oil & filter: replace every 3750 miles.

Ball joints & dust covers: service or inspect every 7500 miles.

Bolts & nuts on chassis & body: service or inspect every 7500 miles.

Brake linings & drums: service or inspect every 7500 miles.

Brake pads & discs (front & rear): service or inspect every 7500 miles.

Steering knuckle & chassis grease: service or inspect every 7500 miles.

Steering linkage: service or inspect every 7500 miles.

Propeller shaft grease: service or inspect every 7500 miles.

Exhaust pipes & mountings: service or inspect every 15,000 miles.

93081CS2

SCHEDULED MAINTENANCE INTERVALS
LEXUS
LX450, LX470
RX300

The following should be used as a guide when determining the amount of work required for a particular service. In estimating how long a particular Scheduled Maintenance Service should take, please observe the following:

- Labor Time is time based on field research and data supplied by the vehicle manufacturer.
- Labor time operations are given in hours and tenths of an hour.
- All labor operations are to be used as a guide.

Mechanic Skill Level Codes:
(A) PRECISION: Highly skilled with multiple certification.
(B) GENERAL: Normally skilled with certification.
(C) MAINTENANCE: Semi-skilled working on certification.

	LABOR TIME		LABOR TIME		LABOR TIME
7500 Mile Service (C)		**37500 Mile Service (C)**		**75000 Mile Service (C)**	
All Models	.4	All Models	.4	RX300	1.6
15000 Mile Service (C)		**45000 Mile Service (B)**		LX450, LX470	1.7
RX300	1.6	RX300	2.1	**82500 Mile Service (C)**	
LX450, LX470	1.7	LX450, LX470	2.2	All Models	.4
22500 Mile Service (C)		**52500 Mile Service (C)**		**90000 Mile Service (B)**	
All Models	.4	All Models	.4	RX300	2.4
LX450, LX470 add	.2	**60000 Mile Service (B)**		LX450, LX470	2.5
30000 Mile Service (B)		RX300	3.9	**97500 Mile Service (C)**	
RX300	2.4	LX450, LX470	4.2	All Models	.4
LX450, LX470	2.5	**67500 Mile Service (C)**			
		All Models	.4		

93081CS3

TIRE, WHEEL AND BALL JOINT SPECIFICATIONS
Lexus

Year	Model	OEM Tires		Tire Pressures (psi)		Wheel Size	Ball Joint Inspection
		Standard	Optional	Front	Rear		
1997	LX450	P275/70HR16	None	32	32	6.5-JJ	①
1998	LX470	P275/70HR16	None	32	32	6.5-JJ	①
1999	LX470	P275/70HR16	None	32	32	6.5-JJ	①
	RX300	P255/70HR16	None	30	30	6.5-JJ	①
2000-01	LX470	P275/70HR16	None	32	32	6.5-JJ	①
	RX300	P255/70HR16	None	30	30	6.5-JJ	①

OEM: Original Equipment Manufacturer

PSI: Pounds Per Square Inch

STD: Standard

OPT: Optional

① Replace if any measurable movement is found.

93081CS4

For brake related suspension and axle service, refer to the model specific sections of this manual

MAZDA
B2300 • B2500 • B3000 • B4000 • MPV

ENGINE AND VEHICLE IDENTIFICATION

		Engine						Model Year	
Code ①	Liters (cc)	Cu. In.	Cyl.	Fuel Sys.	Engine Type	Eng. Mfg.		Code ②	Year
A	2.3 (2298)	140	4	MFI	SOHC	Ford		V	1997
C	2.5 (2500)	152	4	MFI	OHV	Ford		W	1998
GY ③	2.5 (2507)	153	6	SFI	DOHC	Ford		X	1999
JE ④	3.0 (2954)	180	6	MFI	SOHC	Mazda		Y	2000
U	3.0 (2968)	182	6	MFI	OHV	Ford		1	2001
X	4.0 (4016)	245	6	MFI	OHV	Ford			

MFI: Multi-port Fuel Injection
SFI: Sequential Fuel Injection
SOHC: Single Overhead Camshaft
DOHC: Double Overhead Camshaft
OHV: Overhead Valve

93081CS5

GENERAL ENGINE SPECIFICATIONS

Year	Model	Engine Displacement Liters (cc)	Engine ID/VIN	Fuel System Type	Net Horsepower @ rpm	Net Torque @ rpm (ft. lbs.)	Bore x Stroke (in.)	Com-pression Ratio	Oil Pressure @ rpm
1997	B2300	2.3 (2298)	A	EFI	112@4800	135@2400	3.78x3.13	9.2:1	40-60@2000
	B3000	3.0 (2968)	U	EFI	145@4800	165@3000	3.50x3.14	9.3:1	40-60@2500
	B4000	4.0 (4016)	X	EFI	160@4200	220@3000	3.94x3.31	9.0:1	40-60@2000
	MPV	3.0 (2954)	JE	EFI	155@5000	169@4000	3.54x3.05	8.5:1	53-75@3000
1998	B2500	2.5 (2500)	C	MFI	119@5000	146@3000	3.78x3.40	9.4:1	40-60@2000
	B3000	3.0 (2968)	U	MFI	150@5000	185@3750	3.50x3.14	9.1:1	40-60@2500
	B4000	4.0 (4016)	X	MFI	160@4200	225@3000	3.95x3.32	9.0:1	40-60@2000
	MPV	3.0 (2954)	JE	MFI	155@5000	169@4000	3.54x3.05	8.5:1	53-75@3000
1999	B2500	2.5 (2500)	C	MFI	119@5000	146@3000	3.78x3.40	9.4:1	40-60@2000
	B3000	3.0 (2968)	U	MFI	150@5000	185@3750	3.50x3.14	9.1:1	40-60@2000
	B4000	4.0 (4016)	X	MFI	160@4200	225@3000	3.95x3.32	9.0:1	40-60@2000
2000-01	B2500	2.5 (2500)	C	MFI	119@5000	146@3000	3.78x3.40	9.4:1	40-60@2000
	B3000	3.0 (2968)	U	MFI	150@5000	185@3750	3.50x3.14	9.1:1	40-60@2000
	B4000	4.0 (4016)	X	MFI	160@4200	225@3000	3.95x3.32	9.0:1	40-60@2000
	MPV	2.5 (2507)	GY	SFI	170@6250 ①	165@4250	3.25x3.13	9.7:1	20-45@1500

EFI: Electronic fuel injection
MFI: Multi-port Fuel Injection
SFI: Sequential Fuel Injection
① California LEV: 160@6250

93081CS6

ENGINE TUNE-UP SPECIFICATIONS

Year	Engine Displacement Liters (cc)	Engine ID/VIN	Spark Plug Gap (in.)	Ignition Timing (deg.) MT	AT	Fuel Pump (psi)	Idle Speed (rpm) MT	AT	Valve Clearance Intake	Exhaust
1997	2.3 (2298)	A	①	8-12B	8-12B	35-45	475-575	475-575	HYD	HYD
	3.0 (2954)	JE	0.040-0.043	—	10-12B	30-37	—	780-820	HYD	HYD
	3.0 (2968)	U	①	8-12B	8-12B	35-45	①	①	HYD	HYD
	4.0 (4016)	X	①	8-12B	8-12B	35-45	①	①	HYD	HYD
1998	2.5 (2500)	C	0.044	10B	10B	56-72	①	①	HYD	HYD
	3.0 (2954)	JE	0.041	—	10-12B	31-38	—	①	HYD	HYD
	3.0 (2968)	U	0.044	10B	10B	56-72	①	①	HYD	HYD
	4.0 (4016)	X	0.054	NA	NA	56-72	①	①	HYD	HYD
1999	2.5 (2500)	C	0.044	10B	10B	56-72	①	①	HYD	HYD
	3.0 (2968)	U	0.044	10B	10B	56-72	①	①	HYD	HYD
	4.0 (4016)	X	0.054	NA	NA	56-72	①	①	HYD	HYD
2000-01	2.5 (2500)	C	0.044	10B	10B	56-72	①	①	HYD	HYD
	2.5 (2507)	GY	0.054	—	10B	37-41	—	①	HYD	HYD
	3.0 (2968)	U	0.044	10B	10B	56-72	①	①	HYD	HYD
	4.0 (4016)	X	0.054	NA	NA	56-72	①	①	HYD	HYD

NOTE: The Vehicle Emission Control Information label often reflects specification changes made during production. The label figures must be used if they differ from those in this chart.

B: Before top dead center

HYD: Hydraulic

① Refer to Vehicle's Emission Control Information label

93081CS7

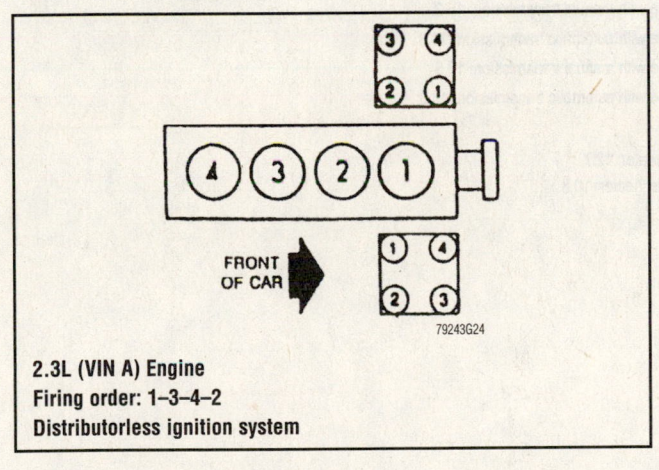

2.3L (VIN A) Engine
Firing order: 1-3-4-2
Distributorless ignition system

79243G24

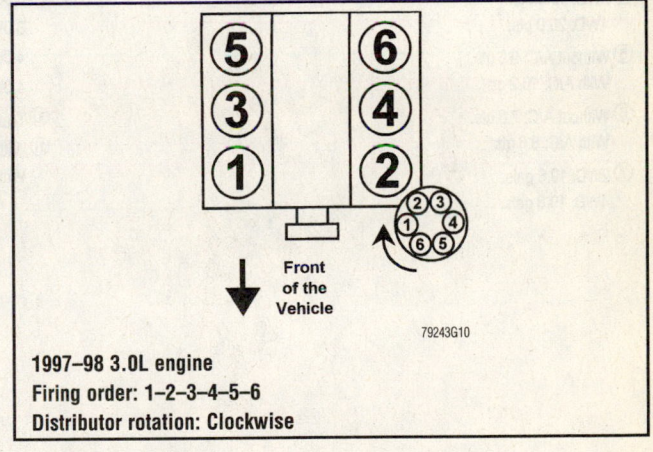

1997-98 3.0L engine
Firing order: 1-2-3-4-5-6
Distributor rotation: Clockwise

79243G10

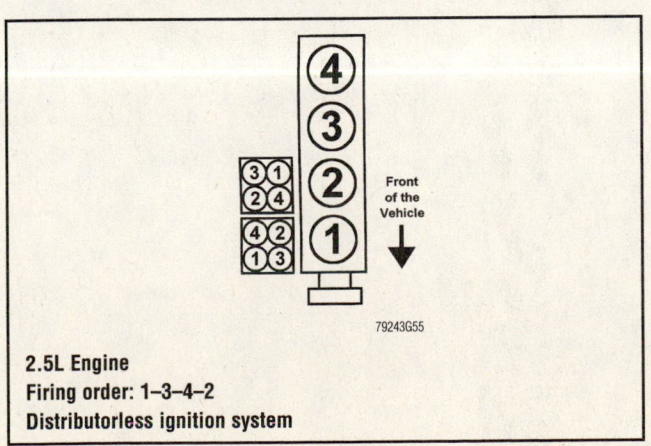

2.5L Engine
Firing order: 1-3-4-2
Distributorless ignition system

79243G55

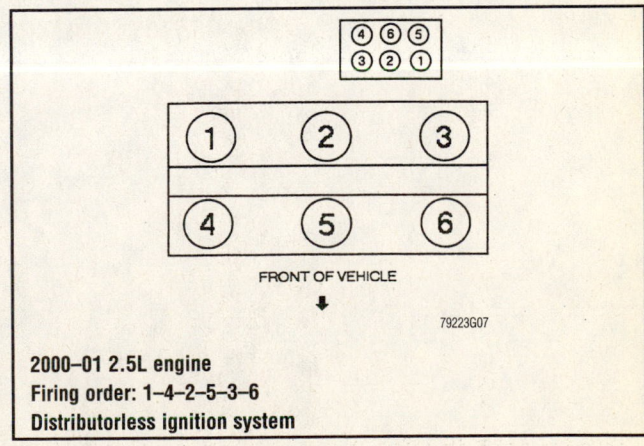

2000-01 2.5L engine
Firing order: 1-4-2-5-3-6
Distributorless ignition system

79223G07

Refer to the model specific sections for driveline service procedures

CAPACITIES

Year	Model	Engine Displacement Liters (cc)	Engine ID/VIN	Engine Oil with Filter (qts.)	Transmission (pts.) Manual	Transmission (pts.) Auto.	Transfer Case (pts.)	Drive Axle Front (pts.)	Drive Axle Rear (pts.)	Fuel Tank (gal.)	Cooling System (qts.)
1997	B2300	2.3 (2298)	A	5.0	5.6	19.0	2.50	①	5.0	16.3②	③
	B3000	3.0 (2968)	U	4.5	5.6	④	2.50	①	5.0	16.3②	⑤
	B4000	4.0 (4016)	X	5.0	5.6	④	2.50	①	5.0	16.3②	⑥
	MPV	3.0 (2954)	JE	5.0	—	18.2	3.20	3.6	3.2	⑦	10.3
1998	B2500	2.5 (2500)	C	4.5	5.6	④	3.25	5.0	⑧	16.3②	⑨
	B3000	3.0 (2968)	U	4.5	5.6	④	3.25	5.0	⑧	16.3②	⑨
	B4000	4.0 (4016)	X	5.0	5.6	④	3.25	5.0	⑧	16.3②	⑨
	MPV	3.0 (2954)	JE	5.0	—	18.2	3.60	3.6	3.2	⑦	10.3
1999	B2500	2.5 (2500)	C	4.5	5.6	④	3.25	5.0	⑧	16.3②	⑨
	B3000	3.0 (2968)	U	4.5	5.6	④	3.25	5.0	⑧	16.3②	⑨
	B4000	4.0 (4016)	X	5.0	5.6	④	3.25	5.0	⑧	16.3②	⑨
2000-01	B2500	2.5 (2500)	C	4.5	5.6	④	3.25	5.0	⑧	16.3②	⑨
	B3000	3.0 (2968)	U	4.5	5.6	④	3.25	5.0	⑧	16.3②	⑨
	B4000	4.0 (4016)	X	5.0	5.6	④	3.25	5.0	⑧	16.3②	⑨
	MPV	2.5 (2507)	GY	6	—	20.6⑩	—	—	—	18.5	⑪

NOTE: All capacities are approximate. Add fluid gradually and ensure a proper fluid level is obtained.

① Dana 28: 3.0 pts.
Dana 35: 3.5 pts.
② Long bed and Supercab: 19.6 gals.
③ Without A/C: 6.5 qts.
With A/C: 7.2 qts.
④ 2WD: 19.4 pts.
4WD: 20.0 pts.
⑤ Without A/C: 9.5 qts.
With A/C: 10.2 qts.
⑥ Without A/C: 7.8 qts.
With A/C: 8.6 qts.
⑦ 2WD: 19.6 gals.
4WD: 19.8 gals.

⑧ Regular cab/short bed: 16.3
Regular cab/long bed: 19.6
Cab Plus: 20.0
⑨ 2.5L engine with manual transmission: 10.5
2.5L engine with automatic transmission: 10.2
3.0L engine with manual transmission: 15.2
3.0L engine with automatic transmission: 14.8
4.0L engine with manual transmission: 13.5
4.0L engine with automatic transmission: 13.2
⑩ Transaxle
⑪ With rear heater: 12.7
Without rear heater: 10.8

93081CS8

VALVE SPECIFICATIONS

Year	Engine Displacement Liters (cc)	Engine ID/VIN	Seat Angle (deg.)	Face Angle (deg.)	Spring Test Pressure (lbs. @ in.)	Spring Installed Height (in.)	Stem-to-Guide Clearance (in.)		Stem Diameter (in.)	
							Intake	Exhaust	Intake	Exhaust
1997	2.3 (2299)	A	45	44	57-63@1.56	1.540-1.580	0.0010-0.0027	0.0015-0.0032	0.2746-0.2754	0.2736-0.2744
	3.0 (2954)	JE	45	45	①	②	0.0010-0.0023	0.0012-0.0025	0.2745-0.2750	0.3160-0.3165
	3.0 (2968)	U	45	44	③	1.736-1.650	0.0010-0.0017	0.0015-0.0032	0.3134-0.3126	0.3129-0.3121
	4.0 (4016)	X	45	44	60-68@1.59	1.910④	0.0008-0.0025	0.0018-0.0035	0.3159-0.3167	0.3149-0.3156
1998	2.5 (2500)	C	45	44	57-63@1.56	1.540-1.580	0.0008-0.0027	0.0018-0.0037	0.2746-0.2754	0.2736-0.2744
	3.0 (2954)	JE	45	45	①	②	0.0010-0.0023	0.0012-0.0025	0.2745-0.2750	0.3160-0.3165
	3.0 (2968)	U	45	44	③	1.736-1.650	0.0010-0.0017	0.0015-0.0032	0.3134-0.3126	0.3129-0.3121
	4.0 (4016)	X	45	44	60-68@1.59	1.910④	0.0008-0.0025	0.0018-0.0035	0.3159-0.3167	0.3149-0.3156
1999	2.5 (2500)	C	45	44	57-63@1.56	1.540-1.580	0.0008-0.0027	0.0018-0.0037	0.2746-0.2754	0.2736-0.2744
	3.0 (2968)	U	45	44	③	1.736-1.650	0.0010-0.0017	0.0015-0.0032	0.3134-0.3126	0.3129-0.3121
	4.0 (4016)	X	45	44	60-68@1.59	1.910④	0.0008-0.0025	0.0018-0.0035	0.3159-0.3167	0.3149-0.3156
2000-01	2.5 (2500)	C	45	44	57-63@1.56	1.540-1.580	0.0008-0.0027	0.0018-0.0037	0.2746-0.2754	0.2736-0.2744
	2.5 (2507)	GY	44.75	45.5	153@1.18	1.570	0.0007-0.0027	0.0017-0.0037	0.2350-0.2358	0.2343-0.2350
	3.0 (2968)	U	45	44	③	1.736-1.650	0.0010-0.0017	0.0015-0.0032	0.3134-0.3126	0.3129-0.3121
	4.0 (4016)	X	45	44	60-68@1.59	1.910④	0.0008-0.0025	0.0018-0.0035	0.3159-0.3167	0.3149-0.3156

NA - Not Available

① Intake:
  Inner: 21-22@1.77
  Outer: 31-33@1.73
  Exhaust:
  Inner: 33-37@1.59
  Outer: 21-22@1.56

② Intake:
  Inner: 1.840
  Outer: 2.004
  Exhaust:
  Inner: 2.092
  Outer: 2.296

③ Loaded: 180@1.16
  Unloaded: 65@1.58
④ Free length only

93081CS9

For exhaust manifold replacement procedures, see the model specific sections of this manual

CRANKSHAFT AND CONNECTING ROD SPECIFICATIONS
All measurements are given in inches.

Year	Engine Displacement Liters (cc)	Engine ID/VIN	Crankshaft				Connecting Rod		
			Main Brg. Journal Dia.	Main Brg. Oil Clearance	Shaft End-play	Thrust on No.	Journal Diameter	Oil Clearance	Side Clearance
1997	2.3 (2299)	A	2.2059-2.2051	0.0008-0.0015	0.0040-0.0080	3	2.0462-2.0472	0.0008-0.0015	0.0035-0.0115
	3.0 (2954)	JE	2.4385-2.4391	0.0010-0.0014	0.0032-0.0111	4	2.0843-2.0848	0.0010-0.0025	0.0071-0.0129
	3.0 (2968)	U	2.5190-2.5198	0.0010-0.0014	0.0040-0.0080	3	2.1253-2.1261	0.0010-0.0014	0.0060-0.0140
	4.0 (4016)	X	2.2433-2.2441	0.0008-0.0015	0.0020-0.0120	3	2.1252-2.1260	0.0003-0.0024	0.0002-0.0025
1998	2.5 (2500)	C	2.2051-2.2059	0.0008-0.0015	0.0040-0.0080	3	2.0464-2.0472	0.0008-0.0015	0.0035-0.0115
	3.0 (2954)	JE	2.4385-2.4391	0.0010-0.0014	0.0032-0.0111	4	2.0843-2.0848	0.0010-0.0025	0.0071-0.0129
	3.0 (2968)	U	2.5190-2.5198	0.0010-0.0014	0.0040-0.0080	3	2.1253-2.1261	0.0010-0.0014	0.0060-0.0140
	4.0 (4016)	X	2.2433-2.2441	0.0008-0.0015	0.0020-0.0120	3	2.1252-2.1260	0.0003-0.0024	0.0002-0.0025
1999	2.5 (2500)	C	2.2051-2.2059	0.0008-0.0015	0.0040-0.0080	3	2.0464-2.0472	0.0008-0.0015	0.0035-0.0115
	3.0 (2968)	U	2.5190-2.5198	0.0010-0.0014	0.0040-0.0080	3	2.1253-2.1261	0.0010-0.0014	0.0060-0.0140
	4.0 (4016)	X	2.2433-2.2441	0.0008-0.0015	0.0020-0.0120	3	2.1252-2.1260	0.0003-0.0024	0.0002-0.0025
2000-01	2.5 (2500)	C	2.2051-2.2059	0.0008-0.0015	0.0040-0.0080	3	2.0464-2.0472	0.0008-0.0015	0.0035-0.0115
	2.5 (2507)	GY	2.4670-2.4790	0.0009-0.0019	0.0040-0.0090	4	1.9670-1.9680	0.0010-0.0025	0.0039-0.0118
	3.0 (2968)	U	2.5190-2.5198	0.0010-0.0014	0.0040-0.0080	3	2.1253-2.1261	0.0010-0.0014	0.0060-0.0140
	4.0 (4016)	X	2.2433-2.2441	0.0008-0.0015	0.0020-0.0120	3	2.1252-2.1260	0.0003-0.0024	0.0002-0.0025

93081CS0

PISTON AND RING SPECIFICATIONS
All measurements are given in inches.

Year	Engine Displacement Liters (cc)	Engine ID/VIN	Piston Clearance	Ring Gap			Ring Side Clearance		
				Top Compression	Bottom Compression	Oil Control	Top Compression	Bottom Compression	Oil Control
1997	2.3 (2299)	A	0.0100-0.0200	0.008-0.016	0.013-0.019	0.010-0.030	0.0016-0.0033	0.0016-0.0033	SNUG
	3.0 (2954)	JE	0.0010-0.0020	0.008-0.013	0.006-0.011	0.008-0.027	0.0012-0.0027	0.0012-0.0027	SNUG
	3.0 (2968)	U	0.0012-0.0023	0.010-0.020	0.010-0.020	0.010-0.049	0.0602-0.0612	0.0602-0.0612	SNUG
	4.0 (4016)	X	0.0008-0.0019	0.015-0.023	0.015-0.023	0.015-0.055	0.0020-0.0033	0.0020-0.0033	SNUG
1998	2.5 (2500)	C	0.0010-0.0020	0.008-0.018	0.013-0.023	0.010-0.035	0.0014-0.0030	0.0014-0.0030	SNUG
	3.0 (2954)	JE	0.0010-0.0020	0.008-0.013	0.006-0.011	0.008-0.027	0.0012-0.0027	0.0012-0.0027	SNUG
	3.0 (2968)	U	0.0012-0.0023	0.010-0.020	0.010-0.020	0.010-0.049	0.0602-0.0612	0.0602-0.0612	SNUG
	4.0 (4016)	X	0.0008-0.0019	0.015-0.023	0.015-0.023	0.015-0.055	0.0020-0.0033	0.0020-0.0033	SNUG
1999	2.5 (2500)	C	0.0010-0.0020	0.008-0.018	0.013-0.023	0.010-0.035	0.0014-0.0030	0.0014-0.0030	SNUG
	3.0 (2968)	U	0.0012-0.0023	0.010-0.020	0.010-0.020	0.010-0.049	0.0602-0.0612	0.0602-0.0612	SNUG
	4.0 (4016)	X	0.0008-0.0019	0.015-0.023	0.015-0.023	0.015-0.055	0.0020-0.0033	0.0020-0.0033	SNUG
2000-01	2.5 (2500)	C	0.0010-0.0020	0.008-0.018	0.013-0.023	0.010-0.035	0.0014-0.0030	0.0014-0.0030	SNUG
	2.5 (2507)	GY	0.0005-0.0009	0.004-0.010	0.011-0.017	0.006-0.026	0.0015-0.0029	0.0015-0.0033	SNUG
	3.0 (2968)	U	0.0012-0.0023	0.010-0.020	0.010-0.020	0.010-0.049	0.0602-0.0612	0.0602-0.0612	SNUG
	4.0 (4016)	X	0.0008-0.0019	0.015-0.023	0.015-0.023	0.015-0.055	0.0020-0.0033	0.0020-0.0033	SNUG

93081CT1

Refer to the model specific sections for cooling system service procedures

TORQUE SPECIFICATIONS
All readings in ft. lbs.

Year	Engine Displacement Liters (cc)	Engine ID/VIN	Cylinder Head Bolts	Main Bearing Bolts	Rod Bearing Bolts	Crankshaft Damper Bolts	Flywheel Bolts	Manifold Intake	Manifold Exhaust	Spark Plugs	Lug Nut
1997	2.3 (2298)	A	①	②	③	92-121	56-64	19-28	③	7-15	100
	3.0 (2954)	JE	⑤	⑥	⑦	116-122	76-81	14-19	16-21	11-16	65-87
	3.0 (2968)	U	⑧	55-62	23-28	92-122	54-64	⑨	15-22	7-14	100
	4.0 (4016)	X	⑩	66-77	18-24	30-37	60	⑪	18	7-15	100
1998	2.5 (2500)	C	①	②	③	92-121	56-64	19-28	④	7-15	100
	3.0 (2954)	JE	⑤	⑥	⑦	116-122	76-81	14-19	16-21	11-16	65-87
	3.0 (2968)	U	⑧	55-62	23-28	92-122	54-64	⑨	15-22	7-14	100
	4.0 (4016)	X	⑩	66-77	18-24	30-37	60	⑪	18	7-15	100
1999	2.5 (2500)	C	①	②	③	92-121	56-64	19-28	④	7-15	100
	3.0 (2968)	U	⑧	55-62	23-28	92-122	54-64	⑨	15-22	7-14	100
	4.0 (4016)	X	⑩	66-77	18-24	30-37	60	⑪	18	7-15	100
2000-01	2.5 (2500)	C	①	②	③	92-121	56-64	19-28	④	7-15	100
	2.5 (2507)	GY	⑫	⑬	⑭	⑮	54-64	6-9	13-16	14	66-86
	3.0 (2968)	U	⑧	55-62	23-28	92-122	54-64	⑨	15-22	7-14	100
	4.0 (4016)	X	⑩	66-77	18-24	30-37	60	⑪	18	7-15	100

① Step 1: 52 ft. lbs.
Step 2: 52 ft. lbs.
Step 3: Plus 90-100 degrees

② Step 1: Tighten by hand until seated
Step 2: 50-60 ft. lbs.
Step 3: 75-85 ft. lbs.

③ Step 1: 25-30 ft. lbs.
Step 2: 30-36 ft. lbs.

④ Step 1: 15-22 ft. lbs.
Step 2: 45-59 ft. lbs.

⑤ Step 1: 13-16 ft. lbs.
Step 2: Plus 85-95 degrees
Step 3: Plus 85-95 degrees

⑥ Step 1: 12.7-16.2 ft. lbs.
Step 2: Plus 90 degrees
Step 3: Plus 45 degrees

⑦ Step 1: 20-23.5 ft. lbs.
Step 2: Plus 90 degrees

⑧ Step 1: 59 ft. lbs.
Step 2: Loosen all bolts 1 turn
Step 3: 33-41 ft. lbs.
Step 4: 63-73 ft. lbs.

⑨ Step 1: 11 ft. lbs.
Step 2: 19-24 ft. lbs.

⑩ Step 1: 22-26 ft. lbs.
Step 2: 52-56 ft. lbs.

⑪ Step 1: 6 ft. lbs.
Step 2: 11 ft. lbs.

⑫ Step 1: 28-31 ft. lbs.
Step 2: Plus 90 degrees
Step 3: Loosen bolts 1 turn
Step 4: 28-31 ft. lbs.
Step 5: Plus 90 degrees
Step 6: Plus 90 degrees

⑬ Step 1: 12-43 inch lbs.
Step 2: Outer cap bolts: 16-21 ft. lbs.
Step 3: Inner cap bolts: 27-32 ft. lbs.
Step 4: All cap bolts: 85-95 degrees
Step 5: Remaining bolts: 15-22 ft. lbs.

⑭ 26-33 ft. lbs. plus 90-120 degrees

⑮ Step 1: 89 ft. lbs.
Step 2: Loosen bolt
Step 3: 35-39 ft. lbs.
Step 4: Plus 85-95 degrees

93081CT2

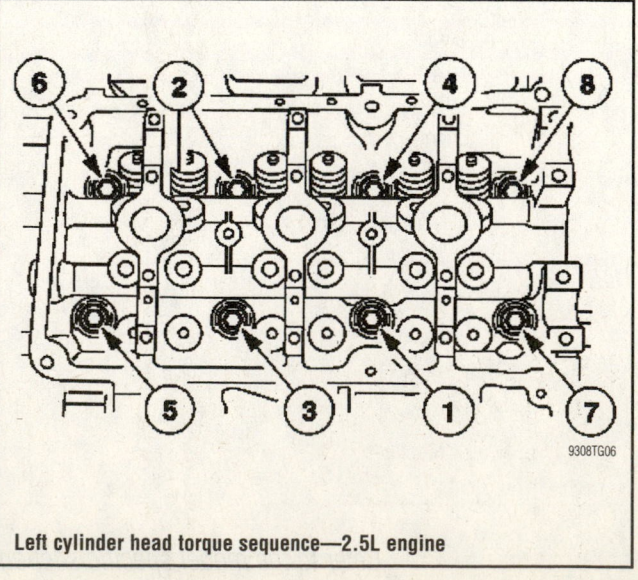

FRONT OF ENGINE

WHEN INSTALLING CYLINDER HEAD, POSITION THE CAMSHAFT AS SHOWN TO AVOID DAMAGE TO PROTRUDING VALVES.

PIN

7924EG02

Cylinder head bolt torque sequence 2.3L engine

9308TG06

Left cylinder head torque sequence—2.5L engine

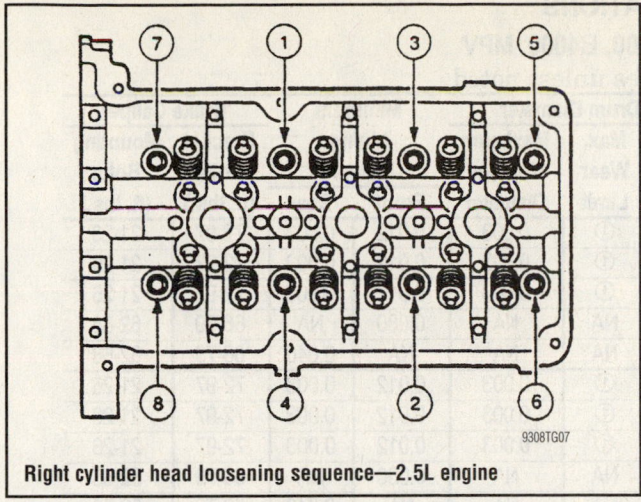

Right cylinder head loosening sequence—2.5L engine

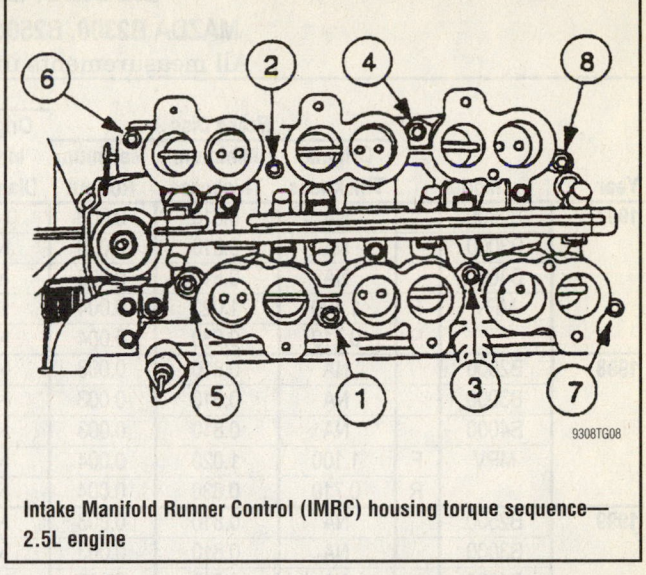

Intake Manifold Runner Control (IMRC) housing torque sequence—2.5L engine

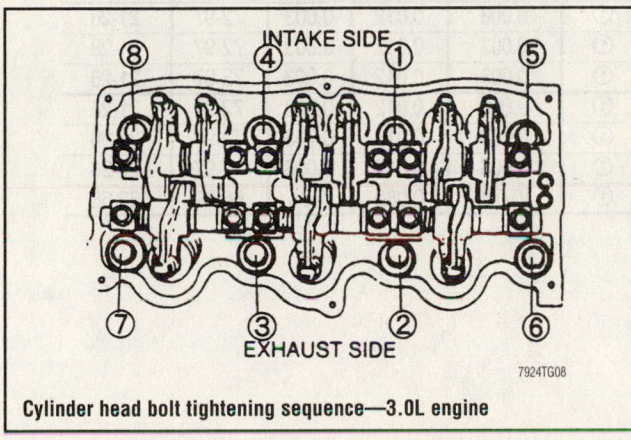

Cylinder head bolt tightening sequence—3.0L engine

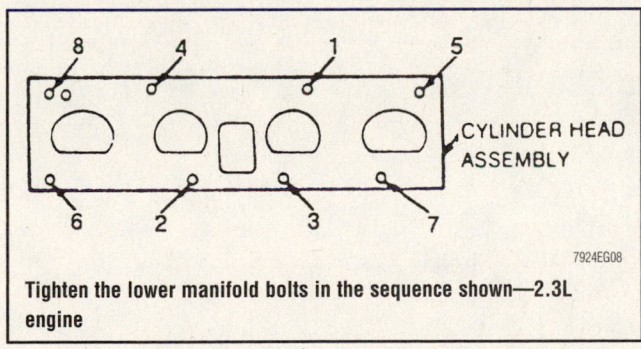

Tighten the lower manifold bolts in the sequence shown—2.3L engine

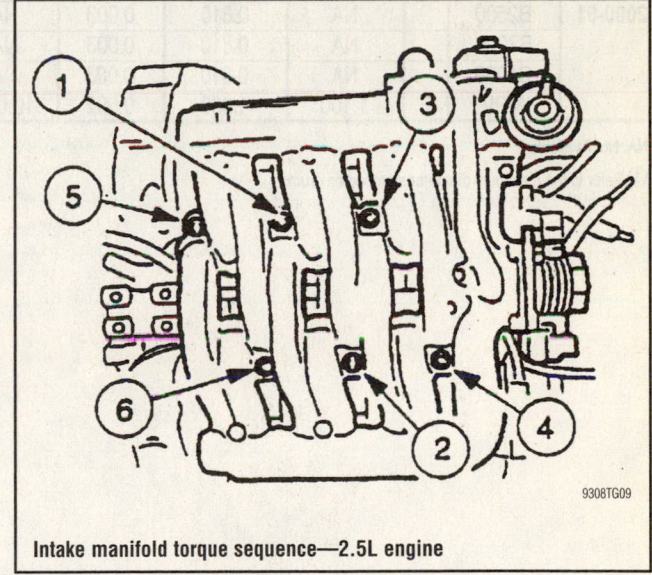

Intake manifold torque sequence—2.5L engine

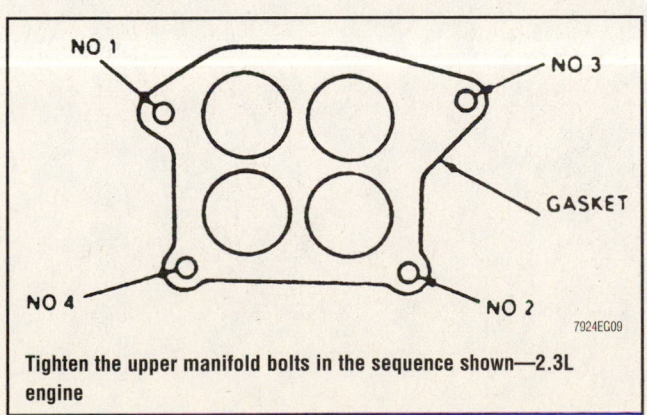

Tighten the upper manifold bolts in the sequence shown—2.3L engine

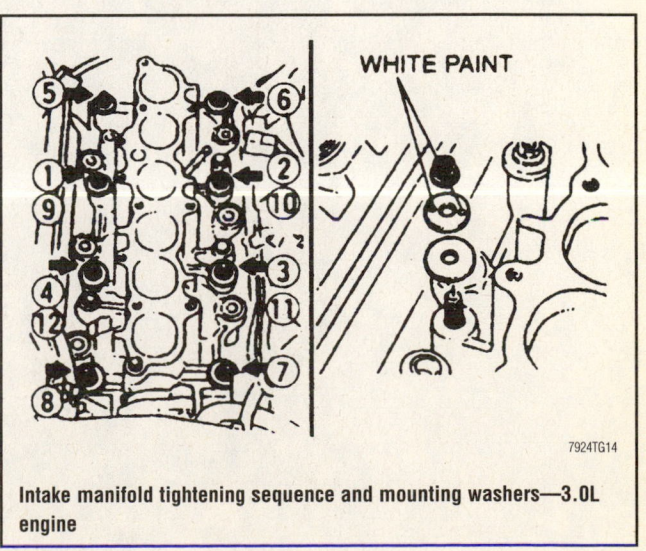

Intake manifold tightening sequence and mounting washers—3.0L engine

BRAKE SPECIFICATIONS
MAZDA B2300, B2500, B3000, B4000, MPV
All measurements in inches unless noted

Year	Model		Brake Disc			Brake Drum Diameter			Minimum Lining Thickness		Brake Caliper	
			Original Thickness	Minimum Thickness	Maximum Runout	Original Inside Diameter	Max. Wear Limit	Maximum Machine Diameter	Front	Rear	Bracket Bolts (ft. lbs.)	Mounting Bolts (ft. lbs.)
1997	B2300		NA	0.810	0.003	NA	①	0.003	0.012	0.003	72-97	21-26
	B3000		NA	0.810	0.003	NA	①	0.003	0.012	0.003	72-97	21-26
	B4000		NA	0.810	0.003	NA	①	0.003	0.012	0.003	72-97	21-26
	MPV	F	1.100	1.020	0.004	NA	NA	NA	0.080	NA	66-79	62-68
		R	0.710	0.630	0.004	NA	NA	NA	NA	0.040	66-79	62-68
1998	B2500		NA	0.810	0.003	NA	①	0.003	0.012	0.003	72-97	21-26
	B3000		NA	0.810	0.003	NA	①	0.003	0.012	0.003	72-97	21-26
	B4000		NA	0.810	0.003	NA	①	0.003	0.012	0.003	72-97	21-26
	MPV	F	1.100	1.020	0.004	NA	NA	NA	0.080	NA	66-79	62-68
		R	0.710	0.630	0.004	NA	NA	NA	NA	0.040	66-79	62-68
1999	B2500		NA	0.810	0.003	NA	①	0.003	0.012	0.003	72-97	21-26
	B3000		NA	0.810	0.003	NA	①	0.003	0.012	0.003	72-97	21-26
	B4000		NA	0.810	0.003	NA	①	0.003	0.012	0.003	72-97	21-26
2000-01	B2500		NA	0.810	0.003	NA	①	0.003	0.012	0.003	72-97	21-26
	B3000		NA	0.810	0.003	NA	①	0.003	0.012	0.003	72-97	21-26
	B4000		NA	0.810	0.003	NA	①	0.003	0.012	0.003	72-97	21-26
	MPV	F	1.100	1.030	0.002	10.000	①	10.050	0.080	0.04	66-79	62-68

NA: Not Available

① Refer to the maximum diameter stamped on drum

93081CT3

SCHEDULED MAINTENANCE INTERVALS
(MAZDA MPV)

TO BE SERVICED	TYPE OF SERVICE	VEHICLE MILEAGE INTERVAL (x1000)												
		7.5	15	22.5	30	37.5	45	52.5	60	67.5	75	82.5	90	97.5
Engine oil & filter	R	✓	✓	✓	✓	✓	✓	✓	✓	✓	✓	✓	✓	✓
Air cleaner filter	R				✓				✓				✓	
Brake fluid	R				✓				✓				✓	
Spark plugs	R				✓				✓				✓	
Bolts & nuts on chassis & body	S/I				✓				✓				✓	
Cooling system	S/I				✓				✓				✓	
Disc brakes, brake lines, hoses & connections	S/I				✓				✓				✓	
Drive belt(s)	S/I			✓					✓					
Driveshaft dust boots (4WD)	S/I				✓				✓				✓	
Exhaust system heat shields	S/I				✓				✓				✓	
Front suspension ball joints	S/I				✓				✓				✓	
Fuel lines & hoses	S/I				✓				✓				✓	
Idle speed	S/I		✓				✓				✓			
Steering operation & linkages	S/I				✓				✓				✓	
Engine coolant	R						✓				✓			
Timing belt (except Calif.)	R								✓					
Timing belt (Calif.)①	S/I								✓				✓	
Automatic transmission fluid & filter	R								✓					
Front & rear axle oil	R								✓					
Fuel filter & PCV valve	R								✓					

93081CT4

Timing chain and gear service is covered in the model specific sections of this manual

SCHEDULED MAINTENANCE INTERVALS
(MAZDA MPV) (Cont.)

TO BE SERVICED	TYPE OF SERVICE	VEHICLE MILEAGE INTERVAL (x1000)												
		7.5	15	22.5	30	37.5	45	52.5	60	67.5	75	82.5	90	97.5
Transfer case oil (4WD)	R								✓					
Emission hoses & tubes②	S/I								✓					
Ignitioin timing	S/I								✓					

R: Replace   S/I: Service or Inspect

① Timing belt (Calif.): replace at 105,000 miles, unless previously replaced.

② Emission hoses & tubes: replace at 80,000 miles.

FREQUENT OPERATION MAINTENANCE (SEVERE SERVICE)

 If a vehicle is operated under any of the following conditions it is considered severe service:

- Extremely dusty areas.

- 50% or more of the vehicle operation is in 32°C (90°F) or higher temperatures, or constant operation in temperatures below 0°C (32°F).

- Prolonged idling (vehicle operation in stop and go traffic).

- Frequent short running periods (engine does not warm to normal operating temperatures).

- Police, taxi, delivery usage or trailer towing usage.

Air cleaner filter: service or inspect every 15,000 miles

Engine oil & filter: replace every 5000 miles.

Ball joints & dust covers: service or inspect every 7500 miles.

Bolts & nuts on chassis & body: tighten every 15,000 miles.

Spark plugs: replace every 15,000 miles.

Automatic transmission fluid & filter: replace every 30,000 miles.

Front & rear axle oil: replace every 30,000 miles.

Transfer case oil (4WD): replace every 30,000 miles.

93081CT5

1997 SCHEDULED MAINTENANCE INTERVALS
(MAZDA B SERIES)

TO BE SERVICED	TYPE OF SERVICE	VEHICLE MILEAGE INTERVAL (x1000)												
		5	10	15	20	25	30	35	40	45	50	55	60	65
Engine oil & filter	R	✓	✓	✓	✓	✓	✓	✓	✓	✓	✓	✓	✓	✓
Automatic transmission shift linkage	S/I	✓		✓		✓		✓		✓		✓		✓
Clutch reservoir fluid	S/I	✓		✓		✓		✓		✓		✓		✓
Exhaust system	S/I	✓		✓		✓		✓		✓		✓		✓
Propeller shaft slip yoke (B Series)	S/I	✓		✓		✓		✓		✓		✓		✓
Propeller shaft U-joints	S/I	✓		✓		✓		✓		✓		✓		✓
Rear propeller shaft double cardan joint centering ball (B Series short bed 4x4)	S/I	✓		✓		✓		✓		✓		✓		✓
Rotate tires	S/I	✓		✓		✓		✓		✓		✓		✓
Steering linkage suspension	S/I	✓		✓		✓		✓		✓		✓		✓
Disc brake system & caliper slide rails	S/I			✓			✓			✓			✓	
Drum brake linings, lines & hoses	S/I			✓			✓			✓			✓	
Engine cooling hoses, clamps & coolant condition	S/I			✓			✓						✓	
Transfer case shift lever pivot bolt & control rod connecting pins (4x4)	S/I			✓			✓			✓			✓	
Air cleaner filter	R						✓						✓	
Automatic transmission fluid & filter (B Series)	R						✓						✓	
Engine coolant ①	R										✓			
Fuel filter	R						✓						✓	
Accessory drive belts	S/I						✓						✓	
Front axle R.H. axle shaft slip yoke (4x4)	S/I						✓						✓	

93081CT6

Ignition system service is covered in the model specific sections of this manual

1997 SCHEDULED MAINTENANCE INTERVALS
(MAZDA B SERIES) (Cont.)

TO BE SERVICED	TYPE OF SERVICE	VEHICLE MILEAGE INTERVAL (x1000)												
		5	10	15	20	25	30	35	40	45	50	55	60	65
Front wheel bearings	S/I						✓						✓	
Hub lock (4x4)	S/I						✓						✓	
Parking brake system	S/I						✓						✓	
Spindle needle bearing spindle thrust bearing (4x4)	S/I						✓						✓	
Manual transmission oil	R												✓	
PCV valve	R												✓	
Spark plugs (Calif.)	R												✓	
Spark plugs (exc. Calif.) ②	R													
Timing belt (B Series 2.3L) ③	S/I													
Transfer case oil (4x4)	R												✓	

R: Replace   S/I: Service or Inspect

① Engine coolant: replace initially at 50,000 miles, and every 30,000 miles thereafter.

② Replace every 100,000 miles.

③ Timing belt (2.3L): service or inspect at 120,000 miles.

FREQUENT OPERATION MAINTENANCE (SEVERE SERVICE)

If a vehicle is operated under any of the following conditions it is considered severe service:

- Extremely dusty areas.

- 50% or more of the vehicle operation is in 32°C (90°F) or higher temperatures, or constant operation in temperatures below 0°C (32°F).

- Prolonged idling (vehicle operation in stop and go traffic).

- Frequent short running periods (engine does not warm to normal operating temperatures).

- Police, taxi, delivery usage or trailer towing usage.

Oil & oil filter: replace every 3000 miles.

Automatic transmission shift linkage: lubricate every 6000 miles.

Exhaust system: service or inspect every 6000 miles.

Clutch reservoir fluid: service or inspect every 6000 miles.

Propeller shaft slip yoke: lubricate every 6000 miles.

Propeller shaft U-joints: lubricate every 6000 miles.

Rear propeller shaft double cardan joint centering ball (short bed 4x4): lubricate every 6000 miles.

Rotate tires: rotate every 6000 miles.

Steering linkage suspension: lubricate every 6000 miles.

Automatic transmission fluid & filter: replace every 21,000 miles.

Manual transmission oil: replace every 30,000 miles.

Rear axle oil: replace at 99,000 miles.

93081CT7

1998-01 SCHEDULED MAINTENANCE INTERVALS
(MAZDA B SERIES)

TO BE SERVICED	TYPE OF SERVICE	VEHICLE MILEAGE INTERVAL (x1000)																		
		5	10	15	20	25	30	35	40	45	50	55	60	65	70	75	80	85	90	95
Accessory drive belts	S/I												✓						✓	
Air cleaner element	R						✓						✓						✓	
Caliper slide rails	L			✓			✓			✓			✓			✓			✓	
Clutch reservoir fluid level	S/I	✓		✓		✓		✓		✓		✓		✓		✓		✓		✓
Cooling system (hoses, clamps, coolant)	S/I			✓			✓			✓			✓			✓			✓	
Disc brake system	S/I			✓				✓		✓			✓			✓			✓	
Driveshaft slip joint (if equipped)	L	✓		✓		✓		✓		✓		✓		✓		✓		✓		✓
Driveshaft U-joints (if equipped w/grease fittings)	L	✓		✓		✓		✓		✓		✓		✓		✓		✓		✓
Drum brake system, lines & hoses	S/I			✓			✓			✓			✓			✓			✓	
Engine coolant	R										✓				✓					
Engine oil & filter	R	✓	✓	✓	✓	✓	✓	✓	✓	✓	✓	✓	✓	✓	✓	✓	✓	✓	✓	✓
Exhaust system	S/I	✓		✓		✓		✓		✓		✓		✓		✓		✓		✓
Exhaust system shielding	S/I	✓		✓		✓		✓		✓		✓		✓		✓		✓		✓
Front axle R.H. axle shaft slip yoke (4x4)	L						✓						✓						✓	
Front wheel bearings	S/I & L						✓						✓						✓	
Fuel filter	R						✓						✓						✓	
Manual transmission fluid	R												✓							
Parking brake system	S/I						✓						✓						✓	
PCV valve	R												✓							
Rear axle lubricant ①	R																			
Rear driveshaft double cardan joint centering ball (short bed 4x4)	L	✓		✓		✓		✓		✓		✓		✓		✓		✓		✓
Rotate tires & check air pressure	S/I	✓		✓		✓		✓		✓		✓		✓		✓		✓		✓

93081CT8

1998-01 SCHEDULED MAINTENANCE INTERVALS
(MAZDA B SERIES) (Cont.)

TO BE SERVICED	TYPE OF SERVICE	VEHICLE MILEAGE INTERVAL (x1000)																		
		5	10	15	20	25	30	35	40	45	50	55	60	65	70	75	80	85	90	95
Spark plugs (2.5L)	R												✓							
Spark plugs (3.0L/4.0L) ②	R																			
Timing belt ③	S/I																			
Transfer case fluid (4x4)	R												✓							

R: Replace   S/I: Service or Inspect   L: Lubricate

① The rear axle lubricant should be replaced every 100,000 miles or whenever the axle housing is submerged beneath water. Otherwise, the lube should not be checked or changed unless there is a leak or service is required.

② The spark plugs should be replaced every 100,000 miles.

③ On the 2.5L engine, the timing belt tension and condition should be inspected at the 120,000 mile mark.

FREQUENT OPERATION MAINTENANCE (SEVERE SERVICE)

If a vehicle is operated under any of the following conditions it is considered severe service:

- Towing a trailer or using a camper or car-top carrier.
- Repeated short trips of less than 5 miles in temperatures below freezing.
- Extensive idling or low-speed driving for long distances as in heavy commercial use, such as delivery, taxi or police cars.
- Operating on rough, muddy or salt-covered roads.
- Operating on unpaved or dusty roads.

Engine oil and filter: replace every 3000 miles or 6 months, whichever occurs first.

Spark plugs: replace every 60,000 miles.

Engine coolant: replace initially at the 48,000 mile mark then every 30,000 miles, or at 48 months, then every 30 months.

Engine cooling system: inspect and service every 15,000 miles or every 12 months, whichever occurs first.

Air cleaner filter: replace every 30,000 miles.

PCV valve: replace every 60,000 miles.

Camshaft drive belt tension (2.5L): inspect and service every 120,000 miles.

Accessory drive belt (2.5L/4.0L): inspect and service initially at the 60,000 mile mark, then every 30,000 miles.

Accessory drive belt (3.0L): inspect and service initially at the 90,000 mile mark, then every 30,000 miles.

Wheel lug nut torque: inspect initially at the 500 mile mark, then every 6000 miles.

Rotate tires and adjust tire pressure: perform initially at the 6000 mile mark, then every 9000 miles.

Clutch reservoir level: inspect every 6000 miles.

Front wheel bearings (4x2 only): inspect and repack every 30,000 miles.

Disc brake system: inspect every 15,000 miles.

Caliper slide rails: lubricate every 15,000 miles.

Brake lines, hoses and linings: inspect every 15,000 miles.

Exhaust system: inspect for leaks, damage or looseness every 6000 miles.

Driveshaft U-joints (if equipped with grease fittings): lubricate every 6000 miles.

Parking brake system: inspect every 30,000 miles.

Rear driveshaft double cardan joint centering ball (short bed 4x4): lubricate every 6000 miles.

Transfer case fluid: replace every 30,000 miles.

Automatic transmission fluid: replace every 51,000 miles.

Fuel filter: replace every 51,000 miles.

Rear axle lubricant: replace every 102,000 miles.

93081CT9

SCHEDULED MAINTENANCE INTERVALS
MAZDA
B SERIES
MPV

The following should be used as a guide when determining the amount of work required for a particular service.
In estimating how long a particular Scheduled Maintenance Service should take, please observe the following:

- Labor Time is time based on field research and data supplied by the vehicle manufacturer.
- Labor time operations are given in hours and tenths of an hour.
- All labor operations are to be used as a guide.

Mechanic Skill Level Codes:
(A) PRECISION: Highly skilled with multiple certification.
(B) GENERAL: Normally skilled with certification.
(C) MAINTENANCE: Semi-skilled working on certification.

	LABOR TIME		LABOR TIME		LABOR TIME
5000 Mile Service (C)		**35000 Mile Service (C)**		w/AT add (B-Series)	.6
1997 B-Series	1.3	1997 B-Series	1.3	w/AT add (98-01 B-Series)	.5
1998-01 B-Series	1.1	1998-01 B-Series	1.1	w/4WD add (B-Series)	.6
w/AT add	.1	w/AT add	.1	**65000 Mile Service (C)**	
w/4WD short bed add	.1	w/4WD add	.1	1997 B-Series	1.3
7500 Mile Service (C)		**37500 Mile Service (C)**		1998-01 B-Series	1.1
MPV	.4	MPV	.4	w/AT add	.1
10000 Mile Service (C)		**40000 Mile Service (C)**		w/4WD add	.1
1997 B-Series	.4	1997 B-Series	.4	**67500 Mile Service (C)**	
1998-01 B-Series	.8	1998-01 B-Series	.8	MPV	.4
15000 Mile Service (C)		**45000 Mile Service (C)**		**75000 Mile Service (C)**	
1997 B-Series	1.9	1997 B-Series	1.9	MPV	1.1
1998-01 B-Series	1.4	1998-01 B-Series	1.4	**80000 Mile Service (C)**	
MPV	.6	MPV	1.1	1996-01 B-Series	1.1
w/AT add	.1	w/AT add (B-Series)	.1	**82500 Mile Service (C)**	
w/4WD short bed add	.1	w/4WD add	.1	MPV	.4
20000 Mile Service (C)		**50000 Mile Service (C)**		**85000 Mile Service (C)**	
1997 B-Series	.4	1997 B-Series	.9	1996-01 B-Series	1.1
1998-01 B-Series	.8	1998-01 B-Series	1.1	**90000 Mile Service (B)**	
22500 Mile Service (C)		**52500 Mile Service (C)**		MPV	2.4
MPV	.4	1996-98 MPV	.4	1998-01 B-Series	
25000 Mile Service (C)		**55000 Mile Service (C)**		AT	
1997 B-Series	1.3	1997 B-Series	1.3	2WD	3.1
1998-01 B-Series	1.1	1998-01 B-Series	1.1	4WD	3.8
w/AT add	.1	w/AT add	.1	MT	
w/4WD add	.1	w/4WD add	.1	2WD	2.4
30000 Mile Service (B)		**60000 Mile Service (B)**		4WD	2.6
1997 B-Series	1.8	1997 B-Series	2.3	Replace timing belt Calif. engs.	
1998-01 B-Series		1998-01 B-Series		(96-98 MPV) add	3.1
AT		AT		w/4WD add (96-98 MPV)	.1
2WD	3.0	2WD	3.1	**95000 Mile Service (C)**	
4WD	3.9	4WD	4.2	1998-01 B-Series	1.1
MT		MT		**97500 Mile Service (C)**	
2WD	2.4	2WD	2.8	MPV	.4
4WD	3.2	4WD	4.1		
MPV	2.4	MPV	6.4		
w/AT add	.5	Replace spark plugs Calif. engs.			
w/4WD add	.6	(B-Series) add	.8		
		Replace timing belt (2.3L) add	2.4		

93081CT0

Refer to the model specific sections for engine mechanical service procedures

TIRE, WHEEL AND BALL JOINT SPECIFICATIONS
Mazda Truck

Year	Model	OEM Tires		Tire Pressures (psi)		Wheel Size	Ball Joint Inspection
		Standard	Optional	Front	Rear		
1997	MPV 2wd	P195/75R15	215/65R15	35	35	6-JJ	18-30 in. ①
	MPV 4wd	P215/70R15	None	32	32	6-JJ	18-30 in. ①
	Navajo	P225/70R15	P235/75R15SL	30	35	7-JJ	0.030 in. ②
			P255/70R16	26	26	7-JJ	
	B-Series 2wd	P195/70R14SL	P215/70R14SL	35	35	6-JJ	0.040 in. ②
			P225/70R14SL				
	B-Series 4wd	P215/75R15SL	P235/75R15SL	30	35	Std: 6-J	0.040 in. ②
			P265/75R15SL			Opt: 7-J	
1998	MPV 2wd	P195/75R15	215/65R15	35	35	6-JJ	18-30 in. ①
	MPV 4wd	P215/70R15	None	32	32	6-JJ	18-30 in. ①
	Navajo	P225/70R15	P235/75R15SL	30	35	7-JJ	0.030 in. ②
			P255/70R16	26	26	7-JJ	
	B-Series 2wd	P205/75R14SL	P225/70R14SL	35	35	6-JJ	0.040 in. ②
	B-Series 4wd	P215/75R15SL	P235/75R15SL	35	35	6-JJ	0.040 in. ②
1999	MPV 2wd	P195/75R15	215/65R15	35	35	6-JJ	18-30 in. ①
	MPV 4wd	P215/70R15	None	32	32	6-JJ	18-30 in. ①
	Navajo	P225/70R15	P235/75R15SL	30	35	7-JJ	0.030 in. ②
			P255/70R16	26	26	7-JJ	
	B-Series 2wd	P205/75R14SL	P225/70R14SL	35	35	6-JJ	0.040 in. ②
	B-Series 4wd	P215/75R15SL	P235/75R15SL	35	35	6-JJ	0.040 in. ②
2000-01	MPV 2wd	P195/75R15	215/65R15	35	35	6-JJ	18-30 in. ①
	MPV 4wd	P215/70R15	None	32	32	6-JJ	18-30 in. ①
	Navajo	P225/70R15	P235/75R15SL	30	35	7-JJ	0.030 in. ②
			P255/70R16	26	26	7-JJ	
	B-Series 2wd	P205/75R14SL	P225/70R14SL	35	35	6-JJ	0.040 in. ②
	B-Series 4wd	P215/75R15SL	P235/75R15SL	35	35	6-JJ	0.040 in. ②

OEM: Original Equipment Manufacturer

PSI: Pounds Per Square Inch

STD: Standard

OPT: Optional

① Torque required in inch lbs. to rotate ball joint when removed from the knuckle

② Both upper and lower

93081CU1

MAZDA
Mazda Tribute

ENGINE AND VEHICLE IDENTIFICATION

Engine							Model Year	
Code ①	Liters (cc)	Cu. In.	Cyl.	Fuel Sys.	Engine Type	Eng. Mfg.	Code ②	Year
B	2.0 (1998)	121	4	SFI	DOHC	Ford	1	2001
1	3.0 (3049)	182	6	SFI	DOHC	Ford		

SFI: Multi-port Fuel Injection

DOHC: Double Overhead Camshafts

① 8th digit of VIN

② 10th digit of VIN

93081CU2

GENERAL ENGINE SPECIFICATIONS

Year	Model	Engine Displacement Liters (cc)	Engine ID/VIN	Fuel System Type	Net Horsepower @ rpm	Net Torque @ rpm (ft. lbs.)	Bore x Stroke (in.)	Compression Ratio	Oil Pressure @ rpm
2001	Tribute	2.0 (1998)	B	SFI	135@5500	135@4500	3.34x3.46	9.6:1	54-80 ①
	Tribute	3.0 (3049)	1	SFI	200@5500	200@4500	3.39x3.39	10.0:1	45 ①

SFI: Multi-port Fuel Injection

① The manufacturer does not provide an engine speed specification for oil pump pressure.

93081CU3

ENGINE TUNE-UP SPECIFICATIONS

Year	Engine Displacement Liters (cc)	Engine ID/VIN	Spark Plug Gap (in.)	Ignition Timing (deg.) MT	Ignition Timing (deg.) AT	Fuel Pump (psi)	Idle Speed (rpm) MT	Idle Speed (rpm) AT	Valve Clearance Intake	Valve Clearance Exhaust
2001	2.0 (1998)	B	0.039-0.043	10 BTDC	—	65	①	—	HYD.	HYD.
	3.0 (3049)	1	0.052-0.056	10 BTDC	10 BTDC	65	①	①	HYD.	HYD.

BTDC: Before Top Dead Center

HYD: Hydraulic lash adjusters

① Refer to Vehicle Emission Control Information Label

93081CU4

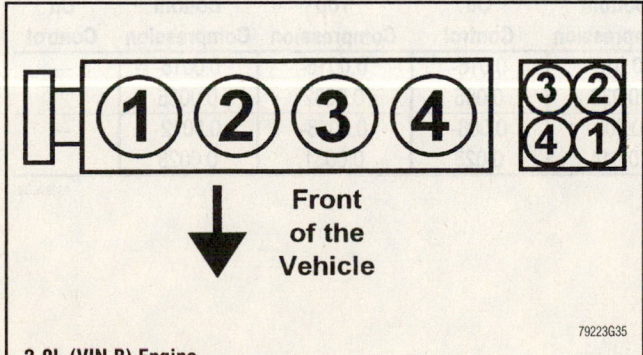

2.0L (VIN B) Engine
Firing order: 1-3-4-2
Distributorless ignition system

79223G35

3.0L (VIN 1) Engine
Firing order: 1-4-2-5-3-6
Distributorless ignition system

79223G26

Refer to the model specific sections for fuel system service procedures

CAPACITIES

Year	Model	Engine Displacement Liters (cc)	Engine ID/VIN	Engine Oil with Filter (qts.)	Transmission (pts.) Manual	Transmission (pts.) Auto.	Transfer Case (pts.)	Drive Axle Front (pts.)	Drive Axle Rear (pts.)	Fuel Tank (gal.)	Cooling System (qts.)
2001	Tribute	2.0 (1998)	B	4.5	5.7	—	3.0	2.6	3.0	15.0	7.0
	Tribute	3.0 (3049)	1	5.8	5.7	2.5	3.0	2.6	3.0	16.0	10.5

NOTE: All capacities are approximate. Add fluid gradually and check to be sure a proper fluid level is obtained.

93081CU5

VALVE SPECIFICATIONS

Year	Engine Displacement Liters (cc)	Engine ID/VIN	Seat Angle (deg.)	Face Angle (deg.)	Spring Test Pressure (lbs. @ in.)	Spring Installed Height (in.)	Stem-to-Guide Clearance (in.) Intake	Stem-to-Guide Clearance (in.) Exhaust	Stem Diameter (in.) Intake	Stem Diameter (in.) Exhaust
2001	2.0 (1998)	B	45	45	82.1@ 0.988	1.420-1.54	0.0007-0.0027	0.0017-0.0037	0.2374	0.2374
	3.0 (3049)	1	44.75	45	153@ 1.18	1.57	0.0010-0.0024	0.0012-0.0026	0.2350-0.2358	0.2343-0.2358

93081CU6

CRANKSHAFT AND CONNECTING ROD SPECIFICATIONS
All measurements are given in inches.

Year	Engine Displacement Liters (cc)	Engine ID/VIN	Crankshaft Main Brg. Journal Dia.	Crankshaft Main Brg. Oil Clearance	Crankshaft Shaft End-play	Crankshaft Thrust on No.	Connecting Rod Journal Diameter	Connecting Rod Oil Clearance	Connecting Rod Side Clearance
2001	2.0 (1998)	B	2.282-2.284	①	0.0035-0.0102	3	1.7279-1.7287	0.0080-0.0026	0.0040-0.0110
	3.0 (3049)	1	2.467-2.479	①	0.0009-0.0019	3	1.9670-1.9680	0.0010-0.0025	0.0039-0.0118

① Journals 1, 2 and 4: 0.0010 - 0.0017 in.
Journal 3: 0.0012 - 0.0019 in.

93081CU7

PISTON AND RING SPECIFICATIONS
All measurements are given in inches.

Year	Engine Displacement Liters (cc)	Engine ID/VIN	Piston Clearance	Ring Gap Top Compression	Ring Gap Bottom Compression	Ring Gap Oil Control	Ring Side Clearance Top Compression	Ring Side Clearance Bottom Compression	Ring Side Clearance Oil Control
2001	2.0 (1998)	B	0.0004-0.0012	0.010-0.030	0.010-0.030	0.016-0.066	0.0015-0.0032	0.0015-0.0035	—
	3.0 (3049)	1	0.0005-0.0009	0.004-0.016	0.008-0.014	0.008-0.028	0.0018-0.0031	0.0012-0.0028	—

93081CU8

TORQUE SPECIFICATIONS
All readings in ft. lbs.

Year	Engine Displacement Liters (cc)	Engine ID/VIN	Cylinder Head Bolts	Main Bearing Bolts	Rod Bearing Bolts	Crankshaft Damper Bolts	Flywheel Bolts	Manifold		Spark Plugs	Lug Nuts
								Intake	Exhaust		
2001	2.0 (1998)	B	①	66-79	26-30	80-87	83	13	8	11	98
	3.0 (3049)	1	②	63	50	11	83	8	15	11	98

① Step 1: 15 ft. lbs. (20 Nm).
　Step 2: 30 ft. lbs. (40 Nm).
　Step 3: Plus an additional 90 degrees.

② Step 1: 30 ft. lbs. (40 Nm).
　Step 2: Tighten the bolts 90 degrees.
　Step 3: Loosen the bolts one full turn.
　Step 4: 30 ft. lbs. (40 Nm).
　Step 5: Tighten the bolts 90 degrees.
　Step 6: Tighten the bolts 90 degrees.

93081CU9

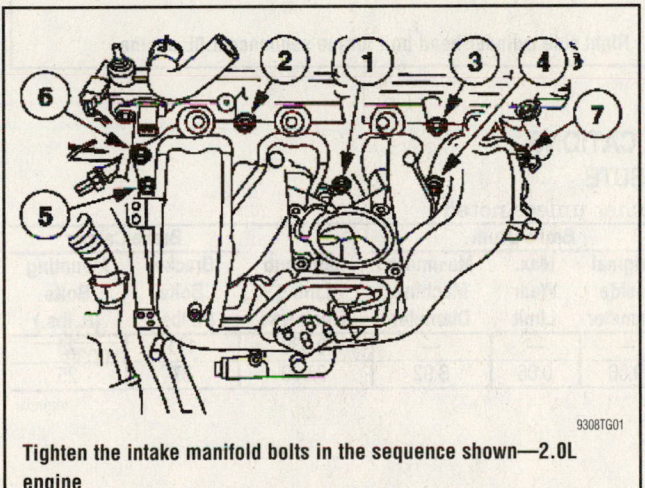

Tighten the intake manifold bolts in the sequence shown—2.0L engine

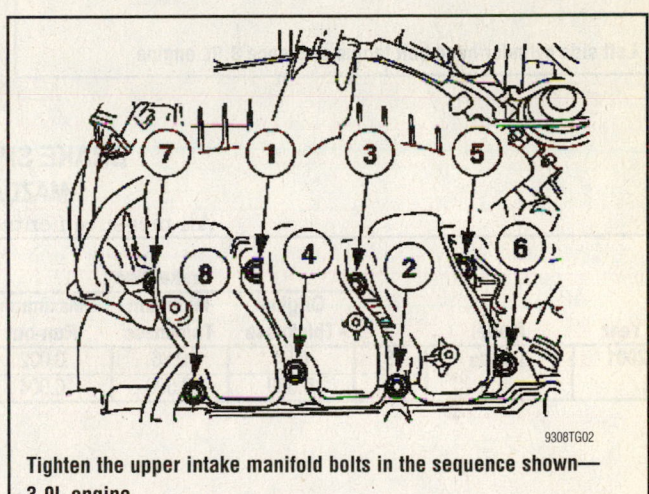

Tighten the upper intake manifold bolts in the sequence shown—3.0L engine

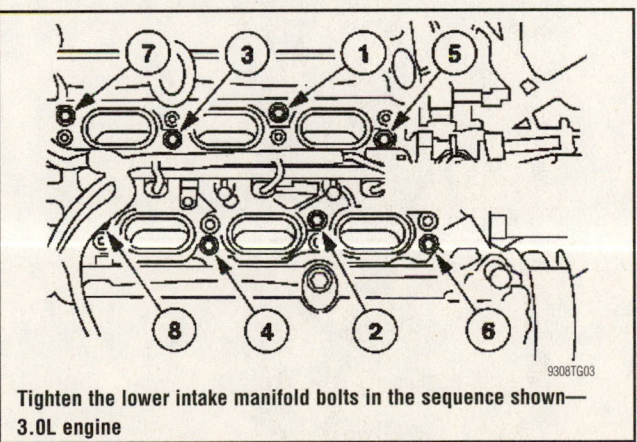

Tighten the lower intake manifold bolts in the sequence shown—3.0L engine

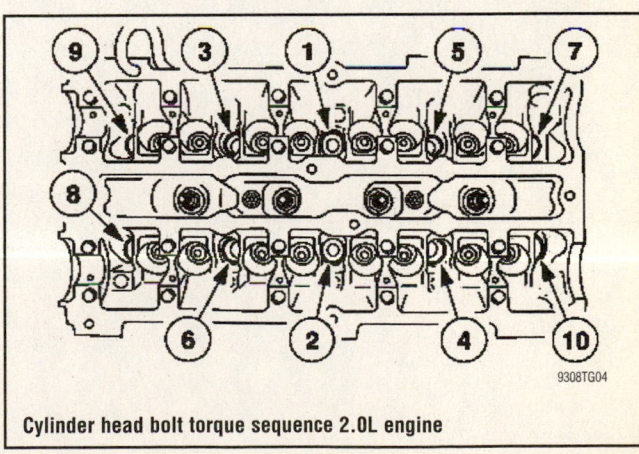

Cylinder head bolt torque sequence 2.0L engine

Refer to the model specific sections for engine electrical system service procedures

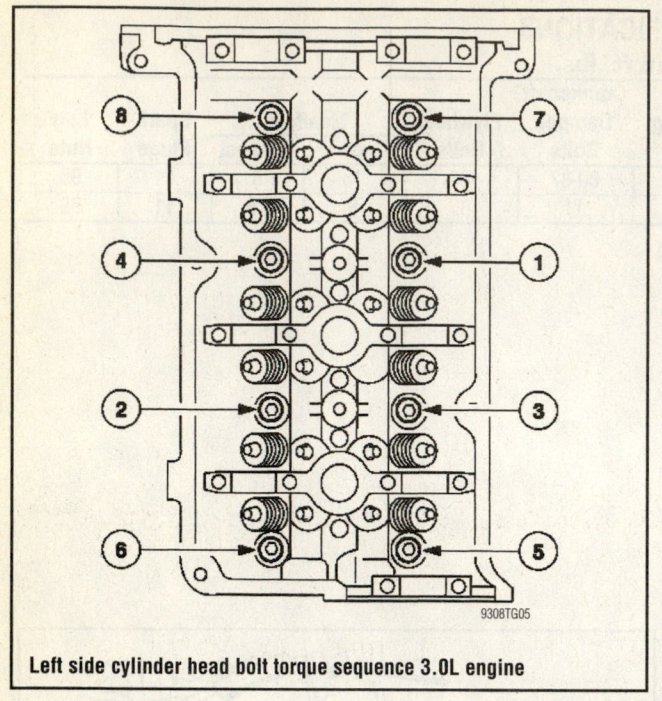

Left side cylinder head bolt torque sequence 3.0L engine

9308TG05

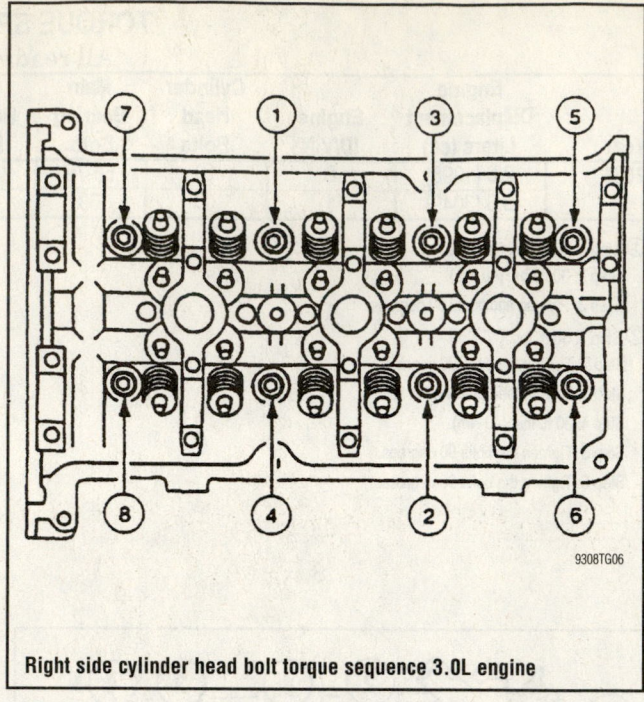

Right side cylinder head bolt torque sequence 3.0L engine

9308TG06

BRAKE SPECIFICATIONS
MAZDA TRIBUTE
All measurements in inches unless noted

Year	Model		Brake Disc			Brake Drum			Minimum Lining Thickness	Brake Caliper	
			Original Thickness	Minimum Thickness	Maximum Run-out	Original Inside Diameter	Max. Wear Limit	Maximum Machine Diameter		Bracket Bolts (ft. lbs.)	Mounting Bolts (ft. lbs.)
2001	Tribute	F	0.94	0.86	0.002	—	—	—	0.039	111	26
		R	0.550	0.500	0.004	9.06	0.06	8.92	0.039	87	25

93081CU0

SCHEDULED MAINTENANCE INTERVALS
(MAZDA TRIBUTE)

TO BE SERVICED	TYPE OF SERVICE	VEHICLE MILEAGE INTERVAL (x1000)												
		5	10	15	20	25	30	35	40	45	50	55	60	65
Air cleaner filter	R						✓						✓	
Accessory drive belt	S/I												✓	
Brake system ①	S/I			✓			✓			✓			✓	
Clutch pedal operation	S/I						✓						✓	
Cooling fan operation	S/I		✓		✓		✓		✓		✓		✓	
Cooling system hoses and clamps	S/I			✓			✓			✓			✓	
CV-joint boots & axle seals	S/I						✓						✓	
Engine coolant	R	Ten years or 150,000 miles												
Engine oil & filter	R	✓	✓	✓	✓	✓	✓	✓	✓	✓	✓	✓	✓	✓
Exterior Lights	S/I	Check monthly												
PCV valve	S/I												✓	
Exhaust system & heat shields	S/I						✓						✓	
Parking brake system	S/I	Every 6 months												
Power steering fluid	S/I	Every 6 months												
Rotate tires	S/I	✓		✓		✓		✓		✓		✓		✓
Steering linkage	S/I						✓						✓	
Spark plugs	R	Change at 100,000 miles												
Suspension components	S/I						✓						✓	

R: Replace   S/I: Inspect and service, if necessary   L: Lubricate   A: Adjust   C: Clean

① Inspect the reservoir fluid level, rotor and or drum, brake lines, hoses, calipers and or wheel cylinders

FREQUENT OPERATION MAINTENANCE (SEVERE SERVICE)

If a vehicle is operated under any of the following conditions it is considered severe service:

- Extremely dusty areas.

- 50% or more of the vehicle operation is in 32°C (90°F) or higher temperatures, or constant operation in temperatures below 0°C (32°F).

- Prolonged idling (vehicle operation in stop and go traffic).

- Frequent short running periods (engine does not warm to normal operating temperatures).

- Police, taxi, delivery usage or trailer towing usage.

Oil & oil filter change: change every 3000 miles.

Air filter element: change every 15,000 miles.

93081CV1

For accessory drive belt replacement procedures see the model specific sections of this manual

SCHEDULED MAINTENANCE INTERVALS
MAZDA
TRIBUTE

The following should be used as a guide when determining the amount of work required for a particular service. In estimating how long a particular Scheduled Maintenance Service should take, please observe the following:

- Labor Time is time based on field research and data supplied by the vehicle manufacturer.
- Labor time operations are given in hours and tenths of an hour.
- All labor operations are to be used as a guide.

Mechanic Skill Level Codes:
(A) PRECISION: Highly skilled with multiple certification.
(B) GENERAL: Normally skilled with certification.
(C) MAINTENANCE: Semi-skilled working on certification.

	LABOR TIME		LABOR TIME		LABOR
5000 Mile Service (C)		**25000 Mile Service (C)**		**50000 Mile Service (C)**	
All Models	.9	All Models	.9	All Models	.7
10000 Mile Service (C)		**30000 Mile Service (B)**		**55000 Mile Service (C)**	
All Models	.5	All Models	1.9	All Models	.9
15000 Mile Service (C)		**35000 Mile Service (C)**		**60000 Mile Service (B)**	
All Models	1.6	All Models	.9	All Models	1.9
20000 Mile Service (C)		**40000 Mile Service (C)**		**65000 Mile Service (C)**	
All Models	.5	All Models	.5	All Models	.9
		45000 Mile Service (C)			
		All Models	1.6		

93081CV2

TIRE, WHEEL AND BALL JOINT SPECIFICATIONS
Mazda Tribute

Year	Model	OEM Tires		Tire Pressures (psi)		Wheel Size	Ball Joint Inspection
		Standard	Optional	Front	Rear		
2001	Tribute	P225/70SR15	P235/70R16	NA	NA	NA	0.030 in.

OEM: Original Equipment Manufacturer

PSI: Pounds Per Square Inch

STD: Standard

OPT: Optional

NA: Not Available

93081CAZ

MERCEDES-BENZ
ML320 • ML430

ENGINE AND VEHICLE IDENTIFICATION CHART

	Engine Code						Model Year	
Code	Liters (cc)	Cu. In.	Cyl.	Fuel Sys.	Eng. Mfg.		Code ①	Year
M112	3.2 (3199)	195	6	SFI	MB		X	1999
M113	4.3 (4266)	262	8	SFI	MB		Y	2000
							1	2001

SFI: Sequential Fuel Injection

MB: Mercedes-Benz

① 10th digit of the VIN

93081CV3

GENERAL ENGINE SPECIFICATIONS

Year	Model	Engine Displacement Liters (cc)	Engine ID/VIN	Fuel System Type	Net Horsepower @ rpm	Net Torque @ rpm (ft. lbs.)	Bore x Stroke (in.)	Compression Ratio	Oil Pressure @ rpm
1998	ML320	3.2 (3199)	M112	SFI	215@5600	233@3000	3.54x3.31	10.0:1	43.5@3000
1999	ML320	3.2 (3199)	M112	SFI	215@5600	233@3000	3.54x3.31	10.0:1	43.5@3000
	ML430	4.3 (4299)	M113	SFI	268@5500	288@3000	3.54x3.31	10.0:1	43.5@3000
2000-01	ML320	3.2 (3199)	M112	SFI	215@5600	233@3000	3.54x3.31	10.0:1	43.5@3000
	ML430	4.3 (4299)	M113	SFI	268@5500	288@3000	3.54x3.31	10.0:1	43.5@3000

SFI: Sequential Fuel Injection

93081CV4

For brake related suspension and axle service, refer to the model specific sections of this manual

ENGINE TUNE-UP SPECIFICATIONS

Year	Engine Displacement Liters (cc)	Engine ID/VIN	Spark Plugs Gap (in.)	Ignition Timing (deg.) MT	Ignition Timing (deg.) AT	Fuel Pump (psi)	Idle Speed (rpm) MT	Idle Speed (rpm) AT	Valve Clearance In.	Valve Clearance Ex.
1998	3.2 (3199)	M112	0.032	—	①	55	—	700	②	②
1999	3.2 (3199)	M112	0.032	—	①	55	—	700	②	②
	4.3 (4299)	M113	0.032	—	①	55	—	700	②	②
2000-01	3.2 (3199)	M112	0.032	—	①	55	—	700	②	②
	4.3 (4299)	M113	0.032	—	①	55	—	700	②	②

① ECM controlled
② Hydraulic lash adjusters

93081CV5

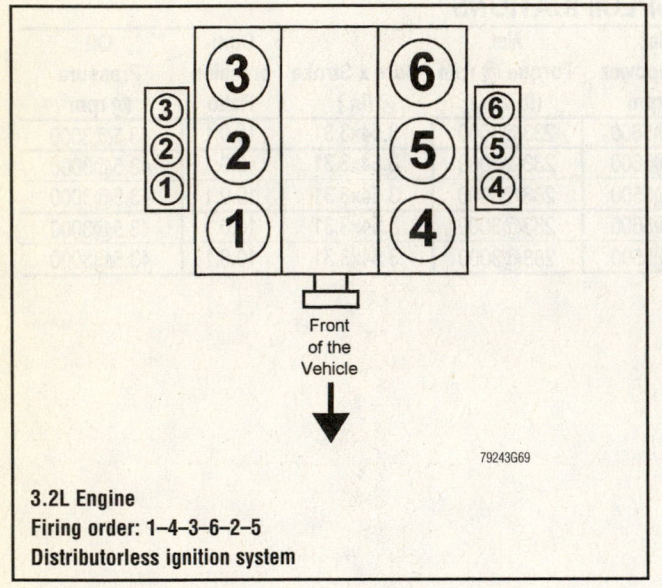

3.2L Engine
Firing order: 1–4–3–6–2–5
Distributorless ignition system

79243G69

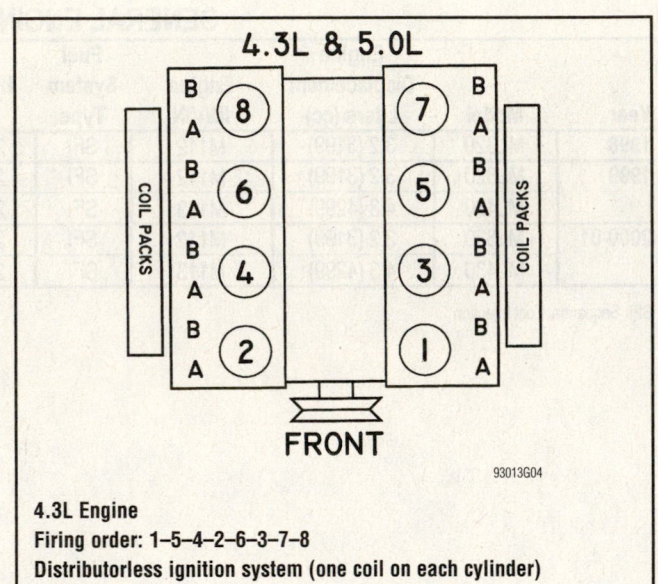

4.3L & 5.0L

4.3L Engine
Firing order: 1–5–4–2–6–3–7–8
Distributorless ignition system (one coil on each cylinder)

93013G04

CAPACITIES

Year	Model	Engine Displacement Liters (cc)	Engine ID/VIN	Engine Oil with Filter	Transmission (pts.) 4-Spd	Transmission (pts.) 5-Spd	Transmission (pts.) Auto.	Transfer Case (pts.)	Drive Axle Front (pts.)	Drive Axle Rear (pts.)	Fuel Tank (gal.)	Cooling System (qts.)
1998	ML320	3.2 (3199)	M112	8.5	—	—	20	3.0	2.4	3.2	19.0	9
1999	ML320	3.2 (3199)	M112	8.5	—	—	20	3.0	2.4	3.2	19.0	9
	ML430	4.3 (4299)	M113	8.5	—	—	20	3.0	2.4	3.2	19.0	9
2000-01	ML320	3.2 (3199)	M112	8.5	—	—	20	3.0	2.4	3.2	19.0	9
	ML430	4.3 (4299)	M113	8.5	—	—	20	3.0	2.4	3.2	19.0	9

Note: All capacities are approximate. Add fluid gradually and check to be sure a proper fluid level is obtained.

93081CV6

TORQUE SPECIFICATIONS
All readings in ft. lbs.

Year	Engine Displacement Liters (cc)	Engine ID/VIN	Cylinder Head Bolts	Main Bearing Bolts	Rod Bearing Bolts	Crankshaft Damper Bolts	Flywheel Bolts	Manifold		Spark Plugs	Lug Nut
								Intake	Exhaust		
1998	3.2 (3199)	M112	①	②	③	④	⑤	15	12	21	111
1999	3.2 (3199)	M112	①	②	③	④	⑤	15	12	21	111
	4.3 (4299)	M113	①	②	③	④	⑤	15	12	21	111
2000-01	3.2 (3199)	M112	①	②	③	④	⑤	15	12	21	111
	4.3 (4299)	M113	①	②	③	④	⑤	15	12	21	111

① Step 1: 15 ft. lbs.
Step 2: 37 ft. lbs.
Step 3: 65 degrees
Step 4: 65 degrees

② M8x40: 18 ft. lbs.
M8x75:
Step 1: 10 ft. lbs.
Step 2: 90-100 degrees
M10x90:
Step 1: 15 ft. lbs.
Step 2: 90-100 degrees

③ Step 1: 44 inch lbs.
Step 2: 18 ft. lbs
Step 3. 90 degrees

④ Step 1: 148 ft. lbs.
Step 2: 95 degrees

⑤ Step 1: 33 ft. lbs.
Step 2: 90 degrees

93081CV7

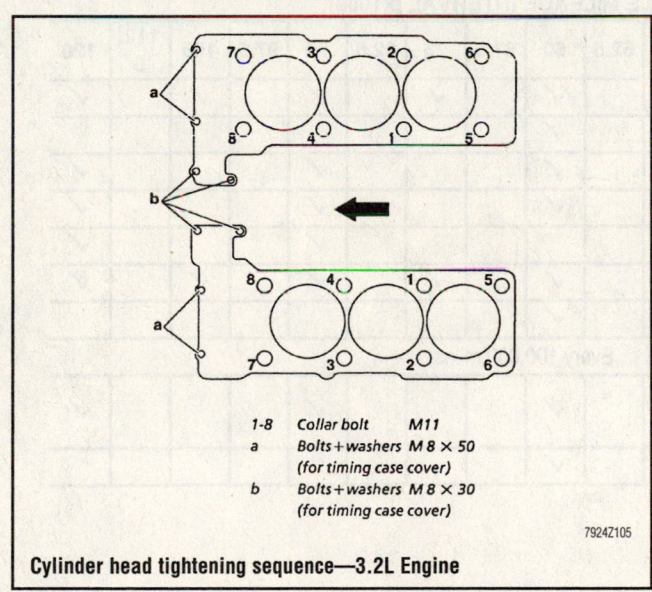

1-8 Collar bolt M11
a Bolts + washers M 8 × 50 (for timing case cover)
b Bolts + washers M 8 × 30 (for timing case cover)

7924Z105

Cylinder head tightening sequence—3.2L Engine

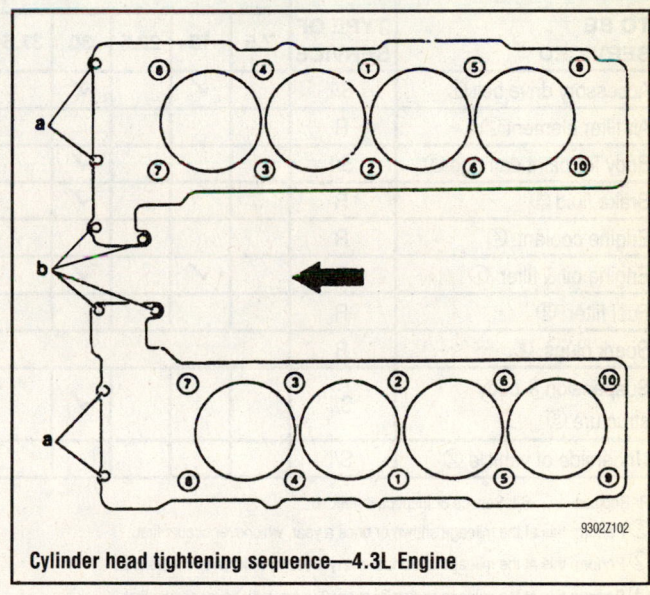

9302Z102

Cylinder head tightening sequence—4.3L Engine

Refer to the model specific sections for driveline service procedures

BRAKE SPECIFICATIONS
All measurements in inches unless noted

Year	Model	Master Cylinder Bore	Front Brake Disc Original Thickness	Front Brake Disc Minimum Thickness	Front Brake Disc Maximum Runout	Rear Brake Disc Original Thickness	Rear Brake Disc Minimum Thickness	Rear Brake Disc Maximum Runout	Minimum Lining Thickness Front	Minimum Lining Thickness Rear	Brake Caliper Bracket Bolts (ft. lbs.)	Brake Caliper Mounting Bolts (ft. lbs.)
1998	ML320	NA	1.02	0.91	NA	0.59	0.49	NA	①	②	26	18
1999	ML320	NA	1.02	0.91	NA	0.59	0.49	NA	①	②	26	18
	ML430	NA	1.02	0.91	NA	0.59	0.49	NA	①	②	26	18
2000-01	ML320	NA	1.02	0.91	NA	0.59	0.49	NA	①	②	26	18
	ML430	NA	1.02	0.91	NA	0.59	0.49	NA	①	②	26	18

NA: Not Available

① New: Inner pad w/backing plate .65 in.
  Wear limit: .47 in
  New: Outter pad w/backing plate .61 in.
  Wear limit: .43 in.

② New: .61 in.
  Wear limit: .43 in.

93081CV8

SCHEDULED MAINTENANCE INTERVALS
(MERCEDES BENZ ML320 & ML430)

TO BE SERVICED	TYPE OF SERVICE	7.5	15	22.5	30	37.5	45	52.5	60	67.5	75	82.5	90	97.5	105	112.5	120
Accessory drive belt ①	S/I		✓		✓		✓		✓		✓		✓		✓		✓
Air filter element ②	R								✓								
Body for paint damage ③	S/I				✓				✓				✓				✓
Brake fluid ③	R				✓				✓				✓				✓
Engine coolant ④	R						✓						✓				✓
Engine oil & filter ①	R		✓		✓		✓		✓		✓		✓		✓		✓
Fuel filter ②	R								✓								
Spark plugs ②	R	Every 100,000 miles															
Suspension & body structure ③	S/I				✓				✓				✓				✓
Underside of vehicle ②	S/I								✓								

R: Replace   S/I: Service or Inspect, if needed

① Perform this at the mileage shown or once a year, whichever occurs first.

② Perform this at the mileage shown, or every 4 years, whichever occurs first.

③ Perform this at the mileage shown or every 2 years, whichever occurs first.

④ Perform this at the mileage shown or every 3 years, whichever occurs first.

93081CV9

SCHEDULED MAINTENANCE INTERVALS
MERCEDES BENZ
ML320 & ML430

The following should be used as a guide when determining the amount of work required for a particular service. In estimating how long a particular Scheduled Maintenance Service should take, please observe the following:

- Labor Time is time based on field research and data supplied by the vehicle manufacturer.
- Labor time operations are given in hours and tenths of an hour.
- All labor operations are to be used as a guide.

Mechanic Skill Level Codes:
(A) PRECISION: Highly skilled with multiple certification.
(B) GENERAL: Normally skilled with certification.
(C) MAINTENANCE: Semi-skilled working on certification.

	LABOR TIME		LABOR TIME		LABOR TIME
15000 Mile Service (B)		**60000 Mile Service (B)**		**90000 Mile Service (B)**	
All Models	1.3	All Models	4.5	All Models	4.0
30000 Mile Service (B)				**105000 Mile Service (B)**	
All Models	2.6	**75000 Mile Service (B)**		All Models	1.3
45000 Mile Service (B)		All Models	1.3	**120000 Mile Service (B)**	
All Models	2.8			All Models	3.5

93081CXX

For exhaust manifold replacement procedures, see the model specific sections of this manual

MITSUBISHI
Montero • Montero Sport

ENGINE AND VEHICLE IDENTIFICATION CHART

Code	Liters (cc)	Cu. In.	Cyl.	Fuel Sys.	Engine Type	Eng. Mfg.		Code	Year
			Engine					**Model Year**	
G	2.4 (2351)	143.4	4	MFI	SOHC	Mitsubishi		V	1997
M	3.5 (3479)	213.4	6	MFI	SOHC	Mitsubishi		W	1998
H	3.0 (2972)	181.4	6	MFI	SOHC	Mitsubishi		X	1999
P	3.0 (2972)	181.4	6	MFI	SOHC	Mitsubishi		Y	2000
								1	2001

MFI: Multi-port Fuel Injection

93081CV0

GENERAL ENGINE SPECIFICATIONS

Year	Engine Displacement Liters (cc)	Engine VIN	Fuel System Type	Net Horsepower @ rpm	Net Torque @ rpm (ft. lbs.)	Bore x Stroke (in.)	Compression Ratio	Oil Pressure @ rpm
1997	2.4 (2350)	G	MFI	132@5500	148@3000	3.41x3.94	9.5:1	41@2000
	3.0 (2972)	H	MFI	173@5250	188@4000	3.59x2.99	9.0:1	30-80@2000
1998	2.4 (2351)	G	MFI	134@5500	148@3000	3.41x3.94	9.5:1	41@2000
	3.0 (2972)	H	MFI	173@5250	188@4000	3.59x2.99	9.0:1	30-80@2000
1999	2.4 (2351)	G	MFI	134@5500	148@3000	3.41x3.94	9.5:1	41@2000
	3.5 (3497)	M	MFI	200@5000	228@3500	3.66x3.38	9.0:1	30-80@2000
	3.0 (2972)	P	MFI	173@5500	188@4500	3.59x2.99	9.0:1	30-80@2000
2000-01	3.5 (3497)	M	MFI	200@5000	228@3500	3.66x3.38	9.0:1	30-80@2000
	3.0 (2972)	P	MFI	173@5500	188@4500	3.59x2.99	9.0:1	30-80@2000

93081CW1

ENGINE TUNE-UP SPECIFICATIONS

Year	Engine Displacement Liters (cc)	Engine VIN	Spark Plugs Gap (in.)	Ignition Timing (deg.) MT	Ignition Timing (deg.) AT	Fuel Pump (psi)		Idle Speed (rpm) MT	Idle Speed (rpm) AT	Valve Clearance In.	Valve Clearance Ex.
1997	2.4 (2350)	G	0.039-0.043	5B	—	38	①	750	—	HYD	HYD
	3.0 (2972)	H	0.039-0.043	5B	5B	38	①	700	700	HYD	HYD
1998	2.4 (2350)	G	0.039-0.043	5B	—	38	①	750	—	HYD	HYD
	3.0 (2972)	H	0.039-0.043	5B	5B	38	①	750	750	HYD	HYD
1999	2.4 (2351)	G	0.039-0.043	5B	—	38	①	750	—	HYD	HYD
	3.5 (3479)	M	0.039-0.043	5B	5B	38	①	700	700	HYD	HYD
	3.0 (2972)	P	0.039-0.043	5B	5B	38	①	750	750	HYD	HYD
2000-01	3.5 (3479)	M	0.039-0.043	5B	5B	38	①	700	700	HYD	HYD
	3.0 (2972)	P	0.039-0.043	5B	5B	38	①	750	750	HYD	HYD

NOTE: The Vehicle Emission Control Information label often reflects specification changes made during production. The label figures must be used if they differ from those in this chart.

B: Before top dead center

HYD: Hydraulic

① With vacuum hose connected

93081CW2

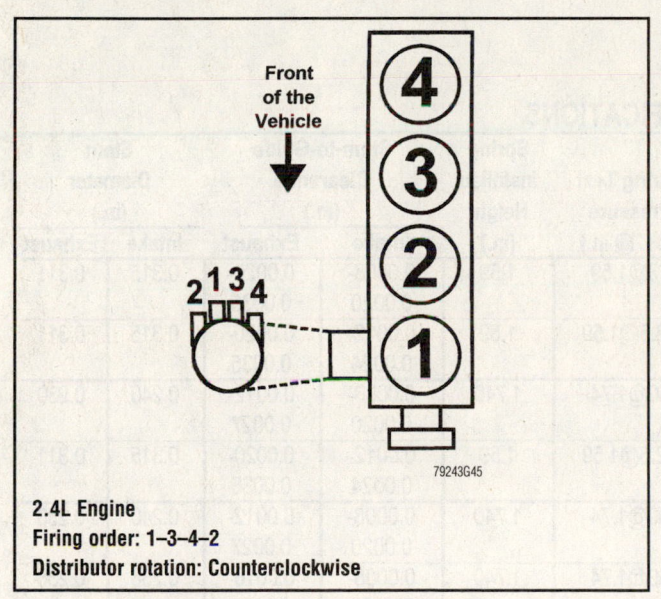

2.4L Engine
Firing order: 1–3–4–2
Distributor rotation: Counterclockwise

79243G45

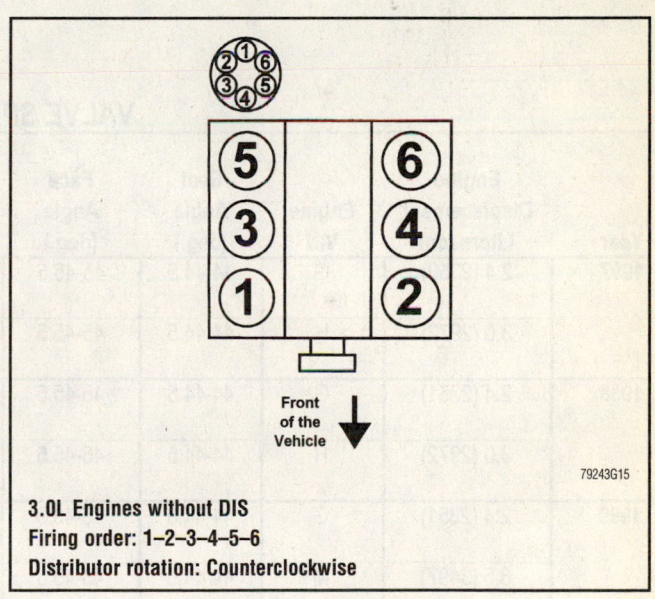

3.0L Engines without DIS
Firing order: 1–2–3–4–5–6
Distributor rotation: Counterclockwise

79243G15

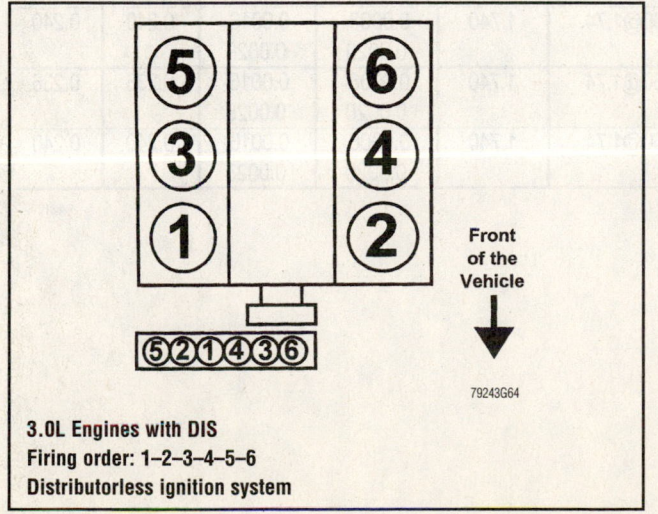

3.0L Engines with DIS
Firing order: 1–2–3–4–5–6
Distributorless ignition system

79243G64

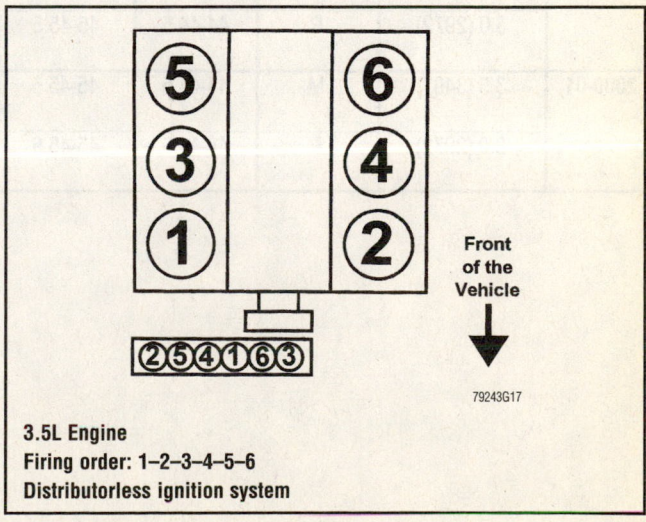

3.5L Engine
Firing order: 1–2–3–4–5–6
Distributorless ignition system

79243G17

Refer to the model specific sections for cooling system service procedures

CAPACITIES

Year	Model	Engine Displacement Liters (cc)	Engine VIN	Engine Oil with Filter (qts.)	Transmission (pts.) 5-Spd	Transmission (pts.) Auto.	Transfer Case (pts.)	Drive Axle Front (pts.)	Drive Axle Rear (pts.)	Fuel Tank (gal.)	Cooling System (qts.)
1997	Montero Sport	3.0 (2972)	H	5.0	5.3	15.2	4.8	2.6	5.5	24.3	10.0
		2.4 (2351)	G	4.5	4.8	—	—	—	3.2	19.5	8.5
1998	Montero Sport	3.0 (2972)	H	5.0	5.3	15.2	4.8	2.6	5.5	24.3	10.0
		2.4 (2351)	G	4.5	4.8	—	—	—	3.2	19.5	8.5
1999	Montero	3.5 (3497)	M	5.5	6.6	17.8	5.2	2.4	6.6	24.3	10.0
	Montero Sport	2.4 (2351)	G	4.5	4.8	—	—	—	3.2	19.5	8.5
		3.0 (2972)	P	5.2	4.8	20.8	4.8	2.4	5.5	19.5	9.5
		3.5 (3497)	M	5.2	4.8	20.8	4.8	2.4	5.5	19.5	9.5
2000-01	Montero	3.5 (3497)	M	5.5	6.6	17.8	5.2	2.4	6.6	24.3	10.0
	Montero Sport	3.5 (3497)	M	5.2	4.8	20.8	4.8	2.4	5.5	19.5	9.5
		3.0 (2972)	P	5.2	4.8	20.8	4.8	2.4	5.5	19.5	9.5

93081CW3

VALVE SPECIFICATIONS

Year	Engine Displacement Liters (cc)	Engine VIN	Seat Angle (deg.)	Face Angle (deg.)	Spring Test Pressure (lbs. @ in.)	Spring Installed Height (in.)	Stem-to-Guide Clearance (in.) Intake	Stem-to-Guide Clearance (in.) Exhaust	Stem Diameter (in.) Intake	Stem Diameter (in.) Exhaust
1997	2.4 (2350)	G	44-44.5	45-45.5	73@1.59	1.59	0.0008-0.0020	0.0020-0.0035	0.315	0.311
	3.0 (2972)	H	44-44.5	45-45.5	72.5@1.59	1.59	0.0012-0.0024	0.0020-0.0035	0.315	0.311
1998	2.4 (2351)	G	44-44.5	45-45.5	60@1.74	1.740	0.0008-0.0020	0.0012-0.0027	0.240	0.230
	3.0 (2972)	H	44-44.5	45-45.5	72.5@1.59	1.59	0.0012-0.0024	0.0020-0.0035	0.315	0.311
1999	2.4 (2351)	G	44-44.5	45-45.5	60@1.74	1.740	0.0008-0.0020	0.0012-0.0027	0.240	0.230
	3.5 (3497)	M	44-44.5	45-45.5	60@1.74	1.740	0.0008-0.0020	0.0016-0.0028	0.236	0.236
	3.0 (2972)	P	44-44.5	45-45.5	60@1.74	1.740	0.0008-0.0020	0.0016-0.0028	0.240	0.240
2000-01	3.5 (3497)	M	44-44.5	45-45.5	60@1.74	1.740	0.0008-0.0020	0.0016-0.0028	0.236	0.236
	3.0 (2972)	P	44-44.5	45-45.5	60@1.74	1.740	0.0008-0.0020	0.0016-0.0028	0.240	0.240

93081CW4

CRANKSHAFT AND CONNECTING ROD SPECIFICATIONS
All measurements are given in inches.

Year	Engine Displacement Liters (cc)	Engine ID/VIN	Crankshaft				Connecting Rod		
			Main Brg. Journal Dia.	Main Brg. Oil Clearance	Shaft End-play	Thrust on No.	Journal Diameter	Oil Clearance	Side Clearance
1997	2.4 (2351)	G	2.2436-2.2441	0.0008-0.0040	0.0020-0.0098	3	1.7709-1.7717	0.0008-0.0040	0.0039-0.0160
	3.0 (2972)	H	2.3614-2.3622	0.0008-0.0040	0.0020-0.0120	3	2.1646-2.1654	0.0008-0.0040	0.0039-0.0160
1998	2.4 (2351)	G	2.2436-2.2441	0.0008-0.0040	0.0020-0.0098	3	1.7709-1.7717	0.0008-0.0040	0.0039-0.0160
	3.0 (2972)	H	2.3614-2.3622	0.0008-0.0040	0.0020-0.0120	3	2.1646-2.1654	0.0008-0.0040	0.0039-0.0160
1999	2.4 (2351)	G	2.2436-2.2441	0.0008-0.0040	0.0020-0.0098	3	1.7709-1.7717	0.0008-0.0040	0.0039-0.0160
	3.0 (2972)	P	2.3614-2.3622	0.0008-0.0040	0.0020-0.0120	3	2.1646-2.1654	0.0008-0.0040	0.0039-0.0160
	3.5 (3497)	M	2.3614-2.3622	0.0008-0.0040	0.0020-0.0120	3	1.9700	0.0008-0.0040	0.0039-0.0160
2000-01	3.0 (2972)	P	2.3614-2.3622	0.0008-0.0040	0.0020-0.0120	3	2.1646-2.1654	0.0008-0.0040	0.0039-0.0160
	3.5 (3497)	M	2.3614-2.3622	0.0008-0.0040	0.0020-0.0120	3	1.9700	0.0008-0.0040	0.0039-0.0160

93081CW5

PISTON AND RING SPECIFICATIONS
All measurements are given in inches.

Year	Engine Displacement Liters (cc)	Engine ID/VIN	Piston Clearance	Ring Gap			Ring Side Clearance		
				Top Compression	Bottom Compression	Oil Control	Top Compression	Bottom Compression	Oil Control
1997	2.4 (2351)	G	0.0008-0.0016	0.0098-0.0310	0.0157-0.0310	0.0039-0.0390	0.0012-0.0040	0.0012-0.0040	Snug
	3.0 (2972)	H	0.0008-0.0020	0.0118-0.0310	0.0177-0.0310	0.0079-0.0390	0.0012-0.0040	0.0008-0.0040	Snug
1998	2.4 (2351)	G	0.0008-0.0016	0.0098-0.0310	0.0157-0.0310	0.0039-0.0390	0.0012-0.0040	0.0012-0.0040	Snug
	3.0 (2972)	H	0.0008-0.0020	0.0118-0.0310	0.0177-0.0310	0.0079-0.0390	0.0012-0.0040	0.0008-0.0040	Snug
1999	2.4 (2351)	G	0.0008-0.0016	0.0098-0.0310	0.0157-0.0310	0.0039-0.0390	0.0012-0.0040	0.0012-0.0040	Snug
	3.0 (2972)	P	0.0008-0.0020	0.0118-0.0310	0.0177-0.0310	0.0079-0.0390	0.0012-0.0040	0.0008-0.0040	Snug
	3.5 (3497)	M	0.0008-0.0020	0.0118-0.0310	0.0177-0.0310	0.0079-0.0390	0.0012-0.0040	0.0008-0.0040	Snug
2000-01	3.0 (2972)	P	0.0008-0.0020	0.0118-0.0310	0.0177-0.0310	0.0079-0.0390	0.0012-0.0040	0.0008-0.0040	Snug
	3.5 (3497)	M	0.0008-0.0020	0.0118-0.0310	0.0177-0.0310	0.0079-0.0390	0.0012-0.0040	0.0008-0.0040	Snug

93081CW6

TORQUE SPECIFICATIONS
All readings in ft. lbs.

Year	Engine ID/VIN	Engine Displacement Liters (cc)	Cylinder Head Bolts	Main Bearing Bolts	Rod Bearing Bolts	Crankshaft Damper Bolts	Flywheel Bolts	Manifold		Spark Plugs	Lug Nut
								Intake *	Exhaust		
1997	G	2.4 (2350)	①	②	③	87	98	13	④	18	100
	H	3.0 (2972)	80	57	38	136	54	10	14	18	100
1998	G	2.4 (2351)	⑤	②	⑥	87	98	14	④	18	100
	H	3.0 (2972)	80	57	38	136	54	10	14	18	100
1999	G	2.4 (2351)	⑤	②	⑥	87	98	14	④	18	100
	M	3.5 (3497)	80	54	38	134	54	16	22	18	100
	P	3.0 (2972)	80	69	37	134	55	16	33	18	100
2000-01	M	3.5 (3497)	80	54	38	134	54	16	22	18	100
	P	3.0 (2972)	80	69	37	134	55	16	33	18	100

* NOTE: Applies to Lower Manifold only.

① Step 1: 54 ft. lbs., then, loosen completely
  Step 2: 14.5 ft. lbs. plus 1/4 turn
  Step 3: Plus an additional 1/4 turn

② Step 1: 18 ft. lbs.
  Step 2: Plus 1/4 turn

③ Step 1: 14.5 ft. lbs.
  Step 2: Plus 1/4 turn

④ M8 fasteners: 22 ft. lbs.
  M10 fasteners: 36 ft. lbs.

⑤ Step 1: 58 ft. lbs., then, loosen completely
  Step 2: 14 ft. lbs. plus 1/4 turn
  Step 3: Plus an additional 1/4 turn

⑥ Step 1: 14 ft. lbs.
  Step 2: Plus 1/4 turn

93081CW7

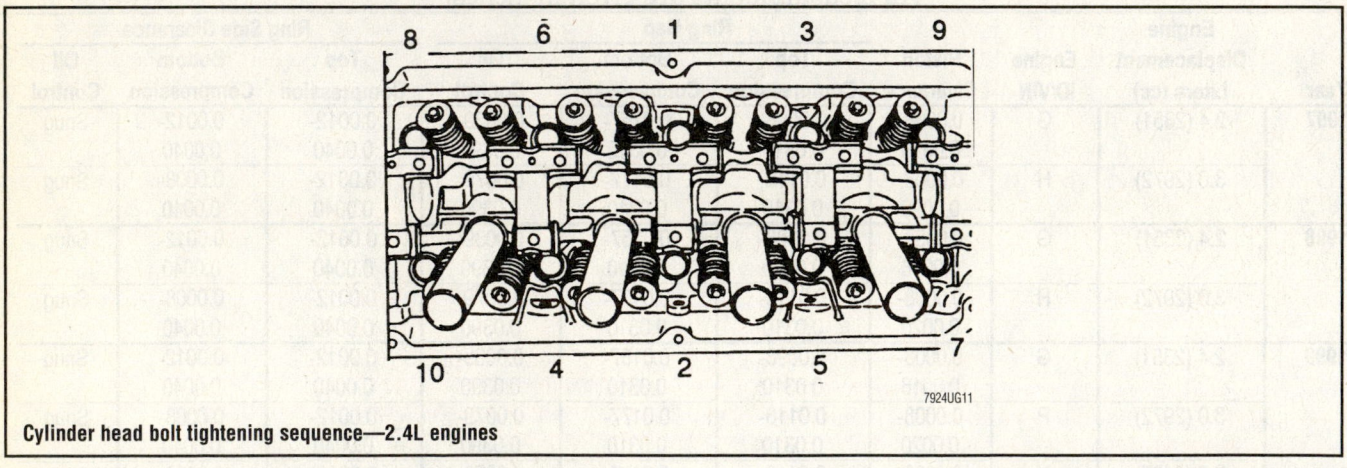

Cylinder head bolt tightening sequence—2.4L engines

7924UG11

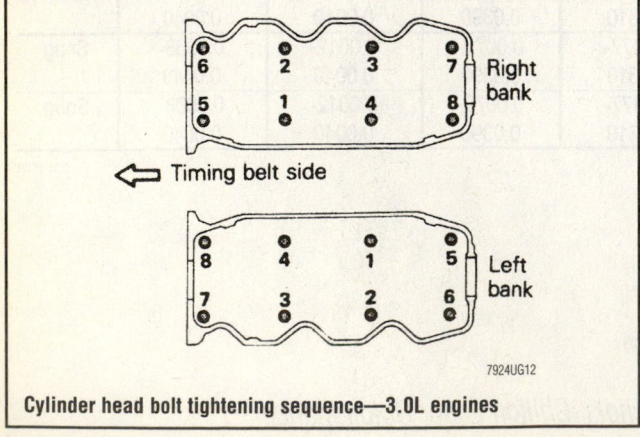

Right bank

Left bank

Timing belt side

Cylinder head bolt tightening sequence—3.0L engines

7924UG12

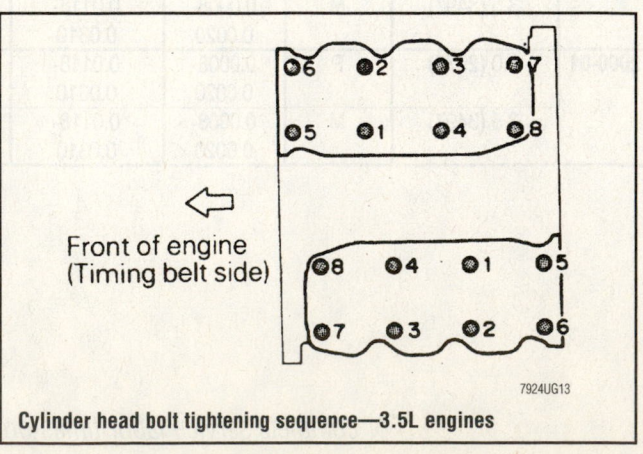

Front of engine (Timing belt side)

Cylinder head bolt tightening sequence—3.5L engines

7924UG13

BRAKE SPECIFICATIONS
MITSUBISHI MONTERO, MONTERO SPORT
All measurements in inches unless noted

Year	Model		Brake Disc Original Thickness	Brake Disc Minimum Thickness	Brake Disc Maximum Runout	Brake Drum Diameter Original Inside Diameter	Brake Drum Diameter Max. Wear Limit	Brake Drum Diameter Maximum Machine Diameter	Minimum Lining Thickness Front	Minimum Lining Thickness Rear	Brake Caliper Bracket Bolts (ft. lbs.)	Brake Caliper Mounting Bolts (ft. lbs.)
1997	Montero Sport	F	0.940	0.880	0.002	—	—	—	0.079	0.040	65	55
		R	0.700	0.650	0.003	10.63	10.71	10.71	—	0.080	94	32
1998	Montero Sport	F	0.940	0.880	0.002	—	—	—	0.079	0.040	65	55
		R	0.700	0.650	0.003	10.63	10.71	10.71	—	0.080	94	32
1999	Montero	F	1.060	1.000	0.002	—	—	—	0.079	—	65	54
		R	0.710	0.646	0.003	—	—	—	—	0.040	65	32
	Montero Sport	F	0.940	0.880	0.002	—	—	—	0.079		65	55
		R	0.700	0.650	0.003	10.63	10.71	10.71	—	0.080	94	32
2000-01	Montero	F	1.060	1.000	0.002	—	—	—	0.079	—	65	54
		R	0.710	0.646	0.003	—	—	—	—	0.040	65	32
	Montero Sport	F	0.940	0.880	0.002	—	—	—	0.079	—	65	55
		R	0.700	0.650	0.003	—	—	—	—	0.080	94	32

93081CW8

Timing chain and gear service is covered in the model specific sections of this manual

SCHEDULED MAINTENANCE INTERVALS
(MITSUBISHI MONTERO & MONTERO SPORT)

TO BE SERVICED	TYPE OF SERVICE	VEHICLE MILEAGE INTERVAL (x1000)												
		7.5	15	22.5	30	37.5	45	52.5	60	67.5	75	82.5	90	97.5
Engine oil & filter	R	✓	✓	✓	✓	✓	✓	✓	✓	✓	✓	✓	✓	✓
Automatic transmission & transfer oil	S/I		✓		✓		✓		✓		✓		✓	
Brake hoses	S/I		✓		✓		✓		✓		✓		✓	
Disc brake pads & rotors	S/I		✓		✓		✓		✓		✓		✓	
Drive shaft boots	S/I		✓		✓		✓		✓		✓		✓	
Air cleaner filter	R				✓				✓				✓	
Automatic transmission & transfer oil (4WD)	R				✓				✓				✓	
Engine coolant	R				✓				✓				✓	
Ball joints & steering linkage seals	S/I				✓				✓				✓	
Drive belt(s)	S/I				✓				✓				✓	
Drum brake linings & wheel cylinders	S/I				✓				✓				✓	
Exhaust system	S/I				✓				✓				✓	
Front & rear axle	S/I				✓				✓				✓	
Fuel hoses	S/I				✓				✓				✓	
Manual transmission & transfer oil (4WD)	S/I				✓				✓				✓	
Propeller shaft joint	S/I				✓				✓				✓	
Spark plugs (Montero)	R				✓				✓				✓	
Spark plugs (Montero Sport w/platinum tip)	R								✓					
Ignition cables	R								✓					
Timing belt	R								✓					
Distributor cap & rotor	S/I								✓					
EVAP system (except EVAP canister)	S/I								✓					

93081CW9

SCHEDULED MAINTENANCE INTERVALS
(MITSUBISHI MONTERO & MONTERO SPORT) (Cont.)

TO BE SERVICED	TYPE OF SERVICE	VEHICLE MILEAGE INTERVAL (x1000)												
		7.5	15	22.5	30	37.5	45	52.5	60	67.5	75	82.5	90	97.5
Fuel system (tank, pipe line connection & fuel tank filler tube cap)	S/I								✓					
EGR valve ①	S/I													
EVAP canister ①	S/I													
PCV system ②	S/I													

R: Replace   S/I: Service or Inspect

① Replace at 100,000 miles.

② PCV system (except EVAP canister): service or inspect at 100,000 miles.

FREQUENT OPERATION MAINTENANCE (SEVERE SERVICE)

If a vehicle is operated under any of the following conditions it is considered severe service:

- Extremely dusty areas.
- 50% or more of the vehicle operation is in 32°C (90°F) or higher temperatures, or constant operation in temperatures below 0°C (32°F).
- Prolonged idling (vehicle operation in stop and go traffic).
- Frequent short running periods (engine does not warm to normal operating temperatures).
- Police, taxi, delivery usage or trailer towing usage.

Oil & oil filter: replace every 3000 miles.

Front disc brake pads (dusty or salty conditions): service or inspect every 6000 miles.

Front disc brake pads: service or inspect every 7500 miles.

Air cleaner filter: service or inspect every 15,000 miles.

Rear drum brake linings & rear wheel cylinders: service or inspect every 15,000 miles.

Spark plugs (except platinum tip): replace every 15,000 miles.

PCV system: service or inspect every 60,000 miles.

93081CW0

Ignition system service is covered in the model specific sections of this manual

SCHEDULED MAINTENANCE INTERVALS
MITSUBISHI
MONTERO
MONTERO SPORT

The following should be used as a guide when determining the amount of work required for a particular service.
In estimating how long a particular Scheduled Maintenance Service should take, please observe the following:

- Labor Time is time based on field research and data supplied by the vehicle manufacturer.
- Labor time operations are given in hours and tenths of an hour.
- All labor operations are to be used as a guide.

Mechanic Skill Level Codes:
(A) PRECISION: Highly skilled with multiple certification.
(B) GENERAL: Normally skilled with certification.
(C) MAINTENANCE: Semi-skilled working on certification.

	LABOR TIME
7500 Mile Service (C)	
All Models	.4
15000 Mile Service (C)	
All Models	.7
w/AT add	.1
w/4WD add	.1
22500 Mile Service (C)	
All Models	.4
30000 Mile Service (B)	
All Models	2.2
Renew spark plugs (Montero)	
add	.6
w/4WD add	1.0
w/AT add	.2

	LABOR TIME
37500 Mile Service (C)	
All Models	.4
45000 Mile Service (C)	
All Models	.7
w/4WD add	.1
w/AT add	.1
52500 Mile Service (C)	
All Models	.4
60000 Mile Service (B)	
All Models	6.2
Renew spark plugs (Montero)	
add	.6
w/4WD add	.5
w/AT add	.6
67500 Mile Service (C)	
All Models	.4

	LABOR TIME
75000 Mile Service (C)	
All Models	.7
w/4WD add	.1
w/AT add	.1
82500 Mile Service (C)	
All Models	.4
90000 Mile Service (B)	
All Models	2.3
Renew spark plugs (Montero)	
add	.6
w/4WD add	.4
w/AT add	.6
97500 Mile Service (C)	
All Models	.4

93081CX1

TIRE, WHEEL AND BALL JOINT SPECIFICATIONS
Mitsubishi Truck

| Year | Model | OEM Tires | | Tire Pressures (psi) | | Wheel Size | Ball Joint Inspection |
		Standard	Optional	Front	Rear		
1997	Montero	P235/75SR15	P265/70HR15 31x10.5R15 LT	P-metric: 26 LT: 30	P235: 35 P265: 29 LT: 40	Std: 6-JJ Opt: 7-JJ	U: 7-30 in. ① L: 0.010 in.
	Montero Sport	P225/75R15	P265/70R15	26	26	Std: 6-JJ Opt: 7-JJ	U: 7-30 in. ① L: 0.010 in.
1998	Montero	P265/70HR15	None	26	26	7-JJ	U: 7-30 in. ① L: 0.010 in.
	Montero Sport	P225/75R15	P265/70R15	26	26	Std: 6-JJ Opt: 7-JJ	U: 7-30 in. ① L: 0.010 in.
1999	Montero	P265/70HR15	None	26	26	7-JJ	U: 7-30 in. ① L: 0.010 in.
	Montero Sport	P225/75R15	P265/70R15	26	26	Std: 6-JJ Opt: 7-JJ	U: 7-30 in. ① L: 0.010 in.
2000-01	Montero	P265/70HR15	None	26	26	7-JJ	U: 7-30 in. ① L: 0.010 in.
	Montero Sport	P225/75R15	P265/70R15	26	26	Std: 6-JJ Opt: 7-JJ	U: 7-30 in. ① L: 0.010 in.

OEM: Original Equipment Manufacturer

PSI: Pounds Per Square Inch

STD: Standard

OPT: Optional

① Torque required in inch lbs. to rotate ball joint when removed from the knuckle

93081CX2

NISSAN
Nissan Frontier • Pathfinder • Pickup • Quest • Xterra

ENGINE AND VEHICLE IDENTIFICATION

			Engine				
Code ①	Liters (cc)	Cu. In.	Cyl.	Fuel Sys.	Engine Type	Eng. Mfg.
KA24E	2.4 (2389)	146	4	MFI	SOHC	Nissan
KA24DE	2.4 (2389)	146	4	MFI	DOHC	Nissan
VG30E	3.0 (2960)	181	6	MFI	SOHC	Nissan
VG33E	3.3 (3277)	199	6	MFI	SOHC	Nissan

Model Year	
Code ②	Year
V	1997
W	1998
X	1999
Y	2000
1	2001

MFI: Multi-port Fuel Injection

SOHC: Single Overhead Camshaft

DOHC: Double Overhead Camshafts

① Located on the timing belt cover

② 10th digit of the Vehicle Identification Number (VIN)

93081CX3

GENERAL ENGINE SPECIFICATIONS

Year	Model	Engine Displacement Liters (cc)	Engine ID/VIN	Fuel System Type	Net Horsepower @ rpm	Net Torque @ rpm (ft. lbs.)	Bore x Stroke (in.)	Compression Ratio	Oil Pressure @ rpm
1997	Pathfinder	3.3 (3277)	VG33E	MFI	168@4800	196@2800	3.60X3.27	8.9:1	53@3200
	Pick-Up	2.4 (2389)	KA24E	MFI	134@5200	154@3600	3.50x3.78	8.6:1	60@3000
	Quest	3.0 (2960)	VG30E	MFI	151@4800	174@4400	3.43x3.27	9.0:1	53@3200
1998	Frontier	2.4 (2389)	KA24DE	MFI	143@5200	154@4000	3.50x3.78	9.2:1	60-70@3000
	Pathfinder	3.3 (3277)	VG33E	MFI	168@4800	196@2800	3.60X3.27	8.9:1	60-65@2000
	Quest	3.0 (2960)	VG30E	MFI	151@4800	174@4400	3.43x3.27	9.0:1	57-70@3200
1999	Frontier	2.4 (2389)	KA24DE	MFI	143@5200	154@4000	3.50x3.78	9.2:1	60-70@3000
	Frontier	3.3 (3277)	VG33E	MFI	170@4800	200@2800	3.60X3.27	8.9:1	60-65@2000
	Pathfinder	3.3 (3277)	VG33E	MFI	170@4800	200@2800	3.60X3.27	8.9:1	60-65@2000
	Quest	3.3 (3277)	VG33E	MFI	170@4800	200@2800	3.60X3.27	8.9:1	60-65@2000
2000-01	Frontier	2.4 (2389)	KA24DE	MFI	143@5200	154@4000	3.50x3.78	9.2:1	60-70@3000
	Frontier	3.3 (3277)	VG33E	MFI	170@4800	200@2800	3.60X3.27	8.9:1	60-65@2000
	Xterra	2.4 (2389)	KA24DE	MFI	143@5200	154@4000	3.50x3.78	9.2:1	60-70@3000
	Xterra	3.3 (3277)	VG33E	MFI	170@4800	200@2800	3.60X3.27	8.9:1	60-65@2000
	Pathfinder	3.3 (3277)	VG33E	MFI	170@4800	200@2800	3.60X3.27	8.9:1	60-65@2000
	Quest	3.3 (3277)	VG33E	MFI	170@4800	200@2800	3.60X3.27	8.9:1	60-65@2000

MFI: Multi-port Fuel Injection

93081CX4

ENGINE TUNE-UP SPECIFICATIONS

Year	Engine Displacement Liters (cc)	Engine ID/VIN	Spark Plug Gap (in.)	Ignition Timing (deg.)		Fuel Pump (psi) ①	Idle Speed (rpm)		Valve Clearance (in.)	
				MT	AT		MT	AT ②	In.	Ex.
1997	2.4 (2389)	KA24E	0.033	10B	10B	36	800	800	HYD	HYD
	3.0 (2960)	VG30E	③	15B	15B	34	700	700	HYD	HYD
	3.3 (3277)	VG33E	0.041	15B	15B	34	750	750	HYD	HYD
1998	2.4 (2389)	KA24DE	0.039-0.043	18-22B	18-22B	34	750-850	750-850	0.012-0.015	0.013-0.016
	3.0 (2960)	VG30E	0.031-0.035	—	13-17B	34	—	700-800	HYD	HYD
	3.3 (3277)	VG33E	0.039-0.043	13-17B	13-17B	34	700-800	700-800	HYD	HYD
1999	2.4 (2389)	KA24DE	0.039-0.043	18-22B	18-22B	34	750-850	750-850	0.012-0.015	0.013-0.016
	3.3 (3277)	VG33E	0.039-0.043	13-17B	13-17B	34	700-800	700-800	HYD	HYD
2000-01	2.4 (2389)	KA24DE	0.039-0.043	18-22B	18-22B	34	750-850	750-850	0.012-0.015	0.013-0.016
	3.3 (3277)	VG33E	0.039-0.043	13-17B	13-17B	34	700-800	700-800	HYD	HYD

NOTE: The Vehicle Emission Control Information label often reflects specification changes made during production. The label figures must be used if they differ from those in this chart.

B: Before top dead center

HYD: Hydraulic

① System pressure at idle with vacuum hose connected
   Should increase to 43 psi when disconnected

② Automatic transmission in Neutral

③ Quest: 0.033
   Pick-Up and Pathfinder: 0.041

93081CX5

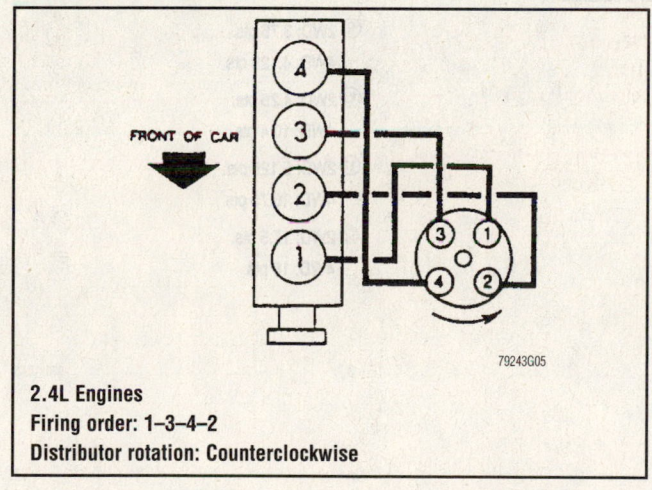

2.4L Engines
Firing order: 1–3–4–2
Distributor rotation: Counterclockwise

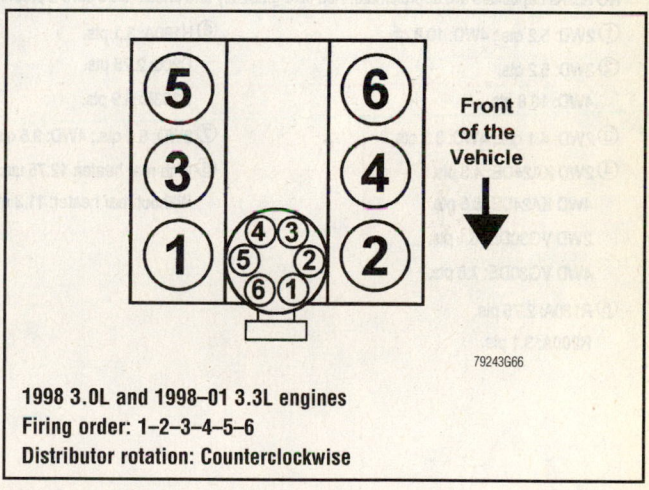

1998 3.0L and 1998–01 3.3L engines
Firing order: 1–2–3–4–5–6
Distributor rotation: Counterclockwise

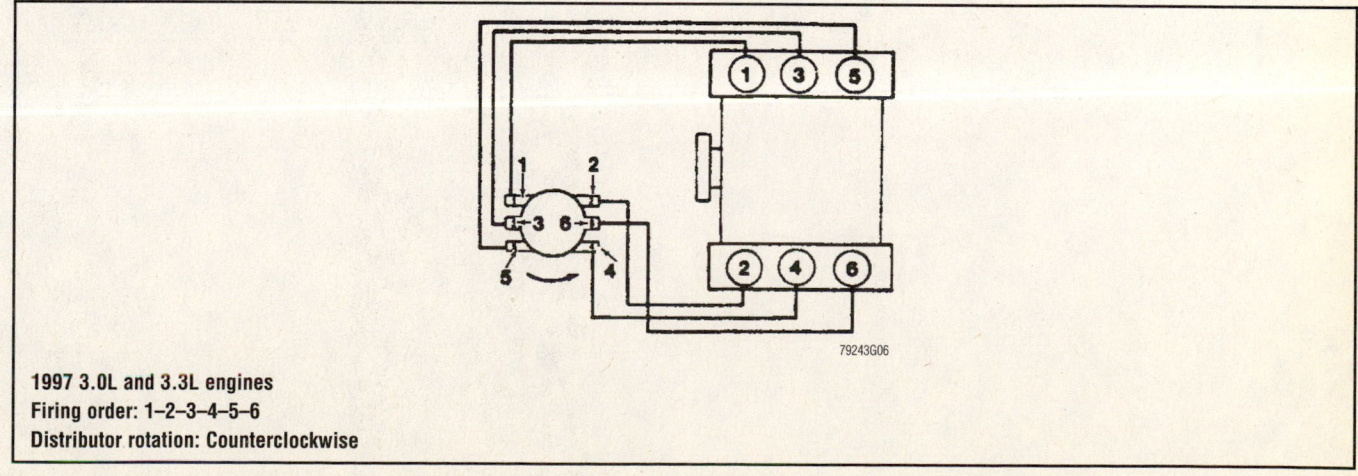

1997 3.0L and 3.3L engines
Firing order: 1–2–3–4–5–6
Distributor rotation: Counterclockwise

Refer to the model specific sections for engine mechanical service procedures

CAPACITIES

Year	Model	Engine Displacement Liters (cc)	Engine ID/VIN	Engine Oil with Filter (qts.)	Transmission (pts.) 5-Spd	Transmission (pts.) Auto.	Transfer Case (pts.)	Drive Axle Front (pts.)	Drive Axle Rear (pts.)	Fuel Tank (gal.)	Cooling System (qts.)
1997	Pathfinder	3.3 (3277)	VG33E	3.8	①	②	2.4	4.4	5.9	21.1	10
	Pick-up	2.4 (2389)	KA24E	③	④	—	—	⑤	⑥	15.9	⑦
	Quest	3.0 (2960)	VG30E	4.3	—	20.0	—	—	—	20.0	⑧
1998	Frontier	2.4 (2389)	KA24DE	⑨	⑩	16.8	4.8	2.8	⑥	15.9	⑦
	Pathfinder	3.3 (3277)	VG33E	3.8	⑪	⑫	4.8	4.4	4.9	21.1	11.25
	Quest	3.0 (2960)	VG30E	4.3	—	20	—	—	—	20.0	⑧
1999	Frontier	2.4 (2389)	KA24DE	⑨	⑩	16.8	4.8	2.8	⑥	15.9	⑦
	Frontier	3.3 (3277)	VG33E	⑨	⑩	16.8	4.8	2.8	⑥	19.4	⑦
	Pathfinder	3.3 (3277)	VG33E	3.8	⑩	⑫	4.8	4.4	4.9	21.1	11.25
	Quest	3.3 (3277)	VG33E	4.3	—	20	—	—	—	20.0	⑧
2000-01	Frontier	2.4 (2389)	KA24DE	⑨	⑩	16.8	4.8	2.8	⑥	15.9	⑦
	Frontier	3.3 (3277)	VG33E	⑨	⑬	16.8	4.8	2.8	⑥	19.4	⑦
	Xterra	2.4 (2389)	KA24DE	3.75	4.25	—	—	—	⑥	15.9	8.6
	Xterra	3.3 (3277)	VG33E	⑨	⑩	16.8	4.8	2.8	⑥	19.4	⑦
	Pathfinder	3.3 (3277)	VG33E	3.8	⑪	⑫	4.8	4.4	4.9	21.1	11.25
	Quest	3.3 (3277)	VG33E	4.3	—	20	—	—	—	20.0	⑧

NOTE: All capacities are approximate. Add fluid gradually and check to be sure a proper fluid level is obtained.

① 2WD: 5.2 qts.; 4WD: 10.8 qts.

② 2WD: 5.2 qts.
   4WD: 10.8 qts.

③ 2WD: 4.1 qts.; 4WD: 3.5 qts.

④ 2WD KA24DE: 4.3 pts.
   4WD KA24DE: 8.5 pts.
   2WD VG30DE: 5.1 pts.
   4WD VG30DE: 7.6 pts.

⑤ R180A: 2.75 pts.
   R200A: 3.1 pts.

⑥ H190A: 3.1 pts.
   C200: 2.75 pts.
   H233B: 5.9 pts.

⑦ 2WD: 8.6 qts.; 4WD: 9.5 qts.

⑧ With rear heater: 12.75 qts.
   Without rear heater: 11.3 qts.

⑨ 2WD: 3.75 qts.
   4WD: 4.125 qts.

⑩ 2WD: 4.25 pts.
   4WD: 10.4 pts.

⑪ 2WD: 5.125 pts.
   4WD: 10.75 pts.

⑫ 2WD: 17.5 pts.
   4WD: 18 pts.

93081CX6

VALVE SPECIFICATIONS

Year	Engine Displacement Liters (cc)	Engine ID/VIN	Seat Angle (deg.)	Face Angle (deg.)	Spring Test Pressure (lbs. @ in.)	Spring Installed Height (in.)	Stem-to-Guide Clearance (in.)		Stem Diameter (in.)	
							Intake	Exhaust	Intake	Exhaust
1997	2.4 (2389)	KA24E	45	45.5	①	NA	0.0008-0.0021	0.0016-0.0029	0.2742-0.2748	0.3129-0.3134
	3.0 (2960)	VG30E	45	45.25-45.75	②	NA	0.0008-0.0021	0.0016-0.0029	0.2742-0.2748	0.3136-0.3138
	3.3 (3277)	VG33E	45	45.25-46.75	②	NA	0.0008-0.0021	0.0016-0.0029	0.2742-0.2748	0.3136-0.3138
1998	2.4 (2389)	KA24DE	45	45.5	93.9@1.15	NA	0.0008-0.0021	0.0016-0.0029	0.2742-0.2748	0.2734-0.2740
	3.0 (2960)	VG30E	45	45.25-45.75	②	NA	0.0008-0.0021	0.0016-0.0029	0.2742-0.2748	0.3136-0.3138
	3.3 (3277)	VG33E	45	45.25-46.75	②	NA	0.0008-0.0021	0.0016-0.0029	0.2742-0.2748	0.3135-0.3138
1999	2.4 (2389)	KA24DE	45	45.5	93.9@1.15	NA	0.0008-0.0021	0.0016-0.0029	0.2742-0.2748	0.2734-0.2740
	3.3 (3277)	VG33E	45	45.25-46.75	②	NA	0.0008-0.0021	0.0016-0.0029	0.2742-0.2748	0.3135-0.3138
2000-01	2.4 (2389)	KA24DE	45	45.5	93.9@1.15	NA	0.0008-0.0021	0.0016-0.0029	0.2742-0.2748	0.2734-0.2740
	3.3 (3277)	VG33E	45	45.25-46.75	②	NA	0.0008-0.0021	0.0016-0.0029	0.2742-0.2748	0.3135-0.3138

NA: Not Available

① Intake:
   Inner: 63.9 @ 1.28
   Outer: 135.2 @ 1.48
  Exhaust:
   Inner: 74 @ 1.15
   Outer: 144 @ 1.34

② Inner: 57.3 @ 0.984
  Outer: 117.7 @ 1.181

93081CX7

Refer to the model specific sections for fuel system service procedures

CRANKSHAFT AND CONNECTING ROD SPECIFICATIONS
All measurements are given in inches.

Year	Engine Displacement Liters (cc)	Engine ID/VIN	Crankshaft				Connecting Rod		
			Main Brg. Journal Dia.	Main Brg. Oil Clearance	Shaft End-play	Thrust on No.	Journal Diameter	Oil Clearance	Side Clearance
1997	2.4 (2389)	KA24E	2.3609-2.3612	0.0008-0.0019	0.0020-0.0071	3	1.9672-1.9675	0.0004-0.0014	0.0080-0.0160
	3.0 (2960)	VG30E	2.4790-2.4793	0.0011-0.0022	0.0020-0.0067	4	1.9967-1.9675	0.0006-0.0021	0.0079-0.0138
	3.3 (3277)	VG33E	2.4790-2.4793	0.0011-0.0022	0.0020-0.0067	4	1.9967-1.9675	0.0006-0.0021	0.0079-0.0138
1998	2.4 (2389)	KA24DE	2.3609-2.3612	0.0008-0.0019	0.0020-0.0071	3	1.9672-1.9675	0.0004-0.0014	0.0080-0.0160
	3.0 (2960)	VG30E	2.4790-2.4793	0.0011-0.0022	0.0020-0.0067	4	1.9967-1.9675	0.0006-0.0021	0.0079-0.0138
	3.3 (3277)	VG33E	2.4790-2.4793	0.0011-0.0022	0.0020-0.0067	4	1.9967-1.9675	0.0006-0.0021	0.0079-0.0138
1999	2.4 (2389)	KA24DE	2.3609-2.3612	0.0008-0.0019	0.0020-0.0071	3	1.9672-1.9675	0.0004-0.0014	0.0080-0.0160
	3.3 (3277)	VG33E	2.4790-2.4793	0.0011-0.0022	0.0020-0.0067	4	1.9967-1.9675	0.0006-0.0021	0.0079-0.0138
2000-01	2.4 (2389)	KA24DE	2.3609-2.3612	0.0008-0.0019	0.0020-0.0071	3	1.9672-1.9675	0.0004-0.0014	0.0080-0.0160
	3.3 (3277)	VG33E	2.4790-2.4793	0.0011-0.0022	0.0020-0.0067	4	1.9967-1.9675	0.0006-0.0021	0.0079-0.0138

93081CX8

PISTON AND RING SPECIFICATIONS
All measurements are given in inches.

Year	Engine Displacement Liters (cc)	Engine ID/VIN	Piston Clearance	Ring Gap			Ring Side Clearance		
				Top Compression	Bottom Compression	Oil Control	Top Compression	Bottom Compression	Oil Control
1997	2.4 (2389)	KA24E	0.0008-0.0016	0.011-0.021	0.018-0.027	0.008-0.027	0.0016-0.0031	0.0012-0.0028	0.0026-0.0053
	3.0 (2960)	VG30E	0.0010-0.0018	0.008-0.017	0.007-0.017	0.008-0.030	0.0016-0.0031	0.0012-0.0025	0.0005-0.0075
	3.3 (3277)	VG33E	①	0.0083-0.0157	0.0197-0.0272	0.0079-0.0272	0.0009-0.0030	0.0012-0.0028	0.0006-0.0073
1998	2.4 (2389)	KA24E	0.0008-0.0016	0.011-0.021	0.018-0.027	0.008-0.027	0.0016-0.0031	0.0012-0.0028	0.0026-0.0053
	3.0 (2960)	VG30E	0.0010-0.0018	0.008-0.017	0.007-0.017	0.008-0.030	0.0016-0.0031	0.0012-0.0025	0.0005-0.0075
	3.3 (3277)	VG33E	①	0.0083-0.0157	0.0197-0.0272	0.0079-0.0272	0.0009-0.0030	0.0012-0.0028	0.0006-0.0073
1999	2.4 (2389)	KA24E	0.0008-0.0016	0.011-0.021	0.018-0.027	0.008-0.027	0.0016-0.0031	0.0012-0.0028	0.0026-0.0053
	3.3 (3277)	VG33E	①	0.0083-0.0157	0.0197-0.0272	0.0079-0.0272	0.0009-0.0030	0.0012-0.0028	0.0006-0.0073
2000-01	2.4 (2389)	KA24E	0.0008-0.0016	0.011-0.021	0.018-0.027	0.008-0.027	0.0016-0.0031	0.0012-0.0028	0.0026-0.0053
	3.3 (3277)	VG33E	①	0.0083-0.0157	0.0197-0.0272	0.0079-0.0272	0.0009-0.0030	0.0012-0.0028	0.0006-0.0073

① Except cylinders 3 and 4: 0.0010 - 0.0018 in.
  Cylinders 3 and 4: 0.0006 - 0.0010 in.

93081CX9

TORQUE SPECIFICATIONS
All readings in ft. lbs.

Year	Engine Displacement Liters (cc)	Engine ID/VIN	Cylinder Head Bolts	Main Bearing Bolts	Rod Bearing Bolts	Crankshaft Damper Bolts	Flywheel Bolts	Manifold Intake	Manifold Exhaust	Spark Plugs	Lug Nuts
1997	2.4 (2389)	KA24E	①	34-38	②	87-116	③	12-14	12-14	18	④
	3.0 (2960)	VG30E	⑤	67-74	②	90-98	72-80	⑥	15	18	80
	3.3 (3277)	VG33E	⑤	67-74	②	141-156	61-69	⑦	21-25	18	87-108
1998	2.4 (2389)	KA24DE	①	34-41	②	105-112	105-112	12-14	27-35	14-22	87-108
	3.0 (2960)	VG30E	⑤	67-74	②	141-156	61-69	⑥	13-16	14-22	72-87
	3.3 (3277)	VG33E	⑧	67-74	②	141-156	61-69	⑨	21-25	14-22	87-108
1999	2.4 (2389)	KA24DE	①	34-41	②	105-112	105-112	12-14	27-35	14-22	87-108
	3.3 (3277)	VG33E	⑧	67-74	②	141-156	61-69	⑥	21-25	14-22	87-108
2000-01	2.4 (2389)	KA24DE	①	34-41	②	105-112	105-112	12-14	27-35	14-22	87-108
	3.3 (3277)	VG33E	⑧	67-74	②	141-156	61-69	⑨	21-25	14-22	87-108

① Step 1: 22 ft. lbs.
  Step 2: 59 ft. lbs.
  Step 3: Loosen completely then retorque to 22 ft. lbs.
  Step 4: 18-25 ft. lbs.
  Step 5: Plus 86-91 degrees

② 10-12 ft. lbs. plus 60-65 degrees or 28-33 ft. lbs.

③ Manual transmission: 105-112 ft. lbs.
  Automatic transmission: 69-76 ft. lbs.

④ Pick-up with single wheels: 87-108 ft. lbs.
  Pick-up with dual wheels: 166-203 ft. lbs.

⑤ Step 1: 22 ft. lbs.
  Step 2: 43 ft. lbs.
  Step 3: Loosen completely then retorque to 22 ft. lbs.
  Step 4: 40-47 ft. lbs. or an additional 60-65 degrees

⑥ Step 1: Tighten nuts and bolts to 3 ft. lbs.
  Step 2: Tighten bolts to 12-14 ft. lbs.; nuts to 17-20 ft. lbs.
  Step 3: Repeat Step 2

⑦ Step 1: All bolts to 26-43 inch lbs.
  Step 2: All nuts to 26-43 inch lbs
  Step 3: All bolts to 13-16 ft. lbs.
  Step 4: All nuts to 13-16 ft. lbs.

⑧ The cylinder heads and the lower intake manifold are installed together
  Step 1: Tighten the cylinder head bolts to 22 ft. lbs.
  Step 2: Tighten the cylinder head bolts to 43 ft. lbs.
  Step 3: Loosen the cylinder head bolts completely
  Step 4: Tighten the cylinder head bolts to 84 inch lbs.
  Step 5: Tighten the intake manifold fasteners to 35 inch lbs.
  Step 6: Tighten the intake manifold fasteners to 13 ft. lbs.
  Step 7: Tighten the intake manifold fasteners to 12-14 ft. lbs.
  Step 8: Loosen all intake manifold fasteners completely
  Step 9: Tighten the cylinder head bolts to 22 ft. lbs.
  Step 10: Tighten the cylinder head bolts 60-65 degrees
  Step 11: Tighten the cylinder head sub-bolts to 80-105 inch lbs.
  Step 12: Tighten the intake manifold fasteners to 35 inch lbs.
  Step 13: Tighten the intake manifold fasteners to 78 inch lbs.
  Step 14: Tighten the intake manifold fasteners to 70-84 inch lbs.

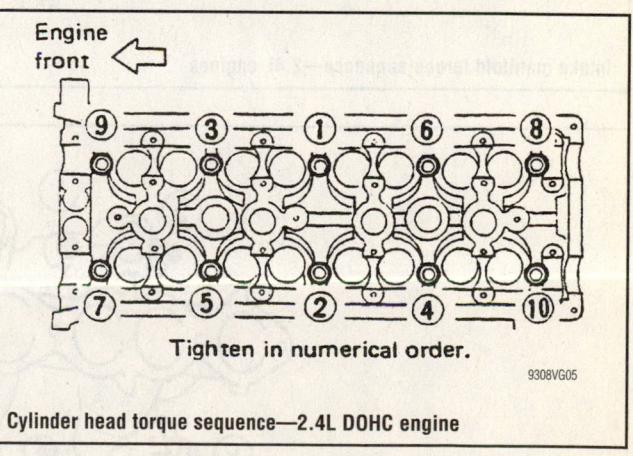

Cylinder head torque sequence—2.4L SOHC engine

7924VG23

Engine front ←

Tighten in numerical order.

Cylinder head torque sequence—2.4L DOHC engine

9308VG05

93081CX0

Refer to the model specific sections for engine electrical system service procedures

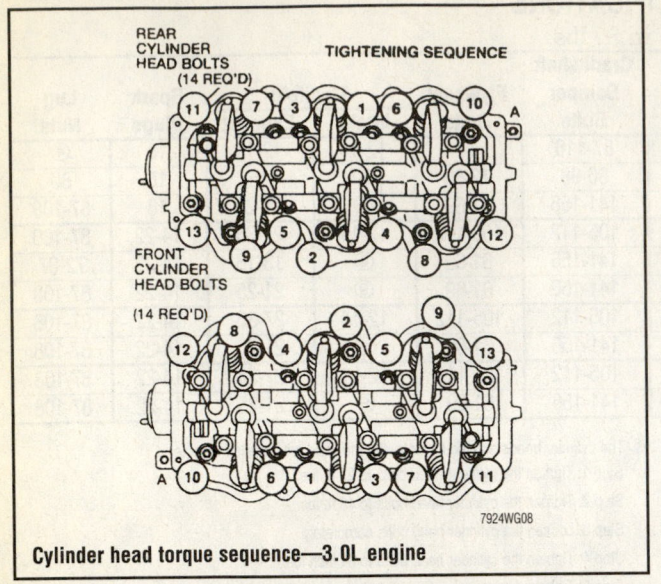

Cylinder head torque sequence—3.0L engine

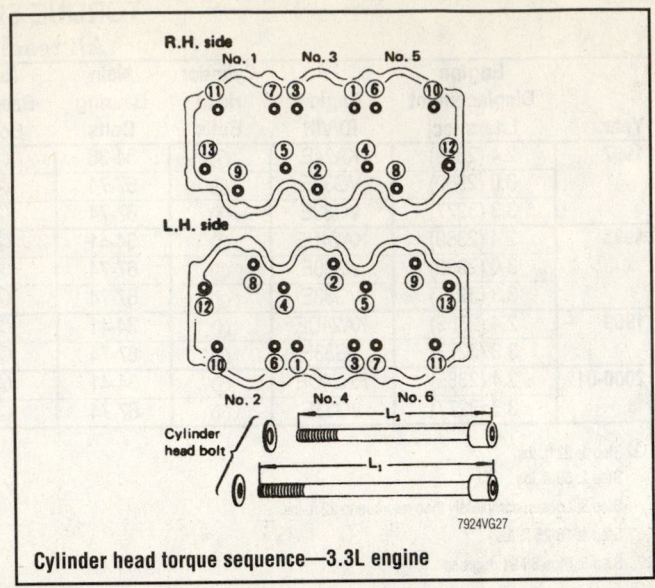

Cylinder head torque sequence—3.3L engine

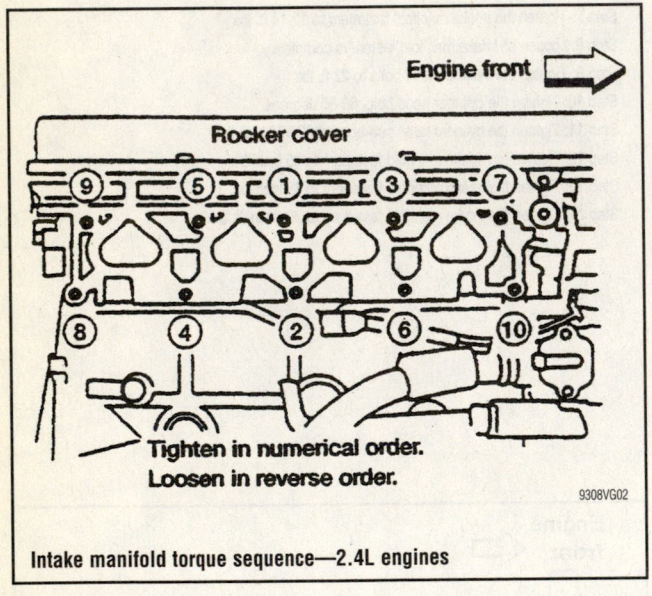

Intake manifold torque sequence—2.4L engines

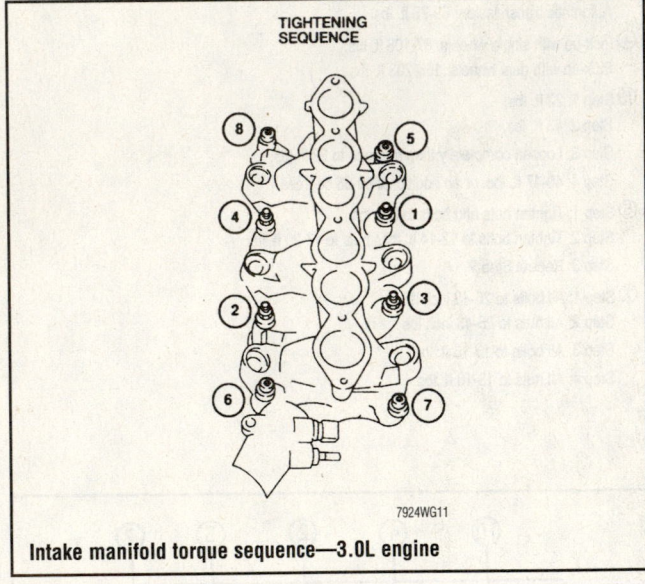

Intake manifold torque sequence—3.0L engine

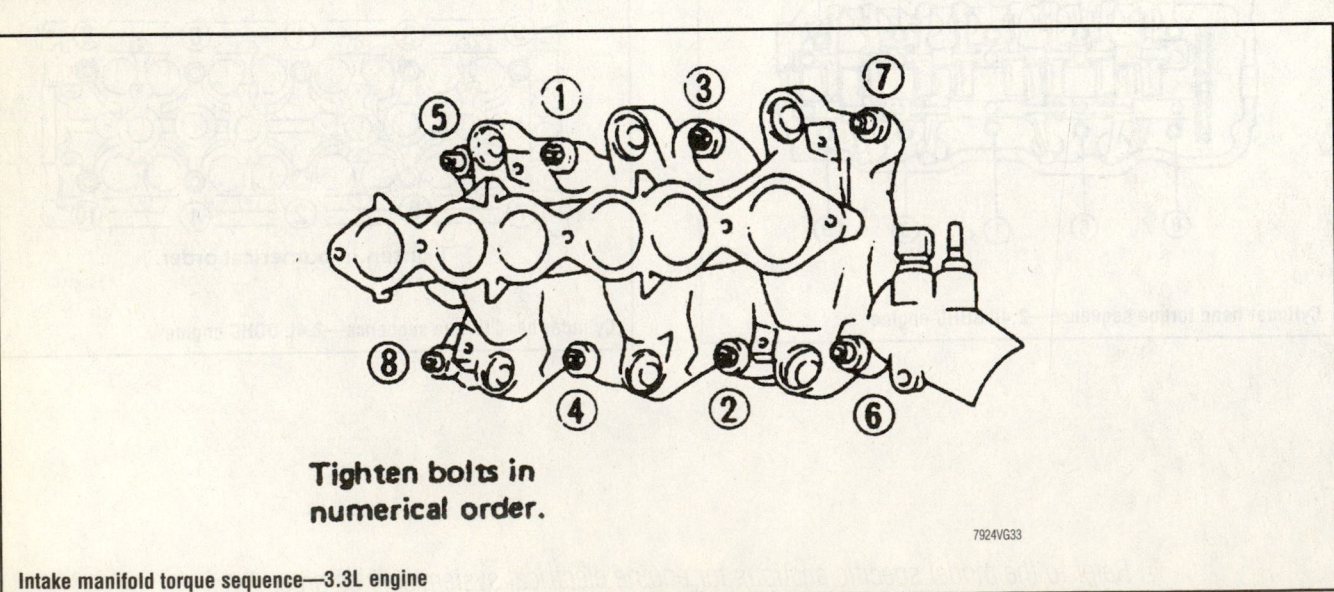

Intake manifold torque sequence—3.3L engine

BRAKE SPECIFICATIONS
NISSAN FRONTIER, PATHFINDER, PICK-UP, QUEST, XTERRA
All measurements in inches unless noted

| Year | Model | Brake Disc | | | Brake Drum Diameter | | | Minimum Lining Thickness | | Brake Caliper | |
		Original Thickness	Minimum Thickness	Maximum Runout	Original Inside Diameter	Max. Wear Limit	Maximum Machine Diameter	Front	Rear	Bracket Bolts (ft. lbs.)	Mounting Bolts (ft. lbs.)
1997	Pathfinder	1.100	1.024	0.003	11.60	NA	11.67	0.079	0.059	53-72	24-31
	Pick-up	①	②	0.003	③	NA	④	0.079	0.059	53-72	16-23
	Quest	1.020	0.945	0.003	9.80	NA	9.90	0.079	0.079	—	12-14
1998	Frontier	①	②	0.003	③	NA	④	0.079	0.059	53-72	24-31
	Pathfinder	1.100	1.024	0.004	11.60	NA	11.67	0.079	0.059	53-72	16-23
	Quest	1.020	0.945	0.003	9.80	NA	9.90	0.079	0.079	—	12-14
1999	Frontier	①	②	0.003	③	NA	④	0.079	0.059	53-72	24-31
	Pathfinder	1.100	1.024	0.004	11.60	NA	11.67	0.079	0.059	53-72	16-23
	Quest	1.020	0.945	0.003	9.80	NA	9.90	0.079	0.079	—	12-14
2000-01	Frontier	①	②	0.003	③	NA	④	0.079	0.059	53-72	24-31
	Xterra	①	②	0.003	③	NA	④	0.079	0.059	53-72	24-31
	Pathfinder	1.100	1.024	0.004	11.60	NA	11.67	0.079	0.059	53-72	16-23
	Quest	1.020	0.945	0.003	9.80	NA	9.90	0.079	0.079	—	12-14

NA: Not Available

① 2WD: 0.870
   4WD: 1.020

② 2WD: 0.787
   4WD: 0.945

③ 2WD: 10.20
   4WD: 11.60

④ 2WD: 10.30
   4WD: 11.67

93081CY1

For accessory drive belt replacement procedures see the model specific sections of this manual

SCHEDULED MAINTENANCE INTERVALS
(NISSAN FRONTIER, PATHFINDER, PICK-UP, QUEST & XTERRA)

TO BE SERVICED	TYPE OF SERVICE	VEHICLE MILEAGE INTERVAL (x1000)												
		7.5	15	22.5	30	37.5	45	52.5	60	67.5	75	82.5	90	97.5
Engine oil & filter	R	✓	✓	✓	✓	✓	✓	✓	✓	✓	✓	✓	✓	✓
Brake lines & cables	S/I		✓		✓		✓		✓		✓		✓	
Brake pads, discs, drums & linings	S/I		✓		✓		✓		✓		✓		✓	
Driveshaft boots (Quest)	S/I		✓		✓		✓		✓		✓		✓	
Driveshaft boots & propeller shaft (1997 4x4 Pathfinder & Pick-Up)	S/I		✓		✓		✓		✓		✓		✓	
Driveshaft boots & propeller shaft (1998-01 4x4 Pathfinder & Frontier)	S/I				✓				✓				✓	
Front wheel bearings (4x2 Pathfinder & Pick-Up)	S/I				✓				✓				✓	
Automatic transaxle oil (Quest)	S/I		✓		✓		✓		✓		✓		✓	
Automatic & manual transmission, transfer & differential gear oil (Pathfinder & Pick-Up) ①	S/I		✓		✓		✓		✓		✓		✓	
Front wheel bearings (1997 4x4 Pathfinder)	S/I		✓		✓		✓		✓		✓		✓	
Front wheel bearings (1998-01 4x4 Pathfinder)	S/I				✓				✓				✓	
Propeller shaft (1997 Pathfinder)	S/I		✓		✓		✓		✓		✓		✓	
Propeller shaft (1998-01 Pathfinder)	S/I	✓		✓		✓		✓		✓		✓		✓
Air cleaner filter	R				✓				✓				✓	
Engine coolant (Quest)	R				✓				✓				✓	
Engine coolant (Pathfinder & Pick-Up)	R				✓				✓				✓	
PCV filter (Pathfinder & Pick-Up KA24E)	R				✓				✓				✓	
Spark plugs	R				✓				✓				✓	
Drive belt(s) (Pathfinder & Pick-Up)	S/I				✓				✓				✓	
Exhaust system	S/I				✓				✓				✓	

93081CY2

SCHEDULED MAINTENANCE INTERVALS
(NISSAN FRONTIER, PATHFINDER, PICK-UP, QUEST & XTERRA) (Cont.)

TO BE SERVICED	TYPE OF SERVICE	VEHICLE MILEAGE INTERVAL (x1000)												
		7.5	15	22.5	30	37.5	45	52.5	60	67.5	75	82.5	90	97.5
Drive belt(s) (Quest)	S/I								✓		✓		✓	
Fuel lines	S/I				✓				✓				✓	
Steering gear (box) & linkage, (steering dumper-4x4), axle & suspension parts (Pathfinder & Pick-Up)	S/I				✓				✓				✓	
Steering gear linkage, axle & suspension parts (Quest)	S/I				✓				✓				✓	
Vapor lines	S/I				✓				✓				✓	
Steering linkage ball joints & front suspension ball joints (Pathfinder & Pick-Up)	S/I								✓					
Timing belt ②	R													

R: Replace   S/I: Service or Inspect

① Differential (w/limited-slip differential) oil: replace oil every 30,000 miles.

② Timing belt: replace at 105,000 miles.

FREQUENT OPERATION MAINTENANCE (SEVERE SERVICE)

If a vehicle is operated under any of the following conditions it is considered severe service:

- Extremely dusty areas.
- 50% or more of the vehicle operation is in 32°C (90°F) or higher temperatures, or constant operation in temperatures below 0°C (32°F).
- Prolonged idling (vehicle operation in stop and go traffic).
- Frequent short running periods (engine does not warm to normal operating temperatures).
- Police, taxi, delivery usage or trailer towing usage.

Oil & oil filter: replace every 3750 miles.

Brake pads, discs, drums & linings: service or inspect every 7500 miles.

Driveshaft boots (Quest): service or inspect every 7500 miles.

Driveshaft boots & propeller shaft (Pathfinder): service or inspect every 7500 miles.

Exhaust system: service or inspect every 7500 miles.

Propeller shaft (Pathfinder): service or inspect every 7500 miles. (If immersed in water, grease daily.)

Steering gear (box) & linkage, (steering damper-4x4), axle & suspension parts (Pathfinder): service or inspect every 7500 miles.

Steering gear linkage, axle & suspension parts (Quest): service or inspect every 7500 miles.

Steering linkage ball joints & front suspension ball joints: service or inspect every 7500 miles.

93081CY3

For brake related suspension and axle service, refer to the model specific sections of this manual

SCHEDULED MAINTENANCE INTERVALS
NISSAN
FRONTIER, PATHFINDER, PICK-UP, QUEST, XTERRA

The following should be used as a guide when determining the amount of work required for a particular service. In estimating how long a particular Scheduled Maintenance Service should take, please observe the following:

- Labor Time is time based on field research and data supplied by the vehicle manufacturer.
- Labor time operations are given in hours and tenths of an hour.
- All labor operations are to be used as a guide.

Mechanic Skill Level Codes:
(A) PRECISION: Highly skilled with multiple certification.
(B) GENERAL: Normally skilled with certification.
(C) MAINTENANCE: Semi-skilled working on certification.

	LABOR TIME
7500 Mile Service (C)	
All Models	.6
15000 Mile Service (C)	
Pick-up, Pathfinder	
Frontier, Xterra	1.0
Quest	1.0
w/4WD add	.3
22500 Mile Service (C)	
All Models	.5
30000 Mile Service (B)	
Pick-up, Pathfinder	
Frontier, Xterra	3.0
Quest	3.2
w/4WD add	.5
w/KA24E engine add	.2

	LABOR TIME
37500 Mile Service (C)	
All Models	.6
45000 Mile Service (C)	
Pick-up, Pathfinder	
Frontier, Xterra	1.0
Quest	1.0
w/4WD add	.3
52500 Mile Service (C)	
All Models	.6
60000 Mile Service (B)	
Pick-up, Pathfinder	
Frontier, Xterra	3.8
Quest	3.3
w/4WD add	.5
w/KA24E engine add	.2
67500 Mile Service (C)	
All Models	.6

	LABOR TIME
75000 Mile Service (C)	
Pick-up, Pathfinder	
Frontier, Xterra	1.0
Quest	1.1
w/4WD add	.3
82500 Mile Service (C)	
All Models	.5
90000 Mile Service (B)	
Pick-up, Pathfinder	
Frontier, Xterra	3.8
Quest	3.3
w/4WD add	.5
97500 Mile Service (C)	
All Models	.6

93081CY4

TIRE, WHEEL AND BALL JOINT SPECIFICATIONS
Nissan Truck

Year	Model	OEM Tires		Tire Pressures (psi)		Wheel Size	Ball Joint Inspection
		Standard	Optional	Front	Rear		
1997	Pickup 2wd	P195/75R14	P215/70R14	30	30	Std: 5-J Opt: 6-JJ	U: 0.021 in. L: 0.018 in.
	Pickup 4wd	P235/75R15	None	30	30	7-JJ	U: 0.021 in. L: 0.018 in.
	Pathfinder 2wd	P235/75R15	None	30	30	6.5-JJ	U: 0.021 in. L: 0.018 in.
	Pathfinder 4wd	P235/75R15	P265/70R15	30	30	7-JJ	U: 0.021 in. L: 0.018 in.
1998	Frontier 2wd	P195/75R14	P215/65R15	30	30	Std: 5-J Opt: 6-JJ	U: 0.020 in. L: ①
	Frontier 4wd	P215/75R15	P235/70R15	30	30	7-JJ	U: 0.020 in. L: ①
	Pathfinder 2wd	P235/75R15	None	30	30	6.5-JJ	U: 0.020 in. L: ①
	Pathfinder 4wd	P235/75R15	P265/70R15	30	30	7-JJ	U: 0.020 in. L: ①
1999	Frontier 2wd	P195/75R14	P215/65R15	30	30	Std: 5-J Opt: 6-JJ	U: 0.020 in. L: ①
	Frontier 4wd	P215/75R15	P235/70R15	30	30	7-JJ	U: 0.020 in. L: ①
	Pathfinder	P235/70R15	P265/70R15	30	30	Std: 6.5-JJ Opt: 7-JJ	U: 0.020 in. L: ①
2000-01	Frontier 2wd	P195/75R14	P215/65R15	30	30	Std: 5-J Opt: 6-JJ	U: 0.020 in. L: ①
	Frontier 4wd	P215/75R15	P235/70R15	30	30	7-JJ	U: 0.020 in. L: ①
	Pathfinder	P235/70R15	P265/70R15	30	30	Std: 6.5-JJ Opt: 7-JJ	U: 0.020 in. L: ①

OEM: Original Equipment Manufacturer

PSI: Pounds Per Square Inch

STD: Standard

OPT: Optional

L: Lower

U: Upper

① Replace if any measurable movement is found.

93081CY5

Refer to the model specific sections for driveline service procedures

SUBARU
Forester

ENGINE AND VEHICLE IDENTIFICATION CHART

			Engine Code						Model Year	
Code ①	Liters (cc)	Cu. In.	Cyl.	Fuel Sys.	Type	Eng. Mfg.		Code ②		Year
6	2.5 (2457)	150	4	MFI	DOHC	Subaru		W		1998
								X		1999
								Y		2000
								1		2001

MFI: Multiport Fuel Injection

DOHC: Double Overhead Camshafts

① 6th digit of the VIN.

② 10th digit of the VIN.

93081CY6

GENERAL ENGINE SPECIFICATIONS

Year	Model	Engine Displacement Liters (cc)	Engine ID/VIN	Fuel System Type	Net Horsepower @ rpm	Net Torque @ rpm (ft. lbs.)	Bore x Stroke (in.)	Compression Ratio	Oil Pressure @ rpm
1998	Forester	2.5 (2457)	6	MFI	165@5600	162@4000	3.92x3.11	9.7:1	14 psi @ 800
1999	Forester	2.5 (2457)	6	MFI	165@5600	162@4000	3.92x3.11	9.7:1	14 psi @ 800
2000-01	Forester	2.5 (2457)	6	MFI	165@5600	162@4000	3.92x3.11	9.7:1	14 psi @ 800

MFI: Multi-port Fuel Injection

93081CY7

ENGINE TUNE-UP SPECIFICATIONS

Year	Engine Displacement Liters (cc)	Engine ID/VIN	Spark Plugs Gap (in.)	Ignition Timing (deg.) ①		Fuel Pump (psi)	Idle Speed (rpm) ②		Valve Clearance ③	
				MT	AT		MT	AT	In.	Ex.
1998	2.5 (2457)	6	0.039-0.043	7-23 BTDC	7-23 BTDC	34-38	600-800	600-800	0.0071-0.0087	0.0090-0.0106
1999	2.5 (2457)	6	0.039-0.043	7-23 BTDC	7-23 BTDC	34-38	600-800	600-800	0.0071-0.0087	0.0090-0.0106
2000-01	2.5 (2457)	6	0.039-0.043	7-23 BTDC	7-23 BTDC	34-38	600-800	600-800	0.0071-0.0087	0.0090-0.0106

BTDC: Before Top Dead Center
① At idle speed.
② With engine under no load.
③ With engine cold.

93081CY8

2.5L engine
Firing order: 1–3–2–4
Distributorless ignition system

79243GA1

CAPACITIES

Year	Model	Engine Displacement Liters (cc)	Engine ID/VIN	Engine Oil with Filter (qts.)	Transmission (pts.)			Transfer Case (pts.)	Drive Axle		Fuel Tank (gal.)	Cooling System (qts.)
					4-Spd	5-Spd	Auto.		Front (pts.)	Rear (pts.)		
1998	Forester	2.5 (2457)	6	4.7	—	7.4	20	—	2.6 ①	1.6	15.9	6.3
1999	Forester	2.5 (2457)	6	4.7	—	7.4	20	—	2.6 ①	1.6	15.9	6.3
2000-01	Forester	2.5 (2457)	6	4.7	—	7.4	20	—	2.6 ①	1.6	15.9	6.3

① A/T differential only.

93081CY9

For exhaust manifold replacement procedures, see the model specific sections of this manual

VALVE SPECIFICATIONS

Year	Engine Displacement Liters (cc)	Engine ID/VIN	Seat Angle (deg.)	Face Angle (deg.)	Spring Test Pressure (lbs. @ in.)	Spring Installed Height (in.)	Stem-to-Guide Clearance (in.)		Stem Diameter (in.)	
							Intake	Exhaust	Intake	Exhaust
1998	2.5 (2457)	6	①	①	33-38@ 1.654 ②	③	0.0014-③ 0.0024	0.0016-④ 0.0026	0.2343-0.2348	0.2343-0.2348
1999	2.5 (2457)	6	①	①	33-38@ 1.654 ②	③	0.0014-③ 0.0024	0.0016-④ 0.0026	0.2343-0.2348	0.2343-0.2348
2000-01	2.5 (2457)	6	①	①	33-38@ 1.654 ②	③	0.0014-③ 0.0024	0.0016-④ 0.0026	0.2343-0.2348	0.2343-0.2348

① Refacing angle: 90 degrees
② 102-118 lbs. @ 1.315 in.
③ Free length: 1.8913 in.
④ Wear limit: 0.0059 in.

93081CY0

CRANKSHAFT AND CONNECTING ROD SPECIFICATIONS
All measurements are given in inches.

Year	Engine Displacement Liters (cc)	Engine ID/VIN	Crankshaft				Connecting Rod		
			Main Brg. Journal Dia.	Main Brg. Oil Clearance	Shaft End-play	Thrust on No.	Journal Diameter	Oil Clearance	Side Clearance
1998	2.5 (2457)	6	2.3619-2.3625	①	0.0012-0.0098	3	1.8891-1.8898	0.0004-0.0020	0.0028-0.0160
1999	2.5 (2457)	6	2.3619-2.3625	①	0.0012-0.0098	3	1.8891-1.8898	0.0004-0.0020	0.0028-0.0160
2000-01	2.5 (2457)	6	2.3619-2.3625	①	0.0012-0.0098	3	1.8891-1.8898	0.0004-0.0020	0.0028-0.0160

① Journals 1 and 5: 0.0001-0.0016
Journals 2 and 4: 0.0004-0.0018
Journal 3: 0.0004-0.0016

93081CZ1

PISTON AND RING SPECIFICATIONS
All measurements are given in inches.

Year	Engine Displacement Liters (cc)	Engine ID/VIN	Piston Clearance	Ring Gap			Ring Side Clearance		
				Top Compression	Bottom Compression	Oil Control	Top Compression	Bottom Compression	Oil Control
1998	2.5 (2457)	6	0.0004-0.0020	0.0079-0.0390	0.0146-0.0390	0.0079-0.0590	0.0016-0.0059	0.0012-0.0059	NA
1999-00	2.5 (2457)	6	0.0004-0.0020	0.0079-0.0390	0.0146-0.0390	0.0079-0.0590	0.0016-0.0059	0.0012-0.0059	NA
2000-01	2.5 (2457)	6	0.0004-0.0020	0.0079-0.0390	0.0146-0.0390	0.0079-0.0590	0.0016-0.0059	0.0012-0.0059	NA

NA: Not Available

93081CZ2

TORQUE SPECIFICATIONS
All readings in ft. lbs.

Year	Engine Displacement Liters (cc)	Engine ID/VIN	Cylinder Head Bolts	Main Bearing Bolts	Rod Bearing Bolts	Crankshaft Damper Bolts	Flywheel Bolts	Manifold Intake	Manifold Exhaust	Spark Plugs	Lug Nut
1998	2.5 (2457)	6	①	②	31-34	123-137	51-55	14-17	19-26 ③	13-17	58-72
1999	2.5 (2457)	6	①	②	31-34	123-137	51-55	14-17	19-26 ③	13-17	58-72
2000-01	2.5 (2457)	6	①	②	31-34	123-137	51-55	14-17	19-26 ③	13-17	58-72

① Step 1: Tighten all bolts, in sequence, to 22 ft. lbs.
  Step 2: Tighten all bolts, in sequence, to 51 ft. lbs.
  Step 3: Loosen all bolts 180 degrees (one-half turn)
  Step 4: Loosen all bolts another 180 degrees (one-half turn)
  Step 5: Tighetn bolts A and B, in sequence, to 25 ft. lbs.
  Step 6: Tighten bolts C, D, E and F, in sequence, to 11 ft. lbs.
  Step 7: Tighten all bolts, in sequence, 80-90 degrees
  Step 8: Tighten all bolts, in sequence, another 80-90 degrees

② Split engine case bolts:
  10mm bolts: 33-37 ft. lbs.
  8mm bolts: A thru G to 17-20 ft. lbs. and H to 5 ft. lbs.

③ No separate exhaust manifold is used, the front pipe bolts directly to the cylinder heads

93081CZ3

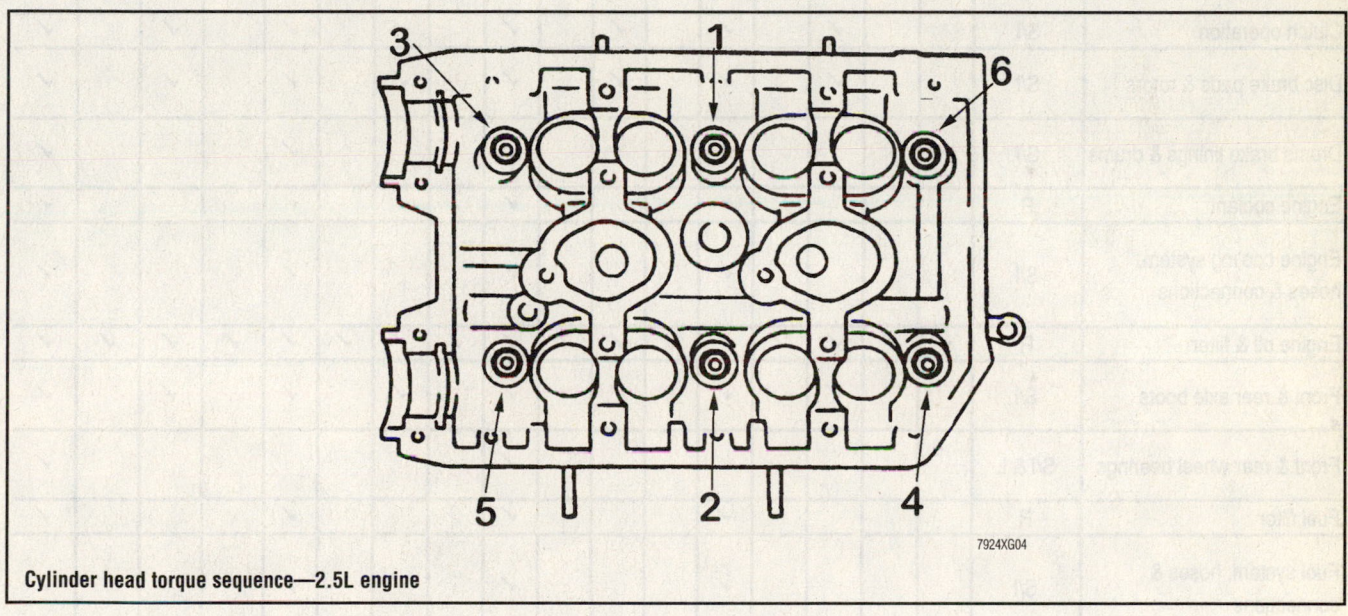

Cylinder head torque sequence—2.5L engine

7924XG04

BRAKE SPECIFICATIONS
SUBARU FORESTER
All measurements in inches unless noted

Year	Model		Brake Disc Original Thickness	Brake Disc Minimum Thickness	Brake Disc Maximum Runout	Brake Drum Diameter Original Inside Diameter	Brake Drum Diameter Max. Wear Limit	Brake Drum Diameter Maximum Machine Diameter	Minimum Lining Thickness Front	Minimum Lining Thickness Rear	Brake Caliper Bracket Bolts (ft. lbs.)	Brake Caliper Mounting Bolts (ft. lbs.)
1998	Forester	F	0.940	0.870	0.003	—	—	—	0.059	—	51-65	25-31
		R	0.390	0.340	0.004	9.00 ①	9.079 ②	NA	—	0.059	—	25-31
1999	Forester	F	0.940	0.870	0.003	—	—	—	0.059	—	51-65	25-31
		R	0.390	0.340	0.004	9.00 ①	9.079 ②	NA	—	0.059	—	25-31
2000-01	Forester	F	0.940	0.870	0.003	—	—	—	0.059	—	51-65	25-31
		R	0.390	0.340	0.004	9.00 ①	9.079 ②	NA	—	0.059	—	25-31

NA: Not Available

① Parking brake drum on vehicles with rear disc brakes: 6.69 in.
② Parking brake drum on vehicles with rear disc brakes: 6.73 in.

93081CZ4

Refer to the model specific sections for cooling system service procedures

SCHEDULED MAINTENANCE INTERVALS
(SUBARU FORESTER)

TO BE SERVICED	TYPE OF SERVICE	VEHICLE MILEAGE INTERVAL (x1000)																
		3	7.5	15	22.5	30	37.5	45	52.5	60	67.5	75	82.5	90	97.5	105	112.5	120
Accessory drive belts	R									✓								✓
Accessory drive belts	S/I					✓								✓				
Air cleaner filter	R					✓				✓				✓				✓
Automatic transmission fluid	S/I					✓				✓				✓				✓
Axle shaft joints	S/I			✓		✓		✓		✓		✓		✓		✓		✓
Brake fluid	R					✓				✓				✓				✓
Brake system lines	S/I			✓		✓		✓		✓		✓		✓		✓		✓
Clutch operation	S/I			✓		✓		✓		✓		✓		✓		✓		✓
Disc brake pads & rotors	S/I			✓		✓		✓		✓		✓		✓		✓		✓
Drums brake linings & drums	S/I					✓				✓				✓				✓
Engine coolant	R					✓				✓				✓				✓
Engine cooling system, hoses & connections	S/I					✓				✓				✓				✓
Engine oil & filter	R	✓	✓	✓	✓	✓	✓	✓	✓	✓	✓	✓	✓	✓	✓	✓	✓	✓
Front & rear axle boots	S/I			✓		✓		✓		✓		✓		✓		✓		✓
Front & rear wheel bearings	S/I & L									✓								✓
Fuel filter	R					✓				✓				✓				✓
Fuel system, hoses & connections	S/I					✓				✓				✓				✓
Parking & service brake systems' operation	S/I			✓		✓		✓		✓		✓		✓		✓		✓
Spark plugs	R									✓								✓
Steering & suspension	S/I			✓		✓		✓		✓		✓		✓		✓		✓
Supplemental Restraint System (SRS)	S/I	Every 10 years																
Timing belt	R															✓		
Timing belt	S/I					✓				✓				✓				

93081CZ5

SCHEDULED MAINTENANCE INTERVALS
(SUBARU FORESTER) (Cont.)

TO BE SERVICED	TYPE OF SERVICE	VEHICLE MILEAGE INTERVAL (x1000)																
		3	7.5	15	22.5	30	37.5	45	52.5	60	67.5	75	82.5	90	97.5	105	112.5	120
Transmission & differential fluid levels	S/I					✓				✓				✓				✓
Valve clearance	S/I															✓		

R: Replace   S/I: Inspect and service, if needed   L: Lubricate

FREQUENT OPERATION MAINTENANCE (SEVERE SERVICE)

If a vehicle is operated under any of the following conditions it is considered severe service:

- Towing a trailer or using a camper or car-top carrier.
- Repeated short trips of less than 5 miles in temperatures below freezing, or trips of less than 10 miles in any temperature.
- Extensive idling or low-speed driving for long distances as in heavy commercial use, such as delivery, taxi or police cars.
- Operating on rough, muddy or salt-covered roads, or extensive mountain driving.
- Operating on unpaved or dusty roads.
- Driving in extremely hot (over 90°) conditions.

Engine oil and filter: replace every 3000 miles or 3 months, whichever occurs first.

Fuel filter: replace every 7500 miles or 7.5 months, whichever occurs first.

Fuel system, hoses & connections: inspect every 7500 miles or 7.5 months, whichever occurs first.

Transmission & differential fluid: replace every 15,000 miles.

Automatic transmission fluid: replace every 15,000 miles.

Brake fluid: replace every 15,000 miles.

Disc brake pads & rotors: inspect every 7500 miles or 7.5 months, whichever occurs first.

Front & rear axle boots: inspect every 7500 miles or 7.5 months, whichever occurs first.

Axle shaft boots: inspect every 7500 miles or 7.5 months, whichever occurs first.

Drum brake linings & drums: inspect every 7500 miles or 7.5 months, whichever occurs first.

Brake lines: inspect every 7500 miles or 7.5 months, whichever occurs first.

Parking & service brake system operation: inspect every 7500 miles or 7.5 months, whichever occurs first.

Clutch operation: inspect every 7500 miles or 7.5 months, whichever occurs first.

Steering & suspension: inspect every 7500 miles or 7.5 months, whichever occurs first.

Valve clearance: inspect every 7500 miles or 7.5 months, whichever occurs first.

93081CZ6

SCHEDULED MAINTENANCE INTERVALS
SUBARU
FORESTER

The following should be used as a guide when determining the amount of work required for a particular service.
In estimating how long a particular Scheduled Maintenance Service should take, please observe the following:

- Labor Time is time based on field research and data supplied by the vehicle manufacturer.
- Labor time operations are given in hours and tenths of an hour.
- All labor operations are to be used as a guide.

Mechanic Skill Level Codes:
(A) PRECISION: Highly skilled with multiple certification.
(B) GENERAL: Normally skilled with certification.
(C) MAINTENANCE: Semi-skilled working on certification.

	LABOR TIME		LABOR TIME		LABOR TIME
3000 Mile Service (C)		**45000 Mile Service (C)**		**90000 Mile Service (B)**	
All Models	.4	All Models	1.0	All Models	6.1
7500 Mile Service (C)		**52500 Mile Service (C)**		**97500 Mile Service (C)**	
All Models	.4	All Models	.4	All Models	.4
15000 Mile Service (C)		**60000 Mile Service (B)**		**105000 Mile Service (C)**	
All Models	1.0	All Models	6.1	All Models	1.0
22500 Mile Service (C)		**67500 Mile Service (C)**		*Replace timing belt add*	2.7
All Models	.4	All Models	.4	**112500 Mile Service (C)**	
30000 Mile Service (B)		**75000 Mile Service (C)**		All Models	.4
All Models	6.1	All Models	1.0	**120000 Mile Service (B)**	
37500 Mile Service (C)		**82500 Mile Service (C)**		All Models	6.1
All Models	.4	All Models	.4		

93081CZ7

TIRE, WHEEL AND BALL JOINT SPECIFICATIONS
Subaru Forester

Year	Model	OEM Tires		Tire Pressures (psi)		Wheel Size	Ball Joint Inspection
		Standard	Optional	Front	Rear		
1998	Forester	P205/70R15 95S	P215/60R16 94H	29	26①	②	0.012 in. ③
1999	Forester	P205/70R15 95S	P215/60R16 94H	29	26①	②	0.012 in. ③
2000-01	Forester	P205/70R15 95S	P215/60R16 94H	29	26①	②	0.012 in. ③

OEM: Original Equipment Manufacturer

PSI: Pounds Per Square Inch

STD: Standard

OPT: Optional

① Wigh full load: 36 psi.

93081CBB

SUZUKI
Sidekick • Sidekick Sport • X90 • Vitara • Grand Vitara

ENGINE AND VEHICLE IDENTIFICATION CHART

		Engine Code						Model Year	
Code	Liters (cc)	Cu. In.	Cyl.	Fuel Sys.	Engine Type	Eng. Mfg.		Code	Year
0	1.6 (1590)	97	4	MFI	SOHC	Suzuki		V	1997
2	1.8 (1843)	112.5	4	MFI	DOHC	Suzuki		W	1998
5	2.0 (1997)	121.8	4	MFI	DOHC	Suzuki		X	1999
6	2.5 (2494)	152	6	MFI	DOHC	Suzuki		Y	2000
								1	2001

MFI: Multiport Fuel Injection
DOHC: Dual Overhead Cam
SOHC: Single Overhead Cam

93081CZ8

GENERAL ENGINE SPECIFICATIONS

Year	Model	Engine Displacement Liters (cc)	Engine ID/VIN	Fuel System Type	Net Horsepower @ rpm	Net Torque @ rpm (ft. lbs.)	Bore x Stroke (in.)	Compression Ratio	Oil Pressure @ rpm
1997	X90	1.6 (1590)	0	MFI	95@5600	98@4000	2.95x3.54	9.5:1	47-61@3000
	Sidekick	1.6 (1590)	0	MFI	95@5600	98@4000	2.95x3.54	9.5:1	47-61@3000
	Sidekick Sport	1.8 (1843)	2	MFI	120@6500	114@3500	3.31x3.27	9.8:1	55-67@4000
1998	X90	1.6 (1590)	0	MFI	95@5600	98@4000	2.95x3.54	9.5:1	47-61@3000
	Sidekick	1.6 (1590)	0	MFI	95@5600	98@4000	2.95x3.54	9.5:1	47-61@3000
	Sidekick Sport	1.8 (1843)	2	MFI	120@6500	114@3500	3.31x3.27	9.8:1	55-67@4000
1999	Vitara	1.6 (1590)	0	MFI	95@5600	98@4000	2.95x3.54	9.5:1	47-61@3000
		2.0 (1997)	5	MFI	127@6000	134@3000	3.31x3.54	NA	55-67@4000
	Grand Vitara	2.5 (2494)	6	MFI	140@6500	151@4000	3.31x2.95	9.5:1	55-67@4000
2000-01	Vitara	1.6 (1590)	0	MFI	95@5600	98@4000	2.95x3.54	9.5:1	47-61@3000
		2.0 (1997)	5	MFI	127@6000	134@3000	3.31x3.54	NA	55-67@4000
	Grand Vitara	2.5 (2494)	6	MFI	140@6500	151@4000	3.31x2.95	9.5:1	55-67@4000

MFI: Multi-port Fuel Injection
NA: Not available

93081CZ9

Timing chain and gear service is covered in the model specific sections of this manual

ENGINE TUNE-UP SPECIFICATIONS

Year	Engine Displacement Liters (cc)	Engine ID/VIN	Spark Plugs Gap (in.)	Ignition Timing (deg.)		Fuel Pump (psi)	Idle Speed (rpm)		Valve Clearance	
				MT	AT		MT	AT	In.	Ex.
1997	1.6 (1590)	0	0.029	5B	5B	28-37	750-850	750-850	0.0050-0.0070	0.0050-0.0070
	1.8 (1843)	2	0.029	5B	5B	31-37	750-850	750-850	HYD	HYD
1998	1.6 (1590)	0	0.029	5B	5B	28-37	750-850	750-850	0.0050-0.0070	0.0050-0.0070
	1.8 (1843)	2	0.029	5B	5B	31-37	750-850	750-850	HYD	HYD
1999	1.6 (1590)	0	0.040	5B	5B	30-37	700-800	700-800	0.0050-0.0070	0.0050-0.0070
	2.0 (1997)	5	0.040	5B	5B	30-37	700-800	700-800	HYD	HYD
	2.5 (2494)	6	0.040	5B	5B	30-45	700-800	700-800	HYD	HYD
2000-01	1.6 (1590)	0	0.040	5B	5B	30-37	700-800	700-800	0.0050-0.0070	0.0050-0.0070
	2.0 (1997)	5	0.040	5B	5B	30-37	700-800	700-800	HYD	HYD
	2.5 (2494)	6	0.040	5B	5B	30-45	700-800	700-800	HYD	HYD

HYD: Hydraulic

93081CZ0

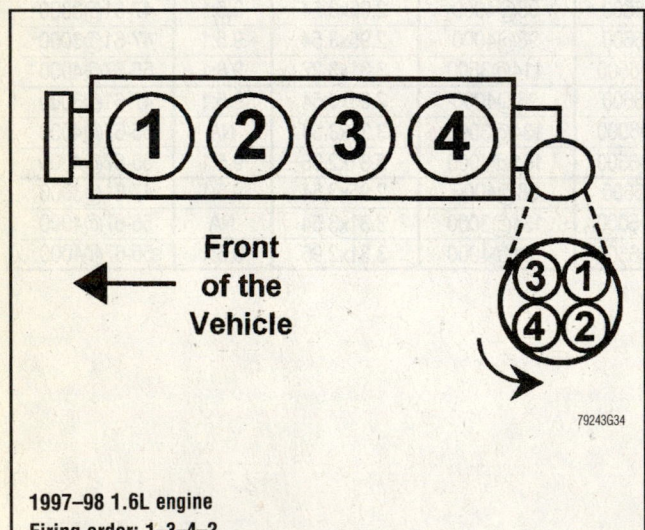

Front of the Vehicle

79243G34

1997–98 1.6L engine
Firing order: 1–3–4–2
Distributor rotation: Counterclockwise

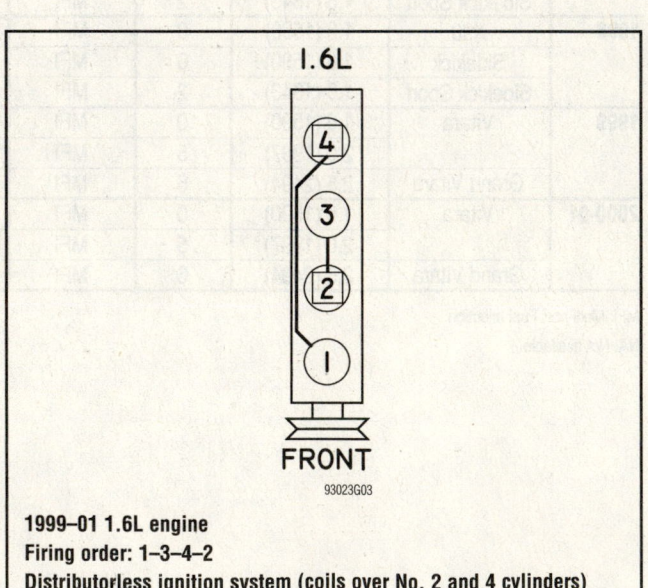

1.6L

FRONT

93023G03

1999–01 1.6L engine
Firing order: 1–3–4–2
Distributorless ignition system (coils over No. 2 and 4 cylinders)

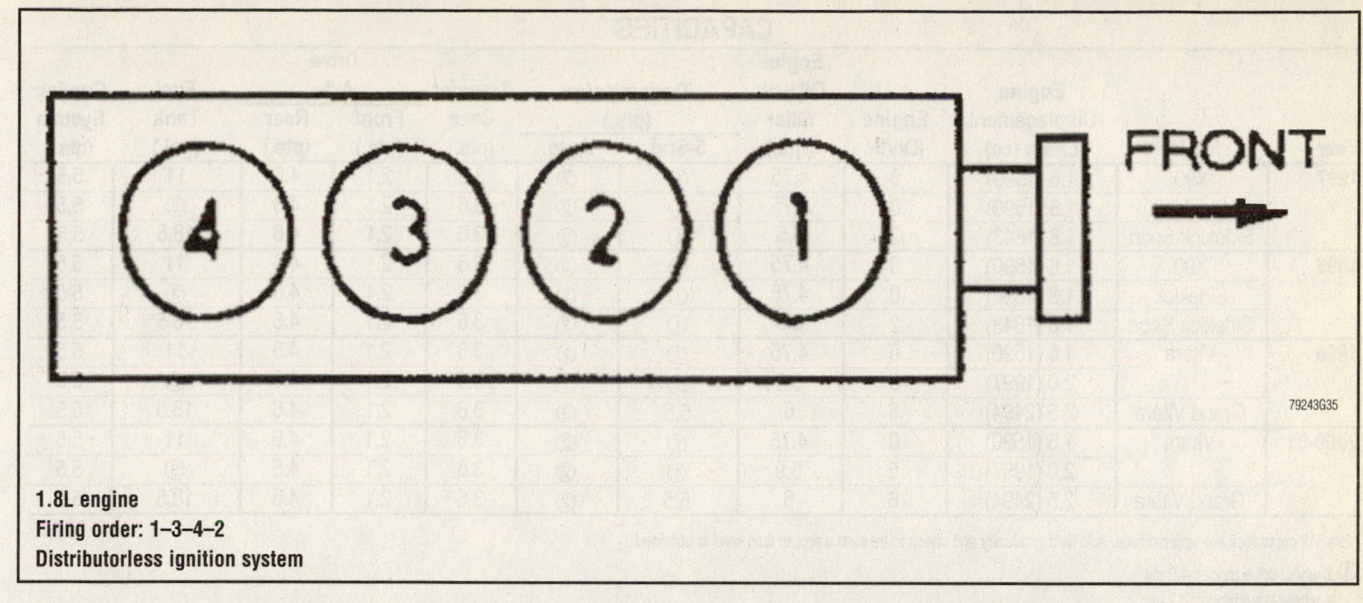

1.8L engine
Firing order: 1–3–4–2
Distributorless ignition system

79243G35

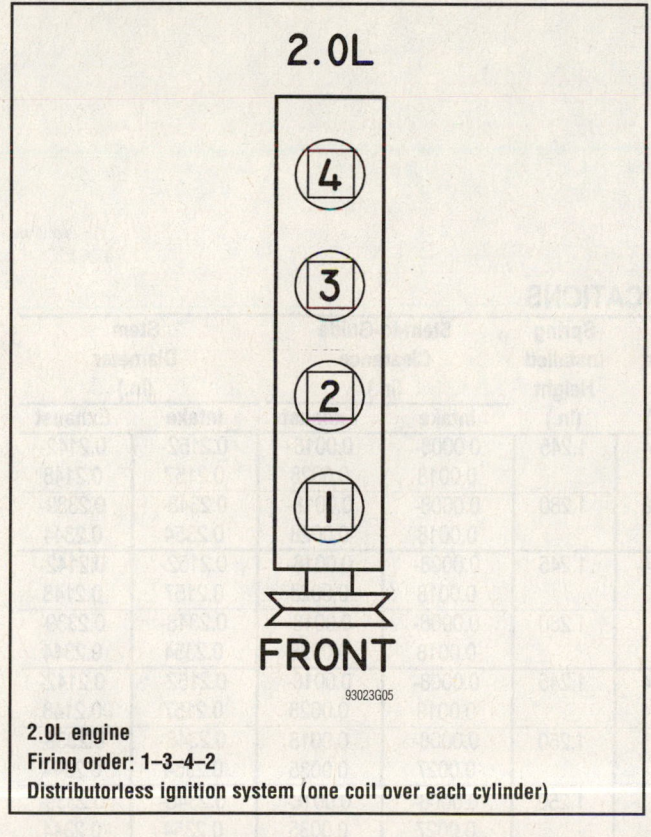

2.0L engine
Firing order: 1–3–4–2
Distributorless ignition system (one coil over each cylinder)

93023G05

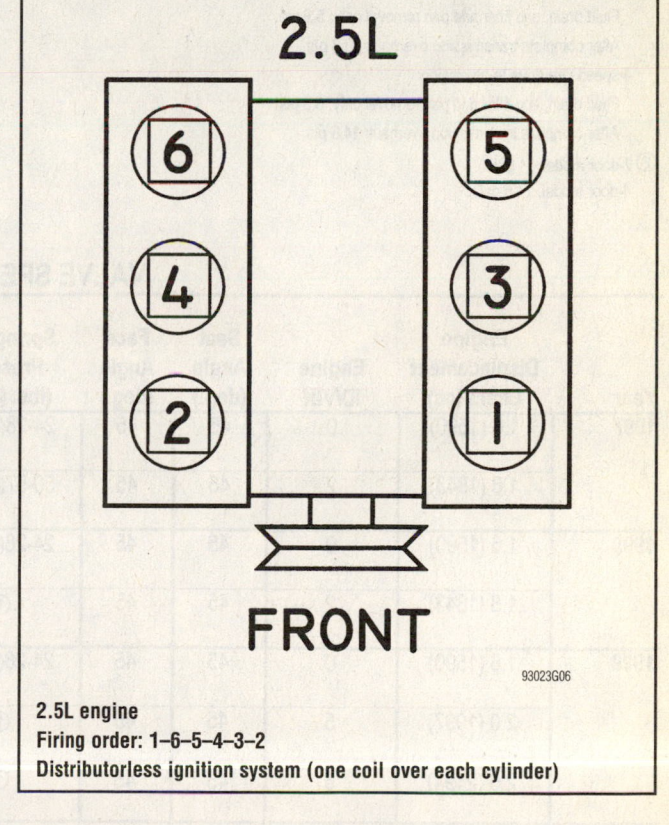

2.5L engine
Firing order: 1–6–5–4–3–2
Distributorless ignition system (one coil over each cylinder)

93023G06

Ignition system service is covered in the model specific sections of this manual

CAPACITIES

Year	Model	Engine Displacement Liters (cc)	Engine ID/VIN	Engine Oil with Filter (qts.)	Transmission (pts.) 5-Spd	Transmission (pts.) Auto.	Transfer Case (pts.)	Drive Axle Front (pts.)	Drive Axle Rear (pts.)	Fuel Tank (gal.)	Cooling System (qts.)
1997	X90	1.6 (1590)	0	4.75	①	②	3.6	2.1	4.6	11	5.5
	Sidekick	1.6 (1590)	0	4.75	①	②	3.6	2.1	4.6	③	5.5
	Sidekick Sport	1.8 (1843)	2	5.5	①	②	3.6	2.1	4.6	18.5	5.5
1998	X90	1.6 (1590)	0	4.75	①	②	3.6	2.1	4.6	11	5.5
	Sidekick	1.6 (1590)	0	4.75	①	②	3.6	2.1	4.6	③	5.5
	Sidekick Sport	1.8 (1843)	2	5.5	①	②	3.6	2.1	4.6	18.5	5.5
1999	Vitara	1.6 (1590)	0	4.75	①	②	3.6	2.1	4.6	11	5.5
		2.0 (1997)	5	5.9	①	②	3.6	2.1	4.6	③	5.5
	Grand Vitara	2.5 (2494)	6	6	5.5	②	3.6	2.1	4.6	18.5	5.5
2000-01	Vitara	1.6 (1590)	0	4.75	①	②	3.6	2.1	4.6	11	5.5
		2.0 (1997)	5	5.9	①	②	3.6	2.1	4.6	③	5.5
	Grand Vitara	2.5 (2494)	6	6	5.5	②	3.6	2.1	4.6	18.5	5.5

Note: All capacities are approximate. Add fluid gradually and check to be sure a proper fluid level is obtained.

① 2-wheel drive model: 4.0 pts.
   4-wheel drive model: 3.2 pts.

② 3-speed transmission:
   Fluid drain, and filter and pan removal only: 5.9 pts.
   After complete transmission overhaul: 10.8 pts.
   4-speed overdrive transmission:
   Fluid drain, and filter and pan removal only: 5.3 pts.
   After complete transmission overhaul: 14.6 pts.

③ 2-door model: 11 gals.
   4-door model: 14.5 gals.

93081CAA

VALVE SPECIFICATIONS

Year	Engine Displacement Liters (cc)	Engine ID/VIN	Seat Angle (deg.)	Face Angle (deg.)	Spring Test Pressure (lbs. @ in.)	Spring Installed Height (in.)	Stem-to-Guide Clearance (in.) Intake	Stem-to-Guide Clearance (in.) Exhaust	Stem Diameter (in.) Intake	Stem Diameter (in.) Exhaust
1997	1.6 (1590)	0	45	45	24-28@1.24	1.245	0.0008-0.0018	0.0018-0.0028	0.2152-0.2157	0.2142-0.2148
	1.8 (1843)	2	45	45	50-57@1.28	1.280	0.0008-0.0018	0.0018-0.0028	0.2348-0.2354	0.2339-0.2344
1998	1.6 (1590)	0	45	45	24-28@1.24	1.245	0.0008-0.0018	0.0018-0.0028	0.2152-0.2157	0.2142-0.2148
	1.8 (1843)	2	45	45	①	1.280	0.0008-0.0018	0.0018-0.0028	0.2348-0.2354	0.2339-0.2344
1999	1.6 (1590)	0	45	45	24-28@1.24	1.245	0.0008-0.0018	0.0018-0.0028	0.2152-0.2157	0.2142-0.2148
	2.0 (1997)	5	45	45	①	1.250	0.0008-0.0027	0.0018-0.0035	0.2348-0.2354	0.2339-0.2344
	2.5 (2494)	6	45	45	①	1.250	0.0008-0.0027	0.0018-0.0035	0.2348-0.2354	0.2339-0.2344
2000-01	1.6 (1590)	0	45	45	24-28@1.24	1.245	0.0008-0.0018	0.0018-0.0028	0.2152-0.2157	0.2142-0.2148
	2.0 (1997)	5	45	45	①	1.250	0.0008-0.0027	0.0018-0.0035	0.2348-0.2354	0.2339-0.2344
	2.5 (2494)	6	45	45	①	1.250	0.0008-0.0027	0.0018-0.0035	0.2348-0.2354	0.2339-0.2344

① Inner: 13.6-17.4@1.08
   Outer: 30.4-39.2@1.25

93081CAB

CRANKSHAFT AND CONNECTING ROD SPECIFICATIONS

All measurements are given in inches.

| Year | Engine Displacement Liters (cc) | Engine ID/VIN | Crankshaft | | | | Connecting Rod | | |
			Main Brg. Journal Dia.	Main Brg. Oil Clearance	Shaft End-play	Thrust on No.	Journal Diameter	Oil Clearance	Side Clearance
1997	1.6 (1590)	0	2.0465-2.0472	0.0006-0.0023	0.0044-0.0149	3	1.7316-1.7322	0.0008-0.0031	NA
	1.8 (1843)	2	2.2828-2.2834	0.0008-0.0023	0.0039-0.0165	3	1.9660-1.9709	0.0008-0.0031	NA
1998	1.6 (1590)	0	2.0465-2.0472	0.0006-0.0023	0.0044-0.0149	3	1.7316-1.7322	0.0008-0.0031	NA
	1.8 (1843)	2	2.2828-2.2834	0.0008-0.0023	0.0039-0.0165	3	1.9660-1.9709	0.0008-0.0031	NA
1999	1.6 (1590)	0	2.0465-2.0472	0.0006-0.0023	0.0044-0.0149	3	1.7316-1.7322	0.0008-0.0031	NA
	2.0 (1997)	5	2.2828-2.2834	0.0008-0.0023	0.0039-0.0165	3	1.9660-1.9709	0.0008-0.0031	NA
	2.5 (2494)	6	2.5583-2.5590	0.0008-0.0023	0.0044-0.0149	2	1.9678-1.9685	0.0016-0.0031	NA
2000-01	1.6 (1590)	0	2.0465-2.0472	0.0006-0.0023	0.0044-0.0149	3	1.7316-1.7322	0.0008-0.0031	NA
	2.0 (1997)	5	2.2828-2.2834	0.0008-0.0023	0.0039-0.0165	3	1.9660-1.9709	0.0008-0.0031	NA
	2.5 (2494)	6	2.5583-2.5590	0.0008-0.0023	0.0044-0.0149	2	1.9678-1.9685	0.0016-0.0031	NA

NA: Not Available

93081CAC

PISTON AND RING SPECIFICATIONS

All measurements are given in inches.

| Year | Engine Displacement Liters (cc) | Engine ID/VIN | Piston Clearance | Ring Gap | | | Ring Side Clearance | | |
				Top Compression	Bottom Compression	Oil Control	Top Compression	Bottom Compression	Oil Control
1997	1.6 (1590)	0	0.0008-0.0015	0.0079-0.0275	0.0138-0.0275	0.0039-0.0669	0.0012-0.0027	0.0008-0.0023	NA
	1.8 (1843)	2	0.0008-0.0015	0.0079-0.0276	0.0138-0.0276	0.0079-0.0709	0.0012-0.0027	0.0008-0.0023	NA
1998	1.6 (1590)	0	0.0008-0.0015	0.0079-0.0275	0.0138-0.0275	0.0039-0.0669	0.0012-0.0027	0.0008-0.0023	NA
	1.8 (1843)	2	0.0008-0.0015	0.0079-0.0276	0.0138-0.0276	0.0079-0.0709	0.0012-0.0027	0.0008-0.0023	NA
1999	1.6 (1590)	0	0.0008-0.0015	0.0079-0.0275	0.0138-0.0275	0.0039-0.0669	0.0012-0.0027	0.0008-0.0023	NA
	2.0 (1997)	5	0.0008-0.0015	0.0079-0.0276	0.0138-0.0276	0.0079-0.0709	0.0012-0.0027	0.0008-0.0023	NA
	2.5 (2494)	6	0.0008-0.0015	0.0079-0.0276	0.0138-0.0276	0.0079-0.0709	0.0012-0.0027	0.0008-0.0023	NA
2000-01	1.6 (1590)	0	0.0008-0.0015	0.0079-0.0275	0.0138-0.0275	0.0039-0.0669	0.0012-0.0027	0.0008-0.0023	NA
	2.0 (1997)	5	0.0008-0.0015	0.0079-0.0276	0.0138-0.0276	0.0079-0.0709	0.0012-0.0027	0.0008-0.0023	NA
	2.5 (2494)	6	0.0008-0.0015	0.0079-0.0276	0.0138-0.0276	0.0079-0.0709	0.0012-0.0027	0.0008-0.0023	NA

NA: Not Available

93081CAD

TORQUE SPECIFICATIONS
All readings in ft. lbs.

Year	Engine Displacement Liters (cc)	Engine ID/VIN	Cylinder Head Bolts	Main Bearing Bolts	Rod Bearing Bolts	Crankshaft Damper Bolts	Flywheel Bolts	Manifold		Spark Plugs	Lug Nut
								Intake	Exhaust		
1997	1.6 (1590)	0	①	36-41	24-26	94 ②	56.5	13-20	13-20	14-21	58-80
	1.8 (1843)	2	③	④	33	109	51	13-20	13-20	14-21	58-80
1998	1.6 (1590)	0	①	36-41	24-26	94 ②	56.5	13-20	13-20	14-21	58-80
	1.8 (1843)	2	③	④	33	109	51	13-20	13-20	14-21	58-80
1999	1.6 (1590)	0	⑤	36-41	24-26	94 ②	56.5	13-20	13-20	14-21	58-80
	2.0 (1997)	5	⑥	④	33	109	51	13-20	13-20	14-21	58-80
	2.5 (2494)	6	⑥	④	33	109	51	16.5	21.5	18	69
2000-01	1.6 (1590)	0	⑤	36-41	24-26	94 ②	56.5	13-20	13-20	14-21	58-80
	2.0 (1997)	5	⑥	④	33	109	51	13-20	13-20	14-21	58-80
	2.5 (2494)	6	⑥	④	33	109	51	16.5	21.5	18	69

① Step 1: 26 ft. lbs.
  Step 2: 41 ft. lbs.
  Step 3: 52 ft. lbs.

② Value shown is for crankshaft timing belt sprocket

③ Step 1: 38 ft. lbs.
  Step 2: 61 ft. lbs.
  Step 3: Loosen in reverse order to 0 ft. lbs.
  Step 4: 27 ft. lbs.
  Step 5: 76 ft. lbs.
  Step 6: Tighten 6mm bolt to 8 ft. lbs.

④ 10mm: 43.5 ft. lbs.
  8mm: 19.5 ft. lbs.

⑤ Step 1: 26 ft. lbs.
  Step 2: 41 ft. lbs.
  Step 3: Loosen in reverse order to 0 ft. lbs.
  Step 4: 26 ft. lbs.
  Step 5: 52 ft. lbs.

⑥ Step 1: 38 ft. lbs.
  Step 2: 61 ft. lbs.
  Step 3: Loosen in reverse order to 0 ft. lbs.
  Step 4: 38 ft. lbs.
  Step 5: 76 ft. lbs.
  Step 6: Tighten 6mm bolt to 8 ft. lbs.

93081CAE

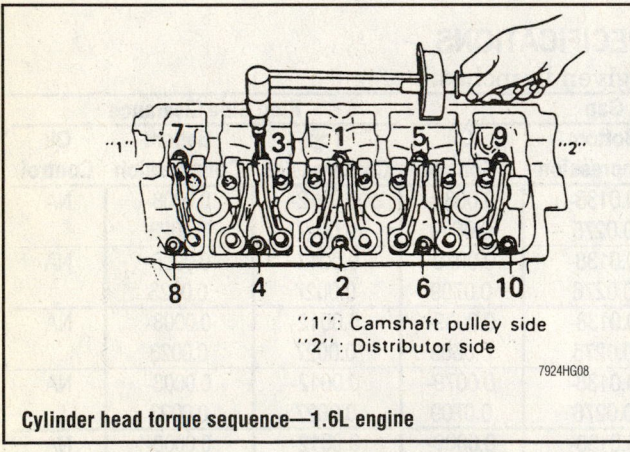

"1": Camshaft pulley side
"2": Distributor side

7924HG08

Cylinder head torque sequence—1.6L engine

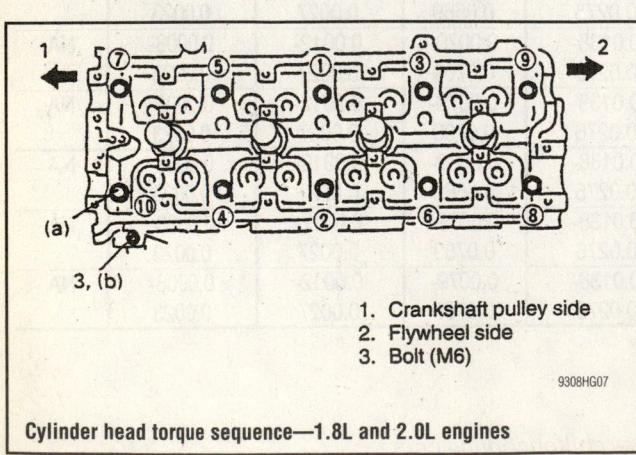

1. Crankshaft pulley side
2. Flywheel side
3. Bolt (M6)

9308HG07

Cylinder head torque sequence—1.8L and 2.0L engines

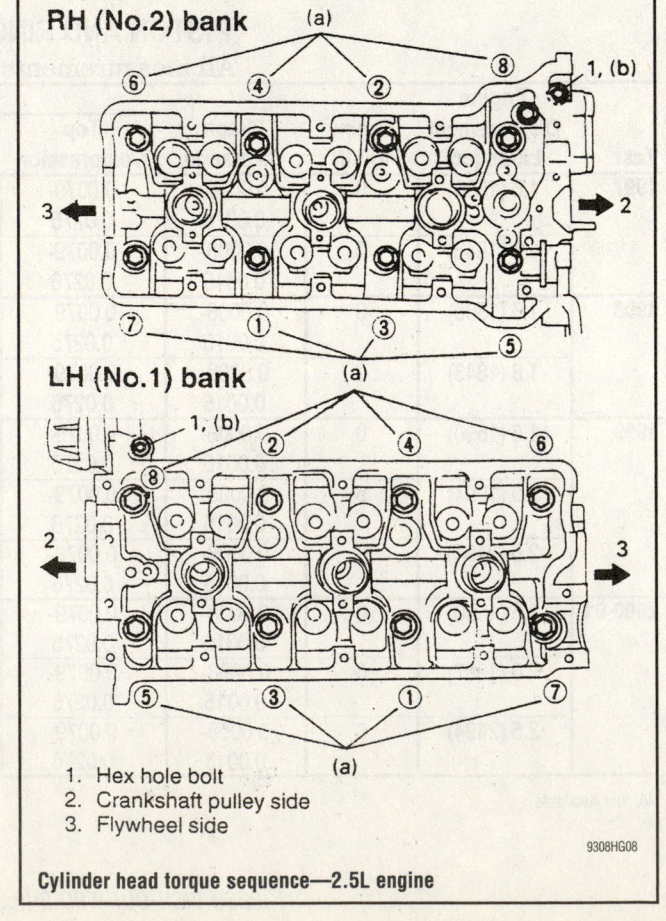

RH (No.2) bank

LH (No.1) bank

1. Hex hole bolt
2. Crankshaft pulley side
3. Flywheel side

9308HG08

Cylinder head torque sequence—2.5L engine

BRAKE SPECIFICATIONS
SUZUKI X-90, SIDEKICK, SIDEKICK SPORT, VITARA, GRAND VITARA
All measurements in inches unless noted

| Year | Model | Brake Disc | | | Brake Drum Diameter | | | Minimum Lining Thickness | | Brake Caliper | |
		Original Thickness	Minimum Thickness	Maximum Runout	Original Inside Diameter	Max. Wear Limit	Maximum Machine Diameter	Front	Rear	Bracket Bolts (ft. lbs.)	Mounting Bolts (ft. lbs.)
1997	X-90	0.394	0.315	0.006	8.66	8.74	8.74	0.08	0.04	51-72	19-21
	Sidekick ①	0.394	0.315	0.006	8.66	8.74	8.74	0.08	0.04	51-72	19-21
	Sidekick ②	0.670	0.590	0.006	10.00	10.07	10.07	0.08	0.04	51-72	19-21
	Sidekick Sport	0.866	0.787	0.006	10.00	10.07	10.07	0.08	0.04	51-72	③
1998	X-90	0.394	0.315	0.006	8.66	8.74	8.74	0.08	0.04	51-72	19-21
	Sidekick ①	0.394	0.315	0.006	8.66	8.74	8.74	0.08	0.04	51-72	19-21
	Sidekick ②	0.670	0.590	0.006	10.00	10.07	10.07	0.08	0.04	51-72	19-21
	Sidekick Sport	0.866	0.787	0.006	10.00	10.07	10.07	0.08	0.04	51-72	③
1999	Vitara	0.670	0.590	0.006	8.66	8.74	8.74	0.08	0.04	51-72	19-21
	Grand Vitara	0.866	0.787	0.006	8.66	8.74	8.74	0.08	0.04	61.5	④
2000-01	Vitara	0.670	0.590	0.006	8.66	8.74	8.74	0.08	0.04	51-72	19-21
	Grand Vitara	0.866	0.787	0.006	8.66	8.74	8.74	0.08	0.04	61.5	④

① 2-door model
② 4-door model
③ 10mm: 37 ft. lbs.
   12mm: 42 ft. lbs.
④ 10mm: 37 ft. lbs.
   12mm: 62 ft. lbs.

93081CAF

Refer to the model specific sections for engine mechanical service procedures

SCHEDULED MAINTENANCE INTERVALS
(SUZUKI GRAND VITARA, SIDEKICK, SIDEKICK SPORT, VITARA & X90)

TO BE SERVICED	TYPE OF SERVICE	VEHICLE MILEAGE INTERVAL (x1000)												
		7.5	15	22.5	30	37.5	45	52.5	60	67.5	75	82.5	90	97.5
Engine oil & filter	R	✓	✓	✓	✓	✓	✓	✓	✓	✓	✓	✓	✓	✓
Automatic transmission fluid (Sidekick) ①	S/I	✓	✓	✓	✓	✓	✓	✓	✓	✓	✓	✓	✓	✓
Manual transmission oil (Sidekick) ②	S/I	✓	✓	✓	✓	✓	✓	✓	✓	✓	✓	✓	✓	✓
Steering system	S/I	✓	✓	✓	✓	✓	✓	✓	✓	✓	✓	✓	✓	✓
Transfer & differential oil (Sidekick) ②	S/I	✓	✓	✓	✓	✓	✓	✓	✓	✓	✓	✓	✓	✓
Wheel discs & free wheeling hubs	S/I	✓	✓	✓	✓	✓	✓	✓	✓	✓	✓	✓	✓	✓
Suspension system (Sidekick)	S/I	✓	✓	✓	✓	✓	✓	✓	✓	✓	✓	✓	✓	✓
Brake discs & pads (front)	S/I		✓		✓		✓		✓		✓		✓	
Brake drums & shoes (rear)	S/I		✓		✓		✓		✓		✓		✓	
Brake fluid ③	S/I		✓		✓		✓		✓		✓		✓	
Brake hoses & pipes	S/I		✓		✓		✓		✓		✓		✓	
Brake pedal	S/I		✓		✓		✓		✓		✓		✓	
Brake lever & cable	S/I		✓		✓		✓		✓		✓		✓	
Clutch	S/I		✓		✓		✓		✓		✓		✓	
Idle speed	S/I		✓		✓		✓		✓		✓		✓	
Propeller shafts	S/I		✓		✓		✓		✓		✓		✓	
Valve lash (clearance)	S/I		✓		✓		✓		✓		✓		✓	
Wheel bearings	S/I		✓		✓		✓		✓		✓		✓	
Air cleaner filter element	R				✓				✓				✓	
Engine coolant	R				✓				✓				✓	
Fuel filter	R				✓				✓				✓	
Spark plugs	R				✓				✓				✓	
Cooling system hoses & connections	S/I				✓				✓				✓	
Drive belt(s)	S/I				✓				✓				✓	
Exhaust pipes & mountings	S/I				✓				✓				✓	
Fuel lines & connections	S/I				✓				✓				✓	
Leaf springs (Samurai)	S/I				✓				✓				✓	
Camshaft timing belt	R								✓				✓	
Distributor cap & rotor	S/I								✓					

93081CAG

SCHEDULED MAINTENANCE INTERVALS
(SUZUKI GRAND VITARA, SIDEKICK, SIDEKICK SPORT, VITARA & X90) (Cont.)

TO BE SERVICED	TYPE OF SERVICE	VEHICLE MILEAGE INTERVAL (x1000)												
		7.5	15	22.5	30	37.5	45	52.5	60	67.5	75	82.5	90	97.5
Emission-related hoses & tubes	S/I								✓					
Oxygen sensor or heated oxygen sensor ④	S/I													
EVAP canister ①	R													
PCV valve ⑤	R													
EGR system ⑥	S/I													
Fuel Injectors ⑦	S/I													
TWC converter ⑦	S/I													

R: Replace   S/I: Service or Inspect

① Replace at 100,000 miles.
② Replace oil every 30,000 miles.
③ Replace every 60,000 miles.
④ Oxygen sensor or heated oxygen sensor: service or inspect at 80,000 miles.
⑤ PCV valve: replace every 50,000 miles.
⑥ EGR system: service or inspect every 50,000 miles.
⑦ Service or inspect at 100,000 miles.

FREQUENT OPERATION MAINTENANCE (SEVERE SERVICE)

If a vehicle is operated under any of the following conditions it is considered severe service:

- Extremely dusty areas.
- 50% or more of the vehicle operation is in 32°C (90°F) or higher temperatures, or constant operation in temperatures below 0°C (32°F).
- Prolonged idling (vehicle operation in stop and go traffic).
- Frequent short running periods (engine does not warm to normal operating temperatures).
- Police, taxi, delivery usage or trailer towing usage.

Oil & oil filter: replace every 3000 miles.

Air cleaner filter element: service or inspect every 3000 miles & replace every 15,000 miles.

Steering wheel free play, gear box oil & linkage: service or inspect every 3000 miles.

Brake & nuts on chassis: tighten every 6000 miles.

Brake discs & pads (front): service or inspect every 6000 miles.

Brake drums & shoes (rear): service or inspect every 6000 miles.

Exhaust pipes & mountings: tighten every 6000 miles.

Propeller shafts: service or inspect every 6000 miles.

Automatic transmission fluid & filter: replace every 15,000 miles.

Distributor cap & ignition wires: service or inspect every 15,000 miles.

Drive belt(s): service or inspect every 15,000 miles.

Manual transmission oil: replace every 15,000 miles.

Transfer & differential oil: replace every 15,000 miles.

93081CAH

Refer to the model specific sections for fuel system service procedures

SCHEDULED MAINTENANCE INTERVALS
SUZUKI
GRAND VITARA, SIDEKICK,
SIDEKICK SPORT VITARA, X90

The following should be used as a guide when determining the amount of work required for a particular service.
In estimating how long a particular Scheduled Maintenance Service should take, please observe the following:

- Labor Time is time based on field research and data supplied by the vehicle manufacturer.
- Labor time operations are given in hours and tenths of an hour.
- All labor operations are to be used as a guide.

Mechanic Skill Level Codes:
(A) PRECISION: Highly skilled with multiple certification.
(B) GENERAL: Normally skilled with certification.
(C) MAINTENANCE: Semi-skilled working on certification.

	LABOR TIME		LABOR TIME		LABOR TIME
7500 Mile Service (C)		**37500 Mile Service (C)**		**75000 Mile Service (B)**	
All Models	.8	All Models	.8	All Models	2.0
w/AT add	.1	w/AT add	.1	w/AT add	.1
w/4WD add	.3	w/4WD add	.3	w/4WD add	.3
15000 Mile Service (B)		**45000 Mile Service (B)**		**82500 Mile Service (C)**	
All Models	2.1	All Models	2.1	All Models	.7
w/AT add	.1	w/AT add	.1	w/AT add	.1
w/4WD add	.3	w/4WD add	.3	w/4WD add	.3
22500 Mile Service (C)		**52500 Mile Service (C)**		**90000 Mile Service (B)**	
All Models	.7	All Models	.7	All Models	7.4
w/AT add	.1	w/AT add	.1	w/AT add	.1
w/4WD add	.3	w/4WD add	.3	w/4WD add	.3
30000 Mile Service (B)		**60000 Mile Service (B)**		**97500 Mile Service (C)**	
All Models	4.5	All Models	7.7	All Models	.7
w/AT add	.1	w/AT add	.1	w/AT add	.1
w/4WD add	.3	w/4WD add	.3	w/4WD add	.3
		67500 Mile Service (C)			
		All Models	.7		
		w/AT add	.1		
		w/4WD add	.3		

93081CAI

TIRE, WHEEL AND BALL JOINT SPECIFICATIONS
Suzuki Sidekick, Sidekick Sport, X-90, Vitara, Grand Vitara

Year	Model	OEM Tires		Tire Pressures (psi)		Wheel Size	Ball Joint Inspection
		Standard	Optional	Front	Rear		
1997	Sidekick	P195/75R15	P205/75R15	23	23	5.5-JJ	①
	Sidekick Sport	P215/65R16	none	23	23	②	①
	X-90	P195/65R15	none	23	23	5.5-JJ	①
1998	Sidekick	P195/75R15	P205/75R15	23	23	5.5-JJ	①
	Sidekick Sport	P215/65R16	none	23	23	②	①
	X-90	P195/65R15	none	23	23	5.5-JJ	①
1999	Vitara	P195/75SR15	P215/65SR16	23	23	6-JJ	①
	Grand Vitara	P235/65SR16	none	23	23	7-JJ	①
2000-01	Vitara	P195/75SR15	P215/65SR16	23	23	6-JJ	①
	Grand Vitara	P235/65SR16	none	23	23	7-JJ	①

OEM: Original Equipment Manufacturer

PSI: Pounds Per Square Inch

STD: Standard

OPT: Optional

① Replace if any measurable movement is found.

93081CBA

Refer to the model specific sections for engine electrical system service procedures

TOYOTA
4runner • Land Cruiser • Previa • RAV4 • Sienna • Sequoia • T100 • Tacoma • Tundra

ENGINE AND VEHICLE IDENTIFICATION

Engine							Model Year	
Code ①	Liters (cc)	Cu. In.	Cyl.	Fuel Sys.	Engine Type	Eng. Mfg.	Code ②	Year
1FZ-FE	4.5 (4477)	273	8	SFI	DOHC	Toyota	V	1997
1MZ-FE	3.0 (2995)	183	6	MFI	DOHC	Toyota	W	1998
2TZ-FE	2.4 (2438)	149	4	MFI	DOHC	Toyota	X	1999
2RZ-FE	2.4 (2438)	149	4	MFI	DOHC	Toyota	Y	2000
2UZ-FE	4.7 (4664)	285	8	SFI	DOHC	Toyota	1	2001
3RZ-FE	2.7 (2693)	164	4	MFI	DOHC	Toyota		
3S-FE	2.0 (1998)	122	4	MFI	DOHC	Toyota		
5VZ-FE	3.4 (3378)	206	6	MFI	DOHC	Toyota		

SFI: Sequential Fuel Injection

MFI: Multi-port Fuel Injection

DOHC: Double Overhead Camshaft

① Stamped on the left side of the engine block

② 10th digit of the Vehicle Identification Number (VIN)

93081CAJ

GENERAL ENGINE SPECIFICATIONS

Year	Model	Engine Displacement Liters (cc)	Engine Series (ID/VIN)	Fuel System	Net Horsepower @ rpm	Net Torque @ rpm (ft. lbs.)	Bore x Stroke (in.)	Compression Ratio	Oil Pressure @ rpm
1997	Previa	2.4 (2438)	2TZ-FE	MFI	161@5000	201@3600	3.74x3.39	8.9:1	36@3000
	4Runner	2.7 (2693)	3RZ-FE	MFI	150@4800	177@4000	3.74x3.74	9.5:1	36-71@3000
		3.4 (3378)	5VZ-FE	MFI	190@4800	220@3600	3.68x3.23	9.6:1	NA
	Land Cruiser	4.5 (4477)	1FZ-FE	SFI	212@4600	275@3200	3.94x3.74	9.0:1	36-71@3000
	RAV4	2.0 (1998)	3S-FE	MFI	120@5400	125@4600	3.40x3.40	9.5:1	NA
	T100	2.7 (2693)	3RZ-FE	MFI	150@4800	177@4000	3.74x3.74	9.5:1	36-71@3000
		3.4 (3378)	5VZ-FE	MFI	190@4800	220@3600	3.68x3.23	9.6:1	NA
	Tacoma	2.4 (2438)	2RZ-FE	MFI	142@5000	160@4000	3.74x3.38	9.5:1	36-71@3000
		2.7 (2693)	3RZ-FE	MFI	150@4800	177@4000	3.74x3.74	9.5:1	36-71@3000
		3.4 (3378)	5VZ-FE	MFI	190@4800	220@3600	3.68x3.23	9.6:1	NA
1998	4Runner	2.7 (2693)	3RZ-FE	MFI	150@4800	177@4000	3.74x3.74	9.5:1	36-71@3000
		3.4 (3378)	5VZ-FE	MFI	190@4800	220@3600	3.68x3.23	9.6:1	NA
	Land Cruiser	4.7 (4664)	2UZ-FE	SFI	230@4800	320@3400	3.70x3.30	9.6:1	45-65@3000
	RAV4	2.0 (1998)	3S-FE	MFI	120@5400	125@4600	3.40x3.40	9.5:1	NA
	Sienna	3.0 (2995)	1MZ-FE	MFI	188@5200	203@4400	3.44x3.27	10.5:1	43-78@3000
	T100	2.7 (2693)	3RZ-FE	MFI	150@4800	177@4000	3.74x3.74	9.5:1	36-71@3000
		3.4 (3378)	5VZ-FE	MFI	190@4800	220@3600	3.68x3.23	9.6:1	NA
	Tacoma	2.4 (2438)	2RZ-FE	MFI	142@5000	160@4000	3.74x3.38	9.5:1	36-71@3000
		2.7 (2693)	3RZ-FE	MFI	150@4800	177@4000	3.74x3.74	9.5:1	36-71@3000
		3.4 (3378)	5VZ-FE	MFI	190@4800	220@3600	3.68x3.23	9.6:1	NA
1999	4Runner	2.7 (2693)	3RZ-FE	MFI	150@4800	177@4000	3.74x3.74	9.5:1	36-71@3000
		3.4 (3378)	5VZ-FE	MFI	183@4800	217@3600	3.68x3.23	9.6:1	NA
	Land Cruiser	4.7 (4664)	2UZ-FE	SFI	230@4800	320@3400	3.70x3.30	9.6:1	45-65@3000
	RAV4	2.0 (1998)	3S-FE	MFI	127@5400	132@4600	3.40x3.40	9.5:1	NA
	Sienna	3.0 (2995)	1MZ-FE	MFI	194@5200	209@4400	3.44x3.27	10.5:1	43-78@3000
	Tacoma	2.4 (2438)	2RZ-FE	MFI	142@5000	160@4000	3.74x3.38	9.5:1	36-71@3000
		2.7 (2693)	3RZ-FE	MFI	150@4800	177@4000	3.74x3.74	9.5:1	36-71@3000
		3.4 (3378)	5VZ-FE	MFI	190@4800	220@3600	3.68x3.23	9.6:1	NA
	Tundra	3.4 (3378)	5VZ-FE	MFI	190@4800	220@3600	3.68x3.23	9.6:1	NA
		4.7 (4664)	2UZ-FE	MFI	245@4800	315@3400	3.70x3.30	9.6:1	45-65@3000
2000-01	4Runner	2.7 (2693)	3RZ-FE	MFI	150@4800	177@4000	3.74x3.74	9.5:1	36-71@3000
		3.4 (3378)	5VZ-FE	MFI	183@4800	217@3600	3.68x3.23	9.6:1	NA
	Land Cruiser	4.7 (4664)	2UZ-FE	SFI	230@4800	320@3400	3.70x3.30	9.6:1	45-65@3000
	RAV4	2.0 (1998)	3S-FE	MFI	127@5400	132@4600	3.40x3.40	9.5:1	NA
	Sienna	3.0 (2995)	1MZ-FE	MFI	194@5200	209@4400	3.44x3.27	10.5:1	43-78@3000
	Sequoia	3.4 (3378)	5VZ-FE	MFI	190@4800	220@3600	3.68x3.23	9.6:1	NA
		4.7 (4664)	2UZ-FE	MFI	245@4800	315@3400	3.70x3.30	9.6:1	45-65@3000
	Tacoma	2.4 (2438)	2RZ-FE	MFI	142@5000	160@4000	3.74x3.38	9.5:1	36-71@3000
		2.7 (2693)	3RZ-FE	MFI	150@4800	177@4000	3.74x3.74	9.5:1	36-71@3000
		3.4 (3378)	5VZ-FE	MFI	190@4800	220@3600	3.68x3.23	9.6:1	NA
	Tundra	3.4 (3378)	5VZ-FE	MFI	190@4800	220@3600	3.68x3.23	9.6:1	NA
		4.7 (4664)	2UZ-FE	MFI	245@4800	315@3400	3.70x3.30	9.6:1	45-65@3000

NA: Not Available

SFI: Sequential Fuel Injection

MFI: Multi-port Fuel Injection

93081CAK

For accessory drive belt replacement procedures see the model specific sections of this manual

ENGINE TUNE-UP SPECIFICATIONS

Year	Engine Displacement Liters (cc)	Engine ID/VIN	Spark Plug Gap (in.)	Ignition Timing (deg.)	Fuel Pump (psi)	Idle Speed (rpm) MT	Idle Speed (rpm) AT	Valve Clearance Intake	Valve Clearance Exhaust
1997	2.0 (1998)	3S-FE	0.043	5B	44-50	700-800	700-800	0.007-0.011	0.011-0.015
	2.4 (2438)	2RZ-FE	0.031	10B	38-44	650-750	—	0.006-0.010	0.010-0.014
	2.4 (2438)	2TZ-FE	0.043	10B	38-44	700-800	700-800	0.006-0.010	0.010-0.014
	2.7 (2693)	3RZ-FE	0.031	10B	38-44	650-750	650-750	0.006-0.010	0.010-0.014
	3.4 (3378)	5VZ-FE	0.043	5B	38-44	650-750	650-750	0.006-0.009	0.011-0.014
	4.5 (4477)	1FZ-FE	0.031	3B	38-44	—	600-700	0.006-0.010	0.010-0.014
1998	2.0 (1998)	3S-FE	0.043	5B	44-50	700-800	700-800	0.007-0.011	0.011-0.015
	2.4 (2438)	2RZ-FE	0.031	10B	38-44	650-750	—	0.006-0.010	0.010-0.014
	2.7 (2693)	3RZ-FE	0.031	10B	38-44	650-750	650-750	0.006-0.010	0.010-0.014
	3.0 (2995)	1MZ-FE	0.043	10B	38-44	—	650-750	0.006-0.010	0.010-0.014
	3.4 (3378)	5VZ-FE	0.043	5B	38-44	650-750	650-750	0.006-0.009	0.011-0.014
	4.7 (4664)	2UZ-FE	0.043	—	38-44	—	650-750	0.006-0.010	0.010-0.014
1999	2.0 (1998)	3S-FE	0.043	5B	44-50	700-800	700-800	0.007-0.011	0.011-0.015
	2.4 (2438)	2RZ-FE	0.031	5B	38-44	650-750	—	0.006-0.010	0.010-0.014
	2.7 (2693)	3RZ-FE	0.031	5B	38-44	650-750	650-750	0.006-0.010	0.010-0.014
	3.0 (2995)	1MZ-FE	0.043	10B	38-44	—	650-750	0.006-0.010	0.010-0.014
	3.4 (3378)	3RZ-FE	0.031	5B	38-44	650-750	650-750	0.006-0.010	0.010-0.014
	4.7 (4664)	2UZ-FE	0.043	5B	38-44	650-750	650-750	0.006-0.009	0.011-0.014
2000-01	2.0 (1998)	3S-FE	0.043	5B	44-50	700-800	700-800	0.007-0.011	0.011-0.015
	2.4 (2438)	2RZ-FE	0.031	5B	38-44	650-750	—	0.006-0.010	0.010-0.014
	2.7 (2693)	3RZ-FE	0.031	5B	38-44	650-750	650-750	0.006-0.010	0.010-0.014
	3.0 (2995)	1MZ-FE	0.043	10B	38-44	—	650-750	0.006-0.010	0.010-0.014
	3.4 (3378)	3RZ-FE	0.031	5B	38-44	650-750	650-750	0.006-0.010	0.010-0.014
	4.7 (4664)	2UZ-FE	0.043	5B	38-44	650-750	650-750	0.006-0.009	0.011-0.014

NOTE: The Vehicle Emission Control Information label often reflects specification changes made during production. The label figures must be used if they differ from those in this chart.

B: Before top dead center

93081CAL

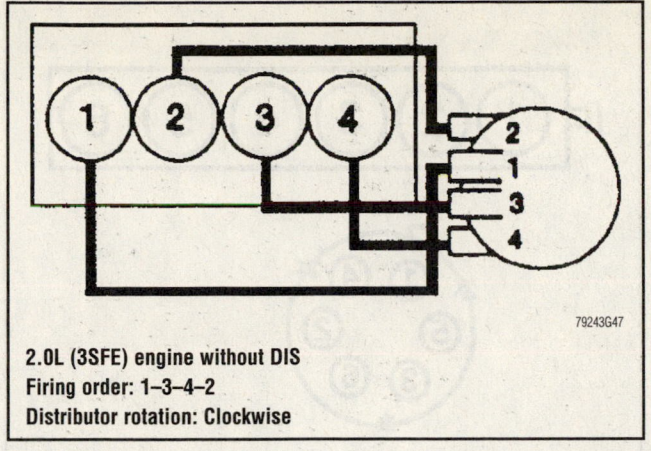

2.0L (3SFE) engine without DIS
Firing order: 1–3–4–2
Distributor rotation: Clockwise

79243G47

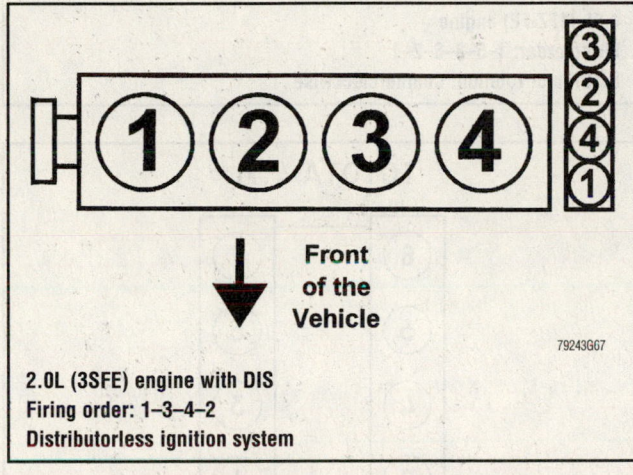

Front
of the
Vehicle

2.0L (3SFE) engine with DIS
Firing order: 1–3–4–2
Distributorless ignition system

79243G67

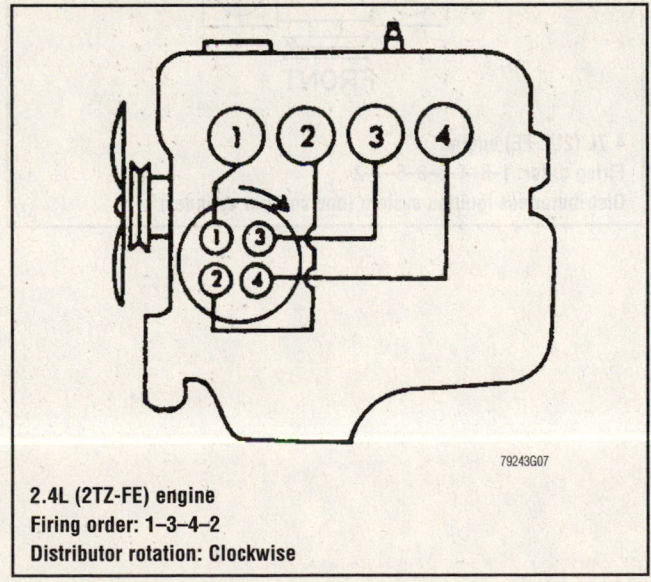

2.4L (2TZ-FE) engine
Firing order: 1–3–4–2
Distributor rotation: Clockwise

79243G07

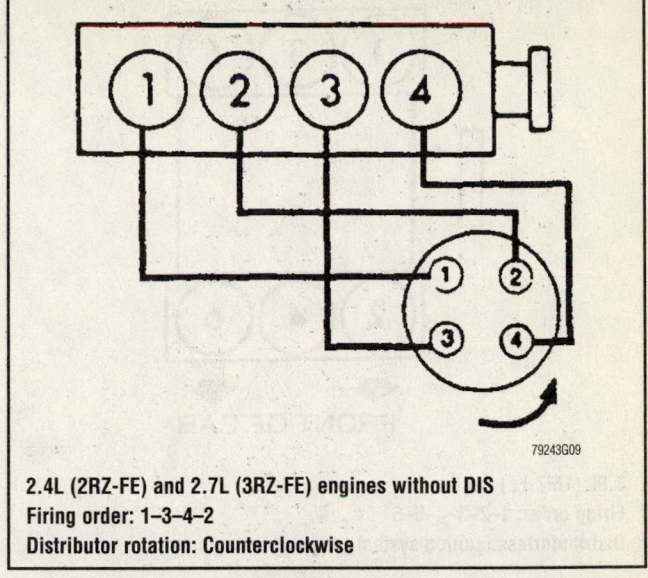

2.4L (2RZ-FE) and 2.7L (3RZ-FE) engines without DIS
Firing order: 1–3–4–2
Distributor rotation: Counterclockwise

79243G09

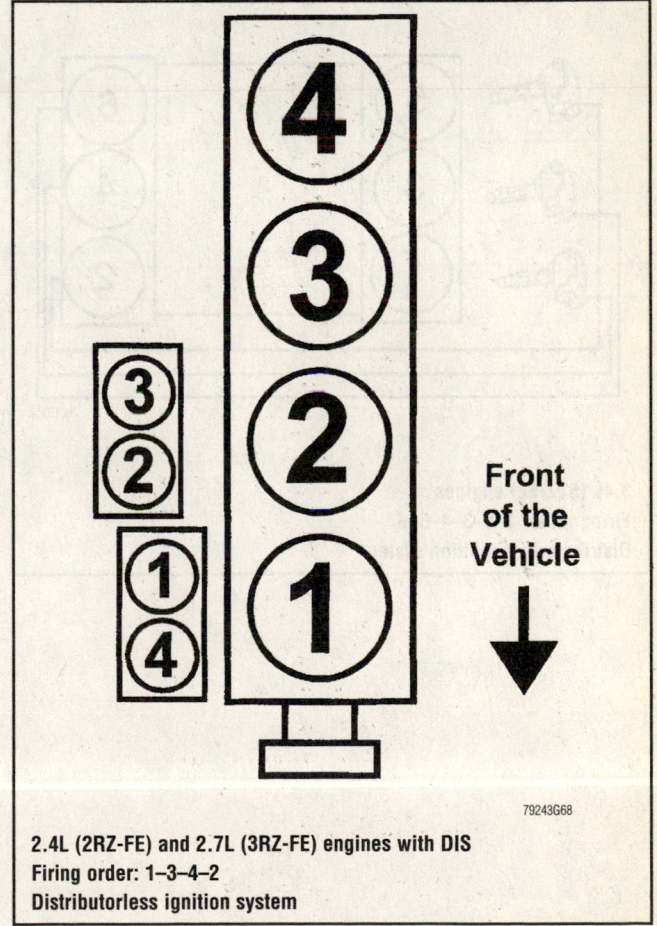

Front
of the
Vehicle

2.4L (2RZ-FE) and 2.7L (3RZ-FE) engines with DIS
Firing order: 1–3–4–2
Distributorless ignition system

79243G68

For brake related suspension and axle service, refer to the model specific sections of this manual

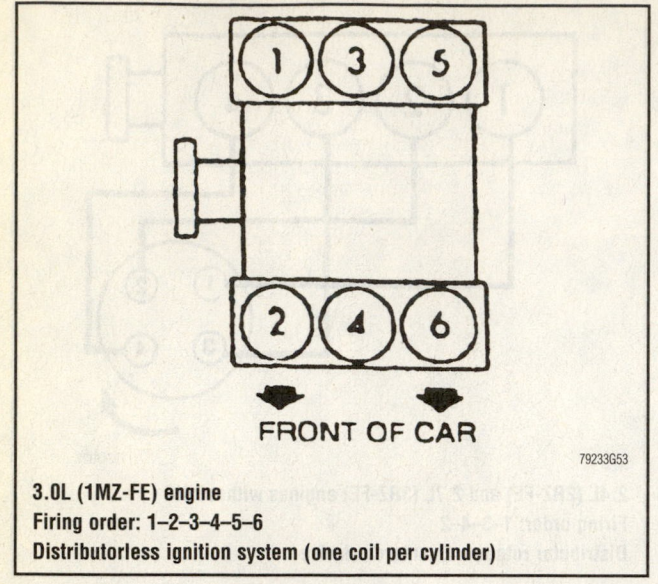

3.0L (1MZ-FE) engine
Firing order: 1–2–3–4–5–6
Distributorless ignition system (one coil per cylinder)

79233G53

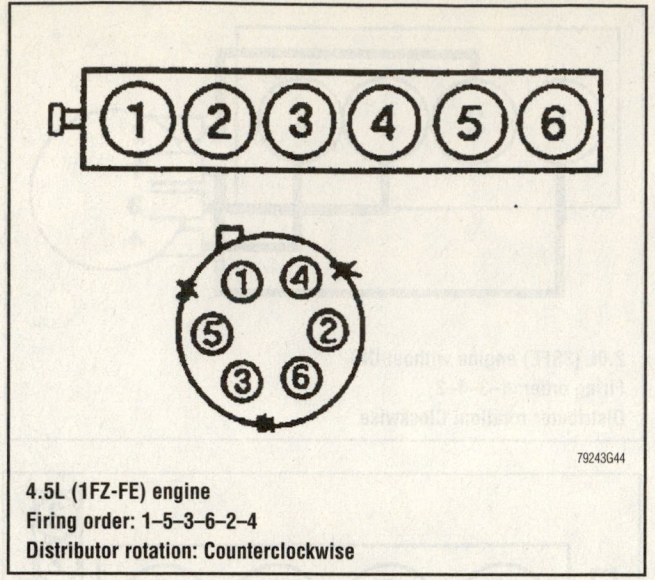

4.5L (1FZ-FE) engine
Firing order: 1–5–3–6–2–4
Distributor rotation: Counterclockwise

79243G44

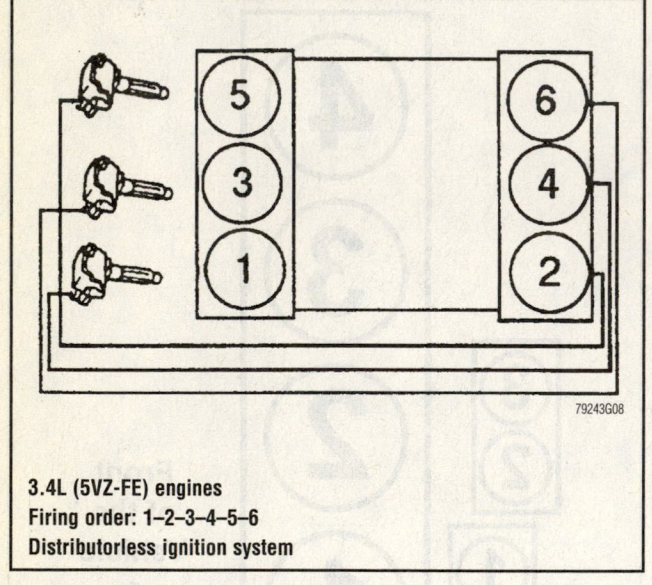

3.4L (5VZ-FE) engines
Firing order: 1–2–3–4–5–6
Distributorless ignition system

79243G08

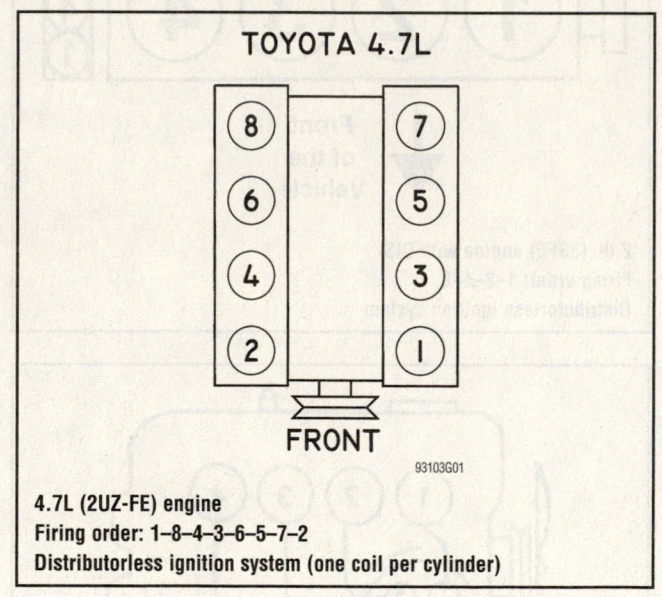

TOYOTA 4.7L

4.7L (2UZ-FE) engine
Firing order: 1–8–4–3–6–5–7–2
Distributorless ignition system (one coil per cylinder)

93103G01

CAPACITIES

Year	Model	Engine Displacement Liters (cc)	Engine ID/VIN	Engine Oil with Filter (qts.)	Transmission (pts.) 5-Spd	Transmission (pts.) Auto.	Transfer Case (pts.)	Drive Axle Front (pts.)	Drive Axle Rear (pts.)	Fuel Tank (gal.)	Cooling System (qts.)
1997	4Runner	2.7 (2693)	3RZ-FE	5.8	①	②	2.4	③	④	18.0	⑤
		3.4 (3378)	5VZ-FE	5.5	①	②	2.4	③	④	18.0	⑥
	Land Cruiser	4.5 (4477)	1FZ-FE	7.8	—	4.0	3.6	⑦	6.8	25.1	38.0
	Previa	2.4 (2438)	2TZ-FE	6.1	—	3.4	2.8	⑧	3.2	19.8	13.0
	RAV4	2.0 (1998)	3S-FE	4.1	⑨	7.0	—	—	—	15.3	⑩
	T100	2.7 (2693)	3RZ-FE	5.8	2.7	—	—	—	3.8	24.0	9.2
		3.4 (3378)	5VZ-FE	⑪	⑫	2.4	3.9	⑬	—	24.0	⑭
	Tacoma	2.4 (2438)	2RZ-FE	5.8	①	②	2.2	③	2.9	15.1	⑮
		2.7 (2693)	3RZ-FE	5.8	①	②	2.2	③	⑯	18.0	⑮
		3.4 (3378)	5VZ-FE	⑰	①	②	2.2	③	⑯	18.0	⑱
1998	4Runner	2.7 (2693)	3RZ-FE	5.8	①	②	2.4	③	④	18.0	⑤
		3.4 (3378)	5VZ-FE	5.5	①	②	2.4	③	④	18.0	⑥
	Land Cruiser	4.7 (4664)	2UZ-FE	7.2	—	4	3.6	3.6	6.8	25.1	38
	RAV4	2.0 (1998)	3S-FE	4.1	⑨	7.0	—	—	—	15.3	⑩
	Sienna	3.0 (2995)	1MZ-FE	5	—	3.7	—	—	—	13.0	⑱
	T100	2.7 (2693)	3RZ-FE	5.8	2.7	—	—	—	3.8	24.0	9.2
		3.4 (3378)	5VZ-FE	⑪	B	2.4	3.9	⑬	—	24.0	⑭
	Tacoma	2.4 (2438)	2RZ-FE	5.8	①	②	2.2	③	2.9	15.1	⑮
		2.7 (2693)	3RZ-FE	5.8	①	②	2.2	③	⑯	18.0	⑮
		3.4 (3378)	5VZ-FE	⑰	①	②	2.2	③	⑯	18.1	⑱
1999	4Runner	2.7 (2693)	3RZ-FE	5.8	①	②	2.3	③	④	18.0	⑤
		3.4 (3378)	5VZ-FE	5.5	①	②	2.4	③	④	18.0	⑥
	Land Cruiser	4.7 (4664)	2UZ-FE	7.2	—	4	3.6	3.6	6.8	25.1	38
	RAV4	2.0 (1998)	3S-FE	4.1	⑨	7.0	—	—	—	15.3	⑩
	Sienna	3.0 (2995)	1MZ-FE	5	—	3.7	—	—	—	13.0	⑱
	Tacoma	2.4 (2438)	2RZ-FE	5.8	①	②	2.2	③	2.9	15.1	⑮
		2.7 (2693)	3RZ-FE	5.8	①	②	2.2	③	⑯	18.0	⑮
		3.4 (3378)	5VZ-FE	⑰	①	②	2.2	③	⑯	18.1	⑲
	Tundra	3.4 (3378)	5VZ-FE	5.5	①	②	2.3	③	⑯	18.0	⑲
		4.7 (4664)	2UZ-FE	6.4	①	②	2.4	③	⑯	18.1	12.3
2000-01	4Runner	2.7 (2693)	3RZ-FE	5.8	①	②	⑳	③	④	18.0	⑤
		3.4 (3378)	5VZ-FE	5.5	①	②	⑳	③	④	18.0	⑥
	Land Cruiser	4.7 (4664)	2UZ-FE	7.2	—	4	3.6	3.6	6.8	25.1	38
	RAV4	2.0 (1998)	3S-FE	4.1	⑨	7.0	—	—	—	15.3	⑩
	Sienna	3.0 (2995)	1MZ-FE	5	—	3.7	—	—	—	13.0	⑱
	Sequoia	3.4 (3378)	5VZ-FE	5.5	①	②	2.3	③	⑯	18.0	⑲
		4.7 (4664)	2UZ-FE	6.4	①	②	2.4	③	⑯	18.1	12.3
	Tacoma	2.4 (2438)	2RZ-FE	5.8	①	②	2.2	③	2.9	15.1	⑮
		2.7 (2693)	3RZ-FE	5.8	①	②	2.2	③	⑯	18.0	⑮
		3.4 (3378)	5VZ-FE	⑰	①	②	2.2	③	⑯	18.1	⑲
	Tundra	3.4 (3378)	5VZ-FE	5.5	①	②	2.3	③	⑯	18.0	⑲
		4.7 (4664)	2UZ-FE	6.4	①	②	2.4	③	⑯	18.1	12.3

① W59:
 2WD: 5.4
 4WD: 5.2
 R150, R150F:
 2WD: 5.4
 4WD: 4.6

② A43D: 5.0
 A340E: 3.4
 A340F: 4.2

③ Without ADD: 2.32
 With ADD: 2.44

④ 2WD: 5.8
 4WD with differential locks: 5.8
 4WD without differential locks: 5.2

⑤ With rear heater: 11.6
 Without rear heater: 10.6

⑥ With rear heater: 9.5
 Without rear heater: 8.5

⑦ With differential lock: 5.6
 Without differential lock: 5.8

⑧ 2WD: 3.2
 4WD: 2.2

⑨ 2WD: 8.2
 4WD: 10.6

⑩ M/T: 8.5
 A/T: 8.1

⑪ 2WD: 5.5
 4WD: 5.0

⑫ Drain and refill:
 A340E: 3.4
 A340F: 4.2

⑬ 2WD: 4.4
 4WD: 4.3

⑭ 2WD M/T: 10.6
 2WD A/T: 10.5
 4WD M/T: 10.6
 4WD A/T: 10.8

⑮ 2WD M/T: 8.5
 2WD A/T: 8.2
 4WD M/T: 8.8
 4WD A/T: 8.7

⑯ Extra long: 4.4
 All others: 5.4

⑰ 2WD: 5.7
 4WD: 5.5

⑱ M/T: 10.7
 A/T: 10.5

⑲ M/T: 10.3
 A/T: 10.0

⑳ VF2A: 2.2
 VF3AM: 2.6

93081CAM

Refer to the model specific sections for driveline service procedures

VALVE SPECIFICATIONS

Year	Engine Displacement Liters (cc)	Engine ID/VIN	Seat Angle (deg.)	Face Angle (deg.)	Spring Test Pressure (lbs. @ in.)	Spring Installed Height (in.)	Stem-to-Guide Clearance (in.) Intake	Stem-to-Guide Clearance (in.) Exhaust	Stem Diameter (in.) Intake	Stem Diameter (in.) Exhaust
1997	2.0 (1998)	3S-FE	45	44.5	36.8-42.5@ 1.366	1.366	0.0010-0.0024	0.0012-0.0026	0.2350-0.2356	0.2348-0.2354
	2.4 (2438)	2RZ-FE	45	44.5	40.0-46.0@ 1.406	1.406	0.0010-0.0024	0.0012-0.0026	0.2350-0.2356	0.2348-0.2354
	2.4 (2438)	2TZ-FZE	45	44.5	38.7-42.8@ 1.594	1.406	0.0010-0.0024	0.0012-0.0026	0.2350-0.2356	0.2348-0.2354
	2.7 (2693)	3RZ-FE	45	44.5	40.0-46.0@ 1.406	1.406	0.0010-0.0024	0.0012-0.0026	0.2350-0.2356	0.2348-0.2354
	3.4 (3378)	5VZ-FE	45	44.5	41.9-46.3@ 1.311	1.311	0.0010-0.0024	0.0012-0.0026	0.2350-0.2356	0.2348-0.2354
	4.5 (4477)	1FZ-FE	45	44.5	48.1-53.4@ 1.437	1.437	0.0010-0.0024	0.0012-0.0026	0.2744-0.2750	0.2742-0.2748
1998	2.0 (1998)	3S-FE	45	44.5	36.8-42.5@ 1.366	1.366	0.0010-0.0024	0.0012-0.0026	0.2350-0.2356	0.2348-0.2354
	2.4 (2438)	2RZ-FE	45	44.5	40.0-46.0@ 1.406	1.406	0.0010-0.0024	0.0012-0.0026	0.2350-0.2356	0.2348-0.2354
	2.7 (2693)	3RZ-FE	45	44.5	40.0-46.0@ 1.406	1.406	0.0010-0.0024	0.0012-0.0026	0.2350-0.2356	0.2348-0.2354
	3.0 (2995)	1MZ-FE	45	44.5	41.9-46.3@ 1.33	1.791	0.0010-0.0024	0.0012-0.0026	0.2154-0.2159	0.2152-0.2157
	3.4 (3378)	5VZ-FE	45	44.5	41.9-46.3@ 1.311	1.311	0.0010-0.0024	0.0012-0.0026	0.2350-0.2356	0.2348-0.2354
	4.7 (4664)	2UZ-FE	45	44.5	45.9-50.7@ 1.378	1.380	0.0010-0.0024	0.0012-0.0026	0.2154-0.2159	0.2152-0.2157
1999	2.0 (1998)	3S-FE	45	44.5	36.8-42.5@ 1.366	1.366	0.0010-0.0024	0.0012-0.0026	0.2350-0.2356	0.2348-0.2354
	2.4 (2438)	2RZ-FE	45	44.5	40.0-46.0@ 1.406	1.406	0.0010-0.0024	0.0012-0.0026	0.2350-0.2356	0.2348-0.2354
	2.7 (2693)	3RZ-FE	45	44.5	40.0-46.0@ 1.406	1.406	0.0010-0.0024	0.0012-0.0026	0.2350-0.2356	0.2348-0.2354
	3.0 (2995)	1MZ-FE	45	44.5	41.9-46.3@ 1.33	1.791	0.0010-0.0024	0.0012-0.0026	0.2154-0.2159	0.2152-0.2157
	3.4 (3378)	5VZ-FE	45	44.5	41.9-46.3@ 1.311	1.311	0.0010-0.0024	0.0012-0.0026	0.2350-0.2356	0.2348-0.2354
	4.7 (4664)	2UZ-FE	45	44.5	45.9-50.7@ 1.378	1.380	0.0010-0.0024	0.0012-0.0026	0.2154-0.2159	0.2152-0.2157
2000-01	2.0 (1998)	3S-FE	45	44.5	36.8-42.5@ 1.366	1.366	0.0010-0.0024	0.0012-0.0026	0.2350-0.2356	0.2348-0.2354
	2.4 (2438)	2RZ-FE	45	44.5	40.0-46.0@ 1.406	1.406	0.0010-0.0024	0.0012-0.0026	0.2350-0.2356	0.2348-0.2354
	2.7 (2693)	3RZ-FE	45	44.5	40.0-46.0@ 1.406	1.406	0.0010-0.0024	0.0012-0.0026	0.2350-0.2356	0.2348-0.2354
	3.0 (2995)	1MZ-FE	45	44.5	41.9-46.3@ 1.33	1.791	0.0010-0.0024	0.0012-0.0026	0.2154-0.2159	0.2152-0.2157
	3.4 (3378)	5VZ-FE	45	44.5	41.9-46.3@ 1.311	1.311	0.0010-0.0024	0.0012-0.0026	0.2350-0.2356	0.2348-0.2354
	4.7 (4664)	2UZ-FE	45	44.5	45.9-50.7@ 1.378	1.380	0.0010-0.0024	0.0012-0.0026	0.2154-0.2159	0.2152-0.2157

93081CAN

CRANKSHAFT AND CONNECTING ROD SPECIFICATIONS
All measurements are given in inches.

Year	Engine Displacement Liters (cc)	Engine ID/VIN	Crankshaft				Connecting Rod		
			Main Brg. Journal Dia.	Main Brg. Oil Clearance	Shaft End-play	Thrust on No.	Journal Diameter	Oil Clearance	Side Clearance
1997	2.0 (1998)	3S-FE	2.1653-2.1655	0.0010-0.0017	0.0008-0.0087	3	2.0466-2.0472	0.0009-0.0022	0.0063-0.0123
	2.4 (2438)	2RZ-FE	2.3617-2.3622	0.0009-0.0022	0.0008-0.0087	2	2.0861-2.0866	0.0012-0.0022	0.0063-0.0123
	2.4 (2438)	2TZ-FE	2.3617-2.3622	0.0009-0.0022	0.0008-0.0087	2	2.0861-2.0866	0.0012-0.0022	0.0063-0.0123
	2.7 (2693)	3RZ-FE	2.2615-2.3620	0.0012-0.0022	0.0008-0.0087	3	2.0861-2.0866	0.0009-0.0022	0.0063-0.0123
	3.4 (3378)	5VZ-FE	2.5191-2.5197	0.0008-0.0015	0.0008-0.0087	2	2.1648-2.1654	0.0009-0.0021	0.0059-0.0130
	4.5 (4477)	1FZ-FE	2.7158-2.7165	0.0017-0.0024	0.0008-0.0087	4	2.2434-2.2441	0.0013-0.0020	0.0063-0.0103
1998	2.0 (1998)	3S-FE	2.1653-2.1655	0.0010-0.0017	0.0008-0.0087	3	2.0466-2.0472	0.0009-0.0022	0.0063-0.0123
	2.4 (2438)	2RZ-FE	2.3617-2.3622	0.0009-0.0022	0.0008-0.0087	2	2.0861-2.0866	0.0012-0.0022	0.0063-0.0123
	2.7 (2693)	3RZ-FE	2.2615-2.3620	0.0012-0.0022	0.0008-0.0087	3	2.0861-2.0866	0.0009-0.0022	0.0063-0.0123
	3.0 (2995)	1MZ-FE	2.4011-2.4016	①	0.0016-0.0095	2	2.0863-2.0866	0.0015-0.0025	0.0059-0.0188
	3.4 (3378)	5VZ-FE	2.5191-2.5197	0.0008-0.0015	0.0008-0.0087	2	2.1648-2.1654	0.0009-0.0021	0.0059-0.0130
	4.7 (4665)	2UZ-FE	2.6373-2.6378	0.0016-0.0023	0.0008-0.0087	3	2.0465-2.0472	0.0011-0.0021	0.0063-0.0138
1999	2.0 (1998)	3S-FE	2.1653-2.1655	0.0010-0.0017	0.0008-0.0087	3	2.0466-2.0472	0.0009-0.0022	0.0063-0.0123
	2.4 (2438)	2RZ-FE	2.3617-2.3622	0.0009-0.0022	0.0008-0.0087	2	2.0861-2.0866	0.0012-0.0022	0.0063-0.0123
	2.7 (2693)	3RZ-FE	2.2615-2.3620	0.0012-0.0022	0.0008-0.0087	3	2.0861-2.0866	0.0009-0.0022	0.0063-0.0123
	3.0 (2995)	1MZ-FE	2.4011-2.4016	①	0.0016-0.0095	2	2.0863-2.0866	0.0015-0.0025	0.0059-0.0188
	3.4 (3378)	5VZ-FE	2.5191-2.5197	0.0008-0.0015	0.0008-0.0087	2	2.1648-2.1654	0.0009-0.0021	0.0059-0.0130
	4.7 (4665)	2UZ-FE	2.6373-2.6378	0.0016-0.0023	0.0008-0.0087	3	2.0465-2.0472	0.0011-0.0021	0.0063-0.0138
2000-01	2.0 (1998)	3S-FE	2.1653-2.1655	0.0010-0.0017	0.0008-0.0087	3	2.0466-2.0472	0.0009-0.0022	0.0063-0.0123
	2.4 (2438)	2RZ-FE	2.3617-2.3622	0.0009-0.0022	0.0008-0.0087	2	2.0861-2.0866	0.0012-0.0022	0.0063-0.0123
	2.7 (2693)	3RZ-FE	2.2615-2.3620	0.0012-0.0022	0.0008-0.0087	3	2.0861-2.0866	0.0009-0.0022	0.0063-0.0123
	3.0 (2995)	1MZ-FE	2.4011-2.4016	①	0.0016-0.0095	2	2.0863-2.0866	0.0015-0.0025	0.0059-0.0188
	3.4 (3378)	5VZ-FE	2.5191-2.5197	0.0008-0.0015	0.0008-0.0087	2	2.1648-2.1654	0.0009-0.0021	0.0059-0.0130
	4.7 (4665)	2UZ-FE	2.6373-2.6378	0.0016-0.0023	0.0008-0.0087	3	2.0465-2.0472	0.0011-0.0021	0.0063-0.0138

① Journals 1 and 4: 0.0006 - 0.0013 in.
 Journals 2 and 3: 0.0010 - 0.0018 in.

93081CAO

For exhaust manifold replacement procedures, see the model specific sections of this manual

PISTON AND RING SPECIFICATIONS

All measurements are given in inches.

Year	Engine Displacement Liters (cc)	Engine ID/VIN	Piston Clearance	Ring Gap Top Compression	Ring Gap Bottom Compression	Ring Gap Oil Control	Ring Side Clearance Top Compression	Ring Side Clearance Bottom Compression	Ring Side Clearance Oil Control
1997	2.0 (1998)	3S-FE	0.0056-0.0064	0.0106-0.0185	0.0177-0.0256	0.0039-0.0177	0.0012-0.0028	0.0012-0.0028	SNUG
	2.4 (2438)	2TZ-FE	0.0012-0.0020	0.0118-0.0169	0.0177-0.0236	0.0051-0.0150	0.0008-0.0028	0.0012-0.0028	SNUG
	2.4 (2438)	2RZ-FE	0.0012-0.0020	0.0118-0.0169	0.0177-0.0236	0.0051-0.0150	0.0008-0.0028	0.0012-0.0028	SNUG
	2.7 (2693)	3RZ-FE	0.0019-0.0028	0.0118-0.0157	0.0157-0.0194	0.0051-0.0150	0.0008-0.0028	0.0012-0.0028	SNUG
	3.4 (3378)	5VZ-FE	0.0053-0.0060	0.0118-0.0197	0.0157-0.0236	0.0059-0.0217	0.0016-0.0031	0.0012-0.0028	SNUG
	4.5 (4477)	1FZ-FE	0.0016-0.0024	0.0118-0.0205	0.0177-0.0264	0.0059-0.0205	0.0016-0.0031	0.0012-0.0028	SNUG
1998	2.0 (1998)	3S-FE	0.0056-0.0064	0.0106-0.0185	0.0177-0.0256	0.0039-0.0177	0.0012-0.0028	0.0012-0.0028	SNUG
	2.4 (2438)	2RZ-FE	0.0012-0.0020	0.0118-0.0169	0.0177-0.0236	0.0051-0.0150	0.0008-0.0028	0.0012-0.0028	SNUG
	2.7 (2693)	3RZ-FE	0.0019-0.0028	0.0118-0.0157	0.0157-0.0194	0.0051-0.0150	0.0008-0.0028	0.0012-0.0028	SNUG
	3.0 (2995)	1MZ-FE	0.0033-0.0042	0.0098-0.0138	0.0138-0.0177	0.0059-0.0157	0.0008-0.0028	0.0008-0.0024	SNUG
	3.4 (3378)	5VZ-FE	0.0053-0.0060	0.0118-0.0197	0.0157-0.0236	0.0059-0.0217	0.0016-0.0031	0.0012-0.0028	SNUG
	4.7 (4665)	2UZ-FE	0.0035-0.0044	0.0118-0.0197	0.0157-0.0256	0.0051-0.0189	0.0012-0.0031	0.0012-0.0028	SNUG
1999	2.0 (1998)	3S-FE	0.0056-0.0064	0.0106-0.0185	0.0177-0.0256	0.0039-0.0177	0.0012-0.0028	0.0012-0.0028	SNUG
	2.4 (2438)	2RZ-FE	0.0012-0.0020	0.0118-0.0169	0.0177-0.0236	0.0051-0.0150	0.0008-0.0028	0.0012-0.0028	SNUG
	2.7 (2693)	3RZ-FE	0.0019-0.0028	0.0118-0.0157	0.0157-0.0194	0.0051-0.0150	0.0008-0.0028	0.0012-0.0028	SNUG
	3.0 (2995)	1MZ-FE	0.0033-0.0042	0.0098-0.0138	0.0138-0.0177	0.0059-0.0157	0.0008-0.0028	0.0008-0.0024	SNUG
	3.4 (3378)	5VZ-FE	0.0053-0.0060	0.0118-0.0197	0.0157-0.0236	0.0059-0.0217	0.0016-0.0031	0.0012-0.0028	SNUG
	4.7 (4665)	2UZ-FE	0.0035-0.0044	0.0118-0.0197	0.0157-0.0256	0.0051-0.0189	0.0012-0.0031	0.0012-0.0028	SNUG
2000-01	2.0 (1998)	3S-FE	0.0056-0.0064	0.0106-0.0185	0.0177-0.0256	0.0039-0.0177	0.0012-0.0028	0.0012-0.0028	SNUG
	2.4 (2438)	2RZ-FE	0.0012-0.0020	0.0118-0.0169	0.0177-0.0236	0.0051-0.0150	0.0008-0.0028	0.0012-0.0028	SNUG
	2.7 (2693)	3RZ-FE	0.0019-0.0028	0.0118-0.0157	0.0157-0.0194	0.0051-0.0150	0.0008-0.0028	0.0012-0.0028	SNUG
	3.0 (2995)	1MZ-FE	0.0033-0.0042	0.0098-0.0138	0.0138-0.0177	0.0059-0.0157	0.0008-0.0028	0.0008-0.0024	SNUG
	3.4 (3378)	5VZ-FE	0.0053-0.0060	0.0118-0.0197	0.0157-0.0236	0.0059-0.0217	0.0016-0.0031	0.0012-0.0028	SNUG
	4.7 (4665)	2UZ-FE	0.0035-0.0044	0.0118-0.0197	0.0157-0.0256	0.0051-0.0189	0.0012-0.0031	0.0012-0.0028	SNUG

93081CAP

TORQUE SPECIFICATIONS
All readings in ft. lbs.

Year	Engine Displacement Liters (cc)	Engine ID/VIN	Cylinder Head Bolts	Main Bearing Bolts	Rod Bearing Bolts	Crankshaft Damper Bolts	Flywheel Bolts	Manifold Intake	Manifold Exhaust	Spark Plugs	Lug Nuts
1997	2.0 (1998)	3S-FE	①	43	②	80	③	14	36	13	76
	2.4 (2438)	2RZ-FE	④	⑤	⑥	193	⑦	22	36	14	83
	2.4 (2438)	2TZ-FE	④	⑤	⑥	192	54	15	36	14	76
	2.7 (2693)	3RZ-FE	④	⑤	⑥	②	⑧	22	36	14	83
	3.4 (3378)	5VZ-FE	⑨	⑩	②	184	63-67	13	30	13	76
	4.5 (4477)	1FZ-FE	④	⑪	①	304	74	15	29	14	⑫
1998	2.0 (1998)	3S-FE	①	43	②	80	③	14	36	13	76
	2.4 (2438)	2RZ-FE	④	⑤	⑥	193	⑦	22	36	14	83
	2.7 (2693)	3RZ-FE	④	⑤	⑥	②	⑧	22	36	14	83
	3.0 (2995)	1MZ-FE	⑬	⑭	⑤	159	61	11	36	13	76
	3.4 (3378)	5VZ-FE	⑨	⑩	②	184	63-67	13	30	13	76
	4.7 (4664)	2UZ-FE	⑮	⑯	②	181	①	13	33	13	97
1999	2.0 (1998)	3S-FE	①	43	②	80	③	14	36	13	76
	2.4 (2438)	2RZ-FE	④	⑤	⑥	193	⑦	22	36	14	83
	2.7 (2693)	3RZ-FE	④	⑤	⑥	②	⑧	22	36	14	83
	3.0 (2995)	1MZ-FE	⑬	⑭	⑤	159	61	11	36	13	76
	3.4 (3378)	5VZ-FE	⑨	⑩	②	184	63-67	13	30	13	76
	4.7 (4664)	2UZ-FE	⑮	⑯	②	181	①	13	33	13	97
2000-01	2.0 (1998)	3S-FE	①	43	②	80	③	14	36	13	76
	2.4 (2438)	2RZ-FE	④	⑤	⑥	193	⑦	22	36	14	83
	2.7 (2693)	3RZ-FE	④	⑤	⑥	②	⑧	22	36	14	83
	3.0 (2995)	1MZ-FE	⑬	⑭	⑤	159	61	11	36	13	76
	3.4 (3378)	5VZ-FE	⑨	⑩	②	184	63-67	13	30	13	76
	4.7 (4664)	2UZ-FE	⑮	⑯	②	181	①	13	33	13	97

① Step 1: 35 ft. lbs.
　Step 2: Plus 90 degrees

② Step 1: 18 ft. lbs.
　Step 2: Plus 90 degrees

③ Manual transmission: 65 ft. lbs.
　Automatic transmission: 61 ft. lbs.

④ Step 1: 29 ft. lbs.
　Step 2: Plus 90 degrees
　Step 3: Plus 90 degrees

⑤ Step 1: 29 ft. lbs.
　Step 2: Plus 90 degrees

⑥ Step 1: 33 ft. lbs.
　Step 2: Plus 90 degrees

⑦ Manual transmission: 65 ft. lbs.
　Automatic transmission: 54 ft. lbs.

⑧ Manual transmission: 19 ft. lbs. + 90°
　Automatic transmission: 54 ft. lbs.

⑨ Step 1: 25 ft. lbs.
　Step 2: Plus 90 degrees
　Recessed head: 13 ft. lbs.

⑩ Step 1: 45 ft. lbs.
　Step 2: Plus 90 degrees

⑪ Step 1: 54 ft. lbs.
　Step 2: Plus 90 degrees

⑫ Steel wheel: 109 ft. lbs.
　Aluminum wheel: 76 ft. lbs.

⑬ Step 1: 40 ft. lbs.
　Step 2: Plus 90 degrees
　Recessed bolt: 13 ft. lbs.

⑭ 6-point bolts: 20 ft. lbs.
　12-point bolts:
　　Step 1: 16 ft. lbs.
　　Step 2: Plus 90 degrees

⑮ Step 1: 24 ft. lbs.
　Step 2: Plus 180 degrees

⑯ Step 1: 20 ft. lbs.
　Step 2: Plus 90 degrees

93081CAQ

Refer to the model specific sections for cooling system service procedures

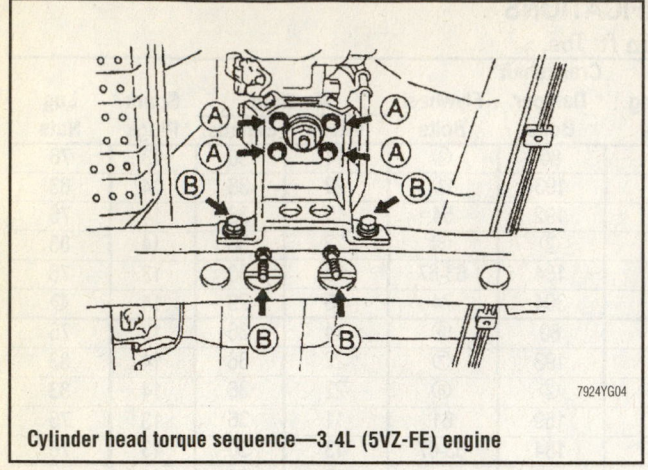

Cylinder head torque sequence—3.4L (5VZ-FE) engine

7924YG04

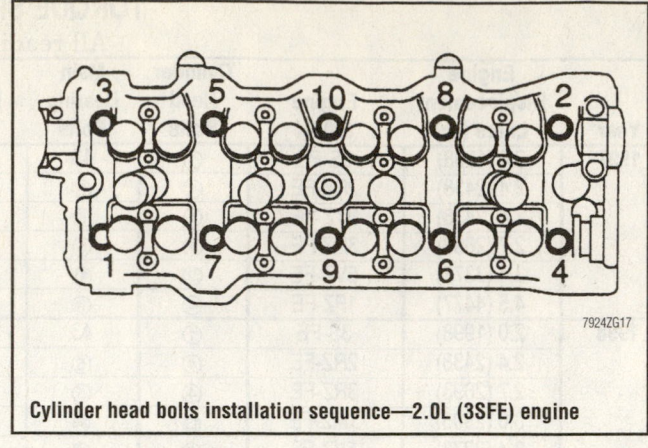

Cylinder head bolts installation sequence—2.0L (3SFE) engine

7924ZG17

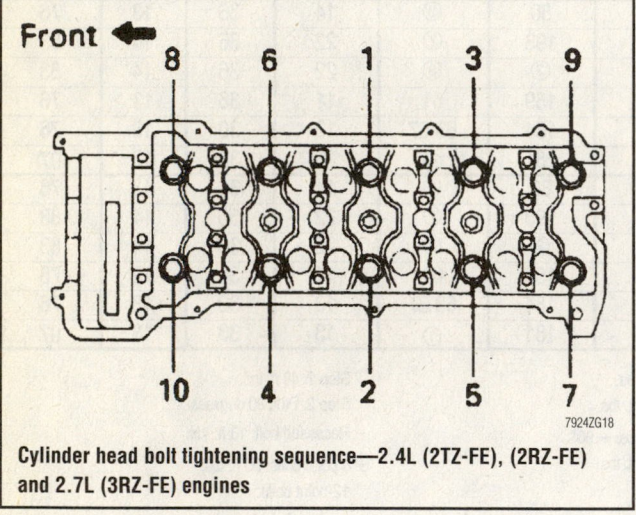

Cylinder head bolt tightening sequence—2.4L (2TZ-FE), (2RZ-FE) and 2.7L (3RZ-FE) engines

7924ZG18

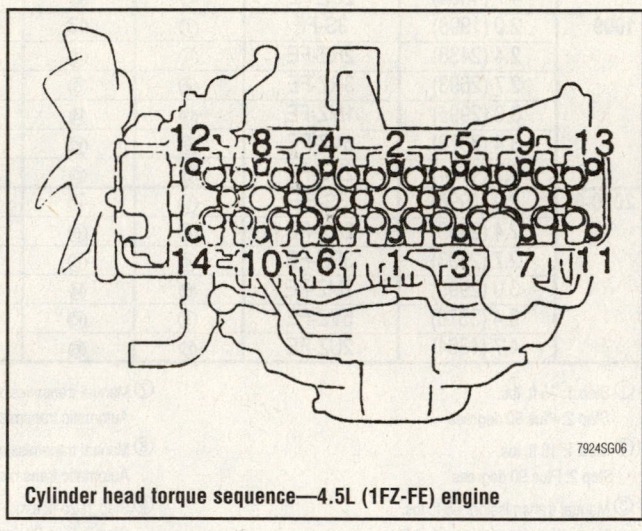

Cylinder head torque sequence—4.5L (1FZ-FE) engine

7924SG06

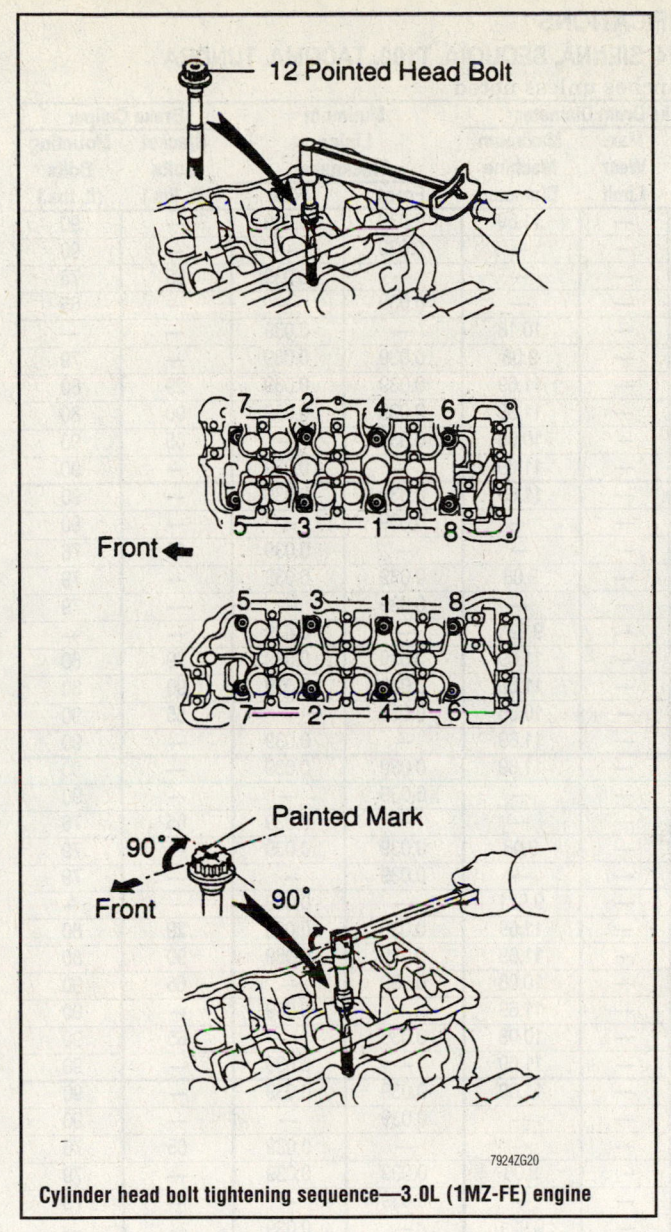

Cylinder head bolt tightening sequence—3.0L (1MZ-FE) engine

7924ZG20

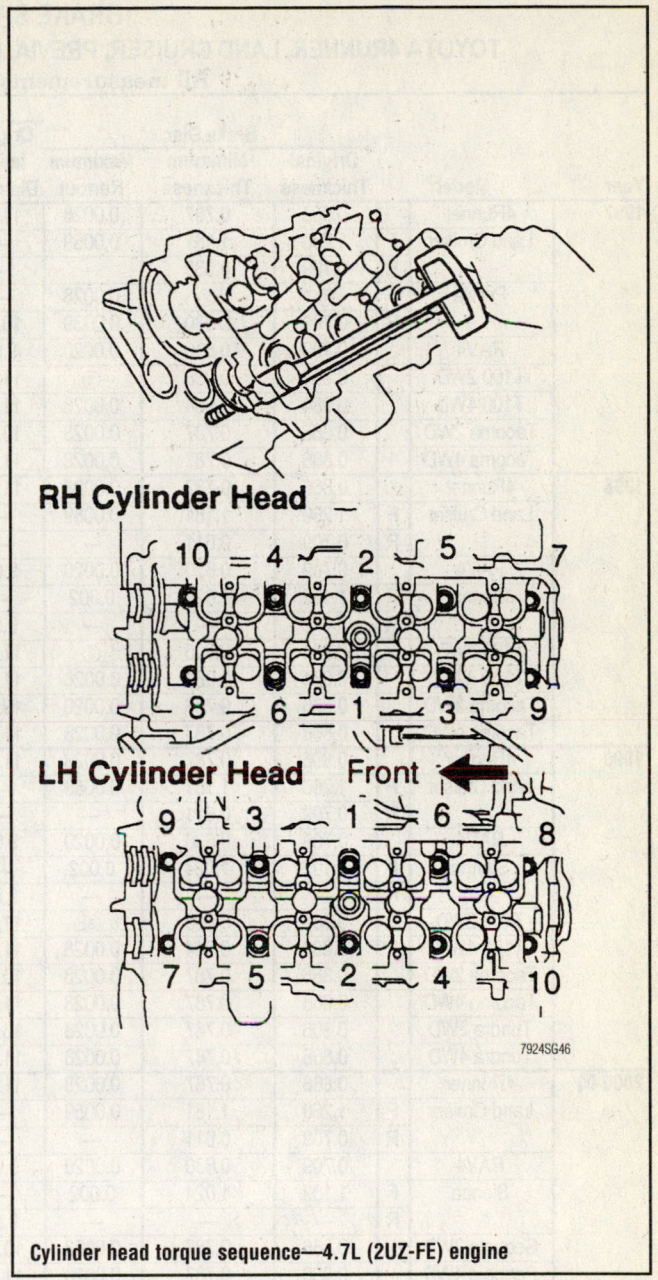

Cylinder head torque sequence—4.7L (2UZ-FE) engine

7924SG46

BRAKE SPECIFICATIONS
TOYOTA 4RUNNER, LAND CRUISER, PREVIA, RAV4, SIENNA, SEQUOIA, T100, TACOMA, TUNDRA
All measurements in inches unless noted

Year	Model		Brake Disc Original Thickness	Brake Disc Minimum Thickness	Maximum Runout	Brake Drum Diameter Original Inside Diameter	Max. Wear Limit	Brake Drum Diameter Maximum Machine Diameter	Minimum Lining Thickness Front	Minimum Lining Thickness Rear	Brake Caliper Bracket Bolts (ft. lbs.)	Brake Caliper Mounting Bolts (ft. lbs.)
1997	4Runner		0.866	0.787	0.0028	11.61	—	11.69	0.039	0.039	—	90
	Land Cruiser	F	1.260	1.181	0.0059	—	—	—	0.039	—	—	90
		R	0.709	0.630	—	—	—	—	—	0.039	65	76
	Previa	F	①	②	0.0028	—	—	—	0.039	—	—	65
		R	0.709	0.630	0.0039	10.00	—	10.18	—	0.039	—	—
	RAV4		0.709	0.630	0.0020	9.00	—	9.08	0.039	0.039	—	79
	T100 2WD		0.984	0.906	③	11.61	—	11.69	0.039	0.039	29	80
	T100 4WD		0.984	0.984	0.0028	11.61	—	11.69	0.039	0.039	90	80
	Tacoma 2WD		0.866	0.787	0.0028	10.00	—	10.08	0.039	—	65	90
	Tacoma 4WD		0.866	0.787	0.0028	11.61	—	11.69	—	0.039	—	90
1998	4Runner		0.866	0.787	0.0028	11.61	—	11.69	0.039	0.039	—	90
	Land Cruiser	F	1.260	1.181	0.0059	—	—	—	0.039	—	—	90
		R	0.709	0.611	—	—	—	—	—	0.039	65	76
	RAV4		0.709	0.630	0.0020	9.00	—	9.08	0.039	0.039	—	79
	Sienna	F	1.102	1.024	0.002	—	—	—	0.039	—	—	79
		R	—	—	—	9.84	—	9.921	—	0.039	—	—
	T100 2WD		0.984	0.906	③	11.61	—	11.69	0.039	0.039	29	80
	T100 4WD		0.984	0.984	0.0028	11.61	—	11.69	0.039	0.039	90	80
	Tacoma 2WD		0.866	0.787	0.0028	10.00	—	10.08	0.039	—	65	90
	Tacoma 4WD		0.866	0.787	0.0028	11.61	—	11.69	—	0.039	—	90
1999	4Runner		0.866	0.787	0.0028	11.61	—	11.69	0.039	0.039	—	90
	Land Cruiser	F	1.260	1.181	0.0059	—	—	—	0.039	—	—	90
		R	0.709	0.611	—	—	—	—	—	0.039	65	76
	RAV4		0.709	0.630	0.0020	9.00	—	9.08	0.039	0.039	—	79
	Sienna	F	1.102	1.024	0.002	—	—	—	0.039	—	—	79
		R	—	—	—	9.84	—	9.921	—	0.039	—	—
	T100 2WD		0.984	0.906	③	11.61	—	11.69	0.039	0.039	29	80
	T100 4WD		0.984	0.984	0.0028	11.61	—	11.69	0.039	0.039	90	80
	Tacoma 2WD		0.866	0.787	0.0028	10.00	—	10.08	0.039	—	65	90
	Tacoma 4WD		0.866	0.787	0.0028	11.61	—	11.69	—	0.039	—	90
	Tundra 2WD		0.866	0.787	0.0028	10.00	—	10.08	0.039	—	65	90
	Tundra 4WD		0.866	0.787	0.0028	11.61	—	11.69	—	0.039	—	90
2000-01	4Runner		0.866	0.787	0.0028	11.61	—	11.69	0.039	0.039	—	90
	Land Cruiser	F	1.260	1.181	0.0059	—	—	—	0.039	—	—	90
		R	0.709	0.611	—	—	—	—	—	0.039	65	76
	RAV4		0.709	0.630	0.0020	9.00	—	9.08	0.039	0.039	—	79
	Sienna	F	1.102	1.024	0.002	—	—	—	0.039	—	—	79
		R	—	—	—	9.84	—	9.921	—	0.039	—	—
	Sequoia 2WD		0.866	0.787	0.0028	10.00	—	10.08	0.039	—	65	90
	Sequoia 4WD		0.866	0.787	0.0028	11.61	—	11.69	—	0.039	—	90
	T100 2WD		0.984	0.906	③	11.61	—	11.69	0.039	0.039	29	80
	T100 4WD		0.984	0.984	0.0028	11.61	—	11.69	0.039	0.039	90	80
	Tacoma 2WD		0.866	0.787	0.0028	10.00	—	10.08	0.039	—	65	90
	Tacoma 4WD		0.866	0.787	0.0028	11.61	—	11.69	—	0.039	—	90
	Tundra 2WD		0.866	0.787	0.0028	10.00	—	10.08	0.039	—	65	90
	Tundra 4WD		0.866	0.787	0.0028	11.61	—	11.69	—	0.039	—	90

F: Front
R: Rear
① With rear drum brake: 0.985
With rear disc brake: 0.866
② With rear drum brake: 0.906
With rear disc brake: 0.787
③ 1 ton: 0.0035
1/2 ton: 0.0028

93081CAR

SCHEDULED MAINTENANCE INTERVALS
(TOYOTA LAND CRUISER, PREVIA, RAV4, SIENNA, T100, TACOMA, TUNDRA & 4RUNNER)

TO BE SERVICED	TYPE OF SERVICE	VEHICLE MILEAGE INTERVAL (x1000)																		
		5	10	15	20	25	30	35	40	45	50	55	60	65	70	75	80	85	90	95
Automatic transmission and differential fluid	S/I			✓			✓			✓			✓			✓			✓	
Ball joints and boots	S/I			✓			✓			✓			✓			✓			✓	
Brake linings, discs/drums, lines & hoses	S/I			✓			✓			✓			✓			✓			✓	
Charcoal canister	S/I												✓							
Drive belts	S/I						✓						✓						✓	
Driveshaft bushing (4WD except Previa)	L						✓						✓						✓	
Engine coolant	R						✓						✓						✓	
Engine oil & filter	R	✓	✓	✓	✓	✓	✓	✓	✓	✓	✓	✓	✓	✓	✓	✓	✓	✓	✓	✓
Exhaust pipes & mounts	S/I			✓			✓			✓			✓			✓			✓	
Fuel lines & connections, fuel tank vapor vent system hoses, fuel tank band	S/I						✓						✓						✓	
Fuel tank cap gasket	S/I						✓						✓						✓	
Halfshaft boots & flange bolts	S/I			✓			✓			✓			✓			✓			✓	
Limited slip differential fluid	R						✓						✓						✓	
Manual transmission and differential fluid	S/I						✓						✓						✓	
Non-platinum spark plugs	R						✓						✓						✓	
Platinum spark plugs	R												✓							
Propeller shaft (4WD models except RAV4)	L			✓			✓			✓			✓			✓			✓	
Propeller shaft bolts	S/I			✓			✓			✓			✓			✓			✓	
Rack and pinion assembly	S/I			✓			✓			✓			✓			✓			✓	
Rear wheel bearing (T100, Tacoma, 4Runner and Land Cruiser)	L						✓						✓						✓	
Steering Knuckle (Land Cruiser)	L			✓			✓			✓			✓			✓			✓	

93081CAS

Timing chain and gear service is covered in the model specific sections of this manual

SCHEDULED MAINTENANCE INTERVALS
(TOYOTA LAND CRUISER, PREVIA, RAV4, SIENNA, T100, TACOMA, TUNDRA & 4RUNNER) (Cont.)

TO BE SERVICED	TYPE OF SERVICE	VEHICLE MILEAGE INTERVAL (x1000)																		
		5	10	15	20	25	30	35	40	45	50	55	60	65	70	75	80	85	90	95
Steering linkage	S/I			✓			✓			✓			✓			✓			✓	
Supercharger gear oil (Previa)	S/I						✓						✓						✓	
Transfer case and differential fluid (RAV4)	S/I			✓			✓			✓			✓			✓			✓	
Valves	S/I												✓							

R: Replace   S/I: Service or Inspect   L: Lubricate

FREQUENT OPERATION MAINTENANCE (SEVERE SERVICE)

 If a vehicle is operated under any of the following conditions it is considered severe service:

- Towing a trailer or using a camper or car-top carrier.

- Repeated short trips of less than 5 miles in temperatures below freezing.

- Excessive idling or low-speed driving for long distances as in heavy commercial use, such as delivery, taxi or police cars.

- Operating on rough, muddy or salt-covered roads.

- Operating on unpaved or dusty roads.

Oil filter: service or inspect every 5000 miles or 4 months, whichever occurs first.

Brake linings and discs or drums: service or inspect every 5000 miles or 4 months, whichever occurs first.

Steering linkage: service or inspect every 5000 miles or 4 months, whichever occurs first.

Ball joints and boots: service or inspect every 5000 miles or 4 months, whichever occurs first.

Brake discs & pads (front): service or inspect every 6000 miles.

Halfshaft boots: service or inspect every 5000 miles or 4 months. Retighten the flange bolts, whichever occurs first.

Body chassis bolts and nuts: service or inspect every 5000 miles or 4 months, whichever occurs first.

Transmission and differential fluid: replace every 15,000 miles or 12 months, whichever occurs first.

Transfer case and differential fluid (Tacoma, T100, 4Runner and Land Cruiser): replace every 15,000 miles or 12 months, whichever occurs first.

Timing belt: replace every 60,000 miles or 48 months, whichever occurs first.

93081CAT

SCHEDULED MAINTENANCE INTERVALS
TOYOTA
LAND CRUISER, PREVIA, RAV4, SIENNA, T100, TACOMA, TUNDRA, 4RUNNER

The following should be used as a guide when determining the amount of work required for a particular service. In estimating how long a particular Scheduled Maintenance Service should take, please observe the following:

● Labor Time is time based on field research and data supplied by the vehicle manufacturer.
● Labor time operations are given in hours and tenths of an hour.
● All labor operations are to be used as a guide.

Mechanic Skill Level Codes:
(A) PRECISION: Highly skilled with multiple certification.
(B) GENERAL: Normally skilled with certification.
(C) MAINTENANCE: Semi-skilled working on certification.

	LABOR TIME
5000 Mile Service (C)	
All Models	.4
10000 Mile Service (C)	
All Models	.4
15000 Mile Service (B)	
Land Cruiser, Tundra	2.1
Previa	
2WD	1.6
4WD	1.9
Sienna	1.7
RAV4	1.9
T100	
4 cyl.	1.8
6 cyl.	
2WD	1.3
4WD	1.8
Tacoma	
2WD	1.8
4WD	1.9
4Runner	
2WD	1.3
4WD	1.8
20000 Mile Service (C)	
All Models	.4
22500 Mile Service (C)	
Land Cruiser, Tundra	.9
Previa	.9
RAV4	.9
T100	1.1
Tacoma	.9
4Runner	1.1
25000 Mile Service (C)	
All Models	.4
30000 Mile Service (B)	
Land Cruiser, Tundra	3.8
Previa	2.9
Sienna	2.7
RAV4	3.7
T100	3.7

	LABOR TIME
Tacoma	3.8
4Runner	4.1
35000 Mile Service (C)	
All Models	.4
37500 Mile Service (C)	
RAV4	.9
40000 Mile Service (C)	
All Models	.4
45000 Mile Service (B)	
Land Cruiser, Tundra	2.1
Previa	
2WD	1.6
4WD	1.9
Sienna	1.7
RAV4	1.9
T100	
4 cyl.	1.8
6 cyl.	
2WD	1.3
4WD	1.8
Tacoma	
2WD	1.8
4WD	1.9
4Runner	
2WD	1.3
4WD	1.8
50000 Mile Service (C)	
All Models	.4
55000 Mile Service (C)	
All Models	.3
60000 Mile Service (B)	
Land Cruiser, Tundra	3.8
Previa	2.9
Sienna	2.7
RAV4	3.7
T100	3.7
Tacoma	3.8

	LABOR TIME
4Runner	4.1
65000 Mile Service (C)	
All Models	.4
70000 Mile Service (C)	
All Models	.4
75000 Mile Service (B)	
Land Cruiser, Tundra	2.1
Previa	
2WD	1.6
4WD	1.9
Sienna	1.7
RAV4	1.9
T100	
4 cyl.	1.8
6 cyl.	
2WD	1.3
4WD	1.8
Tacoma	
2WD	1.8
4WD	1.9
4Runner	
2WD	1.1
4WD	1.8
80000 Mile Service (C)	
All Models	.4
85000 Mile Service (C)	
All Models	.4
90000 Mile Service (B)	
Land Cruiser, Tundra	3.8
Previa	2.9
Sienna	2.7
RAV4	3.7
T100	3.7
Tacoma	3.8
4Runner	4.1
95000 Mile Service (C)	
All Models	.4

93081CAU

Ignition system service is covered in the model specific sections of this manual

TIRE, WHEEL AND BALL JOINT SPECIFICATIONS
Toyota Truck

| Year | Model | OEM Tires | | Tire Pressures (psi) | | Wheel Size | Ball Joint Inspection |
		Standard	Optional	Front	Rear		
1997	Tacoma 2wd	P195/75R14	None	29	35	5-J	①
	Tacoma 2wd Xtracab	P215/70R14	None	29	29	6-JJ	4-30 in. ②
	Tacoma 4wd	P225/75R15	31x10.5R15 LT	26	29	7-JJ	4-30 in. ②
	T100 2wd	P215/75R15	P235/75R15	Std: 33 Opt: 26	Std: 35 Opt: 28	Std: 6-JJ Opt: 7-JJ	①
	T100 4wd	P235/75R15	P265/70R16 31x10.5R15 LT	26	29	7-JJ	①
	T100 1 Ton	P235/75R15	None	26	40	7-JJ	①
	Land Cruiser	P275/70R15	None	32	32	8-JJ	①
	4Runner	P225/75R15	P265/70R16	Std: 29 Opt: 32	Std: 29 Opt: 32	7-JJ	6-39 in. ②
	Rav4	P215/70R16	P235/60HR15	28	28	6.5-JJ	4-30 in. ②
1998	T100 2wd	P215/75R15	P235/75R15	Std: 33 Opt: 26	Std: 35 Opt: 28	Std: 6-JJ Opt: 7-JJ	①
	T100 4wd	P235/75R15	P265/70R16 31x10.5R15 LT	26	29	7-JJ	①
	T100 1 Ton	P235/75R15	None	26	40	7-JJ	①
	Land Cruiser	P275/70R15	None	32	32	8-JJ	①
	4Runner	P225/75R15	P265/70R16	Std: 29 Opt: 32	Std: 29 Opt: 32	7-JJ	4-30 in. ②
	Rav4	P215/70R16	P235/60HR15	28	28	6.5-JJ	4-30 in. ②
	Tacoma 2wd	P195/75R14	None	29	35	5-J	4-30 in. ②
	Tacoma 2wd Xtracab	P215/70R14	None	29	29	6-JJ	4-30 in. ②
	Tacoma 4wd & Prerunner	P225/75R15	31x10.5R15 LT	29	29	7-JJ	4-30 in. ②
1999	Land Cruiser	P275/70R15	None	32	32	8-JJ	4-30 in. ②
	4Runner	P225/75R15	P265/70R16	Std: 29 Opt: 32	Std: 29 Opt: 32	7-JJ	6-39 in. ②
	Rav4	P215/70R16	P235/60HR15	28	28	6.5-JJ	4-30 in. ②
	Tacoma 2wd	P195/75R14	None	29	35	5-J	4-30 in. ②
	Tacoma 2wd Xtracab	P215/70R14	None	29	29	6-JJ	4-30 in. ②
	Tacoma 4wd & Prerunner	P225/75R15	31x10.5R15 LT	26	29	7-JJ	4-30 in. ②
2000-01	Land Cruiser	P275/70R15	None	32	32	8-JJ	①
	4Runner	P225/75R15	P265/70R16	Std: 29 Opt: 32	Std: 29 Opt: 32	7-JJ	6-39 in. ②
	Rav4	P215/70R16	P235/60HR15	28	28	6.5-JJ	4-30 in. ②
	Tacoma 2wd	P195/75R14	None	29	35	5-J	4-30 in. ②
	Tacoma 2wd Xtracab	P215/70R14	None	29	29	6-JJ	4-30 in. ②
	Tacoma 4wd & Prerunner	P225/75R15	31x10.5R15 LT	26	29	7-JJ	4-30 in. ②

OEM: Original Equipment Manufacturer

PSI: Pounds Per Square Inch

STD: Standard

OPT: Optional

① Replace if any measurable movement is found.

② Torque required in inch lbs. to rotate ball joint when removed from the knuckle

93081CAV

MAINTENANCE LIGHT RESETTING AND DTC RETRIEVAL

2

2-2 **MAINTENANCE LIGHT RESETTING AND DTC RETRIEVAL**
CHRYSLER CORP.

ISUZU

MAINTENANCE LIGHT RESETTING

This section describes reset procedures for maintenance lights. Maintenance lights are used to indicate to the operator of the vehicle that some type of routine maintenance should be performed. Unlike a Check Engine light that will be displayed when there is a fault with the engine management system, the maintenance light will be displayed when an engine or transmission oil change is recommended according to driving conditions. Also, the light will be displayed to indicate when the emission control system needs to be serviced.

Chrysler Corp.

RESETTING

The Emission Maintenance Reminder (EMR) light is now referred to as a Service Reminder Indicator (SRI) lamp. It is located

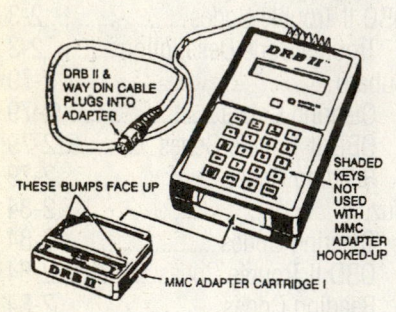

THESE BUMPS FACE UP

MMC ADAPTER CARTRIDGE I

79242G01

The Chrysler second generation Digital Readout Box (DRB-II) scan tool is needed to reset the Service Reminder Light on 5.9L and 8.0L Dodge models

in the dash and is labeled MAINT REQD. It is used on 5.9L V8 HDC engine and 8.0L V10 gas powered engine vehicles only. The SRI lamp will illuminate at the 60,000 and 82,000 mile (96,000 and 131,000 km) marks and will remain ON until it is reset. Perform the required maintenance before resetting the lamp. Failure to adhere to part replacement or service required may be a violation of federal law. Resetting the SRI lamp requires the use of the second generation Digital Readout Box (DRB-II) scan tool or equivalent. Consult the scan tool's instruction guide for this procedure.

Ford Motor Co.

RESETTING

1997 Explorer

The 1997 Explorer is equipped with the CHANGE OIL SOON or OIL CHANGE REQUIRED light. When oil life left is between five percent and zero percent, CHANGE OIL SOON will be displayed on the message center. When oil life reaches zero percent, the OIL CHANGE REQUIRED message will be displayed. The message center indicator will indicate the percent of oil life left during the System Check. This percentage is based on the driver's driving history and the time since the last oil change. In order to ensure oil life left indications, the driver should only perform the OIL CHANGE RESET procedure after every oil change. Reset the system by pressing the OIL CHANGE RESET switch and holding it for 5 seconds. After a successful reset the

Message Center will display oil life indicators. The CHANGE OIL SOON or OIL CHANGE REQUIRED message will disappear after the 5 second interval.

Isuzu

RESETTING

Oasis

The 1997 Oasis is equipped with a maintenance reminder indicator located on the instrument panel. It lets the driver know it is time for a scheduled maintenance. When it is near 7500 miles (12,000 km) since the last maintenance, the indicator will turn yellow. If you exceed 7500 miles (12,000 km), the indicator will turn red. When the required maintenance has been performed, the indicator can be reset by inserting the ignition key or other similar object into the slot below the indicator. This will extinguish the indicator for the next 7500 miles (12,000 km).

The 1998–01 Oasis is equipped with a maintenance reminder indicator located on the instrument panel. It lets the driver know it is time for a scheduled maintenance. The maintenance reminder light will blink for 10 seconds when the ignition is first turned **ON** between 6000–7500 miles (9500–12,000 km) since the last maintenance service, after 7500 miles (12,000 km) the light will stay on for 10 seconds. When the required maintenance has been performed, the indicator can be reset by pushing in and holding the select/reset switch for more than 10 seconds with the ignition switch **ON**.

OBD II DIAGNOSTIC TROUBLE CODE RETRIEVAL

Introduction

To comply with OBD II Regulations, the Control Module is equipped with software designed to allow it to monitor vehicle emission control systems and components. Once the ignition is turned on or the engine is started, and certain test conditions are met, the PCM runs a series of monitors to test the emission control systems and components. Test conditions include different inputs such as time since startup, run-time, engine speed and temperature, transaxle gear position, and the engine open or closed loop status. Once the monitor is started, the control module attempts to run

it to completion. If a particular monitor fails a test, a code is set and operating conditions at that time are recorded in memory. If the same component or system fails twice in succession, the Malfunction Indicator Lamp (MIL) is activated.

Monitors are divided into 2 types: Main Monitors and Comprehensive Component Monitors.

- Catalyst Monitor
- EGR Monitor
- EVAP Monitor
- Fuel System Monitor
- Misfire Monitor
- Oxygen Sensor Monitor
- Oxygen Sensor Heater Monitor

Certain monitors, in particular the fuel system and misfire monitors, have limitations that are different from any of the other monitors. The first time either of these monitors fail, the MIL is activated and engine conditions at the time of the fault are recorded. In order for the control module to turn off, an MIL related to these 2 monitors, must determine that no faults are present with engine operating conditions similar to when it detected the fault. To qualify, the engine must be operated within a specified speed range, engine load range and temperature range.

A warm-up cycle is considered to be a vehicle operation after the engine has been turned off for a period of time, with the ECT input rising a specified amount and reaching normal operating temperature. When the MIL is turned off because a fault is no longer present, most OBD II codes will be erased after a minimum of 40 warm-up cycles. Misfire and fuel system codes require a minimum of 80 warm-up cycles before they clear.

OBD II Systems use a standardized test connector, called the Data Link Connector (DLC); it is located under the left side of the instrument panel. The DLC is located out of the line of sight of vehicle passengers, but is easily viewable from a kneeling position outside the vehicle. The connector is rectangular in design and contains up to 16 terminals. It has keying features to allow for easy connection. Both the DLC and Scan Tool connectors have latching features that ensure the scan tool will remain properly connected.

Some common uses of the Scan Tool are to identify and clear Diagnostic Trouble Codes (DTCs) and to read control module freeze frame.

The Malfunction Indicator Lamp (MIL) looks similar to the "Check Engine" lamp. However, on OBD II Systems, it is controlled under a strict set of guidelines that dictate when the MIL is illuminated. If any of the control module monitors detect a fault that could impact vehicle emissions, a fault code is set. A One-Trip Monitor requires that a test fail once, a Two-Trip Monitor requires a test fail twice in succession, and a Three-Trip Monitor requires that a test fail three times in succession to activate the MIL.

The MIL is mounted in the instrument panel and has 2 functions: To act as a bulb check at key On and to inform the driver that an emissions fault has occurred.

Once the engine is started, if no faults are detected, the control module should extinguish the MIL after a few seconds. If the MIL remains On or flashes with the engine running, a driveability symptom is present.

OBD II Trouble Codes

Federal law required all vehicle manufacturers to meet On Board Diagnostics, Second Generation or OBD II. In order to meet this standard, the automobile's on-board computer must monitor and perform diagnostic tests on vehicle emissions to ensure that the vehicle is operating at an acceptable (legal) emission level. The maximum allowable emission level is set by the Federal Test Procedure (FTP).

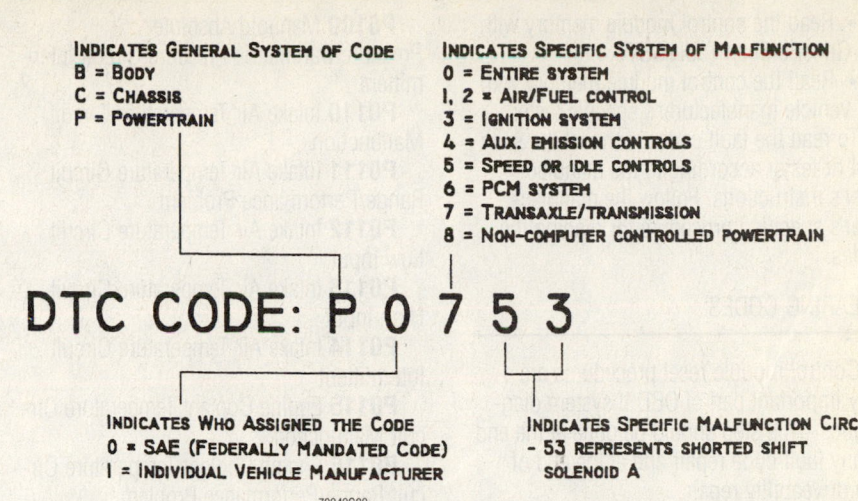

INDICATES GENERAL SYSTEM OF CODE
B = BODY
C = CHASSIS
P = POWERTRAIN

INDICATES SPECIFIC SYSTEM OF MALFUNCTION
0 = ENTIRE SYSTEM
1, 2 = AIR/FUEL CONTROL
3 = IGNITION SYSTEM
4 = AUX. EMISSION CONTROLS
5 = SPEED OR IDLE CONTROLS
6 = PCM SYSTEM
7 = TRANSAXLE/TRANSMISSION
8 = NON-COMPUTER CONTROLLED POWERTRAIN

DTC CODE: P 0 7 5 3

INDICATES WHO ASSIGNED THE CODE
0 = SAE (FEDERALLY MANDATED CODE)
1 = INDIVIDUAL VEHICLE MANUFACTURER

INDICATES SPECIFIC MALFUNCTION CIRCUIT
- 53 REPRESENTS SHORTED SHIFT SOLENOID A

79242G99

OBD II Diagnostic Trouble Code (DTC) break-down

All OBD II vehicles have the same 16 pin diagnostic connector or DLC. This eliminates the need to have a manufacturer specific connector to plug a scan tool into your vehicle.

TROUBLE CODE DESCRIPTION

In the past, trouble code numbers varied between manufacturers, years, makes and models. OBD II requires that all vehicle manufacturers use a common Diagnostic Trouble Code (DTC) numbering system. Since the generic listing was not specific enough, most manufacturers came up with their own DTC listings which are called manufacturer specific codes. Both generic and manufacturer specific codes are 5 digits. The numbers can be decoded as follows:

The first digit is a letter which identifies the function of the device or circuit which has the fault. This digit can be either:
- P—Powertrain
- B—Body
- C—Chassis
- U—Network or data link code

The second digit is either a 0 or 1 and indicates whether the code is generic or manufacturer specific.
- 0—Generic
- 1—Manufacturer Specific

The third digit represents the specific vehicle circuit or system that has the fault. Listed below are the number identifiers for the powertrain system.
- 1—Fuel and Air Metering
- 2—Fuel and Air Metering (Injector Circuit Malfunctions Only)
- 3—Ignition System or Misfire

- 4—Auxiliary Emission Control
- 5—Vehicle Speed Control and Idle Control System
- 6—Computer and Auxiliary Outputs
- 7—Transmission
- 8—Transmission

The last 2 digits indicate the specific trouble code.

On OBD II vehicles there are 2 different types of DTCs: Stored and Pending. For a DTC to become Stored, certain malfunction conditions must occur. The condition(s) required to Store codes are different for every DTC and vary by vehicle manufacturer.

In order for some DTCs to become Stored, a malfunction condition has to happen more than once. If the malfunction conditions are required to occur more than once, the potential malfunction is called a Pending DTC. The DTC remains pending until the malfunction condition occurs the required number of times to make the code stored. If the malfunction condition does not occur again after a set time the pending DTC will be cleared.

Acura

READING CODES

Reading the control module memory is one of the first steps in OBD II system diagnostics. This step should be initially performed to determine the general nature of the fault. Subsequent readings will determine if the fault has been cleared.

Reading codes can be performed by any of the methods below:

• Read the control module memory with the Generic Scan Tool (GST)

• Read the control module memory with the vehicle manufacturer's specific tester

To read the fault codes, connect the scan tool or tester according to the manufacturer's instructions. Follow the manufacturer's specified procedure for reading the codes.

CLEARING CODES

Control module reset procedures are a very important part of OBD II system diagnostics. This step should be done at the end of any fault code repair and at the end of any driveability repair.

Clearing codes can be performed by any of the methods below:

• Clear the control module memory with the Generic Scan Tool (GST)

• Clear the control module memory with the vehicle manufacturer's specific tester

• Turn the ignition OFF and remove the negative battery cable for at least 1 minute.

Removing the negative battery cable may cause other systems in the vehicle to loose their memory. Prior to removing the cable, ensure you have the proper reset codes for radios and alarms.

➡ **The MIL will may also be de-activated for some codes if the vehicle completes three consecutive trips without a fault detected with vehicle conditions similar to those present during the fault.**

OBD II TROUBLE CODES

P0100 Mass or Volume Air Flow Circuit Malfunction

P0101 Mass or Volume Air Flow Circuit Range/Performance Problem

P0102 Mass or Volume Air Flow Circuit Low Input

P0103 Mass or Volume Air Flow Circuit High Input

P0104 Mass or Volume Air Flow Circuit Intermittent

P0105 Manifold Absolute Pressure/Barometric Pressure Circuit Malfunction

P0106 Manifold Absolute Pressure/Barometric Pressure Circuit Range/Performance Problem

P0107 Manifold Absolute Pressure/Barometric Pressure Circuit Low Input

P0108 Manifold Absolute Pressure/Barometric Pressure Circuit High Input

P0109 Manifold Absolute Pressure/Barometric Pressure Circuit Intermittent

P0110 Intake Air Temperature Circuit Malfunction

P0111 Intake Air Temperature Circuit Range/Performance Problem

P0112 Intake Air Temperature Circuit Low Input

P0113 Intake Air Temperature Circuit High Input

P0114 Intake Air Temperature Circuit Intermittent

P0115 Engine Coolant Temperature Circuit Malfunction

P0116 Engine Coolant Temperature Circuit Range/Performance Problem

P0117 Engine Coolant Temperature Circuit Low Input

P0118 Engine Coolant Temperature Circuit High Input

P0119 Engine Coolant Temperature Circuit Intermittent

P0120 Throttle/Pedal Position Sensor/Switch "A" Circuit Malfunction

P0121 Throttle/Pedal Position Sensor/Switch "A" Circuit Range/Performance Problem

P0122 Throttle/Pedal Position Sensor/Switch "A" Circuit Low Input

P0123 Throttle/Pedal Position Sensor/Switch "A" Circuit High Input

P0124 Throttle/Pedal Position Sensor/Switch "A" Circuit Intermittent

P0125 Insufficient Coolant Temperature For Closed Loop Fuel Control

P0126 Insufficient Coolant Temperature For Stable Operation

P0130 O_2 Circuit Malfunction (Bank #1 Sensor #1)

P0131 O_2 Sensor Circuit Low Voltage (Bank #1 Sensor #1)

P0132 O_2 Sensor Circuit High Voltage (Bank #1 Sensor #1)

P0133 O_2 Sensor Circuit Slow Response (Bank #1 Sensor #1)

P0134 O_2 Sensor Circuit No Activity Detected (Bank #1 Sensor #1)

P0135 O_2 Sensor Heater Circuit Malfunction (Bank #1 Sensor #1)

P0136 O_2 Sensor Circuit Malfunction (Bank #1 Sensor #2)

P0137 O_2 Sensor Circuit Low Voltage (Bank #1 Sensor #2)

P0138 O_2 Sensor Circuit High Voltage (Bank #1 Sensor #2)

P0139 O_2 Sensor Circuit Slow Response (Bank #1 Sensor #2)

P0140 O_2 Sensor Circuit No Activity Detected (Bank #1 Sensor #2)

P0141 O_2 Sensor Heater Circuit Malfunction (Bank #1 Sensor #2)

P0142 O_2 Sensor Circuit Malfunction (Bank #1 Sensor #3)

P0143 O_2 Sensor Circuit Low Voltage (Bank #1 Sensor #3)

P0144 O_2 Sensor Circuit High Voltage (Bank #1 Sensor #3)

P0145 O_2 Sensor Circuit Slow Response (Bank #1 Sensor #3)

P0146 O_2 Sensor Circuit No Activity Detected (Bank #1 Sensor #3)

P0147 O_2 Sensor Heater Circuit Malfunction (Bank #1 Sensor #3)

P0150 O_2 Sensor Circuit Malfunction (Bank #2 Sensor #1)

P0151 O_2 Sensor Circuit Low Voltage (Bank #2 Sensor #1)

P0152 O_2 Sensor Circuit High Voltage (Bank #2 Sensor #1)

P0153 O_2 Sensor Circuit Slow Response (Bank #2 Sensor #1)

P0154 O_2 Sensor Circuit No Activity Detected (Bank #2 Sensor #1)

P0155 O_2 Sensor Heater Circuit Malfunction (Bank #2 Sensor #1)

P0156 O_2 Sensor Circuit Malfunction (Bank #2 Sensor #2)

P0157 O_2 Sensor Circuit Low Voltage (Bank #2 Sensor #2)

P0158 O_2 Sensor Circuit High Voltage (Bank #2 Sensor #2)

P0159 O_2 Sensor Circuit Slow Response (Bank #2 Sensor #2)

P0160 O_2 Sensor Circuit No Activity Detected (Bank #2 Sensor #2)

P0161 O_2 Sensor Heater Circuit Malfunction (Bank #2 Sensor #2)

P0162 O_2 Sensor Circuit Malfunction (Bank #2 Sensor #3)

P0163 O_2 Sensor Circuit Low Voltage (Bank #2 Sensor #3)

P0164 O_2 Sensor Circuit High Voltage (Bank #2 Sensor #3)

P0165 O_2 Sensor Circuit Slow Response (Bank #2 Sensor #3)

P0166 O_2 Sensor Circuit No Activity Detected (Bank #2 Sensor #3)

P0167 O_2 Sensor Heater Circuit Malfunction (Bank #2 Sensor #3)

P0170 Fuel Trim Malfunction (Bank #1)

P0171 System Too Lean (Bank #1)

P0172 System Too Rich (Bank #1)

P0173 Fuel Trim Malfunction (Bank #2)

P0174 System Too Lean (Bank #2)

P0175 System Too Rich (Bank #2)

P0176 Fuel Composition Sensor Circuit Malfunction

P0177 Fuel Composition Sensor Circuit Range/Performance

P0178 Fuel Composition Sensor Circuit Low Input

P0179 Fuel Composition Sensor Circuit High Input

P0180 Fuel Temperature Sensor "A" Circuit Malfunction

P0181 Fuel Temperature Sensor "A" Circuit Range/Performance

P0182 Fuel Temperature Sensor "A" Circuit Low Input

P0183 Fuel Temperature Sensor "A" Circuit High Input

P0184 Fuel Temperature Sensor "A" Circuit Intermittent

P0185 Fuel Temperature Sensor "B" Circuit Malfunction

P0186 Fuel Temperature Sensor "B" Circuit Range/Performance

P0187 Fuel Temperature Sensor "B" Circuit Low Input

P0188 Fuel Temperature Sensor "B" Circuit High Input

P0189 Fuel Temperature Sensor "B" Circuit Intermittent

P0190 Fuel Rail Pressure Sensor Circuit Malfunction

P0191 Fuel Rail Pressure Sensor Circuit Range/Performance

P0192 Fuel Rail Pressure Sensor Circuit Low Input

P0193 Fuel Rail Pressure Sensor Circuit High Input

P0194 Fuel Rail Pressure Sensor Circuit Intermittent

P0195 Engine Oil Temperature Sensor Malfunction

P0196 Engine Oil Temperature Sensor Range/Performance

P0197 Engine Oil Temperature Sensor Low

P0198 Engine Oil Temperature Sensor High

P0199 Engine Oil Temperature Sensor Intermittent

P0200 Injector Circuit Malfunction

P0201 Injector Circuit Malfunction—Cylinder #1

P0202 Injector Circuit Malfunction—Cylinder #2

P0203 Injector Circuit Malfunction—Cylinder #3

P0204 Injector Circuit Malfunction—Cylinder #4

P0205 Injector Circuit Malfunction—Cylinder #5

P0206 Injector Circuit Malfunction—Cylinder #6

P0207 Injector Circuit Malfunction—Cylinder #7

P0208 Injector Circuit Malfunction—Cylinder #8

P0209 Injector Circuit Malfunction—Cylinder #9

P0210 Injector Circuit Malfunction—Cylinder #10

P0211 Injector Circuit Malfunction—Cylinder #11

P0212 Injector Circuit Malfunction—Cylinder #12

P0213 Cold Start Injector #1 Malfunction

P0214 Cold Start Injector #2 Malfunction

P0215 Engine Shutoff Solenoid Malfunction

P0216 Injection Timing Control Circuit Malfunction

P0217 Engine Over Temperature Condition

P0218 Transmission Over Temperature Condition

P0219 Engine Over Speed Condition

P0220 Throttle/Pedal Position Sensor/Switch "B" Circuit Malfunction

P0221 Throttle/Pedal Position Sensor/Switch "B" Circuit Range/Performance Problem

P0222 Throttle/Pedal Position Sensor/Switch "B" Circuit Low Input

P0223 Throttle/Pedal Position Sensor/Switch "B" Circuit High Input

P0224 Throttle/Pedal Position Sensor/Switch "B" Circuit Intermittent

P0225 Throttle/Pedal Position Sensor/Switch "C" Circuit Malfunction

P0226 Throttle/Pedal Position Sensor/Switch "C" Circuit Range/Performance Problem

P0227 Throttle/Pedal Position Sensor/Switch "C" Circuit Low Input

P0228 Throttle/Pedal Position Sensor/Switch "C" Circuit High Input

P0229 Throttle/Pedal Position Sensor/Switch "C" Circuit Intermittent

P0230 Fuel Pump Primary Circuit Malfunction

P0231 Fuel Pump Secondary Circuit Low

P0232 Fuel Pump Secondary Circuit High

P0233 Fuel Pump Secondary Circuit Intermittent

P0234 Engine Over Boost Condition

P0261 Cylinder #1 Injector Circuit Low

P0262 Cylinder #1 Injector Circuit High

P0263 Cylinder #1 Contribution/Balance Fault

P0264 Cylinder #2 Injector Circuit Low

P0265 Cylinder #2 Injector Circuit High

P0266 Cylinder #2 Contribution/Balance Fault

P0267 Cylinder #3 Injector Circuit Low

P0268 Cylinder #3 Injector Circuit High

P0269 Cylinder #3 Contribution/Balance Fault

P0270 Cylinder #4 Injector Circuit Low

P0271 Cylinder #4 Injector Circuit High

P0272 Cylinder #4 Contribution/Balance Fault

P0273 Cylinder #5 Injector Circuit Low

P0274 Cylinder #5 Injector Circuit High

P0275 Cylinder #5 Contribution/Balance Fault

P0276 Cylinder #6 Injector Circuit Low

P0277 Cylinder #6 Injector Circuit High

P0278 Cylinder #6 Contribution/Balance Fault

P0279 Cylinder #7 Injector Circuit Low

P0280 Cylinder #7 Injector Circuit High

P0281 Cylinder #7 Contribution/Balance Fault

P0282 Cylinder #8 Injector Circuit Low

P0283 Cylinder #8 Injector Circuit High

P0284 Cylinder #8 Contribution/Balance Fault

P0285 Cylinder #9 Injector Circuit Low

P0286 Cylinder #9 Injector Circuit High

P0287 Cylinder #9 Contribution/Balance Fault

P0288 Cylinder #10 Injector Circuit Low

P0289 Cylinder #10 Injector Circuit High

P0290 Cylinder #10 Contribution/Balance Fault

P0291 Cylinder #11 Injector Circuit Low

P0292 Cylinder #11 Injector Circuit High

P0293 Cylinder #11 Contribution/Balance Fault

P0294 Cylinder #12 Injector Circuit Low

P0295 Cylinder #12 Injector Circuit High

P0296 Cylinder #12 Contribution/Balance Fault

P0300 Random/Multiple Cylinder Misfire Detected

P0301 Cylinder #1—Misfire Detected

P0302 Cylinder #2—Misfire Detected

P0303 Cylinder #3—Misfire Detected

P0304 Cylinder #4—Misfire Detected

P0305 Cylinder #5—Misfire Detected

P0306 Cylinder #6—Misfire Detected

P0307 Cylinder #7—Misfire Detected

P0308 Cylinder #8—Misfire Detected

P0309 Cylinder #9—Misfire Detected

P0310 Cylinder #10—Misfire Detected

P0311 Cylinder #11—Misfire Detected

P0312 Cylinder #12—Misfire Detected

P0320 Ignition/Distributor Engine Speed Input Circuit Malfunction

Ignition system service is covered in the model specific sections of this manual

P0321 Ignition/Distributor Engine Speed Input Circuit Range/Performance

P0322 Ignition/Distributor Engine Speed Input Circuit No Signal

P0323 Ignition/Distributor Engine Speed Input Circuit Intermittent

P0325 Knock Sensor #1—Circuit Malfunction (Bank #1 or Single Sensor)

P0326 Knock Sensor #1—Circuit Range/Performance (Bank #1 or Single Sensor)

P0327 Knock Sensor #1—Circuit Low Input (Bank #1 or Single Sensor)

P0328 Knock Sensor #1—Circuit High Input (Bank #1 or Single Sensor)

P0329 Knock Sensor #1—Circuit Input Intermittent (Bank #1 or Single Sensor)

P0330 Knock Sensor #2—Circuit Malfunction (Bank #2)

P0331 Knock Sensor #2—Circuit Range/Performance (Bank #2)

P0332 Knock Sensor #2—Circuit Low Input (Bank #2)

P0333 Knock Sensor #2—Circuit High Input (Bank #2)

P0334 Knock Sensor #2—Circuit Input Intermittent (Bank #2)

P0335 Crankshaft Position Sensor "A" Circuit Malfunction

P0336 Crankshaft Position Sensor "A" Circuit Range/Performance

P0337 Crankshaft Position Sensor "A" Circuit Low Input

P0338 Crankshaft Position Sensor "A" Circuit High Input

P0339 Crankshaft Position Sensor "A" Circuit Intermittent

P0340 Camshaft Position Sensor Circuit Malfunction

P0341 Camshaft Position Sensor Circuit Range/Performance

P0342 Camshaft Position Sensor Circuit Low Input

P0343 Camshaft Position Sensor Circuit High Input

P0344 Camshaft Position Sensor Circuit Intermittent

P0350 Ignition Coil Primary/Secondary Circuit Malfunction

P0351 Ignition Coil "A" Primary/Secondary Circuit Malfunction

P0352 Ignition Coil "B" Primary/Secondary Circuit Malfunction

P0353 Ignition Coil "C" Primary/Secondary Circuit Malfunction

P0354 Ignition Coil "D" Primary/Secondary Circuit Malfunction

P0355 Ignition Coil "E" Primary/Secondary Circuit Malfunction

P0356 Ignition Coil "F" Primary/Secondary Circuit Malfunction

P0357 Ignition Coil "G" Primary/Secondary Circuit Malfunction

P0358 Ignition Coil "H" Primary/Secondary Circuit Malfunction

P0359 Ignition Coil "I" Primary/Secondary Circuit Malfunction

P0360 Ignition Coil "J" Primary/Secondary Circuit Malfunction

P0361 Ignition Coil "K" Primary/Secondary Circuit Malfunction

P0362 Ignition Coil "L" Primary/Secondary Circuit Malfunction

P0370 Timing Reference High Resolution Signal "A" Malfunction

P0371 Timing Reference High Resolution Signal "A" Too Many Pulses

P0372 Timing Reference High Resolution Signal "A" Too Few Pulses

P0373 Timing Reference High Resolution Signal "A" Intermittent/Erratic Pulses

P0374 Timing Reference High Resolution Signal "A" No Pulses

P0375 Timing Reference High Resolution Signal "B" Malfunction

P0376 Timing Reference High Resolution Signal "B" Too Many Pulses

P0377 Timing Reference High Resolution Signal "B" Too Few Pulses

P0378 Timing Reference High Resolution Signal "B" Intermittent/Erratic Pulses

P0379 Timing Reference High Resolution Signal "B" No Pulses

P0380 Glow Plug/Heater Circuit "A" Malfunction

P0381 Glow Plug/Heater Indicator Circuit Malfunction

P0382 Glow Plug/Heater Circuit "B" Malfunction

P0385 Crankshaft Position Sensor "B" Circuit Malfunction

P0386 Crankshaft Position Sensor "B" Circuit Range/Performance

P0387 Crankshaft Position Sensor "B" Circuit Low Input

P0388 Crankshaft Position Sensor "B" Circuit High Input

P0389 Crankshaft Position Sensor "B" Circuit Intermittent

P0400 Exhaust Gas Recirculation Flow Malfunction

P0401 Exhaust Gas Recirculation Flow Insufficient Detected

P0402 Exhaust Gas Recirculation Flow Excessive Detected

P0403 Exhaust Gas Recirculation Circuit Malfunction

P0404 Exhaust Gas Recirculation Circuit Range/Performance

P0405 Exhaust Gas Recirculation Sensor "A" Circuit Low

P0406 Exhaust Gas Recirculation Sensor "A" Circuit High

P0407 Exhaust Gas Recirculation Sensor "B" Circuit Low

P0408 Exhaust Gas Recirculation Sensor "B" Circuit High

P0410 Secondary Air Injection System Malfunction

P0411 Secondary Air Injection System Incorrect Flow Detected

P0412 Secondary Air Injection System Switching Valve "A" Circuit Malfunction

P0413 Secondary Air Injection System Switching Valve "A" Circuit Open

P0414 Secondary Air Injection System Switching Valve "A" Circuit Shorted

P0415 Secondary Air Injection System Switching Valve "B" Circuit Malfunction

P0416 Secondary Air Injection System Switching Valve "B" Circuit Open

P0417 Secondary Air Injection System Switching Valve "B" Circuit Shorted

P0418 Secondary Air Injection System Relay "A" Circuit Malfunction

P0419 Secondary Air Injection System Relay "B" Circuit Malfunction

P0420 Catalyst System Efficiency Below Threshold (Bank #1)

P0421 Warm Up Catalyst Efficiency Below Threshold (Bank #1)

P0422 Main Catalyst Efficiency Below Threshold (Bank #1)

P0423 Heated Catalyst Efficiency Below Threshold (Bank #1)

P0424 Heated Catalyst Temperature Below Threshold (Bank #1)

P0430 Catalyst System Efficiency Below Threshold (Bank #2)

P0431 Warm Up Catalyst Efficiency Below Threshold (Bank #2)

P0432 Main Catalyst Efficiency Below Threshold (Bank #2)

P0433 Heated Catalyst Efficiency Below Threshold (Bank #2)

P0434 Heated Catalyst Temperature Below Threshold (Bank #2)

P0440 Evaporative Emission Control System Malfunction

P0441 Evaporative Emission Control System Incorrect Purge Flow

P0442 Evaporative Emission Control System Leak Detected (Small Leak)

P0443 Evaporative Emission Control System Purge Control Valve Circuit Malfunction

P0444 Evaporative Emission Control System Purge Control Valve Circuit Open

P0445 Evaporative Emission Control System Purge Control Valve Circuit Shorted

P0446 Evaporative Emission Control System Vent Control Circuit Malfunction

P0447 Evaporative Emission Control System Vent Control Circuit Open

P0448 Evaporative Emission Control System Vent Control Circuit Shorted

P0449 Evaporative Emission Control System Vent Valve/Solenoid Circuit Malfunction

P0450 Evaporative Emission Control System Pressure Sensor Malfunction

P0451 Evaporative Emission Control System Pressure Sensor Range/Performance

P0452 Evaporative Emission Control System Pressure Sensor Low Input

P0453 Evaporative Emission Control System Pressure Sensor High Input

P0454 Evaporative Emission Control System Pressure Sensor Intermittent

P0455 Evaporative Emission Control System Leak Detected (Gross Leak)

P0460 Fuel Level Sensor Circuit Malfunction

P0461 Fuel Level Sensor Circuit Range/Performance

P0462 Fuel Level Sensor Circuit Low Input

P0463 Fuel Level Sensor Circuit High Input

P0464 Fuel Level Sensor Circuit Intermittent

P0465 Purge Flow Sensor Circuit Malfunction

P0466 Purge Flow Sensor Circuit Range/Performance

P0467 Purge Flow Sensor Circuit Low Input

P0468 Purge Flow Sensor Circuit High Input

P0469 Purge Flow Sensor Circuit Intermittent

P0470 Exhaust Pressure Sensor Malfunction

P0471 Exhaust Pressure Sensor Range/Performance

P0472 Exhaust Pressure Sensor Low

P0473 Exhaust Pressure Sensor High

P0474 Exhaust Pressure Sensor Intermittent

P0475 Exhaust Pressure Control Valve Malfunction

P0476 Exhaust Pressure Control Valve Range/Performance

P0477 Exhaust Pressure Control Valve Low

P0478 Exhaust Pressure Control Valve High

P0479 Exhaust Pressure Control Valve Intermittent

P0480 Cooling Fan #1 Control Circuit Malfunction

P0481 Cooling Fan #2 Control Circuit Malfunction

P0482 Cooling Fan #3 Control Circuit Malfunction

P0483 Cooling Fan Rationality Check Malfunction

P0484 Cooling Fan Circuit Over Current

P0485 Cooling Fan Power/Ground Circuit Malfunction

P0500 Vehicle Speed Sensor Malfunction

P0501 Vehicle Speed Sensor Range/Performance

P0502 Vehicle Speed Sensor Circuit Low Input

P0503 Vehicle Speed Sensor Intermittent/Erratic/High

P0505 Idle Control System Malfunction

P0506 Idle Control System RPM Lower Than Expected

P0507 Idle Control System RPM Higher Than Expected

P0510 Closed Throttle Position Switch Malfunction

P0520 Engine Oil Pressure Sensor/Switch Circuit Malfunction

P0521 Engine Oil Pressure Sensor/Switch Range/Performance

P0522 Engine Oil Pressure Sensor/Switch Low Voltage

P0523 Engine Oil Pressure Sensor/Switch High Voltage

P0530 A/C Refrigerant Pressure Sensor Circuit Malfunction

P0531 A/C Refrigerant Pressure Sensor Circuit Range/Performance

P0532 A/C Refrigerant Pressure Sensor Circuit Low Input

P0533 A/C Refrigerant Pressure Sensor Circuit High Input

P0534 A/C Refrigerant Charge Loss

P0550 Power Steering Pressure Sensor Circuit Malfunction

P0551 Power Steering Pressure Sensor Circuit Range/Performance

P0552 Power Steering Pressure Sensor Circuit Low Input

P0553 Power Steering Pressure Sensor Circuit High Input

P0554 Power Steering Pressure Sensor Circuit Intermittent

P0560 System Voltage Malfunction

P0561 System Voltage Unstable

P0562 System Voltage Low

P0563 System Voltage High

P0565 Cruise Control On Signal Malfunction

P0566 Cruise Control Off Signal Malfunction

P0567 Cruise Control Resume Signal Malfunction

P0568 Cruise Control Set Signal Malfunction

P0569 Cruise Control Coast Signal Malfunction

P0570 Cruise Control Accel Signal Malfunction

P0571 Cruise Control/Brake Switch "A" Circuit Malfunction

P0572 Cruise Control/Brake Switch "A" Circuit Low

P0573 Cruise Control/Brake Switch "A" Circuit High

P0574 Through P0580 Reserved for Cruise Codes

P0600 Serial Communication Link Malfunction

P0601 Internal Control Module Memory Check Sum Error

P0602 Control Module Programming Error

P0603 Internal Control Module Keep Alive Memory (KAM) Error

P0604 Internal Control Module Random Access Memory (RAM) Error

P0605 Internal Control Module Read Only Memory (ROM) Error

P0606 PCM Processor Fault

P0608 Control Module VSS Output "A" Malfunction

P0609 Control Module VSS Output "B" Malfunction

P0620 Generator Control Circuit Malfunction

P0621 Generator Lamp "L" Control Circuit Malfunction

P0622 Generator Field "F" Control Circuit Malfunction

P0650 Malfunction Indicator Lamp (MIL) Control Circuit Malfunction

P0654 Engine RPM Output Circuit Malfunction

P0655 Engine Hot Lamp Output Control Circuit Malfunction

P0656 Fuel Level Output Circuit Malfunction

P0700 Transmission Control System Malfunction

P0701 Transmission Control System Range/Performance

P0702 Transmission Control System Electrical

P0703 Torque Converter/Brake Switch "B" Circuit Malfunction

P0704 Clutch Switch Input Circuit Malfunction

P0705 Transmission Range Sensor Circuit Malfunction (PRNDL Input)

P0706 Transmission Range Sensor Circuit Range/Performance

P0707 Transmission Range Sensor Circuit Low Input

P0708 Transmission Range Sensor Circuit High Input

P0709 Transmission Range Sensor Circuit Intermittent

P0710 Transmission Fluid Temperature Sensor Circuit Malfunction

P0711 Transmission Fluid Temperature Sensor Circuit Range/Performance

P0712 Transmission Fluid Temperature Sensor Circuit Low Input

P0713 Transmission Fluid Temperature Sensor Circuit High Input

P0714 Transmission Fluid Temperature Sensor Circuit Intermittent

P0715 Input/Turbine Speed Sensor Circuit Malfunction

P0716 Input/Turbine Speed Sensor Circuit Range/Performance

P0717 Input/Turbine Speed Sensor Circuit No Signal

P0718 Input/Turbine Speed Sensor Circuit Intermittent

P0719 Torque Converter/Brake Switch "B" Circuit Low

P0720 Output Speed Sensor Circuit Malfunction

P0721 Output Speed Sensor Circuit Range/Performance

P0722 Output Speed Sensor Circuit No Signal

P0723 Output Speed Sensor Circuit Intermittent

P0724 Torque Converter/Brake Switch "B" Circuit High

P0725 Engine Speed Input Circuit Malfunction

P0726 Engine Speed Input Circuit Range/Performance

P0727 Engine Speed Input Circuit No Signal

P0728 Engine Speed Input Circuit Intermittent

P0730 Incorrect Gear Ratio

P0731 Gear #1 Incorrect Ratio

P0732 Gear #2 Incorrect Ratio

P0733 Gear #3 Incorrect Ratio

P0734 Gear #4 Incorrect Ratio

P0735 Gear #5 Incorrect Ratio

P0736 Reverse Incorrect Ratio

P0740 Torque Converter Clutch Circuit Malfunction

P0741 Torque Converter Clutch Circuit Performance or Stuck Off

P0742 Torque Converter Clutch Circuit Stuck On

P0743 Torque Converter Clutch Circuit Electrical

P0744 Torque Converter Clutch Circuit Intermittent

P0745 Pressure Control Solenoid Malfunction

P0746 Pressure Control Solenoid Performance or Stuck Off

P0747 Pressure Control Solenoid Stuck On

P0748 Pressure Control Solenoid Electrical

P0749 Pressure Control Solenoid Intermittent

P0750 Shift Solenoid "A" Malfunction

P0751 Shift Solenoid "A" Performance or Stuck Off

P0752 Shift Solenoid "A" Stuck On

P0753 Shift Solenoid "A" Electrical

P0754 Shift Solenoid "A" Intermittent

P0755 Shift Solenoid "B" Malfunction

P0756 Shift Solenoid "B" Performance or Stuck Off

P0757 Shift Solenoid "B" Stuck On

P0758 Shift Solenoid "B" Electrical

P0759 Shift Solenoid "B" Intermittent

P0760 Shift Solenoid "C" Malfunction

P0761 Shift Solenoid "C" Performance Or Stuck Off

P0762 Shift Solenoid "C" Stuck On

P0763 Shift Solenoid "C" Electrical

P0764 Shift Solenoid "C" Intermittent

P0765 Shift Solenoid "D" Malfunction

P0766 Shift Solenoid "D" Performance Or Stuck Off

P0767 Shift Solenoid "D" Stuck On

P0768 Shift Solenoid "D" Electrical

P0769 Shift Solenoid "D" Intermittent

P0770 Shift Solenoid "E" Malfunction

P0771 Shift Solenoid "E" Performance Or Stuck Off

P0772 Shift Solenoid "E" Stuck On

P0773 Shift Solenoid "E" Electrical

P0774 Shift Solenoid "E" Intermittent

P0780 Shift Malfunction

P0781 1–2 Shift Malfunction

P0782 2–3 Shift Malfunction

P0783 3–4 Shift Malfunction

P0784 4–5 Shift Malfunction

P0785 Shift/Timing Solenoid Malfunction

P0786 Shift/Timing Solenoid Range/Performance

P0787 Shift/Timing Solenoid Low

P0788 Shift/Timing Solenoid High

P0789 Shift/Timing Solenoid Intermittent

P0790 Normal/Performance Switch Circuit Malfunction

P0801 Reverse Inhibit Control Circuit Malfunction

P0803 1–4 Upshift (Skip Shift) Solenoid Control Circuit Malfunction

P0804 1–4 Upshift (Skip Shift) Lamp Control Circuit Malfunction

P1106 MAP Sensor Circuit Intermittent High Voltage

P1107 MAP Sensor Circuit Intermittent Low Voltage

P1111 IAT Sensor Circuit Intermittent High Voltage

P1112 IAT Sensor Circuit Intermittent Low Voltage

P1114 ECT Sensor Circuit Intermittent Low Voltage

P1115 ECT Sensor Circuit Intermittent High Voltage

P1121 TP Sensor Circuit Intermittent High Voltage

P1122 TP Sensor Circuit Intermittent Low Voltage

P1133 HO_2 S-11 Insufficient Switching (Bank #1 Sensor #1)

P1134 HO_2 S-11 Transition Time Ratio (Bank #1 Sensor #1)

P1153 HO_2 S-21 Insufficient Switching (Bank #2 Sensor #l)

P1154 HO_2 S-21 Transition Time Ratio (Bank #2 Sensor #1)

P1171 Fuel System Lean During Acceleration

P1391 G-Acceleration Sensor Intermittent Low Voltage

P1390 G-Acceleration (Low G) Sensor Performance

P1392 Rough Road G-Sensor Circuit Low Voltage

P1393 Rough Road G-Sensor Circuit High Voltage

P1394 G-Acceleration Sensor Intermittent High Voltage

P1406 EGR Valve Pintle Position Sensor Circuit Fault

P1441 EVAP System Flow During Non-Purge

P1442 EVAP System Flow During Non-Purge

P1508 Idle Speed Control System-Low

P1509 Idle Speed Control System-High

P1618 Serial Peripheral Interface Communication Error

P1640 Output Driver Module "A" Fault

P1790 PCM ROM (Transmission Side) Check Sum Error

P1792 PCM EEPROM (Transmission Side) Check Sum Error

P1835 Kick Down Switch Always On

P1850 Brake Band Apply Solenoid Electrical Fault

P1860 TCC PWM Solenoid Electrical Fault

P1870 Transmission Component Slipping

Chrysler Corp.

READING CODES

Reading the control module memory is one of the first steps in OBD II system diagnostics. This step should be initially performed to determine the general nature of the fault. Subsequent readings will determine if the fault has been cleared.

Reading codes can be performed by any of the methods below:
- Read the control module memory with the Generic Scan Tool (GST)
- Read the control module memory with the vehicle manufacturer's specific tester

To read the fault codes, connect the scan tool or tester according to the manufacturer's instructions. Follow the manufacturer's specified procedure for reading the codes.

CLEARING CODES

Control module reset procedures are a very important part of OBD II System diagnostics. This step should be done at the end of any fault code repair and at the end of any driveability repair.

Clearing codes can be performed by any of the methods below:
- Clear the control module memory with the Generic Scan Tool (GST)
- Clear the control module memory with the vehicle manufacturer's specific tester
- Turn the ignition OFF and remove the negative battery cable for at least 1 minute.

Removing the negative battery cable may cause other systems in the vehicle to loose their memory. Prior to removing the cable, ensure you have the proper reset codes for radios and alarms.

➡**The MIL will may also be de-activated for some codes if the vehicle completes three consecutive trips without a fault detected with vehicle conditions similar to those present during the fault.**

OBD II TROUBLE CODES

P0100 Mass or Volume Air Flow Circuit Malfunction

P0101 Mass or Volume Air Flow Circuit Range/Performance Problem

P0102 Mass or Volume Air Flow Circuit Low Input

P0103 Mass or Volume Air Flow Circuit High Input

P0104 Mass or Volume Air Flow Circuit Intermittent

P0105 Manifold Absolute Pressure/Barometric Pressure Circuit Malfunction

P0106 Manifold Absolute Pressure/Barometric Pressure Circuit Range/Performance Problem

P0107 Manifold Absolute Pressure/Barometric Pressure Circuit Low Input

P0108 Manifold Absolute Pressure/Barometric Pressure Circuit High Input

P0109 Manifold Absolute Pressure/Barometric Pressure Circuit Intermittent

P0110 Intake Air Temperature Circuit Malfunction

P0111 Intake Air Temperature Circuit Range/Performance Problem

P0112 Intake Air Temperature Circuit Low Input

P0113 Intake Air Temperature Circuit High Input

P0114 Intake Air Temperature Circuit Intermittent

P0115 Engine Coolant Temperature Circuit Malfunction

P0116 Engine Coolant Temperature Circuit Range/Performance Problem

P0117 Engine Coolant Temperature Circuit Low Input

P0118 Engine Coolant Temperature Circuit High Input

P0119 Engine Coolant Temperature Circuit Intermittent

P0120 Throttle/Pedal Position Sensor/Switch "A" Circuit Malfunction

P0121 Throttle/Pedal Position Sensor/Switch "A" Circuit Range/Performance Problem

P0122 Throttle/Pedal Position Sensor/Switch "A" Circuit Low Input

P0123 Throttle/Pedal Position Sensor/Switch "A" Circuit High Input

P0124 Throttle/Pedal Position Sensor/Switch "A" Circuit Intermittent

P0125 Insufficient Coolant Temperature For Closed Loop Fuel Control

P0126 Insufficient Coolant Temperature For Stable Operation

P0130 O_2 Circuit Malfunction (Bank #1 Sensor #1)

P0131 O_2 Sensor Circuit Low Voltage (Bank #1 Sensor #1)

P0132 O_2 Sensor Circuit High Voltage (Bank #1 Sensor #1)

P0133 O_2 Sensor Circuit Slow Response (Bank #1 Sensor #1)

P0134 O_2 Sensor Circuit No Activity Detected (Bank #1 Sensor #1)

P0135 O_2 Sensor Heater Circuit Malfunction (Bank #1 Sensor #1)

P0136 O_2 Sensor Circuit Malfunction (Bank #1 Sensor #2)

P0137 O_2 Sensor Circuit Low Voltage (Bank #1 Sensor #2)

P0138 O_2 Sensor Circuit High Voltage (Bank #1 Sensor #2)

P0139 O_2 Sensor Circuit Slow Response (Bank #1 Sensor #2)

P0140 O_2 Sensor Circuit No Activity Detected (Bank #1 Sensor #2)

P0141 O_2 Sensor Heater Circuit Malfunction (Bank #1 Sensor #2)

P0142 O_2 Sensor Circuit Malfunction (Bank #1 Sensor #3)

P0143 O_2 Sensor Circuit Low Voltage (Bank #1 Sensor #3)

P0144 O_2 Sensor Circuit High Voltage (Bank #1 Sensor #3)

P0145 O_2 Sensor Circuit Slow Response (Bank #1 Sensor #3)

P0146 O_2 Sensor Circuit No Activity Detected (Bank #1 Sensor #3)

P0147 O_2 Sensor Heater Circuit Malfunction (Bank #1 Sensor #3)

P0150 O_2 Sensor Circuit Malfunction (Bank #2 Sensor #1)

P0151 O_2 Sensor Circuit Low Voltage (Bank #2 Sensor #1)

P0152 O_2 Sensor Circuit High Voltage (Bank #2 Sensor #1)

P0153 O_2 Sensor Circuit Slow Response (Bank #2 Sensor #1)

P0154 O_2 Sensor Circuit No Activity Detected (Bank #2 Sensor #1)

P0155 O_2 Sensor Heater Circuit Malfunction (Bank #2 Sensor #1)

P0156 O_2 Sensor Circuit Malfunction (Bank #2 Sensor #2)

P0157 O_2 Sensor Circuit Low Voltage (Bank #2 Sensor #2)

P0158 O_2 Sensor Circuit High Voltage (Bank #2 Sensor #2)

P0159 O_2 Sensor Circuit Slow Response (Bank #2 Sensor #2)

P0160 O_2 Sensor Circuit No Activity Detected (Bank #2 Sensor #2)

P0161 O_2 Sensor Heater Circuit Malfunction (Bank #2 Sensor #2)

P0162 O_2 Sensor Circuit Malfunction (Bank #2 Sensor #3)

P0163 O_2 Sensor Circuit Low Voltage (Bank #2 Sensor #3)

P0164 O_2 Sensor Circuit High Voltage (Bank #2 Sensor #3)

P0165 O_2 Sensor Circuit Slow Response (Bank #2 Sensor #3)

P0166 O_2 Sensor Circuit No Activity Detected (Bank #2 Sensor #3)

P0167 O_2 Sensor Heater Circuit Malfunction (Bank #2 Sensor #3)

Refer to the model specific sections for fuel system service procedures

P0170 Fuel Trim Malfunction (Bank #1)
P0171 System Too Lean (Bank #1)
P0172 System Too Rich (Bank #1)
P0173 Fuel Trim Malfunction (Bank #2)
P0174 System Too Lean (Bank #2)
P0175 System Too Rich (Bank #2)
P0176 Fuel Composition Sensor Circuit Malfunction
P0177 Fuel Composition Sensor Circuit Range/Performance
P0178 Fuel Composition Sensor Circuit Low Input
P0179 Fuel Composition Sensor Circuit High Input
P0180 Fuel Temperature Sensor "A" Circuit Malfunction
P0181 Fuel Temperature Sensor "A" Circuit Range/Performance
P0182 Fuel Temperature Sensor "A" Circuit Low Input
P0183 Fuel Temperature Sensor "A" Circuit High Input
P0184 Fuel Temperature Sensor "A" Circuit Intermittent
P0185 Fuel Temperature Sensor "B" Circuit Malfunction
P0186 Fuel Temperature Sensor "B" Circuit Range/Performance
P0187 Fuel Temperature Sensor "B" Circuit Low Input
P0188 Fuel Temperature Sensor "B" Circuit High Input
P0189 Fuel Temperature Sensor "B" Circuit Intermittent
P0190 Fuel Rail Pressure Sensor Circuit Malfunction
P0191 Fuel Rail Pressure Sensor Circuit Range/Performance
P0192 Fuel Rail Pressure Sensor Circuit Low Input
P0193 Fuel Rail Pressure Sensor Circuit High Input
P0194 Fuel Rail Pressure Sensor Circuit Intermittent
P0195 Engine Oil Temperature Sensor Malfunction
P0196 Engine Oil Temperature Sensor Range/Performance
P0197 Engine Oil Temperature Sensor Low
P0198 Engine Oil Temperature Sensor High
P0199 Engine Oil Temperature Sensor Intermittent
P0200 Injector Circuit Malfunction
P0201 Injector Circuit Malfunction—Cylinder #1
P0202 Injector Circuit Malfunction—Cylinder #2
P0203 Injector Circuit Malfunction—Cylinder #3

P0204 Injector Circuit Malfunction—Cylinder #4
P0205 Injector Circuit Malfunction—Cylinder #5
P0206 Injector Circuit Malfunction—Cylinder #6
P0207 Injector Circuit Malfunction—Cylinder #7
P0208 Injector Circuit Malfunction—Cylinder #8
P0209 Injector Circuit Malfunction—Cylinder #9
P0210 Injector Circuit Malfunction—Cylinder #10
P0211 Injector Circuit Malfunction—Cylinder #11
P0212 Injector Circuit Malfunction—Cylinder #12
P0213 Cold Start Injector #1 Malfunction
P0214 Cold Start Injector #2 Malfunction
P0215 Engine Shutoff Solenoid Malfunction
P0216 Injection Timing Control Circuit Malfunction
P0217 Engine Over Temperature Condition
P0218 Transmission Over Temperature Condition
P0219 Engine Over Speed Condition
P0220 Throttle/Pedal Position Sensor/Switch "B" Circuit Malfunction
P0221 Throttle/Pedal Position Sensor/Switch "B" Circuit Range/Performance Problem
P0222 Throttle/Pedal Position Sensor/Switch "B" Circuit Low Input
P0223 Throttle/Pedal Position Sensor/Switch "B" Circuit High Input
P0224 Throttle/Pedal Position Sensor/Switch "B" Circuit Intermittent
P0225 Throttle/Pedal Position Sensor/Switch "C" Circuit Malfunction
P0226 Throttle/Pedal Position Sensor/Switch "C" Circuit Range/Performance Problem
P0227 Throttle/Pedal Position Sensor/Switch "C" Circuit Low Input
P0228 Throttle/Pedal Position Sensor/Switch "C" Circuit High Input
P0229 Throttle/Pedal Position Sensor/Switch "C" Circuit Intermittent
P0230 Fuel Pump Primary Circuit Malfunction
P0231 Fuel Pump Secondary Circuit Low
P0232 Fuel Pump Secondary Circuit High
P0233 Fuel Pump Secondary Circuit Intermittent
P0234 Engine Over Boost Condition

P0261 Cylinder #1 Injector Circuit Low
P0262 Cylinder #1 Injector Circuit High
P0263 Cylinder #1 Contribution/Balance Fault
P0264 Cylinder #2 Injector Circuit Low
P0265 Cylinder #2 Injector Circuit High
P0266 Cylinder #2 Contribution/Balance Fault
P0267 Cylinder #3 Injector Circuit Low
P0268 Cylinder #3 Injector Circuit High
P0269 Cylinder #3 Contribution/Balance Fault
P0270 Cylinder #4 Injector Circuit Low
P0271 Cylinder #4 Injector Circuit High
P0272 Cylinder #4 Contribution/Balance Fault
P0273 Cylinder #5 Injector Circuit Low
P0274 Cylinder #5 Injector Circuit High
P0275 Cylinder #5 Contribution/Balance Fault
P0276 Cylinder #6 Injector Circuit Low
P0277 Cylinder #6 Injector Circuit High
P0278 Cylinder #6 Contribution/Balance Fault
P0279 Cylinder #7 Injector Circuit Low
P0280 Cylinder #7 Injector Circuit High
P0281 Cylinder #7 Contribution/Balance Fault
P0282 Cylinder #8 Injector Circuit Low
P0283 Cylinder #8 Injector Circuit High
P0284 Cylinder #8 Contribution/Balance Fault
P0285 Cylinder #9 Injector Circuit Low
P0286 Cylinder #9 Injector Circuit High
P0287 Cylinder #9 Contribution/Balance Fault
P0288 Cylinder #10 Injector Circuit Low
P0289 Cylinder #10 Injector Circuit High
P0290 Cylinder #10 Contribution/Balance Fault
P0291 Cylinder #11 Injector Circuit Low
P0292 Cylinder #11 Injector Circuit High
P0293 Cylinder #11 Contribution/Balance Fault
P0294 Cylinder #12 Injector Circuit Low
P0295 Cylinder #12 Injector Circuit High
P0296 Cylinder #12 Contribution/Balance Fault
P0300 Random/Multiple Cylinder Misfire Detected
P0301 Cylinder #1—Misfire Detected
P0302 Cylinder #2—Misfire Detected
P0303 Cylinder #3—Misfire Detected
P0304 Cylinder #4—Misfire Detected
P0305 Cylinder #5—Misfire Detected
P0306 Cylinder #6—Misfire Detected
P0307 Cylinder #7—Misfire Detected
P0308 Cylinder #8—Misfire Detected
P0309 Cylinder #9—Misfire Detected

P0310 Cylinder #10—Misfire Detected

P0311 Cylinder #11—Misfire Detected

P0312 Cylinder #12—Misfire Detected

P0320 Ignition/Distributor Engine Speed Input Circuit Malfunction

P0321 Ignition/Distributor Engine Speed Input Circuit Range/Performance

P0322 Ignition/Distributor Engine Speed Input Circuit No Signal

P0323 Ignition/Distributor Engine Speed Input Circuit Intermittent

P0325 Knock Sensor #1—Circuit Malfunction (Bank #1 or Single Sensor)

P0326 Knock Sensor #1—Circuit Range/Performance (Bank #1 or Single Sensor)

P0327 Knock Sensor #1—Circuit Low Input (Bank #1 or Single Sensor)

P0328 Knock Sensor #1—Circuit High Input (Bank #1 or Single Sensor)

P0329 Knock Sensor #1—Circuit Input Intermittent (Bank #1 or Single Sensor)

P0330 Knock Sensor #2—Circuit Malfunction (Bank #2)

P0331 Knock Sensor #2—Circuit Range/Performance (Bank #2)

P0332 Knock Sensor #2—Circuit Low Input (Bank #2)

P0333 Knock Sensor #2—Circuit High Input (Bank #2)

P0334 Knock Sensor #2—Circuit Input Intermittent (Bank #2)

P0335 Crankshaft Position Sensor "A" Circuit Malfunction

P0336 Crankshaft Position Sensor "A" Circuit Range/Performance

P0337 Crankshaft Position Sensor "A" Circuit Low Input

P0338 Crankshaft Position Sensor "A" Circuit High Input

P0339 Crankshaft Position Sensor "A" Circuit Intermittent

P0340 Camshaft Position Sensor Circuit Malfunction

P0341 Camshaft Position Sensor Circuit Range/Performance

P0342 Camshaft Position Sensor Circuit Low Input

P0343 Camshaft Position Sensor Circuit High Input

P0344 Camshaft Position Sensor Circuit Intermittent

P0350 Ignition Coil Primary/Secondary Circuit Malfunction

P0351 Ignition Coil "A" Primary/Secondary Circuit Malfunction

P0352 Ignition Coil "B" Primary/Secondary Circuit Malfunction

P0353 Ignition Coil "C" Primary/Secondary Circuit Malfunction

P0354 Ignition Coil "D" Primary/Secondary Circuit Malfunction

P0355 Ignition Coil "E" Primary/Secondary Circuit Malfunction

P0356 Ignition Coil "F" Primary/Secondary Circuit Malfunction

P0357 Ignition Coil "G" Primary/Secondary Circuit Malfunction

P0358 Ignition Coil "H" Primary/Secondary Circuit Malfunction

P0359 Ignition Coil "I" Primary/Secondary Circuit Malfunction

P0360 Ignition Coil "J" Primary/Secondary Circuit Malfunction

P0361 Ignition Coil "K" Primary/Secondary Circuit Malfunction

P0362 Ignition Coil "L" Primary/Secondary Circuit Malfunction

P0370 Timing Reference High Resolution Signal "A" Malfunction

P0371 Timing Reference High Resolution Signal "A" Too Many Pulses

P0372 Timing Reference High Resolution Signal "A" Too Few Pulses

P0373 Timing Reference High Resolution Signal "A" Intermittent/Erratic Pulses

P0374 Timing Reference High Resolution Signal "A" No Pulses

P0375 Timing Reference High Resolution Signal "B" Malfunction

P0376 Timing Reference High Resolution Signal "B" Too Many Pulses

P0377 Timing Reference High Resolution Signal "B" Too Few Pulses

P0378 Timing Reference High Resolution Signal "B" Intermittent/Erratic Pulses

P0379 Timing Reference High Resolution Signal "B" No Pulses

P0380 Glow Plug/Heater Circuit "A" Malfunction

P0381 Glow Plug/Heater Indicator Circuit Malfunction

P0382 Glow Plug/Heater Circuit "B" Malfunction

P0385 Crankshaft Position Sensor "B" Circuit Malfunction

P0386 Crankshaft Position Sensor "B" Circuit Range/Performance

P0387 Crankshaft Position Sensor "B" Circuit Low Input

P0388 Crankshaft Position Sensor "B" Circuit High Input

P0389 Crankshaft Position Sensor "B" Circuit Intermittent

P0400 Exhaust Gas Recirculation Flow Malfunction

P0401 Exhaust Gas Recirculation Flow Insufficient Detected

P0402 Exhaust Gas Recirculation Flow Excessive Detected

P0403 Exhaust Gas Recirculation Circuit Malfunction

P0404 Exhaust Gas Recirculation Circuit Range/Performance

P0405 Exhaust Gas Recirculation Sensor "A" Circuit Low

P0406 Exhaust Gas Recirculation Sensor "A" Circuit High

P0407 Exhaust Gas Recirculation Sensor "B" Circuit Low

P0408 Exhaust Gas Recirculation Sensor "B" Circuit High

P0410 Secondary Air Injection System Malfunction

P0411 Secondary Air Injection System Incorrect Flow Detected

P0412 Secondary Air Injection System Switching Valve "A" Circuit Malfunction

P0413 Secondary Air Injection System Switching Valve "A" Circuit Open

P0414 Secondary Air Injection System Switching Valve "A" Circuit Shorted

P0415 Secondary Air Injection System Switching Valve "B" Circuit Malfunction

P0416 Secondary Air Injection System Switching Valve "B" Circuit Open

P0417 Secondary Air Injection System Switching Valve "B" Circuit Shorted

P0418 Secondary Air Injection System Relay "A" Circuit Malfunction

P0419 Secondary Air Injection System Relay "B" Circuit Malfunction

P0420 Catalyst System Efficiency Below Threshold (Bank #1)

P0421 Warm Up Catalyst Efficiency Below Threshold (Bank #1)

P0422 Main Catalyst Efficiency Below Threshold (Bank #1)

P0423 Heated Catalyst Efficiency Below Threshold (Bank #1)

P0424 Heated Catalyst Temperature Below Threshold (Bank #1)

P0430 Catalyst System Efficiency Below Threshold (Bank #2)

P0431 Warm Up Catalyst Efficiency Below Threshold (Bank #2)

P0432 Main Catalyst Efficiency Below Threshold (Bank #2)

P0433 Heated Catalyst Efficiency Below Threshold (Bank #2)

P0434 Heated Catalyst Temperature Below Threshold (Bank #2)

P0440 Evaporative Emission Control System Malfunction

Refer to the model specific sections for engine electrical system service procedurcs

P0441 Evaporative Emission Control System Incorrect Purge Flow

P0442 Evaporative Emission Control System Leak Detected (Small Leak)

P0443 Evaporative Emission Control System Purge Control Valve Circuit Malfunction

P0444 Evaporative Emission Control System Purge Control Valve Circuit Open

P0445 Evaporative Emission Control System Purge Control Valve Circuit Shorted

P0446 Evaporative Emission Control System Vent Control Circuit Malfunction

P0447 Evaporative Emission Control System Vent Control Circuit Open

P0448 Evaporative Emission Control System Vent Control Circuit Shorted

P0449 Evaporative Emission Control System Vent Valve/Solenoid Circuit Malfunction

P0450 Evaporative Emission Control System Pressure Sensor Malfunction

P0451 Evaporative Emission Control System Pressure Sensor Range/Performance

P0452 Evaporative Emission Control System Pressure Sensor Low Input

P0453 Evaporative Emission Control System Pressure Sensor High Input

P0454 Evaporative Emission Control System Pressure Sensor Intermittent

P0455 Evaporative Emission Control System Leak Detected (Gross Leak)

P0460 Fuel Level Sensor Circuit Malfunction

P0461 Fuel Level Sensor Circuit Range/Performance

P0462 Fuel Level Sensor Circuit Low Input

P0463 Fuel Level Sensor Circuit High Input

P0464 Fuel Level Sensor Circuit Intermittent

P0465 Purge Flow Sensor Circuit Malfunction

P0466 Purge Flow Sensor Circuit Range/Performance

P0467 Purge Flow Sensor Circuit Low Input

P0468 Purge Flow Sensor Circuit High Input

P0469 Purge Flow Sensor Circuit Intermittent

P0470 Exhaust Pressure Sensor Malfunction

P0471 Exhaust Pressure Sensor Range/Performance

P0472 Exhaust Pressure Sensor Low

P0473 Exhaust Pressure Sensor High

P0474 Exhaust Pressure Sensor Intermittent

P0475 Exhaust Pressure Control Valve Malfunction

P0476 Exhaust Pressure Control Valve Range/Performance

P0477 Exhaust Pressure Control Valve Low

P0478 Exhaust Pressure Control Valve High

P0479 Exhaust Pressure Control Valve Intermittent

P0480 Cooling Fan #1 Control Circuit Malfunction

P0481 Cooling Fan #2 Control Circuit Malfunction

P0482 Cooling Fan #3 Control Circuit Malfunction

P0483 Cooling Fan Rationality Check Malfunction

P0484 Cooling Fan Circuit Over Current

P0485 Cooling Fan Power/Ground Circuit Malfunction

P0500 Vehicle Speed Sensor Malfunction

P0501 Vehicle Speed Sensor Range/Performance

P0502 Vehicle Speed Sensor Circuit Low Input

P0503 Vehicle Speed Sensor Intermittent/Erratic/High

P0505 Idle Control System Malfunction

P0506 Idle Control System RPM Lower Than Expected

P0507 Idle Control System RPM Higher Than Expected

P0510 Closed Throttle Position Switch Malfunction

P0520 Engine Oil Pressure Sensor/Switch Circuit Malfunction

P0521 Engine Oil Pressure Sensor/Switch Range/Performance

P0522 Engine Oil Pressure Sensor/Switch Low Voltage

P0523 Engine Oil Pressure Sensor/Switch High Voltage

P0530 A/C Refrigerant Pressure Sensor Circuit Malfunction

P0531 A/C Refrigerant Pressure Sensor Circuit Range/Performance

P0532 A/C Refrigerant Pressure Sensor Circuit Low Input

P0533 A/C Refrigerant Pressure Sensor Circuit High Input

P0534 A/C Refrigerant Charge Loss

P0550 Power Steering Pressure Sensor Circuit Malfunction

P0551 Power Steering Pressure Sensor Circuit Range/Performance

P0552 Power Steering Pressure Sensor Circuit Low Input

P0553 Power Steering Pressure Sensor Circuit High Input

P0554 Power Steering Pressure Sensor Circuit Intermittent

P0560 System Voltage Malfunction

P0561 System Voltage Unstable

P0562 System Voltage Low

P0563 System Voltage High

P0565 Cruise Control On Signal Malfunction

P0566 Cruise Control Off Signal Malfunction

P0567 Cruise Control Resume Signal Malfunction

P0568 Cruise Control Set Signal Malfunction

P0569 Cruise Control Coast Signal Malfunction

P0570 Cruise Control Accel Signal Malfunction

P0571 Cruise Control/Brake Switch "A" Circuit Malfunction

P0572 Cruise Control/Brake Switch "A" Circuit Low

P0573 Cruise Control/Brake Switch "A" Circuit High

P0574 Through P0580 Reserved for Cruise Codes

P0600 Serial Communication Link Malfunction

P0601 Internal Control Module Memory Check Sum Error

P0602 Control Module Programming Error

P0603 Internal Control Module Keep Alive Memory (KAM) Error

P0604 Internal Control Module Random Access Memory (RAM) Error

P0605 Internal Control Module Read Only Memory (ROM) Error

P0606 PCM Processor Fault

P0608 Control Module VSS Output "A" Malfunction

P0609 Control Module VSS Output "B" Malfunction

P0620 Generator Control Circuit Malfunction

P0621 Generator Lamp "L" Control Circuit Malfunction

P0622 Generator Field "F" Control Circuit Malfunction

P0650 Malfunction Indicator Lamp (MIL) Control Circuit Malfunction

P0654 Engine RPM Output Circuit Malfunction

P0655 Engine Hot Lamp Output Control Circuit Malfunction

P0656 Fuel Level Output Circuit Malfunction

P0700 Transmission Control System Malfunction

P0701 Transmission Control System Range/Performance

P0702 Transmission Control System Electrical

P0703 Torque Converter/Brake Switch "B" Circuit Malfunction

P0704 Clutch Switch Input Circuit Malfunction

P0705 Transmission Range Sensor Circuit Malfunction (PRNDL Input)

P0706 Transmission Range Sensor Circuit Range/Performance

P0707 Transmission Range Sensor Circuit Low Input

P0708 Transmission Range Sensor Circuit High Input

P0709 Transmission Range Sensor Circuit Intermittent

P0710 Transmission Fluid Temperature Sensor Circuit Malfunction

P0711 Transmission Fluid Temperature Sensor Circuit Range/Performance

P0712 Transmission Fluid Temperature Sensor Circuit Low Input

P0713 Transmission Fluid Temperature Sensor Circuit High Input

P0714 Transmission Fluid Temperature Sensor Circuit Intermittent

P0715 Input/Turbine Speed Sensor Circuit Malfunction

P0716 Input/Turbine Speed Sensor Circuit Range/Performance

P0717 Input/Turbine Speed Sensor Circuit No Signal

P0718 Input/Turbine Speed Sensor Circuit Intermittent

P0719 Torque Converter/Brake Switch "B" Circuit Low

P0720 Output Speed Sensor Circuit Malfunction

P0721 Output Speed Sensor Circuit Range/Performance

P0722 Output Speed Sensor Circuit No Signal

P0723 Output Speed Sensor Circuit Intermittent

P0724 Torque Converter/Brake Switch "B" Circuit High

P0725 Engine Speed Input Circuit Malfunction

P0726 Engine Speed Input Circuit Range/Performance

P0727 Engine Speed Input Circuit No Signal

P0728 Engine Speed Input Circuit Intermittent

P0730 Incorrect Gear Ratio

P0731 Gear #1 Incorrect Ratio

P0732 Gear #2 Incorrect Ratio

P0733 Gear #3 Incorrect Ratio

P0734 Gear #4 Incorrect Ratio

P0735 Gear #5 Incorrect Ratio

P0736 Reverse Incorrect Ratio

P0740 Torque Converter Clutch Circuit Malfunction

P0741 Torque Converter Clutch Circuit Performance or Stuck Off

P0742 Torque Converter Clutch Circuit Stuck On

P0743 Torque Converter Clutch Circuit Electrical

P0744 Torque Converter Clutch Circuit Intermittent

P0745 Pressure Control Solenoid Malfunction

P0746 Pressure Control Solenoid Performance or Stuck Off

P0747 Pressure Control Solenoid Stuck On

P0748 Pressure Control Solenoid Electrical

P0749 Pressure Control Solenoid Intermittent

P0750 Shift Solenoid "A" Malfunction

P0751 Shift Solenoid "A" Performance or Stuck Off

P0752 Shift Solenoid "A" Stuck On

P0753 Shift Solenoid "A" Electrical

P0754 Shift Solenoid "A" Intermittent

P0755 Shift Solenoid "B" Malfunction

P0756 Shift Solenoid "B" Performance or Stuck Off

P0757 Shift Solenoid "B" Stuck On

P0758 Shift Solenoid "B" Electrical

P0759 Shift Solenoid "B" Intermittent

P0760 Shift Solenoid "C" Malfunction

P0761 Shift Solenoid "C" Performance Or Stuck Off

P0762 Shift Solenoid "C" Stuck On

P0763 Shift Solenoid "C" Electrical

P0764 Shift Solenoid "C" Intermittent

P0765 Shift Solenoid "D" Malfunction

P0766 Shift Solenoid "D" Performance Or Stuck Off

P0767 Shift Solenoid "D" Stuck On

P0768 Shift Solenoid "D" Electrical

P0769 Shift Solenoid "D" Intermittent

P0770 Shift Solenoid "E" Malfunction

P0771 Shift Solenoid "E" Performance Or Stuck Off

P0772 Shift Solenoid "E" Stuck On

P0773 Shift Solenoid "E" Electrical

P0774 Shift Solenoid "E" Intermittent

P0780 Shift Malfunction

P0781 1–2 Shift Malfunction

P0782 2–3 Shift Malfunction

P0783 3–4 Shift Malfunction

P0784 4–5 Shift Malfunction

P0785 Shift/Timing Solenoid Malfunction

P0786 Shift/Timing Solenoid Range/Performance

P0787 Shift/Timing Solenoid Low

P0788 Shift/Timing Solenoid High

P0789 Shift/Timing Solenoid Intermittent

P0790 Normal/Performance Switch Circuit Malfunction

P0801 Reverse Inhibit Control Circuit Malfunction

P0803 1–4 Upshift (Skip Shift) Solenoid Control Circuit Malfunction

P0804 1–4 Upshift (Skip Shift) Lamp Control Circuit Malfunction

P1290 CNG Fuel System Pressure Too High (3.3L CNG vehicles only)

P1291 No Temp Rise Seen From Intake Air Heaters

P1292 CNG Pressure Sensor Voltage Too High (3.3L CNG vehicles only)

P1293 CNG Pressure Sensor Voltage Too Low (3.3L CNG vehicles only)

P1294 Target Idle Not Reached

P1296 No 5-Volts To MAP Sensor

P1297 No Change In MAP From Start To Run

P1391 Intermittent Loss Of CMP Or CKP

P1398 Misfire Adaptive Numerator At Limit

P1486 EVAP Leak Monitor Pinched Hose Or Obstruction Found

P1491 Radiator Fan Control Relay Circuit

P1492 Battery Temp Sensor Voltage Too High

P1493 Battery Temp Sensor Voltage Too Low

P1494 Leak Detection Pump Pressure Switch Or Mechanical Fault

P1495 Leak Detection Pump Solenoid Circuit

P1498 Auxiliary 5-Volt Supply Output Too Low

P1697 PCM Failure SRI Mile Not Stored

P1698 PCM Failure EEPROM Write Denied

P1756 Governor Pressure Not Equal To Target @ 15–20 PSI

P1757 Governor Pressure Above 3 PSI In Gear With 0 MPH

P1762 Governor Pressure Sensor Offset Volts Too Low Or High

P1763 Governor Pressure Sensor Volts Too High

P1764 Governor Pressure Sensor Volts Too Low

P1765 Trans 12-Volt Supply Relay Control Circuit

P1899 P/N Switch Stuck In Park Or In Gear

Ford Motor Co.

➡ **The Mercury Villager is covered under the Nissan section since it shares a platform with the Nissan Quest.**

READING CODES

Reading the control module memory is one of the first steps in OBD II system diagnostics. This step should be initially performed to determine the general nature of the fault. Subsequent readings will determine if the fault has been cleared.

Reading codes can be performed by any of the methods below:

• Read the control module memory with the Generic Scan Tool (GST)

• Read the control module memory with the vehicle manufacturer's specific tester

To read the fault codes, connect the scan tool or tester according to the manufacturer's instructions. Follow the manufacturer's specified procedure for reading the codes.

CLEARING CODES

Control module reset procedures are a very important part of OBD II System diagnostics. This step should be done at the end of any fault code repair and at the end of any driveability repair.

Clearing codes can be performed by any of the methods below:

• Clear the control module memory with the Generic Scan Tool (GST)

• Clear the control module memory with the vehicle manufacturer's specific tester

• Turn the ignition OFF and remove the negative battery cable for at least 1 minute.

Removing the negative battery cable may cause other systems in the vehicle to loose their memory. Prior to removing the cable, ensure you have the proper reset codes for radios and alarms.

➡ **The MIL will may also be de-activated for some codes if the vehicle completes three consecutive trips without a fault detected with vehicle conditions similar to those present during the fault.**

OBD II TROUBLE CODES

P0000 No Failures

P0100 Mass or Volume Air Flow Circuit Malfunction

P0101 Mass or Volume Air Flow Circuit Range/Performance Problem

P0102 Mass or Volume Air Flow Circuit Low Input

P0103 Mass or Volume Air Flow Circuit High Input

P0104 Mass or Volume Air Flow Circuit Intermittent

P0105 Manifold Absolute Pressure/Barometric Pressure Circuit Malfunction

P0106 Manifold Absolute Pressure/Barometric Pressure Circuit Range/Performance Problem

P0107 Manifold Absolute Pressure/Barometric Pressure Circuit Low Input

P0108 Manifold Absolute Pressure/Barometric Pressure Circuit High Input

P0109 Manifold Absolute Pressure/Barometric Pressure Circuit Intermittent

P0110 Intake Air Temperature Circuit Malfunction

P0111 Intake Air Temperature Circuit Range/Performance Problem

P0112 Intake Air Temperature Circuit Low Input

P0113 Intake Air Temperature Circuit High Input

P0114 Intake Air Temperature Circuit Intermittent

P0115 Engine Coolant Temperature Circuit Malfunction

P0116 Engine Coolant Temperature Circuit Range/Performance Problem

P0117 Engine Coolant Temperature Circuit Low Input

P0118 Engine Coolant Temperature Circuit High Input

P0119 Engine Coolant Temperature Circuit Intermittent

P0120 Throttle/Pedal Position Sensor/Switch "A" Circuit Malfunction

P0121 Throttle/Pedal Position Sensor/Switch "A" Circuit Range/Performance Problem

P0122 Throttle/Pedal Position Sensor/Switch "A" Circuit Low Input

P0123 Throttle/Pedal Position Sensor/Switch "A" Circuit High Input

P0124 Throttle/Pedal Position Sensor/Switch "A" Circuit Intermittent

P0125 Insufficient Coolant Temperature For Closed Loop Fuel Control

P0126 Insufficient Coolant Temperature For Stable Operation

P0130 O_2 Circuit Malfunction (Bank #1 Sensor #1)

P0131 O_2 Sensor Circuit Low Voltage (Bank #1 Sensor #1)

P0132 O_2 Sensor Circuit High Voltage (Bank #1 Sensor #1)

P0133 O_2 Sensor Circuit Slow Response (Bank #1 Sensor #1)

P0134 O_2 Sensor Circuit No Activity Detected (Bank #1 Sensor #1)

P0135 O_2 Sensor Heater Circuit Malfunction (Bank #1 Sensor #1)

P0136 O_2 Sensor Circuit Malfunction (Bank #1 Sensor #2)

P0137 O_2 Sensor Circuit Low Voltage (Bank #1 Sensor #2)

P0138 O_2 Sensor Circuit High Voltage (Bank #1 Sensor #2)

P0139 O_2 Sensor Circuit Slow Response (Bank #1 Sensor #2)

P0140 O_2 Sensor Circuit No Activity Detected (Bank #1 Sensor #2)

P0141 O_2 Sensor Heater Circuit Malfunction (Bank #1 Sensor #2)

P0142 O_2 Sensor Circuit Malfunction (Bank #1 Sensor #3)

P0143 O_2 Sensor Circuit Low Voltage (Bank #1 Sensor #3)

P0144 O_2 Sensor Circuit High Voltage (Bank #1 Sensor #3)

P0145 O_2 Sensor Circuit Slow Response (Bank #1 Sensor #3)

P0146 O_2 Sensor Circuit No Activity Detected (Bank #1 Sensor #3)

P0147 O_2 Sensor Heater Circuit Malfunction (Bank #1 Sensor #3)

P0150 O_2 Sensor Circuit Malfunction (Bank #2 Sensor #1)

P0151 O_2 Sensor Circuit Low Voltage (Bank #2 Sensor #1)

P0152 O_2 Sensor Circuit High Voltage (Bank #2 Sensor #1)

P0153 O_2 Sensor Circuit Slow Response (Bank #2 Sensor #1)

P0154 O_2 Sensor Circuit No Activity Detected (Bank #2 Sensor #1)

P0155 O_2 Sensor Heater Circuit Malfunction (Bank #2 Sensor #1)

P0156 O_2 Sensor Circuit Malfunction (Bank #2 Sensor #2)

P0157 O_2 Sensor Circuit Low Voltage (Bank #2 Sensor #2)

P0158 O_2 Sensor Circuit High Voltage (Bank #2 Sensor #2)

P0159 O_2 Sensor Circuit Slow Response (Bank #2 Sensor #2)

P0160 O_2 Sensor Circuit No Activity Detected (Bank #2 Sensor #2)

P0161 O_2 Sensor Heater Circuit Malfunction (Bank #2 Sensor #2)

P0162 O_2 Sensor Circuit Malfunction (Bank #2 Sensor #3)

P0163 O_2 Sensor Circuit Low Voltage (Bank #2 Sensor #3)

P0164 O_2 Sensor Circuit High Voltage (Bank #2 Sensor #3)

P0165 O_2 Sensor Circuit Slow Response (Bank #2 Sensor #3)

P0166 O_2 Sensor Circuit No Activity Detected (Bank #2 Sensor #3)

P0167 O_2 Sensor Heater Circuit Malfunction (Bank #2 Sensor #3)

P0170 Fuel Trim Malfunction (Bank #1)

P0171 System Too Lean (Bank #1)

P0172 System Too Rich (Bank #1)

P0173 Fuel Trim Malfunction (Bank #2)

P0174 System Too Lean (Bank #2)

P0175 System Too Rich (Bank #2)

P0176 Fuel Composition Sensor Circuit Malfunction

P0177 Fuel Composition Sensor Circuit Range/Performance

P0178 Fuel Composition Sensor Circuit Low Input

P0179 Fuel Composition Sensor Circuit High Input

P0180 Fuel Temperature Sensor "A" Circuit Malfunction

P0181 Fuel Temperature Sensor "A" Circuit Range/Performance

P0182 Fuel Temperature Sensor "A" Circuit Low Input

P0183 Fuel Temperature Sensor "A" Circuit High Input

P0184 Fuel Temperature Sensor "A" Circuit Intermittent

P0185 Fuel Temperature Sensor "B" Circuit Malfunction

P0186 Fuel Temperature Sensor "B" Circuit Range/Performance

P0187 Fuel Temperature Sensor "B" Circuit Low Input

P0188 Fuel Temperature Sensor "B" Circuit High Input

P0189 Fuel Temperature Sensor "B" Circuit Intermittent

P0190 Fuel Rail Pressure Sensor Circuit Malfunction

P0191 Fuel Rail Pressure Sensor Circuit Range/Performance

P0192 Fuel Rail Pressure Sensor Circuit Low Input

P0193 Fuel Rail Pressure Sensor Circuit High Input

P0194 Fuel Rail Pressure Sensor Circuit Intermittent

P0195 Engine Oil Temperature Sensor Malfunction

P0196 Engine Oil Temperature Sensor Range/Performance

P0197 Engine Oil Temperature Sensor Low

P0198 Engine Oil Temperature Sensor High

P0199 Engine Oil Temperature Sensor Intermittent

P0200 Injector Circuit Malfunction

P0201 Injector Circuit Malfunction—Cylinder #1

P0202 Injector Circuit Malfunction—Cylinder #2

P0203 Injector Circuit Malfunction—Cylinder #3

P0204 Injector Circuit Malfunction—Cylinder #4

P0205 Injector Circuit Malfunction—Cylinder #5

P0206 Injector Circuit Malfunction—Cylinder #6

P0207 Injector Circuit Malfunction—Cylinder #7

P0208 Injector Circuit Malfunction—Cylinder #8

P0209 Injector Circuit Malfunction—Cylinder #9

P0210 Injector Circuit Malfunction—Cylinder #10

P0211 Injector Circuit Malfunction—Cylinder #11

P0212 Injector Circuit Malfunction—Cylinder #12

P0213 Cold Start Injector #1 Malfunction

P0214 Cold Start Injector #2 Malfunction

P0215 Engine Shutoff Solenoid Malfunction

P0216 Injection Timing Control Circuit Malfunction

P0217 Engine Over Temperature Condition

P0218 Transmission Over Temperature Condition

P0219 Engine Over Speed Condition

P0220 Throttle/Pedal Position Sensor/Switch "B" Circuit Malfunction

P0221 Throttle/Pedal Position Sensor/Switch "B" Circuit Range/Performance Problem

P0222 Throttle/Pedal Position Sensor/Switch "B" Circuit Low Input

P0223 Throttle/Pedal Position Sensor/Switch "B" Circuit High Input

P0224 Throttle/Pedal Position Sensor/Switch "B" Circuit Intermittent

P0225 Throttle/Pedal Position Sensor/Switch "C" Circuit Malfunction

P0226 Throttle/Pedal Position Sensor/Switch "C" Circuit Range/Performance Problem

P0227 Throttle/Pedal Position Sensor/Switch "C" Circuit Low Input

P0228 Throttle/Pedal Position Sensor/Switch "C" Circuit High Input

P0229 Throttle/Pedal Position Sensor/Switch "C" Circuit Intermittent

P0230 Fuel Pump Primary Circuit Malfunction

P0231 Fuel Pump Secondary Circuit Low

P0232 Fuel Pump Secondary Circuit High

P0233 Fuel Pump Secondary Circuit Intermittent

P0234 Engine Over Boost Condition

P0261 Cylinder #1 Injector Circuit Low

P0262 Cylinder #1 Injector Circuit High

P0263 Cylinder #1 Contribution/Balance Fault

P0264 Cylinder #2 Injector Circuit Low

P0265 Cylinder #2 Injector Circuit High

P0266 Cylinder #2 Contribution/Balance Fault

P0267 Cylinder #3 Injector Circuit Low

P0268 Cylinder #3 Injector Circuit High

P0269 Cylinder #3 Contribution/Balance Fault

P0270 Cylinder #4 Injector Circuit Low

P0271 Cylinder #4 Injector Circuit High

P0272 Cylinder #4 Contribution/Balance Fault

P0273 Cylinder #5 Injector Circuit Low

P0274 Cylinder #5 Injector Circuit High

P0275 Cylinder #5 Contribution/Balance Fault

P0276 Cylinder #6 Injector Circuit Low

P0277 Cylinder #6 Injector Circuit High

P0278 Cylinder #6 Contribution/Balance Fault

P0279 Cylinder #7 Injector Circuit Low

P0280 Cylinder #7 Injector Circuit High

P0281 Cylinder #7 Contribution/Balance Fault

P0282 Cylinder #8 Injector Circuit Low

P0283 Cylinder #8 Injector Circuit High

P0284 Cylinder #8 Contribution/Balance Fault

P0285 Cylinder #9 Injector Circuit Low

P0286 Cylinder #9 Injector Circuit High

P0287 Cylinder #9 Contribution/Balance Fault

P0288 Cylinder #10 Injector Circuit Low

P0289 Cylinder #10 Injector Circuit High

P0290 Cylinder #10 Contribution/Balance Fault

P0291 Cylinder #11 Injector Circuit Low

P0292 Cylinder #11 Injector Circuit High

P0293 Cylinder #11 Contribution/Balance Fault

P0294 Cylinder #12 Injector Circuit Low

P0295 Cylinder #12 Injector Circuit High

Ignition system service is covered in the model specific sections of this manual

P0296 Cylinder #12 Contribution/Balance Fault

P0300 Random/Multiple Cylinder Misfire Detected

P0301 Cylinder #1—Misfire Detected

P0302 Cylinder #2—Misfire Detected

P0303 Cylinder #3—Misfire Detected

P0304 Cylinder #4—Misfire Detected

P0305 Cylinder #5—Misfire Detected

P0306 Cylinder #6—Misfire Detected

P0307 Cylinder #7—Misfire Detected

P0308 Cylinder #8—Misfire Detected

P0309 Cylinder #9—Misfire Detected

P0310 Cylinder #10—Misfire Detected

P0311 Cylinder #11—Misfire Detected

P0312 Cylinder #12—Misfire Detected

P0320 Ignition/Distributor Engine Speed Input Circuit Malfunction

P0321 Ignition/Distributor Engine Speed Input Circuit Range/Performance

P0322 Ignition/Distributor Engine Speed Input Circuit No Signal

P0323 Ignition/Distributor Engine Speed Input Circuit Intermittent

P0325 Knock Sensor #1—Circuit Malfunction (Bank #1 or Single Sensor)

P0326 Knock Sensor #1—Circuit Range/Performance (Bank #1 or Single Sensor)

P0327 Knock Sensor #1—Circuit Low Input (Bank #1 or Single Sensor)

P0328 Knock Sensor #1—Circuit High Input (Bank #1 or Single Sensor)

P0329 Knock Sensor #1—Circuit Input Intermittent (Bank #1 or Single Sensor)

P0330 Knock Sensor #2—Circuit Malfunction (Bank #2)

P0331 Knock Sensor #2—Circuit Range/Performance (Bank #2)

P0332 Knock Sensor #2—Circuit Low Input (Bank #2)

P0333 Knock Sensor #2—Circuit High Input (Bank #2)

P0334 Knock Sensor #2—Circuit Input Intermittent (Bank #2)

P0335 Crankshaft Position Sensor "A" Circuit Malfunction

P0336 Crankshaft Position Sensor "A" Circuit Range/Performance

P0337 Crankshaft Position Sensor "A" Circuit Low Input

P0338 Crankshaft Position Sensor "A" Circuit High Input

P0339 Crankshaft Position Sensor "A" Circuit Intermittent

P0340 Camshaft Position Sensor Circuit Malfunction

P0341 Camshaft Position Sensor Circuit Range/Performance

P0342 Camshaft Position Sensor Circuit Low Input

P0343 Camshaft Position Sensor Circuit High Input

P0344 Camshaft Position Sensor Circuit Intermittent

P0350 Ignition Coil Primary/Secondary Circuit Malfunction

P0351 Ignition Coil "A" Primary/Secondary Circuit Malfunction

P0352 Ignition Coil "B" Primary/Secondary Circuit Malfunction

P0353 Ignition Coil "C" Primary/Secondary Circuit Malfunction

P0354 Ignition Coil "D" Primary/Secondary Circuit Malfunction

P0355 Ignition Coil "E" Primary/Secondary Circuit Malfunction

P0356 Ignition Coil "F" Primary/Secondary Circuit Malfunction

P0357 Ignition Coil "G" Primary/Secondary Circuit Malfunction

P0358 Ignition Coil "H" Primary/Secondary Circuit Malfunction

P0359 Ignition Coil "I" Primary/Secondary Circuit Malfunction

P0360 Ignition Coil "J" Primary/Secondary Circuit Malfunction

P0361 Ignition Coil "K" Primary/Secondary Circuit Malfunction

P0362 Ignition Coil "L" Primary/Secondary Circuit Malfunction

P0370 Timing Reference High Resolution Signal "A" Malfunction

P0371 Timing Reference High Resolution Signal "A" Too Many Pulses

P0372 Timing Reference High Resolution Signal "A" Too Few Pulses

P0373 Timing Reference High Resolution Signal "A" Intermittent/Erratic Pulses

P0374 Timing Reference High Resolution Signal "A" No Pulses

P0375 Timing Reference High Resolution Signal "B" Malfunction

P0376 Timing Reference High Resolution Signal "B" Too Many Pulses

P0377 Timing Reference High Resolution Signal "B" Too Few Pulses

P0378 Timing Reference High Resolution Signal "B" Intermittent/Erratic Pulses

P0379 Timing Reference High Resolution Signal "B" No Pulses

P0380 Glow Plug/Heater Circuit "A" Malfunction

P0381 Glow Plug/Heater Indicator Circuit Malfunction

P0382 Glow Plug/Heater Circuit "B" Malfunction

P0385 Crankshaft Position Sensor "B" Circuit Malfunction

P0386 Crankshaft Position Sensor "B" Circuit Range/Performance

P0387 Crankshaft Position Sensor "B" Circuit Low Input

P0388 Crankshaft Position Sensor "B" Circuit High Input

P0389 Crankshaft Position Sensor "B" Circuit Intermittent

P0400 Exhaust Gas Recirculation Flow Malfunction

P0401 Exhaust Gas Recirculation Flow Insufficient Detected

P0402 Exhaust Gas Recirculation Flow Excessive Detected

P0403 Exhaust Gas Recirculation Circuit Malfunction

P0404 Exhaust Gas Recirculation Circuit Range/Performance

P0405 Exhaust Gas Recirculation Sensor "A" Circuit Low

P0406 Exhaust Gas Recirculation Sensor "A" Circuit High

P0407 Exhaust Gas Recirculation Sensor "B" Circuit Low

P0408 Exhaust Gas Recirculation Sensor "B" Circuit High

P0410 Secondary Air Injection System Malfunction

P0411 Secondary Air Injection System Incorrect Flow Detected

P0412 Secondary Air Injection System Switching Valve "A" Circuit Malfunction

P0413 Secondary Air Injection System Switching Valve "A" Circuit Open

P0414 Secondary Air Injection System Switching Valve "A" Circuit Shorted

P0415 Secondary Air Injection System Switching Valve "B" Circuit Malfunction

P0416 Secondary Air Injection System Switching Valve "B" Circuit Open

P0417 Secondary Air Injection System Switching Valve "B" Circuit Shorted

P0418 Secondary Air Injection System Relay "A" Circuit Malfunction

P0419 Secondary Air Injection System Relay "B" Circuit Malfunction

P0420 Catalyst System Efficiency Below Threshold (Bank #1)

P0421 Warm Up Catalyst Efficiency Below Threshold (Bank #1)

P0422 Main Catalyst Efficiency Below Threshold (Bank #1)

P0423 Heated Catalyst Efficiency Below Threshold (Bank #1)

P0424 Heated Catalyst Temperature Below Threshold (Bank #1)

P0430 Catalyst System Efficiency Below Threshold (Bank #2)

P0431 Warm Up Catalyst Efficiency Below Threshold (Bank #2)

P0432 Main Catalyst Efficiency Below Threshold (Bank #2)

P0433 Heated Catalyst Efficiency Below Threshold (Bank #2)

P0434 Heated Catalyst Temperature Below Threshold (Bank #2)

P0440 Evaporative Emission Control System Malfunction

P0441 Evaporative Emission Control System Incorrect Purge Flow

P0442 Evaporative Emission Control System Leak Detected (Small Leak)

P0443 Evaporative Emission Control System Purge Control Valve Circuit Malfunction

P0444 Evaporative Emission Control System Purge Control Valve Circuit Open

P0445 Evaporative Emission Control System Purge Control Valve Circuit Shorted

P0446 Evaporative Emission Control System Vent Control Circuit Malfunction

P0447 Evaporative Emission Control System Vent Control Circuit Open

P0448 Evaporative Emission Control System Vent Control Circuit Shorted

P0449 Evaporative Emission Control System Vent Valve/Solenoid Circuit Malfunction

P0450 Evaporative Emission Control System Pressure Sensor Malfunction

P0451 Evaporative Emission Control System Pressure Sensor Range/Performance

P0452 Evaporative Emission Control System Pressure Sensor Low Input

P0453 Evaporative Emission Control System Pressure Sensor High Input

P0454 Evaporative Emission Control System Pressure Sensor Intermittent

P0455 Evaporative Emission Control System Leak Detected (Gross Leak)

P0460 Fuel Level Sensor Circuit Malfunction

P0461 Fuel Level Sensor Circuit Range/Performance

P0462 Fuel Level Sensor Circuit Low Input

P0463 Fuel Level Sensor Circuit High Input

P0464 Fuel Level Sensor Circuit Intermittent

P0465 Purge Flow Sensor Circuit Malfunction

P0466 Purge Flow Sensor Circuit Range/Performance

P0467 Purge Flow Sensor Circuit Low Input

P0468 Purge Flow Sensor Circuit High Input

P0469 Purge Flow Sensor Circuit Intermittent

P0470 Exhaust Pressure Sensor Malfunction

P0471 Exhaust Pressure Sensor Range/Performance

P0472 Exhaust Pressure Sensor Low

P0473 Exhaust Pressure Sensor High

P0474 Exhaust Pressure Sensor Intermittent

P0475 Exhaust Pressure Control Valve Malfunction

P0476 Exhaust Pressure Control Valve Range/Performance

P0477 Exhaust Pressure Control Valve Low

P0478 Exhaust Pressure Control Valve High

P0479 Exhaust Pressure Control Valve Intermittent

P0480 Cooling Fan #1 Control Circuit Malfunction

P0481 Cooling Fan #2 Control Circuit Malfunction

P0482 Cooling Fan #3 Control Circuit Malfunction

P0483 Cooling Fan Rationality Check Malfunction

P0484 Cooling Fan Circuit Over Current

P0485 Cooling Fan Power/Ground Circuit Malfunction

P0500 Vehicle Speed Sensor Malfunction

P0501 Vehicle Speed Sensor Range/Performance

P0502 Vehicle Speed Sensor Circuit Low Input

P0503 Vehicle Speed Sensor Intermittent/Erratic/High

P0505 Idle Control System Malfunction

P0506 Idle Control System RPM Lower Than Expected

P0507 Idle Control System RPM Higher Than Expected

P0510 Closed Throttle Position Switch Malfunction

P0520 Engine Oil Pressure Sensor/ Switch Circuit Malfunction

P0521 Engine Oil Pressure Sensor/ Switch Range/Performance

P0522 Engine Oil Pressure Sensor/ Switch Low Voltage

P0523 Engine Oil Pressure Sensor/ Switch High Voltage

P0530 A/C Refrigerant Pressure Sensor Circuit Malfunction

P0531 A/C Refrigerant Pressure Sensor Circuit Range/Performance

P0532 A/C Refrigerant Pressure Sensor Circuit Low Input

P0533 A/C Refrigerant Pressure Sensor Circuit High Input

P0534 A/C Refrigerant Charge Loss

P0550 Power Steering Pressure Sensor Circuit Malfunction

P0551 Power Steering Pressure Sensor Circuit Range/Performance

P0552 Power Steering Pressure Sensor Circuit Low Input

P0553 Power Steering Pressure Sensor Circuit High Input

P0554 Power Steering Pressure Sensor Circuit Intermittent

P0560 System Voltage Malfunction

P0561 System Voltage Unstable

P0562 System Voltage Low

P0563 System Voltage High

P0565 Cruise Control On Signal Malfunction

P0566 Cruise Control Off Signal Malfunction

P0567 Cruise Control Resume Signal Malfunction

P0568 Cruise Control Set Signal Malfunction

P0569 Cruise Control Coast Signal Malfunction

P0570 Cruise Control Accel Signal Malfunction

P0571 Cruise Control/Brake Switch "A" Circuit Malfunction

P0572 Cruise Control/Brake Switch "A" Circuit Low

P0573 Cruise Control/Brake Switch "A" Circuit High

P0574 Through P0580 Reserved for Cruise Codes

P0600 Serial Communication Link Malfunction

P0601 Internal Control Module Memory Check Sum Error

P0602 Control Module Programming Error

P0603 Internal Control Module Keep Alive Memory (KAM) Error

P0604 Internal Control Module Random Access Memory (RAM) Error

P0605 Internal Control Module Read Only Memory (ROM) Error

P0606 PCM Processor Fault

P0608 Control Module VSS Output "A" Malfunction

P0609 Control Module VSS Output "B" Malfunction

P0620 Generator Control Circuit Malfunction

P0621 Generator Lamp "L" Control Circuit Malfunction

P0622 Generator Field "F" Control Circuit Malfunction

P0650 Malfunction Indicator Lamp (MIL) Control Circuit Malfunction

P0654 Engine RPM Output Circuit Malfunction

P0655 Engine Hot Lamp Output Control Circuit Malfunction

P0656 Fuel Level Output Circuit Malfunction

P0700 Transmission Control System Malfunction

P0701 Transmission Control System Range/Performance

P0702 Transmission Control System Electrical

P0703 Torque Converter/Brake Switch "B" Circuit Malfunction

P0704 Clutch Switch Input Circuit Malfunction

P0705 Transmission Range Sensor Circuit Malfunction (PRNDL Input)

P0706 Transmission Range Sensor Circuit Range/Performance

P0707 Transmission Range Sensor Circuit Low Input

P0708 Transmission Range Sensor Circuit High Input

P0709 Transmission Range Sensor Circuit Intermittent

P0710 Transmission Fluid Temperature Sensor Circuit Malfunction

P0711 Transmission Fluid Temperature Sensor Circuit Range/Performance

P0712 Transmission Fluid Temperature Sensor Circuit Low Input

P0713 Transmission Fluid Temperature Sensor Circuit High Input

P0714 Transmission Fluid Temperature Sensor Circuit Intermittent

P0715 Input/Turbine Speed Sensor Circuit Malfunction

P0716 Input/Turbine Speed Sensor Circuit Range/Performance

P0717 Input/Turbine Speed Sensor Circuit No Signal

P0718 Input/Turbine Speed Sensor Circuit Intermittent

P0719 Torque Converter/Brake Switch "B" Circuit Low

P0720 Output Speed Sensor Circuit Malfunction

P0721 Output Speed Sensor Circuit Range/Performance

P0722 Output Speed Sensor Circuit No Signal

P0723 Output Speed Sensor Circuit Intermittent

P0724 Torque Converter/Brake Switch "B" Circuit High

P0725 Engine Speed Input Circuit Malfunction

P0726 Engine Speed Input Circuit Range/Performance

P0727 Engine Speed Input Circuit No Signal

P0728 Engine Speed Input Circuit Intermittent

P0730 Incorrect Gear Ratio

P0731 Gear #1 Incorrect Ratio

P0732 Gear #2 Incorrect Ratio

P0733 Gear #3 Incorrect Ratio

P0734 Gear #4 Incorrect Ratio

P0735 Gear #5 Incorrect Ratio

P0736 Reverse Incorrect Ratio

P0740 Torque Converter Clutch Circuit Malfunction

P0741 Torque Converter Clutch Circuit Performance or Stuck Off

P0742 Torque Converter Clutch Circuit Stuck On

P0743 Torque Converter Clutch Circuit Electrical

P0744 Torque Converter Clutch Circuit Intermittent

P0745 Pressure Control Solenoid Malfunction

P0746 Pressure Control Solenoid Performance or Stuck Off

P0747 Pressure Control Solenoid Stuck On

P0748 Pressure Control Solenoid Electrical

P0749 Pressure Control Solenoid Intermittent

P0750 Shift Solenoid "A" Malfunction

P0751 Shift Solenoid "A" Performance or Stuck Off

P0752 Shift Solenoid "A" Stuck On

P0753 Shift Solenoid "A" Electrical

P0754 Shift Solenoid "A" Intermittent

P0755 Shift Solenoid "B" Malfunction

P0756 Shift Solenoid "B" Performance or Stuck Off

P0757 Shift Solenoid "B" Stuck On

P0758 Shift Solenoid "B" Electrical

P0759 Shift Solenoid "B" Intermittent

P0760 Shift Solenoid "C" Malfunction

P0761 Shift Solenoid "C" Performance Or Stuck Off

P0762 Shift Solenoid "C" Stuck On

P0763 Shift Solenoid "C" Electrical

P0764 Shift Solenoid "C" Intermittent

P0765 Shift Solenoid "D" Malfunction

P0766 Shift Solenoid "D" Performance Or Stuck Off

P0767 Shift Solenoid "D" Stuck On

P0768 Shift Solenoid "D" Electrical

P0769 Shift Solenoid "D" Intermittent

P0770 Shift Solenoid "E" Malfunction

P0771 Shift Solenoid "E" Performance Or Stuck Off

P0772 Shift Solenoid "E" Stuck On

P0773 Shift Solenoid "E" Electrical

P0774 Shift Solenoid "E" Intermittent

P0780 Shift Malfunction

P0781 1–2 Shift Malfunction

P0782 2–3 Shift Malfunction

P0783 3–4 Shift Malfunction

P0784 4–5 Shift Malfunction

P0785 Shift/Timing Solenoid Malfunction

P0786 Shift/Timing Solenoid Range/Performance

P0787 Shift/Timing Solenoid Low

P0788 Shift/Timing Solenoid High

P0789 Shift/Timing Solenoid Intermittent

P0790 Normal/Performance Switch Circuit Malfunction

P0801 Reverse Inhibit Control Circuit Malfunction

P0803 1–4 Upshift (Skip Shift) Solenoid Control Circuit Malfunction

P0804 1–4 Upshift (Skip Shift) Lamp Control Circuit Malfunction

P1000 OBD II Monitor Testing Not Complete More Driving Required

P1001 Key On Engine Running (KOER) Self-Test Not Able To Complete, KOER Aborted

P1100 Mass Air Flow (MAF) Sensor Intermittent

P1101 Mass Air Flow (MAF) Sensor Out Of Self-Test Range

P1111 System Pass 49 State, Except Econoline

P1112 Intake Air Temperature (IAT) Sensor Intermittent

P1116 Engine Coolant Temperature (ECT) Sensor Out Of Self-Test Range

P1117 Engine Coolant Temperature (ECT) Sensor Intermittent

P1120 Throttle Position (TP) Sensor Out Of Range (Low)

P1121 Throttle Position (TP) Sensor Inconsistent With MAF Sensor

P1124 Throttle Position (TP) Sensor Out Of Self-Test Range

P1125 Throttle Position (TP) Sensor Circuit Intermittent

P1127 Exhaust Not Warm Enough, Downstream Heated Oxygen Sensors (HO2S) Not Tested

P1128 Upstream Heated Oxygen Sensors (HO2 S) Swapped From Bank To Bank

P1129 Downstream Heated Oxygen Sensors (HO2S) Swapped From Bank To Bank

P1130 Lack Of Upstream Heated Oxygen Sensor (HO2S 11) Switch, Adaptive Fuel At Limit (Bank #1)

P1131 Lack Of Upstream Heated Oxygen Sensor (HO2S 11) Switch, Sensor Indicates Lean (Bank #1)

P1132 Lack Of Upstream Heated Oxygen Sensor (HO2S 11) Switch, Sensor Indicates Rich (Bank #1)

P1137 Lack Of Downstream Heated Oxygen Sensor (HO2S 12) Switch, Sensor Indicates Lean (Bank #1)

P1138 Lack Of Downstream Heated

Oxygen Sensor (HO$_2$ 12) Switch, Sensor Indicates Rich (Bank #1)

P1150 Lack Of Upstream Heated Oxygen Sensor (HO2S 21) Switch, Adaptive Fuel At Limit (Bank #2)

P1151 Lack Of Upstream Heated Oxygen Sensor (HO2S 21) Switch, Sensor Indicates Lean (Bank #2)

P1152 Lack Of Upstream Heated Oxygen Sensor (HO2S 21) Switch, Sensor Indicates Rich (Bank #2)

P1157 Lack Of Downstream Heated Oxygen Sensor (HO2S 22) Switch, Sensor Indicates Lean (Bank #2)

P1158 Lack Of Downstream Heated Oxygen Sensor (HO2S 22) Switch, Sensor Indicates Rich (Bank #2)

P1169 (HO2S 12) Signal Remained Unchanged For More Than 20 Seconds After Closed Loop

P1170 (HO2S 11) Signal Remained Unchanged For More Than 20 Seconds After Closed Loop

P1173 Feedback A/F Mixture Control (HO2S 21) Signal Remained Unchanged For More Than 20 Seconds After Closed Loop

P1184 Engine Oil Temp Sensor Circuit Performance

P1195 Barometric (BARO) Pressure Sensor Circuit Malfunction (Signal Is From EGR Boost Sensor)

P1196 Starter Switch Circuit Malfunction

P1209 Injection Control Pressure (ICP) Peak Fault

P1210 Injection Control Pressure (ICP) Above Expected Level

P1211 Injection Control Pressure (ICP) Not Controllable—Pressure Above/Below Desired

P1212 Injection Control Pressure (ICP) Voltage Not At Expected Level

P1218 Cylinder Identification (CID) Stuck High

P1219 Cylinder Identification (CID) Stuck Low

P1220 Series Throttle Control Malfunction (Traction Control System)

P1224 Throttle Position Sensor "B" (TP-B) Out Of Self-Test Range (Traction Control System)

P1230 Fuel Pump Low Speed Malfunction

P1231 Fuel Pump Secondary Circuit Low With High Speed Pump On

P1232 Low Speed Fuel Pump Primary Circuit Malfunction

P1233 Fuel Pump Driver Module Off-line (MIL DTC)

P1234 Fuel Pump Driver Module Disabled Or Off-line (No MIL)

P1235 Fuel Pump Control Out Of Range (MIL DTC)

P1236 Fuel Pump Control Out Of Range (No MIL)

P1237 Fuel Pump Secondary Circuit Malfunction (MIL DTC)

P1238 Fuel Pump Secondary Circuit Malfunction (No DMIL)

P1250 Fuel Pressure Regulator Control (FPRC) Solenoid Malfunction

P1260 THEFT Detected—Engine Disabled

P1261 High To Low Side Short—Cylinder #1 (Indicates Low side Circuit Is Shorted To B+ Or To The High Side Between The IDM And The Injector)

P1262 High To Low Side Short—Cylinder #2 (Indicates Low side Circuit Is Shorted To B+ Or To The High Side Between The IDM And The Injector)

P1263 High To Low Side Short—Cylinder #3 (Indicates Low side Circuit Is Shorted To B+ Or To The High Side Between The IDM And The Injector)

P1264 High To Low Side Short—Cylinder #4 (Indicates Low side Circuit Is Shorted To B+ Or To The High Side Between The IDM And The Injector)

P1265 High To Low Side Short—Cylinder #5 (Indicates Low side Circuit Is Shorted To B+ Or To The High Side Between The IDM And The Injector)

P1266 High To Low Side Short—Cylinder #6 (Indicates Low side Circuit Is Shorted To B+ Or To The High Side Between The IDM And The Injector)

P1267 High To Low Side Short—Cylinder #7 (Indicates Low side Circuit Is Shorted To B+ Or To The High Side Between The IDM And The Injector)

P1268 High To Low Side Short—Cylinder #8 (Indicates Low side Circuit Is Shorted To B+ Or To The High Side Between The IDM And The Injector)

P1270 Engine RPM Or Vehicle Speed Limiter Reached

P1271 High To Low Side Open—Cylinder #1 (Indicates A High To Low Side Open Between The Injector And The IDM)

P1272 High To Low Side Open—Cylinder #2 (Indicates A High To Low Side Open Between The Injector And The IDM)

P1273 High To Low Side Open—Cylinder #3 (Indicates A High To Low Side Open Between The Injector And The IDM)

P1274 High To Low Side Open—Cylinder #4 (Indicates A High To Low Side Open Between The Injector And The IDM)

P1275 High To Low Side Open—Cylinder #5 (Indicates A High To Low Side Open Between The Injector And The IDM)

P1276 High To Low Side Open—Cylinder #6 (Indicates A High To Low Side Open Between The Injector And The IDM)

P1277 High To Low Side Open—Cylinder #7 (Indicates A High To Low Side Open Between The Injector And The IDM)

P1278 High To Low Side Open—Cylinder #8 (Indicates A High To Low Side Open Between The Injector And The IDM)

P1280 Injection Control Pressure (ICP) Circuit Out Of Range Low

P1281 Injection Control Pressure (ICP) Circuit Out Of Range High

P1282 Injection Control Pressure (ICP) Excessive

P1283 Injection Pressure Regulator (IPR) Circuit Failure

P1284 Injection Control Pressure (ICP) Failure—Aborts KOER Or CCT Test

P1285 Cylinder Head Temperature (CHT) Over Temperature Sensed

P1288 Cylinder Head Temperature (CHT) Sensor Out Of Self-Test Range

P1289 Cylinder Head Temperature (CHT) Sensor Circuit Low Input

P1290 Cylinder Head Temperature (CHT) Sensor Circuit High Input

P1291 IDM To Injector High Side Circuit #1 (Right Bank) Short To GND Or B+

P1292 IDM To Injector High Side Circuit #2 (Right Bank) Short To GND Or B+

P1293 IDM To Injector High Side Circuit Open Bank #1 (Right Bank)

P1294 IDM To Injector High Side Circuit Open Bank #2 (Left Bank)

P1295 Multiple IDM/Injector Circuit Faults On Bank #1 (Right)

P1296 Multiple IDM/Injector Circuit Faults On Bank #2 (Left)

P1297 High Sides Shorted Together

P1298 IDM Failure

P1299 Engine Over Temperature Condition

P1309 Misfire Detection Monitor Is Not Enabled

P1316 Injector Circuit/IDM Codes Detected

P1320 Distributor Signal Interrupt

P1336 Crankshaft Position Sensor (Gear)

P1345 No Camshaft Position Sensor Signal

P1351 Ignition Diagnostic Monitor (IDM) Circuit Input Malfunction

Refer to the model specific sections for fuel system service procedures

P1351 Indicates Ignition System Malfunction

P1352 Indicates Ignition System Malfunction

P1353 Indicates Ignition System Malfunction

P1354 Indicates Ignition System Malfunction

P1355 Indicates Ignition System Malfunction

P1356 PIPs Occurred While IDM Pulse width Indicates Engine Not Turning

P1357 Ignition Diagnostic Monitor (IDM) Pulse width Not Defined

P1358 Ignition Diagnostic Monitor (IDM) Signal Out Of Self-Test Range

P1359 Spark Output Circuit Malfunction

P1364 Spark Output Circuit Malfunction

P1390 Octane Adjust (OCT ADJ) Out Of Self-Test Range

P1391 Glow Plug Circuit Low Input Bank #1 (Right)

P1392 Glow Plug Circuit High Input Bank #1 (Right)

P1393 Glow Plug Circuit Low Input Bank #2 (Left)

P1394 Glow Plug Circuit High Input Bank #2 (Left)

P1395 Glow Plug Monitor Fault Bank #1

P1396 Glow Plug Monitor Fault Bank #2

P1397 System Voltage Out Of Self Test Range

P1400 Differential Pressure Feedback EGR (DPFE) Sensor Circuit Low Voltage Detected

P1401 Differential Pressure Feedback EGR (DPFE) Sensor Circuit High Voltage Detected/EGR Temperature Sensor

P1402 EGR Valve Position Sensor Open Or Short

P1403 Differential Pressure Feedback EGR (DPFE) Sensor Hoses Reversed

P1405 Differential Pressure Feedback EGR (DPFE) Sensor Upstream Hose Off Or Plugged

P1406 Differential Pressure Feedback EGR (DPFE) Sensor Downstream Hose Off Or Plugged

P1407 Exhaust Gas Recirculation (EGR) No Flow Detected (Valve Stuck Closed Or Inoperative)

P1408 Exhaust Gas Recirculation (EGR) Flow Out Of Self-Test Range

P1409 Electronic Vacuum Regulator (EVR) Control Circuit Malfunction

P1410 Check That Fuel Pressure Regulator Control Solenoid And The EGR Check Solenoid Connectors Are Not Swapped

P1411 Secondary Air Injection System Incorrect Downstream Flow Detected

P1413 Secondary Air Injection System Monitor Circuit Low Voltage

P1414 Secondary Air Injection System Monitor Circuit High Voltage

P1442 Evaporative Emission Control System Small Leak Detected

P1443 Evaporative Emission Control System—Vacuum System, Purge Control Solenoid Or Purge Control Valve Malfunction

P1444 Purge Flow Sensor (PFS) Circuit Low Input

P1445 Purge Flow Sensor (PFS) Circuit High Input

P1449 Evaporative Emission Control System Unable To Hold Vacuum

P1450 Unable To Bleed Up Fuel Tank Vacuum

P1455 Evaporative Emission Control System Control Leak Detected (Gross Leak)

P1460 Wide Open Throttle Air Conditioning Cut-Off Circuit Malfunction

P1461 Air Conditioning Pressure (ACP) Sensor Circuit Low Input

P1462 Air Conditioning Pressure (ACP) Sensor Circuit High Input

P1463 Air Conditioning Pressure (ACP) Sensor Insufficient Pressure Change

P1464 Air Conditioning (A/C) Demand Out Of Self-Test Range/A/C On During KOER Or CCT Test

P1469 Low Air Conditioning Cycling Period

P1473 Fan Secondary High, With Fan(s) Off

P1474 Low Fan Control Primary Circuit Malfunction

P1479 High Fan Control Primary Circuit Malfunction

P1480 Fan Secondary Low, With Low Fan On

P1481 Fan Secondary Low, With High Fan On

P1483 Power To Fan Circuit Over current

P1484 Open Power/Ground To Variable Load Control Module (VLCM)

P1485 EGR Control Solenoid Open Or Short

P1486 EGR Vent Solenoid Open Or Short

P1487 EGR Boost Check Solenoid Open Or Short

P1500 Vehicle Speed Sensor (VSS) Circuit Intermittent

P1501 Vehicle Speed Sensor (VSS) Out Of Self-Test Range/Vehicle Moved During Test

P1502 Invalid Self Test—Auxiliary Powertrain Control Module (APCM) Functioning

P1504 Idle Air Control (IAC) Circuit Malfunction

P1505 Idle Air Control (IAC) System At Adaptive Clip

P1506 Idle Air Control (IAC) Over-speed Error

P1507 Idle Air Control (IAC) Underspeed Error

P1512 Intake Manifold Runner Control (IMRC) Malfunction (Bank #1 Stuck Closed)

P1513 Intake Manifold Runner Control (IMRC) Malfunction (Bank #2 Stuck Closed)

P1516 Intake Manifold Runner Control (IMRC) Input Error (Bank #1)

P1517 Intake Manifold Runner Control (IMRC) Input Error (Bank #2)

P1518 Intake Manifold Runner Control (IMRC) Malfunction (Stuck Open)

P1519 Intake Manifold Runner Control (IMRC) Malfunction (Stuck Closed)

P1520 Intake Manifold Runner Control (IMRC) Circuit Malfunction

P1521 Variable Resonance Induction System (VRIS) Solenoid #1 Open Or Short

P1522 Variable Resonance Induction System (VRIS) Solenoid #2 Open Or Short

P1523 High Speed Inlet Air (HSIA) Solenoid Open Or Short

P1530 Air Condition (A/C) Clutch Circuit Malfunction

P1531 Invalid Test—Accelerator Pedal Movement

P1536 Parking Brake Applied Failure

P1537 Intake Manifold Runner Control (IMRC) Malfunction (Bank #1 Stuck Open)

P1538 Intake Manifold Runner Control (IMRC) Malfunction (Bank #2 Stuck Open)

P1539 Power To Air Condition (A/C) Clutch Circuit Over-current

P1549 Problem In Intake Manifold Tuning (IMT) Valve System

P1550 Power Steering Pressure (PSP) Sensor Out Of Self-Test Range

P1601 Serial Communication Error

P1605 Powertrain Control Module (PCM)—Keep Alive Memory (KAM) Test Error

P1608 PCM Internal Circuit Malfunction

P1609 PCM Internal Circuit Malfunction (2.5L Only)

P1625 B+ Supply To Variable Load Control Module (VLCM) Fan Circuit Malfunction

P1626 B+ Supply To Variable Load Control Module (VLCM) Air Conditioning (A/C) Circuit

P1650 Power Steering Pressure (PSP) Switch Out Of Self-Test Range

P1651 Power Steering Pressure (PSP) Switch Input Malfunction

P1660 Output Circuit Check Signal High

P1661 Output Circuit Check Signal Low

P1662 Injection Driver Module Enable (IDM EN) Circuit Failure

P1663 Fuel Delivery Command Signal (FDCS) Circuit Failure

P1667 Cylinder Identification (CID) Circuit Failure

P1668 PCM—IDM Diagnostic Communication Error

P1670 EF Feedback Signal Not Detected

P1701 Reverse Engagement Error

P1701 Fuel Trim Malfunction—Villager

P1703 Brake On/Off (BOO) Switch Out Of Self-Test Range

P1704 Digital Transmission Range (TR) Sensor Failed To Transition State

P1705 Transmission Range (TR) Sensor Out Of Self-Test Range

P1705 TP Sensor (AT)—Villager

P1705 Clutch Pedal Position (CPP) Or Park Neutral Position (PNP) Problem

P1706 High Vehicle Speed In Park

P1709 Park Or Neutral Position (PNP) Or Clutch Pedal Position (CPP) Switch Out Of Self-Test Range

P1711 Transmission Fluid Temperature (TFT) Sensor Out Of Self-Test Range

P1714 Shift Solenoid "A" Inductive Signature Malfunction

P1715 Shift Solenoid "B" Inductive Signature Malfunction

P1716 Transmission Malfunction

P1717 Transmission Malfunction

P1719 Transmission Malfunction

P1720 Vehicle Speed Sensor (VSS) Circuit Malfunction

P1727 Coast Clutch Solenoid Inductive Signature Malfunction

P1728 Transmission Slip Error—Converter Clutch Failed

P1729 4x4 Low Switch Error

P1731 Improper 1–2 Shift

P1732 Improper 2–3 Shift

P1733 Improper 3–4 Shift

P1734 Improper 4–5 Shift

P1740 Torque Converter Clutch (TCC) Inductive Signature Malfunction

P1741 Torque Converter Clutch (TCC) Control Error

P1742 Torque Converter Clutch (TCC) Solenoid Failed On (Turns On MIL)

P1743 Torque Converter Clutch (TCC) Solenoid Failed On (Turns On TCIL)

P1744 Torque Converter Clutch (TCC) System Mechanically Stuck In Off Posi-tion

P1744 Torque Converter Clutch (TCC) Solenoid Malfunction (2.5L Only)

P1746 Electronic Pressure Control (EPC) Solenoid Open Circuit (Low Input)

P1747 Electronic Pressure Control (EPC) Solenoid Short Circuit (High Input)

P1748 Electronic Pressure Control (EPC) Malfunction

P1749 Electronic Pressure Control (EPC) Solenoid Failed Low

P1751 Shift Solenoid #1 (SS1) Performance

P1754 Coast Clutch Solenoid (CCS) Circuit Malfunction

P1756 Shift Solenoid #2 (SS2) Performance

P1760 Overrun Clutch SN

P1761 Shift Solenoid #3 (SS3) Performance

P1762 Transmission Malfunction

P1765 3–2 Timing Solenoid Malfunction (2.5L Only)

P1779 TCIL Circuit Malfunction

P1780 Transmission Control Switch (TCS) Circuit Out Of Self-Test Range

P1781 4x4 Low Switch, Out Of Self-Test Range

P1783 Transmission Over Temperature Condition

P1784 Transmission Malfunction

P1785 Transmission Malfunction

P1786 Transmission Malfunction

P1787 Transmission Malfunction

P1788 3–2 Timing/Coast Clutch Solenoid (3–2/CCS) Circuit Open

P1789 3–2 Timing/Coast Clutch Solenoid (3–2/CCS) Circuit Shorted

P1792 Idle (IDL) Switch (Closed Throttle Position Switch) Malfunction

P1794 Loss Of Battery Voltage Input

P1795 EGR Boost Sensor Malfunction

P1797 Clutch Pedal Position (CPP) Switch Or Neutral Switch Circuit Malfunction

P1900 Cooling Fan

U1021 SCP Indicating The Lack Of Air Conditioning (A/C) Clutch Status Response

U1039 Vehicle Speed Signal (VSS) Missing Or Incorrect

U1051 Brake Switch Signal Missing Or Incorrect

U1073 SCP Indicating The Lack Of Engine Coolant Fan Status Response

U1131 SCP Indicating The Lack Of Fuel Pump Status Response

U1135 SCP Indicating The Ignition Switch Signal Missing Or Incorrect

U1256 SCP Indicating A Communications Error

U1451 Lack Of Response From Passive Anti-Theft System (PATS) Module—Engine Disabled

General Motors

READING CODES

Reading the control module memory is one of the first steps in OBD II system diagnostics. This step should be initially performed to determine the general nature of the fault. Subsequent readings will determine if the fault has been cleared.

Reading codes can be performed by any of the methods below:

• Read the control module memory with the Generic Scan Tool (GST)

• Read the control module memory with the vehicle manufacturer's specific tester

To read the fault codes, connect the scan tool or tester according to the manufacturer's instructions. Follow the manufacturer's specified procedure for reading the codes.

CLEARING CODES

Control module reset procedures are a very important part of OBD II System diagnostics. This step should be done at the end of any fault code repair and at the end of any driveability repair.

Clearing codes can be performed by any of the methods below:

• Clear the control module memory with the Generic Scan Tool (GST)

• Clear the control module memory with the vehicle manufacturer's specific tester

• Turn the ignition OFF and remove the negative battery cable for at least 1 minute.

Removing the negative battery cable may cause other systems in the vehicle to loose their memory. Prior to removing the cable, ensure you have the proper reset codes for radios and alarms.

➥**The MIL will may also be de-activated for some codes if the vehicle completes three consecutive trips without a fault detected with vehicle conditions similar to those present during the fault.**

OBD II TROUBLE CODES

P0100 Mass or Volume Air Flow Circuit Malfunction

P0101 Mass or Volume Air Flow Circuit Range/Performance Problem

P0102 Mass or Volume Air Flow Circuit Low Input

P0103 Mass or Volume Air Flow Circuit High Input

P0104 Mass or Volume Air Flow Circuit Intermittent

P0105 Manifold Absolute Pressure/Barometric Pressure Circuit Malfunction

P0106 Manifold Absolute Pressure/Barometric Pressure Circuit Range/Performance Problem

Refer to the model specific sections for engine electrical system service procedures

P0107 Manifold Absolute Pressure/Barometric Pressure Circuit Low Input

P0108 Manifold Absolute Pressure/Barometric Pressure Circuit High Input

P0109 Manifold Absolute Pressure/Barometric Pressure Circuit Intermittent

P0110 Intake Air Temperature Circuit Malfunction

P0111 Intake Air Temperature Circuit Range/Performance Problem

P0112 Intake Air Temperature Circuit Low Input

P0113 Intake Air Temperature Circuit High Input

P0114 Intake Air Temperature Circuit Intermittent

P0115 Engine Coolant Temperature Circuit Malfunction

P0116 Engine Coolant Temperature Circuit Range/Performance Problem

P0117 Engine Coolant Temperature Circuit Low Input

P0118 Engine Coolant Temperature Circuit High Input

P0119 Engine Coolant Temperature Circuit Intermittent

P0120 Throttle/Pedal Position Sensor/Switch "A" Circuit Malfunction

P0121 Throttle/Pedal Position Sensor/Switch "A" Circuit Range/Performance Problem

P0122 Throttle/Pedal Position Sensor/Switch "A" Circuit Low Input

P0123 Throttle/Pedal Position Sensor/Switch "A" Circuit High Input

P0124 Throttle/Pedal Position Sensor/Switch "A" Circuit Intermittent

P0125 Insufficient Coolant Temperature For Closed Loop Fuel Control

P0126 Insufficient Coolant Temperature For Stable Operation

P0130 O_2 Circuit Malfunction (Bank #1 Sensor #1)

P0131 O_2 Sensor Circuit Low Voltage (Bank #1 Sensor #1)

P0132 O_2 Sensor Circuit High Voltage (Bank #1 Sensor #1)

P0133 O_2 Sensor Circuit Slow Response (Bank #1 Sensor #1)

P0134 O_2 Sensor Circuit No Activity Detected (Bank #1 Sensor #1)

P0135 O_2 Sensor Heater Circuit Malfunction (Bank #1 Sensor #1)

P0136 O_2 Sensor Circuit Malfunction (Bank #1 Sensor #2)

P0137 O_2 Sensor Circuit Low Voltage (Bank #1 Sensor #2)

P0138 O_2 Sensor Circuit High Voltage (Bank #1 Sensor #2)

P0139 O_2 Sensor Circuit Slow Response (Bank #1 Sensor #2)

P0140 O_2 Sensor Circuit No Activity Detected (Bank #1 Sensor #2)

P0141 O_2 Sensor Heater Circuit Malfunction (Bank #1 Sensor #2)

P0142 O_2 Sensor Circuit Malfunction (Bank #1 Sensor #3)

P0143 O_2 Sensor Circuit Low Voltage (Bank #1 Sensor #3)

P0144 O_2 Sensor Circuit High Voltage (Bank #1 Sensor #3)

P0145 O_2 Sensor Circuit Slow Response (Bank #1 Sensor #3)

P0146 O_2 Sensor Circuit No Activity Detected (Bank #1 Sensor #3)

P0147 O_2 Sensor Heater Circuit Malfunction (Bank #1 Sensor #3)

P0150 O_2 Sensor Circuit Malfunction (Bank #2 Sensor #1)

P0151 O_2 Sensor Circuit Low Voltage (Bank #2 Sensor #1)

P0152 O_2 Sensor Circuit High Voltage (Bank #2 Sensor #1)

P0153 O_2 Sensor Circuit Slow Response (Bank #2 Sensor #1)

P0154 O_2 Sensor Circuit No Activity Detected (Bank #2 Sensor #1)

P0155 O_2 Sensor Heater Circuit Malfunction (Bank #2 Sensor #1)

P0156 O_2 Sensor Circuit Malfunction (Bank #2 Sensor #2)

P0157 O_2 Sensor Circuit Low Voltage (Bank #2 Sensor #2)

P0158 O_2 Sensor Circuit High Voltage (Bank #2 Sensor #2)

P0159 O_2 Sensor Circuit Slow Response (Bank #2 Sensor #2)

P0160 O_2 Sensor Circuit No Activity Detected (Bank #2 Sensor #2)

P0161 O_2 Sensor Heater Circuit Malfunction (Bank #2 Sensor #2)

P0162 O_2 Sensor Circuit Malfunction (Bank #2 Sensor #3)

P0163 O_2 Sensor Circuit Low Voltage (Bank #2 Sensor #3)

P0164 O_2 Sensor Circuit High Voltage (Bank #2 Sensor #3)

P0165 O_2 Sensor Circuit Slow Response (Bank #2 Sensor #3)

P0166 O_2 Sensor Circuit No Activity Detected (Bank #2 Sensor #3)

P0167 O_2 Sensor Heater Circuit Malfunction (Bank #2 Sensor #3)

P0170 Fuel Trim Malfunction (Bank #1)

P0171 System Too Lean (Bank #1)

P0172 System Too Rich (Bank #1)

P0173 Fuel Trim Malfunction (Bank #2)

P0174 System Too Lean (Bank #2)

P0175 System Too Rich (Bank #2)

P0176 Fuel Composition Sensor Circuit Malfunction

P0177 Fuel Composition Sensor Circuit Range/Performance

P0178 Fuel Composition Sensor Circuit Low Input

P0179 Fuel Composition Sensor Circuit High Input

P0180 Fuel Temperature Sensor "A" Circuit Malfunction

P0181 Fuel Temperature Sensor "A" Circuit Range/Performance

P0182 Fuel Temperature Sensor "A" Circuit Low Input

P0183 Fuel Temperature Sensor "A" Circuit High Input

P0184 Fuel Temperature Sensor "A" Circuit Intermittent

P0185 Fuel Temperature Sensor "B" Circuit Malfunction

P0186 Fuel Temperature Sensor "B" Circuit Range/Performance

P0187 Fuel Temperature Sensor "B" Circuit Low Input

P0188 Fuel Temperature Sensor "B" Circuit High Input

P0189 Fuel Temperature Sensor "B" Circuit Intermittent

P0190 Fuel Rail Pressure Sensor Circuit Malfunction

P0191 Fuel Rail Pressure Sensor Circuit Range/Performance

P0192 Fuel Rail Pressure Sensor Circuit Low Input

P0193 Fuel Rail Pressure Sensor Circuit High Input

P0194 Fuel Rail Pressure Sensor Circuit Intermittent

P0195 Engine Oil Temperature Sensor Malfunction

P0196 Engine Oil Temperature Sensor Range/Performance

P0197 Engine Oil Temperature Sensor Low

P0198 Engine Oil Temperature Sensor High

P0199 Engine Oil Temperature Sensor Intermittent

P0200 Injector Circuit Malfunction

P0201 Injector Circuit Malfunction—Cylinder #1

P0202 Injector Circuit Malfunction—Cylinder #2

P0203 Injector Circuit Malfunction—Cylinder #3

P0204 Injector Circuit Malfunction—Cylinder #4

P0205 Injector Circuit Malfunction—Cylinder #5

P0206 Injector Circuit Malfunction—Cylinder #6

P0207 Injector Circuit Malfunction—Cylinder #7

P0208 Injector Circuit Malfunction—Cylinder #8

P0209 Injector Circuit Malfunction—Cylinder #9

P0210 Injector Circuit Malfunction—Cylinder #10

P0211 Injector Circuit Malfunction—Cylinder #11

P0212 Injector Circuit Malfunction—Cylinder #12

P0213 Cold Start Injector #1 Malfunction

P0214 Cold Start Injector #2 Malfunction

P0215 Engine Shutoff Solenoid Malfunction

P0216 Injection Timing Control Circuit Malfunction

P0217 Engine Over Temperature Condition

P0218 Transmission Over Temperature Condition

P0219 Engine Over Speed Condition

P0220 Throttle/Pedal Position Sensor/Switch "B" Circuit Malfunction

P0221 Throttle/Pedal Position Sensor/Switch "B" Circuit Range/Performance Problem

P0222 Throttle/Pedal Position Sensor/Switch "B" Circuit Low Input

P0223 Throttle/Pedal Position Sensor/Switch "B" Circuit High Input

P0224 Throttle/Pedal Position Sensor/Switch "B" Circuit Intermittent

P0225 Throttle/Pedal Position Sensor/Switch "C" Circuit Malfunction

P0226 Throttle/Pedal Position Sensor/Switch "C" Circuit Range/Performance Problem

P0227 Throttle/Pedal Position Sensor/Switch "C" Circuit Low Input

P0228 Throttle/Pedal Position Sensor/Switch "C" Circuit High Input

P0229 Throttle/Pedal Position Sensor/Switch "C" Circuit Intermittent

P0230 Fuel Pump Primary Circuit Malfunction

P0231 Fuel Pump Secondary Circuit Low

P0232 Fuel Pump Secondary Circuit High

P0233 Fuel Pump Secondary Circuit Intermittent

P0234 Engine Over Boost Condition

P0261 Cylinder #1 Injector Circuit Low

P0262 Cylinder #1 Injector Circuit High

P0263 Cylinder #1 Contribution/Balance Fault

P0264 Cylinder #2 Injector Circuit Low

P0265 Cylinder #2 Injector Circuit High

P0266 Cylinder #2 Contribution/Balance Fault

P0267 Cylinder #3 Injector Circuit Low

P0268 Cylinder #3 Injector Circuit High

P0269 Cylinder #3 Contribution/Balance Fault

P0270 Cylinder #4 Injector Circuit Low

P0271 Cylinder #4 Injector Circuit High

P0272 Cylinder #4 Contribution/Balance Fault

P0273 Cylinder #5 Injector Circuit Low

P0274 Cylinder #5 Injector Circuit High

P0275 Cylinder #5 Contribution/Balance Fault

P0276 Cylinder #6 Injector Circuit Low

P0277 Cylinder #6 Injector Circuit High

P0278 Cylinder #6 Contribution/Balance Fault

P0279 Cylinder #7 Injector Circuit Low

P0280 Cylinder #7 Injector Circuit High

P0281 Cylinder #7 Contribution/Balance Fault

P0282 Cylinder #8 Injector Circuit Low

P0283 Cylinder #8 Injector Circuit High

P0284 Cylinder #8 Contribution/Balance Fault

P0285 Cylinder #9 Injector Circuit Low

P0286 Cylinder #9 Injector Circuit High

P0287 Cylinder #9 Contribution/Balance Fault

P0288 Cylinder #10 Injector Circuit Low

P0289 Cylinder #10 Injector Circuit High

P0290 Cylinder #10 Contribution/Balance Fault

P0291 Cylinder #11 Injector Circuit Low

P0292 Cylinder #11 Injector Circuit High

P0293 Cylinder #11 Contribution/Balance Fault

P0294 Cylinder #12 Injector Circuit Low

P0295 Cylinder #12 Injector Circuit High

P0296 Cylinder #12 Contribution/Balance Fault

P0300 Random/Multiple Cylinder Misfire Detected

P0301 Cylinder #1—Misfire Detected

P0302 Cylinder #2—Misfire Detected

P0303 Cylinder #3—Misfire Detected

P0304 Cylinder #4—Misfire Detected

P0305 Cylinder #5—Misfire Detected

P0306 Cylinder #6—Misfire Detected

P0307 Cylinder #7—Misfire Detected

P0308 Cylinder #8—Misfire Detected

P0309 Cylinder #9—Misfire Detected

P0310 Cylinder #10—Misfire Detected

P0311 Cylinder #11—Misfire Detected

P0312 Cylinder #12—Misfire Detected

P0320 Ignition/Distributor Engine Speed Input Circuit Malfunction

P0321 Ignition/Distributor Engine Speed Input Circuit Range/Performance

P0322 Ignition/Distributor Engine Speed Input Circuit No Signal

P0323 Ignition/Distributor Engine Speed Input Circuit Intermittent

P0325 Knock Sensor #1—Circuit Malfunction (Bank #1 or Single Sensor)

P0326 Knock Sensor #1—Circuit Range/Performance (Bank #1 or Single Sensor)

P0327 Knock Sensor #1—Circuit Low Input (Bank #1 or Single Sensor)

P0328 Knock Sensor #1—Circuit High Input (Bank #1 or Single Sensor)

P0329 Knock Sensor #1—Circuit Input Intermittent (Bank #1 or Single Sensor)

P0330 Knock Sensor #2—Circuit Malfunction (Bank #2)

P0331 Knock Sensor #2—Circuit Range/Performance (Bank #2)

P0332 Knock Sensor #2—Circuit Low Input (Bank #2)

P0333 Knock Sensor #2—Circuit High Input (Bank #2)

P0334 Knock Sensor #2—Circuit Input Intermittent (Bank #2)

P0335 Crankshaft Position Sensor "A" Circuit Malfunction

P0336 Crankshaft Position Sensor "A" Circuit Range/Performance

P0337 Crankshaft Position Sensor "A" Circuit Low Input

P0338 Crankshaft Position Sensor "A" Circuit High Input

P0339 Crankshaft Position Sensor "A" Circuit Intermittent

P0340 Camshaft Position Sensor Circuit Malfunction

P0341 Camshaft Position Sensor Circuit Range/Performance

P0342 Camshaft Position Sensor Circuit Low Input

P0343 Camshaft Position Sensor Circuit High Input

P0344 Camshaft Position Sensor Circuit Intermittent

P0350 Ignition Coil Primary/Secondary Circuit Malfunction

P0351 Ignition Coil "A" Primary/Secondary Circuit Malfunction

P0352 Ignition Coil "B" Primary/Secondary Circuit Malfunction

P0353 Ignition Coil "C" Primary/Secondary Circuit Malfunction

P0354 Ignition Coil "D" Primary/Secondary Circuit Malfunction

P0355 Ignition Coil "E" Primary/Secondary Circuit Malfunction

P0356 Ignition Coil "F" Primary/Secondary Circuit Malfunction

P0357 Ignition Coil "G" Primary/Secondary Circuit Malfunction

P0358 Ignition Coil "H" Primary/Secondary Circuit Malfunction

P0359 Ignition Coil "I" Primary/Secondary Circuit Malfunction

P0360 Ignition Coil "J" Primary/Secondary Circuit Malfunction

P0361 Ignition Coil "K" Primary/Secondary Circuit Malfunction

P0362 Ignition Coil "L" Primary/Secondary Circuit Malfunction

P0370 Timing Reference High Resolution Signal "A" Malfunction

P0371 Timing Reference High Resolution Signal "A" Too Many Pulses

P0372 Timing Reference High Resolution Signal "A" Too Few Pulses

P0373 Timing Reference High Resolution Signal "A" Intermittent/Erratic Pulses

P0374 Timing Reference High Resolution Signal "A" No Pulses

P0375 Timing Reference High Resolution Signal "B" Malfunction

P0376 Timing Reference High Resolution Signal "B" Too Many Pulses

P0377 Timing Reference High Resolution Signal "B" Too Few Pulses

P0378 Timing Reference High Resolution Signal "B" Intermittent/Erratic Pulses

P0379 Timing Reference High Resolution Signal "B" No Pulses

P0380 Glow Plug/Heater Circuit "A" Malfunction

P0381 Glow Plug/Heater Indicator Circuit Malfunction

P0382 Glow Plug/Heater Circuit "B" Malfunction

P0385 Crankshaft Position Sensor "B" Circuit Malfunction

P0386 Crankshaft Position Sensor "B" Circuit Range/Performance

P0387 Crankshaft Position Sensor "B" Circuit Low Input

P0388 Crankshaft Position Sensor "B" Circuit High Input

P0389 Crankshaft Position Sensor "B" Circuit Intermittent

P0400 Exhaust Gas Recirculation Flow Malfunction

P0401 Exhaust Gas Recirculation Flow Insufficient Detected

P0402 Exhaust Gas Recirculation Flow Excessive Detected

P0403 Exhaust Gas Recirculation Circuit Malfunction

P0404 Exhaust Gas Recirculation Circuit Range/Performance

P0405 Exhaust Gas Recirculation Sensor "A" Circuit Low

P0406 Exhaust Gas Recirculation Sensor "A" Circuit High

P0407 Exhaust Gas Recirculation Sensor "B" Circuit Low

P0408 Exhaust Gas Recirculation Sensor "B" Circuit High

P0410 Secondary Air Injection System Malfunction

P0411 Secondary Air Injection System Incorrect Flow Detected

P0412 Secondary Air Injection System Switching Valve "A" Circuit Malfunction

P0413 Secondary Air Injection System Switching Valve "A" Circuit Open

P0414 Secondary Air Injection System Switching Valve "A" Circuit Shorted

P0415 Secondary Air Injection System Switching Valve "B" Circuit Malfunction

P0416 Secondary Air Injection System Switching Valve "B" Circuit Open

P0417 Secondary Air Injection System Switching Valve "B" Circuit Shorted

P0418 Secondary Air Injection System Relay "A" Circuit Malfunction

P0419 Secondary Air Injection System Relay "B" Circuit Malfunction

P0420 Catalyst System Efficiency Below Threshold (Bank #1)

P0421 Warm Up Catalyst Efficiency Below Threshold (Bank #1)

P0422 Main Catalyst Efficiency Below Threshold (Bank #1)

P0423 Heated Catalyst Efficiency Below Threshold (Bank #1)

P0424 Heated Catalyst Temperature Below Threshold (Bank #1)

P0430 Catalyst System Efficiency Below Threshold (Bank #2)

P0431 Warm Up Catalyst Efficiency Below Threshold (Bank #2)

P0432 Main Catalyst Efficiency Below Threshold (Bank #2)

P0433 Heated Catalyst Efficiency Below Threshold (Bank #2)

P0434 Heated Catalyst Temperature Below Threshold (Bank #2)

P0440 Evaporative Emission Control System Malfunction

P0441 Evaporative Emission Control System Incorrect Purge Flow

P0442 Evaporative Emission Control System Leak Detected (Small Leak)

P0443 Evaporative Emission Control System Purge Control Valve Circuit Malfunction

P0444 Evaporative Emission Control System Purge Control Valve Circuit Open

P0445 Evaporative Emission Control System Purge Control Valve Circuit Shorted

P0446 Evaporative Emission Control System Vent Control Circuit Malfunction

P0447 Evaporative Emission Control System Vent Control Circuit Open

P0448 Evaporative Emission Control System Vent Control Circuit Shorted

P0449 Evaporative Emission Control System Vent Valve/Solenoid Circuit Malfunction

P0450 Evaporative Emission Control System Pressure Sensor Malfunction

P0451 Evaporative Emission Control System Pressure Sensor Range/Performance

P0452 Evaporative Emission Control System Pressure Sensor Low Input

P0453 Evaporative Emission Control System Pressure Sensor High Input

P0454 Evaporative Emission Control System Pressure Sensor Intermittent

P0455 Evaporative Emission Control System Leak Detected (Gross Leak)

P0460 Fuel Level Sensor Circuit Malfunction

P0461 Fuel Level Sensor Circuit Range/Performance

P0462 Fuel Level Sensor Circuit Low Input

P0463 Fuel Level Sensor Circuit High Input

P0464 Fuel Level Sensor Circuit Intermittent

P0465 Purge Flow Sensor Circuit Malfunction

P0466 Purge Flow Sensor Circuit Range/Performance

P0467 Purge Flow Sensor Circuit Low Input

P0468 Purge Flow Sensor Circuit High Input

P0469 Purge Flow Sensor Circuit Intermittent

P0470 Exhaust Pressure Sensor Malfunction

P0471 Exhaust Pressure Sensor Range/Performance

P0472 Exhaust Pressure Sensor Low

P0473 Exhaust Pressure Sensor High

P0474 Exhaust Pressure Sensor Intermittent

P0475 Exhaust Pressure Control Valve Malfunction

P0476 Exhaust Pressure Control Valve Range/Performance

P0477 Exhaust Pressure Control Valve Low

P0478 Exhaust Pressure Control Valve High

P0479 Exhaust Pressure Control Valve Intermittent

P0480 Cooling Fan #1 Control Circuit Malfunction

P0481 Cooling Fan #2 Control Circuit Malfunction

P0482 Cooling Fan #3 Control Circuit Malfunction

P0483 Cooling Fan Rationality Check Malfunction

P0484 Cooling Fan Circuit Over Current

P0485 Cooling Fan Power/Ground Circuit Malfunction

P0500 Vehicle Speed Sensor Malfunction

P0501 Vehicle Speed Sensor Range/Performance

P0502 Vehicle Speed Sensor Circuit Low Input

P0503 Vehicle Speed Sensor Intermittent/Erratic/High

P0505 Idle Control System Malfunction

P0506 Idle Control System RPM Lower Than Expected

P0507 Idle Control System RPM Higher Than Expected

P0510 Closed Throttle Position Switch Malfunction

P0520 Engine Oil Pressure Sensor/Switch Circuit Malfunction

P0521 Engine Oil Pressure Sensor/Switch Range/Performance

P0522 Engine Oil Pressure Sensor/Switch Low Voltage

P0523 Engine Oil Pressure Sensor/Switch High Voltage

P0530 A/C Refrigerant Pressure Sensor Circuit Malfunction

P0531 A/C Refrigerant Pressure Sensor Circuit Range/Performance

P0532 A/C Refrigerant Pressure Sensor Circuit Low Input

P0533 A/C Refrigerant Pressure Sensor Circuit High Input

P0534 A/C Refrigerant Charge Loss

P0550 Power Steering Pressure Sensor Circuit Malfunction

P0551 Power Steering Pressure Sensor Circuit Range/Performance

P0552 Power Steering Pressure Sensor Circuit Low Input

P0553 Power Steering Pressure Sensor Circuit High Input

P0554 Power Steering Pressure Sensor Circuit Intermittent

P0560 System Voltage Malfunction

P0561 System Voltage Unstable

P0562 System Voltage Low

P0563 System Voltage High

P0565 Cruise Control On Signal Malfunction

P0566 Cruise Control Off Signal Malfunction

P0567 Cruise Control Resume Signal Malfunction

P0568 Cruise Control Set Signal Malfunction

P0569 Cruise Control Coast Signal Malfunction

P0570 Cruise Control Accel Signal Malfunction

P0571 Cruise Control/Brake Switch "A" Circuit Malfunction

P0572 Cruise Control/Brake Switch "A" Circuit Low

P0573 Cruise Control/Brake Switch "A" Circuit High

P0574 Through P0580 Reserved for Cruise Codes

P0600 Serial Communication Link Malfunction

P0601 Internal Control Module Memory Check Sum Error

P0602 Control Module Programming Error

P0603 Internal Control Module Keep Alive Memory (KAM) Error

P0604 Internal Control Module Random Access Memory (RAM) Error

P0605 Internal Control Module Read Only Memory (ROM) Error

P0606 PCM Processor Fault

P0608 Control Module VSS Output "A" Malfunction

P0609 Control Module VSS Output "B" Malfunction

P0620 Generator Control Circuit Malfunction

P0621 Generator Lamp "L" Control Circuit Malfunction

P0622 Generator Field "F" Control Circuit Malfunction

P0650 Malfunction Indicator Lamp (MIL) Control Circuit Malfunction

P0654 Engine RPM Output Circuit Malfunction

P0655 Engine Hot Lamp Output Control Circuit Malfunction

P0656 Fuel Level Output Circuit Malfunction

P0700 Transmission Control System Malfunction

P0701 Transmission Control System Range/Performance

P0702 Transmission Control System Electrical

P0703 Torque Converter/Brake Switch "B" Circuit Malfunction

P0704 Clutch Switch Input Circuit Malfunction

P0705 Transmission Range Sensor Circuit Malfunction (PRNDL Input)

P0706 Transmission Range Sensor Circuit Range/Performance

P0707 Transmission Range Sensor Circuit Low Input

P0708 Transmission Range Sensor Circuit High Input

P0709 Transmission Range Sensor Circuit Intermittent

P0710 Transmission Fluid Temperature Sensor Circuit Malfunction

P0711 Transmission Fluid Temperature Sensor Circuit Range/Performance

P0712 Transmission Fluid Temperature Sensor Circuit Low Input

P0713 Transmission Fluid Temperature Sensor Circuit High Input

P0714 Transmission Fluid Temperature Sensor Circuit Intermittent

P0715 Input/Turbine Speed Sensor Circuit Malfunction

P0716 Input/Turbine Speed Sensor Circuit Range/Performance

P0717 Input/Turbine Speed Sensor Circuit No Signal

P0718 Input/Turbine Speed Sensor Circuit Intermittent

P0719 Torque Converter/Brake Switch "B" Circuit Low

P0720 Output Speed Sensor Circuit Malfunction

P0721 Output Speed Sensor Circuit Range/Performance

P0722 Output Speed Sensor Circuit No Signal

P0723 Output Speed Sensor Circuit Intermittent

P0724 Torque Converter/Brake Switch "B" Circuit High

P0725 Engine Speed Input Circuit Malfunction

P0726 Engine Speed Input Circuit Range/Performance

P0727 Engine Speed Input Circuit No Signal

P0728 Engine Speed Input Circuit Intermittent

P0730 Incorrect Gear Ratio

P0731 Gear #1 Incorrect Ratio

P0732 Gear #2 Incorrect Ratio

P0733 Gear #3 Incorrect Ratio

P0734 Gear #4 Incorrect Ratio

P0735 Gear #5 Incorrect Ratio

P0736 Reverse Incorrect Ratio

P0740 Torque Converter Clutch Circuit Malfunction

P0741 Torque Converter Clutch Circuit Performance or Stuck Off

P0742 Torque Converter Clutch Circuit Stuck On

Ignition system service is covered in the model specific sections of this manual

2-26 MAINTENANCE LIGHT RESETTING AND DTC RETRIEVAL
GENERAL MOTORS CORP.

GEO/CHEVROLET

P0743 Torque Converter Clutch Circuit Electrical

P0744 Torque Converter Clutch Circuit Intermittent

P0745 Pressure Control Solenoid Malfunction

P0746 Pressure Control Solenoid Performance or Stuck Off

P0747 Pressure Control Solenoid Stuck On

P0748 Pressure Control Solenoid Electrical

P0749 Pressure Control Solenoid Intermittent

P0750 Shift Solenoid "A" Malfunction

P0751 Shift Solenoid "A" Performance or Stuck Off

P0752 Shift Solenoid "A" Stuck On

P0753 Shift Solenoid "A" Electrical

P0754 Shift Solenoid "A" Intermittent

P0755 Shift Solenoid "B" Malfunction

P0756 Shift Solenoid "B" Performance or Stuck Off

P0757 Shift Solenoid "B" Stuck On

P0758 Shift Solenoid "B" Electrical

P0759 Shift Solenoid "B" Intermittent

P0760 Shift Solenoid "C" Malfunction

P0761 Shift Solenoid "C" Performance Or Stuck Off

P0762 Shift Solenoid "C" Stuck On

P0763 Shift Solenoid "C" Electrical

P0764 Shift Solenoid "C" Intermittent

P0765 Shift Solenoid "D" Malfunction

P0766 Shift Solenoid "D" Performance Or Stuck Off

P0767 Shift Solenoid "D" Stuck On

P0768 Shift Solenoid "D" Electrical

P0769 Shift Solenoid "D" Intermittent

P0770 Shift Solenoid "E" Malfunction

P0771 Shift Solenoid "E" Performance Or Stuck Off

P0772 Shift Solenoid "E" Stuck On

P0773 Shift Solenoid "E" Electrical

P0774 Shift Solenoid "E" Intermittent

P0780 Shift Malfunction

P0781 1–2 Shift Malfunction

P0782 2–3 Shift Malfunction

P0783 3–4 Shift Malfunction

P0784 4–5 Shift Malfunction

P0785 Shift/Timing Solenoid Malfunction

P0786 Shift/Timing Solenoid Range/Performance

P0787 Shift/Timing Solenoid Low

P0788 Shift/Timing Solenoid High

P0789 Shift/Timing Solenoid Intermittent

P0790 Normal/Performance Switch Circuit Malfunction

P0801 Reverse Inhibit Control Circuit Malfunction

P0803 1–4 Upshift (Skip Shift) Solenoid Control Circuit Malfunction

P0804 1–4 Upshift (Skip Shift) Lamp Control Circuit Malfunction

P1106 MAP Sensor Voltage Intermittently High (Except 2.2L)

P1107 MAP Sensor Voltage Intermittently Low (Except 2.2L)

P1111 IAT Sensor Circuit Intermittent High Voltage (Except 2.2L)

P1112 IAT Sensor Circuit Intermittent Low Voltage (Except 2.2L)

P1114 ECT Sensor Circuit Intermittent Low Voltage (Except 2.2L)

P1115 ECT Sensor Circuit Intermittent High Voltage (Except 2.2L)

P1121 TP Sensor Voltage Intermittently High (Except 2.2L)

P1122 TP Sensor Voltage Intermittently Low (Except 2.2L)

P1133 HO2S Insufficient Switching Sensor (3.4L)

P1133 HO2S Insufficient Switching Bank #1, Sensor #1 (Except 3.4L & 4.3L)

P1134 HO2S #1 Transition Time Ratio (3.4L)

P1134 HO2S Transition Time Ratio Bank #1, Sensor #1 (4.3L, 5.0L, 5.7L & 7.4L)

P1153 HO2S Insufficient Switching Sensor Bank #2, Sensor #1 (4.3L, 5.0L, 5.7L & 7.4L)

P1154 HO2S Transition Time Ratio Bank #2, Sensor #1 (4.3L, 5.0L, 5.7L & 7.4L)

P1345 Crankshaft/Camshaft (CKP/CMP) Correlation (4.3L, 5.0L, 5.7L & 7.4L)

P1350 Ignition Control (IC) Circuit Malfunction (3.4L)

P1351 Ignition Control (IC) Circuit High Voltage (4.3L, 5.0L, 5.7L & 7.4L)

P1361 Ignition Control (IC) Circuit Not Toggling (3.4L)

P1361 Ignition Control (IC) Circuit Low Voltage (4.3L, 5.0L, 5.7L & 7.4L)

P1380 Electronic Brake Control Module (EBCM) DTC Detected Rough Road Data Unusable

P1381 Misfire Detected, No EBCM/PCM/VCM Serial Data (Except "P" Series)

P1406 EGR Pintle Position Circuit Fault (Except "P" Series)

P1415 AIR System Bank #1 (Except "P" Series)

P1416 AIR System Bank #2 (Except "P" Series)

P1441 EVAP Control System Flow During Non-Purge

P1442 EVAP Vacuum Switch Circuit (3.4L)

P1508 IAC System Low RPM (4.3L, 5.0L, 5.7L & 7.4L)

P1509 IAC System High RPM (4.3L, 5.7L & 7.4L)

P1520 PNP Circuit (2.2L)

P1635 5-Volt Reference "A" Circuit (3.4L)

P1639 5-Volt Reference "B" Circuit (3.4L)

P1641 MIL Control Circuit (3.4L)

P1651 Fan #1 Relay Control Circuit (3.4L)

P1652 Fan #2 Relay Control Circuit (3.4L)

P1654 A/C Relay Control (3.4L)

P1655 EVAP Purge Solenoid Control Circuit (3.4L)

P1672 Low Engine Oil Level Light Control Circuit (3.4L)

Geo/Chevrolet

READING CODES

Reading the control module memory is one of the first steps in OBD II system diagnostics. This step should be initially performed to determine the general nature of the fault. Subsequent readings will determine if the fault has been cleared.

Reading codes can be performed by any of the methods below:

• Read the control module memory with the Generic Scan Tool (GST)

• Read the control module memory with the vehicle manufacturer's specific tester

To read the fault codes, connect the scan tool or tester according to the manufacturer's instructions. Follow the manufacturer's specified procedure for reading the codes.

CLEARING CODES

Control module reset procedures are a very important part of OBD II System diagnostics. This step should be done at the end of any fault code repair and at the end of any driveability repair.

Clearing codes can be performed by any of the methods below:

• Clear the control module memory with the Generic Scan Tool (GST)

• Clear the control module memory with the vehicle manufacturer's specific tester

• Turn the ignition OFF and remove the negative battery cable for at least 1 minute.

Removing the negative battery cable may cause other systems in the vehicle to loose their memory. Prior to removing the cable, ensure you have the proper reset codes for radios and alarms.

➡The MIL will may also be de-activated for some codes if the vehicle completes three consecutive trips without a fault detected with vehicle conditions similar to those present during the fault.

OBD II TROUBLE CODES

P0100 Mass or Volume Air Flow Circuit Malfunction

P0101 Mass or Volume Air Flow Circuit Range/Performance Problem

P0102 Mass or Volume Air Flow Circuit Low Input

P0103 Mass or Volume Air Flow Circuit High Input

P0104 Mass or Volume Air Flow Circuit Intermittent

P0105 Manifold Absolute Pressure/Barometric Pressure Circuit Malfunction

P0106 Manifold Absolute Pressure/Barometric Pressure Circuit Range/Performance Problem

P0107 Manifold Absolute Pressure/Barometric Pressure Circuit Low Input

P0108 Manifold Absolute Pressure/Barometric Pressure Circuit High Input

P0109 Manifold Absolute Pressure/Barometric Pressure Circuit Intermittent

P0110 Intake Air Temperature Circuit Malfunction

P0111 Intake Air Temperature Circuit Range/Performance Problem

P0112 Intake Air Temperature Circuit Low Input

P0113 Intake Air Temperature Circuit High Input

P0114 Intake Air Temperature Circuit Intermittent

P0115 Engine Coolant Temperature Circuit Malfunction

P0116 Engine Coolant Temperature Circuit Range/Performance Problem

P0117 Engine Coolant Temperature Circuit Low Input

P0118 Engine Coolant Temperature Circuit High Input

P0119 Engine Coolant Temperature Circuit Intermittent

P0120 Throttle/Pedal Position Sensor/Switch "A" Circuit Malfunction

P0121 Throttle/Pedal Position Sensor/Switch "A" Circuit Range/Performance Problem

P0122 Throttle/Pedal Position Sensor/Switch "A" Circuit Low Input

P0123 Throttle/Pedal Position Sensor/Switch "A" Circuit High Input

P0124 Throttle/Pedal Position Sensor/Switch "A" Circuit Intermittent

P0125 Insufficient Coolant Temperature For Closed Loop Fuel Control

P0126 Insufficient Coolant Temperature For Stable Operation

P0130 O_2 Circuit Malfunction (Bank #1 Sensor #1)

P0131 O_2 Sensor Circuit Low Voltage (Bank #1 Sensor #1)

P0132 O_2 Sensor Circuit High Voltage (Bank #1 Sensor #1)

P0133 O_2 Sensor Circuit Slow Response (Bank #1 Sensor #1)

P0134 O_2 Sensor Circuit No Activity Detected (Bank #1 Sensor #1)

P0135 O_2 Sensor Heater Circuit Malfunction (Bank #1 Sensor #1)

P0136 O_2 Sensor Circuit Malfunction (Bank #1 Sensor #2)

P0137 O_2 Sensor Circuit Low Voltage (Bank #1 Sensor #2)

P0138 O_2 Sensor Circuit High Voltage (Bank #1 Sensor #2)

P0139 O_2 Sensor Circuit Slow Response (Bank #1 Sensor #2)

P0140 O_2 Sensor Circuit No Activity Detected (Bank #1 Sensor #2)

P0141 O_2 Sensor Heater Circuit Malfunction (Bank #1 Sensor #2)

P0142 O_2 Sensor Circuit Malfunction (Bank #1 Sensor #3)

P0143 O_2 Sensor Circuit Low Voltage (Bank #1 Sensor #3)

P0144 O_2 Sensor Circuit High Voltage (Bank #1 Sensor #3)

P0145 O_2 Sensor Circuit Slow Response (Bank #1 Sensor #3)

P0146 O_2 Sensor Circuit No Activity Detected (Bank #1 Sensor #3)

P0147 O_2 Sensor Heater Circuit Malfunction (Bank #1 Sensor #3)

P0150 O_2 Sensor Circuit Malfunction (Bank #2 Sensor #1)

P0151 O_2 Sensor Circuit Low Voltage (Bank #2 Sensor #1)

P0152 O_2 Sensor Circuit High Voltage (Bank #2 Sensor #1)

P0153 O_2 Sensor Circuit Slow Response (Bank #2 Sensor #1)

P0154 O_2 Sensor Circuit No Activity Detected (Bank #2 Sensor #1)

P0155 O_2 Sensor Heater Circuit Malfunction (Bank #2 Sensor #1)

P0156 O_2 Sensor Circuit Malfunction (Bank #2 Sensor #2)

P0157 O_2 Sensor Circuit Low Voltage (Bank #2 Sensor #2)

P0158 O_2 Sensor Circuit High Voltage (Bank #2 Sensor #2)

P0159 O_2 Sensor Circuit Slow Response (Bank #2 Sensor #2)

P0160 O_2 Sensor Circuit No Activity Detected (Bank #2 Sensor #2)

P0161 O_2 Sensor Heater Circuit Malfunction (Bank #2 Sensor #2)

P0162 O_2 Sensor Circuit Malfunction (Bank #2 Sensor #3)

P0163 O_2 Sensor Circuit Low Voltage (Bank #2 Sensor #3)

P0164 O_2 Sensor Circuit High Voltage (Bank #2 Sensor #3)

P0165 O_2 Sensor Circuit Slow Response (Bank #2 Sensor #3)

P0166 O_2 Sensor Circuit No Activity Detected (Bank #2 Sensor #3)

P0167 O_2 Sensor Heater Circuit Malfunction (Bank #2 Sensor #3)

P0170 Fuel Trim Malfunction (Bank #1)

P0171 System Too Lean (Bank #1)

P0172 System Too Rich (Bank #1)

P0173 Fuel Trim Malfunction (Bank #2)

P0174 System Too Lean (Bank #2)

P0175 System Too Rich (Bank #2)

P0176 Fuel Composition Sensor Circuit Malfunction

P0177 Fuel Composition Sensor Circuit Range/Performance

P0178 Fuel Composition Sensor Circuit Low Input

P0179 Fuel Composition Sensor Circuit High Input

P0180 Fuel Temperature Sensor "A" Circuit Malfunction

P0181 Fuel Temperature Sensor "A" Circuit Range/Performance

P0182 Fuel Temperature Sensor "A" Circuit Low Input

P0183 Fuel Temperature Sensor "A" Circuit High Input

P0184 Fuel Temperature Sensor "A" Circuit Intermittent

P0185 Fuel Temperature Sensor "B" Circuit Malfunction

P0186 Fuel Temperature Sensor "B" Circuit Range/Performance

P0187 Fuel Temperature Sensor "B" Circuit Low Input

P0188 Fuel Temperature Sensor "B" Circuit High Input

P0189 Fuel Temperature Sensor "B" Circuit Intermittent

P0190 Fuel Rail Pressure Sensor Circuit Malfunction

P0191 Fuel Rail Pressure Sensor Circuit Range/Performance

P0192 Fuel Rail Pressure Sensor Circuit Low Input

P0193 Fuel Rail Pressure Sensor Circuit High Input

P0194 Fuel Rail Pressure Sensor Circuit Intermittent

P0195 Engine Oil Temperature Sensor Malfunction

P0196 Engine Oil Temperature Sensor Range/Performance

P0197 Engine Oil Temperature Sensor Low

P0198 Engine Oil Temperature Sensor High

P0199 Engine Oil Temperature Sensor Intermittent

P0200 Injector Circuit Malfunction

P0201 Injector Circuit Malfunction—Cylinder #1

P0202 Injector Circuit Malfunction—Cylinder #2

P0203 Injector Circuit Malfunction—Cylinder #3

P0204 Injector Circuit Malfunction—Cylinder #4

P0205 Injector Circuit Malfunction—Cylinder #5

P0206 Injector Circuit Malfunction—Cylinder #6

P0207 Injector Circuit Malfunction—Cylinder #7

P0208 Injector Circuit Malfunction—Cylinder #8

P0209 Injector Circuit Malfunction—Cylinder #9

P0210 Injector Circuit Malfunction—Cylinder #10

P0211 Injector Circuit Malfunction—Cylinder #11

P0212 Injector Circuit Malfunction—Cylinder #12

P0213 Cold Start Injector #1 Malfunction

P0214 Cold Start Injector #2 Malfunction

P0215 Engine Shutoff Solenoid Malfunction

P0216 Injection Timing Control Circuit Malfunction

P0217 Engine Over Temperature Condition

P0218 Transmission Over Temperature Condition

P0219 Engine Over Speed Condition

P0220 Throttle/Pedal Position Sensor/Switch "B" Circuit Malfunction

P0221 Throttle/Pedal Position Sensor/Switch "B" Circuit Range/Performance Problem

P0222 Throttle/Pedal Position Sensor/Switch "B" Circuit Low Input

P0223 Throttle/Pedal Position Sensor/Switch "B" Circuit High Input

P0224 Throttle/Pedal Position Sensor/Switch "B" Circuit Intermittent

P0225 Throttle/Pedal Position Sensor/Switch "C" Circuit Malfunction

P0226 Throttle/Pedal Position Sensor/Switch "C" Circuit Range/Performance Problem

P0227 Throttle/Pedal Position Sensor/Switch "C" Circuit Low Input

P0228 Throttle/Pedal Position Sensor/Switch "C" Circuit High Input

P0229 Throttle/Pedal Position Sensor/Switch "C" Circuit Intermittent

P0230 Fuel Pump Primary Circuit Malfunction

P0231 Fuel Pump Secondary Circuit Low

P0232 Fuel Pump Secondary Circuit High

P0233 Fuel Pump Secondary Circuit Intermittent

P0234 Engine Over Boost Condition

P0261 Cylinder #1 Injector Circuit Low

P0262 Cylinder #1 Injector Circuit High

P0263 Cylinder #1 Contribution/Balance Fault

P0264 Cylinder #2 Injector Circuit Low

P0265 Cylinder #2 Injector Circuit High

P0266 Cylinder #2 Contribution/Balance Fault

P0267 Cylinder #3 Injector Circuit Low

P0268 Cylinder #3 Injector Circuit High

P0269 Cylinder #3 Contribution/Balance Fault

P0270 Cylinder #4 Injector Circuit Low

P0271 Cylinder #4 Injector Circuit High

P0272 Cylinder #4 Contribution/Balance Fault

P0273 Cylinder #5 Injector Circuit Low

P0274 Cylinder #5 Injector Circuit High

P0275 Cylinder #5 Contribution/Balance Fault

P0276 Cylinder #6 Injector Circuit Low

P0277 Cylinder #6 Injector Circuit High

P0278 Cylinder #6 Contribution/Balance Fault

P0279 Cylinder #7 Injector Circuit Low

P0280 Cylinder #7 Injector Circuit High

P0281 Cylinder #7 Contribution/Balance Fault

P0282 Cylinder #8 Injector Circuit Low

P0283 Cylinder #8 Injector Circuit High

P0284 Cylinder #8 Contribution/Balance Fault

P0285 Cylinder #9 Injector Circuit Low

P0286 Cylinder #9 Injector Circuit High

P0287 Cylinder #9 Contribution/Balance Fault

P0288 Cylinder #10 Injector Circuit Low

P0289 Cylinder #10 Injector Circuit High

P0290 Cylinder #10 Contribution/Balance Fault

P0291 Cylinder #11 Injector Circuit Low

P0292 Cylinder #11 Injector Circuit High

P0293 Cylinder #11 Contribution/Balance Fault

P0294 Cylinder #12 Injector Circuit Low

P0295 Cylinder #12 Injector Circuit High

P0296 Cylinder #12 Contribution/Balance Fault

P0300 Random/Multiple Cylinder Misfire Detected

P0301 Cylinder #1—Misfire Detected

P0302 Cylinder #2—Misfire Detected

P0303 Cylinder #3—Misfire Detected

P0304 Cylinder #4—Misfire Detected

P0305 Cylinder #5—Misfire Detected

P0306 Cylinder #6—Misfire Detected

P0307 Cylinder #7—Misfire Detected

P0308 Cylinder #8—Misfire Detected

P0309 Cylinder #9—Misfire Detected

P0310 Cylinder #10—Misfire Detected

P0311 Cylinder #11—Misfire Detected

P0312 Cylinder #12—Misfire Detected

P0320 Ignition/Distributor Engine Speed Input Circuit Malfunction

P0321 Ignition/Distributor Engine Speed Input Circuit Range/Performance

P0322 Ignition/Distributor Engine Speed Input Circuit No Signal

P0323 Ignition/Distributor Engine Speed Input Circuit Intermittent

P0325 Knock Sensor #1—Circuit Malfunction (Bank #1 or Single Sensor)

P0326 Knock Sensor #1—Circuit Range/Performance (Bank #1 or Single Sensor)

P0327 Knock Sensor #1—Circuit Low Input (Bank #1 or Single Sensor)

P0328 Knock Sensor #1—Circuit High Input (Bank #1 or Single Sensor)

P0329 Knock Sensor #1—Circuit Input Intermittent (Bank #1 or Single Sensor)

P0330 Knock Sensor #2—Circuit Malfunction (Bank #2)

P0331 Knock Sensor #2—Circuit Range/Performance (Bank #2)

P0332 Knock Sensor #2—Circuit Low Input (Bank #2)

P0333 Knock Sensor #2—Circuit High Input (Bank #2)

P0334 Knock Sensor #2—Circuit Input Intermittent (Bank #2)

P0335 Crankshaft Position Sensor "A" Circuit Malfunction

P0336 Crankshaft Position Sensor "A" Circuit Range/Performance

P0337 Crankshaft Position Sensor "A" Circuit Low Input

P0338 Crankshaft Position Sensor "A" Circuit High Input

P0339 Crankshaft Position Sensor "A" Circuit Intermittent

P0340 Camshaft Position Sensor Circuit Malfunction

P0341 Camshaft Position Sensor Circuit Range/Performance

P0342 Camshaft Position Sensor Circuit Low Input

P0343 Camshaft Position Sensor Circuit High Input

P0344 Camshaft Position Sensor Circuit Intermittent

P0350 Ignition Coil Primary/Secondary Circuit Malfunction

P0351 Ignition Coil "A" Primary/Secondary Circuit Malfunction

P0352 Ignition Coil "B" Primary/Secondary Circuit Malfunction

P0353 Ignition Coil "C" Primary/Secondary Circuit Malfunction

P0354 Ignition Coil "D" Primary/Secondary Circuit Malfunction

P0355 Ignition Coil "E" Primary/Secondary Circuit Malfunction

P0356 Ignition Coil "F" Primary/Secondary Circuit Malfunction

P0357 Ignition Coil "G" Primary/Secondary Circuit Malfunction

P0358 Ignition Coil "H" Primary/Secondary Circuit Malfunction

P0359 Ignition Coil "I" Primary/Secondary Circuit Malfunction

P0360 Ignition Coil "J" Primary/Secondary Circuit Malfunction

P0361 Ignition Coil "K" Primary/Secondary Circuit Malfunction

P0362 Ignition Coil "L" Primary/Secondary Circuit Malfunction

P0370 Timing Reference High Resolution Signal "A" Malfunction

P0371 Timing Reference High Resolution Signal "A" Too Many Pulses

P0372 Timing Reference High Resolution Signal "A" Too Few Pulses

P0373 Timing Reference High Resolution Signal "A" Intermittent/Erratic Pulses

P0374 Timing Reference High Resolution Signal "A" No Pulses

P0375 Timing Reference High Resolution Signal "B" Malfunction

P0376 Timing Reference High Resolution Signal "B" Too Many Pulses

P0377 Timing Reference High Resolution Signal "B" Too Few Pulses

P0378 Timing Reference High Resolution Signal "B" Intermittent/Erratic Pulses

P0379 Timing Reference High Resolution Signal "B" No Pulses

P0380 Glow Plug/Heater Circuit "A" Malfunction

P0381 Glow Plug/Heater Indicator Circuit Malfunction

P0382 Glow Plug/Heater Circuit "B" Malfunction

P0385 Crankshaft Position Sensor "B" Circuit Malfunction

P0386 Crankshaft Position Sensor "B" Circuit Range/Performance

P0387 Crankshaft Position Sensor "B" Circuit Low Input

P0388 Crankshaft Position Sensor "B" Circuit High Input

P0389 Crankshaft Position Sensor "B" Circuit Intermittent

P0400 Exhaust Gas Recirculation Flow Malfunction

P0401 Exhaust Gas Recirculation Flow Insufficient Detected

P0402 Exhaust Gas Recirculation Flow Excessive Detected

P0403 Exhaust Gas Recirculation Circuit Malfunction

P0404 Exhaust Gas Recirculation Circuit Range/Performance

P0405 Exhaust Gas Recirculation Sensor "A" Circuit Low

P0406 Exhaust Gas Recirculation Sensor "A" Circuit High

P0407 Exhaust Gas Recirculation Sensor "B" Circuit Low

P0408 Exhaust Gas Recirculation Sensor "B" Circuit High

P0410 Secondary Air Injection System Malfunction

P0411 Secondary Air Injection System Incorrect Flow Detected

P0412 Secondary Air Injection System Switching Valve "A" Circuit Malfunction

P0413 Secondary Air Injection System Switching Valve "A" Circuit Open

P0414 Secondary Air Injection System Switching Valve "A" Circuit Shorted

P0415 Secondary Air Injection System Switching Valve "B" Circuit Malfunction

P0416 Secondary Air Injection System Switching Valve "B" Circuit Open

P0417 Secondary Air Injection System Switching Valve "B" Circuit Shorted

P0418 Secondary Air Injection System Relay "A" Circuit Malfunction

P0419 Secondary Air Injection System Relay "B" Circuit Malfunction

P0420 Catalyst System Efficiency Below Threshold (Bank #1)

P0421 Warm Up Catalyst Efficiency Below Threshold (Bank #1)

P0422 Main Catalyst Efficiency Below Threshold (Bank #1)

P0423 Heated Catalyst Efficiency Below Threshold (Bank #1)

P0424 Heated Catalyst Temperature Below Threshold (Bank #1)

P0430 Catalyst System Efficiency Below Threshold (Bank #2)

P0431 Warm Up Catalyst Efficiency Below Threshold (Bank #2)

P0432 Main Catalyst Efficiency Below Threshold (Bank #2)

P0433 Heated Catalyst Efficiency Below Threshold (Bank #2)

P0434 Heated Catalyst Temperature Below Threshold (Bank #2)

P0440 Evaporative Emission Control System Malfunction

P0441 Evaporative Emission Control System Incorrect Purge Flow

P0442 Evaporative Emission Control System Leak Detected (Small Leak)

P0443 Evaporative Emission Control System Purge Control Valve Circuit Malfunction

P0444 Evaporative Emission Control System Purge Control Valve Circuit Open

P0445 Evaporative Emission Control System Purge Control Valve Circuit Shorted

P0446 Evaporative Emission Control System Vent Control Circuit Malfunction

P0447 Evaporative Emission Control System Vent Control Circuit Open

P0448 Evaporative Emission Control System Vent Control Circuit Shorted

P0449 Evaporative Emission Control System Vent Valve/Solenoid Circuit Malfunction

P0450 Evaporative Emission Control System Pressure Sensor Malfunction

P0451 Evaporative Emission Control System Pressure Sensor Range/Performance

P0452 Evaporative Emission Control System Pressure Sensor Low Input

P0453 Evaporative Emission Control System Pressure Sensor High Input

P0454 Evaporative Emission Control System Pressure Sensor Intermittent

P0455 Evaporative Emission Control System Leak Detected (Gross Leak)

P0460 Fuel Level Sensor Circuit Malfunction

P0461 Fuel Level Sensor Circuit Range/Performance

P0462 Fuel Level Sensor Circuit Low Input

Refer to the model specific sections for fuel system service procedures

P0463 Fuel Level Sensor Circuit High Input

P0464 Fuel Level Sensor Circuit Intermittent

P0465 Purge Flow Sensor Circuit Malfunction

P0466 Purge Flow Sensor Circuit Range/Performance

P0467 Purge Flow Sensor Circuit Low Input

P0468 Purge Flow Sensor Circuit High Input

P0469 Purge Flow Sensor Circuit Intermittent

P0470 Exhaust Pressure Sensor Malfunction

P0471 Exhaust Pressure Sensor Range/Performance

P0472 Exhaust Pressure Sensor Low

P0473 Exhaust Pressure Sensor High

P0474 Exhaust Pressure Sensor Intermittent

P0475 Exhaust Pressure Control Valve Malfunction

P0476 Exhaust Pressure Control Valve Range/Performance

P0477 Exhaust Pressure Control Valve Low

P0478 Exhaust Pressure Control Valve High

P0479 Exhaust Pressure Control Valve Intermittent

P0480 Cooling Fan #1 Control Circuit Malfunction

P0481 Cooling Fan #2 Control Circuit Malfunction

P0482 Cooling Fan #3 Control Circuit Malfunction

P0483 Cooling Fan Rationality Check Malfunction

P0484 Cooling Fan Circuit Over Current

P0485 Cooling Fan Power/Ground Circuit Malfunction

P0500 Vehicle Speed Sensor Malfunction

P0501 Vehicle Speed Sensor Range/Performance

P0502 Vehicle Speed Sensor Circuit Low Input

P0503 Vehicle Speed Sensor Intermittent/Erratic/High

P0505 Idle Control System Malfunction

P0506 Idle Control System RPM Lower Than Expected

P0507 Idle Control System RPM Higher Than Expected

P0510 Closed Throttle Position Switch Malfunction

P0520 Engine Oil Pressure Sensor/Switch Circuit Malfunction

P0521 Engine Oil Pressure Sensor/Switch Range/Performance

P0522 Engine Oil Pressure Sensor/Switch Low Voltage

P0523 Engine Oil Pressure Sensor/Switch High Voltage

P0530 A/C Refrigerant Pressure Sensor Circuit Malfunction

P0531 A/C Refrigerant Pressure Sensor Circuit Range/Performance

P0532 A/C Refrigerant Pressure Sensor Circuit Low Input

P0533 A/C Refrigerant Pressure Sensor Circuit High Input

P0534 A/C Refrigerant Charge Loss

P0550 Power Steering Pressure Sensor Circuit Malfunction

P0551 Power Steering Pressure Sensor Circuit Range/Performance

P0552 Power Steering Pressure Sensor Circuit Low Input

P0553 Power Steering Pressure Sensor Circuit High Input

P0554 Power Steering Pressure Sensor Circuit Intermittent

P0560 System Voltage Malfunction

P0561 System Voltage Unstable

P0562 System Voltage Low

P0563 System Voltage High

P0565 Cruise Control On Signal Malfunction

P0566 Cruise Control Off Signal Malfunction

P0567 Cruise Control Resume Signal Malfunction

P0568 Cruise Control Set Signal Malfunction

P0569 Cruise Control Coast Signal Malfunction

P0570 Cruise Control Accel Signal Malfunction

P0571 Cruise Control/Brake Switch "A" Circuit Malfunction

P0572 Cruise Control/Brake Switch "A" Circuit Low

P0573 Cruise Control/Brake Switch "A" Circuit High

P0574 Through P0580 Reserved for Cruise Codes

P0600 Serial Communication Link Malfunction

P0601 Internal Control Module Memory Check Sum Error

P0602 Control Module Programming Error

P0603 Internal Control Module Keep Alive Memory (KAM) Error

P0604 Internal Control Module Random Access Memory (RAM) Error

P0605 Internal Control Module Read Only Memory (ROM) Error

P0606 PCM Processor Fault

P0608 Control Module VSS Output "A" Malfunction

P0609 Control Module VSS Output "B" Malfunction

P0620 Generator Control Circuit Malfunction

P0621 Generator Lamp "L" Control Circuit Malfunction

P0622 Generator Field "F" Control Circuit Malfunction

P0650 Malfunction Indicator Lamp (MIL) Control Circuit Malfunction

P0654 Engine RPM Output Circuit Malfunction

P0655 Engine Hot Lamp Output Control Circuit Malfunction

P0656 Fuel Level Output Circuit Malfunction

P0700 Transmission Control System Malfunction

P0701 Transmission Control System Range/Performance

P0702 Transmission Control System Electrical

P0703 Torque Converter/Brake Switch "B" Circuit Malfunction

P0704 Clutch Switch Input Circuit Malfunction

P0705 Transmission Range Sensor Circuit Malfunction (PRNDL Input)

P0706 Transmission Range Sensor Circuit Range/Performance

P0707 Transmission Range Sensor Circuit Low Input

P0708 Transmission Range Sensor Circuit High Input

P0709 Transmission Range Sensor Circuit Intermittent

P0710 Transmission Fluid Temperature Sensor Circuit Malfunction

P0711 Transmission Fluid Temperature Sensor Circuit Range/Performance

P0712 Transmission Fluid Temperature Sensor Circuit Low Input

P0713 Transmission Fluid Temperature Sensor Circuit High Input

P0714 Transmission Fluid Temperature Sensor Circuit Intermittent

P0715 Input/Turbine Speed Sensor Circuit Malfunction

P0716 Input/Turbine Speed Sensor Circuit Range/Performance

P0717 Input/Turbine Speed Sensor Circuit No Signal

P0718 Input/Turbine Speed Sensor Circuit Intermittent

P0719 Torque Converter/Brake Switch "B" Circuit Low

P0720 Output Speed Sensor Circuit Malfunction

P0721 Output Speed Sensor Circuit Range/Performance

P0722 Output Speed Sensor Circuit No Signal

P0723 Output Speed Sensor Circuit Intermittent

P0724 Torque Converter/Brake Switch "B" Circuit High

P0725 Engine Speed Input Circuit Malfunction

P0726 Engine Speed Input Circuit Range/Performance

P0727 Engine Speed Input Circuit No Signal

P0728 Engine Speed Input Circuit Intermittent

P0730 Incorrect Gear Ratio

P0731 Gear #1 Incorrect Ratio

P0732 Gear #2 Incorrect Ratio

P0733 Gear #3 Incorrect Ratio

P0734 Gear #4 Incorrect Ratio

P0735 Gear #5 Incorrect Ratio

P0736 Reverse Incorrect Ratio

P0740 Torque Converter Clutch Circuit Malfunction

P0741 Torque Converter Clutch Circuit Performance or Stuck Off

P0742 Torque Converter Clutch Circuit Stuck On

P0743 Torque Converter Clutch Circuit Electrical

P0744 Torque Converter Clutch Circuit Intermittent

P0745 Pressure Control Solenoid Malfunction

P0746 Pressure Control Solenoid Performance or Stuck Off

P0747 Pressure Control Solenoid Stuck On

P0748 Pressure Control Solenoid Electrical

P0749 Pressure Control Solenoid Intermittent

P0750 Shift Solenoid "A" Malfunction

P0751 Shift Solenoid "A" Performance or Stuck Off

P0752 Shift Solenoid "A" Stuck On

P0753 Shift Solenoid "A" Electrical

P0754 Shift Solenoid "A" Intermittent

P0755 Shift Solenoid "B" Malfunction

P0756 Shift Solenoid "B" Performance or Stuck Off

P0757 Shift Solenoid "B" Stuck On

P0758 Shift Solenoid "B" Electrical

P0759 Shift Solenoid "B" Intermittent

P0760 Shift Solenoid "C" Malfunction

P0761 Shift Solenoid "C" Performance Or Stuck Off

P0762 Shift Solenoid "C" Stuck On

P0763 Shift Solenoid "C" Electrical

P0764 Shift Solenoid "C" Intermittent

P0765 Shift Solenoid "D" Malfunction

P0766 Shift Solenoid "D" Performance Or Stuck Off

P0767 Shift Solenoid "D" Stuck On

P0768 Shift Solenoid "D" Electrical

P0769 Shift Solenoid "D" Intermittent

P0770 Shift Solenoid "E" Malfunction

P0771 Shift Solenoid "E" Performance Or Stuck Off

P0772 Shift Solenoid "E" Stuck On

P0773 Shift Solenoid "E" Electrical

P0774 Shift Solenoid "E" Intermittent

P0780 Shift Malfunction

P0781 1–2 Shift Malfunction

P0782 2–3 Shift Malfunction

P0783 3–4 Shift Malfunction

P0784 4–5 Shift Malfunction

P0785 Shift/Timing Solenoid Malfunction

P0786 Shift/Timing Solenoid Range/Performance

P0787 Shift/Timing Solenoid Low

P0788 Shift/Timing Solenoid High

P0789 Shift/Timing Solenoid Intermittent

P0790 Normal/Performance Switch Circuit Malfunction

P0801 Reverse Inhibit Control Circuit Malfunction

P0803 1–4 Upshift (Skip Shift) Solenoid Control Circuit Malfunction

P0804 1–4 Upshift (Skip Shift) Lamp Control Circuit Malfunction

P1450 Barometric Pressure Sensor Circuit Fault

P1451 Barometric Pressure Sensor Performance

P1460 Cooling Fan Control System Fault

P1500 Starter Signal Circuit Fault

P1510 Back-up Power Supply Fault

P1530 Ignition Timing Adjustment Switch Circuit

P1600 PCM Battery Circuit Fault

Honda

➡ **The Honda Passport is covered in the Isuzu section since it shares a platform with the Isuzu Rodeo.**

READING CODES

With Scan Tool

Reading the control module memory is one of the first steps in OBD II system diagnostics. This step should be initially performed to determine the general nature of the fault. Subsequent readings will determine if the fault has been cleared.

Reading codes can be performed by any of the methods below:
- Read the control module memory with the Generic Scan Tool (GST)
- Read the control module memory with the vehicle manufacturer's specific tester

To read the fault codes, connect the scan tool or tester according to the manufacturer's instructions. Follow the manufacturer's specified procedure for reading the codes.

Without Scan Tool

Honda also provides a way of reading OBD II trouble code equivalents using a service connector and viewing the MIL. This method is similar to the flash codes from non-OBD II vehicles.

To read codes, plug the service connector into the service check connector and turn the ignition ON. The MIL will flash any stored trouble codes.

CLEARING CODES

Control module reset procedures are a very important part of OBD II System diagnostics. This step should be done at the end of any fault code repair and at the end of any driveability repair.

Clearing codes can be performed by any of the methods below:
- Clear the control module memory with the Generic Scan Tool (GST)
- Clear the control module memory with the vehicle manufacturer's specific tester
- Turn the ignition OFF and remove the negative battery cable for at least 1 minute.

Removing the negative battery cable may cause other systems in the vehicle to loose their memory. Prior to removing the cable, ensure you have the proper reset codes for radios and alarms.

➡ **The MIL will may also be de-activated for some codes if the vehicle completes three consecutive trips without a fault detected with vehicle conditions similar to those present during the fault.**

OBD II TROUBLE CODES

P0100 Mass or Volume Air Flow Circuit Malfunction

P0101 Mass or Volume Air Flow Circuit Range/Performance Problem

P0102 Mass or Volume Air Flow Circuit Low Input

Refer to the model specific sections for engine electrical system service procedures

P0103 Mass or Volume Air Flow Circuit High Input

P0104 Mass or Volume Air Flow Circuit Intermittent

P0105 Manifold Absolute Pressure/Barometric Pressure Circuit Malfunction

P0106 Manifold Absolute Pressure/Barometric Pressure Circuit Range/Performance Problem

P0107 Manifold Absolute Pressure/Barometric Pressure Circuit Low Input

P0108 Manifold Absolute Pressure/Barometric Pressure Circuit High Input

P0109 Manifold Absolute Pressure/Barometric Pressure Circuit Intermittent

P0110 Intake Air Temperature Circuit Malfunction

P0111 Intake Air Temperature Circuit Range/Performance Problem

P0112 Intake Air Temperature Circuit Low Input

P0113 Intake Air Temperature Circuit High Input

P0114 Intake Air Temperature Circuit Intermittent

P0115 Engine Coolant Temperature Circuit Malfunction

P0116 Engine Coolant Temperature Circuit Range/Performance Problem

P0117 Engine Coolant Temperature Circuit Low Input

P0118 Engine Coolant Temperature Circuit High Input

P0119 Engine Coolant Temperature Circuit Intermittent

P0120 Throttle/Pedal Position Sensor/ Switch "A" Circuit Malfunction

P0121 Throttle/Pedal Position Sensor/ Switch "A" Circuit Range/Performance Problem

P0122 Throttle/Pedal Position Sensor/ Switch "A" Circuit Low Input

P0123 Throttle/Pedal Position Sensor/ Switch "A" Circuit High Input

P0124 Throttle/Pedal Position Sensor/ Switch "A" Circuit Intermittent

P0125 Insufficient Coolant Temperature For Closed Loop Fuel Control

P0126 Insufficient Coolant Temperature For Stable Operation

P0130 O_2 Circuit Malfunction (Bank #1 Sensor #1)

P0131 O_2 Sensor Circuit Low Voltage (Bank #1 Sensor #1)

P0132 O_2 Sensor Circuit High Voltage (Bank #1 Sensor #1)

P0133 O_2 Sensor Circuit Slow Response (Bank #1 Sensor #1)

P0134 O_2 Sensor Circuit No Activity Detected (Bank #1 Sensor #1)

P0135 O_2 Sensor Heater Circuit Malfunction (Bank #1 Sensor #1)

P0136 O_2 Sensor Circuit Malfunction (Bank #1 Sensor #2)

P0137 O_2 Sensor Circuit Low Voltage (Bank #1 Sensor #2)

P0138 O_2 Sensor Circuit High Voltage (Bank #1 Sensor #2)

P0139 O_2 Sensor Circuit Slow Response (Bank #1 Sensor #2)

P0140 O_2 Sensor Circuit No Activity Detected (Bank #1 Sensor #2)

P0141 O_2 Sensor Heater Circuit Malfunction (Bank #1 Sensor #2)

P0142 O_2 Sensor Circuit Malfunction (Bank #1 Sensor #3)

P0143 O_2 Sensor Circuit Low Voltage (Bank #1 Sensor #3)

P0144 O_2 Sensor Circuit High Voltage (Bank #1 Sensor #3)

P0145 O_2 Sensor Circuit Slow Response (Bank #1 Sensor #3)

P0146 O_2 Sensor Circuit No Activity Detected (Bank #1 Sensor #3)

P0147 O_2 Sensor Heater Circuit Malfunction (Bank #1 Sensor #3)

P0150 O_2 Sensor Circuit Malfunction (Bank #2 Sensor #1)

P0151 O_2 Sensor Circuit Low Voltage (Bank #2 Sensor #1)

P0152 O_2 Sensor Circuit High Voltage (Bank #2 Sensor #1)

P0153 O_2 Sensor Circuit Slow Response (Bank #2 Sensor #1)

P0154 O_2 Sensor Circuit No Activity Detected (Bank #2 Sensor #1)

P0155 O_2 Sensor Heater Circuit Malfunction (Bank #2 Sensor #1)

P0156 O_2 Sensor Circuit Malfunction (Bank #2 Sensor #2)

P0157 O_2 Sensor Circuit Low Voltage (Bank #2 Sensor #2)

P0158 O_2 Sensor Circuit High Voltage (Bank #2 Sensor #2)

P0159 O_2 Sensor Circuit Slow Response (Bank #2 Sensor #2)

P0160 O_2 Sensor Circuit No Activity Detected (Bank #2 Sensor #2)

P0161 O_2 Sensor Heater Circuit Malfunction (Bank #2 Sensor #2)

P0162 O_2 Sensor Circuit Malfunction (Bank #2 Sensor #3)

P0163 O_2 Sensor Circuit Low Voltage (Bank #2 Sensor #3)

P0164 O_2 Sensor Circuit High Voltage (Bank #2 Sensor #3)

P0165 O_2 Sensor Circuit Slow Response (Bank #2 Sensor #3)

P0166 O_2 Sensor Circuit No Activity Detected (Bank #2 Sensor #3)

P0167 O_2 Sensor Heater Circuit Malfunction (Bank #2 Sensor #3)

P0170 Fuel Trim Malfunction (Bank #1)

P0171 System Too Lean (Bank #1)

P0172 System Too Rich (Bank #1)

P0173 Fuel Trim Malfunction (Bank #2)

P0174 System Too Lean (Bank #2)

P0175 System Too Rich (Bank #2)

P0176 Fuel Composition Sensor Circuit Malfunction

P0177 Fuel Composition Sensor Circuit Range/Performance

P0178 Fuel Composition Sensor Circuit Low Input

P0179 Fuel Composition Sensor Circuit High Input

P0180 Fuel Temperature Sensor "A" Circuit Malfunction

P0181 Fuel Temperature Sensor "A" Circuit Range/Performance

P0182 Fuel Temperature Sensor "A" Circuit Low Input

P0183 Fuel Temperature Sensor "A" Circuit High Input

P0184 Fuel Temperature Sensor "A" Circuit Intermittent

P0185 Fuel Temperature Sensor "B" Circuit Malfunction

P0186 Fuel Temperature Sensor "B" Circuit Range/Performance

P0187 Fuel Temperature Sensor "B" Circuit Low Input

P0188 Fuel Temperature Sensor "B" Circuit High Input

P0189 Fuel Temperature Sensor "B" Circuit Intermittent

P0190 Fuel Rail Pressure Sensor Circuit Malfunction

P0191 Fuel Rail Pressure Sensor Circuit Range/Performance

P0192 Fuel Rail Pressure Sensor Circuit Low Input

P0193 Fuel Rail Pressure Sensor Circuit High Input

P0194 Fuel Rail Pressure Sensor Circuit Intermittent

P0195 Engine Oil Temperature Sensor Malfunction

P0196 Engine Oil Temperature Sensor Range/Performance

P0197 Engine Oil Temperature Sensor Low

P0198 Engine Oil Temperature Sensor High

P0199 Engine Oil Temperature Sensor Intermittent

P0200 Injector Circuit Malfunction

P0201 Injector Circuit Malfunction— Cylinder #1

P0202 Injector Circuit Malfunction— Cylinder #2

P0203 Injector Circuit Malfunction—Cylinder #3

P0204 Injector Circuit Malfunction—Cylinder #4

P0205 Injector Circuit Malfunction—Cylinder #5

P0206 Injector Circuit Malfunction—Cylinder #6

P0207 Injector Circuit Malfunction—Cylinder #7

P0208 Injector Circuit Malfunction—Cylinder #8

P0209 Injector Circuit Malfunction—Cylinder #9

P0210 Injector Circuit Malfunction—Cylinder #10

P0211 Injector Circuit Malfunction—Cylinder #11

P0212 Injector Circuit Malfunction—Cylinder #12

P0213 Cold Start Injector #1 Malfunction

P0214 Cold Start Injector #2 Malfunction

P0215 Engine Shutoff Solenoid Malfunction

P0216 Injection Timing Control Circuit Malfunction

P0217 Engine Over Temperature Condition

P0218 Transmission Over Temperature Condition

P0219 Engine Over Speed Condition

P0220 Throttle/Pedal Position Sensor/Switch "B" Circuit Malfunction

P0221 Throttle/Pedal Position Sensor/Switch "B" Circuit Range/Performance Problem

P0222 Throttle/Pedal Position Sensor/Switch "B" Circuit Low Input

P0223 Throttle/Pedal Position Sensor/Switch "B" Circuit High Input

P0224 Throttle/Pedal Position Sensor/Switch "B" Circuit Intermittent

P0225 Throttle/Pedal Position Sensor/Switch "C" Circuit Malfunction

P0226 Throttle/Pedal Position Sensor/Switch "C" Circuit Range/Performance Problem

P0227 Throttle/Pedal Position Sensor/Switch "C" Circuit Low Input

P0228 Throttle/Pedal Position Sensor/Switch "C" Circuit High Input

P0229 Throttle/Pedal Position Sensor/Switch "C" Circuit Intermittent

P0230 Fuel Pump Primary Circuit Malfunction

P0231 Fuel Pump Secondary Circuit Low

P0232 Fuel Pump Secondary Circuit High

P0233 Fuel Pump Secondary Circuit Intermittent

P0234 Engine Over Boost Condition

P0261 Cylinder #1 Injector Circuit Low

P0262 Cylinder #1 Injector Circuit High

P0263 Cylinder #1 Contribution/Balance Fault

P0264 Cylinder #2 Injector Circuit Low

P0265 Cylinder #2 Injector Circuit High

P0266 Cylinder #2 Contribution/Balance Fault

P0267 Cylinder #3 Injector Circuit Low

P0268 Cylinder #3 Injector Circuit High

P0269 Cylinder #3 Contribution/Balance Fault

P0270 Cylinder #4 Injector Circuit Low

P0271 Cylinder #4 Injector Circuit High

P0272 Cylinder #4 Contribution/Balance Fault

P0273 Cylinder #5 Injector Circuit Low

P0274 Cylinder #5 Injector Circuit High

P0275 Cylinder #5 Contribution/Balance Fault

P0276 Cylinder #6 Injector Circuit Low

P0277 Cylinder #6 Injector Circuit High

P0278 Cylinder #6 Contribution/Balance Fault

P0279 Cylinder #7 Injector Circuit Low

P0280 Cylinder #7 Injector Circuit High

P0281 Cylinder #7 Contribution/Balance Fault

P0282 Cylinder #8 Injector Circuit Low

P0283 Cylinder #8 Injector Circuit High

P0284 Cylinder #8 Contribution/Balance Fault

P0285 Cylinder #9 Injector Circuit Low

P0286 Cylinder #9 Injector Circuit High

P0287 Cylinder #9 Contribution/Balance Fault

P0288 Cylinder #10 Injector Circuit Low

P0289 Cylinder #10 Injector Circuit High

P0290 Cylinder #10 Contribution/Balance Fault

P0291 Cylinder #11 Injector Circuit Low

P0292 Cylinder #11 Injector Circuit High

P0293 Cylinder #11 Contribution/Balance Fault

P0294 Cylinder #12 Injector Circuit Low

P0295 Cylinder #12 Injector Circuit High

P0296 Cylinder #12 Contribution/Balance Fault

P0300 Random/Multiple Cylinder Misfire Detected

P0301 Cylinder #1—Misfire Detected

P0302 Cylinder #2—Misfire Detected

P0303 Cylinder #3—Misfire Detected

P0304 Cylinder #4—Misfire Detected

P0305 Cylinder #5—Misfire Detected

P0306 Cylinder #6—Misfire Detected

P0307 Cylinder #7—Misfire Detected

P0308 Cylinder #8—Misfire Detected

P0309 Cylinder #9—Misfire Detected

P0310 Cylinder #10—Misfire Detected

P0311 Cylinder #11—Misfire Detected

P0312 Cylinder #12—Misfire Detected

P0320 Ignition/Distributor Engine Speed Input Circuit Malfunction

P0321 Ignition/Distributor Engine Speed Input Circuit Range/Performance

P0322 Ignition/Distributor Engine Speed Input Circuit No Signal

P0323 Ignition/Distributor Engine Speed Input Circuit Intermittent

P0325 Knock Sensor #1—Circuit Malfunction (Bank #1 or Single Sensor)

P0326 Knock Sensor #1—Circuit Range/Performance (Bank #1 or Single Sensor)

P0327 Knock Sensor #1—Circuit Low Input (Bank #1 or Single Sensor)

P0328 Knock Sensor #1—Circuit High Input (Bank #1 or Single Sensor)

P0329 Knock Sensor #1—Circuit Input Intermittent (Bank #1 or Single Sensor)

P0330 Knock Sensor #2—Circuit Malfunction (Bank #2)

P0331 Knock Sensor #2—Circuit Range/Performance (Bank #2)

P0332 Knock Sensor #2—Circuit Low Input (Bank #2)

P0333 Knock Sensor #2—Circuit High Input (Bank #2)

P0334 Knock Sensor #2—Circuit Input Intermittent (Bank #2)

P0335 Crankshaft Position Sensor "A" Circuit Malfunction

P0336 Crankshaft Position Sensor "A" Circuit Range/Performance

P0337 Crankshaft Position Sensor "A" Circuit Low Input

P0338 Crankshaft Position Sensor "A" Circuit High Input

P0339 Crankshaft Position Sensor "A" Circuit Intermittent

P0340 Camshaft Position Sensor Circuit Malfunction

P0341 Camshaft Position Sensor Circuit Range/Performance

P0342 Camshaft Position Sensor Circuit Low Input

P0343 Camshaft Position Sensor Circuit High Input

P0344 Camshaft Position Sensor Circuit Intermittent

P0350 Ignition Coil Primary/Secondary Circuit Malfunction

P0351 Ignition Coil "A" Primary/Secondary Circuit Malfunction

P0352 Ignition Coil "B" Primary/Secondary Circuit Malfunction

P0353 Ignition Coil "C" Primary/Secondary Circuit Malfunction

P0354 Ignition Coil "D" Primary/Secondary Circuit Malfunction

P0355 Ignition Coil "E" Primary/Secondary Circuit Malfunction

P0356 Ignition Coil "F" Primary/Secondary Circuit Malfunction

P0357 Ignition Coil "G" Primary/Secondary Circuit Malfunction

P0358 Ignition Coil "H" Primary/Secondary Circuit Malfunction

P0359 Ignition Coil "I" Primary/Secondary Circuit Malfunction

P0360 Ignition Coil "J" Primary/Secondary Circuit Malfunction

P0361 Ignition Coil "K" Primary/Secondary Circuit Malfunction

P0362 Ignition Coil "L" Primary/Secondary Circuit Malfunction

P0370 Timing Reference High Resolution Signal "A" Malfunction

P0371 Timing Reference High Resolution Signal "A" Too Many Pulses

P0372 Timing Reference High Resolution Signal "A" Too Few Pulses

P0373 Timing Reference High Resolution Signal "A" Intermittent/Erratic Pulses

P0374 Timing Reference High Resolution Signal "A" No Pulses

P0375 Timing Reference High Resolution Signal "B" Malfunction

P0376 Timing Reference High Resolution Signal "B" Too Many Pulses

P0377 Timing Reference High Resolution Signal "B" Too Few Pulses

P0378 Timing Reference High Resolution Signal "B" Intermittent/Erratic Pulses

P0379 Timing Reference High Resolution Signal "B" No Pulses

P0380 Glow Plug/Heater Circuit "A" Malfunction

P0381 Glow Plug/Heater Indicator Circuit Malfunction

P0382 Glow Plug/Heater Circuit "B" Malfunction

P0385 Crankshaft Position Sensor "B" Circuit Malfunction

P0386 Crankshaft Position Sensor "B" Circuit Range/Performance

P0387 Crankshaft Position Sensor "B" Circuit Low Input

P0388 Crankshaft Position Sensor "B" Circuit High Input

P0389 Crankshaft Position Sensor "B" Circuit Intermittent

P0400 Exhaust Gas Recirculation Flow Malfunction

P0401 Exhaust Gas Recirculation Flow Insufficient Detected

P0402 Exhaust Gas Recirculation Flow Excessive Detected

P0403 Exhaust Gas Recirculation Circuit Malfunction

P0404 Exhaust Gas Recirculation Circuit Range/Performance

P0405 Exhaust Gas Recirculation Sensor "A" Circuit Low

P0406 Exhaust Gas Recirculation Sensor "A" Circuit High

P0407 Exhaust Gas Recirculation Sensor "B" Circuit Low

P0408 Exhaust Gas Recirculation Sensor "B" Circuit High

P0410 Secondary Air Injection System Malfunction

P0411 Secondary Air Injection System Incorrect Flow Detected

P0412 Secondary Air Injection System Switching Valve "A" Circuit Malfunction

P0413 Secondary Air Injection System Switching Valve "A" Circuit Open

P0414 Secondary Air Injection System Switching Valve "A" Circuit Shorted

P0415 Secondary Air Injection System Switching Valve "B" Circuit Malfunction

P0416 Secondary Air Injection System Switching Valve "B" Circuit Open

P0417 Secondary Air Injection System Switching Valve "B" Circuit Shorted

P0418 Secondary Air Injection System Relay "A" Circuit Malfunction

P0419 Secondary Air Injection System Relay "B" Circuit Malfunction

P0420 Catalyst System Efficiency Below Threshold (Bank #1)

P0421 Warm Up Catalyst Efficiency Below Threshold (Bank #1)

P0422 Main Catalyst Efficiency Below Threshold (Bank #1)

P0423 Heated Catalyst Efficiency Below Threshold (Bank #1)

P0424 Heated Catalyst Temperature Below Threshold (Bank #1)

P0430 Catalyst System Efficiency Below Threshold (Bank #2)

P0431 Warm Up Catalyst Efficiency Below Threshold (Bank #2)

P0432 Main Catalyst Efficiency Below Threshold (Bank #2)

P0433 Heated Catalyst Efficiency Below Threshold (Bank #2)

P0434 Heated Catalyst Temperature Below Threshold (Bank #2)

P0440 Evaporative Emission Control System Malfunction

P0441 Evaporative Emission Control System Incorrect Purge Flow

P0442 Evaporative Emission Control System Leak Detected (Small Leak)

P0443 Evaporative Emission Control System Purge Control Valve Circuit Malfunction

P0444 Evaporative Emission Control System Purge Control Valve Circuit Open

P0445 Evaporative Emission Control System Purge Control Valve Circuit Shorted

P0446 Evaporative Emission Control System Vent Control Circuit Malfunction

P0447 Evaporative Emission Control System Vent Control Circuit Open

P0448 Evaporative Emission Control System Vent Control Circuit Shorted

P0449 Evaporative Emission Control System Vent Valve/Solenoid Circuit Malfunction

P0450 Evaporative Emission Control System Pressure Sensor Malfunction

P0451 Evaporative Emission Control System Pressure Sensor Range/Performance

P0452 Evaporative Emission Control System Pressure Sensor Low Input

P0453 Evaporative Emission Control System Pressure Sensor High Input

P0454 Evaporative Emission Control System Pressure Sensor Intermittent

P0455 Evaporative Emission Control System Leak Detected (Gross Leak)

P0460 Fuel Level Sensor Circuit Malfunction

P0461 Fuel Level Sensor Circuit Range/Performance

P0462 Fuel Level Sensor Circuit Low Input

P0463 Fuel Level Sensor Circuit High Input

P0464 Fuel Level Sensor Circuit Intermittent

P0465 Purge Flow Sensor Circuit Malfunction

P0466 Purge Flow Sensor Circuit Range/Performance

P0467 Purge Flow Sensor Circuit Low Input

P0468 Purge Flow Sensor Circuit High Input

P0469 Purge Flow Sensor Circuit Intermittent

P0470 Exhaust Pressure Sensor Malfunction

P0471 Exhaust Pressure Sensor Range/Performance

P0472 Exhaust Pressure Sensor Low

P0473 Exhaust Pressure Sensor High

P0474 Exhaust Pressure Sensor Intermittent

P0475 Exhaust Pressure Control Valve Malfunction

P0476 Exhaust Pressure Control Valve Range/Performance

P0477 Exhaust Pressure Control Valve Low

P0478 Exhaust Pressure Control Valve High

P0479 Exhaust Pressure Control Valve Intermittent

P0480 Cooling Fan #1 Control Circuit Malfunction

P0481 Cooling Fan #2 Control Circuit Malfunction

P0482 Cooling Fan #3 Control Circuit Malfunction

P0483 Cooling Fan Rationality Check Malfunction

P0484 Cooling Fan Circuit Over Current

P0485 Cooling Fan Power/Ground Circuit Malfunction

P0500 Vehicle Speed Sensor Malfunction

P0501 Vehicle Speed Sensor Range/Performance

P0502 Vehicle Speed Sensor Circuit Low Input

P0503 Vehicle Speed Sensor Intermittent/Erratic/High

P0505 Idle Control System Malfunction

P0506 Idle Control System RPM Lower Than Expected

P0507 Idle Control System RPM Higher Than Expected

P0510 Closed Throttle Position Switch Malfunction

P0520 Engine Oil Pressure Sensor/Switch Circuit Malfunction

P0521 Engine Oil Pressure Sensor/Switch Range/Performance

P0522 Engine Oil Pressure Sensor/Switch Low Voltage

P0523 Engine Oil Pressure Sensor/Switch High Voltage

P0530 A/C Refrigerant Pressure Sensor Circuit Malfunction

P0531 A/C Refrigerant Pressure Sensor Circuit Range/Performance

P0532 A/C Refrigerant Pressure Sensor Circuit Low Input

P0533 A/C Refrigerant Pressure Sensor Circuit High Input

P0534 A/C Refrigerant Charge Loss

P0550 Power Steering Pressure Sensor Circuit Malfunction

P0551 Power Steering Pressure Sensor Circuit Range/Performance

P0552 Power Steering Pressure Sensor Circuit Low Input

P0553 Power Steering Pressure Sensor Circuit High Input

P0554 Power Steering Pressure Sensor Circuit Intermittent

P0560 System Voltage Malfunction

P0561 System Voltage Unstable

P0562 System Voltage Low

P0563 System Voltage High

P0565 Cruise Control On Signal Malfunction

P0566 Cruise Control Off Signal Malfunction

P0567 Cruise Control Resume Signal Malfunction

P0568 Cruise Control Set Signal Malfunction

P0569 Cruise Control Coast Signal Malfunction

P0570 Cruise Control Accel Signal Malfunction

P0571 Cruise Control/Brake Switch "A" Circuit Malfunction

P0572 Cruise Control/Brake Switch "A" Circuit Low

P0573 Cruise Control/Brake Switch "A" Circuit High

P0574 Through P0580 Reserved for Cruise Codes

P0600 Serial Communication Link Malfunction

P0601 Internal Control Module Memory Check Sum Error

P0602 Control Module Programming Error

P0603 Internal Control Module Keep Alive Memory (KAM) Error

P0604 Internal Control Module Random Access Memory (RAM) Error

P0605 Internal Control Module Read Only Memory (ROM) Error

P0606 PCM Processor Fault

P0608 Control Module VSS Output "A" Malfunction

P0609 Control Module VSS Output "B" Malfunction

P0620 Generator Control Circuit Malfunction

P0621 Generator Lamp "L" Control Circuit Malfunction

P0622 Generator Field "F" Control Circuit Malfunction

P0650 Malfunction Indicator Lamp (MIL) Control Circuit Malfunction

P0654 Engine RPM Output Circuit Malfunction

P0655 Engine Hot Lamp Output Control Circuit Malfunction

P0656 Fuel Level Output Circuit Malfunction

P0700 Transmission Control System Malfunction

P0701 Transmission Control System Range/Performance

P0702 Transmission Control System Electrical

P0703 Torque Converter/Brake Switch "B" Circuit Malfunction

P0704 Clutch Switch Input Circuit Malfunction

P0705 Transmission Range Sensor Circuit Malfunction (PRNDL Input)

P0706 Transmission Range Sensor Circuit Range/Performance

P0707 Transmission Range Sensor Circuit Low Input

P0708 Transmission Range Sensor Circuit High Input

P0709 Transmission Range Sensor Circuit Intermittent

P0710 Transmission Fluid Temperature Sensor Circuit Malfunction

P0711 Transmission Fluid Temperature Sensor Circuit Range/Performance

P0712 Transmission Fluid Temperature Sensor Circuit Low Input

P0713 Transmission Fluid Temperature Sensor Circuit High Input

P0714 Transmission Fluid Temperature Sensor Circuit Intermittent

P0715 Input/Turbine Speed Sensor Circuit Malfunction

P0716 Input/Turbine Speed Sensor Circuit Range/Performance

P0717 Input/Turbine Speed Sensor Circuit No Signal

P0718 Input/Turbine Speed Sensor Circuit Intermittent

P0719 Torque Converter/Brake Switch "B" Circuit Low

P0720 Output Speed Sensor Circuit Malfunction

P0721 Output Speed Sensor Circuit Range/Performance

P0722 Output Speed Sensor Circuit No Signal

P0723 Output Speed Sensor Circuit Intermittent

P0724 Torque Converter/Brake Switch "B" Circuit High

P0725 Engine Speed Input Circuit Malfunction

P0726 Engine Speed Input Circuit Range/Performance

P0727 Engine Speed Input Circuit No Signal

P0728 Engine Speed Input Circuit Intermittent

P0730 Incorrect Gear Ratio

Ignition system service is covered in the model specific sections of this manual

P0731 Gear #1 Incorrect Ratio
P0732 Gear #2 Incorrect Ratio
P0733 Gear #3 Incorrect Ratio
P0734 Gear #4 Incorrect Ratio
P0735 Gear #5 Incorrect Ratio
P0736 Reverse Incorrect Ratio
P0740 Torque Converter Clutch Circuit Malfunction
P0741 Torque Converter Clutch Circuit Performance or Stuck Off
P0742 Torque Converter Clutch Circuit Stuck On
P0743 Torque Converter Clutch Circuit Electrical
P0744 Torque Converter Clutch Circuit Intermittent
P0745 Pressure Control Solenoid Malfunction
P0746 Pressure Control Solenoid Performance or Stuck Off
P0747 Pressure Control Solenoid Stuck On
P0748 Pressure Control Solenoid Electrical
P0749 Pressure Control Solenoid Intermittent
P0750 Shift Solenoid "A" Malfunction
P0751 Shift Solenoid "A" Performance or Stuck Off
P0752 Shift Solenoid "A" Stuck On
P0753 Shift Solenoid "A" Electrical
P0754 Shift Solenoid "A" Intermittent
P0755 Shift Solenoid "B" Malfunction
P0756 Shift Solenoid "B" Performance or Stuck Off
P0757 Shift Solenoid "B" Stuck On
P0758 Shift Solenoid "B" Electrical
P0759 Shift Solenoid "B" Intermittent
P0760 Shift Solenoid "C" Malfunction
P0761 Shift Solenoid "C" Performance Or Stuck Off
P0762 Shift Solenoid "C" Stuck On
P0763 Shift Solenoid "C" Electrical
P0764 Shift Solenoid "C" Intermittent
P0765 Shift Solenoid "D" Malfunction
P0766 Shift Solenoid "D" Performance Or Stuck Off
P0767 Shift Solenoid "D" Stuck On
P0768 Shift Solenoid "D" Electrical
P0769 Shift Solenoid "D" Intermittent
P0770 Shift Solenoid "E" Malfunction
P0771 Shift Solenoid "E" Performance Or Stuck Off
P0772 Shift Solenoid "E" Stuck On
P0773 Shift Solenoid "E" Electrical
P0774 Shift Solenoid "E" Intermittent
P0780 Shift Malfunction
P0781 1–2 Shift Malfunction
P0782 2–3 Shift Malfunction
P0783 3–4 Shift Malfunction
P0784 4–5 Shift Malfunction

P0785 Shift/Timing Solenoid Malfunction
P0786 Shift/Timing Solenoid Range/Performance
P0787 Shift/Timing Solenoid Low
P0788 Shift/Timing Solenoid High
P0789 Shift/Timing Solenoid Intermittent
P0790 Normal/Performance Switch Circuit Malfunction
P0801 Reverse Inhibit Control Circuit Malfunction
P0803 1–4 Upshift (Skip Shift) Solenoid Control Circuit Malfunction
P0804 1–4 Upshift (Skip Shift) Lamp Control Circuit Malfunction
P1106 Barometric Pressure Circuit Range/Performance Problem
P1107 Barometric Pressure Circuit Low Input
P1108 Barometric Pressure Circuit High Input
P1121 Throttle Position Lower Than Expected
P1122 Throttle Position Higher Than Expected
P1128 Manifold Absolute Pressure Lower Than Expected
P1129 Manifold Absolute Pressure Higher Than Expected
P1259 VTEC System Malfunction
P1297 Electrical Load Detector Circuit Low Input
P1298 Electrical Load Detector Circuit High Input
P1297 Electrical Load Detector Circuit Low Input
P1298 Electrical Load Detector Circuit High Input
P1336 Crankshaft Speed Fluctuation Sensor Intermittent Interruption
P1337 Crankshaft Speed Fluctuation Sensor No Signal
P1359 Crankshaft Position Top Dead Center Sensor/Cylinder Position Connector Disconnection
P1361 Top Dead Center Sensor Intermittent Interruption
P1362 Top Dead Center Sensor No Signal
P1381 Cylinder Position Sensor Intermittent Interruption
P1382 Cylinder Position Sensor No Signal
P1456 Evaporative Emission Control System Leak Detected (Fuel Tank System)
P1457 Evaporative Emission Control System Leak Detected (EVAP Control Canister Leak)
P1491 EGR Valve Lift Insufficient Detected
P1498 EGR Valve Lift Sensor High Voltage

P1519 Idle Air Control Valve Circuit Failure
P1508 Idle Air Control Valve Circuit Failure
P1607 Powertrain Control Module Internal Circuit Failure A
P1705 Automatic Transaxle
P1706 Automatic Transaxle
P1753 Automatic Transaxle
P1768 Automatic Transaxle
P1790 Automatic Transaxle
P1791 Automatic Transaxle

OBD II TROUBLE CODE EQUIVALENTS

If a scan tool is not available for code retrieval, the following codes may be retrieved without one.

1 O_2 Sensor Circuit High Voltage (Bank #1 Sensor #1)
1 O_2 Sensor Circuit Low Voltage (Bank #1 Sensor #1)
3 Manifold Absolute Pressure/Barometric Pressure Circuit Low Input
3 Manifold Absolute Pressure/Barometric Pressure Circuit High Input
4 Crankshaft Position Sensor "A" Circuit Malfunction
4 Crankshaft Position Sensor "A" Circuit Range/Performance
5 Manifold Absolute Pressure Higher Than Expected
5 Manifold Absolute Pressure Lower Than Expected
6 Engine Coolant Temperature Circuit High Input
6 Engine Coolant Temperature Circuit Low Input
7 Throttle Position Higher Than Expected
7 Throttle Position Lower Than Expected
7 Throttle/Pedal Position Sensor/Switch "A" Circuit High Input
7 Throttle/Pedal Position Sensor/Switch "A" Circuit Low Input
8 Crankshaft Position Top Dead Center Sensor/Cylinder Position Connector Disconnection
8 Top Dead Center Sensor Intermittent Interruption
8 Top Dead Center Sensor No Signal
9 Cylinder Position Sensor Intermittent Interruption
9 Cylinder Position Sensor No Signal
10 Intake Air Temperature Circuit High Input
10 Intake Air Temperature Circuit Low Input
12 EGR Valve Lift Insufficient Detected
12 EGR Valve Lift Sensor High Voltage
13 Barometric Pressure Circuit High Input

13 Barometric Pressure Circuit Low Input

13 Barometric Pressure Circuit Range/Performance Problem

14 Idle Air Control Valve Circuit Failure

14 Idle Air Control Valve Circuit Failure

14 Idle Control System Malfunction

20 Electrical Load Detector Circuit High Input

20 Electrical Load Detector Circuit High Input

20 Electrical Load Detector Circuit Low Input

20 Electrical Load Detector Circuit Low Input

22 VTEC System Malfunction

23 Knock Sensor #1—Circuit Malfunction (Bank #1 or Single Sensor)

41 O_2 Sensor Heater Circuit Malfunction (Bank #1 Sensor #1)

45 System Too Lean (Bank #1)

45 System Too Rich (Bank #1)

54 Crankshaft Speed Fluctuation Sensor Intermittent Interruption

54 Crankshaft Speed Fluctuation Sensor No Signal

61 O_2 Sensor Circuit Slow Response (Bank #1 Sensor #1)

63 O_2 Sensor Circuit High Voltage (Bank #1 Sensor #2)

63 O_2 Sensor Circuit Low Voltage (Bank #1 Sensor #2)

63 O_2 Sensor Circuit Slow Response (Bank #1 Sensor #2)

65 O_2 Sensor Heater Circuit Malfunction (Bank #1 Sensor #2)

67 Catalyst System Efficiency Below Threshold (Bank #1)

70 Automatic Transaxle

70 Transmission Control System Malfunction

70 Input/Turbine Speed Sensor Circuit Malfunction

70 Output Speed Sensor Circuit Malfunction

70 Incorrect Gear Ratio

70 Torque Converter Clutch Circuit Malfunction

70 Shift Solenoid "A" Electrical

70 Shift Solenoid "B" Electrical

71 Cylinder #1—Misfire Detected

72 Cylinder #2—Misfire Detected

73 Cylinder #3—Misfire Detected

74 Cylinder #4—Misfire Detected

80 Exhaust Gas Recirculation Flow Insufficient Detected

86 Engine Coolant Temperature Circuit Range/Performance Problem

90 Evaporative Emission Control System Leak Detected (EVAP Control Canister Leak)

90 Evaporative Emission Control System Leak Detected (Fuel Tank System)

91 Evaporative Emission Control System Pressure Sensor Low Input

91 Evaporative Emission Control System Pressure Sensor High Input

Isuzu

➡ This section also provides coverage for the Honda Passport since it shares a platform with the Isuzu Rodeo.

READING CODES

Reading the control module memory is one of the first steps in OBD II system diagnostics. This step should be initially performed to determine the general nature of the fault. Subsequent readings will determine if the fault has been cleared.

Reading codes can be performed by any of the methods below:

• Read the control module memory with the Generic Scan Tool (GST)

• Read the control module memory with the vehicle manufacturer's specific tester

To read the fault codes, connect the scan tool or tester according to the manufacturer's instructions. Follow the manufacturer's specified procedure for reading the codes.

CLEARING CODES

Control module reset procedures are a very important part of OBD II System diagnostics. This step should be done at the end of any fault code repair and at the end of any driveability repair.

Clearing codes can be performed by any of the methods below:

• Clear the control module memory with the Generic Scan Tool (GST)

• Clear the control module memory with the vehicle manufacturer's specific tester

• Turn the ignition OFF and remove the negative battery cable for at least 1 minute.

Removing the negative battery cable may cause other systems in the vehicle to loose their memory. Prior to removing the cable, ensure you have the proper reset codes for radios and alarms.

➡ The MIL will may also be de-activated for some codes if the vehicle completes three consecutive trips without a fault detected with vehicle conditions similar to those present during the fault.

OBD II TROUBLE CODES

P0100 Mass or Volume Air Flow Circuit Malfunction

P0101 Mass or Volume Air Flow Circuit Range/Performance Problem

P0102 Mass or Volume Air Flow Circuit Low Input

P0103 Mass or Volume Air Flow Circuit High Input

P0104 Mass or Volume Air Flow Circuit Intermittent

P0105 Manifold Absolute Pressure/Barometric Pressure Circuit Malfunction

P0106 Manifold Absolute Pressure/Barometric Pressure Circuit Range/Performance Problem

P0107 Manifold Absolute Pressure/Barometric Pressure Circuit Low Input

P0108 Manifold Absolute Pressure/Barometric Pressure Circuit High Input

P0109 Manifold Absolute Pressure/Barometric Pressure Circuit Intermittent

P0110 Intake Air Temperature Circuit Malfunction

P0111 Intake Air Temperature Circuit Range/Performance Problem

P0112 Intake Air Temperature Circuit Low Input

P0113 Intake Air Temperature Circuit High Input

P0114 Intake Air Temperature Circuit Intermittent

P0115 Engine Coolant Temperature Circuit Malfunction

P0116 Engine Coolant Temperature Circuit Range/Performance Problem

P0117 Engine Coolant Temperature Circuit Low Input

P0118 Engine Coolant Temperature Circuit High Input

P0119 Engine Coolant Temperature Circuit Intermittent

P0120 Throttle/Pedal Position Sensor/Switch "A" Circuit Malfunction

P0121 Throttle/Pedal Position Sensor/Switch "A" Circuit Range/Performance Problem

P0122 Throttle/Pedal Position Sensor/Switch "A" Circuit Low Input

P0123 Throttle/Pedal Position Sensor/Switch "A" Circuit High Input

P0124 Throttle/Pedal Position Sensor/ Switch "A" Circuit Intermittent

P0125 Insufficient Coolant Temperature For Closed Loop Fuel Control

P0126 Insufficient Coolant Temperature For Stable Operation

P0130 O_2 Circuit Malfunction (Bank #1 Sensor #1)

P0131 O_2 Sensor Circuit Low Voltage (Bank #1 Sensor #1)

P0132 O_2 Sensor Circuit High Voltage (Bank #1 Sensor #1)

P0133 O_2 Sensor Circuit Slow Response (Bank #1 Sensor #1)

P0134 O_2 Sensor Circuit No Activity Detected (Bank #1 Sensor #1)

P0135 O_2 Sensor Heater Circuit Malfunction (Bank #1 Sensor #1)

P0136 O_2 Sensor Circuit Malfunction (Bank #1 Sensor #2)

P0137 O_2 Sensor Circuit Low Voltage (Bank #1 Sensor #2)

P0138 O_2 Sensor Circuit High Voltage (Bank #1 Sensor #2)

P0139 O_2 Sensor Circuit Slow Response (Bank #1 Sensor #2)

P0140 O_2 Sensor Circuit No Activity Detected (Bank #1 Sensor #2)

P0141 O_2 Sensor Heater Circuit Malfunction (Bank #1 Sensor #2)

P0142 O_2 Sensor Circuit Malfunction (Bank #1 Sensor #3)

P0143 O_2 Sensor Circuit Low Voltage (Bank #1 Sensor #3)

P0144 O_2 Sensor Circuit High Voltage (Bank #1 Sensor #3)

P0145 O_2 Sensor Circuit Slow Response (Bank #1 Sensor #3)

P0146 O_2 Sensor Circuit No Activity Detected (Bank #1 Sensor #3)

P0147 O_2 Sensor Heater Circuit Malfunction (Bank #1 Sensor #3)

P0150 O_2 Sensor Circuit Malfunction (Bank #2 Sensor #1)

P0151 O_2 Sensor Circuit Low Voltage (Bank #2 Sensor #1)

P0152 O_2 Sensor Circuit High Voltage (Bank #2 Sensor #1)

P0153 O_2 Sensor Circuit Slow Response (Bank #2 Sensor #1)

P0154 O_2 Sensor Circuit No Activity Detected (Bank #2 Sensor #1)

P0155 O_2 Sensor Heater Circuit Malfunction (Bank #2 Sensor #1)

P0156 O_2 Sensor Circuit Malfunction (Bank #2 Sensor #2)

P0157 O_2 Sensor Circuit Low Voltage (Bank #2 Sensor #2)

P0158 O_2 Sensor Circuit High Voltage (Bank #2 Sensor #2)

P0159 O_2 Sensor Circuit Slow Response (Bank #2 Sensor #2)

P0160 O_2 Sensor Circuit No Activity Detected (Bank #2 Sensor #2)

P0161 O_2 Sensor Heater Circuit Malfunction (Bank #2 Sensor #2)

P0162 O_2 Sensor Circuit Malfunction (Bank #2 Sensor #3)

P0163 O_2 Sensor Circuit Low Voltage (Bank #2 Sensor #3)

P0164 O_2 Sensor Circuit High Voltage (Bank #2 Sensor #3)

P0165 O_2 Sensor Circuit Slow Response (Bank #2 Sensor #3)

P0166 O_2 Sensor Circuit No Activity Detected (Bank #2 Sensor #3)

P0167 O_2 Sensor Heater Circuit Malfunction (Bank #2 Sensor #3)

P0170 Fuel Trim Malfunction (Bank #1)

P0171 System Too Lean (Bank #1)

P0172 System Too Rich (Bank #1)

P0173 Fuel Trim Malfunction (Bank #2)

P0174 System Too Lean (Bank #2)

P0175 System Too Rich (Bank #2)

P0176 Fuel Composition Sensor Circuit Malfunction

P0177 Fuel Composition Sensor Circuit Range/Performance

P0178 Fuel Composition Sensor Circuit Low Input

P0179 Fuel Composition Sensor Circuit High Input

P0180 Fuel Temperature Sensor "A" Circuit Malfunction

P0181 Fuel Temperature Sensor "A" Circuit Range/Performance

P0182 Fuel Temperature Sensor "A" Circuit Low Input

P0183 Fuel Temperature Sensor "A" Circuit High Input

P0184 Fuel Temperature Sensor "A" Circuit Intermittent

P0185 Fuel Temperature Sensor "B" Circuit Malfunction

P0186 Fuel Temperature Sensor "B" Circuit Range/Performance

P0187 Fuel Temperature Sensor "B" Circuit Low Input

P0188 Fuel Temperature Sensor "B" Circuit High Input

P0189 Fuel Temperature Sensor "B" Circuit Intermittent

P0190 Fuel Rail Pressure Sensor Circuit Malfunction

P0191 Fuel Rail Pressure Sensor Circuit Range/Performance

P0192 Fuel Rail Pressure Sensor Circuit Low Input

P0193 Fuel Rail Pressure Sensor Circuit High Input

P0194 Fuel Rail Pressure Sensor Circuit Intermittent

P0195 Engine Oil Temperature Sensor Malfunction

P0196 Engine Oil Temperature Sensor Range/Performance

P0197 Engine Oil Temperature Sensor Low

P0198 Engine Oil Temperature Sensor High

P0199 Engine Oil Temperature Sensor Intermittent

P0200 Injector Circuit Malfunction

P0201 Injector Circuit Malfunction—Cylinder #1

P0202 Injector Circuit Malfunction—Cylinder #2

P0203 Injector Circuit Malfunction—Cylinder #3

P0204 Injector Circuit Malfunction—Cylinder #4

P0205 Injector Circuit Malfunction—Cylinder #5

P0206 Injector Circuit Malfunction—Cylinder #6

P0207 Injector Circuit Malfunction—Cylinder #7

P0208 Injector Circuit Malfunction—Cylinder #8

P0209 Injector Circuit Malfunction—Cylinder #9

P0210 Injector Circuit Malfunction—Cylinder #10

P0211 Injector Circuit Malfunction—Cylinder #11

P0212 Injector Circuit Malfunction—Cylinder #12

P0213 Cold Start Injector #1 Malfunction

P0214 Cold Start Injector #2 Malfunction

P0215 Engine Shutoff Solenoid Malfunction

P0216 Injection Timing Control Circuit Malfunction

P0217 Engine Over Temperature Condition

P0218 Transmission Over Temperature Condition

P0219 Engine Over Speed Condition

P0220 Throttle/Pedal Position Sensor/ Switch "B" Circuit Malfunction

P0221 Throttle/Pedal Position Sensor/ Switch "B" Circuit Range/Performance Problem

P0222 Throttle/Pedal Position Sensor/ Switch "B" Circuit Low Input

P0223 Throttle/Pedal Position Sensor/ Switch "B" Circuit High Input

P0224 Throttle/Pedal Position Sensor/ Switch "B" Circuit Intermittent

P0225 Throttle/Pedal Position Sensor/ Switch "C" Circuit Malfunction

P0226 Throttle/Pedal Position Sensor/ Switch "C" Circuit Range/Performance Problem

P0227 Throttle/Pedal Position Sensor/ Switch "C" Circuit Low Input

P0228 Throttle/Pedal Position Sensor/ Switch "C" Circuit High Input

P0229 Throttle/Pedal Position Sensor/ Switch "C" Circuit Intermittent

P0230 Fuel Pump Primary Circuit Malfunction

P0231 Fuel Pump Secondary Circuit Low

P0232 Fuel Pump Secondary Circuit High

P0233 Fuel Pump Secondary Circuit Intermittent

P0234 Engine Over Boost Condition /Injector)

P0261 Cylinder #1 Injector Circuit Low

P0262 Cylinder #1 Injector Circuit High

P0263 Cylinder #1 Contribution/Balance Fault

P0264 Cylinder #2 Injector Circuit Low

P0265 Cylinder #2 Injector Circuit High

P0266 Cylinder #2 Contribution/Balance Fault

P0267 Cylinder #3 Injector Circuit Low

P0268 Cylinder #3 Injector Circuit High

P0269 Cylinder #3 Contribution/Balance Fault

P0270 Cylinder #4 Injector Circuit Low

P0271 Cylinder #4 Injector Circuit High

P0272 Cylinder #4 Contribution/Balance Fault

P0273 Cylinder #5 Injector Circuit Low

P0274 Cylinder #5 Injector Circuit High

P0275 Cylinder #5 Contribution/Balance Fault

P0276 Cylinder #6 Injector Circuit Low

P0277 Cylinder #6 Injector Circuit High

P0278 Cylinder #6 Contribution/Balance Fault

P0279 Cylinder #7 Injector Circuit Low

P0280 Cylinder #7 Injector Circuit High

P0281 Cylinder #7 Contribution/Balance Fault

P0282 Cylinder #8 Injector Circuit Low

P0283 Cylinder #8 Injector Circuit High

P0284 Cylinder #8 Contribution/Balance Fault

P0285 Cylinder #9 Injector Circuit Low

P0286 Cylinder #9 Injector Circuit High

P0287 Cylinder #9 Contribution/Balance Fault

P0288 Cylinder #10 Injector Circuit Low

P0289 Cylinder #10 Injector Circuit High

P0290 Cylinder #10 Contribution/Balance Fault

P0291 Cylinder #11 Injector Circuit Low

P0292 Cylinder #11 Injector Circuit High

P0293 Cylinder #11 Contribution/Balance Fault

P0294 Cylinder #12 Injector Circuit Low

P0295 Cylinder #12 Injector Circuit High

P0296 Cylinder #12 Contribution/Balance Fault

P0300 Random/Multiple Cylinder Misfire Detected

P0301 Cylinder #1—Misfire Detected

P0302 Cylinder #2—Misfire Detected

P0303 Cylinder #3—Misfire Detected

P0304 Cylinder #4—Misfire Detected

P0305 Cylinder #5—Misfire Detected

P0306 Cylinder #6—Misfire Detected

P0307 Cylinder #7—Misfire Detected

P0308 Cylinder #8—Misfire Detected

P0309 Cylinder #9—Misfire Detected

P0310 Cylinder #10—Misfire Detected

P0311 Cylinder #11—Misfire Detected

P0312 Cylinder #12—Misfire Detected

P0320 Ignition/Distributor Engine Speed Input Circuit Malfunction

P0321 Ignition/Distributor Engine Speed Input Circuit Range/Performance

P0322 Ignition/Distributor Engine Speed Input Circuit No Signal

P0323 Ignition/Distributor Engine Speed Input Circuit Intermittent

P0325 Knock Sensor #1—Circuit Malfunction (Bank #1 or Single Sensor)

P0326 Knock Sensor #1—Circuit Range/Performance (Bank #1 or Single Sensor)

P0327 Knock Sensor #1—Circuit Low Input (Bank #1 or Single Sensor)

P0328 Knock Sensor #1—Circuit High Input (Bank #1 or Single Sensor)

P0329 Knock Sensor #1—Circuit Input Intermittent (Bank #1 or Single Sensor)

P0330 Knock Sensor #2—Circuit Malfunction (Bank #2)

P0331 Knock Sensor #2—Circuit Range/Performance (Bank #2)

P0332 Knock Sensor #2—Circuit Low Input (Bank #2)

P0333 Knock Sensor #2—Circuit High Input (Bank #2)

P0334 Knock Sensor #2—Circuit Input Intermittent (Bank #2)

P0335 Crankshaft Position Sensor "A" Circuit Malfunction

P0336 Crankshaft Position Sensor "A" Circuit Range/Performance

P0337 Crankshaft Position Sensor "A" Circuit Low Input

P0338 Crankshaft Position Sensor "A" Circuit High Input

P0339 Crankshaft Position Sensor "A" Circuit Intermittent

P0340 Camshaft Position Sensor Circuit Malfunction

P0341 Camshaft Position Sensor Circuit Range/Performance

P0342 Camshaft Position Sensor Circuit Low Input

P0343 Camshaft Position Sensor Circuit High Input

P0344 Camshaft Position Sensor Circuit Intermittent

P0350 Ignition Coil Primary/Secondary Circuit Malfunction

P0351 Ignition Coil "A" Primary/Secondary Circuit Malfunction

P0352 Ignition Coil "B" Primary/Secondary Circuit Malfunction

P0353 Ignition Coil "C" Primary/Secondary Circuit Malfunction

P0354 Ignition Coil "D" Primary/Secondary Circuit Malfunction

P0355 Ignition Coil "E" Primary/Secondary Circuit Malfunction

P0356 Ignition Coil "F" Primary/Secondary Circuit Malfunction

P0357 Ignition Coil "G" Primary/Secondary Circuit Malfunction

P0358 Ignition Coil "H" Primary/Secondary Circuit Malfunction

P0359 Ignition Coil "I" Primary/Secondary Circuit Malfunction

P0360 Ignition Coil "J" Primary/Secondary Circuit Malfunction

P0361 Ignition Coil "K" Primary/Secondary Circuit Malfunction

P0362 Ignition Coil "L" Primary/Secondary Circuit Malfunction

P0370 Timing Reference High Resolution Signal "A" Malfunction

P0371 Timing Reference High Resolution Signal "A" Too Many Pulses

P0372 Timing Reference High Resolution Signal "A" Too Few Pulses

P0373 Timing Reference High Resolution Signal "A" Intermittent/Erratic Pulses

P0374 Timing Reference High Resolution Signal "A" No Pulses

P0375 Timing Reference High Resolution Signal "B" Malfunction

P0376 Timing Reference High Resolution Signal "B" Too Many Pulses

P0377 Timing Reference High Resolution Signal "B" Too Few Pulses

P0378 Timing Reference High Resolution Signal "B" Intermittent/Erratic Pulses

Refer to the model specific sections for fuel system service procedures

P0379 Timing Reference High Resolution Signal "B" No Pulses

P0380 Glow Plug/Heater Circuit "A" Malfunction

P0381 Glow Plug/Heater Indicator Circuit Malfunction

P0382 Glow Plug/Heater Circuit "B" Malfunction

P0385 Crankshaft Position Sensor "B" Circuit Malfunction

P0386 Crankshaft Position Sensor "B" Circuit Range/Performance

P0387 Crankshaft Position Sensor "B" Circuit Low Input

P0388 Crankshaft Position Sensor "B" Circuit High Input

P0389 Crankshaft Position Sensor "B" Circuit Intermittent

P0400 Exhaust Gas Recirculation Flow Malfunction

P0401 Exhaust Gas Recirculation Flow Insufficient Detected

P0402 Exhaust Gas Recirculation Flow Excessive Detected

P0403 Exhaust Gas Recirculation Circuit Malfunction

P0404 Exhaust Gas Recirculation Circuit Range/Performance

P0405 Exhaust Gas Recirculation Sensor "A" Circuit Low

P0406 Exhaust Gas Recirculation Sensor "A" Circuit High

P0407 Exhaust Gas Recirculation Sensor "B" Circuit Low

P0408 Exhaust Gas Recirculation Sensor "B" Circuit High

P0410 Secondary Air Injection System Malfunction

P0411 Secondary Air Injection System Incorrect Flow Detected

P0412 Secondary Air Injection System Switching Valve "A" Circuit Malfunction

P0413 Secondary Air Injection System Switching Valve "A" Circuit Open

P0414 Secondary Air Injection System Switching Valve "A" Circuit Shorted

P0415 Secondary Air Injection System Switching Valve "B" Circuit Malfunction

P0416 Secondary Air Injection System Switching Valve "B" Circuit Open

P0417 Secondary Air Injection System Switching Valve "B" Circuit Shorted

P0418 Secondary Air Injection System Relay "A" Circuit Malfunction

P0419 Secondary Air Injection System Relay "B" Circuit Malfunction

P0420 Catalyst System Efficiency Below Threshold (Bank #1)

P0421 Warm Up Catalyst Efficiency Below Threshold (Bank #1)

P0422 Main Catalyst Efficiency Below Threshold (Bank #1)

P0423 Heated Catalyst Efficiency Below Threshold (Bank #1)

P0424 Heated Catalyst Temperature Below Threshold (Bank #1)

P0430 Catalyst System Efficiency Below Threshold (Bank #2)

P0431 Warm Up Catalyst Efficiency Below Threshold (Bank #2)

P0432 Main Catalyst Efficiency Below Threshold (Bank #2)

P0433 Heated Catalyst Efficiency Below Threshold (Bank #2)

P0434 Heated Catalyst Temperature Below Threshold (Bank #2)

P0440 Evaporative Emission Control System Malfunction

P0441 Evaporative Emission Control System Incorrect Purge Flow

P0442 Evaporative Emission Control System Leak Detected (Small Leak)

P0443 Evaporative Emission Control System Purge Control Valve Circuit Malfunction

P0444 Evaporative Emission Control System Purge Control Valve Circuit Open

P0445 Evaporative Emission Control System Purge Control Valve Circuit Shorted

P0446 Evaporative Emission Control System Vent Control Circuit Malfunction

P0447 Evaporative Emission Control System Vent Control Circuit Open

P0448 Evaporative Emission Control System Vent Control Circuit Shorted

P0449 Evaporative Emission Control System Vent Valve/Solenoid Circuit Malfunction

P0450 Evaporative Emission Control System Pressure Sensor Malfunction

P0451 Evaporative Emission Control System Pressure Sensor Range/Performance

P0452 Evaporative Emission Control System Pressure Sensor Low Input

P0453 Evaporative Emission Control System Pressure Sensor High Input

P0454 Evaporative Emission Control System Pressure Sensor Intermittent

P0455 Evaporative Emission Control System Leak Detected (Gross Leak)

P0460 Fuel Level Sensor Circuit Malfunction

P0461 Fuel Level Sensor Circuit Range/Performance

P0462 Fuel Level Sensor Circuit Low Input

P0463 Fuel Level Sensor Circuit High Input

P0464 Fuel Level Sensor Circuit Intermittent

P0465 Purge Flow Sensor Circuit Malfunction

P0466 Purge Flow Sensor Circuit Range/Performance

P0467 Purge Flow Sensor Circuit Low Input

P0468 Purge Flow Sensor Circuit High Input

P0469 Purge Flow Sensor Circuit Intermittent

P0470 Exhaust Pressure Sensor Malfunction

P0471 Exhaust Pressure Sensor Range/Performance

P0472 Exhaust Pressure Sensor Low

P0473 Exhaust Pressure Sensor High

P0474 Exhaust Pressure Sensor Intermittent

P0475 Exhaust Pressure Control Valve Malfunction

P0476 Exhaust Pressure Control Valve Range/Performance

P0477 Exhaust Pressure Control Valve Low

P0478 Exhaust Pressure Control Valve High

P0479 Exhaust Pressure Control Valve Intermittent

P0480 Cooling Fan #1 Control Circuit Malfunction

P0481 Cooling Fan #2 Control Circuit Malfunction

P0482 Cooling Fan #3 Control Circuit Malfunction

P0483 Cooling Fan Rationality Check Malfunction

P0484 Cooling Fan Circuit Over Current

P0485 Cooling Fan Power/Ground Circuit Malfunction

P0500 Vehicle Speed Sensor Malfunction

P0501 Vehicle Speed Sensor Range/Performance

P0502 Vehicle Speed Sensor Circuit Low Input

P0503 Vehicle Speed Sensor Intermittent/Erratic/High

P0505 Idle Control System Malfunction

P0506 Idle Control System RPM Lower Than Expected

P0507 Idle Control System RPM Higher Than Expected

P0510 Closed Throttle Position Switch Malfunction

P0520 Engine Oil Pressure Sensor/Switch Circuit Malfunction

P0521 Engine Oil Pressure Sensor/Switch Range/Performance

P0522 Engine Oil Pressure Sensor/Switch Low Voltage

P0523 Engine Oil Pressure Sensor/Switch High Voltage

P0530 A/C Refrigerant Pressure Sensor Circuit Malfunction

P0531 A/C Refrigerant Pressure Sensor Circuit Range/Performance

P0532 A/C Refrigerant Pressure Sensor Circuit Low Input

P0533 A/C Refrigerant Pressure Sensor Circuit High Input

P0534 A/C Refrigerant Charge Loss

P0550 Power Steering Pressure Sensor Circuit Malfunction

P0551 Power Steering Pressure Sensor Circuit Range/Performance

P0552 Power Steering Pressure Sensor Circuit Low Input

P0553 Power Steering Pressure Sensor Circuit High Input

P0554 Power Steering Pressure Sensor Circuit Intermittent

P0560 System Voltage Malfunction

P0561 System Voltage Unstable

P0562 System Voltage Low

P0563 System Voltage High

P0565 Cruise Control On Signal Malfunction

P0566 Cruise Control Off Signal Malfunction

P0567 Cruise Control Resume Signal Malfunction

P0568 Cruise Control Set Signal Malfunction

P0569 Cruise Control Coast Signal Malfunction

P0570 Cruise Control Accel Signal Malfunction

P0571 Cruise Control/Brake Switch "A" Circuit Malfunction

P0572 Cruise Control/Brake Switch "A" Circuit Low

P0573 Cruise Control/Brake Switch "A" Circuit High

P0574 Through P0580 Reserved for Cruise Codes

P0600 Serial Communication Link Malfunction

P0601 Internal Control Module Memory Check Sum Error

P0602 Control Module Programming Error

P0603 Internal Control Module Keep Alive Memory (KAM) Error

P0604 Internal Control Module Random Access Memory (RAM) Error

P0605 Internal Control Module Read Only Memory (ROM) Error

P0606 PCM Processor Fault

P0608 Control Module VSS Output "A" Malfunction

P0609 Control Module VSS Output "B" Malfunction

P0620 Generator Control Circuit Malfunction

P0621 Generator Lamp "L" Control Circuit Malfunction

P0622 Generator Field "F" Control Circuit Malfunction

P0650 Malfunction Indicator Lamp (MIL) Control Circuit Malfunction

P0654 Engine RPM Output Circuit Malfunction

P0655 Engine Hot Lamp Output Control Circuit Malfunction

P0656 Fuel Level Output Circuit Malfunction

P0700 Transmission Control System Malfunction

P0701 Transmission Control System Range/Performance

P0702 Transmission Control System Electrical

P0703 Torque Converter/Brake Switch "B" Circuit Malfunction

P0704 Clutch Switch Input Circuit Malfunction

P0705 Transmission Range Sensor Circuit Malfunction (PRNDL Input)

P0706 Transmission Range Sensor Circuit Range/Performance

P0707 Transmission Range Sensor Circuit Low Input

P0708 Transmission Range Sensor Circuit High Input

P0709 Transmission Range Sensor Circuit Intermittent

P0710 Transmission Fluid Temperature Sensor Circuit Malfunction

P0711 Transmission Fluid Temperature Sensor Circuit Range/Performance

P0712 Transmission Fluid Temperature Sensor Circuit Low Input

P0713 Transmission Fluid Temperature Sensor Circuit High Input

P0714 Transmission Fluid Temperature Sensor Circuit Intermittent

P0715 Input/Turbine Speed Sensor Circuit Malfunction

P0716 Input/Turbine Speed Sensor Circuit Range/Performance

P0717 Input/Turbine Speed Sensor Circuit No Signal

P0718 Input/Turbine Speed Sensor Circuit Intermittent

P0719 Torque Converter/Brake Switch "B" Circuit Low

P0720 Output Speed Sensor Circuit Malfunction

P0721 Output Speed Sensor Circuit Range/Performance

P0722 Output Speed Sensor Circuit No Signal

P0723 Output Speed Sensor Circuit Intermittent

P0724 Torque Converter/Brake Switch "B" Circuit High

P0725 Engine Speed Input Circuit Malfunction

P0726 Engine Speed Input Circuit Range/Performance

P0727 Engine Speed Input Circuit No Signal

P0728 Engine Speed Input Circuit Intermittent

P0730 Incorrect Gear Ratio

P0731 Gear #1 Incorrect Ratio

P0732 Gear #2 Incorrect Ratio

P0733 Gear #3 Incorrect Ratio

P0734 Gear #4 Incorrect Ratio

P0735 Gear #5 Incorrect Ratio

P0736 Reverse Incorrect Ratio

P0740 Torque Converter Clutch Circuit Malfunction

P0741 Torque Converter Clutch Circuit Performance or Stuck Off

P0742 Torque Converter Clutch Circuit Stuck On

P0743 Torque Converter Clutch Circuit Electrical

P0744 Torque Converter Clutch Circuit Intermittent

P0745 Pressure Control Solenoid Malfunction

P0746 Pressure Control Solenoid Performance or Stuck Off

P0747 Pressure Control Solenoid Stuck On

P0748 Pressure Control Solenoid Electrical

P0749 Pressure Control Solenoid Intermittent

P0750 Shift Solenoid "A" Malfunction

P0751 Shift Solenoid "A" Performance or Stuck Off

P0752 Shift Solenoid "A" Stuck On

P0753 Shift Solenoid "A" Electrical

P0754 Shift Solenoid "A" Intermittent

P0755 Shift Solenoid "B" Malfunction

P0756 Shift Solenoid "B" Performance or Stuck Off

P0757 Shift Solenoid "B" Stuck On

P0758 Shift Solenoid "B" Electrical

P0759 Shift Solenoid "B" Intermittent

P0760 Shift Solenoid "C" Malfunction

P0761 Shift Solenoid "C" Performance Or Stuck Off

P0762 Shift Solenoid "C" Stuck On

P0763 Shift Solenoid "C" Electrical

P0764 Shift Solenoid "C" Intermittent

P0765 Shift Solenoid "D" Malfunction

Refer to the model specific sections for engine electrical system service procedures

P0766 Shift Solenoid "D" Performance Or Stuck Off

P0767 Shift Solenoid "D" Stuck On

P0768 Shift Solenoid "D" Electrical

P0769 Shift Solenoid "D" Intermittent

P0770 Shift Solenoid "E" Malfunction

P0771 Shift Solenoid "E" Performance Or Stuck Off

P0772 Shift Solenoid "E" Stuck On

P0773 Shift Solenoid "E" Electrical

P0774 Shift Solenoid "E" Intermittent

P0780 Shift Malfunction

P0781 1–2 Shift Malfunction

P0782 2–3 Shift Malfunction

P0783 3–4 Shift Malfunction

P0784 4–5 Shift Malfunction

P0785 Shift/Timing Solenoid Malfunction

P0786 Shift/Timing Solenoid Range/Performance

P0787 Shift/Timing Solenoid Low

P0788 Shift/Timing Solenoid High

P0789 Shift/Timing Solenoid Intermittent

P0790 Normal/Performance Switch Circuit Malfunction

P0801 Reverse Inhibit Control Circuit Malfunction

P0803 1–4 Upshift (Skip Shift) Solenoid Control Circuit Malfunction

P0804 1–4 Upshift (Skip Shift) Lamp Control Circuit Malfunction

P1106 MAP Sensor Circuit Intermittent High Voltage

P1107 MAP Sensor Circuit Intermittent Low Voltage

P1111 IAT Sensor Circuit Intermittent High Voltage

P1112 IAT Sensor Circuit Intermittent Low Voltage

P1114 ECT Sensor Circuit Intermittent Low Voltage

P1115 ECT Sensor Circuit Intermittent High Voltage

P1121 TP Sensor Circuit Intermittent High Voltage

P1122 TP Sensor Circuit Intermittent Low Voltage

P1133 HO2S-11 Insufficient Switching (Bank #1 Sensor #1)

P1134 HO2S-11 Transition Time Ratio (Bank #1 Sensor #1)

P1153 HO2S-21 Insufficient Switching (Bank #2 Sensor #I)

P1154 HO2S-21 Transition Time Ratio (Bank #2 Sensor #1)

P1171 Fuel System Lean During Acceleration

P1391 G-Acceleration Sensor Intermittent Low Voltage

P1390 G-Acceleration (Low G) Sensor Performance

P1392 Rough Road G-Sensor Circuit Low Voltage

P1393 Rough Road G-Sensor Circuit High Voltage

P1394 G-Acceleration Sensor Intermittent High Voltage

P1406 EGR Valve Pintle Position Sensor Circuit Fault

P1441 EVAP System Flow During Non-Purge

P1442 EVAP System Flow During Non-Purge

P1508 Idle Speed Control System-Low

P1509 Idle Speed Control System-High

P1618 Serial Peripheral Interface Communication Error

P1640 Output Driver Module "A" Fault

P1790 PCM ROM (Transmission Side) Check Sum Error

P1792 PCM EEPROM (Transmission Side) Check Sum Error

P1835 Kick Down Switch Always On

P1850 Brake Band Apply Solenoid Electrical Fault

P1860 TCC PWM Solenoid Electrical Fault

P1870 Transmission Component Slipping

KIA

READING CODES

Reading the control module memory is one of the first steps in OBD II system diagnostics. This step should be initially performed to determine the general nature of the fault. Subsequent readings will determine if the fault has been cleared.

Reading codes can be performed by any of the methods below:

• Read the control module memory with the Generic Scan Tool (GST)

• Read the control module memory with the vehicle manufacturer's specific tester

To read the fault codes, connect the scan tool or tester according to the manufacturer's instructions. Follow the manufacturer's specified procedure for reading the codes.

CLEARING CODES

Control module reset procedures are a very important part of OBD II System diagnostics. This step should be done at the end of any fault code repair and at the end of any driveability repair.

Clearing codes can be performed by any of the methods below:

• Clear the control module memory with the Generic Scan Tool (GST)

• Clear the control module memory with the vehicle manufacturer's specific tester

• Turn the ignition OFF and remove the negative battery cable for at least 1 minute.

Removing the negative battery cable may cause other systems in the vehicle to loose their memory. Prior to removing the cable, ensure you have the proper reset codes for radios and alarms.

➡**The MIL will may also be de-activated for some codes if the vehicle completes three consecutive trips without a fault detected with vehicle conditions similar to those present during the fault.**

OBD II TROUBLE CODES

P0100 Mass or Volume Air Flow Circuit Malfunction

P0101 Mass or Volume Air Flow Circuit Range/Performance Problem

P0102 Mass or Volume Air Flow Circuit Low Input

P0103 Mass or Volume Air Flow Circuit High Input

P0104 Mass or Volume Air Flow Circuit Intermittent

P0105 Manifold Absolute Pressure/Barometric Pressure Circuit Malfunction

P0106 Manifold Absolute Pressure/Barometric Pressure Circuit Range/Performance Problem

P0107 Manifold Absolute Pressure/Barometric Pressure Circuit Low Input

P0108 Manifold Absolute Pressure/Barometric Pressure Circuit High Input

P0109 Manifold Absolute Pressure/Barometric Pressure Circuit Intermittent

P0110 Intake Air Temperature Circuit Malfunction

P0111 Intake Air Temperature Circuit Range/Performance Problem

P0112 Intake Air Temperature Circuit Low Input

P0113 Intake Air Temperature Circuit High Input

P0114 Intake Air Temperature Circuit Intermittent

P0115 Engine Coolant Temperature Circuit Malfunction

P0116 Engine Coolant Temperature Circuit Range/Performance Problem

P0117 Engine Coolant Temperature Circuit Low Input

P0118 Engine Coolant Temperature Circuit High Input

P0119 Engine Coolant Temperature Circuit Intermittent

P0120 Throttle/Pedal Position Sensor/Switch "A" Circuit Malfunction

P0121 Throttle/Pedal Position Sensor/Switch "A" Circuit Range/Performance Problem

P0122 Throttle/Pedal Position Sensor/Switch "A" Circuit Low Input

P0123 Throttle/Pedal Position Sensor/Switch "A" Circuit High Input

P0124 Throttle/Pedal Position Sensor/Switch "A" Circuit Intermittent

P0125 Insufficient Coolant Temperature For Closed Loop Fuel Control

P0126 Insufficient Coolant Temperature For Stable Operation

P0130 O_2 Circuit Malfunction (Bank #1 Sensor #1)

P0131 O_2 Sensor Circuit Low Voltage (Bank #1 Sensor #1)

P0132 O_2 Sensor Circuit High Voltage (Bank #1 Sensor #1)

P0133 O_2 Sensor Circuit Slow Response (Bank #1 Sensor #1)

P0134 O_2 Sensor Circuit No Activity Detected (Bank #1 Sensor #1)

P0135 O_2 Sensor Heater Circuit Malfunction (Bank #1 Sensor #1)

P0136 O_2 Sensor Circuit Malfunction (Bank #1 Sensor #2)

P0137 O_2 Sensor Circuit Low Voltage (Bank #1 Sensor #2)

P0138 O_2 Sensor Circuit High Voltage (Bank #1 Sensor #2)

P0139 O_2 Sensor Circuit Slow Response (Bank #1 Sensor #2)

P0140 O_2 Sensor Circuit No Activity Detected (Bank #1 Sensor #2)

P0141 O_2 Sensor Heater Circuit Malfunction (Bank #1 Sensor #2)

P0142 O_2 Sensor Circuit Malfunction (Bank #1 Sensor #3)

P0143 O_2 Sensor Circuit Low Voltage (Bank #1 Sensor #3)

P0144 O_2 Sensor Circuit High Voltage (Bank #1 Sensor #3)

P0145 O_2 Sensor Circuit Slow Response (Bank #1 Sensor #3)

P0146 O_2 Sensor Circuit No Activity Detected (Bank #1 Sensor #3)

P0147 O_2 Sensor Heater Circuit Malfunction (Bank #1 Sensor #3)

P0150 O_2 Sensor Circuit Malfunction (Bank #2 Sensor #1)

P0151 O_2 Sensor Circuit Low Voltage (Bank #2 Sensor #1)

P0152 O_2 Sensor Circuit High Voltage (Bank #2 Sensor #1)

P0153 O_2 Sensor Circuit Slow Response (Bank #2 Sensor #1)

P0154 O_2 Sensor Circuit No Activity Detected (Bank #2 Sensor #1)

P0155 O_2 Sensor Heater Circuit Malfunction (Bank #2 Sensor #1)

P0156 O_2 Sensor Circuit Malfunction (Bank #2 Sensor #2)

P0157 O_2 Sensor Circuit Low Voltage (Bank #2 Sensor #2)

P0158 O_2 Sensor Circuit High Voltage (Bank #2 Sensor #2)

P0159 O_2 Sensor Circuit Slow Response (Bank #2 Sensor #2)

P0160 O_2 Sensor Circuit No Activity Detected (Bank #2 Sensor #2)

P0161 O_2 Sensor Heater Circuit Malfunction (Bank #2 Sensor #2)

P0162 O_2 Sensor Circuit Malfunction (Bank #2 Sensor #3)

P0163 O_2 Sensor Circuit Low Voltage (Bank #2 Sensor #3)

P0164 O_2 Sensor Circuit High Voltage (Bank #2 Sensor #3)

P0165 O_2 Sensor Circuit Slow Response (Bank #2 Sensor #3)

P0166 O_2 Sensor Circuit No Activity Detected (Bank #2 Sensor #3)

P0167 O_2 Sensor Heater Circuit Malfunction (Bank #2 Sensor #3)

P0170 Fuel Trim Malfunction (Bank #1)

P0171 System Too Lean (Bank #1)

P0172 System Too Rich (Bank #1)

P0173 Fuel Trim Malfunction (Bank #2)

P0174 System Too Lean (Bank #2)

P0175 System Too Rich (Bank #2)

P0176 Fuel Composition Sensor Circuit Malfunction

P0177 Fuel Composition Sensor Circuit Range/Performance

P0178 Fuel Composition Sensor Circuit Low Input

P0179 Fuel Composition Sensor Circuit High Input

P0180 Fuel Temperature Sensor "A" Circuit Malfunction

P0181 Fuel Temperature Sensor "A" Circuit Range/Performance

P0182 Fuel Temperature Sensor "A" Circuit Low Input

P0183 Fuel Temperature Sensor "A" Circuit High Input

P0184 Fuel Temperature Sensor "A" Circuit Intermittent

P0185 Fuel Temperature Sensor "B" Circuit Malfunction

P0186 Fuel Temperature Sensor "B" Circuit Range/Performance

P0187 Fuel Temperature Sensor "B" Circuit Low Input

P0188 Fuel Temperature Sensor "B" Circuit High Input

P0189 Fuel Temperature Sensor "B" Circuit Intermittent

P0190 Fuel Rail Pressure Sensor Circuit Malfunction

P0191 Fuel Rail Pressure Sensor Circuit Range/Performance

P0192 Fuel Rail Pressure Sensor Circuit Low Input

P0193 Fuel Rail Pressure Sensor Circuit High Input

P0194 Fuel Rail Pressure Sensor Circuit Intermittent

P0195 Engine Oil Temperature Sensor Malfunction

P0196 Engine Oil Temperature Sensor Range/Performance

P0197 Engine Oil Temperature Sensor Low

P0198 Engine Oil Temperature Sensor High

P0199 Engine Oil Temperature Sensor Intermittent

P0200 Injector Circuit Malfunction

P0201 Injector Circuit Malfunction—Cylinder #1

P0202 Injector Circuit Malfunction—Cylinder #2

P0203 Injector Circuit Malfunction—Cylinder #3

P0204 Injector Circuit Malfunction—Cylinder #4

P0205 Injector Circuit Malfunction—Cylinder #5

P0206 Injector Circuit Malfunction—Cylinder #6

P0207 Injector Circuit Malfunction—Cylinder #7

P0208 Injector Circuit Malfunction—Cylinder #8

P0209 Injector Circuit Malfunction—Cylinder #9

P0210 Injector Circuit Malfunction—Cylinder #10

P0211 Injector Circuit Malfunction—Cylinder #11

P0212 Injector Circuit Malfunction—Cylinder #12

P0213 Cold Start Injector #1 Malfunction

P0214 Cold Start Injector #2 Malfunction

P0215 Engine Shutoff Solenoid Malfunction

P0216 Injection Timing Control Circuit Malfunction

P0217 Engine Over Temperature Condition

P0218 Transmission Over Temperature Condition

P0219 Engine Over Speed Condition

P0220 Throttle/Pedal Position Sensor/Switch "B" Circuit Malfunction

P0221 Throttle/Pedal Position Sensor/Switch "B" Circuit Range/Performance Problem

P0222 Throttle/Pedal Position Sensor/Switch "B" Circuit Low Input

P0223 Throttle/Pedal Position Sensor/Switch "B" Circuit High Input

P0224 Throttle/Pedal Position Sensor/Switch "B" Circuit Intermittent

P0225 Throttle/Pedal Position Sensor/Switch "C" Circuit Malfunction

P0226 Throttle/Pedal Position Sensor/Switch "C" Circuit Range/Performance Problem

P0227 Throttle/Pedal Position Sensor/Switch "C" Circuit Low Input

P0228 Throttle/Pedal Position Sensor/Switch "C" Circuit High Input

P0229 Throttle/Pedal Position Sensor/Switch "C" Circuit Intermittent

P0230 Fuel Pump Primary Circuit Malfunction

P0231 Fuel Pump Secondary Circuit Low

P0232 Fuel Pump Secondary Circuit High

P0233 Fuel Pump Secondary Circuit Intermittent

P0234 Engine Over Boost Condition

P0261 Cylinder #1 Injector Circuit Low

P0262 Cylinder #1 Injector Circuit High

P0263 Cylinder #1 Contribution/Balance Fault

P0264 Cylinder #2 Injector Circuit Low

P0265 Cylinder #2 Injector Circuit High

P0266 Cylinder #2 Contribution/Balance Fault

P0267 Cylinder #3 Injector Circuit Low

P0268 Cylinder #3 Injector Circuit High

P0269 Cylinder #3 Contribution/Balance Fault

P0270 Cylinder #4 Injector Circuit Low

P0271 Cylinder #4 Injector Circuit High

P0272 Cylinder #4 Contribution/Balance Fault

P0273 Cylinder #5 Injector Circuit Low

P0274 Cylinder #5 Injector Circuit High

P0275 Cylinder #5 Contribution/Balance Fault

P0276 Cylinder #6 Injector Circuit Low

P0277 Cylinder #6 Injector Circuit High

P0278 Cylinder #6 Contribution/Balance Fault

P0279 Cylinder #7 Injector Circuit Low

P0280 Cylinder #7 Injector Circuit High

P0281 Cylinder #7 Contribution/Balance Fault

P0282 Cylinder #8 Injector Circuit Low

P0283 Cylinder #8 Injector Circuit High

P0284 Cylinder #8 Contribution/Balance Fault

P0285 Cylinder #9 Injector Circuit Low

P0286 Cylinder #9 Injector Circuit High

P0287 Cylinder #9 Contribution/Balance Fault

P0288 Cylinder #10 Injector Circuit Low

P0289 Cylinder #10 Injector Circuit High

P0290 Cylinder #10 Contribution/Balance Fault

P0291 Cylinder #11 Injector Circuit Low

P0292 Cylinder #11 Injector Circuit High

P0293 Cylinder #11 Contribution/Balance Fault

P0294 Cylinder #12 Injector Circuit Low

P0295 Cylinder #12 Injector Circuit High

P0296 Cylinder #12 Contribution/Balance Fault

P0300 Random/Multiple Cylinder Misfire Detected

P0301 Cylinder #1—Misfire Detected

P0302 Cylinder #2—Misfire Detected

P0303 Cylinder #3—Misfire Detected

P0304 Cylinder #4—Misfire Detected

P0305 Cylinder #5—Misfire Detected

P0306 Cylinder #6—Misfire Detected

P0307 Cylinder #7—Misfire Detected

P0308 Cylinder #8—Misfire Detected

P0309 Cylinder #9—Misfire Detected

P0310 Cylinder #10—Misfire Detected

P0311 Cylinder #11—Misfire Detected

P0312 Cylinder #12—Misfire Detected

P0320 Ignition/Distributor Engine Speed Input Circuit Malfunction

P0321 Ignition/Distributor Engine Speed Input Circuit Range/Performance

P0322 Ignition/Distributor Engine Speed Input Circuit No Signal

P0323 Ignition/Distributor Engine Speed Input Circuit Intermittent

P0325 Knock Sensor #1—Circuit Malfunction (Bank #1 or Single Sensor)

P0326 Knock Sensor #1—Circuit Range/Performance (Bank #1 or Single Sensor)

P0327 Knock Sensor #1—Circuit Low Input (Bank #1 or Single Sensor)

P0328 Knock Sensor #1—Circuit High Input (Bank #1 or Single Sensor)

P0329 Knock Sensor #1—Circuit Input Intermittent (Bank #1 or Single Sensor)

P0330 Knock Sensor #2—Circuit Malfunction (Bank #2)

P0331 Knock Sensor #2—Circuit Range/Performance (Bank #2)

P0332 Knock Sensor #2—Circuit Low Input (Bank #2)

P0333 Knock Sensor #2—Circuit High Input (Bank #2)

P0334 Knock Sensor #2—Circuit Input Intermittent (Bank #2)

P0335 Crankshaft Position Sensor "A" Circuit Malfunction

P0336 Crankshaft Position Sensor "A" Circuit Range/Performance

P0337 Crankshaft Position Sensor "A" Circuit Low Input

P0338 Crankshaft Position Sensor "A" Circuit High Input

P0339 Crankshaft Position Sensor "A" Circuit Intermittent

P0340 Camshaft Position Sensor Circuit Malfunction

P0341 Camshaft Position Sensor Circuit Range/Performance

P0342 Camshaft Position Sensor Circuit Low Input

P0343 Camshaft Position Sensor Circuit High Input

P0344 Camshaft Position Sensor Circuit Intermittent

P0350 Ignition Coil Primary/Secondary Circuit Malfunction

P0351 Ignition Coil "A" Primary/Secondary Circuit Malfunction

P0352 Ignition Coil "B" Primary/Secondary Circuit Malfunction

P0353 Ignition Coil "C" Primary/Secondary Circuit Malfunction

P0354 Ignition Coil "D" Primary/Secondary Circuit Malfunction

P0355 Ignition Coil "E" Primary/Secondary Circuit Malfunction

P0356 Ignition Coil "F" Primary/Secondary Circuit Malfunction

P0357 Ignition Coil "G" Primary/Secondary Circuit Malfunction

P0358 Ignition Coil "H" Primary/Secondary Circuit Malfunction

P0359 Ignition Coil "I" Primary/Secondary Circuit Malfunction

P0360 Ignition Coil "J" Primary/Secondary Circuit Malfunction

P0361 Ignition Coil "K" Primary/Secondary Circuit Malfunction

P0362 Ignition Coil "L" Primary/Secondary Circuit Malfunction

P0370 Timing Reference High Resolution Signal "A" Malfunction

P0371 Timing Reference High Resolution Signal "A" Too Many Pulses

P0372 Timing Reference High Resolution Signal "A" Too Few Pulses

P0373 Timing Reference High Resolution Signal "A" Intermittent/Erratic Pulses

P0374 Timing Reference High Resolution Signal "A" No Pulses

P0375 Timing Reference High Resolution Signal "B" Malfunction

P0376 Timing Reference High Resolution Signal "B" Too Many Pulses

P0377 Timing Reference High Resolution Signal "B" Too Few Pulses

P0378 Timing Reference High Resolution Signal "B" Intermittent/Erratic Pulses

P0379 Timing Reference High Resolution Signal "B" No Pulses

P0380 Glow Plug/Heater Circuit "A" Malfunction

P0381 Glow Plug/Heater Indicator Circuit Malfunction

P0382 Glow Plug/Heater Circuit "B" Malfunction

P0385 Crankshaft Position Sensor "B" Circuit Malfunction

P0386 Crankshaft Position Sensor "B" Circuit Range/Performance

P0387 Crankshaft Position Sensor "B" Circuit Low Input

P0388 Crankshaft Position Sensor "B" Circuit High Input

P0389 Crankshaft Position Sensor "B" Circuit Intermittent

P0400 Exhaust Gas Recirculation Flow Malfunction

P0401 Exhaust Gas Recirculation Flow Insufficient Detected

P0402 Exhaust Gas Recirculation Flow Excessive Detected

P0403 Exhaust Gas Recirculation Circuit Malfunction

P0404 Exhaust Gas Recirculation Circuit Range/Performance

P0405 Exhaust Gas Recirculation Sensor "A" Circuit Low

P0406 Exhaust Gas Recirculation Sensor "A" Circuit High

P0407 Exhaust Gas Recirculation Sensor "B" Circuit Low

P0408 Exhaust Gas Recirculation Sensor "B" Circuit High

P0410 Secondary Air Injection System Malfunction

P0411 Secondary Air Injection System Incorrect Flow Detected

P0412 Secondary Air Injection System Switching Valve "A" Circuit Malfunction

P0413 Secondary Air Injection System Switching Valve "A" Circuit Open

P0414 Secondary Air Injection System Switching Valve "A" Circuit Shorted

P0415 Secondary Air Injection System Switching Valve "B" Circuit Malfunction

P0416 Secondary Air Injection System Switching Valve "B" Circuit Open

P0417 Secondary Air Injection System Switching Valve "B" Circuit Shorted

P0418 Secondary Air Injection System Relay "A" Circuit Malfunction

P0419 Secondary Air Injection System Relay "B" Circuit Malfunction

P0420 Catalyst System Efficiency Below Threshold (Bank #1)

P0421 Warm Up Catalyst Efficiency Below Threshold (Bank #1)

P0422 Main Catalyst Efficiency Below Threshold (Bank #1)

P0423 Heated Catalyst Efficiency Below Threshold (Bank #1)

P0424 Heated Catalyst Temperature Below Threshold (Bank #1)

P0430 Catalyst System Efficiency Below Threshold (Bank #2)

P0431 Warm Up Catalyst Efficiency Below Threshold (Bank #2)

P0432 Main Catalyst Efficiency Below Threshold (Bank #2)

P0433 Heated Catalyst Efficiency Below Threshold (Bank #2)

P0434 Heated Catalyst Temperature Below Threshold (Bank #2)

P0440 Evaporative Emission Control System Malfunction

P0441 Evaporative Emission Control System Incorrect Purge Flow

P0442 Evaporative Emission Control System Leak Detected (Small Leak)

P0443 Evaporative Emission Control System Purge Control Valve Circuit Malfunction

P0444 Evaporative Emission Control System Purge Control Valve Circuit Open

P0445 Evaporative Emission Control System Purge Control Valve Circuit Shorted

P0446 Evaporative Emission Control System Vent Control Circuit Malfunction

P0447 Evaporative Emission Control System Vent Control Circuit Open

P0448 Evaporative Emission Control System Vent Control Circuit Shorted

P0449 Evaporative Emission Control System Vent Valve/Solenoid Circuit Malfunction

P0450 Evaporative Emission Control System Pressure Sensor Malfunction

P0451 Evaporative Emission Control System Pressure Sensor Range/Performance

P0452 Evaporative Emission Control System Pressure Sensor Low Input

P0453 Evaporative Emission Control System Pressure Sensor High Input

P0454 Evaporative Emission Control System Pressure Sensor Intermittent

P0455 Evaporative Emission Control System Leak Detected (Gross Leak)

P0460 Fuel Level Sensor Circuit Malfunction

P0461 Fuel Level Sensor Circuit Range/Performance

P0462 Fuel Level Sensor Circuit Low Input

P0463 Fuel Level Sensor Circuit High Input

P0464 Fuel Level Sensor Circuit Intermittent

P0465 Purge Flow Sensor Circuit Malfunction

P0466 Purge Flow Sensor Circuit Range/Performance

P0467 Purge Flow Sensor Circuit Low Input

P0468 Purge Flow Sensor Circuit High Input

P0469 Purge Flow Sensor Circuit Intermittent

P0470 Exhaust Pressure Sensor Malfunction

P0471 Exhaust Pressure Sensor Range/Performance

P0472 Exhaust Pressure Sensor Low

P0473 Exhaust Pressure Sensor High

P0474 Exhaust Pressure Sensor Intermittent

P0475 Exhaust Pressure Control Valve Malfunction

P0476 Exhaust Pressure Control Valve Range/Performance

P0477 Exhaust Pressure Control Valve Low

P0478 Exhaust Pressure Control Valve High

P0479 Exhaust Pressure Control Valve Intermittent

P0480 Cooling Fan #1 Control Circuit Malfunction

P0481 Cooling Fan #2 Control Circuit Malfunction

P0482 Cooling Fan #3 Control Circuit Malfunction

P0483 Cooling Fan Rationality Check Malfunction

P0484 Cooling Fan Circuit Over Current

P0485 Cooling Fan Power/Ground Circuit Malfunction

P0500 Vehicle Speed Sensor Malfunction

P0501 Vehicle Speed Sensor Range/Performance

P0502 Vehicle Speed Sensor Circuit Low Input

Ignition system service is covered in the model specific sections of this manual

P0503 Vehicle Speed Sensor Intermittent/Erratic/High

P0505 Idle Control System Malfunction

P0506 Idle Control System RPM Lower Than Expected

P0507 Idle Control System RPM Higher Than Expected

P0510 Closed Throttle Position Switch Malfunction

P0520 Engine Oil Pressure Sensor/Switch Circuit Malfunction

P0521 Engine Oil Pressure Sensor/Switch Range/Performance

P0522 Engine Oil Pressure Sensor/Switch Low Voltage

P0523 Engine Oil Pressure Sensor/Switch High Voltage

P0530 A/C Refrigerant Pressure Sensor Circuit Malfunction

P0531 A/C Refrigerant Pressure Sensor Circuit Range/Performance

P0532 A/C Refrigerant Pressure Sensor Circuit Low Input

P0533 A/C Refrigerant Pressure Sensor Circuit High Input

P0534 A/C Refrigerant Charge Loss

P0550 Power Steering Pressure Sensor Circuit Malfunction

P0551 Power Steering Pressure Sensor Circuit Range/Performance

P0552 Power Steering Pressure Sensor Circuit Low Input

P0553 Power Steering Pressure Sensor Circuit High Input

P0554 Power Steering Pressure Sensor Circuit Intermittent

P0560 System Voltage Malfunction

P0561 System Voltage Unstable

P0562 System Voltage Low

P0563 System Voltage High

P0565 Cruise Control On Signal Malfunction

P0566 Cruise Control Off Signal Malfunction

P0567 Cruise Control Resume Signal Malfunction

P0568 Cruise Control Set Signal Malfunction

P0569 Cruise Control Coast Signal Malfunction

P0570 Cruise Control Accel Signal Malfunction

P0571 Cruise Control/Brake Switch "A" Circuit Malfunction

P0572 Cruise Control/Brake Switch "A" Circuit Low

P0573 Cruise Control/Brake Switch "A" Circuit High

P0574 Through P0580 Reserved for Cruise Codes

P0600 Serial Communication Link Malfunction

P0601 Internal Control Module Memory Check Sum Error

P0602 Control Module Programming Error

P0603 Internal Control Module Keep Alive Memory (KAM) Error

P0604 Internal Control Module Random Access Memory (RAM) Error

P0605 Internal Control Module Read Only Memory (ROM) Error

P0606 PCM Processor Fault

P0608 Control Module VSS Output "A" Malfunction

P0609 Control Module VSS Output "B" Malfunction

P0620 Generator Control Circuit Malfunction

P0621 Generator Lamp "L" Control Circuit Malfunction

P0622 Generator Field "F" Control Circuit Malfunction

P0650 Malfunction Indicator Lamp (MIL) Control Circuit Malfunction

P0654 Engine RPM Output Circuit Malfunction

P0655 Engine Hot Lamp Output Control Circuit Malfunction

P0656 Fuel Level Output Circuit Malfunction

P0700 Transmission Control System Malfunction

P0701 Transmission Control System Range/Performance

P0702 Transmission Control System Electrical

P0703 Torque Converter/Brake Switch "B" Circuit Malfunction

P0704 Clutch Switch Input Circuit Malfunction

P0705 Transmission Range Sensor Circuit Malfunction (PRNDL Input)

P0706 Transmission Range Sensor Circuit Range/Performance

P0707 Transmission Range Sensor Circuit Low Input

P0708 Transmission Range Sensor Circuit High Input

P0709 Transmission Range Sensor Circuit Intermittent

P0710 Transmission Fluid Temperature Sensor Circuit Malfunction

P0711 Transmission Fluid Temperature Sensor Circuit Range/Performance

P0712 Transmission Fluid Temperature Sensor Circuit Low Input

P0713 Transmission Fluid Temperature Sensor Circuit High Input

P0714 Transmission Fluid Temperature Sensor Circuit Intermittent

P0715 Input/Turbine Speed Sensor Circuit Malfunction

P0716 Input/Turbine Speed Sensor Circuit Range/Performance

P0717 Input/Turbine Speed Sensor Circuit No Signal

P0718 Input/Turbine Speed Sensor Circuit Intermittent

P0719 Torque Converter/Brake Switch "B" Circuit Low

P0720 Output Speed Sensor Circuit Malfunction

P0721 Output Speed Sensor Circuit Range/Performance

P0722 Output Speed Sensor Circuit No Signal

P0723 Output Speed Sensor Circuit Intermittent

P0724 Torque Converter/Brake Switch "B" Circuit High

P0725 Engine Speed Input Circuit Malfunction

P0726 Engine Speed Input Circuit Range/Performance

P0727 Engine Speed Input Circuit No Signal

P0728 Engine Speed Input Circuit Intermittent

P0730 Incorrect Gear Ratio

P0731 Gear #1 Incorrect Ratio

P0732 Gear #2 Incorrect Ratio

P0733 Gear #3 Incorrect Ratio

P0734 Gear #4 Incorrect Ratio

P0735 Gear #5 Incorrect Ratio

P0736 Reverse Incorrect Ratio

P0740 Torque Converter Clutch Circuit Malfunction

P0741 Torque Converter Clutch Circuit Performance or Stuck Off

P0742 Torque Converter Clutch Circuit Stuck On

P0743 Torque Converter Clutch Circuit Electrical

P0744 Torque Converter Clutch Circuit Intermittent

P0745 Pressure Control Solenoid Malfunction

P0746 Pressure Control Solenoid Performance or Stuck Off

P0747 Pressure Control Solenoid Stuck On

P0748 Pressure Control Solenoid Electrical

P0749 Pressure Control Solenoid Intermittent

P0750 Shift Solenoid "A" Malfunction

P0751 Shift Solenoid "A" Performance or Stuck Off

P0752 Shift Solenoid "A" Stuck On

P0753 Shift Solenoid "A" Electrical

P0754 Shift Solenoid "A" Intermittent

P0755 Shift Solenoid "B" Malfunction

P0756 Shift Solenoid "B" Performance or Stuck Off

P0757 Shift Solenoid "B" Stuck On
P0758 Shift Solenoid "B" Electrical
P0759 Shift Solenoid "B" Intermittent
P0760 Shift Solenoid "C" Malfunction
P0761 Shift Solenoid "C" Performance Or Stuck Off
P0762 Shift Solenoid "C" Stuck On
P0763 Shift Solenoid "C" Electrical
P0764 Shift Solenoid "C" Intermittent
P0765 Shift Solenoid "D" Malfunction
P0766 Shift Solenoid "D" Performance Or Stuck Off
P0767 Shift Solenoid "D" Stuck On
P0768 Shift Solenoid "D" Electrical
P0769 Shift Solenoid "D" Intermittent
P0770 Shift Solenoid "E" Malfunction
P0771 Shift Solenoid "E" Performance Or Stuck Off
P0772 Shift Solenoid "E" Stuck On
P0773 Shift Solenoid "E" Electrical
P0774 Shift Solenoid "E" Intermittent
P0780 Shift Malfunction
P0781 1–2 Shift Malfunction
P0782 2–3 Shift Malfunction
P0783 3–4 Shift Malfunction
P0784 4–5 Shift Malfunction
P0785 Shift/Timing Solenoid Malfunction
P0786 Shift/Timing Solenoid Range/Performance
P0787 Shift/Timing Solenoid Low
P0788 Shift/Timing Solenoid High
P0789 Shift/Timing Solenoid Intermittent
P0790 Normal/Performance Switch Circuit Malfunction
P0801 Reverse Inhibit Control Circuit Malfunction
P0803 1–4 Upshift (Skip Shift) Solenoid Control Circuit Malfunction
P0804 1–4 Upshift (Skip Shift) Lamp Control Circuit Malfunction
P0740 Torque Converter Clutch System Fault
P0750 TCM Shift Solenoid "A" Electrical Fault
P0755 TCM Shift Solenoid "B" Electrical Fault
P0760 TCM Shift Solenoid "C" Electrical Fault
P1102 HO₂S-11 Heater Circuit High Voltage
P1105 HO₂S-12 Heater Circuit High Voltage
P1115 HO₂S-11 Heater Circuit Low Voltage
P1117 HO₂S-12 Heater Circuit Low Voltage
P1123 Long Term Fuel Trim Adaptive Air System Low

P1124 Long Term Fuel Trim Adaptive Air System High
P1127 Long Term Fuel Trim Multiplicative Air System Low
P1128 Long Term Fuel Trim Multiplicative Air System High
P1140 Load Calculation Cross Check
P1170 HO₂S-11 Circuit Voltage Stuck At Mid-Range
P1195 EGR Boost Or Pressure Sensor Circuit Fault
P1196 Ignition Switch Start Circuit Fault
P1213 Fuel Injector 1, 2, 3 Or 4 Circuit High Voltage
P1214 Fuel Injector 1, 2, 3 Or 4 Circuit High Voltage
P1215 Fuel Injector 1, 2, 3 Or 4 Circuit High Voltage
P1216 Fuel Injector 1, 2, 3 Or 4 Circuit High Voltage
P1225 Fuel Injector 1, 2, 5 Or 4 Circuit Low Voltage
P1226 Fuel Injector 1, 2, 5 Or 4 Circuit Low Voltage
P1227 Fuel Injector 1, 2, 5 Or 4 Circuit Low Voltage
P1228 Fuel Injector 1, 2, 5 Or 4 Circuit Low Voltage
P1250 Pressure Regulator Control Solenoid Circuit Fault
P1307 Chassis Acceleration Sensor Signal Malfunction
P1308 Chassis Acceleration Sensor Signal Low
P1309 Chassis Acceleration Sensor Signal High
P1345 No SGC (CMP) Signal To PCM
P1386 Knock Sensor Control Zero Test
P1401 EGR Control Solenoid Circuit Signal Low
P1402 EGR Control Solenoid Circuit Signal High
P1402 EGR Valve Position Sensor Circuit Fault
P1410 EVAP Purge Control Solenoid Circuit High Voltage
P1412 EGR Differential Pressure Sensor Signal Low
P1413 EGR Differential Pressure Sensor Signal High
P1425 EVAP Purge Control Solenoid Circuit Low Voltage
P1449 Canister Drain Cut Valve Solenoid Circuit Fault
P1455 Fuel Tank Sending Unit Circuit Fault
P1458 Air Conditioning Compressor Clutch Signal Fault

P1485 EGR Vent Control Solenoid Circuit Fault
P1486 EGR Vacuum Control Solenoid Circuit Fault
P1487 EGR Boost Sensor Solenoid Circuit Fault
P1505 Idle Air Control Valve Opening Coil Low Voltage
P1507 Idle Air Control Valve Opening Coil High Voltage
P1508 Idle Air Control Valve Closing Coil High Voltage
P1510 Idle Air Control Valve Closing Coil High Voltage
P1513 Idle Air Control Valve Closing Coil Low Voltage
P1515 A/T To M/T Codification
P1523 VICS Solenoid Valve Circuit Fault
P1552 Idle Air Control Valve Opening Coil Low Voltage
P1553 Idle Air Control Valve Opening Coil High Voltage
P1586 AT—MT Codification
P1606 Chassis Accelerator Sensor Signal Circuit Fault
P1608 PCM Internal Fault
P1611 MIL Request Circuit Low Voltage
P1614 MIL Request Circuit High Voltage
P1616 Chassis Accelerator Sensor Signal Low Voltage
P1617 Chassis Accelerator Sensor Signal High Voltage
P1624 TCM to PCM MIL Request Circuit Fault
P1655 Unused Power Stage "B"
P1660 Unused Power Stage "A"
P1660 Unused Power Stage "B"
P1665 Power Stage Group "A"
P1743 Torque Converter Clutch Solenoid Circuit Fault
P1794 Battery Or Circuit Fault
P1795 4WD Low Switch Signal Malfunction
P1797 Clutch Pedal Switch (MT) Or PIN Switch Circuit Fault

Land Rover

READING CODES

Reading the control module memory is one of the first steps in OBD II system diagnostics. This step should be initially performed to determine the general nature of the fault. Subsequent readings will determine if the fault has been cleared.

Reading codes can be performed by any of the methods below:

• Read the control module memory with the Generic Scan Tool (GST)

• Read the control module memory with the vehicle manufacturer's specific tester

To read the fault codes, connect the scan tool or tester according to the manufacturer's instructions. Follow the manufacturer's specified procedure for reading the codes.

CLEARING CODES

Control module reset procedures are a very important part of OBD II System diagnostics. This step should be done at the end of any fault code repair and at the end of any driveability repair.

Clearing codes can be performed by any of the methods below:

• Clear the control module memory with the Generic Scan Tool (GST)

• Clear the control module memory with the vehicle manufacturer's specific tester

• Turn the ignition OFF and remove the negative battery cable for at least 1 minute. Removing the negative battery cable may cause other systems in the vehicle to loose their memory. Prior to removing the cable, ensure you have the proper reset codes for radios and alarms.

➡ The MIL will may also be de-activated for some codes if the vehicle completes three consecutive trips without a fault detected with vehicle conditions similar to those present during the fault.

OBD II TROUBLE CODES

P0100 Mass or Volume Air Flow Circuit Malfunction

P0101 Mass or Volume Air Flow Circuit Range/Performance Problem

P0102 Mass or Volume Air Flow Circuit Low Input

P0103 Mass or Volume Air Flow Circuit High Input

P0104 Mass or Volume Air Flow Circuit Intermittent

P0105 Manifold Absolute Pressure/Barometric Pressure Circuit Malfunction

P0106 Manifold Absolute Pressure/Barometric Pressure Circuit Range/Performance Problem

P0107 Manifold Absolute Pressure/Barometric Pressure Circuit Low Input

P0108 Manifold Absolute Pressure/Barometric Pressure Circuit High Input

P0109 Manifold Absolute Pressure/Barometric Pressure Circuit Intermittent

P0110 Intake Air Temperature Circuit Malfunction

P0111 Intake Air Temperature Circuit Range/Performance Problem

P0112 Intake Air Temperature Circuit Low Input

P0113 Intake Air Temperature Circuit High Input

P0114 Intake Air Temperature Circuit Intermittent

P0115 Engine Coolant Temperature Circuit Malfunction

P0116 Engine Coolant Temperature Circuit Range/Performance Problem

P0117 Engine Coolant Temperature Circuit Low Input

P0118 Engine Coolant Temperature Circuit High Input

P0119 Engine Coolant Temperature Circuit Intermittent

P0120 Throttle/Pedal Position Sensor/Switch "A" Circuit Malfunction

P0121 Throttle/Pedal Position Sensor/Switch "A" Circuit Range/Performance Problem

P0122 Throttle/Pedal Position Sensor/Switch "A" Circuit Low Input

P0123 Throttle/Pedal Position Sensor/Switch "A" Circuit High Input

P0124 Throttle/Pedal Position Sensor/Switch "A" Circuit Intermittent

P0125 Insufficient Coolant Temperature For Closed Loop Fuel Control

P0126 Insufficient Coolant Temperature For Stable Operation

P0130 O_2 Circuit Malfunction (Bank #1 Sensor #1)

P0131 O_2 Sensor Circuit Low Voltage (Bank #1 Sensor #1)

P0132 O_2 Sensor Circuit High Voltage (Bank #1 Sensor #1)

P0133 O_2 Sensor Circuit Slow Response (Bank #1 Sensor #1)

P0134 O_2 Sensor Circuit No Activity Detected (Bank #1 Sensor #1)

P0135 O_2 Sensor Heater Circuit Malfunction (Bank #1 Sensor #1)

P0136 O_2 Sensor Circuit Malfunction (Bank #1 Sensor #2)

P0137 O_2 Sensor Circuit Low Voltage (Bank #1 Sensor #2)

P0138 O_2 Sensor Circuit High Voltage (Bank #1 Sensor #2)

P0139 O_2 Sensor Circuit Slow Response (Bank #1 Sensor #2)

P0140 O_2 Sensor Circuit No Activity Detected (Bank #1 Sensor #2)

P0141 O_2 Sensor Heater Circuit Malfunction (Bank #1 Sensor #2)

P0142 O_2 Sensor Circuit Malfunction (Bank #1 Sensor #3)

P0143 O_2 Sensor Circuit Low Voltage (Bank #1 Sensor #3)

P0144 O_2 Sensor Circuit High Voltage (Bank #1 Sensor #3)

P0145 O_2 Sensor Circuit Slow Response (Bank #1 Sensor #3)

P0146 O_2 Sensor Circuit No Activity Detected (Bank #1 Sensor #3)

P0147 O_2 Sensor Heater Circuit Malfunction (Bank #1 Sensor #3)

P0150 O_2 Sensor Circuit Malfunction (Bank #2 Sensor #1)

P0151 O_2 Sensor Circuit Low Voltage (Bank #2 Sensor #1)

P0152 O_2 Sensor Circuit High Voltage (Bank #2 Sensor #1)

P0153 O_2 Sensor Circuit Slow Response (Bank #2 Sensor #1)

P0154 O_2 Sensor Circuit No Activity Detected (Bank #2 Sensor #1)

P0155 O_2 Sensor Heater Circuit Malfunction (Bank #2 Sensor #1)

P0156 O_2 Sensor Circuit Malfunction (Bank #2 Sensor #2)

P0157 O_2 Sensor Circuit Low Voltage (Bank #2 Sensor #2)

P0158 O_2 Sensor Circuit High Voltage (Bank #2 Sensor #2)

P0159 O_2 Sensor Circuit Slow Response (Bank #2 Sensor #2)

P0160 O_2 Sensor Circuit No Activity Detected (Bank #2 Sensor #2)

P0161 O_2 Sensor Heater Circuit Malfunction (Bank #2 Sensor #2)

P0162 O_2 Sensor Circuit Malfunction (Bank #2 Sensor #3)

P0163 O_2 Sensor Circuit Low Voltage (Bank #2 Sensor #3)

P0164 O_2 Sensor Circuit High Voltage (Bank #2 Sensor #3)

P0165 O_2 Sensor Circuit Slow Response (Bank #2 Sensor #3)

P0166 O_2 Sensor Circuit No Activity Detected (Bank #2 Sensor #3)

P0167 O_2 Sensor Heater Circuit Malfunction (Bank #2 Sensor #3)

P0170 Fuel Trim Malfunction (Bank #1)

P0171 System Too Lean (Bank #1)

P0172 System Too Rich (Bank #1)

P0173 Fuel Trim Malfunction (Bank #2)

P0174 System Too Lean (Bank #2)

P0175 System Too Rich (Bank #2)

P0176 Fuel Composition Sensor Circuit Malfunction

P0177 Fuel Composition Sensor Circuit Range/Performance

P0178 Fuel Composition Sensor Circuit Low Input

P0179 Fuel Composition Sensor Circuit High Input

P0180 Fuel Temperature Sensor "A" Circuit Malfunction

P0181 Fuel Temperature Sensor "A" Circuit Range/Performance

P0182 Fuel Temperature Sensor "A" Circuit Low Input

P0183 Fuel Temperature Sensor "A" Circuit High Input

P0184 Fuel Temperature Sensor "A" Circuit Intermittent

P0185 Fuel Temperature Sensor "B" Circuit Malfunction

P0186 Fuel Temperature Sensor "B" Circuit Range/Performance

P0187 Fuel Temperature Sensor "B" Circuit Low Input

P0188 Fuel Temperature Sensor "B" Circuit High Input

P0189 Fuel Temperature Sensor "B" Circuit Intermittent

P0190 Fuel Rail Pressure Sensor Circuit Malfunction

P0191 Fuel Rail Pressure Sensor Circuit Range/Performance

P0192 Fuel Rail Pressure Sensor Circuit Low Input

P0193 Fuel Rail Pressure Sensor Circuit High Input

P0194 Fuel Rail Pressure Sensor Circuit Intermittent

P0195 Engine Oil Temperature Sensor Malfunction

P0196 Engine Oil Temperature Sensor Range/Performance

P0197 Engine Oil Temperature Sensor Low

P0198 Engine Oil Temperature Sensor High

P0199 Engine Oil Temperature Sensor Intermittent

P0200 Injector Circuit Malfunction

P0201 Injector Circuit Malfunction—Cylinder #1

P0202 Injector Circuit Malfunction—Cylinder #2

P0203 Injector Circuit Malfunction—Cylinder #3

P0204 Injector Circuit Malfunction—Cylinder #4

P0205 Injector Circuit Malfunction—Cylinder #5

P0206 Injector Circuit Malfunction—Cylinder #6

P0207 Injector Circuit Malfunction—Cylinder #7

P0208 Injector Circuit Malfunction—Cylinder #8

P0209 Injector Circuit Malfunction—Cylinder #9

P0210 Injector Circuit Malfunction—Cylinder #10

P0211 Injector Circuit Malfunction—Cylinder #11

P0212 Injector Circuit Malfunction—Cylinder #12

P0213 Cold Start Injector #1 Malfunction

P0214 Cold Start Injector #2 Malfunction

P0215 Engine Shutoff Solenoid Malfunction

P0216 Injection Timing Control Circuit Malfunction

P0217 Engine Over Temperature Condition

P0218 Transmission Over Temperature Condition

P0219 Engine Over Speed Condition

P0220 Throttle/Pedal Position Sensor/Switch "B" Circuit Malfunction

P0221 Throttle/Pedal Position Sensor/Switch "B" Circuit Range/Performance Problem

P0222 Throttle/Pedal Position Sensor/Switch "B" Circuit Low Input

P0223 Throttle/Pedal Position Sensor/Switch "B" Circuit High Input

P0224 Throttle/Pedal Position Sensor/Switch "B" Circuit Intermittent

P0225 Throttle/Pedal Position Sensor/Switch "C" Circuit Malfunction

P0226 Throttle/Pedal Position Sensor/Switch "C" Circuit Range/Performance Problem

P0227 Throttle/Pedal Position Sensor/Switch "C" Circuit Low Input

P0228 Throttle/Pedal Position Sensor/Switch "C" Circuit High Input

P0229 Throttle/Pedal Position Sensor/Switch "C" Circuit Intermittent

P0230 Fuel Pump Primary Circuit Malfunction

P0231 Fuel Pump Secondary Circuit Low

P0232 Fuel Pump Secondary Circuit High

P0233 Fuel Pump Secondary Circuit Intermittent

P0234 Engine Over Boost Condition

P0261 Cylinder #1 Injector Circuit Low

P0262 Cylinder #1 Injector Circuit High

P0263 Cylinder #1 Contribution/Balance Fault

P0264 Cylinder #2 Injector Circuit Low

P0265 Cylinder #2 Injector Circuit High

P0266 Cylinder #2 Contribution/Balance Fault

P0267 Cylinder #3 Injector Circuit Low

P0268 Cylinder #3 Injector Circuit High

P0269 Cylinder #3 Contribution/Balance Fault

P0270 Cylinder #4 Injector Circuit Low

P0271 Cylinder #4 Injector Circuit High

P0272 Cylinder #4 Contribution/Balance Fault

P0273 Cylinder #5 Injector Circuit Low

P0274 Cylinder #5 Injector Circuit High

P0275 Cylinder #5 Contribution/Balance Fault

P0276 Cylinder #6 Injector Circuit Low

P0277 Cylinder #6 Injector Circuit High

P0278 Cylinder #6 Contribution/Balance Fault

P0279 Cylinder #7 Injector Circuit Low

P0280 Cylinder #7 Injector Circuit High

P0281 Cylinder #7 Contribution/Balance Fault

P0282 Cylinder #8 Injector Circuit Low

P0283 Cylinder #8 Injector Circuit High

P0284 Cylinder #8 Contribution/Balance Fault

P0285 Cylinder #9 Injector Circuit Low

P0286 Cylinder #9 Injector Circuit High

P0287 Cylinder #9 Contribution/Balance Fault

P0288 Cylinder #10 Injector Circuit Low

P0289 Cylinder #10 Injector Circuit High

P0290 Cylinder #10 Contribution/Balance Fault

P0291 Cylinder #11 Injector Circuit Low

P0292 Cylinder #11 Injector Circuit High

P0293 Cylinder #11 Contribution/Balance Fault

P0294 Cylinder #12 Injector Circuit Low

P0295 Cylinder #12 Injector Circuit High

P0296 Cylinder #12 Contribution/Balance Fault

P0300 Random/Multiple Cylinder Misfire Detected

P0301 Cylinder #1—Misfire Detected

P0302 Cylinder #2—Misfire Detected

P0303 Cylinder #3—Misfire Detected

P0304 Cylinder #4—Misfire Detected

P0305 Cylinder #5—Misfire Detected

P0306 Cylinder #6—Misfire Detected

P0307 Cylinder #7—Misfire Detected

P0308 Cylinder #8—Misfire Detected

P0309 Cylinder #9—Misfire Detected

P0310 Cylinder #10—Misfire Detected

P0311 Cylinder #11—Misfire Detected

P0312 Cylinder #12—Misfire Detected

P0320 Ignition/Distributor Engine Speed Input Circuit Malfunction

Refer to the model specific sections for fuel system service procedures

P0321 Ignition/Distributor Engine Speed Input Circuit Range/Performance

P0322 Ignition/Distributor Engine Speed Input Circuit No Signal

P0323 Ignition/Distributor Engine Speed Input Circuit Intermittent

P0325 Knock Sensor #1—Circuit Malfunction (Bank #1 or Single Sensor)

P0326 Knock Sensor #1—Circuit Range/Performance (Bank #1 or Single Sensor)

P0327 Knock Sensor #1—Circuit Low Input (Bank #1 or Single Sensor)

P0328 Knock Sensor #1—Circuit High Input (Bank #1 or Single Sensor)

P0329 Knock Sensor #1—Circuit Input Intermittent (Bank #1 or Single Sensor)

P0330 Knock Sensor #2—Circuit Malfunction (Bank #2)

P0331 Knock Sensor #2—Circuit Range/Performance (Bank #2)

P0332 Knock Sensor #2—Circuit Low Input (Bank #2)

P0333 Knock Sensor #2—Circuit High Input (Bank #2)

P0334 Knock Sensor #2—Circuit Input Intermittent (Bank #2)

P0335 Crankshaft Position Sensor "A" Circuit Malfunction

P0336 Crankshaft Position Sensor "A" Circuit Range/Performance

P0337 Crankshaft Position Sensor "A" Circuit Low Input

P0338 Crankshaft Position Sensor "A" Circuit High Input

P0339 Crankshaft Position Sensor "A" Circuit Intermittent

P0340 Camshaft Position Sensor Circuit Malfunction

P0341 Camshaft Position Sensor Circuit Range/Performance

P0342 Camshaft Position Sensor Circuit Low Input

P0343 Camshaft Position Sensor Circuit High Input

P0344 Camshaft Position Sensor Circuit Intermittent

P0350 Ignition Coil Primary/Secondary Circuit Malfunction

P0351 Ignition Coil "A" Primary/Secondary Circuit Malfunction

P0352 Ignition Coil "B" Primary/Secondary Circuit Malfunction

P0353 Ignition Coil "C" Primary/Secondary Circuit Malfunction

P0354 Ignition Coil "D" Primary/Secondary Circuit Malfunction

P0355 Ignition Coil "E" Primary/Secondary Circuit Malfunction

P0356 Ignition Coil "F" Primary/Secondary Circuit Malfunction

P0357 Ignition Coil "G" Primary/Secondary Circuit Malfunction

P0358 Ignition Coil "H" Primary/Secondary Circuit Malfunction

P0359 Ignition Coil "I" Primary/Secondary Circuit Malfunction

P0360 Ignition Coil "J" Primary/Secondary Circuit Malfunction

P0361 Ignition Coil "K" Primary/Secondary Circuit Malfunction

P0362 Ignition Coil "L" Primary/Secondary Circuit Malfunction

P0370 Timing Reference High Resolution Signal "A" Malfunction

P0371 Timing Reference High Resolution Signal "A" Too Many Pulses

P0372 Timing Reference High Resolution Signal "A" Too Few Pulses

P0373 Timing Reference High Resolution Signal "A" Intermittent/Erratic Pulses

P0374 Timing Reference High Resolution Signal "A" No Pulses

P0375 Timing Reference High Resolution Signal "B" Malfunction

P0376 Timing Reference High Resolution Signal "B" Too Many Pulses

P0377 Timing Reference High Resolution Signal "B" Too Few Pulses

P0378 Timing Reference High Resolution Signal "B" Intermittent/Erratic Pulses

P0379 Timing Reference High Resolution Signal "B" No Pulses

P0380 Glow Plug/Heater Circuit "A" Malfunction

P0381 Glow Plug/Heater Indicator Circuit Malfunction

P0382 Glow Plug/Heater Circuit "B" Malfunction

P0385 Crankshaft Position Sensor "B" Circuit Malfunction

P0386 Crankshaft Position Sensor "B" Circuit Range/Performance

P0387 Crankshaft Position Sensor "B" Circuit Low Input

P0388 Crankshaft Position Sensor "B" Circuit High Input

P0389 Crankshaft Position Sensor "B" Circuit Intermittent

P0400 Exhaust Gas Recirculation Flow Malfunction

P0401 Exhaust Gas Recirculation Flow Insufficient Detected

P0402 Exhaust Gas Recirculation Flow Excessive Detected

P0403 Exhaust Gas Recirculation Circuit Malfunction

P0404 Exhaust Gas Recirculation Circuit Range/Performance

P0405 Exhaust Gas Recirculation Sensor "A" Circuit Low

P0406 Exhaust Gas Recirculation Sensor "A" Circuit High

P0407 Exhaust Gas Recirculation Sensor "B" Circuit Low

P0408 Exhaust Gas Recirculation Sensor "B" Circuit High

P0410 Secondary Air Injection System Malfunction

P0411 Secondary Air Injection System Incorrect Flow Detected

P0412 Secondary Air Injection System Switching Valve "A" Circuit Malfunction

P0413 Secondary Air Injection System Switching Valve "A" Circuit Open

P0414 Secondary Air Injection System Switching Valve "A" Circuit Shorted

P0415 Secondary Air Injection System Switching Valve "B" Circuit Malfunction

P0416 Secondary Air Injection System Switching Valve "B" Circuit Open

P0417 Secondary Air Injection System Switching Valve "B" Circuit Shorted

P0418 Secondary Air Injection System Relay "A" Circuit Malfunction

P0419 Secondary Air Injection System Relay "B" Circuit Malfunction

P0420 Catalyst System Efficiency Below Threshold (Bank #1)

P0421 Warm Up Catalyst Efficiency Below Threshold (Bank #1)

P0422 Main Catalyst Efficiency Below Threshold (Bank #1)

P0423 Heated Catalyst Efficiency Below Threshold (Bank #1)

P0424 Heated Catalyst Temperature Below Threshold (Bank #1)

P0430 Catalyst System Efficiency Below Threshold (Bank #2)

P0431 Warm Up Catalyst Efficiency Below Threshold (Bank #2)

P0432 Main Catalyst Efficiency Below Threshold (Bank #2)

P0433 Heated Catalyst Efficiency Below Threshold (Bank #2)

P0434 Heated Catalyst Temperature Below Threshold (Bank #2)

P0440 Evaporative Emission Control System Malfunction

P0441 Evaporative Emission Control System Incorrect Purge Flow

P0442 Evaporative Emission Control System Leak Detected (Small Leak)

P0443 Evaporative Emission Control System Purge Control Valve Circuit Malfunction

P0444 Evaporative Emission Control System Purge Control Valve Circuit Open

P0445 Evaporative Emission Control System Purge Control Valve Circuit Shorted

P0446 Evaporative Emission Control System Vent Control Circuit Malfunction

P0447 Evaporative Emission Control System Vent Control Circuit Open

P0448 Evaporative Emission Control System Vent Control Circuit Shorted

P0449 Evaporative Emission Control System Vent Valve/Solenoid Circuit Malfunction

P0450 Evaporative Emission Control System Pressure Sensor Malfunction

P0451 Evaporative Emission Control System Pressure Sensor Range/Performance

P0452 Evaporative Emission Control System Pressure Sensor Low Input

P0453 Evaporative Emission Control System Pressure Sensor High Input

P0454 Evaporative Emission Control System Pressure Sensor Intermittent

P0455 Evaporative Emission Control System Leak Detected (Gross Leak)

P0460 Fuel Level Sensor Circuit Malfunction

P0461 Fuel Level Sensor Circuit Range/Performance

P0462 Fuel Level Sensor Circuit Low Input

P0463 Fuel Level Sensor Circuit High Input

P0464 Fuel Level Sensor Circuit Intermittent

P0465 Purge Flow Sensor Circuit Malfunction

P0466 Purge Flow Sensor Circuit Range/Performance

P0467 Purge Flow Sensor Circuit Low Input

P0468 Purge Flow Sensor Circuit High Input

P0469 Purge Flow Sensor Circuit Intermittent

P0470 Exhaust Pressure Sensor Malfunction

P0471 Exhaust Pressure Sensor Range/Performance

P0472 Exhaust Pressure Sensor Low

P0473 Exhaust Pressure Sensor High

P0474 Exhaust Pressure Sensor Intermittent

P0475 Exhaust Pressure Control Valve Malfunction

P0476 Exhaust Pressure Control Valve Range/Performance

P0477 Exhaust Pressure Control Valve Low

P0478 Exhaust Pressure Control Valve High

P0479 Exhaust Pressure Control Valve Intermittent

P0480 Cooling Fan #1 Control Circuit Malfunction

P0481 Cooling Fan #2 Control Circuit Malfunction

P0482 Cooling Fan #3 Control Circuit Malfunction

P0483 Cooling Fan Rationality Check Malfunction

P0484 Cooling Fan Circuit Over Current

P0485 Cooling Fan Power/Ground Circuit Malfunction

P0500 Vehicle Speed Sensor Malfunction

P0501 Vehicle Speed Sensor Range/Performance

P0502 Vehicle Speed Sensor Circuit Low Input

P0503 Vehicle Speed Sensor Intermittent/Erratic/High

P0505 Idle Control System Malfunction

P0506 Idle Control System RPM Lower Than Expected

P0507 Idle Control System RPM Higher Than Expected

P0510 Closed Throttle Position Switch Malfunction

P0520 Engine Oil Pressure Sensor/Switch Circuit Malfunction

P0521 Engine Oil Pressure Sensor/Switch Range/Performance

P0522 Engine Oil Pressure Sensor/Switch Low Voltage

P0523 Engine Oil Pressure Sensor/Switch High Voltage

P0530 A/C Refrigerant Pressure Sensor Circuit Malfunction

P0531 A/C Refrigerant Pressure Sensor Circuit Range/Performance

P0532 A/C Refrigerant Pressure Sensor Circuit Low Input

P0533 A/C Refrigerant Pressure Sensor Circuit High Input

P0534 A/C Refrigerant Charge Loss

P0550 Power Steering Pressure Sensor Circuit Malfunction

P0551 Power Steering Pressure Sensor Circuit Range/Performance

P0552 Power Steering Pressure Sensor Circuit Low Input

P0553 Power Steering Pressure Sensor Circuit High Input

P0554 Power Steering Pressure Sensor Circuit Intermittent

P0560 System Voltage Malfunction

P0561 System Voltage Unstable

P0562 System Voltage Low

P0563 System Voltage High

P0565 Cruise Control On Signal Malfunction

P0566 Cruise Control Off Signal Malfunction

P0567 Cruise Control Resume Signal Malfunction

P0568 Cruise Control Set Signal Malfunction

P0569 Cruise Control Coast Signal Malfunction

P0570 Cruise Control Accel Signal Malfunction

P0571 Cruise Control/Brake Switch "A" Circuit Malfunction

P0572 Cruise Control/Brake Switch "A" Circuit Low

P0573 Cruise Control/Brake Switch "A" Circuit High

P0574 Through P0580 Reserved for Cruise Codes

P0600 Serial Communication Link Malfunction

P0601 Internal Control Module Memory Check Sum Error

P0602 Control Module Programming Error

P0603 Internal Control Module Keep Alive Memory (KAM) Error

P0604 Internal Control Module Random Access Memory (RAM) Error

P0605 Internal Control Module Read Only Memory (ROM) Error

P0606 PCM Processor Fault

P0608 Control Module VSS Output "A" Malfunction

P0609 Control Module VSS Output "B" Malfunction

P0620 Generator Control Circuit Malfunction

P0621 Generator Lamp "L" Control Circuit Malfunction

P0622 Generator Field "F" Control Circuit Malfunction

P0650 Malfunction Indicator Lamp (MIL) Control Circuit Malfunction

P0654 Engine RPM Output Circuit Malfunction

P0655 Engine Hot Lamp Output Control Circuit Malfunction

P0656 Fuel Level Output Circuit Malfunction

P0700 Transmission Control System Malfunction

P0701 Transmission Control System Range/Performance

P0702 Transmission Control System Electrical

P0703 Torque Converter/Brake Switch "B" Circuit Malfunction

P0704 Clutch Switch Input Circuit Malfunction

P0705 Transmission Range Sensor Circuit Malfunction (PRNDL Input)

P0706 Transmission Range Sensor Circuit Range/Performance

Refer to the model specific sections for engine electrical system service procedures

P0707 Transmission Range Sensor Circuit Low Input

P0708 Transmission Range Sensor Circuit High Input

P0709 Transmission Range Sensor Circuit Intermittent

P0710 Transmission Fluid Temperature Sensor Circuit Malfunction

P0711 Transmission Fluid Temperature Sensor Circuit Range/Performance

P0712 Transmission Fluid Temperature Sensor Circuit Low Input

P0713 Transmission Fluid Temperature Sensor Circuit High Input

P0714 Transmission Fluid Temperature Sensor Circuit Intermittent

P0715 Input/Turbine Speed Sensor Circuit Malfunction

P0716 Input/Turbine Speed Sensor Circuit Range/Performance

P0717 Input/Turbine Speed Sensor Circuit No Signal

P0718 Input/Turbine Speed Sensor Circuit Intermittent

P0719 Torque Converter/Brake Switch "B" Circuit Low

P0720 Output Speed Sensor Circuit Malfunction

P0721 Output Speed Sensor Circuit Range/Performance

P0722 Output Speed Sensor Circuit No Signal

P0723 Output Speed Sensor Circuit Intermittent

P0724 Torque Converter/Brake Switch "B" Circuit High

P0725 Engine Speed Input Circuit Malfunction

P0726 Engine Speed Input Circuit Range/Performance

P0727 Engine Speed Input Circuit No Signal

P0728 Engine Speed Input Circuit Intermittent

P0730 Incorrect Gear Ratio

P0731 Gear #1 Incorrect Ratio

P0732 Gear #2 Incorrect Ratio

P0733 Gear #3 Incorrect Ratio

P0734 Gear #4 Incorrect Ratio

P0735 Gear #5 Incorrect Ratio

P0736 Reverse Incorrect Ratio

P0740 Torque Converter Clutch Circuit Malfunction

P0741 Torque Converter Clutch Circuit Performance or Stuck Off

P0742 Torque Converter Clutch Circuit Stuck On

P0743 Torque Converter Clutch Circuit Electrical

P0744 Torque Converter Clutch Circuit Intermittent

P0745 Pressure Control Solenoid Malfunction

P0746 Pressure Control Solenoid Performance or Stuck Off

P0747 Pressure Control Solenoid Stuck On

P0748 Pressure Control Solenoid Electrical

P0749 Pressure Control Solenoid Intermittent

P0750 Shift Solenoid "A" Malfunction

P0751 Shift Solenoid "A" Performance or Stuck Off

P0752 Shift Solenoid "A" Stuck On

P0753 Shift Solenoid "A" Electrical

P0754 Shift Solenoid "A" Intermittent

P0755 Shift Solenoid "B" Malfunction

P0756 Shift Solenoid "B" Performance or Stuck Off

P0757 Shift Solenoid "B" Stuck On

P0758 Shift Solenoid "B" Electrical

P0759 Shift Solenoid "B" Intermittent

P0760 Shift Solenoid "C" Malfunction

P0761 Shift Solenoid "C" Performance Or Stuck Off

P0762 Shift Solenoid "C" Stuck On

P0763 Shift Solenoid "C" Electrical

P0764 Shift Solenoid "C" Intermittent

P0765 Shift Solenoid "D" Malfunction

P0766 Shift Solenoid "D" Performance Or Stuck Off

P0767 Shift Solenoid "D" Stuck On

P0768 Shift Solenoid "D" Electrical

P0769 Shift Solenoid "D" Intermittent

P0770 Shift Solenoid "E" Malfunction

P0771 Shift Solenoid "E" Performance Or Stuck Off

P0772 Shift Solenoid "E" Stuck On

P0773 Shift Solenoid "E" Electrical

P0774 Shift Solenoid "E" Intermittent

P0780 Shift Malfunction

P0781 1–2 Shift Malfunction

P0782 2–3 Shift Malfunction

P0783 3–4 Shift Malfunction

P0784 4–5 Shift Malfunction

P0785 Shift/Timing Solenoid Malfunction

P0786 Shift/Timing Solenoid Range/Performance

P0787 Shift/Timing Solenoid Low

P0788 Shift/Timing Solenoid High

P0789 Shift/Timing Solenoid Intermittent

P0790 Normal/Performance Switch Circuit Malfunction

P0801 Reverse Inhibit Control Circuit Malfunction

P0803 1–4 Upshift (Skip Shift) Solenoid Control Circuit Malfunction

P0804 1–4 Upshift (Skip Shift) Lamp Control Circuit Malfunction

Lexus

READING CODES

Reading the control module memory is one of the first steps in OBD II system diagnostics. This step should be initially performed to determine the general nature of the fault. Subsequent readings will determine if the fault has been cleared.

Reading codes can be performed by any of the methods below:
- Read the control module memory with the Generic Scan Tool (GST)
- Read the control module memory with the vehicle manufacturer's specific tester

To read the fault codes, connect the scan tool or tester according to the manufacturer's instructions. Follow the manufacturer's specified procedure for reading the codes.

CLEARING CODES

Control module reset procedures are a very important part of OBD II System diagnostics. This step should be done at the end of any fault code repair and at the end of any driveability repair.

Clearing codes can be performed by any of the methods below:
- Clear the control module memory with the Generic Scan Tool (GST)
- Clear the control module memory with the vehicle manufacturer's specific tester
- Turn the ignition OFF and remove the negative battery cable for at least 1 minute.

Removing the negative battery cable may cause other systems in the vehicle to loose their memory. Prior to removing the cable, ensure you have the proper reset codes for radios and alarms.

➡ **The MIL will may also be de-activated for some codes if the vehicle completes three consecutive trips without a fault detected with vehicle conditions similar to those present during the fault.**

OBD II TROUBLE CODES

P0100 Mass or Volume Air Flow Circuit Malfunction

P0101 Mass or Volume Air Flow Circuit Range/Performance Problem

P0102 Mass or Volume Air Flow Circuit Low Input

P0103 Mass or Volume Air Flow Circuit High Input

P0104 Mass or Volume Air Flow Circuit Intermittent

P0105 Manifold Absolute Pressure/Barometric Pressure Circuit Malfunction

P0106 Manifold Absolute Pressure/Barometric Pressure Circuit Range/Performance Problem

P0107 Manifold Absolute Pressure/Barometric Pressure Circuit Low Input

P0108 Manifold Absolute Pressure/Barometric Pressure Circuit High Input

P0109 Manifold Absolute Pressure/Barometric Pressure Circuit Intermittent

P0110 Intake Air Temperature Circuit Malfunction

P0111 Intake Air Temperature Circuit Range/Performance Problem

P0112 Intake Air Temperature Circuit Low Input

P0113 Intake Air Temperature Circuit High Input

P0114 Intake Air Temperature Circuit Intermittent

P0115 Engine Coolant Temperature Circuit Malfunction

P0116 Engine Coolant Temperature Circuit Range/Performance Problem

P0117 Engine Coolant Temperature Circuit Low Input

P0118 Engine Coolant Temperature Circuit High Input

P0119 Engine Coolant Temperature Circuit Intermittent

P0120 Throttle/Pedal Position Sensor/Switch "A" Circuit Malfunction

P0121 Throttle/Pedal Position Sensor/Switch "A" Circuit Range/Performance Problem

P0122 Throttle/Pedal Position Sensor/Switch "A" Circuit Low Input

P0123 Throttle/Pedal Position Sensor/Switch "A" Circuit High Input

P0124 Throttle/Pedal Position Sensor/Switch "A" Circuit Intermittent

P0125 Insufficient Coolant Temperature For Closed Loop Fuel Control

P0126 Insufficient Coolant Temperature For Stable Operation

P0130 O_2 Circuit Malfunction (Bank #1 Sensor #1)

P0131 O_2 Sensor Circuit Low Voltage (Bank #1 Sensor #1)

P0132 O_2 Sensor Circuit High Voltage (Bank #1 Sensor #1)

P0133 O_2 Sensor Circuit Slow Response (Bank #1 Sensor #1)

P0134 O_2 Sensor Circuit No Activity Detected (Bank #1 Sensor #1)

P0135 O_2 Sensor Heater Circuit Malfunction (Bank #1 Sensor #1)

P0136 O_2 Sensor Circuit Malfunction (Bank #1 Sensor #2)

P0137 O_2 Sensor Circuit Low Voltage (Bank #1 Sensor #2)

P0138 O_2 Sensor Circuit High Voltage (Bank #1 Sensor #2)

P0139 O_2 Sensor Circuit Slow Response (Bank #1 Sensor #2)

P0140 O_2 Sensor Circuit No Activity Detected (Bank #1 Sensor #2)

P0141 O_2 Sensor Heater Circuit Malfunction (Bank #1 Sensor #2)

P0142 O_2 Sensor Circuit Malfunction (Bank #1 Sensor #3)

P0143 O_2 Sensor Circuit Low Voltage (Bank #1 Sensor #3)

P0144 O_2 Sensor Circuit High Voltage (Bank #1 Sensor #3)

P0145 O_2 Sensor Circuit Slow Response (Bank #1 Sensor #3)

P0146 O_2 Sensor Circuit No Activity Detected (Bank #1 Sensor #3)

P0147 O_2 Sensor Heater Circuit Malfunction (Bank #1 Sensor #3)

P0150 O_2 Sensor Circuit Malfunction (Bank #2 Sensor #1)

P0151 O_2 Sensor Circuit Low Voltage (Bank #2 Sensor #1)

P0152 O_2 Sensor Circuit High Voltage (Bank #2 Sensor #1)

P0153 O_2 Sensor Circuit Slow Response (Bank #2 Sensor #1)

P0154 O_2 Sensor Circuit No Activity Detected (Bank #2 Sensor #1)

P0155 O_2 Sensor Heater Circuit Malfunction (Bank #2 Sensor #1)

P0156 O_2 Sensor Circuit Malfunction (Bank #2 Sensor #2)

P0157 O_2 Sensor Circuit Low Voltage (Bank #2 Sensor #2)

P0158 O_2 Sensor Circuit High Voltage (Bank #2 Sensor #2)

P0159 O_2 Sensor Circuit Slow Response (Bank #2 Sensor #2)

P0160 O_2 Sensor Circuit No Activity Detected (Bank #2 Sensor #2)

P0161 O_2 Sensor Heater Circuit Malfunction (Bank #2 Sensor #2)

P0162 O_2 Sensor Circuit Malfunction (Bank #2 Sensor #3)

P0163 O_2 Sensor Circuit Low Voltage (Bank #2 Sensor #3)

P0164 O_2 Sensor Circuit High Voltage (Bank #2 Sensor #3)

P0165 O_2 Sensor Circuit Slow Response (Bank #2 Sensor #3)

P0166 O_2 Sensor Circuit No Activity Detected (Bank #2 Sensor #3)

P0167 O_2 Sensor Heater Circuit Malfunction (Bank #2 Sensor #3)

P0170 Fuel Trim Malfunction (Bank #1)

P0171 System Too Lean (Bank #1)

P0172 System Too Rich (Bank #1)

P0173 Fuel Trim Malfunction (Bank #2)

P0174 System Too Lean (Bank #2)

P0175 System Too Rich (Bank #2)

P0176 Fuel Composition Sensor Circuit Malfunction

P0177 Fuel Composition Sensor Circuit Range/Performance

P0178 Fuel Composition Sensor Circuit Low Input

P0179 Fuel Composition Sensor Circuit High Input

P0180 Fuel Temperature Sensor "A" Circuit Malfunction

P0181 Fuel Temperature Sensor "A" Circuit Range/Performance

P0182 Fuel Temperature Sensor "A" Circuit Low Input

P0183 Fuel Temperature Sensor "A" Circuit High Input

P0184 Fuel Temperature Sensor "A" Circuit Intermittent

P0185 Fuel Temperature Sensor "B" Circuit Malfunction

P0186 Fuel Temperature Sensor "B" Circuit Range/Performance

P0187 Fuel Temperature Sensor "B" Circuit Low Input

P0188 Fuel Temperature Sensor "B" Circuit High Input

P0189 Fuel Temperature Sensor "B" Circuit Intermittent

P0190 Fuel Rail Pressure Sensor Circuit Malfunction

P0191 Fuel Rail Pressure Sensor Circuit Range/Performance

P0192 Fuel Rail Pressure Sensor Circuit Low Input

P0193 Fuel Rail Pressure Sensor Circuit High Input

P0194 Fuel Rail Pressure Sensor Circuit Intermittent

P0195 Engine Oil Temperature Sensor Malfunction

P0196 Engine Oil Temperature Sensor Range/Performance

P0197 Engine Oil Temperature Sensor Low

P0198 Engine Oil Temperature Sensor High

P0199 Engine Oil Temperature Sensor Intermittent

P0200 Injector Circuit Malfunction

P0201 Injector Circuit Malfunction—Cylinder #1

P0202 Injector Circuit Malfunction—Cylinder #2

P0203 Injector Circuit Malfunction—Cylinder #3

P0204 Injector Circuit Malfunction—Cylinder #4

P0205 Injector Circuit Malfunction—Cylinder #5

P0206 Injector Circuit Malfunction—Cylinder #6

P0207 Injector Circuit Malfunction—Cylinder #7

P0208 Injector Circuit Malfunction—Cylinder #8

P0209 Injector Circuit Malfunction—Cylinder #9

P0210 Injector Circuit Malfunction—Cylinder #10

P0211 Injector Circuit Malfunction—Cylinder #11

P0212 Injector Circuit Malfunction—Cylinder #12

P0213 Cold Start Injector #1 Malfunction

P0214 Cold Start Injector #2 Malfunction

P0215 Engine Shutoff Solenoid Malfunction

P0216 Injection Timing Control Circuit Malfunction

P0217 Engine Over Temperature Condition

P0218 Transmission Over Temperature Condition

P0219 Engine Over Speed Condition

P0220 Throttle/Pedal Position Sensor/Switch "B" Circuit Malfunction

P0221 Throttle/Pedal Position Sensor/Switch "B" Circuit Range/Performance Problem

P0222 Throttle/Pedal Position Sensor/Switch "B" Circuit Low Input

P0223 Throttle/Pedal Position Sensor/Switch "B" Circuit High Input

P0224 Throttle/Pedal Position Sensor/Switch "B" Circuit Intermittent

P0225 Throttle/Pedal Position Sensor/Switch "C" Circuit Malfunction

P0226 Throttle/Pedal Position Sensor/Switch "C" Circuit Range/Performance Problem

P0227 Throttle/Pedal Position Sensor/Switch "C" Circuit Low Input

P0228 Throttle/Pedal Position Sensor/Switch "C" Circuit High Input

P0229 Throttle/Pedal Position Sensor/Switch "C" Circuit Intermittent

P0230 Fuel Pump Primary Circuit Malfunction

P0231 Fuel Pump Secondary Circuit Low

P0232 Fuel Pump Secondary Circuit High

P0233 Fuel Pump Secondary Circuit Intermittent

P0234 Engine Over Boost Condition

P0261 Cylinder #1 Injector Circuit Low

P0262 Cylinder #1 Injector Circuit High

P0263 Cylinder #1 Contribution/Balance Fault

P0264 Cylinder #2 Injector Circuit Low

P0265 Cylinder #2 Injector Circuit High

P0266 Cylinder #2 Contribution/Balance Fault

P0267 Cylinder #3 Injector Circuit Low

P0268 Cylinder #3 Injector Circuit High

P0269 Cylinder #3 Contribution/Balance Fault

P0270 Cylinder #4 Injector Circuit Low

P0271 Cylinder #4 Injector Circuit High

P0272 Cylinder #4 Contribution/Balance Fault

P0273 Cylinder #5 Injector Circuit Low

P0274 Cylinder #5 Injector Circuit High

P0275 Cylinder #5 Contribution/Balance Fault

P0276 Cylinder #6 Injector Circuit Low

P0277 Cylinder #6 Injector Circuit High

P0278 Cylinder #6 Contribution/Balance Fault

P0279 Cylinder #7 Injector Circuit Low

P0280 Cylinder #7 Injector Circuit High

P0281 Cylinder #7 Contribution/Balance Fault

P0282 Cylinder #8 Injector Circuit Low

P0283 Cylinder #8 Injector Circuit High

P0284 Cylinder #8 Contribution/Balance Fault

P0285 Cylinder #9 Injector Circuit Low

P0286 Cylinder #9 Injector Circuit High

P0287 Cylinder #9 Contribution/Balance Fault

P0288 Cylinder #10 Injector Circuit Low

P0289 Cylinder #10 Injector Circuit High

P0290 Cylinder #10 Contribution/Balance Fault

P0291 Cylinder #11 Injector Circuit Low

P0292 Cylinder #11 Injector Circuit High

P0293 Cylinder #11 Contribution/Balance Fault

P0294 Cylinder #12 Injector Circuit Low

P0295 Cylinder #12 Injector Circuit High

P0296 Cylinder #12 Contribution/Balance Fault

P0300 Random/Multiple Cylinder Misfire Detected

P0301 Cylinder #1—Misfire Detected

P0302 Cylinder #2—Misfire Detected

P0303 Cylinder #3—Misfire Detected

P0304 Cylinder #4—Misfire Detected

P0305 Cylinder #5—Misfire Detected

P0306 Cylinder #6—Misfire Detected

P0307 Cylinder #7—Misfire Detected

P0308 Cylinder #8—Misfire Detected

P0320 Ignition/Distributor Engine Speed Input Circuit Malfunction

P0321 Ignition/Distributor Engine Speed Input Circuit Range/Performance

P0322 Ignition/Distributor Engine Speed Input Circuit No Signal

P0323 Ignition/Distributor Engine Speed Input Circuit Intermittent

P0325 Knock Sensor #1—Circuit Malfunction (Bank #1 or Single Sensor)

P0326 Knock Sensor #1—Circuit Range/Performance (Bank #1 or Single Sensor)

P0327 Knock Sensor #1—Circuit Low Input (Bank #1 or Single Sensor)

P0328 Knock Sensor #1—Circuit High Input (Bank #1 or Single Sensor)

P0329 Knock Sensor #1—Circuit Input Intermittent (Bank #1 or Single Sensor)

P0330 Knock Sensor #2—Circuit Malfunction (Bank #2)

P0331 Knock Sensor #2—Circuit Range/Performance (Bank #2)

P0332 Knock Sensor #2—Circuit Low Input (Bank #2)

P0333 Knock Sensor #2—Circuit High Input (Bank #2)

P0334 Knock Sensor #2—Circuit Input Intermittent (Bank #2)

P0335 Crankshaft Position Sensor "A" Circuit Malfunction

P0336 Crankshaft Position Sensor "A" Circuit Range/Performance

P0337 Crankshaft Position Sensor "A" Circuit Low Input

P0338 Crankshaft Position Sensor "A" Circuit High Input

P0339 Crankshaft Position Sensor "A" Circuit Intermittent

P0340 Camshaft Position Sensor Circuit Malfunction

P0341 Camshaft Position Sensor Circuit Range/Performance

P0342 Camshaft Position Sensor Circuit Low Input

P0343 Camshaft Position Sensor Circuit High Input

P0344 Camshaft Position Sensor Circuit Intermittent

P0350 Ignition Coil Primary/Secondary Circuit Malfunction

P0351 Ignition Coil "A" Primary/Secondary Circuit Malfunction

P0352 Ignition Coil "B" Primary/Secondary Circuit Malfunction

P0353 Ignition Coil "C" Primary/Secondary Circuit Malfunction

P0354 Ignition Coil "D" Primary/Secondary Circuit Malfunction

P0355 Ignition Coil "E" Primary/Secondary Circuit Malfunction

P0356 Ignition Coil "F" Primary/Secondary Circuit Malfunction

P0357 Ignition Coil "G" Primary/Secondary Circuit Malfunction

P0358 Ignition Coil "H" Primary/Secondary Circuit Malfunction

P0359 Ignition Coil "I" Primary/Secondary Circuit Malfunction

P0360 Ignition Coil "J" Primary/Secondary Circuit Malfunction

P0361 Ignition Coil "K" Primary/Secondary Circuit Malfunction

P0362 Ignition Coil "L" Primary/Secondary Circuit Malfunction

P0370 Timing Reference High Resolution Signal "A" Malfunction

P0371 Timing Reference High Resolution Signal "A" Too Many Pulses

P0372 Timing Reference High Resolution Signal "A" Too Few Pulses

P0373 Timing Reference High Resolution Signal "A" Intermittent/Erratic Pulses

P0374 Timing Reference High Resolution Signal "A" No Pulses

P0375 Timing Reference High Resolution Signal "B" Malfunction

P0376 Timing Reference High Resolution Signal "B" Too Many Pulses

P0377 Timing Reference High Resolution Signal "B" Too Few Pulses

P0378 Timing Reference High Resolution Signal "B" Intermittent/Erratic Pulses

P0379 Timing Reference High Resolution Signal "B" No Pulses

P0380 Glow Plug/Heater Circuit "A" Malfunction

P0381 Glow Plug/Heater Indicator Circuit Malfunction

P0382 Glow Plug/Heater Circuit "B" Malfunction

P0385 Crankshaft Position Sensor "B" Circuit Malfunction

P0386 Crankshaft Position Sensor "B" Circuit Range/Performance

P0387 Crankshaft Position Sensor "B" Circuit Low Input

P0388 Crankshaft Position Sensor "B" Circuit High Input

P0389 Crankshaft Position Sensor "B" Circuit Intermittent

P0400 Exhaust Gas Recirculation Flow Malfunction

P0401 Exhaust Gas Recirculation Flow Insufficient Detected

P0402 Exhaust Gas Recirculation Flow Excessive Detected

P0403 Exhaust Gas Recirculation Circuit Malfunction

P0404 Exhaust Gas Recirculation Circuit Range/Performance

P0405 Exhaust Gas Recirculation Sensor "A" Circuit Low

P0406 Exhaust Gas Recirculation Sensor "A" Circuit High

P0407 Exhaust Gas Recirculation Sensor "B" Circuit Low

P0408 Exhaust Gas Recirculation Sensor "B" Circuit High

P0410 Secondary Air Injection System Malfunction

P0411 Secondary Air Injection System Incorrect Flow Detected

P0412 Secondary Air Injection System Switching Valve "A" Circuit Malfunction

P0413 Secondary Air Injection System Switching Valve "A" Circuit Open

P0414 Secondary Air Injection System Switching Valve "A" Circuit Shorted

P0415 Secondary Air Injection System Switching Valve "B" Circuit Malfunction

P0416 Secondary Air Injection System Switching Valve "B" Circuit Open

P0417 Secondary Air Injection System Switching Valve "B" Circuit Shorted

P0418 Secondary Air Injection System Relay "A" Circuit Malfunction

P0419 Secondary Air Injection System Relay "B" Circuit Malfunction

P0420 Catalyst System Efficiency Below Threshold (Bank #1)

P0421 Warm Up Catalyst Efficiency Below Threshold (Bank #1)

P0422 Main Catalyst Efficiency Below Threshold (Bank #1)

P0423 Heated Catalyst Efficiency Below Threshold (Bank #1)

P0424 Heated Catalyst Temperature Below Threshold (Bank #1)

P0430 Catalyst System Efficiency Below Threshold (Bank #2)

P0431 Warm Up Catalyst Efficiency Below Threshold (Bank #2)

P0432 Main Catalyst Efficiency Below Threshold (Bank #2)

P0433 Heated Catalyst Efficiency Below Threshold (Bank #2)

P0434 Heated Catalyst Temperature Below Threshold (Bank #2)

P0440 Evaporative Emission Control System Malfunction

P0441 Evaporative Emission Control System Incorrect Purge Flow

P0442 Evaporative Emission Control System Leak Detected (Small Leak)

P0443 Evaporative Emission Control System Purge Control Valve Circuit Malfunction

P0444 Evaporative Emission Control System Purge Control Valve Circuit Open

P0445 Evaporative Emission Control System Purge Control Valve Circuit Shorted

P0446 Evaporative Emission Control System Vent Control Circuit Malfunction

P0447 Evaporative Emission Control System Vent Control Circuit Open

P0448 Evaporative Emission Control System Vent Control Circuit Shorted

P0449 Evaporative Emission Control System Vent Valve/Solenoid Circuit Malfunction

P0450 Evaporative Emission Control System Pressure Sensor Malfunction

P0451 Evaporative Emission Control System Pressure Sensor Range/Performance

P0452 Evaporative Emission Control System Pressure Sensor Low Input

P0453 Evaporative Emission Control System Pressure Sensor High Input

P0454 Evaporative Emission Control System Pressure Sensor Intermittent

P0455 Evaporative Emission Control System Leak Detected (Gross Leak)

P0460 Fuel Level Sensor Circuit Malfunction

P0461 Fuel Level Sensor Circuit Range/Performance

P0462 Fuel Level Sensor Circuit Low Input

P0463 Fuel Level Sensor Circuit High Input

P0464 Fuel Level Sensor Circuit Intermittent

P0465 Purge Flow Sensor Circuit Malfunction

P0466 Purge Flow Sensor Circuit Range/Performance

P0467 Purge Flow Sensor Circuit Low Input

P0468 Purge Flow Sensor Circuit High Input

P0469 Purge Flow Sensor Circuit Intermittent

P0470 Exhaust Pressure Sensor Malfunction

P0471 Exhaust Pressure Sensor Range/Performance

P0472 Exhaust Pressure Sensor Low

P0473 Exhaust Pressure Sensor High

P0474 Exhaust Pressure Sensor Intermittent

Ignition system service is covered in the model specific sections of this manual

P0475 Exhaust Pressure Control Valve Malfunction

P0476 Exhaust Pressure Control Valve Range/Performance

P0477 Exhaust Pressure Control Valve Low

P0478 Exhaust Pressure Control Valve High

P0479 Exhaust Pressure Control Valve Intermittent

P0480 Cooling Fan #1 Control Circuit Malfunction

P0481 Cooling Fan #2 Control Circuit Malfunction

P0482 Cooling Fan #3 Control Circuit Malfunction

P0483 Cooling Fan Rationality Check Malfunction

P0484 Cooling Fan Circuit Over Current

P0485 Cooling Fan Power/Ground Circuit Malfunction

P0500 Vehicle Speed Sensor Malfunction

P0501 Vehicle Speed Sensor Range/Performance

P0502 Vehicle Speed Sensor Circuit Low Input

P0503 Vehicle Speed Sensor Intermittent/Erratic/High

P0505 Idle Control System Malfunction

P0506 Idle Control System RPM Lower Than Expected

P0507 Idle Control System RPM Higher Than Expected

P0510 Closed Throttle Position Switch Malfunction

P0520 Engine Oil Pressure Sensor/Switch Circuit Malfunction

P0521 Engine Oil Pressure Sensor/Switch Range/Performance

P0522 Engine Oil Pressure Sensor/Switch Low Voltage

P0523 Engine Oil Pressure Sensor/Switch High Voltage

P0530 A/C Refrigerant Pressure Sensor Circuit Malfunction

P0531 A/C Refrigerant Pressure Sensor Circuit Range/Performance

P0532 A/C Refrigerant Pressure Sensor Circuit Low Input

P0533 A/C Refrigerant Pressure Sensor Circuit High Input

P0534 A/C Refrigerant Charge Loss

P0550 Power Steering Pressure Sensor Circuit Malfunction

P0551 Power Steering Pressure Sensor Circuit Range/Performance

P0552 Power Steering Pressure Sensor Circuit Low Input

P0553 Power Steering Pressure Sensor Circuit High Input

P0554 Power Steering Pressure Sensor Circuit Intermittent

P0560 System Voltage Malfunction

P0561 System Voltage Unstable

P0562 System Voltage Low

P0563 System Voltage High

P0565 Cruise Control On Signal Malfunction

P0566 Cruise Control Off Signal Malfunction

P0567 Cruise Control Resume Signal Malfunction

P0568 Cruise Control Set Signal Malfunction

P0569 Cruise Control Coast Signal Malfunction

P0570 Cruise Control Accel Signal Malfunction

P0571 Cruise Control/Brake Switch "A" Circuit Malfunction

P0572 Cruise Control/Brake Switch "A" Circuit Low

P0573 Cruise Control/Brake Switch "A" Circuit High

P0574 Through P0580 Reserved for Cruise Codes

P0600 Serial Communication Link Malfunction

P0601 Internal Control Module Memory Check Sum Error

P0602 Control Module Programming Error

P0603 Internal Control Module Keep Alive Memory (KAM) Error

P0604 Internal Control Module Random Access Memory (RAM) Error

P0605 Internal Control Module Read Only Memory (ROM) Error

P0606 PCM Processor Fault

P0608 Control Module VSS Output "A" Malfunction

P0609 Control Module VSS Output "B" Malfunction

P0620 Generator Control Circuit Malfunction

P0621 Generator Lamp "L" Control Circuit Malfunction

P0622 Generator Field "F" Control Circuit Malfunction

P0650 Malfunction Indicator Lamp (MIL) Control Circuit Malfunction

P0654 Engine RPM Output Circuit Malfunction

P0655 Engine Hot Lamp Output Control Circuit Malfunction

P0656 Fuel Level Output Circuit Malfunction

P0700 Transmission Control System Malfunction

P0701 Transmission Control System Range/Performance

P0702 Transmission Control System Electrical

P0703 Torque Converter/Brake Switch "B" Circuit Malfunction

P0704 Clutch Switch Input Circuit Malfunction

P0705 Transmission Range Sensor Circuit Malfunction (PRNDL Input)

P0706 Transmission Range Sensor Circuit Range/Performance

P0707 Transmission Range Sensor Circuit Low Input

P0708 Transmission Range Sensor Circuit High Input

P0709 Transmission Range Sensor Circuit Intermittent

P0710 Transmission Fluid Temperature Sensor Circuit Malfunction

P0711 Transmission Fluid Temperature Sensor Circuit Range/Performance

P0712 Transmission Fluid Temperature Sensor Circuit Low Input

P0713 Transmission Fluid Temperature Sensor Circuit High Input

P0714 Transmission Fluid Temperature Sensor Circuit Intermittent

P0715 Input/Turbine Speed Sensor Circuit Malfunction

P0716 Input/Turbine Speed Sensor Circuit Range/Performance

P0717 Input/Turbine Speed Sensor Circuit No Signal

P0718 Input/Turbine Speed Sensor Circuit Intermittent

P0719 Torque Converter/Brake Switch "B" Circuit Low

P0720 Output Speed Sensor Circuit Malfunction

P0721 Output Speed Sensor Circuit Range/Performance

P0722 Output Speed Sensor Circuit No Signal

P0723 Output Speed Sensor Circuit Intermittent

P0724 Torque Converter/Brake Switch "B" Circuit High

P0725 Engine Speed Input Circuit Malfunction

P0726 Engine Speed Input Circuit Range/Performance

P0727 Engine Speed Input Circuit No Signal

P0728 Engine Speed Input Circuit Intermittent

P0730 Incorrect Gear Ratio

P0731 Gear #1 Incorrect Ratio

P0732 Gear #2 Incorrect Ratio

P0733 Gear #3 Incorrect Ratio

P0734 Gear #4 Incorrect Ratio

P0735 Gear #5 Incorrect Ratio

P0736 Reverse Incorrect Ratio

P0740 Torque Converter Clutch Circuit Malfunction

P0741 Torque Converter Clutch Circuit Performance or Stuck Off

P0742 Torque Converter Clutch Circuit Stuck On

P0743 Torque Converter Clutch Circuit Electrical

P0744 Torque Converter Clutch Circuit Intermittent

P0745 Pressure Control Solenoid Malfunction

P0746 Pressure Control Solenoid Performance or Stuck Off

P0747 Pressure Control Solenoid Stuck On

P0748 Pressure Control Solenoid Electrical

P0749 Pressure Control Solenoid Intermittent

P0750 Shift Solenoid "A" Malfunction

P0751 Shift Solenoid "A" Performance or Stuck Off

P0752 Shift Solenoid "A" Stuck On

P0753 Shift Solenoid "A" Electrical

P0754 Shift Solenoid "A" Intermittent

P0755 Shift Solenoid "B" Malfunction

P0756 Shift Solenoid "B" Performance or Stuck Off

P0757 Shift Solenoid "B" Stuck On

P0758 Shift Solenoid "B" Electrical

P0759 Shift Solenoid "B" Intermittent

P0760 Shift Solenoid "C" Malfunction

P0761 Shift Solenoid "C" Performance Or Stuck Off

P0762 Shift Solenoid "C" Stuck On

P0763 Shift Solenoid "C" Electrical

P0764 Shift Solenoid "C" Intermittent

P0765 Shift Solenoid "D" Malfunction

P0766 Shift Solenoid "D" Performance Or Stuck Off

P0767 Shift Solenoid "D" Stuck On

P0768 Shift Solenoid "D" Electrical

P0769 Shift Solenoid "D" Intermittent

P0770 Shift Solenoid "E" Malfunction

P0771 Shift Solenoid "E" Performance Or Stuck Off

P0772 Shift Solenoid "E" Stuck On

P0773 Shift Solenoid "E" Electrical

P0774 Shift Solenoid "E" Intermittent

P0780 Shift Malfunction

P0781 1–2 Shift Malfunction

P0782 2–3 Shift Malfunction

P0783 3–4 Shift Malfunction

P0784 4–5 Shift Malfunction

P0785 Shift/Timing Solenoid Malfunction

P0786 Shift/Timing Solenoid Range/Performance

P0787 Shift/Timing Solenoid Low

P0788 Shift/Timing Solenoid High

P0789 Shift/Timing Solenoid Intermittent

P0790 Normal/Performance Switch Circuit Malfunction

P0801 Reverse Inhibit Control Circuit Malfunction

P0803 1–4 Upshift (Skip Shift) Solenoid Control Circuit Malfunction

P0804 1–4 Upshift (Skip Shift) Lamp Control Circuit Malfunction

P1100 Barometric Pressure Sensor Circuit Fault

P1120 Accelerator Pedal Position Sensor Circuit Malfunction

P1121 Accelerator Pedal Position Sensor Range/Performance Problem

P1125 Throttle Control Motor Circuit Malfunction

P1126 Magnetic Clutch Circuit Malfunction

P1127 ETCS Actuator Power Source Circuit Malfunction

P1128 Throttle Control Motor Lock Malfunction

P1129 Electric Throttle Control System Malfunction

P1130 A/F Sensor Circuit Range / Performance Malfunction (Bank #1 Sensor #1)

P1133 A/F Sensor Circuit Response Malfunction (Bank #1 Sensor #1)

P1135 A/F Sensor Heater Circuit Malfunction (Bank #1 Sensor #1)

P1150 A/F Sensor Circuit Range / Performance Malfunction (Bank #2 Sensor #1)

P1153 A/F Sensor Circuit Response Malfunction (Bank #2 Sensor #1)

P1155 A/F Sensor Heater Circuit Malfunction (Bank #2 Sensor #1)

P1200 Fuel Pump Relay Circuit Fault

P1300 Igniter Circuit Fault (Bank #1)

P1305 Igniter Circuit Fault (Bank #2)

P1310 Igniter Circuit Fault (Bank #3)

P1315 Igniter Circuit Fault (Bank #4)

P1320 Igniter Circuit Fault (Bank #5)

P1325 Igniter Circuit Fault (Bank #6)

P1330 Igniter Circuit Fault (Bank #7)

P1335 Crankshaft Position Sensor Circuit Fault (during engine running)

P1340 Igniter Circuit Fault (Bank #8)

P1400 Sub-Throttle Position Sensor Circuit Fault

P1401 Sub-Throttle Position Sensor Performance

P1500 Starter Signal Circuit Fault

P1510 Air Volume Too Low With Supercharger On

P1520 Stop Light Switch Signal Malfunction

P1600 ECM Battery Back-up Circuit Fault

P1633 ECM Malfunction (ETCS Circuit)

P1605 Knock Control CPU Fault

P1700 Vehicle Speed Sensor Circuit Fault

P1705 Direct Clutch Speed Sensor Circuit Fault

P1765 Linear Shift Solenoid Circuit Fault

P1780 Park Neutral Position Switch Fault

Mazda

READING CODES

Reading the control module memory is one of the first steps in OBD II system diagnostics. This step should be initially performed to determine the general nature of the fault. Subsequent readings will determine if the fault has been cleared.

Reading codes can be performed by any of the methods below:

- Read the control module memory with the Generic Scan Tool (GST)
- Read the control module memory with the vehicle manufacturer's specific tester

To read the fault codes, connect the scan tool or tester according to the manufacturer's instructions. Follow the manufacturer's specified procedure for reading the codes.

CLEARING CODES

Control module reset procedures are a very important part of OBD II System diagnostics. This step should be done at the end of any fault code repair and at the end of any driveability repair.

Clearing codes can be performed by any of the methods below:

- Clear the control module memory with the Generic Scan Tool (GST)
- Clear the control module memory with the vehicle manufacturer's specific tester
- Turn the ignition OFF and remove the negative battery cable for at least 1 minute.

Removing the negative battery cable may cause other systems in the vehicle to loose their memory. Prior to removing the cable, ensure you have the proper reset codes for radios and alarms.

➡**The MIL will may also be de-activated for some codes if the vehicle completes three consecutive trips with-**

out a fault detected with vehicle conditions similar to those present during the fault.

OBD II TROUBLE CODES

P0100 Mass or Volume Air Flow Circuit Malfunction

P0101 Mass or Volume Air Flow Circuit Range/Performance Problem

P0102 Mass or Volume Air Flow Circuit Low Input

P0103 Mass or Volume Air Flow Circuit High Input

P0104 Mass or Volume Air Flow Circuit Intermittent

P0105 Manifold Absolute Pressure/Barometric Pressure Circuit Malfunction

P0106 Manifold Absolute Pressure/Barometric Pressure Circuit Range/Performance Problem

P0107 Manifold Absolute Pressure/Barometric Pressure Circuit Low Input

P0108 Manifold Absolute Pressure/Barometric Pressure Circuit High Input

P0109 Manifold Absolute Pressure/Barometric Pressure Circuit Intermittent

P0110 Intake Air Temperature Circuit Malfunction

P0111 Intake Air Temperature Circuit Range/Performance Problem

P0112 Intake Air Temperature Circuit Low Input

P0113 Intake Air Temperature Circuit High Input

P0114 Intake Air Temperature Circuit Intermittent

P0115 Engine Coolant Temperature Circuit Malfunction

P0116 Engine Coolant Temperature Circuit Range/Performance Problem

P0117 Engine Coolant Temperature Circuit Low Input

P0118 Engine Coolant Temperature Circuit High Input

P0119 Engine Coolant Temperature Circuit Intermittent

P0120 Throttle/Pedal Position Sensor/Switch "A" Circuit Malfunction

P0121 Throttle/Pedal Position Sensor/Switch "A" Circuit Range/Performance Problem

P0122 Throttle/Pedal Position Sensor/Switch "A" Circuit Low Input

P0123 Throttle/Pedal Position Sensor/Switch "A" Circuit High Input

P0124 Throttle/Pedal Position Sensor/Switch "A" Circuit Intermittent

P0125 Insufficient Coolant Temperature For Closed Loop Fuel Control

P0126 Insufficient Coolant Temperature For Stable Operation

P0130 O_2 Circuit Malfunction (Bank #1 Sensor #1)

P0131 O_2 Sensor Circuit Low Voltage (Bank #1 Sensor #1)

P0132 O_2 Sensor Circuit High Voltage (Bank #1 Sensor #1)

P0133 O_2 Sensor Circuit Slow Response (Bank #1 Sensor #1)

P0134 O_2 Sensor Circuit No Activity Detected (Bank #1 Sensor #1)

P0135 O_2 Sensor Heater Circuit Malfunction (Bank #1 Sensor #1)

P0136 O_2 Sensor Circuit Malfunction (Bank #1 Sensor #2)

P0137 O_2 Sensor Circuit Low Voltage (Bank #1 Sensor #2)

P0138 O_2 Sensor Circuit High Voltage (Bank #1 Sensor #2)

P0139 O_2 Sensor Circuit Slow Response (Bank #1 Sensor #2)

P0140 O_2 Sensor Circuit No Activity Detected (Bank #1 Sensor #2)

P0141 O_2 Sensor Heater Circuit Malfunction (Bank #1 Sensor #2)

P0142 O_2 Sensor Circuit Malfunction (Bank #1 Sensor #3)

P0143 O_2 Sensor Circuit Low Voltage (Bank #1 Sensor #3)

P0144 O_2 Sensor Circuit High Voltage (Bank #1 Sensor #3)

P0145 O_2 Sensor Circuit Slow Response (Bank #1 Sensor #3)

P0146 O_2 Sensor Circuit No Activity Detected (Bank #1 Sensor #3)

P0147 O_2 Sensor Heater Circuit Malfunction (Bank #1 Sensor #3)

P0150 O_2 Sensor Circuit Malfunction (Bank #2 Sensor #1)

P0151 O_2 Sensor Circuit Low Voltage (Bank #2 Sensor #1)

P0152 O_2 Sensor Circuit High Voltage (Bank #2 Sensor #1)

P0153 O_2 Sensor Circuit Slow Response (Bank #2 Sensor #1)

P0154 O_2 Sensor Circuit No Activity Detected (Bank #2 Sensor #1)

P0155 O_2 Sensor Heater Circuit Malfunction (Bank #2 Sensor #1)

P0156 O_2 Sensor Circuit Malfunction (Bank #2 Sensor #2)

P0157 O_2 Sensor Circuit Low Voltage (Bank #2 Sensor #2)

P0158 O_2 Sensor Circuit High Voltage (Bank #2 Sensor #2)

P0159 O_2 Sensor Circuit Slow Response (Bank #2 Sensor #2)

P0160 O_2 Sensor Circuit No Activity Detected (Bank #2 Sensor #2)

P0161 O_2 Sensor Heater Circuit Malfunction (Bank #2 Sensor #2)

P0162 O_2 Sensor Circuit Malfunction (Bank #2 Sensor #3)

P0163 O_2 Sensor Circuit Low Voltage (Bank #2 Sensor #3)

P0164 O_2 Sensor Circuit High Voltage (Bank #2 Sensor #3)

P0165 O_2 Sensor Circuit Slow Response (Bank #2 Sensor #3)

P0166 O_2 Sensor Circuit No Activity Detected (Bank #2 Sensor #3)

P0167 O_2 Sensor Heater Circuit Malfunction (Bank #2 Sensor #3)

P0170 Fuel Trim Malfunction (Bank #1)

P0171 System Too Lean (Bank #1)

P0172 System Too Rich (Bank #1)

P0173 Fuel Trim Malfunction (Bank #2)

P0174 System Too Lean (Bank #2)

P0175 System Too Rich (Bank #2)

P0176 Fuel Composition Sensor Circuit Malfunction

P0177 Fuel Composition Sensor Circuit Range/Performance

P0178 Fuel Composition Sensor Circuit Low Input

P0179 Fuel Composition Sensor Circuit High Input

P0180 Fuel Temperature Sensor "A" Circuit Malfunction

P0181 Fuel Temperature Sensor "A" Circuit Range/Performance

P0182 Fuel Temperature Sensor "A" Circuit Low Input

P0183 Fuel Temperature Sensor "A" Circuit High Input

P0184 Fuel Temperature Sensor "A" Circuit Intermittent

P0185 Fuel Temperature Sensor "B" Circuit Malfunction

P0186 Fuel Temperature Sensor "B" Circuit Range/Performance

P0187 Fuel Temperature Sensor "B" Circuit Low Input

P0188 Fuel Temperature Sensor "B" Circuit High Input

P0189 Fuel Temperature Sensor "B" Circuit Intermittent

P0190 Fuel Rail Pressure Sensor Circuit Malfunction

P0191 Fuel Rail Pressure Sensor Circuit Range/Performance

P0192 Fuel Rail Pressure Sensor Circuit Low Input

P0193 Fuel Rail Pressure Sensor Circuit High Input

P0194 Fuel Rail Pressure Sensor Circuit Intermittent

P0195 Engine Oil Temperature Sensor Malfunction

P0196 Engine Oil Temperature Sensor Range/Performance

P0197 Engine Oil Temperature Sensor Low

P0198 Engine Oil Temperature Sensor High

P0199 Engine Oil Temperature Sensor Intermittent

P0200 Injector Circuit Malfunction

P0201 Injector Circuit Malfunction—Cylinder #1

P0202 Injector Circuit Malfunction—Cylinder #2

P0203 Injector Circuit Malfunction—Cylinder #3

P0204 Injector Circuit Malfunction—Cylinder #4

P0205 Injector Circuit Malfunction—Cylinder #5

P0206 Injector Circuit Malfunction—Cylinder #6

P0207 Injector Circuit Malfunction—Cylinder #7

P0208 Injector Circuit Malfunction—Cylinder #8

P0209 Injector Circuit Malfunction—Cylinder #9

P0210 Injector Circuit Malfunction—Cylinder #10

P0211 Injector Circuit Malfunction—Cylinder #11

P0212 Injector Circuit Malfunction—Cylinder #12

P0213 Cold Start Injector #1 Malfunction

P0214 Cold Start Injector #2 Malfunction

P0215 Engine Shutoff Solenoid Malfunction

P0216 Injection Timing Control Circuit Malfunction

P0217 Engine Over Temperature Condition

P0218 Transmission Over Temperature Condition

P0219 Engine Over Speed Condition

P0220 Throttle/Pedal Position Sensor/Switch "B" Circuit Malfunction

P0221 Throttle/Pedal Position Sensor/Switch "B" Circuit Range/Performance Problem

P0222 Throttle/Pedal Position Sensor/Switch "B" Circuit Low Input

P0223 Throttle/Pedal Position Sensor/Switch "B" Circuit High Input

P0224 Throttle/Pedal Position Sensor/Switch "B" Circuit Intermittent

P0225 Throttle/Pedal Position Sensor/Switch "C" Circuit Malfunction

P0226 Throttle/Pedal Position Sensor/Switch "C" Circuit Range/Performance Problem

P0227 Throttle/Pedal Position Sensor/Switch "C" Circuit Low Input

P0228 Throttle/Pedal Position Sensor/Switch "C" Circuit High Input

P0229 Throttle/Pedal Position Sensor/Switch "C" Circuit Intermittent

P0230 Fuel Pump Primary Circuit Malfunction

P0231 Fuel Pump Secondary Circuit Low

P0232 Fuel Pump Secondary Circuit High

P0233 Fuel Pump Secondary Circuit Intermittent

P0234 Engine Over Boost Condition

P0261 Cylinder #1 Injector Circuit Low

P0262 Cylinder #1 Injector Circuit High

P0263 Cylinder #1 Contribution/Balance Fault

P0264 Cylinder #2 Injector Circuit Low

P0265 Cylinder #2 Injector Circuit High

P0266 Cylinder #2 Contribution/Balance Fault

P0267 Cylinder #3 Injector Circuit Low

P0268 Cylinder #3 Injector Circuit High

P0269 Cylinder #3 Contribution/Balance Fault

P0270 Cylinder #4 Injector Circuit Low

P0271 Cylinder #4 Injector Circuit High

P0272 Cylinder #4 Contribution/Balance Fault

P0273 Cylinder #5 Injector Circuit Low

P0274 Cylinder #5 Injector Circuit High

P0275 Cylinder #5 Contribution/Balance Fault

P0276 Cylinder #6 Injector Circuit Low

P0277 Cylinder #6 Injector Circuit High

P0278 Cylinder #6 Contribution/Balance Fault

P0279 Cylinder #7 Injector Circuit Low

P0280 Cylinder #7 Injector Circuit High

P0281 Cylinder #7 Contribution/Balance Fault

P0282 Cylinder #8 Injector Circuit Low

P0283 Cylinder #8 Injector Circuit High

P0284 Cylinder #8 Contribution/Balance Fault

P0285 Cylinder #9 Injector Circuit Low

P0286 Cylinder #9 Injector Circuit High

P0287 Cylinder #9 Contribution/Balance Fault

P0288 Cylinder #10 Injector Circuit Low

P0289 Cylinder #10 Injector Circuit High

P0290 Cylinder #10 Contribution/Balance Fault

P0291 Cylinder #11 Injector Circuit Low

P0292 Cylinder #11 Injector Circuit High

P0293 Cylinder #11 Contribution/Balance Fault

P0294 Cylinder #12 Injector Circuit Low

P0295 Cylinder #12 Injector Circuit High

P0296 Cylinder #12 Contribution/Balance Fault

P0300 Random/Multiple Cylinder Misfire Detected

P0301 Cylinder #1—Misfire Detected

P0302 Cylinder #2—Misfire Detected

P0303 Cylinder #3—Misfire Detected

P0304 Cylinder #4—Misfire Detected

P0305 Cylinder #5—Misfire Detected

P0306 Cylinder #6—Misfire Detected

P0307 Cylinder #7—Misfire Detected

P0308 Cylinder #8—Misfire Detected

P0309 Cylinder #9—Misfire Detected

P0310 Cylinder #10—Misfire Detected

P0311 Cylinder #11—Misfire Detected

P0312 Cylinder #12—Misfire Detected

P0320 Ignition/Distributor Engine Speed Input Circuit Malfunction

P0321 Ignition/Distributor Engine Speed Input Circuit Range/Performance

P0322 Ignition/Distributor Engine Speed Input Circuit No Signal

P0323 Ignition/Distributor Engine Speed Input Circuit Intermittent

P0325 Knock Sensor #1—Circuit Malfunction (Bank #1 or Single Sensor)

P0326 Knock Sensor #1—Circuit Range/Performance (Bank #1 or Single Sensor)

P0327 Knock Sensor #1—Circuit Low Input (Bank #1 or Single Sensor)

P0328 Knock Sensor #1—Circuit High Input (Bank #1 or Single Sensor)

P0329 Knock Sensor #1—Circuit Input Intermittent (Bank #1 or Single Sensor)

P0330 Knock Sensor #2—Circuit Malfunction (Bank #2)

P0331 Knock Sensor #2—Circuit Range/Performance (Bank #2)

P0332 Knock Sensor #2—Circuit Low Input (Bank #2)

P0333 Knock Sensor #2—Circuit High Input (Bank #2)

P0334 Knock Sensor #2—Circuit Input Intermittent (Bank #2)

P0335 Crankshaft Position Sensor "A" Circuit Malfunction

P0336 Crankshaft Position Sensor "A" Circuit Range/Performance

P0337 Crankshaft Position Sensor "A" Circuit Low Input

P0338 Crankshaft Position Sensor "A" Circuit High Input

Refer to the model specific sections for fuel system service procedures

P0339 Crankshaft Position Sensor "A" Circuit Intermittent

P0340 Camshaft Position Sensor Circuit Malfunction

P0341 Camshaft Position Sensor Circuit Range/Performance

P0342 Camshaft Position Sensor Circuit Low Input

P0343 Camshaft Position Sensor Circuit High Input

P0344 Camshaft Position Sensor Circuit Intermittent

P0350 Ignition Coil Primary/Secondary Circuit Malfunction

P0351 Ignition Coil "A" Primary/Secondary Circuit Malfunction

P0352 Ignition Coil "B" Primary/Secondary Circuit Malfunction

P0353 Ignition Coil "C" Primary/Secondary Circuit Malfunction

P0354 Ignition Coil "D" Primary/Secondary Circuit Malfunction

P0355 Ignition Coil "E" Primary/Secondary Circuit Malfunction

P0356 Ignition Coil "F" Primary/Secondary Circuit Malfunction

P0357 Ignition Coil "G" Primary/Secondary Circuit Malfunction

P0358 Ignition Coil "H" Primary/Secondary Circuit Malfunction

P0359 Ignition Coil "I" Primary/Secondary Circuit Malfunction

P0360 Ignition Coil "J" Primary/Secondary Circuit Malfunction

P0361 Ignition Coil "K" Primary/Secondary Circuit Malfunction

P0362 Ignition Coil "L" Primary/Secondary Circuit Malfunction

P0370 Timing Reference High Resolution Signal "A" Malfunction

P0371 Timing Reference High Resolution Signal "A" Too Many Pulses

P0372 Timing Reference High Resolution Signal "A" Too Few Pulses

P0373 Timing Reference High Resolution Signal "A" Intermittent/Erratic Pulses

P0374 Timing Reference High Resolution Signal "A" No Pulses

P0375 Timing Reference High Resolution Signal "B" Malfunction

P0376 Timing Reference High Resolution Signal "B" Too Many Pulses

P0377 Timing Reference High Resolution Signal "B" Too Few Pulses

P0378 Timing Reference High Resolution Signal "B" Intermittent/Erratic Pulses

P0379 Timing Reference High Resolution Signal "B" No Pulses

P0380 Glow Plug/Heater Circuit "A" Malfunction

P0381 Glow Plug/Heater Indicator Circuit Malfunction

P0382 Glow Plug/Heater Circuit "B" Malfunction

P0385 Crankshaft Position Sensor "B" Circuit Malfunction

P0386 Crankshaft Position Sensor "B" Circuit Range/Performance

P0387 Crankshaft Position Sensor "B" Circuit Low Input

P0388 Crankshaft Position Sensor "B" Circuit High Input

P0389 Crankshaft Position Sensor "B" Circuit Intermittent

P0400 Exhaust Gas Recirculation Flow Malfunction

P0401 Exhaust Gas Recirculation Flow Insufficient Detected

P0402 Exhaust Gas Recirculation Flow Excessive Detected

P0403 Exhaust Gas Recirculation Circuit Malfunction

P0404 Exhaust Gas Recirculation Circuit Range/Performance

P0405 Exhaust Gas Recirculation Sensor "A" Circuit Low

P0406 Exhaust Gas Recirculation Sensor "A" Circuit High

P0407 Exhaust Gas Recirculation Sensor "B" Circuit Low

P0408 Exhaust Gas Recirculation Sensor "B" Circuit High

P0410 Secondary Air Injection System Malfunction

P0411 Secondary Air Injection System Incorrect Flow Detected

P0412 Secondary Air Injection System Switching Valve "A" Circuit Malfunction

P0413 Secondary Air Injection System Switching Valve "A" Circuit Open

P0414 Secondary Air Injection System Switching Valve "A" Circuit Shorted

P0415 Secondary Air Injection System Switching Valve "B" Circuit Malfunction

P0416 Secondary Air Injection System Switching Valve "B" Circuit Open

P0417 Secondary Air Injection System Switching Valve "B" Circuit Shorted

P0418 Secondary Air Injection System Relay "A" Circuit Malfunction

P0419 Secondary Air Injection System Relay "B" Circuit Malfunction

P0420 Catalyst System Efficiency Below Threshold (Bank #1)

P0421 Warm Up Catalyst Efficiency Below Threshold (Bank #1)

P0422 Main Catalyst Efficiency Below Threshold (Bank #1)

P0423 Heated Catalyst Efficiency Below Threshold (Bank #1)

P0424 Heated Catalyst Temperature Below Threshold (Bank #1)

P0430 Catalyst System Efficiency Below Threshold (Bank #2)

P0431 Warm Up Catalyst Efficiency Below Threshold (Bank #2)

P0432 Main Catalyst Efficiency Below Threshold (Bank #2)

P0433 Heated Catalyst Efficiency Below Threshold (Bank #2)

P0434 Heated Catalyst Temperature Below Threshold (Bank #2)

P0440 Evaporative Emission Control System Malfunction

P0441 Evaporative Emission Control System Incorrect Purge Flow

P0442 Evaporative Emission Control System Leak Detected (Small Leak)

P0443 Evaporative Emission Control System Purge Control Valve Circuit Malfunction

P0444 Evaporative Emission Control System Purge Control Valve Circuit Open

P0445 Evaporative Emission Control System Purge Control Valve Circuit Shorted

P0446 Evaporative Emission Control System Vent Control Circuit Malfunction

P0447 Evaporative Emission Control System Vent Control Circuit Open

P0448 Evaporative Emission Control System Vent Control Circuit Shorted

P0449 Evaporative Emission Control System Vent Valve/Solenoid Circuit Malfunction

P0450 Evaporative Emission Control System Pressure Sensor Malfunction

P0451 Evaporative Emission Control System Pressure Sensor Range/Performance

P0452 Evaporative Emission Control System Pressure Sensor Low Input

P0453 Evaporative Emission Control System Pressure Sensor High Input

P0454 Evaporative Emission Control System Pressure Sensor Intermittent

P0455 Evaporative Emission Control System Leak Detected (Gross Leak)

P0460 Fuel Level Sensor Circuit Malfunction

P0461 Fuel Level Sensor Circuit Range/Performance

P0462 Fuel Level Sensor Circuit Low Input

P0463 Fuel Level Sensor Circuit High Input

P0464 Fuel Level Sensor Circuit Intermittent

P0465 Purge Flow Sensor Circuit Malfunction

P0466 Purge Flow Sensor Circuit Range/Performance

P0467 Purge Flow Sensor Circuit Low Input

P0468 Purge Flow Sensor Circuit High Input

P0469 Purge Flow Sensor Circuit Intermittent

P0470 Exhaust Pressure Sensor Malfunction

P0471 Exhaust Pressure Sensor Range/Performance

P0472 Exhaust Pressure Sensor Low

P0473 Exhaust Pressure Sensor High

P0474 Exhaust Pressure Sensor Intermittent

P0475 Exhaust Pressure Control Valve Malfunction

P0476 Exhaust Pressure Control Valve Range/Performance

P0477 Exhaust Pressure Control Valve Low

P0478 Exhaust Pressure Control Valve High

P0479 Exhaust Pressure Control Valve Intermittent

P0480 Cooling Fan #1 Control Circuit Malfunction

P0481 Cooling Fan #2 Control Circuit Malfunction

P0482 Cooling Fan #3 Control Circuit Malfunction

P0483 Cooling Fan Rationality Check Malfunction

P0484 Cooling Fan Circuit Over Current

P0485 Cooling Fan Power/Ground Circuit Malfunction

P0500 Vehicle Speed Sensor Malfunction

P0501 Vehicle Speed Sensor Range/Performance

P0502 Vehicle Speed Sensor Circuit Low Input

P0503 Vehicle Speed Sensor Intermittent/Erratic/High

P0505 Idle Control System Malfunction

P0506 Idle Control System RPM Lower Than Expected

P0507 Idle Control System RPM Higher Than Expected

P0510 Closed Throttle Position Switch Malfunction

P0520 Engine Oil Pressure Sensor/ Switch Circuit Malfunction

P0521 Engine Oil Pressure Sensor/ Switch Range/Performance

P0522 Engine Oil Pressure Sensor/ Switch Low Voltage

P0523 Engine Oil Pressure Sensor/ Switch High Voltage

P0530 A/C Refrigerant Pressure Sensor Circuit Malfunction

P0531 A/C Refrigerant Pressure Sensor Circuit Range/Performance

P0532 A/C Refrigerant Pressure Sensor Circuit Low Input

P0533 A/C Refrigerant Pressure Sensor Circuit High Input

P0534 A/C Refrigerant Charge Loss

P0550 Power Steering Pressure Sensor Circuit Malfunction

P0551 Power Steering Pressure Sensor Circuit Range/Performance

P0552 Power Steering Pressure Sensor Circuit Low Input

P0553 Power Steering Pressure Sensor Circuit High Input

P0554 Power Steering Pressure Sensor Circuit Intermittent

P0560 System Voltage Malfunction

P0561 System Voltage Unstable

P0562 System Voltage Low

P0563 System Voltage High

P0565 Cruise Control On Signal Malfunction

P0566 Cruise Control Off Signal Malfunction

P0567 Cruise Control Resume Signal Malfunction

P0568 Cruise Control Set Signal Malfunction

P0569 Cruise Control Coast Signal Malfunction

P0570 Cruise Control Accel Signal Malfunction

P0571 Cruise Control/Brake Switch "A" Circuit Malfunction

P0572 Cruise Control/Brake Switch "A" Circuit Low

P0573 Cruise Control/Brake Switch "A" Circuit High

P0574 Through P0580 Reserved for Cruise Codes

P0600 Serial Communication Link Malfunction

P0601 Internal Control Module Memory Check Sum Error

P0602 Control Module Programming Error

P0603 Internal Control Module Keep Alive Memory (KAM) Error

P0604 Internal Control Module Random Access Memory (RAM) Error

P0605 Internal Control Module Read Only Memory (ROM) Error

P0606 PCM Processor Fault

P0608 Control Module VSS Output "A" Malfunction

P0609 Control Module VSS Output "B" Malfunction

P0620 Generator Control Circuit Malfunction

P0621 Generator Lamp "L" Control Circuit Malfunction

P0622 Generator Field "F" Control Circuit Malfunction

P0650 Malfunction Indicator Lamp (MIL) Control Circuit Malfunction

P0654 Engine RPM Output Circuit Malfunction

P0655 Engine Hot Lamp Output Control Circuit Malfunction

P0656 Fuel Level Output Circuit Malfunction

P0700 Transmission Control System Malfunction

P0701 Transmission Control System Range/Performance

P0702 Transmission Control System Electrical

P0703 Torque Converter/Brake Switch "B" Circuit Malfunction

P0704 Clutch Switch Input Circuit Malfunction

P0705 Transmission Range Sensor Circuit Malfunction (PRNDL Input)

P0706 Transmission Range Sensor Circuit Range/Performance

P0707 Transmission Range Sensor Circuit Low Input

P0708 Transmission Range Sensor Circuit High Input

P0709 Transmission Range Sensor Circuit Intermittent

P0710 Transmission Fluid Temperature Sensor Circuit Malfunction

P0711 Transmission Fluid Temperature Sensor Circuit Range/Performance

P0712 Transmission Fluid Temperature Sensor Circuit Low Input

P0713 Transmission Fluid Temperature Sensor Circuit High Input

P0714 Transmission Fluid Temperature Sensor Circuit Intermittent

P0715 Input/Turbine Speed Sensor Circuit Malfunction

P0716 Input/Turbine Speed Sensor Circuit Range/Performance

P0717 Input/Turbine Speed Sensor Circuit No Signal

P0718 Input/Turbine Speed Sensor Circuit Intermittent

P0719 Torque Converter/Brake Switch "B" Circuit Low

P0720 Output Speed Sensor Circuit Malfunction

P0721 Output Speed Sensor Circuit Range/Performance

P0722 Output Speed Sensor Circuit No Signal

P0723 Output Speed Sensor Circuit Intermittent

Refer to the model specific sections for engine electrical system service procedures

P0724 Torque Converter/Brake Switch "B" Circuit High

P0725 Engine Speed Input Circuit Malfunction

P0726 Engine Speed Input Circuit Range/Performance

P0727 Engine Speed Input Circuit No Signal

P0728 Engine Speed Input Circuit Intermittent

P0730 Incorrect Gear Ratio

P0731 Gear #1 Incorrect Ratio

P0732 Gear #2 Incorrect Ratio

P0733 Gear #3 Incorrect Ratio

P0734 Gear #4 Incorrect Ratio

P0735 Gear #5 Incorrect Ratio

P0736 Reverse Incorrect Ratio

P0740 Torque Converter Clutch Circuit Malfunction

P0741 Torque Converter Clutch Circuit Performance or Stuck Off

P0742 Torque Converter Clutch Circuit Stuck On

P0743 Torque Converter Clutch Circuit Electrical

P0744 Torque Converter Clutch Circuit Intermittent

P0745 Pressure Control Solenoid Malfunction

P0746 Pressure Control Solenoid Performance or Stuck Off

P0747 Pressure Control Solenoid Stuck On

P0748 Pressure Control Solenoid Electrical

P0749 Pressure Control Solenoid Intermittent

P0750 Shift Solenoid "A" Malfunction

P0751 Shift Solenoid "A" Performance or Stuck Off

P0752 Shift Solenoid "A" Stuck On

P0753 Shift Solenoid "A" Electrical

P0754 Shift Solenoid "A" Intermittent

P0755 Shift Solenoid "B" Malfunction

P0756 Shift Solenoid "B" Performance or Stuck Off

P0757 Shift Solenoid "B" Stuck On

P0758 Shift Solenoid "B" Electrical

P0759 Shift Solenoid "B" Intermittent

P0760 Shift Solenoid "C" Malfunction

P0761 Shift Solenoid "C" Performance Or Stuck Off

P0762 Shift Solenoid "C" Stuck On

P0763 Shift Solenoid "C" Electrical

P0764 Shift Solenoid "C" Intermittent

P0765 Shift Solenoid "D" Malfunction

P0766 Shift Solenoid "D" Performance Or Stuck Off

P0767 Shift Solenoid "D" Stuck On

P0768 Shift Solenoid "D" Electrical

P0769 Shift Solenoid "D" Intermittent

P0770 Shift Solenoid "E" Malfunction

P0771 Shift Solenoid "E" Performance Or Stuck Off

P0772 Shift Solenoid "E" Stuck On

P0773 Shift Solenoid "E" Electrical

P0774 Shift Solenoid "E" Intermittent

P0780 Shift Malfunction

P0781 1–2 Shift Malfunction

P0782 2–3 Shift Malfunction

P0783 3–4 Shift Malfunction

P0784 4–5 Shift Malfunction

P0785 Shift/Timing Solenoid Malfunction

P0786 Shift/Timing Solenoid Range/Performance

P0787 Shift/Timing Solenoid Low

P0788 Shift/Timing Solenoid High

P0789 Shift/Timing Solenoid Intermittent

P0790 Normal/Performance Switch Circuit Malfunction

P0801 Reverse Inhibit Control Circuit Malfunction

P0803 1–4 Upshift (Skip Shift) Solenoid Control Circuit Malfunction

P0804 1–4 Upshift (Skip Shift) Lamp Control Circuit Malfunction

P1000 OBD II Monitor Testing Not Complete More Driving Required

P1001 Key On Engine Running (KOER) Self-Test Not Able To Complete, KOER Aborted

P1100 Mass Air Flow (MAF) Sensor Intermittent

P1101 Mass Air Flow (MAF) Sensor Out Of Self-Test Range

P1110 Intake Air Temperature (IAT) Sensor Signal Circuit Fault

P1112 Intake Air Temperature (IAT) Sensor Intermittent

P1113 Intake Air Temperature (IAT) Sensor Intermittent

P1116 Engine Coolant Temperature (ECT) Sensor Out Of Self-Test Range

P1117 Engine Coolant Temperature (ECT) Sensor Intermittent

P1120 Throttle Position (TP) Sensor Out Of Range (Low)

P1121 Throttle Position (TP) Sensor Inconsistent With MAF Sensor

P1124 Throttle Position (TP) Sensor Out Of Self-Test Range

P1125 Throttle Position (TP) Sensor Circuit Intermittent

P1127 Exhaust Not Warm Enough, Downstream Heated Oxygen Sensors (HO2S) Not Tested

P1128 Upstream Heated Oxygen Sensors (HO2S) Swapped From Bank To Bank

P1129 Downstream Heated Oxygen Sensors (HO2S) Swapped From Bank To Bank

P1130 Lack Of Upstream Heated Oxygen Sensor (HO2S 11) Switch, Adaptive Fuel At Limit (Bank #1)

P1131 Lack Of Upstream Heated Oxygen Sensor (HO2S 11) Switch, Sensor Indicates Lean (Bank #1)

P1132 Lack Of Upstream Heated Oxygen Sensor (HO2S 11) Switch, Sensor Indicates Rich (Bank #1)

P1137 Lack Of Downstream Heated Oxygen Sensor (HO2S 12) Switch, Sensor Indicates Lean (Bank #1)

P1138 Lack Of Downstream Heated Oxygen Sensor (HO2S 12) Switch, Sensor Indicates Rich (Bank #1)

P1150 Lack Of Upstream Heated Oxygen Sensor (HO2S 21) Switch, Adaptive Fuel At Limit (Bank #2)

P1151 Lack Of Upstream Heated Oxygen Sensor (HO2S 21) Switch, Sensor Indicates Lean (Bank #2)

P1152 Lack Of Upstream Heated Oxygen Sensor (HO2S 21) Switch, Sensor Indicates Rich (Bank #2)

P1170 (HO2S 11) Signal Remained Unchanged For More Than 20 Seconds After Closed Loop

P1173 Feedback A/F Mixture Control (HO2S 21) Signal Remained Unchanged For More Than 20 Seconds After Closed Loop

P1195 Barometric (BARO) Pressure Sensor Circuit Malfunction (Signal Is From EGR Boost Sensor)

P1196 Starter Switch Circuit Malfunction

P1235 Fuel Pump Control Out Of Range (MIL DTC)

P1236 Fuel Pump Control Out Of Range (No MIL)

P1250 Fuel Pressure Regulator Control (FPRC) Solenoid Malfunction

P1252 Fuel Pressure Regulator Control (FPRC) Solenoid Malfunction

P1260 THEFT Detected—Engine Disabled

P1270 Engine RPM Or Vehicle Speed Limiter Reached

P1345 No Camshaft Position Sensor Signal

P1351 Ignition Diagnostic Monitor (IDM) Circuit Input Malfunction

P1352 Indicates Ignition System Malfunction

P1353 Indicates Ignition System Malfunction

P1354 Indicates Ignition System Malfunction

P1358 Ignition Diagnostic Monitor (IDM) Signal Out Of Self-Test Range

P1359 Spark Output Circuit Malfunction

P1360 Ignition Coil "A" Secondary Circuit Fault

P1361 Ignition Coil "A" Secondary Circuit Fault

P1362 Ignition Coil "A" Secondary Circuit Fault

P1364 Spark Output Circuit Malfunction

P1365 Ignition Coil Secondary Circuit Fault

P1390 Octane Adjust (OCT ADJ) Out Of Self-Test Range

P1400 Differential Pressure Feedback EGR (DPFE) Sensor Circuit Low Voltage Detected

P1401 Differential Pressure Feedback EGR (DPFE) Sensor Circuit High Voltage Detected/EGR Temperature Sensor

P1402 EGR Valve Position Sensor Open Or Short

P1405 Differential Pressure Feedback EGR (DPFE) Sensor Upstream Hose Off Or Plugged

P1406 Differential Pressure Feedback EGR (DPFE) Sensor Downstream Hose Off Or Plugged

P1407 Exhaust Gas Recirculation (EGR) No Flow Detected (Valve Stuck Closed Or Inoperative)

P1408 Exhaust Gas Recirculation (EGR) Flow Out Of Self-Test Range

P1409 Electronic Vacuum Regulator (EVR) Control Circuit Malfunction

P1443 Evaporative Emission Control System—Vacuum System, Purge Control Solenoid Or Purge Control Valve Malfunction

P1444 Purge Flow Sensor (PFS) Circuit Low Input

P1445 Purge Flow Sensor (PFS) Circuit High Input

P1449 Evaporative Emission Control System Unable To Hold Vacuum

P1455 Evaporative Emission Control System Control Leak Detected (Gross Leak)

P1460 Wide Open Throttle Air Conditioning Cut-Off Circuit Malfunction

P1464 Air Conditioning (A/C) Demand Out Of Self-Test Range/A/C On During KOER Or CCT Test

P1474 Low Fan Control Primary Circuit Malfunction

P1485 EGR Control Solenoid Open Or Short

P1486 EGR Vent Solenoid Open Or Short

P1487 EGR Boost Check Solenoid Open Or Short

P1500 Vehicle Speed Sensor (VSS) Circuit Intermittent

P1501 Vehicle Speed Sensor (VSS) Out Of Self-Test Range/Vehicle Moved During Test

P1502 Invalid Self Test—Auxiliary Powertrain Control Module (APCM) Functioning

P1504 Idle Air Control (IAC) Circuit Malfunction

P1505 Idle Air Control (IAC) System At Adaptive Clip

P1506 Idle Air Control (IAC) Over-speed Error

P1507 Idle Air Control (IAC) Under-speed Error

P1508 Bypass Air Solenoid "1" Circuit Fault

P1509 Bypass Air Solenoid "2" Circuit Fault

P1521 Variable Resonance Induction System (VRIS) Solenoid #1 Open Or Short

P1522 Variable Resonance Induction System (VRIS) Solenoid #2 Open Or Short

P1523 High Speed Inlet Air (HSIA) Solenoid Open Or Short

P1524 Charge Air Cooler Bypass Solenoid Circuit Fault

P1525 ABV Vacuum Solenoid Circuit Fault

P1526 ABV Vent Solenoid Circuit Fault

P1529 Atmospheric balance Air Control Valve Fault

P1540 ABV System Fault

P1601 Serial Communication Error

P1602 Serial Communication Error

P1605 Powertrain Control Module (PCM)—Keep Alive Memory (KAM) Test Error

P1608 PCM Internal Circuit Malfunction

P1609 PCM Internal Circuit Malfunction

P1627 Serial Communication Error

P1628 Serial Communication Error

P1650 Power Steering Pressure (PSP) Switch Out Of Self-Test Range

P1651 Power Steering Pressure (PSP) Switch Input Malfunction

P1701 Reverse Engagement Error

P1703 Brake On/Off (BOO) Switch Out Of Self-Test Range

P1705 Transmission Range (TR) Sensor Out Of Self-Test Range

P1706 High Vehicle Speed In Park

P1709 Park Or Neutral Position (PNP) Or Clutch Pedal Position (CPP) Switch Out Of Self-Test Range

P1711 Transmission Fluid Temperature (TFT) Sensor Out Of Self-Test Range

P1720 Vehicle Speed Sensor (VSS) Circuit Malfunction

P1729 4x4 Low Switch Error

P1741 Torque Converter Clutch (TCC) Control Error

P1742 Torque Converter Clutch (TCC) Solenoid Failed On (Turns On MIL)

P1743 Torque Converter Clutch (TCC) Solenoid Failed On (Turns On TCIL)

P1746 Electronic Pressure Control (EPC) Solenoid Open Circuit (Low Input)

P1747 Electronic Pressure Control (EPC) Solenoid Short Circuit (High Input)

P1749 Electronic Pressure Control (EPC) Solenoid Failed Low

P1751 Shift Solenoid #1 (SS1) Performance

P1754 Coast Clutch Solenoid (CCS) Circuit Malfunction

P1756 Shift Solenoid #2 (SS2) Performance

P1761 Shift Solenoid #3 (SS3) Performance

P1780 Transmission Control Switch (TCS) Circuit Out Of Self-Test Range

P1781 4x4 Low Switch, Out Of Self-Test Range

P1783 Transmission Over Temperature Condition

P1794 PCM Battery Direct Power Circuit Fault

P1797 P/N Switch Open or Short Circuit Fault

Mercedes-Benz

READING CODES

Reading the control module memory is one of the first steps in OBD II system diagnostics. This step should be initially performed to determine the general nature of the fault. Subsequent readings will determine if the fault has been cleared.

Reading codes can be performed by any of the methods below:
- Read the control module memory with the Generic Scan Tool (GST)
- Read the control module memory with the vehicle manufacturer's specific tester

To read the fault codes, connect the scan tool or tester according to the manufacturer's instructions. Follow the manufacturer's specified procedure for reading the codes.

CLEARING CODES

Control module reset procedures are a very important part of OBD II System diagnostics. This step should be done at the end of any fault code repair and at the end of any driveability repair.

Clearing codes can be performed by any of the methods below:
- Clear the control module memory with the Generic Scan Tool (GST)
- Clear the control module memory with the vehicle manufacturer's specific tester
- Turn the ignition OFF and remove the negative battery cable for at least 1 minute.

Removing the negative battery cable may cause other systems in the vehicle to loose their memory. Prior to removing the cable, ensure you have the proper reset codes for radios and alarms.

➡ **The MIL will may also be de-activated for some codes if the vehicle completes three consecutive trips without a fault detected with vehicle conditions similar to those present during the fault.**

OBD II TROUBLE CODES

P0100 Mass or Volume Air Flow Circuit Malfunction

P0101 Mass or Volume Air Flow Circuit Range/Performance Problem

P0102 Mass or Volume Air Flow Circuit Low Input

P0103 Mass or Volume Air Flow Circuit High Input

P0104 Mass or Volume Air Flow Circuit Intermittent

P0105 Manifold Absolute Pressure/Barometric Pressure Circuit Malfunction

P0106 Manifold Absolute Pressure/Barometric Pressure Circuit Range/Performance Problem

P0107 Manifold Absolute Pressure/Barometric Pressure Circuit Low Input

P0108 Manifold Absolute Pressure/Barometric Pressure Circuit High Input

P0109 Manifold Absolute Pressure/Barometric Pressure Circuit Intermittent

P0110 Intake Air Temperature Circuit Malfunction

P0111 Intake Air Temperature Circuit Range/Performance Problem

P0112 Intake Air Temperature Circuit Low Input

P0113 Intake Air Temperature Circuit High Input

P0114 Intake Air Temperature Circuit Intermittent

P0115 Engine Coolant Temperature Circuit Malfunction

P0116 Engine Coolant Temperature Circuit Range/Performance Problem

P0117 Engine Coolant Temperature Circuit Low Input

P0118 Engine Coolant Temperature Circuit High Input

P0119 Engine Coolant Temperature Circuit Intermittent

P0120 Throttle/Pedal Position Sensor/Switch "A" Circuit Malfunction

P0121 Throttle/Pedal Position Sensor/Switch "A" Circuit Range/Performance Problem

P0122 Throttle/Pedal Position Sensor/Switch "A" Circuit Low Input

P0123 Throttle/Pedal Position Sensor/Switch "A" Circuit High Input

P0124 Throttle/Pedal Position Sensor/Switch "A" Circuit Intermittent

P0125 Insufficient Coolant Temperature For Closed Loop Fuel Control

P0126 Insufficient Coolant Temperature For Stable Operation

P0130 O_2 Circuit Malfunction (Bank #1 Sensor #1)

P0131 O_2 Sensor Circuit Low Voltage (Bank #1 Sensor #1)

P0132 O_2 Sensor Circuit High Voltage (Bank #1 Sensor #1)

P0133 O_2 Sensor Circuit Slow Response (Bank #1 Sensor #1)

P0134 O_2 Sensor Circuit No Activity Detected (Bank #1 Sensor #1)

P0135 O_2 Sensor Heater Circuit Malfunction (Bank #1 Sensor #1)

P0136 O_2 Sensor Circuit Malfunction (Bank #1 Sensor #2)

P0137 O_2 Sensor Circuit Low Voltage (Bank #1 Sensor #2)

P0138 O_2 Sensor Circuit High Voltage (Bank #1 Sensor #2)

P0139 O_2 Sensor Circuit Slow Response (Bank #1 Sensor #2)

P0140 O_2 Sensor Circuit No Activity Detected (Bank #1 Sensor #2)

P0141 O_2 Sensor Heater Circuit Malfunction (Bank #1 Sensor #2)

P0142 O_2 Sensor Circuit Malfunction (Bank #1 Sensor #3)

P0143 O_2 Sensor Circuit Low Voltage (Bank #1 Sensor #3)

P0144 O_2 Sensor Circuit High Voltage (Bank #1 Sensor #3)

P0145 O_2 Sensor Circuit Slow Response (Bank #1 Sensor #3)

P0146 O_2 Sensor Circuit No Activity Detected (Bank #1 Sensor #3)

P0147 O_2 Sensor Heater Circuit Malfunction (Bank #1 Sensor #3)

P0150 O_2 Sensor Circuit Malfunction (Bank #2 Sensor #1)

P0151 O_2 Sensor Circuit Low Voltage (Bank #2 Sensor #1)

P0152 O_2 Sensor Circuit High Voltage (Bank #2 Sensor #1)

P0153 O_2 Sensor Circuit Slow Response (Bank #2 Sensor #1)

P0154 O_2 Sensor Circuit No Activity Detected (Bank #2 Sensor #1)

P0155 O_2 Sensor Heater Circuit Malfunction (Bank #2 Sensor #1)

P0156 O_2 Sensor Circuit Malfunction (Bank #2 Sensor #2)

P0157 O_2 Sensor Circuit Low Voltage (Bank #2 Sensor #2)

P0158 O_2 Sensor Circuit High Voltage (Bank #2 Sensor #2)

P0159 O_2 Sensor Circuit Slow Response (Bank #2 Sensor #2)

P0160 O_2 Sensor Circuit No Activity Detected (Bank #2 Sensor #2)

P0161 O_2 Sensor Heater Circuit Malfunction (Bank #2 Sensor #2)

P0162 O_2 Sensor Circuit Malfunction (Bank #2 Sensor #3)

P0163 O_2 Sensor Circuit Low Voltage (Bank #2 Sensor #3)

P0164 O_2 Sensor Circuit High Voltage (Bank #2 Sensor #3)

P0165 O_2 Sensor Circuit Slow Response (Bank #2 Sensor #3)

P0166 O_2 Sensor Circuit No Activity Detected (Bank #2 Sensor #3)

P0167 O_2 Sensor Heater Circuit Malfunction (Bank #2 Sensor #3)

P0170 Fuel Trim Malfunction (Bank #1)

P0171 System Too Lean (Bank #1)

P0172 System Too Rich (Bank #1)

P0173 Fuel Trim Malfunction (Bank #2)

P0174 System Too Lean (Bank #2)

P0175 System Too Rich (Bank #2)

P0176 Fuel Composition Sensor Circuit Malfunction

P0177 Fuel Composition Sensor Circuit Range/Performance

P0178 Fuel Composition Sensor Circuit Low Input

P0179 Fuel Composition Sensor Circuit High Input

P0180 Fuel Temperature Sensor "A" Circuit Malfunction

P0181 Fuel Temperature Sensor "A" Circuit Range/Performance

P0182 Fuel Temperature Sensor "A" Circuit Low Input

P0183 Fuel Temperature Sensor "A" Circuit High Input

P0184 Fuel Temperature Sensor "A" Circuit Intermittent

P0185 Fuel Temperature Sensor "B" Circuit Malfunction

P0186 Fuel Temperature Sensor "B" Circuit Range/Performance

P0187 Fuel Temperature Sensor "B" Circuit Low Input

P0188 Fuel Temperature Sensor "B" Circuit High Input

P0189 Fuel Temperature Sensor "B" Circuit Intermittent

P0190 Fuel Rail Pressure Sensor Circuit Malfunction

P0191 Fuel Rail Pressure Sensor Circuit Range/Performance

P0192 Fuel Rail Pressure Sensor Circuit Low Input

P0193 Fuel Rail Pressure Sensor Circuit High Input

P0194 Fuel Rail Pressure Sensor Circuit Intermittent

P0195 Engine Oil Temperature Sensor Malfunction

P0196 Engine Oil Temperature Sensor Range/Performance

P0197 Engine Oil Temperature Sensor Low

P0198 Engine Oil Temperature Sensor High

P0199 Engine Oil Temperature Sensor Intermittent

P0200 Injector Circuit Malfunction

P0201 Injector Circuit Malfunction—Cylinder #1

P0202 Injector Circuit Malfunction—Cylinder #2

P0203 Injector Circuit Malfunction—Cylinder #3

P0204 Injector Circuit Malfunction—Cylinder #4

P0205 Injector Circuit Malfunction—Cylinder #5

P0206 Injector Circuit Malfunction—Cylinder #6

P0207 Injector Circuit Malfunction—Cylinder #7

P0208 Injector Circuit Malfunction—Cylinder #8

P0209 Injector Circuit Malfunction—Cylinder #9

P0210 Injector Circuit Malfunction—Cylinder #10

P0211 Injector Circuit Malfunction—Cylinder #11

P0212 Injector Circuit Malfunction—Cylinder #12

P0213 Cold Start Injector #1 Malfunction

P0214 Cold Start Injector #2 Malfunction

P0215 Engine Shutoff Solenoid Malfunction

P0216 Injection Timing Control Circuit Malfunction

P0217 Engine Over Temperature Condition

P0218 Transmission Over Temperature Condition

P0219 Engine Over Speed Condition

P0220 Throttle/Pedal Position Sensor/Switch "B" Circuit Malfunction

P0221 Throttle/Pedal Position Sensor/Switch "B" Circuit Range/Performance Problem

P0222 Throttle/Pedal Position Sensor/Switch "B" Circuit Low Input

P0223 Throttle/Pedal Position Sensor/Switch "B" Circuit High Input

P0224 Throttle/Pedal Position Sensor/Switch "B" Circuit Intermittent

P0225 Throttle/Pedal Position Sensor/Switch "C" Circuit Malfunction

P0226 Throttle/Pedal Position Sensor/Switch "C" Circuit Range/Performance Problem

P0227 Throttle/Pedal Position Sensor/Switch "C" Circuit Low Input

P0228 Throttle/Pedal Position Sensor/Switch "C" Circuit High Input

P0229 Throttle/Pedal Position Sensor/Switch "C" Circuit Intermittent

P0230 Fuel Pump Primary Circuit Malfunction

P0231 Fuel Pump Secondary Circuit Low

P0232 Fuel Pump Secondary Circuit High

P0233 Fuel Pump Secondary Circuit Intermittent

P0234 Engine Over Boost Condition

P0261 Cylinder #1 Injector Circuit Low

P0262 Cylinder #1 Injector Circuit High

P0263 Cylinder #1 Contribution/Balance Fault

P0264 Cylinder #2 Injector Circuit Low

P0265 Cylinder #2 Injector Circuit High

P0266 Cylinder #2 Contribution/Balance Fault

P0267 Cylinder #3 Injector Circuit Low

P0268 Cylinder #3 Injector Circuit High

P0269 Cylinder #3 Contribution/Balance Fault

P0270 Cylinder #4 Injector Circuit Low

P0271 Cylinder #4 Injector Circuit High

P0272 Cylinder #4 Contribution/Balance Fault

P0273 Cylinder #5 Injector Circuit Low

P0274 Cylinder #5 Injector Circuit High

P0275 Cylinder #5 Contribution/Balance Fault

P0276 Cylinder #6 Injector Circuit Low

P0277 Cylinder #6 Injector Circuit High

P0278 Cylinder #6 Contribution/Balance Fault

P0279 Cylinder #7 Injector Circuit Low

P0280 Cylinder #7 Injector Circuit High

P0281 Cylinder #7 Contribution/Balance Fault

P0282 Cylinder #8 Injector Circuit Low

P0283 Cylinder #8 Injector Circuit High

P0284 Cylinder #8 Contribution/Balance Fault

P0285 Cylinder #9 Injector Circuit Low

P0286 Cylinder #9 Injector Circuit High

P0287 Cylinder #9 Contribution/Balance Fault

P0288 Cylinder #10 Injector Circuit Low

P0289 Cylinder #10 Injector Circuit High

P0290 Cylinder #10 Contribution/Balance Fault

P0291 Cylinder #11 Injector Circuit Low

P0292 Cylinder #11 Injector Circuit High

P0293 Cylinder #11 Contribution/Balance Fault

P0294 Cylinder #12 Injector Circuit Low

P0295 Cylinder #12 Injector Circuit High

P0296 Cylinder #12 Contribution/Balance Fault

P0300 Random/Multiple Cylinder Misfire Detected

P0301 Cylinder #1—Misfire Detected

P0302 Cylinder #2—Misfire Detected

P0303 Cylinder #3—Misfire Detected

P0304 Cylinder #4—Misfire Detected

P0305 Cylinder #5—Misfire Detected

P0306 Cylinder #6—Misfire Detected

P0307 Cylinder #7—Misfire Detected

P0308 Cylinder #8—Misfire Detected

P0309 Cylinder #9—Misfire Detected

P0310 Cylinder #10—Misfire Detected

P0311 Cylinder #11—Misfire Detected

P0312 Cylinder #12—Misfire Detected

P0320 Ignition/Distributor Engine Speed Input Circuit Malfunction

P0321 Ignition/Distributor Engine Speed Input Circuit Range/Performance

P0322 Ignition/Distributor Engine Speed Input Circuit No Signal

P0323 Ignition/Distributor Engine Speed Input Circuit Intermittent

P0325 Knock Sensor #1—Circuit Malfunction (Bank #1 or Single Sensor)

P0326 Knock Sensor #1—Circuit Range/Performance (Bank #1 or Single Sensor)

P0327 Knock Sensor #1—Circuit Low Input (Bank #1 or Single Sensor)

P0328 Knock Sensor #1—Circuit High Input (Bank #1 or Single Sensor)

P0329 Knock Sensor #1—Circuit Input Intermittent (Bank #1 or Single Sensor)

P0330 Knock Sensor #2—Circuit Malfunction (Bank #2)

P0331 Knock Sensor #2—Circuit Range/Performance (Bank #2)

P0332 Knock Sensor #2—Circuit Low Input (Bank #2)

P0333 Knock Sensor #2—Circuit High Input (Bank #2)

P0334 Knock Sensor #2—Circuit Input Intermittent (Bank #2)

P0335 Crankshaft Position Sensor "A" Circuit Malfunction

Ignition system service is covered in the model specific sections of this manual

P0336 Crankshaft Position Sensor "A" Circuit Range/Performance

P0337 Crankshaft Position Sensor "A" Circuit Low Input

P0338 Crankshaft Position Sensor "A" Circuit High Input

P0339 Crankshaft Position Sensor "A" Circuit Intermittent

P0340 Camshaft Position Sensor Circuit Malfunction

P0341 Camshaft Position Sensor Circuit Range/Performance

P0342 Camshaft Position Sensor Circuit Low Input

P0343 Camshaft Position Sensor Circuit High Input

P0344 Camshaft Position Sensor Circuit Intermittent

P0350 Ignition Coil Primary/Secondary Circuit Malfunction

P0351 Ignition Coil "A" Primary/Secondary Circuit Malfunction

P0352 Ignition Coil "B" Primary/Secondary Circuit Malfunction

P0353 Ignition Coil "C" Primary/Secondary Circuit Malfunction

P0354 Ignition Coil "D" Primary/Secondary Circuit Malfunction

P0355 Ignition Coil "E" Primary/Secondary Circuit Malfunction

P0356 Ignition Coil "F" Primary/Secondary Circuit Malfunction

P0357 Ignition Coil "G" Primary/Secondary Circuit Malfunction

P0358 Ignition Coil "H" Primary/Secondary Circuit Malfunction

P0359 Ignition Coil "I" Primary/Secondary Circuit Malfunction

P0360 Ignition Coil "J" Primary/Secondary Circuit Malfunction

P0361 Ignition Coil "K" Primary/Secondary Circuit Malfunction

P0362 Ignition Coil "L" Primary/Secondary Circuit Malfunction

P0370 Timing Reference High Resolution Signal "A" Malfunction

P0371 Timing Reference High Resolution Signal "A" Too Many Pulses

P0372 Timing Reference High Resolution Signal "A" Too Few Pulses

P0373 Timing Reference High Resolution Signal "A" Intermittent/Erratic Pulses

P0374 Timing Reference High Resolution Signal "A" No Pulses

P0375 Timing Reference High Resolution Signal "B" Malfunction

P0376 Timing Reference High Resolution Signal "B" Too Many Pulses

P0377 Timing Reference High Resolution Signal "B" Too Few Pulses

P0378 Timing Reference High Resolution Signal "B" Intermittent/Erratic Pulses

P0379 Timing Reference High Resolution Signal "B" No Pulses

P0380 Glow Plug/Heater Circuit "A" Malfunction

P0381 Glow Plug/Heater Indicator Circuit Malfunction

P0382 Glow Plug/Heater Circuit "B" Malfunction

P0385 Crankshaft Position Sensor "B" Circuit Malfunction

P0386 Crankshaft Position Sensor "B" Circuit Range/Performance

P0387 Crankshaft Position Sensor "B" Circuit Low Input

P0388 Crankshaft Position Sensor "B" Circuit High Input

P0389 Crankshaft Position Sensor "B" Circuit Intermittent

P0400 Exhaust Gas Recirculation Flow Malfunction

P0401 Exhaust Gas Recirculation Flow Insufficient Detected

P0402 Exhaust Gas Recirculation Flow Excessive Detected

P0403 Exhaust Gas Recirculation Circuit Malfunction

P0404 Exhaust Gas Recirculation Circuit Range/Performance

P0405 Exhaust Gas Recirculation Sensor "A" Circuit Low

P0406 Exhaust Gas Recirculation Sensor "A" Circuit High

P0407 Exhaust Gas Recirculation Sensor "B" Circuit Low

P0408 Exhaust Gas Recirculation Sensor "B" Circuit High

P0410 Secondary Air Injection System Malfunction

P0411 Secondary Air Injection System Incorrect Flow Detected

P0412 Secondary Air Injection System Switching Valve "A" Circuit Malfunction

P0413 Secondary Air Injection System Switching Valve "A" Circuit Open

P0414 Secondary Air Injection System Switching Valve "A" Circuit Shorted

P0415 Secondary Air Injection System Switching Valve "B" Circuit Malfunction

P0416 Secondary Air Injection System Switching Valve "B" Circuit Open

P0417 Secondary Air Injection System Switching Valve "B" Circuit Shorted

P0418 Secondary Air Injection System Relay "A" Circuit Malfunction

P0419 Secondary Air Injection System Relay "B" Circuit Malfunction

P0420 Catalyst System Efficiency Below Threshold (Bank #1)

P0421 Warm Up Catalyst Efficiency Below Threshold (Bank #1)

P0422 Main Catalyst Efficiency Below Threshold (Bank #1)

P0423 Heated Catalyst Efficiency Below Threshold (Bank #1)

P0424 Heated Catalyst Temperature Below Threshold (Bank #1)

P0430 Catalyst System Efficiency Below Threshold (Bank #2)

P0431 Warm Up Catalyst Efficiency Below Threshold (Bank #2)

P0432 Main Catalyst Efficiency Below Threshold (Bank #2)

P0433 Heated Catalyst Efficiency Below Threshold (Bank #2)

P0434 Heated Catalyst Temperature Below Threshold (Bank #2)

P0440 Evaporative Emission Control System Malfunction

P0441 Evaporative Emission Control System Incorrect Purge Flow

P0442 Evaporative Emission Control System Leak Detected (Small Leak)

P0443 Evaporative Emission Control System Purge Control Valve Circuit Malfunction

P0444 Evaporative Emission Control System Purge Control Valve Circuit Open

P0445 Evaporative Emission Control System Purge Control Valve Circuit Shorted

P0446 Evaporative Emission Control System Vent Control Circuit Malfunction

P0447 Evaporative Emission Control System Vent Control Circuit Open

P0448 Evaporative Emission Control System Vent Control Circuit Shorted

P0449 Evaporative Emission Control System Vent Valve/Solenoid Circuit Malfunction

P0450 Evaporative Emission Control System Pressure Sensor Malfunction

P0451 Evaporative Emission Control System Pressure Sensor Range/Performance

P0452 Evaporative Emission Control System Pressure Sensor Low Input

P0453 Evaporative Emission Control System Pressure Sensor High Input

P0454 Evaporative Emission Control System Pressure Sensor Intermittent

P0455 Evaporative Emission Control System Leak Detected (Gross Leak)

P0460 Fuel Level Sensor Circuit Malfunction

P0461 Fuel Level Sensor Circuit Range/Performance

P0462 Fuel Level Sensor Circuit Low Input

P0463 Fuel Level Sensor Circuit High Input

P0464 Fuel Level Sensor Circuit Intermittent

P0465 Purge Flow Sensor Circuit Malfunction

P0466 Purge Flow Sensor Circuit Range/Performance

P0467 Purge Flow Sensor Circuit Low Input

P0468 Purge Flow Sensor Circuit High Input

P0469 Purge Flow Sensor Circuit Intermittent

P0470 Exhaust Pressure Sensor Malfunction

P0471 Exhaust Pressure Sensor Range/Performance

P0472 Exhaust Pressure Sensor Low

P0473 Exhaust Pressure Sensor High

P0474 Exhaust Pressure Sensor Intermittent

P0475 Exhaust Pressure Control Valve Malfunction

P0476 Exhaust Pressure Control Valve Range/Performance

P0477 Exhaust Pressure Control Valve Low

P0478 Exhaust Pressure Control Valve High

P0479 Exhaust Pressure Control Valve Intermittent

P0480 Cooling Fan #1 Control Circuit Malfunction

P0481 Cooling Fan #2 Control Circuit Malfunction

P0482 Cooling Fan #3 Control Circuit Malfunction

P0483 Cooling Fan Rationality Check Malfunction

P0484 Cooling Fan Circuit Over Current

P0485 Cooling Fan Power/Ground Circuit Malfunction

P0500 Vehicle Speed Sensor Malfunction

P0501 Vehicle Speed Sensor Range/Performance

P0502 Vehicle Speed Sensor Circuit Low Input

P0503 Vehicle Speed Sensor Intermittent/Erratic/High

P0505 Idle Control System Malfunction

P0506 Idle Control System RPM Lower Than Expected

P0507 Idle Control System RPM Higher Than Expected

P0510 Closed Throttle Position Switch Malfunction

P0520 Engine Oil Pressure Sensor/Switch Circuit Malfunction

P0521 Engine Oil Pressure Sensor/Switch Range/Performance

P0522 Engine Oil Pressure Sensor/Switch Low Voltage

P0523 Engine Oil Pressure Sensor/Switch High Voltage

P0530 A/C Refrigerant Pressure Sensor Circuit Malfunction

P0531 A/C Refrigerant Pressure Sensor Circuit Range/Performance

P0532 A/C Refrigerant Pressure Sensor Circuit Low Input

P0533 A/C Refrigerant Pressure Sensor Circuit High Input

P0534 A/C Refrigerant Charge Loss

P0550 Power Steering Pressure Sensor Circuit Malfunction

P0551 Power Steering Pressure Sensor Circuit Range/Performance

P0552 Power Steering Pressure Sensor Circuit Low Input

P0553 Power Steering Pressure Sensor Circuit High Input

P0554 Power Steering Pressure Sensor Circuit Intermittent

P0560 System Voltage Malfunction

P0561 System Voltage Unstable

P0562 System Voltage Low

P0563 System Voltage High

P0565 Cruise Control On Signal Malfunction

P0566 Cruise Control Off Signal Malfunction

P0567 Cruise Control Resume Signal Malfunction

P0568 Cruise Control Set Signal Malfunction

P0569 Cruise Control Coast Signal Malfunction

P0570 Cruise Control Accel Signal Malfunction

P0571 Cruise Control/Brake Switch "A" Circuit Malfunction

P0572 Cruise Control/Brake Switch "A" Circuit Low

P0573 Cruise Control/Brake Switch "A" Circuit High

P0574 Through P0580 Reserved for Cruise Codes

P0600 Serial Communication Link Malfunction

P0601 Internal Control Module Memory Check Sum Error

P0602 Control Module Programming Error

P0603 Internal Control Module Keep Alive Memory (KAM) Error

P0604 Internal Control Module Random Access Memory (RAM) Error

P0605 Internal Control Module Read Only Memory (ROM) Error

P0606 PCM Processor Fault

P0608 Control Module VSS Output "A" Malfunction

P0609 Control Module VSS Output "B" Malfunction

P0620 Generator Control Circuit Malfunction

P0621 Generator Lamp "L" Control Circuit Malfunction

P0622 Generator Field "F" Control Circuit Malfunction

P0650 Malfunction Indicator Lamp (MIL) Control Circuit Malfunction

P0654 Engine RPM Output Circuit Malfunction

P0655 Engine Hot Lamp Output Control Circuit Malfunction

P0656 Fuel Level Output Circuit Malfunction

P0700 Transmission Control System Malfunction

P0701 Transmission Control System Range/Performance

P0702 Transmission Control System Electrical

P0703 Torque Converter/Brake Switch "B" Circuit Malfunction

P0704 Clutch Switch Input Circuit Malfunction

P0705 Transmission Range Sensor Circuit Malfunction (PRNDL Input)

P0706 Transmission Range Sensor Circuit Range/Performance

P0707 Transmission Range Sensor Circuit Low Input

P0708 Transmission Range Sensor Circuit High Input

P0709 Transmission Range Sensor Circuit Intermittent

P0710 Transmission Fluid Temperature Sensor Circuit Malfunction

P0711 Transmission Fluid Temperature Sensor Circuit Range/Performance

P0712 Transmission Fluid Temperature Sensor Circuit Low Input

P0713 Transmission Fluid Temperature Sensor Circuit High Input

P0714 Transmission Fluid Temperature Sensor Circuit Intermittent

P0715 Input/Turbine Speed Sensor Circuit Malfunction

P0716 Input/Turbine Speed Sensor Circuit Range/Performance

P0717 Input/Turbine Speed Sensor Circuit No Signal

P0718 Input/Turbine Speed Sensor Circuit Intermittent

P0719 Torque Converter/Brake Switch "B" Circuit Low

P0720 Output Speed Sensor Circuit Malfunction

P0721 Output Speed Sensor Circuit Range/Performance

P0722 Output Speed Sensor Circuit No Signal

P0723 Output Speed Sensor Circuit Intermittent

P0724 Torque Converter/Brake Switch "B" Circuit High

P0725 Engine Speed Input Circuit Malfunction

P0726 Engine Speed Input Circuit Range/Performance

P0727 Engine Speed Input Circuit No Signal

P0728 Engine Speed Input Circuit Intermittent

P0730 Incorrect Gear Ratio

P0731 Gear #1 Incorrect Ratio

P0732 Gear #2 Incorrect Ratio

P0733 Gear #3 Incorrect Ratio

P0734 Gear #4 Incorrect Ratio

P0735 Gear #5 Incorrect Ratio

P0736 Reverse Incorrect Ratio

P0740 Torque Converter Clutch Circuit Malfunction

P0741 Torque Converter Clutch Circuit Performance or Stuck Off

P0742 Torque Converter Clutch Circuit Stuck On

P0743 Torque Converter Clutch Circuit Electrical

P0744 Torque Converter Clutch Circuit Intermittent

P0745 Pressure Control Solenoid Malfunction

P0746 Pressure Control Solenoid Performance or Stuck Off

P0747 Pressure Control Solenoid Stuck On

P0748 Pressure Control Solenoid Electrical

P0749 Pressure Control Solenoid Intermittent

P0750 Shift Solenoid "A" Malfunction

P0751 Shift Solenoid "A" Performance or Stuck Off

P0752 Shift Solenoid "A" Stuck On

P0753 Shift Solenoid "A" Electrical

P0754 Shift Solenoid "A" Intermittent

P0755 Shift Solenoid "B" Malfunction

P0756 Shift Solenoid "B" Performance or Stuck Off

P0757 Shift Solenoid "B" Stuck On

P0758 Shift Solenoid "B" Electrical

P0759 Shift Solenoid "B" Intermittent

P0760 Shift Solenoid "C" Malfunction

P0761 Shift Solenoid "C" Performance Or Stuck Off

P0762 Shift Solenoid "C" Stuck On

P0763 Shift Solenoid "C" Electrical

P0764 Shift Solenoid "C" Intermittent

P0765 Shift Solenoid "D" Malfunction

P0766 Shift Solenoid "D" Performance Or Stuck Off

P0767 Shift Solenoid "D" Stuck On

P0768 Shift Solenoid "D" Electrical

P0769 Shift Solenoid "D" Intermittent

P0770 Shift Solenoid "E" Malfunction

P0771 Shift Solenoid "E" Performance Or Stuck Off

P0772 Shift Solenoid "E" Stuck On

P0773 Shift Solenoid "E" Electrical

P0774 Shift Solenoid "E" Intermittent

P0780 Shift Malfunction

P0781 1–2 Shift Malfunction

P0782 2–3 Shift Malfunction

P0783 3–4 Shift Malfunction

P0784 4–5 Shift Malfunction

P0785 Shift/Timing Solenoid Malfunction

P0786 Shift/Timing Solenoid Range/Performance

P0787 Shift/Timing Solenoid Low

P0788 Shift/Timing Solenoid High

P0789 Shift/Timing Solenoid Intermittent

P0790 Normal/Performance Switch Circuit Malfunction

P0801 Reverse Inhibit Control Circuit Malfunction

P0803 1–4 Upshift (Skip Shift) Solenoid Control Circuit Malfunction

P0804 1–4 Upshift (Skip Shift) Lamp Control Circuit Malfunction

Mitsubishi

READING CODES

Reading the control module memory is one of the first steps in OBD II system diagnostics. This step should be initially performed to determine the general nature of the fault. Subsequent readings will determine if the fault has been cleared.

Reading codes can be performed by any of the methods below:

• Read the control module memory with the Generic Scan Tool (GST)

• Read the control module memory with the vehicle manufacturer's specific tester

To read the fault codes, connect the scan tool or tester according to the manufacturer's instructions. Follow the manufacturer's specified procedure for reading the codes.

CLEARING CODES

Control module reset procedures are a very important part of OBD II System diagnostics. This step should be done at the end of any fault code repair and at the end of any driveability repair.

Clearing codes can be performed by any of the methods below:

• Clear the control module memory with the Generic Scan Tool (GST)

• Clear the control module memory with the vehicle manufacturer's specific tester

• Turn the ignition OFF and remove the negative battery cable for at least 1 minute.

Removing the negative battery cable may cause other systems in the vehicle to loose their memory. Prior to removing the cable, ensure you have the proper reset codes for radios and alarms.

➡ The MIL will may also be de-activated for some codes if the vehicle completes three consecutive trips without a fault detected with vehicle conditions similar to those present during the fault.

OBD II TROUBLE CODES

P0100 Mass or Volume Air Flow Circuit Malfunction

P0101 Mass or Volume Air Flow Circuit Range/Performance Problem

P0102 Mass or Volume Air Flow Circuit Low Input

P0103 Mass or Volume Air Flow Circuit High Input

P0104 Mass or Volume Air Flow Circuit Intermittent

P0105 Manifold Absolute Pressure/Barometric Pressure Circuit Malfunction

P0106 Manifold Absolute Pressure/Barometric Pressure Circuit Range/Performance Problem

P0107 Manifold Absolute Pressure/Barometric Pressure Circuit Low Input

P0108 Manifold Absolute Pressure/Barometric Pressure Circuit High Input

P0109 Manifold Absolute Pressure/Barometric Pressure Circuit Intermittent

P0110 Intake Air Temperature Circuit Malfunction

P0111 Intake Air Temperature Circuit Range/Performance Problem

P0112 Intake Air Temperature Circuit Low Input

P0113 Intake Air Temperature Circuit High Input

P0114 Intake Air Temperature Circuit Intermittent

P0115 Engine Coolant Temperature Circuit Malfunction

P0116 Engine Coolant Temperature Circuit Range/Performance Problem

P0117 Engine Coolant Temperature Circuit Low Input

P0118 Engine Coolant Temperature Circuit High Input

P0119 Engine Coolant Temperature Circuit Intermittent

P0120 Throttle/Pedal Position Sensor/ Switch "A" Circuit Malfunction

P0121 Throttle/Pedal Position Sensor/ Switch "A" Circuit Range/Performance Problem

P0122 Throttle/Pedal Position Sensor/ Switch "A" Circuit Low Input

P0123 Throttle/Pedal Position Sensor/ Switch "A" Circuit High Input

P0124 Throttle/Pedal Position Sensor/ Switch "A" Circuit Intermittent

P0125 Insufficient Coolant Temperature For Closed Loop Fuel Control

P0126 Insufficient Coolant Temperature For Stable Operation

P0130 O_2 Circuit Malfunction (Bank #1 Sensor #1)

P0131 O_2 Sensor Circuit Low Voltage (Bank #1 Sensor #1)

P0132 O_2 Sensor Circuit High Voltage (Bank #1 Sensor #1)

P0133 O_2 Sensor Circuit Slow Response (Bank #1 Sensor #1)

P0134 O_2 Sensor Circuit No Activity Detected (Bank #1 Sensor #1)

P0135 O_2 Sensor Heater Circuit Malfunction (Bank #1 Sensor #1)

P0136 O_2 Sensor Circuit Malfunction (Bank #1 Sensor #2)

P0137 O_2 Sensor Circuit Low Voltage (Bank #1 Sensor #2)

P0138 O_2 Sensor Circuit High Voltage (Bank #1 Sensor #2)

P0139 O_2 Sensor Circuit Slow Response (Bank #1 Sensor #2)

P0140 O_2 Sensor Circuit No Activity Detected (Bank #1 Sensor #2)

P0141 O_2 Sensor Heater Circuit Malfunction (Bank #1 Sensor #2)

P0142 O_2 Sensor Circuit Malfunction (Bank #1 Sensor #3)

P0143 O_2 Sensor Circuit Low Voltage (Bank #1 Sensor #3)

P0144 O_2 Sensor Circuit High Voltage (Bank #1 Sensor #3)

P0145 O_2 Sensor Circuit Slow Response (Bank #1 Sensor #3)

P0146 O_2 Sensor Circuit No Activity Detected (Bank #1 Sensor #3)

P0147 O_2 Sensor Heater Circuit Malfunction (Bank #1 Sensor #3)

P0150 O_2 Sensor Circuit Malfunction (Bank #2 Sensor #1)

P0151 O_2 Sensor Circuit Low Voltage (Bank #2 Sensor #1)

P0152 O_2 Sensor Circuit High Voltage (Bank #2 Sensor #1)

P0153 O_2 Sensor Circuit Slow Response (Bank #2 Sensor #1)

P0154 O_2 Sensor Circuit No Activity Detected (Bank #2 Sensor #1)

P0155 O_2 Sensor Heater Circuit Malfunction (Bank #2 Sensor #1)

P0156 O_2 Sensor Circuit Malfunction (Bank #2 Sensor #2)

P0157 O_2 Sensor Circuit Low Voltage (Bank #2 Sensor #2)

P0158 O_2 Sensor Circuit High Voltage (Bank #2 Sensor #2)

P0159 O_2 Sensor Circuit Slow Response (Bank #2 Sensor #2)

P0160 O_2 Sensor Circuit No Activity Detected (Bank #2 Sensor #2)

P0161 O_2 Sensor Heater Circuit Malfunction (Bank #2 Sensor #2)

P0162 O_2 Sensor Circuit Malfunction (Bank #2 Sensor #3)

P0163 O_2 Sensor Circuit Low Voltage (Bank #2 Sensor #3)

P0164 O_2 Sensor Circuit High Voltage (Bank #2 Sensor #3)

P0165 O_2 Sensor Circuit Slow Response (Bank #2 Sensor #3)

P0166 O_2 Sensor Circuit No Activity Detected (Bank #2 Sensor #3)

P0167 O_2 Sensor Heater Circuit Malfunction (Bank #2 Sensor #3)

P0170 Fuel Trim Malfunction (Bank #1)

P0171 System Too Lean (Bank #1)

P0172 System Too Rich (Bank #1)

P0173 Fuel Trim Malfunction (Bank #2)

P0174 System Too Lean (Bank #2)

P0175 System Too Rich (Bank #2)

P0176 Fuel Composition Sensor Circuit Malfunction

P0177 Fuel Composition Sensor Circuit Range/Performance

P0178 Fuel Composition Sensor Circuit Low Input

P0179 Fuel Composition Sensor Circuit High Input

P0180 Fuel Temperature Sensor "A" Circuit Malfunction

P0181 Fuel Temperature Sensor "A" Circuit Range/Performance

P0182 Fuel Temperature Sensor "A" Circuit Low Input

P0183 Fuel Temperature Sensor "A" Circuit High Input

P0184 Fuel Temperature Sensor "A" Circuit Intermittent

P0185 Fuel Temperature Sensor "B" Circuit Malfunction

P0186 Fuel Temperature Sensor "B" Circuit Range/Performance

P0187 Fuel Temperature Sensor "B" Circuit Low Input

P0188 Fuel Temperature Sensor "B" Circuit High Input

P0189 Fuel Temperature Sensor "B" Circuit Intermittent

P0190 Fuel Rail Pressure Sensor Circuit Malfunction

P0191 Fuel Rail Pressure Sensor Circuit Range/Performance

P0192 Fuel Rail Pressure Sensor Circuit Low Input

P0193 Fuel Rail Pressure Sensor Circuit High Input

P0194 Fuel Rail Pressure Sensor Circuit Intermittent

P0195 Engine Oil Temperature Sensor Malfunction

P0196 Engine Oil Temperature Sensor Range/Performance

P0197 Engine Oil Temperature Sensor Low

P0198 Engine Oil Temperature Sensor High

P0199 Engine Oil Temperature Sensor Intermittent

P0200 Injector Circuit Malfunction

P0201 Injector Circuit Malfunction— Cylinder #1

P0202 Injector Circuit Malfunction— Cylinder #2

P0203 Injector Circuit Malfunction— Cylinder #3

P0204 Injector Circuit Malfunction— Cylinder #4

P0205 Injector Circuit Malfunction— Cylinder #5

P0206 Injector Circuit Malfunction— Cylinder #6

P0207 Injector Circuit Malfunction— Cylinder #7

P0208 Injector Circuit Malfunction— Cylinder #8

P0209 Injector Circuit Malfunction— Cylinder #9

P0210 Injector Circuit Malfunction— Cylinder #10

P0211 Injector Circuit Malfunction— Cylinder #11

P0212 Injector Circuit Malfunction— Cylinder #12

P0213 Cold Start Injector #1 Malfunction

P0214 Cold Start Injector #2 Malfunction

Refer to the model specific sections for fuel system service procedures

P0215 Engine Shutoff Solenoid Malfunction

P0216 Injection Timing Control Circuit Malfunction

P0217 Engine Over Temperature Condition

P0218 Transmission Over Temperature Condition

P0219 Engine Over Speed Condition

P0220 Throttle/Pedal Position Sensor/Switch "B" Circuit Malfunction

P0221 Throttle/Pedal Position Sensor/Switch "B" Circuit Range/Performance Problem

P0222 Throttle/Pedal Position Sensor/Switch "B" Circuit Low Input

P0223 Throttle/Pedal Position Sensor/Switch "B" Circuit High Input

P0224 Throttle/Pedal Position Sensor/Switch "B" Circuit Intermittent

P0225 Throttle/Pedal Position Sensor/Switch "C" Circuit Malfunction

P0226 Throttle/Pedal Position Sensor/Switch "C" Circuit Range/Performance Problem

P0227 Throttle/Pedal Position Sensor/Switch "C" Circuit Low Input

P0228 Throttle/Pedal Position Sensor/Switch "C" Circuit High Input

P0229 Throttle/Pedal Position Sensor/Switch "C" Circuit Intermittent

P0230 Fuel Pump Primary Circuit Malfunction

P0231 Fuel Pump Secondary Circuit Low

P0232 Fuel Pump Secondary Circuit High

P0233 Fuel Pump Secondary Circuit Intermittent

P0234 Engine Over Boost Condition

P0261 Cylinder #1 Injector Circuit Low

P0262 Cylinder #1 Injector Circuit High

P0263 Cylinder #1 Contribution/Balance Fault

P0264 Cylinder #2 Injector Circuit Low

P0265 Cylinder #2 Injector Circuit High

P0266 Cylinder #2 Contribution/Balance Fault

P0267 Cylinder #3 Injector Circuit Low

P0268 Cylinder #3 Injector Circuit High

P0269 Cylinder #3 Contribution/Balance Fault

P0270 Cylinder #4 Injector Circuit Low

P0271 Cylinder #4 Injector Circuit High

P0272 Cylinder #4 Contribution/Balance Fault

P0273 Cylinder #5 Injector Circuit Low

P0274 Cylinder #5 Injector Circuit High

P0275 Cylinder #5 Contribution/Balance Fault

P0276 Cylinder #6 Injector Circuit Low

P0277 Cylinder #6 Injector Circuit High

P0278 Cylinder #6 Contribution/Balance Fault

P0279 Cylinder #7 Injector Circuit Low

P0280 Cylinder #7 Injector Circuit High

P0281 Cylinder #7 Contribution/Balance Fault

P0282 Cylinder #8 Injector Circuit Low

P0283 Cylinder #8 Injector Circuit High

P0284 Cylinder #8 Contribution/Balance Fault

P0285 Cylinder #9 Injector Circuit Low

P0286 Cylinder #9 Injector Circuit High

P0287 Cylinder #9 Contribution/Balance Fault

P0288 Cylinder #10 Injector Circuit Low

P0289 Cylinder #10 Injector Circuit High

P0290 Cylinder #10 Contribution/Balance Fault

P0291 Cylinder #11 Injector Circuit Low

P0292 Cylinder #11 Injector Circuit High

P0293 Cylinder #11 Contribution/Balance Fault

P0294 Cylinder #12 Injector Circuit Low

P0295 Cylinder #12 Injector Circuit High

P0296 Cylinder #12 Contribution/Balance Fault

P0300 Random/Multiple Cylinder Misfire Detected

P0301 Cylinder #1—Misfire Detected

P0302 Cylinder #2—Misfire Detected

P0303 Cylinder #3—Misfire Detected

P0304 Cylinder #4—Misfire Detected

P0305 Cylinder #5—Misfire Detected

P0306 Cylinder #6—Misfire Detected

P0307 Cylinder #7—Misfire Detected

P0308 Cylinder #8—Misfire Detected

P0309 Cylinder #9—Misfire Detected

P0310 Cylinder #10—Misfire Detected

P0311 Cylinder #11—Misfire Detected

P0312 Cylinder #12—Misfire Detected

P0320 Ignition/Distributor Engine Speed Input Circuit Malfunction

P0321 Ignition/Distributor Engine Speed Input Circuit Range/Performance

P0322 Ignition/Distributor Engine Speed Input Circuit No Signal

P0323 Ignition/Distributor Engine Speed Input Circuit Intermittent

P0325 Knock Sensor #1—Circuit Malfunction (Bank #1 or Single Sensor)

P0326 Knock Sensor #1—Circuit Range/Performance (Bank #1 or Single Sensor)

P0327 Knock Sensor #1—Circuit Low Input (Bank #1 or Single Sensor)

P0328 Knock Sensor #1—Circuit High Input (Bank #1 or Single Sensor)

P0329 Knock Sensor #1—Circuit Input Intermittent (Bank #1 or Single Sensor)

P0330 Knock Sensor #2—Circuit Malfunction (Bank #2)

P0331 Knock Sensor #2—Circuit Range/Performance (Bank #2)

P0332 Knock Sensor #2—Circuit Low Input (Bank #2)

P0333 Knock Sensor #2—Circuit High Input (Bank #2)

P0334 Knock Sensor #2—Circuit Input Intermittent (Bank #2)

P0335 Crankshaft Position Sensor "A" Circuit Malfunction

P0336 Crankshaft Position Sensor "A" Circuit Range/Performance

P0337 Crankshaft Position Sensor "A" Circuit Low Input

P0338 Crankshaft Position Sensor "A" Circuit High Input

P0339 Crankshaft Position Sensor "A" Circuit Intermittent

P0340 Camshaft Position Sensor Circuit Malfunction

P0341 Camshaft Position Sensor Circuit Range/Performance

P0342 Camshaft Position Sensor Circuit Low Input

P0343 Camshaft Position Sensor Circuit High Input

P0344 Camshaft Position Sensor Circuit Intermittent

P0350 Ignition Coil Primary/Secondary Circuit Malfunction

P0351 Ignition Coil "A" Primary/Secondary Circuit Malfunction

P0352 Ignition Coil "B" Primary/Secondary Circuit Malfunction

P0353 Ignition Coil "C" Primary/Secondary Circuit Malfunction

P0354 Ignition Coil "D" Primary/Secondary Circuit Malfunction

P0355 Ignition Coil "E" Primary/Secondary Circuit Malfunction

P0356 Ignition Coil "F" Primary/Secondary Circuit Malfunction

P0357 Ignition Coil "G" Primary/Secondary Circuit Malfunction

P0358 Ignition Coil "H" Primary/Secondary Circuit Malfunction

P0359 Ignition Coil "I" Primary/Secondary Circuit Malfunction

P0360 Ignition Coil "J" Primary/Secondary Circuit Malfunction

P0361 Ignition Coil "K" Primary/Secondary Circuit Malfunction

P0362 Ignition Coil "L" Primary/Secondary Circuit Malfunction

P0370 Timing Reference High Resolution Signal "A" Malfunction

P0371 Timing Reference High Resolution Signal "A" Too Many Pulses

P0372 Timing Reference High Resolution Signal "A" Too Few Pulses

P0373 Timing Reference High Resolution Signal "A" Intermittent/Erratic Pulses

P0374 Timing Reference High Resolution Signal "A" No Pulses

P0375 Timing Reference High Resolution Signal "B" Malfunction

P0376 Timing Reference High Resolution Signal "B" Too Many Pulses

P0377 Timing Reference High Resolution Signal "B" Too Few Pulses

P0378 Timing Reference High Resolution Signal "B" Intermittent/Erratic Pulses

P0379 Timing Reference High Resolution Signal "B" No Pulses

P0380 Glow Plug/Heater Circuit "A" Malfunction

P0381 Glow Plug/Heater Indicator Circuit Malfunction

P0382 Glow Plug/Heater Circuit "B" Malfunction

P0385 Crankshaft Position Sensor "B" Circuit Malfunction

P0386 Crankshaft Position Sensor "B" Circuit Range/Performance

P0387 Crankshaft Position Sensor "B" Circuit Low Input

P0388 Crankshaft Position Sensor "B" Circuit High Input

P0389 Crankshaft Position Sensor "B" Circuit Intermittent

P0400 Exhaust Gas Recirculation Flow Malfunction

P0401 Exhaust Gas Recirculation Flow Insufficient Detected

P0402 Exhaust Gas Recirculation Flow Excessive Detected

P0403 Exhaust Gas Recirculation Circuit Malfunction

P0404 Exhaust Gas Recirculation Circuit Range/Performance

P0405 Exhaust Gas Recirculation Sensor "A" Circuit Low

P0406 Exhaust Gas Recirculation Sensor "A" Circuit High

P0407 Exhaust Gas Recirculation Sensor "B" Circuit Low

P0408 Exhaust Gas Recirculation Sensor "B" Circuit High

P0410 Secondary Air Injection System Malfunction

P0411 Secondary Air Injection System Incorrect Flow Detected

P0412 Secondary Air Injection System Switching Valve "A" Circuit Malfunction

P0413 Secondary Air Injection System Switching Valve "A" Circuit Open

P0414 Secondary Air Injection System Switching Valve "A" Circuit Shorted

P0415 Secondary Air Injection System Switching Valve "B" Circuit Malfunction

P0416 Secondary Air Injection System Switching Valve "B" Circuit Open

P0417 Secondary Air Injection System Switching Valve "B" Circuit Shorted

P0418 Secondary Air Injection System Relay "A" Circuit Malfunction

P0419 Secondary Air Injection System Relay "B" Circuit Malfunction

P0420 Catalyst System Efficiency Below Threshold (Bank #1)

P0421 Warm Up Catalyst Efficiency Below Threshold (Bank #1)

P0422 Main Catalyst Efficiency Below Threshold (Bank #1)

P0423 Heated Catalyst Efficiency Below Threshold (Bank #1)

P0424 Heated Catalyst Temperature Below Threshold (Bank #1)

P0430 Catalyst System Efficiency Below Threshold (Bank #2)

P0431 Warm Up Catalyst Efficiency Below Threshold (Bank #2)

P0432 Main Catalyst Efficiency Below Threshold (Bank #2)

P0433 Heated Catalyst Efficiency Below Threshold (Bank #2)

P0434 Heated Catalyst Temperature Below Threshold (Bank #2)

P0440 Evaporative Emission Control System Malfunction

P0441 Evaporative Emission Control System Incorrect Purge Flow

P0442 Evaporative Emission Control System Leak Detected (Small Leak)

P0443 Evaporative Emission Control System Purge Control Valve Circuit Malfunction

P0444 Evaporative Emission Control System Purge Control Valve Circuit Open

P0445 Evaporative Emission Control System Purge Control Valve Circuit Shorted

P0446 Evaporative Emission Control System Vent Control Circuit Malfunction

P0447 Evaporative Emission Control System Vent Control Circuit Open

P0448 Evaporative Emission Control System Vent Control Circuit Shorted

P0449 Evaporative Emission Control System Vent Valve/Solenoid Circuit Malfunction

P0450 Evaporative Emission Control System Pressure Sensor Malfunction

P0451 Evaporative Emission Control System Pressure Sensor Range/Performance

P0452 Evaporative Emission Control System Pressure Sensor Low Input

P0453 Evaporative Emission Control System Pressure Sensor High Input

P0454 Evaporative Emission Control System Pressure Sensor Intermittent

P0455 Evaporative Emission Control System Leak Detected (Gross Leak)

P0460 Fuel Level Sensor Circuit Malfunction

P0461 Fuel Level Sensor Circuit Range/Performance

P0462 Fuel Level Sensor Circuit Low Input

P0463 Fuel Level Sensor Circuit High Input

P0464 Fuel Level Sensor Circuit Intermittent

P0465 Purge Flow Sensor Circuit Malfunction

P0466 Purge Flow Sensor Circuit Range/Performance

P0467 Purge Flow Sensor Circuit Low Input

P0468 Purge Flow Sensor Circuit High Input

P0469 Purge Flow Sensor Circuit Intermittent

P0470 Exhaust Pressure Sensor Malfunction

P0471 Exhaust Pressure Sensor Range/Performance

P0472 Exhaust Pressure Sensor Low

P0473 Exhaust Pressure Sensor High

P0474 Exhaust Pressure Sensor Intermittent

P0475 Exhaust Pressure Control Valve Malfunction

P0476 Exhaust Pressure Control Valve Range/Performance

P0477 Exhaust Pressure Control Valve Low

P0478 Exhaust Pressure Control Valve High

P0479 Exhaust Pressure Control Valve Intermittent

P0480 Cooling Fan #1 Control Circuit Malfunction

P0481 Cooling Fan #2 Control Circuit Malfunction

P0482 Cooling Fan #3 Control Circuit Malfunction

P0483 Cooling Fan Rationality Check Malfunction

P0484 Cooling Fan Circuit Over Current

P0485 Cooling Fan Power/Ground Circuit Malfunction

P0500 Vehicle Speed Sensor Malfunction

P0501 Vehicle Speed Sensor Range/Performance

Refer to the model specific sections for engine electrical system service procedures

P0502 Vehicle Speed Sensor Circuit Low Input

P0503 Vehicle Speed Sensor Intermittent/Erratic/High

P0505 Idle Control System Malfunction

P0506 Idle Control System RPM Lower Than Expected

P0507 Idle Control System RPM Higher Than Expected

P0510 Closed Throttle Position Switch Malfunction

P0520 Engine Oil Pressure Sensor/ Switch Circuit Malfunction

P0521 Engine Oil Pressure Sensor/ Switch Range/Performance

P0522 Engine Oil Pressure Sensor/ Switch Low Voltage

P0523 Engine Oil Pressure Sensor/ Switch High Voltage

P0530 A/C Refrigerant Pressure Sensor Circuit Malfunction

P0531 A/C Refrigerant Pressure Sensor Circuit Range/Performance

P0532 A/C Refrigerant Pressure Sensor Circuit Low Input

P0533 A/C Refrigerant Pressure Sensor Circuit High Input

P0534 A/C Refrigerant Charge Loss

P0550 Power Steering Pressure Sensor Circuit Malfunction

P0551 Power Steering Pressure Sensor Circuit Range/Performance

P0552 Power Steering Pressure Sensor Circuit Low Input

P0553 Power Steering Pressure Sensor Circuit High Input

P0554 Power Steering Pressure Sensor Circuit Intermittent

P0560 System Voltage Malfunction

P0561 System Voltage Unstable

P0562 System Voltage Low

P0563 System Voltage High

P0565 Cruise Control On Signal Malfunction

P0566 Cruise Control Off Signal Malfunction

P0567 Cruise Control Resume Signal Malfunction

P0568 Cruise Control Set Signal Malfunction

P0569 Cruise Control Coast Signal Malfunction

P0570 Cruise Control Accel Signal Malfunction

P0571 Cruise Control/Brake Switch "A" Circuit Malfunction

P0572 Cruise Control/Brake Switch "A" Circuit Low

P0573 Cruise Control/Brake Switch "A" Circuit High

P0574 Through P0580 Reserved for Cruise Codes

P0600 Serial Communication Link Malfunction

P0601 Internal Control Module Memory Check Sum Error

P0602 Control Module Programming Error

P0603 Internal Control Module Keep Alive Memory (KAM) Error

P0604 Internal Control Module Random Access Memory (RAM) Error

P0605 Internal Control Module Read Only Memory (ROM) Error

P0606 PCM Processor Fault

P0608 Control Module VSS Output "A" Malfunction

P0609 Control Module VSS Output "B" Malfunction

P0620 Generator Control Circuit Malfunction

P0621 Generator Lamp "L" Control Circuit Malfunction

P0622 Generator Field "F" Control Circuit Malfunction

P0650 Malfunction Indicator Lamp (MIL) Control Circuit Malfunction

P0654 Engine RPM Output Circuit Malfunction

P0655 Engine Hot Lamp Output Control Circuit Malfunction

P0656 Fuel Level Output Circuit Malfunction

P0700 Transmission Control System Malfunction

P0701 Transmission Control System Range/Performance

P0702 Transmission Control System Electrical

P0703 Torque Converter/Brake Switch "B" Circuit Malfunction

P0704 Clutch Switch Input Circuit Malfunction

P0705 Transmission Range Sensor Circuit Malfunction (PRNDL Input)

P0706 Transmission Range Sensor Circuit Range/Performance

P0707 Transmission Range Sensor Circuit Low Input

P0708 Transmission Range Sensor Circuit High Input

P0709 Transmission Range Sensor Circuit Intermittent

P0710 Transmission Fluid Temperature Sensor Circuit Malfunction

P0711 Transmission Fluid Temperature Sensor Circuit Range/Performance

P0712 Transmission Fluid Temperature Sensor Circuit Low Input

P0713 Transmission Fluid Temperature Sensor Circuit High Input

P0714 Transmission Fluid Temperature Sensor Circuit Intermittent

P0715 Input/Turbine Speed Sensor Circuit Malfunction

P0716 Input/Turbine Speed Sensor Circuit Range/Performance

P0717 Input/Turbine Speed Sensor Circuit No Signal

P0718 Input/Turbine Speed Sensor Circuit Intermittent

P0719 Torque Converter/Brake Switch "B" Circuit Low

P0720 Output Speed Sensor Circuit Malfunction

P0721 Output Speed Sensor Circuit Range/Performance

P0722 Output Speed Sensor Circuit No Signal

P0723 Output Speed Sensor Circuit Intermittent

P0724 Torque Converter/Brake Switch "B" Circuit High

P0725 Engine Speed Input Circuit Malfunction

P0726 Engine Speed Input Circuit Range/Performance

P0727 Engine Speed Input Circuit No Signal

P0728 Engine Speed Input Circuit Intermittent

P0730 Incorrect Gear Ratio

P0731 Gear #1 Incorrect Ratio

P0732 Gear #2 Incorrect Ratio

P0733 Gear #3 Incorrect Ratio

P0734 Gear #4 Incorrect Ratio

P0735 Gear #5 Incorrect Ratio

P0736 Reverse Incorrect Ratio

P0740 Torque Converter Clutch Circuit Malfunction

P0741 Torque Converter Clutch Circuit Performance or Stuck Off

P0742 Torque Converter Clutch Circuit Stuck On

P0743 Torque Converter Clutch Circuit Electrical

P0744 Torque Converter Clutch Circuit Intermittent

P0745 Pressure Control Solenoid Malfunction

P0746 Pressure Control Solenoid Performance or Stuck Off

P0747 Pressure Control Solenoid Stuck On

P0748 Pressure Control Solenoid Electrical

P0749 Pressure Control Solenoid Intermittent

P0750 Shift Solenoid "A" Malfunction

P0751 Shift Solenoid "A" Performance or Stuck Off

P0752 Shift Solenoid "A" Stuck On

P0753 Shift Solenoid "A" Electrical

P0754 Shift Solenoid "A" Intermittent

P0755 Shift Solenoid "B" Malfunction

P0756 Shift Solenoid "B" Performance or Stuck Off

P0757 Shift Solenoid "B" Stuck On

P0758 Shift Solenoid "B" Electrical

P0759 Shift Solenoid "B" Intermittent

P0760 Shift Solenoid "C" Malfunction

P0761 Shift Solenoid "C" Performance Or Stuck Off

P0762 Shift Solenoid "C" Stuck On

P0763 Shift Solenoid "C" Electrical

P0764 Shift Solenoid "C" Intermittent

P0765 Shift Solenoid "D" Malfunction

P0766 Shift Solenoid "D" Performance Or Stuck Off

P0767 Shift Solenoid "D" Stuck On

P0768 Shift Solenoid "D" Electrical

P0769 Shift Solenoid "D" Intermittent

P0770 Shift Solenoid "E" Malfunction

P0771 Shift Solenoid "E" Performance Or Stuck Off

P0772 Shift Solenoid "E" Stuck On

P0773 Shift Solenoid "E" Electrical

P0774 Shift Solenoid "E" Intermittent

P0780 Shift Malfunction

P0781 1–2 Shift Malfunction

P0782 2–3 Shift Malfunction

P0783 3–4 Shift Malfunction

P0784 4–5 Shift Malfunction

P0785 Shift/Timing Solenoid Malfunction

P0786 Shift/Timing Solenoid Range/Performance

P0787 Shift/Timing Solenoid Low

P0788 Shift/Timing Solenoid High

P0789 Shift/Timing Solenoid Intermittent

P0790 Normal/Performance Switch Circuit Malfunction

P0801 Reverse Inhibit Control Circuit Malfunction

P0803 1–4 Upshift (Skip Shift) Solenoid Control Circuit Malfunction

P0804 1–4 Upshift (Skip Shift) Lamp Control Circuit Malfunction

P1100 Induction Control Motor Position Sensor Fault

P1101 Traction Control Vacuum Solenoid Circuit Fault

P1102 Traction Control Ventilation Solenoid Circuit Fault

P1103 Turbocharger Waste Gate Actuator Circuit Fault

P1104 Turbocharger Waste Gate Solenoid Circuit Fault

P1105 Fuel Pressure Solenoid Circuit Fault

P1294 Target Idle Speed Not Reached

P1295 No 5-Volt Supply To TP Sensor

P1296 No 5-Volt Supply To MAP Sensor

P1297 No Change In MAP From Start To Run

P1300 Ignition Timing Adjustment Circuit

P1390 Timing Belt Skipped One Tooth Or More

P1391 Intermittent Loss Of CMP Or CKP Sensor Signals

P1400 Manifold Differential Pressure Sensor Fault

P1443 EVAP Purge Control Solenoid "2" Circuit Fault

P1486 EVAP Leak Monitor Pinched Hose Detected

P1487 High Speed Radiator Fan Control Relay Circuit Fault

P1989 High Speed Condenser Fan Control Relay Fault

P1490 Low Speed Fan Control Relay Fault

P1492 Battery Temperature Sensor High Voltage

P1494 EVAP Ventilation Switch Or Mechanical Fault

P1495 EVAP Ventilation Solenoid Circuit Fault

P1496 5-Volt Supply Output Too Low

P1500 Generator FR Terminal Circuit Fault

P1600 PCM-TCM Serial Communication Link Circuit Fault

P1696 PCM Failure- EEPROM Write Denied

P1715 No CCD Messages From TCM

P1750 TCM Pulse Generator Circuit Fault

P1791 Pressure Control, Shift Control, TCC Solenoid Fault

P1899 PCM ECT Level Signal to TCM Circuit Fault

Nissan

➡️**This section also provides coverage for the Mercury Villager since it shares a platform with the Nissan Quest**

READING CODES

With Scan Tool

Reading the control module memory is one of the first steps in OBD II system diagnostics. This step should be initially performed to determine the general nature of the fault. Subsequent readings will determine if the fault has been cleared.

Reading codes can be performed by any of the methods below:

• Read the control module memory with the Generic Scan Tool (GST)

• Read the control module memory with the vehicle manufacturer's specific tester

To read the fault codes, connect the scan tool or tester according to the manufacturer's instructions. Follow the manufacturer's specified procedure for reading the codes.

Without Scan Tool

The ECM is capable of outputting data in 4 different modes, depending on the position of the mode switch and the ignition key. Modes are switched by turning the mode screw on the side of the ECM, near the red LED. Additional modes are accessed by turning the ignition key on or off.

With the ECM set in Mode 1 and the ignition in the **ON** position, a malfunction indicator lamp bulb check may be performed. When the engine is started, the ECM will illuminate the indicator lamps as a warning of a fault in the system.

Mode 2 is set by turning the mode selector screw fully clockwise, waiting 2 seconds, then turning the screw fully counterclockwise. With the ignition in the **ON** position, self-diagnostic results will be output as a series of lamp flashes. When the engine is started, the oxygen sensor monitor function is enabled and the red LED on the ECM is used to determine proper oxygen sensor function.

1. Remove the access cover and locate the mode adjusting screw and LED on the ECM.

2. Turn the ignition switch **ON** but do not start the engine. Both the LED and the malfunction indicator lamp on the instrument panel should be illuminated. This is a bulb check.

3. Start the engine.

➡️**Switching modes is not possible while the engine is running.**

4. If the LED or malfunction indicator lamp illuminates, there is a fault in the system.

5. Turn the mode selector screw fully clockwise. Wait 2 seconds, then turn the screw fully counterclockwise.

6. The diagnostic trouble codes will now be read from the ECM memory. They will appear as flashes of the malfunction indicator lamp, or the ECM's LED.

7. After all codes have been read, turn the mode selector screw fully clockwise to erase the codes.

➥**Turn the mode adjusting screw to the fully counterclockwise position whenever the vehicle is in use.**

8. Turn the ignition **OFF**.

➥**When the ignition switch is turned OFF during diagnosis, power to the ECM will drop after approximately 5 seconds. The diagnosis will automatically return to Mode 1 at this time.**

CLEARING CODES

With Scan Tool

Control module reset procedures are a very important part of OBD II System diagnostics. This step should be done at the end of any fault code repair and at the end of any driveability repair.

Clearing codes can be performed by any of the methods below:

• Clear the control module memory with the Generic Scan Tool (GST)

• Clear the control module memory with the vehicle manufacturer's specific tester

➥**The MIL will may also be de-activated for some codes if the vehicle completes three consecutive trips without a fault detected with vehicle conditions similar to those present during the fault.**

Without Scan Tool

The easiest way to clear trouble codes without a scan tool is to turn the mode selector screw fully clockwise after all codes have been read.

➥**Turn the mode adjusting screw to the fully counterclockwise position whenever the vehicle is in use.**

Codes may also be erased by turning the ignition OFF and remove the negative battery cable for at least 1 minute. However, removing the negative battery cable may cause other systems in the vehicle to loose their memory. Prior to removing the cable, ensure you have the proper reset codes for radios and alarms.

OBD II TROUBLE CODES

P0000 No Self Diagnostic Failure Indicated

P0100 Mass or Volume Air Flow Circuit Malfunction

P0101 Mass or Volume Air Flow Circuit Range/Performance Problem

P0102 Mass or Volume Air Flow Circuit Low Input

P0103 Mass or Volume Air Flow Circuit High Input

P0104 Mass or Volume Air Flow Circuit Intermittent

P0105 Manifold Absolute Pressure/Barometric Pressure Circuit Malfunction

P0106 Manifold Absolute Pressure/Barometric Pressure Circuit Range/Performance Problem

P0107 Manifold Absolute Pressure/Barometric Pressure Circuit Low Input

P0108 Manifold Absolute Pressure/Barometric Pressure Circuit High Input

P0109 Manifold Absolute Pressure/Barometric Pressure Circuit Intermittent

P0110 Intake Air Temperature Circuit Malfunction

P0111 Intake Air Temperature Circuit Range/Performance Problem

P0112 Intake Air Temperature Circuit Low Input

P0113 Intake Air Temperature Circuit High Input

P0114 Intake Air Temperature Circuit Intermittent

P0115 Engine Coolant Temperature Circuit Malfunction

P0116 Engine Coolant Temperature Circuit Range/Performance Problem

P0117 Engine Coolant Temperature Circuit Low Input

P0118 Engine Coolant Temperature Circuit High Input

P0119 Engine Coolant Temperature Circuit Intermittent

P0120 Throttle/Pedal Position Sensor/Switch "A" Circuit Malfunction

P0121 Throttle/Pedal Position Sensor/Switch "A" Circuit Range/Performance Problem

P0122 Throttle/Pedal Position Sensor/Switch "A" Circuit Low Input

P0123 Throttle/Pedal Position Sensor/Switch "A" Circuit High Input

P0124 Throttle/Pedal Position Sensor/Switch "A" Circuit Intermittent

P0125 Insufficient Coolant Temperature For Closed Loop Fuel Control

P0126 Insufficient Coolant Temperature For Stable Operation

P0130 O_2 Circuit Malfunction (Bank #1 Sensor #1)

P0131 O_2 Sensor Circuit Low Voltage (Bank #1 Sensor #1)

P0132 O_2 Sensor Circuit High Voltage (Bank #1 Sensor #1)

P0133 O_2 Sensor Circuit Slow Response (Bank #1 Sensor #1)

P0134 O_2 Sensor Circuit No Activity Detected (Bank #1 Sensor #1)

P0135 O_2 Sensor Heater Circuit Malfunction (Bank #1 Sensor #1)

P0136 O_2 Sensor Circuit Malfunction (Bank #1 Sensor #2)

P0137 O_2 Sensor Circuit Low Voltage (Bank #1 Sensor #2)

P0138 O_2 Sensor Circuit High Voltage (Bank #1 Sensor #2)

P0139 O_2 Sensor Circuit Slow Response (Bank #1 Sensor #2)

P0140 O_2 Sensor Circuit No Activity Detected (Bank #1 Sensor #2)

P0141 O_2 Sensor Heater Circuit Malfunction (Bank #1 Sensor #2)

P0142 O_2 Sensor Circuit Malfunction (Bank #1 Sensor #3)

P0143 O_2 Sensor Circuit Low Voltage (Bank #1 Sensor #3)

P0144 O_2 Sensor Circuit High Voltage (Bank #1 Sensor #3)

P0145 O_2 Sensor Circuit Slow Response (Bank #1 Sensor #3)

P0146 O_2 Sensor Circuit No Activity Detected (Bank #1 Sensor #3)

P0147 O_2 Sensor Heater Circuit Malfunction (Bank #1 Sensor #3)

P0150 O_2 Sensor Circuit Malfunction (Bank #2 Sensor #1)

P0151 O_2 Sensor Circuit Low Voltage (Bank #2 Sensor #1)

P0152 O_2 Sensor Circuit High Voltage (Bank #2 Sensor #1)

P0153 O_2 Sensor Circuit Slow Response (Bank #2 Sensor #1)

P0154 O_2 Sensor Circuit No Activity Detected (Bank #2 Sensor #1)

P0155 O_2 Sensor Heater Circuit Malfunction (Bank #2 Sensor #1)

P0156 O_2 Sensor Circuit Malfunction (Bank #2 Sensor #2)

P0157 O_2 Sensor Circuit Low Voltage (Bank #2 Sensor #2)

P0158 O_2 Sensor Circuit High Voltage (Bank #2 Sensor #2)

P0159 O_2 Sensor Circuit Slow Response (Bank #2 Sensor #2)

P0160 O_2 Sensor Circuit No Activity Detected (Bank #2 Sensor #2)

P0161 O_2 Sensor Heater Circuit Malfunction (Bank #2 Sensor #2)

P0162 O_2 Sensor Circuit Malfunction (Bank #2 Sensor #3)

P0163 O_2 Sensor Circuit Low Voltage (Bank #2 Sensor #3)

P0164 O_2 Sensor Circuit High Voltage (Bank #2 Sensor #3)

P0165 O_2 Sensor Circuit Slow Response (Bank #2 Sensor #3)

P0166 O_2 Sensor Circuit No Activity Detected (Bank #2 Sensor #3)

P0167 O$_2$ Sensor Heater Circuit Malfunction (Bank #2 Sensor #3)

P0170 Fuel Trim Malfunction (Bank #1)

P0171 System Too Lean (Bank #1)

P0172 System Too Rich (Bank #1)

P0173 Fuel Trim Malfunction (Bank #2)

P0174 System Too Lean (Bank #2)

P0175 System Too Rich (Bank #2)

P0176 Fuel Composition Sensor Circuit Malfunction

P0177 Fuel Composition Sensor Circuit Range/Performance

P0178 Fuel Composition Sensor Circuit Low Input

P0179 Fuel Composition Sensor Circuit High Input

P0180 Fuel Temperature Sensor "A" Circuit Malfunction

P0181 Fuel Temperature Sensor "A" Circuit Range/Performance

P0182 Fuel Temperature Sensor "A" Circuit Low Input

P0183 Fuel Temperature Sensor "A" Circuit High Input

P0184 Fuel Temperature Sensor "A" Circuit Intermittent

P0185 Fuel Temperature Sensor "B" Circuit Malfunction

P0186 Fuel Temperature Sensor "B" Circuit Range/Performance

P0187 Fuel Temperature Sensor "B" Circuit Low Input

P0188 Fuel Temperature Sensor "B" Circuit High Input

P0189 Fuel Temperature Sensor "B" Circuit Intermittent

P0190 Fuel Rail Pressure Sensor Circuit Malfunction

P0191 Fuel Rail Pressure Sensor Circuit Range/Performance

P0192 Fuel Rail Pressure Sensor Circuit Low Input

P0193 Fuel Rail Pressure Sensor Circuit High Input

P0194 Fuel Rail Pressure Sensor Circuit Intermittent

P0195 Engine Oil Temperature Sensor Malfunction

P0196 Engine Oil Temperature Sensor Range/Performance

P0197 Engine Oil Temperature Sensor Low

P0198 Engine Oil Temperature Sensor High

P0199 Engine Oil Temperature Sensor Intermittent

P0200 Injector Circuit Malfunction

P0201 Injector Circuit Malfunction—Cylinder #1

P0202 Injector Circuit Malfunction—Cylinder #2

P0203 Injector Circuit Malfunction—Cylinder #3

P0204 Injector Circuit Malfunction—Cylinder #4

P0205 Injector Circuit Malfunction—Cylinder #5

P0206 Injector Circuit Malfunction—Cylinder #6

P0207 Injector Circuit Malfunction—Cylinder #7

P0208 Injector Circuit Malfunction—Cylinder #8

P0209 Injector Circuit Malfunction—Cylinder #9

P0210 Injector Circuit Malfunction—Cylinder #10

P0211 Injector Circuit Malfunction—Cylinder #11

P0212 Injector Circuit Malfunction—Cylinder #12

P0213 Cold Start Injector #1 Malfunction

P0214 Cold Start Injector #2 Malfunction

P0215 Engine Shutoff Solenoid Malfunction

P0216 Injection Timing Control Circuit Malfunction

P0217 Engine Over Temperature Condition

P0218 Transmission Over Temperature Condition

P0219 Engine Over Speed Condition

P0220 Throttle/Pedal Position Sensor/Switch "B" Circuit Malfunction

P0221 Throttle/Pedal Position Sensor/Switch "B" Circuit Range/Performance Problem

P0222 Throttle/Pedal Position Sensor/Switch "B" Circuit Low Input

P0223 Throttle/Pedal Position Sensor/Switch "B" Circuit High Input

P0224 Throttle/Pedal Position Sensor/Switch "B" Circuit Intermittent

P0225 Throttle/Pedal Position Sensor/Switch "C" Circuit Malfunction

P0226 Throttle/Pedal Position Sensor/Switch "C" Circuit Range/Performance Problem

P0227 Throttle/Pedal Position Sensor/Switch "C" Circuit Low Input

P0228 Throttle/Pedal Position Sensor/Switch "C" Circuit High Input

P0229 Throttle/Pedal Position Sensor/Switch "C" Circuit Intermittent

P0230 Fuel Pump Primary Circuit Malfunction

P0231 Fuel Pump Secondary Circuit Low

P0232 Fuel Pump Secondary Circuit High

P0233 Fuel Pump Secondary Circuit Intermittent

P0234 Engine Over Boost Condition

P0261 Cylinder #1 Injector Circuit Low

P0262 Cylinder #1 Injector Circuit High

P0263 Cylinder #1 Contribution/Balance Fault

P0264 Cylinder #2 Injector Circuit Low

P0265 Cylinder #2 Injector Circuit High

P0266 Cylinder #2 Contribution/Balance Fault

P0267 Cylinder #3 Injector Circuit Low

P0268 Cylinder #3 Injector Circuit High

P0269 Cylinder #3 Contribution/Balance Fault

P0270 Cylinder #4 Injector Circuit Low

P0271 Cylinder #4 Injector Circuit High

P0272 Cylinder #4 Contribution/Balance Fault

P0273 Cylinder #5 Injector Circuit Low

P0274 Cylinder #5 Injector Circuit High

P0275 Cylinder #5 Contribution/Balance Fault

P0276 Cylinder #6 Injector Circuit Low

P0277 Cylinder #6 Injector Circuit High

P0278 Cylinder #6 Contribution/Balance Fault

P0279 Cylinder #7 Injector Circuit Low

P0280 Cylinder #7 Injector Circuit High

P0281 Cylinder #7 Contribution/Balance Fault

P0282 Cylinder #8 Injector Circuit Low

P0283 Cylinder #8 Injector Circuit High

P0284 Cylinder #8 Contribution/Balance Fault

P0285 Cylinder #9 Injector Circuit Low

P0286 Cylinder #9 Injector Circuit High

P0287 Cylinder #9 Contribution/Balance Fault

P0288 Cylinder #10 Injector Circuit Low

P0289 Cylinder #10 Injector Circuit High

P0290 Cylinder #10 Contribution/Balance Fault

P0291 Cylinder #11 Injector Circuit Low

P0292 Cylinder #11 Injector Circuit High

P0293 Cylinder #11 Contribution/Balance Fault

P0294 Cylinder #12 Injector Circuit Low

P0295 Cylinder #12 Injector Circuit High

P0296 Cylinder #12 Contribution/Balance Fault

Ignition system service is covered in the model specific sections of this manual

P0300 Random/Multiple Cylinder Misfire Detected

P0301 Cylinder #1—Misfire Detected

P0302 Cylinder #2—Misfire Detected

P0303 Cylinder #3—Misfire Detected

P0304 Cylinder #4—Misfire Detected

P0305 Cylinder #5—Misfire Detected

P0306 Cylinder #6—Misfire Detected

P0307 Cylinder #7—Misfire Detected

P0308 Cylinder #8—Misfire Detected

P0309 Cylinder #9—Misfire Detected

P0310 Cylinder #10—Misfire Detected

P0311 Cylinder #11—Misfire Detected

P0312 Cylinder #12—Misfire Detected

P0320 Ignition/Distributor Engine Speed Input Circuit Malfunction

P0321 Ignition/Distributor Engine Speed Input Circuit Range/Performance

P0322 Ignition/Distributor Engine Speed Input Circuit No Signal

P0323 Ignition/Distributor Engine Speed Input Circuit Intermittent

P0325 Knock Sensor #1—Circuit Malfunction (Bank #1 or Single Sensor)

P0326 Knock Sensor #1—Circuit Range/Performance (Bank #1 or Single Sensor)

P0327 Knock Sensor #1—Circuit Low Input (Bank #1 or Single Sensor)

P0328 Knock Sensor #1—Circuit High Input (Bank #1 or Single Sensor)

P0329 Knock Sensor #1—Circuit Input Intermittent (Bank #1 or Single Sensor)

P0330 Knock Sensor #2—Circuit Malfunction (Bank #2)

P0331 Knock Sensor #2—Circuit Range/Performance (Bank #2)

P0332 Knock Sensor #2—Circuit Low Input (Bank #2)

P0333 Knock Sensor #2—Circuit High Input (Bank #2)

P0334 Knock Sensor #2—Circuit Input Intermittent (Bank #2)

P0335 Crankshaft Position Sensor "A" Circuit Malfunction

P0336 Crankshaft Position Sensor "A" Circuit Range/Performance

P0337 Crankshaft Position Sensor "A" Circuit Low Input

P0338 Crankshaft Position Sensor "A" Circuit High Input

P0339 Crankshaft Position Sensor "A" Circuit Intermittent

P0340 Camshaft Position Sensor Circuit Malfunction

P0341 Camshaft Position Sensor Circuit Range/Performance

P0342 Camshaft Position Sensor Circuit Low Input

P0343 Camshaft Position Sensor Circuit High Input

P0344 Camshaft Position Sensor Circuit Intermittent

P0350 Ignition Coil Primary/Secondary Circuit Malfunction

P0351 Ignition Coil "A" Primary/Secondary Circuit Malfunction

P0352 Ignition Coil "B" Primary/Secondary Circuit Malfunction

P0353 Ignition Coil "C" Primary/Secondary Circuit Malfunction

P0354 Ignition Coil "D" Primary/Secondary Circuit Malfunction

P0355 Ignition Coil "E" Primary/Secondary Circuit Malfunction

P0356 Ignition Coil "F" Primary/Secondary Circuit Malfunction

P0357 Ignition Coil "G" Primary/Secondary Circuit Malfunction

P0358 Ignition Coil "H" Primary/Secondary Circuit Malfunction

P0359 Ignition Coil "I" Primary/Secondary Circuit Malfunction

P0360 Ignition Coil "J" Primary/Secondary Circuit Malfunction

P0361 Ignition Coil "K" Primary/Secondary Circuit Malfunction

P0362 Ignition Coil "L" Primary/Secondary Circuit Malfunction

P0370 Timing Reference High Resolution Signal "A" Malfunction

P0371 Timing Reference High Resolution Signal "A" Too Many Pulses

P0372 Timing Reference High Resolution Signal "A" Too Few Pulses

P0373 Timing Reference High Resolution Signal "A" Intermittent/Erratic Pulses

P0374 Timing Reference High Resolution Signal "A" No Pulses

P0375 Timing Reference High Resolution Signal "B" Malfunction

P0376 Timing Reference High Resolution Signal "B" Too Many Pulses

P0377 Timing Reference High Resolution Signal "B" Too Few Pulses

P0378 Timing Reference High Resolution Signal "B" Intermittent/Erratic Pulses

P0379 Timing Reference High Resolution Signal "B" No Pulses

P0380 Glow Plug/Heater Circuit "A" Malfunction

P0381 Glow Plug/Heater Indicator Circuit Malfunction

P0382 Glow Plug/Heater Circuit "B" Malfunction

P0385 Crankshaft Position Sensor "B" Circuit Malfunction

P0386 Crankshaft Position Sensor "B" Circuit Range/Performance

P0387 Crankshaft Position Sensor "B" Circuit Low Input

P0388 Crankshaft Position Sensor "B" Circuit High Input

P0389 Crankshaft Position Sensor "B" Circuit Intermittent

P0400 Exhaust Gas Recirculation Flow Malfunction

P0401 Exhaust Gas Recirculation Flow Insufficient Detected

P0402 Exhaust Gas Recirculation Flow Excessive Detected

P0403 Exhaust Gas Recirculation Circuit Malfunction

P0404 Exhaust Gas Recirculation Circuit Range/Performance

P0405 Exhaust Gas Recirculation Sensor "A" Circuit Low

P0406 Exhaust Gas Recirculation Sensor "A" Circuit High

P0407 Exhaust Gas Recirculation Sensor "B" Circuit Low

P0408 Exhaust Gas Recirculation Sensor "B" Circuit High

P0410 Secondary Air Injection System Malfunction

P0411 Secondary Air Injection System Incorrect Flow Detected

P0412 Secondary Air Injection System Switching Valve "A" Circuit Malfunction

P0413 Secondary Air Injection System Switching Valve "A" Circuit Open

P0414 Secondary Air Injection System Switching Valve "A" Circuit Shorted

P0415 Secondary Air Injection System Switching Valve "B" Circuit Malfunction

P0416 Secondary Air Injection System Switching Valve "B" Circuit Open

P0417 Secondary Air Injection System Switching Valve "B" Circuit Shorted

P0418 Secondary Air Injection System Relay "A" Circuit Malfunction

P0419 Secondary Air Injection System Relay "B" Circuit Malfunction

P0420 Catalyst System Efficiency Below Threshold (Bank #1)

P0421 Warm Up Catalyst Efficiency Below Threshold (Bank #1)

P0422 Main Catalyst Efficiency Below Threshold (Bank #1)

P0423 Heated Catalyst Efficiency Below Threshold (Bank #1)

P0424 Heated Catalyst Temperature Below Threshold (Bank #1)

P0430 Catalyst System Efficiency Below Threshold (Bank #2)

P0431 Warm Up Catalyst Efficiency Below Threshold (Bank #2)

P0432 Main Catalyst Efficiency Below Threshold (Bank #2)

P0433 Heated Catalyst Efficiency Below Threshold (Bank #2)

P0434 Heated Catalyst Temperature Below Threshold (Bank #2)

P0440 Evaporative Emission Control System Malfunction

P0441 Evaporative Emission Control System Incorrect Purge Flow

P0442 Evaporative Emission Control System Leak Detected (Small Leak)

P0443 Evaporative Emission Control System Purge Control Valve Circuit Malfunction

P0444 Evaporative Emission Control System Purge Control Valve Circuit Open

P0445 Evaporative Emission Control System Purge Control Valve Circuit Shorted

P0446 Evaporative Emission Control System Vent Control Circuit Malfunction

P0447 Evaporative Emission Control System Vent Control Circuit Open

P0448 Evaporative Emission Control System Vent Control Circuit Shorted

P0449 Evaporative Emission Control System Vent Valve/Solenoid Circuit Malfunction

P0450 Evaporative Emission Control System Pressure Sensor Malfunction

P0451 Evaporative Emission Control System Pressure Sensor Range/Performance

P0452 Evaporative Emission Control System Pressure Sensor Low Input

P0453 Evaporative Emission Control System Pressure Sensor High Input

P0454 Evaporative Emission Control System Pressure Sensor Intermittent

P0455 Evaporative Emission Control System Leak Detected (Gross Leak)

P0460 Fuel Level Sensor Circuit Malfunction

P0461 Fuel Level Sensor Circuit Range/Performance

P0462 Fuel Level Sensor Circuit Low Input

P0463 Fuel Level Sensor Circuit High Input

P0464 Fuel Level Sensor Circuit Intermittent

P0465 Purge Flow Sensor Circuit Malfunction

P0466 Purge Flow Sensor Circuit Range/Performance

P0467 Purge Flow Sensor Circuit Low Input

P0468 Purge Flow Sensor Circuit High Input

P0469 Purge Flow Sensor Circuit Intermittent

P0470 Exhaust Pressure Sensor Malfunction

P0471 Exhaust Pressure Sensor Range/Performance

P0472 Exhaust Pressure Sensor Low

P0473 Exhaust Pressure Sensor High

P0474 Exhaust Pressure Sensor Intermittent

P0475 Exhaust Pressure Control Valve Malfunction

P0476 Exhaust Pressure Control Valve Range/Performance

P0477 Exhaust Pressure Control Valve Low

P0478 Exhaust Pressure Control Valve High

P0479 Exhaust Pressure Control Valve Intermittent

P0480 Cooling Fan #1 Control Circuit Malfunction

P0481 Cooling Fan #2 Control Circuit Malfunction

P0482 Cooling Fan #3 Control Circuit Malfunction

P0483 Cooling Fan Rationality Check Malfunction

P0484 Cooling Fan Circuit Over Current

P0485 Cooling Fan Power/Ground Circuit Malfunction

P0500 Vehicle Speed Sensor Malfunction

P0501 Vehicle Speed Sensor Range/Performance

P0502 Vehicle Speed Sensor Circuit Low Input

P0503 Vehicle Speed Sensor Intermittent/Erratic/High

P0505 Idle Control System Malfunction

P0506 Idle Control System RPM Lower Than Expected

P0507 Idle Control System RPM Higher Than Expected

P0510 Closed Throttle Position Switch Malfunction

P0520 Engine Oil Pressure Sensor/Switch Circuit Malfunction

P0521 Engine Oil Pressure Sensor/Switch Range/Performance

P0522 Engine Oil Pressure Sensor/Switch Low Voltage

P0523 Engine Oil Pressure Sensor/Switch High Voltage

P0530 A/C Refrigerant Pressure Sensor Circuit Malfunction

P0531 A/C Refrigerant Pressure Sensor Circuit Range/Performance

P0532 A/C Refrigerant Pressure Sensor Circuit Low Input

P0533 A/C Refrigerant Pressure Sensor Circuit High Input

P0534 A/C Refrigerant Charge Loss

P0550 Power Steering Pressure Sensor Circuit Malfunction

P0551 Power Steering Pressure Sensor Circuit Range/Performance

P0552 Power Steering Pressure Sensor Circuit Low Input

P0553 Power Steering Pressure Sensor Circuit High Input

P0554 Power Steering Pressure Sensor Circuit Intermittent

P0560 System Voltage Malfunction

P0561 System Voltage Unstable

P0562 System Voltage Low

P0563 System Voltage High

P0565 Cruise Control On Signal Malfunction

P0566 Cruise Control Off Signal Malfunction

P0567 Cruise Control Resume Signal Malfunction

P0568 Cruise Control Set Signal Malfunction

P0569 Cruise Control Coast Signal Malfunction

P0570 Cruise Control Accel Signal Malfunction

P0571 Cruise Control/Brake Switch "A" Circuit Malfunction

P0572 Cruise Control/Brake Switch "A" Circuit Low

P0573 Cruise Control/Brake Switch "A" Circuit High

P0574 Through P0580 Reserved for Cruise Codes

P0600 Serial Communication Link Malfunction

P0601 Internal Control Module Memory Check Sum Error

P0602 Control Module Programming Error

P0603 Internal Control Module Keep Alive Memory (KAM) Error

P0604 Internal Control Module Random Access Memory (RAM) Error

P0605 Internal Control Module Read Only Memory (ROM) Error

P0606 PCM Processor Fault

P0608 Control Module VSS Output "A" Malfunction

P0609 Control Module VSS Output "B" Malfunction

P0620 Generator Control Circuit Malfunction

P0621 Generator Lamp "L" Control Circuit Malfunction

P0622 Generator Field "F" Control Circuit Malfunction

P0650 Malfunction Indicator Lamp (MIL) Control Circuit Malfunction

P0654 Engine RPM Output Circuit Malfunction

P0655 Engine Hot Lamp Output Control Circuit Malfunction

P0656 Fuel Level Output Circuit Malfunction

P0700 Transmission Control System Malfunction

P0701 Transmission Control System Range/Performance

P0702 Transmission Control System Electrical

P0703 Torque Converter/Brake Switch "B" Circuit Malfunction

P0704 Clutch Switch Input Circuit Malfunction

P0705 Transmission Range Sensor Circuit Malfunction (PRNDL Input)

P0706 Transmission Range Sensor Circuit Range/Performance

P0707 Transmission Range Sensor Circuit Low Input

P0708 Transmission Range Sensor Circuit High Input

P0709 Transmission Range Sensor Circuit Intermittent

P0710 Transmission Fluid Temperature Sensor Circuit Malfunction

P0711 Transmission Fluid Temperature Sensor Circuit Range/Performance

P0712 Transmission Fluid Temperature Sensor Circuit Low Input

P0713 Transmission Fluid Temperature Sensor Circuit High Input

P0714 Transmission Fluid Temperature Sensor Circuit Intermittent

P0715 Input/Turbine Speed Sensor Circuit Malfunction

P0716 Input/Turbine Speed Sensor Circuit Range/Performance

P0717 Input/Turbine Speed Sensor Circuit No Signal

P0718 Input/Turbine Speed Sensor Circuit Intermittent

P0719 Torque Converter/Brake Switch "B" Circuit Low

P0720 Output Speed Sensor Circuit Malfunction

P0721 Output Speed Sensor Circuit Range/Performance

P0722 Output Speed Sensor Circuit No Signal

P0723 Output Speed Sensor Circuit Intermittent

P0724 Torque Converter/Brake Switch "B" Circuit High

P0725 Engine Speed Input Circuit Malfunction

P0726 Engine Speed Input Circuit Range/Performance

P0727 Engine Speed Input Circuit No Signal

P0728 Engine Speed Input Circuit Intermittent

P0730 Incorrect Gear Ratio

P0731 Gear #1 Incorrect Ratio

P0732 Gear #2 Incorrect Ratio

P0733 Gear #3 Incorrect Ratio

P0734 Gear #4 Incorrect Ratio

P0735 Gear #5 Incorrect Ratio

P0736 Reverse Incorrect Ratio

P0740 Torque Converter Clutch Circuit Malfunction

P0741 Torque Converter Clutch Circuit Performance or Stuck Off

P0742 Torque Converter Clutch Circuit Stuck On

P0743 Torque Converter Clutch Circuit Electrical

P0744 Torque Converter Clutch Circuit Intermittent

P0745 Pressure Control Solenoid Malfunction

P0746 Pressure Control Solenoid Performance or Stuck Off

P0747 Pressure Control Solenoid Stuck On

P0748 Pressure Control Solenoid Electrical

P0749 Pressure Control Solenoid Intermittent

P0750 Shift Solenoid "A" Malfunction

P0751 Shift Solenoid "A" Performance or Stuck Off

P0752 Shift Solenoid "A" Stuck On

P0753 Shift Solenoid "A" Electrical

P0754 Shift Solenoid "A" Intermittent

P0755 Shift Solenoid "B" Malfunction

P0756 Shift Solenoid "B" Performance or Stuck Off

P0757 Shift Solenoid "B" Stuck On

P0758 Shift Solenoid "B" Electrical

P0759 Shift Solenoid "B" Intermittent

P0760 Shift Solenoid "C" Malfunction

P0761 Shift Solenoid "C" Performance Or Stuck Off

P0762 Shift Solenoid "C" Stuck On

P0763 Shift Solenoid "C" Electrical

P0764 Shift Solenoid "C" Intermittent

P0765 Shift Solenoid "D" Malfunction

P0766 Shift Solenoid "D" Performance Or Stuck Off

P0767 Shift Solenoid "D" Stuck On

P0768 Shift Solenoid "D" Electrical

P0769 Shift Solenoid "D" Intermittent

P0770 Shift Solenoid "E" Malfunction

P0771 Shift Solenoid "E" Performance Or Stuck Off

P0772 Shift Solenoid "E" Stuck On

P0773 Shift Solenoid "E" Electrical

P0774 Shift Solenoid "E" Intermittent

P0780 Shift Malfunction

P0781 1–2 Shift Malfunction

P0782 2–3 Shift Malfunction

P0783 3–4 Shift Malfunction

P0784 4–5 Shift Malfunction

P0785 Shift/Timing Solenoid Malfunction

P0786 Shift/Timing Solenoid Range/Performance

P0787 Shift/Timing Solenoid Low

P0788 Shift/Timing Solenoid High

P0789 Shift/Timing Solenoid Intermittent

P0790 Normal/Performance Switch Circuit Malfunction

P0801 Reverse Inhibit Control Circuit Malfunction

P0803 1–4 Upshift (Skip Shift) Solenoid Control Circuit Malfunction

P0804 1–4 Upshift (Skip Shift) Lamp Control Circuit Malfunction

P1120 Secondary Throttle Position Sensor Circuit Fault

P1125 Tandem Throttle Position Sensor Circuit Fault

P1210 Traction Control System Signal Fault

P1220 Fuel Pump Control Module Fault

P1320 Ignition Control Signal Fault

P1336 Crankshaft Position Sensor Circuit Fault

P1400 EGR/EVAP Control Solenoid Circuit Fault

P1401 EGR Temperature Sensor Circuit Fault

P1443 EVAP Canister Control Vacuum Switch Circuit Fault

P1445 EVAP Purge Volume Control Valve Circuit Fault

P1605 TCM A/T Diagnosis Communication Line Fault

P1705 Throttle Position Sensor (Switch) Circuit Fault

P1760 Overrun Clutch Solenoid Valve Circuit Fault

P1900 Cooling Fan Control Circuit Fault

OBD II TROUBLE CODE EQUIVALENTS

If a scan tool is not available for code retrieval, the following codes may be retrieved without one.

0101 Camshaft Position Sensor Circuit Malfunction

0102 Mass or Volume Air Flow Circuit Malfunction

0103 Engine Coolant Temperature Circuit Malfunction

0104 Vehicle Speed Sensor Malfunction

0114 System Too Rich (Bank #1)

0115 System Too Lean (Bank #1)

0201 Ignition Control Signal Fault

0205 Idle Control System Malfunction

0301 Internal Control Module Read Only Memory (ROM) Error

0302 Exhaust Gas Recirculation Flow Malfunction

0303 O$_2$ Circuit Malfunction

0304 Knock Sensor #1—Circuit Malfunction (Bank #1 or Single Sensor)

0305 EGR Temperature Sensor Circuit Fault

0306 Exhaust Gas Recirculation Flow Excessive Detected

0307 Closed Loop Control

0401 Intake Air Temperature Circuit Malfunction

0403 Throttle/Pedal Position Sensor/Switch "A" Circuit Malfunction

0505 No Self Diagnostic Failure Indicated

0605 Cylinder #4—Misfire Detected
0606 Cylinder #3—Misfire Detected
0607 Cylinder #2—Misfire Detected
0608 Cylinder #1—Misfire Detected
0701 Random/Multiple Cylinder Misfire Detected

0702 Catalyst System Efficiency Below Threshold (Bank #1)

0707 O₂ Sensor Circuit Malfunction (Bank #1 Sensor #2)

0802 Crankshaft Position Sensor "A" Circuit Malfunction

0804 TCM A/T Diagnosis Communication Line Fault

0901 O₂ Sensor Heater Circuit Malfunction (Bank #1 Sensor #1)

0902 O₂ Sensor Heater Circuit Malfunction (Bank #1 Sensor #2)

0905 Crankshaft Position Sensor Circuit Fault

0908 Insufficient Coolant Temperature For Closed Loop Fuel Control

1003 Transmission Range Sensor Circuit Malfunction (PRNDL Input)

1005 EGR/EVAP Control Solenoid Circuit Fault

1101 Inhibitor Switch Circuit
1102 Output Speed Sensor Circuit Malfunction
1103 Gear #1 Incorrect Ratio
1104 Gear #2 Incorrect Ratio
1105 Gear #3 Incorrect Ratio
1106 Gear #4 Incorrect Ratio
1108 Shift Solenoid "A" Malfunction
1201 Shift Solenoid "B" Malfunction
1203 Overrun Clutch Solenoid Valve Circuit Fault
1204 Torque Converter Clutch Circuit Malfunction
1205 Pressure Control Solenoid Malfunction
1206 Throttle Position Sensor (Switch) Circuit Fault
1207 Engine Speed Input Circuit Malfunction

1208 Transmission Fluid Temperature Sensor Circuit Malfunction

1308 Cooling Fan Control Circuit Fault

Subaru

READING CODES

Reading the control module memory is one of the first steps in OBD II system diagnostics. This step should be initially performed to determine the general nature of the fault. Subsequent readings will determine if the fault has been cleared.

Reading codes can be performed by any of the methods below:
- Read the control module memory with the Generic Scan Tool (GST)
- Read the control module memory with the vehicle manufacturer's specific tester

To read the fault codes, connect the scan tool or tester according to the manufacturer's instructions. Follow the manufacturer's specified procedure for reading the codes.

CLEARING CODES

Control module reset procedures are a very important part of OBD II System diagnostics. This step should be done at the end of any fault code repair and at the end of any driveability repair.

Clearing codes can be performed by any of the methods below:
- Clear the control module memory with the Generic Scan Tool (GST)
- Clear the control module memory with the vehicle manufacturer's specific tester
- Turn the ignition OFF and remove the negative battery cable for at least 1 minute.

Removing the negative battery cable may cause other systems in the vehicle to loose their memory. Prior to removing the cable, ensure you have the proper reset codes for radios and alarms.

➡ **The MIL will may also be de-activated for some codes if the vehicle completes three consecutive trips without a fault detected with vehicle conditions similar to those present during the fault.**

OBD II TROUBLE CODES

P0100 Mass or Volume Air Flow Circuit Malfunction

P0101 Mass or Volume Air Flow Circuit Range/Performance Problem

P0102 Mass or Volume Air Flow Circuit Low Input

P0103 Mass or Volume Air Flow Circuit High Input

P0104 Mass or Volume Air Flow Circuit Intermittent

P0105 Manifold Absolute Pressure/Barometric Pressure Circuit Malfunction

P0106 Manifold Absolute Pressure/Barometric Pressure Circuit Range/Performance Problem

P0107 Manifold Absolute Pressure/Barometric Pressure Circuit Low Input

P0108 Manifold Absolute Pressure/Barometric Pressure Circuit High Input

P0109 Manifold Absolute Pressure/Barometric Pressure Circuit Intermittent

P0110 Intake Air Temperature Circuit Malfunction

P0111 Intake Air Temperature Circuit Range/Performance Problem

P0112 Intake Air Temperature Circuit Low Input

P0113 Intake Air Temperature Circuit High Input

P0114 Intake Air Temperature Circuit Intermittent

P0115 Engine Coolant Temperature Circuit Malfunction

P0116 Engine Coolant Temperature Circuit Range/Performance Problem

P0117 Engine Coolant Temperature Circuit Low Input

P0118 Engine Coolant Temperature Circuit High Input

P0119 Engine Coolant Temperature Circuit Intermittent

P0120 Throttle/Pedal Position Sensor/Switch "A" Circuit Malfunction

P0121 Throttle/Pedal Position Sensor/Switch "A" Circuit Range/Performance Problem

P0122 Throttle/Pedal Position Sensor/Switch "A" Circuit Low Input

P0123 Throttle/Pedal Position Sensor/Switch "A" Circuit High Input

P0124 Throttle/Pedal Position Sensor/Switch "A" Circuit Intermittent

P0125 Insufficient Coolant Temperature For Closed Loop Fuel Control

P0126 Insufficient Coolant Temperature For Stable Operation

P0130 O₂ Circuit Malfunction (Bank #1 Sensor #1)

P0131 O_2 Sensor Circuit Low Voltage (Bank #1 Sensor #1)

P0132 O_2 Sensor Circuit High Voltage (Bank #1 Sensor #1)

P0133 O_2 Sensor Circuit Slow Response (Bank #1 Sensor #1)

P0134 O_2 Sensor Circuit No Activity Detected (Bank #1 Sensor #1)

P0135 O_2 Sensor Heater Circuit Malfunction (Bank #1 Sensor #1)

P0136 O_2 Sensor Circuit Malfunction (Bank #1 Sensor #2)

P0137 O_2 Sensor Circuit Low Voltage (Bank #1 Sensor #2)

P0138 O_2 Sensor Circuit High Voltage (Bank #1 Sensor #2)

P0139 O_2 Sensor Circuit Slow Response (Bank #1 Sensor #2)

P0140 O_2 Sensor Circuit No Activity Detected (Bank #1 Sensor #2)

P0141 O_2 Sensor Heater Circuit Malfunction (Bank #1 Sensor #2)

P0142 O_2 Sensor Circuit Malfunction (Bank #1 Sensor #3)

P0143 O_2 Sensor Circuit Low Voltage (Bank #1 Sensor #3)

P0144 O_2 Sensor Circuit High Voltage (Bank #1 Sensor #3)

P0145 O_2 Sensor Circuit Slow Response (Bank #1 Sensor #3)

P0146 O_2 Sensor Circuit No Activity Detected (Bank #1 Sensor #3)

P0147 O_2 Sensor Heater Circuit Malfunction (Bank #1 Sensor #3)

P0150 O_2 Sensor Circuit Malfunction (Bank #2 Sensor #1)

P0151 O_2 Sensor Circuit Low Voltage (Bank #2 Sensor #1)

P0152 O_2 Sensor Circuit High Voltage (Bank #2 Sensor #1)

P0153 O_2 Sensor Circuit Slow Response (Bank #2 Sensor #1)

P0154 O_2 Sensor Circuit No Activity Detected (Bank #2 Sensor #1)

P0155 O_2 Sensor Heater Circuit Malfunction (Bank #2 Sensor #1)

P0156 O_2 Sensor Circuit Malfunction (Bank #2 Sensor #2)

P0157 O_2 Sensor Circuit Low Voltage (Bank #2 Sensor #2)

P0158 O_2 Sensor Circuit High Voltage (Bank #2 Sensor #2)

P0159 O_2 Sensor Circuit Slow Response (Bank #2 Sensor #2)

P0160 O_2 Sensor Circuit No Activity Detected (Bank #2 Sensor #2)

P0161 O_2 Sensor Heater Circuit Malfunction (Bank #2 Sensor #2)

P0162 O_2 Sensor Circuit Malfunction (Bank #2 Sensor #3)

P0163 O_2 Sensor Circuit Low Voltage (Bank #2 Sensor #3)

P0164 O_2 Sensor Circuit High Voltage (Bank #2 Sensor #3)

P0165 O_2 Sensor Circuit Slow Response (Bank #2 Sensor #3)

P0166 O_2 Sensor Circuit No Activity Detected (Bank #2 Sensor #3)

P0167 O_2 Sensor Heater Circuit Malfunction (Bank #2 Sensor #3)

P0170 Fuel Trim Malfunction (Bank #1)

P0171 System Too Lean (Bank #1)

P0172 System Too Rich (Bank #1)

P0173 Fuel Trim Malfunction (Bank #2)

P0174 System Too Lean (Bank #2)

P0175 System Too Rich (Bank #2)

P0176 Fuel Composition Sensor Circuit Malfunction

P0177 Fuel Composition Sensor Circuit Range/Performance

P0178 Fuel Composition Sensor Circuit Low Input

P0179 Fuel Composition Sensor Circuit High Input

P0180 Fuel Temperature Sensor "A" Circuit Malfunction

P0181 Fuel Temperature Sensor "A" Circuit Range/Performance

P0182 Fuel Temperature Sensor "A" Circuit Low Input

P0183 Fuel Temperature Sensor "A" Circuit High Input

P0184 Fuel Temperature Sensor "A" Circuit Intermittent

P0185 Fuel Temperature Sensor "B" Circuit Malfunction

P0186 Fuel Temperature Sensor "B" Circuit Range/Performance

P0187 Fuel Temperature Sensor "B" Circuit Low Input

P0188 Fuel Temperature Sensor "B" Circuit High Input

P0189 Fuel Temperature Sensor "B" Circuit Intermittent

P0190 Fuel Rail Pressure Sensor Circuit Malfunction

P0191 Fuel Rail Pressure Sensor Circuit Range/Performance

P0192 Fuel Rail Pressure Sensor Circuit Low Input

P0193 Fuel Rail Pressure Sensor Circuit High Input

P0194 Fuel Rail Pressure Sensor Circuit Intermittent

P0195 Engine Oil Temperature Sensor Malfunction

P0196 Engine Oil Temperature Sensor Range/Performance

P0197 Engine Oil Temperature Sensor Low

P0198 Engine Oil Temperature Sensor High

P0199 Engine Oil Temperature Sensor Intermittent

P0200 Injector Circuit Malfunction

P0201 Injector Circuit Malfunction—Cylinder #1

P0202 Injector Circuit Malfunction—Cylinder #2

P0203 Injector Circuit Malfunction—Cylinder #3

P0204 Injector Circuit Malfunction—Cylinder #4

P0205 Injector Circuit Malfunction—Cylinder #5

P0206 Injector Circuit Malfunction—Cylinder #6

P0207 Injector Circuit Malfunction—Cylinder #7

P0208 Injector Circuit Malfunction—Cylinder #8

P0209 Injector Circuit Malfunction—Cylinder #9

P0210 Injector Circuit Malfunction—Cylinder #10

P0211 Injector Circuit Malfunction—Cylinder #11

P0212 Injector Circuit Malfunction—Cylinder #12

P0213 Cold Start Injector #1 Malfunction

P0214 Cold Start Injector #2 Malfunction

P0215 Engine Shutoff Solenoid Malfunction

P0216 Injection Timing Control Circuit Malfunction

P0217 Engine Over Temperature Condition

P0218 Transmission Over Temperature Condition

P0219 Engine Over Speed Condition

P0220 Throttle/Pedal Position Sensor/Switch "B" Circuit Malfunction

P0221 Throttle/Pedal Position Sensor/Switch "B" Circuit Range/Performance Problem

P0222 Throttle/Pedal Position Sensor/Switch "B" Circuit Low Input

P0223 Throttle/Pedal Position Sensor/Switch "B" Circuit High Input

P0224 Throttle/Pedal Position Sensor/Switch "B" Circuit Intermittent

P0225 Throttle/Pedal Position Sensor/Switch "C" Circuit Malfunction

P0226 Throttle/Pedal Position Sensor/Switch "C" Circuit Range/Performance Problem

P0227 Throttle/Pedal Position Sensor/Switch "C" Circuit Low Input

P0228 Throttle/Pedal Position Sensor/Switch "C" Circuit High Input

P0229 Throttle/Pedal Position Sensor/Switch "C" Circuit Intermittent

P0230 Fuel Pump Primary Circuit Malfunction

P0231 Fuel Pump Secondary Circuit Low

P0232 Fuel Pump Secondary Circuit High

P0233 Fuel Pump Secondary Circuit Intermittent

P0261 Cylinder #1 Injector Circuit Low

P0262 Cylinder #1 Injector Circuit High

P0263 Cylinder #1 Contribution/Balance Fault

P0264 Cylinder #2 Injector Circuit Low

P0265 Cylinder #2 Injector Circuit High

P0266 Cylinder #2 Contribution/Balance Fault

P0267 Cylinder #3 Injector Circuit Low

P0268 Cylinder #3 Injector Circuit High

P0269 Cylinder #3 Contribution/Balance Fault

P0270 Cylinder #4 Injector Circuit Low

P0271 Cylinder #4 Injector Circuit High

P0272 Cylinder #4 Contribution/Balance Fault

P0273 Cylinder #5 Injector Circuit Low

P0274 Cylinder #5 Injector Circuit High

P0275 Cylinder #5 Contribution/Balance Fault

P0276 Cylinder #6 Injector Circuit Low

P0277 Cylinder #6 Injector Circuit High

P0278 Cylinder #6 Contribution/Balance Fault

P0279 Cylinder #7 Injector Circuit Low

P0280 Cylinder #7 Injector Circuit High

P0281 Cylinder #7 Contribution/Balance Fault

P0282 Cylinder #8 Injector Circuit Low

P0283 Cylinder #8 Injector Circuit High

P0284 Cylinder #8 Contribution/Balance Fault

P0285 Cylinder #9 Injector Circuit Low

P0286 Cylinder #9 Injector Circuit High

P0287 Cylinder #9 Contribution/Balance Fault

P0288 Cylinder #10 Injector Circuit Low

P0289 Cylinder #10 Injector Circuit High

P0290 Cylinder #10 Contribution/Balance Fault

P0291 Cylinder #11 Injector Circuit Low

P0292 Cylinder #11 Injector Circuit High

P0293 Cylinder #11 Contribution/Balance Fault

P0294 Cylinder #12 Injector Circuit Low

P0295 Cylinder #12 Injector Circuit High

P0296 Cylinder #12 Contribution/Balance Fault

P0300 Random/Multiple Cylinder Misfire Detected

P0301 Cylinder #1—Misfire Detected

P0302 Cylinder #2—Misfire Detected

P0303 Cylinder #3—Misfire Detected

P0304 Cylinder #4—Misfire Detected

P0305 Cylinder #5—Misfire Detected

P0306 Cylinder #6—Misfire Detected

P0307 Cylinder #7—Misfire Detected

P0308 Cylinder #8—Misfire Detected

P0309 Cylinder #9—Misfire Detected

P0310 Cylinder #10—Misfire Detected

P0311 Cylinder #11—Misfire Detected

P0312 Cylinder #12—Misfire Detected

P0320 Ignition/Distributor Engine Speed Input Circuit Malfunction

P0321 Ignition/Distributor Engine Speed Input Circuit Range/Performance

P0322 Ignition/Distributor Engine Speed Input Circuit No Signal

P0323 Ignition/Distributor Engine Speed Input Circuit Intermittent

P0325 Knock Sensor #1—Circuit Malfunction (Bank #1 or Single Sensor)

P0326 Knock Sensor #1—Circuit Range/Performance (Bank #1 or Single Sensor)

P0327 Knock Sensor #1—Circuit Low Input (Bank #1 or Single Sensor)

P0328 Knock Sensor #1—Circuit High Input (Bank #1 or Single Sensor)

P0329 Knock Sensor #1—Circuit Input Intermittent (Bank #1 or Single Sensor)

P0330 Knock Sensor #2—Circuit Malfunction (Bank #2)

P0331 Knock Sensor #2—Circuit Range/Performance (Bank #2)

P0332 Knock Sensor #2—Circuit Low Input (Bank #2)

P0333 Knock Sensor #2—Circuit High Input (Bank #2)

P0334 Knock Sensor #2—Circuit Input Intermittent (Bank #2)

P0335 Crankshaft Position Sensor "A" Circuit Malfunction

P0336 Crankshaft Position Sensor "A" Circuit Range/Performance

P0337 Crankshaft Position Sensor "A" Circuit Low Input

P0338 Crankshaft Position Sensor "A" Circuit High Input

P0339 Crankshaft Position Sensor "A" Circuit Intermittent

P0340 Camshaft Position Sensor Circuit Malfunction

P0341 Camshaft Position Sensor Circuit Range/Performance

P0342 Camshaft Position Sensor Circuit Low Input

P0343 Camshaft Position Sensor Circuit High Input

P0344 Camshaft Position Sensor Circuit Intermittent

P0350 Ignition Coil Primary/Secondary Circuit Malfunction

P0351 Ignition Coil "A" Primary/Secondary Circuit Malfunction

P0352 Ignition Coil "B" Primary/Secondary Circuit Malfunction

P0353 Ignition Coil "C" Primary/Secondary Circuit Malfunction

P0354 Ignition Coil "D" Primary/Secondary Circuit Malfunction

P0355 Ignition Coil "E" Primary/Secondary Circuit Malfunction

P0356 Ignition Coil "F" Primary/Secondary Circuit Malfunction

P0357 Ignition Coil "G" Primary/Secondary Circuit Malfunction

P0358 Ignition Coil "H" Primary/Secondary Circuit Malfunction

P0359 Ignition Coil "I" Primary/Secondary Circuit Malfunction

P0360 Ignition Coil "J" Primary/Secondary Circuit Malfunction

P0361 Ignition Coil "K" Primary/Secondary Circuit Malfunction

P0362 Ignition Coil "L" Primary/Secondary Circuit Malfunction

P0370 Timing Reference High Resolution Signal "A" Malfunction

P0371 Timing Reference High Resolution Signal "A" Too Many Pulses

P0372 Timing Reference High Resolution Signal "A" Too Few Pulses

P0373 Timing Reference High Resolution Signal "A" Intermittent/Erratic Pulses

P0374 Timing Reference High Resolution Signal "A" No Pulses

P0375 Timing Reference High Resolution Signal "B" Malfunction

P0376 Timing Reference High Resolution Signal "B" Too Many Pulses

P0377 Timing Reference High Resolution Signal "B" Too Few Pulses

P0378 Timing Reference High Resolution Signal "B" Intermittent/Erratic Pulses

P0379 Timing Reference High Resolution Signal "B" No Pulses

P0380 Glow Plug/Heater Circuit "A" Malfunction

P0381 Glow Plug/Heater Indicator Circuit Malfunction

P0382 Glow Plug/Heater Circuit "B" Malfunction

P0385 Crankshaft Position Sensor "B" Circuit Malfunction

P0386 Crankshaft Position Sensor "B" Circuit Range/Performance

Refer to the model specific sections for engine electrical system service procedures

P0387 Crankshaft Position Sensor "B" Circuit Low Input

P0388 Crankshaft Position Sensor "B" Circuit High Input

P0389 Crankshaft Position Sensor "B" Circuit Intermittent

P0400 Exhaust Gas Recirculation Flow Malfunction

P0401 Exhaust Gas Recirculation Flow Insufficient Detected

P0402 Exhaust Gas Recirculation Flow Excessive Detected

P0403 Exhaust Gas Recirculation Circuit Malfunction

P0404 Exhaust Gas Recirculation Circuit Range/Performance

P0405 Exhaust Gas Recirculation Sensor "A" Circuit Low

P0406 Exhaust Gas Recirculation Sensor "A" Circuit High

P0407 Exhaust Gas Recirculation Sensor "B" Circuit Low

P0408 Exhaust Gas Recirculation Sensor "B" Circuit High

P0410 Secondary Air Injection System Malfunction

P0411 Secondary Air Injection System Incorrect Flow Detected

P0412 Secondary Air Injection System Switching Valve "A" Circuit Malfunction

P0413 Secondary Air Injection System Switching Valve "A" Circuit Open

P0414 Secondary Air Injection System Switching Valve "A" Circuit Shorted

P0415 Secondary Air Injection System Switching Valve "B" Circuit Malfunction

P0416 Secondary Air Injection System Switching Valve "B" Circuit Open

P0417 Secondary Air Injection System Switching Valve "B" Circuit Shorted

P0418 Secondary Air Injection System Relay "A" Circuit Malfunction

P0419 Secondary Air Injection System Relay "B" Circuit Malfunction

P0420 Catalyst System Efficiency Below Threshold (Bank #1)

P0421 Warm Up Catalyst Efficiency Below Threshold (Bank #1)

P0422 Main Catalyst Efficiency Below Threshold (Bank #1)

P0423 Heated Catalyst Efficiency Below Threshold (Bank #1)

P0424 Heated Catalyst Temperature Below Threshold (Bank #1)

P0430 Catalyst System Efficiency Below Threshold (Bank #2)

P0431 Warm Up Catalyst Efficiency Below Threshold (Bank #2)

P0432 Main Catalyst Efficiency Below Threshold (Bank #2)

P0433 Heated Catalyst Efficiency Below Threshold (Bank #2)

P0434 Heated Catalyst Temperature Below Threshold (Bank #2)

P0440 Evaporative Emission Control System Malfunction

P0441 Evaporative Emission Control System Incorrect Purge Flow

P0442 Evaporative Emission Control System Leak Detected (Small Leak)

P0443 Evaporative Emission Control System Purge Control Valve Circuit Malfunction

P0444 Evaporative Emission Control System Purge Control Valve Circuit Open

P0445 Evaporative Emission Control System Purge Control Valve Circuit Shorted

P0446 Evaporative Emission Control System Vent Control Circuit Malfunction

P0447 Evaporative Emission Control System Vent Control Circuit Open

P0448 Evaporative Emission Control System Vent Control Circuit Shorted

P0449 Evaporative Emission Control System Vent Valve/Solenoid Circuit Malfunction

P0450 Evaporative Emission Control System Pressure Sensor Malfunction

P0451 Evaporative Emission Control System Pressure Sensor Range/Performance

P0452 Evaporative Emission Control System Pressure Sensor Low Input

P0453 Evaporative Emission Control System Pressure Sensor High Input

P0454 Evaporative Emission Control System Pressure Sensor Intermittent

P0455 Evaporative Emission Control System Leak Detected (Gross Leak)

P0460 Fuel Level Sensor Circuit Malfunction

P0461 Fuel Level Sensor Circuit Range/Performance

P0462 Fuel Level Sensor Circuit Low Input

P0463 Fuel Level Sensor Circuit High Input

P0464 Fuel Level Sensor Circuit Intermittent

P0465 Purge Flow Sensor Circuit Malfunction

P0466 Purge Flow Sensor Circuit Range/Performance

P0467 Purge Flow Sensor Circuit Low Input

P0468 Purge Flow Sensor Circuit High Input

P0469 Purge Flow Sensor Circuit Intermittent

P0470 Exhaust Pressure Sensor Malfunction

P0471 Exhaust Pressure Sensor Range/Performance

P0472 Exhaust Pressure Sensor Low

P0473 Exhaust Pressure Sensor High

P0474 Exhaust Pressure Sensor Intermittent

P0475 Exhaust Pressure Control Valve Malfunction

P0476 Exhaust Pressure Control Valve Range/Performance

P0477 Exhaust Pressure Control Valve Low

P0478 Exhaust Pressure Control Valve High

P0479 Exhaust Pressure Control Valve Intermittent

P0480 Cooling Fan #1 Control Circuit Malfunction

P0481 Cooling Fan #2 Control Circuit Malfunction

P0482 Cooling Fan #3 Control Circuit Malfunction

P0483 Cooling Fan Rationality Check Malfunction

P0484 Cooling Fan Circuit Over Current

P0485 Cooling Fan Power/Ground Circuit Malfunction

P0500 Vehicle Speed Sensor Malfunction

P0501 Vehicle Speed Sensor Range/Performance

P0502 Vehicle Speed Sensor Circuit Low Input

P0503 Vehicle Speed Sensor Intermittent/Erratic/High

P0505 Idle Control System Malfunction

P0506 Idle Control System RPM Lower Than Expected

P0507 Idle Control System RPM Higher Than Expected

P0510 Closed Throttle Position Switch Malfunction

P0520 Engine Oil Pressure Sensor/Switch Circuit Malfunction

P0521 Engine Oil Pressure Sensor/Switch Range/Performance

P0522 Engine Oil Pressure Sensor/Switch Low Voltage

P0523 Engine Oil Pressure Sensor/Switch High Voltage

P0530 A/C Refrigerant Pressure Sensor Circuit Malfunction

P0531 A/C Refrigerant Pressure Sensor Circuit Range/Performance

P0532 A/C Refrigerant Pressure Sensor Circuit Low Input

P0533 A/C Refrigerant Pressure Sensor Circuit High Input

P0534 A/C Refrigerant Charge Loss

P0550 Power Steering Pressure Sensor Circuit Malfunction

P0551 Power Steering Pressure Sensor Circuit Range/Performance

P0552 Power Steering Pressure Sensor Circuit Low Input

P0553 Power Steering Pressure Sensor Circuit High Input

P0554 Power Steering Pressure Sensor Circuit Intermittent

P0560 System Voltage Malfunction

P0561 System Voltage Unstable

P0562 System Voltage Low

P0563 System Voltage High

P0565 Cruise Control On Signal Malfunction

P0566 Cruise Control Off Signal Malfunction

P0567 Cruise Control Resume Signal Malfunction

P0568 Cruise Control Set Signal Malfunction

P0569 Cruise Control Coast Signal Malfunction

P0570 Cruise Control Accel Signal Malfunction

P0571 Cruise Control/Brake Switch "A" Circuit Malfunction

P0572 Cruise Control/Brake Switch "A" Circuit Low

P0573 Cruise Control/Brake Switch "A" Circuit High

P0574 Through P0580 Reserved for Cruise Codes

P0600 Serial Communication Link Malfunction

P0601 Internal Control Module Memory Check Sum Error

P0602 Control Module Programming Error

P0603 Internal Control Module Keep Alive Memory (KAM) Error

P0604 Internal Control Module Random Access Memory (RAM) Error

P0605 Internal Control Module Read Only Memory (ROM) Error

P0606 PCM Processor Fault

P0608 Control Module VSS Output "A" Malfunction

P0609 Control Module VSS Output "B" Malfunction

P0620 Generator Control Circuit Malfunction

P0621 Generator Lamp "L" Control Circuit Malfunction

P0622 Generator Field "F" Control Circuit Malfunction

P0650 Malfunction Indicator Lamp (MIL) Control Circuit Malfunction

P0654 Engine RPM Output Circuit Malfunction

P0655 Engine Hot Lamp Output Control Circuit Malfunction

P0656 Fuel Level Output Circuit Malfunction

P0700 Transmission Control System Malfunction

P0701 Transmission Control System Range/Performance

P0702 Transmission Control System Electrical

P0703 Torque Converter/Brake Switch "B" Circuit Malfunction

P0704 Clutch Switch Input Circuit Malfunction

P0705 Transmission Range Sensor Circuit Malfunction (PRNDL Input)

P0706 Transmission Range Sensor Circuit Range/Performance

P0707 Transmission Range Sensor Circuit Low Input

P0708 Transmission Range Sensor Circuit High Input

P0709 Transmission Range Sensor Circuit Intermittent

P0710 Transmission Fluid Temperature Sensor Circuit Malfunction

P0711 Transmission Fluid Temperature Sensor Circuit Range/Performance

P0712 Transmission Fluid Temperature Sensor Circuit Low Input

P0713 Transmission Fluid Temperature Sensor Circuit High Input

P0714 Transmission Fluid Temperature Sensor Circuit Intermittent

P0715 Input/Turbine Speed Sensor Circuit Malfunction

P0716 Input/Turbine Speed Sensor Circuit Range/Performance

P0717 Input/Turbine Speed Sensor Circuit No Signal

P0718 Input/Turbine Speed Sensor Circuit Intermittent

P0719 Torque Converter/Brake Switch "B" Circuit Low

P0720 Output Speed Sensor Circuit Malfunction

P0721 Output Speed Sensor Circuit Range/Performance

P0722 Output Speed Sensor Circuit No Signal

P0723 Output Speed Sensor Circuit Intermittent

P0724 Torque Converter/Brake Switch "B" Circuit High

P0725 Engine Speed Input Circuit Malfunction

P0726 Engine Speed Input Circuit Range/Performance

P0727 Engine Speed Input Circuit No Signal

P0728 Engine Speed Input Circuit Intermittent

P0730 Incorrect Gear Ratio

P0731 Gear #1 Incorrect Ratio

P0732 Gear #2 Incorrect Ratio

P0733 Gear #3 Incorrect Ratio

P0734 Gear #4 Incorrect Ratio

P0735 Gear #5 Incorrect Ratio

P0736 Reverse Incorrect Ratio

P0740 Torque Converter Clutch Circuit Malfunction

P0741 Torque Converter Clutch Circuit Performance or Stuck Off

P0742 Torque Converter Clutch Circuit Stuck On

P0743 Torque Converter Clutch Circuit Electrical

P0744 Torque Converter Clutch Circuit Intermittent

P0745 Pressure Control Solenoid Malfunction

P0746 Pressure Control Solenoid Performance or Stuck Off

P0747 Pressure Control Solenoid Stuck On

P0748 Pressure Control Solenoid Electrical

P0749 Pressure Control Solenoid Intermittent

P0750 Shift Solenoid "A" Malfunction

P0751 Shift Solenoid "A" Performance or Stuck Off

P0752 Shift Solenoid "A" Stuck On

P0753 Shift Solenoid "A" Electrical

P0754 Shift Solenoid "A" Intermittent

P0755 Shift Solenoid "B" Malfunction

P0756 Shift Solenoid "B" Performance or Stuck Off

P0757 Shift Solenoid "B" Stuck On

P0758 Shift Solenoid "B" Electrical

P0759 Shift Solenoid "B" Intermittent

P0760 Shift Solenoid "C" Malfunction

P0761 Shift Solenoid "C" Performance Or Stuck Off

P0762 Shift Solenoid "C" Stuck On

P0763 Shift Solenoid "C" Electrical

P0764 Shift Solenoid "C" Intermittent

P0765 Shift Solenoid "D" Malfunction

P0766 Shift Solenoid "D" Performance Or Stuck Off

P0767 Shift Solenoid "D" Stuck On

P0768 Shift Solenoid "D" Electrical

P0769 Shift Solenoid "D" Intermittent

P0770 Shift Solenoid "E" Malfunction

P0771 Shift Solenoid "E" Performance Or Stuck Off

P0772 Shift Solenoid "E" Stuck On

P0773 Shift Solenoid "E" Electrical

P0774 Shift Solenoid "E" Intermittent

P0780 Shift Malfunction

P0781 1–2 Shift Malfunction

P0782 2–3 Shift Malfunction

P0783 3–4 Shift Malfunction

P0784 4–5 Shift Malfunction

P0785 Shift/Timing Solenoid Malfunction

P0786 Shift/Timing Solenoid Range/Performance

P0787 Shift/Timing Solenoid Low

P0788 Shift/Timing Solenoid High

P0789 Shift/Timing Solenoid Intermittent

P0790 Normal/Performance Switch Circuit Malfunction

P0801 Reverse Inhibit Control Circuit Malfunction

P0803 1–4 Upshift (Skip Shift) Solenoid Control Circuit Malfunction

P0804 1–4 Upshift (Skip Shift) Lamp Control Circuit Malfunction

P1100 Starter Switch Circuit Fault

P1101 Neutral Position Switch Circuit Fault (MT)

Suzuki

READING CODES

Reading the control module memory is one of the first steps in OBD II system diagnostics. This step should be initially performed to determine the general nature of the fault. Subsequent readings will determine if the fault has been cleared.

Reading codes can be performed by any of the methods below:

• Read the control module memory with the Generic Scan Tool (GST)

• Read the control module memory with the vehicle manufacturer's specific tester

To read the fault codes, connect the scan tool or tester according to the manufacturer's instructions. Follow the manufacturer's specified procedure for reading the codes.

CLEARING CODES

Control module reset procedures are a very important part of OBD II System diagnostics. This step should be done at the end of any fault code repair and at the end of any driveability repair.

Clearing codes can be performed by any of the methods below:

• Clear the control module memory with the Generic Scan Tool (GST)

• Clear the control module memory with the vehicle manufacturer's specific tester

• Turn the ignition OFF and remove the negative battery cable for at least 1 minute.

Removing the negative battery cable may cause other systems in the vehicle to loose their memory. Prior to removing the cable,

ensure you have the proper reset codes for radios and alarms.

➡The MIL will may also be de-activated for some codes if the vehicle completes three consecutive trips without a fault detected with vehicle conditions similar to those present during the fault.

OBD II TROUBLE CODES

P0100 Mass or Volume Air Flow Circuit Malfunction

P0101 Mass or Volume Air Flow Circuit Range/Performance Problem

P0102 Mass or Volume Air Flow Circuit Low Input

P0103 Mass or Volume Air Flow Circuit High Input

P0104 Mass or Volume Air Flow Circuit Intermittent

P0105 Manifold Absolute Pressure/Barometric Pressure Circuit Malfunction

P0106 Manifold Absolute Pressure/Barometric Pressure Circuit Range/Performance Problem

P0107 Manifold Absolute Pressure/Barometric Pressure Circuit Low Input

P0108 Manifold Absolute Pressure/Barometric Pressure Circuit High Input

P0109 Manifold Absolute Pressure/Barometric Pressure Circuit Intermittent

P0110 Intake Air Temperature Circuit Malfunction

P0111 Intake Air Temperature Circuit Range/Performance Problem

P0112 Intake Air Temperature Circuit Low Input

P0113 Intake Air Temperature Circuit High Input

P0114 Intake Air Temperature Circuit Intermittent

P0115 Engine Coolant Temperature Circuit Malfunction

P0116 Engine Coolant Temperature Circuit Range/Performance Problem

P0117 Engine Coolant Temperature Circuit Low Input

P0118 Engine Coolant Temperature Circuit High Input

P0119 Engine Coolant Temperature Circuit Intermittent

P0120 Throttle/Pedal Position Sensor/Switch "A" Circuit Malfunction

P0121 Throttle/Pedal Position Sensor/Switch "A" Circuit Range/Performance Problem

P0122 Throttle/Pedal Position Sensor/Switch "A" Circuit Low Input

P0123 Throttle/Pedal Position Sensor/Switch "A" Circuit High Input

P0124 Throttle/Pedal Position Sensor/Switch "A" Circuit Intermittent

P0125 Insufficient Coolant Temperature For Closed Loop Fuel Control

P0126 Insufficient Coolant Temperature For Stable Operation

P0130 O_2 Circuit Malfunction (Bank #1 Sensor #1)

P0131 O_2 Sensor Circuit Low Voltage (Bank #1 Sensor #1)

P0132 O_2 Sensor Circuit High Voltage (Bank #1 Sensor #1)

P0133 O_2 Sensor Circuit Slow Response (Bank #1 Sensor #1)

P0134 O_2 Sensor Circuit No Activity Detected (Bank #1 Sensor #1)

P0135 O_2 Sensor Heater Circuit Malfunction (Bank #1 Sensor #1)

P0136 O_2 Sensor Circuit Malfunction (Bank #1 Sensor #2)

P0137 O_2 Sensor Circuit Low Voltage (Bank #1 Sensor #2)

P0138 O_2 Sensor Circuit High Voltage (Bank #1 Sensor #2)

P0139 O_2 Sensor Circuit Slow Response (Bank #1 Sensor #2)

P0140 O_2 Sensor Circuit No Activity Detected (Bank #1 Sensor #2)

P0141 O_2 Sensor Heater Circuit Malfunction (Bank #1 Sensor #2)

P0142 O_2 Sensor Circuit Malfunction (Bank #1 Sensor #3)

P0143 O_2 Sensor Circuit Low Voltage (Bank #1 Sensor #3)

P0144 O_2 Sensor Circuit High Voltage (Bank #1 Sensor #3)

P0145 O_2 Sensor Circuit Slow Response (Bank #1 Sensor #3)

P0146 O_2 Sensor Circuit No Activity Detected (Bank #1 Sensor #3)

P0147 O_2 Sensor Heater Circuit Malfunction (Bank #1 Sensor #3)

P0150 O_2 Sensor Circuit Malfunction (Bank #2 Sensor #1)

P0151 O_2 Sensor Circuit Low Voltage (Bank #2 Sensor #1)

P0152 O_2 Sensor Circuit High Voltage (Bank #2 Sensor #1)

P0153 O_2 Sensor Circuit Slow Response (Bank #2 Sensor #1)

P0154 O_2 Sensor Circuit No Activity Detected (Bank #2 Sensor #1)

P0155 O_2 Sensor Heater Circuit Malfunction (Bank #2 Sensor #1)

P0156 O_2 Sensor Circuit Malfunction (Bank #2 Sensor #2)

P0157 O_2 Sensor Circuit Low Voltage (Bank #2 Sensor #2)

P0158 O₂ Sensor Circuit High Voltage (Bank #2 Sensor #2)

P0159 O₂ Sensor Circuit Slow Response (Bank #2 Sensor #2)

P0160 O₂ Sensor Circuit No Activity Detected (Bank #2 Sensor #2)

P0161 O₂ Sensor Heater Circuit Malfunction (Bank #2 Sensor #2)

P0162 O₂ Sensor Circuit Malfunction (Bank #2 Sensor #3)

P0163 O₂ Sensor Circuit Low Voltage (Bank #2 Sensor #3)

P0164 O₂ Sensor Circuit High Voltage (Bank #2 Sensor #3)

P0165 O₂ Sensor Circuit Slow Response (Bank #2 Sensor #3)

P0166 O₂ Sensor Circuit No Activity Detected (Bank #2 Sensor #3)

P0167 O₂ Sensor Heater Circuit Malfunction (Bank #2 Sensor #3)

P0170 Fuel Trim Malfunction (Bank #1)

P0171 System Too Lean (Bank #1)

P0172 System Too Rich (Bank #1)

P0173 Fuel Trim Malfunction (Bank #2)

P0174 System Too Lean (Bank #2)

P0175 System Too Rich (Bank #2)

P0176 Fuel Composition Sensor Circuit Malfunction

P0177 Fuel Composition Sensor Circuit Range/Performance

P0178 Fuel Composition Sensor Circuit Low Input

P0179 Fuel Composition Sensor Circuit High Input

P0180 Fuel Temperature Sensor "A" Circuit Malfunction

P0181 Fuel Temperature Sensor "A" Circuit Range/Performance

P0182 Fuel Temperature Sensor "A" Circuit Low Input

P0183 Fuel Temperature Sensor "A" Circuit High Input

P0184 Fuel Temperature Sensor "A" Circuit Intermittent

P0185 Fuel Temperature Sensor "B" Circuit Malfunction

P0186 Fuel Temperature Sensor "B" Circuit Range/Performance

P0187 Fuel Temperature Sensor "B" Circuit Low Input

P0188 Fuel Temperature Sensor "B" Circuit High Input

P0189 Fuel Temperature Sensor "B" Circuit Intermittent

P0190 Fuel Rail Pressure Sensor Circuit Malfunction

P0191 Fuel Rail Pressure Sensor Circuit Range/Performance

P0192 Fuel Rail Pressure Sensor Circuit Low Input

P0193 Fuel Rail Pressure Sensor Circuit High Input

P0194 Fuel Rail Pressure Sensor Circuit Intermittent

P0195 Engine Oil Temperature Sensor Malfunction

P0196 Engine Oil Temperature Sensor Range/Performance

P0197 Engine Oil Temperature Sensor Low

P0198 Engine Oil Temperature Sensor High

P0199 Engine Oil Temperature Sensor Intermittent

P0200 Injector Circuit Malfunction

P0201 Injector Circuit Malfunction—Cylinder #1

P0202 Injector Circuit Malfunction—Cylinder #2

P0203 Injector Circuit Malfunction—Cylinder #3

P0204 Injector Circuit Malfunction—Cylinder #4

P0205 Injector Circuit Malfunction—Cylinder #5

P0206 Injector Circuit Malfunction—Cylinder #6

P0207 Injector Circuit Malfunction—Cylinder #7

P0208 Injector Circuit Malfunction—Cylinder #8

P0209 Injector Circuit Malfunction—Cylinder #9

P0210 Injector Circuit Malfunction—Cylinder #10

P0211 Injector Circuit Malfunction—Cylinder #11

P0212 Injector Circuit Malfunction—Cylinder #12

P0213 Cold Start Injector #1 Malfunction

P0214 Cold Start Injector #2 Malfunction

P0215 Engine Shutoff Solenoid Malfunction

P0216 Injection Timing Control Circuit Malfunction

P0217 Engine Over Temperature Condition

P0218 Transmission Over Temperature Condition

P0219 Engine Over Speed Condition

P0220 Throttle/Pedal Position Sensor/Switch "B" Circuit Malfunction

P0221 Throttle/Pedal Position Sensor/Switch "B" Circuit Range/Performance Problem

P0222 Throttle/Pedal Position Sensor/Switch "B" Circuit Low Input

P0223 Throttle/Pedal Position Sensor/Switch "B" Circuit High Input

P0224 Throttle/Pedal Position Sensor/Switch "B" Circuit Intermittent

P0225 Throttle/Pedal Position Sensor/Switch "C" Circuit Malfunction

P0226 Throttle/Pedal Position Sensor/Switch "C" Circuit Range/Performance Problem

P0227 Throttle/Pedal Position Sensor/Switch "C" Circuit Low Input

P0228 Throttle/Pedal Position Sensor/Switch "C" Circuit High Input

P0229 Throttle/Pedal Position Sensor/Switch "C" Circuit Intermittent

P0230 Fuel Pump Primary Circuit Malfunction

P0231 Fuel Pump Secondary Circuit Low

P0232 Fuel Pump Secondary Circuit High

P0233 Fuel Pump Secondary Circuit Intermittent

P0234 Engine Over Boost Condition

P0261 Cylinder #1 Injector Circuit Low

P0262 Cylinder #1 Injector Circuit High

P0263 Cylinder #1 Contribution/Balance Fault

P0264 Cylinder #2 Injector Circuit Low

P0265 Cylinder #2 Injector Circuit High

P0266 Cylinder #2 Contribution/Balance Fault

P0267 Cylinder #3 Injector Circuit Low

P0268 Cylinder #3 Injector Circuit High

P0269 Cylinder #3 Contribution/Balance Fault

P0270 Cylinder #4 Injector Circuit Low

P0271 Cylinder #4 Injector Circuit High

P0272 Cylinder #4 Contribution/Balance Fault

P0273 Cylinder #5 Injector Circuit Low

P0274 Cylinder #5 Injector Circuit High

P0275 Cylinder #5 Contribution/Balance Fault

P0276 Cylinder #6 Injector Circuit Low

P0277 Cylinder #6 Injector Circuit High

P0278 Cylinder #6 Contribution/Balance Fault

P0279 Cylinder #7 Injector Circuit Low

P0280 Cylinder #7 Injector Circuit High

P0281 Cylinder #7 Contribution/Balance Fault

P0282 Cylinder #8 Injector Circuit Low

P0283 Cylinder #8 Injector Circuit High

P0284 Cylinder #8 Contribution/Balance Fault

P0285 Cylinder #9 Injector Circuit Low

Ignition system service is covered in the model specific sections of this manual

P0286 Cylinder #9 Injector Circuit High

P0287 Cylinder #9 Contribution/Balance Fault

P0288 Cylinder #10 Injector Circuit Low

P0289 Cylinder #10 Injector Circuit High

P0290 Cylinder #10 Contribution/Balance Fault

P0291 Cylinder #11 Injector Circuit Low

P0292 Cylinder #11 Injector Circuit High

P0293 Cylinder #11 Contribution/Balance Fault

P0294 Cylinder #12 Injector Circuit Low

P0295 Cylinder #12 Injector Circuit High

P0296 Cylinder #12 Contribution/Balance Fault

P0300 Random/Multiple Cylinder Misfire Detected

P0301 Cylinder #1—Misfire Detected

P0302 Cylinder #2—Misfire Detected

P0303 Cylinder #3—Misfire Detected

P0304 Cylinder #4—Misfire Detected

P0305 Cylinder #5—Misfire Detected

P0306 Cylinder #6—Misfire Detected

P0307 Cylinder #7—Misfire Detected

P0308 Cylinder #8—Misfire Detected

P0309 Cylinder #9—Misfire Detected

P0310 Cylinder #10—Misfire Detected

P0311 Cylinder #11—Misfire Detected

P0312 Cylinder #12—Misfire Detected

P0320 Ignition/Distributor Engine Speed Input Circuit Malfunction

P0321 Ignition/Distributor Engine Speed Input Circuit Range/Performance

P0322 Ignition/Distributor Engine Speed Input Circuit No Signal

P0323 Ignition/Distributor Engine Speed Input Circuit Intermittent

P0325 Knock Sensor #1—Circuit Malfunction (Bank #1 or Single Sensor)

P0326 Knock Sensor #1—Circuit Range/Performance (Bank #1 or Single Sensor)

P0327 Knock Sensor #1—Circuit Low Input (Bank #1 or Single Sensor)

P0328 Knock Sensor #1—Circuit High Input (Bank #1 or Single Sensor)

P0329 Knock Sensor #1—Circuit Input Intermittent (Bank #1 or Single Sensor)

P0330 Knock Sensor #2—Circuit Malfunction (Bank #2)

P0331 Knock Sensor #2—Circuit Range/Performance (Bank #2)

P0332 Knock Sensor #2—Circuit Low Input (Bank #2)

P0333 Knock Sensor #2—Circuit High Input (Bank #2)

P0334 Knock Sensor #2—Circuit Input Intermittent (Bank #2)

P0335 Crankshaft Position Sensor "A" Circuit Malfunction

P0336 Crankshaft Position Sensor "A" Circuit Range/Performance

P0337 Crankshaft Position Sensor "A" Circuit Low Input

P0338 Crankshaft Position Sensor "A" Circuit High Input

P0339 Crankshaft Position Sensor "A" Circuit Intermittent

P0340 Camshaft Position Sensor Circuit Malfunction

P0341 Camshaft Position Sensor Circuit Range/Performance

P0342 Camshaft Position Sensor Circuit Low Input

P0343 Camshaft Position Sensor Circuit High Input

P0344 Camshaft Position Sensor Circuit Intermittent

P0350 Ignition Coil Primary/Secondary Circuit Malfunction

P0351 Ignition Coil "A" Primary/Secondary Circuit Malfunction

P0352 Ignition Coil "B" Primary/Secondary Circuit Malfunction

P0353 Ignition Coil "C" Primary/Secondary Circuit Malfunction

P0354 Ignition Coil "D" Primary/Secondary Circuit Malfunction

P0355 Ignition Coil "E" Primary/Secondary Circuit Malfunction

P0356 Ignition Coil "F" Primary/Secondary Circuit Malfunction

P0357 Ignition Coil "G" Primary/Secondary Circuit Malfunction

P0358 Ignition Coil "H" Primary/Secondary Circuit Malfunction

P0359 Ignition Coil "I" Primary/Secondary Circuit Malfunction

P0360 Ignition Coil "J" Primary/Secondary Circuit Malfunction

P0361 Ignition Coil "K" Primary/Secondary Circuit Malfunction

P0362 Ignition Coil "L" Primary/Secondary Circuit Malfunction

P0370 Timing Reference High Resolution Signal "A" Malfunction

P0371 Timing Reference High Resolution Signal "A" Too Many Pulses

P0372 Timing Reference High Resolution Signal "A" Too Few Pulses

P0373 Timing Reference High Resolution Signal "A" Intermittent/Erratic Pulses

P0374 Timing Reference High Resolution Signal "A" No Pulses

P0375 Timing Reference High Resolution Signal "B" Malfunction

P0376 Timing Reference High Resolution Signal "B" Too Many Pulses

P0377 Timing Reference High Resolution Signal "B" Too Few Pulses

P0378 Timing Reference High Resolution Signal "B" Intermittent/Erratic Pulses

P0379 Timing Reference High Resolution Signal "B" No Pulses

P0380 Glow Plug/Heater Circuit "A" Malfunction

P0381 Glow Plug/Heater Indicator Circuit Malfunction

P0382 Glow Plug/Heater Circuit "B" Malfunction

P0385 Crankshaft Position Sensor "B" Circuit Malfunction

P0386 Crankshaft Position Sensor "B" Circuit Range/Performance

P0387 Crankshaft Position Sensor "B" Circuit Low Input

P0388 Crankshaft Position Sensor "B" Circuit High Input

P0389 Crankshaft Position Sensor "B" Circuit Intermittent

P0400 Exhaust Gas Recirculation Flow Malfunction

P0401 Exhaust Gas Recirculation Flow Insufficient Detected

P0402 Exhaust Gas Recirculation Flow Excessive Detected

P0403 Exhaust Gas Recirculation Circuit Malfunction

P0404 Exhaust Gas Recirculation Circuit Range/Performance

P0405 Exhaust Gas Recirculation Sensor "A" Circuit Low

P0406 Exhaust Gas Recirculation Sensor "A" Circuit High

P0407 Exhaust Gas Recirculation Sensor "B" Circuit Low

P0408 Exhaust Gas Recirculation Sensor "B" Circuit High

P0410 Secondary Air Injection System Malfunction

P0411 Secondary Air Injection System Incorrect Flow Detected

P0412 Secondary Air Injection System Switching Valve "A" Circuit Malfunction

P0413 Secondary Air Injection System Switching Valve "A" Circuit Open

P0414 Secondary Air Injection System Switching Valve "A" Circuit Shorted

P0415 Secondary Air Injection System Switching Valve "B" Circuit Malfunction

P0416 Secondary Air Injection System Switching Valve "B" Circuit Open

P0417 Secondary Air Injection System Switching Valve "B" Circuit Shorted

P0418 Secondary Air Injection System Relay "A" Circuit Malfunction

P0419 Secondary Air Injection System Relay "B" Circuit Malfunction

P0420 Catalyst System Efficiency Below Threshold (Bank #1)

P0421 Warm Up Catalyst Efficiency Below Threshold (Bank #1)

P0422 Main Catalyst Efficiency Below Threshold (Bank #1)

P0423 Heated Catalyst Efficiency Below Threshold (Bank #1)

P0424 Heated Catalyst Temperature Below Threshold (Bank #1)

P0430 Catalyst System Efficiency Below Threshold (Bank #2)

P0431 Warm Up Catalyst Efficiency Below Threshold (Bank #2)

P0432 Main Catalyst Efficiency Below Threshold (Bank #2)

P0433 Heated Catalyst Efficiency Below Threshold (Bank #2)

P0434 Heated Catalyst Temperature Below Threshold (Bank #2)

P0440 Evaporative Emission Control System Malfunction

P0441 Evaporative Emission Control System Incorrect Purge Flow

P0442 Evaporative Emission Control System Leak Detected (Small Leak)

P0443 Evaporative Emission Control System Purge Control Valve Circuit Malfunction

P0444 Evaporative Emission Control System Purge Control Valve Circuit Open

P0445 Evaporative Emission Control System Purge Control Valve Circuit Shorted

P0446 Evaporative Emission Control System Vent Control Circuit Malfunction

P0447 Evaporative Emission Control System Vent Control Circuit Open

P0448 Evaporative Emission Control System Vent Control Circuit Shorted

P0449 Evaporative Emission Control System Vent Valve/Solenoid Circuit Malfunction

P0450 Evaporative Emission Control System Pressure Sensor Malfunction

P0451 Evaporative Emission Control System Pressure Sensor Range/Performance

P0452 Evaporative Emission Control System Pressure Sensor Low Input

P0453 Evaporative Emission Control System Pressure Sensor High Input

P0454 Evaporative Emission Control System Pressure Sensor Intermittent

P0455 Evaporative Emission Control System Leak Detected (Gross Leak)

P0460 Fuel Level Sensor Circuit Malfunction

P0461 Fuel Level Sensor Circuit Range/Performance

P0462 Fuel Level Sensor Circuit Low Input

P0463 Fuel Level Sensor Circuit High Input

P0464 Fuel Level Sensor Circuit Intermittent

P0465 Purge Flow Sensor Circuit Malfunction

P0466 Purge Flow Sensor Circuit Range/Performance

P0467 Purge Flow Sensor Circuit Low Input

P0468 Purge Flow Sensor Circuit High Input

P0469 Purge Flow Sensor Circuit Intermittent

P0470 Exhaust Pressure Sensor Malfunction

P0471 Exhaust Pressure Sensor Range/Performance

P0472 Exhaust Pressure Sensor Low

P0473 Exhaust Pressure Sensor High

P0474 Exhaust Pressure Sensor Intermittent

P0475 Exhaust Pressure Control Valve Malfunction

P0476 Exhaust Pressure Control Valve Range/Performance

P0477 Exhaust Pressure Control Valve Low

P0478 Exhaust Pressure Control Valve High

P0479 Exhaust Pressure Control Valve Intermittent

P0480 Cooling Fan #1 Control Circuit Malfunction

P0481 Cooling Fan #2 Control Circuit Malfunction

P0482 Cooling Fan #3 Control Circuit Malfunction

P0483 Cooling Fan Rationality Check Malfunction

P0484 Cooling Fan Circuit Over Current

P0485 Cooling Fan Power/Ground Circuit Malfunction

P0500 Vehicle Speed Sensor Malfunction

P0501 Vehicle Speed Sensor Range/Performance

P0502 Vehicle Speed Sensor Circuit Low Input

P0503 Vehicle Speed Sensor Intermittent/Erratic/High

P0505 Idle Control System Malfunction

P0506 Idle Control System RPM Lower Than Expected

P0507 Idle Control System RPM Higher Than Expected

P0510 Closed Throttle Position Switch Malfunction

P0520 Engine Oil Pressure Sensor/Switch Circuit Malfunction

P0521 Engine Oil Pressure Sensor/Switch Range/Performance

P0522 Engine Oil Pressure Sensor/Switch Low Voltage

P0523 Engine Oil Pressure Sensor/Switch High Voltage

P0530 A/C Refrigerant Pressure Sensor Circuit Malfunction

P0531 A/C Refrigerant Pressure Sensor Circuit Range/Performance

P0532 A/C Refrigerant Pressure Sensor Circuit Low Input

P0533 A/C Refrigerant Pressure Sensor Circuit High Input

P0534 A/C Refrigerant Charge Loss

P0550 Power Steering Pressure Sensor Circuit Malfunction

P0551 Power Steering Pressure Sensor Circuit Range/Performance

P0552 Power Steering Pressure Sensor Circuit Low Input

P0553 Power Steering Pressure Sensor Circuit High Input

P0554 Power Steering Pressure Sensor Circuit Intermittent

P0560 System Voltage Malfunction

P0561 System Voltage Unstable

P0562 System Voltage Low

P0563 System Voltage High

P0565 Cruise Control On Signal Malfunction

P0566 Cruise Control Off Signal Malfunction

P0567 Cruise Control Resume Signal Malfunction

P0568 Cruise Control Set Signal Malfunction

P0569 Cruise Control Coast Signal Malfunction

P0570 Cruise Control Accel Signal Malfunction

P0571 Cruise Control/Brake Switch "A" Circuit Malfunction

P0572 Cruise Control/Brake Switch "A" Circuit Low

P0573 Cruise Control/Brake Switch "A" Circuit High

P0574 Through P0580 Reserved for Cruise Codes

P0600 Serial Communication Link Malfunction

P0601 Internal Control Module Memory Check Sum Error

P0602 Control Module Programming Error

P0603 Internal Control Module Keep Alive Memory (KAM) Error

P0604 Internal Control Module Random Access Memory (RAM) Error

P0605 Internal Control Module Read Only Memory (ROM) Error

P0606 PCM Processor Fault

P0608 Control Module VSS Output "A" Malfunction

P0609 Control Module VSS Output "B" Malfunction

P0620 Generator Control Circuit Malfunction

P0621 Generator Lamp "L" Control Circuit Malfunction

P0622 Generator Field "F" Control Circuit Malfunction

P0650 Malfunction Indicator Lamp (MIL) Control Circuit Malfunction

P0654 Engine RPM Output Circuit Malfunction

P0655 Engine Hot Lamp Output Control Circuit Malfunction

P0656 Fuel Level Output Circuit Malfunction

P0700 Transmission Control System Malfunction

P0701 Transmission Control System Range/Performance

P0702 Transmission Control System Electrical

P0703 Torque Converter/Brake Switch "B" Circuit Malfunction

P0704 Clutch Switch Input Circuit Malfunction

P0705 Transmission Range Sensor Circuit Malfunction (PRNDL Input)

P0706 Transmission Range Sensor Circuit Range/Performance

P0707 Transmission Range Sensor Circuit Low Input

P0708 Transmission Range Sensor Circuit High Input

P0709 Transmission Range Sensor Circuit Intermittent

P0710 Transmission Fluid Temperature Sensor Circuit Malfunction

P0711 Transmission Fluid Temperature Sensor Circuit Range/Performance

P0712 Transmission Fluid Temperature Sensor Circuit Low Input

P0713 Transmission Fluid Temperature Sensor Circuit High Input

P0714 Transmission Fluid Temperature Sensor Circuit Intermittent

P0715 Input/Turbine Speed Sensor Circuit Malfunction

P0716 Input/Turbine Speed Sensor Circuit Range/Performance

P0717 Input/Turbine Speed Sensor Circuit No Signal

P0718 Input/Turbine Speed Sensor Circuit Intermittent

P0719 Torque Converter/Brake Switch "B" Circuit Low

P0720 Output Speed Sensor Circuit Malfunction

P0721 Output Speed Sensor Circuit Range/Performance

P0722 Output Speed Sensor Circuit No Signal

P0723 Output Speed Sensor Circuit Intermittent

P0724 Torque Converter/Brake Switch "B" Circuit High

P0725 Engine Speed Input Circuit Malfunction

P0726 Engine Speed Input Circuit Range/Performance

P0727 Engine Speed Input Circuit No Signal

P0728 Engine Speed Input Circuit Intermittent

P0730 Incorrect Gear Ratio

P0731 Gear #1 Incorrect Ratio

P0732 Gear #2 Incorrect Ratio

P0733 Gear #3 Incorrect Ratio

P0734 Gear #4 Incorrect Ratio

P0735 Gear #5 Incorrect Ratio

P0736 Reverse Incorrect Ratio

P0740 Torque Converter Clutch Circuit Malfunction

P0741 Torque Converter Clutch Circuit Performance or Stuck Off

P0742 Torque Converter Clutch Circuit Stuck On

P0743 Torque Converter Clutch Circuit Electrical

P0744 Torque Converter Clutch Circuit Intermittent

P0745 Pressure Control Solenoid Malfunction

P0746 Pressure Control Solenoid Performance or Stuck Off

P0747 Pressure Control Solenoid Stuck On

P0748 Pressure Control Solenoid Electrical

P0749 Pressure Control Solenoid Intermittent

P0750 Shift Solenoid "A" Malfunction

P0751 Shift Solenoid "A" Performance or Stuck Off

P0752 Shift Solenoid "A" Stuck On

P0753 Shift Solenoid "A" Electrical

P0754 Shift Solenoid "A" Intermittent

P0755 Shift Solenoid "B" Malfunction

P0756 Shift Solenoid "B" Performance or Stuck Off

P0757 Shift Solenoid "B" Stuck On

P0758 Shift Solenoid "B" Electrical

P0759 Shift Solenoid "B" Intermittent

P0760 Shift Solenoid "C" Malfunction

P0761 Shift Solenoid "C" Performance Or Stuck Off

P0762 Shift Solenoid "C" Stuck On

P0763 Shift Solenoid "C" Electrical

P0764 Shift Solenoid "C" Intermittent

P0765 Shift Solenoid "D" Malfunction

P0766 Shift Solenoid "D" Performance Or Stuck Off

P0767 Shift Solenoid "D" Stuck On

P0768 Shift Solenoid "D" Electrical

P0769 Shift Solenoid "D" Intermittent

P0770 Shift Solenoid "E" Malfunction

P0771 Shift Solenoid "E" Performance Or Stuck Off

P0772 Shift Solenoid "E" Stuck On

P0773 Shift Solenoid "E" Electrical

P0774 Shift Solenoid "E" Intermittent

P0780 Shift Malfunction

P0781 1–2 Shift Malfunction

P0782 2–3 Shift Malfunction

P0783 3–4 Shift Malfunction

P0784 4–5 Shift Malfunction

P0785 Shift/Timing Solenoid Malfunction

P0786 Shift/Timing Solenoid Range/Performance

P0787 Shift/Timing Solenoid Low

P0788 Shift/Timing Solenoid High

P0789 Shift/Timing Solenoid Intermittent

P0790 Normal/Performance Switch Circuit Malfunction

P0801 Reverse Inhibit Control Circuit Malfunction

P0803 1–4 Upshift (Skip Shift) Solenoid Control Circuit Malfunction

P0804 1–4 Upshift (Skip Shift) Lamp Control Circuit Malfunction

P1250 EFI Heater Circuit Fault

P1408 Manifold Differential Pressure Sensor Circuit Fault

P1410 Fuel Tank Pressure Control Solenoid Circuit Fault

P1450 Barometric Pressure Sensor Circuit Fault

P1451 Barometric Pressure Sensor Performance

P1460 Cooling Fan Control System Fault

P1500 Starter Signal Circuit Fault

P1510 Back-up Power Supply Fault

P1530 Ignition Timing Adjustment Switch Circuit

P1600 PCM Battery Circuit Fault

P1700 TCM Throttle Position Sensor Circuit Fault

P1705 TCM ECT Circuit Fault

P1715 PNP Switch Circuit Fault

P1717 AT Drive Range Signal Circuit Fault

Toyota

READING CODES

Reading the control module memory is one of the first steps in OBD II system diagnostics. This step should be initially performed to determine the general nature of the fault. Subsequent readings will determine if the fault has been cleared.

Reading codes can be performed by any of the methods below:
- Read the control module memory with the Generic Scan Tool (GST)
- Read the control module memory with the vehicle manufacturer's specific tester

To read the fault codes, connect the scan tool or tester according to the manufacturer's instructions. Follow the manufacturer's specified procedure for reading the codes.

CLEARING CODES

Control module reset procedures are a very important part of OBD II System diagnostics. This step should be done at the end of any fault code repair and at the end of any driveability repair.

Clearing codes can be performed by any of the methods below:
- Clear the control module memory with the Generic Scan Tool (GST)
- Clear the control module memory with the vehicle manufacturer's specific tester
- Turn the ignition OFF and remove the negative battery cable for at least 1 minute.

Removing the negative battery cable may cause other systems in the vehicle to loose their memory. Prior to removing the cable, ensure you have the proper reset codes for radios and alarms.

➡️**The MIL will may also be de-activated for some codes if the vehicle completes three consecutive trips without a fault detected with vehicle conditions similar to those present during the fault.**

OBD II TROUBLE CODES

P0100 Mass or Volume Air Flow Circuit Malfunction

P0101 Mass or Volume Air Flow Circuit Range/Performance Problem

P0102 Mass or Volume Air Flow Circuit Low Input

P0103 Mass or Volume Air Flow Circuit High Input

P0104 Mass or Volume Air Flow Circuit Intermittent

P0105 Manifold Absolute Pressure/Barometric Pressure Circuit Malfunction

P0106 Manifold Absolute Pressure/Barometric Pressure Circuit Range/Performance Problem

P0107 Manifold Absolute Pressure/Barometric Pressure Circuit Low Input

P0108 Manifold Absolute Pressure/Barometric Pressure Circuit High Input

P0109 Manifold Absolute Pressure/Barometric Pressure Circuit Intermittent

P0110 Intake Air Temperature Circuit Malfunction

P0111 Intake Air Temperature Circuit Range/Performance Problem

P0112 Intake Air Temperature Circuit Low Input

P0113 Intake Air Temperature Circuit High Input

P0114 Intake Air Temperature Circuit Intermittent

P0115 Engine Coolant Temperature Circuit Malfunction

P0116 Engine Coolant Temperature Circuit Range/Performance Problem

P0117 Engine Coolant Temperature Circuit Low Input

P0118 Engine Coolant Temperature Circuit High Input

P0119 Engine Coolant Temperature Circuit Intermittent

P0120 Throttle/Pedal Position Sensor/Switch "A" Circuit Malfunction

P0121 Throttle/Pedal Position Sensor/Switch "A" Circuit Range/Performance Problem

P0122 Throttle/Pedal Position Sensor/Switch "A" Circuit Low Input

P0123 Throttle/Pedal Position Sensor/Switch "A" Circuit High Input

P0124 Throttle/Pedal Position Sensor/Switch "A" Circuit Intermittent

P0125 Insufficient Coolant Temperature For Closed Loop Fuel Control

P0126 Insufficient Coolant Temperature For Stable Operation

P0130 O_2 Circuit Malfunction (Bank #1 Sensor #1)

P0131 O_2 Sensor Circuit Low Voltage (Bank #1 Sensor #1)

P0132 O_2 Sensor Circuit High Voltage (Bank #1 Sensor #1)

P0133 O_2 Sensor Circuit Slow Response (Bank #1 Sensor #1)

P0134 O_2 Sensor Circuit No Activity Detected (Bank #1 Sensor #1)

P0135 O_2 Sensor Heater Circuit Malfunction (Bank #1 Sensor #1)

P0136 O_2 Sensor Circuit Malfunction (Bank #1 Sensor #2)

P0137 O_2 Sensor Circuit Low Voltage (Bank #1 Sensor #2)

P0138 O_2 Sensor Circuit High Voltage (Bank #1 Sensor #2)

P0139 O_2 Sensor Circuit Slow Response (Bank #1 Sensor #2)

P0140 O_2 Sensor Circuit No Activity Detected (Bank #1 Sensor #2)

P0141 O_2 Sensor Heater Circuit Malfunction (Bank #1 Sensor #2)

P0142 O_2 Sensor Circuit Malfunction (Bank #1 Sensor #3)

P0143 O_2 Sensor Circuit Low Voltage (Bank #1 Sensor #3)

P0144 O_2 Sensor Circuit High Voltage (Bank #1 Sensor #3)

P0145 O_2 Sensor Circuit Slow Response (Bank #1 Sensor #3)

P0146 O_2 Sensor Circuit No Activity Detected (Bank #1 Sensor #3)

P0147 O_2 Sensor Heater Circuit Malfunction (Bank #1 Sensor #3)

P0150 O_2 Sensor Circuit Malfunction (Bank #2 Sensor #1)

P0151 O_2 Sensor Circuit Low Voltage (Bank #2 Sensor #1)

P0152 O_2 Sensor Circuit High Voltage (Bank #2 Sensor #1)

P0153 O_2 Sensor Circuit Slow Response (Bank #2 Sensor #1)

P0154 O_2 Sensor Circuit No Activity Detected (Bank #2 Sensor #1)

P0155 O_2 Sensor Heater Circuit Malfunction (Bank #2 Sensor #1)

P0156 O_2 Sensor Circuit Malfunction (Bank #2 Sensor #2)

P0157 O_2 Sensor Circuit Low Voltage (Bank #2 Sensor #2)

P0158 O_2 Sensor Circuit High Voltage (Bank #2 Sensor #2)

P0159 O_2 Sensor Circuit Slow Response (Bank #2 Sensor #2)

P0160 O_2 Sensor Circuit No Activity Detected (Bank #2 Sensor #2)

P0161 O_2 Sensor Heater Circuit Malfunction (Bank #2 Sensor #2)

P0162 O_2 Sensor Circuit Malfunction (Bank #2 Sensor #3)

P0163 O_2 Sensor Circuit Low Voltage (Bank #2 Sensor #3)

P0164 O_2 Sensor Circuit High Voltage (Bank #2 Sensor #3)

Refer to the model specific sections for fuel system service procedures

P0165 O$_2$ Sensor Circuit Slow Response (Bank #2 Sensor #3)

P0166 O$_2$ Sensor Circuit No Activity Detected (Bank #2 Sensor #3)

P0167 O$_2$ Sensor Heater Circuit Malfunction (Bank #2 Sensor #3)

P0170 Fuel Trim Malfunction (Bank #1)

P0171 System Too Lean (Bank #1)

P0172 System Too Rich (Bank #1)

P0173 Fuel Trim Malfunction (Bank #2)

P0174 System Too Lean (Bank #2)

P0175 System Too Rich (Bank #2)

P0176 Fuel Composition Sensor Circuit Malfunction

P0177 Fuel Composition Sensor Circuit Range/Performance

P0178 Fuel Composition Sensor Circuit Low Input

P0179 Fuel Composition Sensor Circuit High Input

P0180 Fuel Temperature Sensor "A" Circuit Malfunction

P0181 Fuel Temperature Sensor "A" Circuit Range/Performance

P0182 Fuel Temperature Sensor "A" Circuit Low Input

P0183 Fuel Temperature Sensor "A" Circuit High Input

P0184 Fuel Temperature Sensor "A" Circuit Intermittent

P0185 Fuel Temperature Sensor "B" Circuit Malfunction

P0186 Fuel Temperature Sensor "B" Circuit Range/Performance

P0187 Fuel Temperature Sensor "B" Circuit Low Input

P0188 Fuel Temperature Sensor "B" Circuit High Input

P0189 Fuel Temperature Sensor "B" Circuit Intermittent

P0190 Fuel Rail Pressure Sensor Circuit Malfunction

P0191 Fuel Rail Pressure Sensor Circuit Range/Performance

P0192 Fuel Rail Pressure Sensor Circuit Low Input

P0193 Fuel Rail Pressure Sensor Circuit High Input

P0194 Fuel Rail Pressure Sensor Circuit Intermittent

P0195 Engine Oil Temperature Sensor Malfunction

P0196 Engine Oil Temperature Sensor Range/Performance

P0197 Engine Oil Temperature Sensor Low

P0198 Engine Oil Temperature Sensor High

P0199 Engine Oil Temperature Sensor Intermittent

P0200 Injector Circuit Malfunction

P0201 Injector Circuit Malfunction—Cylinder #1

P0202 Injector Circuit Malfunction—Cylinder #2

P0203 Injector Circuit Malfunction—Cylinder #3

P0204 Injector Circuit Malfunction—Cylinder #4

P0205 Injector Circuit Malfunction—Cylinder #5

P0206 Injector Circuit Malfunction—Cylinder #6

P0207 Injector Circuit Malfunction—Cylinder #7

P0208 Injector Circuit Malfunction—Cylinder #8

P0209 Injector Circuit Malfunction—Cylinder #9

P0210 Injector Circuit Malfunction—Cylinder #10

P0211 Injector Circuit Malfunction—Cylinder #11

P0212 Injector Circuit Malfunction—Cylinder #12

P0213 Cold Start Injector #1 Malfunction

P0214 Cold Start Injector #2 Malfunction

P0215 Engine Shutoff Solenoid Malfunction

P0216 Injection Timing Control Circuit Malfunction

P0217 Engine Over Temperature Condition

P0218 Transmission Over Temperature Condition

P0219 Engine Over Speed Condition

P0220 Throttle/Pedal Position Sensor/Switch "B" Circuit Malfunction

P0221 Throttle/Pedal Position Sensor/Switch "B" Circuit Range/Performance Problem

P0222 Throttle/Pedal Position Sensor/Switch "B" Circuit Low Input

P0223 Throttle/Pedal Position Sensor/Switch "B" Circuit High Input

P0224 Throttle/Pedal Position Sensor/Switch "B" Circuit Intermittent

P0225 Throttle/Pedal Position Sensor/Switch "C" Circuit Malfunction

P0226 Throttle/Pedal Position Sensor/Switch "C" Circuit Range/Performance Problem

P0227 Throttle/Pedal Position Sensor/Switch "C" Circuit Low Input

P0228 Throttle/Pedal Position Sensor/Switch "C" Circuit High Input

P0229 Throttle/Pedal Position Sensor/Switch "C" Circuit Intermittent

P0230 Fuel Pump Primary Circuit Malfunction

P0231 Fuel Pump Secondary Circuit Low

P0232 Fuel Pump Secondary Circuit High

P0233 Fuel Pump Secondary Circuit Intermittent

P0234 Engine Over Boost Condition

P0261 Cylinder #1 Injector Circuit Low

P0262 Cylinder #1 Injector Circuit High

P0263 Cylinder #1 Contribution/Balance Fault

P0264 Cylinder #2 Injector Circuit Low

P0265 Cylinder #2 Injector Circuit High

P0266 Cylinder #2 Contribution/Balance Fault

P0267 Cylinder #3 Injector Circuit Low

P0268 Cylinder #3 Injector Circuit High

P0269 Cylinder #3 Contribution/Balance Fault

P0270 Cylinder #4 Injector Circuit Low

P0271 Cylinder #4 Injector Circuit High

P0272 Cylinder #4 Contribution/Balance Fault

P0273 Cylinder #5 Injector Circuit Low

P0274 Cylinder #5 Injector Circuit High

P0275 Cylinder #5 Contribution/Balance Fault

P0276 Cylinder #6 Injector Circuit Low

P0277 Cylinder #6 Injector Circuit High

P0278 Cylinder #6 Contribution/Balance Fault

P0279 Cylinder #7 Injector Circuit Low

P0280 Cylinder #7 Injector Circuit High

P0281 Cylinder #7 Contribution/Balance Fault

P0282 Cylinder #8 Injector Circuit Low

P0283 Cylinder #8 Injector Circuit High

P0284 Cylinder #8 Contribution/Balance Fault

P0285 Cylinder #9 Injector Circuit Low

P0286 Cylinder #9 Injector Circuit High

P0287 Cylinder #9 Contribution/Balance Fault

P0288 Cylinder #10 Injector Circuit Low

P0289 Cylinder #10 Injector Circuit High

P0290 Cylinder #10 Contribution/Balance Fault

P0291 Cylinder #11 Injector Circuit Low

P0292 Cylinder #11 Injector Circuit High

P0293 Cylinder #11 Contribution/Balance Fault

P0294 Cylinder #12 Injector Circuit Low

P0295 Cylinder #12 Injector Circuit High

P0296 Cylinder #12 Contribution/Balance Fault

P0300 Random/Multiple Cylinder Misfire Detected

P0301 Cylinder #1—Misfire Detected

P0302 Cylinder #2—Misfire Detected

P0303 Cylinder #3—Misfire Detected

P0304 Cylinder #4—Misfire Detected

P0305 Cylinder #5—Misfire Detected

P0306 Cylinder #6—Misfire Detected

P0307 Cylinder #7—Misfire Detected

P0308 Cylinder #8—Misfire Detected

P0320 Ignition/Distributor Engine Speed Input Circuit Malfunction

P0321 Ignition/Distributor Engine Speed Input Circuit Range/Performance

P0322 Ignition/Distributor Engine Speed Input Circuit No Signal

P0323 Ignition/Distributor Engine Speed Input Circuit Intermittent

P0325 Knock Sensor #1—Circuit Malfunction (Bank #1 or Single Sensor)

P0326 Knock Sensor #1—Circuit Range/Performance (Bank #1 or Single Sensor)

P0327 Knock Sensor #1—Circuit Low Input (Bank #1 or Single Sensor)

P0328 Knock Sensor #1—Circuit High Input (Bank #1 or Single Sensor)

P0329 Knock Sensor #1—Circuit Input Intermittent (Bank #1 or Single Sensor)

P0330 Knock Sensor #2—Circuit Malfunction (Bank #2)

P0331 Knock Sensor #2—Circuit Range/Performance (Bank #2)

P0332 Knock Sensor #2—Circuit Low Input (Bank #2)

P0333 Knock Sensor #2—Circuit High Input (Bank #2)

P0334 Knock Sensor #2—Circuit Input Intermittent (Bank #2)

P0335 Crankshaft Position Sensor "A" Circuit Malfunction

P0336 Crankshaft Position Sensor "A" Circuit Range/Performance

P0337 Crankshaft Position Sensor "A" Circuit Low Input

P0338 Crankshaft Position Sensor "A" Circuit High Input

P0339 Crankshaft Position Sensor "A" Circuit Intermittent

P0340 Camshaft Position Sensor Circuit Malfunction

P0341 Camshaft Position Sensor Circuit Range/Performance

P0342 Camshaft Position Sensor Circuit Low Input

P0343 Camshaft Position Sensor Circuit High Input

P0344 Camshaft Position Sensor Circuit Intermittent

P0350 Ignition Coil Primary/Secondary Circuit Malfunction

P0351 Ignition Coil "A" Primary/Secondary Circuit Malfunction

P0352 Ignition Coil "B" Primary/Secondary Circuit Malfunction

P0353 Ignition Coil "C" Primary/Secondary Circuit Malfunction

P0354 Ignition Coil "D" Primary/Secondary Circuit Malfunction

P0355 Ignition Coil "E" Primary/Secondary Circuit Malfunction

P0356 Ignition Coil "F" Primary/Secondary Circuit Malfunction

P0357 Ignition Coil "G" Primary/Secondary Circuit Malfunction

P0358 Ignition Coil "H" Primary/Secondary Circuit Malfunction

P0359 Ignition Coil "I" Primary/Secondary Circuit Malfunction

P0360 Ignition Coil "J" Primary/Secondary Circuit Malfunction

P0361 Ignition Coil "K" Primary/Secondary Circuit Malfunction

P0362 Ignition Coil "L" Primary/Secondary Circuit Malfunction

P0370 Timing Reference High Resolution Signal "A" Malfunction

P0371 Timing Reference High Resolution Signal "A" Too Many Pulses

P0372 Timing Reference High Resolution Signal "A" Too Few Pulses

P0373 Timing Reference High Resolution Signal "A" Intermittent/Erratic Pulses

P0374 Timing Reference High Resolution Signal "A" No Pulses

P0375 Timing Reference High Resolution Signal "B" Malfunction

P0376 Timing Reference High Resolution Signal "B" Too Many Pulses

P0377 Timing Reference High Resolution Signal "B" Too Few Pulses

P0378 Timing Reference High Resolution Signal "B" Intermittent/Erratic Pulses

P0379 Timing Reference High Resolution Signal "B" No Pulses

P0380 Glow Plug/Heater Circuit "A" Malfunction

P0381 Glow Plug/Heater Indicator Circuit Malfunction

P0382 Glow Plug/Heater Circuit "B" Malfunction

P0385 Crankshaft Position Sensor "B" Circuit Malfunction

P0386 Crankshaft Position Sensor "B" Circuit Range/Performance

P0387 Crankshaft Position Sensor "B" Circuit Low Input

P0388 Crankshaft Position Sensor "B" Circuit High Input

P0389 Crankshaft Position Sensor "B" Circuit Intermittent

P0400 Exhaust Gas Recirculation Flow Malfunction

P0401 Exhaust Gas Recirculation Flow Insufficient Detected

P0402 Exhaust Gas Recirculation Flow Excessive Detected

P0403 Exhaust Gas Recirculation Circuit Malfunction

P0404 Exhaust Gas Recirculation Circuit Range/Performance

P0405 Exhaust Gas Recirculation Sensor "A" Circuit Low

P0406 Exhaust Gas Recirculation Sensor "A" Circuit High

P0407 Exhaust Gas Recirculation Sensor "B" Circuit Low

P0408 Exhaust Gas Recirculation Sensor "B" Circuit High

P0410 Secondary Air Injection System Malfunction

P0411 Secondary Air Injection System Incorrect Flow Detected

P0412 Secondary Air Injection System Switching Valve "A" Circuit Malfunction

P0413 Secondary Air Injection System Switching Valve "A" Circuit Open

P0414 Secondary Air Injection System Switching Valve "A" Circuit Shorted

P0415 Secondary Air Injection System Switching Valve "B" Circuit Malfunction

P0416 Secondary Air Injection System Switching Valve "B" Circuit Open

P0417 Secondary Air Injection System Switching Valve "B" Circuit Shorted

P0418 Secondary Air Injection System Relay "A" Circuit Malfunction

P0419 Secondary Air Injection System Relay "B" Circuit Malfunction

P0420 Catalyst System Efficiency Below Threshold (Bank #1)

P0421 Warm Up Catalyst Efficiency Below Threshold (Bank #1)

P0422 Main Catalyst Efficiency Below Threshold (Bank #1)

P0423 Heated Catalyst Efficiency Below Threshold (Bank #1)

P0424 Heated Catalyst Temperature Below Threshold (Bank #1)

P0430 Catalyst System Efficiency Below Threshold (Bank #2)

P0431 Warm Up Catalyst Efficiency Below Threshold (Bank #2)

P0432 Main Catalyst Efficiency Below Threshold (Bank #2)

P0433 Heated Catalyst Efficiency Below Threshold (Bank #2)

P0434 Heated Catalyst Temperature Below Threshold (Bank #2)

P0440 Evaporative Emission Control System Malfunction

P0441 Evaporative Emission Control System Incorrect Purge Flow

Refer to the model specific sections for engine electrical system service procedures

P0442 Evaporative Emission Control System Leak Detected (Small Leak)

P0443 Evaporative Emission Control System Purge Control Valve Circuit Malfunction

P0444 Evaporative Emission Control System Purge Control Valve Circuit Open

P0445 Evaporative Emission Control System Purge Control Valve Circuit Shorted

P0446 Evaporative Emission Control System Vent Control Circuit Malfunction

P0447 Evaporative Emission Control System Vent Control Circuit Open

P0448 Evaporative Emission Control System Vent Control Circuit Shorted

P0449 Evaporative Emission Control System Vent Valve/Solenoid Circuit Malfunction

P0450 Evaporative Emission Control System Pressure Sensor Malfunction

P0451 Evaporative Emission Control System Pressure Sensor Range/Performance

P0452 Evaporative Emission Control System Pressure Sensor Low Input

P0453 Evaporative Emission Control System Pressure Sensor High Input

P0454 Evaporative Emission Control System Pressure Sensor Intermittent

P0455 Evaporative Emission Control System Leak Detected (Gross Leak)

P0460 Fuel Level Sensor Circuit Malfunction

P0461 Fuel Level Sensor Circuit Range/Performance

P0462 Fuel Level Sensor Circuit Low Input

P0463 Fuel Level Sensor Circuit High Input

P0464 Fuel Level Sensor Circuit Intermittent

P0465 Purge Flow Sensor Circuit Malfunction

P0466 Purge Flow Sensor Circuit Range/Performance

P0467 Purge Flow Sensor Circuit Low Input

P0468 Purge Flow Sensor Circuit High Input

P0469 Purge Flow Sensor Circuit Intermittent

P0470 Exhaust Pressure Sensor Malfunction

P0471 Exhaust Pressure Sensor Range/Performance

P0472 Exhaust Pressure Sensor Low

P0473 Exhaust Pressure Sensor High

P0474 Exhaust Pressure Sensor Intermittent

P0475 Exhaust Pressure Control Valve Malfunction

P0476 Exhaust Pressure Control Valve Range/Performance

P0477 Exhaust Pressure Control Valve Low

P0478 Exhaust Pressure Control Valve High

P0479 Exhaust Pressure Control Valve Intermittent

P0480 Cooling Fan #1 Control Circuit Malfunction

P0481 Cooling Fan #2 Control Circuit Malfunction

P0482 Cooling Fan #3 Control Circuit Malfunction

P0483 Cooling Fan Rationality Check Malfunction

P0484 Cooling Fan Circuit Over Current

P0485 Cooling Fan Power/Ground Circuit Malfunction

P0500 Vehicle Speed Sensor Malfunction

P0501 Vehicle Speed Sensor Range/Performance

P0502 Vehicle Speed Sensor Circuit Low Input

P0503 Vehicle Speed Sensor Intermittent/Erratic/High

P0505 Idle Control System Malfunction

P0506 Idle Control System RPM Lower Than Expected

P0507 Idle Control System RPM Higher Than Expected

P0510 Closed Throttle Position Switch Malfunction

P0520 Engine Oil Pressure Sensor/Switch Circuit Malfunction

P0521 Engine Oil Pressure Sensor/Switch Range/Performance

P0522 Engine Oil Pressure Sensor/Switch Low Voltage

P0523 Engine Oil Pressure Sensor/Switch High Voltage

P0530 A/C Refrigerant Pressure Sensor Circuit Malfunction

P0531 A/C Refrigerant Pressure Sensor Circuit Range/Performance

P0532 A/C Refrigerant Pressure Sensor Circuit Low Input

P0533 A/C Refrigerant Pressure Sensor Circuit High Input

P0534 A/C Refrigerant Charge Loss

P0550 Power Steering Pressure Sensor Circuit Malfunction

P0551 Power Steering Pressure Sensor Circuit Range/Performance

P0552 Power Steering Pressure Sensor Circuit Low Input

P0553 Power Steering Pressure Sensor Circuit High Input

P0554 Power Steering Pressure Sensor Circuit Intermittent

P0560 System Voltage Malfunction

P0561 System Voltage Unstable

P0562 System Voltage Low

P0563 System Voltage High

P0565 Cruise Control On Signal Malfunction

P0566 Cruise Control Off Signal Malfunction

P0567 Cruise Control Resume Signal Malfunction

P0568 Cruise Control Set Signal Malfunction

P0569 Cruise Control Coast Signal Malfunction

P0570 Cruise Control Accel Signal Malfunction

P0571 Cruise Control/Brake Switch "A" Circuit Malfunction

P0572 Cruise Control/Brake Switch "A" Circuit Low

P0573 Cruise Control/Brake Switch "A" Circuit High

P0574 Through P0580 Reserved for Cruise Codes

P0600 Serial Communication Link Malfunction

P0601 Internal Control Module Memory Check Sum Error

P0602 Control Module Programming Error

P0603 Internal Control Module Keep Alive Memory (KAM) Error

P0604 Internal Control Module Random Access Memory (RAM) Error

P0605 Internal Control Module Read Only Memory (ROM) Error

P0606 PCM Processor Fault

P0608 Control Module VSS Output "A" Malfunction

P0609 Control Module VSS Output "B" Malfunction

P0620 Generator Control Circuit Malfunction

P0621 Generator Lamp "L" Control Circuit Malfunction

P0622 Generator Field "F" Control Circuit Malfunction

P0650 Malfunction Indicator Lamp (MIL) Control Circuit Malfunction

P0654 Engine RPM Output Circuit Malfunction

P0655 Engine Hot Lamp Output Control Circuit Malfunction

P0656 Fuel Level Output Circuit Malfunction

P0700 Transmission Control System Malfunction

P0701 Transmission Control System Range/Performance

P0702 Transmission Control System Electrical

P0703 Torque Converter/Brake Switch "B" Circuit Malfunction

P0704 Clutch Switch Input Circuit Malfunction

P0705 Transmission Range Sensor Circuit Malfunction (PRNDL Input)

P0706 Transmission Range Sensor Circuit Range/Performance

P0707 Transmission Range Sensor Circuit Low Input

P0708 Transmission Range Sensor Circuit High Input

P0709 Transmission Range Sensor Circuit Intermittent

P0710 Transmission Fluid Temperature Sensor Circuit Malfunction

P0711 Transmission Fluid Temperature Sensor Circuit Range/Performance

P0712 Transmission Fluid Temperature Sensor Circuit Low Input

P0713 Transmission Fluid Temperature Sensor Circuit High Input

P0714 Transmission Fluid Temperature Sensor Circuit Intermittent

P0715 Input/Turbine Speed Sensor Circuit Malfunction

P0716 Input/Turbine Speed Sensor Circuit Range/Performance

P0717 Input/Turbine Speed Sensor Circuit No Signal

P0718 Input/Turbine Speed Sensor Circuit Intermittent

P0719 Torque Converter/Brake Switch "B" Circuit Low

P0720 Output Speed Sensor Circuit Malfunction

P0721 Output Speed Sensor Circuit Range/Performance

P0722 Output Speed Sensor Circuit No Signal

P0723 Output Speed Sensor Circuit Intermittent

P0724 Torque Converter/Brake Switch "B" Circuit High

P0725 Engine Speed Input Circuit Malfunction

P0726 Engine Speed Input Circuit Range/Performance

P0727 Engine Speed Input Circuit No Signal

P0728 Engine Speed Input Circuit Intermittent

P0730 Incorrect Gear Ratio

P0731 Gear #1 Incorrect Ratio

P0732 Gear #2 Incorrect Ratio

P0733 Gear #3 Incorrect Ratio

P0734 Gear #4 Incorrect Ratio

P0735 Gear #5 Incorrect Ratio

P0736 Reverse Incorrect Ratio

P0740 Torque Converter Clutch Circuit Malfunction

P0741 Torque Converter Clutch Circuit Performance or Stuck Off

P0742 Torque Converter Clutch Circuit Stuck On

P0743 Torque Converter Clutch Circuit Electrical

P0744 Torque Converter Clutch Circuit Intermittent

P0745 Pressure Control Solenoid Malfunction

P0746 Pressure Control Solenoid Performance or Stuck Off

P0747 Pressure Control Solenoid Stuck On

P0748 Pressure Control Solenoid Electrical

P0749 Pressure Control Solenoid Intermittent

P0750 Shift Solenoid "A" Malfunction

P0751 Shift Solenoid "A" Performance or Stuck Off

P0752 Shift Solenoid "A" Stuck On

P0753 Shift Solenoid "A" Electrical

P0754 Shift Solenoid "A" Intermittent

P0755 Shift Solenoid "B" Malfunction

P0756 Shift Solenoid "B" Performance or Stuck Off

P0757 Shift Solenoid "B" Stuck On

P0758 Shift Solenoid "B" Electrical

P0759 Shift Solenoid "B" Intermittent

P0760 Shift Solenoid "C" Malfunction

P0761 Shift Solenoid "C" Performance Or Stuck Off

P0762 Shift Solenoid "C" Stuck On

P0763 Shift Solenoid "C" Electrical

P0764 Shift Solenoid "C" Intermittent

P0765 Shift Solenoid "D" Malfunction

P0766 Shift Solenoid "D" Performance Or Stuck Off

P0767 Shift Solenoid "D" Stuck On

P0768 Shift Solenoid "D" Electrical

P0769 Shift Solenoid "D" Intermittent

P0770 Shift Solenoid "E" Malfunction

P0771 Shift Solenoid "E" Performance Or Stuck Off

P0772 Shift Solenoid "E" Stuck On

P0773 Shift Solenoid "E" Electrical

P0774 Shift Solenoid "E" Intermittent

P0780 Shift Malfunction

P0781 1–2 Shift Malfunction

P0782 2–3 Shift Malfunction

P0783 3–4 Shift Malfunction

P0784 4–5 Shift Malfunction

P0785 Shift/Timing Solenoid Malfunction

P0786 Shift/Timing Solenoid Range/Performance

P0787 Shift/Timing Solenoid Low

P0788 Shift/Timing Solenoid High

P0789 Shift/Timing Solenoid Intermittent

P0790 Normal/Performance Switch Circuit Malfunction

P0801 Reverse Inhibit Control Circuit Malfunction

P0803 1–4 Upshift (Skip Shift) Solenoid Control Circuit Malfunction

P0804 1–4 Upshift (Skip Shift) Lamp Control Circuit Malfunction

P1100 Barometric Pressure Sensor Circuit Fault

P1120 Accelerator Pedal Position Sensor Circuit Malfunction

P1121 Accelerator Pedal Position Sensor Range/Performance Problem

P1125 Throttle Control Motor Circuit Malfunction

P1126 Magnetic Clutch Circuit Malfunction

P1127 ETCS Actuator Power Source Circuit Malfunction

P1128 Throttle Control Motor Lock Malfunction

P1129 Electric Throttle Control System Malfunction

P1130 A/F Sensor Circuit Range / Performance Malfunction (Bank #1 Sensor #1)

P1133 A/F Sensor Circuit Response Malfunction (Bank #1 Sensor #1)

P1135 A/F Sensor Heater Circuit Malfunction (Bank #1 Sensor #1)

P1150 A/F Sensor Circuit Range / Performance Malfunction (Bank #2 Sensor #1)

P1153 A/F Sensor Circuit Response Malfunction (Bank #2 Sensor #1)

P1155 A/F Sensor Heater Circuit Malfunction (Bank #2 Sensor #1)

P1200 Fuel Pump Relay Circuit Fault

P1300 Igniter Circuit Fault (Bank #1)

P1305 Igniter Circuit Fault (Bank #2)

P1310 Igniter Circuit Fault (Bank #3)

P1315 Igniter Circuit Fault (Bank #4)

P1320 Igniter Circuit Fault (Bank #5)

P1325 Igniter Circuit Fault (Bank #6)

P1330 Igniter Circuit Fault (Bank #7)

P1335 Crankshaft Position Sensor Circuit Fault (during engine running)

P1340 Igniter Circuit Fault (Bank #8)

P1400 Sub-Throttle Position Sensor Circuit Fault

P1401 Sub-Throttle Position Sensor Performance

P1500 Starter Signal Circuit Fault

P1510 Air Volume Too Low With Supercharger On

P1520 Stop Light Switch Signal Malfunction

P1600 ECM Battery Back-up Circuit Fault

P1633 ECM Malfunction (ETCS Circuit)

P1605 Knock Control CPU Fault
P1700 Vehicle Speed Sensor Circuit Fault

P1705 Direct Clutch Speed Sensor Circuit Fault
P1765 Linear Shift Solenoid Circuit Fault

P1780 Park Neutral Position Switch Fault

ACCESSORY DRIVE BELTS

3

ACCESSORY DRIVE BELTS

Accessory drive belts are usually divided into two basic types: V-belts (conventional, cogged, and flat multi-ribbed) and serpentine (multi-ribbed) belts. The flat multi-ribbed V-belt actually resembles a serpentine belt, however, unlike a serpentine belt, only the inner surface of the belt makes contact with the components' pulleys. Rarely, the back of a multi-ribbed belt may ride against an idler or tensioner pulley, however. V-belts ride in pulleys with V-shaped groove(s) and are used to rotate various accessories, such as the power steering pump, air conditioner compressor, alternator/generator, water pump, and air pump. Only the inside of a V-belt is used, unlike a serpentine belt which utilizes both sides. V-belts typically operate one or two accessories per belt, whereas a single serpentine belt can drive all of the accessories. V-belts and a few serpentine belts require periodic adjustment because the belts are under tension and stretch over time. Most serpentine belts utilize an automatic belt tensioner that constantly provides the proper tension to the belt.

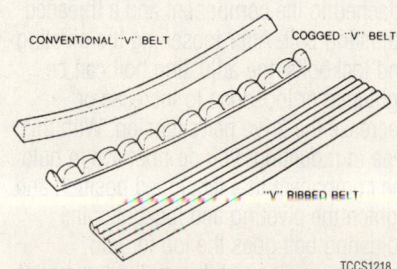

Typical accessory drive belts found on vehicles today

V-Belts

INSPECTION

Although different maintenance intervals are given by each manufacturer, it is a good rule of thumb to inspect the drive belts every 15,000 miles (24,000 km) or 12 months (whichever occurs first). Determine the belt tension at a point half-way between the pulleys by pressing on the belt with moderate thumb pressure. The belt should deflect about ¼–½ in. (6–13mm) at this point. Note that "deflection" is not play, but the ability of the belt, under actual tension, to stretch slightly and give.

Inspect the belts for the following signs of damage or wear: glazing, cracking, fraying, crumbling or missing chunks. A glazed belt will be perfectly smooth from slippage, while a good belt will have a slight texture of fabric visible. Cracks will usually start at the inner edge of the belt and run outward. A belt that is fraying will have the fabric backing de-laminating its self from the belt. A belt that is crumbling or missing chunks will have voids in the cross-section of the belt, some times the section missing chunks will be in the pulley groove and not easily seen. All worn or damaged drive belts should be replaced immediately. It is best to replace all drive belts

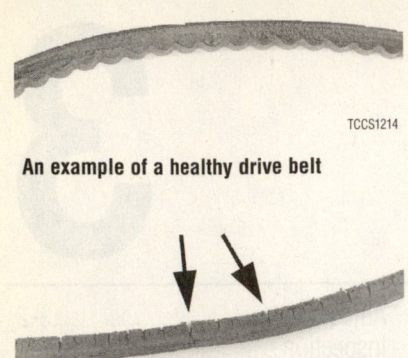

An example of a healthy drive belt

TCCS1214

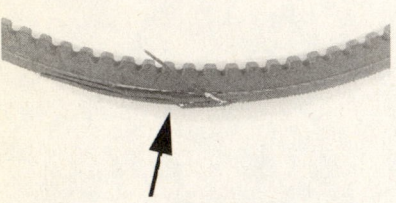

Deep cracks in this belt will cause flex, building up heat that will eventually lead to belt failure

TCCS1215

The cover of this belt is worn, exposing the critical reinforcing cords to excessive wear

TCCS1216

Installing too wide a belt can result in serious belt wear and/or breakage

TCCS1217

at one time, as a preventive maintenance measure.

Although it is generally easier on the component to have the belt too loose than too tight, a very loose belt may place a high impact load on a bearing due to the whipping or snapping action of the belt. A belt that is slightly loose may slip, especially when component loads are high. This slippage may be hard to identify. For example, the generator belt may run okay during the day, and then slip at night when headlights are turned on. Slipping belts wear quickly not only due to the direct effect of slippage but also because of the heat the slippage generates. Extreme slippage may even cause a belt to burn. A very smooth, glazed appearance on the belt's sides, as opposed to the obvious pattern of a fabric cover, indicates that the belt has been slipping.

ADJUSTMENT

✳✳ CAUTION

On vehicles with an electric cooling fan, disable the power to the fan by disengaging the fan motor wiring connector or removing the negative battery cable before replacing or adjusting the drive belts. Otherwise, the fan may engage even though the ignition is OFF.

Belt tension can be checked by pressing on the belt at the center point of its longest straight span. The belt should give approximately ¼–½ in. (6–13mm). If the belt is loose it will slip, whereas if the belt is too tight it will damage the bearings in the driven unit.

For the purposes of V-belt tensioning, there are generally three types of mounting for the various components driven by the drive belt. The first method, referred to as pivoting type without adjuster, is designed so that the component is secured by at least 2 bolts. One of the bolts is a pivoting bolt and the other is the lockbolt. When both bolts are loosened so that the component may move, the component pivots on the pivoting bolt. The lockbolt passes through the component and a slotted bracket, so that when the lockbolt's nut is tightened the component is held in that position. There are not automatic adjusting mechanisms used with this type of mounting.

The second method of component mounting, referred to as pivoting type with adjuster, is almost identical except for the addition of an adjuster of some sort. Usually the adjuster is composed of a bracket attached to the component and a threaded adjusting bolt. After loosening the pivoting and lockbolts, the adjusting bolt can be tightened or loosened to increase or decrease the drive belt's tension. With this type of mounting, you do not have to hold the component in a tensioned position and tighten the pivoting and lockbolts; the adjusting bolt does the job for you.

Some versions of this method of mounting use an adjuster which is built into one of the components mounting braces. The brace attaches the component to the engine and incorporates a threaded adjuster in its mid-span, so that when the threaded adjuster is turned the brace shortens or lengthens. This in turn increases or decreases the amount of tension on the component.

The third type of mounting, referred to as stationary type, is designed so that the com-

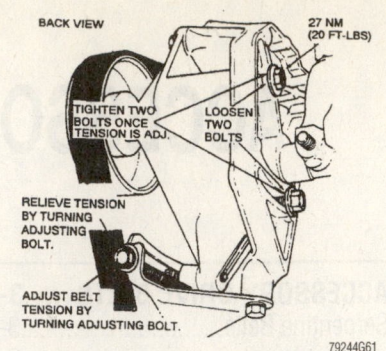

A typical pivoting accessory with an adjusting bolt

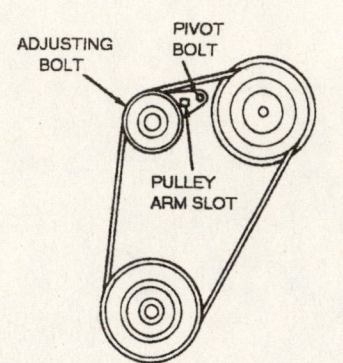

An accessory that is fixed will have an adjustable pulley—notice the square slot to aid the adjustment

ponent is mounted on its brackets. There are no pivots or lockbolts, and the component is not designed to be moved. Rather, this type of mounting uses an extra tensioner idler pulley assembly. The drive belt is tensioned by adjusting the position of the idler pulley, usually accomplished by turning the adjuster bolt on the idler mechanism.

Pivoting Type

WITHOUT ADJUSTER

1. Disconnect the negative battery cable.
2. Loosen the component's lockbolt and pivoting bolt only enough for the component to move.
3. Using a strong wooden, plastic or metal prytool, move the component either closer to, or farther away from, the engine to provide the correct tension on the belt.

✳✳ WARNING

If using a metal prytool, always wrap the end with a rag or towel to prevent accidentally damaging the component from undue stress.

4. Once the proper amount of tension is applied to the drive belt, hold the prytool

with one hand while tightening the lockbolt securely with the other hand.

5. Release the pressure from the prytool and tighten the pivoting bolt securely.

6. Double check the drive belt's tension, in case the component moved slightly while tightening the bolts.

7. Connect the negative battery cable.

WITH ADJUSTER

This type of drive belt is tensioned by a tensioner, which makes precise tension adjustment easy.

1. Disconnect the negative battery cable.

2. loosen the component's pivot and lockbolts.

3. Inspect the tensioner assembly on the component; the tensioner adjusting bolt may use a locknut or screw to prevent it from loosening over time. On the type of adjuster with a threaded mounting brace, there may be two jam nuts used on either side of the threaded coupling. If such locking fasteners are found, loosen them.

4. Turn the tensioner adjusting bolt or threaded coupling to increase or decrease the amount of tension on the drive belt, as necessary.

5. When the belt tension is correct, tighten the lockbolt and the pivot bolt.

6. If equipped, tighten the tension adjusting bolt locknut or screw to prevent the adjuster from slowly loosening over time. If equipped, tighten the two jam nuts.

7. Connect the negative battery cable.

Stationary Type

IDLER PULLEY WITH ADJUSTING BOLT

1. Loosen the idler bracket pivot bolt and locking bolts.

2. Adjust the belt tension by inserting the proper size ratchet in the square slot of the idler bracket and rotating the bracket until tension is applied.

3. While holding the tension on the belt with the ratchet, tighten the locking bolts, then the pivot bolt.

IDLER PULLEY WITHOUT ADJUSTING BOLT

1. Loosen the mounting/pivot bolt behind the idler pulley.

2. Swivel the idler pulley with a pair of pliers or a wrench on the bearing mounting until the proper tension is achieved.

3. While holding the idler pulley, at the proper tension, tighten the mounting/pivot bolt.

REMOVAL & INSTALLATION

If a belt must be replaced, the driven unit or idler pulley must be loosened and moved to its extreme loosest position, generally by moving it toward the center of the motor. After removing the old belt, check the pulleys for dirt or built-up material which could affect belt contact. Carefully install the new belt, remembering that it is new and unused; it may appear to be just a little too small to fit over the pulley flanges. Fit the belt over the largest pulley (usually the crankshaft pulley at the bottom center of the motor) first, then work on the smaller one(s). Gentle pressure in the direction of rotation is helpful. Some belts run around a third, or idler pulley, which acts as an additional pivot in the belt's path. It may be possible to loosen the idler pulley as well as the main component, making your job much easier. Depending on which belt(s) you are changing, it may be necessary to loosen or remove other interfering belts to get at the one(s) you want.

When buying replacement belts, remember that the fit is critical according to the length of the belt ("diameter"), the width of the belt, the depth of the belt and the angle or profile of the V shape or the ribs. The belt shape should match the shape of the pulley exactly; belts that are not an exact match can cause noise, slippage and premature failure.

After the new belt is installed, draw tension on it by moving the driven unit or idler pulley away from the motor and tighten its mounting bolts. This is sometimes a three or four-handed job; you may find an assistant helpful. Make sure that all the bolts you loosened are tightened and that any other loosened belts also have the correct tension. A new belt can be expected to stretch a bit after installation so, be prepared to readjust your new belt, if needed, within the first two hundred miles of use.

Pivoting Type

⁂ **CAUTION**

On vehicles with an electric cooling fan, disable the power to the fan by disengaging the fan motor wiring connector or removing the negative battery cable before replacing or adjusting the drive belts. Otherwise, the fan may engage even though the ignition is OFF.

WITHOUT ADJUSTER

1. Disconnect the negative battery cable.

2. Loosen the accessory's slotted adjust-

ing bracket bolt. If the hinge bolt is excessively tight, it too will have to be loosened.

3. Push the component toward the engine to provide enough slack in the belt so that it will slide over one of the accessory drive pulleys. Remove the drive belt from the accessory drive pulleys and from the vehicle.

To install:

4. Position the new drive belt over the component pulleys. Make sure that it is routed correctly.

5. Adjust the tension of the belt, as described earlier in this section.

6. Connect the negative battery cable.

WITH ADJUSTER

1. Disconnect the negative battery cable.

2. loosen the component's pivot and lockbolts.

3. Inspect the tensioner assembly on the component; the tensioner adjusting bolt may use a locknut or screw to prevent it from loosening over time. On the type of adjuster with a threaded mounting brace, there may be two jam nuts used on either side of the threaded coupling. If such locking fasteners are found, loosen them.

4. Turn the tensioner adjusting bolt or threaded coupling to relieve all tension from the drive belt until the most possible slack is gained from the component.

5. Slip the belt off of the accessory pulley, then remove it from the other pulleys. Remove the belt from the vehicle.

To install:

6. Route the new belt on the component pulleys. Make certain that it is routed correctly; incorrect routing could cause a component to spin backward, possibly damaging it.

7. Once the belt is correctly positioned on all of the pulleys, adjust the tension as described earlier in this section.

8. Connect the negative battery cable.

Stationary Type

IDLER PULLEY WITH ADJUSTING BOLT

1. Disconnect the negative battery cable.

2. Loosen the idler bracket pivot bolt and locking bolts.

3. Move the idler pulley until the most amount of slack is gained.

4. Remove the drive belt from the accessory pulley, then from the other applicable pulleys.

To install:

5. Position the new belt over the crankshaft pulley, the idler pulley and the accessory pulley. Make certain that it is correctly

routed, otherwise it could cause the accessory to be rotated backwards. This could cause damage to the accessory.

6. Adjust the belt tension, as described earlier in this section.

7. While holding the tension on the belt with the ratchet, tighten the locking bolts, then the pivot bolt.

8. Connect the negative battery cable.

IDLER PULLEY WITHOUT ADJUSTING BOLT

1. Disconnect the negative battery cable.

2. Loosen the mounting/pivot bolt behind the idler pulley.

3. Remove the drive belt from the accessory pulley, then from the other applicable pulleys.

To install:

4. Position the new belt over the crankshaft pulley, the idler pulley and the accessory pulley. Make certain that it is correctly routed, otherwise it could cause the accessory to be rotated backwards. This could cause damage to the accessory.

5. Swivel the idler pulley with a pair of pliers or a wrench on the bearing mounting until the proper tension is achieved.

6. While holding the idler pulley, at the proper tension, tighten the mounting/pivot bolt.

7. Connect the negative battery cable.

Serpentine Belts

INSPECTION

Although many manufacturers recommend that the drive belt(s) be inspected every 30,000 miles (48,000 km) or more, it is really a good idea to check them at least once a year, or at every major fluid change. Whichever interval you choose, the belts should be checked for wear or damage. Obviously, a damaged drive belt can cause problems should it give way while the vehicle is in operation. But, improper length belts (too short or long), as well as excessively worn belts, can also cause problems. Loose accessory drive belts can lead to poor engine cooling and diminished output from the alternator, air conditioning compressor or power steering pump. A belt that is too tight places a severe strain on the driven unit and can wear out bearings quickly.

Serpentine drive belts should be inspected for rib chunking (pieces of the ribs breaking off), severe glazing, frayed cords or other visible damage. Any belt which is missing sections of 2 or more adjacent ribs which are ½ in. (13mm) or longer must be replaced. You

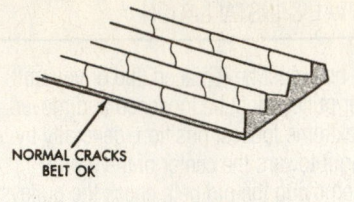

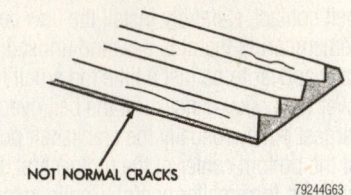

Typical wear patterns for a serpentine drive belt

might want to note that serpentine belts do tend to form small cracks across the backing. If the only wear you find is in the form of one or more cracks are across the backing and NOT parallel to the ribs, the belt is still good and does not need to be replaced.

ADJUSTMENT

Periodic drive belt tensioning is not necessary, because an automatic spring-loaded tensioner is used with these belts to maintain proper adjustment at all times. The tensioner is also useful as a wear indicator. When the belt is properly installed, the arrow on the tensioner housing must point within the acceptable range lines on the tensioner's face. If the arrow falls outside the range, either an improper belt has been installed or the belt is worn beyond its useful life span. In either case, a new belt must be installed immediately to assure proper engine operation and to prevent possible accessory damage.

REMOVAL & INSTALLATION

Because serpentine belts use a spring loaded tensioner for adjustment, belt replacement tends to be somewhat easier than it used to be on engines where accessories were pivoted and bolted in place for tension adjustment. Basically, all belt replacement involves is to pivot the tensioner to loosen the belt, then slide the belt off of the pulleys. The two most important points are to pay CLOSE attention to the proper belt routing (since serpentine belts tend to be "snaked" all different ways through the pulleys) and to make sure the V-ribs are properly seated in all the pulleys.

Although belt routing diagrams have been included in this section, the first places you should check for proper belt routing are the labels in your engine com-

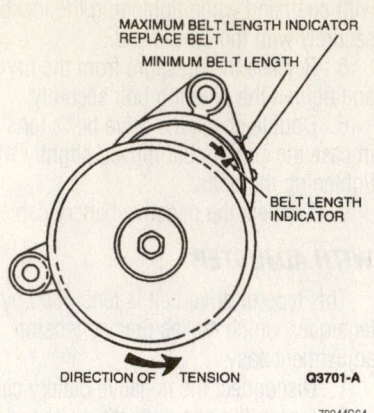

Typical drive belt automatic tensioner wear indicator

partment. These should include a belt routing diagram which may reflect changes made during a production run.

1. Disconnect the negative battery cable for safety. This will help assure that no one mistakenly cranks the engine over with your hands between the pulleys, and that the cooling fan cannot activate while servicing the belt(s).

➡Take a good look at the installed belt and make a note of the routing. Before removing the belt, make sure the routing matches that of the belt routing label or one of the diagrams in this book. If for some reason a diagram does not match (you may not have the original engine or it may have been modified), carefully note the changes on a piece of paper.

2. For tensioners equipped with a ½ in. (13mm) square hole, insert the drive end of a large breaker bar into the hole. Use the breaker bar to pivot the tensioner away from the drive belt. For tensioners not equipped with this hole, use the proper-sized socket and breaker bar (or a large handled wrench) on the tensioner idler pulley center bolt to pivot the tensioner away from the belt. This will loosen the belt sufficiently that it can be pulled off of one or more of the pulleys. It is usually easiest to carefully pull the belt out from underneath the tensioner pulley itself.

3. Once the belt is off one of the pulleys, gently pivot the tensioner back into position. DO NOT allow the tensioner to snap back, as this could damage the tensioner's internal parts.

4. Now finish removing the belt from the other pulleys and remove it from the engine.

To install:

5. While referring to the proper routing diagram (which you identified earlier), begin to route the belt over the pulleys, leaving

Troubleshooting the Serpentine Drive Belt

Problem	Cause	Solution
Tension sheeting fabric failure (woven fabric on outside circumference of belt has cracked or separated from body of belt)	• Grooved or backside idler pulley diameters are less than minimum recommended • Tension sheeting contacting (rubbing) stationary object • Excessive heat causing woven fabric to age • Tension sheeting splice has fractured	• Replace pulley(s) not conforming to specification • Correct rubbing condition • Replace belt • Replace belt
Noise (objectional squeal, squeak, or rumble is heard or felt while drive belt is in operation)	• Belt slippage • Bearing noise • Belt misalignment • Belt-to-pulley mismatch • Driven component inducing vibration • System resonant frequency inducing vibration	• Adjust belt • Locate and repair • Align belt/pulley(s) • Install correct belt • Locate defective driven component and repair • Vary belt tension within specifications. Replace belt.
Rib chunking (one or more ribs has separated from belt body)	• Foreign objects imbedded in pulley grooves • Installation damage • Drive loads in excess of design specifications • Insufficient internal belt adhesion	• Remove foreign objects from pulley grooves • Replace belt • Adjust belt tension • Replace belt
Rib or belt wear (belt ribs contact bottom of pulley grooves)	• Pulley(s) misaligned • Mismatch of belt and pulley groove widths • Abrasive environment • Rusted pulley(s) • Sharp or jagged pulley groove tips • Rubber deteriorated	• Align pulley(s) • Replace belt • Replace belt • Clean rust from pulley(s) • Replace pulley • Replace belt
Longitudinal belt cracking (cracks between two ribs)	• Belt has mistracked from pulley groove • Pulley groove tip has worn away rubber-to-tensile member	• Replace belt • Replace belt
Belt slips	• Belt slipping because of insufficient tension • Belt or pulley subjected to substance (belt dressing, oil, ethylene glycol) that has reduced friction • Driven component bearing failure • Belt glazed and hardened from heat and excessive slippage	• Adjust tension • Replace belt and clean pulleys • Replace faulty component bearing • Replace belt
"Groove jumping" (belt does not maintain correct position on pulley, or turns over and/or runs off pulleys)	• Insufficient belt tension • Pulley(s) not within design tolerance • Foreign object(s) in grooves	• Adjust belt tension • Replace pulley(s) • Remove foreign objects from grooves

TCCS3C09

Troubleshooting the Serpentine Drive Belt

Problem	Cause	Solution
"Groove jumping" (belt does not maintain correct position on pulley, or turns over and/or runs off pulleys)	• Excessive belt speed • Pulley misalignment • Belt-to-pulley profile mismatched • Belt cordline is distorted	• Avoid excessive engine acceleration • Align pulley(s) • Install correct belt • Replace belt
Belt broken (Note: identify and correct problem before replacement belt is installed)	• Excessive tension • Tensile members damaged during belt installation • Belt turnover • Severe pulley misalignment • Bracket, pulley, or bearing failure	• Replace belt and adjust tension to specification • Replace belt • Replace belt • Align pulley(s) • Replace defective component and belt
Cord edge failure (tensile member exposed at edges of belt or separated from belt body)	• Excessive tension • Drive pulley misalignment • Belt contacting stationary object • Pulley irregularities • Improper pulley construction • Insufficient adhesion between tensile member and rubber matrix	• Adjust belt tension • Align pulley • Correct as necessary • Replace pulley • Replace pulley • Replace belt and adjust tension to specifications
Sporadic rib cracking (multiple cracks in belt ribs at random intervals)	• Ribbed pulley(s) diameter less than minimum specification • Backside bend flat pulley(s) diameter less than minimum • Excessive heat condition causing rubber to harden • Excessive belt thickness • Belt overcured • Excessive tension	• Replace pulley(s) • Replace pulley(s) • Correct heat condition as necessary • Replace belt • Replace belt • Adjust belt tension

TCCS3C10

whichever pulley you first released it from for last.

6. Once the belt is mostly in place, carefully pivot the tensioner and position the belt over the final pulley. As you begin to allow the tensioner back into contact with the belt, run your hand around the pulleys and make sure the belt is properly seated in the ribs. If not, release the tension and seat the belt.

7. Once the belt is installed, take another look at all the pulleys to double check your installation.

8. Connect the negative battery cable, then start and run the engine to check belt operation.

9. Once the engine has reached normal operating temperature, turn the ignition **OFF** and check that the belt tensioner arrow is within the proper adjustment range.

Often the underhood label will display the serpentine drive belt routing

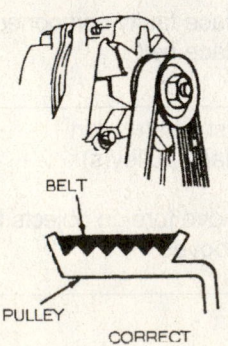

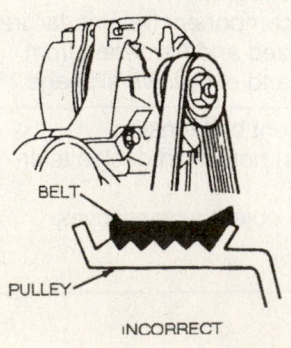

Verifying serpentine belt alignment in the pulley

Relieve the belt tension by pivoting the automatic tensioner away from the belt, then remove the belt

ACCESSORY DRIVE BELT ROUTING INDEX

MANUFACTURER

ENGINES	DESCRIPTION	FIGURE
Acura		
3.2L SLX engine	Accessory V-belt routing	1
3.5L SLX engine	Accessory serpintine belt routing	2
Chrysler		
2.4L engine	Accessory V-belt routing	10
3.0L engine	Accessory V-belt routing	11
3.3L engine	Accessory V-belt routing	12
3.8L engine	Accessory V-belt routing	12
Dodge		
2.5L engines		
Models with A/C	Accessory serpentine belt routing	3
Models without A/C	Accessory serpentine belt routing	4
3.9L, 5.2L and 5.9L gasoline engines	Accessory serpentine belt routing	5
5.9L diesel engines		
Models with A/C	Accessory serpentine belt routing	8
Models without A/C	Accessory serpentine belt routing	9
5.9L HDC gasoline engines		
Models with A/C	Accessory serpentine belt routing	6
Models without A/C	Accessory serpentine belt routing	7
8.0L engines		
Models with A/C	Accessory serpentine belt routing	6
Models without A/C	Accessory serpentine belt routing	7
Ford Motor Co.		
2.3L Ranger engines	Accessory serpentine belt routing	13
2.5L engines	Accessory serpentine belt routing	13
3.0L Aerostar engines		
Models with A/C	Accessory serpentine belt routing	15
Models without A/C	Accessory serpentine belt routing	16
3.0L Ranger engines	Accessory serpentine belt routing	14
3.0L Windstar engine	Accessory serpentine belt routing	29
3.8L Windstar engine	Accessory serpentine belt routing	30
4.0L Ranger engines	Accessory serpentine belt routing	17
4.0L SOHC engines	Accessory serpentine belt routing	27
4.2L engines		
Models with A/C	Accessory serpentine belt routing	25
Models without A/C	Accessory serpentine belt routing	26
4.6L engines		
Models with A/C	Accessory serpentine belt routing	23
Models without A/C	Accessory serpentine belt routing	24
4.9L engine	Accessory serpentine belt routing	18
5.0L (except Explorer) engines	Accessory serpentine belt routing	19
5.0L (Explorer) engines	Accessory serpentine belt routing	28
5.4L engines		
Models with A/C	Accessory serpentine belt routing	23
Models without A/C	Accessory serpentine belt routing	24
5.8L engine	Accessory serpentine belt routing	19

93083C01

Refer to the model specific sections for engine electrical system service procedures

ACCESSORY DRIVE BELT ROUTING INDEX

93083C02

ACCESSORY DRIVE BELT ROUTING INDEX

MANUFACTURER

ENGINES	DESCRIPTION	FIGURE
Jeep (cont.)		
2.5L Wrangler engines		
Models with A/C	Accessory serpentine belt routing	47
Models without A/C	Accessory serpentine belt routing	46
4.0L Cherokee (right-hand drive) engines		
Models with A/C	Accessory serpentine belt routing	48
Models without A/C	Accessory serpentine belt routing	49
4.0L Cherokee engines		
Models with A/C	Accessory serpentine belt routing	51
Models without A/C	Accessory serpentine belt routing	50
4.0L Grand Cherokee engine	Accessory serpentine belt routing	44
4.0L Wrangler engines		
Models with A/C	Accessory serpentine belt routing	47
Models without A/C	Accessory serpentine belt routing	46
4.7L Grand Cherokee engine	Accessory serpentine belt routing	54
5.2L Grand Cherokee engine	Accessory serpentine belt routing	45
5.9L engines	Accessory serpentine belt routing	45
Kia		
2.0L engines	Accessory V-belt routing	55
Land Rover		
4.0L engines		
Models with A/C	Accessory serpentine belt routing	56
Models without A/C	Accessory serpentine belt routing	57
4.6L engines		
Models with A/C	Accessory serpentine belt routing	56
Models without A/C	Accessory serpentine belt routing	57
Lexus		
3.0L engines	Accessory V-belt routing	80
4.5L engines	Accessory V-belt routing	82
4.7L engines	Accessory serpentine belt routing	83
Mazda		
2.3L B-series truck engines	Accessory serpentine belt routing	13
2.5L B-series truck engines	Accessory serpentine belt routing	13
3.0L B-series truck engines	Accessory serpentine belt routing	14
3.0L MPV engines	Accessory V-belt routing (alternator)	58
3.0L MPV engines	Accessory V-belt routing (power steering)	59
3.0L MPV engines	Accessory V-belt routing (A/C compressor)	60
4.0L B-series truck engines	Accessory serpentine belt routing	17
Mercedes-Benz		
3.2L engines	Accessory serpentine belt routing	61
Mercury		
3.0L Villager engines	Accessory V-belt routing	31
3.3L Villager engines	Accessory V-belt routing	31
5.0L Mountaineer engines	Accessory serpentine belt routing	28
Mitsubishi		
2.4L engines	Accessory serpentine belt routing	62
3.0L engines	Accessory serpentine belt routing	63
3.5L engines	Accessory serpentine belt routing	64
Nissan		
2.4L (KA24E & KA24DE) engines	Accessory V-belt routing	65
3.0L (VG30E) engines	Accessory V-belt routing	66
3.3L (VG33E) engines	Accessory V-belt routing	67

93083C03

Refer to the model specific sections for engine electrical system service procedures

ACCESSORY DRIVE BELT ROUTING INDEX

MANUFACTURER ENGINES	DESCRIPTION	FIGURE
Nissan (cont.)		
3.0L and 3.3L Quest engines	Accessory V-belt routing	31
Subaru		
2.5L engines	Accessory V-belt routing	68
Suzuki		
1.6L engines		
Models with A/C	Accessory V-belt routing	69
Models with A/C and P/S	Accessory V-belt routing	70
Models with P/S	Accessory V-belt routing	71
1.8L and 2.0L engines	Accessory serpentine belt routing	72
1.8L and 2.0L engines	Accessory V-belt routing	73
2.5L engines		
Models with P/S	Accessory V-belt routing	74
Models with A/C and P/S	Accessory V-belt routing	75
Toyota		
2.0L (3SFE) engines	Accessory V-belt routing	76
2.4L (2RZFE) engines	Accessory V-belt routing	77
2.4L (2TZFE) engines	Accessory V-belt routing	78
2.7L (3RZFE) engines	Accessory V-belt routing	79
3.0L (1MZFE) engines	Accessory V-belt routing	80
3.4L engines	Accessory V-belt routing	81
4.5L engines	Accessory V-belt routing	82
4.7L engines	Accessory serpentine belt routing	83

93083C04

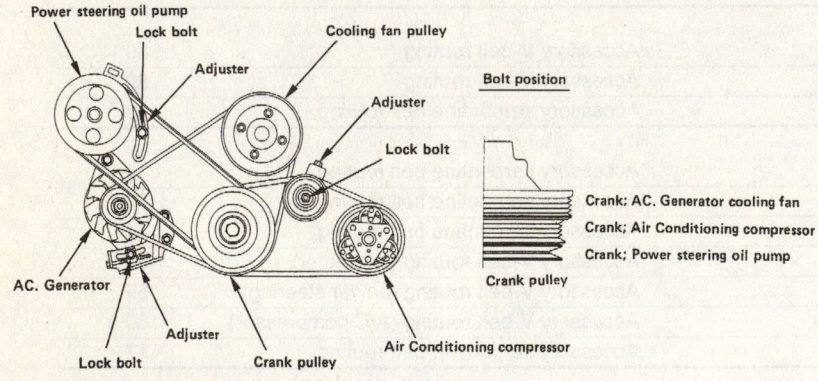

Fig. 1 Accessory V-belt routing—Acura/Isuzu 3.2L engines

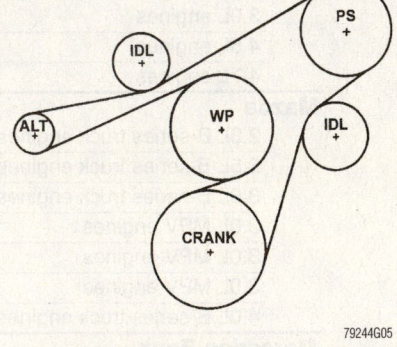

Fig. 4 Accessory serpentine belt routing—Dodge 2.5L engines without A/C

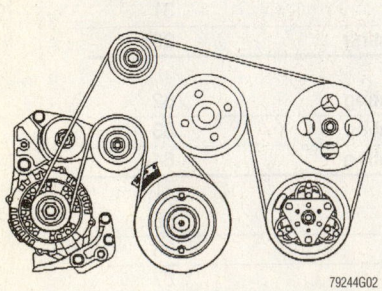

Fig. 2 Accessory serpentine belt routing—Acura/Isuzu 3.5L engines

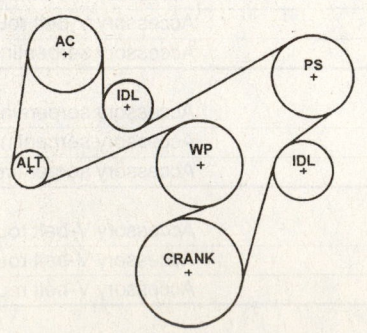

Fig. 3 Accessory serpentine belt routing—Dodge 2.5L engines with A/C

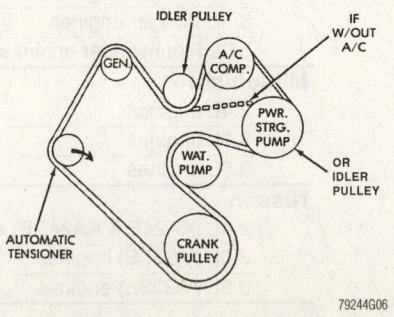

Fig. 5 Accessory serpentine belt routing—Dodge 3.9L, 5.2L and 5.9L LDC gasoline engines

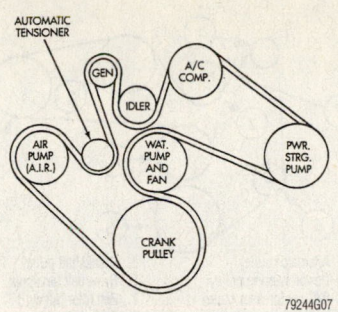

Fig. 6 Accessory serpentine belt routing—Dodge 5.9L HDC and 8.0L gasoline engines with A/C

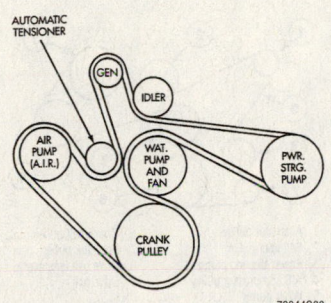

Fig. 7 Accessory serpentine belt routing—Dodge 5.9L HDC and 8.0L gasoline engines without A/C

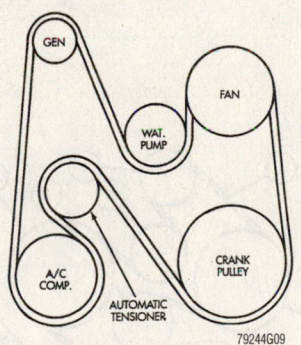

Fig. 8 Accessory serpentine belt routing—Dodge 5.9L Diesel engine with A/C

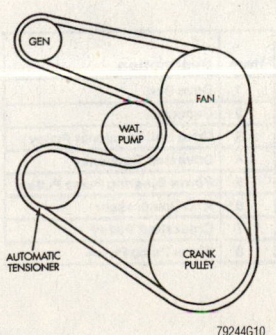

Fig. 9 Accessory serpentine belt routing—Dodge 5.9L Diesel engine without A/C

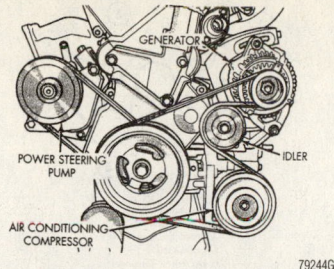

Fig. 10 Accessory V-belt routing—Chrysler 2.4L engine

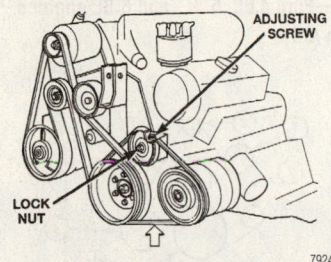

Fig. 11 Accessory V-belt routing—Chrysler 3.0L engine

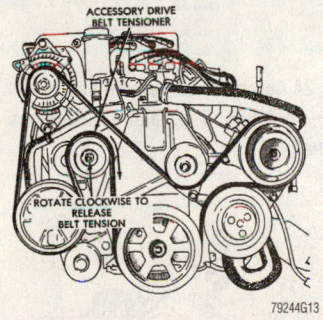

Fig. 12 Accessory V-belt routing—Chrysler 3.3L and 3.8L engines

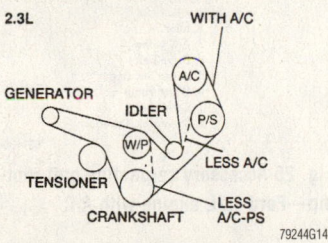

Fig. 13 Accessory serpentine belt routing—Ford/Mazda 2.3L and 2.5L engines

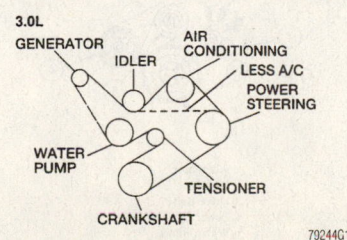

Fig. 14 Accessory serpentine belt routing—Ford/Mazda 3.0L engine (except Aerostar)

Fig. 15 Accessory serpentine belt routing—Ford Aerostar 3.0L engine with A/C

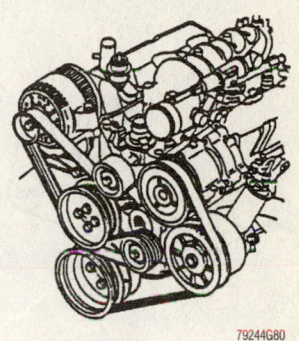

Fig. 16 Accessory serpentine belt routing—Ford Aerostar 3.0L engine without A/C

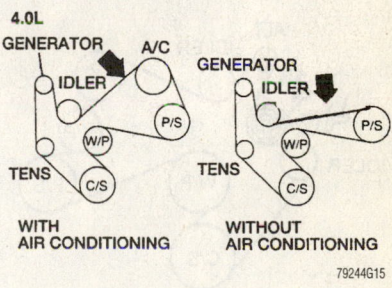

Fig. 17 Accessory serpentine belt routing—Ford/Mazda 4.0L engine

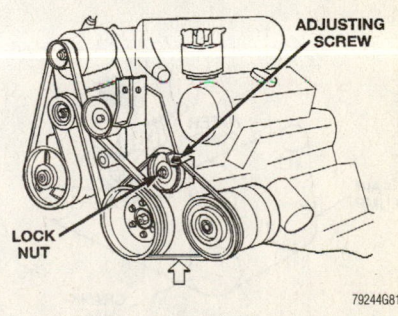

Fig. 18 Accessory serpentine belt routing—Ford 4.9L engine

For accessory drive belt replacement procedures see the model specific sections of this manual

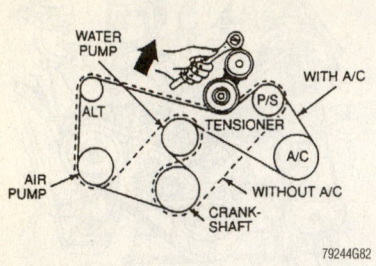

Fig. 19 Accessory serpentine belt routing—Ford 5.0L and 5.8L engines

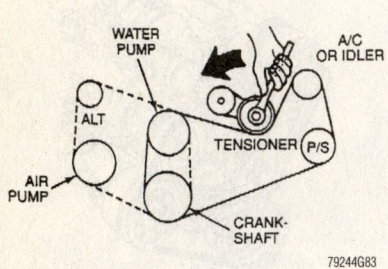

Fig. 20 Accessory serpentine belt routing—Ford 7.5L engine

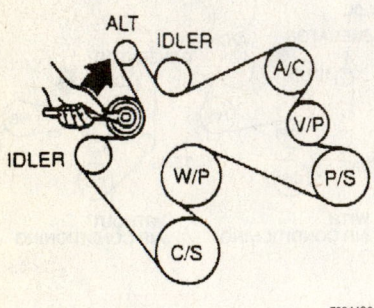

Fig. 21 Accessory serpentine belt routing—Ford 7.3L turbo diesel engine

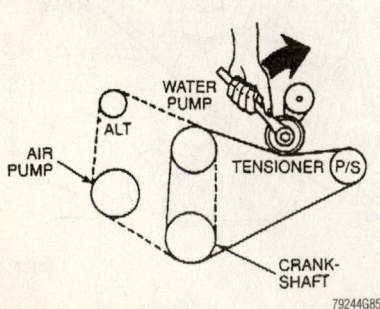

Fig. 22 Accessory serpentine belt routing—Ford 7.5L F-super duty motorhome engine

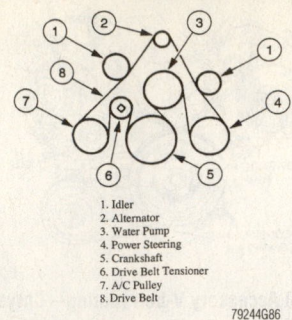

1. Idler
2. Alternator
3. Water Pump
4. Power Steering
5. Crankshaft
6. Drive Belt Tensioner
7. A/C Pulley
8. Drive Belt

Fig. 23 Accessory serpentine belt routing—Ford 4.6L, 5.4L, and 6.8L engines with A/C

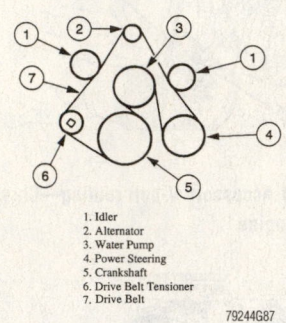

1. Idler
2. Alternator
3. Water Pump
4. Power Steering
5. Crankshaft
6. Drive Belt Tensioner
7. Drive Belt

Fig. 24 Accessory serpentine belt routing—Ford 4.6L, 5.4L, and 6.8L engines without A/C

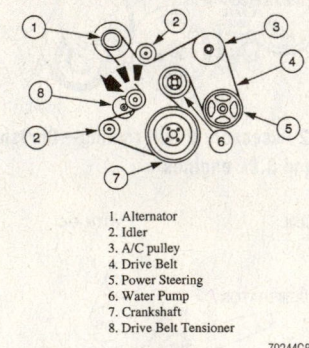

1. Alternator
2. Idler
3. A/C pulley
4. Drive Belt
5. Power Steering
6. Water Pump
7. Crankshaft
8. Drive Belt Tensioner

Fig. 25 Accessory serpentine belt routing—Ford 4.2L engine with A/C

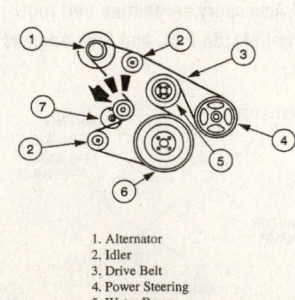

1. Alternator
2. Idler
3. Drive Belt
4. Power Steering
5. Water Pump
6. Crankshaft
7. Drive Belt Tensioner

Fig. 26 Accessory serpentine belt routing—Ford 4.2L engine without A/C

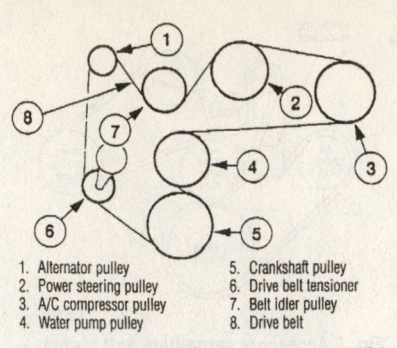

1. Alternator pulley
2. Power steering pulley
3. A/C compressor pulley
4. Water pump pulley
5. Crankshaft pulley
6. Drive belt tensioner
7. Belt idler pulley
8. Drive belt

Fig. 27 Accessory serpentine belt routing—Ford 4.0L SOHC engine

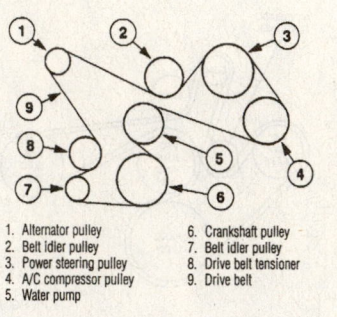

1. Alternator pulley
2. Belt idler pulley
3. Power steering pulley
4. A/C compressor pulley
5. Water pump
6. Crankshaft pulley
7. Belt idler pulley
8. Drive belt tensioner
9. Drive belt

Fig. 28 Accessory serpentine belt routing—Ford Explorer/Mercury Mountaineer 5.0L engine

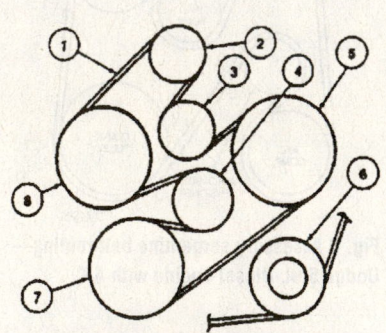

Item	Description
1	Drive Belt
2	Generator
3	Drive Belt Tensioner Pulley
4	Drive Belt Tensioner
5	Power Steering Pump Pulley
6	A/C Compressor
7	Crankshaft Pulley
8	Water Pump Pulley

Fig. 29 Accessory serpentine belt routing—Ford Windstar 3.0L engine

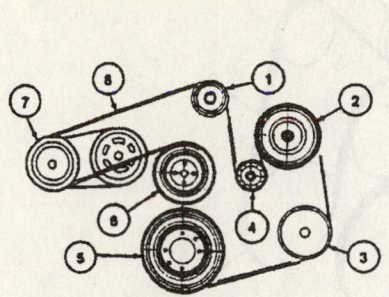

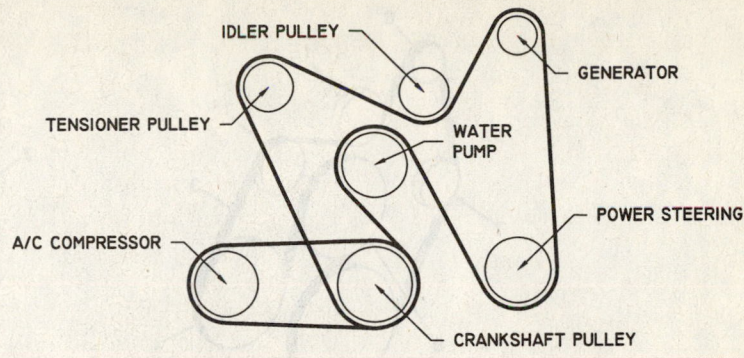

Fig. 31 Accessory serpentine belt routing—GM 4.8L, 5.3L, 6.0L engines

Item	Description
1	Generator
2	Power Steering Pump
3	A/C Compressor
4	Drive Belt Tensioner Pulley
5	Crankshaft Pulley
6	Water Pump Pulley
7	Drive Belt Tensioner
8	Drive Belt

Fig. 30 Accessory serpentine belt routing—Ford Windstar 3.8L engine

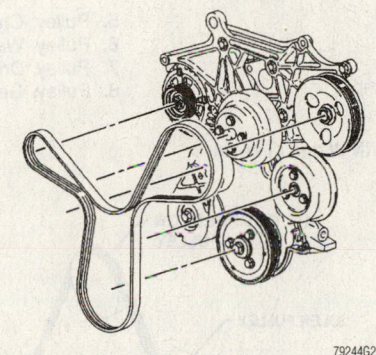

Fig. 32 Accessory serpentine belt routing—GM/Isuzu 2.2L engine without A/C

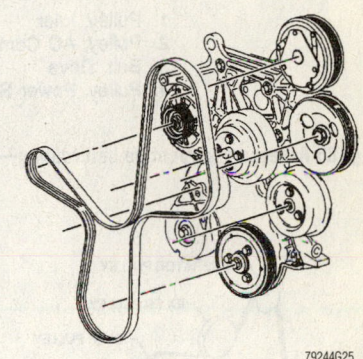

Fig. 33 Accessory serpentine belt routing—GM/Isuzu 2.2L engine with A/C

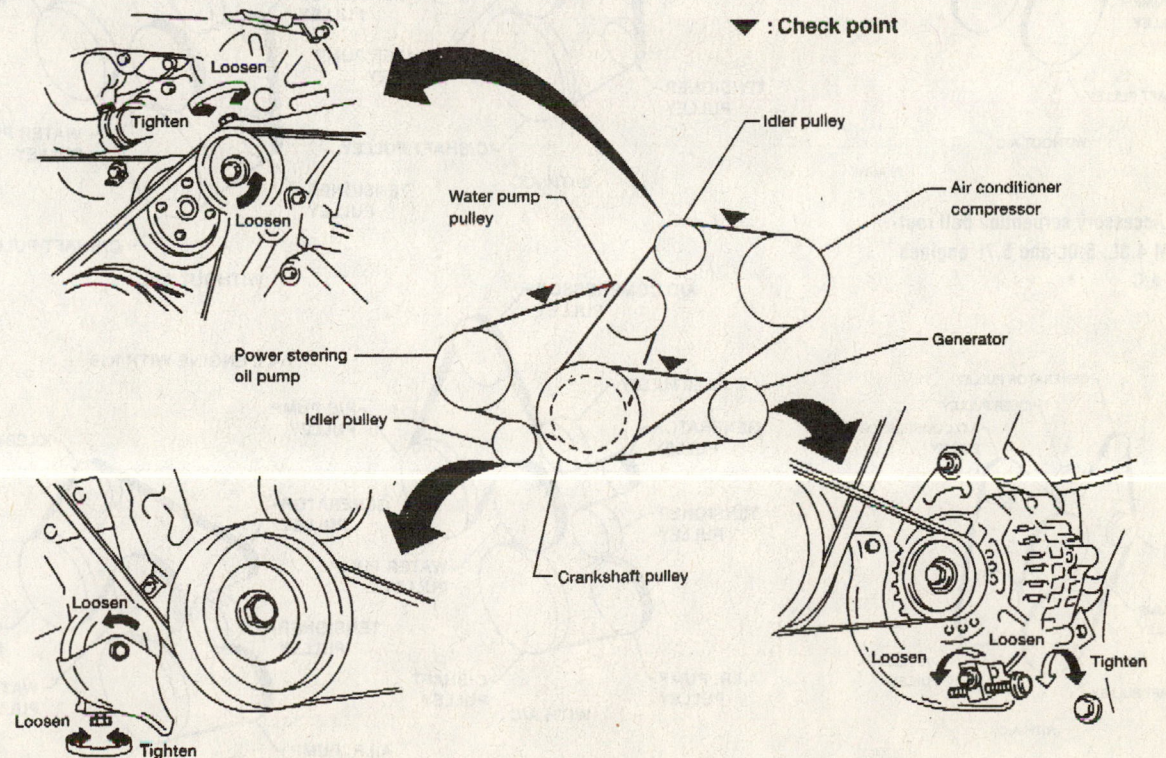

Fig. 34 Accessory V-belt routing—Nissan Quest/Mercury Villager 3.0L and 3.3L engines

Refer to the model specific sections for cooling system service procedures

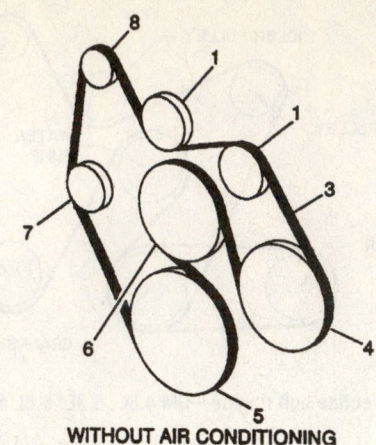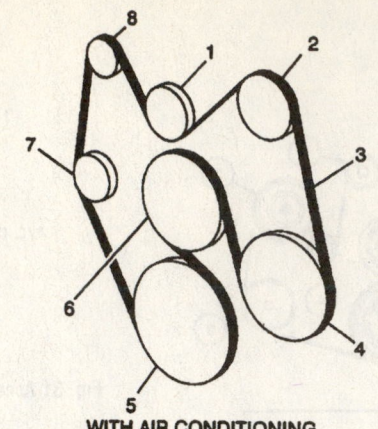

WITHOUT AIR CONDITIONING

WITH AIR CONDITIONING

1. Pulley, Idler
2. Pulley, AC Compressor
3. Belt, Drive
4. Pulley. Power Steering Pump

5. Pulley, Crankshaft
6. Pulley, Water Pump
7. Pulley, Drive Belt Tensioner
8. Pulley, Generator

79244G24

Fig. 35 Accessory serpentine belt routing—GM 4.3L (VIN W and X) engines

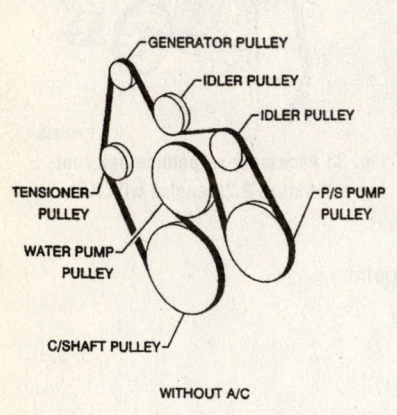

Fig. 36 Accessory serpentine belt routing—GM 4.3L, 5.0L and 5.7L engines without A/C

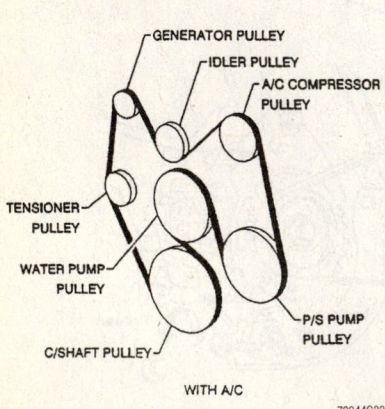

Fig. 37 Accessory serpentine belt routing—GM 4.3L, 5.0L and 5.7L engines with A/C

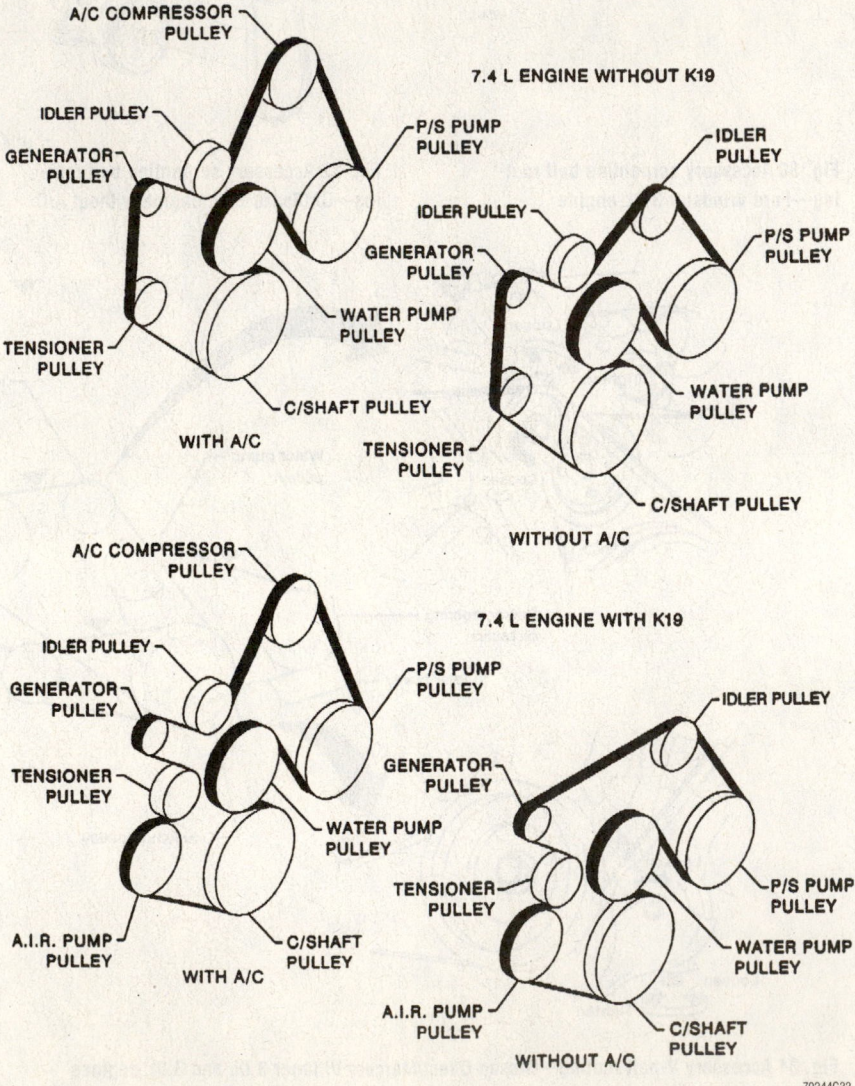

Fig. 38 Accessory serpentine belt routing—GM 7.4L engine

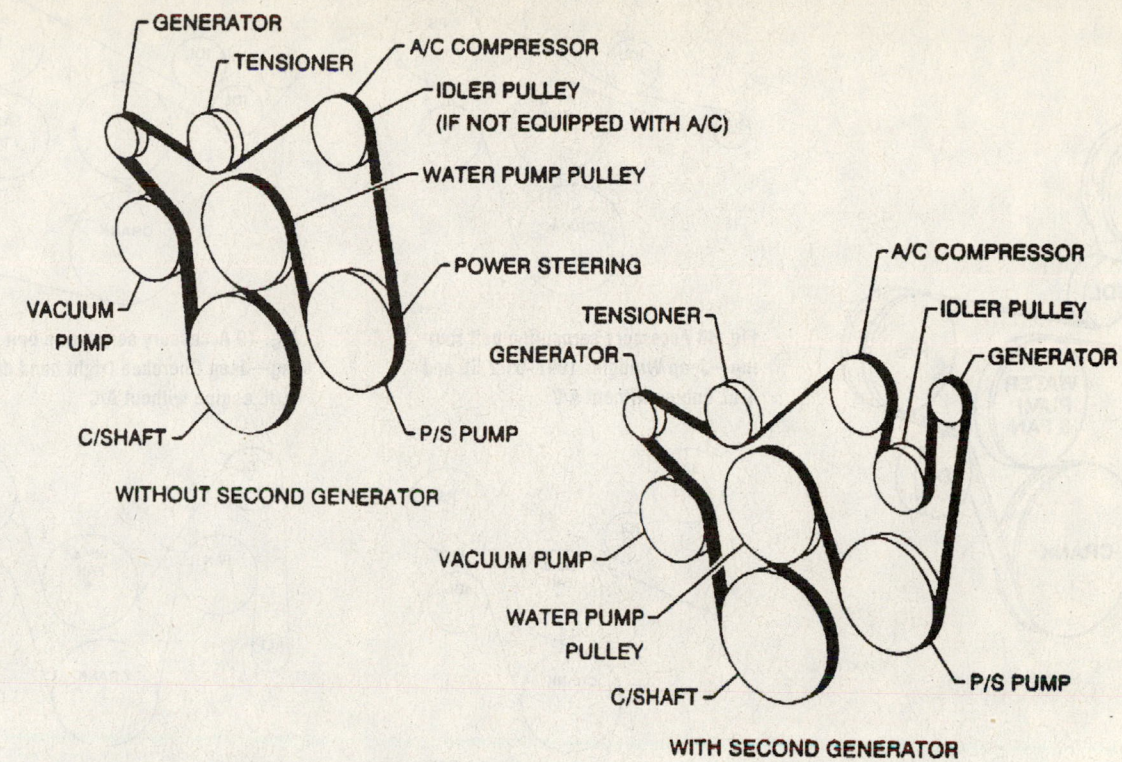

Fig. 39 Accessory serpentine belt routing—GM 6.5L Diesel engines

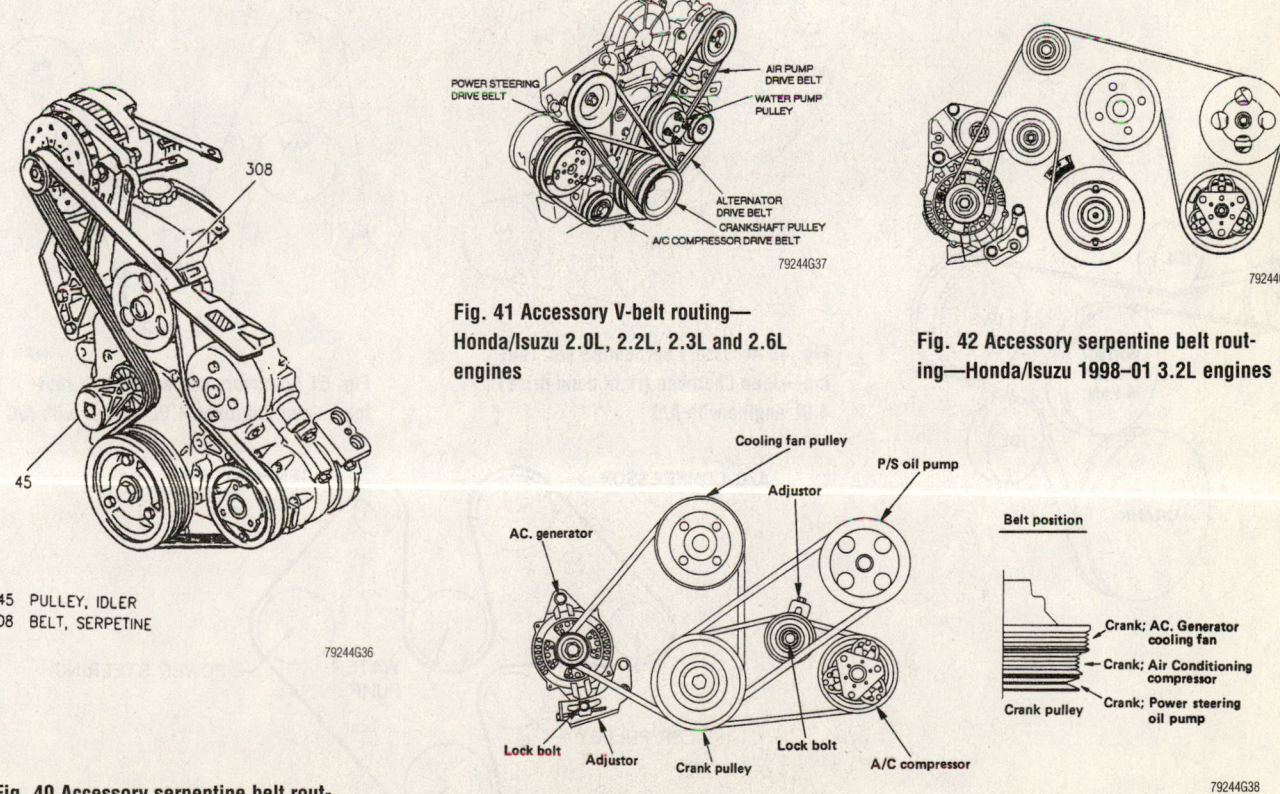

Fig. 40 Accessory serpentine belt routing—GM 3.4L engines

45   PULLEY, IDLER
308 BELT, SERPENTINE

Fig. 41 Accessory V-belt routing—Honda/Isuzu 2.0L, 2.2L, 2.3L and 2.6L engines

Fig. 42 Accessory serpentine belt routing—Honda/Isuzu 1998–01 3.2L engines

Fig. 43 Accessory V-belt routing—Honda/Isuzu 1997 3.2L engine

For complete service labor times order Nichols' Chilton Labor Guide Manual

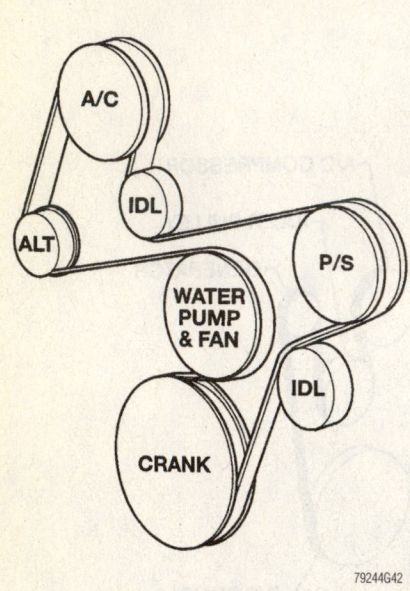

Fig. 44 Accessory serpentine belt routing—Jeep Grand Cherokee 4.0L engine

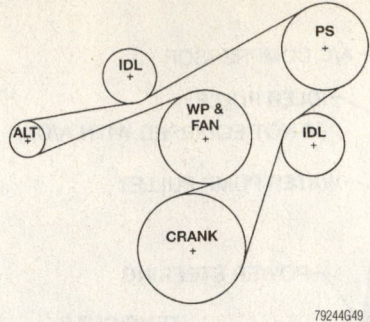

Fig. 46 Accessory serpentine belt routing—Jeep Wrangler 1997–01 2.5L and 4.0L engine without A/C

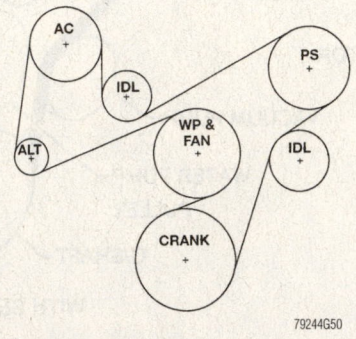

Fig. 47 Accessory serpentine belt routing—Jeep Cherokee 1997–01 2.5L or 4.0L engine with A/C

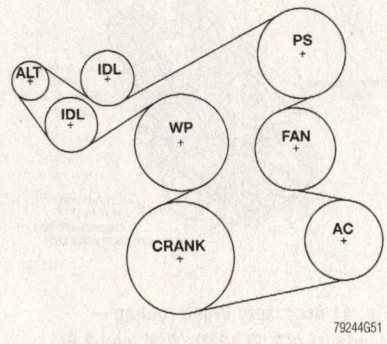

Fig. 48 Accessory serpentine belt routing—Jeep Cherokee (right hand drive) 4.0L engine with A/C

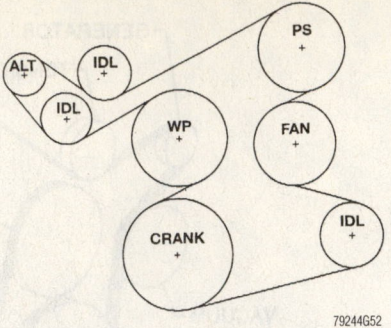

Fig. 49 Accessory serpentine belt routing—Jeep Cherokee (right hand drive) 4.0L engine without A/C

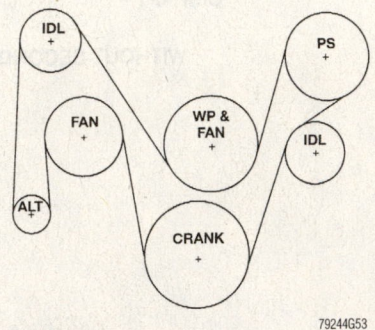

Fig. 50 Accessory serpentine belt routing—Jeep Cherokee 4.0L engine without A/C

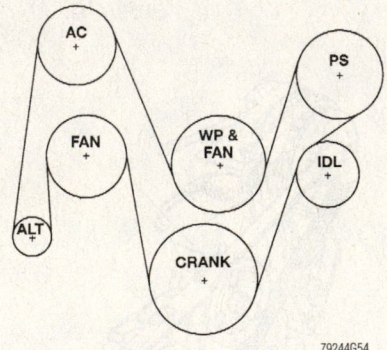

Fig. 51 Accessory serpentine belt routing—Jeep Cherokee 4.0L engine with A/C

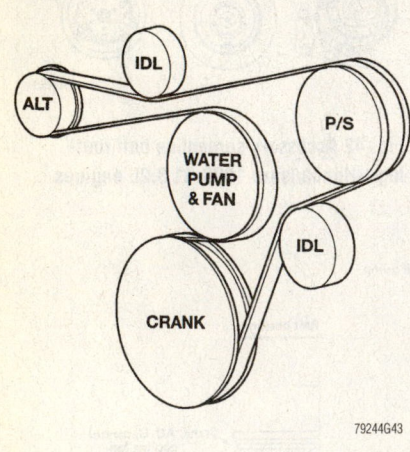

Fig. 45 Accessory serpentine belt routing—Jeep Grand Cherokee 5.2L and 5.9L engines

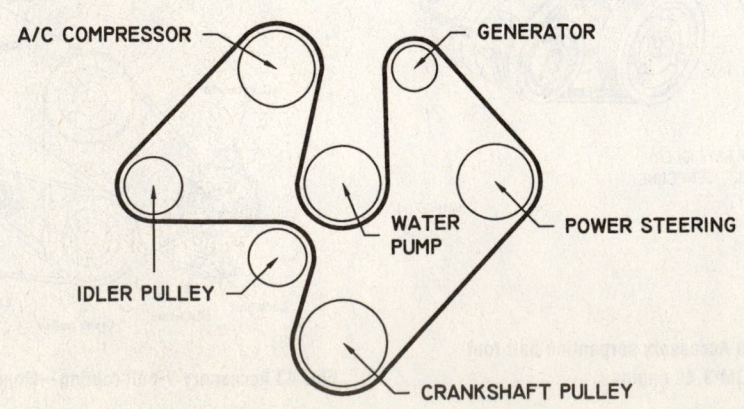

Fig. 52 Accessory serpentine belt routing—Jeep 4.7L Grand Cherokee engine

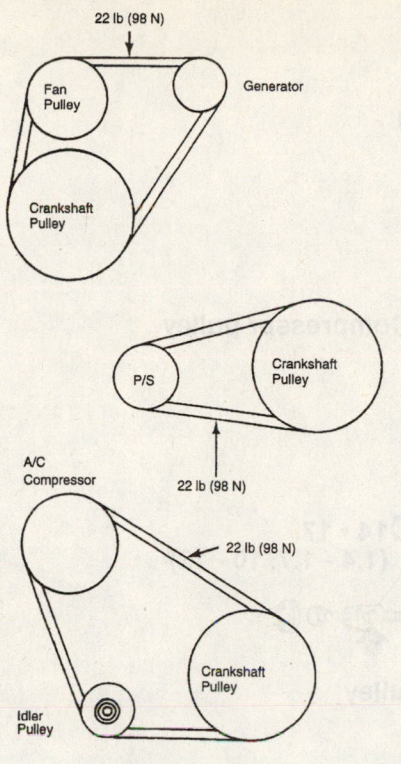

Fan Pulley

Generator

22 lb (98 N)

Crankshaft Pulley

P/S

Crankshaft Pulley

22 lb (98 N)

A/C Compressor

22 lb (98 N)

Crankshaft Pulley

Idler Pulley

79244G57

Fig. 53 Accessory V-belt routing—KIA 2.0L engine

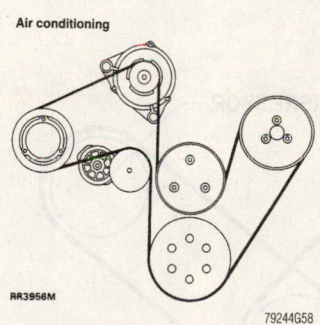

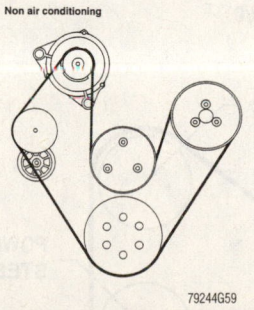

Air conditioning

RR3956M

79244G58

Fig. 54 Accessory serpentine belt routing—Land Rover 4.0L and 4.6L engines with A/C

Non air conditioning

79244G59

Fig. 55 Accessory serpentine belt routing—Land Rover 4.0L and 4.6L engines without A/C

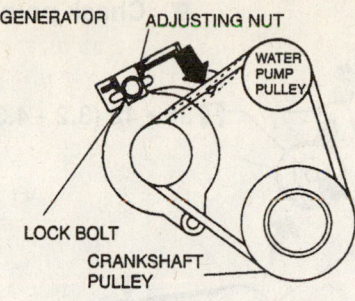

GENERATOR

ADJUSTING NUT

WATER PUMP PULLEY

LOCK BOLT

CRANKSHAFT PULLEY

79244G67

Fig. 56 Accessory V-belt routing (alternator)—Mazda MPV 3.0L engine

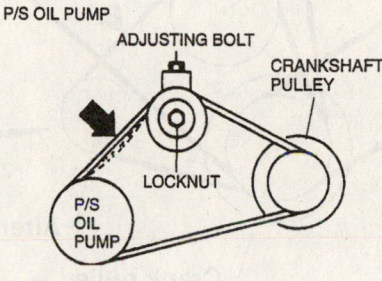

P/S OIL PUMP

ADJUSTING BOLT

CRANKSHAFT PULLEY

LOCKNUT

P/S OIL PUMP

79244G66

Fig. 57 Accessory V-belt routing (power steering)—Mazda MPV 3.0L engine

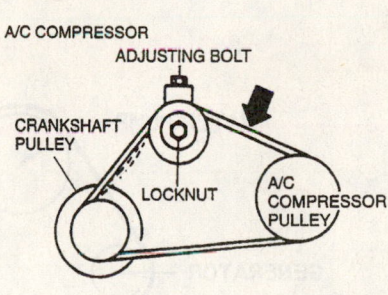

A/C COMPRESSOR

ADJUSTING BOLT

CRANKSHAFT PULLEY

LOCKNUT

A/C COMPRESSOR PULLEY

79244G65

Fig. 58 Accessory V-belt routing (A/C compressor)—Mazda MPV 3.0L engine

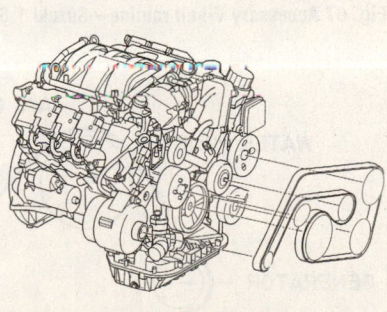

79244G90

Fig. 59 Accessory serpentine belt routing—Mercedes-Benz 3.2L engine

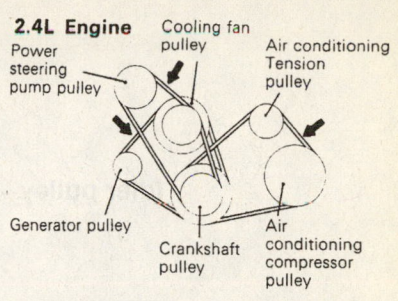

2.4L Engine

Power steering pump pulley

Cooling fan pulley

Air conditioning Tension pulley

Generator pulley

Crankshaft pulley

Air conditioning compressor pulley

79244G68

Fig. 60 Accessory serpentine belt routing—Mitsubishi 2.4L engine

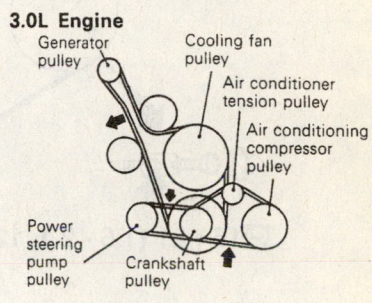

3.0L Engine

Generator pulley

Cooling fan pulley

Air conditioner tension pulley

Air conditioning compressor pulley

Power steering pump pulley

Crankshaft pulley

79244G69

Fig. 61 Accessory serpentine belt routing—Mitsubishi 3.0L engine

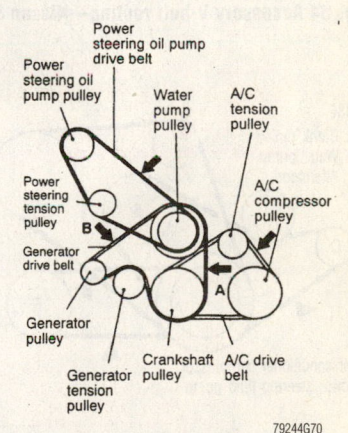

Power steering oil pump drive belt

Power steering oil pump pulley

Water pump pulley

A/C tension pulley

Power steering tension pulley

A/C compressor pulley

Generator drive belt

B

A

Generator pulley

Crankshaft pulley

A/C drive belt

Generator tension pulley

79244G70

Fig. 62 Accessory serpentine belt routing—Mitsubishi 3.5L engine

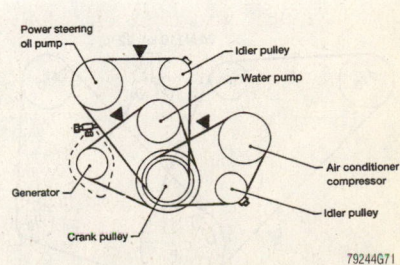

Power steering oil pump

Idler pulley

Water pump

Generator

Air conditioner compressor

Crank pulley

Idler pulley

79244G71

Fig. 63 Accessory V-belt routing—Nissan 2.4L (KA24E and KA24DE) engines

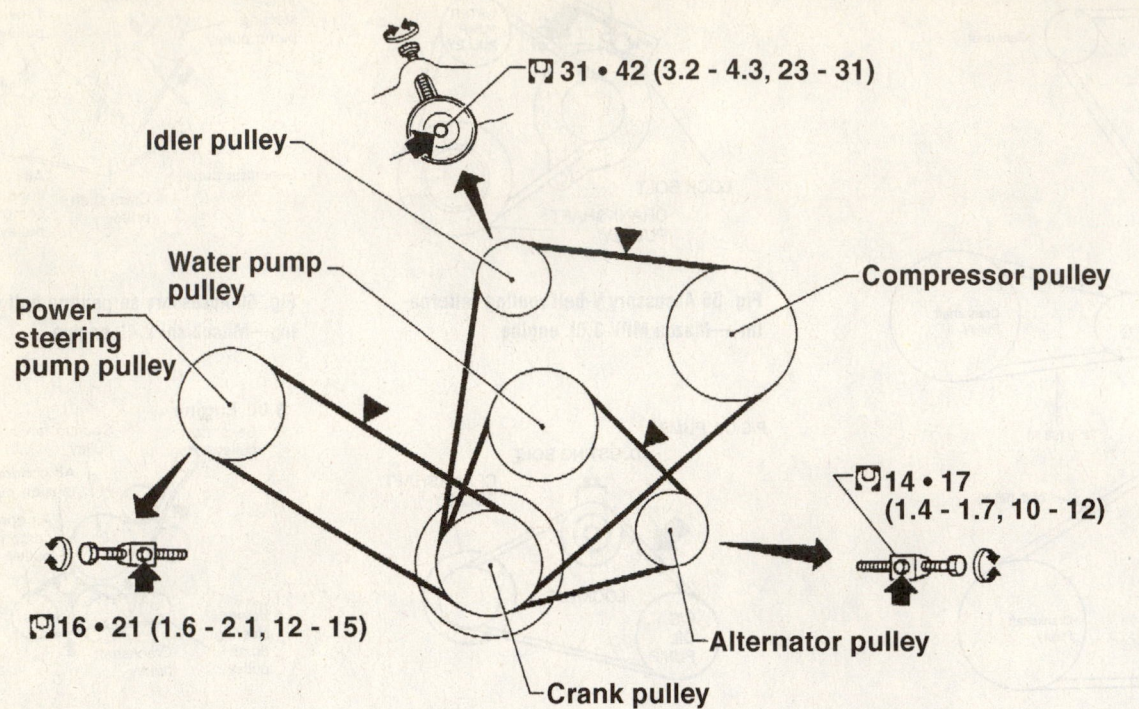

▼ : Check point

⊡ 31 • 42 (3.2 - 4.3, 23 - 31)

Idler pulley

Water pump pulley

Power steering pump pulley

Compressor pulley

⊡ 14 • 17 (1.4 - 1.7, 10 - 12)

⊡ 16 • 21 (1.6 - 2.1, 12 - 15)

Alternator pulley

Crank pulley

⊡ : N•m (kg-m, ft-lb)

79244G72

Fig. 64 Accessory V-belt routing—Nissan 3.0L (VG30E) engine

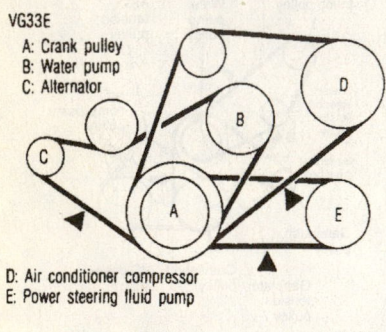

VG33E
A: Crank pulley
B: Water pump
C: Alternator

D: Air conditioner compressor
E: Power steering fluid pump

79244G73

Fig. 65 Accessory V-belt routing—Nissan 3.3L (VG33E) engine

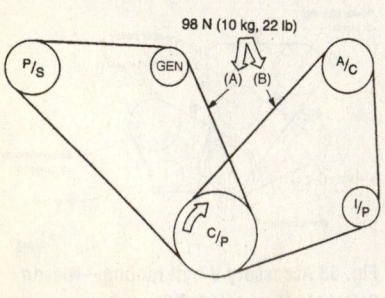

98 N (10 kg, 22 lb)

79244G91

Fig. 66 Accessory V-belt routing—Subaru 2.5L engine

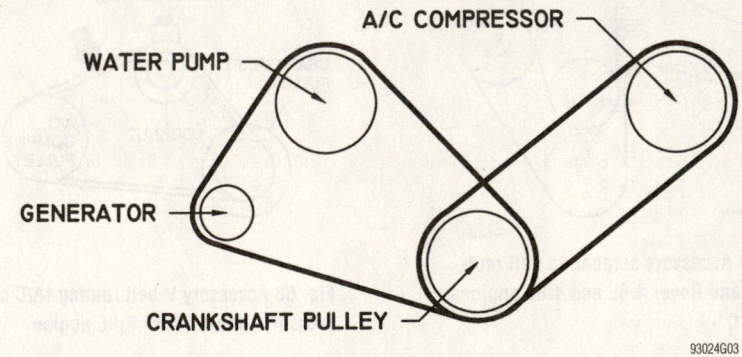

WATER PUMP

A/C COMPRESSOR

GENERATOR

CRANKSHAFT PULLEY

93024G03

Fig. 67 Accessory V-belt routing—Suzuki 1.6L engine with A/C

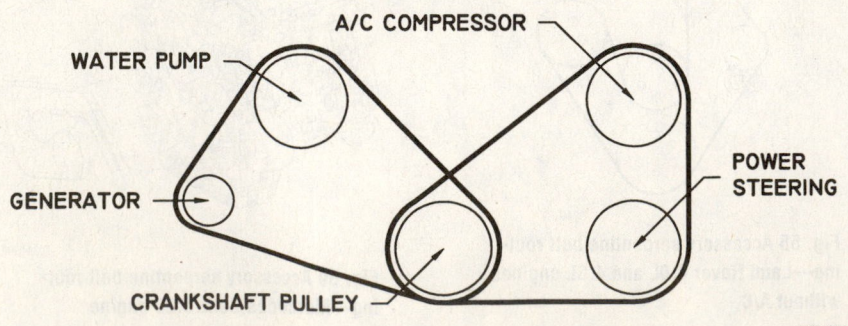

WATER PUMP

A/C COMPRESSOR

GENERATOR

POWER STEERING

CRANKSHAFT PULLEY

93024G04

Fig. 68 Accessory V-belt routing—Suzuki 1.6L engine with A/C and P/S

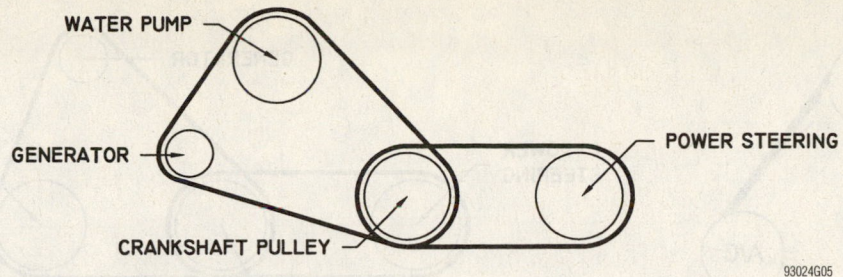

Fig. 69 Accessory V-belt routing—Suzuki 1.6L engine with P/S

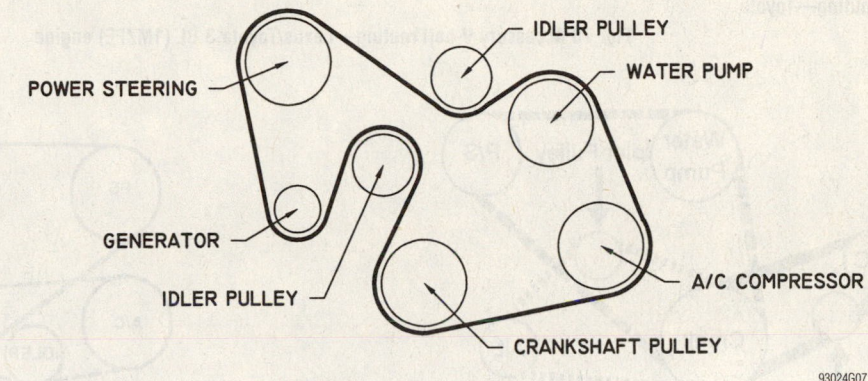

Fig. 70 Accessory serpentine belt routing—Suzuki 1.8L and 2.0L engines

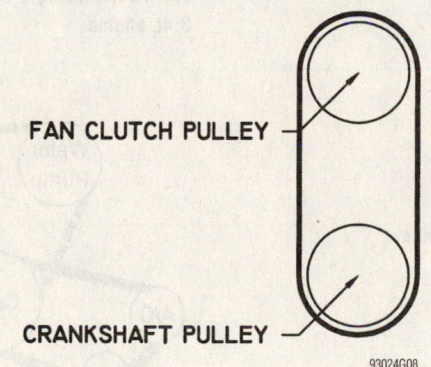

Fig. 71 Accessory V-belt routing—Suzuki 1.8L and 2.0L engines

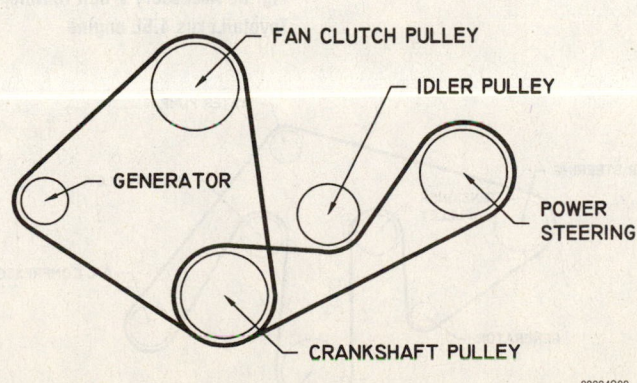

Fig. 72 Accessory V-belt routing—Suzuki 2.5L engine with P/S

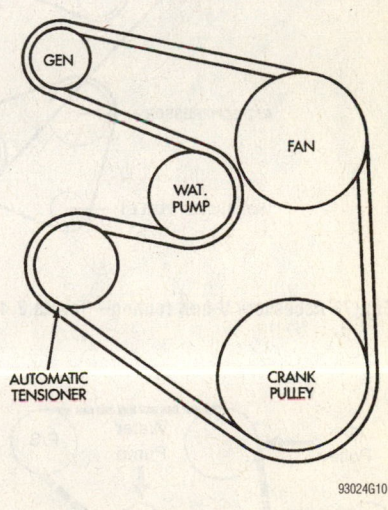

Fig. 73 Accessory V-belt routing—Suzuki 2.5L engine with A/C and P/S

Refer to the model specific sections for engine mechanical system service procedures

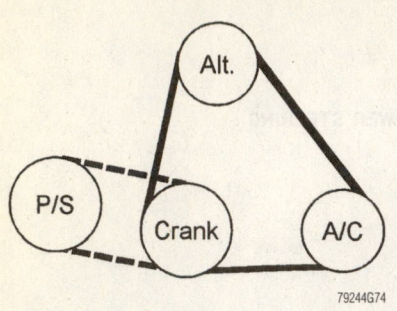

Fig. 74 Accessory V-belt routing—Toyota 2.0L (3SFE) engine

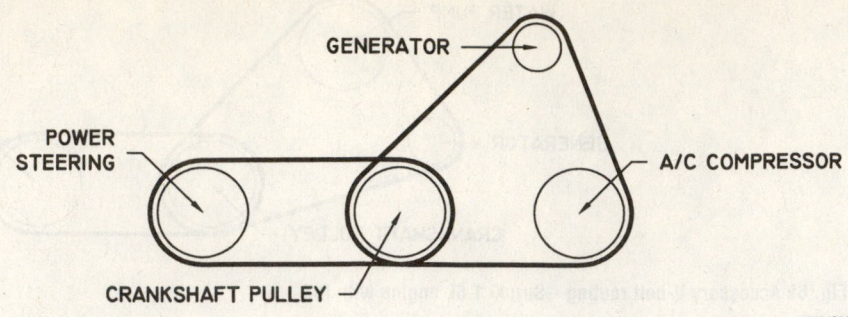

Fig. 78 Accessory V-belt routing—Lexus/Toyota 3.0L (1MZFE) engine

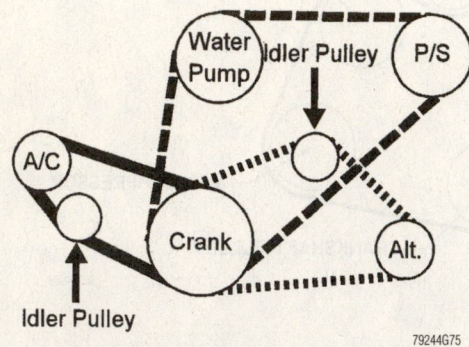

Fig. 75 Accessory V-belt routing—Toyota 2.4L (2RZFE) engine

Fig. 79 Accessory V-belt routing—Toyota 3.4L engine

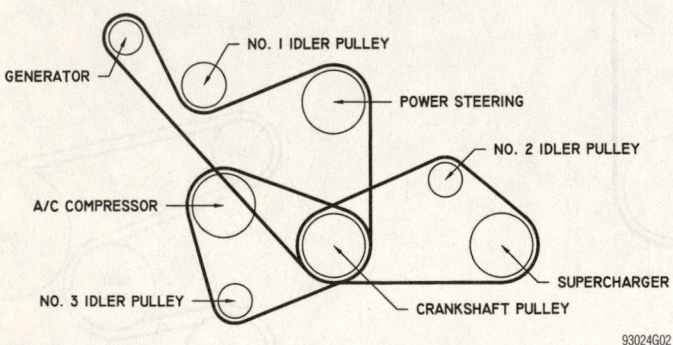

Fig. 76 Accessory V-belt routing—Toyota 2.4L (2TZFE) engine

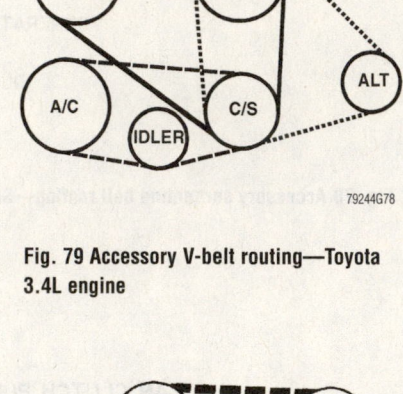

Fig. 80 Accessory V-belt routing—Toyota/Lexus 4.5L engine

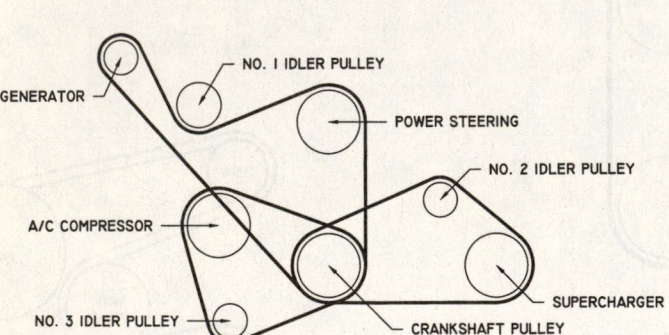

Fig. 77 Accessory V-belt routing—Toyota 2.7L (3RZFE) engine

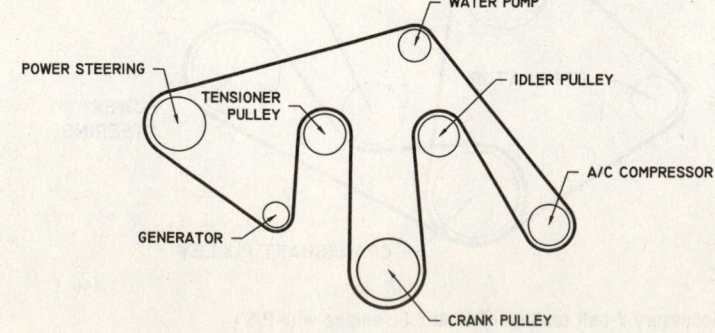

Fig. 81 Accessory serpentine belt routing—Toyota/Lexus 4.7L engine

TIMING BELTS

4

TIMING BELTS

General Information

Timing belts are typically only used on overhead camshaft engines. Timing belts are used to synchronize the crankshaft with the camshaft, similar to a timing chain on an overhead valve (pushrod) engine. Unlike a timing belt, a timing chain will normally last the life of the engine without needing service or replacement. Timing belts use raised teeth to mesh with sprockets to operate the valve train of an overhead camshaft engine.

Whenever a vehicle with an unknown service history comes into your repair facility or is recently purchased, here are some points that should be asked to help prevent costly engine damage:

• Does the owner know if, or when the belt was replaced?

• If the vehicle purchased is used, or the condition and mileage of the last timing belt replacement are unknown, it is recommended to inspect, replace, or at least

inform the owner that the vehicle is equipped with a timing belt.

• Note the mileage of the vehicle. The average replacement interval for a timing belt is approximately 60,000 miles (96,000 km).

Interference Engines

Engines, chain- or belt-driven, can be classified as either free-running or interference, depending on what would happen if the piston-to-valve timing is disrupted. A free-running engine is designed with enough clearance between the pistons and valves to allow the crankshaft to rotate (pistons still moving) while the camshaft stays in one position (several valves fully open). If this condition occurs normally, no internal engine damage will result. In an interference engine, there is not enough clearance between the pistons and valves to allow the crankshaft to turn without the camshaft being in time.

An interference engine can suffer extensive internal damage if a timing belt fails. The piston design does not allow clearance for the valve to be fully open and the piston to be at the top of its stroke. If the belt fails, the piston will collide with the valve and will bend or break the valve, damage the piston, and/or bend a connecting rod. When this type of failure occurs, the engine will need to be replaced or disassembled for further internal inspection; either choice costing many times that of replacing the timing belt.

Timing Belt Service

INSPECTION

➡**For manufacturer's recommended service interval, refer to the maintenance interval chart located in this manual.**

The average replacement interval for a timing belt is approximately 60,000 miles

(96,000 km). If, however, the timing belt is inspected earlier or more frequently than suggested, and shows signs of wear or defects, the belt should be replaced at that time.

✳✳ WARNING

Never allow antifreeze, oil or solvents to come into with a timing belt. If this occurs immediately wash the solution from the timing belt. Also, never excessive bend or twist the timing belt; this can damage the belt so that its lifetime is severely shortened.

Inspect both sides of the timing belt. Replace the belt with a new one if any of the following conditions exist:
- Hardening of the rubber—back side is glossy without resilience and leaves no indentation when pressed with a fingernail

Never bend or twist a timing belt excessively, and do not allow solvents, antifreeze, gasoline, acid or oil to come into contact with the belt

Clean the timing belt before inspection so that imperfections or defects are easier to recognize

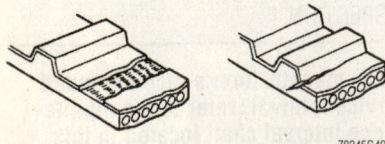

Inspect the timing belt for damage, such as a broken or missing tooth, which may be due to a damaged pulley

- Cracks on the rubber backing
- Cracks or peeling of the canvas backing
- Cracks on rib root
- Cracks on belt sides
- Missing teeth or chunks of teeth
- Abnormal wear of belt sides—the sides are normal if they are sharp, as if cut by a knife.

If none of these conditions exist, the belt does not need replacement unless it is at the recommended interval. The belt MUST be replaced at the recommended interval.

✳✳ WARNING

On interference engines, it is very important to replace the timing belt at the recommended intervals, otherwise expensive engine damage will likely result if the belt fails.

REMOVAL & INSTALLATION

Acura SLX

3.2L AND 3.5L ENGINES

1. Disconnect the negative battery cable.

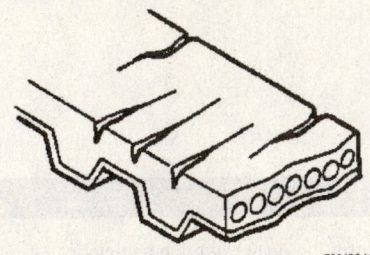

Back surface worn or cracked from a possible overheated engine or interference with the belt cover

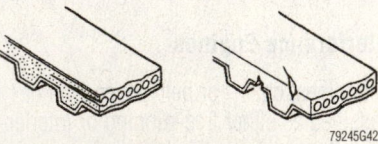

Side wear from improper installation or a defective pulley plate

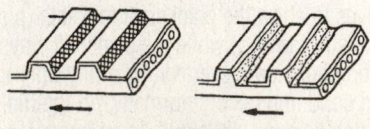

Rotating direction

Worn teeth from excessive belt tension, camshaft or distributor not turning properly, or fluid leaking on the belt

2. Drain the engine coolant into a sealable container.
3. Remove the air cleaner assembly and intake air duct.
4. Disconnect the upper radiator hose from the coolant inlet.
5. Remove the upper fan shroud from the radiator.
6. Remove the 4 nuts retaining the cooling fan assembly. Remove the cooling fan from the fan pulley.
7. Loosen and remove the drive belts.
8. Remove the upper timing belt covers.
9. Remove the fan pulley assembly.
10. Rotate the crankshaft to align the camshaft timing marks with the pointer dots on the back covers. Verify that the pointer on the crankshaft aligns with the mark on the lower timing cover.

➡ **When the timing marks are aligned, the No. 2 piston is at Top Dead Center (TDC) of the compression.**

✳✳ WARNING

Align the camshaft and crankshaft sprockets with their alignment marks before removing the timing belt. Failure to align the belt and sprocket marks may result in valve damage.

11. Use tool No. J-8614-01 or a suitable pulley holding tool to remove the crankshaft pulley center bolt. Remove the crankshaft pulley.
12. If present, disconnect the 2 oil cooler hose bracket bolts on the timing cover. Move the oil cooler hoses and bracket off of the lower timing cover.
13. Remove the lower timing belt cover.
14. Remove the pusher assembly (tensioner) from below the belt tensioner pulley. The pusher rod must always face upward to prevent oil leakage. Depress the pusher rod, and insert a wire pin into the hole to keep the pusher rod retracted.
15. Remove the timing belt.

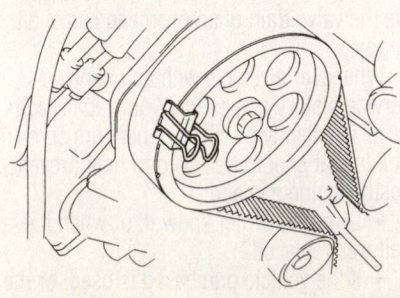

Using a double clip to hold the belt in place—Acura 3.2L and 3.5L engines

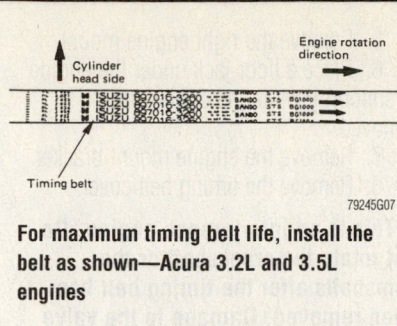

For maximum timing belt life, install the belt as shown—Acura 3.2L and 3.5L engines

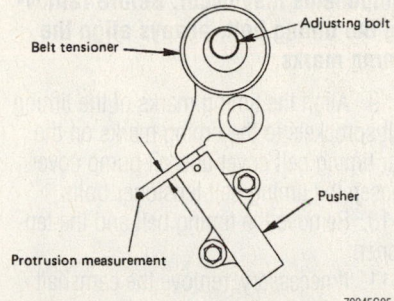

View of timing belt tensioner and pusher—Acura 3.2L and 3.5 engines

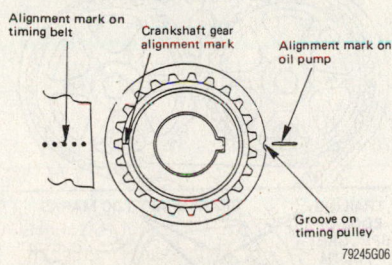

Proper crankshaft alignment marks for timing belt installation—Acura 3.2L and 3.5L engines

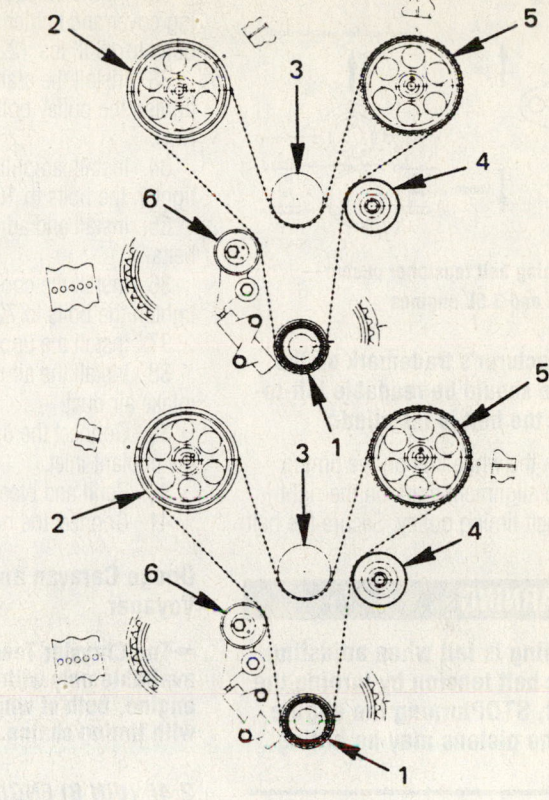

DOHC

SOHC

1) Crankshaft timing pulley
2) RH bank timing pulley
3) Water pump pulley
4) Idler pulley
5) LH bank timing pulley
6) Tension pulley

Timing belt routing—Acura 3.2L and 3.5L engines

Alignment mark on timing belt

Alignment mark on front plate

DOHC

Alignment mark on timing belt

SOHC

Alignment mark on front plate

Proper camshaft alignment marks for timing belt installation—Acura 3.2L and 3.5L engines

16. Inspect the water pump and replace it if there is any doubt about its condition.

17. Repair any oil or coolant leaks before installing a new timing belt. If the timing belt has been contaminated with oil or coolant, or is damaged, it must be replaced.

To install:

18. Verify that the sprocket timing marks are still aligned and that the groove and the keyway on the crankshaft timing sprocket align with the mark on the oil pump. The white pointers on the camshaft timing sprockets should align with the dots on the front plate.

19. Install the timing belt. Use clips to secure the belt onto each sprocket until the installation is complete. Align the dotted marks on the timing belt with the timing mark opposite the groove on the crankshaft sprocket.

➡**The arrows on the timing belt must follow the belt's direction of rotation.**

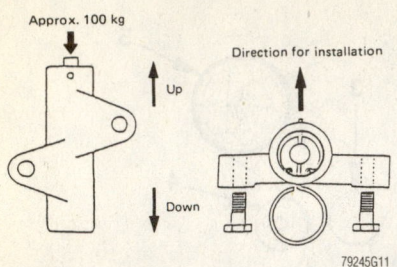

View of timing belt tensioner pusher—
Acura 3.2L and 3.5L engines

The manufacturer's trademark on the belt's spine should be readable left-to-right when the belt is installed.

20. Align the white line on the timing belt with the alignment mark on the right bank camshaft timing pulley. Secure the belt with a clip.

✻✻ WARNING

If any binding is felt when adjusting the timing belt tension by turning the crankshaft, STOPturning the engine, because the pistons may be hitting the valves.

21. Rotate the crankshaft counterclockwise to remove the slack between the crankshaft sprocket and the right camshaft timing belt sprocket.

22. Install the belt around the water pump pulley.

23. Install the belt on the idler pulley.

24. Align the white alignment mark on the timing belt with the alignment mark on the left bank camshaft timing belt sprocket.

25. Install the crankshaft pulley and tighten the center bolt by hand. Rotate the crankshaft pulley clockwise to give slack between the crankshaft timing belt pulley and the right bank camshaft timing belt pulley.

26. Insert a 1.4mm piece of wire through the hole in the pusher to hold the rod in. Install the pusher assembly while pushing the tension pulley toward the belt.

27. Pull the pin out from the pusher to release the rod.

28. Remove the clamps from the sprockets. Rotate the crankshaft pulley clockwise 2 turns. Measure the rod protrusion to ensure it is between 0.16–0.24 in. (4–6mm).

29. If the tensioner pulley bracket pivot bolt was removed, tighten it to 31 ft. lbs. (42 Nm).

30. Tighten the pusher bolts to 14 ft. lbs. (19 Nm).

31. Remove the crankshaft pulley. Install the lower and upper timing belt covers and tighten their bolts to 12 ft. lbs. (17 Nm).

32. Fit the oil cooler hose onto the timing cover and tighten its mounting bracket bolts to 16 ft. lbs. (22 Nm).

33. Install the crankshaft pulley and tighten the pulley bolt to 123 ft. lbs. (167 Nm).

34. Install fan pulley assembly and tighten the bolts to 16 ft. lbs. (22 Nm).

35. Install and adjust the accessory drive belts.

36. Install the cooling fan assembly and tighten the bolts to 72 inch lbs. (8 Nm).

37. Install the upper fan shroud.

38. Install the air cleaner assembly and intake air duct.

39. Connect the upper radiator hose to the coolant inlet.

40. Refill and bleed the cooling system.

41. Connect the negative battery cable.

Dodge Caravan and Plymouth Voyager

➡**The Chrysler Town & Country is available only with a 3.3L or 3.8L engine, both of which are equipped with timing chains.**

2.4L (VIN B) ENGINE

➡**You may need DRB scan tool to perform the crankshaft and camshaft relearn alignment procedure.**

1. Disconnect the negative battery cable remote connector, located on the left strut tower.

2. Remove the right inner splash shield.

3. Remove the accessory drive belts.

4. Remove the crankshaft damper.

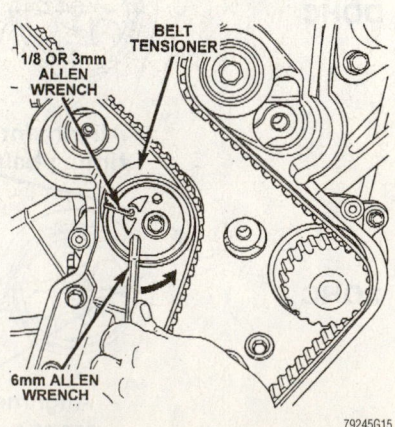

Timing cover and engine mounting bracket bolt locations—Chrysler 2.4L (VIN B) engine

5. Remove the right engine mount.

6. Place a floor jack under the engine to support it while the engine mount is removed.

7. Remove the engine mount bracket.

8. Remove the timing belt cover.

➡**This is an interference engine. Do not rotate the crankshaft or the camshafts after the timing belt has been removed. Damage to the valve components may occur. Before removing the timing belt, always align the timing marks.**

9. Align the timing marks of the timing belt sprockets to the timing marks on the rear timing belt cover and oil pump cover. Loosen the timing belt tensioner bolts.

10. Remove the timing belt and the tensioner.

11. If necessary, remove the camshaft timing belt sprockets.

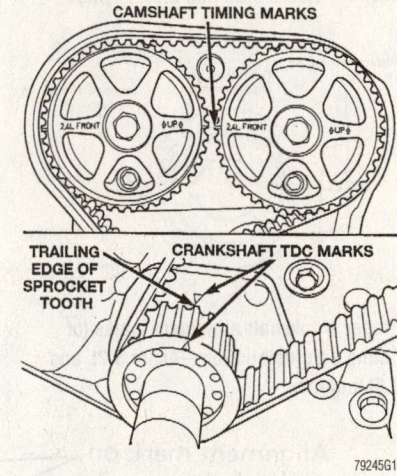

Camshaft and crankshaft alignment marks—Chrysler 2.4L (VIN B) engine

To lock the timing belt tensioner, be sure to fully insert the smaller Allen wrench into the tensioner as shown—Chrysler 2.4L (VIN B) engine

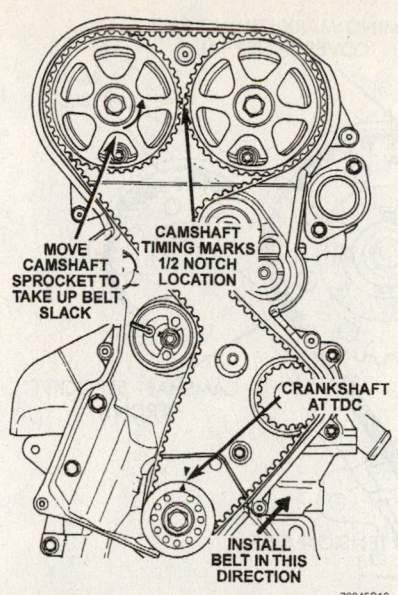

79245G16

Installation of the timing belt, notice the camshaft alignment—Chrysler 2.4L (VIN B) engine

MOVE CAMSHAFT SPROCKET TO TAKE UP BELT SLACK

CAMSHAFT TIMING MARKS 1/2 NOTCH LOCATION

CRANKSHAFT AT TDC

INSTALL BELT IN THIS DIRECTION

12. If necessary, remove the crankshaft timing belt sprocket using removal tool No. 6793, or equivalent.

13. Place the tensioner into a soft-jawed vise to compress the tensioner.

14. After compressing the tensioner, insert a pin (a 5/64 in. Allen wrench will also work) into the plunger side hole to retain the plunger until installation.

To install:

15. If necessary, use tool No. 6792, or equivalent, to install the crankshaft timing belt sprocket onto the crankshaft.

16. If necessary, install the camshaft sprockets onto the camshafts. Install and tighten the camshaft sprocket bolts to 75 ft. lbs. (101 Nm).

17. Set the crankshaft sprocket to Top Dead Center (TDC) by aligning the notch on the sprocket with the arrow on the oil pump housing.

18. Set the camshafts to align the timing marks on the sprockets.

19. Move the crankshaft to 1/2 notch before TDC.

20. Install the timing belt starting at the crankshaft, then around the water pump sprocket, idler pulley, camshaft sprockets and around the tensioner pulley.

21. Move the crankshaft sprocket to TDC to take up the belt slack.

22. Install the tensioner on the engine block but do not tighten.

23. Using a torque wrench on the ten-

sioner pulley, apply 250 inch lbs. (28 Nm) of torque to the tensioner pulley.

24. With torque being applied to the tensioner pulley, move the tensioner up against the tensioner pulley bracket and tighten the fasteners to 23 ft. lbs. (31 Nm).

25. Remove the tensioner plunger pin, the tension is correct when the plunger pin can be removed and reinserted easily.

✷✷ WARNING

If any binding is felt when adjusting the timing belt tension by turning the crankshaft, STOP turning the engine, because the pistons may be hitting the valves.

26. Rotate the crankshaft 2 revolutions and recheck the timing marks. Wait several minutes and then recheck that the plunger pin can easily be removed and installed.

27. Install the front timing belt cover.

28. Install the engine mount bracket.

29. Install the right engine mount.

30. Remove the floor jack from under the vehicle.

31. Install the crankshaft damper and tighten it to 105 ft. lbs. (142 Nm).

32. Install the accessory drive belts and adjust to the proper tension.

33. Install the right inner splash shield.

34. Reconnect the negative battery cable.

35. Perform the crankshaft and camshaft relearn alignment procedure using the DRB scan tool, or equivalent.

3.0L (VIN 3) ENGINE

The timing belt can be inspected by removing the upper front outer timing belt cover.

Working on any engine (especially overhead camshaft engines) requires much care be given to valve timing. It is good practice to set the engine up at TDC No. 1 cylinder firing position before beginning work. Verify that all timing marks on the crankshaft and camshaft sprockets are properly aligned before removing the timing belt and starting camshaft service. This serves as a point of reference for all work that follows. Valve timing is very important and engine damage will result if the work is incorrect.

1. Disconnect the negative battery cable.

2. Remove the accessory drive belts. Remove the engine mount insulator from the engine support bracket.

3. Remove the engine support bracket. Remove the crankshaft pulleys and tor-

sional damper. Remove the timing belt covers.

4. Rotate the crankshaft until the sprocket timing marks are aligned. The crankshaft sprocket timing mark should align with the oil pump timing mark. The rear camshaft sprocket timing mark should align with the generator bracket timing mark and the front camshaft sprocket timing mark should align with the inner timing belt cover timing mark.

5. If the belt is to be reused, mark the direction of rotation on the belt for installation reference.

6. Loosen the timing belt tensioner bolt and remove the timing belt.

7. If necessary, remove the timing belt tensioner.

8. Remove the crankshaft sprocket flange shield and crankshaft sprocket.

9. Hold the camshaft sprocket using spanner tool MB990775, or equivalent, and remove the camshaft sprocket bolt and washer. Remove the camshaft sprocket.

To install:

10. Install the camshaft sprocket on the camshaft with the retaining bolt and washer. Hold the camshaft sprocket using spanner tool MB990775, or equivalent, and tighten the bolt to 70 ft. lbs. (95 Nm).

11. Install the crankshaft sprocket.

12. If removed, install the timing belt tensioner and tensioner spring. Hook the spring upper end to the water pump pin and the lower end to the tensioner bracket with the hook out.

13. Turn the timing belt tensioner counterclockwise full travel in the adjustment slot and tighten the bolt to temporarily hold it in this position.

14. Rotate the crankshaft sprocket until its timing mark is aligned with the oil pump timing mark.

15. Rotate the rear camshaft sprocket until its timing mark is aligned with the timing mark on the generator bracket.

16. Rotate the front (radiator side) camshaft sprocket until its mark is aligned with the timing mark on the inner timing belt cover.

17. Install the timing belt on the crankshaft sprocket while keeping the belt tight on the tension side.

➡**If the original belt is being reused, be sure to install it in the same rotational direction.**

18. Position the timing belt over the front camshaft sprocket (radiator side).

Timing chain and gear service is covered in the model specific sections of this manual

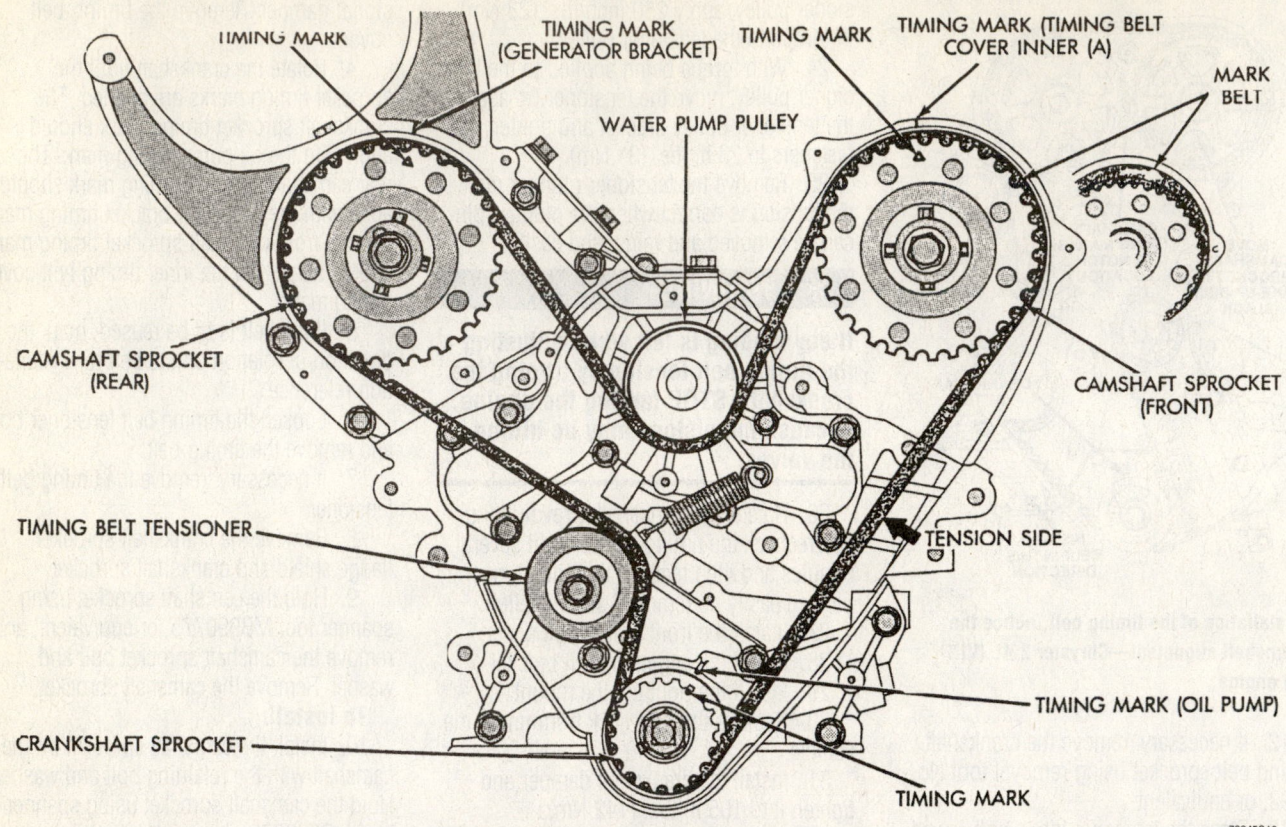

TIMING MARK

TIMING MARK (GENERATOR BRACKET)

TIMING MARK

TIMING MARK (TIMING BELT COVER INNER (A)

MARK BELT

WATER PUMP PULLEY

CAMSHAFT SPROCKET (REAR)

CAMSHAFT SPROCKET (FRONT)

TIMING BELT TENSIONER

TENSION SIDE

TIMING MARK (OIL PUMP)

CRANKSHAFT SPROCKET

TIMING MARK

79245G19

Timing belt sprocket timing marks for proper timing belt installation—Chrysler 3.0L (VIN 3) engine

Next, position the belt under the water pump pulley, then over the rear camshaft sprocket and finally over the tensioner.

✳✳ WARNING

If any binding is felt when adjusting the timing belt tension by turning the crankshaft, STOP turning the engine, because the pistons may be hitting the valves.

19. Apply rotating force in the opposite direction to the front camshaft sprocket (radiator side) to create tension on the timing belt tension side. Check that all timing marks are aligned.

20. Install the crankshaft sprocket flange.

21. Loosen the tensioner bolt and allow the tensioner spring to tension the belt.

22. Rotate the crankshaft 2 full turns in a clockwise direction. Turn the crankshaft smoothly and in a clockwise direction only.

23. Align the timing marks. If all marks are aligned, tighten the tensioner bolt to 250 inch lbs. (28 Nm). Otherwise repeat the installation procedure.

24. Install the timing belt covers. Install the engine support bracket. Tighten the support bracket mounting bolts to 35 ft. lbs. (47 Nm).

25. Install the engine mount insulator, torsional damper and crankshaft pulleys. Tighten the crankshaft pulley bolt to 112 ft. lbs. (151 Nm).

26. Install the accessory drive belts and adjust them to the proper tension.

27. Reconnect the negative battery cable.

28. Run the engine and check for proper operation. Road test the vehicle.

Ford Ranger

2.3L (VIN A) AND 2.5L (VIN C) ENGINES

1. Rotate the engine so that No. 1 cylinder is at Top Dead Center (TDC) on the compression stroke. Check that the timing marks are aligned on the camshaft and crankshaft pulleys. An access plug is provided in the cam belt cover so that the camshaft timing can be checked without removal of the cover or any other parts. Set the crankshaft to TDC by aligning the timing mark on the crank pulley with the TDC mark on the belt cover. Look through the access hole in the belt cover to be sure that the timing mark on the cam drive sprocket is aligned with the pointer on the inner belt cover.

➡ **Always turn the engine in the normal direction of rotation. Backward rotation**

may cause the timing belt to jump time, due to the arrangement of the belt tensioner.

2. Drain cooling system. Remove the upper radiator hose as necessary. Remove the fan blade and water pump pulley bolts.

✳✳ CAUTION

When draining the coolant, keep in mind that cats and dogs are attracted by ethylene glycol antifreeze, and are likely to drink any that is left in an uncovered container or in puddles on the ground. This will prove fatal in sufficient quantity. Always drain the coolant into a sealable container. Coolant should be reused unless it is contaminated or several years old.

3. Loosen the alternator retaining bolts and remove the drive belt from the pulleys. Remove the water pump pulley.

4. Remove the power steering pump and set it aside.

5. Remove the 4 timing belt outer cover retaining bolts and remove the cover. Remove the crankshaft pulley and belt guide.

6. Loosen the belt tensioner pulley assembly, then position a camshaft belt

adjuster tool T74P-6254-A, or equivalent, on the tension spring roll pin and retract the belt tensioner away from the timing belt. Tighten the adjustment bolt to lock the tensioner in the retracted position.

7. If the belt is to be reused, mark the direction of rotation on the belt for installation reference.

8. Remove the timing belt.

To install:

9. Install the new belt over the crankshaft sprocket and then counterclockwise over the auxiliary and camshaft sprockets, making sure the lugs on the belt properly engage the sprocket teeth on the pulleys. Be careful not to rotate the pulleys when installing the belt.

10. Release the timing belt tensioner pulley, allowing the tensioner to take up the belt slack. If the spring does not have enough tension to move the roller against the belt (belt hangs loose), it might be necessary to manually push the roller against the belt and tighten the bolt.

➡ **The spring cannot be used to set belt tension; a wrench must be used on the tensioner assembly.**

✳✳ WARNING

If any binding is felt when adjusting the timing belt tension by turning the crankshaft, STOP turning the engine, because the pistons may be hitting the valves.

11. Rotate the crankshaft 2 complete turns by hand (in the normal direction of rotation) to remove slack from the belt. Tighten the tensioner adjustment to 26–33 ft. lbs. (35–45 Nm) and pivot bolts to 30–40 ft. lbs. (40–55 Nm). Be sure the belt is seated properly on the pulleys and that the timing marks are still in alignment when No. 1 cylinder is again at TDC/compression.

12. Install the crankshaft pulley and belt guide.

13. Install the timing belt cover.

14. Install the water pump pulley and fan blades. Install the upper radiator hose if necessary. Refill the cooling system.

15. Install the accessory drive belts.

16. Start the engine and check the ignition timing. Adjust the timing, if necessary.

GEO/Chevrolet Tracker

1.6L 16-VALVE ENGINE

The 1.6L 16-valve engine is known as an interference motor, because it is fabricated with such close tolerances between the pistons and valves that, if the timing belt is incorrectly positioned, jumps teeth on one of the sprockets or breaks, the valve and pistons will come into contact. This can cause severe internal engine damage

➡ **Do not rotate the crankshaft counterclockwise or attempt to rotate the crankshaft by turning the camshaft sprocket.**

1. Remove the timing belt cover.

2. If the timing belt is not already marked with a directional arrow, use white paint, a grease pencil or correction fluid to do so.

3. Rotate the crankshaft clockwise until the timing mark on the camshaft sprocket and the V mark on the timing belt inside cover are aligned, and the punch mark on the crankshaft sprocket is aligned with the mark on the engine.

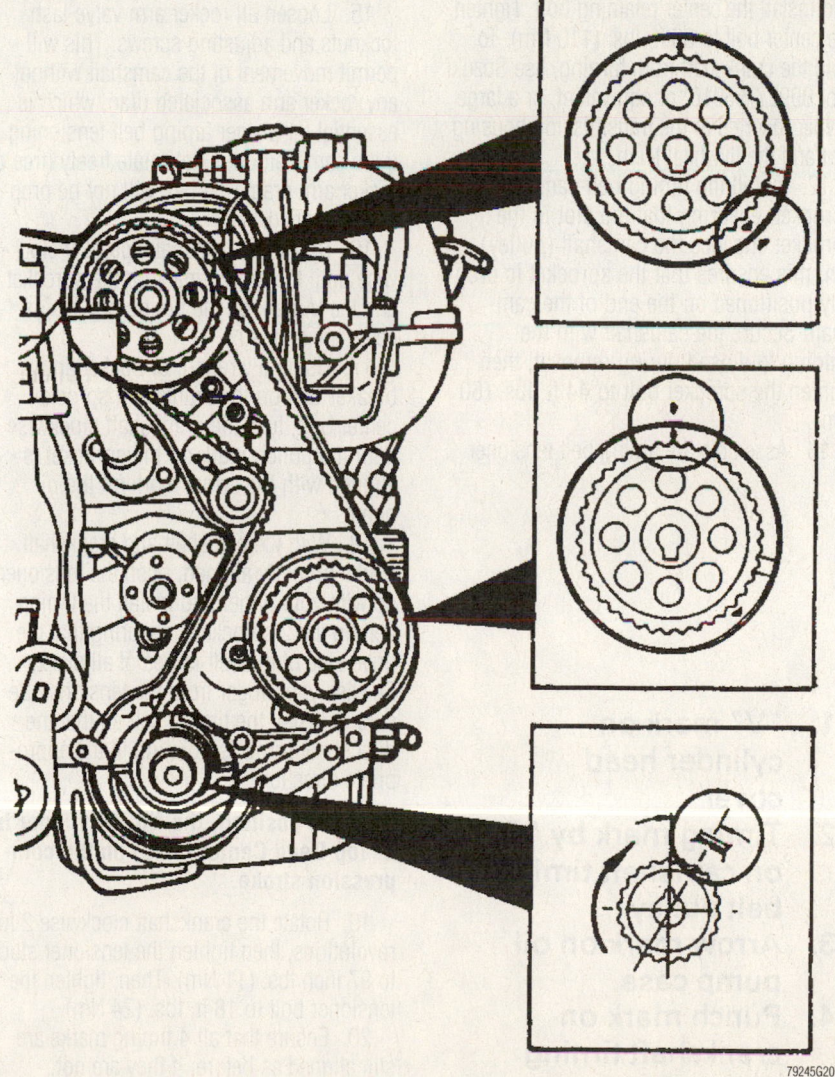

Camshaft, auxiliary shaft and crankshaft timing belt sprocket alignment mark locations—Ford 2.3L and 2.5L engines

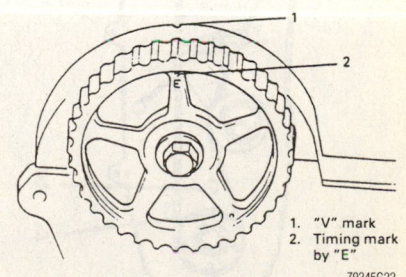

1. "V" mark
2. Timing mark by "E"

Camshaft timing marks—GEO/Chevrolet Tracker 1.6L 16-valve engine

4. Disconnect one end of the tensioner spring. Loosen the timing belt tensioner bolt and stud, then, using your finger, press the tensioner plate up and remove the timing belt from the crankshaft and camshaft sprockets.

5. Remove the timing belt tensioner, tensioner plate and spring from the engine.

6. Install Suzuki tool 09917-68220, or equivalent, onto the camshaft sprocket to hold the camshaft from rotating. Loosen the camshaft sprocket retaining bolt, then pull the camshaft sprocket off of the end of the camshaft.

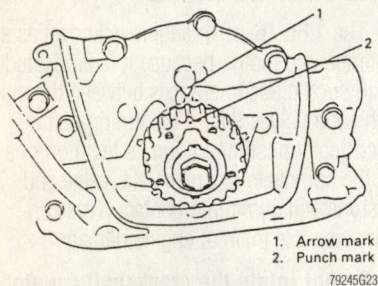

1. Arrow mark
2. Punch mark

79245G23

Align the punch mark with the arrow for proper timing belt installation—GEO/Chevrolet Tracker 1.6L 16-valve engine

7. Remove the crankshaft timing belt sprocket by loosening the center bolt, while preventing the crankshaft from rotating. To hold the crankshaft from turning, use Suzuki tool 09927-56010, or equivalent, or a large prybar inserted in the transmission housing slot and the flywheel teeth. Pull the sprocket off of the end of the crankshaft. Be sure to retain the crankshaft sprocket key and belt guide for assembly.

8. If necessary, remove the timing belt inside cover from the cylinder head.

To install:

9. If necessary, install the timing belt inside cover.

10. Slide the timing belt guide on the crankshaft so that the concave side faces the oil pump, then install the sprocket key in the groove in the crankshaft.

11. Slide the pulley onto the crankshaft, and install the center retaining bolt. Tighten the center bolt to 80 ft. lbs. (110 Nm). To hold the crankshaft from turning, use Suzuki tool 09927-56010, or equivalent, or a large prybar inserted in the transmission housing slot and the flywheel teeth.

12. Install the timing belt camshaft sprocket, ensuring that the slot in the sprocket engages the camshaft (pulley) pin; this ensures that the sprocket is properly positioned on the end of the camshaft. Secure the camshaft with the holding tool used during removal, then tighten the sprocket bolt to 44 ft. lbs. (60 Nm).

13. Assemble the timing belt tensioner

1. "V" mark on cylinder head cover
2. Timing mark by "E" on camshaft timing belt pulley
3. Arrow mark on oil pump case
4. Punch mark on crankshaft timing belt pulley

79245G47

Rotate the crankshaft clockwise until the camshaft and crankshaft timing marks are aligned—GEO/Chevrolet Tracker 1.6L 16-valve engine

plate and the tensioner, making sure that the lug of the tensioner plate engages the tensioner.

14. Install the timing belt tensioner, tensioner plate and spring on the engine. Tighten the mounting bolt and stud only finger-tight at this time. Ensure that when the tensioner is moved in a counterclockwise direction, the tensioner moves in the same direction. If the tensioner does not move, remove it and the tensioner plate to reassemble them properly.

15. Loosen all rocker arm valve lash locknuts and adjusting screws. This will permit movement of the camshaft without any rocker arm associated drag, which is essential for proper timing belt tensioning. If the camshaft does not rotate freely (free of rocker arm drag), the belt will not be properly tensioned.

16. Rotate the camshaft sprocket clockwise until the timing mark on the sprocket and the V mark on the timing belt inside cover are aligned.

17. Using a wrench, or socket and breaker bar, on the crankshaft sprocket center bolt, turn the crankshaft clockwise until the punch mark on the sprocket is aligned with the arrow mark on the oil pump.

18. With the camshaft and crankshaft marks properly aligned, push the tensioner up with your finger and install the timing belt on the 2 sprockets, ensuring that the drive side of the belt is free of all slack. Release your finger from the tensioner. Be sure to install the timing belt so that the directional arrow is pointing in the appropriate direction.

➡**In this position, the No. 4 cylinder is at Top Dead Center (TDC) on the compression stroke.**

19. Rotate the crankshaft clockwise 2 full revolutions, then tighten the tensioner stud to 97 inch lbs. (11 Nm). Then, tighten the tensioner bolt to 18 ft. lbs. (24 Nm).

20. Ensure that all 4 timing marks are still aligned as before; if they are not, remove the timing belt, and install and tension it again.

21. Install the timing belt cover and all related components.

Honda CR-V

2.0L (B20B4) ENGINE

1. Disconnect the negative battery cable.
2. Position crankshaft so that No. 1 piston is at Top Dead Center (TDC).
3. Remove the splash guard.
4. Remove the accessory drive belts.
5. If equipped, remove the cruise control actuator.
6. Place a piece of wood between the oil pan and the jack, support the engine with a jack.
7. Remove upper engine bracket.
8. Remove the valve cover.
9. Remove the timing belt covers.
10. Loosen the adjusting bolt 180 degrees. Release the tension from the belt by pushing on the tensioner, then retighten the adjusting bolt.
11. Remove the timing belt.

To install:

12. Be sure the timing marks are properly aligned.
13. Install the timing belt on the pulleys following this sequence:
   a. Crankshaft pulley.
   b. Adjusting pulley.
   c. Water pump pulley.
   d. Exhaust camshaft pulley.
   e. Intake camshaft pulley.
14. Loosen and retighten the adjusting bolt to allow tension to be applied to the belt.
15. Install the lower and middle timing covers.
16. Install the crankshaft pulley and tighten the bolt to 130 ft. lbs. (177 Nm).

❋❋ WARNING

If any binding is felt when adjusting the timing belt tension by turning the crankshaft, STOP turning the engine, because the pistons may be hitting the valves.

17. Rotate the crankshaft about 5–6 times counterclockwise to seat the timing belt.
18. Position the No. 1 piston to TDC.
19. Loosen the adjusting bolt ½ turn.
20. Rotate the crankshaft counterclockwise 3 teeth on the camshaft pulley.
21. Tighten the adjusting bolt to 40 ft. lbs. (54Nm).
22. Retighten the crankshaft pulley bolt to 130 ft. lbs. (177 Nm).
23. Install the valve cover.
24. Install the engine mounting bracket, then remove the jack.

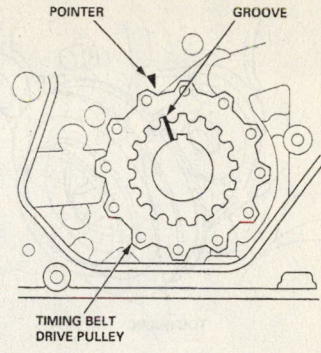

Crankshaft timing mark will be easier to verify when clean—Honda CR-V 2.0L (B20B4) engine

25. If removed, install the cruise control actuator.
26. Install the accessory drive belts.
27. Install the splash guard.
28. Connect the negative battery cable.
29. Check the engine operation and road test.

Honda Odyssey

1997 2.2L (F22B6) AND 1998 2.3L (F23A7) ENGINES

➡The radio may contain a coded theft protection circuit. Always make note the code number before disconnecting the battery.

1. Disconnect the negative and positive battery cables.
2. Remove the cylinder head cover.
3. Remove the upper timing belt cover.
4. Turn the crankshaft to align the timing marks and set cylinder No.1 to Top Dead Center (TDC) for the compression stroke. The white mark on the crankshaft pulley should align with the pointer on the timing belt cover. The words **UP** embossed on the camshaft pulley should be aligned in the upward position and the marks on the edge of the pulley should be aligned with the cylinder head or the back cover upper edge. Once in this position, the engine must NOT be turned or disturbed.
5. Remove the splash shield from below the engine.
6. Remove the wheel well splash shield.
7. Loosen and remove the power steering pump belt. Remove the power steering pump.
8. Loosen the adjusting and mounting bolts for the alternator and remove the drive belt.

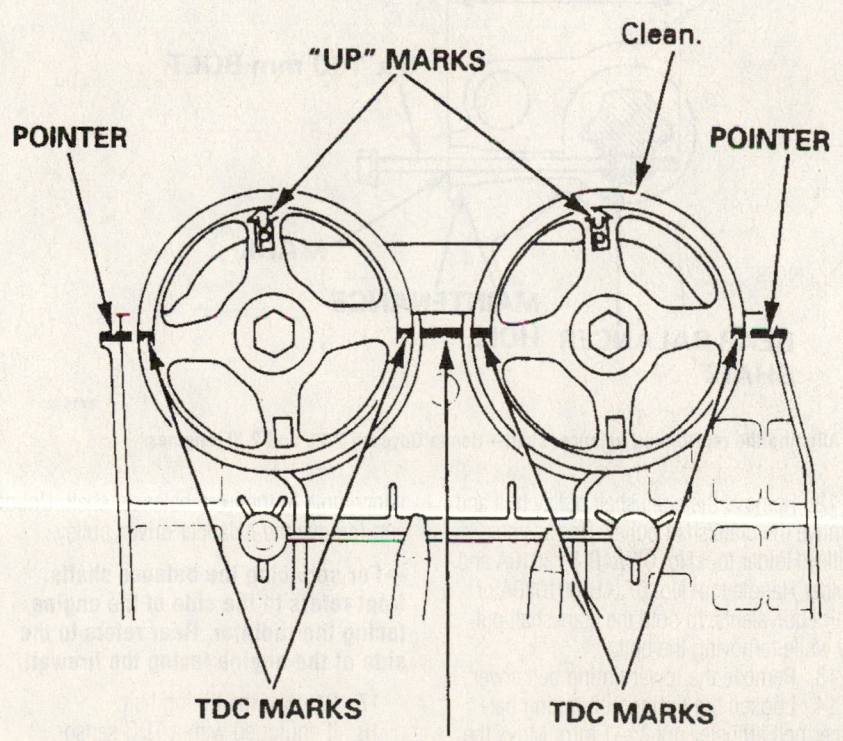

Intake and exhaust camshaft timing marks properly aligned at TDC—Honda CR-V 2.0L (B20B4) engine

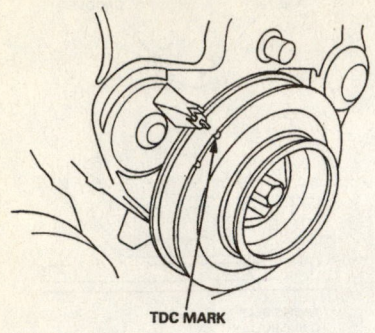

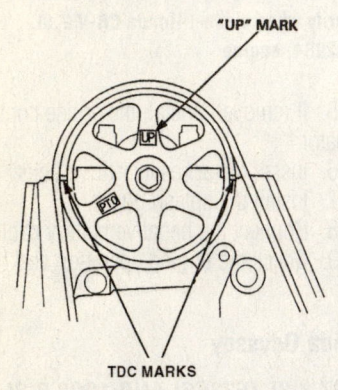

Align the camshaft, crankshaft and engine marks before removing the timing belt and pulleys—Honda Odyssey 2.2L and 2.3L engines

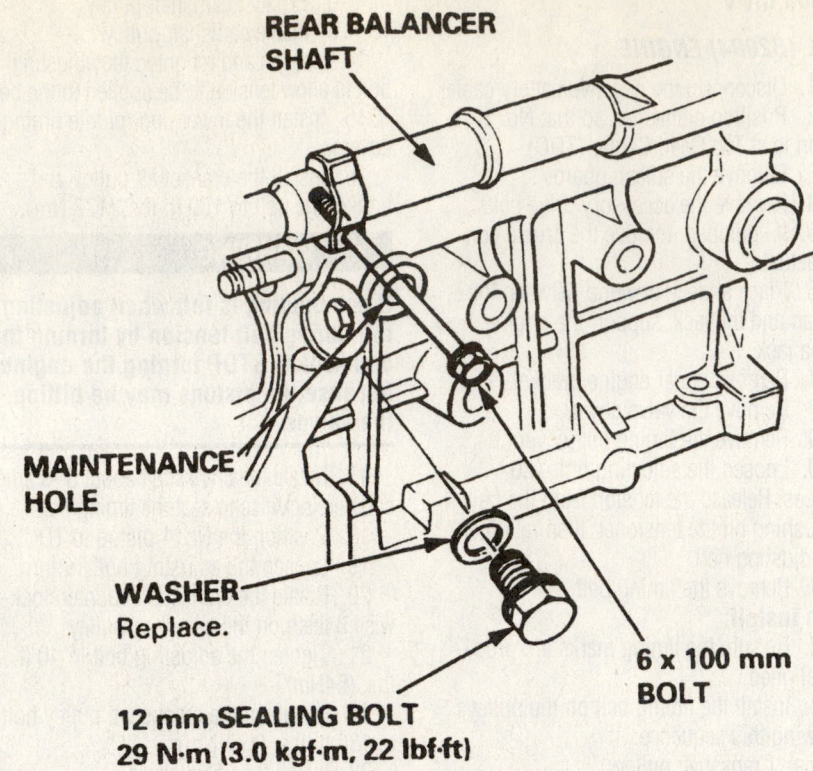

Aligning the rear timing balancer shaft—Honda Odyssey 2.2L and 2.3L engines

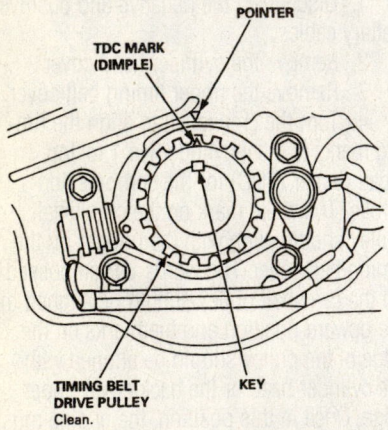

Align the crankshaft sprocket with the oil pump pointer before installing the timing belt—Honda Odyssey 2.2L and 2.3L engines

9. Support the engine with a floor jack cushioned with a piece of wood under the oil pan.

10. Remove the dipstick and the dipstick tube.

11. Remove the through-bolt for the side engine mount and remove the mount.

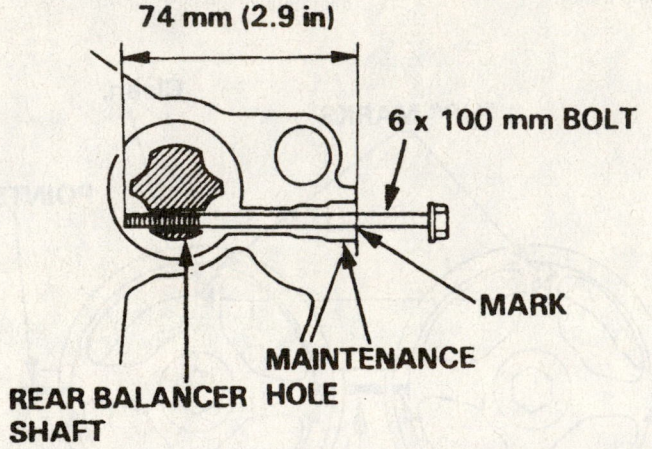

12. Remove the crankshaft pulley bolt and remove the crankshaft pulley. Use a Crank Pulley Holder tool No. 07MAB-PY3010A and Holder Handle tool No. 07JAB-001020A or their equivalents, to hold the crankshaft pulley while removing the bolt.

13. Remove the lower timing belt cover.

14. Loosen the timing belt/timing balancer belt adjuster nut ⅔–1 turn. Move the tension adjuster to release the belt tension and retighten the adjuster nut.

15. Remove the balancer shaft belt and its drive pulley.

16. Insert a suitable tool into the mainte-nance hole in the front balancer shaft. Unbolt and remove the balancer driven pulley.

➡For servicing the balance shafts, front refers to the side of the engine facing the radiator. Rear refers to the side of the engine facing the firewall.

17. Remove the timing belt.

18. If equipped with a TDC sensor assembly at the crankshaft sprocket, unbolt the assembly and move it to the side before removing the sprocket.

19. Remove the key and the spacers to remove the crankshaft timing sprocket.

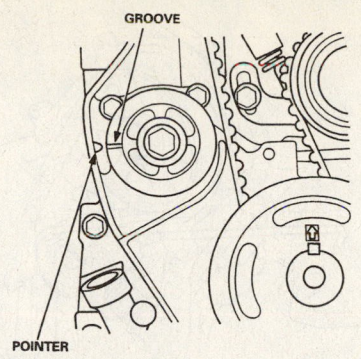

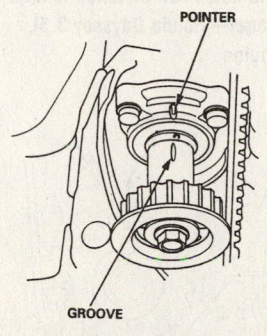

**Aligning the front timing balancer shaft—
Honda Odyssey 2.2L and 2.3L engines**

20. Unbolt and remove the camshaft timing sprocket.

To install:

21. Install the camshaft timing sprocket so that the **UP** mark is up and the TDC marks are parallel to the cylinder head gasket surface. Install the key and tighten the bolt to 27 ft. lbs. (37 Nm).

22. Install the crankshaft sprocket so that the TDC mark aligns with the pointer on the oil pump. Install the spacers with their concave surfaces facing in. Install the key. Install the TDC sensor assembly back into position before installing the timing belt.

23. Install and tension the timing belt.

24. Rotate the crankshaft counterclockwise 5–6 turns to be sure the belt is properly seated.

25. Set the No. 1 piston at TDC for its compression stroke.

❊❊ WARNING

If any binding is felt when adjusting the timing belt tension by turning the crankshaft, STOP turning the engine, because the pistons may be hitting the valves.

26. Rotate the crankshaft counterclockwise so that the camshaft pulley moves only 3 teeth beyond its TDC mark.

27. Tighten the tensioner adjusting nut to 33 ft. lbs. (45 Nm).

28. Tighten the crankshaft pulley bolt to 181 ft. lbs. (245 Nm).

29. Align the rear balancer shaft into position by performing the following procedures:

   a. Scribe a 3 in. (74mm) line from the end of a 6 x 1.0mm bolt.

   b. Remove the maintenance hole sealing bolt and insert the 6 x 1.0mm bolt into the maintenance hole to the scribed line.

30. Install the balancer shaft belt drive pulley.

31. Align the groove on the pulley edge with the pointer on the balancer gear case.

32. Check the alignment of the pointer on the balancer pulley to the pointer on the oil pump.

33. Install and tension the timing balancer shaft belt.

34. Be sure the timing belts have been tensioned correctly and that all TDC and alignment marks are in their proper positions.

35. Install the lower timing cover and the crankshaft pulley. Apply engine oil to the pulley bolt threads and washer surface. Install the pulley bolt and tighten it to 181 ft. lbs. (245 Nm).

36. Install the upper timing cover and the valve cover. Be sure the seals are properly seated.

37. Install the side engine mount. Tighten the through-bolt to 47 ft. lbs. (64 Nm). Tighten the mount nut and bolt to 40 ft. lbs. (55 Nm) each.

38. Remove the floor jack.

39. Install and tension the alternator belt.

40. Install the power steering pump and tension its belt.

41. Install the splash shields.

42. Reconnect the positive and negative battery cables. Enter the radio security code.

43. Check engine operation.

1999–01 3.5L (J35A1) V6 ENGINE

➡ **The radio may contain a coded theft protection circuit. Always make note the code number before disconnecting the battery.**

1. Disconnect the negative battery terminal.

2. Turn the crankshaft so the white mark on the crankshaft pulley aligns with the pointer on the oil pump housing cover.

3. Open the inspection plugs on the upper timing belt covers and check that the camshaft sprocket marks align with the upper cover marks.

❊❊ WARNING

Align the camshaft and crankshaft sprockets with their alignment marks before removing the timing belt. Failure to align the timing marks correctly may result in valve damage.

4. Raise and safely support the vehicle and remove both front tires/wheels.

5. Remove the front lower splash shield.

6. Move the alternator tensioner with a Belt Tensioner Release Arm tool YA9317, or equivalent, to release tension from the belt and remove the alternator drive belt.

7. Remove the alternator belt tensioner release arm.

8. Loosen the power steering pump adjustment nut, adjustment locknut and mounting bolt, then remove the power steering pump with the hoses attached.

9. Support the weight of the engine by placing a wood block on a floor jack and carefully lift on the oil pan.

10. Remove the bolts from the side engine mount bracket and remove the bracket.

11. Remove the dipstick, the dipstick tube and discard the O-ring.

12. Hold the crankshaft pulley with the Handle tool 07JAB-001020A and Crankshaft Holding tool 07MAB-PY3010A, or equivalent. While holding the crankshaft pulley, remove the crankshaft pulley bolt using a heavy duty ¾ in. (19mm) socket and breaker bar.

13. Remove the crankshaft pulley, the upper timing belt covers and the lower timing belt cover.

14. Remove one of the battery clamp fasteners from the battery tray and grind a 45 degree bevel on the threaded end of the battery clamp bolt.

15. Screw in the battery hold-down bolt into the threaded bracket just above the auto-tensioner (automatic timing belt adjuster) and tighten the bolt hand-tight to hold the auto-tensioner adjuster in its current position.

16. Remove the engine mount bracket bolts and the bracket.

17. Loosen the timing belt idler pulley bolt (located on the right side across from the auto-tensioner pulley) about 5–6 revolutions and remove the timing belt.

To install:

18. Clean the timing belt sprockets and the timing belt covers.

Align the camshaft and crankshaft sprockets with their alignment marks before installing the timing belt. Failure to align the timing marks correctly may result in valve damage.

19. Align the timing mark on the crankshaft sprocket with the oil pump pointer.

20. Align the camshaft sprocket TDC timing marks with the pointers on the rear cover.

21. If installing a new belt or if the auto-tensioner has extended or if the timing belt cannot be reinstalled easily, the auto-tensioner must be collapsed before installation of the timing belt, perform the following procedures:

a. Remove the battery hold-down bolt from the auto-tensioner bracket.

b. Remove the timing belt auto-tensioner bolts and the auto-tensioner.

c. Secure the auto-tensioner in a soft jawed vise, clamping onto the flat surface of one of the mounting bolt holes with the maintenance bolt facing upward.

d. Remove the maintenance bolt and use caution not to spill oil from the tensioner assembly.

e. Should oil spill from the tensioner, be sure the tensioner is filled with 0.22 ounces (6.5 ml) of fresh engine oil.

f. Using care not to damage the threads or the gasket sealing surface, insert a flat-blade screwdriver through the tensioner maintenance hole and turn the screwdriver clockwise to compress the auto-tensioner bottom while the Tensioner Holder tool 14540-P8A-A01, or equivalent, is installed on the auto-tensioner assembly.

g. Install the auto-tensioner maintenance bolt with a new gasket and tighten to a torque 72 inch lbs. (8 Nm).

h. Install the auto-tensioner on the engine with the tensioner holder tool installed and torque the mounting bolts to 104 inch lbs. (12 Nm).

22. Install the timing belt in a counterclockwise pattern starting with the crankshaft drive sprocket. Install the timing belt counterclockwise in the following sequence:

- Crankshaft drive sprocket.
- Idler pulley.
- Left side camshaft sprocket.
- Water pump.
- Right side camshaft sprocket.
- Auto-tensioner adjustment pulley.

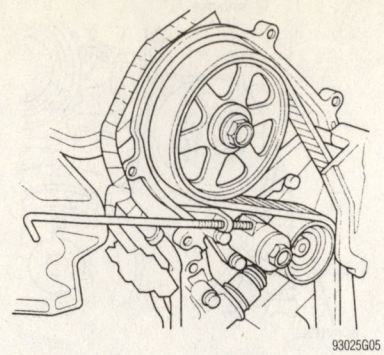

Battery hold-down bolt installed to hold auto-tensioner—Honda Odyssey 3.5L (J35A1) engine

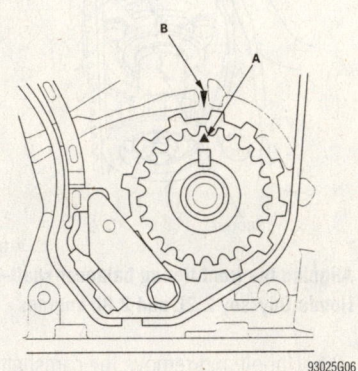

Crankshaft sprocket Top Dead Center (TDC) mark—Honda Odyssey 3.5L (J35A1) engine

FRONT CAMSHAFT PULLEY:

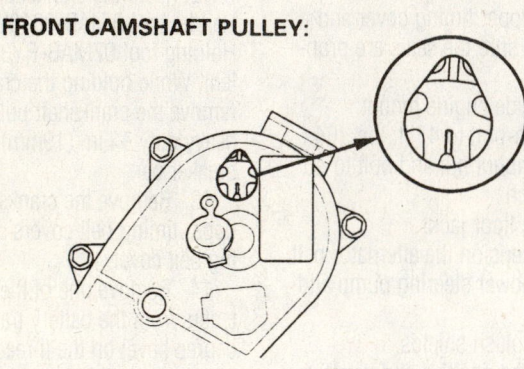

REAR CAMSHAFT PULLEY:

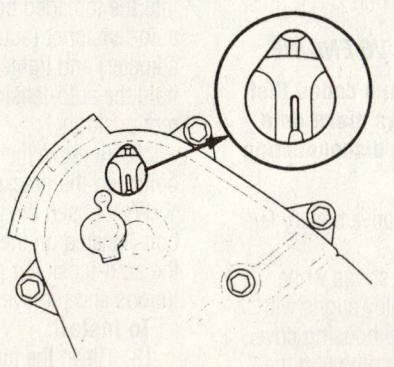

Crankshaft and camshaft timing marks at Top Dead Center (TDC)—Honda Odyssey 3.5L (J35A1) engine

FRONT:

REAR:

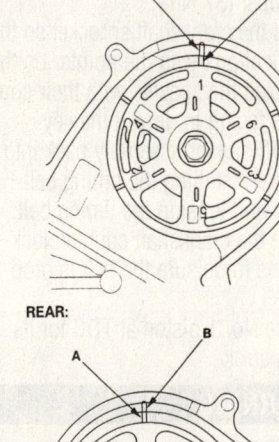

Camshaft sprocket Top Dead Center (TDC) mark—Honda Odyssey 3.5L (J35A1) engine

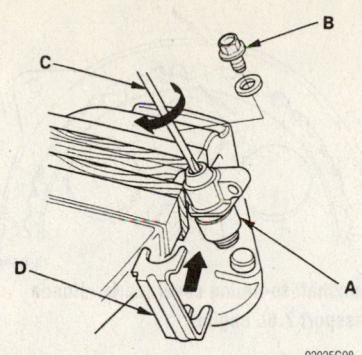

Adjusting the auto-tensioner—Honda Odyssey 3.5L (J35A1) engine

23. Torque the timing belt idler pulley bolt to 33 ft. lbs. (44 Nm).

24. Remove the auto-tensioner holding tool to allow the tensioner to extend.

25. Install the engine mount bracket to the engine and torque the bolts to 33 ft. lbs. (44 Nm).

26. Install the lower timing belt cover and both upper timing belt covers.

27. Hold the crankshaft pulley with special tools 07JAB-001020A handle and 07MAB-PY3010A crankshaft holding tool, or equivalent tools. While holding the crankshaft pulley, install the crankshaft pulley bolt using a heavy duty ¾ in. (19mm) socket and a commercially available torque wrench and torque the bolt to 181 ft. lbs. (245 Nm).

❉❉ WARNING

If any binding is felt while moving the crankshaft pulley, STOP turning the crankshaft pulley immediately because the pistons may be hitting the valves.

28. Rotate the crankshaft pulley clockwise 5–6 revolutions to allow the timing belt to be seated in the pulleys.

29. Move the crankshaft pulley to the white TDC mark and inspect the camshaft TDC marks to ensure proper timing of the camshafts.

❉❉ WARNING

If the timing marks do not align, the timing belt removal and installation procedure must be performed again.

30. Install the engine dipstick tube using a new O-ring.

31. Install the power steering pump, and loosely install the mounting bolt, adjustment locknut and adjustment nut.

32. Adjust the power steering belt to a tension such that a 22 lb. (98 N) pull halfway between the 2 drive pulleys will allow the belt to move 0.51–0.65 in. (13.0–16.5mm).

33. Tighten the power steering pump mounting bolt and adjustment locknut.

➡ **If a new belt is used, set the deflection to 0.33–0.43 in. (8.5–11.0mm) and after engine has run for 5 minutes, readjust the new belt to the used belt specification.**

34. Install the alternator belt tensioner arm.

35. Move the alternator tensioner with a Belt Tensioner Release Arm tool YA9317, or equivalent, to release tension from the belt and install the alternator drive belt.

36. Install both engine mount bracket bolts and torque to 33 ft. lbs. (44 Nm).

37. Install the bushing through bolt and tighten to 40 ft. lbs. (54 Nm).

38. Release and carefully remove the floor jack.

39. Install the front lower splash shield.

40. Install both front tires/wheels.

41. Carefully lower the vehicle.

42. Install the battery hold-down bolt in the battery tray.

43. Install the negative battery cable.

44. Enter the radio security code.

Honda Passport

1997 2.6L (4ZE1/E) ENGINE

1. Disconnect the negative battery cable.

2. Loosen and remove the engine accessory drive belts.

3. Remove the cooling fan assembly and the water pump pulley.

4. Drain the fluid from the power steering reservoir.

5. Unbolt and remove the power steering pump. Unbolt the hydraulic line brackets from the upper timing cover and move the pump from the work area without disconnecting the hydraulic lines.

6. Disconnect and remove the starter motor if a Flywheel Holder tool No. J-38674, or equivalent, is to be used.

7. Remove the upper timing belt cover.

8. Rotate the crankshaft to set the engine at Top Dead Center (TDC) of the compression for the No. 1 cylinder. The arrow mark on the camshaft sprocket will be aligned with the mark on the rear timing cover.

9. Remove the crankshaft pulley.

10. Remove the lower timing belt cover.

11. Verify that the engine is set at TDC/compression for the No. 1 cylinder. The notch on the crankshaft sprocket will be aligned with the pointer on the oil seal retainer.

12. Release and remove the tensioner spring to release the timing belt's tension.

13. Remove the timing belt.

14. Unbolt the tensioner pulley bracket from the engine's front cover.

15. If necessary, unbolt and remove the camshaft sprockets. If necessary, use a puller to remove the crankshaft pulley. Don't lose the crankshaft sprocket key.

To install:

16. If removed, install the camshaft and crankshaft sprockets. Align the camshaft and crankshaft timing marks and be sure to install any keys. Tighten the camshaft sprocket bolt to 43 ft. lbs. (59 Nm).

17. Install the tensioner assembly. Tighten the tensioner mounting bolt to 14 ft. lbs. (19 Nm) and the cap bolt to 108 inch lbs. (13 Nm).

18. Be sure the crankshaft and the camshaft sprockets are aligned with their timing marks. Install the timing belt onto the sprockets using the following sequence:

- Crankshaft sprocket
- Oil pump sprocket
- Camshaft sprocket

19. Loosen the tensioner mounting bolt. This will allow the tensioner spring to apply pressure to the timing belt.

20. After the spring has pulled the timing belt as far as possible, temporarily tighten the tensioner mounting bolt to 14 ft. lbs. (19 Nm).

➡ **Remove the flywheel holder before rotating the crankshaft. Reinstall the holder to tighten the crankshaft pulley bolt.**

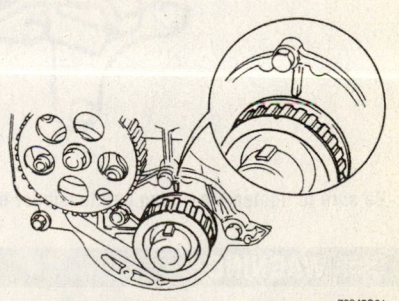

Align the crankshaft pulley timing mark the with oil retainer setting mark—Honda Passport 2.6L engine

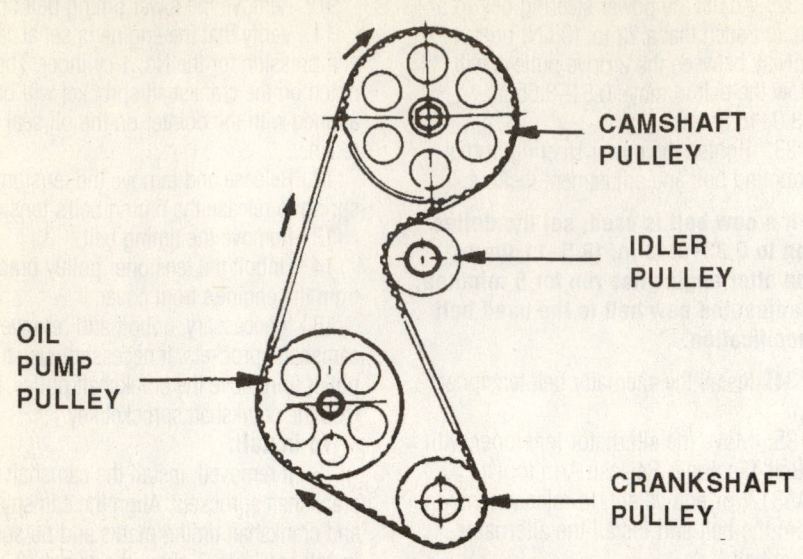

CAMSHAFT PULLEY

IDLER PULLEY

OIL PUMP PULLEY

CRANKSHAFT PULLEY

79245G02

Timing belt direction of travel—Honda Passport 2.6L engine

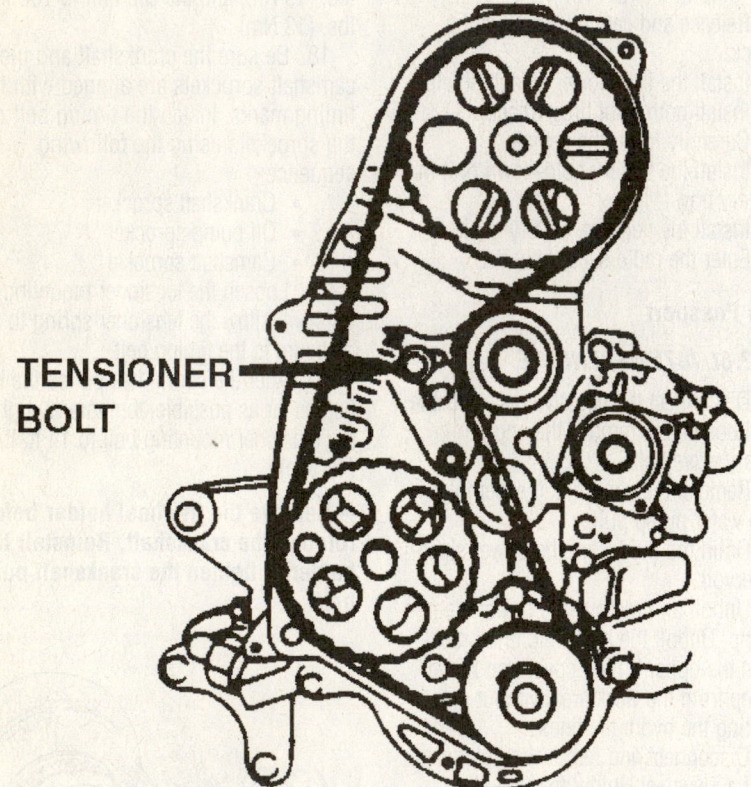

TENSIONER BOLT

79245G03

Be sure to tighten the timing belt tensioner bolt (B)—Honda Passport 2.6L engine

✳✳ WARNING

If any binding is felt when adjusting the timing belt tension by turning the crankshaft, STOP turning the engine, because the pistons may be hitting the valves.

21. Rotate the crankshaft counterclockwise 2 complete revolutions to check the rotation of the belt and the alignment of the timing marks. Listen for any rubbing noises that may mean the belt is binding.

22. Loosen the tensioner pulley bolt to allow the spring to adjust the correct ten-

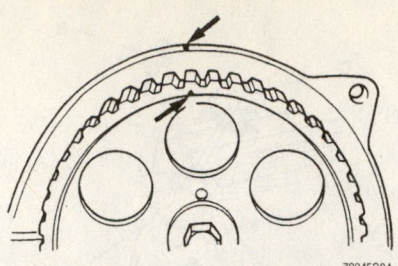

79245G04

Camshaft-to-timing cover mark—Honda Passport 2.6L engine

sion. Then, retighten the tensioner pulley bolt to 14 ft. lbs. (19 Nm).

23. Install the lower timing belt cover and the crankshaft pulley.

24. Tighten the crankshaft pulley bolt to 87 ft. lbs. (118 Nm). Tighten the small pulley bolts to 72 inch lbs. (8 Nm).

25. Install the upper timing cover.

26. If removed, install the starter and tighten the bolts to 30 ft. lbs. (40 Nm).

27. Install the power steering pump. If the hydraulic lines were disconnected, refill and bleed the power steering system.

28. Install the water pump pulley and tighten its nut to 20 ft. lbs. (26 Nm).

29. Install the cooling fan assembly.

30. Install and adjust the accessory drive belts.

31. Connect the negative battery cable.

3.2L (6VD1) ENGINES

1. Disconnect the negative battery cable.

2. Remove the air cleaner assembly and intake air duct.

3. Remove the upper fan shroud from the radiator.

4. Remove the 4 nuts retaining the cooling fan assembly. Remove the cooling fan from the fan pulley.

5. Loosen and remove the drive belts.

6. Remove the upper timing belt covers.

7. Remove the fan pulley assembly.

8. Rotate the crankshaft to align the camshaft timing marks with the pointer dots on the back covers. Verify that the pointer on the crankshaft aligns with the mark on the lower timing cover.

➡ When the timing marks are aligned, the No. 2 piston is at Top Dead Center (TDC) of the compression.

✳✳ WARNING

Align the camshaft and crankshaft sprockets with their alignment marks before removing the timing belt. Failure to align the belt and sprocket marks may result in valve damage.

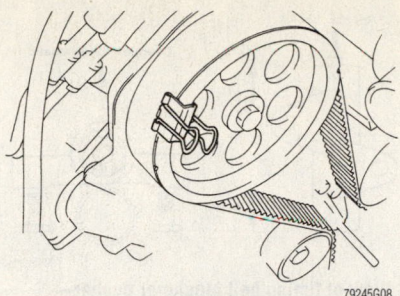

Using a double clip to hold the belt in place—Honda Passport 3.2L engine

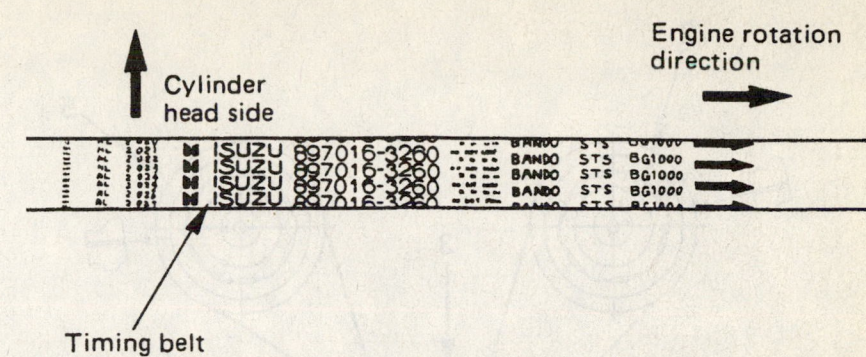

For maximum timing belt life, install the belt as shown—Honda Passport 3.2L engine

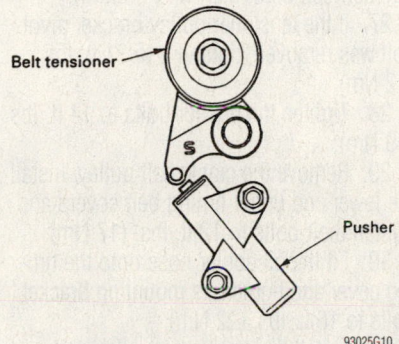

View of timing belt tensioner and pusher—Honda Passport 3.2L engine

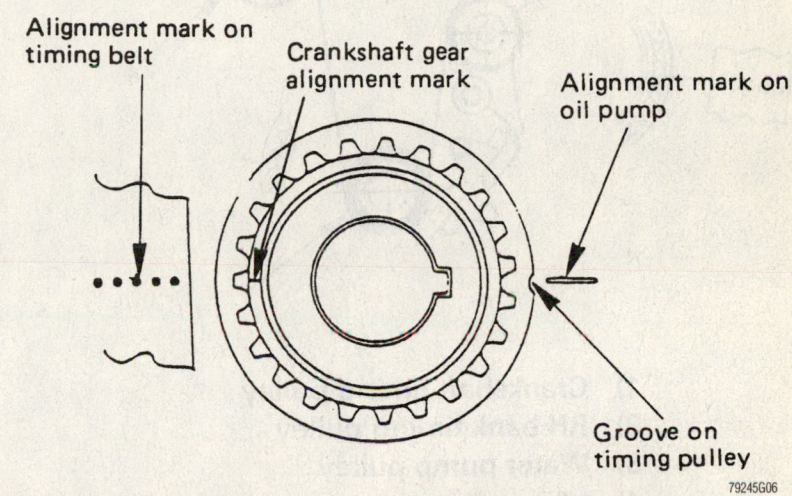

Proper crankshaft alignment marks for timing belt installation—Honda Passport 3.2L SOHC (VIN V) engine

9. Use tool No. J-8614-01 or a suitable pulley holding tool to remove the crankshaft pulley center bolt. Remove the crankshaft pulley.

10. If present, disconnect the 2 oil cooler hose bracket bolts on the timing cover. Move the oil cooler hoses and bracket off of the lower timing cover.

11. Remove the lower timing belt cover.

12. Remove the pusher assembly (tensioner) from below the belt tensioner pulley. The pusher rod must always face upward to prevent oil leakage. Depress the pusher rod and insert a wire pin into the hole to keep the pusher rod retracted.

13. Remove the timing belt.

14. Inspect the water pump and replace it if there is any doubt about its condition.

15. Repair any oil or coolant leaks before installing a new timing belt. If the timing belt has been contaminated with oil or coolant, or is damaged, it must be replaced.

To install:

16. Verify that the sprocket timing marks are still aligned and that the groove and the keyway on the crankshaft timing sprocket align with the mark on the oil pump. The white pointers on the camshaft timing sprockets should align with the dots on the front plate.

17. Install the timing belt. Use clips to secure the belt onto each sprocket until the installation is complete. Align the dotted marks on the timing belt with the timing mark opposite the groove on the crankshaft sprocket.

➡ **The arrows on the timing belt must follow the belt's direction of rotation. The manufacturer's trademark on the belt's spine should be readable left-to-right when the belt is installed.**

18. Align the white line on the timing belt with the alignment mark on the right bank camshaft timing pulley. Secure the belt with a clip.

�֎✖ WARNING

If any binding is felt when adjusting the timing belt tension by turning the crankshaft, STOP turning the engine, because the pistons may be hitting the valves.

19. Rotate the crankshaft counterclockwise to remove the slack between the crankshaft sprocket and the right camshaft timing belt sprocket.

20. Install the belt around the water pump pulley.

21. Install the belt on the idler pulley.

22. Align the white alignment mark on the timing belt with the alignment mark on the left bank camshaft timing belt sprocket.

23. Install the crankshaft pulley and tighten the center bolt by hand. Rotate the crankshaft pulley clockwise to give slack between the crankshaft timing belt pulley and the right bank camshaft timing belt pulley.

24. Insert a 1.4mm piece of wire through the hole in the pusher to hold the rod in. Install the pusher assembly while pushing the tension pulley toward the belt.

25. Pull the pin out from the pusher to release the rod.

26. Remove the clamps from the sprockets. Rotate the crankshaft pulley clockwise 2

Timing chain and gear service is covered in the model specific sections of this manual

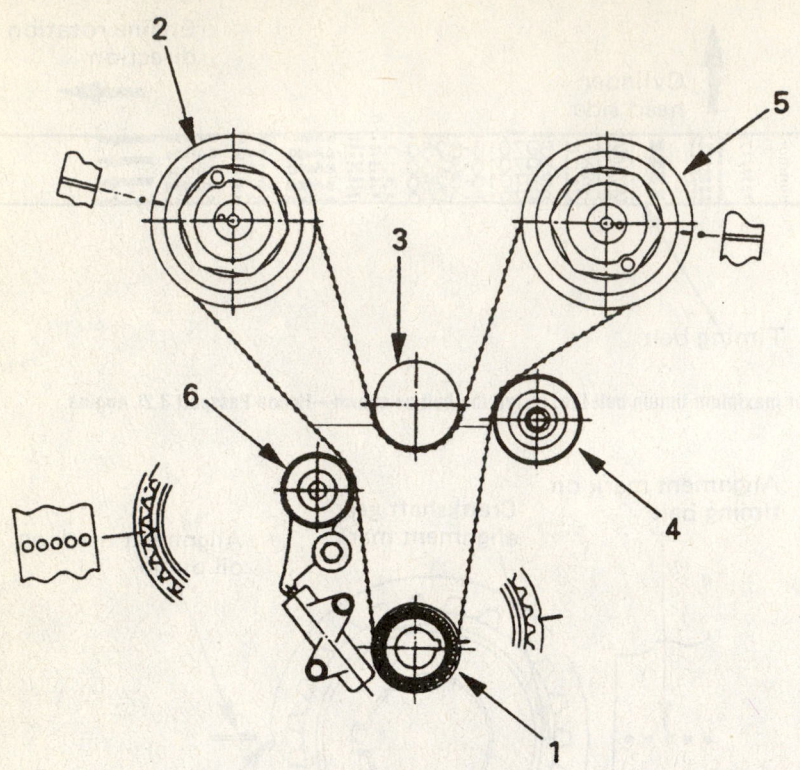

1) **Crankshaft timing pulley**
2) **RH bank timing pulley**
3) **Water pump pulley**
4) **Idler pulley**
5) **LH bank timing pulley**
6) **Tension pulley**

93025G09

Timing mark alignment and timing belt routing—Honda Passport 3.2L SOHC (VIN V) engine

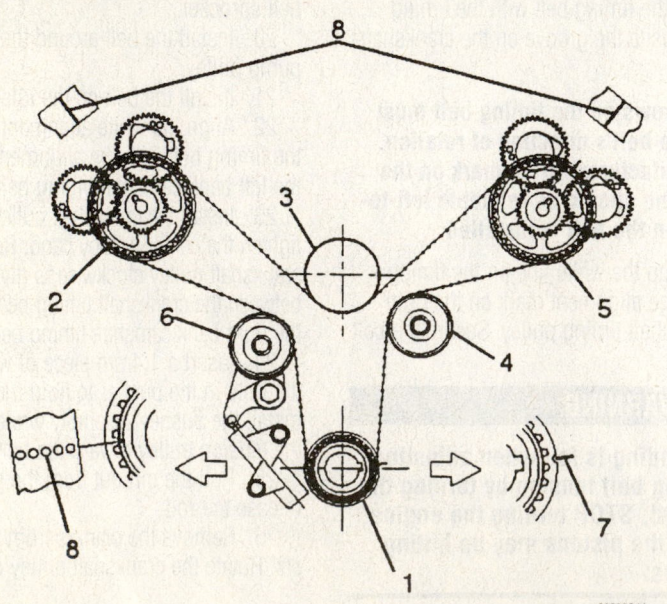

93025G11

Timing mark alignment and timing belt routing—Honda Passport 3.2L DOHC (VIN W) engine

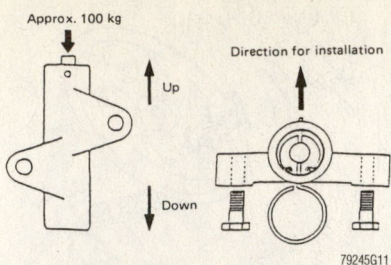

79245G11

View of timing belt tensioner pusher—Honda Passport 3.2L engine

turns. Measure the rod protrusion to ensure it is between 0.16–0.24 in. (4–6mm).

27. If the tensioner pulley bracket pivot bolt was removed, tighten it to 31 ft. lbs. (42 Nm).

28. Tighten the pusher bolts to 14 ft. lbs. (19 Nm).

29. Remove the crankshaft pulley. Install the lower and upper timing belt covers and tighten their bolts to 12 ft. lbs. (17 Nm).

30. Fit the oil cooler hose onto the timing cover and tighten its mounting bracket bolts to 16 ft. lbs. (22 Nm).

31. Install the crankshaft pulley and tighten the pulley bolt to 123 ft. lbs. (167 Nm).

32. Install fan pulley assembly and tighten the bolts to 16 ft. lbs. (22 Nm).

33. Install and adjust the accessory drive belts.

34. Install the cooling fan assembly and tighten the bolts to 72 inch lbs. (8 Nm).

35. Install the upper fan shroud.

36. Install the air cleaner assembly and intake air duct.

37. Connect the negative battery cable.

1998–01 2.2L (X22SE/D) ENGINE

1. Disconnect the negative battery cable.

2. Using a box-end wrench on the drive belt adjuster, turn the adjuster clockwise and remove the drive belt.

3. From the left rear of the engine compartment, disconnect the 3 electrical connectors from the chassis harness.

4. Remove the crankshaft pulley-to-crankshaft bolts and remove the pulley.

5. From the front of the engine, remove the nut and the engine harness cover.

6. Remove the timing belt cover.

7. Rotate the crankshaft to position the timing marks at Top Dead Center (TDC) of the No. 1 cylinder's compression stroke.

➡ **Mark the rotational direction of the timing belt for reinstallation purposes.**

8. Remove the timing belt tensioner adjusting bolt and the tensioner from the engine.

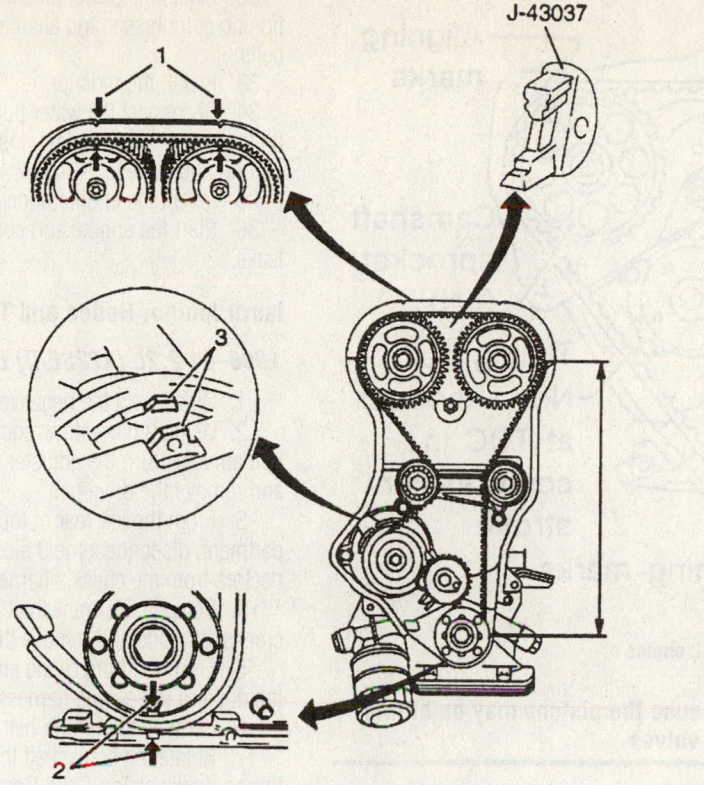

Aligning the timing marks and installing the timing belt—Honda Passport 2.2L (X22SE/D) engine

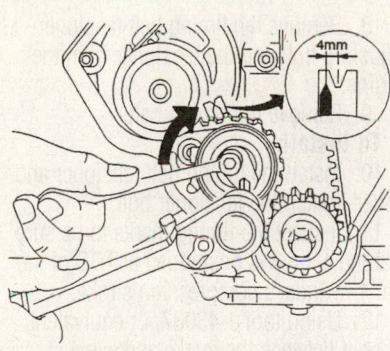

Tensioning the timing belt for a used timing belt—Honda Passport 2.2L (X22SE/D) engine

9. Remove the timing belt.

To install:

10. Install the timing belt tensioner and finger-tighten the tensioner bolt.

11. Inspect the timing marks to be sure that the engine is positioned at TDC of the No. 1 cylinder's compression stroke.

12. Using tool J-43037, or equivalent, place it between the intake and exhaust sprockets to prevent the camshaft gear from moving during the timing belt installation.

13. Install the timing belt.

14. Position the timing belt to ensure that the tension side of the belt is taut and move the timing belt tension adjusting lever clockwise until the tensioner pointer is flowing.

15. If installing a used timing belt (used over 60 min. from new), the pointer should be positioned approximately 0.16 in. (4mm) to the left of the "V" notch when viewed from the front of the engine.

16. If installing a new timing belt, the pointer should be positioned at the center of the "V" notch when viewed from the front of the engine.

17. Torque the timing belt tensioner adjusting bolt to 18 ft. lbs. (25 Nm).

18. Install the timing belt front cover and torque the bolts to 53 inch lbs. (6 Nm).

19. Install the engine harness connectors.

20. Install the crankshaft pulley and toque the pulley-to-crankshaft bolts to 14 ft. lbs. (20 Nm).

21. Move the drive belt tensioner to the loose side and install the drive belt to its normal position.

22. Connect the negative battery cable.

Infiniti QX4

3.3L (VG33E) ENGINE

1. Remove the engine undercover.

2. Remove the radiator shroud, the fan and the pulleys.

3. Drain the coolant from the radiator and remove the water pump hose.

✳✳ CAUTION

When draining the coolant, keep in mind that cats and dogs are attracted by the ethylene glycol antifreeze, and are quite likely to drink any that is left in an uncovered container or in puddles on the ground. This will prove fatal in sufficient quantity. Always drain the coolant into a sealable container. Coolant should be reused unless it is contaminated or several years old.

4. Remove the radiator.

5. Remove the power steering, air conditioning compressor and alternator drive belts.

6. Remove the spark plugs.

7. Remove the distributor protector (dust shield).

8. Remove the air conditioning compressor drive belt idler pulley and bracket.

9. Remove the fresh air intake tube at the cylinder head cover.

10. Disconnect the radiator hose at the thermostat housing.

11. Remove the crankshaft pulley bolt, then pull off the pulley with a suitable puller.

12. Remove the bolts, then remove the front upper and lower timing belt covers.

13. Set the No. 1 piston at Top Dead Center (TDC) of its compression stroke. Align the punchmark on the left camshaft sprocket with the punchmark on the timing belt upper rear cover. Align the punchmark on the crankshaft sprocket with the notch on the oil pump housing. Temporarily install the crank pulley bolt so the crankshaft can be rotated if necessary.

14. Loosen the timing belt tensioner and return spring, then remove the timing belt.

To install:

✳✳ CAUTION

Before installing the timing belt, confirm that the No. 1 cylinder is set at the TDC of the compression stroke.

15. Remove both cylinder head covers and loosen all rocker arm shaft retaining bolts.

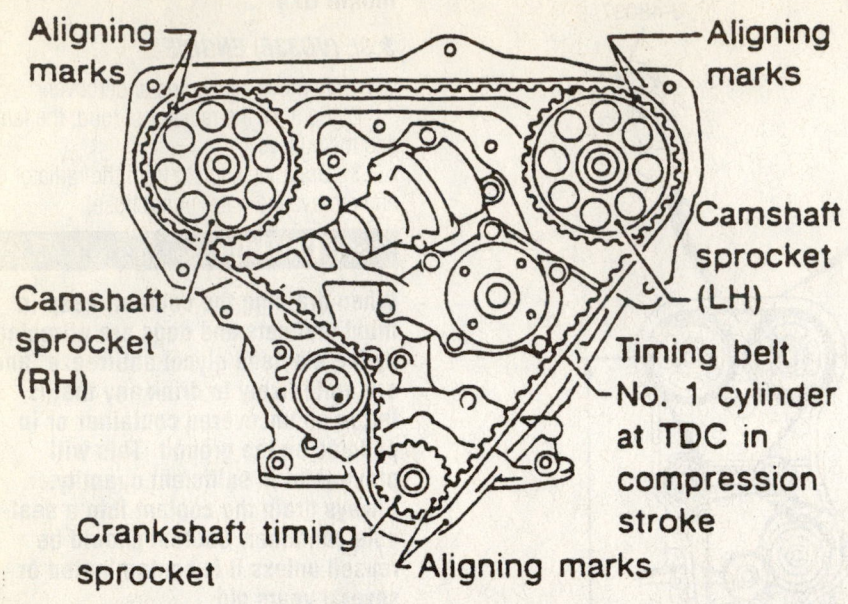

Aligning marks

Aligning marks

Camshaft sprocket (RH)

Camshaft sprocket (LH)

Timing belt No. 1 cylinder at TDC in compression stroke

Crankshaft timing sprocket

Aligning marks

79245G35

Timing belt alignment mark locations—Infiniti QX4 3.3L engine

➡The rocker arm shaft bolts MUST be loosened so that the correct belt tension can be obtained.

16. Install the tensioner and the return spring. Using a hexagon wrench, turn the tensioner clockwise and temporarily tighten the locknut.

17. Be sure that the timing belt is clean and free from oil or water.

18. When installing the timing belt, align the white lines on the belt with the punch-marks on the camshaft and crankshaft sprockets. Have the arrow on the timing belt pointing toward the front belt covers.

➡A good way (although rather tedious!) to check for proper timing belt installation is to count the number of belt teeth between the timing marks. There are 133 teeth on the belt; there should be 40 teeth between the timing marks on the left and right side camshaft sprockets, and 43 teeth between the timing marks on the left side camshaft sprocket and the crankshaft sprocket.

19. While keeping the tensioner steady, loosen the locknut with a hex wrench.

20. Turn the tensioner approximately 70–80 degrees clockwise with the wrench, then tighten the locknut.

✷✷ WARNING

If any binding is felt when adjusting the timing belt tension by turning the crankshaft, STOP turning the engine, because the pistons may be hitting the valves.

21. Turn the crankshaft in a clockwise direction several times, then **slowly** set the No. 1 piston to TDC of the compression stroke.

22. Apply 22 lbs. (10 kg) of pressure (push it in!) to the center span of the timing belt between the right side camshaft sprocket and the tensioner pulley, then loosen the tensioner locknut.

23. Using a 0.0138 in. (0.35mm) thick feeler gauge (the actual width of the blade **must** be ½ in. or 13mm!), turn the crankshaft clockwise (**slowly!**). The timing belt should move approximately 2½ teeth. Tighten the tensioner locknut, turn the crankshaft slightly and remove the feeler gauge.

24. Slowly rotate the crankshaft clockwise several more times, then set the No. 1 piston to TDC of the compression stroke.

25. Position the 2 timing covers on the block, then tighten the mounting bolts to 24 ft. lbs. (35 Nm).

26. Press the crankshaft pulley onto the shaft, then tighten the bolt to 90–98 ft. lbs. (123–132 Nm).

27. Connect the radiator hose to the thermostat housing.

28. Reconnect the fresh air intake tube at the cylinder head cover.

29. Install the air conditioning compressor drive belt idler pulley and bracket.

30. Install the distributor protector (dust shield).

31. Install the spark plugs.

32. Install the power steering, air conditioning compressor and alternator drive belts.

33. Install the radiator.

34. Reconnect the water pump hose and fill the engine with coolant. Install the fan shroud and pulleys.

35. Install the engine undercover.

36. Start the engine and check for any leaks.

Isuzu Amigo, Rodeo and Trooper

1998–01 2.2L (X22SE/D) ENGINE

1. Disconnect the negative battery cable.

2. Using a box-end wrench on the drive belt adjuster, turn the adjuster clockwise and remove the drive belt.

3. From the left rear of the engine compartment, disconnect the 3 electrical connectors from the chassis harness.

4. Remove the crankshaft pulley-to-crankshaft bolts and remove the pulley.

5. From the front of the engine, remove the nut and the engine harness cover.

6. Remove the timing belt cover.

7. Rotate the crankshaft to position the timing marks at Top Dead Center (TDC) of the No. 1 cylinder's compression stroke.

➡Mark the rotational direction of the timing belt for reinstallation purposes.

8. Remove the timing belt tensioner adjusting bolt and the tensioner from the engine.

9. Remove the timing belt.

To install:

10. Install the timing belt tensioner and finger-tighten the tensioner bolt.

11. Inspect the timing marks to be sure that the engine is positioned at TDC of the No. 1 cylinder's compression stroke.

12. Using tool J-43037, or equivalent, place it between the intake and exhaust sprockets to prevent the camshaft gear from moving during the timing belt installation.

13. Install the timing belt.

14. Position the timing belt to ensure that the tension side of the belt is taut and move the timing belt tension adjusting lever clockwise until the tensioner pointer is flowing.

15. If installing a used timing belt (used over 60 min. from new), the pointer should be positioned approximately 0.16 in. (4mm) to the left of the "V" notch when viewed from the front of the engine.

16. If installing a new timing belt, the pointer should be positioned at the center of the "V" notch when viewed from the front of the engine.

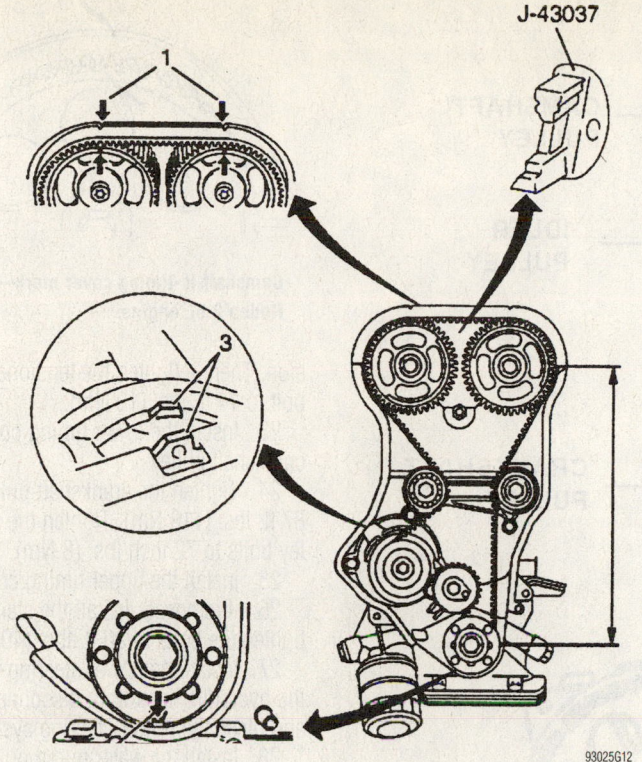

Aligning the timing marks and installing the timing belt—Isuzu Amigo and Rodeo 2.2L (X22SE/D) engine

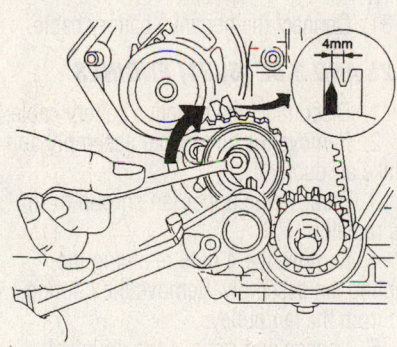

Tensioning the timing belt for a used timing belt—Isuzu Amigo and Rodeo 2.2L (X22SE/D) engine

17. Torque the timing belt tensioner adjusting bolt to 18 ft. lbs. (25 Nm).

18. Install the timing belt front cover and torque the bolts to 53 inch lbs. (6 Nm).

19. Install the engine harness connectors.

20. Install the crankshaft pulley and toque the pulley-to-crankshaft bolts to 14 ft. lbs. (20 Nm).

21. Move the drive belt tensioner to the loose side and install the drive belt to its normal position.

22. Connect the negative battery cable.

2.6L ENGINE

1. Disconnect the negative battery cable.

2. Loosen and remove the engine accessory drive belts.

3. Remove the cooling fan assembly and the water pump pulley.

4. Drain the fluid from the power steering reservoir.

5. Unbolt and remove the power steering pump. Unbolt the hydraulic line brackets from the upper timing cover and move the pump out of the work area without disconnecting the hydraulic lines.

6. Disconnect and remove the starter motor if a flywheel holder tool No. J-38674, or equivalent, is to be used.

7. Remove the upper timing belt cover.

8. Rotate the crankshaft to set the engine at Top Dead Center (TDC) of its compression for the No. 1 cylinder. The arrow mark on the camshaft sprocket will be aligned with the mark on the rear timing cover.

9. Remove the crankshaft pulley.

10. Remove the lower timing belt cover.

11. Verify that the engine is set at TDC/compression for the No. 1 cylinder. The notch on the crankshaft sprocket will be aligned with the pointer on the oil seal retainer.

12. Release and remove the tensioner spring to release the timing belt's tension.

13. Remove the timing belt.

14. Unbolt the tensioner pulley bracket from the engine's front cover.

15. If necessary, unbolt and remove the camshaft sprockets. Use a puller to remove the crankshaft pulley if necessary. Don't lose the crankshaft sprocket key.

To install:

16. If removed, install the camshaft and crankshaft sprockets. Align the camshaft and crankshaft timing marks and be sure to install any keys. Tighten the camshaft sprocket bolt to 43 ft. lbs. (59 Nm).

17. Install the tensioner assembly. Tighten the tensioner mounting bolt to 14 ft. lbs. (19 Nm) and the cap bolt to 108 inch lbs. (13 Nm).

18. Be sure the crankshaft and the camshaft sprockets are aligned with their timing marks. Install the timing belt onto the sprockets using the following sequence: first around the crankshaft sprocket; second around the oil pump sprocket; third around the camshaft sprocket.

19. Loosen the tensioner mounting bolt. This will allow the tensioner spring to apply pressure to the timing belt.

20. After the spring has pulled the timing belt as far as possible, temporarily tighten the tensioner mounting bolt to 14 ft. lbs. (19 Nm).

➡**Remove the flywheel holder before rotating the crankshaft. Reinstall the holder to tighten the crankshaft pulley bolt.**

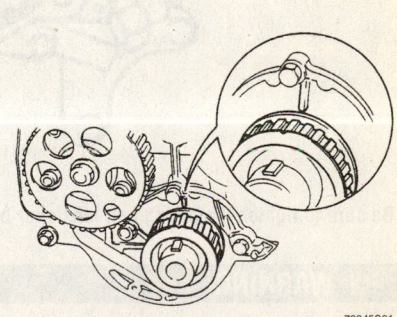

Align the crankshaft pulley timing mark the with oil retainer setting mark—Isuzu Rodeo 2.6L engine

Refer to the model specific sections for engine mechanical service procedures

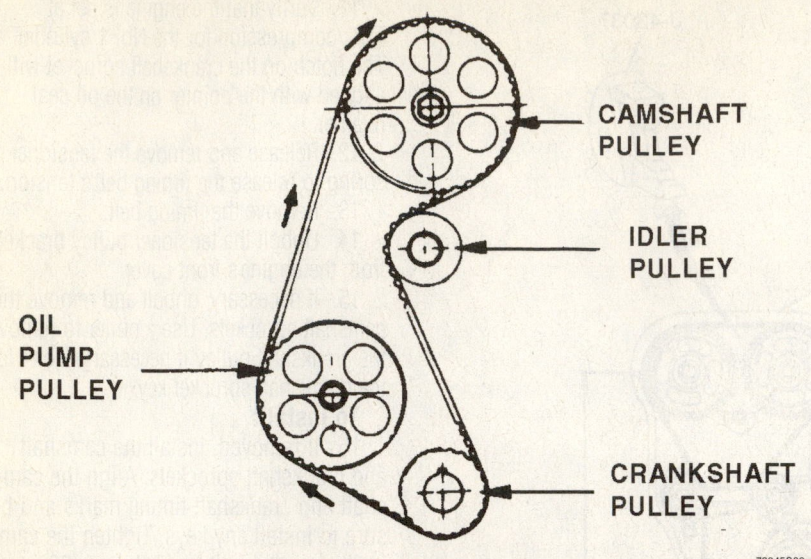

CAMSHAFT PULLEY

IDLER PULLEY

OIL PUMP PULLEY

CRANKSHAFT PULLEY

Timing belt direction of travel—Isuzu Rodeo 2.6L engine

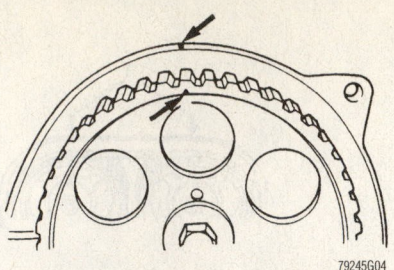

Camshaft-to-timing cover mark—Isuzu Rodeo 2.6L engine

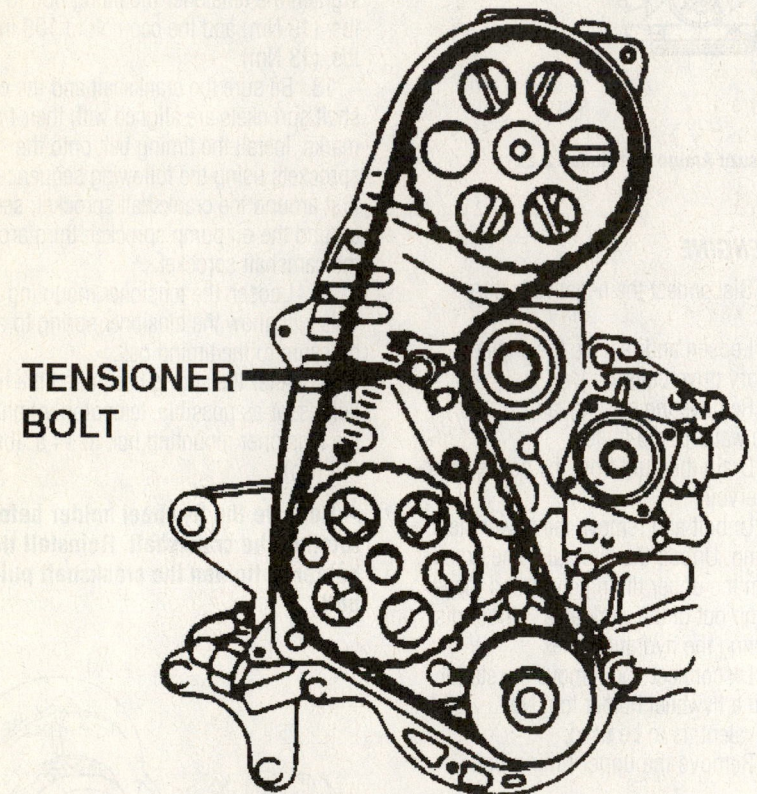

TENSIONER BOLT

Be sure to tighten the timing belt tensioner bolt (B)—Isuzu Rodeo 2.6L engine

❋❋ WARNING

If any binding is felt when adjusting the timing belt tension by turning the crankshaft, STOP turning the engine, because the pistons may be hitting the valves.

21. Rotate the crankshaft counterclockwise 2 complete revolutions to check the rotation of the belt and the alignment of the timing marks. Listen for any rubbing noises which may mean the belt is binding.

22. Loosen the tensioner pulley bolt to allow the spring to adjust the correct tension. Then, retighten the tensioner pulley bolt to 14 ft. lbs. (19 Nm).

23. Install the lower timing cover and the crankshaft pulley.

24. Tighten the crankshaft pulley bolt to 87 ft. lbs. (118 Nm). Tighten the small pulley bolts to 72 inch lbs. (8 Nm).

25. Install the upper timing cover.

26. If removed, install the starter and tighten the bolts to 30 ft. lbs. (40 Nm).

27. Install the power steering pump. If the hydraulic lines were disconnected, refill and bleed the power steering system.

28. Install the water pump pulley and tighten its nut to 20 ft. lbs. (26 Nm).

29. Install the cooling fan assembly.

30. Install and adjust the accessory drive belts.

31. Connect the negative battery cable.

3.2L AND 3.5L (6VE1) ENGINES

1. Disconnect the negative battery cable.

2. Remove the air cleaner assembly and intake air duct.

3. Remove the upper fan shroud from the radiator.

4. Remove the 4 nuts retaining the cooling fan assembly. Remove the cooling fan from the fan pulley.

5. Loosen and remove the drive belts.

6. Remove the upper timing belt covers.

7. Remove the fan pulley assembly.

8. Rotate the crankshaft to align the camshaft timing marks with the pointer dots on the back covers. Verify that the pointer on the crankshaft aligns with the mark on the lower timing cover.

➡**When the timing marks are aligned, the No. 2 piston is at Top Dead Center (TDC) compression.**

❋❋ WARNING

Align the camshaft and crankshaft sprockets with their alignment marks before removing the timing belt. Failure to align the belt and sprocket marks may result in valve damage.

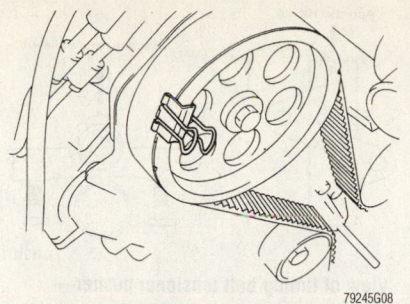

79245G08

Using a double clip to hold the belt in place—Isuzu Amigo, Rodeo and 1997 Trooper 3.2L and 1998–01 Trooper 3.5L (6VE1) engines

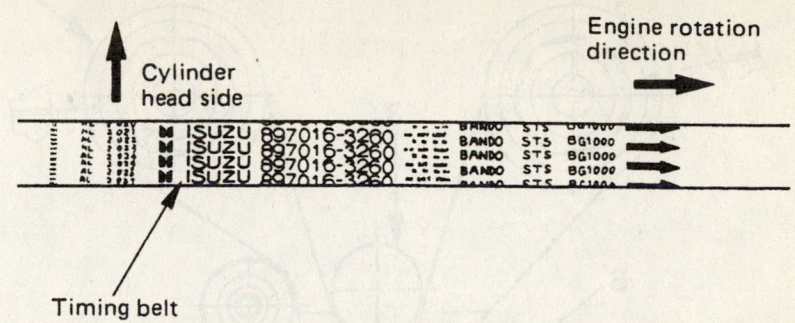

79245G07

For maximum timing belt life, install the belt as shown—Isuzu Amigo, Rodeo and 1997 Trooper 3.2L and 1998–01 Trooper 3.5L (6VE1) engines

9. Use tool No. J-8614-01, or a suitable pulley holding tool to remove the crankshaft pulley center bolt. Remove the crankshaft pulley.

10. If present, disconnect the 2 oil cooler hose bracket bolts on the timing cover. Move the oil cooler hoses and bracket off of the lower timing cover.

11. Remove the lower timing belt cover.

12. Remove the pusher assembly (tensioner) from below the belt tensioner pulley. The pusher rod must always face upward to prevent oil leakage. Depress the pusher rod, and insert a wire pin into the hole to keep the pusher rod retracted.

13. Remove the timing belt.

14. Inspect the water pump and replace it if there is any doubt about its condition.

15. Repair any oil or coolant leaks before installing a new timing belt. If the timing belt has been contaminated with oil or coolant, or is damaged, it must be replaced.

To install:

16. Verify that the sprocket timing marks are still aligned and that the groove and the keyway on the crankshaft timing sprocket align with the mark on the oil pump. The white

pointers on the camshaft timing sprockets should align with the dots on the front plate.

17. Install the timing belt. Use clips to secure the belt onto each sprocket until the installation is complete. Align the dotted marks on the timing belt with the timing mark opposite the groove on the crankshaft sprocket.

➡ **The arrows on the timing belt must follow the belt's direction of rotation. The manufacturer's trademark on the belt's spine should be readable left-to-right when the belt is installed.**

18. Align the white line on the timing belt with the alignment mark on the right bank camshaft timing pulley. Secure the belt with a clip.

✴✴ WARNING

If any binding is felt when adjusting the timing belt tension by turning the

crankshaft, STOP turning the engine, because the pistons may be hitting the valves.

19. Rotate the crankshaft counterclockwise to remove the slack between the crankshaft sprocket and the right camshaft timing belt sprocket.

20. Install the belt around the water pump pulley.

21. Install the belt on the idler pulley.

22. Align the white alignment mark on the timing belt with the alignment mark on the left bank camshaft timing belt sprocket.

23. Install the crankshaft pulley and tighten the center bolt by hand. Rotate the crankshaft pulley clockwise to give slack between the crankshaft timing belt pulley and the right bank camshaft timing belt pulley.

24. Insert a 1.4mm piece of wire through the hole in the pusher to hold the rod in.

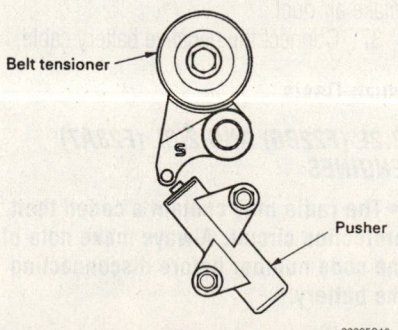

93025G10

View of timing belt tensioner and pusher—Isuzu Amigo, Rodeo and 1997 Trooper 3.2L and 1998–01 Trooper 3.5L (6VE1) engines

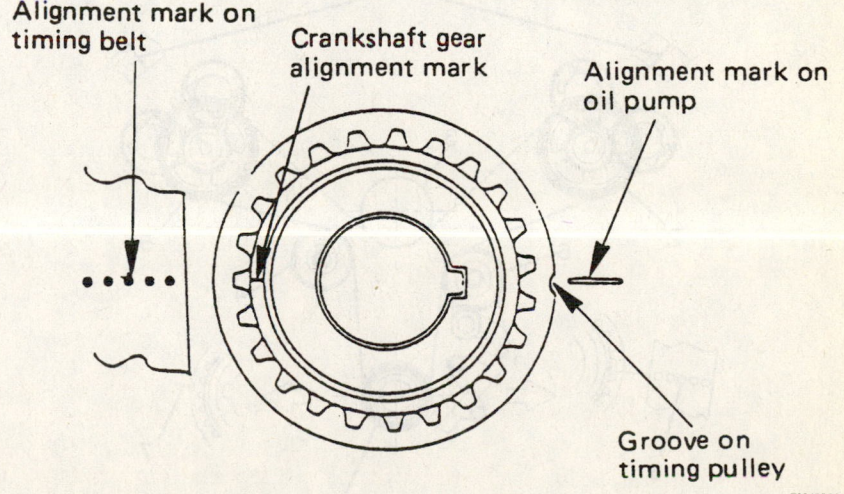

79245G06

Proper crankshaft alignment marks for timing belt installation—Isuzu 1997 Rodeo and Trooper 3.2L SOHC (VIN V) engine

For accessory drive belt replacement procedures see the model specific sections of this manual

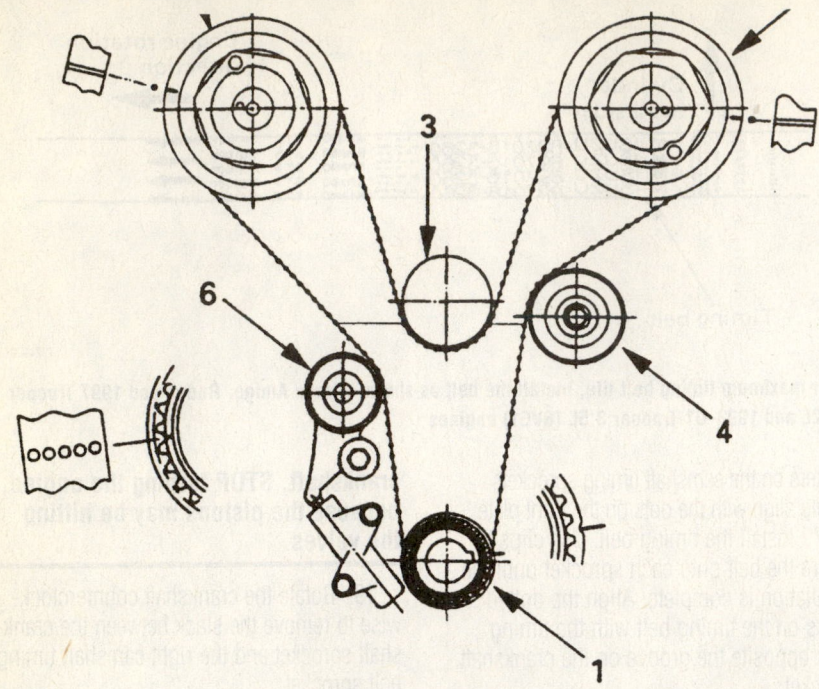

1) **Crankshaft timing pulley**
2) **RH bank timing pulley**
3) **Water pump pulley**
4) **Idler pulley**
5) **LH bank timing pulley**
6) **Tension pulley**

93025G09

Timing mark alignment and timing belt routing—Isuzu 1997 Rodeo and Trooper 3.2L SOHC (VIN V) engine

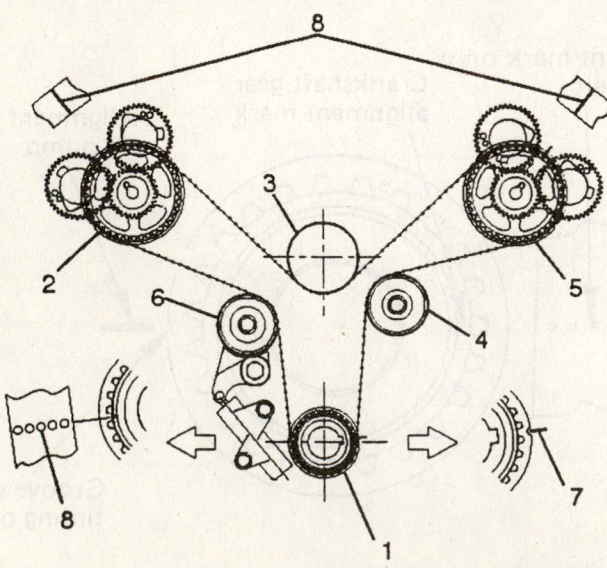

93025G11

Timing mark alignment and timing belt routing—Isuzu 1998–01 Amigo and Rodeo 3.2L DOHC (VIN W) and 1998–01 Trooper 3.5L DOHC (6VE1) engines

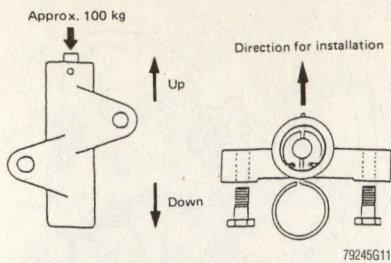

79245G11

View of timing belt tensioner pusher— Isuzu Amigo, Rodeo and 1997 Trooper 3.2L and 1998–01 Trooper 3.5L (6VE1) engines

Install the pusher assembly while pushing the tension pulley toward the belt.

25. Pull the pin out from the pusher to release the rod.

26. Remove the clamps from the sprockets. Rotate the crankshaft pulley clockwise 2 turns. Measure the rod protrusion to ensure it is between 0.16–0.24 in. (4–6mm).

27. If the tensioner pulley bracket pivot bolt was removed, tighten it to 31 ft. lbs. (42 Nm).

28. Tighten the pusher bolts to 14 ft. lbs. (19 Nm).

29. Remove the crankshaft pulley. Install the lower and upper timing belt covers and tighten their bolts to 12 ft. lbs. (17 Nm).

30. Fit the oil cooler hose onto the timing cover and tighten its mounting bracket bolts to 16 ft. lbs. (22 Nm).

31. Install the crankshaft pulley and tighten the pulley bolt to 123 ft. lbs. (167 Nm).

32. Install fan pulley assembly and tighten the bolts to 16 ft. lbs. (22 Nm).

33. Install and adjust the accessory drive belts.

34. Install the cooling fan assembly and tighten the bolts to 72 inch lbs. (8 Nm).

35. Install the upper fan shroud.

36. Install the air cleaner assembly and intake air duct.

37. Connect the negative battery cable.

Isuzu Oasis

2.2L (F22B6) AND 2.3L (F23A7) ENGINES

➡**The radio may contain a coded theft protection circuit. Always make note of the code number before disconnecting the battery.**

1. Disconnect the negative and positive battery cables.

2. Remove the valve cover.

3. Remove the upper timing belt cover.

4. Turn the engine to align the timing marks and set cylinder No.1 to Top Dead

Center (TDC) for the compression stroke. The white mark on the crankshaft pulley should align with the pointer on the timing belt cover. The words **UP** embossed on the camshaft pulley should be aligned in the upward position. The marks on the edge of the pulley should be aligned with the cylinder head or the back cover upper edge. Once in this position, the engine must NOT be turned or disturbed.

5. Remove the splash shield from below the engine.

6. Remove the wheel well splash shield.

7. Loosen and remove the power steering pump belt. Remove the power steering pump.

8. Loosen the adjusting and mounting bolts for the alternator and remove the drive belt.

9. Support the engine with a floor jack cushioned with a piece of wood.

10. Remove the through-bolt for the side engine mount and remove the mount.

11. Remove the crankshaft pulley bolt and remove the crankshaft pulley. Use a Crank Pulley Holder tool No. 07MAB-PY3010A and Holder Handle tool No. 07JAB-001020A or their equivalents, to

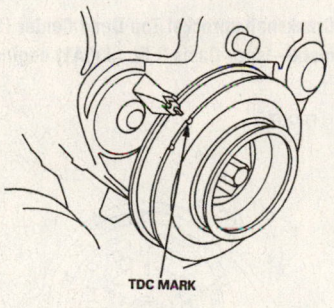

TDC MARK

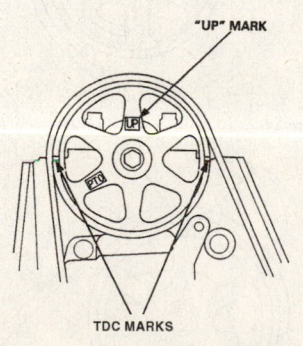

"UP" MARK

TDC MARKS

79245G24

Align the camshaft, crankshaft and engine marks before removing the timing belt and pulleys—Isuzu Oasis 2.2L and 2.3L engines

hold the crankshaft pulley in place while removing the bolt.

12. Remove the lower timing belt cover.

13. Remove the balancer shaft belt and its drive pulley.

14. Insert a suitable tool into the maintenance hole in the front balancer shaft. Unbolt and remove the balancer driven pulley.

➡**For servicing the balance shafts, front refers to the side of the engine facing the radiator. Rear refers to the side of the engine facing the firewall.**

15. Remove the timing belt.

16. If equipped with a TDC sensor assembly at the crankshaft sprocket, unbolt the assembly and move it aside before removing the sprocket.

17. Remove the key and the spacers to remove the crankshaft timing sprocket.

18. Unbolt and remove the camshaft timing sprocket.

To install:

19. Install the camshaft timing sprocket so that the **UP** mark is up and the TDC marks are parallel to the cylinder head gasket surface. Install the key and tighten the bolt to 27 ft. lbs. (37 Nm).

20. Install the crankshaft timing sprocket so that the TDC mark aligns with the pointer on the oil pump. Install the spacers with their concave surfaces facing in. Install the key. Install the TDC sensor assembly back into position before installing the timing belt.

21. Install and tension the timing belt.

22. Rotate the crankshaft counterclockwise 5–6 turns to be sure the belt is properly seated.

23. Set the No. 1 piston at TDC for its compression stroke.

✳✳ **WARNING**

If any binding is felt when adjusting the timing belt tension by turning the crankshaft, STOP turning the engine, because the pistons may be hitting the valves.

24. Rotate the crankshaft counterclockwise so that the camshaft pulley moves only 3 teeth beyond its TDC mark.

25. Tighten the tensioner adjusting nut to 33 ft. lbs. (45 Nm).

26. Tighten the crankshaft pulley bolt to 181 ft. lbs. (245 Nm).

27. Install the balancer shaft belt drive pulley.

28. Align the groove on the pulley edge to the pointer on the balancer gear case.

29. Check the alignment of the pointer on the balancer pulley to the pointer on the oil pump.

30. Install and tension the balancer shaft belt.

31. Be sure the timing belts have been tensioned correctly and that all TDC and alignment marks are in their proper positions.

32. Install the lower timing cover and the crankshaft pulley. Apply engine oil to the pulley bolt threads and washer surface. Install the pulley bolt and tighten it to 181 ft. lbs. (245 Nm).

33. Install the upper timing cover and the valve cover. Be sure the seals are properly seated.

34. Install the side engine mount. Tighten the through-bolt to 47 ft. lbs. (64 Nm). Tighten the mount nut and bolt to 40 ft. lbs. (55 Nm) each.

35. Remove the floor jack.

36. Install and tension the alternator belt.

37. Install the power steering pump and tension its belt.

38. Install the splash shields.

39. Reconnect the positive and negative battery cables. Enter the radio security code.

40. Check engine operation.

1999–01 3.5L (J35A1) V6 ENGINE

➡**The radio may contain a coded theft protection circuit. Always make note the code number before disconnecting the battery.**

1. Disconnect the negative battery terminal.

2. Turn the crankshaft so the white mark on the crankshaft pulley aligns with the pointer on the oil pump housing cover.

3. Open the inspection plug on the upper cover of the cam covers and check that the camshaft sprocket marks align with the upper cover marks.

✳✳ **WARNING**

Align the camshaft and crankshaft sprockets with their alignment marks before removing the timing belt. Failure to align the timing marks correctly may result in valve damage.

4. Raise and safely support the vehicle and remove both front tires/wheels.

5. Remove the front lower splash shield.

6. Move the alternator tensioner with a

Belt Tensioner Release Arm tool YA9317, or equivalent, to release tension from the belt and remove the alternator belt.

7. Remove the alternator belt tensioner release arm.

8. Loosen the power steering pump adjustment nut, adjustment locknut, and mounting bolt, then remove the power steering pump with the hoses attached.

9. Support the weight of the engine by placing a wood block on a floor jack and carefully lift on the oil pan.

10. Remove the bolts from the side engine mount bracket and remove the bracket.

11. Remove the dipstick, the dipstick tube and discard the O-ring.

12. Hold the crankshaft pulley with Handle tool 07JAB-001020A and Crankshaft Holding tool 07MAB-PY3010A, or equivalent. While holding the crankshaft pulley, remove the crankshaft pulley bolt using a heavy duty ¾ in. (19mm) socket and breaker bar.

13. Remove the crankshaft pulley, the upper timing belt covers and the lower timing belt cover.

14. Remove one of the battery hold-down fasteners from the battery tray and grind a 45 degree bevel on the threaded end of the battery hold-down bolt.

15. Screw in the battery hold-down bolt into the threaded bracket just above the auto-tensioner, (automatic timing belt adjuster), and tighten the bolt hand-tight to hold the auto-tensioner adjuster in its current position.

16. Remove the engine mount bracket bolts and the bracket.

17. Loosen the timing belt idler pulley bolt (located on the right side across from the auto-tensioner pulley) about 5–6 revolutions and remove the timing belt.

To install:

18. Clean the timing belt sprockets and the timing belt covers.

✳✳ WARNING

Align the camshaft and crankshaft sprockets with their alignment marks before installing the timing belt. Failure to align the timing marks correctly may result in valve damage.

19. Align the timing mark on the crankshaft sprocket with the oil pump pointer.

20. Align the camshaft sprocket TDC timing marks with the pointers on the rear cover.

21. If installing a new belt or if the auto-

tensioner has extended or if the timing belt cannot be reinstalled easily, the auto-tensioner must be collapsed before installation of the timing belt, perform the following procedures:

a. Remove the battery hold-down bolt from the auto-tensioner bracket.

b. Remove the timing belt auto-tensioner bolts and the auto-tensioner.

c. Secure the auto-tensioner in a soft jawed vise, clamping onto the flat surface of one of the mounting bolt holes with the maintenance bolt facing upward.

d. Remove the maintenance bolt and use caution not to spill oil from the tensioner assembly.

e. Should oil spill from the tensioner, be sure the tensioner is filled with 0.22 ounces (6.5 ml) of fresh engine oil.

f. Using care not to damage the threads or the gasket sealing surface,

FRONT CAMSHAFT PULLEY:

REAR CAMSHAFT PULLEY:

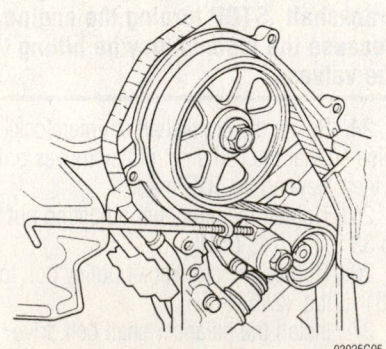

93025G04

Crankshaft and camshaft timing marks at Top Dead Center (TDC)—Isuzu Oasis 3.5L (J35A1) engine

insert a flat-blade screwdriver through the tensioner maintenance hole and turn the screwdriver clockwise to compress the auto-tensioner bottom while the tensioner holder tool 14540-P8A-A01, or equivalent, is installed on the auto-tensioner assembly.

g. Install the auto-tensioner maintenance bolt with a new gasket and tighten to a torque 72 inch lbs. (8 Nm).

h. Install the auto-tensioner on the engine with the tensioner holder tool installed and torque the mounting bolts to 104 inch lbs. (12 Nm).

22. Install the timing belt in a counterclockwise pattern starting with the crankshaft drive sprocket. Install the timing belt counterclockwise in the following sequence:

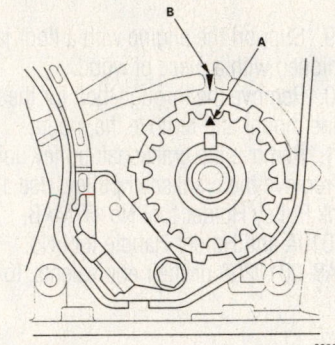

93025G06

Crankshaft sprocket Top Dead Center (TDC) mark—Isuzu Oasis 3.5L (J35A1) engine

FRONT:

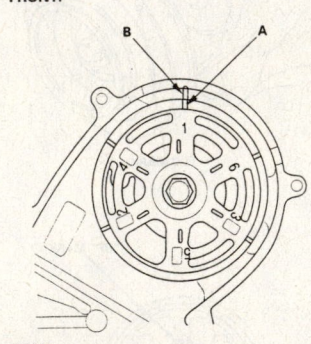

REAR:

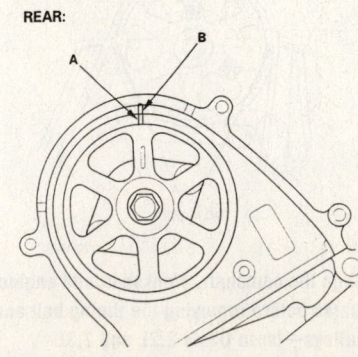

93025G07

Camshaft sprocket Top Dead Center (TDC) mark—Isuzu Oasis 3.5L (J35A1) engine

Battery hold-down bolt installed to hold auto-tensioner—Isuzu Oasis 3.5L (J35A1) engine

93025G05

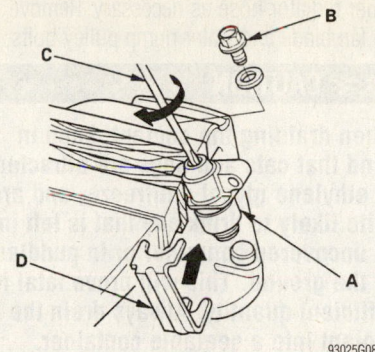

Adjusting the auto-tensioner—Isuzu Oasis 3.5L (J35A1) engine

- Crankshaft drive sprocket.
- Idler pulley.
- Left side camshaft sprocket.
- Water pump.
- Right side camshaft sprocket.
- Auto-tensioner adjustment pulley.

23. Torque the timing belt idler pulley bolt to 33 ft. lbs. (44 Nm).

24. Remove the auto-tensioner holding tool to allow the tensioner to extend.

25. Install the engine mount bracket to the engine and torque the bolts to 33 ft. lbs. (44 Nm).

26. Install the lower timing belt cover and both upper timing belt covers.

27. Hold the crankshaft pulley with Handle tool 07JAB-001020A and Crankshaft Holding tool 07MAB-PY3010A, or equivalent tools. While holding the crankshaft pulley, install the crankshaft pulley bolt using a heavy duty ¾ in. (19mm) socket and a commercially available torque wrench and torque the bolt to 181 ft. lbs. (245 Nm).

✱✱ WARNING

If any binding is felt while moving the crankshaft pulley, STOP turning the crankshaft pulley immediately because the pistons may be hitting the valves.

28. Rotate the crankshaft pulley clockwise 5–6 revolutions to allow the timing belt to be seated in the pulleys.

29. Move the crankshaft pulley to the white TDC mark and inspect the camshaft TDC marks to ensure proper timing of the camshafts.

✱✱ WARNING

If the timing marks do not align, the timing belt removal and installation

procedure must be performed again.

30. Install the engine dipstick tube using a new O-ring.

31. Install the power steering pump, and loosely install the mounting bolt, adjustment locknut and adjustment nut.

32. Adjust the power steering belt to a tension such that a 22 lb. (98 N) pull halfway between the 2 drive pulleys will allow the belt to move 0.51–0.65 in. (13.0–16.5mm).

33. Tighten the power steering pump mounting bolt and adjustment locknut.

➡**If a new belt is used, set the deflection to 0.33–0.43 in. (8.5–11.0mm) and after engine has run for 5 minutes, readjust the new belt to the used belt specification.**

34. Install the alternator belt tensioner arm.

35. Move the alternator tensioner with a Belt Tensioner Release Arm tool YA9317, or equivalent, to release tension from the belt and install the alternator drive belt.

36. Install the 2 bolts for the engine mount bracket and torque to 33 ft. lbs. (44 Nm).

37. Install the bushing through bolt and tighten to 40 ft. lbs. (54 Nm).

38. Release and carefully remove the floor jack.

39. Install the front lower splash shield.

40. Install both front tires/wheels.

41. Carefully lower the vehicle.

42. Install the battery clamp bolt in the battery tray.

43. Install the negative battery cable.

44. Enter the radio security code.

KIA Sportage

2.0L (DOHC) ENGINE

1. Disconnect the negative battery cable.

2. Properly relieve the fuel system pressure.

3. Remove the alternator drive belt.

4. Remove the fresh air duct from the top of the radiator.

5. Remove the upper radiator hose.

6. Remove the 4 attaching nuts to the clutch fan.

7. Remove the 5 fan shroud bolts. Remove the fan and shroud as an assembly.

8. Remove the 4 splash guard mounting bolts and the splash guard.

9. Loosen the lockbolts and loosen the air conditioning drive belt.

10. Loosen the power steering lock and mounting bolt. Remove the power steering belt.

11. Remove the 5 upper timing belt cover bolts and remove the cover.

12. Remove the 2 lower timing belt cover bolts and remove the cover.

13. Align the timing marks.

➡**When aligning the cam pulleys with the seal plate marks, align the left cam pulley I mark and the right cam pulley on the E mark.**

✱✱ WARNING

When aligning the timing marks, do not turn the timing gear counterclockwise. Damage to the engine will occur.

14. Loosen the tensioner bolt. Pry the tensioner away from the belt. Tighten the tensioner bolt to relieve the pressure against the timing belt.

15. Remove the timing belt.

16. Remove the camshaft pulley attaching bolts. Use a driver placed through one

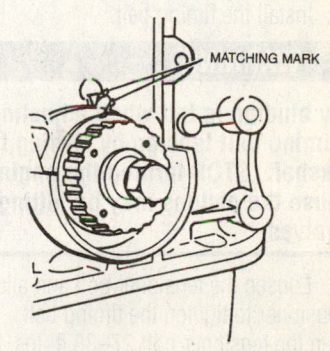

Align the crankshaft marks before removing the timing belt—KIA Sportage 2.0L (DOHC) engine

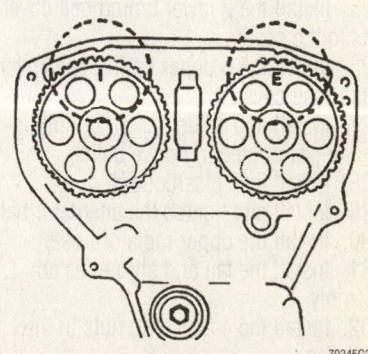

Proper alignment of the intake and exhaust camshaft pulley timing marks—KIA Sportage 2.0L (DOHC) engine

Timing chain and gear service is covered in the model specific sections of this manual

of the holes in the pulley to prevent it from moving when the attaching bolt is removed. Remove and mark the pulleys.

17. Remove the lower timing belt pulley and locking bolt.

To install:

18. Install the camshaft pulleys. Tighten the bolts to 35–48 ft. lbs. (47–65 Nm).

19. Install the lower timing belt pulley and locking bolt. Tighten the bolt to 120 ft. lbs. (162 Nm).

20. If necessary, align the timing marks.

➡When aligning the cam pulleys with the seal plate marks, align the left cam pulley "I" mark and the right cam pulley on the "E" mark.

✳✳ WARNING

When aligning the timing marks, do not turn the timing gear counterclockwise. Damage to the engine will occur.

21. Loosen the tensioner bolt. Pry the tensioner away from the belt. Tighten tensioner bolt to relieve the pressure against the timing belt.

22. Install the timing belt.

✳✳ WARNING

If any binding is felt when adjusting the timing belt tension by turning the crankshaft, STOP turning the engine, because the pistons may be hitting the valves.

23. Loosen the tensioner bolt and allow the tensioner to tighten the timing belt. Tighten the tensioner bolt 27–38 ft. lbs. (37–52 Nm).

24. Check the timing belt deflection. If there is more than 0.30–0.33 in. (7.5–8.5mm) replace the tensioner spring.

25. Install the 2 lower timing belt cover bolts to the cover.

26. Install the 5 upper timing belt cover bolts to the cover.

27. Install and adjust the air conditioning and power steering drive belts.

28. Install the splash guard.

29. Install and tighten the alternator belt.

30. Install the upper radiator hose.

31. Install the fan and shroud as an assembly.

32. Install the 4 attaching nuts to the clutch fan.

33. Install the 5 fan shroud bolts.

34. Install the fresh air duct to the top of the radiator.

35. Properly fill the cooling system.

36. Connect the negative battery cable.

37. Start the engine and check for leaks.

38. Road test the vehicle.

Mazda B-Series Pick-Ups

1997 2.3L (VIN A) AND 1998–01 2.5L (VIN C) ENGINES

1. Rotate the engine so that No. 1 cylinder is at Top Dead Center (TDC) on the compression stroke. Check that the timing marks are aligned on the camshaft and crankshaft pulleys. An access plug is provided in the cam belt cover so that the camshaft timing can be checked without removal of the cover or any other parts. Set the crankshaft to TDC by aligning the timing mark on the crank pulley with the TDC mark on the belt cover. Look through the access hole in the belt cover to be sure that the timing mark on the cam drive sprocket is aligned with the pointer on the inner belt cover.

➡Always turn the engine in the normal direction of rotation. Backward rotation may cause the timing belt to jump time, due to the arrangement of the belt tensioner.

2. Drain cooling system. Remove the upper radiator hose as necessary. Remove the fan blade and water pump pulley bolts.

✳✳ CAUTION

When draining the coolant, keep in mind that cats and dogs are attracted by ethylene glycol antifreeze, and are quite likely to drink any that is left in an uncovered container or in puddles on the ground. This will prove fatal in sufficient quantity. Always drain the coolant into a sealable container. Coolant should be reused unless it is contaminated or several years old.

3. Loosen the alternator retaining bolts and remove the drive belt from the pulleys. Remove the water pump pulley.

4. Remove the power steering pump and set it aside.

5. Remove the 4 timing belt outer cover retaining bolts and remove the cover. Remove the crankshaft pulley and belt guide.

6. Loosen the belt tensioner pulley assembly, then position a Camshaft Belt Adjuster tool T74P-6254-A, or equivalent, on the tension spring roll pin and retract the belt tensioner away from the timing belt.

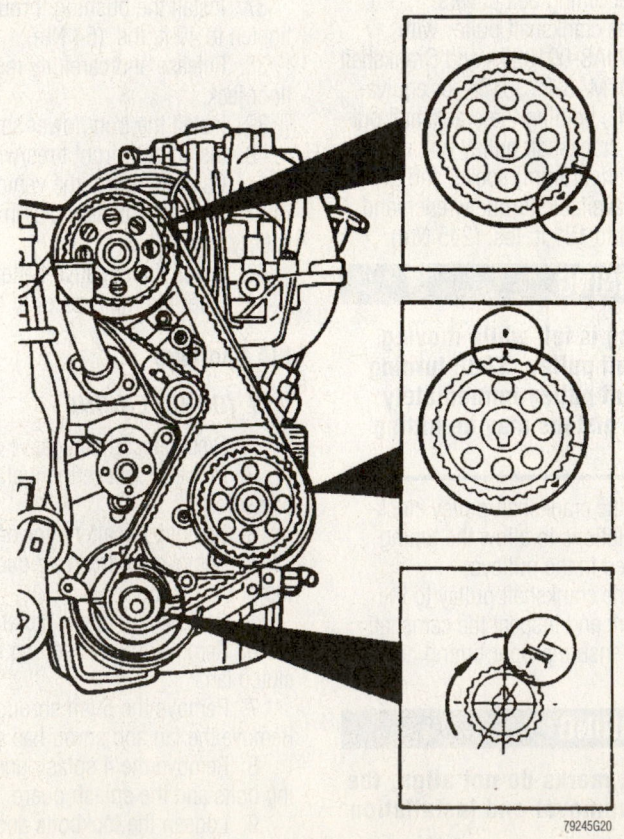

79245G20

Camshaft, auxiliary shaft and crankshaft timing belt sprocket alignment mark locations—Mazda B-Series Pick-Ups 1997 2.3L (VIN A) and 1998–01 2.5L (VIN C) engines

Tighten the adjustment bolt to lock the tensioner in the retracted position.

7. If the belt is to be reused, mark the direction of rotation on the belt for installation reference.

8. Remove the timing belt.

To install:

9. Install the new belt over the crankshaft sprocket and then counterclockwise over the auxiliary and camshaft sprockets, making sure the lugs on the belt properly engage the sprocket teeth on the pulleys. Be careful not to rotate the pulleys when installing the belt.

10. Release the timing belt tensioner pulley, allowing the tensioner to take up the belt slack. If the spring does not have enough tension to move the roller against the belt (belt hangs loose), it might be necessary to manually push the roller against the belt and tighten the bolt.

➡**The spring cannot be used to set belt tension; a wrench must be used on the tensioner assembly.**

✳✳ WARNING

If any binding is felt when adjusting the timing belt tension by turning the crankshaft, STOP turning the engine, because the pistons may be hitting the valves.

11. Rotate the crankshaft 2 complete turns by hand (in the normal direction of rotation) to remove slack from the belt. Tighten the tensioner adjustment to 26–33 ft. lbs. (35–45 Nm) and pivot bolts to 30–40 ft. lbs. (40–55 Nm). Be sure the belt is seated properly on the pulleys and that the timing marks are still in alignment when No. 1 cylinder is again at TDC/compression.

12. Install the crankshaft pulley and belt guide.

13. Install the timing belt cover.

14. Install the water pump pulley and fan blades. Install the upper radiator hose if necessary. Refill the cooling system.

15. Install the accessory drive belts.

16. Start the engine and check the ignition timing. Adjust the timing, if necessary.

Mazda MPV

3.0L (VIN JE) ENGINE

1. Disconnect the negative battery cable, and drain the cooling system.

✳✳ CAUTION

Never open, service or drain the radiator or cooling system when hot; serious burns can occur from the steam and hot coolant. Also, when draining engine coolant, keep in mind that cats and dogs are attracted to ethylene glycol antifreeze and could drink any that is left in an uncovered container or in puddles on the ground. This will prove fatal in sufficient quantities. Always drain coolant into a sealable container. Coolant should be reused unless it is contaminated or is several years old.

2. Remove the timing belt covers.

3. Remove the upper idler pulley.

4. Turn the crankshaft to align the matching marks on the sprockets. If the timing belt is to be reused, draw an arrow on the belt to indicate rotation direction.

5. Remove the timing belt and automatic tensioner.

6. Using SST 49-H012-010 tool or its equivalent, loosen and remove the camshaft sprocket lockbolts. Remove the camshaft sprockets.

7. Using a suitable puller, remove the crankshaft sprocket.

To install:

8. Install the crankshaft sprocket on the crankshaft.

9. Install the camshaft sprockets with the lockbolts and tighten the bolts to 52–59 ft. lbs. (71–80 Nm).

10. Set a plain washer at the bottom of the tensioner body to prevent damage to the body plug. Press in the tensioner rod slowly, using a press or a vise.

➡**Do not press the tensioner rod with more than 2200 lbs. (9800 N).**

11. Insert a pin to hold the tensioner rod in the body. Install the automatic tensioner and tighten the mounting bolts to 14–19 ft. lbs. (19–25 Nm).

12. Install the crankshaft pulley lockbolt and loosely tighten. Check the alignment of the matching marks on the sprockets.

13. With the upper idler pulley removed, install the timing belt, making sure there is no slack between the crankshaft and camshaft sprockets. If the timing belt is being reused, it must be installed in the same direction of rotation.

14. Install the upper idler pulley and

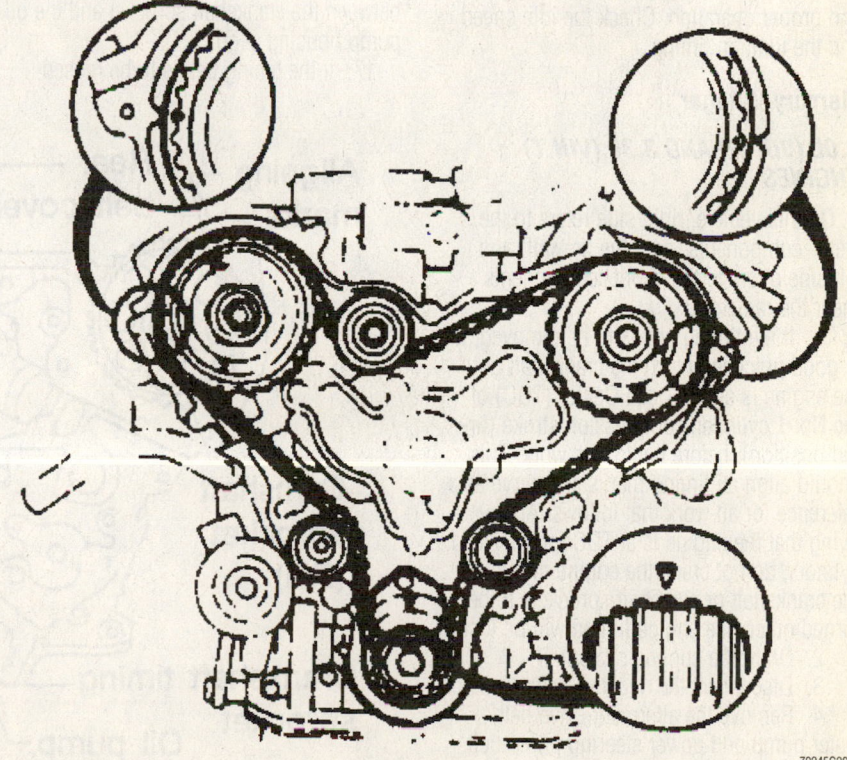

Timing belt routing and timing mark locations—Mazda MPV 3.0L (VIN JE) engine

79245G29

tighten the attaching bolt to 27–38 ft. lbs. (37–52 Nm).

15. Turn the crankshaft twice in the direction of rotation (clockwise) and align the matching marks. If the marks do not align, repeat the previous 3 steps.

✴✴ WARNING

If any binding is felt when adjusting the timing belt tension by turning the crankshaft, STOP turning the engine, because the pistons may be hitting the valves.

16. Remove the pin from the automatic tensioner. Turn the crankshaft twice and align the matching marks. Be sure the marks are aligned.

17. Check the timing belt deflection. The deflection should be 0.20–0.28 in. (5–7mm). Do not apply tension other than that of the automatic tensioner.

18. If the deflection is not correct, repeat the previous 3 steps.

19. Remove the crankshaft pulley lockbolt.

20. Install the timing belt cover, along with the related components.

21. Reinstall the crankshaft pulley and tighten the lockbolt to 116–123 ft. lbs. (37–52 Nm).

22. Fill and bleed the cooling system.

23. Run the engine and check for leaks and proper operation. Check the idle speed and the ignition timing.

Mercury Villager

3.0L (VIN W) AND 3.3L (VIN T) ENGINES

On this vehicle, right side refers to the "rear" components (near the firewall) and left side refers to the "front" components (near the radiator).

1. If the timing belt is to be removed, it is good practice to turn the crankshaft until the engine is at Top Dead Center (TDC) of the No. 1 cylinder, compression stroke (firing position), before beginning work. This should align all timing marks and serve as a reference for all work that follows. After verifying that the engine is at TDC for the No. 1 cylinder, do not crank the engine or allow the crankshaft or camshaft sprockets to be turned otherwise engine timing will be lost.

2. Drain the cooling system.

3. Disconnect the negative battery cable.

4. Remove the alternator drive belt, water pump and power steering pump belt and the air conditioning compressor belt, if equipped, using the recommended drive belt removal procedure.

5. If equipped with air conditioning,

remove the 3 air conditioning compressor drive belt idler pulley bolts and remove the idler pulley.

6. Remove the upper radiator hose bracket bolt. Remove the upper hose with the bracket from the vehicle.

7. Remove the water bypass hose from between the thermostat housing and the lower water hose connection.

8. Remove the main wiring harness from the upper engine front cover.

9. Remove the 8 upper engine front cover bolts and remove the upper cover.

10. Raise and safely support the vehicle.

11. Remove the right side front wheel and tire assembly.

12. Remove the 4 right side engine and transmission splash shield bolts and 2 screws, and remove the right side outer engine and transaxle splash shield.

13. Use a strap wrench to hold the water pump pulley. Remove the 4 pulley bolts, and the water pump pulley.

14. Use a strap wrench to hold the crankshaft pulley. Remove the center pulley bolt, and the crankshaft pulley using a harmonic balancer (damper) puller to draw the pulley from the front of the crankshaft.

15. Remove the 5 lower engine front cover bolts, then remove the lower engine front cover.

16. Be sure that the timing marks between the crankshaft sprocket and the oil pump housing align.

17. If the timing belt is to be reused,

mark an arrow on the belt indicating the direction of rotation. The directional arrow is necessary to ensure that the timing belt, if it to be reused, can reinstalled in the same direction.

18. Loosen the timing belt tensioner nut and slip the timing belt off of the sprockets.

19. If necessary, the camshaft sprockets can be removed. A special spanner tool is designed to hold the sprocket to keep it from turning while the center bolt is being loosened. Use care if using substitutes.

➡ **The sprockets are not interchangeable.**

20. If necessary, the crankshaft sprocket can be removed. The outer timing belt guide (looks like a large washer) and the crankshaft sprocket simply pull off the front of the crankshaft.

➡ **Be careful, there are 2 crankshaft keys. Use care not to loose them.**

To install:

21. Clean all parts well. If removed, inspect the crankshaft sprocket for warping or abnormal wear. Check the sprocket teeth for wear, deformation, chipping or other damage. Replace as necessary. Clean the sprocket mounting surface to ease installation. Install the key. Slip the sprocket onto the crankshaft. Tap it in place with a suitably-sized socket.

22. If removed, inspect the camshaft sprockets for damage and wear. Replace as

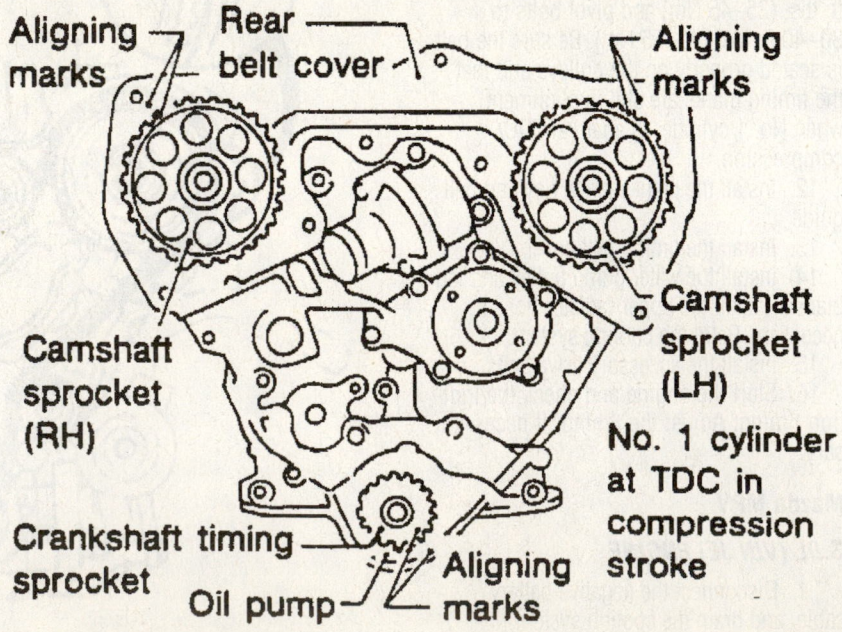

Use a shop rag to clean the alignment marks for the timing belt—Mercury Villager 3.0L (VIN W) and 3.3L (VIN T) engines

79245G21

required. The sprockets should be marked **L3** to designate the front, or left side camshaft and **R3** to designate the rear, or right side camshaft. Use care to install the sprockets properly. A special spanner tool is designed to hold the sprocket to keep it from turning while the center bolt is being tightened. Use care if using a substitute. Tighten the camshaft sprocket center bolts to 58–65 ft. lbs. (78–88 Nm) for 3.0L engine or 61 ft. lbs. (83 Nm) for 3.3L engine. Verify that the timing marks on the camshaft sprockets and the timing marks on the rear cover (called the seal plate) are aligned.

23. Use an Allen wrench to turn the timing belt tensioner clockwise until the belt tensioner spring is fully extended. Temporarily tighten the tensioner nut to 32–43 ft. lbs. (43–58 Nm).

24. If a new timing belt is to be installed, look for a printed arrow on the belt. Be sure the arrow is pointing away from the engine. If the original timing belt is to be reused, be sure that the directional arrow that was marked at disassembly is facing the correct direction.

25. A new Original Equipment Manufacture (OEM) timing belt should have 3 white timing marks on it that indicate the correct timing positions of the camshafts and the crankshaft. These marks are to help ensure that the engine is properly timed. When the engine is properly timed, each white timing mark on the timing belt will be aligned with the corresponding camshaft and crankshaft timing mark on the sprocket. Because the white timing marks are not evenly spaced, the technician needs to use care in installing the belt. There should be 40 timing belt teeth between the timing marks on the front and rear camshaft sprockets and 43 teeth between the timing mark on the front camshaft sprocket and the timing mark on the crankshaft sprocket.

26. Verify that the camshaft timing marks are aligned with the timing marks on the rear cover (seal plate) and that the crankshaft sprocket timing mark is aligned with the timing mark on the oil pump housing.

27. Install the timing belt starting at the crankshaft sprocket and moving around the camshaft sprockets following a counterclockwise path. Do not allow any slack in the timing belt between the sprockets. After all of the timing marks are aligned with the timing belt installed, slip the timing belt onto the belt tensioner.

28. While holding the timing belt tensioner with an Allen wrench, loosen the tensioner nut. Allow the tensioner to put pressure on the timing belt. Use an Allen wrench to turn the timing belt tensioner 70–80 degrees clockwise and tighten the timing belt tensioner nut to 32–43 ft. lbs. (43–58 Nm).

✳✳ WARNING

If any binding is felt when adjusting the timing belt tension by turning the crankshaft, STOP turning the engine, because the pistons may be hitting the valves.

29. Rotate the crankshaft clockwise twice and align the No. 1 piston to TDC on the compression stroke (firing position).

30. Apply 22 lbs. (10kg) of force on the timing belt between the rear camshaft sprocket and the timing belt tensioner. An assistant may be needed. While holding the timing belt tensioner steady with an Allen wrench, loosen the timing belt tensioner nut. Remove the Allen wrench and adjust the timing belt tensioner using the following procedure:

　a. Install a 0.0138 in. (0.35mm) thick and 0.500 in. (12.7mm) wide feeler gauge where the timing belt just starts to go around the tensioner (approximately the 4 o'clock position, looking at the tensioner).

　b. Turn the crankshaft sprocket clockwise, which should force the feeler gauge between the timing belt and the tensioner, up to a position on the tensioner of about 1 o'clock.

　c. Tighten the timing belt tensioner nut to 32–43 ft. lbs. (43–58 Nm) for the 3.0L engine or 61 ft. lbs. (83 Nm) for the 3.3L engine.

　d. Turn the crankshaft clockwise to rotate the feeler gauge out from between the timing belt tensioner and the timing belt.

31. Rotate the crankshaft clockwise twice, and once again align the No. 1 piston to TDC on the compression stroke (firing position).

32. Apply 22 lbs. (10kg) of force on the timing belt between the front and rear camshaft sprockets. Measure the amount of belt deflection. Belt deflection should be between 0.51–0.59 in. (13–15mm). If belt deflection is out of specification, repeat Steps 29 through 33. If the timing belt deflection cannot be adjusted into specification, the timing belt will have to be replaced.

33. Position the lower engine front cover and install the 5 lower cover bolts. Do not over tighten. Tighten to 27–44 inch lbs. (3–5 Nm).

34. Install the outer timing belt guide next to the crankshaft sprocket with the dished side facing away from the cylinder block. Install the crankshaft pulley. Use a strap wrench to keep the crankshaft pulley from turning and tighten the center bolt to 90–98 ft. lbs. (123–132 Nm) for the 3.0L engine or 148 ft. lbs. (201 Nm) for the 3.3L engine.

35. Position the water pump pulley on the pump. Install the 4 bolts. Use a strap wrench to keep the water pump pulley from turning and tighten the 4 water pump pulley bolts to 12–15 ft. lbs. (16–21 Nm) for the 3.0L engine or 89 inch lbs. (10 Nm) for the 3.3L engine.

36. Position the right side outer engine and transaxle splash shield, and secure with the 4 bolts and 2 screws.

37. Install the right side front wheel. Tighten the lug nuts to 72–87 ft. lbs. (98–118 Nm).

38. Lower the vehicle.

39. Position the upper engine timing belt front cover, and tighten the 8 bolts to 27–44 inch lbs. (3–5 Nm).

40. Install the main wiring harness on the upper engine front cover.

41. Position the water bypass hose between the thermostat housing and water connection. Install the upper radiator hose between the radiator and the water hose connection. Secure the hoses with clamps. Install the upper radiator hose bracket. Tighten the bracket bolt to 34–58 ft. lbs. (46–65 Nm).

42. If equipped, position the air conditioning compressor drive belt idler pulley and install the 3 bolts. Tighten to 15 ft. lbs. (21 Nm).

43. Install and adjust the alternator drive belt, the water pump and power steering pump drive belt and the air conditioning compressor drive belt, if equipped.

44. Connect the battery cable.

45. Fill the cooling system.

46. Start the engine and allow it to warm to operating temperature. Check and adjust the ignition timing. Road test to verify correct engine operation.

Mitsubishi Montero Sport

1997 2.4L (VIN G) ENGINE

1. Be sure that the engine's No. 1 piston is at Top Dead Center (TDC) in the compression stroke.

✳✳ CAUTION

Wait at least 90 seconds after the negative battery cable is disconnected to prevent possible deployment of the air bag.

2. Disconnect the negative battery cable.

3. Remove the spark plug wires from the tree on the upper cover.

4. Drain the cooling system.

5. Remove the shroud, fan and accessory drive belts.

6. Remove the radiator as required.

7. Remove the power steering pump, alternator, air conditioning compressor, tension pulley and accompanying brackets, as required.

8. Remove the upper front timing belt cover.

9. Remove the water pump pulley and the crankshaft pulley(s).

10. Remove the lower timing belt cover mounting screws and remove the cover.

11. If the belt(s) are to be reused, mark the direction of rotation on the belt.

12. Remove the timing (outer) belt tensioner and remove the belt. Unbolt the tensioner from the block and remove.

13. Remove the outer crankshaft sprocket and flange.

14. Remove the silent shaft (inner) belt tensioner and remove the inner belt. Unbolt the tensioner from the block and remove it.

15. To remove the camshaft sprockets, use SST MB990767-01 and MIT308239 or their equivalents.

To install:

16. Install the camshaft sprockets and tighten the center bolt to 65 ft. lbs. (90 Nm).

17. Align the timing mark of the silent shaft belt sprockets on the crankshaft and silent shaft with the marks on the front case. Wrap the silent shaft belt around the sprockets so there is no slack in the upper span of the belt and the timing marks are aligned.

18. Install the tensioner initially so the actual center of the pulley is above and to the left of the installation bolt.

19. Move the pulley up by hand so the center span of the long side of the belt deflects about ¼ in. (6mm).

20. Hold the pulley tightly so it does not rotate when the bolt is tightened. Tighten the bolt to 15 ft. lbs. (20 Nm). If the pulley has moved, the belt will be too tight.

21. Install the timing belt tensioner fully toward the water pump and temporarily tighten the bolts. Place the upper end of the spring against the water pump body. Align the timing marks of the cam, crankshaft and oil pump sprockets with the corresponding marks on the front case or head.

➡**If the following steps are not followed exactly, there is a chance that the silent shaft alignment will be 180 degrees off. This will cause a noticeable vibration in the engine and the entire procedure will have to be repeated.**

22. Before installing the timing belt, ensure that the left side silent shaft is in the correct position.

➡**It is possible to align the timing marks on the camshaft sprocket, crankshaft sprocket and the oil pump sprocket with the left balance shaft out of alignment.**

23. With the timing mark on the oil pump pulley aligned with the mark on the front case, check the alignment of the left balance shaft to assure correct shaft timing.

a. Remove the plug located on the left side of the block in the area of the starter.

b. Insert a tool having a shaft diameter of 0.3 in. (8mm) into the hole.

c. With the timing marks still aligned, the tool must be able to go in at least 2⅓ in. If it can only go in about 1 inch, turn the oil pump sprocket one complete revolution.

d. Recheck the position of the balance shaft with the timing marks realigned. Leave the tool in place to hold the silent shaft while continuing.

24. Install the belt to the crankshaft sprocket, oil pump sprocket and the camshaft sprocket, in that order. While doing so, be sure there is no slack between the sprockets except where the tensioner will take it up when released.

25. Recheck the timing marks' alignment.

26. If all are aligned, loosen the ten-

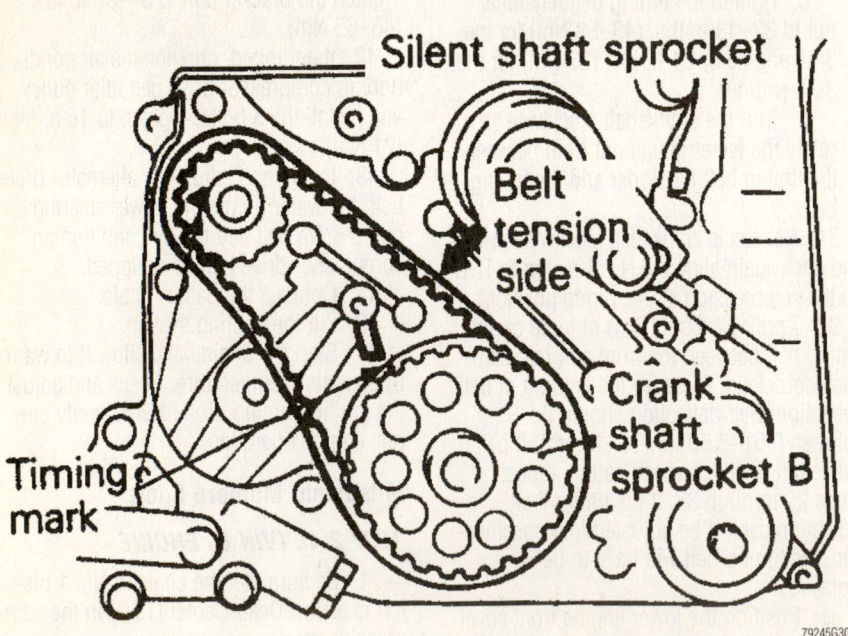

Silent shaft alignment marks. Notice the tension side of the inner (silent shaft) belt—Mitsubishi Montero Sport 2.4L engine

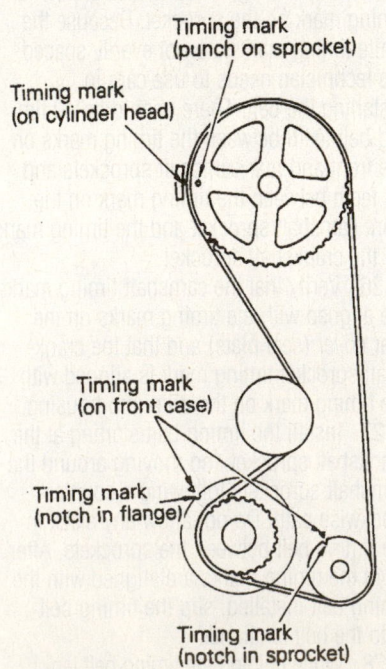

Timing belt pulley alignment marks—Mitsubishi Montero Sport 2.4L engine

sioner mounting bolt and allow the tensioner to apply tension to the belt.

27. Remove the tool that is holding the silent shaft in place and turn the crankshaft clockwise a distance equal to 2 teeth of the camshaft sprocket. This will allow the tensioner to automatically tension the belt the proper amount.

✳ WARNING

Do not manually apply pressure to the tensioner. This will over tighten the belt and will cause a howling noise.

28. First tighten the lower mounting bolt and then tighten the upper spacer bolt.

✳ WARNING

If any binding is felt when adjusting the timing belt tension by turning the crankshaft, STOP turning the engine, because the pistons may be hitting the valves.

29. To verify that belt tension is correct, check that the deflection of the longest span (between the camshaft and oil pump sprockets) is ½ in. (13mm).

30. Install the lower timing belt cover. Be sure the packing is properly positioned in the inner grooves of the covers when installing.

31. Install the water pump pulley and the crankshaft pulley(s).

32. Install the upper front timing belt cover.

33. Install the power steering pump, alternator, air conditioning compressor, tension pulley and accompanying brackets, as required.

34. Install the radiator, shroud, fan and accessory drive belts.

35. Install the spark plug wires to the tree on the upper cover.

36. Refill the cooling system.

37. Connect the negative battery cable. Start the engine and check for leaks.

Mitsubishi Montero

1997–98 3.0L (VIN P) ENGINES

1. Position the engine with No. 1 cylinder at Top Dead Center (TDC) of the compression stroke.

2. Disconnect the negative battery cable.

3. Drain the cooling system. Remove the drive belts.

✳ CAUTION

Never open, service or drain the radiator or cooling system when hot; serious burns can occur from the steam and hot coolant. Also, when draining engine coolant, keep in mind that cats and dogs are attracted to ethylene glycol antifreeze and could drink any that is left in an uncovered container or in puddles on the ground. This will prove fatal in sufficient quantities. Always drain coolant into a sealable container. Coolant should be reused unless it is contaminated or is several years old.

4. Remove the upper radiator shroud.

5. Remove the fan and fan pulley.

6. Without disconnecting the lines, remove the power steering pump from its bracket and position it aside. Remove the pump brackets.

7. Remove the belt tensioner pulley bracket.

8. Without releasing the refrigerant, remove the air conditioning compressor from its bracket and position it aside. Remove the bracket.

9. Remove the cooling fan bracket.

10. On some vehicles, it may be necessary to remove the pulley from the crankshaft to access the lower cover bolts.

11. Remove the timing belt cover bolts, and the upper and lower covers from the engine.

12. If the same timing belt will be reused, mark the direction of the timing belt's rotation, for installation in the same direction. Be sure engine is positioned so that the No. 1 cylinder is at TDC of its compression stroke and the sprockets timing marks are aligned with the engine's timing mark indicators.

13. Loosen the timing belt tensioner bolt and remove the belt. If not removing the tensioner, position it as far away from the center of the engine as possible and tighten the bolt.

14. If tensioner is being removed, mark outside of the spring to ensure that it is not installed backwards. Unbolt the tensioner and remove it along with the spring.

15. Using SST MB990767-01 and MIT308239 or their equivalents, remove the camshaft sprockets.

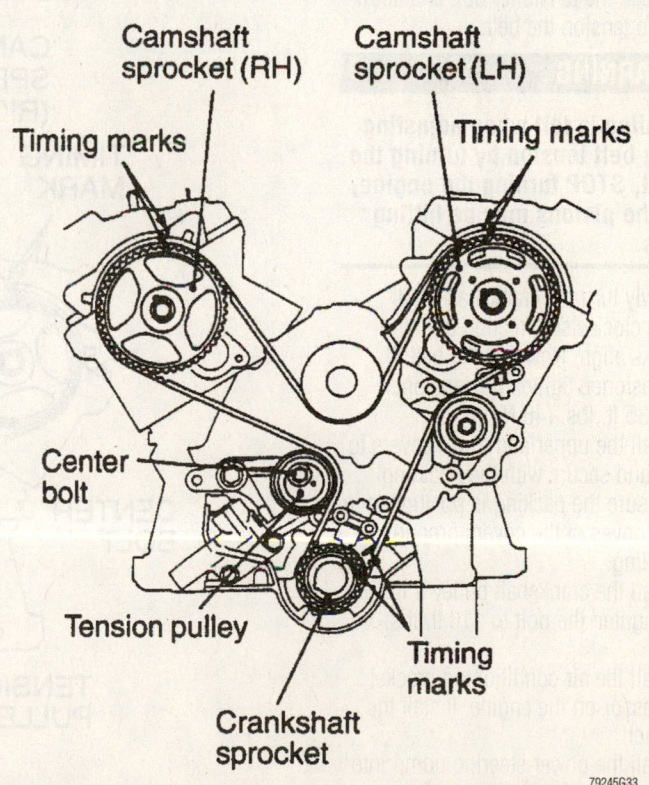

Be sure to align the timing marks before removing or installing the timing belt—Mitsubishi 1999–01 3.0L (VIN H), 1997–98 3.0L (VIN P) and 1997–01 3.5L engines

---

For accessory drive belt replacement procedures see the model specific sections of this manual

To install:

16. Hold the hexagonal portion of the camshaft with a wrench when tightening the camshaft sprocket bolt and tighten to 64 ft. lbs. (88 Nm).

17. If removed, install the tensioner and hook the upper end of the spring to the water pump pin. Install the lower end of the spring to the tensioner in exactly the same position as originally installed.

18. Position both camshafts so the timing marks align with those on the alternator bracket (rear bank) and inner timing cover (front bank). Rotate the crankshaft so the timing mark aligns with the mark on the oil pump.

19. Install the timing belt on the crankshaft sprocket, and while keeping the belt tight on the tension side (right side), install the belt on the front camshaft sprocket.

20. Install the belt on the water pump pulley, then the rear camshaft sprocket and the tensioner.

21. Rotate the front camshaft counterclockwise to tension the belt between the front camshaft and the crankshaft. If the timing marks came out of line, repeat the procedure.

22. Install the crankshaft sprocket flange.

23. Loosen the tensioner bolt and allow the spring to tension the belt.

> **✳✳ WARNING**
>
> **If any binding is felt when adjusting the timing belt tension by turning the crankshaft, STOP turning the engine, because the pistons may be hitting the valves.**

24. Slowly turn the crankshaft 2 full turns in the clockwise direction until the timing marks align. Now that the belt is properly tensioner, tighten the tensioner lockbolt to 35 ft. lbs. (48 Nm).

25. Install the upper and lower covers to the engine and secure with the retaining screws. Be sure the packing is positioned in the inner grooves of the covers properly when installing.

26. Install the crankshaft pulley if it was removed. Tighten the bolt to 110 ft. lbs. (150 Nm).

27. Install the air conditioning bracket and compressor on the engine. Install the belt tensioner.

28. Install the power steering pump into position. Install the fan pulley and fan.

29. Install the fan shroud to the radiator.

30. Refill the cooling system.

31. Connect the negative battery cable. Start the engine and check for fluid leaks.

1999–01 3.0L (VIN H), 1997–98 3.5L (VIN M) AND 1999–01 3.5L (VIN R) ENGINES

1. Disconnect the negative battery cable.

2. Drain the engine coolant and store it for reinstallation. Remove the upper radiator hose.

3. Remove the cooling fan shroud assembly.

4. Remove the cooling fan-to-clutch bolts and the fan.

5. Remove the cooling fan clutch-to-water pump nuts and the clutch assembly.

6. Remove the drive belts for the alter-

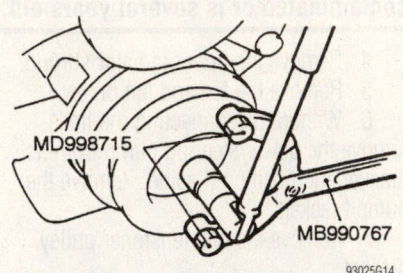

Removing or installing the crankshaft pulley bolt—Mitsubishi 1999–01 3.0L (VIN H), 1997–98 3.5L (VIN M) and 1999–01 3.5L (VIN R) engines

nator, power steering pump and air conditioning compressor.

7. Disconnect the electrical connectors from the alternator.

8. Remove the alternator-to-engine bolts and the alternator bracket-to-engine bolts; then, remove the alternator and bracket from the engine.

9. Remove the power steering pump cover. Remove the power steering pump-to-engine bolts and move the pump aside with the hoses and electrical connector attached.

10. Remove the air conditioning compressor-to-bracket bolts and move the compressor aside with the lines and electrical connector attached.

11. Remove the air conditioning compressor bracket-to-engine bolts and the bracket.

12. Remove the timing indicator bracket (near crankshaft pulley) bolts and the bracket.

13. Remove the accessory mount assembly-to-engine bolts and the mount assembly.

14. Remove the upper timing belt cover assembly.

15. Using the End Yoke Holder tool MD990767 and 2 Crankshaft Pulley Holder Pin tools MD998715, or equivalent to hold

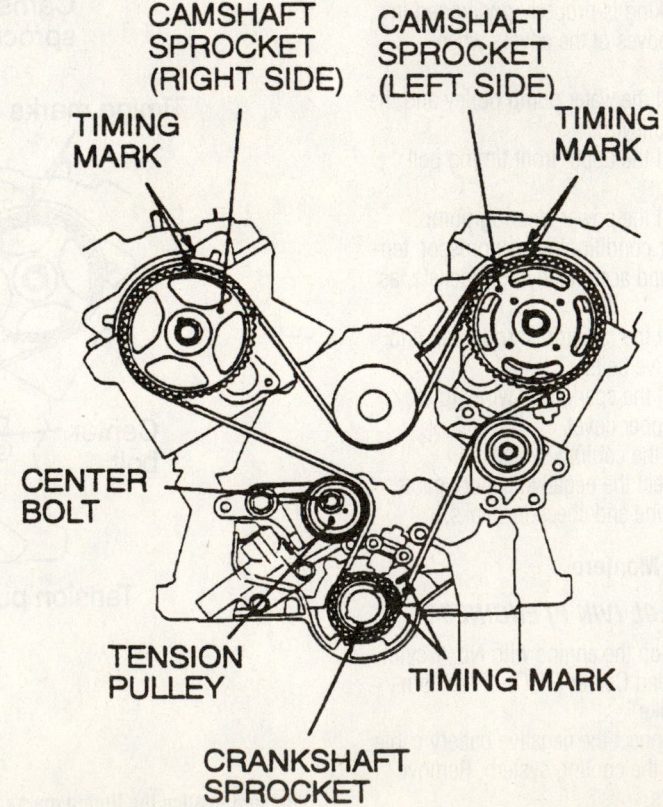

View of the timing belt alignment marks—Mitsubishi 1999–01 3.0L (VIN H), 1997–98 3.5L (VIN M) and 1999–01 3.5L (VIN R) engines

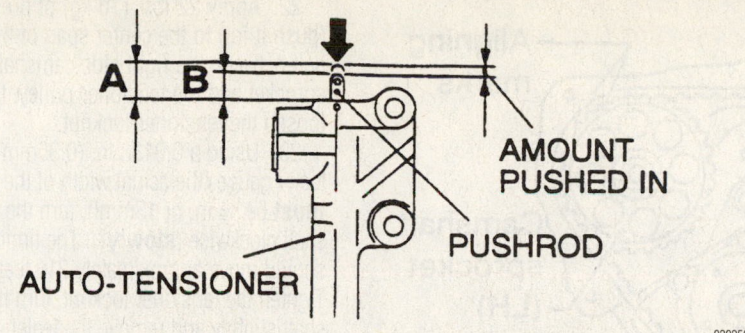

Inspecting the auto-tensioner movement—Mitsubishi 1999–01 3.0L (VIN H), 1997–98 3.5L (VIN M) and 1999–01 3.5L (VIN R) engines

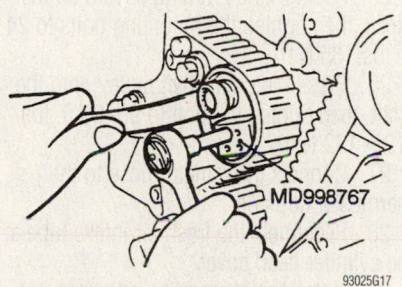

Adjusting the timing belt tensioner pulley—Mitsubishi 1999–01 3.0L (VIN H), 1997–98 3.5L (VIN M) and 1999–01 3.5L (VIN R) engines

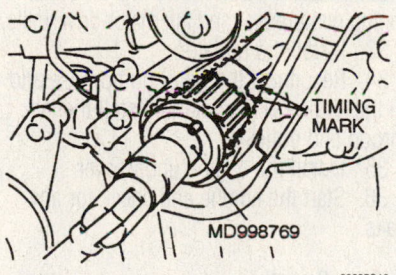

Using crankshaft spacer tool to rotate the crankshaft—Mitsubishi 1999–01 3.0L (VIN H), 1997–98 3.5L (VIN M) and 1999–01 3.5L (VIN R) engines

the crankshaft pulley, and a socket wrench, remove the crankshaft pulley bolt and the pulley.

16. Remove the lower timing belt cover.

17. Rotate the crankshaft clockwise to align the timing marks to position the No. 1 cylinder at the Top Dead Center (TDC) of its compression stroke.

18. Use chalk to mark the rotating (clockwise) direction of the timing belt for reinstallation purposes.

19. Loosen the auto-tensioner pulley center bolt and remove the timing bolt.

20. Remove the auto-tensioner pulley and the auto-tensioner arm assembly.

To install:

21. Press the end of the auto-tensioner inward with 72–145 ft. lbs. (98–196 Nm) of force and measure the distance that the pushrod is pushed in. If the standard distance is not 0.04 in. (1mm), replace the auto-tensioner.

22. Position the auto-tensioner in a soft-jawed vise and SLOWLY compress the pushrod until the pushrod and housing holes align; then, install a setting pin to secure the auto-tensioner in the retracted position.

23. Align the camshaft and crankshaft TDC timing marks.

24. Install the timing belt (noting its rotational direction) so that there is no deflection between the sprockets and pulleys in the following manner:

- Crankshaft sprocket
- Idler pulley
- Left camshaft sprocket
- Water pump pulley
- Right camshaft sprocket
- Tension pulley

25. Turn the camshaft sprocket counterclockwise until the tension side of the timing belt is firmly stretched, then, recheck the timing marks.

26. Using the Tension Pulley Socket Wrench tool MD998767, or equivalent, push the tensioner pulley into the timing belt and secure the center bolt.

27. Using the Crankshaft Pulley Spacer tool MD998769, or equivalent, rotate the crankshaft ¼ turn counterclockwise, then, turn it again clockwise to align the timing marks.

28. Loosen the timing belt tensioner center bolt. Using the Tension Pulley Socket Wrench tool MD998767, or equivalent, and a torque wrench, apply 39 inch lbs. (4.4

Nm) pressure on the timing belt. Torque the tensioner pulley center bolt to 35 ft. lbs. (48 Nm).

29. Remove the setting pin from the auto-tensioner.

30. Rotate the crankshaft 2 complete revolutions and realign the timing marks. Then, wait for 5 minutes until the auto-tensioner's pushrod extends to its standard value. If the standard value is not 0.15–0.20 in. (3.8–5.0mm), repeat the adjustment procedure. If the standard value is still not achieved, replace the auto-tensioner.

31. Install the lower timing belt cover and crankshaft pulley.

32. Using the End Yoke Holder tool MD990767 and 2 Crankshaft Pulley Holder Pin tools MD998715, or equivalent to hold the crankshaft pulley, and a socket torque wrench, torque the crankshaft pulley bolt to 134 ft. lbs. (181 Nm).

33. Install the upper timing belt cover assembly.

34. Install the remaining items by reversing the removal procedures.

35. Refill the cooling system.

36. Connect the negative battery cable.

Nissan Pick-Up and Pathfinder

3.0L (VG30E) AND 3.3L (VG33E) ENGINES

1. Remove the engine undercover.

2. Remove the radiator shroud, the fan and the pulleys.

3. Drain the coolant from the radiator and remove the water pump hose.

✱✱ CAUTION

When draining the coolant, keep in mind that cats and dogs are attracted by the ethylene glycol antifreeze, and are quite likely to drink any that is left in an uncovered container or in puddles on the ground. This will prove fatal in sufficient quantity. Always drain the coolant into a sealable container. Coolant should be reused unless it is contaminated or several years old.

4. Remove the radiator.

5. Remove the power steering, air conditioning compressor and alternator drive belts.

6. Remove the spark plugs.

7. Remove the distributor protector (dust shield).

8. Remove the air conditioning compressor drive belt idler pulley and bracket.

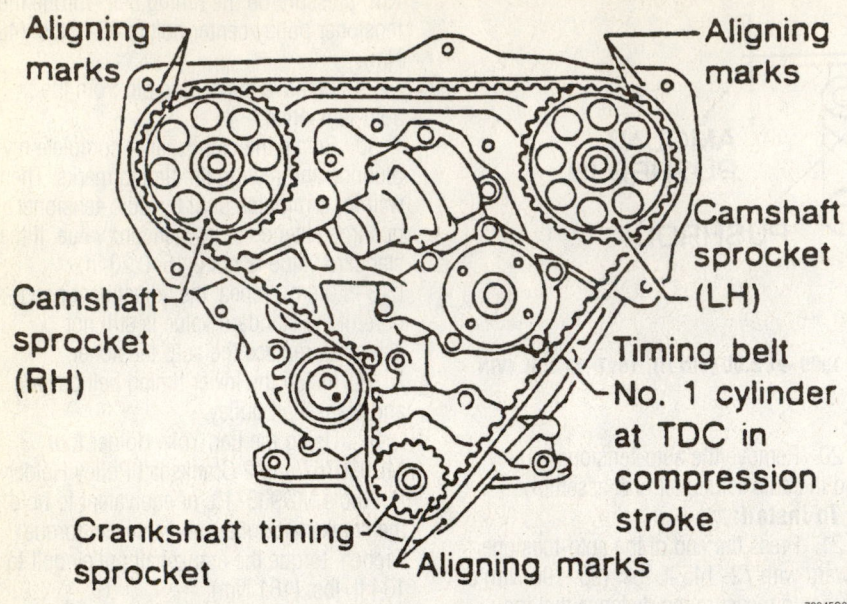

Timing belt alignment mark locations—Nissan Pick-Up and Pathfinder 3.0L (VG30E) and 3.3L (VG33E) engines

9. Remove the fresh air intake tube at the cylinder head cover.

10. Disconnect the radiator hose at the thermostat housing.

11. Remove the crankshaft pulley bolt, then pull off the pulley with a suitable puller.

12. Remove the bolts, then remove the front upper and lower timing belt covers.

13. Set the No. 1 piston at Top Dead Center (TDC) of its compression stroke. Align the punchmark on the left camshaft sprocket with the punchmark on the timing belt upper rear cover. Align the punchmark on the crankshaft sprocket with the notch on the oil pump housing. Temporarily install the crank pulley bolt so the crankshaft can be rotated if necessary.

14. Loosen the timing belt tensioner and return spring, then remove the timing belt.
To install:

✳✳ CAUTION

Before installing the timing belt, confirm that the No. 1 cylinder is set at the TDC of the compression stroke.

15. Remove both cylinder head covers and loosen all rocker arm shaft retaining bolts.

➡**The rocker arm shaft bolts MUST be loosened so that the correct belt tension can be obtained.**

16. Install the tensioner and the return spring. Using a hexagon wrench, turn the tensioner clockwise and temporarily tighten the locknut.

17. Be sure that the timing belt is clean and free from oil or water.

18. When installing the timing belt, align the white lines on the belt with the punchmarks on the camshaft and crankshaft sprockets. Have the arrow on the timing belt pointing toward the front belt covers.

➡**A good way (although rather tedious!) to check for proper timing belt installation is to count the number of belt teeth between the timing marks. There are 133 teeth on the belt; there should be 40 teeth between the timing marks on the left and right side camshaft sprockets, and 43 teeth between the timing marks on the left side camshaft sprocket and the crankshaft sprocket.**

19. While keeping the tensioner steady, loosen the locknut with a hex wrench.

20. Turn the tensioner approximately 70–80 degrees clockwise with the wrench, then tighten the locknut.

✳✳ WARNING

If any binding is felt when adjusting the timing belt tension by turning the crankshaft, STOP turning the engine, because the pistons may be hitting the valves.

21. Turn the crankshaft in a clockwise direction several times, then **slowly** set the No. 1 piston to TDC of the compression stroke.

22. Apply 22 lbs. (10 kg) of pressure (push it in!) to the center span of the timing belt between the right side camshaft sprocket and the tensioner pulley, then loosen the tensioner locknut.

23. Using a 0.0138 in. (0.35mm) thick feeler gauge (the actual width of the blade **must** be ½ in. or 13mm!), turn the crankshaft clockwise (**slowly!**). The timing belt should move approximately 2½ teeth. Tighten the tensioner locknut, turn the crankshaft slightly and remove the feeler gauge.

24. Slowly rotate the crankshaft clockwise several more times, then set the No. 1 piston to TDC of the compression stroke.

25. Position the 2 timing covers on the block, then tighten the mounting bolts to 24 ft. lbs. (35 Nm).

26. Press the crankshaft pulley onto the shaft, then tighten the bolt to 90–98 ft. lbs. (123–132 Nm).

27. Connect the radiator hose to the thermostat housing.

28. Reconnect the fresh air intake tube at the cylinder head cover.

29. Install the air conditioning compressor drive belt idler pulley and bracket.

30. Install the distributor protector (dust shield).

31. Install the spark plugs.

32. Install the power steering, air conditioning compressor and alternator drive belts.

33. Install the radiator.

34. Reconnect the water pump hose and fill the engine with coolant. Install the fan shroud and pulleys.

35. Install the engine undercover.

36. Start the engine and check for any leaks.

Nissan Quest

3.0L (VG30E) AND 3.3L (VG33E) ENGINES

On this vehicle, right side refers to the "rear" components (near the firewall) and left side refers to the "front" components (near the radiator).

1. If the timing belt is to be removed, it is good practice to turn the crankshaft until the engine is at Top Dead Center (TDC) of the No. 1 cylinder, compression stroke (firing position), before beginning work. This should align all timing marks and serve as a reference for all work that follows. After verifying that the engine is at TDC for the No. 1 cylinder, do not crank the engine or allow the crankshaft or camshaft sprockets to be turned otherwise engine timing will be lost.

2. Drain the cooling system.

3. Disconnect the negative battery cable.

4. Remove the alternator drive belt, water pump and power steering pump belt and the air conditioning compressor belt, if equipped, using the recommended drive belt removal procedure.

5. If equipped with air conditioning, remove the 3 air conditioning compressor drive belt idler pulley bolts and remove the idler pulley.

6. Remove the upper radiator hose bracket bolt. Remove the upper hose with the bracket from the vehicle.

7. Remove the water bypass hose from between the thermostat housing and the lower water hose connection.

8. Remove the main wiring harness from the upper engine front cover.

9. Remove the 8 upper engine front cover bolts and remove the upper cover.

10. Raise and safely support the vehicle.

11. Remove the right side front wheel and tire assembly.

12. Remove the 4 right side engine and transmission splash shield bolts and 2 screws, and remove the right side outer engine and transaxle splash shield.

13. Use a strap wrench to hold the water pump pulley. Remove the 4 pulley bolts, and the water pump pulley.

14. Use a strap wrench to hold the crankshaft pulley. Remove the center pulley bolt, and the crankshaft pulley using a har-

monic balancer (damper) puller to draw the pulley from the front of the crankshaft.

15. Remove the 5 lower engine front cover bolts, then remove the lower engine front cover.

16. Be sure that the timing marks between the crankshaft sprocket and the oil pump housing align.

17. If the timing belt is to be reused, mark an arrow on the belt indicating the direction of rotation. The directional arrow is necessary to ensure that the timing belt, if it to be reused, can reinstalled in the same direction.

18. Loosen the timing belt tensioner nut and slip the timing belt off of the sprockets.

19. If necessary, the camshaft sprockets can be removed. A special spanner tool is designed to hold the sprocket to keep it from turning while the center bolt is being loosened. Use care if using substitutes.

➡**The sprockets are not interchangeable.**

20. If necessary, the crankshaft sprocket can be removed. The outer timing belt guide (looks like a large washer) and the crankshaft sprocket simply pull off the front of the crankshaft.

➡**Be careful, there are 2 crankshaft keys. Use care not to loose them.**

To install:

21. Clean all parts well. If removed,

inspect the crankshaft sprocket for warping or abnormal wear. Check the sprocket teeth for wear, deformation, chipping or other damage. Replace as necessary. Clean the sprocket mounting surface to ease installation. Install the key. Slip the sprocket onto the crankshaft. Tap it in place with a suitably-sized socket.

22. If removed, inspect the camshaft sprockets for damage and wear. Replace as required. The sprockets should be marked **L3** to designate the front, or left side camshaft and **R3** to designate the rear, or right side camshaft. Use care to install the sprockets properly. A special spanner tool is designed to hold the sprocket to keep it from turning while the center bolt is being tightened. Use care if using a substitute. Tighten the camshaft sprocket center bolts to 58–65 ft. lbs. (78–88 Nm) for the 3.0L engine or 61 ft. lbs. (83 Nm) for the 3.3L engine. Verify that the timing marks on the camshaft sprockets and the timing marks on the rear cover (called the seal plate) are aligned.

23. Use an Allen wrench to turn the timing belt tensioner clockwise until the belt tensioner spring is fully extended. Temporarily tighten the tensioner nut to 32–43 ft. lbs. (43–58 Nm).

24. If a new timing belt is to be installed, look for a printed arrow on the belt. Be sure the arrow is pointing away from the engine. If the original timing belt is to be reused, be sure that the directional arrow that was marked at disassembly is facing the correct direction.

25. A new Original Equipment Manufacture (OEM) timing belt should have 3 white timing marks on it that indicate the correct timing positions of the camshafts and the crankshaft. These marks are to help ensure that the engine is properly timed. When the engine is properly timed, each white timing mark on the timing belt will be aligned with the corresponding camshaft and crankshaft timing mark on the sprocket. Because the white timing marks are not evenly spaced, the technician needs to use care in installing the belt. There should be 40 timing belt teeth between the timing marks on the front and rear camshaft sprockets and 43 teeth between the timing mark on the front camshaft sprocket and the timing mark on the crankshaft sprocket.

26. Verify that the camshaft timing marks are aligned with the timing marks on the rear cover (seal plate) and that the crank-

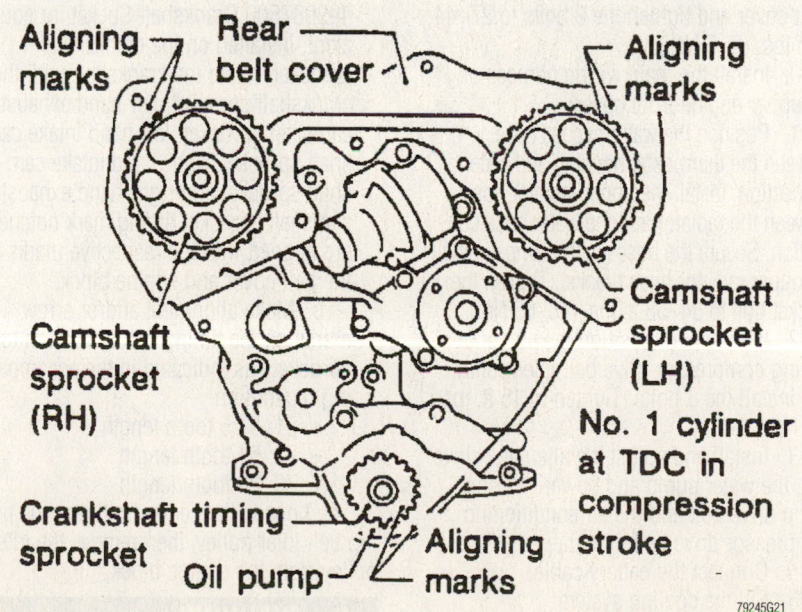

Use a shop rag to clean the alignment marks for the timing belt—Nissan Quest 3.0L (VG30E) and 3.3L (VG33E) engines

Timing chain and gear service is covered in the model specific sections of this manual

shaft sprocket timing mark is aligned with the timing mark on the oil pump housing.

27. Install the timing belt starting at the crankshaft sprocket and moving around the camshaft sprockets following a counter-clockwise path. Do not allow any slack in the timing belt between the sprockets. After all of the timing marks are aligned with the timing belt installed, slip the timing belt onto the belt tensioner.

28. While holding the timing belt tensioner with an Allen wrench, loosen the tensioner nut. Allow the tensioner to put pressure on the timing belt. Use an Allen wrench to turn the timing belt tensioner 70–80 degrees clockwise and tighten the timing belt tensioner nut to 32–43 ft. lbs. (43–58 Nm).

✻✻ WARNING

If any binding is felt when adjusting the timing belt tension by turning the crankshaft, STOP turning the engine, because the pistons may be hitting the valves.

29. Rotate the crankshaft clockwise twice and align the No. 1 piston to TDC on the compression stroke (firing position).

30. Apply 22 lbs. (10kg) of force on the timing belt between the rear camshaft sprocket and the timing belt tensioner. An assistant may be needed. While holding the timing belt tensioner steady with an Allen wrench, loosen the timing belt tensioner nut. Remove the Allen wrench and adjust the timing belt tensioner using the following procedure:

   a. Install a 0.0138 in. (0.35mm) thick and 0.500 in. (12.7mm) wide feeler gauge where the timing belt just starts to go around the tensioner (approximately the 4 o'clock position, looking at the tensioner).

   b. Turn the crankshaft sprocket clockwise, which should force the feeler gauge between the timing belt and the tensioner, up to a position on the tensioner of about 1 o'clock.

   c. Tighten the timing belt tensioner nut to 32–43 ft. lbs. (43–58 Nm) for the 3.0L engine or 61 ft. lbs. (83 Nm) for the 3.3L engine.

   d. Turn the crankshaft clockwise to rotate the feeler gauge out from between the timing belt tensioner and the timing belt.

31. Rotate the crankshaft clockwise twice, and once again align the No. 1 piston to TDC on the compression stroke (firing position).

32. Apply 22 lbs. (10 kg) of force on the timing belt between the front and rear cam-

shaft sprockets. Measure the amount of belt deflection. Belt deflection should be between 0.51–0.59 in. (13–15mm). If belt deflection is out of specification, repeat Steps 29 through 33. If the timing belt deflection cannot be adjusted into specification, the timing belt will have to be replaced.

33. Position the lower engine front cover and install the 5 lower cover bolts. Do not over tighten. Tighten to 27–44 inch lbs. (3–5 Nm).

34. Install the outer timing belt guide next to the crankshaft sprocket with the dished side facing away from the cylinder block. Install the crankshaft pulley. Use a strap wrench to keep the crankshaft pulley from turning and tighten the center bolt to 90–98 ft. lbs. (123–132 Nm) for the 3.0L engine or 148 ft. lbs. (201 Nm) for the 3.3L engine.

35. Position the water pump pulley on the pump. Install the 4 bolts. Use a strap wrench to keep the water pump pulley from turning and tighten the 4 water pump pulley bolts to 12–15 ft. lbs. (16–21 Nm) for the 3.0L engine or 89 inch lbs. (10 Nm) for the 3.3L engine.

36. Position the right side outer engine and transaxle splash shield, and secure with the 4 bolts and 2 screws.

37. Install the right side front wheel and tire assembly. Tighten the lug nuts to 72–87 ft. lbs. (98–118 Nm).

38. Lower the vehicle.

39. Position the upper engine timing belt front cover and tighten the 8 bolts to 27–44 inch lbs. (3–5 Nm).

40. Install the main wiring harness on the upper engine front cover.

41. Position the water bypass hose between the thermostat housing and water connection. Install the upper radiator hose between the radiator and the water hose connection. Secure the hoses with clamps. Install the upper radiator hose bracket. Tighten the bracket bolt to 34–58 ft. lbs. (46–65 Nm).

42. If equipped, position the air conditioning compressor drive belt idler pulley and install the 3 bolts. Tighten to 15 ft. lbs. (21 Nm).

43. Install and adjust the alternator drive belt, the water pump and power steering pump drive belt and the air conditioning compressor drive belt, if equipped.

44. Connect the battery cable.

45. Fill the cooling system.

46. Start the engine and allow it to warm to operating temperature. Check and adjust the ignition timing. Road test to verify correct engine operation.

Subaru Forester

2.5L DOHC ENGINE

When servicing the timing belt, note the following:

• The intake and exhaust camshafts can be rotated independently when the timing belt is removed. If the intake and exhaust valves are lifted off of their seats simultaneously, their heads will contact each other, possibly causing damage.

• When the timing belt is removed, the camshafts are positioned so that none of the valves are lifted off of their seats, resulting in a "zero-lift" position.

• The left-hand cylinder head camshafts must be rotated from the "zero-lift" position as little as possible when orienting it for timing belt installation, otherwise possible valve head interference may occur.

• Never allow the camshafts to rotate in the direction shown in the accompanying illustration, which would cause both the intake and exhaust valves to lift simultaneously, causing interference.

1. Remove all necessary components to gain access to the timing belt.

2. If equipped with manual transmissions, loosen the 2 timing belt guide mounting bolts, then separate the guide from the engine block.

3. If the directional arrow and alignment marks on the timing belt are faded, and the belt is to be reused, remark the belt with white paint or a grease pencil as follows:

   a. Using a Subaru tool No. ST-499987500 Crankshaft Socket, or equivalent, installed on the crankshaft sprocket, rotate the crankshaft until the crankshaft sprocket, left-hand exhaust camshaft sprocket, left-hand intake camshaft sprocket, right-hand intake camshaft sprocket and right-hand exhaust camshaft sprocket timing mark notches are aligned with the respective marks on the belt cover and engine block.

   b. Make alignment and/or arrow marks on the timing belt in relation to the sprockets as indicated in the accompanying illustration.

      • Z1: 54.5 tooth length
      • Z2: 51 tooth length
      • Z3: 28 tooth length

4. Loosen the center bolt from the timing belt idler pulley, then remove the idler pulley from the engine block.

✻✻ WARNING

After removing the timing belt, DO NOT rotate the camshafts. Damage to the valves may occur.

5. Carefully remove the timing belt from all of the sprockets.

6. Remove the automatic belt tension adjuster assembly as follows:

a. Remove the 2 timing belt idler pulleys, as indicated in the accompanying illustration.

b. Loosen the automatic tension

adjuster assembly mounting bolts, then separate the adjuster assembly from the engine block.

To install:

✳✳ WARNING

Do not allow oil, grease, or coolant to come in contact with the timing

belt. If this occurs, quickly and thoroughly remove all traces of the compound. Also, never bend the timing belt sharply; the minimum bending radius is 2.36 in. (60mm).

7. Inspect the camshaft and crankshaft sprocket teeth for abnormal or excessive

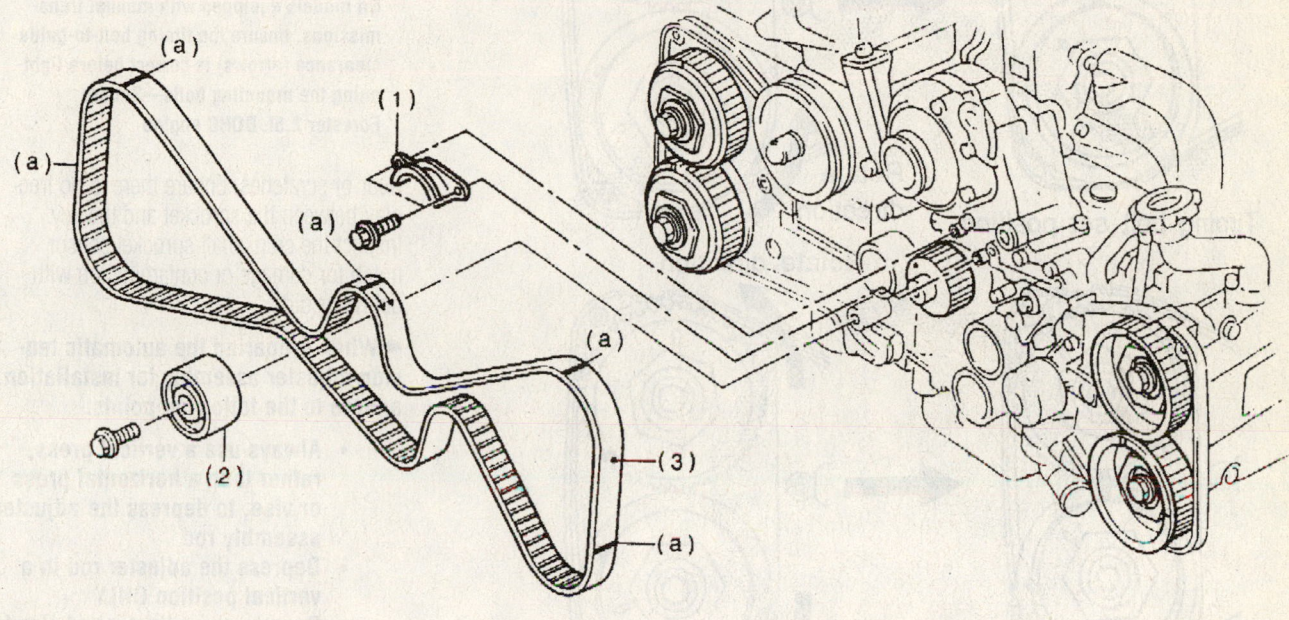

Timing belt guide (MT vehicles only)

(2) Belt idler
(3) Timing belt

(4) Alignment marks

79245G48

Timing belt routing and timing belt guide (manual transmission equipped vehicles only) location—Subaru Forester 2.5L DOHC engine

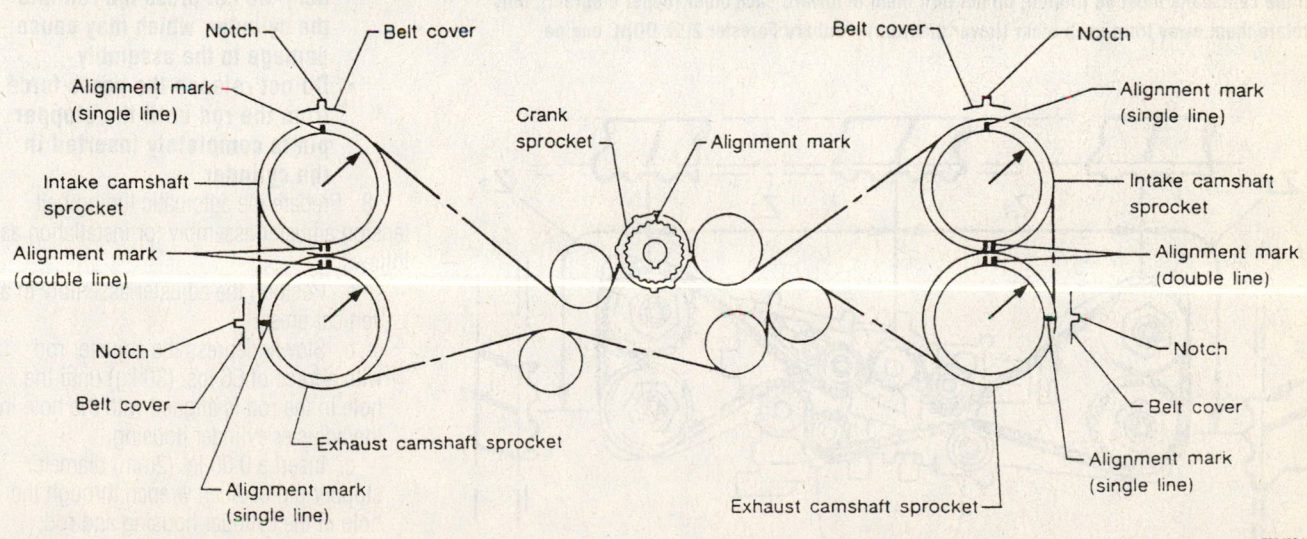

79245G49

Before removing the timing belt, turn the crankshaft sprocket until all of the alignment marks are aligned as indicated—Subaru Forester 2.5L DOHC engine

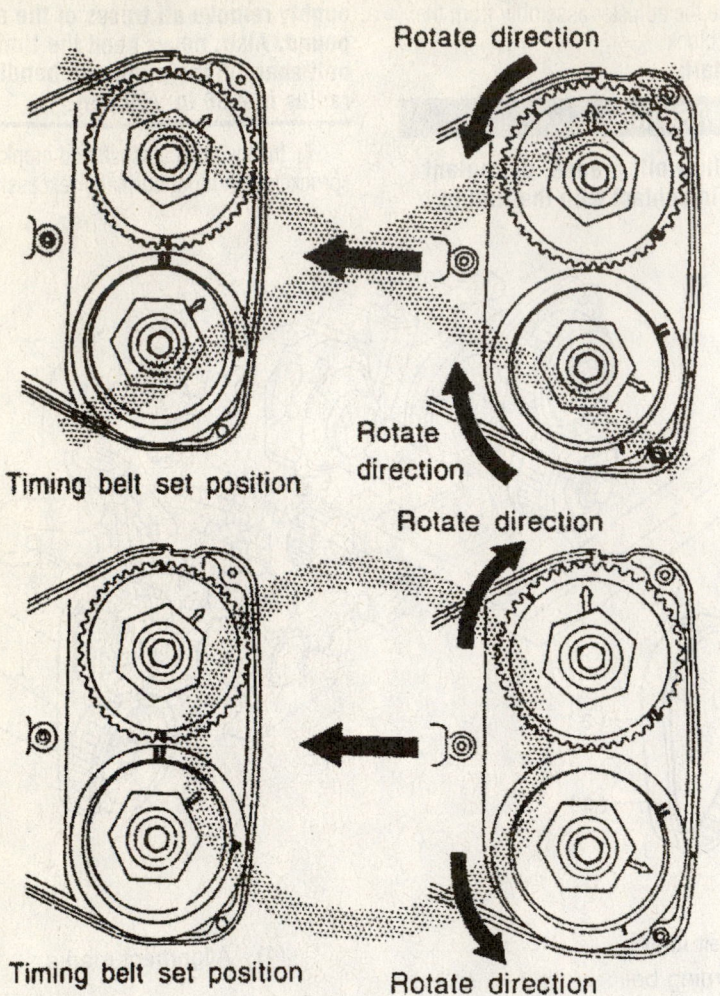

If the camshafts must be rotated, do not turn them in toward each other (upper diagram); only rotate them away from each other (lower diagram)—Subaru Forester 2.5L DOHC engine

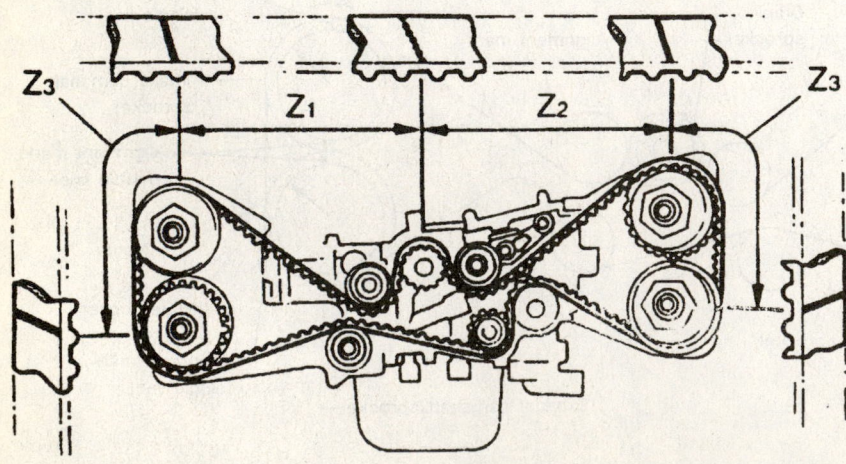

If the original marks on the timing belt are worn or faded, make new alignment marks in the positions indicated—Subaru Forester 2.5L DOHC engine

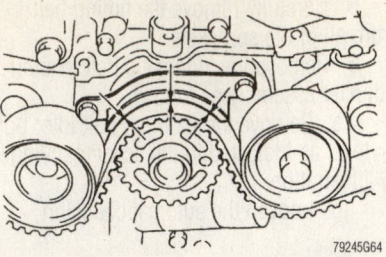

On models equipped with manual transmissions, ensure the timing belt-to-guide clearance (arrows) is correct before tightening the mounting bolts—Subaru Forester 2.5L DOHC engine

wear or scratches. Ensure there is no free-play between the sprocket and the key. Inspect the crankshaft sprocket sensor notch for damage or contamination with debris or dirt.

➡️ **When preparing the automatic tension adjuster assembly for installation, adhere to the following points:**

- **Always use a vertical press, rather than a horizontal press or vise, to depress the adjuster assembly rod**
- **Depress the adjuster rod in a vertical position ONLY**
- **Depress the adjuster rod slowly (taking more than 3 minutes) with a force of 66 lbs. (30 kg)**
- **Do not allow the press force to exceed 2205 lbs. (1000 kg)**
- **Press the adjuster rod in as far as the end surface of the cylinder—do not press the rod into the cylinder, which may cause damage to the assembly**
- **Do not release the press force from the rod until the stopper pin is completely inserted in the cylinder**

8. Prepare the automatic timing belt tension adjuster assembly for installation as follows:

a. Position the adjuster assembly in a vertical press.

b. Slowly depress the adjuster rod with a force of 66 lbs. (30 kg) until the hole in the rod is aligned with the hole in the adjuster cylinder housing.

c. Insert a 0.08 in. (2mm) diameter stopper pin or Allen wrench through the hole in the cylinder housing and rod, then slowly release the press force from the adjuster rod.

9. Install the adjuster assembly onto the engine block.

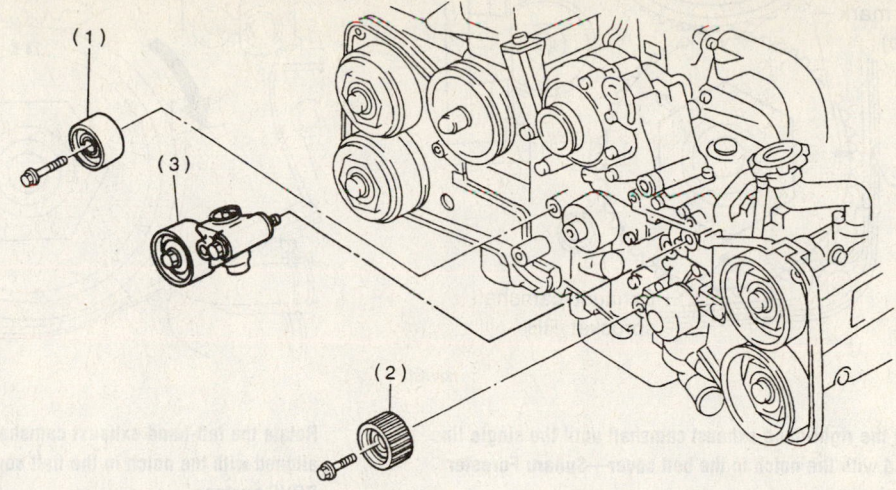

(1) Belt idler
(2) Belt idler No. 2

(3) Automatic belt tension adjuster
ASSY

79245G52

It is necessary to remove the automatic adjuster assembly and reset the pushrod for timing belt installation—Subaru Forester 2.5L DOHC engine

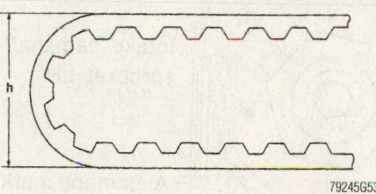

79245G53

Never bend the timing belt into a radius tighter than 2.36 in./60mm (h), otherwise it will be damaged beyond use—Subaru Forester 2.5L DOHC engine

10. Install timing belt idler pulley No. 2 on the engine block.

11. Install the timing belt idler pulley No. 1 on the engine block.

12. If the camshaft and crankshaft timing marks are no longer aligned, perform the following:

   a. Position the crankshaft sprocket so that its mark is aligned with the mark on the oil pump cover on the engine block.

   b. Align the single line mark on the right-hand exhaust camshaft sprocket with the notch on the belt cover.

   c. Rotate the right-hand intake camshaft so that the single line mark is aligned with the notch on the belt cover.

➡**At this point, the double line marks on both right-hand camshaft sprockets should be aligned.**

   d. Turn the left-hand exhaust (lower) camshaft counterclockwise (as viewed from the front of the engine) until the

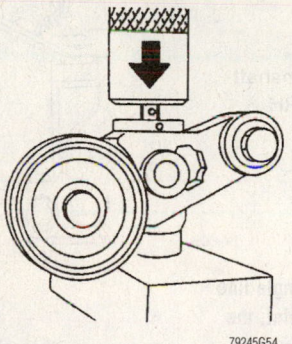

79245G54

Use a vertical press to push the adjuster rod into its housing until it is flush with the assembly's outer surface . . .—Subaru Forester 2.5L DOHC engine

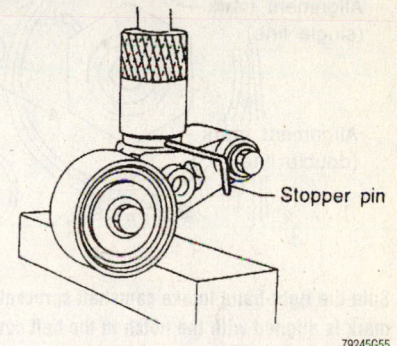

Stopper pin

79245G55

. . . then insert a 0.08 in. (2mm) diameter pin or Allen wrench into the housing and rod holes to hold it in position—Subaru Forester 2.5L DOHC engine

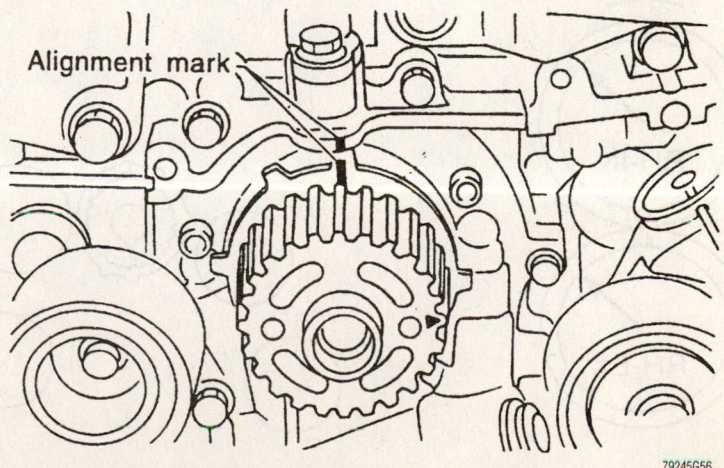

Alignment mark

79245G56

If the camshaft sprockets are no longer aligned, rotate the crankshaft sprocket until the marks are aligned . . .—Subaru Forester 2.5L DOHC engine

Refer to the model specific sections for engine mechanical service procedures

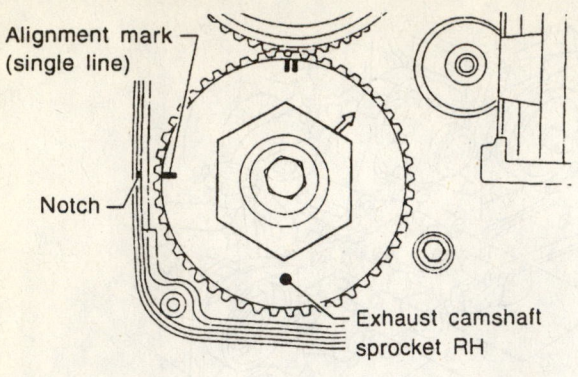

. . . then turn the right-hand exhaust camshaft until the single line mark is aligned with the notch in the belt cover—Subaru Forester 2.5L DOHC engine

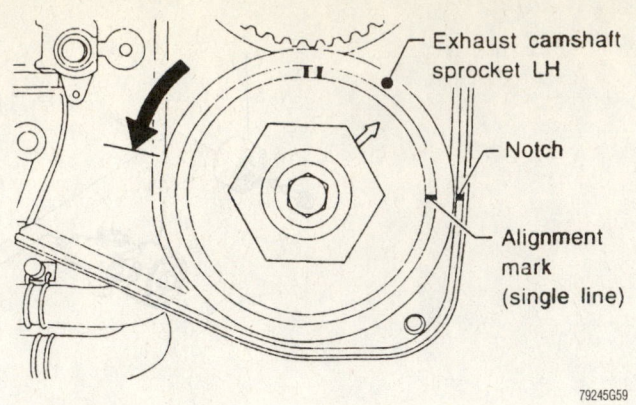

Rotate the left-hand exhaust camshaft until the single line mark is aligned with the notch in the belt cover . . .—Subaru Forester 2.5L DOHC engine

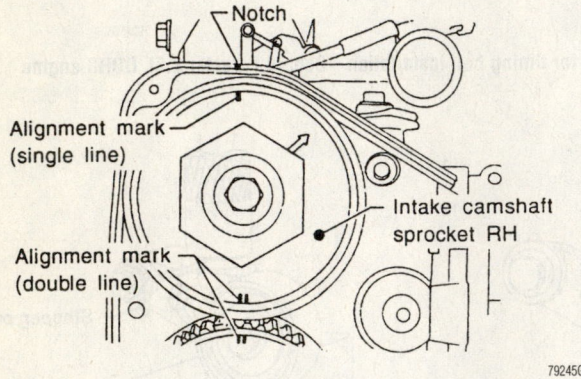

Spin the right-hand intake camshaft sprocket so that the single line mark is aligned with the notch in the belt cover—at this point, the double line marks on both right-hand camshaft sprockets must be aligned—Subaru Forester 2.5L DOHC engine

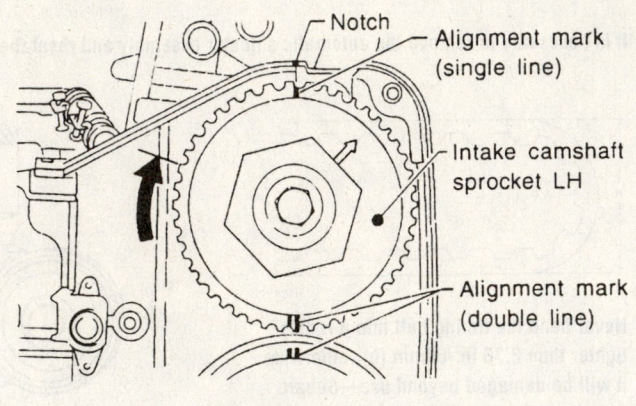

. . . then align the single line mark on the left-hand intake sprocket with the belt cover notch—Subaru Forester 2.5L DOHC engine

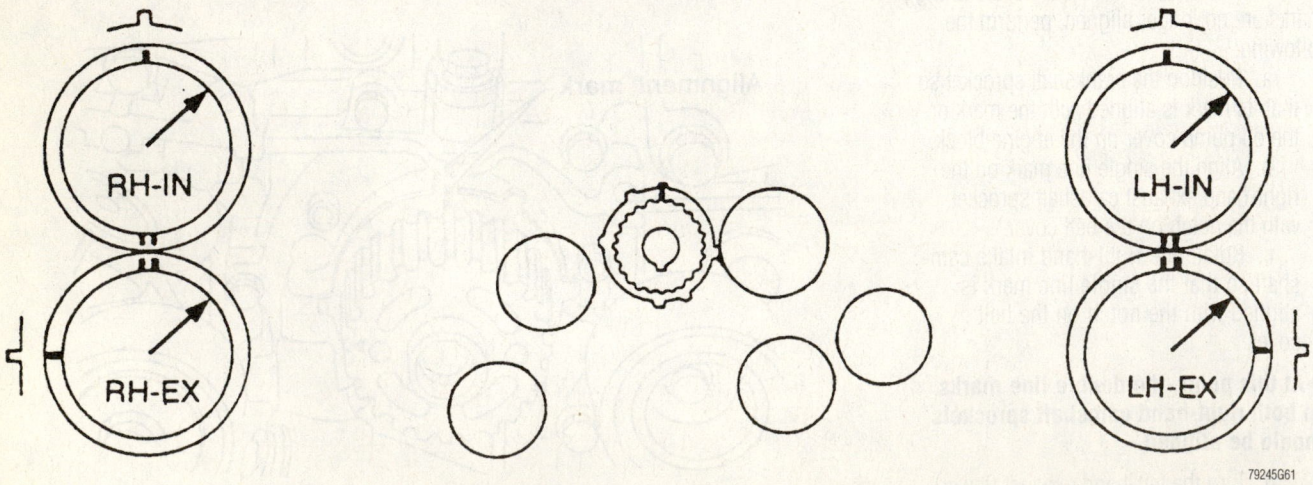

After orienting all 5 sprockets, the alignment marks should be positioned as shown—Subaru Forester 2.5L DOHC engine

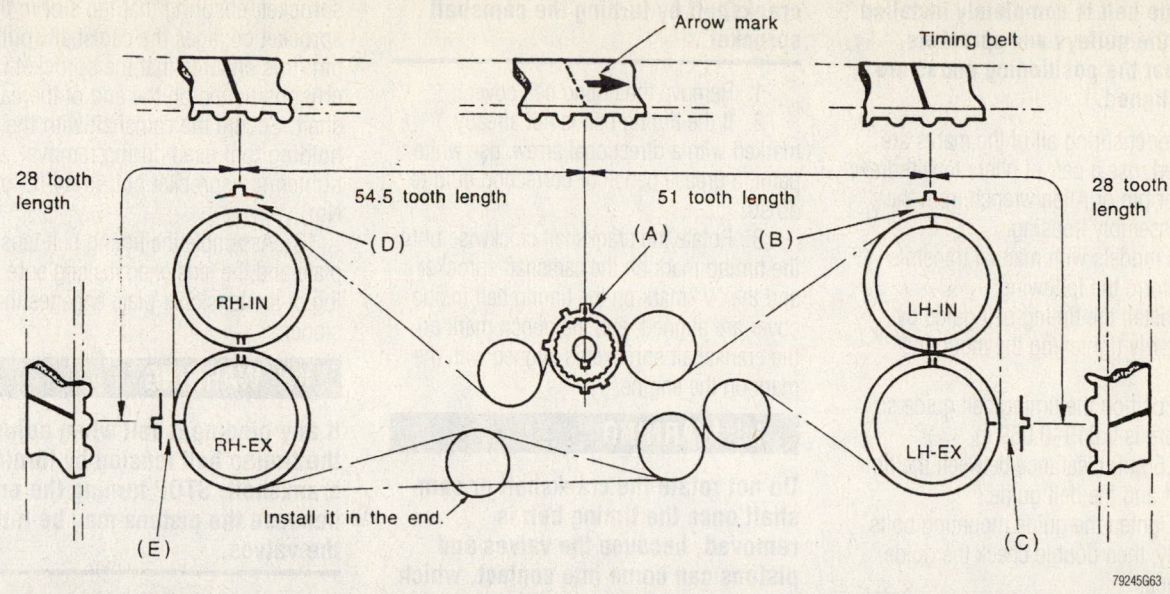

When installing the timing belt, be sure to route it in the proper order (a through e), and ensure that all of the matchmarks are properly aligned—Subaru Forester 2.5L DOHC engine

On models equipped with a manual transmission, loosen the 2 timing belt guide bolts and separate the guide from the engine block—Subaru Forester 2.5L DOHC engine

single line mark is aligned with the notch on the belt cover.

　e. Position the single line mark on the left-hand intake camshaft sprocket so that it is aligned with the notch on the belt cover. When rotating the camshaft, do so only in a clockwise direction (as viewed from the front of the engine).

➡At this point, the double line marks on both left-hand camshaft sprockets should be aligned.

　f. Ensure the timing marks are aligned as shown in the accompanying illustration. If they are not, repeat Substeps 12a through 12e until they are properly aligned.
13. Install the timing belt around the camshaft, crankshaft and idler pulleys so

that the positioning marks on the timing belt are aligned with the marks on the sprockets as follows:

　a. Position the timing belt on the crankshaft sprocket so that the marks are aligned.

　b. Route the belt down and under the left-hand, upper idler pulley, then up and around the left-hand intake camshaft sprocket, ensuring the camshaft sprocket mark is aligned with the mark on the belt.

　c. Route the belt down and around the left-hand exhaust camshaft sprocket, making sure the marks are properly aligned, then up and over the first lower idler pulley and down and around the second lower idler pulley.

　d. While holding the timing belt on the inner, left-hand, lower idler pulley, route the other side of the timing belt (from the crankshaft sprocket) down and under the right-hand upper idler pulley.

　e. Route the timing belt up and around the right-hand intake camshaft sprocket so that the belt and sprocket marks are aligned.

　f. Position the belt down and around the right-hand exhaust camshaft sprocket, ensuring the positioning marks are aligned.
14. Install the right-hand lower idler pulley so that the timing belt is routed over the top side of it.

➡Once the belt is completely installed on all of the pulleys and sprockets, ensure that the positioning marks are still all aligned.

15. After ensuring all of the marks are still aligned, use a pair of pliers to withdraw the stopper pin or Allen wrench from the adjuster assembly housing.

16. On models with manual transmissions, perform the following:

a. Install the timing belt guide by temporarily tightening the mounting bolts.

b. Position the timing belt guide so that there is 0.019–0.059 in. (0.5–1.5mm) clearance between the timing belt and the belt guide.

c. Tighten the guide mounting bolts securely, then double check the guide clearance.

17. Install the timing belt covers and all remaining engine components.

Suzuki Sidekick, Vitara and X-90

➡During these procedures, identify all components removed from the engine so that they may be reinstalled in their original positions. If discarding the old components so that new components can be installed, identifying the old items is not necessary.

1.6L 16-VALVE ENGINE

The 1.6L 16-valve engine is known as an interference motor, because it is fabricated with such close tolerances between the pistons and valves that, if the timing belt is incorrectly positioned, jumps teeth on one of the sprockets or breaks, the valve and pistons will come into contact. This can cause severe internal engine damage.

✳✳ WARNING

Do not rotate the crankshaft counter-clockwise or attempt to rotate the

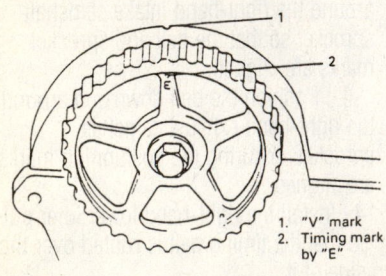

1. "V" mark
2. Timing mark by "E"

79245G22

Camshaft timing marks—Suzuki Sidekick, Vitara and X-90 1.6L 16-valve engine

crankshaft by turning the camshaft sprocket.

1. Remove the timing belt cover.

2. If the timing belt is not already marked with a directional arrow, use white paint, a grease pencil or correction fluid to do so.

3. Rotate the crankshaft clockwise until the timing mark on the camshaft sprocket and the "V" mark on the timing belt inside cover are aligned, and the punch mark on the crankshaft sprocket is aligned with the mark on the engine.

✳✳ WARNING

Do not rotate the crankshaft or camshaft once the timing belt is removed, because the valves and pistons can come into contact, which may cause internal engine damage.

4. Disconnect one end of the tensioner spring. Loosen the timing belt tensioner bolt and stud, then, using your finger, press the tensioner plate up and remove the timing belt from the crankshaft and camshaft sprockets.

5. Remove the timing belt tensioner, tensioner plate and spring from the engine.

6. Install Suzuki tool 09917-68220, or equivalent, onto the camshaft sprocket to hold the camshaft from rotating. Loosen the camshaft sprocket retaining bolt, then pull the camshaft sprocket off of the end of the camshaft.

7. Remove the crankshaft timing belt sprocket by loosening the center bolt, while preventing the crankshaft from rotating. To hold the crankshaft from turning, use Suzuki tool 09927-56010, or equivalent, or a large prybar inserted in the transmission housing slot and the flywheel teeth. Pull the sprocket off of the end of the crankshaft. Be sure to retain the crankshaft sprocket key and belt guide for assembly.

8. If necessary, remove the timing belt inside cover from the cylinder head.

To install:

9. If necessary, install the timing belt inside cover.

10. Slide the timing belt guide on the crankshaft so that the concave side faces the oil pump, then install the sprocket key in the groove in the crankshaft.

11. Slide the pulley onto the crankshaft, and install the center retaining bolt. Tighten the center bolt to 80 ft. lbs. (110 Nm). To hold the crankshaft from turning, use Suzuki tool 09927-56010, or equivalent, or a large prybar inserted in the transmission housing slot and the flywheel teeth.

12. Install the timing belt camshaft

sprocket, ensuring that the slot in the sprocket engages the camshaft (pulley) pin; this ensures that the sprocket is properly positioned on the end of the camshaft. Secure the camshaft with the holding tool used during removal, then tighten the sprocket bolt to 44 ft. lbs. (60 Nm).

13. Assemble the timing belt tensioner plate and the tensioner, making sure that the lug of the tensioner plate engages the tensioner.

✳✳ WARNING

If any binding is felt when adjusting the timing belt tension by turning the crankshaft, STOP turning the engine, because the pistons may be hitting the valves.

14. Install the timing belt tensioner, tensioner plate and spring on the engine. Tighten the mounting bolt and stud only finger-tight at this time. Ensure that when the tensioner is moved in a counterclockwise direction, the tensioner moves in the same direction. If the tensioner does not move, remove it and the tensioner plate to reassemble them properly.

15. Loosen all rocker arm valve lash locknuts and adjusting screws. This will permit movement of the camshaft without any rocker arm associated drag, which is essential for proper timing belt tensioning. If the camshaft does not rotate freely (free of rocker arm drag), the belt will not be properly tensioned.

16. Rotate the camshaft sprocket clockwise until the timing mark on the sprocket and the "V" mark on the timing belt inside cover are aligned.

17. Using a wrench, or socket and breaker bar, on the crankshaft sprocket center bolt, turn the crankshaft clockwise until the punch mark on the sprocket is aligned with the arrow mark on the oil pump.

18. With the camshaft and crankshaft marks properly aligned, push the tensioner up with your finger and install the timing belt on the 2 sprockets, ensuring that the drive side of the belt is free of all slack. Release your finger from the tensioner. Be sure to install the timing belt so that the directional arrow is pointing in the appropriate direction.

➡In this position, the No. 4 cylinder is at Top Dead Center (TDC) on the compression stroke.

19. Rotate the crankshaft clockwise 2 full revolutions, then tighten the tensioner stud

to 97 inch lbs. (11 Nm). Then, tighten the tensioner bolt to 18 ft. lbs. (24 Nm).

20. Ensure that all 4 timing marks are still aligned as before; if they are not, remove the timing belt, and install and tension it again.

21. Install the timing belt cover and all related components.

Toyota Sienna

3.0L (1MZ-FE) ENGINE

1. Disconnect the negative battery cable.

2. Remove the outer front cowl top panel assembly by performing the following procedure:

a. Remove the wiper arm/blade assemblies head caps, nuts and assemblies.

b. Remove the head-to-cowl seal and the cowl panel hole cover.

c. Disconnect the windshield washer clip and hose.

d. Remove both (right and left) cowl top ventilator louvers.

e. Disconnect the electrical connector from the windshield wiper motor.

f. Remove the outer front cowl top panel assembly-to-cowl bolts and the panel.

3. Raise and safely support the vehicle.

4. Remove the right front wheel assembly and apron seal.

5. Remove the alternator by performing the following procedure:

a. Loosen the pivot bolt, adjusting lockbolt and adjusting bolt, then, remove the drive belt.

b. Disconnect the alternator's electrical connector.

c. Remove the nut and the alternator wire.

d. Disconnect the wiring harness from the clip.

e. Remove the alternator-to-bracket pivot bolt, the washer, adjusting lockbolt and alternator.

6. Loosen the power steering pump's mount and adjusting bolt, then, remove the drive belt.

7. Disconnect the hose from the engine coolant reservoir.

8. Disconnect the Diagnostic Link Connector 1 (DLC1) from the No. 2 right side engine mounting bracket.

9. Remove the right side engine mounting stay, the engine moving control rod and the No. 2 right side engine mounting bracket.

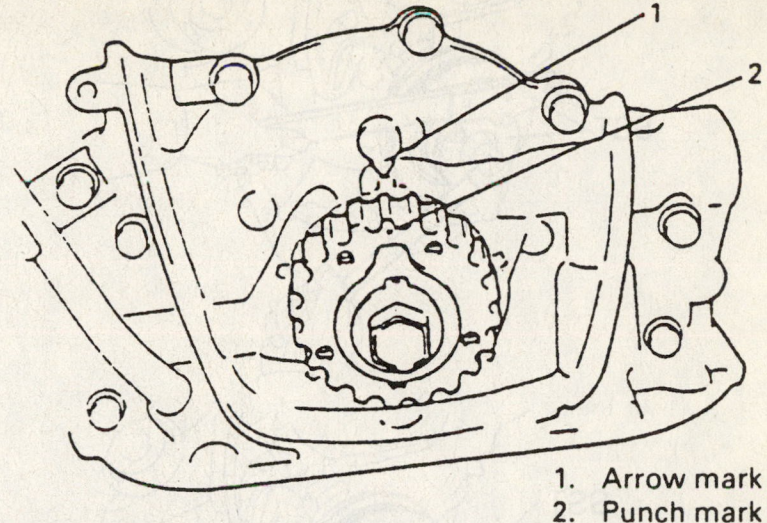

1. Arrow mark
2. Punch mark

79245G23

Align the punch mark with the arrow for proper timing belt installation—Suzuki Sidekick, Vitara and X-90 1.6L 16-valve engine

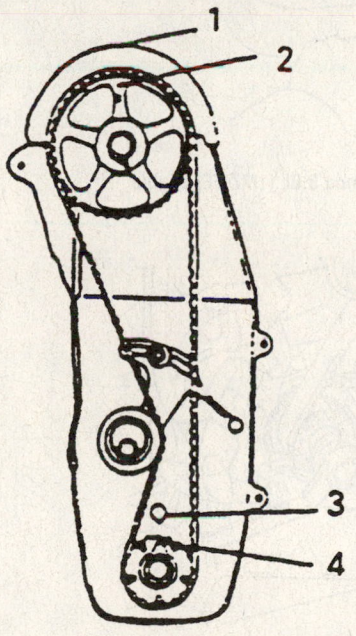

1. "V" mark on cylinder head cover
2. Timing mark by "E" on camshaft timing belt pulley
3. Arrow mark on oil pump case
4. Punch mark on crankshaft timing belt pulley

79245G47

Rotate the crankshaft clockwise until the camshaft and crankshaft timing marks are aligned—Suzuki Sidekick, Vitara and X-90 1.6L 16-valve engine

10. Loosen the alternator's pivot bolt, the nut and the No. 2 alternator bracket.

11. Using the Crankshaft Pulley Holding tool 09213-54015, Bolt tool 91651-60855 and Companion Flange Holding tool 09330-00021, or equivalent, remove the crankshaft pulley bolt.

12. Using a Puller "C" Set 09950-50011 (Hanger 150 tool 09951-05010, Slide Arm tool 09952-5010, Center Bolt 100 tool 09953-05010, Center Bolt 150 tool 09953-05020 and 2 No. 2 Claw tools 09954-05020), pull the crankshaft pulley from the crankshaft.

13. Remove the lower (No. 1) timing belt cover. Remove the timing belt guide from the crankshaft.

14. Remove the engine wire protector clamps from the upper (No. 2) timing belt

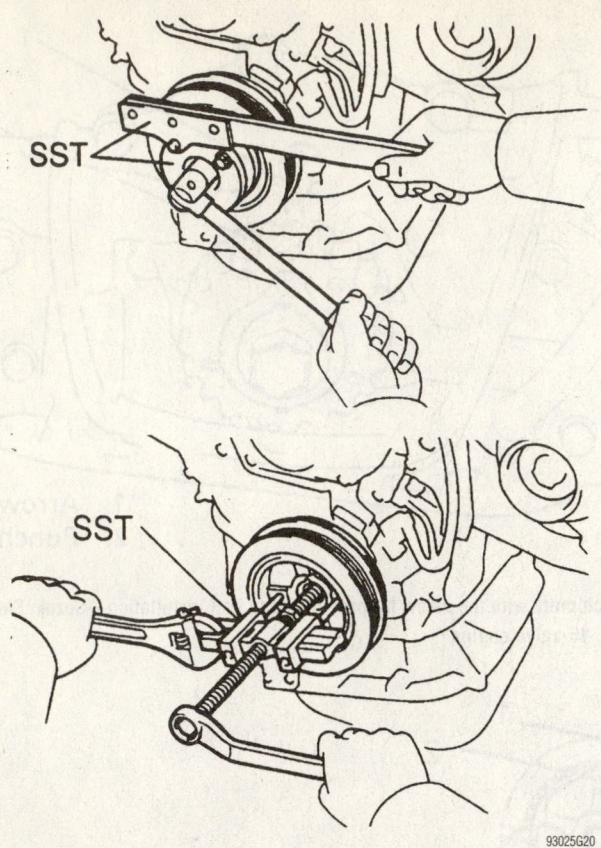

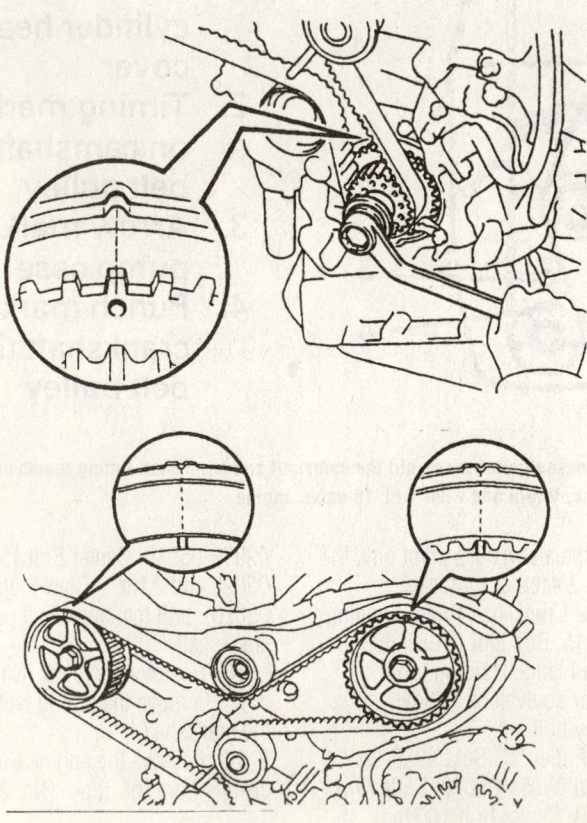

Removing/installing the crankshaft pulley—Toyota Sienna 3.0L (1MZ-FE) engine

View of the timing mark locations—Toyota Sienna 3.0L (1MZ-FE) engine

cover and remove the upper (No. 2) timing belt cover.

15. Remove the right side engine mounting brace

➡**If reusing the timing belt, be sure that you can still read the installation marks. If not, place new installation marks on the timing belt to match the timing marks of the camshaft timing pulleys.**

16. Temporarily install the crankshaft pulley bolt.

17. Set the No. 1 cylinder to Top Dead Center (TDC) of the compression stroke, as follows:

   a. Rotate the crankshaft (CLOCKWISE) to align the timing marks: dimple on the crankshaft timing sprocket with the notch on the oil pump body.

   b. Check that the timing marks on the camshaft sprockets and the rear timing belt cover are aligned; if not, rotate the crankshaft 360 degrees (1 revolution) and align the marks.

18. Remove the timing belt tensioner and the timing belt.

To install:

19. Inspect the timing belt tensioner by performing the following procedures:

   a. Inspect the seal for leakage; if leakage is suspected, replace the tensioner.

   b. Using both hands to hold the tensioner facing upward, strongly press the pushrod against a solid surface. If the pushrod moves, replace the tensioner.

❊❊ **WARNING**

Never hold the tensioner with the pushrod facing downward.

   c. Measure the pushrod's protrusion from the housing end, it should be 0.394–0.425 in. (10.0–10.8mm); if the protrusion is not as specified, replace the tensioner.

20. Set the No. 1 cylinder to Top Dead Center (TDC) of the compression stroke, as follows:

   a. Rotate the crankshaft (CLOCKWISE) to align the timing marks: dimple on the crankshaft timing sprocket with the notch on the oil pump body.

   b. Check that the timing marks on the camshaft sprockets and the rear timing belt cover are aligned; if not, rotate the crankshaft 1 revolution (360 degrees) and align the marks.

21. Install the timing belt in the following order:

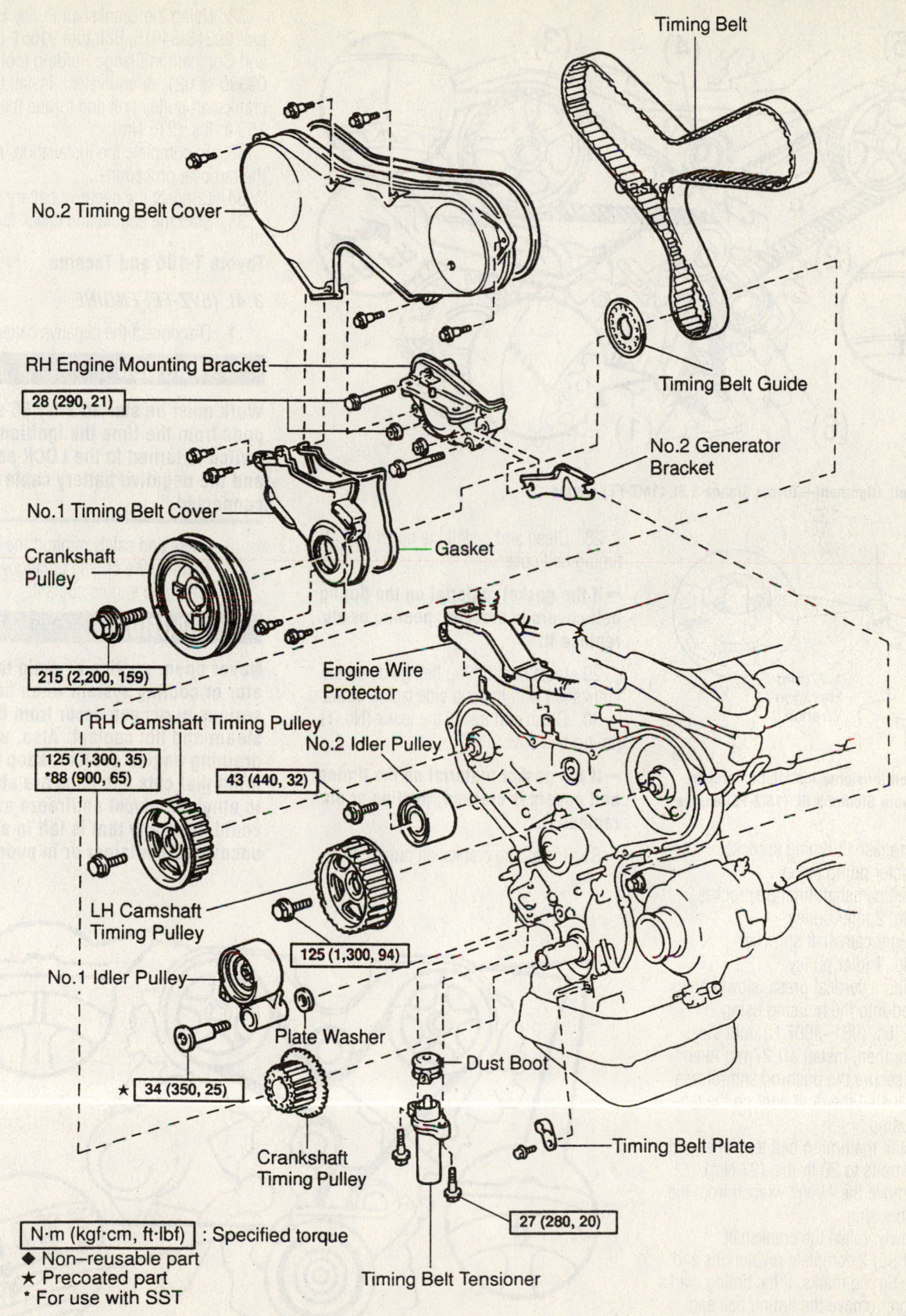

Timing Belt

No.2 Timing Belt Cover

Timing Belt Guide

RH Engine Mounting Bracket

28 (290, 21)

No.2 Generator Bracket

No.1 Timing Belt Cover

Gasket

Crankshaft Pulley

215 (2,200, 159)

Engine Wire Protector

RH Camshaft Timing Pulley

125 (1,300, 35)
*88 (900, 65)

No.2 Idler Pulley

43 (440, 32)

LH Camshaft Timing Pulley

125 (1,300, 94)

No.1 Idler Pulley

Plate Washer

Dust Boot

★ 34 (350, 25)

Crankshaft Timing Pulley

Timing Belt Plate

27 (280, 20)

N·m (kgf·cm, ft·lbf) : Specified torque
◆ Non–reusable part
★ Precoated part
* For use with SST

Timing Belt Tensioner

93025G19

Exploded view of the timing belt assembly—Toyota Sienna 3.0L (1MZ-FE) engine

Timing chain and gear service is covered in the model specific sections of this manual

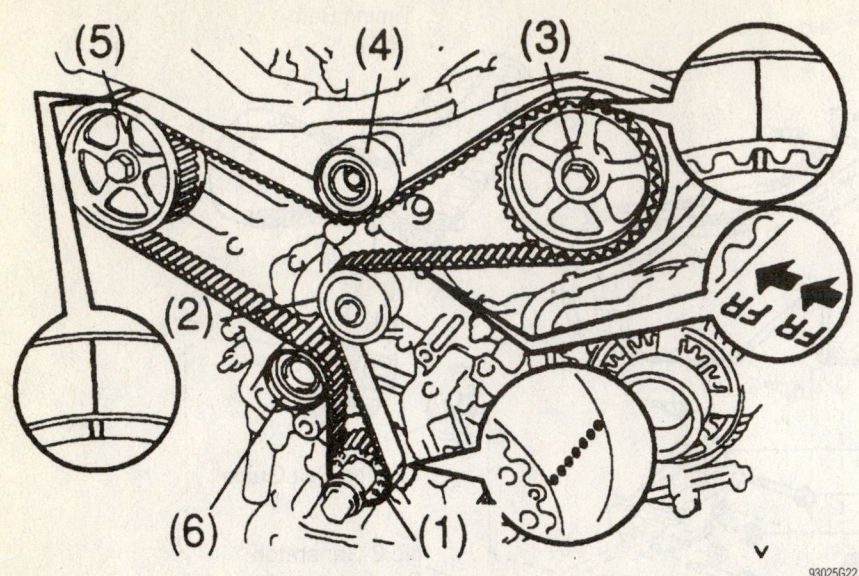

Timing belt alignment—Toyota Sienna 3.0L (1MZ-FE) engine

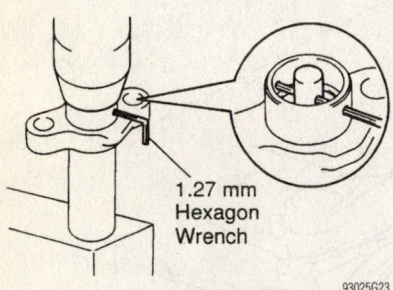

1.27 mm Hexagon Wrench

Timing belt tensioner installation preparation—Toyota Sienna 3.0L (1MZ-FE) engine

a. Crankshaft timing sprocket
b. Water pump pulley
c. Left camshaft timing sprocket
d. No. 2 idler pulley
e. Right camshaft sprocket
f. No. 1 idler pulley

22. Using a vertical press, slowly press the pushrod into the housing using 200–2205 lbs. (981–9807 N) until the holes align, then, install a 1.27mm Allen® wrench to secure the pushrod and release the press. Install the dust boot on the tensioner housing.

23. Install the timing belt tensioner and torque the bolts to 20 ft. lbs. (27 Nm).

24. Remove the Allen® wrench from the tensioner housing.

25. Slowly, rotate the crankshaft (CLOCKWISE) 2 complete revolutions and realign the timing marks. If the timing marks do not align, remove the timing belt and reinstall it.

26. Remove the crankshaft pulley bolt.

27. Install the right side engine mounting bracket and torque the bolts to 21 ft. lbs. (28 Nm).

28. Clean and install the upper (No. 2) timing belt cover.

➡**If the gasket material on the timing belt covers is cracked, peeling or etc., replace it.**

29. Install the timing belt guide on the crankshaft with the cup side facing outward.

30. Clean and install the lower (No. 1) timing belt cover.

➡**If the gasket material on the timing belt covers is cracked, peeling or etc., replace it.**

31. Install the crankshaft pulley.

32. Using the Crankshaft Pulley Holding tool 09213-54015, Bolt tool 91651-60855 and Companion Flange Holding tool 09330-00021, or equivalent, install the crankshaft pulley bolt and torque the bolt to 159 ft. lbs. (215 Nm).

33. To complete the installation, reverse the removal procedures.

34. Connect the negative battery cable.

35. Start the engine and check for leaks.

Toyota T-100 and Tacoma

3.4L (5VZ-FE) ENGINE

1. Disconnect the negative battery cable.

✷✷ CAUTION

Work must be started after 90 seconds from the time the ignition switch is turned to the LOCK position and the negative battery cable is disconnected.

2. Raise and safely support the vehicle.
3. Remove the engine undercover.
4. Drain the engine coolant.

✷✷ CAUTION

Never open, service or drain the radiator or cooling system when hot; serious burns can occur from the steam and hot coolant. Also, when draining engine coolant, keep in mind that cats and dogs are attracted to ethylene glycol antifreeze and could drink any that is left in an uncovered container or in puddles on

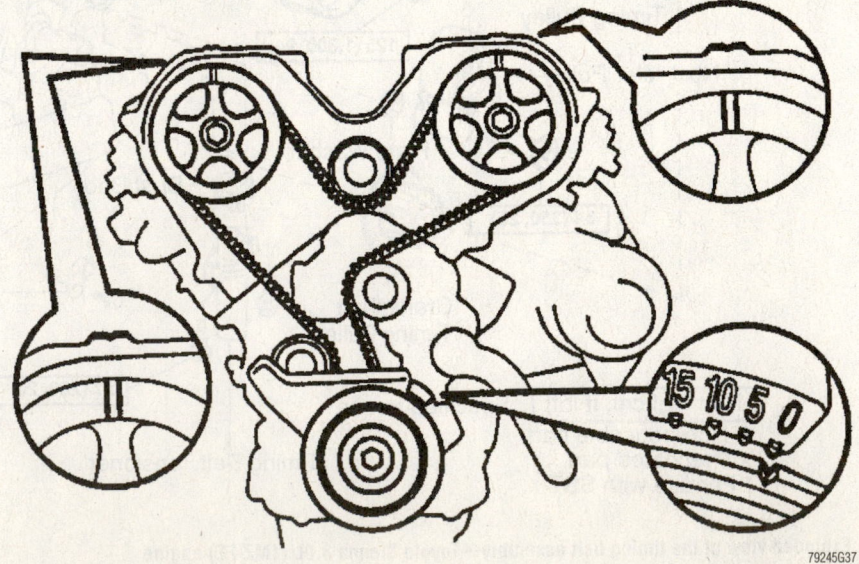

Turn the crankshaft clockwise to align the timing marks before removing the timing belt—Toyota T-100 and Tacoma 3.4L (5VZ-FE) engine

the ground. **This will prove fatal in sufficient quantities. Always drain coolant into a sealable container. Coolant should be reused unless it is contaminated or is several years old.**

5. Disconnect the upper radiator hose from the engine.

6. Remove the power steering drive belt.

7. Remove the air conditioning drive belt by loosening the idler pulley nut and the adjusting bolt.

8. Loosen the lockbolt, pivot bolt, and the adjusting bolt and the alternator drive belt.

9. Remove the No. 2 fan shroud by removing the 2 clips.

10. Remove the fan with the fluid coupling and fan pulleys.

11. Disconnect the power steering pump from the engine and set aside. Do not disconnect the lines from the pump.

12. If equipped with air conditioning, disconnect the compressor from the engine and set aside. Do not disconnect the lines from the compressor.

13. If equipped with air conditioning, disconnect the air conditioning bracket.

14. Remove the No. 2 timing belt cover, as follows:

   a. Detach the camshaft position sensor connector from the No. 2 timing belt cover.

   b. Disconnect the 3 spark plug wire clamps from the No. 2 timing belt cover.

   c. Remove the 6 bolts and remove the timing belt cover.

15. Remove the fan bracket, as follows:

   a. Remove the power steering adjusting strut by removing the nut.

   b. Remove the fan bracket by removing the bolt and nut.

16. Set the No. 1 cylinder at Top Dead Center (TDC) of the compression stroke, as follows:

   a. Turn the crankshaft pulley and align its groove with the timing mark **0** of the No. 1 timing belt cover.

   b. Check that the timing marks of the camshaft timing pulleys and the No. 3 timing belt cover are aligned. If not, turn the crankshaft pulley one revolution (360 degrees).

➡**If reusing the timing belt, be sure that you can still read the installation marks. If not, place new installation marks on the timing belt to match the timing marks of the camshaft timing pulleys.**

17. Remove the timing belt tensioner by alternately loosening the 2 bolts.

18. Remove the camshaft timing pulleys, as follows:

   a. Using SST 09960-10010, or equivalent, remove the pulley bolt, the timing pulley and the knock pin. Remove the 2 timing pulleys with the timing belt.

19. Remove the crankshaft pulley, as follows:

   a. Using SST 09213-54015 and 09330-00021 or their equivalents, loosen the pulley bolt.

   b. Remove the SST tool, the pulley bolt and the pulley.

20. Remove the starter wire bracket and the No. 1 timing belt cover.

21. Remove the timing belt guide and remove the timing belt.

22. Remove the bolt and the No. 2 idler pulley.

23. Remove the pivot bolt, the No. 1 idler pulley and the plate washer.

24. Remove the crankshaft gear.

To install:

25. Install the crankshaft timing gear.

   a. Align the timing pulley set key with the key groove of the gear.

   b. Using SST 09214-60010, or equivalent, and a hammer, tap in the timing gear with the flange side facing inward.

26. Install the plate washer and the No. 1 idler pulley with the pivot bolt and tighten it to 26 ft. lbs. (35 Nm). Check that the pulley bracket moves smoothly.

27. Install the No. 2 timing belt idler with the bolt. Tighten the bolt to 30 ft. lbs. (40 Nm). Check that the pulley bracket moves smoothly.

28. Temporarily install the timing belt, as follows:

   a. Using the crankshaft pulley bolt, turn the crankshaft and align the timing marks of the crankshaft timing pulley and the oil pump body.

   b. Align the installation mark on the timing belt with the dot mark of the crankshaft timing pulley.

   c. Install the timing belt on the crankshaft timing pulley, No. 1 idler pulley and the water pump pulleys.

29. Install the timing belt guide with the cup side facing outward.

30. Install the No. 1 timing belt cover and starter wire bracket. Tighten the timing belt cover bolts to 80 inch lbs. (9 Nm).

✳✳ WARNING

If any binding is felt when adjusting the timing belt tension by turning the

crankshaft, **STOP turning the engine, because the pistons may be hitting the valves.**

31. Install the crankshaft pulley, as follows:

   a. Align the pulley set key with the key groove of the crankshaft pulley.

   b. Install the pulley bolt and tighten it to 184 ft. lbs. (250 Nm).

32. Install the left camshaft timing pulley.

   a. Install the knock pin to the camshaft.

   b. Align the knock pin hose of the camshaft with the knock pin groove of the timing pulley.

   c. Slide the timing belt pulley on the camshaft with the flange side facing outward. Tighten the pulley bolt to 81 ft. lbs. (110 Nm).

33. Set the No. 1 cylinder to TDC of the compression stroke, as follows:

   a. Turn the crankshaft pulley, and align its groove with the timing mark **0** of the No. 1 timing belt cover.

   b. Turn the camshaft to align the knock pin hole of the camshaft with the timing mark of the No. 3 timing belt cover.

   c. Turn the camshaft timing pulley, and align the timing marks of the camshaft timing pulley and the No. 3 timing belt cover.

34. Connect the timing belt to the left camshaft timing pulley, as follows:

➡**Check that the installation mark on the timing belt is aligned with the end of the No. 1 timing belt cover.**

   a. Using SST 09960-01000, or equivalent, slightly turn the left camshaft timing pulley clockwise. Align the installation mark on the timing belt with the timing mark of the camshaft timing pulley and hang the timing belt on the left camshaft timing pulley.

   b. Align the timing marks of the left camshaft pulley and the No. 3 timing belt cover.

   c. Check that the timing belt has tension between the crankshaft timing pulley and the left camshaft timing pulley.

35. Install the right camshaft timing pulley and the timing belt, as follows:

   a. Align the installation mark on the timing belt with the timing mark of the right camshaft timing pulley and hang the timing belt on the right camshaft timing pulley with the flange side facing inward.

   b. Slide the right camshaft timing

pulley on the camshaft. Align the timing marks on the right camshaft timing pulley and the No. 3 timing belt cover.

    c. Align the knock pin hole of the camshaft with the knock pin groove of the pulley and install the knock pin. Install the bolt and tighten it to 81 ft. lbs. (110 Nm).

36. Set the timing belt tensioner, as follows:

    a. Using a press, slowly press in the pushrod using 220–2205 lbs. (981–9807 N) of force.

    b. align the holes of the pushrod and housing, pass a 1.5mm hex wrench through the holes to keep the setting position of the pushrod.

    c. Release the press and install the dust boot on the tensioner.

37. Install the timing belt tensioner and alternately tighten the bolts to 20 ft. lbs. (28 Nm). Using pliers, remove the 1.5mm hex wrench from the belt tensioner.

38. Check the valve timing, as follows:

    a. Slowly turn the crankshaft pulley 2 revolutions from TDC to TDC. Always turn the crankshaft pulley clockwise.

    b. Check that each pulley aligns with the timing marks. If the timing marks do not align, remove the timing belt and reinstall it.

39. Install the fan bracket with the bolt and nut.

40. Install the power steering adjusting strut with the nut.

41. Install the No. 2 timing belt cover. Tighten the bolts to 80 inch lbs. (9 Nm). Install the remaining components.

42. Fill the cooling system with coolant.

43. Connect the negative battery cable.

44. Start the engine and check for leaks.

Toyota 4Runner

3.4L (5VZ-FE) ENGINE

1. Disconnect the negative battery cable.

❋❋ CAUTION

Wait 90 seconds from the time the key is turned to LOCK and the negative battery cable is disconnected to begin work. This allows the SRS capacitor to discharge and prevent deployment of the air bag(s).

2. Raise and safely support the vehicle.
3. Remove the engine undercover.
4. Drain the engine coolant.

❋❋ CAUTION

Never open, service or drain the radiator or cooling system when hot; serious burns can occur from the steam and hot coolant. Also, when draining engine coolant, keep in mind that cats and dogs are attracted to ethylene glycol antifreeze and could drink any that is left in an uncovered container or in puddles on the ground. This will prove fatal in sufficient quantities. Always drain coolant into a sealable container. Coolant should be reused unless it is contaminated or is several years old.

5. Disconnect the upper radiator hose from the engine.

6. Remove the power steering drive belt.

7. Remove the air conditioning drive belt by loosening the idler pulley nut and the adjusting bolt.

8. If equipped with air conditioning, disconnect the compressor from the engine and set aside. Do not disconnect the lines from the compressor.

9. If equipped with air conditioning, disconnect the air conditioning bracket.

10. Remove the fan with the fluid coupling and fan pulleys.

11. Loosen the lockbolt, pivot bolt, and the adjusting bolt and the alternator drive belt.

12. Remove the No. 2 fan shroud by removing the 2 clips.

13. Disconnect the power steering pump

from the engine and set aside. Do not disconnect the lines from the pump.

14. Remove the oil dipstick and the guide.

15. Remove the No. 2 timing belt cover as follows:

    a. Detach the camshaft position sensor connector from the No. 2 timing belt cover.

    b. Disconnect the 4 spark plug wire clamps from the No. 2 timing belt cover.

    c. Remove the 6 bolts and remove the timing belt cover.

16. Remove the fan bracket as follows:

    a. Remove the power steering adjusting strut by removing the nut.

    b. Remove the fan bracket by removing the bolt and nut.

17. Using SST 09213-54015, or equivalent, remove the crankshaft pulley.

18. Remove the starter wire bracket and the No. 1 timing belt cover.

19. Remove the timing belt guide.

20. Set the No. 1 cylinder at Top Dead Center (TDC) of the compression stroke, as follows:

    a. Temporarily install the crankshaft pulley bolt to the crankshaft.

    b. Turn the crankshaft and align the timing marks of the crankshaft timing pulley and the oil pump body.

    c. Check that the timing marks of the camshaft timing pulleys and the No. 3 timing belt cover are aligned. If not, turn the crankshaft pulley one revolution (360 degrees).

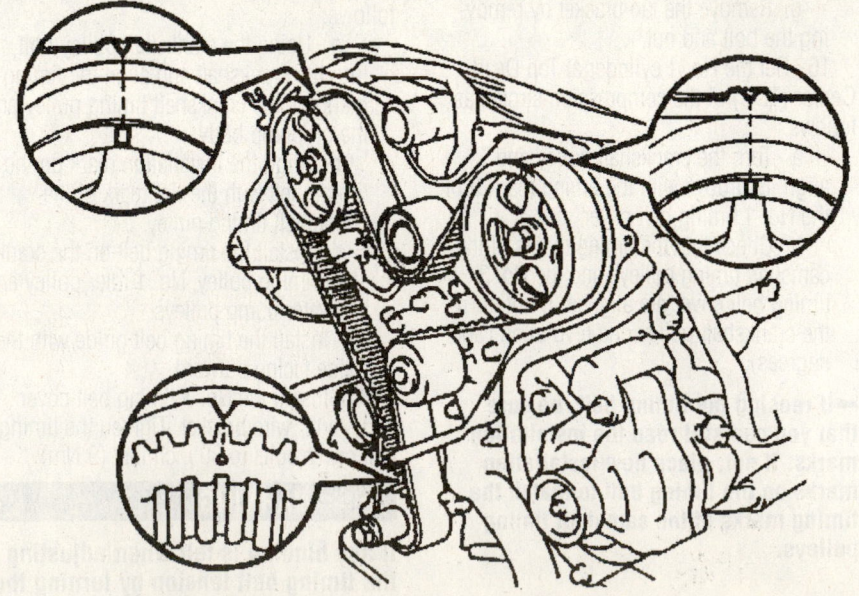

Crankshaft and camshaft timing mark locations—Toyota 4Runner 3.4L (5VZ-FE) engine

79245G38

➡️**If reusing the timing belt, be sure that you can still read the installation marks. If not, place new installation marks on the timing belt to match the timing marks of the camshaft timing pulleys.**

21. Remove the timing belt tensioner by alternately loosening the 2 bolts.

22. Remove the right and left camshaft pulleys.

23. Remove the No. 2 idler pulley.

24. Using a 10mm hex wrench, remove the pivot bolt, No.1 idler pulley and the plate washer.

25. Remove the timing belt guide and remove the timing belt.

26. Remove the crankshaft timing pulley.

To install:

27. Install the crankshaft timing belt pulley, as follows:

a. Align the timing belt pulley set key with the key groove of the timing pulley and slide on the timing pulley.

b. Slide on the timing belt pulley with the flange side facing inward.

28. Install the plate washer and the No. 1 idler pulley with the pivot bolt and tighten it to 26 ft. lbs. (35 Nm). Check that the pulley bracket moves smoothly.

29. Install the No. 2 timing belt idler with the bolt. Tighten the bolt to 30 ft. lbs. (40 Nm). Check that the pulley bracket moves smoothly.

30. Install the left and right camshaft timing pulleys.

31. Set the No. 1 cylinder to TDC of the compression stroke, as follows:

a. Using the crankshaft pulley bolt, turn the crankshaft and align the timing marks of the crankshaft timing pulley and the oil pump body.

b. Using SST 09960-10010, or equivalent, to turn the camshaft pulley to align the marks of the camshaft timing belt pulley and the No. 3 timing belt cover.

32. Install the timing belt, as follows:

➡️**The engine should be cold.**

a. Face the front mark on the timing belt forward.

b. Align the installation mark on the timing belt with the timing mark of the crankshaft timing pulley.

c. Align the installation marks on the timing belt with the timing marks of the camshaft pulleys.

33. Install the timing belt in the following order:

- Left camshaft pulley
- No. 2 idler pulley
- Right camshaft pulley
- Water pump pulley
- Crankshaft pulley
- No. 1 idler pulley

✱✱ WARNING

If any binding is felt when adjusting the timing belt tension by turning the crankshaft, STOP turning the engine, because the pistons may be hitting the valves.

34. Set the timing belt tensioner as follows:

a. Using a press, slowly press in the pushrod using 220–2205 lbs. (981–9807 N) of force.

b. Align the holes of the pushrod and housing, pass a 1.27mm wrench through the holes to keep the setting position of the pushrod.

c. Release the press and install the dust boot to the tensioner.

35. Install the timing belt tensioner and alternately tighten the bolts to 20 ft. lbs. (27 Nm). Using pliers, remove the 1.27mm wrench from the belt tensioner.

36. Check the valve timing, as follows:

a. Slowly turn the crankshaft and align the timing marks of the crankshaft timing pulley and the oil pump body. Always turn the crankshaft pulley clockwise.

b. Check that the timing marks of the right and left timing pulleys align with the timing marks of the No. 3 timing belt cover. If the marks do not align, remove the timing belt and reinstall it.

37. Install the timing belt guide with the cup side facing outward.

38. Install the No. 1 timing belt cover and starter wire bracket. Tighten the timing belt cover fasteners to 80 inch lbs. (9 Nm).

39. Install the crankshaft pulley, as follows:

a. Align the pulley set key with the key groove of the pulley and slide the pulley.

b. Using SST 09213-54014, or equivalent, tighten the bolt to 184 ft. lbs. (250 Nm).

40. Install the fan bracket with the bolt and nut.

41. Install the No. 2 timing belt cover, and tighten the bolts to 80 inch lbs. (9 Nm). Install the remaining components.

42. Fill the cooling system with coolant.

43. Connect the negative battery cable.

44. Start the engine and check for leaks.

45. Check the ignition timing.

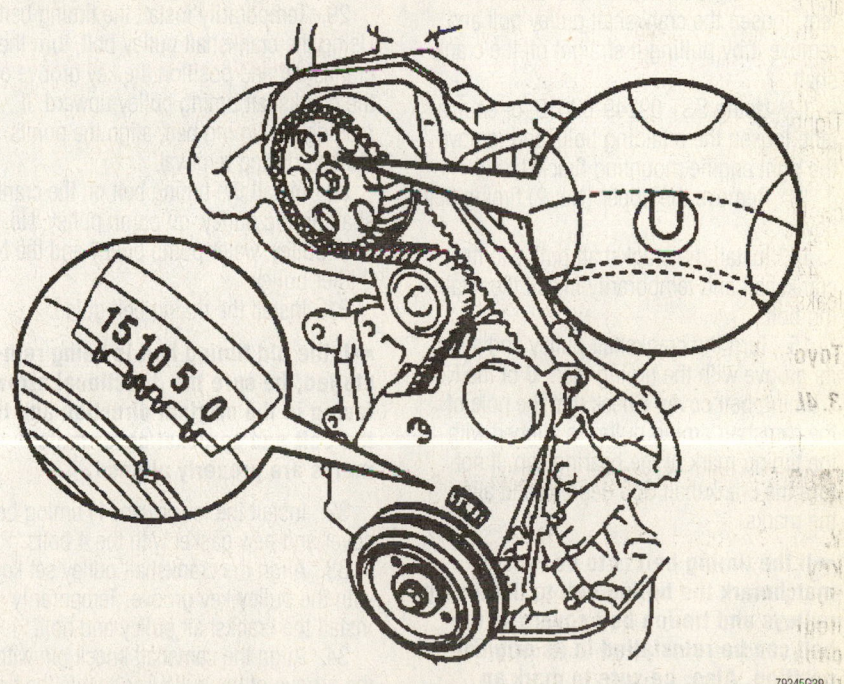

It is necessary to align the timing reference indicators prior to removing the timing belt—Toyota RAV4 2.0L (3S-FE) engine

Refer to the model specific sections for engine mechanical service procedures

Toyota RAV4

2.0L (3S-FE) ENGINE

The timing belt is not adjustable.

1. Disconnect the negative battery cable.

※ CAUTION

To avoid air bag deployment, if equipped, work must be started after approximately 90 seconds or longer from the time the ignition switch is turned to the LOCK position and the negative battery cable is disconnected from the battery.

2. Disconnect the power steering reservoir tank and remove the reservoir bracket.

3. Detach the wiring harness bracket for the Data Link Connector 1 (DLC1).

4. Remove the alternator and alternator bracket.

5. If equipped with ABS brakes, remove the ABS actuator.

6. Remove the right front wheel and the fender apron seal.

7. Remove the power steering drive belt.

8. Slightly raise the engine using a block of wood and floor jack under the oil pan to prevent damage.

9. Remove the 4 bolts, 2 nuts, and right-hand mounting bracket.

10. Remove the spark plugs.

11. Using SST 09213-54015, or equivalent, loosen the crankshaft pulley bolt and remove it by pulling it straight off the crankshaft.

12. Using SST 09249-63010, or equivalent, loosen the retaining bolts and remove the right engine mounting bracket.

13. Remove the upper (No. 2) timing belt cover.

14. Install the crankshaft pulley to the crankshaft and temporarily install the retaining bolt.

15. Turn the crankshaft pulley and align its groove with the timing mark **0** of the No. 1 timing belt cover. Check that the hole of the camshaft timing pulley is aligned with the timing mark of the bearing cap. If not, turn the crankshaft 360 degrees and align the marks.

➡**If the timing belt is to be reused, matchmark the timing belt to the timing pulleys and timing belt covers so the belt can be reinstalled in its original position. Also, be sure to mark an arrow on the belt to indicate which direction it was turning.**

16. Remove the timing belt from the camshaft timing pulley.

17. Hold the camshaft sprocket with a spanner wrench and remove the mounting bolt. Remove the camshaft pulley.

18. Remove the crankshaft pulley bolt and remove the crankshaft pulley.

19. Remove the No. 1 timing belt cover.

20. Remove the timing belt guide and the timing belt.

21. Remove the No. 1 idler pulley and tension spring.

22. Remove the No. 2 idler pulley.

23. Remove the crankshaft timing pulley.

24. Support the oil pump sprocket with a spanner wrench, then remove the mounting bolt and remove the sprocket.

To install:

25. Install the oil pump pulley. Tighten the nut to 18 ft. lbs. (24 Nm).

26. Install the crankshaft timing pulley. Align the pulley set key with the key groove of the pulley. Slide on the pulley facing the flange side inward.

27. Install the No. 2 idler pulley and tighten the mounting bolt to 31 ft. lbs. (42 Nm). Be sure that the pulley moves smoothly.

28. Install the No. 1 idler pulley with the bolt and the tension spring. Pry the pulley toward the left as far as it will go and tighten the bolt. Make sure that the pulley moves smoothly.

29. Temporarily install the timing belt. Using the crankshaft pulley bolt, turn the crankshaft and position the key groove of the crankshaft timing pulley upward. If reusing the timing belt, align the points marked during removal.

30. Install the timing belt on the crankshaft timing pulley, oil pump pulley, No. 1 idler pulley, water pump pulley and the No. 2 idler pulley.

31. Install the timing belt guide.

➡**If the old timing belt is being reinstalled, be sure the directional arrow is facing in the original direction and that the belt and sprocket/cover matchmarks are properly aligned.**

32. Install the lower (No. 1) timing belt cover and new gasket with the 4 bolts.

33. Align the crankshaft pulley set key with the pulley key groove. Temporarily install the crankshaft pulley and bolt.

34. Align the camshaft knock pin with the groove of the pulley, and slide the timing pulley onto the camshaft with the plate washer and set bolt.

35. Tighten the pulley set bolt to 40 ft. lbs. (54 Nm).

※※ WARNING

If any binding is felt when adjusting the timing belt tension by turning the crankshaft, STOP turning the engine, because the pistons may be hitting the valves.

36. Turn the crankshaft pulley and align the **0** mark on the lower (No. 1) timing belt cover.

37. Finish installing the timing belt and check the valve timing, as follows:

a. If reusing the old timing belt, align the matchmarks made previously and install the timing belt onto the camshaft pulley.

b. Align the marks on the timing belt with the marks on the camshaft pulley.

c. Loosen the No. 1 idler pulley set bolt ½ turn.

d. Turn the crankshaft pulley 2 complete revolutions TDC to TDC. ALWAYS turn the crankshaft CLOCKWISE. Check that the pulleys are still in alignment with the timing marks.

e. If the No. 1 idler pulley uses a green tension spring, slowly turn the crankshaft pulley 1⅞ revolutions, and align its groove with the mark at 45 degrees BTDC (for the No. 1 cylinder) of the No. 1 timing belt cover.

f. Tighten the No. 1 idler pulley set bolt to 31 ft. lbs. (42 Nm).

g. Be sure there is belt tension between the crankshaft and camshaft timing pulleys.

38. Place the right-hand engine mounting bracket in position but do not install the bolts.

39. Install the upper (No. 2) timing cover with a new gasket(s).

40. Remove the engine crankshaft pulley bolt and pulley.

41. Using SST 09249-63010, or equivalent, install the mounting bolts for the right-hand mounting bracket. Tighten the mounting bolts to 38 ft. lbs. (52 Nm).

42. Align the crankshaft pulley set key with the pulley key groove. Install the pulley. Tighten the pulley bolt to 80 ft. lbs. (108 Nm).

43. Install the spark plugs.

44. Install the right-hand mounting insulator, as follows:

a. Attach the mounting insulator to the body and mounting bracket with the 4 bolts and 2 nuts.

b. Tighten the 3 bolts to hold the mounting insulator to the body. Tighten the bolts to 47 ft. lbs. (64 Nm).

c. Tighten the 2 nuts and bolt to hold the mounting insulator to the mounting bracket. Tighten the bolt to 27 ft. lbs. (37 Nm) and the nut to 38 ft. lbs. (52 Nm).

45. Install and adjust the power steering pump drive belt.

46. Install the right-hand engine under-cover.

47. Install the right front wheel.

48. Lower the engine.

49. If equipped, install the ABS actuator.

50. Install the alternator and alternator bracket.

51. Install the wiring harness bracket for the DLC1.

52. Install the power steering reservoir bracket and reservoir.

53. Connect the negative battery cable.

54. Start the engine and check the timing.

Toyota Land Cruiser

4.7L (2UZ-FE) ENGINE

1. Disconnect the negative battery cable.

2. Raise and safely support the vehicle.

3. Remove the oil pan protector and the engine under cover.

4. Drain the cooling system and store the coolant for refilling purposes.

5. Lower the vehicle and remove the battery clamp cover.

6. From the top of the engine, remove the fuel return hose, the engine cover nuts/bolts and the cover.

7. Remove the air cleaner and the intake air connector assembly.

8. Remove the cooling fan pulley by performing the following procedures:

   a. Loosen the 4 fan clutch-to-fan pulley nuts.

   b. Using a box-end wrench on the serpentine drive belt tensioner bolt, rotate the tensioner counterclockwise and remove the drive belt.

➡ **The serpentine drive belt tensioner bolt is a left-hand thread.**

   c. Remove the fan clutch-to-fan pulley nuts, the fan, the clutch assembly and the fan pulley.

9. Remove the radiator by performing the following procedures:

   a. Disconnect the upper, lower and reservoir hoses from the radiator.

   b. Disconnect and plug the automatic transmission oil cooler at the radiator. Disconnect the automatic transmission

oil cooler hoses from the fan shroud clamp.

   c. Remove the radiator reservoir tank.

   d. Remove the fan shroud-to-radiator bolts and the shroud.

   e. Remove the 2 upper radiator-to-chassis nuts.

   f. Remove the middle radiator-to-chassis nut/bolts and brackets.

   g. Carefully, lift the radiator from the vehicle.

10. Remove the serpentine drive belt idler pulley bolt, cover plate and pulley.

11. Remove the right side (No. 3) timing belt cover.

12. Remove the left side (No. 3) timing belt cover by performing the following procedures:

   a. Disconnect the engine wire from both wire clamps.

   b. Disconnect the camshaft position sensor wire from the wire clamp on the left-side (No.3) timing belt cover.

   c. Disconnect the sensor connector from the connector bracket.

   d. Disconnect the sensor connector.

   e. Remove the wire grommet from the left-side (No. 3) timing belt cover.

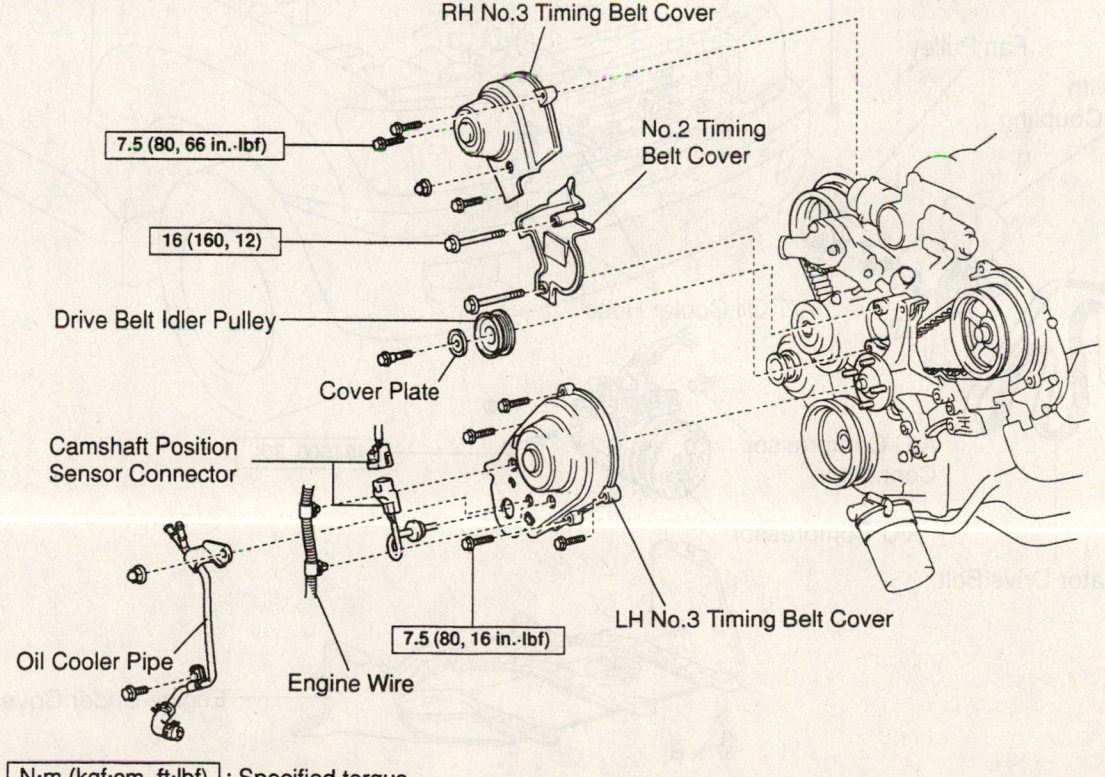

RH No.3 Timing Belt Cover

No.2 Timing Belt Cover

7.5 (80, 66 in.·lbf)

16 (160, 12)

Drive Belt Idler Pulley

Cover Plate

Camshaft Position Sensor Connector

7.5 (80, 16 in.·lbf)

LH No.3 Timing Belt Cover

Oil Cooler Pipe

Engine Wire

N·m (kgf·cm, ft·lbf) : Specified torque

Exploded view of upper timing belt covers—Toyota Land Cruiser 4.7L (2UZ-FE) engine

93025G25

For accessory drive belt replacement procedures see the model specific sections of this manual

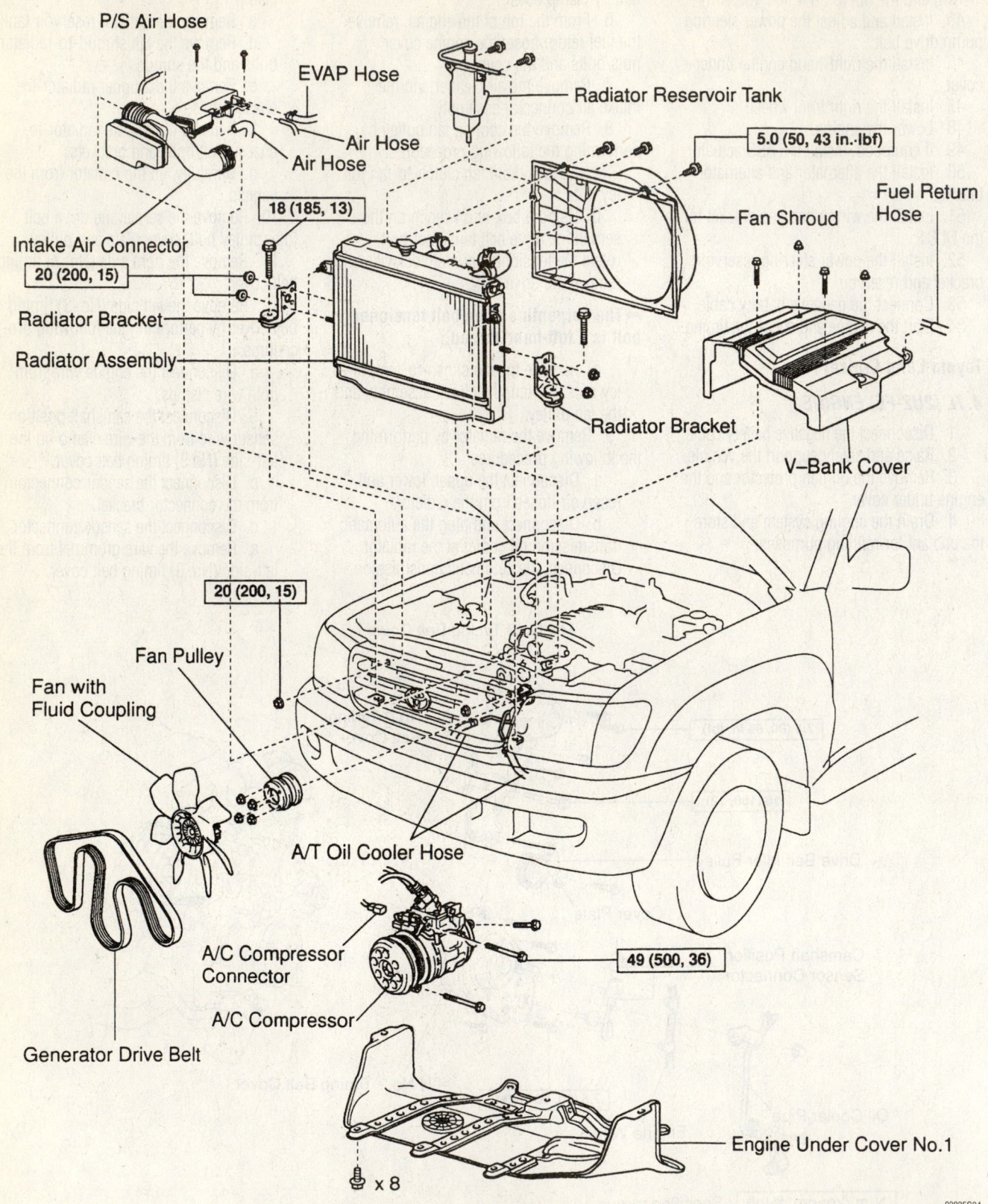

P/S Air Hose

EVAP Hose

Air Hose

Air Hose

Radiator Reservoir Tank

Fan Shroud

5.0 (50, 43 in.-lbf)

Fuel Return Hose

Intake Air Connector

18 (185, 13)

20 (200, 15)

Radiator Bracket

Radiator Assembly

Radiator Bracket

V–Bank Cover

20 (200, 15)

Fan Pulley

Fan with Fluid Coupling

A/T Oil Cooler Hose

A/C Compressor Connector

49 (500, 36)

A/C Compressor

Generator Drive Belt

Engine Under Cover No.1

x 8

93025G24

Exploded view of vehicle components for timing belt replacement—Toyota Land Cruiser 4.7L (2UZ-FE) engine

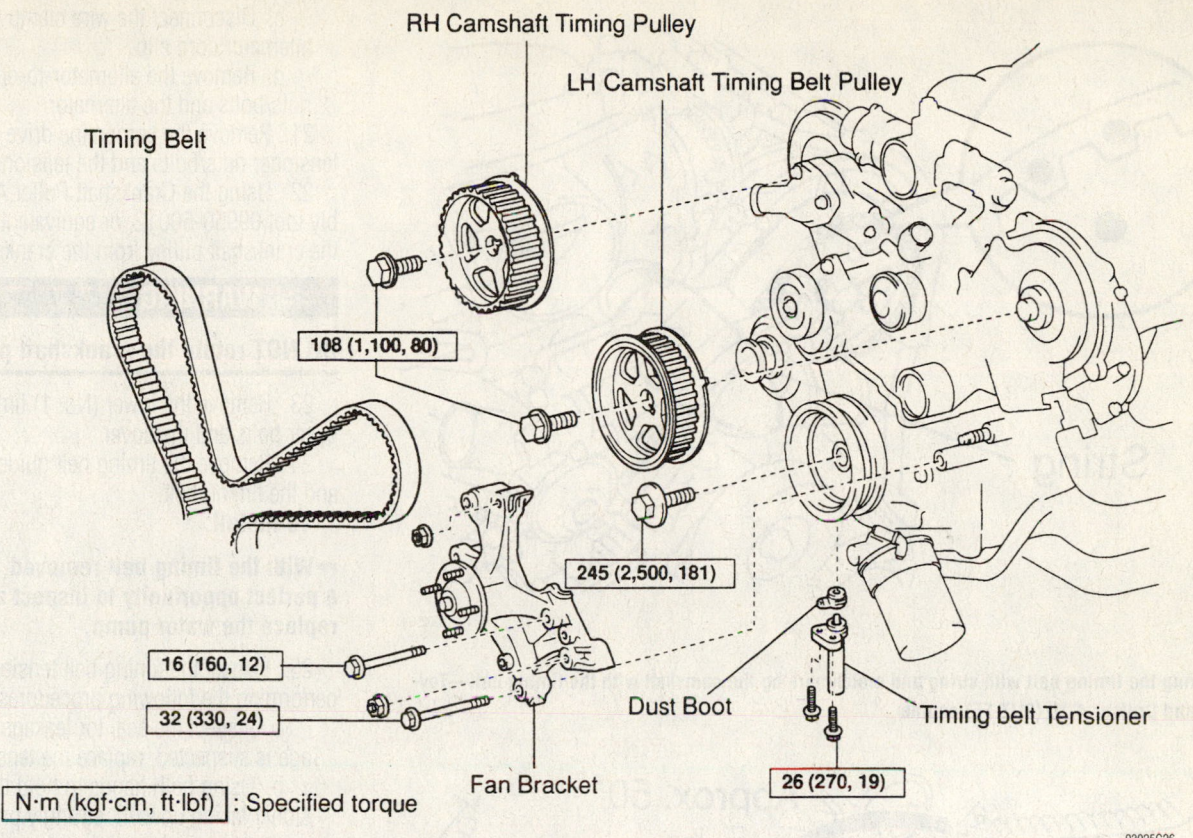

RH Camshaft Timing Pulley

LH Camshaft Timing Belt Pulley

Timing Belt

108 (1,100, 80)

245 (2,500, 181)

16 (160, 12)

32 (330, 24)

Dust Boot

Timing belt Tensioner

26 (270, 19)

Fan Bracket

N·m (kgf·cm, ft·lbf) : Specified torque

93025G26

Exploded view of upper timing sprockets and components—Toyota Land Cruiser 4.7L (2UZ-FE) engine

f. Remove the oil cooler tube bolts and tube.

13. Remove the middle (No. 2) timing belt cover bolts and cover.

14. Remove the cooling fan bracket nuts/bolts and bracket.

➡**If reusing the timing belt, make sure that there are 3 installation marks on the belt; if there are none, install them.**

15. Using the Crankshaft Pulley Holding tool 09213-70010, Bolt tool 90105-08076 and Companion Flange Holding tool

09330-00021, or equivalent, loosen the crankshaft pulley bolt.

16. Position the No. 1 cylinder to approximately 50 degrees After Top Dead Center (ATDC) of the compression stroke by performing the following procedures:

a. Rotate the crankshaft pulley (CLOCKWISE) to align its groove with the timing mark "0" on the lower (No. 1) timing belt cover.

b. Check that the camshaft sprocket timing marks are aligned with the rear timing belt plate marks; if not, rotate the crankshaft 1 revolution (360 degrees).

c. Rotate the crankshaft pulley approximately 50 degrees (CLOCKWISE) and align the crankshaft pulley timing mark between the centers of the crankshaft pulley bolt and the idler pulley bolt.

※※ **WARNING**

If the timing belt is disengaged, having the crankshaft pulley in the wrong angle can cause the valve to come into contact with the piston when removing the camshaft pulley.

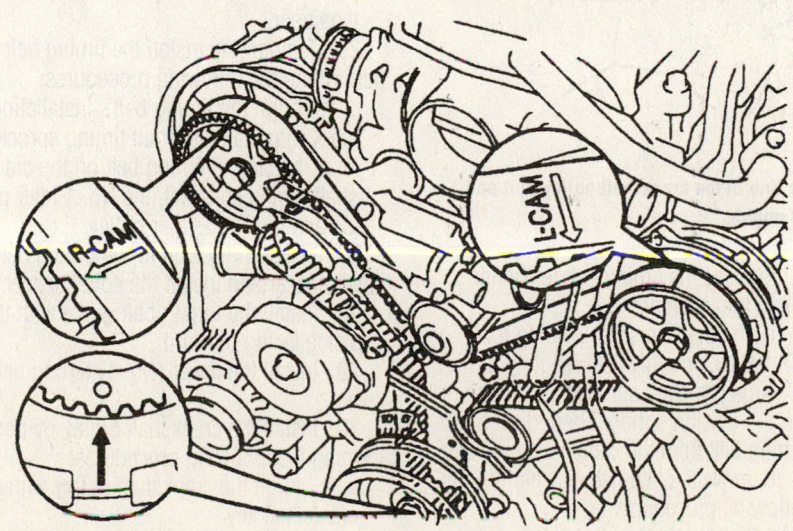

93025G28

Alignment of timing belt with the timing sprockets—Toyota Land Cruiser 4.7L (2UZ-FE) engine

For complete service labor times order Nichols' Chilton Labor Guide Manual

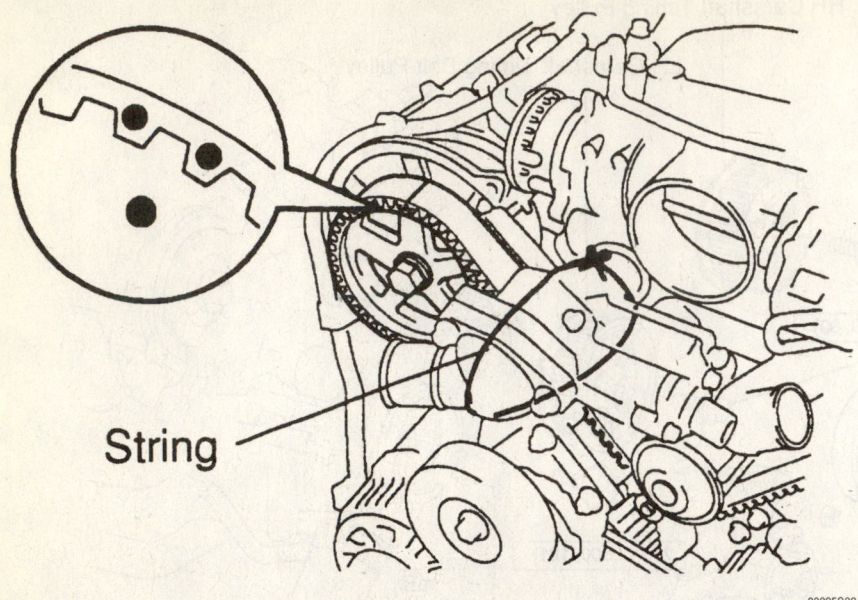

Securing the timing belt with string and matchmarking the camshaft with the timing belt—Toyota Land Cruiser 4.7L (2UZ-FE) engine

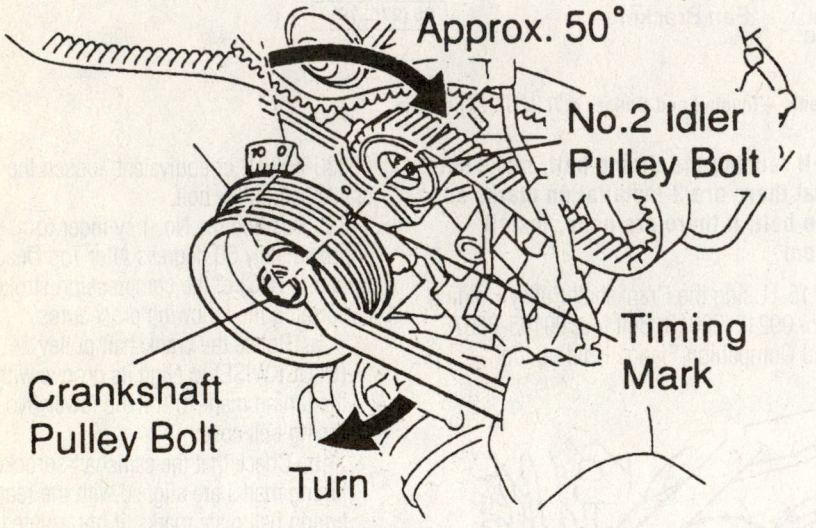

Aligning of crankshaft pulley timing mark with the center line of the crankshaft pulley bolt and the idler pulley bolt—Toyota Land Cruiser 4.7L (2UZ-FE) engine

17. Remove the crankshaft pulley bolt.

➡ If reusing the timing belt and the installation marks have disappeared, place new installation marks on the timing belt to match the camshaft timing sprocket marks.

➡ To avoid meshing the timing sprocket and the timing belt, secure one with a string; then, place matchmarks on the timing belt and the right-side camshaft timing sprocket.

18. Remove the timing belt tensioner bolts and the tensioner.

19. Using the Camshaft Holding tool 09960-10010, or equivalent, slightly turn the left-side camshaft sprocket clockwise to loosen the tension spring. Then, disconnect the timing belt from the camshaft sprockets.

20. Remove the alternator by performing the following procedures:
    a. Disconnect the electrical connector from the alternator.
    b. Remove the rubber cap/nut and disconnect the battery wire from the alternator.

c. Disconnect the wire clamp from the alternator cord clip.
    d. Remove the alternator-to-engine nuts/bolts and the alternator.

21. Remove the serpentine drive belt tensioner nuts/bolts and the tensioner.

22. Using the Crankshaft Puller Assembly tool 09950-50012, or equivalent, press the crankshaft pulley from the crankshaft.

✲✲ WARNING

DO NOT rotate the crankshaft pulley.

23. Remove the lower (No. 1) timing belt cover bolts and the cover.

24. Remove the timing belt guide, spacer and the timing belt.

To install:

➡ **With the timing belt removed, this is a perfect opportunity to inspect and/or replace the water pump.**

25. Inspect the timing belt tensioner by performing the following procedures:
    a. Inspect the seal for leakage; if leakage is suspected, replace the tensioner.
    b. Using both hands to hold the tensioner facing upward, strongly press the pushrod against a solid surface. If the pushrod moves, replace the tensioner.

✲✲ WARNING

Never hold the tensioner with the pushrod facing downward.

c. Measure the pushrod's protrusion from the housing end, it should be 0.413–0.453 in. (10.5–11.5mm). If the protrusion is not as specified, replace the tensioner.

26. Temporarily install the timing belt by performing the following procedures:
    a. Align the timing belt's installation mark with the crankshaft timing sprocket.
    b. Install the timing belt on the crankshaft timing sprocket, the No. 1 idler pulley and the No. 2 idler pulley.

27. Install the gasket to the timing belt cover spacer and install the cover spacer.

28. Install the timing belt guide with the cup side facing outward.

29. Install the lower (No. 1) timing belt cover.

30. Install the crankshaft pulley by performing the following procedures:
    a. Align the crankshaft pulley with the crankshaft key.
    b. Using the Crankshaft Installer tool 09223-46011, or equivalent, and a hammer, tap the crankshaft pulley into position.

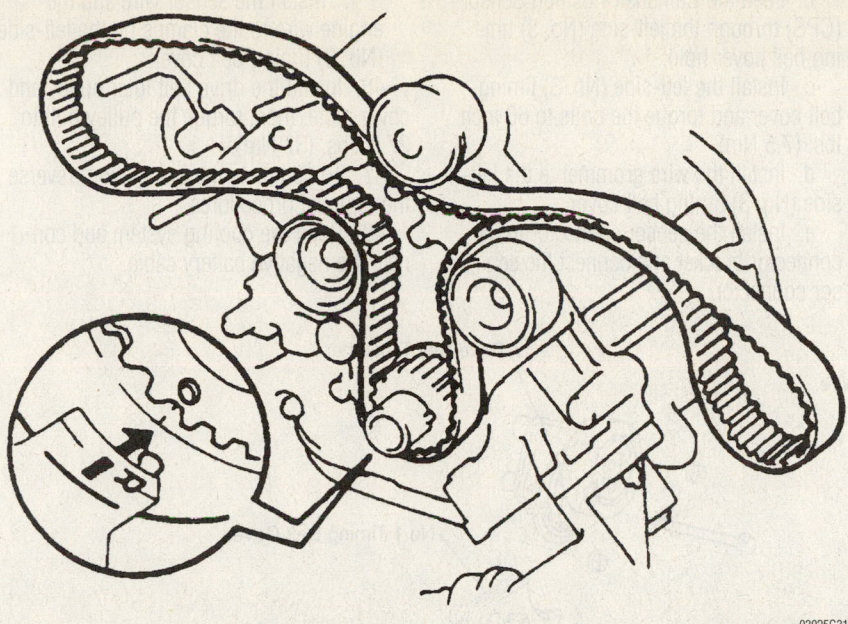

Installing the timing belt on the crankshaft sprocket—Toyota Land Cruiser 4.7L (2UZ-FE) engine

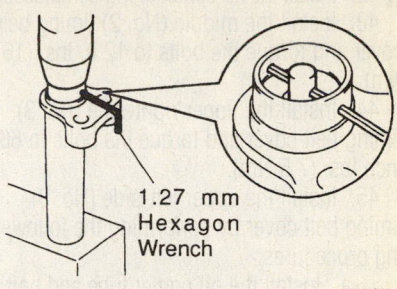

Securing the timing belt tensioner pushrod—Toyota Land Cruiser 4.7L (2UZ-FE) engine

and slide the belt onto the camshaft timing sprocket.

b. Using the Camshaft Holding tool 09960-10010, or equivalent, slightly turn the left-side camshaft sprocket counterclockwise to place tension on the timing belt between the crankshaft sprocket and the camshaft sprocket.

35. Rotate the right-side camshaft pulley to align the timing belt installation mark with the camshaft sprocket's timing mark and slide the belt onto the camshaft timing sprocket.

36. Using a vertical press, slowly press the pushrod into the housing using 200–2205 lbs. (981–9807 N) until the holes align, then, install a 1.27mm Allen® wrench to secure the pushrod and release the press. Install the dust boot on the tensioner housing.

37. Install the timing belt tensioner and torque the bolts to 19 ft. lbs. (26 Nm).

38. Using a pair of pliers, remove the Allen® wrench from the tensioner housing.

39. Check the valve timing by performing the following procedure:

a. Temporarily install the crankshaft pulley bolt.

b. Slowly, rotate the crankshaft pulley 2 revolutions (CLOCKWISE) and realign the TDC marks.

➡**If the pulley/sprocket timing marks do not realign, remove the timing belt and reinstall it.**

40. Using the Crankshaft Pulley Holding tool 09213-70010, Bolt tool 90105-08076 and Companion Flange Holding tool 09330-00021, or equivalent, torque the crankshaft pulley bolt to 181 ft. lbs. (245 Nm).

41. Install the cooling fan bracket and torque the 12mm (head size) bolt to 12 ft. lbs. (16 Nm) and the 14mm (head size) bolt to 24 ft. lbs. (32 Nm).

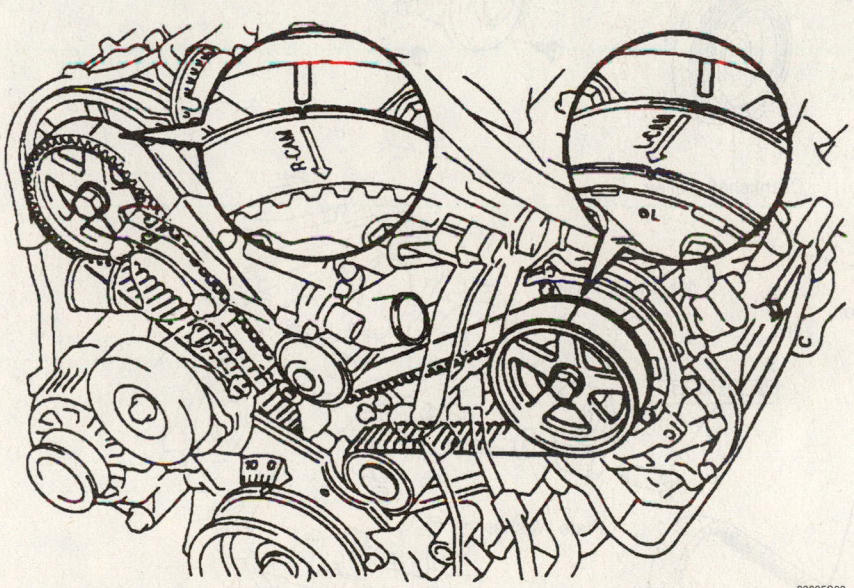

Checking the TDC alignment marks after rotating the crankshaft 2 revolutions—Toyota Land Cruiser 4.7L (2UZ-FE) engine

31. Install the serpentine drive belt tensioner and torque the tensioner-to-engine bolts to 12 ft. lbs. (16 Nm).

➡**To install the serpentine drive belt tensioner, use a bolt 4.18 in. (106mm) in length.**

32. Check that the crankshaft pulley's timing mark is aligned with the centers of the idler pulley and crankshaft pulley bolts.

33. Install the alternator and torque the alternator-to-engine nuts/bolts to 29 ft. lbs. (39 Nm). Connect the alternator's electrical connectors and clip.

34. Install the timing belt to the left-side camshaft by performing the following procedures:

a. Rotate the left-side camshaft pulley to align the timing belt installation mark with the camshaft sprocket's timing mark

Timing chain and gear service is covered in the model specific sections of this manual

42. Install the air conditioning compressor.

43. Install the middle (No. 2) timing belt cover and torque the bolts to 12 ft. lbs. (16 Nm).

44. Install the upper right-side (No. 3) timing belt cover and torque the bolts to 66 inch lbs. (7.5 Nm).

45. Install the upper left-side (No. 3) timing belt cover by performing the following procedures:

   a. Install the oil cooler tube and bolt.

   b. Feed the Camshaft Position Sensor (CPS) through the left-side (No. 3) timing belt cover hole.

   c. Install the left-side (No. 3) timing belt cover and torque the bolts to 66 inch lbs. (7.5 Nm).

   d. Install the wire grommet to the left-side (No. 3) timing belt cover.

   e. Install the sensor connector to the connector bracket and connect the sensor connector.

   f. Install the sensor wire and the engine wire to the clamps on the left-side (No. 3) timing belt cover.

46. Install the drive belt idler pulley and cover plate; then, torque the pulley bolt to 27 ft. lbs. (37 Nm).

47. To complete the installation, reverse the removal procedures.

48. Refill the cooling system and connect the negative battery cable.

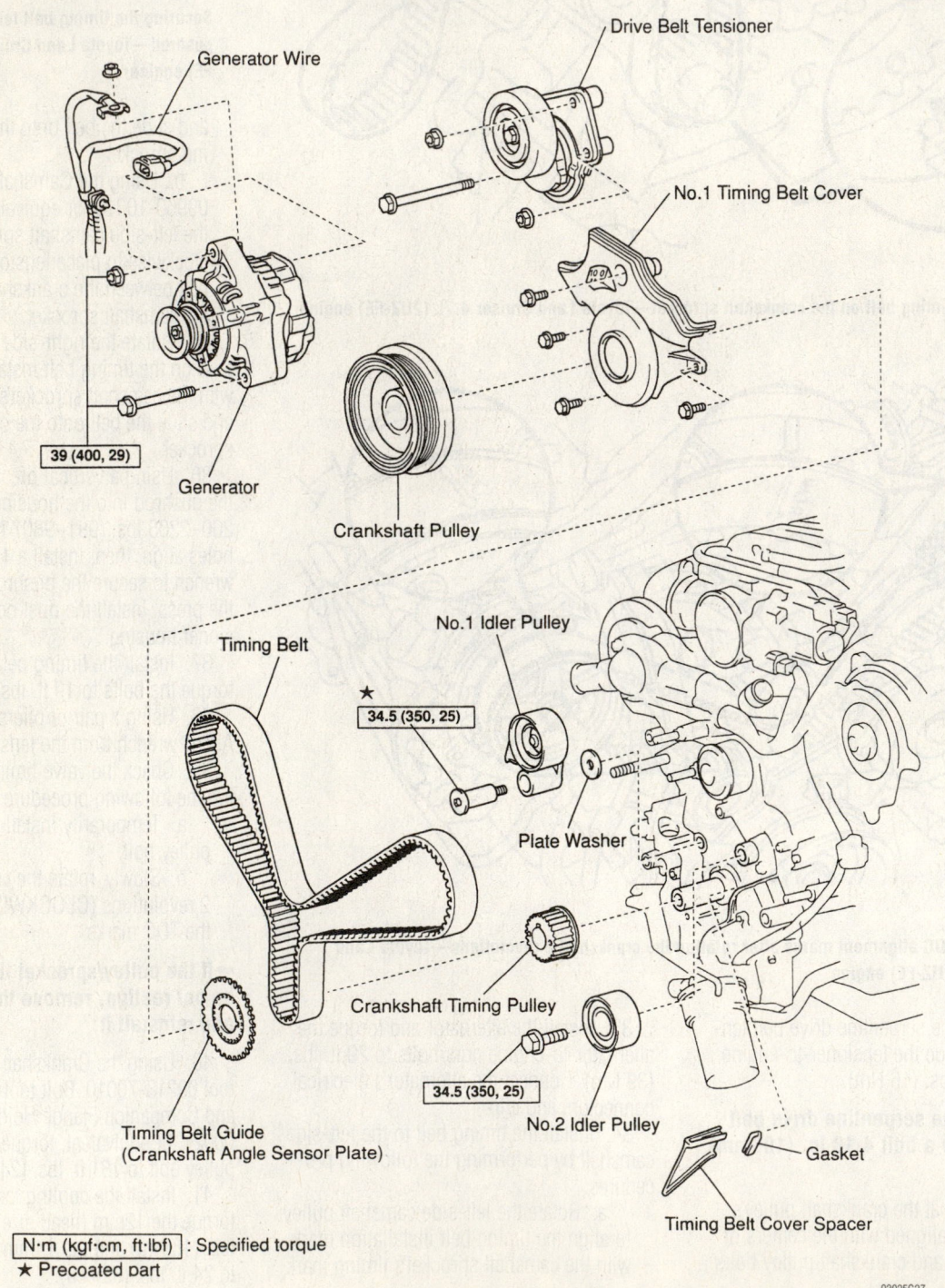

N·m (kgf·cm, ft·lbf) : Specified torque
★ Precoated part

Exploded view of lower timing belt cover, sprockets and components—Toyota Land Cruiser 4.7L (2UZ-FE) engine

93025G27

BRAKES

5

ACURA

Brake Caliper

REMOVAL & INSTALLATION

SLX

FRONT

1. Raise and safely support the vehicle.
2. Remove some brake fluid from the reservoir.
3. Remove the front wheels.
4. Disconnect the brake fluid line from the caliper. Plug the line to prevent fluid loss.
5. Loosen the brake caliper mounting bolt and guide bolt. Remove the caliper from the mount.
6. Remove the brake pads and clips from the caliper. Inspect the brake pads for wear and replace them if necessary.

To install:

7. Fill the brake caliper with clean brake fluid and connect the fluid line to the caliper using new washers. Tighten the brake line banjo fitting to 26 ft. lbs. (35 Nm). Install the brake pads and clips onto the caliper.
8. Install the caliper onto the mounting bracket. Lubricate the caliper bolts and their boots. Then, install the caliper mounting bolts and tighten them to 54 ft. lbs. (74 Nm).
9. Refill and bleed the brake system.
10. Install the front wheels and lower the vehicle.

REAR

1. Raise and safely support the vehicle.
2. Remove some brake fluid from the reservoir.
3. Remove the rear wheels.
4. Disconnect the brake fluid line from the caliper. Plug the line to prevent fluid loss.
5. Loosen the brake caliper mounting bolt and guide bolt. Remove the caliper from the mount bracket.
6. Remove the brake pads and clips from the caliper. Inspect the brake pads for wear; replace them if necessary.
7. If necessary for servicing, unbolt the caliper mounting bracket from the backing plate.

To install:

8. If removed, install the caliper mounting bracket and tighten its bolts to 76 ft. lbs. (103 Nm).

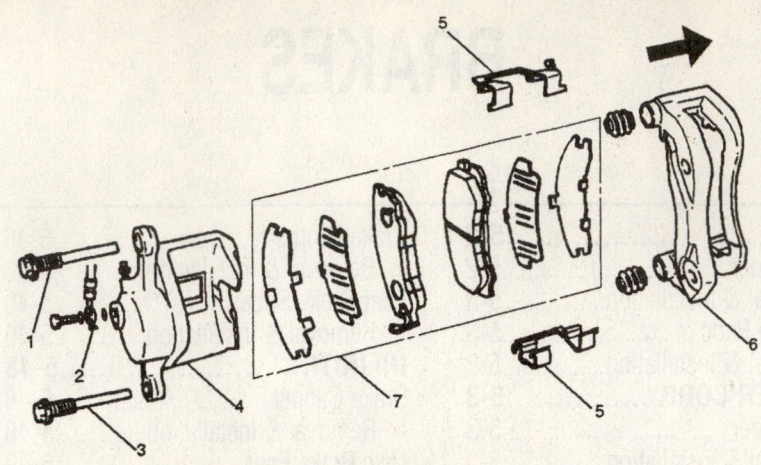

(1) Guide Bolt
(2) Brake Flexible Hose
(3) Lock Bolt
(4) Caliper Assembly
(5) Clip
(6) Support Bracket with Pad Assembly
(7) Pad Assembly

93026G02

Front caliper assembly—SLX

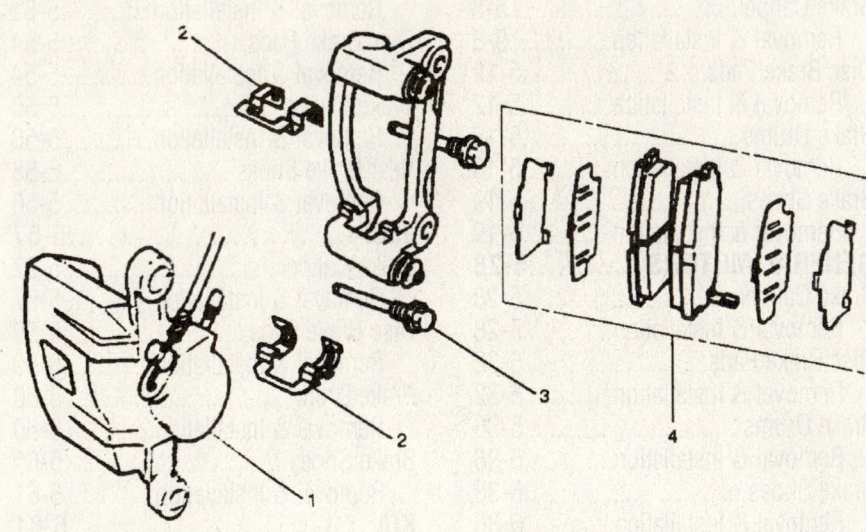

(1) Caliper Assembly
(2) Clip
(3) Lock Bolt
(4) Pad Assembly

93026G01

Rear caliper assembly—SLX

9. Fill the brake caliper with clean brake fluid and connect the fluid line to the caliper using new washers. Tighten the brake line banjo fitting to 26 ft. lbs. (35 Nm). Install the brake pads and clips onto the caliper.
10. Install the caliper on the mounting bracket. Lubricate the caliper bolts and their boots. Then, install the caliper mounting bolts. Tighten them to 32 ft. lbs. (44 Nm).
11. Refill and bleed the brake system.
12. Install the rear wheels and lower the vehicle.

Disc Brake Pads

REMOVAL & INSTALLATION

SLX

FRONT

1. Remove about ½ of the brake fluid from the master cylinder reservoir to prevent overflow when the caliper piston is compressed.
2. Raise and safely support the vehicle.
3. Remove the front wheels.
4. Remove the brake caliper from the caliper bracket without disconnecting the brake line. Support the caliper with a length of wire. Do not let the caliper hang from the brake hose.
5. Remove the brake pads and shims. Inspect the brake rotor and machine or replace as necessary. Check the minimum thickness (specification is cast into the rotor) before machining.

To install:

6. Use a large C-clamp or brake piston tool to push the caliper piston into its bore.

7. Apply a thin coat of brake grease to both sides of both inner shims. Assemble the pads and shims, then install them into the caliper. The wear indicator on the inner pad must face down.
8. Install the calipers. Clean and lubricate the caliper mounting bolts and lubricate the mounting bolt boots. Install the mounting bolts and tighten them to 54 ft. lbs. (74 Nm).
9. Install the front wheels and lower the vehicle.
10. Apply the brakes several times to seat the pads before moving the vehicle. Check the fluid level in the master cylinder reservoir and add as necessary.

REAR

1. Use a vacuum pump to remove some brake fluid from the master cylinder reservoir to prevent overflow when the caliper piston is compressed.
2. Raise and safely support the vehicle.
3. Remove the rear wheels.
4. Remove the brake caliper from the caliper bracket without disconnecting the brake line. Support the caliper with a length

of wire. Do not let the caliper hang from the brake hose.
5. Remove the brake pads and shims. Inspect the brake rotor and machine or replace as necessary. Check the minimum thickness (specification is cast into the rotor) before machining.

To install:

6. Use a large C-clamp or brake piston tool to push the caliper piston into its bore.
7. Apply a thin coat of brake grease to both sides of both inner shims. Assemble the pads and shims, then install them into the caliper. The wear indicator on the inner pad must face down.
8. Install the calipers. Clean and lubricate the caliper mounting bolts and lubricate the mounting bolt boots. Install the mounting bolts and tighten them to 32 ft. lbs. (44 Nm).
9. Install the rear wheels and lower the vehicle.
10. Apply the brakes several times to seat the pads before moving the vehicle. Check the fluid level in the master cylinder reservoir and add as necessary.

CHRYSLER CORP.

Brake Caliper

REMOVAL & INSTALLATION

Caravan, Town & Country and Voyager

1. Raise and safely support the front of the vehicle. Remove the front wheels.
2. If the caliper is only being removed from the bracket (as for a brake pad change), move to Step 3. If the caliper is being removed from the vehicle (as for replacement or an overhaul and reseal), remove the brake hose attaching bolt from the caliper. Remove the hose from the caliper and discard the washers. New seal washers will be required at assembly. Plug the brake hose to prevent fluid leakage.
3. Remove the caliper guide pin bolts that secure the caliper to the steering knuckle.
4. Remove the caliper by slowly sliding it away from the steering knuckle. Slide the opposite end of the brake caliper out from under the machined abutment on the steering knuckle.
5. Using a strong piece of wire, support

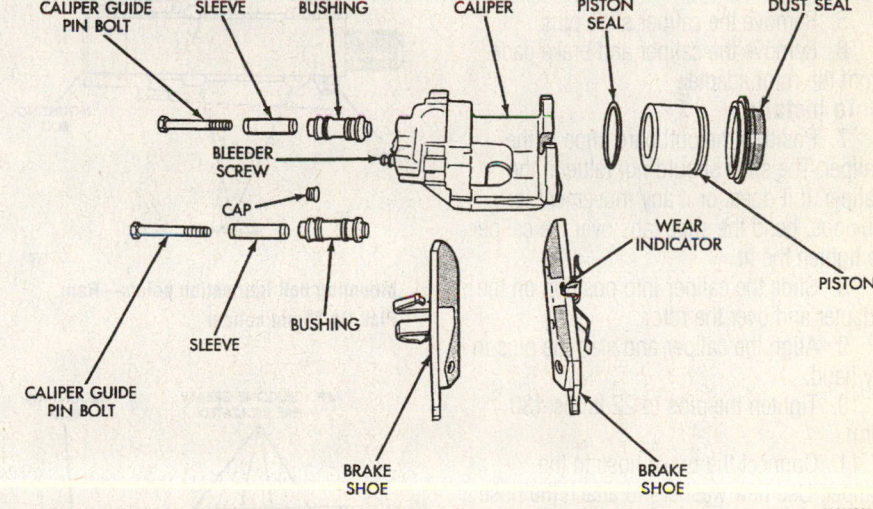

Front brake caliper assembly—Caravan, Town & Country and Voyager

the brake caliper assembly off the strut unit. Do NOT allow the caliper to hang from the brake fluid flex hose or damage to the hose will result.

To install:

6. Clean both steering knuckle abutment surfaces of any dirt, grease or corrosion. Then lubricate the abutment surfaces

with a liberal amount of MOPAR® Multipurpose Lubricant or equivalent.
7. Properly position the brake caliper over the brake pads and disc rotor. Be careful not to allow the caliper seals or guide pin bushings to get damaged by the steering knuckle bosses. Install the caliper guide pin bolts and torque to: 30 ft. lbs. (41 Nm)

for 1997–99 or 195 inch lbs. (22 Nm) for 2000–01 for front caliper; 30 ft. lbs. (41 Nm) for 1997 or 192 inch lbs. (22 Nm) for 1998–01 for rear calipers. Be careful not to cross thread the guide pin bolts.

8. If removed, attach the brake hose to the caliper using new washers. Tighten the banjo bolt to 35 ft. lbs. (47 Nm).

9. Bleed the brake system.

10. Install the front wheels and lug nuts. Torque the lug nuts, in a star pattern sequence, to ½ torque specifications. Then repeat the tightening sequence to the full torque specification of 100 ft. lbs. (135 Nm). Lower the vehicle.

11. Pump the brake pedal several times to insure that the brake pedal is firm. Road-test the vehicle.

Dakota and Durango

1. Raise and support the front end on jackstands.

2. Remove the wheels.

3. Disconnect the rubber brake hose from the tubing at the frame mount. If the pistons are to be removed from the caliper, leave the brake hose connected to the caliper. Check the rubber hose for cracks or chafed spots.

4. Plug the brake line to prevent loss of fluid.

5. Remove the caliper slide pins.

6. Remove the caliper and brake pads from the rotor adapter.

To install:

7. Position the outboard shoe in the caliper. The shoe should not rattle in the caliper. If it does, or if any movement is obvious, bend the shoe tabs over the caliper to tighten the fit.

8. Slide the caliper into position on the adapter and over the rotor.

9. Align the caliper and start the pins in by hand.

10. Tighten the pins to 22 ft. lbs. (30 Nm).

11. Connect the brake hose to the caliper. Use new washers to attach the hose fitting if the original washers are scored, worn or damaged.

12. Fill and bleed the brake system.

13. Install the wheels.

14. Lower the vehicle.

B-Series Van and Ram Pick-Up

1. Raise and support the front end on jackstands.

2. Remove the wheels.

3. Press the caliper piston back into the bore with a suitable prytool. Use a large C-clamp to drive the piston into the bore of additional force is required.

4. Remove the caliper mounting bolts with a ⅜ in. hex wrench or socket.

5. Loosen the bolt that secures the front brake hose fitting bolt in the caliper.

6. Rotate the caliper rearward off the rotor and out from its mount.

7. Remove the front brake hose fitting bolt completely, then remove the caliper with the pads installed as an assembly. Take care not to drip fluid onto the pad surfaces.

8. Cover the open end of the front brake hose fitting to prevent dirt entry.

To install:

9. Clean the caliper and steering knuckle sliding surfaces with a wire brush. Then, apply a coat of Mopar® multi-mileage grease or equivalent.

10. Lubricate the caliper mounting bolts, collars, bushings and bores with Dow 111® or GE 661® silicone grease or equivalent.

11. Install the caliper over the rotor and seat it in its original position until flush.

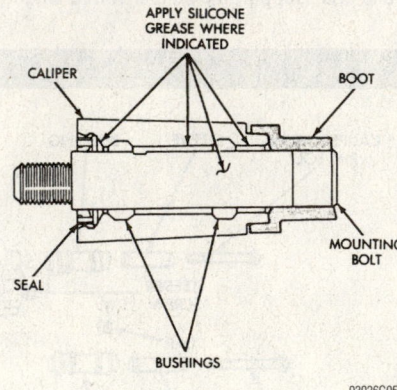

Mounting bolt lubrication points—Ram Pick-Up 75mm caliper

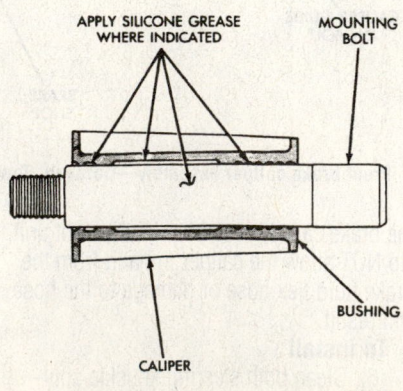

Mounting bolt lubrication points—Ram Pick-Up 80 or 86mm caliper

12. Install the mounting bolts by hand, then tighten them to 38 ft. lbs. (51 Nm).

13. Install the wheels.

14. Lower the vehicle.

15. Pump the brakes several times to seat the pads.

Disc Brake Pads

REMOVAL & INSTALLATION

Caravan, Town & Country and Voyager

1. Remove brake fluid from the master cylinder brake fluid reservoir until the reservoir is approximately ½ full. Discard the removed fluid.

2. Raise and safely support the front of the vehicle. Remove the front wheels.

3. Remove the front brake caliper guide pin bolts.

4. Remove the brake caliper by slowly sliding it up and off the adapter and brake rotor. Support the caliper out of the way with a strong piece of wire. Do not let the caliper hang by the brake hose or damage to the brake hose will result.

5. If necessary, compress the caliper piston into the bore using a C-clamp. Insert a suitable piece of wood between the C-clamp and caliper piston to protect the piston.

6. Remove the outboard disc brake pad from the caliper by prying the brake pad retaining clip over the raised area on the caliper. Slide the brake pad down and off the caliper.

7. Remove the inboard disc brake pad from the caliper by pulling the brake pad away from the caliper piston until the retaining clip on the pad is free from the caliper piston cavity.

To install:

8. Be sure the caliper piston has been completely retracted into the piston bore of the caliper assembly. This is required when installing the brake caliper equipped with new brake pads.

9. If equipped, remove the protective paper from the noise suppression gaskets on the new disc brake pads.

10. Install the new inboard disc brake pad into the caliper piston by pressing the pad firmly into the cavity of the caliper piston. Be sure the new inboard brake pad is seated squarely against the face of the brake caliper piston.

11. Install the outboard disc brake pad by sliding it onto the caliper assembly.

12. Install the brake caliper assembly over the brake rotor and onto the steering knuckle adapter. Install the caliper guide pin bolts and torque to: 30 ft. lbs. (41 Nm) for 1997–99 or 195 inch lbs. (22 Nm) for 2000–01 for front caliper; 30 ft. lbs. (41 Nm) for 1997 or 192 inch lbs. (22 Nm) for 1998–01 for rear calipers.

13. Install the front wheels and lug nuts. Torque the lug nuts, in a star pattern sequence, to 95 ft. lbs. (129 Nm). Apply the brake pedal several times until a firm pedal is obtained.

14. Check the fluid level in the master cylinder and add fluid as necessary. Road-test the vehicle.

Dakota and Durango

1. Raise and support the front end on jackstands.

2. Remove the wheels.

3. Press the caliper piston back into the bore with a suitable prytool. Use a large C-clamp to drive the piston into the bore of additional force is required.

4. Remove the caliper mounting bolts with a ⅜ in. hex wrench or socket.

5. Rotate the caliper rearward off the rotor and out from its mount.

6. Set the caliper on a crate or sturdy box, then remove the inboard and outboard brake pads. The inboard pad has a spring clip that holds it in the caliper. Tilt this pad out at the top to unseat the clip. The outboard pad has a retaining spring that secures it in the caliper. Unseat 1 spring end and rotate the pad out of the caliper.

7. Secure the caliper to a chassis or suspension component with a sturdy wire. Do not let it hang from the hose.

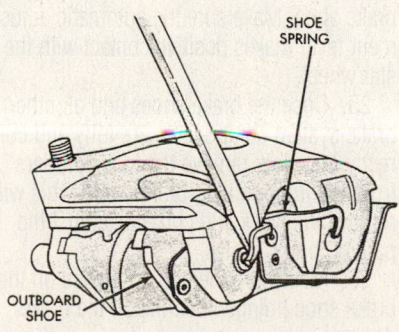

SHOE SPRING

OUTBOARD SHOE

93026G08

Prying the disc brake from the 4WD front brake caliper assembly—1997–98 Dakota—Durango and 1999–01 Dakota similar

To install:

8. Clean the caliper and steering knuckle sliding surfaces with a wire brush. Then, apply a coat of Mopar® multi-mileage grease or equivalent.

9. Clean the caliper slide pins with brake cleaner or brake fluid. Then apply a light coating of silicone grease to the pins.

➡️**If there is minor rust or corrosion on the pins, first polish them with a crocus cloth. If they are severely rusted, replace them.**

10. Install the inboard pad and its spring clip.

11. Install the outboard brake pad.

12. Install the caliper over the rotor and seat it in its original position until flush.

13. Final tighten the caliper slide pins to 18–26 ft. lbs. (25–35 Nm).

14. Install the wheels.

15. Lower the vehicle.

16. Pump the brakes several times to seat the pads.

B-Series Van and Ram Pick-Up

1. Raise and support the front end on jackstands.

2. Remove the wheels.

3. Press the caliper piston back into the bore with a suitable prytool. Use a large C-clamp to drive the piston into the bore of additional force is required.

4. Remove the caliper mounting bolts with a ⅜ in. hex wrench or socket.

5. Rotate the caliper rearward off the rotor and out from its mount.

6. Set the caliper on a crate or sturdy box, then remove the inboard and outboard brake pads. The inboard pad has a spring clip that holds it in the caliper. Tilt this pad out at the top to unseat the clip. The outboard pad has a retaining spring that secures it in the caliper. Unseat 1 spring end and rotate the pad out of the caliper.

7. Secure the caliper to a chassis or suspension component with a sturdy wire. Do not let it hang from the hose.

To install:

8. Clean the caliper and steering knuckle sliding surfaces with a wire brush. Then, apply a coat of Mopar® multi-mileage grease or equivalent.

➡️**If there is minor rust or corrosion on the pins, first polish them with a crocus cloth. If they are severely rusted, replace them.**

9. Lubricate the caliper mounting bolts,

collars, bushings and bores with Dow 111® or GE 661® silicone grease or equivalent.

10. Install the inboard pad and its spring clip.

11. Install the outboard brake pad.

12. Install the caliper over the rotor and seat it until flush in its original position.

13. Install the mounting bolts by hand, then tighten them to 38 ft. lbs. (51 Nm).

14. Install the wheels.

15. Lower the vehicle.

16. Pump the brakes several times to seat the pads.

Brake Drums

REMOVAL & INSTALLATION

Caravan, Town & Country and Voyager

1. Raise and safely support the vehicle.

2. Remove the rear wheels.

3. Remove the brake drum from the hub assembly by pulling the drum straight off the wheel studs.

4. Inspect the brake drum for thickness and runout. Replace or machine as necessary.

To install:

5. Install the brake drum to the hub assembly.

6. Adjust the brake shoes.

7. Install the rear wheel and lug nuts. Torque the lug nuts, in a star pattern sequence, to 95 ft. lbs. (129 Nm). Lower the vehicle.

B-Series Van, Dakota, Durango and Ram Pick-Up

CHRYSLER SERVO TYPE WITH SINGLE ANCHOR

1. Raise and safely support the truck.

2. Remove the plug from the brake adjustment access hole.

3. Insert a thin bladed screwdriver through the adjusting hole and hold the adjusting lever away from the starwheel.

4. Release the brake by prying down against the starwheel with a brake spoon.

5. Remove the rear wheel and clips from the wheel studs. Remove the brake drum.

6. .Installation is the reverse of removal. Adjust the brakes.

BENDIX DUO-SERVO TYPE

1. Raise and safely support the vehicle.

2. Remove the rear wheel and tire.

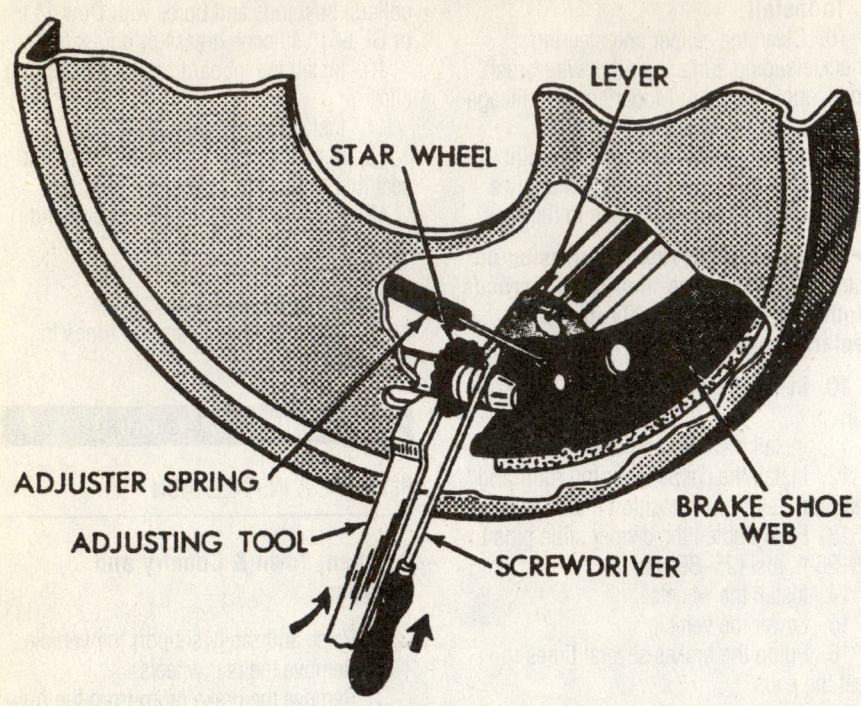

LEVER

STAR WHEEL

ADJUSTER SPRING

ADJUSTING TOOL

BRAKE SHOE WEB

SCREWDRIVER

93026G04

Use a lever releasing tool to depress the adjuster lever while turning the starwheel with a pry-tool—Bendix brakes

3. Remove the axle shaft nuts, washers and cones. If the cones do not readily release, rap the axle shaft sharply in the center.

4. Remove the axle shaft.

5. Remove the outer hub nut.

6. Straighten the lockwasher tab and remove it along with the inner nut and bearing.

7. Carefully remove the drum.

To install:

8. Position the drum on the axle housing.

9. Install the bearing and inner nut. While rotating the wheel and tire, tighten the adjusting nut until a slight drag is felt.

10. Back off the adjusting nut ⅙ turn so that the wheel rotates freely without excessive end-play.

11. Install the lockrings and nut. Place a new gasket on the hub and install the axle shaft, cones, lockwashers and nuts.

12. Install the wheel and tire.

13. Road-test the vehicle.

Brake Shoes

REMOVAL & INSTALLATION

Caravan, Town & Country and Voyager

1. Raise and safely support the vehicle.

2. Remove the rear wheels and the brake drums.

3. Be sure the parking brake pedal is in the released position. Create slack in the rear parking brake cables by grasping an exposed section of the front parking brake cable, pulling it down and rearward. Maintain the slack in the brake cable by clamping a pair of locking pliers onto the parking brake cable just rearward of the rear body outrigger bracket.

4. Remove the adjustment lever spring from the automatic adjustment lever and front brake shoe (leading brake shoe).

5. Remove the automatic adjustment lever from the front brake shoe (leading brake shoe).

6. Remove the brake shoe-to-brake shoe lower return spring.

7. Remove the tension clip that secures the upper return spring to the automatic adjuster assembly.

8. Remove the brake shoe-to-brake shoe upper return spring.

9. Remove the rear brake shoe (trailing brake shoe) hold-down clip and pin.

10. Remove the trailing brake shoe, parking brake actuating lever and parking brake actuator strut from the brake support plate.

11. Remove the automatic adjuster assembly from the leading brake shoe.

12. Remove the leading brake shoe hold-down clip and pin. Remove the leading brake shoe.

13. Remove the parking brake actuator plate from the leading brake shoe and install onto the replacement brake shoe.

To install:

14. Thoroughly clean and dry the backing plate. To prepare the backing plate, lubricate the 8 brake shoe contact areas and brake shoe anchor, using suitable grease.

15. Install the leading brake shoe into position on the brake shoe support plate. Secure the leading brake shoe by installing the brake shoe hold-down clip and pin.

16. Install the parking brake actuating strut onto the leading brake shoe and then install the parking brake actuating lever onto the strut.

17. Lubricate the shaft threads of the automatic adjuster screw assembly with anti-seize lubricant. Install the automatic adjuster screw assembly onto the leading brake shoe.

18. Install the trailing brake shoe onto the parking brake actuating lever and parking brake actuating strut.

19. Place the trailing brake shoe into position on the brake support plate and install the brake shoe hold-down clip and pin.

20. Install the brake shoe-to-brake shoe upper return spring.

21. Install the tension clip that secures the upper return spring to the automatic adjuster assembly. Be sure the tension clip is positioned on the threaded area of the adjuster assembly or the function of the automatic adjuster will be affected.

22. Install the brake shoe-to-brake shoe lower return spring.

23. Install the automatic adjustment lever onto the leading brake shoe.

24. Install the actuating spring onto the automatic adjustment lever and leading brake shoe. Make sure the automatic adjustment lever makes positive contact with the star wheel.

25. Once the brake shoes and all other brake system components are fully and correctly installed, remove the locking pliers from the front parking brake cable. This will remove the slack and correctly adjust the parking brake cables.

26. Make sure there is no grease on the brake shoe linings, then install the brake drums.

27. Adjust the rear brakes, then lower the vehicle and check the brakes for proper operation.

28. Install the wheel and lug nuts. Torque the lug nuts, in a star pattern sequence, to 95 ft. lbs. (129 Nm).

29. Road-test the vehicle. The automatic adjuster will continue to adjust the brake shoes during the road-test.

B-Series Van, Dakota, Durango and Ram Pick-Up

SERVO TYPE WITH SINGLE ANCHOR

1. Raise and support the vehicle.
2. Remove the rear wheel, drum retaining clips and the brake drum.
3. Remove the brake shoe return springs, noting how the secondary spring overlaps the primary spring.
4. Remove the brake shoe retainer, springs and nails.
5. Disconnect the automatic adjuster cable from the anchor and unhook it from the lever. Remove the cable, cable guide, and anchor plate.
6. Remove the spring and lever from the shoe web.
7. Spread the anchor ends of the primary and secondary shoes and remove the parking brake spring and strut.
8. Disconnect the parking brake cable and remove the brake assembly.

9. Remove the primary and secondary brake shoe assemblies and the star adjuster as an assembly. Block the wheel cylinders to retain the pistons.

To install:

10. Measure the drum as described in this section.
11. Apply a thin coat of lubricant to the support platforms.
12. Attach the parking brake lever to the rear of the secondary shoe.
13. Place the primary and secondary shoes in their relative positions on a workbench.
14. Lubricate the adjuster screw threads. Install it between the primary and secondary shoes with the star wheel next to the secondary shoe. The star wheels are stamped with an L (left) and R (right).
15. Overlap the ends of the primary and second brake shoes and install the adjusting spring and lever at the anchor end.
16. Hold the shoes in position and install the parking brake cable into the lever.
17. Install the parking brake strut and spring between the parking brake lever and primary shoe.

18. Place the brake shoes on the support and install the retainer nails and springs.
19. Install the anchor pin plate.
20. Install the eye of the adjusting cable over the anchor pin and install the return spring between the anchor pin and primary shoe.
21. Install the cable guide in the secondary shoe and install the secondary return spring. Be sure that the primary spring overlaps the secondary spring.
22. Position the adjusting cable in the groove of the cable guide and engage the hook of the cable in the adjusting lever.
23. Install the brake drum and retaining clips. Install the wheel and tire.
24. Adjust the brakes and road-test the truck.

BENDIX DUO-SERVO TYPE

1. Unhook and remove the adjusting lever return spring.
2. Remove the lever from the lever pivot pin.
3. Unhook the adjuster lever from the adjuster cable.

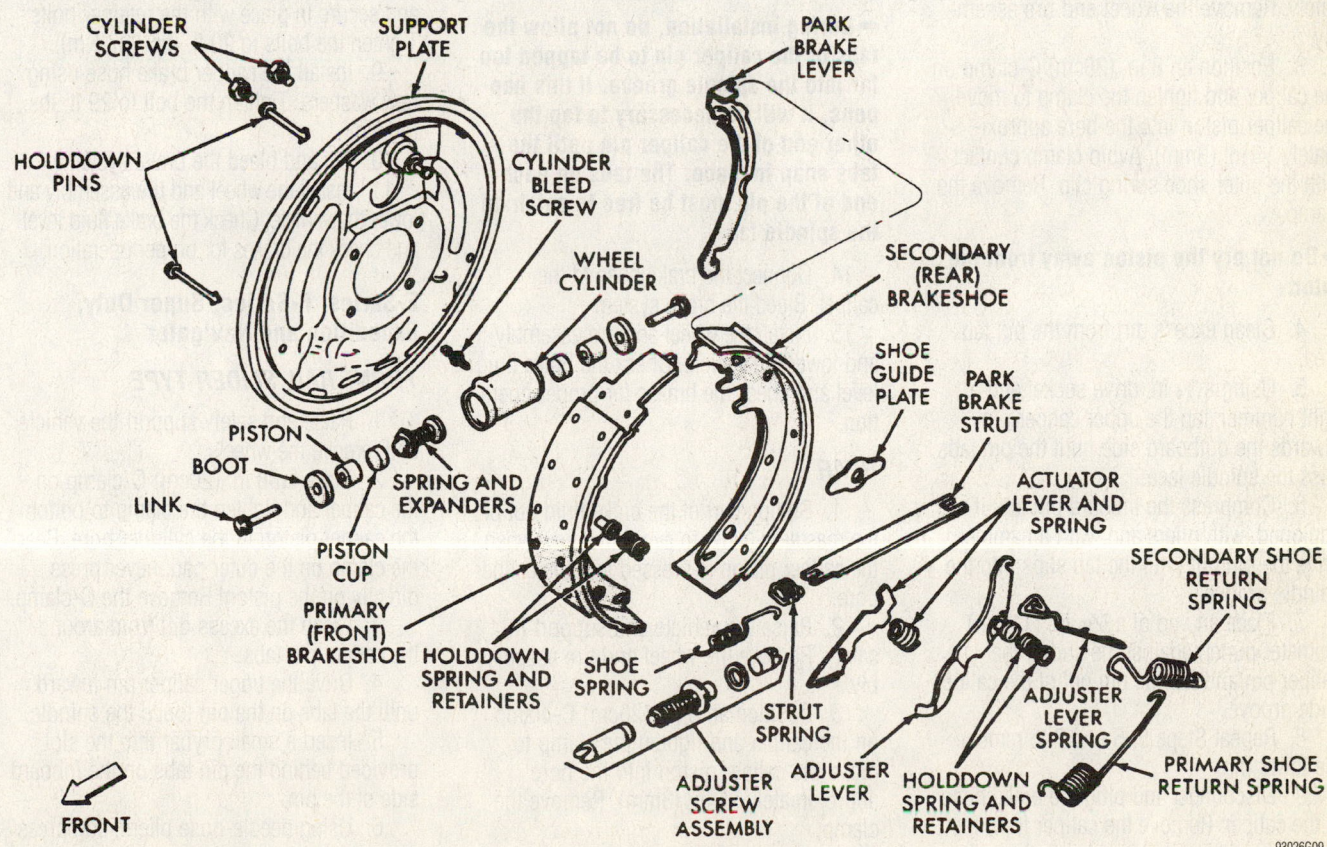

Exploded view of the rear brake components—B-Series Van, Dakota, Durango and Ram Pick-Up

For brake related suspension and axle service, refer to the model specific sections of this manual

4. Unhook the upper shoe-to-shoe spring.

5. Unhook and remove the shoe hold-down springs.

6. Disconnect the parking brake cable from the parking brake lever.

7. Remove the shoes with the lower shoe-to-shoe spring and star wheel as an assembly.

To install:

8. The pivot screw and adjusting nut on the left side have left-hand threads and right-hand threads on the right side.

9. Lubricate and assemble the star wheel assembly. Lubricate the guide pads on the support plates.

10. Assemble the star wheel, lower shoe-to-shoe spring, and the primary and secondary shoes. Position this assembly on the support plate.

11. Install and hook the hold-down springs.

12. Install the upper shoe-to-shoe spring.

13. Install the cable and retaining clip.

14. Position the adjuster lever return spring on the pivot (green springs on left brakes and red springs on right brakes).

15. Install the adjuster lever. Route the adjuster cable and connect it to the adjuster.

16. Install the brake drum and adjust the brakes.

FORD

Brake Caliper

REMOVAL & INSTALLATION

Aerostar, Explorer, Ranger and Mountaineer

FRONT

1. Siphon part of the brake fluid out of the master cylinder to avoid overflow when the caliper piston is pressed into the caliper bore.

2. Raise the vehicle and support it safely. Remove the wheel and tire assembly.

3. Position an 8 in. (20cm) C-clamp on the caliper and tighten the clamp to move the caliper piston into the bore approximately 1/8 in. (3mm). Avoid clamp contact with the outer shoe spring clip. Remove the clamp.

➡ Do not pry the piston away from the rotor.

4. Clean excess dirt from the pin tab area.

5. Using a 1/4 in. drive socket and a light hammer, tap the upper caliper pin towards the outboard side until the pin tabs pass the spindle face.

6. Compress the inboard pin tab, if equipped, with pliers and, with a hammer, drive the pin out until the tab slips into the spindle groove.

7. Place an end of a 7/16 in. (11mm) diameter punch against the end of the caliper pin and tap the pin out of the caliper slide groove.

8. Repeat Steps 5, 6 and 7 to remove the lower pin.

9. Disconnect and plug the brake hose at the caliper. Remove the caliper from the rotor.

To install:

10. Make sure the caliper mounting surfaces are free of dirt. Lubricate the caliper grooves with disc brake caliper grease and install the caliper.

11. From the caliper outboard side, position the pin between the caliper and spindle grooves. The pin must be positioned so the tabs will be installed against the spindle outer face.

12. Tap the pin on the outboard end with a hammer until the retention tabs on the sides of the pin contact the spindle face.

13. Repeat Steps 11 and 12 for the lower pin.

➡ During installation, do not allow the tabs of the caliper pin to be tapped too far into the spindle groove. If this happens, it will be necessary to tap the other end of the caliper pin until the tabs snap in place. The tabs on each end of the pin must be free to catch on the spindle face.

14. Connect the brake hose to the caliper. Bleed the brake system.

15. Install the wheel and tire assembly and lower the vehicle. Check the brake fluid level and check the brakes for proper operation.

REAR

1. Siphon part of the brake fluid out of the master cylinder to avoid overflow when the caliper piston is pressed into the caliper bore.

2. Raise the vehicle and support it safely. Remove the wheel and tire assembly.

3. Position an 8 in. (20cm) C-clamp on the caliper and tighten the clamp to move the caliper piston into the bore approximately 1/8 in. (3mm). Remove the clamp.

➡ Do not pry the piston away from the rotor.

4. Clean excess dirt from the retainer bolt area.

5. Using a Torx® socket, remove the 2 retainer bolts securing the caliper to the bracket and adapter plate.

6. Disconnect and plug the brake hose at the caliper. Remove the caliper from the rotor.

To install:

7. Make sure the caliper mounting surfaces are free of dirt. Lubricate the caliper grooves with disc brake caliper grease and install the caliper.

8. Position the caliper to the bracket and secure in place with the retainer bolts. Tighten the bolts to 20 ft. lbs. (27 Nm).

9. Install the caliper brake hose using new washers. Tighten the bolt to 29 ft. lbs. (40 Nm).

10. Fill and bleed the brake system.

11. Install the wheel and tire assembly and lower the vehicle. Check the brake fluid level and check the brakes for proper operation.

E-Series, F-Series, Super Duty, Expedition and Navigator

FRONT RAIL SLIDER TYPE

1. Raise and safely support the vehicle and remove the wheels.

2. Place an 8 in. (20cm) C-clamp on the caliper and tighten the clamp to bottom the caliper piston in the cylinder bore. Bear the clamp on the outer pad; never press directly on the piston! Remove the C-clamp.

3. Clean the excess dirt from around the caliper pin tabs.

4. Drive the upper caliper pin inward until the tabs on the pin touch the spindle.

5. Insert a small prybar into the slot provided behind the pin tabs on the inboard side of the pin.

6. Using needle-nose pliers, compress the outboard end of the pin while, at the same time, prying with the prybar until the tabs slip into the groove in the spindle.

7. Place the end of a $7/16$ in. (11mm) punch against the end of the caliper pin and drive the pin out of the caliper slide groove.

8. Repeat this procedure for the lower pin.

9. Lift the caliper off of the rotor.

10. Remove the brake pads from the caliper.

11. Disconnect the brake hose from the caliper, then plug the brake line to prohibit contamination of the brake fluid by water or dirt.

To install:

12. Connect the brake hose to the caliper. When connecting the brake fluid hose to the caliper, it is recommended that a new copper washer be used at the connection of the brake hose and caliper.

13. Thoroughly clean the areas of the caliper and spindle assembly which contact each other during the sliding action of the caliper.

14. Install the brake pads onto the caliper.

15. Position the caliper on the spindle assembly. Lightly lubricate the caliper sliding grooves with caliper pin grease.

16. Position a new upper pin with the retention tabs next to the spindle groove.

➡**Don't use the bolt and nut with the new pin.**

17. Carefully drive the pin, at the outboard end, inward until the tabs contact the spindle face.

18. Repeat the procedure for the lower pin.

❋❋ WARNING

Don't drive the pins in too far or it will be necessary to drive them back out until the tabs snap into place. The tabs on each end of the pin must be free to catch on the spindle sides!

19. Install the wheels.

FRONT PIN SLIDER TYPE

1. Break the front wheel lug nuts loose, then raise and support the front of the vehicle safely on jackstands.

2. Remove the front wheels.

3. Remove the front brake hose bolt, then remove the copper washers and plug the front brake hose.

4. Remove the 2 front disc brake caliper slide pins, then lift the caliper off of the front caliper anchor plate.

To install:

5. Install the front disc brake caliper onto the caliper anchor plate. Install the 2 slide pins. Tighten the slider pins/bolts to the following values:

- All except F- and E-250/350: 21–26 ft. lbs. (28–36 Nm)
- F-250, F-350, E-250 and E-350: 141–190 ft. lbs. (191–259 Nm)

6. Using new copper washers, attach the front brake hose to the brake caliper. Install and tighten the retaining bolt to 23–29 ft. lbs. (30–40 Nm)

7. Bleed the brake system.

8. Clean the wheel hub mounting surface.

9. Install the front wheels and snug the lug nuts to fully seat the wheel against the hub.

10. Lower the vehicle until some of the vehicle's weight rests on the front tires, then tighten the lug nuts to 83–112 ft. lbs. (113–153 Nm).

11. Lower the vehicle completely.

12. Make sure that the brakes are operating correctly.

Rear Brake Caliper

F-SUPER DUTY

1. Remove sufficient brake fluid from the brake master cylinder reservoir to allow for pressing the caliper pistons into the bores. Discard the used brake fluid.

2. Raise and safely support the vehicle.

3. Remove the wheels.

4. Place an 8 in. (20cm) C-clamp on the caliper, with the clamp frame on the disc brake caliper and the clamp screw on the outboard brake hoes and lining backing plate. Tighten the clamp to press the caliper pistons in the cylinder bores only enough to give removal clearance. Remove the C-clamp.

5. Remove the rear brake hose-to-caliper flow bolt and discard the used copper washers. Plug the brake hose so that contamination of the brake fluid does not occur.

6. Using the Hydraulic Caliper Pin Remover D89T-2196-A or equivalent, drive the upper and lower caliper locking pins out.

7. Remove the disc brake caliper from the vehicle.

To install:

8. If necessary, install the brake shoe and anti-rattle clip.

9. Position the disc brake caliper in the support bracket.

10. Lubricate the caliper locking pins with Ford Silicone Dielectric Compound D7AZ-19A331-A or equivalent.

11. Drive the locking pins into the caliper/support bracket assembly until the tabs at each end of the pin snap into place.

12. Using new copper washers, attach the rear brake hose to the disc brake caliper. Tighten the rear brake hose-to-caliper flow bolt to 22–29 ft. lbs. (30–39 Nm).

13. Install the wheel, then lower the vehicle.

14. Pump the brake pedal several times to drive the caliper pistons into contact with the brake shoe and lining.

15. Fill the brake master cylinder reservoir with new DOT 3 brake fluid.

16. Bleed the brake system and test the brakes for proper operation.

EXPEDITION, F-450 AND NAVIGATOR

1. Remove enough brake fluid from the brake master cylinder reservoir until it is ½ full.

2. Raise and safely support the vehicle.

3. Remove the wheel and tire assembly.

4. Remove the hollow bolt connecting the brake hose to the disc brake caliper and plug the brake hose. Discard 2 copper sealing washers.

5. Remove 2 brake caliper slide pins and lift the caliper off the anchor plate.

To install:

6. Retract the disc brake caliper pistons fully in the piston bores using an old brake pad or block of wood and a C-clamp or equivalent.

7. Place the disc brake caliper above the rotor and install it with a rotating motion. Make sure the inner and outer pads are properly positioned and the anti-rattle clips are correctly installed. The brake caliper bleed screw should be positioned on top of the caliper when assembled on the vehicle.

8. Lubricate the locating pins and the inside of the insulators with silicone grease. Install the locating pins through the caliper insulators and hand-start the threads into the steering knuckle attaching holes. Tighten the locating pins to 25 ft. lbs. (34 Nm).

9. Remove the plug and install the brake hose to the disc brake caliper using 2 new copper sealing washers. Tighten the hollow bolt to 29 ft. lbs. (40 Nm).

10. Bleed the brake system, filling the brake master cylinder reservoir as required.

11. Install the wheel and tire assembly. Tighten the lug nuts in a star pattern to 83–112 ft. lbs. (113–153 Nm).

12. Lower the vehicle.

13. Pump the brake pedal several times to position the brake pads prior to moving the vehicle.

14. Road-test the vehicle and check for proper brake system operation.

Mercury Villager

The front disc brake caliper slides on 2 stainless steel locating pins. The front disc brakes use a conventional pin slider-type front disc brake caliper with a 10.875 inch (27.6cm) front disc rotor. The front disc brake caliper is attached to the front suspension with 2 Torx® head brake caliper bolts. Rubber insulators isolate the stainless steel locating pins from direct contact with the front disc brake caliper. The front disc brake calipers must be removed to replace the front brake pads.

1. Raise and safely support the vehicle.

2. Remove the wheel and tire.

3. If the brake caliper is being removed for brake pad replacement only, DO NOT disconnect the brake hose.

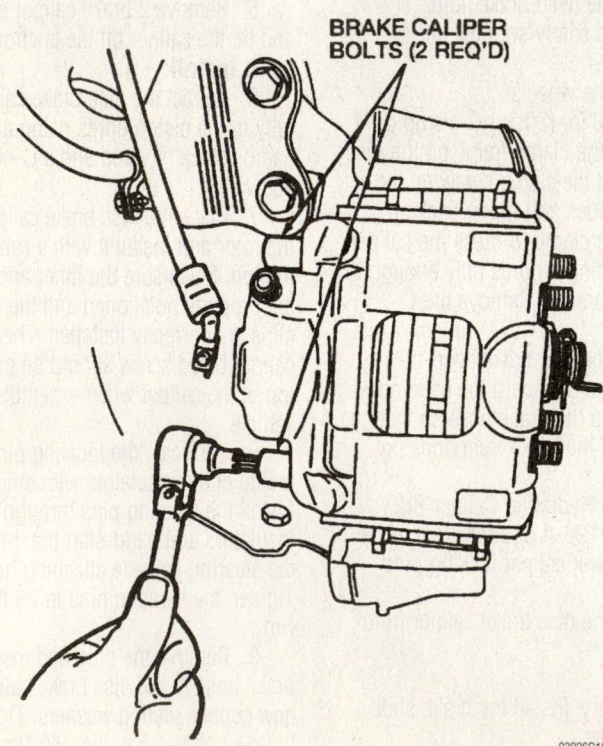

Caliper pin bolt removal—Mercury Vil-

4. Remove the 2 caliper pin bolts. Most applications will require a Torx® T-40 bit to remove the 2 brake caliper bolts.

5. If the brake caliper is being removed just for brake service, with the brake hose still attached to the caliper, use a length of wire to support the caliper from the front shock absorber. Do not let the caliper hang by the brake hose. If the caliper is being completely removed from the vehicle for overhaul, use care not to drip brake fluid on the paint.

➡If both calipers are being completely removed from the vehicle at the same time, mark them Left and Right so the calipers can be reinstalled to their original locations. The reason for this is that the bleeder screws must be positioned on the top of the front disc brake caliper when installed on the vehicle.

To install:

6. Clean all parts well. Use a C-clamp and a used brake pad to push the caliper piston fully in the piston bore. Inspect the caliper pins and clean any dirt and debris.

7. Install the caliper onto the rotor. Make sure the inboard and outboard brake pads are properly positioned.

8. Lubricate the stainless steel locating pins with a Silicone Dielectric Compound such as Ford DZAZ-19A331-A or equivalent

BRAKE CALIPER BOLTS (2 REQ'D)

93026G10

silicone grease. Install the 2 caliper pin bolts and torque to 18–25 ft. lbs. (24–34 Nm).

9. If disconnected, install the brake hose using a new replacement copper washer, install the banjo bolt and torque to 12–14 ft. lbs. (17–20 Nm).

10. If the brake hose had been disconnected, bleed the brake system.

11. Install the wheel and tire.

12. Torque the lug nuts to 72–87 ft. lbs. (98–118 Nm).

13. Check the master cylinder reservoir and add fresh DOT 3 brake fluid as required.

14. Lower the vehicle. Pump the brake pedal slowly until a firm brake pedal is obtained, indicating that the brake pads are properly seated, before attempting to move the vehicle. Road-test and check for proper brake operation.

Windstar

FRONT

1. Raise and safely support the vehicle.

2. Remove the wheel and tire assembly.

3. Mark the disc brake caliper to avoid mixing the left-hand and right-hand components.

4. Disconnect the brake hose from the disc brake caliper by loosening and removing the hollow retaining bolt. Discard the 2 copper sealing washers and plug the brake hose.

5. Remove the 2 brake pin retainer bolts.

6. Lift the disc brake caliper off of the disc brake rotor using a rotating motion. Do not pry against the caliper piston. Prying may damage the piston or seals.

7. Remove the disc brake caliper from the vehicle.

To install:

8. Retract the caliper piston fully into the caliper bore using a C-clamp and block of wood or equivalent.

9. Ensure that the disc brake pads are properly positioned and that the lining material is facing the rotor.

10. Place the disc brake caliper over the rotor and hand-start 2 brake pin retainer bolts. Tighten the brake pin retainer bolts to guide pin bolts to 23–28 ft. lbs. (31–38 Nm).

➡If both disc brake calipers were removed, make sure that they are mounted to the proper side. The brake bleeder on the caliper when properly installed should be on top of the caliper for proper bleeding of air.

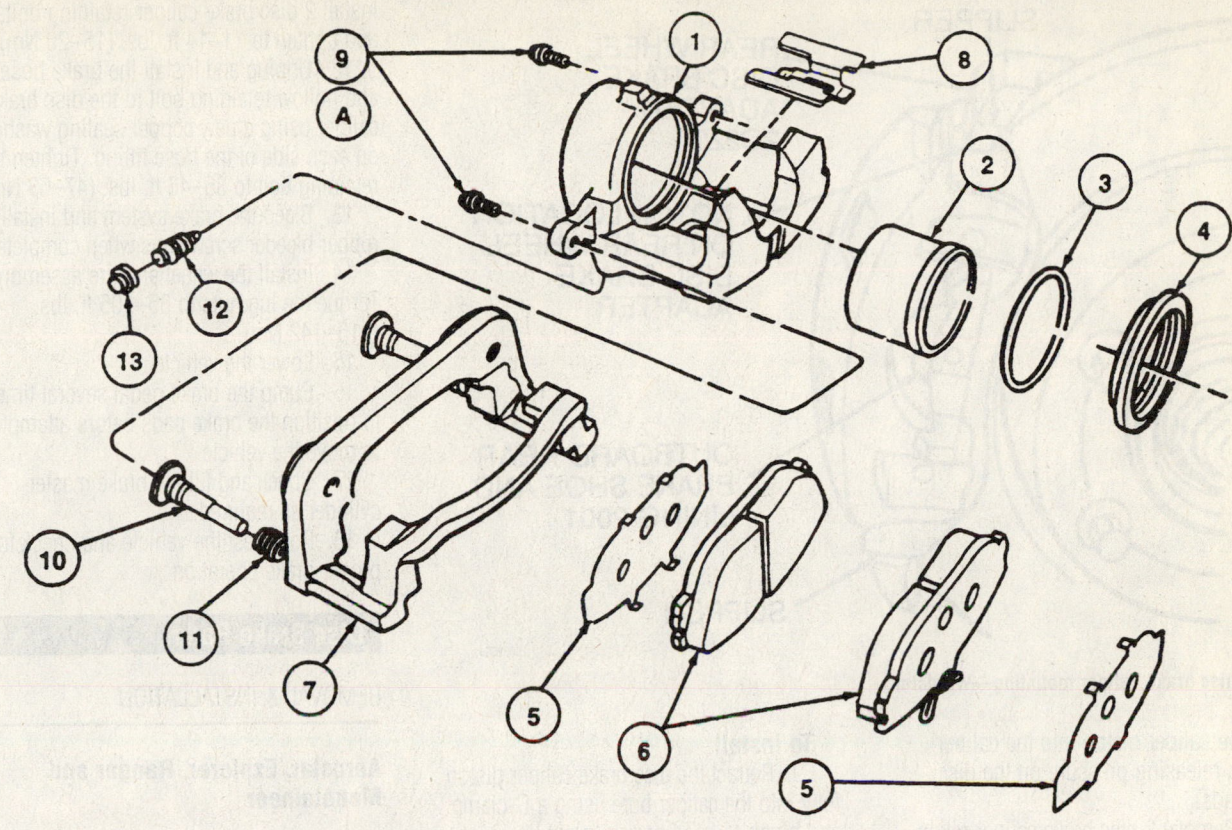

1 Disc Brake Caliper Housing

2 Caliper Piston

3 Brake Piston Seal

4 Piston Boot

5 Front Wheel Disc Brake Shoe Insulator

6 Brake Shoe and Lining

7 Front Disc Brake Caliper Anchor Plate

8 Disc Brake Pad Anti-Rattle Clip

9 Brake Pin Retainer

10 Disc Brake Caliper Locating Pin

11 Retainer Boot

12 Wheel Cylinder Bleeder Screw

13 Bleed Screw Cap

A Tighten to 31-38 N·m (23-28 Lb-Ft)

93026G11

Exploded view of the front disc brake caliper assembly—Windstar

11. Unplug and install the brake hose and hollow retaining bolt to the disc brake caliper using a new copper sealing washer on each side of the hose fitting. Tighten the retaining bolt to 35–46 ft. lbs. (47–63 Nm).

12. Bleed the brake system and install the rubber bleeder screw caps when complete.

13. Install the wheel and tire assembly. Torque the lug nuts to 85–105 ft. lbs. (115–142 Nm).

14. Lower the vehicle.

15. Pump the brake pedal several times to position the brake pads before attempting to move the vehicle.

16. Check and fill the brake master cylinder as required.

17. Road-test the vehicle and check for proper brake operation.

REAR

1. Remove and discard ½ of the brake fluid from the brake master cylinder reservoir.

2. Raise and safely support the vehicle.

3. Remove the wheel and tire assembly.

4. Disconnect the brake hose from the disc brake caliper by loosening and removing the hollow retaining bolt. Discard 2 copper sealing washers and plug the brake hose.

5. Using a C-clamp or equivalent, position the clamp frame on the inboard side of the disc brake caliper housing. Place the clamp screw on the outboard disc brake pad and tighten the clamp enough to

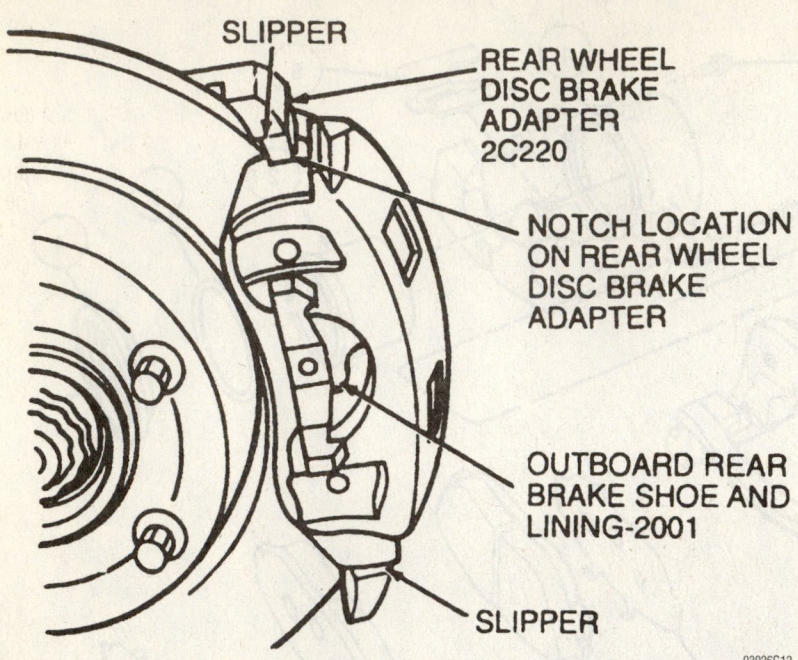

Rear disc brake caliper mounting—Windstar

press the caliper piston into the caliper housing releasing pressure on the disc brake pads.

6. Remove 2 disc brake caliper retaining bolts.

7. Remove the caliper by swinging out the bottom of the caliper first.

8. Remove the disc brake pads, if necessary.

To install:

9. Retract the disc brake caliper piston fully into the caliper bore using a C-clamp and block of wood or equivalent.

10. Ensure that the disc brake pads are properly positioned and that the lining material is facing the rotor.

11. Install the caliper over the disc brake rotor and position on the brake adapter.

Install 2 disc brake caliper retaining bolts and tighten to 11–14 ft. lbs. (15–20 Nm).

12. Unplug and install the brake hose and hollow retaining bolt to the disc brake caliper using a new copper sealing washer on each side of the hose fitting. Tighten the retaining bolt to 35–46 ft. lbs. (47–63 Nm).

13. Bleed the brake system and install the rubber bleeder screw caps when complete.

14. Install the wheel and tire assembly. Torque the lug nuts to 85–105 ft. lbs. (115–142 Nm).

15. Lower the vehicle.

16. Pump the brake pedal several times to position the brake pads before attempting to move the vehicle.

17. Check and fill the brake master cylinder as required.

18. Road-test the vehicle and check for proper brake operation.

Disc Brake Pads

REMOVAL & INSTALLATION

Aerostar, Explorer, Ranger and Mountaineer

FRONT

1. Siphon part of the brake fluid out of the master cylinder to avoid overflow when the caliper piston is pressed into the caliper bore.

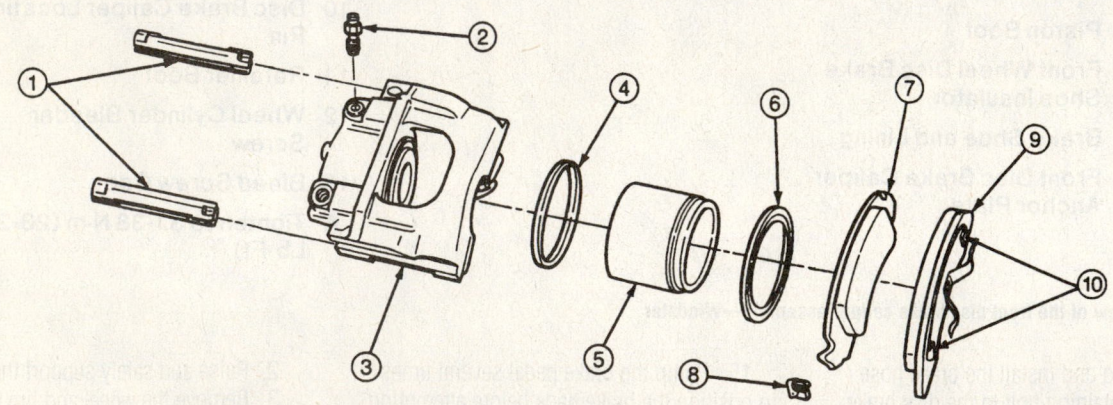

1 Caliper Pins
2 Bleeder Screw
3 Front Disc Brake Caliper
4 Piston Seal
5 Caliper Piston
6 Dust Boot
7 Inner Shoe and Lining (RH)
8 Brake Shoe Hold-Down Spring
9 Outer Shoe and Lining (RH)
10 Torque Buttons

Exploded view of the front brake caliper assembly—1997 Aerostar, Ranger, Explorer and Mountaineer

2. Raise the vehicle and support it safely. Remove the wheel and tire assembly.

3. Remove the brake caliper, but do not disconnect the brake hose. Secure the caliper aside with mechanic's wire.

4. Compress the anti-rattle clip and remove the inner brake pad from the caliper.

5. Press each ear of the outer brake pad

away from the caliper and slide the torque buttons out of the retention notches.

To install:

6. Bottom out the caliper piston in the caliper bore using an 8 in. (20cm) C-clamp or equivalent and a worn out inner brake pad or block of wood to push against the piston. Do not attempt to bottom out the piston with the outer brake pad installed.

7. Place a new anti-rattle clip on the

lower end of the inner brake pad. Make sure the tabs on the clip are properly positioned and the clip is fully seated.

8. Position the inner brake pad and anti-rattle clip in the pad abutment with the ant-rattle clip tab against the pad abutment and the loop-type spring away from the rotor. Compress the anti-rattle clip and slide the upper end of the pad in position.

9. Install the outer pad, making sure the

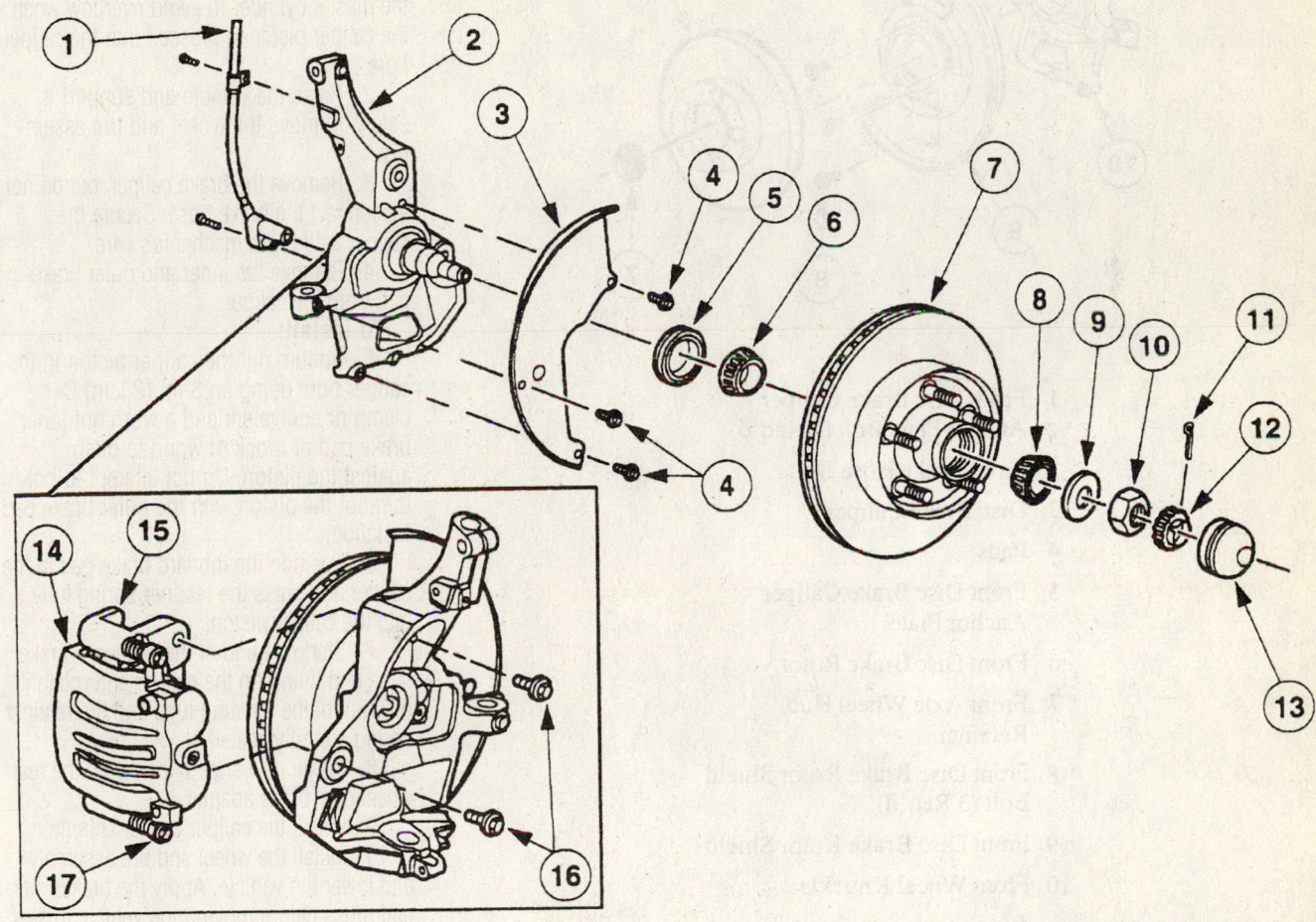

1 Front Brake Anti-Lock Sensor	7 Front Disc Brake Hub and Rotor	12 Nut Retainer
2 Front Wheel Spindle	8 Front Wheel Bearing	13 Hub Grease Cap
3 Front Disc Brake Rotor Shield	9 Front Wheel Outer Bearing Retainer Washer	14 Disc Brake Caliper
4 Rotor Shield Bolt	10 Hub Spindle Nut	15 Front Disc Brake Caliper Anchor Plate
5 Grease Seal	11 Cotter Pin	16 Caliper Anchor Plate Bolts
6 Front Wheel Bearing		17 Disc Brake Caliper Bolt

93026G22

Exploded view of the 2WD front disc brake assembly—1998–01 Explorer, Ranger and Mountaineer

For brake related suspension and axle service, refer to the model specific sections of this manual

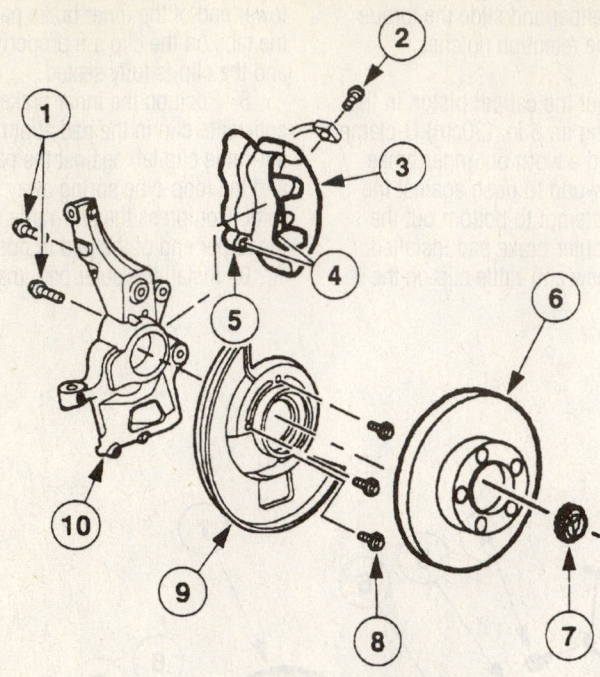

1 Front Disc Brake Caliper
  Anchor Plate Bolt (2 Req'd)

2 Front Brake Hose Bolt

3 Disc Brake Caliper

4 Pads

5 Front Disc Brake Caliper
  Anchor Plate

6 Front Disc Brake Rotor

7 Front Axle Wheel Hub
  Retainer

8 Front Disc Brake Rotor Shield
  Bolt (3 Req'd)

9 Front Disc Brake Rotor Shield

10 Front Wheel Knuckle

93026G23

Exploded view of the 4WD front disc brake assembly—1998–01 Explorer, Ranger and Mountaineer

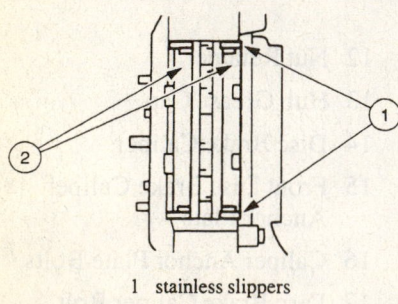

1 stainless slippers
2 pads

93026G24

Position of the front disc brake components—1998–01 Explorer, Ranger and Mountaineer

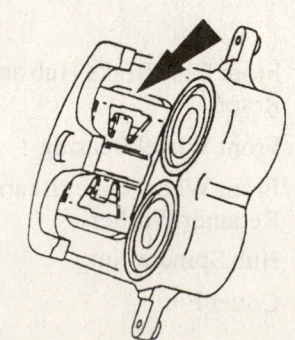

93026G25

View of the front disc brake anti-rattle spring—1998–01 Explorer, Ranger and Mountaineer

torque buttons on the pad are seated solidly in the matching holes in the caliper.

10. Install the caliper on the spindle.

11. Install the wheel and tire assembly and lower the vehicle. Apply the brakes several times before moving the vehicle to seat the pads.

12. Check the brake fluid level. Check the brakes for proper operation.

REAR

1. Siphon part of the brake fluid out of the master cylinder to avoid overflow when the caliper piston is pressed into the caliper bore.

2. Raise the vehicle and support it safely. Remove the wheel and tire assembly.

3. Remove the brake caliper, but do not disconnect the brake hose. Secure the caliper aside with mechanic's wire.

4. Remove the inner and outer brake pad from the caliper.

To install:

5. Bottom out the caliper piston in the caliper bore using an 8 in. (20cm) C-clamp or equivalent and a worn out inner brake pad or block of wood to push against the piston. Do not attempt to bottom out the piston with the outer brake pad installed.

6. Position the inboard brake pad in the caliper and press the retainer spring fully into the caliper piston.

7. Start one end of the outboard brake shoe and lining on the caliper and rotate it down until the locating lugs and the retainer spring are fully seated.

8. Install new shoe slippers on the rear wheel disc brake adapter.

9. Install the caliper on the spindle.

10. Install the wheel and tire assembly and lower the vehicle. Apply the brakes several times before moving the vehicle to seat the pads.

11. Check the brake fluid level. Check the brakes for proper operation.

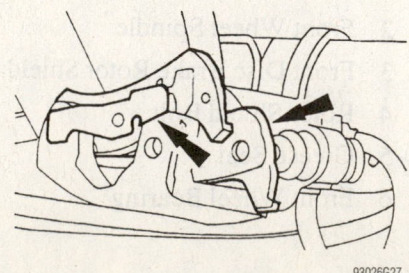

93026G27

Installing the rear disc brake pads—Explorer and Mountaineer

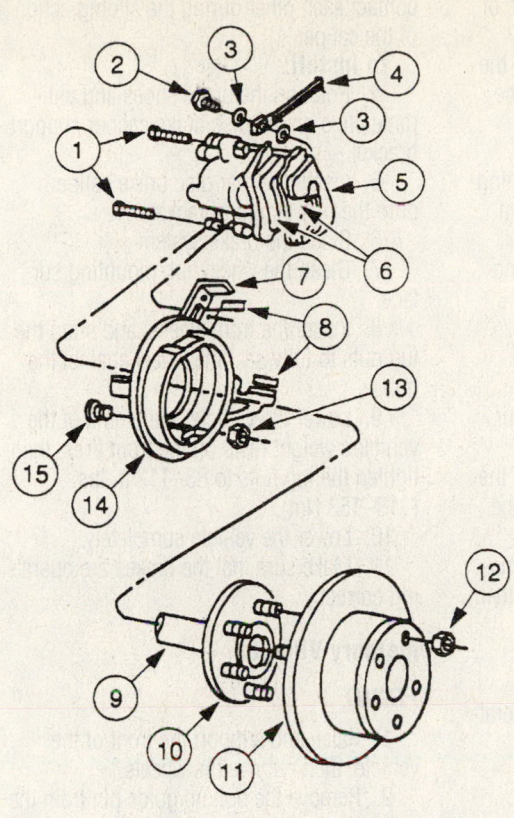

1 Brake Caliper Bolt
2 Flow Bolt
3 Copper Washer (2 Req'd)
4 Rear Wheel Brake Hose
5 Rear Disc Brake Caliper
6 Brake Pads
7 Rear Disc Brake Caliper Anchor Plate
8 Shoe Slippers
9 Axle Shaft
10 Lug Bolt (5 Req'd)
11 Rear Disc Brake Rotor
12 Keeper Nut
13 Rear Wheel Disc Brake Adapter Nut
14 Rear Wheel Disc Brake Adapter
15 Rear Wheel Disc Brake Adapter Bolt

93026G26

Exploded view of the rear disc brake assembly—Explorer and Mountaineer

1997 F-250HD, F-350 and F-Super Duty

E-Series

SINGLE PISTON CALIPER

1. Jack up the front of the truck, support it on jackstands, and remove the wheels.

2. Place an 8 in. (20cm) C-clamp on the caliper and tighten the clamp to bottom the caliper piston in the cylinder bore. Press the clamp on the outer pad. Do not press directly on the composite piston or it may break. Remove the C-clamp.

3. Clean the excess dirt from around the caliper pin tabs.

4. Drive the upper caliper pin inward until the tabs on the pin touch the spindle.

5. Insert a small prybar into the slot provided behind the pin tabs on the inboard side of the pin.

6. Using needle-nose pliers, compress the outboard end of the pin while, at the same time, prying with the prybar until the tabs slip into the groove in the spindle.

7. Place the end of a 7/16 in. (11mm) punch against the end of the caliper pin and drive the pin out of the caliper slide groove.

8. Repeat this procedure for the lower pin.

9. Lift the caliper off of the rotor.

10. Remove the brake pads and anti-rattle spring.

To install:

11. Thoroughly clean the caliper and spindle sliding areas.

12. Place a new anti-rattle clip on the lower end of the inboard pad. Make sure that the tabs on the clip are positioned correctly and the loop-type spring is away from the rotor.

13. Place the lower end of the inner brake pad in the spindle assembly pad abutment, against the anti-rattle clip, and slide the upper end of the pad into position. Be sure that the clip is still in position.

14. Make sure that the caliper piston is fully bottomed in the cylinder bore.

15. Position the outer brake pad on the caliper and press the pad tabs into place by hand. If the pad cannot be pressed into place by hand, use a C-clamp. Be careful not to damage the brake lining with the clamp. Bend the tabs to prevent rattling.

16. Position the caliper on the spindle assembly. Lightly lubricate the caliper sliding grooves with caliper pin grease.

17. Position a new upper pin with the retention tabs next to the spindle groove. Don't use the bolt and nut with the new pin.

18. Carefully drive the pin, at the outboard end, inward until the tabs contact the spindle face.

19. Repeat the procedure for the lower pin.

➥**Do not drive the pins in too far, or it will be necessary to drive them back out until the tabs snap into place. The tabs on each end of the pin must be free to catch on the spindle sides.**

20. Install the wheels.

DUAL PISTON CALIPER

1. Raise and support the front end on jackstands.

2. Remove the wheels.

3. Place an 8 in. (20cm) C-clamp on the caliper and, with the clamp bearing on the outer pad, tighten the clamp to bottom the caliper pistons in the cylinder bores. Do not press directly on the composite piston or it may break. Remove the C-clamp.

4. Clean the excess dirt from around the caliper pin tabs.

5. Drive the upper caliper pin inward until the tabs on the pin touch the spindle.

6. Insert a small prybar into the slot provided behind the pin tabs on the inboard side of the pin.

7. Using needle-nose pliers, compress the outboard end of the pin while, at the same time, prying with the prybar until the tabs slip into the groove in the spindle.

8. Place the end of a 7/16 in. (11mm) punch against the end of the caliper pin and drive the pin out of the caliper slide groove.

9. Repeat this procedure for the lower pin.

10. Lift the caliper off of the rotor.

11. Remove the brake pads and anti-rattle spring.

To install:

12. Thoroughly clean the areas of the caliper and spindle assembly which contact each other during the sliding action of the caliper.

13. Place a new anti-rattle clip on the lower end of the inboard pad. Make sure that the tabs on the clip are positioned correctly and the loop-type spring is away from the rotor.

14. Place the lower end of the inner brake pad in the spindle assembly pad abut-

ment, against the anti-rattle clip, and slide the upper end of the pad into position. Be sure that the clip is still in position.

15. Make sure that the caliper piston is fully bottomed in the cylinder bore.

16. Position the outer brake pad on the caliper, and press the pad tabs into place by hand. If the pad cannot be pressed into place by hand, use a C-clamp. Be careful not to damage the brake lining with the clamp. Bend the tabs to prevent rattling.

17. Position the caliper on the spindle assembly. Lightly lubricate the caliper sliding grooves with caliper pin grease.

18. Position a new upper pin with the retention tabs next to the spindle groove. Do not use the bolt and nut with the new pin.

19. Carefully drive the pin, at the outboard end, inward until the tabs contact the spindle face.

20. Repeat the procedure for the lower pin.

➡️**Do not drive the pins in too far, or it will be necessary to drive them back out until the tabs snap into place. The tabs on each end of the pin must be free to catch on the spindle sides.**

21. Install the wheels.

F-150, F-250 and Expedition 1998–01 F-250HD, F-350, F-450 and Navigator

FRONT

1. Break the front wheel lug nuts loose, then raise and support the front of the vehicle safely on jackstands.

2. Remove the front wheels.

3. Remove the front disc brake calipers.

4. Note the position and orientation of the brake pads and anti-rattle clip. Remove the brake shoes and lings from the front disc brake caliper anchor plate, then remove the anti-rattle clips.

To install:

5. Thoroughly clean the caliper and spindle sliding areas.

6. Place a new anti-rattle clip on the lower end of the inboard shoe. Make sure the tabs on the clip are positioned correctly and the loop-type spring is away from the rotor.

7. Place the lower end of the inner brake pad in the spindle assembly pad abutment, against the anti-rattle clip and slide the upper end of the pad into position. Be sure the clip is still in position.

8. Check and make sure the caliper piston is fully bottomed in the cylinder bore.

Use a large C-clamp, bearing on a piece of wood, to bottom the piston, if necessary.

9. Position the outer brake pad on the caliper and press the pad tabs into place with your fingers. If the pad cannot be pressed into place by hand, use a C-clamp. Be careful not to damage the lining with the clamp. Bend the tabs to prevent rattling.

10. Lightly lubricate the caliper sliding grooves with caliper pin grease.

11. Install the brake caliper onto the anchor plate.

12. Bleed the brake system.

13. Clean the wheel hub mounting surface.

14. Install the front wheels and snug the lug nuts to fully seat the wheel against the hub.

15. Lower the vehicle until some of the vehicle's weight rests on the front tires, then tighten the lug nuts to 83–112 ft. lbs. (113–153 Nm).

16. Lower the vehicle completely.

17. Make sure that the brakes are operating correctly.

REAR

1. Remove the rear brake caliper from the rear hub without disconnecting the brake hose.

2. Remove the brake pads and anti-rattle spring.

3. Thoroughly clean the areas of the caliper and caliper support assembly which

contact each other during the sliding action of the caliper.

To install:

4. Position the brake shoes and anti-rattle clips on the disc brake caliper support bracket.

5. Install the rear disc brake caliper onto the rear support bracket.

6. Bleed the brake system.

7. Clean the wheel hub mounting surface.

8. Install the front wheels and snug the lug nuts to fully seat the wheel against the hub.

9. Lower the vehicle until some of the vehicle's weight rests on the front tires, then tighten the lug nuts to 83–112 ft. lbs. (113–153 Nm).

10. Lower the vehicle completely.

11. Make sure that the brakes are operating correctly.

Mercury Villager

FRONT

1. Raise and support the front of the vehicle, then remove the wheels.

2. Remove the bottom guide pin from the caliper and swing the caliper cylinder body upward; support the caliper with a wire.

3. Remove the brake pad retainers and the pads.

To install:

4. Compress the piston of the disc brake caliper.

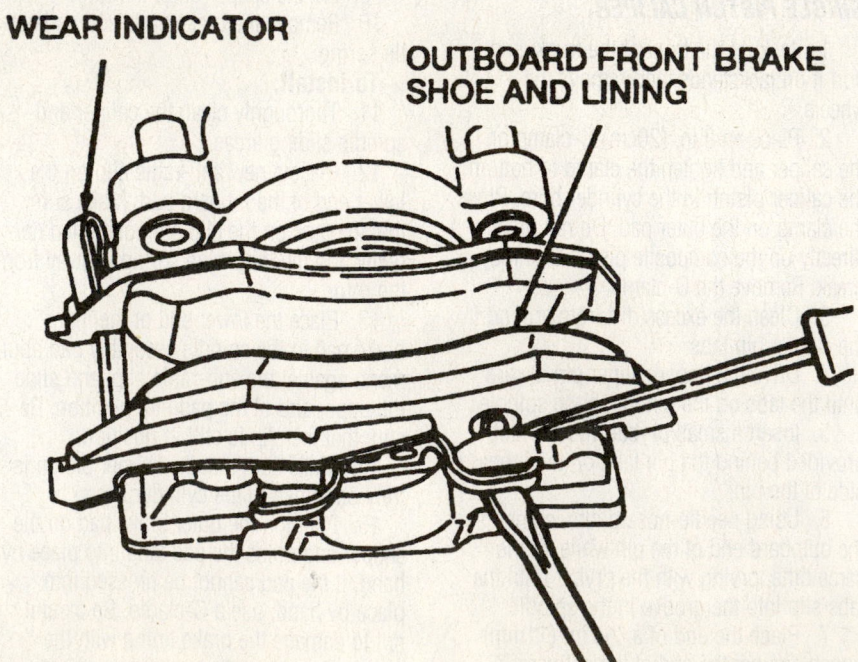

WEAR INDICATOR

OUTBOARD FRONT BRAKE SHOE AND LINING

93026G33

Replacing the disc brake pads—Mercury Villager

5. Install the brake pads and caliper assembly. Torque the guide pin to 23–30 ft. lbs. (31–41 Nm).

6. Install the wheels.

7. Apply the brakes a few times to seat the pads. Check the master cylinder and add fluid if necessary. Bleed the brakes, if necessary.

REAR

➡ Do not press the piston into the bore as performed on the front disc brakes. Due to the parking brake mechanism, the caliper piston must be turned into the bore using a special tool.

1. Raise and support the vehicle safely.

2. Remove the rear wheels.

3. Release the parking brake and remove the cable bracket bolt.

4. Remove the pin bolts and lift off the caliper body.

5. Pull out the pad springs and then remove the pads and shims.

To install:

6. Clean the piston end of the caliper body and the area around the pin holes. Be careful not to get oil on the rotor.

7. Using the proper tool, carefully turn the piston clockwise back into the caliper body. Take care not to damage the piston boot.

8. Coat the pad contact area on the mounting support with a silicone based grease.

9. Install the pads, shims, and the pad springs. Always use new shims.

10. Position the caliper body in the mounting support and tighten the pin bolts to 28–38 ft. lbs. (38–52 Nm).

11. Mount the wheels, lower the vehicle, and bleed the system if necessary.

Windstar

FRONT

1. Remove ½ of the brake fluid from the brake master cylinder reservoir. Properly dispose of the brake fluid.

2. Raise and safely support the vehicle.

3. Remove the wheel and tire assembly.

4. Remove 2 disc brake caliper brake pin retainers. Do not remove the brake hose from the caliper.

5. Lift the disc brake caliper off of the disc brake rotor using a rotating motion. Do not pry against the caliper piston. Prying may damage the piston or seals.

6. Hang the disc brake caliper with a length of wire or equivalent to prevent damage to the brake hose.

7. Remove the inner and outer disc brake pads and the anti-rattle clip.

8. Inspect the disc brake rotor surfaces for grooves, cracks or glazing. Resurface or replace as required. If resurfacing, observe the minimum thickness specification.

To install:

9. Retract the caliper piston fully into the caliper bore using a C-clamp and wood block or equivalent. This will allow room for the new disc brake pads.

10. Install new inner and outer disc brake pads and the anti-rattle clip. Ensure that the disc brake pads are properly positioned and that the lining material is facing the rotor.

11. Place the disc brake caliper over the rotor and install 2 disc brake caliper brake pin retainers. Tighten the brake pin retainers to 23–28 ft. lbs. (31–38 Nm).

12. Install the wheel and tire assembly. Torque the lug nuts to 85–105 ft. lbs. (115–142 Nm).

13. Lower the vehicle.

14. Pump the brake pedal to position the brake pads before attempting to move the vehicle.

15. Check and fill the brake master cylinder reservoir, as required.

16. Road-test the vehicle and check for proper brake system operation.

REAR

1. Remove ½ of the brake fluid from the brake master cylinder reservoir. Properly dispose of the brake fluid.

2. Raise and safely support the vehicle.

3. Remove the wheel and tire assembly.

4. Using a C-clamp or equivalent, position the clamp frame on the inboard side of the disc brake caliper housing. Place the clamp screw on the outboard disc brake pad and tighten the clamp enough to press the caliper piston into the caliper housing releasing pressure on the disc brake pads.

5. Remove 2 disc brake caliper retaining bolts. Do not remove the disc brake caliper brake hose from the caliper.

6. Work the disc brake caliper off the brake rotor and disc brake adapter. Move the disc brake caliper aside and secure with wire or equivalent to prevent damage to the brake hose.

7. Remove the slippers from the anchor plate abutments by gently prying them off the rails and discard the slippers.

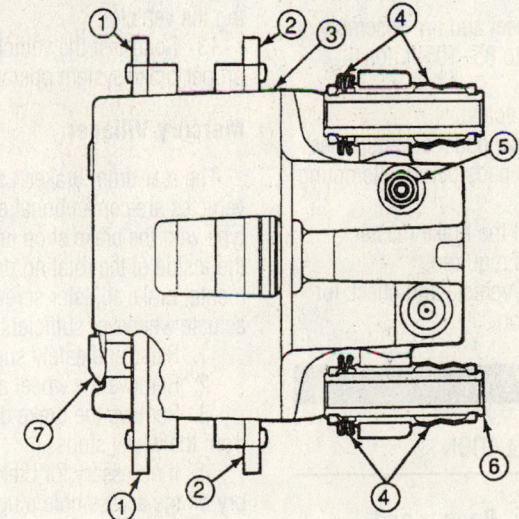

1	Rear Brake Shoe and Lining
2	Rear Brake Shoe and Lining
3	Rear Disc Brake Caliper
4	Caliper Bolt Bushing Dust Boot
5	Wheel Cylinder Bleeder Screw
6	Caliper Bolt Bushing
7	Spring Clip

93026G13

Rear disc brake components—Windstar

8. Remove the inner and outer disc brake pads.

9. Inspect the disc brake rotor surfaces for grooves, cracks or glazing. Resurface or replace as required. If resurfacing, observe the minimum thickness specification.

To install:

10. Retract the disc brake caliper piston fully into the caliper bore using a C-clamp and block of wood or equivalent. This will make room for the new disc brake pads.

11. Install new anti-wear slippers on the rail abutments by snapping them in place.

12. Install new inner and outer disc brake pads. Ensure that the disc brake pads are properly positioned and that the lining material is facing the rotor.

13. Install the disc brake caliper over the brake rotor and place on the brake adapter. Ensure that the notches on the upper ends of the brake pads are seated over the upper ledge of the disc brake adapter and the lower tabs are placed on the lower ledge of the disc brake adapter.

14. Lubricate 2 disc brake caliper retaining bolts with a suitable grease and install. Tighten the retaining bolts to 11–14 ft. lbs. (15–20 Nm).

15. Install the wheel and tire assembly. Torque the lug nuts to 85–105 ft. lbs. (115–142 Nm).

16. Lower the vehicle.

17. Pump the brake pedal several times to position the brake pads before attempting to move the vehicle.

18. Check and fill the brake master cylinder reservoir, as required.

19. Road-test the vehicle and check for proper brake operation.

Brake Drums

REMOVAL & INSTALLATION

Aerostar, Explorer, Ranger and Mountaineer

1. Raise and safely support the vehicle. Remove the wheel and tire assembly.

2. Remove the retaining nuts, if equipped, and remove the brake drum.

3. Inspect the brake drum surface for wear, scoring and runout. Machine or replace, as necessary.

To install:

4. Install the brake drum and secure in place with the retainer nuts, if equipped.

5. Adjust the rear brakes.

6. Install the wheel. Lower the vehicle.

E-Series, Expedition, F-Series and Navigator

1. Ensure that the parking brake control is fully released.

2. Raise and safely support the vehicle.

3. Remove the wheel and tire assembly.

4. If equipped, remove the retaining clips securing the brake drum to the axle.

5. Remove the brake drum and, if equipped, the centering ring.

6. Inspect the brake drum for scoring and/or wear. Machine or replace, as necessary. If machining, observe the maximum permissible drum diameter specification.

To install:

7. Before installing a new brake drum, be sure to remove the protective coating with a brake cleaning solvent.

8. If needed, adjust the rear brake shoes to fit the drum using Brake Adjustment Gauge D81L-1103-C or equivalent.

9. Position the brake drum on the axle hub and if equipped, the centering ring.

10. Install the wheel and tire assembly. Tighten the lug nuts in a star pattern to 84–112 ft. lbs. (113–153 Nm).

11. Lower the vehicle.

12. Pump the brake pedal several times to position the rear brake shoes before moving the vehicle.

13. Road-test the vehicle and check for proper brake system operation.

Mercury Villager

The rear drum brakes used on these vehicles are conventional expanding shoe-type with the brake shoe lining applied to the inside of the rotating drum. An incremental brake adjuster screw is designed to actuate whenever sufficient wear occurs.

1. Raise and safely support the vehicle.

2. Remove the wheel and tire.

3. Remove the brake drum by pulling it from the wheel studs.

4. If necessary for brake drum removal, pry off the access hole plug from the access

hole. Insert a screwdriver and a brake adjustment tool. Press the screwdriver against the adjusting lever to disengage it from the adjuster. Loosen the adjuster using the brake adjusting tool.

To install:

5. Clean all parts well. It is good practice to inspect the wheel cylinder for leaks anytime the brake drum is removed. If a new replacement brake drum is being installed, inspect it for a protective coating on the machined inside braking surface. Remove any coating with suitable solvent.

6. Install the brake drum onto the wheel studs.

7. In most all cases, manual brake adjustment IS NOT recommended. Adjustment is performed by driving the vehicle and applying the brakes.

8. Install the tire and wheel and torque the fasteners to 72–87 ft. lbs. (98–118 Nm).

9. Lower the vehicle.

10. Adjust the rear brake shoes by sharply applying the brakes several times while driving the vehicle alternately forwards and backwards. Check the brake operation by making several stops while driving forward.

Windstar

1. Raise and safely support the vehicle.

2. Remove the wheel and tire assembly.

3. Remove the retainers holding the drum to the hub, if installed and discard.

4. Grasp the drum and remove.

5. If the drum will not slide off with light force, the brake shoes will need to be backed off. Remove the rubber plug on the backing plate and insert a screwdriver and a brake adjusting tool into the slot. Hold the adjuster lever away from the adjuster wheel with the screwdriver and back of the adjuster wheel with the brake adjusting tool.

6. Remove the brake drum. Inspect the drum for wear and/or damage. Machine or replace as necessary. If machining, observe the maximum diameter specification.

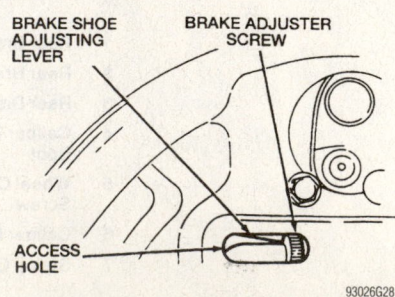

BRAKE SHOE ADJUSTING LEVER
BRAKE ADJUSTER SCREW
ACCESS HOLE
93026G28

Brake shoe adjustment may need to be loosened to remove the brake drum—Mercury Villager

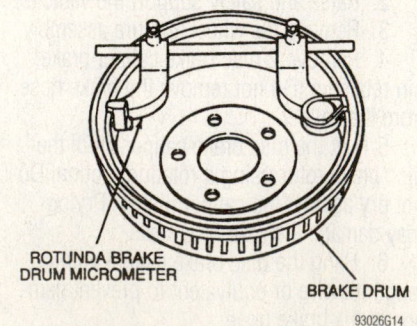

ROTUNDA BRAKE DRUM MICROMETER
BRAKE DRUM
93026G14

Measuring the brake shoes and drum

To install:

7. If a new brake drum is being installed, remove the protective coating from the inner brake surface.

8. Use a suitable brake adjustment gauge to measure the inside diameter of the brake drum.

9. Adjust the brake shoes to match the inside diameter of the brake drum.

10. Slide the brake drum onto the hub. Make sure that the brake shoes are not tight to the brake drum.

11. Install the rubber plug in the access hole. Retainers do not need to be reused to hold the drum.

12. Install the wheel and tire assembly. Torque the lug nuts to 85–105 ft. lbs. (115–142 Nm).

13. Lower the vehicle.

14. Check and fill the brake master cylinder as required.

15. Road-test the vehicle and check for proper brake operation.

Brake Shoes

REMOVAL & INSTALLATION

Aerostar, Explorer, Ranger and Mountaineer

1. Raise and safely support the vehicle. Remove the wheel and tire assembly and the brake drum.

2. Pull backward on the adjusting lever cable to disengage the adjusting lever from the adjusting screw. Move the outboard side of the adjusting screw upward and back off the pivot nut as far as it will go.

3. Pull the adjusting lever, cable and automatic adjuster spring down and toward the rear to unhook the pivot hook from the large hole in the secondary shoe web. Do not pry the pivot hook from the hole.

4. Remove the automatic adjuster spring and adjusting lever.

5. Remove the secondary shoe-to-anchor spring using a suitable brake spring removal/installation tool. Using the tool, remove the primary shoe-to-anchor spring and unhook the cable anchor. Remove the anchor pin plate, if equipped.

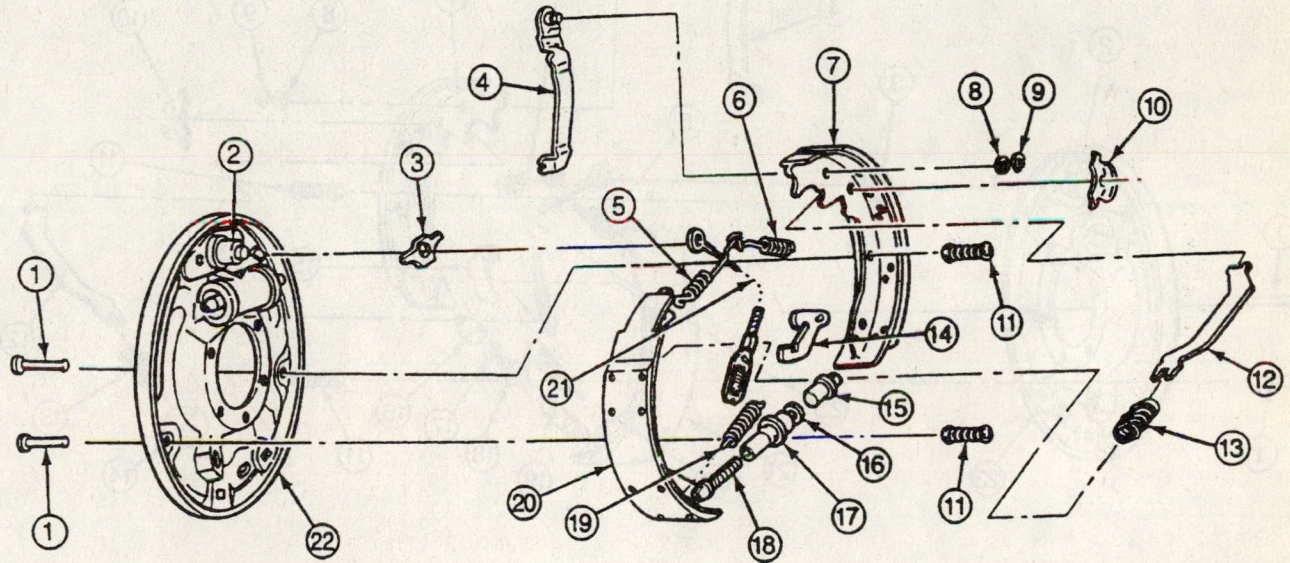

1 Brake Shoe Hold-Down Spring Pin	12 Primary Brake Shoe Parking Brake Lever Link
2 Anchor Pin	13 Parking Brake Link Spring
3 Brake Shoe Anchor Pin Guide Plate	14 Brake Shoe Adjusting Lever
4 Parking Brake Lever	15 Brake Shoe Adjusting Screw Stud
5 Brake Shoe Retracting Spring (Short)	16 Thrust Washer
6 Brake Shoe Retracting Spring (Long)	17 Brake Shoe Adjusting Screw Nut
7 Rear Brake Shoe and Lining (Secondary)	18 Brake Adjuster Screw
8 Washer	19 Brake Shoe Adjusting Screw Spring
9 Parking Brake Lever Pin Retainer	20 Rear Brake Shoe and Lining (Primary)
10 Cable Guide	21 Brake Shoe Adjusting Lever Cable
11 Brake Shoe Hold-Down Spring	22 Brake Backing Plate

93026G19

Exploded view of the rear brake shoes and components—E-150, F-150 and 1997 Ranger

For brake related suspension and axle service, refer to the model specific sections of this manual

6. Remove the cable guide from the secondary shoe.

7. Remove the shoe hold-down springs, shoes, adjusting screw, pivot nut and socket. Note the color and position of each hold-down spring so they can be reassembled in the same position.

8. Remove the parking brake link and spring. Disconnect the parking brake cable from the parking brake lever.

9. Remove the secondary brake shoe. On 9 in. (22.8cm) rear brakes, remove the parking brake lever from the shoe. On 10 in. (25.4cm) rear brakes, remove the retainer clip and spring washer and remove the parking brake lever.

To install:

10. Clean the backing plate ledge pads and sand lightly. Apply a light coating of high temperature lithium grease to the points where the brake shoes touch the backing plate. Lubricate the adjusting cable eye and the anchor pin area.

11. Install the parking brake lever on the secondary shoe. On 10 in. (25.4cm) brakes, secure with the spring washer and retaining clip.

12. Position the brake shoes on the backing plate and install the hold-down spring pins, springs and cups. Install the parking brake link, spring and washer. Connect the parking brake cable to the parking brake lever.

13. Install the anchor pin plate, if equipped, and place the cable anchor over the anchor pin with the crimped side toward the backing plate.

14. Install the primary shoe-to-anchor spring using the brake spring removal/installation tool.

15. Install the cable guide on the secondary shoe with the flanged hole fitted into

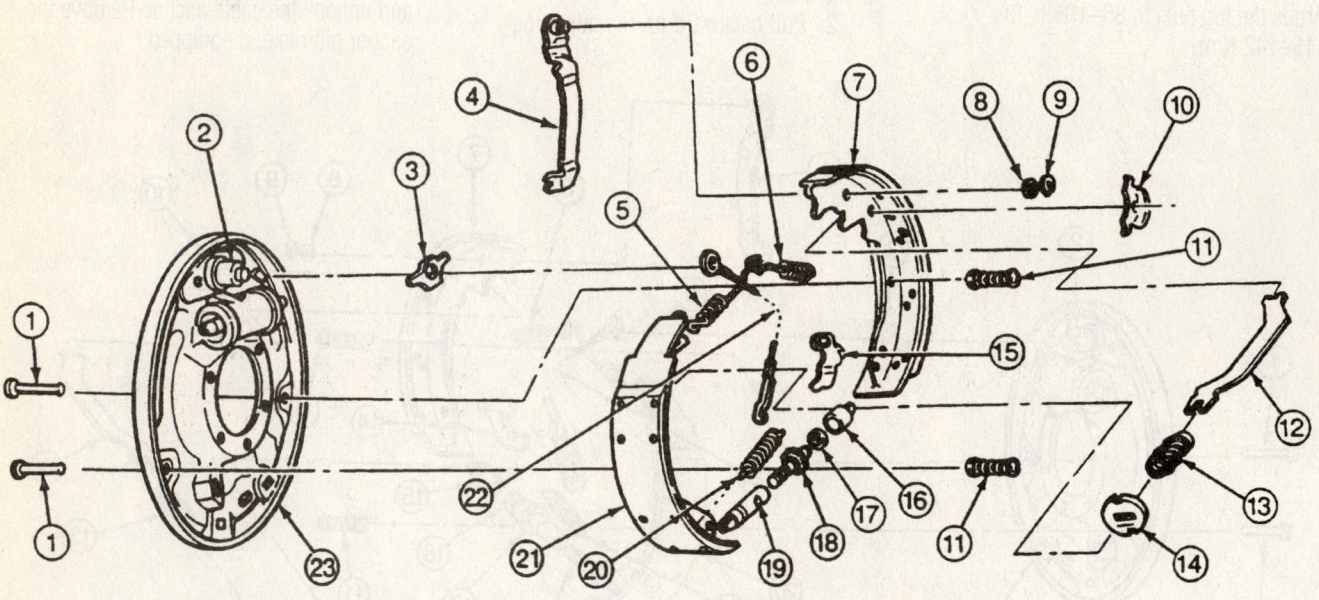

1 Brake Shoe Hold-Down Spring Pin	12 Primary Brake Shoe Parking Brake Lever Link
2 Anchor Pin	13 Parking Brake Link Spring
3 Brake Shoe Anchor Pin Guide Plate	14 Parking Brake Spring Retainer
4 Parking Brake Lever	15 Brake Shoe Adjusting Lever
5 Brake Shoe Retracting Spring (Short)	16 Brake Shoe Adjusting Screw Socket
6 Brake Shoe Retracting Spring (Long)	17 Thrust Washer
7 Rear Brake Shoe and Lining (Secondary)	18 Brake Adjuster Screw
8 Washer	19 Brake Shoe Adjusting Screw Nut
9 Parking Brake Lever Pin Retainer	20 Brake Shoe Adjusting Screw Spring
10 Cable Guide	21 Rear Brake Shoe and Lining (Primary)
11 Brake Shoe Hold-Down Spring	22 Brake Shoe Adjusting Lever Cable
	23 Brake Backing Plate

Exploded view of the rear brake shoes and components—Aerostar

93026G20

the hole in the secondary shoe. Thread the cable around the cable guide groove.

➡ **Make sure the cable is positioned in the groove and not between the guide and shoe web.**

16. Install the secondary shoe-to-anchor (long) spring.

➡ **Make sure the cable end is not cocked or binding on the anchor pin when installed. All parts should be flat on the anchor pin.**

17. Apply high temperature lithium grease to the threads and the socket end of the adjusting screw. Turn the adjusting screw into the adjusting pivot nut to the end of the threads and then loosen, ½ turn.

18. Place the adjusting socket on the screw and install the assembly between the shoe ends with the adjusting screw nearest the secondary shoe.

➡ **Be sure to install the adjusting screw on the same side of the vehicle from**

which it came. To prevent incorrect installation, the socket end of each adjusting screw is stamped with R or L, to indicate installation on the right or left side of the vehicle. The adjusting pivot nuts have lines machined around the body of the nut, 2 lines indicating the right side nut and 1 line indicating the left side nut.

19. Hook the cable hook into the hole in the adjusting lever from the outboard plate side. The adjusting levers are also stamped

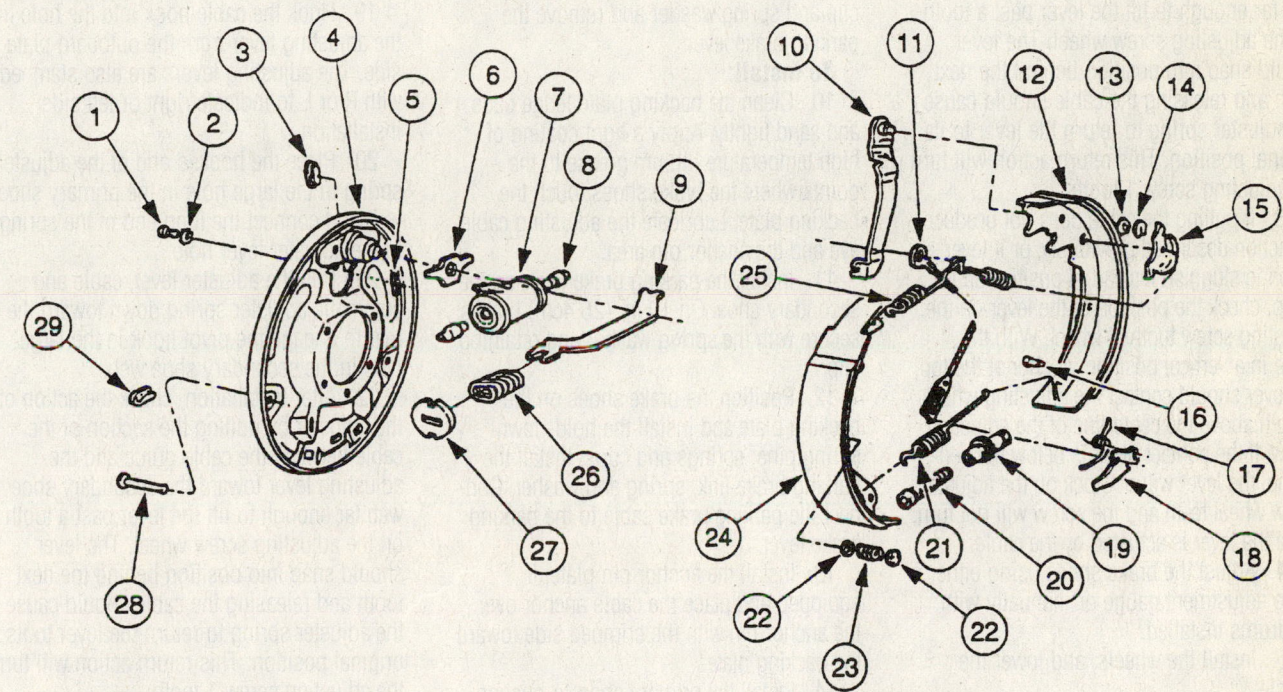

1 Wheel Cylinder-to-Backing Plate Bolt (2 Req'd)	12 Rear Brake Shoe and Lining, Secondary	22 Brake Shoe Hold-Down Spring Cup
2 Washer	13 Washer	23 Brake Shoe Hold-Down Spring
3 Inspection Hole Cover	14 Parking Brake Lever Pin Retainer	24 Rear Brake Shoe and Lining, Primary
4 Brake Backing Plate	15 Cable Guide	25 Brake Shoe Retracting Spring, Short
5 Lining Inspection Hole	16 Adjusting Lever Pin	
6 Anchor Pin Guide Plate	17 Adjusting Lever Return Spring	26 Parking Brake Link Spring
7 Rear Wheel Cylinder	18 Brake Shoe Adjusting Lever	27 Parking Brake Spring Retainer
8 Wheel Cylinder Brake Shoe Link	19 Brake Shoe Adjusting Screw Nut	28 Brake Shoe Hold-Down Spring Pin
9 Parking Brake Strut	20 Brake Adjuster Screw	29 Brake Adjusting Hole Cover
10 Parking Brake Lever	21 Brake Shoe Adjusting Screw Spring	
11 Brake Shoe Adjusting Lever Cable		

93026G21

Exploded view of the rear brake shoes and components—1998–01 Ranger

with an R or L to indicate right or left side installation.

20. Place the hooked end of the adjuster spring in the large hole in the primary shoe web and connect the loop end of the spring to the adjuster lever hole.

21. Pull the adjuster lever, cable and automatic adjuster spring down toward the rear to engage the pivot hook in the large hole in the secondary shoe web.

22. After installation, check the action of the adjuster by pulling the section of the cable between the cable guide and the adjusting lever toward the secondary shoe web far enough to lift the lever past a tooth on the adjusting screw wheel. The lever should snap into position behind the next tooth and releasing the cable should cause the adjuster spring to return the lever to its original position. This return action will turn the adjusting screw 1 tooth.

23. If pulling the cable does not produce the action described previously, or if lever action is sluggish instead of positive and sharp, check the position of the lever on the adjusting screw toothed wheel. With the brake in a vertical position, anchor at the top, the lever should contact the adjusting wheel 1 tooth above the centerline of the adjusting screw. If the contact point is below the centerline, the lever will not lock on the adjusting screw wheel teeth and the screw will not turn, since the lever is actuated by the cable.

24. Adjust the brake shoes using either a brake adjustment gauge or manually with the drums installed.

25. Install the wheels, and lower the vehicle.

F-150 and E-150

1. Raise and safely support the vehicle. Remove the wheel and tire assembly and the brake drum.

2. Pull backward on the adjusting lever cable to disengage the adjusting lever from the adjusting screw. Move the outboard side of the adjusting screw upward and back off the pivot nut as far as it will go.

3. Pull the adjusting lever, cable and automatic adjuster spring down and toward the rear to unhook the pivot hook from the large hole in the secondary shoe web. Do not pry the pivot hook from the hole.

4. Remove the automatic adjuster spring and adjusting lever.

5. Remove the secondary shoe-to-anchor spring using a suitable brake spring removal/installation tool. Using the tool, remove the primary shoe-to-anchor spring and unhook the cable anchor. Remove the anchor pin plate, if equipped.

6. Remove the cable guide from the secondary shoe.

7. Remove the shoe hold-down springs, shoes, adjusting screw, pivot nut and socket. Note the color and position of each hold-down spring so they can be reassembled in the same position.

8. Remove the parking brake link and spring. Disconnect the parking brake cable from the parking brake lever.

9. Remove the secondary brake shoe. On 9 in. (22.8cm) rear brakes, remove the parking brake lever from the shoe. On 10 in. (25.4cm) rear brakes, remove the retainer clip and spring washer and remove the parking brake lever.

To install:

10. Clean the backing plate ledge pads and sand lightly. Apply a light coating of high temperature lithium grease to the points where the brake shoes touch the backing plate. Lubricate the adjusting cable eye and the anchor pin area.

11. Install the parking brake lever on the secondary shoe. On 10 in. (25.4cm) brakes, secure with the spring washer and retaining clip.

12. Position the brake shoes on the backing plate and install the hold-down spring pins, springs and cups. Install the parking brake link, spring and washer. Connect the parking brake cable to the parking brake lever.

13. Install the anchor pin plate, if equipped and place the cable anchor over the anchor pin with the crimped side toward the backing plate.

14. Install the primary shoe-to-anchor spring using the brake spring removal/installation tool.

15. Install the cable guide on the secondary shoe with the flanged hole fitted into the hole in the secondary shoe. Thread the cable around the cable guide groove.

➡**Make sure the cable is positioned in the groove and not between the guide and shoe web.**

16. Install the secondary shoe-to-anchor (long) spring.

➡**Make sure the cable end is not cocked or binding on the anchor pin when installed. All parts should be flat on the anchor pin.**

17. Apply high temperature lithium grease to the threads and the socket end of the adjusting screw. Turn the adjusting screw into the adjusting pivot nut to the end of the threads and then loosen, ½ turn.

18. Place the adjusting socket on the screw and install the assembly between the

shoe ends with the adjusting screw nearest the secondary shoe.

➡**Be sure to install the adjusting screw on the same side of the vehicle from which it came. To prevent incorrect installation, the socket end of each adjusting screw is stamped with R or L, to indicate installation on the right or left side of the vehicle. The adjusting pivot nuts have lines machined around the body of the nut, 2 lines indicating the right side nut and 1 line indicating the left side nut.**

19. Hook the cable hook into the hole in the adjusting lever from the outboard plate side. The adjusting levers are also stamped with R or L to indicate right or left side installation.

20. Place the hooked end of the adjuster spring in the large hole in the primary shoe web and connect the loop end of the spring to the adjuster lever hole.

21. Pull the adjuster lever, cable and automatic adjuster spring down toward the rear to engage the pivot hook in the large hole in the secondary shoe web.

22. After installation, check the action of the adjuster by pulling the section of the cable between the cable guide and the adjusting lever toward the secondary shoe web far enough to lift the lever past a tooth on the adjusting screw wheel. The lever should snap into position behind the next tooth and releasing the cable should cause the adjuster spring to return the lever to its original position. This return action will turn the adjusting screw 1 tooth.

23. If pulling the cable does not produce the action described in Step 22 or if lever action is sluggish instead of positive and sharp, check the position of the lever on the adjusting screw toothed wheel. With the brake in a vertical position, anchor at the top, the lever should contact the adjusting wheel 1 tooth above the centerline of the adjusting screw. If the contact point is below the centerline, the lever will not lock on the adjusting screw wheel teeth and the screw will not turn, as the lever is actuated by the cable.

24. To find the cause of the condition described above, proceed as follows:

a. Check the cable and fittings. The cable should completely fill or extend slightly beyond the crimped section of the fittings. If this does not happen, the cable assembly may be damaged and should be replaced.

b. Check the cable guide for damage. The cable groove should be parallel to the shoe web and the body of the guide should lie flat against the web. Replace the guide if it shows damage.

c. Check the pivot hook on the lever. The hook surfaces should be square with the body on the lever for proper pivoting. Repair the hook or replace the lever if the hook shows damage.

d. Be sure the adjusting screw socket is properly seated in the notch in the shoe web.

25. Adjust the brake shoes using either a brake adjustment gauge or manually with the drums installed.

26. If using a brake adjustment gauge, proceed as follows:

a. Measure the inside diameter of the brake drum with the gauge.

b. Reverse the tool and adjust the brake shoes until they touch the gauge. The gauge contact points on the shoes must be parallel to the vehicle with the centerline through the center of the axle.

c. Install the drum and wheel and tire assembly. Lower the vehicle.

d. Apply the brakes sharply several times while driving the vehicle in reverse. Check brake operation by making several stops while driving forward.

27. If manually adjusting the brakes, proceed as follows:

a. Install the brake drum and wheel and tire assembly.

b. Remove the cover from the adjusting hole at the bottom of the backing plate and turn the adjusting screw to expand the brake shoes until they drag against the brake drum.

c. When the shoes are against the drum, loosen the adjusting screw with the brake adjusting tool, until the drum rotates freely without drag.

d. Install the adjusting hole cover and lower the vehicle.

e. Apply the brakes. If the pedal travels more than halfway to the floor, there is too much clearance between the brake shoes and drums. Repeat the adjustment procedure.

F-250, F-350, E-250 and E-350

1. Raise and support the vehicle.
2. Remove the wheel and drum.

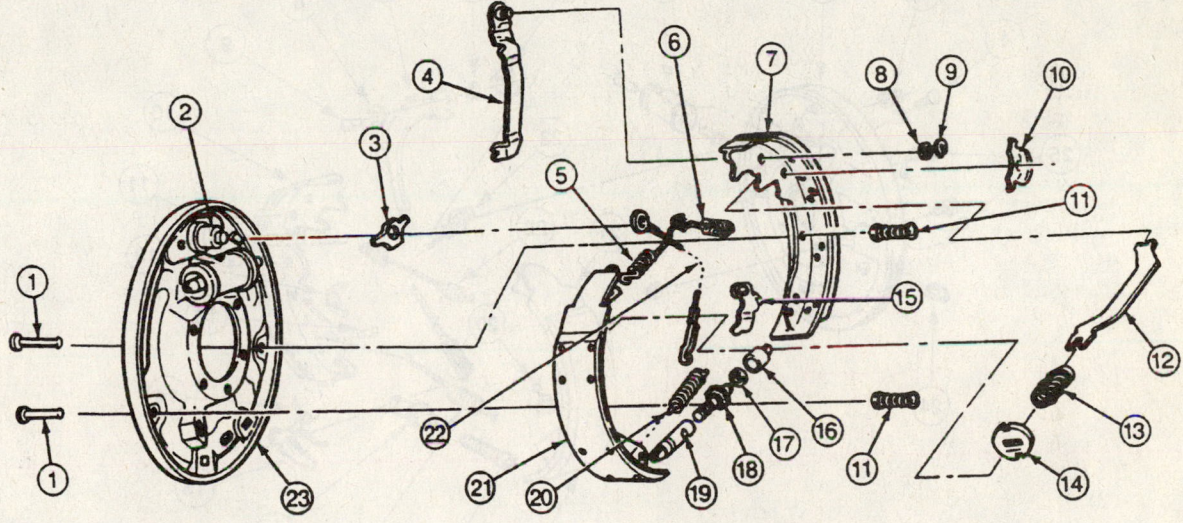

1	Brake Shoe Hold-Down Spring Pin
2	Anchor Pin
3	Brake Shoe Anchor Pin Guide Plate
4	Parking Brake Lever
5	Brake Shoe Retracting Spring (Short)
6	Brake Shoe Retracting Spring (Long)
7	Rear Brake Shoe and Lining (Secondary)
8	Washer
9	Parking Brake Lever Pin Retainer
10	Cable Guide
11	Brake Shoe Hold-Down Spring
12	Primary Brake Shoe Parking Brake Lever Link
13	Parking Brake Link Spring
14	Parking Brake Spring Retainer
15	Brake Shoe Adjusting Lever
16	Brake Shoe Adjusting Screw Socket
17	Thrust Washer
18	Brake Adjuster Screw
19	Brake Shoe Adjusting Screw Nut
20	Brake Shoe Adjusting Screw Spring
21	Rear Brake Shoe and Lining (Primary)
22	Brake Shoe Adjusting Lever Cable
23	Brake Backing Plate

93026G20

Rear brake shoe assembly—F-250, F-350, E-250 and E-350

3. Remove the parking brake lever assembly retaining nut from behind the backing plate and remove the parking brake lever assembly.

4. Remove the adjusting cable assembly from the anchor pin, cable guide and adjusting lever.

5. Remove the brake shoe retracting springs.

6. Remove the brake shoe hold-down spring from each shoe.

7. Remove the brake shoes and adjusting screw assembly.

8. Disassemble the adjusting screw assembly.

9. Clean the ledge pads on the backing plate. Apply a light coat of Lubriplate® to the ledge pads.

To install:

10. Apply Lubriplate® to the adjusting screw assembly and the hold-down and retracting spring contacts on the brake shoes.

11. Install the upper retracting spring on the primary and secondary shoes and position the shoe assembly on the backing plate with the wheel cylinder pushrods in the shoe slots.

12. Install the brake shoe hold-down springs.

13. Install the brake shoe adjustment screw assembly with the slot in the head of the adjusting screw toward the primary shoe, lower retracting spring, adjusting lever spring, adjusting lever assembly and connect the adjusting cable to the adjusting lever. Position the cable in the cable guide and install the cable anchor fitting on the anchor pin.

14. Install the adjusting screw assemblies in the same locations from which they were removed. Interchanging the brake shoe adjusting screws from one side of the vehicle to the other will cause the brake shoes to retract rather than expand each time the automatic adjusting mechanism is operated. To prevent incorrect installation, the socket end of each adjusting screw is stamped with R or

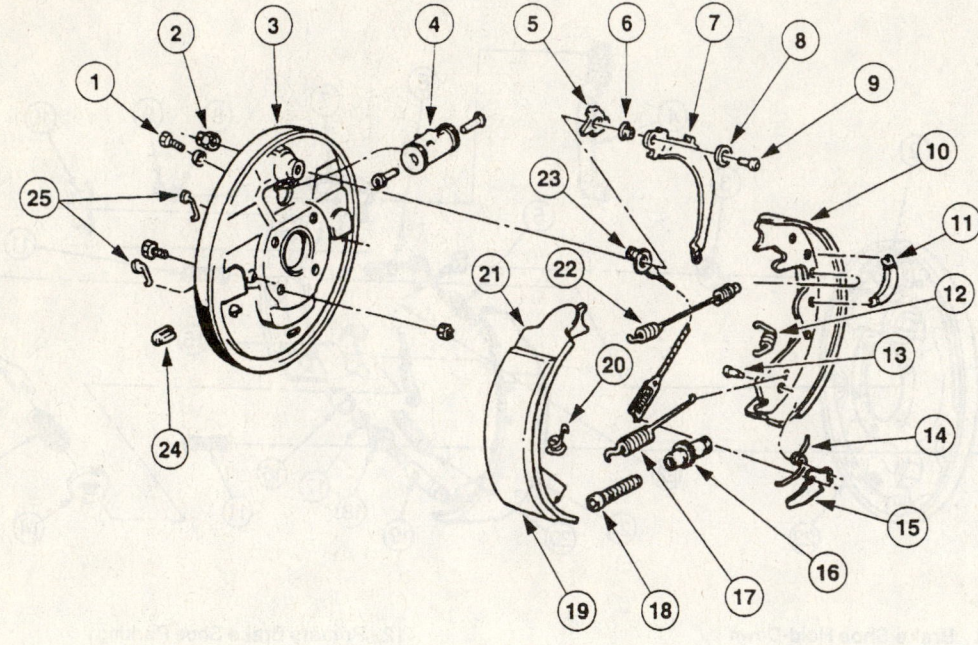

1 Rear Wheel Cylinder Retaining Bolt	13 Adjusting Lever Pin
2 Lock Nut	14 Adjusting Lever Return Spring
3 Rear Brake Backing Plate	15 Brake Shoe Adjusting Lever
4 Rear Wheel Cylinder	16 Brake Shoe Adjusting Screw Nut
5 Primary Brake Shoe Parking Brake Lever Link	17 Brake Shoe Adjusting Screw Spring
6 Parking Brake Link Spring	18 Brake Adjuster Screw
7 Parking Brake Lever	19 Primary Shoe Assembly
8 Parking Brake Lever Pin Retainer	20 Brake Shoe Hold-Down Spring
9 Parking Brake Lever Bolt	21 Rear Brake Shoe and Lining
10 Secondary Shoe Assembly	22 Brake Shoe Retracting Spring
11 Brake Shoe Adjusting Lever Cable Guide	23 Brake Shoe Adjusting Lever Cable
12 Brake Shoe Hold-Down Spring	24 Brake Adjusting Hole Cover
	25 Brake Shoe Hold-Down Spring Pin

93026G34

Exploded view of the rear brake assembly—F-250 HD, F-350 HD, E-250 HD and E-350 HD

L to indicate their installation on the right or left side of the vehicle. The adjusting pivot nuts can be distinguished by the number of lines machined around the body of the nut. Two lines indicate a right-hand nut; 1 line indicates a left-hand nut.

15. Install the parking brake assembly in the anchor pin and secure with the retaining nut behind the backing plate.

16. Adjust the brakes before installing the brake drums and wheels. Install the brake drums and wheels.

17. Lower the vehicle and road-test the brakes. New brakes may pull to one side or the other before they are seated. Continued pulling or erratic braking should not occur.

Mercury Villager

The rear drum brakes use an internal rear wheel cylinder with expanding shoes and lining that are applied against a rotating brake drum. An incremental brake adjuster screw is actuated whenever sufficient wear occurs. Brake adjustment takes place in for-ward or reverse braking but not with parking brake application.

1. Raise and safely support the vehicle.

2. Remove the wheel and tire assembly. Remove the brake drum using the recommended procedure.

3. Disconnect the parking brake rear cable and conduit from the parking brake lever.

4. Remove the 2 brake shoe hold-down springs and the 2 brake shoe hold-down pins.

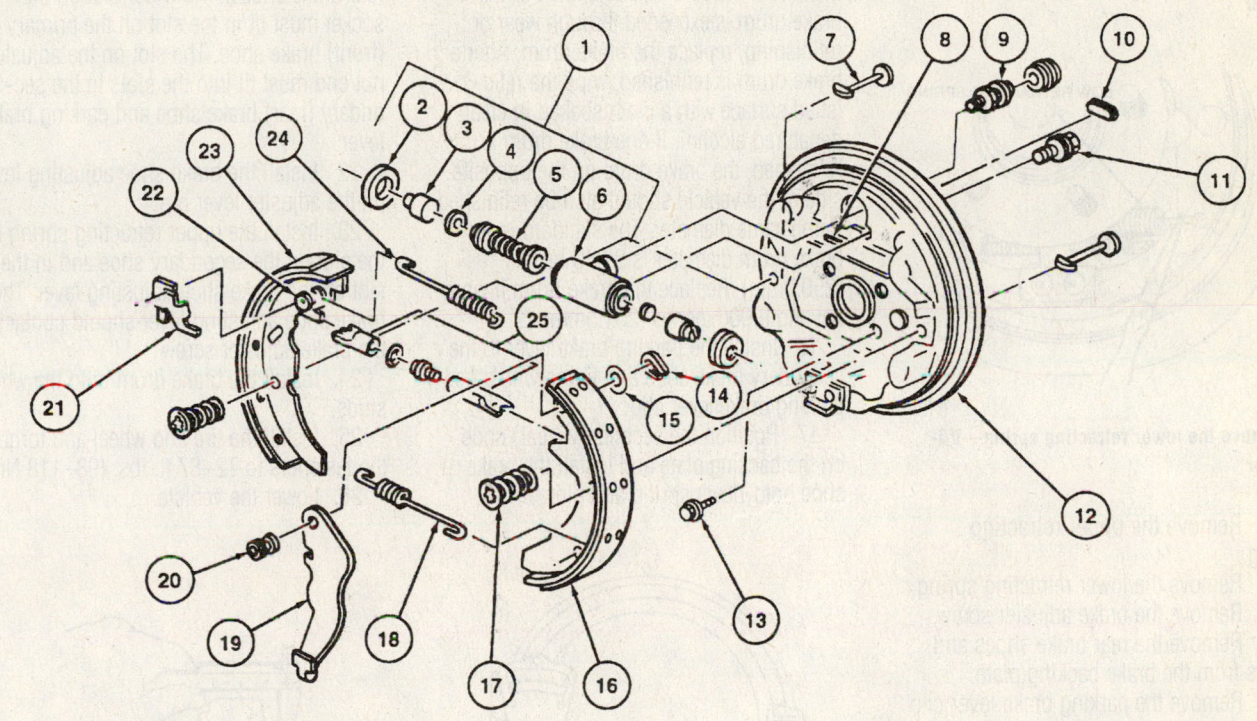

1	Rear Wheel Cylinder
2	Dust Boot (2 Req'd)
3	Wheel Cylinder Piston (2 Req'd)
4	Cup (2 Req'd)
5	Wheel Cylinder Piston Cup Spring
6	Wheel Cylinder Housing
7	Brake Shoe Hold-Down Pin (2 Req'd)
8	Access Hole
9	Rear Brake Bleeder Screw
10	Access Hole Plug
11	Rear Wheel Cylinder Bolt (2 Req'd)
12	Rear Brake Backing Plate

13	Rear Brake Backing Plate Bolts (4 Req'd)
14	Parking Brake Lever Clip
15	Spring Washer
16	Secondary Brake Shoe and Lining
17	Brake Shoe Hold-Down Spring
18	Lower Retracting Spring
19	Parking Brake Lever
20	Parking Brake Lever Pin
21	Brake Shoe Adjusting Lever
22	Adjuster Lever Pin
23	Primary Brake Shoe and Lining
24	Upper Retracting Spring
29	Brake Adjuster Screw

93026G29

Rear drum brake assembly and related components—Villager

For brake related suspension and axle service, refer to the model specific sections of this manual

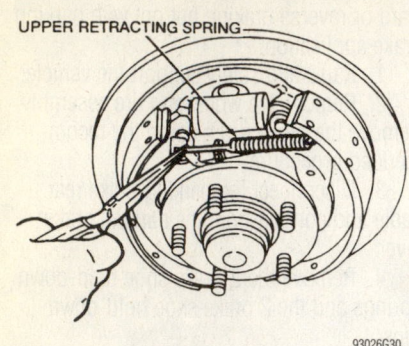

Remove the upper retracting spring—Villager

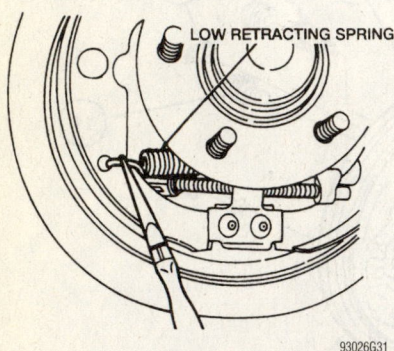

Remove the lower retracting spring—Villager

5. Remove the upper retracting spring.

6. Remove the lower retracting spring.

7. Remove the brake adjuster screw.

8. Remove the rear brake shoes and linings from the brake backing plate.

9. Remove the parking brake lever clip and washer.

10. Remove the parking brake lever from the secondary brake shoe and lining.

To install:

11. Clean all parts well.

12. Inspect the wheel cylinder for signs of leaking. Service as required.

13. Inspect the retracting springs for heat damage, bends or damage to the coils or shank or loss of tension. A good retracting spring will make a full thud when dropped on a concrete floor. A heat-damaged retracting spring that has lost tension will make a distinctive ringing sound when dropped on a concrete floor.

14. Check the brake backing plate for signs of scoring. The shoe contact points must be smooth and have a light coating of lithium grease. Verify that the brake lining thickness is between 0.059–0.232 in. (1.5–5.9mm). Failure to replace worn rear brake shoes will result in a scored drum.

15. Inspect the brake drum for scratches, scoring, bell mouth and out-of-round conditions. Remove minor scores on a brake drum with sandpaper. Do not refinish brake drums to remove scoring marks. A brake drum surface that is highly polished can cause the brakes to lock up. Remove polished surfaces with sandpaper or refinish the brake drum. Refinish a brake drum that is out-of-round enough to cause vehicle vibration or noise when braking. Remove only enough surface metal to true-up the brake drum. Brake drum maximum inside diameter is shown on each drum. If the maximum inside diameter shown on the brake drum is exceeded through wear or refinishing, replace the brake drum. After a brake drum is refinished, wipe the refinished surface with a cloth soaked in clean denatured alcohol. If one brake drum is refinished, the brake drum on the opposite side of the vehicle should also be refinished to the same diameter. The standard inner brake drum diameter is 9.840 inches (250.0mm). Replace the brake drum if worn beyond 9.900 inches (251.5mm).

16. Install the parking brake lever to the secondary brake shoe and lining with a new parking brake lever clip.

17. Position the secondary (rear) shoe on the backing plate and install the brake shoe hold-down spring and pin.

18. Position the primary (front) shoe on the backing plate and install the brake shoe hold-down spring and pin.

19. Attach the parking brake rear cable and conduit to the parking brake lever.

20. Attach the lower retracting spring to the rear brake shoes.

21. Apply a light coat of high-quality grease to the threaded areas of the adjuster nut and adjuster socket. Turn the adjuster nut all the way down on the brake adjuster screw, then loosen the adjuster ½ turn. Install the adjuster screw in the slots on the rear brake shoes. The wider slot on the socket must fit in the slot on the primary (front) brake shoe. The slot on the adjuster nut end must fit into the slots in the secondary (rear) brake shoe and parking brake lever.

22. Install the brake shoe adjusting lever on the adjuster lever pin.

23. Install the upper retracting spring in the slot on the secondary shoe and in the slot on the brake shoe adjusting lever. The brake shoe adjusting lever should contact the brake adjuster screw.

24. Install the brake drum onto the wheel studs.

25. Install the tire and wheel and torque the fasteners to 72–87 ft. lbs. (98–118 Nm).

26. Lower the vehicle.

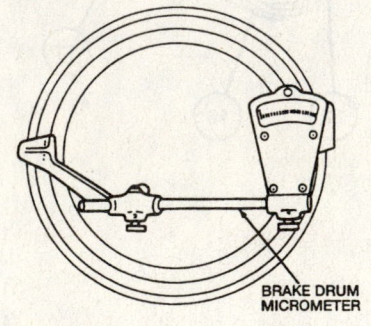

BRAKE DRUM MICROMETER

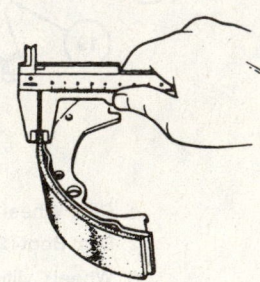

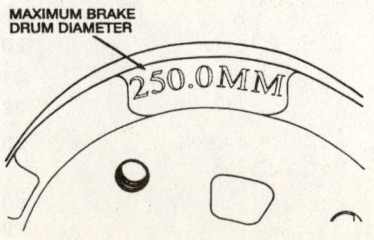

MAXIMUM BRAKE DRUM DIAMETER

250.0MM

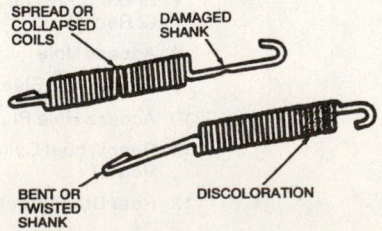

SPREAD OR COLLAPSED COILS — DAMAGED SHANK — BENT OR TWISTED SHANK — DISCOLORATION

These size checks should be made and the retracting springs' condition checked. Replace questionable parts—Villager

➡️ In most all cases, manual brake adjustment IS NOT recommended. Adjustment is performed by driving the vehicle and applying the brakes.

27. The rear brakes do not require adjustment when being serviced to obtain a firm brake pedal feel. To achieve a firm brake pedal after servicing the rear brakes, sharply apply the brake pedal several times while driving the vehicle alternately forwards and backwards. Check the brake operation by making several stops while driving forward. The self-adjusting mechanism will

sufficiently adjust the rear brake shoes without any manual tightening at the brake shoe adjuster. If the rear brake shoes are manually adjusted, the additional action of the brake shoe adjuster can cause the brakes to become over-tightened and result in binding or overheated rear brakes.

Windstar

1. Raise and safely support the vehicle.
2. Remove the wheel and tire assembly.
3. Remove the brake drum.
4. Disconnect the parking brake cable

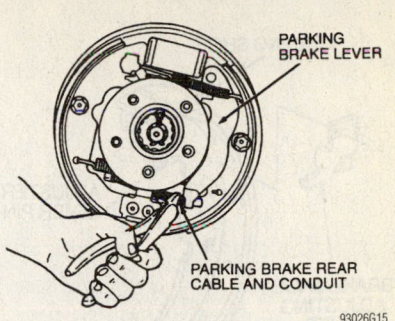

Removing the parking brake cable from the lever—Windstar

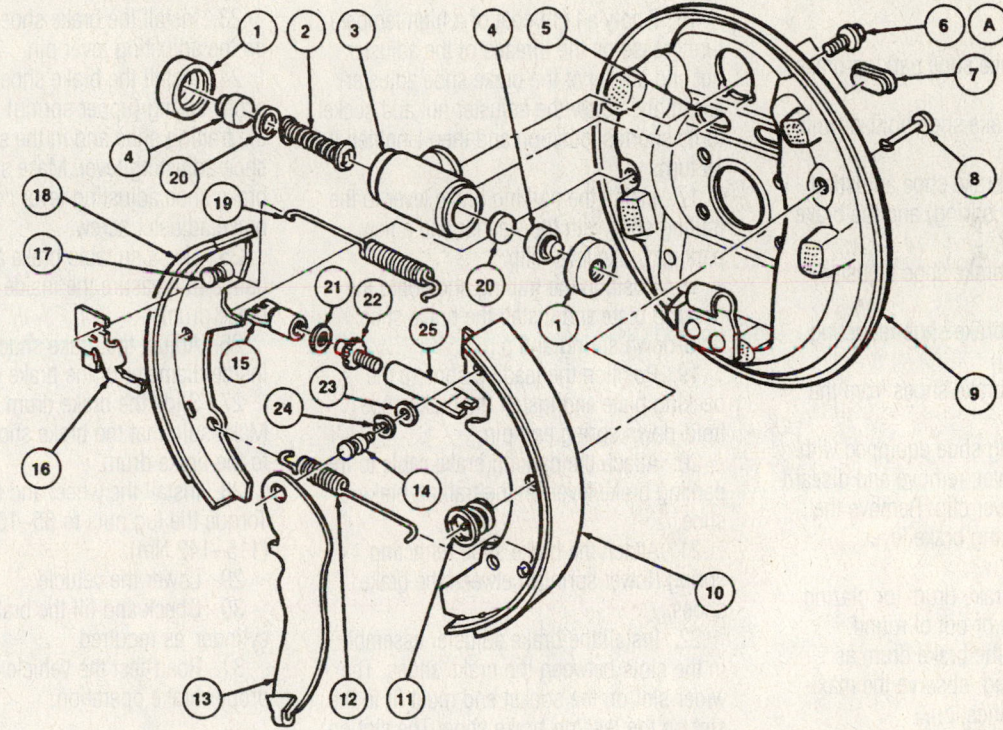

1 Boot	14 Parking Brake Lever Pin (Inner)
2 Spring Expander	15 Brake Shoe Adjusting Screw Socket
3 Rear Wheel Cylinder	16 Brake Shoe Adjusting Lever
4 Piston and Insert	17 Parking Brake Lever Pin (Outer)
5 Shoe and Adjustment Access Hole	18 Leading Shoe and Lining
6 Wheel Cylinder Retaining Screw (2 Req'd)	19 Brake Shoe Adjusting Screw Spring
7 Brake Adjusting Hole Cover	20 Cup
8 Brake Shoe Hold-Down Spring Pin	21 Washer
9 Brake Backing Plate	22 Adjusting Screw
10 Trailing Shoe and Lining	23 Washer
11 Brake Shoe Hold-Down Spring	24 Parking Brake Lever Pin Retainer
12 Brake Shoe Retracting Spring	25 Adjusting Pivot Nut
13 Parking Brake Lever	A Tighten to 12-18 N·m (9-13 Lb-Ft)

Parking brake lever and clip (pin not shown)—Windstar

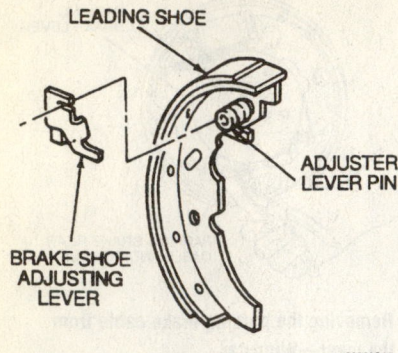

Brake shoe adjusting lever and pin—Windstar

from the trailing brake shoe parking brake lever.

5.   Remove 2 brake shoe hold-down springs and pins.

6.   Remove the brake shoe adjusting screw spring (upper spring) and the brake shoe adjusting lever.

7.   Remove the brake shoe adjuster assembly.

8.   Remove the brake shoe retracting spring (lower spring).

9.   Remove the brake shoes from the backing plate.

10.   On the trailing shoe equipped with the parking brake lever, remove and discard the parking brake lever clip. Remove the washer and the parking brake lever.

To install:

11.   Inspect the brake drum for glazing, cracks, uneven wear or out of round. Machine or replace the brake drum as required. If machining, observe the maximum diameter specification.

12.   Inspect the wheel cylinder for leakage. Gently work the wheel cylinder pistons to make sure that they move without binding. Replace the wheel cylinder, as needed.

13.   Check the new brake shoes that they are correct for the application.

14.   Swap over or install new pins into the leading and trailing shoes for the parking brake lever and the brake shoe adjusting lever using the old shoes as a guide.

15.   Apply a high temperature grease to the backing plate/brake shoe contact areas.

16.   Apply a light coat of a high temperature grease on the threads of the adjuster nut and socket of the brake shoe adjuster assembly. Screw the adjuster nut and socket to its shortest position and then lengthen it ½ turn.

17.   Install the parking brake lever to the trailing shoe with the washer and a new parking brake lever clip.

18.   Position the trailing shoe onto the backing plate and install the brake shoe hold-down spring and pin.

19.   Position the leading shoe to the backing plate and install the brake shoe hold-down spring and pin.

20.   Attach the parking brake cable to the parking brake lever on the trailing brake shoe.

21.   Attach the brake shoe retracting spring (lower spring) between the brake shoes.

22.   Install the brake adjuster assembly in the slots between the brake shoes. The wider slot on the socket end must fit in the slot on the leading brake shoe. The slot on

the adjuster nut end must fit in the slots on the trailing shoe and the parking brake lever.

➡The socket end of each brake adjuster screw is marked with an R or L indicating the right or left side of the vehicle. The adjuster nuts can also be identified for which side they belong to by the number of grooves machined around the body of the adjuster nut. Two grooves indicate a right-hand adjuster nut (right-hand thread) while 1 groove indicates a left-hand adjuster nut (left-hand thread).

23.   Install the brake shoe adjusting lever on the adjusting lever pin.

24.   Install the brake shoe adjusting screw spring (upper spring) in the slot on the trailing shoe and in the slot on the brake shoe adjusting lever. Make sure that the brake shoe adjusting lever contacts the brake adjuster screw.

25.   Use a suitable brake adjustment gauge to measure the inside diameter of the brake drum.

26.   Adjust the brake shoes to match the inside diameter of the brake drum.

27.   Slide the brake drum onto the hub. Make sure that the brake shoes are not tight to the brake drum.

28.   Install the wheel and tire assembly. Torque the lug nuts to 85–105 ft. lbs. (115–142 Nm).

29.   Lower the vehicle.

30.   Check and fill the brake master cylinder, as required.

31.   Road-test the vehicle and check for proper brake operation.

GENERAL MOTORS

Brake Caliper

REMOVAL & INSTALLATION

Astro, Blazer, Bravada, Envoy, Jimmy, Safari, S-series Pick-Up and Sonoma

FRONT

1.   Remove ⅔ of the brake fluid from the master cylinder reservoir.

2.   Raise and support the vehicle safely. Remove the tire and wheel assembly.

3.   Disconnect and plug the caliper fluid line. Remove the bolts retaining the caliper to the rotor. Remove the caliper from the rotor.

4.   Remove the disc brake pads from the caliper. Remove the disc brake pad retaining clips from inside the caliper.

To install:

5.   Clean and lubricate the sleeves and bushings with silicon grease. Install the pads in the caliper.

6.   Install the caliper in position over the rotor and install the mounting bolts. Tighten the mounting bolts to 38 ft. lbs. (51 Nm).

7.   Connect the fluid lines to the caliper, if disconnected, and tighten to 33 ft. lbs. (45 Nm).

8.   Install the wheel and tire assembly.

9.   Lower the vehicle and refill the master cylinder to the correct level. Bleed the brake system if the fluid lines were disconnected from the caliper.

REAR

1.   Raise and safely support the vehicle.

2.   Remove rear wheels.

3.   Remove brake hose and cap line.

4.   Remove retainers from caliper and remove caliper.

To install:

5.   Install brake pads if removed.

6.   Install caliper over rotor, and onto mounts.

7.   Install retainers, and tighten to 23 ft. lbs. or (31 Nm).

8.   Install brake hose, and tighten to 20 ft. lbs. (27 Nm).

9.   Bleed brake system.

10.   Install tires.

11.   Lower the vehicle.

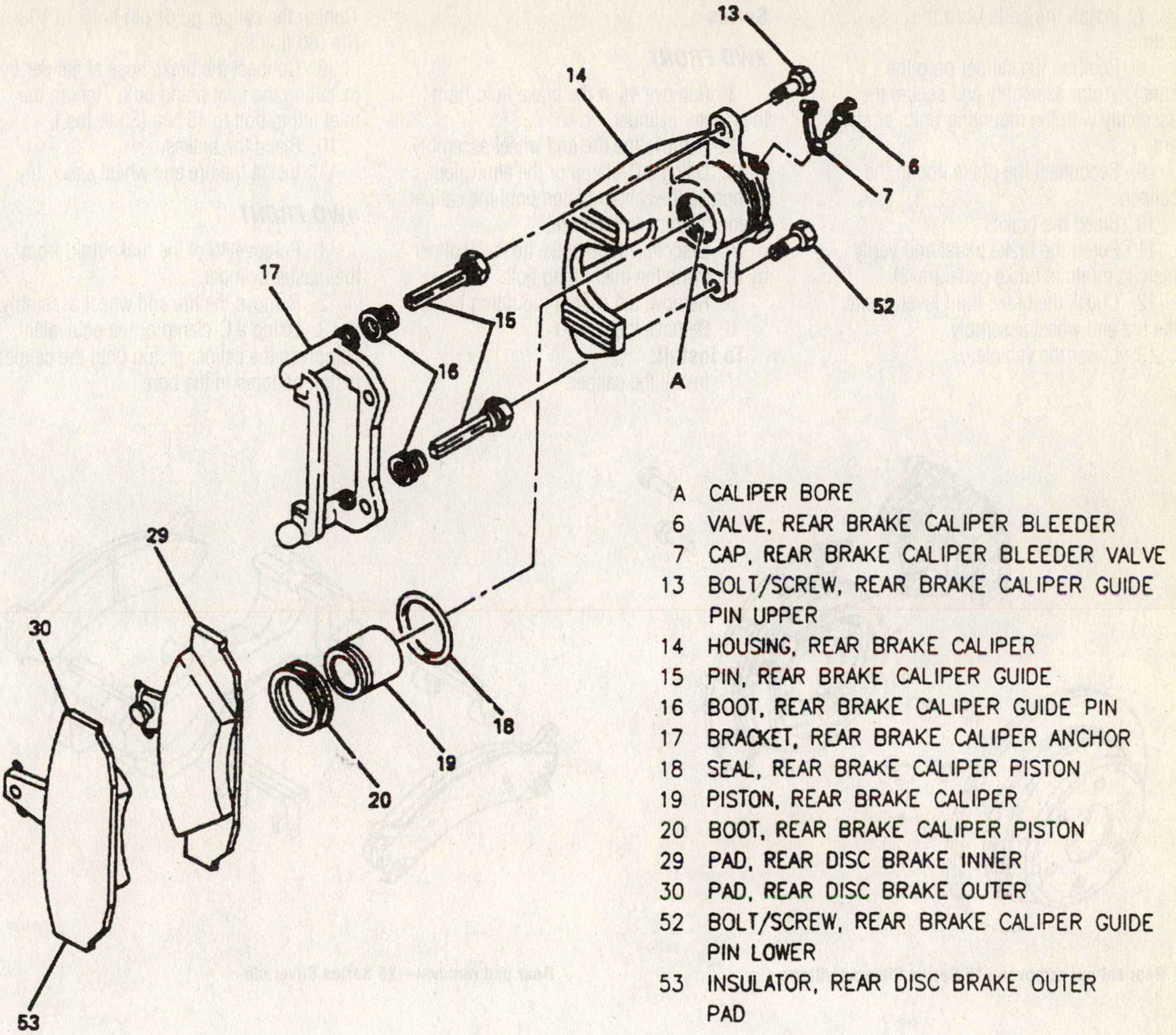

A   CALIPER BORE
6   VALVE, REAR BRAKE CALIPER BLEEDER
7   CAP, REAR BRAKE CALIPER BLEEDER VALVE
13   BOLT/SCREW, REAR BRAKE CALIPER GUIDE
     PIN UPPER
14   HOUSING, REAR BRAKE CALIPER
15   PIN, REAR BRAKE CALIPER GUIDE
16   BOOT, REAR BRAKE CALIPER GUIDE PIN
17   BRACKET, REAR BRAKE CALIPER ANCHOR
18   SEAL, REAR BRAKE CALIPER PISTON
19   PISTON, REAR BRAKE CALIPER
20   BOOT, REAR BRAKE CALIPER PISTON
29   PAD, REAR DISC BRAKE INNER
30   PAD, REAR DISC BRAKE OUTER
52   BOLT/SCREW, REAR BRAKE CALIPER GUIDE
     PIN LOWER
53   INSULATOR, REAR DISC BRAKE OUTER
     PAD

93026G44

Rear Brake Caliper—Bravada

12. Lower the vehicle, refill the master cylinder and pump pedal to attain full brake pedal before Road-testing the vehicle.

C/K Pick-Up, Denali, Escalade, G-Series Van, Savana, Suburban, Tahoe and Yukon

➥There are 2 caliper designs and they can be identified by the method used to secure the assembly to the spindle bracket. The Delco caliper is secured by a bolt and sleeve combination. The Bendix caliper assembly is secured by a slider, spring and bolt.

1. Remove the cover on the master cylinder and siphon enough fluid out of the reservoirs to bring the level to ⅓ full. This step prevents spilling fluid when the piston is pushed back.

2. Raise and support the vehicle safely. Remove the front wheels and tires.

3. Position a C-clamp around the outside pad and caliper; tighten the C-clamp until the caliper piston bottoms in its bore.

4. Remove the brake hose from the caliper by removing the inlet fitting.

5. Remove the bolt and sleeve or bolt and slider assemblies that hold the caliper and then lift the caliper off the rotor.

6. Remove the inboard and outboard pad.

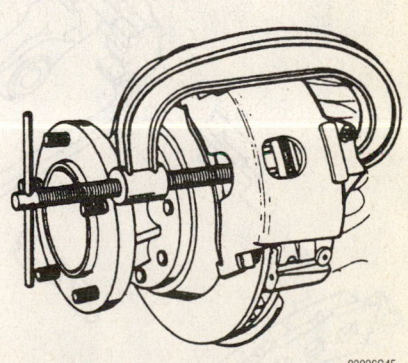

93026G45

Compressing the caliper piston—C/K Pick-Up, Denali, Escalade, G-Series Van, Savana, Suburban, Tahoe and Yukon

To install:

7. Install the pads onto the caliper.

8. Position the caliper onto the knuckle/rotor assembly and secure the assembly with the mounting bolts or sliders.

9. Reconnect the brake line to the caliper.

10. Bleed the brakes

11. Pump the brake pedal and verify there is minimal brake pedal travel.

12. Check the brake fluid level. Install the tire and wheel assembly.

13. Lower the vehicle.

Silverado and 2000–01 Sierra 15 Series

2WD FRONT

1. Remove ⅔ of the brake fluid from the master cylinder.

2. Remove the tire and wheel assembly.

3. Using a C-clamp or the equivalent, compress the caliper piston until the caliper piston bottoms in the bore.

4. Disconnect the brake hose at caliper by removing the inlet fitting bolt.

5. Remove the caliper mounting bolts.

6. Remove the caliper.

To install:

7. Install the caliper.

8. Install the caliper mounting bolts. Tighten the caliper guide pin bolts to 108 Nm (80 ft. lbs.).

9. Connect the brake hose at caliper by installing the inlet fitting bolt. Tighten the inlet fitting bolt to 45 Nm (33 ft. lbs.).

10. Bleed the brakes.

11. Install the tire and wheel assembly.

4WD FRONT

1. Remove ⅔ of the brake fluid from the master cylinder.

2. Remove the tire and wheel assembly.

3. Using a C-clamp or the equivalent, compress the caliper piston until the caliper piston bottoms in the bore.

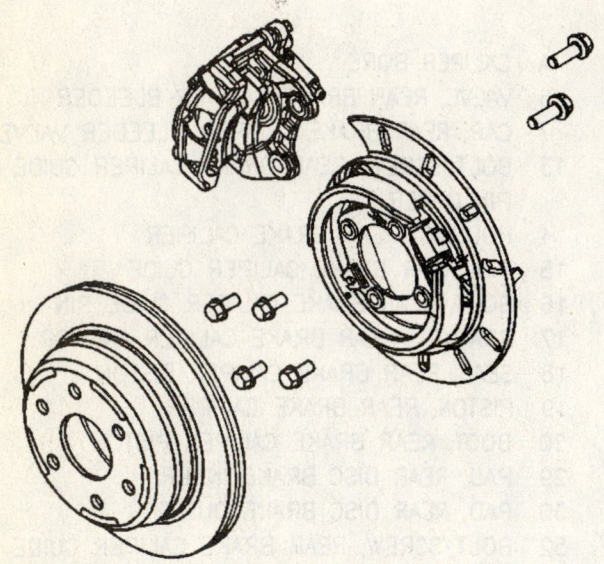

Rear caliper removal—15 Series Silverado/Sierra

93086G96

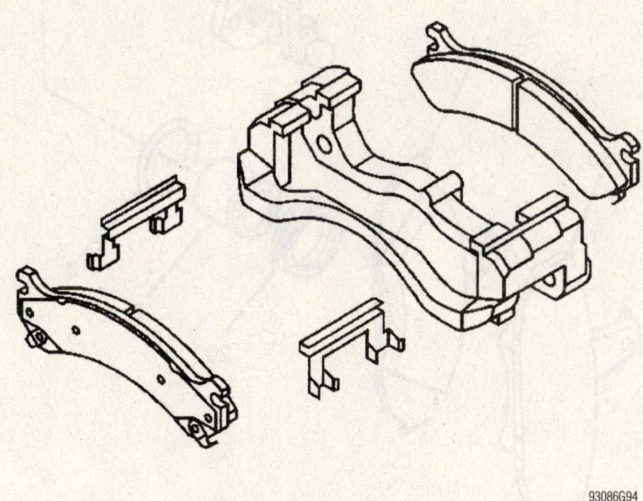

Rear pad removal—25 Series Silverado

93086G94

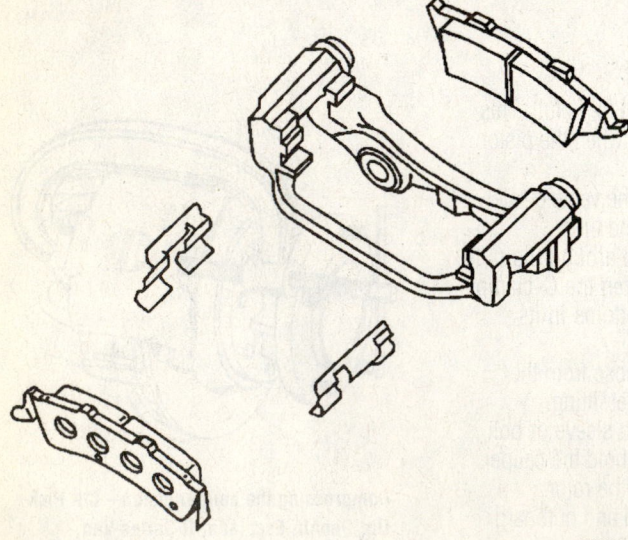

Rear pad removal—15 Series Silverado/Sierra

93086G95

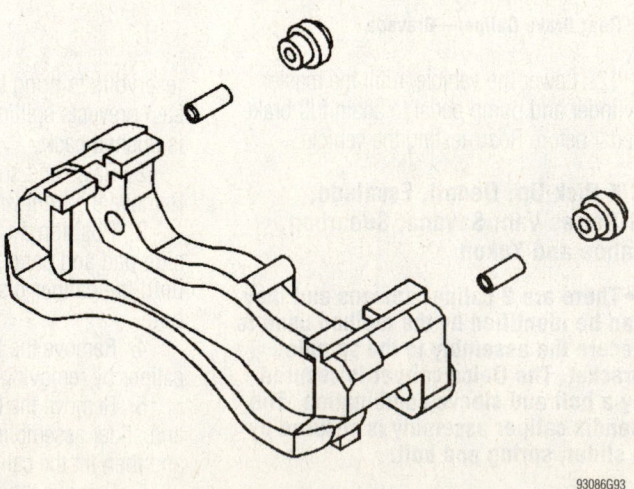

Sleeve and bushing removal—15 Series Silverado/Sierra

93086G93

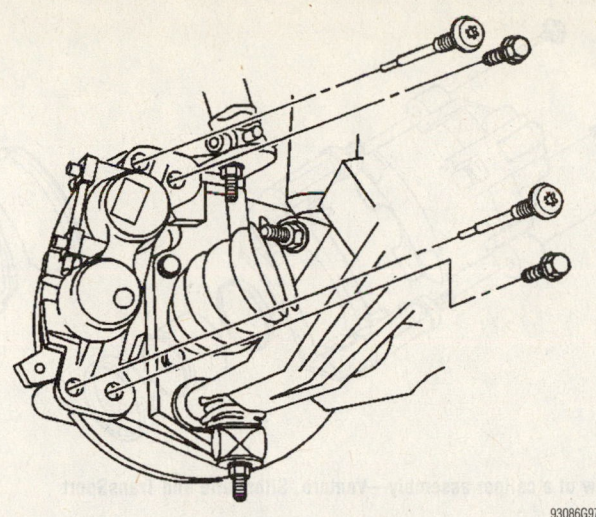

Front caliper removal—Silverado/Sierra

93086G97

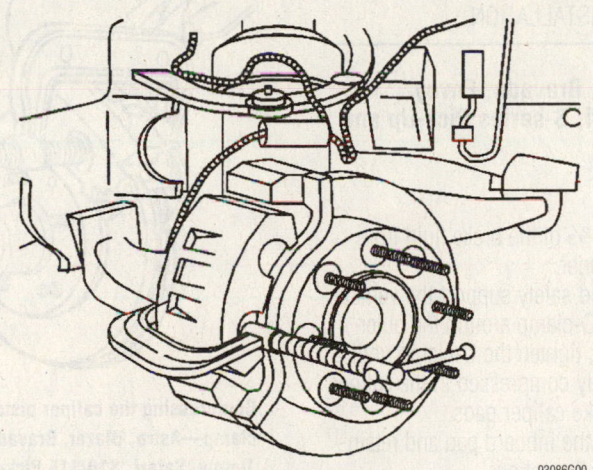

Compressing the rear caliper piston—Series Silverado/Sierra

93086G00

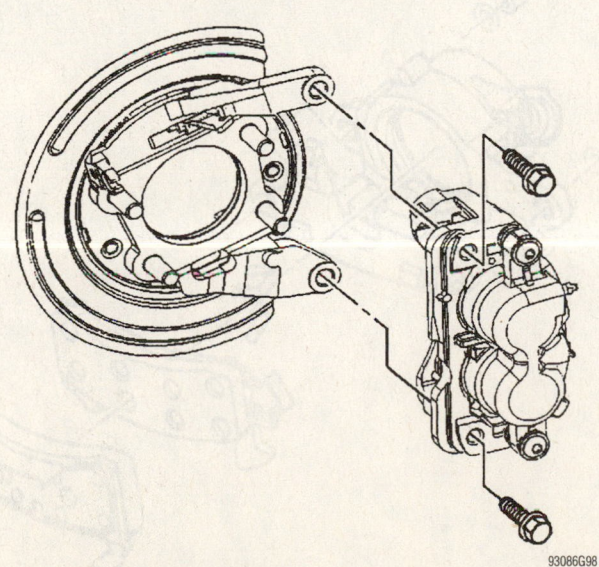

Rear caliper removal—25 Series Silverado

93086G98

4. Disconnect the brake hose at caliper by removing the inlet fitting bolt.

5. Remove the caliper mounting bolts.

6. Remove the caliper. Inspect the caliper assembly.

To install:

7. Install the caliper.

8. Install the caliper mounting bolts. Tighten the caliper guide pin bolts to 108 Nm (80 ft. lbs.).

9. Connect the brake hose at caliper by installing the inlet fitting bolt. Tighten the inlet fitting bolt to 45 Nm (33 ft. lbs.).

10. Bleed the brakes.

11. Install the tire and wheel assembly.

2WD REAR

1. Remove ⅔ of the brake fluid from the master cylinder.

2. Remove the tire and wheel assembly.

3. Using a C-clamp or the equivalent, compress the caliper piston until the caliper piston bottoms in the bore.

4. Disconnect the brake hose at the caliper by removing the inlet fitting bolt.

5. Remove the caliper mounting bolts.

6. Remove the caliper.

7. Inspect the caliper assembly.

To install:

8. Install the caliper.

9. Install the caliper mounting bolts. Perform the following procedure before installing the caliper guide pin bolts (15 Series only).

    a. Remove all traces of the original adhesive patch.

    b. Clean the threads of the bolt with brake parts cleaner or the equivalent and allow to dry.

    c. Apply Red Loctite✱✱272 to the threads of the bolt.

10. Install the caliper mounting bolts. Tighten the caliper guide pin bolts to 42 Nm (31 ft. lbs.) on the 15 series; 108 Nm (80 ft. lbs.) on the 25 series.

11. Connect the brake hose at the caliper by installing the inlet fitting bolt. Tighten the inlet fitting bolt to 45 Nm (33 ft. lbs.).

12. Bleed the brakes.

13. Install the tire and wheel assembly.

14. Refill the brake master cylinder to the proper level with fresh brake fluid.

4WD REAR

1. Remove ⅔ of the brake fluid from the master cylinder.

2. Remove the tire and wheel assembly.

3. Using a C-clamp or the equivalent, compress the caliper piston until the caliper piston bottoms in the bore.

For brake related suspension and axle service, refer to the model specific sections of this manual

4. Disconnect the brake hose at the caliper by removing the inlet fitting bolt.

5. Remove the caliper mounting bolts.

6. Remove the caliper.

7. Inspect the caliper assembly.

8. Install the caliper.

9. Install the caliper mounting bolts. Perform the following procedure before installing the caliper guide pin bolts (15 Series only).

   a. Remove all traces of the original adhesive patch.

   b. Clean the threads of the bolt with brake parts cleaner or the equivalent and allow to dry.

   c. Apply Red Loctite® 272 to the threads of the bolt.

10. Install the caliper mounting bolts (25 series). Tighten the caliper guide pin bolts to 42 Nm (31 ft. lbs.) on the 15 series; 108 Nm (80 ft. lbs.) on the 25 series.

11. Connect the brake hose at the caliper by installing the inlet fitting bolt. Tighten the inlet fitting bolt to 45 Nm (33 ft. lbs.).

12. Bleed the brakes.

13. Install the tire and wheel assembly.

14. Refill the brake master cylinder to the proper level with fresh brake fluid.

Chevrolet Venture
Oldsmobile Silhouette
Pontiac TransSport

1. Remove ⅔ of the brake fluid from the master cylinder reservoir.

2. Raise and support the vehicle safely. Remove the tire and wheel assembly.

3. Retract caliper piston into bore.

4. Disconnect and plug the caliper fluid line. Remove the bolts retaining the caliper to the rotor. Remove the caliper from the rotor.

5. Remove the disc brake pads from the caliper. Remove the disc brake pad retaining clips from inside the caliper.

To install:

6. Clean and lubricate the sleeves and bushings with silicon grease. Install the pads in the caliper.

7. Install the caliper in position over the rotor and install the mounting bolts. Torque to 63 ft. lbs. (54 Nm).

8. If disconnected, connect the fluid lines to the caliper and torque to 33 ft. lbs. (45 Nm).

9. Install the wheel and tire assembly.

10. Lower the vehicle and refill the master cylinder to the correct level. Bleed the brake system if the fluid lines were disconnected from the caliper.

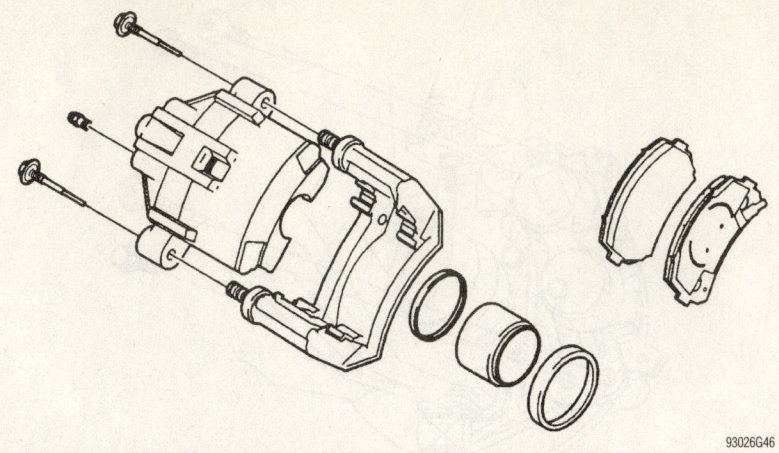

Exploded view of a caliper assembly—Venture, Silhouette and TransSport

93026G46

Disc Brake Pads

REMOVAL & INSTALLATION

Astro, Blazer, Bravada, Envoy, Jimmy, Safari, S-series Pick-Up and Sonoma

FRONT

1. Remove ⅔ of the brake fluid from the master cylinder.

2. Raise and safely support the vehicle.

3. Place a C-clamp around the outer pad and caliper; tighten the C-clamp until the piston is fully compressed in the caliper. Remove the brake caliper pads.

4. Remove the inboard pad and retaining spring from the caliper.

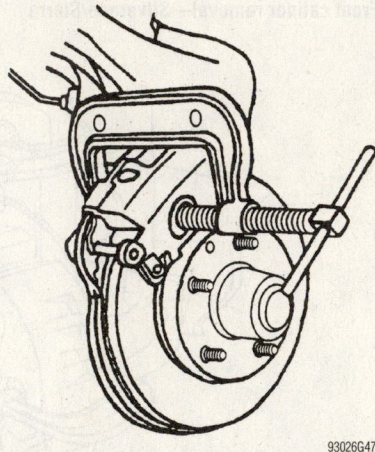

Compressing the caliper piston with a C-clamp—Astro, Blazer, Bravada, Envoy, Jimmy, Safari, S10/S15 Pick-Up, Sonoma

93026G47

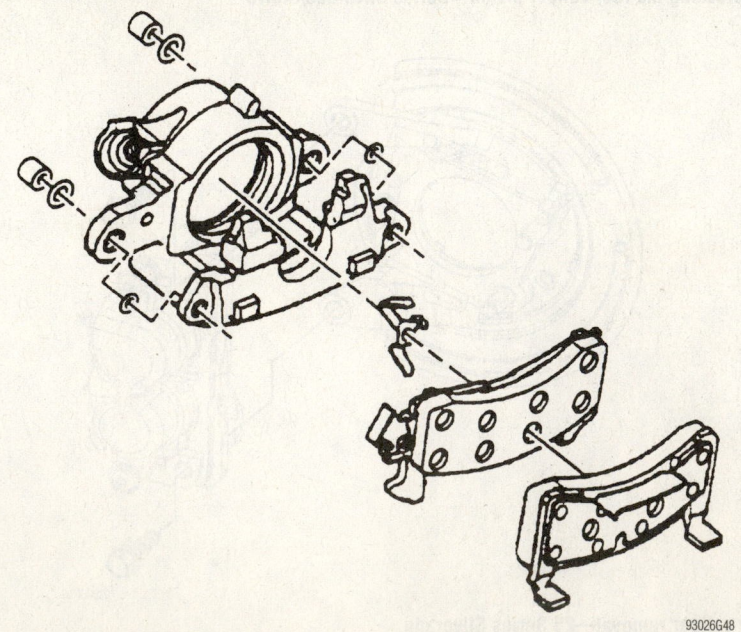

93026G48

Exploded view of the disc brake assembly—Astro, Blazer, Bravada, Envoy, Jimmy, Safari, S10/S15 Pick-Up and Sonoma

5. Remove the outboard pad from the caliper.

6. Remove the sleeves and bushings.

To install:

7. Clean and lubricate the sleeves and bushing with silicone lubricant and install them in the caliper.

8. Clip the retaining spring onto the inboard pad and install the pad in the caliper.

9. Install the outboard pad into the caliper.

10. Install the caliper in position over the rotor and install the mounting bolts. Bend the tabs, on the outboard brake pad, over the caliper.

11. Install the wheel and tire assemblies.

12. Lower the vehicle, refill the master cylinder and pump pedal to attain full brake pedal before Road-testing the vehicle.

REAR

1. Remove ⅔ of the brake fluid from the master cylinder.

2. Raise and safely support the vehicle.

3. Remove wheels

4. Place a C-clamp around the outer pad and caliper; tighten the C-clamp until the piston is fully compressed in the caliper. Remove top caliper retainer, and rotate caliper away from rotor.

5. Remove the inboard pad and retaining spring from the caliper.

6. Remove the outboard pad from the caliper.

To install:

7. Clean and lubricate the sleeves and bushing with silicone lubricant and install them in the caliper.

8. Clip the retaining spring onto the inboard pad and install the pad in the caliper.

9. Install the outboard pad into the caliper.

10. Install the caliper in position over the rotor and install the mounting bolts.

11. Install the wheel and tire assemblies.

12. Lower the vehicle, refill the master cylinder and pump pedal to attain full brake pedal before Road-testing the vehicle.

C/K Pick-Up, Denali, Escalade, G-Series Van, Savana, Suburban, Tahoe and Yukon

DELCO TYPE

1. Remove the cover on the master cylinder and siphon out ⅔ of the fluid. This step prevents spilling fluid when the piston is pushed back into the caliper bore.

2. Raise and support the vehicle safely.

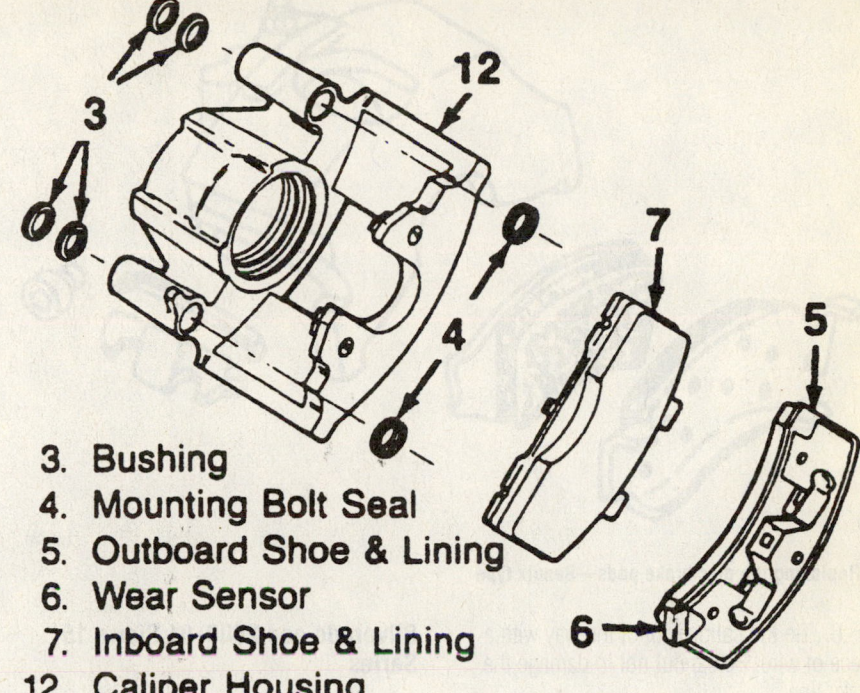

3. **Bushing**
4. **Mounting Bolt Seal**
5. **Outboard Shoe & Lining**
6. **Wear Sensor**
7. **Inboard Shoe & Lining**
12. **Caliper Housing**

93026G49

Replacing the disc brake pads—Delco type

3. Remove the wheels.

4. Compress the brake piston back into its bore using a C-clamp.

5. Remove the 2 bolts holding the caliper and then lift the caliper off the disc.

6. Remove the inboard and outboard shoe.

7. Remove the pad support spring from the piston, if equipped.

To install:

8. Thoroughly inspect, clean and lubricate all caliper slide points, bolts and hardware.

9. Position the retainer spring on the inner pad and insert the assembly into the center cavity of the piston.

10. Push down on the inner pad until it lays flat against the caliper. It is important to push the piston all the way into the caliper if new linings are installed or the caliper will not fit over the rotor.

11. Position the outboard pad with the ears of the pad over the caliper ears and the tab at the bottom engaged in the caliper cutout.

12. With the 2 pads in position, place the caliper over the brake disc and align the holes in the caliper with those of the mounting bracket.

13. Install the mounting bracket bolts through the sleeves in the inboard caliper ears and through the mounting bracket,

making sure the ends of the bolts pass under the retaining ears on the inboard pad.

14. Tighten the mounting bolts to 38 ft. lbs. (51 Nm). After both calipers are mounted pump the brake pedal to seat the pad against the rotor. Use a pair of channel lock pliers to bend over the upper ears of the outer pad so it isn't loose.

15. Install the wheels and lower the vehicle.

16. Add fluid to the master cylinder reservoirs so they are ¼ in. (6.35mm) from the top.

17. Test the brake pedal by pumping it to obtain a hard pedal. Check the fluid level again and add fluid as necessary. Do not move the vehicle until a pedal is obtained.

BENDIX TYPE

1. Remove approximately ⅓ of the brake fluid from the master cylinder. Discard the used brake fluid.

2. Raise and support the vehicle safely and remove the wheel.

3. Push the piston back into its bore. This can be done by using a C-clamp.

4. Remove the bolt at the caliper slider. Use a brass drift pin to remove the slider and spring.

5. Rotate the caliper up and forward from the bottom and lift it off the caliper support.

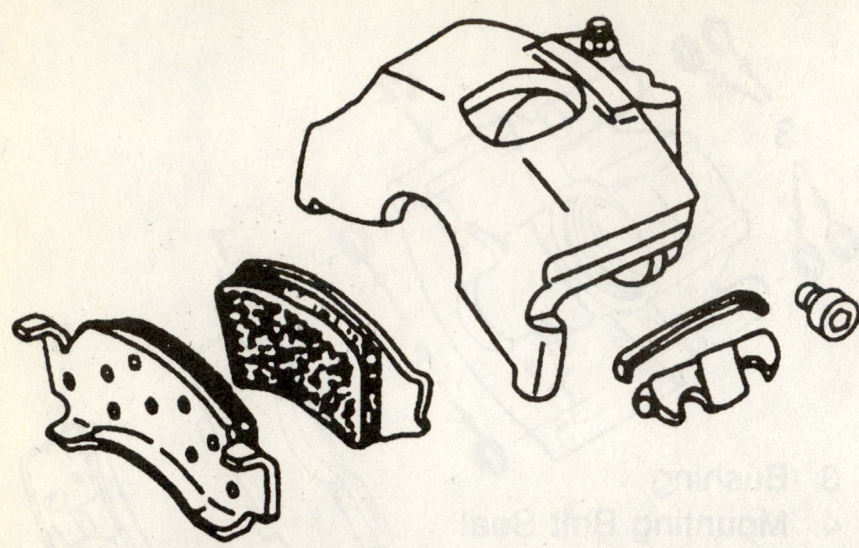

Replacing the disc brake pads—Bendix type

93026G50

6. Tie the caliper out of the way with a piece of wire. Be careful not to damage the brake line.

7. Remove the inner shoe from the caliper support. Discard the inner shoe clip.

8. Remove the outer shoe from the caliper.

To install:

9. Thoroughly clean, inspect and lubricate the caliper, slider and spring with silicone.

10. Install a new inboard shoe clip on the shoe.

11. Install the lower end of the inboard shoe into the groove provided in the support. Slide the upper end of the shoe into position. Be sure the clip remains in position.

12. Position the outboard shoe in the caliper, with the ears at the top of the shoe over the caliper ears and the tab at the bottom of the shoe engaged in the caliper cutout. If assembly is difficult, a C-clamp may be used. Be careful not to damage the lining.

13. Position the caliper over the brake disc, top edge first. Rotate the caliper downward onto the support.

14. Place the spring over the caliper support key, install the assembly between the support and lower caliper groove. Tap into place until the key retaining screw can be installed.

15. Install the screw and torque to 15 ft. lbs. (20 Nm). The boss must fit fully into the circular cutout in the key.

16. Install the wheel and add brake fluid as necessary.

Silverado and 2000–01 Sierra 15 Series

2WD FRONT

1. Remove ⅔ of the brake fluid from the master cylinder.

2. Raise and support the vehicle.

3. Remove the wheel.

4. Remove the caliper. Suspend caliper from the frame with mechanic's wire. Do not allow the caliper to hang from the brake hose.

5. Remove the caliper mounting bracket bolts.

6. Remove the caliper mounting bracket from the steering knuckle assembly.

7. Remove the brake pads from the caliper mounting bracket.

8. Remove the clips from the inside ends of the caliper mounting bracket and discard.

To install:

9. Install the clips to the inside ends of the caliper mounting bracket.

10. Install the brake pads to the caliper mounting bracket.

11. Install the inner pad (1 wear indicator).

12. Install the outer pad (2 wear indicators).

13. Install the caliper mounting bracket to the steering knuckle assembly. Perform the following procedure before installing the caliper mounting bracket bolts.

   a. Remove all traces of the original adhesive patch.

   b. Clean the threads of the bolt with brake parts cleaner or the equivalent and allow to dry.

   c. Apply red Loctite® 272 to the threads of the bolt.

➡Use the correct fastener in the correct location. Replacement fasteners must be the correct part number for that application. Fasteners requiring replacement or fasteners requiring the use of thread locking compound or sealant are identified in the service procedure. Do not use paints, lubricants, or corrosion inhibitors on fasteners or fastener joint surfaces unless specified. These coatings affect fastener torque and joint clamping force and may damage the fastener. Use the correct tightening sequence and specifications when installing fasteners in order to avoid damage to parts and systems.

14. Install the caliper mounting bracket bolts to the steering knuckle.

15. Tighten the brake caliper mounting bracket to 129 ft. lbs. (175 Nm) on the 15 series; 221 ft. lbs. (300 Nm) on the 25 series.

16. Install the caliper.

17. Install the tire and wheel assembly.

18. Remove the safety stands.

19. Lower the vehicle.

20. Refill the master cylinder to the proper level with fresh brake fluid. Pump the brake pedal slowly and firmly in order to seat the brake pads. Burnish the brakes as needed.

4WD FRONT

1. Remove ⅔ of the brake fluid from the master cylinder.

2. Remove the tire and wheel assembly.

3. Inspect the caliper operation.

4. Remove the caliper.

5. Suspend the caliper from the frame with mechanic's wire. Do not allow the caliper to hang from the brake hose.

6. Remove the caliper mounting bracket bolts.

7. Remove the caliper mounting bracket from the steering knuckle assembly.

8. Remove the brake pads from the caliper mounting bracket.

9. Remove the clips from the inside ends of the caliper mounting bracket and discard.

10. Inspect the caliper and mounting bracket.

To install:

11. Install the clips to the inside ends of the caliper mounting bracket.

12. Install the inner pad with 1 wear indicator.

13. Install the outer pad with 2 wear indicators.

14. Install the caliper mounting bracket to the steering knuckle assembly.

15. Perform the following procedure before installing the caliper mounting bracket bolts:

  a. Remove all traces of the original adhesive patch.

  b. Clean the threads of the bolt with brake parts cleaner or the equivalent and allow to dry.

  c. Apply Red LOCTITE® 272 to the threads of the bolt.

16. Install the caliper mounting bracket bolts to the steering knuckle. Tighten the brake caliper mounting bracket to 175 Nm (129 ft. lbs.) on the 15 series, or, 300 Nm (221 ft. lbs.) on the 25 series.

17. Install the caliper.

18. Install the tire and wheel assembly.

19. Refill the master cylinder to the proper level with fresh brake fluid. Pump the brake pedal slowly and firmly in order to seat the brake pads. Burnish the brakes as needed.

2WD REAR

1. Remove ⅔ of the brake fluid from the master cylinder.

2. Raise and support the vehicle.

3. Remove the tire and wheel assembly.

4. Remove the caliper. Suspend the caliper from the frame with mechanic's wire. Do not allow the caliper to hang from the brake hose.

5. Remove the caliper mounting bracket bolts from the backing plate (15 series).

6. Remove the caliper mounting bracket bolts from the backing plate (25 series).

7. Remove the brake pads from the caliper mounting bracket (15 series). Remove the clips from the inside ends of the caliper mounting bracket and discard.

8. Remove the brake pads from the caliper mounting bracket (25 series). Remove the clips from the inside ends of the caliper mounting bracket and discard.

To install:

9. Install the clips to the inside ends of the caliper mounting bracket.

10. Install the brake pads to the caliper mounting bracket (15 series).

11. Install the inner pad (1 wear indicator).

12. Install the outer pad (2 wear indicators).

13. Install the clips to the inside ends of the caliper mounting bracket.

14. Install the brake pads to the caliper mounting bracket (25 series).

15. Install the inner pad (1 wear indicator).

16. Install the outer pad (2 wear indicators).

17. Install the caliper mounting bracket to the backing plate assembly (15 series).

18. Install the caliper mounting bracket to the backing plate assembly (25 series). Perform the following procedure before installing the caliper mounting bracket bolts.

  a. Remove all traces of the original adhesive patch.

  b. Clean the threads of the bolt with brake parts cleaner or the equivalent and allow to dry.

  c. Apply red Loctite® 272 to the threads of the bolt.

➠Use the correct fastener in the correct location. Replacement fasteners must be the correct part number for that application. Fasteners requiring replacement or fasteners requiring the use of thread locking compound or sealant are identified in the service procedure. Do not use paints, lubricants, or corrosion inhibitors on fasteners or fastener joint surfaces unless specified. These coatings affect fastener torque and joint clamping force and may damage the fastener. Use the correct tightening sequence and specifications when installing fasteners in order to avoid damage to parts and systems.

19. Install the caliper mounting bracket bolts to the steering knuckle.

20. Tighten the brake caliper mounting bracket to 148 ft. lbs. (200 Nm) on the 15 series; 122 ft. lbs. (165 Nm on the 25 series.

21. Install the caliper.

22. Install the tire and wheel assembly.

23. Lower the vehicle.

24. Refill the master cylinder to the proper level with fresh brake fluid. Pump the brake pedal slowly and firmly in order to seat the brake pads. Burnish the brakes as needed.

4WD REAR

1. Remove ⅔ of the brake fluid from the master cylinder.

2. Remove the tire and wheel assembly.

3. Inspect the caliper operation.

4. Remove the caliper.

5. Suspend the caliper from the frame with mechanic's wire. Do not allow the caliper to hang from the brake hose.

6. Remove the caliper mounting bracket bolts from the backing plate (15 series).

7. Remove the caliper mounting bracket bolts from the backing plate (25 series).

8. Remove the brake pads from the caliper mounting bracket.

9. Remove the clips from the inside ends of the caliper mounting bracket and discard.

10. Inspect the caliper and mounting bracket.

To install:

11. Install the clips to the inside ends of the caliper mounting bracket. Install the brake pads to the caliper mounting bracket (15 series). The inner pad has 1 wear indicator; the outer pad has 2 wear indicators.

12. Install the caliper mounting bracket to the backing plate assembly.

13. Install the caliper mounting bracket to the backing plate assembly. Perform the following procedure before installing the caliper mounting bracket bolts.

  a. Remove all traces of the original adhesive patch.

  b. Clean the threads of the bolt with brake parts cleaner or the equivalent and allow to dry.

  c. Apply Red Loctite® 272 to the threads of the bolt.

14. Install the caliper mounting bracket bolts to the steering knuckle. Tighten the brake caliper mounting bracket to 200 Nm (148 ft. lbs.) on the 15 series, or, 165 Nm (122 ft. lbs.) on the 25 series.

15. Install the caliper.

16. Install the tire and wheel assembly.

17. Refill the master cylinder to the proper level with fresh brake fluid. Pump the brake pedal slowly and firmly in order to seat the brake pads. Burnish the brakes as needed.

**Chevrolet Venture
Oldsmobile Silhouette
Pontiac TransSport**

1. Remove ⅔ of the brake fluid from the master cylinder.
2. Raise and safely support the vehicle.
3. Place a C-clamp around the outer pad and caliper; tighten the C-clamp until the piston is fully compressed in the caliper. If needed, completely remove the caliper from the spindle or, on some models, remove the lower bolt and swing the caliper up.
4. Remove the inboard pad and retaining spring from the caliper.
5. Remove the outboard pad from the caliper.
6. Remove the sleeves and bushings.

To install:

7. Clean and lubricate the sleeves and bushing with silicon lubricant and install them in the caliper.
8. Clip the retaining spring onto the inboard pad and install the pad in the caliper.
9. Install the outboard pad into the caliper.
10. If completely removed, install the caliper in position over the rotor and install the mounting bolts. Bend the tabs, on the outboard brake pad, over the caliper.
11. Install the wheel and tire assemblies.
12. Lower the vehicle, refill the master cylinder and pump pedal to attain full brake pedal before Road-testing the vehicle.

Brake Drums

REMOVAL & INSTALLATION

Astro, Blazer, Bravada, Envoy, Jimmy, Safari, S-series Pick-Up and Sonoma

1. Raise and safely support the vehicle.
2. Remove the wheel and tire assembly.
3. Remove the brake drum. If the drum will not pull of the axle, use a rubber mallet and tap it around the edge.

To install:

4. Install the drum on the axle and install the wheel and tire assembly.
5. Lower the vehicle.
6. Refill the master cylinder and pump pedal to attain full brake pedal before road-testing the vehicle.

C/K Pick-Up, Denali, Escalade, G-Series Van, Savana, Suburban, Tahoe and Yukon

W/SEMI-FLOATING AXLES

1. Raise and support the vehicle safely.
2. Mark the relationship of the wheel to the hub and remove the wheel.
3. Mark the relationship of the drum to the hub and pull the drum from the brake assembly. If the brake drums have been scored from worn linings, the brake adjuster must be backed off so the brake shoes will retract from the drum. The adjuster can be backed off by inserting a brake adjusting tool through the access hole provided. In some cases the access hole is provided in the brake drum. A metal cover plate is over the hole. This may be removed by using a hammer and chisel.

To install:

4. Align the mark on the drum to mark on hub and install drum
5. Align the mark on the wheel to mark on drum and install wheel
6. Adjust brake lining as needed. Pump brakes

W/FULL FLOATING AXLES

To remove the drums from full floating rear axles, the axle shaft will have to be removed. Full-floating rear axles can be identified by a bearing housing that protrudes through the center of the wheel.

1. Raise and support the vehicle safely.
2. Remove the wheel.
3. Remove the axle shaft.
4. Remove the retaining ring, key and adjusting nut.
5. Remove the hub and drum.

To install:

6. Install the hub and drum to the tube.
7. Install the adjusting nut and torque to specification.
8. Install the key and retaining ring.
9. Install the axle shaft and wheel.

**Chevrolet Venture
Oldsmobile Silhouette
Pontiac TransSport**

1. Raise and safely support the vehicle.
2. Remove the wheel and tire assembly.
3. Remove the brake drum. If drum is hard to remove back off the brake adjustment screw. Penetrating may be used around the drum pilot hole.

To install:

4. Install brake drum

5. Install the tire and wheel assembly and adjust brake lining.
6. Lower the vehicle.

Brake Shoes

REMOVAL & INSTALLATION

Astro, Blazer, Bravada, Envoy, Jimmy, Safari, S-series Pick-Up and Sonoma

1. Raise and safely support the vehicle.
2. Remove the wheel and tire assembly.
3. Remove the brake drum.
4. Remove the return springs from the brake shoes. Remove the shoe guide.
5. Remove the hold-down springs and pins. Remove the actuator lever and pivot.
6. Remove the lever return spring. Remove the actuator link.
7. Remove the parking brake strut and spring. Remove the parking brake lever.
8. Remove the brake shoes and the adjuster assembly.

To install:

9. Lubricate the contact points on the backing plate and the adjuster with lithium grease.
10. Install the parking brake lever, adjusting screw and spring assembly.
11. Install the shoe assembly onto the backing plate.
12. Install the parking brake lever, strut and strut spring.
13. Install the actuator lever and lever pivot. Install the actuator link.
14. Install the lever spring, the hold-down pins and springs.
15. Install the shoe guide. Install the return springs and install the brake drum in position.
16. Adjust the brakes as follows:
   a. Remove the knockout area in the backing plate, behind the adjuster assembly.
   b. Ensure the parking brake system is adjusted properly with no tension on the cables or parking brake lever. The tops of the shoes should be firmly seated against the upper spring retaining anchor, if not as specified, loosen the parking brake cables.
   c. Install the drum and turn the brake adjuster until the wheels can just be turned by hand.
   d. Then, back the adjuster off 24 notches. No brake drag should be felt after 12 notches.
   e. Install an adjusting hole plug in the

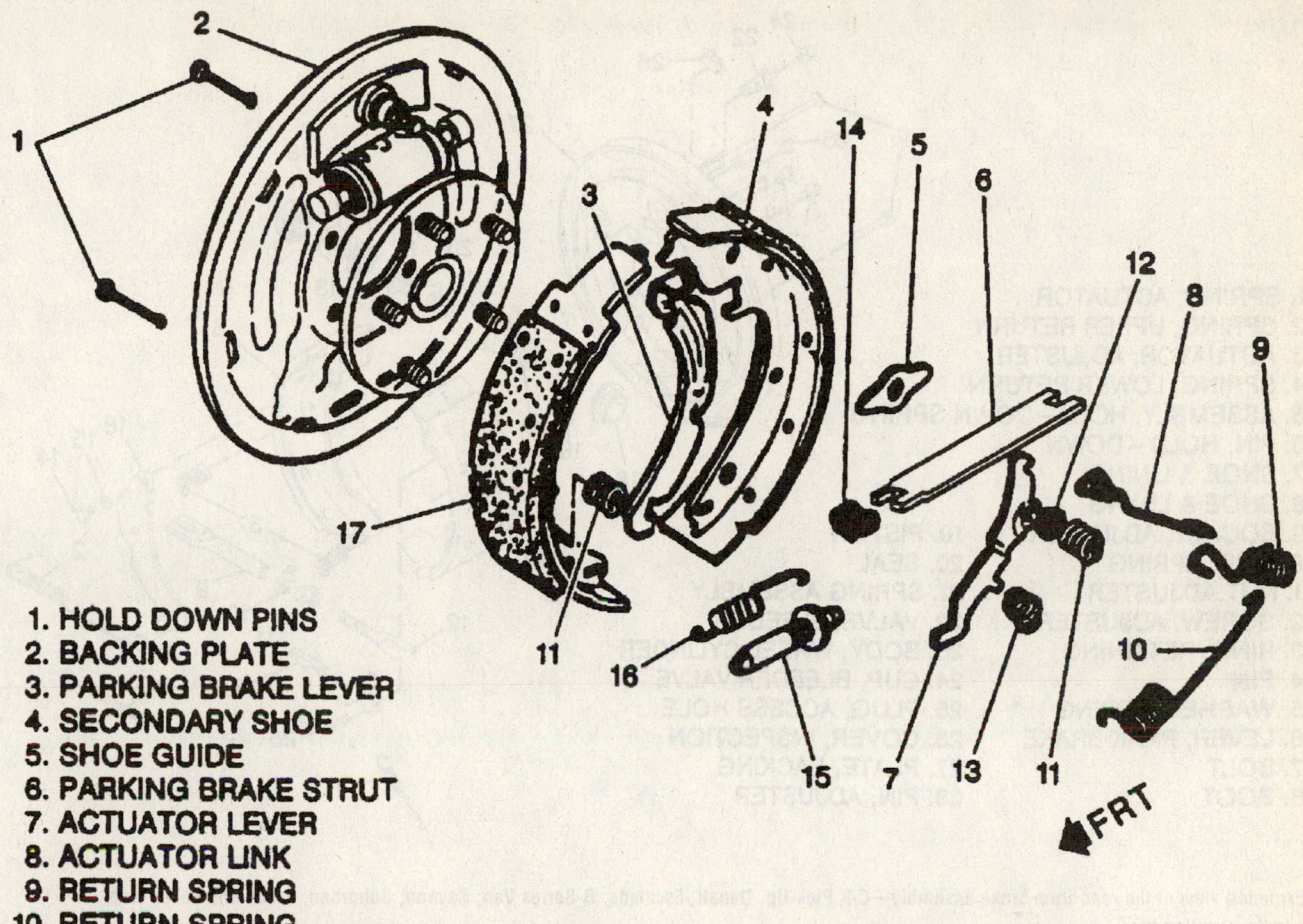

1. **HOLD DOWN PINS**
2. **BACKING PLATE**
3. **PARKING BRAKE LEVER**
4. **SECONDARY SHOE**
5. **SHOE GUIDE**
6. **PARKING BRAKE STRUT**
7. **ACTUATOR LEVER**
8. **ACTUATOR LINK**
9. **RETURN SPRING**
10. **RETURN SPRING**
11. **HOLD DOWN SPRING**
12. **LEVER PIVOT**
13. **LEVER RETURN SPRING**
14. **STRUT SPRING**
15. **ADJUSTING SCREW ASSEMBLY**
16. **ADJUSTING SCREW SPRING**
17. **PRIMARY SHOE**

93026G51

Exploded view of the drum brake components—Astro, Blazer, Bravada, Envoy, Jimmy, Safari, S10/S15 Pick-Up, Sonoma

backing plate to prevent dirt and moisture from entering.

f. Readjust the parking brake cable as necessary.

17. Install the wheel and tire assemblies.

18. Lower the vehicle, refill the master cylinder and pump pedal to attain full brake pedal before Road-testing the vehicle.

C/K Pick-Up, Denali, Escalade, G-Series Van, Savana, Suburban, Tahoe and Yukon

LEADING/TRAILING BRAKES

1. Raise the vehicle and support it safely.
2. Remove the tire and wheel assembly.

3. Remove the brake drums.

4. Raise the lever arm of the actuator until the upper end is clear of the slot in the adjuster screw.

5. Slide the actuator off the adjuster pin. Disconnect the actuator spring from the shoe.

6. Remove the hold-down spring assemblies and pins.

7. Pull the bottom ends of the shoes apart and lift the lower return spring over the anchor plate. Allow the shoe ends to come together and remove the spring.

8. Remove the shoe assembly, along with the upper return spring and the adjusting screw assembly.

9. Remove the upper return spring and the adjusting screw assembly from the shoes.

10. Remove the retaining ring, pin, spring washer, and parking brake lever.

To install:

11. Clean adjuster wheel and the backing plates with a suitable cleaner. Lubricate the backing plate contact points, levers and adjuster with a suitable lubricant.

12. Assemble the parking lever, spring washer (concave side facing the brake lever), pin, and retaining ring onto the rearward shoe.

13. Install the adjuster pin in the forward shoe with the pin projecting 0.276 in.

For brake related suspension and axle service, refer to the model specific sections of this manual

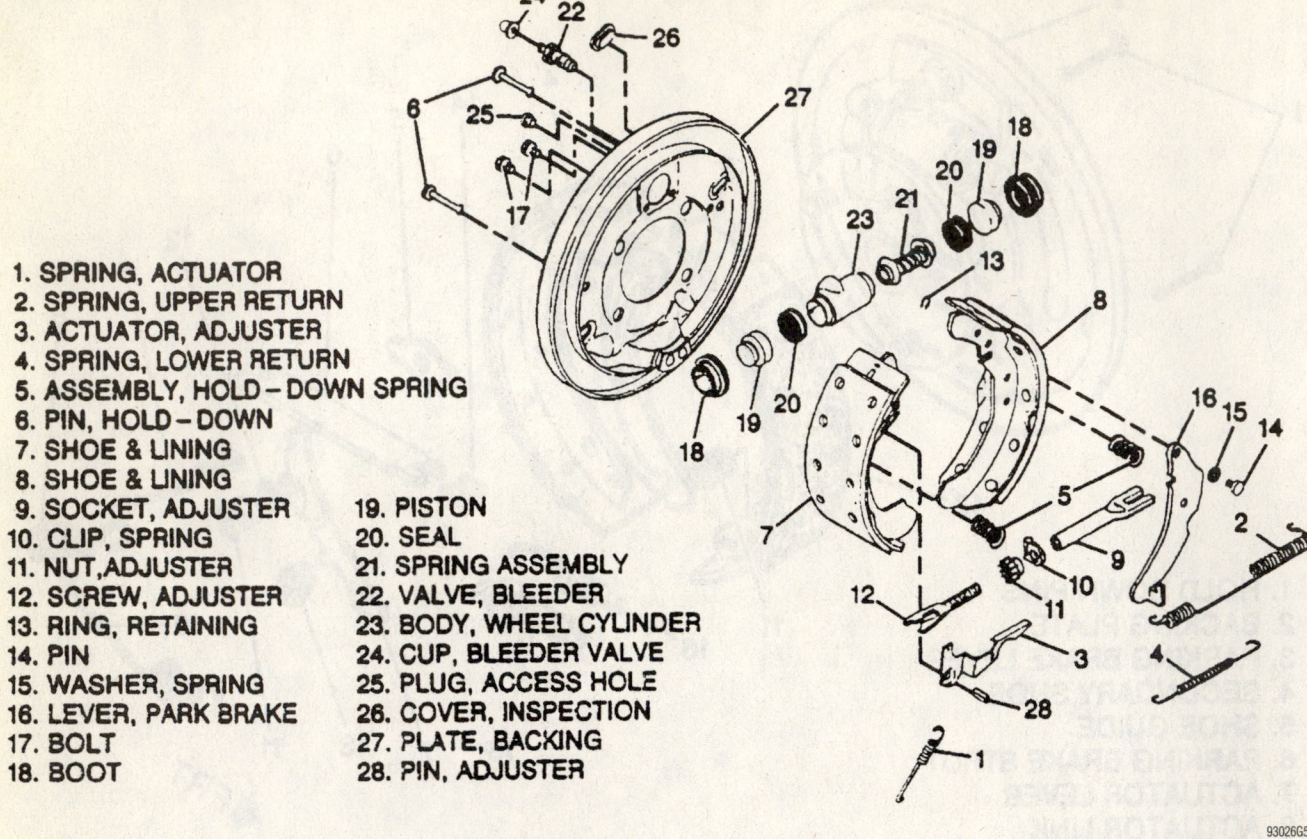

1. SPRING, ACTUATOR
2. SPRING, UPPER RETURN
3. ACTUATOR, ADJUSTER
4. SPRING, LOWER RETURN
5. ASSEMBLY, HOLD—DOWN SPRING
6. PIN, HOLD—DOWN
7. SHOE & LINING
8. SHOE & LINING
9. SOCKET, ADJUSTER
10. CLIP, SPRING
11. NUT, ADJUSTER
12. SCREW, ADJUSTER
13. RING, RETAINING
14. PIN
15. WASHER, SPRING
16. LEVER, PARK BRAKE
17. BOLT
18. BOOT
19. PISTON
20. SEAL
21. SPRING ASSEMBLY
22. VALVE, BLEEDER
23. BODY, WHEEL CYLINDER
24. CUP, BLEEDER VALVE
25. PLUG, ACCESS HOLE
26. COVER, INSPECTION
27. PLATE, BACKING
28. PIN, ADJUSTER

Exploded view of the rear drum brake assembly—C/K Pick-Up, Denali, Escalade, G-Series Van, Savana, Suburban, Tahoe and Yukon with Leading/Trailing type

(7mm) from the side of the shoe web where the adjuster actuator is installed.

14. With the brake shoes resting on a flat surface (the shoe with the parking lever to the rear of the vehicle), install the upper return spring.

15. Install the adjuster screw assembly with the spring clip facing the backing plate.

16. Place the shoes in position on the backing plate. Do not place the lower shoe webs under the anchor plate.

17. Install the lower return spring, spread the bottom of the shoes and position the shoe against the backing plate.

18. Install the hold-down pins and spring assemblies.

19. Install the adjuster actuator over the end of the adjuster pin so the top leg engages the notch in the adjuster screw.

20. Install the actuator spring, being careful not to over-stretch it more than 3.27 in. (83mm).

21. Install the parking brake cable to the lever.

22. Adjust the parking brake if the shoes will not totally retract.

23. Install the drum, tire and wheel assembly. Adjust the rear brakes and lower the vehicle.

DUO-SERVO BRAKES

1. Raise the vehicle and support it safely.
2. Remove the tire and wheel assembly.
3. Remove the brake drums.
4. Using a brake tool, remove the shoe return springs.
5. Remove the shoe guide.
6. Remove the hold-down springs and pins.
7. Remove the actuator lever and pivot.
8. Remove the lever return spring.
9. Remove the actuator link, parking brake strut, spring retaining ring.
10. Remove the parking brake lever and washer.
11. Remove the shoe assemblies.
12. Remove the adjuster screw and spring from the shoe assembly.

To install:

13. Use a brake cleaning fluid to remove dirt from the brake drum. Check the drums

for scoring, cracks and for out-of-round; service the drums as necessary.

14. Check the wheel cylinders by carefully pulling the lower edges of the wheel cylinder boots away from the cylinders. If there is excessive leakage, the inside of the cylinder will drip fluid; repair or replace as necessary.

15. Check the flange plate, which is located around the axle, for leakage of differential lubricant.

16. Lightly lubricate the parking brake cable, parking brake lever where it enters the shoe and the backing plate-to-shoe contact points. Use high temperature, waterproof, grease or special brake lube.

17. Install the parking brake lever into the secondary shoe with the attaching bolt, spring washer, lockwasher, and nut. It is important that the lever move freely before the shoe is attached. Move the assembly and check for proper action.

18. Lubricate the adjusting screw and make sure it works freely.

19. Connect the adjuster screw and

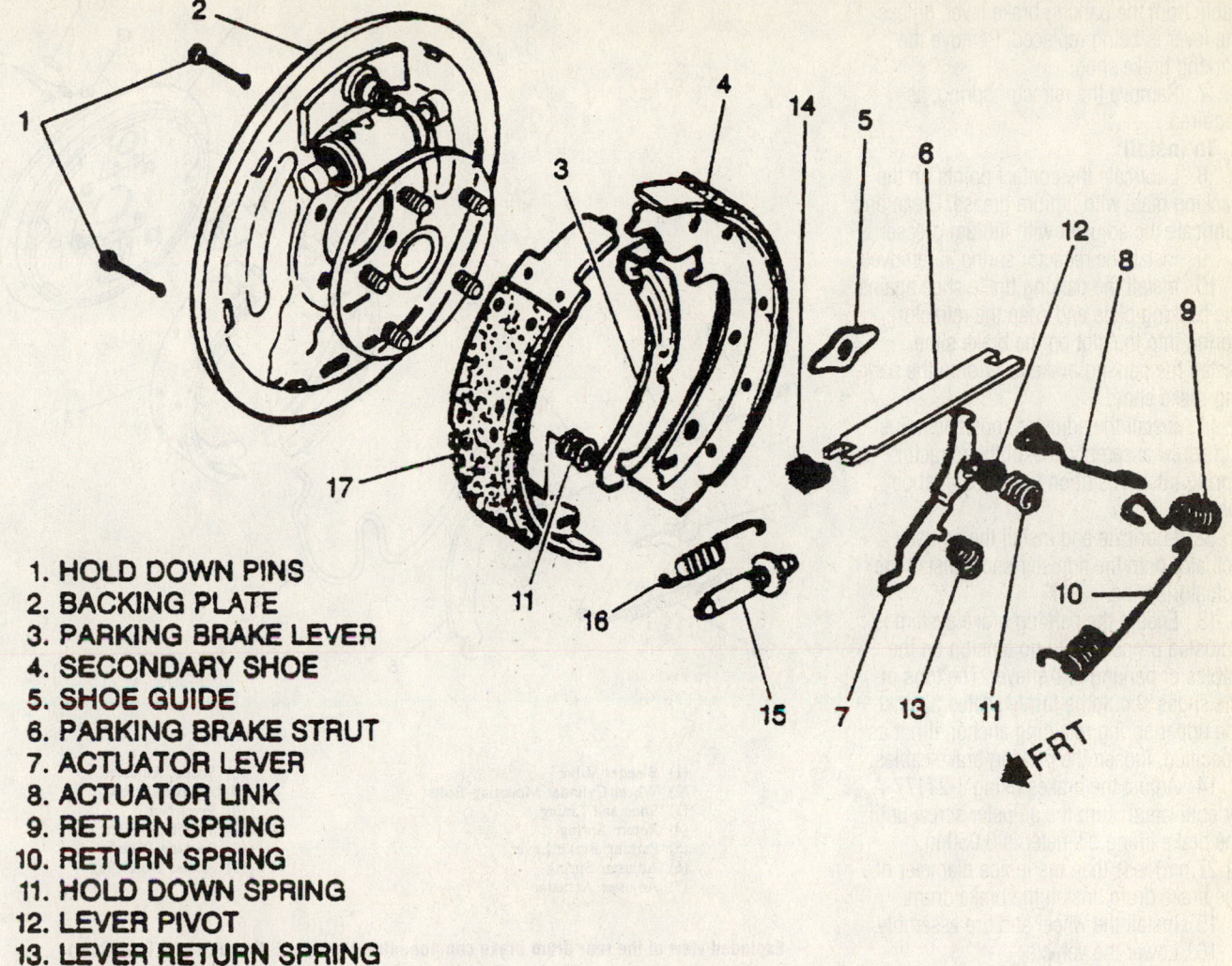

1. HOLD DOWN PINS
2. BACKING PLATE
3. PARKING BRAKE LEVER
4. SECONDARY SHOE
5. SHOE GUIDE
6. PARKING BRAKE STRUT
7. ACTUATOR LEVER
8. ACTUATOR LINK
9. RETURN SPRING
10. RETURN SPRING
11. HOLD DOWN SPRING
12. LEVER PIVOT
13. LEVER RETURN SPRING
14. STRUT SPRING
15. ADJUSTING SCREW ASSEMBLY
16. ADJUSTING SCREW SPRING
17. PRIMARY SHOE

93026G53

Exploded view of the rear drum brake assembly—C/K Pick-Up, Denali, Escalade, G-Series Van, Savana, Suburban, Tahoe and Yukon with Duo-Servo type

spring to the bottom portion of both shoes. Ensure the spring does not interfere with the adjuster rotation when installed. The primary (smaller shoe pad area) to the front and secondary shoe (larger shoe pad area) to the rear of the vehicle.

20. Install the shoe assembly. Ensuring the shoe webs are positioned correctly against the wheel cylinder.

21. Install the parking brake cable.

22. Secure the primary shoes with the hold-down pin and spring.

23. Install the parking brake strut and the strut spring.

24. Install the actuator lever and pivot, securing the assembly with the hold-down pin and spring. Install the actuator link and spring.

25. Install the return springs.

26. Check the operation of the self-adjusting mechanism by moving the actuating lever by hand.

27. Adjust the brakes and install the drum.

28. Adjust the parking brake.

29. Install the tire and wheel assembly.

30. Lower the vehicle.

Chevrolet Venture
Oldsmobile Silhouette
Pontiac TransSport

1. Raise and safely support the vehicle.

2. Remove the wheel and tire assembly.

3. Remove the brake drum.

4. Remove the actuator spring from the brake shoes. Remove the retractor spring from the shoe web, being careful not to over stretch the spring.

5. Remove the adjuster shoe, adjuster actuator and adjusting screw assembly.

6. Do not remove the parking brake cable from the parking brake lever, unless the lever is being replaced. Remove the parking brake shoe.

7. Remove the retractor spring, as required.

To install:

8. Lubricate the contact points on the backing plate with lithium grease. Clean and lubricate the adjuster with lithium grease.

9. Install the retractor spring, if removed.

10. Install the parking brake shoe against the backing plate and snap the retractor spring into the slot on the brake shoe. Install the parking brake lever onto the parking brake shoe.

11. Install the adjuster shoe and adjusting screw assembly. Install the retractor spring into the slot on the adjuster shoe web.

12. Lubricate and install the adjuster actuator onto the adjuster shoe. Install the actuator spring.

13. Ensure the parking brake system is adjusted properly with no tension on the cables or parking brake lever. The tops of the shoes should be firmly seated against the upper spring retaining anchor, if not as specified, loosen the parking brake cables.

14. Adjust the brakes using J-21177-A or equivalent. Turn the adjuster screw until the brake lining diameter is 0.050 in. (1.27mm) less than the inside diameter of the brake drum. Install the brake drum.

15. Install the wheel and tire assembly.

16. Lower the vehicle.

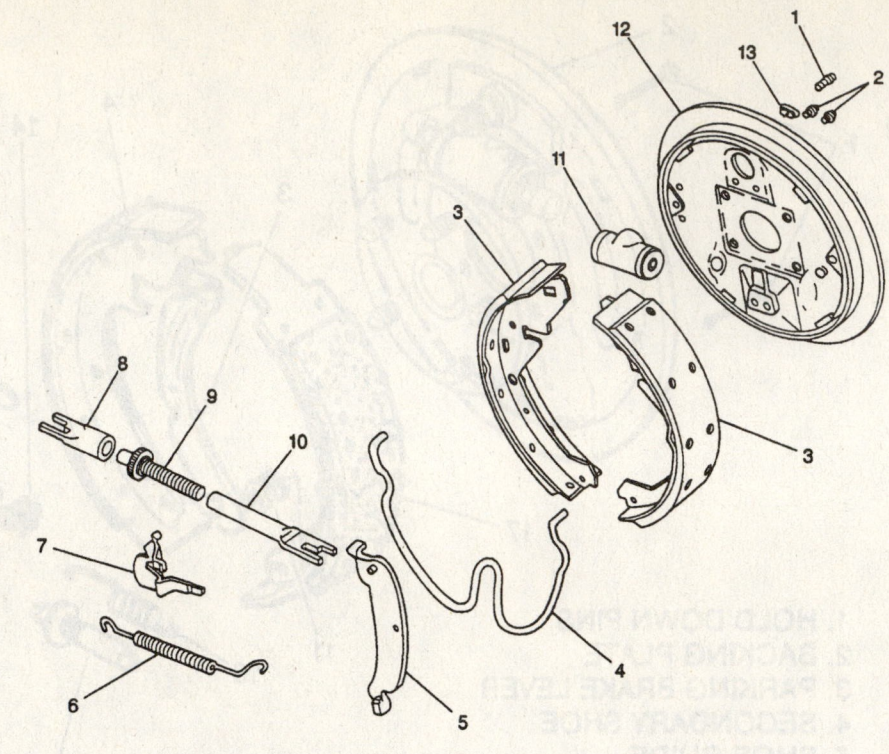

(1) Bleeder Valve
(2) Wheel Cylinder Mounting Bolts
(3) Shoe and Lining
(4) Return Spring
(5) Parking Brake Lever
(6) Adjuster Spring
(7) Adjuster Actuator

(8) Socket Adjuster
(9) Adjuster Screw
(10) Pivot Nut
(11) Wheel Cylinder
(12) Backing Plate
(13) Access Hole Plug

93026G96

Exploded view of the rear drum brake components—Venture, Silhouette and TransSport

GEO/CHEVY TRACKER

Brake Caliper

REMOVAL & INSTALLATION

1. Raise and safely support the vehicle.
2. Remove the wheels.
3. Disconnect and plug the brake line.
4. Remove the caliper mounting bolts (guide pins) and remove the caliper from the vehicle.

To install:

5. Install the caliper on the vehicle. Tighten the mounting bolts to 20 ft. lbs. (27 Nm).

6. Connect the hydraulic brake line, using 2 new washers. Torque the union bolt to 17 ft. lbs. (23 Nm).

7. Replace the front wheels.

8. Lower the vehicle.
9. Fill the brake reservoir and bleed the hydraulic brake system.

Disc Brake Pads

REMOVAL & INSTALLATION

1. Siphon about ⅔ of the fluid out of the master cylinder.
2. Raise and safely support the vehicle.
3. Remove the wheels.
4. Remove the brake caliper mounting bolts and remove the caliper from the mounting bracket.
5. Support the caliper with a wire.
6. Using a large pair of plies or a C-clamp compress the caliper piston back into the bore.

7. Remove the disc brake pads and any shims from the caliper mounting bracket.

To install:

8. Install the brake pads and any shims removed from the caliper mounting bracket.

9. Install the caliper on the mounting bracket and install the mounting bolts. Tighten the mounting bolts to 20 ft. lbs. (27 Nm).

10. Install the front wheels and lower the vehicle.

❋❋ CAUTION

Do not attempt to drive the vehicle until after the following step is performed.

11. Depress the brake pedal repeatedly until a firm pedal is obtained. Do not

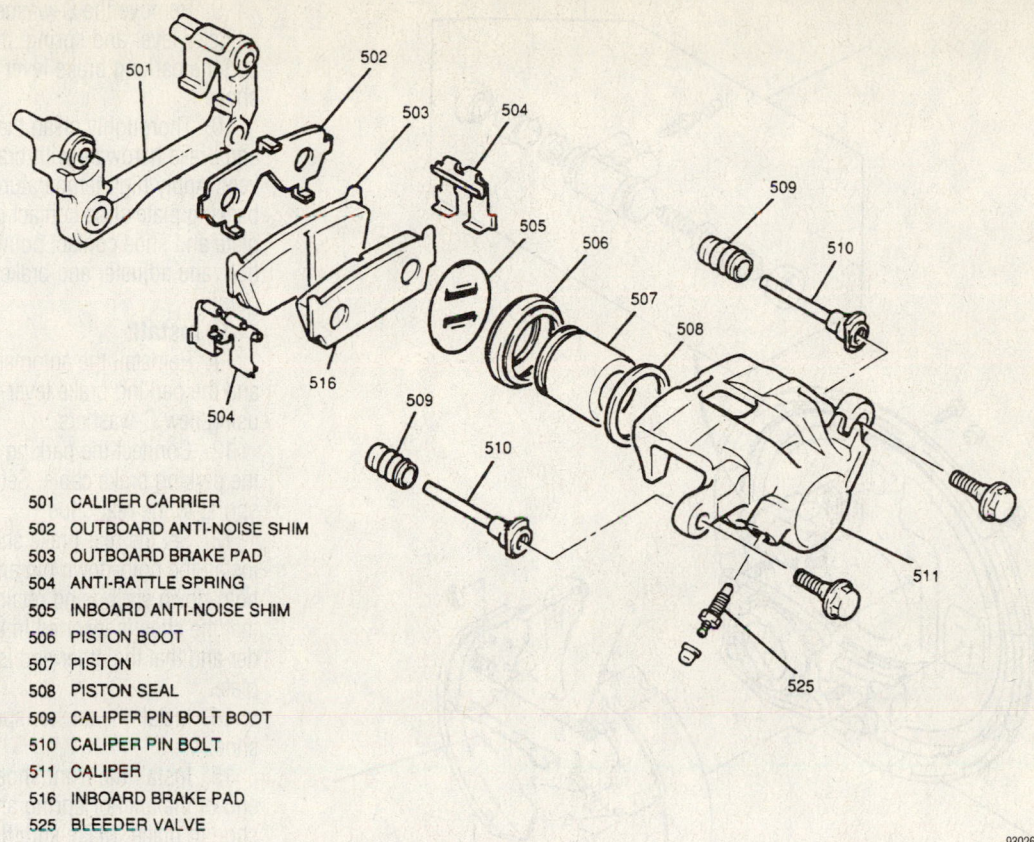

501	CALIPER CARRIER
502	OUTBOARD ANTI-NOISE SHIM
503	OUTBOARD BRAKE PAD
504	ANTI-RATTLE SPRING
505	INBOARD ANTI-NOISE SHIM
506	PISTON BOOT
507	PISTON
508	PISTON SEAL
509	CALIPER PIN BOLT BOOT
510	CALIPER PIN BOLT
511	CALIPER
516	INBOARD BRAKE PAD
525	BLEEDER VALVE

93026G37

Front disc brake components—Tracker

attempt to drive the vehicle unless a firm pedal is obtained.

12. Check the fluid level in the master cylinder. Add fresh brake fluid, as necessary.

13. Road-test the vehicle.

Brake Drums

REMOVAL & INSTALLATION

1. Raise and safely support the vehicle.

2. Remove the rear wheel(s).

3. Release the parking brake.

4. Remove the parking brake lever cover screws and loosen the brake cable locking nut.

5. Install 2, 8mm bolts into the brake drum holes and uniformly tighten each bolt. Tighten each bolt until the brake drum is removed from the vehicle. If there is difficulty in removing the drum, insert a small tool through the hole in the rear of the backing plate, and hold the automatic adjusting lever away from the adjuster. Using another narrow, flat tool at the same time, reduce the brake shoe adjuster by turning the adjusting wheel.

To install:

6. Install the brake drum and pull the parking brake lever all the way up until a clicking sound can no longer be heard.

7. Verify that the rear wheels will not turn. If the rear wheels turn, adjust the parking brake cable as necessary.

8. Release the parking brake and remove the brake drum. Measure the diameter of the brake shoes. Outer diameter should be as follows:

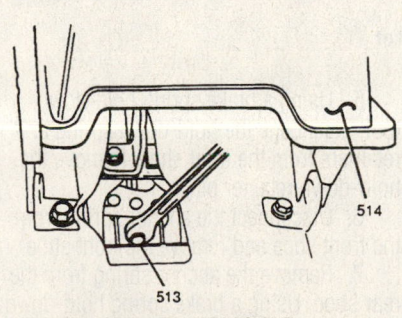

513	PARKING BRAKE CABLE LOCKNUT
514	PARKING BRAKE LEVER COVER

93026G38

Reducing the adjuster to remove the brake drum—Tracker

- 2 door models: 8.638 (0.0012 inches (219 (0.3mm)
- 4 door models: 9.980 (0.0079 inches (253.5 (0.2mm)

9. If the brake shoe clearance is not correct, adjust the brake shoes until the clearance is correct.

10. Reinstall the brake drum, replace the wheel(s), and safely lower the vehicle.

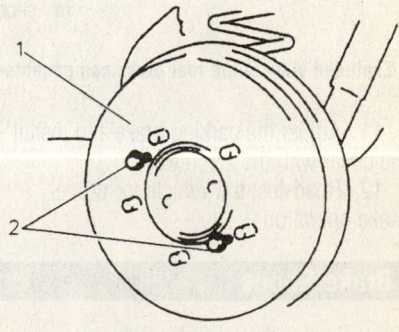

1	DRUM
2	TWO 8mm BOLTS

93026G39

Removing the brake drum with the 2, 8mm bolts—Tracker

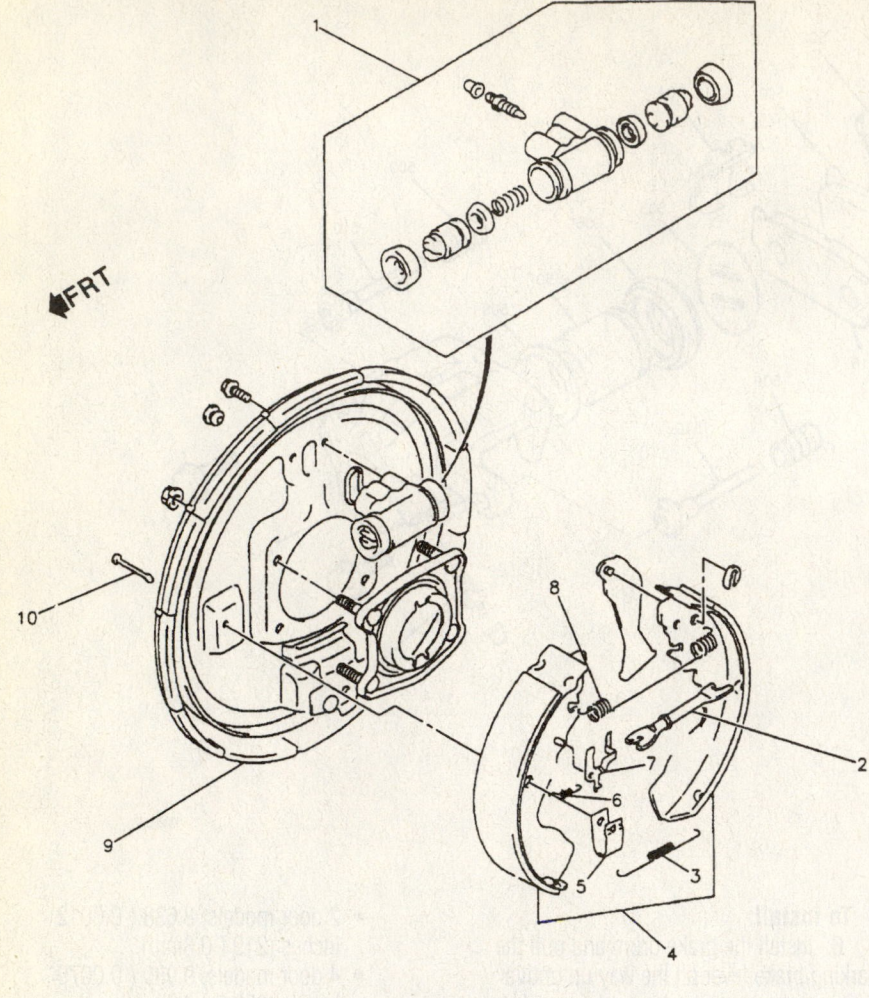

1 WHEEL CYLINDER
2 ADJUSTER
3 SHOE RETURN LOWER SPRING
4 BRAKE SHOES
5 SHOE HOLD DOWN SPRING
6 ADJUSTER SPRING
7 PAWL LEVER
8 SHOE RETURN UPPER SPRING
9 BACKING PLATE
10 SHOE HOLD DOWN PIN

93026G40

Exploded view of the rear brake components—Tracker

11. Adjust the parking brake and install the cover with the 2 screws.

12. Road-test the vehicle for proper brake operation.

Brake Shoes

REMOVAL & INSTALLATION

1. Raise and safely support the vehicle.
2. Remove the rear wheel(s).
3. Remove the brake drum.
4. Using a suitable tool, remove the brake shoe return spring.

5. Using a brake spring hold-down tool, disengage the hold-down spring and retainers from the front shoe. Remove the hold-down retainer pinch

6. Disconnect the anchor spring from the front shoe and remove the front shoe.

7. Remove the anchor spring from the rear shoe. Using a brake spring hold-down tool, disengage the hold-down spring and retainers from the rear shoe. Remove the hold-down pinch

8. Disengage the parking brake lever from the parking brake cable and remove the rear shoe.

9. Remove the C-washer, the automatic adjuster lever and spring, the C-washer, and the parking brake lever from the rear shoe.

10. Thoroughly clean the backing plate and brake hardware with brake cleaning solvent. Apply high temperature grease to the backing plate shoe contact points, anchor plate and shoe contact points, adjusting bolt, and adjuster and brake shoe contact points.

To install:

11. Reinstall the automatic adjuster lever and the parking brake lever to the rear shoe using new C-washers.

12. Connect the parking brake lever to the parking brake cable. Set the adjuster and spring to the rear shoe.

13. Set the rear brake shoe in place, install the hold-down pin and install the hold-down spring and retainers. Make sure that the shoe is inserted in the wheel cylinder and that the other end is in the anchor plate.

14. Install the anchor spring to the rear shoe.

15. Install the front shoe to the other end of the anchor spring and set the front shoe in place. Make sure that the front shoe engages the wheel cylinder, adjuster mechanism and spring, and the anchor plate.

16. Reinstall the front brake shoe hold-down pin and secure with the hold-down spring and retainers using a suitable tool.

17. Install the return spring.

18. Install the brake drum and pull the parking brake lever all the way up until a clicking sound can no longer be heard.

19. Verify that the rear wheels will not turn. If the rear wheels turn, adjust the parking brake cable as necessary.

20. Release the parking brake and remove the brake drum. Measure the diameter of the brake shoes. Brake diameter should be as follows:

- 2 door models: 8.638 (0.0012 inches (219 (0.3mm)
- 4 door models: 9.980 (0.0079 inches (253.5 (0.2mm)

21. If the brake shoe clearance is not correct, adjust the brake shoes until the clearance is correct.

22. Reinstall the brake drum, replace the wheel(s), and safely lower the vehicle.

23. Road-test the vehicle for proper brake operation.

HONDA

Brake Caliper

REMOVAL & INSTALLATION

CR-V and Passport

FRONT

1. Raise and safely support the vehicle. Remove the front wheels.
2. Remove some brake fluid from the master cylinder reservoir.
3. Disconnect and plug the brake fluid line from the caliper.
4. Remove the brake caliper mounting bolt and guide bolt and remove the caliper from the mount. The brackets can be remove for additional work space.
5. Remove the brake pads and clips from the caliper. Inspect the brake pads for wear; replace them, if necessary.

To install:

6. Install the brake pads and clips onto the caliper.
7. If the caliper bracket was removed, tighten the bolts to 103–126 ft. lbs. (139–171 Nm).
8. Install the caliper on the mounting bracket. Torque the caliper-to-mounting bracket bolts to:
   - 4-cylinder models: 20–27 ft. lbs. (27–37 Nm)
   - 6-cylinder models: 54 ft. lbs. (74 Nm)
9. Connect the fluid line to the caliper

using new washers. Torque the brake line banjo fitting to 26 ft. lbs. (35 Nm).

✶✶ WARNING

Be sure the hook end of the flexible brake line is positioned in the anti-rotation cavity.

10. Refill the master cylinder reservoir and bleed the brake system.
11. Install the front wheels and lower the vehicle.

REAR

1. Raise and safely support the vehicle. Remove the rear wheels.
2. Remove some fluid from the master cylinder reservoir.
3. Disconnect and plug the brake fluid line from the caliper.

➡**Discard the parking brake cable mounting pin after removal.**

4. If equipped with caliper actuated

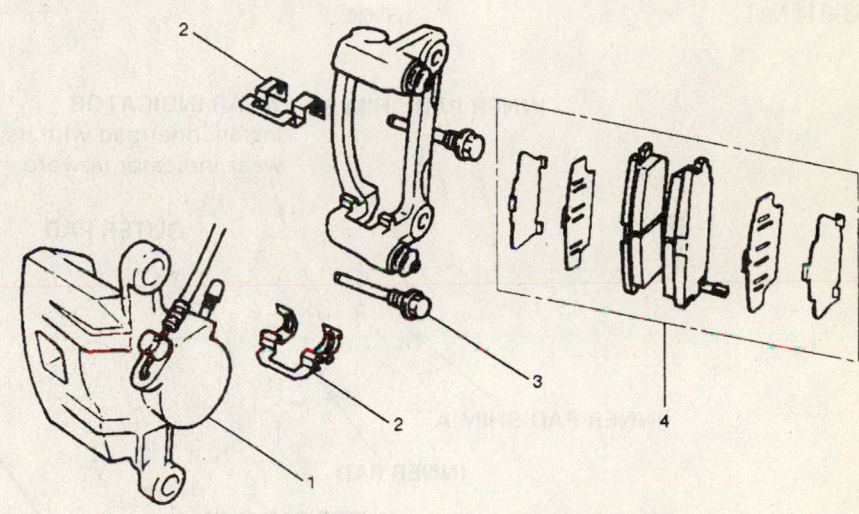

(1) Caliper Assembly
(2) Clip
(3) Lock Bolt
(4) Pad Assembly

93026G55

Exploded view of the rear caliper components—Passport

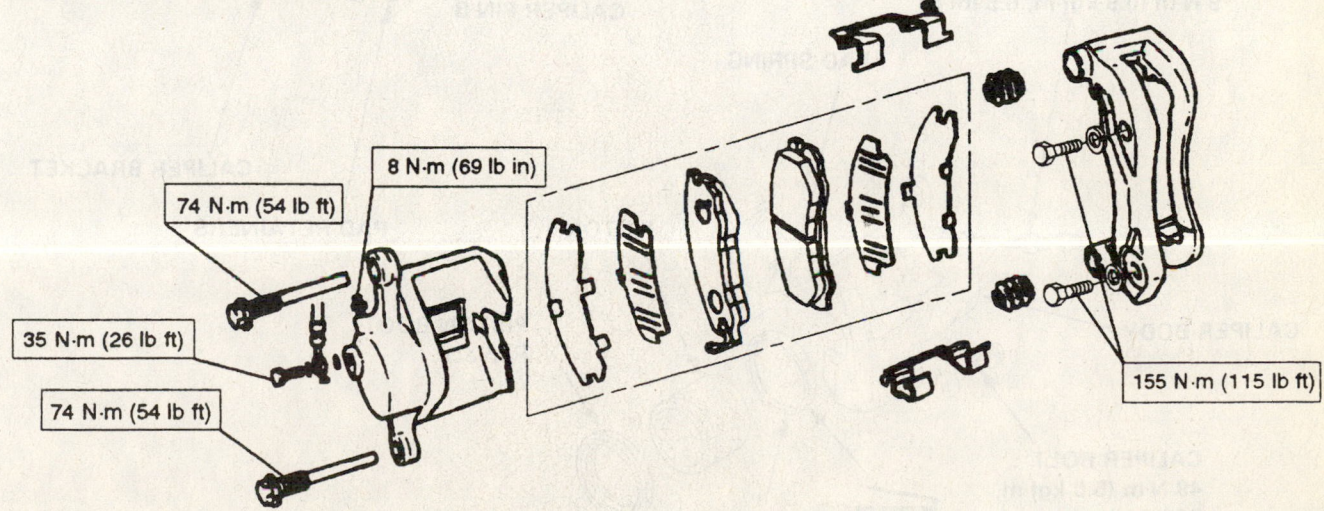

74 N·m (54 lb ft)

8 N·m (69 lb in)

35 N·m (26 lb ft)

74 N·m (54 lb ft)

155 N·m (115 lb ft)

93026G54

Exploded view of the front caliper components—Passport

For brake related suspension and axle service, refer to the model specific sections of this manual

parking brakes; remove the mounting pin from the parking brake cable and disconnect the parking cable from the disc caliper.

5. Remove the brake caliper mounting bolt and guide bolt and remove the caliper from the mount.

6. Remove the brake pads and clips from the caliper. Inspect the brake pads for wear; replace them, if necessary.

To install:

7. Install the brake pads and clips onto the caliper.

8. If the mounting bracket was removed, tighten the bolts to 69–84 ft. lbs. (93–114 Nm).

9. Install the caliper on the mounting bracket. Torque the caliper-to-mounting bracket bolts to 12–17 ft. lbs. (16–24 Nm), or 32 ft. lbs. (43 Nm) on vehicles with shoe-type parking brakes.

10. Connect the parking brake cable to the caliper and install a new mounting pin.

11. Connect the fluid line to the caliper using new washers. Torque the brake line banjo fitting to 26 ft. lbs. (35 Nm).

12. Refill the master cylinder reservoir and bleed the brake system.

13. Install the rear wheels and lower the vehicle.

Odyssey

FRONT

1. Remove some fluid from the reservoir with a suction pump.

2. Raise and safely support the vehicle.

3. Remove the front wheels.

4. Remove the banjo bolt and disconnect the brake hose from the caliper. Plug the hose to prevent fluid loss and contamination.

5. Remove the mounting bolts and remove the caliper from its mounting bracket.

To install:

6. Fit the caliper over the pads and onto its mounting bracket.

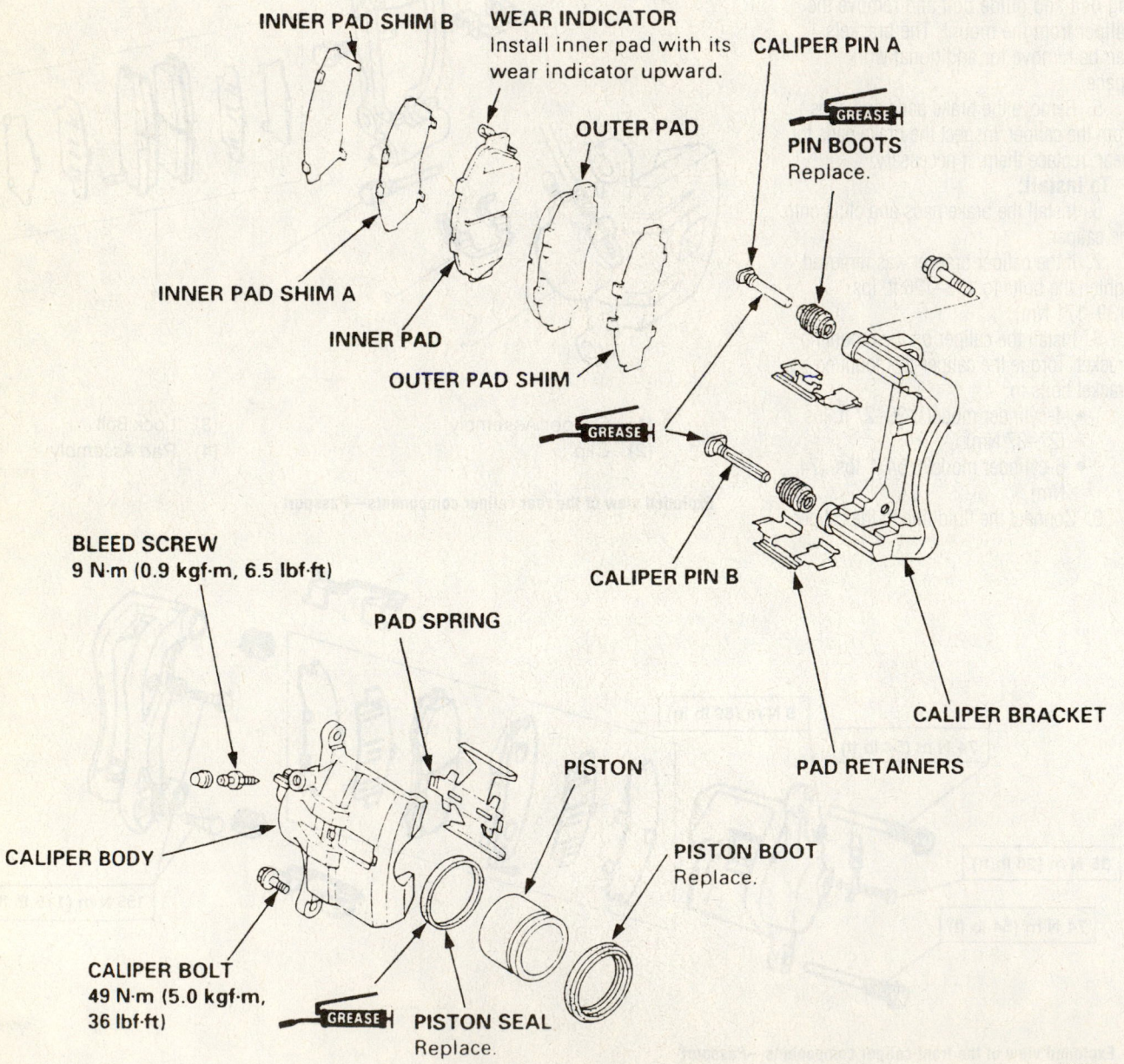

Exploded view of the front caliper components—CR-V and Odyssey

93026G57

7. Torque both caliper bolts to 36 ft. lbs. (49 Nm).

8. Reconnect the brake hose to the caliper using new sealing washers. Carefully torque the banjo bolt to 25 ft. lbs. (35 Nm).

9. Fill the reservoir with fluid and bleed the brakes.

10. Install the front wheels and lower the vehicle.

REAR

1. Remove some fluid from the reservoir with a suction pump.

2. Raise and safely support the vehicle.

3. Remove the rear wheels.

4. Remove the banjo bolt and disconnect the brake hose from the caliper. Plug the hose to prevent fluid loss and contamination.

5. Remove the 2 caliper mounting bolts. Remove the caliper from its mounting bracket.

To install:

6. Fit the caliper over the pads and onto its mounting bracket.

7. Tighten the caliper bolts to 17 ft. lbs. (23 Nm).

8. Reconnect the brake hose with new sealing washers. Tighten the banjo bolt to 17 ft. lbs. (34 Nm).

9. Fill the reservoir with fluid and bleed the brake system. Adjust the parking brake if necessary.

10. Install the rear wheels and lower the vehicle.

Disc Brake Pads

REMOVAL & INSTALLATION

CR-V and Passport

FRONT

Most disc brake pads are equipped with wear indicators. If a squealing noise occurs from the brakes while driving, check the pad wear indicator plate. If there is evidence of the indicator plate contacting the brake disc, the brake pad should be replaced.

1. Remove ½ of the volume of brake fluid from the master cylinder to prevent overflow when the caliper piston is compressed.

2. Raise and safely support the vehicle.

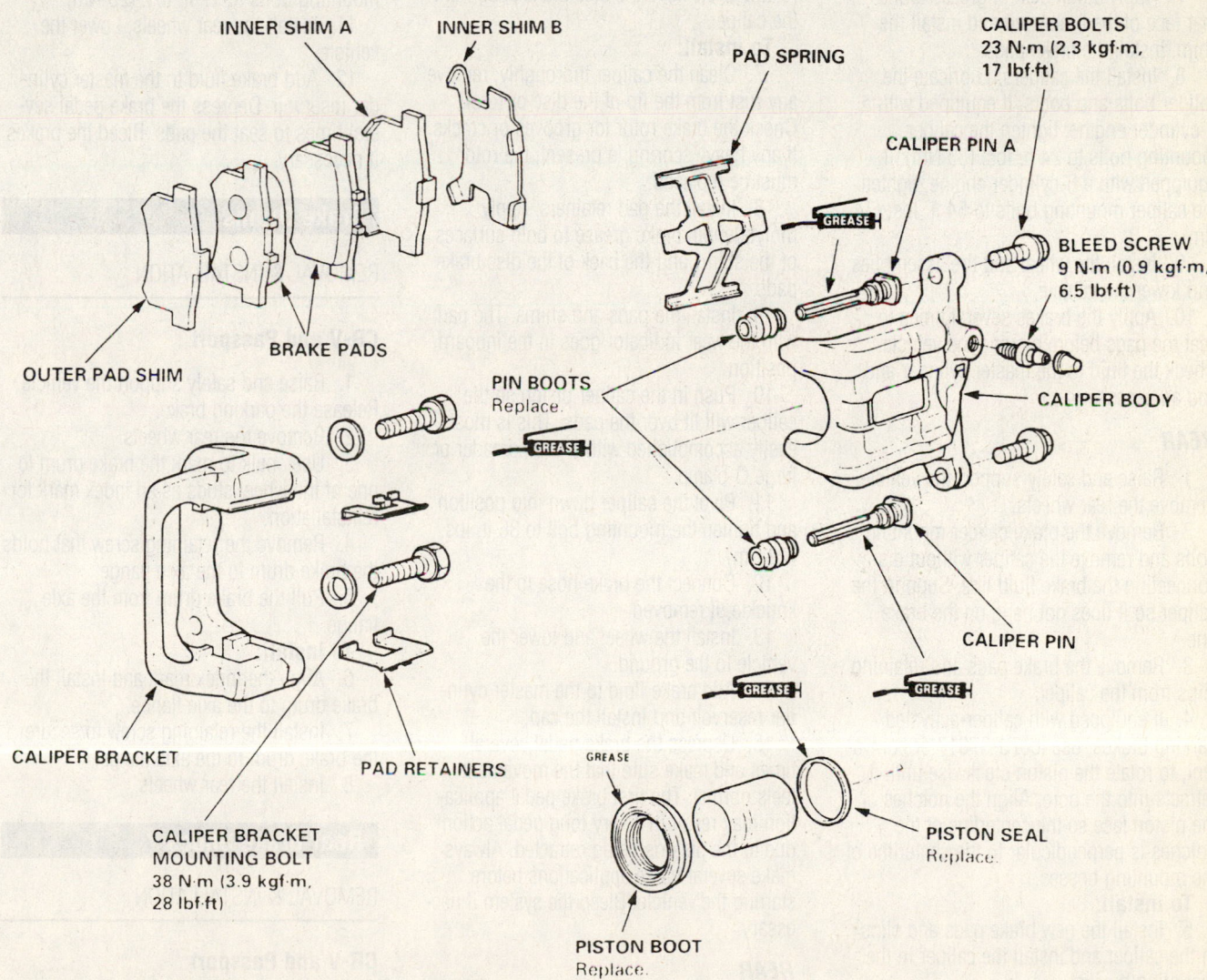

INNER SHIM A

INNER SHIM B

PAD SPRING

CALIPER BOLTS
23 N·m (2.3 kgf·m, 17 lbf·ft)

CALIPER PIN A

BLEED SCREW
9 N·m (0.9 kgf·m, 6.5 lbf·ft)

OUTER PAD SHIM

BRAKE PADS

PIN BOOTS
Replace.

CALIPER BODY

CALIPER PIN

CALIPER BRACKET

PAD RETAINERS

GREASE

PISTON SEAL
Replace.

CALIPER BRACKET
MOUNTING BOLT
38 N·m (3.9 kgf·m, 28 lbf·ft)

PISTON BOOT
Replace.

93026G58

Exploded view of the rear caliper components—CR-V and Odyssey

3. Remove the wheel and tire assemblies.

4. Remove the brake caliper without disconnecting the brake line. Support the caliper with a length of wire. Do not let the caliper hang from the brake hose.

➡ **On some disc brake systems it is not necessary to remove the caliper when installing new brake pads. Remove the lower slide bolt and rotate the caliper upward to remove the pads.**

5. Remove the brake pads and shims. Inspect the brake rotor and machine or replace as necessary. Check the minimum thickness (specification is cast into the rotor) before machining.

To install:

6. Use a suitable tool to push the caliper piston into its bore.

7. Apply a thin coat of grease to the rear face of the brake pad and install the shim. Install the brake pads.

8. Install the calipers. Lubricate the caliper bolts and boots. If equipped with a 4-cylinder engine, tighten the caliper mounting bolts to 24 ft. lbs. (33 Nm). If equipped with a 6-cylinder engine, tighten the caliper mounting bolts to 54 ft. lbs. (74 Nm).

9. Install the wheel and tire assemblies and lower the vehicle.

10. Apply the brakes several times to seat the pads before moving the vehicle. Check the fluid in the master cylinder and add as necessary.

REAR

1. Raise and safely support the vehicle. Remove the rear wheels.

2. Remove the brake caliper mounting bolts and remove the caliper without disconnecting the brake fluid line. Support the caliper so it does not hang on the brake line.

3. Remove the brake pads and retaining clips from the caliper.

4. If equipped with caliper-activated parking brakes; use tool J-37617 or equivalent, to rotate the piston clockwise until it retracts into the bore. Align the notches of the piston face so the centerline of the notches is perpendicular to the centerline of the mounting bosses.

To install:

5. Install the new brake pads and clips in the caliper and install the caliper in the mounting bracket.

6. Tighten the caliper mounting bolts to 12–17 ft. lbs. (16–24 Nm), or 32 ft. lbs. (43 Nm) on vehicles with shoe-type parking brakes.

7. Install the rear wheels. Check the brake fluid level.

8. Pump the brake pedal until pressure is felt before moving the vehicle.

Odyssey

FRONT

1. Raise and support the vehicle safely.

2. Remove the front wheels.

3. Remove a small amount of brake fluid from the reservoir using a suction pump.

4. Unbolt the brake hose clamp from the knuckle by removing the retaining bolts.

5. Remove the lower caliper retaining bolt and pivot the caliper upward, off of the pads.

6. Remove the pad shim and pad retainers. Remove the disc brake pads from the caliper.

To install:

7. Clean the caliper thoroughly; remove any rust from the lip of the disc or rotor. Check the brake rotor for grooves or cracks. If any heavy scoring is present, the rotor must be replaced.

8. Install the pad retainers. Apply molybdenum brake grease to both surfaces of the shims and the back of the disc brake pads.

9. Install the pads and shims. The pad with the wear indicator goes in the inboard position.

10. Push in the caliper piston so the caliper will fit over the pads. This is most easily accomplished with a pad spreader or large C-clamp.

11. Pivot the caliper down into position and tighten the mounting bolt to 36 ft. lbs. (49 Nm).

12. Connect the brake hose to the knuckle, if removed.

13. Install the wheel and lower the vehicle to the ground.

14. Add brake fluid to the master cylinder reservoir and install the cap.

15. Depress the brake pedal several times and make sure that the movement feels normal. The first brake pedal application may result in a very long pedal action due to the pistons being retracted. Always make several brake applications before starting the vehicle. Bleed the system if necessary.

REAR

1. Raise and safely support the vehicle.

2. Remove a small amount of brake fluid from the reservoir using a suction pump.

3. Remove the rear wheels.

4. Remove the 2 caliper mounting bolts and remove the caliper from the bracket.

5. Remove the pads, shims, and pad retainers.

To install:

6. Clean the caliper thoroughly; remove any dirt or dust. Check the brake rotor for grooves or cracks and machine or replace, as necessary.

7. Install the pad retainers. Apply molybdenum brake grease to both surfaces of the shims and the back of the disc brake pads.

8. Install the pads and shims. The wear retainer on the inboard pad faces down.

9. Use a suitable tool to push caliper piston into its bore and enable the caliper to fit over the pads. Lubricate the piston boot with silicon grease. Avoid twisting the boot.

10. Install the brake caliper. Tighten the mounting bolts to 17 ft. lbs. (23 Nm).

11. Install the rear wheels. Lower the vehicle.

12. Add brake fluid to the master cylinder reservoir. Depress the brake pedal several times to seat the pads. Bleed the brakes if necessary.

Brake Drums

REMOVAL & INSTALLATION

CR-V and Passport

1. Raise and safely support the vehicle. Release the parking brake.

2. Remove the rear wheels.

3. Use chalk to mark the brake drum to one of the wheel studs as an index mark for reinstallation.

4. Remove the retaining screw that holds the brake drum to the axle flange.

5. Pull the brake drum from the axle flange.

To install:

6. Align the index mark and install the brake drum to the axle flange.

7. Install the retaining screw to secure the brake drum to the axle flange.

8. Install the rear wheels.

Rear Brake Shoes

REMOVAL & INSTALLATION

CR-V and Passport

1. Raise and safely support the vehicle.

2. Remove the rear wheels.

3. Remove the brake drums.

4. Remove the brake return springs.

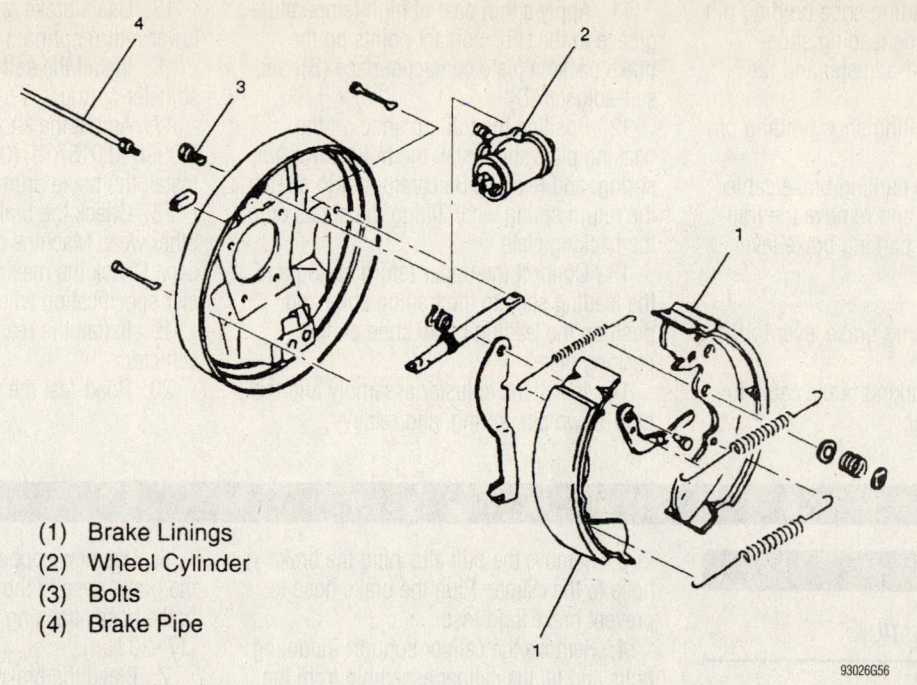

(1) Brake Linings
(2) Wheel Cylinder
(3) Bolts
(4) Brake Pipe

93026G56

Exploded view of the rear drum brakes—Passport

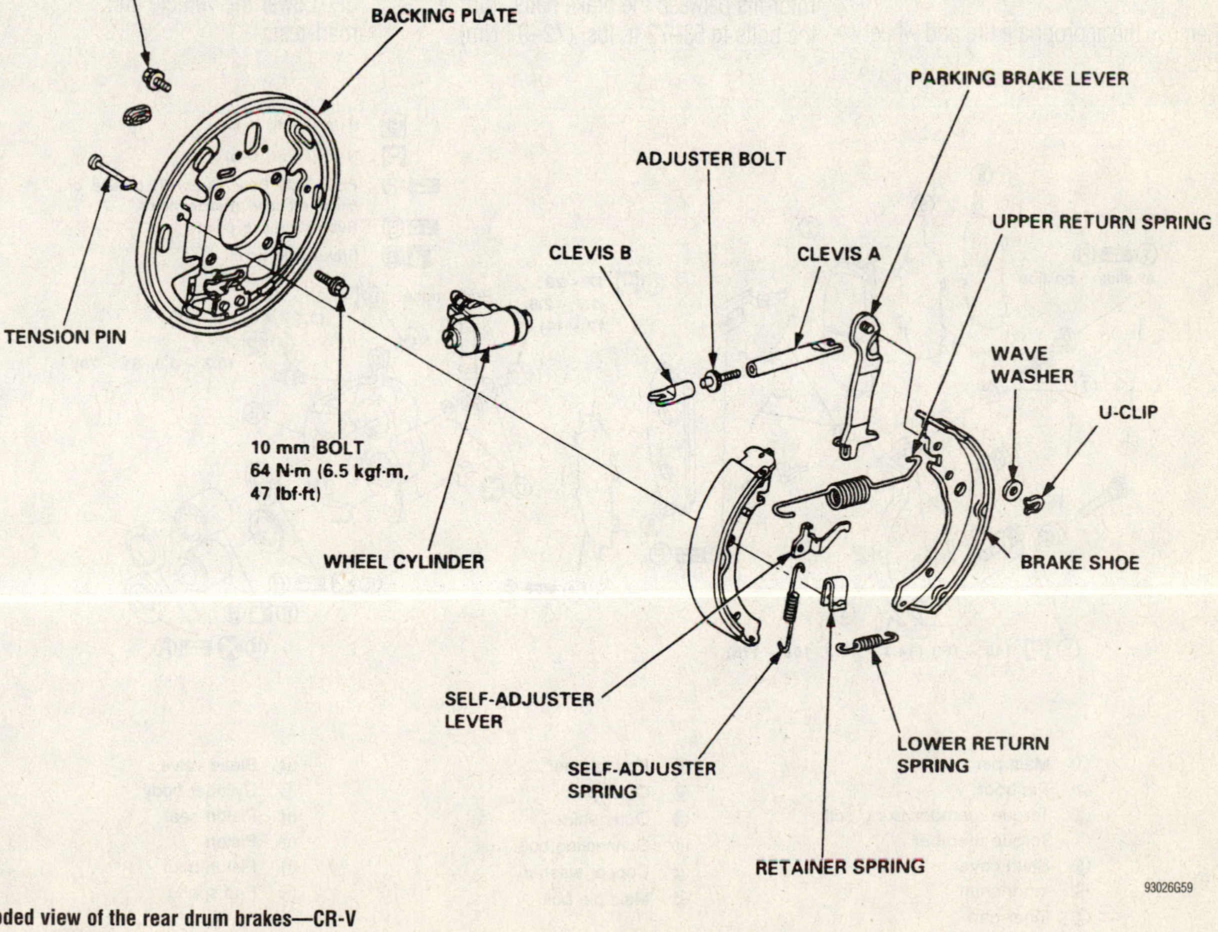

9 N·m (0.9 kgf·m, 6.5 lbf·ft)

BACKING PLATE

PARKING BRAKE LEVER

ADJUSTER BOLT

UPPER RETURN SPRING

CLEVIS B

CLEVIS A

WAVE WASHER

U-CLIP

TENSION PIN

10 mm BOLT
64 N·m (6.5 kgf·m, 47 lbf·ft)

WHEEL CYLINDER

BRAKE SHOE

SELF-ADJUSTER LEVER

SELF-ADJUSTER SPRING

LOWER RETURN SPRING

RETAINER SPRING

93026G59

Exploded view of the rear drum brakes—CR-V

5. Remove the leading shoe holding pin and spring, and then the leading shoe.

6. Remove the self-adjuster and the adjuster lever.

7. Remove the trailing shoe holding pin and spring.

8. Disconnect the parking brake cable from the trailing shoe and remove the trailing shoe. Remove the parking brake lever from the trailing shoe.

To install:

9. Attach the parking brake lever to the trailing shoe.

10. Connect the parking brake cable to the parking brake lever.

11. Apply a thin coat of high temperature grease to the shoe contact points on the brake backing plate contact surface (B), and self-adjuster (D).

12. Position the trailing shoe on the backing plate and install the hold-down pin, spring, and retainer. Be careful not to stretch the return spring when fitting the shoes onto the backing plate.

13. Connect the upper return spring and the leading shoe to the trailing shoe and position the leading brake shoe on the backing plate.

14. Install the adjuster assembly and the hold-down pin, spring, and retainer.

15. Use a brake spring tool to install the lower return spring.

16. Install the self-adjuster lever and adjuster spring.

17. Adjust the shoe-to-drum clearance to 0.0098–0.0157 in. (0.25–0.40mm) and install the brake drum.

18. Check the brake drum for scoring or other wear. Machine or replace as necessary. Check the maximum brake drum diameter specification when machining.

19. Install the rear wheels. Lower the vehicle.

20. Road-test the vehicle.

INFINITI

Brake Caliper

REMOVAL & INSTALLATION

QX4

FRONT

1. Raise the vehicle and support safely.

2. Remove the appropriate tire and wheel assembly.

3. Remove the bolt attaching the brake hose to the caliper. Plug the brake hose to prevent brake fluid loss.

4. Remove the caliper support mounting bolts and lift the caliper assembly from the knuckle.

To install:

5. Position caliper assembly onto the knuckle and install the bolts. Make sure the rotor fits between the brake pads. Torque the bolts to 53–72 ft. lbs. (72–97 Nm).

6. Use new copper washers and connect the brake hose to the caliper. Torque the brake hose attaching bolt to 12–14 ft. lbs. (17–20 Nm).

7. Bleed the brake system.

8. Apply the brake pedal and inspect the system. Ensure proper operation and no leakage.

9. Install tire and wheel assembly. Lower the vehicle and road-test.

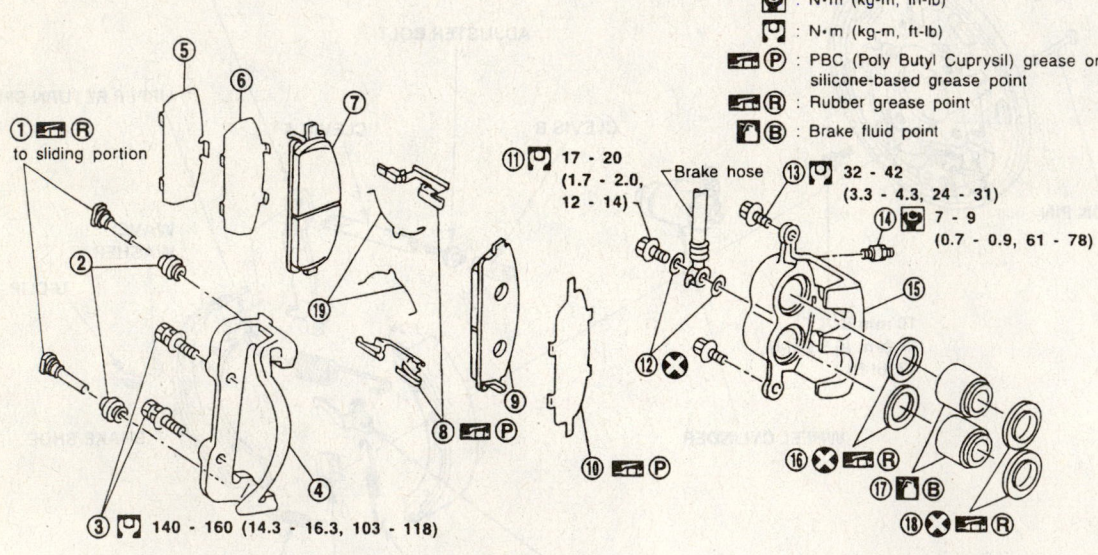

: N·m (kg-m, in-lb)

: N·m (kg-m, ft-lb)

(P) : PBC (Poly Butyl Cuprysil) grease or silicone-based grease point

(R) : Rubber grease point

(B) : Brake fluid point

① Main pin	⑧ Pad retainer
② Pin boot	⑨ Outer pad
③ Torque member fixing bolt	⑩ Outer shim
④ Torque member	⑪ Connecting bolt
⑤ Shim cover	⑫ Copper washer
⑥ Inner shim	⑬ Main pin bolt
⑦ Inner pad	⑭ Bleed valve
	⑮ Cylinder body
	⑯ Piston seal
	⑰ Piston
	⑱ Piston boot
	⑲ Pad spring

Exploded view of the dual piston caliper front brake components—QX4

93026G60

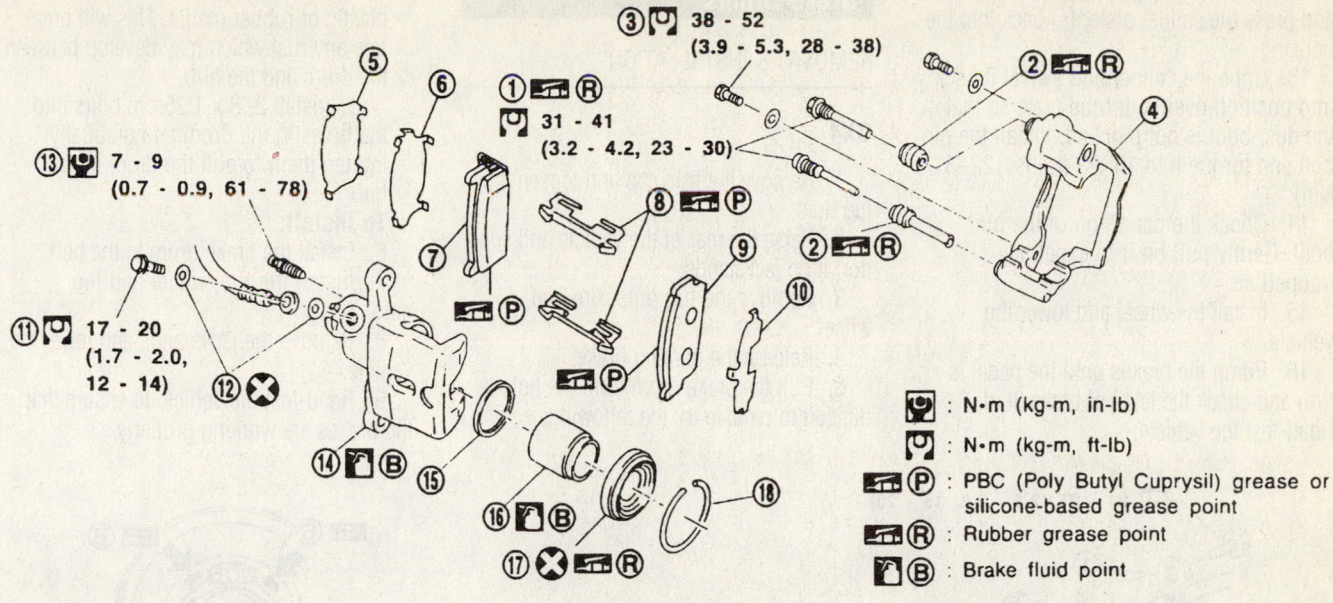

③	38 - 52 (3.9 - 5.3, 28 - 38)
①	31 - 41 (3.2 - 4.2, 23 - 30)
⑬	7 - 9 (0.7 - 0.9, 61 - 78)
⑪	17 - 20 (1.7 - 2.0, 12 - 14)

⬛ : N·m (kg-m, in-lb)

⬛ : N·m (kg-m, ft-lb)

⬛ P : PBC (Poly Butyl Cuprysil) grease or silicone-based grease point

⬛ R : Rubber grease point

⬛ B : Brake fluid point

① Main pin bolt
② Pin boot
③ Torque member fixing bolt
④ Torque member
⑤ Shim cover
⑥ Inner shim
⑦ Inner pad
⑧ Pad retainer
⑨ Outer pad
⑩ Outer shim
⑪ Connecting bolt
⑫ Copper washer
⑬ Bleed valve
⑭ Cylinder body
⑮ Piston seal
⑯ Piston
⑰ Piston boot
⑱ Retainer

93026G61

Exploded view of the rear disc brake components—QX4

REAR

➡**Unlike most rear disc brake designs, this system does not incorporate the parking brake system into the rear brake caliper. The rear brake system is serviced in the same manner as the front system.**

1. Raise the vehicle and support safely.
2. Remove the appropriate tire and wheel assembly.
3. Remove the caliper support mounting bolts and lift the caliper assembly from the baffle plate.
4. Loosen the brake fluid hose with a wrench and turn the caliper to disconnect it from the brake hose. Plug the brake hose to prevent brake fluid loss.
   To install:
5. Use a new copper washer and connect the brake hose to the caliper. Torque the hose fitting to 11 ft. lbs. (15 Nm).
6. Position the caliper assembly over the

baffle plate and install the bolts. Make sure the rotor fits between the brake pads. Torque the bolts to 28–38 ft. lbs. (38–52 Nm).
7. Bleed the brake system.
8. Apply the brake pedal and inspect the system. Ensure proper operation and no leakage.
9. Install tire and wheel assembly. Lower the vehicle and road-test.

Disc Brake Pads

REMOVAL & INSTALLATION

QX4

➡**Both the front and rear disc brake pads can be serviced using the same procedure.**

1. Using a syringe, siphon brake fluid from the reservoir, leaving reservoir approximately ½ full.

2. Raise and properly support the vehicle.
3. Remove the wheel assemblies.
4. Remove the lower pin bolt from the brake caliper.
5. Swivel the caliper up and away from the torque member. Tie the caliper to a suspension member so that it is out of the way.
6. Lift the 2 brake pads out of the torque member.
7. Remove the inner and outer shims. Remove the 2 pad retainers if they are not still attached to the pads.
8. Check the pad thickness and replace the pads if they are less than 0.079 in. (2mm) thick.
   To install:
9. Install the inner and outer shims into the torque member.
10. Install a pad retainer to the bottom of each pad.
11. Install the pads into the torque member.

For brake related suspension and axle service, refer to the model specific sections of this manual

12. Use a C-clamp or hammer handle and press the caliper piston(s) back into the housing.

13. Untie the caliper and swivel it back into position overthe torque plate so that the dust boot is not pinched. Install the pin bolt and torque it to 16–23 ft. lbs. (22–31 Nm).

14. Check the condition of the pin boot. Gently pull on it to expel any trapped air.

15. Install the wheel and lower the vehicle.

16. Pump the brakes until the pedal is firm and check the level of brake fluid. Road-test the vehicle.

Brake Drums

REMOVAL & INSTALLATION

QX4

1. Remove the hub cap and loosen the lug nuts.

2. Raise the rear of the vehicle and support it on jackstands.

3. Remove the lug nuts, tire and wheel.

4. Release the parking brake.

5. Pull the brake drum from the hub. If difficult to remove try the following:

a. Strike the face of the drum with a plastic or rubber mallet. This will break free any rust which may develop between the drum and the hub.

b. Install 2, 8 x 1.25mm bolts into the holes in the drum and gradually tighten them to pull the drum off the hub.

To install:

6. Install the brake drum to the hub.

7. Install the tire, wheel and lug nuts.

8. Remove the jackstands and lower the vehicle.

9. Road-test the vehicle to ensure that the brakes are working properly.

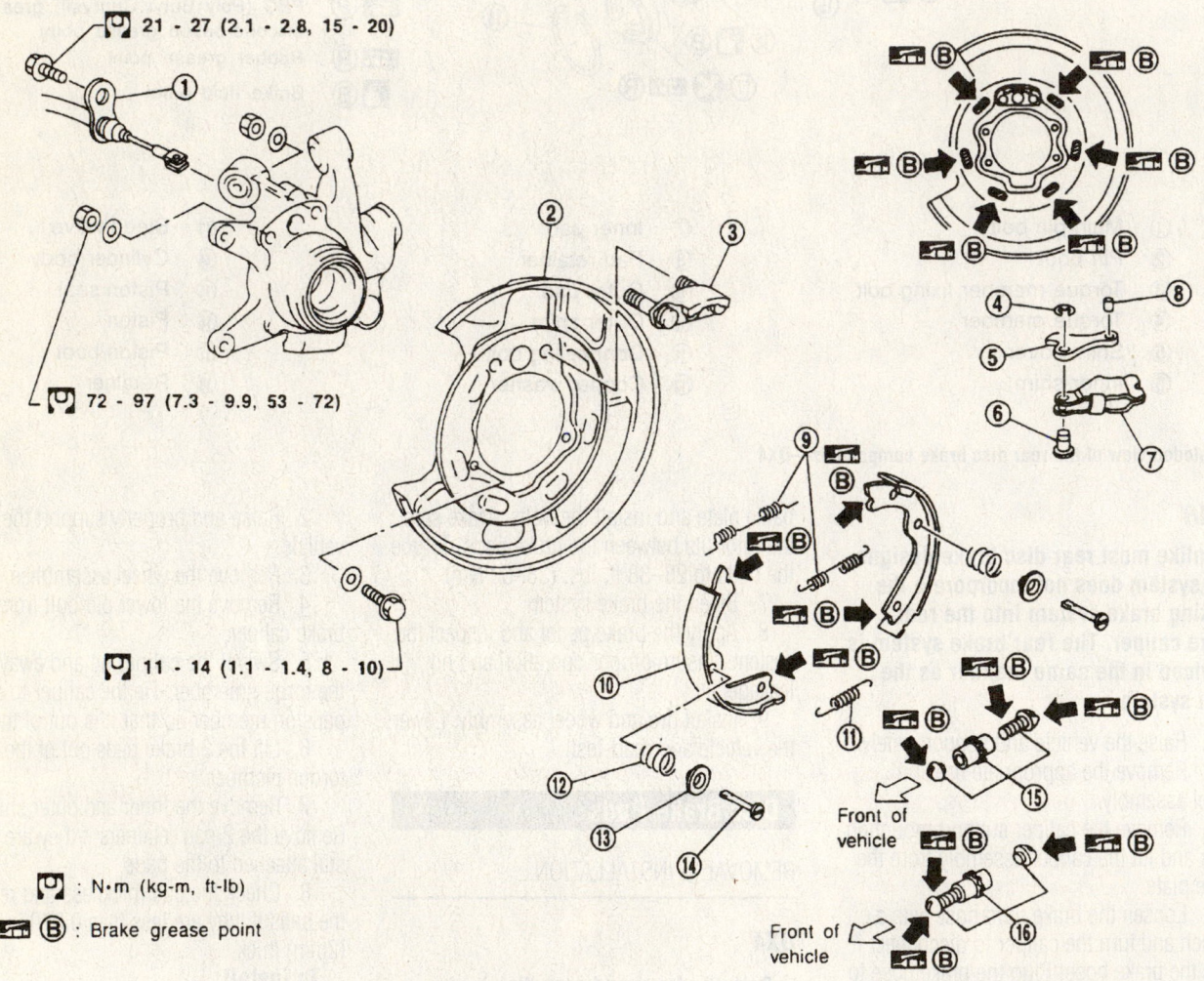

🔩 21 - 27 (2.1 - 2.8, 15 - 20)

🔩 72 - 97 (7.3 - 9.9, 53 - 72)

🔩 11 - 14 (1.1 - 1.4, 8 - 10)

🔩 : N·m (kg-m, ft-lb)

🔧Ⓑ : Brake grease point

①	Parking brake cable	⑦	Toggle lever	⑫	Anti-rattle spring
②	Back plate	⑧	Stopper pin	⑬	Retainer
③	Anchor block	⑨	Return spring	⑭	Anti-rattle pin
④	E-ring	⑩	Shoe	⑮	Adjuster assembly LH
⑤	Lever	⑪	Adjuster spring	⑯	Adjuster assembly RH
⑥	Pin				

Front of vehicle

Front of vehicle

93026G62

Exploded view of the rear disc brake drum assembly—QX4

Brake Shoes

REMOVAL & INSTALLATION

QX4

1. Release the parking brake.
2. Safely raise and support the vehicle.
3. Remove the rear wheel and drum.
4. Remove the hold-down pin retainers.
5. Remove the leading shoe and then the trailing shoe.
6. Remove the adjuster.
7. Disconnect the parking brake cable from the toggle lever on the rear shoe.

To install:

8. Transfer the toggle lever to the new rear shoe.
9. Apply a small amount of brake grease to the tips of the shoes and the 6 pads on the backing plate that contact the brake shoe.
10. Shorten the adjuster by turning it.
11. Connect the parking brake cable to the toggle lever on the rear shoe.
12. Install the lower return spring to both shoes and install the shoes on the backing plate with the hold down pins and retainers.
13. Install the adjuster and the remaining springs. Pay attention to the direction of the adjuster assembly.
14. Inspect the complete assembly and install the brake drum.

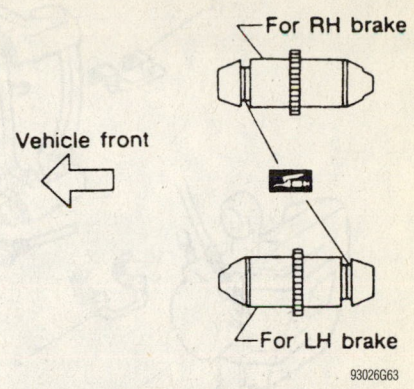

Correct direction of brake shoe adjuster— QX4

15. Adjust the shoe to drum clearance.
16. Install the wheel assembly and lower the vehicle to the floor.

ISUZU

Brake Caliper

REMOVAL & INSTALLATION

Trooper

FRONT

1. Raise and safely support the vehicle.
2. Remove some brake fluid from the reservoir.
3. Remove the front wheels.
4. Disconnect the brake fluid line from the caliper. Plug the line to prevent fluid loss.
5. Loosen the brake caliper mounting bolt and guide bolt. Remove the caliper from the mount.
6. Remove the brake pads and clips from the caliper. Inspect the brake pads for wear and replace them if necessary.

To install:

7. Fill the brake caliper with clean brake fluid and connect the fluid line to the caliper using new washers. Tighten the brake line banjo fitting to 26 ft. lbs. (35 Nm). Install the brake pads and clips onto the caliper.
8. Install the caliper onto the mounting bracket. Lubricate the caliper bolts and their boots. Then, install the caliper mounting bolts and tighten them to 54 ft. lbs. (74 Nm).
9. Refill and bleed the brake system.
10. Install the front wheels and lower the vehicle.

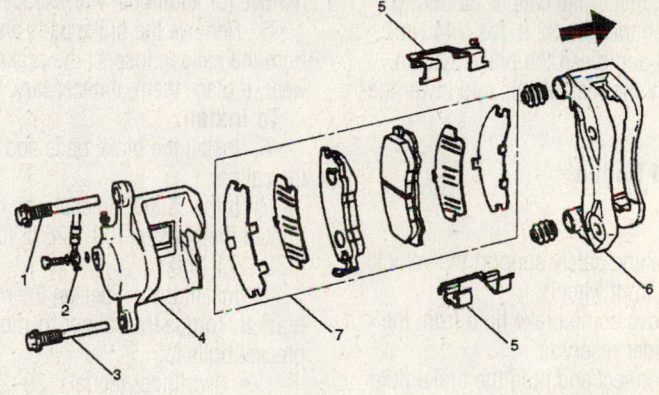

(1) Guide Bolt
(2) Brake Flexible Hose
(3) Lock Bolt
(4) Caliper Assembly
(5) Clip
(6) Support Bracket with Pad Assembly
(7) Pad Assembly

Front caliper assembly—Trooper

REAR

1. Raise and safely support the vehicle.
2. Remove some brake fluid from the reservoir.
3. Remove the rear wheels.
4. Disconnect the brake fluid line from the caliper. Plug the line to prevent fluid loss.
5. Loosen the brake caliper mounting bolt and guide bolt. Remove the caliper from the mount bracket.
6. Remove the brake pads and clips from the caliper. Inspect the brake pads for wear; replace them if necessary.

7. If necessary for servicing, unbolt the caliper mounting bracket from the backing plate.

To install:

8. If removed, install the caliper mounting bracket and tighten its bolts to 76 ft. lbs. (103 Nm).
9. Fill the brake caliper with clean brake fluid and connect the fluid line to the caliper using new washers. Tighten the brake line banjo fitting to 26 ft. lbs. (35 Nm). Install the brake pads and clips onto the caliper.
10. Install the caliper on the mounting

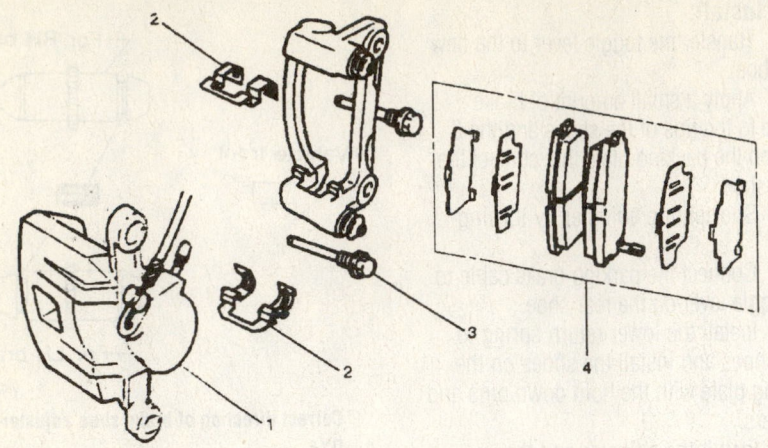

(1) Caliper Assembly
(2) Clip
(3) Lock Bolt
(4) Pad Assembly

93026G01

Rear caliper assembly—Trooper

bracket. Lubricate the caliper bolts and their boots. Then, install the caliper mounting bolts. Tighten them to 32 ft. lbs. (44 Nm).

11. Refill and bleed the brake system.

12. Install the rear wheels and lower the vehicle.

Amigo and Rodeo

FRONT

1. Raise and safely support the vehicle. Remove the front wheels.

2. Remove some brake fluid from the master cylinder reservoir.

3. Disconnect and plug the brake fluid line from the caliper.

4. Remove the brake caliper mount-ing bolt and guide bolt and remove the caliper

from the mount. The brackets can be remove for additional work space.

5. Remove the brake pads and clips from the caliper. Inspect the brake pads for wear; replace them, if necessary.

To install:

6. Install the brake pads and clips onto the caliper.

7. If the caliper bracket was removed, tighten the bolts to 103–126 ft. lbs. (139–171 Nm).

8. Install the caliper on the mounting bracket. Torque the caliper-to-mounting bracket bolts to:

- 4-cylinder models: 20–27 ft. lbs. (27–37 Nm)
- 6-cylinder models: 54 ft. lbs. (74 Nm)

9. Connect the fluid line to the caliper using new washers. Torque the brake line banjo fitting to 26 ft. lbs. (35 Nm).

✳✳ WARNING

Be sure the hook end of the flexible brake line is positioned in the anti-rotation cavity.

10. Refill the master cylinder reservoir and bleed the brake system.

11. Install the front wheels and lower the vehicle.

REAR

1. Raise and safely support the vehicle. Remove the rear wheels.

2. Remove some fluid from the master cylinder reservoir.

3. Disconnect and plug the brake fluid line from the caliper.

➡**Discard the parking brake cable mounting pin after removal.**

4. If equipped with caliper actuated parking brakes; remove the mounting pin from the parking brake cable and discon-nect the parking cable from the disc caliper.

5. Remove the brake caliper mounting bolt and guide bolt and remove the caliper from the mount.

6. Remove the brake pads and clips from the caliper. Inspect the brake pads for wear; replace them, if necessary.

To install:

7. Install the brake pads and clips onto the caliper.

8. If the mounting bracket was removed, tighten the bolts to 69–84 ft. lbs. (93–114 Nm).

9. Install the caliper on the mounting

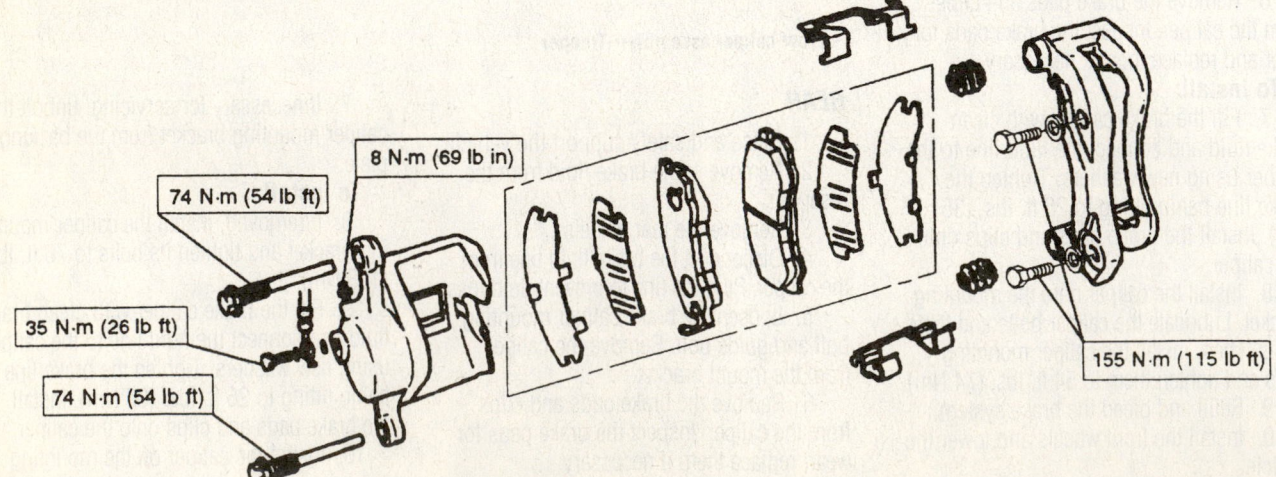

Exploded view of the front caliper components—Rodeo

93026G54

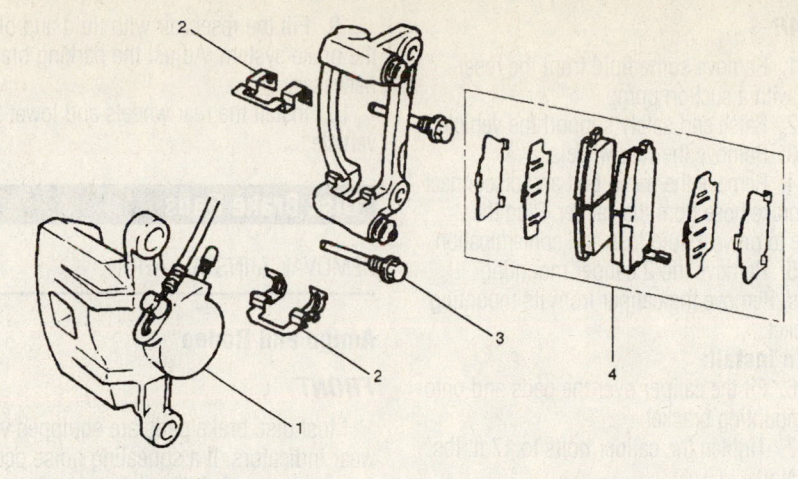

(1) Caliper Assembly
(2) Clip
(3) Lock Bolt
(4) Pad Assembly

93026G55

Exploded view of the rear caliper components—Rodeo

bracket. Torque the caliper-to-mounting bracket bolts to 12–17 ft. lbs. (16–24 Nm), or 32 ft. lbs. (43 Nm) on vehicles with shoe-type parking brakes.

10. Connect the parking brake cable to the caliper and install a new mounting pin.

11. Connect the fluid line to the caliper using new washers. Torque the brake line banjo fitting to 26 ft. lbs. (35 Nm).

12. Refill the master cylinder reservoir and bleed the brake system.

13. Install the rear wheels and lower the vehicle.

Oasis

FRONT

1. Remove some fluid from the reservoir with a suction pump.

2. Raise and safely support the vehicle.

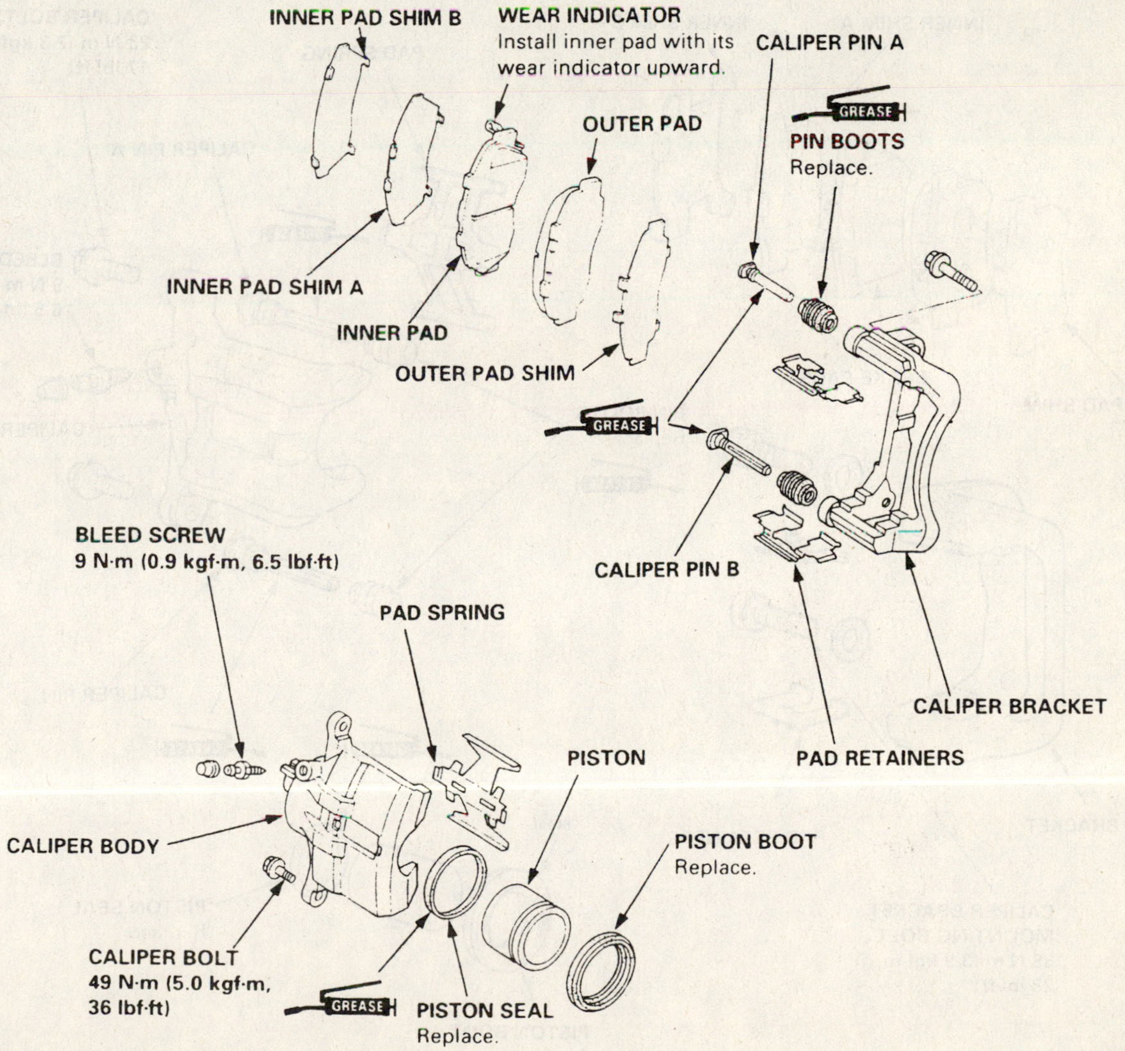

INNER PAD SHIM B

WEAR INDICATOR
Install inner pad with its wear indicator upward.

CALIPER PIN A

OUTER PAD

GREASE
PIN BOOTS
Replace.

INNER PAD SHIM A

INNER PAD

OUTER PAD SHIM

GREASE

CALIPER PIN B

BLEED SCREW
9 N·m (0.9 kgf·m, 6.5 lbf·ft)

PAD SPRING

PISTON

PAD RETAINERS

CALIPER BRACKET

CALIPER BODY

PISTON BOOT
Replace.

CALIPER BOLT
49 N·m (5.0 kgf·m, 36 lbf·ft)

GREASE

PISTON SEAL
Replace.

93026G57

Exploded view of the front caliper components—Oasis

3. Remove the front wheels.

4. Remove the banjo bolt and disconnect the brake hose from the caliper. Plug the hose to prevent fluid loss and contamination.

5. Remove the mounting bolts and remove the caliper from its mounting bracket.

To install:

6. Fit the caliper over the pads and onto its mounting bracket.

7. Torque both caliper bolts to 36 ft. lbs. (49 Nm).

8. Reconnect the brake hose to the caliper using new sealing washers. Carefully torque the banjo bolt to 25 ft. lbs. (35 Nm).

9. Fill the reservoir with fluid and bleed the brakes.

10. Install the front wheels and lower the vehicle.

REAR

1. Remove some fluid from the reservoir with a suction pump.

2. Raise and safely support the vehicle.

3. Remove the rear wheels.

4. Remove the banjo bolt and disconnect the brake hose from the caliper. Plug the hose to prevent fluid loss and contamination.

5. Remove the 2 caliper mounting bolts. Remove the caliper from its mounting bracket.

To install:

6. Fit the caliper over the pads and onto its mounting bracket.

7. Tighten the caliper bolts to 17 ft. lbs. (23 Nm).

8. Reconnect the brake hose with new sealing washers. Tighten the banjo bolt to 17 ft. lbs. (34 Nm).

9. Fill the reservoir with fluid and bleed the brake system. Adjust the parking brake if necessary.

10. Install the rear wheels and lower the vehicle.

Disc Brake Pads

REMOVAL & INSTALLATION

Amigo and Rodeo

FRONT

Most disc brake pads are equipped with wear indicators. If a squealing noise occurs from the brakes while driving, check the pad wear indicator plate. If there is evidence of the indicator plate contacting the

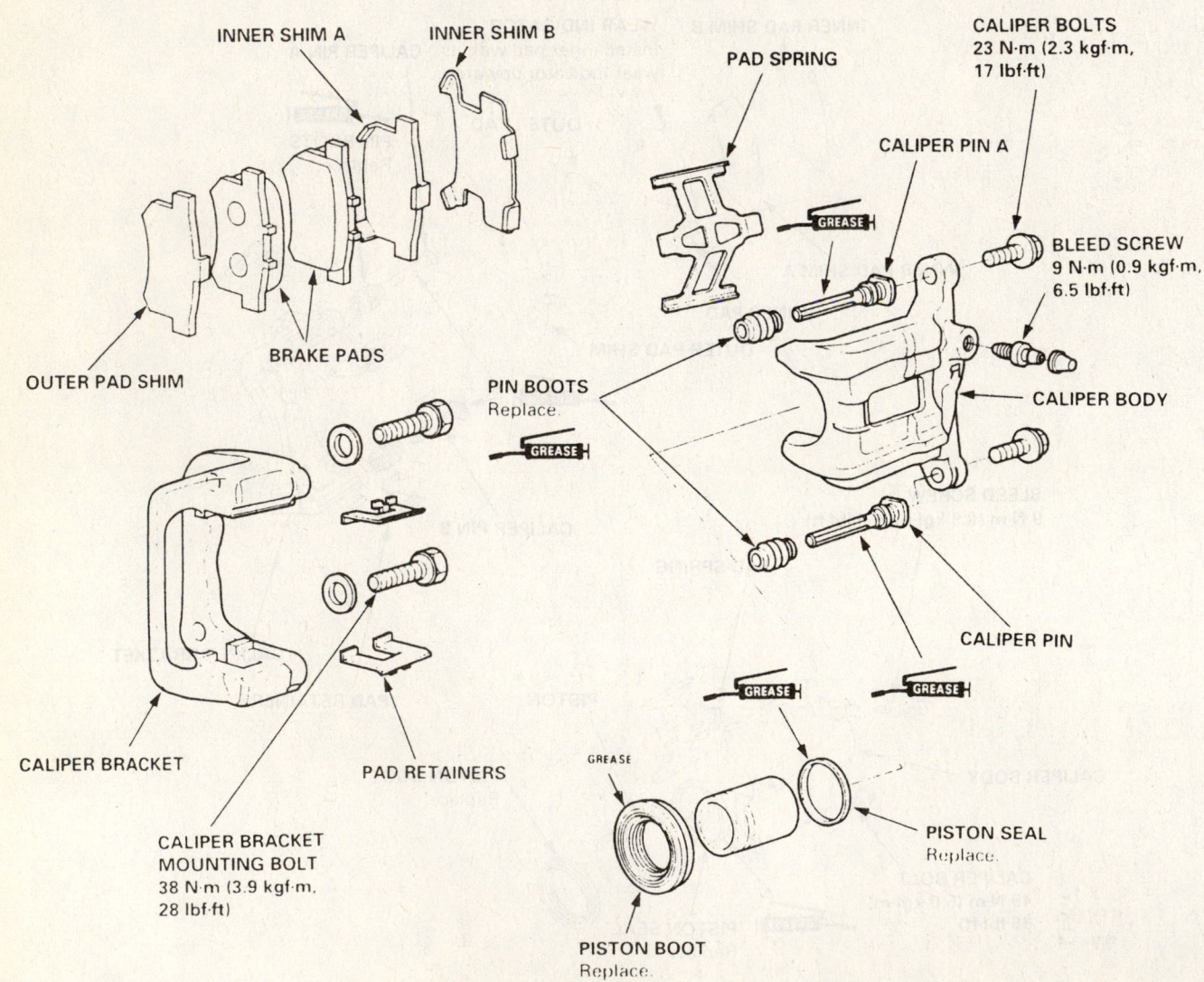

INNER SHIM A
INNER SHIM B
OUTER PAD SHIM
BRAKE PADS
CALIPER BRACKET
CALIPER BRACKET MOUNTING BOLT
38 N·m (3.9 kgf·m, 28 lbf·ft)
PAD RETAINERS
PIN BOOTS
Replace.
GREASE
PAD SPRING
CALIPER PIN A
CALIPER BOLTS
23 N·m (2.3 kgf·m, 17 lbf·ft)
BLEED SCREW
9 N·m (0.9 kgf·m, 6.5 lbf·ft)
CALIPER BODY
CALIPER PIN
GREASE
GREASE
PISTON SEAL
Replace.
PISTON BOOT
Replace.
GREASE

93026G58

Exploded view of the rear caliper components—Oasis

brake disc, the brake pad should be replaced.

1. Remove ½ of the volume of brake fluid from the master cylinder to prevent overflow when the caliper piston is compressed.

2. Raise and safely support the vehicle.

3. Remove the wheel and tire assemblies.

4. Remove the brake caliper without disconnecting the brake line. Support the caliper with a length of wire. Do not let the caliper hang from the brake hose.

➡ **On some disc brake systems it is not necessary to remove the caliper when installing new brake pads. Remove the lower slide bolt and rotate the caliper upward to remove the pads.**

5. Remove the brake pads and shims. Inspect the brake rotor and machine or replace as necessary. Check the minimum thickness (specification is cast into the rotor) before machining.

To install:

6. Use a suitable tool to push the caliper piston into its bore.

7. Apply a thin coat of grease to the rear face of the brake pad and install the shim. Install the brake pads.

8. Install the calipers. Lubricate the caliper bolts and boots. If equipped with a 4-cylinder engine, tighten the caliper mounting bolts to 24 ft. lbs. (33 Nm). If equipped with a 6-cylinder engine, tighten the caliper mounting bolts to 54 ft. lbs. (74 Nm).

9. Install the wheel and tire assemblies and lower the vehicle.

10. Apply the brakes several times to seat the pads before moving the vehicle. Check the fluid in the master cylinder and add as necessary.

REAR

1. Raise and safely support the vehicle. Remove the rear wheels.

2. Remove the brake caliper mounting bolts and remove the caliper without disconnecting the brake fluid line. Support the caliper so it does not hang on the brake line.

3. Remove the brake pads and retaining clips from the caliper.

4. If equipped with caliper-activated parking brakes; use tool J-37617 or equivalent to rotate the piston clockwise until it retracts into the bore. Align the notches of the piston face so the centerline of the notches is perpendicular to the centerline of the mounting bosses.

To install:

5. Install the new brake pads and clips in the caliper and install the caliper in the mounting bracket.

6. Tighten the caliper mounting bolts to 12–17 ft. lbs. (16–24 Nm), or 32 ft. lbs. (43 Nm) on vehicles with shoe-type parking brakes.

7. Install the rear wheels. Check the brake fluid level.

8. Pump the brake pedal until pressure is felt before moving the vehicle.

Oasis

FRONT

1. Raise and support the vehicle safely.

2. Remove the front wheels.

3. Remove a small amount of brake fluid from the reservoir using a suction pump.

4. Unbolt the brake hose clamp from the knuckle by removing the retaining bolts.

5. Remove the lower caliper retaining bolt and pivot the caliper upward, off of the pads.

6. Remove the pad shim and pad retainers. Remove the disc brake pads from the caliper.

To install:

7. Clean the caliper thoroughly; remove any rust from the lip of the disc or rotor. Check the brake rotor for grooves or cracks. If any heavy scoring is present, the rotor must be replaced.

8. Install the pad retainers. Apply molybdenum brake grease to both surfaces of the shims and the back of the disc brake pads.

9. Install the pads and shims. The pad with the wear indicator goes in the inboard position.

10. Push in the caliper piston so the caliper will fit over the pads. This is most easily accomplished with a pad spreader or large C-clamp.

11. Pivot the caliper down into position and tighten the mounting bolt to 36 ft. lbs. (49 Nm).

12. Connect the brake hose to the knuckle, if removed.

13. Install the wheel and lower the vehicle to the ground.

14. Add brake fluid to the master cylinder reservoir and install the cap.

15. Depress the brake pedal several times and make sure that the movement feels normal. The first brake pedal application may result in a very long pedal action due to the pistons being retracted. Always

make several brake applications before starting the vehicle. Bleed the system if necessary.

REAR

1. Raise and safely support the vehicle.

2. Remove a small amount of brake fluid from the reservoir using a suction pump.

3. Remove the rear wheels.

4. Remove the 2 caliper mounting bolts and remove the caliper from the bracket.

5. Remove the pads, shims, and pad retainers.

To install:

6. Clean the caliper thoroughly; remove any dirt or dust. Check the brake rotor for grooves or cracks and machine or replace, as necessary.

7. Install the pad retainers. Apply molybdenum brake grease to both surfaces of the shims and the back of the disc brake pads.

8. Install the pads and shims. The wear retainer on the inboard pad faces down.

9. Use a suitable tool to push caliper piston into its bore and enable the caliper to fit over the pads. Lubricate the piston boot with silicon grease. Avoid twisting the boot.

10. Install the brake caliper. Tighten the mounting bolts to 17 ft. lbs. (23 Nm).

11. Install the rear wheels. Lower the vehicle.

12. Add brake fluid to the master cylinder reservoir. Depress the brake pedal several times to seat the pads. Bleed the brakes if necessary.

Trooper

FRONT

1. Remove about ½ of the brake fluid from the master cylinder reservoir to prevent overflow when the caliper piston is compressed.

2. Raise and safely support the vehicle.

3. Remove the front wheels.

4. Remove the brake caliper from the caliper bracket without disconnecting the brake line. Support the caliper with a length of wire. Do not let the caliper hang from the brake hose.

5. Remove the brake pads and shims. Inspect the brake rotor and machine or replace as necessary. Check the minimum thickness (specification is cast into the rotor) before machining.

To install:

6. Use a large C-clamp or brake piston tool to push the caliper piston into its bore.

7. Apply a thin coat of brake grease to both sides of both inner shims. Assemble the pads and shims, then install them into the caliper. The wear indicator on the inner pad must face down.

8. Install the calipers. Clean and lubricate the caliper mounting bolts and lubricate the mounting bolt boots. Install the mounting bolts and tighten them to 54 ft. lbs. (74 Nm).

9. Install the front wheels and lower the vehicle.

10. Apply the brakes several times to seat the pads before moving the vehicle. Check the fluid level in the master cylinder reservoir and add as necessary.

REAR

1. Use a vacuum pump to remove some brake fluid from the master cylinder reservoir to prevent overflow when the caliper piston is compressed.

2. Raise and safely support the vehicle.

3. Remove the rear wheels.

4. Remove the brake caliper from the caliper bracket without disconnecting the brake line. Support the caliper with a length of wire. Do not let the caliper hang from the brake hose.

5. Remove the brake pads and shims. Inspect the brake rotor and machine or replace as necessary. Check the minimum thickness (specification is cast into the rotor) before machining.

To install:

6. Use a large C-clamp or brake piston tool to push the caliper piston into its bore.

7. Apply a thin coat of brake grease to both sides of both inner shims. Assemble the pads and shims, then install them into the caliper. The wear indicator on the inner pad must face down.

8. Install the calipers. Clean and lubricate the caliper mounting bolts and lubricate the mounting bolt boots. Install the mounting bolts and tighten them to 32 ft. lbs. (44 Nm).

9. Install the rear wheels and lower the vehicle.

10. Apply the brakes several times to seat the pads before moving the vehicle. Check the fluid level in the master cylinder reservoir and add as necessary.

Brake Drums

REMOVAL & INSTALLATION

Amigo and Rodeo

1. Raise and safely support the vehicle. Release the parking brake.

2. Remove the rear wheels.

3. Use chalk to mark the brake drum to one of the wheel studs as an index mark for reinstallation.

4. Remove the retaining screw that holds the brake drum to the axle flange.

5. Pull the brake drum from the axle flange.

To install:

6. Align the index mark and install the brake drum to the axle flange.

7. Install the retaining screw to secure the brake drum to the axle flange.

8. Install the rear wheels.

Rear Brake Shoes

REMOVAL & INSTALLATION

Amigo and Rodeo

1. Raise and safely support the vehicle.

2. Remove the rear wheels.

3. Remove the brake drums.

4. Remove the brake return springs.

5. Remove the leading shoe holding pin and spring, and then the leading shoe.

6. Remove the self-adjuster and the adjuster lever.

7. Remove the trailing shoe holding pin and spring.

8. Disconnect the parking brake cable from the trailing shoe and remove the trailing shoe. Remove the parking brake lever from the trailing shoe.

To install:

9. Attach the parking brake lever to the trailing shoe.

10. Connect the parking brake cable to the parking brake lever.

11. Apply a thin coat of high temperature grease to the shoe contact points on the brake backing plate (locations A and C in the accompanying illustration), piston contact surface (B), and self-adjuster (D).

12. Position the trailing shoe on the backing plate and install the hold-down pin, spring, and retainer. Don't stretch the return spring when fitting the shoes onto the backing plate.

13. Connect the upper return spring and the leading shoe to the trailing shoe and position the leading brake shoe on the backing plate.

14. Install the adjuster assembly and the hold-down pin, spring, and retainer.

15. Use a brake spring tool to install the lower return spring.

16. Install the self-adjuster lever and adjuster spring.

17. Adjust the shoe-to-drum clearance to 0.0098–0.0157 in. (0.25–0.40mm) and install the brake drum.

18. Check the brake drum for scoring or other wear. Machine or replace as necessary. Check the maximum brake drum diameter specification when machining.

19. Install the rear wheels. Lower the vehicle.

20. Road-test the vehicle.

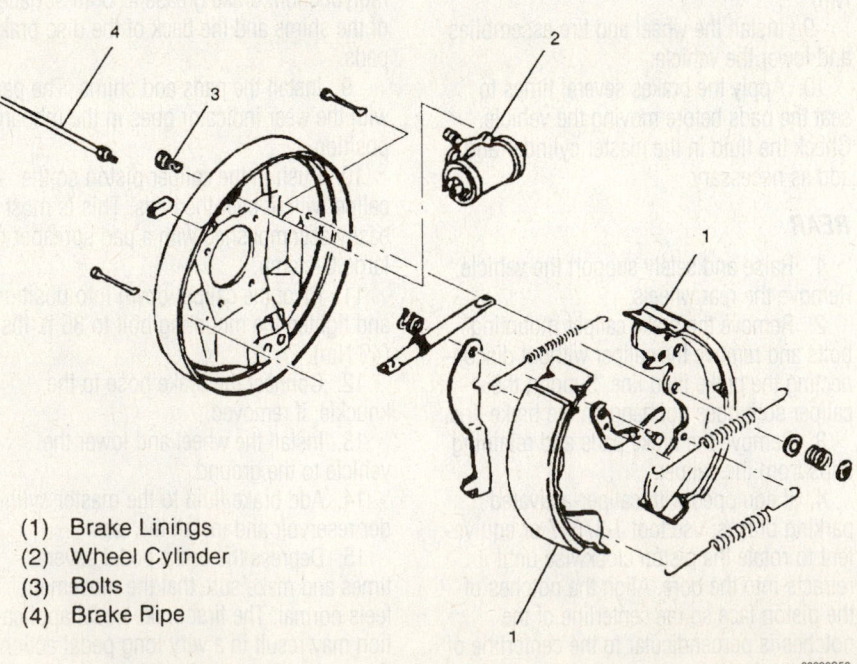

(1) Brake Linings
(2) Wheel Cylinder
(3) Bolts
(4) Brake Pipe

93026G56

Exploded view of the rear drum brakes—Amigo and Rodeo

JEEP

Brake Caliper

REMOVAL & INSTALLATION

Cherokee, Wrangler and 1997–98 Grand Cherokee

1. Drain ⅔ of the brake fluid from the front reservoir. Use the bleeder screw at the front outlet port to drain the fluid. If equipped with anti-lock brakes, relieve the system pressure.

2. Raise and safely support the vehicle.

3. Remove the wheels.

4. Place a C-clamp on the caliper so the solid end contacts the back of the caliper and screw end contacts the metal part of the outboard brake pad.

5. Tighten the clamp until the caliper moves far enough to force the piston to the bottom of the piston bore. This will back the brake pads off of the rotor surface to facilitate the removal and installation of the caliper assembly.

6. Remove the C-clamp.

7. Remove both of the mounting bolts and lift the caliper off the rotor.

8. If the caliper is being removed, it is necessary to disconnect the brake fluid hose. Clean the brake fluid hose-to-caliper connection thoroughly. Remove the hose-to-caliper bolt. Cap or tape the open ends to keep dirt out. Discard the copper gaskets.

To install:

9. Connect the brake line to the caliper with new sealing washers and fitting bolt. Hand-tighten the fitting bolt.

10. Position the caliper into place over the rotor.

11. Coat the caliper mounting bolt with silicone grease and torque them to 84–180 inch lbs. (10–20 Nm).

12. Position the brake line clear of all chassis components, untwisted and free of kinks. Torque the fitting bolt to 23 ft. lbs. (31 Nm).

13. Install the wheels.

14. Fill the master cylinder with fluid and bleed the brake system.

15. Before driving the vehicle, pump the brakes several times to seat the pads.

1999–01 Grand Cherokee

FRONT

1. Drain ⅔ of the brake fluid from the front reservoir. Use the bleeder screw at the front outlet port to drain the fluid. If equipped with anti-lock brakes, relieve the system pressure.

2. Raise and safely support the vehicle.

3. Remove the wheels.

4. Insert a small prybar through the caliper opening and pry the caliper (using the outboard brake pad) to bottom the pistons in the caliper bore.

➡ **This will back the brake pads off of the rotor surface to facilitate the removal and installation of the caliper assembly.**

5. Remove the brake hose-to-caliper bolt, hose and washers.

6. Pry the caliper support spring out of the caliper.

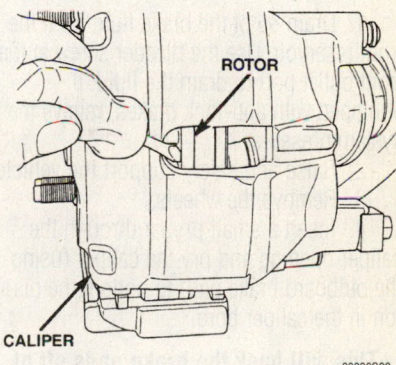

Bottoming the pistons in the front caliper—1999–01 Grand Cherokee

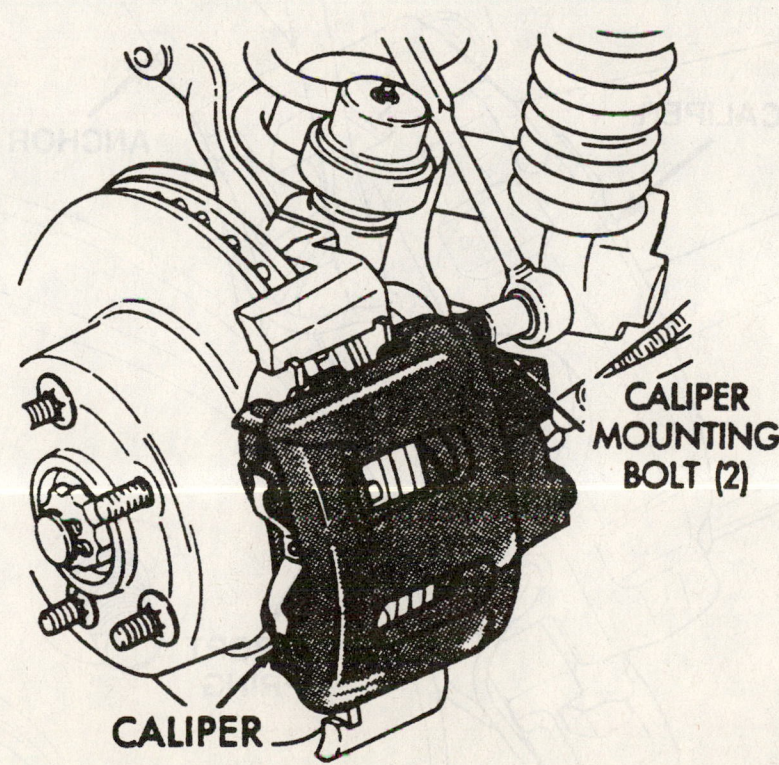

Front caliper mounting—Cherokee, Wrangler and 1997–98 Grand Cherokee

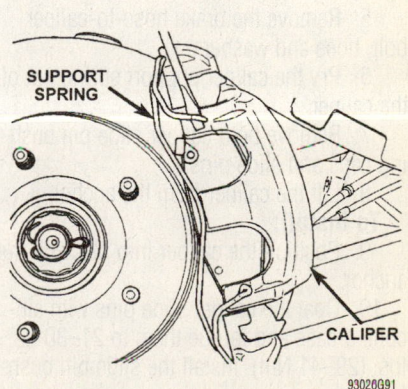

View of the support springs on the front caliper—1999–01 Grand Cherokee

7. Remove both caliper slide pin bushing caps and slide pins.

8. Lift the caliper from the anchor.

To install:

9. Position the caliper into place on the anchor.

10. Coat the caliper slide pins with silicone grease and torque them to 21–30 ft. lbs. (29–41 Nm). Install the slide pin bushing caps.

11. Install the caliper support spring in the top of the caliper under the anchor; then, install the other end into the lower caliper hole.

➡**Hold the spring in the caliper hole with your thumb while prying the spring end out and under the anchor.**

12. Using new gasket washers, install the brake line and torque the fitting bolt to 23 ft. lbs. (31 Nm).

13. Fill the master cylinder with fluid and bleed the brake system.

14. Before driving the vehicle, pump the brakes several times to seat the pads.

15. Install the wheels.

REAR

1. Drain ⅔ of the brake fluid from the front reservoir. Use the bleeder screw at the front outlet port to drain the fluid. If equipped with anti-lock brakes, relieve the system pressure.

2. Raise and safely support the vehicle.

3. Remove the wheels.

4. Insert a small prybar through the caliper opening and pry the caliper (using the outboard brake pad) to bottom the piston in the caliper bore.

➡**This will back the brake pads off of the rotor surface to facilitate the removal and installation of the caliper assembly.**

5. Remove the brake hose-to-caliper bolt, hose and washers.

6. Pry the caliper support spring out of the caliper.

7. Remove both caliper slide pin bushing caps and slide pins.

8. Lift the caliper from the anchor.

To install:

9. Position the caliper into place on the anchor.

10. Coat the caliper slide pins with silicone grease and torque them to 21–30 ft. lbs. (29–41 Nm). Install the slide pin bushing caps.

11. Install the caliper support spring in the top of the caliper under the anchor; then, install the other end into the lower caliper hole.

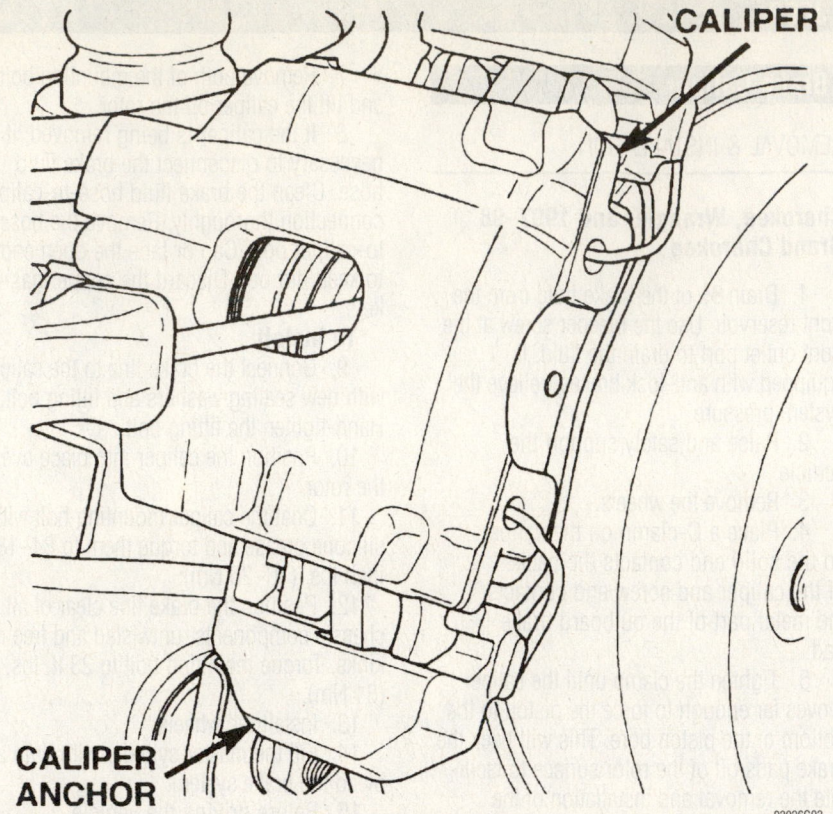

Bottoming the piston in the rear caliper—1999–01 Grand Cherokee

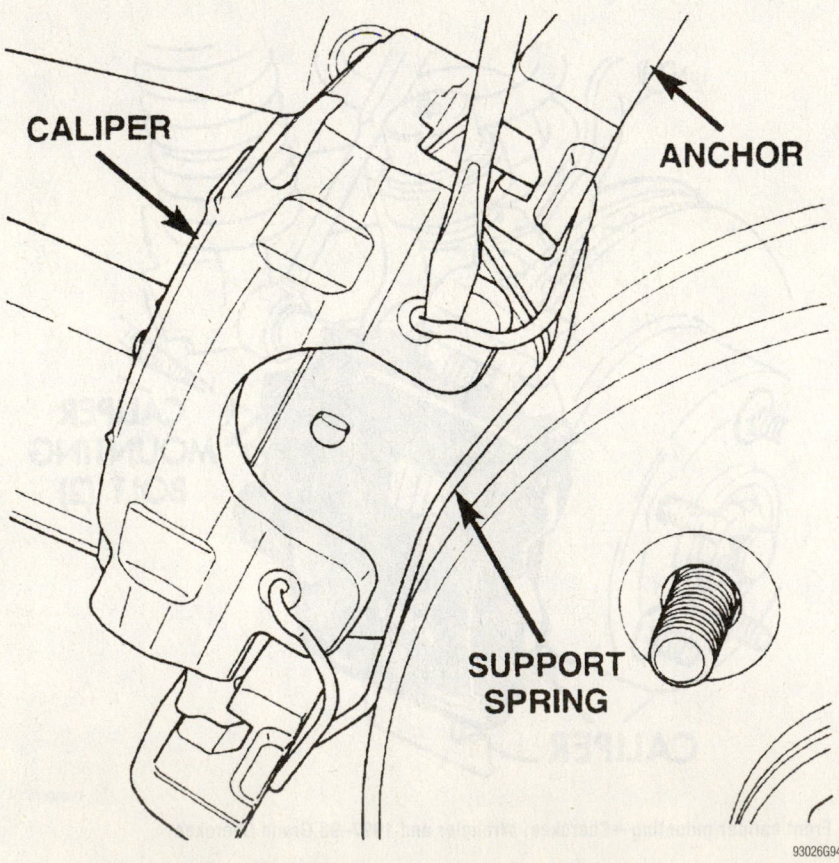

View of the support springs on the rear caliper—1999–01 Grand Cherokee

→Hold the spring in the caliper hole with your thumb while prying the spring end out and under the anchor.

12. Using new gasket washers, install the brake line and torque the fitting bolt to 23 ft. lbs. (31 Nm).

13. Fill the master cylinder with fluid and bleed the brake system.

14. Before driving the vehicle, pump the brakes several times to seat the pads.

15. Install the wheels.

Disc Brake Pads

REMOVAL & INSTALLATION

Cherokee, Wrangler and 1997–98 Grand Cherokee

1. Raise and safely support the vehicle.
2. Drain ⅔ of the brake fluid from the front reservoir. Use the bleeder screw at the front outlet port to drain the fluid.
3. Raise and support the vehicle safely.
4. Remove the wheels.
5. Remove the brake caliper. Use a suitable tool to compress the caliper piston into the bore.
6. Hold the anti-rattle clip against the caliper anchor plate and remove the outboard brake pad.
7. Remove the inboard pad and its anti-rattle clip.

To install:

8. Clean all the mounting holes and bushing grooves in the caliper ears. Clean the mounting bolts. Replace the bolts if they are corroded or if the threads are damaged. Wipe the inside of the caliper clean, including the exterior of the dust boot. Inspect the dust boot for cuts or cracks and for proper seating in the piston bore. If evidence of fluid leakage is noted, the caliper should be rebuilt.

→Do not use abrasives on the bolts. This will destroy their protective plating.

9. Install the inboard anti-rattle clip on the trailing end of the anchor plate. The split end of the clip must face away from the rotor.

10. Install the inboard pad in the caliper. The pad must lay flat against the piston.

11. Install the outboard pad in the caliper while holding the anti-rattle clip.

12. With the pads installed, position the caliper over the rotor. Line up the mounting holes in the caliper and the support bracket and insert the mounting bolts. Make sure the bolts pass under the retaining ears on

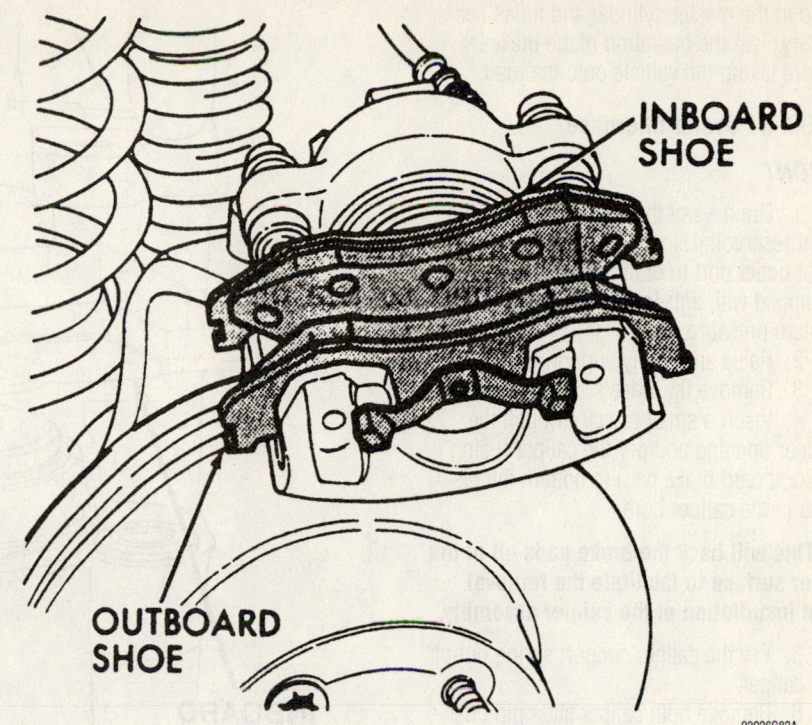

Front disc brake pad installation—Cherokee, Wrangler and 1997–98 Grand Cherokee

the inboard shoes. Push the bolts through until they engage the holes of the outboard pad and caliper ears. Thread the bolts into the support bracket and tighten them to 11 ft. lbs. (15 Nm).

13. Fill the master cylinder with brake fluid and pump the brake pedal to seat the pads.

14. Install the wheel assembly and lower the vehicle. Check the level of the brake

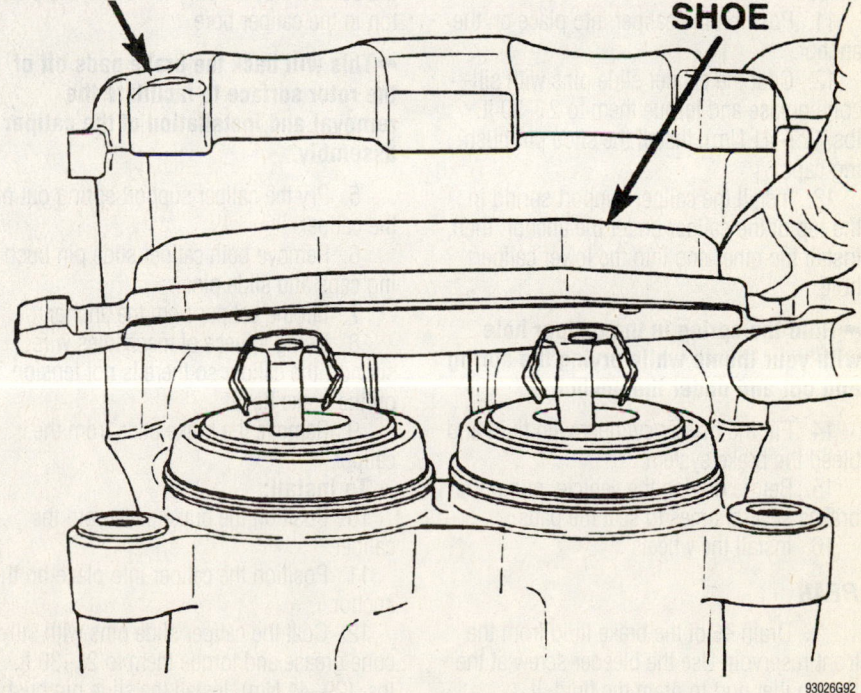

Installing the inward brake pad on the front caliper pistons—1999–01 Grand Cherokee

fluid in the master cylinder and fill as necessary. Test the operation of the brakes before taking the vehicle onto the road.

1999–01 Grand Cherokee

FRONT

1. Drain ⅔ of the brake fluid from the front reservoir. Use the bleeder screw at the front outlet port to drain the fluid. If equipped with anti-lock brakes, relieve the system pressure.
2. Raise and safely support the vehicle.
3. Remove the wheels.
4. Insert a small prybar through the caliper opening and pry the caliper (using the outboard brake pad) to bottom the pistons in the caliper bore.

➡This will back the brake pads off of the rotor surface to facilitate the removal and installation of the caliper assembly.

5. Pry the caliper support spring out of the caliper.
6. Remove both caliper slide pin bushing caps and slide pins.
7. Lift the caliper from the anchor.
8. Using a piece of mechanics wire, support the caliper so there is not tension on the brake hose.
9. Remove the brake pads from the caliper.

To install:

10. Position the brake pads onto the caliper.
11. Position the caliper into place on the anchor.
12. Coat the caliper slide pins with silicone grease and torque them to 21–30 ft. lbs. (29–41 Nm). Install the slide pin bushing caps.
13. Install the caliper support spring in the top of the caliper under the anchor; then, install the other end into the lower caliper hole.

➡Hold the spring in the caliper hole with your thumb while prying the spring end out and under the anchor.

14. Fill the master cylinder with fluid and bleed the brake system.
15. Before driving the vehicle, pump the brakes several times to seat the pads.
16. Install the wheels.

REAR

1. Drain ⅔ of the brake fluid from the front reservoir. Use the bleeder screw at the front outlet port to drain the fluid. If equipped with anti-lock brakes, relieve the system pressure.

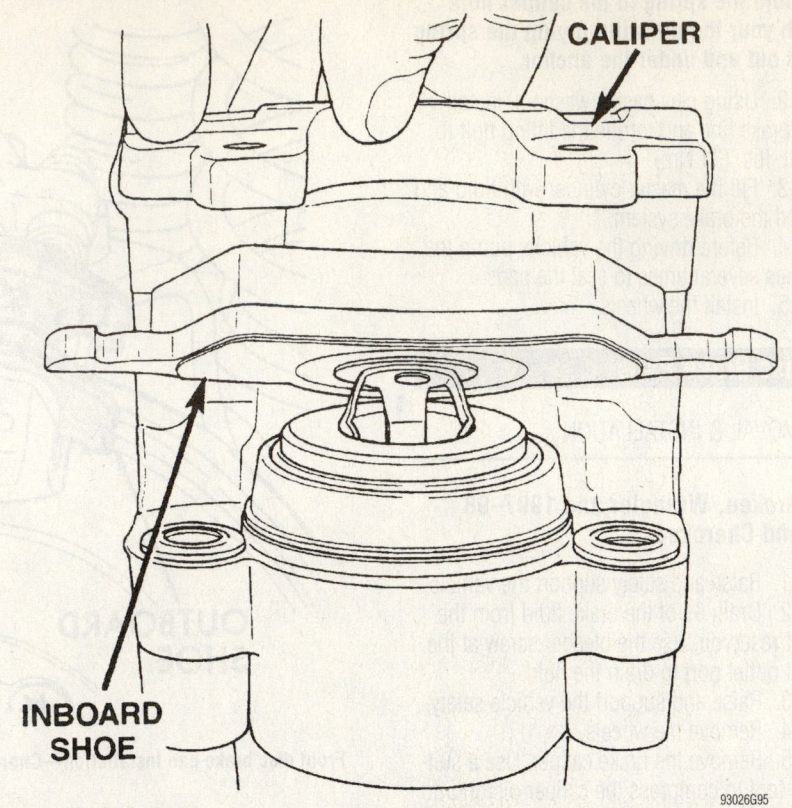

Installing the inward brake pad on the rear caliper piston—1999–01 Grand Cherokee

2. Raise and safely support the vehicle.
3. Remove the wheels.
4. Insert a small prybar through the caliper opening and pry the caliper (using the outboard brake pad) to bottom the piston in the caliper bore.

➡This will back the brake pads off of the rotor surface to facilitate the removal and installation of the caliper assembly.

5. Pry the caliper support spring out of the caliper.
6. Remove both caliper slide pin bushing caps and slide pins.
7. Lift the caliper from the anchor.
8. Using a piece of mechanics wire, support the caliper so there is not tension on the brake hose.
9. Remove the brake pads from the caliper.

To install:

10. Position the brake pads onto the caliper.
11. Position the caliper into place on the anchor.
12. Coat the caliper slide pins with silicone grease and torque them to 21–30 ft. lbs. (29–41 Nm). Install the slide pin bushing caps.
13. Install the caliper support spring in

the top of the caliper under the anchor; then, install the other end into the lower caliper hole.

➡Hold the spring in the caliper hole with your thumb while prying the spring end out and under the anchor.

14. Fill the master cylinder with fluid and bleed the brake system.
15. Before driving the vehicle, pump the brakes several times to seat the pads.
16. Install the wheels.

Brake Drum

REMOVAL & INSTALLATION

Cherokee and Wrangler

1. Raise and safely support the vehicle.
2. Remove the wheel.
3. Remove the spring nuts (if installed) from the lug bolts and remove the drum from the vehicle.

To install:

4. Ensure the contacting surfaces are clean and flat. Install the drum on the hub.
5. Adjust the brake shoes, if necessary.
6. Install the spring nuts on the lug bolts.
7. Install the wheel.

Brake Shoes

REMOVAL & INSTALLATION

Cherokee and Wrangler

1. Raise and safely support the vehicle.
2. Remove the wheel and brake drum.
3. Remove the U-clip and washer securing the adjuster cable to the parking brake lever.
4. Remove the primary and secondary return springs from the anchor pin.
5. Remove the hold-down springs, retainers and pins.
6. Install spring clamps on the wheel cylinders to hold the pistons in place.
7. Remove the adjuster lever, adjuster screw and spring.

8. Remove the adjuster cable and cable guide.
9. Remove the brake shoes and parking brake strut.
10. Disconnect the cable from the parking brake lever and remove the lever.

To install:

11. Clean the support plate with brake cleaner.
12. Apply multi-purpose grease to the brake shoe contact surfaces on the backing plate.
13. Lubricate the adjuster screw threads.
14. Attach the parking brake lever to the secondary brake shoe. Use a new washer and U-clip.
15. Remove the wheel cylinder clamps.
16. Attach the parking brake cable to the lever.

17. Install the brake shoes on the support plate. Secure the shoes with new hold-down springs, pins and retainers.
18. Install the parking brake strut and spring.
19. Install the guide plate and adjuster cable to the anchor pin.
20. Install the return springs.
21. Install the adjuster cable guide on the secondary shoe.
22. Install the adjuster screw, spring and lever. Connect to the adjuster cable.
23. Adjust the shoes to the drum. Install the drum.
24. Install the wheel/tire assemblies and lower the vehicle.
25. Verify a firm brake pedal before moving the vehicle.

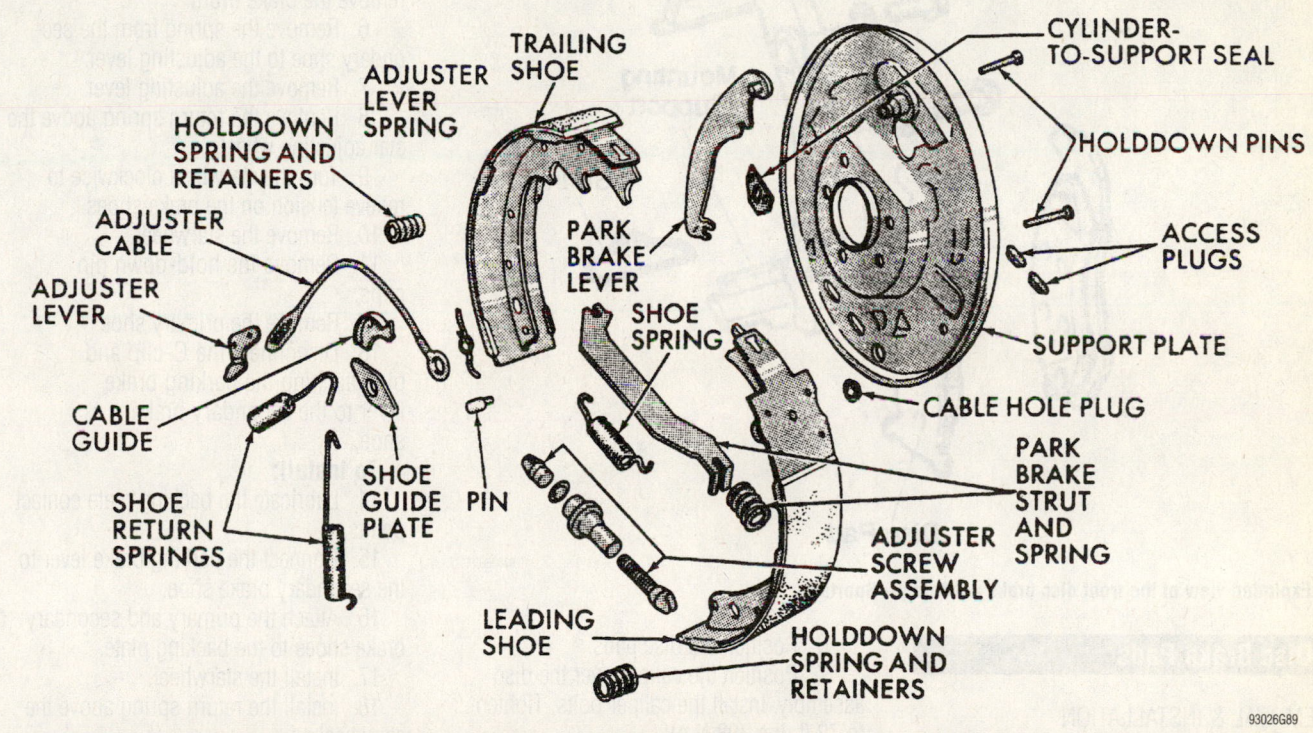

Exploded view of the rear drum brake components—Cherokee and Wrangler

93026G89

KIA

Brake Caliper

REMOVAL & INSTALLATION

Sportage

1. Raise and safely support the vehicle.
2. Remove the front wheels.
3. Remove the 2 caliper bolts and lift the caliper from the disc.
4. Disconnect the brake fluid flex line by removing the retaining bolt if the caliper is to be replaced.

To install:

5. Seat the caliper piston using a C-clamp.
6. Connect the brake fluid flex line bolt to the caliper. Tighten the bolt to 17 ft. lbs. (23.5 Nm).

7. Position the caliper over the disc assembly. Install the caliper bolts. Tighten to 72 ft. lbs. (98 Nm).
8. Install the front wheels. Tighten the lug nuts 77 ft. lbs. (99 Nm).
9. Bleed the hydraulic system if the flex hoses were removed.
10. Lower the vehicle.

For brake related suspension and axle service, refer to the model specific sections of this manual

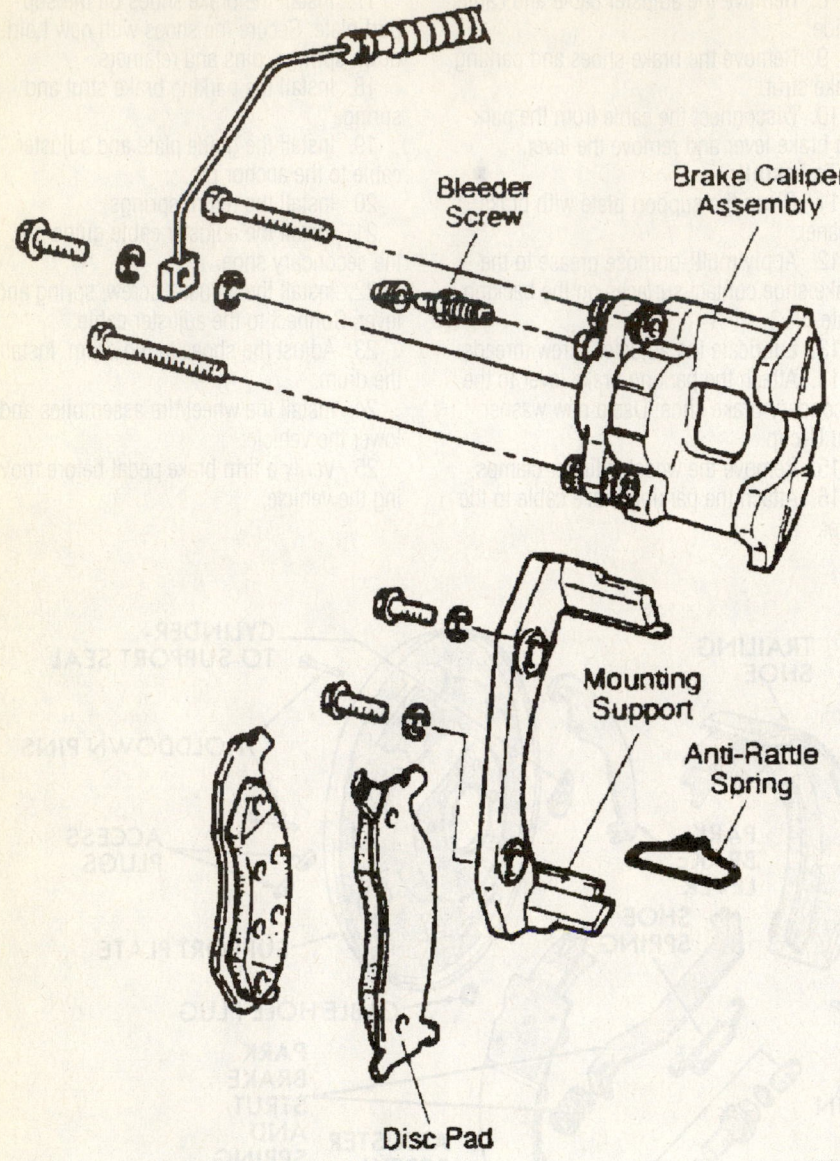

Bleeder Screw

Brake Caliper Assembly

Mounting Support

Anti-Rattle Spring

Disc Pad

93026G87

Exploded view of the front disc brake assembly—Sportage

Disc Brake Pads

REMOVAL & INSTALLATION

Sportage

1. Raise and safely support the vehicle.
2. Remove the front wheels.
3. Remove the 2 caliper bolts and lift the caliper from the disc.
4. Slide the disc pads off the caliper bracket.
   To install:
5. Clean the caliper bracket contact surface with a wire brush and lightly coat with assembly lube.

6. Position the disc pads.
7. Position the caliper over the disc assembly. Install the caliper bolts. Tighten to 72 ft. lbs. (98 Nm).
8. Install the front wheels. Tighten the lug nuts 77 ft. lbs. (99 Nm).
9. Bleed the hydraulic system if the flex hoses were removed.
10. Lower the vehicle.

Brake Drums

REMOVAL & INSTALLATION

Sportage

1. Raise and safely support the vehicle.

2. Remove the rear wheels.
3. Apply the parking brake.
4. Remove the 4 attaching nuts.
5. Release the parking brake and remove the brake drum.
   Installation is the reverse of the removal procedure.

Brake Shoes

REMOVAL & INSTALLATION

Sportage

1. Raise and safely support the vehicle.
2. Remove the rear wheels.
3. Apply the parking brake.
4. Remove the 4 attaching nuts.
5. Release the parking brake and remove the brake drum.
6. Remove the spring from the secondary shoe to the adjusting lever.
7. Remove the adjusting lever.
8. Remove the return spring above the star adjusting wheel.
9. Turn the starwheel clockwise to relieve tension on the brake shoes.
10. Remove the starwheel.
11. Remove the hold-down pin clips.
12. Remove the primary shoe.
13. Disconnect the C-clip and pin attaching the parking brake lever to the secondary brake shoe.
    To install:
14. Lubricate the backing plate contact points.
15. Connect the parking brake lever to the secondary brake shoe.
16. Attach the primary and secondary brake shoes to the backing plate.
17. Install the starwheel.
18. Install the return spring above the starwheel.
19. Install the adjusting lever.
20. Install the spring from the secondary shoe to the adjusting lever. Be sure the lever contacts the starwheel.
21. Install the brake drum and retaining nuts.
22. Adjust the rear brakes through the slot in the rear of the backing plate.
23. Install the wheels. Tighten the wheel lugs to 77 ft. lbs. (99 Nm).
24. Lower the vehicle.

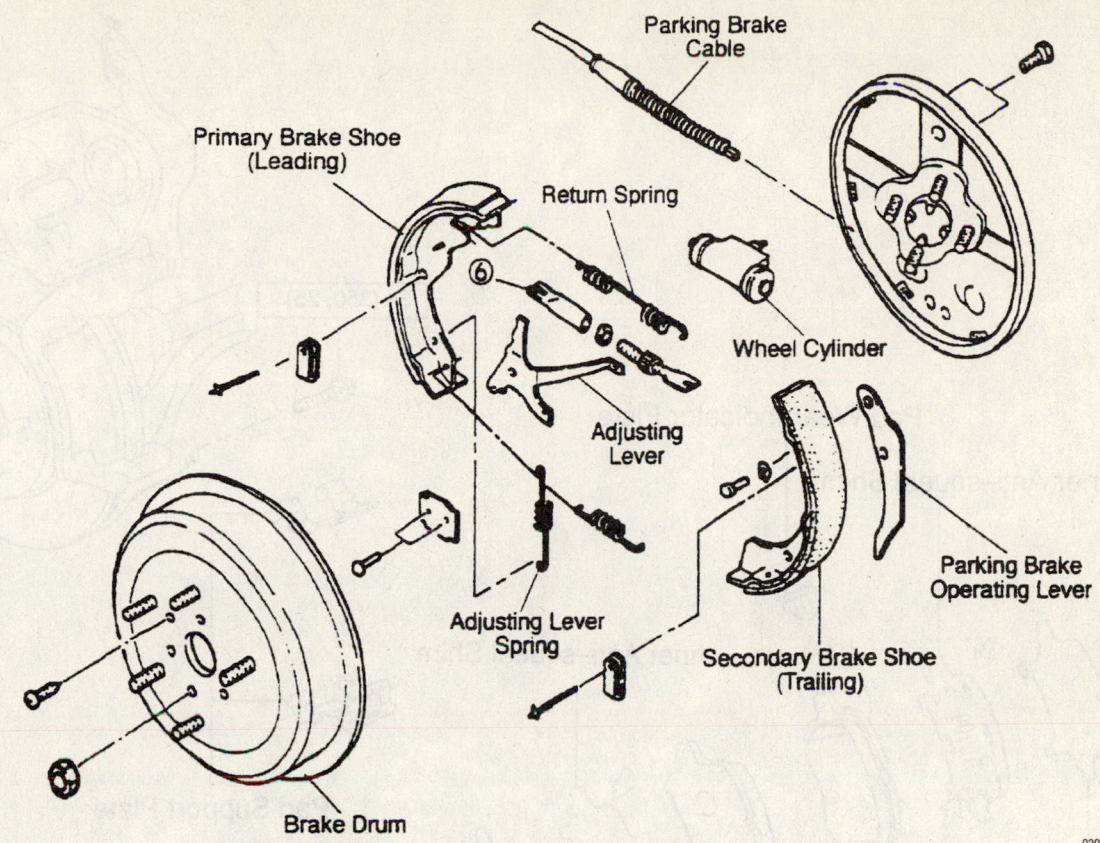

Exploded view of the rear drum brake assembly—Sportage

93026G88

LEXUS

Brake Caliper

REMOVAL & INSTALLATION

LX450, LX470

FRONT

1. Disconnect the negative battery cable from the battery.
2. Raise and support the vehicle safely.
3. Remove the wheels.
4. Disconnect the brake hose from the caliper by removing the union bolt and 2 gaskets. Plug the end of the hose to prevent loss of fluid.
5. Remove the bolts that attach the caliper to the torque plate.
6. Lift the bottom of the caliper up and remove the caliper assembly.

To install:

7. Grease the caliper slides and bolts with lithium grease or equivalent. Install the caliper and secure with the bolts. Torque the bolts to 90 ft. lbs. (123 Nm).

8. Connect the brake hose to the caliper, using 2 new washers. Make sure the flexible hose lock is securely in the lock hole of the caliper. Torque the union bolt to 22 ft. lbs. (30 Nm).
9. Fill the brake system to the proper level and bleed the brake system.
10. Install the tire and wheel assembly.
11. Top off the brake fluid level in the master cylinder. Check for leaks and proper brake operation.
12. Connect the negative battery cable to the battery.

REAR

1. Remove the brake line from the caliper.
2. Hold the siding pin and remove the 2 bolts.
3. Remove the caliper from the torque plate.
4. Remove the pads and shims.
5. Remove the pad support plates.
6. Installation is the reverse of removal. Torque the caliper bolts to 20 ft. lbs. (26 Nm). Torque the brake line union bolt to 22 ft. lbs. (30 Nm).

RX300

FRONT

1. Disconnect the negative battery cable from the battery.
2. Raise and support the vehicle safely.
3. Remove the wheels.
4. Disconnect the brake hose from the caliper by removing the union bolt and 2 gaskets. Plug the end of the hose to prevent loss of fluid.
5. Remove the caliper mounting bolts.
6. Remove the caliper, pads, shims and support plates.

To install:

7. Grease the caliper slides and bolts with lithium grease or equivalent. Install the support plates, shims, pads and caliper and secure with the bolts. Torque the bolts to 25 ft. lbs. (34 Nm).

8. Connect the brake hose to the caliper, using 2 new washers. Make sure the flexible hose lock is securely in the lock hole of the caliper. Torque the union bolt to 21 ft. lbs. (29 Nm).

For complete service labor times order Nichols' Chilton Labor Guide Manual

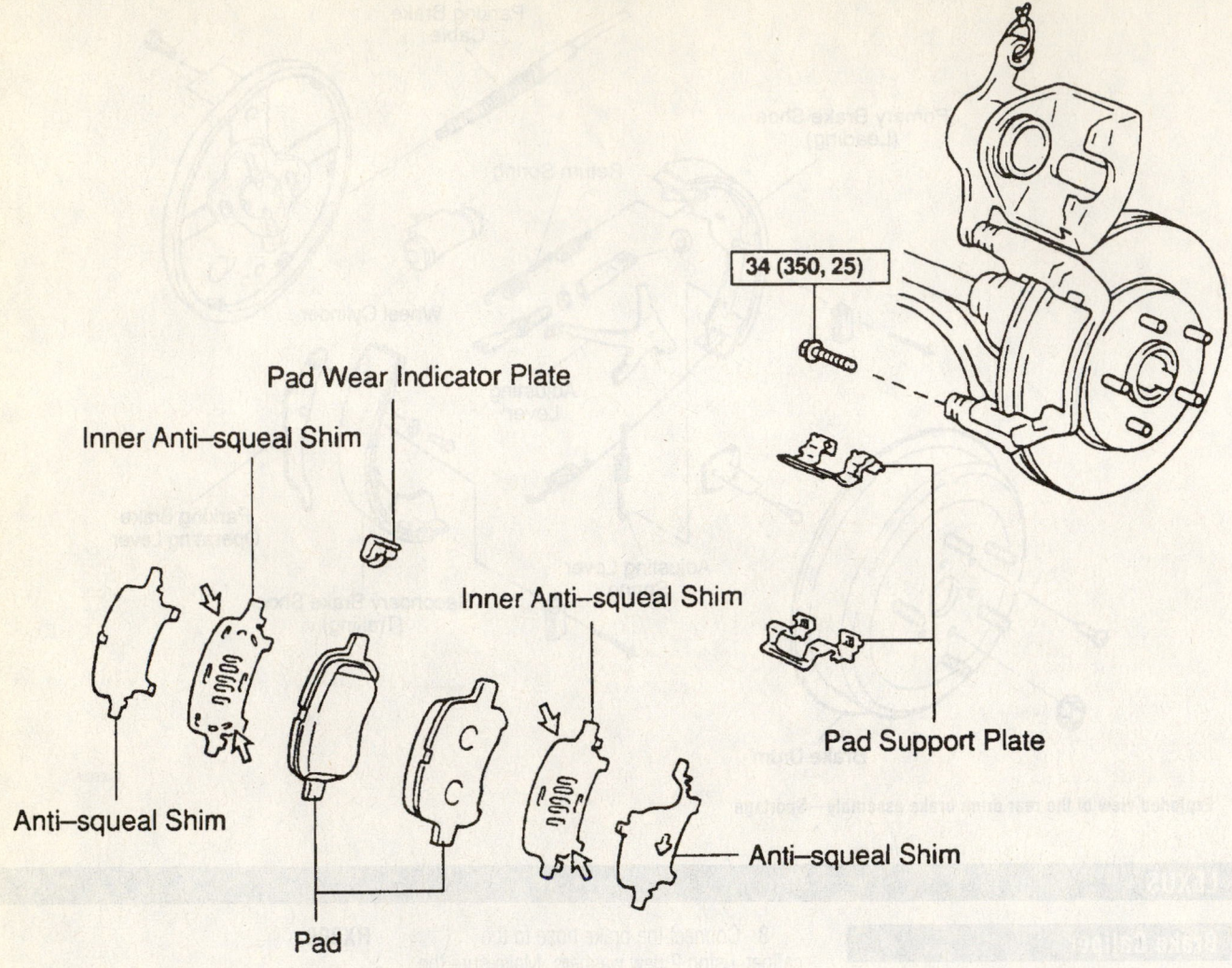

34 (350, 25)

Pad Wear Indicator Plate

Inner Anti–squeal Shim

Inner Anti–squeal Shim

Anti–squeal Shim

Pad Support Plate

Pad

Anti–squeal Shim

N·m (kgf·cm, ft·lbf) : Specified torque

◁ Disc brake grease

Exploded view of the front disc brake components—RX300

93026G86

9. Fill the brake system to the proper level and bleed the brake system.

10. Install the tire and wheel assembly.

11. Top off the brake fluid level in the master cylinder. Check for leaks and proper brake operation.

12. Connect the negative battery cable to the battery.

REAR

1. Disconnect the brake line from the caliper.

2. Remove the caliper mounting bolt.

3. Remove the caliper, pads, shims and support plates.

4. Remove the main pin.

5. Installation is the reverse of removal. Torque the main pin to 20 ft. lbs. (26 Nm),

the caliper bolt to 14 ft. lbs. (20 Nm), and the union bolt to 21 ft. lbs. (29 Nm).

Disc Brake Pads

REMOVAL & INSTALLATION

LX450, LX470

FRONT

1. Raise the vehicle and support it safely.

2. Remove the wheels.

3. Remove the clip, pins and anti-rattle spring.

4. Withdraw the pads and remove the anti-squeal shims.

To install:

5. Before installing the new pads, check the disc thickness and disc runout.

6. Siphon out a small amount of brake fluid from the reservoir.

7. Press in the pistons with a hammer handle or equivalent.

8. Apply disc brake grease to both sides of the inner anti-squeal shim. Install the anti-squeal shims to the new pads.

9. Install the pads.

10. Install the anti-rattle springs and pins. Install the clip.

11. Install the wheels.

12. Check and adjust the fluid level. Apply the brake pedal several times.

13. Road-test the vehicle for proper operation.

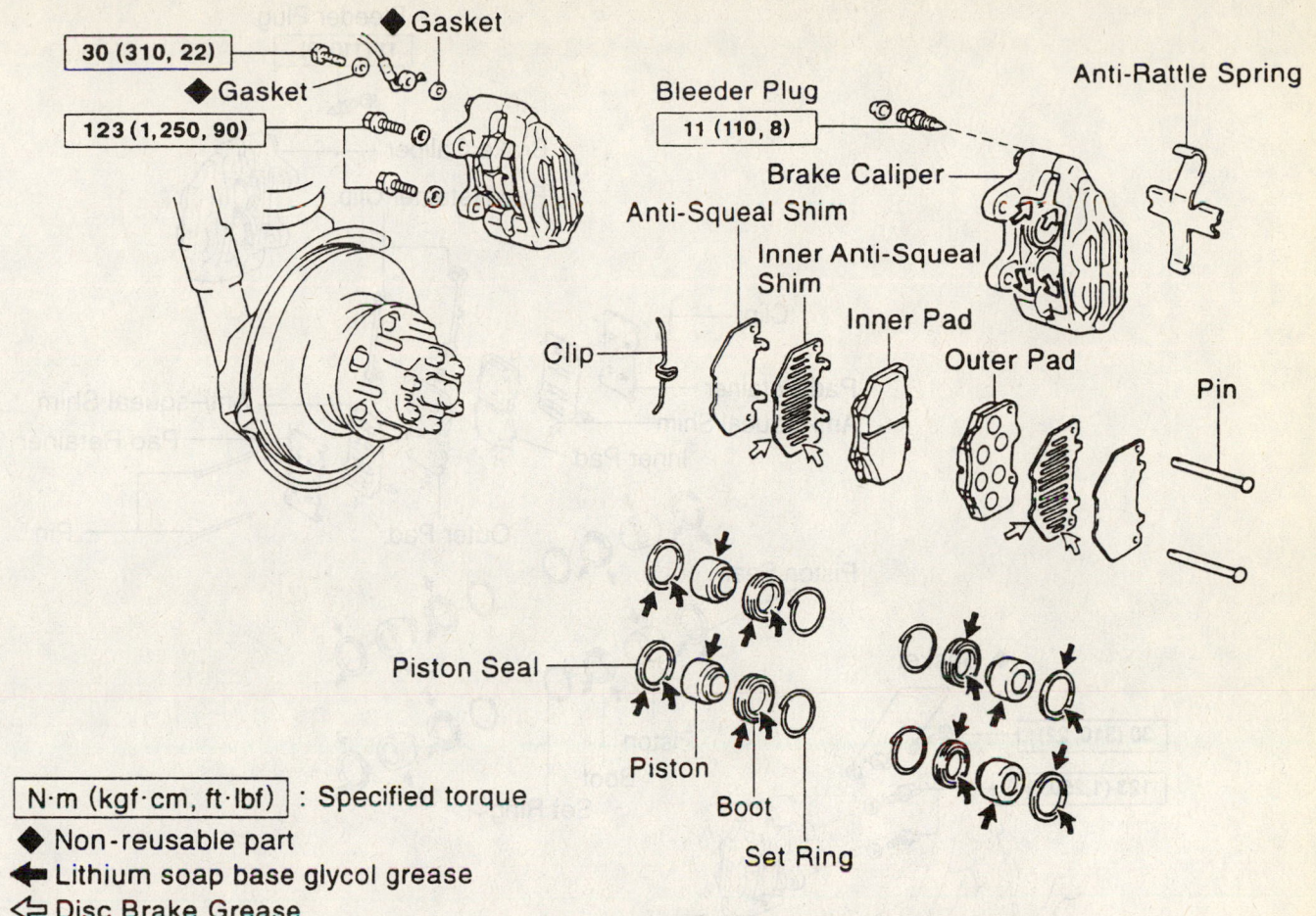

30 (310, 22)
◆ Gasket
◆ Gasket
123 (1,250, 90)

Gasket

Bleeder Plug
11 (110, 8)
Anti-Rattle Spring
Brake Caliper
Anti-Squeal Shim
Inner Anti-Squeal Shim
Inner Pad
Outer Pad
Clip
Pin

Piston Seal
Piston
Boot
Set Ring

N·m (kgf·cm, ft·lbf) : Specified torque
◆ Non-reusable part
◄ Lithium soap base glycol grease
⇐ Disc Brake Grease

93026G81

Exploded view of the front disc brake components—LX450

REAR

1. Raise the vehicle and support it safely.
2. Remove the wheels.
3. Remove the brake caliper and suspend it so the hose is not stretched.
4. Remove the brake pads, anti-squeal shim, pad support plates and wear indicators.

To install:
5. Before installing the new pads, check the disc thickness and disc runout.
6. Install the pad support plates.
7. Install the pad wear indicator plate to each pads.
8. Install the anti-squeal shim to the outer pad. Install the pads so the wear indicator plate is facing up-ward.
9. Install the brake caliper.

10. Install the wheels.
11. Apply the brake pedal several times.
12. Road-test the vehicle for proper operation.

RX300

FRONT

1. Hold the sliding pin and remove the lower bolt.
2. Lift the caliper up and secure it.
3. Remove the pads, 4 shims and wear indicator plate. Remove the 2 pad support plates.

➡ **The support plates can be reused, provided they have sufficient rebound, are not deformed or cracked, show no signs of wear and are cleaned of all rust and debris.**

To install:

➡ **Always use new shims and wear indicators, even when re-installing the original pads.**

4. Install a wear indicator plate on the inner pad.
5. Apply disc brake grease to both sides of the inner anti-squeal shims and install the shims.
6. Install the inner pad with the wear indicator plate facing upwards.
7. Install the outer pad.
8. Install the caliper. Torque the bolt to 25 ft. lbs.

REAR

1. On 2WD, unbolt the brake hose from the shock absorber.
2. Remove the caliper installation bolt from the torque plate.

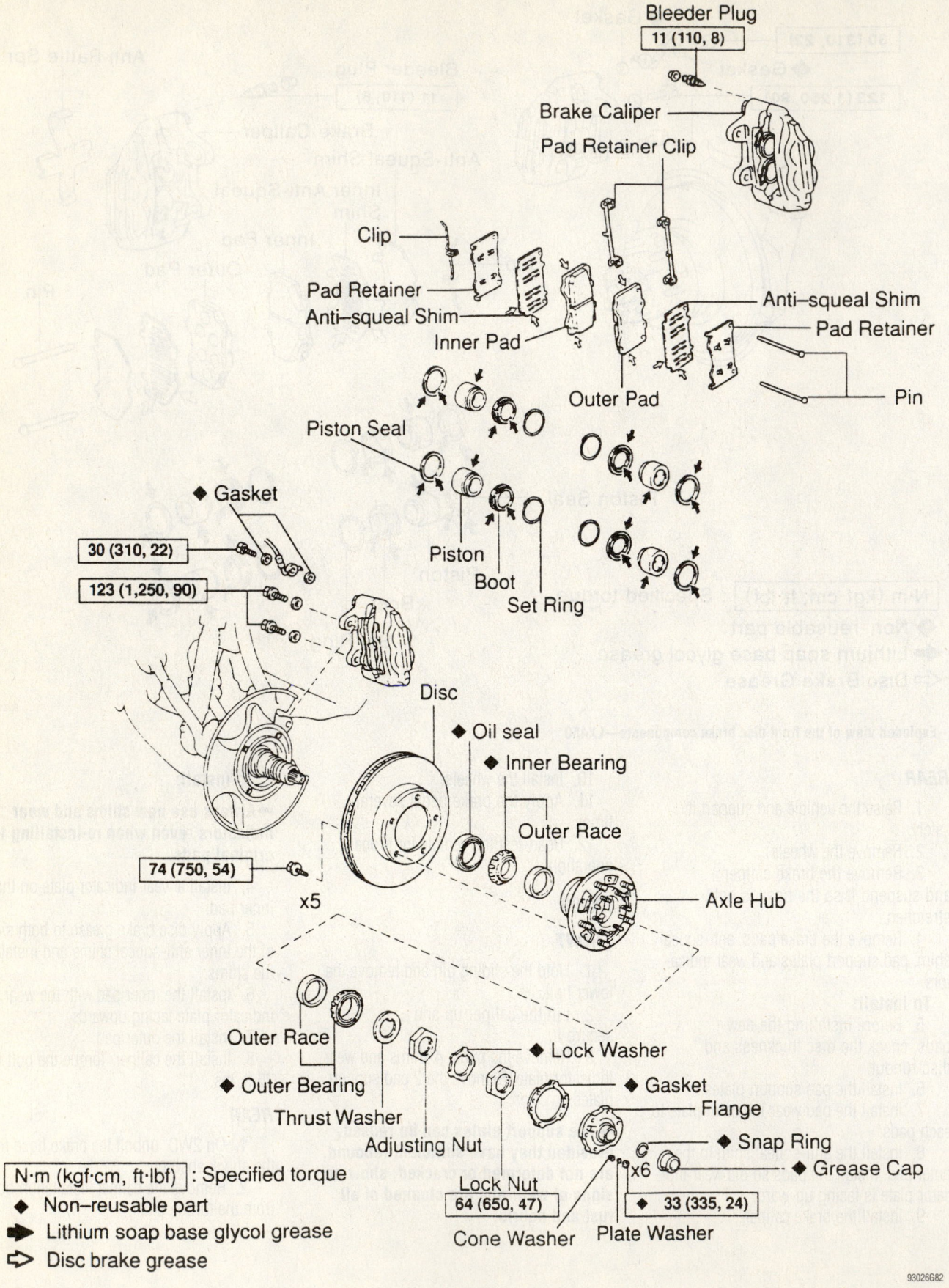

Bleeder Plug
11 (110, 8)

Brake Caliper

Pad Retainer Clip

Clip

Pad Retainer

Anti–squeal Shim

Inner Pad

Anti–squeal Shim

Pad Retainer

Outer Pad

Pin

Piston Seal

Piston

Boot

Set Ring

Gasket

30 (310, 22)

123 (1,250, 90)

Disc

Oil seal

Inner Bearing

Outer Race

Axle Hub

74 (750, 54)

x5

Outer Race

Outer Bearing

Thrust Washer

Adjusting Nut

Lock Washer

Gasket

Flange

Snap Ring

x6

Grease Cap

Lock Nut
64 (650, 47)

Cone Washer

Plate Washer

33 (335, 24)

N·m (kgf·cm, ft·lbf) : Specified torque

◆ Non–reusable part

➤ Lithium soap base glycol grease

⇨ Disc brake grease

Exploded view of the front disc brake components—LX470

93026G82

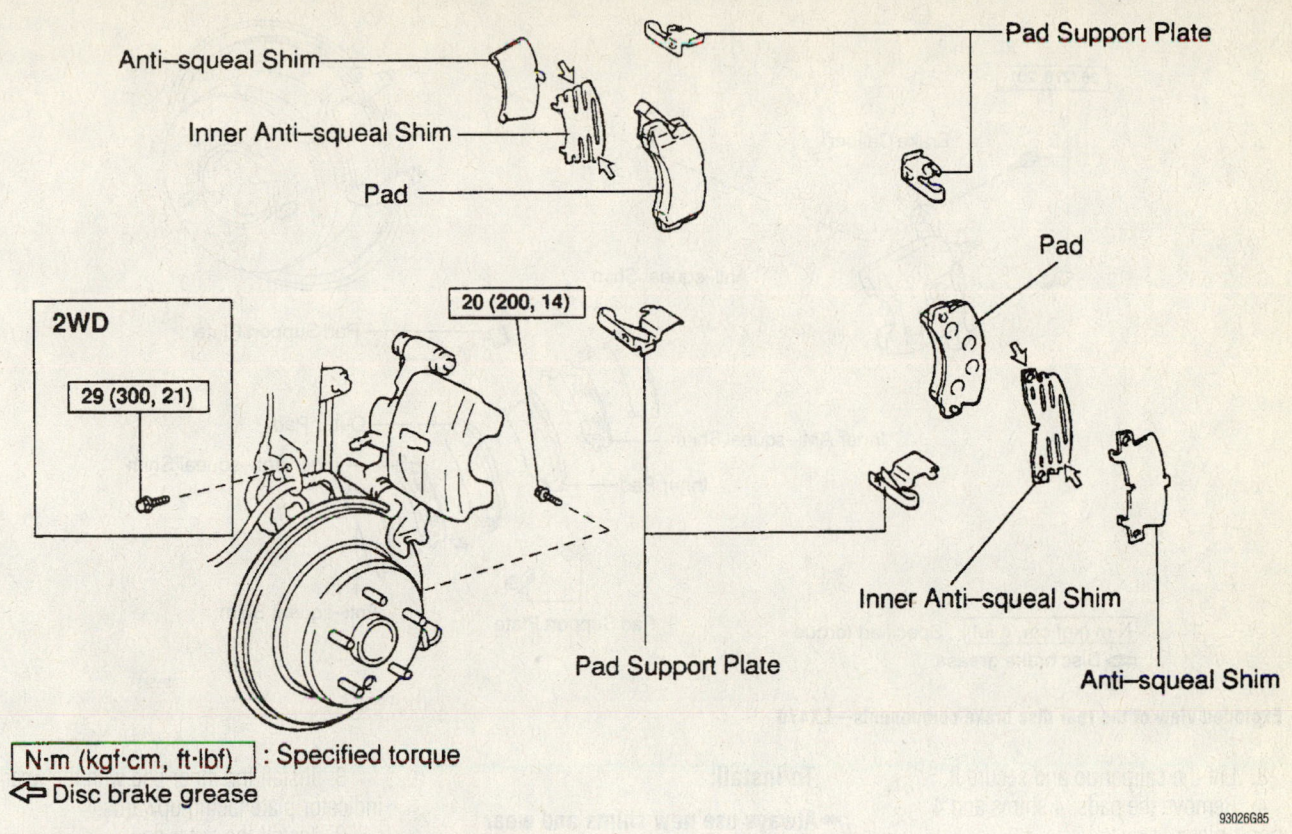

Anti–squeal Shim

Inner Anti–squeal Shim

Pad

Pad Support Plate

Pad

Inner Anti–squeal Shim

Anti–squeal Shim

2WD

29 (300, 21)

20 (200, 14)

Pad Support Plate

N·m (kgf·cm, ft·lbf) : Specified torque

⟸ Disc brake grease

93026G85

Exploded view of the rear disc brake components—RX300

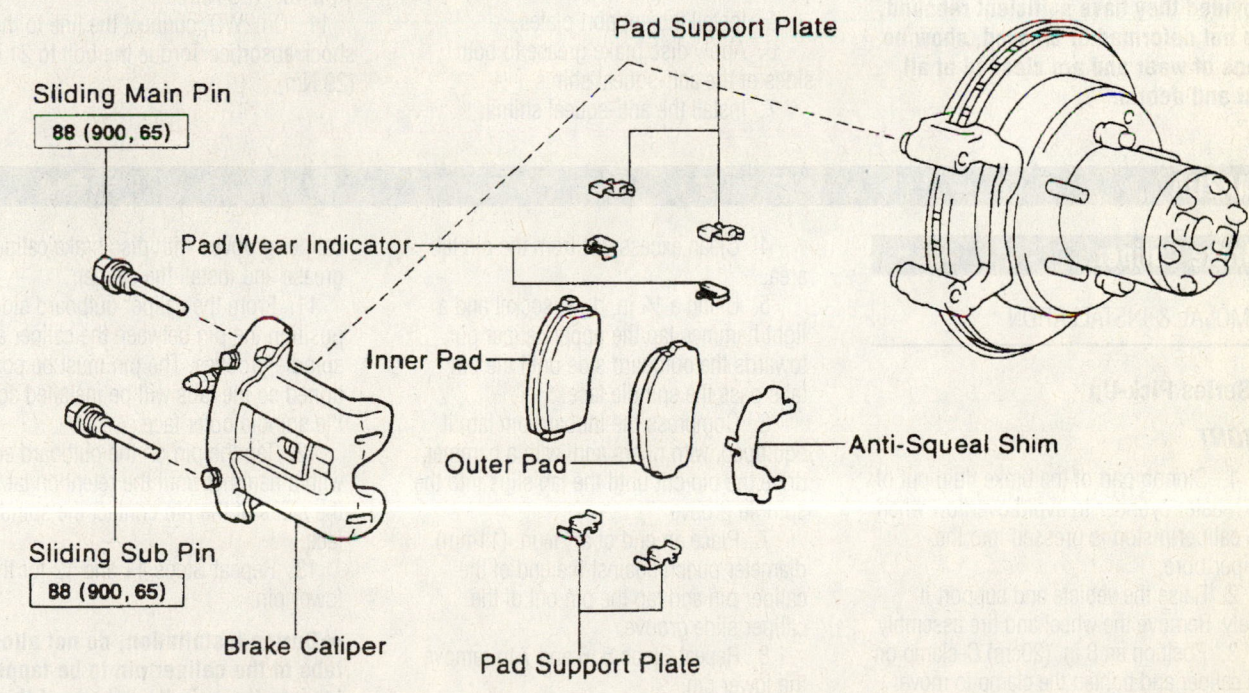

Pad Support Plate

Sliding Main Pin

88 (900, 65)

Pad Wear Indicator

Inner Pad

Outer Pad

Anti-Squeal Shim

Sliding Sub Pin

88 (900, 65)

Brake Caliper

Pad Support Plate

N·m (kgf·cm, ft·lbf) : Specified torque

93026G84

Exploded view of the rear disc brake components—LX450

For brake related suspension and axle service, refer to the model specific sections of this manual

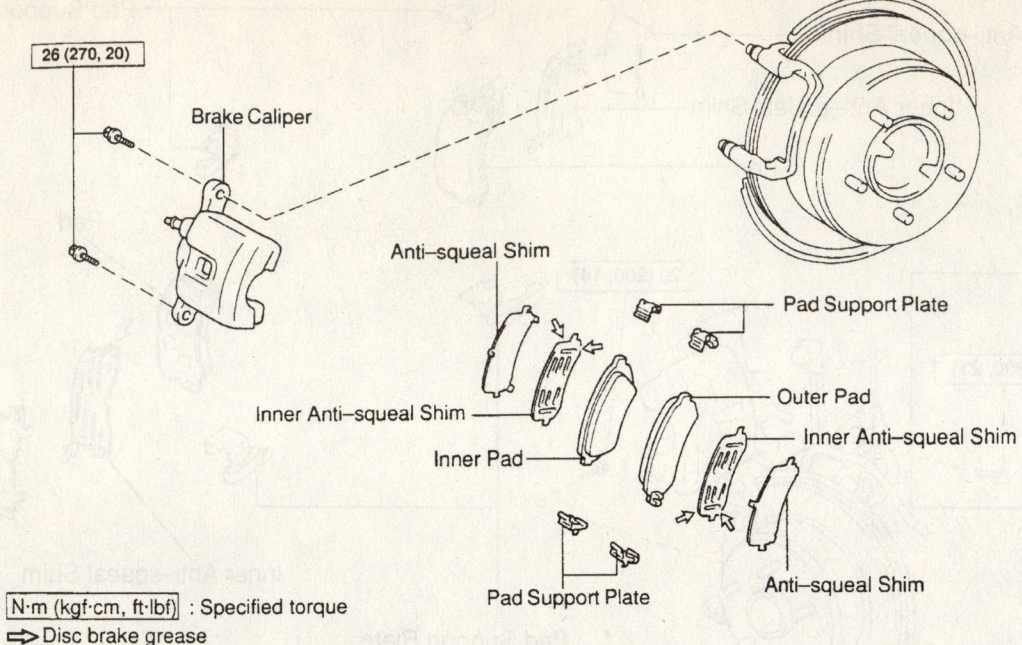

26 (270, 20)

Brake Caliper

Anti-squeal Shim

Pad Support Plate

Inner Anti-squeal Shim

Inner Pad

Outer Pad

Inner Anti-squeal Shim

Pad Support Plate

Anti-squeal Shim

N·m (kgf·cm, ft·lbf) : Specified torque
⇨ Disc brake grease

93026G83

Exploded view of the rear disc brake components—LX470

3. Lift the caliper up and secure it.

4. Remove the pads, 4 shims and 4 support plates.

➡**The support plates can be reused, provided they have sufficient rebound, are not deformed or cracked, show no signs of wear and are cleaned of all rust and debris.**

To install:

➡**Always use new shims and wear indicators, even when re-installing the original pads.**

5. Install the support plates.

6. Apply disc brake grease to both sides of the anti-squeal shims.

7. Install the anti-squeal shims.

8. Install the inner pad with the wear indicator plate facing upwards.

9. Install the outer pad.

10. Install the caliper. Torque the bolt to 14 ft. lbs. (20 Nm).

11. On 2WD, connect the line to the shock absorber. Torque the bolt to 21 ft. lbs. (29 Nm).

MAZDA

Brake Caliper

REMOVAL & INSTALLATION

B-Series Pick-Up

FRONT

1. Siphon part of the brake fluid out of the master cylinder to avoid overflow when the caliper piston is pressed into the caliper bore.

2. Raise the vehicle and support it safely. Remove the wheel and tire assembly.

3. Position an 8 in. (20cm) C-clamp on the caliper and tighten the clamp to move the caliper piston into the bore approximately 1/8 in. (3mm). Avoid clamp contact with the outer shoe spring clip. Remove the clamp.

➡**Do not pry the piston away from the rotor.**

4. Clean excess dirt from the pin tab area.

5. Using a 1/4 in. drive socket and a light hammer, tap the upper caliper pin towards the outboard side until the pin tabs pass the spindle face.

6. Compress the inboard pin tab, if equipped, with pliers and, with a hammer, drive the pin out until the tab slips into the spindle groove.

7. Place an end of a 7/16 in. (11mm) diameter punch against the end of the caliper pin and tap the pin out of the caliper slide groove.

8. Repeat Steps 5, 6 and 7 to remove the lower pin.

9. Disconnect and plug the brake hose at the caliper. Remove the caliper from the rotor.

To install:

10. Make sure the caliper mounting surfaces are free of dirt. Lubricate the caliper grooves with disc brake caliper grease and install the caliper.

11. From the caliper outboard side, position the pin between the caliper and spindle grooves. The pin must be positioned so the tabs will be installed against the spindle outer face.

12. Tap the pin on the outboard end with a hammer until the retention tabs on the sides of the pin contact the spindle face.

13. Repeat Steps 11 and 12 for the lower pin.

➡**During installation, do not allow the tabs of the caliper pin to be tapped too far into the spindle groove. If this happens, it will be necessary to tap the other end of the caliper pin until the tabs snap in place. The tabs on each end of the pin must be free to catch on the spindle face.**

14. Connect the brake hose to the caliper. Bleed the brake system.

15. Install the wheel and tire assembly and lower the vehicle. Check the brake fluid level and check the brakes for proper operation.

REAR

1. Siphon part of the brake fluid out of the master cylinder to avoid overflow when the caliper piston is pressed into the caliper bore.

2. Raise the vehicle and support it safely. Remove the wheel and tire assembly.

3. Position an 8 in. (20cm) C-clamp on the caliper and tighten the clamp to move the caliper piston into the bore approximately ⅛ in. (3mm). Remove the clamp.

➡ **Do not pry the piston away from the rotor.**

4. Clean excess dirt from the retainer bolt area.

5. Using a Torx® socket, remove the 2 retainer bolts securing the caliper to the bracket and adapter plate.

6. Disconnect and plug the brake hose at the caliper. Remove the caliper from the rotor.

To install:

7. Make sure the caliper mounting surfaces are free of dirt. Lubricate the caliper grooves with disc brake caliper grease and install the caliper.

8. Position the caliper to the bracket and secure in place with the retainer bolts. Tighten the bolts to 20 ft. lbs. (27 Nm)

9. Install the caliper brake hose using new washers. Tighten the bolt to 29 ft. lbs. (40 Nm)

10. Fill and bleed the brake system.

11. Install the wheel and tire assembly and lower the vehicle. Check the brake fluid level and check the brakes for proper operation.

MPV

FRONT OR REAR

1. Raise and safely support the vehicle. Remove the wheel and tire assembly.

2. Remove the banjo bolt and disconnect the brake hose from the caliper. Plug the hose to prevent fluid leakage.

3. Remove the caliper mounting bolt and pivot the caliper about the mounting pin and off the brake rotor. Remove the caliper from the pin.

4. Installation is the reverse of the removal procedure. Lubricate the caliper mounting bolts or bolt and pin prior to installation.

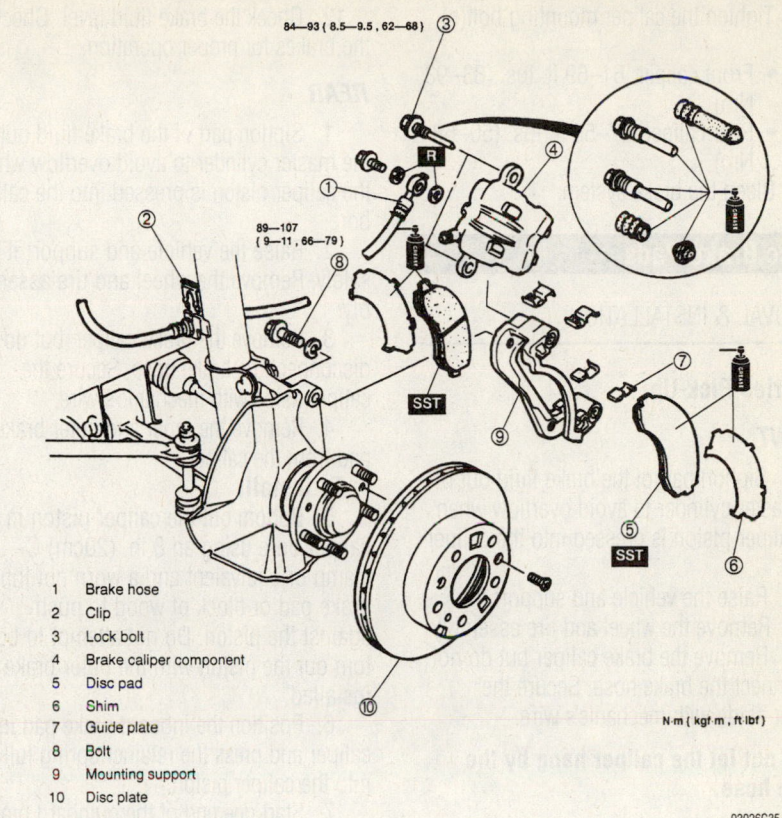

84—93 (8.5—9.5 , 62—68)

89—107 (9—11 , 66—79)

1	Brake hose
2	Clip
3	Lock bolt
4	Brake caliper component
5	Disc pad
6	Shim
7	Guide plate
8	Bolt
9	Mounting support
10	Disc plate

N·m (kgf·m , ft·lbf)

Front disc brake assembly—MPV

93026G35

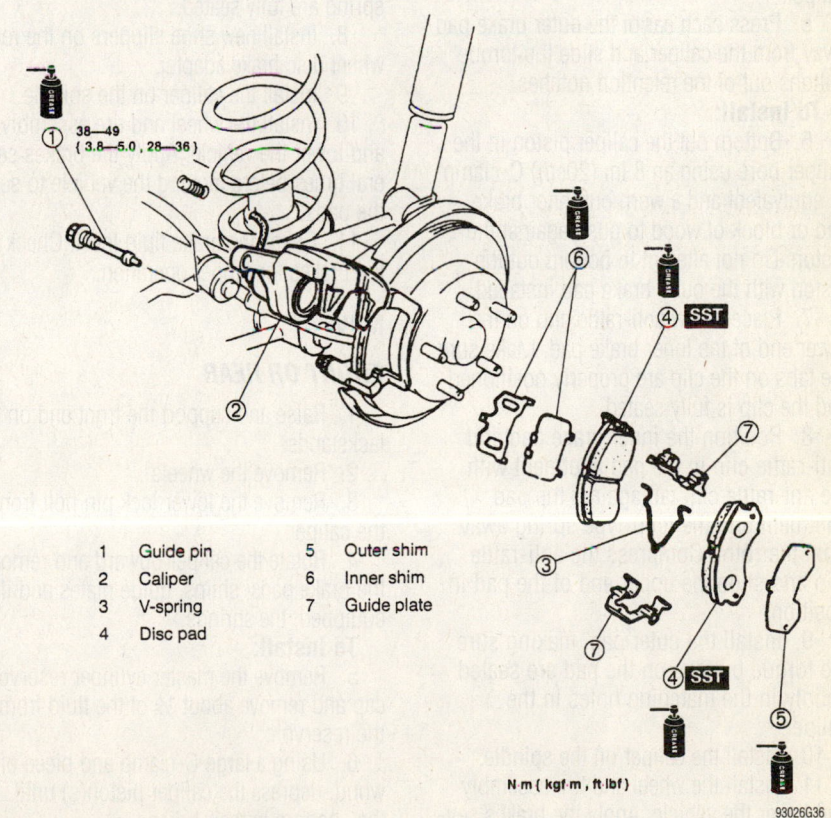

38—49 (3.8—5.0 , 28—36)

1	Guide pin	5	Outer shim
2	Caliper	6	Inner shim
3	V-spring	7	Guide plate
4	Disc pad		

N·m (kgf·m , ft·lbf)

Rear disc brake assembly—MPV

93026G36

5. Tighten the caliper mounting bolt(s) to:

- Front caliper: 61–69 ft. lbs. (83–93 Nm)
- Rear caliper: 37–50 ft. lbs. (50–68 Nm)

6. Bleed the brake system.

Disc Brake Pads

REMOVAL & INSTALLATION

B-Series Pick-Up

FRONT

1. Siphon part of the brake fluid out of the master cylinder to avoid overflow when the caliper piston is pressed into the caliper bore.
2. Raise the vehicle and support it safely. Remove the wheel and tire assembly.
3. Remove the brake caliper but do not disconnect the brake hose. Secure the caliper aside with mechanic's wire.

➡ **Do not let the caliper hang by the brake hose.**

4. Compress the anti-rattle clip and remove the inner brake pad from the caliper.
5. Press each ear of the outer brake pad away from the caliper and slide the torque buttons out of the retention notches.

To install:

6. Bottom out the caliper piston in the caliper bore using an 8 in. (20cm) C-clamp or equivalent and a worn out inner brake pad or block of wood to push against the piston. Do not attempt to bottom out the piston with the outer brake pad installed.
7. Place a new anti-rattle clip on the lower end of the inner brake pad. Make sure the tabs on the clip are properly positioned and the clip is fully seated.
8. Position the inner brake pad and anti-rattle clip in the pad abutment with the ant-rattle clip tab against the pad abutment and the loop-type spring away from the rotor. Compress the anti-rattle clip and slide the upper end of the pad in position.
9. Install the outer pad, making sure the torque buttons on the pad are seated solidly in the matching holes in the caliper.
10. Install the caliper on the spindle.
11. Install the wheel and tire assembly and lower the vehicle. Apply the brakes several times before moving the vehicle to seat the pads.

12. Check the brake fluid level. Check the brakes for proper operation.

REAR

1. Siphon part of the brake fluid out of the master cylinder to avoid overflow when the caliper piston is pressed into the caliper bore.
2. Raise the vehicle and support it safely. Remove the wheel and tire assembly.
3. Remove the brake caliper, but do not disconnect the brake hose. Secure the caliper aside with mechanic's wire.
4. Remove the inner and outer brake pad from the caliper.

To install:

5. Bottom out the caliper piston in the caliper bore using an 8 in. (20cm) C-clamp or equivalent and a worn out inner brake pad or block of wood to push against the piston. Do not attempt to bottom out the piston with the outer brake pad installed.
6. Position the inboard brake pad in the caliper and press the retainer spring fully into the caliper piston.
7. Start one end of the outboard brake shoe and lining on the caliper and rotate it down until the locating lugs and the retainer spring are fully seated.
8. Install new shoe slippers on the rear wheel disc brake adapter.
9. Install the caliper on the spindle.
10. Install the wheel and tire assembly and lower the vehicle. Apply the brakes several times before moving the vehicle to seat the pads.
11. Check the brake fluid level. Check the brakes for proper operation.

MPV

FRONT OR REAR

1. Raise and support the front end on jackstands.
2. Remove the wheels.
3. Remove the lower lock pin bolt from the caliper.
4. Rotate the caliper upward and remove the brake pads, shims, guide plates and if equipped, the springs.

To install:

5. Remove the master cylinder reservoir cap and remove about ½ of the fluid from the reservoir.
6. Using a large C-clamp and piece of wood, depress the caliper piston(s) until they bottom in their bores.
7. Install the shims, guide plates, new pads and if removed, the springs.

8. Reposition the caliper and install the lock pin bolt. Torque the lockbolt to:

- Front caliper: 62–68 ft. lbs. (84–93 Nm)
- Rear caliper: 28–36 ft. lbs. (38–49 Nm)

9. Install the wheels, lower the vehicle, refill the master cylinder and depress the brake pedal a few times to restore pressure. Bleed the system if required.

Brake Drum

REMOVAL & INSTALLATION

B-Series Pick-Up

1. Raise and safely support the vehicle. Remove the wheel and tire assembly.
2. Remove the retaining nuts, if equipped, and remove the brake drum.
3. Inspect the brake drum surface for wear, scoring and runout. Machine or replace, as necessary.

To install:

4. Install the brake drum and secure in place with the retainer nuts, if equipped.
5. Adjust the rear brakes.
6. Install the wheel. Lower the vehicle.

Brake Shoes

REMOVAL & INSTALLATION

B-Series Pick-Up

1. Raise and safely support the vehicle. Remove the wheel and tire assembly and the brake drum.
2. Pull backward on the adjusting lever cable to disengage the adjusting lever from the adjusting screw. Move the outboard side of the adjusting screw upward and back off the pivot nut as far as it will go.
3. Pull the adjusting lever, cable and automatic adjuster spring down and toward the rear to unhook the pivot hook from the large hole in the secondary shoe web. Do not pry the pivot hook from the hole.
4. Remove the automatic adjuster spring and adjusting lever.
5. Remove the secondary shoe-to-anchor spring using a suitable brake spring removal/installation tool. Using the tool, remove the primary shoe-to-anchor spring and unhook the cable anchor. Remove the anchor pin plate, if equipped.
6. Remove the cable guide from the secondary shoe.
7. Remove the shoe hold-down

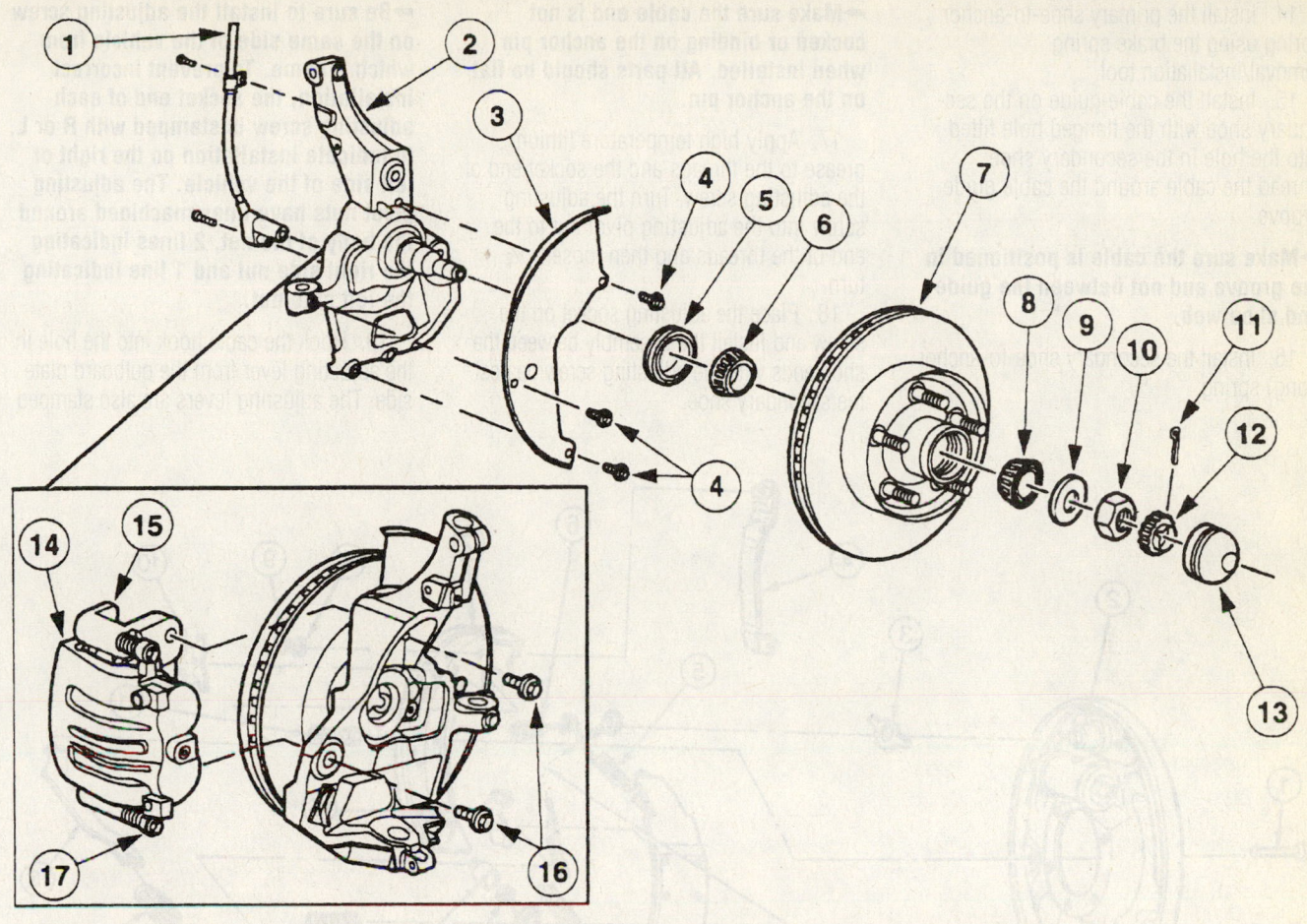

1   Front Brake Anti-Lock Sensor

2   Front Wheel Spindle

3   Front Disc Brake Rotor Shield

4   Rotor Shield Bolt

5   Grease Seal

6   Front Wheel Bearing

7   Front Disc Brake Hub and Rotor

8   Front Wheel Bearing

9   Front Wheel Outer Bearing Retainer Washer

10 Hub Spindle Nut

11 Cotter Pin

12 Nut Retainer

13 Hub Grease Cap

14 Disc Brake Caliper

15 Front Disc Brake Caliper Anchor Plate

16 Caliper Anchor Plate Bolts

17 Disc Brake Caliper Bolt

93026G22

Exploded view of the front disc brake assembly—1998–01 B-Series Pick-Up—1997 B-Series Pick-Up Similar

springs, shoes, adjusting screw, pivot nut and socket. Note the color and position of each hold-down spring so they can be reassembled in the same position.

8. Remove the parking brake link and spring. Disconnect the parking brake cable from the parking brake lever.

9. Remove the secondary brake shoe. On 9 in. (22.8cm) rear brakes, remove the parking brake lever from the shoe. On 10 in. (25.4cm) rear brakes, remove the retainer

clip and spring washer and remove the parking brake lever.

To install:

10. Clean the backing plate ledge pads and sand lightly. Apply a light coating of high temperature lithium grease to the points where the brake shoes touch the backing plate. Lubricate the adjusting cable eye and the anchor pin area.

11. Install the parking brake lever on the secondary shoe. On 10 in. (25.4cm) brakes,

secure with the spring washer and retaining clip.

12. Position the brake shoes on the backing plate and install the hold-down spring pins, springs and cups. Install the parking brake link, spring and washer. Connect the parking brake cable to the parking brake lever.

13. Install the anchor pin plate, if equipped, and place the cable anchor over the anchor pin with the crimped side toward the backing plate.

14. Install the primary shoe-to-anchor spring using the brake spring removal/installation tool.

15. Install the cable guide on the secondary shoe with the flanged hole fitted into the hole in the secondary shoe. Thread the cable around the cable guide groove.

➡**Make sure the cable is positioned in the groove and not between the guide and shoe web.**

16. Install the secondary shoe-to-anchor (long) spring.

➡**Make sure the cable end is not cocked or binding on the anchor pin when installed. All parts should be flat on the anchor pin.**

17. Apply high temperature lithium grease to the threads and the socket end of the adjusting screw. Turn the adjusting screw into the adjusting pivot nut to the end of the threads and then loosen, ½ turn.

18. Place the adjusting socket on the screw and install the assembly between the shoe ends with the adjusting screw nearest the secondary shoe.

➡**Be sure to install the adjusting screw on the same side of the vehicle from which it came. To prevent incorrect installation, the socket end of each adjusting screw is stamped with R or L, to indicate installation on the right or left side of the vehicle. The adjusting pivot nuts have lines machined around the body of the nut, 2 lines indicating the right side nut and 1 line indicating the left side nut.**

19. Hook the cable hook into the hole in the adjusting lever from the outboard plate side. The adjusting levers are also stamped

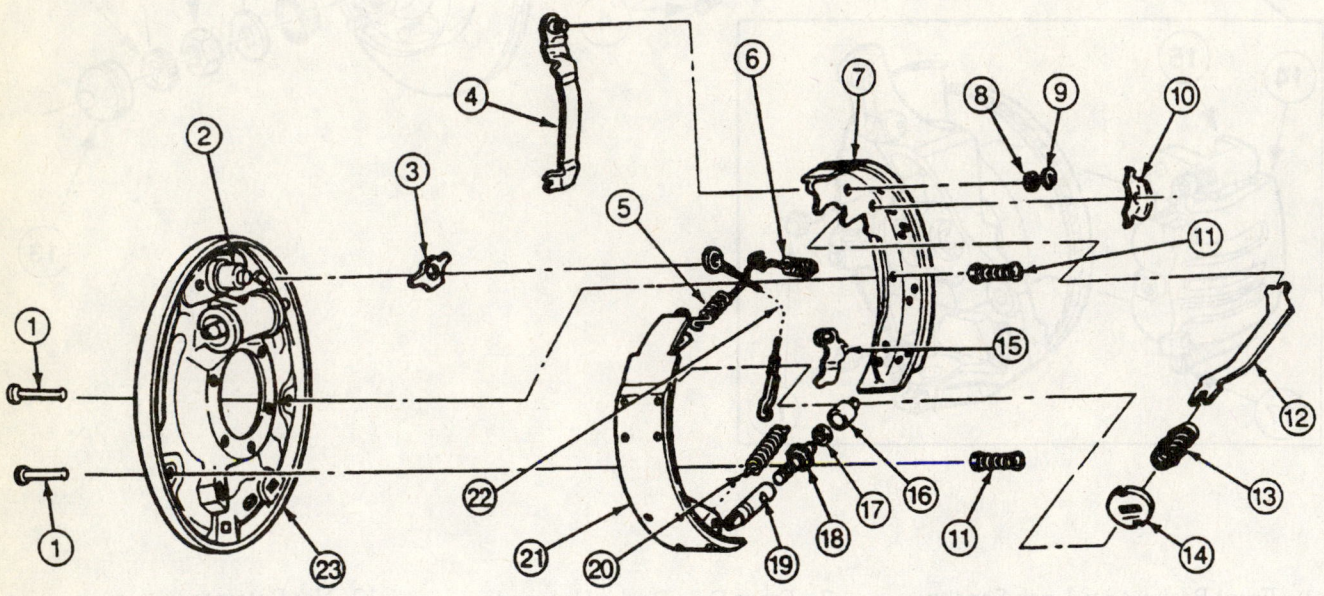

1 Brake Shoe Hold-Down Spring Pin	**12** Primary Brake Shoe Parking Brake Lever Link
2 Anchor Pin	**13** Parking Brake Link Spring
3 Brake Shoe Anchor Pin Guide Plate	**14** Parking Brake Spring Retainer
4 Parking Brake Lever	**15** Brake Shoe Adjusting Lever
5 Brake Shoe Retracting Spring (Short)	**16** Brake Shoe Adjusting Screw Socket
6 Brake Shoe Retracting Spring (Long)	**17** Thrust Washer
7 Rear Brake Shoe and Lining (Secondary)	**18** Brake Adjuster Screw
8 Washer	**19** Brake Shoe Adjusting Screw Nut
9 Parking Brake Lever Pin Retainer	**20** Brake Shoe Adjusting Screw Spring
10 Cable Guide	**21** Rear Brake Shoe and Lining (Primary)
11 Brake Shoe Hold-Down Spring	**22** Brake Shoe Adjusting Lever Cable
	23 Brake Backing Plate

93026G20

Exploded view of the rear brake shoes and components—1997 B-Series Pick-Up

with an R or L to indicate right or left side installation.

20. Place the hooked end of the adjuster spring in the large hole in the primary shoe web and connect the loop end of the spring to the adjuster lever hole.

21. Pull the adjuster lever, cable and automatic adjuster spring down toward the rear to engage the pivot hook in the large hole in the secondary shoe web.

22. After installation, check the action of the adjuster by pulling the section of the cable between the cable guide and the

adjusting lever toward the secondary shoe web far enough to lift the lever past a tooth on the adjusting screw wheel. The lever should snap into position behind the next tooth and releasing the cable should cause the adjuster spring to return the lever to its original position. This return action will turn the adjusting screw 1 tooth.

23. If pulling the cable does not produce the action described previously, or if lever action is sluggish instead of positive and sharp, check the position of the lever on the adjusting screw toothed wheel. With the

brake in a vertical position, anchor at the top, the lever should contact the adjusting wheel 1 tooth above the centerline of the adjusting screw. If the contact point is below the centerline, the lever will not lock on the adjusting screw wheel teeth and the screw will not turn, since the lever is actuated by the cable.

24. Adjust the brake shoes using either a brake adjustment gauge or manually with the drums installed.

25. Install the wheels, and lower the vehicle.

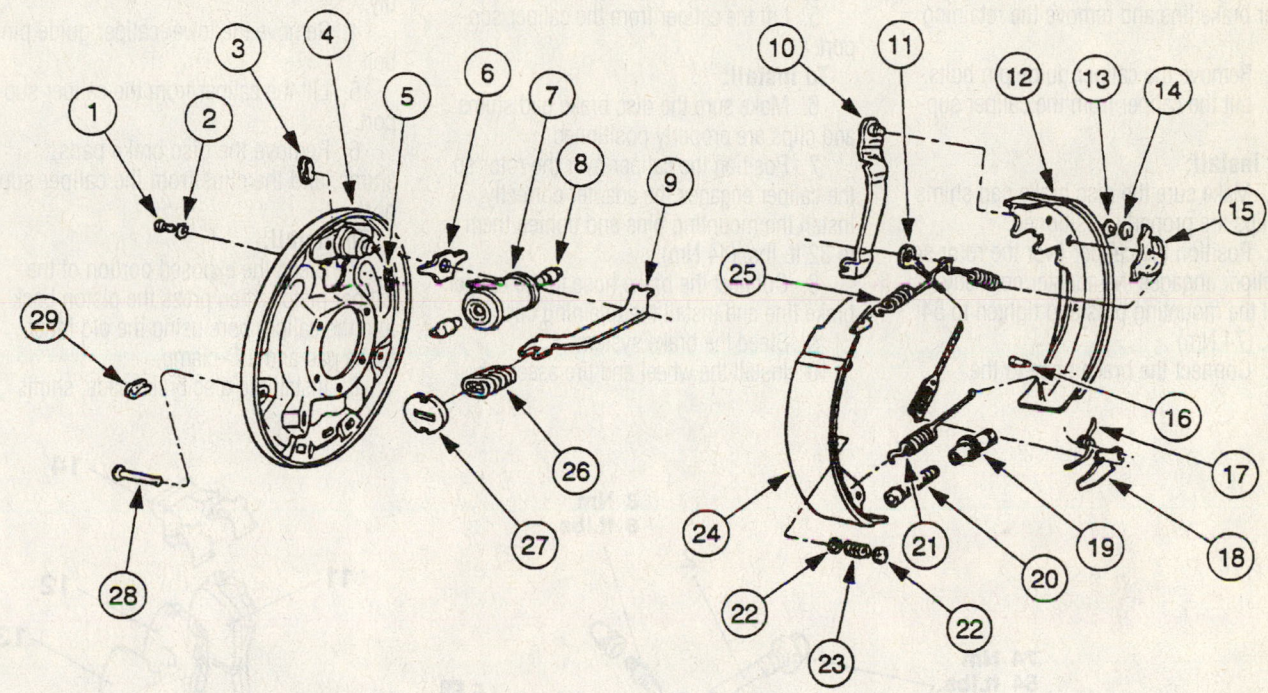

1	Wheel Cylinder-to-Backing Plate Bolt (2 Req'd)	12	Rear Brake Shoe and Lining, Secondary	22	Brake Shoe Hold-Down Spring Cup
2	Washer	13	Washer	23	Brake Shoe Hold-Down Spring
3	Inspection Hole Cover	14	Parking Brake Lever Pin Retainer	24	Rear Brake Shoe and Lining, Primary
4	Brake Backing Plate	15	Cable Guide	25	Brake Shoe Retracting Spring, Short
5	Lining Inspection Hole	16	Adjusting Lever Pin		
6	Anchor Pin Guide Plate	17	Adjusting Lever Return Spring	26	Parking Brake Link Spring
7	Rear Wheel Cylinder	18	Brake Shoe Adjusting Lever	27	Parking Brake Spring Retainer
8	Wheel Cylinder Brake Shoe Link	19	Brake Shoe Adjusting Screw Nut	28	Brake Shoe Hold-Down Spring Pin
9	Parking Brake Strut	20	Brake Adjuster Screw	29	Brake Adjusting Hole Cover
10	Parking Brake Lever	21	Brake Shoe Adjusting Screw Spring		
11	Brake Shoe Adjusting Lever Cable				

93026G21

Exploded view of the rear brake shoes and components—1998–01 B-Series Pick-Up

For brake related suspension and axle service, refer to the model specific sections of this manual

MITSUBISHI

Brake Caliper

REMOVAL & INSTALLATION

Montero and Montero Sport

FRONT

1. Raise and safely support the vehicle.
2. Remove the wheel and tire assembly.
3. Disconnect the brake hose from the caliper brake line and remove the retaining clip.
4. Remove the caliper guide pin bolts.
5. Lift the caliper from the caliper support.

To install:

6. Make sure the disc brake pad shims and clips are properly positioned.
7. Position the caliper over the rotor so the caliper engages the adapter correctly. Install the mounting pins and tighten to 54 ft. lbs. (74 Nm) .
8. Connect the brake hose to the caliper brake line and install the retaining clip.
9. Bleed the brake system.
10. Install the wheel and tire assembly.

REAR

1. Raise and safely support the vehicle.
2. Remove the wheel and tire assembly.
3. Disconnect the brake hose from the caliper brake line and remove the retaining clip.
4. Remove the caliper guide pin bolts.
5. Lift the caliper from the caliper support.

To install:

6. Make sure the disc brake pad shims and clips are properly positioned.
7. Position the caliper over the rotor so the caliper engages the adapter correctly. Install the mounting pins and tighten them to 32 ft. lbs. (44 Nm).
8. Connect the brake hose to the caliper brake line and install the retaining clip.
9. Bleed the brake system.
10. Install the wheel and tire assembly.

Disc Brake Pads

REMOVAL & INSTALLATION

Montero and Montero Sport

1. Remove ½ of the brake fluid from the master cylinder.
2. Raise and safely support the vehicle.
3. Remove the wheel and tire assembly.
4. Remove the lower caliper guide pin bolt.
5. Lift the caliper from the caliper support.
6. Remove the disc brake pads, shims, and the clips from the caliper support.

To install:

7. Clean the exposed portion of the caliper piston, then press the piston back into the caliper bore using the old inner brake pad and a C-clamp.
8. Install the disc brake pads, shims,

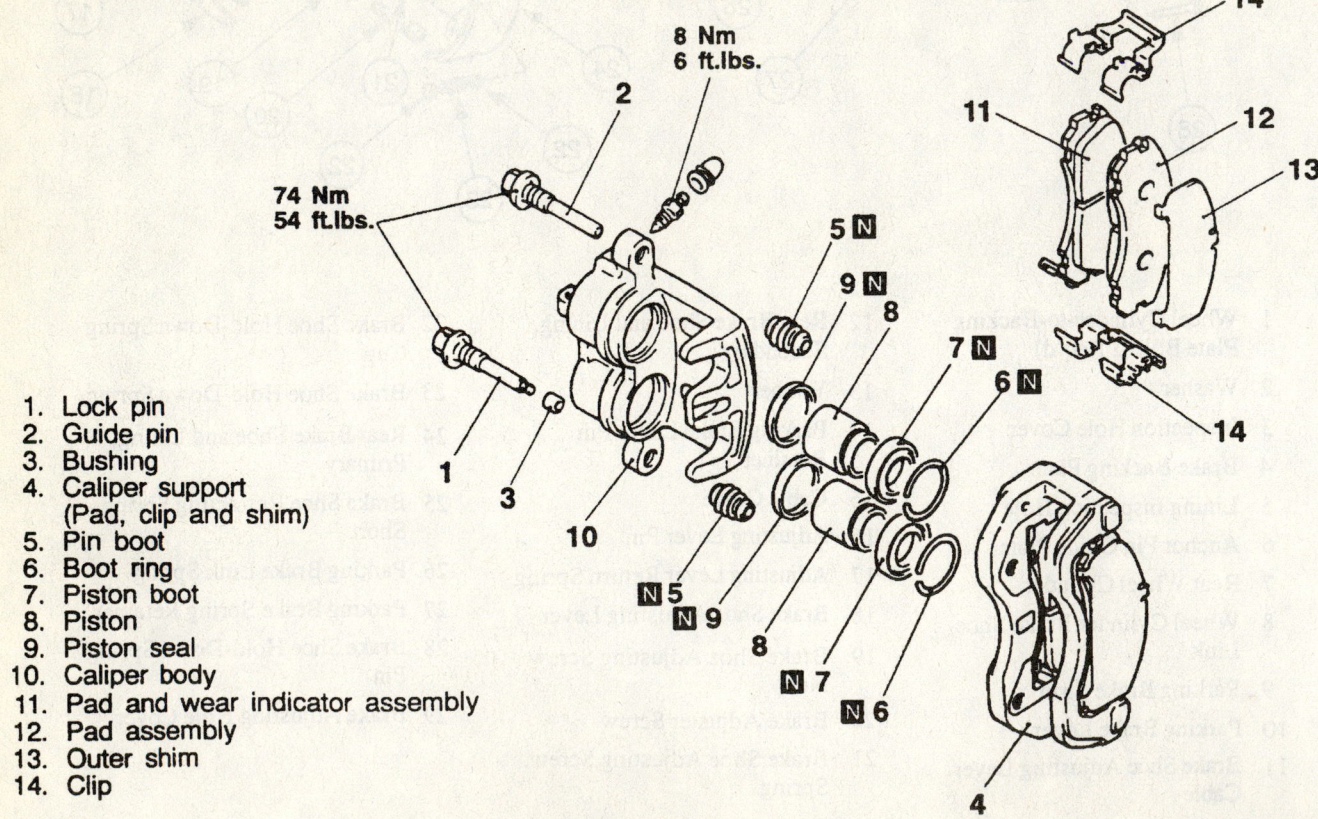

1. Lock pin
2. Guide pin
3. Bushing
4. Caliper support
   (Pad, clip and shim)
5. Pin boot
6. Boot ring
7. Piston boot
8. Piston
9. Piston seal
10. Caliper body
11. Pad and wear indicator assembly
12. Pad assembly
13. Outer shim
14. Clip

Exploded view of the front disc brake assembly—Montero and Montero Sport

93026G99

and the clips. Make sure the shims and clips are properly positioned.

9. Position the caliper over the rotor so the caliper engages the adapter correctly. Install the mounting pin(s) and

tighten the front caliper to 54 ft. lbs. (74 Nm) and the rear caliper to 32 ft. lbs. (44 Nm).

10. Install the wheel and tire assembly and lower the vehicle.

11. Apply the brake pedal several times until a firm pedal is obtained. Check the fluid level in the master cylinder and add fluid, as necessary.

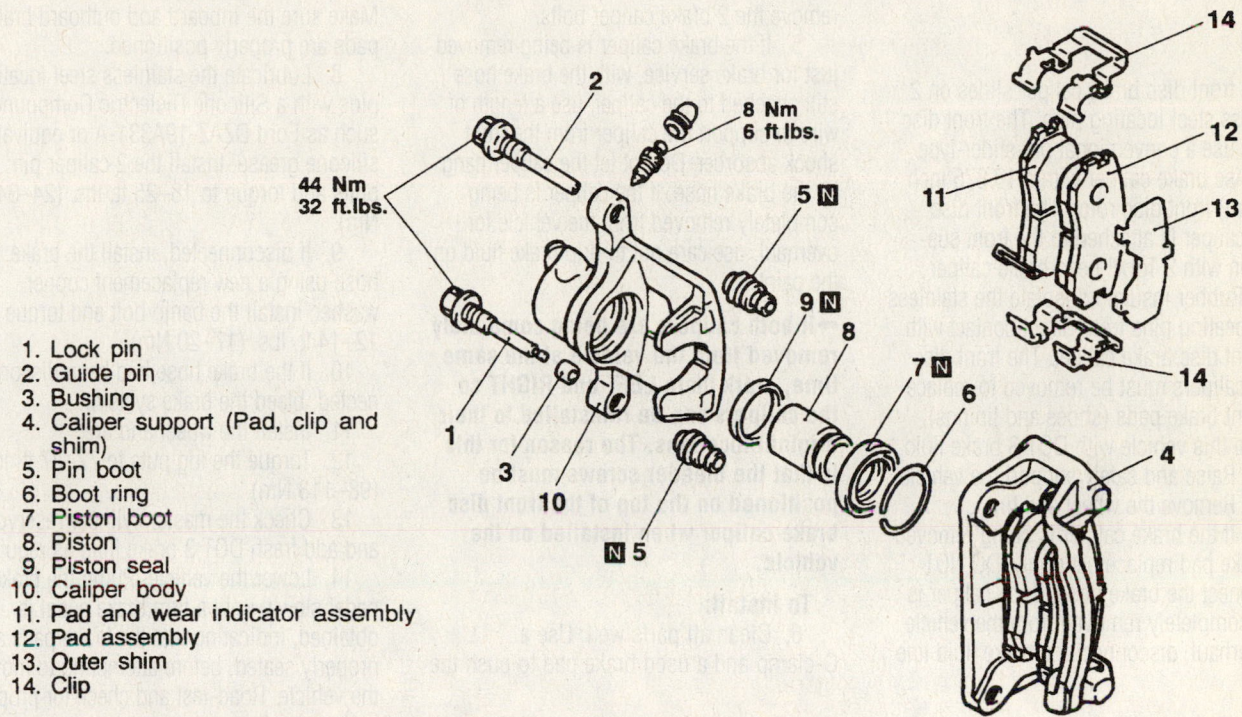

1. Lock pin
2. Guide pin
3. Bushing
4. Caliper support (Pad, clip and shim)
5. Pin boot
6. Boot ring
7. Piston boot
8. Piston
9. Piston seal
10. Caliper body
11. Pad and wear indicator assembly
12. Pad assembly
13. Outer shim
14. Clip

Exploded view of the rear disc brake assembly—Montero

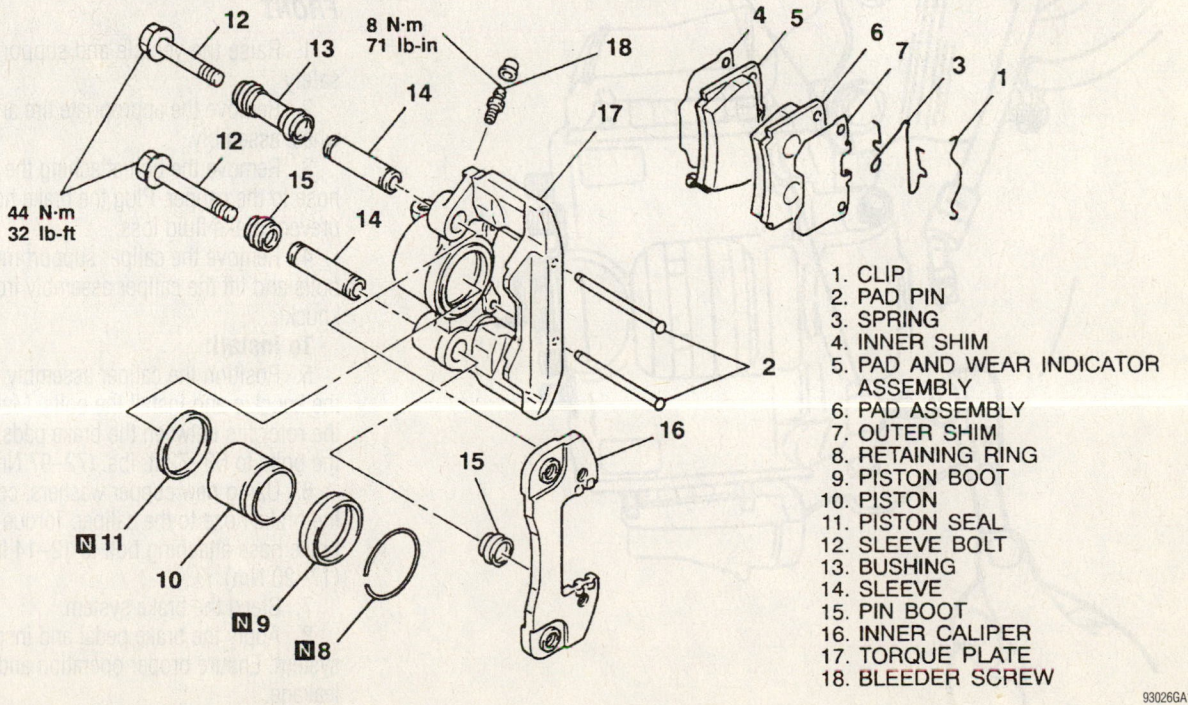

1. CLIP
2. PAD PIN
3. SPRING
4. INNER SHIM
5. PAD AND WEAR INDICATOR ASSEMBLY
6. PAD ASSEMBLY
7. OUTER SHIM
8. RETAINING RING
9. PISTON BOOT
10. PISTON
11. PISTON SEAL
12. SLEEVE BOLT
13. BUSHING
14. SLEEVE
15. PIN BOOT
16. INNER CALIPER
17. TORQUE PLATE
18. BLEEDER SCREW

Exploded view of the rear disc brake assembly—Montero Sport

For complete service labor times order Nichols' Chilton Labor Guide Manual

Brake Caliper

REMOVAL & INSTALLATION

Quest

The front disc brake caliper slides on 2 stainless steel locating pins. The front disc brakes use a conventional pin slider-type front disc brake caliper with a 10.875 inch (27.6cm) front disc rotor. The front disc brake caliper is attached to the front suspension with 2 Torx® head brake caliper bolts. Rubber insulators isolate the stainless steel locating pins from direct contact with the front disc brake caliper. The front disc brake calipers must be removed to replace the front brake pads (shoes and linings). Service this vehicle with DOT 3 brake fluid.

1. Raise and safely support the vehicle.
2. Remove the wheel and tire.
3. If the brake caliper is being removed for brake pad replacement only, DO NOT disconnect the brake hose. If the caliper is to be completely removed from the vehicle for overhaul, disconnect the brake fluid line

by removing the banjo bolt. Discard the copper washer.

4. Remove the 2 caliper pin bolts. Most applications will require a Torx® T-40 bit to remove the 2 brake caliper bolts.

5. If the brake caliper is being removed just for brake service, with the brake hose still attached to the caliper, use a length of wire to support the caliper from the front shock absorber. Do not let the caliper hang by the brake hose. If the caliper is being completely removed from the vehicle for overhaul, use care not to drip brake fluid on the paint.

➡**If both calipers are being completely removed from the vehicle at the same time, mark them LEFT and RIGHT so the calipers can be reinstalled to their original locations. The reason for this is that the bleeder screws must be positioned on the top of the front disc brake caliper when installed on the vehicle.**

To install:

6. Clean all parts well. Use a C-clamp and a used brake pad to push the

caliper piston fully in the piston bore. Inspect the caliper pins and clean any dirt and debris.

7. Install the caliper onto the rotor. Make sure the inboard and outboard brake pads are properly positioned.

8. Lubricate the stainless steel locating pins with a Silicone Dielectric Compound such as Ford DZAZ-19A331-A or equivalent silicone grease. Install the 2 caliper pin bolts and torque to 18–25 ft. lbs. (24–34 Nm).

9. If disconnected, install the brake hose using a new replacement copper washer, install the banjo bolt and torque to 12–14 ft. lbs. (17–20 Nm).

10. If the brake hose had been disconnected, bleed the brake system.

11. Install the wheel and tire.

12. Torque the lug nuts to 72–87 ft. lbs. (98–118 Nm).

13. Check the master cylinder reservoir and add fresh DOT 3 brake fluid as required.

14. Lower the vehicle. Pump the brake pedal slowly until a firm brake pedal is obtained, indicating that the brake pads are properly seated, before attempting to move the vehicle. Road-test and check for proper brake operation.

Pathfinder and Pick-Up

FRONT

1. Raise the vehicle and support safely.

2. Remove the appropriate tire and wheel assembly.

3. Remove the bolt attaching the brake hose to the caliper. Plug the brake hose to prevent brake fluid loss.

4. Remove the caliper support mounting bolts and lift the caliper assembly from the knuckle.

To install:

5. Position the caliper assembly onto the knuckle and install the bolts. Make sure the rotor fits between the brake pads. Torque the bolts to 53–72 ft. lbs. (72–97 Nm).

6. Using new copper washers, connect the brake hose to the caliper. Torque the brake hose attaching bolt to 12–14 ft. lbs. (17–20 Nm).

7. Bleed the brake system.

8. Apply the brake pedal and inspect the system. Ensure proper operation and no leakage.

9. Install tire and wheel assembly. Lower the vehicle and road-test.

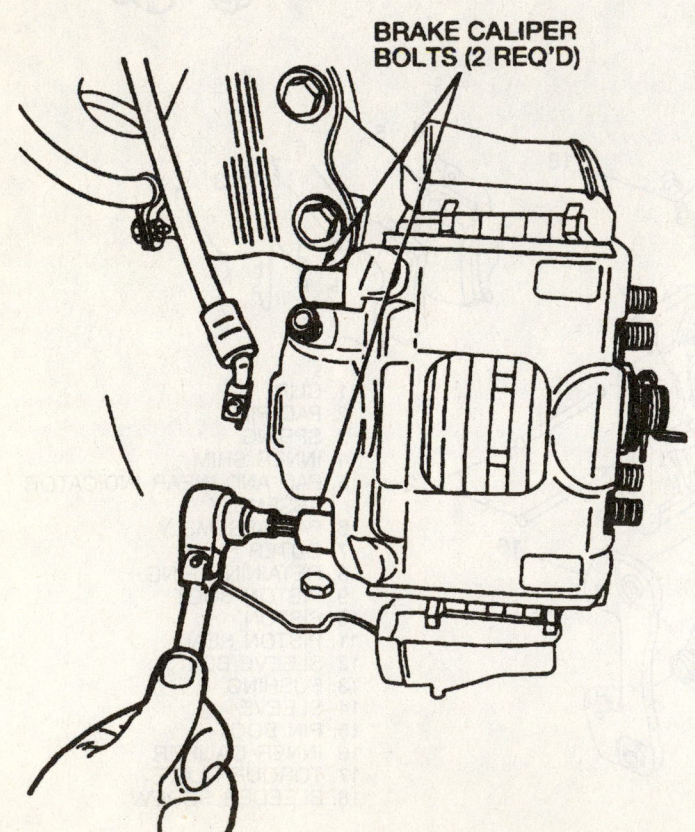

BRAKE CALIPER BOLTS (2 REQ'D)

93026G10

Caliper pin bolt removal—Quest

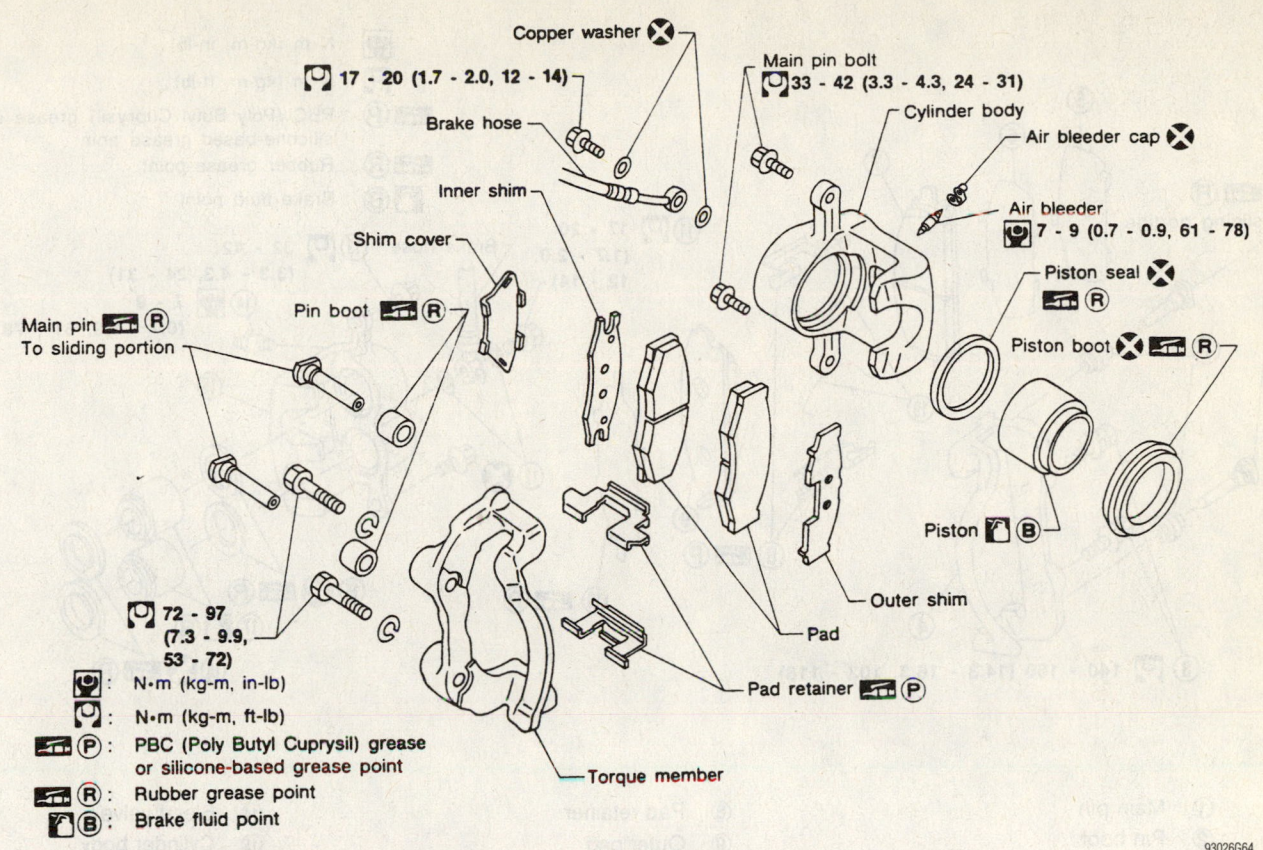

Single piston caliper front brake components—Pick-Up

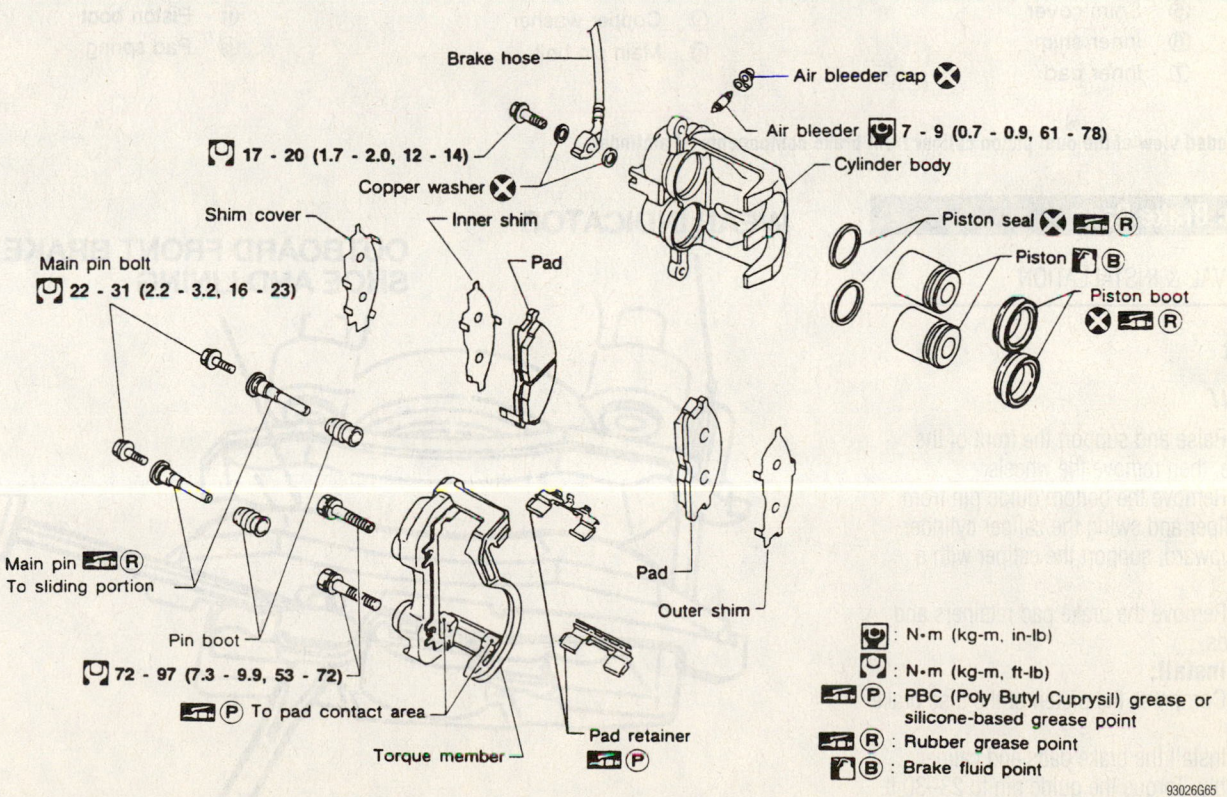

Dual piston caliper front brake components—Pick-Up

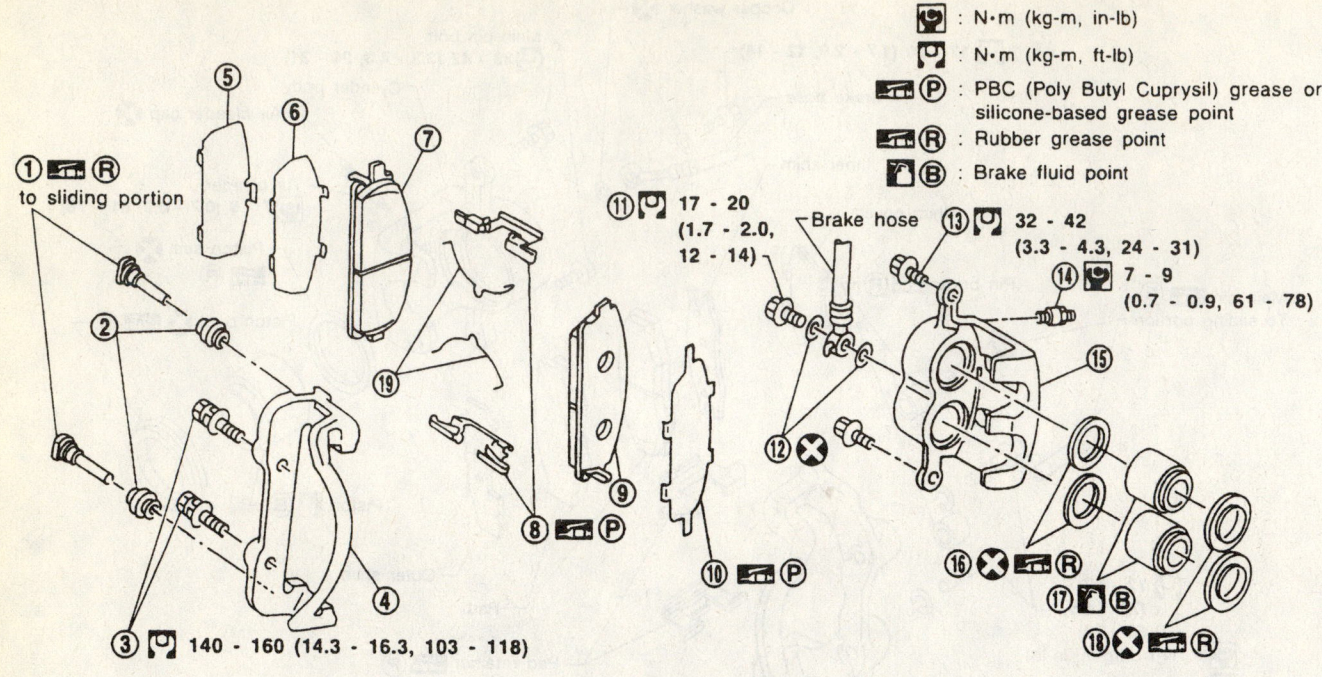

: N·m (kg-m, in-lb)

: N·m (kg-m, ft-lb)

(P) : PBC (Poly Butyl Cuprysil) grease or silicone-based grease point

(R) : Rubber grease point

(B) : Brake fluid point

① (R) to sliding portion

⑪ 17 - 20 (1.7 - 2.0, 12 - 14)

Brake hose

⑬ 32 - 42 (3.3 - 4.3, 24 - 31)

⑭ 7 - 9 (0.7 - 0.9, 61 - 78)

⑧ (P)

⑩ (P)

③ 140 - 160 (14.3 - 16.3, 103 - 118)

⑯ (R)

⑰ (B)

⑱ (R)

①	Main pin	⑧	Pad retainer	⑭	Bleed valve
②	Pin boot	⑨	Outer pad	⑮	Cylinder body
③	Torque member fixing bolt	⑩	Outer shim	⑯	Piston seal
④	Torque member	⑪	Connecting bolt	⑰	Piston
⑤	Shim cover	⑫	Copper washer	⑱	Piston boot
⑥	Inner shim	⑬	Main pin bolt	⑲	Pad spring
⑦	Inner pad				

93026G60

Exploded view of the dual piston caliper front brake components—Pathfinder

Disc Brake Pads

REMOVAL & INSTALLATION

Quest

FRONT

1. Raise and support the front of the vehicle, then remove the wheels.

2. Remove the bottom guide pin from the caliper and swing the caliper cylinder body upward; support the caliper with a wire.

3. Remove the brake pad retainers and the pads.

To install:

4. Compress the piston of the disc brake caliper.

5. Install the brake pads and caliper assembly. Torque the guide pin to 23–30 ft. lbs. (31–41 Nm).

6. Install the wheels.

7. Apply the brakes a few times to seat

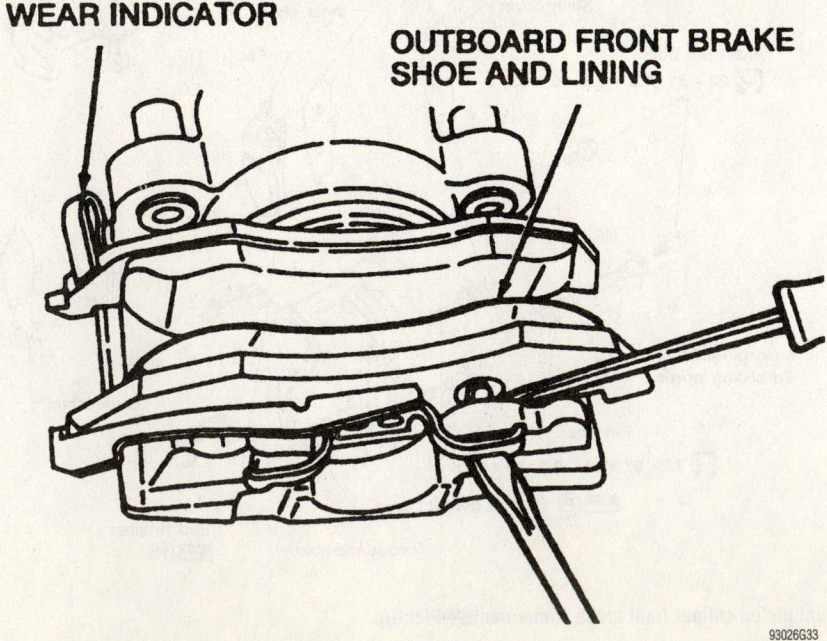

WEAR INDICATOR

OUTBOARD FRONT BRAKE SHOE AND LINING

93026G33

Replacing the disc brake pads—Quest

the pads. Check the master cylinder and add fluid if necessary. Bleed the brakes, if necessary.

REAR

➡ **Do not press the piston into the bore as performed on the front disc brakes. Due to the parking brake mechanism, the caliper piston must be turned into the bore using a special tool.**

1. Raise and support the vehicle safely.
2. Remove the rear wheels.
3. Release the parking brake and remove the cable bracket bolt.
4. Remove the pin bolts and lift off the caliper body.
5. Pull out the pad springs and then remove the pads and shims.

To install:

6. Clean the piston end of the caliper body and the area around the pin holes. Be careful not to get oil on the rotor.
7. Using the proper tool, carefully turn the piston clockwise back into the caliper body. Take care not to damage the piston boot.
8. Coat the pad contact area on the mounting support with a silicone based grease.
9. Install the pads, shims, and the pad springs. Always use new shims.
10. Position the caliper body in the mounting support and tighten the pin bolts to 28–38 ft. lbs. (38–52 Nm).
11. Mount the wheels, lower the vehicle, and bleed the system if necessary.

Pathfinder and Pick-Up

➡ **Both the front and rear disc brake pads can be serviced using the same procedure.**

1. Using a syringe, siphon brake fluid from the reservoir, leaving reservoir approximately ½ full.
2. Raise and properly support the vehicle.
3. Remove the wheel assemblies.
4. Remove the lower pin bolt from the brake caliper.
5. Swivel the caliper up and away from the torque member. Tie the caliper to a suspension member so that it is out of the way.
6. Lift the 2 brake pads out of the torque member.
7. Remove the inner and outer shims. Remove the 2 pad retainers if they are not attached to the pads.
8. Check the pad thickness and replace

the pads if they are less than 0.079 in. (2mm) thick.

To install:

9. Install the inner and outer shims into the torque member.
10. Install a pad retainer to the bottom of each pad.
11. Install the pads into the torque member.
12. Use a C-clamp or hammer handle and press the caliper piston(s) back into the housing.
13. Untie the caliper and swivel it back into position over the torque plate so that the dust boot is not pinched. Install the pin bolt and torque it to 16–23 ft. lbs. (22–31 Nm).
14. Check the condition of the pin boot. Gently pull on it to expel any trapped air.
15. Install the wheel and lower the vehicle.
16. Pump the brakes until the pedal is firm and check the level of brake fluid. Road-test the vehicle.

Brake Drums

REMOVAL & INSTALLATION

Quest

The rear drum brakes used on these vehicles are conventional expanding shoe-type with the brake shoe lining applied to the inside of the rotating drum. An incremental brake adjuster screw is designed to actuate whenever sufficient wear occurs.

1. Raise and safely support the vehicle.
2. Remove the wheel and tire.
3. Remove the brake drum by pulling it from the wheel studs.
4. If necessary for brake drum removal, pry off the access hole plug from the access

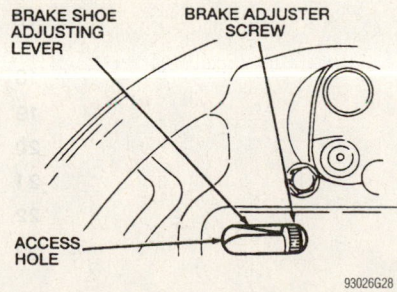

Brake shoe adjustment may need to be loosened to remove the brake drum—Quest

hole. Insert a screwdriver and a brake adjustment tool. Press the screwdriver against the adjusting lever to disengage it from the adjuster. Loosen the adjuster using the brake adjusting tool.

To install:

5. Clean all parts well. It is good practice to inspect the wheel cylinder for leaks anytime the brake drum is removed. If a new replacement brake drum is being installed, inspect it for a protective coating on the machined inside braking surface. Remove any coating with suitable solvent.
6. Install the brake drum onto the wheel studs.
7. In most all cases, manual brake adjustment IS NOT recommended. Adjustment is performed by driving the vehicle and applying the brakes.
8. Install the tire and wheel and torque the fasteners to 72–87 ft. lbs. (98–118 Nm).
9. Lower the vehicle.
10. Adjust the rear brake shoes by sharply applying the brakes several times while driving the vehicle alternately forwards and backwards. Check the brake operation by making several stops while driving forward.

Pathfinder and Pick-Up

1. Remove the hub cap and loosen the lug nuts.
2. Raise the rear of the vehicle and support it on jackstands.
3. Remove the lug nuts, tire and wheel.
4. Release the parking brake.
5. Pull the brake drum from the hub. If difficult to remove try the following:
   a. Strike the face of the drum with a plastic or rubber mallet. This will break free any rust that may develop between the drum and the hub.
   b. Install 2, M8x1.25mm bolts into

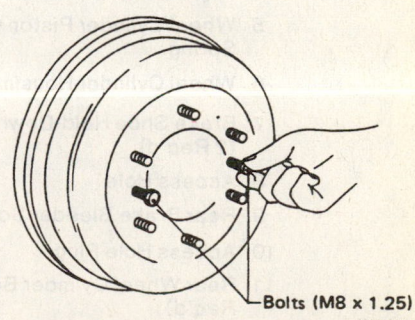

Install and tighten 2 bolts to remove a stubborn brake drum—Pathfinder and Pick-Up

---

For brake related suspension and axle service, refer to the model specific sections of this manual

the holes in the drum and gradually tighten them to pull the drum off the hub.

To install:

6. Install the brake drum to the hub.

7. Install the wheel.

8. Remove the jackstands and lower the vehicle.

9. Road-test the vehicle to ensure that the brakes are working properly.

Brake Shoes

REMOVAL & INSTALLATION

Quest

The rear drum brakes use an internal rear wheel cylinder with expanding shoes and lining that are applied against a rotating brake drum. An incremental brake adjuster screw is actuated whenever sufficient wear occurs. Brake adjustment takes place in forward or reverse braking but not with parking brake application.

1. Raise and safely support the vehicle.

2. Remove the wheel and tire assembly. Remove the brake drum using the recommended procedure.

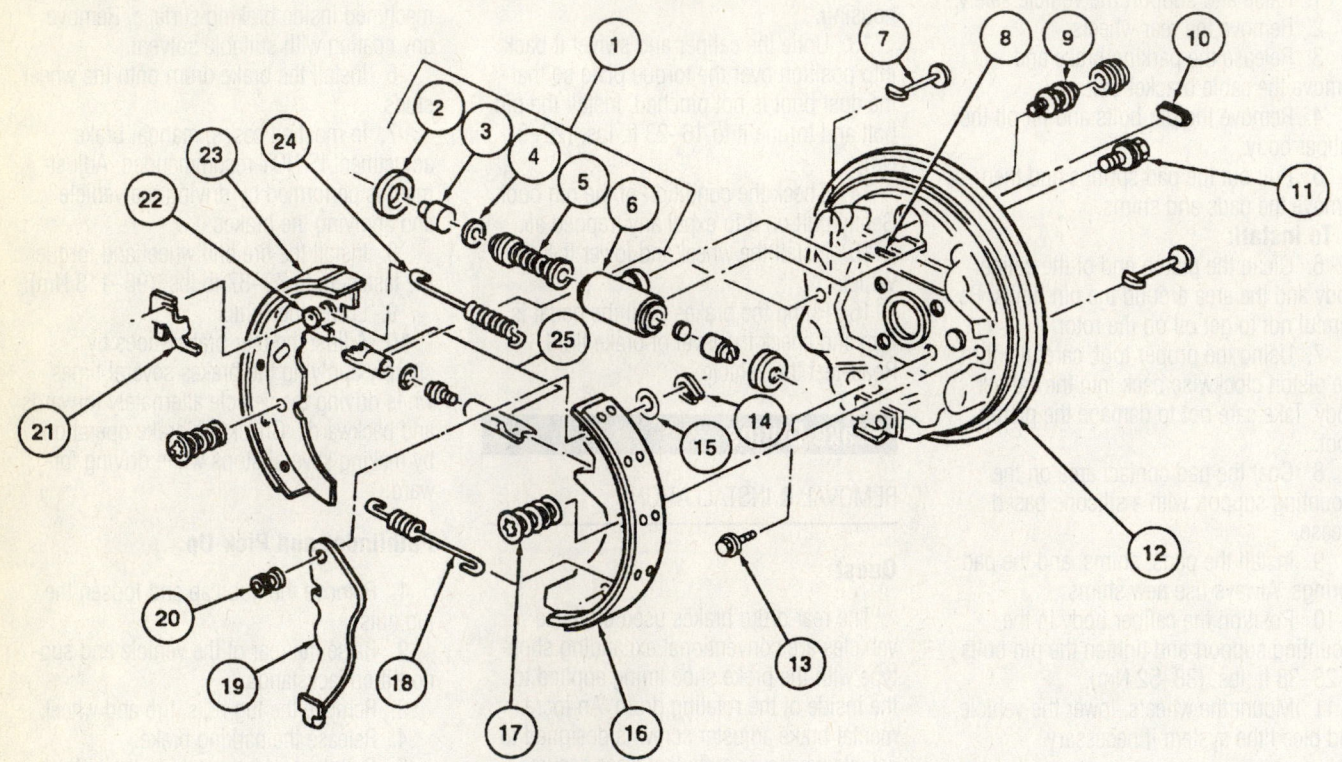

1	Rear Wheel Cylinder
2	Dust Boot (2 Req'd)
3	Wheel Cylinder Piston (2 Req'd)
4	Cup (2 Req'd)
5	Wheel Cylinder Piston Cup Spring
6	Wheel Cylinder Housing
7	Brake Shoe Hold-Down Pin (2 Req'd)
8	Access Hole
9	Rear Brake Bleeder Screw
10	Access Hole Plug
11	Rear Wheel Cylinder Bolt (2 Req'd)
12	Rear Brake Backing Plate

13	Rear Brake Backing Plate Bolts (4 Req'd)
14	Parking Brake Lever Clip
15	Spring Washer
16	Secondary Brake Shoe and Lining
17	Brake Shoe Hold-Down Spring
18	Lower Retracting Spring
19	Parking Brake Lever
20	Parking Brake Lever Pin
21	Brake Shoe Adjusting Lever
22	Adjuster Lever Pin
23	Primary Brake Shoe and Lining
24	Upper Retracting Spring
29	Brake Adjuster Screw

93026G29

Rear drum brake assembly and related components—Quest

3. Disconnect the parking brake rear cable and conduit from the parking brake lever.

4. Remove the 2 brake shoe hold-down springs and the 2 brake shoe hold-down pins.

5. Remove the upper retracting spring.

6. Remove the lower retracting spring.

7. Remove the brake adjuster screw.

8. Remove the rear brake shoes and linings from the brake backing plate.

9. Remove the parking brake lever clip and washer.

10. Remove the parking brake lever from the secondary brake shoe and lining.

To install:

11. Install the parking brake lever to the secondary brake shoe and lining with a new parking brake lever clip.

12. Position the secondary (rear) shoe on the backing plate and install the brake shoe hold-down spring and pin.

13. Position the primary (front) shoe on the backing plate and install the brake shoe hold-down spring and pin.

14. Attach the parking brake rear cable and conduit to the parking brake lever.

15. Attach the lower retracting spring to the rear brake shoes.

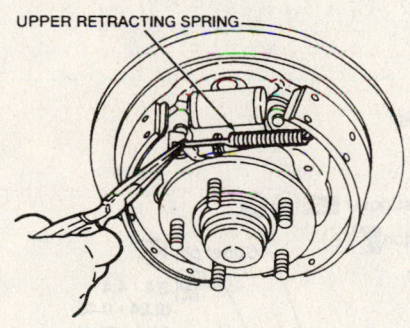

**Remove the upper retracting spring—
Quest**

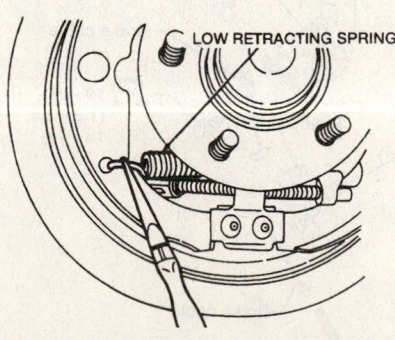

**Remove the lower retracting spring—
Quest**

16. Apply a light coat of high-quality grease to the threaded areas of the adjuster nut and adjuster socket. Turn the adjuster nut all the way down on the brake adjuster screw, then loosen the adjuster ½ turn. Install the adjuster screw in the slots on the rear brake shoes. The wider slot on the socket must fit in the slot on the primary (front) brake shoe. The slot on the adjuster nut end must fit into the slots in the secondary (rear) brake shoe and parking brake lever.

17. Install the brake shoe adjusting lever on the adjuster lever pin.

18. Install the upper retracting spring in the slot on the secondary shoe and in the slot on the brake shoe adjusting lever. The brake shoe adjusting lever should contact the brake adjuster screw.

19. Install the brake drum onto the wheel studs.

20. Install the tire and wheel and torque the fasteners to 72–87 ft. lbs. (98–118 Nm).

21. Lower the vehicle.

➡ **In most all cases, manual brake adjustment IS NOT recommended. Adjustment is performed by driving the vehicle and applying the brakes.**

22. The rear brakes do not require adjustment when being serviced to obtain a firm brake pedal feel. To achieve a firm brake pedal after servicing the rear brakes, sharply apply the brake pedal several times while driving the vehicle alternately forwards and backwards. Check the brake operation by making several stops while driving forward. The self-adjusting mechanism will sufficiently adjust the rear brake shoes without any manual tightening at the brake shoe adjuster. If the rear brake shoes are manually adjusted, the additional action of the brake shoe adjuster can cause the brakes to become over-tightened and result in binding or overheated rear brakes.

Pick-Up

1. Raise and support the vehicle until the axle to be serviced is off the ground.

2. Remove the wheels and brake drums.

3. With a pair of pliers, remove the brake shoe hold-down anti-rattle spring retainers. Depress the retainer while rotating it 90° to align the slot in the retainer with the flanged end of the pin. Remove the retainers, springs, spring seats, and pins.

4. Open the brake shoes outward against the return springs and remove the parking brake extension link.

5. Disconnect the brake shoe return springs.

6. Remove the brake shoes from the backing plate. The secondary (after) brake shoe must be disconnected from the parking brake toggle lever after withdrawing the toggle lever clevis pin.

7. Remove the rubber boot from behind the brake backing plate and slide the adjuster shim, lockplate, and adjuster springs off the back of the adjuster assembly. Remove the adjuster assembly from the backing plate.

To install:

8. Clean the backing plate and adjuster assembly so they are free of all dust and dirt.

9. Check the wheel cylinders.

10. Apply brake grease to the adjuster assembly housing bore, adjuster wheel, and adjuster screw. Assemble the adjuster assemble with the adjuster screw turned all the way in. Apply brake grease to the sliding surfaces of the adjuster assembly, brake backing plate, and the retaining spring. Install the adjuster assembly to the backing plate.

11. On models with 4WD, after installing the crank lever on the back plate, make sure there is no play between the crank lever and the back plate when pulling the crank lever. If play exists, adjust bolt A and locknut B.

12. Assemble the secondary (after) brake shoe to the parking brake toggle lever and adjust the clearance between the toggle lever and the brake shoe.

13. Before assembling the brake shoes to the backing plate apply brake grease to the following areas: the brake shoe grooves in the parking brake extension link, the inside surfaces of the anti-rattle (retaining) spring seats, and the contact surfaces between the brake backing plate and the brake shoes.

14. Assemble the brake shoes to the backing plate. Measure the inner diameter of the brake drum and then measure the outer diameter of the shoes (at the center). The shoe outer diameter should be 0.0098–0.0157 in. (0.25–0.40mm) less than the drum inner diameter; if not, adjust it by rotating the star wheel adjuster.

15. Install the brake drum and the wheel.

16. Adjust the brakes and lower the vehicle.

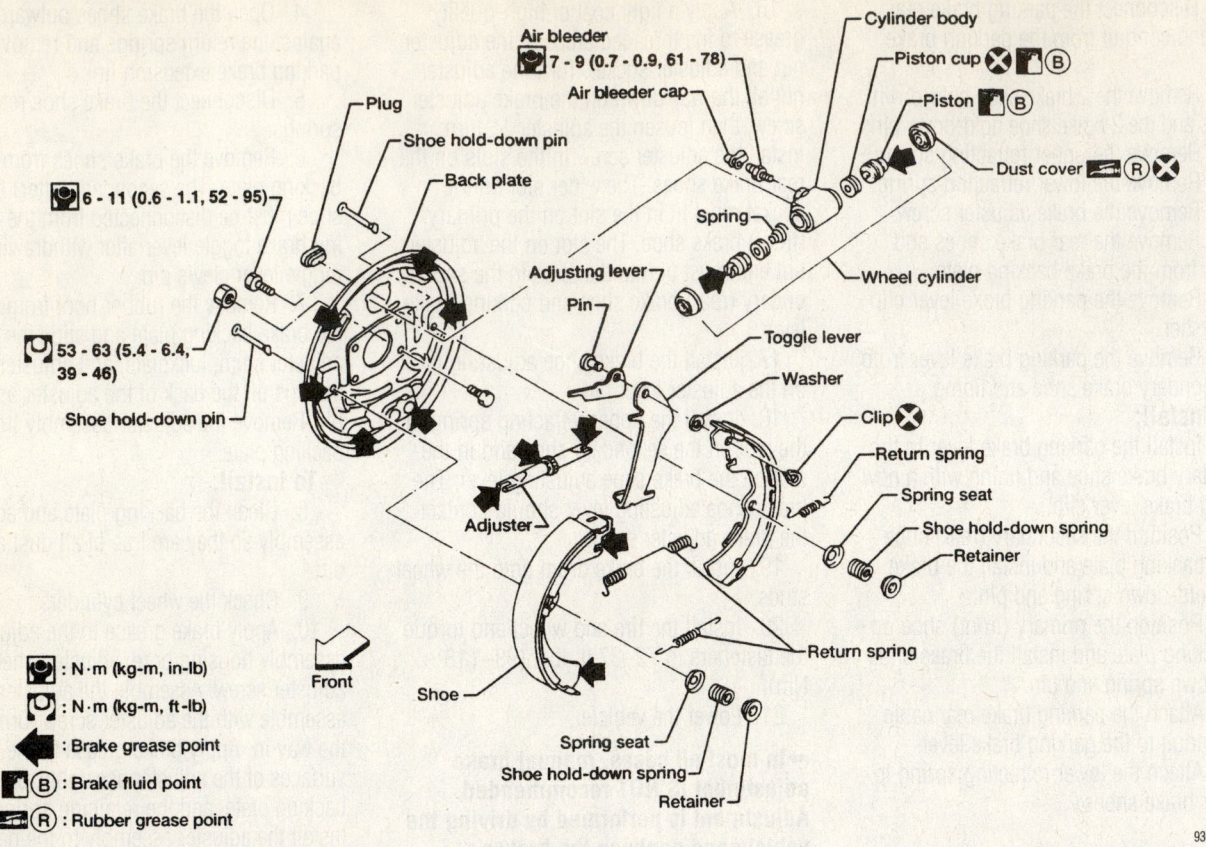

Rear brake shoes and related components—LT26B (2WD) system—Pick-Up

Air bleeder
7 - 9 (0.7 - 0.9, 61 - 78)

Air bleeder cap

Cylinder body

Piston cup

Piston

Dust cover R

Spring

Wheel cylinder

Plug

Shoe hold-down pin

Back plate

6 - 11 (0.6 - 1.1, 52 - 95)

Adjusting lever

Pin

Toggle lever

Washer

Clip

Return spring

Spring seat

Shoe hold-down spring

Retainer

53 - 63 (5.4 - 6.4, 39 - 46)

Shoe hold-down pin

Adjuster

Return spring

Shoe

Spring seat

Shoe hold-down spring

Retainer

: N·m (kg-m, in-lb)

: N·m (kg-m, ft-lb)

: Brake grease point

B : Brake fluid point

R : Rubber grease point

Front

93026G67

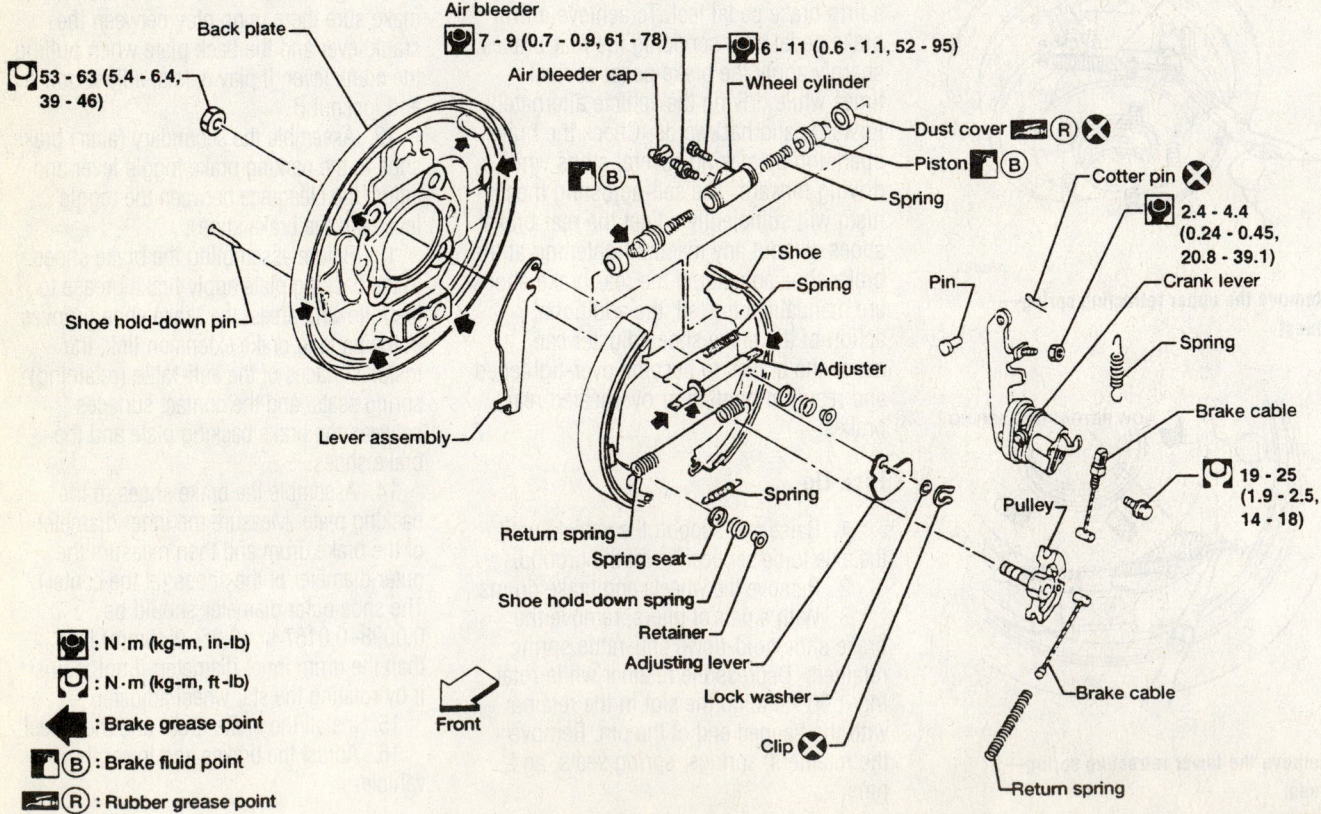

Rear brake shoes and related components—LT30A (4WD) system—Pick-Up

Back plate

Air bleeder
7 - 9 (0.7 - 0.9, 61 - 78)

6 - 11 (0.6 - 1.1, 52 - 95)

Air bleeder cap

Wheel cylinder

53 - 63 (5.4 - 6.4, 39 - 46)

Dust cover R

B

Piston B

Spring

Cotter pin

2.4 - 4.4 (0.24 - 0.45, 20.8 - 39.1)

Shoe hold-down pin

Shoe

Spring

Pin

Crank lever

Spring

Adjuster

Brake cable

Lever assembly

Spring

Pulley

19 - 25 (1.9 - 2.5, 14 - 18)

Return spring

Spring seat

Shoe hold-down spring

Retainer

Adjusting lever

Lock washer

Clip

Brake cable

Return spring

: N·m (kg-m, in-lb)

: N·m (kg-m, ft-lb)

: Brake grease point

B : Brake fluid point

R : Rubber grease point

Front

93026G68

Pathfinder

1. Release the parking brake.
2. Safely raise and support the vehicle.
3. Remove the rear wheel and drum.
4. Remove the hold-down pin retainers.
5. Remove the leading shoe and then the trailing shoe.
6. Remove the adjuster.
7. Disconnect the parking brake cable from the toggle lever on the rear shoe.

To install:

8. Transfer the toggle lever to the new rear shoe.
9. Apply a small amount of brake grease to the tips of the shoes and the 6 pads on the backing plate that contact the brake shoe.
10. Shorten the adjuster by turning it.
11. Connect the parking brake cable to the toggle lever on the rear shoe.

12. Install the lower return spring to both shoes and install the shoes on the backing plate with the hold down pins and retainers.
13. Install the adjuster and the remaining springs. Pay attention to the direction of the adjuster assembly.
14. Inspect the complete assembly and install the brake drum.
15. Adjust the shoe to drum clearance.
16. Install the wheel assembly and lower the vehicle to the floor.

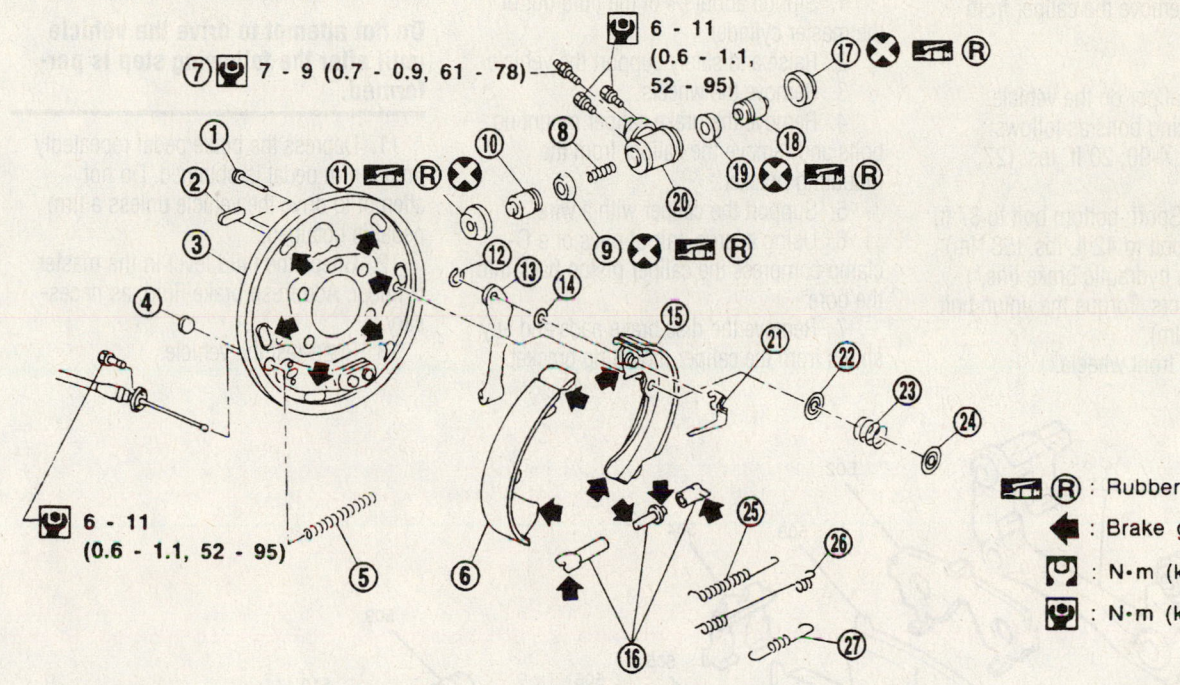

1.	Shoe hold pin
2.	Plug
3.	Back plate
4.	Check plug
5.	Spring
6.	Shoe (leading side)
7.	Air bleeder
8.	Spring
9.	Piston cup
10.	Piston
11.	Boot
12.	Retainer ring
13.	Toggle lever
14.	Wave washer
15.	Shoe (trailing side)
16.	Adjuster
17.	Boot
18.	Piston
19.	Piston cup
20.	Wheel cylinder
21.	Adjuster lever
22.	Spring seat
23.	Shoe hold spring
24.	Retainer
25.	Adjuster spring
26.	Return spring (upper)
27.	Return spring (lower)

93026G69

Drum brake assembly exploded view—Pathfinder w/LT30C system

Brake Caliper

REMOVAL & INSTALLATION

Sidekick, Sidekick Sport, Vitara, Grand Vitara and X-90

1. Raise and safely support the vehicle.
2. Remove the wheels.
3. Disconnect and plug the brake line.
4. Remove the caliper mounting bolts (guide pins) and remove the caliper from the vehicle.

To install:

5. Install the caliper on the vehicle. Tighten the mounting bolts as follows:
   - Sidekick, X-90: 20 ft. lbs. (27 Nm).
   - Sidekick Sport: bottom bolt to 37 ft. lbs.; top bolt to 42 ft. lbs. (58 Nm)
6. Connect the hydraulic brake line, using 2 new washers. Torque the union bolt to 17 ft. lbs. (23 Nm).
7. Replace the front wheels.

8. Lower the vehicle.
9. Fill the brake reservoir and bleed the hydraulic brake system.

Disc Brake Pads

REMOVAL & INSTALLATION

Sidekick, Sidekick Sport, Vitara, Grand Vitara and X-90

1. Siphon about ⅔ of the fluid out of the master cylinder.
2. Raise and safely support the vehicle.
3. Remove the wheels.
4. Remove the brake caliper mounting bolts and remove the caliper from the mounting bracket.
5. Support the caliper with a wire.
6. Using a large pair of plies or a C-clamp compress the caliper piston back into the bore.
7. Remove the disc brake pads and any shims from the caliper mounting bracket.

To install:

8. Install the brake pads and any shims removed from the caliper mounting bracket.
9. Install the caliper on the mounting bracket and install the mounting bolts. Tighten the mounting bolts to 20 ft. lbs. (27 Nm).
10. Install the front wheels and lower the vehicle.

❊❊ CAUTION

Do not attempt to drive the vehicle until after the following step is performed.

11. Depress the brake pedal repeatedly until a firm pedal is obtained. Do not attempt to drive the vehicle unless a firm pedal is obtained.
12. Check the fluid level in the master cylinder. Add fresh brake fluid, as necessary.
13. Road-test the vehicle.

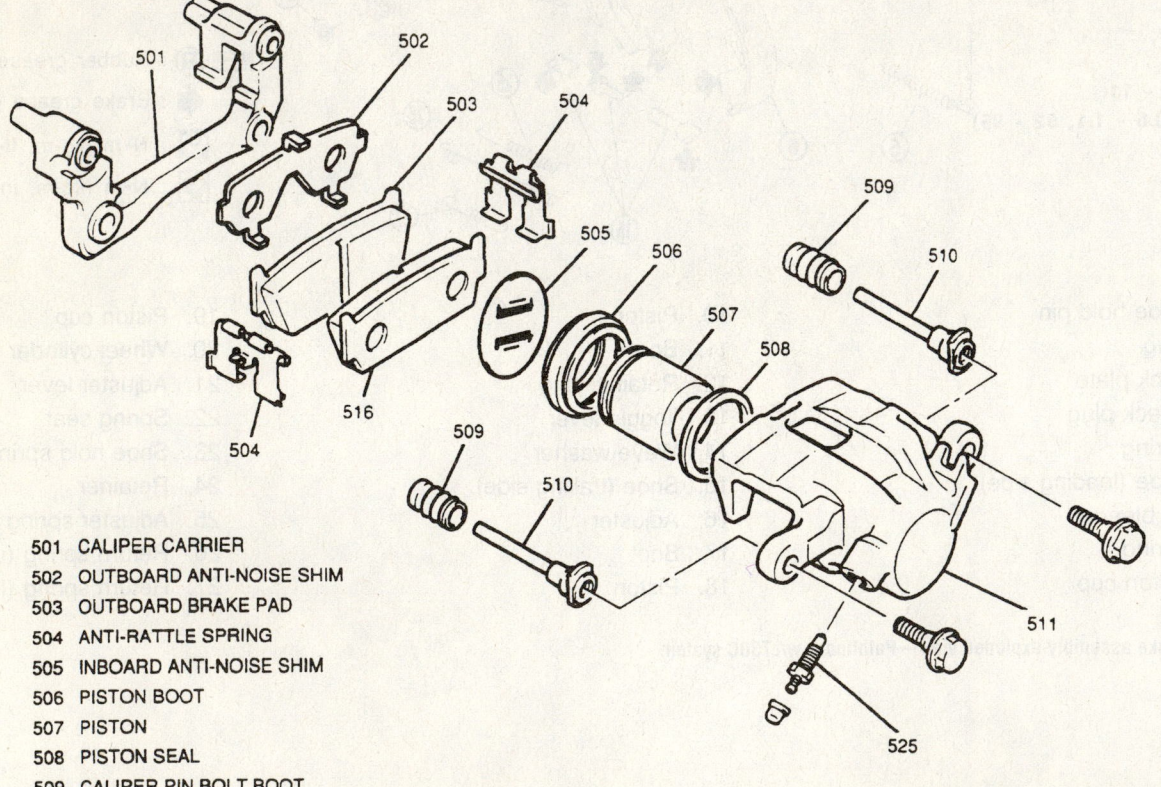

501	CALIPER CARRIER
502	OUTBOARD ANTI-NOISE SHIM
503	OUTBOARD BRAKE PAD
504	ANTI-RATTLE SPRING
505	INBOARD ANTI-NOISE SHIM
506	PISTON BOOT
507	PISTON
508	PISTON SEAL
509	CALIPER PIN BOLT BOOT
510	CALIPER PIN BOLT
511	CALIPER
516	INBOARD BRAKE PAD
525	BLEEDER VALVE

Front disc brake components—Sidekick, Sidekick Sport and X-90 models

93026G37

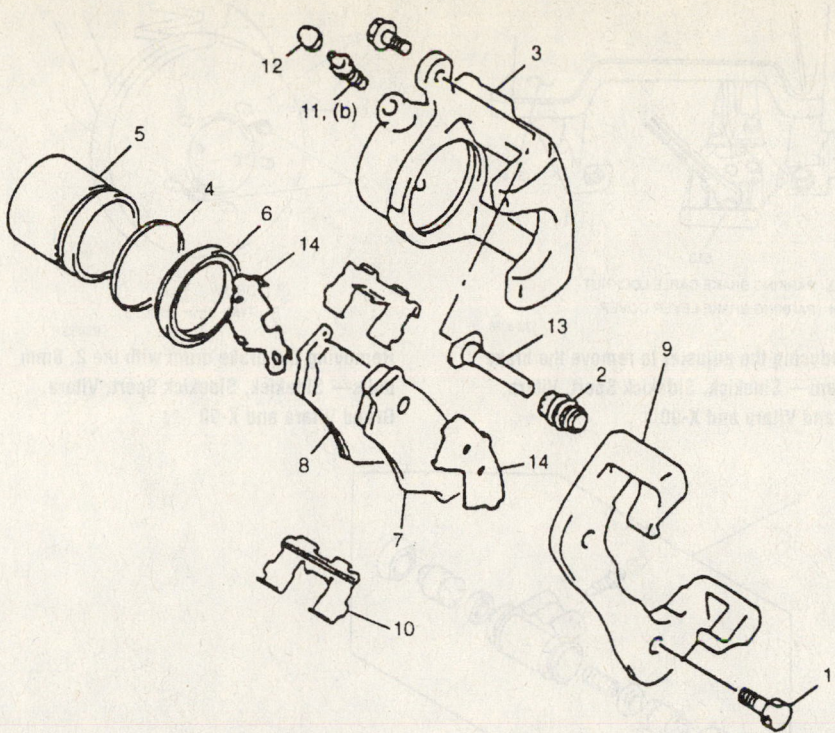

1. Caliper (slide) pin bolt
2. Boot
3. Disc brake caliper
   (disc brake cylinder)
4. Piston seal
5. Disc brake piston
6. Cylinder boot
7. Disc brake inner pad
8. Disc brake outer pad
9. Brake caliper carrier
10. Pad spring
11. Bleeder plug
12. Bleeder plug cap
13. Caliper pin
14. Anti noise shim
15. Inner shim

Tightening torque
(a): 8.0 N·m (0.80 kg-m, 6.0 lb-ft)
(b): 8.5 N·m (0.85 kg-m, 6.5 lb-ft)

93026G41

Front disc brake components—Vitara

1. Caliper (slide) pin bolt
2. Boot
3. Disc brake caliper
   (disc brake cylinder)
4. Piston seal
5. Disc brake piston
6. Cylinder boot
7. Disc brake inner pad
8. Disc brake outer pad
9. Brake caliper carrier
10. Pad spring
11. Bleeder plug
12. Bleeder plug cap
13. Caliper pin
14. Anti noise shim
15. Inner shim

Tightening torque
(a): 8.0 N·m (0.80 kg-m, 6.0 lb-ft)

93026G42

Front disc brake components—Grand Vitara

For brake related suspension and axle service, refer to the model specific sections of this manual

Brake Drums

REMOVAL & INSTALLATION

Sidekick

1. Raise and safely support the vehicle.
2. Remove the rear wheel(s).
3. Release the parking brake.
4. Remove the parking brake lever cover screws and loosen the brake cable locking nut.
5. Install 2, 8mm bolts into the brake drum holes and uniformly tighten each bolt.

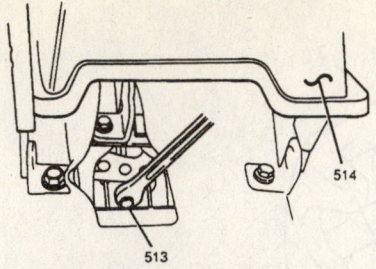

513 PARKING BRAKE CABLE LOCKNUT
514 PARKING BRAKE LEVER COVER

93026G38

Reducing the adjuster to remove the brake drum— Sidekick, Sidekick Sport, Vitara, Grand Vitara and X-90

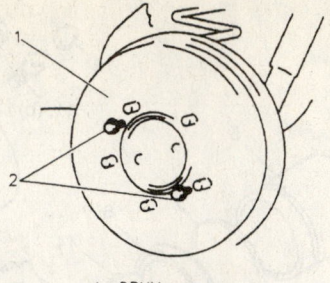

1 DRUM
2 TWO 8mm BOLTS

93026G39

Removing the brake drum with the 2, 8mm bolts— Sidekick, Sidekick Sport, Vitara, Grand Vitara and X-90

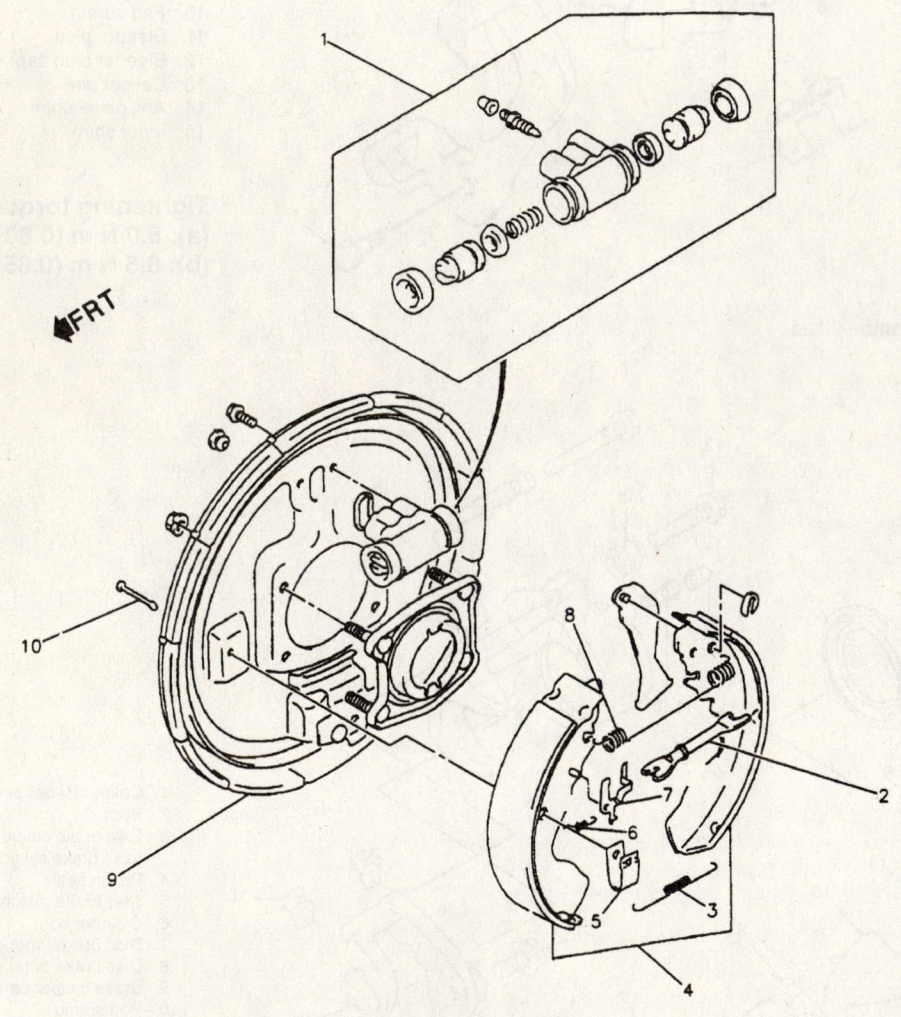

◀FRT

1 WHEEL CYLINDER
2 ADJUSTER
3 SHOE RETURN LOWER SPRING
4 BRAKE SHOES
5 SHOE HOLD DOWN SPRING
6 ADJUSTER SPRING
7 PAWL LEVER
8 SHOE RETURN UPPER SPRING
9 BACKING PLATE
10 SHOE HOLD DOWN PIN

93026G40

Exploded view of the rear brake components—Sidekick, Sidekick Sport and X-90 models

Tighten each bolt until the brake drum is removed from the vehicle. If there is difficulty in removing the drum, insert a small tool through the hole in the rear of the backing plate, and hold the automatic adjusting lever away from the adjuster. Using another narrow, flat tool at the same time, reduce the brake shoe adjuster by turning the adjusting wheel.

To install:

6. Install the brake drum and pull the parking brake lever all the way up until a clicking sound can no longer be heard.

7. Verify that the rear wheels will not turn. If the rear wheels turn, adjust the parking brake cable as necessary.

8. Release the parking brake and remove the brake drum. Measure the diameter of the brake shoes. Outer diameter should be as follows:

- For 2 door models: 8.638 (0.0012 inches (219 (0.3mm)

- For 4 door models: 9.980 (0.0079 inches (253.5 (0.2mm)

9. If the brake shoe clearance is not correct, adjust the brake shoes until the clearance is correct.

10. Reinstall the brake drum, replace the wheel(s), and safely lower the vehicle.

11. Adjust the parking brake and install the cover with the 2 screws.

12. Road-test the vehicle for proper brake operation.

Brake Shoes

REMOVAL & INSTALLATION

Sidekick

1. Raise and safely support the vehicle.
2. Remove the rear wheel(s).
3. Remove the brake drum.

4. Using a suitable tool, remove the brake shoe return spring.

5. Using a brake spring hold-down tool, disengage the hold-down spring and retainers from the front shoe. Remove the hold-down retainer pinch

6. Disconnect the anchor spring from the front shoe and remove the front shoe.

7. Remove the anchor spring from the rear shoe. Using a brake spring hold-down tool, disengage the hold-down spring and retainers from the rear shoe. Remove the hold-down pinch

8. Disengage the parking brake lever from the parking brake cable and remove the rear shoe.

9. Remove the C-washer, the automatic adjuster lever and spring, the C-washer, and the parking brake lever from the rear shoe.

10. Thoroughly clean the backing plate and brake hardware with brake cleaning solvent. Apply high temperature grease to the

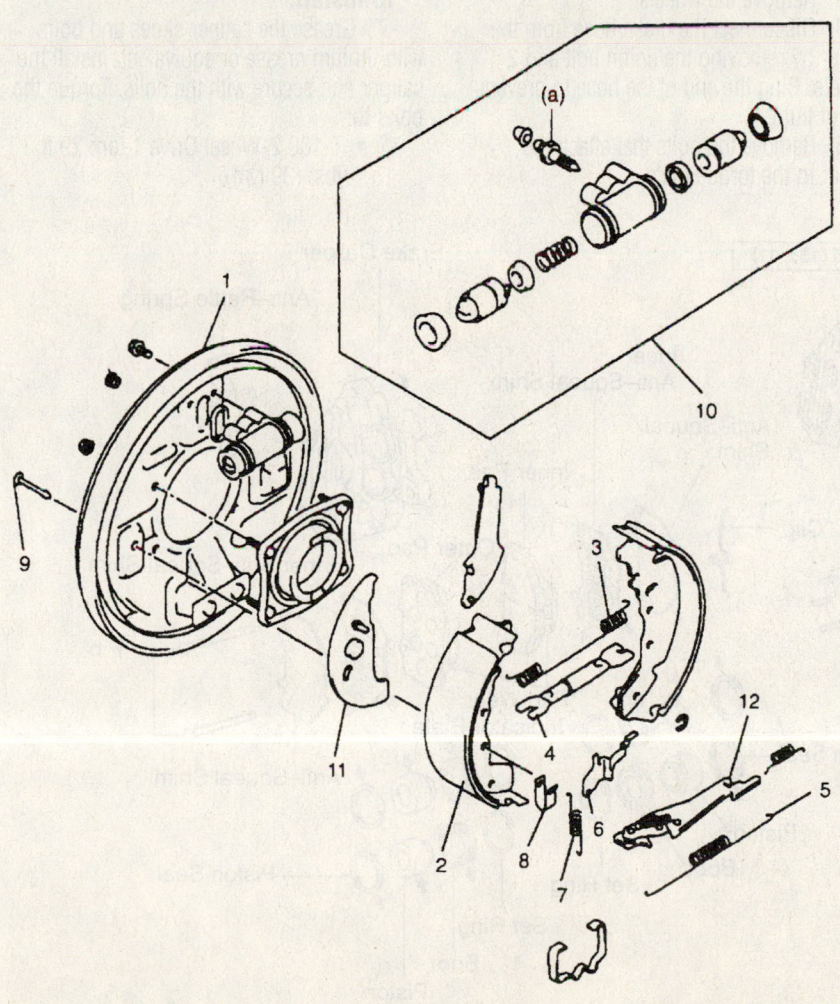

1. Brake back plate
2. Brake shoe
3. Shoe return upper spring
4. Adjuster
5. Shoe return lower spring
6. Adjuster lever
7. Adjuster spring
8. Shoe hold down spring
9. Shoe hold down pin
10. Wheel cylinder
11. Link
12. Brake strut

**Tightening torque
(a): 7.5 N·m (0.75 kg-m, 5.5 lb-ft)**

93026G43

Exploded view of the rear brake components—Vitara and Grand Vitara

backing plate shoe contact points, anchor plate and shoe contact points, adjusting bolt, and adjuster and brake shoe contact points.

To install:

11. Reinstall the automatic adjuster lever and the parking brake lever to the rear shoe using new C-washers.

12. Connect the parking brake lever to the parking brake cable. Set the adjuster and spring to the rear shoe.

13. Set the rear brake shoe in place, install the hold-down pin and install the hold-down spring and retainers. Make sure that the shoe is inserted in the wheel cylinder and that the other end is in the anchor plate.

14. Install the anchor spring to the rear shoe.

15. Install the front shoe to the other end of the anchor spring and set the front shoe in place. Make sure that the front shoe engages the wheel cylinder, adjuster mechanism and spring, and the anchor plate.

16. Reinstall the front brake shoe hold-down pin and secure with the hold-down spring and retainers using a suitable tool.

17. Install the return spring.

18. Install the brake drum and pull the parking brake lever all the way up until a clicking sound can no longer be heard.

19. Verify that the rear wheels will not turn. If the rear wheels turn, adjust the parking brake cable as necessary.

20. Release the parking brake and remove the brake drum. Measure the diameter of the brake shoes. Brake diameter should be as follows:

- For 2 door models: 8.638 (0.0012 inches (219 (0.3mm)
- For 4 door models: 9.980 (0.0079 inches (253.5 (0.2mm)

21. If the brake shoe clearance is not correct, adjust the brake shoes until the clearance is correct.

22. Reinstall the brake drum, replace the wheel(s), and safely lower the vehicle.

23. Road-test the vehicle for proper brake operation.

TOYOTA

Brake Caliper

REMOVAL & INSTALLATION

T-100, Tacoma and 4Runner

1. Disconnect the negative battery cable from the battery.

2. Raise and support the vehicle safely.

3. Remove the wheels.

4. Disconnect the brake hose from the caliper by removing the union bolt and 2 gaskets. Plug the end of the hose to prevent loss of fluid.

5. Remove the bolts that attach the caliper to the torque plate.

6. Lift the bottom of the caliper up and remove the caliper assembly.

To install:

7. Grease the caliper slides and bolts with lithium grease or equivalent. Install the caliper and secure with the bolts. Torque the bolts to:

- T-100 2-Wheel Drive 1 ton: 29 ft. lbs. (39 Nm)

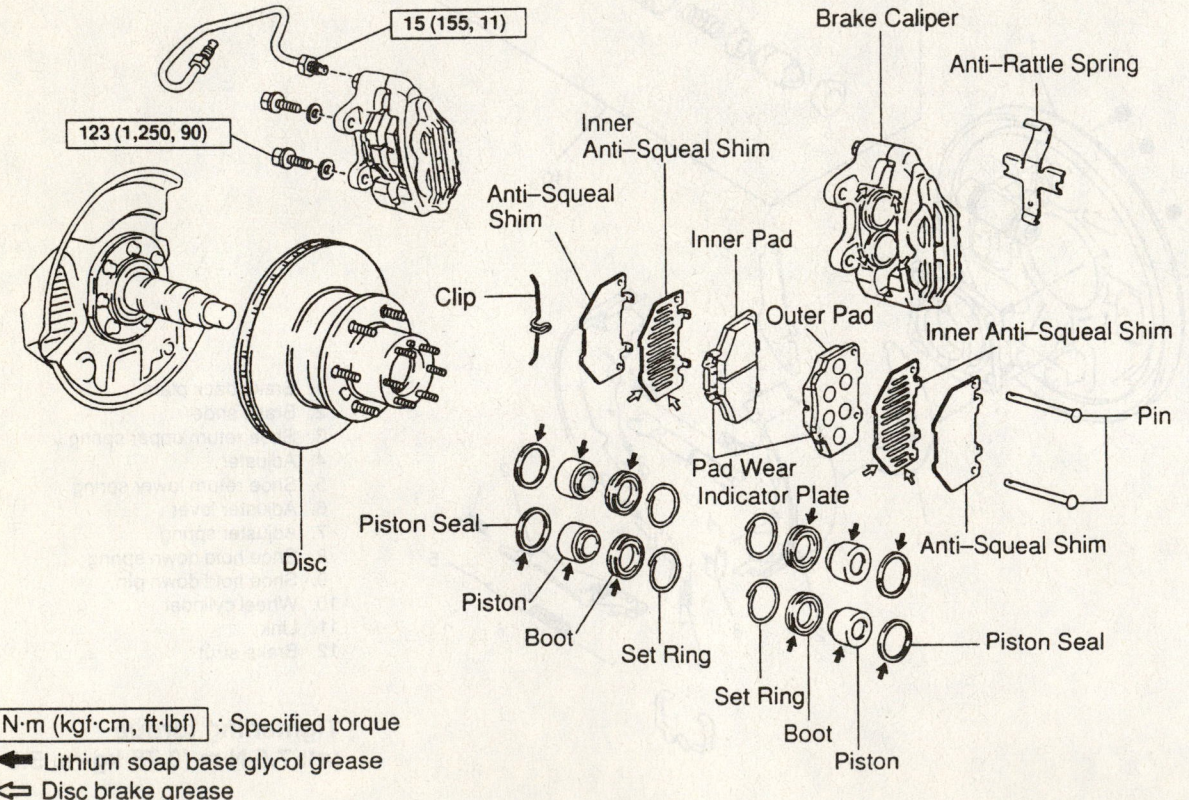

N·m (kgf·cm, ft·lbf) : Specified torque
⬅ Lithium soap base glycol grease
⬅ Disc brake grease

93026G71

Dual piston type caliper assembly—4WD T-100, Tacoma and 4Runner

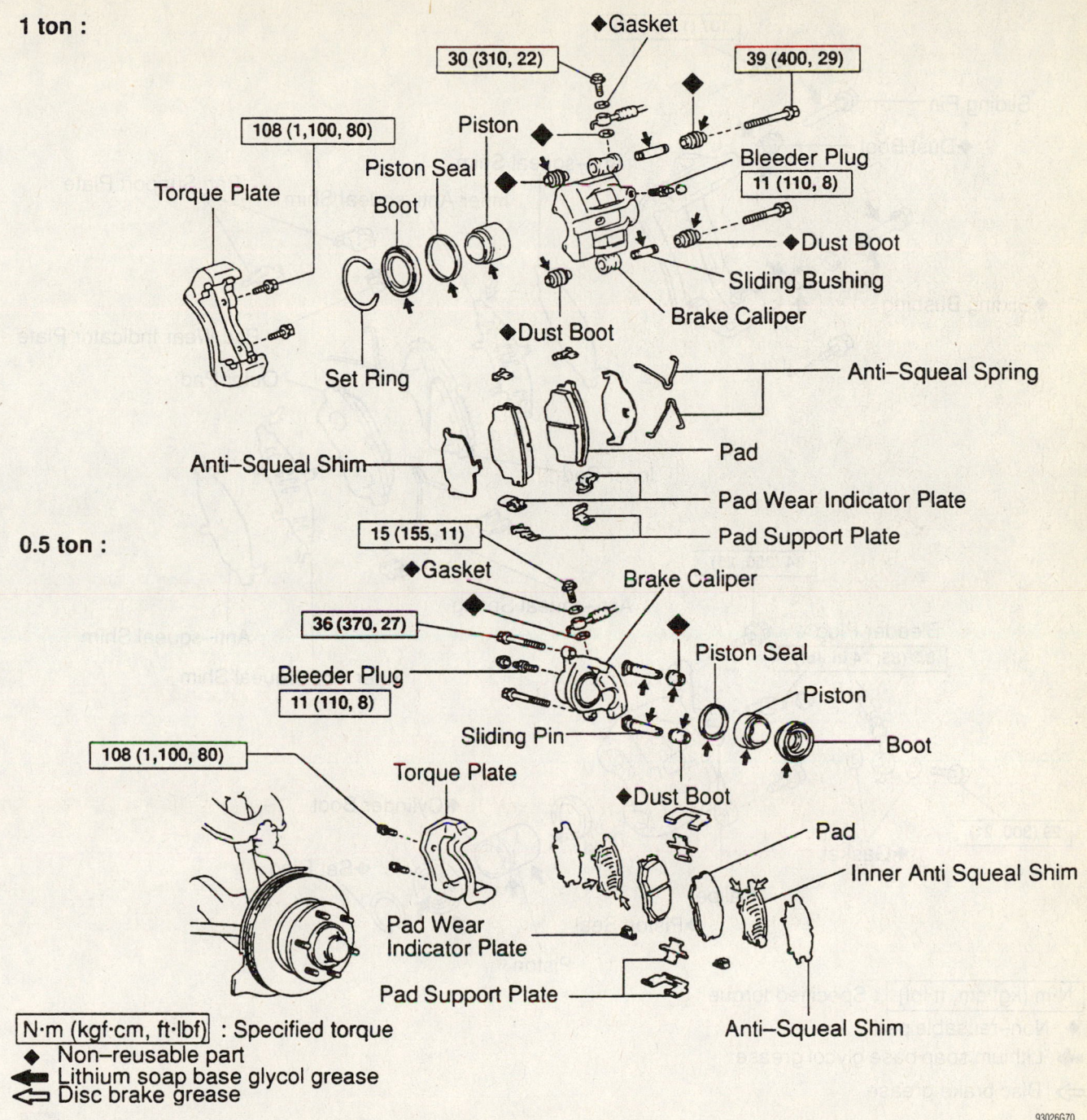

1 ton :

Gasket

30 (310, 22)

39 (400, 29)

108 (1,100, 80)

Piston

Torque Plate

Piston Seal

Boot

Bleeder Plug

11 (110, 8)

◆Dust Boot

Sliding Bushing

Brake Caliper

◆Dust Boot

Set Ring

Anti–Squeal Spring

Anti–Squeal Shim

Pad

Pad Wear Indicator Plate

Pad Support Plate

0.5 ton :

15 (155, 11)

◆Gasket

Brake Caliper

36 (370, 27)

Bleeder Plug

11 (110, 8)

Piston Seal

Piston

Sliding Pin

Boot

108 (1,100, 80)

Torque Plate

◆Dust Boot

Pad

Inner Anti Squeal Shim

Pad Wear
Indicator Plate

Pad Support Plate

Anti–Squeal Shim

N·m (kgf·cm, ft·lbf) : Specified torque
◆ Non–reusable part
◀ Lithium soap base glycol grease
◁ Disc brake grease

93026G70

Single piston type caliper assembly—2WD T-100, Tacoma and 4Runner

- T-100 2-Wheel Drive ½ ton, Tacoma: 65 ft. lbs. (88 Nm)
- 4Runner: 90 ft. lbs. (123 Nm)
- 4-wheel drive: 65 ft. lbs. (88 Nm)

8. Connect the brake hose to the caliper, using 2 new washers. Make sure the flexible hose lock is securely in the lock hole of the caliper. Torque the union bolt to:

- Tacoma: 22 ft. lbs. (30 Nm).

- T-100, and 4Runner: 11 ft. lbs. (15 Nm)

9. Fill the brake system to the proper level and bleed the brake system.

10. Install the tire and wheel assembly.

11. Top off the brake fluid level in the master cylinder. Check for leaks and proper brake operation.

12. Connect the negative battery cable to the battery.

Previa and Sienna

1. Disconnect the negative battery cable from the battery.

2. Raise and support the vehicle safely.

3. Remove the wheels.

4. Disconnect the brake hose from the

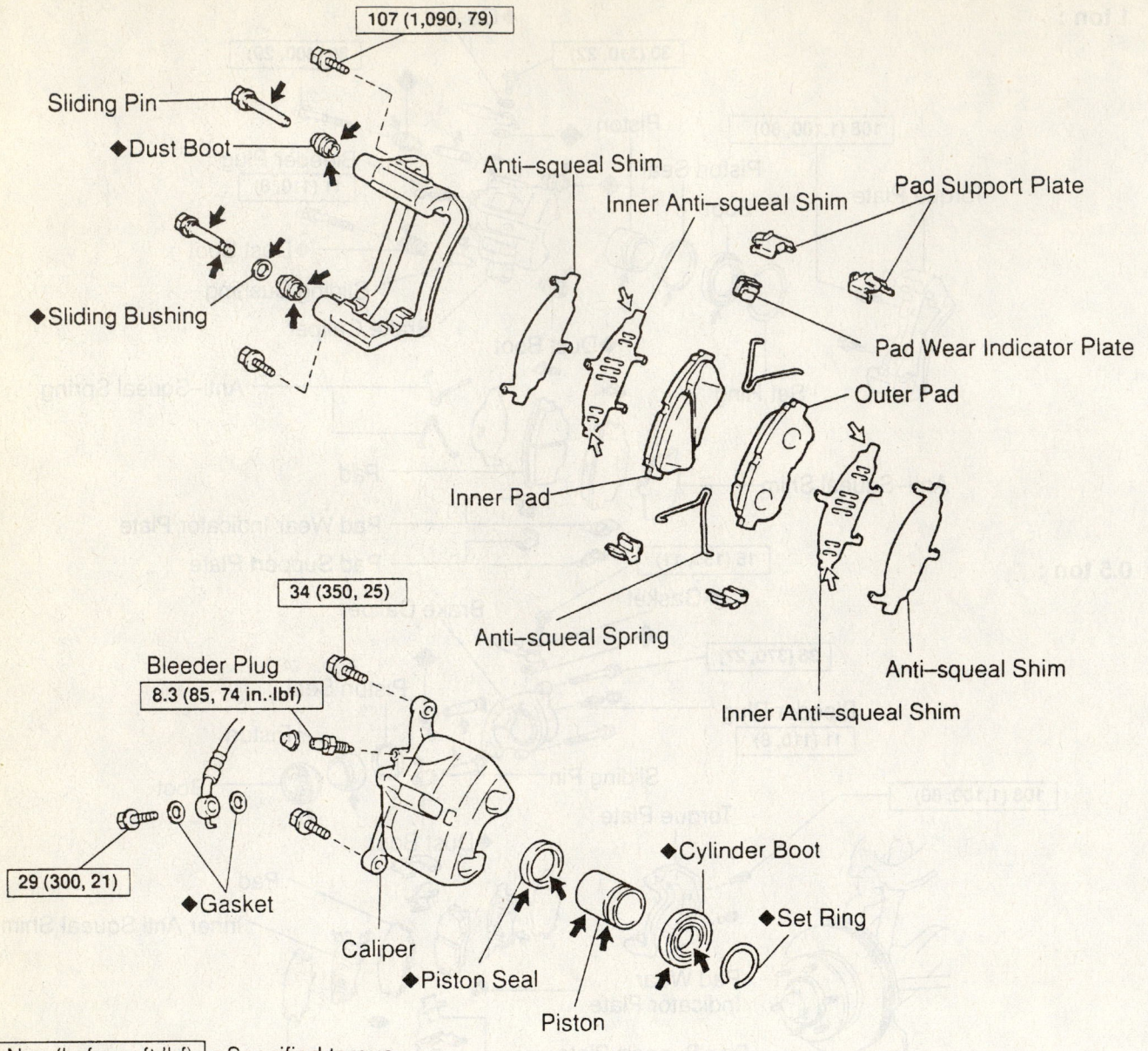

107 (1,090, 79)

Sliding Pin

◆Dust Boot

◆Sliding Bushing

Anti–squeal Shim

Inner Anti–squeal Shim

Pad Support Plate

Pad Wear Indicator Plate

Outer Pad

Inner Pad

Anti–squeal Spring

Anti–squeal Shim

Inner Anti–squeal Shim

34 (350, 25)

Bleeder Plug

8.3 (85, 74 in.·lbf)

29 (300, 21)

◆Gasket

Caliper

◆Piston Seal

Piston

◆Cylinder Boot

◆Set Ring

N·m (kgf·cm, ft·lbf) : Specified torque

◆ Non–reusable part

➡ Lithium soap base glycol grease

➪ Disc brake grease

93026G72

Exploded view of the front disc brake caliper assembly—Sienna

caliper by removing the union bolt and 2 gaskets. Plug the end of the hose to prevent loss of fluid.

5. Remove the bolts that attach the caliper to the torque plate.

6. Lift the bottom of the caliper up and remove the caliper assembly.

To install:

7. Grease the caliper slides and bolts with lithium grease or equivalent. Install the caliper and secure with the bolts. Torque the bolts to 27 ft. lbs. (36 Nm).

8. Reconnect the brake hose to the caliper, using 2 new washers. Make sure the flexible hose lock is securely in the lock hole of the caliper. Torque the union bolt to 22 ft. lbs. (30 Nm). Also, verify that the brake hose is not twisted.

9. Fill the brake system to the proper level and bleed the brake system.

10. Install the tire and wheel assem-bly.

11. Top off the brake fluid level in the master cylinder. Check for leaks and proper brake operation.

12. Connect the negative battery cable to the battery.

RAV4

1. Raise and safely support the vehicle.

2. Remove the wheel(s).

3. Remove the union bolt and 2 gaskets and remove the flexible brake hose from the caliper. Use a suitable con-tainer to catch the brake fluid as it drains out.

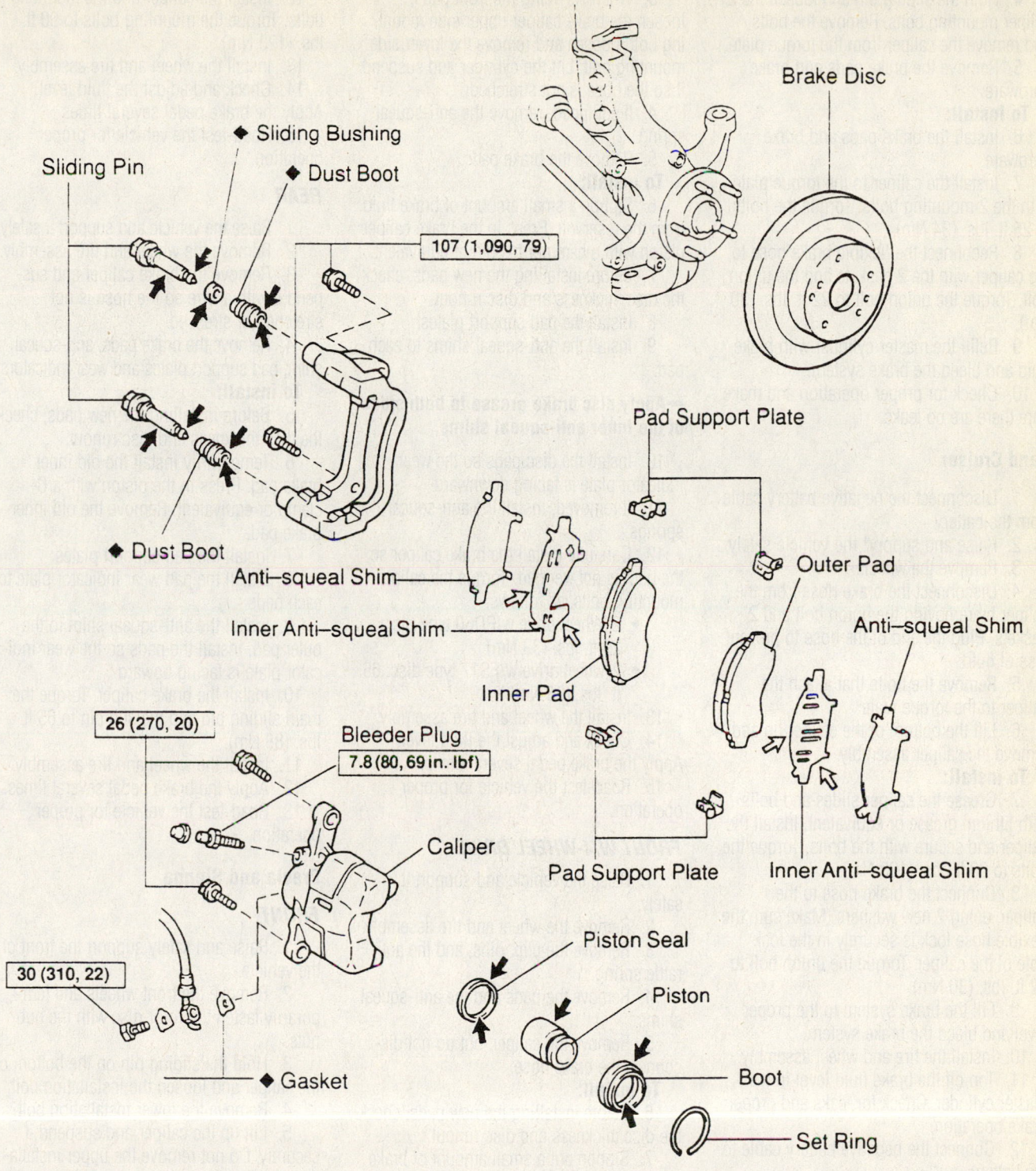

Brake Disc

Sliding Bushing

Sliding Pin

Dust Boot

107 (1,090, 79)

Pad Support Plate

Dust Boot

Anti-squeal Shim

Inner Anti-squeal Shim

Inner Pad

Outer Pad

Anti-squeal Shim

26 (270, 20)

Bleeder Plug

7.8 (80, 69 in.·lbf)

Caliper

Pad Support Plate

Inner Anti-squeal Shim

Piston Seal

Piston

30 (310, 22)

Gasket

Boot

Set Ring

N·m (kgf·cm, ft·lbf) : Specified torque

◆ Non-reusable part

➡ Lithium soap base glycol grease

⇨ Disc brake grease

93026G73

Exploded view of the front brake components—RAV4

For brake related suspension and axle service, refer to the model specific sections of this manual

4. Hold the sliding pin and loosen the 2 caliper mounting bolts. Remove the bolts and remove the caliper from the torque plate.

5. Remove the brake pads and brake hardware.

To install:

6. Install the brake pads and brake hardware.

7. Install the caliper to the torque plate with the 2 mounting bolts. Torque the bolts to 25 ft. lbs. (34 Nm).

8. Reconnect the flexible brake hose to the caliper with the 2 gaskets and the union bolt. Torque the union bolt to 22 ft. lbs. (30 Nm).

9. Refill the master cylinder with brake fluid and bleed the brake system.

10. Check for proper operation and make sure there are no leaks.

Land Cruiser

1. Disconnect the negative battery cable from the battery.

2. Raise and support the vehicle safely.

3. Remove the wheels.

4. Disconnect the brake hose from the caliper by removing the union bolt and 2 gaskets. Plug the end of the hose to prevent loss of fluid.

5. Remove the bolts that attach the caliper to the torque plate.

6. Lift the bottom of the caliper up and remove the caliper assembly.

To install:

7. Grease the caliper slides and bolts with lithium grease or equivalent. Install the caliper and secure with the bolts. Torque the bolts to 90 ft. lbs. (123 Nm).

8. Connect the brake hose to the caliper, using 2 new washers. Make sure the flexible hose lock is securely in the lock hole of the caliper. Torque the union bolt to 22 ft. lbs. (30 Nm).

9. Fill the brake system to the proper level and bleed the brake system.

10. Install the tire and wheel assembly.

11. Top off the brake fluid level in the master cylinder. Check for leaks and proper brake operation.

12. Connect the negative battery cable to the battery.

Disc Brake Pads

REMOVAL & INSTALLATION

T-100, Tacoma and 4Runner

FRONT W/2-WHEEL DRIVE

1. Raise the vehicle and support it safely.
2. Remove the wheel and tire assembly.

3. When servicing the front pads, loosen the brake caliper upper side mounting bolt. Loosen and remove the lower side mounting bolt. Lift the cylinder and suspend it so the hose is not stretched.

4. If equipped, remove the anti-squeal spring.

5. Remove the brake pads.

To install:

6. Siphon a small amount of brake fluid from the reservoir. Press in the brake caliper piston with a hammer handle or equivalent.

7. Before installing the new pads, check the disc thickness and disc runout.

8. Install the pad support plates.

9. Install the anti-squeal shims to each pad.

➡ **Apply disc brake grease to both sides of the inner anti-squeal shims.**

10. Install the disc pads so the wear indicator plate is facing downward.

11. If removed, install the anti-squeal springs.

12. Carefully install the brake caliper so the boot is not wedged. Torque the caliper mounting bolts, as follows:
- 2-Wheel drive w/PD60 type disc: 29 ft. lbs. (39 Nm)
- 2-wheel drive w/FS17 type disc: 65 ft. lbs. (88 Nm)

13. Install the wheel and tire assembly.

14. Check and adjust the fluid level. Apply the brake pedal several times.

15. Road-test the vehicle for proper operation.

FRONT W/4-WHEEL DRIVE

1. Raise the vehicle and support it safely.

2. Remove the wheel and tire assembly.

3. Remove the clip, pins, and the anti-rattle spring.

4. Remove the pads and the anti-squeal shims.

5. Remove the caliper, but do not disconnect the brake hose.

To install:

6. Before installing the new pads, check the disc thickness and disc runout.

7. Siphon out a small amount of brake fluid from the reservoir.

8. Temporarily install the old inner brake pad. Press in the pistons with a C-clamp or equivalent. Remove the old inner brake pad.

9. Apply disc brake grease to both sides of the inner anti-squeal shim. Install the anti-squeal shims to the new pads.

10. Install the pads.

11. Install the anti-rattle springs and pins. Install the clip.

12. Install the caliper and the mounting bolts. Torque the mounting bolts to 90 ft. lbs. (123 Nm).

13. Install the wheel and tire assembly.

14. Check and adjust the fluid level. Apply the brake pedal several times.

15. Road-test the vehicle for proper operation.

REAR

1. Raise the vehicle and support it safely.

2. Remove the wheel and tire assembly.

3. Remove the brake caliper and suspend it with a wire so the hose is not stretched or stressed.

4. Remove the brake pads, anti-squeal shim, pad support plates and wear indicators.

To install:

5. Before installing the new pads, check the disc thickness and disc runout.

6. Temporarily install the old inner brake pad. Press in the piston with a C-clamp or equivalent. Remove the old inner brake pad.

7. Install the pad support plates.

8. Install the pad wear indicator plate to each pads.

9. Install the anti-squeal shim to the outer pad. Install the pads so the wear indicator plate is facing upward.

10. Install the brake caliper. Torque the main sliding pin and the sub pin to 65 ft. lbs. (88 Nm).

11. Install the wheel and tire assembly.

12. Apply the brake pedal several times.

13. Road-test the vehicle for proper operation.

Previa and Sienna

FRONT

1. Raise and safely support the front of the vehicle.

2. Remove the front wheels and temporarily fasten the rotor disc with the hub nuts.

3. Hold the sliding pin on the bottom of the caliper and loosen the installation bolt.

4. Remove the lower installation bolt.

5. Lift up the caliper and suspend it securely. Do not remove the upper installation bolt.

6. Remove the following parts:
- The 2 anti-squeal springs.
- The 2 brake pads.
- The 4 anti-squeal shims.
- The 4 pad support plates.

To install:

7. Install the pad support plates.

8. Install a pad wear indicator plate to the pad. Install the anti-squeal shims and support plates to each pad.

Single-Piston Type:

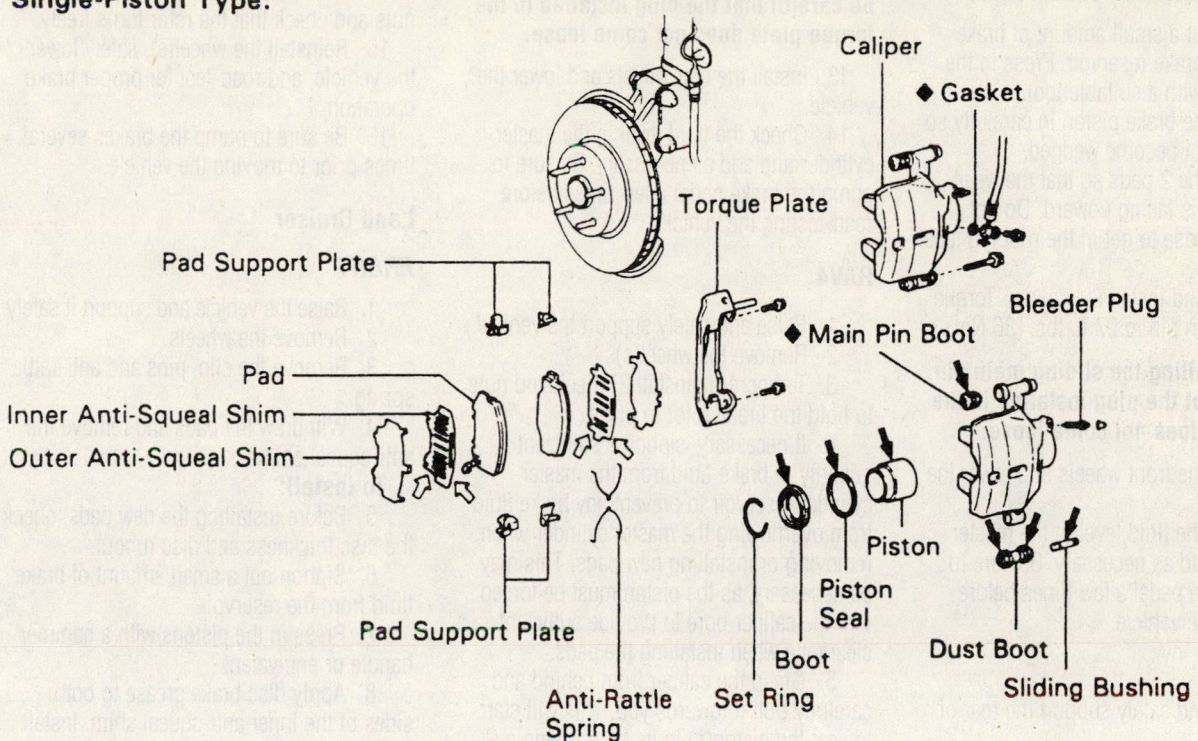

Caliper

◆ Gasket

Torque Plate

Pad Support Plate

◆ Main Pin Boot

Bleeder Plug

Pad

Inner Anti-Squeal Shim

Outer Anti-Squeal Shim

Piston

Piston Seal

Boot

Dust Boot

Sliding Bushing

Pad Support Plate

Set Ring

Anti-Rattle Spring

2-Piston Type:

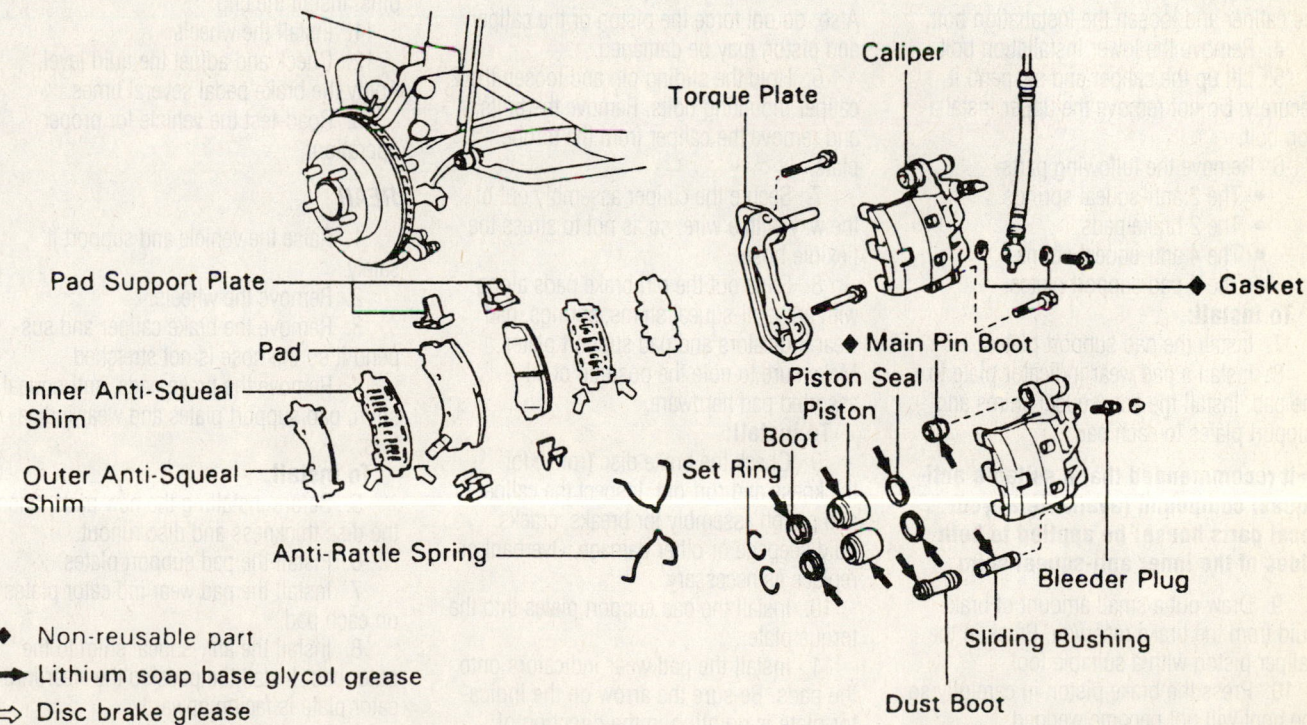

Torque Plate

Caliper

Pad Support Plate

◆ Main Pin Boot

Gasket

Pad

Piston Seal

Piston

Inner Anti-Squeal Shim

Boot

Set Ring

Outer Anti-Squeal Shim

Bleeder Plug

Anti-Rattle Spring

Sliding Bushing

Dust Boot

◆ Non-reusable part

Lithium soap base glycol grease

Disc brake grease

93026G74

Exploded view of the rear disc brake components—single and dual piston—Previa

➡**It recommended that a suitable anti-squeal compound be applied to both sides of the inner anti-squeal shim.**

9. Draw out a small amount of brake fluid from the brake reservoir. Press in the caliper piston with a suitable tool.

10. Press the brake piston in carefully so the boot will not become wedged.

11. Install the 2 pads so that the wear indicator plate is facing upward. Do not allow oil or grease to get in the rubbing face of the pads.

12. Lower and install the caliper. Torque the sliding main pin to 27 ft. lbs. (36 Nm).

➡**When installing the sliding main pin, be careful that the plug installed in the torque plate does not come loose.**

13. Install the front wheels and lower the vehicle.

14. Check the fluid level in the master cylinder and add as necessary. Be sure to pump the brake pedal a few times before road-testing the vehicle.

REAR

1. Raise and safely support the rear of the vehicle.

2. Remove the rear wheels and temporarily fasten the rotor disc with the hub nuts.

3. Hold the sliding pin on the bottom of the caliper and loosen the installation bolt.

4. Remove the lower installation bolt.

5. Lift up the caliper and suspend it securely. Do not remove the upper installation bolt.

6. Remove the following parts:
   - The 2 anti-squeal springs.
   - The 2 brake pads.
   - The 4 anti-squeal shims.
   - The 4 pad support plates.

   To install:

7. Install the pad support plates.

8. Install a pad wear indicator plate to the pad. Install the anti-squeal shims and support plates to each pad.

➡**It recommended that a suitable anti-squeal compound (available at your local parts house) be applied to both sides of the inner anti-squeal shim.**

9. Draw out a small amount of brake fluid from the brake reservoir. Press in the caliper piston with a suitable tool.

10. Press the brake piston in carefully so the boot will not become wedged.

11. Install the 2 pads so that the wear indicator plate is facing upward. Do not allow oil or grease to get in the rubbing face of the pads.

12. Lower and install the caliper. Torque the sliding main pin to 25 ft. lbs. (34 Nm).

➡**When installing the sliding main pin, be careful that the plug installed in the torque plate does not come loose.**

13. Install the rear wheels and lower the vehicle.

14. Check the fluid level in the master cylinder and add as necessary. Be sure to pump the brake pedal a few times before road-testing the vehicle.

RAV4

1. Raise and safely support the vehicle.

2. Remove the wheel(s).

3. Temporarily install 2 wheel stud nuts to hold the brake rotor in place.

4. If necessary, siphon a sufficient quantity of brake fluid from the master cylinder reservoir to prevent any brake fluid from overflowing the master cylinder when removing or installing new pads. This may be necessary, as the piston must be forced into the caliper bore to provide sufficient clearance when installing the pads.

5. Grasp the caliper from behind and carefully pull it towards you. This will start to seat the piston(s) in its bore. Using a C-clamp or other suitable tool, press the piston the remaining way into the caliper. Be careful not to cock the piston in the bore. Also, do not force the piston or the caliper and piston may be damaged.

6. Hold the sliding pin and loosen the 2 caliper mounting bolts. Remove the bolts and remove the caliper from the torque plate.

7. Secure the caliper assembly out of the way with a wire; so as not to stress the flexible hose.

8. Slide out the old brake pads along with any anti-squeal shims, springs, pad wear indicators and pad support plates. Make sure to note the position of all assorted pad hardware.

   To install:

9. Check the brake disc (rotor) for thickness and run-out. Inspect the caliper and piston assembly for breaks, cracks, fluid seepage or other damage. Overhaul or replace as necessary.

10. Install the pad support plates into the torque plate.

11. Install the pad wear indicators onto the pads. Be sure the arrow on the indicator plate is pointing in the direction of rotation.

12. Install the anti-squeal shims on the outside of each pad and then install the pad assemblies into the torque plate.

13. Install the caliper to the torque plate with the 2 mounting bolts. Torque the bolts to 20 ft. lbs. (26 Nm).

14. Remove the 2 temporary wheel stud nuts and check that the rotor turns freely.

15. Reinstall the wheel(s), safely lower the vehicle, and road-test for proper brake operation.

16. Be sure to pump the brakes several times prior to moving the vehicle.

Land Cruiser

FRONT

1. Raise the vehicle and support it safely.

2. Remove the wheels.

3. Remove the clip, pins and anti-rattle spring.

4. Withdraw the pads and remove the anti-squeal shims.

   To install:

5. Before installing the new pads, check the disc thickness and disc runout.

6. Siphon out a small amount of brake fluid from the reservoir.

7. Press in the pistons with a hammer handle or equivalent.

8. Apply disc brake grease to both sides of the inner anti-squeal shim. Install the anti-squeal shims to the new pads.

9. Install the pads.

10. Install the anti-rattle springs and pins. Install the clip.

11. Install the wheels.

12. Check and adjust the fluid level. Apply the brake pedal several times.

13. Road-test the vehicle for proper operation.

REAR

1. Raise the vehicle and support it safely.

2. Remove the wheels.

3. Remove the brake caliper and suspend it so the hose is not stretched.

4. Remove the brake pads, anti-squeal shim, pad support plates and wear indicators.

   To install:

5. Before installing the new pads, check the disc thickness and disc runout.

6. Install the pad support plates.

7. Install the pad wear indicator plates on each pad.

8. Install the anti-squeal shim to the outer pad. Install the pads so the wear indicator plate is facing upward.

9. Install the brake caliper.

10. Install the wheels.

11. Apply the brake pedal several times.

12. Road-test the vehicle for proper operation.

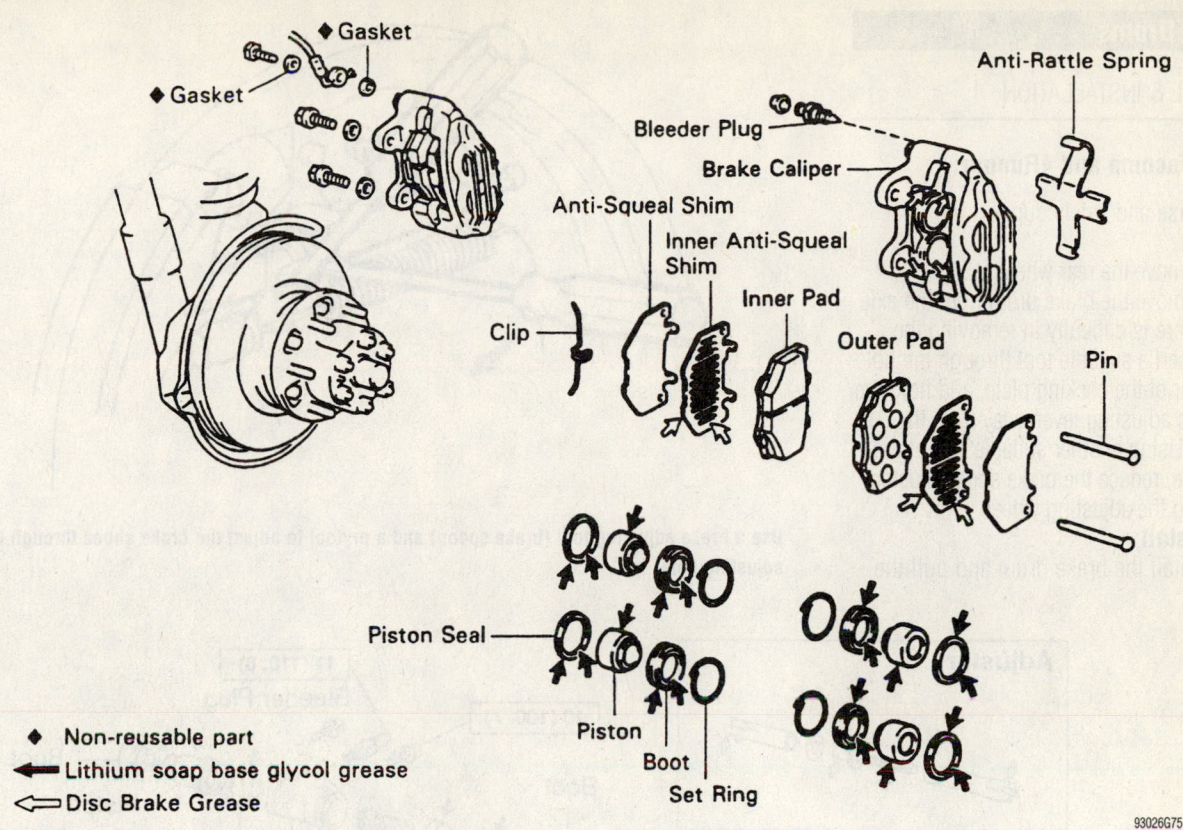

Gasket
Gasket
Gasket
Bleeder Plug
Brake Caliper
Anti-Rattle Spring
Anti-Squeal Shim
Inner Anti-Squeal Shim
Inner Pad
Outer Pad
Clip
Pin
Piston Seal
Piston
Boot
Set Ring

◆ Non-reusable part
← Lithium soap base glycol grease
⇐ Disc Brake Grease

Exploded view of the front disc brake components—Land Cruiser

93026G75

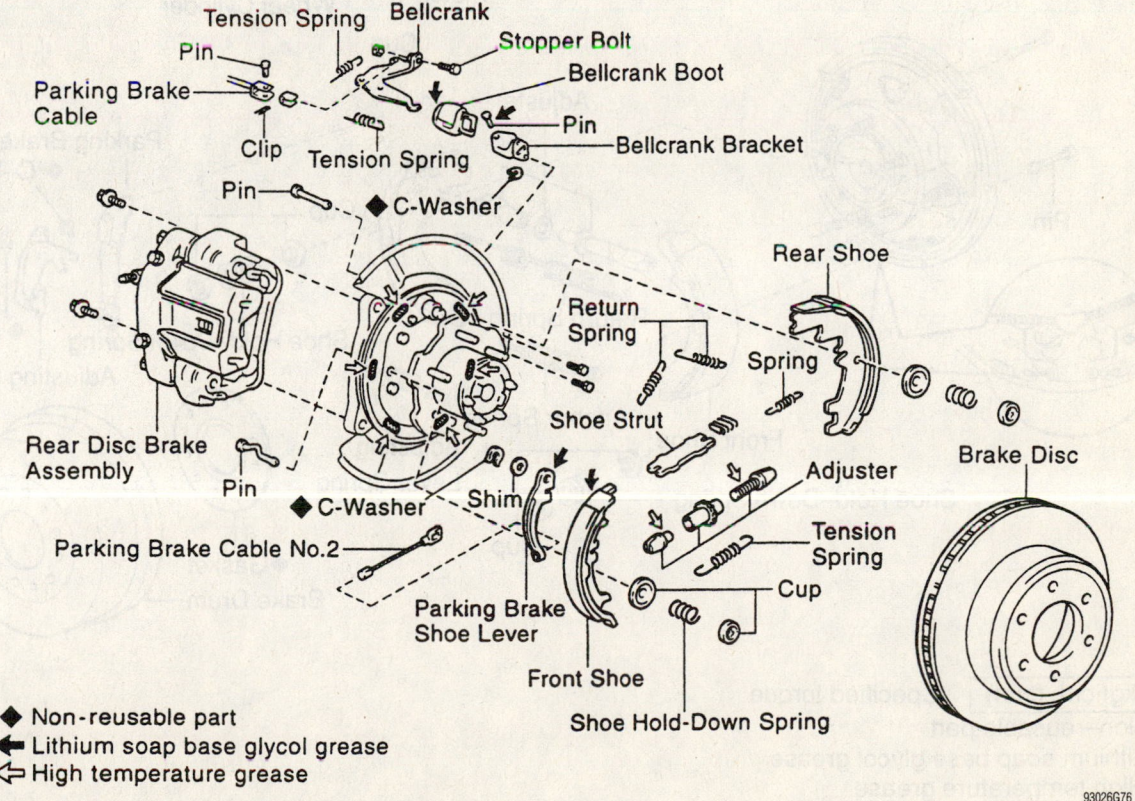

Tension Spring
Bellcrank
Stopper Bolt
Pin
Bellcrank Boot
Parking Brake Cable
Pin
Bellcrank Bracket
Clip
Tension Spring
Pin
◆ C-Washer
Rear Shoe
Return Spring
Spring
Shoe Strut
Rear Disc Brake Assembly
Pin
Brake Disc
◆ C-Washer
Shim
Adjuster
Parking Brake Cable No.2
Tension Spring
Cup
Parking Brake Shoe Lever
Front Shoe
Shoe Hold-Down Spring

◆ Non-reusable part
← Lithium soap base glycol grease
⇐ High temperature grease

Exploded view of the rear disc brake components—Land Cruiser

93026G76

Brake Drums

REMOVAL & INSTALLATION

T-100, Tacoma and 4Runner

1. Raise and safely support the vehicle.
2. Remove the rear wheel(s).
3. Remove the brake drum from the axle hub. If there is difficulty in removing the drum, insert a suitable tool through the hole in the rear of the backing plate, and hold the automatic adjusting lever away from the adjuster. Using another suitable tool at the same time, reduce the brake shoe adjuster by turning the adjusting wheel.

To install:

4. Install the brake drum and pull the

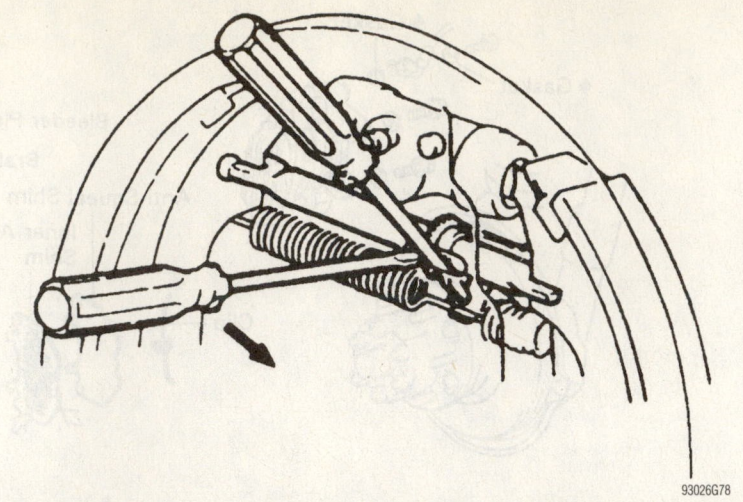

93026G78

Use a brake adjusting tool (brake spoon) and a prytool to adjust the brake shoes through the adjusting hole

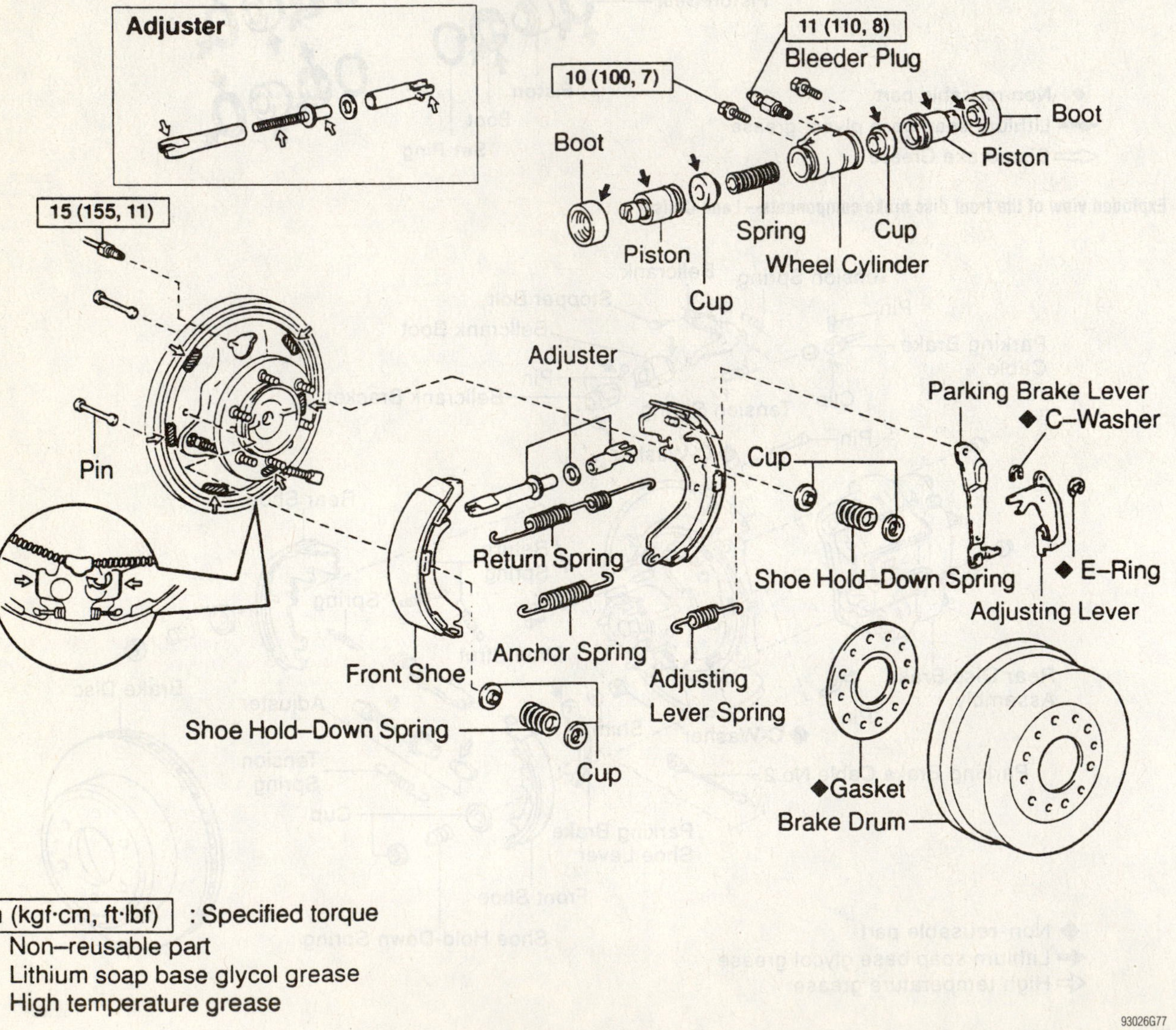

Adjuster

15 (155, 11)

Pin

10 (100, 7)

11 (110, 8)
Bleeder Plug

Boot

Boot
Piston

Piston

Spring
Cup

Cup
Wheel Cylinder

Adjuster

Parking Brake Lever
◆ C–Washer

Cup

Return Spring

Shoe Hold–Down Spring

◆ E–Ring

Adjusting Lever

Anchor Spring

Adjusting Lever Spring

Front Shoe

Shoe Hold–Down Spring

Cup

◆Gasket
Brake Drum

| N·m (kgf·cm, ft·lbf) | : Specified torque
◆ Non–reusable part
➡ Lithium soap base glycol grease
⇨ High temperature grease

93026G77

Exploded view of the rear brake drums components—2-WD T-100 and Tacoma models shown, others similar

parking brake lever all the way up until a clicking sound can no longer be heard.

5. Verify that the rear wheels will not turn. If the rear wheels turn, adjust the parking brake cable as necessary.

6. Release the parking brake and remove the brake drum. Measure the brake drum inside diameter and diameter of the brake shoes. Check that the difference between the diameters is the correct shoe clearance. Clearance is 0.024 in. (6mm).

7. If the brake shoe clearance is not correct, adjust the brake shoes until the clearance is correct.

8. Install the brake drum, replace the wheel(s), and safely lower the vehicle.

9. Road-test the vehicle for proper brake operation.

RAV4

1. Raise and safely support the vehicle.
2. Remove the wheel(s).
3. Temporarily install 2 wheel stud nuts to hold the brake rotor in place.
4. If necessary, siphon a sufficient quantity of brake fluid from the master cylinder reservoir to prevent any brake fluid from overflowing the master cylinder when removing or installing new pads. This may be necessary, as the piston must be forced into the caliper bore to provide sufficient clearance when installing the pads.
5. Grasp the caliper from behind and carefully pull it towards you. This will start to seat the piston(s) in its bore. Using a C-clamp or other suitable tool, press the piston the remaining way into the caliper. Be careful not to cock the piston in the bore. Also, do not force the piston or the caliper and piston may be damaged.
6. Hold the sliding pin and loosen the 2 caliper mounting bolts. Remove the bolts and remove the caliper from the torque plate.
7. Secure the caliper assembly out of the way with a wire, to avoid stressing the flexible hose.
8. Slide out the old brake pads along with any anti-squeal shims, springs, pad wear indicators and pad support plates. Make sure to note the position of all assorted pad hardware.

To install:
9. Check the brake disc (rotor) for thickness and run-out. Inspect the caliper

and piston assembly for breaks, cracks, fluid seepage or other damage. Overhaul or replace as necessary.

10. Install the pad support plates into the torque plate.

11. Install the pad wear indicators onto the pads. Be sure the arrow on the indicator plate is pointing in the direction of rotation.

12. Install the anti-squeal shims on the outside of each pad and then install the pad assemblies into the torque plate.

13. Install the caliper to the torque plate with the 2 mounting bolts. Torque the bolts to 20 ft. lbs. (26 Nm).

14. Remove the 2 temporary wheel stud nuts and check that the rotor turns freely.

15. Reinstall the wheel(s), safely lower the vehicle, and road-test for proper brake operation.

16. Be sure to pump the brakes several times prior to moving the vehicle.

Brake Shoes

REMOVAL & INSTALLATION

T-100, Tacoma and 4Runner

1. Loosen the rear wheel lug nuts slightly.
2. Block the front wheels, raise the rear of the vehicle, and safely support it with jackstands.
3. Remove the wheel lug nuts and the wheel.
4. Remove the brake drum.
5. If the drum is difficult to remove, perform the following:
   a. Insert a flat prying tool through the hole in the brake drum and hold the automatic adjusting lever away from the adjuster.
   b. Reduce the brake shoe adjustment by turning the adjuster bolt with a brake tool.
   c. The drum should now be loose enough to remove without much effort.
6. Remove the rear shoe.
   a. Carefully unhook the return spring from the brake shoe.
   b. Remove the shoe hold-down spring, cups and the pin.
   c. Disconnect the anchor spring from the rear shoe and remove the rear shoe.

d. Disconnect the anchor spring from the front shoe.
7. Remove the front shoe.
   a. Remove the shoe hold-down spring, cups and pin.
   b. Remove the return spring from the front shoe.
   c. Remove the front shoe with the adjuster.
   d. Disconnect the parking brake cable from the front shoe.

To install:
8. Inspect the shoes for signs of unusual wear or scoring.
9. Check the wheel cylinder for any sign of fluid seepage or frozen pistons.
10. Clean and inspect the brake backing plate and all other components. Check that the brake drum inner diameter is within specified limits. Lubricate the backing plate at the positions the brakes come in contact with the backing plate. Also lubricate the anchor plate.
11. Mount the automatic adjuster assembly onto a new rear brake shoe.
12. Install the front shoe.
   a. Install the parking brake cable to the front shoe.
   b. Install the front shoe with the adjuster.
   c. Install the return spring to the front shoe.
   d. Install the shoe hold-down spring, cups and pin.
13. Install the rear shoe.
   a. Install the anchor spring to the front shoe.
   b. Install the anchor spring to the rear shoe and install the rear shoe.
   c. Install the shoe hold-down spring, cups and the pin.
   d. Hook the return spring to the brake shoe.
14. Install the brake drum.
15. Adjust the brake shoes until a slight drag is felt when the drum is spun by hand.
16. Remove the brake drum and check the clearance between brake shoes and brake drum. Adjust the clearance to specification.
17. Pull the parking lever all the way up until a clicking sound can no longer be heard. Verify that the drum doesn't turn. If the drum turns, adjust the parking brake cable.
18. Install the rear wheels, tighten the wheel lug nuts and lower the vehicle.

19. Retighten the wheel lug nuts and pump the brake pedal a few times before moving the vehicle. Adjust the rear brakes again if necessary.

20. Check the level of brake fluid in the master cylinder, then perform a test drive.

21. Connect the negative battery cable to the battery.

Previa, RAV4 and Sienna

1. Disconnect the negative battery cable from the battery.

2. Loosen the rear wheel lug nuts slightly. Release the parking brake.

3. Block the front wheels, raise the rear of the vehicle, and safely support it with jackstands.

4. Remove the wheel lug nuts and the wheel.

5. Remove the brake drum retaining screws, if equipped. Remove the brake drum.

6. If the drum is difficult to remove, perform the following:

a. Insert the end of a bent wire (a coat hanger will do nicely) through the hole in the brake drum and hold the automatic adjusting lever away from the adjuster.

b. Reduce the brake shoe adjustment by turning the adjuster bolt with a brake tool.

c. The drum should now be loose enough to remove without much effort.

7. Carefully unhook the return spring from the leading (front) brake shoe.

8. Press the hold down spring retainer in and turn the pin on the front brake shoe.

9. Remove the hold down spring, retainers and the pin for the front brake shoe.

10. Pull out the brake shoe and unhook the anchor spring from the lower edge.

11. Remove the hold down spring from the trailing (rear) shoe. Pull the shoe out

with the adjuster, automatic adjuster assembly and springs attached. Disconnect the parking brake cable. Remove the tension/return and anchor springs from the rear shoe.

12. Unhook the adjusting lever spring from the rear shoe and then remove the automatic adjuster assembly.

To install:

13. Inspect the shoes for signs of unusual wear or scoring.

14. Check the wheel cylinder for any sign of fluid seepage or frozen pistons.

15. Clean and inspect the brake backing plate and all other components. Check that the brake drum inner diameter is within specified limits. Lubricate the backing plate at the positions the brakes come in contact with the backing plate. Also lubricate the anchor plate.

16. Mount the automatic adjuster assembly onto a new rear brake shoe.

17. Connect the parking brake cable to the rear shoe and then install the automatic

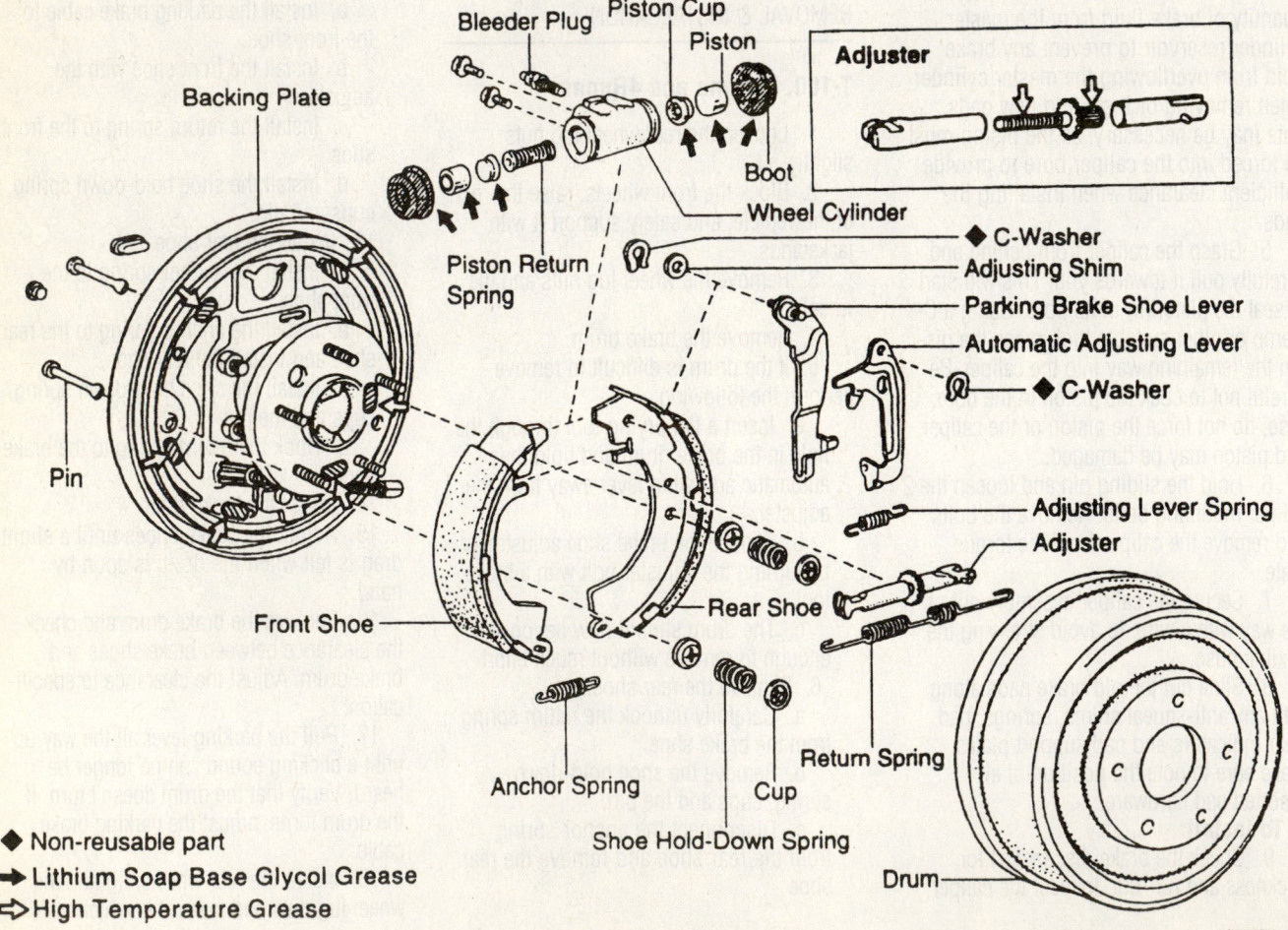

◆ Non-reusable part

➡ Lithium Soap Base Glycol Grease

⇨ High Temperature Grease

Exploded view of the rear drum brake components—Previa

93026G79

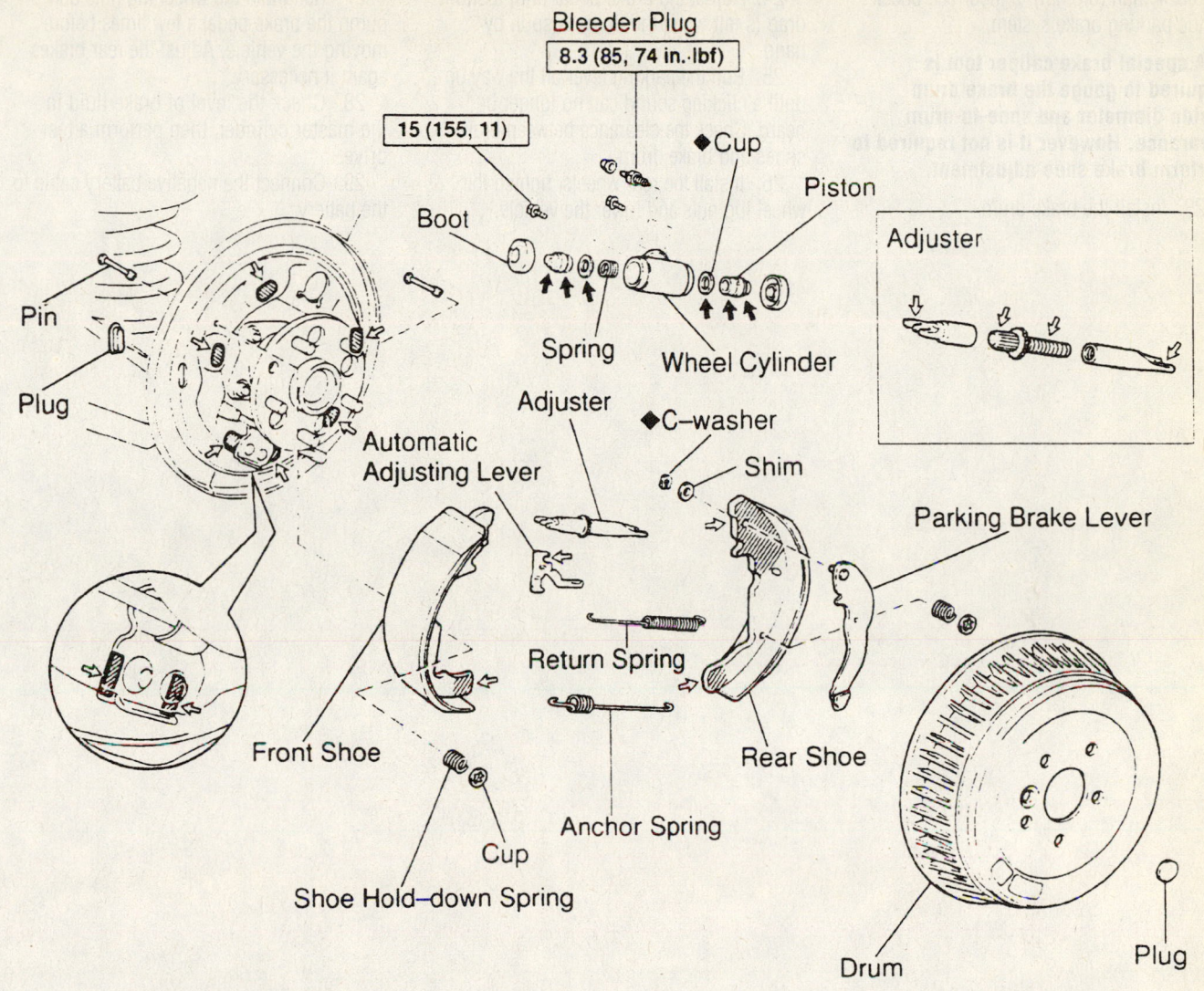

Bleeder Plug
8.3 (85, 74 in.·lbf)

15 (155, 11)

Boot

Cup

Piston

Spring

Wheel Cylinder

Adjuster

Pin

Plug

Automatic
Adjusting Lever

Adjuster

◆ C-washer

Shim

Parking Brake Lever

Return Spring

Front Shoe

Rear Shoe

Anchor Spring

Cup

Shoe Hold—down Spring

Drum

Plug

N·m (kgf·cm, ft·lbf) : Specified torque

◆ Non—reusable part

➡ Lithium soap base glycol grease

⇨ High temperature grease

93026G80

Exploded view of the rear drum brake components—Sienna

adjusting lever, spring and E-ring. Position the rear shoe so the lower end rides in the anchor plate and the upper end is against the boot of the wheel cylinder.

18. Install the pin and the hold down spring. Press the retainer down over the pin and rotate the pin so the crimped edge is held by the retainer.

19. Place the front brake into position and install the anchor spring between the front and rear shoes. Stretch the spring

enough so the front shoe will fit as the rear did. Install the hold down spring, pin and retainer to the front brake shoe.

20. Connect the return spring to the front brake shoe.

21. Check the operation of the automatic adjuster mechanism:

   a. Apply the parking brake lever and verifying the adjusting bolt turns.

   b. Adjust the strut to where it is the shortest possible length.

c. Install the brake drum.

d. Apply the parking brake lever until the clicking sound can no longer be heard.

22. Check the clearance between the brake shoes and drum:

   a. Remove the brake drum.

   b. Measure the brake drum inside diameter and diameter of the brake shoes. The difference is "Shoe-to-drum clearance" and should be approximately

0.024 inch (0.6mm). If incorrect, check the parking brake system.

➡**A special brake caliper tool is required to gauge the brake drum inside diameter and shoe-to-drum clearance. However it is not required to perform brake shoe adjustment.**

23. Install the brake drum.

24. Adjust the brake pedal until a slight drag is felt when the drum is spun by hand.

25. Pull the parking lever all the way up until a clicking sound can no longer be heard. Check the clearance between brake shoes and brake drum.

26. Install the rear wheels, tighten the wheel lug nuts and lower the vehicle.

27. Retighten the wheel lug nuts and pump the brake pedal a few times before moving the vehicle. Adjust the rear brakes again if necessary.

28. Check the level of brake fluid in the master cylinder, then perform a test drive.

29. Connect the negative battery cable to the battery.

WINDSHIELD WIPER SYSTEMS

6

ACURA

SLX

GENERAL DESCRIPTION

The windshield wiper circuit is comprised of the starter switch, wiper and washer switches, wiper motor, washer motors and relays for the intermittent function. Some models include intermittent rear window wipers and therefore have relays to control this function as well.

When the windshield wiper switch is turned on and the starter switch is in the **ON** position, battery voltage is applied to the wiper motor to activate the wiper. A fuse, located in the fuse block, protects the circuitry of the wiper system and the vehicle.

The wiper motor has permanent magnet fields. The speeds are determined by current flow to the appropriate set of brushes.

The wiper system completes the wipe cycle when the switch is turned **OFF**. The wiper blades park in the lowest portion of the wiping pattern.

TESTING

Utilize the flowcharts in conjunction with the circuit wiring diagram to systematically locate the problem (if any) in the wiper circuit. The key to troubleshooting is an organized, logical approach. Do not proceed to the next step until each step has been completed.

If you locate a problem, follow the chart's recommendation to remedy it, then test the system for proper function.

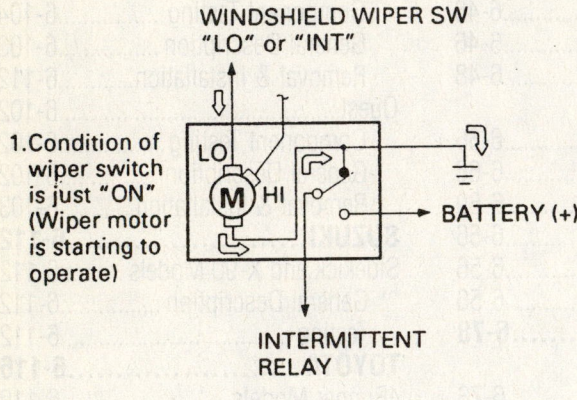

1. Condition of wiper switch is just "ON" (Wiper motor is starting to operate)

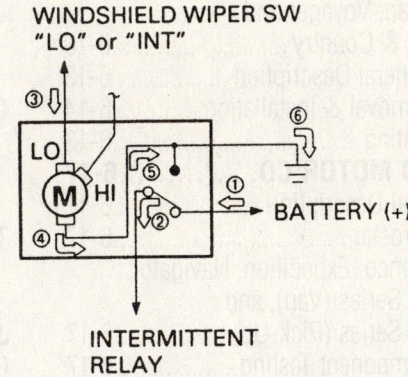

3. Condition of wiper switch is just "OFF" (Wiper motor is still operating)

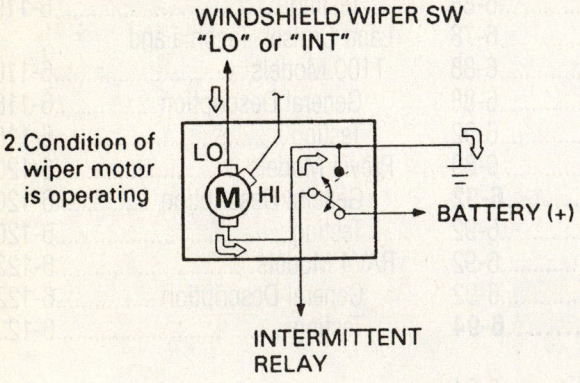

2. Condition of wiper motor is operating

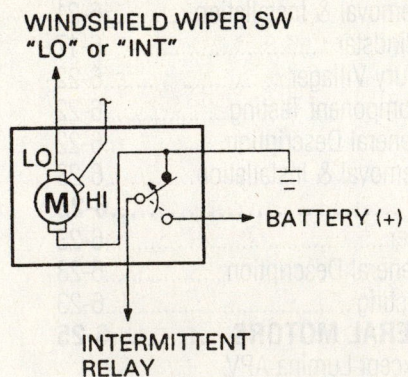

4. Wiper motor stops at auto-stop position

NOTE: Arrow marks " ⇨ " indicate the direction of current

Windshield wiper motor current flow (when switch is at "LO" or "INT")—SLX

7921ZG26

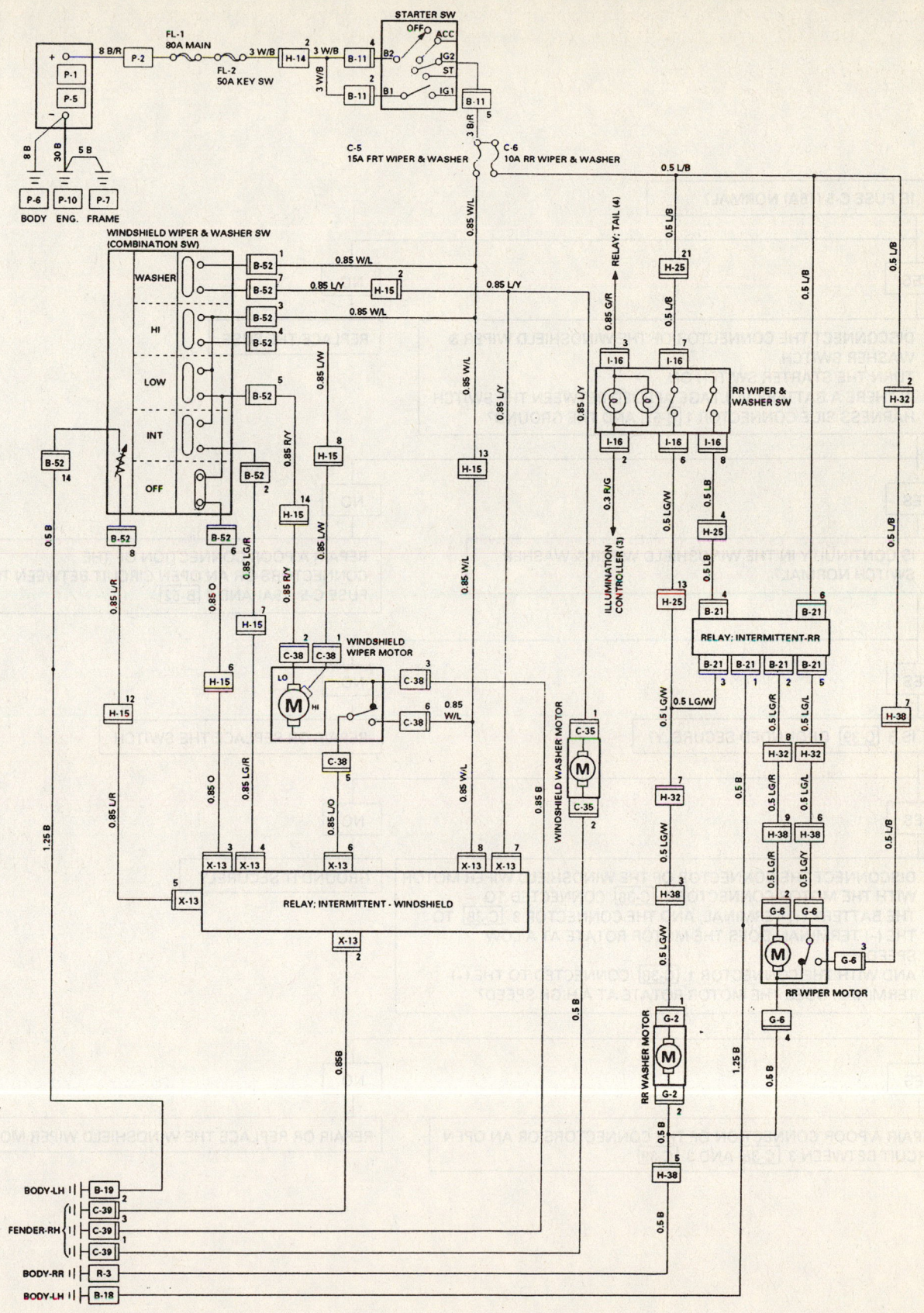

Windshield wiper system circuit wiring diagram—SLX

7921ZG27

For complete service labor times order Nichols' Chilton Labor Guide Manual

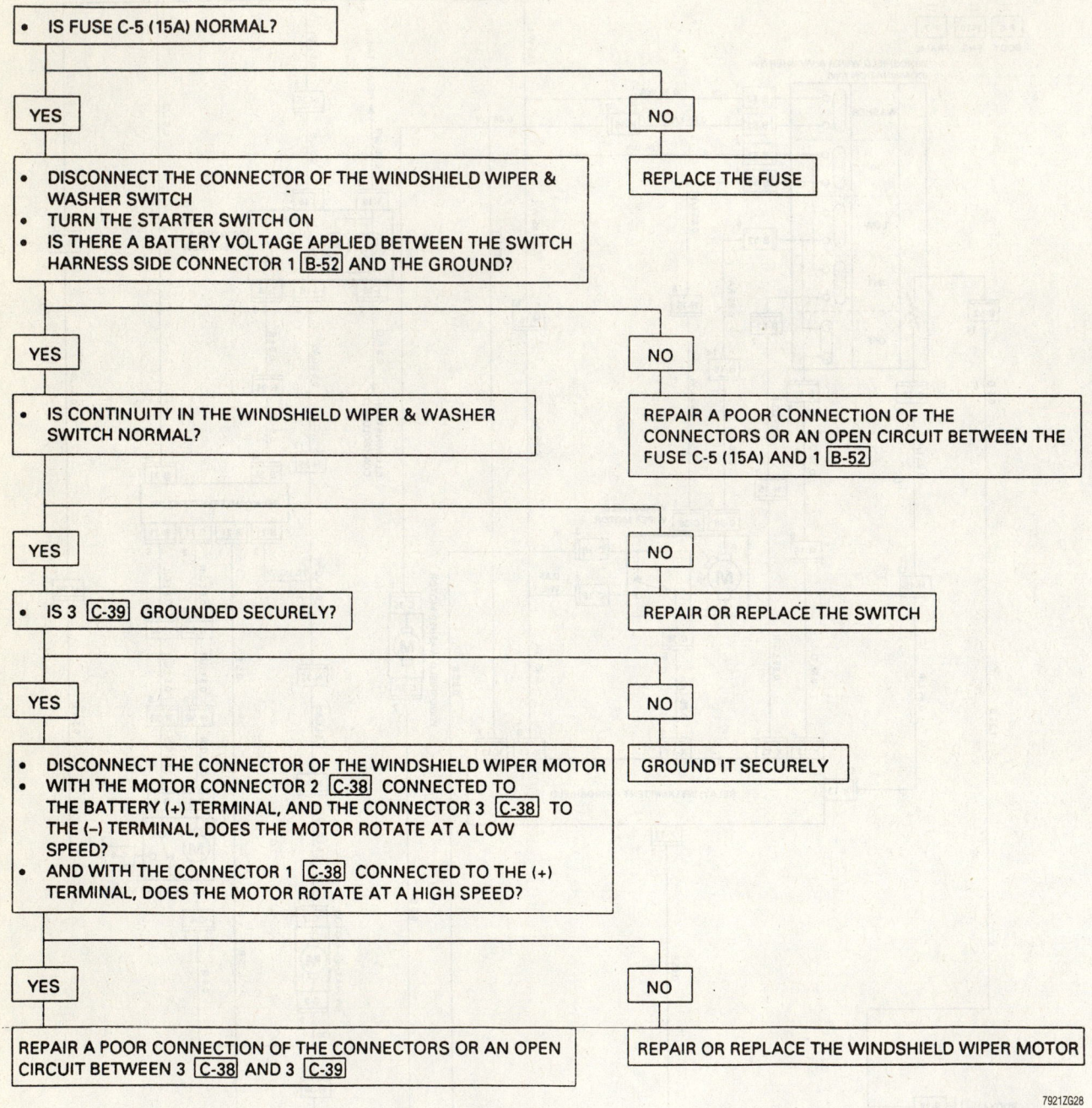

- IS FUSE C-5 (15A) NORMAL?

YES

- DISCONNECT THE CONNECTOR OF THE WINDSHIELD WIPER & WASHER SWITCH
- TURN THE STARTER SWITCH ON
- IS THERE A BATTERY VOLTAGE APPLIED BETWEEN THE SWITCH HARNESS SIDE CONNECTOR 1 B-52 AND THE GROUND?

NO

REPLACE THE FUSE

YES

- IS CONTINUITY IN THE WINDSHIELD WIPER & WASHER SWITCH NORMAL?

NO

REPAIR A POOR CONNECTION OF THE CONNECTORS OR AN OPEN CIRCUIT BETWEEN THE FUSE C-5 (15A) AND 1 B-52

YES

- IS 3 C-39 GROUNDED SECURELY?

NO

REPAIR OR REPLACE THE SWITCH

YES

- DISCONNECT THE CONNECTOR OF THE WINDSHIELD WIPER MOTOR
- WITH THE MOTOR CONNECTOR 2 C-38 CONNECTED TO THE BATTERY (+) TERMINAL, AND THE CONNECTOR 3 C-38 TO THE (–) TERMINAL, DOES THE MOTOR ROTATE AT A LOW SPEED?
- AND WITH THE CONNECTOR 1 C-38 CONNECTED TO THE (+) TERMINAL, DOES THE MOTOR ROTATE AT A HIGH SPEED?

NO

GROUND IT SECURELY

YES

REPAIR A POOR CONNECTION OF THE CONNECTORS OR AN OPEN CIRCUIT BETWEEN 3 C-38 AND 3 C-39

NO

REPAIR OR REPLACE THE WINDSHIELD WIPER MOTOR

7921ZG28

Troubleshooting flowchart: front wiper does not operate in any switch position

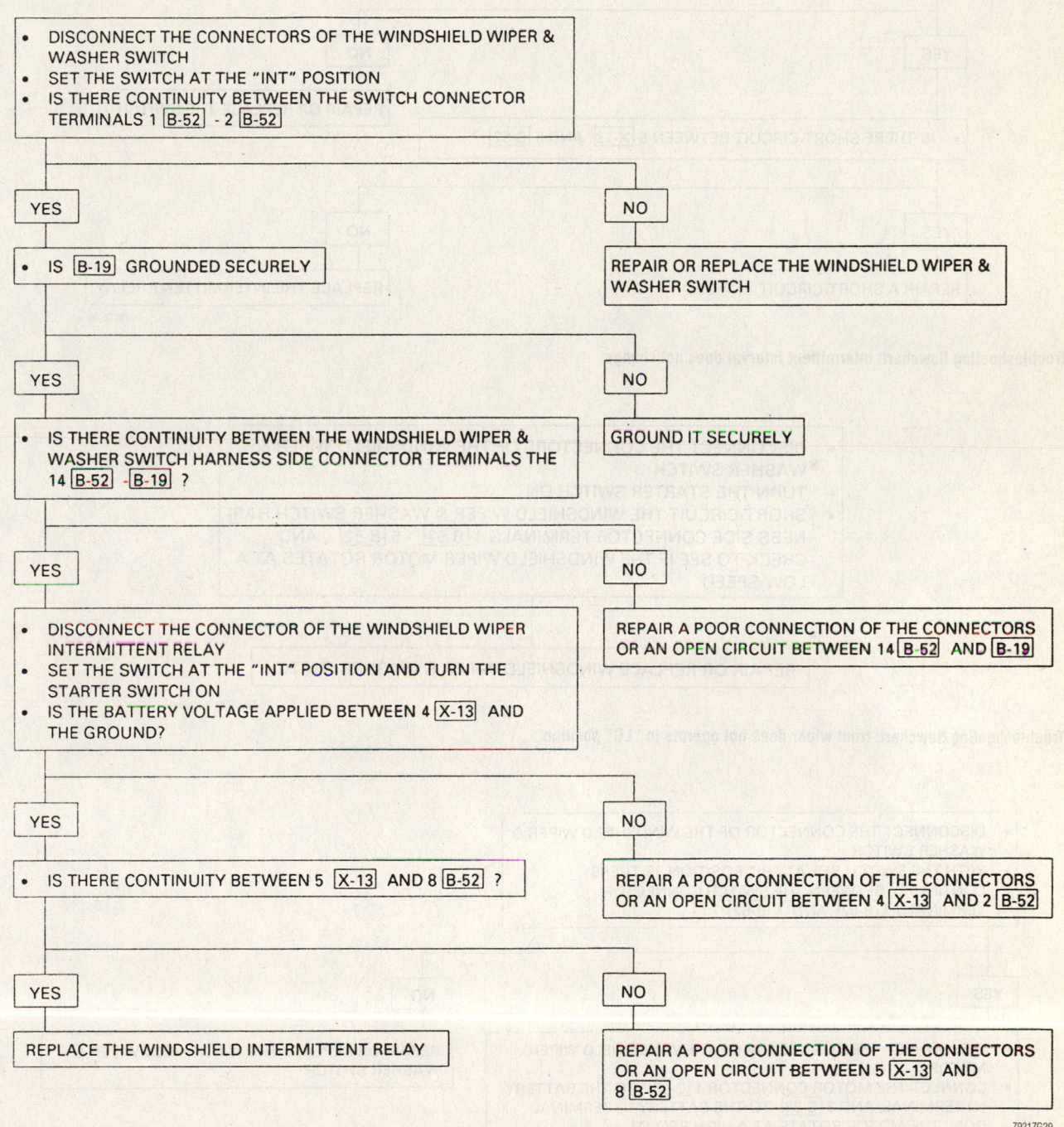

- DISCONNECT THE CONNECTORS OF THE WINDSHIELD WIPER & WASHER SWITCH
- SET THE SWITCH AT THE "INT" POSITION
- IS THERE CONTINUITY BETWEEN THE SWITCH CONNECTOR TERMINALS 1 B-52 - 2 B-52

YES → **NO** → REPAIR OR REPLACE THE WINDSHIELD WIPER & WASHER SWITCH

- IS B-19 GROUNDED SECURELY

YES → **NO** → GROUND IT SECURELY

- IS THERE CONTINUITY BETWEEN THE WINDSHIELD WIPER & WASHER SWITCH HARNESS SIDE CONNECTOR TERMINALS THE 14 B-52 - B-19 ?

YES → **NO** → REPAIR A POOR CONNECTION OF THE CONNECTORS OR AN OPEN CIRCUIT BETWEEN 14 B-52 AND B-19

- DISCONNECT THE CONNECTOR OF THE WINDSHIELD WIPER INTERMITTENT RELAY
- SET THE SWITCH AT THE "INT" POSITION AND TURN THE STARTER SWITCH ON
- IS THE BATTERY VOLTAGE APPLIED BETWEEN 4 X-13 AND THE GROUND?

YES → **NO** → REPAIR A POOR CONNECTION OF THE CONNECTORS OR AN OPEN CIRCUIT BETWEEN 4 X-13 AND 2 B-52

- IS THERE CONTINUITY BETWEEN 5 X-13 AND 8 B-52 ?

YES → **NO** → REPAIR A POOR CONNECTION OF THE CONNECTORS OR AN OPEN CIRCUIT BETWEEN 5 X-13 AND 8 B-52

REPLACE THE WINDSHIELD INTERMITTENT RELAY

7921ZG29

Troubleshooting flowchart: front wiper does not operate in "INT" position

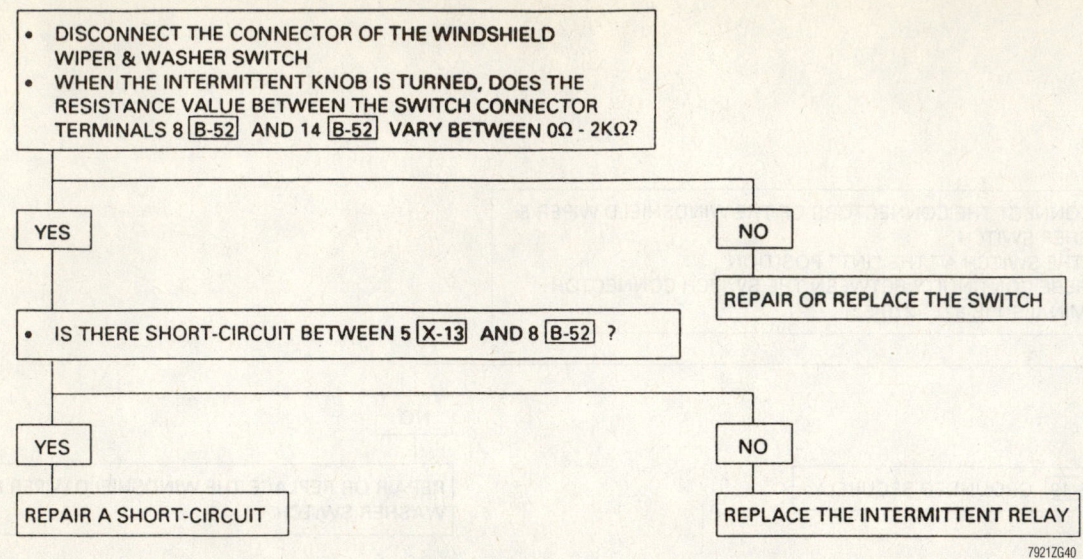

- DISCONNECT THE CONNECTOR OF THE WINDSHIELD WIPER & WASHER SWITCH
- WHEN THE INTERMITTENT KNOB IS TURNED, DOES THE RESISTANCE VALUE BETWEEN THE SWITCH CONNECTOR TERMINALS 8 [B-52] AND 14 [B-52] VARY BETWEEN 0Ω - 2KΩ?

YES

NO

REPAIR OR REPLACE THE SWITCH

- IS THERE SHORT-CIRCUIT BETWEEN 5 [X-13] AND 8 [B-52] ?

YES

NO

REPAIR A SHORT-CIRCUIT

REPLACE THE INTERMITTENT RELAY

7921ZG40

Troubleshooting flowchart: intermittent interval does not change

- DISCONNECT THE CONNECTORS OF THE WINDSHIELD WIPER & WASHER SWITCH
- TURN THE STARTER SWITCH ON
- SHORT-CIRCUIT THE WINDSHIELD WIPER & WASHER SWITCH HARNESS SIDE CONNECTOR TERMINALS 1 [B-52] - 5 [B-52] , AND CHECK TO SEE IF THE WINDSHIELD WIPER MOTOR ROTATES AT A LOW SPEED.

REPAIR OR REPLACE WINDSHIELD WIPER & WASHER SWITCH

7921ZG30

Troubleshooting flowchart: front wiper does not operate in "LO" position

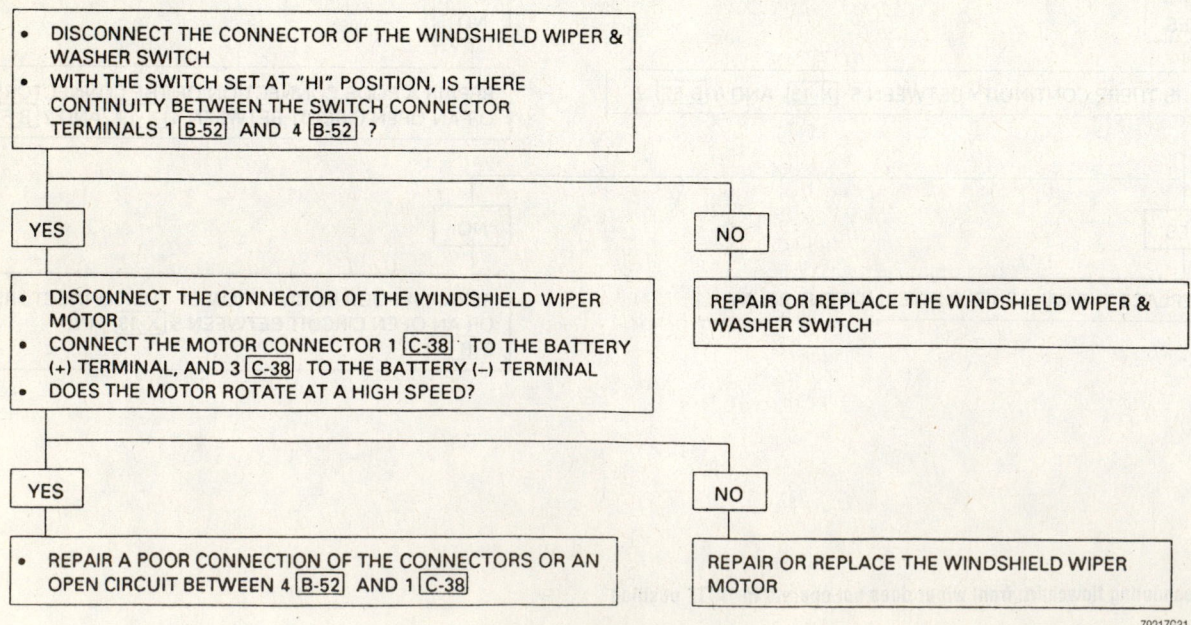

- DISCONNECT THE CONNECTOR OF THE WINDSHIELD WIPER & WASHER SWITCH
- WITH THE SWITCH SET AT "HI" POSITION, IS THERE CONTINUITY BETWEEN THE SWITCH CONNECTOR TERMINALS 1 [B-52] AND 4 [B-52] ?

YES

NO

- DISCONNECT THE CONNECTOR OF THE WINDSHIELD WIPER MOTOR
- CONNECT THE MOTOR CONNECTOR 1 [C-38] TO THE BATTERY (+) TERMINAL, AND 3 [C-38] TO THE BATTERY (–) TERMINAL
- DOES THE MOTOR ROTATE AT A HIGH SPEED?

REPAIR OR REPLACE THE WINDSHIELD WIPER & WASHER SWITCH

YES

NO

- REPAIR A POOR CONNECTION OF THE CONNECTORS OR AN OPEN CIRCUIT BETWEEN 4 [B-52] AND 1 [C-38]

REPAIR OR REPLACE THE WINDSHIELD WIPER MOTOR

7921ZG31

Troubleshooting flowchart: front wiper does not operate in the "HI" position

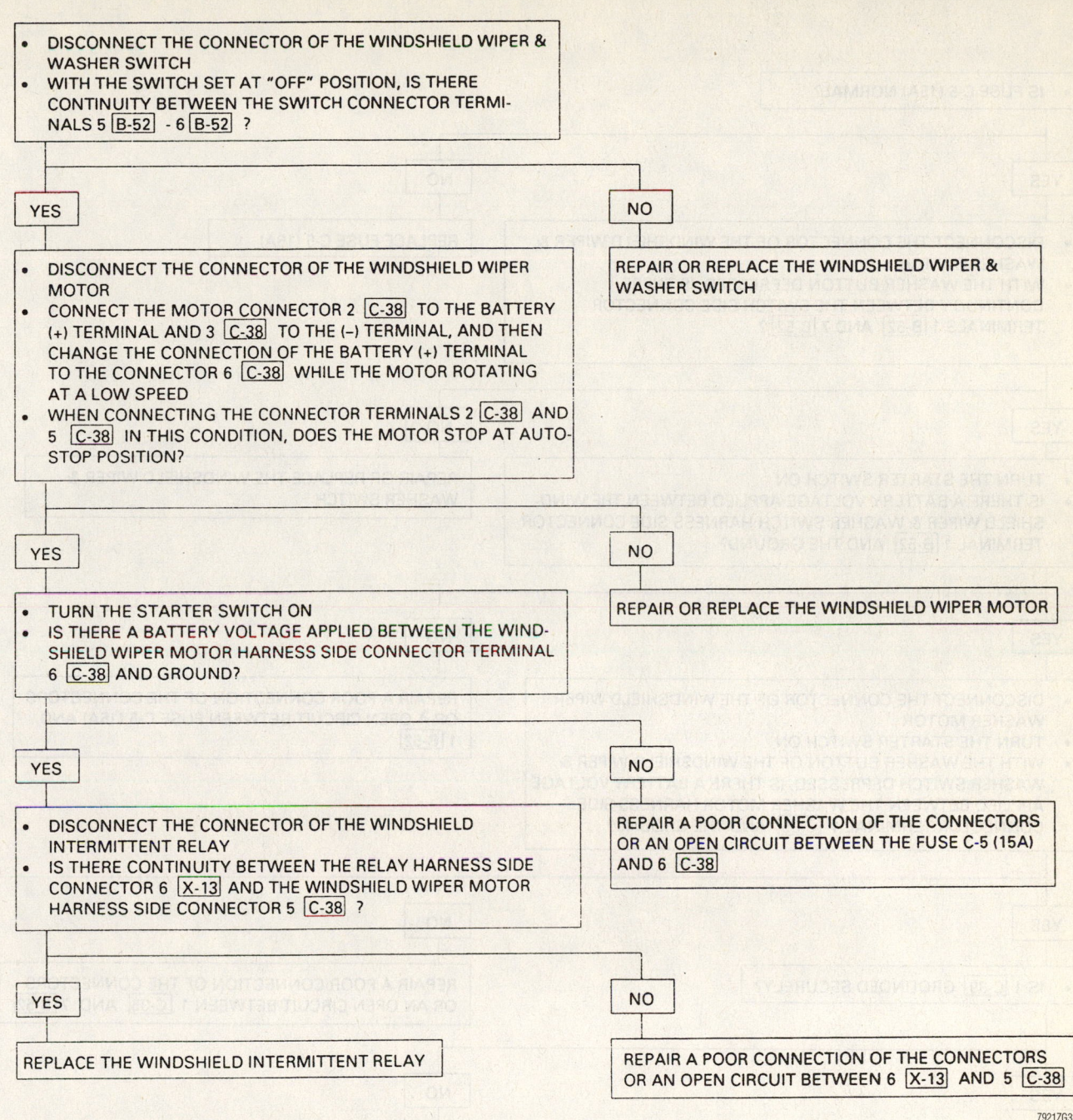

- DISCONNECT THE CONNECTOR OF THE WINDSHIELD WIPER & WASHER SWITCH
- WITH THE SWITCH SET AT "OFF" POSITION, IS THERE CONTINUITY BETWEEN THE SWITCH CONNECTOR TERMINALS 5 [B-52] - 6 [B-52] ?

YES

NO

- DISCONNECT THE CONNECTOR OF THE WINDSHIELD WIPER MOTOR
- CONNECT THE MOTOR CONNECTOR 2 [C-38] TO THE BATTERY (+) TERMINAL AND 3 [C-38] TO THE (–) TERMINAL, AND THEN CHANGE THE CONNECTION OF THE BATTERY (+) TERMINAL TO THE CONNECTOR 6 [C-38] WHILE THE MOTOR ROTATING AT A LOW SPEED
- WHEN CONNECTING THE CONNECTOR TERMINALS 2 [C-38] AND 5 [C-38] IN THIS CONDITION, DOES THE MOTOR STOP AT AUTO-STOP POSITION?

REPAIR OR REPLACE THE WINDSHIELD WIPER & WASHER SWITCH

YES

NO

- TURN THE STARTER SWITCH ON
- IS THERE A BATTERY VOLTAGE APPLIED BETWEEN THE WINDSHIELD WIPER MOTOR HARNESS SIDE CONNECTOR TERMINAL 6 [C-38] AND GROUND?

REPAIR OR REPLACE THE WINDSHIELD WIPER MOTOR

YES

NO

- DISCONNECT THE CONNECTOR OF THE WINDSHIELD INTERMITTENT RELAY
- IS THERE CONTINUITY BETWEEN THE RELAY HARNESS SIDE CONNECTOR 6 [X-13] AND THE WINDSHIELD WIPER MOTOR HARNESS SIDE CONNECTOR 5 [C-38] ?

REPAIR A POOR CONNECTION OF THE CONNECTORS OR AN OPEN CIRCUIT BETWEEN THE FUSE C-5 (15A) AND 6 [C-38]

YES

NO

REPLACE THE WINDSHIELD INTERMITTENT RELAY

REPAIR A POOR CONNECTION OF THE CONNECTORS OR AN OPEN CIRCUIT BETWEEN 6 [X-13] AND 5 [C-38]

7921ZG32

Troubleshooting flowchart: auto-stop function of the front wiper motor does not operate

- IS THE CONTINUITY IN THE WINDSHIELD WIPER & WASHER SWITCH NORMAL?

YES

NO

REPAIR OR REPLACE THE WINDSHIELD WIPER MOTOR

REPAIR OR REPLACE THE WINDSHIELD WIPER & WASHER SWITCH

7921ZG33

Troubleshooting flowchart: rotation of the front wiper motor does not stop

Refer to the model specific sections for driveline service procedures

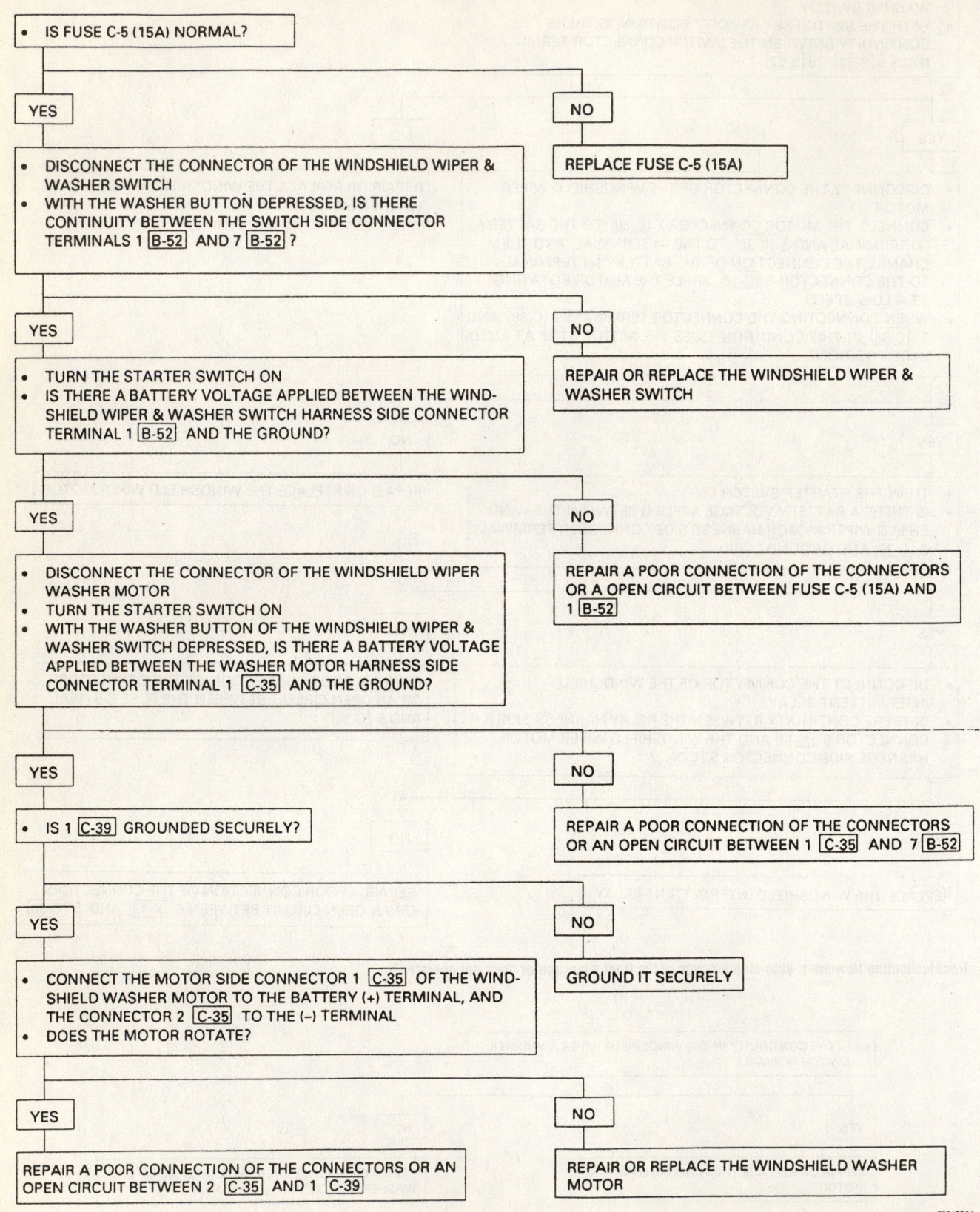

- IS FUSE C-5 (15A) NORMAL?

YES

- DISCONNECT THE CONNECTOR OF THE WINDSHIELD WIPER & WASHER SWITCH
- WITH THE WASHER BUTTON DEPRESSED, IS THERE CONTINUITY BETWEEN THE SWITCH SIDE CONNECTOR TERMINALS 1 B-52 AND 7 B-52 ?

NO

REPLACE FUSE C-5 (15A)

YES

- TURN THE STARTER SWITCH ON
- IS THERE A BATTERY VOLTAGE APPLIED BETWEEN THE WINDSHIELD WIPER & WASHER SWITCH HARNESS SIDE CONNECTOR TERMINAL 1 B-52 AND THE GROUND?

NO

REPAIR OR REPLACE THE WINDSHIELD WIPER & WASHER SWITCH

YES

- DISCONNECT THE CONNECTOR OF THE WINDSHIELD WIPER WASHER MOTOR
- TURN THE STARTER SWITCH ON
- WITH THE WASHER BUTTON OF THE WINDSHIELD WIPER & WASHER SWITCH DEPRESSED, IS THERE A BATTERY VOLTAGE APPLIED BETWEEN THE WASHER MOTOR HARNESS SIDE CONNECTOR TERMINAL 1 C-35 AND THE GROUND?

NO

REPAIR A POOR CONNECTION OF THE CONNECTORS OR A OPEN CIRCUIT BETWEEN FUSE C-5 (15A) AND 1 B-52

YES

- IS 1 C-39 GROUNDED SECURELY?

NO

REPAIR A POOR CONNECTION OF THE CONNECTORS OR AN OPEN CIRCUIT BETWEEN 1 C-35 AND 7 B-52

YES

- CONNECT THE MOTOR SIDE CONNECTOR 1 C-35 OF THE WINDSHIELD WASHER MOTOR TO THE BATTERY (+) TERMINAL, AND THE CONNECTOR 2 C-35 TO THE (–) TERMINAL
- DOES THE MOTOR ROTATE?

NO

GROUND IT SECURELY

YES

REPAIR A POOR CONNECTION OF THE CONNECTORS OR AN OPEN CIRCUIT BETWEEN 2 C-35 AND 1 C-39

NO

REPAIR OR REPLACE THE WINDSHIELD WASHER MOTOR

7921ZG34

Troubleshooting flowchart: front washer motor does not operate

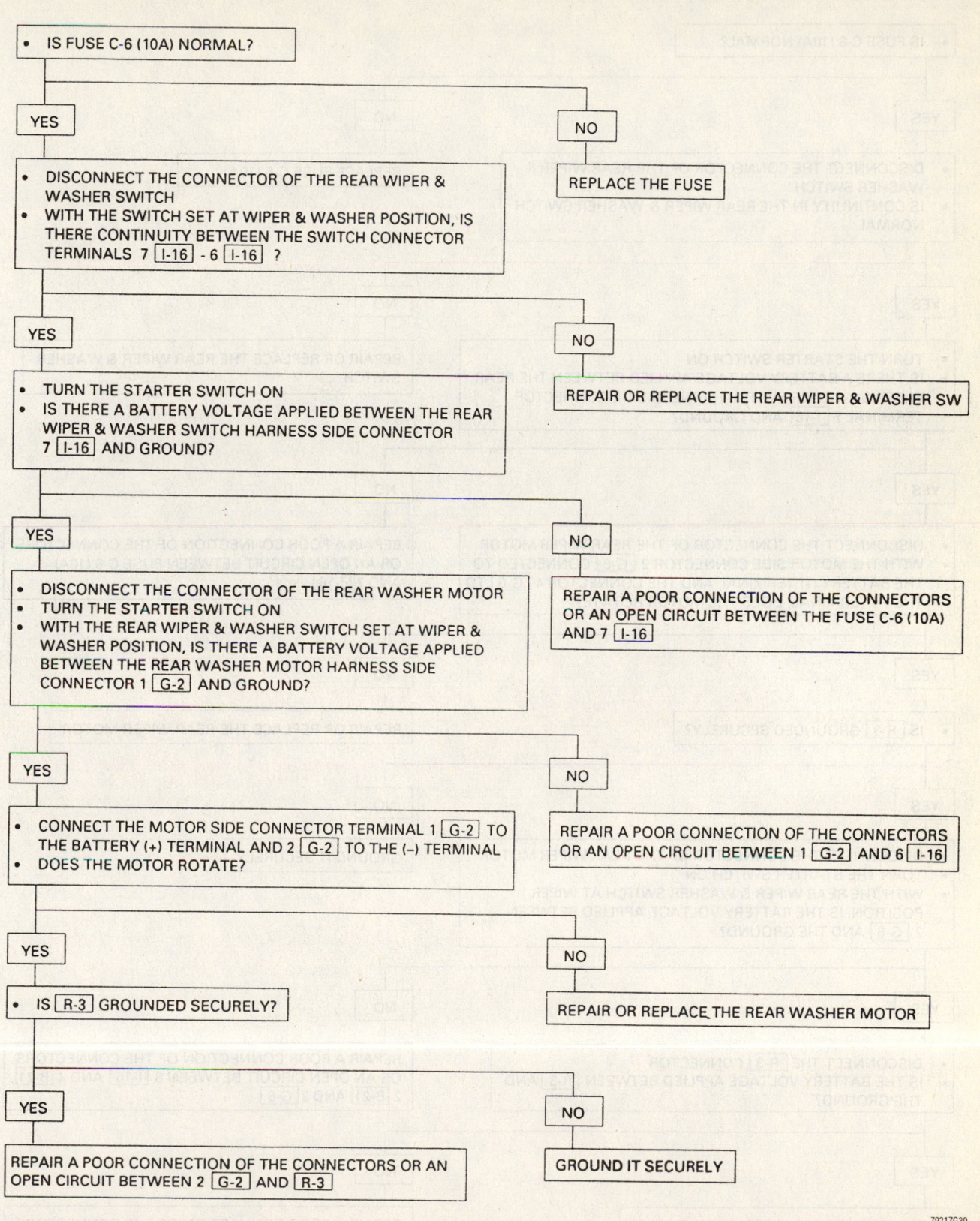

- IS FUSE C-6 (10A) NORMAL?

YES

- DISCONNECT THE CONNECTOR OF THE REAR WIPER & WASHER SWITCH
- WITH THE SWITCH SET AT WIPER & WASHER POSITION, IS THERE CONTINUITY BETWEEN THE SWITCH CONNECTOR TERMINALS 7 I-16 - 6 I-16 ?

NO

REPLACE THE FUSE

YES

- TURN THE STARTER SWITCH ON
- IS THERE A BATTERY VOLTAGE APPLIED BETWEEN THE REAR WIPER & WASHER SWITCH HARNESS SIDE CONNECTOR 7 I-16 AND GROUND?

NO

REPAIR OR REPLACE THE REAR WIPER & WASHER SW

YES

- DISCONNECT THE CONNECTOR OF THE REAR WASHER MOTOR
- TURN THE STARTER SWITCH ON
- WITH THE REAR WIPER & WASHER SWITCH SET AT WIPER & WASHER POSITION, IS THERE A BATTERY VOLTAGE APPLIED BETWEEN THE REAR WASHER MOTOR HARNESS SIDE CONNECTOR 1 G-2 AND GROUND?

NO

REPAIR A POOR CONNECTION OF THE CONNECTORS OR AN OPEN CIRCUIT BETWEEN THE FUSE C-6 (10A) AND 7 I-16

YES

- CONNECT THE MOTOR SIDE CONNECTOR TERMINAL 1 G-2 TO THE BATTERY (+) TERMINAL AND 2 G-2 TO THE (–) TERMINAL
- DOES THE MOTOR ROTATE?

NO

REPAIR A POOR CONNECTION OF THE CONNECTORS OR AN OPEN CIRCUIT BETWEEN 1 G-2 AND 6 I-16

YES

- IS R-3 GROUNDED SECURELY?

NO

REPAIR OR REPLACE THE REAR WASHER MOTOR

YES

REPAIR A POOR CONNECTION OF THE CONNECTORS OR AN OPEN CIRCUIT BETWEEN 2 G-2 AND R-3

NO

GROUND IT SECURELY

7921ZG39

Troubleshooting flowchart: rear washer motor does not operate

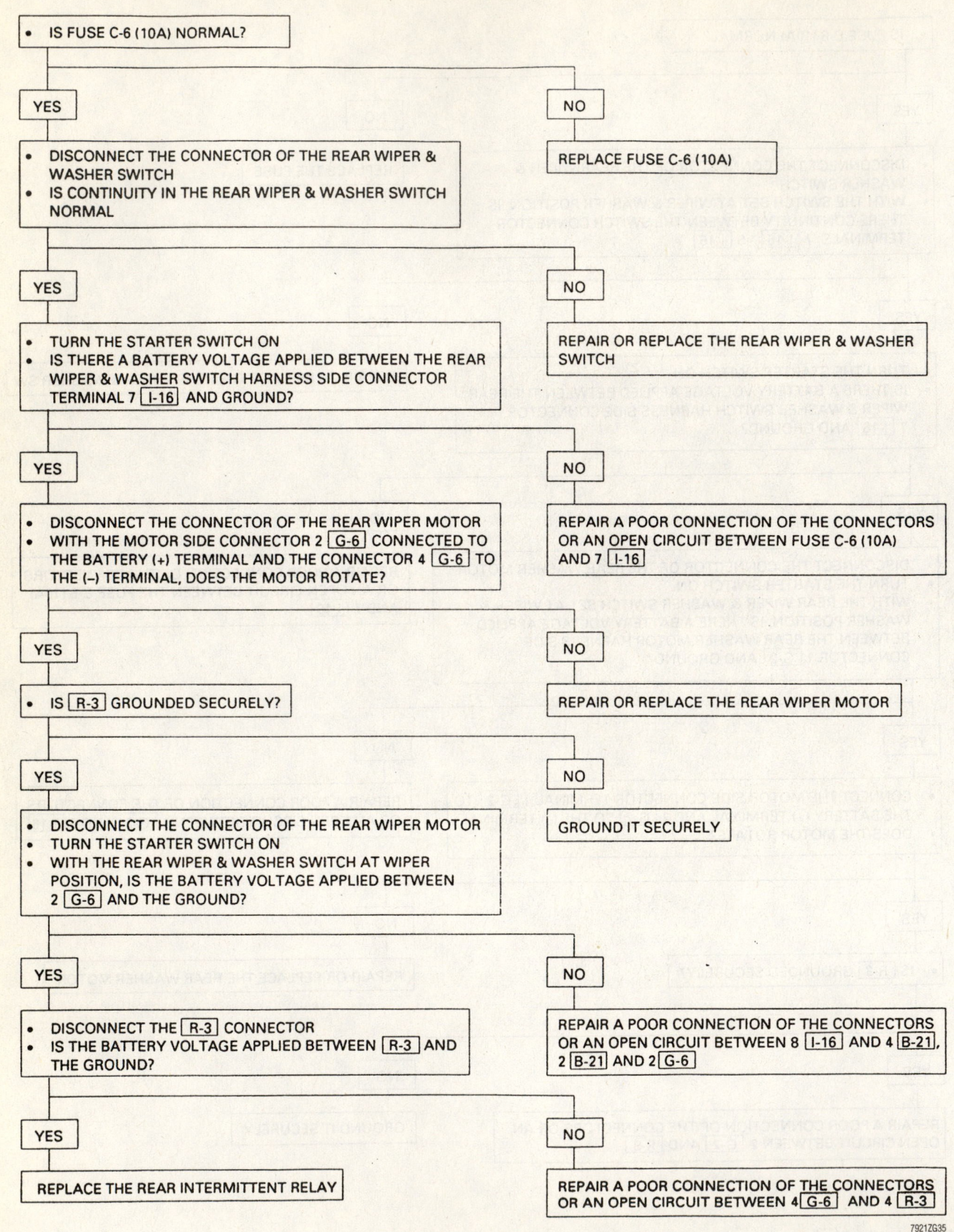

- IS FUSE C-6 (10A) NORMAL?

YES

- DISCONNECT THE CONNECTOR OF THE REAR WIPER & WASHER SWITCH
- IS CONTINUITY IN THE REAR WIPER & WASHER SWITCH NORMAL

NO

REPLACE FUSE C-6 (10A)

YES

- TURN THE STARTER SWITCH ON
- IS THERE A BATTERY VOLTAGE APPLIED BETWEEN THE REAR WIPER & WASHER SWITCH HARNESS SIDE CONNECTOR TERMINAL 7 I-16 AND GROUND?

NO

REPAIR OR REPLACE THE REAR WIPER & WASHER SWITCH

YES

- DISCONNECT THE CONNECTOR OF THE REAR WIPER MOTOR
- WITH THE MOTOR SIDE CONNECTOR 2 G-6 CONNECTED TO THE BATTERY (+) TERMINAL AND THE CONNECTOR 4 G-6 TO THE (–) TERMINAL, DOES THE MOTOR ROTATE?

NO

REPAIR A POOR CONNECTION OF THE CONNECTORS OR AN OPEN CIRCUIT BETWEEN FUSE C-6 (10A) AND 7 I-16

YES

- IS R-3 GROUNDED SECURELY?

NO

REPAIR OR REPLACE THE REAR WIPER MOTOR

YES

- DISCONNECT THE CONNECTOR OF THE REAR WIPER MOTOR
- TURN THE STARTER SWITCH ON
- WITH THE REAR WIPER & WASHER SWITCH AT WIPER POSITION, IS THE BATTERY VOLTAGE APPLIED BETWEEN 2 G-6 AND THE GROUND?

NO

GROUND IT SECURELY

YES

- DISCONNECT THE R-3 CONNECTOR
- IS THE BATTERY VOLTAGE APPLIED BETWEEN R-3 AND THE GROUND?

NO

REPAIR A POOR CONNECTION OF THE CONNECTORS OR AN OPEN CIRCUIT BETWEEN 8 I-16 AND 4 B-21, 2 B-21 AND 2 G-6

YES

REPLACE THE REAR INTERMITTENT RELAY

NO

REPAIR A POOR CONNECTION OF THE CONNECTORS OR AN OPEN CIRCUIT BETWEEN 4 G-6 AND 4 R-3

7921ZG35

Troubleshooting flowchart: rear wiper motor does not operate

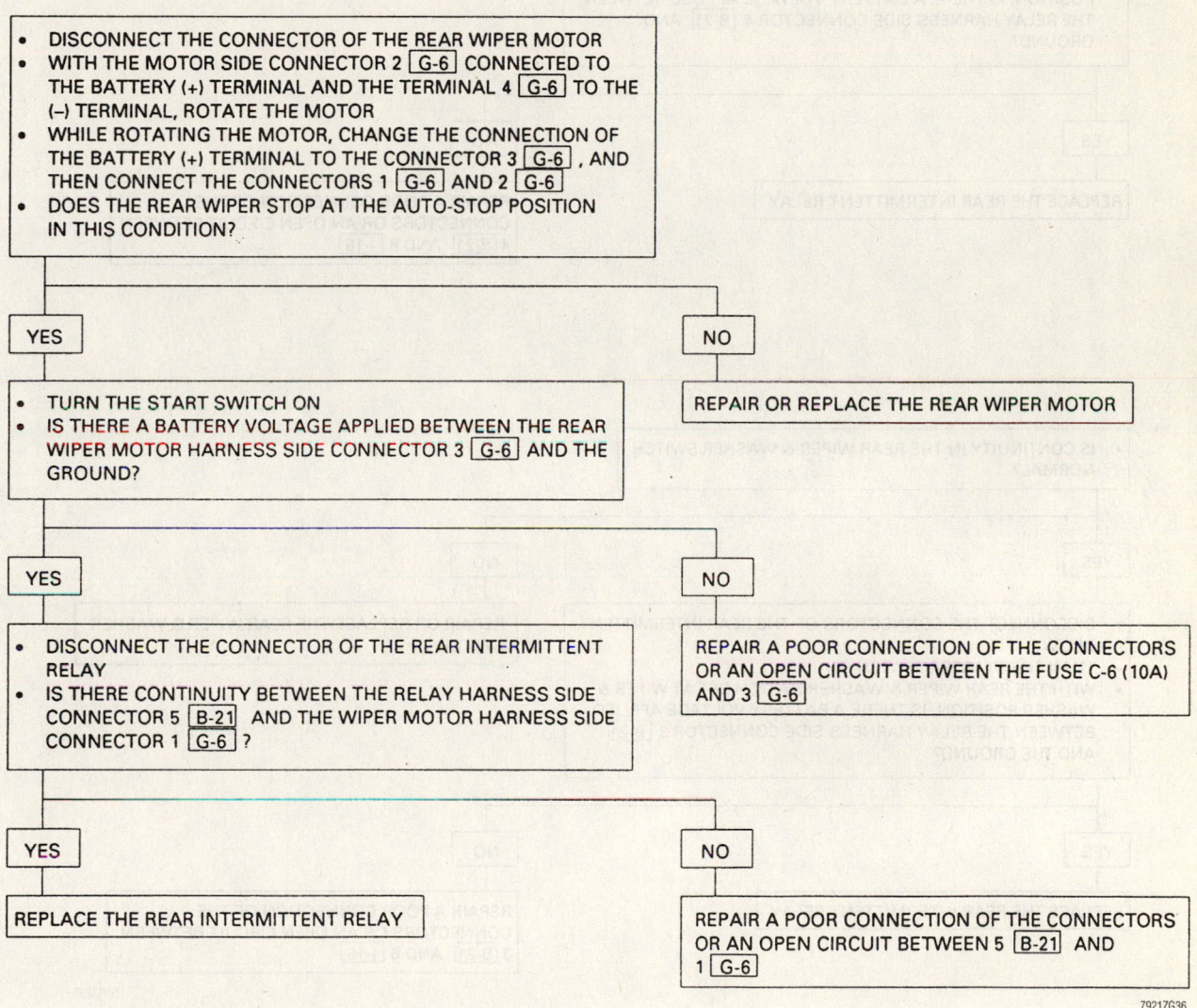

- DISCONNECT THE CONNECTOR OF THE REAR WIPER MOTOR
- WITH THE MOTOR SIDE CONNECTOR 2 G-6 CONNECTED TO THE BATTERY (+) TERMINAL AND THE TERMINAL 4 G-6 TO THE (–) TERMINAL, ROTATE THE MOTOR
- WHILE ROTATING THE MOTOR, CHANGE THE CONNECTION OF THE BATTERY (+) TERMINAL TO THE CONNECTOR 3 G-6 , AND THEN CONNECT THE CONNECTORS 1 G-6 AND 2 G-6
- DOES THE REAR WIPER STOP AT THE AUTO-STOP POSITION IN THIS CONDITION?

YES | **NO**

- TURN THE START SWITCH ON
- IS THERE A BATTERY VOLTAGE APPLIED BETWEEN THE REAR WIPER MOTOR HARNESS SIDE CONNECTOR 3 G-6 AND THE GROUND?

REPAIR OR REPLACE THE REAR WIPER MOTOR

YES | **NO**

- DISCONNECT THE CONNECTOR OF THE REAR INTERMITTENT RELAY
- IS THERE CONTINUITY BETWEEN THE RELAY HARNESS SIDE CONNECTOR 5 B-21 AND THE WIPER MOTOR HARNESS SIDE CONNECTOR 1 G-6 ?

REPAIR A POOR CONNECTION OF THE CONNECTORS OR AN OPEN CIRCUIT BETWEEN THE FUSE C-6 (10A) AND 3 G-6

YES | **NO**

REPLACE THE REAR INTERMITTENT RELAY

REPAIR A POOR CONNECTION OF THE CONNECTORS OR AN OPEN CIRCUIT BETWEEN 5 B-21 AND 1 G-6

7921ZG36

Troubleshooting flowchart: auto-stop function of the rear wiper motor does not operate

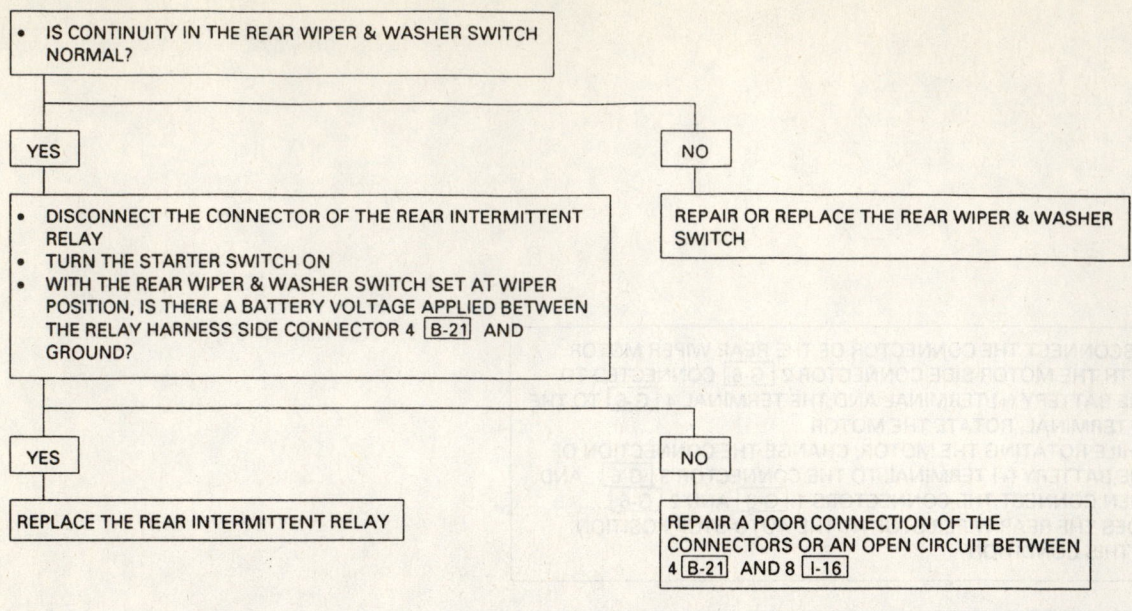

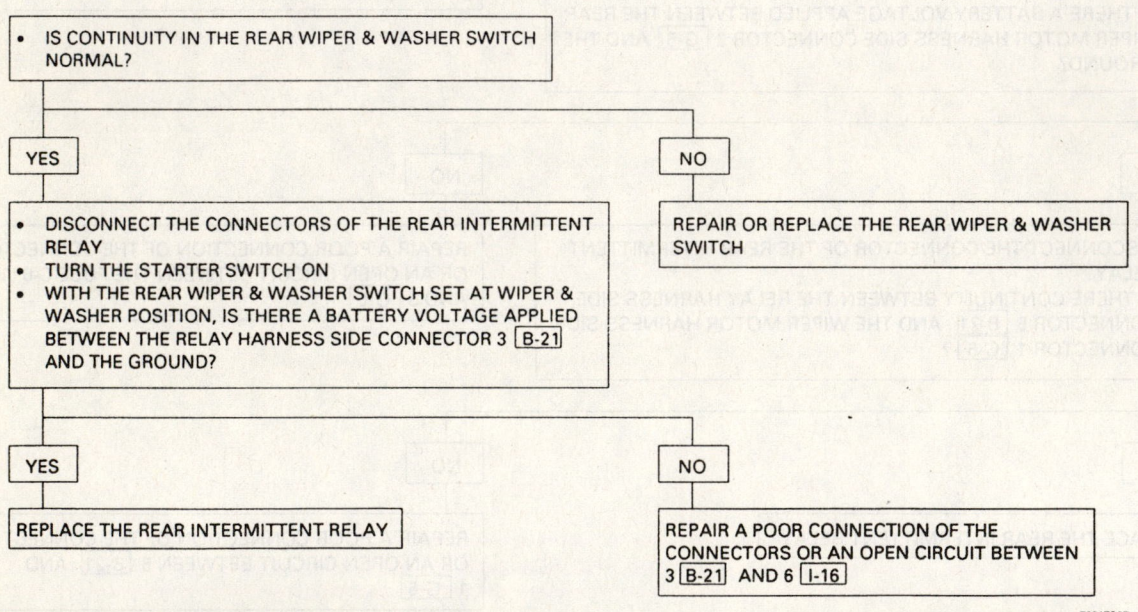

Troubleshooting flowchart: rear wiper motor does not operate at wiper position

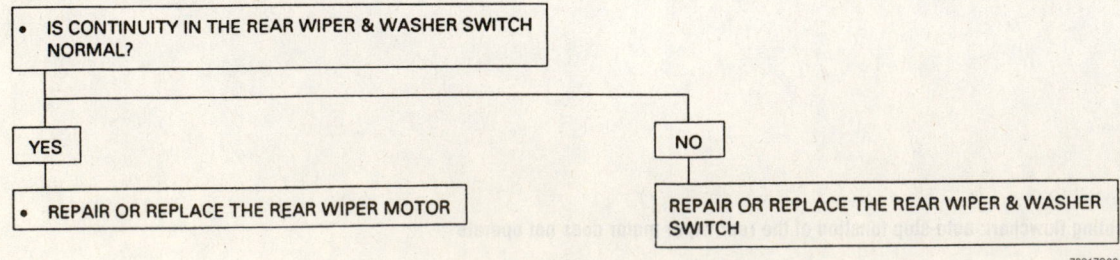

Troubleshooting flowchart: rotation of the rear wiper motor does not stop

CHRYSLER CORPORATION

Caravan, Voyager and Town & Country

GENERAL DESCRIPTION

The windshield wipers can be operated by the windshield wiper switch only when the ignition switch is in the **ACC** or **IGN** position. A fuse, located in the fuse block, protects the circuitry of the wiper system and the vehicle.

The wiper motor has permanent magnet fields. The speeds are determined by current flow to the appropriate set of brushes.

The intermittent wipe system, in addition to low and high speed, has a delay mode. The delay mode has a range of 2–15 seconds. This is accomplished by a variable resistor in the wiper switch and is controlled electrically by a relay.

The wiper system completes the wipe cycle when the switch is turned **OFF**. The wiper blades park in the lowest portion of the wiping pattern.

TESTING

Wiper System

WILL NOT RUN IN ANY SWITCH POSITION

1. Check for blown fuse in fuse block.
   a. If fuse is good, proceed to Step 2.
   b. If fuse is bad, replace and check motor operation in all switch positions.
   c. If motor is still inoperative and the fuse does not blow, proceed to Step 2.
   d. If replacement fuse blows, disconnect motor wiring connector and replace fuse. If fuse does not blow, motor is defective. If fuse blows, switch or wiring is at fault.
2. Place switch in **LOW** speed position. Listen to motor. If motor cannot be heard running, proceed to Step 3. If it is running, check motor output shaft. If output shaft is not turning, replace motor. If it is turning, drive link to output shaft or linkage is disconnected. Replace worn parts.
3. If motor could not be heard running, connect a voltmeter between motor terminal **3** and the ground strap. If there is no voltage or less than 1 volt, move the negative test lead from the ground to the negative battery terminal.
   a. If an increase in voltage is noticed,

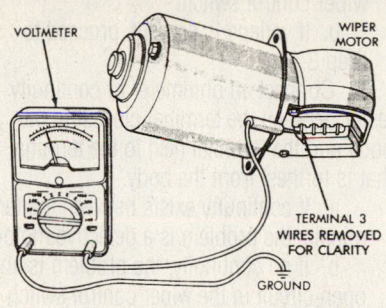

Voltmeter hook-up between terminal 3 and ground—Caravan, Voyager and Town & Country

the problem is a bad ground circuit. Make sure the motor mounting is free of paint and that the nuts or bolts are tight.
   b. If there still is no indication of voltage, the problem is an open circuit in the wiring harness or wiper switch.
   c. If no noticeable increase (greater then 3 volts) in voltage is observed, the problem is a faulty motor assembly.

MOTOR RUNS SLOWLY AT ALL SPEEDS

1. Disconnect the wiring harness connector at the motor. Remove the wiper arms and blades. Connect an ammeter between the battery and terminal **3** on the motor.
   a. If the motor runs and average ammeter reading is more than 6 amps, proceed to Step 2.
   b. If the motor runs and average ammeter reading is less than 6 amps, proceed to Step 3.
2. Check to see if the wiper linkage or pivots are binding or caught. Disconnect the drive link from the motor.
   a. If the motor now runs and draws less than 3 amps, repair wiper linkage system.
   b. If motor continues to draw more than 3 amps, replace the motor assembly.
3. Check the motor wiring harness for shorting between high and low speed as follows:
   a. Connect a voltmeter or test light to motor ground strap.
   b. Set wiper switch to **LOW** position.
   c. Connect other lead of voltmeter or test light to terminal **4** of the wiring harness.
   d. If voltage is present, there is a

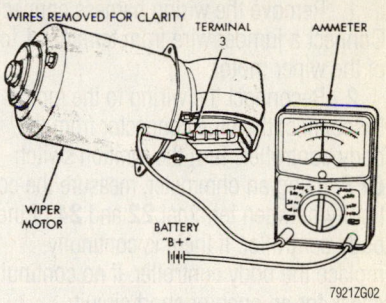

Ammeter hook-up between terminal 3 and battery—Caravan, Voyager and Town & Country

short in the wiring or wiper switch. If no voltage is present, proceed to the next step.
   e. Set wiper switch to **HIGH** position.
   f. Move voltmeter or test light lead from terminal **4** to terminal **3** of the wiring harness.
   g. If voltage is present, check for a short in the wiring or wiper switch.

MOTOR WILL RUN AT HIGH SPEED BUT NOT LOW SPEED, OR MOTOR WILL RUN AT LOW SPEED BUT NOT HIGH SPEED

1. If motor will not run on high speed, put the switch in **HIGH** position and connect a test light between motor terminal **4** and ground. If the motor will not run on low speed, put the switch in **LOW** position and connect a test light between motor terminal **3** and ground.
2. If a test light will not light at the motor terminal, there is an open in the wiring or switch. If the test light turns **ON** at the motor terminal, replace the motor assembly.

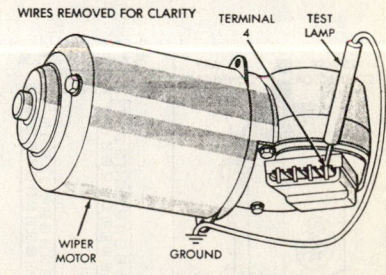

Test lamp hook-up between terminal 4 and ground—Caravan, Voyager and Town & Country

Refer to the model specific sections for driveline service procedures

MOTOR WILL KEEP RUNNING WITH SWITCH IN OFF POSITION

1. Remove the wiring harness connector. Connect a jumper wire from terminal **1** to **3** of the wiper motor.

2. Reconnect the wiring to the motor. Disconnect the blue connector from the body controller. Turn the ignition switch **OFF**, using an ohmmeter, measure the continuity between terminal **22** and **24** of the body controller. If there is continuity, replace the body controller. If no continuity, check for an open or short circuit.

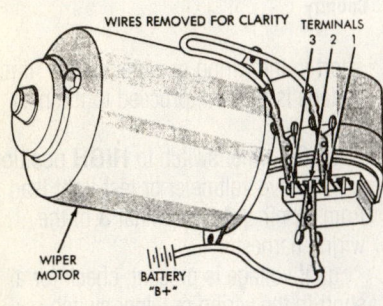

WIRES REMOVED FOR CLARITY — TERMINALS 3 2 1

WIPER MOTOR — BATTERY "B+"

7921ZG04

Jumper wire between terminal 1 and 3— Caravan, Voyager and Town & Country

MOTOR WILL STOP WHEREVER IT IS WHEN THE SWITCH IS TURNED OFF; WIPERS DO NOT PARK

1. Remove the motor wiring connector and clean the terminals. Reconnect electrical connector and clean the terminals. Reconnect electrical connector and test motor. If problem persists, proceed to Step 2.

2. Set wiper switch to **OFF** position. Disconnect motor wiring connector. Connect a voltmeter or test light to the motor ground strap. Connect the other lead to terminal **2** of the wiring connector.

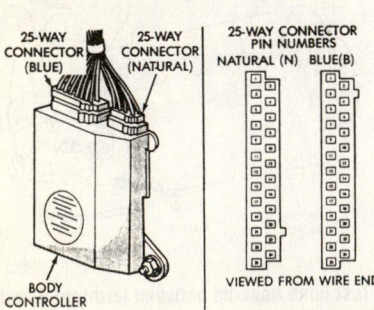

25-WAY CONNECTOR (BLUE) — 25-WAY CONNECTOR (NATURAL) — 25-WAY CONNECTOR PIN NUMBERS NATURAL (N) BLUE(B)

BODY CONTROLLER — VIEWED FROM WIRE END

7921ZG05

Combination controller 25-way connectors—Caravan, Voyager and Town & Country

a. If voltage is not present, check for an open circuit in the wiring harness or wiper control switch.

b. If voltage is present, proceed to Step 3.

3. Connect an ohmmeter or continuity tester between the terminal closest to the body and the terminal next to the terminal that is furthest from the body.

a. If continuity exists between the terminals, the problem is a defective motor.

b. If no continuity, the problem is an open circuit in the wiper control switch or wiring harness.

Intermittent Function Tests

※※ CAUTION

If equipped with the air bag restraint system, follow proper procedures to disarm the system when working around the steering column, checking or servicing the intermittent wiper module. Failure to do so could cause accidental deployment of the air bag and possible personal injury.

The intermittent wipe function is controlled by the body controller located in the passenger compartment behind the right side kick panel.

Disconnect the wires from the body wiring in the steering column. Using an ohmmeter, test for continuity between the terminals of the multi-function switch.

1. In switch position **OFF**, there should be continuity between pin **6** and **7**.

2. In switch position **DELAY**, there should be continuity between pin **8** and **9**, **2** and **4**, **1** and **2**, and **1** and **4**.

3. In switch position **LOW**, there should be continuity between pin **4** and **6**.

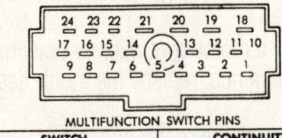

24 23 22 21 20 19 18
17 16 15 14 13 12 11 10
9 8 7 6 5 4 3 2 1

MULTIFUNCTION SWITCH PINS

SWITCH POSITION	CONTINUITY BETWEEN
OFF	PIN 6 AND PIN 7
DELAY	PIN 8 AND PIN 9
	PIN 2 AND PIN 4
	PIN 1 AND PIN 2
	PIN 1 AND PIN 4
LOW	PIN 4 AND PIN 6
HIGH	PIN 4 AND PIN 5
WASH	PIN 3 AND PIN 4

* RESISTANCE AT MAXIMUM DELAY POSITION SHOULD BE BETWEEN 210,000 OHMS AND 390,000 OHMS
* RESISTANCE AT MINIMUM DELAY POSITION SHOULD BE ZERO WITH OHMMETER SET ON HIGH OHM SCALE

7921ZG06

Multi-function switch connector and intermittent wipe continuity—Caravan, Voyager and Town & Country

4. In switch position **HIGH**, there should be continuity between pin **4** and **5**.

5. In switch position **WASH**, there should be continuity between pin **3** and **4**.

REMOVAL & INSTALLATION

Washer Reservoir and Pump

1. Drain the washer fluid from the reservoir.

2. Remove the mounting screws and the reservoir and pump as an assembly.

3. Disconnect the electrical connector and the rubber hose from the bottom of the pump.

4. Carefully pry the pump away from the reservoir and out of the grommet.

※※ WARNING

Care must be taken not to puncture the reservoir.

5. Remove and discard the grommet.
To install:
6. Install a new rubber grommet on the reservoir.

7. Position the pump into place on the reservoir and push in until the pump locks into place.

8. Connect the electrical connector and hose to the pump.

9. Install the reservoir and pump assembly and secure the mounting screws.

10. Fill the reservoir.

Washer Nozzle

The washer nozzles are hood-mounted. The nozzles do not require adjustment. If nozzle performance is unsatisfactory, it should be replaced. The left and right nozzles are identical.

1. Disconnect the hose from the nozzle.

2. Using needle nose pliers, squeeze together the locking tabs on the nozzle.
To install:
3. Snap the nozzle into place and connect the hose.

All Except Caravan, Voyager and Town & Country

GENERAL DESCRIPTION

The windshield wipers can be operated by the windshield wiper switch only when the ignition switch is in the **ACC** or **IGN** position. A fuse, located in the fuse block, protects the circuitry of the wiper system and the vehicle.

The wiper motor has permanent magnet

fields. The speeds are determined by current flow to the appropriate set of brushes.

The intermittent wipe system, in addition to low and high speed, has a delay mode. The delay mode has a range of 2–15 seconds. This is accomplished by a variable resistor in the wiper switch and is controlled electrically by a relay.

The wiper system completes the wipe cycle when the switch is turned **OFF**. The wiper blades park in the lowest portion of the wiping pattern.

TESTING

Wiper System

WILL NOT RUN IN ANY SWITCH POSITION

1. Check for blown fuse in fuse block.

   a. If fuse is good, proceed to Step 2.

   b. If fuse is bad, replace and check motor operation in all switch positions.

   c. If motor is still inoperative and the fuse does not blow, proceed to Step 2.

   d. If replacement fuse blows, disconnect motor wiring connector and replace fuse. If fuse does not blow, motor is defective. If fuse blows, switch or wiring is at fault.

2. Place switch in **LOW** speed position. Listen to motor. If motor cannot be heard running, proceed to Step 3. If it is running, check motor output shaft. If output shaft is not turning, replace motor. If it is turning, drive link to output shaft or linkage is disconnected. Replace worn parts.

3. If motor could not be heard running, connect a voltmeter between motor terminal **L** and the ground strap. If there is no voltage or less than 1 volt, move the negative test lead from the ground to the negative battery terminal.

   a. If an increase in voltage is noticed,

the problem is a bad ground circuit. Make sure the motor mounting is free of paint and that the nuts or bolts are tight.

   b. If there still is no indication of voltage, the problem is an open circuit in the wiring harness or wiper switch.

   c. If no noticeable increase (greater then 3 volts) in voltage is observed, the problem is a faulty motor assembly.

MOTOR RUNS SLOWLY AT ALL SPEEDS

1. Disconnect the wiring harness connector at the motor. Remove the wiper arms and blades. Connect an ammeter between the battery and terminal **L** on the motor.

   a. If the motor runs and average ammeter reading is more than 6 amps, proceed to Step 2.

   b. If the motor runs and average ammeter reading is less than 6 amps, proceed to Step 3.

2. Check to see if the wiper linkage or pivots are binding or caught. Disconnect the drive link from the motor.

   a. If the motor now runs and draws less than 3 amps, repair wiper linkage system.

   b. If motor continues to draw more than 3 amps, replace the motor assembly.

3. Check the motor wiring harness for shorting between high and low speed as follows:

   a. Connect a voltmeter or test light to motor ground strap.

   b. Set wiper switch to **LOW** position.

   c. Connect other lead of voltmeter or test light to terminal **H** of the wiring harness.

   d. If voltage is present, there is a short in the wiring or wiper switch. If no voltage is present, proceed to the next step.

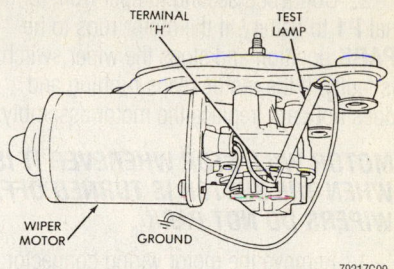

Test lamp hook-up between terminal H and ground—All except Caravan, Voyager and Town & Country

   e. Set wiper switch to **HIGH** position.

   f. Move voltmeter or test light lead from terminal **H** to terminal **L** of the wiring harness.

   g. If voltage is present, check for a short in the wiring or wiper switch.

MOTOR WILL RUN AT HIGH SPEED BUT NOT LOW SPEED, OR MOTOR WILL RUN AT LOW SPEED BUT NOT HIGH SPEED

1. If motor will not run on high speed, put the switch in **HIGH** position and connect a test light between motor terminal **H** and ground. If the motor will not run on low speed, put the switch in **LOW** position and connect a test light between motor terminal **L** and ground.

2. If a test light will not light at the motor terminal, there is an open in the wiring or switch. If the test light turns **ON** at the motor terminal, replace the motor assembly.

MOTOR WILL KEEP RUNNING WITH SWITCH IN OFF POSITION

1. Remove the wiring harness connector. Connect a jumper wire from terminal **P2** to **L** of the wiper motor.

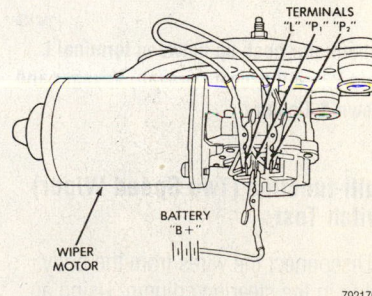

One jumper wire between terminal P2 and L. One jumper wire between terminal P1 and B+—All except Caravan, Voyager and Town & Country

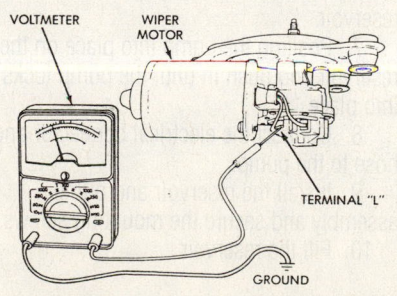

Voltmeter hook-up between terminal L and ground—All except Caravan, Voyager and Town & Country

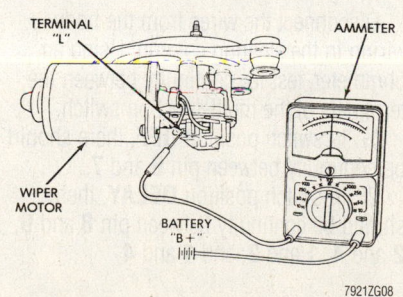

Ammeter hook-up between terminal L and battery—All except Caravan, Voyager and Town & Country

2. Connect a second jumper from terminal **P1** to battery. If the motor runs to he **PARK** position and stops the wiper switch is faulty. If the motor keeps running and does not park, replace the motor assembly.

MOTOR WILL STOP WHEREVER IT IS WHEN THE SWITCH IS TURNED OFF; WIPERS DO NOT PARK

1. Remove the motor wiring connector and clean the terminals. Reconnect electrical connector and clean the terminals. Reconnect electrical connector and test motor. If problem persists, proceed to Step 2.

2. Set wiper switch to **OFF** position and the ignition switch to the **ACC** position. Disconnect motor wiring connector. Connect a voltmeter or test light to the motor ground strap. Connect the other lead to terminal **P1** of the wiring connector.

   a. If voltage is not present, check for an open circuit in the wiring harness or wiper control switch.

   b. If voltage is present, proceed to Step 3.

3. Connect an ohmmeter or continuity tester between terminals **L** and **P2**.

   a. If continuity exists between the terminals, the problem is a defective motor.

   b. If no continuity, the problem is an open circuit in the wiper control switch or wiring harness.

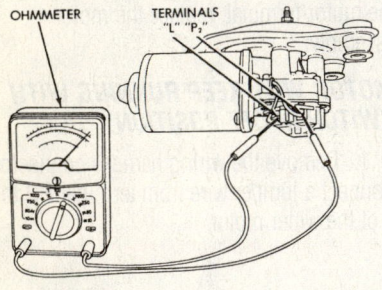

OHMMETER   TERMINALS "L" "P"

7921ZG11

Ohmmeter hook-up between terminal L and P2—All except Caravan, Voyager and Town & Country

Multi-function (Two Speed Wiper) Switch Test

Disconnect the wires from the body wiring in the steering column. Using an

MULTIFUNCTION SWITCH PINS

TWO SPEED WIPER SWITCH CONTINUITY CHART	
SWITCH POSITION	CONTINUITY BETWEEN
OFF & PARK	PIN 1 & PIN 2
LOW	PIN 1 & PIN 4
HIGH	PIN 4 & PIN 5
WASH	PIN 3 & PIN 4

7921ZG12

Standard two speed wiper switch continuity chart—All except Caravan, Voyager and Town & Country

ohmmeter, test for continuity between the terminals of the multi-function switch.

1. In switch position **OFF and PARK**, there should be continuity between pin **1** and **2**.

2. In switch position **LOW**, there should be continuity between pin **1** and **4**.

3. In switch position **HIGH**, there should be continuity between pin **4** and **5**.

4. In switch position **WASH**, there should be continuity between pin **3** and **4**.

Intermittent Function Tests

> **✳✳ CAUTION**
>
> **If equipped with the air bag restraint system, follow proper procedures to disarm the system when working around the steering column, checking or servicing the intermittent wiper module. Failure to do so could cause accidental deployment of the air bag and possible personal injury.**

Disconnect the wires from the body wiring in the steering column. Using an ohmmeter, test for continuity between the terminals of the multi-function switch.

1. In switch position **OFF**, there should be continuity between pin **6** and **7**.

2. In switch position **DELAY**, there should be continuity between pin **8** and **9**, **2** and **4**, **1** and **2**, and **1** and **4**.

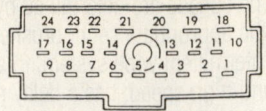

MULTIFUNCTION SWITCH PINS

SWITCH POSITION	CONTINUITY BETWEEN
OFF	PIN 6 AND PIN 7
DELAY	PIN 8 AND PIN 9
	PIN 2 AND PIN 4
	PIN 1 AND PIN 2
	PIN 1 AND PIN 4
LOW	PIN 4 AND PIN 6
HIGH	PIN 4 AND PIN 5
WASH	PIN 3 AND PIN 4

*RESISTANCE AT MAXIMUM DELAY POSITION SHOULD BE BETWEEN 270,000 OHMS AND 330,000 OHMS.
*RESISTANCE AT MINIMUM DELAY POSITION SHOULD BE ZERO WITH OHMMETER SET ON HIGH OHM SCALE.

7921ZG13

Multi-function switch connector and intermittent wipe continuity—all except Caravan, Voyager and Town & Country

3. In switch position **LOW**, there should be continuity between pin **4** and **6**.

4. In switch position **HIGH**, there should be continuity between pin **4** and **5**.

5. In switch position **WASH**, there should be continuity between pin **3** and **4**.

REMOVAL & INSTALLATION

Washer Reservoir and Pump

1. Drain the washer fluid from the reservoir.

2. Remove the mounting screws and the reservoir and pump as an assembly.

3. Disconnect the electrical connector and the rubber hose from the bottom of the pump.

4. Carefully pry the pump away from the reservoir and out of the grommet.

> **✳✳ WARNING**
>
> **Care must be taken not to puncture the reservoir.**

5. Remove and discard the grommet.

To install:

6. Install a new rubber grommet on the reservoir.

7. Position the pump into place on the reservoir and push in until the pump locks into place.

8. Connect the electrical connector and hose to the pump.

9. Install the reservoir and pump assembly and secure the mounting screws.

10. Fill the reservoir.

FORD MOTOR CO.

General Description

AEROSTAR

The wiper motor is located under the wiper assembly. A drive link connects the motor directly to the lever of the right hand pivot shaft.

The 2-speed, permanent magnet, 3 brush electric windshield wiper motor has a brush rigging that permits a selection of low or high speeds. An internal wiper and washer system is part of the steering column multi-function switch.

EXPLORER, MOUNTAINEER AND RANGER

The windshield wipers are actuated by a permanent magnet, rotary-type electric motor. These vehicle are equipped with an internal wiper and washer system featuring a lever-type wiper and washer switch, mounted on the steering column. The system governor uses a relay contact to control current to the wiper motor. The governor electronic circuitry controls the contact to supply wiper motor current.

BRONCO, EXPEDITION, NAVIGATOR, E SERIES (VAN) F SERIES (PICK-UP)

The windshield wiper control module, an electric wiper motor, a washer system and wiper/washer switch integral with the turn signal lever.

The permanent magnet, 3 brush windshield wiper motor permits a selection of low or high speeds. An internal wiper and washer system is part of the steering column multi-function switch.

WINDSTAR

The windshield wiper assembly consists of the following components:
- Windshield wiper assembly
- Generic Electronic Module (GEM), located in the instrument panel between the radio and the steering column
- Windshield wiper motor, mounted on the cowl top extension
- Windshield wiper left and right pivot arms and blades
- Multi-function switch which features a rotary wiper switch and a push-type washer actuator

The wiper system is driven by three GEM controlled relays. The wiper motor is controlled by two relays and the washer fluid pump is driven by a third relay. One wiper relay switches between **HI** and **LO** speeds. The second wiper motor relay switches between **RUN** and a dynamic brake (armature short circuit) and is used in interval (INT) mode of operation.

The GEM receives motor and fluid pump actuation input commands from the multi-function switch. One input selects interval **INT**, **HI**, **LO** or **WASH** mode request. The second input selects INT delay.

COMPONENT TESTING

- On all vehicles, when trouble shooting the wiper system, test the motor first, then work back towards the switch to test the interval governor or module (depending on the vehicle), power circuits and the switch itself.
- In most of the tests, a volt-ohmmeter is required, although a test light can also be useful. For testing the motor, a 0–15 amp DC ammeter is required.
- When the test calls for a voltage check, the ignition switch must be in the **ON** position.
- When testing for continuity or resistance values, turn the ignition switch to the **OFF** position and/or disconnect the negative battery cable.
- Improper or careless testing can cause permanent damage to the vehicle's electronic circuits and to test equipment. Carefully follow the test equipment manufacturer's instructions.

Wiper Motor Test

ALL EXCEPT WINDSTAR

1. Disconnect the positive cable from the battery.
2. Remove the wiper motor linkage and electrical connectors from the windshield wiper motor.

➡**If the electrical connector is not accessible, the motor may need to be removed.**

3. Using a suitable starting charging tester, connect the power lead (green) of the tester to the positive battery terminal.
4. Connect the positive (red) lead from the tester to the low speed connection and high-speed connection at the connector plug.

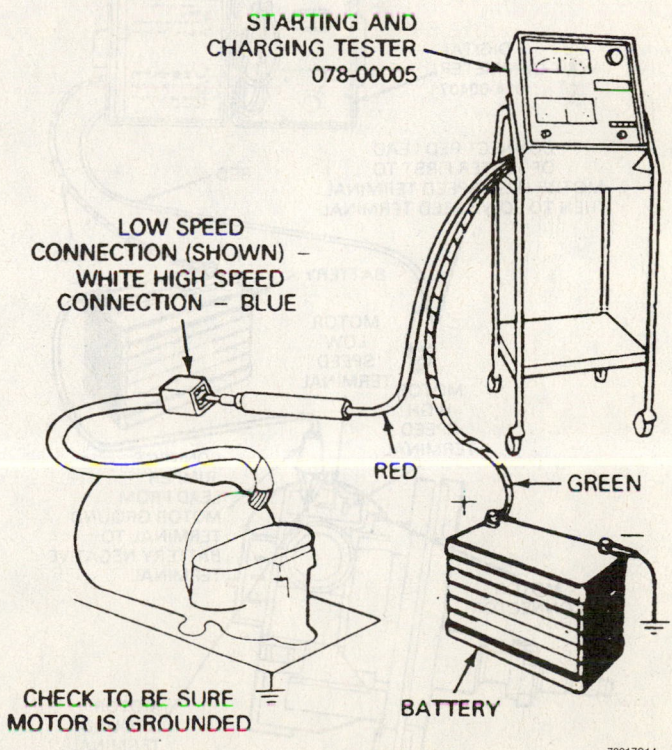

STARTING AND CHARGING TESTER 078-00005

LOW SPEED CONNECTION (SHOWN) – WHITE HIGH SPEED CONNECTION – BLUE

RED

GREEN

BATTERY

CHECK TO BE SURE MOTOR IS GROUNDED

7921ZG14

Wiper motor current draw test—Ford Explorer, Mountaineer and Ranger

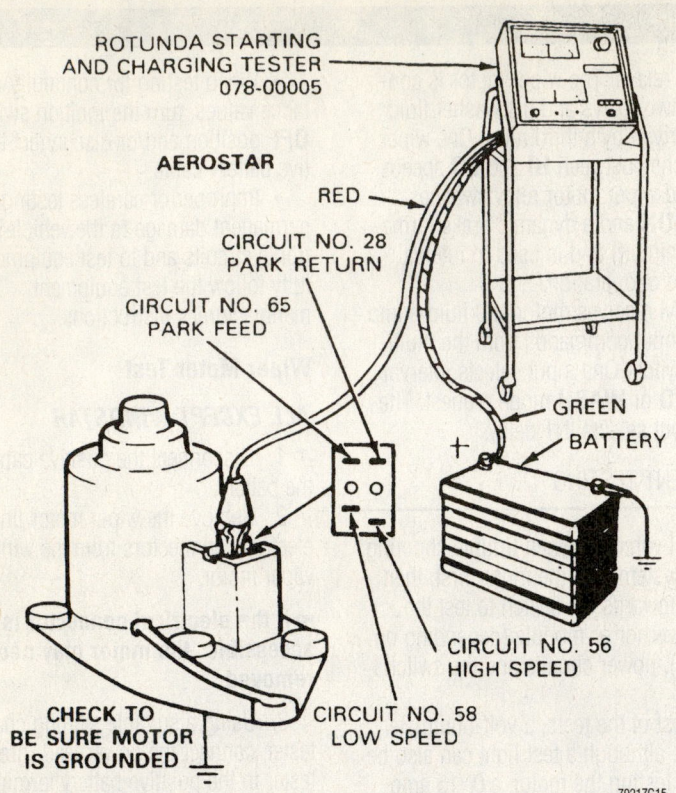

Wiper motor current draw test—Aerostar

ROTUNDA STARTING
AND CHARGING TESTER
078-00005

AEROSTAR

RED

CIRCUIT NO. 28
PARK RETURN

CIRCUIT NO. 65
PARK FEED

GREEN

BATTERY

CIRCUIT NO. 56
HIGH SPEED

CHECK TO
BE SURE MOTOR
IS GROUNDED

CIRCUIT NO. 58
LOW SPEED

7921ZG15

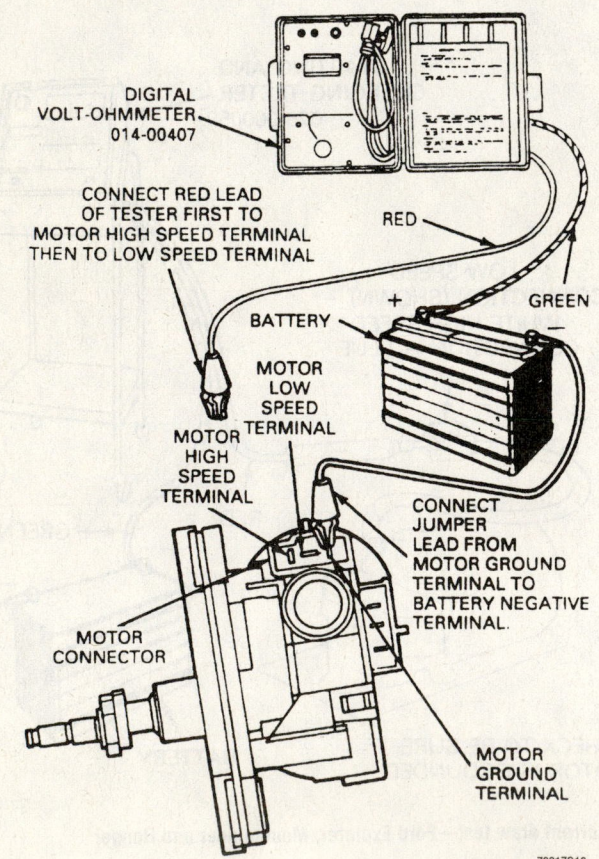

DIGITAL
VOLT-OHMMETER
014-00407

CONNECT RED LEAD
OF TESTER FIRST TO
MOTOR HIGH SPEED TERMINAL
THEN TO LOW SPEED TERMINAL

RED

GREEN

BATTERY

MOTOR
LOW
SPEED
TERMINAL

MOTOR
HIGH
SPEED
TERMINAL

CONNECT
JUMPER
LEAD FROM
MOTOR GROUND
TERMINAL TO
BATTERY NEGATIVE
TERMINAL.

MOTOR
CONNECTOR

MOTOR
GROUND
TERMINAL

7921ZG16

Wiper motor current draw test—Bronco, Expedition, Navigator, E Series (van) F Series (Pick-up)

5. The draw should be no more than 3.0 amps on the (Ford) Aerostar, Ranger, Explorer and Mountaineer, and 3.5 amps on all others, at either speed. Repairs to the motor itself are not possible.

WINDSTAR

1. Remove the wiper motor linkage and electrical connectors from the windshield wiper motor.

➡ **If the electrical connector is not accessible, the motor may need to be removed.**

2. Using a suitable starting charging tester, connect the power lead (green) of the tester to the negative battery terminal.

3. Connect the positive (red) lead from the tester to the common brush terminal. Connect a jumper from the battery positive post first to the low speed connection at the connector plug and ten to the high speed connection at the connector plug.

4. The draw should be no more than 3.5 amps at low and 5.5 amps at high.

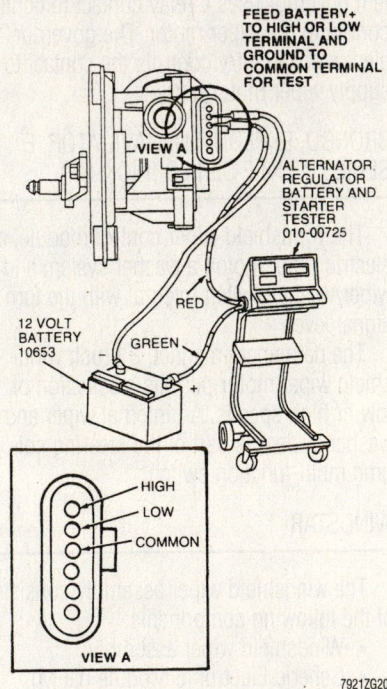

FEED BATTERY+
TO HIGH OR LOW
TERMINAL AND
GROUND TO
COMMON TERMINAL
FOR TEST

VIEW A

ALTERNATOR,
REGULATOR
BATTERY AND
STARTER
TESTER
010-00725

RED

12 VOLT
BATTERY
10653

GREEN

HIGH
LOW
COMMON

VIEW A

7921ZG20

Wiper motor test—Windstar

Washer Pump Current Draw Test

ALL EXCEPT WINDSTAR

1. Attach the leads of a digital volt/ohmmeter or suitable starting charging tester as shown. The current draw should not exceed 4 amps or be less than 1.7 amps while the windshield washer pump is pumping fluid.

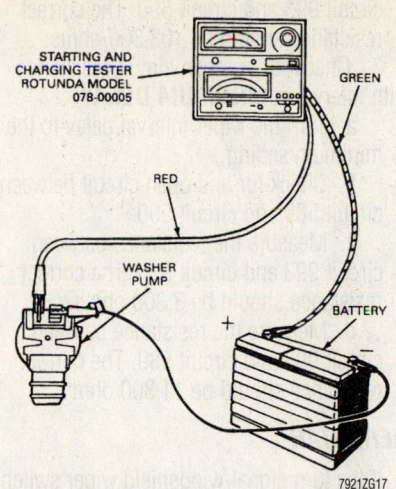

Wiper washer pump current draw test—all except Windstar

WINDSTAR

1. Attach the leads of a digital volt/ohm-meter tester as shown. The current draw should not exceed 4 amps or be less than 2.0 amps while the windshield washer pump is pumping fluid.

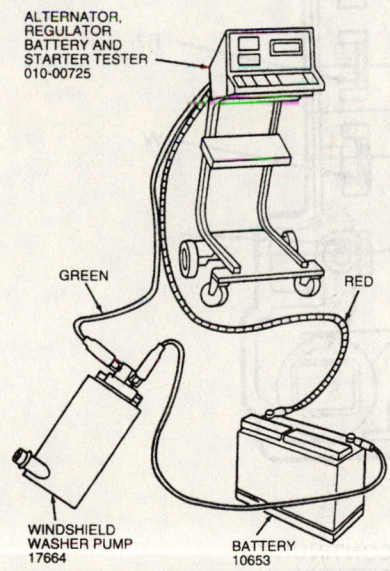

Wiper washer pump current draw test— Windstar

Circuit Breaker Test

ALL EXCEPT WINDSTAR

The front wipers and washers use the same 6 amp circuit breaker (Aerostar and Ranger), 8.25 amps (all other models) located in the fuse panel. Two separate tests

are necessary to check for correct circuit breaker operation.

1. Remove the circuit breaker from the fuse panel.

2. Using a suitable volt-amp tester, touch the test leads together and adjust the current draw until it equals the circuit breaker rating.

3. Connect the test leads to the circuit breaker, hold the current reading on the ammeter at the rated current and leave it connected for 10 minutes.

4. If the circuit breaker opens during the 10 minutes, replace the circuit breaker.

5. Touch the tester's leads together and adjust the current draw until it is twice the rated current.

6. Connect the circuit breaker to the tester and hold the current rating on twice the rated current.

7. The current reading on the ammeter should drop to 0 within 30 seconds.

8. If it takes longer than 30 seconds for the ammeter to drop to 0 (circuit breaker to open), replace the circuit breaker.

Wiper Interval Governor Test

ALL EXCEPT WINDSTAR

If interval operation is unsatisfactory, first check the motor current draw, the control switch and all the connecting wires for continuity. If the motor, switch and connecting wires are OK, replace the electronic governor.

Wiper Switch Test

ALL EXCEPT AEROSTAR AND WINDSTAR

1. Check for an open circuit with the wiper/washer switch **OFF**.
   a. Turn the washer **OFF**.
   b. Check for an open circuit between Circuit 993 and Circuit 590.
2. Check for an closed circuit with the wiper/washer switch **ON**.
   a. Turn the washer **ON**.
   b. Check for continuity between Circuit 993 and Circuit 590.
3. Check for an open circuit/resistance with the wiper on **OFF** and the washer on **OFF**.

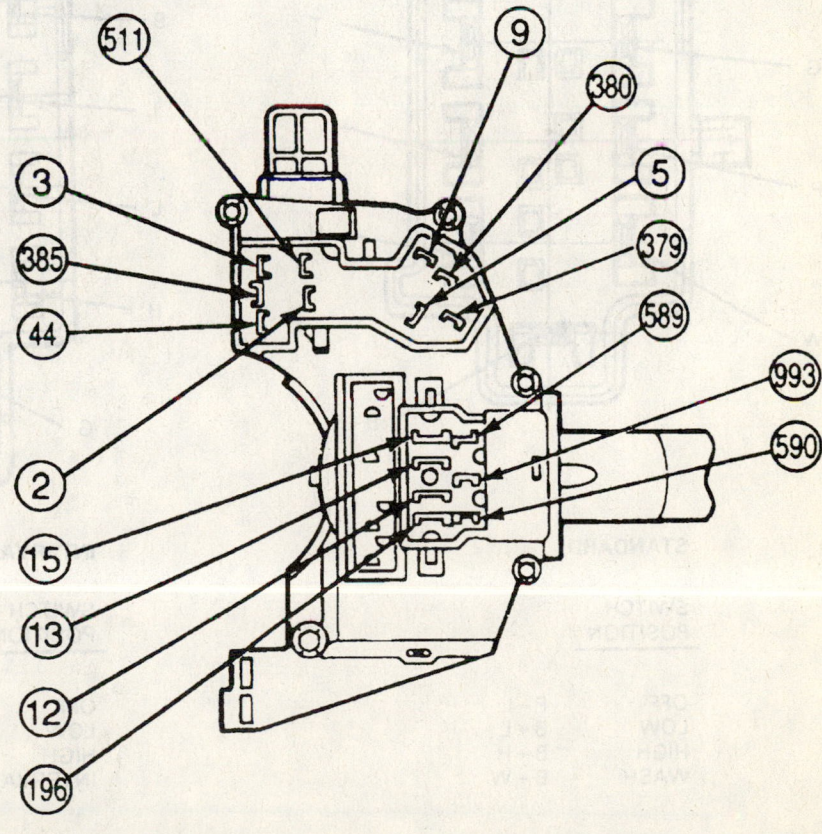

Turn signal/wiper/washer switch terminal locations for switch continuity test—all except Aerostar and Windstar

Refer to the model specific sections for driveline service procedures

a. Turn the wiper **OFF**.

b. Turn the washer **OFF**.

c. Check for and open circuit between circuit 589 and circuit 590.

d. Measure the resistance between circuit 993 and circuit 590. The correct resistance should be 103,000 ohms.

e. Measure the resistance between circuit 993 and circuit 589. The correct resistance should be 47,600 ohms.

4. Check for an open circuit/resistance with the wiper on **LOW** and the washer on **OFF**.

a. Turn the wiper **LOW**.

b. Turn the washer **OFF**.

c. Check for and open circuit between circuit 589 and circuit 590.

d. Measure the resistance between circuit 993 and circuit 590. The correct resistance should be 3,300 ohms.

e. Measure the resistance between circuit 993 and circuit 589. The correct resistance should be 4,100 ohms.

5. Check for an open circuit/resistance with the wiper on **HIGH** and the washer on **OFF**.

a. Turn the wiper **HIGH**.

b. Turn the washer **OFF**.

c. Check for and open circuit between circuit 993 and circuit 589.

d. Measure the resistance between circuit 993 and circuit 590. The correct resistance should be 3,300 ohms.

6. Check for an open circuit/resistance with interval at **MAXIMUM DELAY**.

a. Turn the wiper interval delay to the maximum setting.

b. Check for and open circuit between circuit 589 and circuit 590.

c. Measure the resistance between

circuit 993 and circuit 590. The correct resistance should be 103,300 ohms.

7. Check for an open circuit/resistance with interval at **MINIMUM DELAY**.

a. Turn the wiper interval delay to the minimum setting.

b. Check for and open circuit between circuit 589 and circuit 590.

c. Measure the resistance between circuit 993 and circuit 590. The correct resistance should be 3,300 ohms.

d. Measure the resistance between circuit 993 and circuit 589. The correct resistance should be 11,300 ohms.

AEROSTAR

If the turn signal/windshield wiper switch does not exhibit continuity or if poor continuity exists in any switch position replace the switch assembly. On these models the

FRONT TURN SIGNAL AND WINDSHIELD WIPER SWITCH CONTINUITY TEST

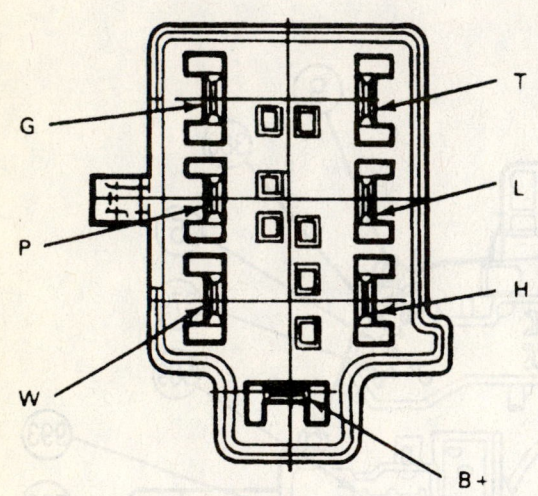

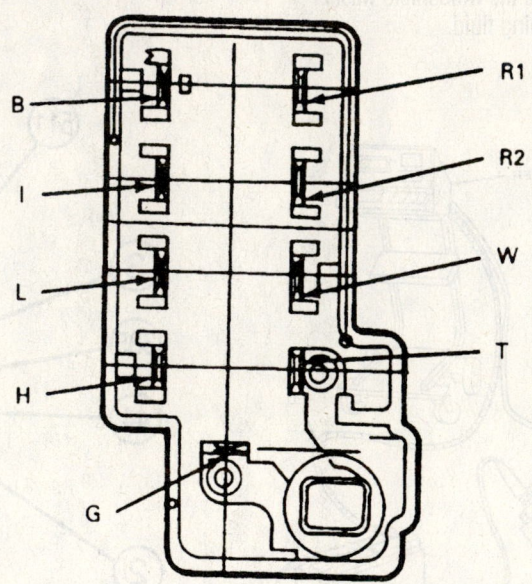

STANDARD		
SWITCH POSITION		
OFF	P – L	
LOW	B + L	
HIGH	B + H	
WASH	B + W	

INTERVAL	
SWITCH POSITION	CONTINUITY BETWEEN TERMINALS
OFF	–
LOW	B + L
HIGH	B + H – L
INTERVAL	B + I
	VARIABLE RESISTANCE BETWEEN R1 AND R2 MIN. 420 TO 880 OHMS MAX. 7,000 TO 13,000 OHMS
WASH	B + W

7921ZG18

Wiper switch test—Aerostar

switch can be tested independently using a powered test light to check for continuity. Interval systems must be tested with an ohmmeter. A defective switch or interval governor cannot be repaired and must be replaced.

WINDSTAR

Using a digital volt/ohmmeter tester, test terminals 1, 4 and 6 for the resistance values shown.

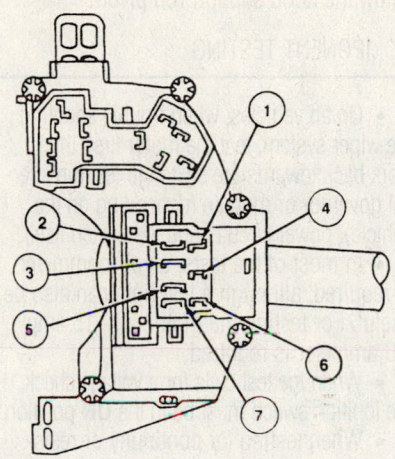

7921ZG22

Wiper/washer switch terminal locations—Windstar

Switch Position	Resistance by Pin Number
Interval Wiper/Washer Switching:	
• Wash ON	Closed Pin 4 to Pin 6
• Wash OFF	Resistance Pin 4 to Pin 6, 103.3 K ohms
	Resistance Pin 4 to Pin 1, 47.6 K ohms
• Wiper Interval at MAX.	Resistance Pin 4 to Pin 1, 11.33 K ohms
• Delay (Closest Position to OFF) to MIN. Delay (Closest Position to LO)	Resistance Pin 4 to Pin 6 linear decreasing from 103.3 K ohms to 3.3 K ohms
• Wiper LO, Wash OFF	Resistance Pin 4 to Pin 6, 3.3 K ohms
	Resistance Pin 4 to Pin 1, 4.08 K ohms
• Wiper HI, Wash OFF	Resistance Pin 4 to Pin 6, 3.3 K ohms
	Closed Pin 4 to Pin 1

7921ZG23

Wiper/washer switch continuity test—Windstar

REMOVAL & INSTALLATION

Aerostar

WIPER CONTROL MODULE

1. Disconnect the negative battery cable.
2. Remove the steering column lower trim panel.
3. Remove the wiper control module from the bracket.
4. Installation is the reverse of removal.

WINDSHIELD WASHER NOZZLES

1. Remove the right and left wiper pivot arms.
2. Remove the cowl top vent grille.
3. Disconnect the washer hoses.
4. Remove the screw retaining the windshield washer nozzle jet and bracket to cowl top vent grille.
5. Installation is the reverse of removal. Tighten the retaining screw to 8–15 inch lbs. (1–1.7 Nm).

WINDSHIELD WASHER PUMP AND RESERVOIR

1. Disconnect the headlamp dash panel junction wire from the windshield washer pump.
2. Remove the retaining screws and lift out the assembly.

3. Disconnect the hoses and drain the contents of the reservoir.
4. Installation is the reverse of removal. Refill the reservoir first then reconnect the electrical connections.

Windstar

WIPER CONTROL MODULE

➤The windshield wiper control module is integral with the generic electronic module, and is located to the right of the steering column under the instrument.

1. Disconnect the negative battery cable.
2. Remove the screw retaining the generic electronic module to the vehicle.
3. Slide the generic electronic module forward and off of the retaining tabs.
4. Disconnect the electrical connectors and remove the generic electronic module from the vehicle.
5. Installation is the reverse of removal. Tighten the retaining screw to 18–27 inch lbs. (2–3 Nm).

WINDSHIELD WASHER PUMP AND SEAL

1. Remove the two retaining screws.
2. Remove the right side inner splash shield.
3. Disconnect the electrical connectors.
4. Disconnect the hose, drain the contents of the reservoir and remove the assembly from the vehicle.
5. Installation is the reverse of removal. Refill the reservoir first then reconnect the electrical connections.

WINDSHIELD WASHER NOZZLES

1. Remove the right and left wiper arm and blade assemblies.
2. Remove the cowl top vent panel retaining screws.
3. Disconnect the washer hose at the left side of the vehicle just ahead of where it enters the cowl top.
4. Disconnect the hood to cowl seal.
5. Remove the cowl top vent panel.
6. Disconnect the washer hose from the windshield washer nozzle and brackets.

➤The windshield washer nozzle jet and brackets are an integral part of the cowl top vent panel. If the windshield washer nozzle jet and bracket requires replacement, replace the cowl top vent panel.

7. Installation is the reverse of removal.

Ford Ranger, Explorer and Mountaineer

WINDSHIELD WASHER PUMP AND SEAL

1. Remove the windshield washer reservoir from the vehicle.

2. Disconnect the headlamp dash panel junction wire plug and windshield washer hose.

3. Using a suitable small prying tool, remove the pump retaining ring.

4. Using a pliers to grip one wall around the electrical terminals, pull out the windshield washer pump, seal and impeller assembly.

To Install:

5. Lubricate the outside diameter of the seal with a dry lubricant such as powered graphite, before installing the assembly to prevent the seal from sticking to the wall of the reservoir motor cavity and make assembly easier.

6. Align the small projection on the end of the pump with the slot in the windshield washer reservoir and assemble so the seal seats against the bottom of the motor cavity.

7. Using a 1 inch socket (preferable 12 point) hand press the retaining ring securely against the motor and plate.

8. Connect the electrical plug and washer hose and replace the reservoir in the vehicle.

WINDSHIELD WASHER GOVERNOR

1. Disconnect the negative battery cable.

2. Remove the steering column shroud.

3. Unplug the governor electrical connector from the turn signal and windshield wiper switch.

4. Unplug the instrument panel wiring harness electrical connector from the windshield wiper governor.

5. Remove the two mounting screws.

6. Installation is the reverse of removal. Tighten the mounting screws to 13–17 inch lbs. (1.5–2.0 Nm).

Bronco, Expedition, Navigator, E Series (Van) F Series (Pick-up)

WIPER CONTROL MODULE (E SERIES VAN)

1. Disconnect the negative battery cable.

2. Remove the right lower trim panel.

3. Disconnect the module electrical connector.

4. Remove the wiper control module and bracket.

5. Installation is the reverse of removal.

WIPER CONTROL MODULE (EXCEPT E SERIES VAN)

1. Disconnect the negative battery cable.

2. Remove the glove box.

3. Accessing through the glove box, disconnect the main wiring.

4. From under the instrument panel, use a flat edge tool and remove the wiper control module from the tabs on the bracket.

5. Installation is the reverse of removal.

WINDSHIELD WASHER JET NOZZLES AND BRACKETS (E SERIES VAN)

1. Remove the right and left wiper pivot arms and blades.

2. Remove the cowl top vent seal.

3. Remove the right and left cowl top panels and disconnect the windshield washer hoses.

4. Remove the windshield washer nozzle jet and bracket from the cowl top vent panel.

5. Installation is the reverse of removal.

WINDSHIELD WASHER JET NOZZLES AND BRACKETS (EXCEPT E SERIES VAN)

1. Disconnect the washer nozzle using a suitable long blade tool.

2. Squeeze the locking tabs and push the windshield washer nozzle jet and bracket up through the cowl top outer panel.

3. Installation is the reverse of removal.

WINDSHIELD WASHER PUMP AND RESERVOIR

1. Disconnect the negative battery cable.

2. Disconnect the headlamp dash panel junction wire from the windshield washer pump by unlocking the tabs.

3. Disconnect the hose from the windshield washer nozzle jet and bracket.

4. Remove the retaining screws and lift out the assembly.

5. Disconnect the hoses and drain the contents of the reservoir.

6. Installation is the reverse of removal. Refill the reservoir first then reconnect the electrical connections.

Mercury Villager

GENERAL DESCRIPTION

The windshield wiper assembly consists of the following components:
- Windshield wiper governor
- Windshield wiper motor, located in the engine compartment
- Windshield wiper pivot arms
- Windshield wiper linkage and pivot shaft

- Multi-function turn signal and windshield wiper switch

The wiper system is a two speed, permanent magnet motor. The windshield wiper motor has brush rigging that permits the selection of **LO** or **HI** speed.

The windshield wiper governor is wired in series between the turn signal and the windshield wiper switch and the windshield wiper motor. It operates as a timer mechanism for the interval wiper function. It is located on the Left side strut tower, directly below the hood support rod pivot.

COMPONENT TESTING

- On all vehicles, when trouble shooting the wiper system, test the motor first, then work back towards the switch to test the interval governor or module (depending on the vehicle), power circuits and the switch itself.

- In most of the tests, a volt-ohmmeter is required, although a test light can also be useful. For testing the motor, a 0–15 amp DC ammeter is required.

- When the test calls for a voltage check, the ignition switch must be in the **ON** position.

- When testing for continuity or resistance values, turn the ignition switch to the **OFF** position and/or disconnect the negative battery cable.

- Improper or careless testing can cause permanent damage to the vehicle's electronic circuits and to test equipment. Carefully follow the test equipment manufacturer's instructions.

Wiper Motor Test

1. Turn the key **OFF**.

2. Disconnect the windshield wiper motor connector, located behind the cowl top vent panel.

3. Connect a jumper between **BK/W** wire terminal at the windshield wiper motor connector (component side) to the battery positive terminal **BK/W** wire terminal at the windshield wiper motor connector (component side) to the battery positive terminal.

4. Connect a jumper between **BR/W** wire terminal at the windshield wiper motor connector (component side) to the battery negative terminal and verify low speed operation of the wiper motor.

5. Connect a jumper between **BK/W** wire terminal at the windshield wiper motor connector (component side) to the battery positive terminal.

6. Connect a jumper between **BL/O** wire terminal at the windshield wiper motor connector (component side) to the battery negative terminal and verify high speed operation of the wiper motor.

Windshield Wiper Position	Resistance Between Wires	
	BK/W to R	R to BK
Park	Less than 5 ohms	Greater than 10,000 ohms
Run	Greater than 10,000 ohms	Less than 5 ohms

7921ZG25

Wiper motor resistance test—Villager

7. Reconnect the windshield wiper motor connector, located behind the cowl top vent panel.

8. Turn the key **ON** and cycle the windshield wipers until they reach the fully parked position.

9. Turn the key **OFF**.

10. Disconnect the windshield wiper motor connector.

11. Verify the resistance between the **BK/W** wire terminal and the **R** wire terminal, at the connector leading to the windshield wiper motor.

12. Verify the resistance between the **R** wire terminal and the **BK** wire terminal, at the connector leading to the windshield wiper motor.

Wiper/Washer Switch Test

1. Turn the key **OFF**.

2. Disconnect the ten pin turn signal and windshield wiper connector located on the steering column.

3. Verify the resistance shown in the chart.

REMOVAL & INSTALLATION

Windshield Wiper Governor

➡ **The windshield wiper governor is located on the left side of the engine compartment behind the battery.**

Windshield Wiper/Washer Switch Position	Resistance Between Wire Terminals	
	3A to 2A	1A to 2A
OFF	47,600 ohms	103,300 ohms
S	11,300 ohms	103,300 ohms
F	11,300 ohms	3,300 ohms
LO	4,080 ohms	3,300 ohms
HI	0 ohms	3,300 ohms
WASH	NA	Less than 5 ohms

* Resistance may vary by ± 15%.

7921ZGA1

Wiper/washer switch resistance test—Villager

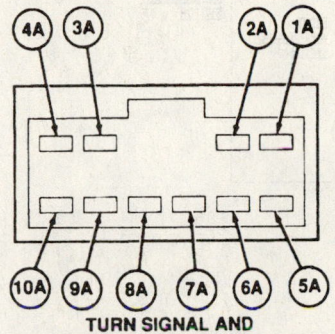

TURN SIGNAL AND WINDSHIELD WIPER SWITCH

7921ZGA2

Wiper/washer switch terminal identification for resistance test (connector shown from component side)—Villager

1. Remove the two windshield wiper governor retaining screws.

2. Disconnect the two windshield wiper governor electrical connectors and remove the governor.

3. Installation is the reverse of removal.

Windshield Washer Jet Nozzle and Bracket

1. Remove the wiper pivot arm.

2. Raise or lower the hood as necessary and remove the cowl top vent panel.

3. Use a suitable prying tool and to loosen the retaining clip and remove the windshield washer nozzle jet and bracket and from the cowl top vent panel.

4. Installation is the reverse of removal.

Windshield Washer Pump and Reservoir

1. Disconnect the negative battery cable.

2. Raise and safely support the vehicle.

3. Remove the right front wheel.

4. Remove the right front fender splash shield.

5. Remove the windshield washer reservoir top bolt.

6. Disconnect the windshield washer reservoir fluid level sensor electrical connector.

7. Disconnect the rear window washer pump electrical connector from the rear window washer pump.

8. Disconnect the windshield washer pump electrical connector from the windshield washer pump.

9. Drain the fluid from the reservoir.

10. Disconnect the hoses from the rear window washer pump and the windshield washer pump. The hoses are color coded for proper installation.

11. Loosen the two windshield washer reservoir side bolts and remove the reservoir by sliding it out of the slots.

12. Remove the windshield washer pump.

13. Installation is the reverse of removal.

GEO

Tracker

GENERAL DESCRIPTION

The windshield wiper circuit consists of the ignition switch, wiper and washer switches, wiper motor, washer motors and relays for the intermittent function. Some models include intermittent rear window wipers and therefore have relays to control this function as well.

When the windshield wiper switch is turned on and the ignition switch is in the **ON** position, battery voltage is applied to the wiper/washer fuse to the front wiper/washer switch (in the combination switch) and front wiper motor pawl and switch contacts. A fuse, located in the fuse block, protects the circuitry of the wiper system and the vehicle.

The wiper motor has permanent magnet fields. The speeds are determined by current flow to the appropriate set of brushes.

The wiper system completes the wipe cycle when the wiper switch is turned off. The wiper blades park in the lowest portion of the wiping pattern.

TESTING

Utilize the accompanying flowcharts and/or drawings in conjunction with the circuit wiring diagram to systematically locate the problem (if any) in the wiper circuit. The key to troubleshooting is an organized, logical approach. Do not proceed to the next step until each step has been completed.

If you locate the problem, follow the chart's recommendation to remedy it, then test the system for proper function.

Tracker Models

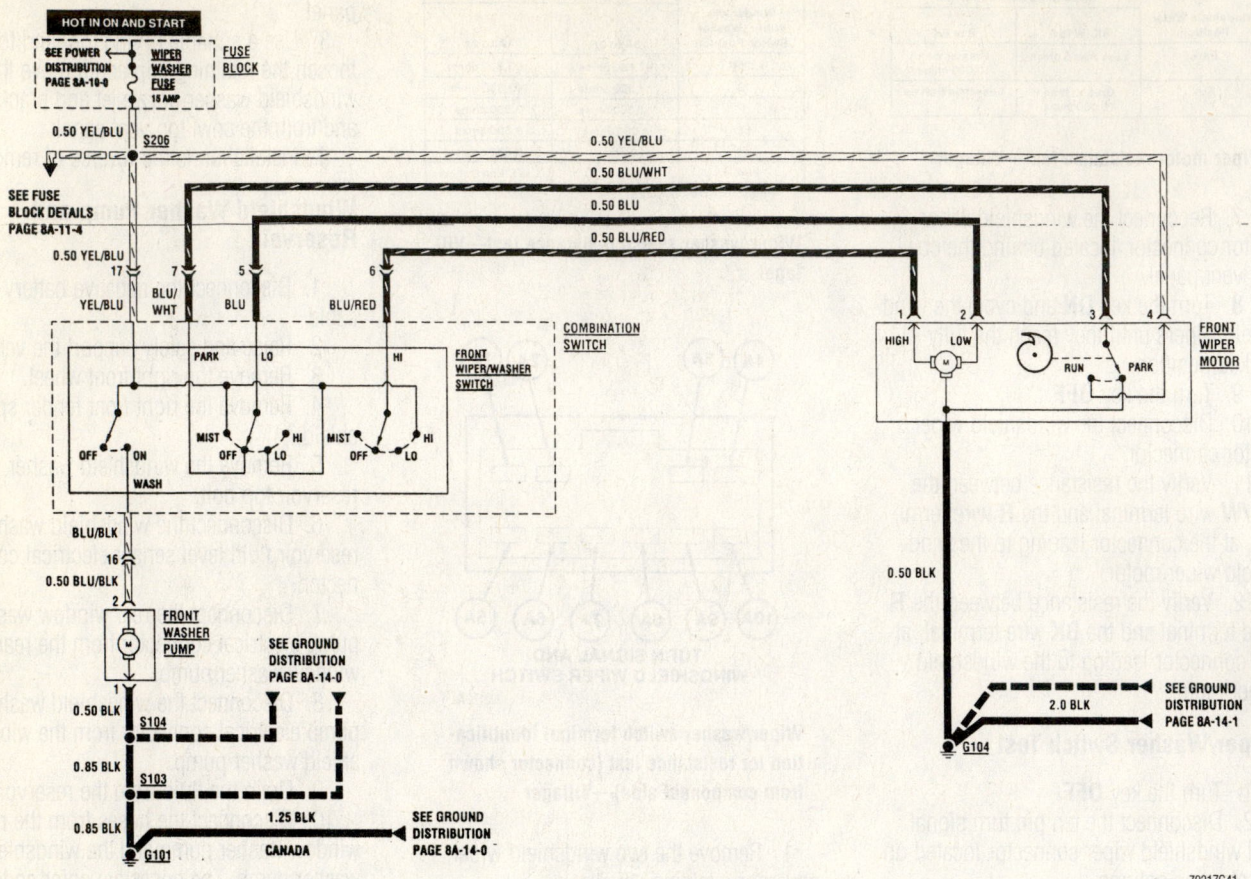

Circuit wiring diagram—Tracker models

WIPER/WASHER	DIAGNOSTIC CHART A		
	TEST	**RESULT**	**ACTION**
A1.	Turn ignition switch to "ON." Pull Front Wiper/Washer Switch back.	FRONT WASHER PUMP operates.	GO TO **A2.**
		FRONT WASHER PUMP does not operate.	GO TO **A5.**
A2.	Press Front Wiper/Washer Switch down to the "MIST" position and release.	Wipers sweep once and stop.	GO TO **A3.**
		Wipers do not sweep.	GO TO **A9.**
		Wipers sweep more than once.	GO TO **A11.**
		Wipers do not complete at least one full sweep.	GO TO **A19.**
A3.	Turn Front Wiper/Washer Switch to the "LO" position.	Wipers do not sweep.	Replace COMBINATION SWITCH.
		Wipers operate at low speed.	GO TO **A4.**
		Wipers operate at high speed.	GO TO **A13.**
A4.	Turn Front Wiper/Washer Switch to the "HI" position.	Wipers operate at high speed.	All systems diagnosed in this cell are functioning normally.
		Wipers do not sweep.	GO TO **A15.**
		Wipers operate at low speed.	GO TO **A17.**
A5.	Backprobe COMBINATION SWITCH connector with a test lamp from cavity 17 to chassis ground.	Test lamp does not light.	Repair open in YEL/BLU wire between FUSE BLOCK and COMBINATION SWITCH.
		Test lamp lights.	GO TO **A6.**
A6.	Backprobe COMBINATION SWITCH connector with a test lamp from cavity 16 to chassis ground. Pull Front Wiper/Washer Switch back.	Test lamp does not light.	Replace COMBINATION SWITCH.
		Test lamp lights.	GO TO **A7.**
A7.	Turn ignition switch to "LOCK." Disconnect FRONT WASHER PUMP connector. Connect a test lamp from connector cavity 2 to chassis ground. Turn ignition switch to "ON" and pull Front Wiper/Washer Switch back.	Test lamp does not light.	Repair open in BLU/BLK wire between FRONT WASHER PUMP and COMBINATION SWITCH.
		Test lamp lights.	GO TO **A8.**
A8.	Connect a digital multimeter from FRONT WASHER PUMP connector cavity 1 to chassis ground. Measure resistance.	More than 1.0 ohm.	Repair BLK ground wire between FRONT WASHER PUMP and G101.
		Less than 1.0 ohm.	Replace FRONT WASHER PUMP.
A9.	Backprobe COMBINATION SWITCH connector with a test lamp from cavity 5 to chassis ground while holding Front Wiper/Washer Switch in the "MIST" position.	Test lamp does not light.	Replace COMBINATION SWITCH.
		Test lamp lights.	GO TO **A10.**

Troubleshooting flowchart: wiper/washer system—Tracker models

WIPER/WASHER	DIAGNOSTIC CHART A (CONT'D)	
TEST	**RESULT**	**ACTION**
A10. Backprobe FRONT WIPER MOTOR connector with a test lamp from cavity 2 to chassis ground while holding Front Wiper/Washer Switch in the "MIST" position.	Test lamp does not light.	Repair open in BLU wire between FRONT WIPER MOTOR and COMBINATION SWITCH.
	Test lamp lights.	Replace FRONT WIPER MOTOR.
A11. Backprobe FRONT WIPER MOTOR connector with a test lamp from cavity 2 to chassis ground. Press Front Wiper/Washer Switch to the "MIST" position and release.	Test lamp lights and goes out.	Replace FRONT WIPER MOTOR.
	Test lamp remains lit.	GO TO **A12.**
A12. Disconnect COMBINATION SWITCH connector. Connect a test lamp from connector terminal 5 (harness side) to chassis ground.	Test lamp lights.	Repair short to voltage in BLU wire between FRONT WIPER MOTOR and COMBINATION SWITCH.
	Test lamp does not light.	Replace COMBINATION SWITCH.
A13. Backprobe FRONT WIPER MOTOR connector with a test lamp from cavity 1 to chassis ground.	Test lamp does not light.	Replace FRONT WIPER MOTOR.
	Test lamp lights.	GO TO **A14.**
A14. Disconnect COMBINATION SWITCH connector. Connect a test lamp from connector terminal 6 (switch side) to chassis ground.	Test lamp lights.	Repair short to voltage in BLU/RED wire between COMBINATION SWITCH and FRONT WIPER MOTOR.
	Test lamp does not light.	Replace COMBINATION SWITCH.
A15. Backprobe FRONT WIPER MOTOR connector with a test lamp from cavity 1 to chassis ground.	Test lamp lights.	Replace FRONT WIPER MOTOR.
	Test lamp does not light.	GO TO **A16.**
A16. Backprobe COMBINATION SWITCH connector with a test lamp from cavity 6 to chassis ground.	Test lamp lights.	Repair open in BLU/RED wire between COMBINATION SWITCH and FRONT WIPER MOTOR.
	Test lamp does not light.	Replace COMBINATION SWITCH.
A17. Backprobe FRONT WIPER MOTOR connector with a test lamp from cavity 2 to chassis ground.	Test lamp does not light.	Check BLU/RED wire for high resistance (more than 3.0 ohms). If OK, replace FRONT WIPER MOTOR.
	Test lamp lights.	GO TO **A18.**
A18. Disconnect COMBINATION SWITCH connector. Connect a test lamp from connector terminal 5 (harness side) to chassis ground.	Test lamp lights.	Repair short to voltage in BLU wire between COMBINATION SWITCH and FRONT WIPER MOTOR.
	Test lamp does not light.	Replace COMBINATION SWITCH.

7921ZG43

Troubleshooting flowchart (cont'd): wiper/washer system—Tracker models

WIPER/WASHER	DIAGNOSTIC CHART A (CONT'D)	
TEST	**RESULT**	**ACTION**
A19. Manually move wipers out of park position. Backprobe FRONT WIPER MOTOR connector with a test lamp from cavity 3 to chassis ground.	Test lamp does not light.	Check for an open in YEL/BLU wire between S206 and FRONT WIPER MOTOR. If OK, replace FRONT WIPER MOTOR.
	Test lamp lights.	Check for an open in BLU/WHT wire between COMBINATION SWITCH and FRONT WIPER MOTOR. If OK, replace COMBINATION SWITCH.

7921ZG44

Troubleshooting flowchart (cont'd): wiper/washer system—Tracker models

GENERAL MOTORS

Lumina APV, Silhouette and Trans Sport

GENERAL DESCRIPTION

A modular, positive park, non-articulating arm, pulse wiper/washer system is used on these vehicles. A wiper/washer switch assembly, washer pump and washer reservoir also are components of this system.

The wiper drive system is installed in the vehicle as a module which includes the wiper motor and linkage assemblies, attached to a tubular frame and bracket assembly.

The pulse and timing functions, along with the demand wash function, are controlled by printed circuit in the wiper motor assembly.

COMPONENT TESTING

Testing Hints

The following procedures assume that the technician has checked the following:

1. Continuity of all harness wires.
2. Wiper motor and wiper/washer switch connectors are mated correctly.
3. If the wiper motor operates but the wipers do not; check the wiper linkage and wiper motor crank arm.

4. Wiper motor-to-dash mounting screws tight for good ground.
5. Fuses are good.
6. Washer hoses clear, fluid in tank.

➡ Prior to starting the diagnosis procedure, it is very important to confirm the reported condition with a complete operational check including the washer system.

Symptom Test

1. Wipers do not operate in any mode? Perform test Chart 1.
2. Wipers run at high speed only, low speed inoperative? Perform test Chart 2.

Refer to the model specific sections for driveline service procedures

CHART 1
WIPERS DO NOT OPERATE IN ANY MODE

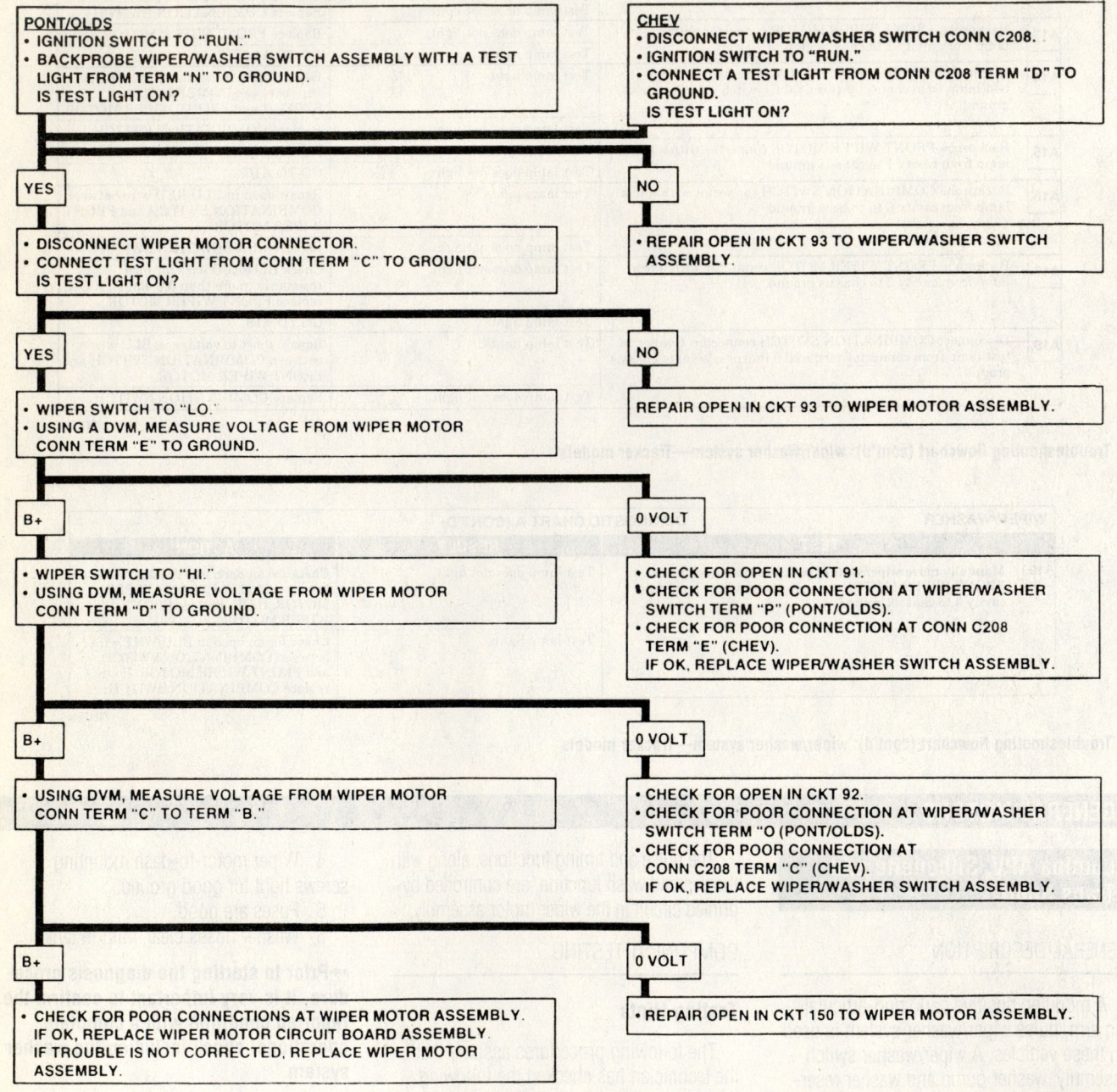

PONT/OLDS
- IGNITION SWITCH TO "RUN."
- BACKPROBE WIPER/WASHER SWITCH ASSEMBLY WITH A TEST LIGHT FROM TERM "N" TO GROUND. IS TEST LIGHT ON?

CHEV
- DISCONNECT WIPER/WASHER SWITCH CONN C208.
- IGNITION SWITCH TO "RUN."
- CONNECT A TEST LIGHT FROM CONN C208 TERM "D" TO GROUND. IS TEST LIGHT ON?

YES

NO

- DISCONNECT WIPER MOTOR CONNECTOR.
- CONNECT TEST LIGHT FROM CONN TERM "C" TO GROUND. IS TEST LIGHT ON?

- REPAIR OPEN IN CKT 93 TO WIPER/WASHER SWITCH ASSEMBLY.

YES

NO

- WIPER SWITCH TO "LO."
- USING A DVM, MEASURE VOLTAGE FROM WIPER MOTOR CONN TERM "E" TO GROUND.

REPAIR OPEN IN CKT 93 TO WIPER MOTOR ASSEMBLY.

B+

0 VOLT

- WIPER SWITCH TO "HI."
- USING DVM, MEASURE VOLTAGE FROM WIPER MOTOR CONN TERM "D" TO GROUND.

- CHECK FOR OPEN IN CKT 91.
- CHECK FOR POOR CONNECTION AT WIPER/WASHER SWITCH TERM "P" (PONT/OLDS).
- CHECK FOR POOR CONNECTION AT CONN C208 TERM "E" (CHEV). IF OK, REPLACE WIPER/WASHER SWITCH ASSEMBLY.

B+

0 VOLT

- USING DVM, MEASURE VOLTAGE FROM WIPER MOTOR CONN TERM "C" TO TERM "B."

- CHECK FOR OPEN IN CKT 92.
- CHECK FOR POOR CONNECTION AT WIPER/WASHER SWITCH TERM "O (PONT/OLDS).
- CHECK FOR POOR CONNECTION AT CONN C208 TERM "C" (CHEV). IF OK, REPLACE WIPER/WASHER SWITCH ASSEMBLY.

B+

0 VOLT

- CHECK FOR POOR CONNECTIONS AT WIPER MOTOR ASSEMBLY. IF OK, REPLACE WIPER MOTOR CIRCUIT BOARD ASSEMBLY. IF TROUBLE IS NOT CORRECTED, REPLACE WIPER MOTOR ASSEMBLY.

- REPAIR OPEN IN CKT 150 TO WIPER MOTOR ASSEMBLY.

7921ZGA3

Wiper/washer symptom test—Lumina APV, Silhouette and Trans Sport

CHART 2
WIPERS RUN AT HIGH SPEED ONLY
(LOW SPEED INOPERATIVE)

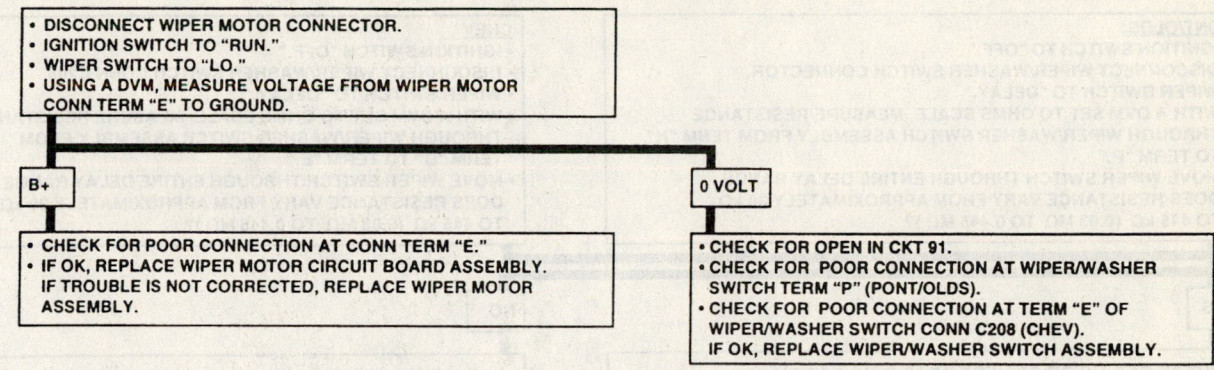

- DISCONNECT WIPER MOTOR CONNECTOR.
- IGNITION SWITCH TO "RUN."
- WIPER SWITCH TO "LO."
- USING A DVM, MEASURE VOLTAGE FROM WIPER MOTOR CONN TERM "E" TO GROUND.

B+

- CHECK FOR POOR CONNECTION AT CONN TERM "E."
- IF OK, REPLACE WIPER MOTOR CIRCUIT BOARD ASSEMBLY. IF TROUBLE IS NOT CORRECTED, REPLACE WIPER MOTOR ASSEMBLY.

0 VOLT

- CHECK FOR OPEN IN CKT 91.
- CHECK FOR POOR CONNECTION AT WIPER/WASHER SWITCH TERM "P" (PONT/OLDS).
- CHECK FOR POOR CONNECTION AT TERM "E" OF WIPER/WASHER SWITCH CONN C208 (CHEV). IF OK, REPLACE WIPER/WASHER SWITCH ASSEMBLY.

CHART 3
WIPERS RUN AT LOW SPEED ONLY
(HIGH SPEED INOPERATIVE)

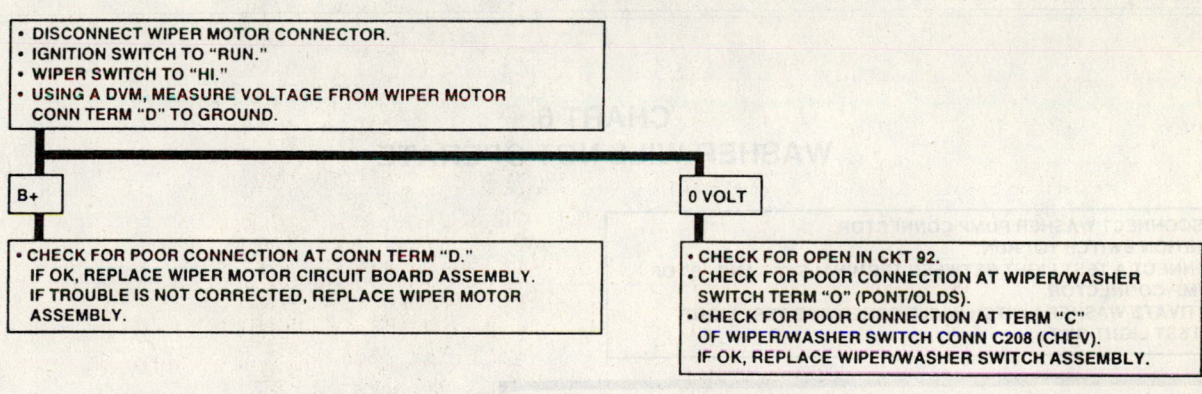

- DISCONNECT WIPER MOTOR CONNECTOR.
- IGNITION SWITCH TO "RUN."
- WIPER SWITCH TO "HI."
- USING A DVM, MEASURE VOLTAGE FROM WIPER MOTOR CONN TERM "D" TO GROUND.

B+

- CHECK FOR POOR CONNECTION AT CONN TERM "D." IF OK, REPLACE WIPER MOTOR CIRCUIT BOARD ASSEMBLY. IF TROUBLE IS NOT CORRECTED, REPLACE WIPER MOTOR ASSEMBLY.

0 VOLT

- CHECK FOR OPEN IN CKT 92.
- CHECK FOR POOR CONNECTION AT WIPER/WASHER SWITCH TERM "O" (PONT/OLDS).
- CHECK FOR POOR CONNECTION AT TERM "C" OF WIPER/WASHER SWITCH CONN C208 (CHEV). IF OK, REPLACE WIPER/WASHER SWITCH ASSEMBLY.

CHART 4
WIPERS WILL NOT TURN OFF

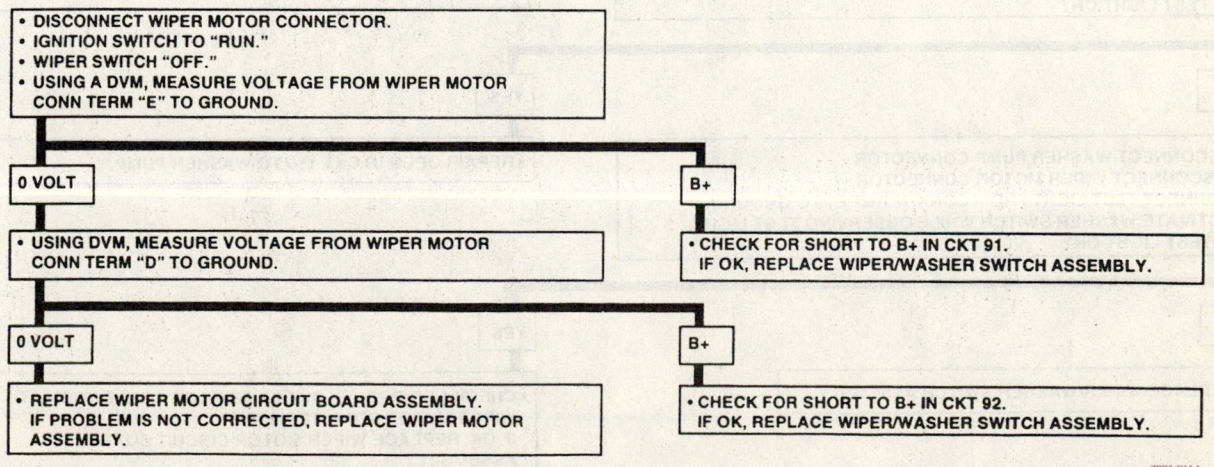

- DISCONNECT WIPER MOTOR CONNECTOR.
- IGNITION SWITCH TO "RUN."
- WIPER SWITCH "OFF."
- USING A DVM, MEASURE VOLTAGE FROM WIPER MOTOR CONN TERM "E" TO GROUND.

0 VOLT

- USING DVM, MEASURE VOLTAGE FROM WIPER MOTOR CONN TERM "D" TO GROUND.

B+

- CHECK FOR SHORT TO B+ IN CKT 91. IF OK, REPLACE WIPER/WASHER SWITCH ASSEMBLY.

0 VOLT

- REPLACE WIPER MOTOR CIRCUIT BOARD ASSEMBLY. IF PROBLEM IS NOT CORRECTED, REPLACE WIPER MOTOR ASSEMBLY.

B+

- CHECK FOR SHORT TO B+ IN CKT 92. IF OK, REPLACE WIPER/WASHER SWITCH ASSEMBLY.

7921ZGA4

Wiper/washer symptom test—Lumina APV, Silhouette and Trans Sport

CHART 5
PULSE DELAY OPERATES INCORRECTLY OR NOT AT ALL

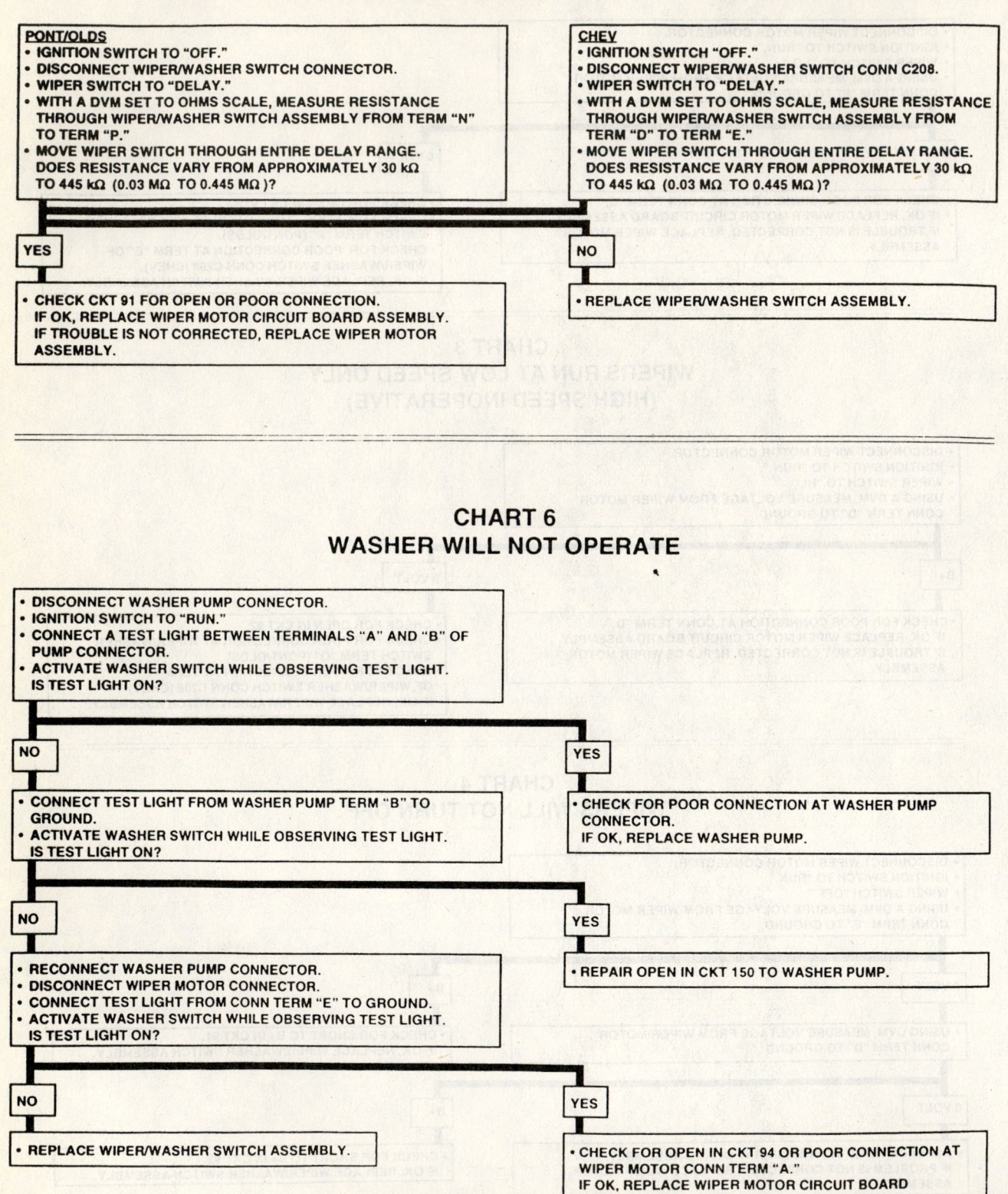

PONT/OLDS
- IGNITION SWITCH TO "OFF."
- DISCONNECT WIPER/WASHER SWITCH CONNECTOR.
- WIPER SWITCH TO "DELAY."
- WITH A DVM SET TO OHMS SCALE, MEASURE RESISTANCE THROUGH WIPER/WASHER SWITCH ASSEMBLY FROM TERM "N" TO TERM "P."
- MOVE WIPER SWITCH THROUGH ENTIRE DELAY RANGE. DOES RESISTANCE VARY FROM APPROXIMATELY 30 kΩ TO 445 kΩ (0.03 MΩ TO 0.445 MΩ)?

CHEV
- IGNITION SWITCH "OFF."
- DISCONNECT WIPER/WASHER SWITCH CONN C208.
- WIPER SWITCH TO "DELAY."
- WITH A DVM SET TO OHMS SCALE, MEASURE RESISTANCE THROUGH WIPER/WASHER SWITCH ASSEMBLY FROM TERM "D" TO TERM "E."
- MOVE WIPER SWITCH THROUGH ENTIRE DELAY RANGE. DOES RESISTANCE VARY FROM APPROXIMATELY 30 kΩ TO 445 kΩ (0.03 MΩ TO 0.445 MΩ)?

YES
- CHECK CKT 91 FOR OPEN OR POOR CONNECTION. IF OK, REPLACE WIPER MOTOR CIRCUIT BOARD ASSEMBLY. IF TROUBLE IS NOT CORRECTED, REPLACE WIPER MOTOR ASSEMBLY.

NO
- REPLACE WIPER/WASHER SWITCH ASSEMBLY.

CHART 6
WASHER WILL NOT OPERATE

- DISCONNECT WASHER PUMP CONNECTOR.
- IGNITION SWITCH TO "RUN."
- CONNECT A TEST LIGHT BETWEEN TERMINALS "A" AND "B" OF PUMP CONNECTOR.
- ACTIVATE WASHER SWITCH WHILE OBSERVING TEST LIGHT. IS TEST LIGHT ON?

NO
- CONNECT TEST LIGHT FROM WASHER PUMP TERM "B" TO GROUND.
- ACTIVATE WASHER SWITCH WHILE OBSERVING TEST LIGHT. IS TEST LIGHT ON?

YES
- CHECK FOR POOR CONNECTION AT WASHER PUMP CONNECTOR. IF OK, REPLACE WASHER PUMP.

NO
- RECONNECT WASHER PUMP CONNECTOR.
- DISCONNECT WIPER MOTOR CONNECTOR.
- CONNECT TEST LIGHT FROM CONN TERM "E" TO GROUND.
- ACTIVATE WASHER SWITCH WHILE OBSERVING TEST LIGHT. IS TEST LIGHT ON?

YES
- REPAIR OPEN IN CKT 150 TO WASHER PUMP.

NO
- REPLACE WIPER/WASHER SWITCH ASSEMBLY.

YES
- CHECK FOR OPEN IN CKT 94 OR POOR CONNECTION AT WIPER MOTOR CONN TERM "A." IF OK, REPLACE WIPER MOTOR CIRCUIT BOARD ASSEMBLY.

7921ZGA5

Wiper/washer symptom test—Lumina APV, Silhouette and Trans Sport

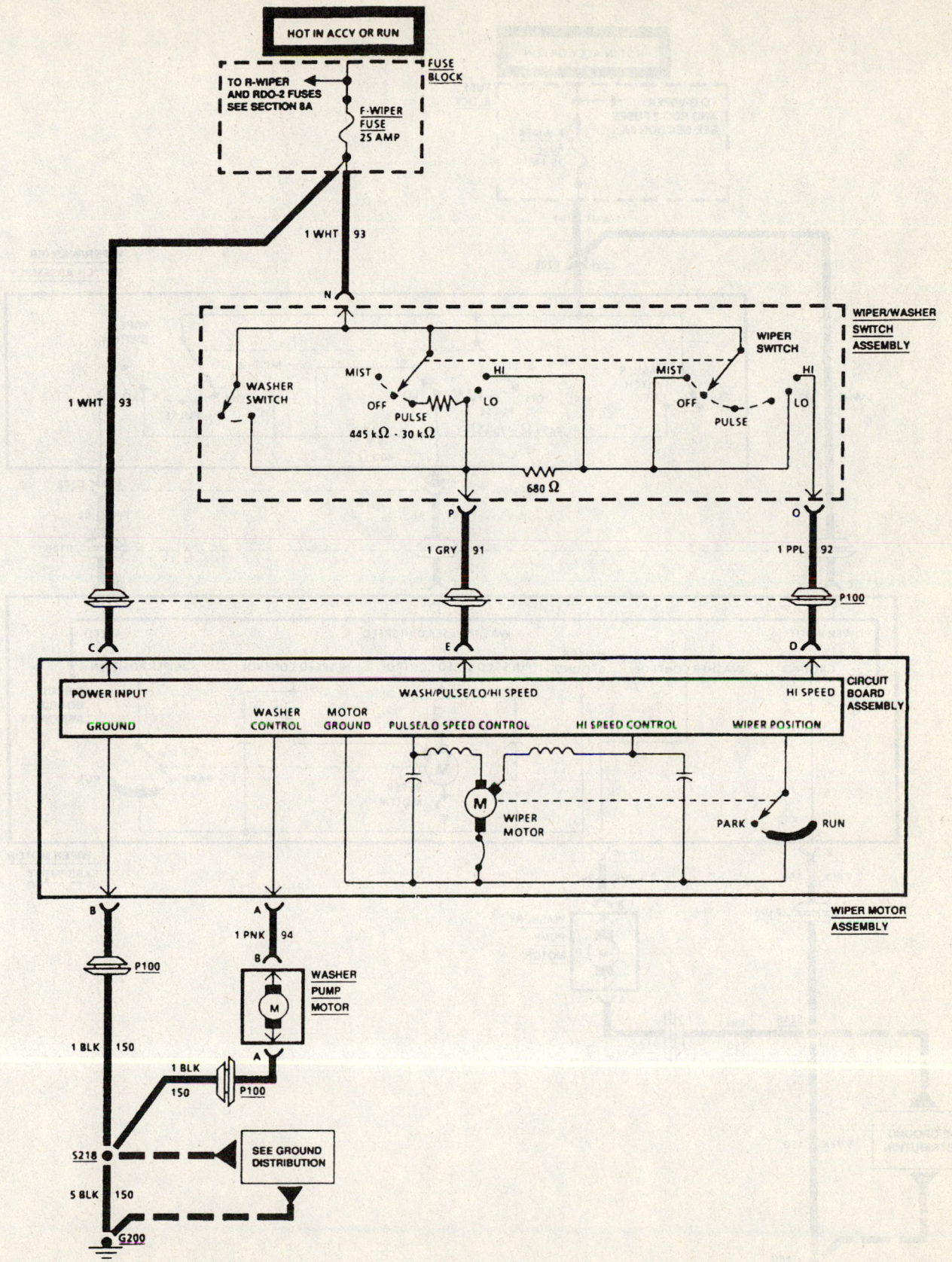

Windshield wiper/washer system electrical schematic—Silhouette and Trans Sport

7921ZGA6

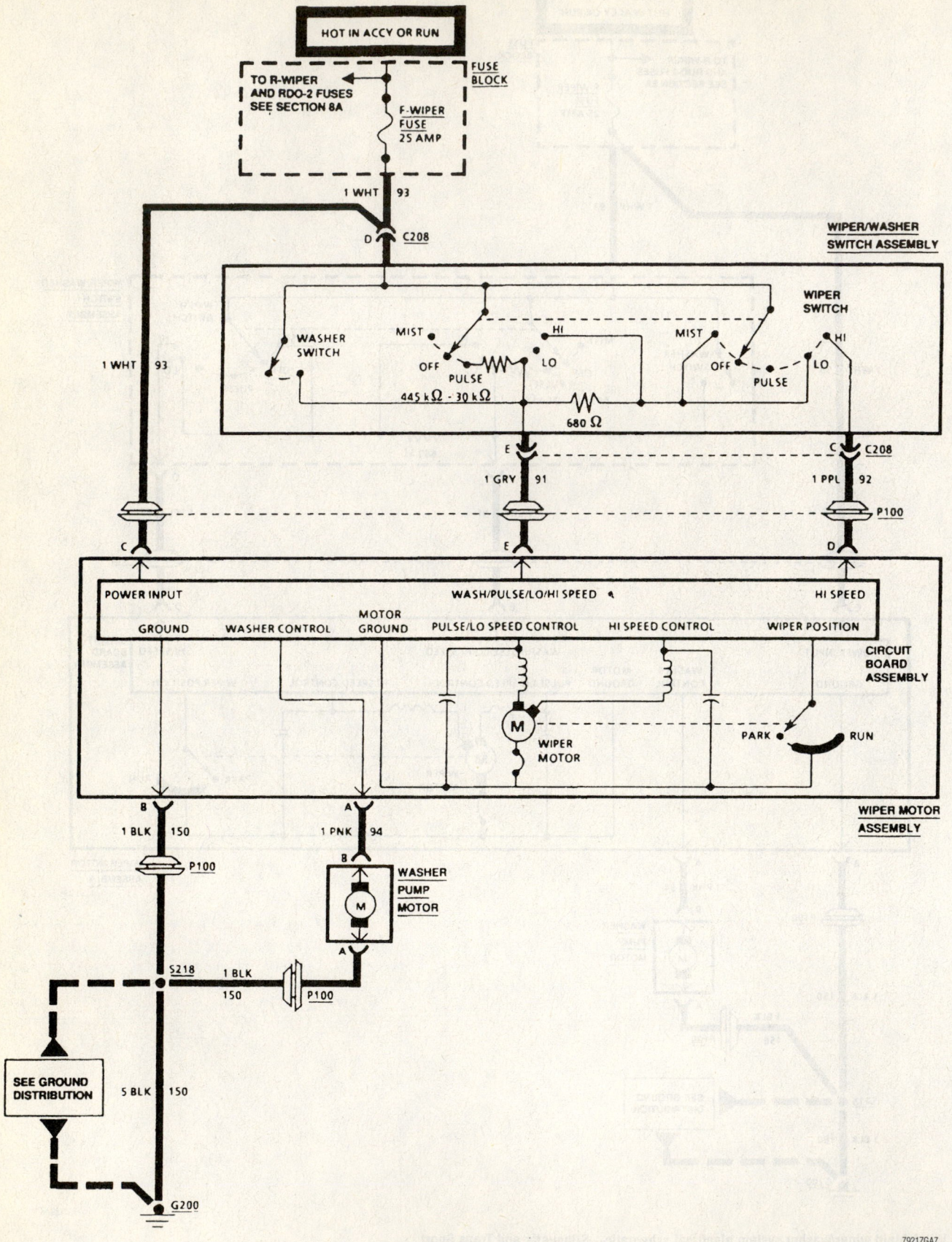

Windshield wiper/washer system electrical schematic—Lumina APV

7921ZGA7

3. Wipers run at low speed only, high speed inoperative? Perform test Chart 3.

4. Wipers will not turn off? Perform test Chart 4.

5. Pulse delay operates incorrectly or not at all? Perform test Chart 5.

6. Washers inoperative? Perform test Chart 6.

REMOVAL & INSTALLATION

Washer Pump

1. Disconnect the negative battery cable.

2. Remove the washer solvent from the reservoir.

3. Disconnect the electrical connector and washer hose from the washer pump.

4. Remove the washer pump from the reservoir.

5. Installation is the reverse of removal. Fill the reservoir and check for correct operation.

Circuit Board

1. Disconnect the negative battery cable.

2. Using a Torx screwdriver, remove the three retaining screws attaching the cover on the windshield wiper motor assembly.

3. Lift up by the terminal and remove the circuit board assembly from the housing.

4. Installation is the reverse of removal.

All Except Lumina APV, Silhouette and Trans Sport

GENERAL DESCRIPTION

The windshield wire/washer system consists of a permanent magnet, positive-park wiper motor assembly, a transmission assembly, wiper arm and blade assemblies, a washer pump mounted on the side of the reservoir and a combination turn signal/wiper/washer switch assembly.

The wiper motor assembly includes a **DELAY** (pulse) mode in addition to three modes of standard system— **HI, LO, MIST**.

A circuit board assembly in the wiper motor assembly and variable resistor (rheostat) in the turn signal/wiper/washer switch control the rate of pulse to the wiper motor.

The wiper motor is sealed and no parts are available. The motor must be replaced if found defective.

The delay module is also sealed and attached directly to the wiper motor. It is also replaced as a unit during service.

COMPONENT TESTING

Testing Hints

The following procedures assume that the technician has checked the following:

1. Continuity of all harness wires.

2. Wiper motor and wiper/washer switch connectors are mated correctly.

3. If the wiper motor operates but the wipers do not; check the wiper linkage and wiper motor crank arm.

4. Wiper motor-to-dash mounting screws tight for good ground.

5. Fuses are good.

6. Washer hoses clear, fluid in tank.

➡**Prior to starting the diagnosis procedure, it is very important to confirm the reported condition with a complete operational check including the washer system.**

All Models

➡**The following procedures assume that the technician has checked the items listed in Testing Hints, outlined earlier in this section:**

WIPER MOTOR ON-VEHICLE TEST

Before performing the following wiper motor test, check motor operation, then disconnect all wiring from the wiper and using a powered test lamp perform the following checks in order as they appear in the illustration.

WASHER PUMP ON-VEHICLE TEST

1. Before performing the following washer pump test, check pump operation, then disconnect the wiring connector from the pump and using a powered test lamp perform the following check as illustrated.

2. If the motor does not run or pump solvent, replace the washer pump.

3. If the motor runs and pumps solvent, the problem is in the circuit board, motor park switch or wiper switch.

WIPER/WASHER SWITCH TEST

Disconnect the wiring harnesses from the wiper motor, turn the ignition switch to the **ON,** position and perform the following switch test as illustrated, using a digital voltmeter.

WIPER MOTOR

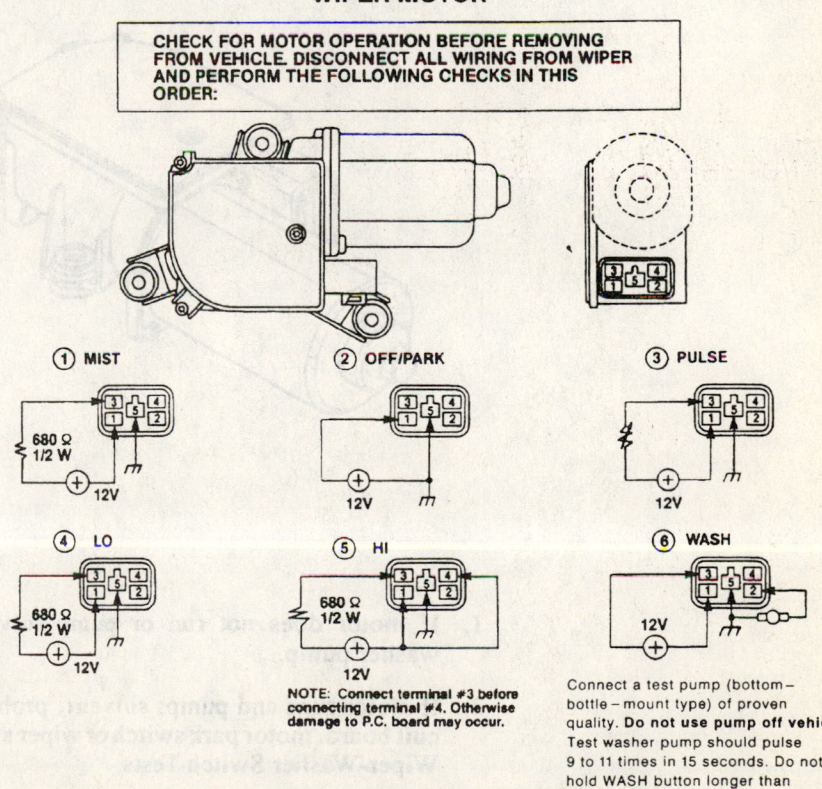

CHECK FOR MOTOR OPERATION BEFORE REMOVING FROM VEHICLE. DISCONNECT ALL WIRING FROM WIPER AND PERFORM THE FOLLOWING CHECKS IN THIS ORDER:

① MIST   680 Ω 1/2 W   12V

② OFF/PARK   12V

③ PULSE   12V

④ LO   680 Ω 1/2 W   12V

⑤ HI   680 Ω 1/2 W   12V

NOTE: Connect terminal #3 before connecting terminal #4. Otherwise damage to P.C. board may occur.

⑥ WASH   12V

Connect a test pump (bottom—bottle – mount type) of proven quality. **Do not use pump off vehicle.** Test washer pump should pulse 9 to 11 times in 15 seconds. Do not hold WASH button longer than this without a 2 minute pause.

7921ZGB1

Windshield wiper motor on-vehicle test—all models

DIAGNOSTIC PROCEDURES (CONT'D)

WASHER PUMP

> CHECK FOR WASHER PUMP OPERATION BEFORE REMOVING FROM VEHICLE. REMOVE CONNECTOR AND APPLY B(+) TO #2 WIRING HARNESS TERMINAL AS SHOWN.

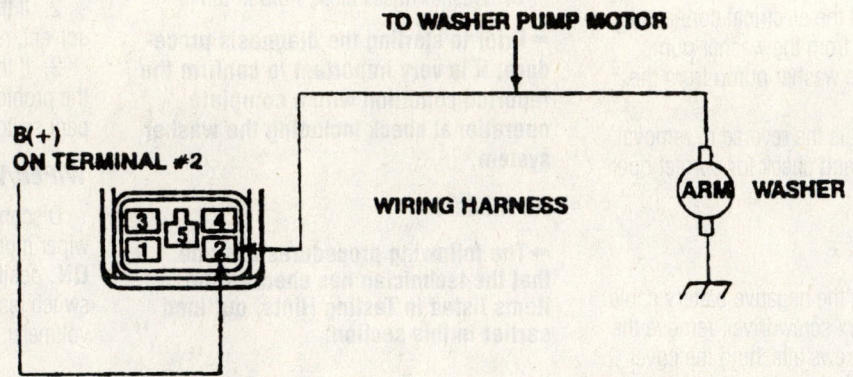

B(+)
ON TERMINAL #2

WIRING HARNESS

TO WASHER PUMP MOTOR

ARM WASHER

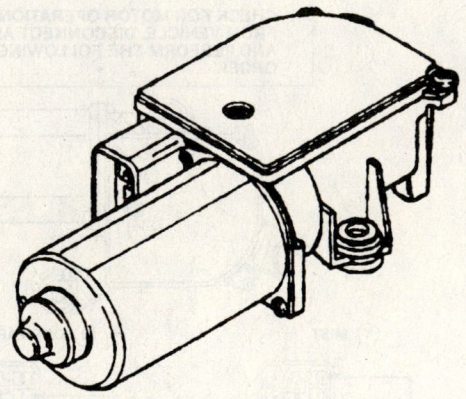

1. If motor does not run or pump solvent, replace washer pump.

2. If motor runs and pumps solvent, problem is in circuit board, motor park switch or wiper switch. Refer to Wiper-Washer Switch Tests.

WIPER-WASHER SWITCH TESTS

Disconnect wiring harnesses from wiper motor and perform the following switch tests using a digital voltmeter and ignition switch on:

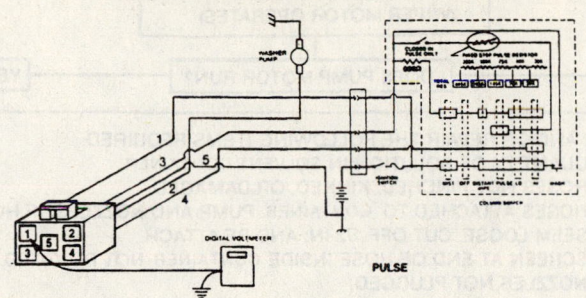

SWITCH MODE TERMINAL		MIST	OFF	PULSE	LO	HI	WASH
PULSE	1	B+	B+	B+	B+	B+	B+
	2	—	—	—	—	—	C
	3	B+	—	B+	B+	C	C
	4	—	—	—	—	C	—
	5	—	—	—	—	—	—

NOTE: All voltage readings taken with respect to vehicle ground.

C = Continuity between terminals

To use Wiper-Washer Switch Check chart, probe terminals 1 thru 5 with digital voltmeter and wiper switch in various positions.

7921ZGB3

Windshield/washer switch test—all models

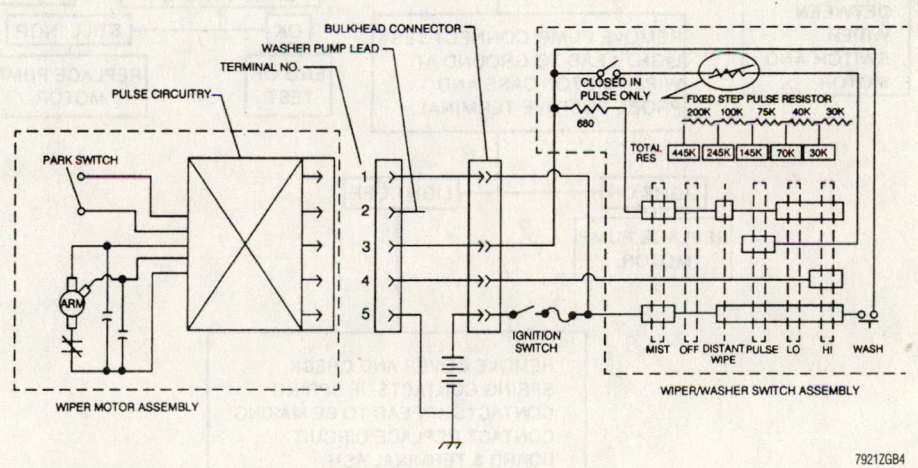

7921ZGB4

Windshield wiper circuit—all models

SYMPTOM DIAGNOSIS TEST

➡ The following procedures assume that the technician has checked the items listed in Testing Hints, outlined earlier in this section. In most of the test an volt-ohmmeter or test light is required.

SYMPTOM	PROCEDURE NO.
1. Pump inoperative—wiper motor operates	1
2. Washer pumps continuously	2
3. Wiper motor inoperative (all modes)	3
4. "Lo" speed only—inoperative in "Hi"	4
5. "Hi" speed only—inoperative in "Lo"	5
6. One speed only—runs the same in both speeds	6
7. Wiper shuts off but blades don't park	7
8. Wiper will not shut off	8
9. Intermittent inoperative	9
10. Wiper motor runs but blades don't move	10
11. Wiper parks above park position	11

7921ZGB5

Windshield wiper/washer symptom diagnosis chart—all models

For complete service labor times order Nichols' Chilton Labor Guide Manual

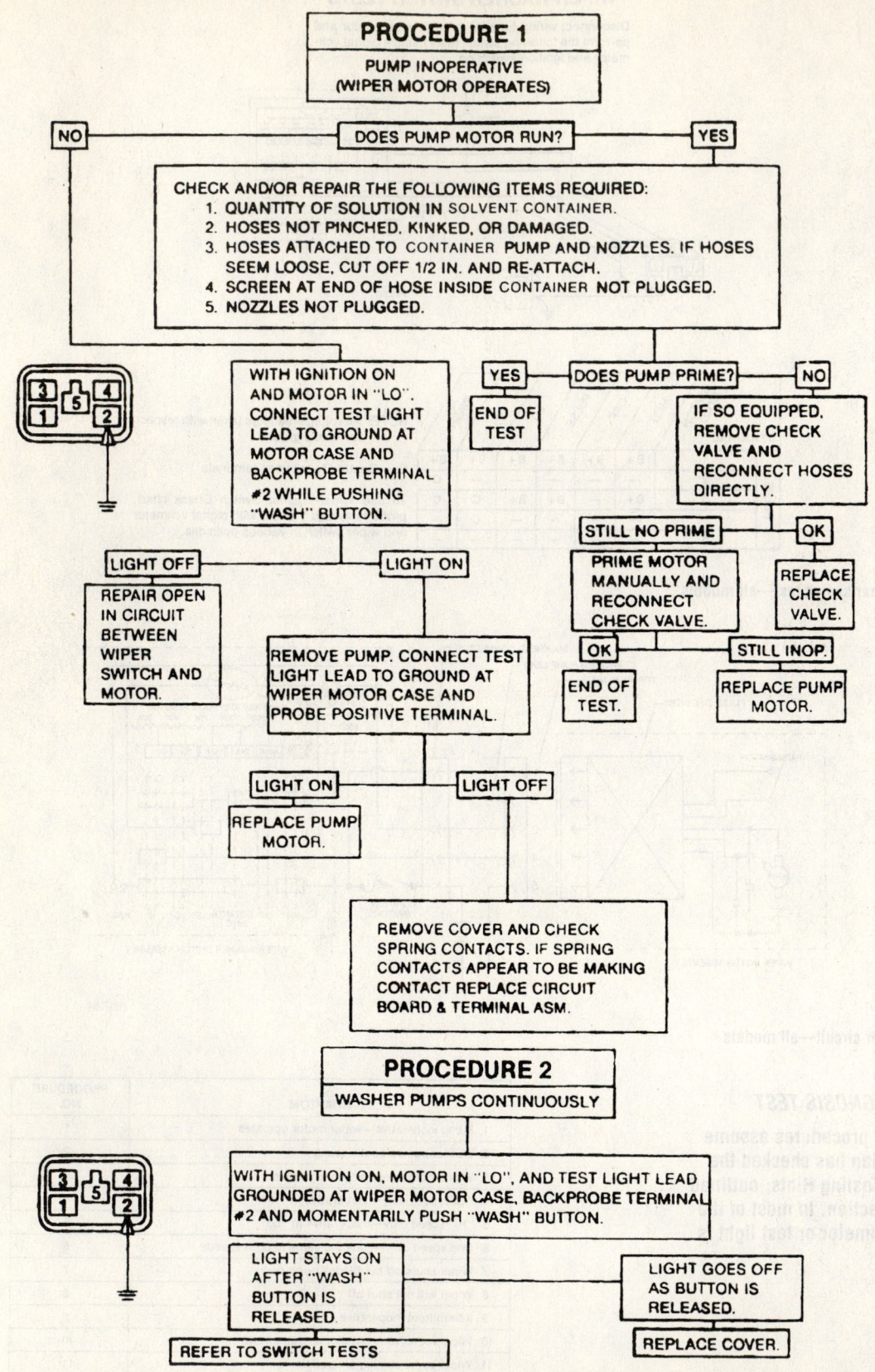

PROCEDURE 1

PUMP INOPERATIVE (WIPER MOTOR OPERATES)

NO — DOES PUMP MOTOR RUN? — YES

CHECK AND/OR REPAIR THE FOLLOWING ITEMS REQUIRED:
1. QUANTITY OF SOLUTION IN SOLVENT CONTAINER.
2. HOSES NOT PINCHED, KINKED, OR DAMAGED.
3. HOSES ATTACHED TO CONTAINER PUMP AND NOZZLES. IF HOSES SEEM LOOSE, CUT OFF 1/2 IN. AND RE-ATTACH.
4. SCREEN AT END OF HOSE INSIDE CONTAINER NOT PLUGGED.
5. NOZZLES NOT PLUGGED.

WITH IGNITION ON AND MOTOR IN "LO", CONNECT TEST LIGHT LEAD TO GROUND AT MOTOR CASE AND BACKPROBE TERMINAL #2 WHILE PUSHING "WASH" BUTTON.

YES — END OF TEST

DOES PUMP PRIME? — NO

IF SO EQUIPPED, REMOVE CHECK VALVE AND RECONNECT HOSES DIRECTLY.

LIGHT OFF — LIGHT ON

REPAIR OPEN IN CIRCUIT BETWEEN WIPER SWITCH AND MOTOR.

STILL NO PRIME — OK

PRIME MOTOR MANUALLY AND RECONNECT CHECK VALVE.

REPLACE CHECK VALVE.

REMOVE PUMP. CONNECT TEST LIGHT LEAD TO GROUND AT WIPER MOTOR CASE AND PROBE POSITIVE TERMINAL.

OK — STILL INOP.

END OF TEST.

REPLACE PUMP MOTOR.

LIGHT ON — LIGHT OFF

REPLACE PUMP MOTOR.

REMOVE COVER AND CHECK SPRING CONTACTS. IF SPRING CONTACTS APPEAR TO BE MAKING CONTACT REPLACE CIRCUIT BOARD & TERMINAL ASM.

PROCEDURE 2

WASHER PUMPS CONTINUOUSLY

WITH IGNITION ON, MOTOR IN "LO", AND TEST LIGHT LEAD GROUNDED AT WIPER MOTOR CASE, BACKPROBE TERMINAL #2 AND MOMENTARILY PUSH "WASH" BUTTON.

LIGHT STAYS ON AFTER "WASH" BUTTON IS RELEASED.

LIGHT GOES OFF AS BUTTON IS RELEASED.

REFER TO SWITCH TESTS

REPLACE COVER.

7921ZGB6

Windshield wiper/washer diagnosis—all models

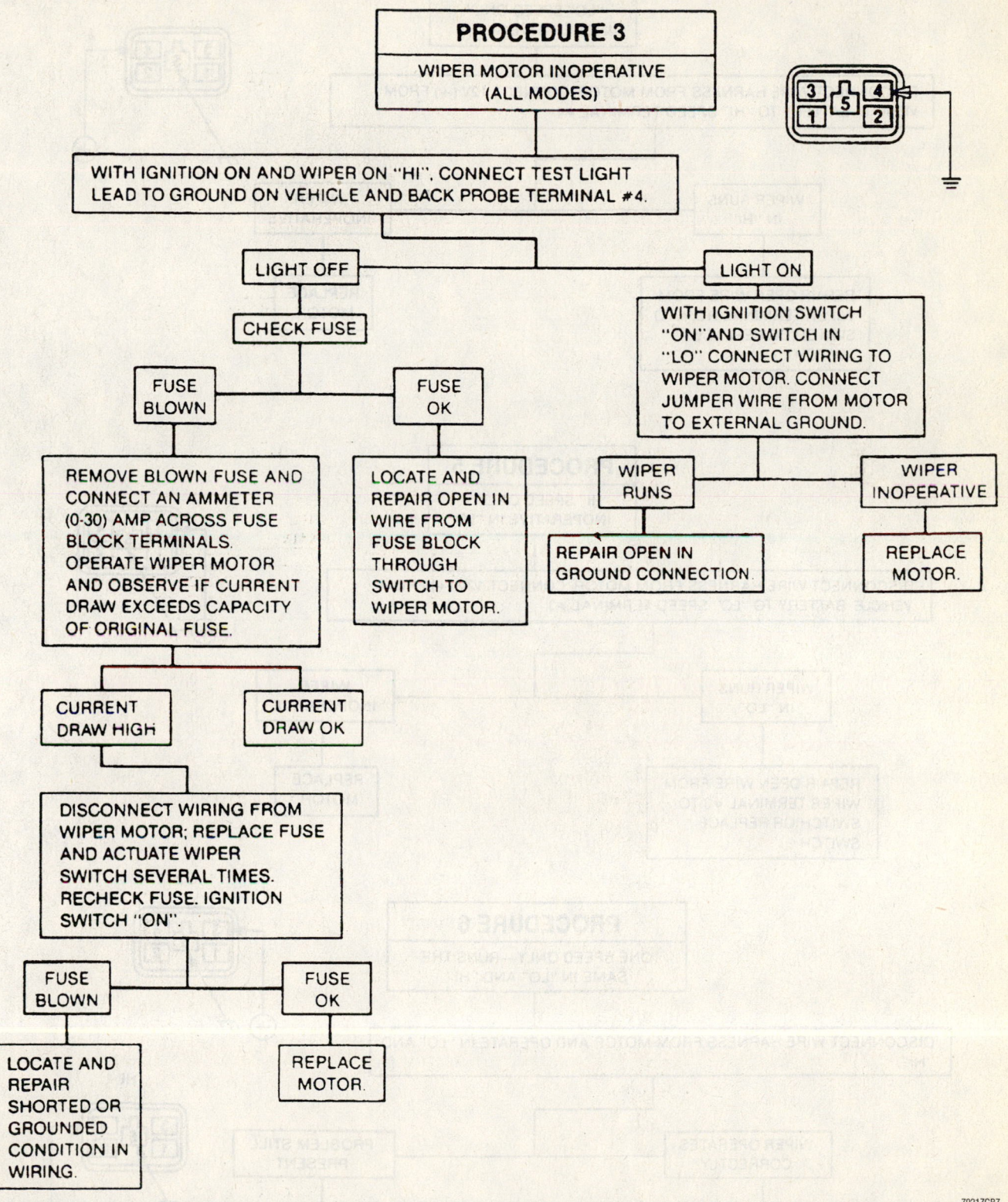

PROCEDURE 3

WIPER MOTOR INOPERATIVE (ALL MODES)

WITH IGNITION ON AND WIPER ON "HI", CONNECT TEST LIGHT LEAD TO GROUND ON VEHICLE AND BACK PROBE TERMINAL #4.

LIGHT OFF

LIGHT ON

CHECK FUSE

WITH IGNITION SWITCH "ON" AND SWITCH IN "LO" CONNECT WIRING TO WIPER MOTOR. CONNECT JUMPER WIRE FROM MOTOR TO EXTERNAL GROUND.

FUSE BLOWN

FUSE OK

WIPER RUNS

WIPER INOPERATIVE

REMOVE BLOWN FUSE AND CONNECT AN AMMETER (0-30) AMP ACROSS FUSE BLOCK TERMINALS. OPERATE WIPER MOTOR AND OBSERVE IF CURRENT DRAW EXCEEDS CAPACITY OF ORIGINAL FUSE.

LOCATE AND REPAIR OPEN IN WIRE FROM FUSE BLOCK THROUGH SWITCH TO WIPER MOTOR.

REPAIR OPEN IN GROUND CONNECTION.

REPLACE MOTOR.

CURRENT DRAW HIGH

CURRENT DRAW OK

DISCONNECT WIRING FROM WIPER MOTOR; REPLACE FUSE AND ACTUATE WIPER SWITCH SEVERAL TIMES. RECHECK FUSE. IGNITION SWITCH "ON".

FUSE BLOWN

FUSE OK

LOCATE AND REPAIR SHORTED OR GROUNDED CONDITION IN WIRING.

REPLACE MOTOR.

7921ZGB7

Windshield wiper/washer diagnosis—all models

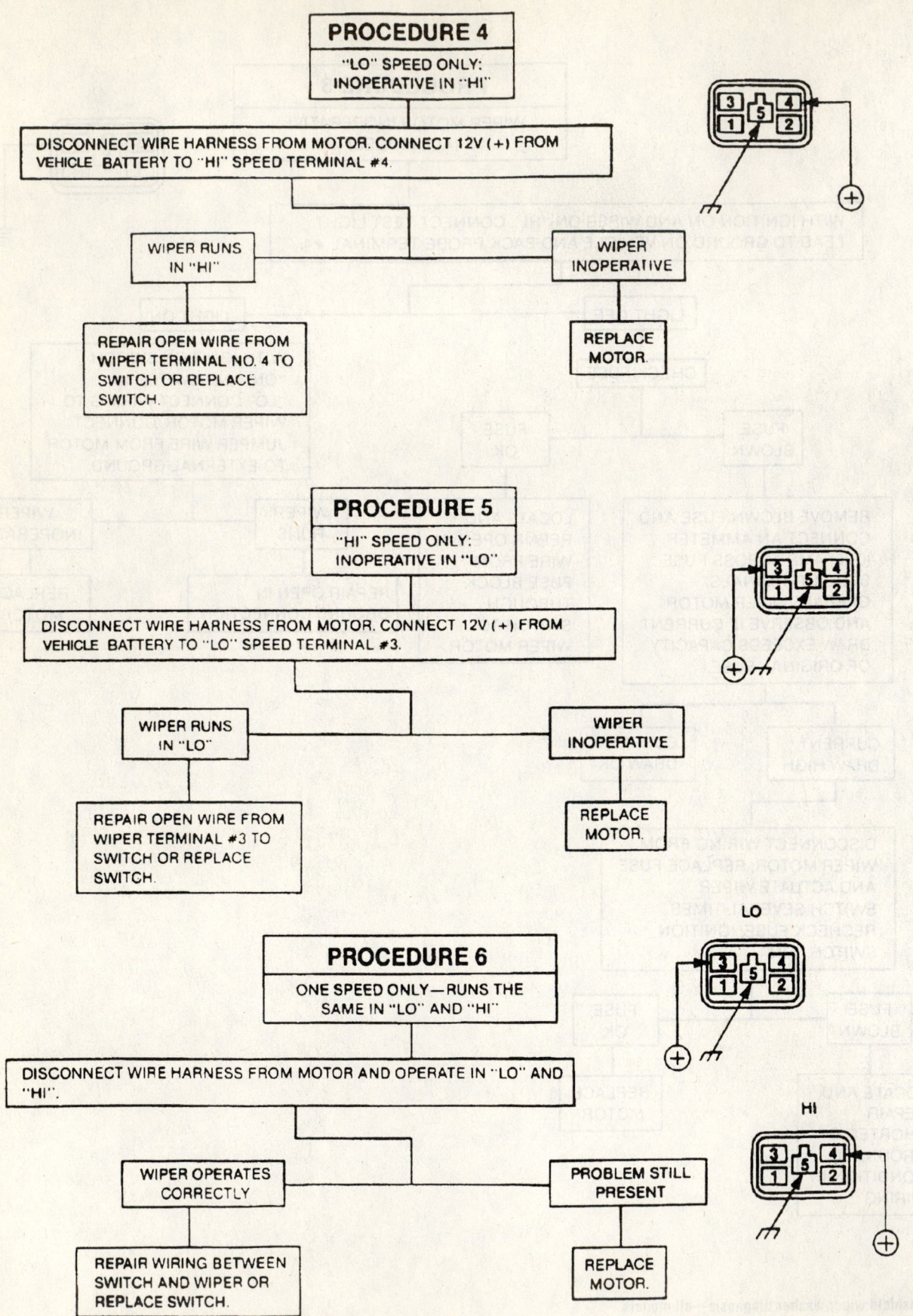

PROCEDURE 4

"LO" SPEED ONLY:
INOPERATIVE IN "HI"

DISCONNECT WIRE HARNESS FROM MOTOR. CONNECT 12V (+) FROM VEHICLE BATTERY TO "HI" SPEED TERMINAL #4.

WIPER RUNS IN "HI"

WIPER INOPERATIVE

REPAIR OPEN WIRE FROM WIPER TERMINAL NO. 4 TO SWITCH OR REPLACE SWITCH.

REPLACE MOTOR.

PROCEDURE 5

"HI" SPEED ONLY:
INOPERATIVE IN "LO"

DISCONNECT WIRE HARNESS FROM MOTOR. CONNECT 12V (+) FROM VEHICLE BATTERY TO "LO" SPEED TERMINAL #3.

WIPER RUNS IN "LO"

WIPER INOPERATIVE

REPAIR OPEN WIRE FROM WIPER TERMINAL #3 TO SWITCH OR REPLACE SWITCH.

REPLACE MOTOR.

LO

PROCEDURE 6

ONE SPEED ONLY—RUNS THE SAME IN "LO" AND "HI"

DISCONNECT WIRE HARNESS FROM MOTOR AND OPERATE IN "LO" AND "HI".

WIPER OPERATES CORRECTLY

PROBLEM STILL PRESENT

REPAIR WIRING BETWEEN SWITCH AND WIPER OR REPLACE SWITCH.

REPLACE MOTOR.

HI

Windshield wiper/washer diagnosis—all models

7921ZGB8

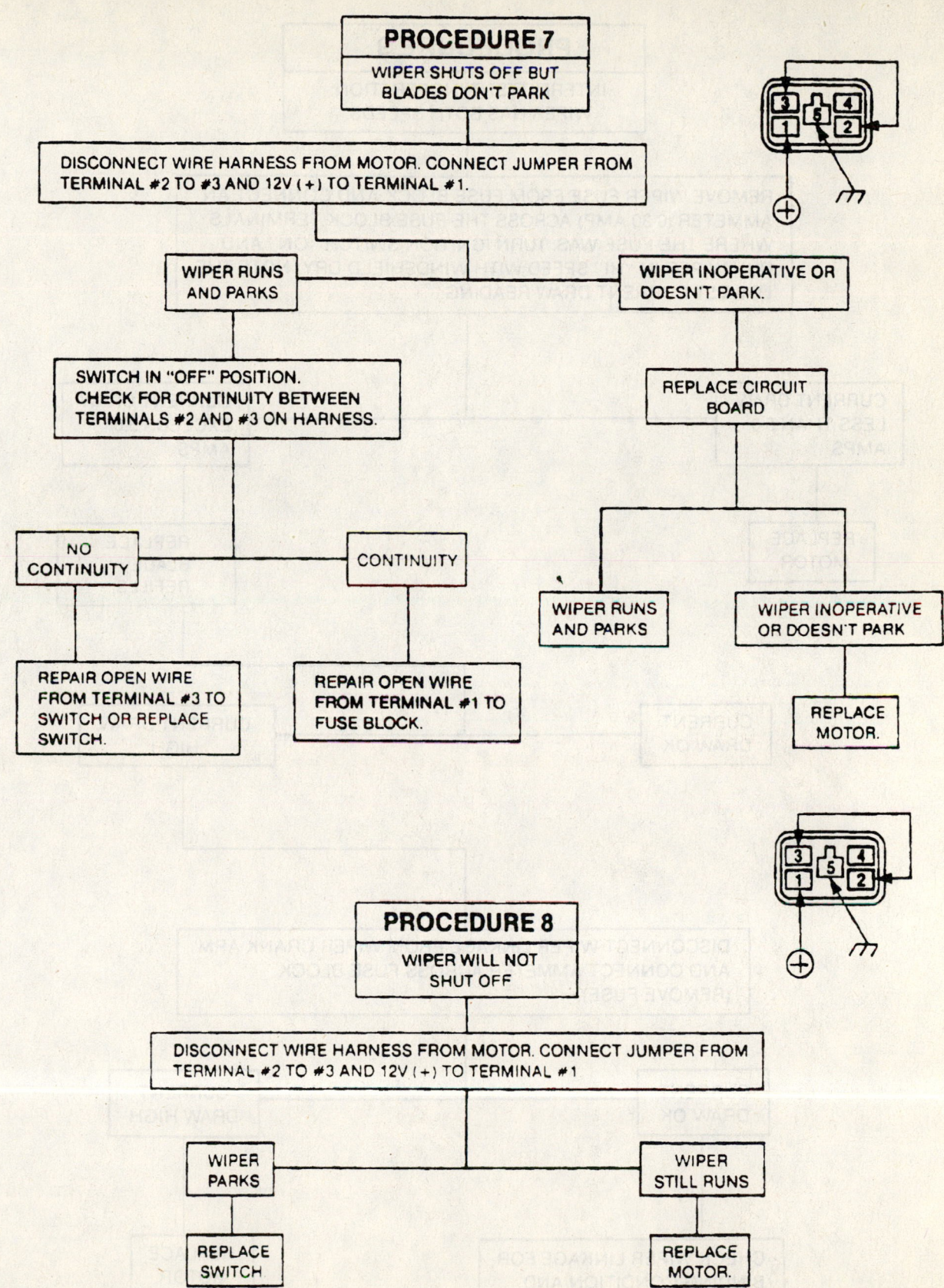

PROCEDURE 7

WIPER SHUTS OFF BUT
BLADES DON'T PARK

DISCONNECT WIRE HARNESS FROM MOTOR. CONNECT JUMPER FROM
TERMINAL #2 TO #3 AND 12V (+) TO TERMINAL #1.

WIPER RUNS
AND PARKS

WIPER INOPERATIVE OR
DOESN'T PARK.

SWITCH IN "OFF" POSITION.
CHECK FOR CONTINUITY BETWEEN
TERMINALS #2 AND #3 ON HARNESS.

REPLACE CIRCUIT
BOARD

NO
CONTINUITY

CONTINUITY

WIPER RUNS
AND PARKS

WIPER INOPERATIVE
OR DOESN'T PARK

REPAIR OPEN WIRE
FROM TERMINAL #3 TO
SWITCH OR REPLACE
SWITCH.

REPAIR OPEN WIRE
FROM TERMINAL #1 TO
FUSE BLOCK.

REPLACE
MOTOR.

PROCEDURE 8

WIPER WILL NOT
SHUT OFF

DISCONNECT WIRE HARNESS FROM MOTOR. CONNECT JUMPER FROM
TERMINAL #2 TO #3 AND 12V (+) TO TERMINAL #1

WIPER
PARKS

WIPER
STILL RUNS

REPLACE
SWITCH

REPLACE
MOTOR.

7921ZGB9

Windshield wiper/washer diagnosis—all models

Refer to the model specific sections for driveline service procedures

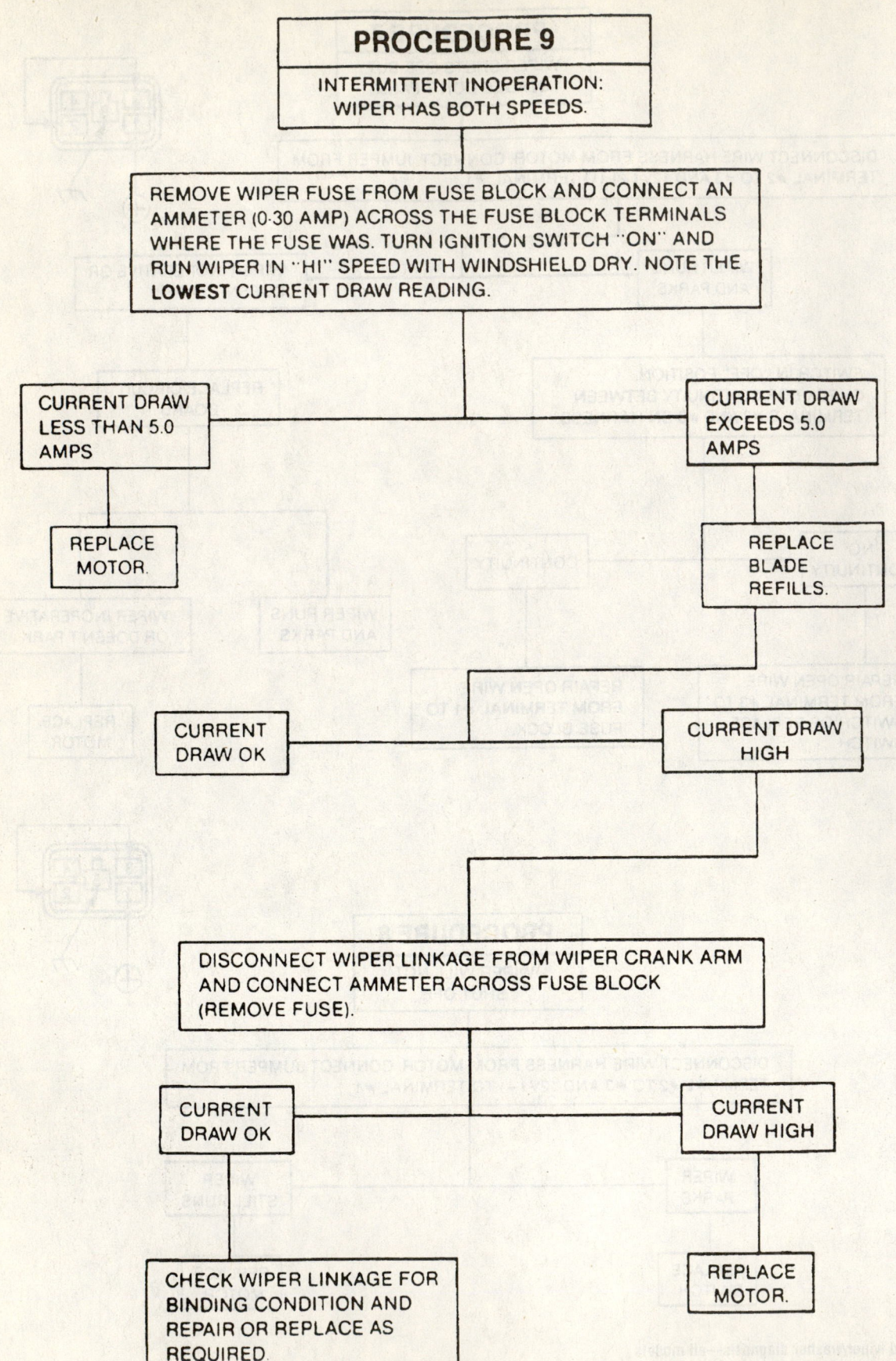

PROCEDURE 9

INTERMITTENT INOPERATION:
WIPER HAS BOTH SPEEDS.

REMOVE WIPER FUSE FROM FUSE BLOCK AND CONNECT AN
AMMETER (0-30 AMP) ACROSS THE FUSE BLOCK TERMINALS
WHERE THE FUSE WAS. TURN IGNITION SWITCH "ON" AND
RUN WIPER IN "HI" SPEED WITH WINDSHIELD DRY. NOTE THE
LOWEST CURRENT DRAW READING.

CURRENT DRAW
LESS THAN 5.0
AMPS

CURRENT DRAW
EXCEEDS 5.0
AMPS

REPLACE
MOTOR.

REPLACE
BLADE
REFILLS.

CURRENT
DRAW OK

CURRENT DRAW
HIGH

DISCONNECT WIPER LINKAGE FROM WIPER CRANK ARM
AND CONNECT AMMETER ACROSS FUSE BLOCK
(REMOVE FUSE).

CURRENT
DRAW OK

CURRENT
DRAW HIGH

CHECK WIPER LINKAGE FOR
BINDING CONDITION AND
REPAIR OR REPLACE AS
REQUIRED.

REPLACE
MOTOR.

7921ZGC1

Windshield wiper/washer diagnosis—all models

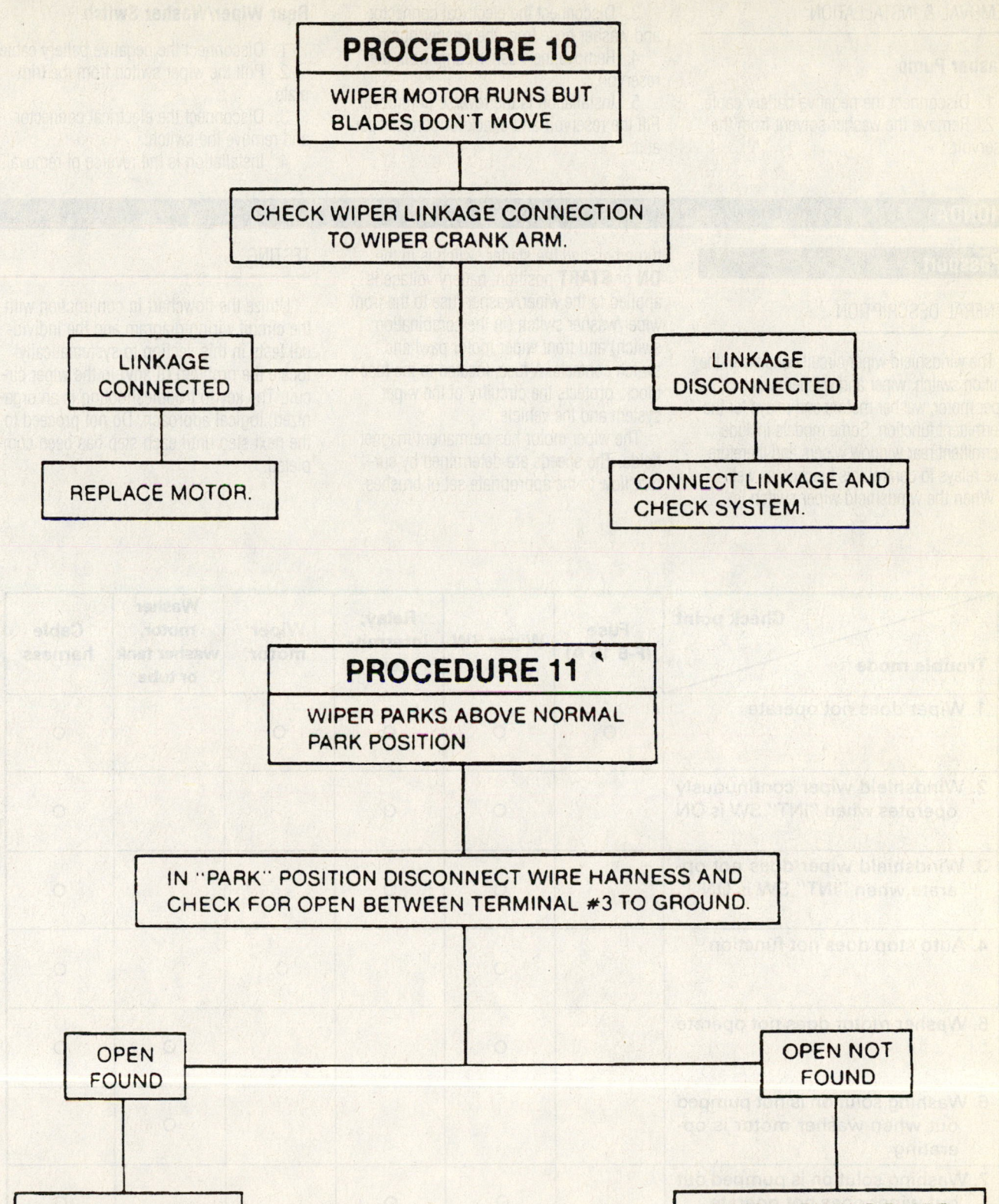

PROCEDURE 10

WIPER MOTOR RUNS BUT
BLADES DON'T MOVE

CHECK WIPER LINKAGE CONNECTION
TO WIPER CRANK ARM.

LINKAGE
CONNECTED

LINKAGE
DISCONNECTED

REPLACE MOTOR.

CONNECT LINKAGE AND
CHECK SYSTEM.

PROCEDURE 11

WIPER PARKS ABOVE NORMAL
PARK POSITION

IN "PARK" POSITION DISCONNECT WIRE HARNESS AND
CHECK FOR OPEN BETWEEN TERMINAL #3 TO GROUND.

OPEN
FOUND

OPEN NOT
FOUND

REPLACE MOTOR.

CHECK ARM AND BLADE
LOCATION AND/OR
LINKAGE.

7921ZGC2

Windshield wiper/washer diagnosis—all models

REMOVAL & INSTALLATION

Washer Pump

1. Disconnect the negative battery cable.
2. Remove the washer solvent from the reservoir.

3. Disconnect the electrical connector and washer hose from the washer pump.
4. Remove the washer pump from the reservoir.
5. Installation is the reverse of removal. Fill the reservoir and check for correct operation.

Rear Wiper/Washer Switch

1. Disconnect the negative battery cable.
2. Pull the wiper switch from the trim plate.
3. Disconnect the electrical connector and remove the switch.
4. Installation is the reverse of removal.

HONDA

Passport

GENERAL DESCRIPTION

The windshield wiper circuit consists of the ignition switch, wiper and washer switches, wiper motor, washer motors and relays for the intermittent function. Some models include intermittent rear window wipers and therefore have relays to control this function as well.

When the windshield wiper switch is turned on and the starter switch is in the **ON** or **START** position, battery voltage is applied to the wiper/washer fuse to the front wiper/washer switch (in the combination switch) and front wiper motor pawl and switch contacts. A fuse, located in the fuse block, protects the circuitry of the wiper system and the vehicle.

The wiper motor has permanent magnet fields. The speeds are determined by current flow to the appropriate set of brushes.

TESTING

Utilize the flowchart in conjunction with the circuit wiring diagram and the individual tests in this section to systematically locate the problem (if any) in the wiper circuit. The key to troubleshooting is an organized, logical approach. Do not proceed to the next step until each step has been completed.

Check point / Trouble mode	Fuse (F-6 15 A)	Wiper SW	Relay; intermittent	Wiper motor	Washer motor, washer tank or tube	Cable harness
1. Wiper does not operate	O	O	O	O		O
2. Windshield wiper continuously operates when "INT" SW is ON		O	O			O
3. Windshield wiper does not operate when "INT" SW is ON		O				O
4. Auto stop does not function		O		O		O
5. Washer motor does not operate		O			O	O
6. Washing solution is not pumped out when washer motor is operating					O	
7. Washing solution is pumped out but wiper does not operate		O	O			O

7921ZG69

Windshield wiper system quick chart for system troubleshooting—Passport

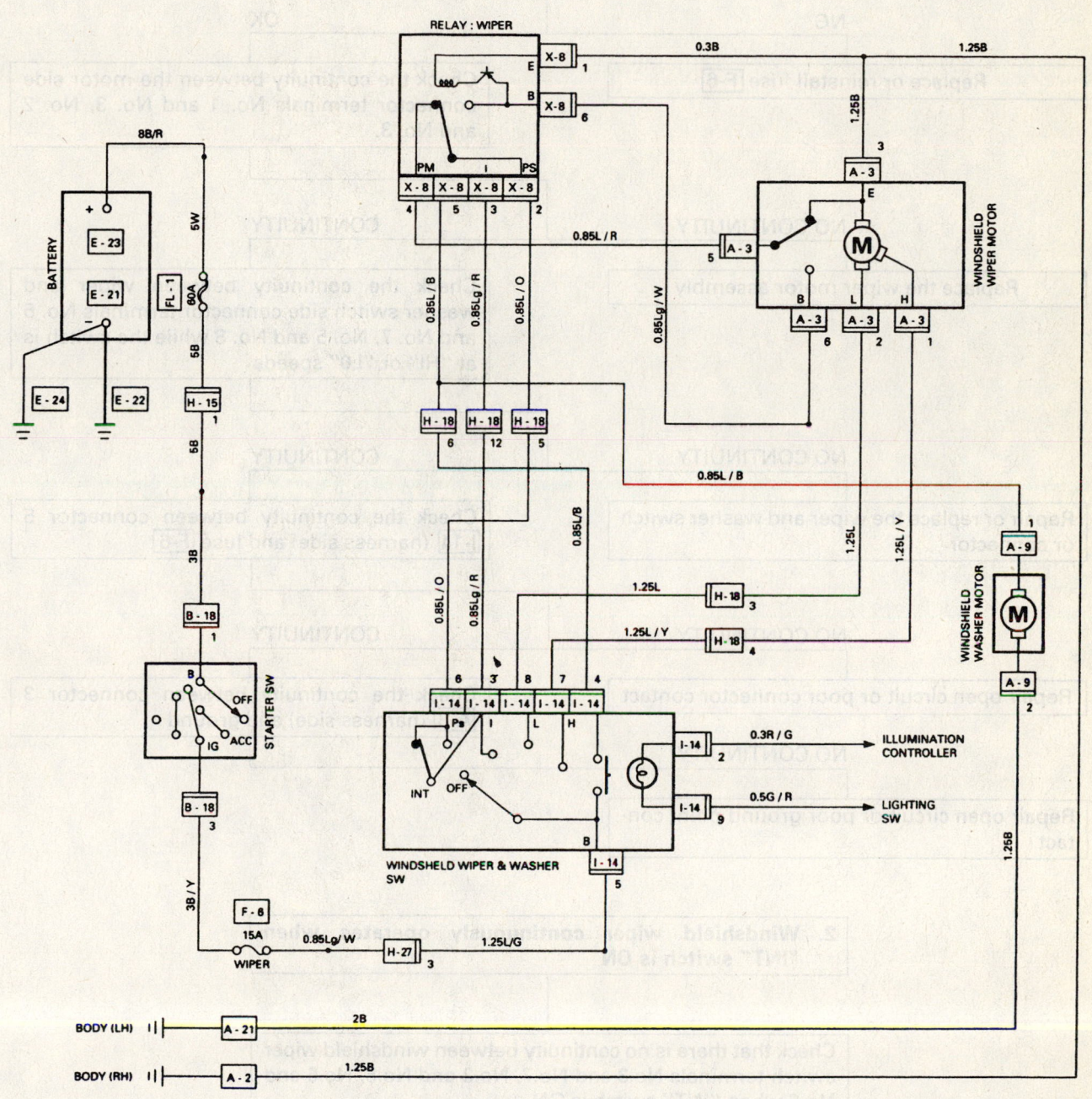

Front wiper circuit wiring diagram—Passport

7921ZG68

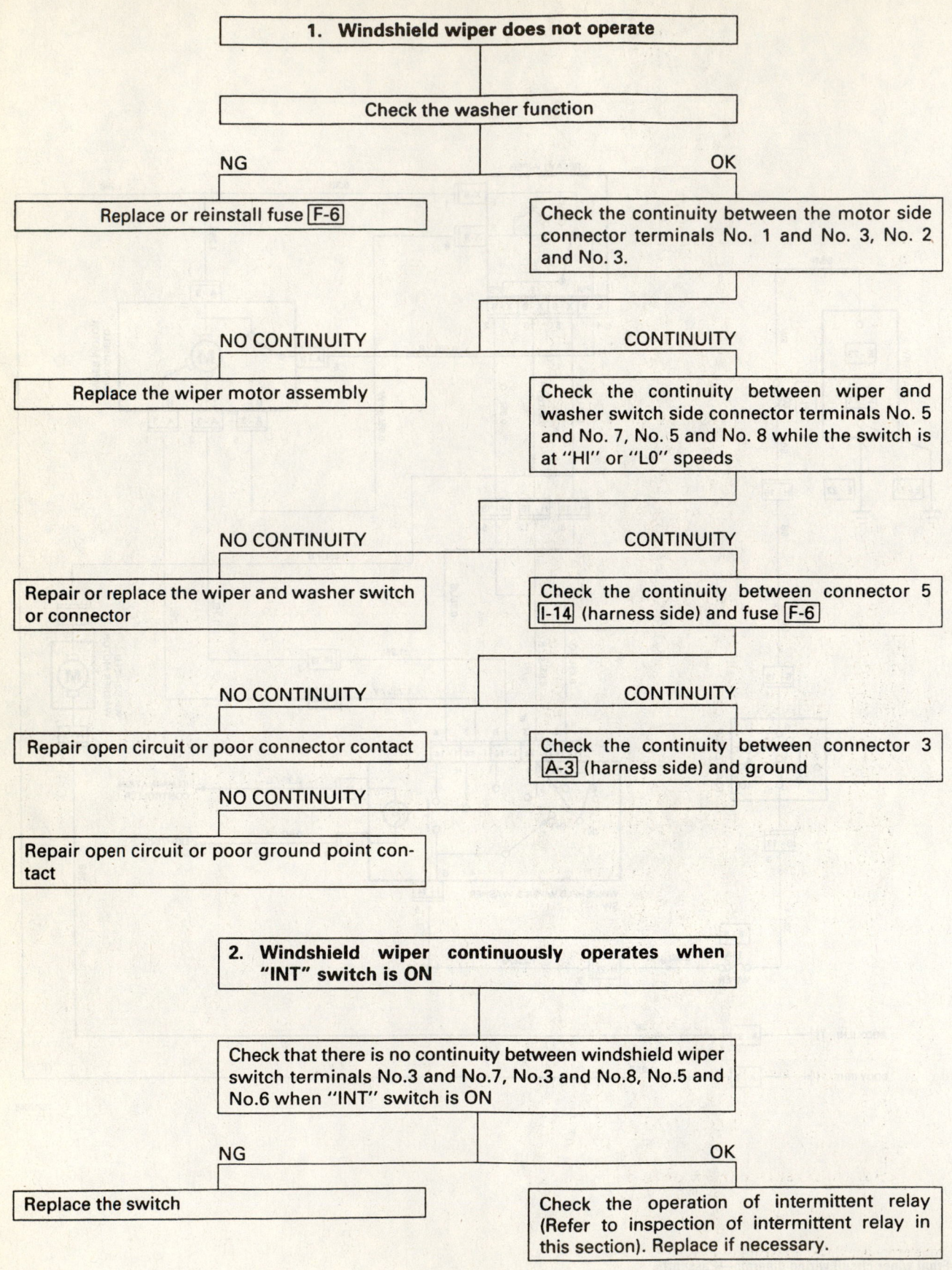

1. Windshield wiper does not operate

Check the washer function

NG

Replace or reinstall fuse F-6

OK

Check the continuity between the motor side connector terminals No. 1 and No. 3, No. 2 and No. 3.

NO CONTINUITY

Replace the wiper motor assembly

CONTINUITY

Check the continuity between wiper and washer switch side connector terminals No. 5 and No. 7, No. 5 and No. 8 while the switch is at "HI" or "LO" speeds

NO CONTINUITY

Repair or replace the wiper and washer switch or connector

CONTINUITY

Check the continuity between connector 5 I-14 (harness side) and fuse F-6

NO CONTINUITY

Repair open circuit or poor connector contact

CONTINUITY

Check the continuity between connector 3 A-3 (harness side) and ground

NO CONTINUITY

Repair open circuit or poor ground point contact

2. Windshield wiper continuously operates when "INT" switch is ON

Check that there is no continuity between windshield wiper switch terminals No.3 and No.7, No.3 and No.8, No.5 and No.6 when "INT" switch is ON

NG

Replace the switch

OK

Check the operation of intermittent relay (Refer to inspection of intermittent relay in this section). Replace if necessary.

Troubleshooting flowchart—Passport

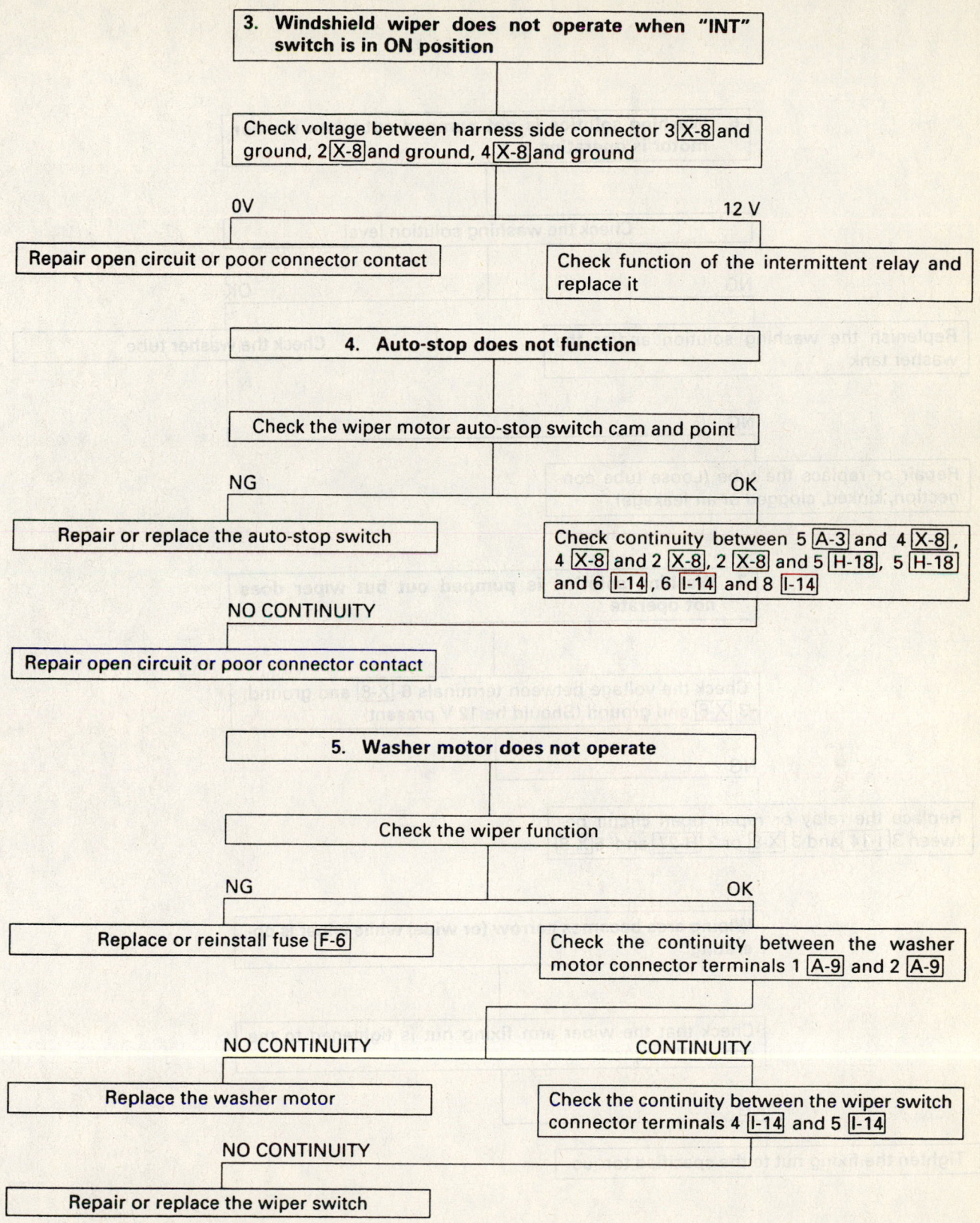

3. Windshield wiper does not operate when "INT" switch is in ON position

Check voltage between harness side connector 3 X-8 and ground, 2 X-8 and ground, 4 X-8 and ground

0V → Repair open circuit or poor connector contact

12 V → Check function of the intermittent relay and replace it

4. Auto-stop does not function

Check the wiper motor auto-stop switch cam and point

NG → Repair or replace the auto-stop switch

OK → Check continuity between 5 A-3 and 4 X-8, 4 X-8 and 2 X-8, 2 X-8 and 5 H-18, 5 H-18 and 6 I-14, 6 I-14 and 8 I-14

NO CONTINUITY → Repair open circuit or poor connector contact

5. Washer motor does not operate

Check the wiper function

NG → Replace or reinstall fuse F-6

OK → Check the continuity between the washer motor connector terminals 1 A-9 and 2 A-9

NO CONTINUITY → Replace the washer motor

CONTINUITY → Check the continuity between the wiper switch connector terminals 4 I-14 and 5 I-14

NO CONTINUITY → Repair or replace the wiper switch

7921ZG71

Troubleshooting flowchart (cont'd)—Passport

Refer to the model specific sections for driveline service procedures

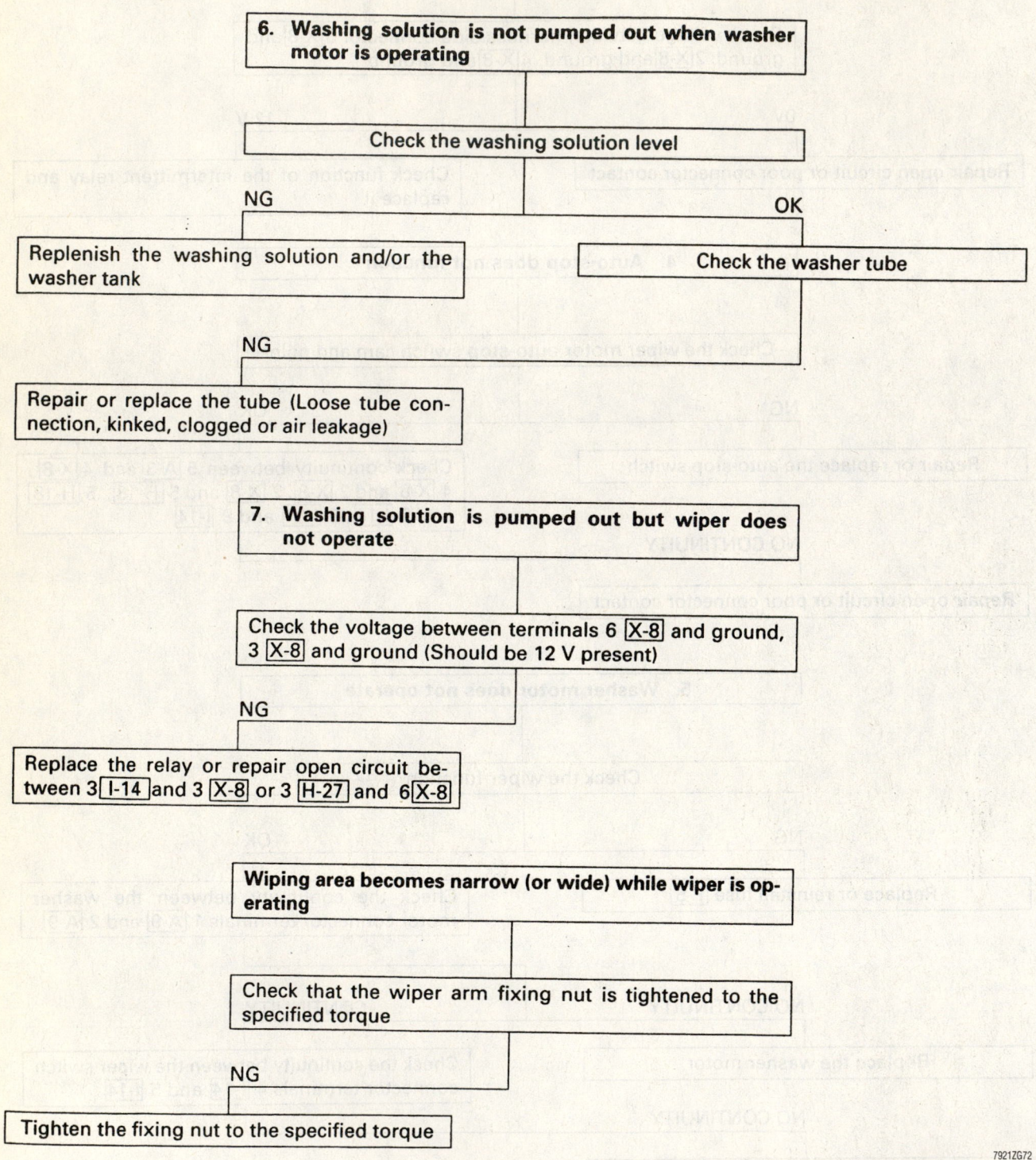

6. Washing solution is not pumped out when washer motor is operating

Check the washing solution level

NG → **Replenish the washing solution and/or the washer tank**

OK → **Check the washer tube**

NG → **Repair or replace the tube (Loose tube connection, kinked, clogged or air leakage)**

7. Washing solution is pumped out but wiper does not operate

Check the voltage between terminals 6 X-8 and ground, 3 X-8 and ground (Should be 12 V present)

NG → **Replace the relay or repair open circuit between 3 I-14 and 3 X-8 or 3 H-27 and 6 X-8**

Wiping area becomes narrow (or wide) while wiper is operating

Check that the wiper arm fixing nut is tightened to the specified torque

NG → **Tighten the fixing nut to the specified torque**

7921ZG72

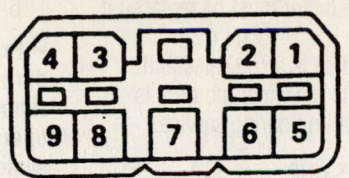

I-14

Switch side

(W/Intermittent)

SW position \ Terminal	5	3	6	8	7	4	9	2
OFF			O—	—O				
INT	O—	—O	O—	—O				
↕	X—		—X				O—	—O
LO	O—			—O				
HI	O—				—O			
WASHER	O—					—O		

(W/O Intermittent)

SW position \ Terminal	5	6	8	7	4	9	2
OFF		O—	—O				
	X—	—X					
LO	O—		—O				
HI	O—			—O		O—	—O
MIST	O—		—O				
WASHER	O—				—O		

7921ZG73

Windshield wiper switch connector—Passport

ISUZU

Hombre

GENERAL DESCRIPTION

The windshield wire/washer system consists of a permanent magnet, positive-park wiper motor assembly, a transmission assembly, wiper arm and blade assemblies, a washer pump mounted on the side of the reservoir and a combination turn signal/wiper/washer switch assembly.

The wiper motor assembly includes a **DELAY** (pulse) mode in addition to three modes of standard system— **HI, LO, MIST**.

A circuit board assembly in the wiper motor assembly and variable resistor (rheostat) in the turn signal/wiper/washer switch control the rate of pulse to the wiper motor.

The wiper motor is sealed and no parts are available. The motor must be replaced if found defective.

The delay module is also sealed and attached directly to the wiper motor. It is also replaced as a unit during service.

COMPONENT TESTING

Testing Hints

The following procedures assume that the technician has checked the following:

1. Continuity of all harness wires.
2. Wiper motor and wiper/washer switch connectors are mated correctly.
3. If the wiper motor operates but the wipers do not; check the wiper linkage and wiper motor crank arm.
4. Wiper motor-to-dash mounting screws tight for good ground.
5. Fuses are good.
6. Washer hoses clear, fluid in tank.

➡**Prior to starting the diagnosis procedure, it is very important to confirm the reported condition with a complete operational check including the washer system.**

All Models

➡**The following procedures assume that the technician has checked the items listed in Testing Hints, outlined earlier in this section:**

WIPER MOTOR ON-VEHICLE TEST

Before performing the following wiper motor test, check motor operation, then disconnect all wiring from the wiper and using a powered test lamp perform the following checks in order as they appear in the illustration.

WIPER MOTOR

CHECK FOR MOTOR OPERATION BEFORE REMOVING FROM VEHICLE. DISCONNECT ALL WIRING FROM WIPER AND PERFORM THE FOLLOWING CHECKS IN THIS ORDER:

① MIST   ② OFF/PARK   ③ PULSE

④ LO   ⑤ HI   ⑥ WASH

NOTE: Connect terminal #3 before connecting terminal #4. Otherwise damage to P.C. board may occur.

Connect a test pump (bottom—bottle—mount type) of proven quality. **Do not use pump off vehicle.** Test washer pump should pulse 9 to 11 times in 15 seconds. Do not hold WASH button longer than this without a 2 minute pause.

7921ZGB1

Windshield wiper motor on-vehicle test—Hombre

WASHER PUMP ON-VEHICLE TEST

1. Before performing the following washer pump test, check pump operation, then disconnect the wiring connector from the pump and using a powered test lamp perform the following check as illustrated.

2. If the motor does not run or pump solvent, replace the washer pump.

3. If the motor runs and pumps solvent, the problem is in the circuit board, motor park switch or wiper switch.

DIAGNOSTIC PROCEDURES (CONT'D)

WASHER PUMP

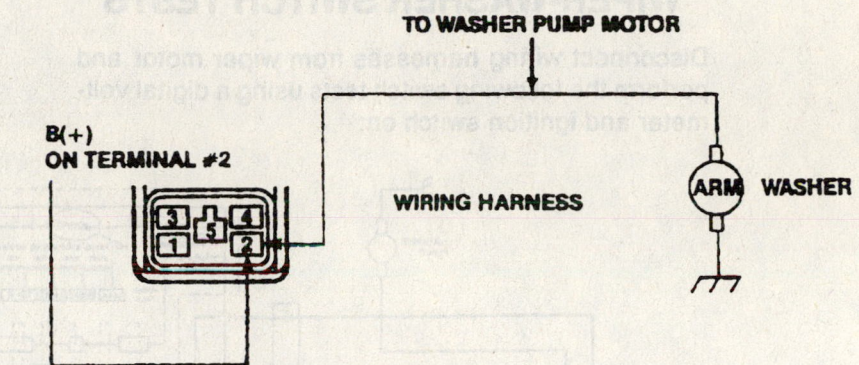

CHECK FOR WASHER PUMP OPERATION BEFORE REMOVING FROM VEHICLE. REMOVE CONNECTOR AND APPLY B(+) TO #2 WIRING HARNESS TERMINAL AS SHOWN.

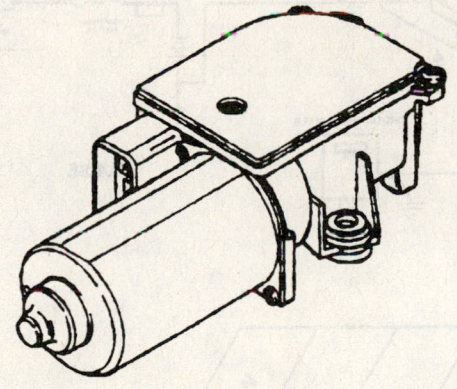

1. If motor does not run or pump solvent, replace washer pump.

2. If motor runs and pumps solvent, problem is in circuit board, motor park switch or wiper switch. Refer to Wiper-Washer Switch Tests.

7921ZGD2

Windshield washer pump on-vehicle test—Hombre

WIPER/WASHER SWITCH TEST

Disconnect the wiring harnesses from the wiper motor, turn the ignition switch to the **ON,** position and perform the following switch test as illustrated, using a digital voltmeter.

SYMPTOM DIAGNOSIS TEST

➡ **The following procedures assume that the technician has checked the items listed in Testing Hints, outlined** earlier in this section. In most of the test an volt-ohmmeter or test light is required.

REMOVAL & INSTALLATION

Washer Pump

1. Disconnect the negative battery cable.
2. Remove the washer solvent from the reservoir.

3. Disconnect the electrical connector and washer hose from the washer pump.
4. Remove the washer pump from the reservoir.
5. Installation is the reverse of removal. Fill the reservoir and check for correct operation.

Rear Wiper/Washer Switch

1. Disconnect the negative battery cable.
2. Pull the wiper switch from the trim plate.

WIPER-WASHER SWITCH TESTS

Disconnect wiring harnesses from wiper motor and perform the following switch tests using a digital voltmeter and ignition switch on:

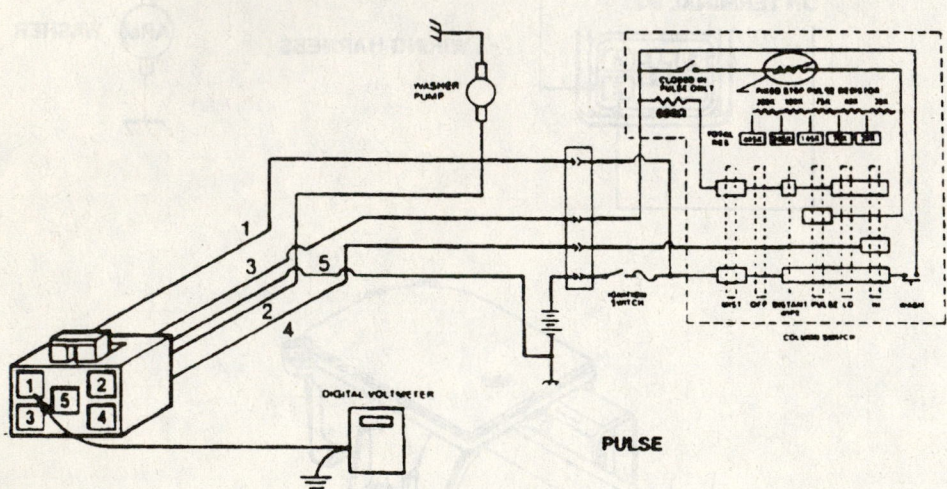

PULSE

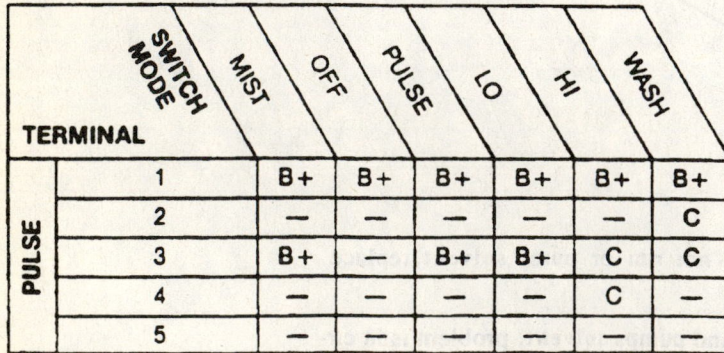

	SWITCH MODE / TERMINAL	MIST	OFF	PULSE	LO	HI	WASH
PULSE	1	B+	B+	B+	B+	B+	B+
	2	—	—	—	—	—	C
	3	B+	—	B+	B+	C	C
	4	—	—	—	—	C	—
	5	—	—	—	—	—	—

NOTE: All voltage readings taken with respect to vehicle ground.

C = Continuity between terminals

To use Wiper-Washer Switch Check chart, probe terminals 1 thru 5 with digital voltmeter and wiper switch in various positions.

Windshield/washer switch test—Hombre

7921ZGB3

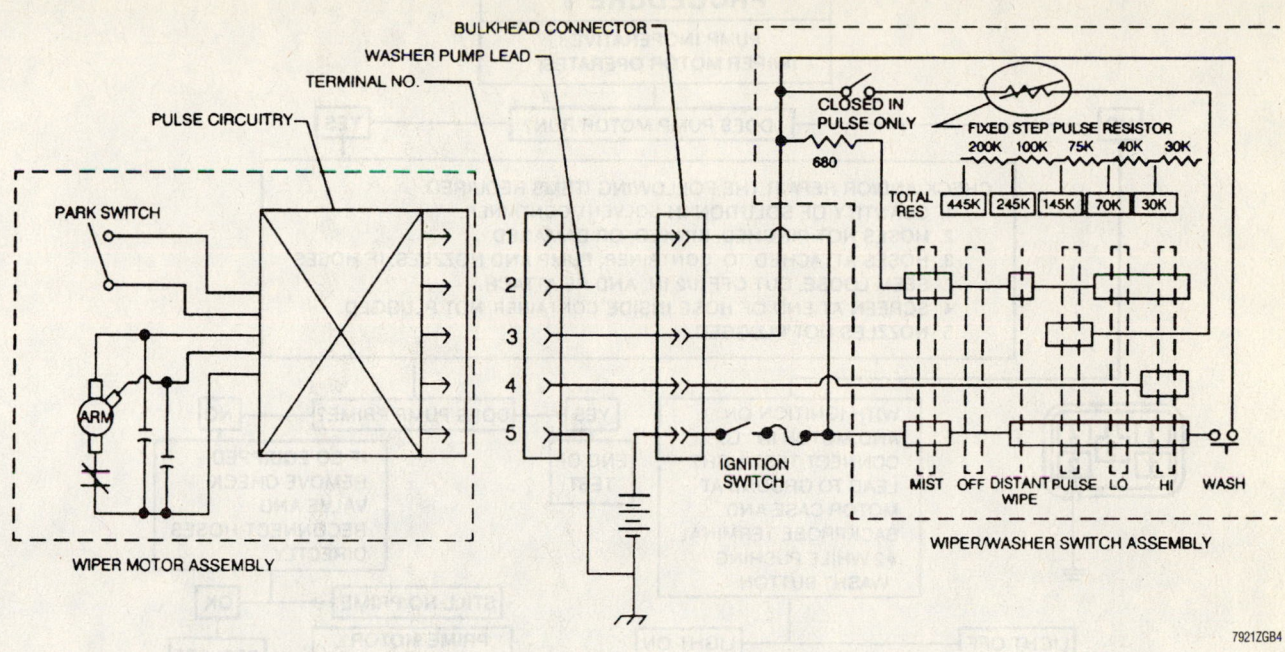

Windshield wiper circuit—Hombre

SYMPTOM	PROCEDURE NO.
1. Pump inoperative—wiper motor operates	1
2. Washer pumps continuously	2
3. Wiper motor inoperative (all modes)	3
4. "Lo" speed only—inoperative in "Hi"	4
5. "Hi" speed only—inoperative in "Lo"	5
6. One speed only—runs the same in both speeds	6
7. Wiper shuts off but blades don't park	7
8. Wiper will not shut off	8
9. Intermittent inoperative	9
10. Wiper motor runs but blades don't move	10
11. Wiper parks above park position	11

7921ZGB5

Windshield wiper/washer symptom diagnosis chart—Hombre

Refer to the model specific sections for driveline service procedures

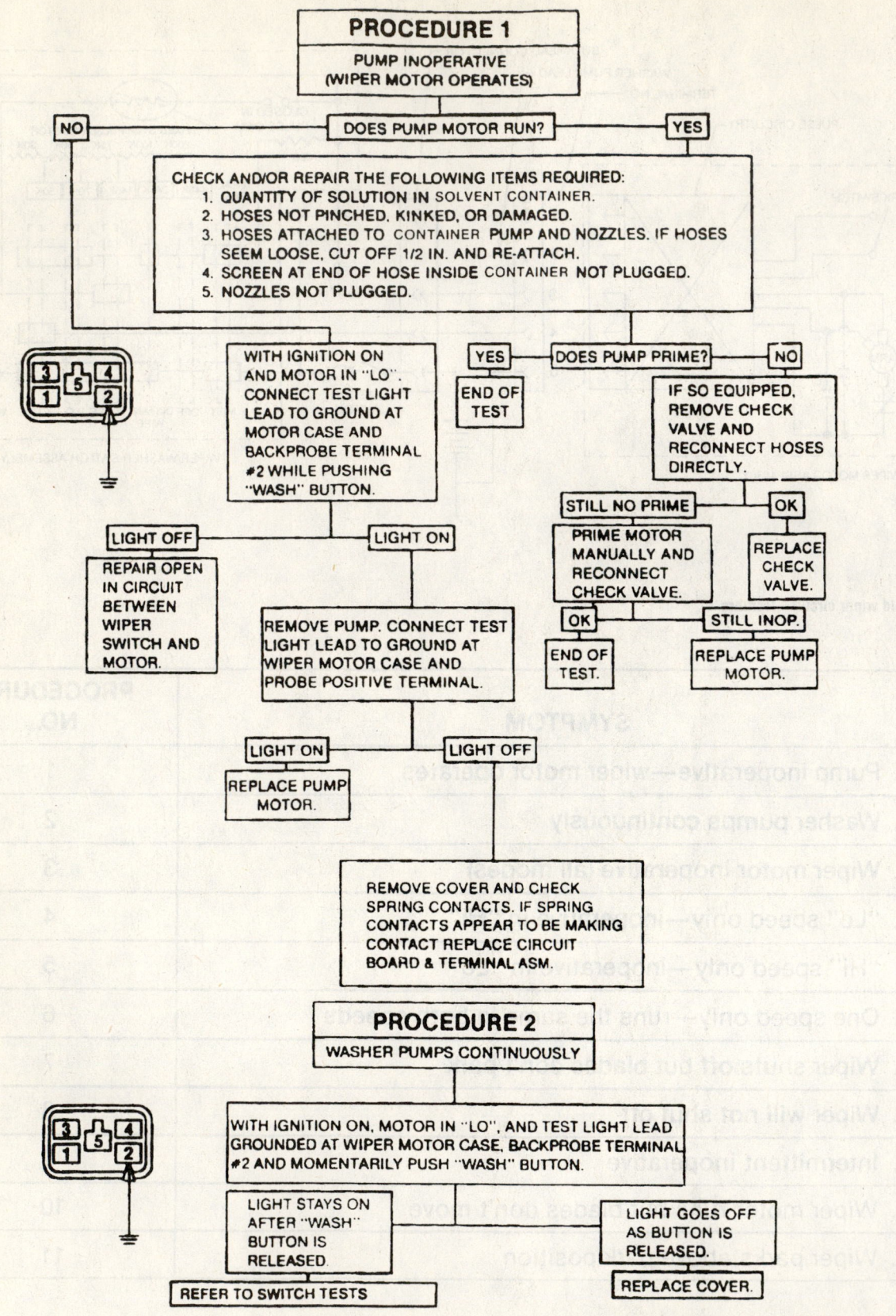

PROCEDURE 1

**PUMP INOPERATIVE
(WIPER MOTOR OPERATES)**

DOES PUMP MOTOR RUN? — NO / YES

CHECK AND/OR REPAIR THE FOLLOWING ITEMS REQUIRED:
1. QUANTITY OF SOLUTION IN SOLVENT CONTAINER.
2. HOSES NOT PINCHED, KINKED, OR DAMAGED.
3. HOSES ATTACHED TO CONTAINER PUMP AND NOZZLES. IF HOSES SEEM LOOSE, CUT OFF 1/2 IN. AND RE-ATTACH.
4. SCREEN AT END OF HOSE INSIDE CONTAINER NOT PLUGGED.
5. NOZZLES NOT PLUGGED.

WITH IGNITION ON AND MOTOR IN "LO". CONNECT TEST LIGHT LEAD TO GROUND AT MOTOR CASE AND BACKPROBE TERMINAL #2 WHILE PUSHING "WASH" BUTTON.

DOES PUMP PRIME? — YES / NO

YES → END OF TEST

NO → IF SO EQUIPPED, REMOVE CHECK VALVE AND RECONNECT HOSES DIRECTLY.

STILL NO PRIME / OK

PRIME MOTOR MANUALLY AND RECONNECT CHECK VALVE.

REPLACE CHECK VALVE.

LIGHT OFF / LIGHT ON

REPAIR OPEN IN CIRCUIT BETWEEN WIPER SWITCH AND MOTOR.

REMOVE PUMP. CONNECT TEST LIGHT LEAD TO GROUND AT WIPER MOTOR CASE AND PROBE POSITIVE TERMINAL.

OK → END OF TEST.

STILL INOP. → REPLACE PUMP MOTOR.

LIGHT ON / LIGHT OFF

REPLACE PUMP MOTOR.

REMOVE COVER AND CHECK SPRING CONTACTS. IF SPRING CONTACTS APPEAR TO BE MAKING CONTACT REPLACE CIRCUIT BOARD & TERMINAL ASM.

PROCEDURE 2

WASHER PUMPS CONTINUOUSLY

WITH IGNITION ON, MOTOR IN "LO", AND TEST LIGHT LEAD GROUNDED AT WIPER MOTOR CASE, BACKPROBE TERMINAL #2 AND MOMENTARILY PUSH "WASH" BUTTON.

LIGHT STAYS ON AFTER "WASH" BUTTON IS RELEASED.

LIGHT GOES OFF AS BUTTON IS RELEASED.

REFER TO SWITCH TESTS

REPLACE COVER.

7921ZGB6

Windshield wiper/washer diagnosis—Hombre

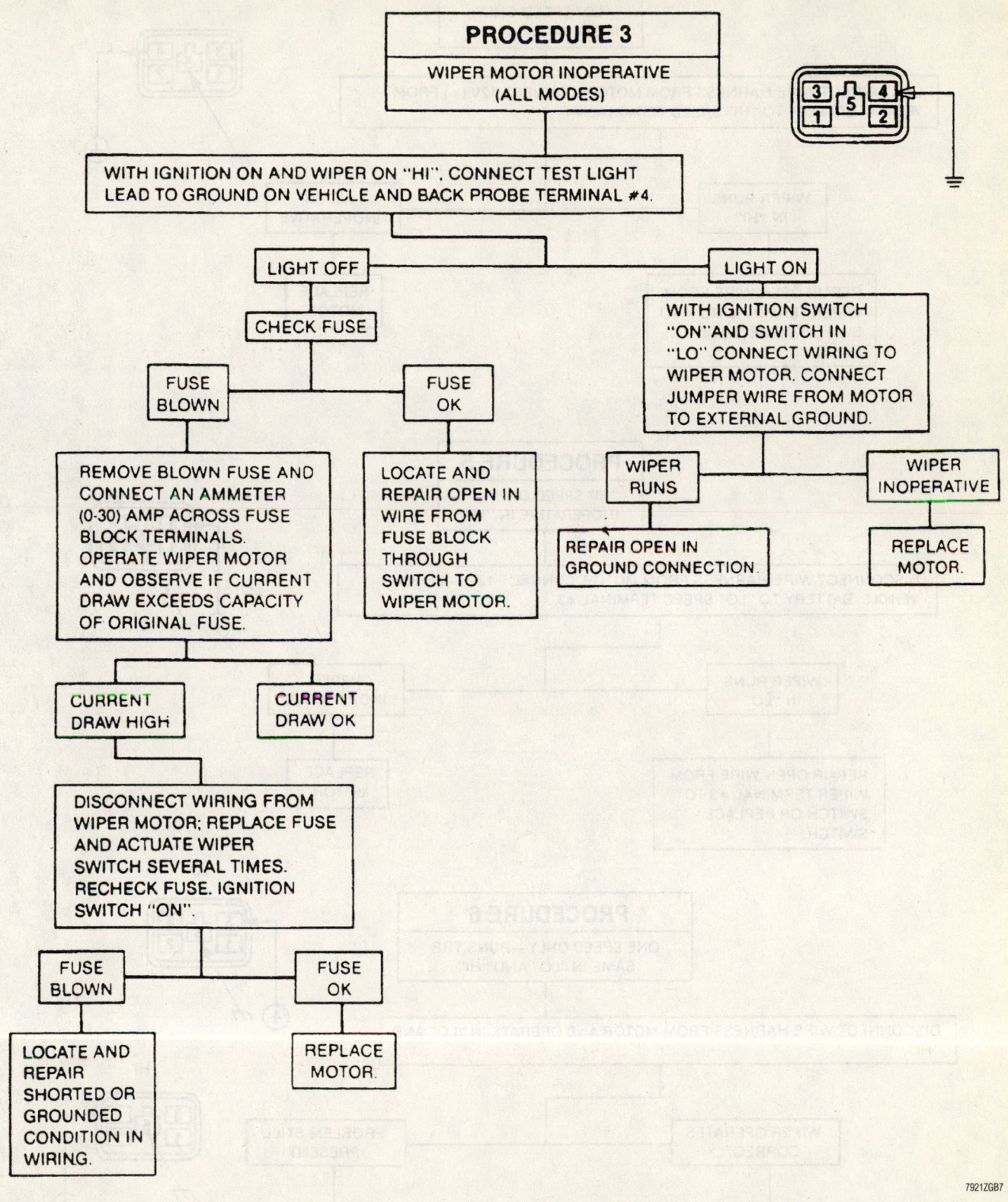

PROCEDURE 3

WIPER MOTOR INOPERATIVE
(ALL MODES)

WITH IGNITION ON AND WIPER ON "HI", CONNECT TEST LIGHT LEAD TO GROUND ON VEHICLE AND BACK PROBE TERMINAL #4.

LIGHT OFF

LIGHT ON

CHECK FUSE

WITH IGNITION SWITCH "ON" AND SWITCH IN "LO" CONNECT WIRING TO WIPER MOTOR. CONNECT JUMPER WIRE FROM MOTOR TO EXTERNAL GROUND.

FUSE BLOWN

FUSE OK

WIPER RUNS

WIPER INOPERATIVE

REMOVE BLOWN FUSE AND CONNECT AN AMMETER (0-30) AMP ACROSS FUSE BLOCK TERMINALS. OPERATE WIPER MOTOR AND OBSERVE IF CURRENT DRAW EXCEEDS CAPACITY OF ORIGINAL FUSE.

LOCATE AND REPAIR OPEN IN WIRE FROM FUSE BLOCK THROUGH SWITCH TO WIPER MOTOR.

REPAIR OPEN IN GROUND CONNECTION.

REPLACE MOTOR.

CURRENT DRAW HIGH

CURRENT DRAW OK

DISCONNECT WIRING FROM WIPER MOTOR; REPLACE FUSE AND ACTUATE WIPER SWITCH SEVERAL TIMES. RECHECK FUSE. IGNITION SWITCH "ON".

FUSE BLOWN

FUSE OK

LOCATE AND REPAIR SHORTED OR GROUNDED CONDITION IN WIRING.

REPLACE MOTOR.

7921ZGB7

Windshield wiper/washer diagnosis—Hombre

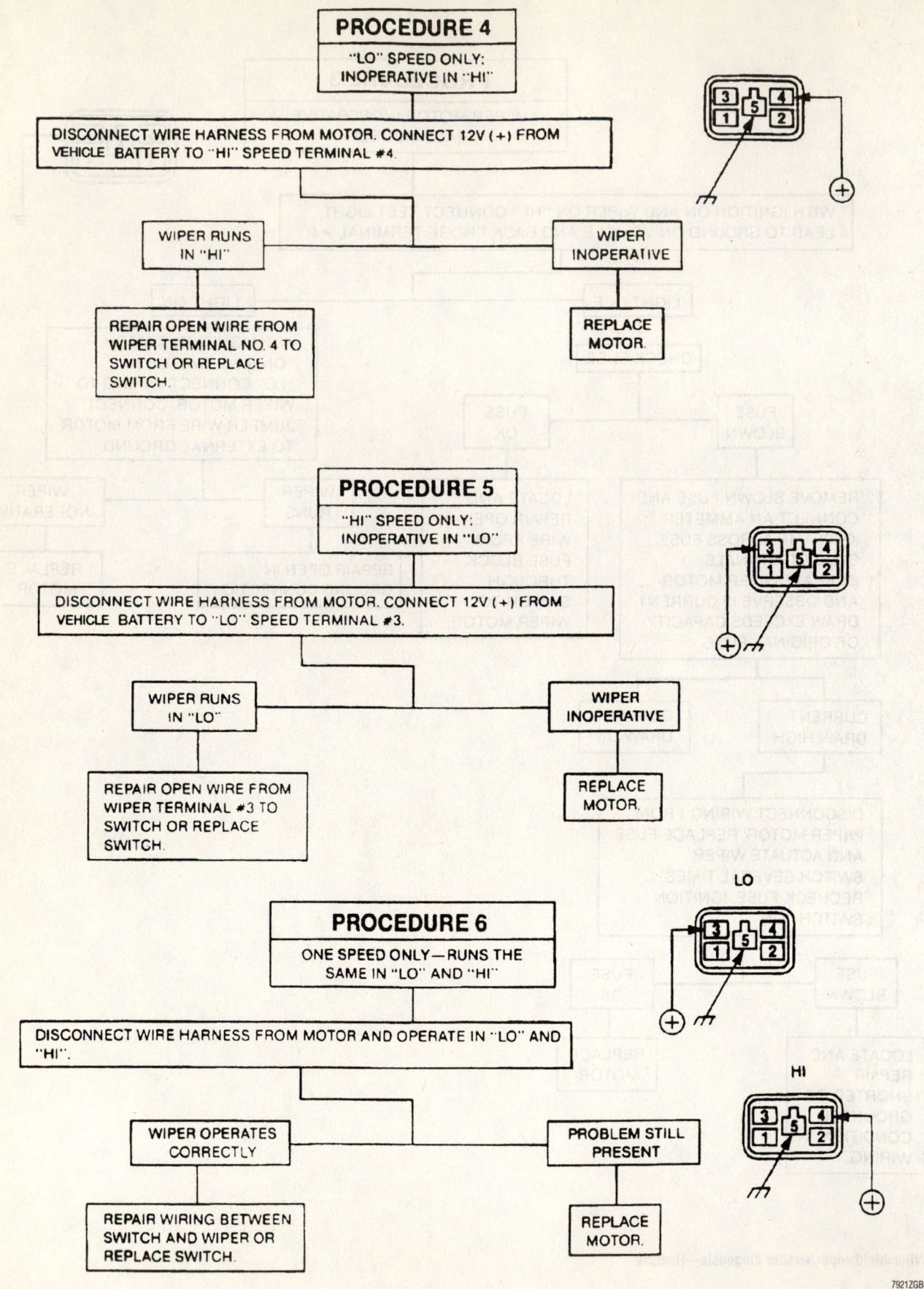

PROCEDURE 4

"LO" SPEED ONLY:
INOPERATIVE IN "HI"

DISCONNECT WIRE HARNESS FROM MOTOR. CONNECT 12V (+) FROM VEHICLE BATTERY TO "HI" SPEED TERMINAL #4.

WIPER RUNS IN "HI"

WIPER INOPERATIVE

REPAIR OPEN WIRE FROM WIPER TERMINAL NO. 4 TO SWITCH OR REPLACE SWITCH.

REPLACE MOTOR.

PROCEDURE 5

"HI" SPEED ONLY:
INOPERATIVE IN "LO"

DISCONNECT WIRE HARNESS FROM MOTOR. CONNECT 12V (+) FROM VEHICLE BATTERY TO "LO" SPEED TERMINAL #3.

WIPER RUNS IN "LO"

WIPER INOPERATIVE

REPAIR OPEN WIRE FROM WIPER TERMINAL #3 TO SWITCH OR REPLACE SWITCH.

REPLACE MOTOR.

PROCEDURE 6

ONE SPEED ONLY—RUNS THE SAME IN "LO" AND "HI"

DISCONNECT WIRE HARNESS FROM MOTOR AND OPERATE IN "LO" AND "HI".

WIPER OPERATES CORRECTLY

PROBLEM STILL PRESENT

REPAIR WIRING BETWEEN SWITCH AND WIPER OR REPLACE SWITCH.

REPLACE MOTOR.

LO

HI

Windshield wiper/washer diagnosis—Hombre

7921ZGB8

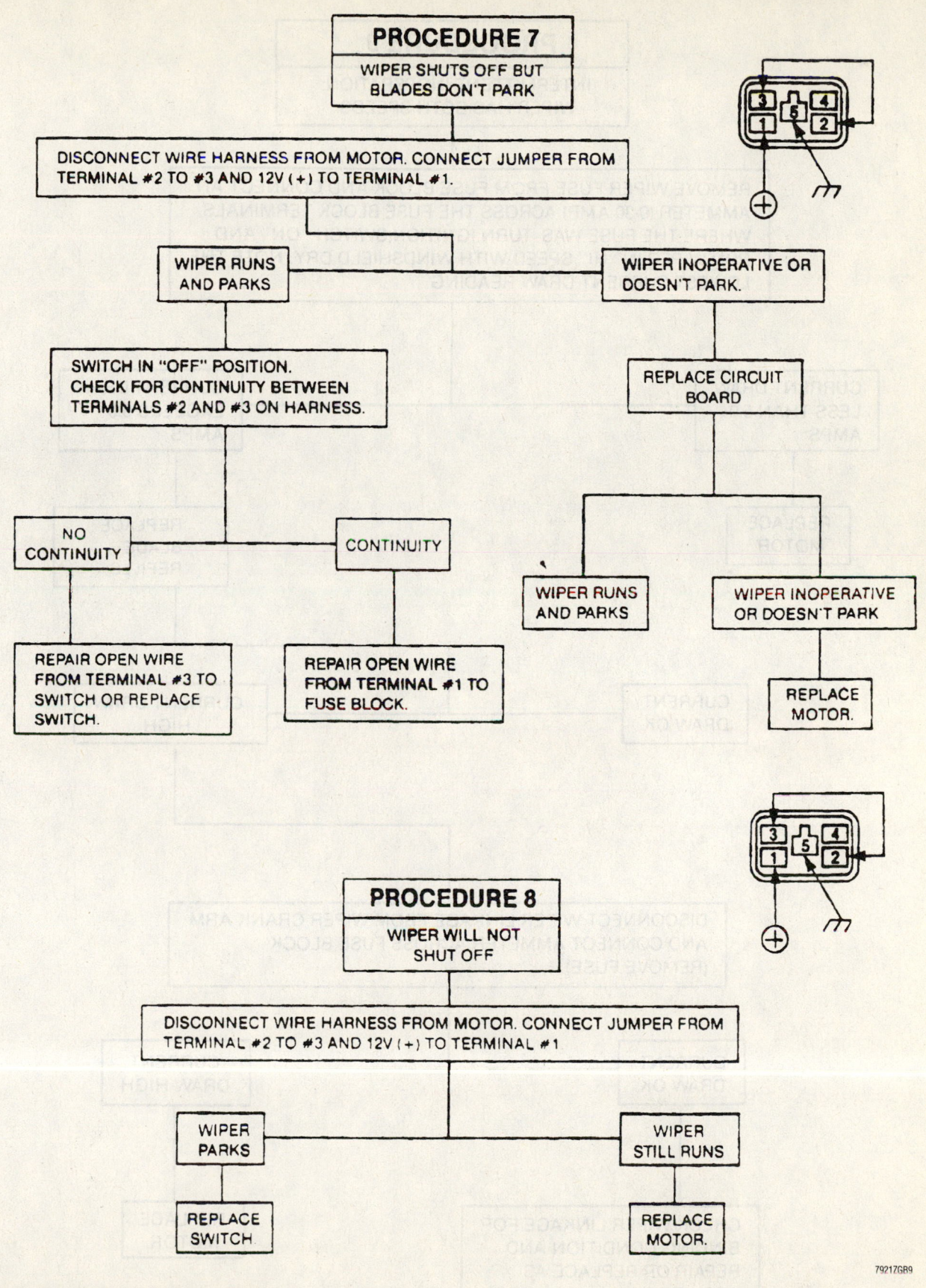

PROCEDURE 7

WIPER SHUTS OFF BUT BLADES DON'T PARK

DISCONNECT WIRE HARNESS FROM MOTOR. CONNECT JUMPER FROM TERMINAL #2 TO #3 AND 12V (+) TO TERMINAL #1.

WIPER RUNS AND PARKS

WIPER INOPERATIVE OR DOESN'T PARK.

SWITCH IN "OFF" POSITION. CHECK FOR CONTINUITY BETWEEN TERMINALS #2 AND #3 ON HARNESS.

REPLACE CIRCUIT BOARD

NO CONTINUITY

CONTINUITY

WIPER RUNS AND PARKS

WIPER INOPERATIVE OR DOESN'T PARK

REPAIR OPEN WIRE FROM TERMINAL #3 TO SWITCH OR REPLACE SWITCH.

REPAIR OPEN WIRE FROM TERMINAL #1 TO FUSE BLOCK.

REPLACE MOTOR.

PROCEDURE 8

WIPER WILL NOT SHUT OFF

DISCONNECT WIRE HARNESS FROM MOTOR. CONNECT JUMPER FROM TERMINAL #2 TO #3 AND 12V (+) TO TERMINAL #1

WIPER PARKS

WIPER STILL RUNS

REPLACE SWITCH.

REPLACE MOTOR.

79217GB9

Windshield wiper/washer diagnosis—Hombre

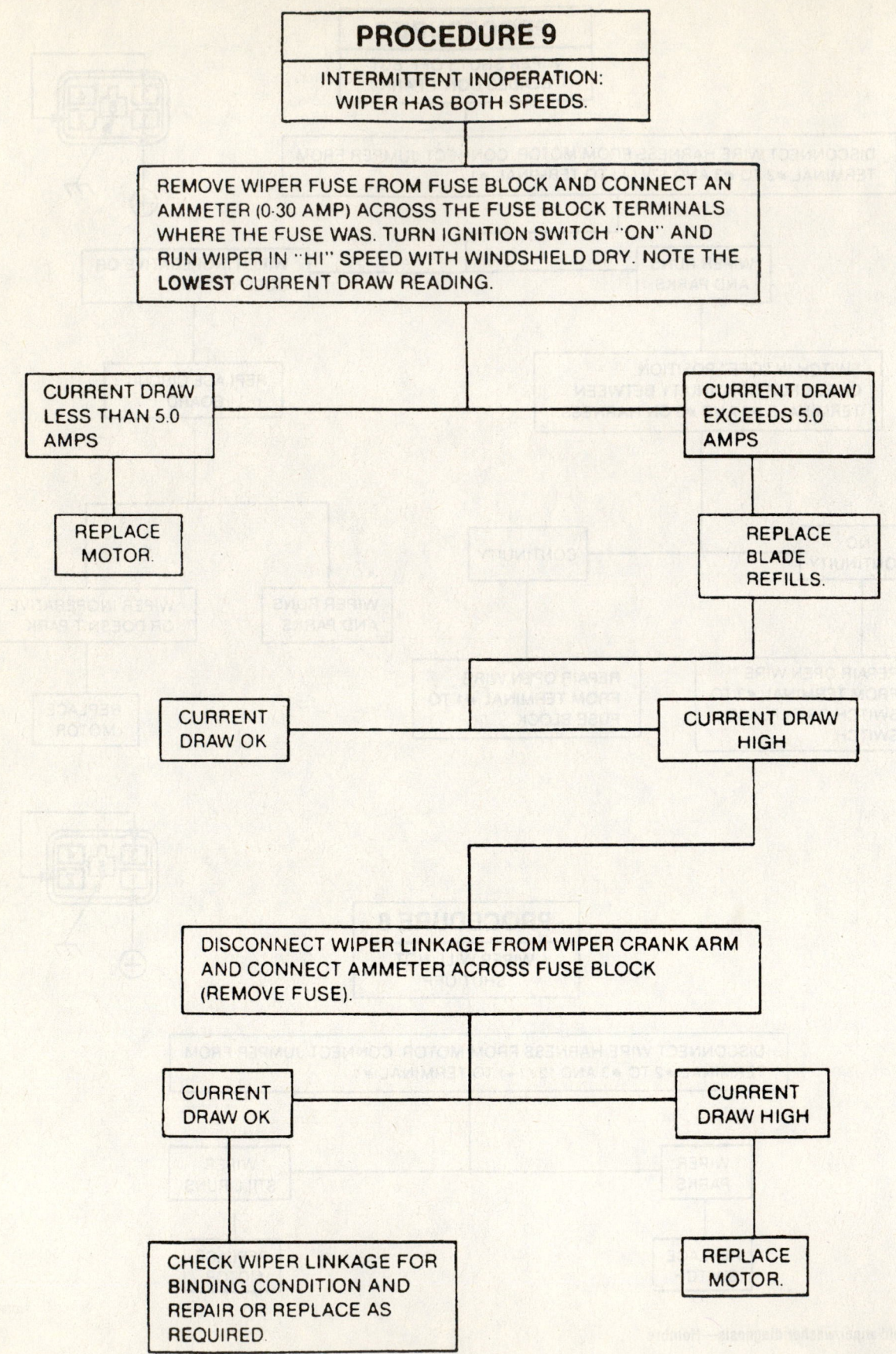

PROCEDURE 9

INTERMITTENT INOPERATION:
WIPER HAS BOTH SPEEDS.

REMOVE WIPER FUSE FROM FUSE BLOCK AND CONNECT AN AMMETER (0-30 AMP) ACROSS THE FUSE BLOCK TERMINALS WHERE THE FUSE WAS. TURN IGNITION SWITCH "ON" AND RUN WIPER IN "HI" SPEED WITH WINDSHIELD DRY. NOTE THE **LOWEST** CURRENT DRAW READING.

CURRENT DRAW LESS THAN 5.0 AMPS

CURRENT DRAW EXCEEDS 5.0 AMPS

REPLACE MOTOR.

REPLACE BLADE REFILLS.

CURRENT DRAW OK

CURRENT DRAW HIGH

DISCONNECT WIPER LINKAGE FROM WIPER CRANK ARM AND CONNECT AMMETER ACROSS FUSE BLOCK (REMOVE FUSE).

CURRENT DRAW OK

CURRENT DRAW HIGH

CHECK WIPER LINKAGE FOR BINDING CONDITION AND REPAIR OR REPLACE AS REQUIRED.

REPLACE MOTOR.

Windshield wiper/washer diagnosis—Hombre

7921ZGC1

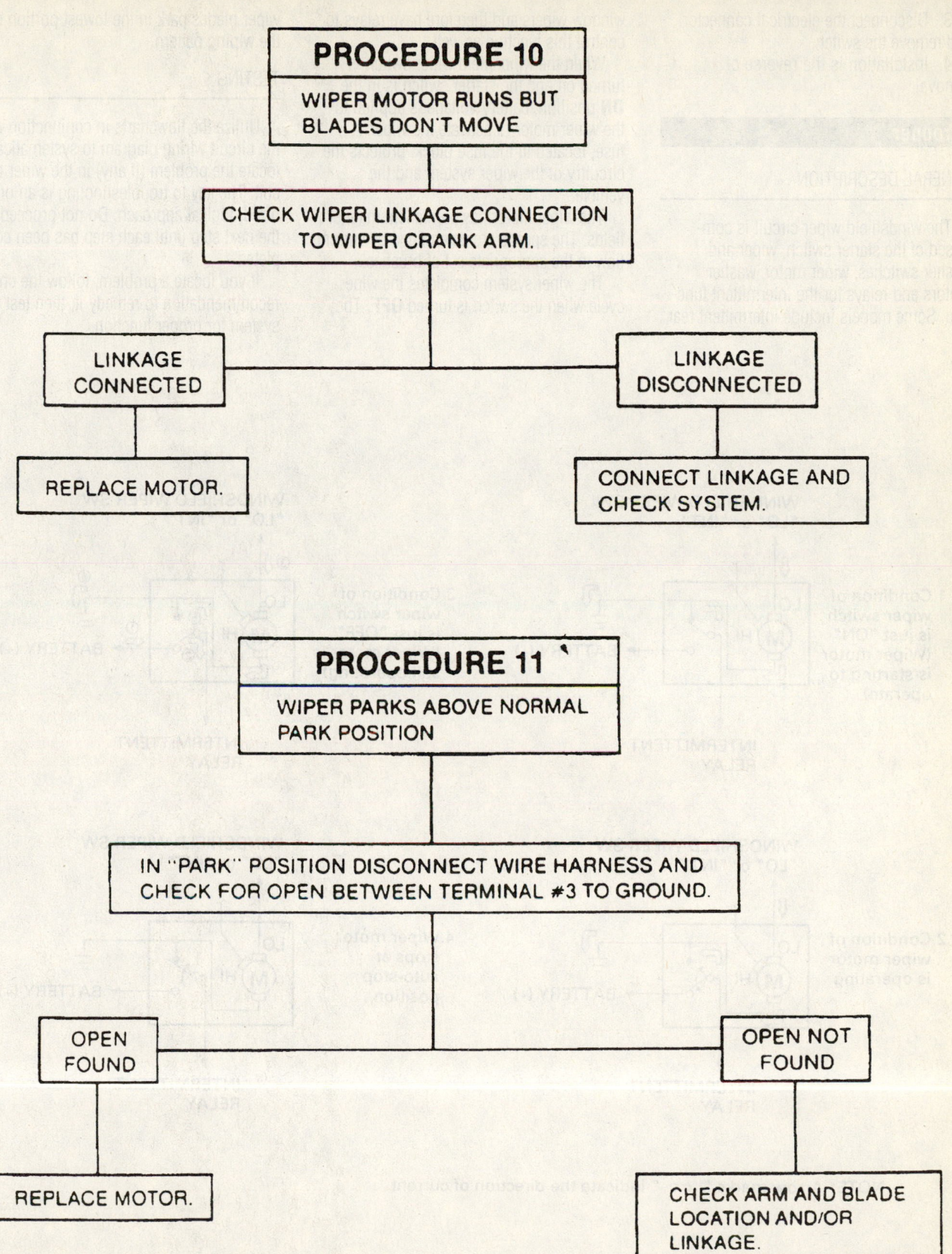

PROCEDURE 10

WIPER MOTOR RUNS BUT BLADES DON'T MOVE

CHECK WIPER LINKAGE CONNECTION TO WIPER CRANK ARM.

LINKAGE CONNECTED

LINKAGE DISCONNECTED

REPLACE MOTOR.

CONNECT LINKAGE AND CHECK SYSTEM.

PROCEDURE 11

WIPER PARKS ABOVE NORMAL PARK POSITION

IN "PARK" POSITION DISCONNECT WIRE HARNESS AND CHECK FOR OPEN BETWEEN TERMINAL #3 TO GROUND.

OPEN FOUND

OPEN NOT FOUND

REPLACE MOTOR.

CHECK ARM AND BLADE LOCATION AND/OR LINKAGE.

7921ZGC2

Windshield wiper/washer diagnosis—Hombre

Refer to the model specific sections for driveline service procedures

3. Disconnect the electrical connector and remove the switch.

4. Installation is the reverse of removal.

Trooper

GENERAL DESCRIPTION

The windshield wiper circuit is comprised of the starter switch, wiper and washer switches, wiper motor, washer motors and relays for the intermittent function. Some models include intermittent rear window wipers and therefore have relays to control this function as well.

When the windshield wiper switch is turned on and the starter switch is in the **ON** position, battery voltage is applied to the wiper motor to activate the wiper. A fuse, located in the fuse block, protects the circuitry of the wiper system and the vehicle.

The wiper motor has permanent magnet fields. The speeds are determined by current flow to the appropriate set of brushes.

The wiper system completes the wipe cycle when the switch is turned **OFF.** The wiper blades park in the lowest portion of the wiping pattern.

TESTING

Utilize the flowcharts in conjunction with the circuit wiring diagram to systematically locate the problem (if any) in the wiper circuit. The key to troubleshooting is an organized, logical approach. Do not proceed to the next step until each step has been completed.

If you locate a problem, follow the chart's recommendation to remedy it, then test the system for proper function.

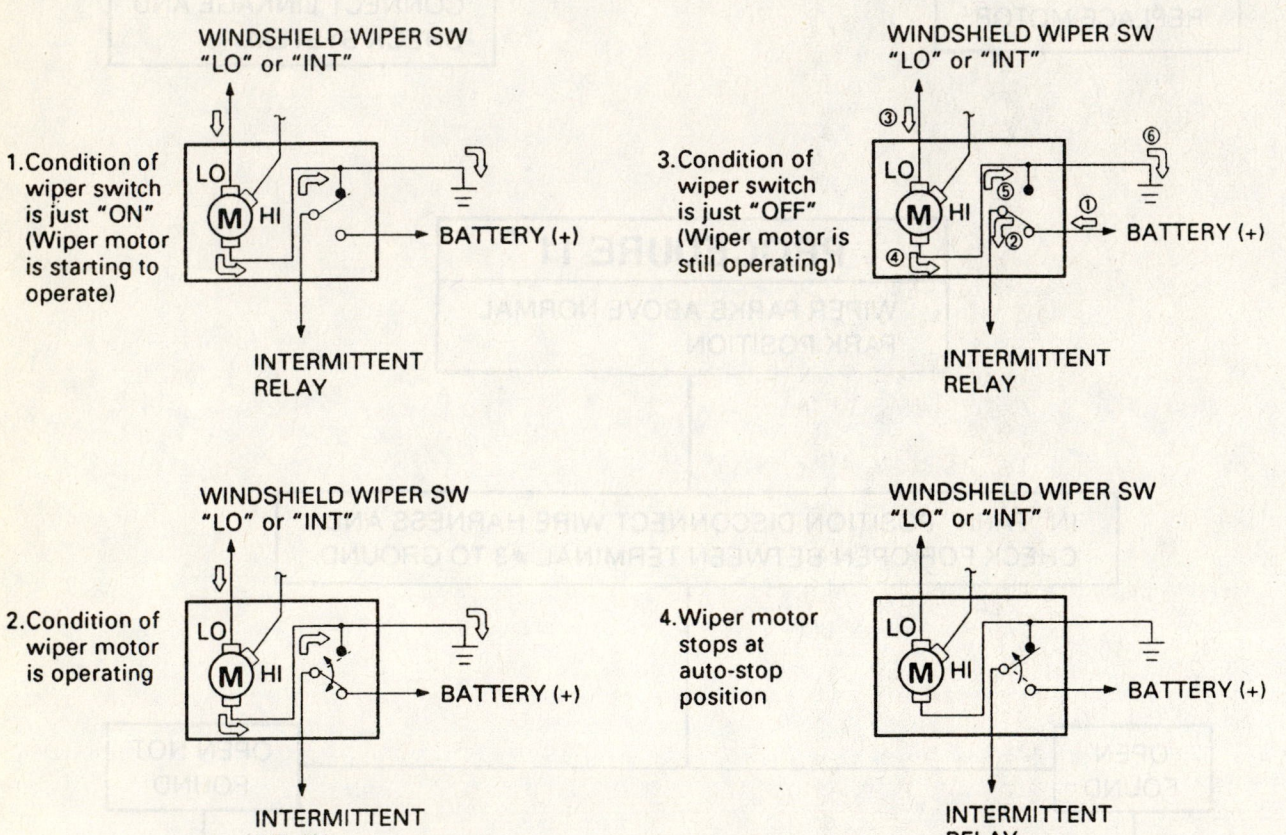

NOTE: Arrow marks " ⇨ " indicate the direction of current

Windshield wiper motor current flow (when switch is at "LO" or "INT")—Trooper

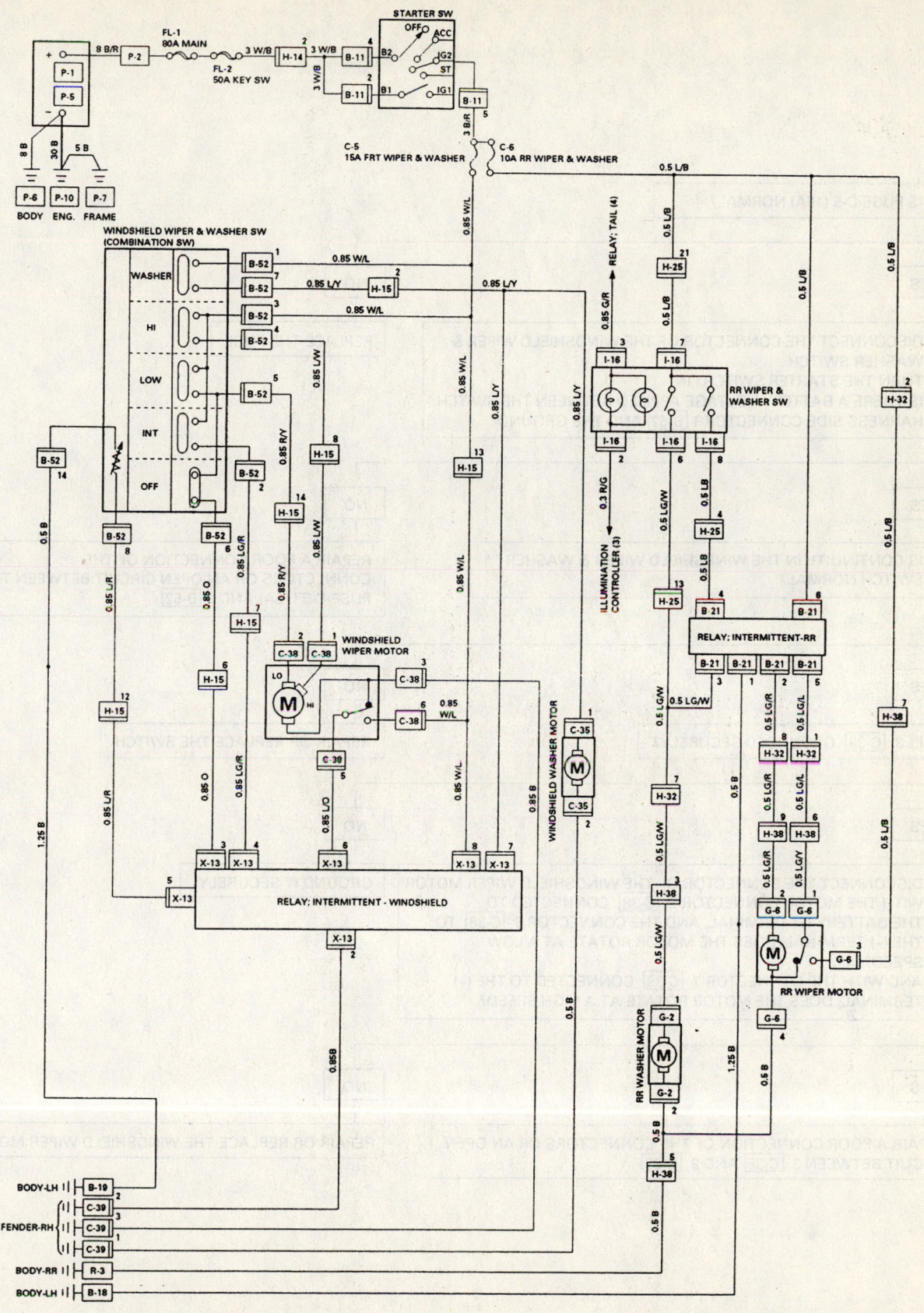

Windshield wiper system circuit wiring diagram—Trooper

7021ZG27

For complete service labor times order Nichols' Chilton Labor Guide Manual

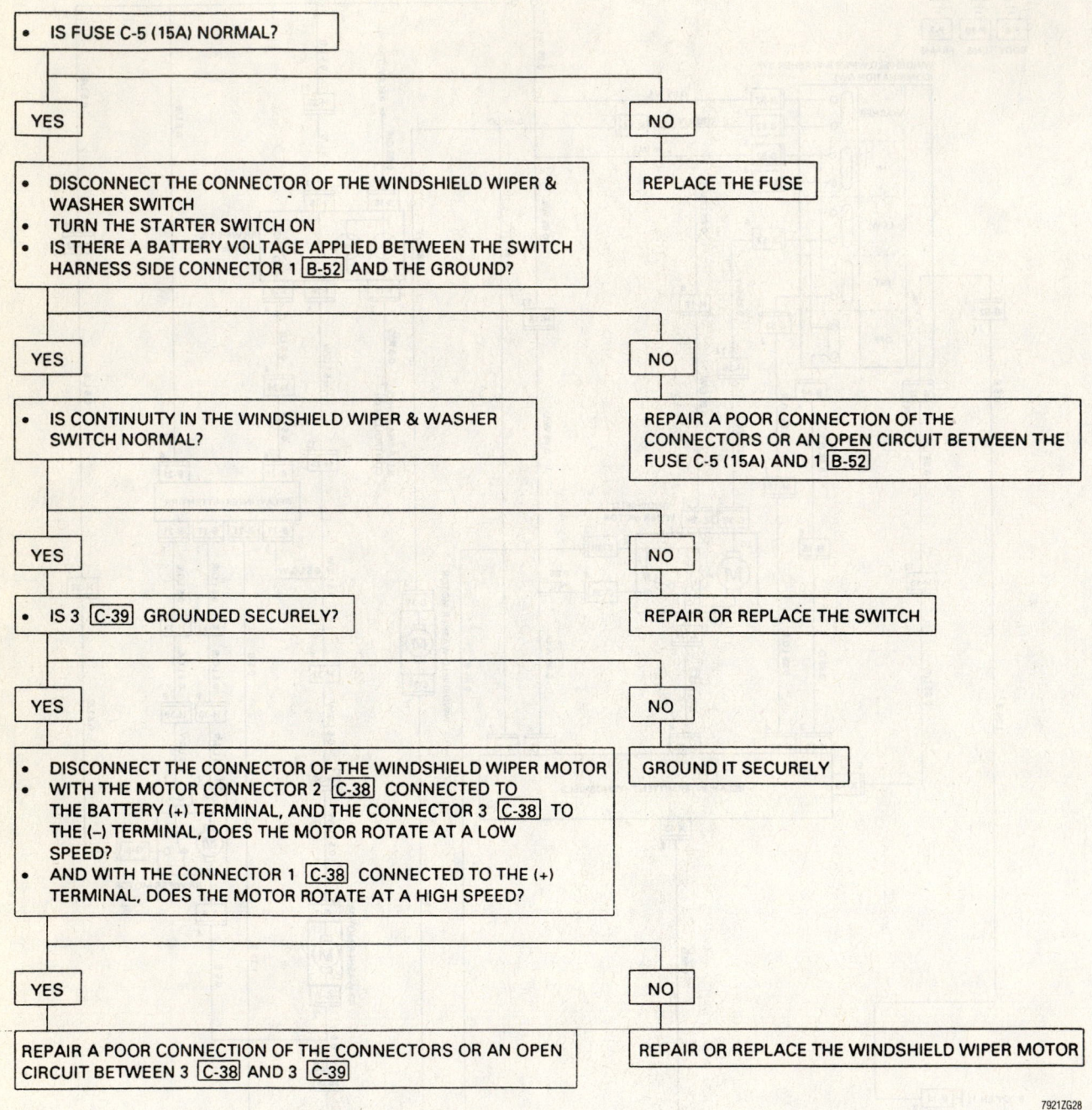

- IS FUSE C-5 (15A) NORMAL?

YES → NO → REPLACE THE FUSE

- DISCONNECT THE CONNECTOR OF THE WINDSHIELD WIPER & WASHER SWITCH
- TURN THE STARTER SWITCH ON
- IS THERE A BATTERY VOLTAGE APPLIED BETWEEN THE SWITCH HARNESS SIDE CONNECTOR 1 B-52 AND THE GROUND?

YES → NO → REPAIR A POOR CONNECTION OF THE CONNECTORS OR AN OPEN CIRCUIT BETWEEN THE FUSE C-5 (15A) AND 1 B-52

- IS CONTINUITY IN THE WINDSHIELD WIPER & WASHER SWITCH NORMAL?

YES → NO → REPAIR OR REPLACE THE SWITCH

- IS 3 C-39 GROUNDED SECURELY?

YES → NO → GROUND IT SECURELY

- DISCONNECT THE CONNECTOR OF THE WINDSHIELD WIPER MOTOR
- WITH THE MOTOR CONNECTOR 2 C-38 CONNECTED TO THE BATTERY (+) TERMINAL, AND THE CONNECTOR 3 C-38 TO THE (–) TERMINAL, DOES THE MOTOR ROTATE AT A LOW SPEED?
- AND WITH THE CONNECTOR 1 C-38 CONNECTED TO THE (+) TERMINAL, DOES THE MOTOR ROTATE AT A HIGH SPEED?

YES → NO → REPAIR OR REPLACE THE WINDSHIELD WIPER MOTOR

REPAIR A POOR CONNECTION OF THE CONNECTORS OR AN OPEN CIRCUIT BETWEEN 3 C-38 AND 3 C-39

7921ZG28

Troubleshooting flowchart: front wiper does not operate in any switch position—Trooper

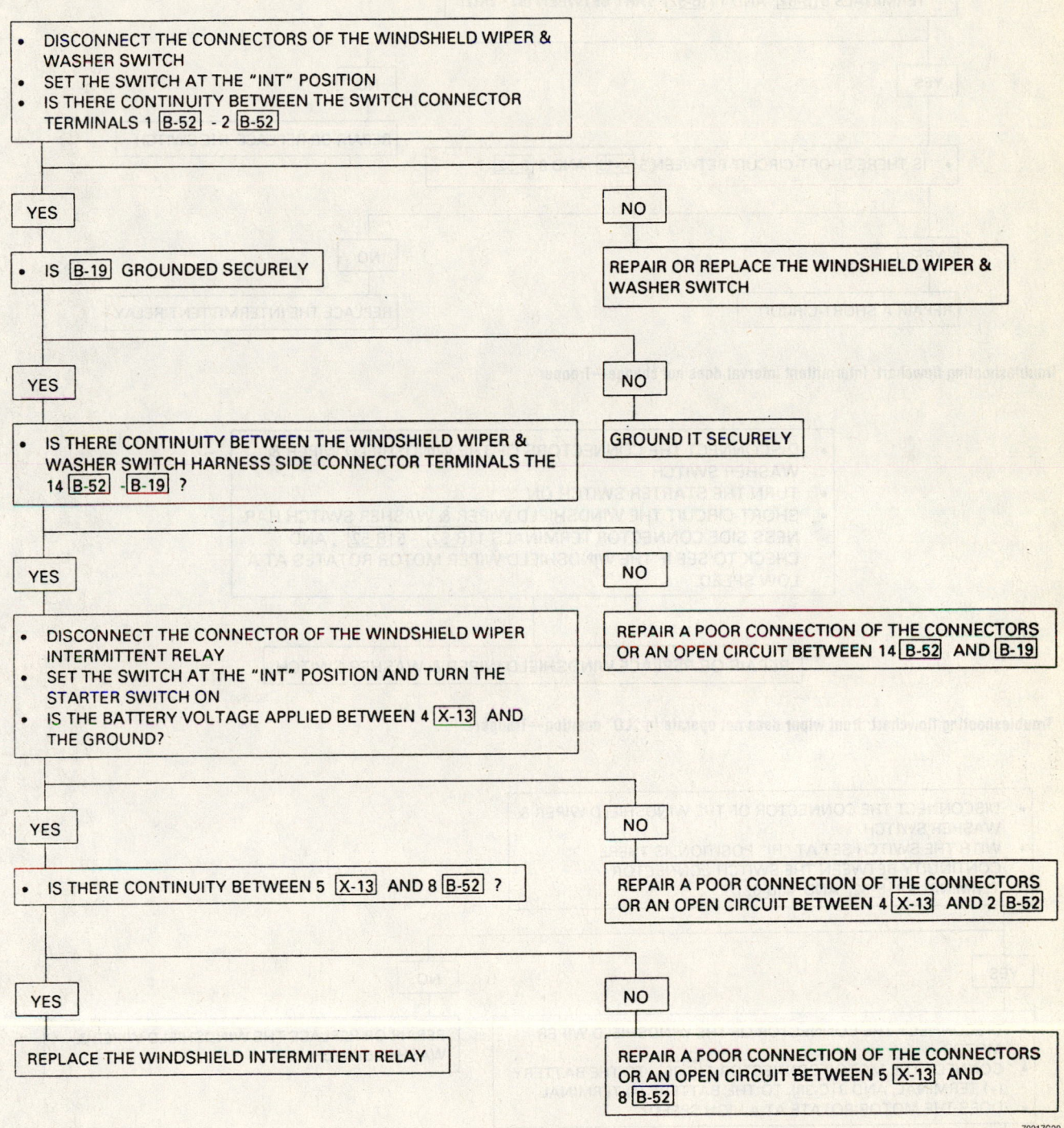

- DISCONNECT THE CONNECTORS OF THE WINDSHIELD WIPER & WASHER SWITCH
- SET THE SWITCH AT THE "INT" POSITION
- IS THERE CONTINUITY BETWEEN THE SWITCH CONNECTOR TERMINALS 1 B-52 - 2 B-52

YES / **NO**

NO → REPAIR OR REPLACE THE WINDSHIELD WIPER & WASHER SWITCH

- IS B-19 GROUNDED SECURELY

YES / **NO**

NO → GROUND IT SECURELY

- IS THERE CONTINUITY BETWEEN THE WINDSHIELD WIPER & WASHER SWITCH HARNESS SIDE CONNECTOR TERMINALS THE 14 B-52 - B-19 ?

YES / **NO**

NO → REPAIR A POOR CONNECTION OF THE CONNECTORS OR AN OPEN CIRCUIT BETWEEN 14 B-52 AND B-19

- DISCONNECT THE CONNECTOR OF THE WINDSHIELD WIPER INTERMITTENT RELAY
- SET THE SWITCH AT THE "INT" POSITION AND TURN THE STARTER SWITCH ON
- IS THE BATTERY VOLTAGE APPLIED BETWEEN 4 X-13 AND THE GROUND?

YES / **NO**

NO → REPAIR A POOR CONNECTION OF THE CONNECTORS OR AN OPEN CIRCUIT BETWEEN 4 X-13 AND 2 B-52

- IS THERE CONTINUITY BETWEEN 5 X-13 AND 8 B-52 ?

YES / **NO**

NO → REPAIR A POOR CONNECTION OF THE CONNECTORS OR AN OPEN CIRCUIT BETWEEN 5 X-13 AND 8 B-52

REPLACE THE WINDSHIELD INTERMITTENT RELAY

7921ZG29

Troubleshooting flowchart: front wiper does not operate in "INT" position—Trooper

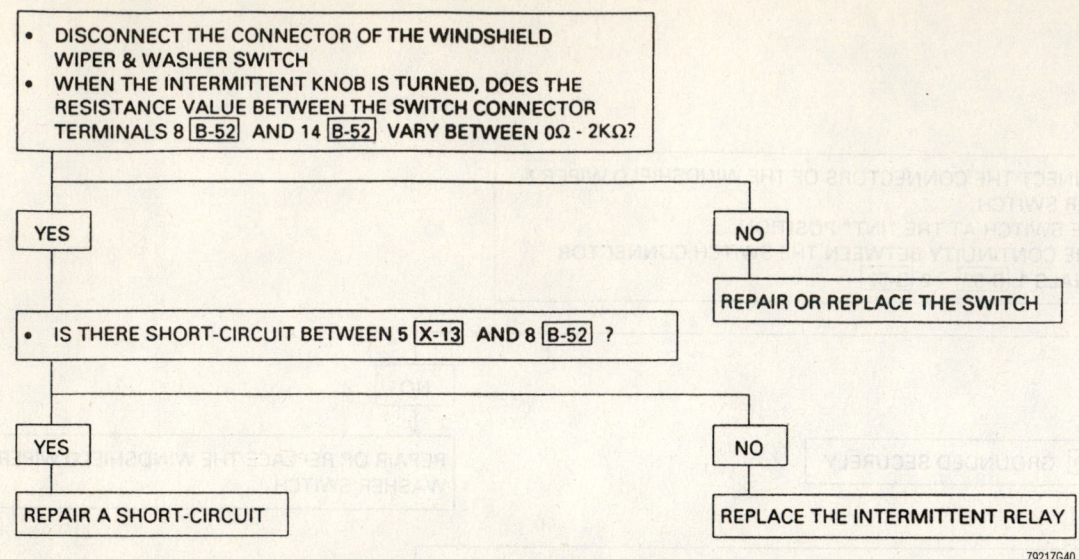

- DISCONNECT THE CONNECTOR OF THE WINDSHIELD WIPER & WASHER SWITCH
- WHEN THE INTERMITTENT KNOB IS TURNED, DOES THE RESISTANCE VALUE BETWEEN THE SWITCH CONNECTOR TERMINALS 8 $\boxed{\text{B-52}}$ AND 14 $\boxed{\text{B-52}}$ VARY BETWEEN 0Ω - 2KΩ?

YES → IS THERE SHORT-CIRCUIT BETWEEN 5 $\boxed{\text{X-13}}$ AND 8 $\boxed{\text{B-52}}$?

NO → REPAIR OR REPLACE THE SWITCH

YES → REPAIR A SHORT-CIRCUIT

NO → REPLACE THE INTERMITTENT RELAY

7921ZG40

Troubleshooting flowchart: intermittent interval does not change—Trooper

- DISCONNECT THE CONNECTORS OF THE WINDSHIELD WIPER & WASHER SWITCH
- TURN THE STARTER SWITCH ON
- SHORT-CIRCUIT THE WINDSHIELD WIPER & WASHER SWITCH HARNESS SIDE CONNECTOR TERMINALS 1 $\boxed{\text{B-52}}$ - 5 $\boxed{\text{B-52}}$, AND CHECK TO SEE IF THE WINDSHIELD WIPER MOTOR ROTATES AT A LOW SPEED.

REPAIR OR REPLACE WINDSHIELD WIPER & WASHER SWITCH

7921ZG30

Troubleshooting flowchart: front wiper does not operate in "LO" position—Trooper

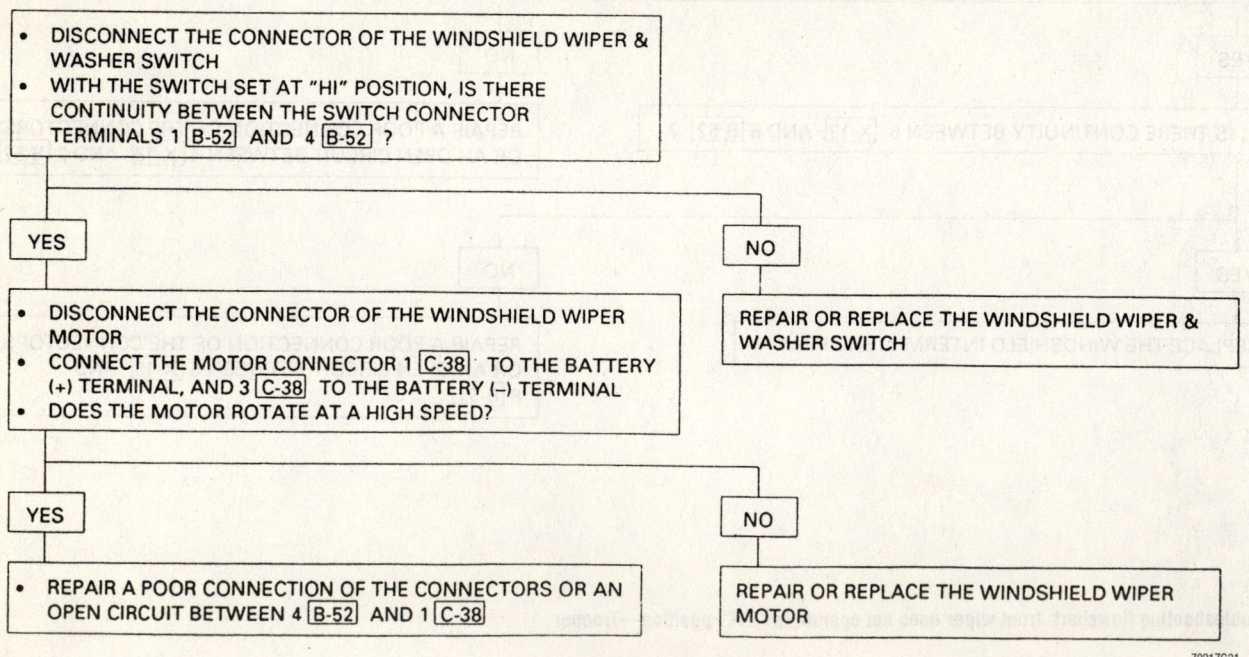

- DISCONNECT THE CONNECTOR OF THE WINDSHIELD WIPER & WASHER SWITCH
- WITH THE SWITCH SET AT "HI" POSITION, IS THERE CONTINUITY BETWEEN THE SWITCH CONNECTOR TERMINALS 1 $\boxed{\text{B-52}}$ AND 4 $\boxed{\text{B-52}}$?

YES
- DISCONNECT THE CONNECTOR OF THE WINDSHIELD WIPER MOTOR
- CONNECT THE MOTOR CONNECTOR 1 $\boxed{\text{C-38}}$ TO THE BATTERY (+) TERMINAL, AND 3 $\boxed{\text{C-38}}$ TO THE BATTERY (–) TERMINAL
- DOES THE MOTOR ROTATE AT A HIGH SPEED?

NO → REPAIR OR REPLACE THE WINDSHIELD WIPER & WASHER SWITCH

YES → REPAIR A POOR CONNECTION OF THE CONNECTORS OR AN OPEN CIRCUIT BETWEEN 4 $\boxed{\text{B-52}}$ AND 1 $\boxed{\text{C-38}}$

NO → REPAIR OR REPLACE THE WINDSHIELD WIPER MOTOR

7921ZG31

Troubleshooting flowchart: front wiper does not operate in the "HI" position—Trooper

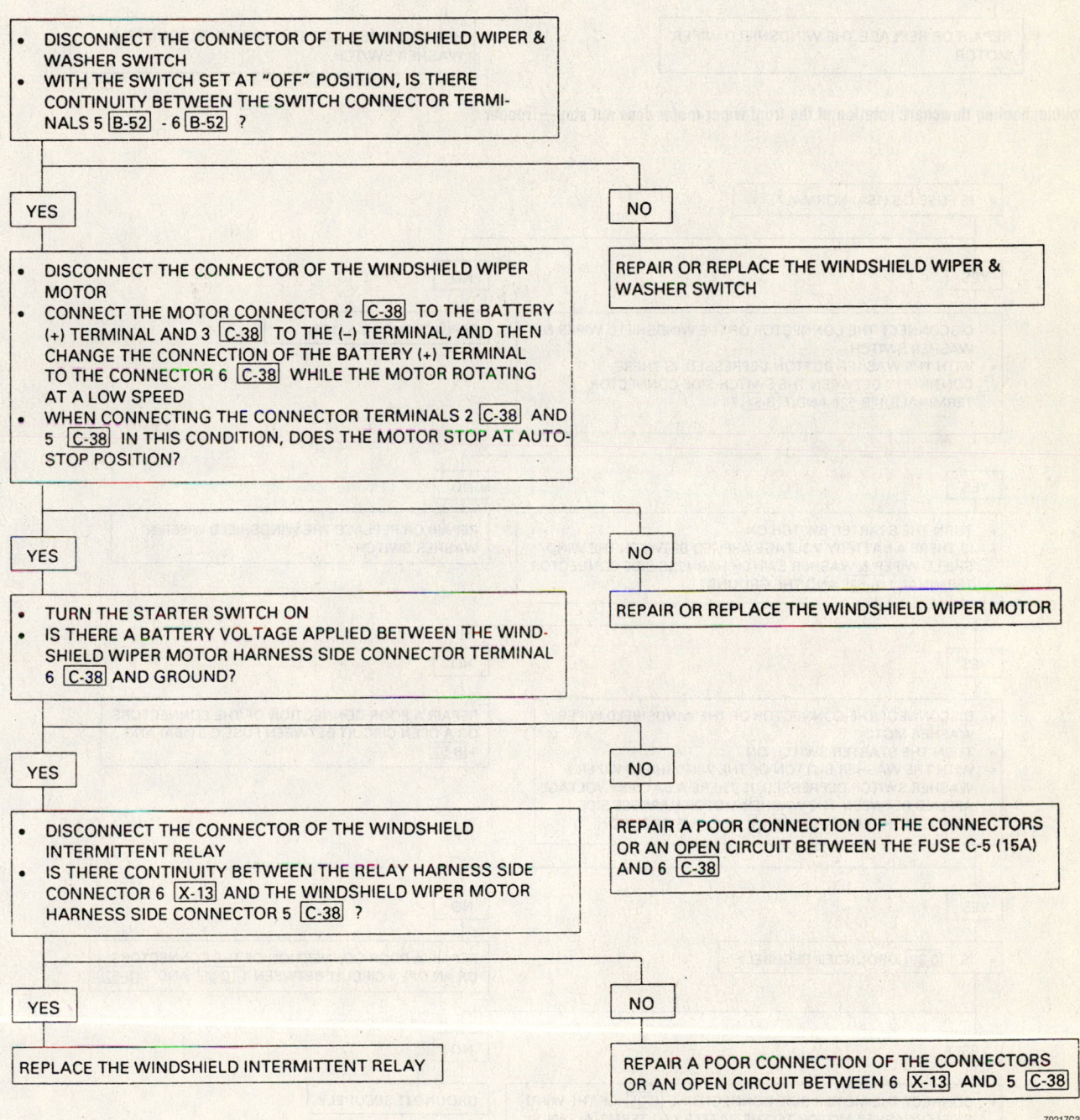

- DISCONNECT THE CONNECTOR OF THE WINDSHIELD WIPER & WASHER SWITCH
- WITH THE SWITCH SET AT "OFF" POSITION, IS THERE CONTINUITY BETWEEN THE SWITCH CONNECTOR TERMINALS 5 [B-52] - 6 [B-52] ?

YES →

- DISCONNECT THE CONNECTOR OF THE WINDSHIELD WIPER MOTOR
- CONNECT THE MOTOR CONNECTOR 2 [C-38] TO THE BATTERY (+) TERMINAL AND 3 [C-38] TO THE (–) TERMINAL, AND THEN CHANGE THE CONNECTION OF THE BATTERY (+) TERMINAL TO THE CONNECTOR 6 [C-38] WHILE THE MOTOR ROTATING AT A LOW SPEED
- WHEN CONNECTING THE CONNECTOR TERMINALS 2 [C-38] AND 5 [C-38] IN THIS CONDITION, DOES THE MOTOR STOP AT AUTO-STOP POSITION?

NO → REPAIR OR REPLACE THE WINDSHIELD WIPER & WASHER SWITCH

YES →

- TURN THE STARTER SWITCH ON
- IS THERE A BATTERY VOLTAGE APPLIED BETWEEN THE WINDSHIELD WIPER MOTOR HARNESS SIDE CONNECTOR TERMINAL 6 [C-38] AND GROUND?

NO → REPAIR OR REPLACE THE WINDSHIELD WIPER MOTOR

YES →

- DISCONNECT THE CONNECTOR OF THE WINDSHIELD INTERMITTENT RELAY
- IS THERE CONTINUITY BETWEEN THE RELAY HARNESS SIDE CONNECTOR 6 [X-13] AND THE WINDSHIELD WIPER MOTOR HARNESS SIDE CONNECTOR 5 [C-38] ?

NO → REPAIR A POOR CONNECTION OF THE CONNECTORS OR AN OPEN CIRCUIT BETWEEN THE FUSE C-5 (15A) AND 6 [C-38]

YES → REPLACE THE WINDSHIELD INTERMITTENT RELAY

NO → REPAIR A POOR CONNECTION OF THE CONNECTORS OR AN OPEN CIRCUIT BETWEEN 6 [X-13] AND 5 [C-38]

7921ZG32

Troubleshooting flowchart: auto-stop function of the front wiper motor does not operate—Trooper

Refer to the model specific sections for driveline service procedures

- IS THE CONTINUITY IN THE WINDSHIELD WIPER & WASHER SWITCH NORMAL?

YES

NO

REPAIR OR REPLACE THE WINDSHIELD WIPER MOTOR

REPAIR OR REPLACE THE WINDSHIELD WIPER & WASHER SWITCH

7921ZG33

Troubleshooting flowchart: rotation of the front wiper motor does not stop—Trooper

- IS FUSE C-5 (15A) NORMAL?

YES

NO

REPLACE FUSE C-5 (15A)

- DISCONNECT THE CONNECTOR OF THE WINDSHIELD WIPER & WASHER SWITCH
- WITH THE WASHER BUTTON DEPRESSED, IS THERE CONTINUITY BETWEEN THE SWITCH SIDE CONNECTOR TERMINALS 1 B-52 AND 7 B-52 ?

YES

NO

REPAIR OR REPLACE THE WINDSHIELD WIPER & WASHER SWITCH

- TURN THE STARTER SWITCH ON
- IS THERE A BATTERY VOLTAGE APPLIED BETWEEN THE WINDSHIELD WIPER & WASHER SWITCH HARNESS SIDE CONNECTOR TERMINAL 1 B-52 AND THE GROUND?

YES

NO

REPAIR A POOR CONNECTION OF THE CONNECTORS OR A OPEN CIRCUIT BETWEEN FUSE C-5 (15A) AND 1 B-52

- DISCONNECT THE CONNECTOR OF THE WINDSHIELD WIPER WASHER MOTOR
- TURN THE STARTER SWITCH ON
- WITH THE WASHER BUTTON OF THE WINDSHIELD WIPER & WASHER SWITCH DEPRESSED, IS THERE A BATTERY VOLTAGE APPLIED BETWEEN THE WASHER MOTOR HARNESS SIDE CONNECTOR TERMINAL 1 C-35 AND THE GROUND?

YES

NO

REPAIR A POOR CONNECTION OF THE CONNECTORS OR AN OPEN CIRCUIT BETWEEN 1 C-35 AND 7 B-52

- IS 1 C-39 GROUNDED SECURELY?

YES

NO

GROUND IT SECURELY

- CONNECT THE MOTOR SIDE CONNECTOR 1 C-35 OF THE WINDSHIELD WASHER MOTOR TO THE BATTERY (+) TERMINAL, AND THE CONNECTOR 2 C-35 TO THE (–) TERMINAL
- DOES THE MOTOR ROTATE?

YES

NO

REPAIR A POOR CONNECTION OF THE CONNECTORS OR AN OPEN CIRCUIT BETWEEN 2 C-35 AND 1 C-39

REPAIR OR REPLACE THE WINDSHIELD WASHER MOTOR

7921ZG34

Troubleshooting flowchart: front washer motor does not operate—Trooper

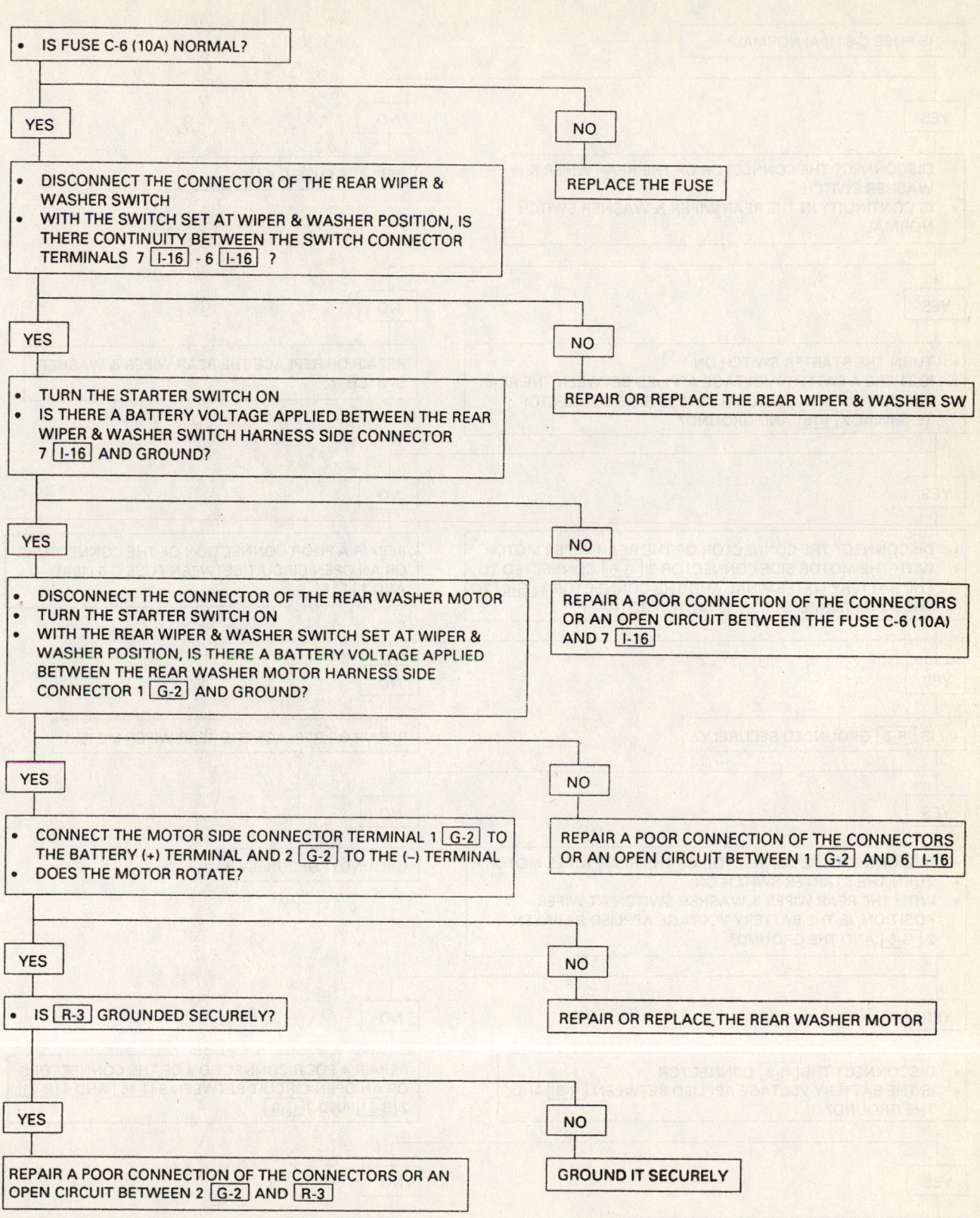

- IS FUSE C-6 (10A) NORMAL?

YES

- DISCONNECT THE CONNECTOR OF THE REAR WIPER & WASHER SWITCH
- WITH THE SWITCH SET AT WIPER & WASHER POSITION, IS THERE CONTINUITY BETWEEN THE SWITCH CONNECTOR TERMINALS 7 I-16 - 6 I-16 ?

NO → REPLACE THE FUSE

YES

- TURN THE STARTER SWITCH ON
- IS THERE A BATTERY VOLTAGE APPLIED BETWEEN THE REAR WIPER & WASHER SWITCH HARNESS SIDE CONNECTOR 7 I-16 AND GROUND?

NO → REPAIR OR REPLACE THE REAR WIPER & WASHER SW

YES

- DISCONNECT THE CONNECTOR OF THE REAR WASHER MOTOR
- TURN THE STARTER SWITCH ON
- WITH THE REAR WIPER & WASHER SWITCH SET AT WIPER & WASHER POSITION, IS THERE A BATTERY VOLTAGE APPLIED BETWEEN THE REAR WASHER MOTOR HARNESS SIDE CONNECTOR 1 G-2 AND GROUND?

NO → REPAIR A POOR CONNECTION OF THE CONNECTORS OR AN OPEN CIRCUIT BETWEEN THE FUSE C-6 (10A) AND 7 I-16

YES

- CONNECT THE MOTOR SIDE CONNECTOR TERMINAL 1 G-2 TO THE BATTERY (+) TERMINAL AND 2 G-2 TO THE (–) TERMINAL
- DOES THE MOTOR ROTATE?

NO → REPAIR A POOR CONNECTION OF THE CONNECTORS OR AN OPEN CIRCUIT BETWEEN 1 G-2 AND 6 I-16

YES

- IS R-3 GROUNDED SECURELY?

NO → REPAIR OR REPLACE THE REAR WASHER MOTOR

YES

REPAIR A POOR CONNECTION OF THE CONNECTORS OR AN OPEN CIRCUIT BETWEEN 2 G-2 AND R-3

NO → GROUND IT SECURELY

7921ZG39

Troubleshooting flowchart: rear washer motor does not operate—Trooper

For complete service labor times order Nichols' Chilton Labor Guide Manual

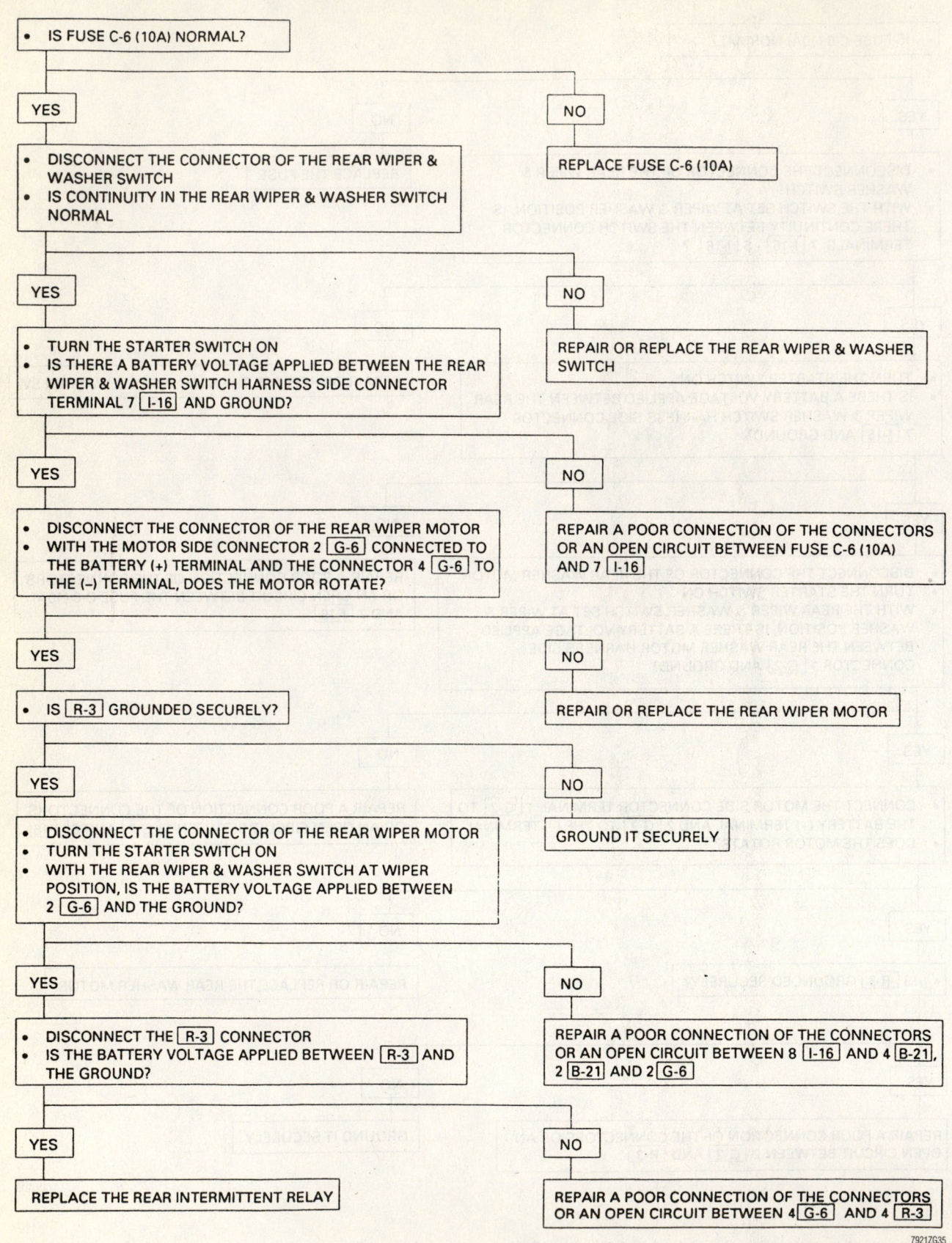

- IS FUSE C-6 (10A) NORMAL?

YES / **NO**

NO → REPLACE FUSE C-6 (10A)

YES:
- DISCONNECT THE CONNECTOR OF THE REAR WIPER & WASHER SWITCH
- IS CONTINUITY IN THE REAR WIPER & WASHER SWITCH NORMAL

NO → REPAIR OR REPLACE THE REAR WIPER & WASHER SWITCH

YES:
- TURN THE STARTER SWITCH ON
- IS THERE A BATTERY VOLTAGE APPLIED BETWEEN THE REAR WIPER & WASHER SWITCH HARNESS SIDE CONNECTOR TERMINAL 7 I-16 AND GROUND?

NO → REPAIR A POOR CONNECTION OF THE CONNECTORS OR AN OPEN CIRCUIT BETWEEN FUSE C-6 (10A) AND 7 I-16

YES:
- DISCONNECT THE CONNECTOR OF THE REAR WIPER MOTOR
- WITH THE MOTOR SIDE CONNECTOR 2 G-6 CONNECTED TO THE BATTERY (+) TERMINAL AND THE CONNECTOR 4 G-6 TO THE (–) TERMINAL, DOES THE MOTOR ROTATE?

NO → REPAIR OR REPLACE THE REAR WIPER MOTOR

YES:
- IS R-3 GROUNDED SECURELY?

NO → GROUND IT SECURELY

YES:
- DISCONNECT THE CONNECTOR OF THE REAR WIPER MOTOR
- TURN THE STARTER SWITCH ON
- WITH THE REAR WIPER & WASHER SWITCH AT WIPER POSITION, IS THE BATTERY VOLTAGE APPLIED BETWEEN 2 G-6 AND THE GROUND?

NO → REPAIR A POOR CONNECTION OF THE CONNECTORS OR AN OPEN CIRCUIT BETWEEN 8 I-16 AND 4 B-21, 2 B-21 AND 2 G-6

YES:
- DISCONNECT THE R-3 CONNECTOR
- IS THE BATTERY VOLTAGE APPLIED BETWEEN R-3 AND THE GROUND?

NO → REPAIR A POOR CONNECTION OF THE CONNECTORS OR AN OPEN CIRCUIT BETWEEN 4 G-6 AND 4 R-3

YES → REPLACE THE REAR INTERMITTENT RELAY

7921ZG35

Troubleshooting flowchart: rear wiper motor does not operate—Trooper

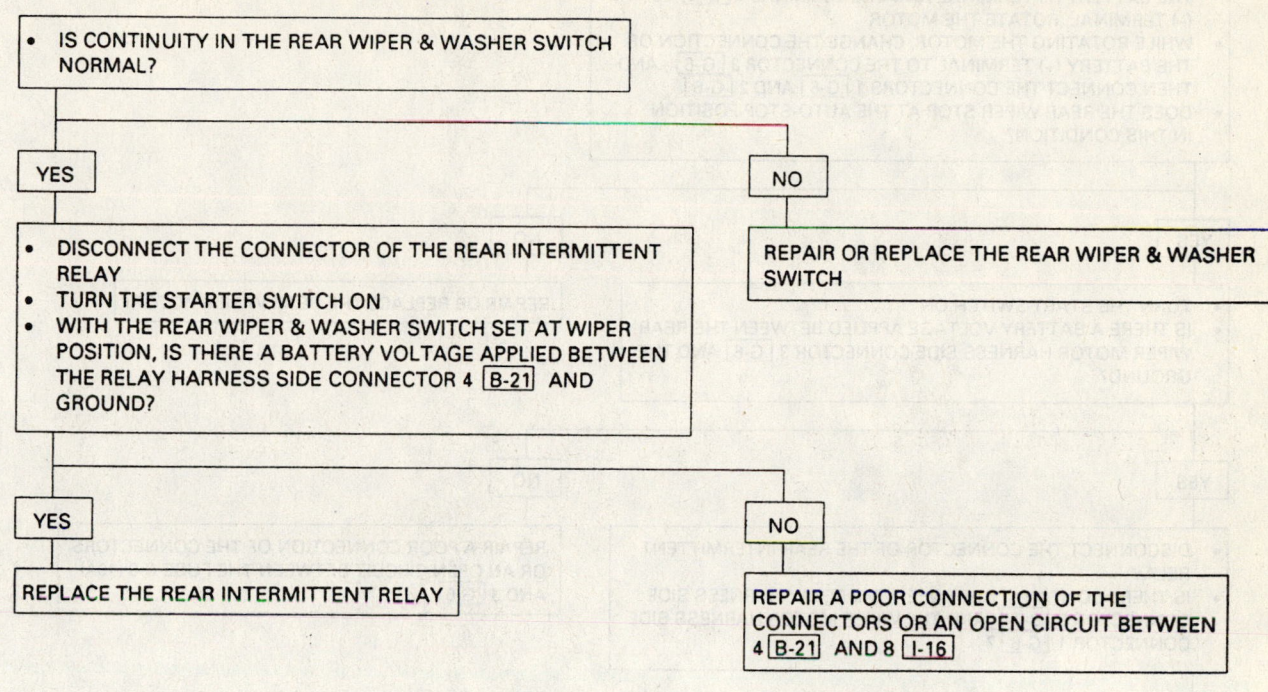

- IS CONTINUITY IN THE REAR WIPER & WASHER SWITCH NORMAL?

YES

- DISCONNECT THE CONNECTOR OF THE REAR INTERMITTENT RELAY
- TURN THE STARTER SWITCH ON
- WITH THE REAR WIPER & WASHER SWITCH SET AT WIPER POSITION, IS THERE A BATTERY VOLTAGE APPLIED BETWEEN THE RELAY HARNESS SIDE CONNECTOR 4 [B-21] AND GROUND?

NO

REPAIR OR REPLACE THE REAR WIPER & WASHER SWITCH

YES

REPLACE THE REAR INTERMITTENT RELAY

NO

REPAIR A POOR CONNECTION OF THE CONNECTORS OR AN OPEN CIRCUIT BETWEEN 4 [B-21] AND 8 [I-16]

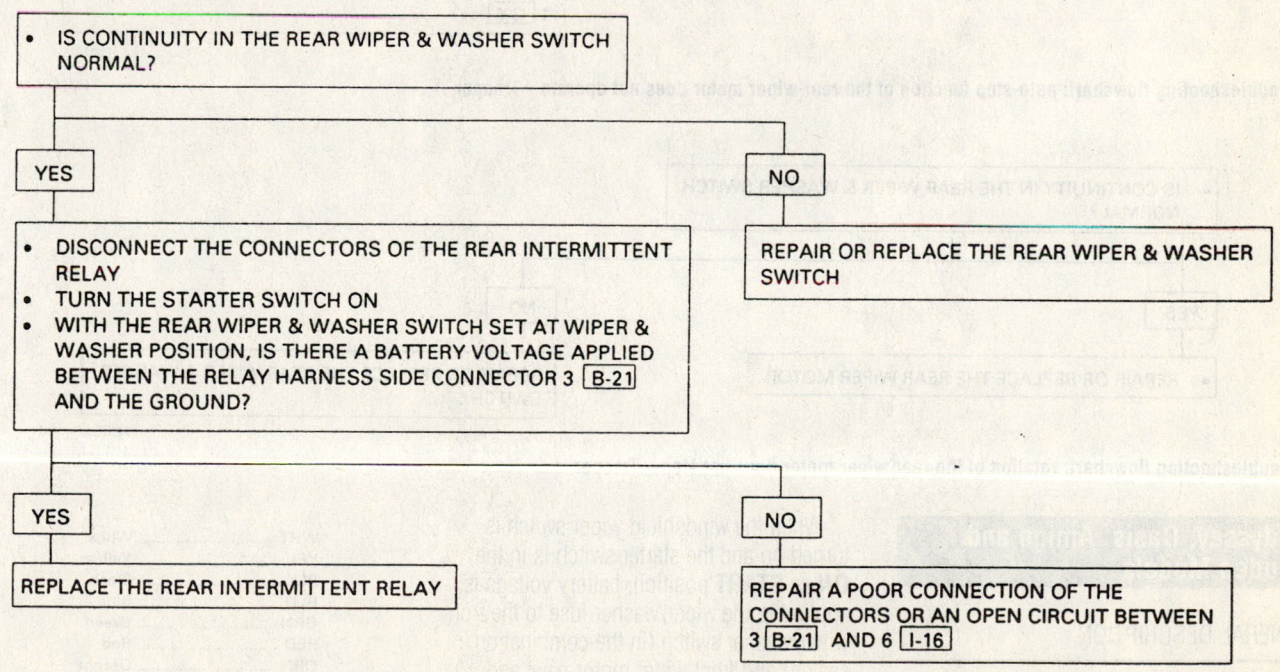

- IS CONTINUITY IN THE REAR WIPER & WASHER SWITCH NORMAL?

YES

- DISCONNECT THE CONNECTORS OF THE REAR INTERMITTENT RELAY
- TURN THE STARTER SWITCH ON
- WITH THE REAR WIPER & WASHER SWITCH SET AT WIPER & WASHER POSITION, IS THERE A BATTERY VOLTAGE APPLIED BETWEEN THE RELAY HARNESS SIDE CONNECTOR 3 [B-21] AND THE GROUND?

NO

REPAIR OR REPLACE THE REAR WIPER & WASHER SWITCH

YES

REPLACE THE REAR INTERMITTENT RELAY

NO

REPAIR A POOR CONNECTION OF THE CONNECTORS OR AN OPEN CIRCUIT BETWEEN 3 [B-21] AND 6 [I-16]

7921ZG37

Troubleshooting flowchart: rear wiper motor does not operate at wiper position—Trooper

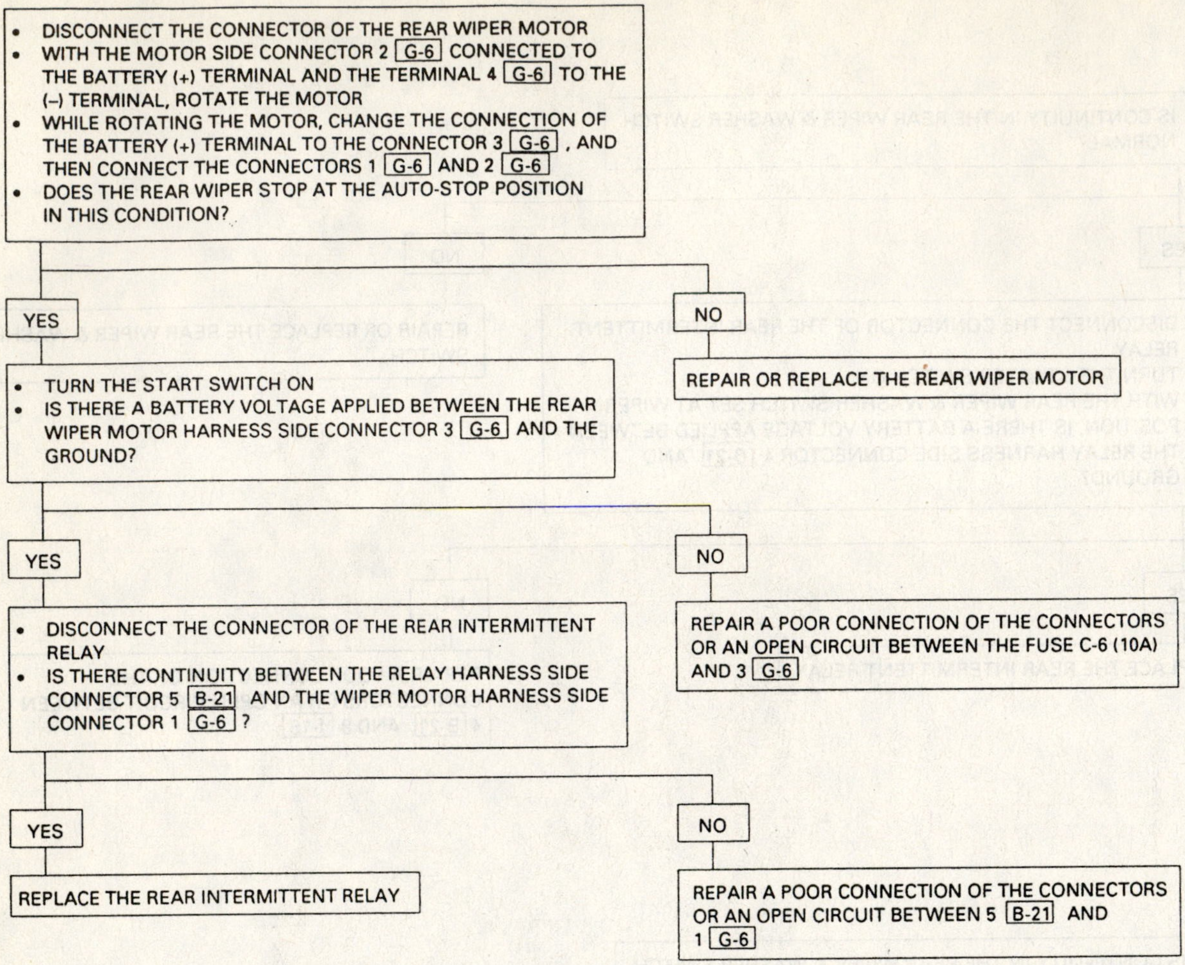

- DISCONNECT THE CONNECTOR OF THE REAR WIPER MOTOR
- WITH THE MOTOR SIDE CONNECTOR 2 [G-6] CONNECTED TO THE BATTERY (+) TERMINAL AND THE TERMINAL 4 [G-6] TO THE (−) TERMINAL, ROTATE THE MOTOR
- WHILE ROTATING THE MOTOR, CHANGE THE CONNECTION OF THE BATTERY (+) TERMINAL TO THE CONNECTOR 3 [G-6], AND THEN CONNECT THE CONNECTORS 1 [G-6] AND 2 [G-6]
- DOES THE REAR WIPER STOP AT THE AUTO-STOP POSITION IN THIS CONDITION?

YES

- TURN THE START SWITCH ON
- IS THERE A BATTERY VOLTAGE APPLIED BETWEEN THE REAR WIPER MOTOR HARNESS SIDE CONNECTOR 3 [G-6] AND THE GROUND?

NO

REPAIR OR REPLACE THE REAR WIPER MOTOR

YES

- DISCONNECT THE CONNECTOR OF THE REAR INTERMITTENT RELAY
- IS THERE CONTINUITY BETWEEN THE RELAY HARNESS SIDE CONNECTOR 5 [B-21] AND THE WIPER MOTOR HARNESS SIDE CONNECTOR 1 [G-6]?

NO

REPAIR A POOR CONNECTION OF THE CONNECTORS OR AN OPEN CIRCUIT BETWEEN THE FUSE C-6 (10A) AND 3 [G-6]

YES

REPLACE THE REAR INTERMITTENT RELAY

NO

REPAIR A POOR CONNECTION OF THE CONNECTORS OR AN OPEN CIRCUIT BETWEEN 5 [B-21] AND 1 [G-6]

7921ZG36

Troubleshooting flowchart: auto-stop function of the rear wiper motor does not operate—Trooper

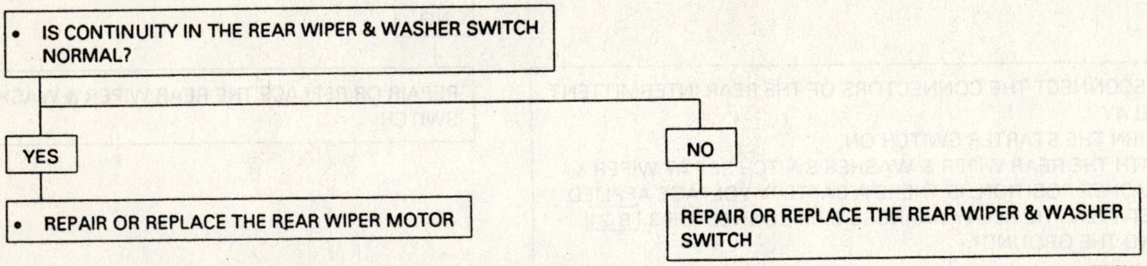

- IS CONTINUITY IN THE REAR WIPER & WASHER SWITCH NORMAL?

YES

- REPAIR OR REPLACE THE REAR WIPER MOTOR

NO

REPAIR OR REPLACE THE REAR WIPER & WASHER SWITCH

7921ZG38

Troubleshooting flowchart: rotation of the rear wiper motor does not stop—Trooper

Odyssey, Oasis, Amigo and Rodeo Models

GENERAL DESCRIPTION

The windshield wiper circuit consists of the ignition switch, wiper and washer switches, wiper motor, washer motors and relays for the intermittent function. Some models include intermittent rear window wipers and therefore have relays to control this function as well.

When the windshield wiper switch is turned on and the starter switch is in the **ON** or **START** position, battery voltage is applied to the wiper/washer fuse to the front wiper/washer switch (in the combination switch) and front wiper motor pawl and switch contacts. A fuse, located in the fuse block, protects the circuitry of the wiper system and the vehicle.

The wiper motor has permanent magnet fields. The speeds are determined by current flow to the appropriate set of brushes.

WHT .... White
YEL .... Yellow
BLK .... Black
BLU .... Blue
GRN .... Green
RED .... Red
ORN .... Orange
PNK .... Pink
BRN .... Brown
GRY .... Gray
PUR .... Purple
LT BLU .... Light Blue
LT GRN .... Light Green

7921ZG49

Wire color codes—Odyssey and Oasis models

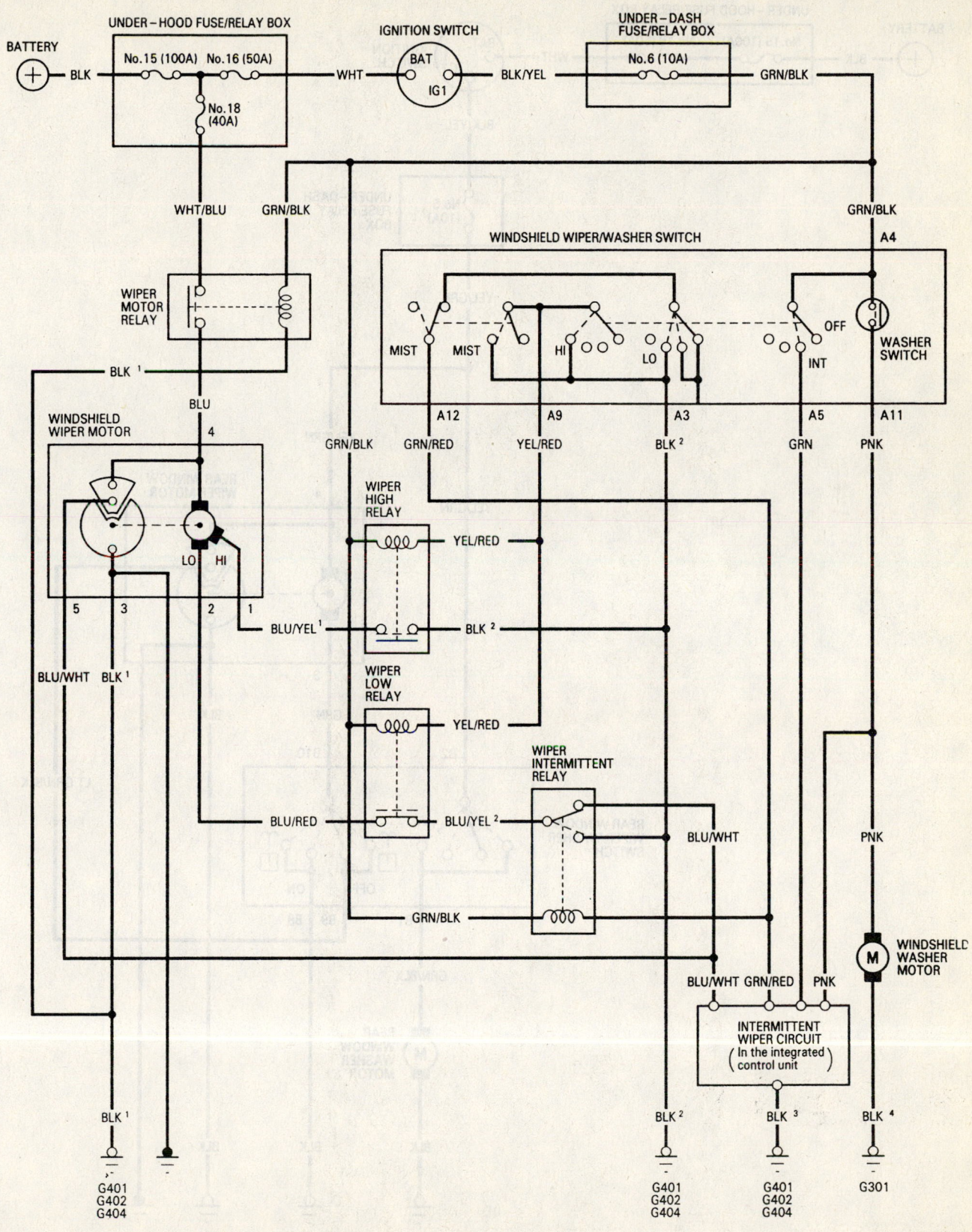

Circuit wiring diagram: front wiper/washer system—Odyssey and Oasis models

Refer to the model specific sections for driveline service procedures

7921ZG45

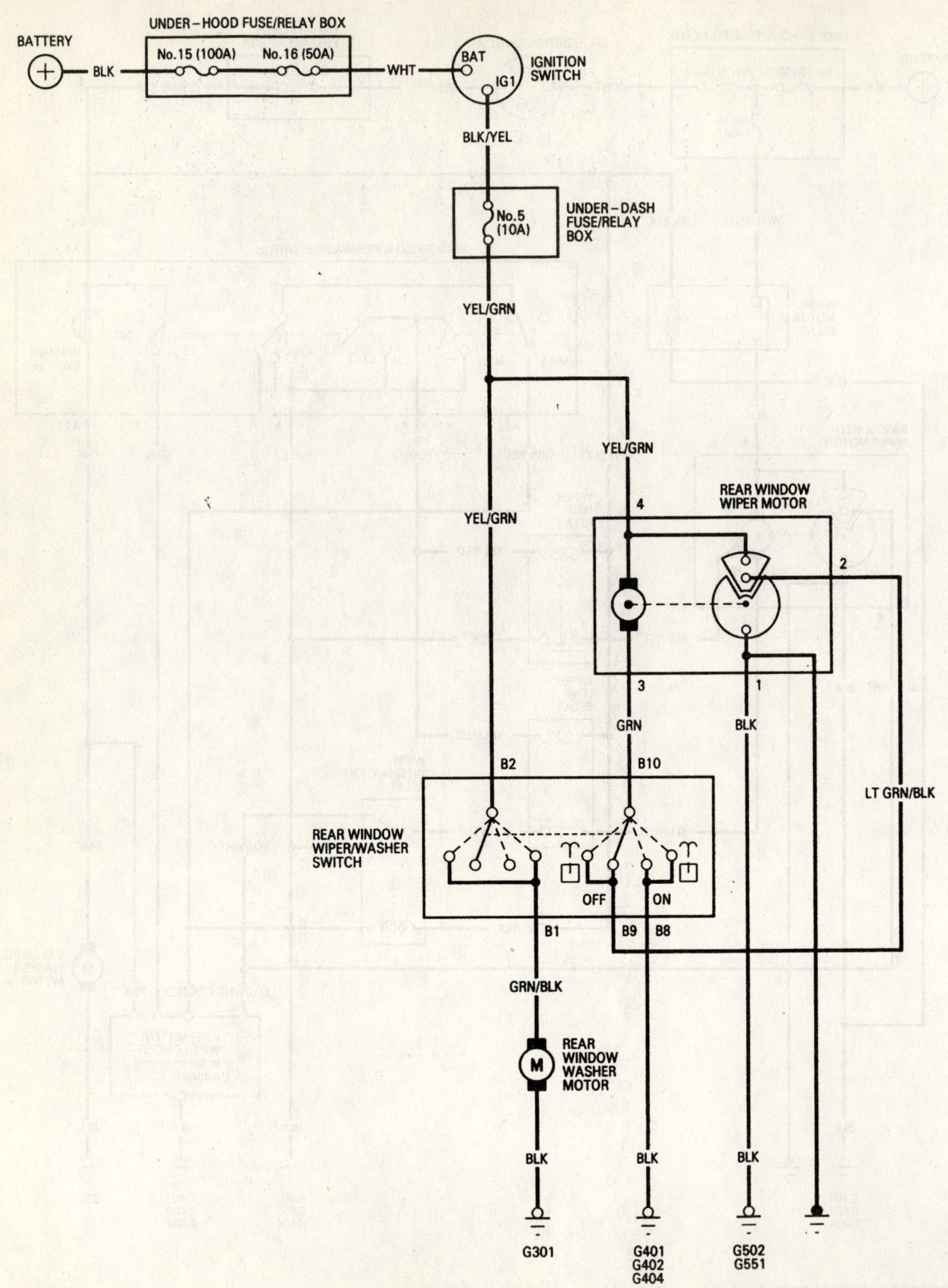

Circuit wiring diagram: rear wiper/washer system—Odyssey and Oasis models

7921ZG46

TESTING

Utilize the flowchart in conjunction with the circuit wiring diagram and the individual tests in this section to systematically locate the problem (if any) in the wiper circuit. The key to troubleshooting is an organized, logical approach. Do not proceed to the next step until each step has been completed.

Odyssey and Oasis

WIPER/WASHER SWITCH TEST

1. Remove the lower dashboard cover and the knee bolster.
2. Unplug terminal 12P and 16P from the main wire harness.
3. Use the accompanying tables to check for continuity between the terminals in each switch position.

WINDSHIELD WIPER MOTOR TEST

1. Remove the cap nuts and the wiper arms.
2. Open the hood, then disconnect the 5P connector from the windshield wiper motor.
3. Test the motor by connecting battery cable and the ground according to the table.
4. If the motor does not run or fails to run smoothly, replace it.

NOTE: The numbers in the table show the troubleshooting sequence.

Symptom	Item to be inspected	Blown No. 6 (10 A) fuse (In the under-dash fuse/relay box)	Blown No. 5 (10 A) fuse (In the under-dash fuse/relay box)	Wiper switch	Washer switch	Windshield wiper motor	Rear window wiper motor	Washer motor	Wiper motor relay	Wiper high relay	Wiper low relay	Intermittent wiper relay	Intermittent wiper circuit (In the integrated control unit)	Combined operation with wiper/washer (In the integrated control unit)	Insufficient washer fluid in reservoir	Disconnected or blocked washer hose or clogged outlet	Disconnected wiper linkages	Poor ground	Open circuit in wires, loose or disconnected terminals
Windshield wipers do not operate.	In all positions	1		4		2			3								5	G401 G402 G404	GRN/BLK
	In INT			1		4					3	2		5				G401 G402 G404	GRN/BLK, GRN, BLU/WHT
	In LO			1		4					2	3		5				G401 G402 G404	GRN/BLK, BLU/YEL[2], GRN/RED, BLU/RED
	In HI			1		3				2								G401 G402 G404	GRN/BLK, YEL/RED, BLU/YEL[2]
	In MIST			1							2							G401 G402 G404	GRN/BLK, GRN/RED, YEL/RED
Rear wiper does not operate.			1	3			2												YEL/GRN
Blades do not return to park position when wipers are turned OFF.	Windshield					2	1					3	4						BLU/WHT
	Rear window					2	1												LT GRN/BLK
Erratic intermittent cycle or wipers do not operate intermittently.												1	2						GRN/RED
Little or no washer fluid is pumped.		2			5			4							1	3		G301	PNK
Wipers do not operate simultaneously with washer.														1					GRN/RED

Troubleshooting flowchart: front and rear wiper/washer system—Odyssey and Oasis models

7921ZG47

For complete service labor times order Nichols' Chilton Labor Guide Manual

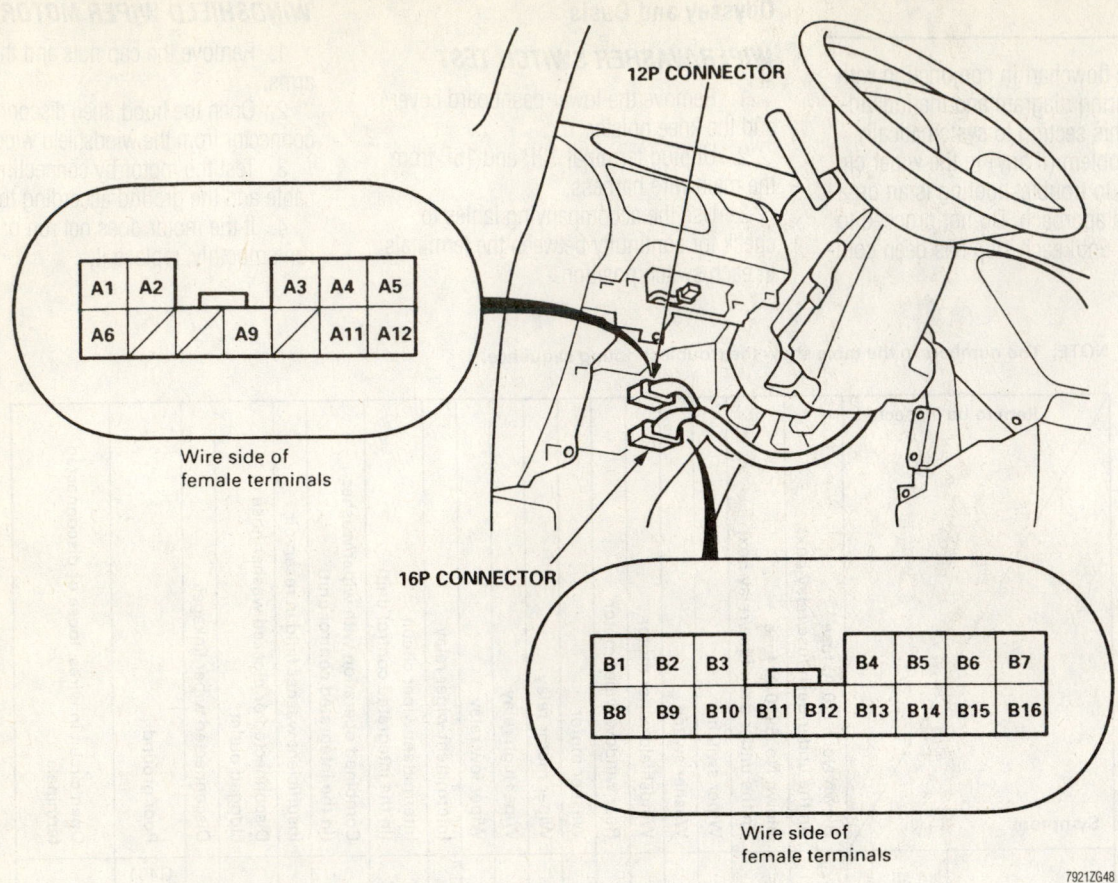

Wire side of female terminals

Wire side of female terminals

7921ZG48

Check for continuity at the wiper/washer switch terminals—Odyssey and Oasis models

Front:

Position \ Terminal	A3	A4	A5	A9	A11	A12
OFF						
INT		○——○				
LO	○					○
HI	○			○		
Mist switch "ON"	○			○		
Washer switch "ON"		○——————————○			○	

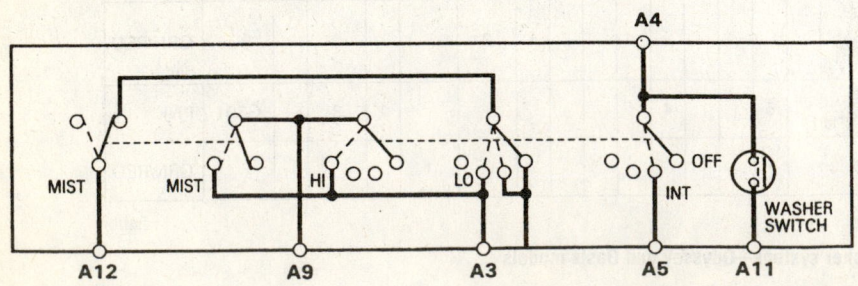

Wiper/washer switch table—Odyssey and Oasis models

7921ZG50

Rear:

Terminal Position	B1	B2	B8	B9	B10
Washer switch "ON" (Wiper switch OFF)	○───	─○		○───	─○
OFF				○───	─○
ON			○───		─○
Washer switch "ON" (Wiper switch "ON")	○───	─○	○───		─○

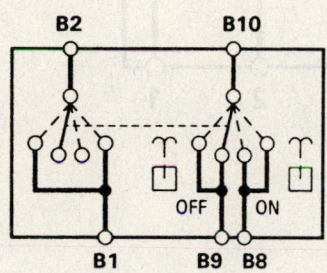

7921ZG51

Wiper/washer switch table—Odyssey and Oasis models

Terminal Position	1	2	4
LOW SPEED		⊖	⊕
HIGH SPEED	⊖		⊕

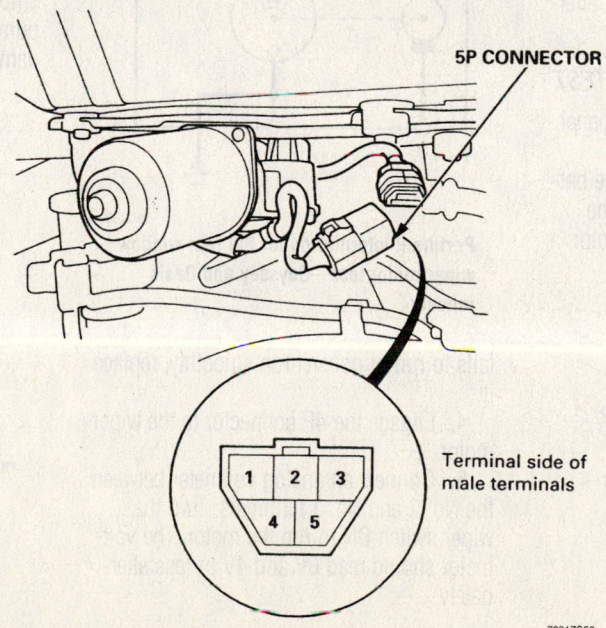

5P CONNECTOR

Terminal side of
male terminals

7921ZG52

Pertinent information for the windshield wiper motor test—Odyssey and Oasis models

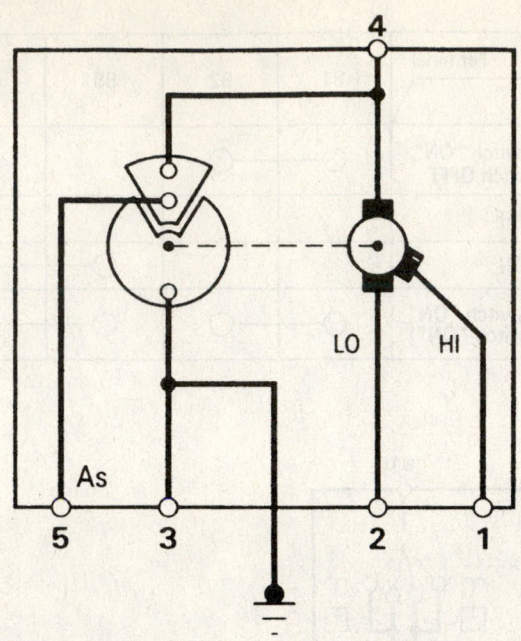

NOTE: "As" means "Automatic stop".
This is sometimes refered to as a "Park switch".

7921ZG53

Pertinent information for the windshield wiper motor test—Odyssey and Oasis models

5. Reconnect the 5P connector to the wiper motor.

6. Connect an analog voltmeter between the No. 3 and No. 5 terminals. Run the motor at low or high speed. The voltage reading should be between 0V and 4V alternately.

REAR WINDOW WIPER MOTOR TEST

1. Remove the tailgate lower trim panel.
2. Disconnect the 4P connector.
3. Test the motor by connecting the battery power to the No. 4 terminal and the ground to the No. 3 terminal. If the motor

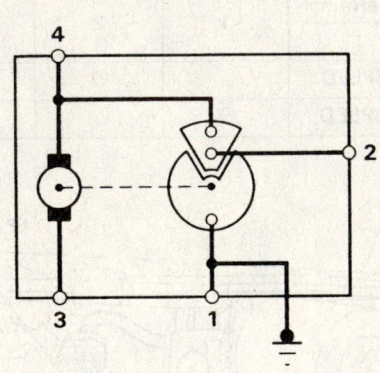

7921ZG55

Pertinent information for the rear window wiper motor test—Odyssey and Oasis models

fails to run or doesn't run smoothly, replace it.

4. Engage the 4P connector to the wiper motor.

5. Connect an analog voltmeter between the No. 2 and No. 1 terminals. Turn the wiper switch ON to run the motor. The voltmeter should read 0V and 4V or less alternately.

WINDSHIELD WASHER MOTOR TEST

1. Remove the left inner fender.
2. Disengage the 2P connectors from the washer motors.

3. Test the washer motors by connecting the battery power to the No. 1 terminals and ground to the No. 2 terminals. If the motors fail to run smoothly, or does not operate at all, replace them. If the motors run smoothly, but there is not enough fluid pumped, check for disconnected, blocked or damaged washer hoses.

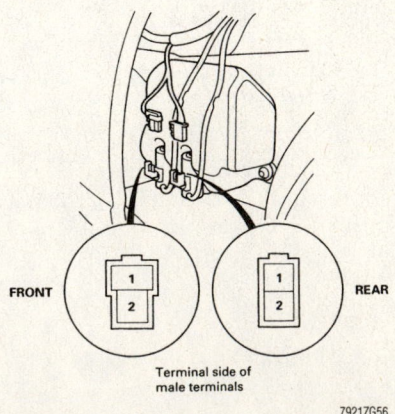

7921ZG56

Pertinent information for the rear window wiper motor test—Odyssey and Oasis models

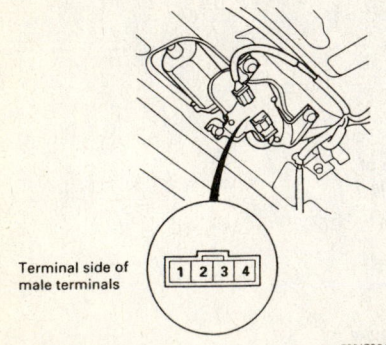

Terminal side of male terminals

7921ZG54

Pertinent information for the rear window wiper motor test—Odyssey and Oasis models

Amigo and Rodeo Models

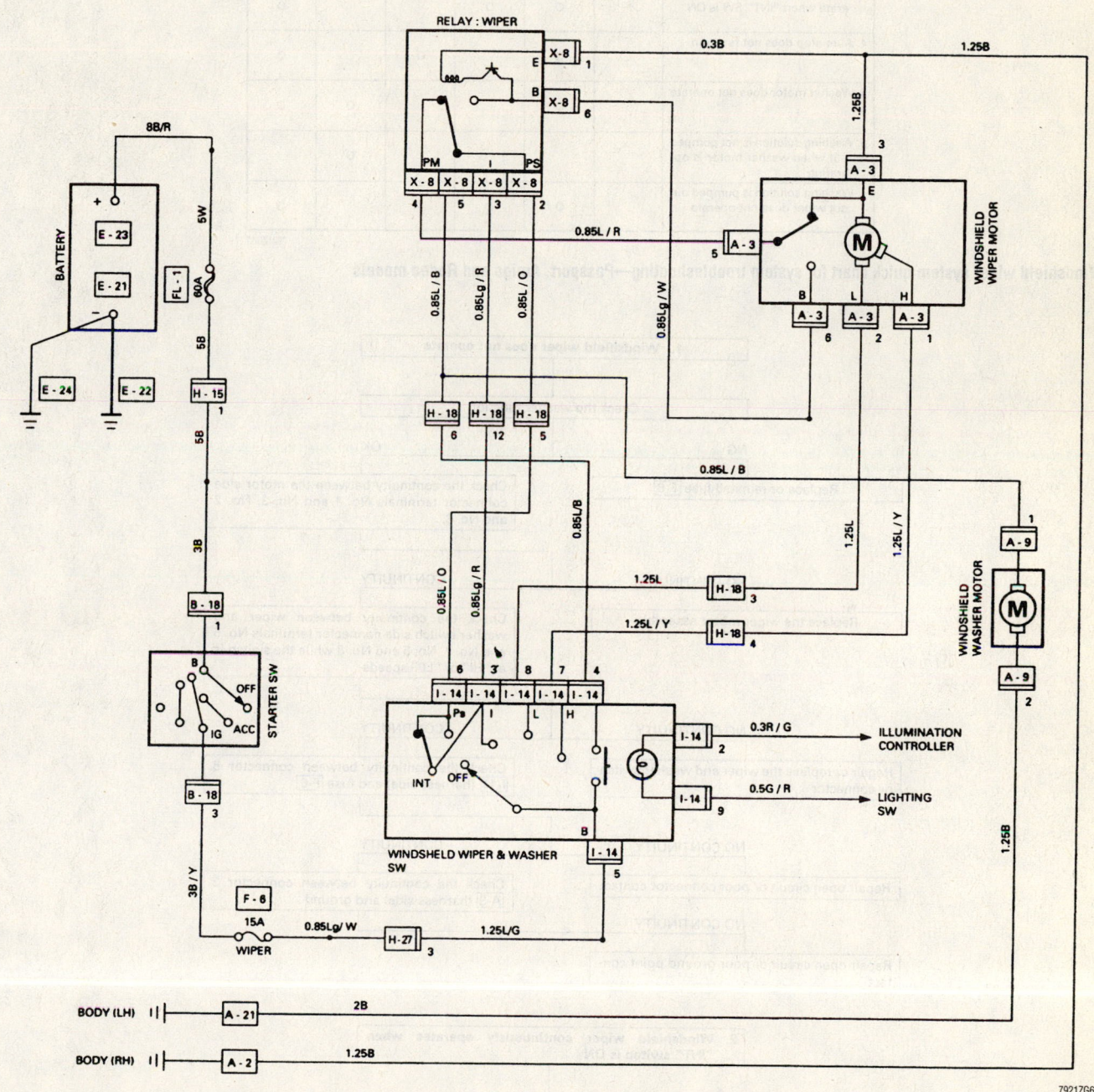

Front wiper circuit wiring diagram—Passport, Amigo and Rodeo models

Refer to the model specific sections for driveline service procedures

Check point / Trouble mode	Fuse (F-6 15 A)	Wiper SW	Relay; intermittent	Wiper motor	Washer motor, washer tank or tube	Cable harness
1. Wiper does not operate	○	○	○	○		○
2. Windshield wiper continuously operates when "INT" SW is ON		○	○			○
3. Windshield wiper does not operate when "INT" SW is ON		○	○			○
4. Auto stop does not function		○		○		○
5. Washer motor does not operate		○			○	○
6. Washing solution is not pumped out when washer motor is operating					○	
7. Washing solution is pumped out but wiper does not operate		○	○			○

7921ZG69

Windshield wiper system quick chart for system troubleshooting—Passport, Amigo and Rodeo models

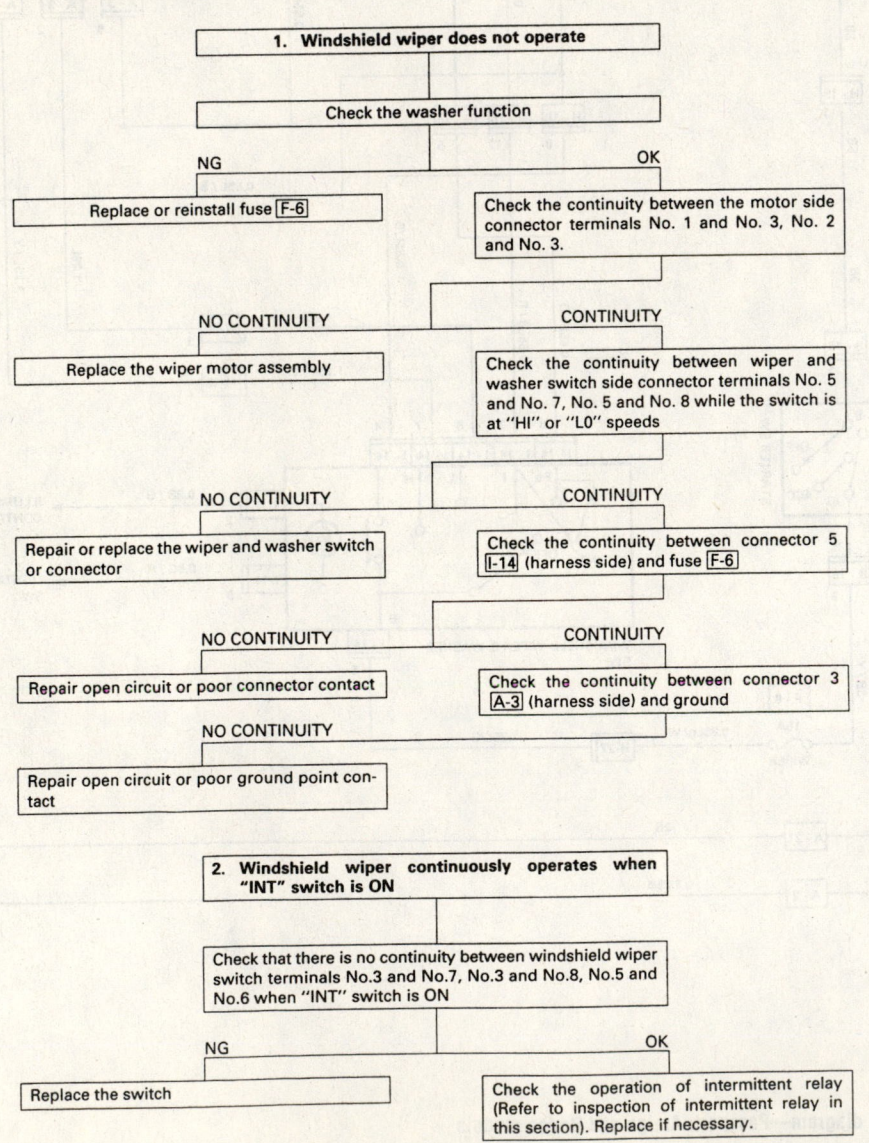

7921ZG70

Troubleshooting flowchart—Passport, Amigo and Rodeo models

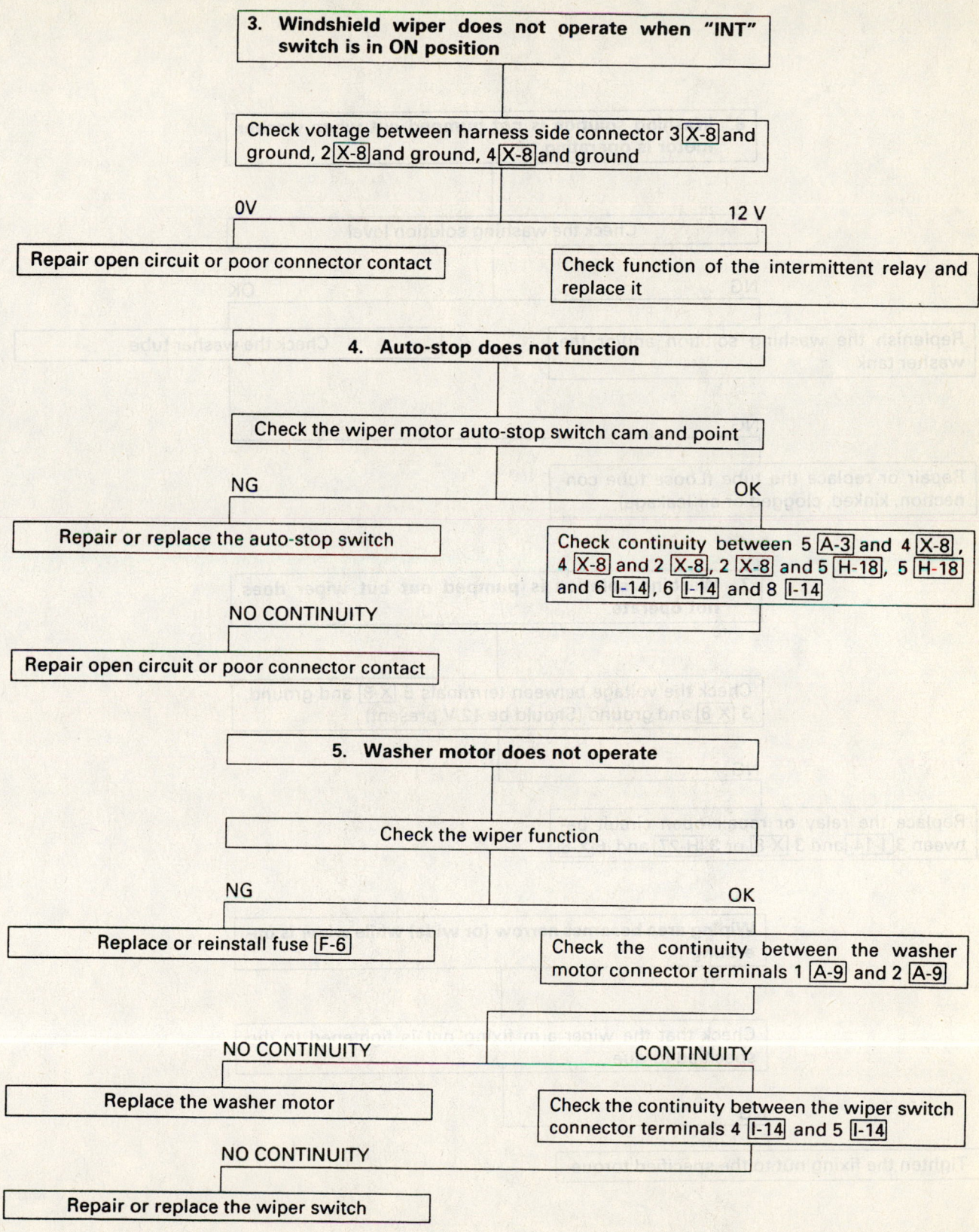

3. Windshield wiper does not operate when "INT" switch is in ON position

Check voltage between harness side connector 3 X-8 and ground, 2 X-8 and ground, 4 X-8 and ground

0V — Repair open circuit or poor connector contact

12 V — Check function of the intermittent relay and replace it

4. Auto-stop does not function

Check the wiper motor auto-stop switch cam and point

NG — Repair or replace the auto-stop switch

OK — Check continuity between 5 A-3 and 4 X-8, 4 X-8 and 2 X-8, 2 X-8 and 5 H-18, 5 H-18 and 6 I-14, 6 I-14 and 8 I-14

NO CONTINUITY — Repair open circuit or poor connector contact

5. Washer motor does not operate

Check the wiper function

NG — Replace or reinstall fuse F-6

OK — Check the continuity between the washer motor connector terminals 1 A-9 and 2 A-9

NO CONTINUITY — Replace the washer motor

CONTINUITY — Check the continuity between the wiper switch connector terminals 4 I-14 and 5 I-14

NO CONTINUITY — Repair or replace the wiper switch

7921ZG71

Troubleshooting flowchart (cont'd)—Passport, Amigo and Rodeo models

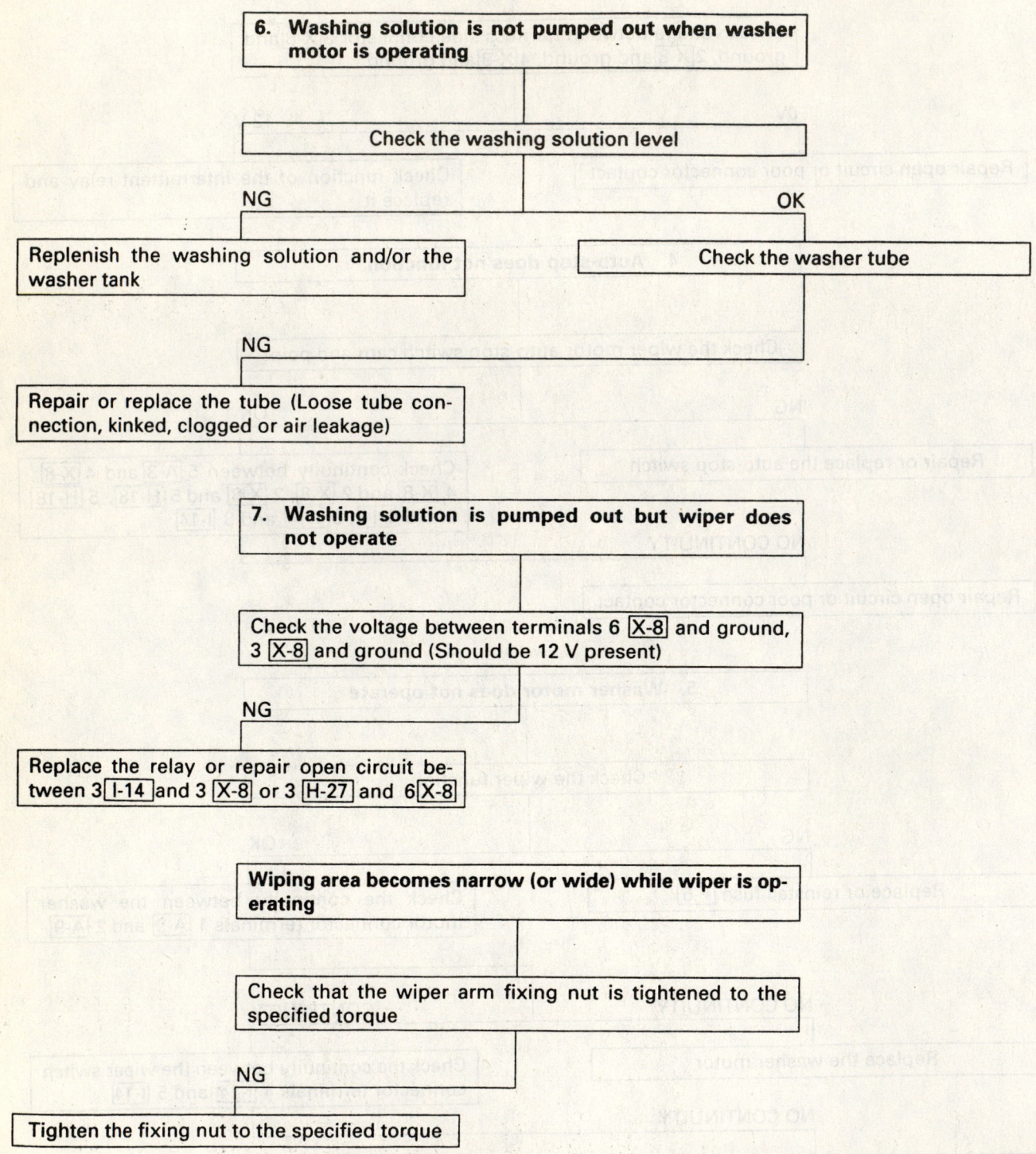

6. Washing solution is not pumped out when washer motor is operating

Check the washing solution level

NG   OK

Replenish the washing solution and/or the washer tank

Check the washer tube

NG

Repair or replace the tube (Loose tube connection, kinked, clogged or air leakage)

7. Washing solution is pumped out but wiper does not operate

Check the voltage between terminals 6 X-8 and ground, 3 X-8 and ground (Should be 12 V present)

NG

Replace the relay or repair open circuit between 3 I-14 and 3 X-8 or 3 H-27 and 6 X-8

Wiping area becomes narrow (or wide) while wiper is operating

Check that the wiper arm fixing nut is tightened to the specified torque

NG

Tighten the fixing nut to the specified torque

7921ZG72

Troubleshooting flowchart (cont'd)—Passport, Amigo and Rodeo models

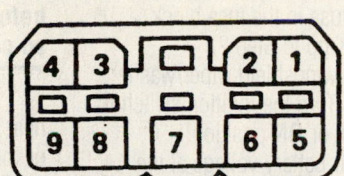

I-14

Switch side

(W/Intermittent)

Terminal / SW position	5	3	6	8	7	4	9	2
OFF			O—O					
INT	O—O		O—O					
↕	X———X							
							O—O	
LO	O———————————O							
HI	O———————————O							
WASHER	O———————————————O							

(W/O Intermittent)

Terminal / SW position	5	6	8	7	4	9	2
OFF		O—O					
		X—X					
LO	O—————O						
HI	O———————————O						
						O—O	
MIST	O—————O						
WASHER	O———————————O						

7921ZG73

Windshield wiper switch connector—Passport, Amigo and Rodeo models

Please visit our web site at www.chiltononline.com

Cherokee, Grand Cherokee, and Wrangler

GENERAL DESCRIPTION

Front Windshield Wiper System

The windshield wipers can be operated by the windshield wiper switch only when the ignition switch is in the **ACC** or **IGN** position. A circuit breaker, located in the fuse block, protects the circuitry of the wiper system and the vehicle.

The wiper motor has permanent magnet fields. The speeds are determined by current flow to the appropriate set of brushes.

The intermittent wipe system, in addition to low and high speed, has a delay mode. The delay mode has a range of 2–15 seconds. This is accomplished by a variable resistor in the wiper switch and is controlled electrically by a relay.

The wiper system completes the wipe cycle when the switch is turned **OFF**. The wiper blades park in the lowest portion of the wiping pattern.

Rear Windshield Wiper System

The rear wiper motor contains electronic controls to provide 3 operating modes. The first is an intermittent wipe with a 5–8 second delay between sweeps. The second is a constant wipe that operates in conjunction with a washer. And the third is a park mode that operates when the ignition or rear wiper switch is turned **OFF**.

The rear wiper switch is located in the instrument panel and is supplied current when the ignition switch is in the **ON** position. When the switch is placed in the intermittent wipe position it provides current to the rear wiper motor. When it is held in the wash/wipe position it provides current to both the motor and the rear washer pump. The switch is spring loaded in the wash/wipe position.

TESTING

Front Wiper System Tests

WRANGLER

> ※ **CAUTION**
>
> On vehicles equipped with an air bag, be sure to disarm the system before starting repairs. Failure to do so could result in personal injury

1. Check the fuse in the fuse block module, and if OK go to Step 2.

2. Unplug the windshield wiper/washer switch connector. Turn the ignition switch to the **ACCESSORY** or **ON** position.

   a. Check for battery voltage at the fused ignition switch output (run/acc) circuit cavity of the wiper/washer switch connector. If OK, go to Step 3. If not OK, repair the open circuit to the fuse block module as required.

3. If the vehicle is equipped with an intermittent wiper system and the problem being diagnosed involves only the pulse wipe, wipe-after-wash, or intermittent wipe models, go to Step 4. If not go to Step 5.

4. Turn the ignition switch to the **OFF** position. Check for continuity between the ground circuit cavity of the wiper/washer switch connector. There should be continuity. If OK, replace the faulty switch. If not OK, repair the circuit to ground as required.

5. Turn the ignition switch to the **OFF** position. Check for windshield wiper/washer switch continuity as described in this section. If OK, go to Step 6. If not OK, replace the faulty switch.

6. Unplug the wiper motor connector. Check for continuity between the ground circuit cavity in the body half of the wiper motor connector and a good ground. There should be continuity. If OK, go to Step 7. If not OK, repair the open circuit to ground as required.

7. Turn the ignition switch to the **ACCESSORY** or **ON** position.

   a. Check for battery voltage at the fused ignition switch output (run/acc) circuit cavity in the body half of the wiper motor connector and a good ground. If OK, go to Step 8. If not OK, repair the open circuit to the fuse block module as required.

8. With the ignition switch still in the **OFF** position, check the cavities for the wiper park switch sense, and the wiper switch low and high speed output circuits in the body half of the wiper motor connector for continuity and the cavities in the wiper/washer switch connector. In each case there should be continuity. If OK, replace the faulty wiper motor. If not OK, repair the open circuit as required

CHEROKEE

> ※ **CAUTION**
>
> On vehicles equipped with an air bag, be sure to disarm the system

before starting repairs. Failure to do so could result in personal injury

1. Remove the in-line circuit breaker near the fuse block module (LHD models), or the fuse from the fuse block module (RHD models), and turn the ignition switch to the **ACCESSORY** or **ON** position.

   a. Measure the voltage at the battery side of the circuit breaker or fuse. The meter should read battery voltage. If OK, go to Step 2. If not OK, repair the circuit. If not OK, repair the circuit from the ignition switch as required.

   b. Measure the voltage at the wiper system side of the circuit breaker or fuse. The meter should read battery voltage. If OK, go to Step 2. If not OK, replace the faulty circuit breaker or fuse.

2. Unplug the wiper motor side of the wiring harness connector (gray) from the intermittent wipe module. Turn the ignition switch to the **ACCESSORY** or **ON** position.

   a. Measure the voltage at the fused ignition switch output circuit cavity of the unplugged wiring connector. The meter should read battery voltage. If OK, go to Step 3. If not OK, repair the circuit as required.

   b. Turn the ignition switch to the **OFF** position. Measure the resistance between the ground circuit cavity of the unplugged wiring harness connector and a good ground. The meter should read zero ohms. If OK, go to Step 3. If not OK, repair the circuit to ground as required.

3. Leave the ignition switch to the **OFF** position. Back-probe the wiring harness connector at the wiper motor. Measure the resistance between the ground circuit cavity of the wiper motor connector and a good ground. The meter should read zero ohms. If OK, go to Step 4. If not OK, repair circuit to ground as required.

4. Replace the intermittent wipe module with a known good unit. Test the wiper system operation in all modes. If OK, replace the intermittent wipe module. If not OK, reinstall the original module and go to Step 5.

5. Test the multi-function switch, as outlined in the test below. If the switch test OK, go to Step 6. If not OK, replace the faulty switch and go to Step 7.

6. Turn the ignition switch to the **ACCESSORY** or **ON** position. Place the multi-function switch in the positions indicated in the test below, and back-probe the switch side of the wiring harness connector (black).

a. Measure the voltage at the wiper switch low speed output circuit cavity of the connector with the wiper switch in the **LOW** and **MIST** positions, and the washer switch depressed. The meter should read battery voltage. If OK, go to Step 2. If not OK, repair the open circuit, as required.

b. Measure the voltage at the wiper switch high speed output circuit cavity of the connector with the wiper switch in the **HIGH** position. The meter should read battery voltage. If OK, go to Step 3. If not OK, repair the open circuit, as required.

c. Measure the voltage at the wiper motor park signal circuit cavity of the connector with the wiper switch in the **LOW** or **HIGH** position, then move the switch to the **OFF** position. The meter should read battery voltage until the wipers park, and then read zero volts. If OK, go to Step 7. If not OK, repair the open circuit, as required and then go to Step 7.

7. To test the wiper motor, turn the ignition switch to the **ACCESSORY** or **ON**

position. Place the multi-function switch in the positions indicated in the test below, and back-probe the motor connector.

a. Measure the voltage at the fused ignition switch output circuit cavity of the connector with the wiper switch in the **LOW** position. The meter should read battery voltage. If OK, go to Step 2. If not OK, repair the open circuit, as required.

b. Measure the voltage at the wiper switch low speed output circuit cavity of the connector with the wiper switch in the **LOW** position. The meter should read battery voltage. If OK, but the wipers do not operate, replace the faulty wiper motor. If not OK, repair the open circuit, as required.

c. Measure the voltage at the wiper park switch sense circuit cavity of the connector with the wiper switch in the **HIGH** position. The meter should read battery voltage. If OK, but the wipers do not operate, replace the faulty wiper motor. If not OK, repair the open circuit, as required.

d. Measure the voltage at the wiper switch high speed output circuit cavity of

the connector with the wiper switch in the **LOW** or **HIGH** position, then move the switch to the **OFF** position. The meter should read battery voltage when the switched is turned to the **OFF** position, then zero volts after the wipers park. If battery voltage is present, but the wipers fail to park; or, if no battery voltage is present, replace the faulty wiper motor.

Wiper Switch Test

CHEROKEE

※ CAUTION

On vehicles equipped with an air bag, be sure to disarm the system before starting repairs. Failure to do so could result in personal injury

➡Perform the washer and wiper system test before testing the multi-function switch test.

1. Disconnect the multi-function switch connector.

2. Using an ohmmeter, perform the

MULTIFUNCTION SWITCH PINS

SWITCH POSITION	CONTINUITY BETWEEN
OFF	PIN 6 AND PIN 7
DELAY	PIN 8 AND PIN 9 PIN 2 AND PIN 4 PIN 1 AND PIN 2 PIN 1 AND PIN 4
LOW	PIN 4 AND PIN 6
HIGH	PIN 4 AND PIN 5
WASH	PIN 3 AND PIN 4

*RESISTANCE AT MAXIMUM DELAY POSITION SHOULD BE BETWEEN 270,000 OHMS AND 330,000 OHMS.

*RESISTANCE AT MINIMUM DELAY POSITION SHOULD BE ZERO WITH OHMMETER SET ON HIGH OHM SCALE.

7921ZGJ1

Multi-function switch continuity test—Cherokee

switch continuity test at the switch terminals as shown in the illustration.

3. If the switch fails in any of the continuity test, replace the faulty switch.

WRANGLER

✷✷ CAUTION

On vehicles equipped with an air bag, be sure to disarm the system before starting repairs. Failure to do so could result in personal injury

➡Perform the washer and wiper system test before testing the multi-function switch test.

1. Disconnect the negative battery cable.
2. Unplug the windshield wiper/washer switch connector.

3. Using an ohmmeter, perform the switch continuity test at the switch terminals as shown in the illustration.

4. If the switch fails in any of the continuity test, replace the faulty switch.

Wiper Motor Test

1. Turn the ignition switch to **ACC** or **ON**. Position the wiper switch and backprobe the motor connector as indicated.

   a. Place the wiper switch in any position, measure voltage at terminal **1** for Cherokee or terminal **B** for Wrangler. Meter should read battery voltage. If not, repair wiring from circuit breaker.

   b. Place wiper switch in **LOW**, measure voltage at terminal **5** for Cherokee or terminal **A** for Wrangler. Meter should read battery voltage. If ok, but wipers do

not operate, replace failed wiper motor. If not, repair wiring from switch or intermittent wiper module connector.

   c. Place wiper switch in **HIGH**, measure voltage at terminal **6** for Cherokee or terminal **H** for Wrangler. Meter should read battery voltage. If ok, but wipers do not operate, replace failed wiper motor. If not, repair wiring from switch or intermittent wiper module connector.

   d. Place wiper switch in **LOW** or **HIGH**, voltmeter connected to terminal **2** for Cherokee or terminal **D** for Wrangler. Turn wiper switch to **OFF** and observe meter. Meter should read battery voltage when switch goes to **OFF**, then zero volts after wipers park. If battery voltage is present, but wipers fail to park; or, if no battery voltage is present, replace failed wiper motor.

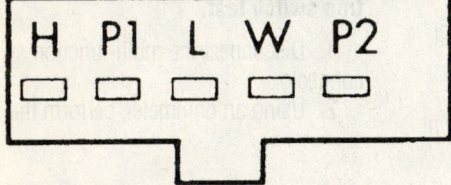

TWO SPEED WIPER
SWITCH PINS

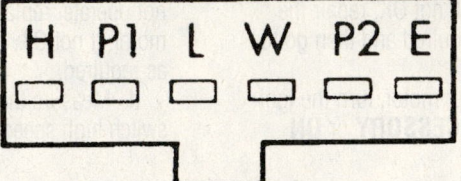

INTERMITTENT WIPER
SWITCH PINS

SWITCH POSITION	CONTINUITY BETWEEN
OFF	PIN P2 and PIN L
LOW	PIN P1 and PIN L
HIGH	PIN P1 and PIN H
WASH	PIN P1 and PIN W
INTERMITTENT	CANNOT BE CHECKED

Windshield wiper/washer switch continuity test—Wrangler

7921ZGJ2

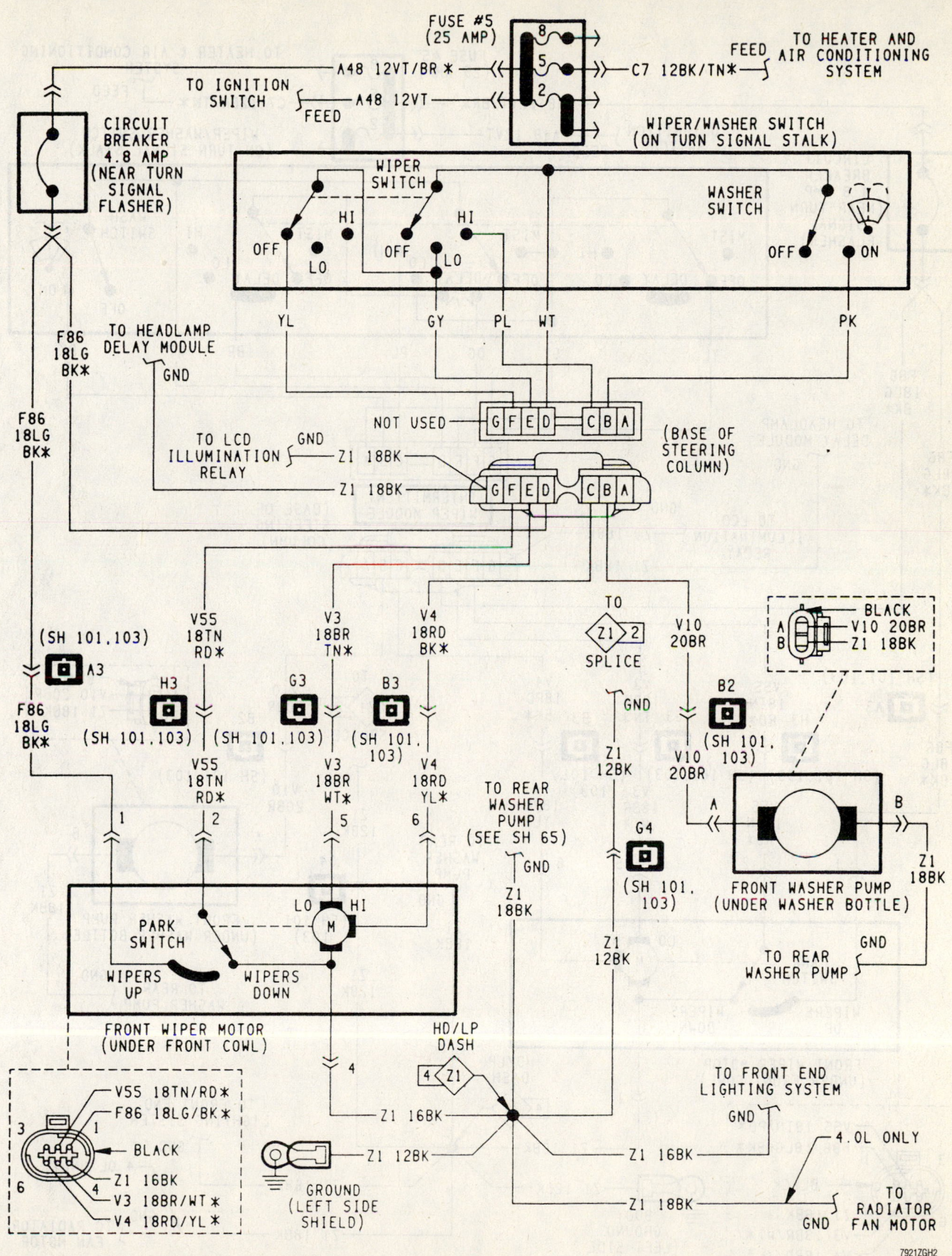

Wiper motor wiring schematic—Without Intermittent wiper circuit for Cherokee

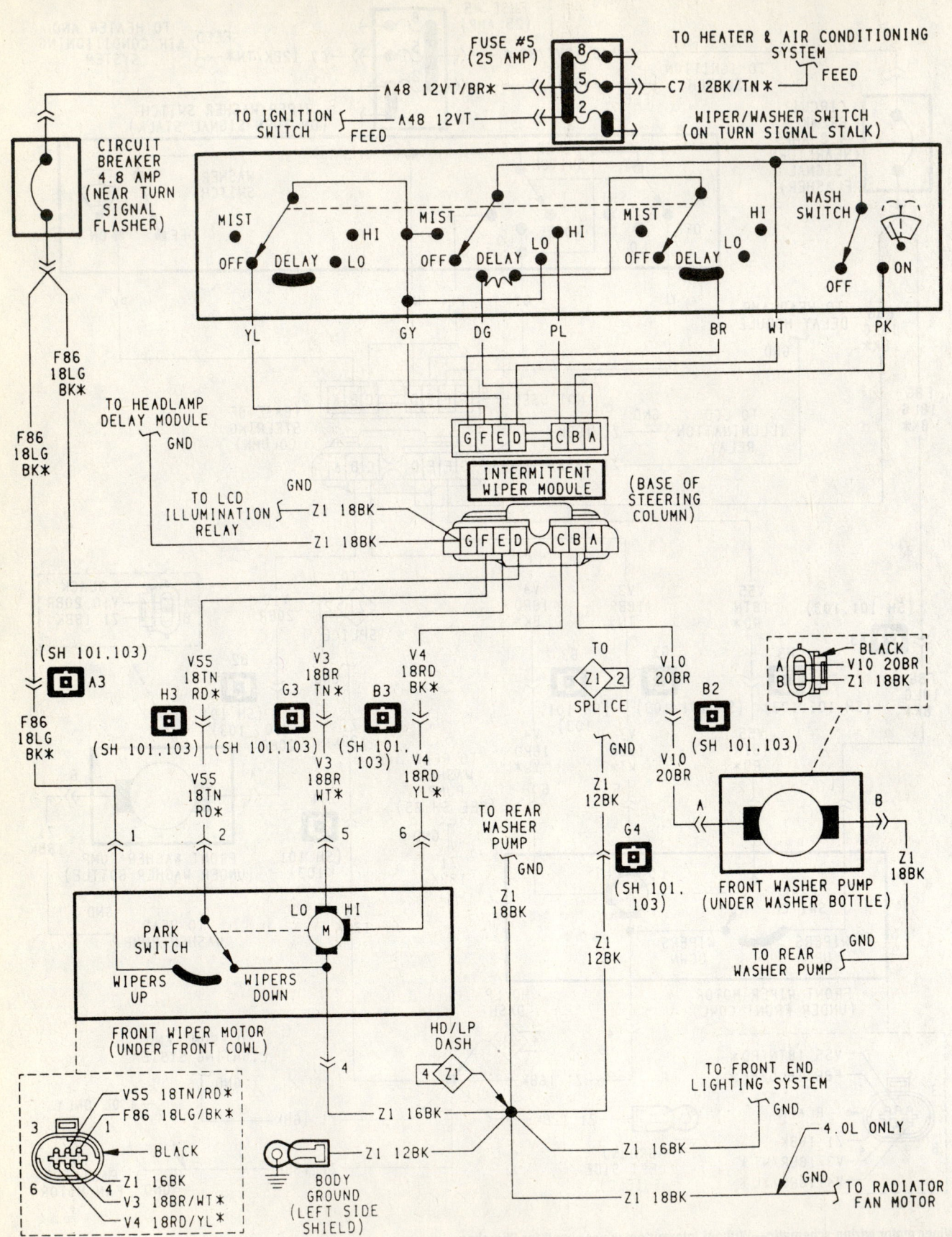

Wiper motor wiring schematic—With Intermittent wiper circuit for Cherokee

7921ZGH3

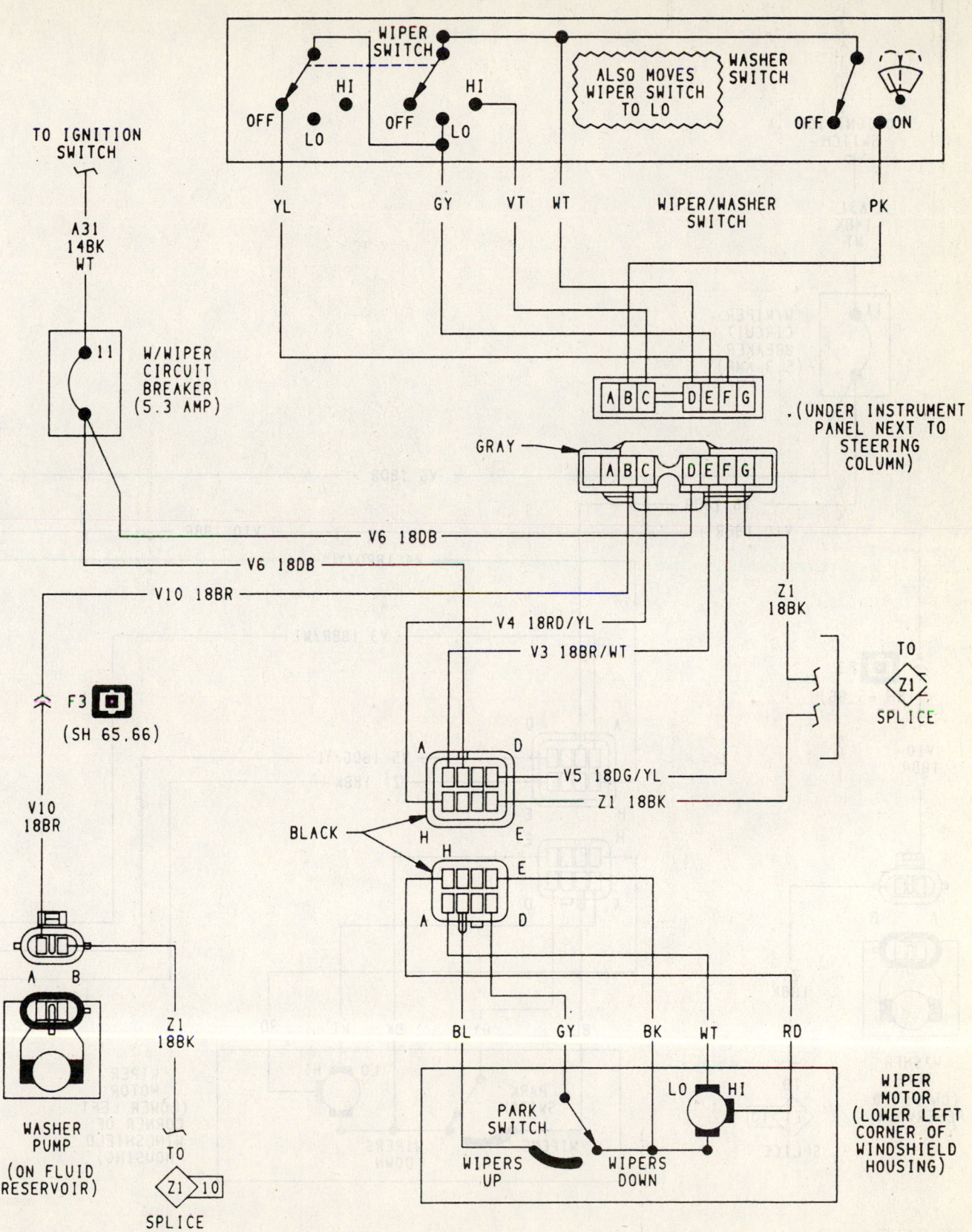

Wiper motor wiring schematic—Without Intermittent wiper circuit for Wrangler

7921ZGH6

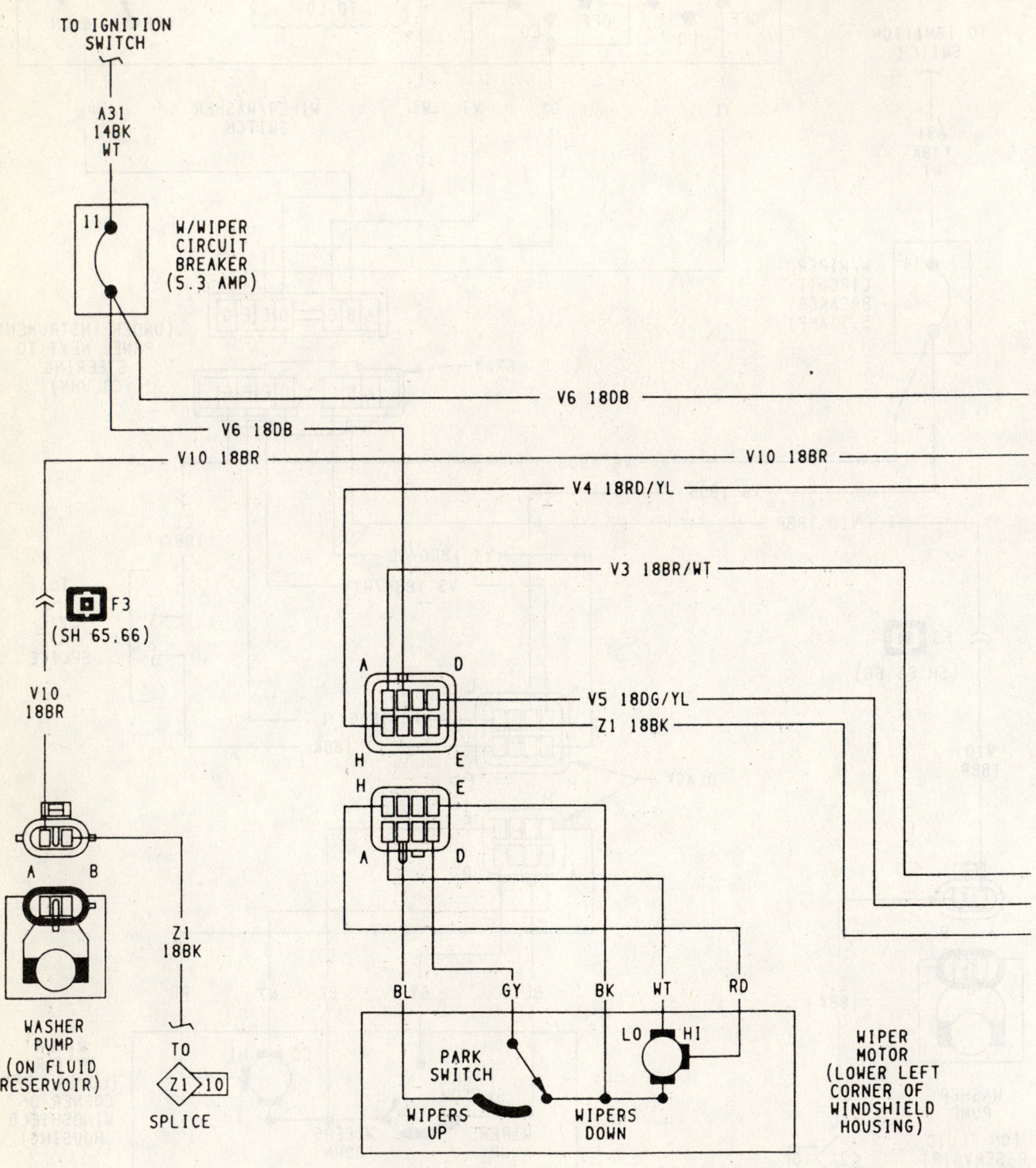

Wiper motor wiring schematic—With Intermittent wiper circuit for Wrangler

7921ZGH7

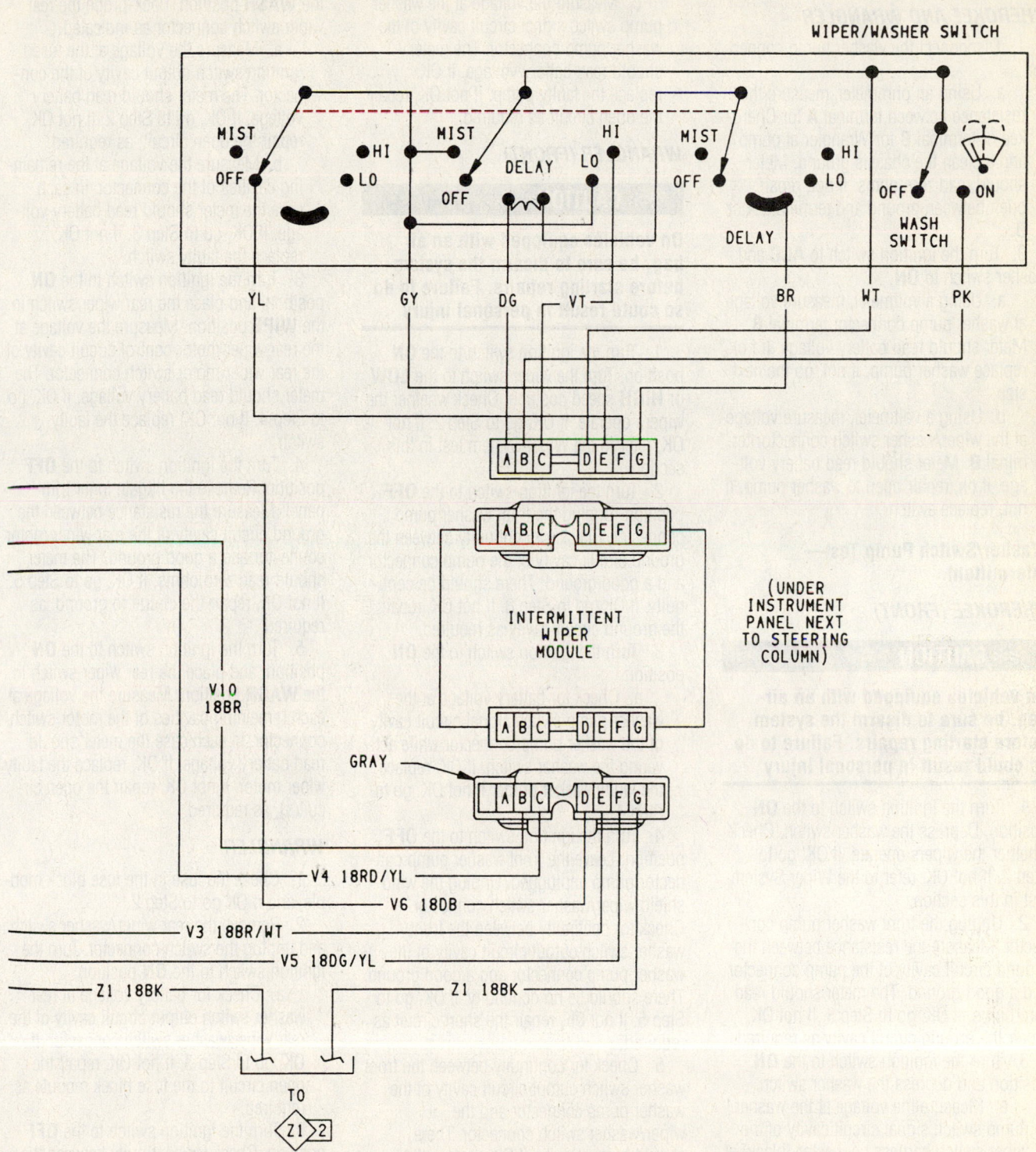

Wiper motor wiring schematic—With Intermittent wiper circuit for Wrangler, cont.

Refer to the model specific sections for driveline service procedures

Washer Switch/Pump Test—Non-Intermittent

CHEROKEE AND WRANGLER

1. Disconnect the washer pump connector.

   a. Using an ohmmeter, measure the resistance between terminal **A** for Cherokee or terminal **B** for Wrangler at pump and a clean the chassis ground. Meter should read zero ohms. If not, repair open between ground and terminals **A** or **B**.

2. Turn the ignition switch to **ACC** and washer switch to **ON**.

   a. Using a voltmeter, measure voltage at washer pump connector terminal **B**. Meter should read battery voltage. If f ok, replace washer pump. If not, go the next step.

   b. Using a voltmeter, measure voltage at the wiper/washer switch connector terminal **B**. Meter should read battery voltage. If ok, repair open to washer pump. If not, replace switch.

Washer/Switch Pump Test—Intermittent

CHEROKEE (FRONT)

⁂ CAUTION

On vehicles equipped with an air bag, be sure to disarm the system before starting repairs. Failure to do so could result in personal injury

1. Turn the ignition switch to the **ON** position. Depress the washer switch. Check whether the wipers operate. If OK, go to Step 2. If not OK, refer to the Wiper System test in this section.

2. Unplug the front washer pump connector. Measure the resistance between the ground circuit cavity of the pump connector and a good ground. The meter should read zero ohms. If OK, go to Step 3. If not OK, repair the ground circuit cavity as required.

3. Turn the ignition switch to the **ON** position and depress the washer switch.

   a. Measure the voltage at the washer pump switch signal circuit cavity of the wiper switch harness connector (black) at the intermittent wipe module. The meter should read battery voltage. If OK, go to Step 2. If not OK, repair the open circuit as required.

   b. Measure the voltage at the washer pump switch signal circuit cavity of the wiper motor harness connector (gray) at the intermittent wipe module. The meter should read battery voltage. If OK, go to

Step 3. If not OK, replace the faulty module.

   c. Measure the voltage at the washer pump switch signal circuit cavity of the washer pump connector. The meter should read battery voltage. If OK, replace the faulty pump. If not OK, repair the open circuit as required.

WRANGLER (FRONT)

⁂ CAUTION

On vehicles equipped with an air bag, be sure to disarm the system before starting repairs. Failure to do so could result in personal injury

1. Turn the ignition switch to the **ON** position. Turn the wiper switch to the **LOW** or **HIGH** speed position. Check whether the wipers operate. If OK, go to Step 2. If not OK, refer to the Wiper System test in this section.

2. Turn the ignition switch to the **OFF** position. Unplug the front washer pump connector. Check for continuity between the ground circuit cavity of the pump connector and a good ground. There should be continuity. If OK, go to Step 3. If not OK, repair the ground circuit cavity as required.

3. Turn the ignition switch to the **ON** position.

   a. Check for battery voltage at the washer pump switch signal circuit cavity of the washer pump connector while activating the washer switch. If OK, replace the faulty washer pump. If not OK, go to Step 4.

4. Turn the ignition switch to the **OFF** position. Leave the front washer pump connector pump unplugged. Unplug the windshield wiper/washer switch connector. Check for continuity between the front washer switch output circuit cavity of the washer pump connector and a good ground. There should be no continuity. If OK, go to Step 5. If not OK, repair the short circuit as required.

5. Check for continuity between the front washer switch output circuit cavity of the washer pump connector and the wiper/washer switch connector. There should be continuity. If OK, replace the faulty switch. If not OK, repair the open circuit as required.

Rear Wiper System Test

CHEROKEE

1. Check the fuse in the fuse block module. If OK, go to Step 2. I not OK, replace the faulty fuse.

2. Turn the ignition switch to the **ON** position, and place the rear wiper switch in the **WASH** position. Back-probe the rear wiper switch connector as indicated.

   a. Measure the voltage at the fused ignition switch output cavity of the connector. The meter should read battery voltage. If OK, go to Step 2. If not OK, repair the open circuit, as required.

   b. Measure the voltage at the remaining cavities of the connector. In each case the meter should read battery voltage. If OK, go to Step 3. If not OK, replace the faulty switch.

3. Turn the ignition switch to the **ON** position, and place the rear wiper switch in the **WIPE** position. Measure the voltage at the rear wiper motor control circuit cavity of the rear wiper motor switch connector. The meter should read battery voltage. If OK, go to Step 4. If not OK, replace the faulty switch.

4. Turn the ignition switch to the **OFF** position. Remove the liftgate inner trim panel. Measure the resistance between the ground circuit cavity of the rear wiper motor connector and a good ground. The meter should read zero ohms. If OK, go to Step 5. If not OK, repair the circuit to ground, as required.

5. Turn the ignition switch to the **ON** position, and place the rear wiper switch in the **WASH** position. Measure the voltage at each remaining cavities of the motor switch connector. In each case the meter should read battery voltage. If OK, replace the faulty wiper motor. If not OK, repair the open circuit(s), as required.

WRANGLER

1. Check the fuse in the fuse block module, and if OK go to Step 2.

2. Remove the rear wiper/washer switch and unplug the switch connector. Turn the ignition switch to the **ON** position.

   a. Check for battery voltage at rear washer switch output circuit cavity of the rear wiper/washer switch connector. If OK, go to Step 3. If not OK, repair the open circuit to the fuse block module as required.

3. Turn the ignition switch to the **OFF** position. Check for continuity between the ground circuit cavity of the rear wiper/washer switch connector. There should be continuity. If OK, go to Step 4. If not OK, repair the circuit to ground as required.

4. Check for rear wiper/washer switch continuity as described in this section. If OK, go to Step 5. If not OK, replace the faulty switch.

5. Remove the rear wiper motor cover and unplug the wiper motor connector. Turn the ignition switch to the **ON** position. Check for continuity between the fused ignition switch output (run) circuit cavity of the rear wiper motor connector. If OK, go to Step 6. If not OK, repair the open circuit to the fuse block module as required.

6. Turn the ignition switch to the **OFF** position. Check for continuity between the ground circuit cavity of the rear wiper motor connector and a good ground. There should be continuity. If OK, go to Step 7. If not OK, repair the open circuit to ground as required.

7. With the ignition switch still in the **OFF** position, and the rear wiper switch still unplugged, check for continuity between the rear wiper motor control circuit cavity of the rear wiper motor connector and a good ground. There should be no continuity. If OK, go to Step 8. If not OK, repair the short circuit as required

8. Check for continuity between the rear wiper motor control circuit cavity of the rear wiper motor connector and the rear wiper switch connector. There should be continuity. If OK, replace the faulty rear wiper motor. If not OK, repair the open circuit as required

Rear Wiper Washer Switch Test

CHEROKEE

➡**Perform the washer and wiper system test before testing the rear wiper/washer switch test.**

SWITCH TEST		
SWITCH POSITION	TERMINALS	ZERO OHMS
OFF (NORMAL)	B AND A	NO
	B AND C	NO
WIPE	B AND C	YES
	B AND A	NO
WASH	A AND B	YES
	B AND C	YES

7921ZGJ4

Rear wiper and washer switch continuity test—Cherokee

1. Remove the rear wiper and washer switch.

2. Using an ohmmeter, perform the switch continuity test at the switch terminals as shown in the illustration.

3. If the switch fails in any of the continuity test, replace the faulty switch.

WRANGLER

➡**Perform the washer and wiper system test before testing the rear wiper/washer switch test.**

1. Remove the rear wiper/washer switch.

2. Using an ohmmeter, perform the switch continuity test at the switch terminals as shown in the illustration.

3. If the switch fails in any of the continuity test, replace the faulty switch.

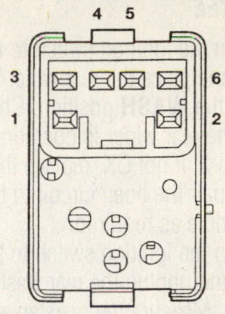

SWITCH POSITION	CONTINUITY BETWEEN
OFF	1 AND 4
WIPE	4 AND 5
WASH	2 AND 5, 4 AND 5
ILLUMINATION LAMP	1 AND 3

7921ZGJ5

Rear wiper/washer switch continuity test—Wrangler

Rear Wiper/Washer System Test

WRANGLER

1. Turn the ignition switch to the **ON** position and place the rear wiper/washer switch in the **WIPE** position. Check whether the rear wiper is operating. If OK, go to Step 2. If not OK, refer to the Rear Wiper test in this section

2. Turn the ignition switch to the **OFF** position and unplug the rear washer pump connector. Check for continuity between the ground circuit cavity of the pump connector and a good ground. There should be continuity. If OK, go to Step 3. If not OK, repair the ground circuit cavity as required.

3. Turn the ignition switch to the **ON** position and place the rear wiper/washer switch in the **WASH** position. Measure the voltage at the rear washer pump motor control circuit cavity of the rear washer pump connector. If OK, replace the faulty pump. If not OK, go to Step 4.

4. Turn the ignition switch to the **OFF** position. Leave the rear washer pump connector unplugged. Remove the rear wiper/washer switch and unplug the wiring connector. Check for continuity between the rear washer motor control circuit cavity of the rear washer pump connector and a good ground. There should be no continuity. If OK, go to Step 5. If not OK, repair the short circuit as required.

5. Check for continuity between the rear washer motor control circuit cavity of the rear washer pump connector and the rear wiper/washer switch connector. There should be continuity. If OK, replace the faulty switch. If not OK, repair the open circuit as required.

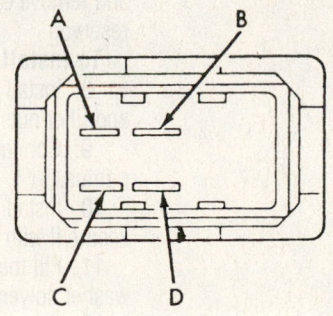

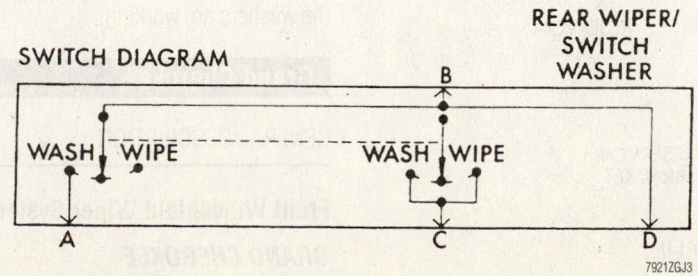

Rear wiper and washer switch circuit—Cherokee

7921ZGJ3

CHEROKEE

1. Turn the ignition switch to the **ON** position and place the rear wiper/washer switch in the **WASH** position. Check whether the rear wiper is operating. If OK, go to Step 2. If not OK, replace the faulty fuse or repair the open circuit to the fuse block module as required.

2. Turn the ignition switch to the **OFF** position and unplug the rear washer pump connector. Measure the resistance between the ground circuit cavity of the pump connector and a good ground. The meter should read zero ohms. If OK, go to Step 3. If not OK, repair the ground circuit cavity as required.

3. Turn the ignition switch to the **ON** position and place the rear wiper/washer switch in the **WASH** position. Measure the voltage at the rear washer pump motor control circuit cavity of the rear washer pump connector. If OK, replace the faulty pump. If not OK, go to Step 4.

4. Remove the rear wiper/washer switch and reconnect it below the instrument panel. Back-probe the switch connector with the ignition switch in the **ON** position.

   a. Measure the voltage at the fused ignition switch output circuit cavity of the switch connector. The meter should read

battery voltage. If OK, go to Step 2. If not OK, repair the open circuit, as required.

   b. Measure the voltage at the rear washer pump motor control circuit cavity of the switch connector; while holding the switch in the **WASH** position. The meter should read battery voltage. If OK, repair the open circuit to the pump as required. If not OK, replace the faulty switch.

REMOVAL & INSTALLATION

Front Washer Reservoir and Pump

CHEROKEE AND WRANGLER

1. Disconnect the negative battery cable.

2. Remove the 2 upper washer reservoir attaching screws.

3. Remove the 1 lower washer reservoir attaching screw.

4. Have a clean container close by to drain the washer solvent into.

5. Disconnect the hoses from the washer pumps and remove the reservoir.

6. Drain the washer reservoir into the clean container.

7. Using a deep socket, remove the filter nuts from the bottom inside the reservoir

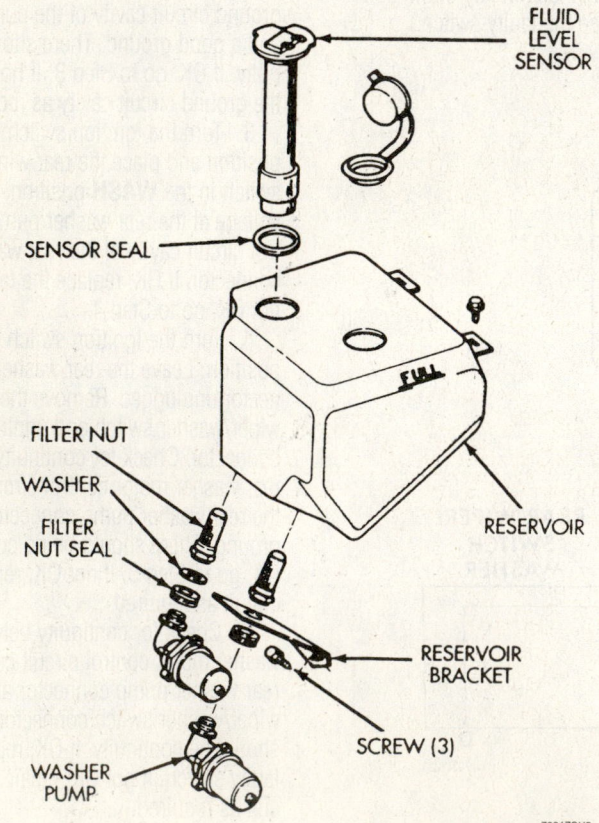

Typical washer reservoir and pumps—Cherokee

and remove each pump and filter from the reservoir.

To install:

8. Install the pumps, seals. washers and filter nuts to the reservoir.

9. Connect the hoses to the washer pumps.

10. Install the washer reservoir and secure it with 3 attaching screws.

11. Fill the washer reservoir with clean washer solvent.

12. Connect the negative battery cable.

13. Operate the washer system to insure the washers are working.

Rear Washer Reservoir and Pump

CHEROKEE AND WRANGLER

The rear washer reservoir and pump is located in the engine compartment next to the front washer reservoir. Pump replacement is virtually the same.

1. Disconnect the negative battery cable.

2. Remove the 2 upper washer reservoir attaching screws.

3. Remove the 1 lower washer reservoir attaching screw.

4. Have a clean container close by to drain the washer solvent into.

5. Disconnect the hoses from the washer pumps and remove the reservoir.

6. Drain the washer reservoir into the clean container.

7. Using a deep socket, remove the filter nuts from the bottom inside the reservoir and remove each pump and filter from the reservoir.

To install:

8. Install the pumps, seals. washers and filter nuts to the reservoir.

9. Connect the hoses to the washer pumps.

10. Install the washer reservoir and secure it with 3 attaching screws.

11. Fill the washer reservoir with clean washer solvent.

12. Connect the negative battery cable.

13. Operate the washer system to insure the washers are working.

Grand Cherokee

GENERAL DESCRIPTION

Front Windshield Wiper System

GRAND CHEROKEE

An Intermittent windshield wiper system is standard equipment. This system incorporates the use of 2 wiper speeds and an intermittent wipe mode. The intermittent wipe mode is provided by the Body Control Module (BCM) and an intermittent wipe relay.

The intermittent wipe mode delay times are speed sensitive. Above 10 miles per hour the delay is driver adjustable

from ½–18 seconds. Below 10 miles per hour the BCM doubles the delay time, or provides delays of about 1–36 seconds.

Vehicles equipped with optional automatic headlamp system have a programmable feature in the BCM that will energize the headlamps automatically whenever the windshield wipers are turned ON. The windshield wipers will operate only when the ignition switch is in the **ACC** or **IGN** positions. A circuit breaker, located in the fuse block, protects the circuitry of the wiper system.

Rear Windshield Wiper System

GRAND CHEROKEE

The rear wiper motor contains electronic controls to provide 4 operating modes. The first is an intermittent wipe with a 5–8 second delay between sweeps. The second is a continuous wipe. The third is a park mode that operates when the ignition or rear wiper switch is turned **OFF**. And the fourth mode is a rear washer mode that provides 2–4 wiper sweeps before returning to 2 of the 3 previously selected operating modes.

The rear wiper switch is located in the instrument panel and is supplied current when the ignition switch is in the **ACC** or **ON** position. When the switch is held in the wash/wipe position it provides current to both the motor and the rear washer pump. The switch is spring loaded in the wash/wipe position. A fuse in the fuse block module protects the circuitry of both the liftgate wiper and washer systems.

TESTING

Front Wiper System Diagnosis

GRAND CHEROKEE

If the problem being diagnosed involves only the pulse wipe or wipe after wash modes, see Washer System Diagnosis.

✳✳ CAUTION

Vehicles equipped with airbags, the passive restraint system must be properly disarmed before attempting removal of the steering wheel, steer-

ing column or instrument panel. Failure to take proper precautions could result in accidental airbag deployment and possible personal injury.

1. Remove the circuit breaker from the junction block and turn the ignition switch to the **ACC** or **ON** position. Measure the voltage at the battery side of the circuit breaker. The meter should read battery voltage. If ok, reinstall the circuit breaker and go to the next step. If not, repair the circuit from the ignition switch.

2. Measure the voltage at the wiper system side of the circuit breaker. The meter should read battery voltage. If ok, go the next step. If not ok, replace the faulty circuit breaker.

3. Unplug the multi-function switch wire harness connector. Turn the ignition switch to the **ON** position. Measure the voltage at the fused ignition switch output (F86) circuit cavity of the multi-function switch wire harness connector. The meter should read battery voltage. If ok, go to the next step. If not, repair open circuit.

4. If the problem being diagnosed involves only the intermittent wipe feature, go to the next step. If the problem being diagnosed involves all wiper modes, or only the **LOW** or **HIGH** speed modes go to step 7.

5. Turn the ignition switch to the **OFF** position. Disconnect and isolate the battery negative cable. Unplug the white 24-way Body Control Module (BCM) wire harness connector. Check for continuity between the wiper switch mode sense cavities of the multi-function switch wire harness connector and the BCM white 24-way wire harness connector. There should be continuity. If ok, go to the next step. If not, repair the open circuit.

6. Unplug the black 24-way BCM wire harness connector. Check for continuity between the windshield wiper switch signal cavities of the multi-function switch wire harness connector and the BCM black 24-way wire harness connector. There should be continuity. If ok, see Intermittent Wipe Relay Testing.

7. Turn the ignition switch to the **OFF** position. Check for continuity between the 2 wiper switch low speed output cavities of the multi-function switch wire harness connector. There should be continuity. If ok, go to the next step. If not, repair open circuit.

8. Test the multi-function switch, as

described. If the switch tests ok, plug in the switch wire harness connector and go the next step. If not ok, replace the faulty switch and test the wiper system operation. If still not ok, go to next step.

9. Measure the voltage at the wiper switch low speed output circuit cavity of the wiper motor wire harness connector and a good ground. The meter should read zero ohms. If ok, go to the next step. If not, repair the circuit to ground.

10. Turn the ignition switch to the **ACC** or **ON** position. Place the multi-function switch in the positions indicated in the tests below and check for voltage at the wiper motor harness connector.

   a. Measure the voltage at the fused ignition switch output circuit cavity of the wiper motor wire harness connector with the wiper switch in any position. The meter should read battery voltage. If ok, go to the next step. If not ok, repair the open circuit.

   b. Measure the voltage at the wiper switch low speed output circuit cavity of the wiper motor wire harness connector with switch in the **LOW** position. The meter should read battery voltage. If ok, got the next step. If not ok, repair the open circuit.

   c. Measure the voltage at the wiper switch high speed circuit cavity of the wiper motor wiper harness connector with the wiper switch in the **HIGH** position. The meter should read battery voltage. If ok, go to the next step. If not, repair open circuit.

   d. Measure the voltage at the wiper park switch sense circuit cavity of the wiper motor wire harness connector with the wiper switch in the **LOW** or **HIGH** position, then move the switch to the **OFF** position. The meter should switch between battery voltage and zero volts while the wipers are cycling. The meter should read battery voltage when the switch is moved to the **OFF** position until the wipers park and then read a steady zero volts. If not, replace the faulty wiper motor.

Rear Wiper System Test

GRAND CHEROKEE

1. Remove and inspect the fuse in the fuse block module. If checks good, move the next step. If blown, replace it.

2. Turn the ignition switch to the **ON** position. Check for battery voltage at the

fused ignition switch output cavity of the rear wiper switch wire harness connector. If ok, go to the next step. If not, repair the circuit.

3. Test the rear wiper switch, as described. If ok, go to the next step. If not, replace the faulty switch.

4. Turn the ignition switch to the **OFF** position. Remove the liftgate inner trim panel Measure the resistance between the ground circuit cavity of the rear wiper motor wire harness connector and a good ground. The meter should read zero ohms. If ok, go to the next step. If not, repair the circuit to ground.

5. Check for continuity between the liftgate ajar switch sense cavity of the wiper motor wire harness connector and a good ground. There should be continuity with the liftgate and liftgate glass closed. If ok, go to the next step. If not ok, repair the liftgate and liftgate glass ajar circuit or switch as required.

6. Turn the ignition switch to the **ON** position and place the rear wiper switch in the **WIPE** position. Measure the voltage at the rear wiper motor control circuit cavity of the rear wiper motor wire harness connector. Repeat the test for the rear wiper motor control (intermittent) circuit cavity with the rear wiper switch in the Intermittent position, then at the rear washer motor control circuit cavity with the rear wiper switch in the **WASH** position. In each case, the meter should read battery voltage. If ok, replace the faulty rear wiper motor. If not ok, repair the open circuit(s).

Front Washer System Test

GRAND CHEROKEE

The diagnosis below addresses an inoperative washer pump or wipe after wash feature. If the washer pump operates, but no washer fluid is emitted from the nozzles, check the fluid level in the reservoir. If weather conditions are freezing, check for ice or other foreign material in the reservoir and for pinched, disconnected, broken, or incorrectly routed washer system plumbing.

> ❇❇ **CAUTION**

Vehicles equipped with airbags, the passive restraint system must be properly disarmed before attempting removal of the steering wheel, steering column or instrument panel. Failure to take proper precautions could result in accidental airbag deployment and possible personal injury.

1. Turn the ignition switch to the **ON** position. Turn the wipers switch to the **LOW** or **HIGH** speed position. Check whether the wipers operate. If ok, go to the next step. If not, see Wiper System Diagnosis.

2. Turn the wiper switch to the **OFF** position. Depress the washer switch for less than ½ second. The wipers should operate for 1 sweep cycle and then park. Depress the washer switch for more than ½ second. The washer pump should operate and the wipers should operate for 2 sweep cycles after the switch is released before they park. If the wipers are ok, but the washers are not, go to the next step. If the washers are ok, but the wipers are not go to step 5.

3. Turn the ignition switch to the **OFF** position. Unplug the front washer pump wire harness connector. Measure the resistance between the ground circuit cavity of the front washer pump wire harness connector and a good ground. The meter should read zero ohms. If ok, go to the next step . If not, repair the ground circuit.

4. Turn the ignition switch to the **ON** position. Depress the washer switch. Measure the voltage at the washer switch output circuit cavity of the front washer pump wire harness connector. The meter should read battery voltage. If ok, replace the faulty pump. If not, repair open circuit.

5. Disconnect and isolate the battery negative cable. Unplug the white 24-way wire harness connector from the Body Control Module (BCM). Connect the battery negative cable. Turn the ignition switch to the **ON** position. Depress the washer switch. Check for battery voltage at the washer switch output circuit cavity of the white 24-way BCM wire harness connector. If ok, see the Intermittent Wipe Relay Testing. If not ok, repair open circuit.

Rear Washer System Test

GRAND CHEROKEE

The diagnosis below addresses an inoperative washer pump or wipe after wash feature. If the washer pump operates, but no washer fluid is emitted from the nozzles, check the fluid level in the reservoir. If weather conditions are freezing, check for ice or other foreign material in the reservoir and for pinched, disconnected, broken, or incorrectly routed washer system plumbing.

> ❇❇ **CAUTION**

Vehicles equipped with airbags, the passive restraint system must be properly disarmed before attempting removal of the steering wheel, steer-

ing column or instrument panel. Failure to take proper precautions could result in accidental airbag deployment and possible personal injury.

1. Turn the ignition switch to the **ON** position. Place the rear wipe/washer switch in the **WIPE** position. Check whether rear wiper is operating. If ok, go to the next step. If not, see Wiper System Diagnosis.

2. Turn the wiper switch to the **OFF** position and unplug the rear washer pump wire harness connector. Measure the resistance between the ground circuit cavity of the rear washer pump wire harness connector and a good ground. The meter should read zero ohms. If ok, go to the next step . If not, repair the ground circuit.

3. Turn the ignition switch to the **ON** position. Depress the rear washer switch. Measure the voltage at rear washer motor control circuit cavity of the rear washer pump wire harness connector. The meter should read battery voltage. If ok, replace the faulty pump. If not, repair the open circuit.

Front Wiper Switch Test

GRAND CHEROKEE

The front wiper switch is a multi-function switch lever. Before testing this switch perform Wiper System Diagnosis first.

1. Unplug the multi-function switch wire harness connector.

2. Using and ohmmeter, perform switch continuity checks at the switch terminals as shown in the Multi-function Switch Continuity Chart.

3. If the switch fails any of the continuity checks, replace faulty switch.

Rear Wiper Switch Test

GRAND CHEROKEE

The rear wiper switch is a single 2 function wiper switch that is a part of the inboard switch pod unit. It is located on the instrument panel just inboard of the steering column. Before testing this switch perform Wiper System Diagnosis first.

1. Remove the rear wiper/washer switch.

2. Using and ohmmeter, check the switch continuity at the switch terminals as follows.

a. With the switch in the **OFF** position, there should be no continuity between any 2 switch terminals.

b. With the switch knob depressed in the **WASH** position, there should be continuity between the fused ignition switch output circuit and the rear washer motor control circuit terminals.

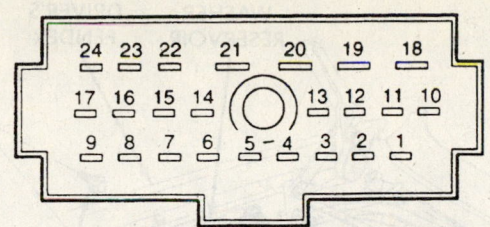

MULTIFUNCTION SWITCH PINS

SWITCH POSITION	CONTINUITY BETWEEN
OFF	PIN 6 AND PIN 7
DELAY	PIN 8 AND PIN 9 PIN 2 AND PIN 4 PIN 1 AND PIN 2 PIN 1 AND PIN 4
LOW	PIN 4 AND PIN 6
HIGH	PIN 4 AND PIN 5
WASH	PIN 3 AND PIN 4

*RESISTANCE AT MAXIMUM DELAY POSITION SHOULD BE BETWEEN 210,000 OHMS ABD 390,000 OHMS.

*RESISTANCE AT MINIMUM DELAY POSITION SHOULD BE ZERO WITH OHMMETER SET ON HIGH OHM SCALE.

7921ZGI8

Multi-function Continuity Chart—Grand Cherokee

c. With the switch in the Intermittent position, there should be continuity between the fused ignition switch output circuit and the rear wiper motor control (intermittent) circuit terminals.

d. With the switch in the **ON** position, there should be continuity between the fused ignition switch output circuit and the rear wiper motor control circuit terminals.

e. If the switch fails any of the continuity checks, replace the faulty switch.

Intermittent Wipe Relay Test

GRAND CHEROKEE

The intermittent wipe relay is located in the Power Distribution Center (PDC) in the engine compartment. Refer to the PDC label for intermittent wipe relay identification and location.

1. Remove the intermittent wipe relay from the PDC.

2. A relay in the de-energized position should have continuity between terminals 87A and 30. If ok, go the next step. If not, replace the faulty relay.

3. Resistance between terminals 85 and 86 (electromagnet) should be 75 plus or minus 5 ohms. If ok, go to the next step. If not, replace faulty relay.

4. Connect a battery terminal to terminal 85 and 86. There should now be continuity between terminals 87A and 30. If ok, see Relay Test. If not, replace faulty relay.

Relay Test

GRAND CHEROKEE

1. The relay common feed terminal cavity (30) is connected to the wiper (multi-function) switch. There should be continuity between the cavity for relay terminal 30 and the 2 fused ignition switch output (V6) circuit cavities of the multi-function switch connector at all times. If ok, go to the next step. If not, repair the open circuit(s) to the multi-function switch.

2. The relay normally closed terminal (87A) is connected to terminal 30 in the de-energized position. There should be continuity between the cavity for relay terminal 87A and wiper park switch sense circuit cavities of the wiper motor wire harness connector and the white 24-way Body Control Module (BCM) wire harness connector at all times. If ok, go to the next step. If not, repair the open circuit(s) to the wiper motor and BCM as required.

3. The relay normally open terminal (87) is connected to the common feed terminal (30) in the energized position. There should be battery voltage at the cavity for relay terminal 87 with the ignition switch in the **ON** or **ACC** positions. If ok, go to the next step. If not, repair the open circuit to the ignition switch.

4. The coil ground terminal (85) is connected to the electromagnet in the relay. It is grounded by the BCM to energize the relay and cycle the wiper motor. Check for continuity between the cavity for relay terminal

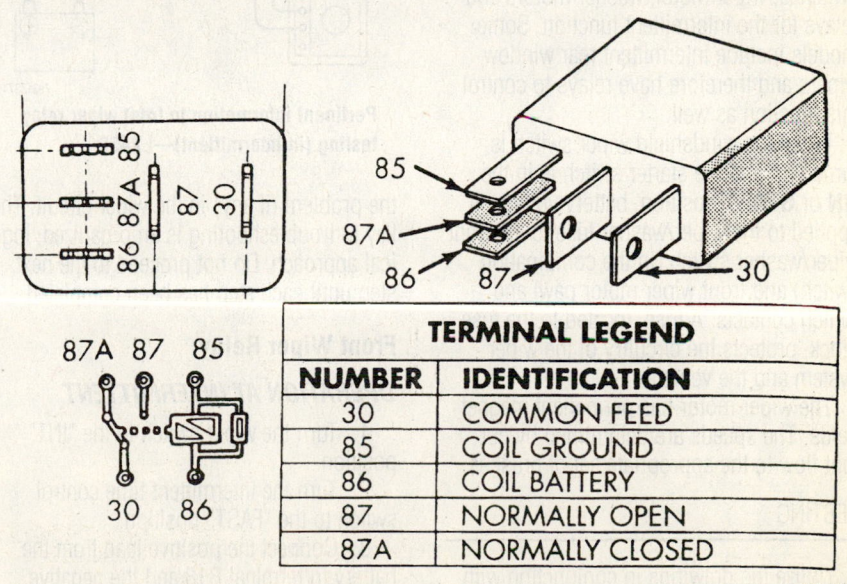

TERMINAL LEGEND

NUMBER	IDENTIFICATION
30	COMMON FEED
85	COIL GROUND
86	COIL BATTERY
87	NORMALLY OPEN
87A	NORMALLY CLOSED

7921ZGI9

Intermittent Wipe Relay Terminal Identification—Grand Cherokee

Refer to the model specific sections for driveline service procedures

(85) and the intermittent wiper relay control circuit cavity of the white 24-way BCM wire harness connector. There should be continuity. If ok, there may be a problem in the BCM or circuit to it.

REMOVAL & INSTALLATION

Front Washer Reservoir and Pump

GRAND CHEROKEE

1. Disconnect the negative battery cable.
2. Remove the 2 upper washer reservoir attaching screws.
3. Remove the 1 lower washer reservoir attaching screw.
4. Have a clean container close by to drain the washer solvent into.
5. Disconnect the hoses from the washer pumps and remove the reservoir.
6. Drain the washer reservoir into the clean container.
7. Using a deep socket, remove the filter nuts from the bottom inside the reservoir and remove each pump and filter from the reservoir.

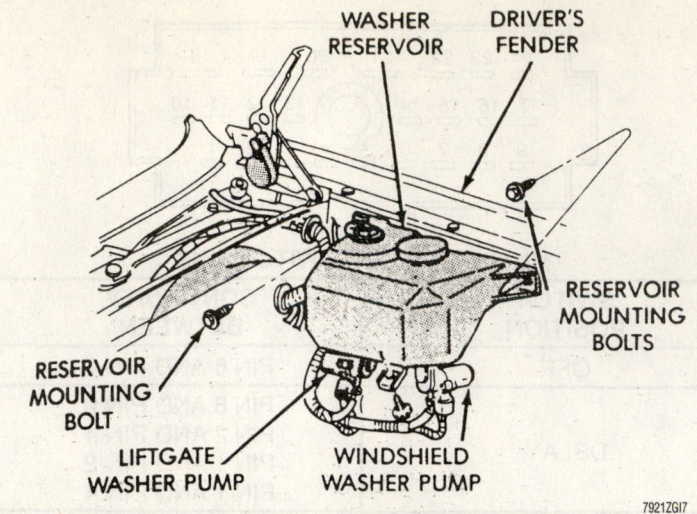

Removal and installation of the washer reservoir/pump assembly—Grand Cherokee

To install:
8. Install the pumps, seals, washers and filter nuts to the reservoir.
9. Connect the hoses to the washer pumps.
10. Install the washer reservoir and secure it with 3 attaching screws.
11. Fill the washer reservoir with clean washer solvent.
12. Connect the negative battery cable.
13. Operate the washer system to insure the washers are working.

LEXUS

LX450/470

GENERAL DESCRIPTION

The windshield wiper circuit consists of the ignition switch, wiper and washer switches, wiper motor, washer motors and relays for the intermittent function. Some models include intermittent rear window wipers and therefore have relays to control this function as well.

When the windshield wiper switch is turned on and the starter switch is in the **ON** or **START** position, battery voltage is applied to the wiper/washer fuse to the front wiper/washer switch (in the combination switch) and front wiper motor pawl and switch contacts. A fuse, located in the fuse block, protects the circuitry of the wiper system and the vehicle.

The wiper motor has permanent magnet fields. The speeds are determined by current flow to the appropriate set of brushes.

TESTING

Utilize the drawings in conjunction with the circuit wiring diagram and the individual tests in this section to systematically locate

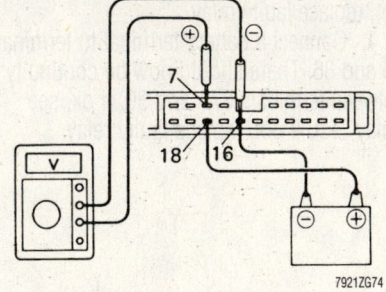

Pertinent information to front wiper relay testing (in intermittent)—LX450

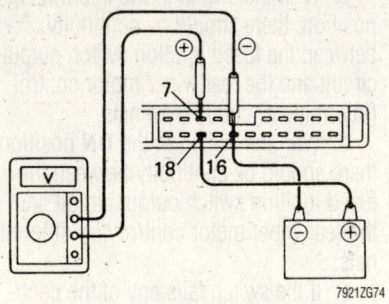

Pertinent information to front wiper relay testing (in intermittent)—LX450

the problem (if any) in the wiper circuit. The key to troubleshooting is an organized, logical approach. Do not proceed to the next step until each step has been completed.

Front Wiper Relay

OPERATION AT INTERMITTENT

1. Turn the wiper switch to the "INT" position.
2. Turn the intermittent time control switch to the "FAST" position.
3. Connect the positive lead from the battery to terminal B18 and the negative lead to terminal B16.
4. Connect the positive lead from the

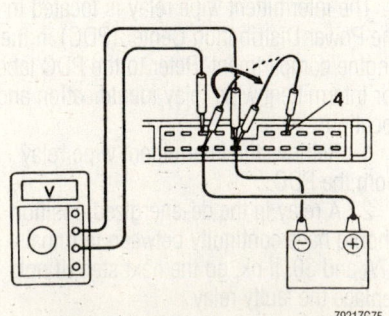

Pertinent information to front wiper relay testing (in intermittent)—LX450

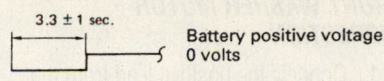

Pertinent information to front wiper relay testing (in intermittent)—LX450

voltmeter to terminal B7 and the negative lead to terminal B16. Check that the meter indicates 12V positive voltage.

5. After connecting terminal B4 to B18, connect to terminal B16. Then check that the voltage within the times as shown in the accompanying table.

OPERATION AS WASHER LINKED

1. Connect the positive lead from the battery to terminal B18 and the negative lead to terminal B16.

2. Connect the positive lead from the voltmeter to terminal B7 and the negative lead to terminal B16.

3. Push in the washer switch. Check that the voltage changes as shown in the table. If the operation is not as specified, replace the switch.

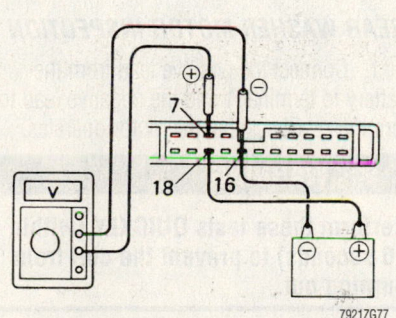

Pertinent information to front wiper relay testing (as washer linked)—LX450

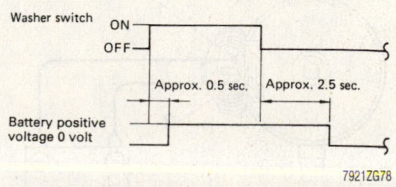

Pertinent Information to front wiper relay testing (as washer linked)—LX450

Rear Wiper Relay Inspection

CONTINUITY

1. Check that there is no continuity between terminals 1 and 3.

2. Check that there is continuity between terminals 2 and 3. If the continuity is not as specified, replace the relay.

Relay Side

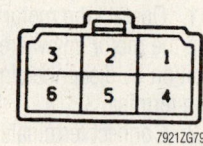

Rear wiper relay terminals—LX450

OPERATION

1. Connect the positive lead from the battery to terminal 1 and the negative lead to terminal 6.

2. Connect the positive lead from the voltmeter to terminal 2 and the negative lead to terminal 6. Check that the meter indicates 0V.

3. Connect the positive lead from the voltmeter to terminal 3 and the negative lead to terminal 6. Check that the meter indicates 12V positive voltage. If the operation is not as specified, replace the relay.

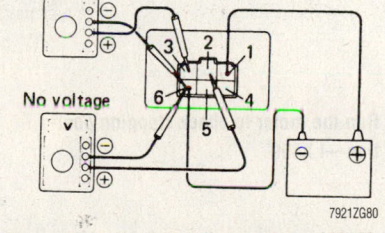

Rear wiper relay operation testing—LX450

INTERMITTENT OPERATION

1. Connect the positive lead from the battery to terminal 2 and the negative lead to terminal 4.

2. Connect the positive lead from the voltmeter to terminal 3 and the negative lead to terminal 4.

3. After disconnecting the positive lead from terminal 2, connect it to terminal 1.

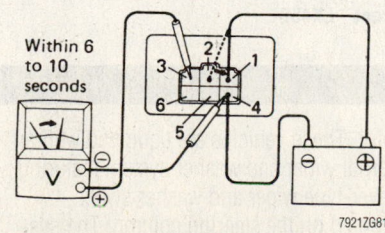

Rear wiper relay intermittent operation testing—LX450

Check that the meter rises from 0V to 12V within 6–8 seconds. If operation is not as specified, replace the relay.

Front Wiper Motor Inspection

LOW SPEED OPERATION

1. Connect the positive lead from the battery to terminal 3 and the negative lead to terminal 1 (for T100, connect to the motor body). Check that the motor operates at low speed.

2. If operation is not as specified, replace the motor.

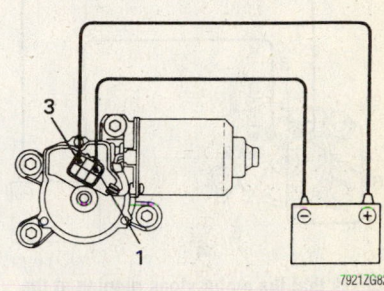

Low speed front wiper motor testing—LX450

HIGH SPEED OPERATION

1. Connect the positive lead from the battery to terminal 2 and the negative lead to terminal 1 (for T100, connect to the motor body). Check that the motor operates at high speed.

2. If the operation is not as specified, replace the motor.

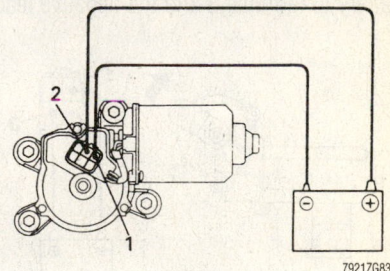

High speed front wiper motor testing—LX450

STOPPING AT THE STOP POSITION TEST

1. Operate the motor at low speed and stop the motor operation anywhere except at the stop position by disengaging the positive lead from terminal 3.

2. Connect terminal 3 and 5.

3. Connect the battery positive lead to

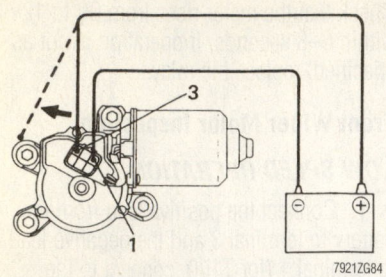

Operate the motor at low speed and stop the motor operation anywhere except at the stop position—LX450

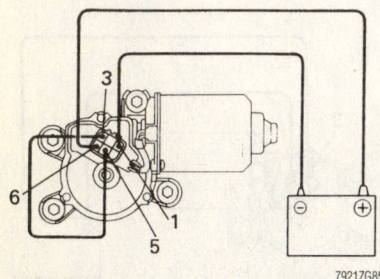

Check that the motor stops running at the stop position after the motor operates again—LX450

terminal 6 and the battery negative lead to terminal 1. Check that the motor stops running at the stop position after the motor operates again. If the motor does not operate as specified, replace it.

Rear Wiper Motor Inspection

LOW SPEED OPERATION

1. Connect the positive lead from the battery to terminal 3 and the negative lead

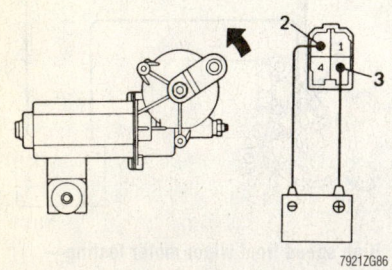

Rear wiper motor low speed operation inspection—LX450

to terminal 2. Check that the motor operates at low speed. If not, replace the motor.

STOPPING AT THE STOP POSITION

1. Operate the motor at low speed, then stop the motor anywhere except at the stop position by disconnecting the positive lead from terminal 3.

2. Connect terminals 3 and 4.

3. Connect the positive lead from the battery to terminal 1 and the negative lead to terminal 2. Check that the motor stops running at the stop position after the motor operates again. If the motor does not function as specified, replace it.

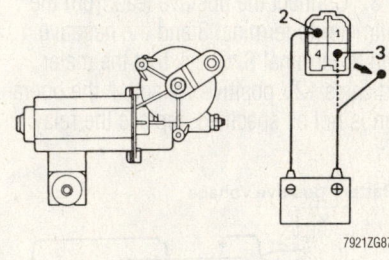

Run the motor to check stopping position—LX450

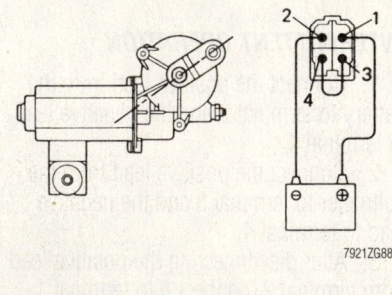

Check that the stopping position is correct—LX450

FRONT WASHER MOTOR INSPECTION

1. Connect the positive lead from the battery to terminal 2 and the negative lead to terminal 1. Check that the motor operates.

❋❋ WARNING

Perform these tests QUICKLY (within 20 seconds) to prevent the coil from burning out.

2. If the motor does not function correctly, replace it.

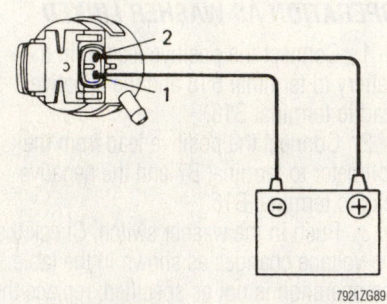

Front washer motor inspection—LX450

REAR WASHER MOTOR INSPECTION

1. Connect the positive lead from the battery to terminal 1 and the negative lead to terminal 2. Check that the motor operates.

❋❋ WARNING

Perform these tests QUICKLY (within 20 seconds) to prevent the coil from burning out.

2. If the motor does not function correctly, replace it.

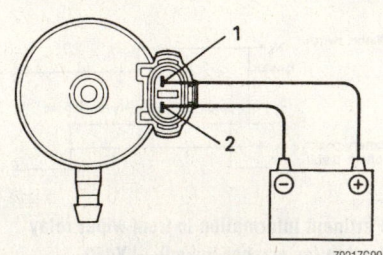

Rear washer motor inspection—LX450

MAZDA

B2300, B3000, B4000 and Navajo

GENERAL DESCRIPTION

The windshield wipers are actuated by a permanent magnet, rotary-type electric motor. These vehicles are equipped with an internal wiper and washer system featuring a lever-type wiper and washer switch, mounted on the steering column. The system governor uses a relay contact to control current to the wiper motor. The governor electronic circuitry controls the contact to supply wiper motor current.

COMPONENT TESTING

• On all vehicles, when trouble shooting the wiper system, test the motor first, then work back towards the switch to test the interval governor or module (depending on the vehicle), power circuits and the switch itself.

• In most of the tests, a volt-ohmmeter is required, although a test light can also be useful. For testing the motor, a 0–15 amp DC ammeter is required.

• When the test calls for a voltage check, the ignition switch must be in the **ON** position.

• When testing for continuity or resistance values, turn the ignition switch to the **OFF** position and/or disconnect the negative battery cable.

• Improper or careless testing can cause permanent damage to the vehicle's electronic circuits and to test equipment. Carefully follow the test equipment manufacturer's instructions.

Wiper Motor Test

1. Disconnect the positive cable from the battery.

2. Remove the wiper motor linkage and electrical connectors from the windshield wiper motor.

➡**If the electrical connector is not accessible, the motor may need to be removed.**

3. Using a suitable starting charging tester, connect the power lead (green) of the tester to the positive battery terminal.

4. Connect the positive (red) lead from the tester to the low speed connection and high speed connection at the connector plug.

5. The draw should be no more than 3.0 amps at either speed. Repairs to the motor itself are not possible.

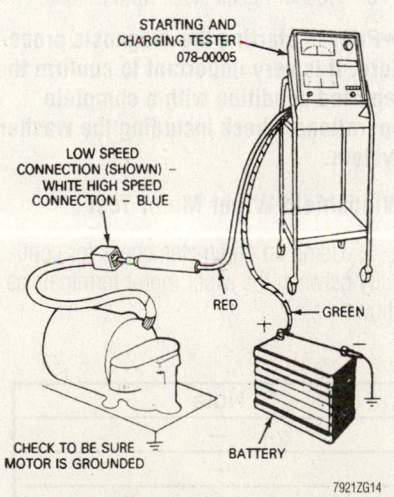

Wiper motor current draw test— Navajo, B2300, B3000, B4000

Washer Pump Current Draw Test

1. Attach the leads of a digital volt/ohmmeter or suitable starting charging tester as shown. The current draw should not exceed 4 amps or be less than 1.7 amps while the windshield washer pump is pumping fluid.

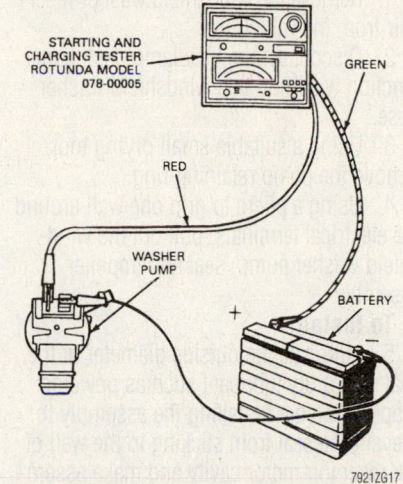

Wiper washer pump current draw test

Circuit Breaker Test

The front wipers and washers use the same 6 amp circuit breaker (B-Series), 8.25 amps (Navajo), located in the fuse panel. Two separate tests are necessary to check for correct circuit breaker operation.

1. Remove the circuit breaker from the fuse panel.

2. Using a suitable volt-amp tester, touch the test leads together and adjust the current draw until it equals the circuit breaker rating.

3. Connect the test leads to the circuit breaker, hold the current reading on the ammeter at the rated current and leave it connected for 10 minutes.

4. If the circuit breaker opens during the 10 minutes, replace the circuit breaker.

5. Touch the tester's leads together and adjust the current draw until it is twice the rated current.

6. Connect the circuit breaker to the tester and hold the current rating on twice the rated current.

7. The current reading on the ammeter should drop to 0 within 30 seconds.

8. If it takes longer than 30 seconds for the ammeter to drop to 0 (circuit breaker to open), replace the circuit breaker.

Wiper Interval Governor Test

If interval operation is unsatisfactory, first check the motor current draw, the control switch and all the connecting wires for continuity. If the motor, switch and connecting wires are OK, replace the electronic governor.

Wiper Switch Test

1. Check for an open circuit with the wiper/washer switch **OFF**.

   a. Turn the washer **OFF**.

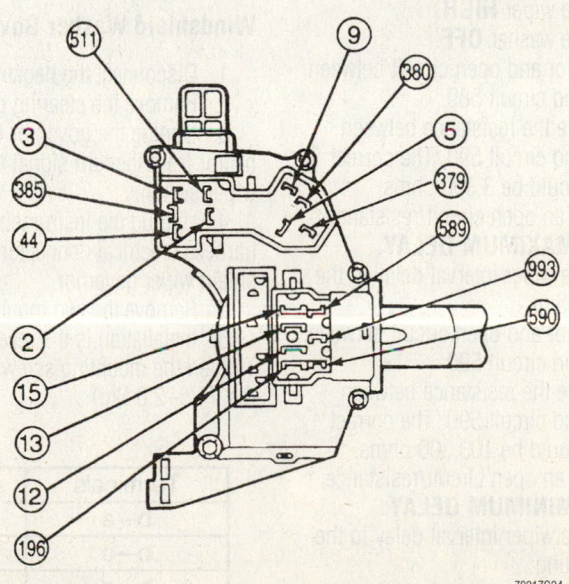

Turn signal/wiper/washer switch terminal locations for switch continuity test— B2300, B3000, B4000 and Navajo

b. Check for an open circuit between Circuit 993 and Circuit 590.

2. Check for an closed circuit with the wiper/washer switch **ON**.

a. Turn the washer **ON**.

b. Check for continuity between Circuit 993 and Circuit 590.

3. Check for an open circuit/resistance with the wiper on **OFF** and the washer on **OFF**.

a. Turn the wiper **OFF**.

b. Turn the washer **OFF**.

c. Check for and open circuit between circuit 589 and circuit 590.

d. Measure the resistance between circuit 993 and circuit 590. The correct resistance should be 103,000 ohms.

e. Measure the resistance between circuit 993 and circuit 589. The correct resistance should be 47,600 ohms.

4. Check for an open circuit/resistance with the wiper on **LOW** and the washer on **OFF**.

a. Turn the wiper **LOW**.

b. Turn the washer **OFF**.

c. Check for and open circuit between circuit 589 and circuit 590.

d. Measure the resistance between circuit 993 and circuit 590. The correct resistance should be 3,300 ohms.

e. Measure the resistance between circuit 993 and circuit 589. The correct resistance should be 4,100 ohms.

5. Check for an open circuit/resistance with the wiper on **HIGH** and the washer on **OFF**.

a. Turn the wiper **HIGH**.

b. Turn the washer **OFF**.

c. Check for and open circuit between circuit 993 and circuit 589.

d. Measure the resistance between circuit 993 and circuit 590. The correct resistance should be 3,300 ohms.

6. Check for an open circuit/resistance with interval at **MAXIMUM DELAY**.

a. Turn the wiper interval delay to the maximum setting.

b. Check for and open circuit between circuit 589 and circuit 590.

c. Measure the resistance between circuit 993 and circuit 590. The correct resistance should be 103,300 ohms.

7. Check for an open circuit/resistance with interval at **MINIMUM DELAY**.

a. Turn the wiper interval delay to the minimum setting.

b. Check for and open circuit between circuit 589 and circuit 590.

c. Measure the resistance between circuit 993 and circuit 590. The correct resistance should be 3,300 ohms.

d. Measure the resistance between circuit 993 and circuit 589. The correct resistance should be 11,300 ohms.

REMOVAL & INSTALLATION

Windshield Washer Pump and Seal

1. Remove the windshield washer reservoir from the vehicle.

2. Disconnect the headlamp dash panel junction wire plug and windshield washer hose.

3. Using a suitable small prying tool, remove the pump retaining ring.

4. Using a pliers to grip one wall around the electrical terminals, pull out the windshield washer pump, seal and impeller assembly.

To Install:

5. Lubricate the outside diameter of the seal with a dry lubricant such as powered graphite, before installing the assembly to prevent the seal from sticking to the wall of the reservoir motor cavity and make assembly easier.

6. Align the small projection on the end of the pump with the slot in the windshield washer reservoir and assemble so the seal seats against the bottom of the motor cavity.

7. Using a 1 inch socket (preferable 12 point) hand press the retaining ring securely against the motor and plate.

8. Connect the electrical plug and washer hose and replace the reservoir in the vehicle.

Windshield Washer Governor

1. Disconnect the negative battery cable.

2. Remove the steering column shroud.

3. Unplug the governor electrical connector from the turn signal and windshield wiper switch.

4. Unplug the instrument panel wiring harness electrical connector from the windshield wiper governor.

5. Remove the two mounting screws.

6. Installation is the reverse of removal. Tighten the mounting screws to 13–17 inch lbs. (1.5–2.0 Nm).

MPV

GENERAL DESCRIPTION

The windshield wiper circuit consists of the ignition switch, wiper and washer switches, wiper motor, washer motors and relays for the intermittent function. Some models include intermittent rear window wipers and therefore have relays to control this function as well.

When the windshield wiper switch is turned on and the ignition switch is in the **ON** or **START** position, battery voltage is applied to the wiper/washer fuse to the front wiper/washer switch (in the combination switch) and front wiper motor pawl and switch contacts. A fuse, located in the fuse block, protects the circuitry of the wiper system and the vehicle.

The wiper motor has permanent magnet fields. The speeds are determined by current flow to the appropriate set of brushes.

COMPONENT TESTING

Testing Hints

The following procedures assume that the technician has checked the following:

1. Continuity of all harness wires.

2. Wiper motor and wiper/washer switch connectors are mated correctly.

3. If the wiper motor operates but the wipers do not; check the wiper linkage and wiper motor crank arm.

4. Wiper motor-to-dash mounting screws tight for good ground.

5. Fuses are good.

6. Washer hoses clear, fluid in tank.

➡ **Prior to starting the diagnosis procedure, it is very important to confirm the reported condition with a complete operational check including the washer system.**

Windshield Wiper Motor Test

1. Using an ohmmeter, check for continuity between the wiper motor terminals as shown.

Terminals	Continuity	Note
b—a	Conductive	—
b—c	Conductive	—
b—d	Conductive	Normal resting position
e—d	Conductive	Except for normal resting position

Windshield wiper motor continuity test—B series pick-ups

79212GD7

V$_B$: Battery voltage

Terminal		Operation speed
V$_B$	Ground	
b	a	Low
	c	High

Windshield wiper motor operational check—B series pick-ups

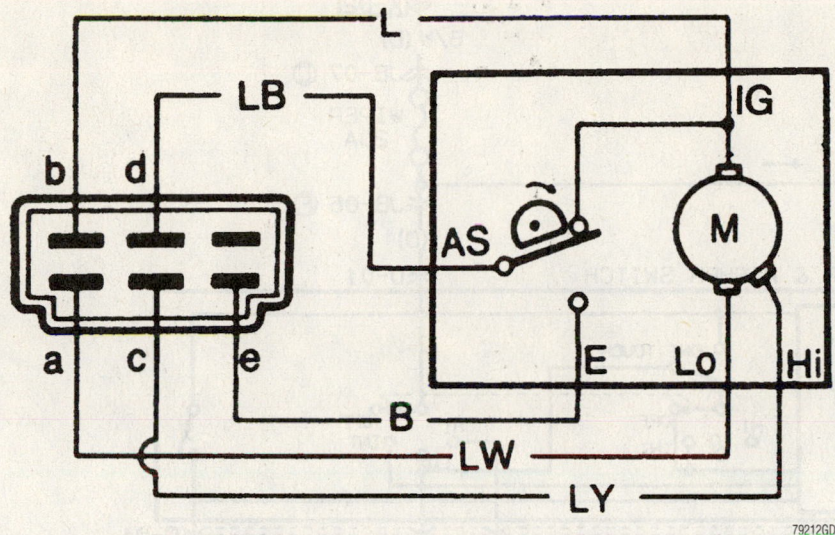

Windshield wiper motor terminal identification and continuity check—B series pick-ups

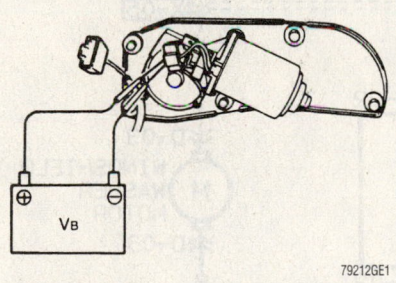

Windshield wiper motor operational check—B series pick-ups

2. Apply battery voltage and check the operation of the wiper motor as indicated.

3. Replace the wiper motor, if not as specified.

Rear Wiper Motor Test

1. Using an ohmmeter, check for continuity between the wiper motor terminals **a** and **b**.

2. Verify operation of the motor when battery voltage is connected to terminal **a** and terminal **b** is connected to ground.

3. Disconnect the ground from terminal **b**, and immediately connect the ground to the motor body. Check that the motor shaft reaches the park position and that there is continuity.

4. Replace the wiper motor, if not as specified.

Windshield Washer Motor Test

1. Using an ohmmeter, check for continuity between the washer motor terminals.

2. Apply battery voltage to terminal **b** and ground to terminal **a**, and verify the operation of the motor.

3. Replace the wiper motor, if not as specified.

Rear Washer Motor Test

1. Using an ohmmeter, check for continuity between the washer motor terminals **a** and **b**.

2. Verify operation of the motor when battery voltage is connected to terminal b and terminal a is connected to ground.

3. Replace the washer motor, if not as specified.

Windshield Wiper Switch Test

1. Using an ohmmeter, check for continuity between the front wiper/washer switch terminals as shown.

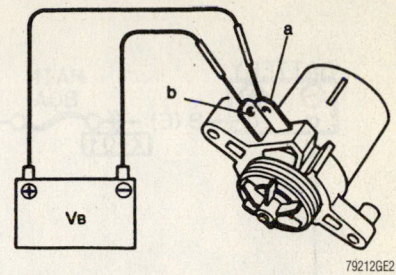

Windshield washer motor terminals—B series pick-ups

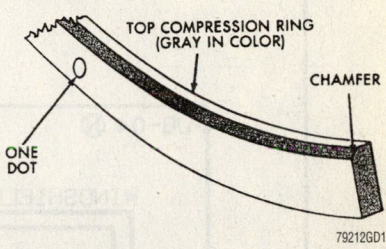

Front windshield wiper/washer switch continuity test—MPV

Rear Wiper Switch Test

1. Using an ohmmeter, check for continuity between the rear wiper/washer switch terminals as shown.

REMOVAL & INSTALLATION

Washer Motor

1. Disconnect the negative battery cable.

2. Remove the washer solvent from the reservoir.

3. Disconnect the electrical connector and washer hose from the washer motor.

4. Remove the washer motor from the reservoir.

5. Installation is the reverse of removal. Fill the reservoir and check for correct operation.

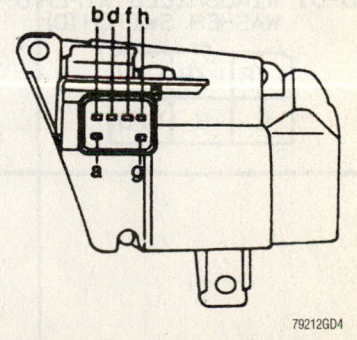

Rear wiper/washer switch continuity test—MPV

Refer to the model specific sections for driveline service procedures

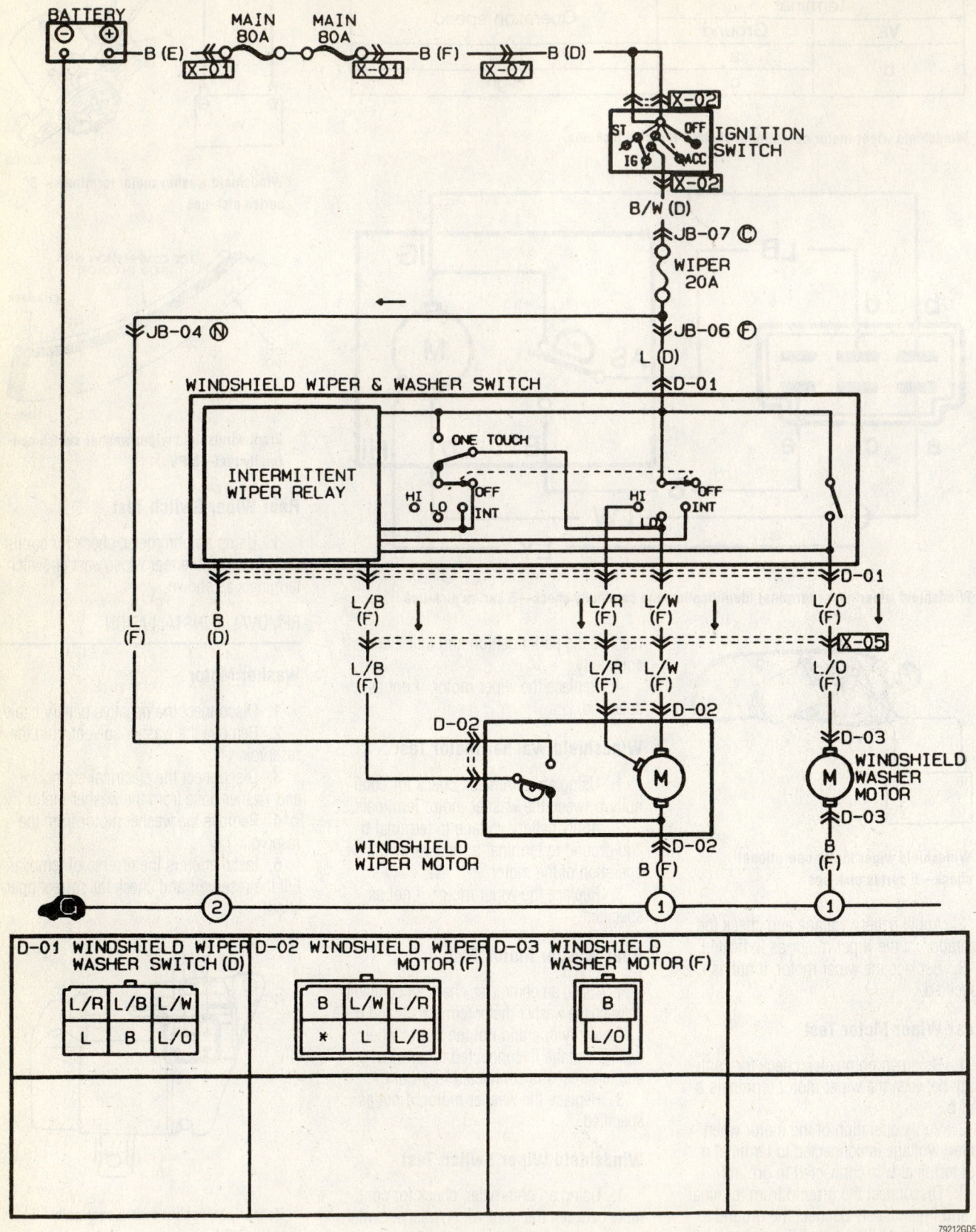

Windshield washer/wiper electrical schematic—MPV

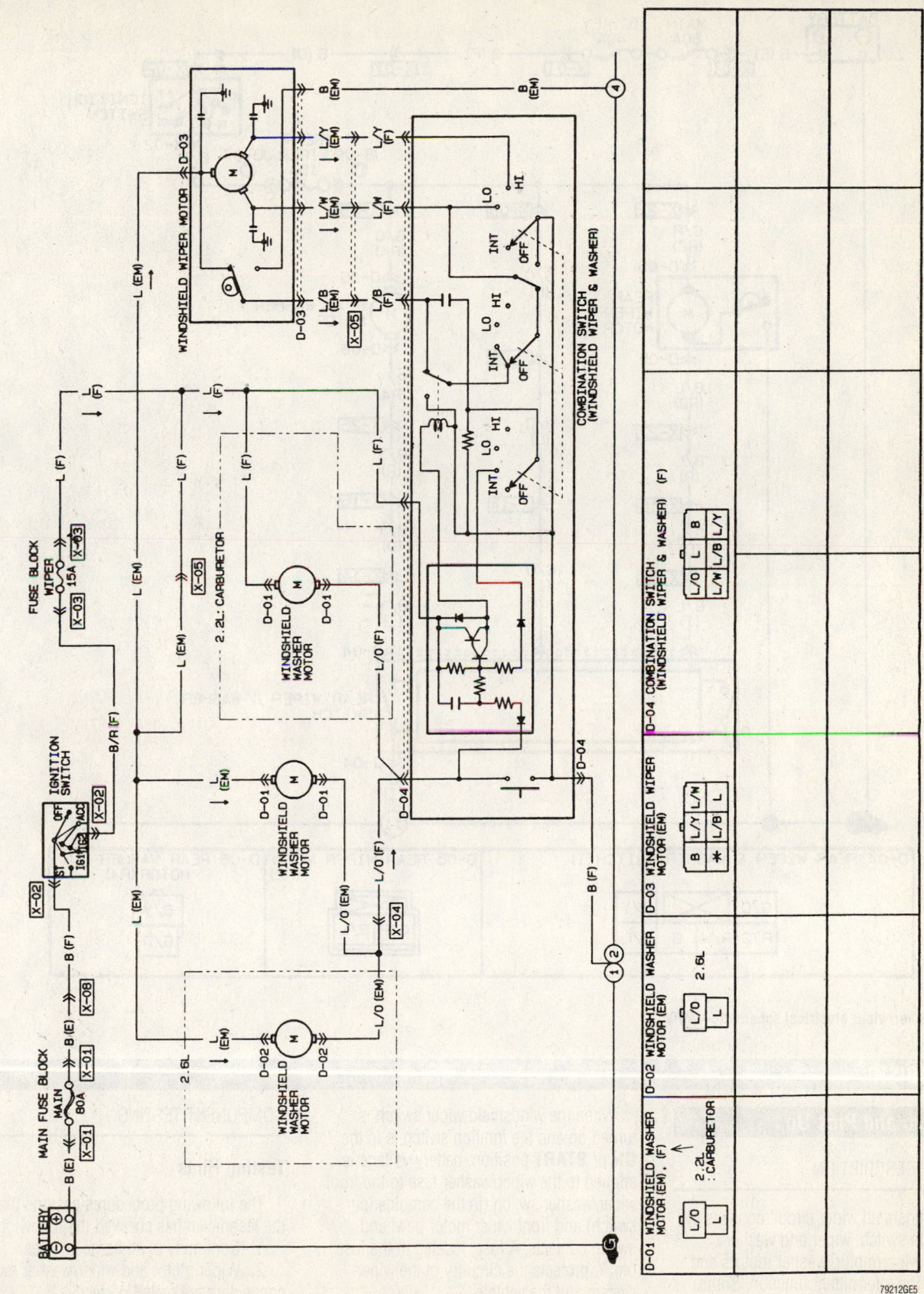

Windshield washer/wiper electrical schematic—B series pick-ups

79212GE5

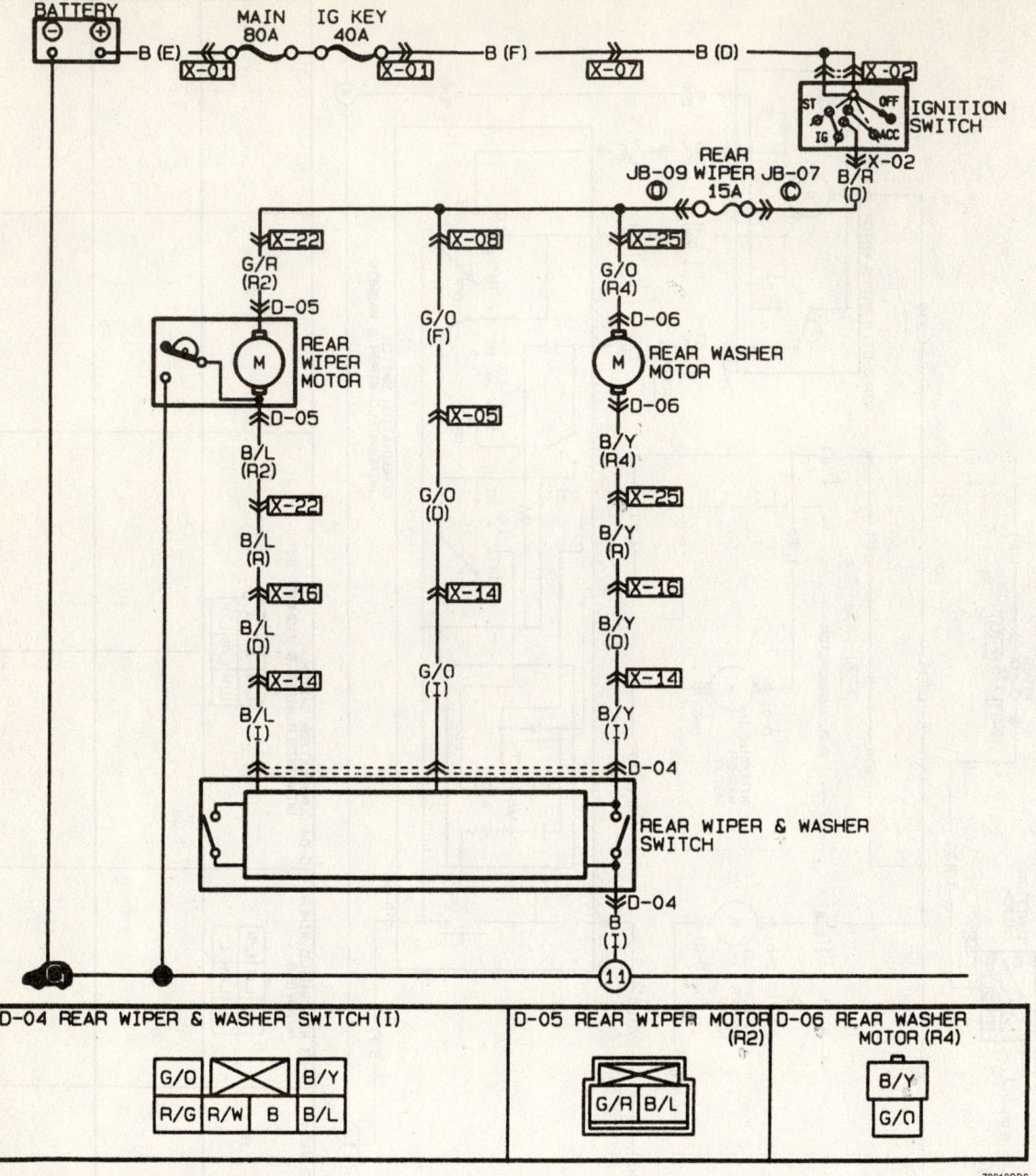

Rear washer/wiper electrical schematic—MPV

MITSUBISHI

Montero and Pick-Up

GENERAL DESCRIPTION

The windshield wiper circuit consists of the ignition switch, wiper and washer switches, wiper motor, washer motors and relays for the intermittent function. Some models include intermittent rear window wipers and therefore have relays to control this function as well.

When the windshield wiper switch is turned on and the ignition switch is in the **ON** or **START** position, battery voltage is applied to the wiper/washer fuse to the front wiper/washer switch (in the combination switch) and front wiper motor pawl and switch contacts. A fuse, located in the fuse block, protects the circuitry of the wiper system and the vehicle.

The wiper motor has permanent magnet fields. The speeds are determined by current flow to the appropriate set of brushes.

COMPONENT TESTING

Testing Hints

The following procedures assume that the technician has checked the following:
1. Continuity of all harness wires.
2. Wiper motor and wiper/washer switch connectors are mated correctly.
3. If the wiper motor operates but the wipers do not; check the wiper linkage and wiper motor crank arm.

4. Wiper motor-to-dash mounting screws tight for good ground.

5. Fuses are good.

6. Washer hoses clear, fluid in tank.

➡ **Prior to starting the diagnosis procedure, it is very important to confirm the reported condition with a complete operational check including the washer system.**

Windshield Wiper Motor Test

MONTERO

1. With the wiper motor installed in vehicle, disconnect the wiring harness connector.

2. Connect a battery to the wiper motor as shown and check the motor operation at both low and high speeds.

Inspection while operating

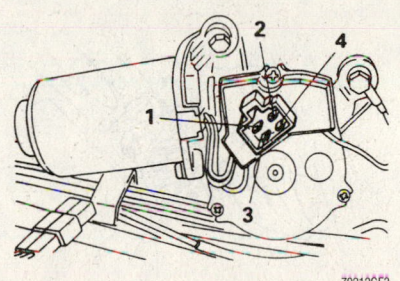

Windshield wiper motor test—Montero

3. Run the motor low speed, disconnect the battery and stop the motor.

4. Reconnect the battery as shown in the illustration confirm that the motor starts operating at the low speed and it stops at the automatic stop position.

PICK-UP

1. With the wiper motor installed in vehicle, disconnect the wiring harness connector.

2. Connect a battery to the wiper motor connector and check the motor operation.

3. Connect the battery positive (+) terminal to terminal **3** and the battery negative (-) terminal to terminal **1** and check that the motor runs at low speed.

4. Connect the battery positive (+) terminal to terminal **3** and the battery negative (-) terminal to terminal **2** and check that the motor runs at high speed.

5. Check the automatic stop operation by connecting the battery positive (+) terminal the terminal **3** and the battery negative (-) terminal to terminal **1** to run the motor at low speed. Then disconnect terminal **3** during operation to stop the motor.

6. Connect terminal **1** to terminal **4** and connect the battery positive (+) terminal to terminal **3** and the battery negative (-) terminal to the wiper motor bracket and check that the motor starts to run at low speed and then stops.

Windshield wiper motor terminal identification—Pick-Up

Windshield Washer Motor Test

MONTERO

1. With the washer motor installed in vehicle and the reservoir filled, disconnect the wiring harness connector.

2. Connect a battery to the wiper motor as shown and check the operation of the washer.

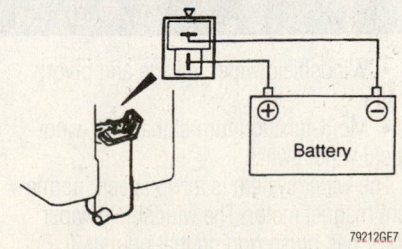

Windshield washer motor test—Montero

Windshield Wiper and Washer Switch Test

MONTERO

1. Remove the column lower and upper covers.

2. Loosen the two retaining screws and remove the wiper and washer switch.

3. Operate the switch and using an ohmmeter, check for continuity between the terminals as shown

Switch position		Terminal				
		6	7	8	9	10
	OFF		○	○		
Wiper switch	1 (LO)			○		○
	2 (HI)				○	○
Washer switch	ON	○				○

79212GF1

Windshield wiper and washer switch continuity test—Montero

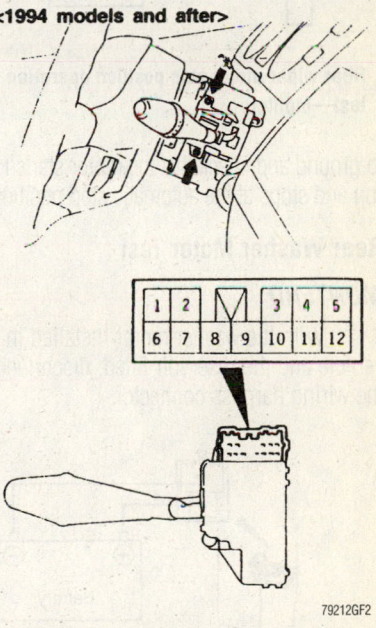

Windshield wiper and washer switch continuity test—Montero

Rear Wiper Motor Test

MONTERO

1. With the wiper motor installed in vehicle, disconnect the wiring harness connector.

2. Connect the battery positive (+) terminal to terminal **3** and the battery negative (-) terminal to ground and check the motor operation.

3. Connect terminal **2** to terminal **3** and connect the battery positive (+) terminal to terminal **1** and the battery negative (-) terminal

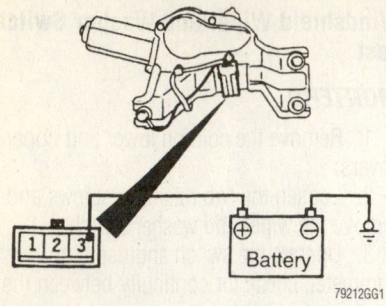

Rear wiper motor operation test—Montero

79212GG1

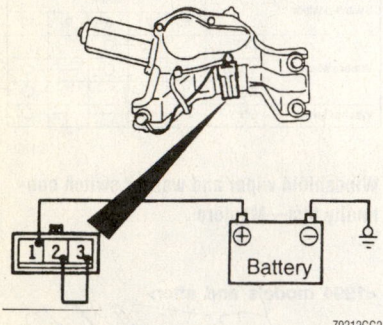

Rear wiper motor stop position operation test—Montero

79212GG2

to ground and check that the motor starts to run and stops at the automatic stop position.

Rear Washer Motor Test

MONTERO

1. With the washer motor installed in vehicle and the reservoir filled, disconnect the wiring harness connector.

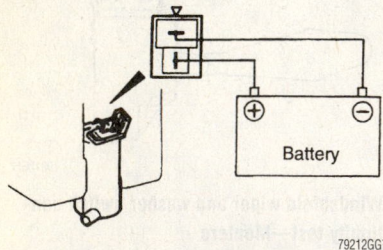

Rear washer motor test—Montero

79212GG7

2. Connect a battery to the wiper motor as shown and check the operation of the washer.

Rear Wiper and Washer Switch Test

MONTERO

1. Remove the column lower and upper covers.
2. Loosen the two retaining screws and remove the wiper and washer switch.
3. Operate the switch and using an

Switch position		Terminal			
		2	3	4	10
Wiper switch	OFF				
	INT		○—	—	—○
	ON			○—	—○
Washer switch	ON	○—	—	—○	

79212GG5

Rear wiper and washer switch continuity test—Montero

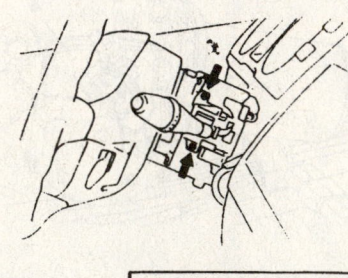

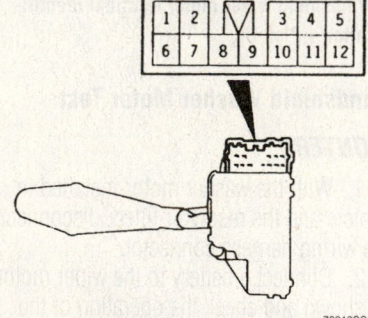

79212GG6

Rear wiper and washer switch continuity test—Montero

ohmmeter, check for continuity between the terminals as shown

REMOVAL & INSTALLATION

Windshield Washer Motor

MONTERO

1. Disconnect the negative battery cable.
2. Remove the fender splash shield.
3. Drain and remove the washer reservoir.
4. Disconnect the washer motor electrical connector.
5. Disconnect the washer motor hose.
6. Remove the motor from the vehicle.
7. Installation is the reverse of removal.

PICK-UP

1. Disconnect the negative battery cable.
2. Drain and remove the washer reservoir.
3. Disconnect the washer motor electrical connector.
4. Remove the motor from the vehicle.
5. Installation is the reverse of removal.

Rear Washer Motor

MONTERO

1. Disconnect the negative battery cable.
2. Remove the back door trim and waterproof shield.
3. Drain and remove the washer reservoir.
4. Disconnect the washer motor electrical connector.
5. Disconnect the washer motor hose.
6. Remove the motor from the vehicle.
7. Installation is the reverse of removal.

NISSAN

Quest

GENERAL DESCRIPTION

The windshield wiper assembly consists of the following components:
- Windshield wiper governor
- Windshield wiper motor, located in the engine compartment
- Windshield wiper pivot arms

- Windshield wiper linkage and pivot shaft
- Multi-function turn signal and windshield wiper switch

The wiper system is a two speed, permanent magnet motor. The windshield wiper motor has brush rigging that permits the selection of **LO** or **HI** speed.

The windshield wiper governor is wired in series between the turn signal and the windshield wiper switch and the windshield

wiper motor. It operates as a timer mechanism for the interval wiper function. It is located on the Left side strut tower, directly below the hood support rod pivot.

COMPONENT TESTING

- On all vehicles, when trouble shooting the wiper system, test the motor first, then work back towards the switch to test the interval governor or module (depending on the vehicle), power circuits and the switch itself.

• In most of the tests, a volt-ohmmeter is required, although a test light can also be useful. For testing the motor, a 0–15 amp DC ammeter is required.

• When the test calls for a voltage check, the ignition switch must be in the **ON** position.

• When testing for continuity or resistance values, turn the ignition switch to the **OFF** position and/or disconnect the negative battery cable.

• Improper or careless testing can cause permanent damage to the vehicle's electronic circuits and to test equipment. Carefully follow the test equipment manufacturer's instructions.

Wiper Motor Test

QUEST

1. Turn the key **OFF**.
2. Disconnect the windshield wiper motor connector, located behind the cowl top vent panel.
3. Connect a jumper between **BK/W** wire terminal at the windshield wiper motor connector (component side) to the battery positive terminal **BK/W** wire terminal at the windshield wiper motor connector (component side) to the battery positive terminal.
4. Connect a jumper between **BR/W** wire terminal at the windshield wiper motor connector (component side) to the battery negative terminal and verify low speed operation of the wiper motor.
5. Connect a jumper between **BK/W** wire terminal at the windshield wiper motor connector (component side) to the battery positive terminal.
6. Connect a jumper between **BL/O** wire terminal at the windshield wiper motor connector (component side) to the battery negative terminal and verify high speed operation of the wiper motor.
7. Reconnect the windshield wiper motor connector, located behind the cowl top vent panel.
8. Turn the key **ON** and cycle the windshield wipers until they reach the fully parked position.
9. Turn the key **OFF**.
10. Disconnect the windshield wiper motor connector.
11. Verify the resistance between the **BK/W** wire terminal and the **R** wire terminal, at the connector leading to the windshield wiper motor.

Windshield Wiper Position	Resistance Between Wires	
	BK/W to R	R to BK
Park	Less than 5 ohms	Greater than 10,000 ohms
Run	Greater than 10,000 ohms	Less than 5 ohms

7921ZG25

Wiper motor resistance test—Quest

12. Verify the resistance between the **R** wire terminal and the **BK** wire terminal, at the connector leading to the windshield wiper motor.

Wiper/Washer Switch Test

1. Turn the key **OFF**.
2. Disconnect the ten pin turn signal and windshield wiper connector located on the steering column.
3. Verify the resistance shown in the chart.

Windshield Wiper/Washer Switch Position	Resistance Between Wire Terminals	
	3A to 2A	1A to 2A
OFF	47,600 ohms	103,300 ohms
S	11,300 ohms	103,300 ohms
F	11,300 ohms	3,300 ohms
LO	4,080 ohms	3,300 ohms
HI	0 ohms	3,300 ohms
WASH	NA	Less than 5 ohms

* Resistance may vary by ± 15%.

7921ZGA1

Wiper/washer switch resistance test—Quest

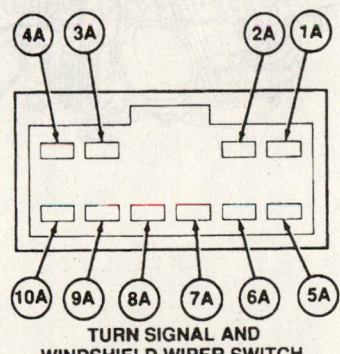

TURN SIGNAL AND WINDSHIELD WIPER SWITCH

7921ZGA2

Wiper/washer switch terminal identification for resistance test (connector shown from component side)—Quest

REMOVAL & INSTALLATION

Windshield Wiper Governor

➡ **The windshield wiper governor is located on the left side of the engine compartment behind the battery.**

1. Remove the two windshield wiper governor retaining screws.
2. Disconnect the two windshield wiper governor electrical connectors and remove the governor.
3. Installation is the reverse of removal.

Windshield Washer Jet Nozzle and Bracket

1. Remove the wiper pivot arm.
2. Raise or lower the hood as necessary and remove the cowl top vent panel.
3. Use a suitable prying tool and to loosen the retaining clip and remove the windshield washer nozzle jet and bracket and from the cowl top vent panel.
4. Installation is the reverse of removal.

Windshield Washer Pump and Reservoir

1. Disconnect the negative battery cable.
2. Raise and safely support the vehicle.
3. Remove the right front wheel.
4. Remove the right front fender splash shield.
5. Remove the windshield washer reservoir top bolt.
6. Disconnect the windshield washer reservoir fluid level sensor electrical connector.
7. Disconnect the rear window washer pump electrical connector from the rear window washer pump.
8. Disconnect the windshield washer pump electrical connector from the windshield washer pump.
9. Drain the fluid from the reservoir.
10. Disconnect the hoses from the rear window washer pump and the windshield washer pump. The hoses are color coded for proper installation.
11. Loosen the two windshield washer reservoir side bolts and remove the reservoir by sliding it out of the slots.
12. Remove the windshield washer pump.
13. Installation is the reverse of removal.

Pathfinder and Pick-Up

GENERAL DESCRIPTION

The windshield wiper circuit consists of the ignition switch, wiper and washer switch, wiper motor, washer motor and amplifier for intermittent operation.

Refer to the model specific sections for driveline service procedures

When the windshield wiper switch is turned on and the ignition switch is in the **ON** or **START** position, battery voltage is applied to the wiper/washer fuse to the front wiper/washer switch (in the combination switch) and wiper motor terminal. A 20 amp fuse, located in the fuse block, protects the circuitry of the wiper system and the vehicle.

The wiper motor has permanent magnet fields. The speeds are determined by current flow to the appropriate set of brushes.

COMPONENT TESTING

Testing Hints

The following procedures assume that the technician has checked the following:

1. Continuity of all harness wires.
2. Wiper motor and wiper/washer switch connectors are mated correctly.
3. If the wiper motor operates but the wipers do not; check the wiper linkage and wiper motor crank arm.
4. Wiper motor-to-dash mounting screws tight for good ground.

5. Fuses are good.
6. Washer hoses clear, fluid in tank.

➡**Prior to starting the diagnosis procedure, it is very important to confirm the reported condition with a complete operational check including the washer system.**

Windshield Wiper and Washer Switch Test

ALL MODELS

1. Disconnect the column switch connector, and using an ohmmeter, check for

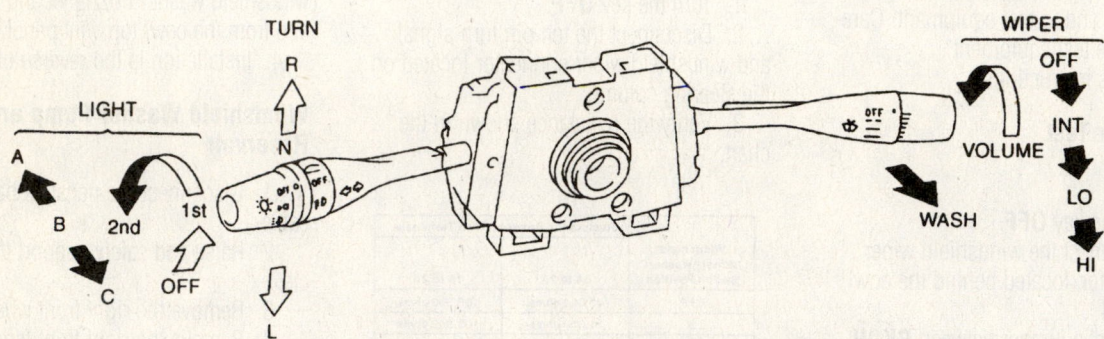

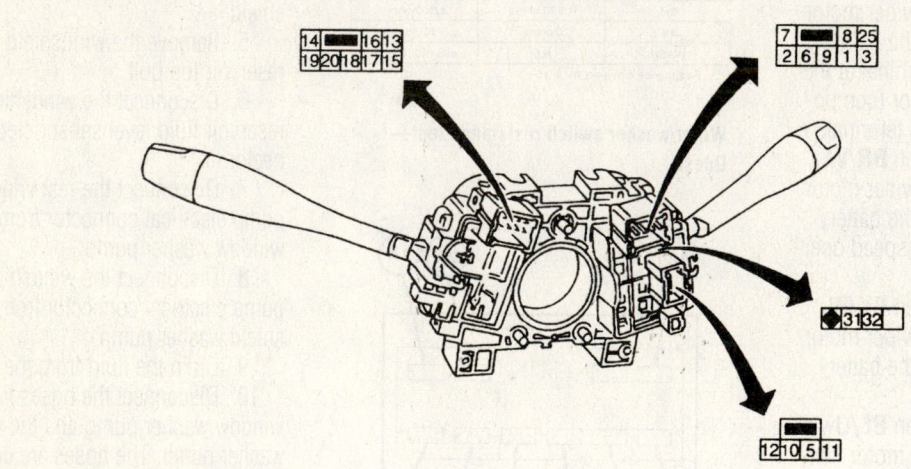

LIGHTING SWITCH

	OFF			1			2		
	A	B	C	A	B	C	A	B	C
5				○			○		
6				○	○		○	○	
7									
8						○	○	○	○
9						○			○
10									
11				○	○	○	○	○	○
12				○	○	○	○	○	○

WIPER SWITCH

	OFF	INT	LO	HI	WASH
13	○	○			
14	○	○	○		
15		○			
16				○	○
17		○	○	○	○
18					○

VARIABLE INTERMITTENT WIPER VOLUME

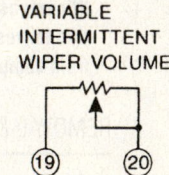

	L	N	R	TURN
1	○			SIGNAL
2			○	SWITCH
3				

FOG LAMP SWITCH

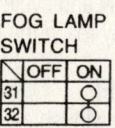

	OFF	ON
31		○
32		○

Windshield wiper and washer switch continuity test—Pathfinder

79212GGC

continuity between the terminals for each switch as shown.

Windshield Wiper Amplifier Test

PICK-UP

1. Connect a test lamp as shown.
2. If the test lamp comes ON when connected to terminal **6** and battery ground, the wiper amplifier is normal.

PATHFINDER

1. Connect a test lamp as shown.
2. If the test lamp comes ON when connected to terminals **1** or **6** and battery ground, the wiper amplifier is normal.

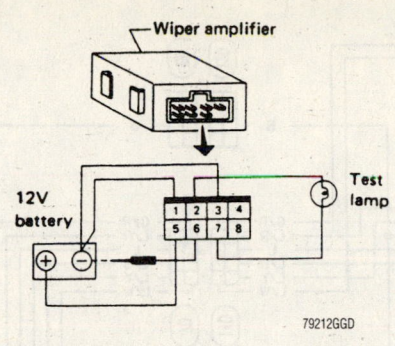

Windshield wiper amplifier test—Pick-up

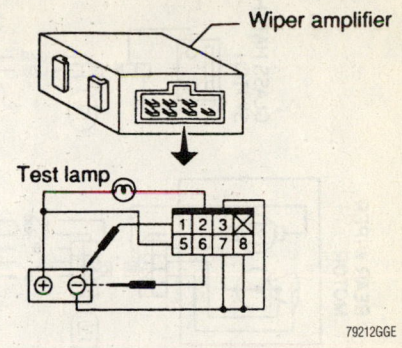

Windshield wiper amplifier test—Pathfinder

WITHOUT INTERMITTENT WIPER

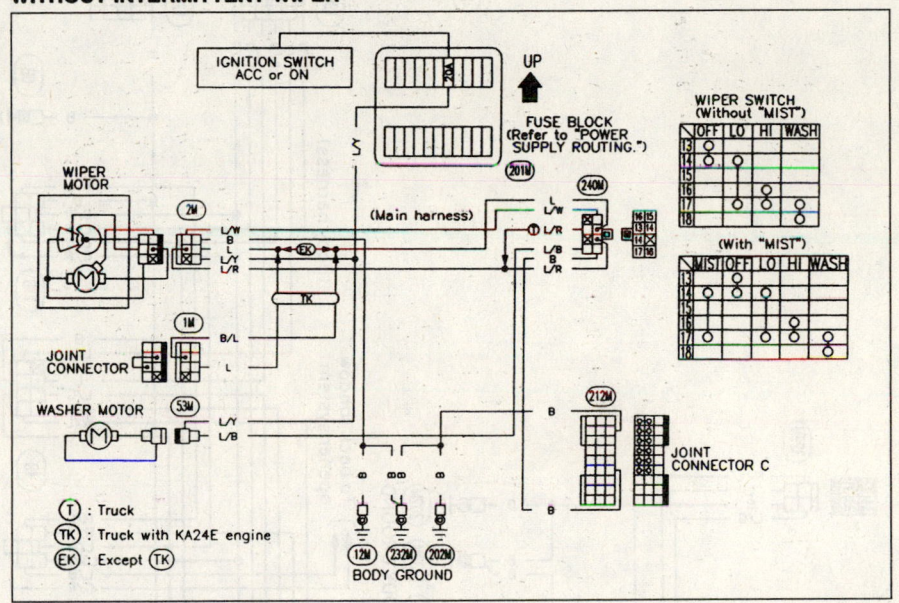

WITH INTERMITTENT WIPER

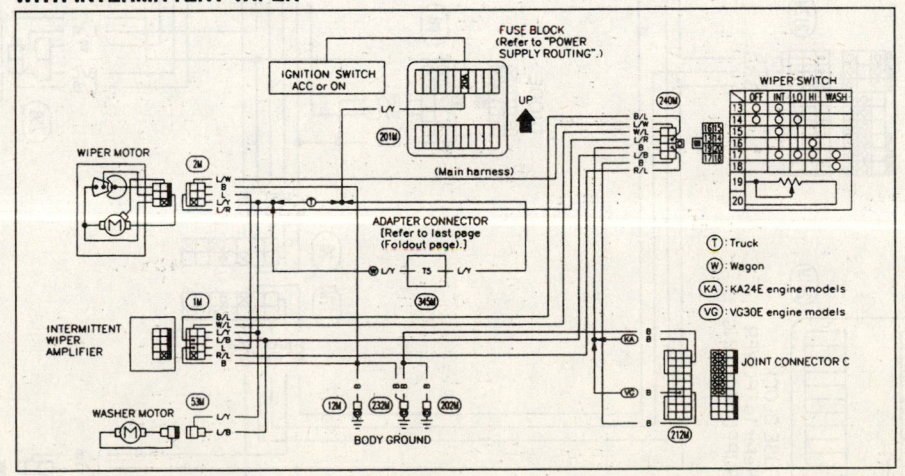

Windshield wiper/washer wiring schematic—Pick-ups

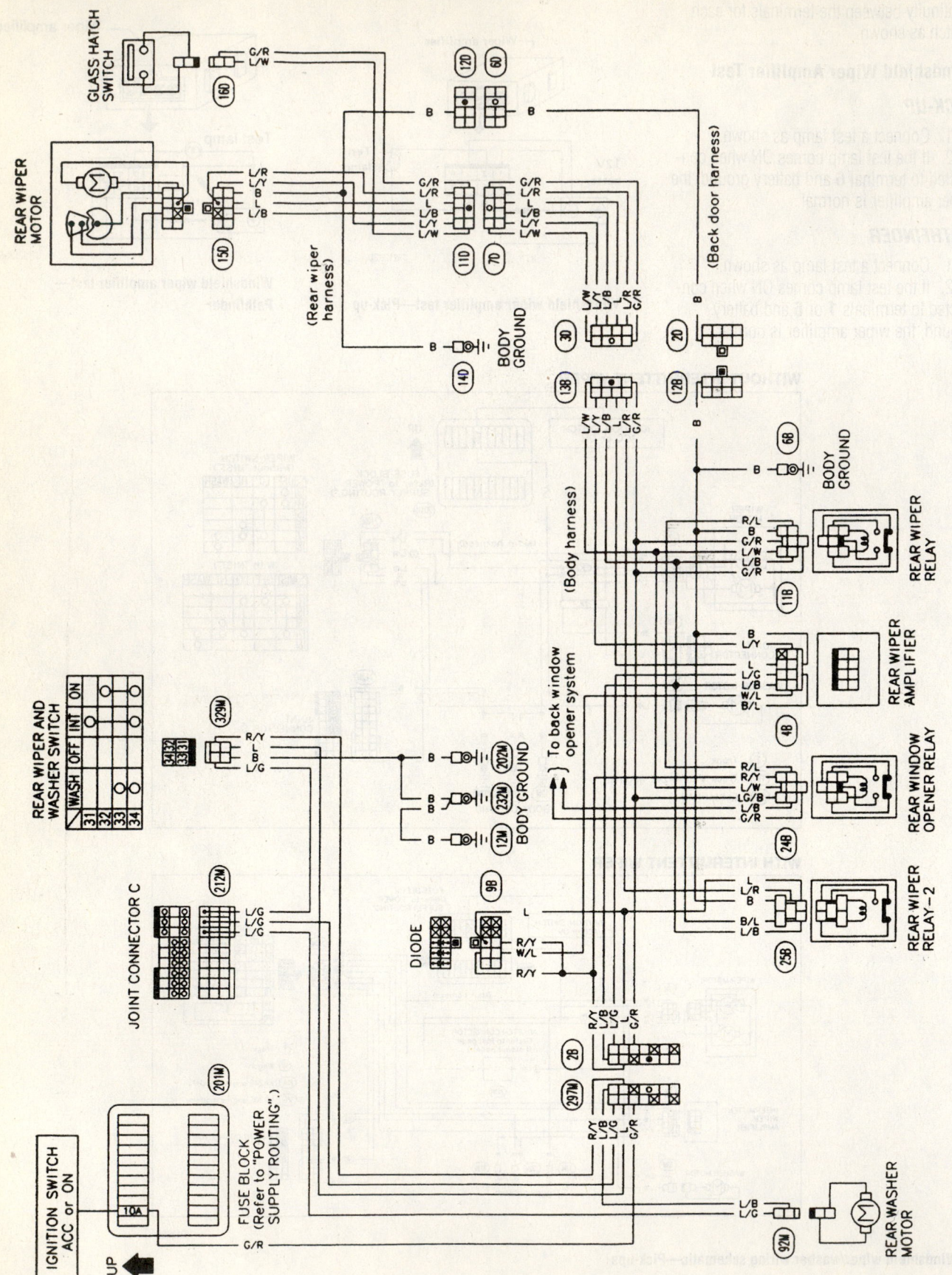

Rear wiper/washer wiring schematic—Pick-ups

79212GGG

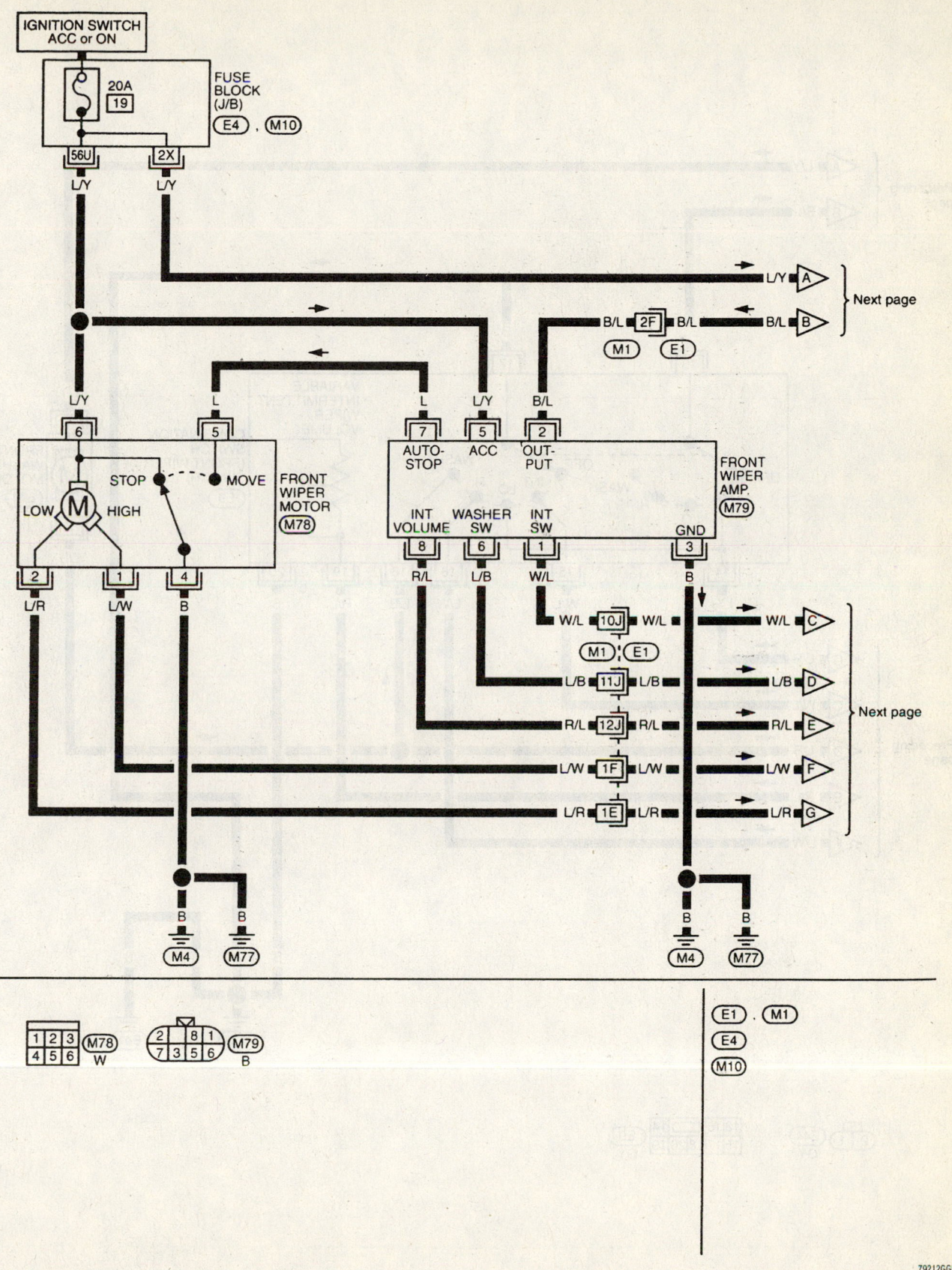

Windshield wiper/washer wiring schematic—Pathfinder

79212GGH

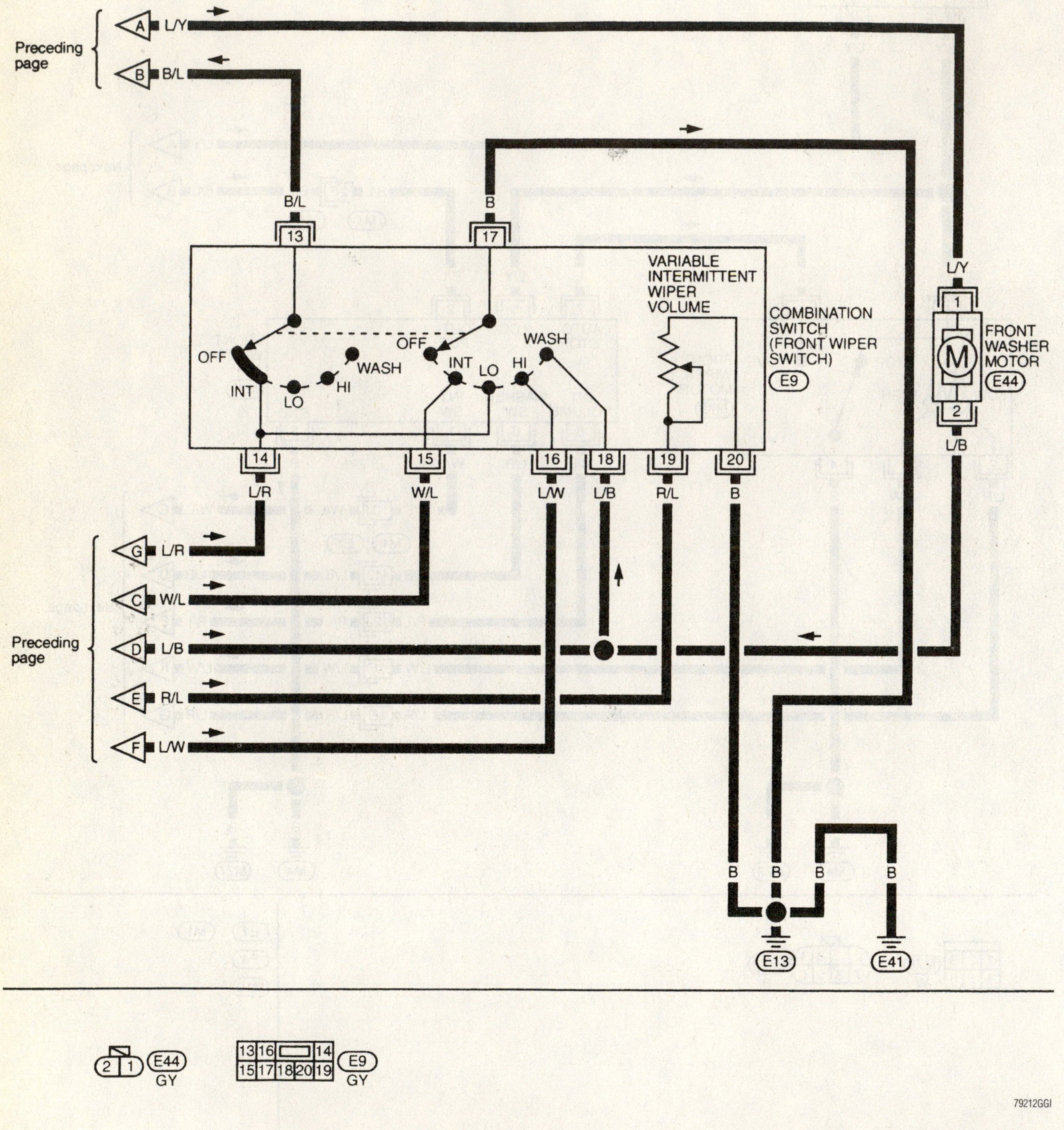

Preceding page

A L/Y

B B/L

B/L **13**

B **17**

OFF

INT   LO   HI   WASH

OFF   INT   LO   HI   WASH

VARIABLE INTERMITTENT WIPER VOLUME

COMBINATION SWITCH (FRONT WIPER SWITCH) (E9)

14 L/R

15 W/L

16 L/W

18 L/B

19 R/L

20 B

L/Y **1**

(M) FRONT WASHER MOTOR (E44)

2 L/B

Preceding page

G L/R

C W/L

D L/B

E R/L

F L/W

B   B   B   B

(E13)   (E41)

 (E44) GY

 (E9) GY

79212GGI

Windshield wiper/washer wiring schematic (cont.)—Pathfinder

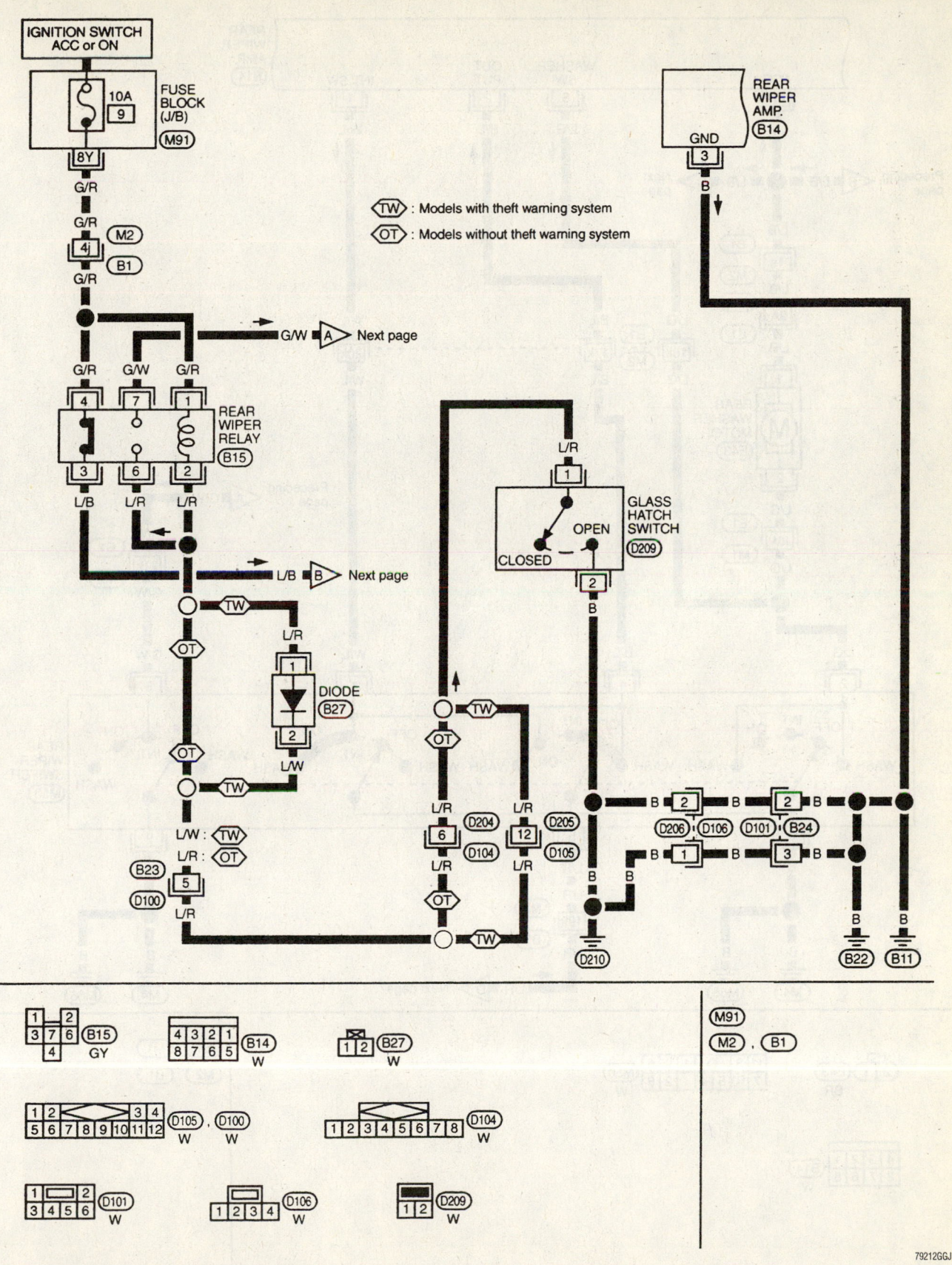

Rear wiper/washer wiring schematic—Pathfinder

Refer to the model specific sections for driveline service procedures

79212GGJ

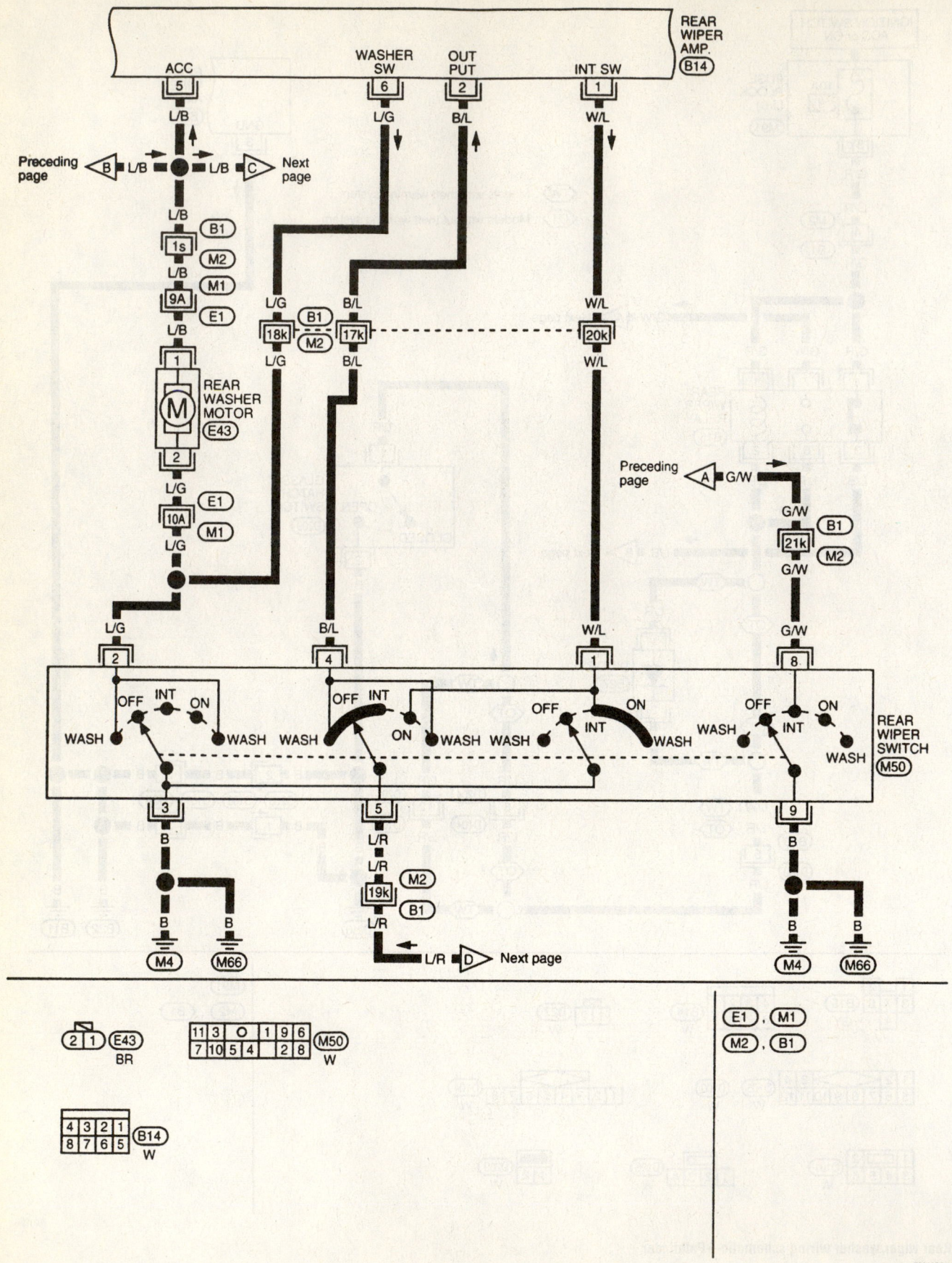

Rear wiper/washer wiring schematic (cont.)—Pathfinder

79212GGK

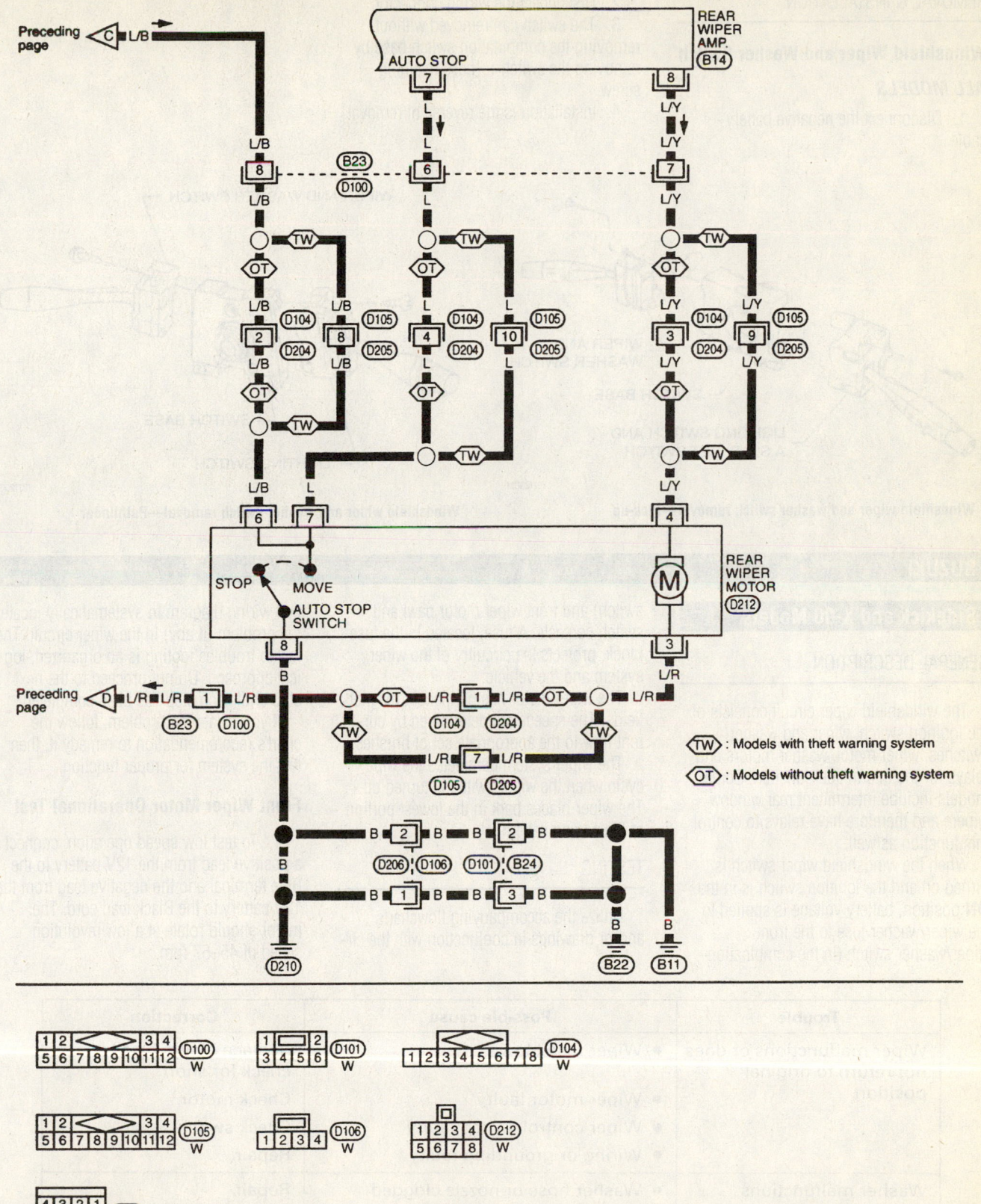

Rear wiper/washer wiring schematic (cont.)—Pathfinder

79212GGL

REMOVAL & INSTALLATION

Windshield Wiper and Washer Switch

ALL MODELS

1. Disconnect the negative battery cable.

2. Disconnect the wiring connector.
3. The switch can removed without removing the combination switch base by removing the switch-to-base retaining screw.
4. Installation is the reverse of removal.

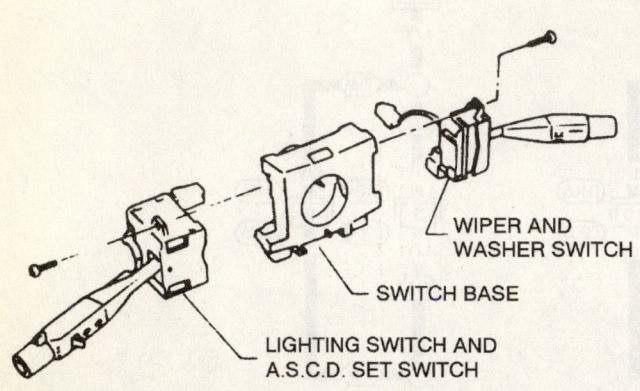

Windshield wiper and washer switch removal—Pick-up

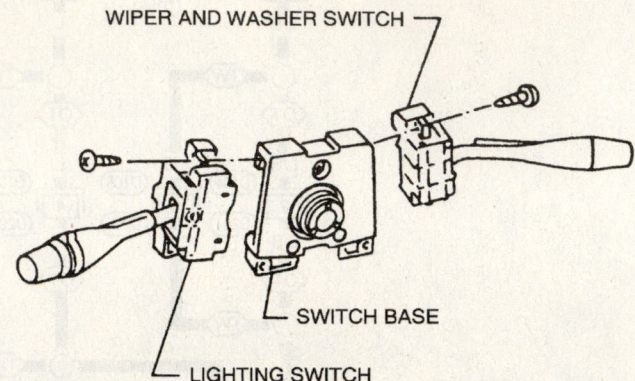

Windshield wiper and washer switch removal—Pathfinder

SUZUKI

Sidekick and X-90 Models

GENERAL DESCRIPTION

The windshield wiper circuit consists of the ignition switch, wiper and washer switches, wiper motor, washer motors and relays for the intermittent function. Some models include intermittent rear window wipers and therefore have relays to control this function as well.

When the windshield wiper switch is turned on and the ignition switch is in the **ON** position, battery voltage is applied to the wiper/washer fuse to the front wiper/washer switch (in the combination switch) and front wiper motor pawl and switch contacts. A fuse, located in the fuse block, protects the circuitry of the wiper system and the vehicle.

The wiper motor has permanent magnet fields. The speeds are determined by current flow to the appropriate set of brushes.

The wiper system completes the wipe cycle when the wiper switch is turned off. The wiper blades park in the lowest portion of the wiping pattern.

TESTING

Utilize the accompanying flowcharts and/or drawings in conjunction with the circuit wiring diagram to systematically locate the problem (if any) in the wiper circuit. The key to troubleshooting is an organized, logical approach. Do not proceed to the next step until each step has been completed.

If you locate the problem, follow the chart's recommendation to remedy it, then test the system for proper function.

Front Wiper Motor Operational Test

1. To test low speed operation, connect a positive lead from the 12V battery to the Blue terminal and the negative lead from the 12V battery to the Black lead cord. The motor should rotate at a low revolution speed of 45–57 rpm.

Trouble	Possible cause	Correction
Wiper malfunctions or does not return to original position.	• Wiper fuse blown	Replace blown fuse to check for short.
	• Wiper motor faulty	Check motor.
	• Wiper control switch faulty	Check switch.
	• Wiring or grounding faulty	Repair.
Washer malfunctions.	• Washer hose or nozzle clogged	Repair.
	• Washer motor faulty	Check motor.
	• Wiper control switch faulty	Check switch.
	• Wiring faulty	Repair.

General diagnostic chart—Sidekick and X-90 models

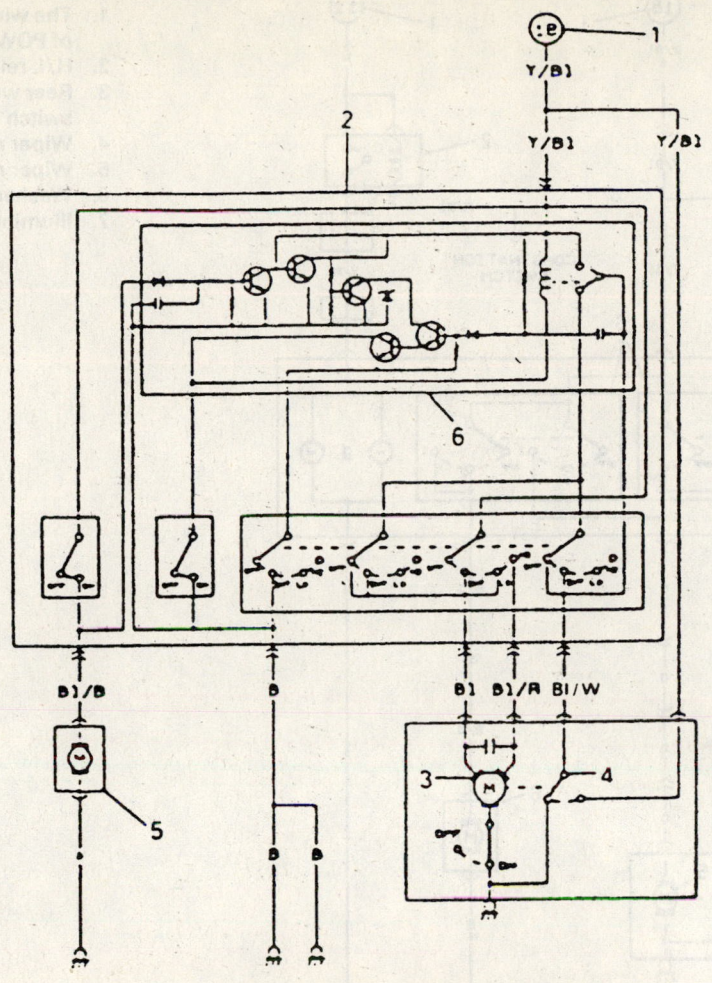

1. The wire No.s are same No.
   as figure of POWER SUPPLY DIAGRAM
2. Combination switch
3. Wiper motor
4. Wiper return switch
5. Washer motor
6. Wiper intermittent relay

7921ZG57

Circuit wiring diagram—Sidekick and X-90 models

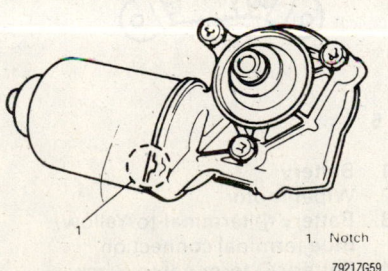

1. Notch

7921ZG59

The wiper motor cover notches into position—Sidekick and X-90 models

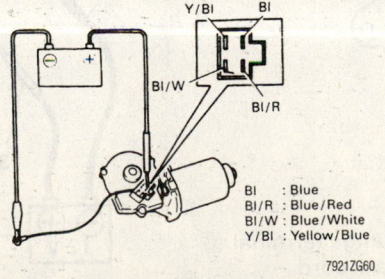

Bl : Blue
Bl/R : Blue/Red
Bl/W : Blue/White
Y/Bl : Yellow/Blue

7921ZG60

Test the front wiper motor operation as shown—Sidekick and X-90 models

2. To test high speed operation, connect the positive lead from the 12V battery to the Blue/Red terminal, and it's negative terminal to the black lead cord. For Samurai models, the motor should rotate at a speed of 67–81 rpm. For Sidekick and X-90 models, the motor should rotate at a speed of 68–78 rpm.

Rear Wiper Motor Operational Test

1. Connect the 12V battery positive and negative terminals to the Orange terminal

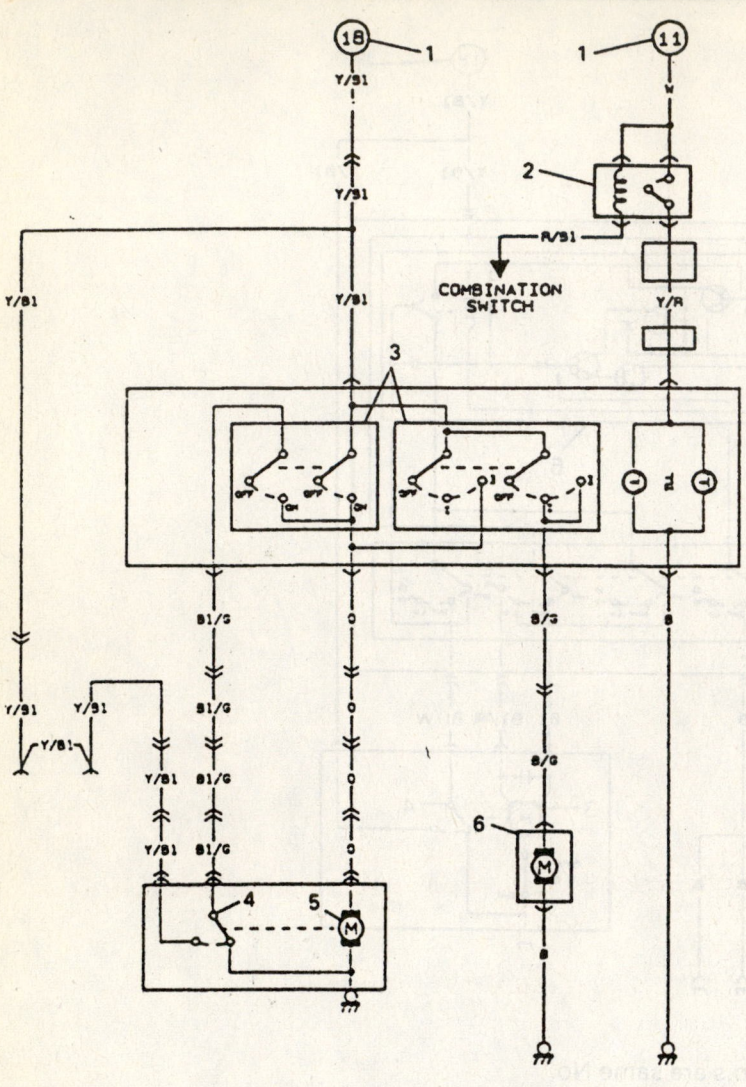

1. The wire No.s are same No. as figure of POWER SUPPLY DIAGRAM
2. H/L relay #2
3. Rear wiper and washer switch
4. Wiper return switch
5. Wiper motor
6. Washer motor
7. Illumination controller (If equipped)

Rear window wiper wiring diagram—Sidekick and X-90 models

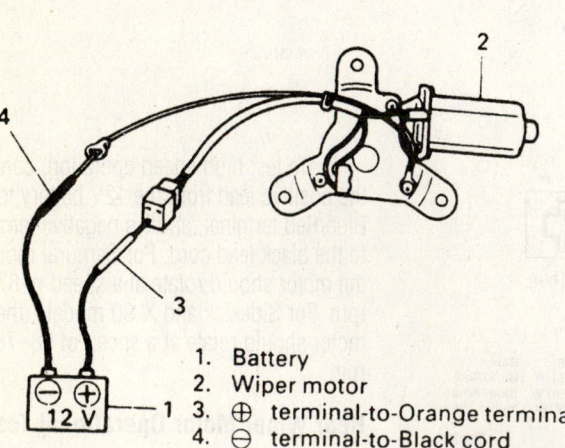

1. Battery
2. Wiper motor
3. ⊕ terminal-to-Orange terminal
4. ⊖ terminal-to-Black cord

Test the rear wiper motor as shown—Sidekick and X-90 models

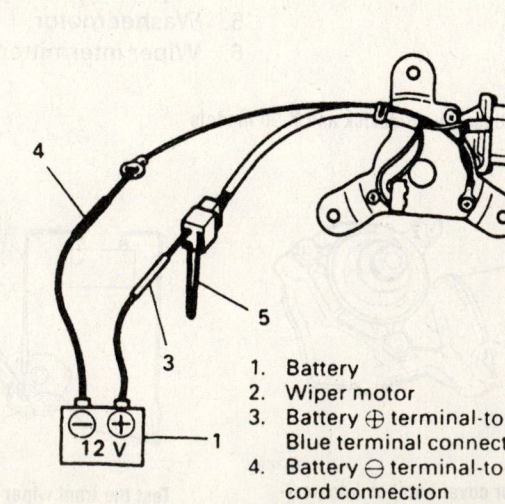

1. Battery
2. Wiper motor
3. Battery ⊕ terminal-to-Yellow/Blue terminal connection
4. Battery ⊖ terminal-to-Black cord connection
5. Jumper (Orange terminal-to-Blue/Green terminal connecting)

Test the automatic stop function as shown—Sidekick and X-90 models

and black lead cord respectively. If the motor rotates at a range of 38–46 rpm, it is correct.

Front Automatic Stop Action Test

1. Connect the battery positive terminal to the motor's Yellow terminal, and use a jumper to short the Blue/White (Blue/Black) and Blue terminals to each other to check whether the motor shaft stops at a given position. This position must conform to the start position. Stop the motor again and again use the jumper to confirm that it stops in the same position.

Rear Automatic Stop Test

1. Connect the battery positive and negative terminals to the motor Yellow terminal and black lead cord respectively.

2. Use a jumper wire to short the Orange and Green terminals to each other to check whether the motor shaft stops at a given position. use the jumper to make sure again and again that the shaft stops at the same position.

Brush and Commutator Test

1. Use a circuit tester to check the Blue terminal to Black lead cord continuity. If the continuity is poor, check the brush to commutator contact area for proper condition.

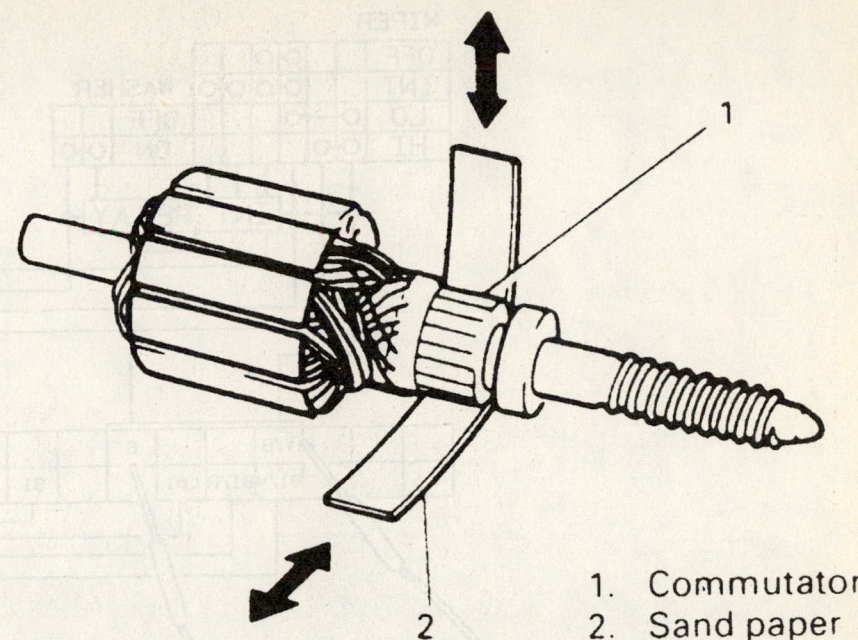

1. Commutator
2. Sand paper

7921ZG62

Restore the commutator with sandpaper as shown—Sidekick and X-90 models

2. When the area is fouled, use a cloth wetted with a suitable solvent to clean the area. When the area is coarse or burnt, use sandpaper to smooth it.

Washer Pump

➡**This procedure applies to front and rear pumps.**

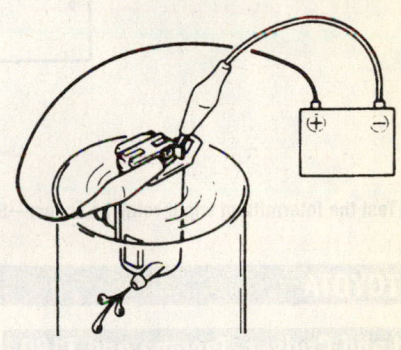

7921ZG63

Test the washer pump as shown—Sidekick and X-90 models

1. Connect the battery positive and negative terminals to the pump positive and negative terminals respectively to check the pumping rate.

Intermittent Wiper Relay Test

1. Disconnect the wiper/washer switch coupler.

2. Connect the positive battery terminal to the Yellow/White coupler terminal and the negative battery terminal to the Black terminal. If an operating sound is heard, the relay is working correctly.

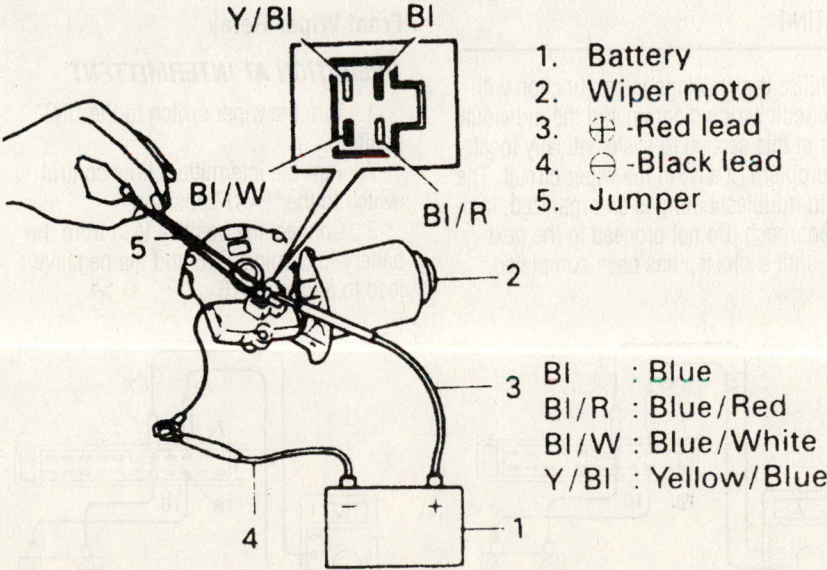

1. Battery
2. Wiper motor
3. ⊕ -Red lead
4. ⊖ -Black lead
5. Jumper

Bl : Blue
Bl/R : Blue/Red
Bl/W : Blue/White
Y/Bl : Yellow/Blue

7921ZG61

Test the automatic stop function as shown—Sidekick and X-90 models

Refer to the model specific sections for driveline service procedures

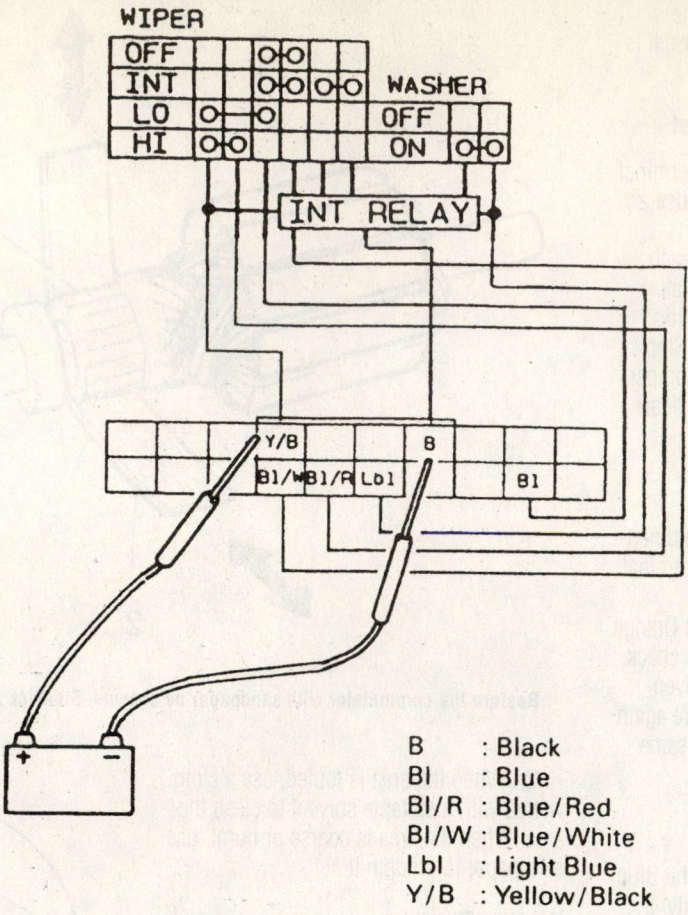

B : Black
Bl : Blue
Bl/R : Blue/Red
Bl/W : Blue/White
Lbl : Light Blue
Y/B : Yellow/Black

7921ZG64

Test the intermittent wiper relay as shown—Sidekick and X-90 shown

TOYOTA

Land Cruiser, Tacoma and T100 Models

GENERAL DESCRIPTION

The windshield wiper circuit consists of the ignition switch, wiper and washer switches, wiper motor, washer motors and relays for the intermittent function. Some models include intermittent rear window wipers and therefore have relays to control this function as well.

When the windshield wiper switch is turned on and the starter switch is in the **ON** or **START** position, battery voltage is applied to the wiper/washer fuse to the front wiper/washer switch (in the combination switch) and front wiper motor pawl and switch contacts. A fuse, located in the fuse block, protects the circuitry of the wiper system and the vehicle.

The wiper motor has permanent magnet fields. The speeds are determined by current flow to the appropriate set of brushes.

TESTING

Utilize the drawings in conjunction with the circuit wiring diagram and the individual tests in this section to systematically locate the problem (if any) in the wiper circuit. The key to troubleshooting is an organized, logical approach. Do not proceed to the next step until each step has been completed.

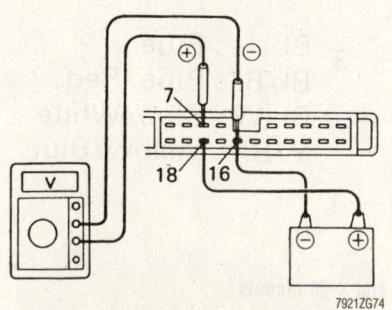

7921ZG74

Pertinent information to front wiper relay testing (in intermittent)—Land Cruiser, Tacoma and T100 models

Front Wiper Relay

OPERATION AT INTERMITTENT

1. Turn the wiper switch to the "INT" position.
2. Turn the intermittent time control switch to the "FAST" position.
3. Connect the positive lead from the battery to terminal B18 and the negative lead to terminal B16.

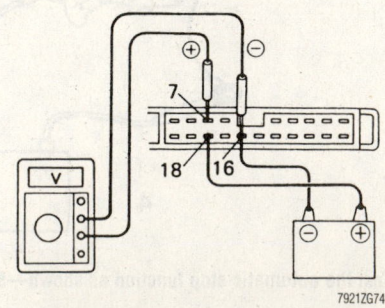

7921ZG74

Pertinent information to front wiper relay testing (in intermittent)—Land Cruiser, Tacoma and T100 models

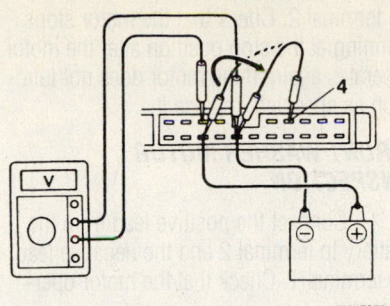

Pertinent information to front wiper relay testing (in intermittent)—Land Cruiser, Tacoma and T100 models

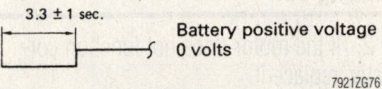

Pertinent information to front wiper relay testing (in intermittent)—Land Cruiser, Tacoma and T100 models

4. Connect the positive lead from the voltmeter to terminal B7 and the negative lead to terminal B16. Check that the meter indicates 12V positive voltage.

5. After connecting terminal B4 to B18, connect to terminal B16. Then check that the voltage within the times as shown in the accompanying table.

OPERATION AS WASHER LINKED

1. Connect the positive lead from the battery to terminal B18 and the negative lead to terminal B16.

2. Connect the positive lead from the voltmeter to terminal B7 and the negative lead to terminal B16.

3. Push in the washer switch. Check that the voltage changes as shown in the table. If the operation is not as specified, replace the switch.

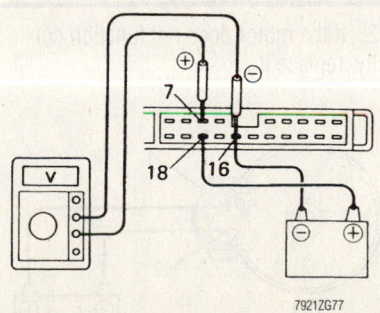

Pertinent information to front wiper relay testing (as washer linked)—Land Cruiser, Tacoma and T100 models

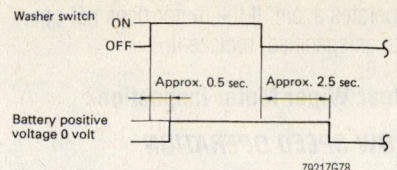

Pertinent information to front wiper relay testing (as washer linked)—Land Cruiser, Tacoma and T100 models

Rear Wiper Relay Inspection

CONTINUITY

1. Check that there is no continuity between terminals 1 and 3.

2. Check that there is continuity between terminals 2 and 3. If the continuity is not as specified, replace the relay.

Relay Side

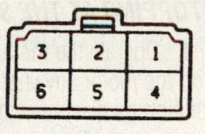

Rear wiper relay terminals—Land Cruiser, Tacoma and T100 models

OPERATION

1. Connect the positive lead from the battery to terminal 1 and the negative lead to terminal 6.

2. Connect the positive lead from the voltmeter to terminal 2 and the negative lead to terminal 6. Check that the meter indicates 0V.

3. Connect the positive lead from the voltmeter to terminal 3 and the negative lead to terminal 6. Check that the meter

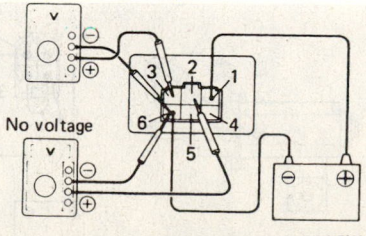

Rear wiper relay operation testing—Land Cruiser, Tacoma and T100 models

indicates 12V positive voltage. If the operation is not as specified, replace the relay.

INTERMITTENT OPERATION

1. Connect the positive lead from the battery to terminal 2 and the negative lead to terminal 4.

2. Connect the positive lead from the voltmeter to terminal 3 and the negative lead to terminal 4.

3. After disconnecting the positive lead from terminal 2, connect it to terminal 1. Check that the meter rises from 0V to 12V within 6–8 seconds. If operation is not as specified, replace the relay.

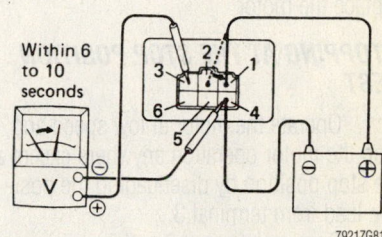

Rear wiper relay intermittent operation testing—Land Cruiser, Tacoma and T100 models

Front Wiper Motor Inspection

LOW SPEED OPERATION

1. Connect the positive lead from the battery to terminal 3 and the negative lead to terminal 1 (for T100, connect to the motor body). Check that the motor operates at low speed.

2. If operation is not as specified, replace the motor.

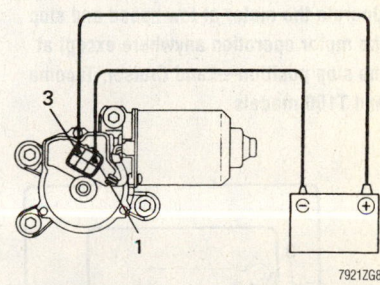

Low speed front wiper motor testing—Land Cruiser, Tacoma and T100 models

HIGH SPEED OPERATION

1. Connect the positive lead from the battery to terminal 2 and the negative lead to terminal 1 (for T100, connect to the

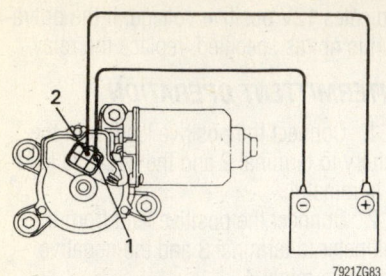

High speed front wiper motor testing—Land Cruiser, Tacoma and T100 models

motor body). Check that the motor operates at high speed.

2. If the operation is not as specified, replace the motor.

STOPPING AT THE STOP POSITION TEST

1. Operate the motor at low speed and stop the motor operation anywhere except at the stop position by disengaging the positive lead from terminal 3.

2. Connect terminal 3 and 5.

3. Connect the battery positive lead to terminal 6 and the battery negative lead to terminal 1. Check that the motor stops running at the stop position after the motor

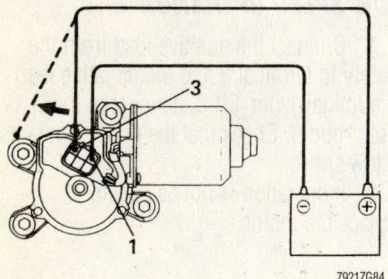

Operate the motor at low speed and stop the motor operation anywhere except at the stop position—Land Cruiser, Tacoma and T100 models

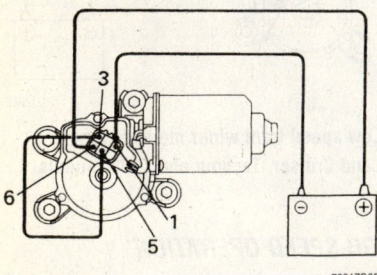

Check that the motor stops running at the stop position after the motor operates again—Land Cruiser, Tacoma and T100 models

operates again. If the motor does not operate as specified, replace it.

Rear Wiper Motor Inspection

LOW SPEED OPERATION

Connect the positive lead from the battery to terminal 3 and the negative lead to terminal 2. Check that the motor operates at low speed. If not, replace the motor.

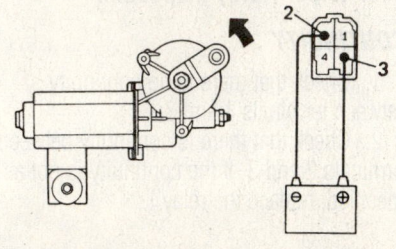

Rear wiper motor low speed operation inspection—Land Cruiser, Tacoma and T100 models

STOPPING AT THE STOP POSITION

1. Operate the motor at low speed, then stop the motor anywhere except at the stop position by disconnecting the positive lead from terminal 3.

2. Connect terminals 3 and 4.

3. Connect the positive lead from the battery to terminal 1 and the negative lead

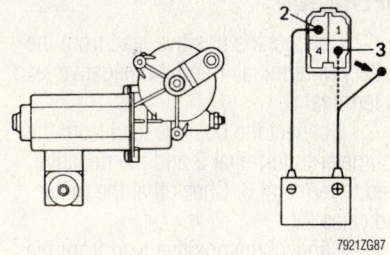

Run the motor to check stopping position—Land Cruiser, Tacoma and T100 models

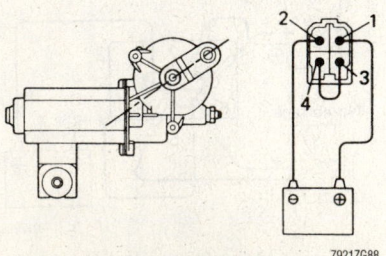

Check that the stopping position is correct—Land Cruiser, Tacoma and T100 models

to terminal 2. Check that the motor stops running at the stop position after the motor operates again. If the motor does not function as specified, replace it.

FRONT WASHER MOTOR INSPECTION

1. Connect the positive lead from the battery to terminal 2 and the negative lead to terminal 1. Check that the motor operates.

✳✳ WARNING

Perform these tests QUICKLY (within 20 seconds) to prevent the coil from burning out.

2. If the motor does not function correctly, replace it.

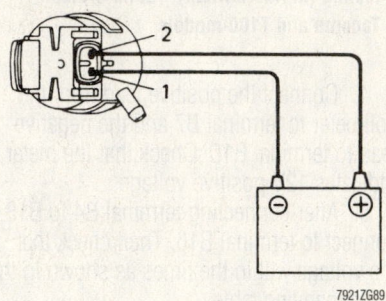

Front washer motor inspection—Land Cruiser, Tacoma and T100 models

REAR WASHER MOTOR INSPECTION

1. Connect the positive lead from the battery to terminal 1 and the negative lead to terminal 2. Check that the motor operates.

✳✳ WARNING

Perform these tests QUICKLY (within 20 seconds) to prevent the coil from burning out.

2. If the motor does not function correctly, replace it.

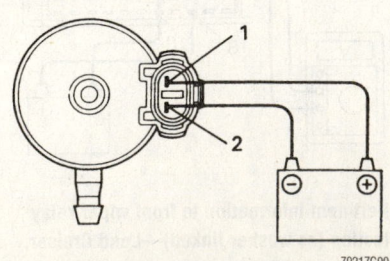

Rear washer motor inspection—Land Cruiser, Tacoma and T100 models

4Runner Models

GENERAL DESCRIPTION

The windshield wiper circuit consists of the ignition switch, wiper and washer switches, wiper motor, washer motors and relays for the intermittent function. Some models include intermittent rear window wipers and therefore have relays to control this function as well.

When the windshield wiper switch is turned on and the starter switch is in the **ON** or **START** position, battery voltage is applied to the wiper/washer fuse to the front wiper/washer switch (in the combination switch) and front wiper motor pawl and switch contacts. A fuse, located in the fuse block, protects the circuitry of the wiper system and the vehicle.

The wiper motor has permanent magnet fields. The speeds are determined by current flow to the appropriate set of brushes.

TESTING

Utilize the drawings in conjunction with the circuit wiring diagram and the individual tests in this section to systematically locate the problem (if any) in the wiper circuit. The key to troubleshooting is an organized, logical approach. Do not proceed to the next step until each step has been completed.

Front Wiper Inspection

INTERMITTENT OPERATION

1. Turn the wiper switch to the "INT" position.
2. If testing a variable type, turn the intermittent time control switch to FAST.
3. Connect the positive lead from the battery to terminal A4 and the negative lead to terminal A1.
4. Connect the positive lead from the voltmeter to terminal A8 and the negative lead to terminal A1. Check that the meter reads 12V positive voltage.
5. After connecting terminal A7 to terminal A4, connect to terminal A1.
6. Check that the voltage rises from 0V to 12V as shown in the table. If operation is not within specification, replace the switch.

LOW SPEED OPERATION

1. Connect the positive lead from the battery to terminal 2 and the negative lead to the motor body. Check that the motor operates at low speed.
2. If operation is not as specified, replace the motor.

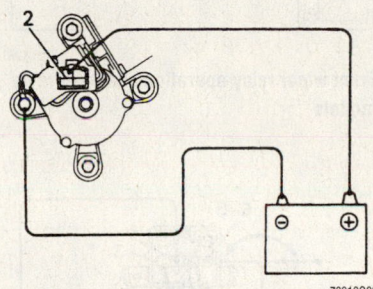

79212G93

Front wiper motor low speed operation inspection—4Runner models

HIGH SPEED OPERATION

1. Connect the positive lead from the battery to terminal 1 and the negative lead to the motor body. Check that the motor operates at high speed.
2. If the operation is not as specified, replace the motor.

STOPPING AT THE STOP POSITION TEST

1. Operate the motor at low speed and stop the motor operation anywhere except at the stop position by disengaging the positive lead from terminal 2.
2. Connect terminal 2 and 3.
3. Connect the battery positive lead to terminal 4 and the battery negative lead to the motor body. Check that the motor stops running at the stop position after the motor operates again. If the motor does not operate as specified, replace it.

Rear Wiper Motor Inspection

OPERATION

1. Connect the positive lead from the battery to terminal 1 and the negative lead to terminal 3. Check that the motor turns clockwise.
2. Reverse polarity. Check that the motor turns counterclockwise. If not, replace the motor.

CONTINUITY

1. Connect the battery positive lead to terminal 3 and the negative lead to terminal 1. Inspect the continuity and compare to the specifications on the table. If not within specification, replace the motor.

Front Washer Motor Inspection

1. Connect the battery positive lead to terminal 2 and the negative lead to terminal 1. Check that the motor operates.

✷✷ WARNING

Perform this test QUICKLY (within 20 seconds) to prevent the coil from burning out.

2. If the operation is not as specified, replace the motor.

Rear Washer Motor Inspection

1. Connect the battery positive lead to terminal 3 and the negative lead to terminal 1. Check that the motor operates.

Non Variable Type

Switch position	Specified condition	
INT	3.3 ± 1 sec.	Battery positive voltage / 0 volts

Variable Type

Switch position		Specified condition	
INT	FAST	1.6 ± 1 sec.	Battery positive voltage / 0 volts
	LOW	10.7 ± 5 sec.	Battery positive voltage / 0 volts

79212GZA

Front wiper motor intermittent testing—4Runner models

Motor link position	Tester connection to terminal number	Specified condition
A	5 — 6	Continuity
B	4 — 5 — 6	Continuity
C	5 — 6	Continuity
Except A, B or C	—	No continuity

79212GM0

Rear wiper motor continuity check—4Runner models

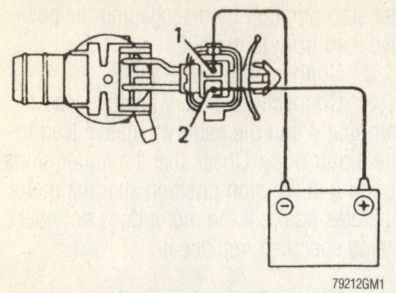

Rear washer motor inspection—4Runner models

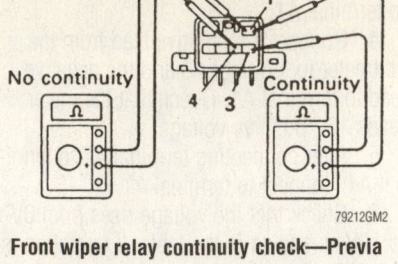

Front wiper relay continuity check—Previa models

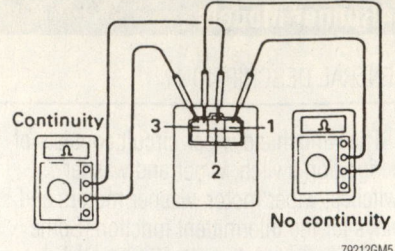

Rear wiper relay continuity check—Previa models

✳✳ WARNING

Perform this test QUICKLY (within 20 seconds) to prevent the coil from burning out.

2. If the operation is not as specified, replace the motor.

Previa Models

GENERAL DESCRIPTION

The windshield wiper circuit consists of the ignition switch, wiper and washer switches, wiper motor, washer motors and relays for the intermittent function. Some models include intermittent rear window wipers and therefore have relays to control this function as well.

When the windshield wiper switch is turned on and the starter switch is in the **ON** or **START** position, battery voltage is applied to the wiper/washer fuse to the front wiper/washer switch (in the combination switch) and front wiper motor pawl and switch contacts. A fuse, located in the fuse block, protects the circuitry of the wiper system and the vehicle.

The wiper motor has permanent magnet fields. The speeds are determined by current flow to the appropriate set of brushes.

TESTING

Front Wiper Relay

CONTINUITY

1. Check that there is no continuity between terminals 1 and 4.
2. Check that there is continuity between terminals 1 and 3. If not as specified, replace the relay.

OPERATION AT WIPER LINKED

1. Connect the positive lead from the battery to terminal 4 and the negative lead to terminal 5.

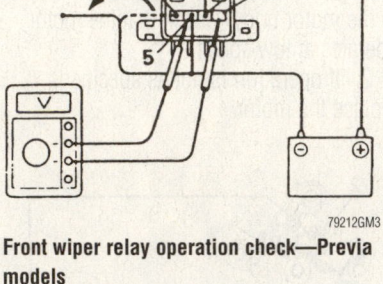

Front wiper relay operation check—Previa models

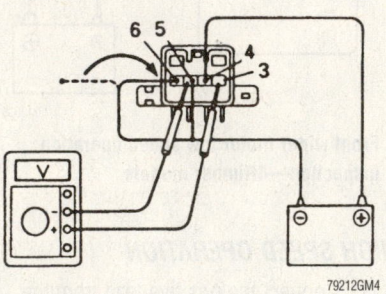

Front wiper relay operation check—Previa models

2. Connect the positive lead from the voltmeter to terminal 3 and the negative lead to terminal 5.

3. Connect the negative lead from the battery to terminal 6. Check that the voltage changes soon to 12V (battery positive voltage) from 0V (no voltage).

4. Disconnect the negative lead from terminal 6. Check that the voltage changes to 0V from 12V approximately 2.5 seconds later. If not as specified, replace the relay.

Rear Wiper Relay Inspection

CONTINUITY

1. Check that there is no continuity between terminals 1 and 3.
2. Check that there is continuity between terminals 2 and 3. If not as specified, replace the relay.

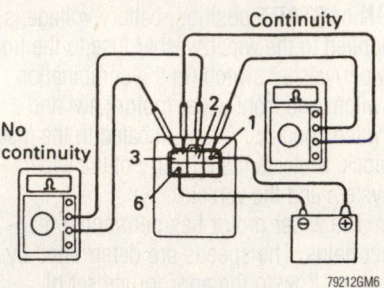

Rear wiper relay continuity check—Previa models

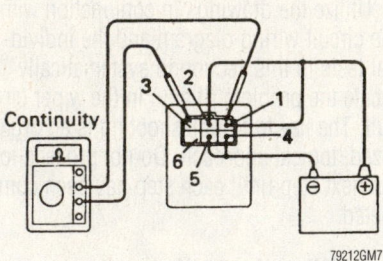

Rear wiper relay continuity check—Previa models

OPERATION

1. Connect the positive lead from the battery to terminal 1 and the negative lead to terminal 6.

2. Check that there is continuity between terminal 1 and 3.

3. Check that there is no continuity between terminal 2 and 3.

4. Connect the battery positive leads to terminals 1 and 2 and check that there is no continuity between terminals 1 and 3 for 3–5 seconds, then there is no continuity.

5. Disconnect the positive lead from terminal 2, check that there is no continuity between terminals 1 and 3 for 9–15 seconds, then there is continuity. If the relay does not function as specified, replace it.

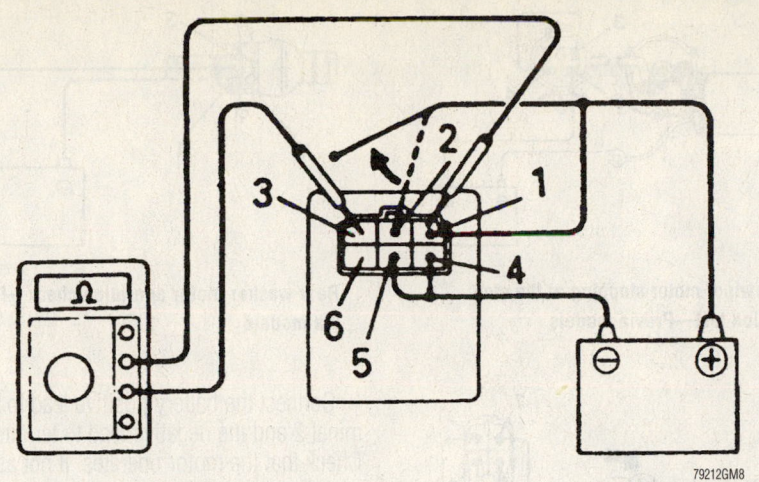

Rear wiper relay operational check—Previa models

Front Wiper Motor

LOW SPEED OPERATION

1. Connect the battery positive lead to terminal 3 and the negative lead to the lead wire, then check that the motor operates at low speed. If the motor does not operate as specified, replace it.

HIGH SPEED OPERATION

1. Connect the positive lead from the battery to terminal 2 and the negative lead to the lead wire. Check that the motor runs at high speed. If not as specified, replace the motor.

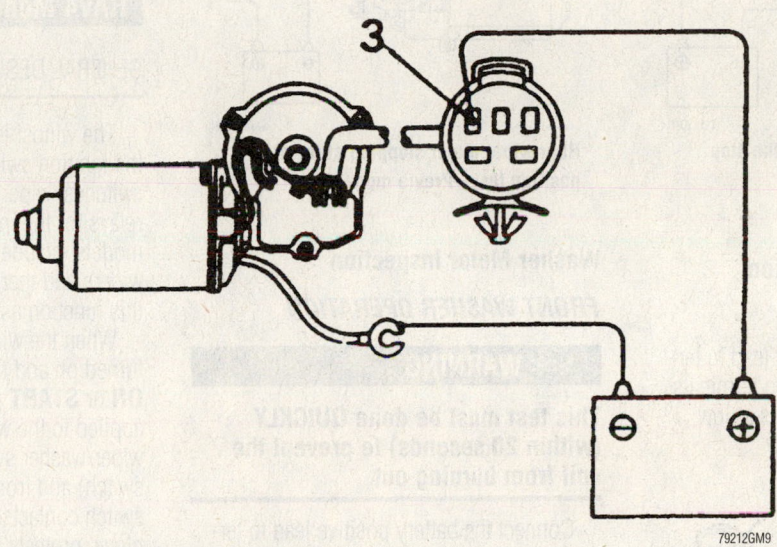

Front wiper motor low speed operation check—Previa models

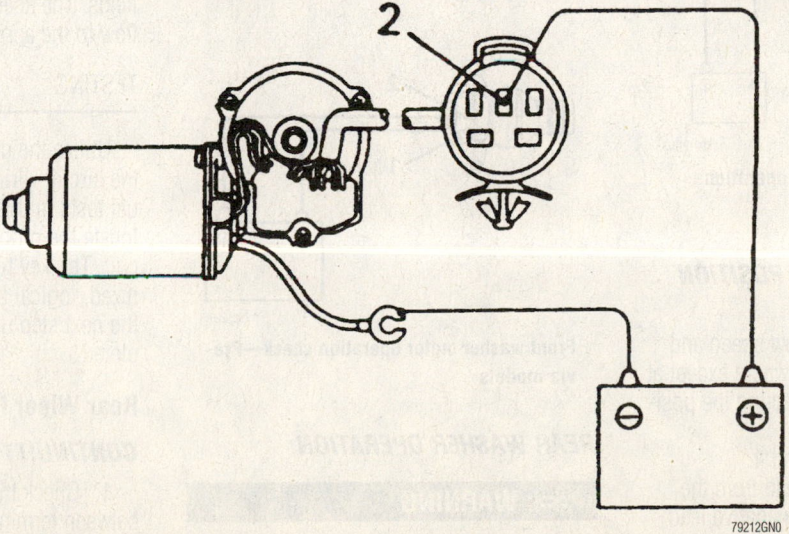

Front wiper motor high speed operation check—Previa models

Refer to the model specific sections for driveline service procedures

STOPPING AT THE STOP POSITION TEST

1. Operate the motor at low speed and stop the motor operation anywhere except at the stop position by disconnecting the positive lead from terminal 3.

2. Connect terminals 3 and 4.

3. Connect the battery positive lead to terminal 5 and the negative lead to the lead wire. Check that the motor stops running at the stop position after the motor operates again. If not as specified, replace the motor.

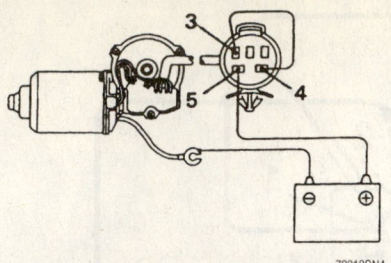

Rear wiper motor stopping at the stop position test—Previa models

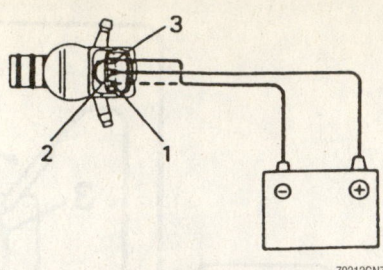

Rear washer motor operation check—Previa models

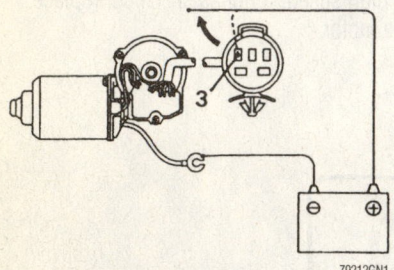

Front wiper motor stopping at the stop position test—Previa models

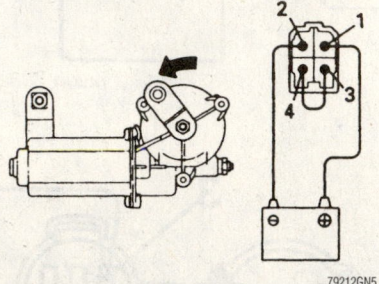

Rear wiper motor stopping at the stop position test—Previa models

Connect the battery positive lead to terminal 2 and the negative lead to terminal 3. Check that the motor operates. If not as specified, replace the motor.

RAV4 Models

GENERAL DESCRIPTION

The windshield wiper circuit consists of the ignition switch, wiper and washer switches, wiper motor, washer motors and relays for the intermittent function. Some models include intermittent rear window wipers and therefore have relays to control this function as well.

When the windshield wiper switch is turned on and the starter switch is in the **ON** or **START** position, battery voltage is applied to the wiper/washer fuse to the front wiper/washer switch (in the combination switch) and front wiper motor pawl and switch contacts. A fuse, located in the fuse block, protects the circuitry of the wiper system and the vehicle.

The wiper motor has permanent magnet fields. The speeds are determined by current flow to the appropriate set of brushes.

TESTING

Utilize the drawings in conjunction with the circuit wiring diagram and the individual tests in this section to systematically locate the problem (if any) in the wiper circuit. The key to troubleshooting is an organized, logical approach. Do not proceed to the next step until each step has been completed.

Rear Wiper Motor Inspection

LOW SPEED OPERATION

Connect the battery positive lead to terminal 3 and the negative lead to terminals 2. Check that the motor operates at low speed. If not, replace the motor.

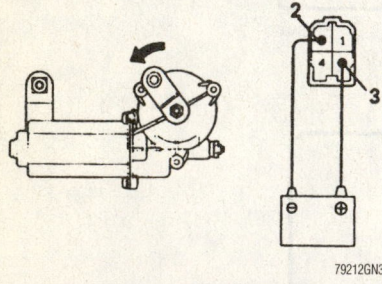

Rear wiper motor low speed operation check—Previa models

STOPPING AT THE STOP POSITION TEST

1. Operate the motor at low speed and stop the motor operation anywhere except at the stop position by disconnecting the positive lead from terminal 3.

2. Connect terminals 3 and 4.

3. Connect the positive lead from the battery to terminal 1 and the negative lead to terminal 2. Check that the motor stops at the stop position after the motor operates again. If not as specified, replace the motor.

Washer Motor Inspection

FRONT WASHER OPERATION

✳✳ WARNING

This test must be done QUICKLY (within 20 seconds) to prevent the coil from burning out.

Connect the battery positive lead to terminal 2 and the negative lead to terminal 1. Check that the motor operates. If not as specified, replace the motor.

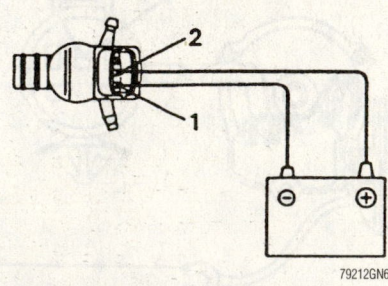

Front washer motor operation check—Previa models

REAR WASHER OPERATION

✳✳ WARNING

This test must be done QUICKLY (within 20 seconds) to prevent the coil from burning out.

Rear Wiper Relay Inspection

CONTINUITY

1. Check that there is no continuity between terminals 3 and 4.

2. Check that there is continuity between terminals 4 and 5. If not as specified, replace the relay.

Relay Side

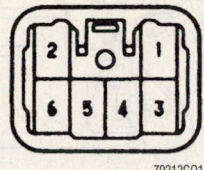

Rear wiper relay continuity check—RAV4 models

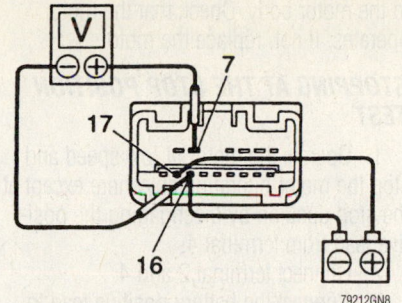

Front wiper motor intermittent testing—RAV4 models

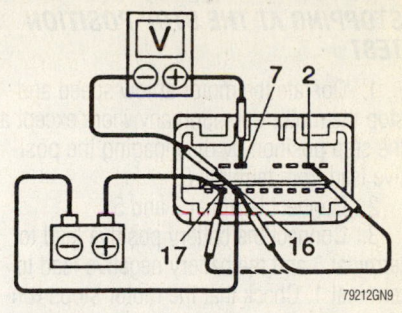

Front wiper motor intermittent testing—RAV4 models

OPERATION

1. Connect the positive lead from the battery to terminal 3 and the negative lead to terminal 6.

2. Connect the positive lead from the voltmeter to terminal 5 and the negative lead to terminal 6. Check that the meter indicates 0V.

3. Connect the positive lead from the voltmeter to terminal 4 and the negative lead to terminal 6. Check that the meter indicates 12V positive voltage. If the operation is not as specified, replace the relay.

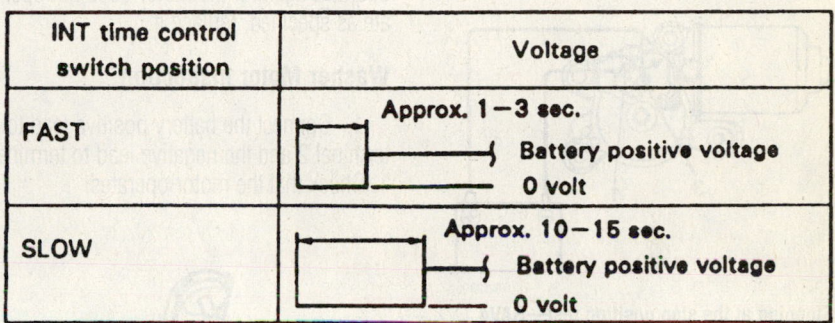

Front wiper motor intermittent testing—RAV4 models

INT time control switch position	Voltage
FAST	Approx. 1–3 sec. Battery positive voltage 0 volt
SLOW	Approx. 10–15 sec. Battery positive voltage 0 volt

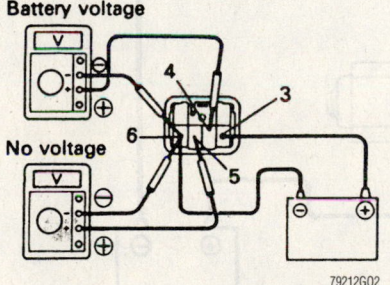

Rear wiper relay operation testing—RAV4 models

INTERMITTENT OPERATION

1. Connect the positive lead from the battery to terminal 5 and the negative lead to terminal 4 more than 2 seconds.

2. Connect the positive lead from the voltmeter to terminal 4 and the negative lead to terminal 2.

3. After disconnecting the positive lead from terminal 5, connect it to terminal 3. Check that the meter rises from 0V to 12V within 9–15 seconds. If operation is not as specified, replace the relay.

Front Wiper Inspection

INTERMITTENT OPERATION

1. Turn the wiper switch to the "INT" position.

2. Turn the intermittent time control switch to FAST.

3. Connect the positive lead from the battery to terminal 17 and the negative lead to terminal 16.

4. Connect the positive lead from the voltmeter to terminal 7 and the negative lead to terminal 16. Check that the meter reads 12V positive voltage.

5. After connecting terminal 2 to terminal 17, connect to terminal 16.

6. Check that the voltage rises from 0V to 12V as shown in the table. If operation is not within specification, replace the switch.

LOW SPEED OPERATION

1. Connect the positive lead from the battery to terminal 3 and the negative lead to terminal 1. Check that the motor operates at low speed.

2. If operation is not as specified, replace the motor.

HIGH SPEED OPERATION

1. Connect the positive lead from the battery to terminal 2 and the negative lead to terminal 1. Check that the motor operates at high speed.

2. If the operation is not as specified, replace the motor.

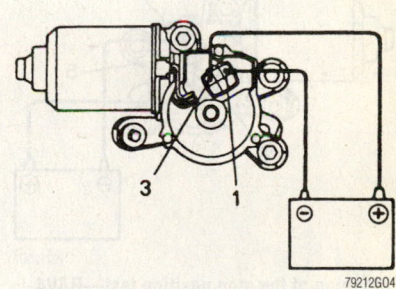

Front wiper motor low speed operation inspection—RAV4 models

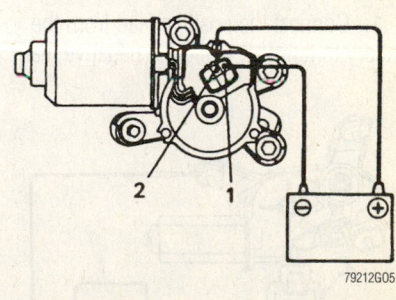

Front wiper motor high speed operation inspection—RAV4 models

STOPPING AT THE STOP POSITION TEST

1. Operate the motor at low speed and stop the motor operation anywhere except at the stop position by disengaging the positive lead from terminal 3.

2. Connect terminal 3 and 5.

3. Connect the battery positive lead to terminal 6 and the battery negative lead to terminal 1. Check that the motor stops running at the stop position after the motor operates again. If the motor does not operate as specified, replace it.

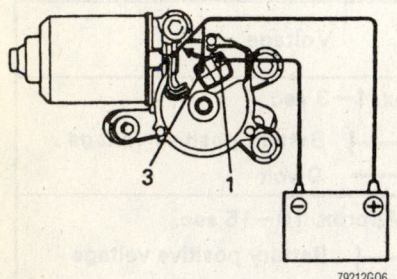

Stopping at the stop position test—RAV4 models

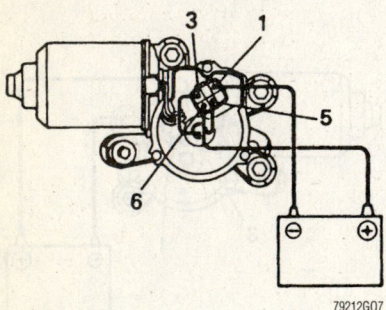

Stopping at the stop position test—RAV4 models

Rear Wiper Motor Inspection

OPERATION

1. Connect the positive lead from the battery to terminal 4 and the negative lead

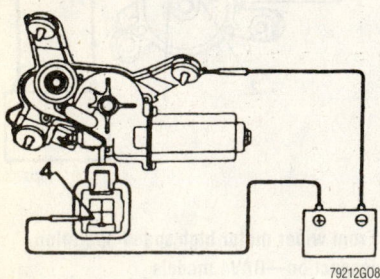

Rear wiper motor operation inspection—RAV4 models

to the motor body. Check that the motor operates. If not, replace the motor.

STOPPING AT THE STOP POSITION TEST

1. Operate the motor at low speed and stop the motor operation anywhere except at the stop position by disengaging the positive lead from terminal 4.

2. Connect terminal 2 and 4.

3. Connect the battery positive lead to terminal 1 and the battery negative lead to the motor body. Check that the motor stops running at the stop position after the motor operates again. If the motor does not operate as specified, replace it.

Washer Motor Inspection

1. Connect the battery positive lead to terminal 2 and the negative lead to terminal 1. Check that the motor operates.

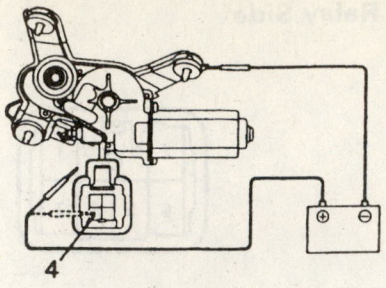

Rear wiper motor stopping at the stop position test—RAV4 models

✳✳ WARNING

Perform this test QUICKLY (within 20 seconds) to prevent the coil from burning out.

2. If the operation is not as specified, replace the motor.

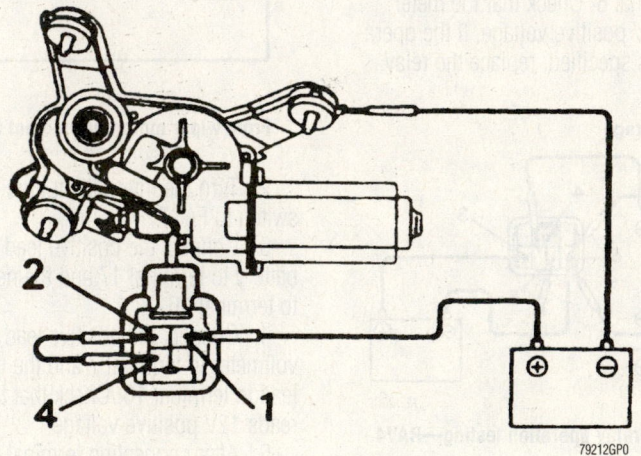

Rear wiper motor stopping at the stop position test—RAV4 models

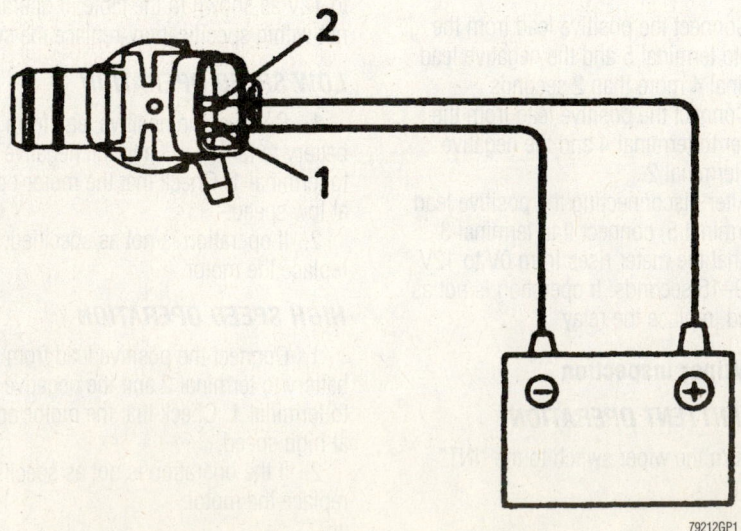

Front washer motor inspection—RAV4 models

OXYGEN (O₂) SENSORS

7

OXYGEN (O₂) SENSORS

General Information

An Oxygen (O₂) sensor is an input device used by the engine control computer to monitor the amount of oxygen in the exhaust gas stream. This information is used by the computer, along with other inputs, to fine-tune the air/fuel mixture so that the engine can run with the greatest efficiency in all conditions. The O₂ sensor sends this information to the computer in the form of a 100–900 millivolt (mV) reference signal, which is actually created by the O₂ sensor itself through chemical interactions between the sensor tip material (zirconium dioxide in almost all cases), the oxygen levels in the exhaust gas stream, and ambient atmosphere gas. At operating temperatures, approximately 1100°F (600°C), the element becomes a semiconductor. Essentially, through the differing levels of oxygen in the exhaust gas stream and in the surrounding atmosphere, the sensor creates a voltage signal which is directly and consistently related to the concentration of oxygen in the exhaust stream. Typically, a higher than normal amount of oxygen in the exhaust stream indicates that not all of the available oxygen was used in the combustion process, because there was not enough

fuel (lean condition) present. Inversely, a lower than normal concentration of oxygen in the exhaust stream indicates that a large amount was used in the combustion process, because a larger than necessary amount of fuel was present (rich condition). Thus, the engine control computer can correct the amount of fuel introduced into the combustion chambers.

Since the control computer uses the O₂ sensor output voltage as an indication of the oxygen concentration, and the oxygen concentration directly affects O₂ sensor output, the signal voltage from the sensor to the computer fluctuates constantly. This fluctuation is caused by the nature of the interaction between the computer and the O₂ sensor, which follows a general pattern: detect, compare, compensate, detect, compare, compensate, etc. This means that when the computer detects a lean signal from the O₂ sensor, it compares the reading with known parameters stored within its memory. It calculates that there is too much oxygen present in the exhaust gases, so it compensates by adding more fuel to the air/fuel mixture. This, in turn, causes the O₂ sensor to send a rich signal to the computer, which then compares this new signal, and adjusts the air/fuel mixture again. This

pattern constantly repeats itself: detect rich, compare, compensate lean, detect lean, compare, compensate rich, etc. Since the O₂ sensor fluctuates between rich and lean, and because the lean limit for sensor output is 100 mV and the rich limit is 900 mV, the proper voltage signal from a normally functioning O₂ sensor consistently fluctuates between 100–300 and 700–900 mV.

➡ **The sensor voltage may never quite reach 100 or 900 mV, but it should fluctuate from at least below 300 mV to above 700 mV, and the mid-point of the fluctuations should be centered around 500 mV.**

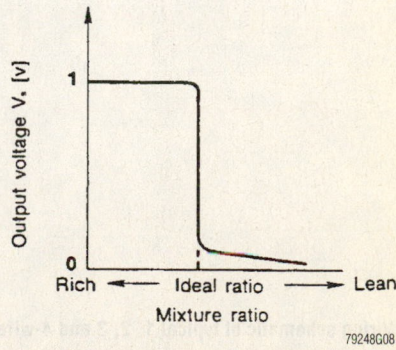

O₂ sensor output voltage vs. mixture ratio

79248G08

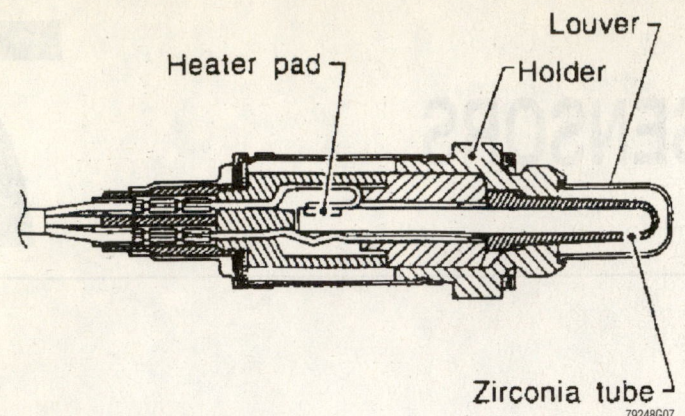

Heater pad — Louver —

Holder

Zirconia tube

79248G07

A cut away view of a heated oxygen sensor

To improve O₂ sensor efficiency, newer O₂ sensors were designed with a built-in heating element, and were called Heated Oxygen (HO₂) sensors. This heating element was incorporated into the sensor so that the sensor would reach optimal operating temperature quicker, meaning that the O₂ sensor output signal could be used by the engine control computer sooner. Because the sensor reaches optimal temperature quicker, modern vehicles enjoy improved driveability and fuel economy even before the engine reaches normal operating temperature.

On-Board Diagnostics second generation (OBD-II), an updated system based on the former OBD-I, calls for additional O₂ sensors to be used after the catalytic converter, so that catalytic converter efficiency can be measured by the vehicle's engine control computer. The O₂ sensors mounted in the exhaust system after the catalytic converters are not used to affect air/fuel mixture; they are used solely to monitor catalytic converter efficiency.

O2 (Oxygen Sensors) Service

PRECAUTIONS

When testing or servicing an O₂ sensor you will need to start and warm the engine to operating temperature in order to either perform the necessary testing procedures or to easily remove the sensor from its fitting. This will create a situation in which you will be working around a **HOT** exhaust system. The following is a list of precautions to consider during this service:

• Do not pierce any wires when testing an O₂ sensor, as this can lead to wiring harness damage. Backprobe the connector, when necessary.

• While testing the sensor, be sure to keep out of the way of moving engine components, such as the cooling fan. Refrain from wearing loose clothing which may

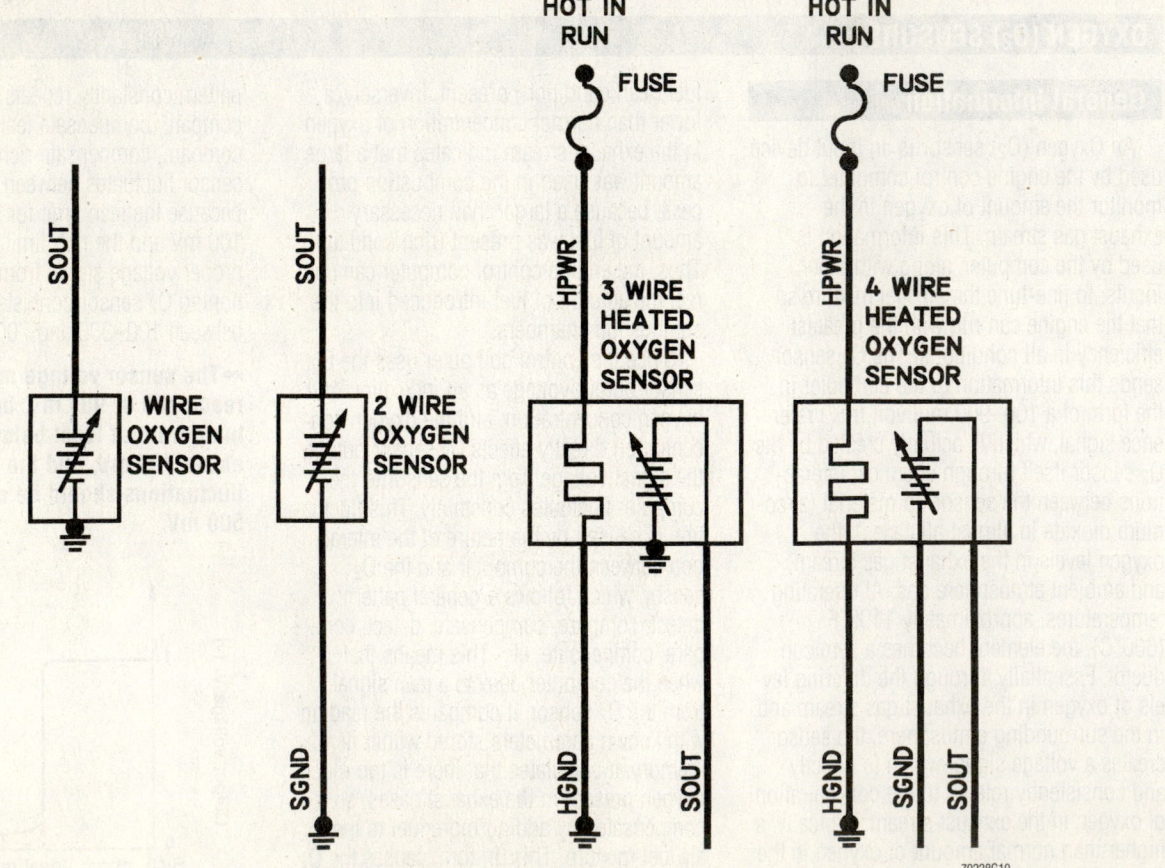

Wiring schematic of typical 1, 2, 3 and 4-wire oxygen sensor circuits

become tangled in moving engine components.

• Safety glasses must be worn at all times when working on or near the exhaust system. Older exhaust systems may be covered with loose rust particles which can shower you when disturbed. These particles are more than a nuisance and can injure your eye.

• Be cautious when working on and around the hot exhaust system. Painful burns will result if skin is exposed to the exhaust system pipes or manifolds.

• The O₂ sensor may be difficult to remove when the engine temperature is below 120°F (48°C). Excessive force may damage the threads in the exhaust manifold or pipe, therefore always start the engine and allow it to reach normal operating temperature prior to removal.

• Since O₂ sensors are usually designed with a permanently-attached wiring pigtail (this allows the wiring harness and sensor connectors to be positioned away from the hot exhaust system), it may be necessary to use a socket or wrench that is designed specifically for this purpose.

TESTING

The best, and most accurate method to test the operation of an O₂ sensor is with the use of either an oscilloscope or a Diagnostic Scan Tool (DST), following their specific instructions for testing. It is possible, however, to test whether the O₂ sensor is functioning properly within general parameters using a Digital Volt-Ohmmeter (DVOM), also referred to as a Digital Multi-Meter (DMM). Newer DMM's are often designed to perform many advanced diagnostic functions, and some are even constructed to be used as an oscilloscope. Two in-vehicle testing procedures, and one bench test procedure, will be provided for the common zirconium dioxide oxygen sensor. The first in-vehicle test makes use of a standard DVOM with a 10 megohms impedance, whereas the second in-vehicle test presented necessitates the usage of an advanced DMM with MIN/MAX/Average functions. Both of these in-vehicle test procedures are likely to set Diagnostic Trouble Codes (DTC's) in the engine control computer. Therefore, after testing, be sure to clear all DTC's before retesting the sensor, if necessary.

These are some of the common DTC's which may be set during testing:

• Open in the O₂ sensor circuit
• Constant low voltage in the O₂ sensor circuit
• Constant high voltage in the O₂ sensor circuit
• Other fuel system problems could set a O₂ sensor code

➡**Because an improperly functioning fuel delivery and/or control system can adversely affect the O₂ sensor voltage output signal, testing only the O₂ sensor is an inaccurate method for diagnosing an engine driveability problem.**

If after testing the sensor, the sensor is thought to be defective because of high or low readings, be sure to check that the fuel delivery and engine management system is working properly before condemning the O₂ sensor. Otherwise, the new O₂ sensor may continue to register the same high or low readings.

Often, by testing the O₂ sensor, another problem in the engine control management system can be diagnosed. If the sensor appears to be defective while installed in the vehicle, perform the bench test. If the sensor functions properly during the bench test, chances are that there may be a larger problem in the vehicle's fuel delivery and/or control system.

Many things can cause an O₂ sensor to fail, including old age, antifreeze contamination, physical damage, prolonged exposure to overly-rich exhaust gases, and exposure to silicone sealant fumes. Be sure to remedy any such condition prior to installing a new sensor, otherwise the new sensor may be damaged as well.

➡**Perform a visual inspection of the sensor. black sooty deposits may indicate a rich air/fuel mixture, brown deposits may indicate an oil consumption problem, and white gritty deposits may indicate an internal coolant leak. All of these conditions can destroy a new sensor if not corrected before installation.**

O₂ Sensor Terminal Identification

The easiest method for determining sensor terminal identification is to use a wiring diagram for the vehicle and engine in question. However, if a wiring diagram is not available there is a method for determining terminal identification. Throughout the testing procedures, the following terms will be used for clarity:

• Vehicle harness connector—this refers to the connector on the wires which are attached to the vehicle; NOT the connector at the end of the sensor pigtail.
• Sensor pigtail connector—this refers to the connector attached to the sensor itself.
• O₂ circuit—this refers to the circuit in a Heated Oxygen (HO₂) sensor which corresponds to the oxygen-sensing function of the sensor; NOT the heating element circuit.
• Heating circuit—this refers to the circuit in a HO₂ sensor which is designed to warm the HO₂ sensor quickly to improve driveability.
• Sensor Output (SOUT) terminal—this is the terminal which corresponds to the O₂ circuit output. This is the terminal which will register the millivolt signals created by the sensor based upon the amount of oxygen in the exhaust gas stream.
• Sensor Ground (SGND) terminal—when a sensor is so equipped, this refers to the O₂ circuit ground terminal. Many O₂ sensors are not equipped with a ground wire, rather they utilize the exhaust system for the ground circuit.
• Heating Power (HPWR) terminal—this terminal corresponds to the circuit which provides the O₂ sensor heating circuit with power when the ignition key is turned to the **ON** or **RUN** positions.
• Heating Ground (HGND) terminal—this is the terminal connected to the heating circuit ground wire.

1-WIRE SENSOR

1-wire sensors are by far the easiest to determine sensor terminal identification, but this is self-evident. On 1-wire O₂ sensors, the single wire terminal is the SOUT and the exhaust system is used to provide the sensor ground pathway. Proceed to the test procedures.

2-WIRE SENSOR

On 2-wire sensors, one of the connector terminals is the SOUT and the other is the SGND. To determine which one is which, perform the following:

1. Locate the O₂ sensor and its pigtail connector. It may be necessary to raise and safely support the vehicle to gain access to the connector.

2. Start the engine and allow it to warm up to normal operating temperature, then turn the engine **OFF**.

3. Using a DVOM set to read 100–900

mV (millivolts) DC, backprobe the positive DVOM lead to one of the unidentified terminals and attach the negative lead to a good engine ground.

✳✳ CAUTION

While the engine is running, keep clear of all moving and hot components. Do not wear loose clothing. Otherwise severe personal injury or death may occur.

4. Have an assistant restart the engine and allow it to idle.

5. Check the DVOM for voltage.

6. If no voltage is evident, check your DVOM leads to ensure that they are properly connected to the terminal and engine ground. If still no voltage is evident at the first terminal, move the positive meter lead to backprobe the second terminal.

7. If voltage is now present, the positive meter lead is attached to the SOUT terminal. The remaining terminal is the SGND terminal. If still no voltage is evident, either the O₂ sensor is defective or the meter leads are not making adequate contact with the engine ground and terminal contacts; clean the contacts and retest. If still no voltage is evident, the sensor is defective.

8. Have your assistant turn the engine **OFF**.

9. Label the sensor pigtail SOUT and SGND terminals.

10. Proceed to the test procedures.

3-WIRE SENSOR

➡ **3-wire sensors are HO₂ sensors.**

On 3-wire sensors, one of the connector terminals is the SOUT, one of the terminals is the HPWR and the other is the HGND. The SGND is achieved through the exhaust system, as with the 1-wire O₂ sensor. To identify the 3 terminals, perform the following:

1. Locate the O₂ sensor and its pigtail connector. It may be necessary to raise and safely support the vehicle to gain access to the connector.

2. Disengage the sensor pigtail connector from the vehicle harness connector.

3. Using a DVOM set to read 12 volts, attach the DVOM ground lead to a good engine ground.

4. Have an assistant turn the ignition switch **ON** without actually starting the engine.

5. Probe all 3 terminals in the vehicle harness connector. One of the terminals should exhibit 12 volts of power with the ignition key **ON**; this is the HPWR terminal.

a. If the HPWR terminal was identified, note which of the sensor harness connector terminals is the HPWR, then match the vehicle harness connector to the sensor pigtail connector. Label the corresponding sensor pigtail connector terminal with HPWR.

b. If none of the terminals showed 12 volts of power, locate and test the heater relay or fuse. Then, perform Steps 3–6 again.

6. Start the engine and allow it to warm up to normal operating temperature, then turn the engine **OFF**.

7. Have your assistant turn the ignition **OFF**.

8. Using the DVOM set to measure resistance (ohms), attach one of the leads to the HPWR terminal of the sensor pigtail connector. Use the other lead to probe the 2 remaining terminals of the sensor pigtail connector, one at a time. The DVOM should show continuity with only one of the remaining unidentified terminals; this is the HGND terminal. The remaining terminal is the SOUT.

a. If continuity was found with only 1 of the 2 unidentified terminals, label the HGND and SOUT terminals on the sensor pigtail connector.

b. If no continuity was evident, or if continuity was evident from both unidentified terminals, the O₂ sensor is defective.

9. All 3 wire terminals should now be labeled on the sensor pigtail connector. Proceed with the test procedures.

4-WIRE SENSOR

➡ **4-wire sensors are HO₂ sensors.**

On 4-wire sensors, one of the connector terminals is the SOUT, one of the terminals is the SGND, one of the terminals is the HPWR and the other is the HGND. To identify the 4 terminals, perform the following:

1. Locate the O₂ sensor and its pigtail connector. It may be necessary to raise and safely support the vehicle to gain access to the connector.

2. Disengage the sensor pigtail connector from the vehicle harness connector.

3. Using a DVOM set to read 12 volts, attach the DVOM ground lead to a good engine ground.

4. Have an assistant turn the ignition switch **ON** without actually starting the engine.

5. Probe all 4 terminals in the vehicle harness connector. One of the terminals should exhibit 12 volts of power with the ignition key **ON**; this is the HPWR terminal.

a. If the HPWR terminal was identified, note which of the sensor harness connector terminals is the HPWR, then match the vehicle harness connector to the sensor pigtail connector. Label the corresponding sensor pigtail connector terminal with HPWR.

b. If none of the terminals showed 12 volts of power, locate and test the heater relay or fuse. Then, perform Steps 2–6 again.

6. Have your assistant turn the ignition **OFF**.

7. Using the DVOM set to measure resistance (ohms), attach one of the leads to the HPWR terminal of the sensor pigtail connector. Use the other lead to probe the 3 remaining terminals of the sensor pigtail connector, one at a time. The DVOM should show continuity with only one of the remaining unidentified terminals; this is the HGND terminal.

a. If continuity was found with only 1 of the 2 unidentified terminals, label the HGND terminal on the sensor pigtail connector.

b. If no continuity was evident, or if continuity was evident from all unidentified terminals, the O₂ sensor is defective.

c. If continuity was found at 2 of the other terminals, the sensor is probably defective. However, the sensor may not necessarily be defective, because it may have been designed with the 2 ground wires joined inside the sensor in case one of the ground wires is damaged; the other circuit could still function properly. Though, this is highly unlikely. A wiring diagram is necessary in this particular case to know whether the sensor was so designed.

8. Reattach the sensor pigtail connector to the vehicle harness connector.

9. Start the engine and allow it to warm up to normal operating temperature, then turn the engine **OFF**.

10. Using a DVOM set to read 100–900 mV (millivolts) DC, backprobe the negative DVOM lead to one of the unidentified terminals and the positive lead to the other unidentified terminal.

✳✳ CAUTION

While the engine is running, keep clear of all moving and hot components. Do not wear loose clothing. Otherwise severe personal injury or death may occur.

11. Have an assistant restart the engine and allow it to idle.

12. Check the DVOM for voltage.

a. If no voltage is evident, check your DVOM leads to ensure that they are properly connected to the terminals. If still no voltage is evident at either of the terminals, either the terminals were accidentally marked incorrectly or the sensor is defective.

b. If voltage is present, but the polarity is reversed (the DVOM will show a negative voltage amount), turn the engine **OFF** and swap the 2 DVOM leads on the terminals. Start the engine and ensure that the voltage now shows the proper polarity.

c. If voltage is evident and is the proper polarity, the positive DVOM lead is attached to the SOUT and the negative lead to the SGND terminals.

13. Have your assistant turn the engine **OFF**.

14. Label the sensor pigtail SOUT and SGND terminals.

In-Vehicle Tests

Never apply voltage to the O₂ circuit of the sensor, otherwise it may be damaged. Also, never connect an ohmmeter (or a DVOM set on the ohm function) to both of the O₂ circuit terminals (SOUT and SGND) of the sensor pigtail connector; it may damage the sensor.

Test 1 makes use of a standard DVOM with a 10 megohms impedance, whereas Test 2 necessitates the usage of an advanced Digital Multi-Meter (DMM) with MIN/MAX/Average functions or a sliding bar graph function. Both of these in-vehicle test procedures are likely to set Diagnostic Trouble Codes (DTC's) in the engine control computer. Therefore, after testing, be sure to clear all DTC's before retesting the sensor, if necessary. The third in-vehicle test is designed for the use of a scan tool or oscilloscope. The 4th test (Heating Circuit Test) is designed to check the function of the heating circuit in a HO₂ sensor.

➡️**If the O₂ sensor being tested is designed to use the exhaust system for the SGND, excessive corrosion between the exhaust and the O₂ sensor may affect sensor functioning.**

The in-vehicle tests may be performed for O₂ sensors located in the exhaust sys-

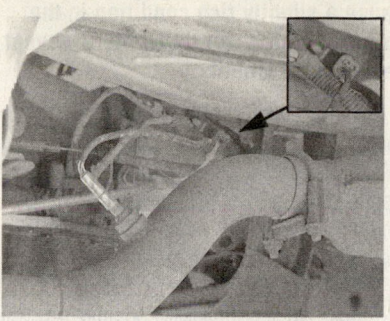

89664P30

To test the O₂ sensor, locate it and its connector (inset), which should be positioned away from the exhaust system to prevent heat damage.

tem after the catalytic converter. However, the O₂ sensors located behind the catalytic converter will not fluctuate like the sensors mounted before the converter, because the converter, when functioning properly, emits a steady amount of oxygen. If the O₂ sensor mounted after the catalytic converter exhibits a fluctuating signal (like other O₂ sensors), the catalytic converter is most likely defective.

TEST 1—DIGITAL VOLT-OHMMETER

This test will not only verify proper sensor functioning, but is also designed to ensure the engine control computer and associated wiring is functioning properly as well.

1. Start the engine and allow it to warm up to normal operating temperature.

➡️**If you are using the opening of the thermostat to gauge normal operating temperature, be forewarned: a defective thermostat can open too early and prevent the engine from reaching normal operating temperature. This can cause a slightly rich condition in the exhaust, which can throw the O₂sensor readings off slightly.**

2. Turn the ignition switch **OFF**, then locate the O₂ sensor pigtail connector.

3. Perform a visual inspection of the connector to ensure it is properly engaged and all terminals are straight, tight and free from corrosion or damage.

4. Disengage the sensor pigtail connector from the vehicle harness connector.

5. On sensors equipped with a SGND terminal (sensors which do not use the exhaust system for the sensor ground pathway), connect a jumper wire to the SGND terminal and to a good, clean engine ground

(preferably the negative terminal of the battery).

6. Using a DVOM set to read DC voltage, attach the positive lead to the SOUT terminal of the sensor pigtail connector, and the DVOM negative lead to a good engine ground.

While the engine is running, keep clear of all moving and hot components. Do not wear loose clothing. Otherwise severe personal injury or death may occur.

7. Have an assistant start the engine and hold it at approximately 2000 rpm. Wait at least 1 minute before commencing with the test to allow the O₂ sensor to sufficiently warm up.

8. Using a jumper wire, connect the SOUT terminal of the **vehicle harness connector** to a good engine ground. This will fool the engine control computer into thinking it is receiving a lean signal from the O₂ sensor, and, therefore, the computer will richen the air/fuel ratio. With the SOUT terminal so grounded, the DVOM should register at least 800 mV, as the control computer adds additional fuel to the air/fuel ratio.

9. While observing the DVOM, disconnect the vehicle harness connector SOUT jumper wire from the engine ground. Use the jumper wire to apply slightly less than 1 volt to the SOUT terminal of the vehicle harness connector. One method to do this is by grasping and squeezing the end of the jumper between your forefinger and thumb of one hand while touching the positive terminal of the battery post with your other hand. This allows your body to act as a resistor for the battery positive voltage, and fools the engine control computer into thinking it is receiving a rich signal. Or, use a mostly-drained AA battery by connecting the positive terminal of the AA battery to the jumper wire and the negative terminal of the battery to a good engine ground. (Another jumper wire may be necessary to do this.) The computer should lean the air/fuel mixture out. This lean mixture should register as 150 mV or less on the DVOM.

10. If the DVOM did not register millivoltages as indicated, the problem may be either the sensor, the engine control computer or the associated wiring. Perform the following to determine which is the defective component:

a. Remove the vehicle harness connector SOUT jumper wire.

b. While observing the DVOM, artificially enrich the air/fuel charge using propane. The DVOM reading should register higher than normal millivoltages. (Normal voltage for an ideal air/fuel mixture is approximately 450–550 mV DC). Then, lean the air/fuel intake charger by either disconnecting one of the fuel injector wiring harness connectors (to prevent the injector from delivering fuel) or by detaching 1 or 2 vacuum lines (to add additional non-metered air into the engine). The DVOM should now register lower than normal millivoltages. If the DVOM functioned as indicated, the problem lies elsewhere in the fuel delivery and control system. If the DVOM readings were still unresponsive, the O₂ sensor is defective; replace the sensor and retest.

→Poor wire connections and/or ground circuits may shift a normal O₂ sensor's millivoltage readings up into the rich range or down into the lean range. It is a good idea to check the wire condition and continuity before replacing a component which will not fix the problem. A voltage drop test between the sensor case and ground which reveals 14–16 mV or more, indicates a probable bad ground.

11. Turn the engine OFF, remove the DVOM and all associated jumper wires. Reattach the vehicle harness connector to the sensor pigtail connector. If applicable, reattach the fuel injector wiring connector and/or the vacuum line(s).

12. Clear any DTC's present in the engine control computer memory, as necessary.

TEST 2—DIGITAL MULTI-METER

This test method is a more straight-forward O₂ sensor test, and does not test the engine control computer's response to the O₂ sensor signal. The use of a DMM with the MIN/MAX/Average function or sliding bar graph/wave function is necessary for this test. Don't forget that the O₂ sensor mounted after the catalytic converter (if equipped) will not fluctuate like the other O₂ sensor(s) will.

1. Start the engine and allow it to warm up to normal operating temperature.

→If you are using the opening of the thermostat to gauge normal operating temperature, be forewarned: a defective thermostat can open too early and prevent the engine from reaching normal operating temperature. This can

cause a slightly rich condition in the exhaust, which can throw the O₂sensor readings off slightly.

2. Turn the ignition switch OFF, then locate the O₂ sensor pigtail connector.

3. Perform a visual inspection of the connector to ensure it is properly engaged and all terminals are straight, tight and free from corrosion or damage.

4. Backprobe the O₂ sensor connector terminals. Attach the DMM positive test lead to the SOUT terminal of the sensor pigtail connector. Connect the negative lead to either the SGND terminal of the sensor pigtail connector (if equipped—refer to the terminal identification procedures earlier in this section for clarification) or to a good, clean engine ground.

5.Activate the MIN/MAX/Average or sliding bar graph/wave function on the DMM.

☀☀ CAUTION

While the engine is running, keep clear of all moving and hot components. Do not wear loose clothing. Otherwise severe personal injury or death may occur.

6. Have an assistant start the engine and wait a few minutes before commencing with the test to allow the O₂ sensor to sufficiently warm up.

7. Read the minimum, maximum and average readings exhibited by the O₂ sensor or observe the bar graph/wave form. The average reading for a properly functioning O₂ sensor is be approximately 450–550 mV DC. The minimum and maximum readings should vary more than 300–600 mV. A typical O₂ sensor can fluctuate from as low as 100 mV to as high as 900 mV; if the sensor range of fluctuation is not large enough, the sensor is defective. Also, if the fluctuation range is biased up or down in the scale. For example, if the fluctuation range is 400 mV to 900 mV the sensor is defective, because the readings are pushed up into the rich range (as long as the fuel delivery system is functioning properly). The same goes for a fluctuation range pushed down into the lean range. The mid-point of the fluctuation range should be around 400–500 mV. Finally, if the O₂ sensor voltage fluctuates too slowly (usually the voltage wave should oscillate past the mid-way point of 500 mV several times per second) the sensor is defective. (Technician's refer to this state as "lazy.")

→Poor wire connections and/or ground circuits may shift a normal O₂ sensor's millivoltage readings up into the rich range or down into the lean range. It is

a good idea to check the wire condition and continuity before replacing a component that will not fix the problem. A voltage drop test between the sensor case and ground which reveals 14–16 mV or more, indicates a probable bad ground.

8. Using the propane method, richen the air/fuel mixture and observe the DMM readings. The average O₂ sensor output signal voltage should rise into the rich range.

9. Lean the air/fuel mixture by either disconnecting a fuel injector wiring harness connector or by disconnecting a vacuum line. The O₂ sensor average output signal voltage should drop into the lean range.

10. If the O₂ sensor did not react as indicated, the sensor is defective and should be replaced.

11. Turn the engine OFF, remove the DMM and all associated jumper wires. Reattach the vehicle harness connector to the sensor pigtail connector. If applicable, reattach the fuel injector wiring connector and/or the vacuum line(s).

12. Clear any DTC's present in the engine control computer memory, as necessary.

TEST 3—OSCILLOSCOPE

This test is designed for the use of an oscilloscope to test the functioning of an O₂ sensor.

→This test is only applicable for O₂ sensors mounted in the exhaust system before the catalytic converter.

1. Start the engine and allow it to reach normal operating temperature.

2. Turn the engine OFF, and locate the O₂ sensor connector. Backprobe the scope lead to the O₂ sensor connector SOUT terminal. Refer to the manufacturer's instructions for more information on attaching the scope to the vehicle.

3. Turn the scope ON.

4. Set the oscilloscope amplitude to 200 mV per division, and the time to 1 second per division. Use the 1:1 setting of the probe, and be sure to connect the scope's ground lead to a good, clean engine ground. Set the signal function to automatic or internal triggering.

5. Start the engine and run it at 2000 rpm.

6. The oscilloscope should display a wave form, representative of the O₂ sensor switching between lean (100–300 mV) and rich (700–900 mV). The sensor should switch between rich and lean, or lean and rich (crossing the mid-point of 500 mV)

several times per second. Also, the range of each wave should reach at least above 700 mV and below 300 mV. However, an occasional low peak is acceptable.

7. Force the air/fuel mixture rich by introducing propane into the engine, then observe the oscilloscope readings. The fluctuating range of the O_2 sensor should climb into the rich range.

8. Lean the air/fuel mixture out by either detaching a vacuum line or by disengaging one of the fuel injector's wiring connectors. Watch the scope readings; the O_2 sensor wave form should drop toward the lean range.

9. If the O_2 sensor's wave form does not fluctuate adequately, is not centered around 500 mV during normal engine operation, does not climb toward the rich range when propane is added to the engine, or does not drop toward the lean range when a vacuum hose or fuel injector connector is detached, the sensor is defective.

10. Reattach the fuel injector connector or vacuum hose.

11. Disconnect the oscilloscope from the vehicle.

HEATING CIRCUIT TEST

The heating circuit in an O_2 sensor is designed only to heat the sensor quicker than a non-heated sensor. This provides an advantage of increased engine driveability and fuel economy while the engine temperature is still below normal operating temperature, because the fuel management system can enter closed loop operation (more efficient than open loop operation) sooner.

Therefore, if the heating element goes bad, the O_2 sensor may still function properly once the sensor warms up to its normal temperature. This will take longer than normal and may cause mild driveability-related problems while the engine has not reached normal operating temperature.

If the heating element is found to be defective, replace the O_2 sensor without wasting your time testing the O_2 circuit. If necessary, you can perform the O_2 circuit test with the new O_2 sensor and save yourself some time.

1. Locate the O_2 sensor pigtail connector.

2. Perform a visual inspection of the

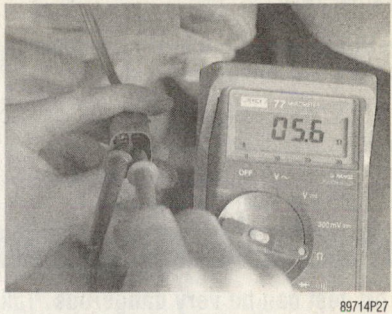

89714P27

The heating circuit of the O₂sensor can be tested with a DMM set to measure resistance

connector to ensure it is properly engaged and all terminals are straight, tight and free from corrosion or damage.

3. Disengage the sensor pigtail connector from the vehicle harness connector.

4. Using a DVOM set to read resistance (ohms), attach one DVOM test lead to the HPWR terminal, and the other lead to the HGND terminal, of the sensor pigtail connector, then observe the resistance readings.

   a. If there is no continuity between the HPWR and HGND terminals, the sensor is defective. Replace it with a new one and retest.

   b. If there is continuity between the 2 terminals, but the resistance is greater than approximately 20 ohms, the sensor is defective. Replace it with a new one and retest.

➡ **For the following step, the HO₂ sensor should be approximately 75°F (23°C) for the proper resistance values.**

   c. If there is continuity between the 2 terminals and it is less than 20 ohms, the sensor is probably not defective. Because of the large diversity of engine control systems used in vehicles today, O_2 sensor heating circuit resistance specifications change often. Generally, the amount of resistance an O_2 sensor heating circuit should exhibit is between 2–9 ohms. However, some manufacturer's O_2 sensors may show resistance as high as 15–20 ohms. As a rule of thumb, 20 ohms of resistance is the upper limit allowable.

5. Turn the engine **OFF**, remove the DVOM and all associated jumper wires. Reattach the vehicle harness connector to the sensor pigtail connector.

6. Clear any DTC's present in the engine control computer memory, as necessary.

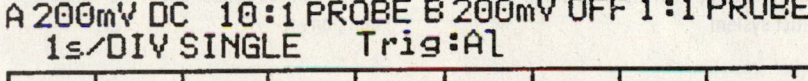

A 200mV DC 10:1 PROBE B 200mV OFF 1:1 PROBE
1s/DIV SINGLE   Trig:A1

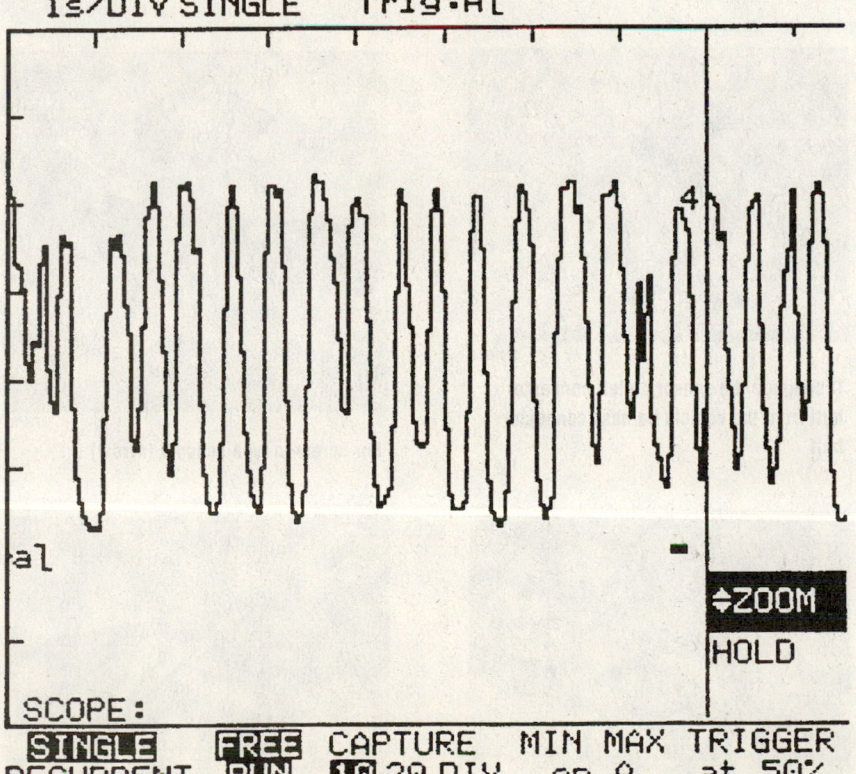

An oscilloscope wave form of a typical good O₂ sensor as it fluctuates from rich to lean

79248G09

Bench Test

➡ **Utilize one of the in-vehicle tests before performing this test.**

This test is designed to test an O₂ sensor which does not seem to fluctuate fully beyond 400–700 mV. The sensor is to be secured in a table-mounted vise.

✳✳ CAUTION

This test can be very dangerous. Take the necessary precautions when working with a propane torch. Ensure that all combustible substances are removed from the work area and have a fire extinguisher ready at all times. Be sure to wear the appropriate protective clothing as well.

1. Remove the O₂ sensor.

➡ **Perform a visual inspection of the sensor. black sooty deposits may indicate a rich air/fuel mixture, brown deposits may indicate an oil consumption problem, and white gritty deposits may indicate an internal coolant leak. All of these conditions can destroy a new sensor if not corrected before installation.**

2. Position the sensor in a vise so that the vise holds the sensor by the hex portion of its case.

3. Attach one lead of a DVOM set to read DC millivoltages to the sensor case and the other lead to the SOUT terminal of the sensor pigtail connector.

4. Carefully use a propane torch to heat the tip (and ONLY the tip) of the sensor. Once the sensor reaches close to normal operating temperature range, alternately heat the sensor up and allow it to cool down; the sensor output voltage signal should change with the temperature change.

➡ **This may also clean a sensor covered with a heavy coat of carbon.**

5. If the sensor voltage does not change with the fluctuation in temperature, replace the sensor with a new one. Install the new sensor and perform one of the in-vehicle tests to rule out additional fuel management system faults.

REMOVAL & INSTALLATION

1. Start the engine and allow it to reach normal operating temperature, then turn the ignition switch **OFF**.

2. Disconnect the negative battery cable.

3. Open the hood and locate the O₂ sensor connector. It may be necessary to

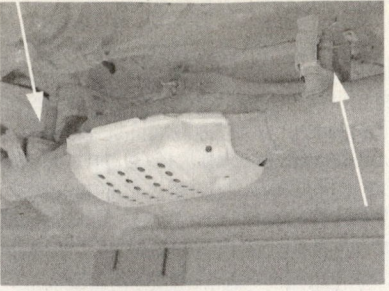

Since sensor locations vary between vehicles, the first step in removal is to locate the O₂ sensors (arrows) . . .

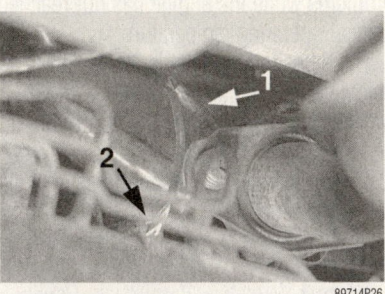

. . . and the sensor connector (2), which is usually near the O₂ sensor (1), but removed enough from the heat of the exhaust system

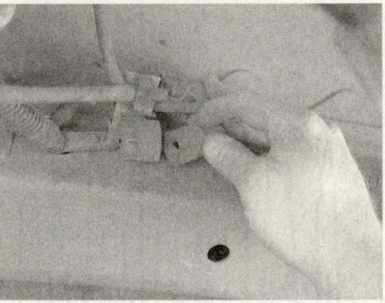

Disengage the sensor pigtail connector half from the vehicle harness connector half

For flange type sensors, loosen the hold-down fasteners . . .

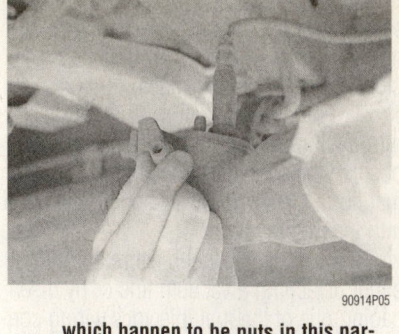

. . . which happen to be nuts in this particular case—some models may use bolts rather than nuts

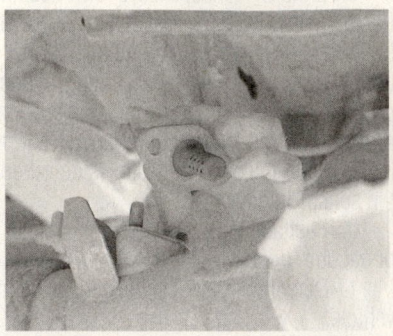

Then, pull the sensor out of the exhaust component

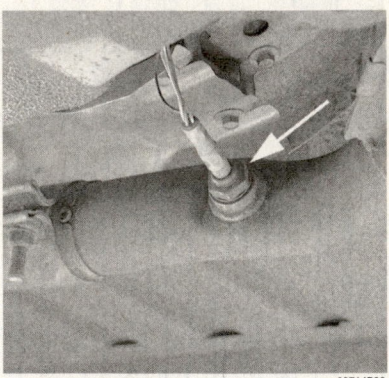

For screw-in type sensors (arrow) . . .

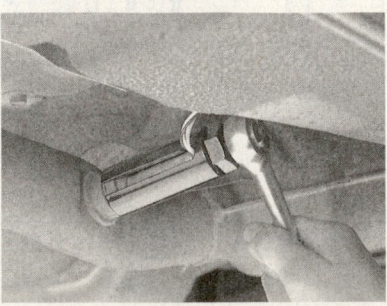

. . . either use a box end wrench to loosen the sensor or a socket designed expressly for this purpose . . .

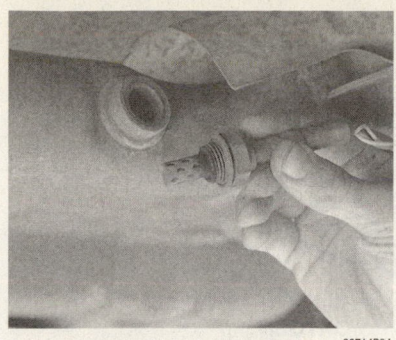

. . . then remove the sensor from the exhaust component

raise and safely support the vehicle for access to the sensor and its connector.

➡ **On a few models, it may be necessary to remove the passenger seat and lift the carpeting in order to access the connector for a downstream O₂ sensor.**

4. Disengage the O₂ sensor pigtail connector from the vehicle harness connector.

➡ **There are generally 2 methods used to mount an O₂ sensor in the exhaust system. Either the O₂ sensor is threaded directly into the exhaust component (screw-in type) or the O₂ sensor is retained by a flange and 2 nuts or bolts (flange type).**

❊❊ WARNING

To prevent damaging a screw-in type O₂ sensor, if excessive force is needed to remove the sensor lubricate it with penetrating oil prior to removal. Also, be sure to protect the tip of the sensor; O₂ sensor tips are very sensitive and may be easily damaged if allowed to strike or come in contact with other objects.

5. Remove the sensor, as follows:
- Screw-in type sensors: Since O₂ sensors are usually designed with a permanently-attached wiring pigtail, it may be necessary to use a socket or wrench that is designed specifically for this purpose. Before purchasing such a socket, be sure that you can't save some money by using a box end wrench for sensor removal.
- Flange type sensors: Loosen the hold-down nuts or bolts and pull the sensor out of the exhaust component. Be sure to remove and dis-

card the old sensor gasket, if equipped. You will need a new gasket for installation.

6. Perform a visual inspection of the sensor. black sooty deposits may indicate a rich air/fuel mixture, brown deposits may indicate an oil consumption problem, and white gritty deposits may indicate an internal coolant leak. All of these conditions can destroy a new sensor if not corrected before installation.

To install:

7. Install the sensor, as follows:

➡ **A special anti-seize compound is used on most screw-in type O₂ sensor threads, and is designed to ease O₂ sensor removal. New sensors usually have the compound already applied to the threads. However, if installing the old O₂ sensor or the new sensor did not come with compound, apply a thin coating of electrically conductive anti-seize compound to the sensor threads.**

❊❊ WARNING

Be sure to prevent any of the anti-seize compound from coming in contact with the O₂ sensor tip. Also, take precautions to protect the sensor tip from physical damage during installation.

- Screw-in type sensors: Install the sensor in the mounting boss, then tighten it securely.
- Flange type sensors: Position a new sensor gasket on the exhaust component and insert the sensor. Tighten the hold-down fasteners securely and evenly.

8. Reattach the sensor pigtail connector to the vehicle harness connector.

9. Lower the vehicle.

10. Connect the negative battery cable.

11. Start the engine and ensure no Diagnostic Trouble Codes (DTC's) are set.

LOCATIONS

There are different locations in the exhaust system where O₂ sensors are positioned. The locations have been given numbers and will be used in the accompanying charts to identify the positions of O₂ sensors in most vehicles.

Due to mid-year production changes or factory inconsistencies, all models may not be covered. If a vehicle being serviced

is not covered in the charts, inspect the exhaust system (while cold!) in the general locations to find the applicable O₂ sensors.

➡ **If equipped with dual exhaust systems, there may be up to 4 or 5 O₂ sensors in the exhaust system. Be sure to locate all of them before commencing with any testing or service.**

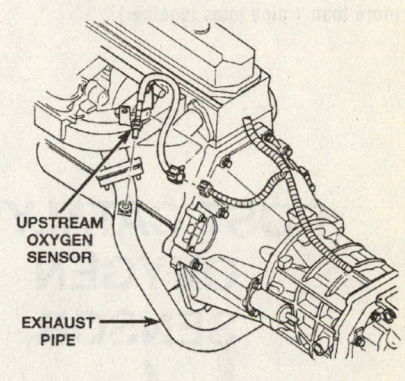

Location No. 1—down pipe

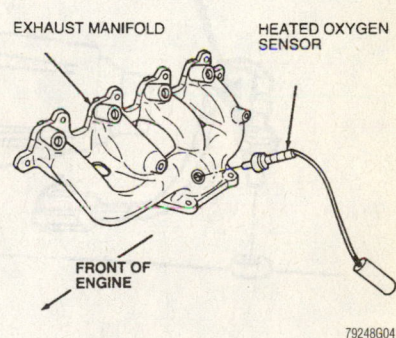

Location No. 1—typical O₂ sensor located in the exhaust manifold

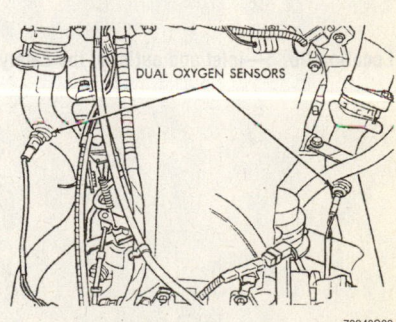

Location No. 2—left and right banks of a V-type engine

For exhaust manifold replacement procedures, see the model specific sections of this manual

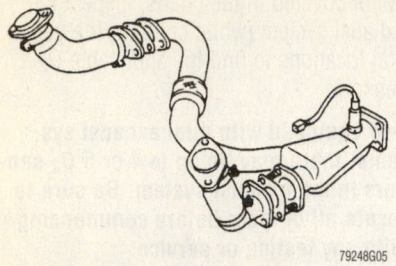

Location No. 3—exhaust collector (where more than 1 pipe joins together)

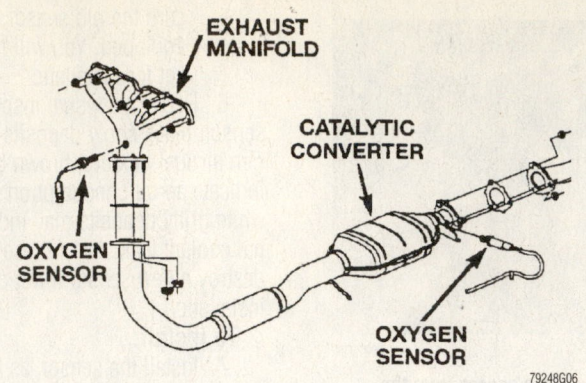

Location No. 4—outlet of the catalytic converter

POST CATALYST OXYGEN SENSOR

PRE-CATALYST OXYGEN SENSOR

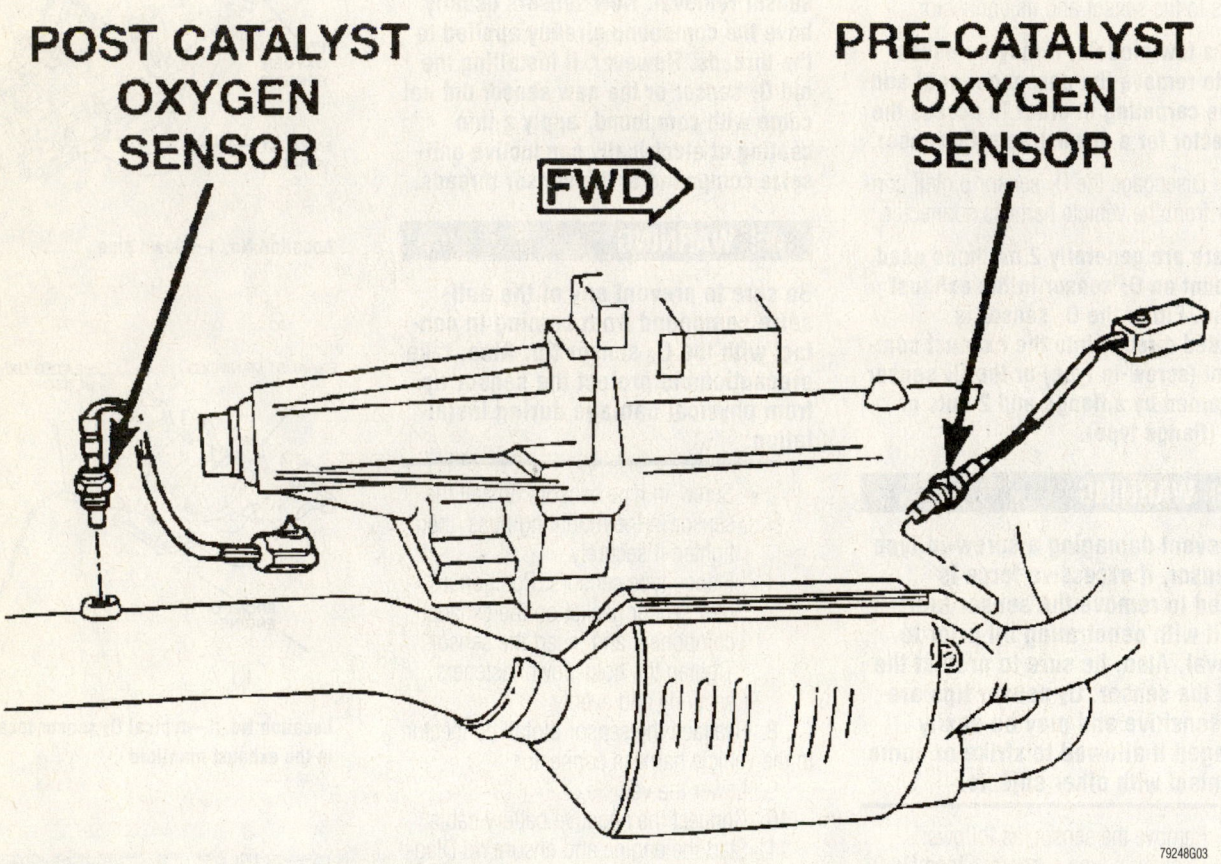

Location No. 5—inlet and outlet of the catalytic converter

OXYGEN SENSOR LOCATIONS

Manufacturer Year	Engines	No. of Sensors	Location
Acura Sport Utility Vehicles			
	3.2L	4	2, 5
	3.5L	4	2, 5
Chrysler Minivans			
	2.4L	2	1, 4
	3.0L	2	1, 4
	3.3L	2	1, 4
	3.8L	2	1, 4
Dodge Trucks and Vans			
	2.3L	2	1, 4
	2.5L	2	1, 4
	5.2L	2	1, 4
	5.9L	2	1, 4
	5.9L HDC	4	2, 5
	8.0L HDC	4	2, 5
Ford Small Trucks and Vans			
	2.3L	2	1, 4
	2.5L	2	1, 4
	3.0L	3	2, 4
	4.0L (E)	4	2, 4
	4.0L (X)	4	2, 4
	5.0L	4	2, 4
Ford Minivans			
	3.0L	4	2, 4
	3.8L	4	2, 4
Ford Full-size Trucks and Vans			
	4.2L	2	3, 4
	4.6L	4	2, 4
	4.9L	1	1
	5.0L	3	2, 4
	5.4L	4	2, 4
	5.8L	3	2, 4
	6.8L	4	2, 4
	7.5L	4	2, 4
GEO Sport Utility Vehicles			
	1.6L	2	1, 4
GM Small Trucks and Vans			
	2.2L	2	1, 4
	4.3L	4	2, 5
GM Minivans			
	3.4L	2	1, 4
GM Full-size Trucks and Vans			
	4.3L	4	2, 5
	4.8L	4	2, 5
	5.0L	4	2, 5
	5.3L	4	2, 5

Manufacturer Year	Engines	No. of Sensors	Location
GM Full-size Trucks and Vans (cont.)			
	5.7L	4	2, 5
	6.0L	4	2, 5
	7.4L	4	2, 5
Honda Sport Utility Vehicles			
	2.0L	2	3, 4
	2.2L	2	3, 4
	2.6L	2	3, 4
	3.2L	4	2, 5
Infiniti Sport Utility Vehicles			
	3.3L	4	2, 4
Isuzu Sport Utility Vehicles			
	2.0L	2	3, 4
	2.2L	2	3, 4
	2.6L	2	3, 4
	3.2L	4	2, 5
	3.5L	4	2, 5
	4.3L	4	2, 5
Jeep Sport Utility Vehicles			
	2.5L	2	1, 4
	4.0L	2	1, 4
	4.7L	2, 4(CA)	4(CA), 5
	5.2L	3	1, 5
	5.9L	3	1, 5
Kia Sport Utility Vehicles			
	2.0L	2	1, 4
Land Rover Sport Utility Vehicles			
	4.0L	4	2, 4
	4.6L	4	2, 4
Lexus Sport Utility Vehicles			
	3.0L	2	3+J54, 4
	4.5L	2	1, 4
	4.7L	4	1, 4
Mazda Trucks			
	2.3L	2	1, 4
	2.5L	2	1, 4
	3.0L	3	2, 4
	4.0L (X)	4	2, 4
Mazda Minivans			
	3.0L	2	1, 4
Mercedes-Benz Sport Utility Vehicles			
	3.2L	4	5
	4.3L	4	5
Mercury Sport Utility Vehicles			
	3.0L	2	1, 4
	3.3L	2	1, 4

93028C01

For complete service labor times order Nichols' Chilton Labor Guide Manual

OXYGEN SENSOR LOCATIONS

Manufacturer Year	Engines	No. of Sensors	Location
Mitsubishi Sport Utility Vehicles			
	2.4L	2	1, 4
	3.0L	3	2, 4
	3.5L	3	2, 4
Nissan Trucks and Sport Utility Vehicles			
	2.4L	2	1, 4
	3.0L	4	2, 4
	3.3L	4	2, 4
Subaru Sport Utility Vehicles			
	2.5L	3	3, 4
Suzuki Sport Utility Vehicles			
	1.6L	2	1, 4

Manufacturer Year	Engines	No. of Sensors	Location
Suzuki Sport Utility Vehicles (cont.)			
	1.8L	2	1, 4
	2.0L	2	1, 4
	2.5L	2	3, 4
Toyota Sport Utility Vehicles			
	2.0L	2	1, 4
	2.4L	2	3, 4
	2.7L	2	3, 4
	3.0L	2	3, 4
	3.4L	2	3, 4
	4.5L	2	1, 4
	4.7L	4	1, 4

CA - California

93028C02

ELECTRIC COOLING FANS

8

ELECTRIC COOLING FANS

General Information

A basic vehicle cooling system consists of a radiator, water pump, thermostat, electric or engine-driven cooling fan, and hoses. Electric cooling fans are common on today's vehicles due to engine compartment space limitations or engine layout. Electric cooling fans operate in either a pusher or a puller capacity. A pusher type fan is typically mounted on the front of the radiator assembly and forces air through the radiator, whereas a puller type fan is mounted on the engine side of the radiator and draws air through the grill and radiator assembly. Vehicles that utilize a transversely-mounted engine will always be equipped with at least 1 electric cooling fan (most having 2), because none of the engine pulleys are in-line with the radiator air-flow.

There are generally 2 types of electric cooling fans: primary cooling fans and secondary cooling fans. Primary cooling fans are typically of the puller style. Vehicles that do not incorporate an engine-driven mechanical cooling fan will utilize a primary cooling fan. The secondary cooling fan, also known as an air conditioning condenser fan or auxiliary cooling fan by certain manufacturers, could be of either a pusher or a puller style. Vehicles equipped with air conditioning will either utilize the radiator cooling fan or a separate fan as the air conditioning condenser cooling fan (which performs the same function as an auxiliary cooling fan on vehicles with a primary mechanical fan). The engine control computer that receives inputs from various sensors in the engine compartment commonly controls electric cooling fans. The engine control computer receives inputs from the engine coolant temperature sensors and air conditioning system pressure switches, then actuates the necessary cooling fan relays to engage the applicable cooling fan for the condition. On models equipped with only 1 electric primary cooling fan, the fan can operate at 2 speeds: low speed and high speed. The low speed condition is enabled when the engine begins to heat up or when the air conditioning is engaged. As the engine demands more cooling, the cooling fan will be stepped-up to high speed.

Electric Cooling Fan Service

Due to the wide variety of vehicle manufacturers and suppliers of electric cooling fans it is almost impossible to cover every specific combination of cooling fan and model. The following procedures will cover the most common types of mountings and troubleshooting techniques.

REMOVAL & INSTALLATION

Puller Type

➡**It may be simpler to remove the cooling fan(s) with the radiator as an assembly.**

1. Disconnect the negative battery cable.
2. Inspect the cooling fan and take note of any wires, hoses or air conditioning lines that may hamper fan removal. Also at this time, decide whether it is necessary to remove the fan along with the radiator or not.
3. Position aside all wires, hoses and air conditioning lines for fan removal. It may not always be possible to create enough clearance for fan removal by simply moving these obstructions aside; often they must be disconnected. If any cooling system lines must be disconnected, drain and recycle the engine coolant. If any of the air conditioning lines must be disconnected, the air conditioning system will need to be discharged and evacuated by an MVAC-trained technician using an approved recovery machine.

To remove a puller type cooling fan, first detach any braces (1), wires (2) or other obstructions . . .

. . . including cooling system hoses, to allow fan removal

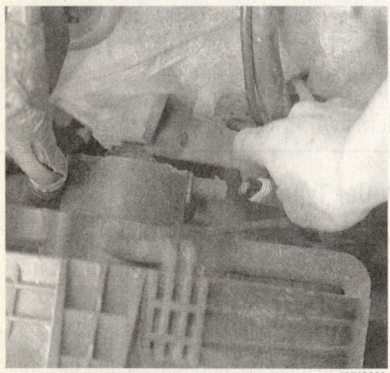

Disengage the fan wiring connector(s) . . .

. . . and loosen all fan mounting fasteners

Separate the fan from the radiator . . .

. . . then lift the fan up and out of the engine compartment

4. Disengage the cooling fan wiring harness connector.

5. If the fan can be removed without the radiator, perform the following:

a. Loosen the mounting fasteners. Usually there are 2 nuts or bolts along the top edge of the cooling fan shroud and either 2 retaining clips or bolts along the bottom edge.

b. Carefully lift the fan up and out of the engine compartment, making sure that no wires or hoses get hung up on it.

6. If it is necessary to remove the radiator for fan removal, perform the following:

a. Disconnect all cooling system hoses from it after draining the cooling system.

b. Locate the radiator mounting fasteners (usually 2 or more nuts or bolts along the top and, possibly 2 along the bottom).

➡Quite a few radiators are secured along the bottom by 2 posts that fit into rubber grommets. The rubber grommets help isolate the radiator from harsh vibrations in the frame. If no nuts or bolts can be located along the bottom of the radiator, chances are that the radiator is secured with the posts and grommets.

c. Lift the radiator and cooling fan up and out of the engine compartment together.

d. Separate the cooling fan from the radiator by removing the attaching fasteners.

To install:

7. If applicable, install the cooling fan on the radiator.

8. Install the cooling fan and shroud assembly (also the radiator if necessary). Tighten the fan shroud mounting bolts.

9. Reattach all wires, hoses and air conditioning lines as applicable. If the air

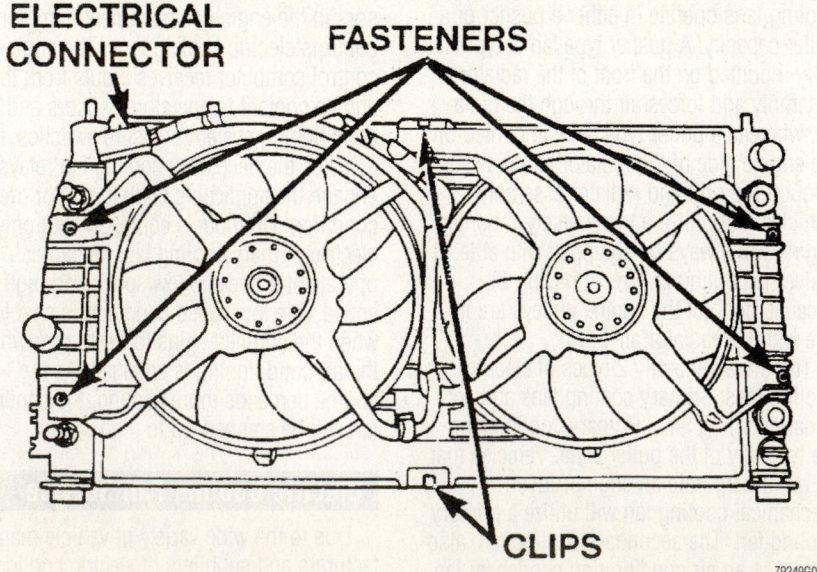

Typical mounting of a puller type cooling fan assembly utilizing retaining clips and screws—note that this particular model uses a dual puller fan setup

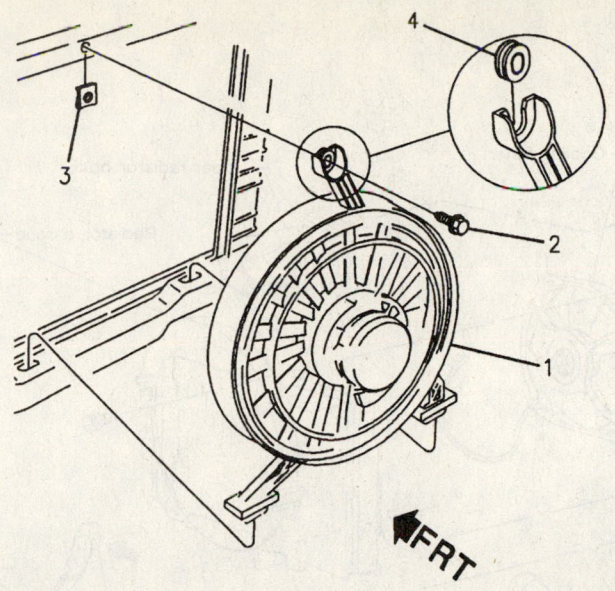

1 FAN ASSEMBLY
2 BOLT
3 CLIP
4 INSULATOR, ENGINE COOLING FAN

79249G10

Notice the slots in the bottom of the radiator, in which the fan housing posts rest—common mounting of a puller type cooling fan.

conditioning lines were detached, the system must be evacuated and recharged by an MVAC-trained technician.

10. If drained, refill and bleed the cooling system.

11. Reattach the cooling fan electrical harness connector.

12. Connect the negative battery cable.

13. Start the engine and check for leaks.

14. Verify the operation of the cooling fan(s).

Pusher Type

Vehicles that utilize the pusher type of electric cooling fan may require the removal of the grilles and/or upper radiator shroud in order to gain access the fasteners that mount the fan assembly in the vehicle.

1. Disconnect the negative battery cable.
2. Access the cooling fan.
3. Label and disconnect the cooling fan electrical harness.

➡ **It may be necessary to loosen the mounting bolts for the air conditioning condenser to the body**

4. Remove the fasteners that mount the cooling fan to the air conditioning condenser or radiator.

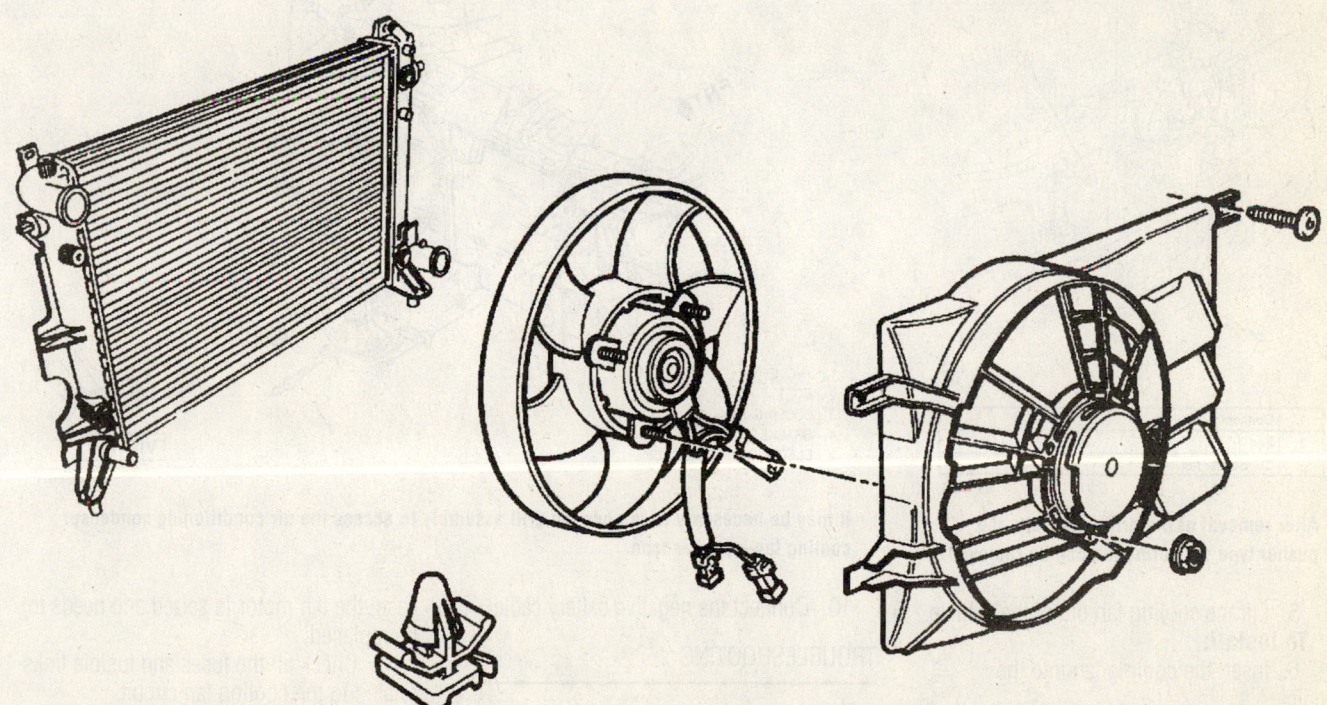

79249G11

This fan mounts to the fan shroud, then the shroud mounts to the radiator—molded clips in the radiator hold the bottom in place and screws at the top.

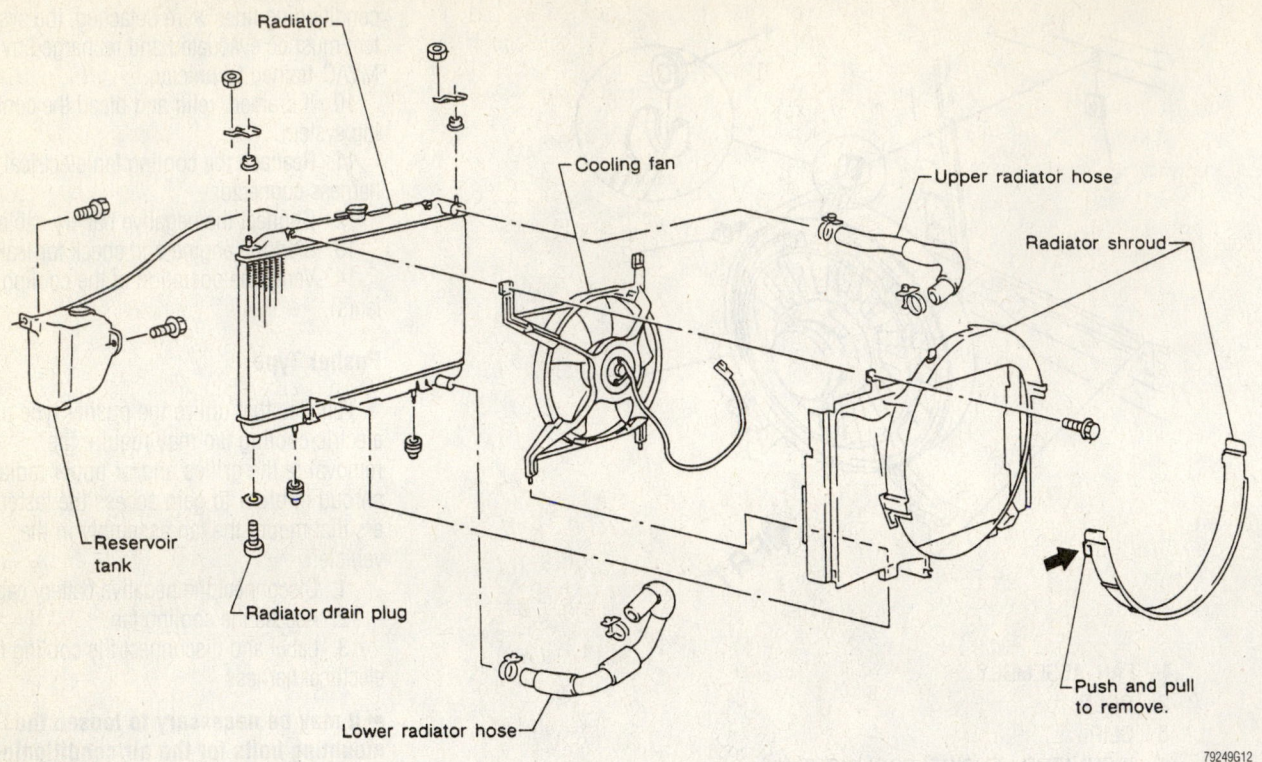

Typically the cooling fan is rubber mounted to isolate vibration and noise—usually the rubber grommets are located at the mount, verify their position before installation

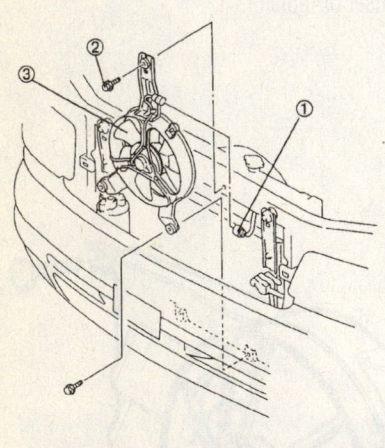

1	Connector
2	Bolt
3	Condenser fan

79249G13

After removal of the grill assembly, the pusher type of cooling fan can be removed

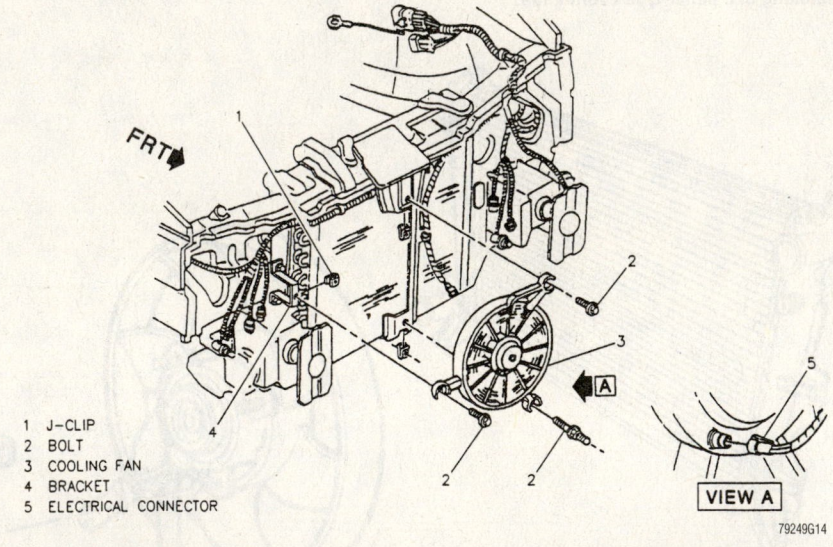

1 J–CLIP
2 BOLT
3 COOLING FAN
4 BRACKET
5 ELECTRICAL CONNECTOR

79249G14

It may be necessary to remove the grill assembly to access the air conditioning condenser cooling fan—pusher type

5. Lift the cooling fan out of the vehicle.
To install:
6. Insert the cooling fan into the vehicle.
7. Mount the cooling fan to the air conditioning condenser or radiator
8. Connect the cooling fan electrical harness.
9. If removed, install any shrouding or grills.

10. Connect the negative battery cable.

TROUBLESHOOTING

When diagnosing an inoperative cooling fan it may be necessary to use a diagnostic scan tool to monitor engine coolant temperature and the engine control computer.

1. Perform a visual inspection of the cooling fan. If the fan does not turn with

ease, the fan motor is seized and needs to be replaced.

2. Check all the fuses and fusible links related to the cooling fan circuit.

3. Check the integrity of the electrical connections related to the cooling fan circuit.

4. Check the cooling fan motor.

5. Check the relays associated with the cooling fan circuit.

6. Using a scan tool, determine if the

engine control computer is calling for the fan to activate.

Cooling Fan Motor

1. Disconnect the negative battery cable.
2. Disengage the cooling fan motor connector.
3. Identify and label the ground and the power terminals of the cooling fan connector using the wiring diagrams provided.
4. Using jumper leads with a fuse in series, apply battery voltage to the appropriate terminals of the cooling fan.
5. The cooling fan should operate. If not, replace the cooling fan.

If the cooling fan functions properly during this test, proceed to the cooling fan relay test.

Cooling Fan Relay

1. Turn the ignition OFF.

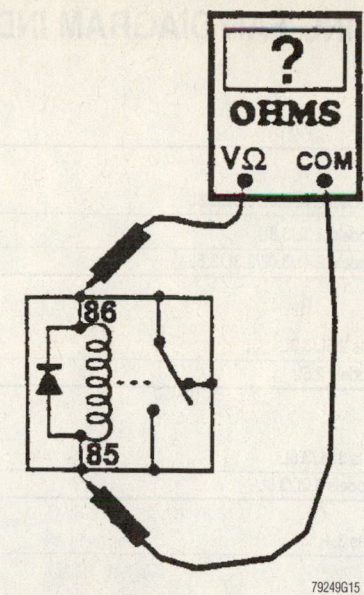

79249G15

Use an ohmmeter to check for circuit continuity of the coil in the relay

2. Remove the relay.
3. Locate the 2 terminals on the relay, which are connected to the coil windings. Check the relay coil for continuity. Connect the common meter lead to terminal 85 and positive meter lead to terminal 86. There should be continuity. If not, replace the relay.
4. Check the operation of the internal relay contacts.

a. Connect the meter leads to terminals 30 and 87. Meter polarity does not matter for this step.

b. Apply positive battery voltage to terminal 86 and ground to terminal 85. The relay should click as the contacts are drawn toward the coil and the meter should indicate continuity. Replace the relay if your results are different.

If the relay functions properly during this test, inspect the coolant temperature sensor and the cooling fan system wiring for defects.

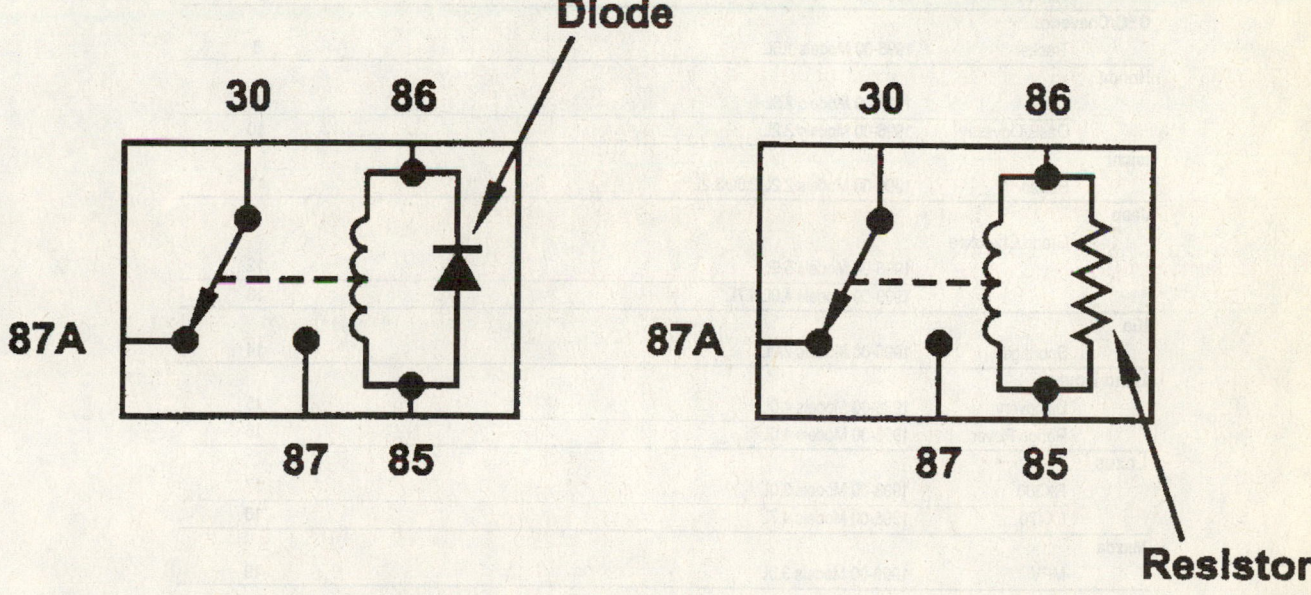

79249G16

Terminal identification of the most common types of relays. Diodes and resistors in the relay prevent voltage spikes induced when the current is removed from the coil from damaging electronic components

COOLING FAN DIAGRAM INDEX

MANUFACTURER MODEL AND ENGINE		DIAGRAM
Chrysler		
Caravan	1996-00 Models 2.4L/3.0L/3.3L/3.8L	1
Town & Country	1996-00 Models 3.3L/3.8L	1
Voyager	1996-00 Models 2.4L/3.0L/3.3L/3.8L	1
Dodge		
Dakota	1996 Models 2.5L/3.9L	2
	1997-00 Models 2.5L	3
Ford		
Windstar	1996 Models 3.0L/3.8L	4
	1997-00 Models 3.0L/3.8L	5
General Motors		
Lumina APV	1996 Models 3.4L	6
Silhouette	1996 Models 3.4L	6
	1997-00 Models 2.0L	7
Trans Sport	1996 Models 3.4L	6
	1997-00 Models 2.0L	7
Venture	1997-00 Models 3.4L	7
GEO/Cheverlot		
Tracker	1996-00 Models 1.6L	8
Honda		
CR-V	1997-00 Models 2.0L	9
Oasis/Odyssey	1996-00 Models 2.2L	10
Isuzu		
Rodeo	1996-00 Models 2.2L/2.6L/3.2L	11
Jeep		
Grand Cherokee	1996-98 Models 5.9L	12
	1999-00 Models 4.0L/4.7L	13
Kia		
Sportage	1996-00 Models 2.0L	14
Land Rover		
Discovery	1996-00 Models 4.0L	15
Range Rover	1996-00 Models 4.0L	16
Lexus		
RX300	1998-00 Models 3.0L	17
LX470	1998-00 Models 4.7L	18
Mazda		
MPV	1996-00 Models 3.0L	19
Mercury		
Villager	1996-00 Models 3.0L/3.3L	20
Mitsubishi		
Montero	1996-00 Models 3.0L/3.5L	21
Montero Sport	1997-00 Models 2.4L/3.0L	22
Nissan		
Quest	1996-97 Models 3.0L/3.3L	23
	1998-00 Models 3.0L/3.3L	24
Subaru		
Forester	1998-00 Models 2.2L/2.5L	25
Suzuki		
Sidekick	1996-00 Models 1.6L	26
Toyota		
RAV4	1996-00 Models 2.0L	27
Sienna	1998-00 Models 3.0L	28

93029C01

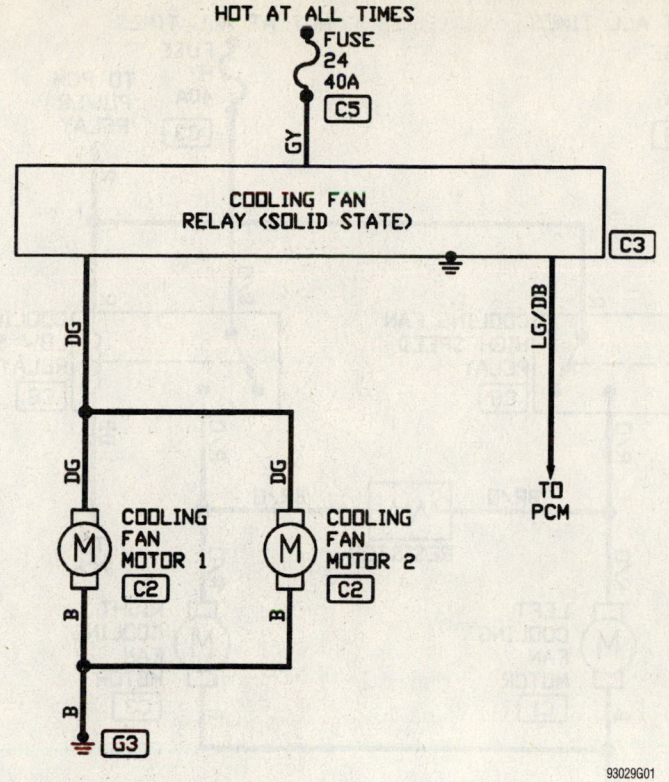

DIA. 1—Chrysler Caravan/Town & Country/Voyager 2.4L/3.0L/3.3L/3.8L

93029G01

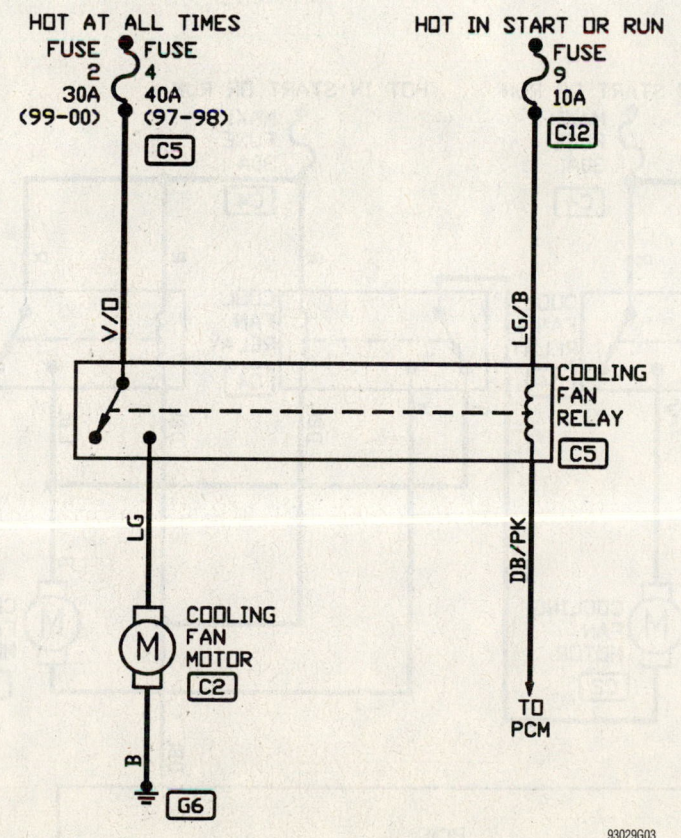

DIA. 2—Dodge Dakota 2.5L

93029G03

Refer to the model specific sections for engine mechanical service procedures

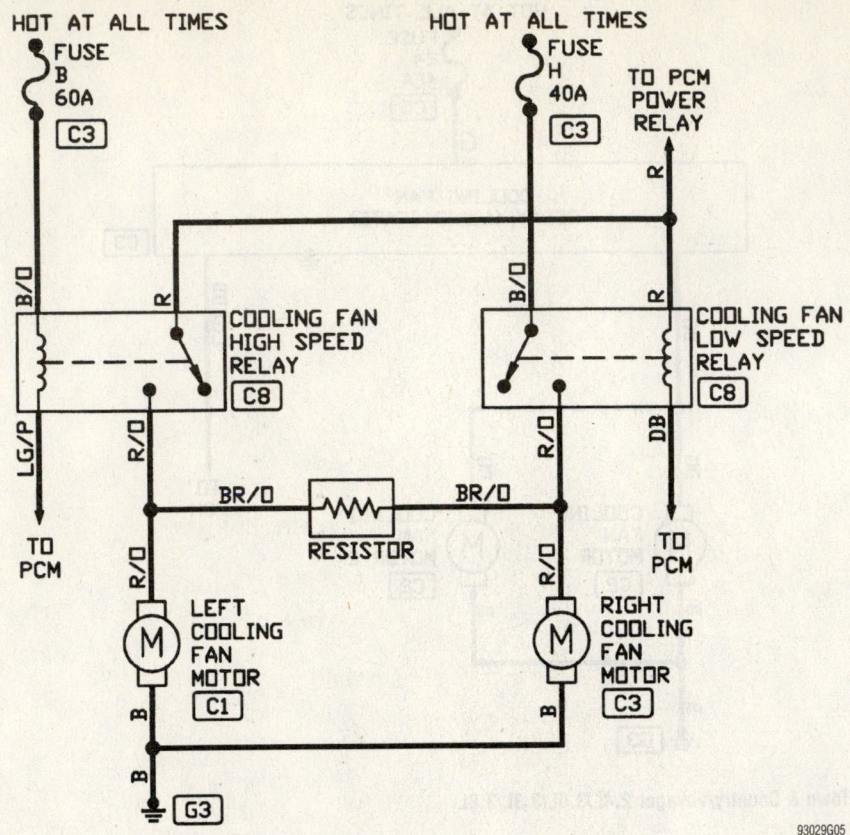

DIA. 3—Ford Windstar 3.0L/3.8L

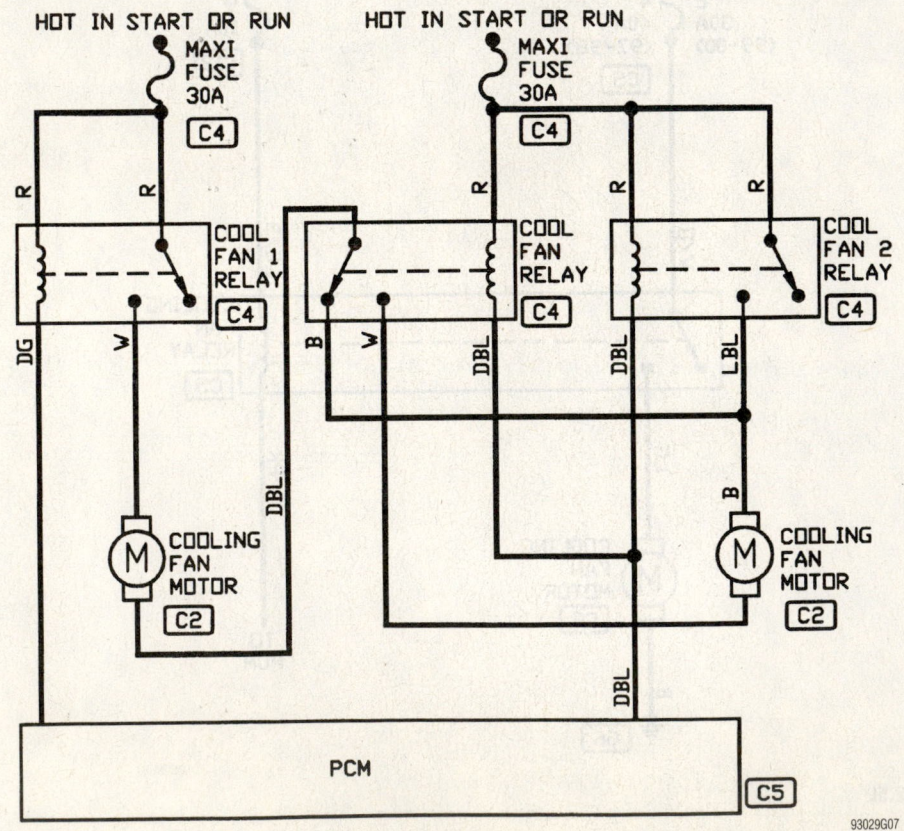

DIA. 4—General Motors Silhouette/Trans Sport/Venture 3.4L

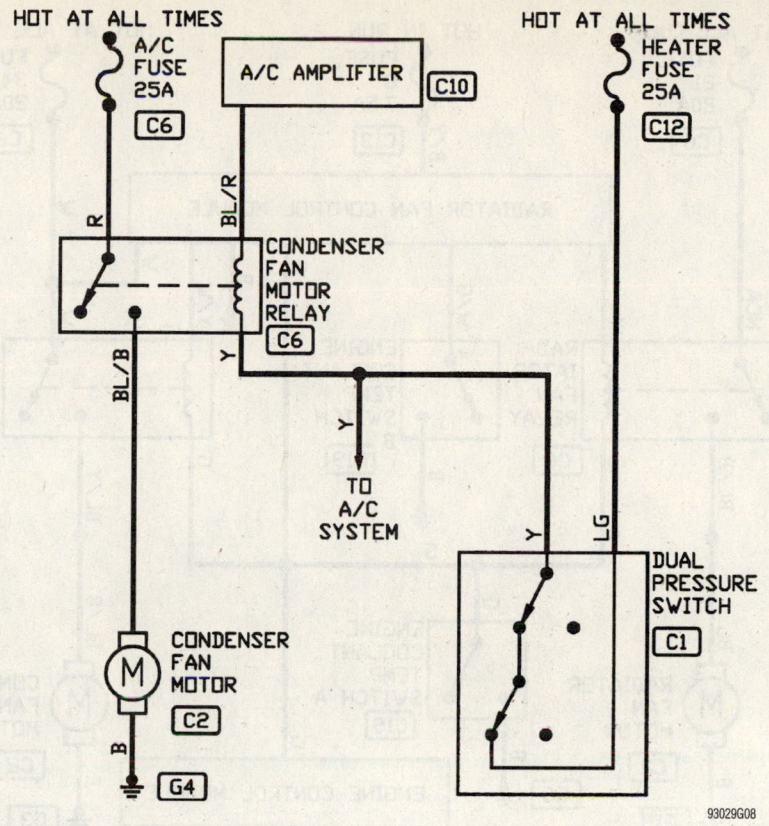

DIA. 5—GEO/Chevrolet Tracker 1.6L

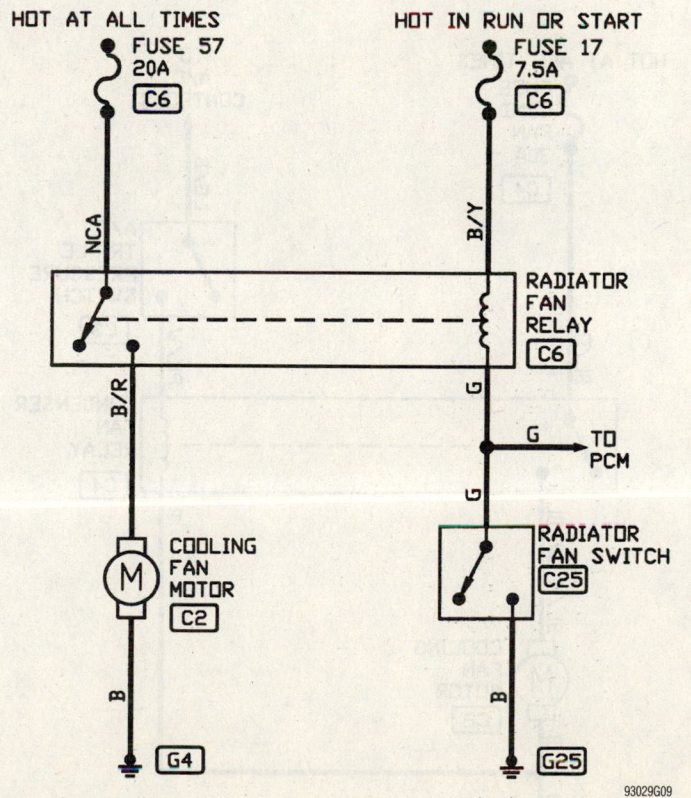

DIA. 6—Honda CR-V 2.0L

Refer to the model specific sections for cooling system service procedures

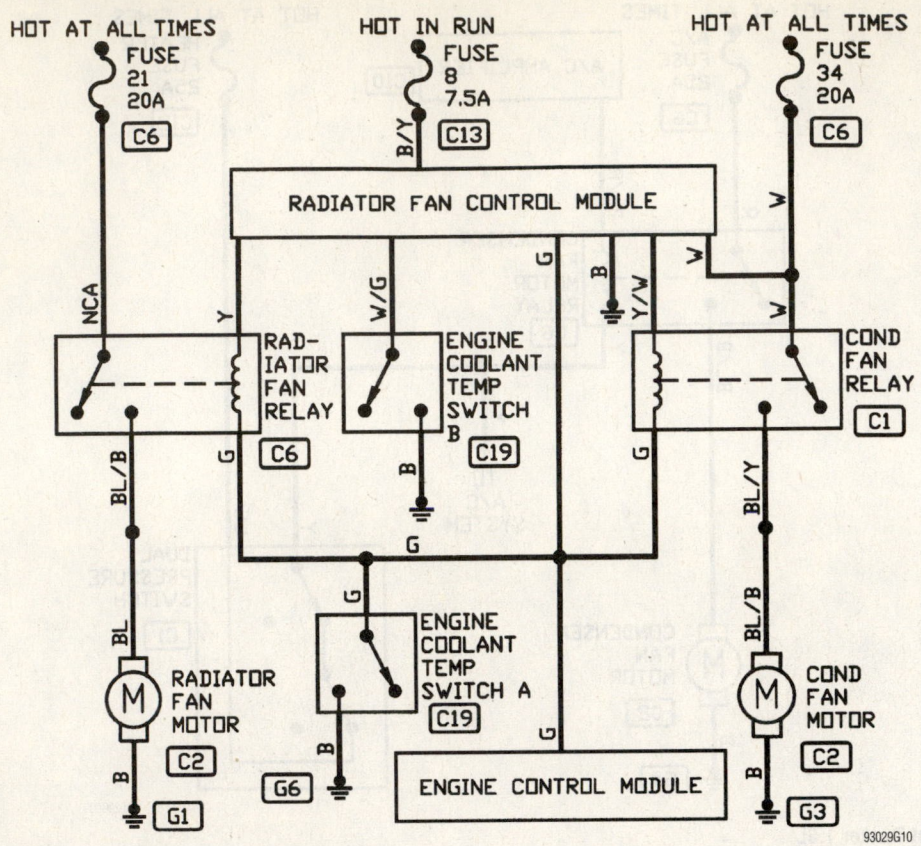

DIA. 7—Honda/Isuzu Oasis/Odyssey 2.2L

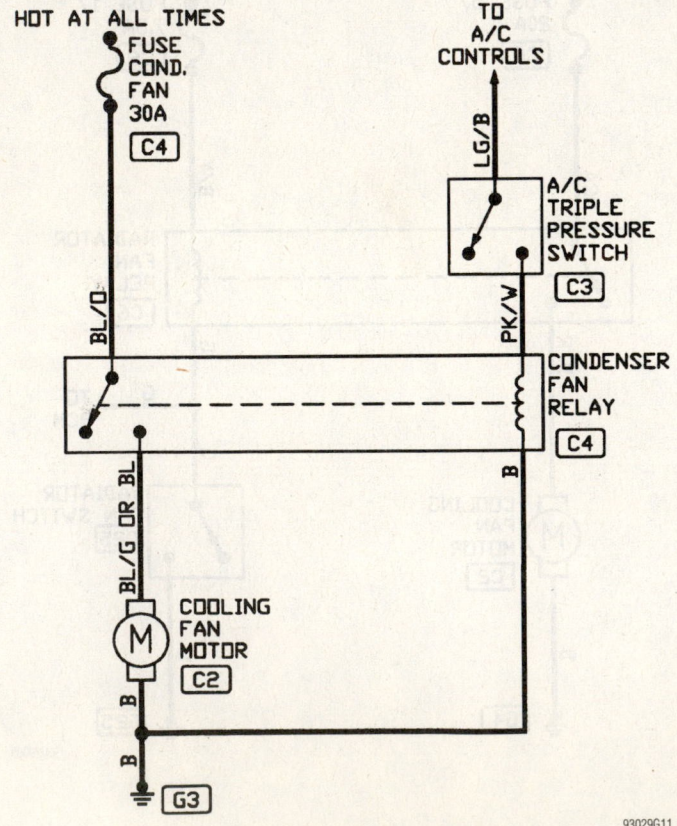

DIA. 8—Isuzu Rodeo 2.2L/2.6L/3.2L

PRECAUTIONS

Test Equipment

Never use jumper wires made from a thinner gauge wire than the circuit being tested. If the jumper wire is of too small a gauge, it may overheat and possibly melt. Never use jumpers to bypass high resistance loads in a circuit. Bypassing resistances, in effect, creates a short circuit. This may, in turn, cause damage and fire. Jumper wires should only be used to bypass lengths of wire or to simulate switches.

Do not use a test light to probe electronic ignition, spark plug or coil wires. Never use a pick-type test light to probe wiring on computer controlled systems unless specifically instructed to do so. Any wire insulation that is pierced by the test light probe should be taped and sealed with silicone after testing.

Never use an ohmmeter to check the resistance of a component or wire while there is voltage applied to the circuit.

A self-powered test light should not be used on any computer controlled system or component. The small amount of electricity transmitted by the test light is enough to damage many electronic automotive components.

Never disengage any sensor while the ignition is ON.

Always replace fuses, circuit breakers and fusible links with identically rated components. Under no circumstances should a component of higher or lower amperage rating be substituted.

Electronic Control Systems

Electronic control systems are very delicate and complicated. To save yourself aggravation, money and time, be sure to adhere to the following points when working on a vehicle's control system:

- Unless otherwise instructed, always disconnect the battery cables when servicing the electronic system.
- When disconnecting the battery, always be sure to detach the negative battery cable FIRST, then the positive cable. This simple practice will almost completely prevent the chance of arcing or shorting the system.
- Never pierce, or cut the insulation off of, a wire for testing purposes. Many of the control system's wires are designed to handle a precise amount of electrical resistance, and the computer expects to see a certain predetermined amount of resistance. If you pierce, or cut the insulation off of a wire, corrosion can build up in the wiring, leading to decreased control system efficiency, DTC storing or possibly even component damage.
- Never subject any control computer to excessive jolts (such as dropping).
- If welding on the vehicle, always disconnect the computer from the vehicle's wiring harness.
- Never detach a wiring harness connector when the ignition switch is turned ON.

Handling Electrostatic Discharge (ESD) Sensitive Parts

Electronic modules are very sensitive to Electrostatic Static Discharge (ESD). If the modules are exposed to these charges, they may be damaged. While most vehicles display a label informing you that their electronic components may be damaged by ESD, some do not have labels, but they may be damaged also. To avoid possible damage to any of these components, follow the steps outlined below.

1. Body movement produces an electrostatic charge. To discharge personal static electricity, touch a ground point (metal) on the vehicle. This should be performed any time you:
- Slide across the vehicle seat
- Sit down or get up
- Do any walking
- Touch an ESD sensitive part

2. Do not touch any exposed terminals on components or connectors with your fingers or any tools.

3. Never use jumper wires, ground a terminal on a component, use test equipment on any component or terminal unless instructed to in a diagnostic or testing procedure. When using test equipment, always connect the ground lead first.

4. Do not remove the part from its protective packing until it's time to install it.

5. Before removing the part from its protective packing, ground the packing to a known good ground on the vehicle.

Air Bags

When working on the air bag system or any components which require the removal of the air bag, adhere to all of the following precautions to minimize the risks of personal injury or component damage:

1. Before attempting to diagnose, remove or install air bag system components, you must first disconnect and isolate the negative (-) battery cable. Failure to do so could result in accidental deployment and possible personal injury.

2. When an undeployed air bag assembly is to be removed from the steering wheel, after disconnecting the negative battery cable, allow the system capacitor to discharge for two minutes before commencing with the air bag system component removal.

3. Replace the air bag system components only with specified replacement parts, or equivalent. Substitute parts may visually appear interchangeable, but internal differences may result in inferior occupant protection.

4. The fasteners, screws, and bolts originally used for the air bag system have special coatings and are specifically designed for the system. They must never be replaced with any substitutes. Anytime a new fastener is needed, replace with the correct fasteners provided in the service package or fasteners listed in the parts books.

BLACK	B	PINK	PK
BROWN	BR	PURPLE	P
RED	R	GREEN	G
ORANGE	O	WHITE	W
YELLOW	Y	LIGHT BLUE	LBL
GRAY	GY	LIGHT GREEN	LG
BLUE	BL	DARK GREEN	DG
VIOLET	V	DARK BLUE	DBL
NO COLOR AVAILABLE			NCA

WIRE COLOR ABREVIATIONS

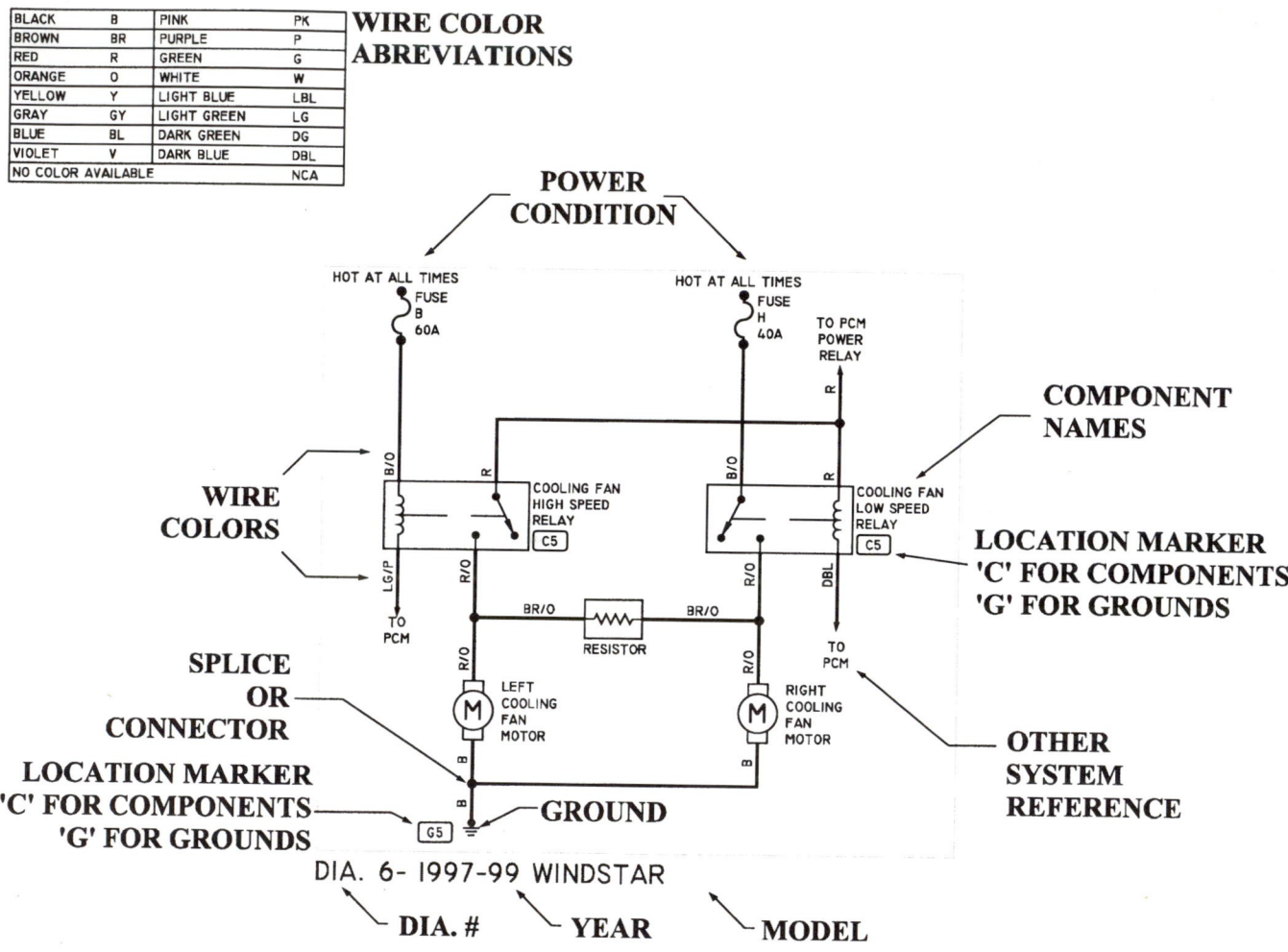

POWER CONDITION

COMPONENT NAMES

WIRE COLORS

LOCATION MARKER 'C' FOR COMPONENTS 'G' FOR GROUNDS

SPLICE OR CONNECTOR

LOCATION MARKER 'C' FOR COMPONENTS 'G' FOR GROUNDS

GROUND

OTHER SYSTEM REFERENCE

DIA. 6- 1997-99 WINDSTAR

DIA. #   **YEAR**   **MODEL**

WIRING DIAGRAM SYMBOLS

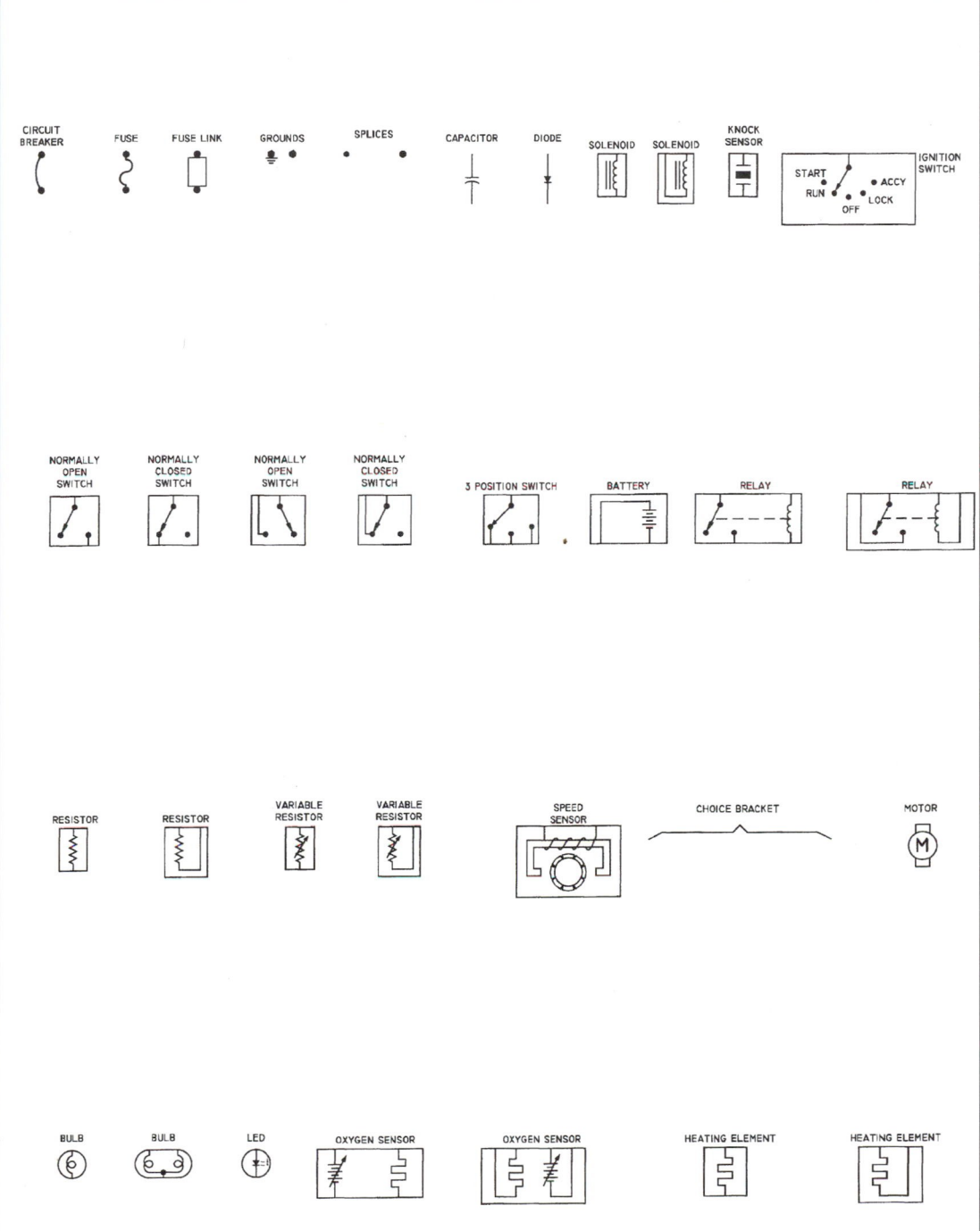

LOCATION SCHEMATIC

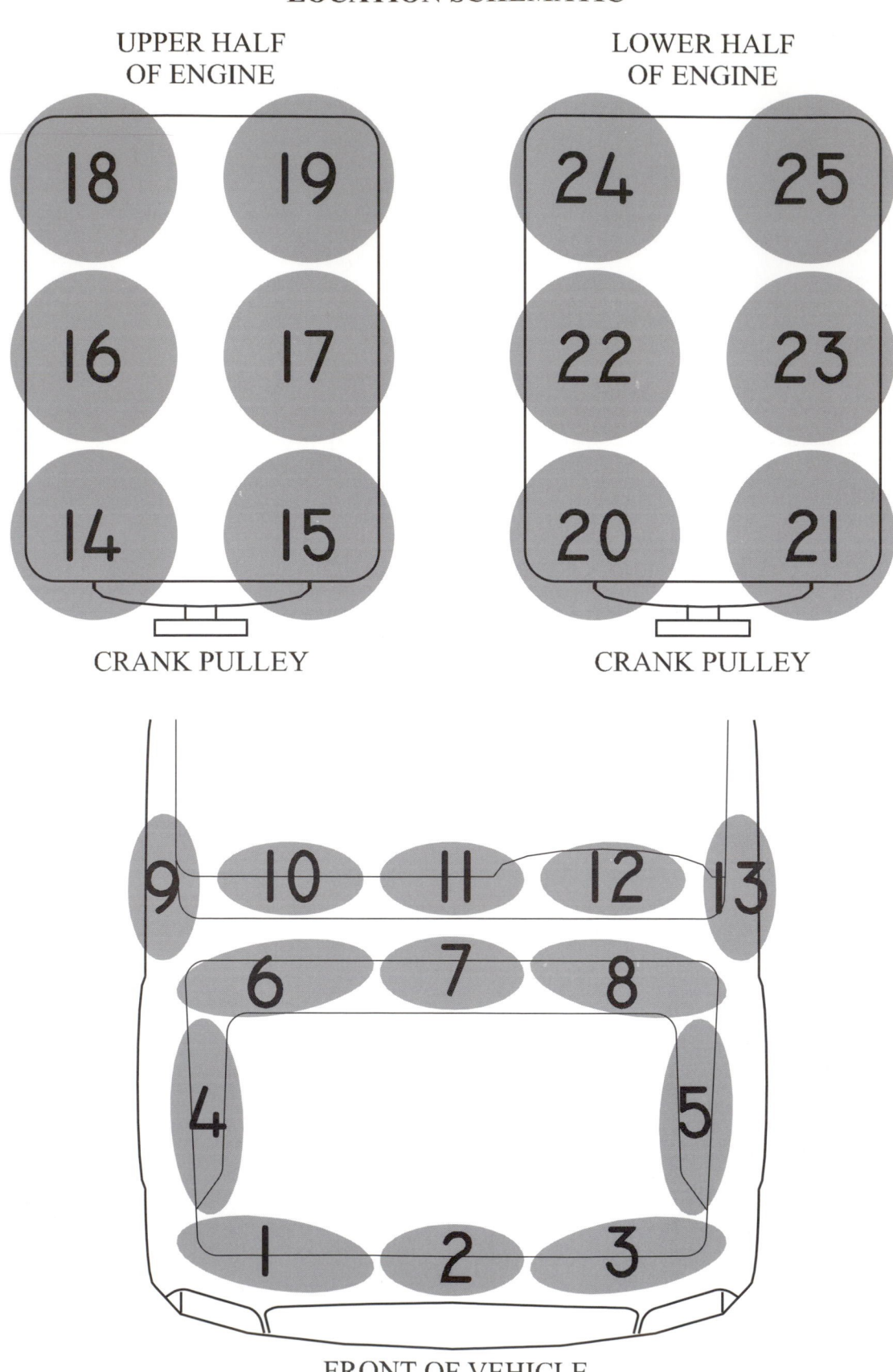

UPPER HALF
OF ENGINE

LOWER HALF
OF ENGINE

CRANK PULLEY

CRANK PULLEY

FRONT OF VEHICLE

DIAGRAM X

Location Number	Location Description
1	Engine compartment - Front right
2	Engine compartment - Front middle
3	Engine compartment - Front left
4	Engine compartment - Right inner fender
5	Engine compartment - Left inner fender
6	Engine compartment - Firewall right
7	Engine compartment - Firewall middle
8	Engine compartment - Firewall left
9	Passenger compartment - Right kick panel
10	Passenger compartment - Underdash right
11	Passenger compartment - Underdash middle
12	Passenger compartment - Underdash left
13	Passenger compartment - Left kick panel
14	Facing Crank Pulley - Upper Engine - Front left
15	Facing Crank Pulley - Upper Engine - Front right
16	Facing Crank Pulley - Upper Engine - Middle left
17	Facing Crank Pulley - Upper Engine - Middle right
18	Facing Crank Pulley - Upper Engine - Rear left
19	Facing Crank Pulley - Upper Engine - Rear right
20	Facing Crank Pulley - Lower Engine - Front left
21	Facing Crank Pulley - Lower Engine - Front right
22	Facing Crank Pulley - Lower Engine - Middle left
23	Facing Crank Pulley - Lower Engine - Middle right
24	Facing Crank Pulley - Lower Engine - Rear left
25	Facing Crank Pulley - Lower Engine - Rear right

NOTES

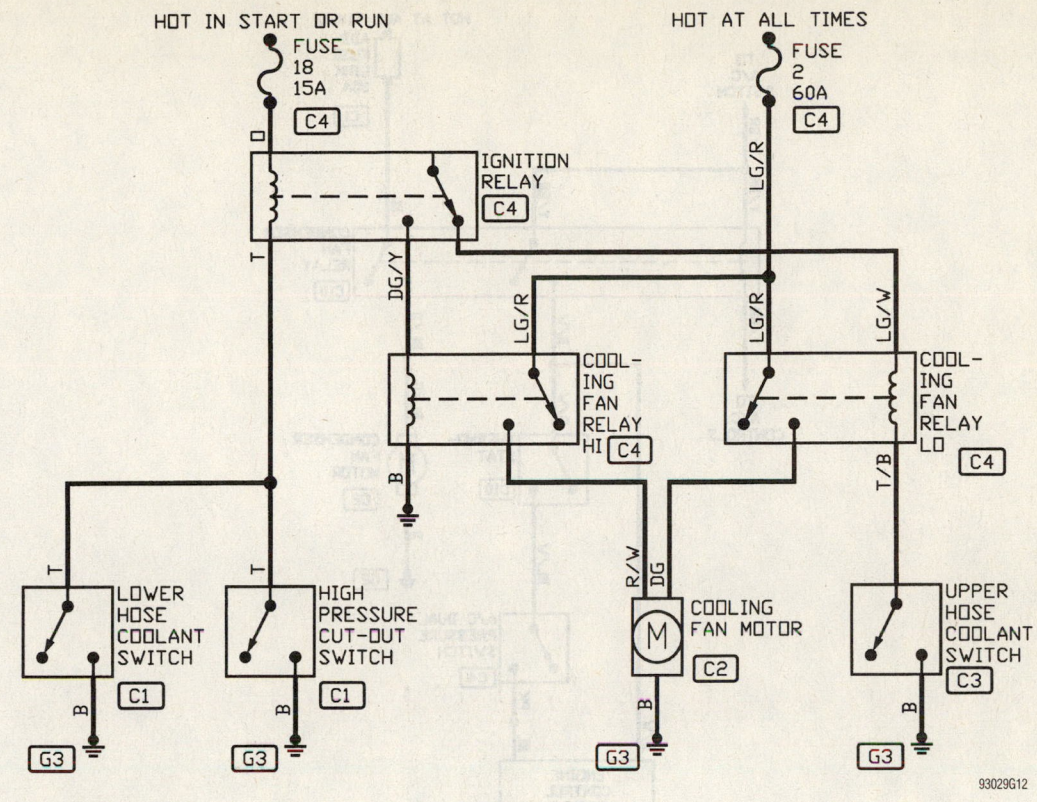

DIA. 9—Jeep Grand Cherokee 5.9L

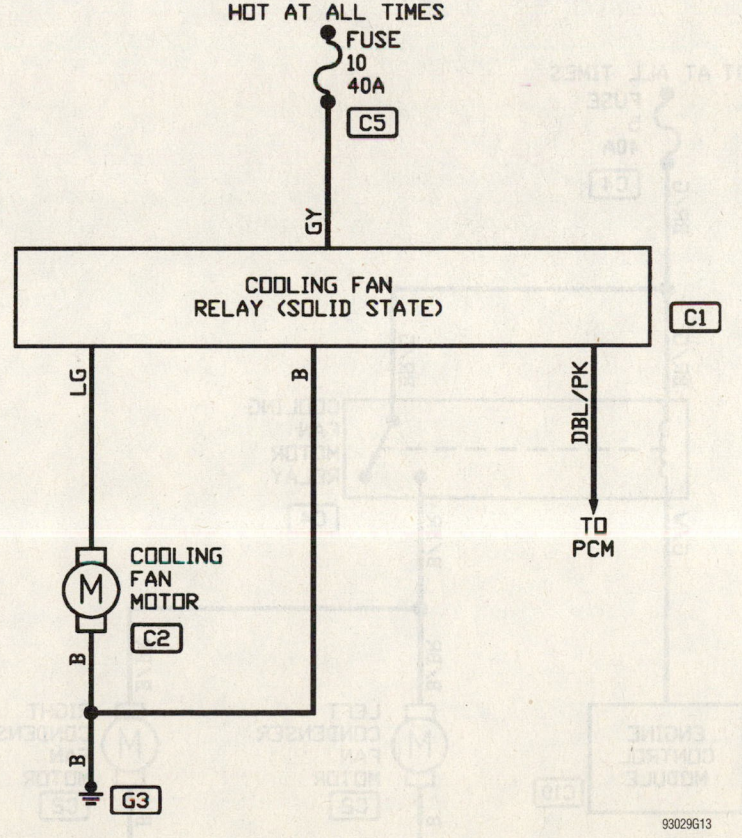

DIA. 10—Jeep Grand Cherokee 4.0L/4.7L

For complete service labor times order Nichols' Chilton Labor Guide Manual

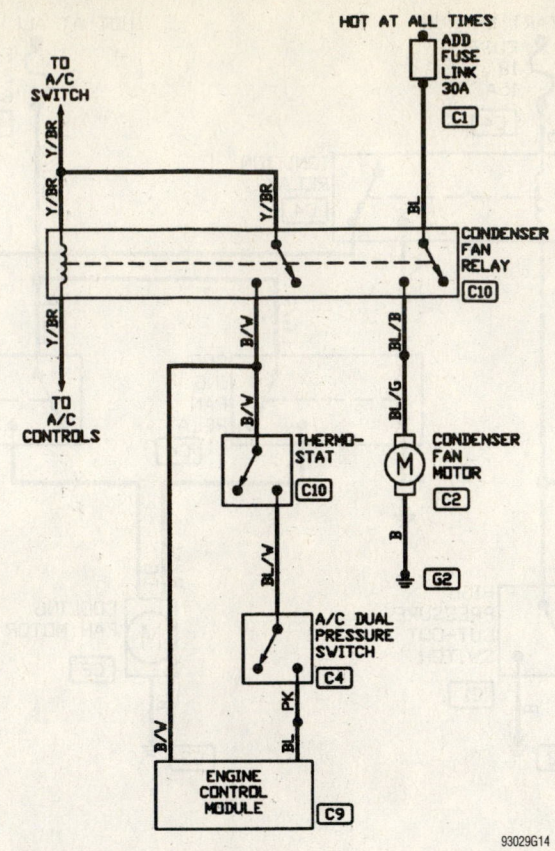

DIA. 11—Kia Sportage 2.0L

93029G14

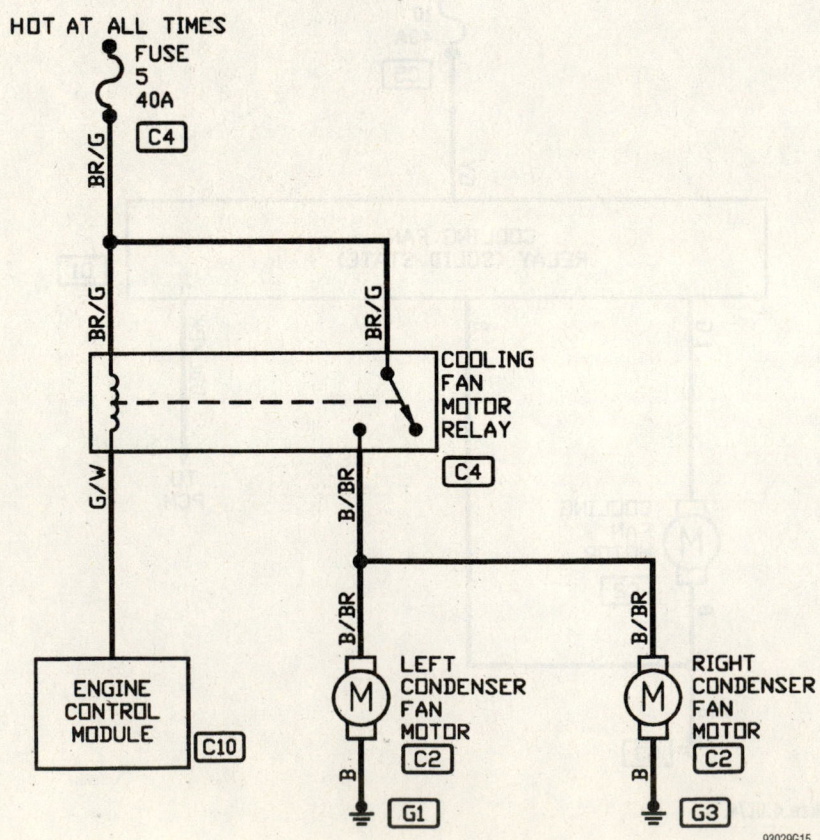

DIA. 12—Land Rover Discovery 4.0L

93029G15

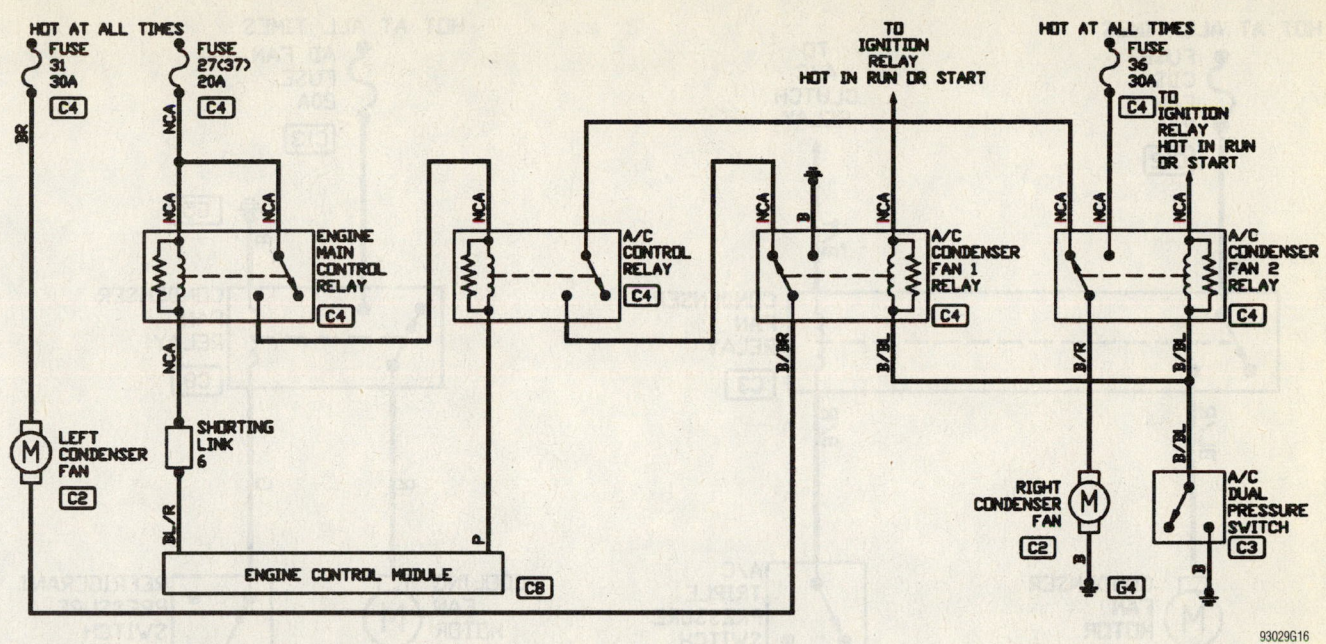

HOT AT ALL TIMES
FUSE 31 30A
C4

FUSE 27(37) 20A
C4

ENGINE MAIN CONTROL RELAY
C4

A/C CONTROL RELAY
C4

TO IGNITION RELAY
HOT IN RUN OR START

A/C CONDENSER FAN 1 RELAY
C4

HOT AT ALL TIMES
FUSE 36 30A
C4
TO IGNITION RELAY
HOT IN RUN OR START

A/C CONDENSER FAN 2 RELAY
C4

LEFT CONDENSER FAN
C2

SHORTING LINK 6

ENGINE CONTROL MODULE
C8

RIGHT CONDENSER FAN
C2
G4

A/C DUAL PRESSURE SWITCH
C3

93029G16

DIA. 13—Land Rover Range Rover 4.0L

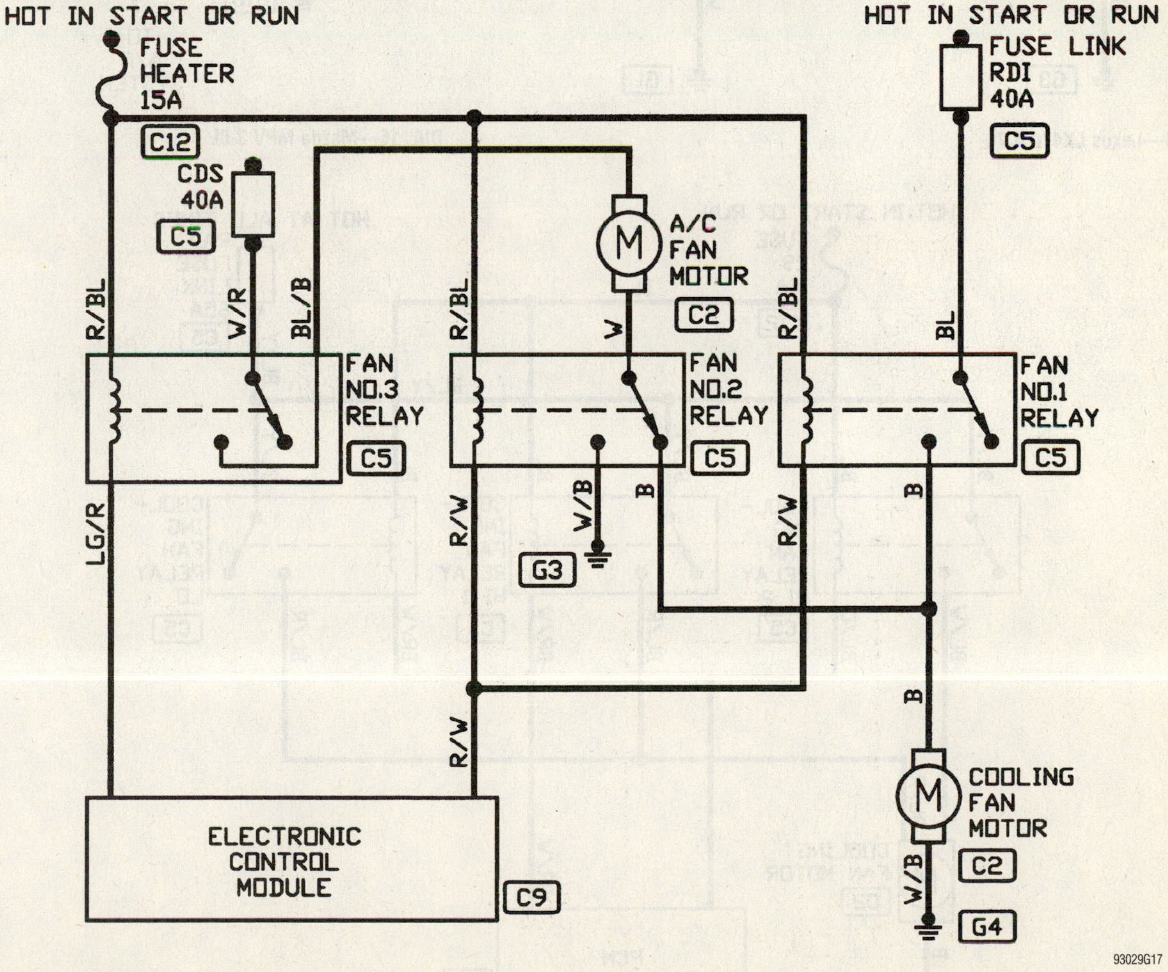

HOT IN START OR RUN
FUSE HEATER 15A
C12

CDS 40A
C5

FAN NO.3 RELAY
C5

A/C FAN MOTOR
C2

FAN NO.2 RELAY
C5

G3

HOT IN START OR RUN
FUSE LINK RDI 40A
C5

FAN NO.1 RELAY
C5

ELECTRONIC CONTROL MODULE
C9

COOLING FAN MOTOR
C2
G4

93029G17

DIA. 14—Lexus RX300 3.0L

Please visit our web site at www.chiltononline.com

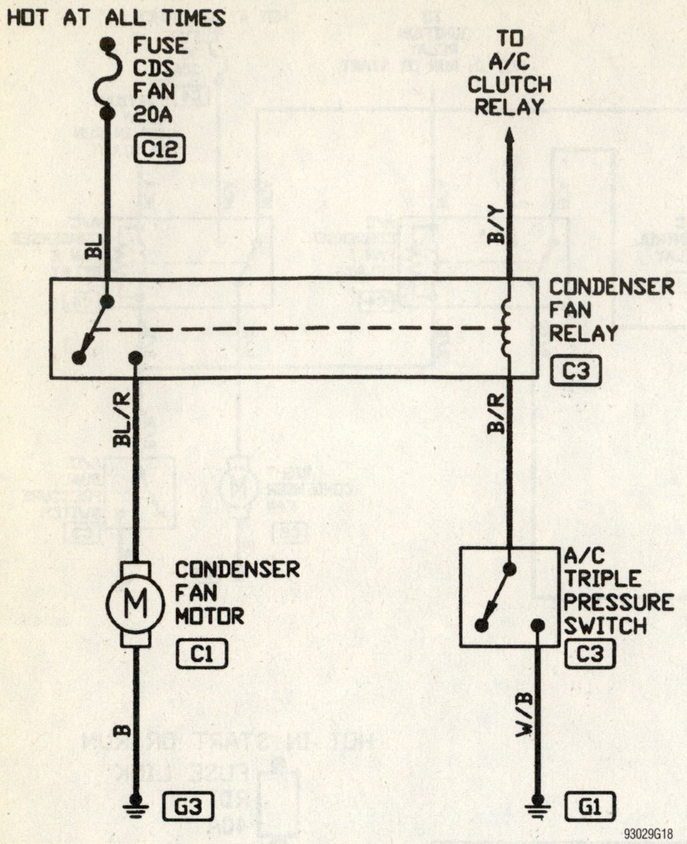

HOT AT ALL TIMES

FUSE
CDS
FAN
20A
[C12]

TO
A/C
CLUTCH
RELAY

B/Y

BL

CONDENSER
FAN
RELAY
[C3]

B/R

BL/R

M CONDENSER
FAN
MOTOR
[C1]

A/C
TRIPLE
PRESSURE
SWITCH
[C3]

B

W/B

[G3]

[G1]

93029G18

DIA. 15—Lexus LX470 4.7L

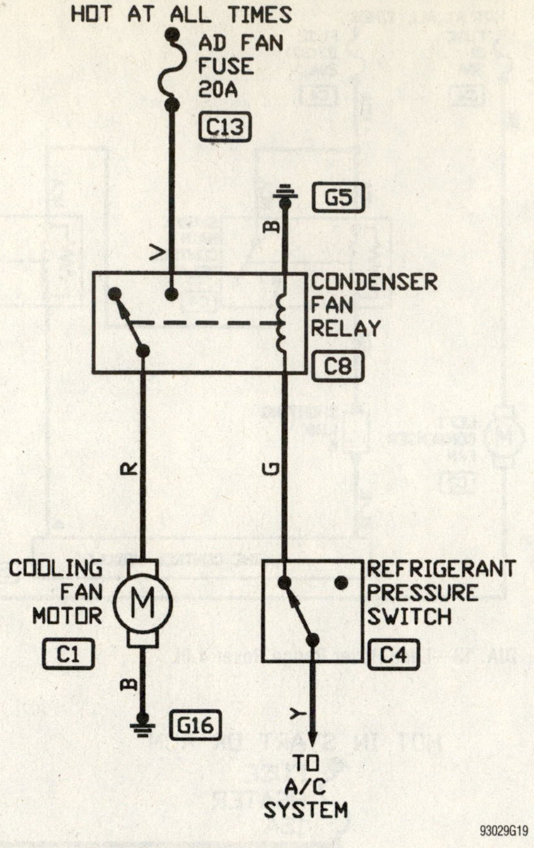

HOT AT ALL TIMES

AD FAN
FUSE
20A
[C13]

[G5]

B

V

CONDENSER
FAN
RELAY
[C8]

R

G

COOLING
FAN
MOTOR
[C1]

M

REFRIGERANT
PRESSURE
SWITCH
[C4]

B

[G16]

Y

TO
A/C
SYSTEM

93029G19

DIA. 16—Mazda MPV 3.0L

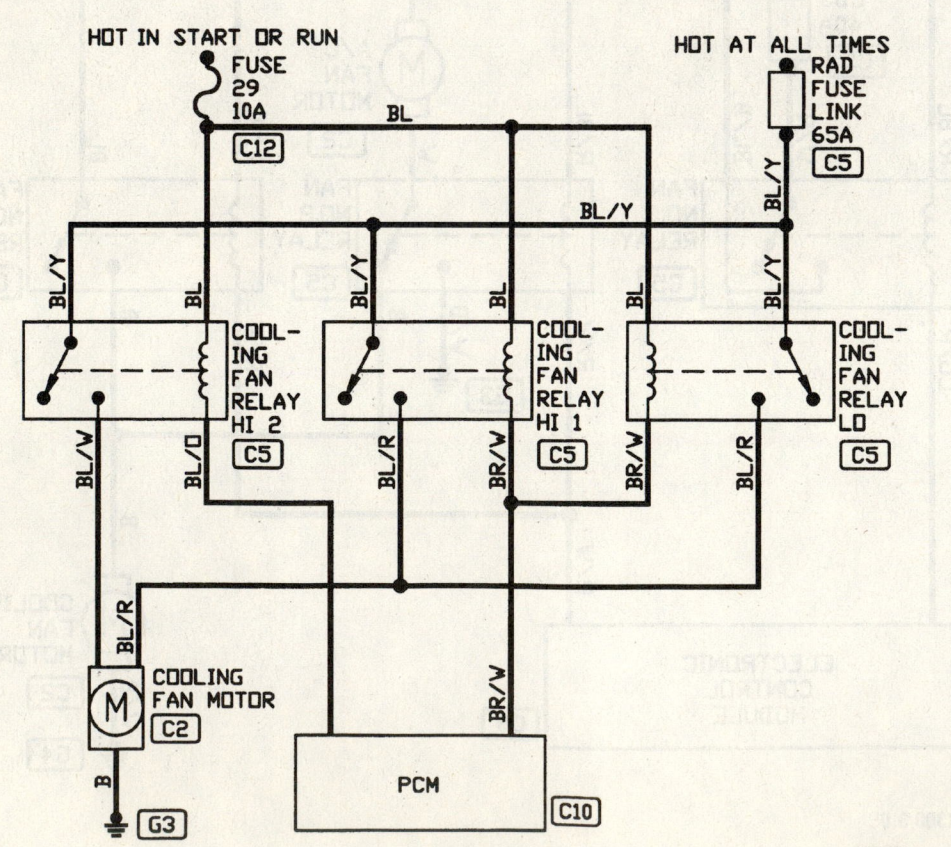

HOT IN START OR RUN

FUSE
29
10A
[C12]

BL

HOT AT ALL TIMES

RAD
FUSE
LINK
65A
[C5]

BL/Y

BL/Y

BL/Y

BL/Y

BL/Y

BL/Y

BL

BL

BL

COOL-
ING
FAN
RELAY
HI 2
[C5]

COOL-
ING
FAN
RELAY
HI 1
[C5]

COOL-
ING
FAN
RELAY
LO
[C5]

BL/W

BL/O

BL/R

BR/W

BR/W

BL/R

BL/R

M COOLING
FAN MOTOR
[C2]

B

[G3]

BR/W

PCM
[C10]

93029G20

DIA. 17—Mercury Villager 3.0L/3.3L

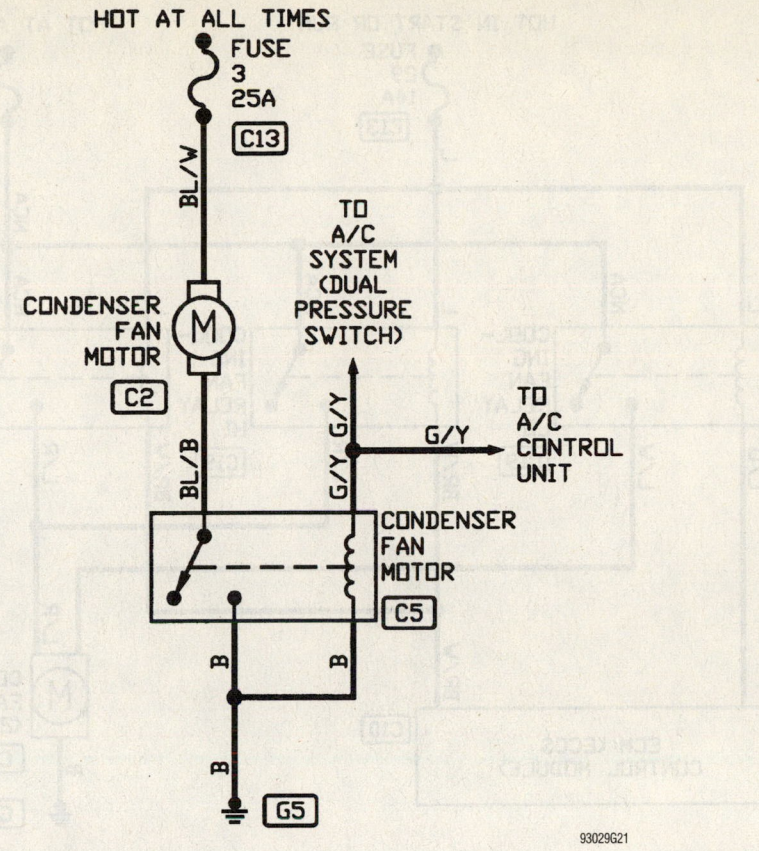

DIA. 18—Mitsubishi Montero 3.0L/3.5L

93029G21

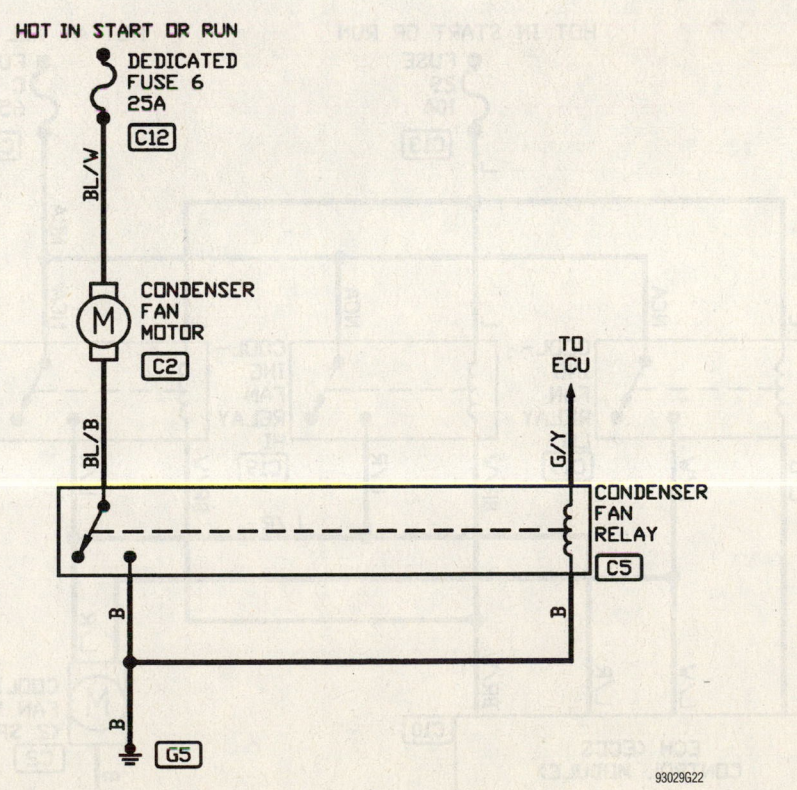

DIA. 19—Mitsubishi Montero Sport 2.4L/3.0L

93029G22

Refer to the model specific sections for engine mechanical service procedures

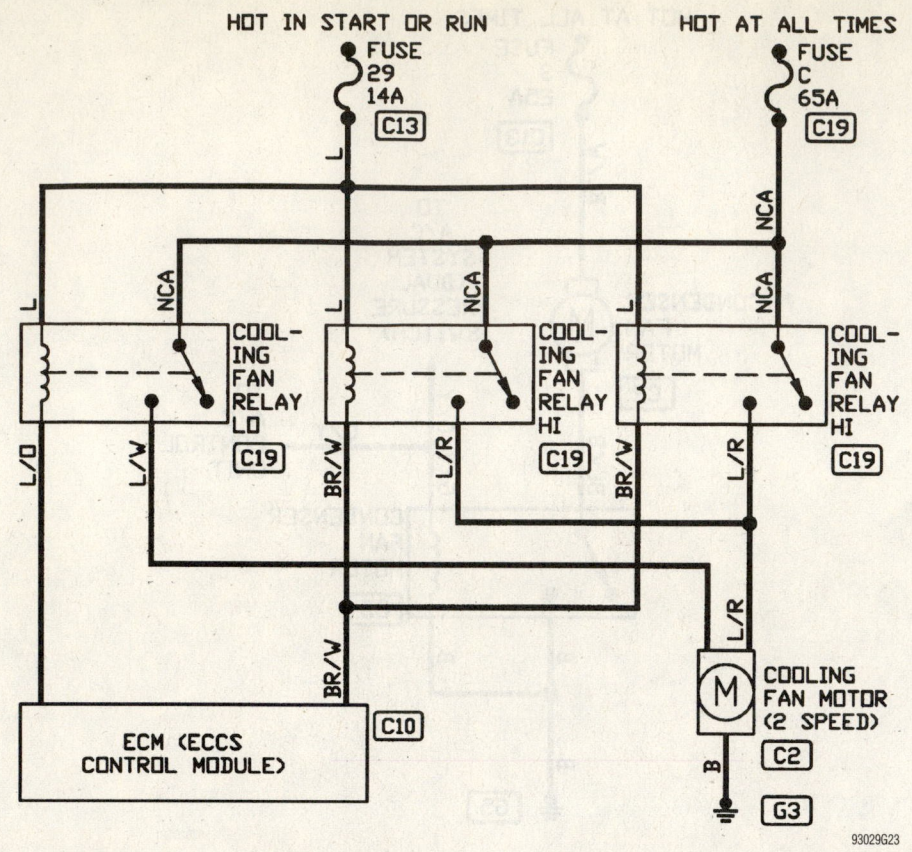

DIA. 20—1997 Nissan Quest 3.0L/3.3L

93029G23

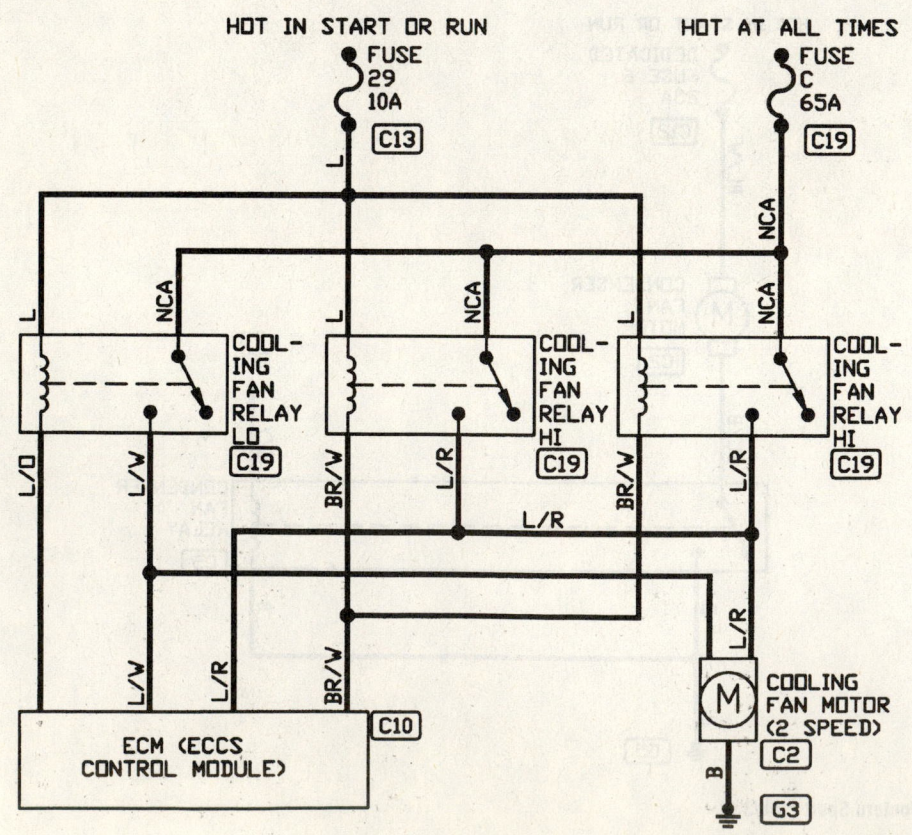

DIA. 21—1998—01 Nissan Quest 3.0L/3.3L

93029G24

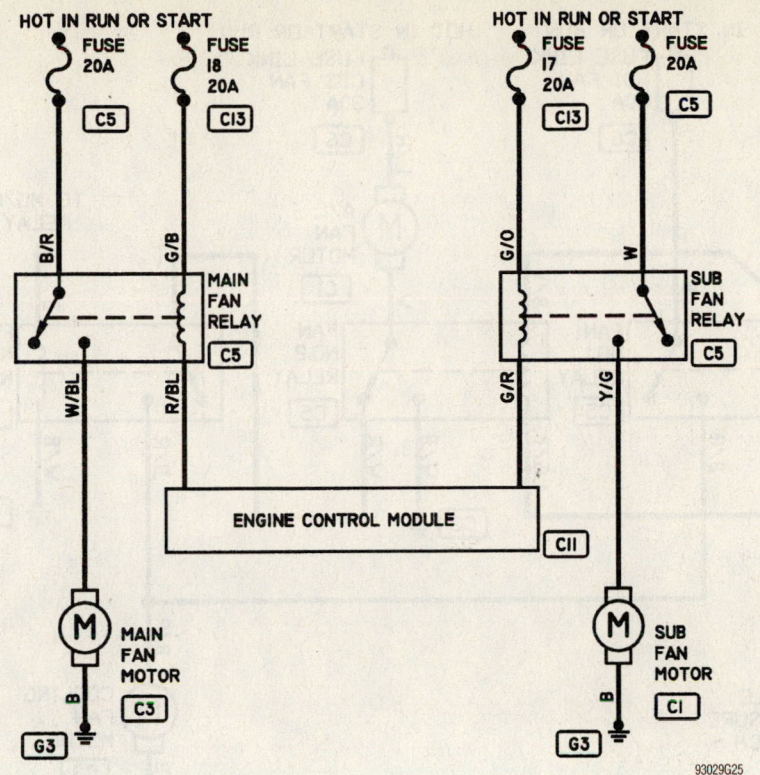

DIA. 22—Subaru Forester 2.2L/2.5L

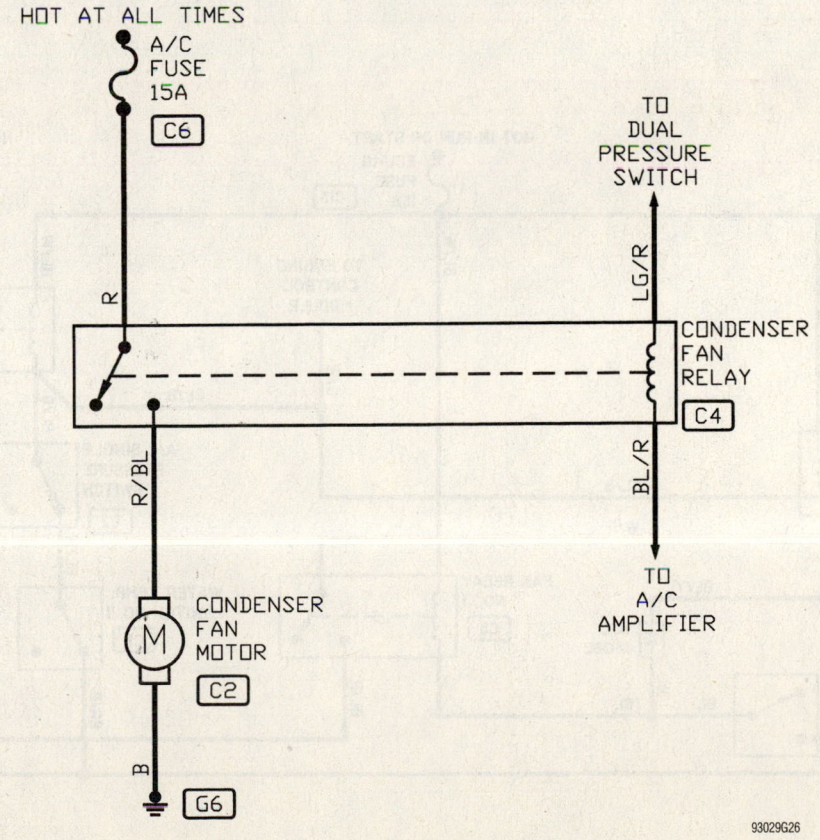

DIA. 23—Suzuki Sidekick 1.6L/1.8L

Refer to the model specific sections for cooling system service procedures

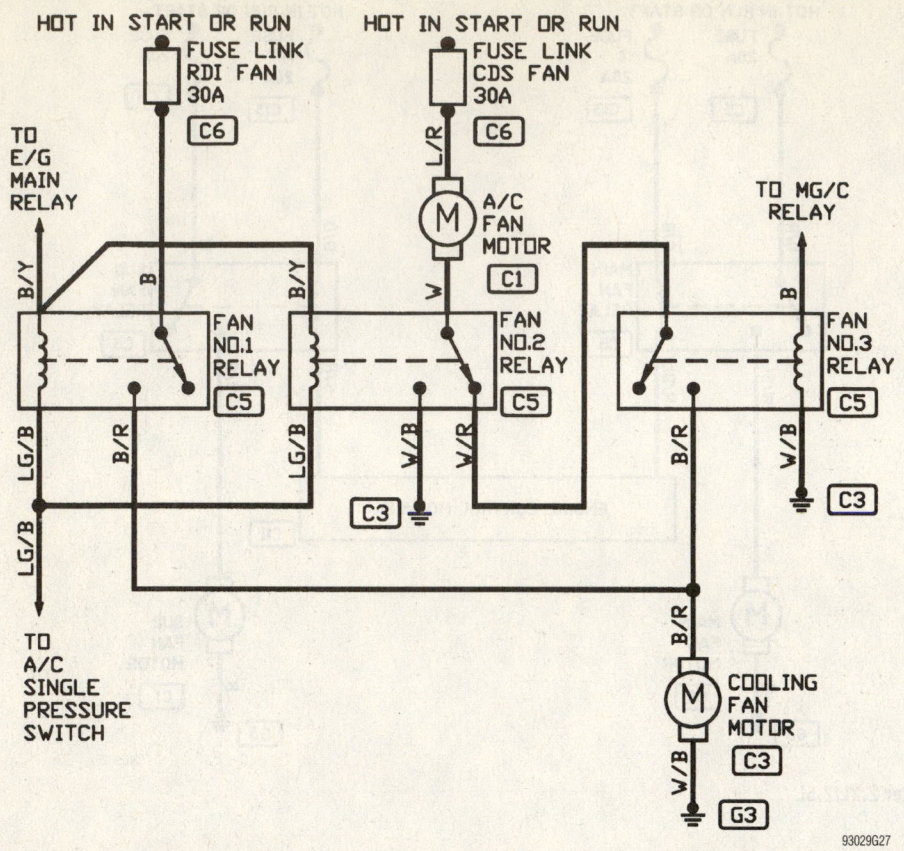

DIA. 24—Toyota RAV4 2.0L

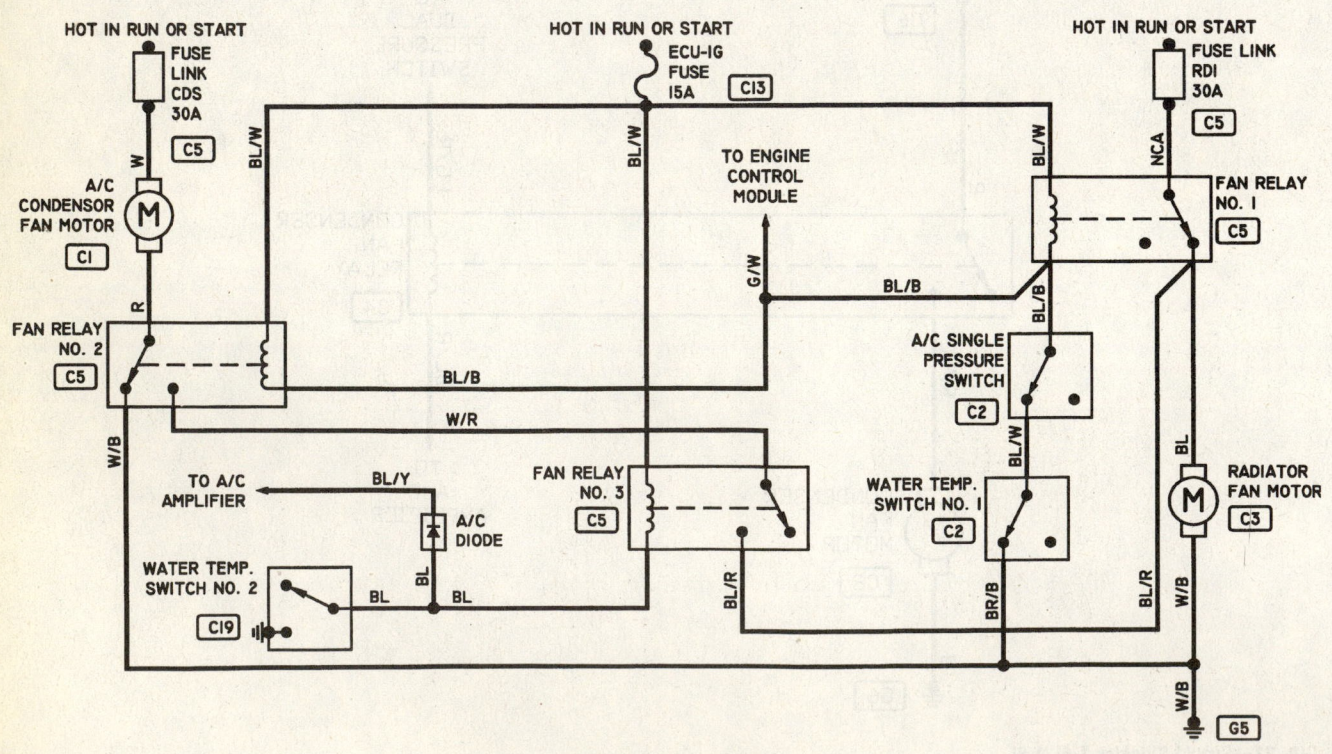

DIA. 25—Toyota Sienna 3.0L

HEATER CORES

9

SLX

REMOVAL & INSTALLATION

✳✳ CAUTION

The vehicle is equipped with a driver's side and a passenger's side air bag. Before starting service procedures on components, especially under the instrument panel and/or near the steering column, disable the air bag systems. There is sufficient voltage in the system to cause a deployment for up to 15 seconds after the battery has been disconnected, the ignition turned OFF or fuse C-21 is removed from the fuse panel.

1. If equipped with an air bag, perform the following procedures:
   a. Disconnect the negative battery cable, then disconnect the positive battery cable.
   b. Disconnect the yellow 2-pin connector located at the base of the steering column.
   c. Remove the glove box and disconnect the yellow 2-pin connector located behind the glove box.
2. Disconnect the negative battery cable.
3. Drain the cooling system.
4. If equipped with air conditioning, discharge and recover the refrigerant.

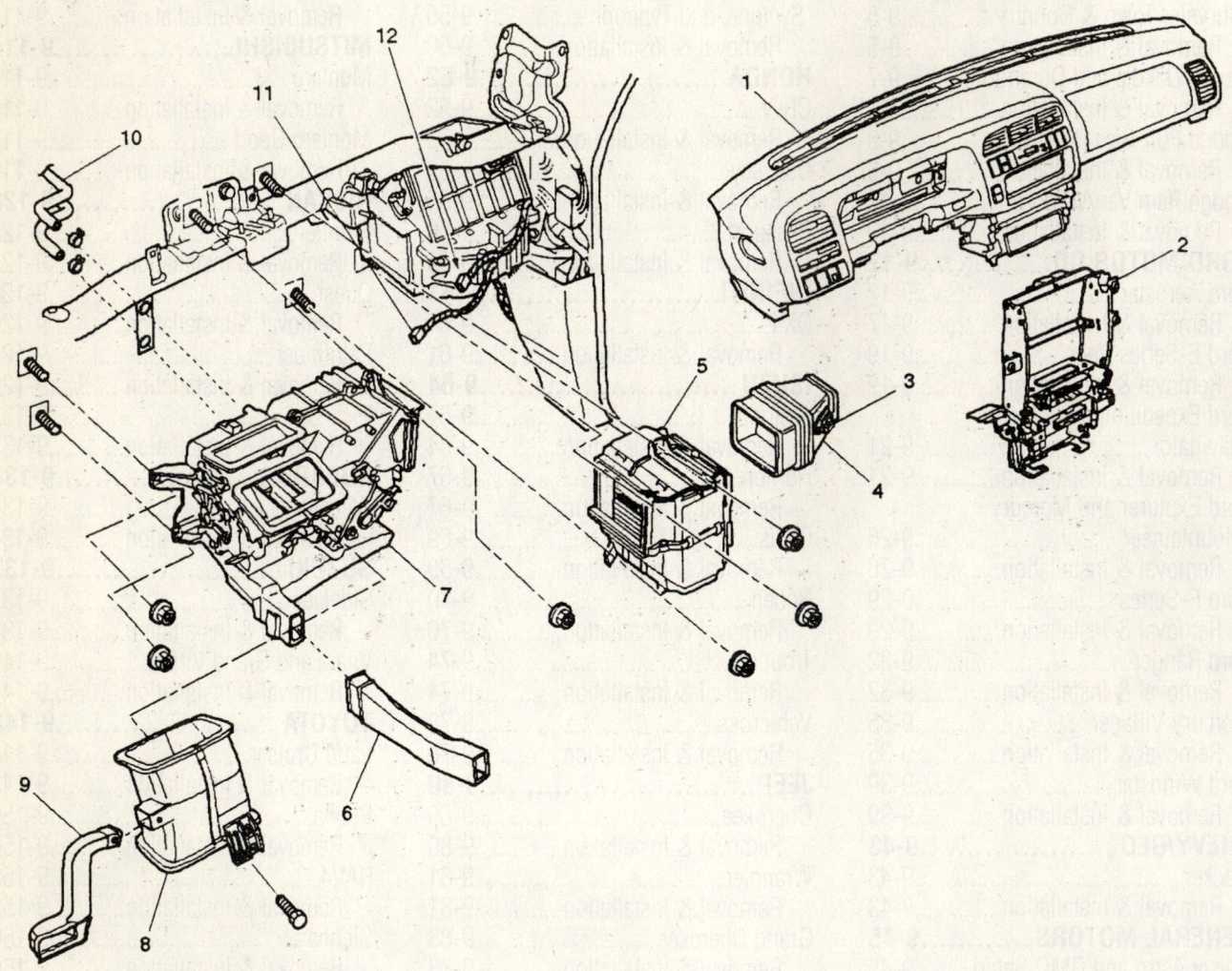

(1) Instrument Panel Assembly
(2) Instrument Panel Center Bracket
(3) Resistor
(4) Duct
(5) Evaporator Assembly (A/C only)
(6) Rear Heater Duct
(7) Heater Unit Assembly
(8) Center Ventilation Lower Duct
(9) Driver Lap Vent Nozzle
(10) Water Hose
(11) Electro Thermo Connector (With A/C)
(12) Resistor Connector

93113G01

Exploded view of the heater unit and related components—Acura SLX

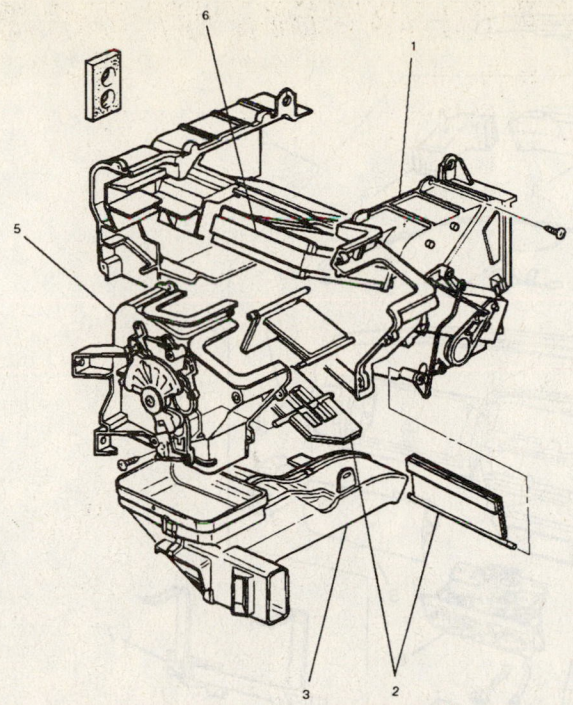

(1) Case (Temperature Control)
(2) Mode Door
(3) Duct

(5) Case (Mode Control)
(6) Heater Core

93113G02

Exploded view of the heater unit—Acura SLX

5. Remove the instrument panel assembly by performing the following procedure:

a. At the front console assembly, disconnect the switch connectors; then, remove the console-to-chassis screws and the console.

b. At the lower cluster assembly, remove the cluster-to-instrument panel screws, disconnect the cigarette lighter and light connectors and remove the lower cluster.

c. Remove the glove box and the instrument panel lower cover and the passenger knee bolster reinforcement.

d. At the left side, remove the instrument panel lower cover and the knee bolster assembly.

e. At the top of the instrument panel, pry the 8 claws on the front side toward you, raise the defroster grille and remove it.

f. At the SRS adjust bracket and cross beam, under the passenger air bag module, remove the 2 attaching bolts and remove the instrument panel assembly.

g. Disconnect the air conditioning control cables from the unit.

h. Remove the instrument harness connectors (5 on the driver's side and 3 on the passenger's side), the passenger air bag

module connector, the radio antenna plug and the center bracket ground cable bolt.

i. Remove the passenger's air bag module nuts, disconnect the connectors and remove the module.

j. Remove the instrument panel cluster assembly screws, disconnect the switch connectors and the instrument panel assembly.

6. Disconnect the heater hoses from the heater unit.

7. Disconnect the heater resistor connector and the electro-thermo connector (if equipped with air conditioning).

8. Remove the heater duct.

9. If equipped with air conditioning, remove the evaporator assembly by performing the following procedure:

a. Disconnect the drain hose.

b. Using a backup wrench, disconnect the refrigerant lines from the evaporator.

c. Plug or cap the refrigerant lines.

d. Remove the evaporator assembly.

10. Remove the instrument panel center bracket (crossbeam assembly) by performing the following procedure:

a. Remove the side support bracket bolts and brackets from both sides of the vehicle.

b. Remove the crossbeam center

bracket nuts, disconnect the electrical connectors and the center bracket.

11. Remove the rear heater duct and heater assembly.

12. Disassemble the heater unit assembly by performing the following procedure:

a. Remove the lower air duct; do not remove the link unit.

b. Remove the temperature control case screws and lift the case from the heater unit.

c. Remove the heater core.

To install:

13. Assemble the heater unit assembly by performing the following procedure:

a. Install the heater core into the heater unit.

b. Install the temperature control case onto the unit and secure with screws.

c. Install the lower air duct.

14. Install the heater unit assembly into the vehicle.

15. Install the rear heater duct.

16. Install the instrument panel cross beam assembly by reversing the removal procedures.

17. If equipped with air conditioning, install the evaporator assembly by performing the following procedures:

a. If installing a new evaporator assembly, add 1.7 fl. oz. (50mL) of refrigerant oil to the evaporator.

b. Using new O-rings and a backup wrench, install the refrigerant lines and torque the outlet line to 18 ft. lbs. (25 Nm) and the inlet line to 11 ft. lbs. (15 Nm).

18. Install the heater duct.

19. Connect the heater resistor connector and the electro-thermo connector (if equipped with air conditioning).

20. Connect the heater hoses to the heater unit.

21. Install the instrument panel assembly by reversing the removal procedures.

22. If equipped with air conditioning, evacuate, charge and leak test the system.

23. Refill the cooling system.

24. Connect the negative battery cable.

✳✳ CAUTION

Never use an air bag assembly from another vehicle and/or different model year. Starting in 1999, the air bag assemblies are equipped with identification colors on the bar code label as follows: YELLOW for the driver's air bag assembly, WHITE for the passenger's air bag assembly.

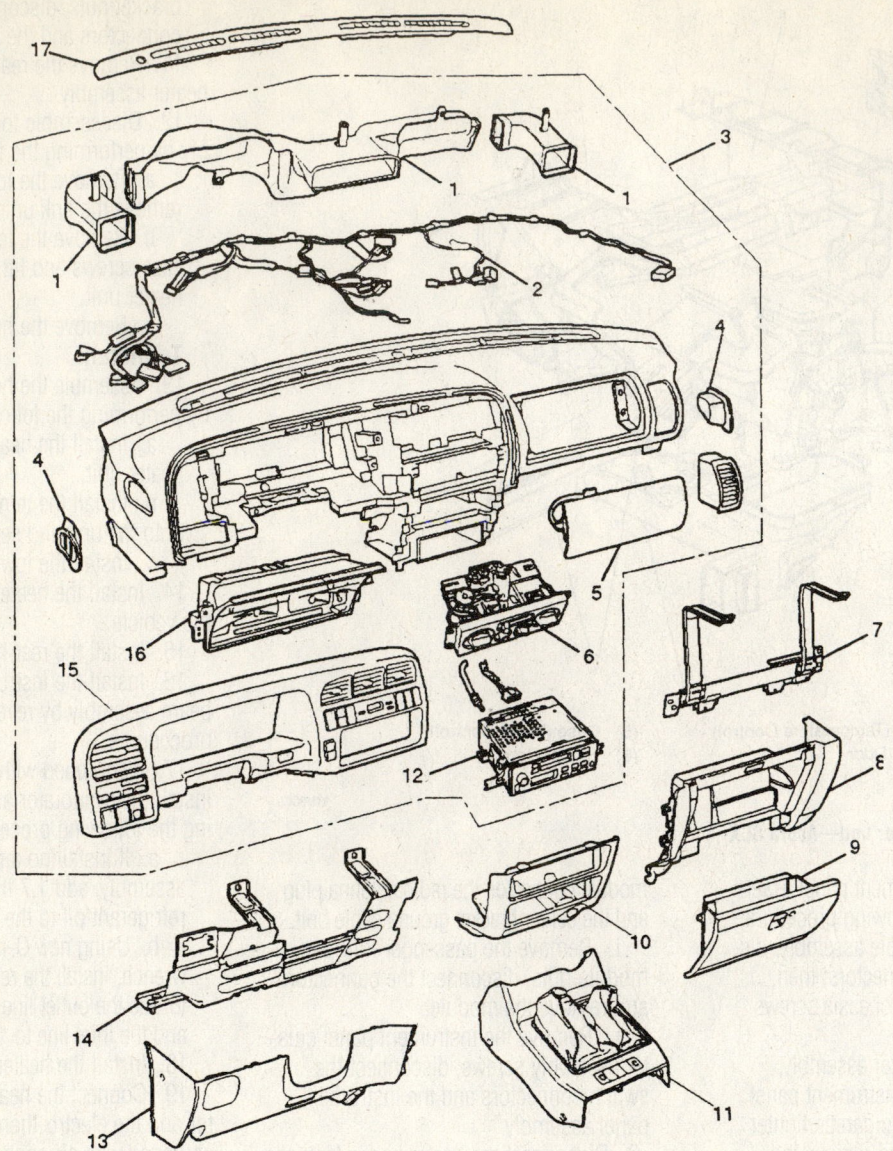

(1) Vent Duct Assembly
(2) Instrument Harness Assembly
(3) Instrument Panel Assembly
(4) Side Defroster Grille
(5) Passenger Inflator Module
(6) Control Lever Assembly
(7) Passenger Knee Bolster Reinforcement Assembly
(8) Instrument Panel Passenger Lower Cover Assembly
(9) Glove Box
(10) Lower Cluster Assembly
(11) Front Console Assembly
(12) Radio Assembly
(13) Instrument Panel Driver Lower Cover Assembly
(14) Driver Knee Bolster Assembly
(15) Instrument Panel Cluster Assembly
(16) Meter Assembly
(17) Front Defroster Grille

93113G03

Exploded view of the instrument panel and accessories—Acura SLX

25. Enable the air bags by performing the following procedure:
 a. Connect the passenger's side air bag yellow 2-pin connector.
 b. Install the glove box.
 c. At the base of the steering column, connect the yellow 2-pin connector.
 d. Install the air bag fuse C-21 (if removed) or connect the negative battery cable.
 e. Turn the ignition switch ON and verify that the AIR BAG warning light flashes 7 times and then turns OFF.

26. Run the engine to normal operating temperatures and check for leaks. Check the systems for correct operation.

CHRYSLER CORPORATION

Dodge Caravan, Plymouth Voyager and Chrysler Town & Country

REMOVAL & INSTALLATION

Front System

1. Align the wheels in the straight-ahead position.
2. Disconnect the negative battery cable.

❄❄ CAUTION

Before working around the steering wheel or the instrument panel all 2

minutes to pass to allow the air bag module to discharge.

3. Drain the cooling system into a clean container for reuse.
4. Remove the steering column assembly by performing the following procedure:

   a. Remove the lower left side steering column cover.

   b. Remove the parking brake release cable from the parking brake lever.

   c. Remove the 10 steering column cover liner-to-instrument panel bolts and the cover liner.

   d. Rotate the key to the LOCK position; then, rotate the steering wheel to the LOCKED position.

   e. Remove the gear selector cable and its mounting bracket as an assembly from the upper steering column mounting bracket.

   f. Remove the 2 instrument cluster trim bezel-to-instrument panel screws, retaining clips and bezel.

   g. Remove the 2 steering column shroud-to-steering column screws and the shroud.

   h. Remove the steering column-to-intermediate steering shaft coupler.

   i. Loosen but do not remove the 2 lower steering column mounting bracket nuts/washers; then, remove the 2 upper steering column mounting bracket nuts/washers.

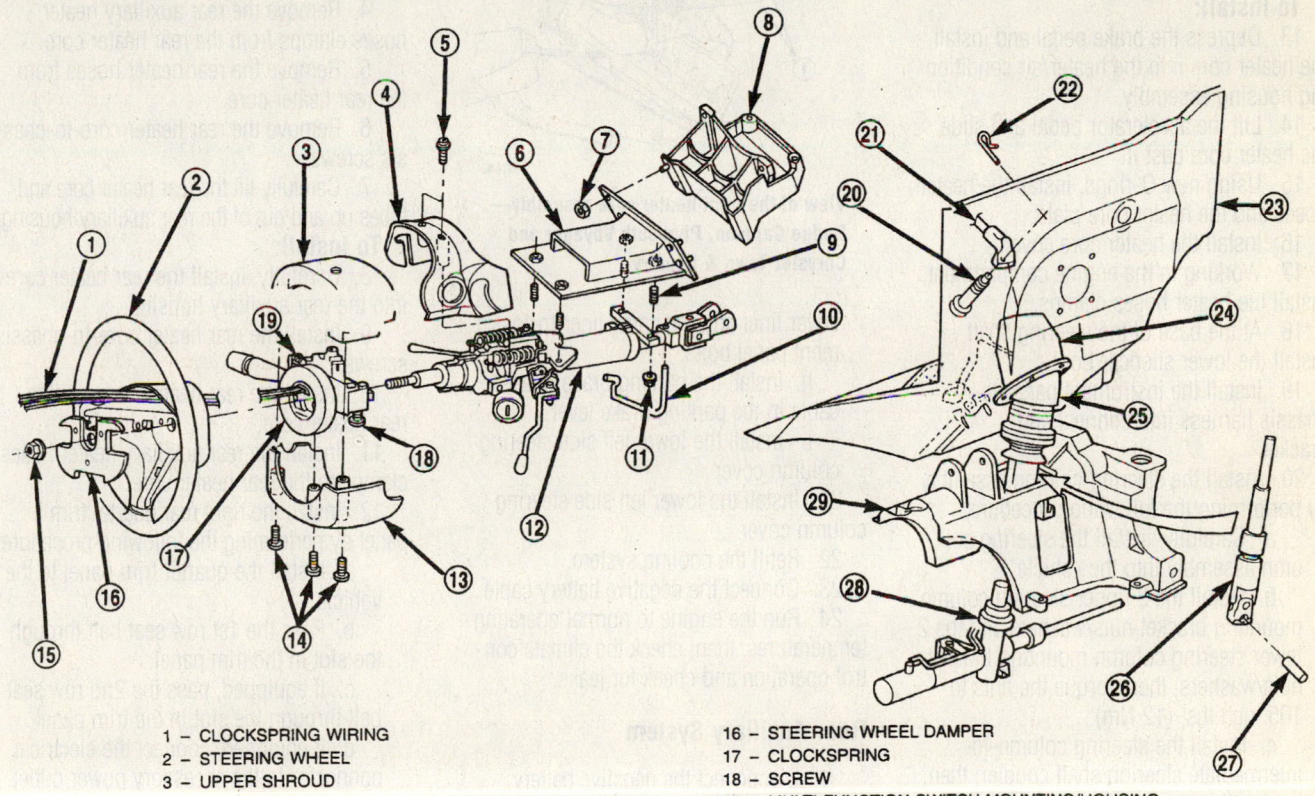

1 – CLOCKSPRING WIRING	16 – STEERING WHEEL DAMPER
2 – STEERING WHEEL	17 – CLOCKSPRING
3 – UPPER SHROUD	18 – SCREW
4 – FIXED SHROUD	19 – MULTI-FUNCTION SWITCH MOUNTING/HOUSING
5 – SCREW	20 – PINCH BOLT
6 – STEERING COLUMN MOUNTING PLATE	21 – STEERING COLUMN COUPLER
7 – NUT	22 – PINCH BOLT RETAINING PIN
8 – DASH PANEL STEERING COLUMN MOUNTING BRACKET	23 – DASH PANEL
9 – STUDS 4	24 – SILENCER SHELL
10 – STEERING COLUMN LOCKING PIN	25 – INTERMEDIATE SHAFT SHIELD AND SEAL
11 – NUT/WASHER ASSEMBLY	26 – INTERMEDIATE SHAFT
12 – STEERING COLUMN ASSEMBLY	27 – ROLL PIN
13 – LOWER SHROUD	28 – STEERING GEAR
14 – SCREWS	29 – FRONT SUSPENSION CRADLE
15 – STEERING WHEEL RETAINING NUT	

93113G95

View of the steering column assembly—Dodge Caravan, Plymouth Voyager and Chrysler Town & Country

j. Carefully, remove the steering column assembly from the vehicle.

5. Remove the instrument panel-to-chassis harness interconnect and bracket.

6. At the base of the steering shaft, remove the lower silencer boot.

7. Working in the engine compartment, pinch of the heater hoses.

8. Remove the heater core cover. Position some towels under the heater core hoses.

9. Remove the heater core plate and the hoses.

10. Depress the heater core retaining clips.

11. Lift the accelerator pedal and slide the heater core past it.

12. Depress the brake pedal and remove the heater core from the heater/air conditioning housing assembly.

To install:

13. Depress the brake pedal and install the heater core into the heater/air conditioning housing assembly.

14. Lift the accelerator pedal and slide the heater core past it.

15. Using new O-rings, install the heater hoses and the heater core plate.

16. Install the heater core cover.

17. Working in the engine compartment, install the heater hoses clamps.

18. At the base of the steering shaft, install the lower silencer boot.

19. Install the instrument panel-to-chassis harness interconnect and bracket.

20. Install the steering column assembly by performing the following procedure:

a. Carefully, install the steering column assembly into the vehicle.

b. Install the 2 upper steering column mounting bracket nuts/washers and the 2 lower steering column mounting bracket nuts/washers; then, torque the nuts to 105 inch lbs. (12 Nm).

c. Install the steering column-to-intermediate steering shaft coupler; then, tighten the pinch bolt to 21 ft. lbs. (28 Nm).

d. Install the 2 steering column shroud and the shroud-to-steering column screws.

e. Install the bezel, the retaining clips and the 2 instrument cluster trim bezel-to-instrument panel screws.

f. Install the gear selector cable and its mounting bracket as an assembly to the upper steering column mounting bracket.

g. Install the 10 steering column

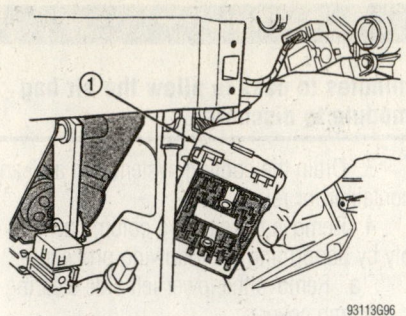

View of the interconnect and bracket—Dodge Caravan, Plymouth Voyager and Chrysler Town & Country

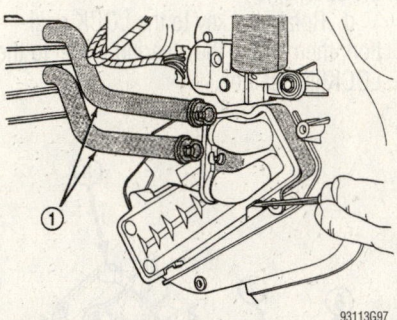

View of the front heater core assembly—Dodge Caravan, Plymouth Voyager and Chrysler Town & Country

cover liner and the cover liner-to-instrument panel bolts.

h. Install the parking brake release cable to the parking brake lever.

i. Install the lower left side steering column cover.

21. Install the lower left side steering column cover.

22. Refill the cooling system.

23. Connect the negative battery cable.

24. Run the engine to normal operating temperatures; then, check the climate control operation and check for leaks.

Rear Auxiliary System

1. Disconnect the negative battery cable.

2. Partially drain the cooling system into a clean container for reuse.

3. Remove the right rear quarter trim panel by performing the following procedure:

a. Remove the 1st row seat.

b. If equipped, remove the 2nd row seat.

c. Remove the sliding door sill trim panel and the quarter trim bolster.

d. Remove the C-pillar and D-pillar trim panels.

e. Remove the 1st row seat belt anchor and the 2nd row seat anchor, if equipped.

f. From the bolster area, remove the quarter trim-to-quarter panel screws.

g. Remove the quarter trim's rear edge-to-bracket screws.

h. Rearward of the sliding door, disconnect the quarter trim-to-quarter panel hidden clips.

i. Remove the quarter trim from the quarter panel.

j. If equipped, disconnect the electrical connector from the accessory power outlet.

k. If equipped, pass the 2nd row seat belt through the slot in the trim panel.

l. Pass the 1st row seat belt through the slot in the trim panel.

m. Remove the quarter trim panel from the vehicle.

4. Remove the rear auxiliary heater hoses clamps from the rear heater core.

5. Remove the rear heater hoses from the rear heater core.

6. Remove the rear heater core-to-chassis screws.

7. Carefully lift the rear heater core and tubes up and out of the rear auxiliary housing.

To install:

8. Carefully, install the rear heater core into the rear auxiliary housing.

9. Install the rear heater core-to-chassis screws.

10. Install the rear heater hoses to the rear heater core.

11. Install the rear auxiliary heater hoses clamps to the rear heater core.

12. Install the right rear quarter trim panel by performing the following procedure:

a. Install the quarter trim panel to the vehicle.

b. Pass the 1st row seat belt through the slot in the trim panel.

c. If equipped, pass the 2nd row seat belt through the slot in the trim panel.

d. If equipped, connect the electrical connector to the accessory power outlet.

e. Install the quarter trim to the quarter panel.

f. Rearward of the sliding door, connect the quarter trim-to-quarter panel hidden clips.

g. Install the quarter trim's rear edge-to-bracket screws.

h. At the bolster area, install the quarter trim-to-quarter panel screws.

i. Install the 1st row seat belt anchor and the 2nd row seat anchor, if equipped.

j. Install the C-pillar and D-pillar trim panels.

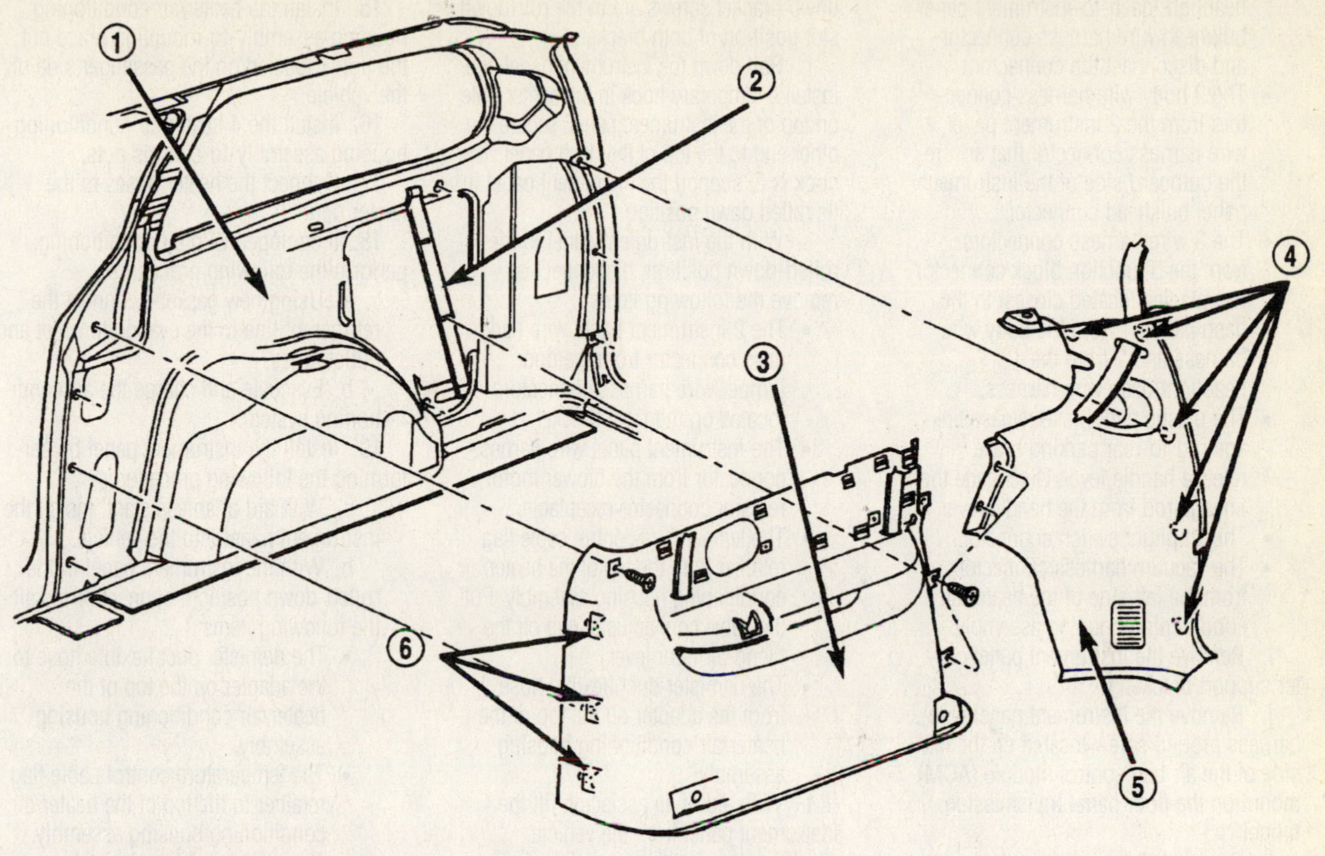

1 – INNER QUARTER PANEL
2 – QUARTER TRIM PANEL ATTACHING BRACKET
3 – QUARTER TRIM PANEL
4 – CLIPS
5 – D-PILLAR TRIM PANEL
6 – CLIPS

93113G98

View of the right quarter and D-trim panels—Dodge Caravan, Plymouth Voyager and Chrysler Town & Country

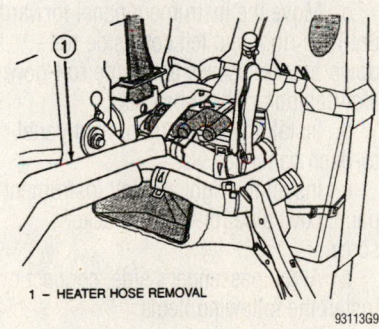

1 – HEATER HOSE REMOVAL

93113G99

View of the rear heater core—Dodge Caravan, Plymouth Voyager and Chrysler Town & Country

k. Install the quarter trim bolster and the sliding door sill trim panel.
l. If equipped, install the 2nd row seat.
m. Install the 1st row seat.
13. Refill the cooling system.
14. Connect the negative battery cable.

15. Run the engine to normal operating temperatures; then, check the climate control operation and check for leaks.

➡ **If the rear heater core was emptied and not refilled, it will be necessary to thermal cycle the vehicle twice. Run the engine until the thermostat opens; then, turn the engine OFF and allow it to cool.**

Dodge Dakota and Durango

REMOVAL & INSTALLATION

1. Disconnect the negative battery cable.

❋❋ CAUTION

After disconnecting the negative battery cable, wait 2 minutes for the driver's/passenger's air bag system capacitor to discharge before attempting to do any work around the steering column or instrument

2. Remove the instrument panel by performing the following procedure:
a. Remove the trim from the right and left door sills.
b. Remove the trim from the right and left cowl side inner panels.
c. Remove the steering column opening cover from the instrument panel.
d. Remove the 2 hood latch release handle-to-instrument panel lower reinforcement screws and lower the release handle to the floor.
e. Disconnect the driver's side air bag module wire harness connector.
f. If equipped, disconnect the overdrive lockout switch harness connector.
g. Do not disassemble the steering column but remove the assembly from the vehicle.
h. From under the driver's side of the instrument panel, disconnect or remove the following items:
• The screw from the center of the

Refer to the model specific sections for engine mechanical service procedures

headlight/dash-to-instrument panel bulkhead wire harness connector and disconnect the connector.

• The 2 body wire harness connectors from the 2 instrument panel wire harness connector that secure the outboard side of the instrument panel bulkhead connector.

• The 3 wire harness connectors from the 3 junction block connector receptacles located closest to the dash panel; 1 from the body wire harness and 2 from the headlight/dash wire harness.

• The plastic park brake release linkage rod-to-rear parking brake release handle lever. Disengage the linkage rod from the handle lever.

• The stoplight switch connector.

• The vacuum harness connector from the left side of the heater/air conditioning housing assembly.

i. Remove the instrument panel center support bracket.

j. Remove the instrument panel wire harness ground screw located on the left side of the air bag control module (ACM) mount on the floor panel transmission tunnel.

k. Disconnect the instrument panel wiring harness-to-ACM connector receptacle.

l. Remove the glove box.

m. Working through the glove box opening, disconnect or remove the following items:

• The 2 halves of the radio antenna coaxial cable connector near the center of the lower instrument panel.

• The antenna half of the radio antenna coaxial cable from the retainer clip near the outboard side of the lower instrument panel.

• The blower motor wire harness connector located near the heater/air conditioning housing assembly support brace.

n. From the passenger's side, disconnect or remove the following items:

• The 2 instrument panel wire harness connectors from the infinity speaker amplifier connector receptacles on the right cowl.

• The instrument panel wire harness radio ground eyelet-to-stud nut on the right cowl.

o. Loosen the right and left instrument panel cowl side roll-down bracket screws.

p. Remove the 5 top instrument panel-to-dash panel screws.

q. Pull the instrument panel rearward until the right and left cowl side roll-

down bracket screws are in the roll-down slot position of both brackets.

r. Roll down the instrument panel and install a temporary hook in the center hole on top of the instrument panel; secure the other end to the top of the dash panel. The hook is to support the instrument panel in its rolled down position.

s. With the instrument panel in the rolled-down position, disconnect or remove the following items:

• The 2 instrument panel wire harness connector from the door jumper wire harness connectors located on the right bracket.

• The instrument panel wire harness connector from the blower motor resistor connector receptacle.

• The temperature control cable flag retainer from the top of the heater/air conditioning housing assembly. Pull the cable core adjuster clip off the blend-air door lever.

• The demister duct flexible hose from the adapter on the top of the heater/air conditioning housing assembly.

t. With aid of an assistant, lift the instrument panel from the vehicle.

3. If equipped with air conditioning, perform the following procedure:

a. Discharge and recover the air conditioning system refrigerant.

b. Disconnect the refrigerant line from the evaporator inlet and outlet tubes. Plug the openings to prevent contamination.

4. Drain the cooling system into a clean container for reuse.

5. Disconnect the heater hoses from the heater core. Plug the openings.

6. Remove the 4 heater/air conditioning housing assembly-to-chassis nuts.

7. Remove the heater/air conditioning housing assembly-to-mounting brace nut; the nut is located on the passenger side of the vehicle.

8. Pull the heater/air conditioning housing assembly rearward for the studs and drain tube to clear the dash panel hole.

9. Remove the heater/air conditioning housing assembly from the vehicle.

10. Remove the heater housing cover screws and the cover.

11. Remove the heater core from the heater/air conditioning housing assembly.

To install:

12. Install the heater core to the heater/air conditioning housing assembly.

13. Install the heater housing cover and the cover screws.

14. Install the heater/air conditioning housing assembly.

15. Install the heater/air conditioning housing assembly-to-mounting brace nut; the nut is located on the passenger side of the vehicle.

16. Install the 4 heater/air conditioning housing assembly-to-chassis nuts.

17. Connect the heater hoses to the heater core.

18. If equipped with air conditioning, perform the following procedure:

a. Using new gaskets, connect the refrigerant line to the evaporator inlet and outlet tubes.

b. Evacuate and charge the air conditioning system.

19. Install the instrument panel by performing the following procedures:

a. With aid of an assistant, install the instrument panel into the vehicle.

b. With the instrument panel in the rolled-down position, connect or install the following items:

• The demister duct flexible hose to the adapter on the top of the heater/air conditioning housing assembly.

• The temperature control cable flag retainer to the top of the heater/air conditioning housing assembly.

• The instrument panel wire harness connector to the blower motor resistor connector receptacle.

• The 2 instrument panel wire harness connector to the door jumper wire harness connectors located on the right bracket.

c. Move the instrument panel forward until the right and left cowl side roll-down bracket screws are in the roll-down slot position of both brackets.

d. Install the 5 top instrument panel-to-dash panel screws.

e. Install the right and left instrument panel cowl side roll-down bracket screws.

f. At the passenger's side, connect or install the following items:

• The instrument panel wire harness radio ground eyelet-to-stud nut on the right cowl.

• The 2 instrument panel wire harness connectors to the infinity speaker amplifier connector receptacles on the right cowl.

g. Working through the glove box opening, connect or install the following items:

• The blower motor wire harness connector located near the heater/air conditioning housing assembly support brace.

• The antenna half of the radio

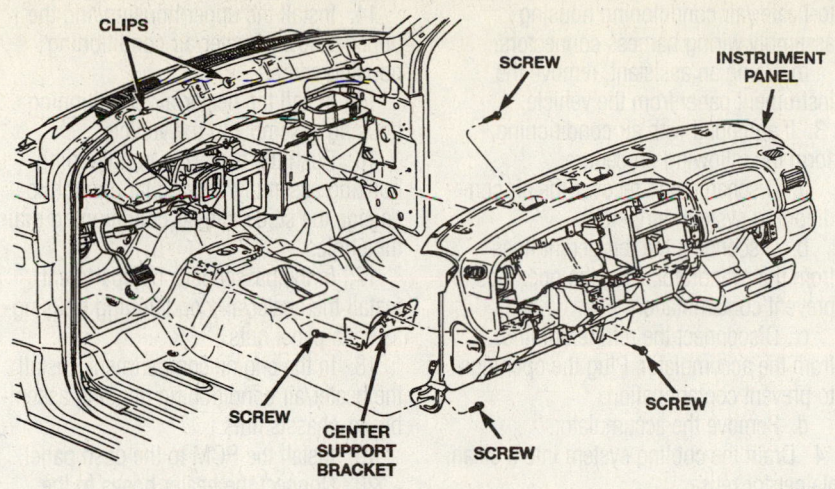

View of the instrument panel assembly—Dodge Dakota and Durango

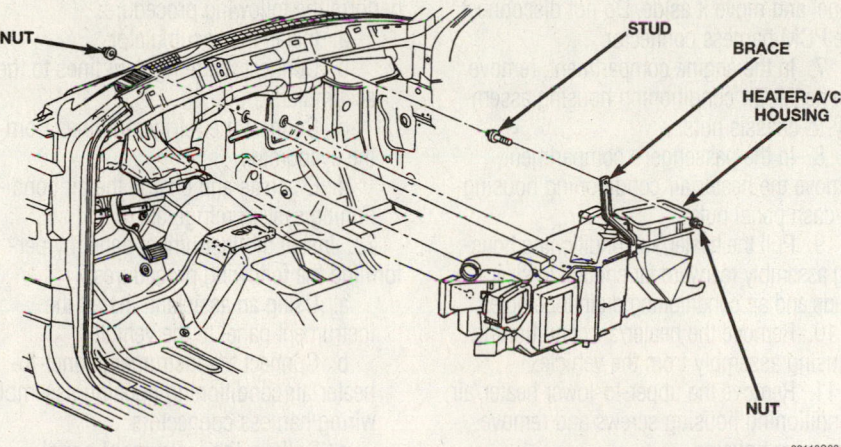

View of the heater/air conditioning assembly—Dodge Dakota and Durango

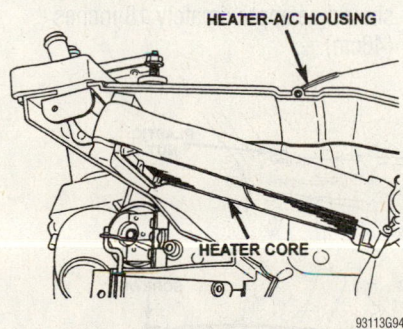

View of the heater core—Dodge Dakota and Durango

antenna coaxial cable to the retainer clip near the outboard side of the lower instrument panel.

• The 2 halves of the radio antenna coaxial cable connector near the center of the lower instrument panel.

h. Install the glove box.

i. Connect the instrument panel wiring harness-to-ACM connector receptacle.

j. Install the instrument panel wire harness ground screw located on the left side of the air bag control module (ACM) mount on the floor panel transmission tunnel.

k. Install the instrument panel center support bracket.

l. Under the driver's side of the instrument panel, connect or install the following items:

• The vacuum harness connector to the left side of the heater/air conditioning housing assembly.
• The stoplight switch connector.
• Engage the linkage rod to the

handle lever. Install the plastic park brake release linkage rod-to-rear parking brake release handle lever.

• The 3 wire harness connectors to the 3 junction block connector receptacles located closest to the dash panel; 1 at the body wire harness and 2 at the headlight/dash wire harness.

• The 2 body wire harness connectors to the 2 instrument panel wire harness connector that secure the outboard side of the instrument panel bulkhead connector.

• Connect the connector. Install the screw at the center of the headlight/dash-to-instrument panel bulkhead wire harness connector.

m. Install the steering column assembly.

n. If equipped, connect the overdrive lockout switch harness connector.

o. Connect the driver's side air bag module wire harness connector.

p. Install the 2 hood latch release handle-to-instrument panel lower reinforcement screws and lower the release handle to the floor.

q. Install the steering column opening cover to the instrument panel.

r. Install the trim to the right and left cowl side inner panels.

s. Install the trim to the right and left door sills.

20. Refill the cooling system.

21. Connect the negative battery cable.

22. Run the engine to normal operating temperatures; then, check the climate control operation and check for leaks.

Dodge Full-Size Pick-Up

REMOVAL & INSTALLATION

1. Disconnect the negative battery cable.

⁂ CAUTION

After disconnecting the negative battery cable, wait 2 minutes for the driver's/passenger's air bag system capacitor to discharge before attempting to do any work around the steering column or instrument

2. Remove the instrument panel by performing the following procedures:

a. Remove the air bag control module (ACM) and bracket from the floor panel tunnel.

b. Remove the trim from both cowl side inner panels.

c. Remove the steering column-to-instrument panel opening cover.

d. Remove the 2 hood latch release handle-to-instrument panel lower reinforcement screws and lower the handle to the floor.

e. Disconnect the driver's side air bag module wiring harness connector from the lower instrument panel reinforcement.

f. Place the wheels in the straight-ahead position and lock the steering wheel. Remove the steering column without disassembling it.

g. From under the driver's side of the instrument, disconnect or remove the following items:

- Parking brake release handle linkage rod from the parking brake mechanism located on the left cowl side inner panel.
- Instrument panel wiring harness connector from the parking brake switch located on the parking brake mechanism.
- Three wiring harness connectors (body wiring harness, headlight, dash) from the 3 junction block connector receptacles located closest to the dash panel.
- Head light/dash-to-instrument panel bulkhead wiring harness connector screw and disconnect the connector.
- Instrument panel-to-door wiring harness connector located directly below the bulkhead wiring harness connector.
- Infinity sound system wiring harness connector (if equipped), located at the outboard side of the instrument panel bulkhead connector.
- Stop light switch electrical connector.
- Vacuum harness connector located near the left side of the heater/air conditioning housing.

h. Under the passenger's side of the instrument panel, disconnect the radio antenna coaxial cable connector.

i. Loosen both sides of the instrument panel cowl side roll-down bracket screws about ½ inch (13mm).

j. Remove the 5 upper instrument panel-to-upper dash panel screws; remove the center screw last.

k. Roll down the instrument panel and install a temporary hook in the center hole on top of the panel. Attach the other end to the center hole in the top of the dash panel. The opening should be approximately 18 inches (46cm).

l. Disconnect the instrument panel-to-heater/air conditioning housing assembly wiring harness connectors.

m. Using an assistant, remove the instrument panel from the vehicle.

3. If equipped with air conditioning, perform the following procedure:

a. Discharge and recover the air conditioning system refrigerant.

b. Disconnect the refrigerant lines from the evaporator. Plug the openings to prevent contamination.

c. Disconnect the refrigerant lines from the accumulator. Plug the openings to prevent contamination.

d. Remove the accumulator.

4. Drain the cooling system into a clean container for reuse.

5. Disconnect the heater hoses from the heater core tubes.

6. Remove the PCM from the dash panel and move it aside. Do not disconnect the PCM harness connector.

7. In the engine compartment, remove the heater/air conditioning housing assembly-to-chassis nuts.

8. In the passenger's compartment, remove the heater/air conditioning housing-to-dash panel nuts.

9. Pull the heater/air conditioning housing assembly rearward far enough to clear the studs and air conditioning drain tube holes.

10. Remove the heater/air conditioning housing assembly from the vehicle.

11. Remove the upper-to-lower heater/air conditioning housing screws and remove the upper housing.

12. Remove the heater core from the lower housing.

To install:

13. Install the heater core in the lower housing.

14. Install the upper housing and the upper-to-lower heater/air conditioning housing screws.

15. Install the heater/air conditioning housing assembly to the vehicle.

16. Push the heater/air conditioning housing assembly forward far enough to engage the studs and air conditioning drain tube holes.

17. In the passenger's compartment, install the heater/air conditioning housing-to-dash panel nuts.

18. In the engine compartment, install the heater/air conditioning housing assembly-to-chassis nuts.

19. Install the PCM to the dash panel.

20. Connect the heater hoses to the heater core tubes.

21. Refill the cooling system.

22. If equipped with air conditioning, perform the following procedure:

a. Install the accumulator.

b. Connect the refrigerant lines to the accumulator.

c. Connect the refrigerant lines from the evaporator.

d. Evacuate and charge the air conditioning system refrigerant.

23. Install the instrument panel by performing the following procedures:

a. Using an assistant, install the instrument panel to the vehicle.

b. Connect the instrument panel-to-heater/air conditioning housing assembly wiring harness connectors.

c. Roll-up the instrument panel and install a temporary hook in the center hole on top of the panel and the top of the dash panel. The opening should be approximately 18 inches (46cm).

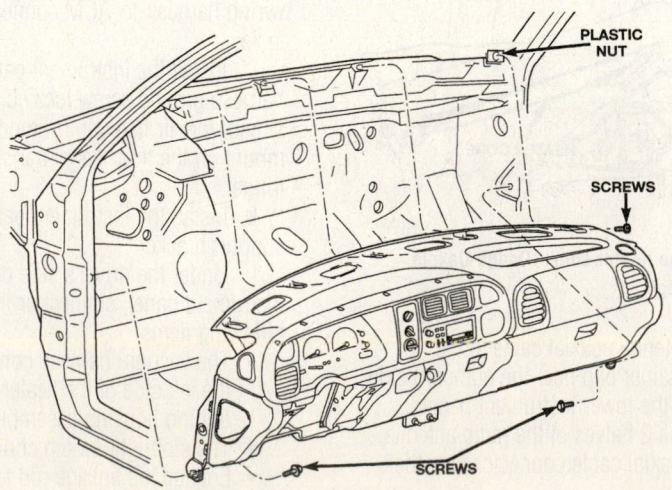

View of the instrument panel—Dodge Ram Pick-Up

93113GB5

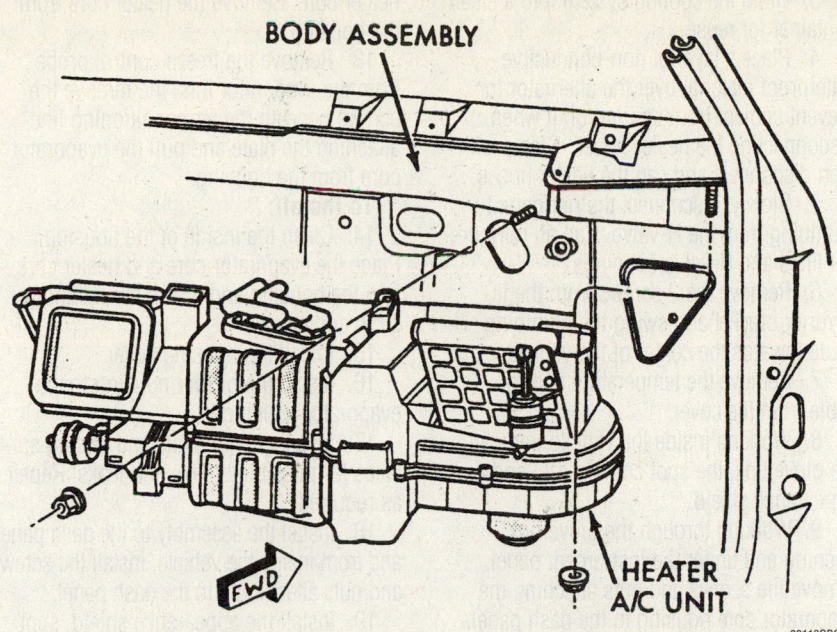

BODY ASSEMBLY

HEATER A/C UNIT

FWD

93113GB6

View of the heater/air conditioning housing assembly—Dodge Ram Pick-Up

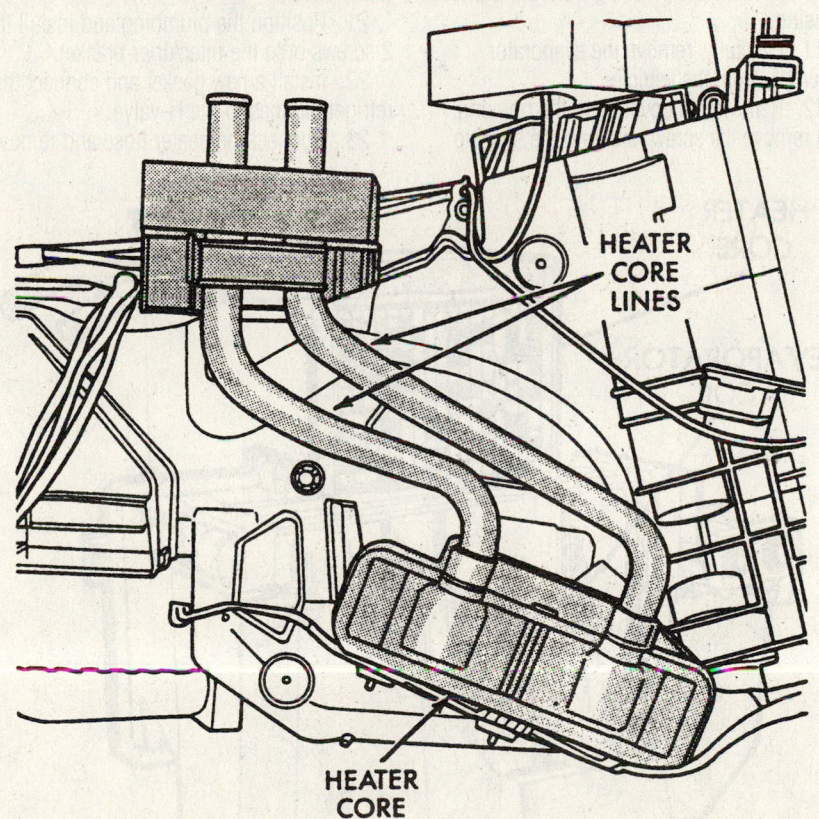

HEATER CORE LINES

HEATER CORE

93113GB7

View of the heater core—Ram Pick-Up

f. Under the passenger's side of the instrument panel, connect the radio antenna coaxial cable connector.

g. Under the driver's side of the instrument, connect or install the following items:

- Vacuum harness connector located near the left side of the heater/air conditioning housing.
- Stoplight switch electrical connector.
- Infinity sound system wiring harness connector (if equipped), located at the outboard side of the instrument panel bulkhead connector.
- Infinity sound system wiring harness connector (if equipped), located at the outboard side of the instrument panel bulkhead connector.
- Instrument panel-to-door wiring harness connector located directly below the bulkhead wiring harness connector.
- Headlight/dash-to-instrument panel bulkhead wiring harness connector and install the screw.
- Three wiring harness connectors (body wiring harness, headlight, dash) from the 3 junction block connector receptacles located closest to the dash panel.
- Instrument panel wiring harness connector to the parking brake switch located on the parking brake mechanism.
- Parking brake release handle linkage rod to the parking brake mechanism located on the left cowl side inner panel.

h. Install the steering column.

i. Connect the driver's side air bag module wiring harness connector to the lower instrument panel reinforcement.

j. Install the 2 hood latch release handle and the handle-to-instrument panel lower reinforcement screws.

k. Install the steering column-to-instrument panel opening cover.

l. Install the trim to both cowl side inner panels.

m. Install the air bag control module (ACM) and bracket to the floor panel tunnel.

24. Connect the negative battery cable.

25. Run the engine to normal operating temperatures; then, check the climate control operation and check for leaks.

d. Install the 5 upper instrument panel-to-upper dash panel screws; install the center screw first.

e. Install both sides of the instrument panel cowl side roll-down bracket screws to about ½ inch (13mm).

Dodge Ram Van/Wagon

REMOVAL & INSTALLATION

1997

FRONT SYSTEM WITHOUT AIR CONDITIONING

1. Disconnect the negative battery cable.
2. Drain the cooling system. Disconnect and plug the heater hoses.
3. Disconnect the temperature control cable from the heater core cover and the blend door crank. Disconnect the vent cable.
4. Disconnect the blower motor connector.
5. Remove the screws retaining the heater assembly to the side cowl and the nuts fastening the heater assembly to the dash panel.
6. Remove the heater unit from the vehicle.
7. Remove the back plate and remove the screws holding the heater core cover to the heater housing.
8. Remove the heater core retaining screws from the heater core and remove the core from the heater housing.

To install:

9. Clean out the inside of the housing. Place the heater core into the housing and fasten.
10. Position the blend air door and the right vent door in the housing and fasten the heater core cover to the housing.
11. Check the dash panel and side cowl seals for breaks and lack of adhesion. Repair as required.
12. Install the heater assembly into the vehicle.
13. Connect the heater blower motor connector.
14. Connect the cables.
15. Connect the heater hose to the heater core.
16. Refill the cooling system.
17. Connect the negative battery cable.
18. Run the engine to normal operating temperatures, until the thermostat opens; then refill the cooling system and check the system operation. Check for leaks.
19. Once the vehicle has cooled, recheck the coolant level.

FRONT SYSTEM WITH AIR CONDITIONING

1. Disconnect the negative battery cable. Properly discharge and recover the air conditioning system refrigerant.
2. Disconnect the freeze control connector from the wire harness at the H-valve.

3. Drain the cooling system into a clean container for reuse.
4. Place a layer of non-conductive waterproof material over the alternator to prevent coolant from spilling on it when disconnecting the heater hoses. Clamp off, then disconnect and cap the heater hoses.
5. Slowly, disconnect the refrigerant plumbing from the H-valve. Cap all refrigerant lines and H-valve openings.
6. Remove the 2 screws from the filter/drier bracket and swing the plumbing aside towards the center of the vehicle.
7. Remove the temperature control cable from the cover.
8. Working inside the vehicle, remove the glove box, the spot cooler bezel and the appearance shield.
9. Working through the glove box opening and under the instrument panel, remove the screws and nuts attaching the evaporator core housing to the dash panel.
10. Remove the 2 screws from the flange connection to the blower housing. Separate the evaporator core housing from the blower housing.
11. Carefully, remove the evaporator assembly from the vehicle.
12. Remove the cover from the housing and remove the screw retaining the strap to

heater core. Remove the heater core from the housing.
13. Remove the freeze control probe from the evaporator fins, the remove the screws beneath the air conditioning line attaching the plate and pull the evaporator core from the housing.

To install:

14. Clean the inside of the housing. Place the evaporator core and heater core into the housing and install the retaining strap and screw.
15. Install the housing cover.
16. Install the blower housing to the evaporator housing.
17. Inspect all air seals and mating surfaces for possible breaks and leaks. Repair as required.
18. Install the assembly to the dash panel and from inside the vehicle, install the screws and nuts attaching it to the dash panel.
19. Install the appearance shield, spot cooler bezel and glove box.
20. Attach the temperature control cable to the cover.
21. Position the plumbing and install the 2 screws onto the filter/drier bracket.
22. Install a new gasket and connect the refrigerant lines to the H-valve.
23. Connect the heater hose and remove

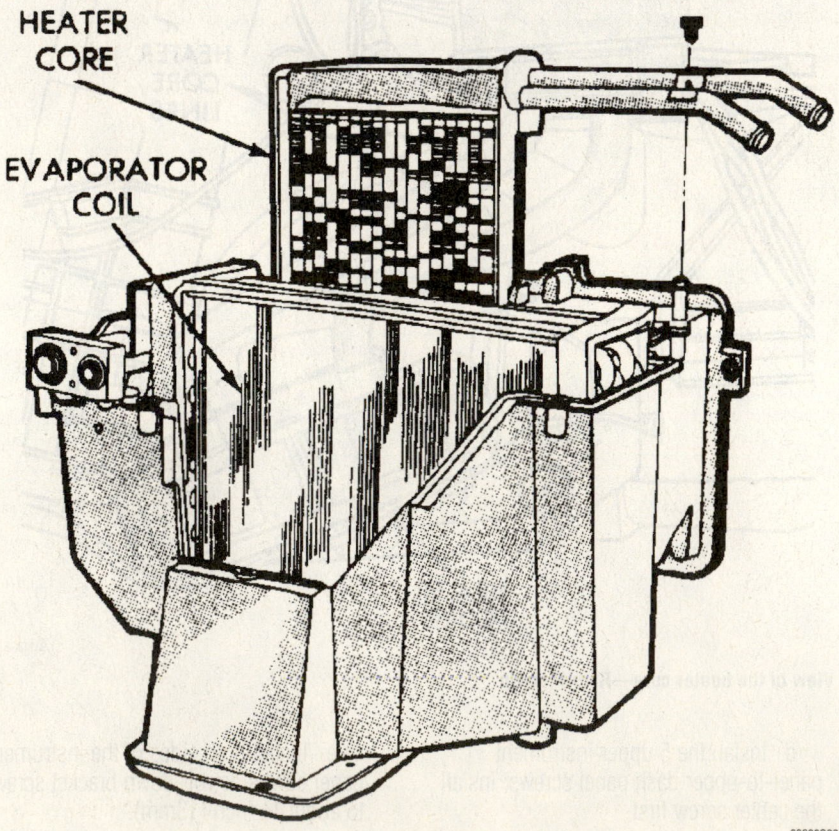

The heater core is mounted adjacent to the evaporator coil—1997 Dodge Ram Van

89666G22

the waterproof material from the alternator. Connect the freeze control wire harness, if equipped.

24. Evacuate, charge and leak test the air conditioning system. Refill the cooling system.

25. Connect the negative battery cable. Run the engine to normal operating temperatures, until the thermostat opens.

26. Refill the radiator completely and check the operation of the entire climate control system.

27. Once the vehicle has cooled, recheck the coolant.

REAR AUXILIARY SYSTEM

1. Disconnect the negative battery cable.

2. Drain the cooling system into a clean container for reuse.

3. Raise and safely support the vehicle. From underneath the vehicle, disconnect the inlet and outlet hoses from the heater core tubes.

4. Remove the auxiliary unit lower cover.

5. Remove the heater core tube seal and mounting plate.

6. Remove the screws from the support bracket and remove the heater core from the housing.

To install:

7. Install the heater core to the housing.

8. Install the mounting plate and the heater core tube seal.

9. Install the auxiliary unit lower cover.

10. Connect the inlet and outlet hoses to the heater core tubes.

11. Lower the vehicle.

12. Refill the cooling system.

13. Connect the negative battery cable.

14. Run the engine to normal operating temperatures; then, check the heater/air conditioning system operation and check for leaks.

1998–00

FRONT HEATER

1. Disconnect the negative battery cable.

✳✳ CAUTION

After disconnecting the negative battery cable, wait 2 minutes for the driver's/passenger's air bag system capacitor to discharge before attempting to do any work around the steering column or instrument

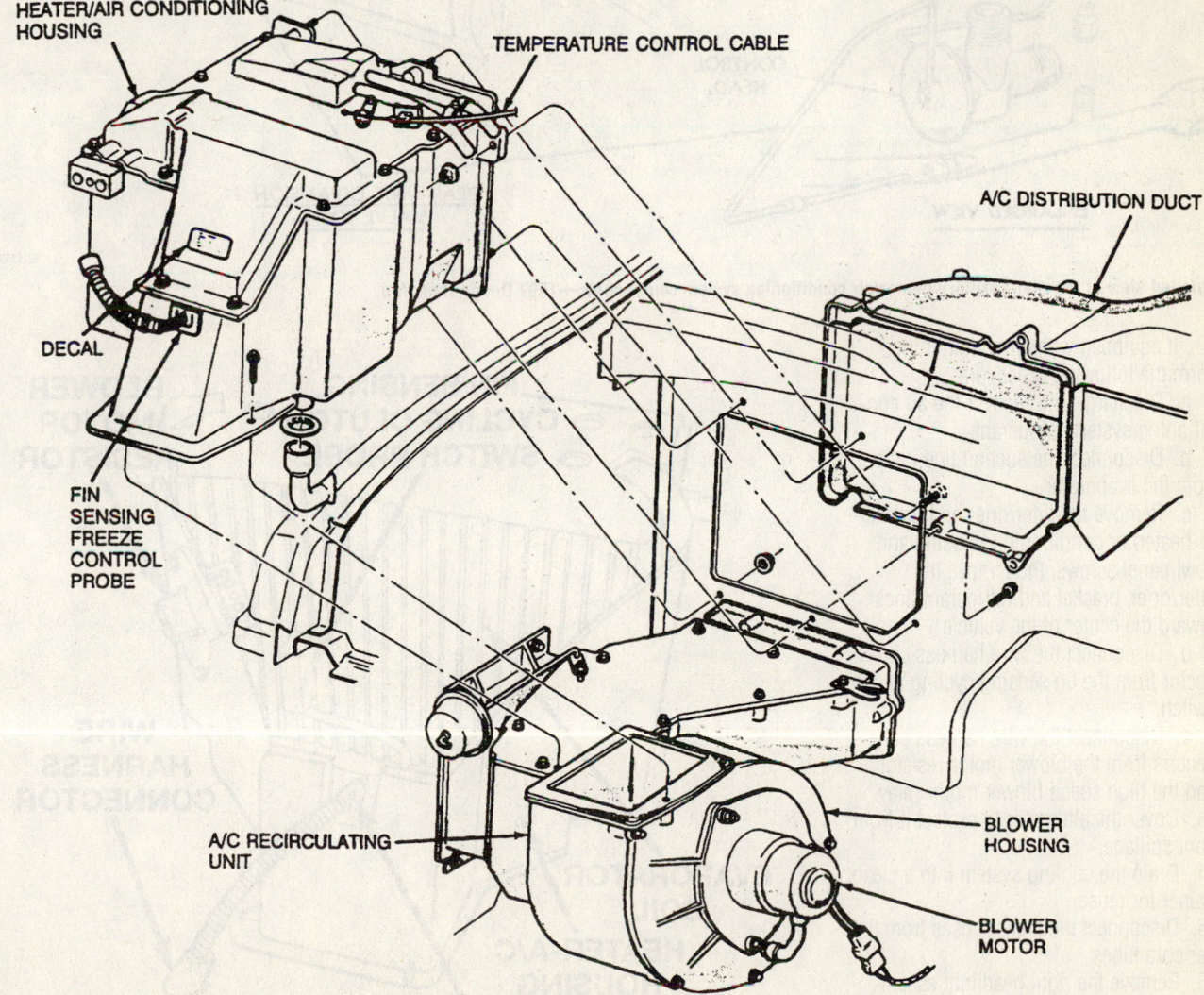

View of the heater/air conditioning housing assembly and blower motor—1997 Dodge Ram Van

93113G31

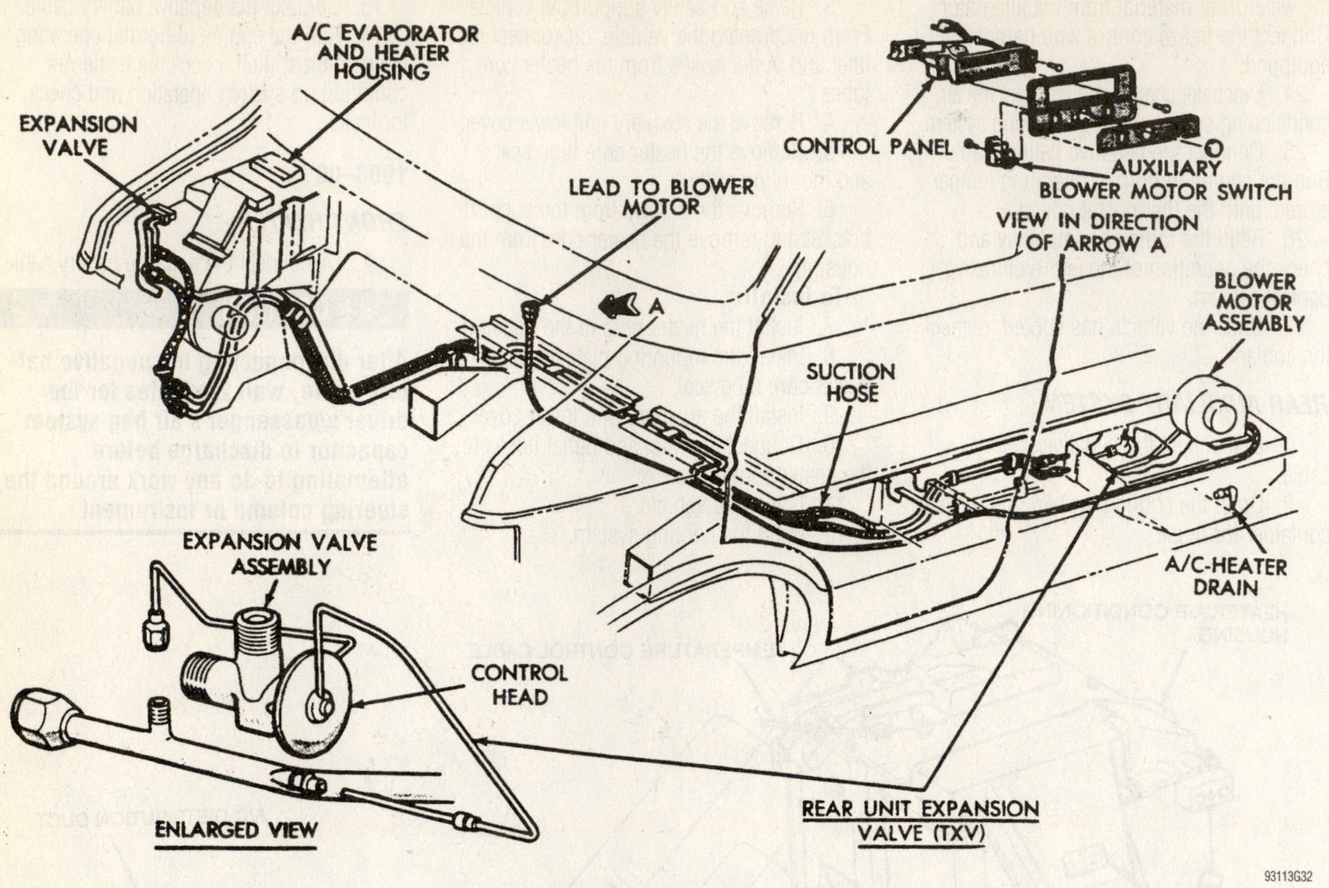

A/C EVAPORATOR
AND HEATER
HOUSING

EXPANSION
VALVE

LEAD TO BLOWER
MOTOR

CONTROL PANEL

AUXILIARY
BLOWER MOTOR SWITCH

VIEW IN DIRECTION
OF ARROW A

◄ A

BLOWER
MOTOR
ASSEMBLY

SUCTION
HOSE

EXPANSION VALVE
ASSEMBLY

CONTROL
HEAD

A/C-HEATER
DRAIN

ENLARGED VIEW

REAR UNIT EXPANSION
VALVE (TXV)

93113G32

Exploded view of the rear auxiliary heater/air conditioning system components—1997 Dodge Ram Van

2. If equipped with air conditioning, perform the following procedure:

a. Discharge and recover the air conditioning system refrigerant.

b. Disconnect the suction line jumper from the evaporator

c. Remove the filter/drier and bracket-to-heater/air conditioning housing and cowl panel screws; then, move the filter/drier, bracket and refrigerant lines toward the center of the vehicle.

d. Disconnect the wire harness connector from the fin sensing cycling clutch switch.

e. Disconnect the wire harness connectors from the blower motor resistor and the high speed blower motor relay.

3. Cover the alternator to protect it from coolant spillage.

4. Drain the cooling system into a clean container for reuse.

5. Disconnect the heater hoses from the heater core tubes.

6. Remove the right headlight assembly, the grille panel, the right cowl grille support panel and the right radiator core support assembly.

7. Remove both lower heater/air condi-

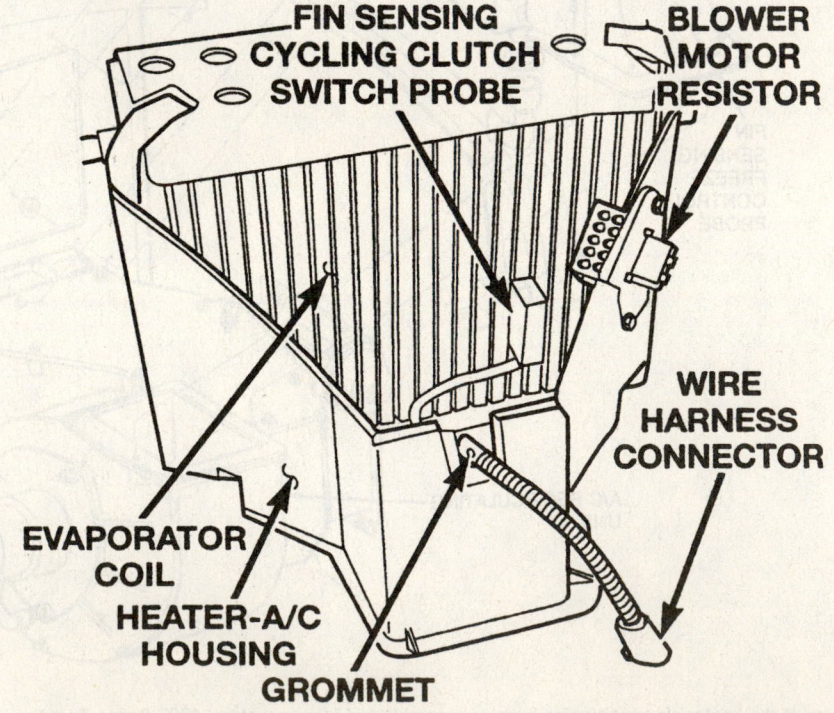

FIN SENSING
CYCLING CLUTCH
SWITCH PROBE

BLOWER
MOTOR
RESISTOR

WIRE
HARNESS
CONNECTOR

EVAPORATOR
COIL

HEATER-A/C
HOUSING

GROMMET

93113GA9

View of the air conditioning fin sensing cycling clutch switch—1998–00 Dodge Ram Van/Wagon

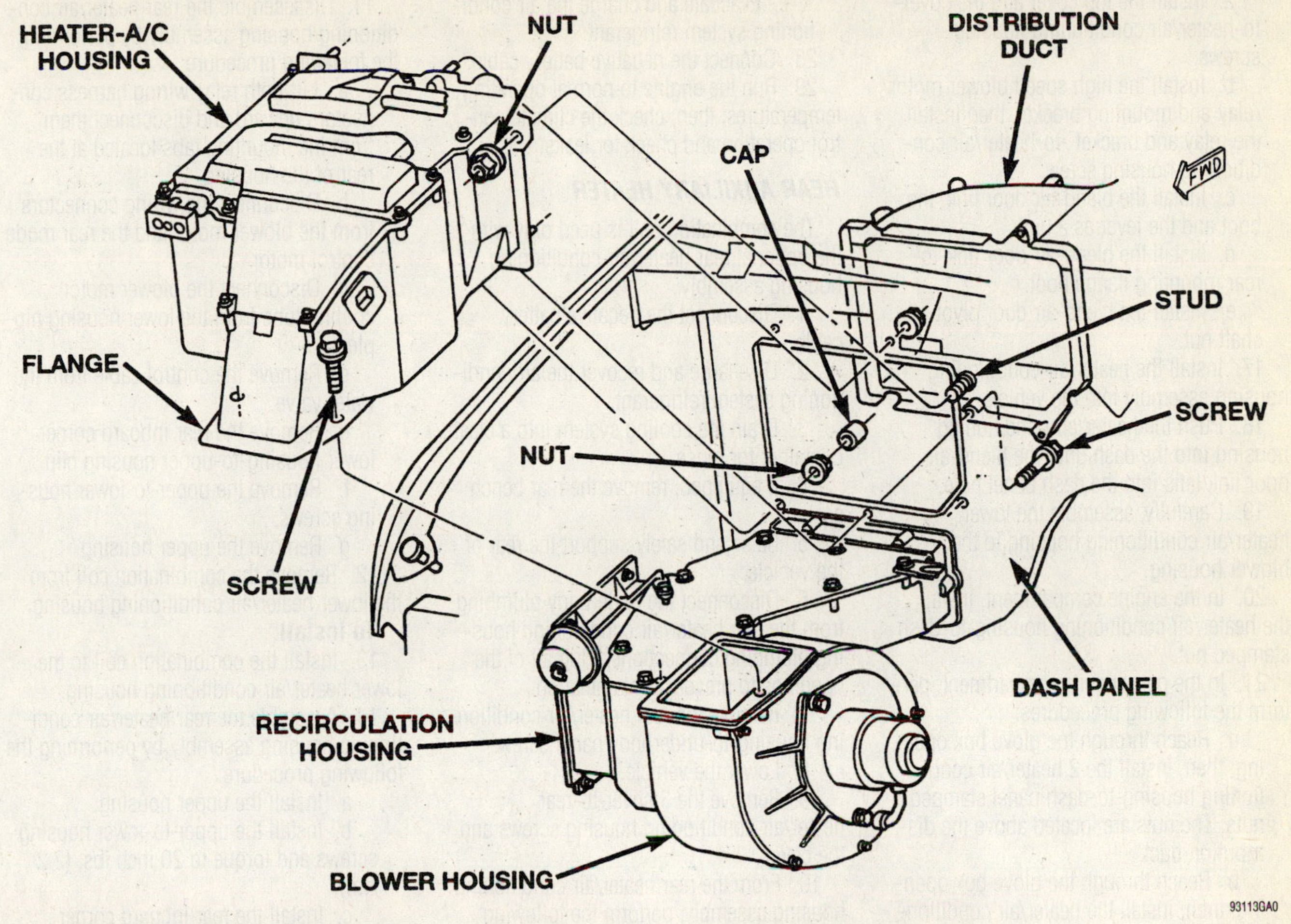

HEATER-A/C HOUSING

NUT

DISTRIBUTION DUCT

CAP

FWD

STUD

FLANGE

SCREW

NUT

SCREW

DASH PANEL

RECIRCULATION HOUSING

BLOWER HOUSING

93113GA0

Exploded view of the heater/air conditioning housing and related components—1998–00 Dodge Ram Van/Wagon

tioning housing flange-to-blower housing screws.

8. In the passenger's compartment, perform the following procedures:

a. From the top of the distribution duct, disconnect the blend-air door motor link.

b. Reach through the glove box opening and remove the heater/air conditioning housing-to-dash panel stamped nuts (2) and screw (1). The fasteners are located below the distribution duct.

c. Reach through the glove box opening; then, remove the 2 heater/air conditioning housing-to-dash panel stamped nuts. The nuts are located above the distribution duct.

9. In the engine compartment, remove the heater/air conditioning housing-to-dash stamped nut.

10. Carefully, separate the lower heater/air conditioning housing from the blower housing.

11. Pull the heater/air conditioning housing from the dash until the blend-air door link is clear of the dash panel hole.

12. Remove the heater/air conditioning housing assembly from the vehicle and place it on a bench with the top cover facing upward.

13. Disassemble the heater/air conditioning housing assembly by performing the following procedure:

a. Remove the blend-air door pivot shaft nut.

b. Remove the blend-air door link-to-rear mounting flange boot.

c. Remove the blend-air door link, the boot and the lever as a unit.

d. Remove the high speed blower motor relay mounting bracket-to-heater/air conditioning housing screw and remove the relay and bracket.

e. Remove the top cover-to-heater/air conditioning housing screws and the cover.

14. Remove the heater core tube support bracket-to-mounting boss screw and remove the heater core from the heater/air conditioning housing assembly.

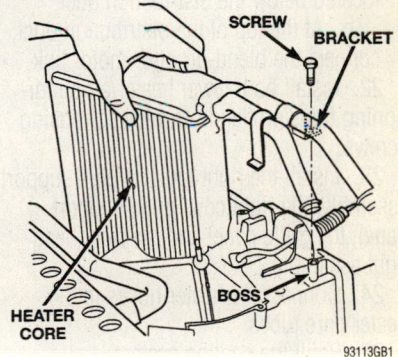

SCREW

BRACKET

HEATER CORE

BOSS

93113GB1

View of the heater core—1998–00 Dodge Ram Van/Wagon

To install:

15. Install the heater core to the heater/air conditioning housing assembly and heater core tube support bracket-to-mounting boss screw, then, tighten the screw to 20 inch lbs. (2.2 Nm).

16. Assemble the heater/air conditioning housing assembly by performing the following procedure:

Refer to the model specific sections for engine mechanical service procedures

a. Install the top cover and the cover-to-heater/air conditioning housing screws.

b. Install the high speed blower motor relay and mounting bracket, then install the relay and bracket -to-heater/air conditioning housing screw.

c. Install the blend-air door link, the boot and the lever as a unit.

d. Install the blend-air door link-to-rear mounting flange boot.

e. Install the blend-air door pivot shaft nut.

17. Install the heater/air conditioning housing assembly into the vehicle.

18. Push the heater/air conditioning housing into the dash until the blend-air door link falls into the dash panel hole.

19. Carefully, assemble the lower heater/air conditioning housing to the blower housing.

20. In the engine compartment, install the heater/air conditioning housing-to-dash stamped nut.

21. In the passenger's compartment, perform the following procedures:

a. Reach through the glove box opening; then, install the 2 heater/air conditioning housing-to-dash panel stamped nuts. The nuts are located above the distribution duct.

b. Reach through the glove box opening; then, install the heater/air conditioning housing-to-dash panel stamped nuts (2) and screw (1). The fasteners are located below the distribution duct.

c. At the top of the distribution duct, connect the blend-air door motor link.

22. Install both lower heater/air conditioning housing flange-to-blower housing screws.

23. Install the right radiator core support assembly, the right cowl grille support panel, the grille panel and the right headlight assembly.

24. Connect the heater hoses to the heater core tubes.

25. Refill the cooling system.

26. Uncover the alternator.

27. If equipped with air conditioning, perform the following procedure:

a. Connect the wire harness connectors to the blower motor resistor and the high-speed blower motor relay.

b. Connect the wire harness connector to the fin sensing cycling clutch switch.

c. Install the filter/drier and bracket-to-heater/air conditioning housing and cowl panel screws.

d. Connect the suction line jumper to the evaporator

e. Evacuate and charge the air conditioning system refrigerant.

28. Connect the negative battery cable.

29. Run the engine to normal operating temperatures; then, check the climate control operation and check for leaks.

REAR AUXILIARY HEATER

The combination coil is used only with the optional rear heater/air conditioning housing assembly.

1. Disconnect the negative battery cable.

2. Discharge and recover the air conditioning system refrigerant.

3. Drain the cooling system into a clean container for reuse.

4. If equipped, remove the rear bench seat.

5. Raise and safely support the rear of the vehicle.

6. Disconnect the underbody plumbing from the rear heater/air conditioning housing plumbing connections. Plug all of the openings to prevent contamination.

7. Remove the rear heater/air conditioning housing-to-underbody panel screw.

8. Lower the vehicle.

9. Remove the 3 cover-to-rear heater/air conditioning housing screws and the cover.

10. From the rear heater/air conditioning housing assembly, perform the following procedures:

a. Remove the vertical duct.

b. Remove the horizontal duct.

c. From behind the unit, remove the ground wire eyelet-to-left side panel strainer screw.

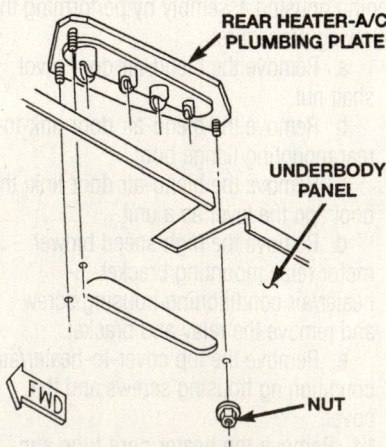

View of the rear heater/air conditioning housing assembly plumbing plate—1998–00 Dodge Ram Van/Wagon

11. Disassemble the rear heater/air conditioning housing assembly by performing the following procedure:

a. Lift both relay wiring harness connectors upward and disconnect them from the mounting tabs located at the rear of the housing.

b. Disconnect the wiring connectors from the blower motor and the rear mode control motor.

c. Disconnect the blower motor cooling tube from the lower housing nipple.

d. Remove the control cable from the water valve.

e. Remove the rear inboard corner lower housing-to-upper housing clip.

f. Remove the upper-to-lower housing screws.

g. Remove the upper housing.

12. Remove the combination coil from the lower heater/air conditioning housing.

To install:

13. Install the combination coil to the lower heater/air conditioning housing.

14. Assemble the rear heater/air conditioning housing assembly by performing the following procedure:

a. Install the upper housing.

b. Install the upper-to-lower housing screws and torque to 20 inch lbs. (2.2 Nm).

c. Install the rear inboard corner lower housing-to-upper housing clip.

d. Install the control cable to the water valve.

e. Connect the blower motor cooling tube to the lower housing nipple.

f. Connect the wiring connectors to the blower motor and the rear mode control motor.

g. Connect them to the mounting tabs located at the rear of the housing.

15. At the rear heater/air conditioning housing assembly, perform the following procedures:

a. Behind the unit, install the ground wire eyelet-to-left side panel strainer screw.

b. Install the horizontal duct.

c. Install the vertical duct.

16. Install the 3 cover-to-rear heater/air conditioning housing screws and the cover.

17. Raise and safely support the rear of the vehicle.

18. Install the rear heater/air conditioning housing-to-underbody panel screw.

19. Connect the underbody plumbing to the rear heater/air conditioning housing plumbing connections.

20. Lower the vehicle.

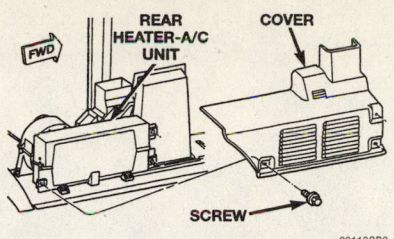

View of the rear heater/air conditioning housing assembly—1998–00 Dodge Ram Van/Wagon

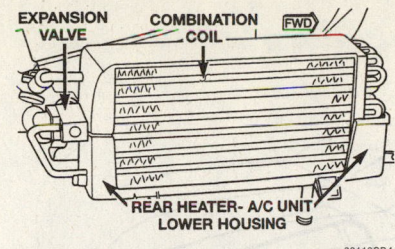

View of the combination coil—1998–00 Dodge Ram Van/Wagon

21. If equipped, install the rear bench seat.

22. Refill the cooling system.

23. Connect the negative battery cable.

24. Evacuate and charge the air conditioning system refrigerant.

25. Run the engine to normal operating temperatures; then, check the climate control operation and check for leaks.

FORD MOTOR CO.

Ford Aerostar

REMOVAL & INSTALLATION

Front System

1. Disconnect the negative battery cable.

2. Drain the cooling system into a clean container for reuse.

3. Disconnect the heater hoses from the heater core tube. Plug the hoses to prevent loss of coolant.

4. In the passenger compartment, remove the screws attaching the heater core access cover to the plenum assembly. Remove the access cover.

5. Pull the heater core rearward and down, removing it from the plenum assembly.

To install:

6. Position the heater core and seal in the plenum assembly.

7. Install the heater core access cover to the plenum assembly and secure it with the screws.

8. Connect the heater hoses to the heater core tubes.

9. Refill the cooling system.

10. Connect the negative battery cable.

11. Run the engine to normal operating temperatures; then, check the climate control operation and check for leaks.

Rear Auxiliary System

1. Disconnect the negative battery cable. With the engine temperature cold and the temperature control at the FULL HEAT position, back off the radiator cap to the first detent to relieve the system pressure. Retighten the cap. This will prevent excess coolant loss when detaching the heater hoses.

2. Remove the first seat behind the driver as follows:

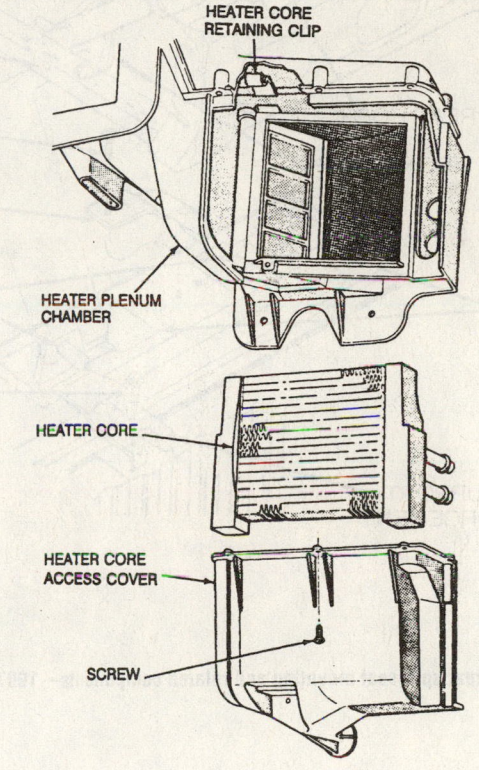

Exploded view of the front heater assembly—1997 Ford Aerostar

a. Rotate the latch handles upward simultaneously.

b. Lift the rear of the seat, causing the seat to rotate about the forward attachment until the seat latches are clear of the rear floor attachments.

c. With an assistant, pull the seat rearward to disengage it from the front floor pins.

3. Remove the auxiliary heater/air conditioning cover attaching the screws and remove the cover.

4. Remove the auxiliary unit floor duct by removing 1–2 attaching screws and rotating the duct gently downward.

5. Remove the remaining 16 screws from the heater assembly cover and remove the cover from the case.

6. Disconnect the heater hoses from the auxiliary heater core by depressing the white tabs while pulling the connectors apart (quick disconnect couplings), then plug the hoses.

7. Slide the heater core and seal assembly out of the housing slot.

To install:

8. Slide the heater core and seal assembly into the housing slot.

9. Connect the heater hoses to the heater core tubes.

10. Refill the cooling system.

Refer to the model specific sections for cooling system service procedures

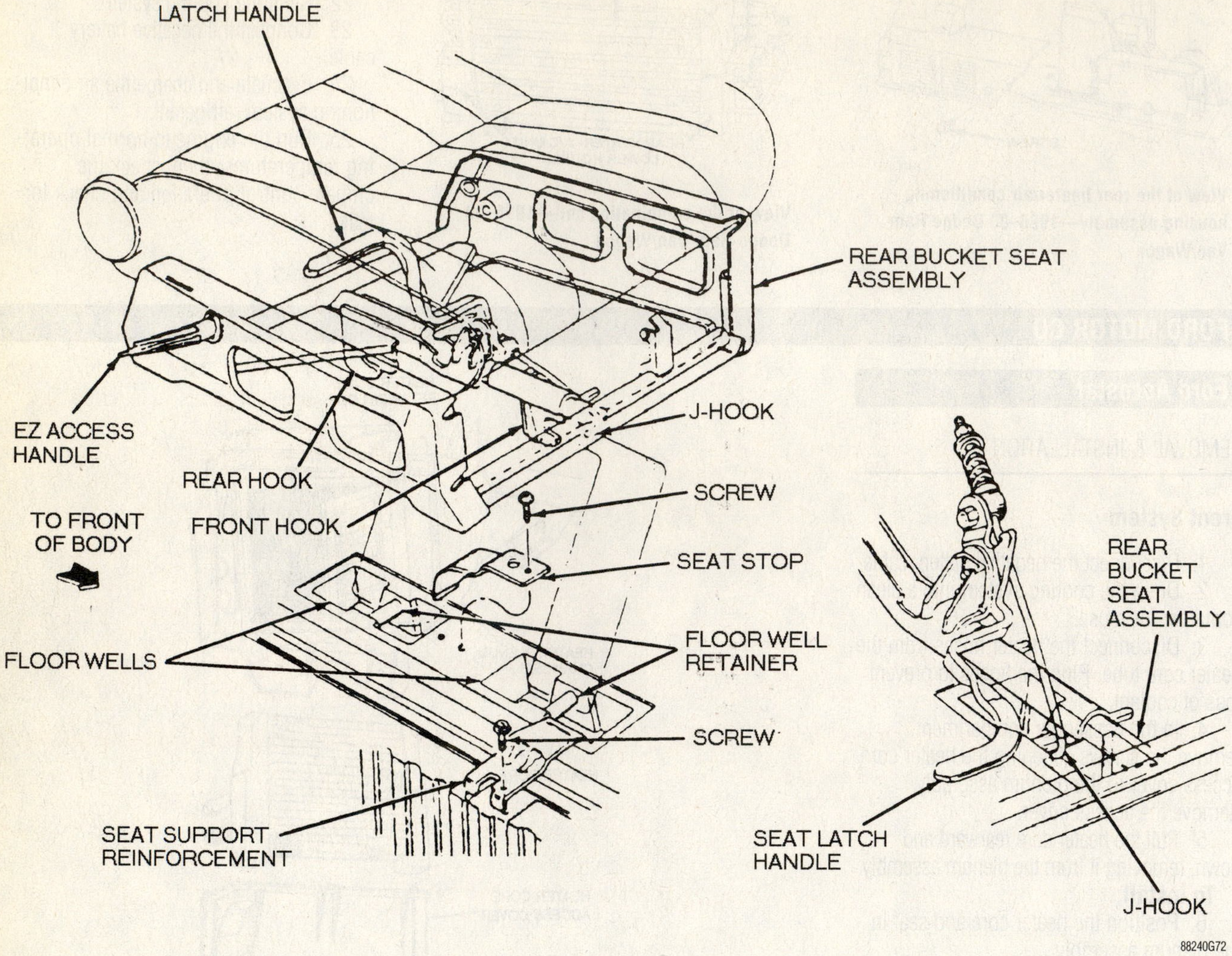

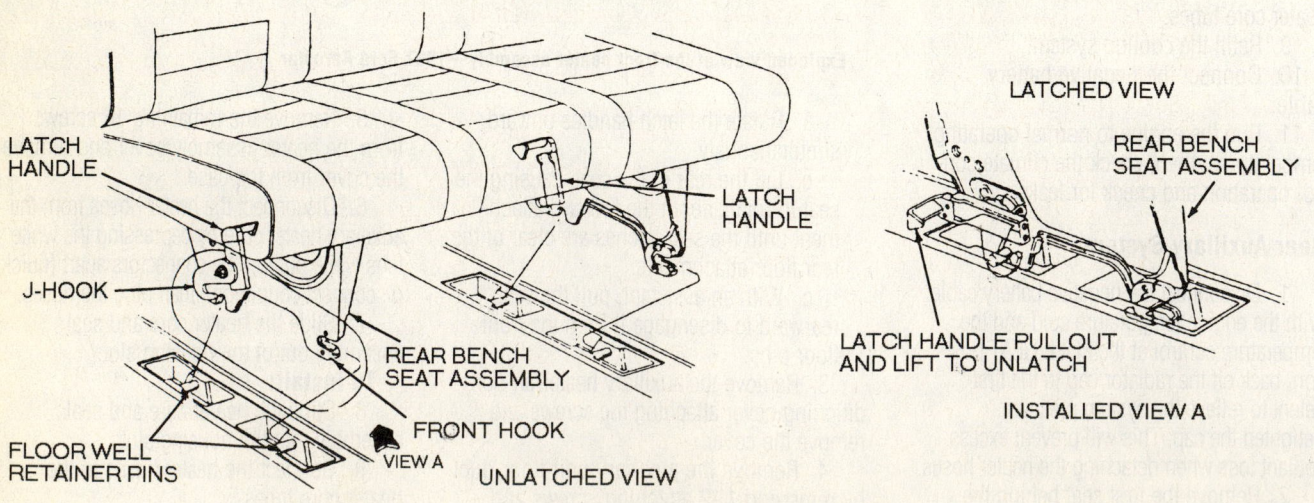

LATCH HANDLE

REAR BUCKET SEAT ASSEMBLY

J-HOOK

EZ ACCESS HANDLE

REAR HOOK

FRONT HOOK

TO FRONT OF BODY

SCREW

SEAT STOP

FLOOR WELL RETAINER

FLOOR WELLS

SCREW

SEAT SUPPORT REINFORCEMENT

REAR BUCKET SEAT ASSEMBLY

SEAT LATCH HANDLE

J-HOOK

88240G72

Exploded view of the rear split seat mounting and related components—1997 Ford Aerostar

LATCH HANDLE

LATCH HANDLE

J-HOOK

REAR BENCH SEAT ASSEMBLY

FRONT HOOK

VIEW A

FLOOR WELL RETAINER PINS

UNLATCHED VIEW

LATCHED VIEW

REAR BENCH SEAT ASSEMBLY

LATCH HANDLE PULLOUT AND LIFT TO UNLATCH

INSTALLED VIEW A

88240G75

Exploded view of the rear bench mounting and quick release components—1997 Ford Aerostar

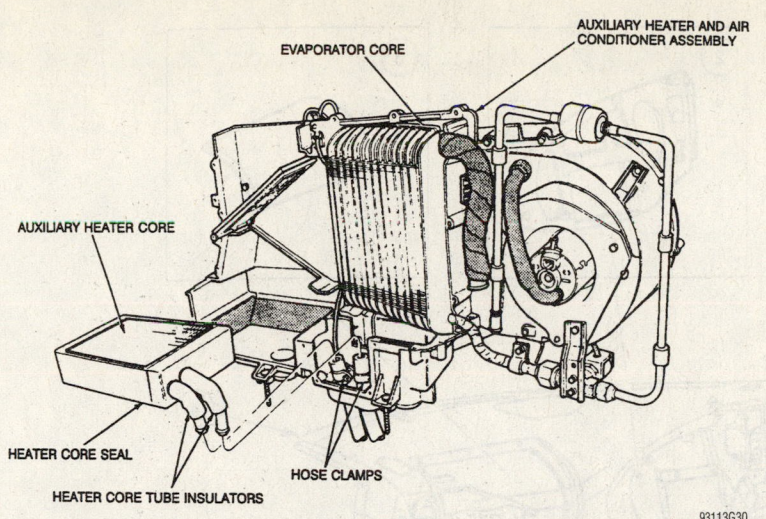

Exploded view of the rear auxiliary heater/air conditioning assembly—1997 Ford Aerostar

11. Install the auxiliary heater/air conditioning cover.

12. Install the floor duct.

13. Install the service cover and passenger seat.

14. Connect the negative battery cable.

15. Run the engine to normal operating temperatures; then, check the climate control operation and check for leaks.

Ford E-Series Vans

REMOVAL & INSTALLATION

1. Drain the cooling system into a clean container for reuse.

2. Disconnect the battery ground cable.

3. Disconnect the quick disconnect heater hose couplings at the heater core by performing the following procedure:

❊❊ WARNING

The engine must be off, fully cool and the cooling system fully depressurized before attempting to disconnect any heater water hoses. Failure to comply with this warning can result in serious injury or burns from hot liquid escaping out of the engine cooling system.

a. Depressurize the engine cooling system.

b. Push the heater water hose toward the tube to fully expose the locking tabs.

➥**When compressing the white coupling retainer, the quick disconnect tool must be perpendicular to and on the highest point of the coupling.**

c. Push the quick disconnect tool over the coupling retainer windows to compress the retainer locking tabs.

d. A slight twisting motion while pulling on the heater water hose may be necessary to assist in the removal.

e. Pull the heater water hose away from the heater core tube.

f. Plug the heater water hose.

g. Remove the white coupling retainer from the tube.

h. Spread the retainer tabs apart and slide the retainer off the tube.

i. Discard the retainer.

4. Plug the heater water hoses with a suitable ⅝ or ¾ inch plug.

5. Remove the engine cover.

6. Remove the instrument panel finish panel by performing the following procedure:

❊❊ CAUTION

Electronic modules are sensitive to static electrical charges. If exposed to these charges, damage may result.

a. Remove the driver's side air bag module by removing or disconnecting the following items:

➥**To deplete the backup power supply energy, disconnect the battery ground cable and wait at least 1 minute. Be sure to disconnect auxiliary batteries and power supplies (if equipped).**

- Make sure the wheels are in the straight-ahead position.
- Driver's air bag module.

- Both back cover plugs.
- Both driver's air bag module screws.
- Horn electrical connector.
- Air bag sliding contact electrical connector.
- Driver's air bag module.

b. Remove the passenger's side air bag modules by removing or disconnecting the following items:

- Instrument panel finish panel and reinforcement.
- Passenger's air bag module retaining nuts.

➥**Using a ⅜ inch x 4 inch slotted screwdriver, carefully slide the head of the screwdriver under the right bottom edge of the door and lift upward, separating the door from the clip. Separate the rest of the door from the clips by lifting the door with your hands.**

- Passenger's air bag module electrical connector and module.
- The 6 offset fasteners used for retaining the air bag module door from the instrument panel.

c. Remove the steering column

d. Remove the engine cover.

e. Unfasten the engine cover latches and remove the engine cover.

f. Remove the instrument panel cowl top screws.

g. Remove the upper center instrument panel access panel.

h. Disconnect the climate control vacuum harness connector.

i. Remove the left-hand upper access panel.

j. Remove the instrument panel cowl top nut.

k. Remove the alternative fuel control module (AFCM).

l. Remove the instrument panel dash brace.

m. Remove the 6 dash brace bolts.

n. Remove the instrument panel dash brace.

o. From under the hood, position the coolant reservoir aside.

p. Remove the bolts.

q. Position the coolant reservoir aside.

r. Remove the main wiring assembly/lower bulkhead connector by performing the following:

- Loosen the bulkhead connector bolt.
- Disconnect the bulkhead connector clips.

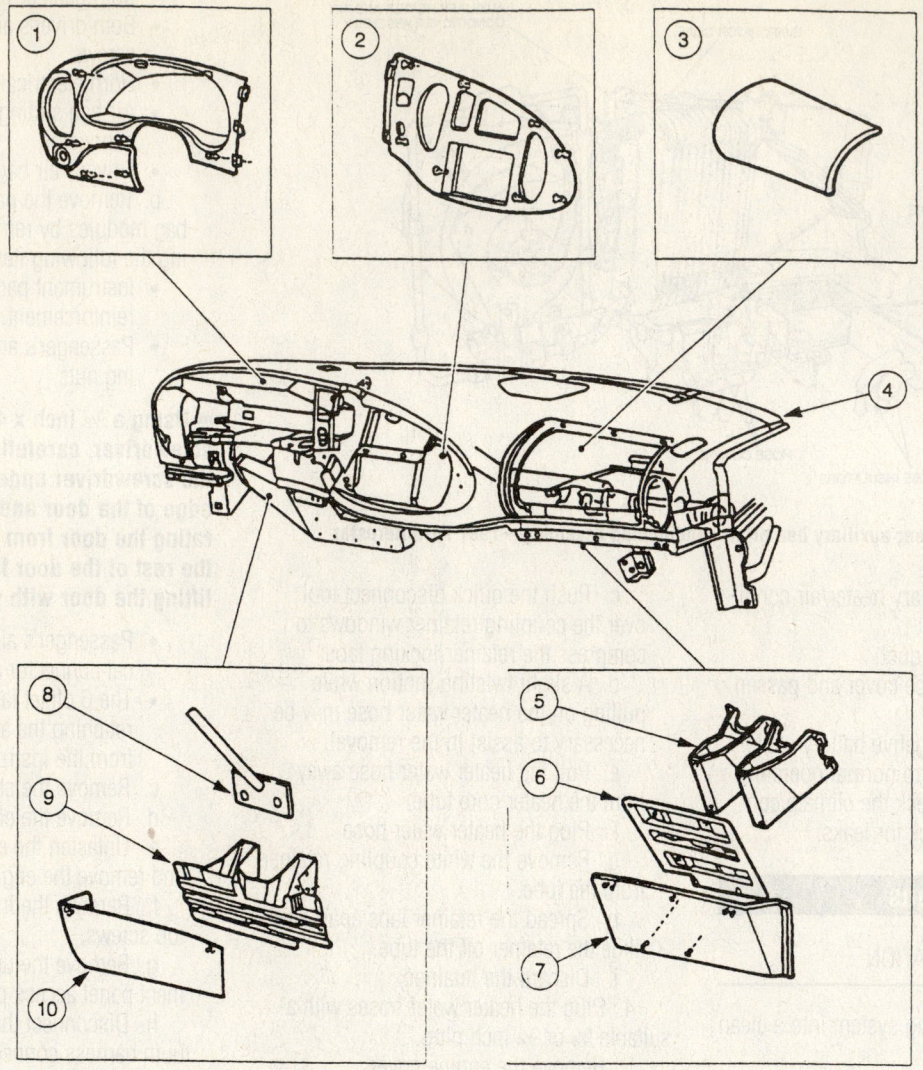

1. Instrument panel cluster finish panel
2. Instrument panel center finsh panel
3. passenger air bag opening cover
4. Instrument panel
5. Instrument panel dash brace
6. Instrument panel finsh panel reinforcement
7. Instrument panel finsh panel
8. Instrument panel steering column opening cover reinforcement
9. Driver side knee brace
10. Instrument panel steering column cover

Exploded view of the instrument panel—Ford Econoline

- Remove the bulkhead connector.
- s. Remove the right-hand A-pillar lower trim panel.
- t. Disconnect the electronic crash sensor (ECS) module electrical connector by performing the following:
  - Remove the locking clip.
  - Disconnect the connector.
- u. Disconnect the right-hand instrument panel cowl side wiring electrical connectors.
- v. Disconnect the antenna cable from the radio and release the cable locators from the instrument panel.
  - w. Remove the right-hand instrument panel bolts.
  - x. Remove the left-hand instrument panel bolts.

➡Removing the instrument panel from the vehicle requires 2 technicians.

y. Remove the instrument panel from the vehicle through the passenger side door.

7. Remove the heater core cover.

8. Remove the 7 screws.
9. Remove the heater core cover.
10. Remove and discard the heater core case seal.

➡Use care not to spill the coolant remaining in the heater core during removal.

11. Remove the heater core.

To install:

12. Install the instrument panel finish panel by performing the following procedure:

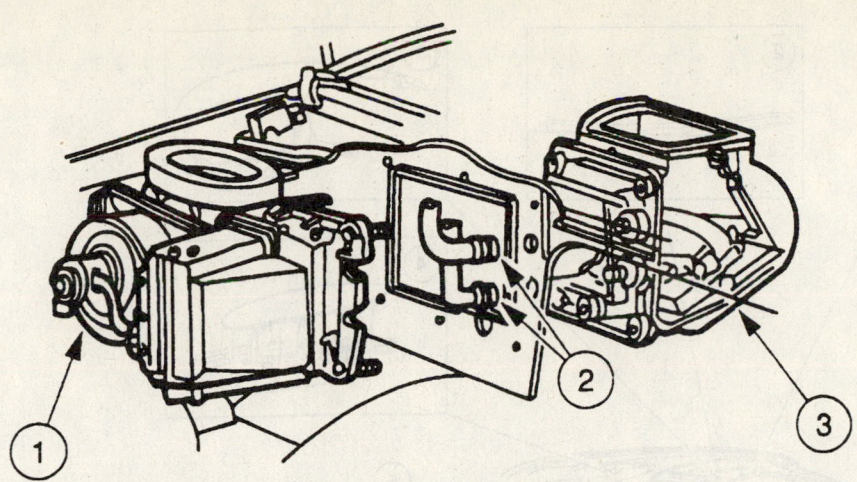

1. A/C evaporator core housing
2. Heater water hoses
3. Heater core housing

93113GM5

View of the heater housing and evaporator housing—Ford Econoline

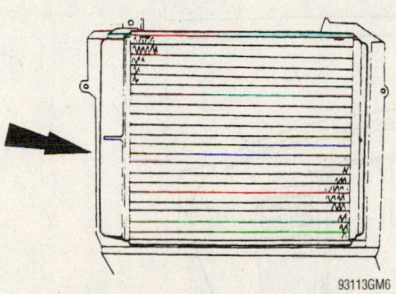

93113GM6

View of the heater core—Ford Econoline

> **✳✳ CAUTION**

Electronic modules are sensitive to static electrical charges. If exposed to these charges, damage may result.

➡**Verify that the 4-way locator on the left-hand side is properly seated.**

a. Position the instrument panel on the center dash panel.

b. Install the left-hand instrument panel bolts.

c. Install the right-hand instrument panel bolts.

d. Engage the antenna cable locators into the instrument panel and connect it to the radio.

e. Connect the right-hand instrument panel cowl side wiring electrical connectors.

f. Connect the ECS module electrical connector by performing the following:
- Connect the connector.
- Install the locking clip.

g. Install the right-hand A-pillar lower trim panel.

h. From inside the engine compartment, install the main wiring assembly/lower bulkhead connector by performing the following:
- Position the bulkhead connector.
- Secure the clips.
- Tighten the bolt.

i. Install the coolant reservoir by performing the following:
- Position the reservoir.
- Install the bolts.

j. Install the instrument panel dash brace by performing the following:
- Position the instrument panel dash brace.
- Install the 6 bolts.

k. Install the AFCM.

l. Install the instrument panel cowl top nut.

m. Install the left-hand upper access panel.

n. Connect the climate control vacuum harness connector.

o. Install the upper center instrument panel access panel.

p. Install the instrument panel cowl top screws.

q. Install the engine cover.

r. Position the engine cover in the vehicle and fasten the cover latches.

s. Install the steering column.

t. Install the driver's side air bag module by installing or connecting the following items:
- Driver's air bag module.
- Air bag sliding contact electrical connector.
- Horn electrical connector.
- Both driver's air bag module screws.
- Both back cover plugs.

u. Install the passenger's side air bag modules by installing or connecting the following items:
- The 6 offset fasteners used for retaining the air bag module door from the instrument panel.
- Passenger's air bag module electrical connector and module.
- Passenger's air bag module retaining nuts.
- Instrument panel finish panel and reinforcement.

13. Connect the quick disconnect heater hose couplings at the heater core by performing the following procedure:

a. Clean the tubes and lubricate them with rubber insulator lube.

b. Install a new coupling retainer, spacer, and lubricated O-ring seals into the quick disconnect coupling housing.

c. Push the heater water hose with a quick disconnect coupling onto the tube.

d. Make sure the coupling is fully engaged by lightly pulling on the heater water hose.

14. Refill the cooling system.

15. Connect the battery ground cable.

16. Run the engine to normal operating temperatures; then, check the climate control operation and check for leaks.

> **Ford Expedition and Lincoln Navigator**

REMOVAL & INSTALLATION

1. Disconnect the negative battery cable.

> **✳✳ CAUTION**

After disconnecting the negative battery cable, wait 1 minute for the SRS module to deplete its energy.

2. Drain the cooling system into a clean container for reuse.

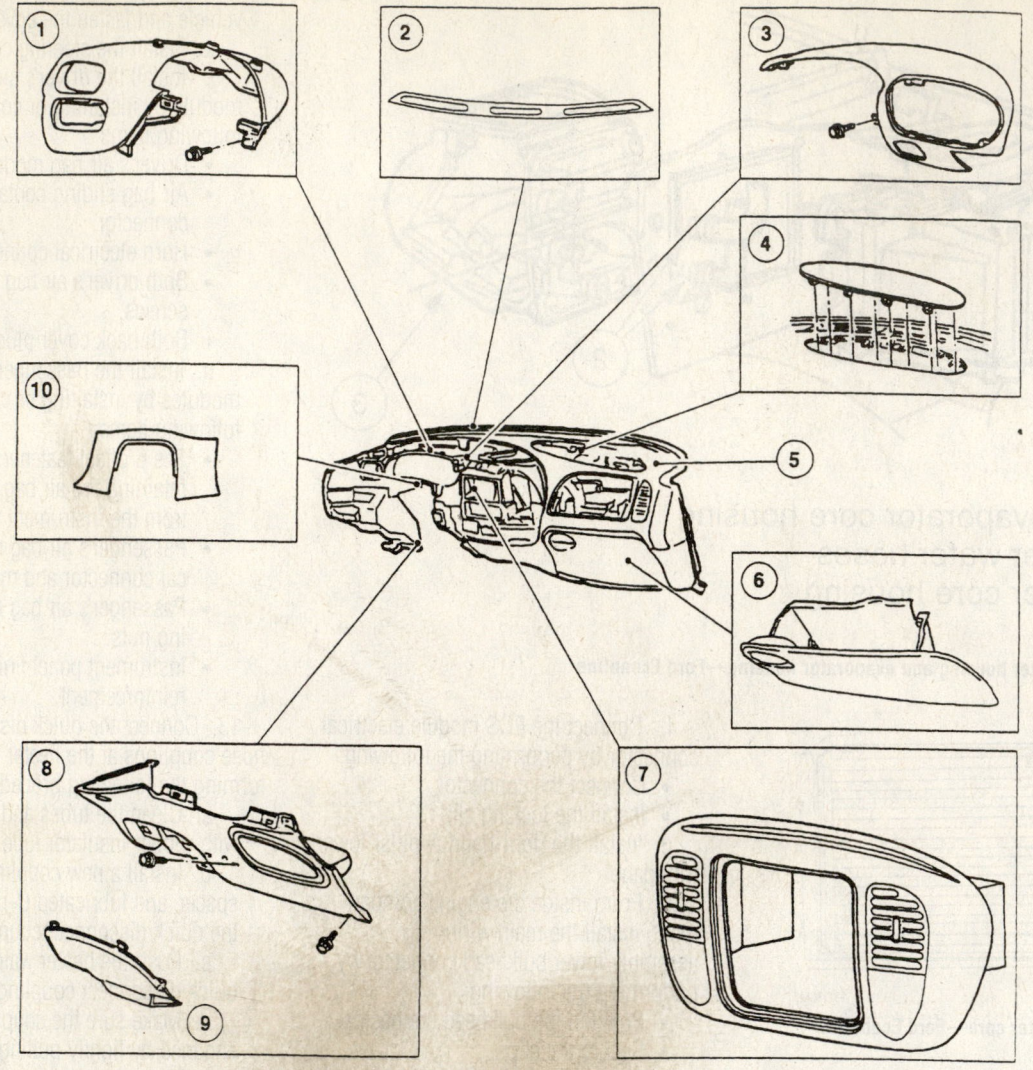

1. Instrument panel finish panel
2. Instrument panel defroster opening grille assembly
3. Instrument cluster panel
4. Instrument panel relay cover
5. Instrument panel
6. Glove compartment
7. Center instrument panel finish panel
8. Instrument panel steering column cover
9. Instrument panel fuse door
10. Steering column opening cover

93113GM2

Exploded view of the instrument panel components—Ford Expedition and Lincoln Navigator

3. Remove the instrument panel by performing the following procedure:

a. If equipped, remove the floor console assembly.

b. Remove the lower steering column cover bolts and the cover.

c. Remove both front door scuff plates.

d. Remove both side cowl trim panels.

e. Disconnect the electrical connector from the Brake Pedal Position (BPP) switch.

f. Remove the radio ground and the GEM/CTM ground bolts.

g. Disconnect the left side instrument panel main wiring harness connector.

h. In the engine compartment, remove the bulkhead wiring harness connector bolts and disconnect the wiring connectors.

i. In the driver's compartment, release the 6 locking tabs and remove the bulkhead electrical connector from the instrument panel.

j. Disconnect the air bag diagnostic monitor electrical connector.

k. Disconnect the inertia fuel shutoff switch electrical connector.

l. Remove the right side ground bolts.

m. Disconnect the right side instrument panel wiring harness connectors.

n. Disconnect the electronic blend door actuator electrical connector.

o. Disconnect the climate control head vacuum harness connector.

p. Remove the steering column opening cover reinforcement nuts and the cover reinforcement.

q. At the base of the steering column,

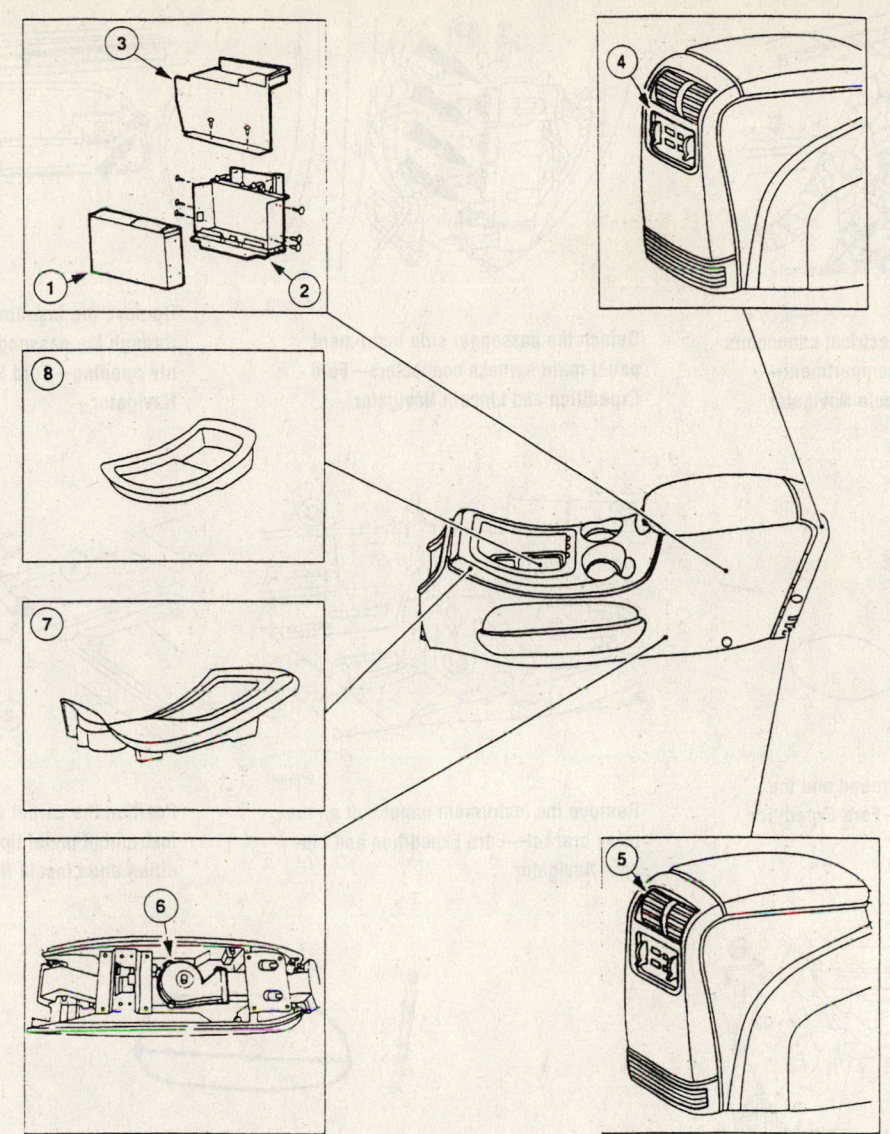

1. Digital audio compact disc player
2. Compact disc player mounting bracket
3. Compact disc player compartment trim panel
4. Radio and A/C integral control assembly
5. A/C register (upper)
6. Blower assembly
7. Center console finish panel
8. Console finish panel mat

93113GM3

Exploded view of the floor console components—Ford Expedition and Lincoln Navigator

disconnect the air bag sliding contact and the anti-theft sensor electrical connectors.

r. At the steering column, disconnect the remaining electrical connectors.

s. If equipped with a transmission range indicator, remove the bolt and disconnect the cable.

t. Remove the steering column-to-instrument panel nuts and lower the steering column.

u. Remove the right side front fender splash shield screws and move the shield away from the panel.

v. Disconnect the antenna cable from the antenna base.

w. Remove the instrument panel relay cover and disconnect the autolamp sensor electrical connector and/or the sun-load sensor connector.

x. Remove the glove box.

y. At the passenger's air bag module,

remove the screws, disconnect the electrical connector and remove the air bag module.

➡ **Place the air bag module in a safe place with the front facing upward.**

z. Remove the right side assist handle screw covers, the screws and the handle.

aa. At both doors, pull back the weatherstrip seals and remove the windshield garnish moldings.

Refer to the model specific sections for engine mechanical service procedures

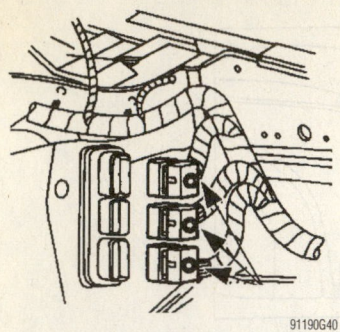

91190G40

Remove the bulkhead electrical connectors from inside the engine compartment—Ford Expedition and Lincoln Navigator

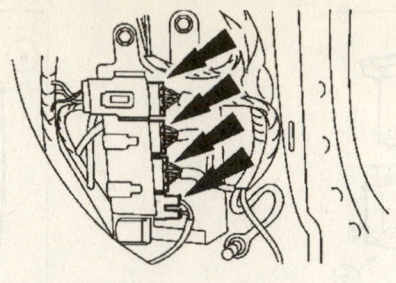

91190G44

Detach the passenger side instrument panel main harness connectors—Ford Expedition and Lincoln Navigator

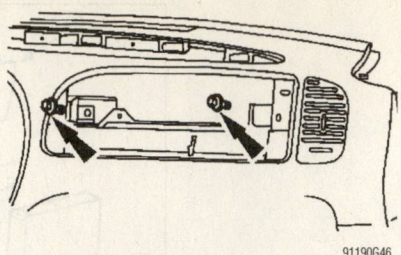

91190G46

Remove the instrument panel bolts through the passenger side air bag module opening—Ford Expedition and Lincoln Navigator

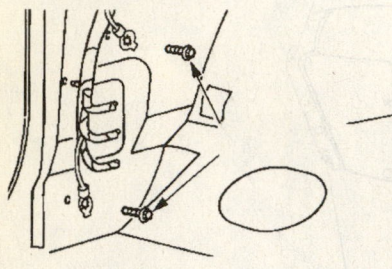

91190G41

Remove the audio unit ground and the GEM/CTM ground bolts—Ford Expedition and Lincoln Navigator

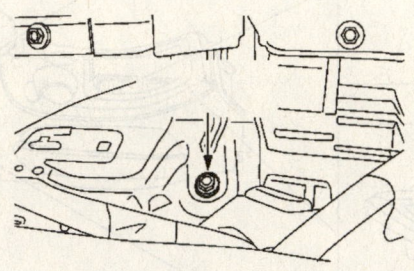

91190G45

Remove the instrument panel bolt on the relay bracket—Ford Expedition and Lincoln Navigator

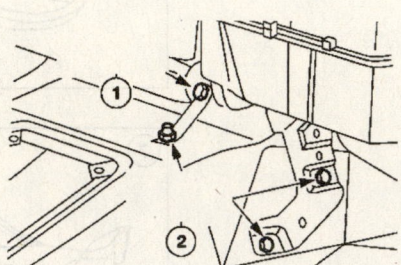

91190G48

Position the carpet aside and loosen the instrument panel floor brace—Ford Expedition and Lincoln Navigator

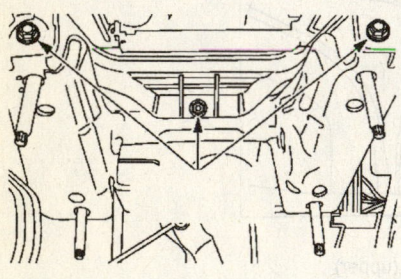

91190G42

Remove the instrument panel bolts through the steering column opening—Ford Expedition and Lincoln Navigator

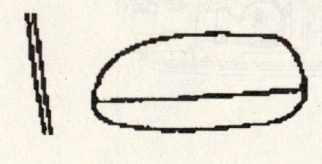

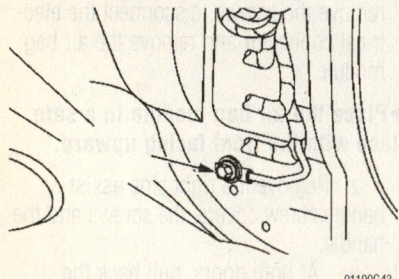

91190G43

Remove the passenger side ground bolt—Ford Expedition and Lincoln Navigator

91190G47

Remove the instrument panel reinforcement bolt below the driver's side corner of the glove compartment—Ford Expedition and Lincoln Navigator

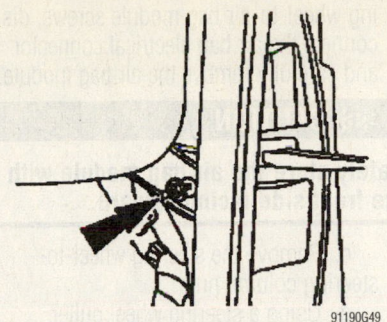

Remove the passenger side instrument panel cowl side nut—Ford Expedition and Lincoln Navigator

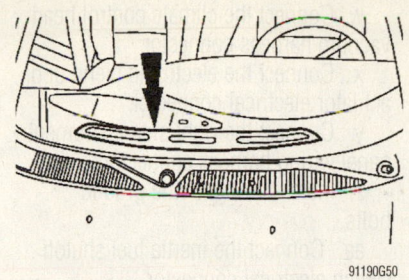

On Navigator, remove the defroster grille assembly—Ford Expedition and Lincoln Navigator

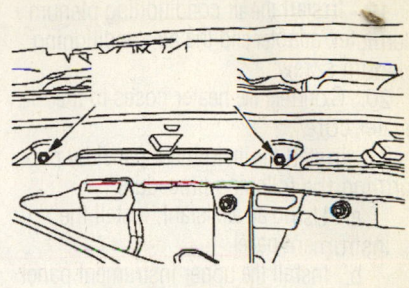

Remove the cowl panel mounting bolts—Ford Expedition and Lincoln Navigator

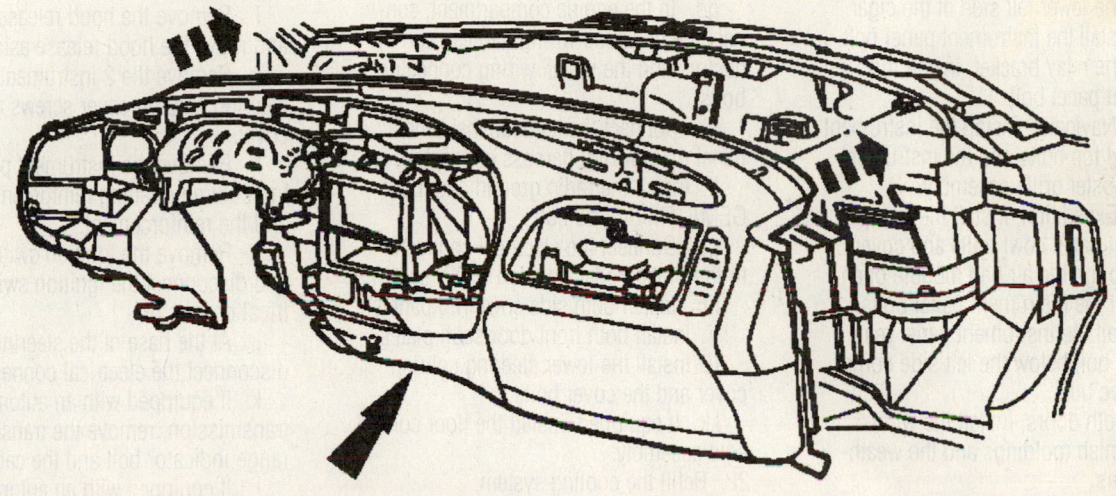

Remove the instrument panel —Ford Expedition and Lincoln Navigator

bb. Remove the instrument panel reinforcement bolt below the left side corner of the glove box.

cc. Through the air bag module opening, remove the instrument panel bolts.

dd. On Expedition, remove the upper instrument panel cowl covers and bolts.

ee. On Navigator, remove the instrument panel defroster grille assembly and the instrument panel cowl top bolts.

ff. At the relay bracket, remove the instrument panel bolt.

gg. At the lower left side of the cigar lighter, remove the instrument panel bolt.

hh. At the both sides, remove the instrument panel-to-cowl side nuts.

ii. At the steering column opening, remove the instrument panel bolts.

jj. Remove the upper instrument panel floor brace bolt.

kk. Using an assistant, remove the instrument panel.

4. If equipped with the 5.4L 4V engine, remove the junction block splash shield.

5. If equipped with the 5.4L 4V engine, remove the bolts and disconnect the cable ends from the starter relay.

6. If equipped with the 5.4L 4V engine, remove the junction block bracket.

7. Compress the holding tabs and disconnect the heater hoses from the heater core.

8. Remove the air conditioning plenum screw and the air conditioning plenum demister adapter.

9. Disconnect the vacuum line.

10. Remove the heater core bracket screws and the bracket.

11. Remove the 13 heater housing plenum camber cover screws and the heater housing plenum chamber cover.

12. Remove the blend door assembly from the heater housing.

13. Remove the heater core.

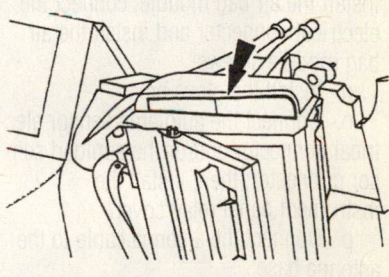

View of the heater core—Ford Expedition and Lincoln Navigator

To install:

14. Install the heater core.

15. Install the blend door assembly to the heater housing.

16. Install the 13 heater housing plenum camber cover and the heater housing plenum chamber cover screws.

17. Install the heater core bracket and the bracket screws.

Refer to the model specific sections for cooling system service procedures

18. Connect the vacuum line.

19. Install the air conditioning plenum demister adapter and the air conditioning plenum screw.

20. Connect the heater hoses to the heater core.

21. Install the instrument panel by performing the following procedure:

a. Using an assistant, install the instrument panel.

b. Install the upper instrument panel floor brace bolt.

c. At the steering column opening, install the instrument panel bolts.

d. At the both sides, install the instrument panel-to-cowl side nuts.

e. At the lower left side of the cigar lighter, install the instrument panel bolt.

f. At the relay bracket, install the instrument panel bolt.

g. On Navigator, install the instrument panel cowl top bolts and the instrument panel defroster grille assembly.

h. On Expedition, install the upper instrument panel cowl bolts and covers.

i. Through the air bag module opening, install the instrument panel bolts.

j. Install the instrument panel reinforcement bolt below the left side corner of the glove box.

k. At both doors, install the windshield garnish moldings and the weatherstrip seals.

l. Install the right side assist handle, the screws and the handle screw covers.

m. At the passenger's air bag module, install the air bag module, connect the electrical connector and install the air bag module screws.

n. Install the glove box.

o. Connect the autolamp sensor electrical connector and/or the sunload sensor connector; then, install the instrument panel relay cover.

p. Connect the antenna cable to the antenna base.

q. Install the right side front fender splash shield and screws.

r. Install the steering column and the steering column-to-instrument panel nuts.

s. If equipped with a transmission range indicator, connect the cable and install the bolt.

t. At the steering column, connect the remaining electrical connectors.

u. At the base of the steering column, connect the air bag sliding contact and the anti-theft sensor electrical connectors.

v. Install the steering column opening cover reinforcement and the cover reinforcement nuts.

w. Connect the climate control head vacuum harness connector.

x. Connect the electronic blend door actuator electrical connector.

y. Connect the right side instrument panel wiring harness connectors.

z. Install the right side ground bolts.

aa. Connect the inertia fuel shutoff switch electrical connector.

bb. Connect the air bag diagnostic monitor electrical connector.

cc. In the driver's compartment, install the bulkhead electrical connector to the instrument panel.

dd. In the engine compartment, connect the bulkhead wiring harness connectors and the install wiring connector bolts.

ee. Connect the left side instrument panel main wiring harness connector.

ff. Install the radio ground and the GEM/CTM ground bolts.

gg. Connect the electrical connector to the Brake Pedal Position (BPP) switch.

hh. Install both side cowl trim panels.

ii. Install both front door scuff plates.

jj. Install the lower steering column cover and the cover bolts.

kk. If equipped, install the floor console assembly.

22. Refill the cooling system.

23. Connect the negative battery cable.

24. Run the engine to normal operating temperatures; then, check the climate control operation and check for leaks.

Ford Explorer and Mercury Mountaineer

REMOVAL & INSTALLATION

1. Disconnect the negative battery cable.

✳✳ CAUTION

After disconnecting the negative battery cable, wait for 1 minute for the SRS module to deplete its energy.

2. Drain the cooling system into a clean container for reuse.

3. Disconnect the heater hoses from the heater core.

4. Remove the steering column by performing the following procedure:

a. Position the front wheels in the straight-ahead direction.

b. At the both sides of the steering wheel, remove the cover plugs, the steering wheel-to-air bag module screws, disconnect the air bag electrical connector and carefully remove the air bag module.

✳✳ CAUTION

Safely store the air bag module with the front side facing upward.

c. Remove the steering wheel-to-steering column nut.

d. Using a steering wheel puller, press the steering wheel from the steering column.

e. Remove the parking brake release handle screws and move the release handle aside.

f. Remove the hood release screws and move the hood release aside.

g. Remove the 2 instrument panel-to-steering column cover screws and the cover.

h. Remove the instrument panel steering column opening reinforcement bolts and the reinforcement.

i. Remove the ignition switch bolt and disconnect the ignition switch electrical connector.

j. At the base of the steering column, disconnect the electrical connectors.

k. If equipped with an automatic transmission, remove the transmission range indicator bolt and the cable.

l. If equipped with an automatic transmission, disconnect the shift cable from the steering column shift tube lever and the steering column bracket.

m. Disconnect the brake shift interlock solenoid electrical connector.

n. Remove the air bag sliding contact.

o. Remove the upper intermediate steering shaft-to-column shaft bolt and discard the bolt.

p. Remove the lower steering column-to-instrument panel nuts and the steering column.

5. Remove the instrument panel by performing the following procedure:

a. Disconnect the Brake Pedal Position (BPP) switch electrical connector.

b. Remove the push pins and remove both cowl side trim panels.

c. At the right side cowl panel, disconnect the electrical connectors and ground wires.

d. Remove both sides windshield garnish moldings.

e. Disconnect the power distribution box from its bracket and move it aside.

f. In the engine compartment, loosen the bulkhead wiring harness bolts and disconnect the electrical connectors.

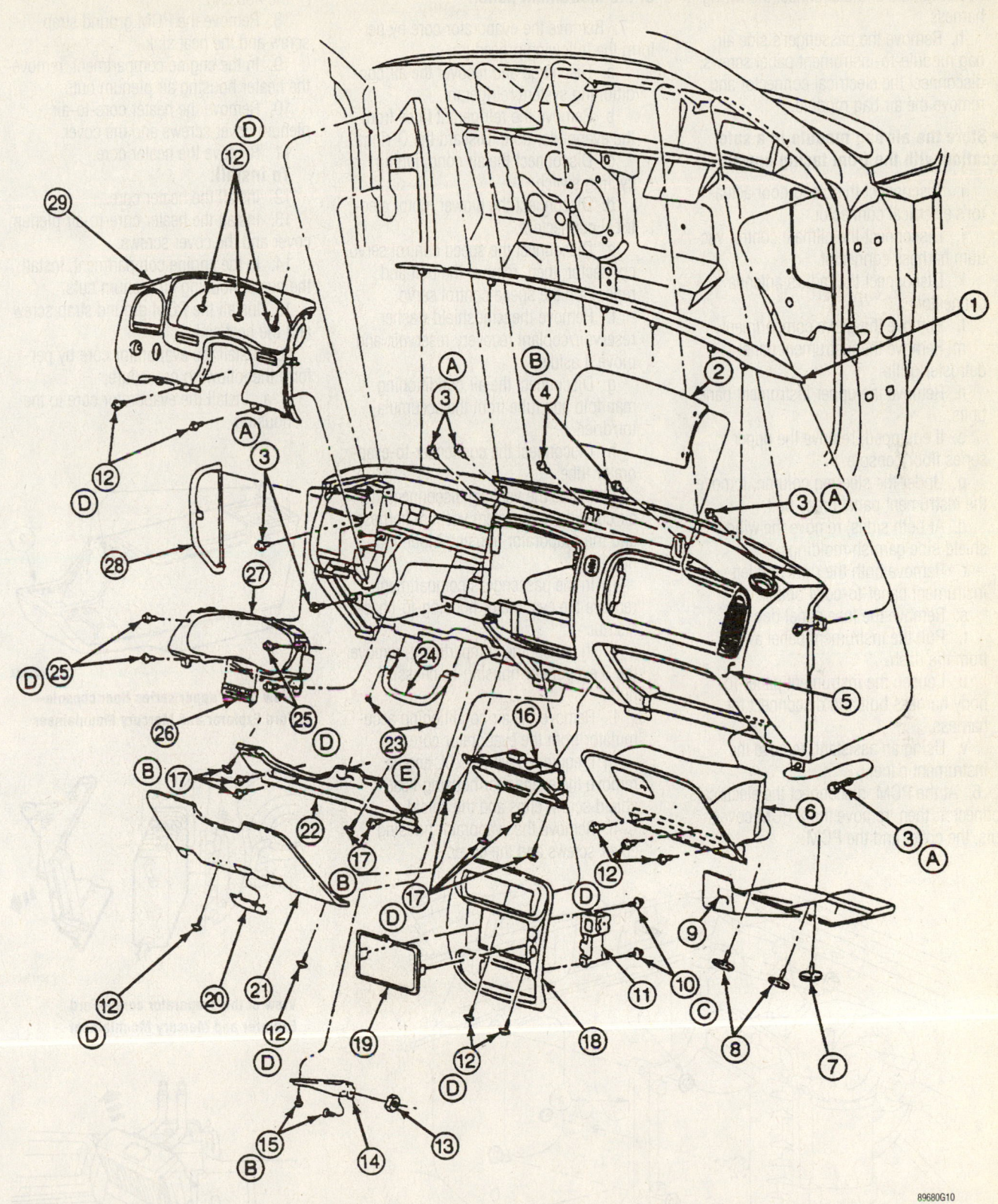

Exploded view of the instrument panel assembly—Ford Explorer and Mercury Mountaineer

89680G10

g. Pull the bulkhead electrical connector handle and disconnect the wiring harness.

h. Remove the passenger's side air bag module-to-instrument panel screws, disconnect the electrical connector and remove the air bag module.

➡ **Store the air bag module in a safe location with the front facing upward.**

i. Disconnect the blend door actuator's electrical connector.

j. Disconnect the climate control vacuum harness connector.

k. Disconnect the radio's antenna connector.

l. Remove the glove compartment.

m. Remove the instrument panel defroster grille.

n. Remove the upper instrument panel bolts.

o. If equipped, remove the upper series floor console.

p. Under the steering column, remove the instrument panel brace bolt.

q. At both sides, remove the windshield side garnish moldings.

r. Remove both the right and left instrument panel-to-cowl bolts.

s. Remove the fuse panel door.

t. Pull the instrument panel away from the dash.

u. Loosen the instrument panel-to-body harness bolt and disconnect the harness.

v. Using an assistant, remove the instrument panel.

6. At the PCM, disconnect the electrical connector; then, remove the 2 PCM cover nuts, the cover and the PCM.

➡ **The PCM is located at the right side of the instrument panel.**

7. Remove the evaporator core by perform the following procedure:

a. Discharge and recover the air conditioning system refrigerant.

b. Remove the refrigerant lines from the evaporator core. Discard the O-rings.

c. Disconnect the air conditioning cycling switch.

d. Disconnect the blower motor electrical connectors.

e. Disconnect the speed control servo connector; then, remove the bolt and reposition the speed control servo.

f. Remove the windshield washer reservoir/coolant recovery reservoir, and move it aside.

g. Disconnect the air conditioning manifold and tube from the accumulator/drier.

h. Disconnect the condenser-to-evaporator tube.

i. Inside the vehicle, disconnect the air conditioning system vacuum harness and the evaporator housing mounting nut.

j. In the passenger's compartment, remove the evaporator housing-to-chassis nut.

k. In the engine compartment, remove the 3 evaporator housing-to-chassis nuts.

l. Remove the air conditioning accumulator from the evaporator core.

m. If equipped with a 5.0L engine, remove the evaporator housing heat shield screw, clips and the shield.

n. Remove the evaporator housing cover screws and the cover.

o. Remove the evaporator core from the housing.

8. Remove the PCM ground strap screw and the heat sink.

9. In the engine compartment, remove the heater housing air plenum nuts.

10. Remove the heater core-to-air plenum cover screws and the cover.

11. Remove the heater core.

To install:

12. Install the heater core.

13. Install the heater core-to-air plenum cover and the cover screws.

14. In the engine compartment, install the heater housing air plenum nuts.

15. Install the PCM ground strap screw and the heat sink.

16. Install the evaporator core by perform the following procedure:

a. Install the evaporator core to the housing.

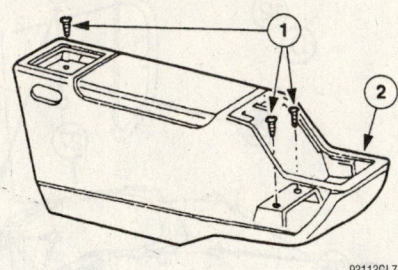

View of the upper series floor console—Ford Explorer and Mercury Mountaineer

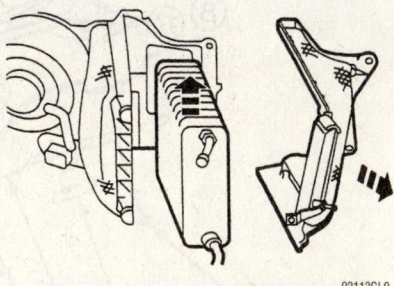

View of the evaporator core—Ford Explorer and Mercury Mountaineer

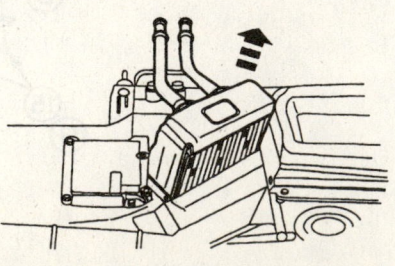

View of the heater core—Ford Explorer and Mercury Mountaineer

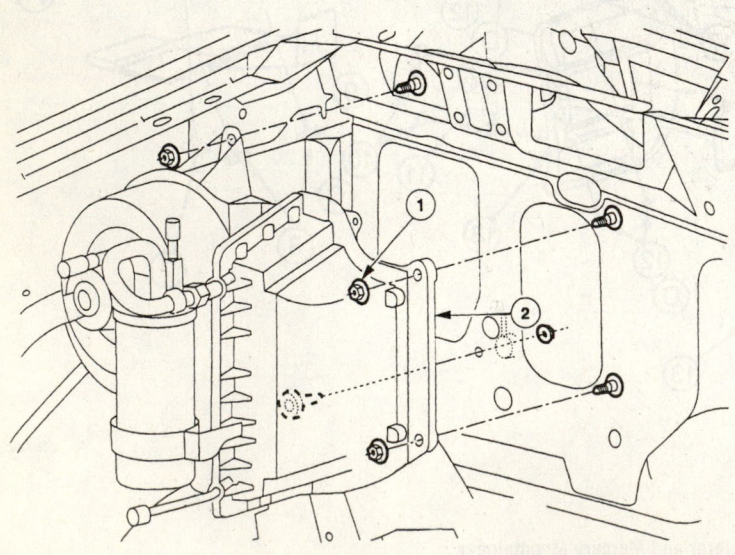

View of the evaporator housing—Ford Explorer and Mercury Mountaineer

b. Install the evaporator housing cover and the cover screws.

c. If equipped with a 5.0L engine, install the evaporator housing heat shield, clips and the shield screw.

d. Install the air conditioning accumulator to the evaporator core.

e. In the engine compartment, install the 3 evaporator housing-to-chassis nuts.

f. In the passenger's compartment, install the evaporator housing-to-chassis nut.

g. Inside the vehicle, connect the air conditioning system vacuum harness and the evaporator housing mounting nut.

h. Connect the condenser-to-evaporator tube.

i. Connect the air conditioning manifold and tube to the accumulator/drier.

j. Install the windshield washer reservoir/coolant recovery reservoir.

k. Install the speed control servo, the bolt and connect the speed control servo connector.

l. Connect the blower motor electrical connectors.

m. Connect the air conditioning cycling switch.

n. Using new O-rings, install the refrigerant lines to the evaporator core.

17. Install the PCM, the cover and the PCM cover nuts; then, disconnect the electrical connector.

18. Install the instrument panel by performing the following procedure:

a. Using an assistant, install the instrument panel.

b. Connect the harness and tighten the instrument panel-to-body harness bolt.

c. Push the instrument panel away toward the dash.

d. Install the fuse panel door.

e. Install both the right and left instrument panel-to-cowl bolts.

f. At both sides, install the windshield side garnish moldings.

g. Under the steering column, install the instrument panel brace bolt.

h. If equipped, install the upper series floor console.

i. Install the upper instrument panel bolts.

j. Install the instrument panel defroster grille.

k. Install the glove compartment.

l. Connect the radio's antenna connector.

m. Connect the climate control vacuum harness connector.

n. Connect the blend door actuator's electrical connector.

o. Install the passenger's side air bag module, connect the electrical connector and install the air bag module-to-instrument panel screws.

p. Connect the bulkhead electrical connector wiring harness.

q. In the engine compartment, connect the electrical connectors and tighten the bulkhead wiring harness bolts.

r. Connect the power distribution box to its bracket.

s. Install both sides windshield garnish moldings.

t. At the right side cowl panel, connect the electrical connectors and ground wires.

u. Install both cowl side trim panels and the push pins.

v. Connect the Brake Pedal Position (BPP) switch electrical connector.

19. Install the steering column by performing the following procedure:

a. Install the lower steering column and the steering column-to-instrument panel nuts; then, torque the nuts to 10–13 ft. lbs. (13–17 Nm).

b. Using a new bolt, install the upper intermediate steering shaft-to-column shaft bolt and torque to 19–25 ft. lbs. (26–34 Nm).

c. Install the air bag sliding contact.

d. Connect the brake shift interlock solenoid electrical connector.

e. If equipped with an automatic transmission, connect the shift cable from the steering column shift tube lever and the steering column bracket.

f. If equipped with an automatic transmission, install the transmission range indicator cable and bolt.

g. At the base of the steering column, connect the electrical connectors.

h. Connect the ignition switch electrical connector and install the ignition switch bolt.

i. Install the instrument panel steering column opening reinforcement and the reinforcement bolts.

j. Install the instrument panel-to-steering column cover and the 2 cover screws.

k. Install the hood release and the hood release screws.

l. Install the parking brake release handle and the release handle screws.

m. Install the steering wheel to the steering column.

n. Install the steering wheel-to-steering column nut and torque the nut to 25–34 ft. lbs. (34–46 Nm).

o. At the both sides of the steering wheel, install the air bag module, connect the air bag electrical connector, install the steering wheel-to-air bag module screws and the cover plugs.

20. Connect the heater hoses to the heater core.

21. Refill the cooling system.

22. Connect the negative battery cable.

23. Evacuate and charge the air conditioning system.

24. Run the engine to normal operating temperatures; then, check the climate control operation and check for leaks.

Ford F-Series

REMOVAL & INSTALLATION

1. If equipped with power seats, move the seats fully rearward.

2. Disconnect the negative battery cable.

✷✷ CAUTION

After disconnecting the negative battery cable, wait for 1 minute for the SRS module to deplete its energy.

3. Drain the cooling system into a clean container for reuse.

4. Remove the instrument panel by performing the following procedure:

a. If equipped with automatic transmission, move the shift lever to the **1** position to ease removal.

b. At the lower driver's side instrument panel, release the electrical connector push button clip and move the connector aside.

c. Remove the fuse panel door.

d. Remove the hood latch release handle screws and move the hood release handle aside.

e. Remove the parking brake release handle screws and move the parking brake release handle aside.

f. If equipped, remove the 2 instrument panel floor duct panel push clips and release the expander clip.

g. Remove the lower steering column cover bolts and the cover.

h. Remove both front door scuff plates.

i. Remove both side cowl trim panels.

j. Disconnect the electrical connector from the Brake Pedal Position (BPP) switch.

k. Remove the radio ground and the GEM/CTM ground bolts.

l. Disconnect the left side instrument panel main wiring harness connector.

m. In the engine compartment, remove the bulkhead wiring harness connector bolts and disconnect the wiring connectors.

n. In the engine compartment, release the 6 locking tabs and remove the bulkhead electrical connector from the instrument panel.

o. Disconnect the air bag diagnostic monitor electrical connector.

p. Disconnect the inertia fuel shutoff switch electrical connector.

q. Remove the right side ground bolts.

r. Disconnect the right side instrument panel wiring harness connectors.

s. Disconnect the electronic blend door actuator electrical connector.

t. Disconnect the climate control head vacuum harness connector.

u. Remove the steering column opening cover reinforcement nuts and the cover reinforcement.

v. At the base of the steering column, disconnect the air bag sliding contact and the anti-theft sensor electrical connectors.

w. At the steering column, disconnect the remaining electrical connectors.

x. If equipped with a transmission range indicator, remove the bolt and disconnect the cable.

y. Remove the steering column-to-instrument panel nuts and lower the steering column.

z. Remove and disconnect the r adio.

aa. Remove the instrument panel

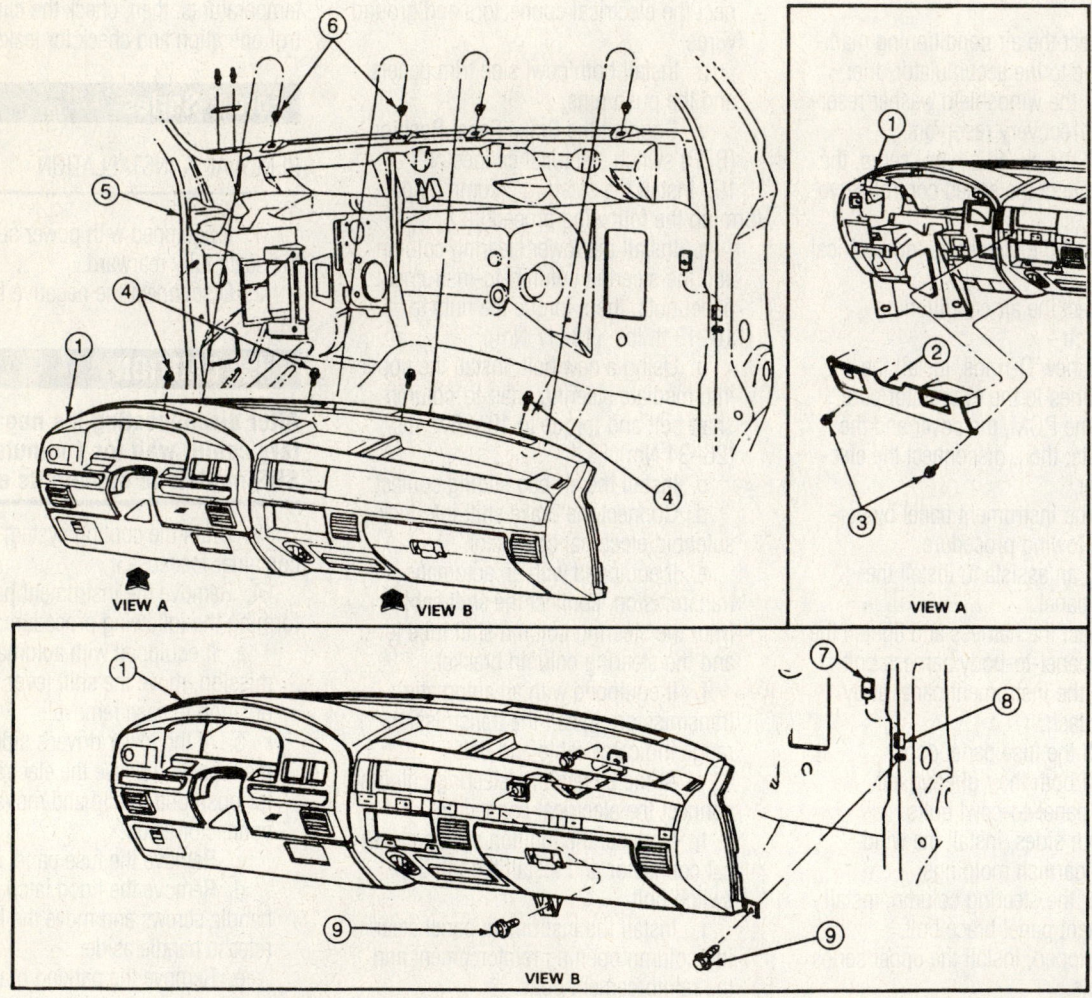

Item	Description
1	Instrument Panel
2	Steering Column Opening Cover
3	Screw(s) 2.0-3.0 N•m (19.0-26.0 In-Lb)
4	Screw(s) 2.0-2.4 N•m (18.0-21.0 In-Lb)

Item	Description
5	Cowl Side Panel (LH)
6	Nut Insert (4 Req'd)
7	U-Nut
8	Cowl Side Panel (RH)
9	Screw(s) 2.0-2.4 N•m (18.0-21.0 In-Lb)

Instrument panel installation—F-250HD, F-350 and F-Super Duty

88280G13

relay cover and disconnect the autolamp sensor electrical connector.

bb. Remove the glove box.

cc. At the passenger's air bag module, remove the screws, disconnect the electrical connector and remove the air bag module.

➡**Place the air bag module in a safe place with the front facing upward.**

dd. Remove the right side assist handle screw covers, the screws and the handle.

ee. At both doors, pull back the weatherstrip seals and remove the windshield garnish moldings.

ff. Remove the instrument panel reinforcement bolt below the left side corner of the glove box.

gg. Through the air bag module opening, remove the instrument panel bolts.

hh. Remove the upper instrument panel cowl covers and bolts.

ii. At the relay bracket, remove the instrument panel bolt.

jj. At the lower left side of the cigar lighter, remove the instrument panel bolt.

kk. At the both sides, remove the instrument panel-to-cowl side nuts.

ll. At the steering column opening, remove the instrument panel bolts.

mm. Remove the upper instrument panel floor brace bolt.

nn. Loosen the instrument panel brace bolts and nut.

➡**Using an assistant, remove the instrument panel.**

5. Compress the holding tabs and disconnect the heater hoses from the heater core.

6. Remove the air conditioning plenum screw and the air conditioning plenum demister adapter.

7. Disconnect the vacuum line.

8. Remove the heater core bracket screws and the bracket.

9. Remove the 13 heater housing plenum camber cover screws and the heater housing plenum chamber cover.

10. Remove the blend door assembly from the heater housing.

11. Remove the heater core.

To install:

12. Install the heater core.

13. Install the blend door assembly to the heater housing.

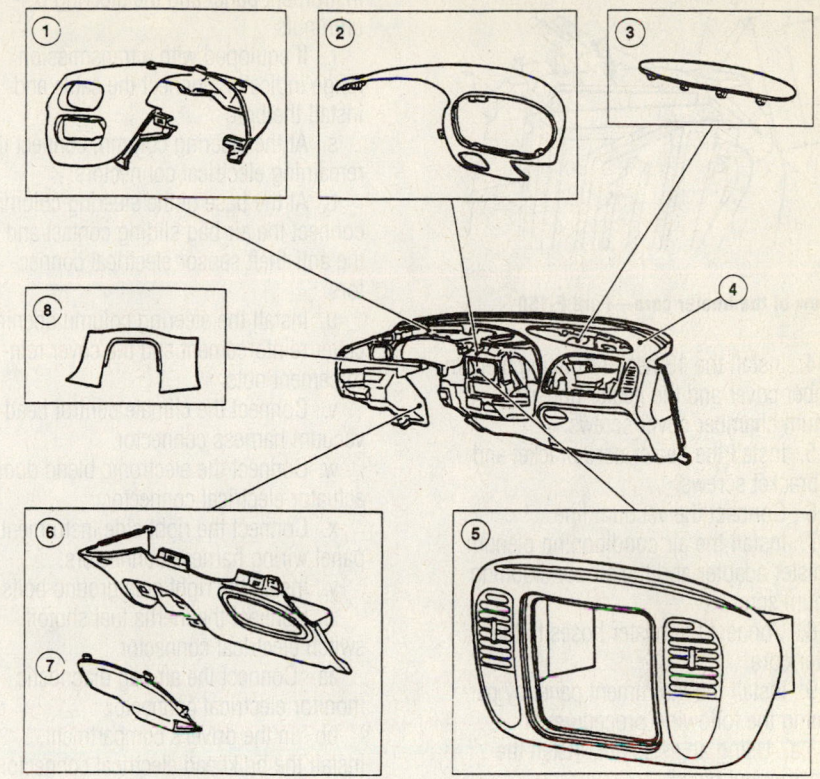

1. Instrument panel finish panel
2. Instrument cluster panel
3. Instrument panel relay cover
4. Instrument panel
5. Center instrument panel finish panel
6. Instrument panel steering column cover, lower
7. Instrument panel fuse door
8. Steering column opening cover

93113GL0

Exploded view of the instrument panel components—Ford F-150, F-250

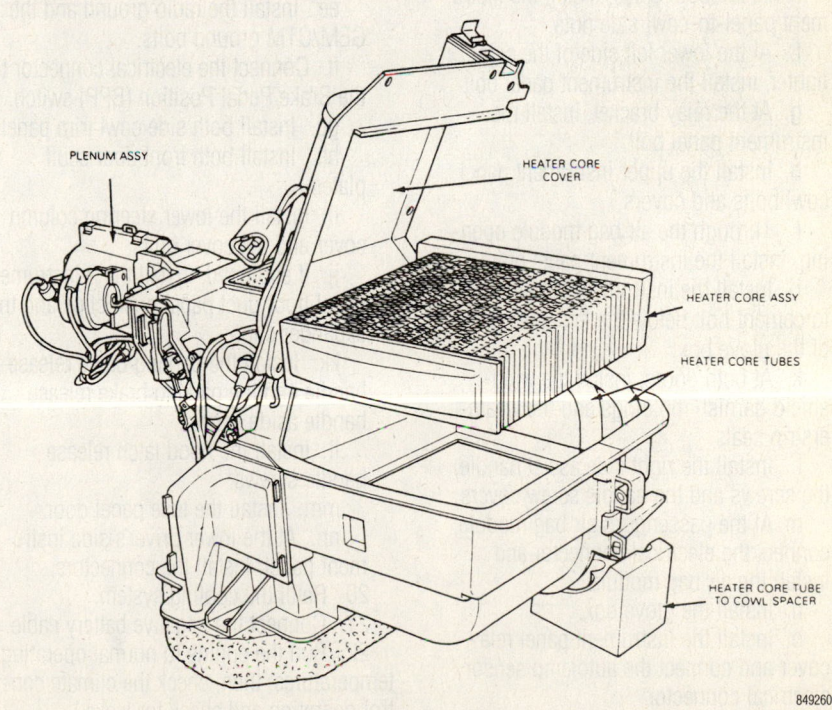

PLENUM ASSY

HEATER CORE COVER

HEATER CORE ASSY

HEATER CORE TUBES

HEATER CORE TUBE TO COWL SPACER

84926007

Heater core removal—F-250, F-350 and F-Super Duty models

Refer to the model specific sections for engine mechanical service procedures

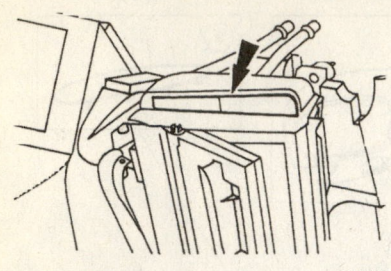

View of the heater core—Ford F-150

93113GM1

14. Install the 13 heater housing plenum camber cover and the heater housing plenum chamber cover screws.

15. Install the heater core bracket and the bracket screws.

16. Connect the vacuum line.

17. Install the air conditioning plenum demister adapter and the air conditioning plenum screw.

18. Connect the heater hoses to the heater core.

19. Install the instrument panel by performing the following procedure:

a. Using an assistant, install the instrument panel.

b. Tighten the instrument panel brace bolts and nut.

c. Install the upper instrument panel floor brace bolt.

d. At the steering column opening, install the instrument panel bolts.

e. At the both sides, install the instrument panel-to-cowl side nuts.

f. At the lower left side of the cigar lighter, install the instrument panel bolt.

g. At the relay bracket, install the instrument panel bolt.

h. Install the upper instrument panel cowl bolts and covers.

i. Through the air bag module opening, install the instrument panel bolts.

j. Install the instrument panel reinforcement bolt below the left side corner of the glove box.

k. At both doors, install the windshield garnish moldings and the weatherstrip seals.

l. Install the right side assist handle, the screws and the handle screw covers.

m. At the passenger's air bag module, connect the electrical connector and install the air bag module.

n. Install the glove box.

o. Install the instrument panel relay cover and connect the autolamp sensor electrical connector.

p. Install and connect the radio.

q. Install the steering column-to-

instrument panel and the steering column nuts.

r. If equipped with a transmission range indicator, connect the cable and install the bolt.

s. At the steering column, connect the remaining electrical connectors.

t. At the base of the steering column, connect the air bag sliding contact and the anti-theft sensor electrical connectors.

u. Install the steering column opening cover reinforcement and the cover reinforcement nuts.

v. Connect the climate control head vacuum harness connector.

w. Connect the electronic blend door actuator electrical connector.

x. Connect the right side instrument panel wiring harness connectors.

y. Install the right side ground bolts.

z. Connect the inertia fuel shutoff switch electrical connector.

aa. Connect the air bag diagnostic monitor electrical connector.

bb. In the driver's compartment, install the bulkhead electrical connector to the instrument panel.

cc. In the engine compartment, install the bulkhead wiring harness connector bolts and connect the wiring connectors.

dd. Connect the left side instrument panel main wiring harness connector.

ee. Install the radio ground and the GEM/CTM ground bolts.

ff. Connect the electrical connector to the Brake Pedal Position (BPP) switch.

gg. Install both side cowl trim panels.

hh. Install both front door scuff plates.

ii. Install the lower steering column cover and the cover bolts.

jj. If equipped, install the 2 instrument panel floor duct panel push clips and the expander clip.

kk. Install the parking brake release handle and the parking brake release handle aside screws.

ll. Install the hood latch release handle screws.

mm. Install the fuse panel door.

nn. At the lower driver's side instrument panel, install the connectors.

20. Refill the cooling system.

21. Connect the negative battery cable.

22. Run the engine to normal operating temperatures; then, check the climate control operation and check for leaks.

Ford Ranger

REMOVAL & INSTALLATION

1997

1. Disconnect the negative battery cable.

2. Drain the cooling system into a clean container for reuse.

3. Disconnect the heater hoses from the heater core tube. Plug the hoses to prevent loss of coolant.

4. In the passenger compartment, remove the screws attaching the heater core access cover to the plenum assembly. Remove the access cover.

5. Pull the heater core rearward and down, removing it from the plenum assembly.

To install:

6. Position the heater core and seal in the plenum assembly.

7. Install the heater core access cover to the plenum assembly and secure it with the screws.

8. Connect the heater hoses to the heater core tubes.

9. Refill the cooling system.

10. Connect the negative battery cable.

11. Run the engine to normal operating temperatures; then, check the climate control operation and check for leaks.

1998–00

1. Disconnect the negative battery cable.

> **⁑ CAUTION**
>
> **After disconnecting the negative battery cable, wait for 1 minute for the SRS module to deplete its energy.**

2. Drain the cooling system into a clean container for reuse.

3. Remove the steering column by performing the following procedure:

a. Position the front wheels in the straight-ahead direction.

b. At the both sides of the steering wheel, remove the cover plugs, the steering wheel-to-air bag module screws, disconnect the air bag electrical connector and carefully remove the air bag module.

> **⁑ CAUTION**
>
> **Safely store the air bag module with the front side facing upward.**

c. Remove the steering wheel-to-steering column nut.

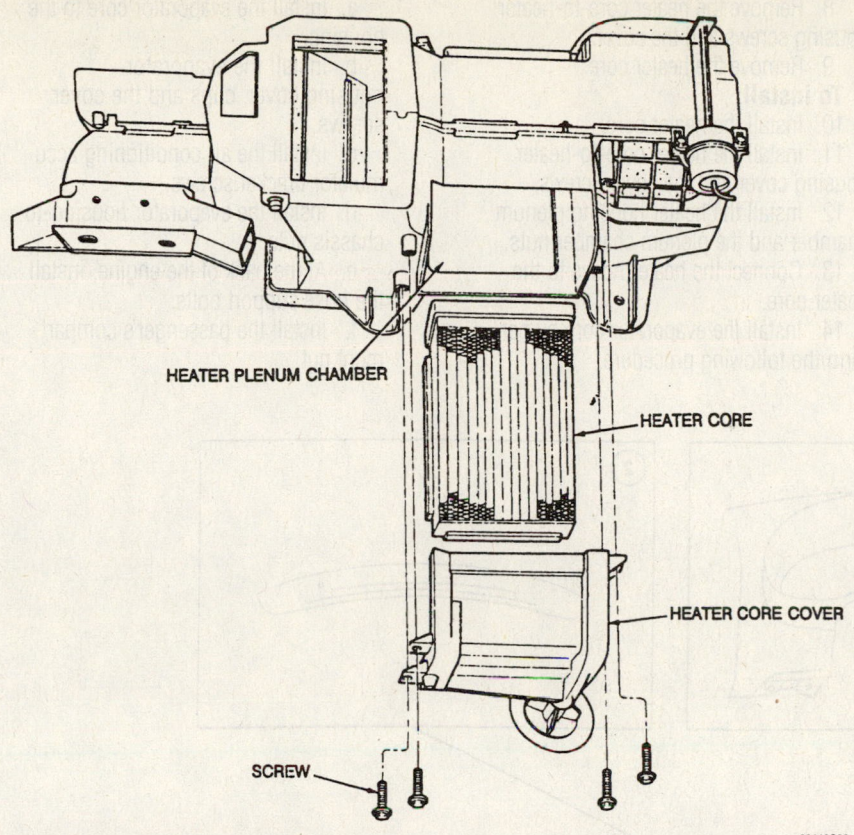

HEATER PLENUM CHAMBER

HEATER CORE

HEATER CORE COVER

SCREW

93113G29

Exploded view of the heater assembly—1990–97 Ford Ranger

d. Using a steering wheel puller, press the steering wheel from the steering column.

e. Remove the parking brake release handle screws and move the release handle aside.

f. Remove the hood release screws and move the hood release aside.

g. Remove the 2 instrument panel-to-steering column cover screws and the cover.

h. Remove the instrument panel steering column opening reinforcement bolts and the reinforcement.

i. Remove the ignition switch bolt and disconnect the ignition switch electrical connector.

j. At the base of the steering column, disconnect the electrical connectors.

k. If equipped with an automatic transmission, remove the transmission range indicator bolt and the cable.

l. If equipped with an automatic transmission, disconnect the shift cable from the steering column shift tube lever and the steering column bracket.

m. Disconnect the brake shift interlock solenoid electrical connector.

n. Remove the air bag sliding contact.

o. Remove the upper intermediate steering shaft-to-column shaft bolt and discard the bolt.

p. Remove the lower steering column-to-instrument panel nuts and the steering column.

4. Remove the instrument panel by performing the following procedure:

a. Remove the parking brake release handle screws and move the release handle aside.

b. Disconnect the Brake Pedal Position (BPP) switch electrical connector.

c. Remove both front door scuff plates.

d. Remove the push pins and remove both cowl side trim panels.

e. At the right side cowl panel, disconnect the electrical connectors and ground wires.

f. Remove both sides windshield garnish moldings.

g. Remove the instrument panel fuse door.

h. Disconnect the power distribution box from its bracket and move it aside.

i. In the engine compartment, loosen the bulkhead wiring harness bolts and disconnect the electrical connectors.

j. Pull the bulkhead electrical connector handle and disconnect the wiring harness.

k. Remove the passenger's side air bag module-to-instrument panel screws, disconnect the electrical connector and remove the air bag module.

➡ **Store the air bag module in a safe location with the front facing upward.**

l. Disconnect the blend door actuator's electrical connector.

m. Disconnect the climate control vacuum harness connector.

n. Disconnect the radio's antenna connector.

o. Remove the glove compartment.

p. Remove the instrument panel defroster grille.

q. Remove the upper instrument panel bolts.

r. Under the steering column, remove the instrument panel brace bolt.

s. Remove both the right and left instrument panel-to-cowl bolts.

t. Pull the instrument panel away from the dash.

u. Loosen the instrument panel-to-body harness bolt and disconnect the harness.

v. Using an assistant, remove the instrument panel.

5. Remove the evaporator core by performing the following procedure:

a. Discharge and recover the air conditioning system refrigerant.

b. Remove the refrigerant lines from the evaporator core. Discard the O-rings.

c. If equipped, remove the air conditioning vacuum reservoir tank/bracket screws and reposition the tank.

d. If equipped, disconnect the speed control servo connector; then, remove the bolt and reposition the speed control servo.

e. If equipped with a 3.0L or 4.0L engine, remove the support bracket.

f. Disengage the windshield washer hose retainer and move it aside.

g. Disconnect the vacuum hose and the retainer; then, move the hose aside.

h. Remove the passenger's compartment nut.

i. At the back of the engine, remove the hose support bolts.

Refer to the model specific sections for cooling system service procedures

j. Remove the evaporator housing-to-chassis nuts.

k. Remove the air conditioning accumulator bracket screws.

l. Remove the evaporator housing cover screws, clips and the cover.

m. Remove the evaporator core from the housing.

6. Disconnect the heater hoses from the heater core.

7. Remove the heater housing plenum chamber nuts and the plenum chamber.

8. Remove the heater core-to-heater housing screws and the cover.

9. Remove the heater core.

To install:

10. Install the heater core.

11. Install the heater core-to-heater housing cover and the cover screws.

12. Install the heater housing plenum chamber and the plenum chamber nuts.

13. Connect the heater hoses to the heater core.

14. Install the evaporator core by perform the following procedure:

a. Install the evaporator core to the housing.

b. Install the evaporator housing cover, clips and the cover screws.

c. Install the air conditioning accumulator bracket screws.

d. Install the evaporator housing-to-chassis nuts.

e. At the back of the engine, install the hose support bolts.

f. Install the passenger's compartment nut.

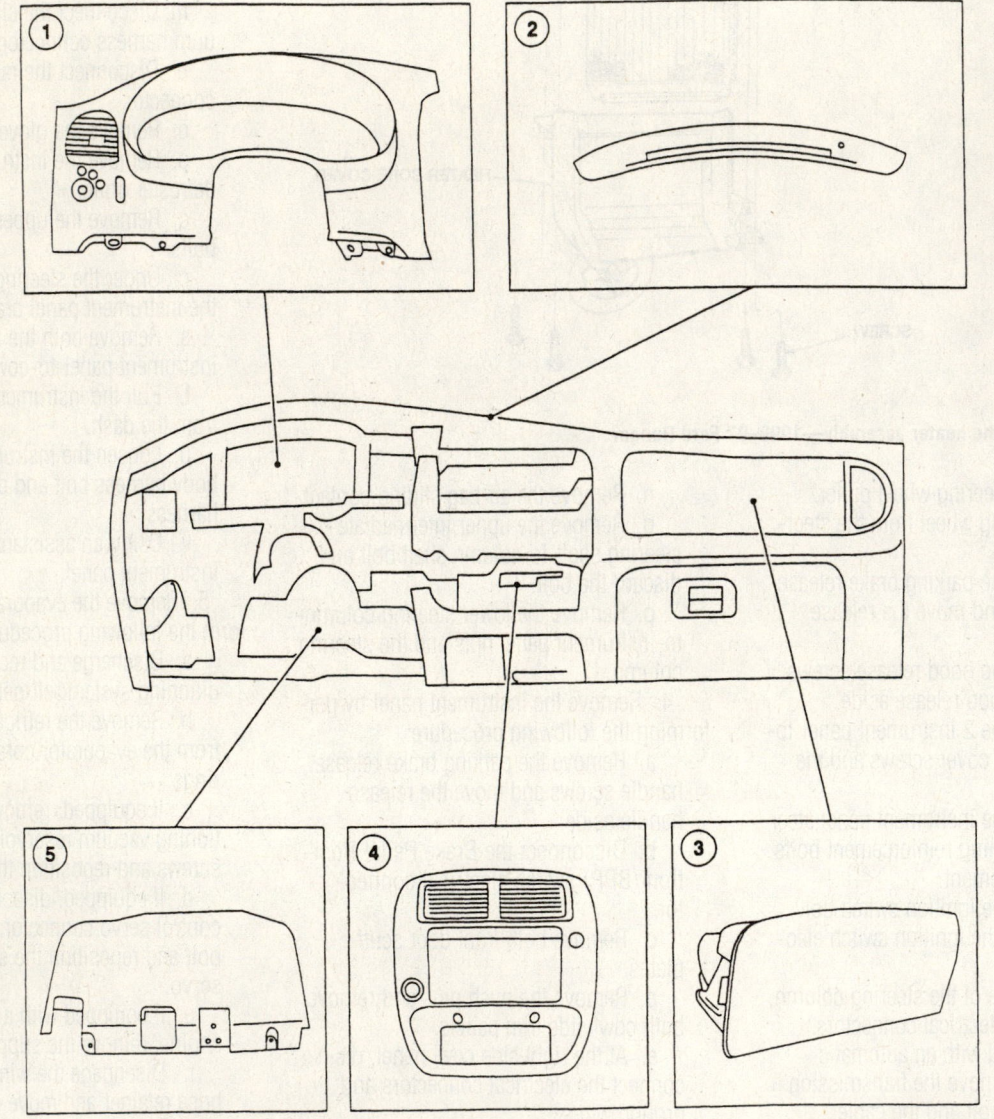

1 Instrument Panel Finish Panel
2 Instrument Panel Defroster
  Opening Grille Assembly
3 Passenger Side Air Bag Module
4 Instrument Panel Center Finish Panel
5 Instrument Panel Steering
  Column Cover

93113GL3

View of the instrument panel components—1998–00 Ford Ranger

g. Connect the vacuum hose and the retainer.

h. Engage the windshield washer hose retainer.

i. If equipped with a 3.0L or 4.0L engine, install the support bracket.

j. If equipped, install the speed control servo bolt and connect the connector.

k. If equipped, install the air conditioning vacuum reservoir tank and the bracket screws.

l. Using new O-rings, install the refrigerant lines to the evaporator core.

15. Install the instrument panel by performing the following procedure:

a. Using an assistant, install the instrument panel.

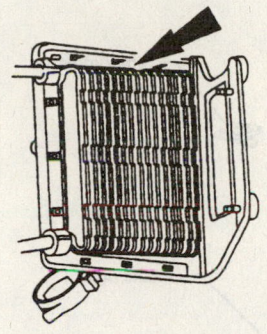

View of the evaporator core—1998–00 Ford Ranger

93113GL4

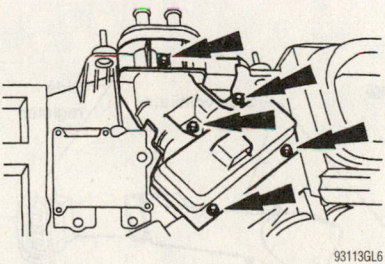

View of the heater core cover—1998–00 Ford Ranger

93113GL6

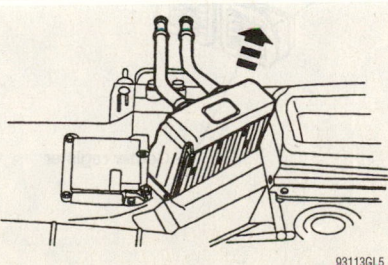

View of the heater core—1998–00 Ford Ranger

93113GL5

b. Connect the harness and tighten the instrument panel-to-body harness bolt.

c. Push the instrument panel toward the dash.

d. Install both the right and left instrument panel-to-cowl bolts.

e. Under the steering column, install the instrument panel brace bolt.

f. Install the upper instrument panel bolts.

g. Install the instrument panel defroster grille.

h. Install the glove compartment.

i. Connect the radio's antenna connector.

j. Connect the climate control vacuum harness connector.

k. Connect the blend door actuator's electrical connector.

l. Install the passenger's side air bag module, connect the electrical connector and torque the air bag module-to-instrument panel screws to 67–92 inch lbs. (7.6–10.4 Nm).

m. Connect the bulkhead electrical connector handle wiring harness.

n. In the engine compartment, connect the electrical connectors and tighten the bulkhead wiring harness bolts.

o. Connect the power distribution box to its bracket.

p. Install the instrument panel fuse door.

q. Install both sides windshield garnish moldings.

r. At the right side cowl panel, connect the electrical connectors and ground wires.

s. Install both cowl side trim panels and the push pins.

t. Install both front door scuff plates.

u. Connect the Brake Pedal Position (BPP) switch electrical connector.

v. Install the parking brake release handle and the release handle aside screws.

16. Install the steering column by performing the following procedure:

17. Install the steering column by performing the following procedure:

a. Install the lower steering column and the steering column-to-instrument panel nuts; then, torque the nuts to 10–13 ft. lbs. (13–17 Nm).

b. Using a new bolt, install the upper intermediate steering shaft-to-column shaft bolt and torque to 19–25 ft. lbs. (26–34 Nm).

c. Install the air bag sliding contact.

d. Connect the brake shift interlock solenoid electrical connector.

e. If equipped with an automatic transmission, connect the shift cable from the steering column shift tube lever and the steering column bracket.

f. If equipped with an automatic transmission, install the transmission range indicator cable and bolt.

g. At the base of the steering column, connect the electrical connectors.

h. Connect the ignition switch electrical connector and install the ignition switch bolt.

i. Install the instrument panel steering column opening reinforcement and the reinforcement bolts.

j. Install the instrument panel-to-steering column cover and the 2 cover screws.

k. Install the hood release and the hood release screws.

l. Install the parking brake release handle and the release handle screws.

m. Install the steering wheel to the steering column.

n. Install the steering wheel-to-steering column nut and torque the nut to 25–34 ft. lbs. (34–46 Nm).

o. At the both sides of the steering wheel, install the air bag module, connect the air bag electrical connector, install the steering wheel-to-air bag module screws and the cover plugs.

18. Refill the cooling system.

19. Connect the negative battery cable.

20. Evacuate and charge the air conditioning system.

21. Run the engine to normal operating temperatures; then, check the climate control operation and check for leaks.

Mercury Villager

REMOVAL & INSTALLATION

Front System

1. Disconnect the negative battery cable.

2. Drain the cooling system into a clean container for reuse.

3. Disconnect and plug the heater hoses at the bulkhead.

4. Remove the storage bin, then remove both side covers by the bin and the foot-lamp, if equipped.

5. Remove the control console bezel (1 screw in the center), then remove the ashtray assembly.

6. Remove the climate control console screws, pull the console rearward and detach the electrical connectors. Remove the 4 radio assembly screws and take the radio out of the vehicle.

7. Remove the floor duct and the right and left knee reinforcement plates. Remove the ABS control module.

8. The speed control module, keyless entry module (if equipped) and the passive restraint (air bag) module are all located behind the center console and can be removed after detaching the respective connectors and removing the retaining nuts or screws.

✳✳ WARNING

The control modules are very sensitive to static electricity and can be damaged if exposed to static or stray electrical impulses.

9. Remove the center air duct.

10. Remove the 2 ground wire bolts. Remove the U-bracket and the 2 console brackets.

11. Remove the glove box and lamp.

12. Remove the accelerator pedal and pedal stop.

13. Remove the floor air duct.

14. Remove the temperature blend sir door actuator and mode door actuator by removing the attaching bracket bolts and detaching the electrical connections.

15. Remove the center distribution duct.

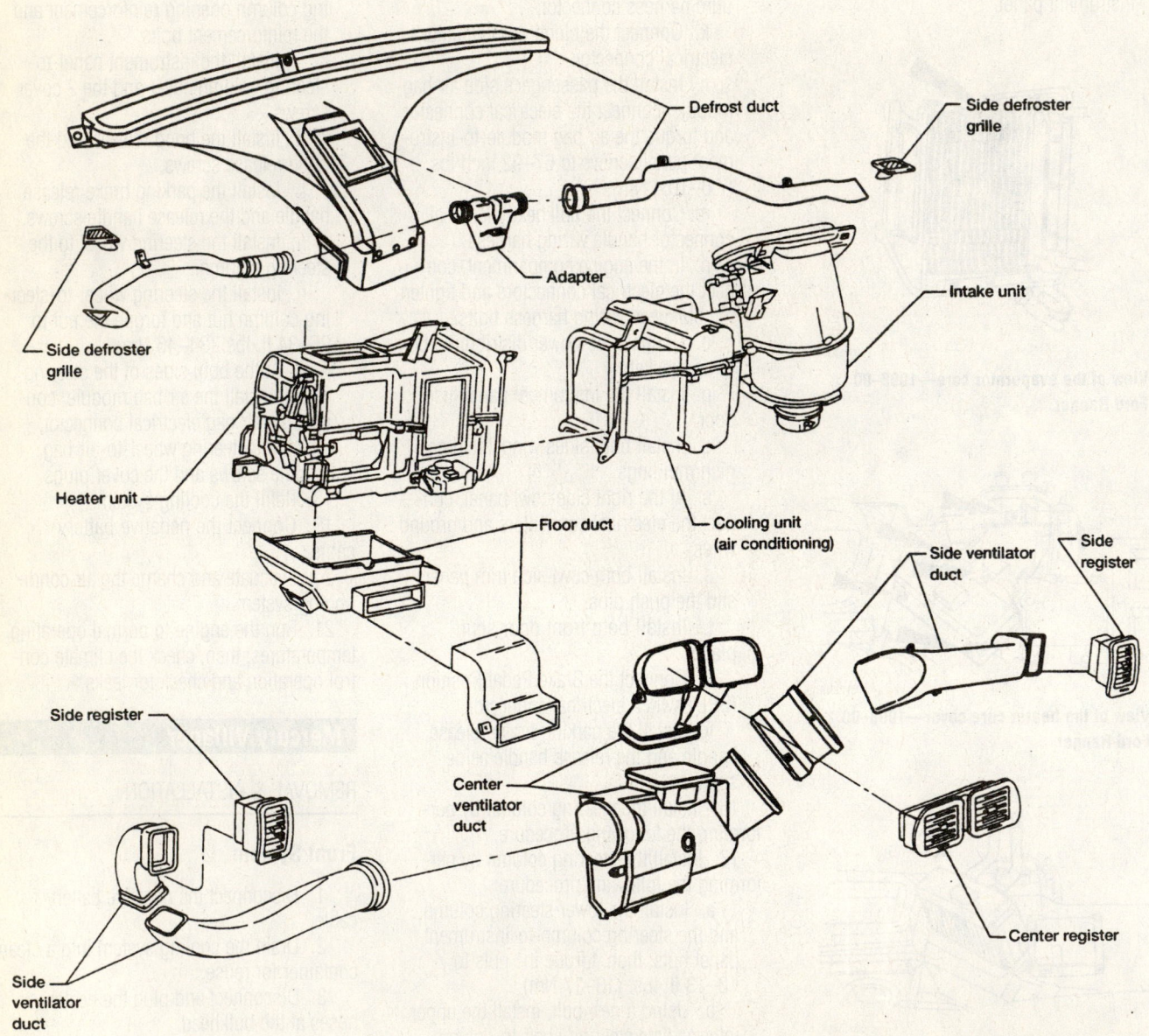

Exploded view the front heater/air conditioning assembly—1997–98 Mercury Villager

93113GC1

16. Remove the 4 evaporator/blower assembly screws, then the 4 heater assembly screws and remove the heater assembly.

17. Remove the heater pipe plate from the assembly.

18. Remove the heater core retainer, disengage the shut-off valve control rod and remove the heater core from the assembly.

To install:

19. Reassemble the heater core to the case, install the retainer and pipe plate.

20. Position the heater assembly in the vehicle and attach the 4 retaining screws.

21. Install the center distribution duct, the blend air and mode door actuators. Install the floor air duct.

22. Install the accelerator stop and pedal.

23. Install the glove box and lamp, then the center console and U-brackets.

24. Install the center air duct, the passive restraint, the keyless entry, the speed control and the ABS modules, as removed.

25. Reassemble the rest of the center console components.

26. Connect the heater hoses to the heater core.

27. Refill the cooling system.

28. Connect the negative battery cable.

29. Run the engine to normal operating temperatures; then, check the climate control operation and check for leaks.

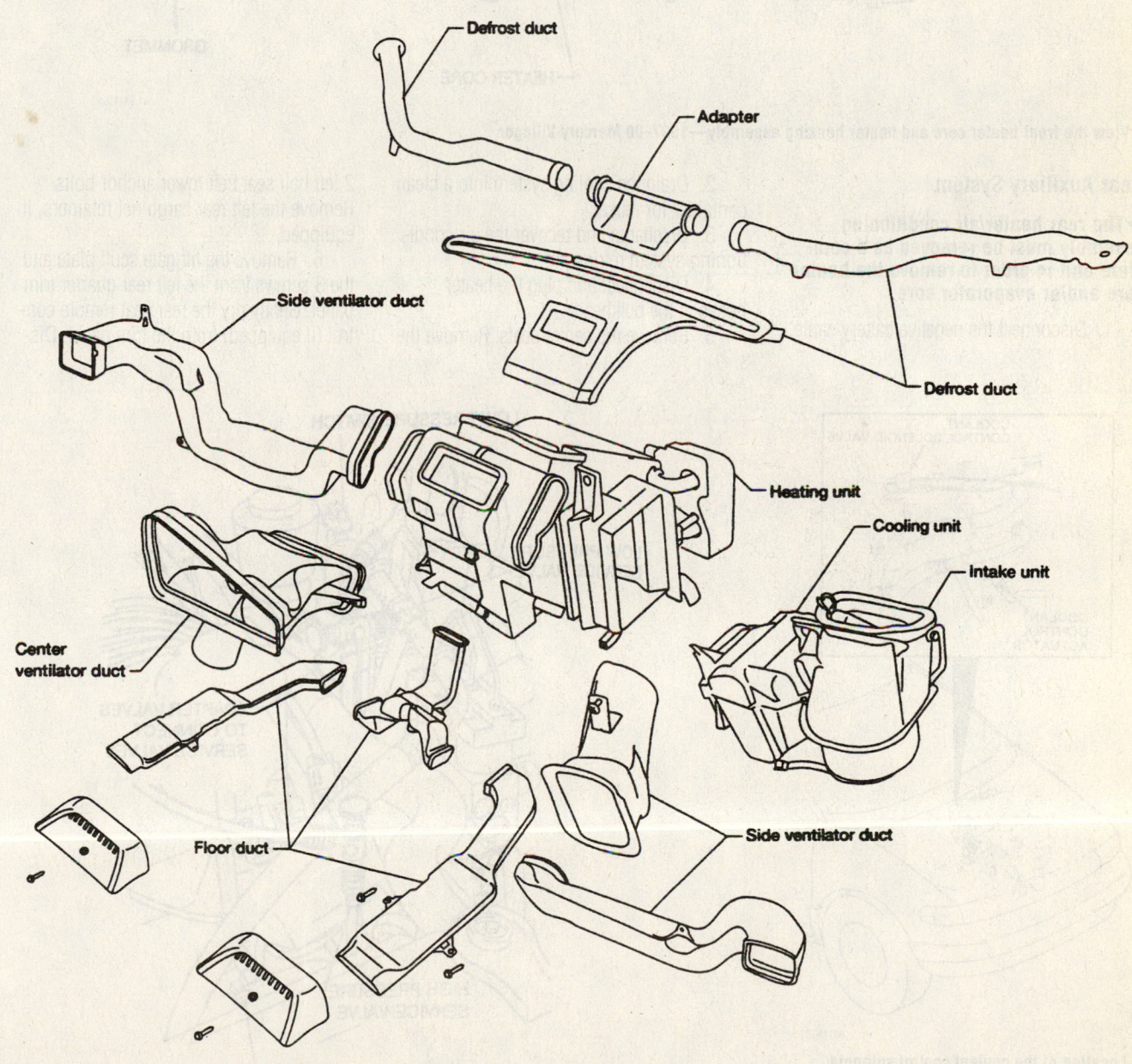

Exploded view the front heater/air conditioning assembly—1999–00 Mercury Villager

93113GC2

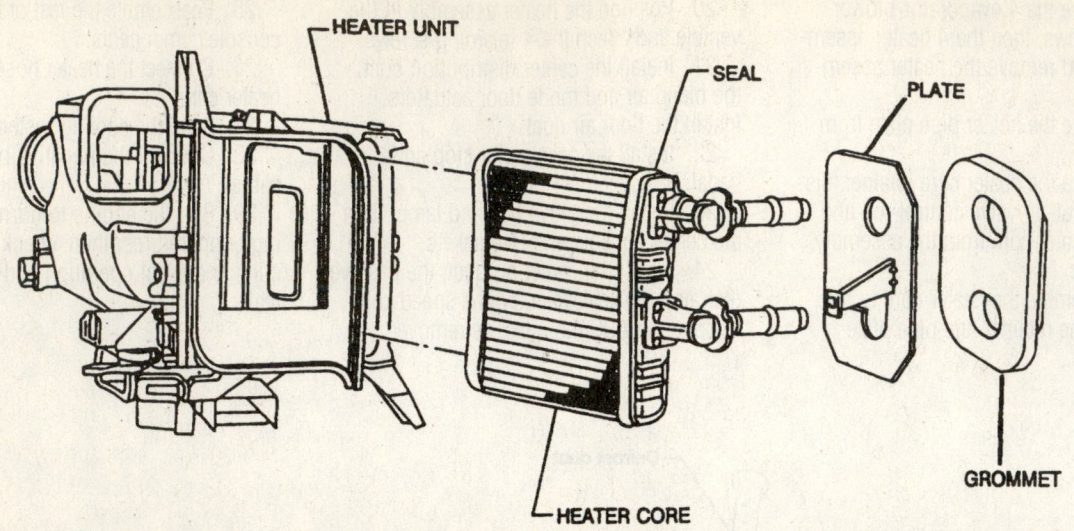

View the front heater core and heater housing assembly—1997–00 Mercury Villager

Rear Auxiliary System

➡The rear heater/air conditioning assembly must be removed as a complete unit in order to remove the heater core and/or evaporator core.

1. Disconnect the negative battery cable.

2. Drain the cooling system into a clean container for reuse.

3. Discharge and recover the air conditioning system refrigerant.

4. Disconnect and plug the heater hoses at the bulkhead.

5. Remove the center seats. Remove the 2 left half seat belt lower anchor bolts. Remove the left rear cargo net retainers, if equipped.

6. Remove the lift gate scuff plate and the 3 screws from the left rear quarter trim panel. Gently pry the rear seat remote control (if equipped) from the trim panel. Dis-

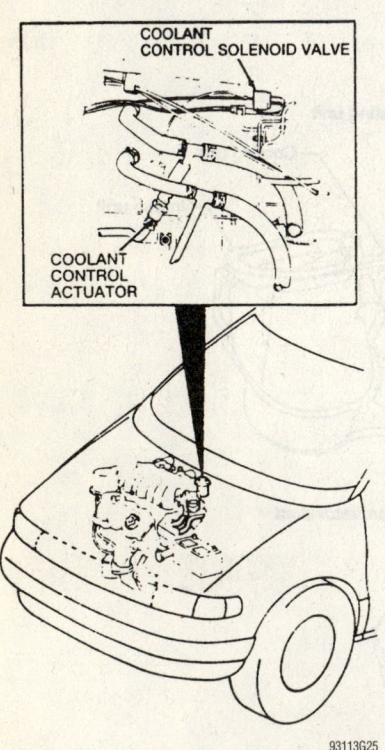

Location of the coolant control solenoid and coolant control actuator for the rear auxiliary heater/air conditioning system— 1997–98 Mercury Villager

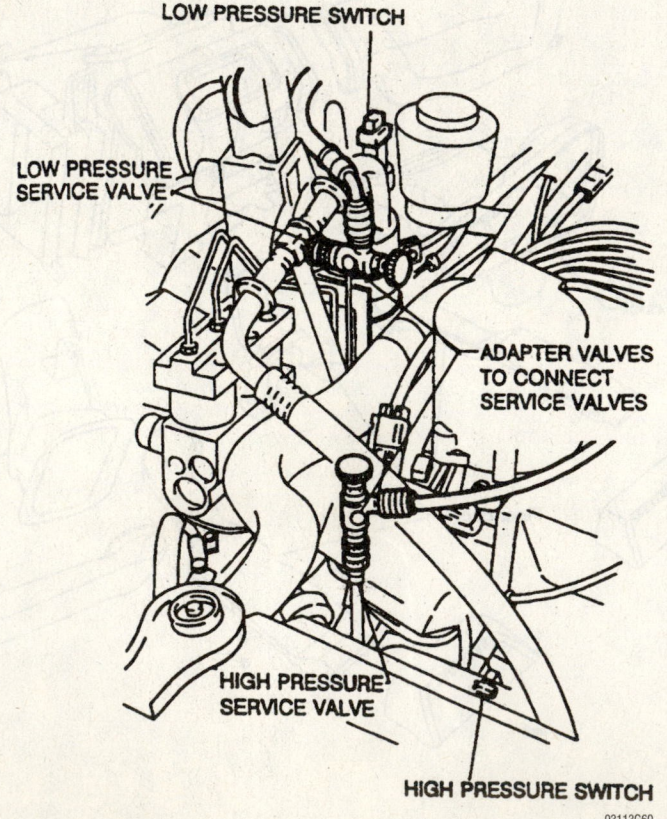

View the air conditioning service valve locations—1997–98 Mercury Villager

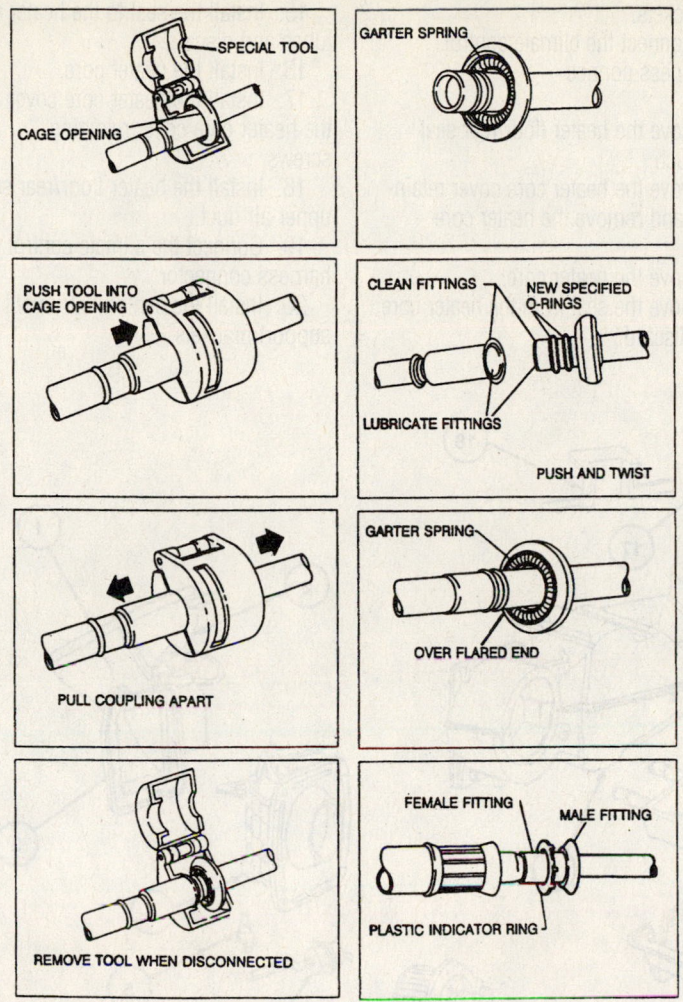

Spring lock coupling disconnect/connect procedures—1997–98 Mercury Villager

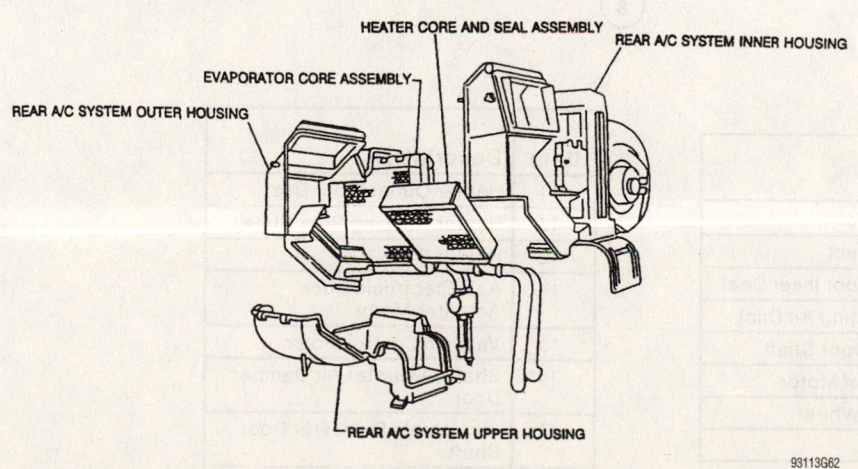

Exploded view the rear auxiliary heater/air conditioning system components—1997–98 Mercury Villager

connect the remote control wiring connector and remove the rear radio control panel. Pull the top of the trim panel away from the body.

7. Disconnect the rear climate control panel wiring, if equipped.

8. Release the left front lap belt guide from the left quarter trim panel and pass the belt through the trim panel. Remove the trim panel from the vehicle.

9. Remove the upper duct from the assembly (6 screws).

10. Disconnect the blower motor and resistor wiring. Detach the temperature blend and vent door actuator connectors.

11. Raise and safely support the vehicle. Use the spring lock coupling tool to disconnect and plug the refrigerant line connections from beneath the vehicle.

12. Lower the vehicle.

13. Remove the 4 heater/air conditioning assembly bolts and remove the assembly from the vehicle. Remove the heater core and/or evaporator core from the assembly.

To install:

14. Install the heater core and/or evaporator core into the assembly. Install the 4 retaining bolts.

15. Raise and safely support the vehicle.

16. Using new O-rings, reconnect the refrigerant lines to the evaporator.

17. Lower the vehicle. Connect all wiring connectors. Install the upper air duct with the 6 screws.

18. Reposition the trim panel and pass the lap seat belt through the panel slot.

19. Connect the rear climate control panel. Install the rear radio and rear remote control.

20. Reinstall the rest of the trim panel and components.

21. Refill the cooling system.

22. Connect the negative battery cable.

23. Evacuate and charge the air conditioning system.

24. Run the engine to normal operating temperatures; then, check the climate control operation and check for leaks.

Ford Windstar

REMOVAL & INSTALLATION

Front System

1. Disconnect the negative battery cable.

2. Drain the cooling system into a clean container for reuse.

Refer to the model specific sections for engine mechanical service procedures

3. Remove the cowl top vent panel for clearance.

4. Disconnect the heater hoses from the heater core inlet and outlet tubes in the engine compartment.

5. Remove the cassette box/center instrument support trim.

6. Pull out and remove the ashtray cup holder by depressing the service lever.

7. Remove the floor/rear seat lower air duct.

8. Disconnect the keyless entry wiring harness, if equipped.

9. Remove the center instrument panel support brackets.

10. Disconnect the climate control vacuum harness connector.

11. Remove the heater floor/rear seat upper air duct.

12. Remove the heater core cover retaining screws and remove the heater core cover.

13. Remove the heater core.

14. Remove the seal from the heater core tubes and discard.

To install:

15. Install the seal to the heater core tubes and discard.

16. Install the heater core.

17. Install the heater core cover and the heater core cover retaining screws.

18. Install the heater floor/rear seat upper air duct.

19. Connect the climate control vacuum harness connector.

20. Install the center instrument panel support brackets.

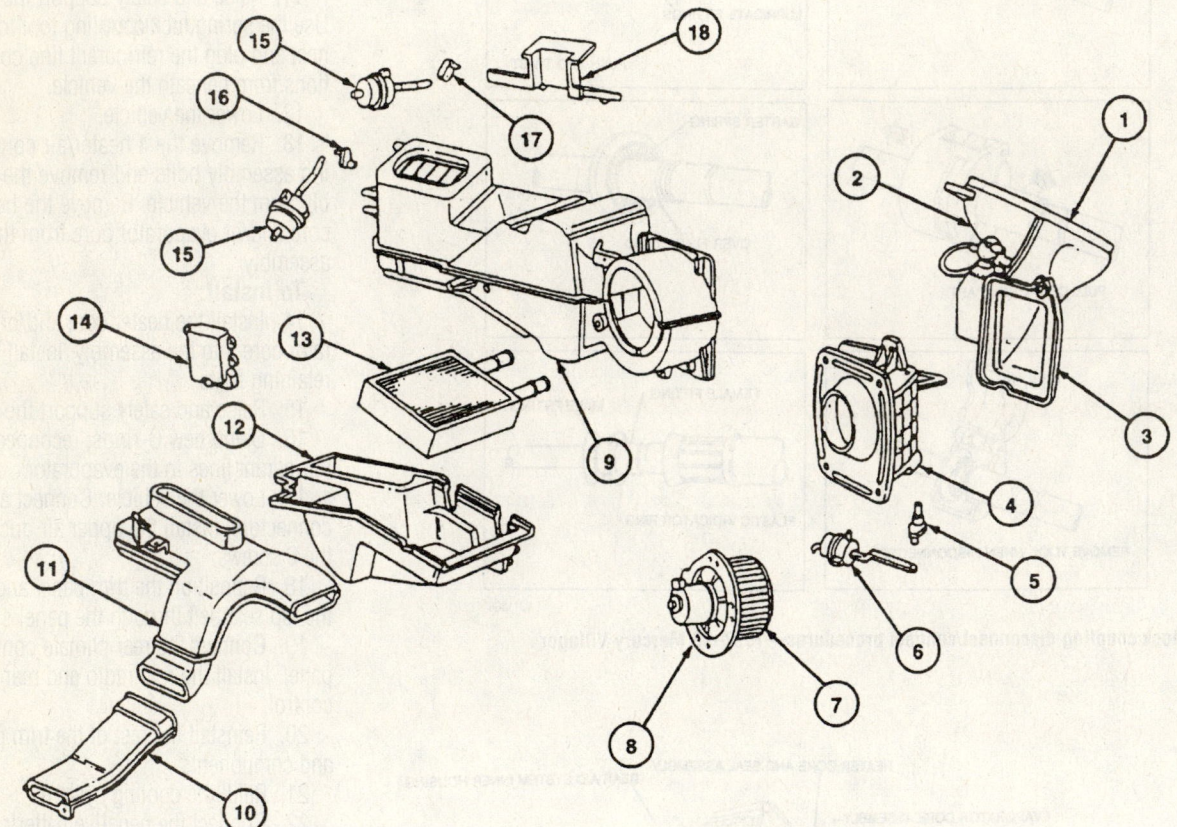

Item	Description
1	Outside Air Seal
2	A/C Air Inlet Duct
3	A/C Air Inlet Door Inner Seal
4	A/C Recirculating Air Duct
5	A/C Damper Door Shaft
6	Vacuum Control Motor
7	Blower Motor Wheel
8	Blower Motor
9	A/C Evaporator Housing
10	Rear Seat Airflow Duct

Item	Description
11	Heater Outlet Floor Duct
12	Heater Housing Core Plate
13	Heater Core
14	A/C Electronic Door Actuator Motor
15	Vacuum Control Motor
16	Shaft — Heater Air Damper Door
17	Windshield Defroster Door Shaft
18	Windshield Defroster Duct Connector

Front heater housing assembly—Ford Windstar

89696G06

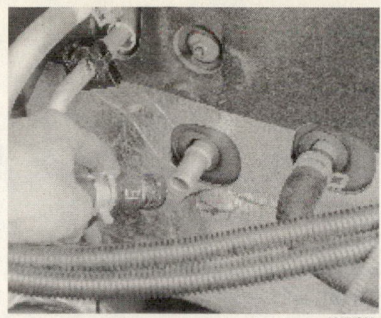

Be careful when removing the hoses from the heater core, as the tubes are easily damaged—Ford Windstar

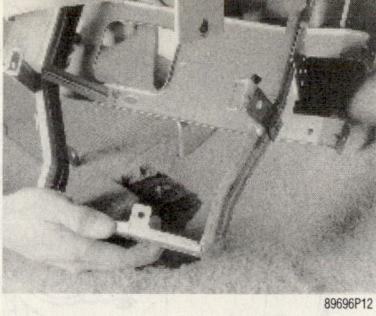

The instrument panel support bracket must be removed to lower the heater core—Ford Windstar

A foam liner is used to cushion the heater core—Ford Windstar

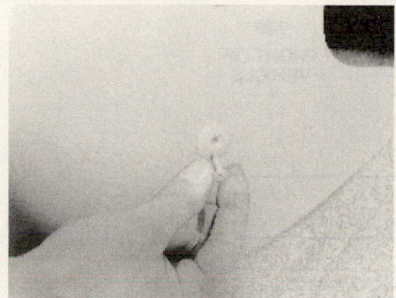

The center instrument panel is attached using special plastic screws—Ford Windstar

The heater outlet floor duct is attached to the bottom of the housing core—Ford Windstar

4. Raise and support the vehicle safely.

5. Place a drain pan under the heater water hose connections for the rear heater assembly.

6. Drain and recycle the engine coolant from the auxiliary heater core and hoses.

7. Disconnect the 2 air conditioning spring lock couplings using a quick disconnect coupling tool.

8. Lower the vehicle.

9. Remove all rear passenger's seating.

10. Remove the 3 push pin retainers from the lower edge of the auxiliary heater and air conditioning service cover.

11. Lift the service cover outward and upward to remove.

12. Label and disconnect the electrical harnesses.

13. Label and disconnect the vacuum lines.

14. Remove the body side trim panels.

15. Disconnect and plug all air conditioning refrigerant lines.

➡ **It is extremely important that the air conditioning lines be plugged to prevent the entry of dirt or moisture.**

16. Remove the lower air conditioning recirculation air duct and heater extension air duct.

17. Remove the auxiliary heater and air conditioning assembly.

18. Remove the housing cover screws and the cover.

19. Remove the heater core and the heater core case seal.

To install:

20. Install the heater core and the heater core case seal.

21. Install the housing cover and screws.

22. Position the auxiliary heater and air conditioning assembly in the vehicle. Guide the heater water hoses through the floor

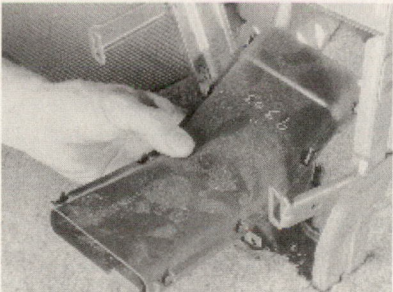

The rear seat airflow duct carries air to the rear of the passenger compartment—Ford Windstar

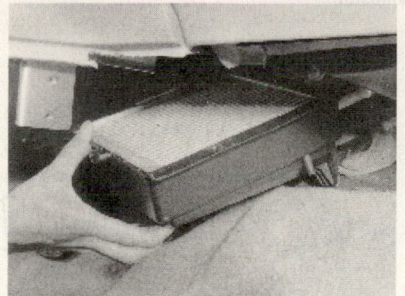

The heater core is located in a box at the bottom of the housing core—Ford Windstar

21. Connect the keyless entry wiring harness, if equipped.

22. Install the floor/rear seat lower air duct.

23. Install the ashtray cup holder by depressing the service lever.

24. Install the cassette box/center instrument support trim.

25. Connect the heater hoses to the heater core inlet and outlet tubes in the engine compartment.

26. Install the cowl top vent panel for clearance.

27. Refill the cooling system.

28. Connect the negative battery cable.

29. Run the engine to normal operating temperatures; then, check the climate control operation and check for leaks.

Rear Auxiliary System

1. Disconnect the negative battery cable.

2. Drain the cooling system into a clean container for reuse.

3. Discharge and recover the rear auxiliary air conditioning refrigerant.

Refer to the model specific sections for cooling system service procedures

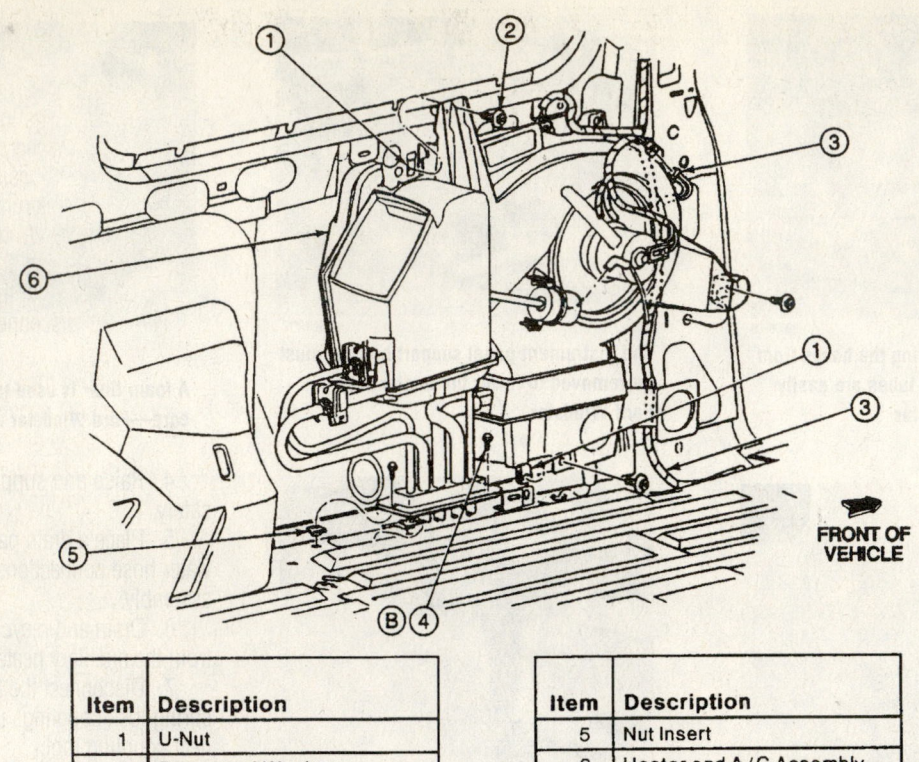

Item	Description
1	U-Nut
2	Screw and Washer Assembly
3	Body Main Wiring
4	Screw and Washer Assembly

Item	Description
5	Nut Insert
6	Heater and A/C Assembly

89696G04

Rear heater and air conditioning assembly—Ford Windstar

grommet. Tighten the retaining screws to 16–23 inch lbs. (2–3 Nm).

23. Connect all air conditioning refrigerant lines.

24. Install the lower air conditioning recirculation air duct and heater extension air duct. Tighten the retaining screws to 16–23 inch lbs. (2–3 Nm).

25. Install the body side trim panels.

26. Connect the vacuum lines.

27. Connect the electrical harnesses.

28. Install the auxiliary heater and air conditioning service cover and secure with 3 push pin retainers.

29. Install all rear passenger's seating.

30. Raise and support the vehicle safely.

31. Connect the heater water hoses to the heater core tubes.

32. Lower the vehicle.

33. Refill the cooling system.

34. Connect the negative battery cable.

35. Evacuate and charge the rear auxiliary air conditioning refrigerant.

36. Run the engine to normal operating temperatures; then, check the climate control operation and check for leaks.

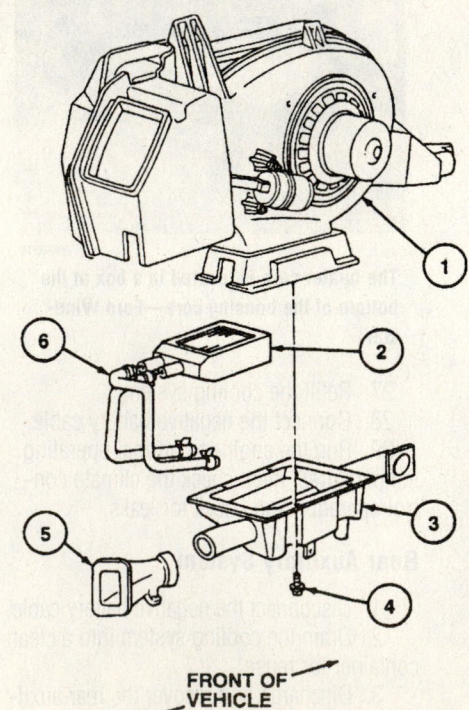

Item	Description
1	A/C Evaporator Housing Assy
2	Heater Core
3	Heater Housing Core Plate
4	Screw
5	Rear Seat Airflow Duct
6	Heater Water Hose

89696G05

Rear heater housing assembly—Ford Windstar

CHEVY/GEO

Tracker

REMOVAL & INSTALLATION

1. Disconnect the negative battery cable.

2. Disable the SIR by performing the following procedure:

a. From the fuse box, located near the base of the steering column, remove the AIR BAG fuse.

b. Remove the steering wheel side cap, disconnect the Connector Positive Assurance (CPA) and the yellow 2-way driver's inflator module connectors.

c. Pull the instrument panel compartment out by pushing the right-side and left-side stoppers (located on both sides) inward.

d. Disconnect the CPA and the yellow 4-way passenger's inflator module connectors.

➡ **With the AIR BAG fuse removed and the ignition switch turned ON, the AIR BAG warning light will be ON; this is normal operation and does not indicate a SIR system malfunction.**

3. Drain the cooling system into a clean container for reuse.

4. Remove the instrument panel as follows:

a. Remove the center console.

b. Remove the lower steering column cover by loosening the mounting screws.

c. Remove the glove box.

d. Detach the wiring harness connectors from the heater unit and the blower motor assembly.

e. Detach the wiring harness connectors from the ignition switch, contact coil and combination switch.

f. Open the hood.

g. Remove the steering column shaft joint bolt, then separate the steering column shaft from the lower steering shaft.

h. Loosen all of the steering column-to-firewall and instrument panel brace bolts.

i. If equipped, remove the shift (key) interlock cable screw. Disconnect the cable from the ignition switch.

j. Remove the steering column from the vehicle.

✳✳ **WARNING**

Do not rest the steering column assembly on the steering wheel with the air bag module facing downward and the column vertical—personal injury may be the result.

k. Disconnect the speedometer cable from the speedometer, then remove the instrument cluster.

l. Remove the hood latch handle.

m. Remove the radio, the heater control panel and the heater control cables from the instrument panel.

n. Disconnect and label all wiring harness connectors from the instrument panel.

o. Remove the instrument panel mounting screws and bolts. Remove the side cover plates and the instrument panel mounting fasteners from the side of the assembly. Then, remove the upper cover plates and loosen the remaining mounting fasteners

p. Have an assistant help you carefully lift the instrument panel up and out of the vehicle. When separating the instrument panel from the firewall, ensure that all of the cables, wires and hoses are disconnected form the instrument panel.

5. Remove the 2 bolts and the right-side instrument panel center support.

6. If equipped with air conditioning, remove the evaporator.

7. Remove the 2 screws securing the SIR harness clip on the Sensing and Diagnostic Module (SDM) bracket.

8. Disconnect the SDM electrical connector.

9. Remove the 4 screws and the SDM bracket from the vehicle.

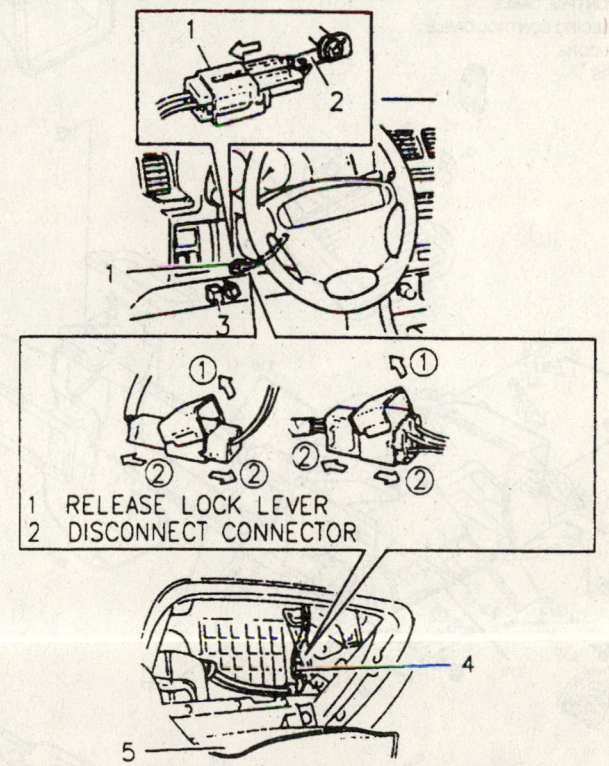

1 RELEASE LOCK LEVER
2 DISCONNECT CONNECTOR

1 YELLOW 2-WAY SIR CONNECTOR (DRIVER)
2 CONNECTOR POSITION ASSURANCE (CPA)
3 AIR BAG FUSE
4 YELLOW 4-WAY SIR CONNECTOR (PASSENGER)
5 GLOVE BOX

93113G90

Disabling the air bag system—Tracker

10. Remove the speedometer cable and antenna cable (if equipped) from the heater case.

11. Remove the floor duct from the heater case.

12. If equipped with air conditioning, disconnect the electrical jumper harness for the air conditioning amplifier.

13. Remove the relay bracket screws and the relay bracket.

14. From the engine compartment, remove the 2 heater assembly-to-chassis nuts and the 2 bolts.

15. Remove the heater case from the vehicle.

16. Remove the dampers and linkages from the heater case.

17. Remove the heater core bracket screw and the bracket.

18. Remove the heater core from the heater case.

To install:

19. Install the heater core to the heater case.

20. Install the heater core bracket and the bracket screw.

21. Install the dampers and linkages to the heater case.

22. Install the heater case to the vehicle.

23. In the engine compartment, install the 2 heater assembly-to-chassis nuts and the 2 bolts. Torque the nuts/bolts to 89 inch lbs. (10 Nm).

24. Install the relay bracket and the relay bracket screws.

25. If equipped with air conditioning, connect the electrical jumper harness for the air conditioning amplifier.

26. Install the floor duct to the heater case.

27. Install the speedometer cable and antenna cable (if equipped) to the heater case.

28. Install the SDM bracket and the 4 screws to the vehicle. Torque the screws to 49 inch lbs. (5.5 Nm).

29. Connect the SDM electrical connector.

30. Install the 2 screws securing the SIR harness clip on the Sensing and Diagnostic Module (SDM) bracket. Torque the screws to 49 inch lbs. (5.5 Nm)

31. If equipped with air conditioning, install the evaporator.

32. Install the 2 bolts and the right-side instrument panel center support.

33. Install the instrument panel as follows:

a. Have an assistant help you position the instrument panel in the vehicle. When installing the instrument panel on the firewall, ensure that all of the cables, wires and hoses are routed properly.

b. Install and tighten the instrument panel mounting screws and bolts.

c. Reattach all wiring harness connectors to the instrument panel.

d. Install the radio, the heater control panel and the heater control cables. Be sure to adjust the heater control cables.

e. Install the hood latch handle.

f. Install the instrument cluster, then connect the cable to the speedometer.

g. Install the steering column in the vehicle.

h. If equipped, connect the cable from the ignition switch, then install the shift (key) interlock cable screw.

i. Install and tighten all of the steering column-to-firewall and instrument panel brace bolts to 221 inch lbs. (25 Nm).

j. Install and tighten the steering column shaft joint bolt to 221 inch lbs. (25 Nm).

k. Reattach the wiring harness connectors to the ignition switch, contact coil and combination switch.

l. Reattach the wiring harness connectors to the heater unit and the blower motor assembly.

m. Install the glove box.

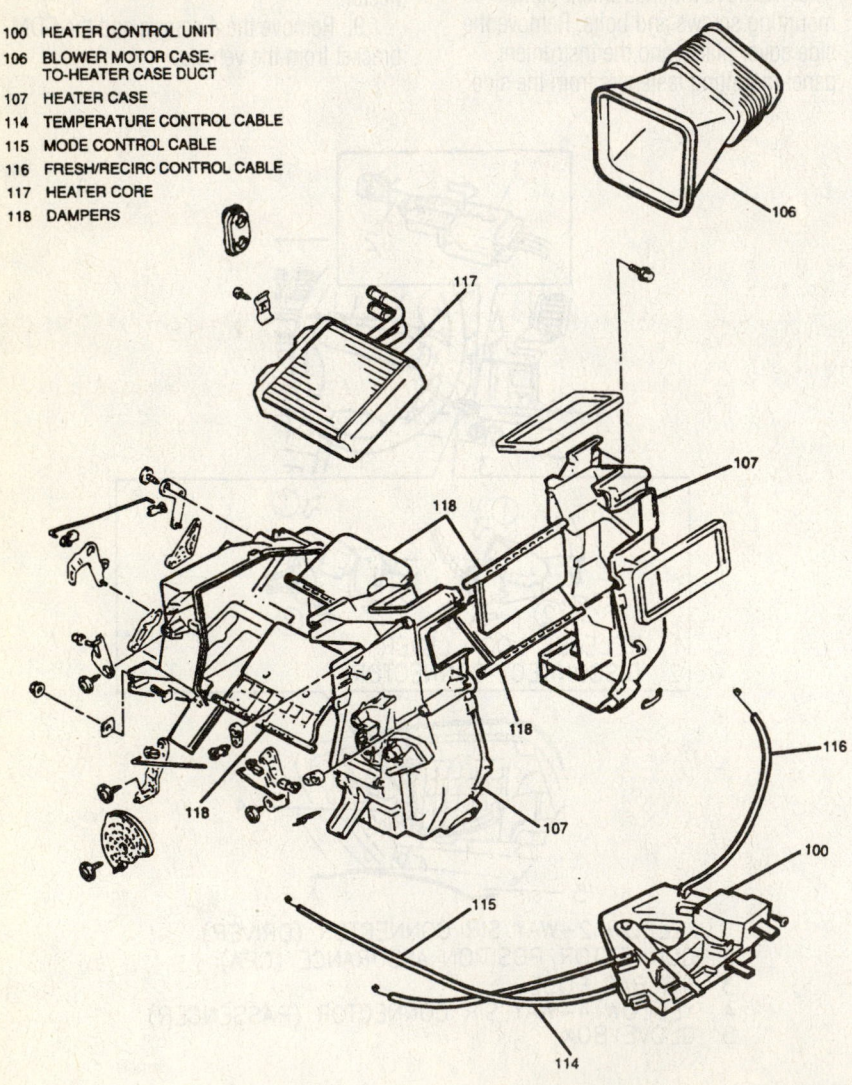

100	HEATER CONTROL UNIT
106	BLOWER MOTOR CASE-TO-HEATER CASE DUCT
107	HEATER CASE
114	TEMPERATURE CONTROL CABLE
115	MODE CONTROL CABLE
116	FRESH/RECIRC CONTROL CABLE
117	HEATER CORE
118	DAMPERS

93113G89

Exploded view of the heater case assembly and related components—Tracker

n. Install the lower steering column cover.

o. Install the center console.

34. Refill the cooling system.

35. Enable the SIR by performing the following procedure:

a. Turn the ignition switch to LOCK and remove the key.

b. Connect the Connector Positive Assurance (CPA) and the yellow 4-way passenger's inflator module connectors.

c. Close the instrument panel compartment.

d. Connect the Connector Positive Assurance (CPA) and the yellow 2-way driver Inflator module connectors and install the steering wheel side cap.

e. At the fuse box, located near the base of the steering column, install the AIR BAG fuse.

36. Connect the negative battery cable.

37. Run the engine to normal operating temperatures; then, check the climate control operation and check for leaks.

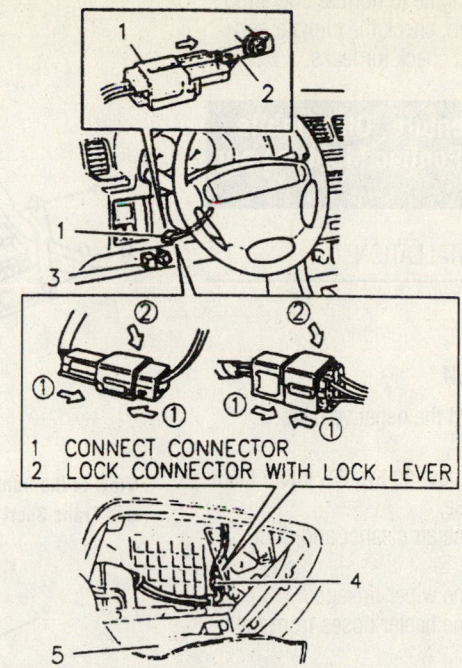

1 YELLOW 2-WAY SIR CONNECTOR (DRIVER)
2 CONNECTOR POSITION ASSURANCE (CPA)
3 AIR BAG-IG FUSE
4 YELLOW 4-WAY SIR CONNECTOR (PASSENGER)
5 GLOVE BOX

93113G91

Enabling the air bag system—Tracker

GENERAL MOTORS

Chevy Astro and GMC Safari

REMOVAL & INSTALLATION

1997–00

FRONT SYSTEM

1. Disconnect the negative battery cable.

2. Drain the engine cooling system into a clean container for reuse.

3. Disconnect the heater hoses from the heater core.

4. Remove the heater core cover-to-heater assembly screws and the cover.

5. Remove the heater core-to-heater assembly strap screws and the straps.

6. Remove the heater core.

To install:

7. Install the heater core.

8. Install the heater core straps and the straps-to-heater assembly screws, then tighten the screws to 18 inch lbs. (2 Nm).

9. Install the heater core cover and the cover-to-heater assembly screws, then tighten the screws to 18 inch lbs. (2 Nm).

10. Connect the heater hoses to the heater core.

11. Refill the cooling system.

12. Connect the negative battery cable.

13. Run the engine to normal operating temperatures; then, check the climate control operation and check for leaks.

REAR AUXILIARY SYSTEM

1. Disconnect the negative battery cable.

2. Drain the engine cooling system into a clean container for reuse.

3. Remove the body side front lower interior trim panel.

4. Remove the clamps from the rear auxiliary heater hoses.

5. Disconnect the heater hoses from the rear auxiliary heater case.

6. From the right side of the heater core, remove the screws and band clamp.

7. From the left side of the heater core, remove the screw and band clamp.

→Place a cloth on the floor to catch any coolant that may spill from the heater core.

8. Remove the heater core from the rear auxiliary case assembly.

9. Remove the seals from the heater core.

To install:

10. Install new seals to the heater core.

11. Install the heater core to the rear auxiliary case assembly.

12. To the left side of the heater core, install the screw and band clamp, then tighten to 18 inch lbs. (2 Nm).

13. To the right side of the heater core, install the screws and band clamp, then tighten to 18 inch lbs. (2 Nm).

14. Connect the heater hoses to the rear auxiliary heater case.

15. Install the clamps to the rear auxiliary heater hoses.

16. Install the body side front lower interior trim panel.

17. Refill the engine cooling system.

18. Connect the negative battery cable.

19. Run the engine to normal operating temperatures; then, check the climate control operation and check for leaks.

Chevrolet Venture, Oldsmobile Silhouette, Pontiac Montana and Trans Sport

REMOVAL & INSTALLATION

1997–00

FRONT SYSTEM

1. Disconnect the negative battery cable.
2. Drain the cooling system into a clean container for reuse.
3. Remove the air cleaner and duct assembly.
4. Remove the wiper linkage.
5. Remove the heater hoses from the heater core.
6. Remove the lower center console.
7. Remove both instrument panel insulators.
8. Remove the heater outlet module screws.
9. Remove the heater cover.
10. Remove the heater core mounting clip and line clamp screws.
11. Remove the heater core.

To install:

12. Install the heater core.
13. Install the heater core mounting clip and line clamp screws.
14. Install the heater cover.
15. Install the heater outlet module screws.
16. Install both instrument panel insulators.
17. Install the lower center console.
18. Install the heater hoses from the heater core.
19. Install the wiper linkage.
20. Install the air cleaner and duct assembly.
21. Refill the cooling system.
22. Connect the negative battery cable.
23. Run the engine to normal operating temperatures; then, check the climate control operation and check for leaks.

REAR AUXILIARY SYSTEM

1. Disconnect the negative battery cable.

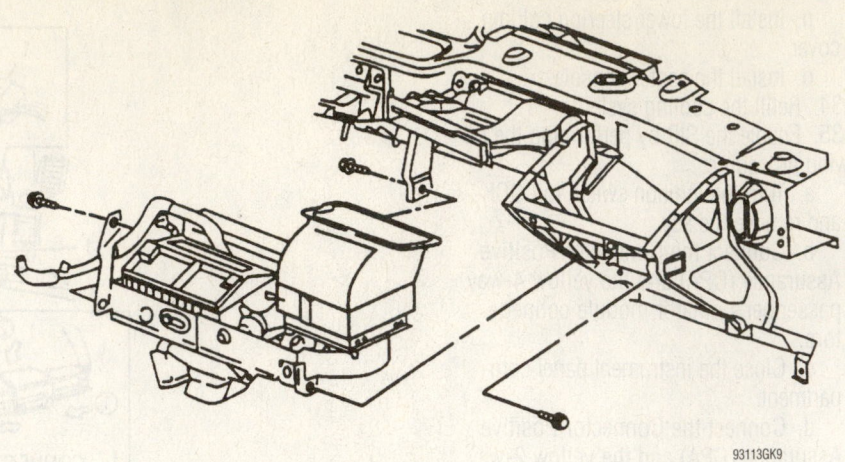

View of the front heater assembly—Chevrolet Venture, Oldsmobile Silhouette, Pontiac Montana and Trans Sport

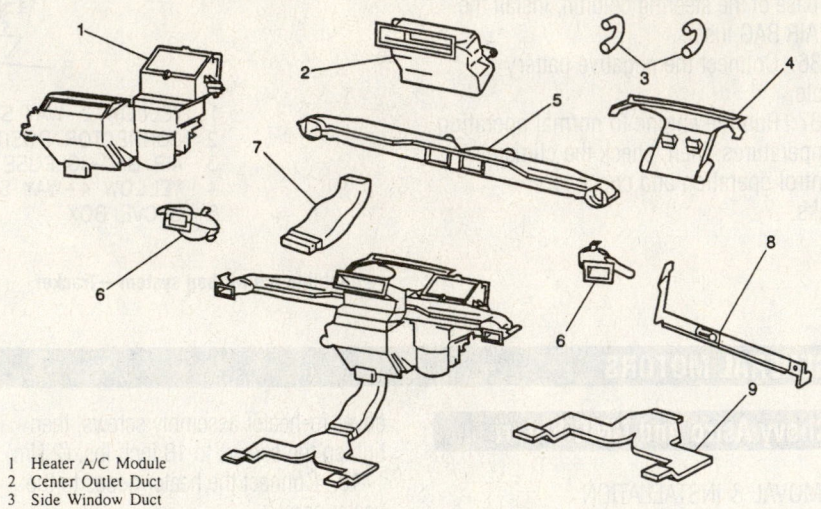

1 Heater A/C Module
2 Center Outlet Duct
3 Side Window Duct
4 Side Window Nozzle
5 Main Duct
6 Side Window Outlet Duct
7 Floor Duct
8 Module Bracket
9 Lower Floor Duct

Exploded view of the front heater ventilation system—Chevrolet Venture, Oldsmobile Silhouette, Pontiac Montana and Trans Sport

2. Drain the cooling system into a clean container for reuse.
3. Remove the left rear side quarter trim.
4. Remove the rear heater hoses from the rear heater core.
5. Remove the bracket bolt securing the hoses to the heater core.
6. Release the rear heater core-to-rear heater housing tabs.
7. Remove the heater core.

To install:

8. Install the heater core.
9. Connect the rear heater core-to-rear heater housing tabs.
10. Install the bracket bolt securing the hoses to the heater core.
11. Install the rear heater hoses from the rear heater core.
12. Install the left rear side quarter trim.
13. Refill the cooling system.
14. Connect the negative battery cable.

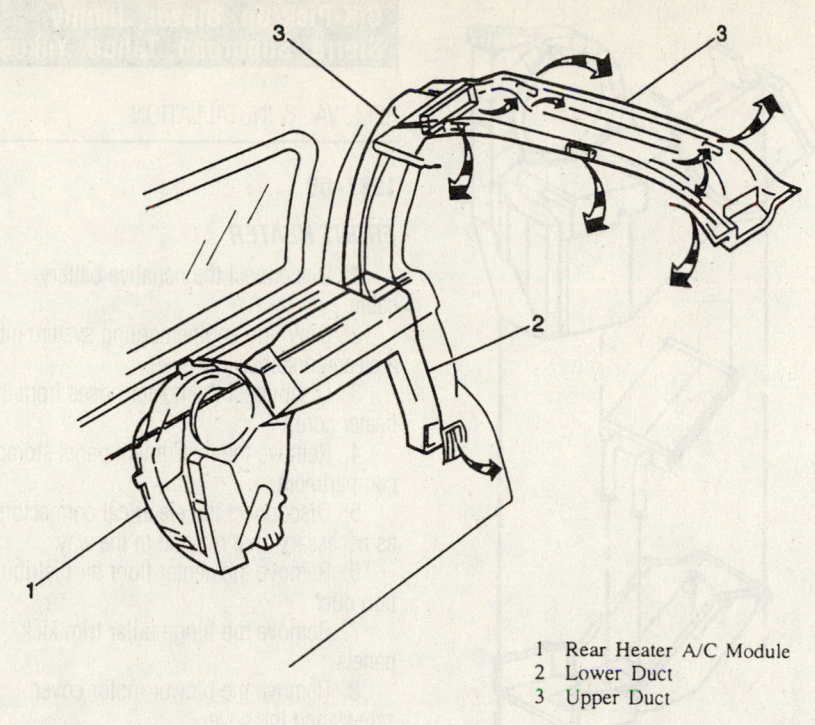

1 Rear Heater A/C Module
2 Lower Duct
3 Upper Duct

93113GL1

View of the rear auxiliary heater assembly ventilation system—Chevrolet Venture, Oldsmobile Silhouette, Pontiac Montana and Trans Sport

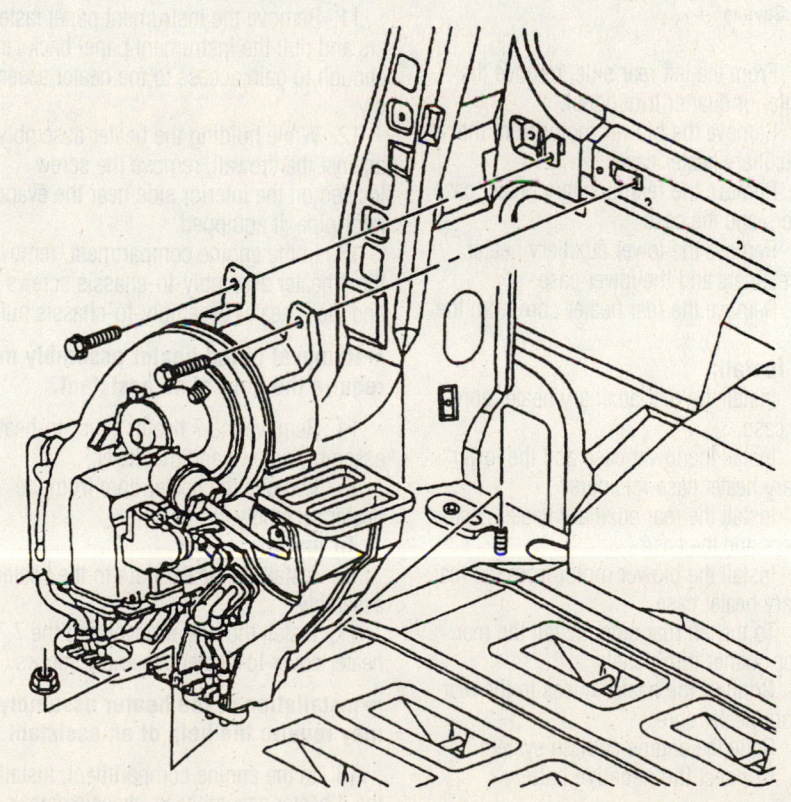

93113GL2

View of the rear auxiliary heater assembly—Chevrolet Venture, Oldsmobile Silhouette, Pontiac Montana and Trans Sport

G-Series Van, Express and Savana

REMOVAL & INSTALLATION

1997–00

FRONT HEATER

1. Disconnect the negative battery cable.
2. Drain the engine cooling system into a clean container for reuse.
3. Disconnect the heater hoses from the heater core.
4. Discharge and recover the air conditioning system refrigerant.
5. Remove the surge tank (diesel) or the coolant recovery reservoir (except diesel).
6. Remove the positive battery cable, the battery hold-down and the battery.
7. Disconnect the refrigeration lines from the air conditioning accumulator and discard the gaskets.
8. Remove the air conditioning accumulator.
9. From the right side, remove the lower right kick panel and the knee bolster.
10. Remove the lower outer floor air outlet duct.
11. Remove the heater case screws.
12. Carefully open the heater core access door.
13. Remove the heater core-to-heater case retainers and the heater core.

To install:

14. Install the heater core and the heater core-to-heater case retainers.
15. Carefully, close the heater core access door.
16. Install the heater case screws.
17. Install the lower outer floor air outlet duct.

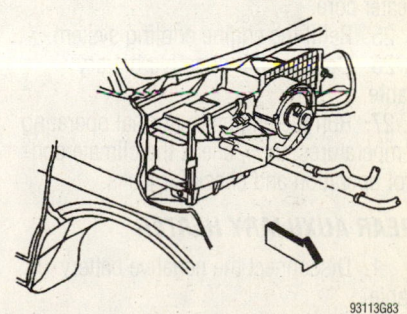

93113G83

Underhood view of the heater assembly—Chevy/GMC Express and Savana

Refer to the model specific sections for engine mechanical service procedures

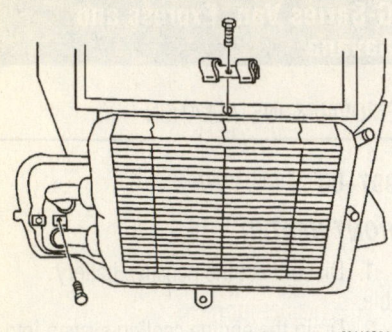

**View of the heater case screws—
Chevy/GMC Express and Savana**

93113G84

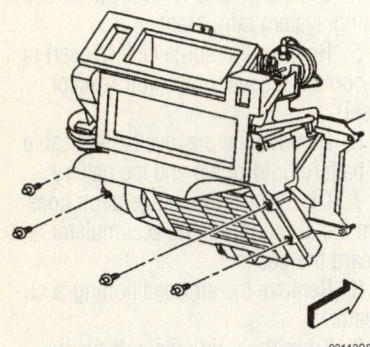

**View of the heater core and retainers—
Chevy/GMC Express and Savana**

93113G85

18. To the right side, install the knee bolster and the lower right kick panel.

19. Install the air conditioning accumulator.

20. Using new gaskets, connect the refrigeration lines to the air conditioning accumulator.

21. Install the battery, the battery hold-down and the positive battery cable.

22. Install the surge tank (diesel) or the coolant recovery reservoir (except diesel).

23. Evacuate and charge the air conditioning system.

24. Connect the heater hoses to the heater core.

25. Refill the engine cooling system.

26. Connect the negative battery cable.

27. Run the engine to normal operating temperatures; then, check the climate control operation and check for leaks.

REAR AUXILIARY HEATER

1. Disconnect the negative battery cable.

2. Drain the engine cooling system into a clean container for reuse.

3. Disconnect the heater hoses from the rear auxiliary heater core.

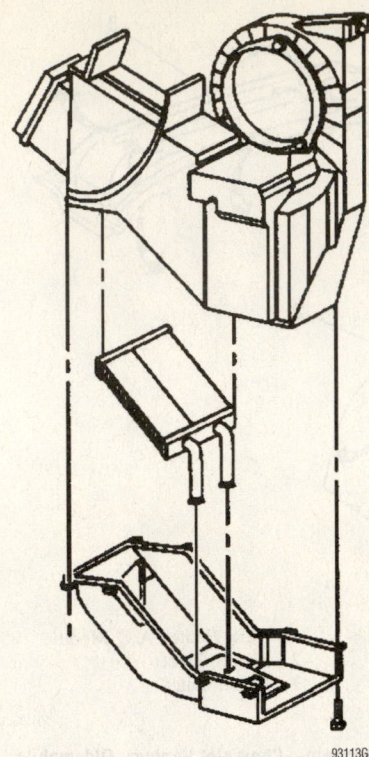

93113G86

**View of the rear auxiliary heater core,
case and retainers—Chevy/GMC Express
and Savana**

4. From the left rear side, remove the rear interior quarter trim panel.

5. Remove the blower motor from the rear auxiliary heater case.

6. Remove the rear auxiliary heater case retainers and the case.

7. Remove the lower auxiliary heater case retainers and the lower case.

8. Remove the rear heater core from the case.

To install:

9. Install the rear auxiliary heater core to the case.

10. Install the lower case and the lower auxiliary heater case retainers.

11. Install the rear auxiliary heater case retainers and the case.

12. Install the blower motor from the rear auxiliary heater case.

13. To the left rear side, install the rear interior quarter trim panel.

14. Connect the heater hoses to the rear auxiliary heater core.

15. Refill the engine cooling system.

16. Connect the negative battery cable.

C/K-Pick-Up, Blazer, Jimmy, Sierra, Suburban, Tahoe, Yukon

REMOVAL & INSTALLATION

1997–00

FRONT HEATER

1. Disconnect the negative battery cable.

2. Drain the engine cooling system into a clean container for reuse.

3. Disconnect the heater hoses from the heater core.

4. Remove the instrument panel storage compartment.

5. Disconnect the electrical connectors, as necessary, that may be in the way.

6. Remove the center floor air distribution duct.

7. Remove the hinge pillar trim kick panels.

8. Remove the blower motor cover screws and the cover.

9. Remove the blower motor screws and the blower motor.

10. Remove the steering wheel and the steering column (standard & tilt).

11. Remove the instrument panel fasteners and pull the instrument panel back far enough to gain access to the heater assembly.

12. While holding the heater assembly against the firewall, remove the screw located on the interior side near the evaporator pipe, if equipped.

13. In the engine compartment, remove the 4 heater assembly-to-chassis screws and the 2 heater assembly-to-chassis nuts.

➡**Removal of the heater assembly may require the help of an assistant.**

14. Remove the 7 heater cover-to-heater assembly screws and the cover.

15. Remove the heater core from the heater assembly.

To install:

16. Install the heater core to the heater assembly.

17. Install the heater cover and the 7 heater cover-to-heater assembly screws.

➡**Installation of the heater assembly may require the help of an assistant.**

18. In the engine compartment, install the 4 heater assembly-to-chassis screws and the 2 heater assembly-to-chassis nuts. Torque the screws to 17 inch lbs. (1.9 Nm) and the nuts to 25 inch lbs. (2.8 Nm).

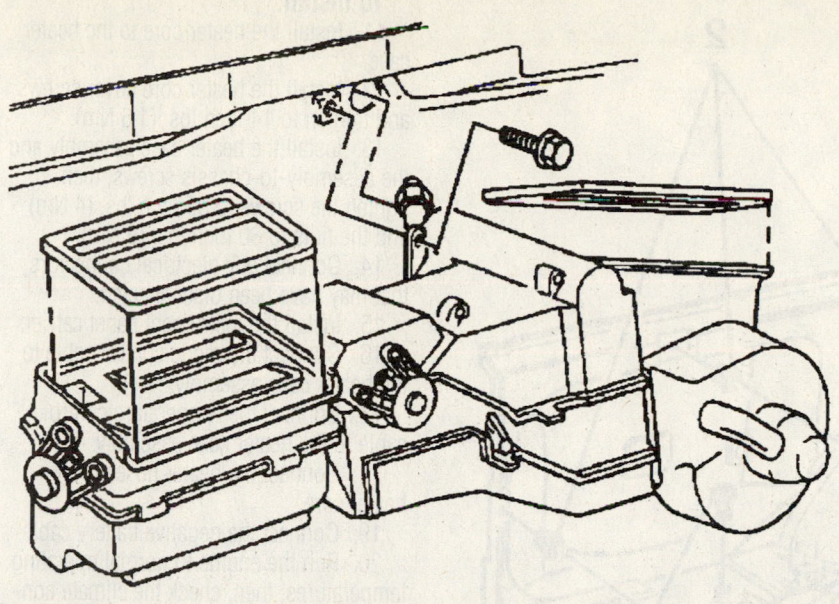

View of the front heater assembly—Chevy/GMC C/K-Series, Blazer, Jimmy, Sierra, Suburban, Tahoe, Yukon

93113G80

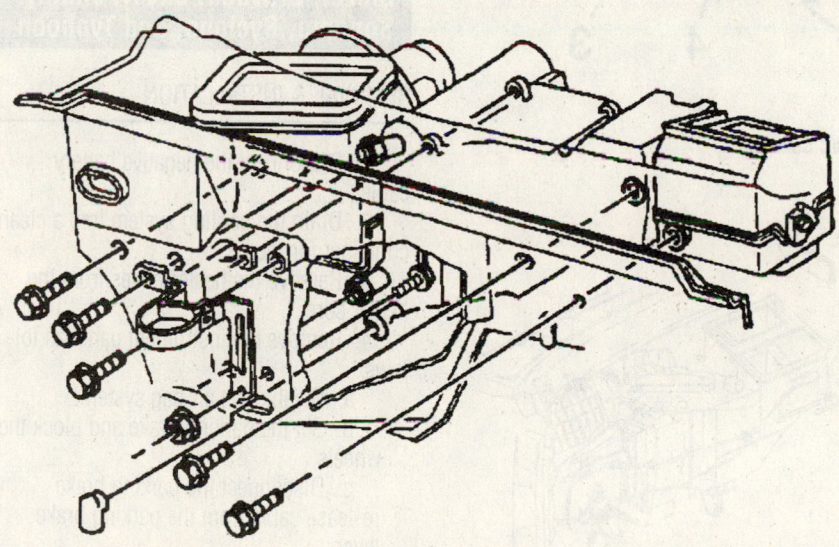

Location of the front heater assembly-to-chassis fasteners—Chevy/GMC C/K-Series, Blazer, Jimmy, Sierra, Suburban, Tahoe, Yukon

93113G81

19. While holding the heater assembly against the firewall, install the screw located on the interior side near the evaporator pipe, if equipped. Torque the screw to 97 inch lbs. (11 Nm).

20. Install the instrument panel and the instrument panel fasteners.

21. Install the steering column (standard & tilt) and the steering wheel.

22. Install the blower motor and the blower motor screws.

23. Install the blower motor the cover and the cover screws.

24. Install the hinge pillar trim kick panels.

25. Install the center floor air distribution duct.

26. Connect the electrical connectors that were disconnected.

27. Install the instrument panel storage compartment.

28. Disconnect the heater hoses to the heater core.

29. Refill the engine cooling system.

30. Connect the negative battery cable.

31. Run the engine to normal operating temperatures; then, check the climate control operation and check for leaks.

REAR AUXILIARY HEATER

1. Disconnect the negative battery cable.

2. Drain the engine cooling system into a clean container for reuse.

3. Remove the rear quarter trim panel, as necessary.

4. Remove the right rear quarter trim panel.

5. Remove the right rear wheelhouse.

6. Disconnect the heater hoses from the rear auxiliary heater core.

7. Disconnect the electrical connectors, as necessary.

8. Remove the drain valve.

9. Remove the rear auxiliary heater assembly-to-chassis nuts and bolts.

10. Remove the rear auxiliary heater assembly.

11. If necessary, remove the blower motor from the heater assembly.

12. Remove the rear auxiliary heater assembly cover.

13. Remove the heater core from the rear auxiliary assembly.

To install:

14. Install the heater core to the rear auxiliary assembly.

15. Install the rear auxiliary heater assembly cover.

16. If removed, install the blower motor to the heater assembly.

17. Install the rear auxiliary heater assembly.

18. Install the rear auxiliary heater assembly-to-chassis nuts and bolts. Torque the bolts to 13 inch lbs. (1.5 Nm) and the nuts to 89 inch lbs. (10 Nm).

19. Install the drain valve.

20. Connect the electrical connectors, as necessary.

21. Connect the heater hoses from the rear auxiliary heater core.

22. Install the right rear wheelhouse.

23. Install the right rear quarter trim panel.

24. Install the rear quarter trim panel, as necessary.

25. Refill the engine cooling system.

26. Connect the negative battery cable.

27. Run the engine to normal operating temperatures; then, check the climate control operation and check for leaks.

Refer to the model specific sections for cooling system service procedures

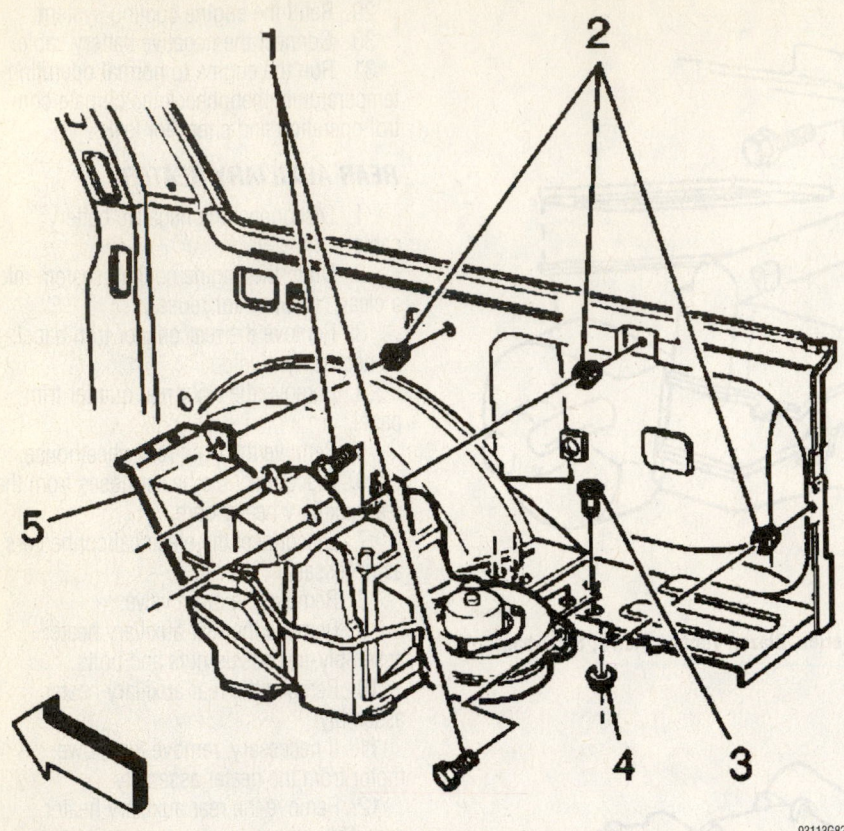

View of the rear auxiliary heater assembly—Chevy/GMC Suburban

93113G82

Chevy/GMC Silverado

REMOVAL & INSTALLATION

1. Disconnect the negative battery cable.

2. Drain the engine cooling system into a clean container for reuse.

3. Disconnect the heater hoses from the heater core.

4. Disconnect the temperature control cable from the heater case assembly.

5. Disconnect the mode control cable from the heater case assembly.

6. Remove the instrument panel carrier to provide access to the heater case assembly.

7. Disconnect any electrical connectors that may interfere with the heater case assembly removal.

8. Remove the heater case assembly-to-chassis screws/nuts and the assembly.

9. Place the heater case assembly on a bench and remove the heater core cover screws.

10. Remove the heater core from the heater case.

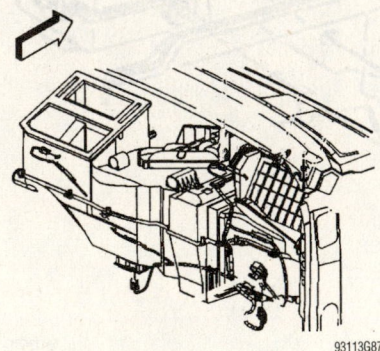

View of the heater case assembly — Chevy/GMC Silverado

93113G87

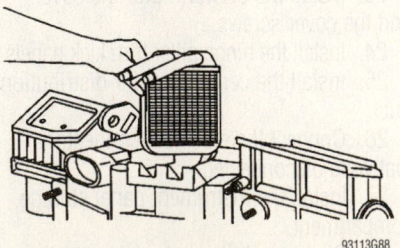

View of the heater core—Chevy/GMC Silverado

93113G88

To install:

11. Install the heater core to the heater case.

12. Install the heater core cover screws and tighten to 14 inch lbs. (1.6 Nm).

13. Install the heater case assembly and the assembly-to-chassis screws, then, tighten the screws to 35 inch lbs. (4 Nm) and the nuts to 80 inch lbs. (9 Nm).

14. Connect any electrical connectors that may have been disconnected.

15. Install the instrument panel carrier.

16. Connect the mode control cable to the heater case assembly.

17. Connect the temperature control cable to the heater case assembly.

18. Connect the heater hoses to the heater core.

19. Connect the negative battery cable.

20. Run the engine to normal operating temperatures; then, check the climate control operation and check for leaks.

Chevy/GMC S-Series Pick-Up, Blazer, Bravada, Envoy, Jimmy, Sonoma, Syclone, and Typhoon

REMOVAL & INSTALLATION

1. Disconnect the negative battery cable.

2. Drain the cooling system into a clean container for reuse.

3. Remove the heater hoses from the heater core.

4. Remove the instrument panel as follows:

   a. Disable the air bag system.

   b. Set the parking brake and block the wheels.

   c. Disconnect the parking brake re-lease cable from the parking brake lever.

   d. Unfasten the screws that retain the DLC instrument panel left side sound insulator. Feed the DLC through the hole in the sound insulator.

   e. Unfasten the right side sound insulator panel screws and remove the panel.

   f. Unfasten the screws that attach the instrument panel left side sound insulator to the knee bolster and cowl panel.

   g. Unfasten the nut that attaches the left side sound insulator to the accelerator pedal bracket.

   h. Unplug the remote control door lock receiver module electrical connector.

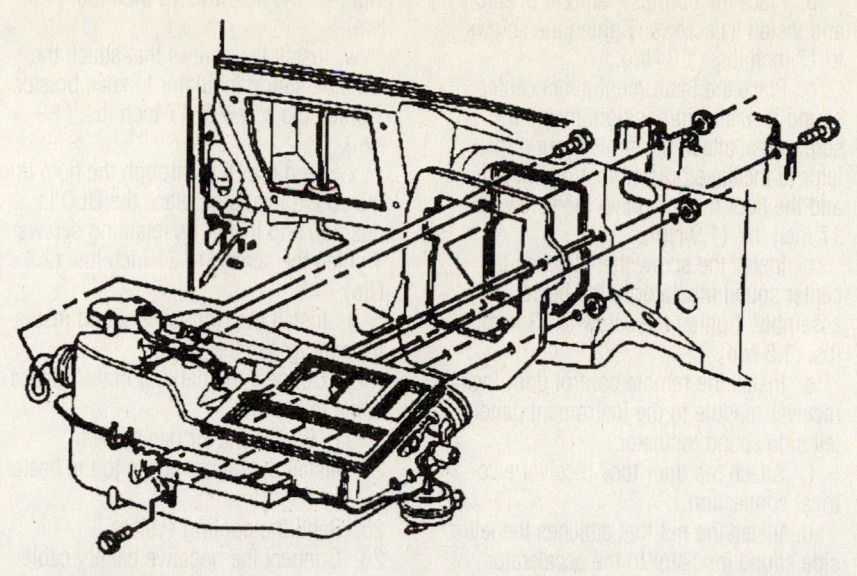

View of the heater case assembly—Chevy/GMC S-Series Pick-up, Bravada, Sonoma and Envoy

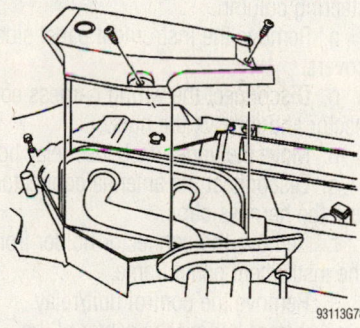

View of the heater case cover—Chevy/GMC S-Series Pick-up, Bravada, Sonoma and Envoy

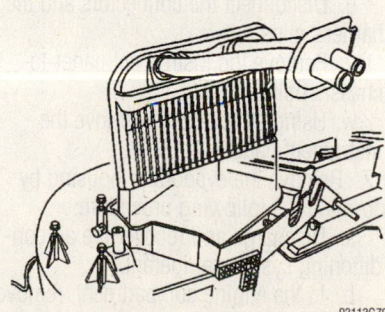

View of the heater core—Chevy/GMC S-Series Pick-up, Bravada, Sonoma and Envoy

i. Remove the door lock receiver module from the left side sound insulator. Remove the left side sound insulator.

j. Unfasten the screws that attach the instrument panel center sound insulator to the knee bolster, instrument panel, heater assembly and floor duct.

k. Remove the center sound insulator.

l. Unfasten the screws that attach the courtesy lamp to the knee bolster.

m. Unfasten the screws that attach the knee bolster to the instrument panel.

n. Disconnect the lap cooler duct from the knee bolster.

o. Unplug the lighter electrical connection and remove the knee bolster.

p. Unfasten the steering column-to-instrument panel nuts and lower the column.

q. Unfasten the screws that attach the instrument panel accessory trim plate to the instrument panel.

r. Remove the trim plate and unplug all necessary electrical connection.

s. Remove the heater and/or air conditioning control assembly.

t. Remove the radio and the storage compartment assembly (if equipped).

u. If necessary, remove the instrument cluster.

v. Unfasten the left and right instrument panel pivot bolts and the panel lower support bolt.

w. Unfasten the speaker grilles retaining screws and remove the speaker grilles.

x. Remove the windshield defroster grille using a flat-bladed prytool. Start at one end of the grille and work your way down the grille.

y. Unfasten the 4 instrument panel upper support screws.

z. Tag and unplug all necessary electrical connections.

aa. Remove the instrument panel from the vehicle.

5. Remove the air inlet assembly, if equipped.

6. Remove the vacuum hoses.

7. From inside the engine compartment, remove the heater assembly studs.

8. Remove the blower motor resistor.

9. From inside the heater case assembly, remove the stud; the stud is located behind the blower motor resistor.

10. Remove the heater assembly-to-chassis screws.

11. Remove the heater assembly from the vehicle.

12. Remove the access cover screws and cover from the heater assembly.

13. Remove the heater core from the heater case assembly.

To install:

14. Install the heater core to the heater case assembly.

15. Install the access cover to the heater assembly and the cover screws.

16. Install the heater assembly to the vehicle.

17. Install the heater assembly-to-chassis screws and torque them to 40 inch lbs. (4.5 Nm).

18. Working inside the heater case assembly, install the stud; the stud is located behind the blower motor resistor.

19. Install the blower motor resistor.

20. Working inside the engine compartment, install the heater assembly studs and torque them to 17 inch lbs. (1.9 Nm).

21. Install the vacuum hoses.

22. Install the air inlet assembly, if equipped.

23. Install the instrument panel as follows:

a. Rest the instrument panel on the lower pivot studs.

b. Attach the electrical connections.

c. Install but do not tighten the 4 upper instrument panel support screws.

d. Install the left and right panel pivot bolts. Tighten the bolts to 102 inch lbs. (11.5 Nm).

e. Install the panel lower support bolt. Tighten the bolt to 102 inch lbs. (11.5 Nm).

f. Tighten the upper support screws to 17 inch lbs. (1.9 Nm).

g. Install the windshield defroster grille and the speaker grilles.

h. Install the radio and storage compartment assembly (if equipped).

i. If removed, install the instrument cluster.

j. Install the heater and/or air conditioning control assembly.

k. attach the electrical connections to the instrument panel accessory trim plate.

l. Place the trim plate in position and install its retaining screws. Tighten the screws to 17 inch lbs. (1.9 Nm).

m. Place the steering column into position and install its retaining nuts. Tighten the nuts to 22 ft. lbs. (30 Nm).

n. Attach the lighter electrical connection and the lap cooler duct to the knee bolster.

o. Place the knee bolster into position and install its retaining screws. Tighten the Torx● head screws to 80 inch lbs. (9 Nm) and the hex head screws to 17 inch lbs. (1.9 Nm).

p. Place the courtesy lamp in position and install its screws. Tighten the screws to 17 inch lbs. (1.9 Nm).

q. Place the instrument panel center sound insulator in position. Install the screws that attach the center sound insulator to the knee bolster, instrument panel and the floor duct. Tighten the screws to 17 inch lbs. (1.9 Nm).

r. Install the screw that attaches the center sound insulator to the heater assembly. Tighten the screw to 13 inch lbs. (1.5 Nm).

s. Install the remote control door lock receiver module to the instrument panel left side sound insulator.

t. Attach the door lock receiver electrical connection.

u. Install the nut that attaches the left side sound insulator to the accelerator pedal bracket. Tighten the nut to 35 inch lbs. (4 Nm).

v. Install the screw that attaches the left side sound insulator to cowl panel.

Tight-en the screw to 13 inch lbs. (1.5 Nm).

w. Install the screws that attach the left side sound insulator to knee bolster. Tighten the screw to 17 inch lbs. (1.9 Nm).

x. Feed the DLC through the hole in the sound insulator, place the DLC in position and install its retaining screws. Tighten the screws to 21 inch lbs. (2.4 Nm).

y. Install the right side sound insulator and tighten the screws

z. Connect the parking brake release cable to the lever.

aa. Enable the air bag system.

24. Install the heater hoses to the heater core.

25. Refill the cooling system.

26. Connect the negative battery cable.

27. Run the engine to normal operating temperatures; then, check the climate control operation and check for leaks.

HONDA

CR-V

REMOVAL & INSTALLATION

1. Disconnect the negative battery cable.

2. Drain the cooling system into a clean container for reuse.

3. In the engine compartment, open the heater valve cable clamp and disconnect the cable from the heater valve arm. Then, turn the heater valve to the fully opened position.

4. Disconnect the heater hoses from the heater core.

5. Remove the heater housing-to-chassis nut.

➡**When removing the heater housing nut, be careful not to damage or bend the fuel lines, the brake lines, etc.**

6. Remove the instrument panel by performing the following procedure:

a. Remove the driver's side lower instrument panel cover screws, disengage the clips and remove the lower cover.

b. Remove the knee bolster bolts and the knee bolster.

c. Remove the glove box stops from each side of the glove box.

d. Remove the glove box-to-instrument panel bolts and the glove box.

e. Remove the lower console cover by disengaging the 4 clips and removing the cover.

f. Remove the 6 center pocket-to-instrument panel screws; then, insert a flat tipped screwdriver at the upper right side corner of the center pocket, push down on the top of the hook and remove the center pocket/beverage holder assembly.

g. Remove the center instrument panel lower cover screws and disengage the clips on the upper left side; then, disconnect the electrical connectors and remove the cover.

h. Gently, push the power window switch from the instrument panel's lower cover opening by hand. Disconnect the electrical connectors and remove the power window switch.

i. Close the driver's side air vent; then, gently, push out the clips and pull out the vent. Disconnect the electrical connectors and remove the vent.

j. Gently, push out the driver's side defogger trim; then, disconnect the electrical connector and remove the side defogger trim.

k. At the base of the steering wheel, remove the access panel and disconnect the air bag electrical connector.

l. Remove the steering column covers screws and the covers.

m. Remove the steering column-to-instrument panel nuts/bolts and lower the steering column.

n. Remove the instrument panel side covers.

o. Disconnect the wiring harness connector and remove the nuts.

p. Move the under-dash fuse/relay box.

q. Disconnect the antenna connector and the harness clips.

r. Remove the connector holder from the instrument panel frame.

s. Remove the control unit/relay bracket from behind the center of the instrument panel.

t. Remove the passenger's side lower instrument panel cover.

u. Disconnect the connectors and the harness clips.

v. Remove the instrument panel-to-chassis bolts.

w. Using an assistant, remove the instrument panel.

7. Remove the evaporator housing by performing the following procedure:

a. Discharge and recover the air conditioning system refrigerant.

b. In the engine compartment, remove the refrigerant lines-to-evaporator housing bolts.

c. Separate the lines, discard the grommets and plug the openings to prevent contamination.

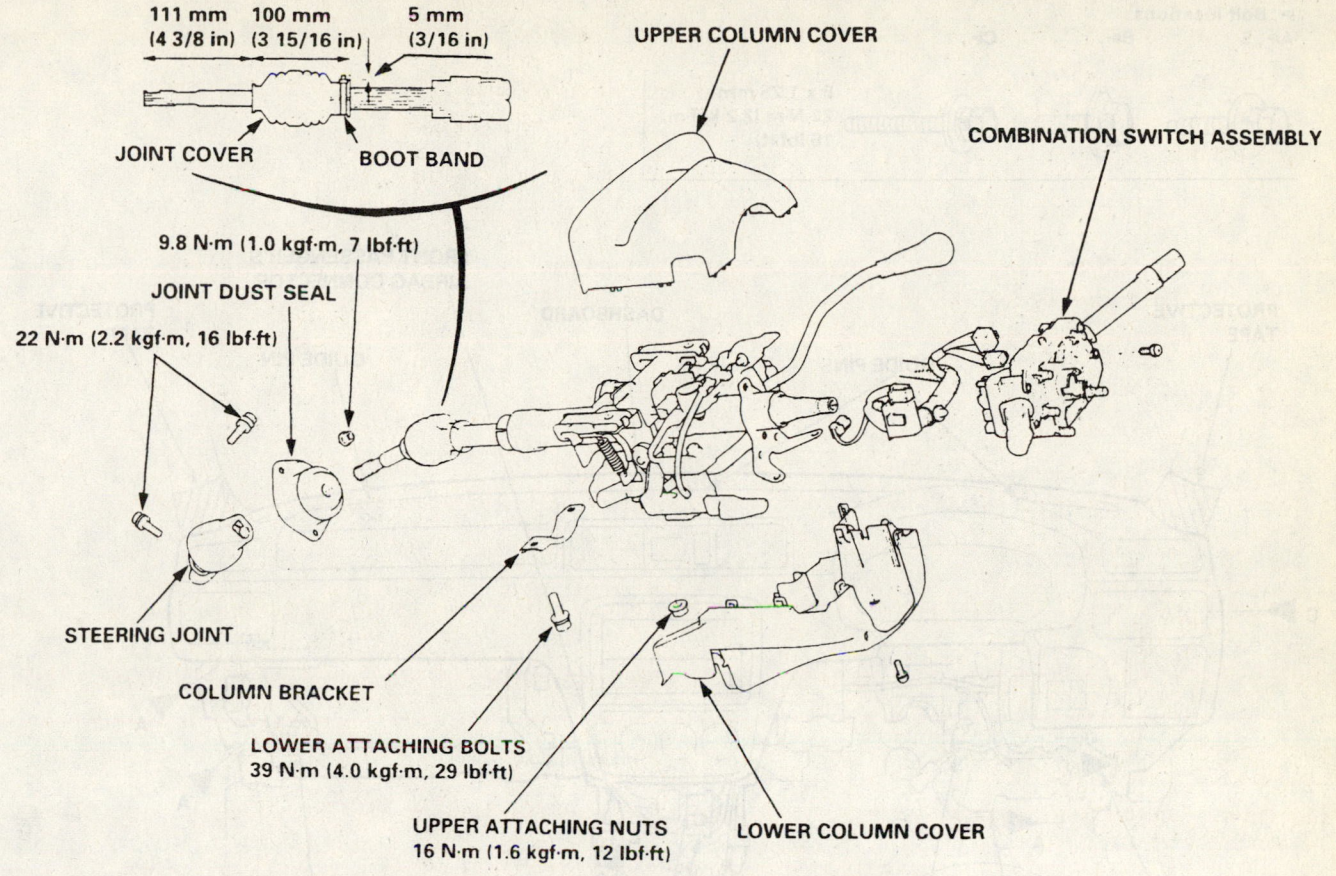

111 mm (4 3/8 in)   **100 mm (3 15/16 in)**   **5 mm (3/16 in)**

JOINT COVER   BOOT BAND

UPPER COLUMN COVER

COMBINATION SWITCH ASSEMBLY

9.8 N·m (1.0 kgf·m, 7 lbf·ft)

JOINT DUST SEAL

22 N·m (2.2 kgf·m, 16 lbf·ft)

STEERING JOINT

COLUMN BRACKET

LOWER ATTACHING BOLTS
39 N·m (4.0 kgf·m, 29 lbf·ft)

UPPER ATTACHING NUTS
16 N·m (1.6 kgf·m, 12 lbf·ft)

LOWER COLUMN COVER

93113GI2

Exploded view of the steering column and related components—Honda CR-V

d. Disconnect the evaporator housing's temperature sensor connector.

e. Remove the evaporator housing-to-chassis screws/nut and remove the evaporator housing.

8. Disconnect the mode control motor and the air mix control motor electrical connectors and remove the wiring harness clips and the wiring harness from the heater housing.

9. Remove the heater duct clip, the heater housing-to-chassis nuts and the heater housing.

10. Remove the heater core cover screws and the cover.

11. Remove the heater core pipe clamp screws and the clamp.

12. Remove the heater core from the heater housing.

To install:

13. Install the heater core in the heater housing.

14. Install the heater core pipe clamp and the clamp screws.

15. Install the heater core cover and the cover screws.

16. Install the heater housing, the heater housing-to-chassis nuts and the heater duct clip.

17. Install the wiring harness clips and the wiring harness to the heater housing and connect the mode control motor and the air mix control motor electrical connectors.

18. Install the evaporator housing by performing the following procedure:

a. Install the evaporator housing and the evaporator housing-to-chassis screws/nut.

b. Connect the evaporator housing's temperature sensor connector.

c. Using new grommets, connect the refrigerant lines.

d. In the engine compartment, install the refrigerant lines-to-evaporator housing bolts.

19. Install the instrument panel by performing the following procedure:

a. Using an assistant, install the instrument panel.

b. Install the instrument panel-to-chassis bolts.

c. Connect the connectors and the harness clips.

d. Install the passenger's side lower instrument panel cover.

e. Install the control unit/relay bracket to the center of the instrument panel.

f. Install the connector holder to the instrument panel frame.

g. Connect the antenna connector and the harness clips.

h. Install the under-dash fuse/relay box.

i. Connect the wiring harness connector and install the nuts.

j. Install the instrument panel side covers.

k. Install the steering column and the column-to-instrument panel nuts/bolts. Torque the nuts to 12 ft. lbs. (16 Nm) and the bolts to 29 ft. lbs. (39 Nm).

l. Install the steering column covers and the cover screws.

m. At the base of the steering wheel, connect the air bag electrical connector and install the access panel.

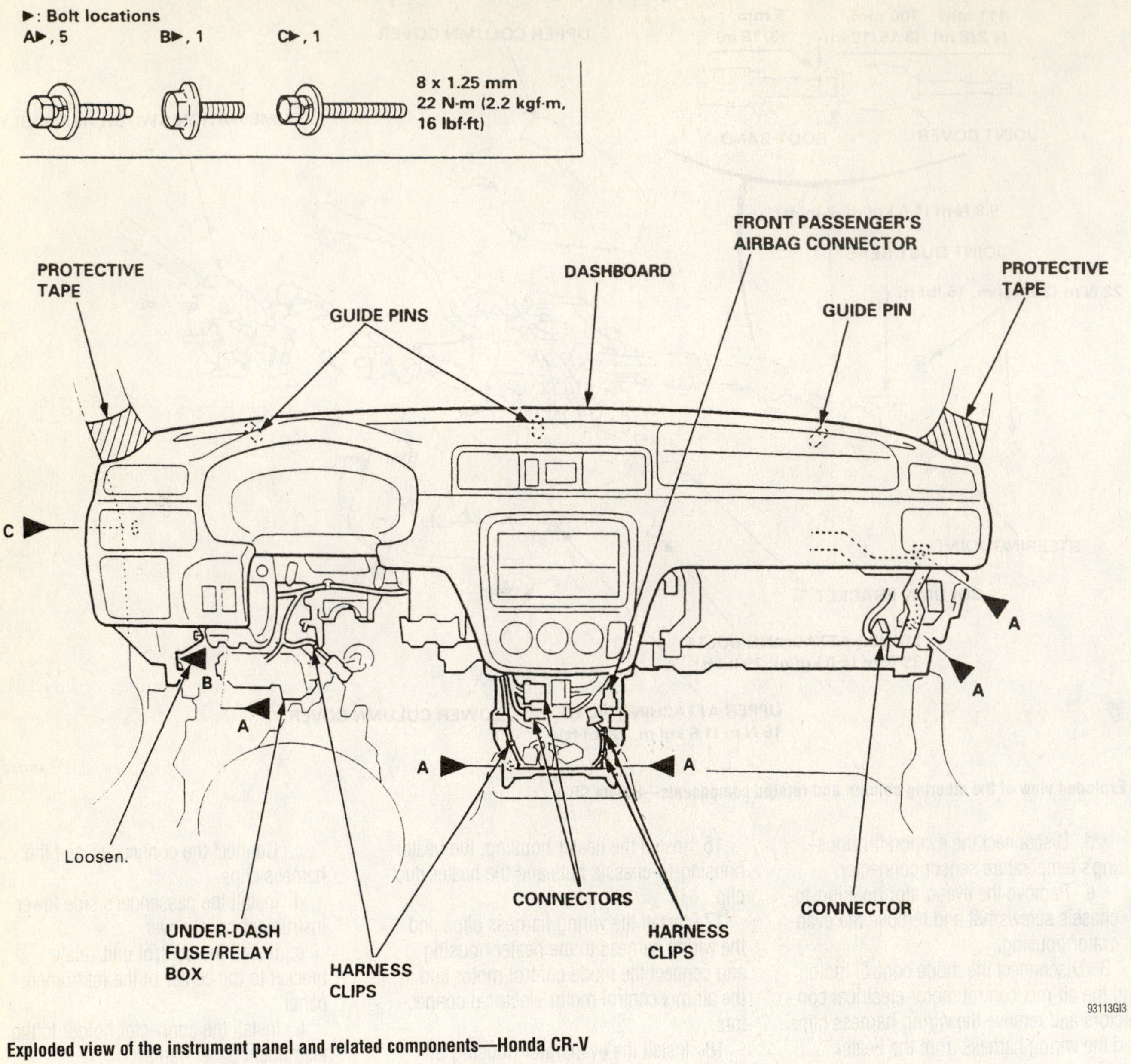

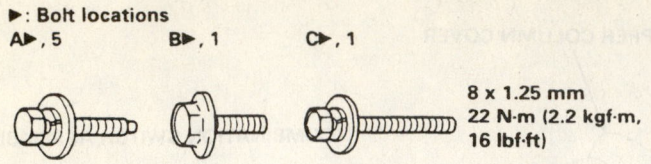

▶: Bolt locations
A▶, 5   B▶, 1   C▶, 1

8 x 1.25 mm
22 N·m (2.2 kgf·m,
16 lbf·ft)

PROTECTIVE
TAPE

GUIDE PINS

DASHBOARD

FRONT PASSENGER'S
AIRBAG CONNECTOR

GUIDE PIN

PROTECTIVE
TAPE

C ▶

A
A
A

B
A

Loosen.

UNDER-DASH
FUSE/RELAY
BOX

HARNESS
CLIPS

CONNECTORS

HARNESS
CLIPS

CONNECTOR

A ▶   ◀ A

93113GI3

Exploded view of the instrument panel and related components—Honda CR-V

n. Connect the electrical connector and install the driver's side defogger trim.

o. Connect the electrical connectors and install driver's side air vent.

p. Connect the electrical connectors and install the power window switch to the instrument panel's lower cover opening.

q. Install the center instrument panel lower cover and engage the clips on the upper left side; then, connect the electrical connectors and Install the cover screws.

r. Install the center pocket/beverage holder assembly and the 6 center pocket-to-instrument panel screws.

s. Install the lower console cover by engaging the 4 clips.

t. Install the glove box and the glove box-to-instrument panel bolts.

u. Install the glove box stops to each side of the glove box.

v. Install the knee bolster and the knee bolster bolts.

w. Install the driver's side lower instrument panel cover, engage the clips and install the lower cover screws.

➡**When installing the heater housing nut, be careful not to damage or bend the fuel lines, the brake lines or etc.**

20. Install the heater housing-to-chassis nut.

21. Connect the heater hoses to the heater core.

22. In the engine compartment, connect the cable to the heater valve arm and close the heater valve cable clamp.

23. Refill the cooling system.

24. Connect the negative battery cable.

25. Evacuate and charge and leak test the air conditioning system refrigerant.

26. Run the engine to normal operating temperatures; then, check the climate control operation and check for leaks.

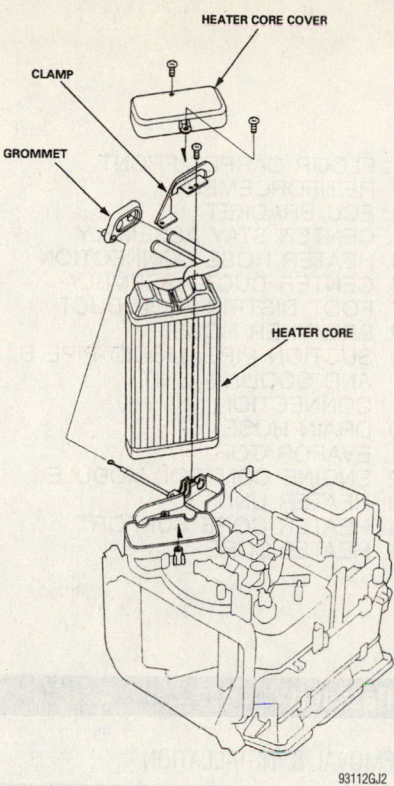

HEATER CORE COVER

CLAMP

GROMMET

HEATER CORE

93112GJ2

Exploded view of the heater core and housing—Honda CR-V

Odyssey

REMOVAL & INSTALLATION

➡**Make sure to acquire the anti-theft code for the radio and write down the frequencies for the radio's preset buttons.**

1. Disconnect the negative battery cable.

✱✱ CAUTION

Wait at least 3 minutes for the air bag to deplete its energy before working on the steering wheel or instrument panel.

2. In the engine compartment, remove the heater valve cable clamp; then, disconnect the heater valve cable and rotate the heater valve to the fully open position.

3. Drain the engine coolant into a clean container for reuse.

4. Disconnect the heater hoses from the heater unit.

5. Remove the heater housing-to-chassis nuts.

6. Remove the center console.

7. Remove the instrument panel.

8. Remove the steering hanger beam mounting bolts and the steering hanger beam.

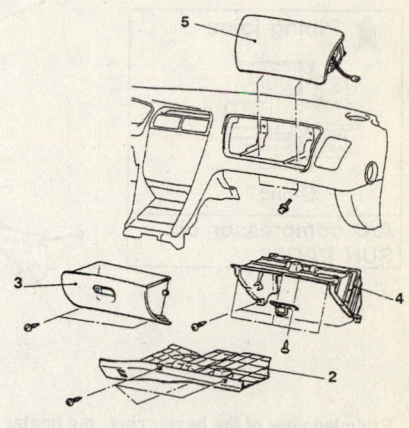

2. UNDERCOVER
3. GLOVE BOX ASSEMBLY
4. GLOVE BOX CASE
5. AIR BAG MODULE

93112GG1

View of the heater housing, evaporator housing and related components—Honda Odyssey

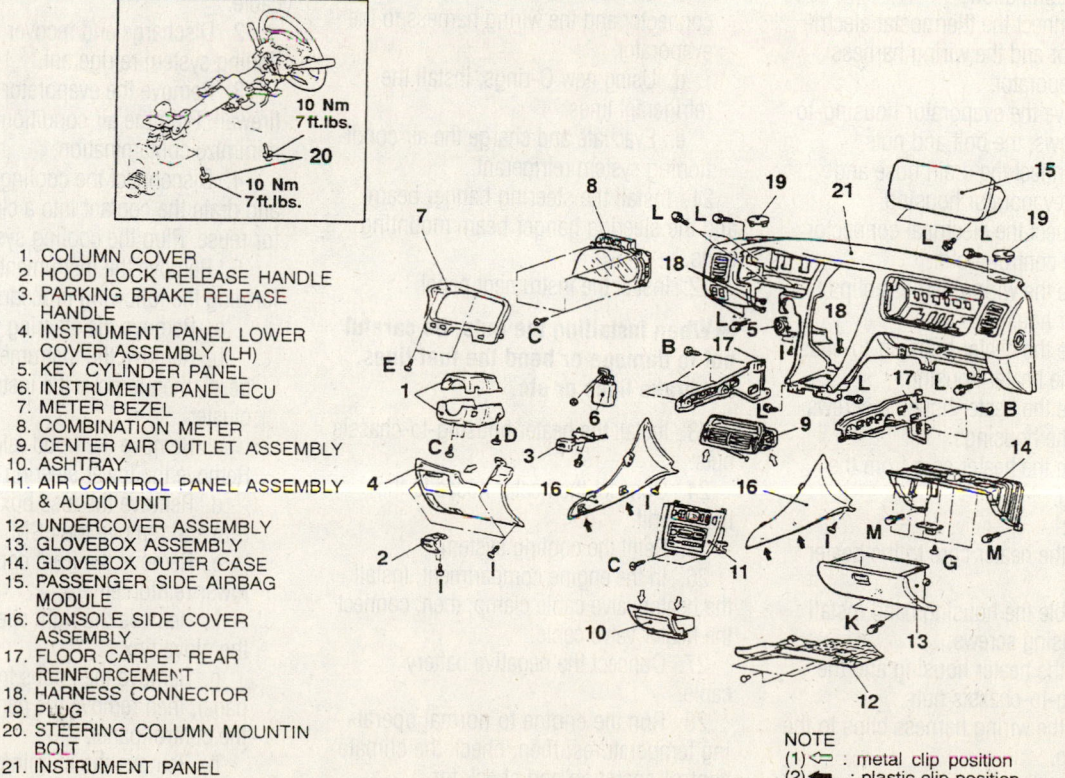

10 Nm
7 ft.lbs.

20

10 Nm
7 ft.lbs.

1. COLUMN COVER
2. HOOD LOCK RELEASE HANDLE
3. PARKING BRAKE RELEASE HANDLE
4. INSTRUMENT PANEL LOWER COVER ASSEMBLY (LH)
5. KEY CYLINDER PANEL
6. INSTRUMENT PANEL ECU
7. METER BEZEL
8. COMBINATION METER
9. CENTER AIR OUTLET ASSEMBLY
10. ASHTRAY
11. AIR CONTROL PANEL ASSEMBLY & AUDIO UNIT
12. UNDERCOVER ASSEMBLY
13. GLOVEBOX ASSEMBLY
14. GLOVEBOX OUTER CASE
15. PASSENGER SIDE AIRBAG MODULE
16. CONSOLE SIDE COVER ASSEMBLY
17. FLOOR CARPET REAR REINFORCEMENT
18. HARNESS CONNECTOR
19. PLUG
20. STEERING COLUMN MOUNTIN BOLT
21. INSTRUMENT PANEL

NOTE
(1) ⇨ : metal clip position
(2) ◄ : plastic clip position

93112GG2

View of the steering hanger beam and related components—Honda Odyssey

Refer to the model specific sections for engine mechanical service procedures

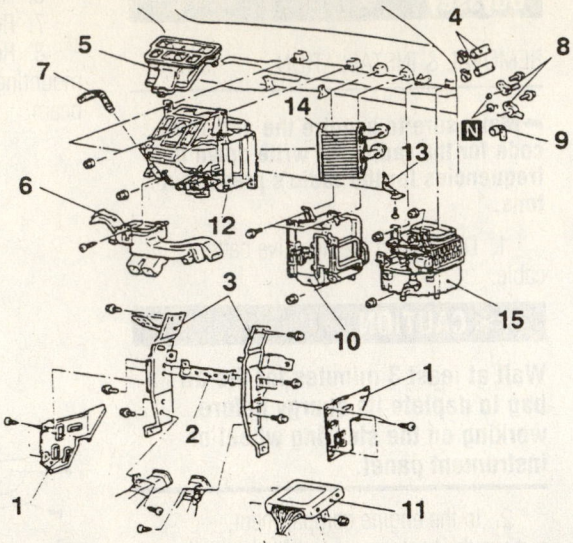

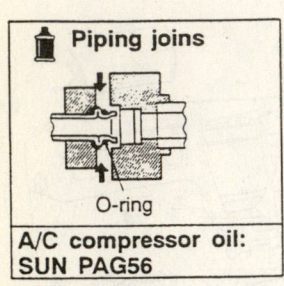

Piping joins

O-ring

A/C compressor oil:
SUN PAG56

1. FLOOR CARPET FRONT
   REINFORCEMENT
3. ECU BRACKET
4. CENTER STAY ASSEMBLY
5. HEATER HOSE CONNECTION
6. CENTER DUCT ASSEMBLY
7. FOOT DISTRIBUTION DUCT
8. BREATHER HOSE
9. SUCTION PIPE, LIQUID PIPE B
   AND COOLING UNIT
   CONNECTION
10. DRAIN HOSE
11. EVAPORATOR
12. ENGINE CONTROL MODULE
13. HEATER UNIT
14. HEATER CORE SUPPORT
15. HEATER CORE

93112GG3

Exploded view of the heater core, the heater housing and related components—Honda Odyssey

9. Remove the evaporator housing by performing the following procedure:

  a. Discharge and recover the air conditioning system refrigerant.

  b. Remove the refrigerant lines. Discard the O-rings. Plug the openings to prevent contamination.

  c. Disconnect the thermostat electrical connector and the wiring harness from the evaporator.

  d. Remove the evaporator housing-to-chassis screws, the bolt and nuts.

  e. Disconnect the drain hose and remove the evaporator housing.

10. Disconnect the electrical connector from the mode control motor.

11. Remove the wiring harness clips from the heater housing.

12. Remove the heater housing-to-chassis nuts and the heater housing.

13. Remove the heater housing screws and separate the housings.

14. Remove the heater core from the heater housing.

To install:

15. Install the heater core to the heater housing.

16. Assemble the housings and install the heater housing screws.

17. Install the heater housing and the heater housing-to-chassis nuts.

18. Install the wiring harness clips to the heater housing.

19. Connect the electrical connector to the mode control motor.

20. Install the evaporator housing by performing the following procedure:

  a. Install the evaporator housing and connect the drain hose.

  b. Install the evaporator housing-to-chassis screws, the bolt and nuts.

  c. Connect the thermostat electrical connector and the wiring harness to the evaporator.

  d. Using new O-rings, install the refrigerant lines.

  e. Evacuate and charge the air conditioning system refrigerant.

21. Install the steering hanger beam and the steering hanger beam mounting bolts.

22. Install the instrument panel.

➡**When installing the nuts, be careful not to damage or bend the fuel lines, the brake lines or etc.**

23. Install the heater housing-to-chassis nuts.

24. Connect the heater hoses to the heater unit.

25. Refill the cooling system.

26. In the engine compartment, Install the heater valve cable clamp; then, connect the heater valve cable.

27. Connect the negative battery cable.

28. Run the engine to normal operating temperatures; then, check the climate control operation and check for leaks.

Passport

REMOVAL & INSTALLATION

1997

1. Disconnect the negative battery cable.

2. Discharge and recover the air conditioning system refrigerant.

3. Remove the evaporator lines at the firewall. Plug the air conditioning lines to minimize contamination.

4. Disconnect the cooling system hoses and drain the coolant into a clean container for reuse. Plug the cooling system hoses.

5. Remove the instrument panel by performing the following procedure:

  a. Remove the steering wheel.

  b. Remove the instrument cluster bezel, then remove the instrument cluster.

  c. Remove the hood release handle. Remove the lower steering column cover.

  d. Remove the fuse box, the left side trim and remove the ECM, if applicable.

  e. Remove the front console and the lower reinforcement.

  f. Remove the right speaker grille and the glove box.

  g. Remove the knobs from the control panel, then remove the panel bezel and the control panel.

  h. Remove the illumination controller (to the right of the steering column).

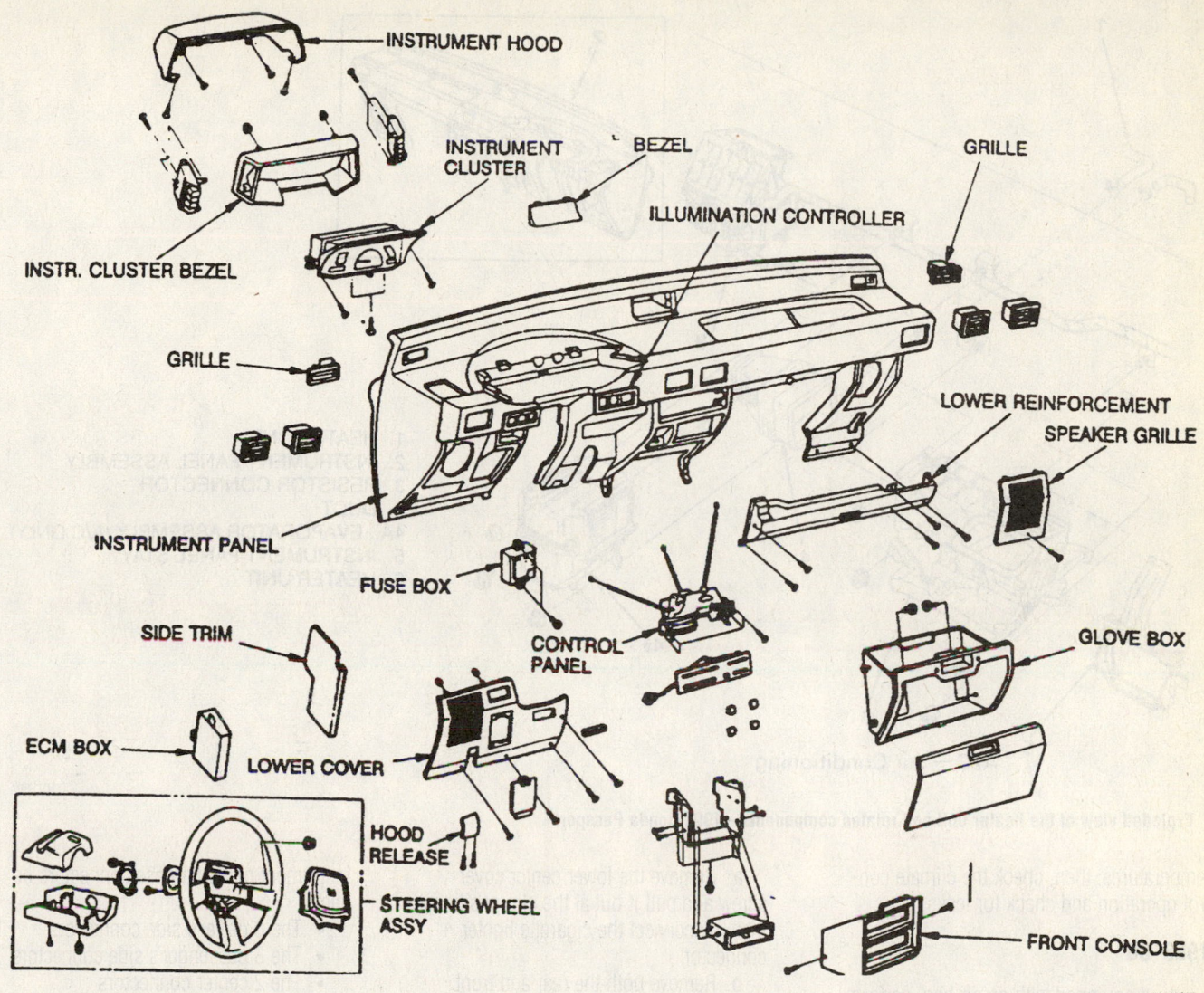

Exploded view of the instrument panel—1997 Honda Passport

i. Remove the instrument panel.

6. Remove the resistor connector.

7. If not equipped with air conditioning, remove the heater-to-blower air duct.

8. If equipped with air conditioning, remove the evaporator assembly.

9. Remove the instrument panel support.

10. Remove the heater unit attaching nuts and remove the assembly.

11. Disassemble the heater unit case and remove the heater core.

To install:

12. Assemble the heater unit case and install the heater core.

13. Install the assembly and the heater unit attaching nuts.

14. Install the instrument panel support.

15. If equipped with air conditioning, install the evaporator assembly.

16. If not equipped with air conditioning, install the heater-to-blower air duct.

17. Install the resistor connector.

18. Install the instrument panel by performing the following procedure:

a. Install the instrument panel.

b. Install the illumination controller (to the right of the steering column).

c. Install the panel bezel and the control panel, then the knobs to the control panel.

d. Install the right speaker grille and the glove box.

e. Install the lower reinforcement and the front console.

f. Install the ECM (if applicable), the fuse box and the left side trim.

g. Install the lower steering column cover and the hood release handle.

h. Install the instrument cluster and the instrument cluster bezel.

i. Install the steering wheel.

19. Install the evaporator lines at the firewall.

20. Refill the cooling system.

21. Evacuate and charge the air conditioning system.

22. Connect the negative battery cable.

23. Run the engine to normal operating

Refer to the model specific sections for cooling system service procedures

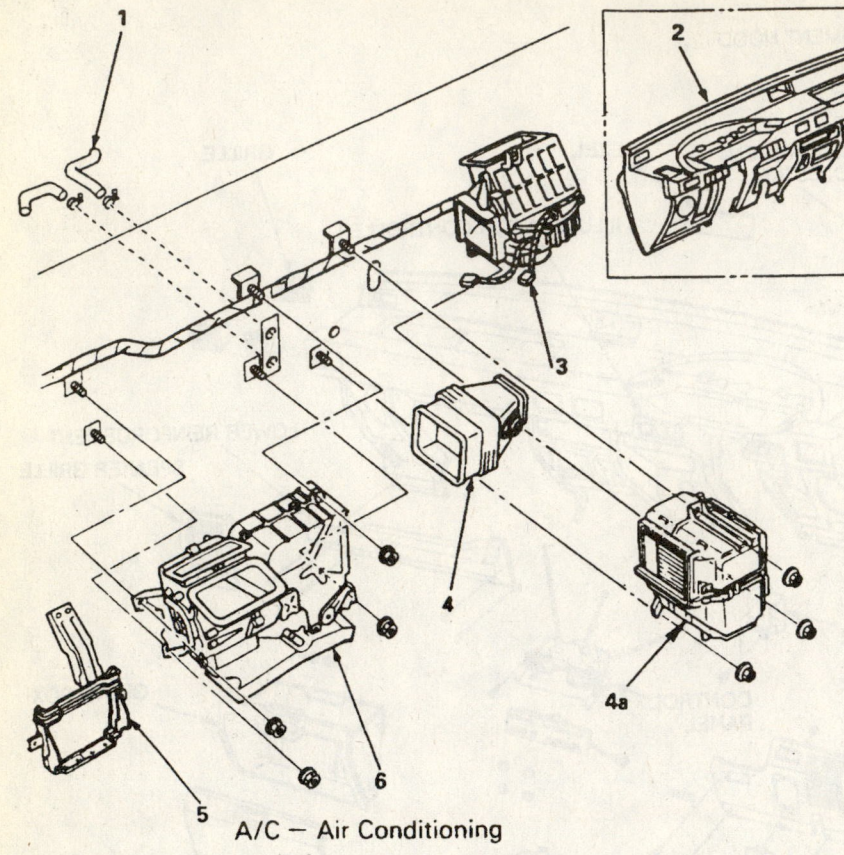

1. HEATER UNIT
2. INSTRUMENT PANEL ASSEMBLY
3. RESISTOR CONNECTOR
4. DUCT
4A. EVAPORATOR ASSEMBLY (A/C ONLY)
5. INSTRUMENT PANEL STAY
6. HEATER UNIT

A/C — Air Conditioning

93113G76

Exploded view of the heater unit and related components—1997 Honda Passport

temperatures; then, check the climate control operation and check for leaks.

1998–00

1. If equipped with an air bag, perform the following procedure:

a. Turn the ignition to the LOCK position and remove the key.

b. From the lower left dash side fuse block, remove the SRS-1 fuse.

c. Disconnect the 2-pin yellow connector located at the base of the steering column.

d. Remove the glove box assembly.

e. Disconnect the 2-pin yellow connector located behind the glove box.

2. Disconnect the negative battery cable.

3. If equipped, discharge and recover the air conditioning system refrigerant.

4. Remove the evaporator lines at the firewall. Plug the air conditioning lines to minimize contamination.

5. Disconnect the cooling system hoses and drain the coolant into a clean container for reuse. Plug the cooling system hoses.

6. Remove the instrument panel by performing the following procedure:

a. Remove the lower center cover screw and pull it out at the clip positions; then, disconnect the cigarette lighter connector.

b. Remove both the rear and front console.

c. Remove the dash side trim panel sill plates and the panels.

d. Remove the 2 glove box screws and the glove box.

e. Remove the 2 hood release screws, the 6 instrument panel driver's lower cover assembly screws and the cover assembly.

f. Remove the 5 instrument cluster screws and the 2 clips. Disconnect the 8 switch connectors and remove the instrument cluster assembly.

g. Remove the 6 driver's knee bolster assembly bolts and screws and the knee bolster assembly.

h. Remove the 4 control lever assembly bolts; then, disconnect the 3 control cables (unit side) and the 3 harness connectors.

i. Remove the 4 radio/audio sub box assembly screws and the radio/audio sub box assembly.

j. Disconnect or remove the following

instrument panel harness connectors or items:

- The 6 driver's side connectors
- The 3 passenger's side connectors
- The 2 center connectors
- Passenger's inflator module connector
- Radio antenna cable plug
- Ground cable bolt on the left dash side panel
- The 8 instrument panel-to-chassis bolts and the 3 nuts.

k. Remove the instrument panel assembly.

7. Remove the instrument panel bracket by performing the following procedure:

a. Remove the 2 passenger's inflator module bolts and 4 nuts.

b. Remove the 4 meter assembly screws. Then, disconnect the meter wiring harness connectors and remove the meter assembly.

c. Remove the 5 vent duct assembly screws and the assembly.

d. Remove the 3 lower passenger's bracket screws and the bracket.

e. Remove the 9 passenger's knee bolster reinforcement screws and the reinforcement.

f. Remove the 6 instrument panel center reinforcement screws and the reinforcement.

g. Remove the instrument panel wiring harness assembly clips and the wiring harness.

h. Remove the 2 instrument panel bracket nuts and 2 bolts for each bracket; then, remove the bracket(s).

8. Remove the 5 cross beam assembly nuts, 2 bolts and the 6 lower bolts; then, remove the crossbeam.

9. Disconnect the resistor wiring connector.

10. Remove the duct from the heater assembly.

11. If equipped with air conditioning, remove the evaporator assembly.

12. Remove the driver's lap vent.

13. Remove the lower ventilation duct.

14. Remove the footrest, the carpet, the 3 clips and the rear heater duct.

15. Remove the heater assembly.

16. Remove the mode control case-to-temperature control case screws and remove the mode control case; do not remove the link unit.

17. Remove the temperature control case screws and separate the cases.

18. Remove the heater core from the case.

To install:

19. Install the heater core to the case.

20. Assemble the temperature control cases and install the case screws.

21. Install the mode control case and the mode control case-to-temperature control case screws.

22. Install the heater assembly.

23. Install the rear heater duct, the footrest, the carpet, and the 3 clips.

24. Install the lower ventilation duct.

25. Install the driver's lap vent.

26. If equipped with air conditioning, install the evaporator assembly.

27. Install the duct to the heater assembly.

28. Connect the resistor wiring connector.

29. Install the crossbeam, the 5 cross beam assembly nuts, 2 bolts and the 6 lower bolts.

30. Install the instrument panel bracket by performing the following procedure:

a. Install the instrument panel bracket and the 2 nuts and 2 bolts for each bracket.

b. Install the instrument panel wiring harness assembly and the wiring harness clips.

c. Install the instrument panel center reinforcement and the 6 reinforcement screws.

d. Install the passenger knee bolster reinforcement and the 9 reinforcement screws.

e. Install the lower passenger bracket and the 3 bracket screws.

f. Install the vent duct assembly and the 5 vent duct assembly screws.

g. Install the meter assembly and the 4 meter assembly screws; then, connect the meter wiring harness connectors.

h. Install the 2 passenger's inflator module bolts and 4 nuts.

31. Install the instrument panel by performing the following procedure:

a. Install the instrument panel assembly.

b. Connect or install the following instrument panel harness connectors or items:

- The 6 driver's side connectors
- The 3 passenger's side connectors
- The 2 center connectors
- Passenger's inflator module connector
- Radio antenna cable plug
- Ground cable bolt on the left dash side panel

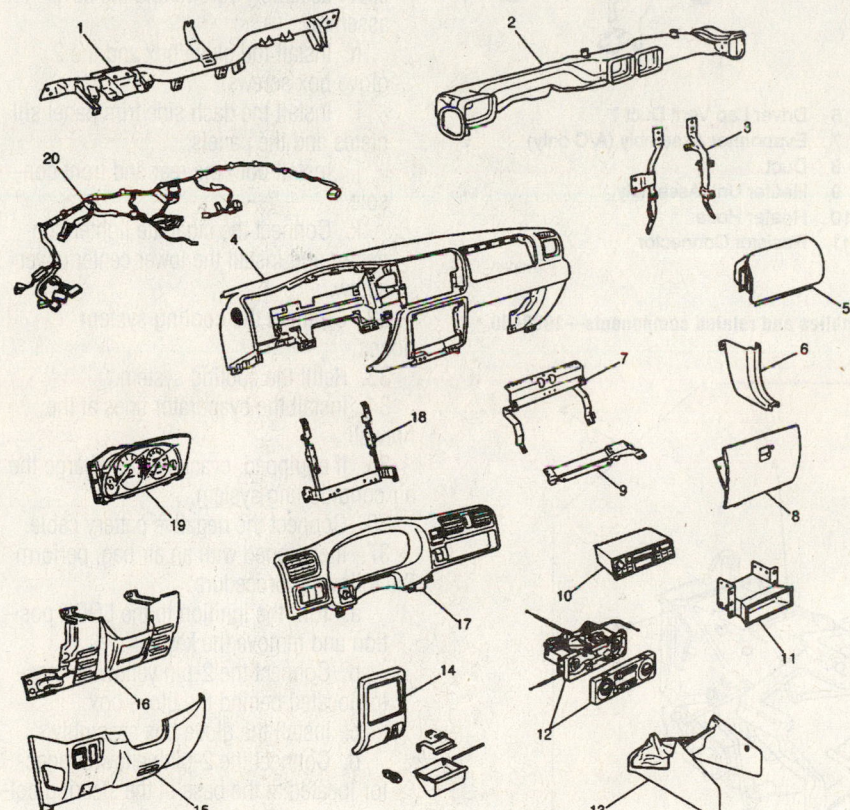

1 Cross Beam	11 Audio Sub Box
2 Vent Duct Assembly	12 Control Lever Assembly
3 Instrument Panel Bracket	13 Front Console Assembly
4 Instrument Panel Assembly	14 Lower Center Cover
5 Passenger Inflator Module	15 Instrument Panel Driver Lower Cover Assembly
6 Dash Side Trim Panel	16 Driver Knee Bolster Assembly
7 Passenger Knee Bolster Reinforcement Assembly	17 Meter Cluster Assembly
8 Glove Box	18 Instrument Panel Center Reinforcement
9 Passenger Lower Bracket	19 Meter Assembly
10 Radio Assembly	20 Instrument Harness Assembly

93113GB8

Exploded view of the instrument panel—1998–00 Honda Passport

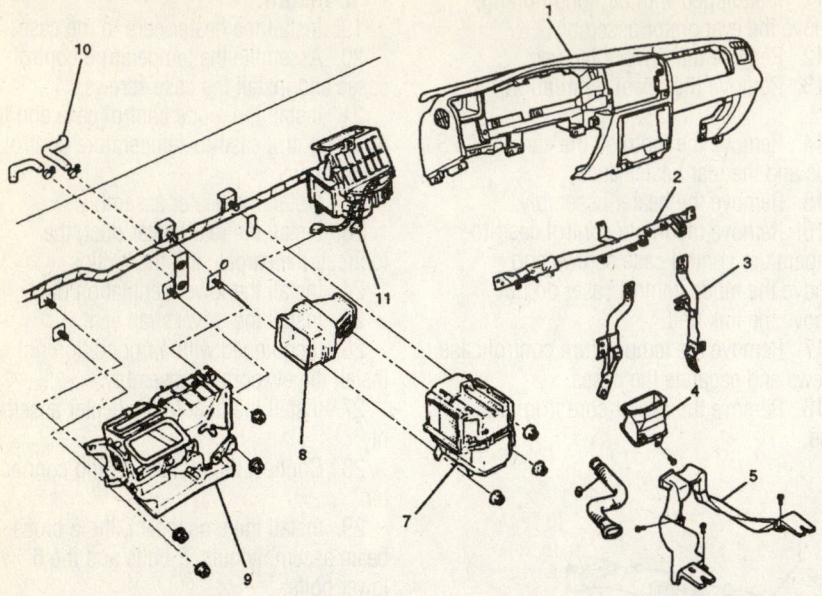

1 Instrument Panel Assembly
2 Cross Beam Assembly
3 Instrument Panel Bracket
4 Ventilation Lower Duct
5 Rear Heater Duct
6 Driver Lap Vent Duct
7 Evaporator Assembly (A/C only)
8 Duct
9 Heater Unit Assembly
10 Heater Hose
11 Resistor Connector

93113GB9

View of the heater and air conditioning housing assemblies and related components—1998–00

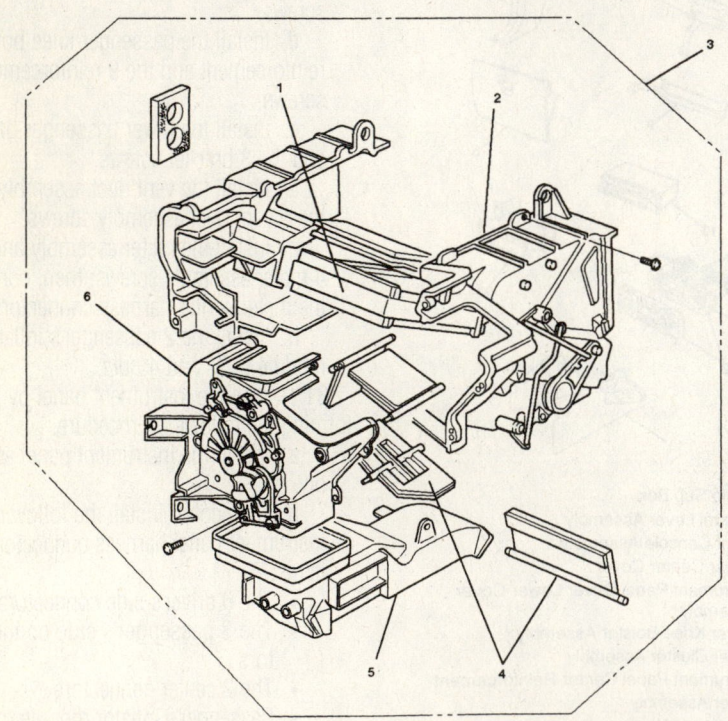

1 Heater Core
2 Case (Temperature Control)
3 Heater Unit
4 Mode Door
5 Duct
6 Case (Mode Control)

93113GB0

Exploded view of the heater housing assembly—1998–00 Honda Passport

• The 8 instrument panel-to-chassis bolts and the 3 nuts.

c. Install the radio/audio sub box assembly and the 4 radio/audio sub box assembly screws.

d. Connect the 3 control cables (unit side) and the 3 harness connectors. Install the 4 control lever assembly bolts.

e. Install the knee bolster assembly and the 6 driver's knee bolster assembly bolts and screws.

f. Install the instrument cluster assembly. Connect the 8 switch connectors. Install 5 instrument cluster screws and the 2 clips.

g. Install the 2 hood release screws, the 6 instrument panel driver's lower cover assembly screws and the cover assembly.

h. Install the glove box and the 2 glove box screws.

i. Install the dash side trim panel sill plates and the panels.

j. Install both the rear and front console.

k. Connect the cigarette lighter connector and install the lower center cover screw.

32. Connect the cooling system hoses.

33. Refill the cooling system.

34. Install the evaporator lines at the firewall.

35. If equipped, evacuate and charge the air conditioning system.

36. Connect the negative battery cable.

37. If equipped with an air bag, perform the following procedure:

a. Turn the ignition to the LOCK position and remove the key.

b. Connect the 2-pin yellow connector located behind the glove box.

c. Install the glove box assembly.

d. Connect the 2-pin yellow connector located at the base of the steering column.

e. At the lower left dash side fuse block, install the SRS-1 fuse.

f. Turn the ignition switch to ON and verify that the AIR BAG warning light flashes 7 times and turns OFF.

38. Run the engine to normal operating temperatures; then, check the climate control operation and check for leaks.

INFINITI

QX4

REMOVAL & INSTALLATION

1. Disconnect the negative battery cable.

✳✳ CAUTION

After disconnecting the negative battery cable, wait for at least 3 minutes before working on the steering column or instrument panel.

2. Drain the cooling system into a clean container for reuse.

3. Disconnect the heater hoses from the heater core.

4. Remove the driver's side air bag and steering wheel by performing the following procedure:

  a. Place the front wheels in the straight-ahead position.

  b. Remove the lower lid from the steering wheel and disconnect the air bag module connector.

  c. Remove the side lids from both sides of the steering wheel.

  d. Using the Tamper Resistant Torx® tool T50, remove the left and right Torx® bolts.

  e. Carefully, remove the air bag module.

✳✳ CAUTION

Place the air bag module in safe place with the front facing upward.

  f. Remove the steering wheel nut.

  g. Using a steering wheel puller, press the steering wheel from the steering column.

5. Remove the passenger's side air bag by performing the following procedure:

  a. Remove the glove box clips and disconnect the passenger's side air bag module connector.

  b. Remove the lower panel screws; then, disconnect the harness connector and remove the air bag module bracket.

  c. Using the Tamper Resistant Torx® tool T50, remove the passenger's side air bag module bolts.

  d. Carefully, remove the air bag module.

✳✳ CAUTION

Place the air bag module in safe place with the front facing upward.

6. Remove the instrument panel by performing the following procedure:

  a. Remove the steering column cover and the combination switch.

  b. Remove the instrument panel side lower finisher.

  c. At the driver's side, remove the lower panel screws, disconnect the electrical harness connectors and remove the panel.

  d. Remove the cluster lid "A" screws and the cluster lid "A".

  e. Remove the combination meter screws, disconnect the electrical harness connectors and remove the combination meter.

  f. Remove the cluster lid "C" screws, disconnect the electrical harness connectors and remove the cluster lid "C".

  g. Remove the audio assembly screws and the audio assembly.

  h. Remove the air conditioning control unit screws, disconnect the electrical harness connectors and the air conditioning control unit.

  i. Remove the ashtray.

  j. Remove the shifter (automatic transmission) or shift lever boot (manual transmission); then, remove the screw and disconnect the harness connector.

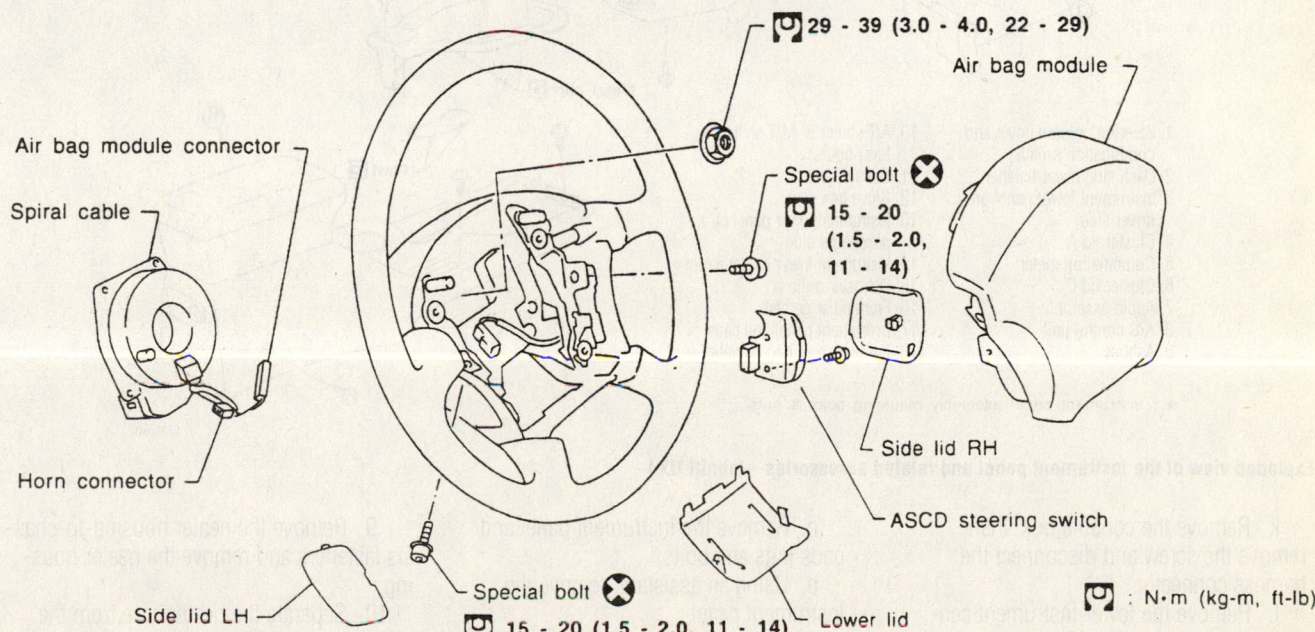

Exploded view of the driver's side air bag module and steering wheel—Infiniti QX4

93113GH8

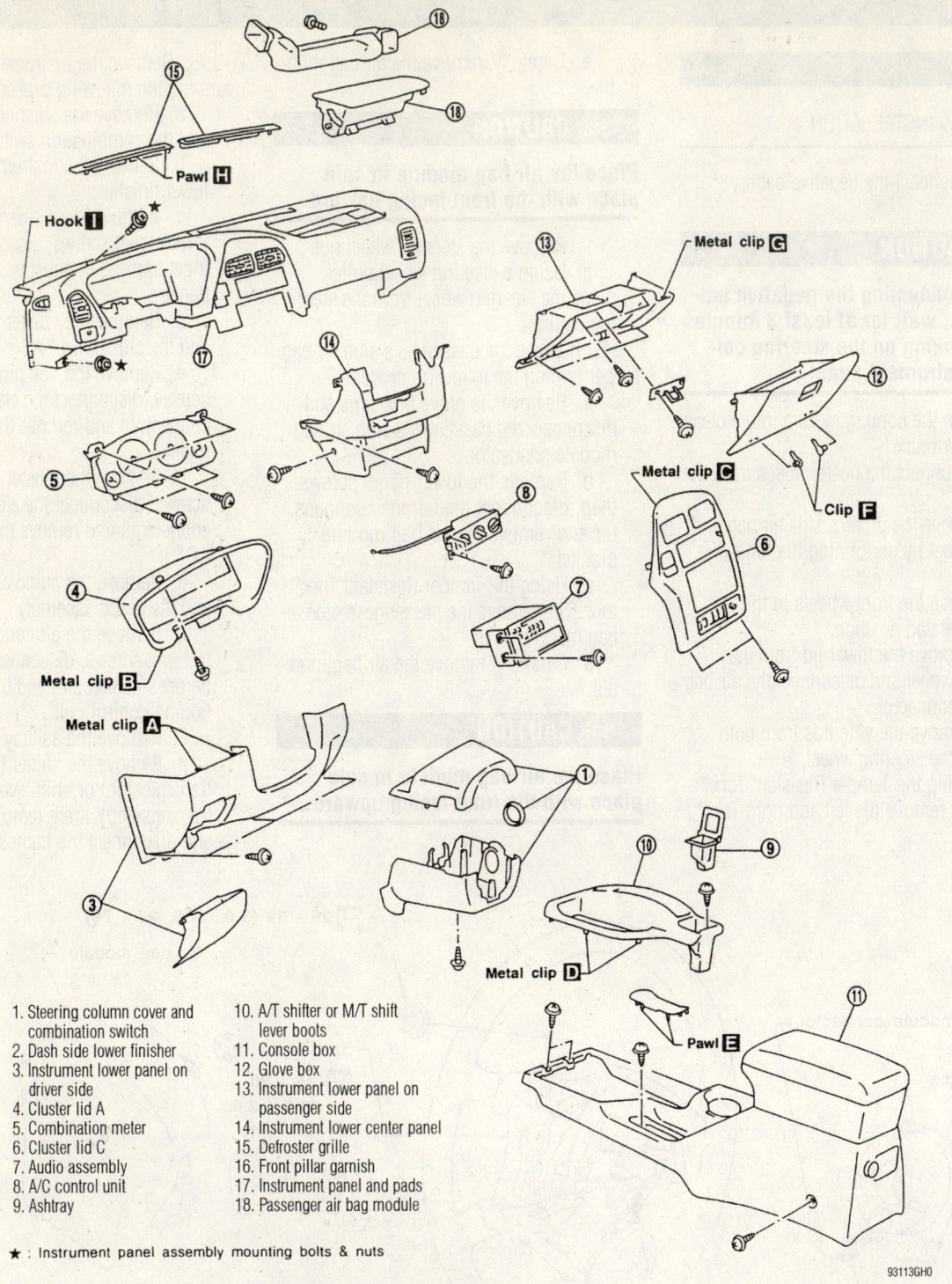

Hook (labels within image) — Pawl H, Hook I, Metal clip G, Metal clip C, Clip F, Metal clip B, Metal clip A, Metal clip D, Pawl E

1. Steering column cover and combination switch
2. Dash side lower finisher
3. Instrument lower panel on driver side
4. Cluster lid A
5. Combination meter
6. Cluster lid C
7. Audio assembly
8. A/C control unit
9. Ashtray
10. A/T shifter or M/T shift lever boots
11. Console box
12. Glove box
13. Instrument lower panel on passenger side
14. Instrument lower center panel
15. Defroster grille
16. Front pillar garnish
17. Instrument panel and pads
18. Passenger air bag module

★ : Instrument panel assembly mounting bolts & nuts

93113GH0

Exploded view of the instrument panel and related accessories—Infiniti QX4

k. Remove the console box; then, remove the screw and disconnect the harness connector.

l. Remove the lower instrument center panel screws and the lower instrument center panel.

m. Remove the defroster grille.

n. At both sides, remove the pillar garnishes.

o. Remove the instrument panel and pads nuts and bolts.

p. Using an assistant, remove the instrument panel.

7. Remove the defroster nozzle and the heater nozzle from the heater housing.

8. Disconnect the electrical connector and/or control cable from the heater housing.

9. Remove the heater housing-to-chassis fasteners and remove the heater housing.

10. Separate the heater core from the heater housing and remove the heater core.

To install:

11. Install the heater core and assemble the heater housing.

12. Install the heater housing and the heater housing-to-chassis fasteners.

13. Connect the electrical connector and/or control cable to the heater housing.

14. Install the defroster nozzle and the heater nozzle to the heater housing.

15. Install the passenger's side air bag by performing the following procedure:

a. Carefully, install the air bag module.

b. Using the Tamper Resistant Torx® tool T50, install the passenger's side air bag module bolts. Torque the bolts to 11–18 ft. lbs. (15–25 Nm).

c. Connect the harness connector and install the air bag module bracket; then, install the lower panel screws.

d. Connect the passenger's side air bag module connector and install the glove box clips.

16. Install the instrument panel by performing the following procedure:

a. Using an assistant, install the instrument panel.

b. Install the instrument panel and pads nuts and bolts.

c. At both sides, install the pillar garnishes.

d. Install the defroster grille.

e. Install the lower instrument center panel and the lower instrument center panel screws.

f. Install the console box; then, install the screw and connect the harness connector.

g. Connect the harness connector and install the screw; then, install the shifter (automatic transmission) or shift lever boot (manual transmission).

h. Install the ashtray.

i. Install the air conditioning control unit, connect the electrical harness connectors and the air conditioning control unit screws.

j. Install the audio assembly and the audio assembly screws.

k. Install the cluster lid **"C"**, connect the electrical harness connectors and install the cluster lid **"C"** screws.

l. Install the combination meter, connect the electrical harness connectors and install the combination meter screws.

m. Install the cluster lid **"A"** and the cluster lid **"A"** screws.

n. At the driver's side, install the lower panel, connect the electrical harness connectors and install the panel screws.

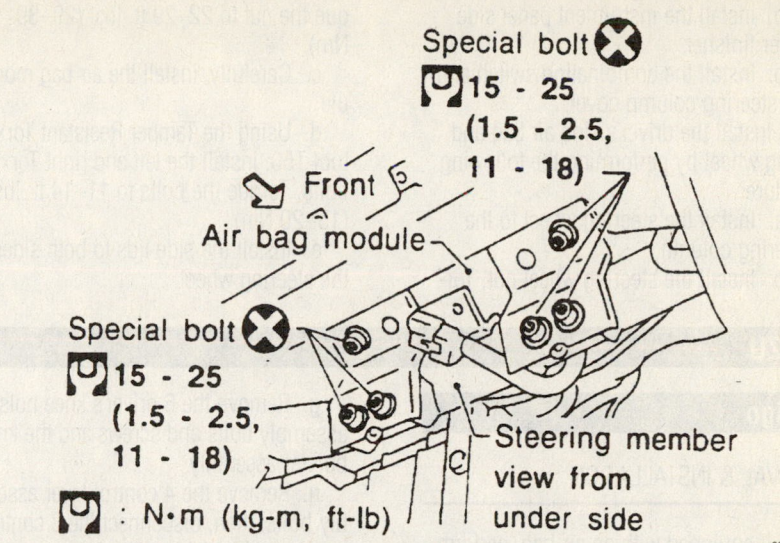

Special bolt ⊗
15 - 25
(1.5 - 2.5,
11 - 18)

Front

Air bag module

Special bolt ⊗
15 - 25
(1.5 - 2.5,
11 - 18)

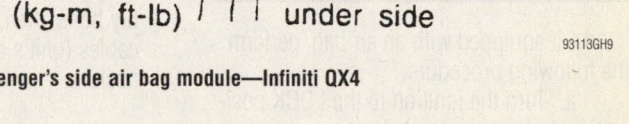
: N•m (kg-m, ft-lb)

Steering member view from under side

93113GH9

Exploded view of the passenger's side air bag module—Infiniti QX4

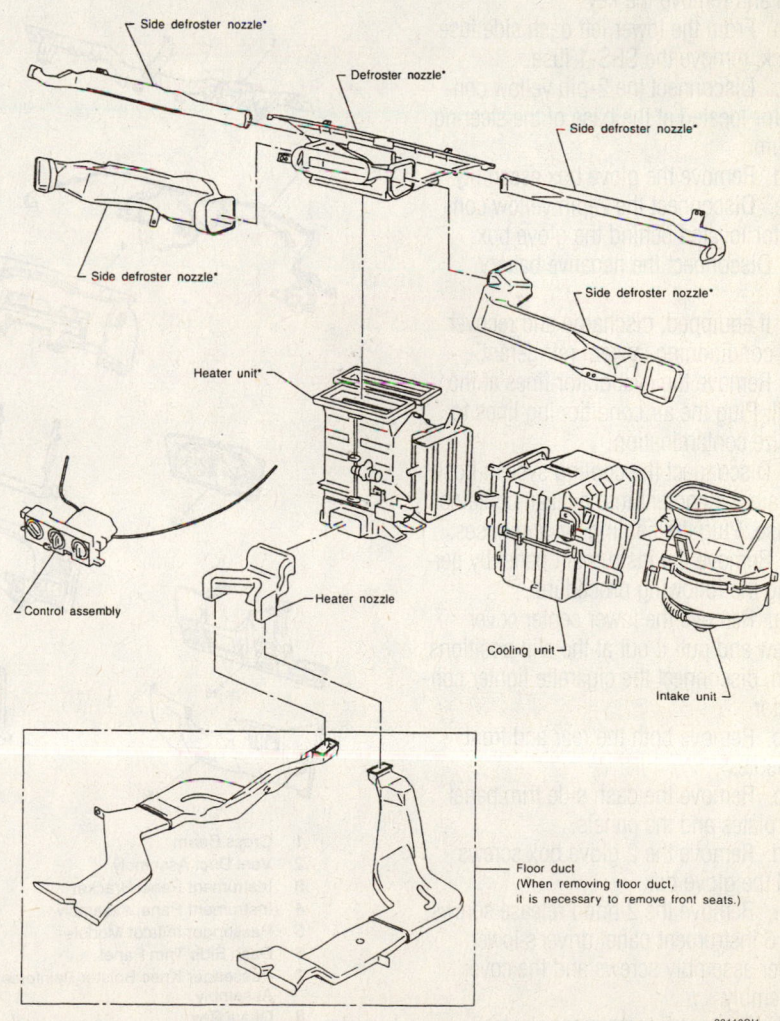

Side defroster nozzle*

Defroster nozzle*

Side defroster nozzle*

Side defroster nozzle*

Side defroster nozzle*

Heater unit*

Control assembly

Heater nozzle

Cooling unit

Intake unit

Floor duct
(When removing floor duct, it is necessary to remove front seats.)

93113GI1

Exploded view of the heater housing, the evaporator housing, the ventilation dusts and related accessories—Infiniti QX4

Refer to the model specific sections for engine mechanical service procedures

o. Install the instrument panel side lower finisher.

p. Install the combination switch and the steering column cover.

17. Install the driver's side air bag and steering wheel by performing the following procedure:

a. Install the steering wheel to the steering column.

b. Install the steering wheel nut. Torque the nut to 22–29 ft. lbs. (29–39 Nm).

c. Carefully, install the air bag module.

d. Using the Tamper Resistant Torx® tool T50, install the left and right Torx® bolts. Torque the bolts to 11–14 ft. lbs. (15–20 Nm).

e. Install the side lids to both sides of the steering wheel.

f. Connect the air bag module connector and install the lower lid to the steering wheel.

18. Connect the heater hoses to the heater core.

19. Refill the cooling system.

20. Connect the negative battery cable.

21. Run the engine to normal operating temperatures; then, check the climate control operation and check for leaks.

ISUZU

Amigo

REMOVAL & INSTALLATION

1. If equipped with an air bag, perform the following procedure:

a. Turn the ignition to the LOCK position and remove the key.

b. From the lower left dash side fuse block, remove the SRS-1 fuse.

c. Disconnect the 2-pin yellow connector located at the base of the steering column.

d. Remove the glove box assembly.

e. Disconnect the 2-pin yellow connector located behind the glove box.

2. Disconnect the negative battery cable.

3. If equipped, discharge and recover the air conditioning system refrigerant.

4. Remove the evaporator lines at the firewall. Plug the air conditioning lines to minimize contamination.

5. Disconnect the cooling system hoses and drain the coolant into a clean container for reuse. Plug the cooling system hoses.

6. Remove the instrument panel by performing the following procedure:

a. Remove the lower center cover screw and pull it out at the clip positions; then, disconnect the cigarette lighter connector.

b. Remove both the rear and front console.

c. Remove the dash side trim panel sill plates and the panels.

d. Remove the 2 glove box screws and the glove box.

e. Remove the 2 hood release screws, the 6 instrument panel driver's lower cover assembly screws and the cover assembly.

f. Remove 5 instrument cluster screws, the 2 clips; then, disconnect the 8 switch connectors and remove the instrument cluster assembly.

g. Remove the 6 driver's knee bolster assembly bolts and screws and the knee bolster assembly.

h. Remove the 4 control lever assembly bolts; then, disconnect the 3 control cables (unit side) and the 3 harness connectors.

i. Remove the 4 radio/audio sub box assembly screws and the radio/audio sub box assembly.

j. Disconnect or remove the following instrument panel harness connectors or items:

• The 6 driver's side connectors

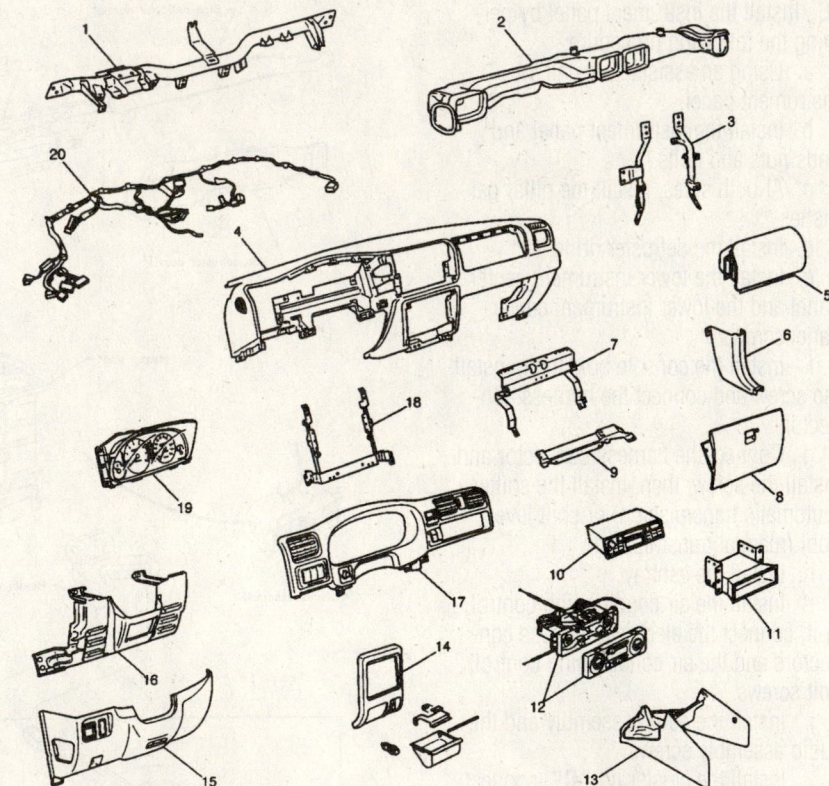

1	Cross Beam
2	Vent Duct Assembly
3	Instrument Panel Bracket
4	Instrument Panel Assembly
5	Passenger Inflator Module
6	Dash Side Trim Panel
7	Passenger Knee Bolster Reinforcement Assembly
8	Glove Box
9	Passenger Lower Bracket
10	Radio Assembly
11	Audio Sub Box
12	Control Lever Assembly
13	Front Console Assembly
14	Lower Center Cover
15	Instrument Panel Driver Lower Cover Assembly
16	Driver Knee Bolster Assembly
17	Meter Cluster Assembly
18	Instrument Panel Center Reinforcement
19	Meter Assembly
20	Instrument Harness Assembly

93113GB8

Exploded view of the instrument panel—Isuzu Amigo

- The 3 passenger's side connectors
- The 2 center connectors
- Passenger's inflator module connector
- Radio antenna cable plug
- Ground cable bolt on the left dash side panel
- The 8 instrument panel-to-chassis bolts and the 3 nuts.

k. Remove the instrument panel assembly.

7. Remove the instrument panel bracket by performing the following procedure:

a. Remove the 2 passenger's inflator module bolts and 4 nuts.

b. Remove the 4 meter assembly screws; then, disconnect the meter wiring harness connectors and remove the meter assembly.

c. Remove the 5 vent duct assembly screws and the assembly.

d. Remove the 3 lower passenger bracket screws and the bracket.

e. Remove the 9 passenger knee bolster reinforcement screws and the reinforcement.

f. Remove the 6 instrument panel

center reinforcement screws and the reinforcement.

g. Remove the instrument panel wiring harness assembly clips and the wiring harness.

h. Remove the 2 instrument panel bracket nuts and 2 bolts for each bracket; then, remove the bracket(s).

8. Remove the 5 cross beam assembly nuts, 2 bolts and the 6 lower bolts; then, remove the crossbeam.

9. Disconnect the resistor wiring connector.

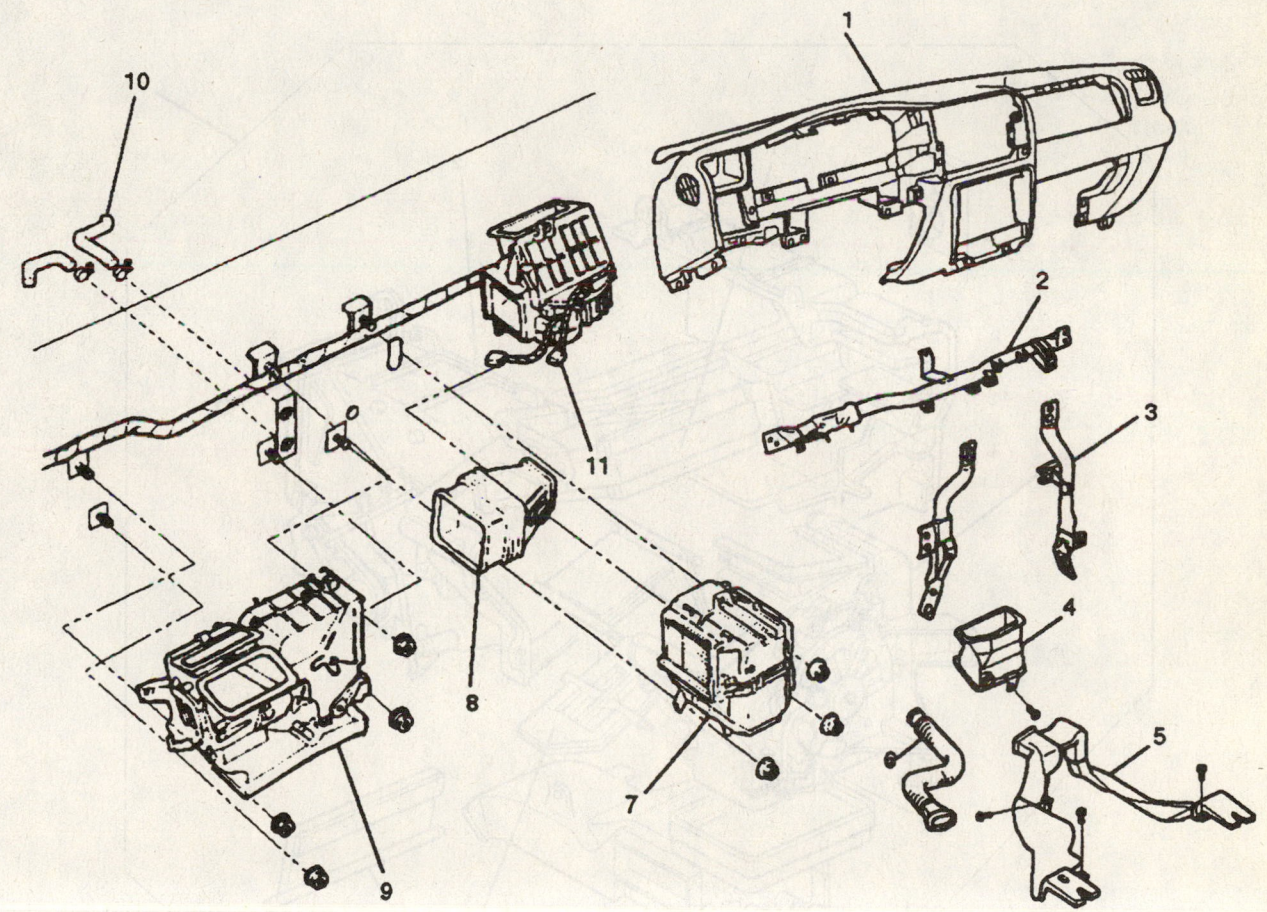

1	Instrument Panel Assembly	6	Driver Lap Vent Duct
2	Cross Beam Assembly	7	Evaporator Assembly (A/C only)
3	Instrument Panel Bracket	8	Duct
4	Ventilation Lower Duct	9	Heater Unit Assembly
5	Rear Heater Duct	10	Heater Hose
		11	Resistor Connector

93113GB9

View of the heater and air conditioning housing assemblies and related components—Isuzu Amigo

Refer to the model specific sections for cooling system service procedures

10. Remove the duct from the heater assembly.

11. If equipped with air conditioning, remove the evaporator assembly.

12. Remove the driver's lap vent.

13. Remove the lower ventilation duct.

14. Remove the footrest, the carpet, the 3 clips and the rear heater duct.

15. Remove the heater assembly.

16. Remove the mode control case-to-temperature control case screws and remove the mode control case; do not remove the link unit.

17. Remove the temperature control case screws and separate the cases.

18. Remove the heater core from the case.

To install:

19. Install the heater core to the case.

20. Assemble the temperature control cases and install the case screws.

21. Install the mode control case and the mode control case-to-temperature control case screws.

22. Install the heater assembly.

23. Install the rear heater duct, the footrest, the carpet, and the 3 clips.

24. Install the lower ventilation duct.

25. Install the driver's lap vent.

26. If equipped with air conditioning, install the evaporator assembly.

27. Install the duct to the heater assembly.

28. Connect the resistor wiring connector.

29. Install the crossbeam, the 5 crossbeam assembly nuts, 2 bolts and the 6 lower bolts.

30. Install the instrument panel bracket by performing the following procedure:

   a. Install the instrument panel bracket and the 2 nuts and 2 bolts for each bracket.

   b. Install the instrument panel wiring harness assembly and the wiring harness clips.

   c. Install the instrument panel center reinforcement and the 6 reinforcement screws.

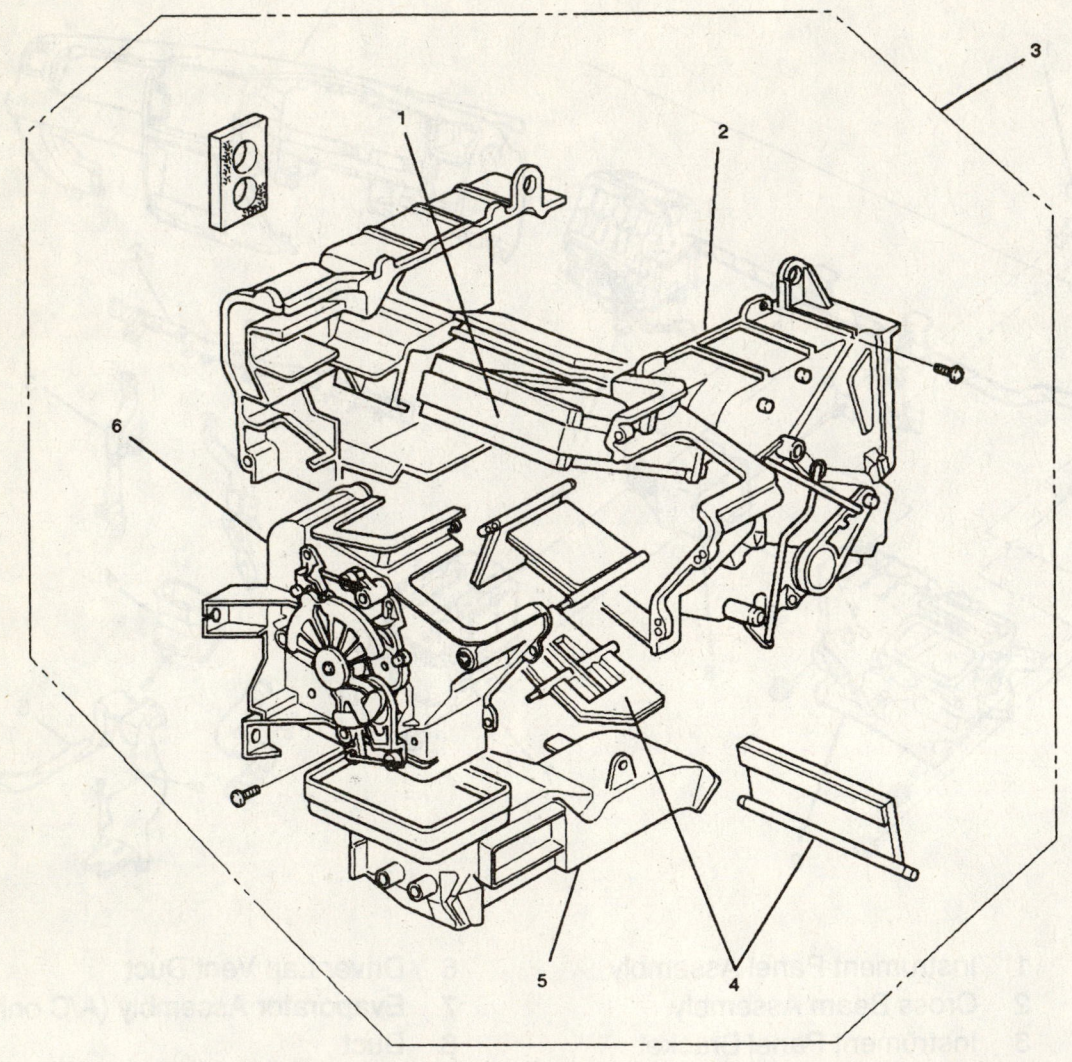

1	Heater Core	4	Mode Door
2	Case (Temperature Control)	5	Duct
3	Heater Unit	6	Case (Mode Control)

93113GB0

Exploded view of the heater housing assembly—Isuzu Amigo

d. Install the passenger knee bolster reinforcement and the 9 reinforcement screws.

e. Install the lower passenger bracket and the 3 bracket screws.

f. Install the vent duct assembly and the 5 vent duct assembly screws.

g. Install the meter assembly and the 4 meter assembly screws; then, connect the meter wiring harness connectors.

h. Install the 2 passenger's inflator module bolts and 4 nuts.

31. Install the instrument panel by performing the following procedure:

a. Install the instrument panel assembly.

b. Connect or install the following instrument panel harness connectors or items:

- The 6 driver's side connectors
- The 3 passenger's side connectors
- The 2 center connectors
- Passenger's inflator module connector
- Radio antenna cable plug
- Ground cable bolt on the left dash side panel
- The 8 instrument panel-to-chassis bolts and the 3 nuts.

c. Install the radio/audio sub box assembly and the 4 radio/audio sub box assembly screws.

d. Connect the 3 control cables (unit side) and the 3 harness connectors. Install the 4 control lever assembly bolts.

e. Install the knee bolster assembly and the 6 driver's knee bolster assembly bolts and screws.

f. Install the instrument cluster assembly. Connect the 8 switch connectors. Install 5 instrument cluster screws and the 2 clips.

g. Install the 2 hood release screws, the 6 instrument panel driver's lower cover assembly screws and the cover assembly.

h. Install the glove box and the 2 glove box screws.

i. Install the dash side trim panel sill plates and the panels.

j. Install both the rear and front console.

k. Connect the cigarette lighter connector and install the lower center cover screw.

32. Connect the cooling system hoses.

33. Refill the cooling system.

34. Install the evaporator lines at the firewall.

35. If equipped, evacuate and charge the air conditioning system.

36. Connect the negative battery cable.

37. If equipped with an air bag, perform the following procedure:

a. Turn the ignition to the LOCK position and remove the key.

b. Connect the 2-pin yellow connector located behind the glove box.

c. Install the glove box assembly.

d. Connect the 2-pin yellow connector located at the base of the steering column.

e. At the lower left dash side fuse block, install the SRS-1 fuse.

f. Turn the ignition switch to ON and verify that the AIR BAG warning light flashes 7 times and turns OFF.

38. Run the engine to normal operating temperatures; then, check the climate control operation and check for leaks.

Hombre

REMOVAL & INSTALLATION

1. Disconnect the negative battery cable.

2. Drain the cooling system into a clean container for reuse.

3. Remove the heater hoses from the heater core.

4. Remove the instrument panel as follows:

a. Disable the air bag system.

b. Set the parking brake and block the wheels.

c. Disconnect the parking brake release cable from the parking brake lever.

d. Unfasten the screws that retain the DLC instrument panel left side sound insulator. Feed the DLC through the hole in the sound insulator.

e. Unfasten the right side sound insulator panel screws and remove the panel.

f. Unfasten the screws that attach the instrument panel left side sound insulator to the knee bolster and cowl panel.

g. Unfasten the nut that attaches the left side sound insulator to the accelerator pedal bracket.

h. Unplug the remote control door lock receiver module electrical connector.

i. Remove the door lock receiver module from the left side sound insulator. Remove the left side sound insulator.

j. Unfasten the screws that attach the instrument panel center sound insulator

to the knee bolster, instrument panel, heater assembly and floor duct.

k. Remove the center sound insulator.

l. Unfasten the screws that attach the courtesy lamp to the knee bolster.

m. Unfasten the screws that attach the knee bolster to the instrument panel.

n. Disconnect the lap cooler duct from the knee bolster.

o. Unplug the lighter electrical connection and remove the knee bolster.

p. Unfasten the steering column-to-instrument panel nuts and lower the column.

q. Unfasten the screws that attach the instrument panel accessory trim plate to the instrument panel.

r. Remove the trim plate and unplug all necessary electrical connection.

s. Remove the heater and/or air conditioning control assembly.

t. Remove the radio and the storage compartment assembly (if equipped).

u. If necessary, remove the instrument cluster.

v. Unfasten the left and right instrument panel pivot bolts and the panel lower support bolt.

w. Unfasten the speaker grilles retaining screws and remove the speaker grilles.

x. Remove the windshield defroster grille using a flat-bladed prytool. Start at one end of the grille and work your way down the grille.

y. Unfasten the four instrument panel upper support screws.

z. Tag and unplug all necessary electrical connections.

aa. Remove the instrument panel from the vehicle.

5. Remove the air inlet assembly, if equipped.

6. Remove the vacuum hoses.

7. From inside the engine compartment, remove the heater assembly studs.

8. Remove the blower motor resistor.

9. From inside the heater case assembly, remove the stud; the stud is located behind the blower motor resistor.

10. Remove the heater assembly-to-chassis screws.

11. Remove the heater assembly from the vehicle.

12. Remove the access cover screws and cover from the heater assembly.

13. Remove the heater core from the heater case assembly.

To install:

14. Install the heater core to the heater case assembly.

15. Install the access cover to the heater assembly and the cover screws.

16. Install the heater assembly to the vehicle.

17. Install the heater assembly-to-chassis screws and torque them to 40 inch lbs. (4.5 Nm).

18. Working inside the heater case assembly, install the stud; the stud is located behind the blower motor resistor.

19. Install the blower motor resistor.

20. Working inside the engine compartment, install the heater assembly studs and torque them to 17 inch lbs. (1.9 Nm).

21. Install the vacuum hoses.

22. Install the air inlet assembly, if equipped.

23. Install the instrument panel as follows:

　a. Rest the instrument panel on the lower pivot studs.

　b. Attach the electrical connections.

　c. Install but do not tighten the four upper instrument panel support screws.

　d. Install the left and right panel pivot bolts. Tighten the bolts to 102 inch lbs. (11.5 Nm).

　e. Install the panel lower support bolt. Tighten the bolt to 102 inch lbs. (11.5 Nm).

　f. Tighten the upper support screws to 17 inch lbs. (1.9 Nm).

　g. Install the windshield defroster grille and the speaker grilles.

　h. Install the radio and storage compartment assembly (if equipped).

　i. If removed, install the instrument cluster.

　j. Install the heater and/or air conditioning control assembly.

　k. attach the electrical connections to the instrument panel accessory trim plate.

　l. Place the trim plate in position and install its retaining screws. Tighten the screws to 17 inch lbs. (1.9 Nm).

　m. Place the steering column into position and install its retaining nuts. Tighten the nuts to 22 ft. lbs. (30 Nm).

　n. Attach the lighter electrical connection and the lap cooler duct to the knee bolster.

　o. Place the knee bolster into position and install its retaining screws. Tighten the Torx• head screws to 80 inch lbs. (9 Nm) and the hex head screws to 17 inch lbs. (1.9 Nm).

　p. Place the courtesy lamp in position and install its screws. Tighten the screws to 17 inch lbs. (1.9 Nm).

　q. Place the instrument panel center sound insulator in position. Install the screws that attach the center sound insulator to the knee bolster, instrument panel and the floor duct. Tighten the screws to 17 inch lbs. (1.9 Nm).

　r. Install the screw that attaches the center sound insulator to the heater assembly. Tighten the screw to 13 inch lbs. (1.5 Nm).

　s. Install the remote control door lock receiver module to the instrument panel left side sound insulator.

　t. Attach the door lock receiver electrical connection.

　u. Install the nut that attaches the left side sound insulator to the accelerator pedal bracket. Tighten the nut to 35 inch lbs. (4 Nm).

　v. Install the screw that attaches the left side sound insulator to cowl panel. Tighten the screw to 13 inch lbs. (1.5 Nm).

　w. Install the screws that attach the left side sound insulator to knee bolster. Tighten the screw to 17 inch lbs. (1.9 Nm).

　x. Feed the DLC through the hole in the sound insulator, place the DLC in position and install its retaining screws. Tighten the screws to 21 inch lbs. (2.4 Nm).

　y. Install the right side sound insulator and tighten the screws

　z. Connect the parking brake release cable to the lever.

　aa. Enable the air bag system.

24. Install the heater hoses to the heater core.

25. Refill the cooling system.

26. Connect the negative battery cable.

27. Run the engine to normal operating temperatures; then, check the climate control operation and check for leaks.

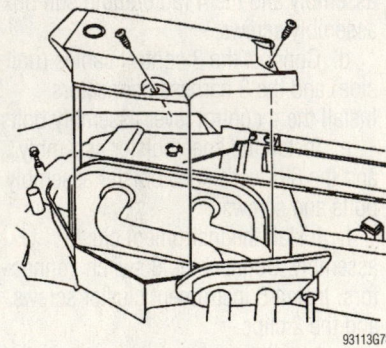

View of the heater case cover—Isuzu Hombre

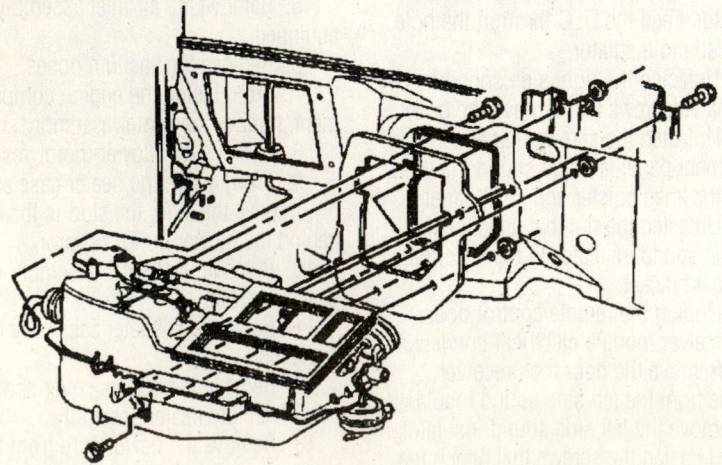

View of the heater case assembly—Isuzu Hombre

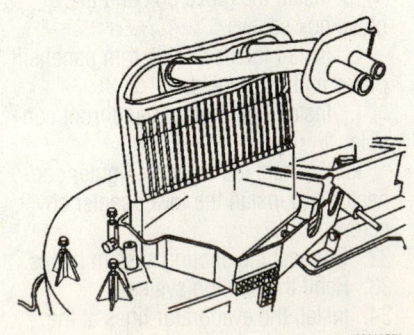

View of the heater core—Isuzu Hombre

Oasis

REMOVAL & INSTALLATION

➡️**Make sure to acquire the anti-theft code for the radio and write down the frequencies for the radio's preset buttons.**

1. Disconnect the negative battery cable.

❊❊ CAUTION

Wait at least 3 minutes for the air bag to deplete its energy before working on the steering wheel or instrument panel.

2. In the engine compartment, remove the heater valve cable clamp; then, disconnect the heater valve cable and rotate the heater valve to the fully open position.

3. Drain the engine coolant into a clean container for reuse.

4. Disconnect the heater hoses from the heater unit.

5. Remove the heater housing-to-chassis nuts.

➡️**When removing the nuts, be careful not to damage or bend the fuel lines, the brake lines or etc.**

6. Remove the center console.

7. Remove the instrument panel

8. Remove the steering hanger beam mounting bolts and the steering hanger beam.

9. Remove the evaporator housing by performing the following procedure:

   a. Discharge and recover the air conditioning system refrigerant.

   b. Remove the refrigerant lines. Discard the O-rings. Plug the openings to prevent contamination.

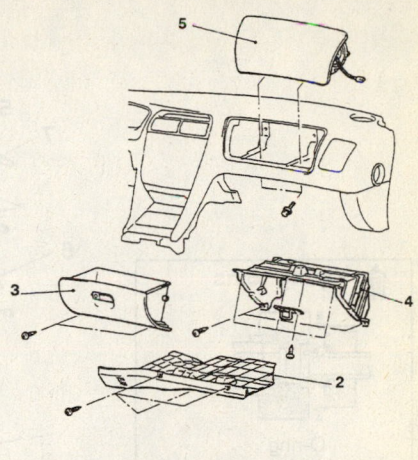

2. UNDERCOVER
3. GLOVE BOX ASSEMBLY
4. GLOVE BOX CASE
5. AIR BAG MODULE

93112GG1

View of the heater housing, evaporator housing and related components—Isuzu Oasis

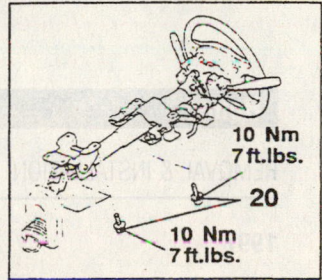

10 Nm
7 ft.lbs.

20

10 Nm
7 ft.lbs.

1. COLUMN COVER
2. HOOD LOCK RELEASE HANDLE
3. PARKING BRAKE RELEASE HANDLE
4. INSTRUMENT PANEL LOWER COVER ASSEMBLY (LH)
5. KEY CYLINDER PANEL
6. INSTRUMENT PANEL ECU
7. METER BEZEL
8. COMBINATION METER
9. CENTER AIR OUTLET ASSEMBLY
10. ASHTRAY
11. AIR CONTROL PANEL ASSEMBLY & AUDIO UNIT
12. UNDERCOVER ASSEMBLY
13. GLOVEBOX ASSEMBLY
14. GLOVEBOX OUTER CASE
15. PASSENGER SIDE AIRBAG MODULE
16. CONSOLE SIDE COVER ASSEMBLY
17. FLOOR CARPET REAR REINFORCEMENT
18. HARNESS CONNECTOR
19. PLUG
20. STEERING COLUMN MOUNTIN BOLT
21. INSTRUMENT PANEL

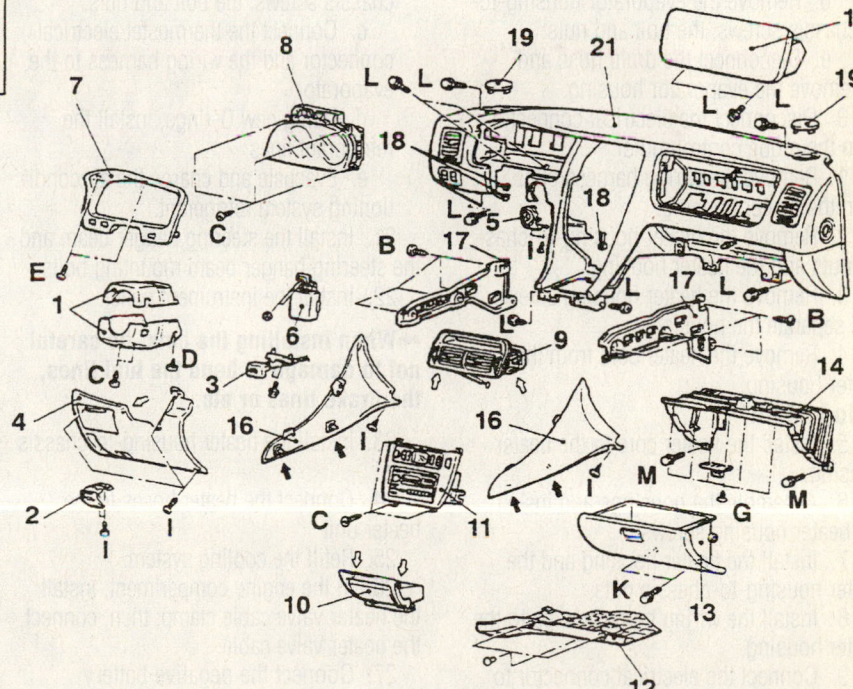

NOTE
(1) ⇦ : metal clip position
(2) ⬅ : plastic clip position

93112GG2

View of the steering hanger beam and related components—Isuzu Oasis

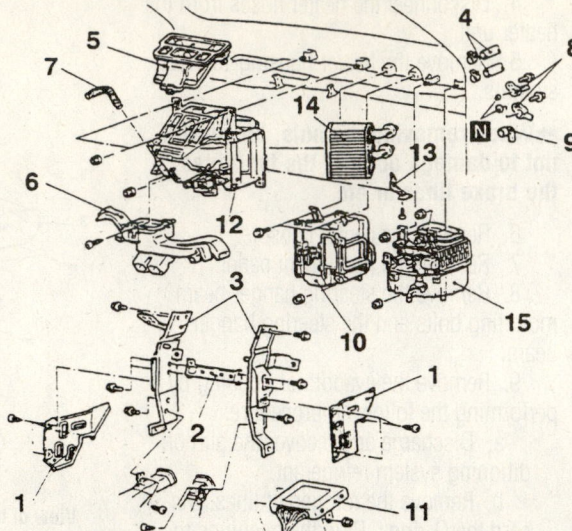

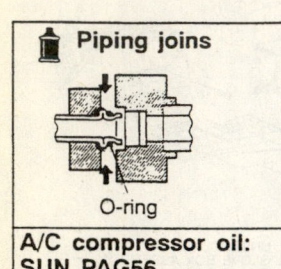

Piping joins

O-ring

A/C compressor oil:
SUN PAG56

1. FLOOR CARPET FRONT
   REINFORCEMENT
3. ECU BRACKET
4. CENTER STAY ASSEMBLY
5. HEATER HOSE CONNECTION
6. CENTER DUCT ASSEMBLY
7. FOOT DISTRIBUTION DUCT
8. BREATHER HOSE
9. SUCTION PIPE, LIQUID PIPE B
   AND COOLING UNIT
   CONNECTION
10. DRAIN HOSE
11. EVAPORATOR
12. ENGINE CONTROL MODULE
13. HEATER UNIT
14. HEATER CORE SUPPORT
15. HEATER CORE

93112GG3

Exploded view of the heater core, the heater housing and related components—Isuzu Oasis

c. Disconnect the thermostat electrical connector and the wiring harness from the evaporator.

d. Remove the evaporator housing-to-chassis screws, the bolt and nuts.

e. Disconnect the drain hose and remove the evaporator housing.

10. Disconnect the electrical connector from the mode control motor.

11. Remove the wiring harness clips from the heater housing.

12. Remove the heater housing-to-chassis nuts and the heater housing.

13. Remove the heater housing screws and separate the housings.

14. Remove the heater core from the heater housing.

To install:

15. Install the heater core to the heater housing.

16. Assemble the housings and install the heater housing screws.

17. Install the heater housing and the heater housing-to-chassis nuts.

18. Install the wiring harness clips to the heater housing.

19. Connect the electrical connector to the mode control motor.

20. Install the evaporator housing by performing the following procedure:

a. Install the evaporator housing and connect the drain hose.

b. Install the evaporator housing-to-chassis screws, the bolt and nuts.

c. Connect the thermostat electrical connector and the wiring harness to the evaporator.

d. Using new O-rings, install the refrigerant lines.

e. Evacuate and charge the air conditioning system refrigerant.

21. Install the steering hanger beam and the steering hanger beam mounting bolts.

22. Install the instrument panel.

➡**When installing the nuts, be careful not to damage or bend the fuel lines, the brake lines or etc.**

23. Install the heater housing-to-chassis nuts.

24. Connect the heater hoses to the heater unit.

25. Refill the cooling system.

26. In the engine compartment, Install the heater valve cable clamp; then, connect the heater valve cable.

27. Connect the negative battery cable.

28. Run the engine to normal operating temperatures; then, check the climate control operation and check for leaks.

Rodeo

REMOVAL & INSTALLATION

1997

1. Disconnect the negative battery cable.

2. Discharge and recover the air conditioning system refrigerant.

3. Remove the evaporator lines at the firewall. Plug the air conditioning lines to minimize contamination.

4. Disconnect the cooling system hoses and drain the coolant into a clean container for reuse. Plug the cooling system hoses.

5. Remove the instrument panel by performing the following procedure:

a. Remove the steering wheel.

b. Remove the instrument cluster bezel, then remove the instrument cluster.

c. Remove the hood release handle. Remove the lower steering column cover.

d. Remove the fuse box, the left side trim and remove the ECM, if applicable.

e. Remove the front console and the lower reinforcement.

f. Remove the right speaker grille and the glove box.

g. Remove the knobs from the control

panel, then remove the panel bezel and the control panel.

h. Remove the illumination controller (to the right of the steering column).

i. Remove the instrument panel.

6. Remove the resistor connector.

7. If not equipped with air conditioning, remove the heater-to-blower air duct.

8. If equipped with air conditioning, remove the evaporator assembly.

9. Remove the instrument panel support.

10. Remove the heater unit attaching nuts and remove the assembly.

11. Disassemble the heater unit case and remove the heater core.

To install:

12. Assemble the heater unit case and install the heater core.

13. Install the assembly and the heater unit attaching nuts.

14. Install the instrument panel support.

15. If equipped with air conditioning, install the evaporator assembly.

16. If not equipped with air conditioning, install the heater-to-blower air duct.

17. Install the resistor connector.

18. Install the instrument panel by performing the following procedure:

a. Install the instrument panel.

b. Install the illumination controller (to the right of the steering column).

c. Install the panel bezel and the control panel, then the knobs to the control panel.

d. Install the right speaker grille and the glove box.

e. Install the lower reinforcement and the front console.

f. Install the ECM (if applicable), the fuse box and the left side trim.

g. Install the lower steering column cover and the hood release handle.

h. Install the instrument cluster and the instrument cluster bezel.

i. Install the steering wheel.

19. Install the evaporator lines at the firewall.

20. Refill the cooling system.

21. Evacuate and charge the air conditioning system.

22. Connect the negative battery cable.

23. Run the engine to normal operating temperatures; then, check the climate control operation and check for leaks.

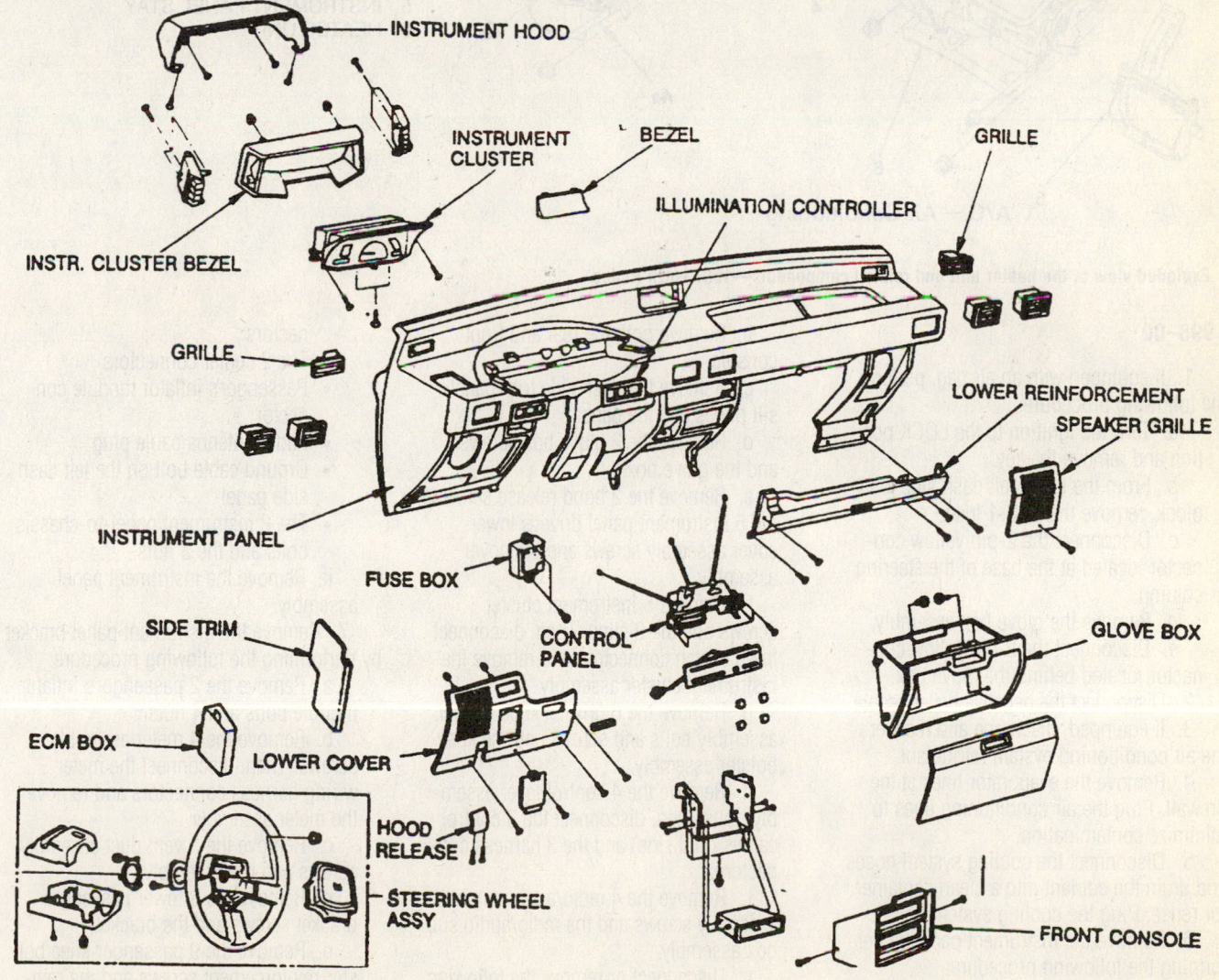

Exploded view of the instrument panel—1997 Isuzu Rodeo

93113G75

Refer to the model specific sections for engine mechanical service procedures

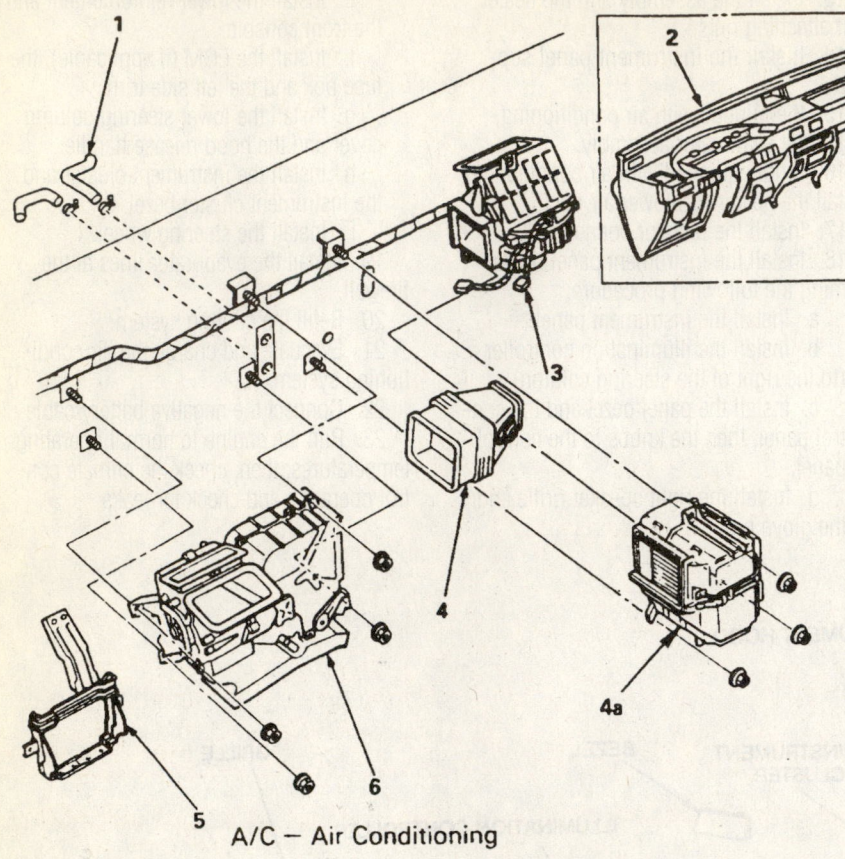

1. HEATER UNIT
2. INSTRUMENT PANEL ASSEMBLY
3. RESISTOR CONNECTOR
4. DUCT
4A. EVAPORATOR ASSEMBLY (A/C ONLY)
5. INSTRUMENT PANEL STAY
6. HEATER UNIT

A/C – Air Conditioning

93113G76

Exploded view of the heater unit and related components—1997 Isuzu Rodeo

1998–00

1. If equipped with an air bag, perform the following procedure:

a. Turn the ignition to the LOCK position and remove the key.

b. From the lower left dash side fuse block, remove the SRS-1 fuse.

c. Disconnect the 2-pin yellow connector located at the base of the steering column.

d. Remove the glove box assembly.

e. Disconnect the 2-pin yellow connector located behind the glove box.

2. Disconnect the negative battery cable.

3. If equipped, discharge and recover the air conditioning system refrigerant.

4. Remove the evaporator lines at the firewall. Plug the air conditioning lines to minimize contamination.

5. Disconnect the cooling system hoses and drain the coolant into a clean container for reuse. Plug the cooling system hoses.

6. Remove the instrument panel by performing the following procedure:

a. Remove the lower center cover screw and pull it out at the clip positions; then, disconnect the cigarette lighter connector.

b. Remove both the rear and front console.

c. Remove the dash side trim panel sill plates and the panels.

d. Remove the 2 glove box screws and the glove box.

e. Remove the 2 hood release screws, the 6 instrument panel driver's lower cover assembly screws and the cover assembly.

f. Remove 5 instrument cluster screws and the 2 clips. Then, disconnect the 8 switch connectors and remove the instrument cluster assembly.

g. Remove the 6 driver's knee bolster assembly bolts and screws and the knee bolster assembly.

h. Remove the 4 control lever assembly bolts; then, disconnect the 3 control cables (unit side) and the 3 harness connectors.

i. Remove the 4 radio/audio sub box assembly screws and the radio/audio sub box assembly.

j. Disconnect or remove the following instrument panel harness connectors or items:

• The 6 driver's side connectors
• The 3 passenger's side connectors

• The 2 center connectors
• Passenger's inflator module connector
• Radio antenna cable plug
• Ground cable bolt on the left dash side panel
• The 8 instrument panel-to-chassis bolts and the 3 nuts.

k. Remove the instrument panel assembly.

7. Remove the instrument panel bracket by performing the following procedure:

a. Remove the 2 passenger's inflator module bolts and 4 nuts.

b. Remove the 4 meter assembly screws. Then, disconnect the meter wiring harness connectors and remove the meter assembly.

c. Remove the 5 vent duct assembly screws and the assembly.

d. Remove the 3 lower passenger bracket screws and the bracket.

e. Remove the 9 passenger knee bolster reinforcement screws and the reinforcement.

f. Remove the 6 instrument panel center reinforcement screws and the reinforcement.

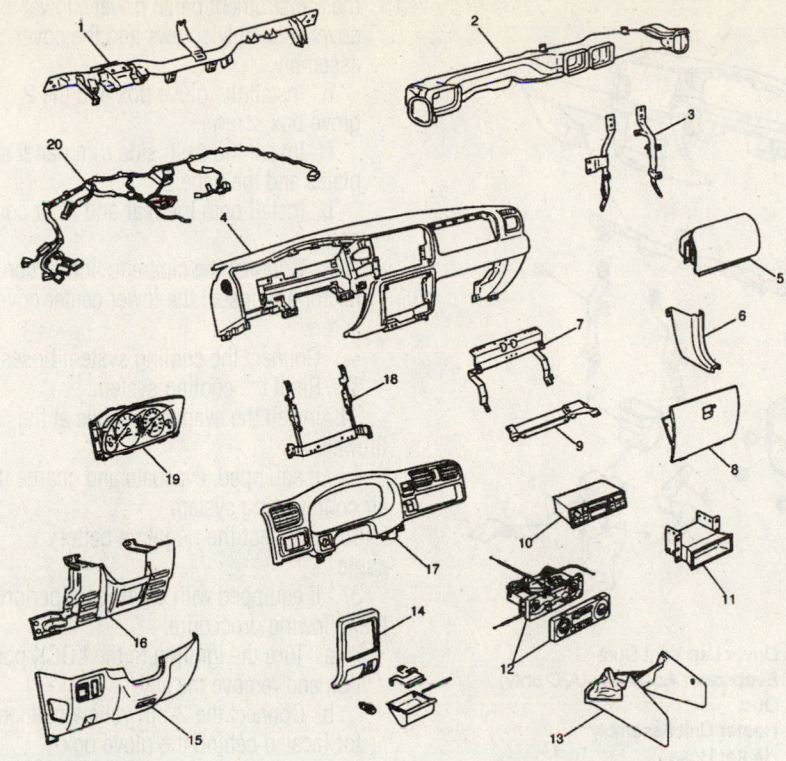

1	Cross Beam	11	Audio Sub Box
2	Vent Duct Assembly	12	Control Lever Assembly
3	Instrument Panel Bracket	13	Front Console Assembly
4	Instrument Panel Assembly	14	Lower Center Cover
5	Passenger Inflator Module	15	Instrument Panel Driver Lower Cover
6	Dash Side Trim Panel		Assembly
7	Passenger Knee Bolster Reinforcement	16	Driver Knee Bolster Assembly
	Assembly	17	Meter Cluster Assembly
8	Glove Box	18	Instrument Panel Center Reinforcement
9	Passenger Lower Bracket	19	Meter Assembly
10	Radio Assembly	20	Instrument Harness Assembly

93113GB8

Exploded view of the instrument panel—1998–00 Isuzu Rodeo

g. Remove the instrument panel wiring harness assembly clips and the wiring harness.

h. Remove the 2 instrument panel bracket nuts and 2 bolts for each bracket; then, remove the bracket(s).

8. Remove the 5 cross beam assembly nuts, 2 bolts and the 6 lower bolts; then, remove the crossbeam.

9. Disconnect the resistor wiring connector.

10. Remove the duct from the heater assembly.

11. If equipped with air conditioning, remove the evaporator assembly.

12. Remove the driver's lap vent.

13. Remove the lower ventilation duct.

14. Remove the footrest, the carpet, the 3 clips and the rear heater duct.

15. Remove the heater assembly.

16. Remove the mode control case-to-temperature control case screws and

remove the mode control case; do not remove the link unit.

17. Remove the temperature control case screws and separate the cases.

18. Remove the heater core from the case.

To install:

19. Install the heater core to the case.

20. Assemble the temperature control cases and install the case screws.

21. Install the mode control case and the mode control case-to-temperature control case screws.

22. Install the heater assembly.

23. Install the rear heater duct, the footrest, the carpet, and the 3 clips.

24. Install the lower ventilation duct.

25. Install the driver's lap vent.

26. If equipped with air conditioning, install the evaporator assembly.

27. Install the duct to the heater assembly.

28. Connect the resistor wiring connector.

29. Install the crossbeam, the 5 crossbeam assembly nuts, 2 bolts and the 6 lower bolts.

30. Install the instrument panel bracket by performing the following procedure:

a. Install the instrument panel bracket and the 2 nuts and 2 bolts for each bracket.

b. Install the instrument panel wiring harness assembly and the wiring harness clips.

c. Install the instrument panel center reinforcement and the 6 reinforcement screws.

d. Install the passenger knee bolster reinforcement and the 9 reinforcement screws.

e. Install the lower passenger bracket and the 3 bracket screws.

f. Install the vent duct assembly and the 5 vent duct assembly screws.

g. Install the meter assembly and the 4 meter assembly screws. Then, connect the meter wiring harness connectors.

h. Install the 2 passenger's inflator module bolts and 4 nuts.

31. Install the instrument panel by performing the following procedure:

a. Install the instrument panel assembly.

b. Connect or install the following instrument panel harness connectors or items:

- The 6 driver's side connectors
- The 3 passenger's side connectors
- The 2 center connectors
- Passenger's inflator module connector
- Radio antenna cable plug
- Ground cable bolt on the left dash side panel
- The 8 instrument panel-to-chassis bolts and the 3 nuts.

c. Install the radio/audio sub box assembly and the 4 radio/audio sub box assembly screws.

d. Connect the 3 control cables (unit side) and the 3 harness connectors. Install the 4 control lever assembly bolts.

e. Install the knee bolster assembly and the 6 driver's knee bolster assembly bolts and screws.

f. Install the instrument cluster assembly. Connect the 8 switch connectors. Install 5 instrument cluster screws and the 2 clips.

g. Install the 2 hood release screws,

Refer to the model specific sections for cooling system service procedures

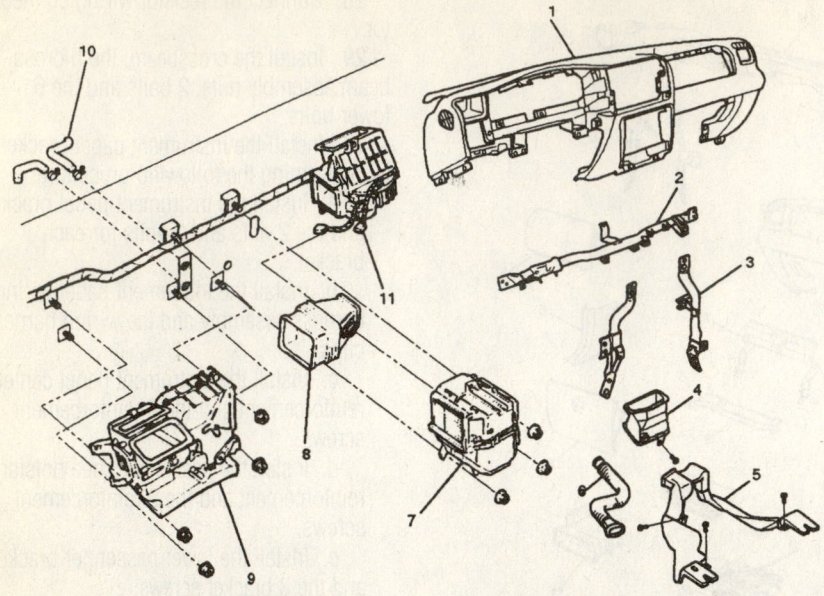

1 Instrument Panel Assembly
2 Cross Beam Assembly
3 Instrument Panel Bracket
4 Ventilation Lower Duct
5 Rear Heater Duct
6 Driver Lap Vent Duct
7 Evaporator Assembly (A/C only)
8 Duct
9 Heater Unit Assembly
10 Heater Hose
11 Resistor Connector

93113GB9

View of the heater and air conditioning housing assemblies and related components—1998–00 Isuzu Rodeo

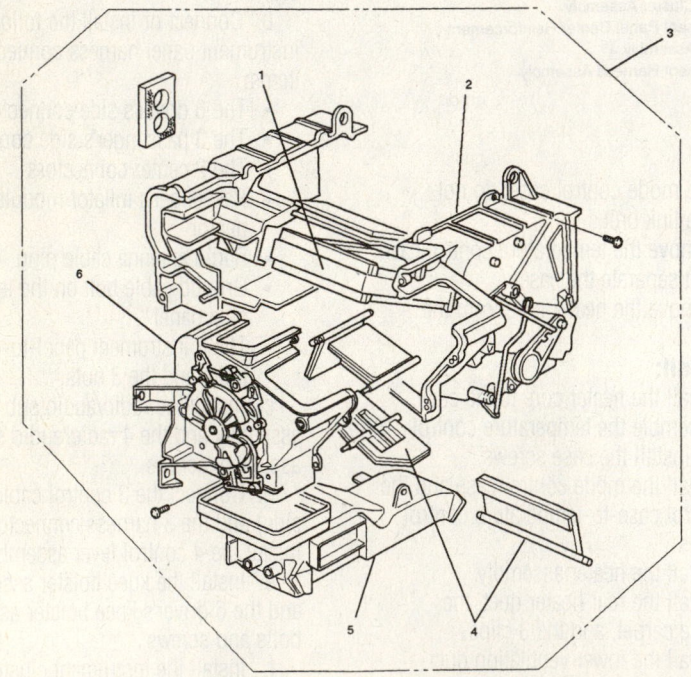

1 Heater Core
2 Case (Temperature Control)
3 Heater Unit
4 Mode Door
5 Duct
6 Case (Mode Control)

93113GB0

Exploded view of the heater housing assembly—1998–00 Isuzu Rodeo

the 6 instrument panel driver's lower cover assembly screws and the cover assembly.

h. Install the glove box and the 2 glove box screws.

i. Install the dash side trim panel sill plates and the panels.

j. Install both the rear and front console.

k. Connect the cigarette lighter connector and install the lower center cover screw.

32. Connect the cooling system hoses.

33. Refill the cooling system.

34. Install the evaporator lines at the firewall.

35. If equipped, evacuate and charge the air conditioning system.

36. Connect the negative battery cable.

37. If equipped with an air bag, perform the following procedure:

a. Turn the ignition to the LOCK position and remove the key.

b. Connect the 2-pin yellow connector located behind the glove box.

c. Install the glove box assembly.

d. Connect the 2-pin yellow connector located at the base of the steering column.

e. At the lower left dash side fuse block, install the SRS-1 fuse.

f. Turn the ignition switch to ON and verify that the AIR BAG warning light flashes 7 times and turns OFF.

38. Run the engine to normal operating temperatures; then, check the climate control operation and check for leaks.

Trooper

REMOVAL & INSTALLATION

✳✳ CAUTION

The vehicle is equipped with a driver's side and a passenger's side air bag. Before starting service procedures on components, especially under the instrument panel and/or near the steering column, disable the air bag systems. There is sufficient voltage in the system to cause a deployment for up to 15 seconds after the battery has been disconnected, the ignition turned OFF or fuse C-21 is removed from the fuse panel.

1. If equipped with an air bag, perform the following procedures:

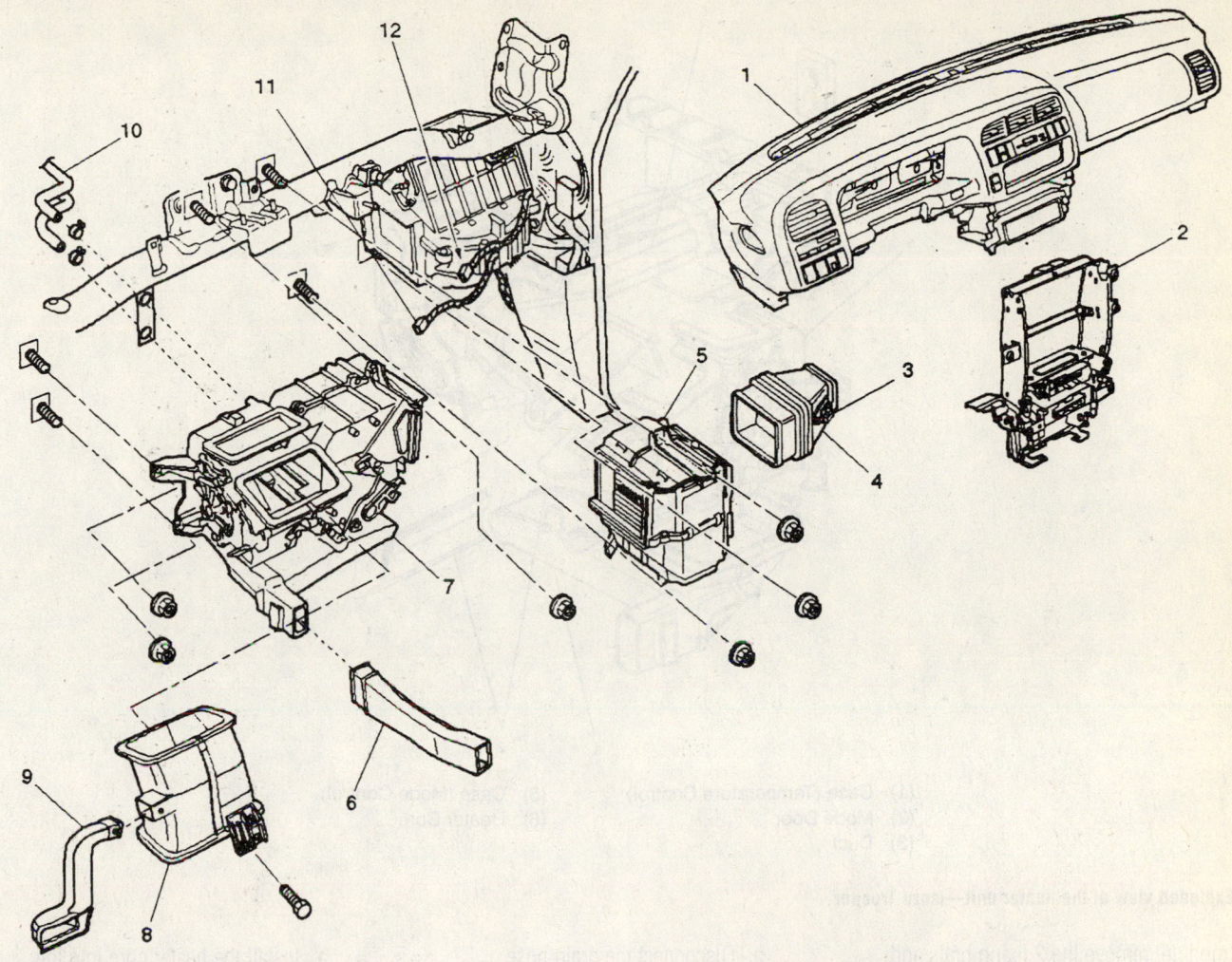

(1) Instrument Panel Assembly
(2) Instrument Panel Center Bracket
(3) Resistor
(4) Duct
(5) Evaporator Assembly (A/C only)
(6) Rear Heater Duct
(7) Heater Unit Assembly
(8) Center Ventilation Lower Duct
(9) Driver Lap Vent Nozzle
(10) Water Hose
(11) Electro Thermo Connector (With A/C)
(12) Resistor Connector

93113G01

Exploded view of the heater unit and related components—Isuzu Trooper

a. Disconnect the negative battery cable, then disconnect the positive battery cable.

b. Disconnect the yellow 2-pin connector located at the base of the steering column.

c. Remove the glove box and disconnect the yellow 2-pin connector located behind the glove box.

2. Disconnect the negative battery cable.

3. Drain the cooling system.

4. If equipped with air conditioning, discharge and recover the refrigerant.

5. Remove the instrument panel assembly by performing the following procedure:

a. At the front console assembly, disconnect the switch connectors; then, remove the console-to-chassis screws and the console.

b. At the lower cluster assembly, remove the cluster-to-instrument panel screws, disconnect the cigarette lighter and light connectors and remove the lower cluster.

c. Remove the glove box and the instrument panel lower cover and the passenger knee bolster reinforcement.

d. At the left side, remove the instrument panel lower cover and the knee bolster assembly.

e. At the top of the instrument panel, pry the 8 claws on the front side toward you, raise the defroster grille and remove it.

f. At the SRS adjust bracket and cross beam under the passenger air bag

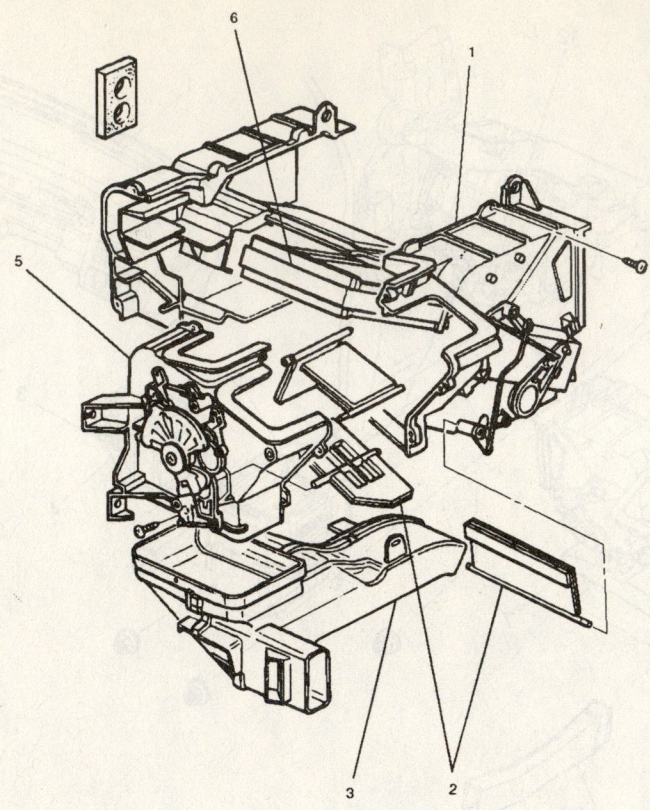

(1) Case (Temperature Control)   (5) Case (Mode Control)
(2) Mode Door   (6) Heater Core
(3) Duct

93113G02

Exploded view of the heater unit—Isuzu Trooper

module, remove the 2 fixing bolts and remove the instrument panel assembly.

g. Disconnect the air conditioning control cables from the unit.

h. Remove the instrument panel harness connectors (5 on the driver's side and 3 on the passenger's side), the passenger air bag module connector, the radio antenna plug and the center bracket ground cable bolt.

i. Remove the passenger's air bag module nuts, disconnect the connectors and remove the module.

j. Remove the instrument panel cluster assembly screws, disconnect the switch connectors and the instrument panel assembly.

6. Disconnect the heater hoses from the heater unit.

7. Disconnect the heater resistor connector and the electro thermo connector (if equipped with air conditioning).

8. Remove the heater duct.

9. If equipped with air conditioning, remove the evaporator assembly by performing the following procedure:

a. Disconnect the drain hose.

b. Using a backup wrench, disconnect the refrigerant lines from the evaporator.

c. Plug or cap the refrigerant lines.

d. Remove the evaporator assembly.

10. Remove the instrument panel center bracket (crossbeam assembly) by performing the following procedure:

a. Remove the side support bracket bolts and brackets from both sides of the vehicle.

b. Remove the crossbeam center bracket nuts, disconnect the electrical connectors and the center bracket.

11. Remove the rear heater duct and heater assembly.

12. Disassemble the heater unit assembly by performing the following procedure:

a. Remove the lower air duct; do not remove the link unit.

b. Remove the temperature control case screws and lift the case from the heater unit.

c. Remove the heater core.

To install:

13. Assemble the heater unit assembly by performing the following procedure:

a. Install the heater core into the heater unit.

b. Install the temperature control case onto the unit and secure with screws.

c. Install the lower air duct.

14. Install the heater unit assembly into the vehicle.

15. Install the rear heater duct.

16. Install the instrument panel cross beam assembly by reversing the removal procedures.

17. If equipped with air conditioning, install the evaporator assembly by performing the following procedures:

a. If installing a new evaporator assembly, add 1.7 fl. oz. (50mL) of refrigerant oil to the evaporator.

b. Using new O-rings and a backup wrench, install the refrigerant lines and torque the outlet line to 18 ft. lbs. (25 Nm) and the inlet line to 11 ft. lbs. (15 Nm).

18. Install the heater duct.

19. Connect the heater resistor connector and the electro-thermo connector (if equipped with air conditioning).

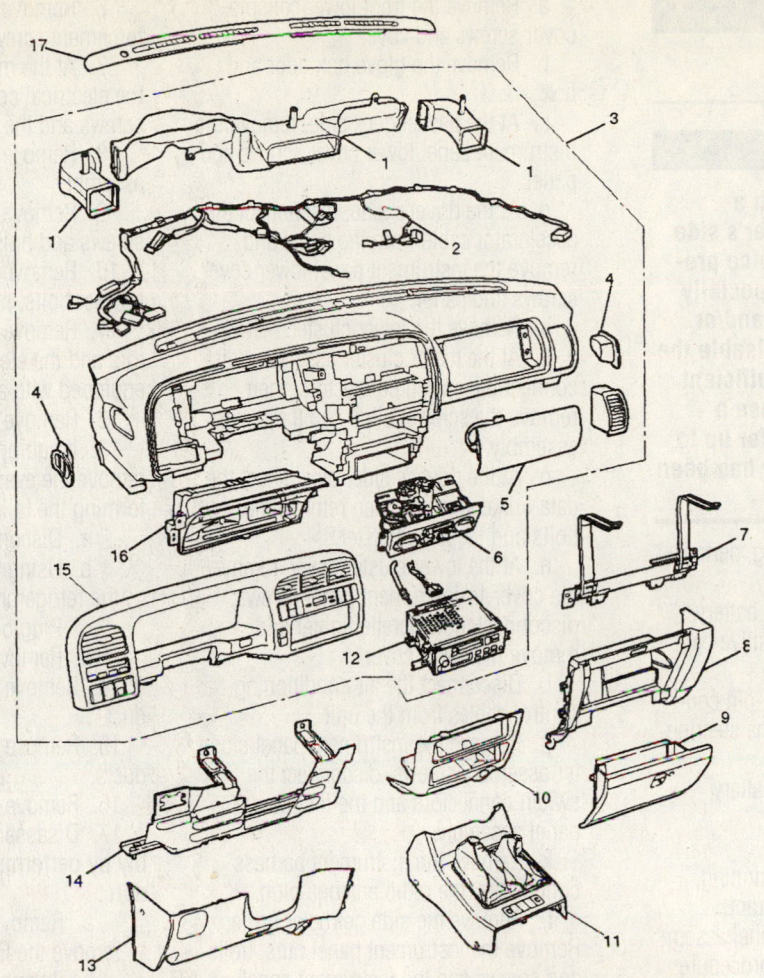

(1) Vent Duct Assembly
(2) Instrument Harness Assembly
(3) Instrument Panel Assembly
(4) Side Defroster Grille
(5) Passenger Inflator Module
(6) Control Lever Assembly
(7) Passenger Knee Bolster Reinforcement Assembly
(8) Instrument Panel Passenger Lower Cover Assembly

(9) Glove Box
(10) Lower Cluster Assembly
(11) Front Console Assembly
(12) Radio Assembly
(13) Instrument Panel Driver Lower Cover Assembly
(14) Driver Knee Bolster Assembly
(15) Instrument Panel Cluster Assembly
(16) Meter Assembly
(17) Front Defroster Grille

93113G03

Exploded view of the instrument panel and accessories—Isuzu Trooper

20. Connect the heater hoses to the heater unit.

21. Install the instrument panel assembly by reversing the removal procedures.

22. If equipped with air conditioning, evacuate and charge and leak-test the system.

23. Refill the cooling system.

24. Connect the negative battery cable.

✴✴ CAUTION

Never use an air bag assembly from another vehicle and/or different

model year. Starting in 1999, the air bag assemblies are equipped with identification colors on the bar code label as follows: YELLOW for the driver's air bag assembly, WHITE for the passenger's air bag assembly.

25. Enable the air bags by performing the following procedure:

a. Connect the passenger's side air bag yellow 2-pin connector.

b. Install the glove box.

c. At the base of the steering column, connect the yellow 2-pin connector.

d. Install the air bag fuse C-21 (if removed) or connect the negative battery cable.

e. Turn the ignition switch ON and verify that the AIR BAG warning light flashes 7 times and then turns OFF.

26. Run the engine to normal operating temperatures and check for leaks. Check the systems for correct operation.

VehiCROSS

REMOVAL & INSTALLATION

✳✳ CAUTION

The vehicle is equipped with a driver's side and a passenger's side air bag. Before starting service procedures on components, especially under the instrument panel and/or near the steering column, disable the air bag systems. There is sufficient voltage in the system to cause a deployment of the air bags for up to 15 seconds after the battery has been disconnected.

1. If equipped with an air bag, perform the following procedures:

   a. Disconnect the negative battery cable, then disconnect the positive battery cable.

   b. Disconnect the yellow 3-pin connector located at the base of the steering column.

2. Disconnect the negative battery cable.

3. Drain the cooling system.

4. If equipped with air conditioning, discharge and recover the refrigerant.

5. Remove the instrument panel assembly by performing the following procedure:

a. Remove the front lower console cover screws and cover.

b. Remove the glove box door and box.

c. At the passenger's side, remove the instrument panel lower cover screws and panel.

d. At the driver's side, disconnect the accelerator cable from the pedal and remove the instrument panel lower cover screws and panel.

e. Remove the lower cluster.

f. At the meter cluster assembly, disconnect the switch connectors, then remove the screws, clips and the meter assembly.

g. At the driver's side, disconnect the data link connector, then remove the bolts and the knee bolster.

h. At the lower cluster cover, remove the cover-to-instrument panel screws, disconnect the cigarette lighter and remove the lower cover.

i. Disconnect the air conditioning control cables from the unit.

j. Remove the instrument panel cluster assembly screws, disconnect the switch connectors and the instrument panel assembly.

k. Remove the instrument harness connectors, the radio antenna plug.

l. Remove the side defroster grille. Remove the instrument panel nuts, bolts and screws and the instrument panel.

6. Remove the passenger's air bag reinforcement screws and the reinforcement.

7. At the meter assembly, disconnect the electrical connector, then remove the screws and the meter assembly.

8. Remove the radio and the vent duct assembly.

9. Remove the passenger's knee bolster screws and bolster.

10. Remove the instrument panel center bracket bolts, nuts and bracket.

11. Remove the heater resistor connectors and the electro thermo connector (if equipped with air conditioning).

12. Remove the blower motor assembly.

13. If equipped with air conditioning, remove the evaporator assembly by performing the following procedure:

   a. Disconnect the drain hose.

   b. Using a backup wrench, disconnect the refrigerant lines from the evaporator.

   c. Plug or cap the refrigerant lines.

   d. Remove the evaporator assembly.

14. Remove the driver's side lap vent duct.

15. Remove the center and lower vent ducts.

16. Remove the heater assembly.

17. Disassemble the heater unit assembly by performing the following procedure:

   a. Remove the lower air duct; do not remove the link unit.

   b. Remove the temperature control

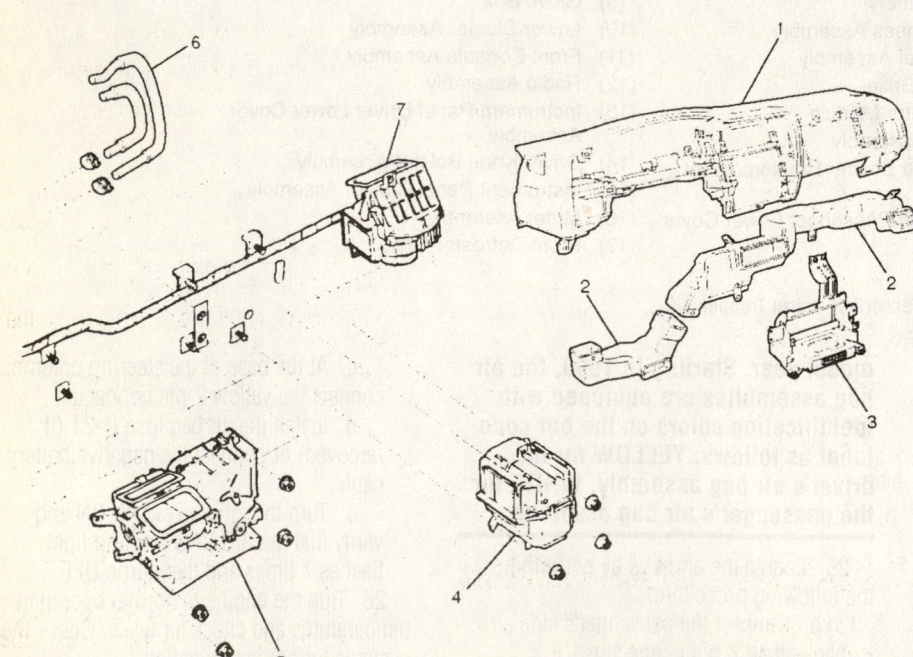

1 Instrument Panel Assembly
2 Center & Lower Vent Duct
3 Instrument Panel Center Bracket
4 Evaporator Assembly
5 Heater Unit Assembly
6 Heater Hose
7 Blower Unit

Exploded view of the heater unit and related components—Isuzu VehiCROSS

93113G04

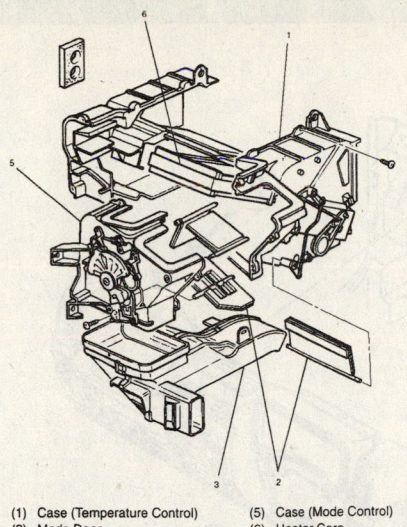

(1) Case (Temperature Control) (5) Case (Mode Control)
(2) Mode Door   (6) Heater Core
(3) Duct

93113G02

Exploded view of the heater unit—Isuzu VehiCROSS

case screws and lift the case from the heater unit.

   c. Remove the heater core.

To install:

18. Assemble the heater unit assembly by performing the following procedure:

   a. Install the heater core into the heater unit.

   b. Install the temperature control case onto the unit and secure with screws.

   c. Install the lower air duct.

19. Install the heater unit assembly into the vehicle.

20. Install the center and lower vent ducts.

21. Install the driver's side lap vent duct.

22. Install the instrument panel cross beam assembly by reversing the removal procedures.

23. If equipped with air conditioning, install the evaporator assembly by performing the following procedures:

   a. If installing a new evaporator assembly, add 1.7 fl. oz. (50mL) of refrigerant oil to the evaporator.

   b. Using new O-rings and a backup wrench, install the refrigerant lines and torque the outlet line to 18 ft. lbs. (25 Nm) and the inlet line to 11 ft. lbs. (15 Nm).

24. Install the blower motor.

25. Connect the heater resistor connectors and the electro-thermo connector (if equipped with air conditioning).

26. Connect the heater hoses to the heater unit.

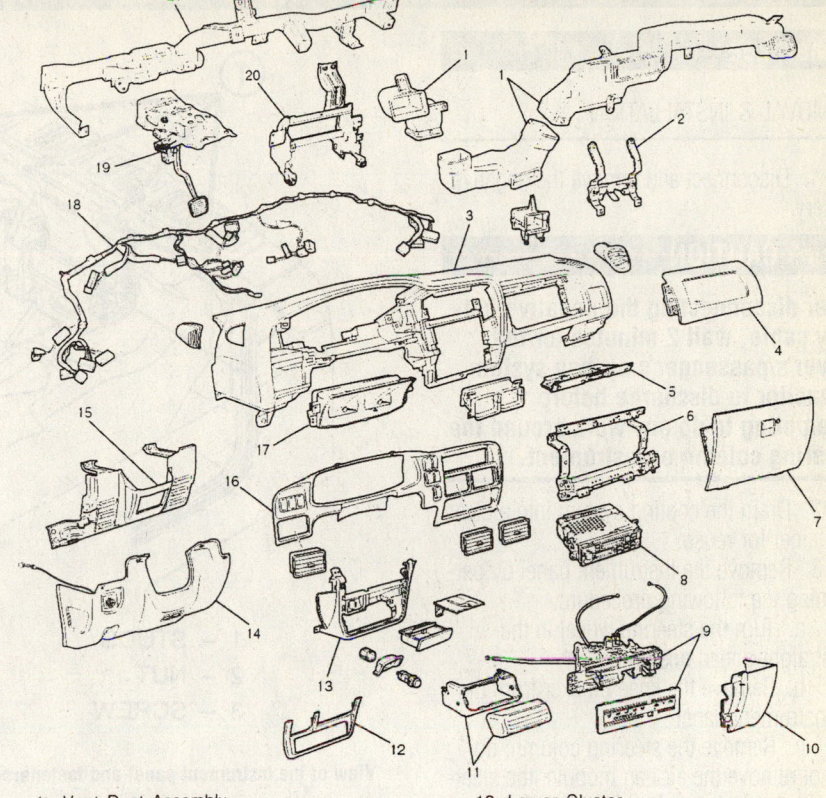

1	Vent Duct Assembly	12	Lower Cluster
2	Passenger Air Bag Reinforcement	13	Instrument Panel Lower Center Cover
3	Instrument Panel Assembly	14	Instrument Panel Driver Lower Cover
4	Passenger Air Bag Assembly	15	Driver Knee Bolster
5	Glove Box Cover	16	Meter Cluster Assembly
6	Passenger Knee Bolster	17	Meter Assembly
7	Glove Box Assembly	18	Instrument Harness Assembly
8	Radio Assembly	19	Brake Pedal & Bracket Assembly
9	Air Conditioner Control Lever Assembly	20	Instrument Panel Center Bracket
10	Instrument Panel Passenger Lower Cover	21	Cross Beam Assembly
11	Front Lower Console Cover		

93113G05

Exploded view of the instrument panel and accessories—Isuzu VehiCROSS

27. Install the instrument panel assembly by reversing the removal procedures.

28. If equipped with air conditioning, evacuate and recharge the system.

29. Refill the cooling system.

30. Connect the negative battery cable.

✳✳ CAUTION

Never use an air bag assembly from another vehicle and/or different model year.

31. Enable the air bag by performing the following procedure:

   a. At the base of the steering column, connect the yellow 3-pin connector.

   b. Connect the negative battery cable.

   c. Turn the ignition switch ON and verify that the AIR BAG warning light flashes 7 times and then turns OFF.

32. Run the engine to normal operating temperatures and check for leaks. Check the systems for correct operation.

Refer to the model specific sections for engine mechanical service procedures

JEEP

Cherokee

REMOVAL & INSTALLATION

1. Disconnect and remove the negative battery.

> ✳✳ **CAUTION**
>
> **After disconnecting the negative battery cable, wait 2 minutes for the driver's/passenger's air bag system capacitor to discharge before attempting to do any work around the steering column or instrument.**

2. Drain the cooling system into a clean container for reuse.

3. Remove the instrument panel by performing the following procedure:

   a. Turn the steering wheel in the straight-ahead position.

   b. Remove the knee blocker from the instrument panel.

   c. Remove the steering column; do not remove the air bag module, the steering wheel or switches from the steering column.

   d. From under the driver's side of the instrument panel, disconnect the following items:

- Instrument panel wiring harness connector from the 100-way wiring harness connector at the left side of the inner panel.
- Side window demister hose at the heater/air conditioning housing demister/defroster duct on the driver's side.

   e. Remove the glove box.

   f. Reaching through the glove box opening, disconnect the following items:

- Two halves of the heater/air conditioning system vacuum harness connector.
- Instrument panel wiring harness connector from the heater/air conditioning system wiring harness connector.
- Instrument panel wiring harness connector from the passenger's side air bag module wiring harness connector.
- Side window demister hose at the heater/air conditioning housing demister/defroster duct (passenger's side).
- Two halves of the radio antenna coaxial cable connector.

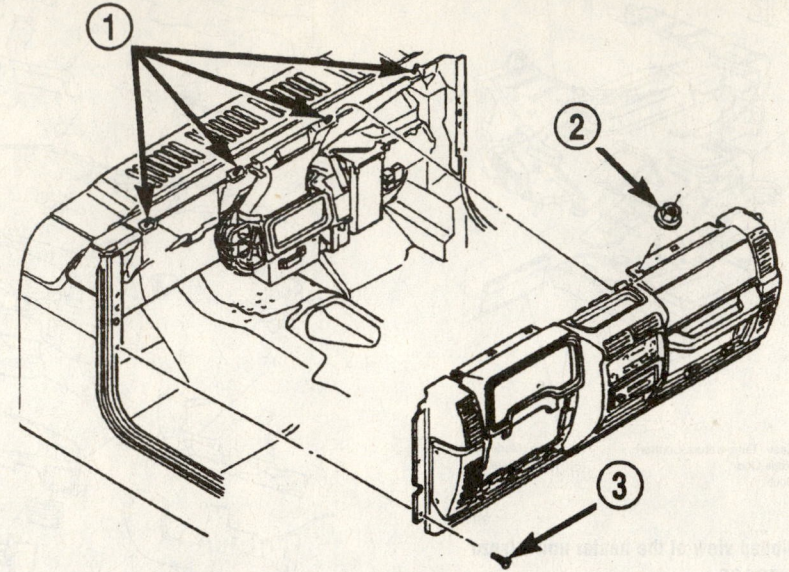

1 – STUDS
2 – NUT
3 – SCREW

View of the instrument panel and fasteners—Jeep Cherokee

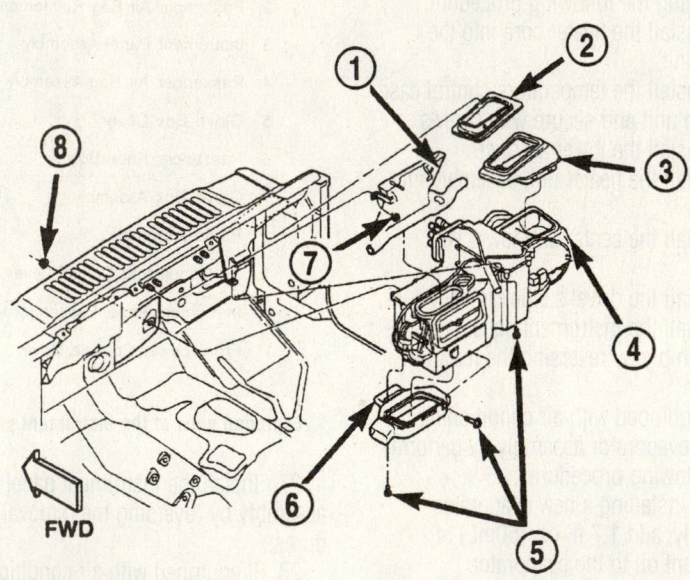

1 – DEFROST/DEMIST DUCT
2 – COLLAR
3 – FRESH AIR DUCT
4 – HEATER-A/C HOUSING
5 – SCREWS
6 – FLOOR DUCT
7 – NUT
8 – NUT

Exploded view of the heater core assembly—Jeep Cherokee

- Two instrument panel wiring harness connectors from the passenger air bag ON/OFF switch wiring harness connector.
- Passenger's side air bag ON/OFF switch wiring harness from the retainer clip on the plenum bracket that supports the heater/air conditioning housing just inboard of the fuse block module.
- Two lower passenger's side air bag module bracket-to-dash panel nuts.

g. Remove the upper cover from the instrument panel.

h. Remove the 3 instrument panel-to-door hinge pillar screws.

i. Remove the 4 upper instrument panel-to-dash nuts.

j. Using an assistant, remove the instrument panel from the vehicle.

4. If equipped with air conditioning, discharge and recover the air conditioning system refrigerant.

5. Disconnect the refrigerant lines from the evaporator. Plug the refrigerant openings to prevent evaporation.

6. Disconnect the heater hoses from the heater core tubes.

7. Disconnect the heater/air conditioning system vacuum supply line connector from the T-fitting near the heater core tubes.

8. In the engine compartment, remove the 5 heater/air conditioning housing-to-chassis nuts. If necessary, loosen the battery hold-downs and reposition the battery for access.

9. Remove the cowl plenum drain tube from the heater/air conditioning housing stud; it's located behind the cylinder head on the cowl.

10. From the bottom of the heater/air conditioning housing, remove the floor duct.

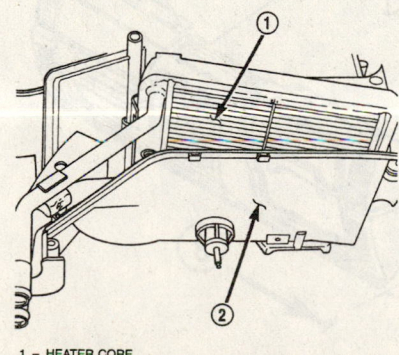

1 – HEATER CORE
2 – LOWER HEATER-A/C HOUSING

93113GA8

View of the heater core—Jeep Cherokee

11. On the passenger side, remove the heater/air conditioning housing-to-plenum bracket screw.

12. Pull the heater/air conditioning housing down far enough to clear the defrost/demist and fresh air ducts, then, rearward far enough to clear the mounting studs and the evaporator drain tube to clear the dash panel holes.

13. Remove the heater/air conditioning housing assembly from the vehicle.

14. Remove the heater/air conditioning housing upper case.

15. Lift the heater core from the lower half of the heater/air conditioning housing.

To install:

16. Assemble the heater core into the lower half of the heater/air conditioning housing.

17. Install the heater/air conditioning housing upper case.

18. Install the heater/air conditioning housing assembly to the vehicle.

19. On the passenger's side, install the heater/air conditioning housing-to-plenum bracket screw.

20. At the bottom of the heater/air conditioning housing, install the floor duct.

21. Install the cowl plenum drain tube to the heater/air conditioning housing stud; it's located behind the cylinder head on the cowl.

22. In the engine compartment, install the 5 heater/air conditioning housing-to-chassis nuts.

23. Connect the heater/air conditioning system vacuum supply line connector to the T-fitting near the heater core tubes.

24. Connect the heater hoses to the heater core tubes.

25. Connect the refrigerant lines to the evaporator.

26. If equipped with air conditioning, evacuate and charge the air conditioning system refrigerant.

27. Install the instrument panel by performing the following procedure:

a. Using an assistant, install the instrument panel to the vehicle.

b. Install the 4 upper instrument panel-to-dash nuts.

c. Install the 3 instrument panel-to-door hinge pillar screws.

d. Install the upper cover to the instrument panel.

e. Reaching through the glove box opening, connect the following items:

- Two lower passenger's side air bag module bracket-to-dash panel nuts.
- Passenger's side air bag ON/OFF switch wiring harness to the retainer clip on the plenum bracket that supports the heater/air conditioning housing just inboard of the fuse block module.
- Two instrument panel wiring harness connectors to the passenger air bag ON/OFF switch wiring harness connector.
- Two halves of the radio antenna coaxial cable connector.
- Side window demister hose at the heater/air conditioning housing demister/defroster duct (passenger's side).
- Instrument panel wiring harness connector to the passenger's side air bag module wiring harness connector.
- Instrument panel wiring harness connector to the heater/air conditioning system wiring harness connector.
- Two halves of the heater/air conditioning system vacuum harness connector.

f. Install the glove box.

g. Under the driver's side of the instrument panel, connect the following items:

- Side window demister hose at the heater/air conditioning housing demister/defroster duct on the driver's side.
- Instrument panel wiring harness connector to the 100-way wiring harness connector at the left side of the inner panel.

h. Install the steering column.

i. Install the knee blocker to the instrument panel.

28. Connect and remove the negative battery.

29. Refill the cooling system.

30. Run the engine to normal operating temperatures; then, check the climate control operation and check for leaks.

Wrangler

REMOVAL & INSTALLATION

1. Disconnect and remove the negative battery.

Refer to the model specific sections for cooling system service procedures

❈❈ CAUTION

After disconnecting the negative battery cable, wait 2 minutes for the driver's/passenger's air bag system capacitor to discharge before attempting to do any work around the steering column or instrument.

2. Drain the cooling system into a clean container for reuse.

3. Remove the instrument panel by performing the following procedure:

   a. Turn the steering wheel in the straight-ahead position.

   b. Remove the knee blocker from the instrument panel.

   c. Remove the steering column; do not remove the air bag module, the steering wheel or switches from the steering column.

   d. From under the driver's side of the instrument panel, disconnect the following items:

- Instrument panel wiring harness connector from the 100-way wiring harness connector at the left side of the inner panel.
- Side window demister hose at the heater/air conditioning housing demister/defroster duct on the driver's side.

   e. Remove the glove box.

   f. Reaching through the glove box opening, disconnect the following items:

- Two halves of the heater/air conditioning system vacuum harness connector.
- Instrument panel wiring harness connector from the heater/air conditioning system wiring harness connector.
- Instrument panel wiring harness connector from the passenger's side air bag module wiring harness connector.
- Side window demister hose at the heater/air conditioning housing demister/defroster duct (passenger's side).
- Two halves of the radio antenna coaxial cable connector.
- Two instrument panel wiring harness connectors from the passenger air bag ON/OFF switch wiring harness connector.
- Passenger's side air bag ON/OFF switch wiring harness from the retainer clip on the plenum bracket that supports the heater/air conditioning housing just inboard of the fuse block module.

- Two lower passenger's side air bag module bracket-to-dash panel nuts.

   g. Remove the upper cover from the instrument panel.

   h. Remove the 3 instrument panel-to-door hinge pillar screws.

   i. Remove the 4 upper instrument panel-to-dash nuts.

   j. Using an assistant, remove the instrument panel from the vehicle.

4. If equipped with air conditioning, discharge and recover the air conditioning system refrigerant.

5. Disconnect the refrigerant lines from the evaporator. Plug the refrigerant openings to prevent evaporation.

6. Disconnect the heater hoses from the heater core tubes.

7. Disconnect the heater/air conditioning system vacuum supply line connector from the T-fitting near the heater core tubes.

8. In the engine compartment, remove the 5 heater/air conditioning housing-to-chassis nuts. If necessary, loosen the battery hold-downs and reposition the battery for access.

9. Remove the cowl plenum drain tube from the heater/air conditioning housing stud; it's located behind the cylinder head on the cowl.

10. From the bottom of the heater/air conditioning housing, remove the floor duct.

11. On the passenger side, remove the heater/air conditioning housing-to-plenum bracket screw.

12. Pull the heater/air conditioning housing down far enough to clear the defrost/demist and fresh air ducts, then, rearward far enough to clear the mounting studs and the evaporator drain tube to clear the dash panel holes.

13. Remove the heater/air conditioning housing assembly from the vehicle.

14. Remove the heater/air conditioning housing upper case.

15. Lift the heater core from the lower half of the heater/air conditioning housing.

To install:

16. Assemble the heater core into the lower half of the heater/air conditioning housing.

17. Install the heater/air conditioning housing upper case.

18. Install the heater/air conditioning housing assembly to the vehicle.

19. On the passenger's side, install the heater/air conditioning housing-to-plenum bracket screw.

20. At the bottom of the heater/air conditioning housing, install the floor duct.

21. Install the cowl plenum drain tube to the heater/air conditioning housing stud; it's located behind the cylinder head on the cowl.

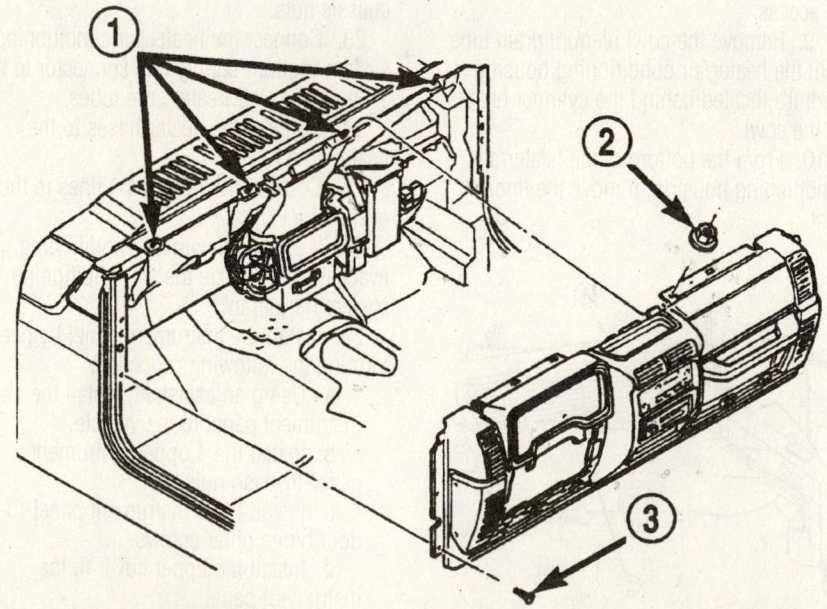

1 — STUDS
2 — NUT
3 — SCREW

93113GA6

View of the instrument panel and fasteners—Jeep Wrangler

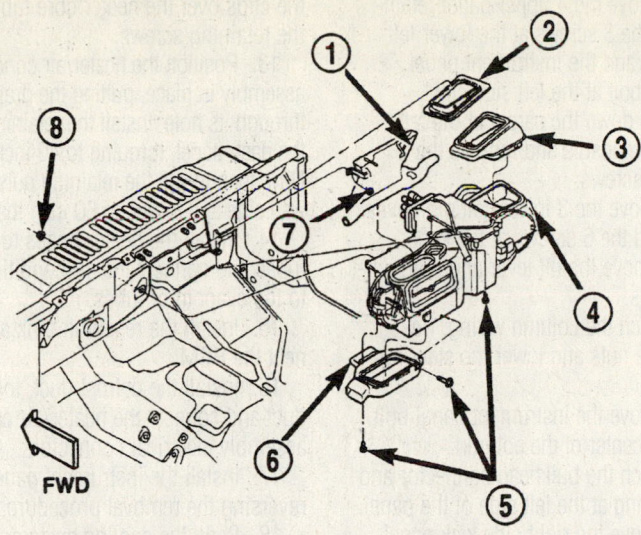

1 – DEFROST/DEMIST DUCT
2 – COLLAR
3 – FRESH AIR DUCT
4 – HEATER-A/C HOUSING
5 – SCREWS
6 – FLOOR DUCT
7 – NUT
8 – NUT

93113GA7

Exploded view of the heater core assembly—Jeep Wrangler

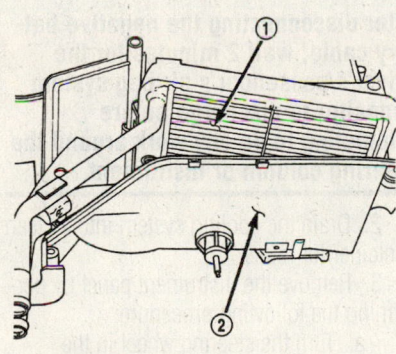

1 – HEATER CORE
2 – LOWER HEATER-A/C HOUSING

93113GA8

View of the heater core—Jeep Cherokee Wrangler

22. In the engine compartment, install the 5 heater/air conditioning housing-to-chassis nuts.

23. Connect the heater/air conditioning system vacuum supply line connector to the T-fitting near the heater core tubes.

24. Connect the heater hoses to the heater core tubes.

25. Connect the refrigerant lines to the evaporator.

26. If equipped with air conditioning, evacuate and charge the air conditioning system refrigerant.

27. Install the instrument panel by performing the following procedure:

   a. Using an assistant, install the instrument panel to the vehicle.

   b. Install the 4 upper instrument panel-to-dash nuts.

   c. Install the 3 instrument panel-to-door hinge pillar screws.

   d. Install the upper cover to the instrument panel.

   e. Reaching through the glove box opening, connect the following items.

   • Two lower passenger's side air bag module bracket-to-dash panel nuts.

   • Passenger's side air bag ON/OFF switch wiring harness to the retainer clip on the plenum bracket that supports the heater/air conditioning housing just inboard of the fuse block module.

   • Two instrument panel wiring harness connectors to the passenger air bag ON/OFF switch wiring harness connector.

   • Two halves of the radio antenna coaxial cable connector.

   • Side window demister hose at the heater/air conditioning housing demister/defroster duct (passenger's side).

   • Instrument panel wiring harness connector to the passenger's side air bag module wiring harness connector.

   • Instrument panel wiring harness connector to the heater/air conditioning system wiring harness connector.

   • Two halves of the heater/air conditioning system vacuum harness connector.

   f. Install the glove box.

   g. Under the driver's side of the instrument panel, connect the following items:

   • Side window demister hose at the heater/air conditioning housing demister/defroster duct on the driver's side.

   • Instrument panel wiring harness connector to the 100-way wiring harness connector at the left side of the inner panel.

   h. Install the steering column.

   i. Install the knee blocker to the instrument panel.

28. Connect and remove the negative battery.

29. Refill the cooling system.

30. Run the engine to normal operating temperatures; then, check the climate control operation and check for leaks.

Grand Cherokee

REMOVAL & INSTALLATION

1997

➡**This procedure requires discharging and recharging of the air conditioning system, if equipped. This model operates with R-134a refrigerant and special components with R-134a refrigerant and special components for this application. Use only dedicated service equipment, replacement parts, refrigerant and refrigerant oil when servicing the system or replacing the components.**

   1. Disconnect the negative battery cable.

   2. Properly discharge and recover the air conditioning system refrigerant.

3. Disconnect and plug the air conditioning lines from the evaporator, using the spring lock disconnect tool.

4. Drain the cooling system into a clean container for reuse.

5. Disconnect the heater hoses from the heater core tubes. Plug the openings to prevent coolant leakage. Remove the coolant reservoir tank.

6. Remove the PCM and set it aside. Do not disconnect the 60-way connector.

7. Remove the heater/air conditioning unit attaching nuts from the firewall.

8. Remove the instrument panel by performing the following procedures:

  a. Remove the defroster duct grille and the speaker grilles.

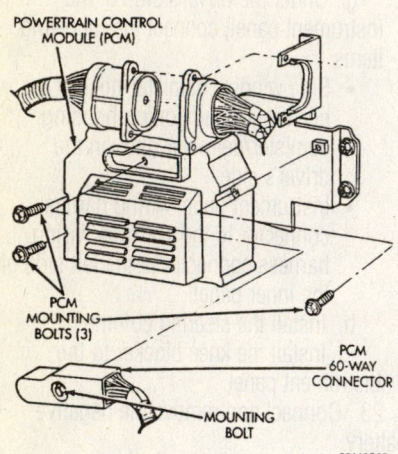

View of the PCM—1997 Jeep Grand Cherokee

  b. Remove the 4 upper panel retaining nuts, the 3 screws at the lower left side panel and the instrument panel mounting bolt at the left side cowl.

  c. Fold down the carpet at the left side of the console and remove the 2 mounting screws.

  d. Remove the 3 lower column cover screws and the 6 screws at the knee panel. Remove the tilt lever and both column covers.

  e. Detach the column wiring. Remove the 2 nuts and lower the steering column.

  f. Remove the instrument panel bolt above the center of the column.

  g. Detach the bulkhead connector and cluster wiring at the left side of the panel.

  h. Remove the right side kick panel door and detach the wiring.

  i. Pull back and lower the instrument panel. Disconnect the air conditioning vacuum lines and antenna. Remove the instrument panel.

9. Remove the defroster duct and disconnect the rear floor duct from the center duct connector.

10. Disconnect the electrical connections, remove the attaching nuts at the dash panel and remove the heater/air conditioning assembly.

11. Remove the heater core retaining screws and pull the heater core out of its housing.

To install:

12. Install the heater core and position

the clips over the heater core tubes. Install the retaining screws.

13. Position the heater/air conditioning assembly in place, putting the drain tube through its hole. Install the retaining nuts at the dash panel, torquing to 40 inch lbs. (4.5 Nm), then install the retaining nuts to the firewall side and torque to 60 inch lbs. (7 Nm).

14. Install the heater hoses to the heater tubes and connect the air conditioning lines to the evaporator tubes.

15. Install the reservoir tank and reconnect the PCM.

16. Install the defrost duct, the rear floor duct and connect the heater/air conditioning assembly electrical connectors.

17. Install the instrument panel by reversing the removal procedure.

18. Refill the cooling system.

19. Connect the negative battery cable.

20. Evacuate, charge and leak test the air conditioning system.

21. Run the engine to normal operating temperatures; then, check the climate control operation and check for leaks.

1998–00

1. Disconnect and remove the negative battery.

❄❄ CAUTION

After disconnecting the negative battery cable, wait 2 minutes for the driver's/passenger's air bag system capacitor to discharge before attempting to do any work around the steering column or instrument.

2. Drain the cooling system into a clean container for reuse.

3. Remove the instrument panel by performing the following procedure:

  a. Turn the steering wheel in the straight-ahead position.

  b. Remove the A-pillar trim from both sides of the vehicle.

  c. Remove the top cover from the instrument panel.

  d. Near the windshield line, remove the 4 instrument panel-to-chassis nuts.

  e. Remove the scuff plates from both front door sills.

  f. Remove the trim panels from both sides of the inner cowl.

  g. Remove the floor console.

  h. Remove the fuse cover from the junction box.

  i. Remove the instrument panel cluster bezel.

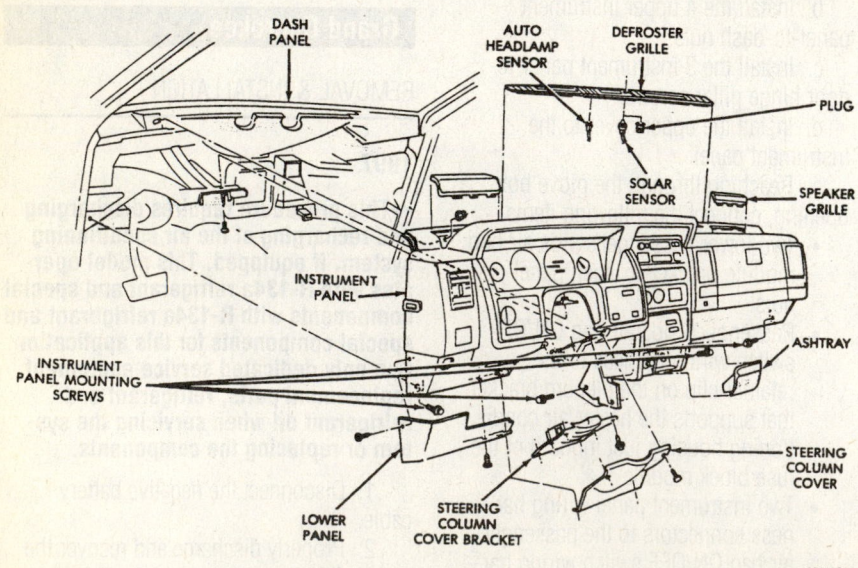

Exploded view of the instrument panel assembly—1997 Jeep Grand Cherokee

j. Remove the steering column opening cover from the instrument panel.

k. Remove the steering column bracket from the instrument panel column support bracket.

l. Remove the lower steering column shroud cover-to-multifunction switch screw; then, unsnap both halves of the shroud cover from the steering column.

m. Disconnect the instrument panel wiring harness connectors from the following steering column components:

- Both lower clockspring connector receptacles
- Left multifunction switch receptacle
- Right multifunction switch receptacle
- Both ignition switch receptacles
- Shifter interlock solenoid receptacle
- Sentry Key Immobilizer Module (SKIM) receptacle, if equipped

n. Turn the ignition switch to ON position; then, release and remove the shifter interlock cable connector from the ignition lock housing receptacle.

o. Turn the ignition switch to OFF position; this will prevent the steering wheel from turning and the loss of the clockspring centering following steering column removal.

p. Remove the 4 steering column-to-instrument panel steering column bracket nuts.

q. Remove the steering column from the instrument panel.

r. Disconnect both side body wiring harness bulkhead connectors, the Ignition Off Draw (IOD) wiring harness connector and the fused wiring harness connector from the junction block connector receptacles.

s. Disconnect the instrument panel

wiring harness-to-floor console component connectors:

- Air bag control module connector receptacle
- Parking brake switch terminal
- Transmission shifter connector receptacle

t. Remove the 2 instrument panel wiring harness-to-floor console ground terminals located behind the air bag control module.

u. Disconnect the instrument panel wiring harness-to-floor console retainers.

v. Remove the instrument panel-to-floor console bracket screws and the bracket.

w. Remove the driver's side floor duct-to-heater/air conditioning housing assembly screw and remove the duct.

x. If equipped with a manual heating-air conditioning system, disconnect the vacuum harness connector from behind the driver's side floor duct.

y. Remove the instrument panel steering column support bracket-to-driver's side of the heater/air conditioning housing assembly screw

z. Remove the instrument panel steering column support bracket-to-intermediate bracket screw.

aa. Remove the instrument panel steering column support bracket-to-driver's side cowl plenum panel nut.

bb. Remove the 2 instrument panel-to-driver's side cowl side inner panel screws.

cc. Remove the instrument panel end cap.

dd. Remove the lower right center bezel from the instrument panel.

ee. At the passenger's side cowl side inner panel, disconnect the instrument panel wiring harness bulkhead connector from the lower cavity of the inline connector.

ff. Near the right side cowl inner panel, located under the end of the instrument panel, disconnect both halves of the radio antenna coaxial cable connector.

gg. Disconnect the 2 instrument panel-to-heater/air conditioning assembly wiring harness connectors.

hh. At the passenger's side, remove the 2 instrument panel structural duct-to-heater/air conditioning housing assembly screws.

ii. At the passenger's side cowl side inner panel, remove the 2 instrument

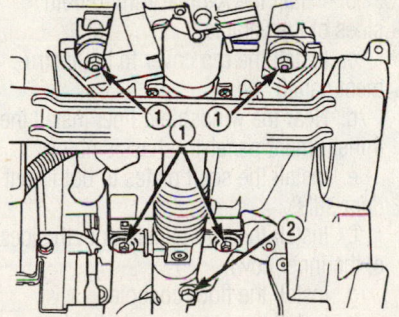

1 – COLUMN MOUNTING NUTS
2 – COUPLER BOLT

93113GA1

View of the steering column mounting nuts—1998–00 Jeep Grand Cherokee

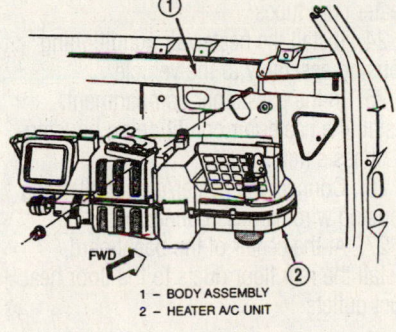

FWD

1 – BODY ASSEMBLY
2 – HEATER A/C UNIT

93113GA3

View of the heater/air conditioning housing assembly—1998–00 Jeep Grand Cherokee

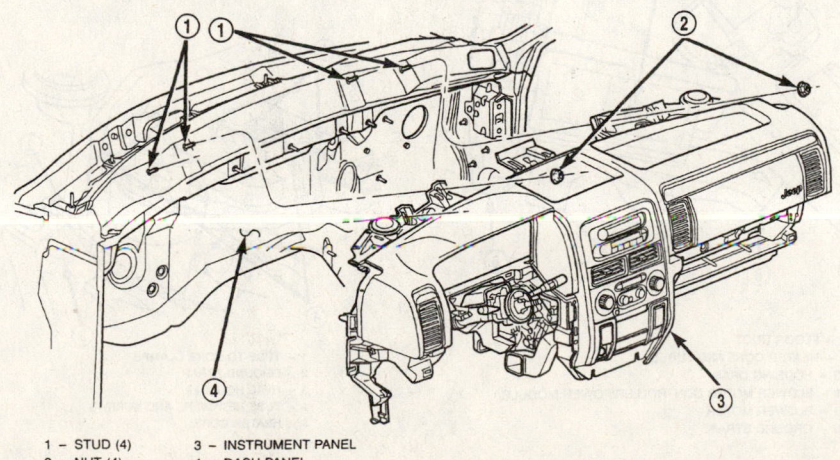

1 – STUD (4)   3 – INSTRUMENT PANEL
2 – NUT (4)   4 – DASH PANEL

93113GA2

View of the instrument panel assembly—1998–00 Jeep Grand Cherokee

panel-to-passenger's side cowl side inner panel screws.

jj. With the help of an assistant, lift the instrument panel from the vehicle.

4. Discharge and recover the air conditioning system refrigerant.

5. Disconnect the air conditioning system lines at the evaporator. Plug the openings to prevent contamination.

6. Disconnect the heater hoses from the heater core. Plug the openings to prevent coolant loss.

7. If equipped with a manual temperature control system, unplug the heater/air conditioning system vacuum supply line connector from the T-fitting located near the heater core tubes.

8. From the passenger's side inner fender shield, remove the coolant reservoir/overflow bottle.

9. From the passenger's side in the engine compartment dash panel, remove the PCM; DO NOT unplug it, just move it aside.

10. In the engine compartment, remove the heater/air conditioning housing-to-chassis nuts.

11. At the center of the dashboard, remove the rear floor ducts from the floor heat duct outlets.

12. Disconnect the heater/air conditioning housing wire harness connectors.

13. In the passenger compartment, remove the heater/air conditioning housing-to-chassis nuts.

14. Place covers inside the vehicle to catch any spilt coolant.

15. Remove the heater/air conditioning housing assembly from the vehicle.

16. Remove the foam gasket from around the heater core tubes.

➡ **Note the position of the irregular shaped gasket so that it may be reinstalled in its correct position.**

17. Remove the heater core retainers and screws.

18. If necessary, remove the mode door actuator for clearance to remove the core.

19. Remove the heater core from the heater/air conditioning housing assembly.

To install:

20. Install the heater core tom the heater/air conditioning housing assembly.

21. If removed, install the mode door actuator.

22. Install the heater core retainers and screws.

23. Install the foam gasket around the heater core tubes.

24. Install the heater/air conditioning housing assembly to the vehicle.

25. In the passenger compartment, install the heater/air conditioning housing-to-chassis nuts.

26. Connect the heater/air conditioning housing wire harness connectors.

27. At the center of the dashboard, install the rear floor ducts to the floor heat duct outlets.

28. In the engine compartment, install the heater/air conditioning housing-to-chassis nuts.

29. At the passenger's side in the engine compartment dash panel, install the PCM.

30. At the passenger's side inner fender shield, install the coolant reservoir/overflow bottle.

31. If equipped with a manual temperature control system, plug the heater/air conditioning system vacuum supply line connector to the T-fitting located near the heater core tubes.

32. Connect the heater hoses to the heater core.

33. Connect the air conditioning system lines to the evaporator.

34. Evacuate and charge the air conditioning system refrigerant.

35. Remove the instrument panel by performing the following procedure:

a. Turn the steering wheel in the straight-ahead position.

b. Install the A-pillar trim to both sides of the vehicle.

c. Install the top cover to the instrument panel.

d. Near the windshield line, install the 4 instrument panel-to-chassis nuts.

e. Install the scuff plates to both front door sills.

f. Install the trim panels to both sides of the inner cowl.

g. Install the floor console.

h. Install the fuse cover to the junction box.

i. Install the instrument panel cluster bezel.

j. Install the steering column opening cover to the instrument panel.

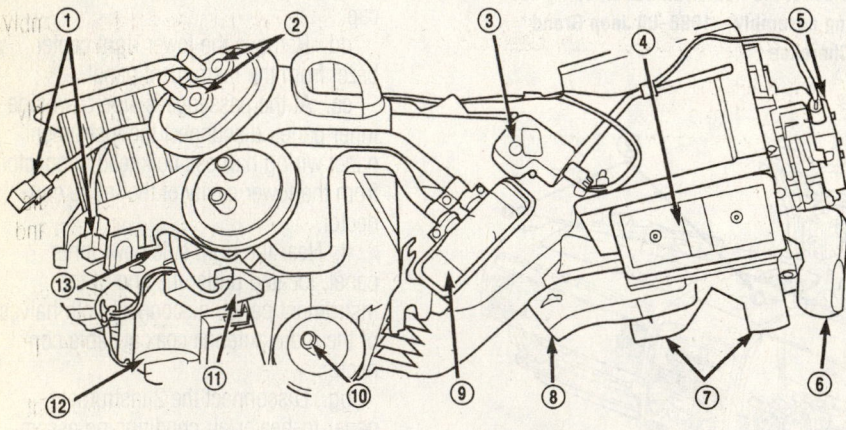

1 – ELECTRICAL CONNECTORS
2 – EVAPORATOR FITTINGS (CAPPED)
3 – ELECTRIC ACTUATOR
4 – OUTLET TO DEFROSTER DUCTS
5 – ELECTRIC ACTUATOR
6 – FLOOR DUCT
7 – TO REAR PASSENGER FLOOR AIR DUCTS
8 – FLOOR DUCT
9 – HEATER CORE AND TUBES
10 – HOUSING DRAIN
11 – BLOWER MOTOR CONTROLLER/POWER MODULE
12 – BLOWER MOTOR
13 – GROUND STRAP

93113GA4

View of the heater core, the heater/air conditioning housing and related components—1998–00 Jeep Grand Cherokee

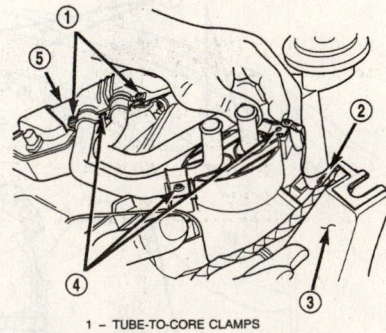

1 – TUBE-TO-CORE CLAMPS
2 – GROUND STRAP
3 – HVAC HOUSING
4 – TUBE RETAINERS AND SCREWS
5 – HEATER CORE

93113GA5

View of the heater core screws, gasket and retainers—1998–00 Jeep Grand Cherokee

k. Install the steering column bracket to the instrument panel column support bracket.

l. Install the lower steering column shroud cover-to-multifunction switch screw; then, snap both halves of the shroud cover to the steering column.

m. Connect the instrument panel wiring harness connectors to the following steering column components:

- Sentry Key Immobilizer Module (SKIM) receptacle, if equipped
- Shifter interlock solenoid receptacle
- Both ignition switch receptacles
- Right multifunction switch receptacle
- Left multifunction switch receptacle
- Both lower clockspring connector receptacles

n. Turn the ignition switch to ON position; then, release and install the shifter interlock cable connector to the ignition lock housing receptacle.

o. Install the 4 steering column-to-instrument panel steering column bracket nuts.

p. Install the steering column to the instrument panel.

q. Connect both side body wiring harness bulkhead connectors, the Ignition Off Draw (IOD) wiring harness connector and the fused wiring harness connector to the junction block connector receptacles.

r. Disconnect the instrument panel wiring harness-to-floor console component connectors:

- Transmission shifter connector receptacle
- Parking brake switch terminal
- Air bag control module connector receptacle

s. Install the 2 instrument panel wiring harness-to-floor console ground terminals located behind the air bag control module.

t. Connect the instrument panel wiring harness-to-floor console retainers.

u. Install the instrument panel-to-floor console bracket and the screws.

v. Install the driver's side floor duct and the duct-to-heater/air conditioning housing assembly screw.

w. If equipped with a manual heating-air conditioning system, connect the vacuum harness connector behind the driver's side floor duct.

x. Install the instrument panel steering column support bracket-to-driver's side of the heater/air conditioning housing assembly screw.

y. Install the instrument panel steering column support bracket-to-intermediate bracket screw.

z. Install the instrument panel steering column support bracket-to-driver's side cowl plenum panel nut.

aa. Install the 2 instrument panel-to-

driver's side cowl side inner panel screws.

bb. Install the instrument panel end cap.

cc. Install the lower right center bezel to the instrument panel.

dd. At the passenger's side cowl side inner panel, connect the instrument panel wiring harness bulkhead connector to the lower cavity of the inline connector.

ee. Near the right cowl side inner panel located under the end of the instrument panel, connect both halves of the radio antenna coaxial cable connector.

ff. Connect the 2 instrument panel-to-heater/air conditioning assembly wiring harness connectors.

gg. At the passenger's side, install the 2 instrument panel structural duct-to-heater/air conditioning housing assembly screws.

hh. At the passenger's side cowl side inner panel, install the 2 instrument panel-to-passenger's side cowl side inner panel screws.

ii. With the help of an assistant, lift the instrument panel into the vehicle.

36. Refill the cooling system.

37. Connect the negative battery.

38. Run the engine to normal operating temperatures. Check the climate control operation and check for leaks.

KIA

Sportage

REMOVAL & INSTALLATION

1. Disconnect the negative battery cable.

✳✳ CAUTION

After disconnecting the negative battery cable, wait for at least 10 minutes for the air bag module to deplete its stored energy.

2. Remove the driver's side air bag and steering wheel by performing the following procedure:

a. Position the front wheels in the straight-ahead position.

b. Remove the 4 steering wheel-to-air bag module bolts.

c. Carefully, lift the air bag module and disconnect the electrical connector.

✳✳ CAUTION

Place the air bag module in a safe location with the front facing upward.

d. Remove the steering wheel-to-steering column nut.

➡**It may be necessary to mark the steering wheel to steering column alignment.**

e. Using a steering wheel puller, press the steering wheel from the steering column.

3. Drain the cooling system into a clean container for reuse.

4. Discharge and recover the air conditioning system refrigerant.

5. Remove the instrument panel by performing the following procedure:

a. Remove both the rear and front consoles.

b. Remove the knee bolster assembly.

c. Remove the "T" bar section.

d. Remove the relay bracket.

e. Remove the turn signal assembly and the upper/lower steering column covers.

f. Remove the hood release handle lockscrew, the hood release handle and the cable assembly nut.

g. Remove the left side front pillar trim and the lower left side cover.

h. Remove the 2 left side of the "T" bar-to-chassis bolts.

i. At the left side of the instrument panel, remove the 3 instrument panel-to-chassis bolts.

j. Remove the ashtray.

k. Remove the center panel trim.

l. Remove the ventilation control panel.

m. At the center of the windshield next to the windshield, remove the cap and the mounting bolt.

Refer to the model specific sections for engine mechanical service procedures

n. Remove the right side front pillar trim and the lower right side cover.

o. Remove the 2 right side of the "T" bar-to-chassis bolts.

p. At the right side of the instrument panel, remove the 3 instrument panel-to-chassis bolts.

q. Remove the steering column-to-instrument panel bolts and lower the steering column.

r. Disconnect the instrument panel electrical connectors.

s. Remove the instrument panel.

6. Remove the blower/evaporator housing by performing the following procedure:

a. Disconnect the air conditioning refrigerant lines from the evaporator core and discard the gaskets. Plug the openings to prevent contamination.

b. Disconnect the fresh air control cable from the blower/evaporator housing inlet duct.

c. Disconnect the 5 connectors from the bottom of the blower/evaporator housing.

d. Move the carpeting from the bulkhead to gain access to the hole cover plate.

e. Remove the 4 hole cover plate nuts and the plate.

f. Remove the 2 upper blower/evaporator housing bolts.

g. Remove the 2 lower blower/evaporator housing-to-bulkhead nuts.

h. Remove the blower/evaporator housing.

7. Disconnect the heater hoses from the heater core.

8. Remove the temperature control cable from the heater housing.

9. Remove the 2 lower heater housing nuts and the upper heater housing-to-bulkhead nut.

10. Remove the heater housing.

11. Disassemble the heater housing by performing the following procedure:

a. Remove the seal from the heater core tube connections.

b. Remove the vent seal.

c. Remove the 2 wiring harness-to-heater servo screws.

d. Remove the 8 heater housing clips located on the servo side (left side).

e. Remove the left side of the heater housing.

f. Remove the 6 heater housing assembly clips.

g. Remove the 4 heater core tube mounting bracket screws and the bracket.

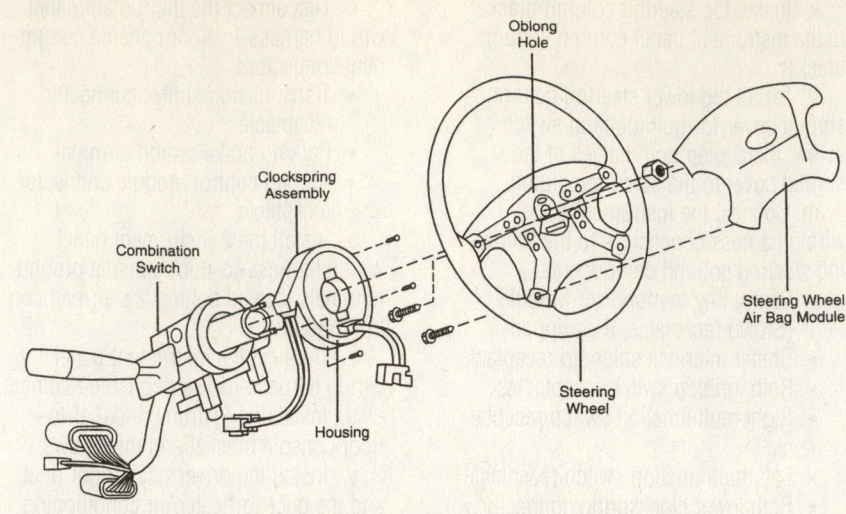

Exploded view of the steering wheel and air bag module assembly—Kia Sportage

h. Remove the 8 remaining heater housing clips and disassemble the housings.

i. Remove the heater core from the housing.

To install:

12. Assemble the heater housing by performing the following procedure:

a. Install the heater core to the housing.

b. Assemble the housings and install the 8 remaining heater housing clips.

c. Install the heater core tube mounting bracket and the 4 bracket screws.

d. Install the 6 heater housing assembly clips.

e. Install the left side of the heater housing.

f. Install the 8 heater housing clips located on the servo side (left side).

g. Install the 2 wiring harness-to-heater servo screws.

h. Install the vent seal.

i. Install the seal to the heater core tube connections.

13. Install the heater housing.

14. Install the 2 lower heater housing nuts and the upper heater housing-to-bulkhead nut.

15. Install the temperature control cable to the heater housing.

16. Connect the heater hoses to the heater core.

17. Install the blower/evaporator housing by performing the following procedure:

a. Install the blower/evaporator housing.

b. Install the 2 lower blower/evaporator housing-to-bulkhead nuts.

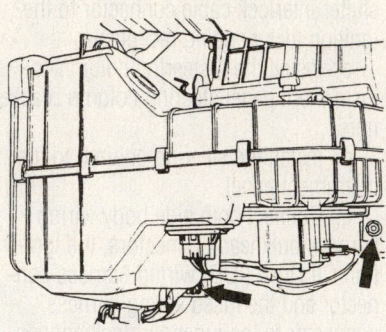

View of the blower/evaporator housing assembly—Kia Sportage

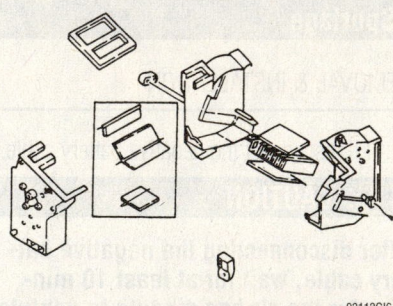

Exploded view of the heater core and heater housing assembly—Kia Sportage

c. Install the 2 upper blower/evaporator housing bolts.

d. Install the hole cover plate and the 4 plate nuts.

e. Move the carpeting over the bulkhead.

f. Connect the 5 connectors to the bottom of the blower/evaporator housing.

g. Connect the fresh air control cable

to the blower/evaporator housing inlet duct.

h. Using new gaskets, connect the air conditioning refrigerant lines to the evaporator core.

18. Install the instrument panel by performing the following procedure:

a. Install the instrument panel.

b. Connect the instrument panel electrical connectors.

c. Install the steering column and lower the steering column-to-instrument panel bolts. Torque the bolts to 15 ft. lbs. (20 Nm).

d. At the right side of the instrument panel, install the 3 instrument panel-to-chassis bolts.

e. Install the 2 right side of the "T" bar-to-chassis bolts.

f. Install the right side front pillar trim and the lower right side cover.

g. At the center of the windshield next

to the windshield, install the cap and the mounting bolt.

h. Install the ventilation control panel.

i. Install the center panel trim.

j. Install the ashtray.

k. At the left side of the instrument panel, install the 3 instrument panel-to-chassis bolts.

l. Install the 2 left side of the "T" bar-to-chassis bolts.

m. Install the lower left side cover and the left side front pillar trim.

n. Install the cable assembly nut, the hood release handle and the hood release handle lockscrew.

o. Install the turn signal assembly and the upper/lower steering column covers.

p. Install the relay bracket.

q. Install the "T" bar section.

r. Install the knee bolster assembly.

s. Install both the rear and front consoles.

19. Evacuate and charge the air conditioning system refrigerant.

20. Refill the cooling system.

21. Install the driver's side air bag and steering wheel by performing the following procedure:

a. Install the steering wheel to the steering column.

b. Install the steering wheel-to-steering column nut and torque the nut to 33 ft. lbs. (45 Nm).

c. Carefully, install the air bag module and connect the electrical connector.

d. Install the 4 steering wheel-to-air bag module bolts and torque to 72–106 inch lbs. (8–12 Nm).

22. Connect the negative battery cable.

23. Run the engine to normal operating temperatures; then, check the climate control operation and check for leaks.

LAND ROVER

Discovery

1. Turn the steering wheel 90° from horizontal.

2. Turn the ignition switch OFF.

3. Disconnect the negative (-) battery cable and then the positive (+) battery cable.

➡ **Wait at least 20 minutes for the air bag(s) to discharge before performing any work on the system(s).**

4. Drain the cooling system into a clean container for reuse.

5. Discharge and recover the air conditioning system refrigerant.

6. Remove the dash panel assembly by performing the following procedure:

a. Move the seats rearward.

b. Working under the dash panel assembly, disconnect the air bag multiplug electrical connectors.

c. Remove the glove box.

d. Remove the center console assembly.

e. Remove the driver's SRS module, by disconnecting or removing following items:

- Under the steering wheel, release the lower dash panel cover turnbuckles and remove the lower dash panel.
- Disconnect the air bag harness connector from the yellow air bag column harness.

- Using a special socket, remove the 2 tamper-proof resistor air bag module-to-steering wheel screws.
- Remove the air bag module from the steering wheel.

✳✳ CAUTION

Do not allow the air bag module to hang by electrical harness.

- Disconnect the air bag harness connector.
- Remove the air bag module.

f. Remove the passenger's SRS module, by disconnecting or removing following items:

- Open the glove box door and disconnect the air bag module electrical connector.
- Using a special socket and a long extension, remove both front air bag module-to-dash panel screws.
- Using a Torx® socket, remove both rear air bag module-to-dash panel screws.
- Remove the air bag module from the dash panel.

✳✳ CAUTION

Do not allow the air bag module to hang by electrical harness.

- Disconnect the air bag harness connector.

g. Release the clamp and lower the steering column.

h. Remove the steering wheel and the steering column switch.

i. Remove the instrument housing.

j. Disconnect the electrical connectors and remove the radio.

k. Remove the exterior mirrors switch panel and the coin tray.

l. Remove the switch panel and the clock.

m. Remove the passenger's side relay assembly mounting bracket screw and move the assembly aside.

n. Turn the heater controls fully clockwise. Noting the position of the levers, disconnect the heater control cables from the levers and outer cable from the retaining clips.

o. Remove the 4 dash panel-to-center lower mounting bracket bolts.

p. Remove the 4 dash panel-to-side lower mounting bracket bolts.

q. Working below the steering column, remove the 4 driver's knee bolster pads screws and both knee bolster pads.

r. Remove the 4 instrument bracket-to-dash panel nuts.

s. Using an assistant, partially maneuver the dash panel rearward.

t. At the driver's side, disconnect the

Refer to the model specific sections for cooling system service procedures

6 dash harness-to-main harness multi-plugs connectors.

u. Disconnect the 3 dash harness-to-fusebox multi-plug connectors.

v. Using an assistant, remove the dash panel assembly from the vehicle.

7. In the engine compartment, disconnect the heater hoses from the heater tubes.

8. Release the P-clip securing both the high and low air conditioning pressure tubes.

9. Remove both the high and low pressure tubes-to-evaporator bolts; then, separate the tubes from the evaporator and discard the O-rings.

10. At the lower right side of the heater/air conditioning housing, disconnect the heater-to-blower motor multi-plug connector.

11. Remove the 3 blower motor housing screws and remove the blower motor housing.

12. Remove the 5 heater/air conditioning housing-to-chassis screws.

13. Remove the 2 center console front mounting bracket-to-chassis bolts and remove the center console front mounting bracket.

14. Disconnect both drain tubes.

15. Carefully, remove the heater/air conditioning housing from the vehicle.

16. Remove both right side footwell outlet-to-heater/air conditioning housing screws and the outlet.

17. Remove the heater hoses-to-heater assembly clip.

18. Slide the heater core from the heater/air conditioning housing.

To install:

19. If installing a new heater core, transfer the heater hoses to the new heater core.

20. Slide the heater core into the heater/air conditioning housing.

21. Install the heater hoses-to-heater assembly clip.

22. Install the right side footwell outlet and both outlet-to-heater/air conditioning housing screws.

23. Carefully, install the heater/air conditioning housing to the vehicle.

24. Connect both drain tubes.

25. Install the center console front mounting bracket and the 2 center console front mounting bracket-to-chassis bolts.

26. Install the 5 heater/air conditioning housing-to-chassis screws.

27. Install the blower motor housing and the 3 blower motor housing screws.

28. At the lower right side of the heater/air conditioning housing, connect the heater-to-blower motor multi-plug connector.

29. Using new O-rings, assemble the tubes to the evaporator and install both the high and low pressure tubes-to-evaporator bolts.

30. Install the P-clip securing both the high and low air conditioning pressure tubes.

31. In the engine compartment, connect the heater hoses to the heater tubes.

32. Install the dash panel assembly by performing the following procedure:

a. Using an assistant, install the dash panel assembly to the vehicle.

b. Connect the 3 dash harness-to-fuse box multi-plug connectors.

c. At the driver's side, connect the 6 dash harness-to-main harness multi-plugs connectors.

d. Using an assistant, partially maneuver the dash panel forward.

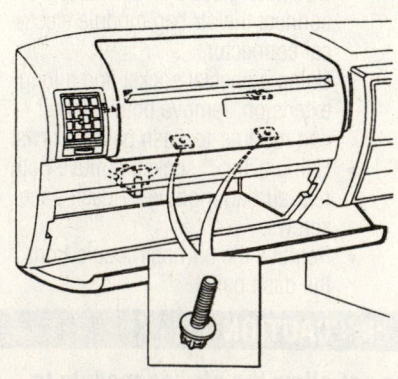

View of the steering wheel, SRS module and special tool—Land Rover Discovery

93113GC8

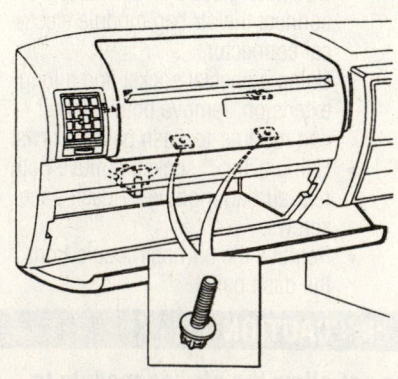

View of the passenger's side SRS module and special screws—Land Rover Discovery

93113GC9

e. Install the 4 instrument bracket-to-dash panel nuts.

f. Working below the steering column, install both knee bolster pads and the 4 driver's knee bolster pads screws.

g. Install the 4 dash panel-to-side lower mounting bracket bolts.

h. Install the 4 dash panel-to-center lower mounting bracket bolts.

i. Noting the position of the levers, connect the heater control cables to the levers and outer cable to the retaining clips.

j. Install the passenger's side relay assembly mounting bracket and the assembly screw.

k. Install the switch panel and the clock.

l. Install the exterior mirrors switch panel and the coin tray.

m. Connect the electrical connectors and install the radio.

n. Install the instrument housing.

o. Install the steering column switch and the steering wheel.

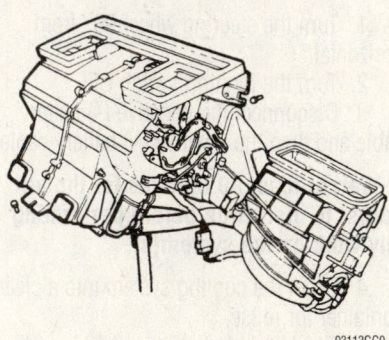

View of the heater/air conditioning housing assembly—Land Rover Discovery

93113GC0

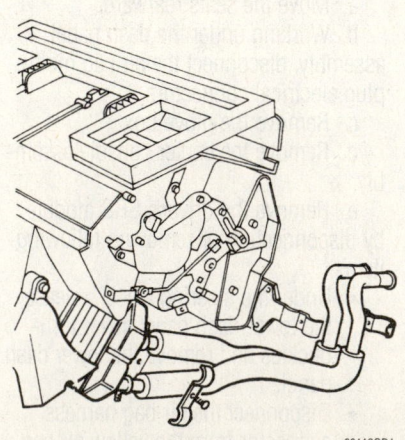

View of the heater core and related components—Land Rover Discovery

93113GD1

p. Raise the steering column and install the clamp.

q. Install the passenger's SRS module, by connecting or installing following items:

- Connect the air bag harness connector.
- Install the air bag module to the dash panel.
- Using a Torx® socket, install both rear air bag module-to-dash panel screws.
- Using a special socket and a long extension, install both front air bag module-to-dash panel screws.
- Open the glove box door and connect the air bag module electrical connector.

r. Install the driver's SRS module, by connecting or installing following items:

- Install the air bag module.
- Connect the air bag harness connector.
- Install the air bag module to the steering wheel.
- Using a special socket, install the 2 tamper-proof resistor air bag module-to-steering wheel screws.
- Connect the air bag harness connector to the yellow air bag column harness.
- Under the steering wheel, install the lower dash panel and install the lower dash panel cover turnbuckles.

s. Install the center console assembly.

t. Install the glove box.

u. Working under the dash panel assembly, connect the air bag multi-plug electrical connectors.

v. Move the seats forward.

33. Refill the cooling system.

34. Connect the positive (+) battery cable and then the negative (-) battery cable.

35. Evacuate and charge the air conditioning system.

36. Run the engine to normal operating temperatures; then, check the climate control operation and check for leaks.

Range Rover

1. Disconnect the negative (-) battery cable; then the positive (+) battery cable.

➥**Wait at least 20 minutes for the air bag(s) to discharge before performing any work on the system(s).**

2. If equipped with SRS, remove the battery.

3. Drain the cooling system into a clean container for reuse.

4. Loosen the hose clips and disconnect the heater hoses from the heater tubes.

5. If equipped with air conditioning, perform the following procedure:

a. Discharge and recover the air conditioning refrigerant.

b. Remove the refrigerant pipes mount-to-evaporator bolt

c. Disconnect the pipes and discard the O-rings.

d. Plug the openings to prevent contamination.

6. Remove the dash panel assembly by performing the following procedures:

a. Remove the center console.

b. Remove the wiper motor and linkage.

c. Remove the steering column.

d. At the passenger's side, remove the clip and disconnect the heated front screen multi-plug connector.

e. Remove the 6 scuttle side panel-to-chassis bolts and the side panel.

f. Remove the heater intake pollen filters.

g. Remove the 8 pollen filter housing screws from each housing and remove both housings.

h. Remove the radio.

i. Near the A-post lower trim panels, remove the door aperture seal.

j. If equipped with a footrest on the driver's side, remove the 3 foot rest-to-A-post lower trim bolts and remove the foot rest.

k. At each A-post's lower trim panel, remove the screw and release the spring clip and remove both trim panels.

l. At the driver's seat base trim, remove the fuse cover.

m. Remove the screw, the 2 trim studs and the seat base trim.

n. At the driver's side, release the 4 spring clips and remove the carpet retainer.

o. Remove the 2 lower closing panel-to-passenger side scrivet fasteners and the panel.

p. Release the closing panel, disconnect the footwell lamp and the diagnostic multi-plug connector; then, remove the closing panel.

q. Remove the 4 dash center bracket bolts and the bracket.

r. Disconnect the 4 multi-plug connectors from the Body Control Module (BCM).

s. At the base of the A-post on the driver's side, remove the ground wires from the stud.

t. Disconnect the multi-plug electrical connectors at the base of each A-post.

u. Disconnect the BCM electrical harness from the sill and move it into the dash panel so it will not hamper removal of the dash panel.

v. At the brake and clutch switches, disconnect the multi-plug electrical connectors and vacuum hose.

w. If equipped with SRS, disconnect the following items:

- The SRS harness connector from the main wiring harness
- The SRS harness connector from the control module

x. Remove both front wheel arch liners.

y. At the left wheel arch, remove the 2 air cleaner baffle scrivet fasteners and the baffle.

z. If equipped with SRS, disconnect both SRS crash sensor electrical connectors.

aa. Remove the 4 battery tray bolts and the 2 air cleaner-to-valance bolts.

bb. Raise the air cleaner and battery tray to access the crash sensor harness clips.

cc. Disconnect the crash sensor harness-to-valance clips; then, move the harnesses into the wheel arches.

dd. Disconnect the 3 crash sensor harness-to-underside wheel arches; then,

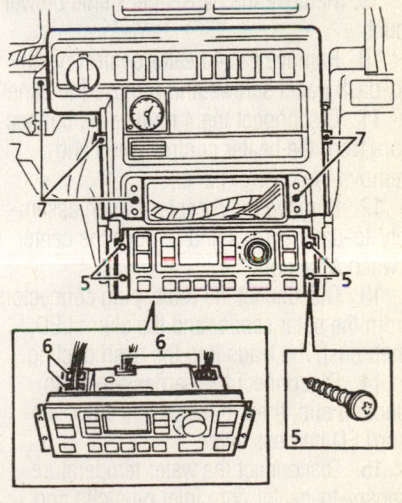

93113GD2

View of the center switch assembly—
Range Rover

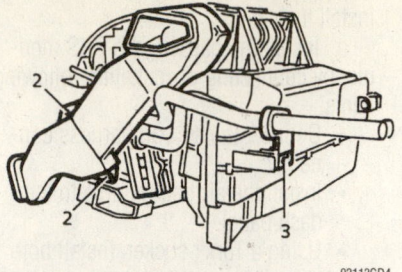

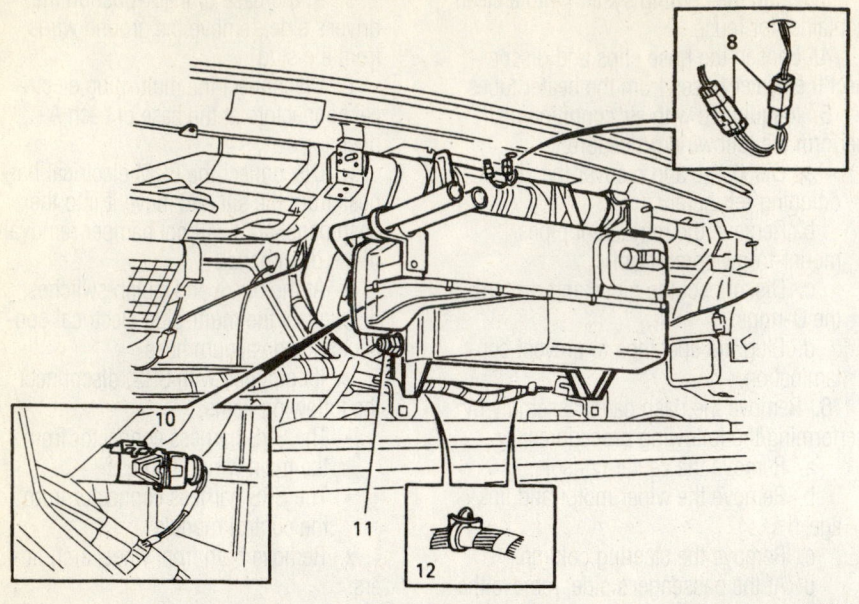

View of the heater/air conditioning housing assembly and related components—Range Rover

View of the heater/air conditioning housing—Range Rover

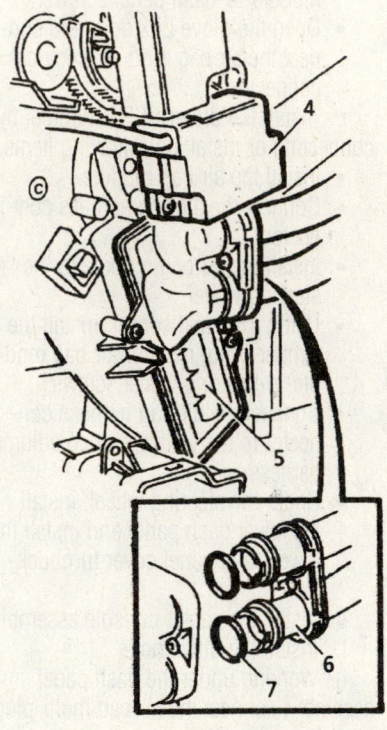

View of the heater core, heater tubes and seals—Range Rover

move the harness through the bulkhead and into the dash.

ee. At the top of the dash panel, remove the 4 dash panel-to-scuttle panel tube bolts.

ff. Remove the dash panel-to-chassis bolts. Pull the panel rearward and support it on 50mm deep wooden blocks.

7. With the dash panel supported on 50mm deep wooden blocks, remove the face level vent ducts-to-dash screws; there is a vent duct located on both sides of the dash.

8. Remove the face level vent ducts inserts from the heater unit.

9. Remove the passenger's side blower duct.

10. Remove the 4 heater control panel-to-dash panel screws and remove the panel.

11. Disconnect the 4 multi-plug connectors from the heater control panel and remove the control panel.

12. Remove the 5 center switch assembly-to-dash screws and remove the center switch assembly.

13. Disconnect the multi-plug connectors from the solar sensor and the alarm LED; then push the leads into the dash ducting.

14. Disconnect the harness-to-dash ducting clip; then, position the solar sensor/LED harness aside.

15. Disconnect the water temperature sensor-to-heater core inlet pipe clip and position the sensor aside.

16. Disconnect the multi-plug connector from the evaporator sensor.

17. Disconnect the 2 harness-to-heater base clips.

18. Remove the 4 heater housing-to-dash frame bolts.

19. Using an assistant, hold the harness away and remove the heater housing.

20. Remove the right side duct-to-heater/air conditioning housing screws and the duct.

21. Remove the heater pipe bracket screw.

22. Remove the 2 right side servo-to-heater/air conditioning housing screws and the servo.

23. Remove the heater core/pipe assembly-to-heater/air conditioning housing clips and the heater core/pipe assembly.

24. If installing a new heater core, remove the 2 heater core-to-heater pipe assembly screws and separate the heater pipe assembly. Discard the O-rings.

To install:

25. If installing a new heater core, install new O-rings, the heater pipe assembly and the 2 heater core-to-heater pipe assembly screws.

26. Install the heater core/pipe assembly and the heater core/pipe assembly-to-heater/air conditioning housing clips.

27. Install the right side servo and the 2 servo-to-heater/air conditioning housing screws.

28. Install the heater pipe bracket screw.

29. Install the right side duct and the

duct-to-heater/air conditioning housing screws.

30. Using an assistant, install the heater housing.

31. Install the 4 heater housing-to-dash frame bolts.

32. Connect the 2 harness-to-heater base clips.

33. Connect the multi-plug connector to the evaporator sensor.

34. Connect the water temperature sensor-to-heater core inlet pipe clip.

35. Connect the harness-to-dash ducting clip.

36. Connect the multi-plug connectors to the solar sensor and the alarm LED.

37. Install the center switch assembly

and the 5 center switch assembly-to-dash screws.

38. Install the control panel and connect the 4 multi-plug connectors to the heater control panel.

39. Install the heater control panel and the 4 panel-to-dash panel screws.

40. Install the passenger's side blower duct.

41. Install the face level vent ducts inserts to the heater unit.

42. With the dash panel supported on 50mm deep wooden blocks, install the face level vent ducts-to-dash screws; there is a vent duct located on both sides of the dash.

43. Install the dash panel assembly by performing the following procedures:

a. Push the panel forward and support it on 50mm deep wooden blocks. Install the dash panel-to-chassis bolts.

b. At the top of the dash panel, install the 4 dash panel-to-scuttle panel tube bolts.

c. Connect the 3 crash sensor harness-to-underside wheel arches.

d. Connect the crash sensor harness-to-valance clips.

e. Install the 4 battery tray bolts and the 2 air cleaner-to-valance bolts.

f. If equipped with SRS, connect both SRS crash sensor electrical connectors.

g. At the left wheel arch, install the air cleaner baffle and the 2 baffle scrivet fasteners.

h. Install both front wheel arch liners.

i. If equipped with SRS, connect the following items:
- The SRS harness connector to the main wiring harness
- The SRS harness connector to the control module

j. At the brake and clutch switches, connect the multi-plug electrical connectors and vacuum hose.

k. Connect the BCM electrical harness to the sill.

l. Connect the multi-plug electrical connectors at the base of each A-post.

m. At the base of the A-post on the driver's side, install the ground wires to the stud.

n. Connect the 4 multi-plug connectors to the Body Control Module (BCM).

o. Install the dash center bracket and the 4 bracket bolts.

p. Install the closing panel; then, connect the footwell lamp and the diagnostic multi-plug connector.

q. Install the lower closing panel and the 2 panel-to-passenger side scrivet fasteners.

r. At the driver's side, install the carpet retainer and the 4 spring clips.

s. Install the seat base trim, the 2 trim studs and the screw.

t. At the driver's seat base trim, install the fuse cover.

u. At each A-post's lower trim panel, install both trim panels, the screw and the spring clip.

v. If equipped with a foot rest on the driver's side, install the foot rest and the 3 foot rest-to-A-post lower trim bolts.

w. Near the A-post lower trim panels, install the door aperture seal.

x. Install the radio.

y. Install the both pollen filter housings and the 8 housing screws to each housing.

z. Install the heater intake pollen filters.

aa. Install the scuttle side panel and the 6 side panel-to-chassis bolts.

bb. At the passenger's side, connect the heated front screen multi-plug connector and install the clip.

cc. Install the steering column.

dd. Install the wiper motor and linkage.

ee. Install the center console.

44. If equipped with air conditioning, perform the following procedure:

a. Lubricate and install new O-rings and connect the pipes.

b. Install the refrigerant pipes mount-to-evaporator bolt.

45. Connect the heater hoses to the heater tubes and install the hose clips.

46. Refill the cooling system.

47. If the battery was removed, install it.

48. Connect the positive (+) battery cable; then, the negative (-) battery cable.

49. Evacuate and charge the air conditioning system.

50. Run the engine to normal operating temperatures; then, check the climate control operation and check for leaks.

LEXUS

LX 450 and LX 470

REMOVAL & INSTALLATION

Front Heater

1. Disconnect the negative battery cable.
2. Drain the cooling system into a clean container for reuse.
3. Disconnect the heater hoses from the heater core.
4. Remove the steering wheel by performing the following procedure:

a. Position the front wheels facing straight-ahead.

b. Remove the steering wheel side covers.

c. Using a Torx® wrench, loosen the 2 screws located at each side of the steering wheel until the screw's circumference groove catches on the screw case.

d. Pull the air bag module from the steering wheel and disconnect the electrical connector.

✳✳ CAUTION

Place the air bag module in a safe place with the front side facing upward.

e. Remove the steering wheel nut.

f. Place alignment marks on the steering wheel and the main shaft.

g. Using a steering wheel puller, press the steering wheel from the steering column.

5. Remove the instrument panel and reinforcement by performing the following procedure:

a. Remove the front door scuff plates, the cowl side trim and the front door opening trim.

b. At the driver's side, remove the 2 assist grip plugs, the 2 screws and assist grip and the front pillar garnish.

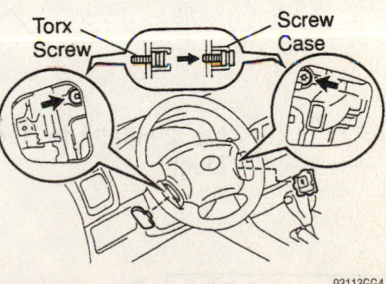

View the steering wheel's Torx® bolts— Lexus LX 450 and LX 470

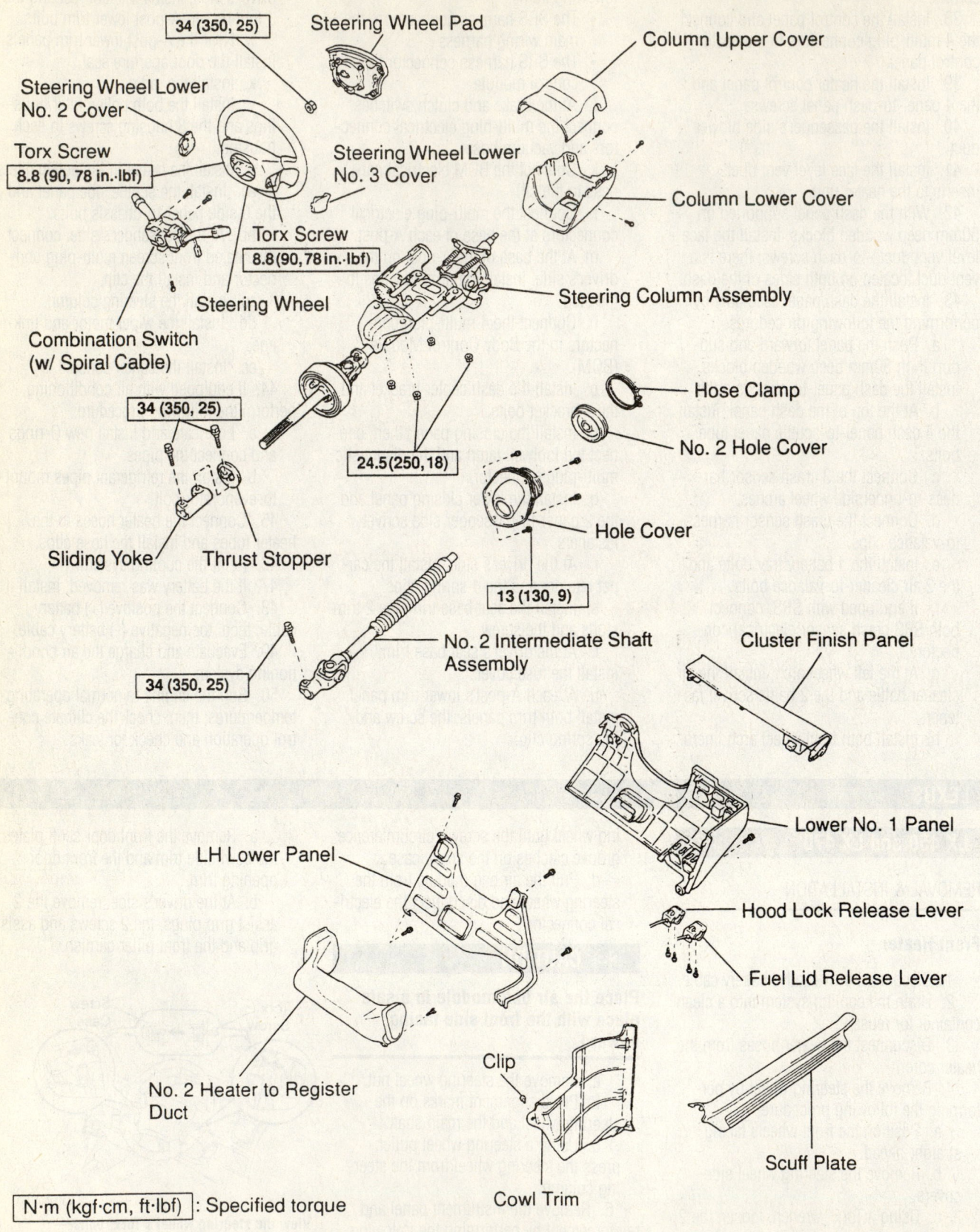

34 (350, 25)

Steering Wheel Pad

Column Upper Cover

Steering Wheel Lower
No. 2 Cover

Torx Screw
8.8 (90, 78 in.·lbf)

Steering Wheel Lower
No. 3 Cover

Column Lower Cover

Torx Screw
8.8 (90, 78 in.·lbf)

Steering Wheel

Steering Column Assembly

Combination Switch
(w/ Spiral Cable)

Hose Clamp

34 (350, 25)

No. 2 Hole Cover

24.5 (250, 18)

Hole Cover

Sliding Yoke   Thrust Stopper

13 (130, 9)

Cluster Finish Panel

34 (350, 25)

No. 2 Intermediate Shaft
Assembly

Lower No. 1 Panel

LH Lower Panel

Hood Lock Release Lever

Fuel Lid Release Lever

No. 2 Heater to Register
Duct

Clip

Scuff Plate

Cowl Trim

N·m (kgf·cm, ft·lbf) : Specified torque

Exploded view the steering column—LX 450 and Lexus LX 470 (Part 1 of 2)

93113GG5

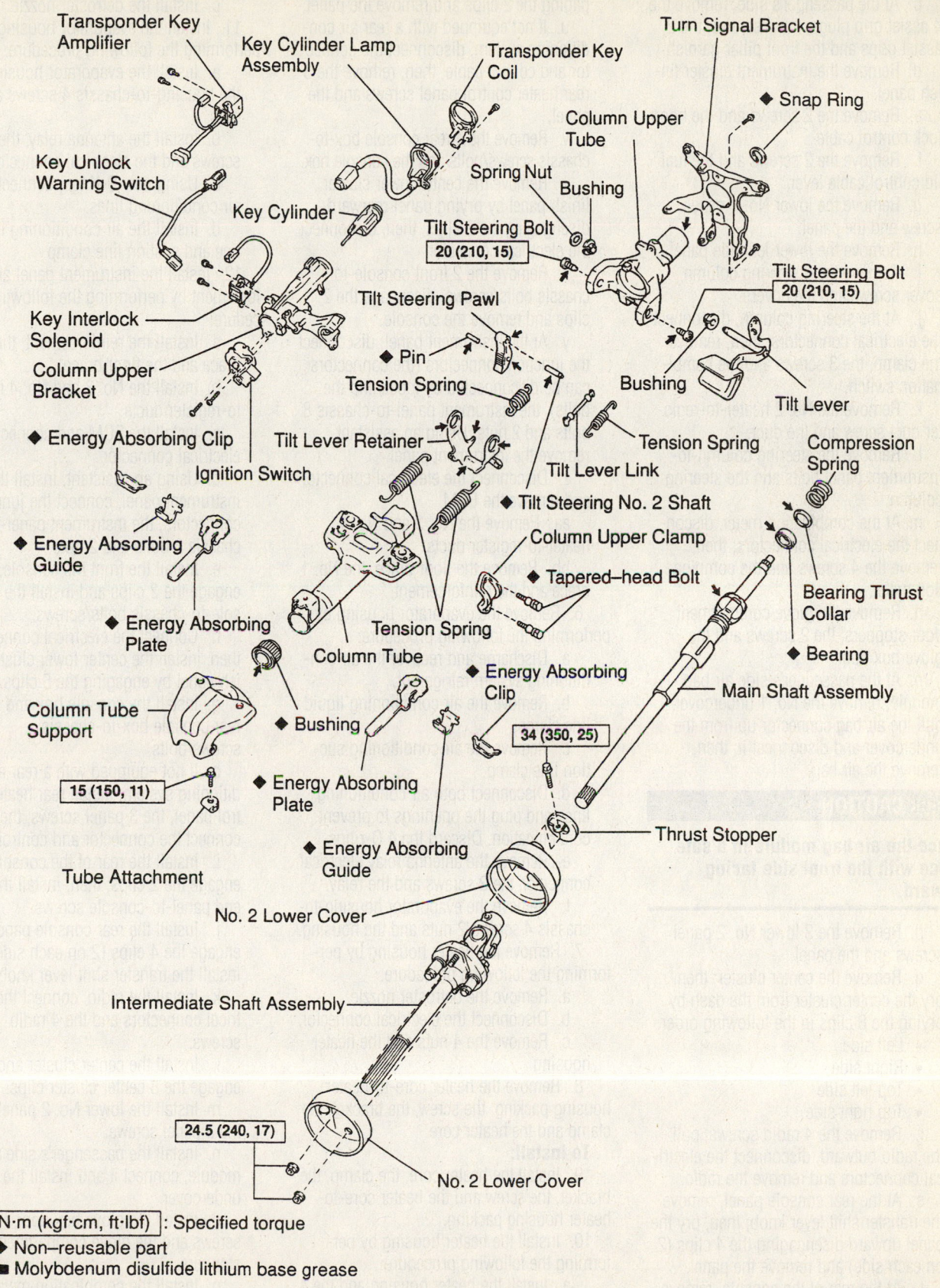

Transponder Key
Amplifier

Key Cylinder Lamp
Assembly

Transponder Key
Coil

Turn Signal Bracket

◆ Snap Ring

Column Upper
Tube

Key Unlock
Warning Switch

Spring Nut

Bushing

Key Cylinder

Tilt Steering Bolt

20 (210, 15)

Tilt Steering Bolt

20 (210, 15)

Key Interlock
Solenoid

Tilt Steering Pawl

Bushing

Tilt Lever

Column Upper
Bracket

◆ Pin

Tension Spring

Tension Spring

Compression
Spring

◆ Energy Absorbing Clip

Tilt Lever Retainer

Tilt Lever Link

Ignition Switch

Tilt Steering No. 2 Shaft

Bearing Thrust
Collar

◆ Energy Absorbing
Guide

Column Upper Clamp

◆ Tapered–head Bolt

◆ Bearing

◆ Energy Absorbing
Plate

Tension Spring

Main Shaft Assembly

Column Tube

◆ Energy Absorbing
Clip

Column Tube
Support

◆ Bushing

34 (350, 25)

15 (150, 11)

◆ Energy Absorbing
Plate

Thrust Stopper

Tube Attachment

◆ Energy Absorbing
Guide

No. 2 Lower Cover

Intermediate Shaft Assembly

24.5 (240, 17)

No. 2 Lower Cover

N·m (kgf·cm, ft·lbf) : Specified torque

◆ Non–reusable part

◀ Molybdenum disulfide lithium base grease

93113GG6

Exploded view the steering column—LX 450 and Lexus LX 470 (Part 2 of 2)

Refer to the model specific sections for engine mechanical service procedures

c. At the passenger's side, remove the 4 assist grip plugs, the 4 screws, the 2 assist grips and the front pillar garnish.

d. Remove the instrument cluster finish panel.

e. Remove the 2 screws and the hood lock control cable.

f. Remove the 2 screws and the fuel lid control cable lever.

g. Remove the lower No. 1 panel screw and the panel.

h. Remove the lower left side panel.

i. Remove the 3 steering column cover screws and the covers.

j. At the steering column, disconnect the electrical connectors; then, remove the clamp, the 3 screws and the combination switch.

k. Remove the No. 2 heater-to-register duct screw and the duct.

l. Remove the steering column-to-instrument panel bolts and the steering column.

m. At the combination meter, disconnect the electrical connectors; then, remove the 4 screws and the combination meter.

n. Remove the glove compartment door stoppers, the 2 screws and the glove box door.

o. At the passenger's side air bag module, remove the No. 1 undercover, pull the air bag connector up from the undercover and disconnect it; then, remove the air bag.

✳✳ CAUTION

Place the air bag module in a safe place with the front side facing upward.

p. Remove the 3 lower No. 2 panel screws and the panel.

q. Remove the center cluster; then, pry the center cluster from the dash by prying the 8 clips in the following order:
- Left side
- Right side
- Top left side
- Top right side

r. Remove the 4 radio screws, pull the radio outward, disconnect the electrical connectors and remove the radio.

s. At the rear console panel, remove the transfer shift lever knob; then, pry the panel upward disengaging the 4 clips (2 on each side) and remove the panel.

t. At the rear of the console, remove the 2 rear end panel-to-console screws; then, pry the end panel rearward disen-

gaging the 2 clips and remove the panel.

u. If not equipped with a rear air conditioning system, disconnect the connector and control cable; then, remove the 3 rear heater control panel screws and the panel.

v. Remove the 4 rear console box-to-chassis screws/bolts and the console box.

w. Remove the center lower cluster finish panel by prying panel rearward disengaging the 5 clips; then, disconnect the electrical connector.

x. Remove the 2 front console-to-chassis bolts/screws, disengage the 2 clips and remove the console.

y. At the instrument panel, disconnect the junction connectors (the connectors can be disconnected by loosening the bolts), the instrument panel-to-chassis 8 bolts and 2 nuts. Using an assistant, remove the instrument panel.

z. Disconnect the electrical connector and remove the ECM.

aa. Remove the No. 3 and No. 4 heater-to-register ducts.

bb. Remove the floor brace, the No. 1 brace and the reinforcement.

6. Remove the evaporator housing by performing the following procedure:

a. Discharge and recover the air conditioning system refrigerant.

b. Remove the air conditioning liquid line clamp.

c. Remove the air conditioning suction line clamp.

d. Disconnect both air conditioning lines and plug the openings to prevent contamination. Discard the 4 O-rings.

e. Remove the antenna relay electrical connector, the 2 screws and the relay.

f. Remove the evaporator housing-to-chassis 4 screws/2 nuts and the housing.

7. Remove the heater housing by performing the following procedure:

a. Remove the defroster nozzle.

b. Disconnect the electrical connector.

c. Remove the 4 nuts and the heater housing.

8. Remove the heater core-to-heater housing packing, the screw, the bracket, the clamp and the heater core.

To install:

9. Install the heater core, the clamp, the bracket, the screw and the heater core-to-heater housing packing.

10. Install the heater housing by performing the following procedure:

a. Install the heater housing and the 4 nuts.

b. Connect the electrical connector.

c. Install the defroster nozzle.

11. Install the evaporator housing by performing the following procedure:

a. Install the evaporator housing and the housing-to-chassis 4 screws and 2 nuts.

b. Install the antenna relay, the 2 screws and the electrical connector.

c. Using new O-rings, connect both air conditioning lines.

d. Install the air conditioning liquid line and suction line clamp.

12. Install the instrument panel and reinforcement by performing the following procedure:

a. Install the reinforcement, the No. 1 brace and the floor brace.

b. Install the No. 3 and No. 4 heater-to-register ducts.

c. Install the ECM and connect the electrical connector.

d. Using an assistant, install the instrument panel, connect the junction connectors, the instrument panel-to-chassis 8 bolts and 2 nuts.

e. Install the front the console, engage the 2 clips and install the 2 console-to-chassis bolts/screws.

f. Connect the electrical connector; then, install the center lower cluster finish panel by engaging the 5 clips.

g. Install the console box and the 4 rear console box-to-chassis screws/bolts.

h. If not equipped with a rear air conditioning system, install rear heater control panel, the 3 panel screws; then, connect the connector and control cable.

i. Install the rear of the console and engage the 2 clips; then, install the 2 rear end panel-to-console screws.

j. Install the rear console panel and engage the 4 clips (2 on each side); then, install the transfer shift lever knob.

k. Install the radio, connect the electrical connectors and the 4 radio screws.

l. Install the center cluster and engage the 8 center cluster clips.

m. Install the lower No. 2 panel and the 3 panel screws.

n. Install the passenger's side air bag module, connect it and install the No. 1 undercover.

o. Install the glove box door, the 2 screws and the glove compartment door stoppers.

p. Install the combination meter and the 4 screws; then, connect the electrical connectors.

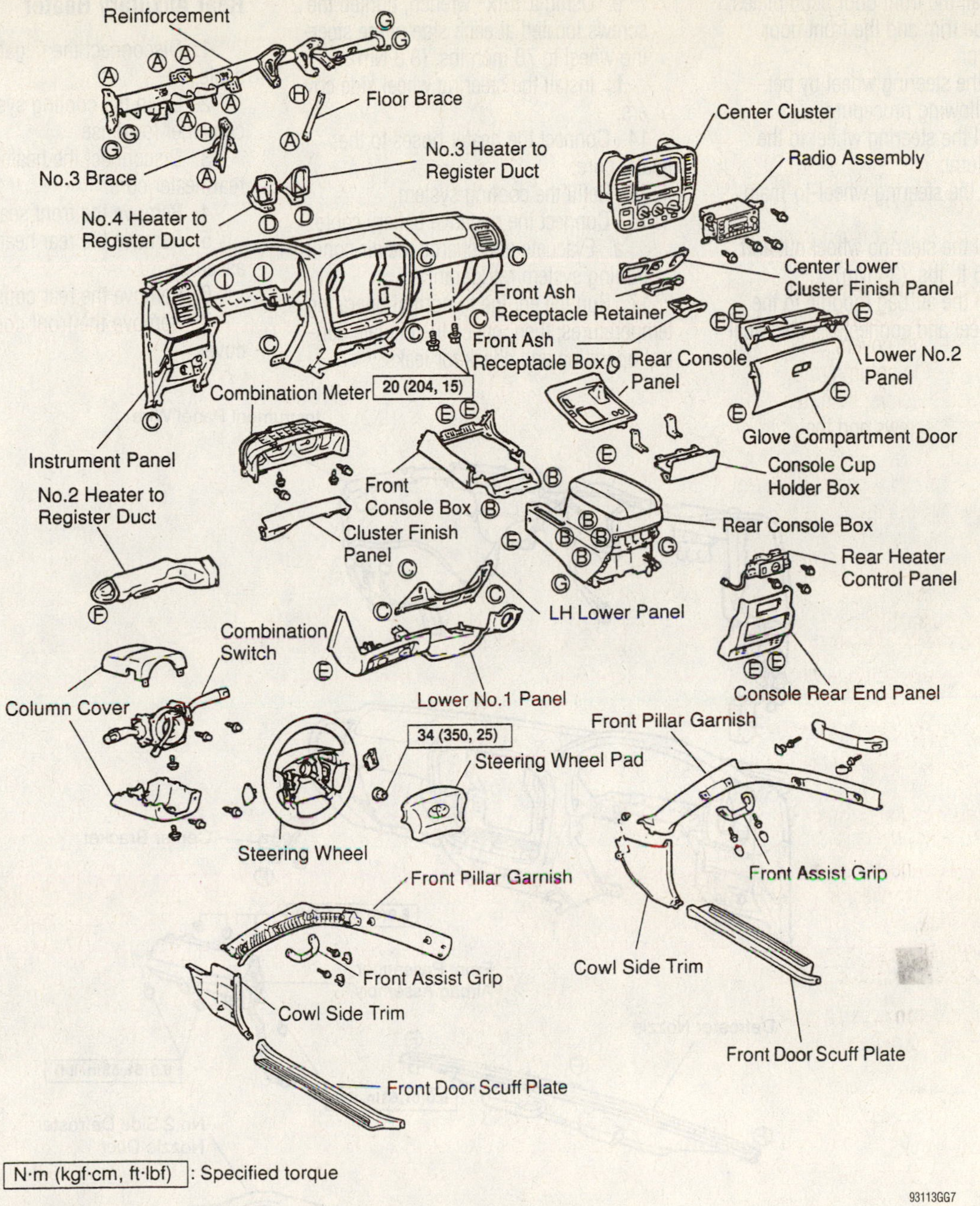

Reinforcement

Floor Brace

No.3 Heater to Register Duct

No.3 Brace

No.4 Heater to Register Duct

Center Cluster

Radio Assembly

Center Lower Cluster Finish Panel

Front Ash Receptacle Retainer

Front Ash Receptacle Box

Rear Console Panel

Lower No.2 Panel

Glove Compartment Door

Combination Meter   20 (204, 15)

Instrument Panel

No.2 Heater to Register Duct

Front Console Box

Cluster Finish Panel

Rear Console Box

Console Cup Holder Box

Rear Heater Control Panel

Combination Switch

LH Lower Panel

Column Cover

Lower No.1 Panel

Console Rear End Panel

Front Pillar Garnish

34 (350, 25)

Steering Wheel Pad

Front Assist Grip

Steering Wheel

Front Pillar Garnish

Cowl Side Trim

Front Door Scuff Plate

Front Assist Grip

Cowl Side Trim

Front Door Scuff Plate

N·m (kgf·cm, ft·lbf) : Specified torque

93113GG7

Exploded view the instrument panel and related components—Lexus LX 450 and LX 470

q. Install the steering column and the steering column-to-instrument panel bolts.

r. Install the No. 2 heater-to-register duct and the duct screw.

s. At the steering column, install the combination switch, the 3 screws and the clamp; then, connect the electrical connectors.

t. Install the steering column covers and the 3 covers screws.

u. Install the lower left side panel.

v. Install the lower No. 1 panel and the panel screw.

w. Install the fuel lid control cable lever and the 2 screws.

x. Install the hood lock control cable and the 2 screws.

y. Install the instrument cluster finish panel.

z. At the passenger's side, install the front pillar garnish, the 2 assist grips, the 4 screws and the 4 assist grip plugs.

aa. At the driver's side, install the front pillar garnish, assist grip, the 2 screws and the 2 assist grip plugs.

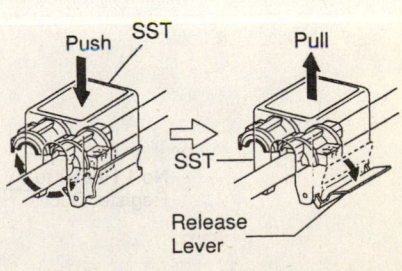

Push   SST

Pull

SST

Release Lever

93113GG9

View the air conditioning line clamp removal tool—Lexus LX 450 and LX 470

Refer to the model specific sections for cooling system service procedures

bb. Install the front door scuff plates, the cowl side trim and the front door opening trim.

13. Install the steering wheel by performing the following procedure:

a. Install the steering wheel to the steering column.

b. Align the steering wheel-to-main shaft marks.

c. Install the steering wheel nut and torque to 25 ft. lbs. (34 Nm).

d. Install the air bag module to the steering wheel and connect the electrical connector.

e. Using a Torx® wrench, tighten the 2 screws located at each side of the steering wheel to 78 inch lbs. (8.8 Nm).

f. Install the steering wheel side covers.

14. Connect the heater hoses to the heater core.

15. Refill the cooling system.

16. Connect the negative battery cable.

a. Evacuate and charge the air conditioning system refrigerant.

17. Run the engine to normal operating temperatures; then, check the climate control operation and check for leaks.

Rear Auxiliary Heater

1. Disconnect the negative battery cable.

2. Drain the cooling system into a clean container for reuse.

3. Disconnect the heater hoses from the rear heater core.

4. Remove the front seats.

5. Remove the rear heater control assembly.

6. Remove the rear console box.

7. Remove the front console box cover.

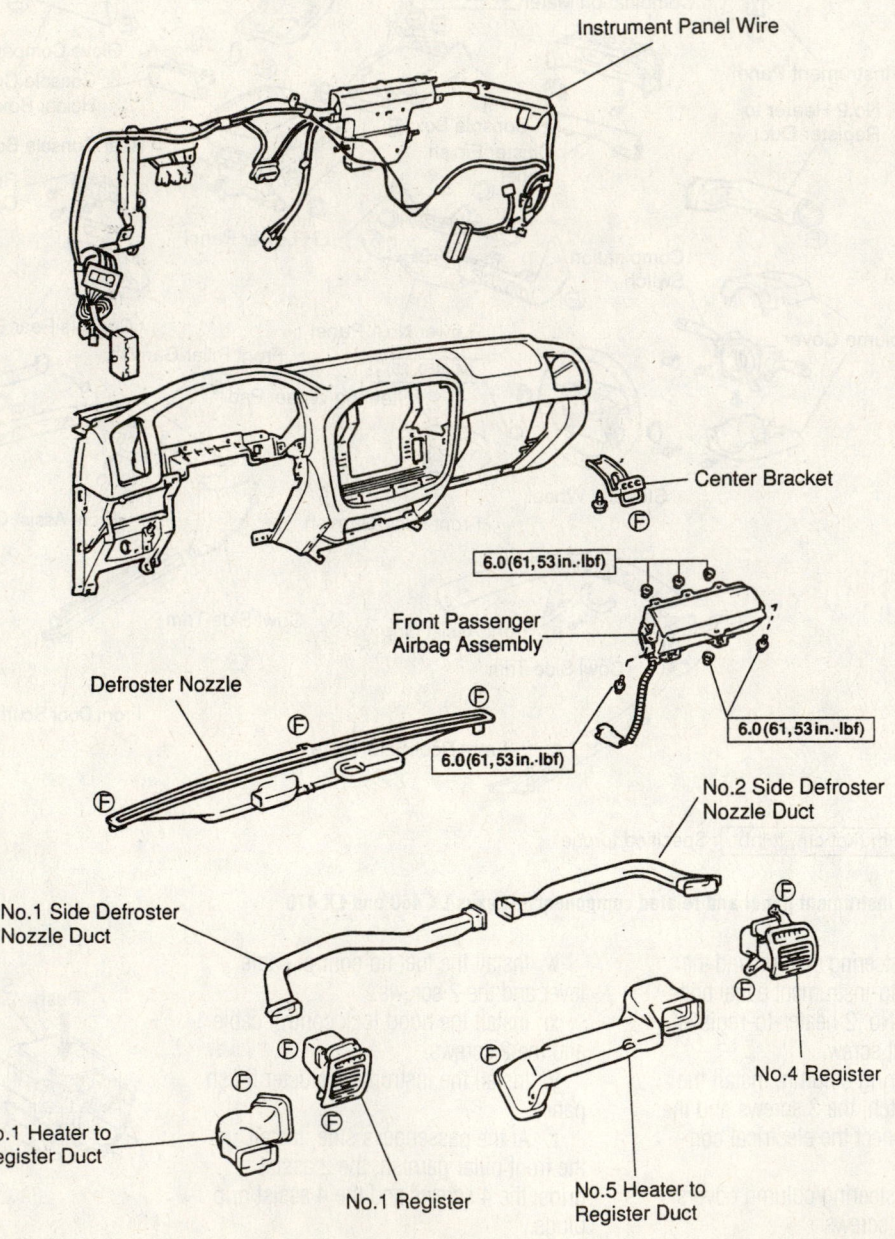

Instrument Panel Wire

Center Bracket

6.0 (61, 53 in.·lbf)

Front Passenger Airbag Assembly

6.0 (61, 53 in.·lbf)

Defroster Nozzle

6.0 (61, 53 in.·lbf)

No.2 Side Defroster Nozzle Duct

No.1 Side Defroster Nozzle Duct

No.4 Register

No.1 Heater to Register Duct

No.1 Register

No.5 Heater to Register Duct

N·m (kgf·cm, ft·lbf) : Specified torque

93113GG8

Exploded view the front ventilation ducts and related components—Lexus LX 450 and LX 470

8. Remove the lower center cluster finish panel.

9. Remove the front door scuff plates.

10. Remove the cowl side trim.

11. Remove the rear door scuff plates.

12. Remove the center pillar garnishes.

13. Slide the carpet rearward.

14. Remove the cooler bracket bolts and the bracket.

15. Remove the rear heater duct bolt/screw and the duct.

16. Disconnect the rear heater housing electrical connector.

17. Remove the 3 rear heater housing-to-chassis bolts and the heater housing.

18. Remove the heater core-to-heater housing 3 screws and 2 clamps.

19. Remove the heater core from the heater housing.

To install:

20. Install the heater core to the heater housing.

21. Install the heater core-to-heater housing 3 screws and 2 clamps.

22. Install the heater housing and the 3 rear heater housing-to-chassis bolts.

23. Connect the rear heater housing electrical connector.

24. Install the rear heater duct and the duct bolt/screw.

25. Install the cooler bracket and the bracket bolts.

26. Slide the carpet rearward.

27. Install the center pillar garnishes.

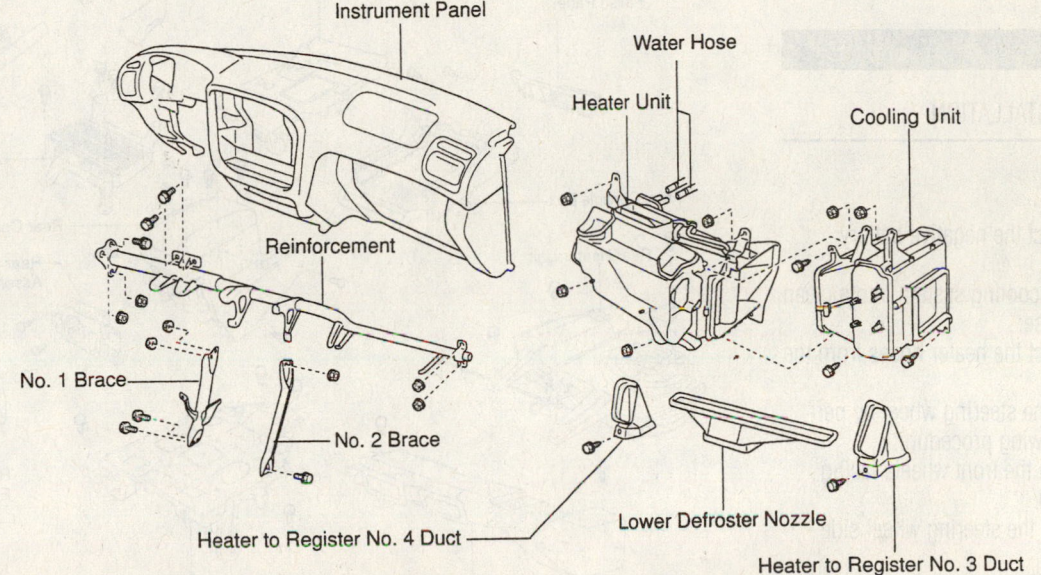

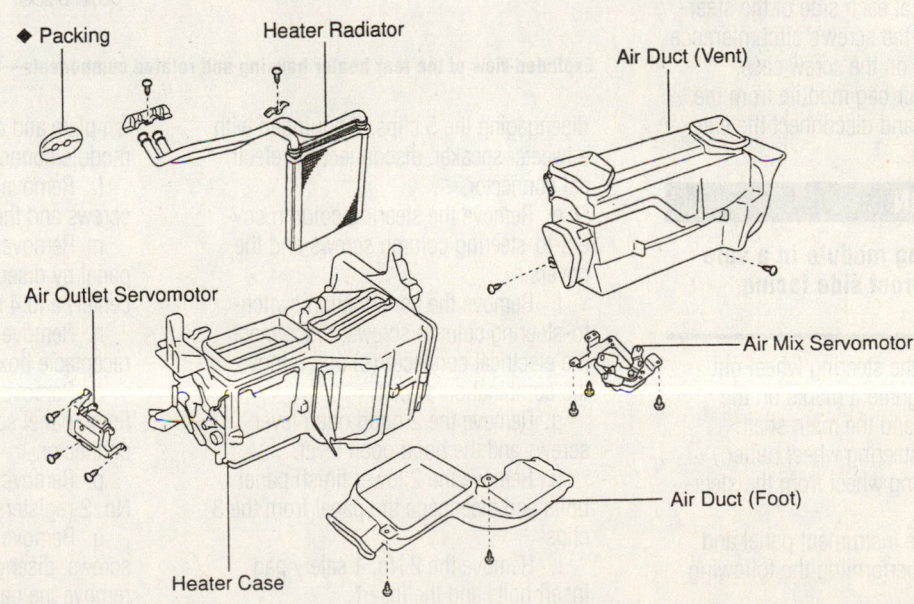

Exploded view the front heater core, heater housing, evaporator housing and related components—Lexus LX 450 and LX 470

93113GG0

28. Install the rear door scuff plates.
29. Install the cowl side trim.
30. Install the front door scuff plates.
31. Install the lower center cluster finish panel.
32. Install the front console box cover.
33. Install the rear console box.
34. Install the rear heater control assembly.
35. Install the front seats.
36. Connect the heater hoses to the rear heater core.
37. Refill the cooling system.
38. Connect the negative battery cable.

RX 300

REMOVAL & INSTALLATION

Front Heater

1. Disconnect the negative battery cable.
2. Drain the cooling system into a clean container for reuse.
3. Disconnect the heater hoses from the heater core.
4. Remove the steering wheel by performing the following procedure:
   a. Position the front wheels facing straight-ahead.
   b. Remove the steering wheel side covers.
   c. Using a Torx® wrench, loosen the 2 screws located at each side of the steering wheel until the screw's circumference groove catches on the screw case.
   d. Pull the air bag module from the steering wheel and disconnect the electrical connector.

✳✳ CAUTION

Place the air bag module in a safe place with the front side facing upward.

   e. Remove the steering wheel nut.
   f. Place alignment marks on the steering wheel and the main shaft.
   g. Using a steering wheel puller, press the steering wheel from the steering column.
5. Remove the instrument panel and reinforcement by performing the following procedure:
   a. Remove the front door scuff plates.
   b. Remove the cowl side boards.
   c. Remove the front door trim covers.
   d. Remove the front pillar garnish by

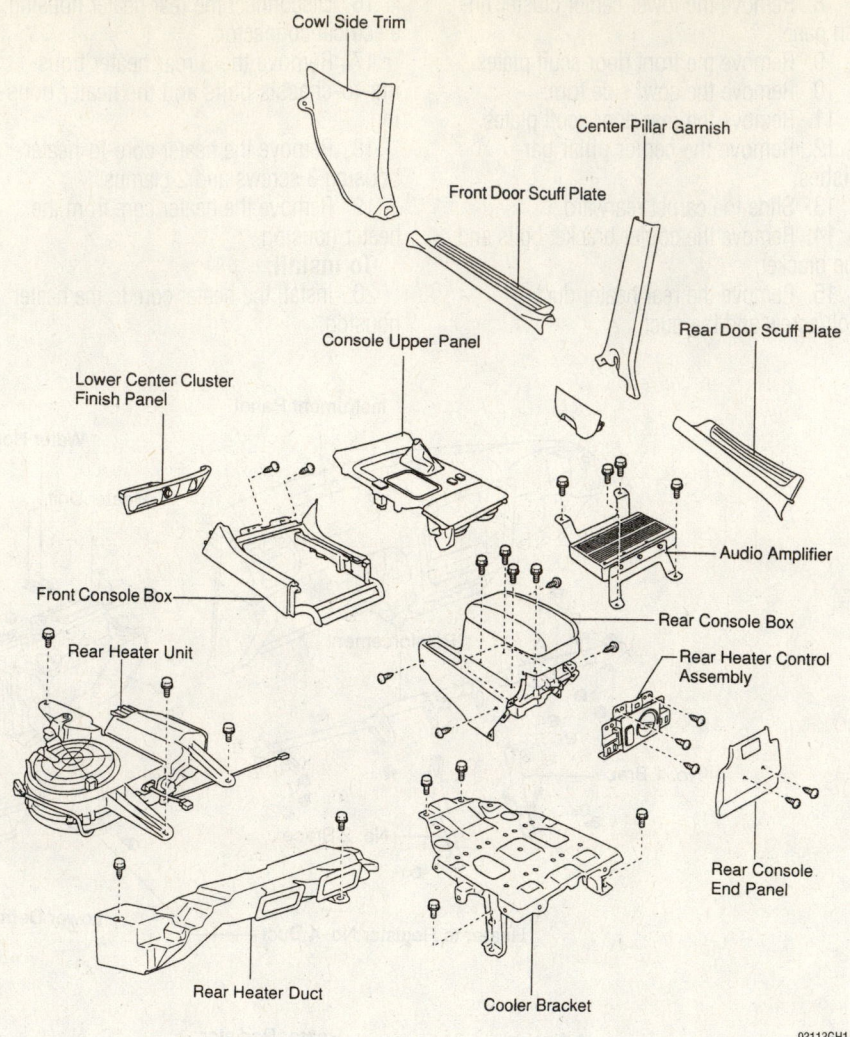

Exploded view of the rear heater housing and related components—Lexus LX 450 and LX 470

Labels in figure: Cowl Side Trim; Center Pillar Garnish; Front Door Scuff Plate; Rear Door Scuff Plate; Console Upper Panel; Lower Center Cluster Finish Panel; Audio Amplifier; Front Console Box; Rear Console Box; Rear Heater Unit; Rear Heater Control Assembly; Rear Console End Panel; Rear Heater Duct; Cooler Bracket

93113GH1

disengaging the 5 clips. If equipped with a tweeter speaker, disconnect the electrical connector.
   e. Remove the steering column covers-to-steering column screws and the covers.
   f. Remove the combination switch-to-steering column screws, disconnect the electrical connector(s) and remove the combination switch.
   g. Remove the 2 hood open lever screws and the hood open lever.
   h. Remove the 2 lower finish panel bolts and disengage the panel from the 3 clips.
   i. Remove the 2 No. 1 safety pad insert bolts and the insert.
   j. Remove the 2 No. 2 finish panel bolts and disengage the panel from the 4 clips.
   k. In the left side of the glove compartment, pry out the glove box door fin-

ish plate and disconnect the air bag module connector.
   l. Remove the glove box 3 nuts and 2 screws and the glove box.
   m. Remove the center cluster finish panel by disengaging the claw (bottom center) and 4 clips (1 at each corner).
   n. Remove the ashtray, the 2 ashtray receptacle box screws.
   o. Remove the 4 lower center cluster finish panel screws and disconnect the connector.
   p. Remove the clock, the No. 1 and No. 2 registers from the panel.
   q. Remove the 3 cluster finish panel screws, disengage the 8 clips and remove the panel.
   r. Remove the combination meter.
   s. Remove the radio assembly.
   t. Remove the heater control assembly.
   u. Remove 2 passenger's side air bag

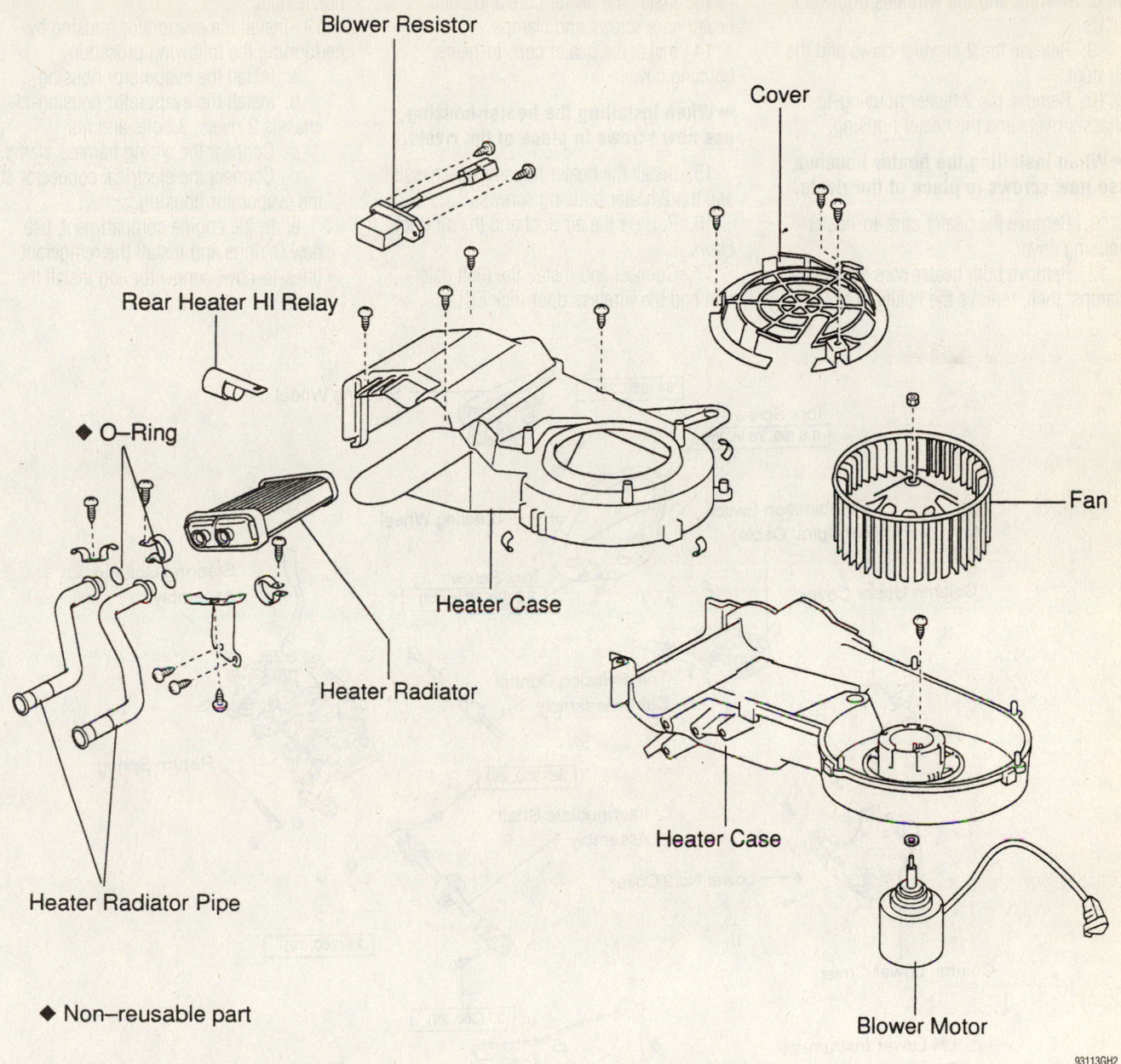

Blower Resistor

Cover

Rear Heater HI Relay

◆ O–Ring

Fan

Heater Case

Heater Radiator

Heater Case

Heater Radiator Pipe

◆ Non–reusable part

Blower Motor

93113GH2

Exploded view of the rear heater core, heater housing and related components—Lexus LX 450 and LX 470

module bolts; then, disconnect and remove the air bag module.

❊❊ CAUTION

Place the air bag module in a safe place with the front side facing upward.

v. Remove the instrument panel-to-chassis 5 bolts and nut.

w. Remove the audio amplifier.

x. Remove the No. 1 and No. 2 braces.

y. Remove the No. 2 cowl brace.

z. Remove the instrument panel reinforcement.

6. Remove the evaporator housing by performing the following procedure:

a. Discharge and recover the air conditioning system refrigerant.

b. In the engine compartment, remove the refrigerant lines-to-cowl connector

bolts; then, disconnect the lines and discard the O-rings.

c. Disconnect the electrical connector at the evaporator housing.

d. Disconnect the wiring harness clamp.

e. Remove the evaporator housing-to-chassis 2 rivets, 3 bolts and nut.

f. Remove the evaporator housing.

7. Remove the 4 defroster nozzle nuts and the nozzle.

8. Disconnect and remove the theft deterrent and the wireless door lock ECUs.

9. Release the 2 air duct claws and the air duct.

10. Remove the 2 heater housing-to-chassis rivets and the heater housing.

➡ **When installing the heater housing, use new screws in place of the rivets.**

11. Remove the heater core-to-heater housing cover.

12. Remove both heater core screws and clamps; then, remove the heater core.

To install:

13. Install the heater core and both heater core screws and clamps.

14. Install the heater core-to-heater housing cover.

➡ **When installing the heater housing, use new screws in place of the rivets.**

15. Install the heater housing-to-chassis and the 2 heater housing screws.

16. Release the air duct and the air duct claws.

17. Connect and install the theft deterrent and the wireless door lock ECUs.

18. Install the defroster nozzle and the 4 nozzle nuts.

19. Install the evaporator housing by performing the following procedure:

a. Install the evaporator housing.

b. Install the evaporator housing-to-chassis 2 rivets, 3 bolts and nut.

c. Connect the wiring harness clamp.

d. Connect the electrical connector at the evaporator housing.

e. In the engine compartment, use new O-rings and install the refrigerant lines-to-cowl connector and install the bolts.

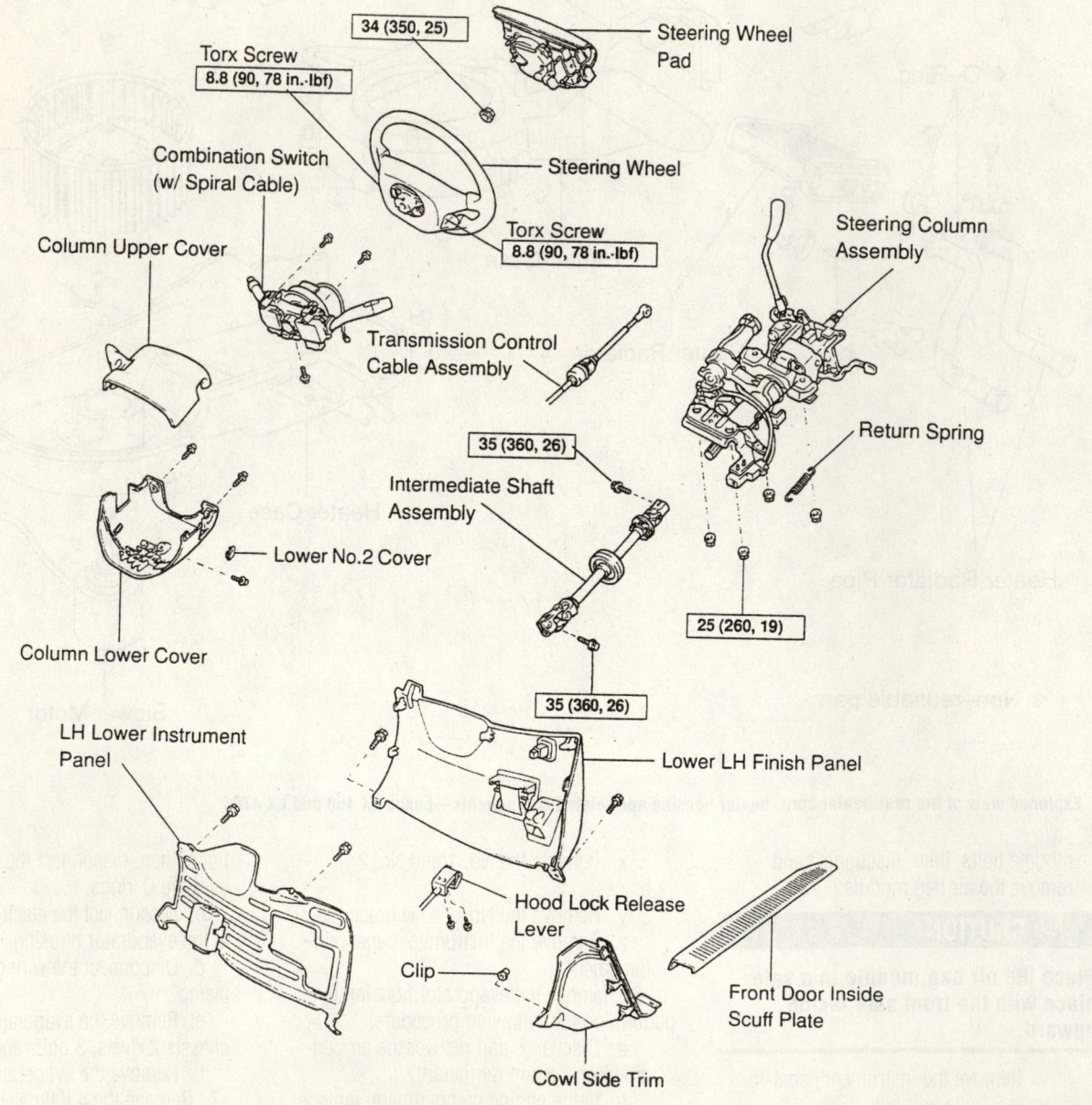

34 (350, 25)

Torx Screw
8.8 (90, 78 in.·lbf)

Steering Wheel Pad

Combination Switch (w/ Spiral Cable)

Steering Wheel

Torx Screw
8.8 (90, 78 in.·lbf)

Column Upper Cover

Steering Column Assembly

Transmission Control Cable Assembly

35 (360, 26)

Intermediate Shaft Assembly

Return Spring

Lower No.2 Cover

25 (260, 19)

Column Lower Cover

LH Lower Instrument Panel

35 (360, 26)

Lower LH Finish Panel

Hood Lock Release Lever

Clip

Front Door Inside Scuff Plate

Cowl Side Trim

N·m (kgf·cm, ft·lbf) : Specified torque

93113GH3

Exploded view of the steering wheel, steering column and related components—Lexus RX 300

20. Install the instrument panel and reinforcement by performing the following procedure:

a. Install the instrument panel reinforcement.

b. Install the No. 2 cowl brace.

c. Install the No. 1 and No. 2 braces.

d. Install the audio amplifier.

e. Install the instrument panel-to-chassis 5 bolts and nut.

f. Connect and install the air bag module and the 2 passenger's side air bag module bolts.

g. Install the heater control assembly.

h. Install the radio assembly.

i. Install the combination meter.

j. Install the cluster finish panel, engage the 8 clips and install the panel screws.

k. Install the No. 1 and No. 2 registers and the clock to the panel.

l. Connect the lower center cluster finish panel connector and install the 4 lower center cluster finish panel screws.

m. Install the 2 ashtray receptacle box screws and the ashtray.

n. Install the center cluster finish panel by engaging the 4 clips (1 at each corner) and the claw (bottom center).

o. Install the glove box and the glove box 3 nuts and 2 screws.

p. In the left side of the glove compartment, connect the air bag module

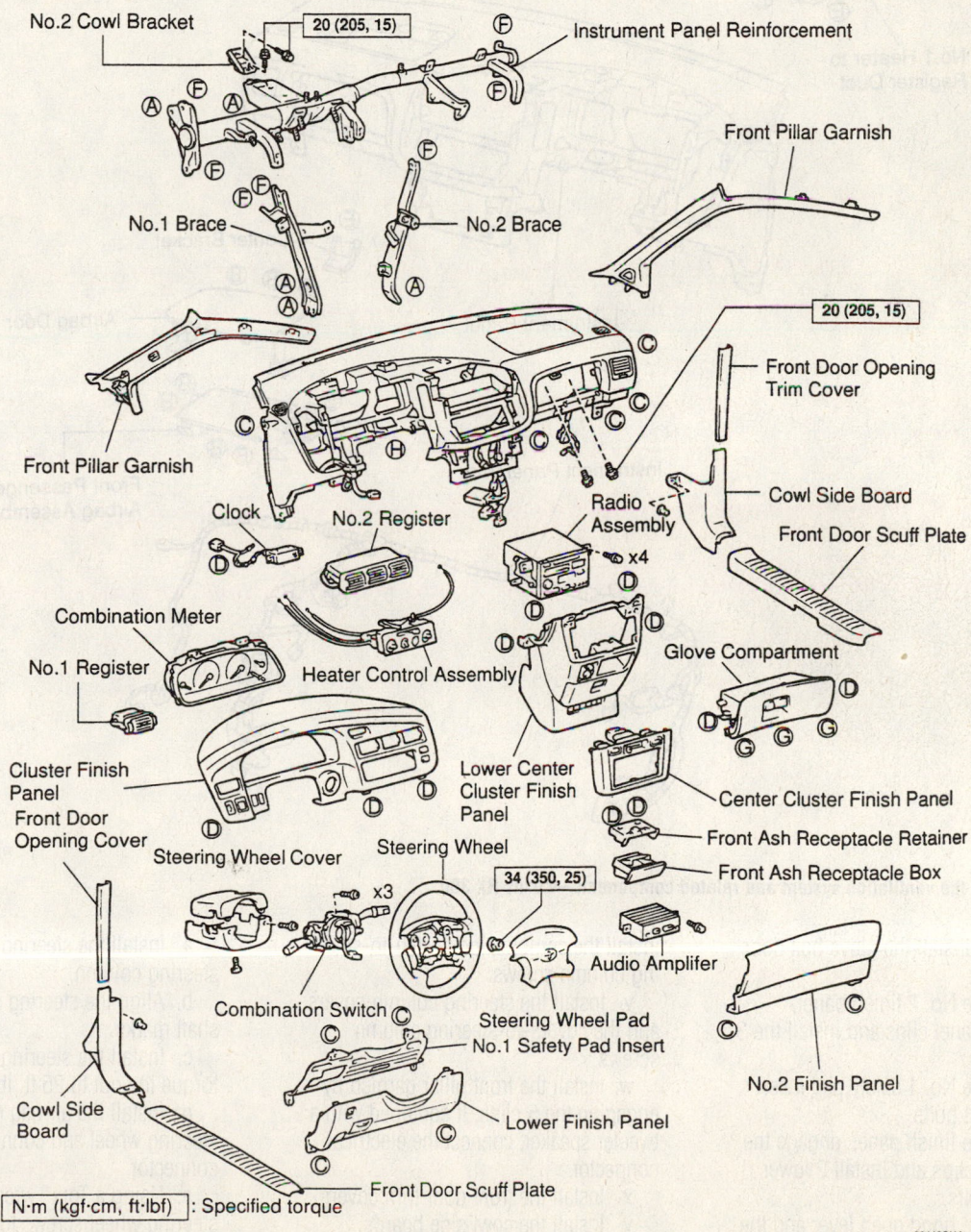

Exploded view of the instrument panel and related components—Lexus RX 300

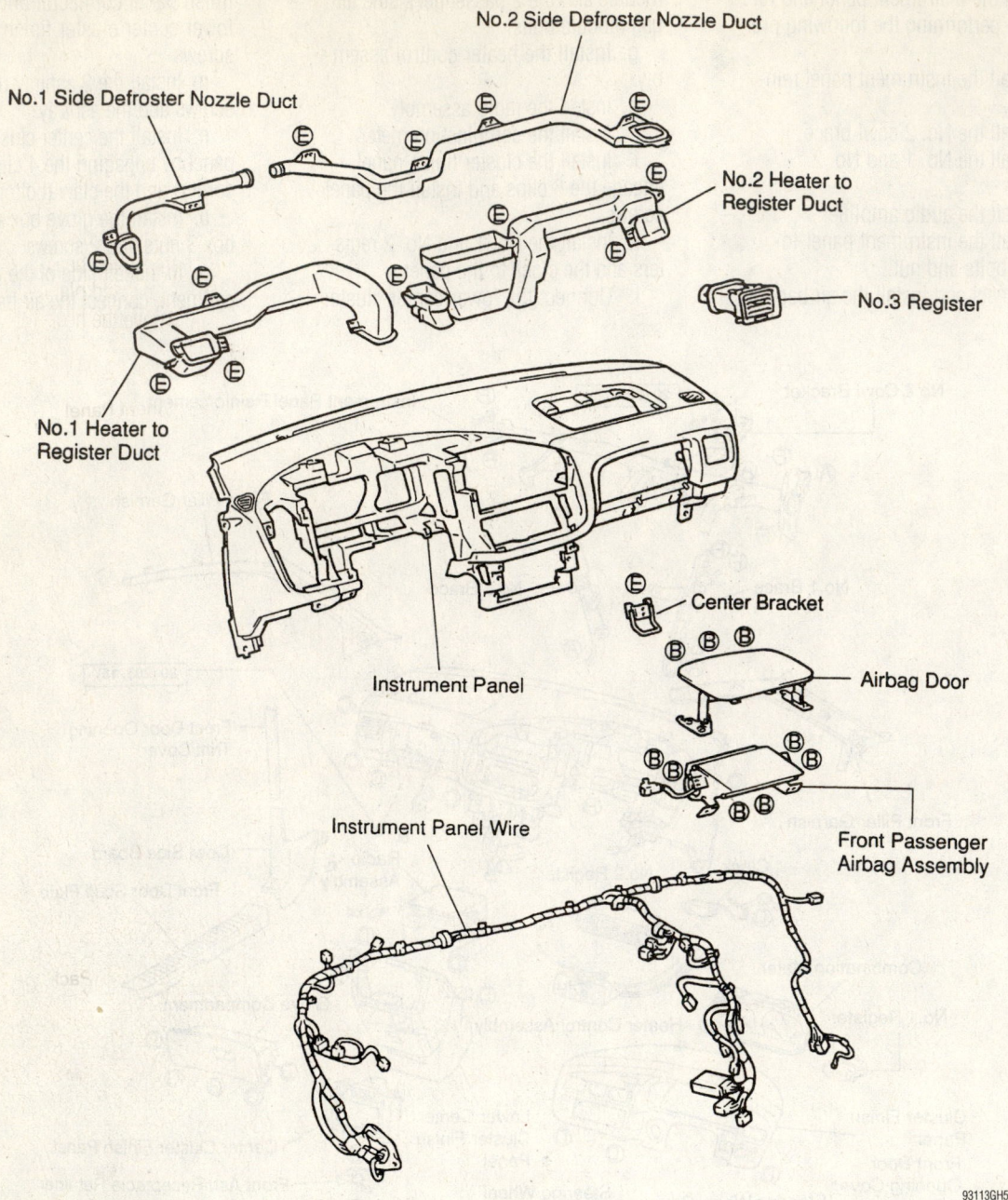

No.2 Side Defroster Nozzle Duct

No.1 Side Defroster Nozzle Duct

No.2 Heater to Register Duct

No.3 Register

No.1 Heater to Register Duct

Center Bracket

Instrument Panel

Airbag Door

Instrument Panel Wire

Front Passenger Airbag Assembly

93113GH5

Exploded view of the ventilation system and related components—Lexus RX 300

connector and install the glove box door finish plate.

q. Install the No. 2 finish panel, engage the 4 panel clips and install the 3 panel bolts.

r. Install the No. 1 safety pad insert and the 2 insert bolts.

s. Install the finish panel, engage the 3 finish panel clips and install 2 lower finish panel bolts.

t. Install the hood open lever and the 2 hood open lever screws.

u. Install the combination switch, connect the electrical connector(s) and

install the combination switch-to-steering column screws.

v. Install the steering column covers and the covers-to-steering column screws.

w. Install the front pillar garnish by engaging the 5 clips. If equipped with a tweeter speaker, connect the electrical connector.

x. Install the front door trim covers.

y. Install the cowl side boards.

z. Install the front door scuff plates.

21. Install the steering wheel by performing the following procedure:

a. Install the steering wheel to the steering column.

b. Align the steering wheel-to-main shaft marks.

c. Install the steering wheel nut and torque the nut to 25 ft. lbs. (34 Nm).

d. Install the air bag module to the steering wheel and connect the electrical connector.

e. Using a Torx® wrench, tighten the steering wheel screws to 78 inch lbs. (8.8 Nm).

f. Install the steering wheel side covers.

22. Connect the heater hoses to the heater core.
23. Refill the cooling system.
24. Connect the negative battery cable.
25. Evacuate and charge the air conditioning system.
26. Run the engine to normal operating temperatures; then, check the climate control operation and check for leaks.

Rear Auxiliary Heater

1. Disconnect the negative battery cable.

2. Drain the cooling system into a clean container for reuse.
3. Disconnect the heater hoses from the rear heater core.
4. Remove the front seats.
5. Remove the front door scuff plates.
6. Remove the cowl side trim.
7. Remove the rear door scuff plates.
8. Remove the lower door scuff plates.
9. Remove the rear console box.
10. Remove the left side air outlet grille.
11. Pull the carpet rearward.

12. Remove the 3 clips and the air outlet grille.
13. Remove the rear air duct 2 bolts, 2 clips and the duct.
14. Disconnect the electrical connectors.
15. Remove the 3 rear heater housing bolts and the housing.
16. Remove both heater core-to-heater housing screws and clamps.
17. Remove the heater core-to-heater housing screw and plate.
18. Remove the heater core.

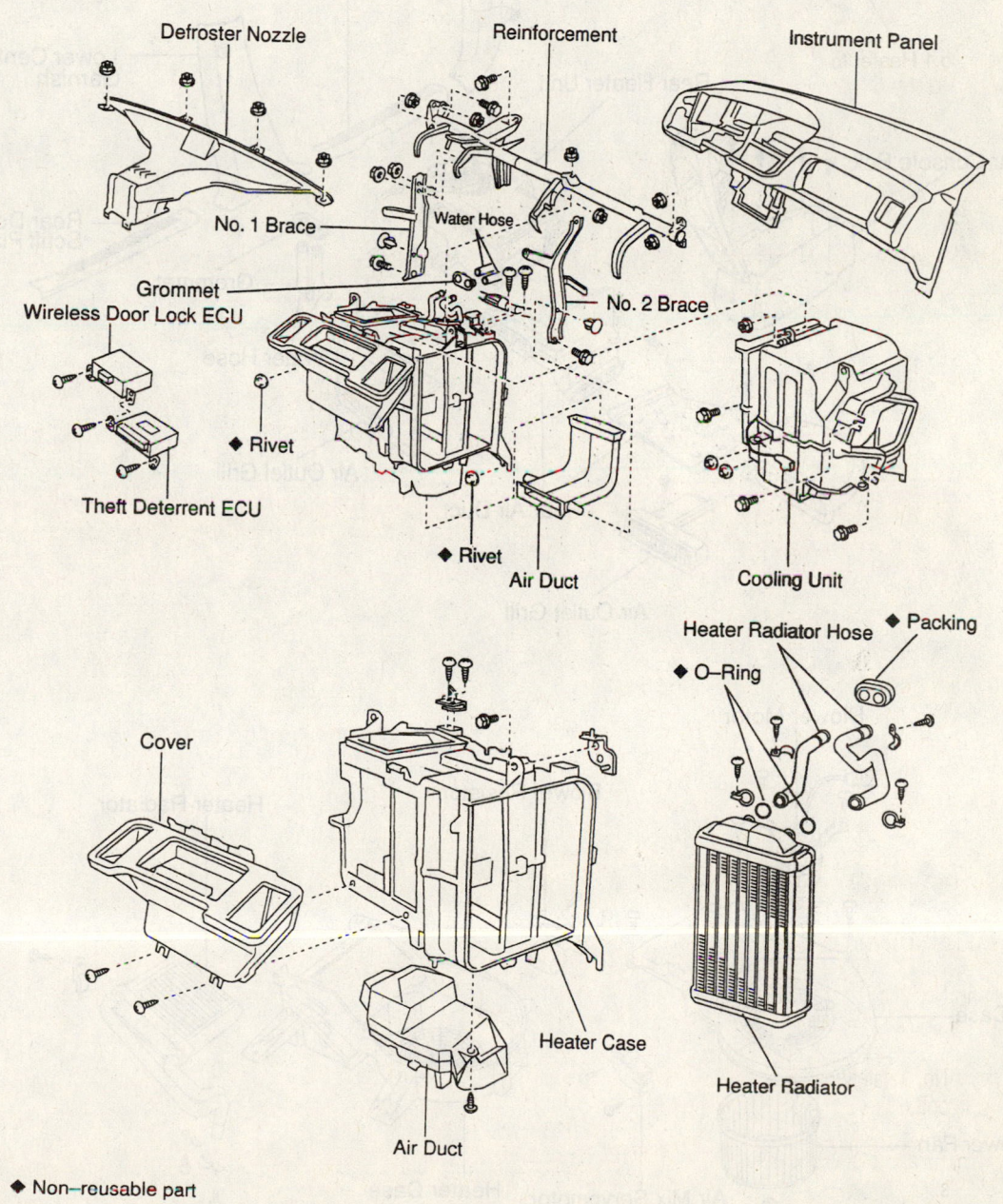

Exploded view of the heater core, heater housing, evaporator housing and related components—Lexus RX 300

93113GH6

Refer to the model specific sections for cooling system service procedures

To install:

19. Install the heater core.
20. Install the heater core-to-heater housing screw and plate.
21. Install both heater core-to-heater housing screws and clamps.
22. Install the rear heater housing and the 3 housing bolts.
23. Connect the electrical connectors.

24. Install the rear air duct and the duct 2 bolts and 2 clips.
25. Install the 3 clips and the air outlet grille.
26. Move the carpet forward.
27. Install the left side air outlet grille.
28. Install the rear console box.
29. Install the lower door scuff plates.
30. Install the rear door scuff plates.

31. Install the cowl side trim.
32. Install the front door scuff plates.
33. Install the front seats.
34. Connect the heater hoses to the rear heater core.
35. Refill the cooling system.
36. Connect the negative battery cable.

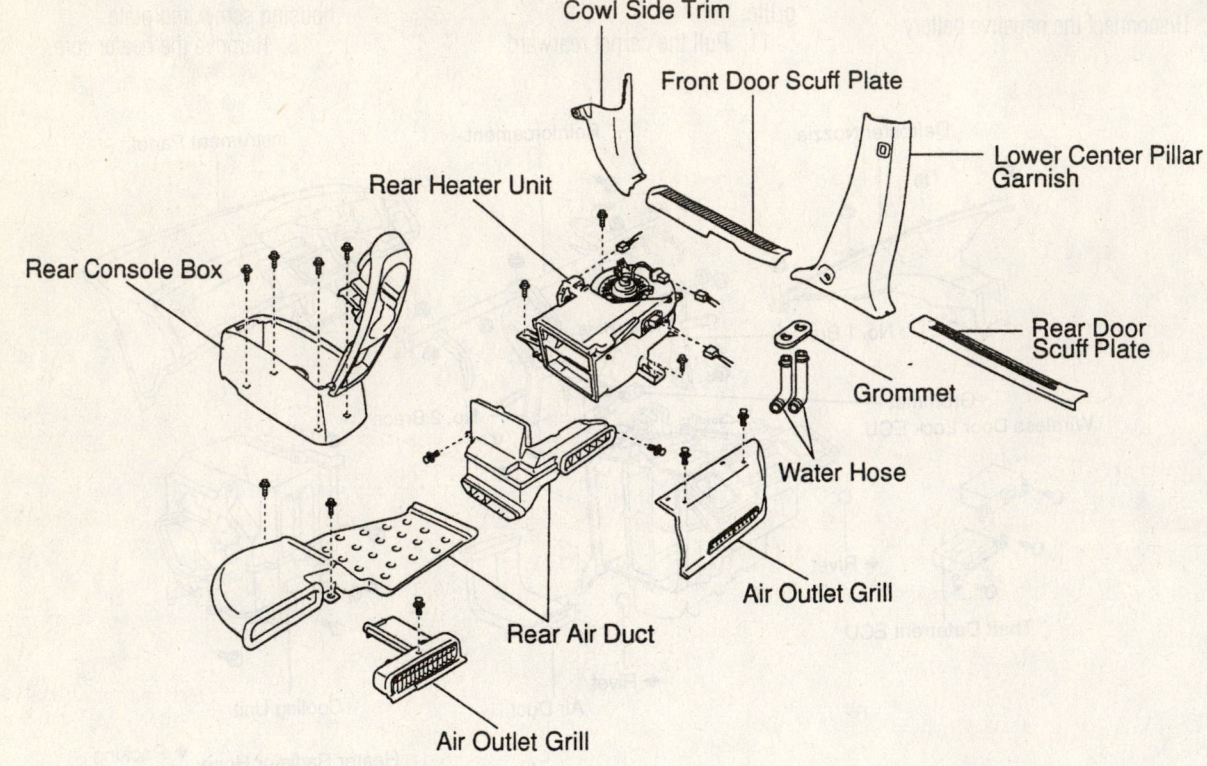

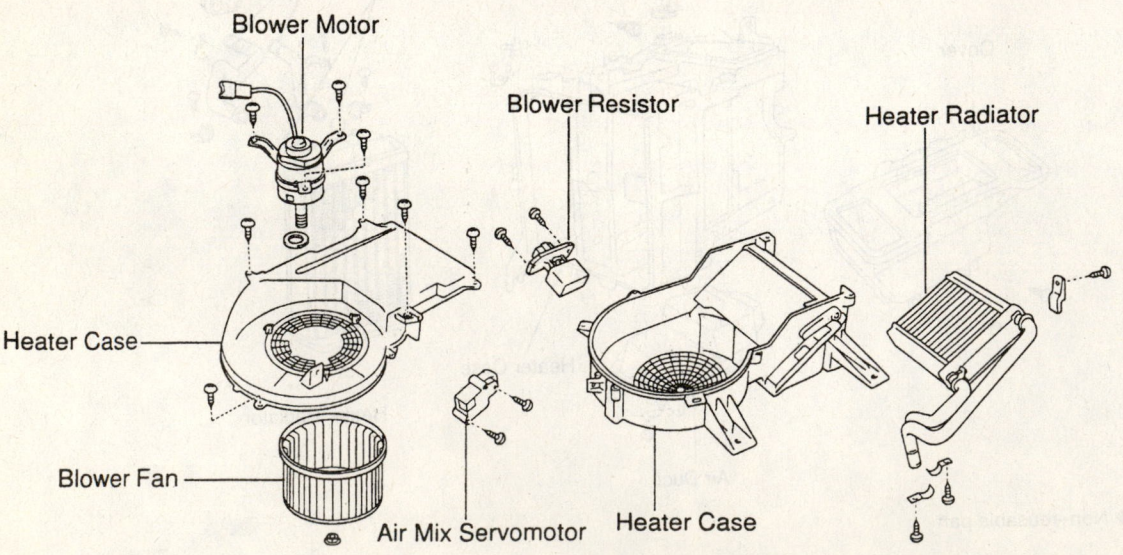

Exploded view of the rear heater core, the rear heater housing and related components—Lexus RX 300

MAZDA

MPV

REMOVAL & INSTALLATION

Front System

1. Disconnect the negative battery cable.

❄❄ CAUTION

After disconnecting the battery, wait for more than 1 minute for the air bag system to deplete its stored energy.

2. Drain the cooling system into a clean container for reuse.

3. Disconnect the heater hoses from the heater core.

4. Discharge and recover the air conditioning system refrigerant.

5. At the driver's side, remove the SAS module and the steering wheel by performing the following procedure:

   a. Place the wheel in the straight-ahead position and turn the ignition switch to LOCK.

   b. Remove the lower steering column cover.

   c. Disconnect the clock spring connector.

   d. Remove the steering wheel-to-SAS module bolts.

   e. Carefully, lift the SAS module from the steering wheel.

❄❄ CAUTION

Place the SAS in a safe place with the module facing upward.

   f. Remove the steering wheel-to-column nut.

   g. Using a steering wheel puller, press the steering wheel from the steering column.

6. At the passenger's side, remove the SAS module by performing the following procedure:

   a. Remove the glove compartment by sliding it to the left; then, pull the right side forward to remove the stopper and the pin, then, move it to the right to remove it.

   b. Remove the SAS module-to-dash bolts.

   c. Carefully, lift the SAS module and disconnect the electrical connector.

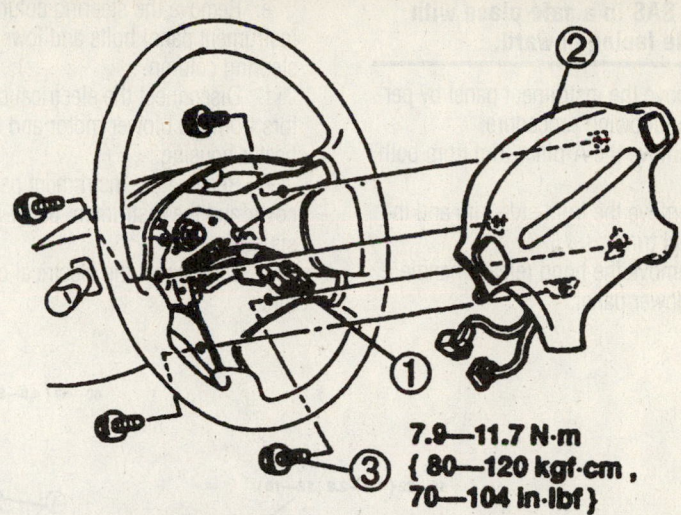

7.9—11.7 N·m
{ 80—120 kgf·cm ,
70—104 in·lbf }

1   **Connector**

2   **Driver-side air bag module**

3   **Bolt**

931136FG1

Exploded view of the steering wheel and SAS module—Mazda MPV

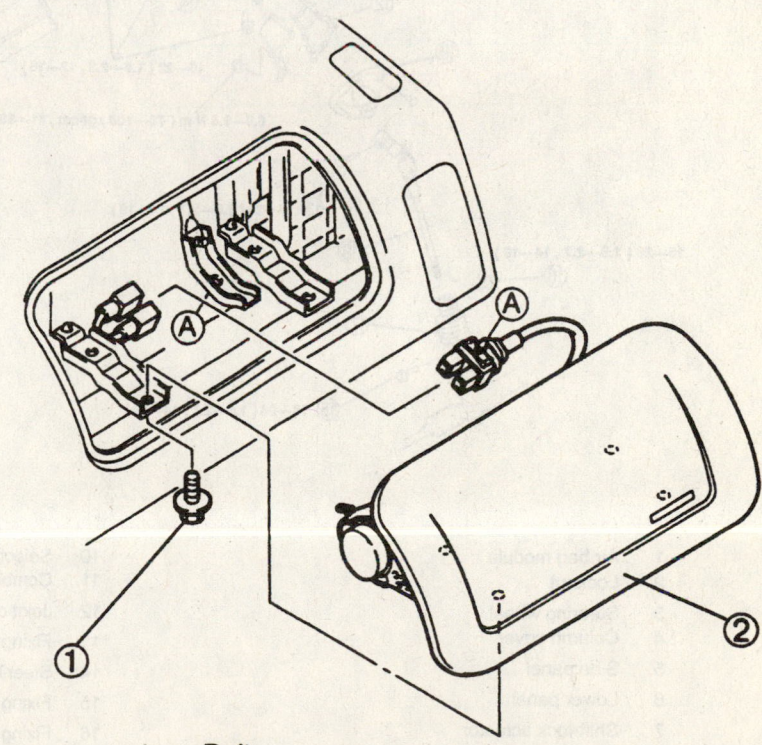

1   **Bolt**

2   **Passenger-side air bag module**

93113GF2

Exploded view of the passenger's side SAS module—Mazda MPV

✳✳ CAUTION

Place the SAS in a safe place with the module facing upward.

7. Remove the instrument panel by performing the following procedure:

a. Remove the A-pillar trim from both sides.

b. Remove the front side trim and the side panel trim.

c. Remove the hood release handle and the lower panel.

d. Remove the meter hood and the instrument cluster.

e. Remove the steering column-to-instrument panel bolts and lower the steering column.

f. Disconnect the electrical connectors from the blower motor and the heater housing.

g. Remove the instrument panel hole cover and the instrument panel-to-chassis bolts.

h. Disconnect the electrical connectors.

i. Using an assistant, carefully remove the instrument panel.

8. Remove the heater housing-to-chassis nuts.

9. Remove the heater housing-to-air conditioning housing fastener and seal plate.

10. Remove the heater housing.

11. Disassemble the heater housing and remove the heater core.

To install:

12. Install the heater core and assemble the heater housing.

13. Install the heater housing.

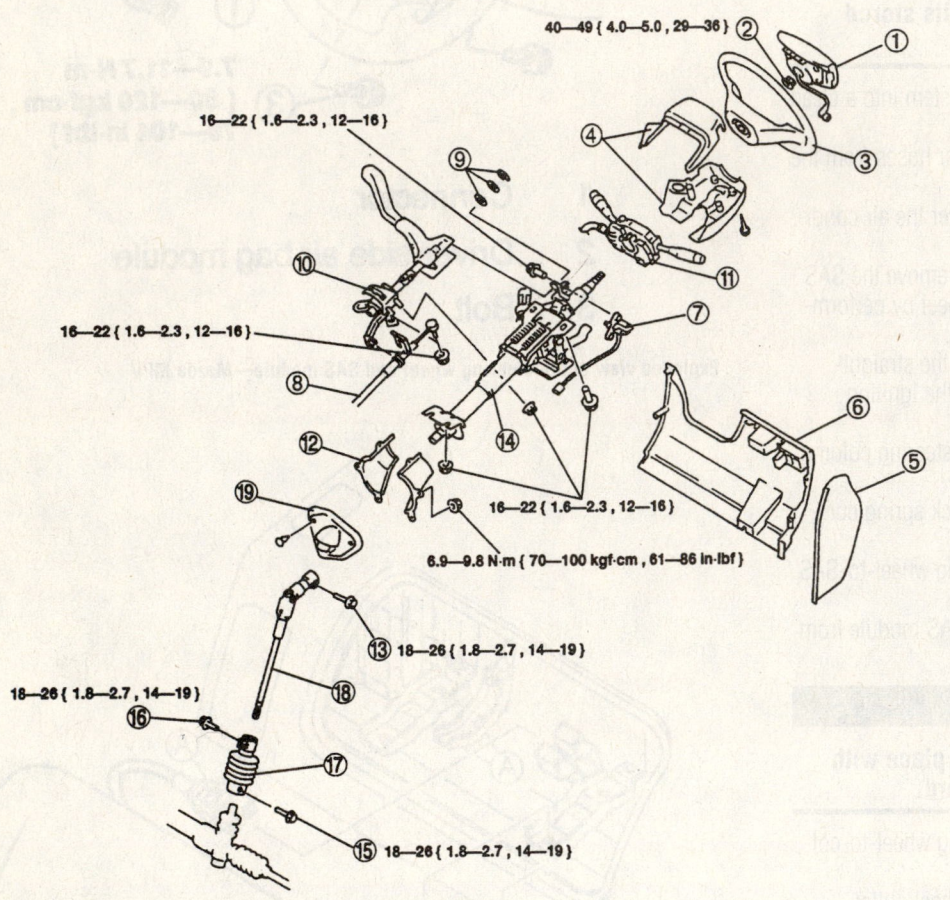

1	Air bag module
2	Locknut
3	Steering wheel
4	Column cover
5	Side panel
6	Lower panel
7	Shift-lock actuator
8	Selector cable
9	Retaining ring, wave washer, adjustment washer(s)
10	Selector lever component
11	Combination switch
12	Joint cover
13	Fixing bolt (steering shaft/intermediate shaft)
14	Steering shaft
15	Fixing bolt (universal joint/pinion shaft)
16	Fixing bolt (intermediate shaft/universal joint)
17	Universal joint
18	Intermediate shaft
19	Dust cover

N·m { kgf·m , ft·lbf }

93113GF3

Exploded view of the steering column and related components—Mazda MPV

14. Install the heater housing-to-air conditioning housing seal plate and fastener.

15. Install the heater housing-to-chassis nuts.

16. Install the instrument panel by performing the following procedure:

    a. Using an assistant, carefully, install the instrument panel.

    b. Connect the electrical connectors.

    c. Install the instrument panel-to-chassis bolts and the instrument panel hole cover.

    d. Connect the electrical connectors to the blower motor and the heater housing.

    e. Install the steering column and the steering column-to-instrument panel bolts. Torque the bolts to 12–16 ft. lbs. (16–22 Nm).

    f. Install the instrument cluster and the meter hood.

    g. Install the hood release handle and the lower panel.

    h. Install the front side trim and the side panel trim.

    i. Install the A-pillar trim to both sides.

17. At the passenger's side, install the

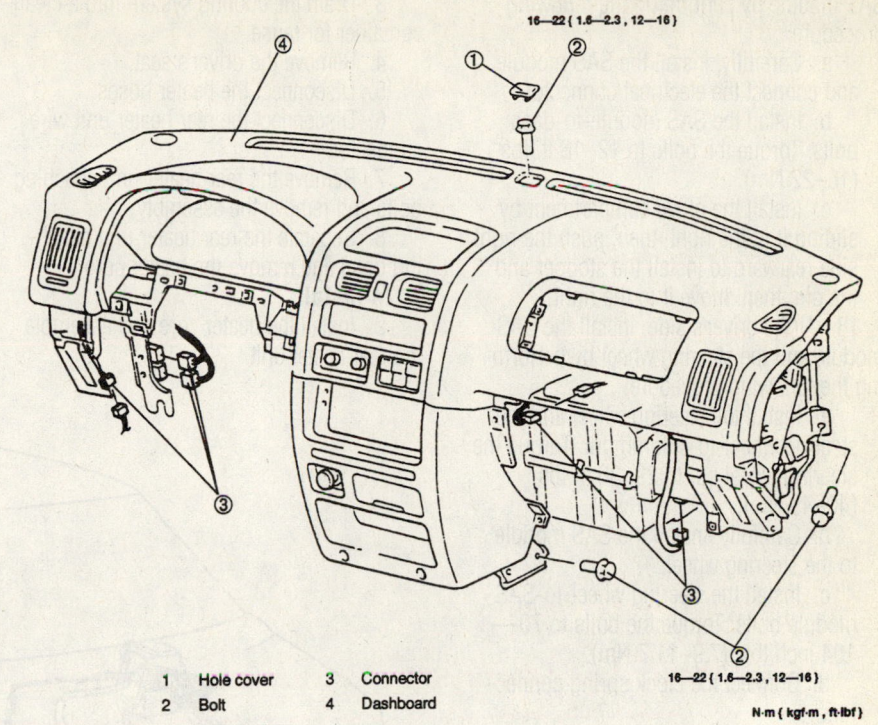

1	Hole cover	3	Connector
2	Bolt	4	Dashboard

16—22 { 1.6—2.3 , 12—16 }

N·m { kgf·m , ft-lbf }

93113GF4

View of the instrument panel and related components—Mazda MPV

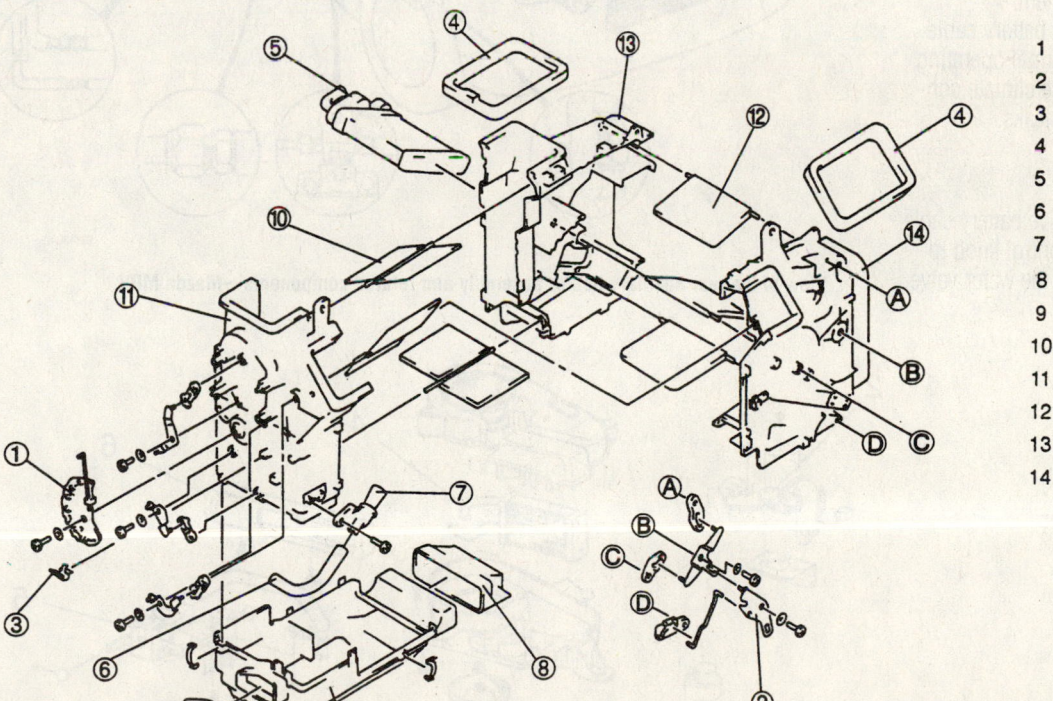

1	Air mix link
2	Airflow mode link
3	Wire clamp
4	Polyurethane protector
5	Front heater core
6	Drain hose
7	Joint
8	Duct
9	Case (bottom)
10	Airflow mode door
11	Case (left)
12	Air mix door
13	Case (right No.1)
14	Case (right No.2)

93113GF5

Exploded view of the heater core, heater housing and related components—Mazda MPV

SAS module by performing the following procedure:

   a. Carefully, install the SAS module and connect the electrical connector.

   b. Install the SAS module-to-dash bolts. Torque the bolts to 12–16 ft. lbs. (16–22 Nm).

   c. Install the glove compartment by sliding it to the right; then, push the right side rearward to install the stopper and the pin, then, move it to the right.

18. At the driver's side, install the SAS module and the steering wheel by performing the following procedure:

   a. Install the steering wheel and the steering wheel-to-column nut. Torque the steering wheel nut to 29–36 ft. lbs. (40–49 Nm).

   b. Carefully, install the SAS module to the steering wheel.

   c. Install the steering wheel-to-SAS module bolts. Torque the bolts to 70—104 inch lbs. (7.9–11.7 Nm).

   d. Connect the clock spring connector.

   e. Install the lower steering column cover.

19. Connect the heater hoses to the heater core.

20. Refill the cooling system.

21. Connect the negative battery cable.

22. Run the engine to normal operating temperatures; then, check the climate control operation and check for leaks.

Rear Auxiliary System

1. Disconnect the negative battery cable.

2. Set the rear heater control knob to the WARM position to open the water valve.

3. Drain the cooling system into a clean container for reuse.

4. Remove the driver's seat.

5. Disconnect the heater hoses.

6. Disconnect the rear heater unit wire connector.

7. Remove the rear heater unit attaching bolts and remove the assembly.

8. Separate the rear heater unit attaching bolts and remove the heater core.

To install:

9. Install the heater core and assemble the rear heater unit.

10. Install the assembly and the rear heater unit.

11. Connect the rear heater unit wire connector.

12. Connect the heater hoses to the heater core.

13. Install the driver's seat.

14. Refill the cooling system.

15. Connect the negative battery cable.

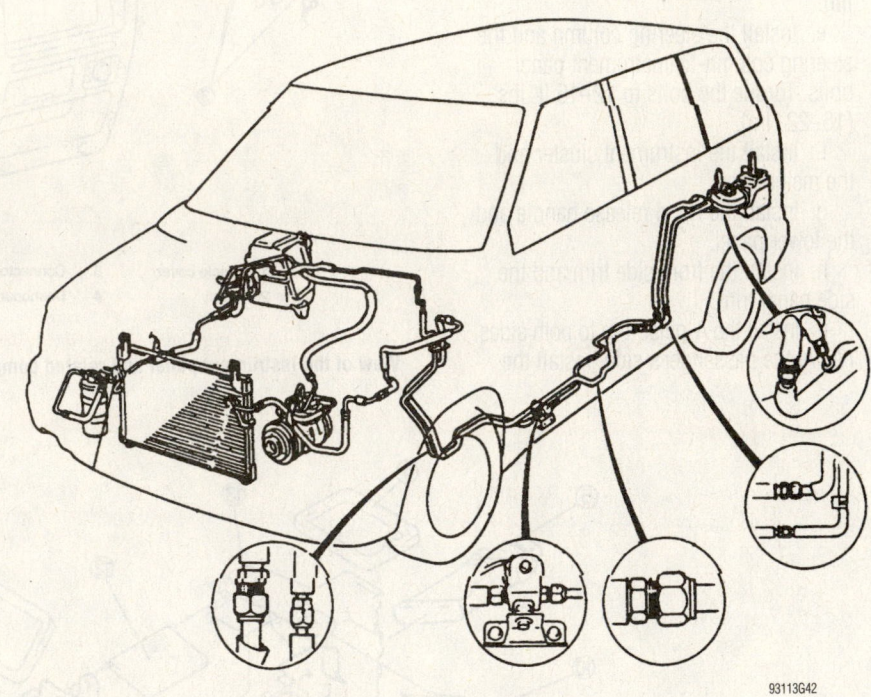

93113G42

View of the rear auxiliary heater assembly and related components—Mazda MPV

1. **Rear heater blower motor**
2. **Resistor assembly**
3. **Rear heater relay**
4. **Heater core**
5. **Water valve**
6. **Switch panel**

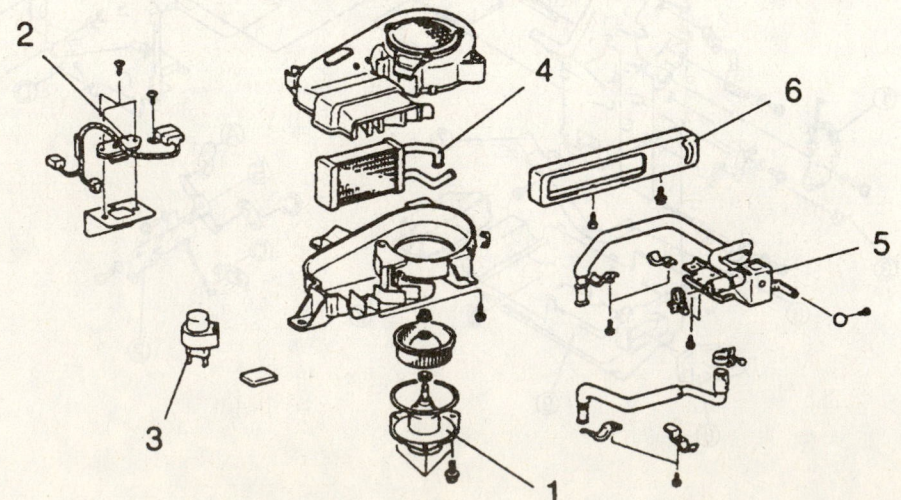

93113G43

Exploded view of the rear auxiliary heater unit—Mazda MPV

Pick-Ups

REMOVAL & INSTALLATION

1. Disconnect the negative battery cable.

❋❋ CAUTION

After disconnecting the battery, wait for more than 1 minute for the air bag system to deplete its stored energy.

2. Drain the cooling system into a clean container for reuse.

3. Disconnect the heater hoses from the heater core.

4. Discharge and recover the air conditioning system refrigerant.

5. At the driver's side, remove the SAS module and the steering wheel by performing the following procedure:

a. Place the wheel in the straight-ahead position and turn the ignition switch to LOCK.

b. At both sides of the steering wheel, remove the cover clips.

c. Remove the steering wheel-to-SAS module bolts.

d. Carefully, lift the SAS module from the steering wheel and disconnect the electrical connector.

❋❋ CAUTION

Place the SAS in a safe place with the module facing upward.

e. Remove the steering wheel-to-column nut.

f. Using a steering wheel puller, press the steering wheel from the steering column.

6. At the passenger's side, remove the SAS module by performing the following procedure:

a. Remove the glove compartment and the glove compartment cover.

b. Remove the SAS module-to-dash bolts.

c. Carefully, lift the SAS module and disconnect the electrical connector.

❋❋ CAUTION

Place the SAS in a safe place with the module facing upward.

7. Remove the steering column by performing the following procedure:

a. Remove the parking brake release handle.

b. Remove the hood release lever.

c. Remove the instrument panel steering column cover and the cover reinforcement.

d. Remove and disconnect the ignition switch electrical connector.

e. Disconnect the electrical harness connectors.

f. If equipped with an automatic transmission, remove the shift indicator cable bolt and the cable.

g. Remove the air bag sliding contact.

h. Remove the upper intermediate steering shaft-to-column shaft bolt; then, discard the bolt.

i. Remove the lower steering column nuts.

j. Remove the steering column nuts, column support and the column.

8. Remove the instrument panel by performing the following procedures:

a. Disconnect the Brake Pedal Position (BPP) switch connector.

b. If equipped, disconnect the Clutch Pedal Position (CPP) switch connector.

c. Remove the right and left hand scuff plates.

d. Remove both A-pillar trim plates.

e. Remove both front side trim panels.

f. Remove the fuse panel opening door.

g. In the engine compartment, disconnect the fuse box and position it aside.

h. In the engine compartment, remove and disconnect the bulkhead wiring harness connector.

i. Remove the valance panel.

j. Disconnect the following items:
- Air bag diagnostic monitor locking tab and connector
- Blend door actuator connector
- Climate control vacuum harness connector
- Radio antenna cable in-line connector

k. At the right cowl panel, disconnect the electrical connectors and the ground.

l. Under the steering column, remove the instrument panel brace bolt.

m. Remove the right and left instrument panel cowl sides.

n. Pull the instrument panel away from the cowl.

o. Disconnect the instrument panel-to-main electrical harness connector.

p. Using an assistant, remove the instrument panel.

9. Remove the evaporator core housing by performing the following procedure:

a. Disconnect the refrigerant lines from the evaporator core. Discard the O-rings.

b. Remove the engine air cleaner.

c. Remove the windshield washer reservoir/coolant recovery reservoir and move them aside.

d. Remove the vacuum reservoir tank and bracket; then, move it aside.

e. Disconnect the cruise control servo electrical connector.

f. Disconnect the manifold/tube assembly from the receiver drier.

g. Disconnect the air conditioning cycling switch connector.

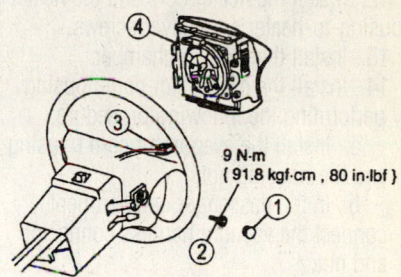

9 N·m
{ 91.8 kgf·cm , 80 in·lbf }

1	Cover Plugs
2	Screws
3	Connector
4	Driver-Side Air Bag Module

93113GF6

View of the SAS module and steering wheel—Mazda Pick-Ups

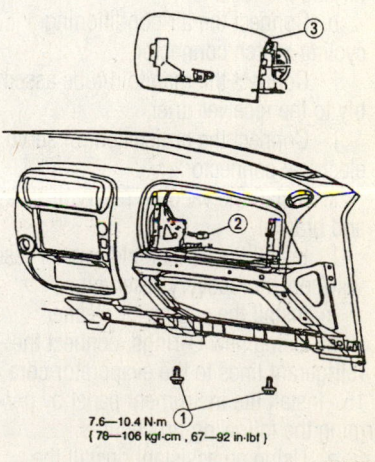

7.6—10.4 N·m
{ 78—106 kgf·cm , 67—92 in·lbf }

93113GF7

View of the passenger's side SAS module—Mazda Pick-Ups

Refer to the model specific sections for engine mechanical service procedures

h. Disconnect the blower motor connector and the resistor.

i. If equipped with a 3.0L or 4.0L engine, remove the support bracket.

j. Disconnect the windshield washer hose retainer and move it aside.

k. Disconnect the vacuum hose.

l. If equipped with a 4.0L engine, remove the air conditioning hose support retaining bolts from the back of the engine.

m. In the passenger compartment, disconnect the vacuum harness connector and nut.

n. Remove the evaporator core housing nuts and remove the housing.

10. Remove the plenum chamber.

11. Remove the heater housing-to-heater core cover screws and the heater core.

To install:

12. Install the heater core and the heater housing-to-heater core cover screws.

13. Install the plenum chamber.

14. Install the evaporator core housing by performing the following procedure:

a. Install the evaporator core housing and the housing nuts.

b. In the passenger compartment, connect the vacuum harness connector and nut.

c. If equipped with a 4.0L engine, install the air conditioning hose support retaining bolts to the back of the engine.

d. Connect the vacuum hose.

e. Connect the windshield washer hose retainer.

f. If equipped with a 3.0L or 4.0L engine, install the support bracket.

g. Connect the blower motor connector and the resistor.

h. Connect the air conditioning cycling switch connector.

i. Connect the manifold/tube assembly to the receiver drier.

j. Connect the cruise control servo electrical connector.

k. Install the vacuum reservoir tank and bracket.

l. Install the windshield washer reservoir/coolant recovery reservoir.

m. Install the engine air cleaner.

n. Using new O-rings, connect the refrigerant lines to the evaporator core.

15. Install the instrument panel by performing the following procedures:

a. Using an assistant, install the instrument panel.

b. Connect the instrument panel-to-main electrical harness connector.

c. Push the instrument panel toward from the cowl.

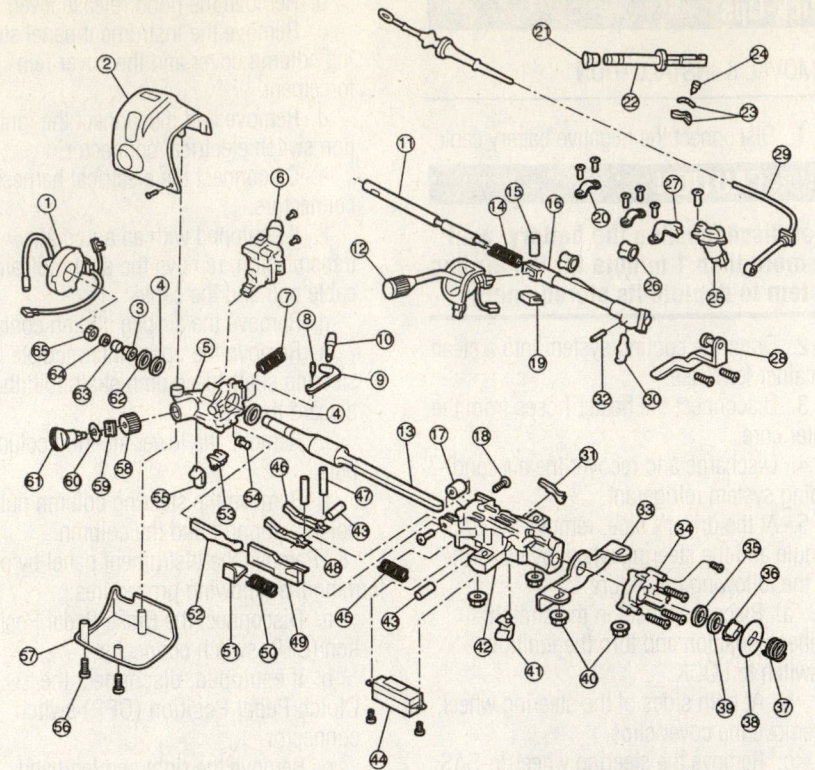

1	Air Bag Sliding Contact
2	Upper Steering Column Shroud
3	Steering Column Bearing Sleeve
4	Steering Column Bearing
5	Steering Column Lock Cylinder Housing
6	Multi-Function Switch
7	Pin
8	Steering Column Release Lever Pin
9	Steering Column Release Lever
10	Tilt Wheel Handle and Shank
11	Column Shift Selector Lever Plunger
12	Gearshift Lever
13	Steering Column Shaft
14	Transmission Control Selector Lever Plunger Spring
15	Gearshift Lever Pin
16	Transmission Column Shift Selector Tube
17	Steering Column Spacer (Fixed Column)
18	Tilt Column Pivot Screw
19	Transmission Control Selector Lever Spring Clip
20	Gearshift Tube Bushing Clamp
21	Spacer (Fixed Column)
22	Steering Shaft (Fixed Column)
23	Lever Assembly (Manual Transmission)
24	Pin (Manual Transmission)
25	Brake Shift Interlock Solenoid
26	Gearshift Lever Socket Bushing
27	Transmission Shift Selector Position Insert
28	Transmission Selector Lever Arm and Support
29	Shift Cable and Bracket
30	Gearshift Lever
31	Steering Column Lock Pawl
32	Gearshift Lever Pin
33	Steering Column Instrument Panel Bracket
34	Steering Column Lower Bearing Retainer
35	Steering Column Bearing Sleeve
36	Steering Column Bearing Tolerance Ring
37	Steering Column Lower Bearing Spring
38	Suspension Height Sensor Control Ring
39	Steering Column Bearing
40	Steering Column Retaining Nuts
41	Wiring Harness Retainer
42	Steering Actuator Housing
43	Steering Column Lock Lever Pin
44	Ignition Switch
45	Steering Column Position Spring
46	Steering Column Lock Lever
47	Steering Column Position Lock Spring
48	Steering Column Locking Lever
49	Lower Steering Column Lock Actuator
50	Steering Column Lock Spring
51	Steering Column Lock Pawl
52	Upper Steering Column Lock Lever Actuator
53	Steering Column Lock Cam
54	Steering Column Tilt Flange Bumper
55	Wiring Harness Retainer
56	Shroud Screws
57	Steering Column Shroud
58	Steering Column Lock Gear
59	Steering Column Lock Housing Bearing
60	Bearing Retainer
61	Ignition Switch Lock Cylinder
62	Steering Column Tolerance Ring
63	Steering Column Upper Bearing Spring
64	Snap Ring
65	Turn Signal Cancel Cam

93113GF8

Exploded view of the steering column assembly—Mazda Pick-Ups

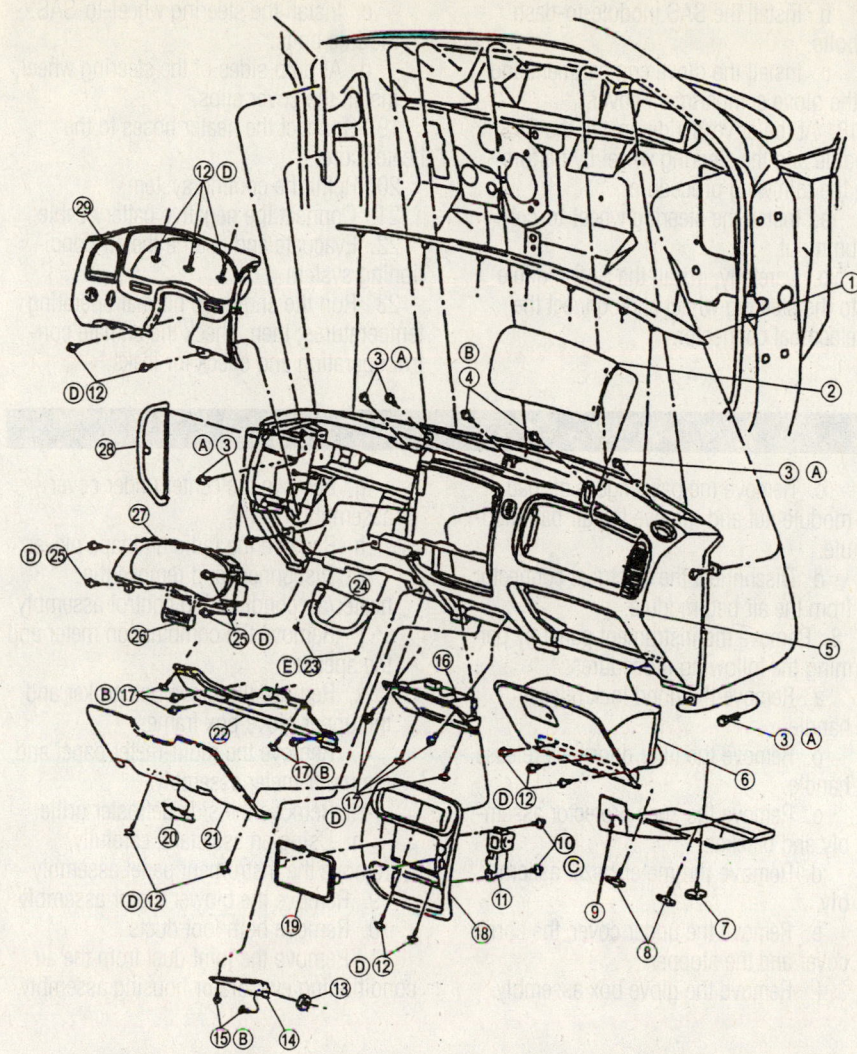

d. Install the right and left instrument panel cowl sides.

e. Under the steering column, install the instrument panel brace bolt.

f. At the right cowl panel, connect the electrical connectors and the ground.

g. Connect the following items:
- Air bag diagnostic monitor locking tab and connector
- Blend door actuator connector
- Climate control vacuum harness connector
- Radio antenna cable in-line connector

h. Install the valance panel.

i. In the engine compartment, install and connect the bulkhead wiring harness connector.

j. In the engine compartment, connect the fuse box.

k. Install the fuse panel opening door.

l. Install both front side trim panels.

m. Install both A-pillar trim plates.

n. Install the right and left hand scuff plates.

o. If equipped, connect the Clutch Pedal Position (CPP) switch connector.

p. Connect the Brake Pedal Position (BPP) switch connector.

16. Install the steering column by performing the following procedure:

a. Install the steering column, column support and the column nuts.

b. Install the lower steering column nuts.

c. Using a new bolt, install the upper intermediate steering shaft-to-column shaft bolt.

d. Install the air bag sliding contact.

e. If equipped with an automatic transmission, install the shift indicator cable bolt and the cable.

f. Connect the electrical harness connectors.

1	Defroster opening grille
2	Passenger-side airbag module
3	Screws (6)
4	Screws (2)
5	Instrument panel
6	Glove compartment
7	Pushpin (2)
8	Rivets (2)
9	Instrument panel sound insulation
10	Screws (2)
11	Instrument panel sound insulation
12	Screws (12)
13	Nut (1)
14	Instrument panel brace
15	Screws (2)
16	Ash tray
17	Screws (10)
18	Center trim finish panel
19	Instrument panel radio opening panel
20	Instrument panel cover access cover
21	Instrument panel steering column cover
22	Instrument panel steering column opening cover reinforcement
23	Nut (2)
24	Instrument panel steering column opening cover brace
25	Screw (4)
26	PRNDL indicator
27	Instrument cluster
28	Instrument panel fuse panel opening door
29	Instrument cluster finish panel
A	Tighten to 25.5 — 34.5 N•m {2.6 — 3.5 kgf•m, 19 — 25 ft•lbf}
B	Tighten to 7.2 — 10.8 N•m {73 — 110 kgf•cm, 64 — 96 in•lbf}
C	Tighten to 1 — 2 N•m {10 — 20 kgf•cm, 9 — 18 in•lbf}
D	Tighten to 2 — 3 N•m {20 — 31 kgf•cm, 18 — 26 in•lbf}

93113GF9

Exploded view of the instrument panel assembly—Mazda Pick-Ups

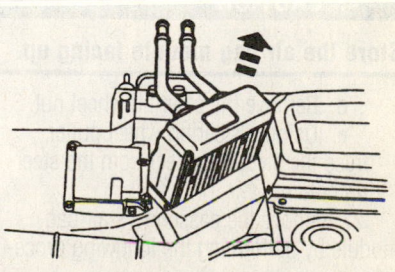

93113GF0

View of the heater housing and heater core—Mazda Pick-Ups

Refer to the model specific sections for cooling system service procedures

g. Install and connect the ignition switch electrical connector.

h. Install the instrument panel steering column cover reinforcement and the cover.

i. Install the hood release lever.

j. Install the parking brake release handle.

17. At the passenger's side, install the SAS module by performing the following procedure:

a. Carefully, install the SAS module and connect the electrical connector.

b. Install the SAS module-to-dash bolts.

c. Install the glove compartment and the glove compartment cover.

18. At the driver's side, install the SAS module and the steering wheel by performing the following procedure:

a. Install the steering wheel-to-column nut.

b. Carefully, install the SAS module to the steering wheel and connect the electrical connector.

c. Install the steering wheel-to-SAS module bolts.

d. At both sides of the steering wheel, install the cover clips.

19. Connect the heater hoses to the heater core.

20. Refill the cooling system.

21. Connect the negative battery cable.

22. Evacuate and charge the air conditioning system.

23. Run the engine to normal operating temperatures; then, check the climate control operation and check for leaks.

MITSUBISHI

Montero

REMOVAL & INSTALLATION

1. Place the wheels in the straight-ahead position.
2. Disconnect the negative battery.

❋❋ CAUTION

Wait at least 60 seconds after disconnecting the battery cable before performing any work on the air bag or instrument panel.

3. Drain the cooling system into a clean container for reuse.
4. Discharge and recover the air conditioning system refrigerant.
5. Remove the floor console assembly.
6. Remove the air bag module, column covers and the steering wheel by performing the following procedure:

a. Remove the steering column-to-instrument panel cover screws and the cover.

b. Carefully, remove the air bag module from the steering wheel.

c. Disconnect the electrical connectors from the air bag module.

❋❋ CAUTION

Store the air bag module facing up.

d. Remove the steering wheel nut.

e. Using a steering wheel puller, press the steering wheel from the steering column.

7. Remove the passenger's air bag module by performing the following procedure:

a. Remove the foot shower duct.

b. Remove the glove box stoppers and the glove box.

c. Remove the passenger's air bag module nut and remove the air bag module.

d. Disconnect the electrical connector from the air bag module.

8. Remove the instrument panel by performing the following procedures:

a. Remove the hood lock release handle.

b. Remove the filler door lock release handle.

c. Remove the knee protector assembly and bracket.

d. Remove the meter bezel assembly.

e. Remove the under cover, the corner cover and the stopper.

f. Remove the glove box assembly.

g. Remove the center under cover assembly.

h. Remove the radio and tape player.

i. Disconnect and remove the heater/air conditioning control assembly.

j. Remove the combination meter and the speaker.

k. Remove the glove box striker and the upper glove box frame.

l. Remove the multi-meter panel and the multi-meter assembly.

m. Remove the side defroster grille.

n. Using an assistant, carefully, remove the instrument panel assembly.

9. Remove the blower motor assembly.
10. Remove both foot ducts.
11. Remove the joint duct from the air conditioning evaporator housing assembly.

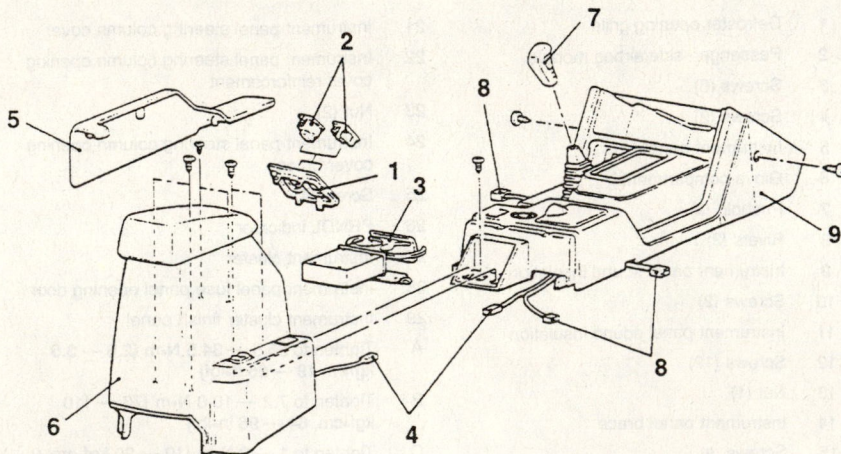

1. Switch panel
2. Suspension control switch or hole cover
3. Cup holder assembly
4. Rear console harness connector
5. Side panel A
6. Rear console assembly
7. Transfer shift lever knob
8. Floor console harness connector
9. Front console assembly

93113GE2

Exploded view of the floor console and related components—Mitsubishi Montero

12. Remove the foot distribution duct.
13. Remove the center reinforcement.
14. Remove the center ventilation duct.
15. Remove the drain hose from the air conditioning evaporator housing assembly.

16. Disconnect the heater hoses from the heater housing assembly.

17. Disconnect the refrigerant lines from the air conditioning evaporator housing assembly and discard the O-rings.
18. Remove the heater housing assembly.
19. Remove the center duct assembly.
20. Remove the heater core from the heater housing.

To install:

21. Install the heater core to the heater housing.
22. Install the center duct assembly.
23. Install the heater housing assembly.
24. Using new O-rings, connect the refrigerant lines to the air conditioning evaporator housing assembly.
25. Connect the heater hoses to the heater housing assembly.
26. Install the drain hose to the air conditioning evaporator housing assembly.
27. Install the center ventilation duct.
28. Install the center reinforcement.
29. Install the foot distribution duct.
30. Install the joint duct to the air conditioning evaporator housing assembly.
31. Install both foot shower ducts.
32. Install the blower motor assembly.
33. Install the instrument panel by performing the following procedures:
   a. Using an assistant, carefully, install the instrument panel assem-bly.
   b. Install the side defroster grille.

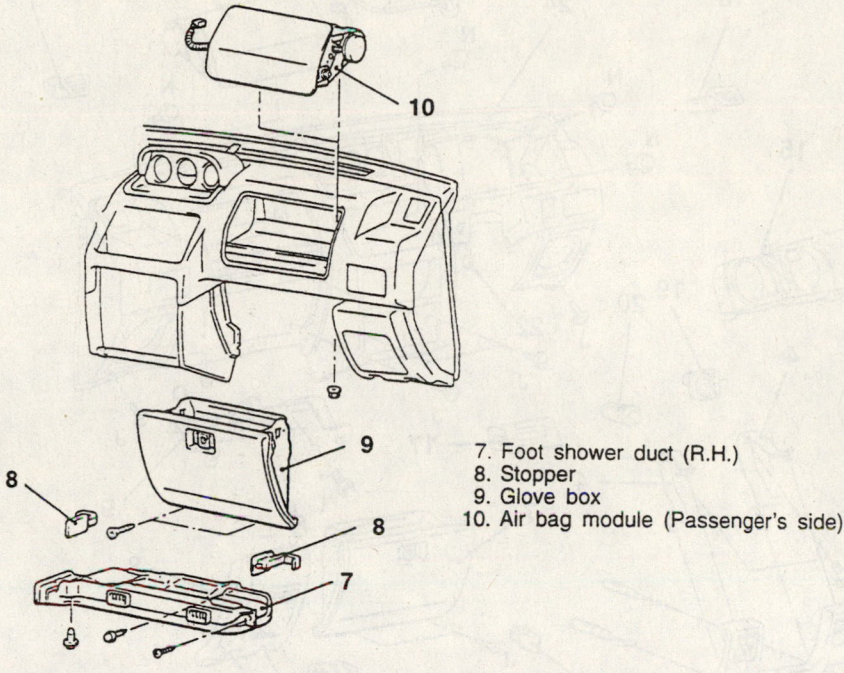

7. Foot shower duct (R.H.)
8. Stopper
9. Glove box
10. Air bag module (Passenger's side)

93113GE3

Exploded view of the passenger's side air bag module—Mitsubishi Montero

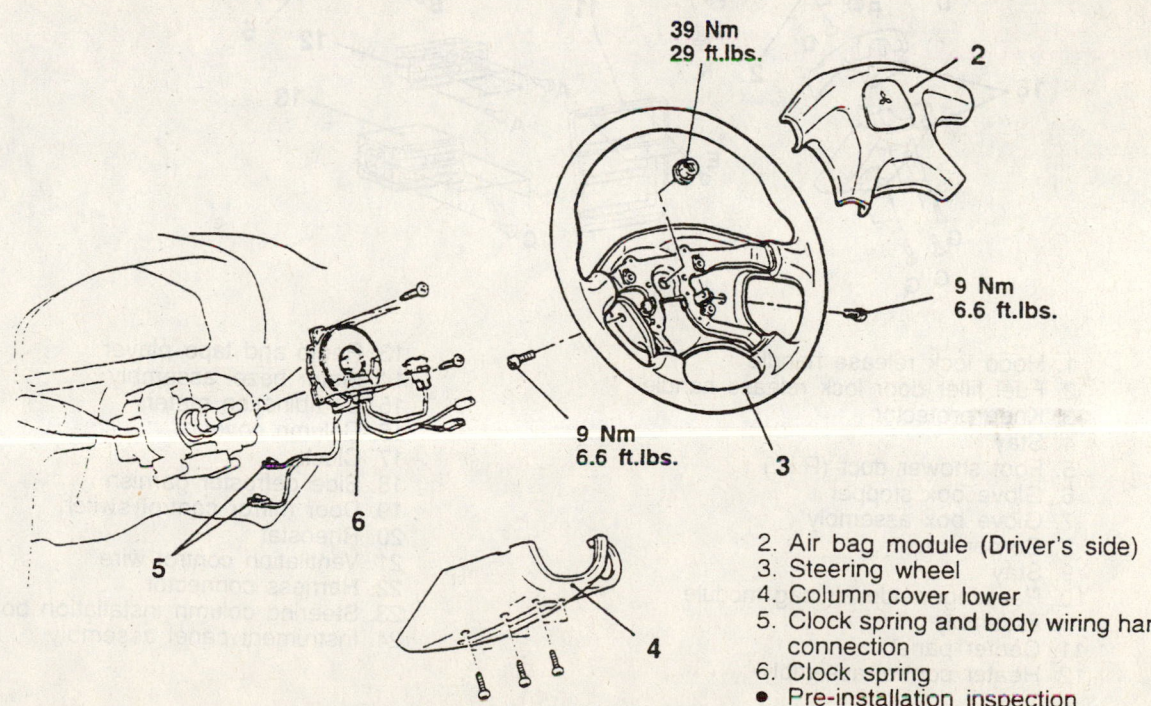

39 Nm
29 ft.lbs.

9 Nm
6.6 ft.lbs.

9 Nm
6.6 ft.lbs.

2. Air bag module (Driver's side)
3. Steering wheel
4. Column cover lower
5. Clock spring and body wiring harness connection
6. Clock spring
• Pre-installation inspection

93113GE4

Exploded view of the steering wheel and air bag module—Mitsubishi Montero

For complete service labor times order Nichols' Chilton Labor Guide Manual

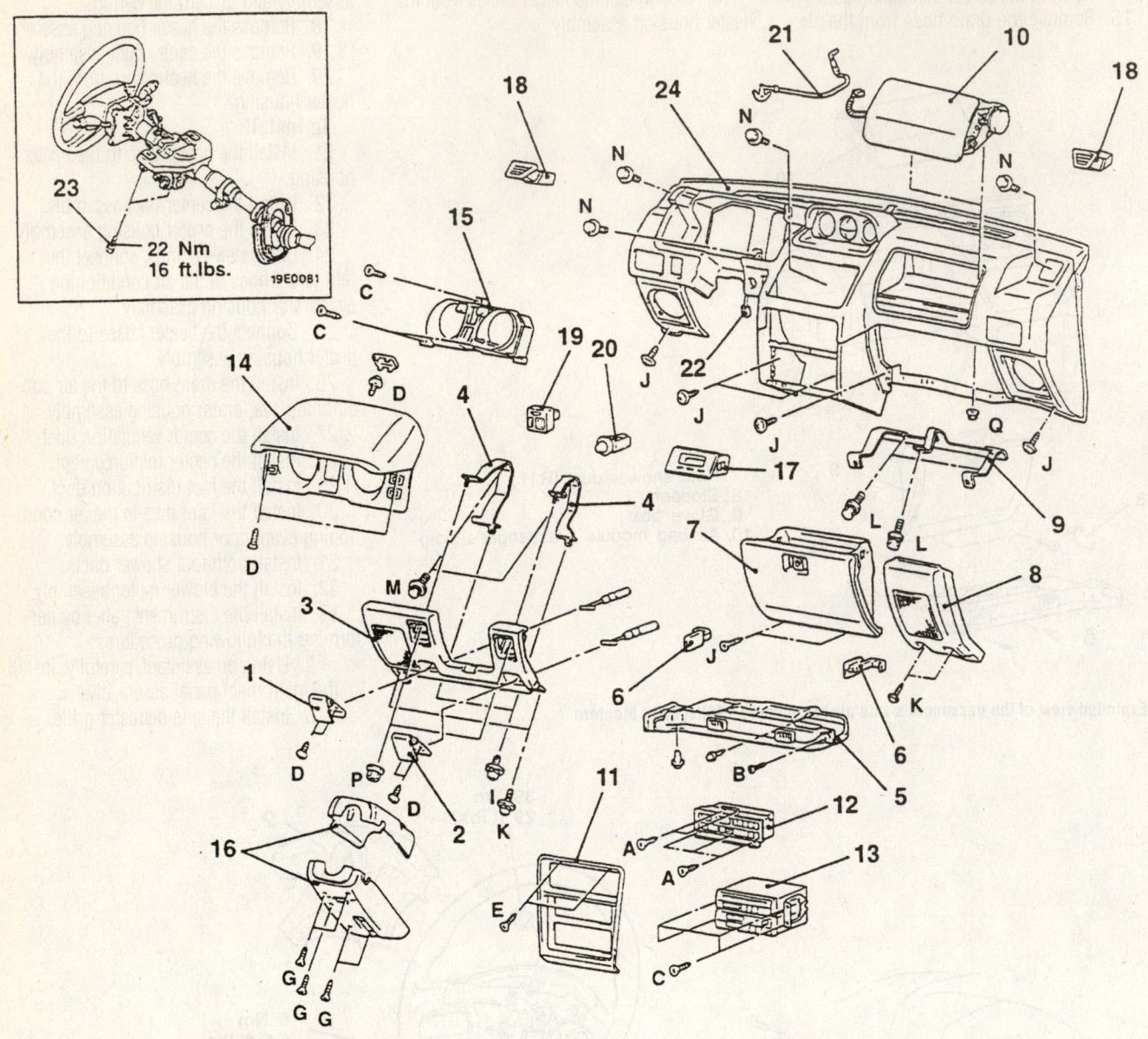

22 Nm
16 ft.lbs.

19E00B1

1. Hood lock release handle
2. Fuel filler door lock release handle
3. Knee protector
4. Stay
5. Foot shower duct (R.H.)
6. Glove box stopper
7. Glove box assembly
8. Corner cover
9. Stay
10. Passenger-side air bag module assembly
11. Center panel
12. Heater control assembly
13. Radio and tape player
14. Meter bezel assembly
15. Combination meter
16. Column cover
17. Clock
18. Side defroster garnish
19. Door mirror control switch
20. Rheostat
21. Ventilation control wire
22. Harness connector
23. Steering column installation bolts
24. Instrument panel assembly

93113GE5

Exploded view of the instrument panel and related components—Mitsubishi Montero

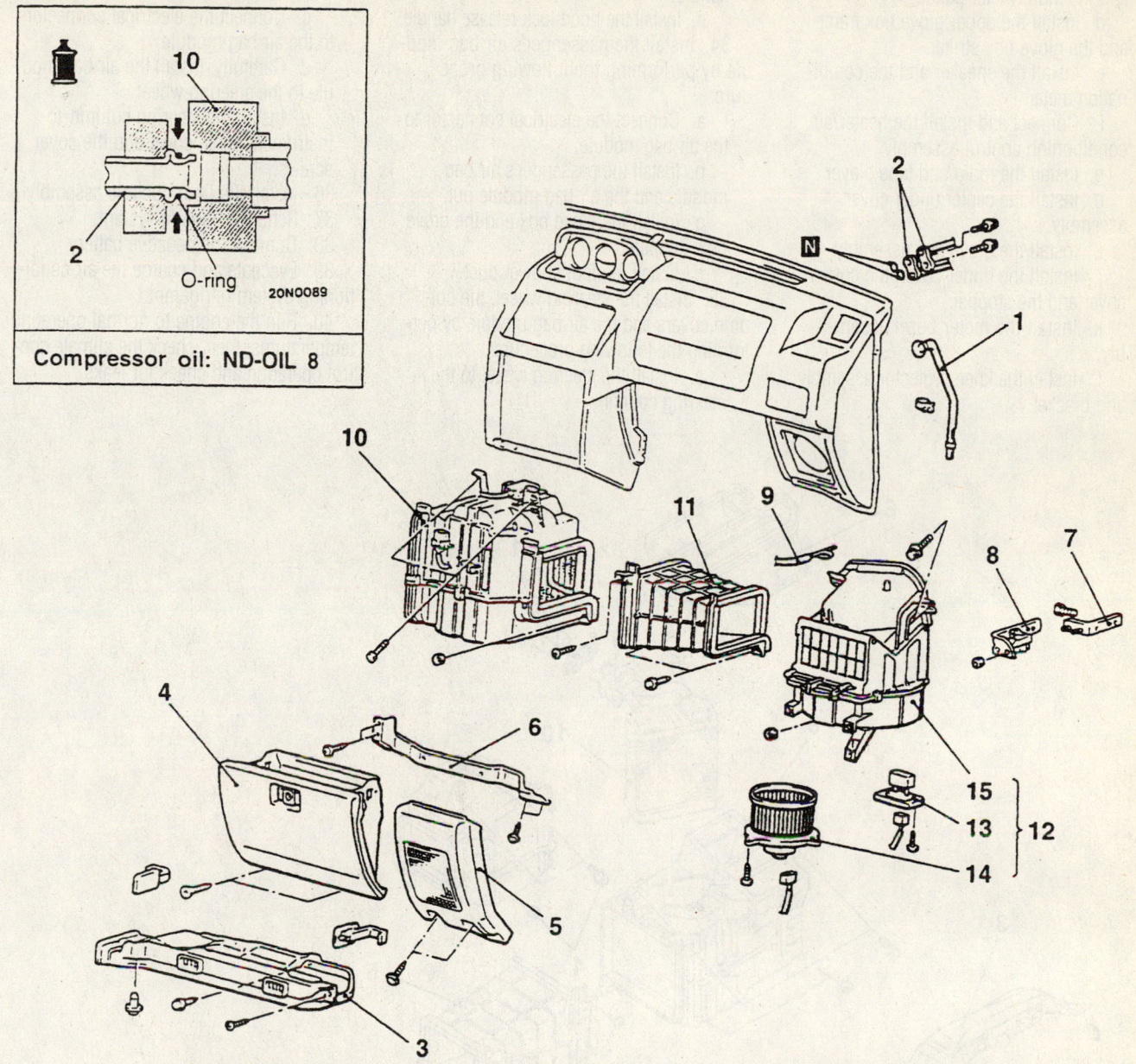

Compressor oil: ND-OIL 8

O-ring

20N0089

1. Drain hose
2. Liquid pipe and suction hose connection
3. Foot shower duct (R.H.)
4. Glove box
5. Corner cover
6. Lower frame
7. Engine control relay assembly
8. Bracket
9. Air selection control wire connection
10. Evaporator
11. Duct joint
12. Blower assembly
13. Resistor
14. Blower motor assembly
15. Blower case assembly

93113GE6

Exploded view of the air conditioning evaporator housing, blower motor assembly and related components—Mitsubishi Montero

c. Install the multi-meter assembly and the multi-meter panel.

d. Install the upper glove box frame and the glove box striker.

e. Install the speaker and the combination meter.

f. Connect and install the heater/air conditioning control assembly.

g. Install the radio and tape player.

h. Install the center under cover assembly.

i. Install the glove box assembly.

j. Install the under cover, the corner cover and the stopper.

k. Install the meter bezel assembly.

l. Install the knee protector assembly and bracket.

m. Install the filler door lock release handle.

n. Install the hood lock release handle.

34. Install the passenger's air bag module by performing the following procedure:

a. Connect the electrical connector to the air bag module.

b. Install the passenger's air bag module and the air bag module nut.

c. Install the glove box and the glove box stoppers.

d. Install the foot shower duct.

35. Install the steering wheel, the column covers and the air bag module by performing the following procedure:

a. Install the steering wheel to the steering column.

b. Install the steering wheel nut and torque the nut to 29 ft. lbs. (39 Nm).

c. Connect the electrical connectors to the air bag module.

d. Carefully, install the air bag module to the steering wheel.

e. Install the steering column-to-instrument panel cover and the cover screws.

36. Install the floor console assembly.

37. Refill the cooling system.

38. Connect the negative battery.

39. Evacuate and charge the air conditioning system refrigerant.

40. Run the engine to normal operating temperatures; then, check the climate control operation and check for leaks.

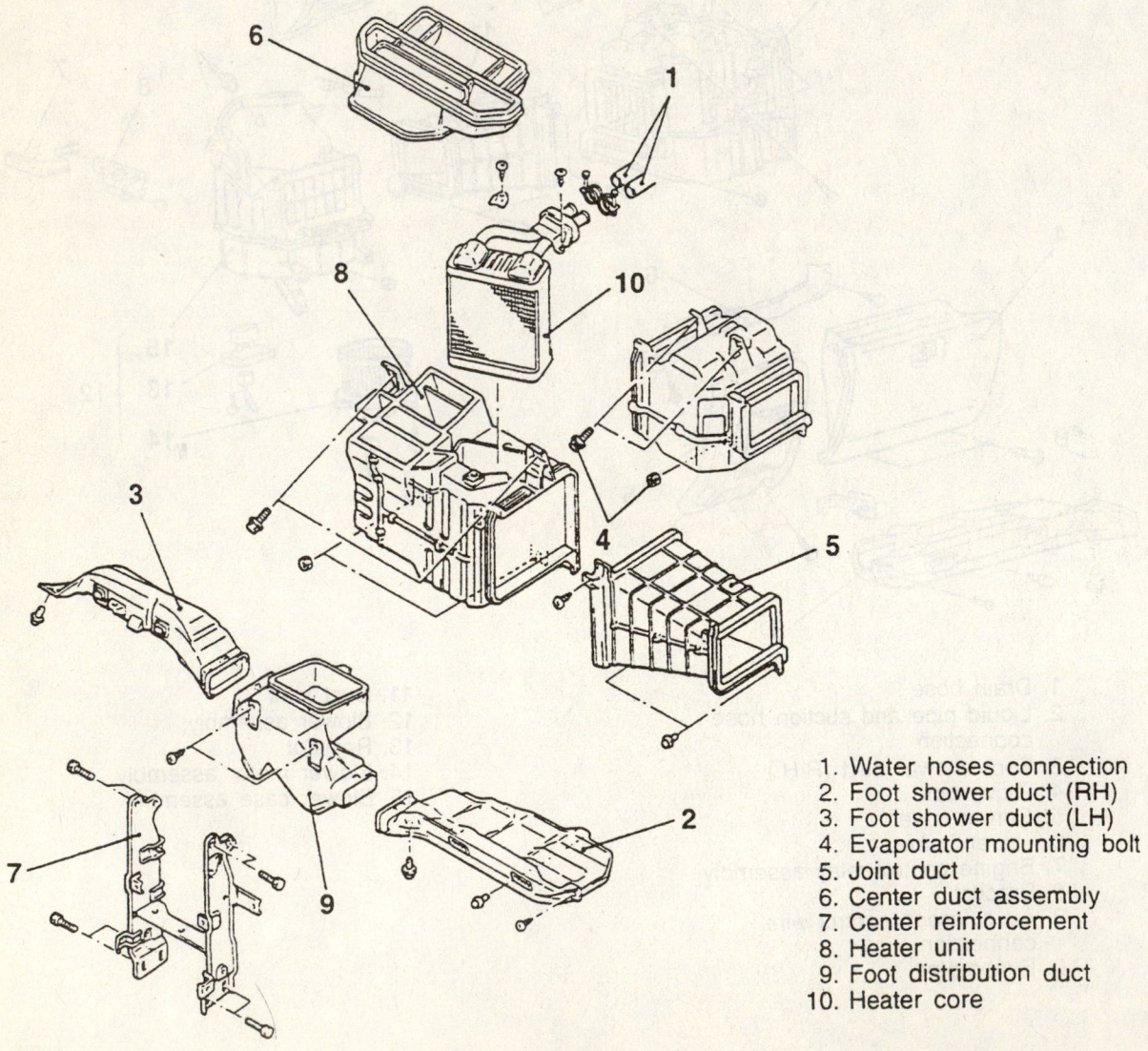

1. Water hoses connection
2. Foot shower duct (RH)
3. Foot shower duct (LH)
4. Evaporator mounting bolt and nut
5. Joint duct
6. Center duct assembly
7. Center reinforcement
8. Heater unit
9. Foot distribution duct
10. Heater core

93113GE7

Exploded view of the heater housing, air conditioning evaporator housing and related components—Mitsubishi Montero

Montero Sport

REMOVAL & INSTALLATION

Front Heater System

1. Place the wheels in the straight-ahead position.
2. Disconnect the negative battery.

✳✳ CAUTION

Wait at least 60 seconds after disconnecting the battery cable before performing any work on the air bag or instrument panel.

3. Drain the cooling system into a clean container for reuse.
4. Discharge and recover the air conditioning system refrigerant.
5. Remove the floor console assembly.
6. Remove the air bag module, column covers and the steering wheel by performing the following procedure:

    a. Remove the steering column-to-instrument panel cover screws and the cover.

    b. Carefully, remove the air bag module from the steering wheel.

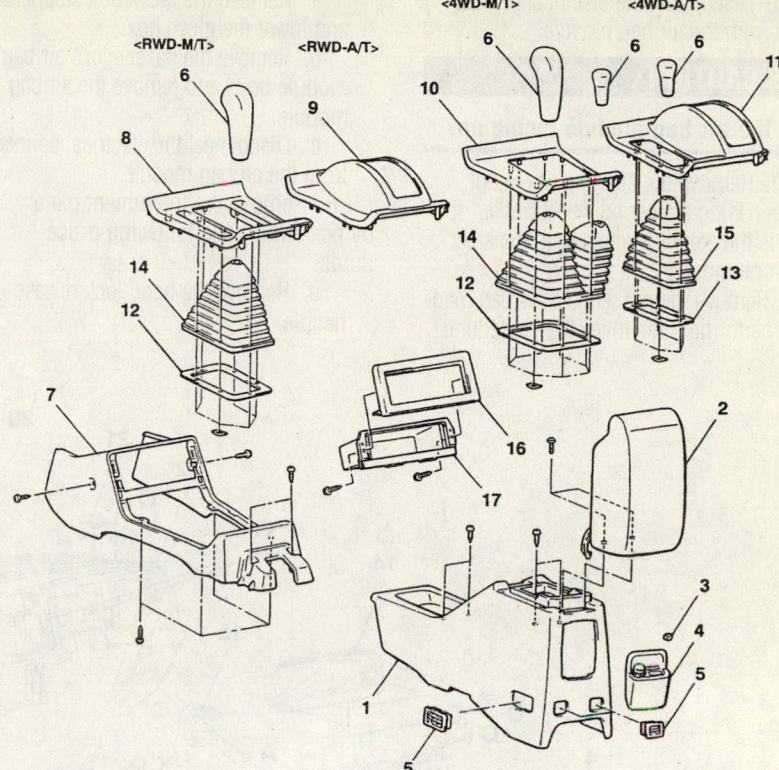

1. REAR FLOOR CONSOLE ASSEMBLY
2. CONSOLE LID ASSEMBLY
3. KNOB
4. REAR HEATER CONTROL PANEL ASSEMBLY
5. FOOT GRILL
6. SHIFT LEVER KNOB
7. FRONT FLOOR CONSOLE ASSEMBLY
8. CONSOLE PANEL A <RWD-M/T>
9. CONSOLE PANEL B <RWD-A/T>
10. CONSOLE PANEL C <4WD-M/T>
11. CONSOLE PANEL D <4WD-A/T>
12. SHIFT LEVER BOOT REINFORCEMENT <M/T>
13. TRANSFER LEVER BOOT REINFORCEMENT <4WD-A/T>
14. SHIFT LEVER BOOT <M/T>
15. TRANSFER LEVER BOOT <4WD-A/T>
16. CONSOLE PANEL
17. BOX

93113GD6

Exploded view of the floor console and related components—Mitsubishi Montero Sport

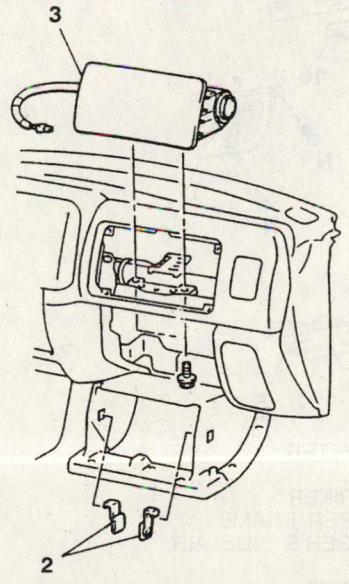

1. NEGATIVE (-) BATTERY CABLE CONNECTION
2. STOPPER
3. AIR BAG MODULE
● PRE-INSTALLATION INSPECTION

93113GD7

Exploded view of the passenger's side air bag module—Mitsubishi Montero Sport

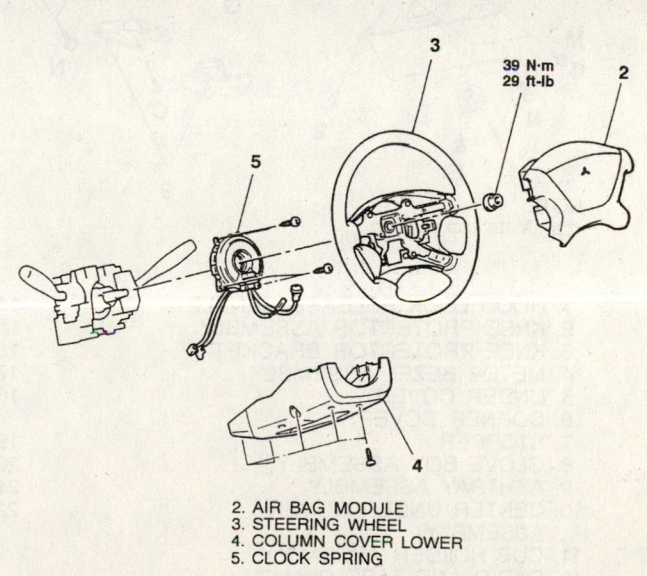

39 N·m
29 ft-lb

2. AIR BAG MODULE
3. STEERING WHEEL
4. COLUMN COVER LOWER
5. CLOCK SPRING

93113GD8

Exploded view of the steering wheel and air bag module—Mitsubishi Montero Sport

Refer to the model specific sections for engine mechanical service procedures

c. Disconnect the electrical connectors from the air bag module.

✳✳ CAUTION

Store the air bag module facing up.

d. Remove the steering wheel nut.

e. Using a steering wheel puller, press the steering wheel from the steering column.

7. Remove the passenger's air bag module by performing the following procedure:

a. Remove the glove box stoppers and lower the glove box.

b. Remove the passenger's air bag module bolts and remove the air bag module.

c. Disconnect the electrical connector from the air bag module.

8. Remove the instrument panel by performing the following procedures:

a. Remove the hood lock release handle.

b. Remove the knee protector assembly and bracket.

c. Remove the meter bezel assembly.

d. Remove the under cover, the corner cover and the stopper.

e. Remove the glove box assembly and the ashtray.

f. Remove the center under cover assembly and the cup holder assembly.

g. Remove the radio and tape player.

h. Disconnect and remove the heater/air conditioning control assembly.

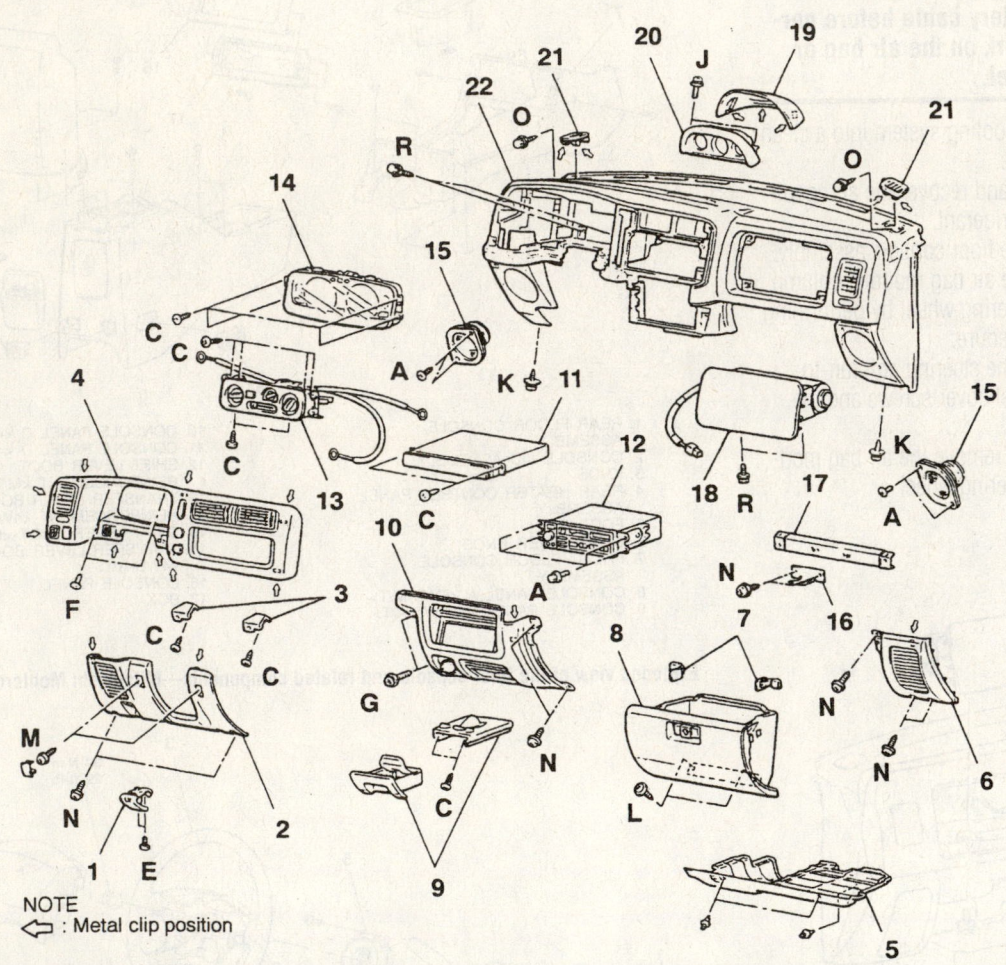

NOTE
⬅ : Metal clip position

1. HOOD LOCK RELEASE HANDLE
2. KNEE PROTECTOR ASSEMBLY
3. KNEE PROTECTOR BRACKET
4. METER BEZEL ASSEMBLY
5. UNDER COVER
6. CORNER COVER
7. STOPPER
8. GLOVE BOX ASSEMBLY
9. ASHTRAY ASSEMBLY
10. CENTER UNDER COVER ASSEMBLY
11. CUP HOLDER ASSEMBLY
12. RADIO AND TAPE PLAYER
13. HEATER CONTROL ASSEMBLY

14. COMBINATION METER
15. SPEAKER
16. GLOVE BOX STRIKER
17. GLOVE BOX UPPER FRAME
18. FRONT PASSENGER'S SIDE AIR BAG MODULE
19. MULTI-METER PANEL
20. MULTI-METER ASSEMBLY
21. SIDE DEFROSTER GRILL
22. INSTRUMENT PANEL ASSEMBLY

93113GD9

Exploded view of the instrument panel and related components—Mitsubishi Montero Sport

i. Remove the combination meter and the speaker.

j. Remove the glove box striker and the upper glove box frame.

k. Remove the multi-meter panel and the multimeter assembly.

l. Remove the side defroster grille.

m. Using an assistant, carefully, remove the instrument panel assembly.

9. Remove the blower motor assembly.

10. Remove the joint duct from the air conditioning evaporator housing assembly.

11. Remove the center reinforcement.

12. Remove the center ventilation duct.

13. Remove the drain hose from the air conditioning evaporator housing assembly.

14. Disconnect the heater hoses from the heater housing assembly.

15. Disconnect the refrigerant lines from the air conditioning evaporator housing assembly and discard the O-rings.

16. Remove the heater housing assembly.

17. Remove the heater core from the heater housing.

To install:

18. Install the heater core to the heater housing.

19. Install the heater housing assembly.

20. Using new O-rings, connect the refrigerant lines to the air conditioning evaporator housing assembly.

21. Connect the heater hoses to the heater housing assembly.

22. Install the drain hose to the air conditioning evaporator housing assembly.

23. Install the center ventilation duct.

PIPING CONNECTION

COMPRESSOR OIL: SUN PAG56

20Z0006

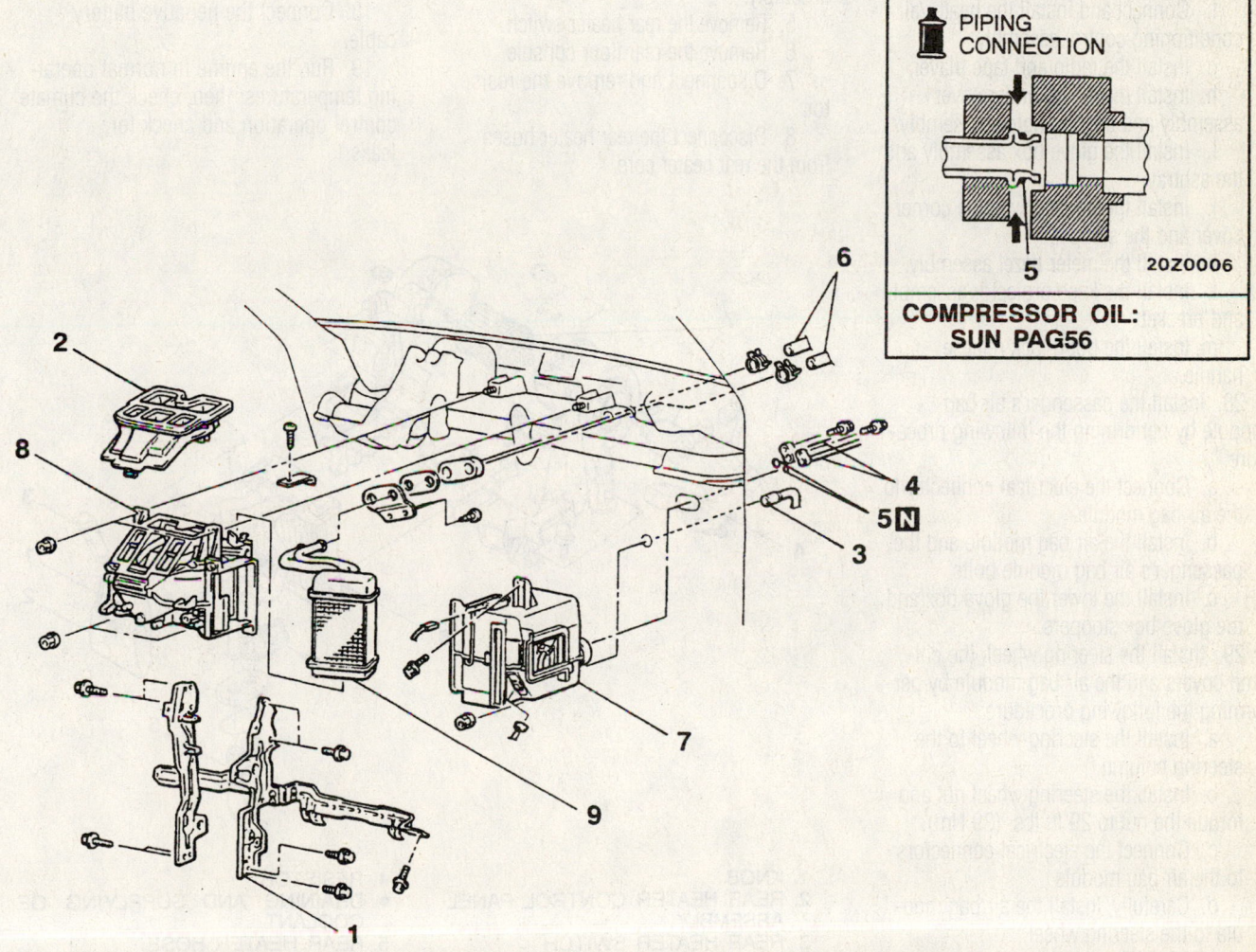

1. CENTER REINFORCEMENT
2. CENTER VENTILATION DUCT
3. DRAIN HOSE <VEHICLES WITH A/C>
4. SUCTION PIPE OR HOSE AND DISCHARGE PIPE CONNECTION <VEHICLES WITH A/C>
5. O-RING
6. HEATER HOSE CONNECTION
7. EVAPORATOR <VEHICLES WITH A/C>
8. HEATER UNIT
9. HEATER CORE

93113GD0

Exploded view of the heater housing, air conditioning evaporator housing and related components—Mitsubishi Montero Sport

Refer to the model specific sections for cooling system service procedures

24. Install the center reinforcement.
25. Install the joint duct to the air conditioning evaporator housing assembly.
26. Install the blower motor assembly.
27. Install the instrument panel by performing the following procedures:

a. Using an assistant, carefully, install the instrument panel assembly.

b. Install the side defroster grille.

c. Install the multi-meter assembly and the multimeter panel.

d. Install the upper glove box frame and the glove box striker.

e. Install the speaker and the combination meter.

f. Connect and install the heater/air conditioning control assembly.

g. Install the radio and tape player.

h. Install the center under cover assembly and the cup holder assembly.

i. Install the glove box assembly and the ashtray.

j. Install the under cover, the corner cover and the stopper.

k. Install the meter bezel assembly.

l. Install the knee protector assembly and bracket.

m. Install the hood lock release handle.

28. Install the passenger's air bag module by performing the following procedure:

a. Connect the electrical connector to the air bag module.

b. Install the air bag module and the passenger's air bag module bolts.

c. Install the lower the glove box and the glove box stoppers.

29. Install the steering wheel, the column covers and the air bag module by performing the following procedure:

a. Install the steering wheel to the steering column.

b. Install the steering wheel nut and torque the nut to 29 ft. lbs. (39 Nm).

c. Connect the electrical connectors to the air bag module.

d. Carefully, install the air bag module to the steering wheel.

e. Install the steering column-to-instrument panel cover and the cover screws.

30. Install the floor console assembly.
31. Refill the cooling system.
32. Connect the negative battery.

33. Evacuate and charge the air conditioning system refrigerant.
34. Run the engine to normal operating temperatures; then, check the climate control operation and check for leaks.

Rear Auxiliary System

1. Disconnect the negative battery cable.
2. Drain the cooling system into a clean container for reuse.
3. Remove the rear heater unit switch knob.
4. Remove the rear heater control panel assembly.
5. Remove the rear heater switch.
6. Remove the rear floor console.
7. Disconnect and remove the resistor.
8. Disconnect the rear heater hoses from the rear heater core.

9. Remove the rear heater core from the rear heater housing.

To install:

10. Install the rear heater core to the rear heater housing.
11. Connect the rear heater hoses to the rear heater core.
12. Install and connect the resistor.
13. Install the rear floor console.
14. Install the rear heater switch.
15. Install the rear heater control panel assembly.
16. Install the rear heater unit switch knob.
17. Refill the cooling system.
18. Connect the negative battery cable.
19. Run the engine to normal operating temperatures; then, check the climate control operation and check for leaks.

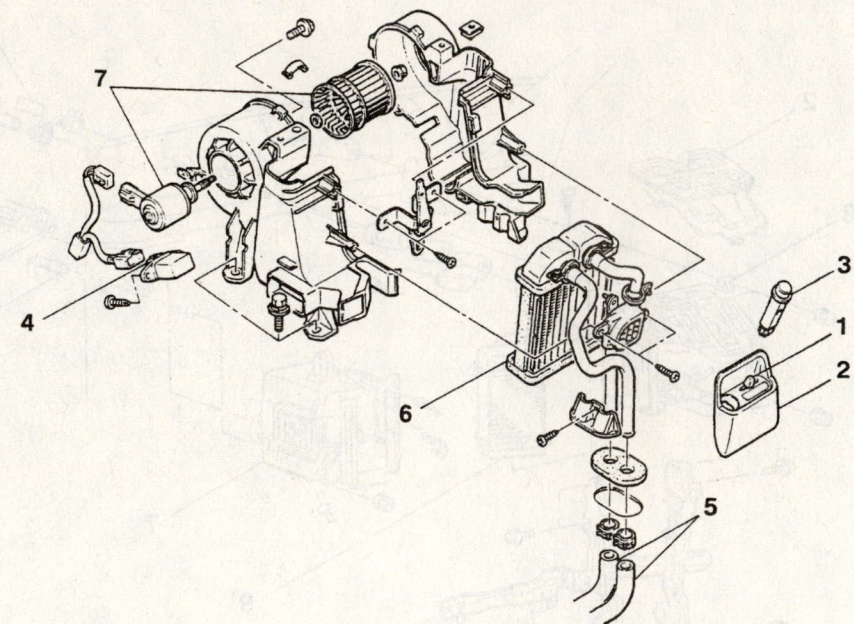

1. KNOB
2. REAR HEATER CONTROL PANEL ASSEMBLY
3. REAR HEATER SWITCH
4. RESISTOR
● DRAINING AND SUPPLYING OF COOLANT
5. REAR HEATER HOSE CONNECTION
6. REAR HEATER CORE ASSEMBLY
7. REAR BLOWER MOTOR ASSEMBLY

93113GE1

Exploded view of the rear heater core and related components—Mitsubishi Montero Sport

NISSAN

Frontier

REMOVAL & INSTALLATION

1. Disconnect both the negative (1st) and positive (2nd) battery cables.
2. Remove the steering wheel by performing the following procedure:
    a. Turn the ignition switch to the OFF position.

✳✳ CAUTION

Wait 3 minutes after disconnecting the battery cables and turning the ignition switch to the OFF position before servicing the air bag system.

b. Remove the lower lid and disconnect the driver's air bag module connector.
c. Remove both side lids.
d. Using the Tamper Resistant Torx® Wrench size T50, remove the special bolts from both sides of the steering wheel and discard them.
e. Remove the SRS module from the steering wheel.

✳✳ CAUTION

Always store the SRS module face up.

f. Position the steering wheel in the straight-ahead position.
g. Disconnect the horn connector and remove the steering wheel nut.
h. Using a steering wheel puller, press the steering wheel from the steering column.

3. Remove the passenger's side air bag by disconnecting or removing the following items:
    a. Turn the ignition switch to the OFF position.

✳✳ CAUTION

Wait 3 minutes after disconnecting the battery cables and turning the ignition switch to the OFF position before servicing the air bag system.

b. Open the glove box door.
c. Working inside the glove box, open the lower instrument panel lid.
d. Remove the passenger's air bag module connector clip from the lid.

e. Disconnect the passenger's SRS module connector.
f. Remove the glove box and the lower passenger's side instrument panel.
g. Using the Tamper Resistant Torx® Wrench size T50, remove the SRS module-to-instrument panel special bolts and discard them.
h. Remove the 4 SRS module-to-instrument panel mounting nuts.
i. Release the SRS module-to-instrument panel clips and remove the SRS module.

✳✳ CAUTION

Always store the SRS module face up.

4. Drain the cooling system into a clean container for reuse.
5. Working inside the engine compartment, disconnect the 2 heater hoses from the heater core.
6. Discharge and recover the air conditioning system refrigerant.
7. Disconnect both refrigerant lines from the evaporator core. Plug the lines to prevent moisture from entering the system.

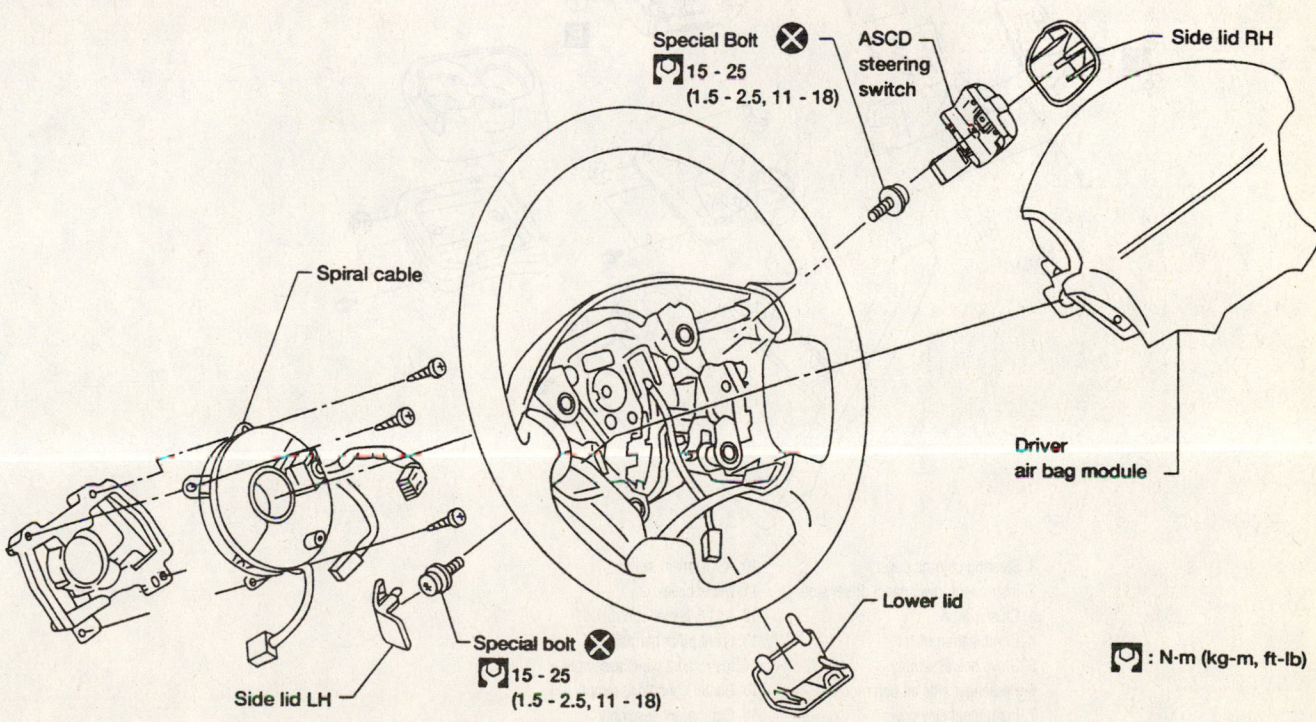

Spiral cable

Special Bolt ⊗
🔧 15 - 25
(1.5 - 2.5, 11 - 18)

ASCD steering switch

Side lid RH

Driver air bag module

Lower lid

Side lid LH

Special bolt ⊗
🔧 15 - 25
(1.5 - 2.5, 11 - 18)

🔧 : N-m (kg-m, ft-lb)

93113GC3

Exploded view of the steering wheel and SRS module and related components—Nissan Frontier

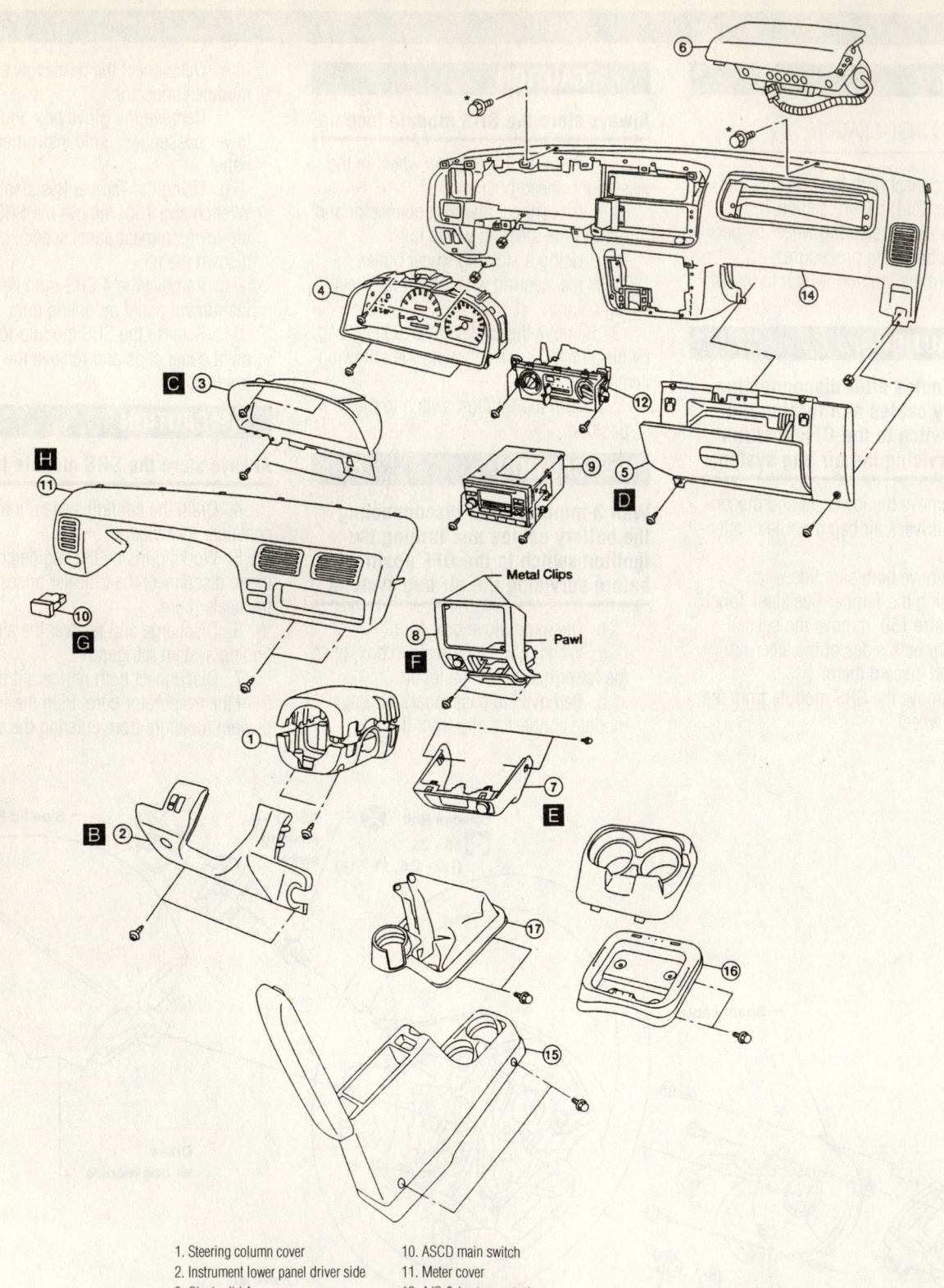

Metal Clips

Pawl

1. Steering column cover
2. Instrument lower panel driver side
3. Cluster lid A
4. Combination meter
5. Glove box assembly
6. Passenger side air bag module
7. Instrument stay cover
8. Cluster lid C
9. Audio and deck pocket
10. ASCD main switch
11. Meter cover
12. A/C & heater control
13. Front pillar garnish
14. Instrument panel assembly
15. Center console assembly
16. Cup holder assembly
17. M/T boot assembly

93113GC5

Exploded view of the instrument panel and related components—Nissan Frontier

8. Remove the glove box and the mating trim.

9. Disconnect the thermal amp connector.

10. Remove the air conditioning housing assembly from the vehicle.

11. Remove the instrument panel assembly by performing the following procedure:

 a. Remove the 4 steering column cover screws; then, separate and remove the steering column covers.

 b. Remove the 2 driver's side lower instrument panel screws and the lower instrument panel.

 c. Remove the 4 cluster cover screws and the cluster cover.

 d. Remove the 6 combination meter screws; then, disconnect the combination meter electrical connector and remove the meter.

 e. Remove the 2 glove box screws and the glove box.

 f. Remove the 2 instrument stay cover screws; then, disconnect the electrical harness connectors and remove the stay cover.

 g. Remove the 2 cluster lid "C" screws; then, disconnect the electrical harness connectors and remove the cluster lid "C".

 h. Remove the 4 audio and deck pocket screws; then, disconnect the electrical harness connectors and remove the audio and deck pocket.

 i. Disconnect the ASCD main switch connector.

 j. Remove the 2 meter cover screws; then, disconnect the electrical harness connectors and remove the meter cover.

 k. Remove the 4 air conditioning-heater control screws; then, disconnect the control cables and remove the air conditioning-heater control.

 l. Remove the front pillar garnish.

 m. Remove the 3 instrument panel assembly nuts and 2 bolts; then, remove the instrument panel.

12. Remove the heater housing assembly.

13. Remove the heater core from the heater housing assembly.

To install:

14. Install the heater core to the heater housing assembly.

15. Install the heater housing assembly.

16. Install the instrument panel assembly by performing the following procedure:

 a. Install the instrument panel and the 3 instrument panel assembly nuts and 2 bolts.

 b. Install the front pillar garnish.

 c. Install the air conditioning-heater control, connect the control cables and install the 4 air conditioning/heater control screws.

 d. Install the meter cover, connect the electrical harness connectors and install the 2 meter cover screws.

 e. Connect the ASCD main switch connector.

 f. Install the audio and deck pocket, connect the electrical harness connectors and install the 4 audio and deck pocket screws.

 g. Install the cluster lid "C", con-nect the electrical harness connectors and install the 2 cluster lid "C" screws.

 h. Install the stay cover, connect the electrical harness connectors and the 2 instrument stay cover screws.

 i. Install the glove box and the 2 glove box screws.

 j. Install the meter, connect the combination meter electrical connector and install the 6 combination meter screws.

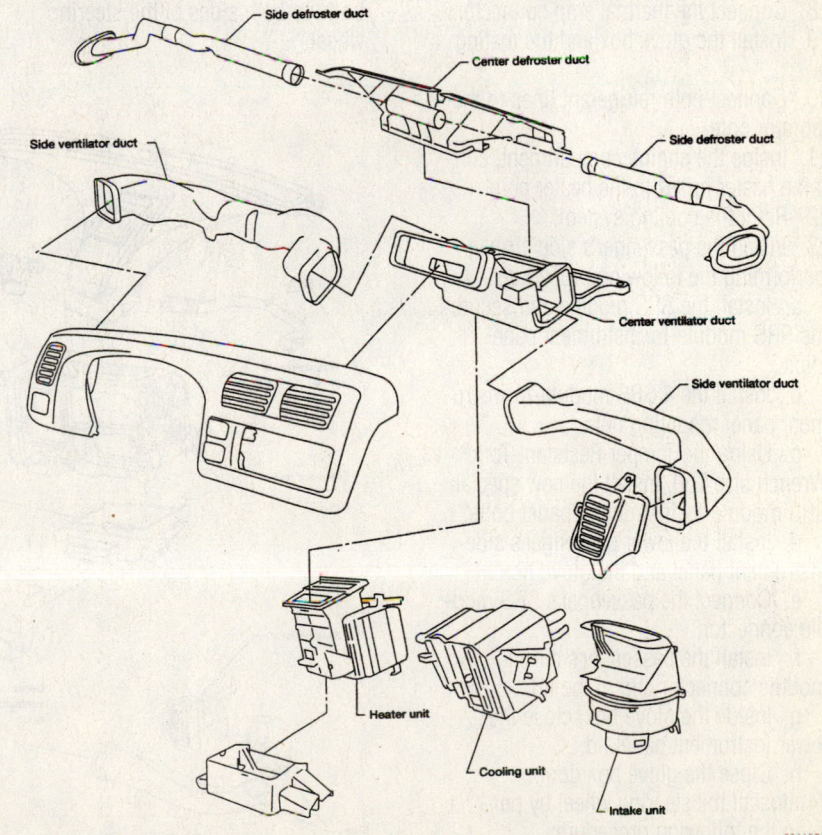

Nut (4)
5.2 – 7.0
(0.53 – 0.71,
46.0 – 61.6)

Clips

Special bolt

: N·m (kg-m, ft-lb)
: N·m (kg-m, in-lb)
: Insert front edge first

15 – 25
(1.5 – 2.5,
11 – 18)

93113GC4

View of the passenger's side SRS module and related components—Nissan Frontier

Side defroster duct
Center defroster duct
Side defroster duct
Side ventilator duct
Center ventilator duct
Side ventilator duct
Heater unit
Cooling unit
Intake unit

93113GC6

Exploded view of the heater housing, air conditioning housing and related components—Nissan Frontier

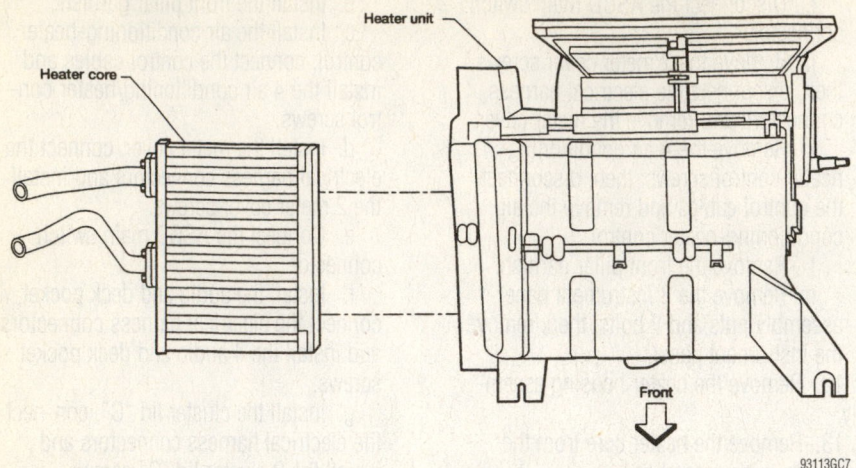

View of the heater core and heater housing—Nissan Frontier

k. Install the cluster cover and the 4 cluster cover screws.

l. Install the lower instrument panel and the 2 driver's side lower instrument panel screws.

m. Install the steering column covers and the 4 steering column cover screws.

17. Install the air conditioning housing assembly to the vehicle.

18. Connect the thermal amp connector.

19. Install the glove box and the mating trim.

20. Connect both refrigerant lines to the evaporator core.

21. Inside the engine compartment, connect the heater hoses to the heater core.

22. Refill the cooling system.

23. Install the passenger's side air bag by performing the following procedure:

a. Install the SRS module and secure the SRS module-to-instrument panel clips.

b. Install the 4 SRS module-to-instrument panel mounting nuts.

c. Using the Tamper Resistant Torx® Wrench size T50, install the new special SRS module-to-instrument panel bolts.

d. Install the lower passenger's side instrument panel and the glove box.

e. Connect the passenger's SRS module connector.

f. Install the passenger's air bag module connector clip to the lid.

g. Inside the glove box, close the lower instrument panel lid.

h. Close the glove box door.

24. Install the steering wheel by performing the following procedure:

a. Align the spiral cable pin guide and install the steering wheel by pulling the spiral cable connectors through it.

b. Connect the horn connector and connect the spiral cable by aligning the pawls in the steering wheel.

c. Install the steering wheel nut and torque it to 22–29 ft. lbs. (29–39 Nm).

d. Install the SRS module to the steering wheel.

e. Using the Tamper Resistant Torx® Wrench size T50, install the new special bolts to both sides of the steering wheel.

f. Install the lower lid and disconnect the driver's air bag module connector.

g. Install both side lids.

h. Rotate the steering wheel fully right and left to make sure that the spiral cable is set in the neutral position.

25. Connect both the positive (1st) and negative (2nd) battery cables.

26. Evacuate and charge the air conditioning system refrigerant.

27. Run the engine to normal operating temperatures; then, check the climate control operation and check for leaks.

Quest

REMOVAL & INSTALLATION

Front System

1. Disconnect the negative battery cable.

2. Drain the cooling system into a clean container for reuse.

3. Disconnect the heater hoses from the heater core tubes in the engine compartment.

4. Disconnect the heater unit air ducts.

5. Remove the 2 heater retaining bolts.

6. Disconnect the electrical connector from the door motors.

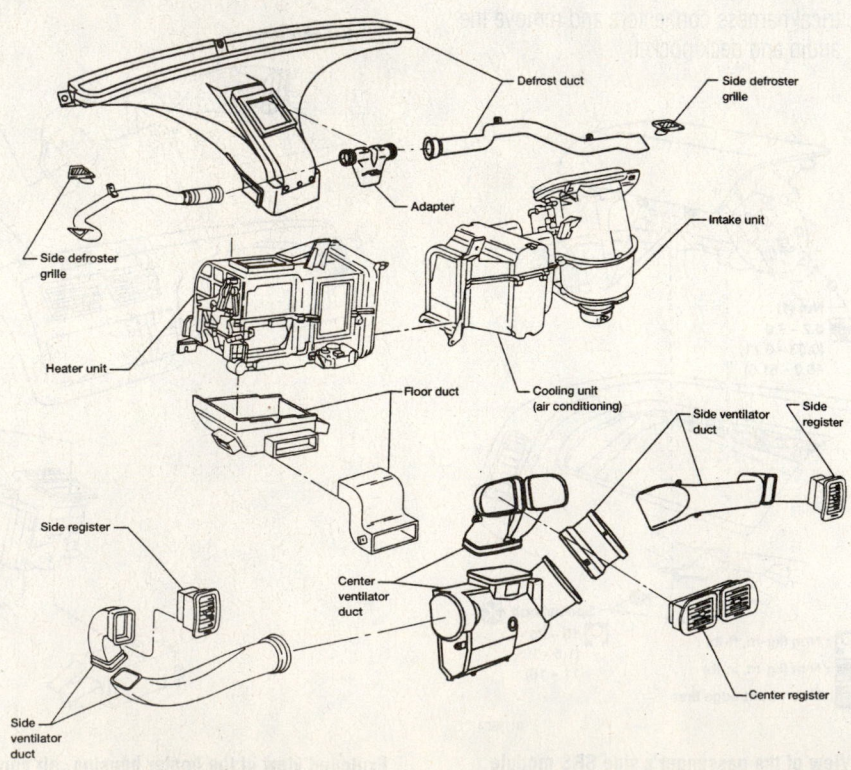

Exploded view of the front heater assembly—1997—98 Nissan Quest

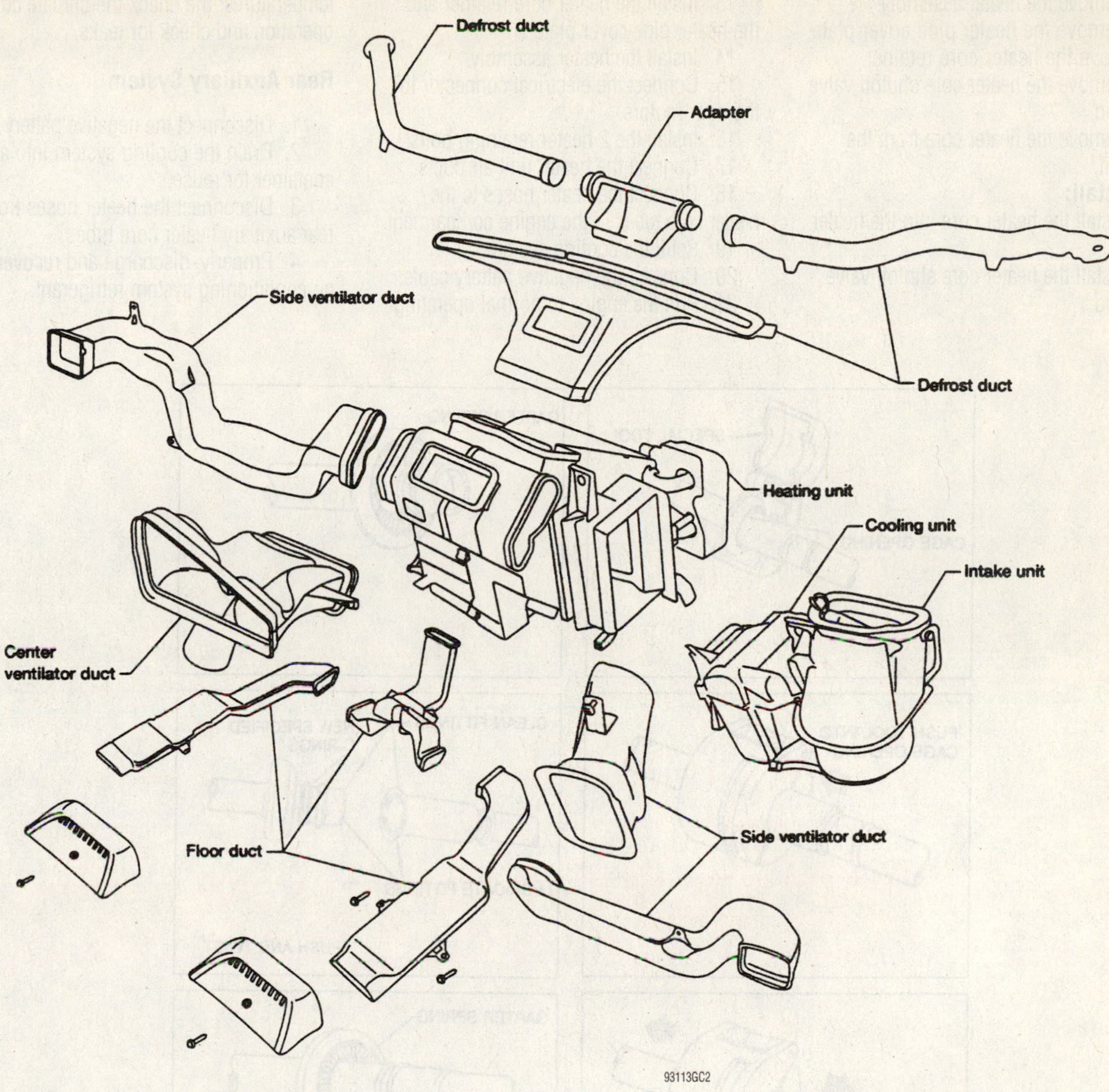

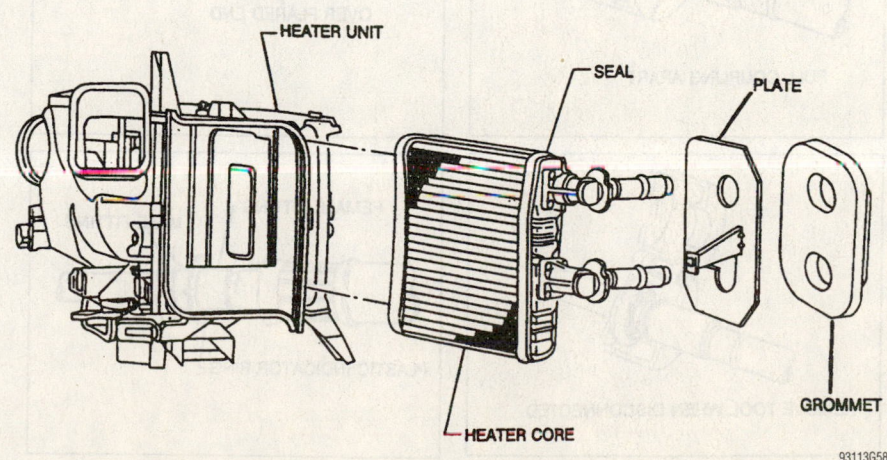

Defrost duct

Adapter

Side ventilator duct

Defrost duct

Heating unit

Cooling unit

Intake unit

Center
ventilator duct

Floor duct

Side ventilator duct

93113GC2

Exploded view of the front heater assembly—1999—00 Nissan Quest

HEATER UNIT

SEAL

PLATE

HEATER CORE

GROMMET

93113G58

View of the front heater core and heater housing assembly—1997—00 Nissan Quest

Refer to the model specific sections for engine mechanical service procedures

7. Remove the heater assembly.

8. Remove the heater pipe cover plate, then remove the heater core retainer.

9. Remove the heater core shutoff valve control rod.

10. Remove the heater core from the heater unit.

To install:

11. Install the heater core into the heater unit.

12. Install the heater core shutoff valve control rod.

13. Install the heater core retainer and the heater pipe cover plate.

14. Install the heater assembly.

15. Connect the electrical connector to the door motors.

16. Install the 2 heater retaining bolts.

17. Connect the heater unit air ducts.

18. Connect the heater hoses to the heater core tubes in the engine comparment.

19. Refill the cooling system.

20. Connect the negative battery cable.

21. Run the engine to normal operating temperatures; the check the climate control operation and check for leaks.

Rear Auxiliary System

1. Disconnect the negative battery cable.

2. Drain the cooling system into a clean container for reuse.

3. Disconnect the heater hoses from the rear auxiliary heater core tubes.

4. Properly, discharge and recover the air conditioning system refrigerant.

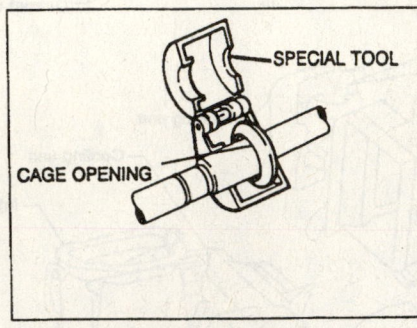

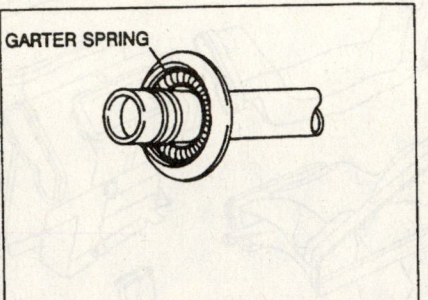

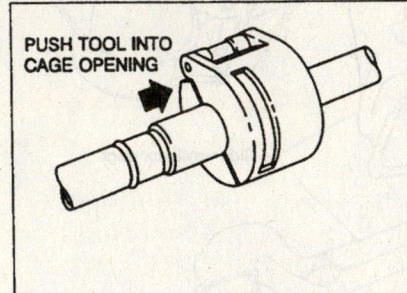

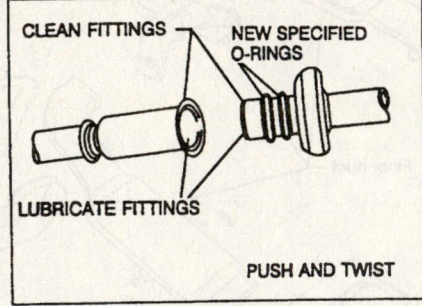

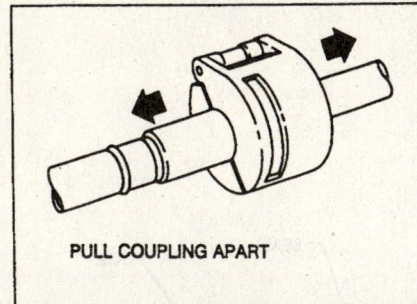

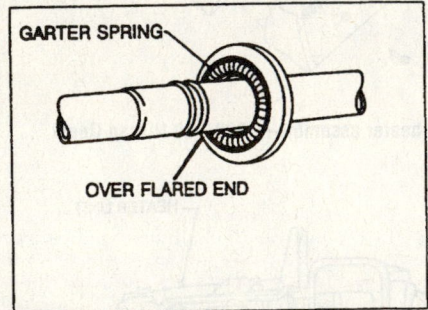

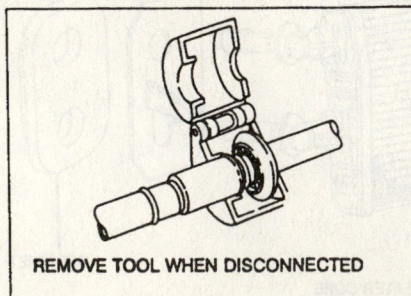

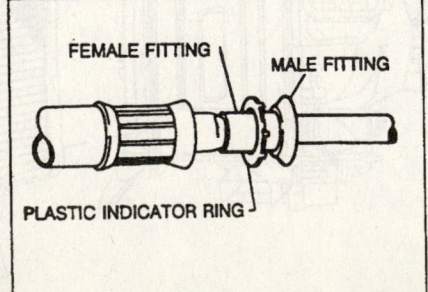

93113G61

Spring lock coupling disconnect/connect procedures—1997—98 Nissan Quest

5. Remove the driver's side rear trim panel and remove the bolts retaining the rear auxiliary heater/air conditioning housing.

6. Remove the upper housing and the outer housing.

7. Remove the evaporator core and the heater core.

To install:

8. Install the heater core and the evaporator core.

9. Install the outer housing and the upper housing.

10. Install the bolts retaining the rear auxiliary heater/air conditioning housing and the driver's side rear trim panel.

11. Evacuate and charge and the air conditioning system.

12. Connect the heater hoses to the rear auxiliary heater core tubes.

13. Refill the cooling system.

14. Connect the negative battery cable.

15. Run the engine to normal operating temperatures; then, check the climate control operation and check for leaks.

Pathfinder

REMOVAL & INSTALLATION

1. Disconnect the negative battery cable.

✳✳ CAUTION

After disconnecting the negative battery cable, wait for at least 3 minutes before working on the steering column or instrument panel.

2. Drain the cooling system into a clean container for reuse.

3. Disconnect the heater hoses from the heater core.

4. Remove the driver's side air bag and steering wheel by performing the following procedure:

a. Place the front wheels in the straight-ahead position.

b. Remove the lower lid from the steering wheel and disconnect the air bag module connector.

c. Remove the side lids from both sides of the steering wheel.

d. Using the Tamper Resistant Torx® tool T50, remove the left and right Torx® bolts.

e. Carefully, remove the air bag module.

✳✳ CAUTION

Place the air bag module in safe place with the front facing upward.

f. Remove the steering wheel nut.

g. Using a steering wheel puller, press the steering wheel from the steering column.

5. Remove the passenger's side air bag by performing the following procedure:

a. Remove the glove box clips and disconnect the passenger's side air bag module connector.

b. Remove the lower panel screws; then, disconnect the harness connector and remove the air bag module bracket.

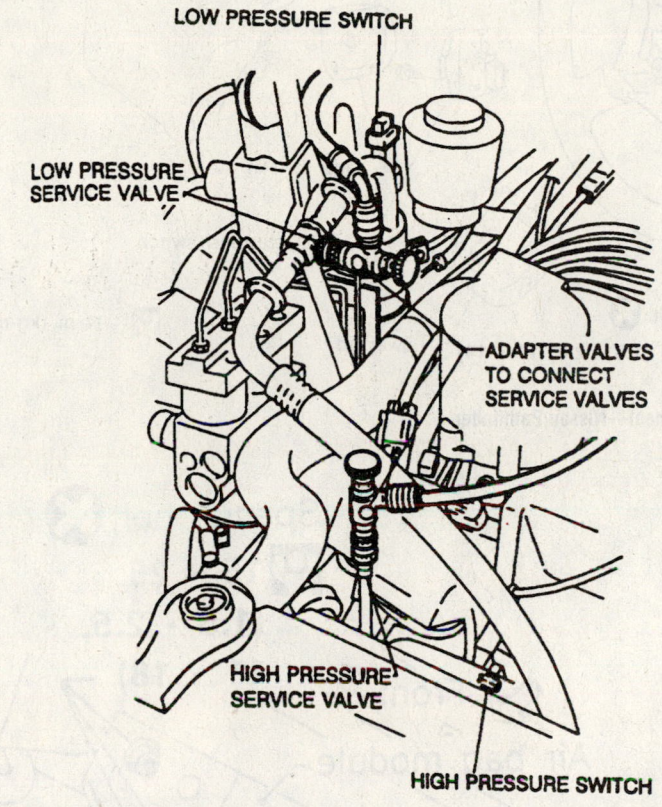

View of the air conditioning service valve locations—1997–98 Nissan Quest

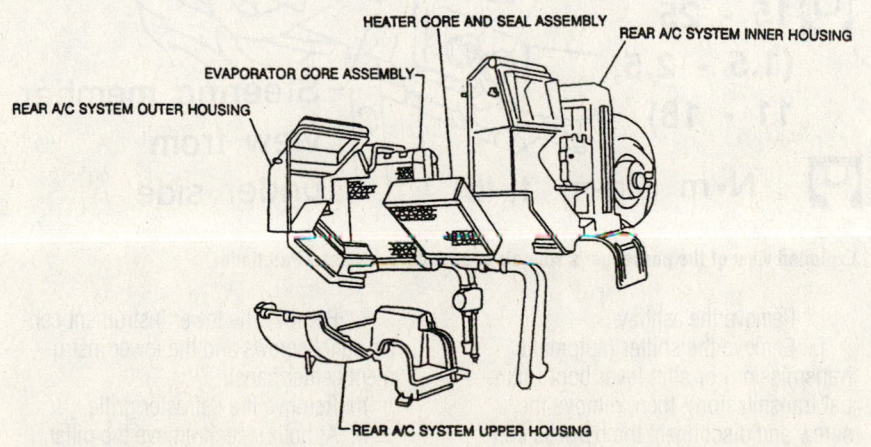

Exploded view of the rear auxiliary heater/air conditioning system components—1997–98 Nissan Quest

Refer to the model specific sections for cooling system service procedures

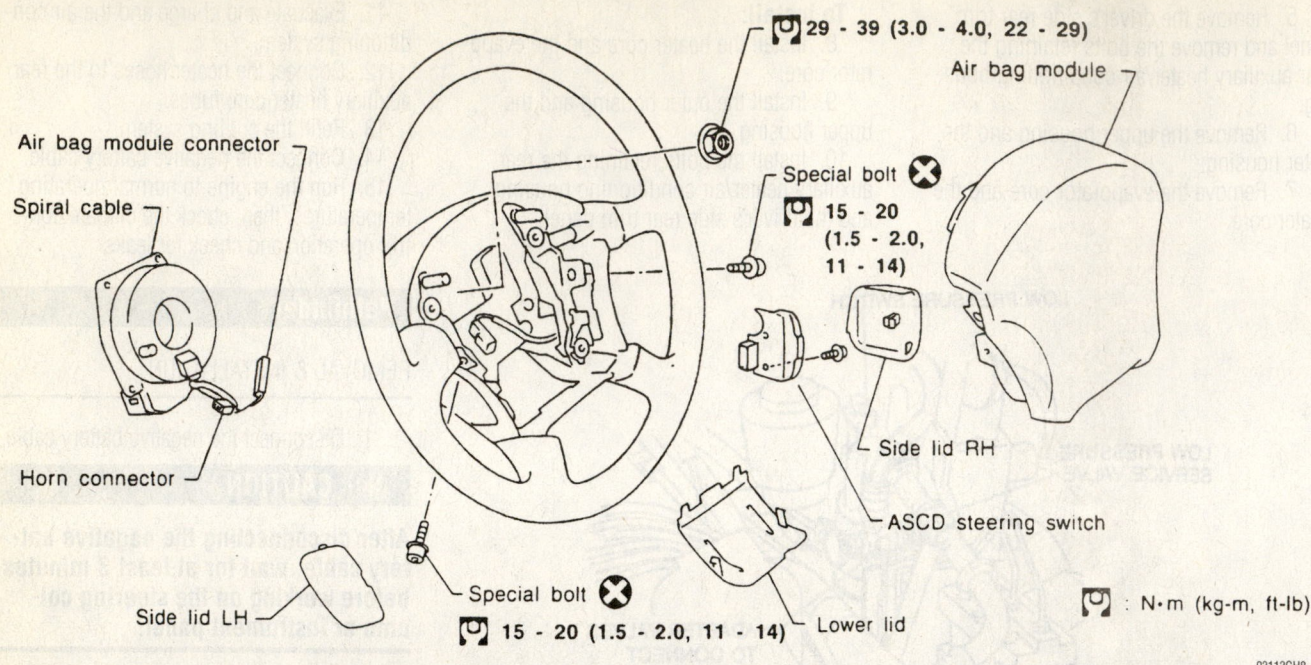

Exploded view of the driver's side air bag module and steering wheel—Nissan Pathfinder

c. Using the Tamper Resistant Torx® tool T50, remove the passenger's side air bag module bolts.

d. Carefully, remove the air bag module.

✳✳ CAUTION

Place the air bag module in safe place with the front facing upward.

6. Remove the instrument panel by performing the following procedure:

a. Remove the steering column cover and the combination switch.

b. Remove the instrument panel side lower finisher.

c. At the driver's side, remove the lower panel screws, disconnect the electrical harness connectors and remove the panel.

d. Remove the cluster lid "A" screws and the cluster lid "A".

e. Remove the combination meter screws, disconnect the electrical harness connectors and remove the combination meter.

f. Remove the cluster lid "C" screws, disconnect the electrical harness connectors and remove the cluster lid "C".

g. Remove the audio assembly screws and the audio assembly.

h. Remove the air conditioning control unit screws, disconnect the electrical harness connectors and the air conditioning control unit.

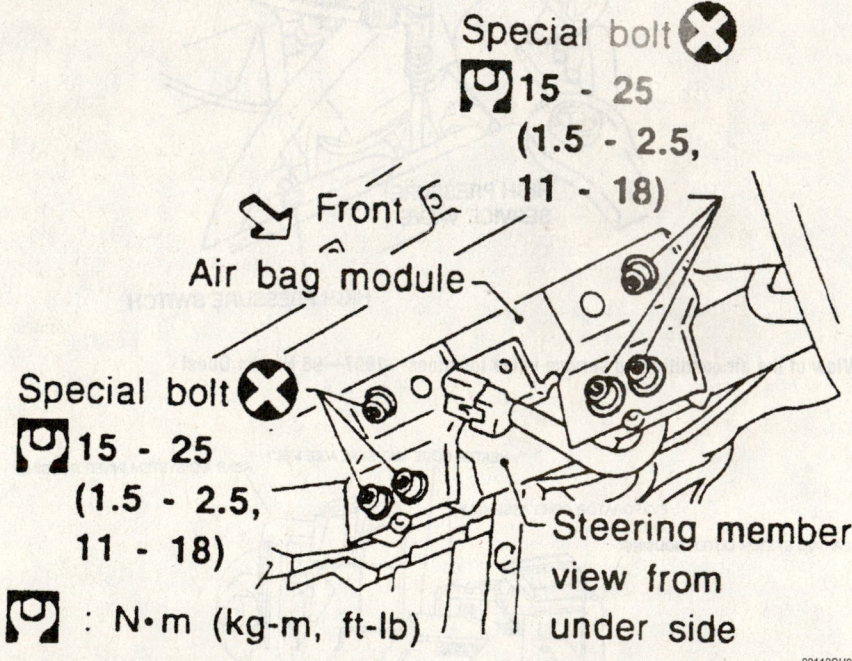

Exploded view of the passenger's side air bag module—Nissan Pathfinder

i. Remove the ashtray.

j. Remove the shifter (automatic transmission) or shift lever boot (manual transmission); then, remove the screw and disconnect the harness connector.

k. Remove the console box; then, remove the screw and disconnect the harness connector.

l. Remove the lower instrument center panel screws and the lower instrument center panel.

m. Remove the defroster grille.

n. At both sides, remove the pillar garnishes.

o. Remove the instrument panel and pads nuts and bolts.

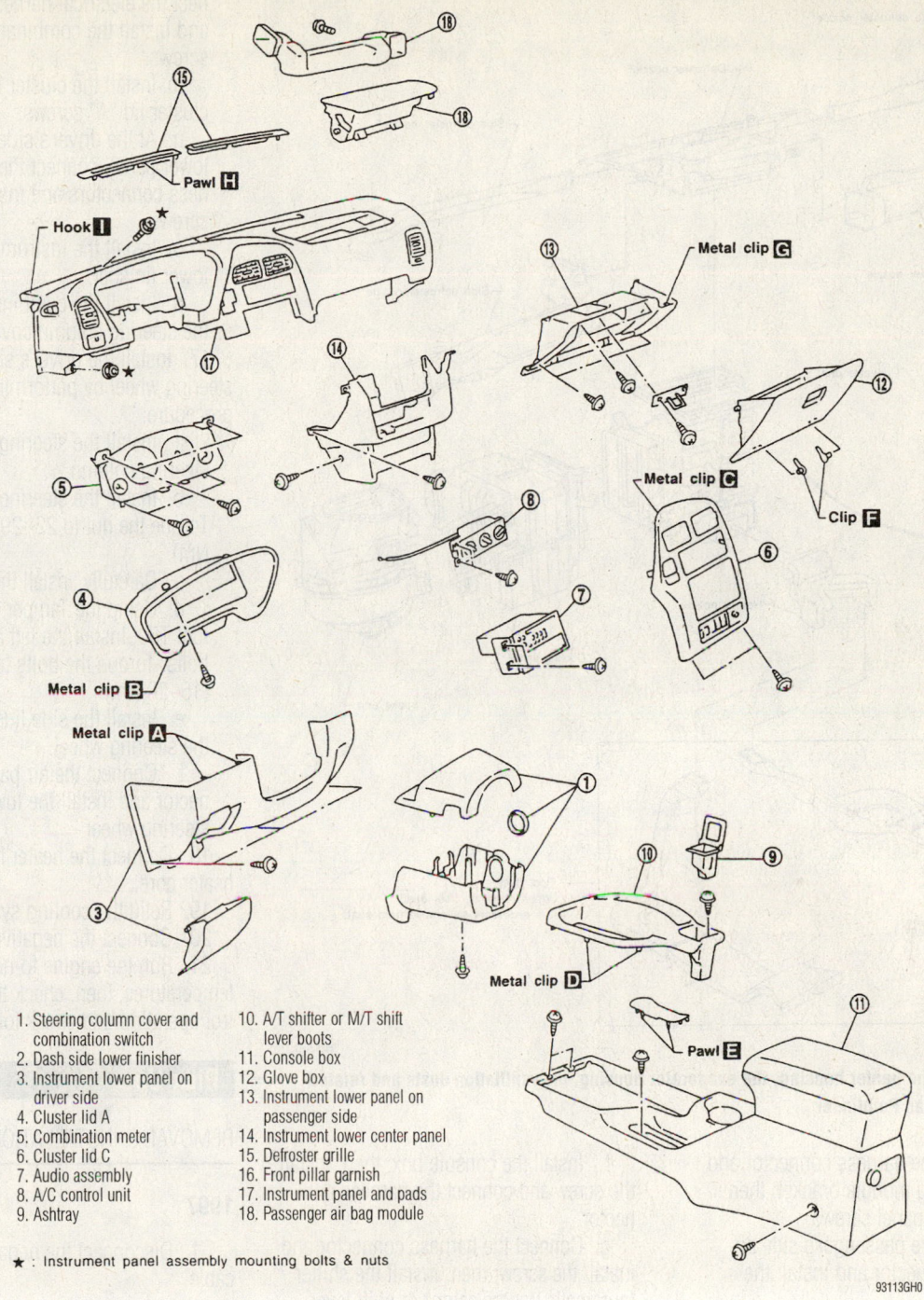

1. Steering column cover and combination switch
2. Dash side lower finisher
3. Instrument lower panel on driver side
4. Cluster lid A
5. Combination meter
6. Cluster lid C
7. Audio assembly
8. A/C control unit
9. Ashtray
10. A/T shifter or M/T shift lever boots
11. Console box
12. Glove box
13. Instrument lower panel on passenger side
14. Instrument lower center panel
15. Defroster grille
16. Front pillar garnish
17. Instrument panel and pads
18. Passenger air bag module

★ : Instrument panel assembly mounting bolts & nuts

Exploded view of the instrument panel and related accessories—Nissan Pathfinder

p. Using an assistant, remove the instrument panel.

7. Remove the defroster nozzle and the heater nozzle from the heater housing.

8. Disconnect the electrical connector and/or control cable from the heater housing.

9. Remove the heater housing-to-chassis fasteners and remove the heater housing.

10. Separate the heater core from the heater housing and remove the heater core.

To install:

11. Install the heater core and assemble the heater housing.

12. Install the heater housing and the heater housing-to-chassis fasteners.

13. Connect the electrical connector and/or control cable to the heater housing.

14. Install the defroster nozzle and the heater nozzle to the heater housing.

15. Install the passenger's side air bag by performing the following procedure:

a. Carefully, install the air bag module.

b. Using the Tamper Resistant Torx® tool T50, install the passenger's side air bag module bolts. Torque the bolts to 11–18 ft. lbs. (15–25 Nm).

For complete service labor times order Nichols' Chilton Labor Guide Manual

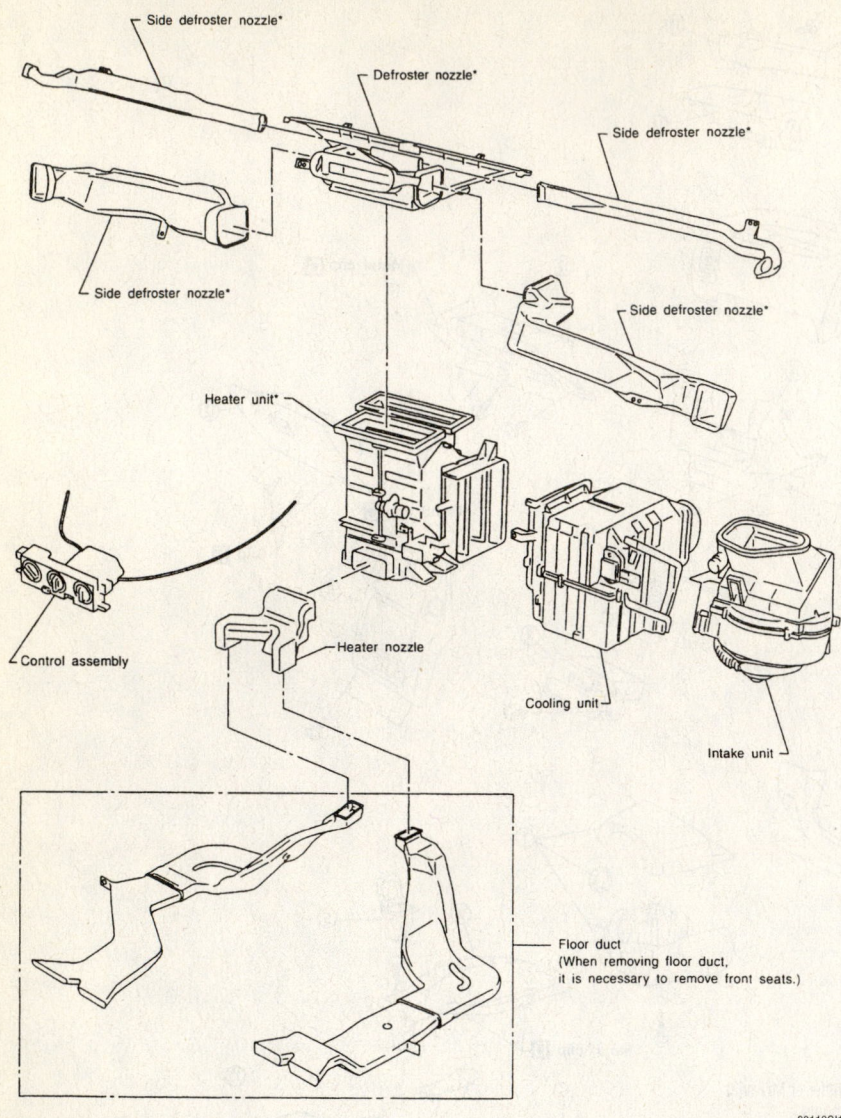

Side defroster nozzle*

Defroster nozzle*

Side defroster nozzle*

Side defroster nozzle*

Side defroster nozzle*

Heater unit*

Control assembly

Heater nozzle

Cooling unit

Intake unit

Floor duct
(When removing floor duct,
it is necessary to remove front seats.)

93113GI1

Exploded view of the heater housing, the evaporator housing, the ventilation dusts and related accessories—Nissan Pathfinder

c. Connect the harness connector and install the air bag module bracket; then, install the lower panel screws.

d. Connect the passenger's side air bag module connector and install the glove box clips.

16. Install the instrument panel by performing the following procedure:

a. Using an assistant, position the instrument panel.

b. Install the instrument pads, nuts and bolts.

c. At both sides, install the pillar garnishes.

d. Install the defroster grille.

e. Install the lower instrument center panel and the lower instrument center panel screws.

f. Install the console box; then, install the screw and connect the harness connector.

g. Connect the harness connector and install the screw; then, install the shifter (automatic transmission) or shift lever boot (manual transmission).

h. Install the ashtray.

i. Install the air conditioning control unit, connect the electrical harness connectors and the air conditioning control unit screws.

j. Install the audio assembly and the audio assembly screws.

k. Install the cluster lid "C", connect the electrical harness connectors and install the cluster lid "C" screws.

l. Install the combination meter, connect the electrical harness connectors and install the combination meter screws.

m. Install the cluster lid "A" and the cluster lid "A" screws.

n. At the driver's side, install the lower panel, connect the electrical harness connectors and install the panel screws.

o. Install the instrument panel side lower finisher.

p. Install the combination switch and the steering column cover.

17. Install the driver's side air bag and steering wheel by performing the following procedure:

a. Install the steering wheel to the steering column.

b. Install the steering wheel nut. Torque the nut to 22–29 ft. lbs. (29–39 Nm).

c. Carefully, install the air bag module.

d. Using the Tamper Resistant Torx® tool T50, install the left and right Torx® bolts. Torque the bolts to 11–14 ft. lbs. (15–20 Nm).

e. Install the side lids to both sides of the steering wheel.

f. Connect the air bag module connector and install the lower lid to the steering wheel.

18. Connect the heater hoses to the heater core.

19. Refill the cooling system.

20. Connect the negative battery cable.

21. Run the engine to normal operating temperatures; then, check the climate control operation and check for leaks.

Pick-Up

REMOVAL & INSTALLATION

1997

1. Disconnect the negative battery cable.

➡**If equipped with a theft-protected radio, obtain the owner's security code.**

2. Set the TEMP lever to the maximum **HOT** position and drain the cooling system into a clean container for reuse.

3. Disconnect the heater hoses at the engine compartment.

4. Remove the instrument panel by performing the following procedure:

a. Remove the ashtray.

b. Remove the screw holding the center console face cover.

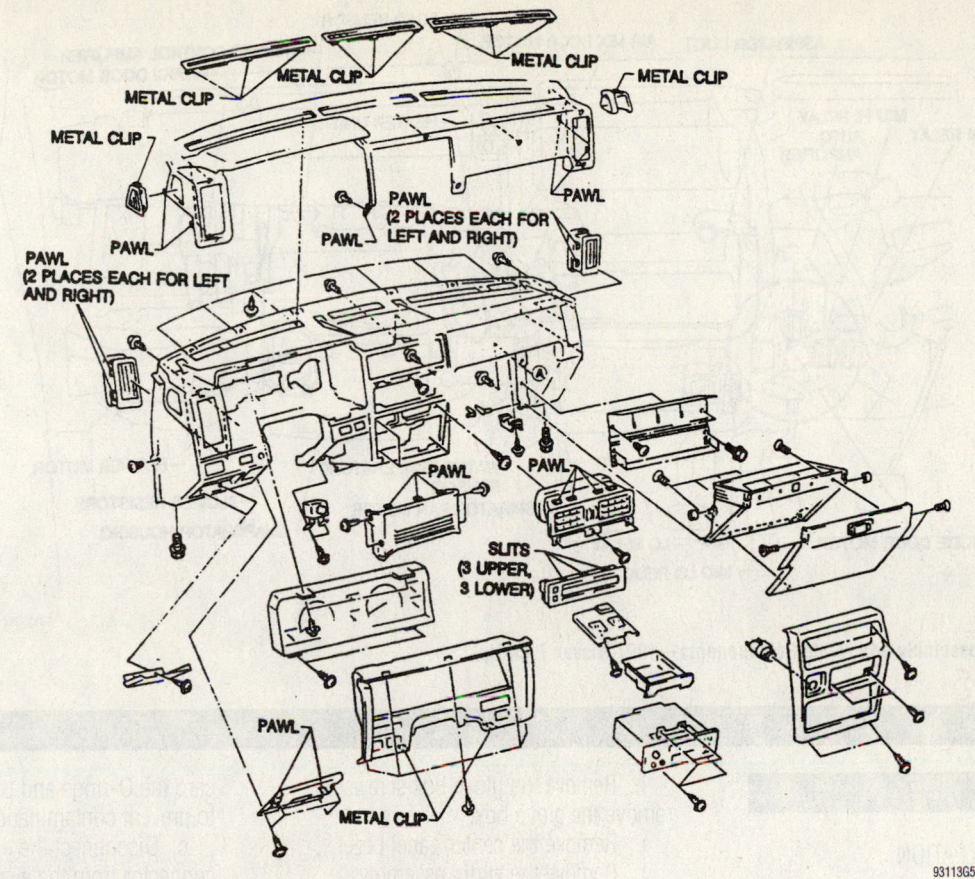

93113G55

Exploded view of the instrument panel assembly—1997 Nissan Pick-Up

c. Remove the cover, the heater controls, the radio and the center vent.

d. Disconnect the control cables and wiring as needed and remove the instrument panel.

5. Disconnect the ducts and remove the heater unit.

6. Remove the case clips and split the case to remove the heater core.

To install:

7. Install the heater core and assemble the heater core halves. Use a new gasket and seal as required.

8. Always check for smooth operation of the air mix door when reattaching the heater case halves.

9. Install the heater unit and use a new gasket to connect it to the heater unit.

10. Install the instrument panel by performing the following procedure:

a. Install the instrument panel and connect the control cables and wiring as needed.

b. Install the center vent, the cover, the radio and the heater controls.

c. Install the screw holding the center console face cover.

d. Install the ashtray.

11. Install the heater control assembly, the center vent and the radio.

12. Adjust the heater controls and the air flow doors, as required.

13. Connect the heater hose to the heater core.

14. Refill the cooling system.

15. Connect the negative battery cable.

16. Run the engine to normal operating temperatures; then check the climate control system and check for leaks.

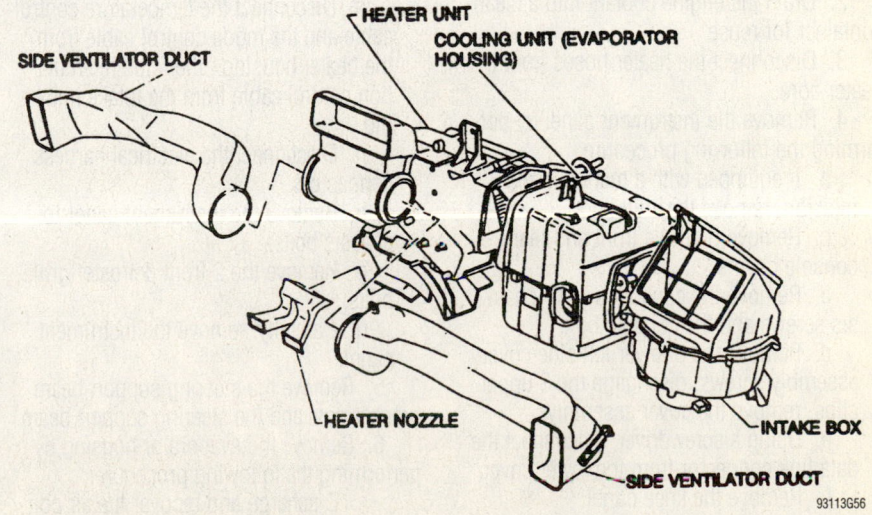

93113G56

View of the heater/air conditioning housing assembly—1997 Nissan Pick-Up

Please visit our web site at www.chiltononline.com

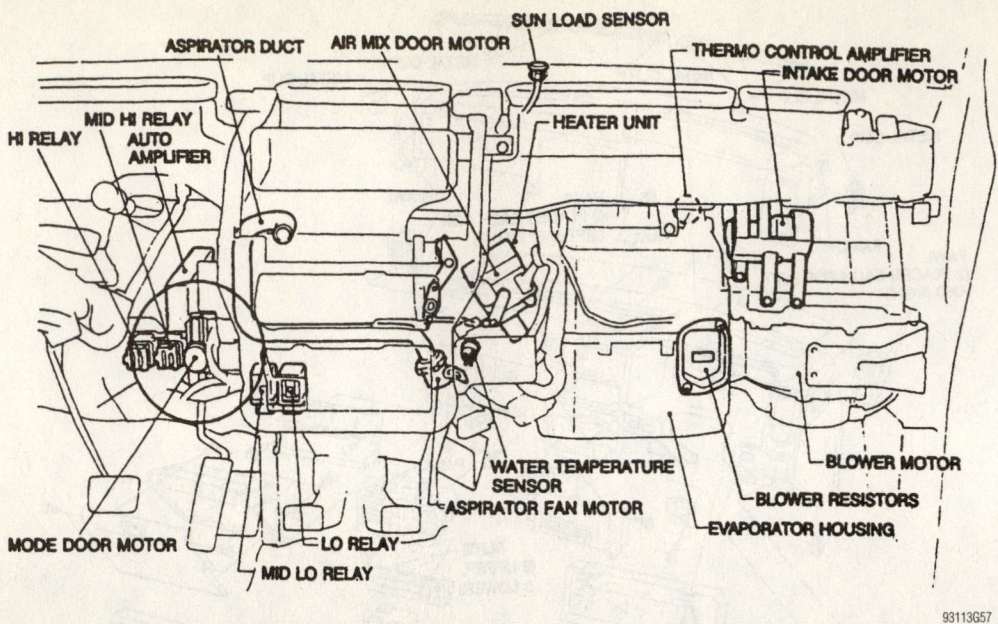

View of the heater assembly and related components—1997 Nissan Pick-Up

SUBARU

Forester

REMOVAL & INSTALLATION

1. Disconnect the negative battery cable.

✱✱ CAUTION

After disconnecting the negative battery cable, wait for at least 20 seconds for the air bag module to deplete its energy.

2. Drain the engine coolant into a clean container for reuse.

3. Disconnect the heater hoses from the heater core.

4. Remove the instrument panel by performing the following procedure:

   a. If equipped with a manual transmission, remove the shift knob.

   b. Remove both the front and rear console covers.

   c. Remove the console box-to-chassis screws and the console box.

   d. Remove the 3 lower left side cover assembly screws, disengage the 3 upper clips, remove the cover assembly.

   e. Using a screwdriver, disconnect the data link connector from the lower cover.

   f. Remove the knee panel.

   g. At the glove box, remove the right side cover screw, the clip and the side cover.

   h. Remove the glove box screws and remove the glove box.

   i. Remove the center panel bezel.

   j. Remove the audio assembly screws, disconnect the electrical connectors and remove the audio assembly.

   k. Remove the 2 steering column-to-instrument panel bolts and lower the steering column.

   l. Move the temperature control switch to FULL HOT, the mode selector switch to DEF and the recirculation switch to FRESH positions.

   m. Disconnect the temperature control cable and the mode control cable from the heater housing.; then, the recirculation control cable from the intake housing.

   n. Disconnect the electrical harness connectors.

   o. Remove the instrument panel-to-chassis bolts.

   p. Remove the 2 front defroster grille bolts.

   q. Carefully, remove the instrument panel.

5. Remove the steering support beam bracket nuts and the steering support beam.

6. Remove the evaporator housing by performing the following procedure:

   a. Discharge and recover the air conditioning system refrigerant.

   b. Remove the refrigerant line-to-cowl connector bolt, separate the lines, discard the O-rings and plug the openings to prevent contamination.

   c. Disconnect the electrical harness connector from the evaporator housing.

   d. Disconnect the drain hose.

   e. Remove the evaporator housing nut/bolts and the evaporator housing.

7. Remove the heater housing-to-chassis bolts and the heater housing.

8. Remove the heater core from the heater housing.

   To install:

9. Install the heater core to the heater housing.

10. Install the heater housing and the heater housing-to-chassis bolts.

11. Install the steering support beam and the steering support beam bracket nuts.

12. Install the evaporator housing by performing the following procedure:

   a. Install the evaporator housing and the evaporator housing nut/bolts.

   b. Connect the drain hose.

   c. Connect the electrical harness connector to the evaporator housing.

   d. Using new O-rings, assemble the refrigerant lines and install the refrigerant line-to-cowl connector bolt.

13. Install the instrument panel by performing the following procedure:

   a. Carefully, install the instrument panel.

   b. Install the 2 front defroster grille bolts.

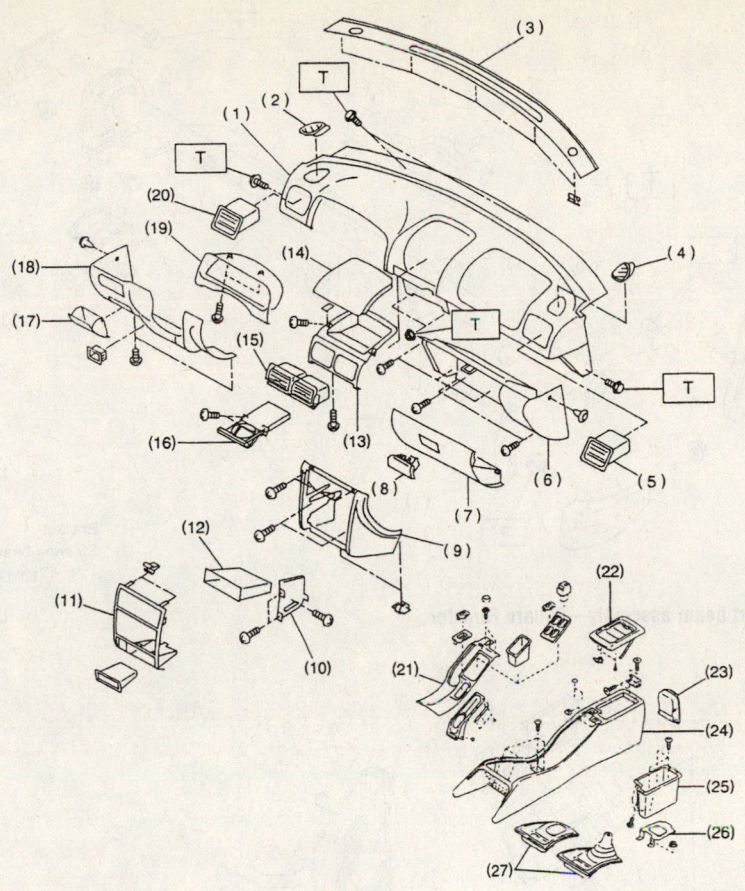

1 Pad & frame
2 Grille side (D)
3 Front def. grille
4 Grille side (P)
5 Grille vent (P)
6 Glove box panel
7 Glove box lid
8 Knob
9 Instrument panel center console
10 BRKT (Radio)
11 Center console cover

12 Pocket
13 Panel center
14 Center pocket lid
15 Grille center
16 Cup holder
17 Side pocket
18 Lower cover ASSY
19 Meter visor
20 Grille vent (D)
21 Console cover
22 Console lid

23 Rear cup holder
24 Console box
25 Console pocket
26 Rear console BRKT
27 Front cover

Tightening torque: N·m (kg-m, ft-lb)
  T: 7±1 (0.7±0.1, 5.1±0.7)

93113GI8

Exploded view of the instrument panel assembly—Subaru Forester

c. Install the instrument panel-to-chassis bolts.

d. Connect the electrical harness connectors.

e. Connect the temperature control cable and the mode control cable to the heater housing. Then, the recirculation control cable to the intake housing.

f. Install the steering column and lower the 2 steering column-to-instrument panel bolts and torque to 14–21 ft. lbs. (20–30 Nm).

g. Install the audio assembly, connect the electrical connectors and install the audio assembly screws.

h. Install the center panel bezel.

i. Install the glove box and the glove box screws.

j. At the glove box, install the right side cover, the clip and the side cover screw.

k. Install the knee panel.

l. Connect the data link connector to the lower cover.

m. Install the lower left side cover assembly, engage the 3 upper clips and install the cover assembly screws.

n. Install the console box and the console box-to-chassis screws.

o. Install both the front and rear console covers.

p. If equipped with a manual transmission, install the shift knob.

14. Connect the heater hoses to the heater core.

15. Refill the cooling system.

16. Connect the negative battery cable.

17. Evacuate and charge the air conditioning system refrigerant.

18. Run the engine to normal operating temperatures; then, check the climate control operation and check for leaks.

Refer to the model specific sections for engine mechanical service procedures

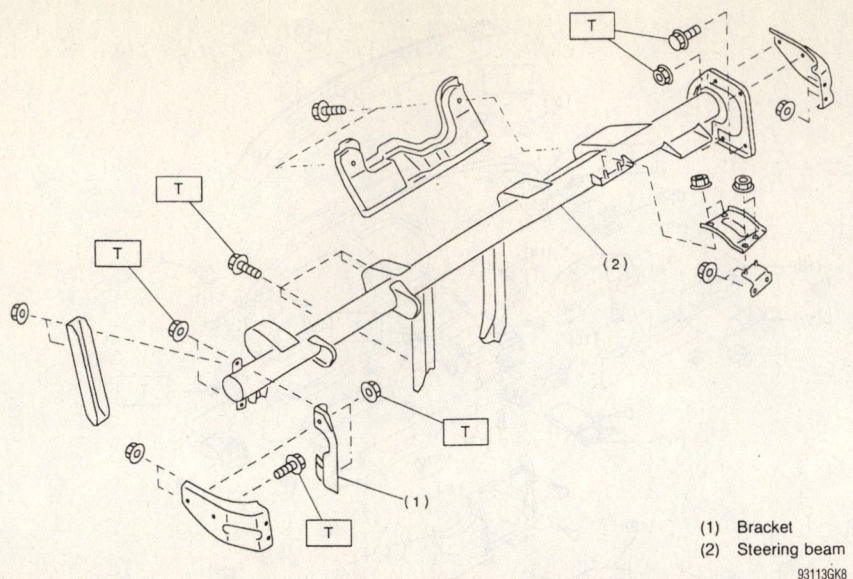

(1) Bracket
(2) Steering beam

93113GK8

Exploded view of the steering support beam assembly—Subaru Forester

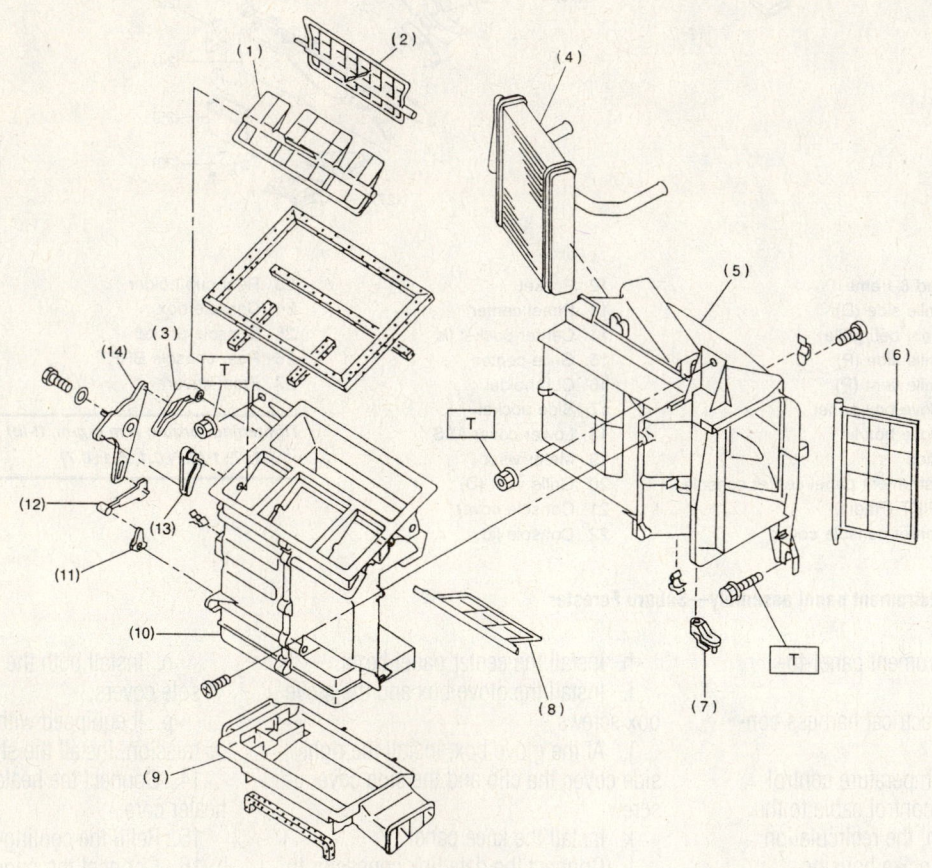

1 Vent door	7 **Mix lever**	13 Vent lever
2 DEF door	8 Foot door	14 Side link
3 DEF lever	9 Foot duct	
4 Heater core	10 Heater case REAR	
5 Heater case FRONT	11 Foot lever lower	
6 Mix door	12 Foot lever upper	

Tightening torque: N·m (kg-m, ft-lb)
T: 7.35±1.96
(0.750±0.200, 5.421±1.446)

93113GI7

Exploded view of the heater core, heater housing and related components—Subaru Forester

SUZUKI

Sidekick

REMOVAL & INSTALLATION

1. Disconnect the negative battery cable.
2. Drain the engine cooling system into a large, clean catch pan.

✳✳ CAUTION

The air bag system must be disarmed before performing service around air bag components or air bag wiring. Failure to do so may cause accidental deployment of the air bag, resulting in unnecessary air bag system repairs and/or personal injury.

3. Disable the air bag system by performing the following procedure:
   a. Turn the steering wheel so the front wheels are in the straight-ahead position.
   b. Turn the ignition switch to the **LOCK** position and remove the key.
   c. Remove the AIR BAG fuse from the air bag fuse box.
   d. Remove the steering wheel side cap and disengage the yellow connector inside the inflator module housing.
   e. Remove the glove box, by disengaging both glove box stoppers from each side, then unplug the yellow passenger air bag inflator module connector.
4. Remove the steering column as follows:
   a. Detach the wiring harness connectors from the ignition switch, contact coil and combination switch.
   b. Open the hood.
   c. Remove the steering column shaft joint bolt, then separate the steering column shaft from the lower steering shaft.
   d. Loosen all of the steering column-to-firewall and instrument panel brace bolts.
   e. If equipped, remove the shift (key) interlock cable screw. Disconnect the cable from the ignition switch.
   f. Remove the steering column from the vehicle.

✳✳ CAUTION

Do not rest the steering column assembly on the steering wheel with

the air bag module facing downward and the column vertical. Personal injury may be the result!

5. Remove the center console.
6. Remove the instrument panel by performing the following procedure:
   a. Remove the lower steering column cover by loosening the mounting screws.
   b. Remove the glove box.
   c. Detach the wiring harness connectors from the heater unit and the blower motor assembly.
   d. Disconnect the speedometer cable from the speedometer, then remove the instrument cluster.
   e. Remove the hood latch handle.
   f. Remove the radio, the heater control panel and the heater control cables from the instrument panel.

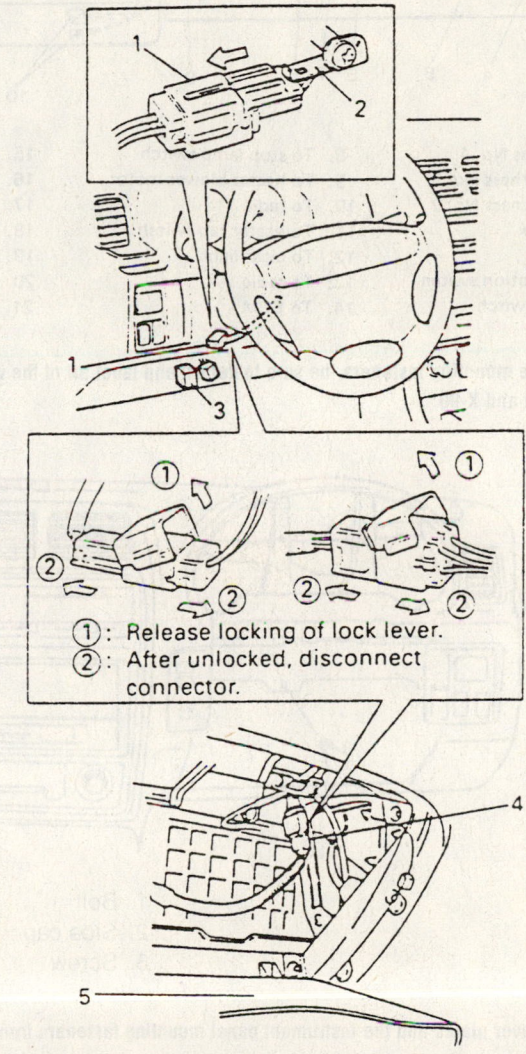

① : Release locking of lock lever.
② : After unlocked, disconnect connector.

1. Yellow connector of driver air bag (inflator) module
2. Connector stay
3. Air bag fuse box
4. Yellow connector of passenger air bag (inflator) module
5. Glove box

90886G00

To disable the air bag system, the air bag fuse must be removed and the yellow air bag module connector disengaged—Suzuki Sidekick, Sidekick Sport and X-90

Refer to the model specific sections for cooling system service procedures

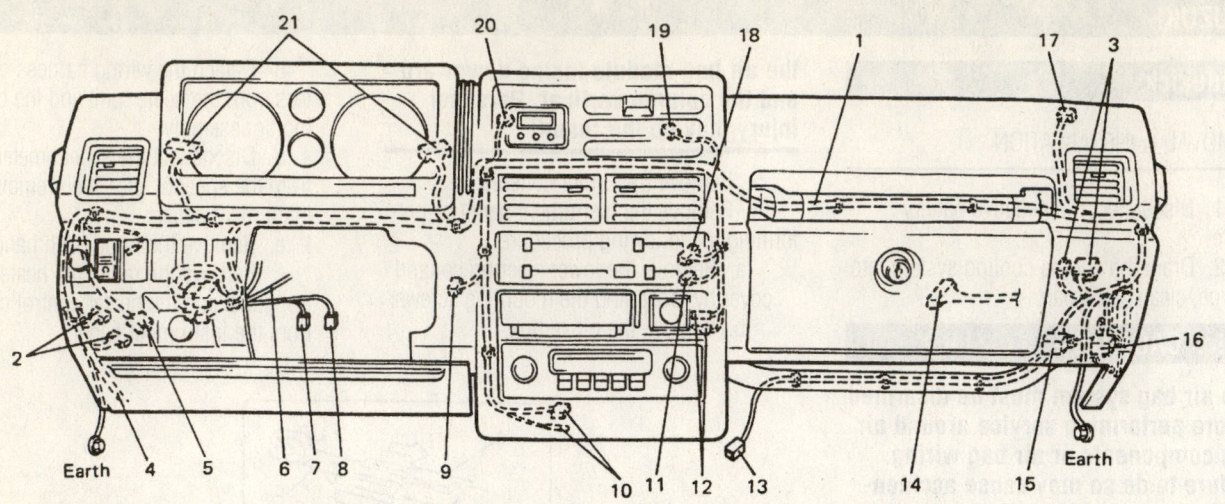

1. Wire harness No. 1
2. To wire harness No. 2
3. To wire harness No. 2
4. To fuse box
5. Horn relay
6. To combination switch
7. To clutch switch
8. To stop lamp switch
9. To heater blower motor
10. To radio
11. To heater fan switch
12. To cigar light
13. To radio
14. To ECM
15. Door warning buzzer
16. Check relay
17. To wiper motor
18. To illumination lamp
19. To optional meter
20. To clock
21. To meter

Before removing the mounting fasteners, be sure to detach and label all of the wiring harness connectors from the instrument panel—Suzuki Sidekick, Sidekick Sport and X-90

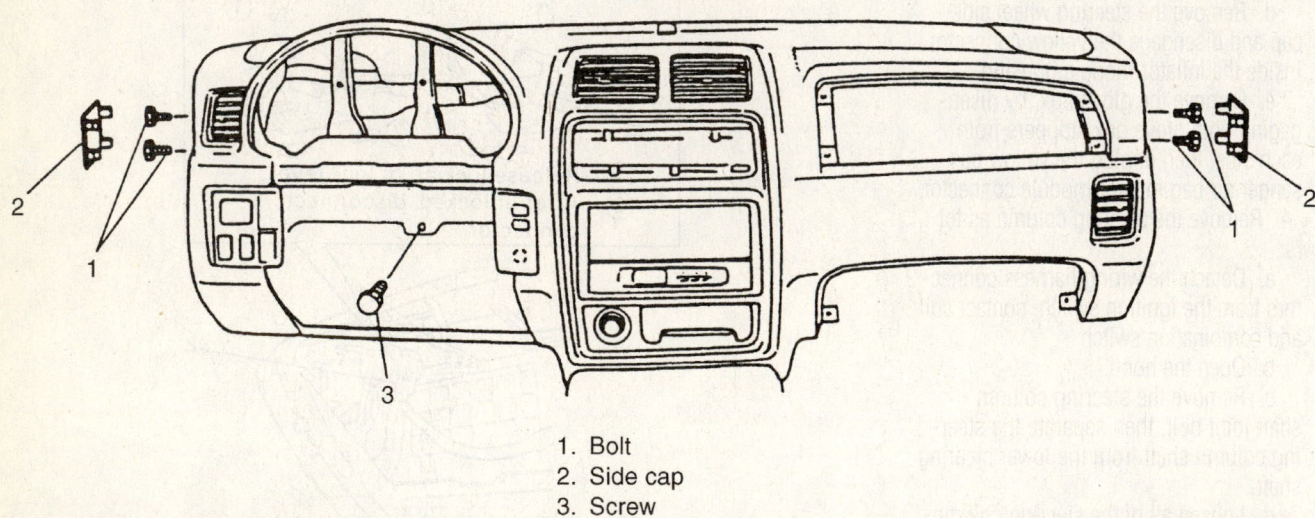

1. Bolt
2. Side cap
3. Screw

Remove the side cover plates and the instrument panel mounting fasteners from the side of the assembly . . . .—Suzuki Sidekick, Sidekick Sport and X-90

g. Disconnect and label all wiring harness connectors from the instrument panel.

h. Remove the instrument panel mounting screws and bolts. Remove the side cover plates and the instrument panel mounting fasteners from the side of the assembly. Then, remove the upper cover plates and loosen the remaining mounting fasteners

i. Using an assistant, remove the instrument panel. Make sure that all of the cables, wires and hoses are disconnected form the instrument panel.

7. Remove the instrument panel center support from the firewall.

8. Detach and label all wiring harness connectors from the heater case.

9. Disconnect all of the cables from the heater case.

10. Detach the 2 heater hoses from the heater case.

11. Remove the defroster duct and speedometer cable retaining bracket from the heater case.

12. Remove the grommets and floor duct from the case.

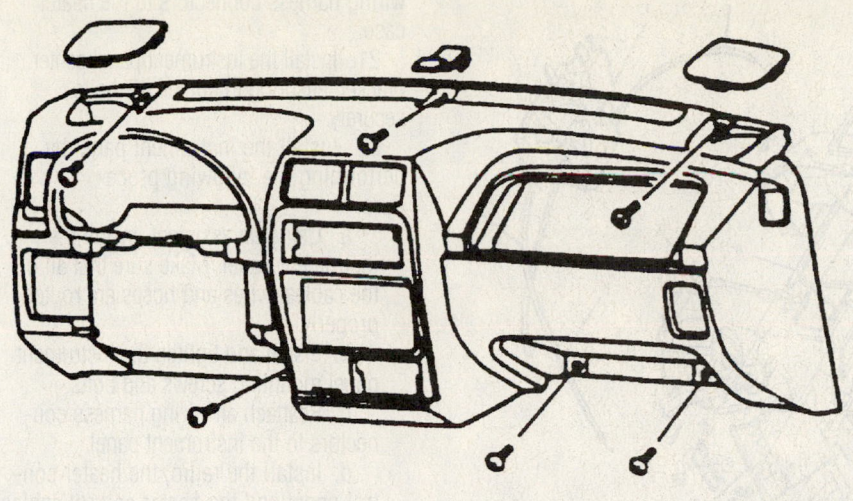

... then remove the upper cover plates and loosen the remaining mounting fasteners—
Suzuki Sidekick, Sidekick Sport and X-90

13. Open the hood, then remove the heater case-to-firewall mounting nuts from the engine side of the firewall.

14. Remove the 2 mounting bolts from inside the passengers' compartment, then remove the case from the vehicle.

15. Loosen the heater core retaining bolts, then slide the heater core out of the heater case.

To install:

16. Install the heater core in the heater case, then tighten the retaining bolts securely.

17. Position the heater case in the vehicle, against the firewall, and install the mounting bolts. Tighten them securely.

18. From the engine compartment, install and tighten the heater case mounting nuts securely.

19. Install the floor duct and grommets, then reattach the speedometer cable retaining bracket and defroster duct to the heater case.

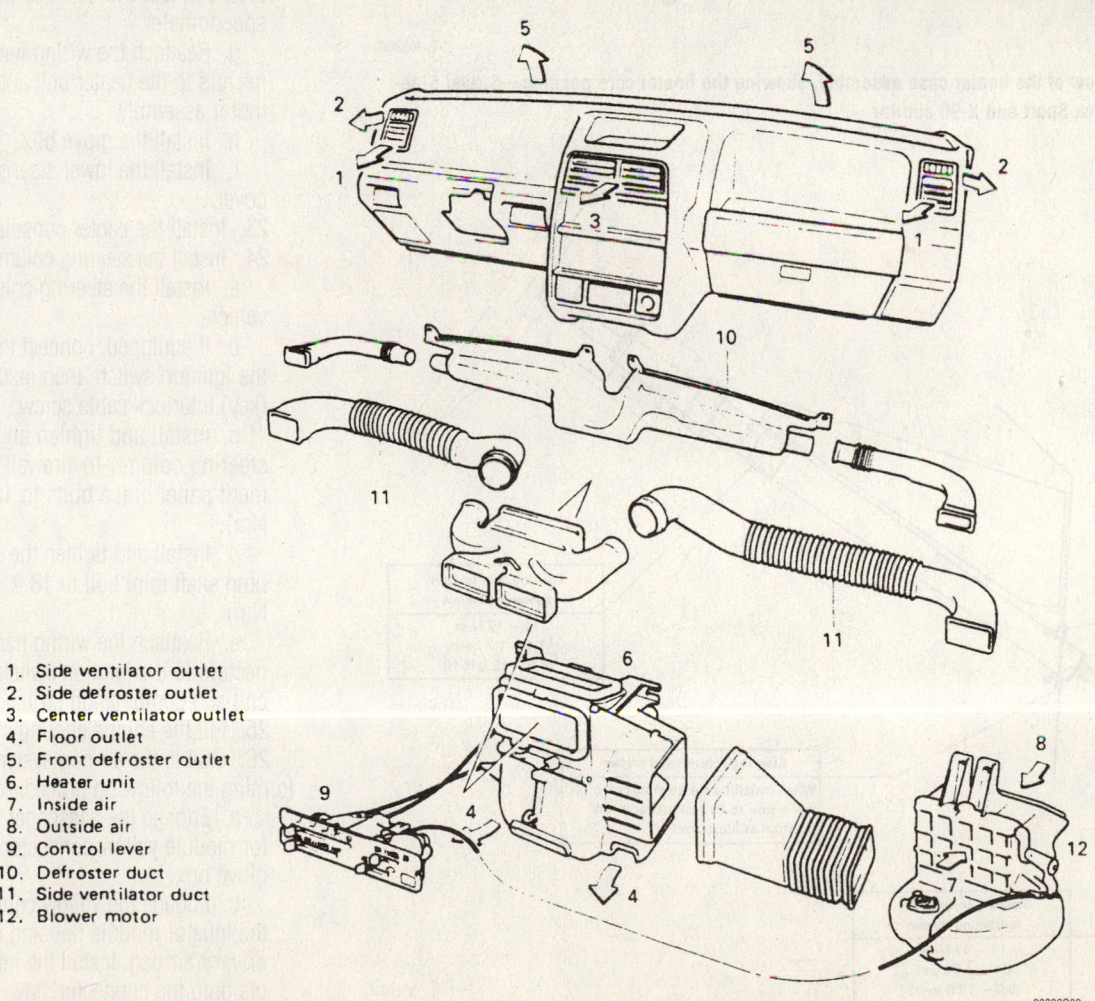

1. Side ventilator outlet
2. Side defroster outlet
3. Center ventilator outlet
4. Floor outlet
5. Front defroster outlet
6. Heater unit
7. Inside air
8. Outside air
9. Control lever
10. Defroster duct
11. Side ventilator duct
12. Blower motor

Exploded view of the air distribution (ducting) system—Suzuki Sidekick, Sidekick Sport and X-90 similar

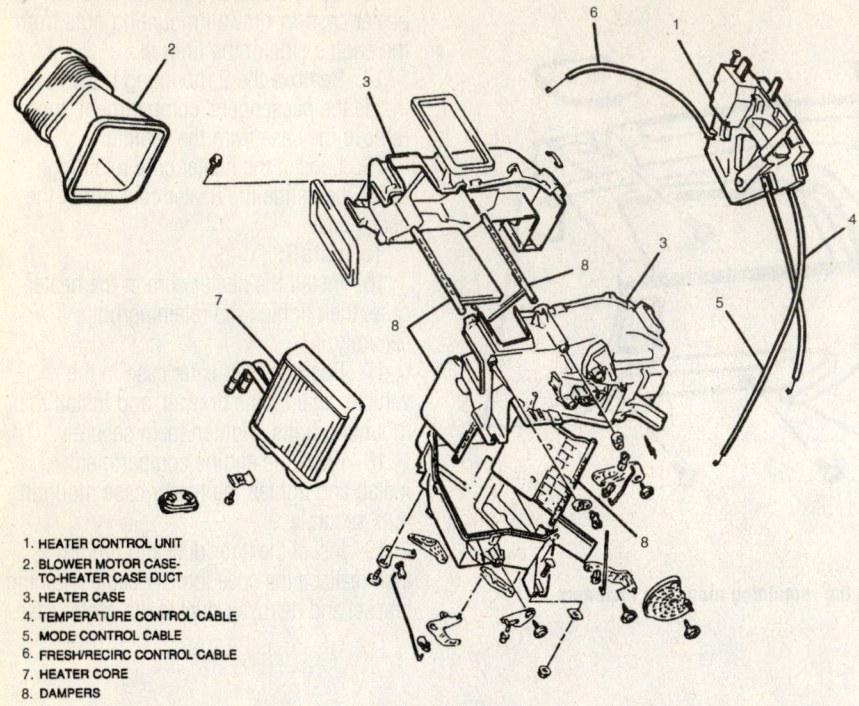

1. HEATER CONTROL UNIT
2. BLOWER MOTOR CASE-TO-HEATER CASE DUCT
3. HEATER CASE
4. TEMPERATURE CONTROL CABLE
5. MODE CONTROL CABLE
6. FRESH/RECIRC CONTROL CABLE
7. HEATER CORE
8. DAMPERS

90886G08

Exploded view of the heater case assembly, showing the heater core position—Suzuki Sidekick, Sidekick Sport and X-90 similar

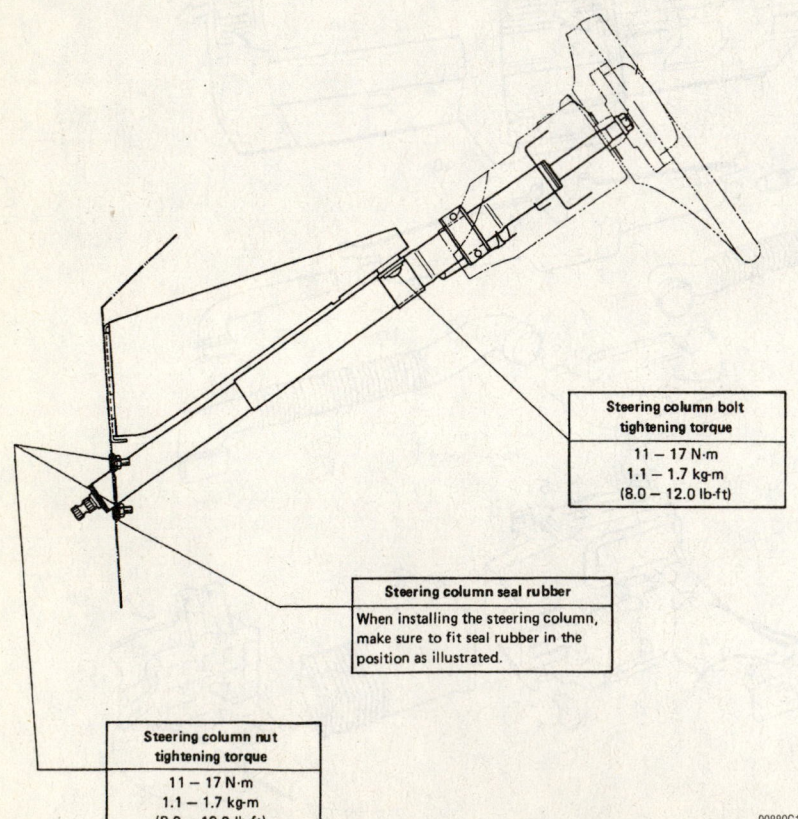

Steering column bolt tightening torque
11 – 17 N·m
1.1 – 1.7 kg-m
(8.0 – 12.0 lb-ft)

Steering column seal rubber
When installing the steering column, make sure to fit seal rubber in the position as illustrated.

Steering column nut tightening torque
11 – 17 N·m
1.1 – 1.7 kg-m
(8.0 – 12.0 lb-ft)

90880G15

During steering column installation, ensure that the mounting bolts are tightened to the proper torque values—Suzuki Sidekick, Sidekick Sport and X-90 similar

20. Reattach all of the cables, hoses and wiring harness connectors to the heater case.

21. Install the instrument panel center bracket, ensuring to tighten the bolts securely.

22. Install the instrument panel by performing the following procedure:

a. Using an assistant, install the instrument panel. Make sure that all of the cables, wires and hoses are routed properly.

b. Install and tighten the instrument panel mounting screws and bolts.

c. Reattach all wiring harness connectors to the instrument panel.

d. Install the radio, the heater control panel and the heater control cables. Be sure to adjust the heater control cables.

e. Install the hood latch handle.

f. Install the instrument cluster, then connect the cable to the speedometer.

g. Reattach the wiring harness connectors to the heater unit and the blower motor assembly.

h. Install the glove box.

i. Install the lower steering column cover.

23. Install the center console.

24. Install the steering column as follows:

a. Install the steering column in the vehicle.

b. If equipped, connect the cable from the ignition switch, then install the shift (key) interlock cable screw.

c. Install and tighten all of the steering column-to-firewall and instrument panel brace bolts to 18 ft. lbs. (25 Nm).

d. Install and tighten the steering column shaft joint bolt to 18 ft. lbs. (25 Nm).

e. Reattach the wiring harness connectors to the ignition switch, contact coil and combination switch.

25. Fill the engine cooling system.

26. Enable the air bag system by performing the following procedure:

a. Engage the passenger air bag inflator module yellow connector. Install glove box.

b. Engage the yellow connector inside the inflator module housing on the driver's air bag. Install the inflator module onto the connector stay.

c. Install the plastic access cover.

d. Turn the ignition switch to the **ON**

position. Verify that the air bag indicator lamp flashes 7 times and then turns OFF. If the lamp does not function as specified, there is a malfunction in the SIR system.

27. Connect the negative battery cable, then start the engine and ensure that the heater system works properly.

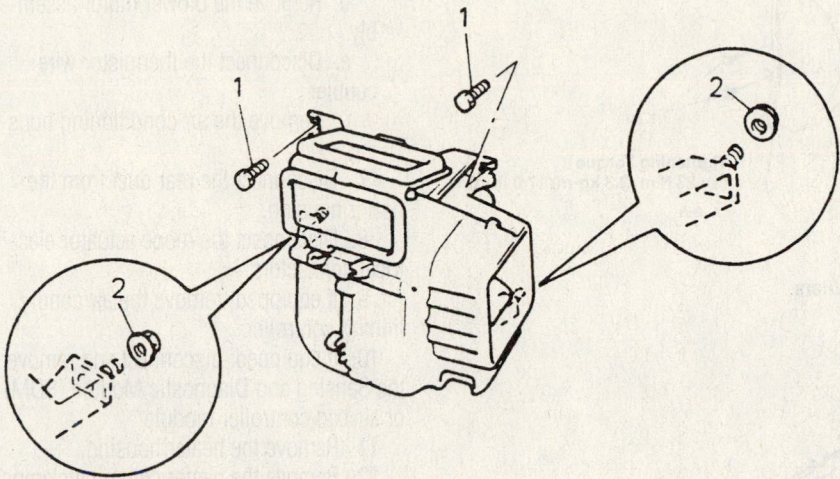

1. **Fastening bolts**
2. **Fastening nuts**

90886G04

To separate the heater case assembly from the firewall, remove the 2 nuts from the engine compartment, and the 2 bolts from inside the passengers' compartment—Suzuki Sidekick, Sidekick Sport and X-90 similar

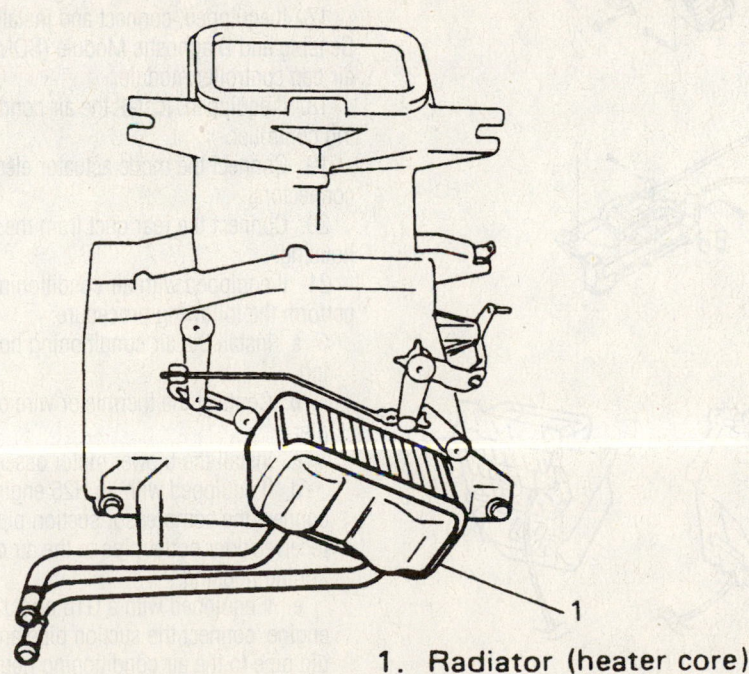

1. **Radiator (heater core)**

90886G05

Remove the heater core retaining fasteners, then slide the core out of the heater case assembly—Suzuki Sidekick, Sidekick Sport and X-90 similar

Vitara and Grand Vitara

REMOVAL & INSTALLATION

1. Disconnect the negative battery cable.

2. To disable the air bag system, perform the following procedure:

   a. Position the front wheels so that they are pointing straight ahead.

   b. Turn the ignition switch to the LOCK position.

   c. In the fuse box, remove the AIR BAG fuse.

   d. Under the steering column, locate the contact coil/combination switch assembly's yellow connector; then, unlock and disconnect the connector.

   e. Pull outward on the glove box while pushing the stopper located at both sides and locate the passenger's side air bag module yellow connector; then, unlock and disconnect the connector.

➡**With the AIR BAG fuse removed and the ignition switch turned ON; the air bag warning light may be ON; this is normal operation and does not indicate an air bag malfunction.**

3. Drain the cooling system into a clean container for reuse.

4. Disconnect the heater hoses from the heater core.

5. Remove the instrument panel by performing the following procedure:

   a. Remove the console.

   b. Remove the glove box and the column hole cover.

   c. Disconnect the electrical connector and cables from the heater housing and blower motor assembly.

   d. Remove the steering column.

   e. Disconnect the speedometer connector and the speedometer assembly.

   f. Remove the hood opener.

   g. Disconnect the instrument panel electrical connectors.

   h. Remove the instrument panel-to-chassis screws and bolts.

   i. Using an assistant, remove the instrument panel.

6. If equipped with air conditioning, perform the following procedure:

   a. Discharge and recover the air conditioning refrigerant.

   b. If equipped with a G16 or a J20 engine, disconnect the suction pipe and liquid pipe from the air conditioning

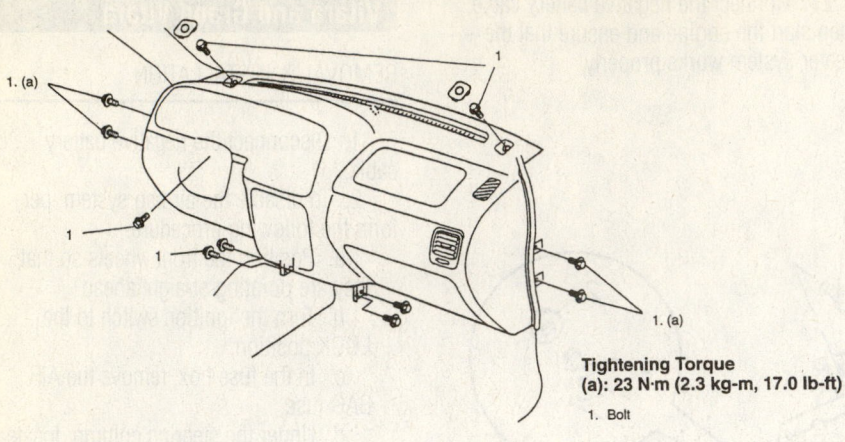

Tightening Torque
(a): 23 N·m (2.3 kg-m, 17.0 lb-ft)
1. Bolt

93113GE8

View of the instrument panel and fasteners—Suzuki Vitara

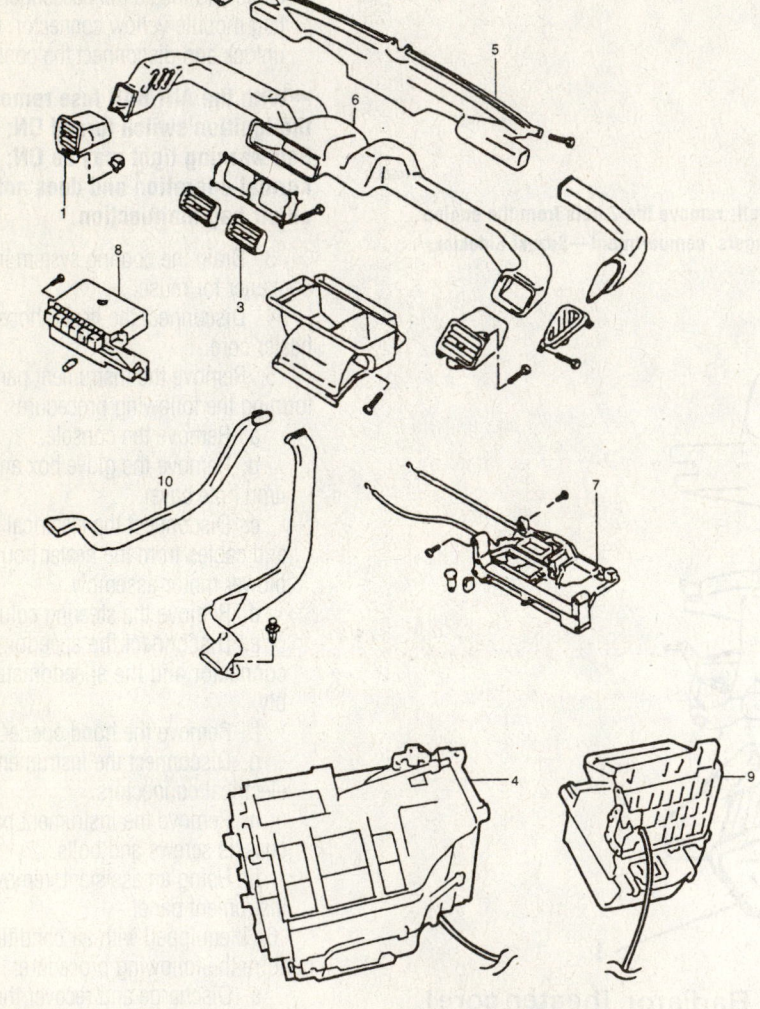

1. Side ventilator outlet
2. Side defroster outlet
3. Center ventilatior outlet
4. Heater unit
5. Defroster duct
6. Ventilator duct
7. Control lever
8. Mode control switch
9. Blower unit
10. Rear duct

93113GE9

Exploded view of the heater housing and ventilation ducts—Suzuki Vitara

housing. Plug the openings to prevent contamination.

c. If equipped with an H25 engine, disconnect the compressor suction pipe and receiver/drier outlet pipe from the air conditioning housing. Plug the openings to prevent contamination.

d. Remove the blower motor assembly.

e. Disconnect the thermistor wire coupler.

f. Remove the air conditioning housing.

7. Disconnect the rear duct from the heater housing.

8. Disconnect the mode actuator electrical connectors.

9. If equipped, remove the air conditioning controller.

10. If equipped, disconnect and remove the Sensing and Diagnostic Module (SDM) or air bag controller module.

11. Remove the heater housing.

12. Remove the heater core pipe clamps and grommet.

13. Remove the heater core from the heater housing.

To install:

14. Install the heater core to the heater housing.

15. Install the heater core pipe clamps and grommet.

16. Install the heater housing.

17. If equipped, connect and install the Sensing and Diagnostic Module (SDM) or air bag controller module.

18. If equipped, install the air conditioning controller.

19. Connect the mode actuator electrical connectors.

20. Connect the rear duct from the heater housing.

21. If equipped with air conditioning, perform the following procedure:

a. Install the air conditioning housing.

b. Connect the thermistor wire coupler.

c. Install the blower motor assembly.

d. If equipped with an H25 engine, connect the compressor suction pipe and receiver/drier outlet pipe to the air conditioning housing.

e. If equipped with a G16 or a J20 engine, connect the suction pipe and liquid pipe to the air conditioning housing.

f. Evacuate and charge the air conditioning system.

22. Install the instrument panel by performing the following procedure:

a. Using an assistant, install the instrument panel.

b. Install the instrument panel-to-chassis screws and bolts.

c. Connect the instrument panel electrical connectors.

d. Install the hood opener.

e. Connect the speedometer connector and the speedometer assembly.

f. Install the steering column.

g. Connect the electrical connector and cables to the heater housing and blower motor assembly.

h. Install the glove box and the column hole cover.

i. Install the console.

23. Connect the heater hoses to the heater core.

24. Refill the cooling system.

25. To enable the air bag system, perform the following procedure:

a. Push inward on the glove box while pushing the stopper located at both sides and connect the passenger's side air bag module yellow connector and lock it.

b. Under the steering column, connect the contact coil/combina-tion switch assembly's yellow connector.

c. In the fuse box, install the AIR BAG fuse.

d. Turn the ignition switch ON and verify that the AIR BAG warning light flashes 7 times and turns OFF; if the system does not operate as described, perform the Air Bad Diagnostic System Check.

26. Connect the negative battery cable.

27. Run the engine to normal operating temperatures; then, check the climate control operation and check for leaks.

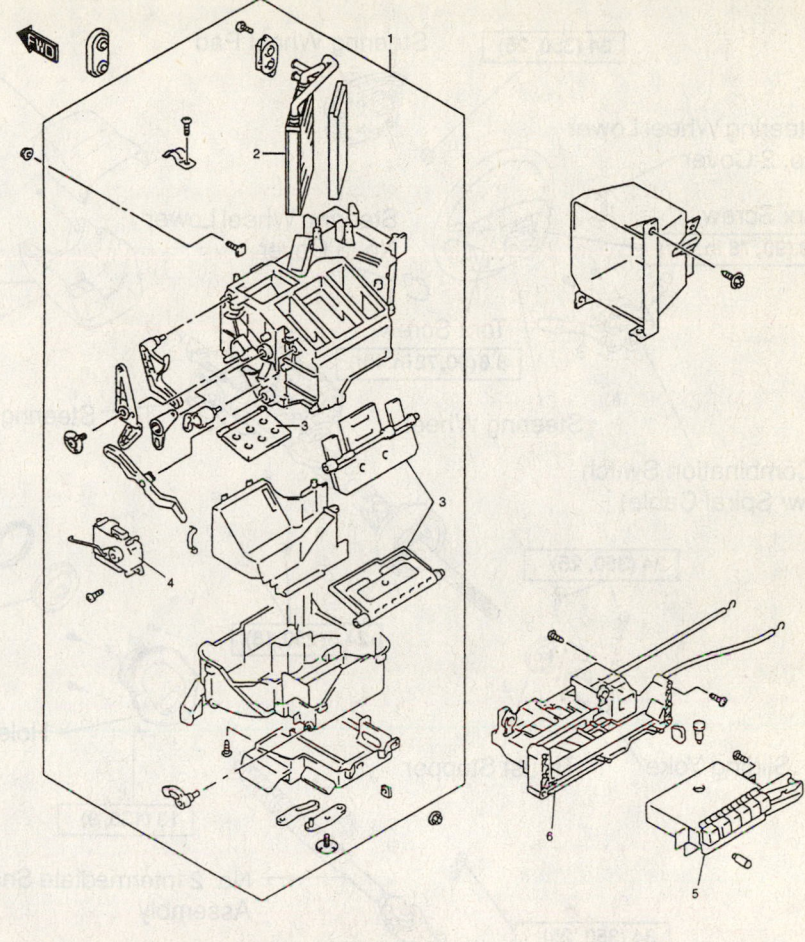

1. Heater assembly
2. Heater core
3. Damper
4. Mode actuator
5. Mode control switch
6. Control lever assembly

93113GE0

Exploded view of the heater core, heater housing and related components—Suzuki Vitara

TOYOTA

Land Cruiser

REMOVAL & INSTALLATION

Front Heater

1. Disconnect the negative battery cable.
2. Drain the cooling system into a clean container for reuse.
3. Disconnect the heater hoses from the heater core.
4. Remove the steering wheel by performing the following procedure:

a. Position the front wheels facing straight-ahead.

b. Remove the steering wheel side covers.

c. Using a Torx® wrench, loosen the 2 screws located at each side of the steering wheel until the screw's circumference groove catches on the screw case.

d. Pull the air bag module from the steering wheel and disconnect the electrical connector.

✳✳ CAUTION

Place the air bag module in a safe place with the front side facing upward.

e. Remove the steering wheel nut.

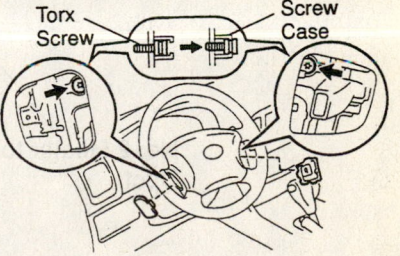

93113GG4

View the steering wheel's Torx® bolts—Toyota Land Cruiser

Refer to the model specific sections for engine mechanical service procedures

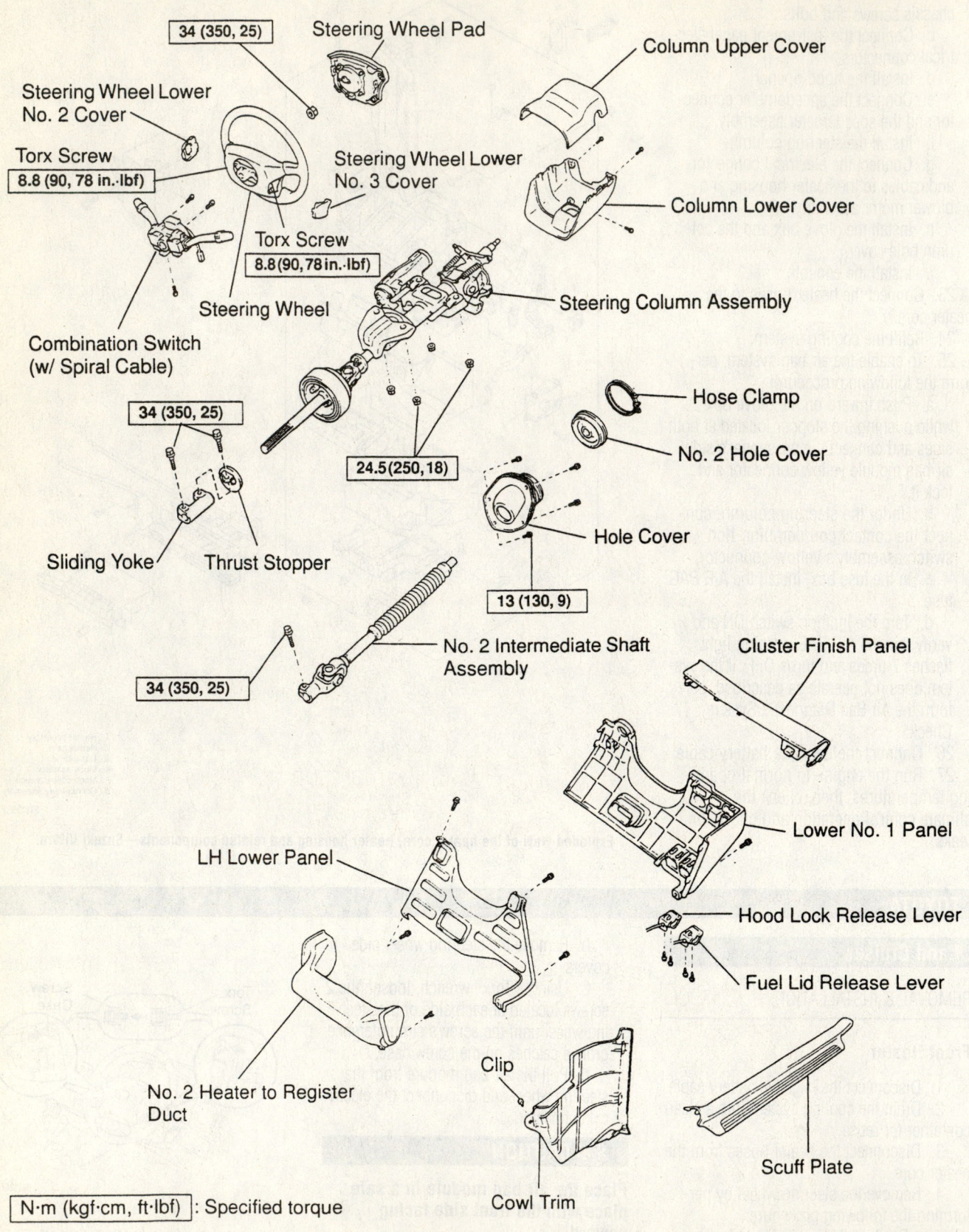

34 (350, 25)

Steering Wheel Pad

Column Upper Cover

Steering Wheel Lower No. 2 Cover

Torx Screw
8.8 (90, 78 in.·lbf)

Steering Wheel Lower No. 3 Cover

Column Lower Cover

Torx Screw
8.8 (90, 78 in.·lbf)

Steering Wheel

Steering Column Assembly

Combination Switch (w/ Spiral Cable)

Hose Clamp

No. 2 Hole Cover

34 (350, 25)

24.5 (250, 18)

Hole Cover

Sliding Yoke

Thrust Stopper

13 (130, 9)

34 (350, 25)

No. 2 Intermediate Shaft Assembly

Cluster Finish Panel

Lower No. 1 Panel

LH Lower Panel

Hood Lock Release Lever

Fuel Lid Release Lever

No. 2 Heater to Register Duct

Clip

Scuff Plate

Cowl Trim

N·m (kgf·cm, ft·lbf) : Specified torque

93113GG5

Exploded view the steering column—Toyota Land Cruiser (Part 1 of 2)

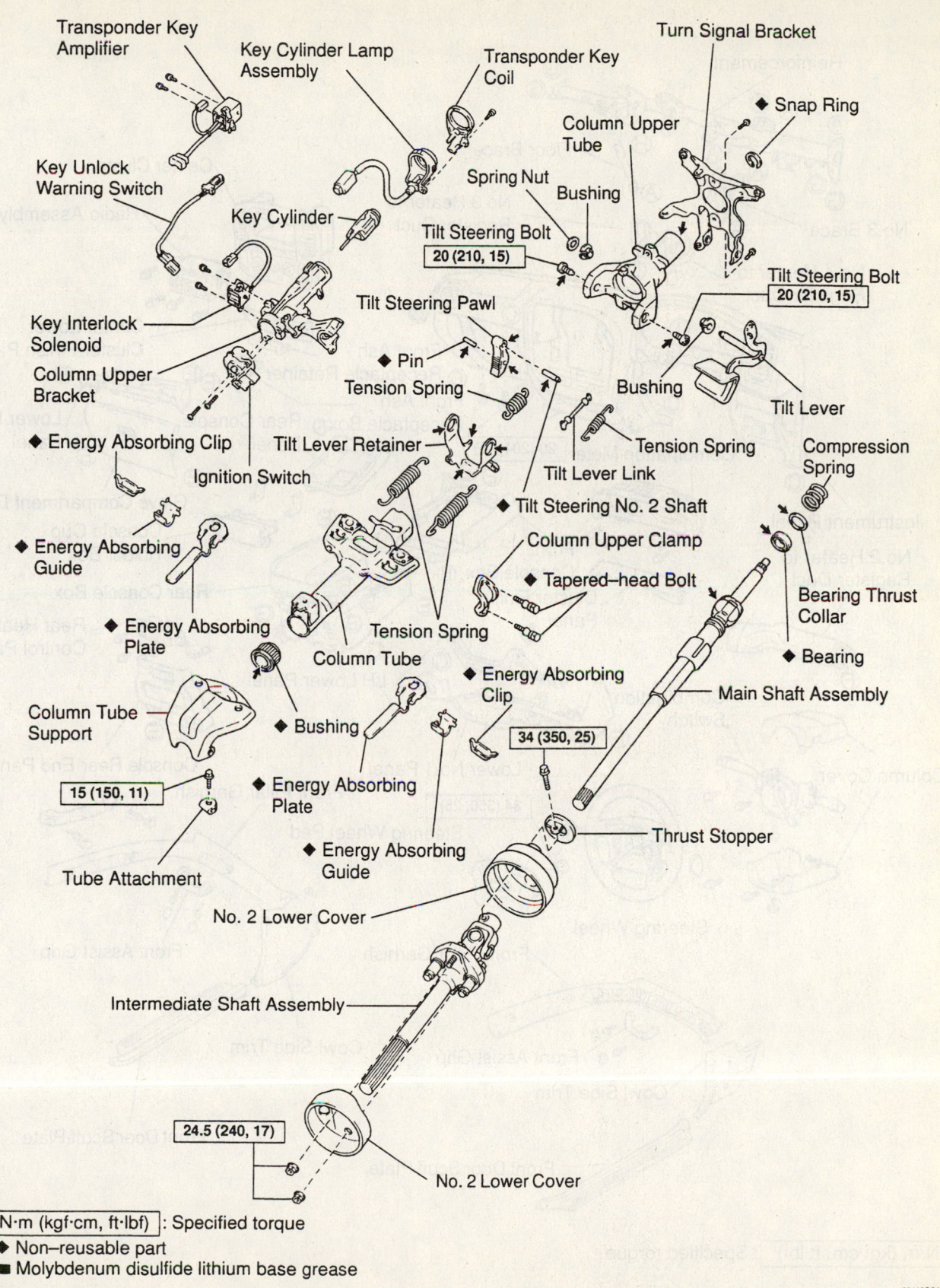

Transponder Key Amplifier

Key Cylinder Lamp Assembly

Transponder Key Coil

Turn Signal Bracket

◆ Snap Ring

Column Upper Tube

Key Unlock Warning Switch

Spring Nut

Bushing

Key Cylinder

Tilt Steering Bolt
20 (210, 15)

Tilt Steering Bolt
20 (210, 15)

Tilt Steering Pawl

Key Interlock Solenoid

◆ Pin

Tension Spring

Bushing

Tilt Lever

Column Upper Bracket

◆ Energy Absorbing Clip

Tilt Lever Retainer

Tension Spring

Compression Spring

Ignition Switch

Tilt Lever Link

◆ Energy Absorbing Guide

◆ Tilt Steering No. 2 Shaft

Column Upper Clamp

◆ Energy Absorbing Plate

◆ Tapered–head Bolt

Bearing Thrust Collar

Tension Spring

◆ Bearing

Column Tube Support

Column Tube

◆ Energy Absorbing Clip

Main Shaft Assembly

◆ Bushing

34 (350, 25)

15 (150, 11)

◆ Energy Absorbing Plate

Thrust Stopper

Tube Attachment

◆ Energy Absorbing Guide

No. 2 Lower Cover

Intermediate Shaft Assembly

24.5 (240, 17)

No. 2 Lower Cover

N·m (kgf·cm, ft·lbf) : Specified torque

◆ Non–reusable part

Molybdenum disulfide lithium base grease

93113GG6

Exploded view the steering column—Toyota Land Cruiser (Part 2 of 2)

Refer to the model specific sections for cooling system service procedures

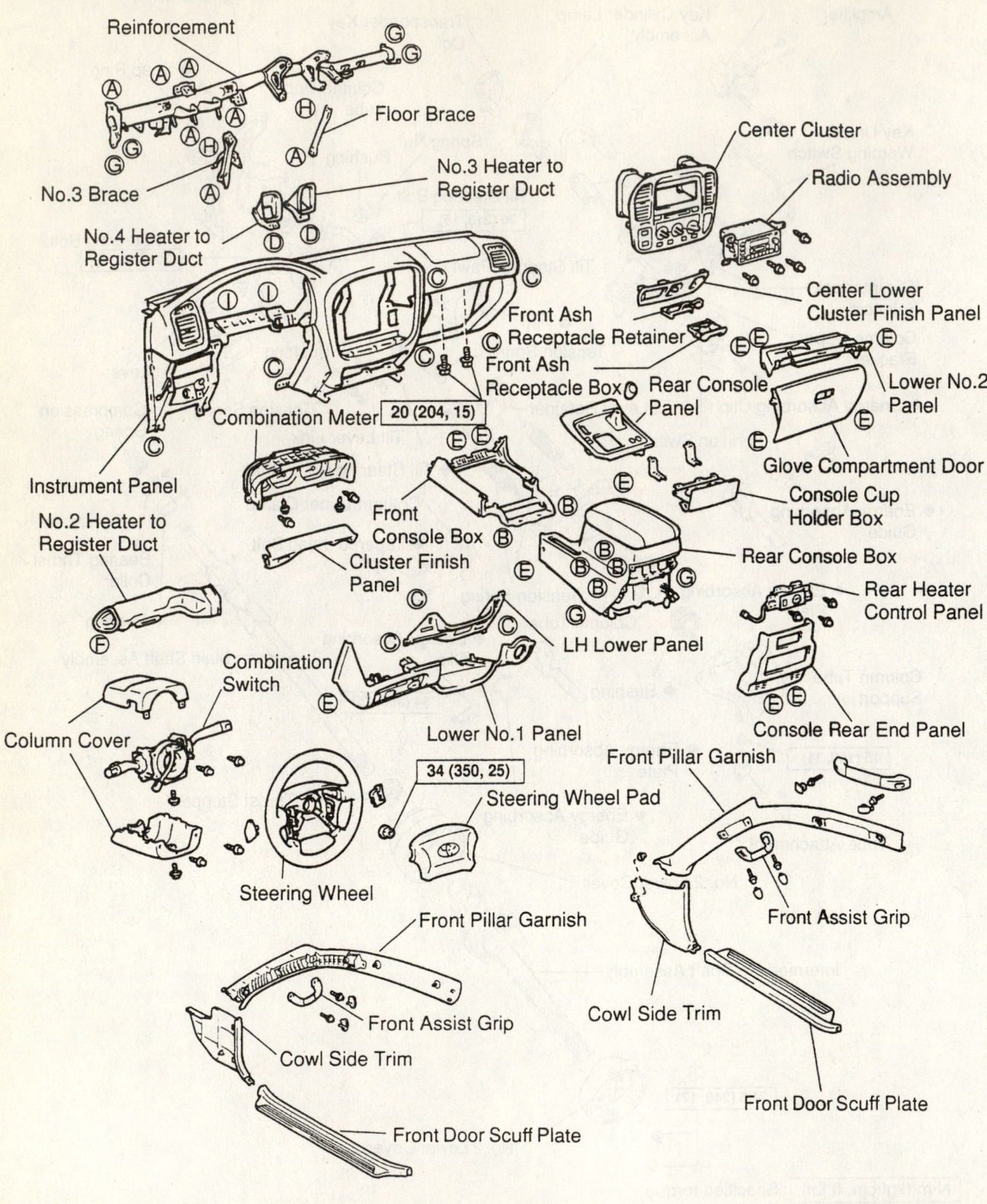

Reinforcement

No.3 Brace

No.4 Heater to Register Duct

Floor Brace

No.3 Heater to Register Duct

Center Cluster

Radio Assembly

Center Lower Cluster Finish Panel

Front Ash Receptacle Retainer

Front Ash Receptacle Box

Lower No.2 Panel

Glove Compartment Door

Rear Console Panel

Combination Meter   20 (204, 15)

Console Cup Holder Box

Instrument Panel

No.2 Heater to Register Duct

Front Console Box

Cluster Finish Panel

Rear Console Box

LH Lower Panel

Rear Heater Control Panel

Combination Switch

Column Cover

Lower No.1 Panel

34 (350, 25)

Steering Wheel Pad

Console Rear End Panel

Front Pillar Garnish

Front Assist Grip

Steering Wheel

Front Pillar Garnish

Cowl Side Trim

Front Door Scuff Plate

Front Assist Grip

Cowl Side Trim

Front Door Scuff Plate

N·m (kgf·cm, ft·lbf) : Specified torque

93113GG7

Exploded view the instrument panel and related components—Toyota Land Cruiser

f. Place alignment marks on the steering wheel and the main shaft.

g. Using a steering wheel puller, press the steering wheel from the steering column.

5. Remove the instrument panel and reinforcement by performing the following procedure:

a. Remove the front door scuff plates, the cowl side trim and the front door opening trim.

b. At the driver's side, remove the 2 assist grip plugs, the 2 screws and assist grip and the front pillar garnish.

c. At the passenger's side, remove the 4 assist grip plugs, the 4 screws, the 2 assist grips and the front pillar garnish.

d. Remove the instrument cluster finish panel.

e. Remove the 2 screws and the hood lock control cable.

f. Remove the 2 screws and the fuel lid control cable lever.

g. Remove the lower No. 1 panel screw and the panel.

h. Remove the lower left side panel.

i. Remove the 3 steering column cover screws and the covers.

j. At the steering column, disconnect the electrical connectors; then, remove the clamp, the 3 screws and the combination switch.

k. Remove the No. 2 heater-to-register duct screw and the duct.

l. Remove the steering column-to-

instrument panel bolts and the steering column.

m. At the combination meter, disconnect the electrical connectors; then, remove the 4 screws and the combination meter.

n. Remove the glove compartment door stoppers, the 2 screws and the glove box door.

o. At the passenger's side air bag module, remove the No. 1 undercover, pull the air bag connector up from the undercover and disconnect it; then, remove the air bag.

※※ CAUTION

Place the air bag module in a safe place with the front side facing upward.

p. Remove the 3 lower No. 2 panel screws and the panel.

q. Remove the center cluster; then, pry the center cluster from the dash by prying the 8 clips in the following order:
- Left side
- Right side
- Top left side
- Top right side

r. Remove the 4 radio screws, pull the radio outward, disconnect the electrical connectors and remove the radio.

s. At the rear console panel, remove the transfer shift lever knob. Pry the panel upward disengaging the 4 clips (2 on each side) and remove the panel.

t. At the rear of the console, remove the 2 rear end panel-to-console screws; then, pry the end panel rearward disengaging the 2 clips and remove the panel.

u. If not equipped with a rear air conditioning system, disconnect the connector and control cable; then, remove the 3 rear heater control panel screws and the panel.

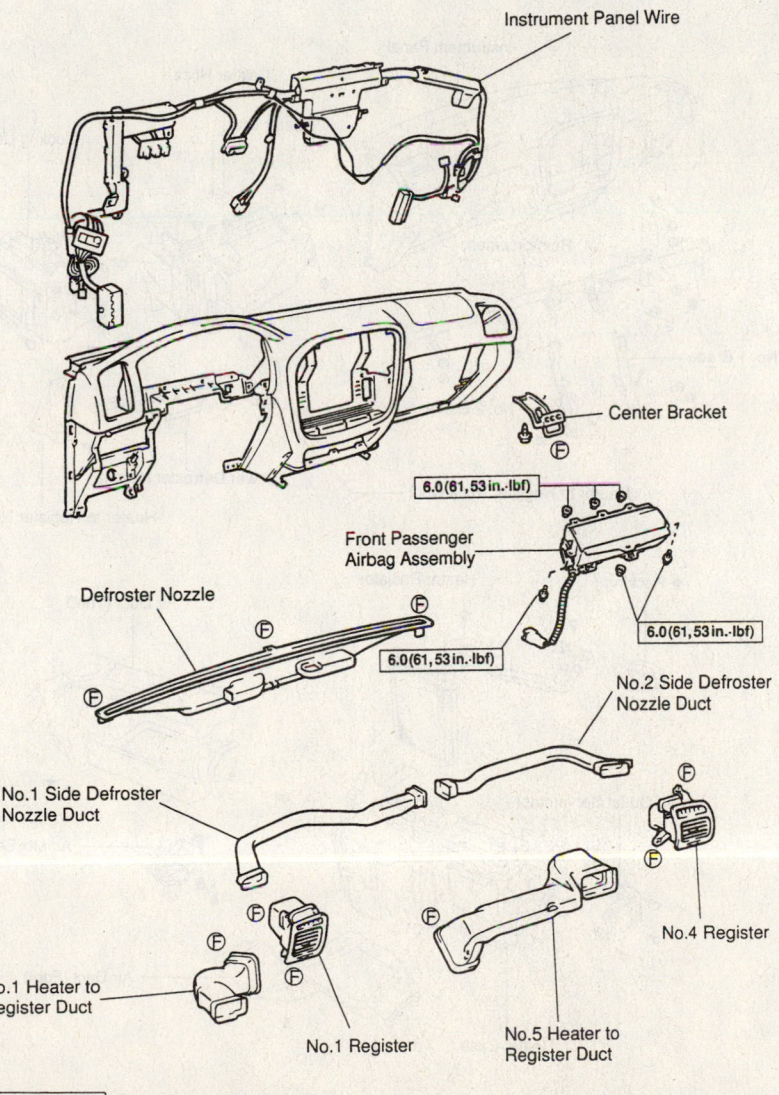

Instrument Panel Wire

Center Bracket

6.0 (61, 53 in.-lbf)

Front Passenger Airbag Assembly

6.0 (61, 53 in.-lbf)

Defroster Nozzle

6.0 (61, 53 in.-lbf)

No.2 Side Defroster Nozzle Duct

No.1 Side Defroster Nozzle Duct

No.4 Register

No.1 Heater to Register Duct

No.1 Register

No.5 Heater to Register Duct

N·m (kgf·cm, ft·lbf) : Specified torque

93113GG8

Exploded view the front ventilation ducts and related components—Toyota Land Cruiser

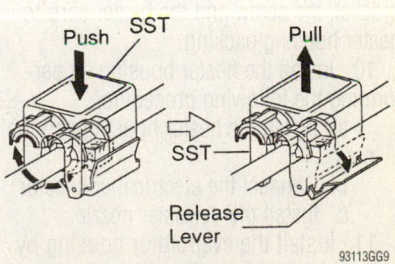

Push   SST   Pull

SST

Release Lever

93113GG9

View the air conditioning line clamp removal tool—Toyota Land Cruiser

For complete service labor times order Nichols' Chilton Labor Guide Manual

v. Remove the 4 rear console box-to-chassis screws/bolts and the console box.

w. Remove the center lower cluster finish panel by prying panel rearward disengaging the 5 clips; then, disconnect the electrical connector.

x. Remove the 2 front console-to-chassis bolts/screws, disengage the 2 clips and remove the console.

y. At the instrument panel, disconnect the junction connectors (the connectors can be disconnected by loosening the bolts), the instrument panel-to-chassis 8 bolts and 2 nuts. Using an assistant, remove the instrument panel.

z. Disconnect the electrical connector and remove the ECM.

aa. Remove the No. 3 and No. 4 heater-to-register ducts.

bb. Remove the floor brace, the No. 1 brace and the reinforcement.

6. Remove the evaporator housing by performing the following procedure:

a. Discharge and recover the air conditioning system refrigerant.

b. Remove the air conditioning liquid line clamp.

c. Remove the air conditioning suction line clamp.

d. Disconnect both air conditioning lines and plug the openings to prevent contamination. Discard the 4 O-rings.

e. Remove the antenna relay electrical connector, the 2 screws and the relay.

f. Remove the evaporator housing-to-chassis 4 screws/2 nuts and the housing.

7. Remove the heater housing by performing the following procedure:

a. Remove the defroster nozzle.

b. Disconnect the electrical connector.

c. Remove the 4 nuts and the heater housing.

8. Remove the heater core-to-heater housing packing, the screw, the bracket, the clamp and the heater core.

To install:

9. Install the heater core, the clamp, the bracket, the screw and the heater core-to-heater housing packing.

10. Install the heater housing by performing the following procedure:

a. Install the heater housing and the 4 nuts.

b. Connect the electrical connector.

c. Install the defroster nozzle.

11. Install the evaporator housing by performing the following procedure:

a. Install the evaporator housing and the housing-to-chassis 4 screws and 2 nuts.

b. Install the antenna relay, the 2 screws and the electrical connector.

c. Using new O-rings, connect both air conditioning lines.

d. Install the air conditioning liquid line and suction line clamp.

12. Install the instrument panel and reinforcement by performing the following procedure:

a. Install the reinforcement, the No. 1 brace and the floor brace.

b. Install the No. 3 and No. 4 heater-to-register ducts.

c. Install the ECM and connect the electrical connector.

d. Using an assistant, install the instrument panel, connect the junction connectors, the instrument panel-to-chassis 8 bolts and 2 nuts.

e. Install the front the console, engage the 2 clips and install the 2 console-to-chassis bolts/screws.

f. Connect the electrical connector; then, install the center lower cluster finish panel by engaging the 5 clips.

g. Install the console box and the 4 rear console box-to-chassis screws/bolts.

h. If not equipped with a rear air conditioning system, install rear heater control panel, the 3 panel screws; then, connect the connector and control cable.

i. Install the rear of the console and engage the 2 clips; then, install the 2 rear end panel-to-console screws.

j. Install the rear console panel and engage the 4 clips (2 on each side); then, install the transfer shift lever knob.

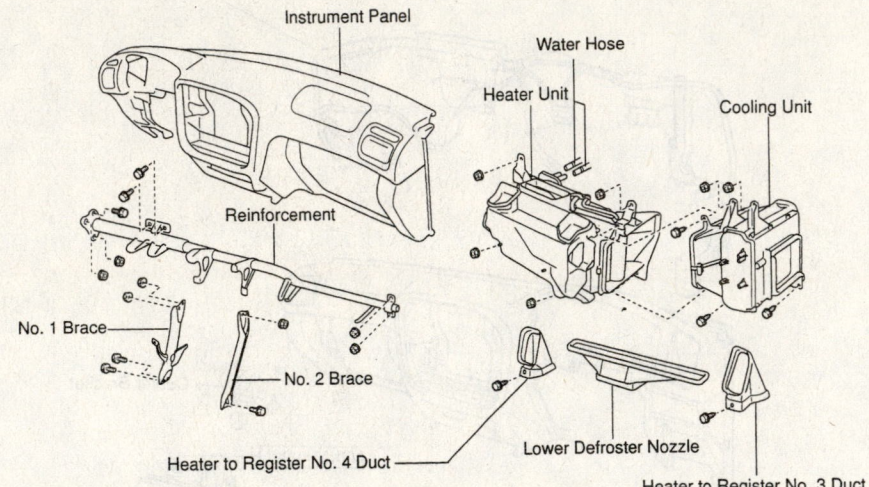

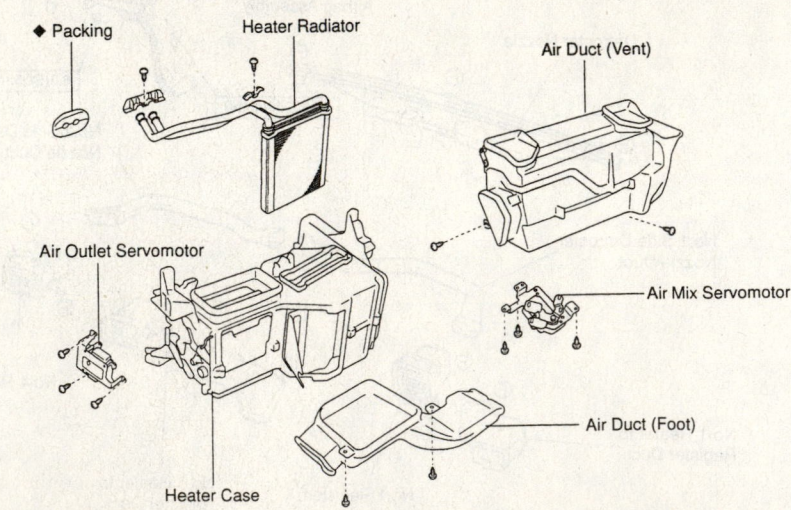

♦ Non-reusable part

93113GG0

Exploded view of the front heater core, heater housing, evaporator housing and related components—Toyota Land Cruiser

k. Install the radio, connect the electrical connectors and the 4 radio screws.

l. Install the center cluster and engage the 8 center cluster clips.

m. Install the lower No. 2 panel and the 3 panel screws.

n. Install the passenger's side air bag module, connect it and install the No. 1 undercover.

o. Install the glove box door, the 2 screws and the glove compartment door stoppers.

p. Install the combination meter and the 4 screws; then, connect the electrical connectors.

q. Install the steering column and the steering column-to-instrument panel bolts.

r. Install the No. 2 heater-to-register duct and the duct screw.

s. At the steering column, install the combination switch, the 3 screws and the clamp; then, connect the electrical connectors.

t. Install the steering column covers and the 3 covers screws.

u. Install the lower left side panel.

v. Install the lower No. 1 panel and the panel screw.

w. Install the fuel lid control cable lever and the 2 screws.

x. Install the hood lock control cable and the 2 screws.

y. Install the instrument cluster finish panel.

z. At the passenger's side, install the front pillar garnish, the 2 assist grips, the 4 screws and the 4 assist grip plugs.

aa. At the driver's side, install the front pillar garnish, assist grip, the 2 screws and the 2 assist grip plugs.

bb. Install the front door scuff plates, the cowl side trim and the front door opening trim.

13. Install the steering wheel by performing the following procedure:

a. Install the steering wheel to the steering column.

b. Align the steering wheel-to-main shaft marks.

c. Install the steering wheel nut and torque to 25 ft. lbs. (34 Nm).

d. Install the air bag module to the steering wheel and connect the electrical connector.

e. Using a Torx® wrench, tighten the 2 screws located at each side of the steering wheel to 78 inch lbs. (8.8 Nm).

f. Install the steering wheel side covers.

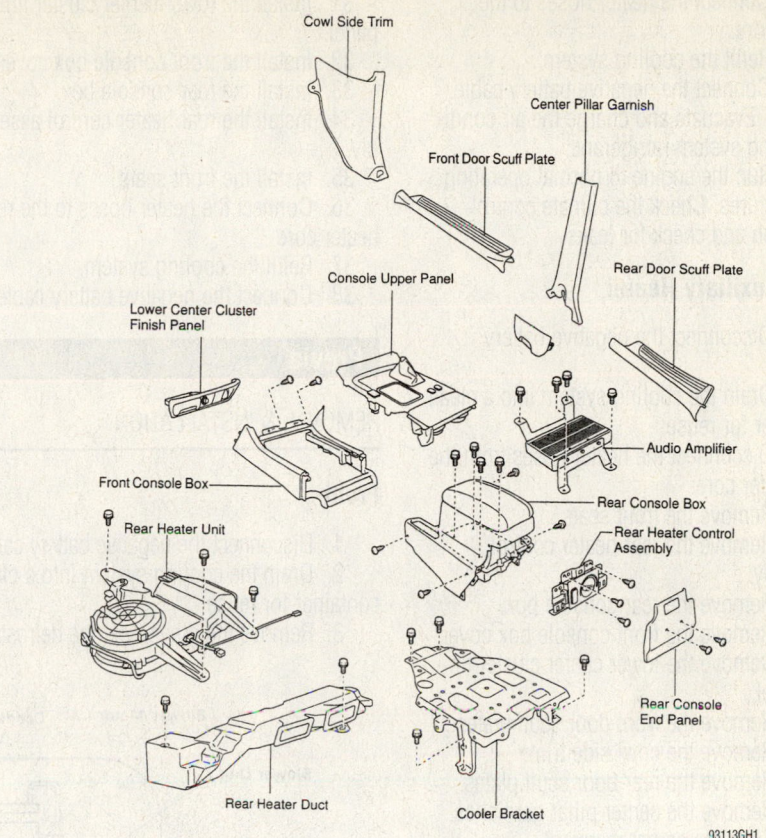

Exploded view of the rear heater housing and related components—Toyota Land Cruiser

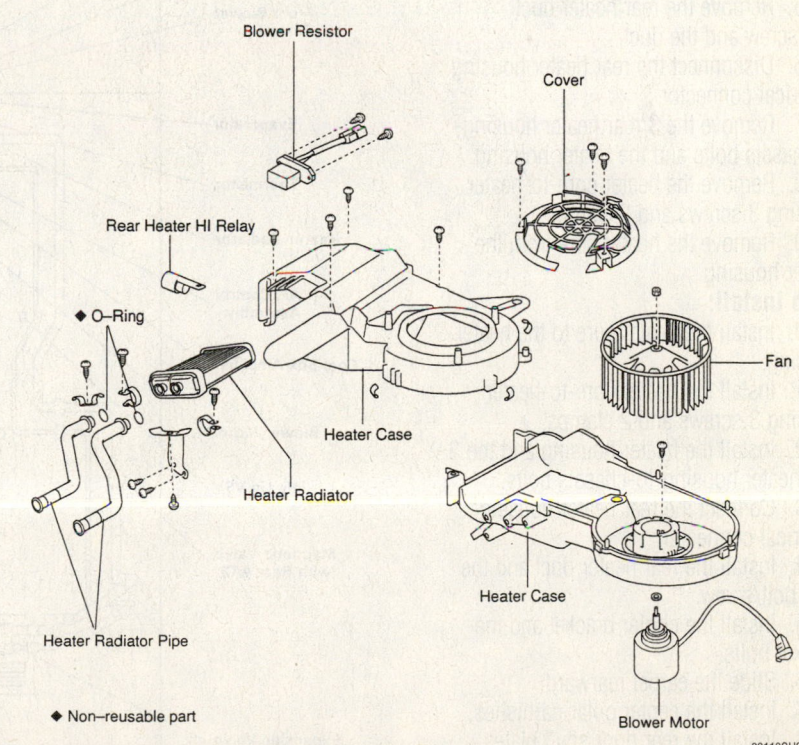

Exploded view of the rear heater core, heater housing and related components—Toyota Land Cruiser

14. Connect the heater hoses to the heater core.

15. Refill the cooling system.

16. Connect the negative battery cable.

a. Evacuate and charge the air conditioning system refrigerant.

17. Run the engine to normal operating temperatures. Check the climate control operation and check for leaks.

Rear Auxiliary Heater

1. Disconnect the negative battery cable.

2. Drain the cooling system into a clean container for reuse.

3. Disconnect the heater hoses from the rear heater core.

4. Remove the front seats.

5. Remove the rear heater control assembly.

6. Remove the rear console box.

7. Remove the front console box cover.

8. Remove the lower center cluster finish panel.

9. Remove the front door scuff plates.

10. Remove the cowl side trim.

11. Remove the rear door scuff plates.

12. Remove the center pillar garnishes.

13. Slide the carpet rearward.

14. Remove the cooler bracket bolts and the bracket.

15. Remove the rear heater duct bolt/screw and the duct.

16. Disconnect the rear heater housing electrical connector.

17. Remove the 3 rear heater housing-to-chassis bolts and the heater housing.

18. Remove the heater core-to-heater housing 3 screws and 2 clamps.

19. Remove the heater core from the heater housing.

To install:

20. Install the heater core to the heater housing.

21. Install the heater core-to-heater housing 3 screws and 2 clamps.

22. Install the heater housing and the 3 rear heater housing-to-chassis bolts.

23. Connect the rear heater housing electrical connector.

24. Install the rear heater duct and the duct bolt/screw.

25. Install the cooler bracket and the bracket bolts.

26. Slide the carpet rearward.

27. Install the center pillar garnishes.

28. Install the rear door scuff plates.

29. Install the cowl side trim.

30. Install the front door scuff plates.

31. Install the lower center cluster finish panel.

32. Install the front console box cover.

33. Install the rear console box.

34. Install the rear heater control assembly.

35. Install the front seats.

36. Connect the heater hoses to the rear heater core.

37. Refill the cooling system.

38. Connect the negative battery cable.

Previa

REMOVAL & INSTALLATION

Front

1. Disconnect the negative battery cable.

2. Drain the cooling system into a clean container for reuse.

3. Remove the glove box, the defroster hoses, the air damper, the air duct and the 2 defroster ducts.

4. Remove the control unit from the instrument panel.

5. Remove the blower motor.

6. Disconnect any necessary electrical connectors.

7. If equipped with air conditioning, it may be necessary to remove the air conditioning evaporator by performing the following procedure:

a. Discharge and recover the air conditioning refrigerant.

b. Disconnect the suction and liquid lines from the evaporator.

c. Remove the 2 nuts, the bolt and the cover from the evaporator.

d. Remove the evaporator.

8. Disconnect the heater hoses from the heater core tubes.

9. Remove the retaining bolts and lift out the heater unit.

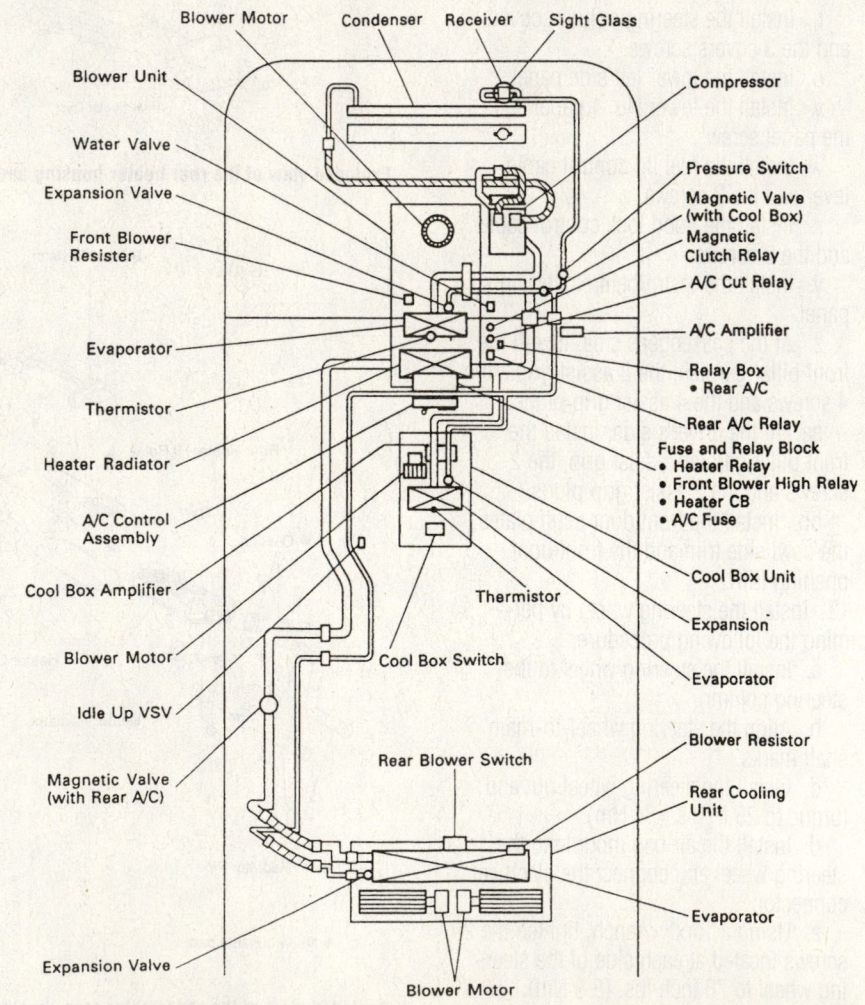

View of the heating/air conditioning system and related components—Toyota Previa

93113G73

10. Remove the heater core from the heater unit.

To install:

11. Install the heater core to the heater unit.

12. Install the heater unit and the retaining bolts.

13. Connect the heater hoses to the heater core tubes.

14. If equipped with air conditioning, install the air conditioning evaporator by performing the following procedure:

  a. Install the cover and the 2 nuts and bolt to the evaporator.

  b. Using new gaskets, connect the suction and liquid lines to the evaporator.

15. Connect any necessary electrical connectors.

16. Install the blower motor.

17. Install the control unit to the instrument panel.

18. Install the 2 defroster ducts, the air duct, the air damper, the defroster hoses and the glove box.

19. Refill the cooling system.

20. Connect the negative battery cable.

21. Evacuate and charge the air conditioning system.

22. Run the engine to normal operating temperatures; then, check the climate control operation and check for leaks.

Rear

NIPPONDENSO

1. Disconnect the negative battery cable and wait at least 90 seconds to proceed working on the vehicle.

2. Remove the right and left air inlet grilles and air outlet grilles.

3. Remove the filter.

4. Unbolt and remove the lower case.

5. Disengage the rear air conditioning switch.

6. Extract the evaporator assembly.

7. Remove the right and left blower motor assemblies.

8. Remove the blower resistor.

9. Disassemble the blower motor assemblies to access the motors.

To install:

10. Assemble the blower motor assemblies.

11. Install the blower resistor to the upper case.

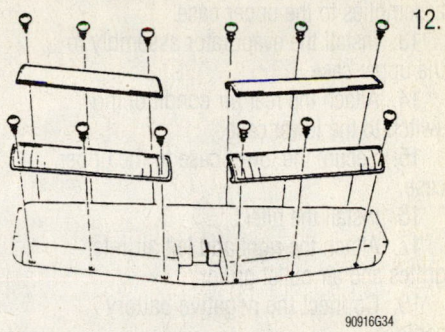

90916G34

Unscrew and remove the right and left suction grilles—1997 Toyota Previa

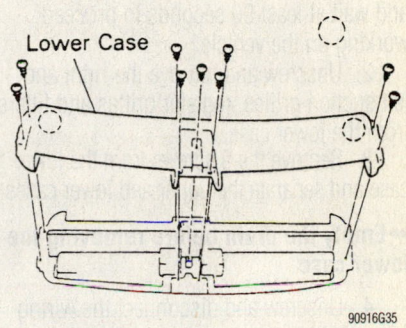

90916G35

Remove the 9 screws from the lower case and extract the case—1997 Toyota Previa

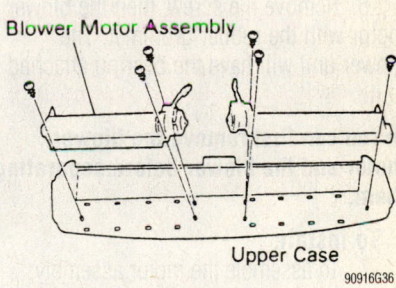

90916G36

Unbolt and extract the 2 blower motor assemblies from the upper case—1997 Toyota Previa

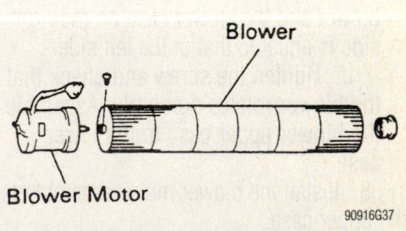

90916G37

Fig. 36 Remove the screw then extract the motor with rubber mount—1997 Toyota Previa

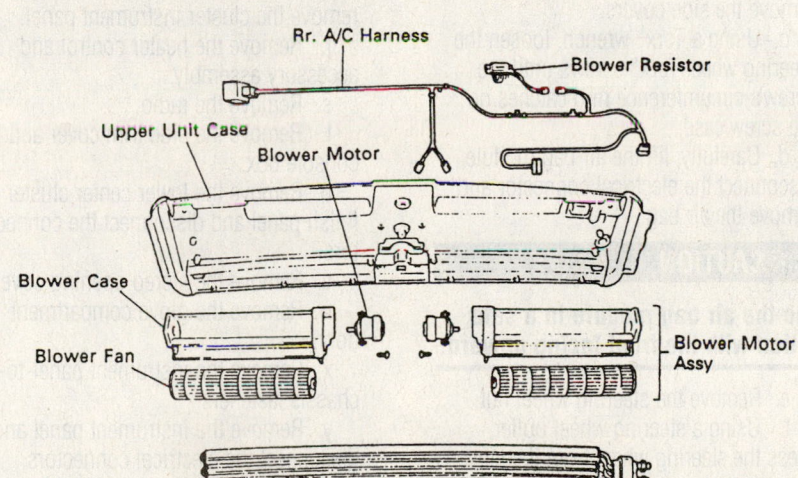

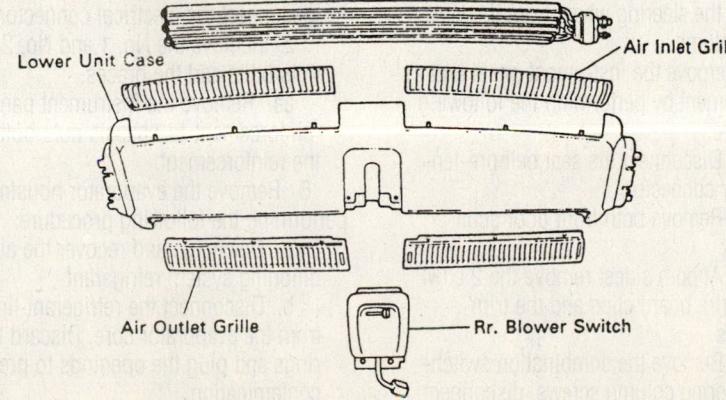

90916G21

Exploded view of the common rear heating and cooling unit—1997 Toyota Previa

Refer to the model specific sections for engine mechanical service procedures

Install the right and left blower motor assemblies to the upper case.

13. Install the evaporator assembly to the upper case.

14. Attach the rear air conditioning switch to the lower case.

15. Secure the lower case to the upper case.

16. Install the filter.

17. Attach the right and left air inlet grilles and air outlet grilles.

18. Connect the negative battery cable.

PANASONIC

1. Disconnect the negative battery cable and wait at least 90 seconds to proceed working on the vehicle.

2. Unscrew and remove the right and left suction grilles, register grilles and filters from the lower case.

3. Remove the 9 screws from the lower case and separate the upper and lower cases.

➡ **Empty the drain before removing the lower case.**

4. Unscrew and disconnect the wiring from the blower motor assemblies, then extract them.

5. Disengage the 8 pawls of the blower case and separate the blower motor assembly into an upper and lower piece.

6. Remove the screw, then the blower motor with the rubber grommet. The blower unit will have the bearing attached to it.

➡ **You can first remove the blower motor and the blower before separating them.**

To install:

7. To assemble the motor assembly:

a. Temporarily secure the blower to the blower motor.

b. Place the blower motor unit on the blower lower case.

c. Visually adjust the blower protrusion so that the clearance between the blower and the blower case on the right side is equal to that of the left side.

d. Tighten the screw and check that the blower rotates smoothly. Assemble the blower upper case to the lower case.

8. Install the blower motor assembly to the upper case.

9. Install the lower case and secure it to the upper case.

10. install the right and left air filters to the lower case.

11. Install the right and left suction grills, and the register grill to the lower case.

12. Connect the negative battery cable.

RAV4

REMOVAL & INSTALLATION

1. Disconnect the negative battery cable.

❄❄ CAUTION

After the negative battery cable has been disconnected, wait at least 1½ minutes for the air bag module to deplete its energy.

2. Drain the cooling system into a clean container for reuse.

3. Disconnect the heater hoses from the heater core.

4. Remove the steering wheel by performing the following procedure:

a. Position the front wheels in the straight-ahead position.

b. At both sides of the steering wheel, remove the side covers.

c. Using a Torx® wrench, loosen the steering wheel Torx® screws until the screw's circumference ring catches on the screw case.

d. Carefully, lift the air bag module, disconnect the electrical connector and remove the air bag.

❄❄ CAUTION

Place the air bag module in a safe location with the front facing upward.

e. Remove the steering wheel nut.

f. Using a steering wheel puller, press the steering wheel from the steering column.

5. Remove the instrument panel and reinforcement by performing the following procedure:

a. Disconnect the seat belt pre-tensioner connector.

b. Remove both front door scuff plates.

c. At both sides, remove the 2 cowl side trim board clips and the trim boards.

d. Remove the combination switch-to-steering column screws, disconnect the electrical connectors and remove the combination switch.

e. Remove the 4 steering column cover screws and the cover.

f. Remove the cluster finish panel screw and the panel.

g. Remove the 4 combination meter screws, disconnect the electrical connectors and the meter.

h. Remove the hood lock release lever.

i. Remove the 2 lower finish panel screws and the panel.

j. For USA models, remove the lower panel insert.

k. Remove the No. 2 heater-to-register duct.

l. Remove the steering column-to-instrument panel nuts/bolts and the lower steering column bolt; then carefully, remove the steering column.

m. Remove the 2 center cluster finish panel screws and the panel.

n. Pull off the heater control knobs.

➡ **For Canada models, remove the 2 screws.**

o. Pry off the heater control name plate and the cluster instrument panel.

p. Remove the 3 heater control assembly screws and the assembly.

q. Disconnect the connectors and remove the cluster instrument panel.

r. Remove the heater control and accessory assembly.

s. Remove the radio.

t. Remove the side trim cover and the console box.

u. Remove the lower center cluster finish panel and disconnect the connectors.

v. Remove the stereo opening cover.

w. Remove the glove compartment door.

x. Remove the instrument panel-to-chassis fasteners.

y. Remove the instrument panel and disconnect the electrical connectors.

z. Remove the No. 1 and No. 2 brace nuts/bolts and the braces.

aa. Remove the instrument panel reinforcement-to-chassis nuts/bolts and the reinforcement.

6. Remove the evaporator housing by performing the following procedure:

a. Discharge and recover the air conditioning system refrigerant.

b. Disconnect the refrigerant lines from the evaporator core. Discard the O-rings and plug the openings to prevent contamination.

c. Disconnect the electrical connectors.

d. Remove the 3 evaporator housing-to-chassis nuts/bolts and the housing.

7. Remove the rear heater duct from the heater housing.

8. Remove the heater housing-to-chassis nuts and the housing.

9. Remove the 2 defroster nozzle-to-heater housing screws and the nozzle.

10. Remove the 2 heater core-to-heater housing screws, clamps and the heater core.

To install:

11. Install the heater core and the 2 heater core-to-heater housing screws and clamps.

12. Install the defroster nozzle and the 2 nozzle-to-heater housing screws.

13. Install the heater housing and the housing-to-chassis nuts.

14. Install the rear heater duct to the heater housing.

15. Install the evaporator housing by performing the following procedure:

a. Install the evaporator housing and the 3 housing-to-chassis nuts/bolts.

b. Connect the electrical connectors.

c. Using new O-rings, connect the refrigerant lines to the evaporator core.

16. Install the instrument panel and reinforcement by performing the following procedure:

a. Install the instrument panel reinforcement and the reinforcement-to-chassis nuts/bolts.

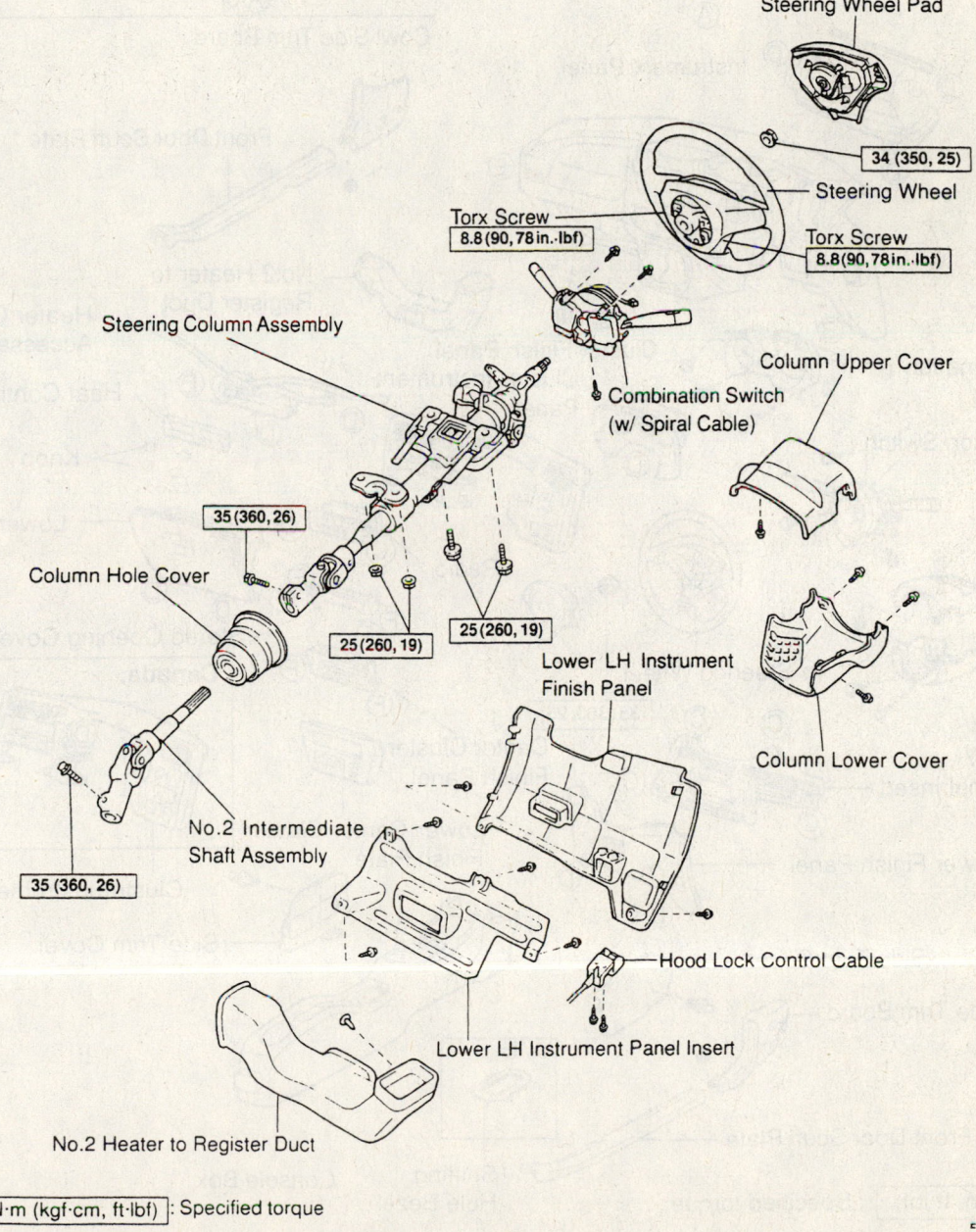

Exploded view of the steering wheel, air bag module, steering column and related components—Toyota RAV4

Refer to the model specific sections for cooling system service procedures

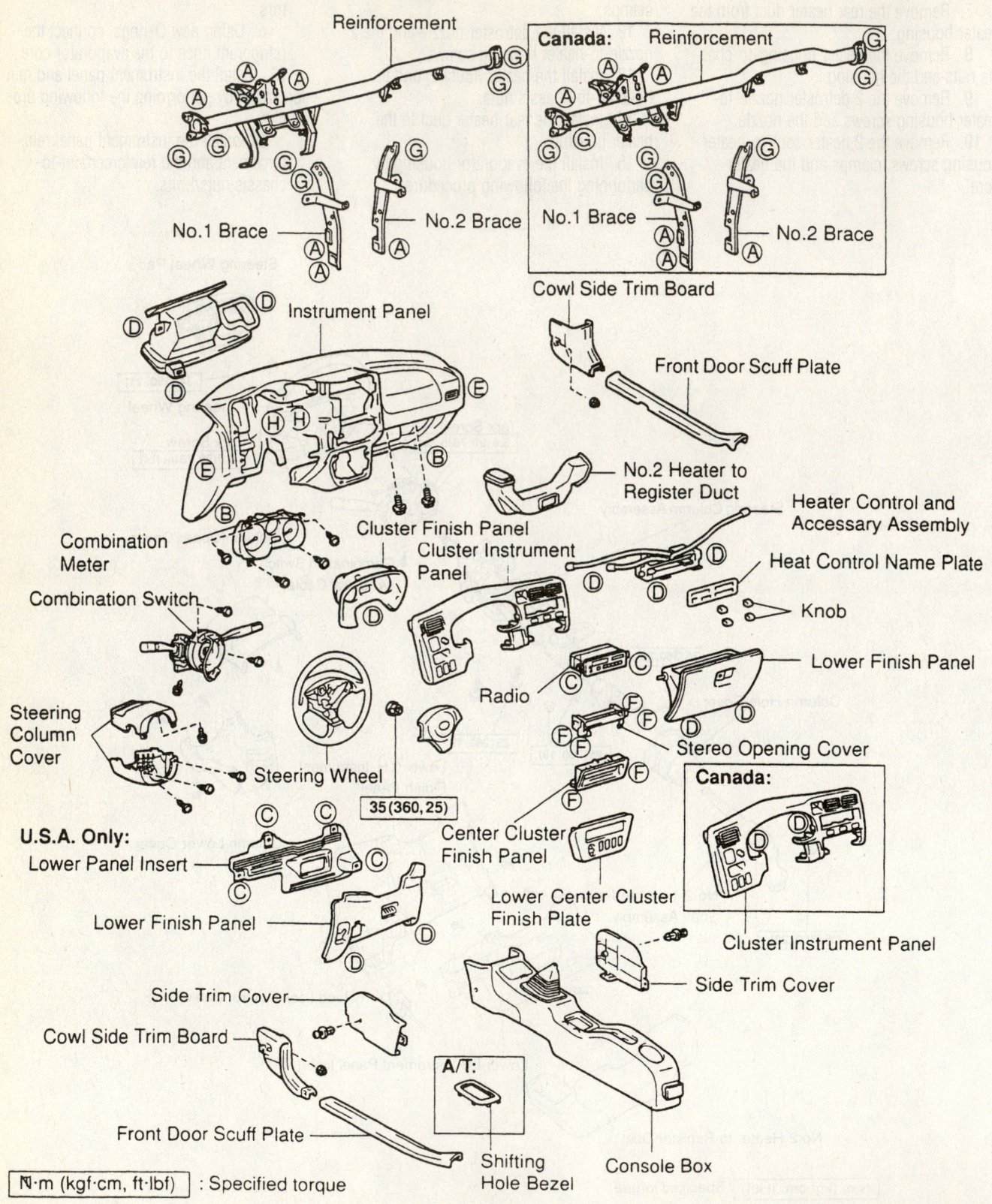

Reinforcement

Canada: Reinforcement

No.1 Brace

No.2 Brace

No.1 Brace

No.2 Brace

Cowl Side Trim Board

Front Door Scuff Plate

Instrument Panel

No.2 Heater to Register Duct

Heater Control and Accessary Assembly

Combination Meter

Cluster Finish Panel
Cluster Instrument Panel

Heat Control Name Plate

Knob

Combination Switch

Lower Finish Panel

Steering Column Cover

Radio

Steering Wheel

35 (360, 25)

Stereo Opening Cover

Canada:

U.S.A. Only:

Center Cluster Finish Panel

Lower Panel Insert

Lower Center Cluster Finish Plate

Cluster Instrument Panel

Lower Finish Panel

Side Trim Cover

Side Trim Cover

Cowl Side Trim Board

A/T:

Console Box

Front Door Scuff Plate

Shifting Hole Bezel

N·m (kgf·cm, ft·lbf) : Specified torque

93113GK5

Exploded view of the instrument panel and related components—Toyota RAV4

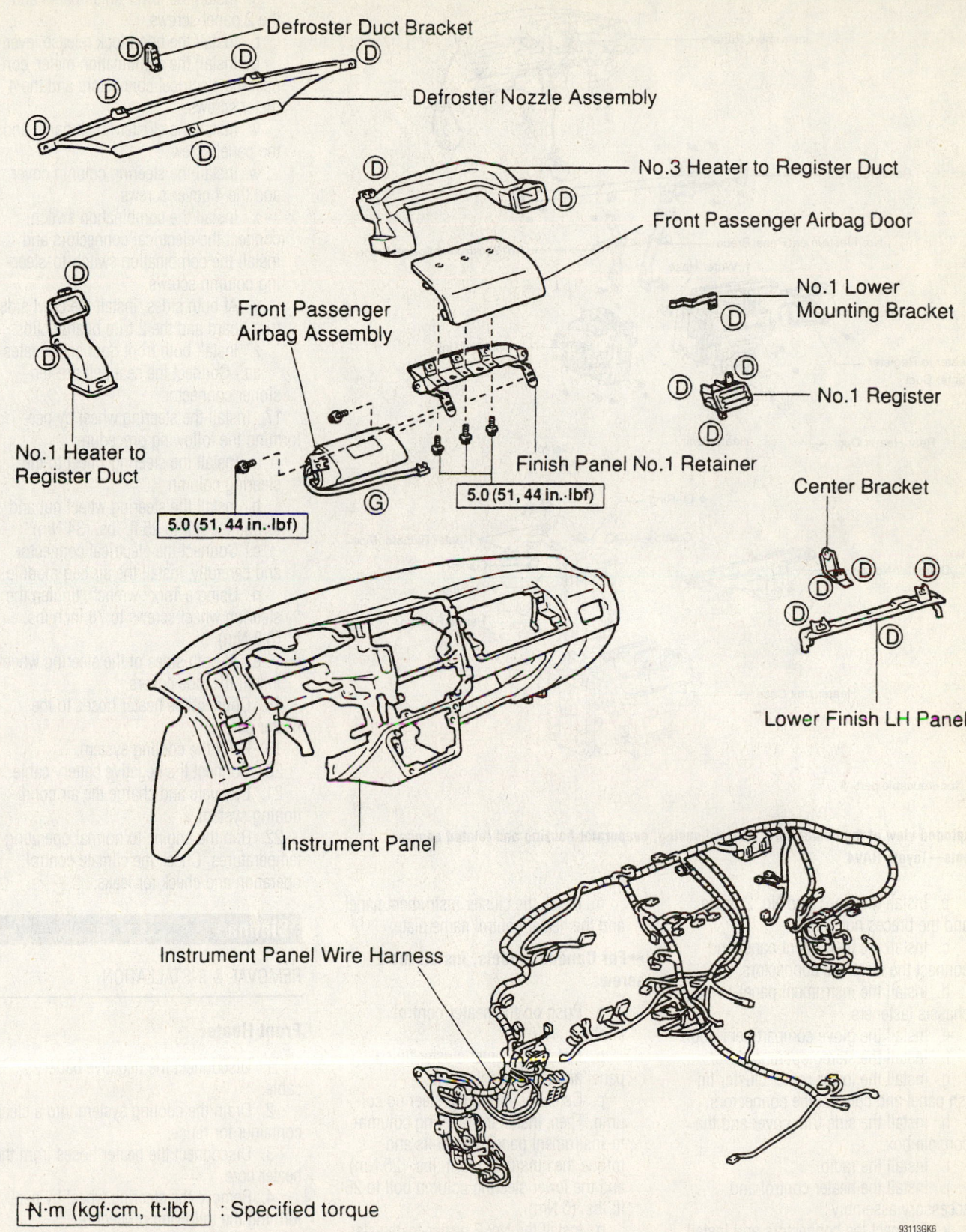

Defroster Duct Bracket

Defroster Nozzle Assembly

No.3 Heater to Register Duct

Front Passenger Airbag Door

Front Passenger Airbag Assembly

No.1 Lower Mounting Bracket

No.1 Register

No.1 Heater to Register Duct

Finish Panel No.1 Retainer

5.0 (51, 44 in.·lbf)

5.0 (51, 44 in.·lbf)

Center Bracket

Lower Finish LH Panel

Instrument Panel

Instrument Panel Wire Harness

Ṅ·m (kgf·cm, ft·lbf) : Specified torque

93113GK6

Exploded view of the instrument panel air bag module, ventilation components and wiring harness—Toyota RAV4

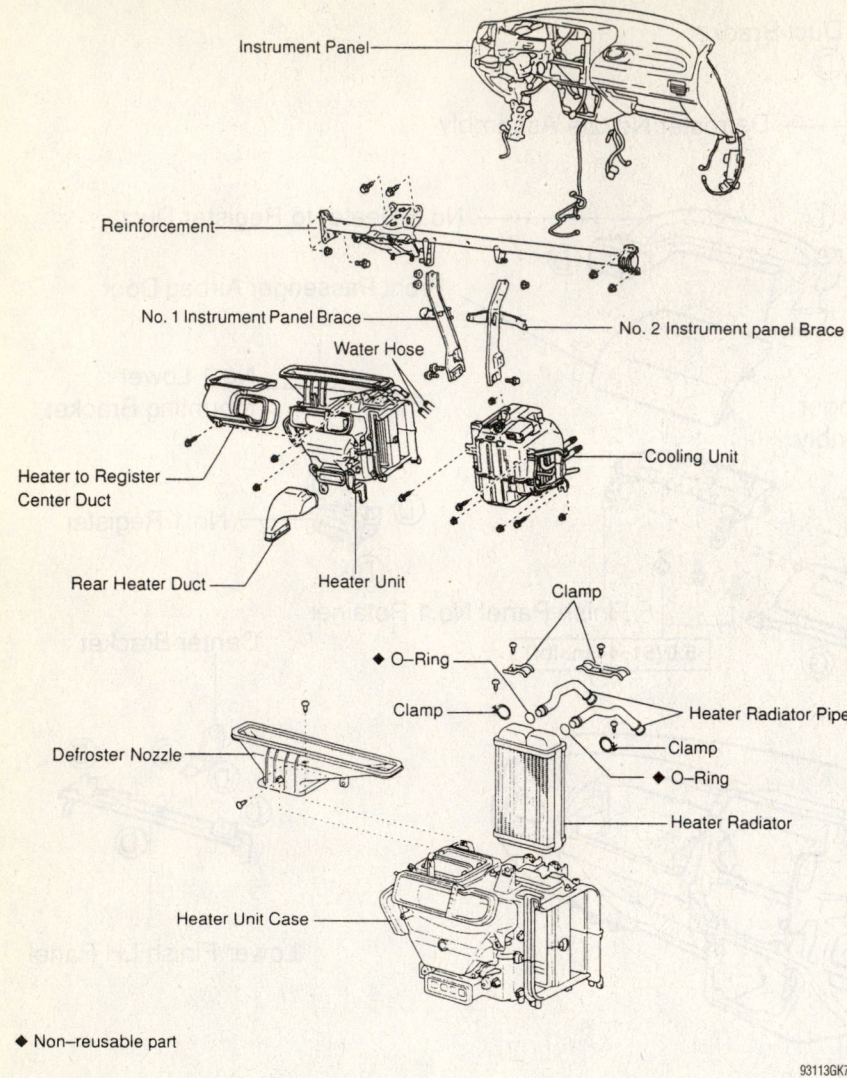

Instrument Panel

Reinforcement

No. 1 Instrument Panel Brace

No. 2 Instrument panel Brace

Water Hose

Heater to Register Center Duct

Cooling Unit

Rear Heater Duct

Heater Unit

Clamp

◆ O–Ring

Clamp

Heater Radiator Pipe

Clamp

Defroster Nozzle

◆ O–Ring

Heater Radiator

Heater Unit Case

◆ Non–reusable part

93113GK7

Exploded view of the heater core, heater housing, evaporator housing and related components—Toyota RAV4

b. Install the No. 1 and No. 2 brace and the braces nuts/bolts.

c. Install the instrument panel and connect the electrical connectors.

d. Install the instrument panel-to-chassis fasteners.

e. Install the glove compartment door.

f. Install the stereo opening cover.

g. Install the lower center cluster finish panel and connect the connectors.

h. Install the side trim cover and the console box.

i. Install the radio.

j. Install the heater control and accessory assembly.

k. Connect the connectors and install the cluster instrument panel.

l. Install the heater control assembly and the 3 assembly screws.

m. Install the cluster instrument panel and the heater control name plate.

➡**For Canada models, install the 2 screws.**

n. Push on the heater control knobs.

o. Install the center cluster finish panel and the 2 panel screws.

p. Carefully, install the steering column. Then, install the steering column-to-instrument panel nuts/bolts and torque the nuts/bolts 19 ft. lbs. (25 Nm) and the lower steering column bolt to 26 ft. lbs. (5 Nm).

q. Install the No. 2 heater-to-register duct.

r. For USA models, install the lower panel insert.

s. Install the lower finish panel and the 2 panel screws.

t. Install the hood lock release lever.

u. Install the combination meter, connect the electrical connectors and the 4 meter screws.

v. Install the cluster finish panel and the panel screw.

w. Install the steering column cover and the 4 cover screws.

x. Install the combination switch, connect the electrical connectors and install the combination switch-to-steering column screws.

y. At both sides, install the cowl side trim board and the 2 trim boards clips.

z. Install both front door scuff plates.

aa. Connect the seat belt pre-tensioner connector.

17. Install the steering wheel by performing the following procedure:

a. Install the steering wheel to the steering column.

b. Install the steering wheel nut and torque the nut to 25 ft. lbs. (34 Nm).

c. Connect the electrical connector and carefully, install the air bag module.

d. Using a Torx® wrench, tighten the steering wheel screws to 78 inch lbs. (8.8 Nm).

e. At both sides of the steering wheel, install the side covers.

18. Connect the heater hoses to the heater core.

19. Refill the cooling system.

20. Connect the negative battery cable.

21. Evacuate and charge the air conditioning system.

22. Run the engine to normal operating temperatures. Check the climate control operation and check for leaks.

Sienna

REMOVAL & INSTALLATION

Front Heater

1. Disconnect the negative battery cable.

2. Drain the cooling system into a clean container for reuse.

3. Disconnect the heater hoses from the heater core.

4. Remove the steering wheel by performing the following procedure:

a. Position the front wheels facing straight-ahead.

b. Remove the steering wheel side covers.

c. Using a Torx® wrench, loosen the 2 screws located at each side of the steering wheel until the screw's circumference groove catches on the screw case.

d. Pull the air bag module from the steering wheel and disconnect the electrical connector.

✳✳ CAUTION

Place the air bag module in a safe place with the front side facing upward.

e. Remove the steering wheel nut.

f. Place alignment marks on the steering wheel and the main shaft.

g. Using a steering wheel puller, press the steering wheel from the steering column.

5. Remove the instrument panel and reinforcement by performing the following procedure:

a. Remove the front door scuff plates.

b. Remove the cowl side boards.

c. Remove the front door trim covers.

d. Remove the front pillar garnish by disengaging the 5 clips. If equipped with a tweeter speaker, disconnect the electrical connector.

e. Remove the steering column covers-to-steering column screws and the covers.

f. Remove the combination switch-to-steering column screws, disconnect the electrical connector(s) and remove the combination switch.

g. Remove the 2 hood open lever screws and the hood open lever.

h. Remove the 2 lower finish panel bolts and disengage the panel from the 3 clips.

i. Remove the 2 No. 1 safety pad insert bolts and the insert.

j. Remove the 2 No. 2 finish panel bolts and disengage the panel from the 4 clips.

k. In the left side of the glove compartment, pry out the glove box door finish plate and disconnect the air bag module connector.

l. Remove the glove box 3 nuts and 2 screws and the glove box.

m. Remove the center cluster finish panel by disengaging the claw (bottom center) and 4 clips (one at each corner).

n. Remove the ashtray, the 2 ashtray receptacle box screws.

o. Remove the 4 lower center cluster finish panel screws and disconnect the connector.

p. Remove the clock, the No. 1 and No. 2 registers from the panel.

q. Remove the 3 cluster finish panel screws, disengage the 8 clips and remove the panel.

r. Remove the combination meter.

s. Remove the radio assembly.

t. Remove the heater control assembly.

u. Remove 2 passenger's side air bag module bolts; then, disconnect and remove the air bag module.

✳✳ CAUTION

Place the air bag module in a safe place with the front side facing upward.

v. Remove the instrument panel-to-chassis 5 bolts and nut.

w. Remove the audio amplifier.

x. Remove the No. 1 and No. 2 braces.

y. Remove the No. 2 cowl brace.

z. Remove the instrument panel reinforcement.

6. Remove the evaporator housing by performing the following procedure:

a. Discharge and recover the air conditioning system refrigerant.

b. In the engine compartment, remove the refrigerant lines-to-cowl connector bolts; then, disconnect the lines and discard the O-rings.

c. Disconnect the electrical connector at the evaporator housing.

d. Disconnect the wiring harness clamp.

e. Remove the evaporator housing-to-chassis 2 rivets, 3 bolts and nut.

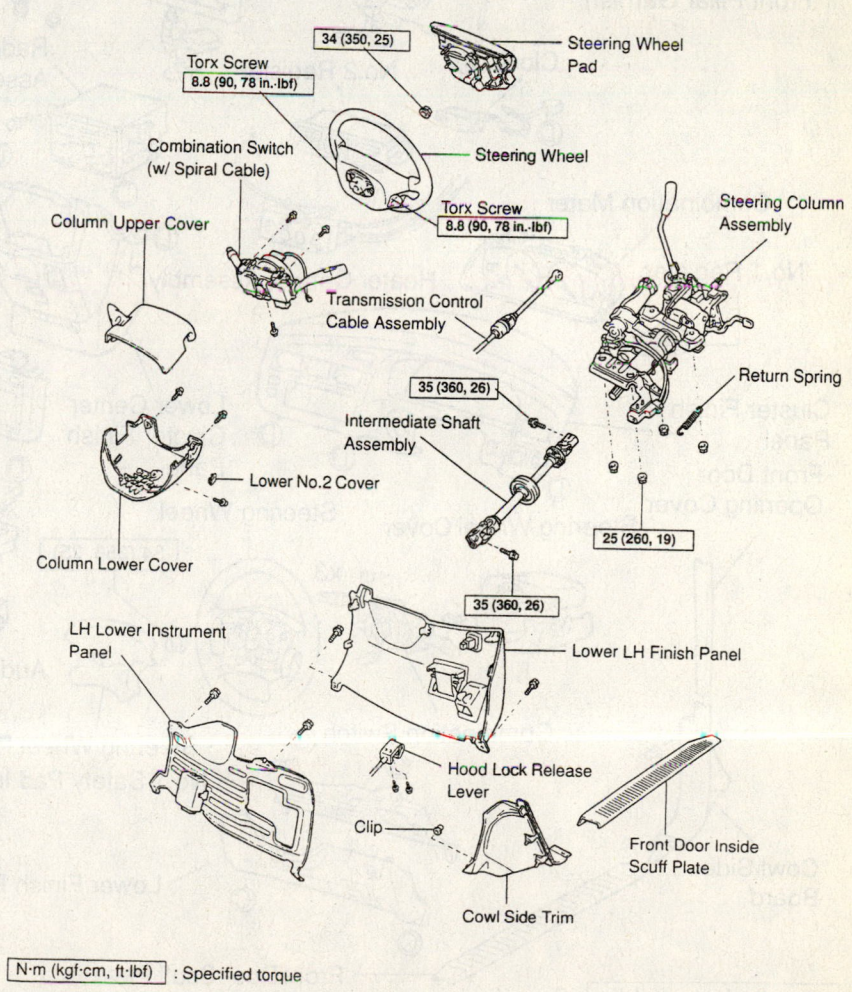

| 34 (350, 25) | — Steering Wheel Pad

Torx Screw 8.8 (90, 78 in.·lbf)

Combination Switch (w/ Spiral Cable)

Column Upper Cover

— Steering Wheel

Torx Screw 8.8 (90, 78 in.·lbf)

Steering Column Assembly

Transmission Control Cable Assembly

| 35 (360, 26) |

Intermediate Shaft Assembly

Return Spring

Lower No.2 Cover

| 25 (260, 19) |

Column Lower Cover

| 35 (360, 26) |

LH Lower Instrument Panel

Lower LH Finish Panel

Hood Lock Release Lever

Clip

Front Door Inside Scuff Plate

Cowl Side Trim

| N·m (kgf·cm, ft·lbf) | : Specified torque

93113GH3

Exploded view of the steering wheel, steering column and related components—Toyota Sienna

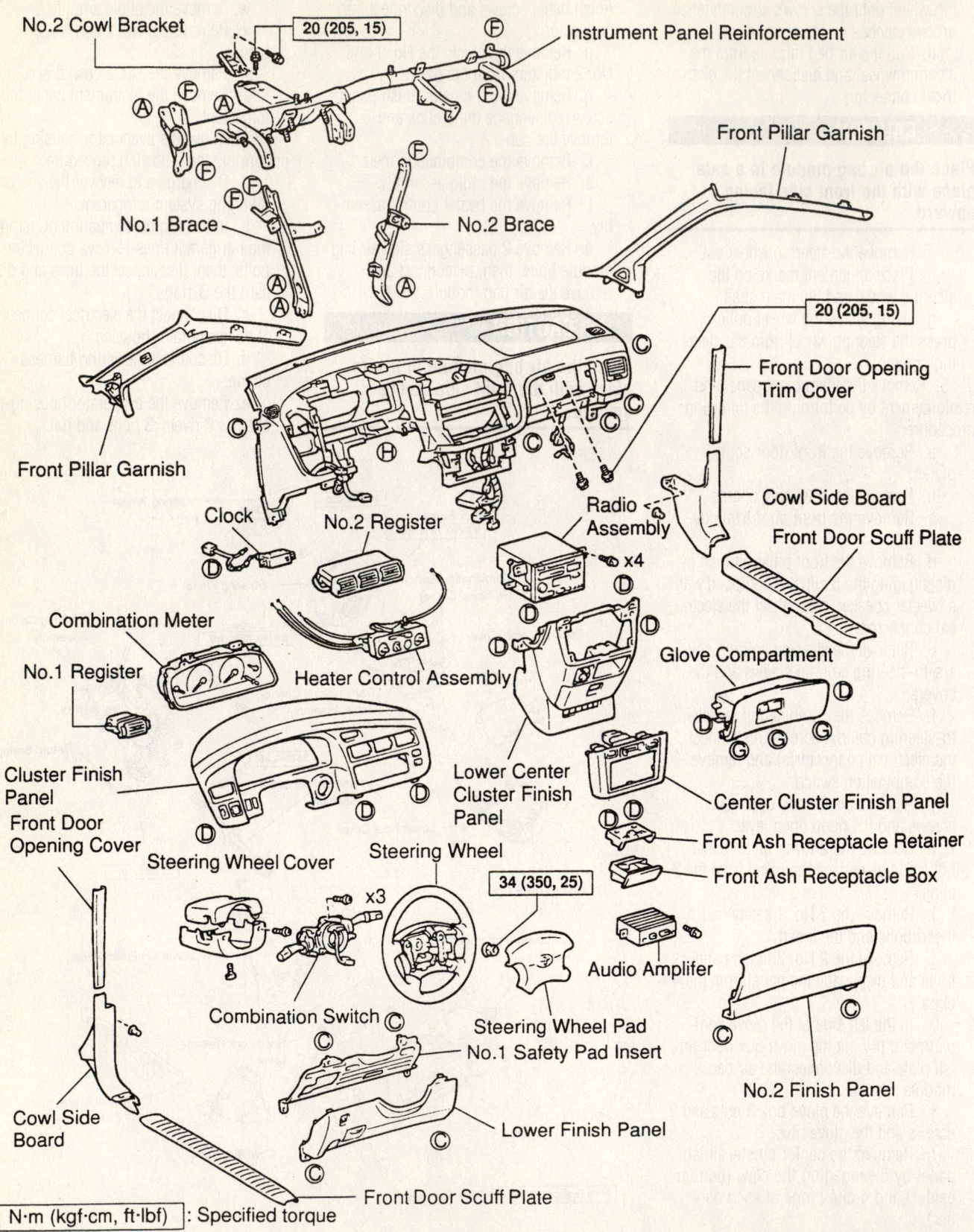

No.2 Cowl Bracket

20 (205, 15)

Instrument Panel Reinforcement

Front Pillar Garnish

No.1 Brace

No.2 Brace

20 (205, 15)

Front Door Opening Trim Cover

Front Pillar Garnish

Radio Assembly

Cowl Side Board

Front Door Scuff Plate

Clock

No.2 Register

Combination Meter

No.1 Register

Heater Control Assembly

Glove Compartment

Cluster Finish Panel

Front Door Opening Cover

Steering Wheel Cover

Steering Wheel

Lower Center Cluster Finish Panel

Center Cluster Finish Panel

Front Ash Receptacle Retainer

Front Ash Receptacle Box

34 (350, 25)

x3

Audio Amplifer

Combination Switch

Steering Wheel Pad

No.1 Safety Pad Insert

Cowl Side Board

Lower Finish Panel

No.2 Finish Panel

Front Door Scuff Plate

N·m (kgf·cm, ft·lbf) : Specified torque

93113GH4

Exploded view of the instrument panel and related components—Toyota Sienna

f. Remove the evaporator housing.

7. Remove the 4 defroster nozzle nuts and the nozzle.

8. Disconnect and remove the theft deterrent and the wireless door lock ECUs.

9. Release the 2 air duct claws and the air duct.

10. Remove the 2 heater housing-to-chassis rivets and the heater housing.

➡**When installing the heater housing, use new screws in place of the rivets.**

11. Remove the heater core-to-heater housing cover.

12. Remove both heater core screws and clamps; then, remove the heater core.

To install:

13. Install the heater core and both heater core screws and clamps.

14. Install the heater core-to-heater housing cover.

➡**When installing the heater housing, use new screws in place of the rivets.**

15. Install the heater housing-to-chassis and the 2 heater housing screws.

16. Release the air duct and the air duct claws.

17. Connect and install the theft deterrent and the wireless door lock ECUs.

18. Install the defroster nozzle and the 4 nozzle nuts.

19. Install the evaporator housing by performing the following procedure:

a. Install the evaporator housing.

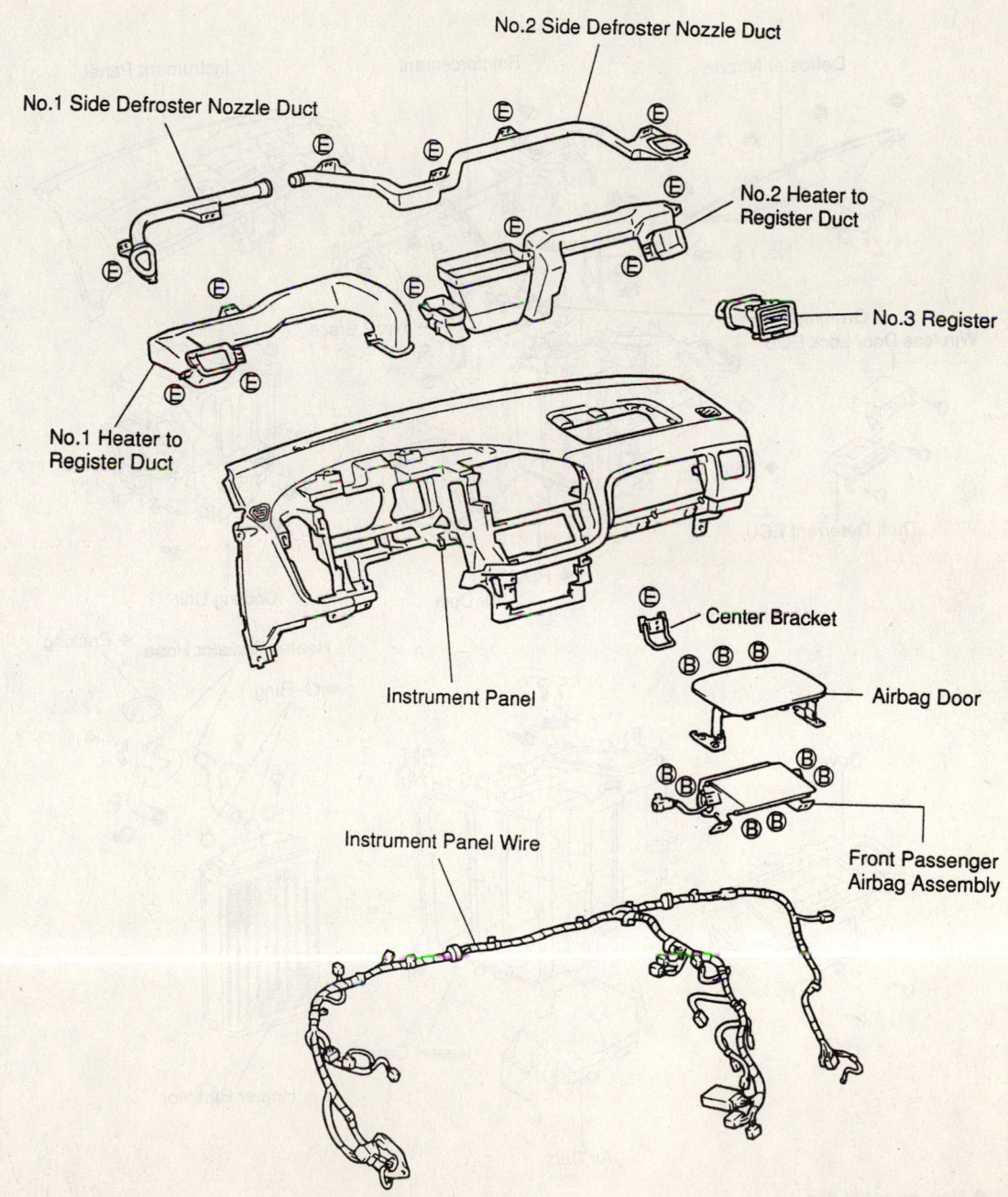

Exploded view of the ventilation system and related components—Toyota Sienna

Refer to the model specific sections for engine mechanical service procedures

b. Install the evaporator housing-to-chassis 2 rivets, 3 bolts and nut.

c. Connect the wiring harness clamp.

d. Connect the electrical connector at the evaporator housing.

e. In the engine compartment, use new O-rings and install the refrigerant lines-to-cowl connector and install the bolts.

20. Install the instrument panel and reinforcement by performing the following procedure:

a. Install the instrument panel reinforcement.

b. Install the No. 2 cowl brace.

c. Install the No. 1 and No. 2 braces.

d. Install the audio amplifier.

e. Install the instrument panel-to-chassis 5 bolts and nut.

f. Connect and install the air bag module and the 2 passenger's side air bag module bolts.

g. Install the heater control assembly.

h. Install the radio assembly.

i. Install the combination meter.

j. Install the cluster finish panel, engage the 8 clips and install the panel screws.

k. Install the No. 1 and No. 2 registers and the clock to the panel.

l. Connect the lower center cluster finish panel connector and install the 4 lower center cluster finish panel screws.

m. Install the 2 ashtray receptacle box screws and the ashtray.

n. Install the center cluster finish panel by engaging the 4 clips (1 at each corner) and the claw (bottom center).

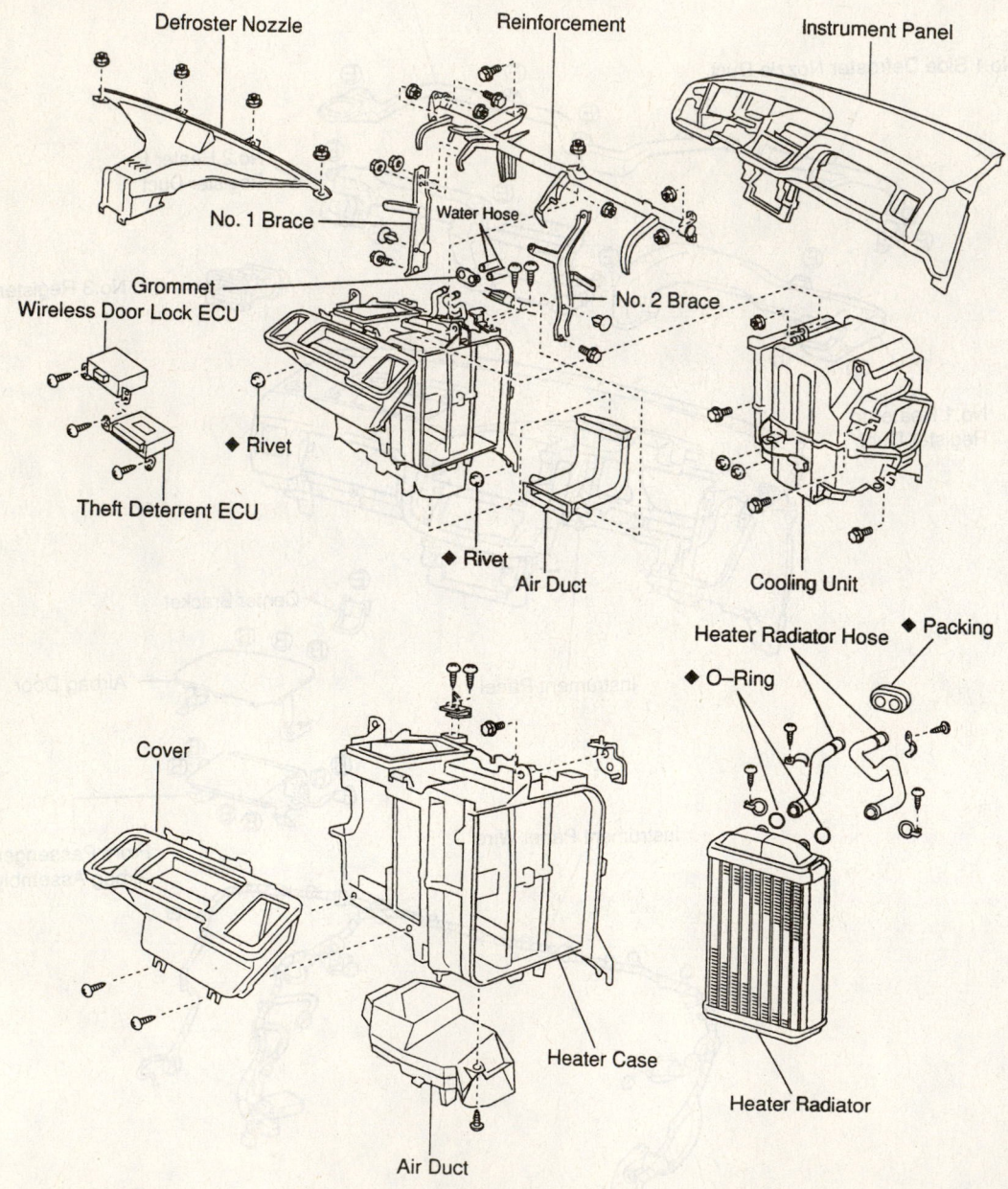

Defroster Nozzle

Reinforcement

Instrument Panel

No. 1 Brace

Water Hose

No. 2 Brace

Grommet
Wireless Door Lock ECU

◆ Rivet

Theft Deterrent ECU

◆ Rivet

Air Duct

Cooling Unit

Heater Radiator Hose

◆ Packing

◆ O–Ring

Cover

Heater Case

Heater Radiator

Air Duct

◆ Non–reusable part

Exploded view of the heater core, heater housing, evaporator housing and related components—Toyota Sienna

93113GH6

o. Install the glove box and the glove box 3 nuts and 2 screws.

p. In the left side of the glove compartment, connect the air bag module connector and install the glove box door finish plate.

q. Install the No. 2 finish panel, engage the 4 panel clips and install the 3 panel bolts.

r. Install the No. 1 safety pad insert and the 2 insert bolts.

s. Install the finish panel, engage the

3 finish panel clips and install 2 lower finish panel bolts.

t. Install the hood open lever and the 2 hood open lever screws.

u. Install the combination switch, connect the electrical connector(s) and install the combination switch-to-steering column screws.

v. Install the steering column covers and the covers-to-steering column screws.

w. Install the front pillar garnish by

engaging the 5 clips. If equipped with a tweeter speaker, connect the electrical connector.

x. Install the front door trim covers.

y. Install the cowl side boards.

z. Install the front door scuff plates.

21. Install the steering wheel by performing the following procedure:

a. Install the steering wheel to the steering column.

b. Align the steering wheel-to-main shaft marks.

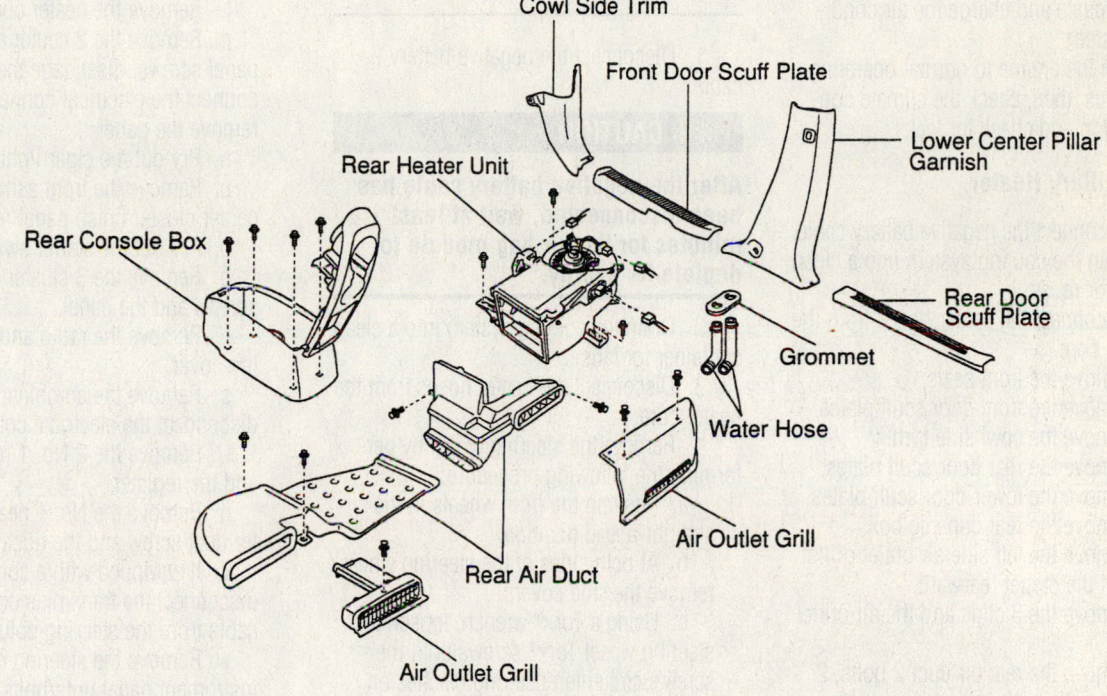

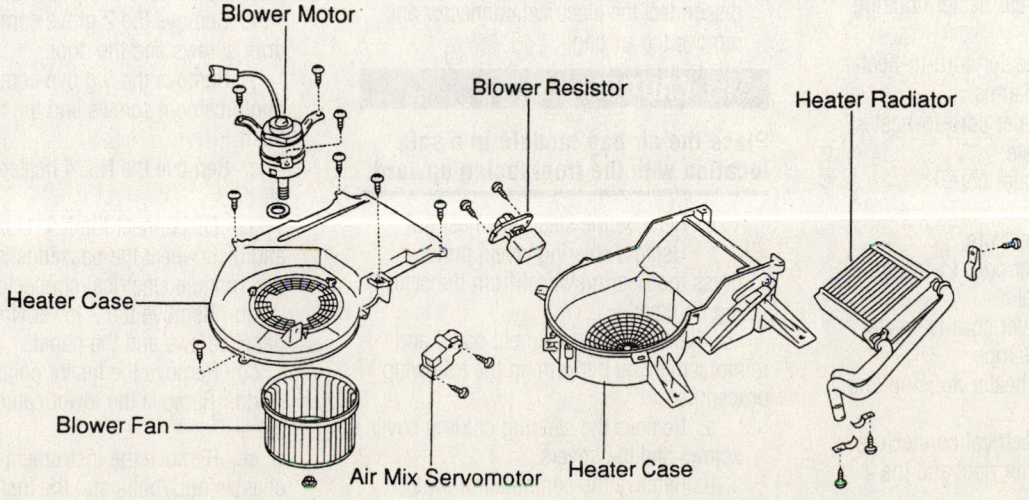

Exploded view of the rear heater core, the rear heater housing and related components—1998–00 Toyota Sienna

93113GH7

Refer to the model specific sections for cooling system service procedures

c. Install the steering wheel nut and torque the nut to 25 ft. lbs. (34 Nm).

d. Install the air bag module to the steering wheel and connect the electrical connector.

e. Using a Torx® wrench, tighten the steering wheel screws to 78 inch lbs. (8.8 Nm).

f. Install the steering wheel side covers.

22. Connect the heater hoses to the heater core.

23. Refill the cooling system.

24. Connect the negative battery cable.

25. Evacuate and charge the air conditioning system.

26. Run the engine to normal operating temperatures; then, check the climate control operation and check for leaks.

Rear Auxiliary Heater

1. Disconnect the negative battery cable.

2. Drain the cooling system into a clean container for reuse.

3. Disconnect the heater hoses from the rear heater core.

4. Remove the front seats.

5. Remove the front door scuff plates.

6. Remove the cowl side trim.

7. Remove the rear door scuff plates.

8. Remove the lower door scuff plates.

9. Remove the rear console box.

10. Remove the left side air outlet grille.

11. Pull the carpet rearward.

12. Remove the 3 clips and the air outlet grille.

13. Remove the rear air duct 2 bolts, 2 clips and the duct.

14. Disconnect the electrical connectors.

15. Remove the 3 rear heater housing bolts and the housing.

16. Remove both heater core-to-heater housing screws and clamps.

17. Remove the heater core-to-heater housing screw and plate.

18. Remove the heater core.

To install:

19. Install the heater core.

20. Install the heater core-to-heater housing screw and plate.

21. Install both heater core-to-heater housing screws and clamps.

22. Install the rear heater housing and the 3 housing bolts.

23. Connect the electrical connectors.

24. Install the rear air duct and the 2 bolts and 2 clips.

25. Install the 3 clips and the air outlet grille.

26. Move the carpet forward.

27. Install the left side air outlet grille.

28. Install the rear console box.

29. Install the lower door scuff plates.

30. Install the rear door scuff plates.

31. Install the cowl side trim.

32. Install the front door scuff plates.

33. Install the front seats.

34. Connect the heater hoses to the rear heater core.

35. Refill the cooling system.

36. Connect the negative battery cable.

Tacoma

REMOVAL & INSTALLATION

1. Disconnect the negative battery cable.

✳✳ CAUTION

After the negative battery cable has been disconnected, wait at least 1½ minutes for the air bag module to deplete its energy.

2. Drain the cooling system into a clean container for reuse.

3. Disconnect the heater hoses from the heater core.

4. Remove the steering wheel by performing the following procedure:

a. Position the front wheels in the straight-ahead position.

b. At both sides of the steering wheel, remove the side covers.

c. Using a Torx® wrench, loosen the steering wheel Torx® screws until the screw's circumference ring catches on the screw case.

d. Carefully, lift the air bag module, disconnect the electrical connector and remove the air bag.

✳✳ CAUTION

Place the air bag module in a safe location with the front facing upward.

e. Remove the steering wheel nut.

f. Using a steering wheel puller, press the steering wheel from the steering column.

5. Remove the instrument panel and reinforcement by performing the following procedure:

a. Remove the steering column cover screws and the covers.

b. Remove the combination switch-to-steering column screws and the combination switch.

c. Remove the 2 hood lock release lever screws and the hood lock release lever.

d. Remove the fuse box opening cover.

e. Remove the 4 lower left side finish panel bolts, the screw and the panel.

f. If equipped, remove the 2 rear console box bolts/screws and the rear console box.

g. Remove the front console box.

h. Remove the 2 upper console box mounting bracket screws and the bracket.

i. Remove the 2 lower center cover clips and the cover.

j. Remove the No. 2 heater-to-register duct screw and the duct.

k. Remove the heater control knobs.

l. Remove the heater control panel.

m. Remove the 2 center cluster finish panel screws, disengage the 5 clips, disconnect the electrical connectors and remove the panel.

n. Pry out the cigar lighter hole bezel.

o. Remove the front ashtray and the center cluster finish panel retainer.

p. Pry out the starter switch bezel.

q. Remove the 3 cluster finish panel screws and the panel.

r. Remove the radio and stereo opening cover.

s. Remove the combination meter and disconnect the electrical connectors.

t. Remove the 2 No. 1 register screws and the register.

u. Remove the No. 1 heater-to-register duct screw and the duct.

v. If equipped with a column shifter, disconnect the transmission control cable from the steering column.

w. Remove the steering column-to-instrument panel nuts/bolts and the lower steering column joint bolt; then, carefully, remove the steering column.

x. Remove the 2 glove compartment door screws and the door.

y. Remove the 3 glove compartment reinforcement screws and the reinforcement.

z. Remove the No. 4 heater-to-register duct.

aa. Disconnect the No. 1 under-cover and disconnect the passenger's side air bag module electrical connector.

bb. Remove the 3 lower No. 2 finish panel screws and the panel.

cc. Remove the heater control screws.

dd. Remove the lower center finish panel.

ee. Remove the instrument panel-to-chassis nuts/bolts and the instrument panel.

ff. Remove the 3 No. 1 brace bolts and the brace.

gg. Remove the 2 No. 2 brace bolts and the brace.

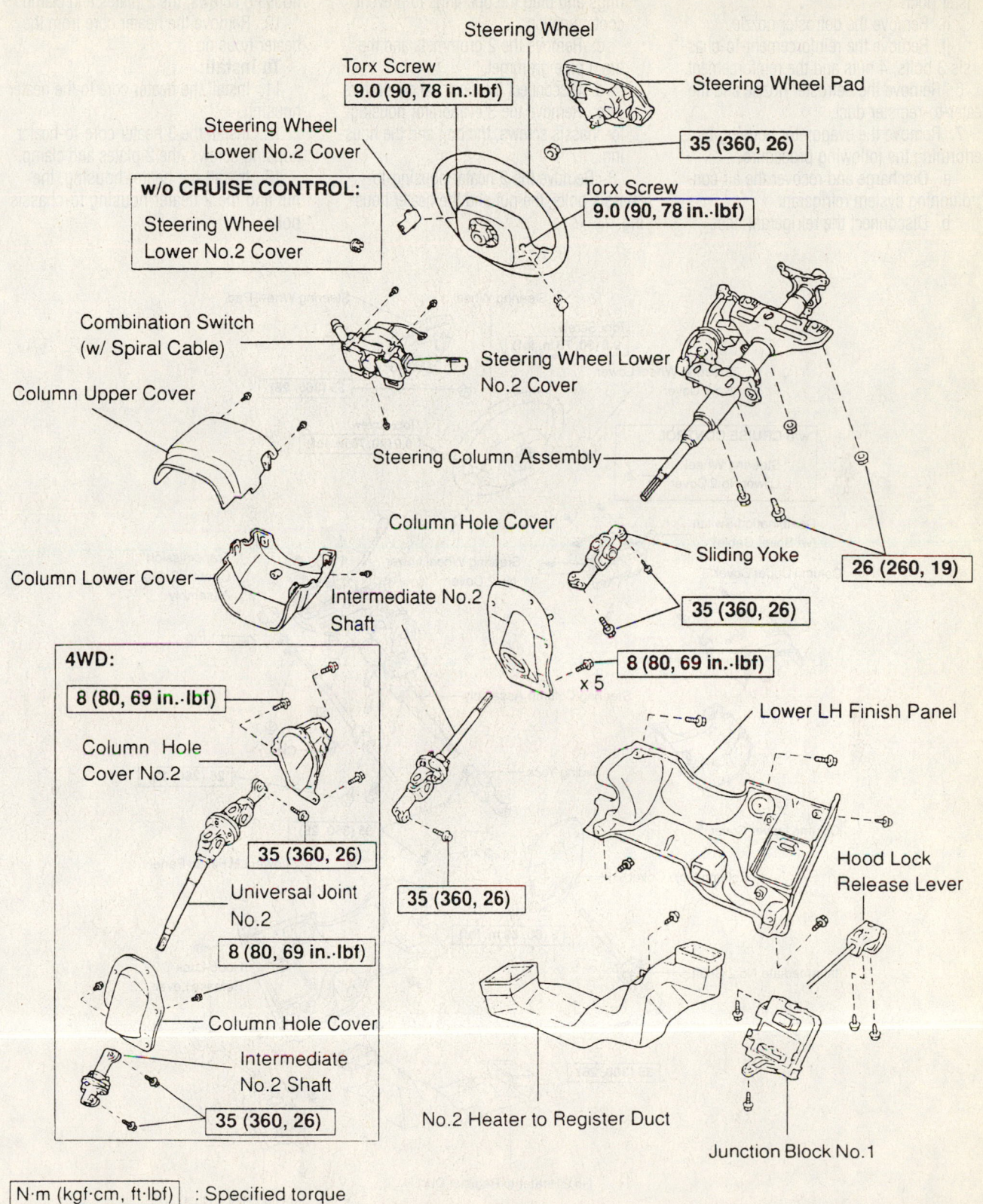

Exploded view of the steering wheel, air bag module, floor shift steering column and related components—Toyota Tacoma

hh. Remove the center heater-to-register duct.

ii. Remove the defroster nozzle.

jj. Remove the reinforcement-to-chassis 3 bolts, 4 nuts and the reinforcement.

6. Remove the defroster nozzle and the heater-to-register duct.

7. Remove the evaporator housing by performing the following procedure:

a. Discharge and recover the air conditioning system refrigerant.

b. Disconnect the refrigerant lines from the evaporator core. Discard the O-rings and plug the openings to prevent contamination.

c. Remove the 2 grommets and the drain pipe grommet.

d. Disconnect the electrical connectors.

e. Remove the 3 evaporator housing-to-chassis screws, the bolt and the housing.

8. Remove the 2 heater housing-to-chassis bolts, the nut and the heater housing.

9. Remove the 3 heater core-to-heater housing screws, the 2 plates and clamp.

10. Remove the heater core from the heater housing.

To install:

11. Install the heater core to the heater housing.

12. Install the 3 heater core-to-heater housing screws, the 2 plates and clamp.

13. Install the heater housing, the nut and the 2 heater housing to-chassis bolts.

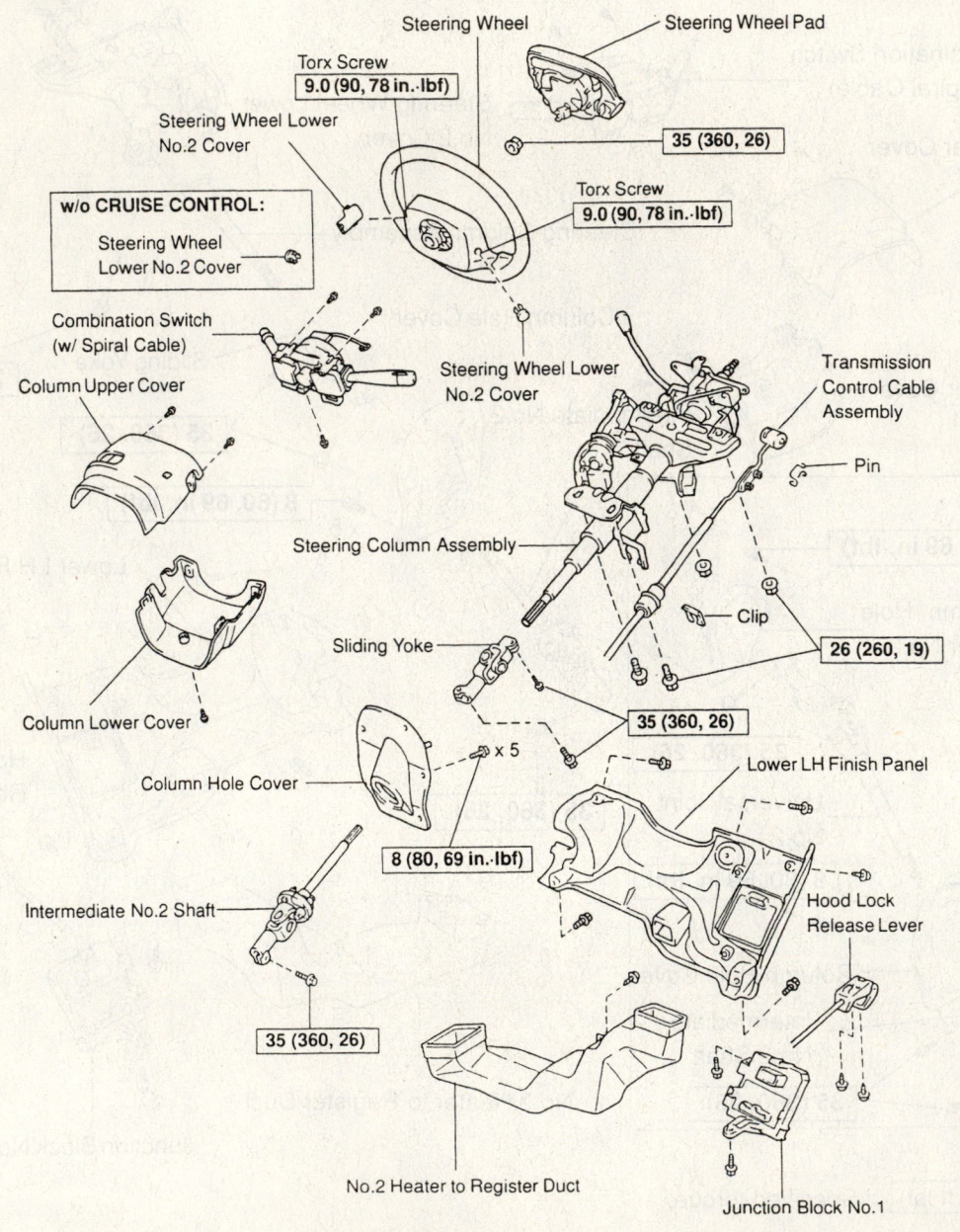

Exploded view of the steering wheel, air bag module, column shift steering column and related components—Toyota Tacoma

Steering Wheel

Steering Wheel Pad

Torx Screw
9.0 (90, 78 in.·lbf)

Steering Wheel Lower No.2 Cover

35 (360, 26)

Torx Screw
9.0 (90, 78 in.·lbf)

w/o CRUISE CONTROL:
Steering Wheel Lower No.2 Cover

Combination Switch (w/ Spiral Cable)

Column Upper Cover

Steering Wheel Lower No.2 Cover

Column Lower Cover

Steering Column Assembly

Transmission Control Cable Assembly

Pin

Clip

26 (260, 19)

Column Hole Cover

Sliding Yoke

35 (360, 26)

Lower LH Finish Panel

8 (80, 69 in.·lbf)

Intermediate No.2 Shaft

Hood Lock Release Lever

35 (360, 26)

No.2 Heater to Register Duct

Junction Block No.1

N·m (kgf·cm, ft·lbf) : Specified torque

93113GI0

14. Install the evaporator housing by performing the following procedure:

    a. Install the evaporator housing, the bolt and the 3 housing-to-chassis screws.

    b. Connect the electrical connectors.

    c. Install the 2 grommets and the drain pipe grommet.

    d. Using new O-rings, connect the refrigerant lines to the evaporator core.

15. Install the defroster nozzle and the heater-to-register duct.

16. Install the instrument panel and reinforcement by performing the following procedure:

    a. Install the reinforcement-to-chassis 3 bolts, 4 nuts and the reinforcement.

    b. Install the defroster nozzle.

    c. Install the center heater-to-register duct.

    d. Install the No. 2 brace and the 2 brace bolts.

    e. Install the No. 1 brace and the 3 brace bolts.

    f. Install the instrument panel and the instrument panel-to-chassis nuts/bolts.

    g. Install the lower center finish panel.

    h. Install the heater control screws.

    i. Install the lower No. 2 finish panel and the 3 panel screws.

    j. Connect the passenger's side air bag module electrical connector and the No. 1 undercover.

    k. Install the No. 4 heater-to-register duct.

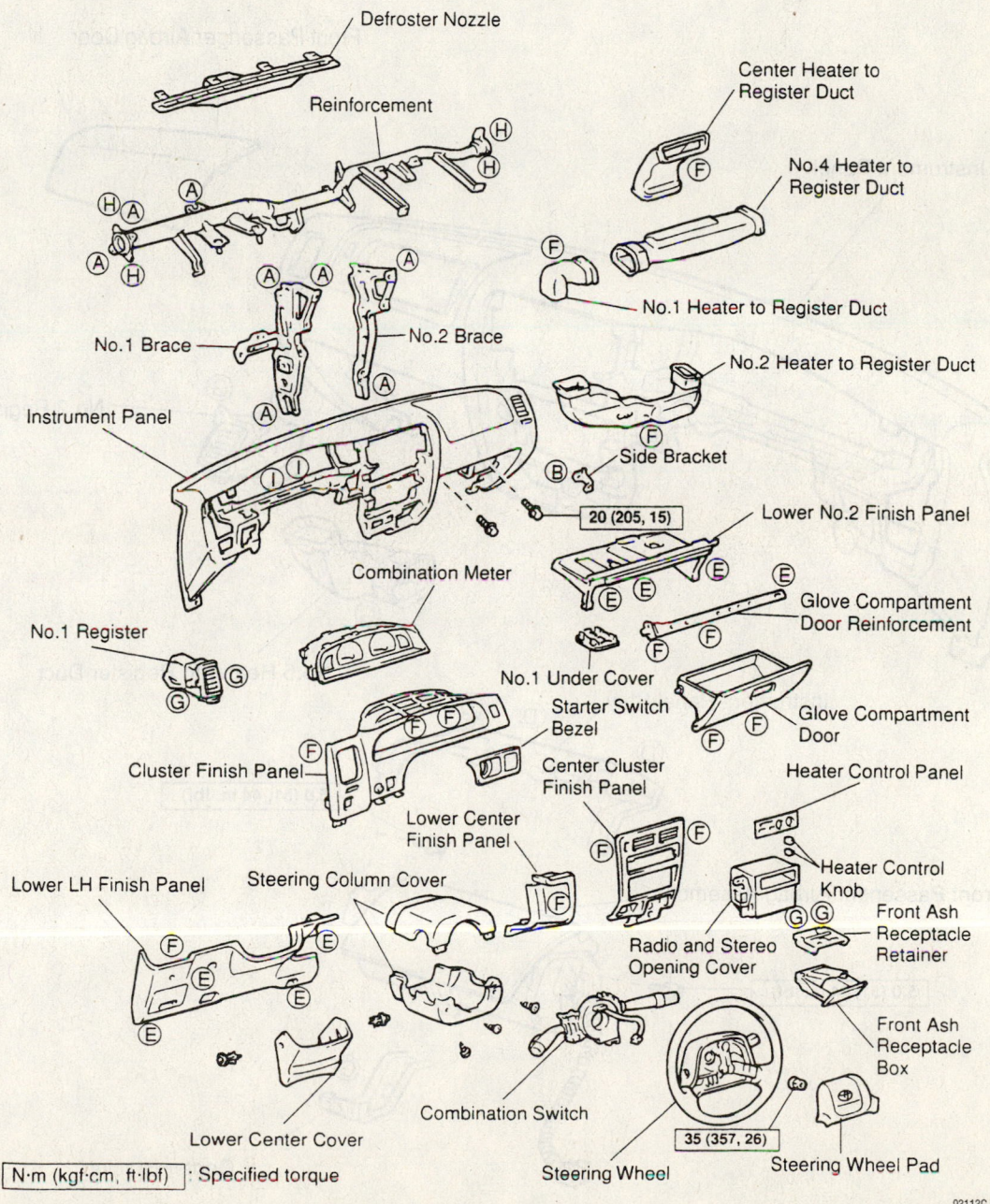

Exploded view of the instrument panel and related components—Toyota Tacoma

93113GJ1

l. Install the glove compartment reinforcement and the 3 reinforcement screws.

m. Install the glove compartment door and the 2 door screws.

n. Install the steering column and torque the steering column-to-instrument panel nuts/bolts to 19 ft. lbs. (26 Nm) and the lower steering column joint bolt to 26 ft. lbs. (35 Nm).

o. If equipped with a column shifter, connect the transmission control cable to the steering column.

p. Install the No. 1 heater-to-register

duct and the duct screw.

q. Install the No. 1 register and the 2 register screws.

r. Install the combination meter and connect the electrical connectors.

s. Install the radio and stereo opening cover.

t. Install the cluster finish panel and the 3 panel screws.

u. Pry out the starter switch bezel.

v. Install the front ashtray and the center cluster finish panel retainer.

w. Install the cigar lighter hole bezel.

x. Install the center cluster finish panel, engage the 5 clips, connect the electrical connectors and install the 2 panel screws.

y. Install the heater control panel.

z. Install the heater control knobs.

aa. Install the No. 2 heater-to-register duct and the duct screw.

bb. Install the lower center cover and engage the 2 clips.

cc. Install the upper console box mounting bracket and the 2 bracket screws.

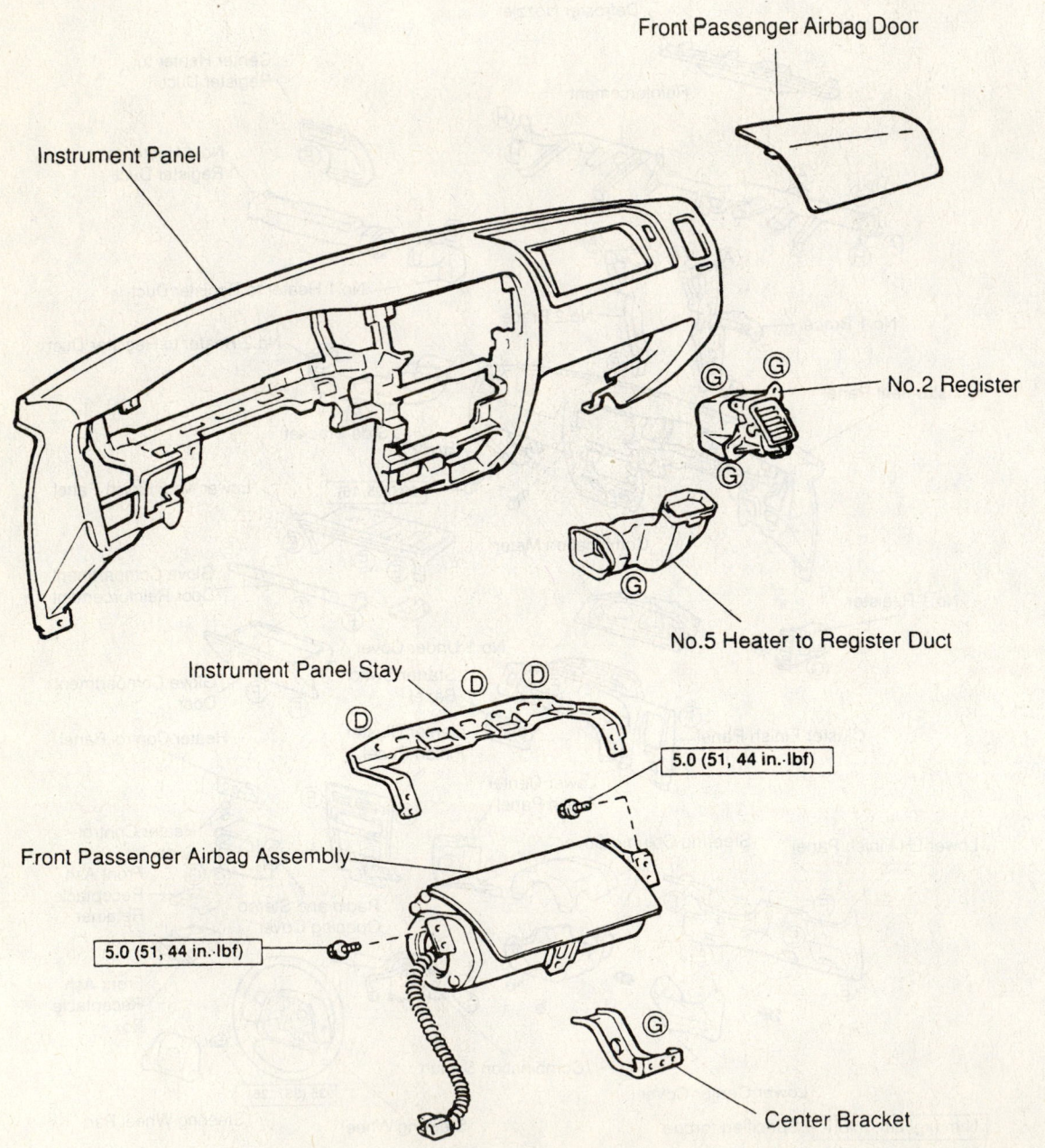

Front Passenger Airbag Door

Instrument Panel

No.2 Register

No.5 Heater to Register Duct

Instrument Panel Stay

5.0 (51, 44 in. lbf)

Front Passenger Airbag Assembly

5.0 (51, 44 in. lbf)

Center Bracket

93113GJ2

Exploded view of the instrument panel air bag module, ventilation components and brackets—Toyota Tacoma

dd. Install the front console box.

ee. If equipped, install the rear console box and the 2 rear console box bolts/screws.

ff. Install the lower left side finish panel, the 4 bolts and the screw.

gg. Install the fuse box opening cover.

hh. Install the hood lock release lever and the 2 hood lock release lever screws.

ii. Install the combination switch-to-steering column and the combination switch screws.

jj. Install the steering column cover and the covers screws.

17. Install the steering wheel by performing the following procedure:

a. Install the steering wheel from the steering column.

b. Install the steering wheel nut and torque to 26 ft. lbs. (35 Nm).

c. Carefully, install the air bag module and connect the electrical connector.

d. Using a Torx® wrench, tighten the steering wheel screws to 78 inch lbs. (8.8 Nm).

e. At both sides of the steering wheel, install the side covers.

18. Connect the heater hoses to the heater core.

19. Refill the cooling system.

20. Connect the negative battery cable.

21. Evacuate and charge the air conditioning system refrigerant.

22. Run the engine to normal operating temperatures; then, check the climate control operation and check for leaks.

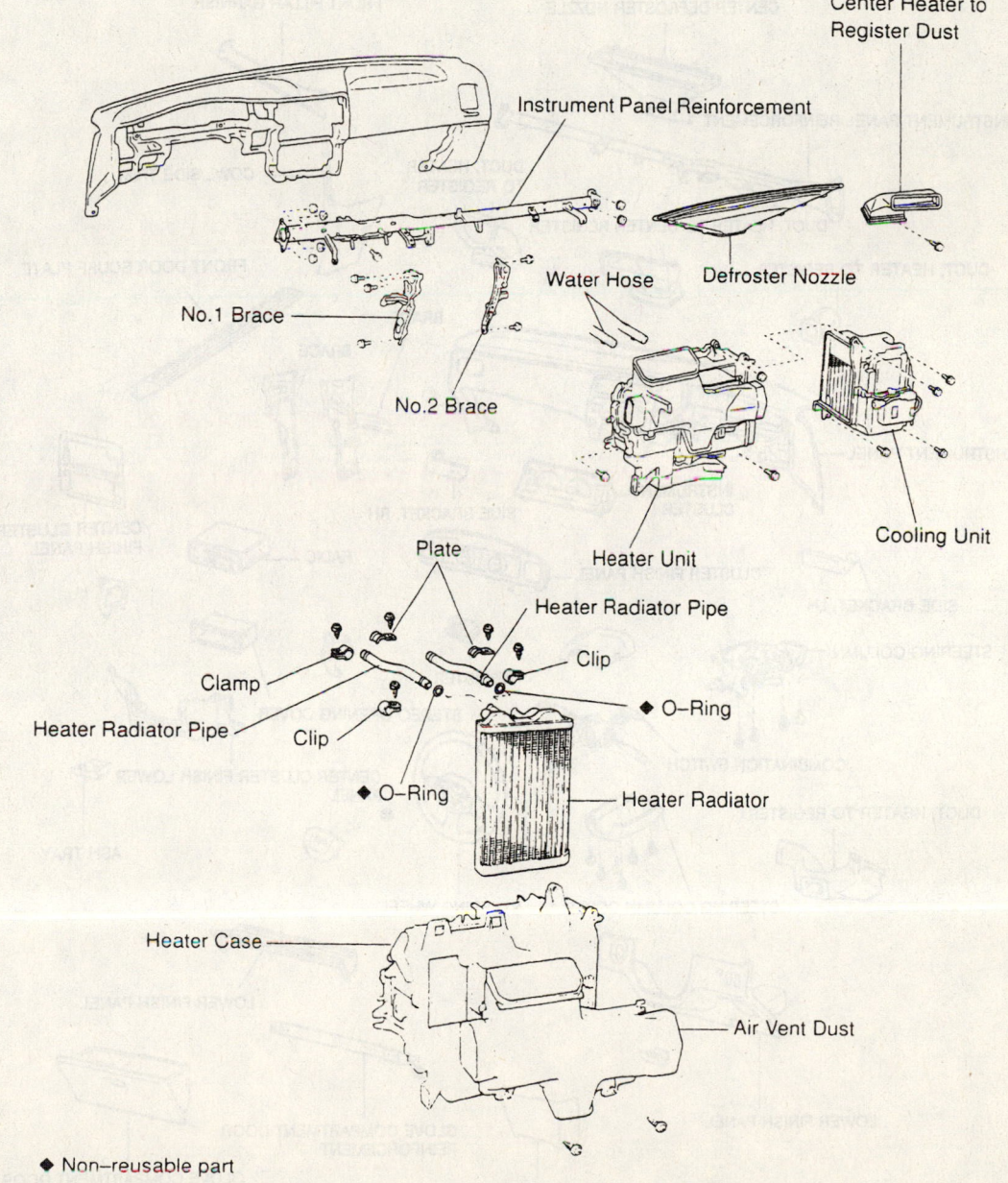

Exploded view of the front heater core, heater housing, evaporator housing and related components—Toyota Tacoma

Refer to the model specific sections for engine mechanical service procedures

T-100

REMOVAL & INSTALLATION

1997

1. Disconnect the negative battery cable.
2. Discharge and recover the air conditioning system refrigerant.
3. Disconnect the suction and discharge lines from the tube connections at the firewall. Cap all openings immediately to minimize contamination. Remove the grommets around the tubes.
4. Remove the evaporator drain pipe grommet.
5. Remove the glove box door (2 screws), the lower trim panel and the door reinforcement.
6. Remove the evaporator housing assembly (4 screws and 1 nut) after detaching the electrical connectors.
7. Drain the cooling system into a clean container for reuse.
8. Disconnect the heater hoses from the heater core tubes at the firewall. Remove the pipe grommets.
9. Remove the instrument panel, starting with the front pillar trim, the door scuff plates and the cowl side trim.
10. Remove the steering wheel, the column cover, the hood lock release lever (detach from the panel only), the lower panel trim and the combination switch on the column.
11. Remove the lower center instrument panel cover. Remove the heater control knobs and gently pry off the finish panel.

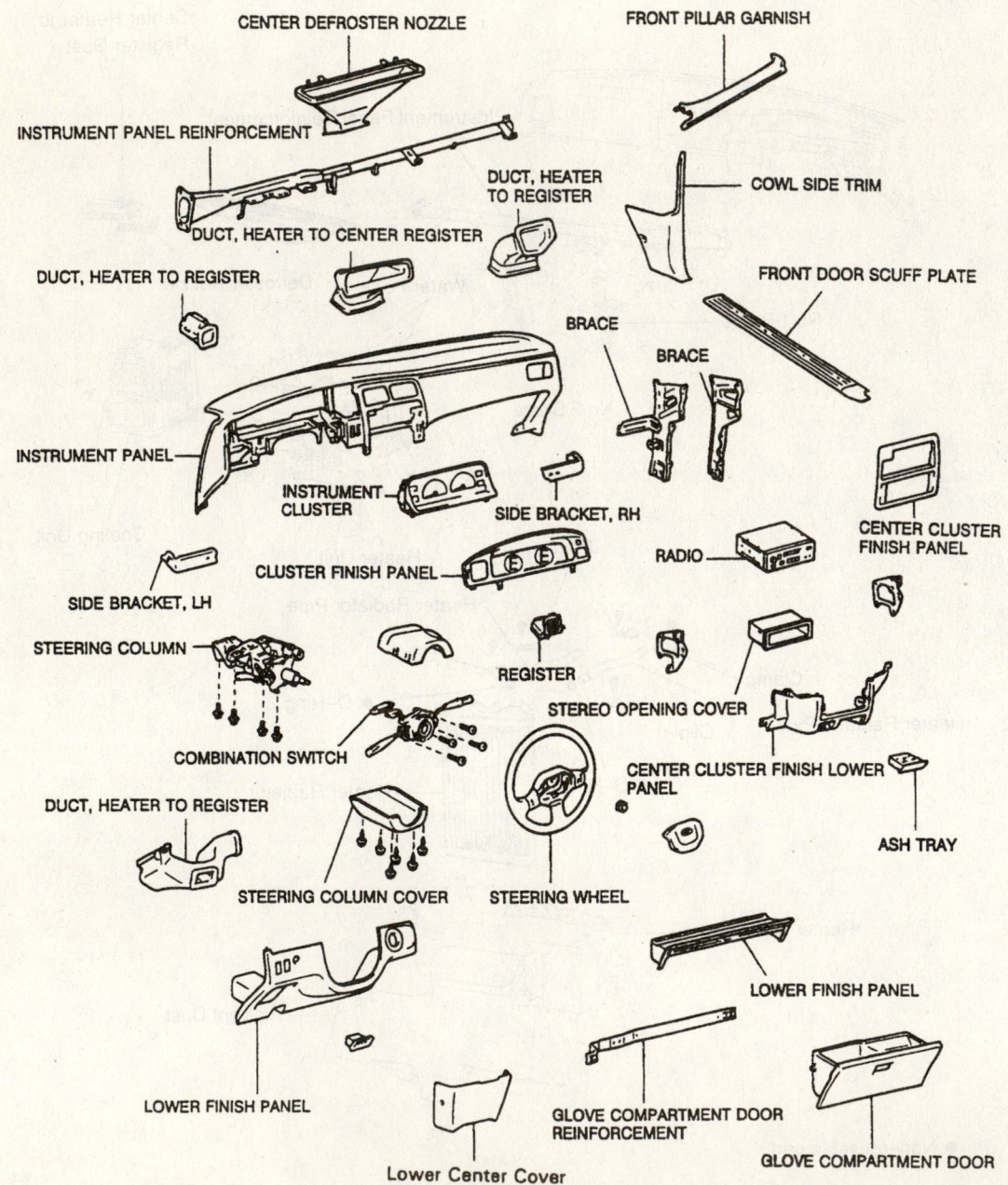

Exploded view of the instrument panel—1997 Toyota T-100

93113G66

12. Remove the radio assembly, disconnect the climate control panel cables from the heater unit, then remove the climate control assembly.

13. Remove the 2 screws now accessible in the center panel, then pry the panel off gently (tape the screwdriver tip first).

14. Remove the instrument cluster trim and the cluster.

15. Remove the small center air outlet register, the left side heater duct, then the glove box reinforcement and the 2 center braces.

16. Detach the instrument panel wiring harness connectors, remove the 2 bolts from the instrument panel on either side of the steering column location and remove the instrument panel assembly with the remaining components attached.

17. Remove the right side, center and floor air ducts.

18. Remove the 2 bolts and 1 nut holding the heater assembly in place and remove the assembly from the vehicle.

19. Remove the heater core from the assembly.

To install:

20. Assemble the heater core into the heater case assembly.

21. Install the heater case assembly into the vehicle.

22. Attach the air ducts, as removed.

23. Install the instrument panel assembly, attaching the wiring harness.

24. Install the center braces, the glove box reinforcement, the left heater duct and the small center air outlet register.

25. Install the instrument cluster and the trim panel.

26. Attach the cables and connections and install the climate control panel, the radio and the center panel trim.

27. Install the steering column and column components, as removed.

28. Install the evaporator assembly, making all connections. Install the glove box, the reinforcement and trim.

29. Connect the heater hoses and the air conditioning refrigerant lines (as removed) from the connections at the firewall.

30. Refill the cooling system.

31. Evacuate and charge the air conditioning system with R-134-a refrigerant and any appropriate refrigerant oil, as needed.

32. Connect the negative battery cable.

33. Run the engine to normal operating temperatures; then, check the climate control operation and check for leaks.

1998–00

➥If equipped with a theft-deterrent system, be sure to acquire code. Also, write down the frequencies of the preset radio push buttons so the audio system may be reprogrammed.

1. Disconnect the negative battery cable.

✳✳ CAUTION

After disconnecting the negative battery cable, be sure to wait at least 1½ minutes so that the air bag module can deplete its energy.

2. Drain the cooling system into a clean container for reuse.

3. Disconnect the heater hoses from the heater core.

4. Discharge and recover the air conditioning system refrigerant.

5. Remove the front pillar garnish, the front door scuff plate and the cowl side trim.

6. Remove the steering wheel by performing the following procedure:

a. Position the front wheels in the straight-ahead position.

b. At both sides of the steering wheel, remove the side covers.

c. Using a Torx® wrench, loosen the steering wheel Torx® screws until the screw's circumference ring catches on the screw case.

d. Carefully, lift the air bag module, disconnect the electrical connector and remove the air bag.

✳✳ CAUTION

Place the air bag module in a safe location with the front facing upward.

e. Remove the steering wheel nut.

f. Using a steering wheel puller, press the steering wheel from the steering column.

7. Remove the instrument panel by performing the following procedure:

a. Remove the steering column cover screws and the cover.

b. Remove the hood lock release lever.

c. Remove the No. 1 lower finish panel.

d. Remove the combination switch.

e. Remove the glove compartment door.

f. Remove the No. 2 lower finish panel.

g. Remove the lower center cover.

h. Remove the rear console box.

i. Remove the heater control knobs; then, pry out the center cluster finish panel.

j. Remove the radio and the heater control assembly.

k. Remove the 2 center cluster finish lower panel screws and the panel; then, disconnect the connector.

l. Remove the stereo opening cover.

m. Remove the 5 cluster finish panel screws and the combination meter.

n. Remove the No. 1 register.

o. Remove the heater ducts from the No.1 and No. 2 registers.

p. Remove the glove compartment door reinforcement.

q. Remove the No. 1 and No. 2 brace.

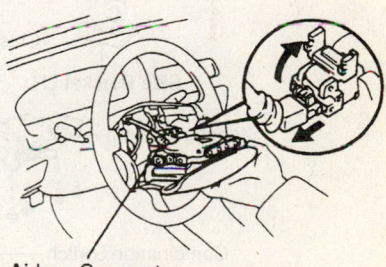

Airbag Connector

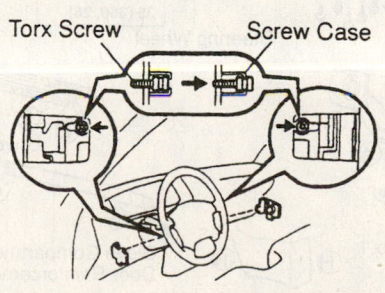

View of the driver's side air bag module Torx® screws—1998–00 Toyota T-100

Exploded view of the steering wheel and air bag module assembly—1998–00 Toyota T-100

Refer to the model specific sections for cooling system service procedures

r. Remove the instrument panel electrical connectors.

s. Remove the 2 instrument panel bolts and the instrument panel.

t. Remove the instrument panel reinforcement.

8. Remove the evaporator housing by performing the following procedure:

a. Disconnect the refrigerant lines from the evaporator housing; then, discard the O-rings and plug the openings to prevent contamination.

b. Remove the evaporator-to-chassis grommets.

c. Remove the drain pipe grommet.

d. Disconnect the connectors to the evaporator housing.

e. Remove the 5 evaporator housing-to-chassis screws, the nut and the evaporator housing.

9. Disconnect the control cables from the heater housing.

10. Remove the heater housing-to-No. 4 register duct screw and the duct.

11. Remove the heater housing-to-center register duct screw and the duct.

12. Remove the heater housing-to-foot air duct screw and the duct.

13. Remove the 2 heater housing-to-chassis bolts/nut and the heater housing.

14. Remove the 3 heater core-to-heater housing screws, plates and clamp.

15. Remove the heater core from the heater housing.

To install:

16. Install the heater core to the heater housing.

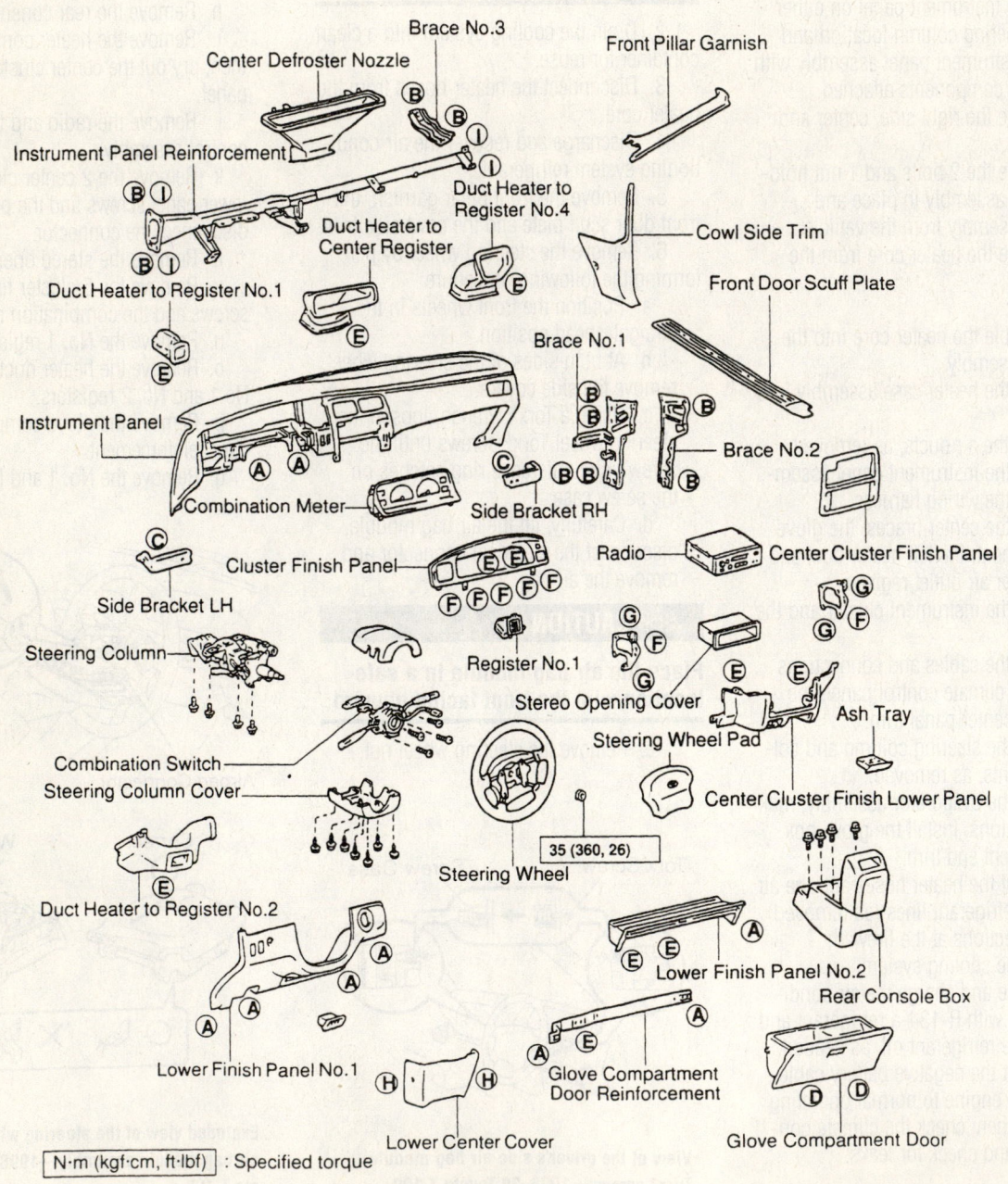

N·m (kgf·cm, ft·lbf) : Specified torque

Exploded view of the instrument panel assembly—1998–00 Toyota T-100

93113GJ6

17. Install the 3 heater core-to-heater housing screws, plates and clamp.

18. Install the heater housing and the 2 heater housing-to-chassis bolts/nut.

19. Install the heater housing-to-foot air duct and the duct screw.

20. Install the heater housing-to-center register duct and the duct screw.

21. Install the heater housing-to-No. 4 register duct and the duct screw.

22. Connect the control cables to the heater housing.

23. Install the evaporator housing by performing the following procedure:

    a. Install the evaporator housing, the nut and the 5 evaporator housing-to-chassis screws.

    b. Connect the connectors to the evaporator housing.

    c. Install the drain pipe grommet.

    d. Install the evaporator-to-chassis grommets.

    e. Using new O-rings, connect the refrigerant lines to the evaporator housing.

24. Install the instrument panel by performing the following procedure:

    a. Install the instrument panel reinforcement.

    b. Install the instrument panel and the 2 instrument panel bolts.

    c. Install the instrument panel electrical connectors.

    d. Install the No. 1 and No. 2 brace.

    e. Install the glove compartment door reinforcement.

    f. Install the heater ducts to the No.1 and No. 2 registers.

    g. Install the No. 1 register.

    h. Install the combination meter and the 5 cluster finish panel screws.

    i. Install the stereo opening cover.

    j. Connect the connector; then, install the center cluster finish lower panel and the 2 panel screws.

    k. Install the heater control assembly and the radio.

    l. Install the center cluster finish panel and the heater control knobs.

    m. Install the rear console box.

    n. Install the lower center cover.

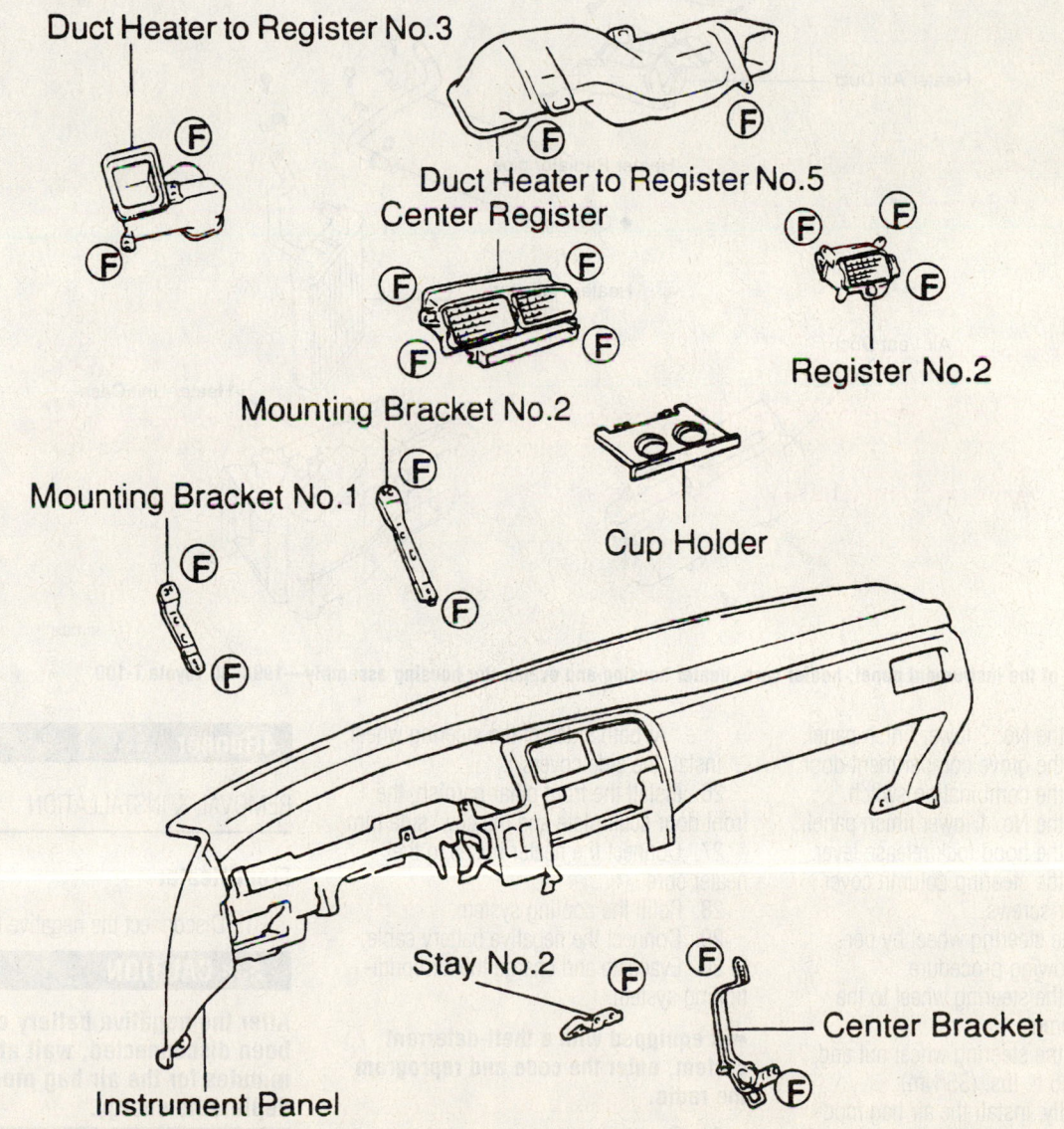

Exploded view of the instrument panel registers and braces—1998–00 Toyota T-100

93113GJ7

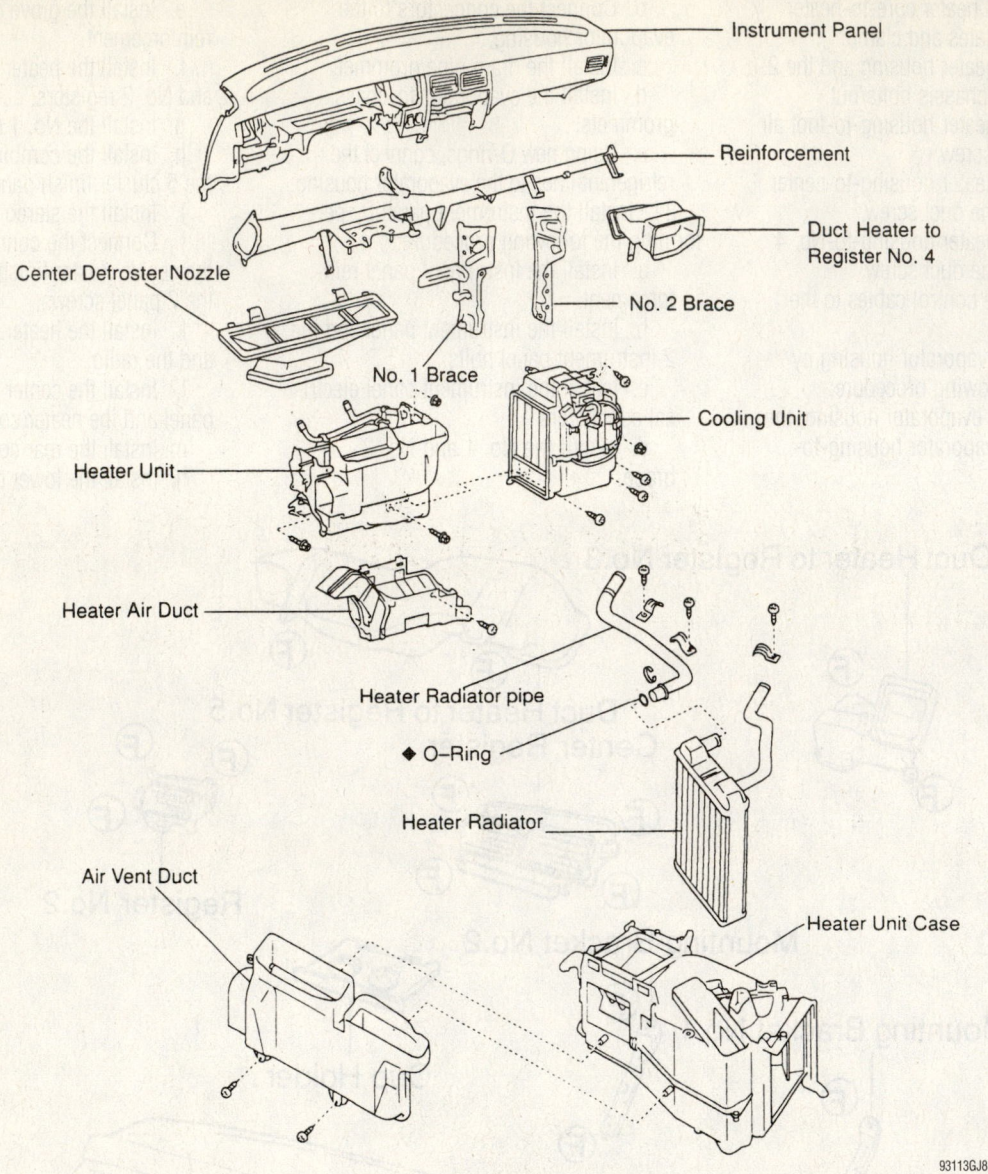

Instrument Panel

Reinforcement

Duct Heater to Register No. 4

No. 2 Brace

Center Defroster Nozzle

No. 1 Brace

Cooling Unit

Heater Unit

Heater Air Duct

Heater Radiator pipe

◆ O–Ring

Heater Radiator

Air Vent Duct

Heater Unit Case

93113GJ8

Exploded view of the instrument panel, heater core, heater housing and evaporator housing assembly—1998–00 Toyota T-100

o. Install the No. 2 lower finish panel.

p. Install the glove compartment door.

q. Install the combination switch.

r. Install the No. 1 lower finish panel.

s. Install the hood lock release lever.

t. Install the steering column cover and the cover screws.

25. Install the steering wheel by performing the following procedure:

a. Install the steering wheel to the steering column.

b. Install the steering wheel nut and torque it to 26 ft. lbs. (35 Nm).

c. Carefully, install the air bag module and connect the electrical connector.

d. Using a Torx® wrench, tighten the steering wheel screws to 78 inch lbs. (9.0 Nm).

e. At both sides of the steering wheel, install the side covers.

26. Install the front pillar garnish, the front door scuff plate and the cowl side trim.

27. Connect the heater hoses to the heater core.

28. Refill the cooling system.

29. Connect the negative battery cable.

30. Evacuate and charge the air conditioning system.

➡ **If equipped with a theft-deterrent system, enter the code and reprogram the radio.**

31. Run the engine to normal operating temperatures; then, check the climate control operation and check for leaks.

4Runner

REMOVAL & INSTALLATION

Front Heater

1. Disconnect the negative battery cable.

✳✳ CAUTION

After the negative battery cable has been disconnected, wait at least 1½ minutes for the air bag module to deplete its energy.

2. Drain the cooling system into a clean container for reuse.

3. Disconnect the heater hoses from the heater core.

4. Remove the steering wheel by performing the following procedure:

a. Position the front wheels in the straight-ahead position.

b. At both sides of the steering wheel, remove the side covers.

c. Using a Torx® wrench, loosen the steering wheel screws until the screw's circumference ring catches on the screw case.

d. Carefully, lift the air bag module, disconnect the electrical connector and remove the air bag.

❊❊ CAUTION

Place the air bag module in a safe location with the front facing upward.

e. Remove the steering wheel nut.

f. Using a steering wheel puller, press the steering wheel from the steering column.

5. Remove the instrument panel and reinforcement by performing the following procedure:

a. Remove both front door scuff plates.

b. Remove both cowl side trims.

c. Remove the 2 hood lock release lever screws and the hood lock release lever.

d. Remove the 2 fuel lid release lever screws and the fuel lid release lever.

e. Remove the 4 lower finish panel bolts and the panel.

f. Remove the No. 1 and No. 2 heater-to-register duct screw and the ducts.

g. Pry out the starter switch bezel.

h. Remove the steering column cover screws and the covers.

i. Remove the combination switch-to-steering column screws, disconnect the electrical connector and the combination switch.

j. Remove the steering column-to-instrument panel nuts/bolts and the lower steering column bolt; then carefully, remove the steering column.

k. Remove the 4 cluster finish panel screws and the panel.

l. Remove the 4 combination meter screws, disconnect the electrical connectors and remove the combination meter.

m. Pry out the parking brake hole cover.

n. Pry out the upper console panel.

o. Disengage the 7 center cluster finish panel clips and remove the panel.

➡**Remove the center cluster finish panel clips by starting at the bottom and working toward the top.**

p. Remove the heater control knobs.

q. Remove the 2 rear console box bolts/screws and the rear console box.

r. Remove the upper console panel garnish.

s. Remove the 2 glove compartment door screws and the door.

t. Disconnect the passenger's side air bag module electrical connector.

u. Remove the glove box light.

v. Remove the 3 lower No. 2 finish panel bolts and the panel.

w. Remove the 3 glove compartment door reinforcement bolts and the reinforcement.

x. Remove the No. 4 heater-to-register duct.

y. Remove the radio assembly.

z. Remove the side bracket bolt and the bracket.

aa. If equipped with manual air conditioning, remove the heater control assembly.

bb. If equipped with automatic air conditioning, remove the air conditioning control assembly.

cc. Remove the instrument panel-to-chassis nut and 2 bolts; then, remove the instrument panel.

dd. Remove the instrument panel reinforcement-to-chassis nuts/bolts and the reinforcement.

6. Remove the defroster nozzle and heater-to-register duct.

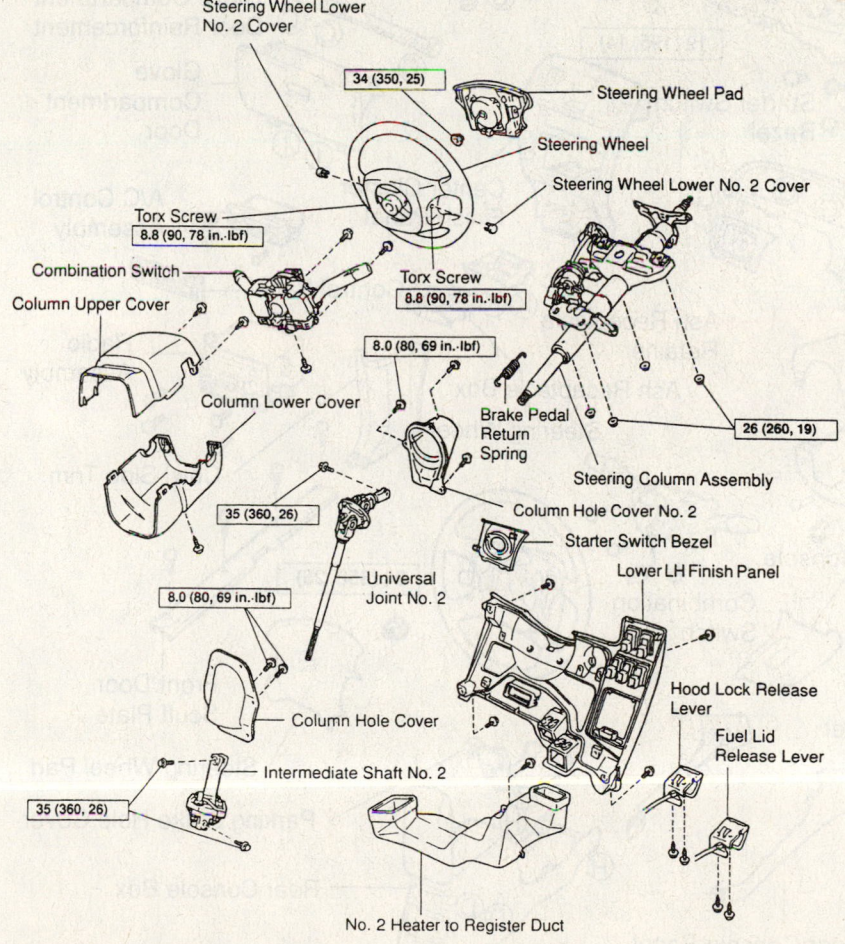

Steering Wheel Lower No. 2 Cover
34 (350, 25)
Steering Wheel Pad
Steering Wheel
Torx Screw
8.8 (90, 78 in.-lbf)
Combination Switch
Column Upper Cover
Steering Wheel Lower No. 2 Cover
Torx Screw
8.8 (90, 78 in.-lbf)
8.0 (80, 69 in.-lbf)
Column Lower Cover
Brake Pedal Return Spring
26 (260, 19)
35 (360, 26)
Steering Column Assembly
Column Hole Cover No. 2
Starter Switch Bezel
Lower LH Finish Panel
Universal Joint No. 2
8.0 (80, 69 in.-lbf)
Column Hole Cover
Hood Lock Release Lever
Fuel Lid Release Lever
Intermediate Shaft No. 2
35 (360, 26)
No. 2 Heater to Register Duct

N·m (kgf·cm, ft·lbf) : Specified torque

93113GJ9

Exploded view of the steering wheel, air bag module, steering column and related components—Toyota 4Runner

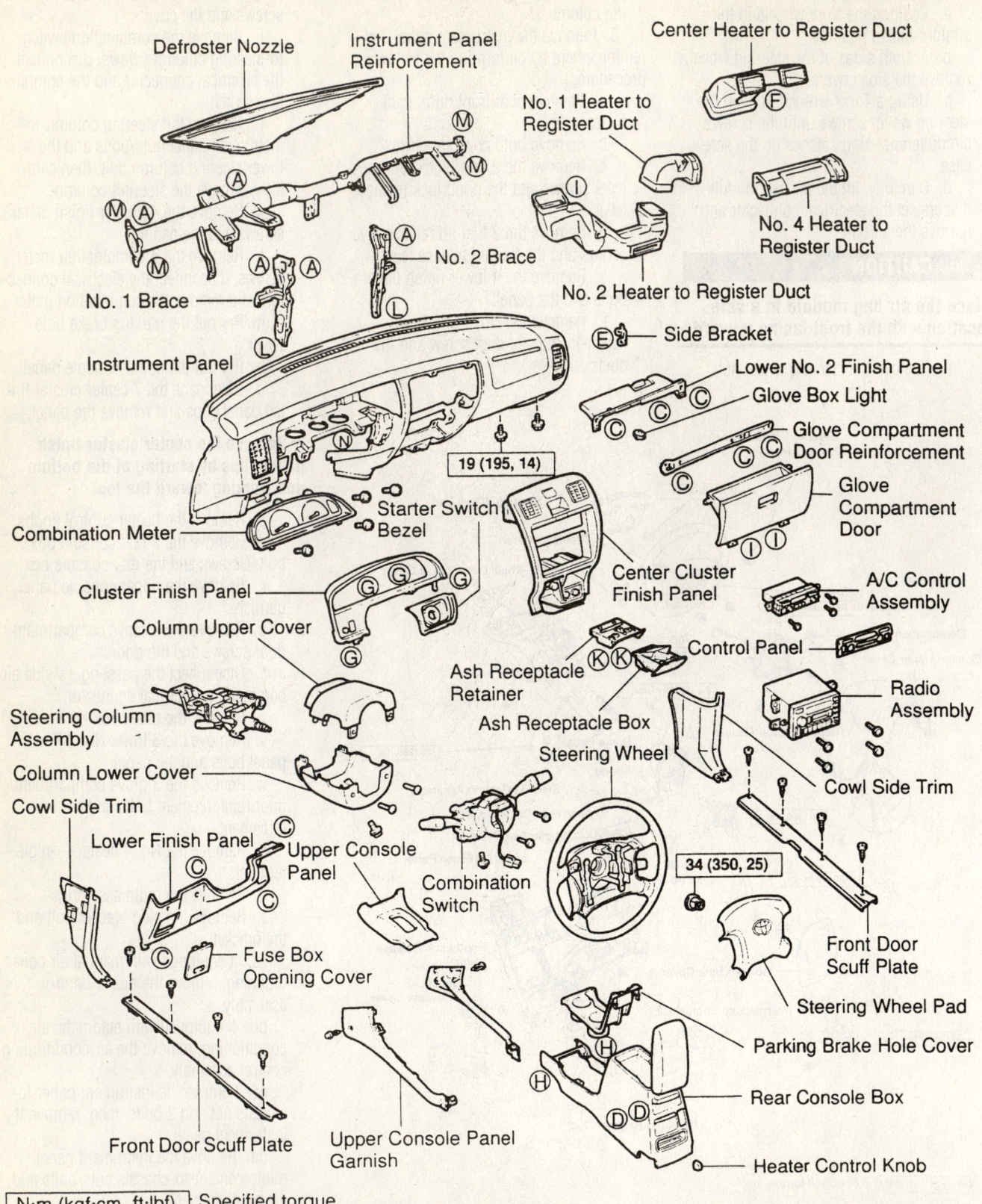

Defroster Nozzle

Instrument Panel Reinforcement

Center Heater to Register Duct

No. 1 Heater to Register Duct

No. 4 Heater to Register Duct

No. 2 Brace

No. 2 Heater to Register Duct

No. 1 Brace

Side Bracket

Instrument Panel

Lower No. 2 Finish Panel

Glove Box Light

Glove Compartment Door Reinforcement

Glove Compartment Door

19 (195, 14)

Combination Meter

Starter Switch Bezel

Cluster Finish Panel

Center Cluster Finish Panel

A/C Control Assembly

Control Panel

Column Upper Cover

Ash Receptacle Retainer

Radio Assembly

Steering Column Assembly

Ash Receptacle Box

Column Lower Cover

Steering Wheel

Cowl Side Trim

Cowl Side Trim

Lower Finish Panel

Upper Console Panel

34 (350, 25)

Front Door Scuff Plate

Combination Switch

Steering Wheel Pad

Fuse Box Opening Cover

Parking Brake Hole Cover

Rear Console Box

Front Door Scuff Plate

Upper Console Panel Garnish

Heater Control Knob

N·m (kgf·cm, ft·lbf) : Specified torque

93113GJ0

Exploded view of the instrument panel and related components—Toyota 4Runner

7. Remove the evaporator housing by performing the following procedure:

a. Discharge and recover the air conditioning system refrigerant.

b. Disconnect the refrigerant lines from the evaporator core. Discard the O-rings and plug the openings to prevent contamination.

c. Disconnect the electrical connectors.

d. Remove the 3 evaporator housing-to-chassis screws and the housing.

8. Disconnect the mode control servomotor connector.

9. Disconnect the aspirator hose from the room temperature sensor.

10. Disconnect the heater valve control cable.

11. Remove the heater housing-to-chassis nuts and the heater housing.

12. Remove the 3 heater core-to-heater housing screws, the 2 clips and clamp.

13. Remove the heater core from the heater housing.

To install:

14. Install the 3 heater core-to-heater housing screws, the 2 clips and clamp.

15. Install the heater housing and the heater housing-to-chassis nuts.

16. Connect the heater valve control cable.

17. Connect the aspirator hose to the room temperature sensor.

18. Connect the mode control servomotor connector.

19. Install the defroster nozzle and heater-to-register duct.

20. Install the evaporator housing by performing the following procedure:

a. Install the evaporator housing and the 3 housing-to-chassis screws.

b. Connect the electrical connectors.

c. Using new O-rings, connect the refrigerant lines to the evaporator core.

21. Install the instrument panel and reinforcement by performing the following procedure:

a. Install the instrument panel reinforcement and the reinforcement-to-chassis nuts/bolts.

b. Install the instrument panel and the instrument panel-to-chassis nut and 2 bolts.

c. If equipped with automatic air conditioning, install the air conditioning control assembly.

d. If equipped with manual air conditioning, install the heater control assembly.

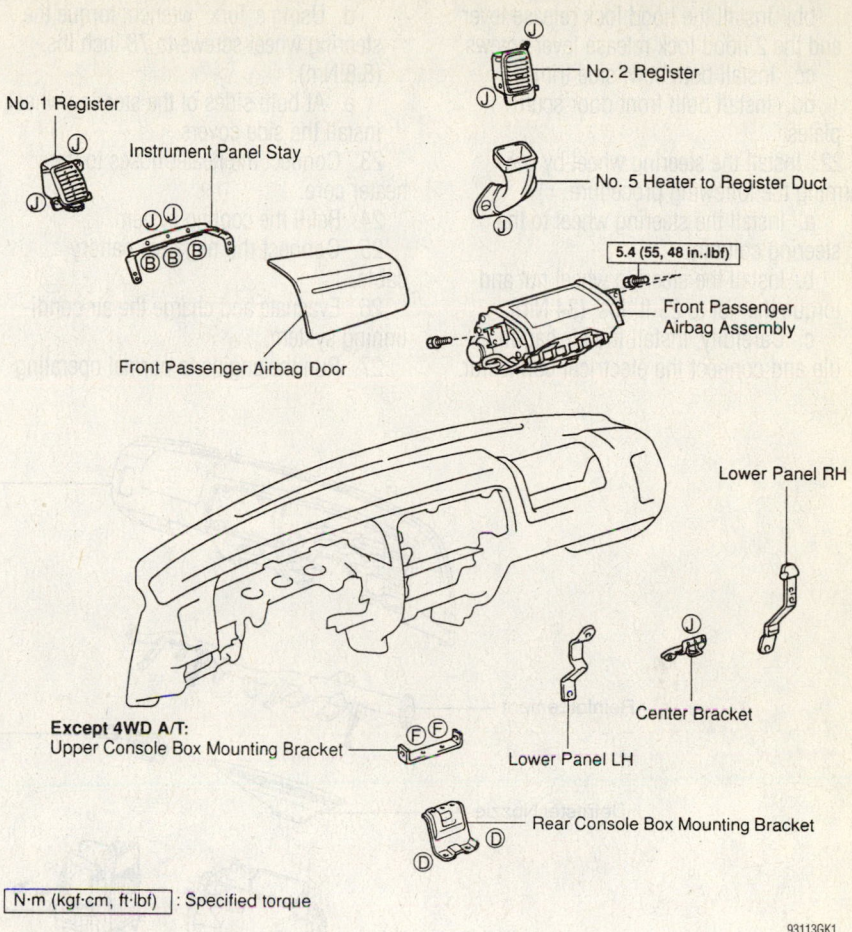

Exploded view of the instrument panel air bag module, ventilation components and brackets—Toyota 4Runner

e. Install the side bracket and the bracket bolt.

f. Install the radio assembly.

g. Install the No. 4 heater-to-register duct.

h. Install the glove compartment door reinforcement and the 3 reinforcement bolts.

i. Install the lower No. 2 finish panel and the 3 panel bolts.

j. Install the glove box light.

k. Connect the passenger's side air bag module electrical connector.

l. Install the glove compartment door and the 2 door screws.

m. Install the upper console panel garnish.

n. Install the rear console box and the 2 rear console box bolts/screws.

o. Install the heater control knobs.

p. Install the center cluster finish panel and engage the 7 panel clips.

q. Install the upper console panel.

r. Install the parking brake hole cover.

s. Install the combination meter, connect the electrical connectors and install the 4 combination meter screws.

t. Install the cluster finish panel and the 4 panel screws.

u. Install the steering column and torque the steering column-to-instrument panel nuts to 19 ft. lbs. (26 Nm) and the lower steering column bolt to 26 ft. lbs. (35 Nm).

v. Install the combination switch-to-steering column, connect the electrical connector and the combination switch screws.

w. Install the steering column cover and the cover screws.

x. Pry out the starter switch bezel.

y. Install the No. 1 and No. 2 heater-to-register duct and the duct screws.

z. Install the lower finish panel and the 4 panel bolts.

aa. Install the fuel lid release lever and the 2 fuel lid release lever screws.

Refer to the model specific sections for engine mechanical service procedures

bb. Install the hood lock release lever and the 2 hood lock release lever screws.

cc. Install both cowl side trims.

dd. Install both front door scuff plates.

22. Install the steering wheel by performing the following procedure:

a. Install the steering wheel to the steering column.

b. Install the steering wheel nut and torque the nut to 25 ft. lbs. (34 Nm).

c. Carefully, install the air bag module and connect the electrical connector.

d. Using a Torx® wrench, torque the steering wheel screws to 78 inch lbs. (8.8 Nm).

e. At both sides of the steering wheel, install the side covers.

23. Connect the heater hoses to the heater core.

24. Refill the cooling system.

25. Connect the negative battery cable.

26. Evacuate and charge the air conditioning system.

27. Run the engine to normal operating temperatures; then, check the climate control operation and check for leaks.

Rear Auxiliary Heater

1. Disconnect the negative battery cable.

2. Drain the cooling system into a clean container for reuse.

3. Remove the front seats.

4. Remove the center console box.

5. Move the floor carpet backward.

6. Disconnect the rear heater hoses from the rear heater core.

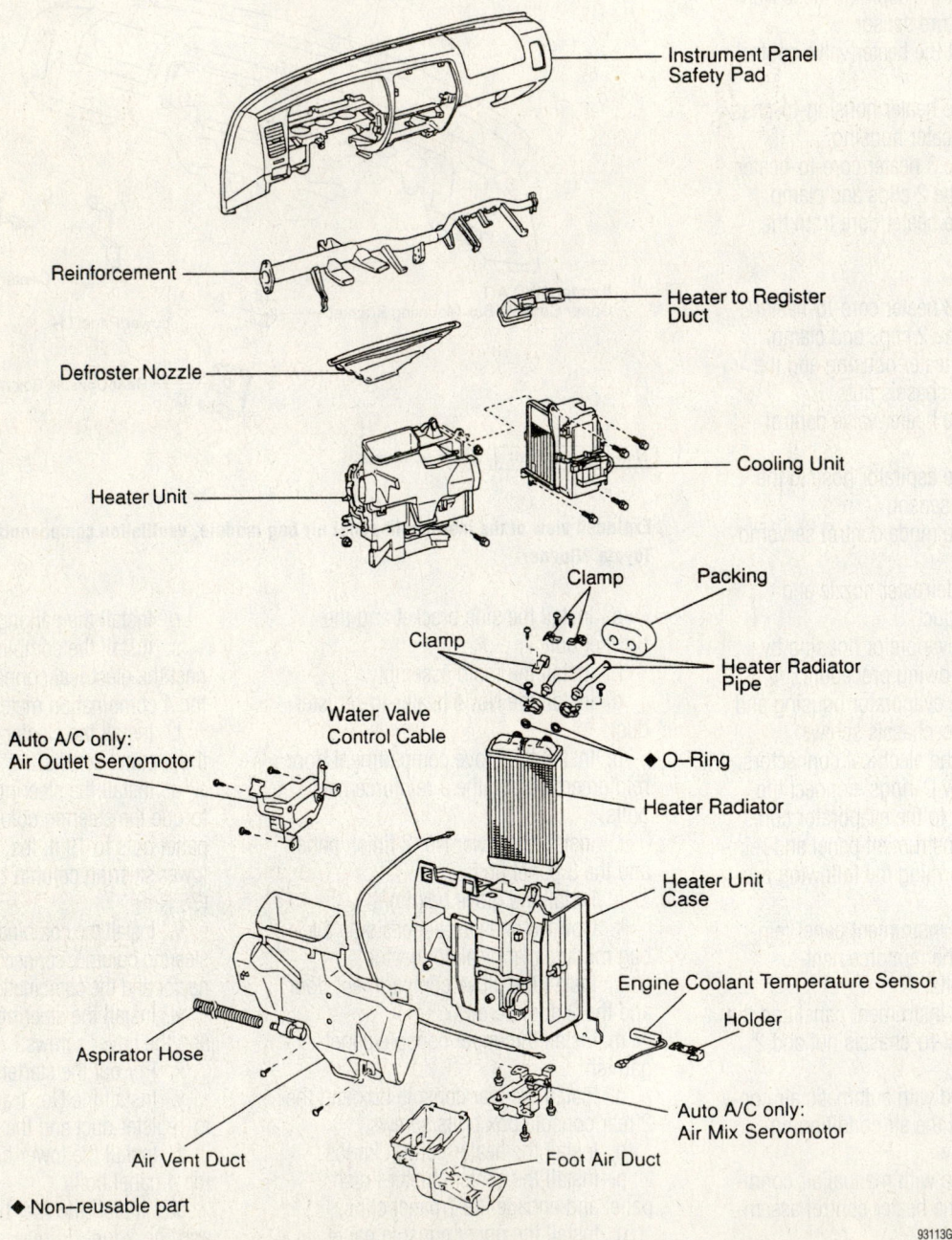

Instrument Panel Safety Pad

Reinforcement

Heater to Register Duct

Defroster Nozzle

Heater Unit

Cooling Unit

Clamp

Clamp

Clamp

Packing

Heater Radiator Pipe

◆ O—Ring

Heater Radiator

Water Valve Control Cable

Auto A/C only: Air Outlet Servomotor

Heater Unit Case

Engine Coolant Temperature Sensor

Holder

Aspirator Hose

Auto A/C only: Air Mix Servomotor

Air Vent Duct

Foot Air Duct

◆ Non—reusable part

93113GK2

Exploded view of the front heater core, heater housing, evaporator housing and related components—Toyota 4Runner

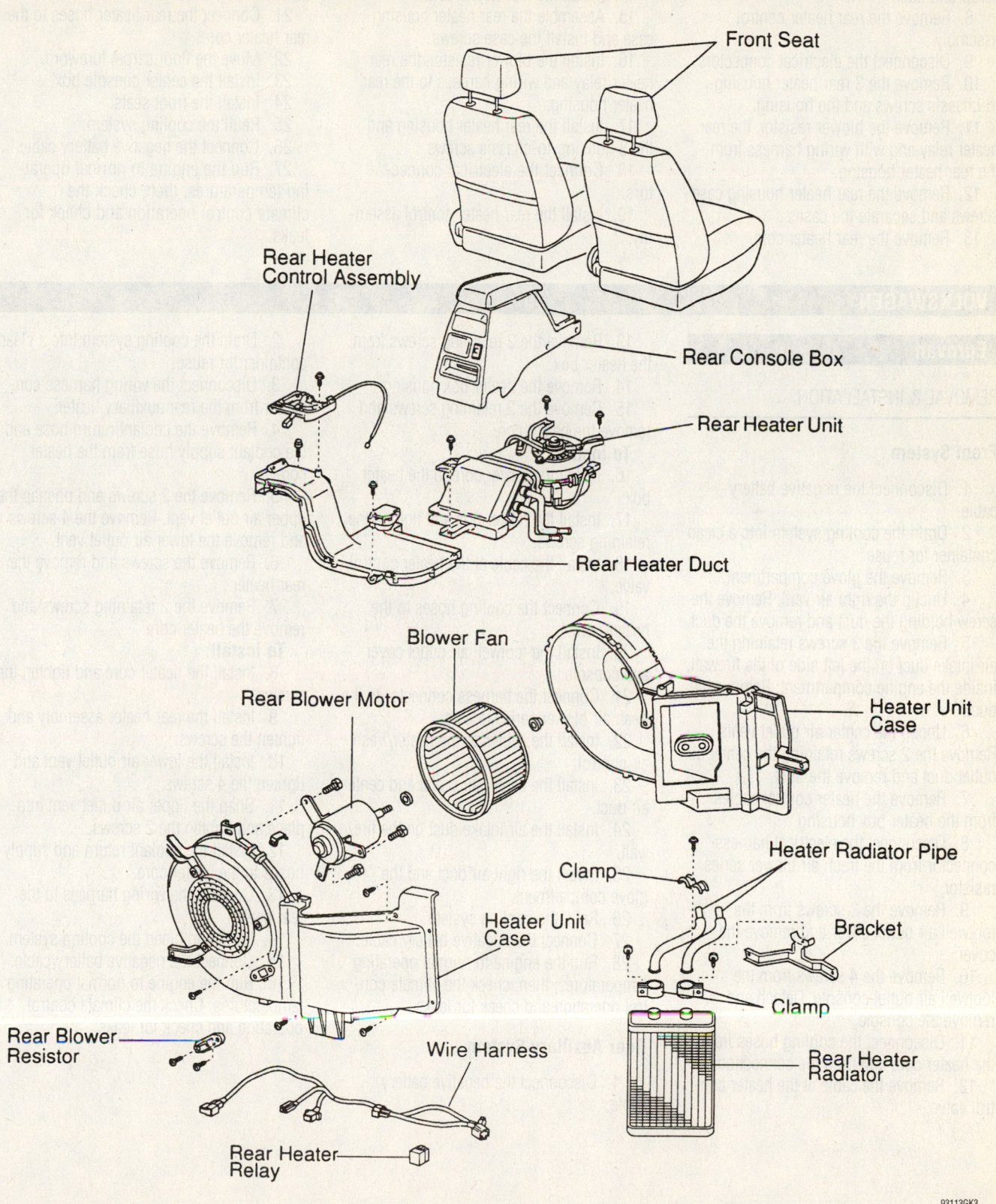

Front Seat

Rear Console Box

Rear Heater
Control Assembly

Rear Heater Unit

Rear Heater Duct

Blower Fan

Rear Blower Motor

Heater Unit
Case

Heater Radiator Pipe

Clamp

Bracket

Clamp

Rear Heater
Radiator

Heater Unit
Case

Rear Blower
Resistor

Wire Harness

Rear Heater
Relay

93113GK3

Exploded view of the rear heater housing and heater core—Toyota 4Runner

Refer to the model specific sections for cooling system service procedures

7. Remove the rear heater duct bolt, screw and duct.

8. Remove the rear heater control assembly.

9. Disconnect the electrical connectors.

10. Remove the 3 rear heater housing-to-chassis screws and the housing.

11. Remove the blower resistor, the rear heater relay and with wiring harness from the rear heater housing.

12. Remove the rear heater housing case screws and separate the cases.

13. Remove the rear heater core.

To install:

14. Install the rear heater core.

15. Assemble the rear heater housing case and install the case screws.

16. Install the blower resistor, the rear heater relay and wiring harness to the rear heater housing.

17. Install the rear heater housing and the 3 housing-to-chassis screws.

18. Connect the electrical connectors.

19. Install the rear heater control assembly.

20. Install the rear heater duct, bolt and screw.

21. Connect the rear heater hoses to the rear heater core.

22. Move the floor carpet foreword.

23. Install the center console box.

24. Install the front seats.

25. Refill the cooling system.

26. Connect the negative battery cable.

27. Run the engine to normal operating temperatures; then, check the climate control operation and check for leaks.

VOLKSWAGEN

Eurovan

REMOVAL & INSTALLATION

Front System

1. Disconnect the negative battery cable.

2. Drain the cooling system into a clean container for reuse.

3. Remove the glove compartment.

4. Unclip the right air vent. Remove the screw holding the duct and remove the duct.

5. Remove the 3 screws retaining the air intake duct on the left side of the firewall, inside the engine compartment. Remove the duct.

6. Unclip the center air outlet vents. Remove the 2 screws retaining the center air outlet duct and remove the duct.

7. Remove the heater control cables from the heater box housing.

8. Disconnect the electrical harness connector from the fresh air blower series resistor.

9. Remove the 3 screws from the footwell air outlet cover and remove the cover.

10. Remove the 4 screws from the footwell air outlet console. Detach and remove the console.

11. Disconnect the cooling hoses from the heater core and plug the connections.

12. Remove the cable at the heater control valve.

13. Remove the 2 retaining screws from the heater box.

14. Remove the heater box housing.

15. Remove the 2 retaining screws and remove the heater core.

To install:

16. Install the heater core to the heater box.

17. Install the heater box and tighten the retaining screws.

18. Install the cable at the heater control valve.

19. Connect the cooling hoses to the heater core.

20. Install the footwell air outlet cover and console.

21. Connect the harness connector to the fresh air blower series resistor.

22. Install the cables to the heater/fresh air control.

23. Install the center air outlet and center air duct.

24. Install the air intake duct on the firewall.

25. Install the right air duct and the glove compartment.

26. Refill the cooling system.

27. Connect the negative battery cable.

28. Run the engine to normal operating temperatures; then, check the climate control operation and check for leaks.

Rear Auxiliary System

1. Disconnect the negative battery cable.

2. Drain the cooling system into a clean container for reuse.

3. Disconnect the wiring harness connector from the rear auxiliary heater.

4. Remove the coolant return hose and the coolant supply hose from the heater core.

5. Remove the 2 screws and unsnap the upper air outlet vent. Remove the 4 screws and remove the lower air outlet vent.

6. Remove the screws and remove the rear heater.

7. Remove the 2 retaining screws and remove the heater core.

To install:

8. Install the heater core and tighten the screws.

9. Install the rear heater assembly and tighten the screws.

10. Install the lower air outlet vent and tighten the 4 screws.

11. Snap the upper air outlet vent into place and tighten the 2 screws.

12. Install the coolant return and supply hoses to the heater core.

13. Connect the wiring harness to the rear heater.

14. Refill and bleed the cooling system.

15. Connect the negative battery cable.

16. Run the engine to normal operating temperatures. Check the climate control operation and check for leaks.

PRECAUTIONS

Before servicing any vehicle, please be sure to read all of the following precautions, which deal with personal safety, prevention of component damage and important points to take into consideration when servicing a motor vehicle:

• Never open, service or drain the radiator or cooling system when the engine is hot; serious burns can occur from the steam and hot coolant.

• Observe all applicable safety precautions when working around fuel. Whenever servicing the fuel system, always work in a well-ventilated area. Do not allow fuel spray or vapors to come in contact with a spark, open flame, or excessive heat (a hot drop light, for example). Keep a dry chemical fire extinguisher near the work area. Always keep fuel in a container specifically designed for fuel storage; also, always properly seal fuel containers to avoid the possibility of fire or explosion. Refer to the additional fuel system precautions later in this section.

• Fuel injection systems often remain pressurized, even after the engine has been turned **OFF**. The fuel system pressure must be relieved before disconnecting any fuel lines. Failure to do so may result in fire and/or personal injury.

• Brake fluid often contains polyglycol ethers and polyglycols. Avoid contact with the eyes and wash your hands thoroughly after handling brake fluid. If you do get brake fluid in your eyes, flush your eyes with clean, running water for 15 minutes. If eye irritation persists, or if you have taken brake fluid internally, seek medical assistance IMMEDIATELY.

• The EPA warns that prolonged contact with used engine oil may cause a number of skin disorders, including cancer. You should make every effort to minimize your exposure to used engine oil. Protective gloves should be worn when changing oil. Wash your hands and any other exposed skin areas as soon as possible after exposure to used engine oil. Soap and water, or waterless hand cleaner should be used.

• All new vehicles are now equipped with an air bag system, often referred to as a Supplemental Restraint System (SRS) or Supplemental Inflatable Restraint (SIR) system. The system must be disabled before performing service on or around system components, steering column, instrument panel components, wiring and sensors. Failure to follow safety and disabling procedures could result in accidental air bag deployment, possible personal injury and unnecessary system repairs.

• Always wear safety goggles when working with, or around, the air bag system. When carrying a non-deployed air bag, be sure the bag and trim cover are pointed away from your body. When placing a non-deployed air bag on a work surface, always face the bag and trim cover upward, away from the surface. This will reduce the motion of the module if it is accidentally deployed. Refer to the additional air bag system precautions later in this section.

• Clean, high quality brake fluid from a sealed container is essential to the safe and proper operation of the brake system. You should always buy the correct type of brake fluid for your vehicle. If the brake fluid becomes contaminated, completely flush the system with new fluid. Never reuse any brake fluid. Any brake fluid that is removed from the system should be discarded. Also, do not allow any brake fluid to come in contact with a painted surface; it will damage the paint.

• Never operate the engine without the proper amount and type of engine oil; doing so WILL result in severe engine damage.

• Timing belt maintenance is extremely important. Many models utilize an interference-type, non-freewheeling engine. If the timing belt breaks, the valves in the cylinder head may strike the pistons, causing potentially serious (also time-consuming and expensive) engine damage. Refer to the maintenance interval charts in the front of this manual for the recommended replacement interval for the timing belt and to the timing belt section for belt replacement and inspection.

• Disconnecting the negative battery cable on some vehicles may interfere with the functions of the on-board computer system(s) and may require the computer to undergo a relearning process once the negative battery cable is reconnected.

• When servicing drum brakes, only disassemble and assemble one side at a time, leaving the remaining side intact for reference.

• Only an MVAC-trained, EPA-certified automotive technician should service the air conditioning system or its components.

ENGINE REPAIR

➡ **Disconnecting the negative battery cable on some vehicles may interfere with the functions of the on board computer system. The computer may undergo a relearning process once the negative battery cable is reconnected.**

Alternator

REMOVAL

3.2L Engine

1. Before servicing the vehicle, refer to the precautions in the beginning of this section.
2. Remove or disconnect the following:
   • Negative battery cable
   • Front splash shield
   • Alternator drive belt
   • Adjuster
   • Top alternator bolt
   • Alternator wiring connectors
   • Alternator

3.5L Engine

1. Before servicing the vehicle, refer to the precautions in the beginning of this section.
2. Remove or disconnect the following:
   • Negative battery cable
   • Accessory drive belt
   • Alternator wiring connectors
   • Alternator

INSTALLATION

3.2L Engine

1. Install or connect the following:
   • Alternator
   • Alternator wiring connectors
   • Top alternator bolt
   • Adjuster
   • Alternator drive belt. Tighten the alternator top bolt to 16 ft. lbs. (22 Nm) and the adjuster lock bolt to 17 ft. lbs. (24 Nm).
   • Front splash shield
   • Negative battery cable

3.5L Engine

1. Before servicing the vehicle, refer to the precautions in the beginning of this section.

2. Install or connect the following:
- Alternator. Tighten the 10mm bolts to 30 ft. lbs. (41 Nm) and the 8mm bolts to 15 ft. lbs. (21 Nm).
- Alternator wiring connectors
- Accessory drive belt
- Negative battery cable

Ignition Timing

ADJUSTMENT

Ignition timing is controlled by the Powertrain Control Module (PCM) and is not adjustable.

Engine Assembly

REMOVAL & INSTALLATION

1. Before servicing the vehicle, refer to the precautions in the beginning of this section.
2. Drain the cooling system.
3. Remove or disconnect the following:
- Battery
- Hood
- Air cleaner assembly
- Accelerator cable
- Cruise control cable
- Canister vacuum line
- Brake booster vacuum line
- Engine wiring harness connectors
- Transmission harness connectors and bracket
- Engine ground cable
- Starter harness connector
- Alternator harness connector
- Coolant reservoir tank hose
- Radiator hoses
- Heater hoses
- Upper fan shroud
- Radiator
- Cooling fan
- Accessory drive belt
- Power steering pump
- A/C compressor
- Heated Oxygen (HO$_2$S) sensor connectors
- Left and right exhaust front pipes
- Fuel lines
- Flywheel dust cover
- Transmission. Refer to the transmission procedure in this section.
- Left and right engine mounts
- Engine

To install:

4. Install or connect the following:

- Engine
- Left and right engine mounts. Tighten the bolts to 30 ft. lbs. (41 Nm).
- Transmission
- Flywheel dust cover
- Fuel lines
- Left and right exhaust front pipes
- HO$_2$S sensor connectors
- A/C compressor
- Power steering pump
- Accessory drive belt
- Cooling fan. Tighten the nuts to 16 ft. lbs. (22 Nm).
- Radiator
- Upper fan shroud
- Heater hoses
- Radiator hoses
- Coolant reservoir tank hose
- Alternator harness connector
- Starter harness connector
- Engine ground cable
- Transmission harness connectors and bracket
- Engine wiring harness connectors
- Brake booster vacuum line
- Canister vacuum line
- Cruise control cable
- Accelerator cable
- Air cleaner assembly
- Hood
- Battery

5. Fill the cooling system. Check all fluid levels and adjust as necessary.

6. Start the engine and check for leaks.

Water Pump

REMOVAL & INSTALLATION

1. Before servicing the vehicle, refer to the precautions in the beginning of this section.

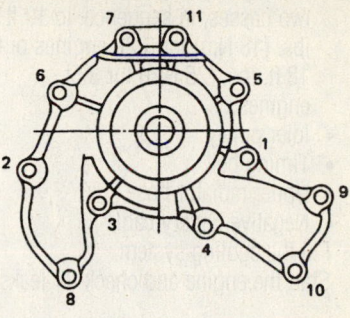

Water pump torque sequence—3.2L engine

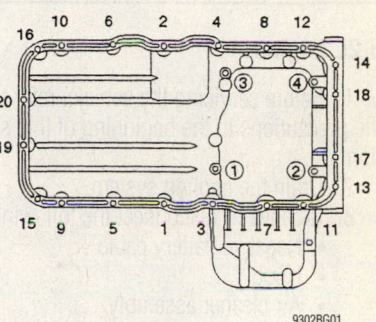

**Water pump torque sequence.
Apply LOCTITE® 262 to bolt number 3 (arrow)—3.5L engine**

2. Drain the cooling system.
3. Remove or disconnect the following:
- Negative battery cable
- Upper radiator hose
- Timing belt. Refer to the Timing Belt Unit Repair Section.
- Idler pulley
- Water pump

To install:

➡ On 3.5L engines, apply Loctite® 262 to bolt number 3 prior to installation.

4. Install or connect the following:

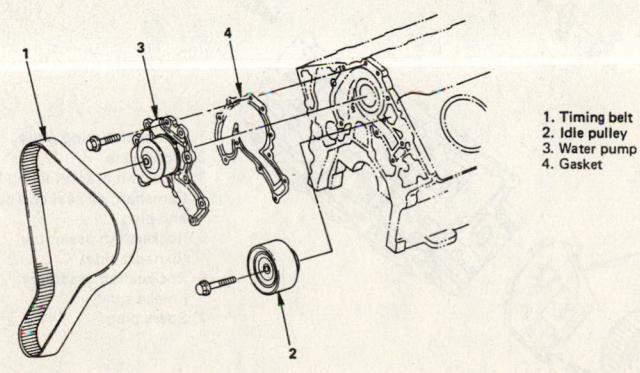

1. Timing belt
2. Idle pulley
3. Water pump assembly
4. Gasket

Exploded view of the water pump mounting

- Water pump. Tighten the bolts in two passes, in sequence, to 13 ft. lbs. (18 Nm) for 3.2L engines or to 18 ft. lbs. (25 Nm) for 3.5L engines.
- Idler pulley
- Timing belt
- Upper radiator hose
- Negative battery cable

5. Fill the cooling system.
6. Start the engine and check for leaks.

Cylinder Head

REMOVAL & INSTALLATION

3.2L Engine

1. Before servicing the vehicle, refer to the precautions in the beginning of this section.
2. Drain the cooling system.
3. Remove or disconnect the following:
   - Negative battery cable
   - Hood
   - Air cleaner assembly

- Fuel lines
- Upper intake manifold
- Lower intake manifold
- Ignition coils
- Valve covers
- Engine coolant manifold
- Accessory drive belts
- Power steering pump and bracket
- Cooling fan and pulley
- Crankshaft pulley
- Oil cooler hoses
- Timing belt cover
- Timing belt. Refer to the Timing Belt Unit Repair Section.
- Left and right exhaust front pipes
- Oil dipstick tube
- Cylinder heads

To install:

➡**Use new head bolts when installing the cylinder head. Do not apply oil to the head bolt threads.**

➡**Refer to Section 1 of this manual for the cylinder head torque sequence illustration. The illustration is located after the Torque Specification Chart.**

4. Install the cylinder heads with new gaskets. Tighten the 11mm bolts to 47 ft. lbs. (64 Nm) and the 8mm bolts to 15 ft. lbs. (21 Nm).
5. Install or connect the following:
   - Oil dipstick tube
   - Left and right exhaust front pipes
   - Timing belt
   - Timing belt cover
   - Oil cooler hoses
   - Crankshaft pulley. Tighten the pulley bolt to 123 ft. lbs. (167 Nm).
   - Cooling fan and pulley
   - Power steering pump and bracket. Tighten the bolts to 34 ft. lbs. (46 Nm).
   - Accessory drive belts
   - Engine coolant manifold
   - Valve covers
   - Ignition coils
   - Lower intake manifold
   - Upper intake manifold
   - Fuel lines
   - Air cleaner assembly
   - Hood
   - Negative battery cable
6. Fill the cooling system.
7. Start the engine. Check for leaks and proper operation.

3.5L Engine

1. Before servicing the vehicle, refer to the precautions in the beginning of this section.
2. Drain the cooling system.
3. Remove or disconnect the following:
   - Negative battery cable
   - Hood
   - Engine cover
   - Mass Air Flow (MAF) sensor connector
   - Intake Air Temperature (IAT) sensor connector
   - Positive Crankcase Ventilation (PCV) valve and hose
   - Air cleaner assembly
   - Manifold Absolute Pressure (MAP) sensor connector
   - Vacuum Switching Valve (VSV) connector and vacuum line
   - Fuel injector connectors
   - Throttle Position (TP) sensor connector
   - Idle Air Control (IAC) valve connector
   - Ignition coils
   - Brake booster vacuum line
   - Canister purge vacuum line
   - Duty solenoid valve
   - Fuel lines
   - Intake manifold

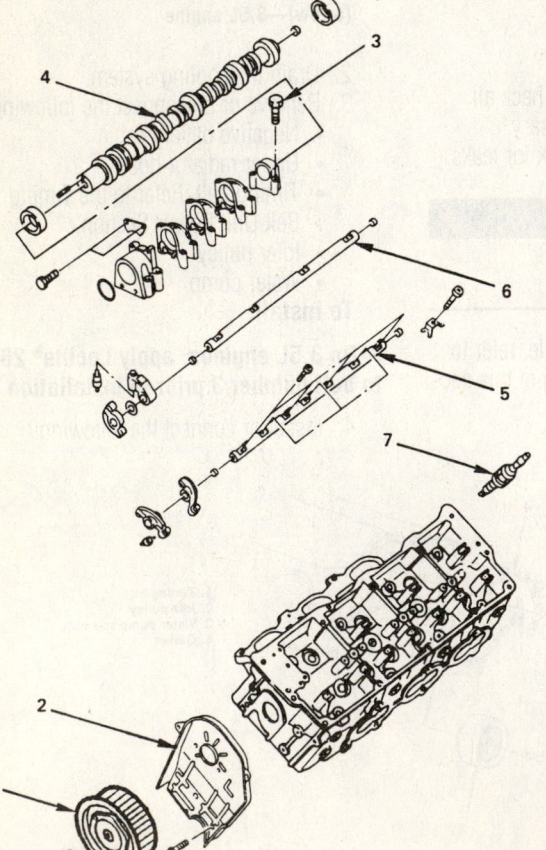

1. Camshaft timing pulley
2. Front plate
3. Camshaft bracket fixing bolts
4. Camshaft, oil seal and camshaft end plug
5. Rockershaft assembly (Exhaust side)
6. Rockershaft assembly (Intake side)
7. Spark plug

7924BG42

Exploded view of the cylinder head components—3.2L engines

- Radiator hoses
- Engine coolant manifold
- Upper fan shroud
- Accessory drive belt and tensioner
- Cooling fan and pulley
- Alternator
- Idler pulley
- Power steering pump and bracket
- A/C compressor
- Crankshaft pulley
- Oil cooler hoses
- Timing belt cover
- Valve covers
- Timing belt. Refer to the Timing Belt Unit Repair Section.
- Left and right exhaust front pipes
- Oil dipstick tube
- Cylinder heads

To install:

➡ **Use new head bolts when installing the cylinder head. Do not apply oil to the head bolt threads.**

➡ **The left and right cylinder head gaskets are not interchangeable.**

➡ **Refer to Section 1 of this manual for the cylinder head torque sequence illustration. The illustration is located after the Torque Specification Chart.**

4. Install the cylinder heads with new gaskets. Tighten the bolts to 47 ft. lbs. (64 Nm).

5. Install or connect the following:
- Oil dipstick tube
- Left and right exhaust front pipes
- Timing belt
- Valve covers
- Timing belt cover
- Oil cooler hoses
- Crankshaft pulley. Tighten the pulley bolt to 123 ft. lbs. (167 Nm).
- A/C compressor
- Power steering pump and bracket.

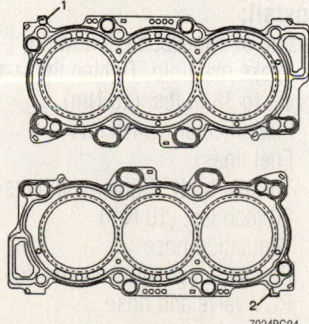

Right (1) and left (2) head gasket identification mark locations—3.5L engine

Tighten the bolts to 34 ft. lbs. (46 Nm).
- Idler pulley
- Alternator
- Cooling fan and pulley
- Accessory drive belt and tensioner
- Upper fan shroud
- Engine coolant manifold
- Radiator hoses
- Intake manifold
- Fuel lines
- Duty solenoid valve
- Canister purge vacuum line
- Brake booster vacuum line
- Ignition coils
- IAC valve connector
- TP sensor connector
- Fuel injector connectors
- VSV connector and vacuum line
- MAP sensor connector
- Air cleaner assembly
- PCV valve and hose
- IAT sensor connector
- MAF sensor connector
- Engine cover
- Hood
- Negative battery cable

6. Fill the cooling system.
7. Start the engine. Check for leaks and proper operation.

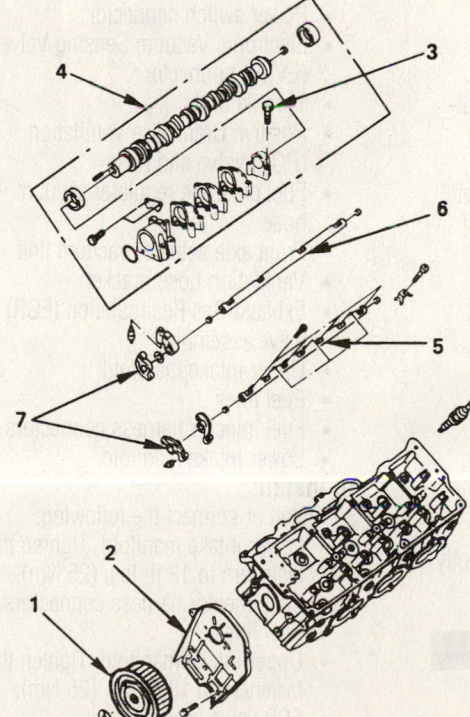

Exploded view of the rocker arm/shaft assembly mounting—3.2L engines

Rocker Arms/Shafts

REMOVAL & INSTALLATION

3.2L Engine

1. Before servicing the vehicle, refer to the precautions in the beginning of this section.

2. Remove or disconnect the following:
- Negative battery cable
- Air cleaner assembly
- Fuel lines
- Upper intake manifold
- Ignition coils
- Valve covers
- Upper fan shroud
- Accessory drive belts
- Power steering pump and bracket
- Cooling fan and pulley
- Crankshaft pulley
- Oil cooler hoses
- Timing belt cover
- Timing belt. Refer to the Timing Belt Unit Repair Section.
- Camshaft sprockets
- Cylinder head front plates
- Camshafts
- Rocker arm shafts

1. Camshaft timing pulley
2. Front plate
3. Camshaft bracket housing fixing bolts
4. Camshaft assembly
5. Rockershaft assembly (Exhaust side)
6. Rockershaft assembly (Intake side)
7. Rocker arm

Timing belt service is covered in Section 4 of this manual

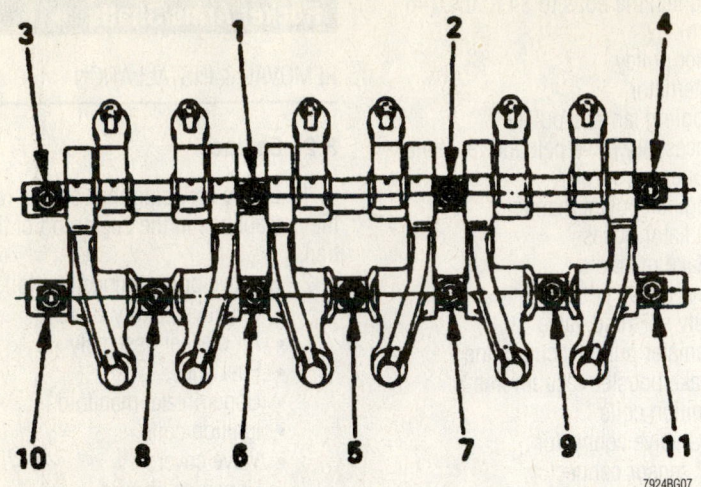

Rocker shaft bolt tightening pattern—3.2L engines

- Rocker arms from the shafts

To install:

3. Install or connect the following:
   - Rocker arms
   - Rocker arm shafts. Tighten the bolts, in sequence, to 13 ft. lbs. (18 Nm).
   - Camshafts
   - Cylinder head front plates. Tighten the bolts to 12 ft. lbs. (17 Nm).
   - Camshaft sprockets. Tighten the bolts to 46 ft. lbs. (64 Nm).
   - Timing belt
   - Timing belt cover
   - Oil cooler hoses
   - Crankshaft pulley. Tighten the pulley bolt to 123 ft. lbs. (167 Nm).
   - Cooling fan and pulley
   - Power steering pump and bracket
   - Accessory drive belts
   - Upper fan shroud
   - Valve covers
   - Ignition coils
   - Upper intake manifold
   - Fuel lines
   - Air cleaner assembly
   - Negative battery cable

3.5L Engine

The 3.5L engine is not equipped with rocker arms. The camshaft lobes act directly on the valve shims.

Intake Manifold

REMOVAL & INSTALLATION

3.2L Engine

1. Before servicing the vehicle, refer to the precautions in the beginning of this section.

2. Remove or disconnect the following:
   - Negative battery cable
   - Air cleaner assembly
   - Accelerator cable
   - Cruise control cable
   - Brake booster vacuum line
   - Manifold Absolute Pressure (MAP) sensor connector
   - Idle Air Control (IAC) valve connector
   - Throttle Position (TP) sensor connector
   - Power switch connector
   - Electronic Vacuum Sensing Valve (EVSV) connector
   - Throttle body
   - Positive Crankcase Ventilation (PCV) valve and hose
   - Fuel pressure regulator vacuum hose
   - Front axle actuator vacuum line
   - Ventilation hose bracket
   - Exhaust Gas Recirculation (EGR) valve assembly
   - Upper intake manifold
   - Fuel lines
   - Fuel injector harness connectors
   - Lower intake manifold

To install:

3. Install or connect the following:
   - Lower intake manifold. Tighten the fasteners to 18 ft. lbs. (25 Nm).
   - Fuel injector harness connectors
   - Fuel lines
   - Upper intake manifold. Tighten the fasteners to 18 ft. lbs. (25 Nm).
   - EGR valve assembly
   - Ventilation hose bracket
   - Front axle actuator vacuum line
   - Fuel pressure regulator vacuum hose
   - PCV valve and hose

- Throttle body. Tighten the bolts to 10 ft. lbs. (13.5 Nm).
- EVSV connector
- Power switch connector
- TP sensor connector
- IAC valve connector
- MAP sensor connector
- Brake booster vacuum line
- Cruise control cable
- Accelerator cable
- Air cleaner assembly
- Negative battery cable

4. Start the engine and check for proper operation.

3.5L Engine

1. Before servicing the vehicle, refer to the precautions in the beginning of this section.

2. Remove or disconnect the following:
   - Negative battery cable
   - Engine cover
   - Air cleaner assembly
   - Accelerator cable
   - Cruise control cable
   - Brake booster vacuum line
   - Manifold Absolute Pressure (MAP) sensor connector
   - Idle Air Control (IAC) valve connector
   - Throttle Position (TP) sensor connector
   - Canister purge solenoid connector
   - Electronic Vacuum Sensing Valve (EVSV) connector and vacuum line
   - Exhaust Gas Recirculation (EGR) valve
   - Positive Crankcase Ventilation (PCV) valve and hose
   - Pressure regulator vacuum line
   - Ventilation hose
   - Throttle body
   - Fuel lines
   - Fuel injector connectors
   - Intake manifold

To install:

3. Install or connect the following:
   - Intake manifold. Tighten the fasteners to 18 ft. lbs. (25 Nm).
   - Fuel injector connectors
   - Fuel lines
   - Throttle body. Tighten the bolts to 88 inch lbs. (10 Nm).
   - Ventilation hose
   - Pressure regulator vacuum line
   - PCV valve and hose
   - EGR valve
   - EVSV connector and vacuum line
   - Canister purge solenoid connector
   - TP sensor connector
   - IAC valve connector

- MAP sensor connector
- Brake booster vacuum line
- Cruise control cable
- Accelerator cable
- Air cleaner assembly
- Engine cover
- Negative battery cable

4. Start the engine and check for proper operation.

Exhaust Manifold

REMOVAL & INSTALLATION

3.2L Engine

1. Before servicing the vehicle, refer to the precautions in the beginning of this section.

2. Remove or disconnect the following:

- Negative battery cable
- Air cleaner assembly
- Exhaust Gas Recirculation (EGR) pipe
- 3rd crossmember
- Transfer case skid plate
- Heated Oxygen (HO$_2$S) sensor connectors
- Left and right exhaust front pipes
- Heat shields
- Exhaust manifolds

To install:

➡**Use new nuts when installing the exhaust manifolds.**

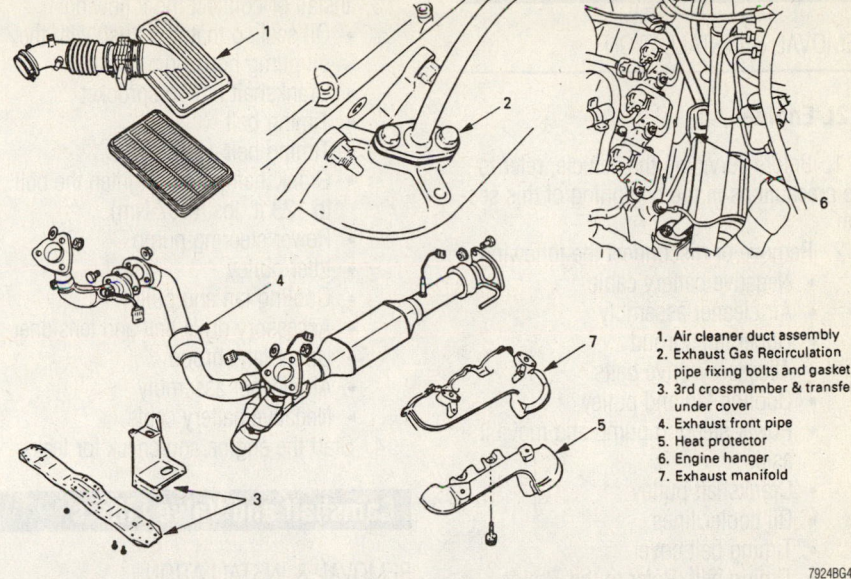

1. Air cleaner duct assembly
2. Exhaust Gas Recirculation pipe fixing bolts and gasket
3. 3rd crossmember & transfer under cover
4. Exhaust front pipe
5. Heat protector
6. Engine hanger
7. Exhaust manifold

7924BG45

Identification of the left-hand exhaust manifold and related components—3.2L engine

3. Install or connect the following:
- Exhaust manifolds. Tighten the nuts to 42 ft. lbs. (57 Nm).
- Heat shields
- Left and right exhaust front pipes
- HO$_2$S sensor connectors
- Transfer case skid plate
- 3rd crossmember
- EGR pipe
- Air cleaner assembly
- Negative battery cable
4. Start the engine and check for leaks.

3.5L Engine

1. Before servicing the vehicle, refer to the precautions in the beginning of this section.

2. Remove or disconnect the following:

- Negative battery cable
- Air cleaner assembly
- Heated Oxygen (HO$_2$S) sensor connectors
- Right torsion bar
- Exhaust Gas Recirculation (EGR) pipe and bracket
- Left and right exhaust front pipes
- Heat shields
- Accessory drive belt
- A/C compressor and bracket
- Exhaust manifolds

To install:

3. Install or connect the following:
- Exhaust manifolds. Tighten the bolts to 38 ft. lbs. (52 Nm).
- A/C compressor and bracket
- Accessory drive belt
- Heat shields
- Left and right exhaust front pipes
- EGR pipe and bracket
- Right torsion bar
- HO$_2$S sensor connectors
- Air cleaner assembly
- Negative battery cable
4. Start the engine and check for leaks.

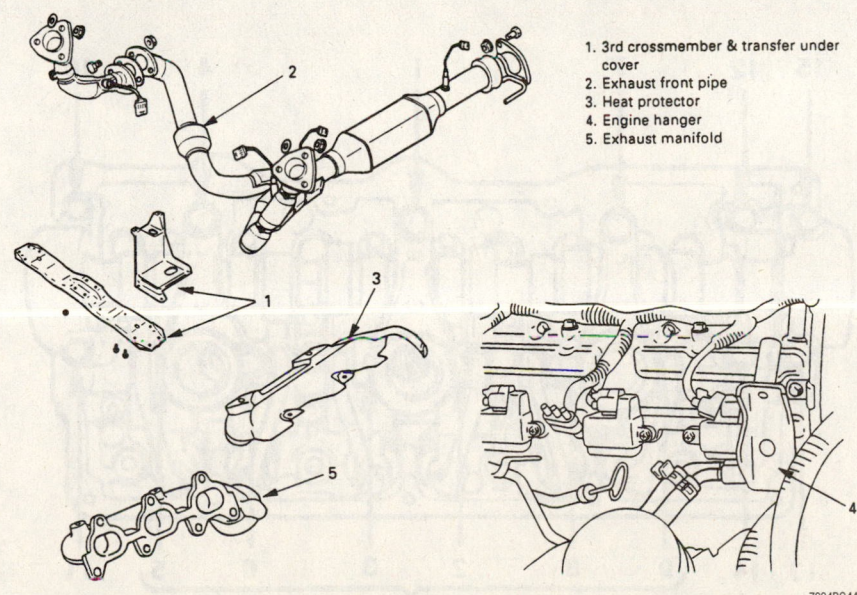

1. 3rd crossmember & transfer under cover
2. Exhaust front pipe
3. Heat protector
4. Engine hanger
5. Exhaust manifold

7924BG44

Identification of the right-hand exhaust manifold and related components—3.2L engine

Front Crankshaft Seal

REMOVAL & INSTALLATION

3.2L Engine

1. Before servicing the vehicle, refer to the precautions in the beginning of this section.
2. Remove or disconnect the following:
   - Negative battery cable
   - Air cleaner assembly
   - Upper fan shroud
   - Accessory drive belts
   - Cooling fan and pulley
   - Power steering pump and move it aside
   - Crankshaft pulley
   - Oil cooler lines
   - Timing belt cover
   - Timing belt. Refer to the Timing Belt Unit Repair Section.
   - Crankshaft timing sprocket
   - Oil seal

To install:

3. Install or connect the following:
   - Oil seal so that it is flush with the oil pump housing
   - Crankshaft timing sprocket
   - Timing belt
   - Timing belt cover
   - Oil cooler lines
   - Crankshaft pulley. Tighten the bolt to 123 ft. lbs. (167 Nm).
   - Power steering pump
   - Cooling fan and pulley
   - Accessory drive belts
   - Upper fan shroud
   - Air cleaner assembly
   - Negative battery cable
4. Start the engine and check for leaks.

3.5L Engine

1. Before servicing the vehicle, refer to the precautions in the beginning of this section.
2. Remove or disconnect the following:
   - Negative battery cable
   - Air cleaner assembly
   - Upper fan shroud
   - Accessory drive belt and tensioner
   - Cooling fan and pulley
   - Idler pulley
   - Power steering pump and move it aside
   - Crankshaft pulley
   - Timing belt cover
   - Timing belt. Refer to the Timing Belt Unit Repair Section.
   - Crankshaft timing sprocket
   - Oil seal

To install:

3. Install or connect the following:
   - Oil seal so that it is flush with the oil pump housing
   - Crankshaft timing sprocket
   - Timing belt
   - Timing belt cover
   - Crankshaft pulley. Tighten the bolt to 123 ft. lbs. (167 Nm).
   - Power steering pump
   - Idler pulley
   - Cooling fan and pulley
   - Accessory drive belt and tensioner
   - Upper fan shroud
   - Air cleaner assembly
   - Negative battery cable
4. Start the engine and check for leaks.

Camshaft and Valve Lifters

REMOVAL & INSTALLATION

3.2L Engine

➡**The hydraulic lifters are attached to the rocker arms. Refer to the rocker arm procedure for rocker arm removal.**

1. Before servicing the vehicle, refer to the precautions in the beginning of this section.
2. Relieve the fuel pressure.
3. Remove or disconnect the following:
   - Negative battery cable
   - Upper intake manifold
   - Upper fan shroud
   - Accessory drive belts
   - Cooling fan and pulley
   - Fuel lines
   - Power steering pump and move it aside
   - Crankshaft pulley
   - Oil cooler lines
   - Timing belt cover
   - Timing belt. Refer to the Timing Belt Unit Repair Section.
   - Ignition coils
   - Valve covers
   - Camshaft pulleys
   - Cylinder head front plates
   - Camshaft oil seals
   - Camshafts

To install:

4. Apply a bead of sealant to the front and rear camshaft holder mating surfaces on the cylinder head.
5. Install the camshaft and holder assembly onto the cylinder head. Tighten the bolts in sequence to the following specifications:
   - 6mm bolts: 69 inch lbs. (8 Nm)
   - 8mm bolts: 13 ft. lbs. (18 Nm)
6. Install or connect the following:
   - Camshaft oil seals
   - Cylinder head front plates. Tighten the bolts to 12 ft. lbs. (17 Nm).
   - Camshaft pulleys. Tighten the bolts to 41 ft. lbs. (55 Nm).
   - Valve covers
   - Ignition coils
   - Timing belt
   - Timing belt cover
   - Oil cooler lines
   - Crankshaft pulley. Tighten the bolt to 123 ft. lbs. (167 Nm).

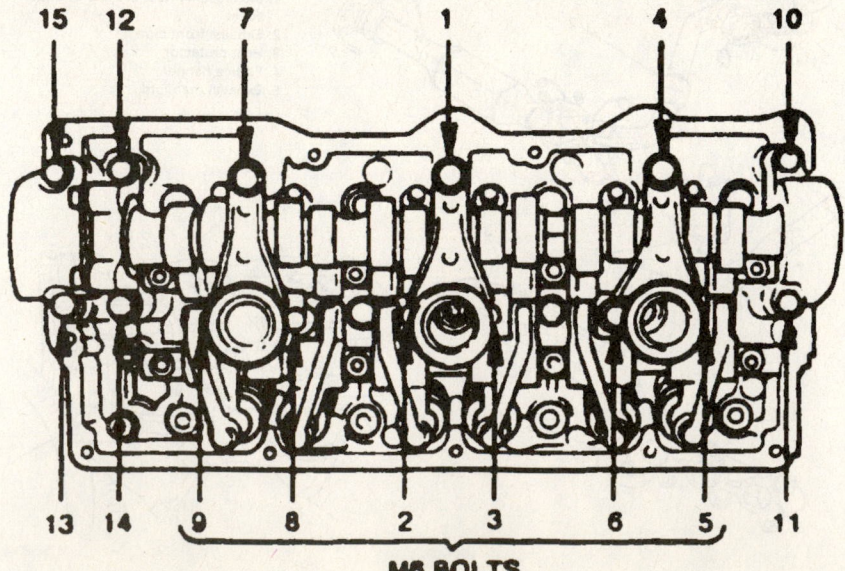

Camshaft mounting bolt tightening sequence—3.2L engines

7924BG08

- Power steering pump
- Fuel lines
- Cooling fan and pulley
- Accessory drive belts
- Upper fan shroud
- Upper intake manifold
- Negative battery cable

3.5L Engine

1. Before servicing the vehicle, refer to the precautions in the beginning of this section.

2. Remove or disconnect the following:
- Negative battery cable
- Air cleaner assembly
- Upper fan shroud
- Accessory drive belt and tensioner
- Cooling fan and pulley
- Idler pulley
- Power steering pump and move it aside
- Crankshaft pulley
- Timing belt cover
- Timing belt. Refer to the Timing Belt Unit Repair Section.
- Ignition coils
- Valve covers

- Camshafts
- Valve shims and tappets

➡ **Keep the valve shims and tappets in order for installation.**

To install:

3. Install the valve tappets and shims in their original locations.

4. Using Gear Spring Lever J-42686, turn the sub gear clockwise to align the 5mm bolt holes in the sub gear and the camshaft driven gear. Tighten the 5mm bolt.

5. Install the camshafts. Align the timing marks as shown. Tighten the bolts in sequence to 89 inch lbs. (10 Nm).

6. Install or connect the following:
- Valve covers
- Ignition coils
- Timing belt. Refer to the Timing Belt Unit Repair Section.
- Timing belt cover
- Crankshaft pulley
- Power steering pump
- Idler pulley
- Cooling fan and pulley
- Accessory drive belt and tensioner
- Upper fan shroud

- Air cleaner assembly
- Negative battery cable

Valve Lash

ADJUSTMENT

3.2L Engine

This engine is equipped with hydraulic lifters. No adjustment is necessary.

3.5L Engine

➡ **Measure valve clearance with the engine cold.**

1. Before servicing the vehicle, refer to the precautions in the beginning of this section.

2. Remove the valve covers.

3. Check the valve clearance with the camshafts positioned as shown. Intake valve clearance should be 0.0091–0.0130 inches. Exhaust valve clearance should be 0.0098–0.0138 inches.

4. If adjustment is required, replace the shims as follows:

   a. Step 1: Position special tool J–42689 on the edge of the tappet.

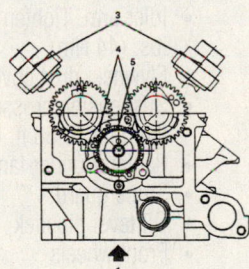 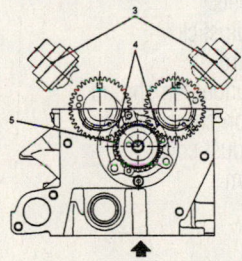

| 1 | Right Bank |
| 2 | Left Bank |

3	Alignment Mark on Camshaft Drive Gear
4	Alignment Mark on Camshaft
5	Alignment Mark on Retainer

7924BG11

Camshaft alignment marks for the left and right cylinder heads—3.5L engine

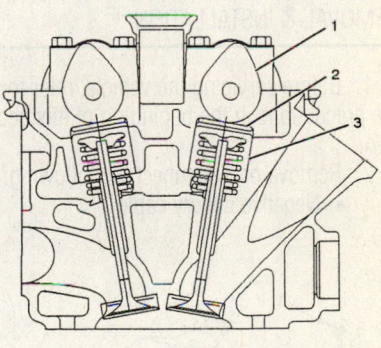

9302BG02

Cross section of the 3.5L cylinder head. Note the position of the camshaft lobe (1), adjustment shim (2) and the tappet (3)

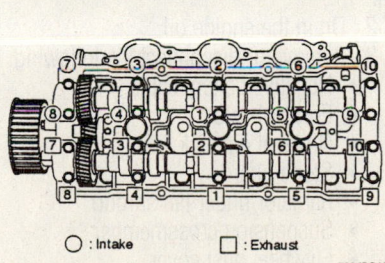

○ : Intake   □ : Exhaust

7924BG12

Camshaft retaining bracket tightening sequence—3.5L engine

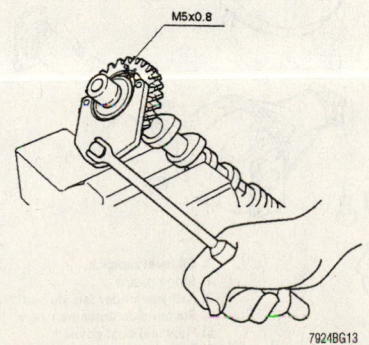

M5x0.8

7924BG13

Aligning the sub gear with the Gear Spring Lever J-42686—3.5L engine

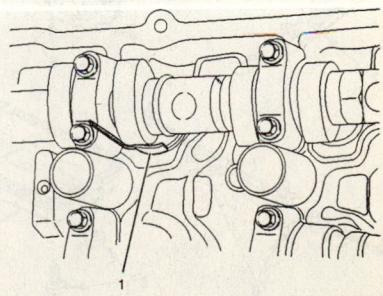

9302BG03

Valve clearance adjusting tool J-42689 (1)

Refer to Section 1 for engine rebuilding specifications

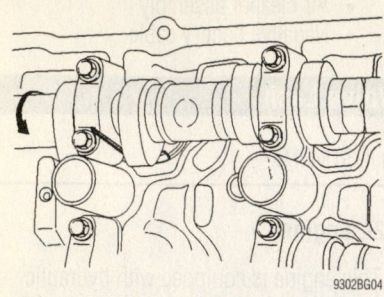

9302BG04

Using the valve clearance adjusting tool to hold the tappet for shim replacement

b. Step 2: Rotate the crankshaft until the maximum lift portion of the camshaft lobe contacts the upper edge of the special tool and presses the tappet down to create enough clearance between the adjustment shim and the camshaft for the shim to be removed.

c. Step 3: Replace shims as necessary to achieve correct valve clearance.

d. Step 4: Repeat for each valve to be adjusted.

5. Replace the valve covers. Tighten the bolts to 80 inch lbs. (9 Nm).

Starter Motor

REMOVAL & INSTALLATION

1. Before servicing the vehicle, refer to the precautions in the beginning of this section.

2. Remove or disconnect the following:
   - Negative battery cable

- Heated Oxygen (HO2S) sensor connectors
- Exhaust front pipe
- Heat shield
- Starter wiring connectors
- Starter motor

To install:

3. Install or connect the following:
   - Starter motor. Tighten the bolts to 30 ft. lbs. (40 Nm).
   - Starter wiring connectors
   - Heat shield
   - Exhaust front pipe
   - Heated Oxygen (HO2S) sensor connectors
   - Negative battery cable

Oil Pan

REMOVAL & INSTALLATION

3.2L Engine

1. Before servicing the vehicle, refer to the precautions in the beginning of this section.

2. Drain the engine oil.

3. Remove or disconnect the following:
   - Negative battery cable
   - Front wheels
   - Oil level dipstick
   - Stone guard
   - Radiator under fan shroud
   - Suspension crossmember
   - Flywheel dust cover
   - Pitman arm
   - Idler arm

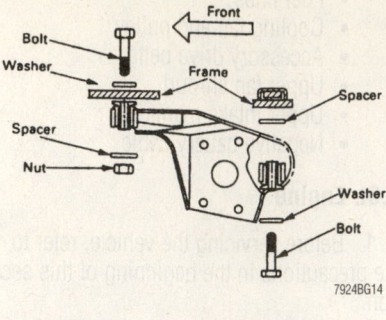

7924BG14

Exploded view of the axle bracket mounting bolt, spacer, and nut locations

4. Unbolt and lower the front axle housing assembly for clearance.

5. Remove the oil pan.

To install:

6. Apply a bead of silicone sealant to the oil pan flange and install the oil pan. Tighten the fasteners to 89 inch lbs. (10 Nm).

7. Raise the axle housing assembly into position. Tighten the bolts to 61 ft. lbs. (82 Nm) and the nuts to 112 ft. lbs. (152 Nm).

8. Install or connect the following:
   - Pitman arm. Tighten the nut to 159 ft. lbs. (216 Nm).
   - Idler arm. Tighten the bolt to 33 ft. lbs. (44 Nm).
   - Flywheel dust cover
   - Suspension crossmember. Tighten the bolts to 58 ft. lbs. (78 Nm).
   - Radiator under fan shroud
   - Stone guard
   - Oil level dipstick
   - Front wheels
   - Negative battery cable

9. Fill the crankcase with engine oil.

10. Start the engine and check for leaks.

3.5L Engine

1. Before servicing the vehicle, refer to the precautions in the beginning of this section.

2. Drain the engine oil.

3. Remove or disconnect the following:
   - Negative battery cable
   - Front wheels
   - Oil level dipstick
   - Stone guard
   - Radiator under fan shroud
   - Suspension crossmember
   - Flywheel dust cover
   - Pitman arm
   - Idler arm

4. If equipped with 4 wheel drive, unbolt and lower the front axle housing assembly for clearance.

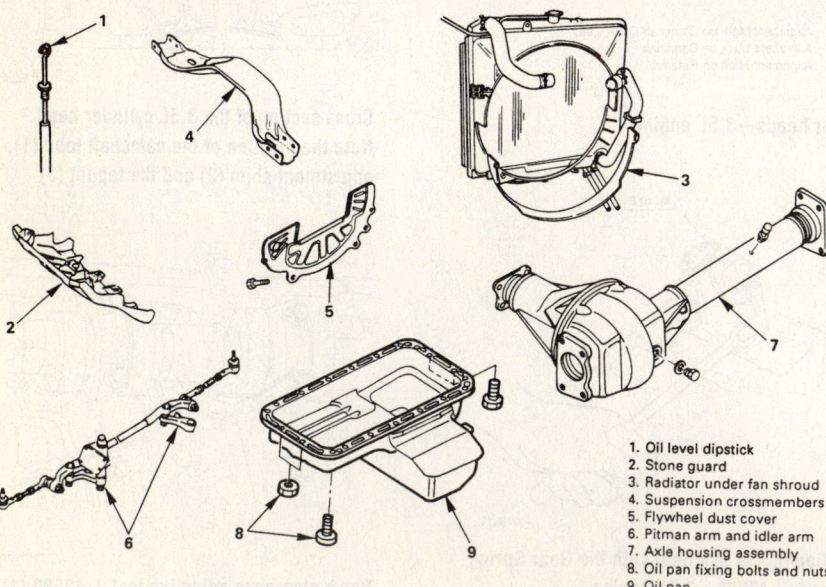

1. Oil level dipstick
2. Stone guard
3. Radiator under fan shroud
4. Suspension crossmembers
5. Flywheel dust cover
6. Pitman arm and idler arm
7. Axle housing assembly
8. Oil pan fixing bolts and nuts
9. Oil pan

7924BG46

Identification of the oil pan (9) and related service components

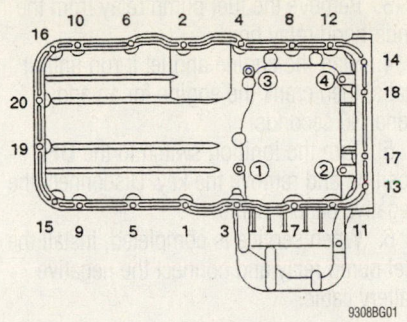

Lower crankcase torque sequence—3.5L engine

5. Remove or disconnect the following:

- Oil pan
- Lower crankcase

To install:

6. Apply a bead of silicone sealant to the crankcase flange and install the crankcase. Tighten the fasteners in sequence to 89 inch lbs. (10 Nm).

7. Apply a bead of silicone sealant to the oil pan flange and install the oil pan. Tighten the fasteners to 89 inch lbs. (10 Nm).

8. If equipped, raise the axle housing assembly into position. Tighten the axle case bolts to 61 ft. lbs. (82 Nm) and the mounting bolts to 112 ft. lbs. (152 Nm).

9. Install or connect the following:

- Pitman arm. Tighten the nut to 159 ft. lbs. (216 Nm).
- Idler arm. Tighten the bolt to 33 ft. lbs. (44 Nm).
- Flywheel dust cover
- Suspension crossmember. Tighten the bolts to 58 ft. lbs. (78 Nm).
- Radiator under fan shroud
- Stone guard
- Oil level dipstick
- Front wheels
- Negative battery cable

10. Fill the crankcase with engine oil.

11. Start the engine and check for leaks.

Oil Pump

REMOVAL & INSTALLATION

1. Before servicing the vehicle, refer to the precautions in the beginning of this section.

2. Remove or disconnect the following:

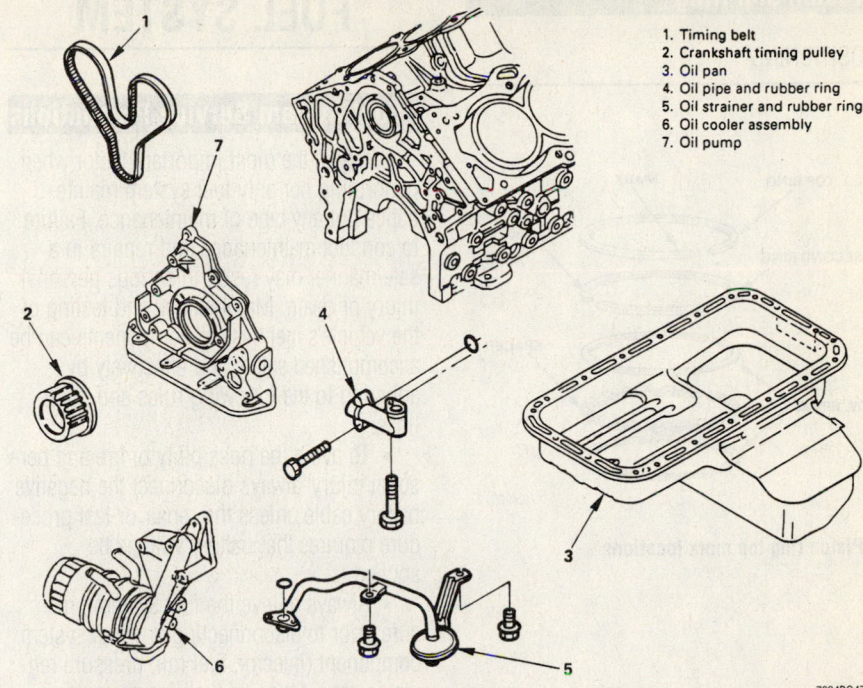

1. Timing belt
2. Crankshaft timing pulley
3. Oil pan
4. Oil pipe and rubber ring
5. Oil strainer and rubber ring
6. Oil cooler assembly
7. Oil pump

Oil pump and related components—3.2L engine shown

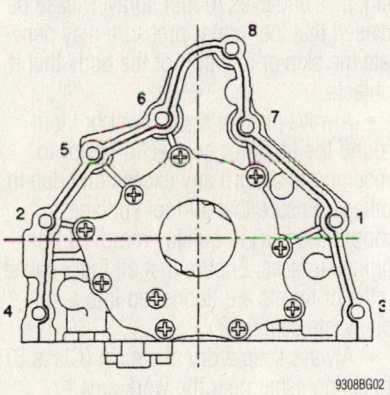

Oil pump torque sequence

- Timing belt
- Oil pan
- Oil pick-up tube
- Oil filter adapter
- Oil pump

To install:

3. Apply silicone sealant to the oil pump mounting surface and install the oil pump. Tighten the bolts in sequence to 13 ft. lbs. (18 Nm) for 3.2L engines or to 18 ft. lbs. (25 Nm) for 3.5L engines.

4. Install or connect the following:

- Oil filter adapter
- Oil pickup tube
- Oil pan
- Timing belt

Rear Main Seal

REMOVAL & INSTALLATION

1. Before servicing the vehicle, refer to the precautions in the beginning of this section.

2. Remove or disconnect the following:

- Negative battery cable
- Transmission
- Clutch assembly, if equipped with a manual transmission
- Flywheel by loosening the flywheel bolts in a 2-step crisscross sequence
- Rear main seal, using a seal puller

➡**Do not damage the crankshaft sealing surface.**

To install:

3. Install or connect the following:

- New rear main seal, by lubricating it with engine oil
- Flywheel, using new flywheel bolts. Tighten the bolts, in a 2-step crisscross pattern, to 40 ft. lbs. (54 Nm).
- Clutch assembly, if removed
- Transmission
- Negative battery cable

4. Check the oil and refill as necessary.

For engine torque specifications, refer to Section 1 of this manual

Piston and Ring

POSITIONING

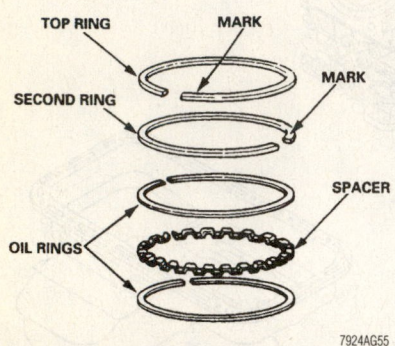

Piston ring top mark locations

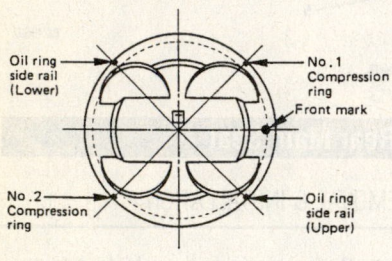

Piston ring end-gap spacing

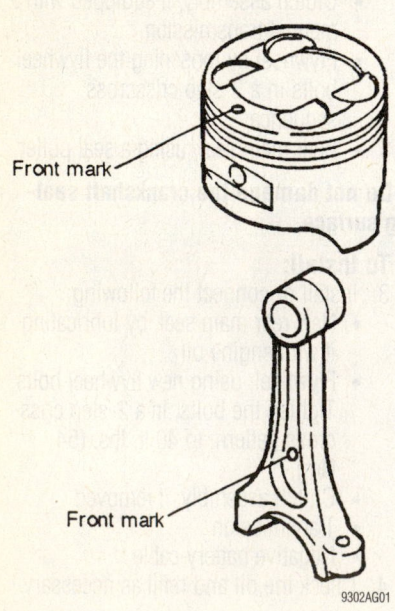

Piston and rod front marks

FUEL SYSTEM

Fuel System Service Precautions

Safety is the most important factor when performing not only fuel system maintenance but any type of maintenance. Failure to conduct maintenance and repairs in a safe manner may result in serious personal injury or death. Maintenance and testing of the vehicle's fuel system components can be accomplished safely and effectively by adhering to the following rules and guidelines:

• To avoid the possibility of fire and personal injury, always disconnect the negative battery cable unless the repair or test procedure requires that battery voltage be applied.

• Always relieve the fuel system pressure prior to disconnecting any fuel system component (injector, fuel rail, pressure regulator, etc.), fitting or fuel line connection. Exercise extreme caution whenever relieving fuel system pressure, to avoid exposing skin, face and eyes to fuel spray. Please be advised that fuel under pressure may penetrate the skin or any part of the body that it contacts.

• Always place a shop towel or cloth around the fitting or connection prior to loosening to absorb any excess fuel due to spillage. Ensure that all fuel spillage (should it occur) is quickly removed from engine surfaces. Ensure that all fuel soaked cloths or towels are deposited into a suitable waste container.

• Always keep a dry chemical (Class B) fire extinguisher near the work area.

• Do not allow fuel spray or fuel vapors to come into contact with a spark or open flame.

• Always use a backup wrench when loosening and tightening fuel line connection fittings. This will prevent unnecessary stress and torsion to fuel line piping. Always follow the proper tightening specifications.

• Always replace worn fuel fitting O-rings with new. Do not substitute fuel hose or equivalent, where fuel pipe is installed.

Fuel System Pressure

RELIEVING

1. Before servicing the vehicle, refer to the precautions in the beginning of this section.

2. Remove the fuel filler cap.

3. Remove the fuel pump relay from the underhood relay box.

4. Start the engine and let it run until it stalls, then crank the engine for an additional 30 seconds.

5. Turn the ignition switch to the **OFF** position and remove the key. Disconnect the negative battery cable.

6. When service is completed, install the fuel pump relay and connect the negative battery cable.

Fuel Filter

REMOVAL & INSTALLATION

1. Before servicing the vehicle, refer to the precautions in the beginning of this section.

2. Relieve the fuel system pressure.

3. Remove or disconnect the following:
   • Fuel lines from the fuel filter
   • Fuel filter

To install:

4. Install or connect the following:
   • Fuel filter and tighten the bracket bolt. Note the fuel flow directional arrow.
   • Fuel lines to the fuel filter
   • Negative battery cable

5. Start the engine and inspect the fuel filter connections for leaks.

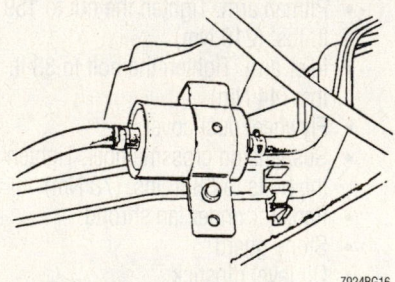

Fuel filter mounting location

Fuel Pump

REMOVAL & INSTALLATION

1. Before servicing the vehicle, refer to the precautions in the beginning of this section.

2. Relieve fuel system pressure.

3. Drain the fuel tank.

4. Remove or disconnect the following:
   • Negative battery cable
   • Right rear inner fender liner
   • Fuel filler and vent hoses

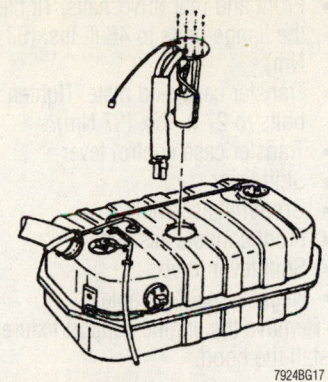

Fuel pump assembly mounting

- Fuel tank skid plate
- Fuel tank wiring connectors
- Fuel supply and return lines
- Fuel tank
- Fuel pump assembly

To install:

5. Install or connect the following:
- Fuel pump assembly
- Fuel tank. Tighten the bolts to 27 ft. lbs. (36 Nm).
- Fuel supply and return lines
- Fuel tank wiring connectors
- Fuel tank skid plate
- Fuel filler and vent hoses
- Right rear inner fender liner
- Negative battery cable

6. Start the engine and check for leaks.

Fuel Injector

REMOVAL & INSTALLATION

3.2L Engine

1. Before servicing the vehicle, refer to the precautions in the beginning of this section.
2. Relieve fuel system pressure.
3. Remove or disconnect the following:
- Negative battery cable
- Air cleaner assembly
- Accelerator cable
- Cruise control cable
- Brake booster vacuum line
- Manifold Absolute Pressure (MAP) sensor connector
- Idle Air Control (IAC) valve connector
- Throttle Position (TP) sensor connector
- Power switch connector
- Electronic Vacuum Sensing Valve (EVSV) connector
- Throttle body

- Positive Crankcase Ventilation (PCV) valve and hose
- Fuel pressure regulator vacuum hose
- Front axle actuator vacuum line
- Ventilation hose bracket
- Exhaust Gas Recirculation (EGR) valve assembly
- Upper intake manifold
- Fuel lines
- Fuel injector harness connectors
- Fuel supply manifold with injectors attached
- Clips
- Injectors from the supply manifold

To install:

4. Install or connect the following:
- New O-rings on the fuel injectors
- Fuel injectors
- Fuel supply manifold with injectors attached. Tighten the bolts to 75 inch lbs. (7 Nm).
- Fuel injector harness connectors
- Fuel lines
- Upper intake manifold. Tighten the fasteners to 18 ft. lbs. (25 Nm).
- EGR valve assembly
- Ventilation hose bracket
- Front axle actuator vacuum line
- Fuel pressure regulator vacuum hose
- PCV valve and hose
- Throttle body. Tighten the bolts to 10 ft. lbs. (13.5 Nm).
- EVSV connector
- Power switch connector
- TP sensor connector
- IAC valve connector
- MAP sensor connector
- Brake booster vacuum line
- Cruise control cable
- Accelerator cable
- Air cleaner assembly
- Negative battery cable

5. Start the engine and check for leaks.

3.5L Engine

1. Before servicing the vehicle, refer to the precautions in the beginning of this section.
2. Relieve fuel system pressure.
3. Remove or disconnect the following:
- Negative battery cable
- Engine cover
- Fuel injector wiring connectors
- Fuel lines
- Fuel supply manifold with injectors attached
- Clips

- Injectors from the supply manifold

To install:

4. Install or connect the following:
- New O-rings on the fuel injectors
- Fuel injectors
- Fuel supply manifold with injectors attached. Tighten the bolts to 60 inch lbs. (6.5 Nm).
- Fuel lines
- Fuel injector wiring connectors
- Engine cover
- Negative battery cable

5. Start the engine and check for leaks.

DRIVE TRAIN

Transmission Assembly

REMOVAL & INSTALLATION

Manual

1. Before servicing the vehicle, refer to the precautions in the beginning of this section.
2. Remove the hood.
3. Install a support fixture to the engine lifting eyes.
4. Remove or disconnect the following:
- Negative battery cable
- Shift lever knob
- Front console assembly
- Grommet assembly
- Shift lever
- Transfer case control lever
- Transfer case skid plate
- Front and rear driveshafts
- Reverse lamp switch connector
- Indicator switch connectors
- Vehicle Speed (VSS) sensor con-

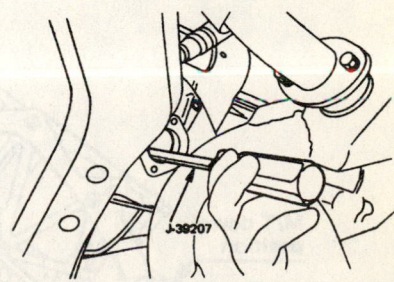

Insert the release bearing remover J-39207 or equivalent, through the hole in the bell housing

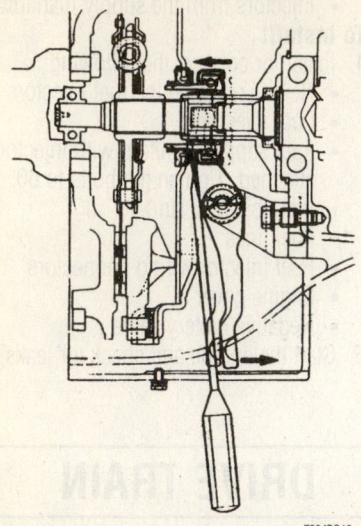

7924BG19

Pull the release bearing fork toward the transmission to release the bearing from the pressure plate

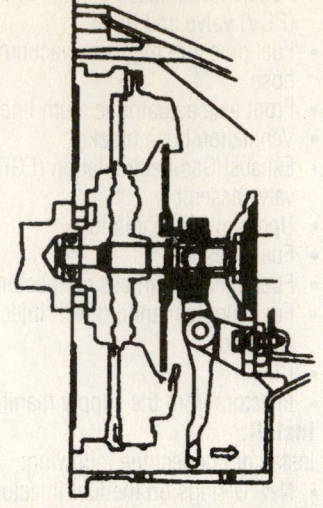

7924BG21

Push the release bearing fork toward the transmission to engage the release bearing with the pressure plate

nector
- 4WD actuator connector
- Transmission harness clamps
- Fuel pipe bracket
- Clutch slave cylinder and heat shield
- Transmission mount and cross-member
- Heated Oxygen (HO2S) sensor connectors
- Right exhaust front pipe
- Wiring harness heat shield
- Flywheel under cover

5. Release the throw out bearing from the pressure plate as shown.

6. Remove the transmission flange bolts and remove the transmission.

To install:

7. Install the transmission. Tighten the large bolts to 56 ft. lbs. (76 Nm) and the small bolts to 52 inch lbs. (6 Nm).

8. Apply 13–18 lbs. (59–78 N) of force

to the clutch fork to engage the throw out bearing to the pressure plate.

9. Install or connect the following:
- Flywheel under cover
- Wiring harness heat shield
- Right exhaust front pipe. Tighten the manifold flange fasteners to 49 ft. lbs. (67 Nm), and the exhaust flange bolts to 32 ft. lbs. (43 Nm).
- HO2S sensor connectors
- Crossmember. Tighten the bolts to 37 ft. lbs. (50 Nm).
- Transmission mount. Tighten the bolts to 30 ft. lbs. (41 Nm).
- Clutch slave cylinder and heat shield
- Fuel pipe bracket
- Transmission harness clamps
- 4WD actuator connector
- VSS sensor connector
- Indicator switch connectors
- Reverse lamp switch connector

- Front and rear driveshafts. Tighten the flange bolts to 46 ft. lbs. (63 Nm).
- Transfer case skid plate. Tighten the bolts to 27 ft. lbs. (37 Nm).
- Transfer case control lever
- Shift lever
- Grommet assembly
- Front console assembly
- Shift lever knob
- Negative battery cable

10. Remove the engine support fixture and install the hood.

Automatic

2 WHEEL DRIVE

1. Before servicing the vehicle, refer to the precautions in the beginning of this section.

2. Remove the hood.

3. Install a support fixture to the engine lifting eyes.

4. Remove or disconnect the following:
- Negative battery cable
- Front console assembly and wiring connectors
- Shift lock cable
- Shift control rod
- Selector lever assembly
- Driveshaft
- Wiring harness heat shield
- Transmission mount and cross-member
- Heated Oxygen (HO2S) sensor connectors
- Left and right exhaust front pipes
- Transmission oil cooler lines
- Starter motor
- Fuel line bracket
- Transmission harness connectors
- Flywheel under covers
- Torque converter
- Transmission flange bolts
- Transmission

To install:

➡**Use new torque converter bolts.**

5. Install or connect the following:
- Transmission. Tighten the large bolts to 56 ft. lbs. (76 Nm) and the small bolts to 69 inch lbs. (8 Nm).
- Torque converter. Tighten the bolts to 40 ft. lbs. (54 Nm).
- Flywheel under covers
- Transmission harness connectors
- Fuel line bracket
- Starter motor. Tighten the bolts to 30 ft. lbs. (40 Nm).
- Transmission oil cooler lines
- Left and right exhaust front pipes. Tighten the manifold flange fasten-

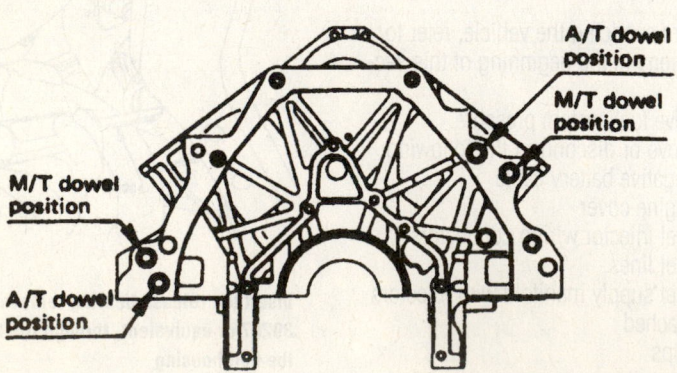

7924BG15

Transmission mounting dowel position

ers to 49 ft. lbs. (67 Nm), and the exhaust flange bolts to 32 ft. lbs. (43 Nm).
- HO$_2$S sensor connectors
- Crossmember. Tighten the bolts to 37 ft. lbs. (50 Nm).
- Transmission mount. Tighten the bolts to 30 ft. lbs. (41 Nm).
- Wiring harness heat shield
- Driveshaft. Tighten the flange bolts to 46 ft. lbs. (63 Nm).
- Selector lever assembly
- Shift control rod
- Shift lock cable
- Front console assembly and wiring connectors
- Negative battery cable

6. Remove the engine support fixture and install the hood.

4 WHEEL DRIVE

1. Before servicing the vehicle, refer to the precautions in the beginning of this section.
2. Remove the hood.
3. Install a support fixture to the engine lifting eyes.
4. Remove or disconnect the following:
- Negative battery cable
- Transfer case shift lever knob
- Front console assembly and wiring connectors
- Shift lock cable
- Shift control rod
- Selector lever assembly
- Transfer case shift lever
- Transfer case skid plate
- Front and rear driveshafts
- Wiring harness heat shield
- Transmission mount and cross-member
- Right torsion bar, if equipped with Torque On Demand (TOD) system
- Heated Oxygen (HO$_2$S) sensor connectors
- Left and right exhaust front pipes
- Transmission oil cooler lines
- Starter motor
- Fuel line bracket
- Transmission harness connectors
- Flywheel under covers
- Torque converter
- Transmission flange bolts
- Transmission

To install:

➡**Use new torque converter bolts.**

5. Install or connect the following:
- Transmission. Tighten the large bolts to 56 ft. lbs. (76 Nm) and the small bolts to 69 inch lbs. (8 Nm).

- Torque converter. Tighten the bolts to 40 ft. lbs. (54 Nm).
- Flywheel under covers
- Transmission harness connectors
- Fuel line bracket
- Starter motor. Tighten the bolts to 30 ft. lbs. (40 Nm).
- Transmission oil cooler lines
- Left and right exhaust front pipes. Tighten the manifold flange fasteners to 49 ft. lbs. (67 Nm), and the exhaust flange bolts to 32 ft. lbs. (43 Nm).
- HO$_2$S sensor connectors
- Right torsion bar, if removed
- Crossmember. Tighten the bolts to 37 ft. lbs. (50 Nm).
- Transmission mount. Tighten the bolts to 30 ft. lbs. (41 Nm).
- Wiring harness heat shield
- Front and rear driveshafts. Tighten the flange bolts to 46 ft. lbs. (63 Nm).
- Transfer case skid plate. Tighten the bolts to 27 ft. lbs. (37 Nm).
- Transfer case shift lever
- Selector lever assembly
- Shift control rod
- Shift lock cable
- Front console assembly and wiring connectors
- Transfer case shift lever knob
- Negative battery cable

6. Remove the engine support fixture and install the hood.

Clutch Assembly

ADJUSTMENTS

➡**This vehicle is equipped with a hydraulic clutch linkage. No adjustment is necessary.**

REMOVAL & INSTALLATION

1. Before servicing the vehicle, refer to the precautions in the beginning of this section.
2. Remove the transmission.
3. Loosen the pressure plate mounting bolts in a 2-step crisscross sequence until the spring tension is relieved.
4. Remove the pressure plate and the clutch disc.

To install:
5. Install a new wedge collar and wire snaping into the pressure plate.
6. Using a clutch alignment tool, assemble the clutch disc and pressure plate onto the flywheel.

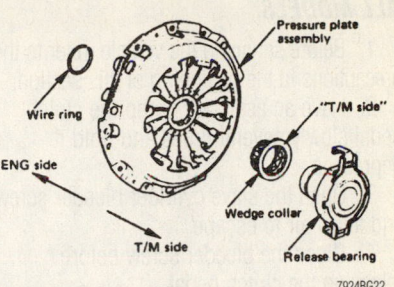

Exploded view of the pressure plate and release bearing components

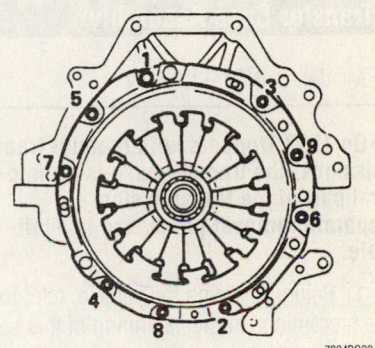

Pressure plate mounting bolt tightening sequence

7. Tighten the pressure plate bolts in sequence and in two passes to 13 ft. lbs. (8 Nm).
8. Install the transmission.
9. Road test the vehicle and check for proper clutch operation.

Hydraulic Clutch System

BLEEDING

Damping Cylinder

1997 TROOPER

1. Before servicing the vehicle, refer to the precautions in the beginning of this section.
2. Have an assistant pump the clutch pedal slowly several times and hold it depressed.
3. Open the damping cylinder bleeder screw and allow air to escape.
4. Close the bleeder screw before releasing the clutch pedal.
5. Repeat until all air is purged from the damping cylinder.
6. Refill the reservoir to the full mark.

Slave Cylinder

ALL MODELS

1. Before servicing the vehicle, refer to the precautions in the beginning of this section.

2. Have an assistant pump the clutch pedal slowly several times and hold it depressed.

3. Open the slave cylinder bleeder screw and allow air to escape.

4. Close the bleeder screw before releasing the clutch pedal.

5. Repeat until all air is purged from the clutch hydraulic system.

6. Refill the reservoir to the full mark.

Transfer Case Assembly

REMOVAL & INSTALLATION

➡**On 1997 Troopers with manual transmissions, the transfer case is an integral part of the transmission. No separate removal procedure is available.**

1. Before servicing the vehicle, refer to the precautions in the beginning of this section.

2. Remove or disconnect the following:
- Negative battery cable
- Transfer case skid plate
- Front and rear driveshafts
- Heated Oxygen (HO2S) sensor connectors
- Left and right exhaust front pipes
- Transfer case control lever knob
- Selector lever assembly
- Transfer case control lever
- Vehicle Speed (VSS) sensor connector
- 4 wheel drive switch connector
- 4 wheel drive actuator connector
- Transfer case flange fasteners
- Transfer case

To install:

3. Install or connect the following:
- Transfer case. Tighten the flange fasteners to 34 ft. lbs. (46 Nm).
- 4 wheel drive actuator connector
- 4 wheel drive switch connector
- VSS sensor connector
- Transfer case control lever
- Selector lever assembly
- Transfer case control lever knob
- Left and right exhaust front pipes
- HO2S sensor connectors
- Front and rear driveshafts. Tighten the bolts to 46 ft. lbs. (63 Nm).
- Transfer case skid plate. Tighten the bolts to 27 ft. lbs. (37 Nm).
- Negative battery cable

Halfshaft

REMOVAL & INSTALLATION

1. Before servicing the vehicle, refer to the precautions in the beginning of this section.

2. Remove or disconnect the following:
- Negative battery cable
- Front wheel
- Radiator skid plate
- Transfer case skid plate
- Brake calipers and mounting bracket
- Brake rotor
- Wheel speed sensor
- Steering knuckle

3. Support the axle housing with a jack. Unbolt the axle mounting bracket and remove the halfshaft/bracket assembly.

To install:

4. Install or connect the following:
- Axle/bracket assembly. Tighten the bracket flange bolts to 85 ft. lbs. (116 Nm) and the bracket mounting bolts to 112 ft. lbs. (152 Nm).
- Steering knuckle
- Wheel speed sensor

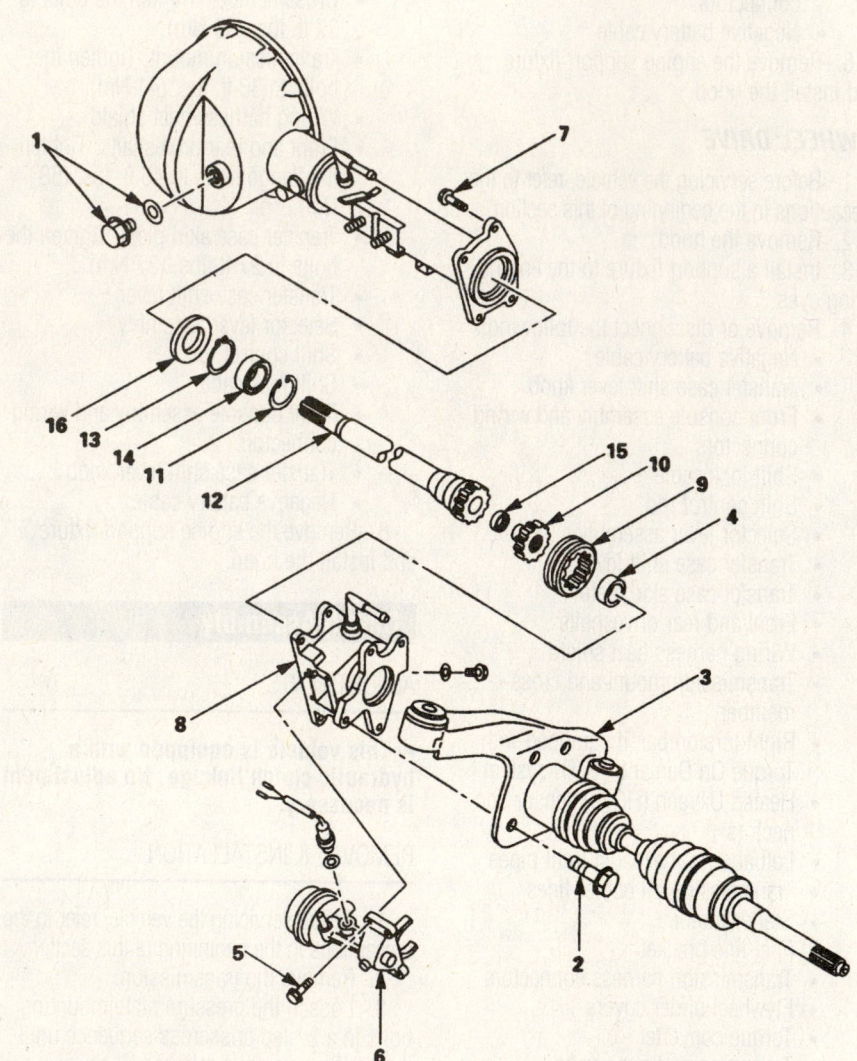

1. Filler plug
2. Bolt
3. Front axle drive shaft (LH side)
4. Spacer
5. Bolt
6. Actuator assembly
7. Bolt
8. Housing
9. Sleeve
10. Clutch gear
11. Snap ring
12. Inner shaft
13. Snap ring
14. Inner shaft bearing
15. Needle bearing
16. Oil seal

Exploded view of the left halfshaft, axle shaft, and axle disconnect

7924BG26

- Brake rotor
- Brake caliper and mounting bracket. Tighten the bracket bolts to 115 ft. lbs. (155 Nm).
- Transfer case skid plate. Tighten the bolts to 27 ft. lbs. (37 Nm).
- Radiator skid plate. Tighten the bolts to 58 ft. lbs. (78 Nm).
- Front wheel
- Negative battery cable

5. Check the wheel alignment and adjust as necessary.

CV-Joints

OVERHAUL

Outer CV-Joint

The outer CV-joint is serviced with the axle shaft as an assembly. The outer CV-joint boot can be serviced by removing the inner CV-joint.

Inner CV-Joint

1. Before servicing the vehicle, refer to the precautions in the beginning of this section.
2. Remove or disconnect the following:
   - Halfshaft from the vehicle
   - Snapring and bearing
   - Snapring and oil seal
   - Mounting bracket
   - CV-joint boot
   - Circlip and inner joint housing
   - Snapring and spacer
   - Inner joint balls
   - Snapring and inner CV-joint

To install:

3. Install or connect the following:
   - Inner CV-joint and snapring
   - Inner joint balls
   - Spacer and snapring
   - Inner joint housing and circlip. Add 150 grams CV-joint grease.
   - CV-joint boot
   - Mounting bracket
   - Oil seal and snapring
   - Bearing and snapring

4. Install the halfshaft and mounting bracket to the vehicle.

5. Check the wheel alignment and adjust as necessary.

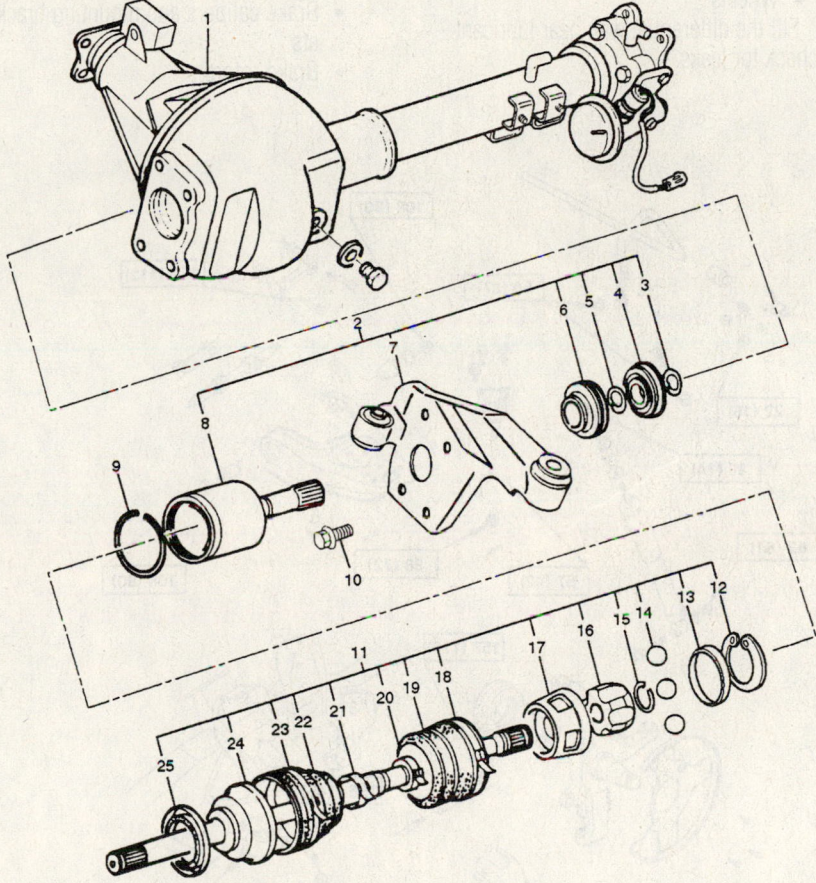

1 Axle Case and Differential
2 DOJ Case Assembly
3 Snap Ring
4 Bearing
5 Snap Ring
6 Oil Seal
7 Bracket
8 DOJ Case
9 Circlip
10 Bolt
11 Drive Shaft Joint Assembly
12 Snap Ring
13 Spacer
14 Ball
15 Snap Ring
16 Ball Retainer
17 Ball Guide
18 Band
19 Bellows
20 Band
21 Band
22 Bellows
23 Band
24 BJ Shaft
25 Dust Seal

9308BG03

Exploded view of the right halfshaft and mounting bracket

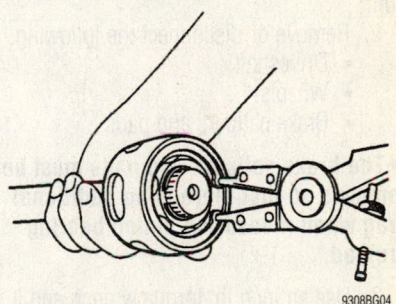

9308BG04

CV-joint spacer snapring—Inner CV-Joint

Axle Shaft, Bearing and Seal

REMOVAL & INSTALLATION

1. Before servicing the vehicle, refer to the precautions in the beginning of this section.
2. Remove or disconnect the following:
   - Rear wheel
   - Disc brake caliper and bracket
   - Disc brake rotor
   - Wheel speed sensor bracket
   - Parking brake cable and bracket
   - Parking brake shoes
   - Axle shaft

Turn to Section 5 for brake system applications

- Snapring and discard it
- Bearing, press it off the axle shaft with the bearing holder and oil seal

To install:

3. Install or connect the following:
- New oil seal into the bearing housing
- Bearing housing onto the axle shaft
- Bearing, press it onto the axle shaft
- New snapring
- Axle shaft. Use new lock washers and tighten the bearing holder nuts to 54 ft. lbs. (74 Nm).
- Parking brake shoes
- Parking brake cable and bracket
- Wheel speed sensor bracket
- Disc brake rotor
- Disc brake caliper and bracket. Tighten the bracket bolts to 76 ft. lbs. (103 Nm).
- Rear wheel

4. Check the rear axle oil level and adjust as necessary.

Pinion Seal

REMOVAL & INSTALLATION

1. Before servicing the vehicle, refer to the precautions in the beginning of this section.

2. Remove or disconnect the following:
- Driveshaft
- Wheels
- Brake calipers and pads

➡ **The brake calipers and pads must be removed so that there is no additional drag when measuring pinion bearing preload.**

3. Use an inch lb. torque wrench and measure and record the amount of torque required to maintain pinion rotation through several revolutions.

4. Remove or disconnect the following:
- Pinion flange
- Pinion seal
- Pinion bearing
- Collapsible spacer

To install:

➡ **Use a new collapsible spacer and flange nut for assembly.**

5. Install or connect the following:
- Collapsible spacer
- Pinion bearing
- Pinion seal
- Pinion flange

6. Rotate the pinion flange occasionally while tightening the flange nut to make sure the pinion bearings seat correctly.

7. Take frequent bearing preload torque readings. Tighten the flange nut to achieve the preload torque readings originally recorded.

✳✳ CAUTION

Never loosen the pinion nut to reduce bearing preload. If it is necessary to reduce bearing preload, install a new collapsible spacer and pinion nut.

8. Install or connect the following:
- Driveshaft
- Brake calipers and pads
- Wheels

9. Fill the differential with gear lubricant and check for leaks.

Axle Housing Assembly

REMOVAL & INSTALLATION

Front

1. Before servicing the vehicle, refer to the precautions in the beginning of this section.

2. Remove or disconnect the following:
- Negative battery cable
- Front wheels
- Radiator skid plate
- Transfer case skid plate
- Brake calipers and mounting brackets
- Brake rotors

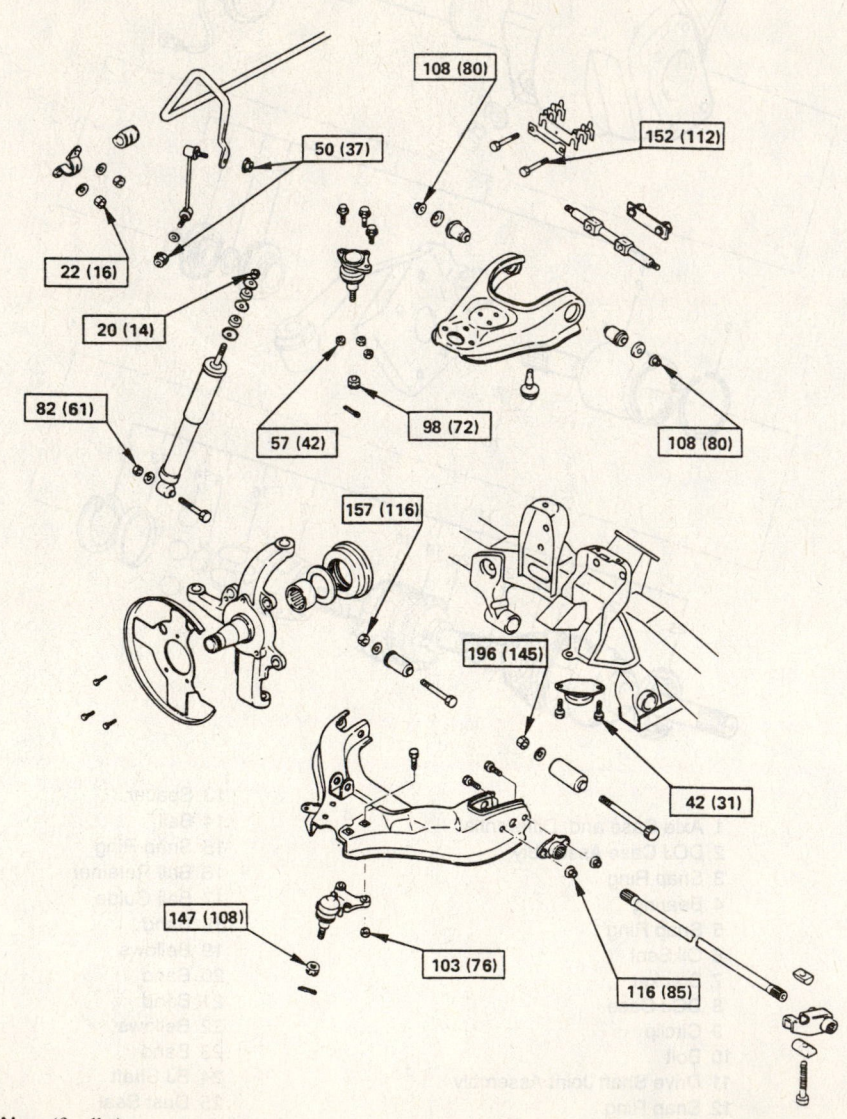

N•m (ft • lbs)

7924BG48

Exploded view of the front suspension, showing the tightening specifications

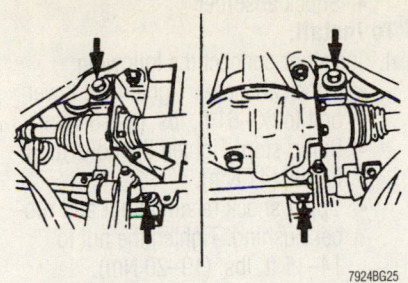

Axle assembly mounting bracket bolt locations

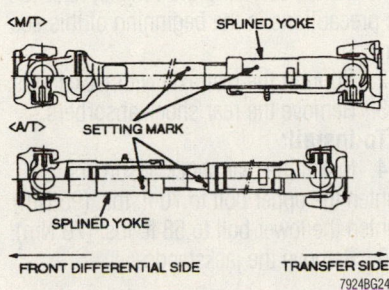

Driveshaft alignment mark locations

- Wheel speed sensors
- Axle disconnect actuator
- Vacuum Switching (VSV) valve
- Steering knuckles
- Idler arm
- Pitman arm
- Front suspension crossmember
- Front driveshaft
- Front axle bracket mounting bolts
- Right halfshaft and mounting bracket from the axle
- Axle assembly from the vehicle with the left halfshaft and bracket attached
- Left halfshaft and bracket from the axle disconnect housing

To install:

➡**Use new nuts, bolts and snaprings for assembly.**

3. Install or connect the following:
- Left halfshaft and mounting bracket. Tighten the bracket flange bolts to 85 ft. lbs. (116 Nm).
- Axle housing. Tighten the bracket mounting bolts to 112 ft. lbs. (152 Nm).
- Right halfshaft and mounting bracket. Tighten the bracket flange bolts to 85 ft. lbs. (116 Nm).
- Front driveshaft. Tighten the bolts to 46 ft. lbs. (63 Nm).
- Front suspension crossmember.

Tighten the bolts to 58 ft. lbs. (78 Nm).
- Pitman arm
- Idler arm
- Steering knuckles
- VSV valve
- Axle disconnect actuator
- Wheel speed sensors
- Brake rotors
- Brake calipers and mounting brackets. Tighten the bracket bolts to 115 ft. lbs. (155 Nm).
- Transfer case skid plate. Tighten the bolts to 27 ft. lbs. (37 Nm).
- Radiator skid plate. Tighten the bolts to 58 ft. lbs. (78 Nm).
- Front wheels
- Negative battery cable

4. Check the wheel alignment and adjust as necessary.

Rear

1. Before servicing the vehicle, refer to the precautions in the beginning of this section.
2. Support the rear axle with a jack.
3. Remove or disconnect the following:
- Rear wheels
- Rear driveshaft

- Parking brake cables
- Axle breather hose
- Wheel speed sensor connectors and bracket
- Brake fluid hose
- Shock absorbers
- Coil springs
- Stabilizer bar linkage
- Lateral rod
- Center link
- Trailing links
- Axle housing from the vehicle

To install:

4. Install or connect the following:
- Axle housing, raise it into position
- Trailing links
- Center link
- Lateral rod
- Stabilizer bar linkage
- Coil springs
- Shock absorbers
- Brake fluid hose
- Wheel speed sensor connectors and bracket
- Axle breather hose
- Parking brake cables
- Rear driveshaft
- Rear wheels

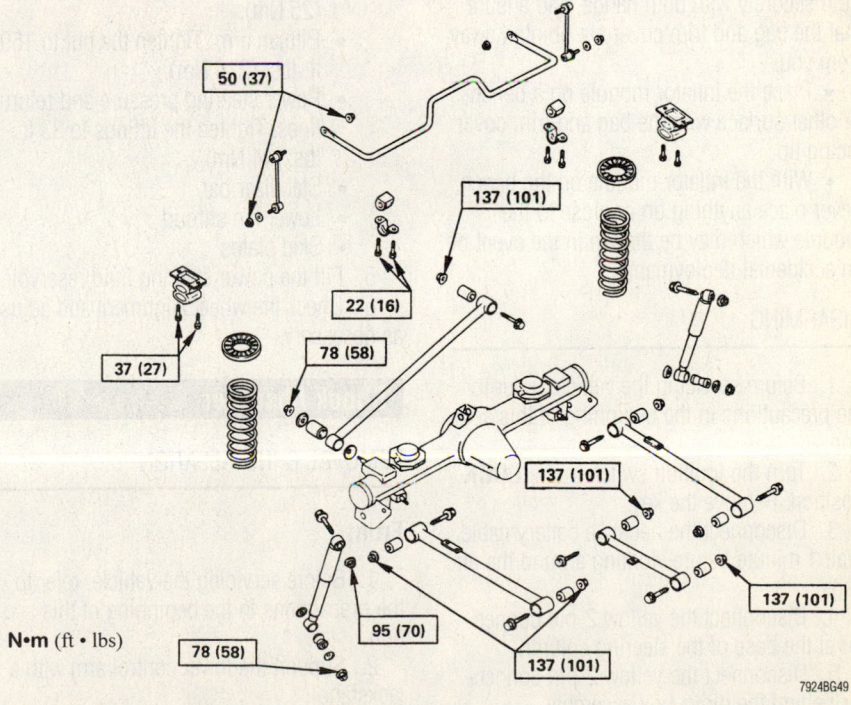

N•m (ft • lbs)

Exploded view of the rear suspension

For complete service labor times order Nichols' Chilton Labor Guide Manual

STEERING AND SUSPENSION

Air Bag

✳✳ CAUTION

Some vehicles are equipped with an air bag system. The system must be disarmed before performing service on, or around, system components, the steering column, instrument panel components, wiring and sensors. Failure to follow the safety precautions and the disarming procedure could result in accidental air bag deployment, possible injury and unnecessary system repairs.

PRECAUTIONS

Several precautions must be observed when handling the inflator module to avoid accidental deployment and possible personal injury.

- Never carry the inflator module by the wires or connector on the underside of the module.
- When carrying a live inflator module, hold securely with both hands, and ensure that the bag and trim cover are pointed away from you.
- Place the inflator module on a bench or other surface with the bag and trim cover facing up.
- With the inflator module on the bench, never place anything on or close to the module which may be thrown in the event of an accidental deployment.

DISARMING

1. Before servicing the vehicle, refer to the precautions in the beginning of this section.
2. Turn the ignition switch to the **LOCK** position. Remove the key.
3. Disconnect the negative battery cable. Wait 1 minute before working around the air bags.
4. Disconnect the yellow 2-pin connector at the base of the steering column.
5. Disconnect the yellow 2-pin connector behind the glove box assembly.
6. When repairs are completed, connect the yellow 2-pin connectors.
7. Connect the negative battery cable.
8. Turn the ignition to the **ON** position,

but don't start the engine. The AIR BAG warning light should turn ON and flash ON and OFF 7 times, and then turn OFF. This light sequence indicates that the SRS system is functioning normally. If the AIR BAG light doesn't come ON, or stays ON longer than 7 seconds, the system must be diagnosed.

Recirculating Ball Steering Gear

REMOVAL & INSTALLATION

1. Before servicing the vehicle, refer to the precautions in the beginning of this section.
2. Disable the air bag system.
3. Remove or disconnect the following:
   - Skid plates
   - Lower fan shroud
   - Stabilizer bar
   - Power steering pressure and return lines
   - Pitman arm
   - Steering column intermediate shaft
   - Steering gear

To install:
4. Install or connect the following:
   - Steering gear. Tighten the bolts to 33 ft. lbs. (44 Nm).
   - Steering column intermediate shaft. Tighten the pinch bolt to 18 ft. lbs. (25 Nm).
   - Pitman arm. Tighten the nut to 159 ft. lbs. (216 Nm).
   - Power steering pressure and return lines. Tighten the fittings to 33 ft. lbs. (44 Nm).
   - Stabilizer bar
   - Lower fan shroud
   - Skid plates
5. Fill the power steering fluid reservoir.
6. Check the wheel alignment and adjust as necessary.

Shock Absorber

REMOVAL & INSTALLATION

Front

1. Before servicing the vehicle, refer to the precautions in the beginning of this section.
2. Support the lower control arm with a jackstand.
3. Remove or disconnect the following:
   - Front wheels
   - Upper shock retaining nut and rubber bushing
   - Suspension bump stops

- Shock absorber

To install:
4. Install or connect the following:
   - Shock absorber. Tighten the lower bolt to 60–61 ft. lbs. (82–84 Nm).
   - Bump stop. Tighten the bolts to 30 ft. lbs. (41 Nm).
   - Upper shock retaining nut and rubber bushing. Tighten the nut to 14–15 ft. lbs. (19–20 Nm).
   - Front wheels

Rear

1. Before servicing the vehicle, refer to the precautions in the beginning of this section.
2. Support the rear axle with jackstands.
3. Remove the rear shock absorbers.

To install:
4. Install the rear shock absorbers. Tighten the upper bolt to 70 ft. lbs. (95 Nm). Tighten the lower bolt to 58 ft. lbs. (78 Nm).
5. Remove the jackstands.

Coil Spring

REMOVAL & INSTALLATION

1. Before servicing the vehicle, refer to the precautions in the beginning of this section.
2. Support the vehicle under the frame.
3. Support the rear axle with a jack.
4. Remove or disconnect the following:
   - Rear wheels
   - Stabilizer bar links
   - Parking brake cable brackets
   - Shock absorbers
5. Lower the rear axle with the jack to release the coil spring tension. Remove the coil springs and insulators.

To install:
6. Place the coil springs on the axle assembly and the insulators on top of the springs.
7. Raise the axle assembly into position.
8. Install or connect the following:
   - Shock absorbers
   - Parking brake cable brackets
   - Stabilizer bar links. Tighten the nuts to 37 ft. lbs. (50 Nm).
   - Rear wheels

Torsion Bar

REMOVAL & INSTALLATION

1. Before servicing the vehicle, refer to the precautions in the beginning of this section.

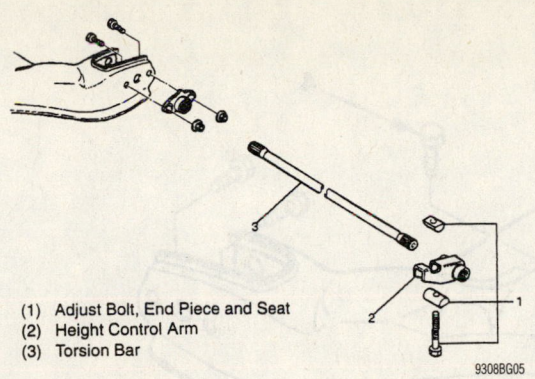

(1) Adjust Bolt, End Piece and Seat
(2) Height Control Arm
(3) Torsion Bar

9308BG05

Exploded view of the torsion bar assembly

2. Matchmark the adjusting bolt and end piece, then remove the bolt, end piece, and seat.

3. Matchmark the height control arm to the torsion bar, then remove the height control arm.

4. Matchmark the torsion bar to the lower control arm, then remove the torsion bar.

To install:

5. Apply grease to the torsion bar splines.

6. Apply grease to the contact points of the height control arm, adjusting bolt end piece and seat.

7. Align the matchmarks and install the torsion bar.

8. Align the matchmarks and install the height control arm.

9. Install the adjusting bolt, seat and end piece.

10. Tighten the adjusting bolt to align the matchmarks.

Upper Ball Joint

REMOVAL & INSTALLATION

1. Before servicing the vehicle, refer to the precautions in the beginning of this section.

2. Support the lower control arm with a floor jack.

3. Remove or disconnect the following:

- Front wheel
- Wheel speed sensor
- Upper ball joint

To install:

➡ **Use new nuts, bolts and split pins for assembly.**

4. Install or connect the following:

- Upper ball joint. Tighten the mounting bolts to 42 ft. lbs. (57 Nm) and the nut to 72 ft. lbs. (96 Nm).
- Wheel speed sensor
- Front wheel

Lower Ball Joint

REMOVAL & INSTALLATION

1. Before servicing the vehicle, refer to the precautions in the beginning of this section.

2. Support the lower control arm with a jackstand.

3. Remove or disconnect the following:

- Front wheel
- Disc brake caliper and support
- Brake rotor and backing plate

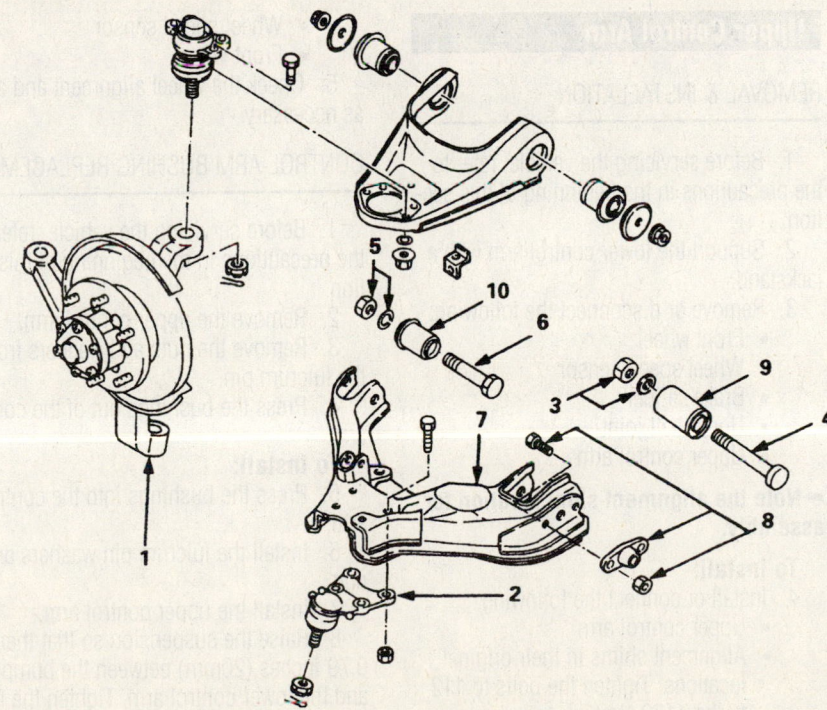

1. Knuckle
2. Lower end
3. Nut and washer, rear
4. Bolt, rear
5. Nut and washer, front
6. Bolt, front
7. Lower control arm assembly
8. Torsion bar arm bracket
9. Bushing, rear
10. Bushing, front

7924BG34

Exploded view of the control arm and ball joint components

For complete service labor times order Nichols' Chilton Labor Guide Manual

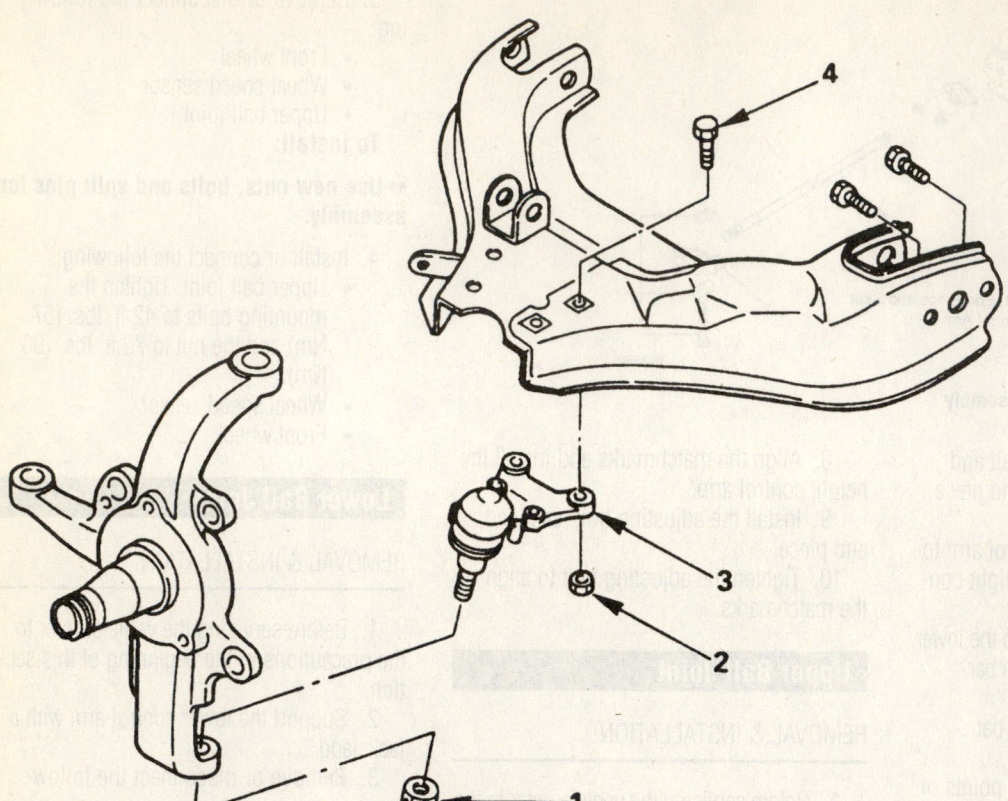

1. Nut and cotter pin
2. Nut
3. Lower ball joint
4. Bolt

7924BG35

Exploded view of the lower ball joint mounting and related components

- Wheel speed sensor
- Outer tie rod end
- Upper ball joint
- Steering knuckle
- Lower ball joint

To install:

➡**Use new nuts, bolts and split pins for assembly.**

4. Install or connect the following:
   - Lower ball joint. Tighten the mounting bolts to 76 ft. lbs. (103 Nm).
   - Steering knuckle. Tighten the lower ball joint nut to 108 ft. lbs. (147 Nm).
   - Upper ball joint. Tighten the nut to 72 ft. lbs. (96 Nm).
   - Outer tie rod end. Tighten the nut to 72 ft. lbs. (98 Nm).
   - Wheel speed sensor
   - Brake rotor and backing plate
   - Disc brake caliper and support. Tighten the support bolts to 115 ft. lbs. (155 Nm).
   - Front wheel

5. Check the wheel alignment and adjust as necessary.

Upper Control Arm

REMOVAL & INSTALLATION

1. Before servicing the vehicle, refer to the precautions in the beginning of this section.
2. Support the lower control arm with a jackstand.
3. Remove or disconnect the following:
   - Front wheel
   - Wheel speed sensor
   - Brake caliper
   - Upper ball joint
   - Upper control arm

➡**Note the alignment shim location for assembly.**

To install:

4. Install or connect the following:
   - Upper control arm
   - Alignment shims in their original locations. Tighten the bolts to 112 ft. lbs. (152 Nm).
   - Upper ball joint. Tighten the nut to 72 ft. lbs. (98 Nm).
   - Brake caliper

- Wheel speed sensor
- Front wheel

5. Check the wheel alignment and adjust as necessary.

CONTROL ARM BUSHING REPLACEMENT

1. Before servicing the vehicle, refer to the precautions in the beginning of this section.
2. Remove the upper control arm.
3. Remove the nuts and washers from the fulcrum pin.
4. Press the bushings out of the control arm.

To install:

5. Press the bushings into the control arm.
6. Install the fulcrum pin washers and nuts.
7. Install the upper control arm.
8. Raise the suspension so that there is 0.79 inches (20mm) between the bump stop and the lower control arm. Tighten the fulcrum pin nuts to 80 ft. lbs. (108 Nm).
9. Check the wheel alignment and adjust as necessary.

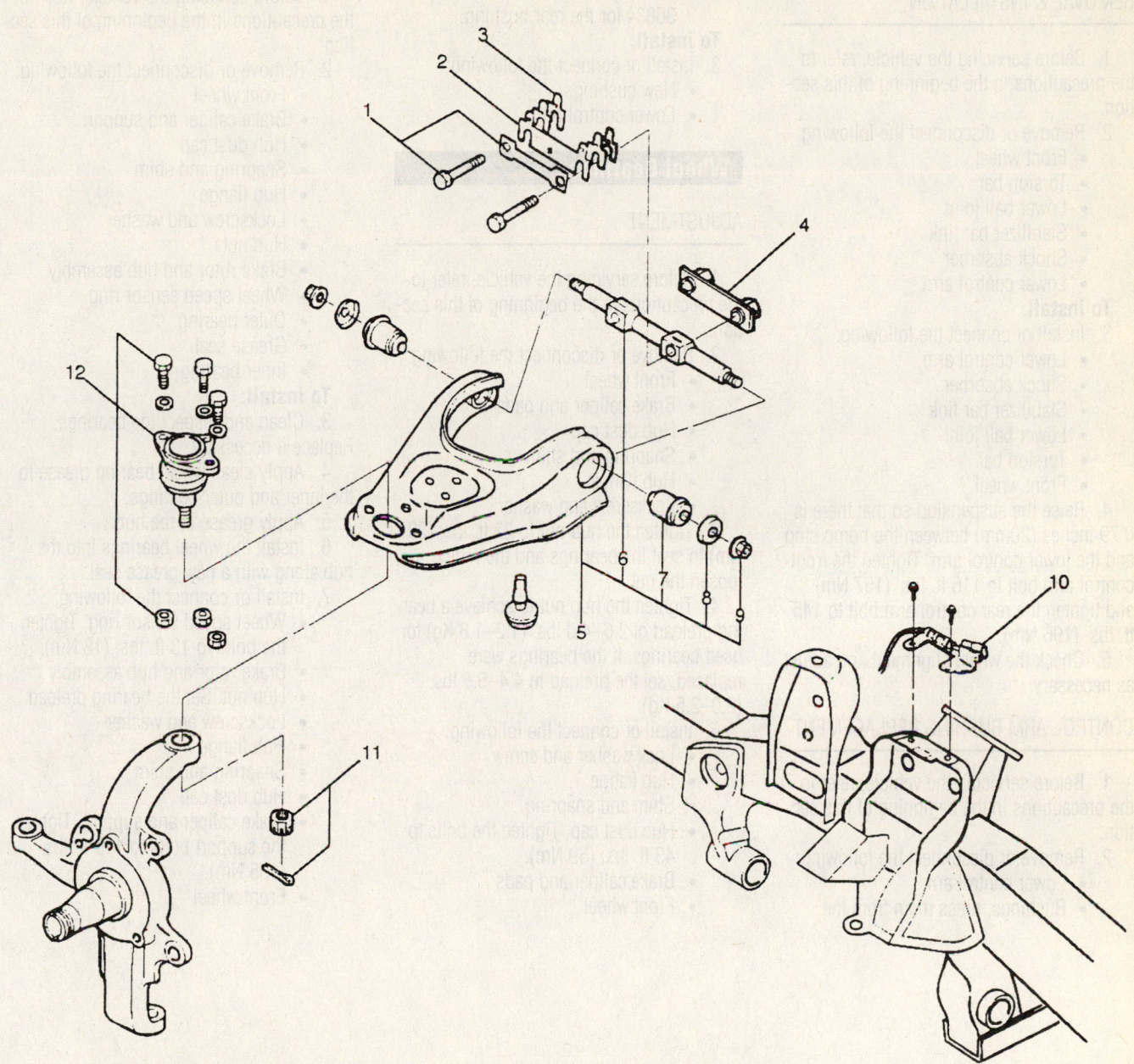

1	Bolt and Plate	7	Bushing
2	Camber Shims	8	Plate
3	Caster Shims	9	Nut
4	Nut Assembly	10	Speed Sensor Cable
5	Upper Control Arm Assembly	11	Nut and Cotter Pin
6	Fulcrum Pin	12	Upper Ball Joint

9308BG06

Upper control arm and related parts

Lower Control Arm

REMOVAL & INSTALLATION

1. Before servicing the vehicle, refer to the precautions in the beginning of this section.

2. Remove or disconnect the following:
   - Front wheel
   - Torsion bar
   - Lower ball joint
   - Stabilizer bar link
   - Shock absorber
   - Lower control arm

To install:

3. Install or connect the following:
   - Lower control arm
   - Shock absorber
   - Stabilizer bar link
   - Lower ball joint
   - Torsion bar
   - Front wheel

4. Raise the suspension so that there is 0.79 inches (20mm) between the bump stop and the lower control arm. Tighten the front control arm bolt to 116 ft. lbs. (157 Nm) and tighten the rear control arm bolt to 145 ft. lbs. (196 Nm).

5. Check the wheel alignment and adjust as necessary.

CONTROL ARM BUSHING REPLACEMENT

1. Before servicing the vehicle, refer to the precautions in the beginning of this section.

2. Remove or disconnect the following:
   - Lower control arm
   - Bushings, press them from the control arm, using Remover/Installer J-36833 for the front bushing and Remover/Installer J-36834 for the rear bushing.

To install:

3. Install or connect the following:
   - New bushings
   - Lower control arm

Wheel Bearings

ADJUSTMENT

1. Before servicing the vehicle, refer to the precautions in the beginning of this section.

2. Remove or disconnect the following:
   - Front wheel
   - Brake caliper and pads
   - Hub dust cap
   - Snapring and shim
   - Hub flange
   - Lockscrew and washer

3. Tighten the hub nut to 22 ft. lbs. (29 Nm) to seat the bearings and then fully loosen the nut.

4. Tighten the hub nut to achieve a bearing preload of 2.6–4.0 lbs. (1.2–1.8 Kg) for used bearings. If the bearings were replaced, set the preload to 4.4–5.5 lbs. (2.0–2.5 Kg).

5. Install or connect the following:
   - Lock washer and screw
   - Hub flange
   - Shim and snapring
   - Hub dust cap. Tighten the bolts to 43 ft. lbs. (59 Nm).
   - Brake caliper and pads
   - Front wheel

REMOVAL & INSTALLATION

1. Before servicing the vehicle, refer to the precautions in the beginning of this section.

2. Remove or disconnect the following:
   - Front wheel
   - Brake caliper and support
   - Hub dust cap
   - Snapring and shim
   - Hub flange
   - Lockscrew and washer
   - Hub nut
   - Brake rotor and hub assembly
   - Wheel speed sensor ring
   - Outer bearing
   - Grease seal
   - Inner bearing

To install:

3. Clean and inspect the bearings. Replace if necessary.

4. Apply clean wheel bearing grease to the inner and outer bearings.

5. Apply grease in the hub.

6. Install the wheel bearings into the hub along with a new grease seal.

7. Install or connect the following:
   - Wheel speed sensor ring. Tighten the bolts to 13 ft. lbs. (18 Nm).
   - Brake rotor and hub assembly
   - Hub nut. Set the bearing preload.
   - Lockscrew and washer
   - Hub flange
   - Snapring and shim
   - Hub dust cap
   - Brake caliper and support. Tighten the support bolts to 115 ft. lbs. (155 Nm).
   - Front wheel

11

BMW

X5

PRECAUTIONS

Before servicing any vehicle, please be sure to read all of the following precautions, which deal with personal safety, prevention of component damage and important points to take into consideration when servicing a motor vehicle:

• Never open, service or drain the radiator or cooling system when the engine is hot; serious burns can occur from the steam and hot coolant.

• Observe all applicable safety precautions when working around fuel. Whenever servicing the fuel system, always work in a well-ventilated area. Do not allow fuel spray or vapors to come in contact with a spark, open flame, or excessive heat (a hot drop light, for example). Keep a dry chemical fire extinguisher near the work area. Always keep fuel in a container specifically designed for fuel storage; also, always properly seal fuel containers to avoid the possibility of fire or explosion. Refer to the additional fuel system precautions later in this section.

• Fuel injection systems often remain pressurized, even after the engine has been turned **OFF**. The fuel system pressure must be relieved before disconnecting any fuel lines. Failure to do so may result in fire and/or personal injury.

• Brake fluid often contains polyglycol ethers and polyglycols. Avoid contact with the eyes and wash your hands thoroughly after handling brake fluid. If you do get brake fluid in your eyes, flush your eyes with clean, running water for 15 minutes. If eye irritation persists, or if you have taken brake fluid internally, seek medical assistance IMMEDIATELY.

• The EPA warns that prolonged contact with used engine oil may cause a number of skin disorders, including cancer! You should make every effort to minimize your exposure to used engine oil. Protective gloves should be worn when changing oil. Wash your hands and any other exposed skin areas as soon as possible after exposure to used engine oil. Soap and water, or waterless hand cleaner should be used.

• All new vehicles are now equipped with an air bag system. The system must be disabled before performing service on or around system components, steering column, instrument panel components, wiring and sensors. Failure to follow safety and disabling procedures could result in accidental air bag deployment, possible personal injury and unnecessary system repairs.

• Always wear safety goggles when working with, or around, the air bag system. When carrying a non-deployed air bag, be sure the bag and trim cover are pointed away from your body. When placing a non-deployed air bag on a work surface, always face the bag and trim cover upward, away from the surface. This will reduce the motion of the module if it is accidentally deployed. Refer to the additional air bag system precautions later in this section.

• Clean, high quality brake fluid from a sealed container is essential to the safe and proper operation of the brake system. You should always buy the correct type of brake fluid for your vehicle. If the brake fluid becomes contaminated, completely flush the system with new fluid. Never reuse any brake fluid. Any brake fluid that is removed from the system should be discarded. Also, do not allow any brake fluid to come in contact with a painted surface; it will damage the paint.

• Never operate the engine without the proper amount and type of engine oil; doing so WILL result in severe engine damage.

• Timing belt maintenance is extremely important! Many models utilize an interference-type, non-freewheeling engine. If the timing belt breaks, the valves in the cylinder head may strike the pistons, causing potentially serious (also time-consuming and expensive) engine damage. Refer to the maintenance interval charts in the front of this manual for the recommended replacement interval for the timing belt and to the timing belt section for belt replacement and inspection.

• Disconnecting the negative battery cable on some vehicles may interfere with the functions of the on-board computer system(s) and may require the computer to undergo a relearning process once the negative battery cable is reconnected.

• When servicing drum brakes, only disassemble and assemble one side at a time, leaving the remaining side intact for reference.

• Only an MVAC-trained, EPA-certified automotive technician should service the air conditioning system or its components.

ENGINE REPAIR

➡**Disconnecting the negative battery cable on some vehicles may interfere with the functions of the on-board computer systems and may require the computer to undergo a relearning process.**

ADJUSTMENT

The Digital Motor Electronics (DME) control, unit controls all ignition and fuel injection functions. Ignition timing is fully electronically controlled; there is no vacuum advance or manual adjustment. Ignition functions are calculated from internal maps and from the same sensors used for the fuel injection system. On vehicles with an automatic transmission, the control unit will retard ignition timing briefly when the transmission is about to shift up or down. For this reason, there is a data link between the DME control unit and the transmission control unit.

Since the ignition timing is controlled by the DME, checking and adjusting the timing is impossible. There is no method of setting dynamic or static timing.

REMOVAL & INSTALLATION

➡**When the battery is disconnected the radio code, on-board computer and clock settings will be lost. The radio code should be obtained before disconnecting the battery or radio. Once the battery has been reconnected, the radio will not function unless the code is keyed in.**

1. Before servicing the vehicle, refer to the precautions in the beginning of this section.

2. Drain the cooling system.

3. Remove or disconnect the following:
   • Negative battery cable
   • Drive belt
   • Fan cowling
   • Alternator bolts
   • Alternator electrical connectors
   • Alternator roller by releasing the screw
   • Alternator

To install:

4. Replace the sealing ring for the alternator.

5. Install or connect the following:
   • Alternator. Torque the bolts to 31 ft. lbs. (43 Nm).
   • Alternator roller
   • Alternator electrical connectors
   • Fan cowling
   • Drive belt
   • Negative battery cable

6. Fill the cooling system to the proper level.

7. Start the vehicle and check for leaks, repair if necessary.

Engine Assembly

REMOVAL & INSTALLATION

1. Fully open the hood and properly secure it in place.

2. Properly relieve the fuel system pressure.

3. Evacuate and recover the A/C system.

4. Drain the cooling system.

5. Drain the engine oil.

6. Drain the power steering fluid.

7. Before servicing the vehicle, refer to the precautions in the beginning of this section.

8. Remove or disconnect the following:

- Negative battery cable
- Engine cover
- Throttle cable from the intake filter housing
- Intake filter housing
- Mass Air Flow (MAF) sensor
- Windshield washer reservoir
- Brake booster hose from the suction jet pump
- Fuel feed line from the injection pipe
- Engine splash shield and reinforcement plate
- Drive belt
- Power steering pump
- A/C system lines between the compressor and condenser
- A/C suction line
- Transmission
- Starter electrical connectors and heat shield
- Starter
- Oil lines to the transmission on the heat exchanger
- Radiator
- Coolant hoses on the alternator and thermostat housing
- Coolant hoses from the coolant manifold
- Heating valve and hoses
- Fuel tank vent hose
- Engine wire harness from the control unit box
- Transmission wire harness from the control unit box

- Oxygen (O$_2$S) sensor wiring and place all wires on top of the engine
- Expansion tank
- Supply reservoir from the carrier
- Ground strap from the oil filter housing
- Left and right swivel bearings
- Output shafts
- Propeller shaft
- Partition wall
- Ground tape from the right side engine support
- Upper nuts from the left and right side engine mounts and install an engine removal tool to the locating lugs
- Engine from the vehicle

To install:

9. Carefully lower the engine into the engine compartment.

10. Install or connect the following:

- Engine mounts. Torque the bolts to 32 ft. lbs. (45 Nm).
- Ground tape
- Partition wall
- Propeller shafts
- Output shafts
- Left and right swivel bearings
- Ground strap to the oil filter housing
- Supply reservoir
- Expansion tank
- O$_2$S sensor electrical connector
- Engine and transmission wire harness to the control unit box
- Fuel tank vent hose
- Heater valve and hoses
- Coolant hoses to the manifold and thermostat housing
- Radiator
- Transmission
- Oil lines to the transmission. Torque the nuts to 25 ft. lbs. (34 Nm).
- Starter and electrical connectors
- A/C lines
- Power steering pump
- Drive belt
- Engine splash shield and reinforcement plate
- Fuel feed line to the injection pipe
- Brake booster vacuum hose
- Windshield washer reservoir
- MAF sensor
- Intake filter housing
- Throttle cable to the filter housing

- Engine cover
- Negative battery cable

11. Fill and bleed the power steering system.

12. Fill and bleed the coolant system.

13. Recharge the A/C system.

14. Fill the engine with clean oil.

15. Start the vehicle and check for leaks, repair if necessary.

Water Pump

REMOVAL & INSTALLATION

1. Before servicing the vehicle, refer to the precautions in the beginning of this section.

2. Drain the cooling system.

3. Remove or disconnect:

- Negative battery cable
- Vibration damper
- Thermostat housing
- Water pump pulley
- Coolant hoses
- Water pump and discard the seal

To install:

4. Clean and remove any residual debris or gasket material from the engine mounting surface for the water pump.

5. Install the water pump with a new gasket. Torque the bolts as follows:

a. M6 bolts: 78 inch lbs. (9 Nm).
b. M7 bolts: 89 inch lbs. (10 Nm).
c. M8 bolts: 16 ft. lbs. (22 Nm).

6. Install or connect the following:

- Coolant hoses to the water pump
- Water pump pulley
- Thermostat housing
- Vibration damper
- Negative battery cable

7. Fill and bleed the cooling system.

8. Start the vehicle, check for leaks and repair as necessary.

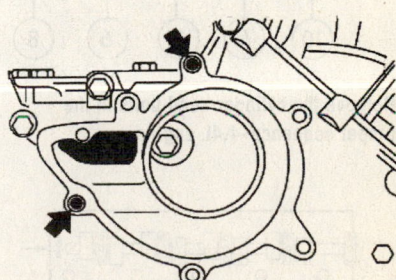

9308KG01

Exploded view of the water pump—4.4L engine

Cylinder Head

REMOVAL & INSTALLATION

LEFT SIDE

1. Before servicing the vehicle, refer to the precautions in the beginning of this section.

2. Properly relieve the fuel system pressure.

3. Drain the cooling system.

4. Remove or disconnect the following:
   - Negative battery cable
   - Left side exhaust manifold
   - Cylinder head cover
   - Spark plugs
   - Intake manifold
   - Coolant manifold
   - Left side camshaft adjustment unit

5. Install special tool 11–5–180 and pull back until the flywheel is no longer secured.

6. Lift the timing chain and hold it under tension.

7. Crank the engine at the central bolt against the direction of rotation to 45 degrees Before Top Dead Center (BTDC).

8. Remove the special tools.

9. Remove or disconnect the following:
   - Guide rail from the cylinder head
   - Cylinder head bolts in the proper sequence

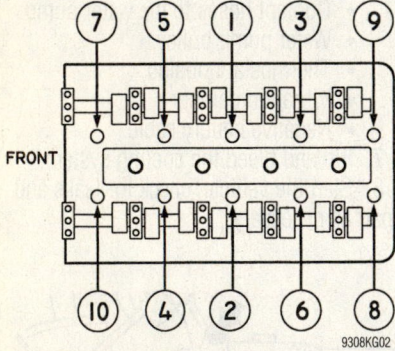

Remove the cylinder head bolts in the proper sequence—4.4L engine

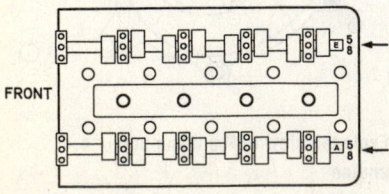

Rotate the camshafts until the markings face upward—4.4L engine

   - Cylinder head

To install:

10. Thoroughly clean all mounting surfaces and check the head for warpage. Take care not to drop any pieces of gasket or debris into the oil or coolant passages. Check the condition of the head locating dowel sleeves and clean out the bolt threads with a tap.

➡ **Refer to Section 1 of this manual for the cylinder head torque sequence illustration. The illustration is located after the Torque Specification Chart.**

11. Mount the cylinder head on the block and use new bolts. Do not remove the coating on the head bolts, apply oil to the threads and torque the bolts in the following sequence:
   a. Step 1: 22 ft. lbs. (30 Nm).
   b. Step 2: 80 degrees.
   c. Step 3: 80 degrees.

12. Install or connect the following:
   - Guide rail screw and rotate the camshafts until the markings face upward
   - Camshaft sprockets and the timing chain tensioner. Torque the bolts to 11 ft. lbs. (15 Nm).
   - Left side camshaft adjustment unit
   - Coolant manifold
   - Spark plugs
   - Cylinder head cover. Torque the bolts to 10 ft. lbs. (15 Nm).
   - Left side exhaust manifold
   - Negative battery cable

13. Fill and bleed the cooling system.

14. Change the engine oil and filter.

15. Start the vehicle, check for leaks and repair as necessary.

RIGHT SIDE

1. Before servicing the vehicle, refer to the precautions in the beginning of this section.

2. Properly relieve the fuel system pressure.

3. Drain the cooling system.

4. Remove or disconnect the following:
   - Negative battery cable
   - Right side exhaust manifold
   - Cylinder head cover
   - Spark plugs
   - Fan clutch and impeller
   - Intake manifold
   - Coolant manifold
   - Right side cam adjustment unit

5. Install special tool 11–5–180 and pull back until the flywheel is no longer secured.

6. Lift the timing chain and hold it under tension.

7. Crank the engine at the central bolt against the direction of rotation to 45 degrees Before Top Dead Center (BTDC).

8. Remove the special tools.

9. Remove or disconnect the following:
   - Guide rail from the cylinder head
   - Cylinder head bolts in the proper sequence
   - Cylinder head

To install:

10. Thoroughly clean all mounting surfaces and check the head for warpage. Take care not to drop any pieces of gasket or debris into the oil or coolant passages. Check the condition of the head locating dowel sleeves and clean out the bolt threads with a tap.

➡ **Refer to Section 1 of this manual for the cylinder head torque sequence illustration. The illustration is located after the Torque Specification Chart.**

11. Mount the cylinder head on the block and use new bolts. Do not remove the coating on the head bolts, apply oil to the threads and torque the bolts in the following sequence:
   a. Step 1: 22 ft. lbs. (30 Nm).
   b. Step 2: 80 degrees.
   c. Step 3: 80 degrees.

12. Install or connect the following:
   - Guide rail screw and rotate the camshafts until the markings face upward
   - Camshaft sprockets and the timing chain tensioner. Torque the bolts to 11 ft. lbs. (15 Nm).
   - Left side camshaft adjustment unit
   - Coolant manifold
   - Spark plugs
   - Cylinder head cover. Torque the bolts to 10 ft. lbs. (15 Nm).
   - Left side exhaust manifold
   - Negative battery cable

13. Fill and bleed the cooling system.

14. Change the engine oil and filter.
   - Start the vehicle and check for leaks, repair if necessary.

Intake Manifold

REMOVAL & INSTALLATION

1. Before servicing the vehicle, refer to the precautions in the beginning of this section.

2. Properly relieve the fuel system pressure.

3. Remove or disconnect the following:
   - Both battery cables
   - Acoustic cover
   - Ignition coil electrical connectors

- Throttle bellows
- Intake filter housing
- Mass Air Flow (MAF) sensor
- Wiring harness from the intake manifold
- Air injection vacuum control hoses
- Throttle body vacuum hose
- Fuel feed line from the injection pipe
- Engine ventilation hose from the cylinder head cover
- Engine ventilation hose from the oil separator
- Brake booster vacuum hose
- Oil separator from the cover
- Decoupling elements from under the intake manifold
- Oil drain hose from the rear cover after raising the intake manifold slightly
- Intake manifold

➥The intake manifold is vibrationally **separated from the cylinder head by decoupling elements and gaskets.**

To install:
4. Install or connect the following:
- Decoupling elements to the cylinder head
- Intake manifold
- Remaining components of the decoupling elements. Torque the M6 nuts to 89 inch lbs. (10 Nm), the M7 nuts to 10 ft. lbs. (15 Nm) and the M8 nuts to 16 ft. lbs. (22 Nm).
- Oil drain hose to the rear cover

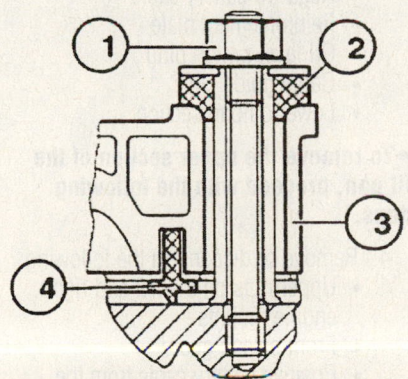

(1)   Nut
(2)   Decoupling element
(3)   Intake air manifold
(4)   Seal

9308KG04

Separating the intake manifold from the cylinder head

- Oil separator
- Brake booster vacuum hose
- Engine vent hose to the oil separator and the cylinder head
- Fuel feed line to the injection pipe
- Throttle body vacuum hose
- Air injection vacuum control hoses
- Wiring harness to the intake manifold
- MAF sensor
- Intake filter housing
- Throttle bellows
- Ignition coil electrical connectors
- Acoustic cover
- Both battery cables

Exhaust Manifold

REMOVAL & INSTALLATION

1. Before servicing the vehicle, refer to the precautions in the beginning of this section.
2. Remove or disconnect the following:
- Negative battery cable
- Exhaust system
- Reinforcement plate
- Propeller shaft, left side manifold only
- Screw connection at the exhaust manifold
- Exhaust manifold downward and discard the gaskets

To install:
3. Remove the old gasket off of the cylinder head and exhaust manifold and replace the gasket. The gasket beads face the exhaust manifolds.
4. Install or connect the following:
- Exhaust manifold with new gaskets. Torque the bolts to 10 ft. lbs. (15 Nm).
- Screw connection at the exhaust manifold
- Propeller shaft, left side manifold only
- Reinforcement plate
- Exhaust system
- Negative battery cable

Camshaft and Valve Lifters

REMOVAL & INSTALLATION

LEFT CAMSHAFT (CYLINDER BANK 5–8)

1. Before servicing the vehicle, refer to the precautions in the beginning of this section.

---

2. Remove or disconnect the following:
- Negative battery cable
- Splash guard
- Left and right cylinder head covers
- Spark plugs
- Timing chain tensioning piston
- Top left timing case cover
- Left camshaft adjustment unit and distributor
- Oil lines to the left and right cylinder head
3. Install special tool 11–2–300 and pull back on it until the flywheel is no longer secured in position.
4. Lift the timing chain and hold it under tension.
5. Crank the engine counter-engine wise on the central screw into the 45 degrees Before Top Dead Center (BTDC) position.
6. Rotate the exhaust camshaft at the hex head until the cam at cylinder No. 6 faces upward.
7. Rotate the inlet camshaft at the hex head until the cam at cylinder No. 8 faces upward.
8. Evenly release the bearing covers on the exhaust and inlet camshafts in ½ turn steps from the outside working in.
9. Remove the bearing covers and remove the camshafts.
10. Remove the hydraulic valve lifters. To remove, use tool No. 11-3-250 to pull them out of the cylinder head. Be sure that no damage occurs to the guides in the head. Inspect the bearing surfaces of the tappets for wear and scoring.

To install:
11. If the lifters were removed, install them with tool No. 11-32-250.
12. Lubricate and install the camshafts in their correct position.
13. Install or connect the following:
- Exhaust and inlet camshafts and rotate them until exhaust cam at cylinder No. 6 faces up and inlet cam at cylinder No. 8 faces up
- Bearing caps. The exhaust camshaft bearing covers are marked A1 to A5 and the inlet covers are marked E1 to E5. Evenly tighten the bearing covers in ½ turn steps from the outside working in.
14. Torque the camshaft bearing covers as follows:
  a. M6 to 89 inch lbs. (10 Nm).
  b. M7 to 9 ft. lbs. (14 Nm).
  c. M8 to 15 ft. lbs. (20 Nm).
15. Rotate the camshafts until the markings face upwards.

Timing belt service is covered in Section 4 of this manual

16. Using special tools 11–2–446 and 11–2–442 align the inlet and exhaust camshafts with an open-end wrench so the tools rest without a gap on the cylinder head.

17. Crank the engine from the 45 degrees BTDC position in the direction of rotation up to the TDC position.

18. Hold the crankshaft and install the distributor on the camshaft adjustment unit.

19. Install or connect the following:
- Camshaft adjustment unit
- Left timing case cover
- Timing chain tensioning piston
- Spark plugs
- Cylinder head covers
- Splash guard
- Negative battery cable

RIGHT CAMSHAFT (CYLINDER BANK 1–4)

1. Before servicing the vehicle, refer to the precautions in the beginning of this section.

2. Remove or disconnect the following:
- Negative battery cable
- Splash guard
- Left and right cylinder head covers
- Spark plugs
- Timing chain tensioning piston
- Top right timing case cover
- Right camshaft adjustment unit and distributor
- Oil lines to the left and right cylinder head

3. Install special tool 11–2–300 and pull back on it until the flywheel is no longer secured in position.

4. Lift the timing chain and hold it under tension.

5. Crank the engine counter-engine wise on the central screw into the 45 degrees Before Top Dead Center (BTDC) position.

6. Rotate the exhaust camshaft at the hex head until the cam at cylinder No. 6 faces upward.

7. Rotate the inlet camshaft at the hex head until the cam at cylinder No. 8 faces upward.

8. Evenly release the bearing covers on the exhaust and inlet camshafts in ½turn steps from the outside working in.

9. Remove the bearing covers and remove the camshafts.

10. Remove the hydraulic valve lifters. To remove, use tool No. 11-3-250 to pull them out of the cylinder head. Be sure that no damage occurs to the guides in the head. Inspect the bearing surfaces of the tappets for wear and scoring.

To install:
11. If the lifters were removed, install them with tool No. 11-32-250.

12. Lubricate and install the camshafts in their correct position.

13. Install or connect the following:
- Exhaust and inlet camshafts and rotate them until exhaust cam at cylinder No. 6 faces up and inlet cam at cylinder No. 8 faces up
- Bearing caps. The exhaust camshaft bearing covers are marked A1 to A5 and the inlet covers are marked E1 to E5. Evenly tighten the bearing covers in ½ turn steps from the outside working in.

14. Torque the camshaft bearing covers as follows:
   a. M6 to 89 inch lbs. (10 Nm).
   b. M7 to 9 ft. lbs. (14 Nm).
   c. M8 to 15 ft. lbs. (20 Nm).

15. Rotate the camshafts until the markings face upwards.

16. Using special tools 11–2–446 and 11–2–442 align the inlet and exhaust camshafts with an open-end wrench so the tools rest without a gap on the cylinder head.

17. Crank the engine from the 45 degrees BTDC position in the direction of rotation up to the TDC position.

18. Hold the crankshaft and install the distributor on the camshaft adjustment unit.

19. Install or connect the following:
- Camshaft adjustment unit
- Both timing case covers
- Timing chain tensioning piston
- Spark plugs
- Cylinder head covers
- Splash guard
- Negative battery cable

Valve Lash

ADJUSTMENT

All engines are equipped with hydraulic valve lash adjusters. This design does not permit adjustments nor are adjustments possible.

Starter

REMOVAL & INSTALLATION

➡When the battery is disconnected, the radio code, on-board computer and clock settings will be lost. The radio code should be obtained before disconnecting the battery or radio. Once the battery has been reconnected, the radio will not function unless the code is keyed in.

1. If needed, read the stored fault memories from the control module.

2. Relieve the fuel system pressure.

3. Set the ignition switch to the **OFF** position.

4. Before servicing the vehicle, refer to the precautions in the beginning of this section.

5. Remove or disconnect the following:
- Negative battery cable
- Reinforcement plate
- Positive battery cable from the starter
- Starter electrical connectors
- Heat shield
- Starter from the transmission mount
- Starter

To install:
6. Install or connect the following:
- Starter to the transmission mount
- Heat shield. Torque the bolts to 38 ft. lbs. (47 Nm).
- Starter electrical connectors
- Positive battery cable to the starter
- Reinforcement plate
- Negative battery cable

Oil Pan

REMOVAL & INSTALLATION

1. Before servicing the vehicle, refer to the precautions in the beginning of this section.

2. Drain the engine oil.

3. Remove or disconnect the following:
- Negative battery cable
- Reinforcement plate
- Oil level switch plug
- Cable guide clips
- Lower oil pan section

➡**To remove the upper section of the oil pan, proceed with the following steps.**

4. Remove or disconnect the following:
- Upper nuts on the left and right engine mounts
- Front splash guard
- Positive battery cable from the starter
- Left and right swivel bearings
- Output shafts
- Bearing pedestal from the right output shaft
- Propeller shaft
- Steering spindle from the steering gear and support the front axle
- Front axle support from the engine carrier and slightly lower the axle support
- Drive belt

- Vane pump from the oil pan
- Adjustable plate from the oil pan after releasing the tension from the A/C compressor belt
- Guide tube for the oil dipstick
- Oil return line from the oil separator to the oil pan
- Oil pump snorkel
- Cable guide for the positive lead
- Upper oil pan section towards the rear of the vehicle

To install:

5. Clean the mounting surfaces.
6. Check the seals on the oil pipes and replace it if necessary. Lubricate the seals with oil.
7. Install or connect the following:
- Install upper oil pan. Torque the bolts to 89 inch lbs. (10 Nm) and lower the engine
- Cable guide for the positive lead
- Banjo bolt for the oil return pipe from the oil filter at the oil pan
- Drive belt
- Left and right engine mounts Torque the bottom bolts to 32 ft. lbs. (43 Nm).
- Lower oil pan with a new gasket. Torque the bolts, beginning in the middle and working to the outside to 89 inch lbs. (10 Nm).
- Plug for the level switch, making sure to replace the O-ring
- Steering spindle to the steering gear
- Propeller shaft
- Bearing pedestal
- Output shafts
- Positive battery cable
- Engine splash guards
- Oil dipstick guide tube, making sure to replace the O-ring
- Reinforcement plate
- Negative battery cable

8. Fill the engine with clean oil.
9. Start the vehicle and check for leaks, repair if necessary.

Oil Pump

REMOVAL & INSTALLATION

1. Before servicing the vehicle, refer to the precautions in the beginning of this section.
2. Drain the engine oil.
3. Remove or disconnect the following:
- Negative battery cable
- Oil pan
- Oil pump sprocket wheel and chain
- Oil pump

To install:

4. Check the seals on the oil pipes and replace it if necessary. Lubricate the seals with oil.
5. Check the seal in the oil pump and replace it if necessary. Screw the hexagon adapter back into the oil pump until it stops.
6. Install or connect the following:
- Oil pump. Torque the bolts to 17 ft. lbs. (22 Nm).
- Oil pump sprocket wheel and chain. Torque the nut to 35 ft. lbs. (47 Nm).
- Oil pan
- Negative battery cable

7. Fill the engine with clean oil.
8. Start the vehicle and check for leaks, repair if necessary.

Rear Main Seal

REMOVAL & INSTALLATION

The rear main bearing oil seal can be replaced after the transmission and flywheel has been removed from the engine.

1. Before servicing the vehicle, refer to the precautions in the beginning of this section.
2. Drain the transmission fluid.
3. Remove or disconnect the following:
- Negative battery cable
- Transmission
- Flywheel assembly
- Oil seal, using a suitable seal removal tool

To install:

4. Coat the sealing lips of the new seal with oil.
5. Install or connect the following:
- New seal into the end cover housing with a suitable seal installation tool
- Flywheel
- Transmission
- Negative battery cable

6. Fill the transmission with new fluid.
7. Start the engine and check that oil pressure is present; if the oil pressure lamp does not extinguish within 5–7 seconds of starting the engine, turn the engine **OFF**.
8. Check and top off all fluid levels.

Timing Chain, Sprockets, Front Cover and Seal

REMOVAL & INSTALLATION

1. Before servicing the vehicle, refer to the precautions in the beginning of this section.

2. Drain the engine oil.
3. Remove or disconnect the following:
- Negative battery cable
- Spark plugs
- Cylinder head covers

➡**In the Top Dead Center (TDC) firing position, the inlet camshaft twists in the splines of the camshaft adjustment unit.**

4. Remove or disconnect the following:
- Oil lines from the cylinder head
- Vibration damper and rotate the engine at the central bolt so that the first cylinder is at the TDC position.
- Timing chain tensioning piston
- Both top timing case covers
- Left hand threaded nut from the sensor gear on cylinder bank 1–4
- Left hand threaded nut from the sensor gear on cylinder bank 5–8

5. Slacken the screw connection for the exhaust camshaft on cylinder bank 5–8 by ½ turn.
6. Slacken the screw connection for the exhaust camshaft on cylinder bank 1–4 by ½ turn.
7. Slacken the screw connection for the inlet camshaft on cylinder bank 5–8 by ½ turn.
8. Slacken the screw connection for the inlet camshaft on cylinder bank 1–4 by ½ turn.
9. Align the camshafts and install special tool 11–2–445/441 to the camshafts on cylinder back 1–4.
10. Align the camshafts and install special tool 11–2–446/442 to the camshafts on cylinder back 5–8.
11. Remove or disconnect the following:
- Central bolt and hub from the vibration damper
- Oil pump
- Water pump and thermostat housing
- Bottom timing case cover
- Tensioning rail and oil guide
- Timing chain from the camshaft adjustment unit

To install:

12. Install or connect the following:
- Timing chain over the reversing rail, camshaft adjustment unit and crankshaft sprocket wheel for cylinder bank 5–8
- Timing chain inside screw-in pin
- Timing chain onto the camshaft adjustment unit for cylinder bank 1–4

13. Raise the timing chain slightly by the guide rail and slide the rail over the pin until the retaining lug can be heard snapping into place on the lower guide pin.

14. Align the timing chain to the guide rail.

15. Install the oil guide for the bow cover in the pivot rail.

16. Install the tensioning rail screw. Press the cover against the timing chain and secure the cover with the plastic strap.

17. Install or connect the following:
- Upper oil pan section and secure the crankshaft in the TDC position with special tool 11–5–180
- Special tool 11–7–380 to the right side cylinder bank and install special tool 11–4–230
- Adjustment screw into the tensioning rail and hand tighten
- Special tool 11–6–440 to the camshaft adjustment unit on cylinder bank 5–8 and move it 31 ft. lbs. (40 Nm) to the left hand stop.

18. Tighten the screw connection on the inlet camshaft on cylinder bank 5–8 to 10 ft. lbs. (15 Nm) and back off by ¼ turn.

19. Tighten the screw connection on the exhaust camshaft on cylinder bank 5–8 to 10 ft. lbs. (15 Nm) and back off by ¼ turn.

20. Special tool 11–6–440 to the camshaft adjustment unit on cylinder bank 1–4 and move it 31 ft. lbs. (40 Nm) to the left hand stop.

21. Tighten the screw connection on the inlet camshaft on cylinder bank 1–4 to 10 ft. lbs. (15 Nm) and back off by ¼ turn.

22. Tighten the screw connection on the exhaust camshaft on cylinder bank 1–4 to 10 ft. lbs. (15 Nm) and back off by ¼ turn.

23. Tighten the tensioning rail by turning the adjusting screw on special tool 11–4–230.

➡ When the timing chain is pretensioned, the camshaft adjustment unit moves and must be reset to the left hand stop.

24. Tighten the inlet camshaft screw connection on cylinder bank 5–8 to 85 ft. lbs. (110 Nm).

25. Tighten the exhaust camshaft screw connection on cylinder bank 5–8 to 85 ft. lbs. (110 Nm).

26. Install special tool 11–6–451 to the camshaft adjustment unit on cylinder bank 1–4 and move it 31 ft. lbs. (40 Nm) to the left hand stop.

27. Tighten the inlet camshaft screw connection on cylinder bank 1–4 to 85 ft. lbs. (110 Nm).

28. Tighten the exhaust camshaft screw connection on cylinder bank 1–4 to 85 ft. lbs. (110 Nm).

29. Install the sensor gear to cylinder bank 1–4 and hand tighten the nut.

30. Align the locating bore on the sensor gear to the positioning pin on special tool 11–6–451. Press the tool downward and align it to the cylinder head. Torque the sensor gear screw to 30 ft. lbs. (40 Nm). Remove the special tool.

31. Install special tool 11–6–452 to the camshaft adjustment unit on cylinder bank 5–8 and move it 31 ft. lbs. (40 Nm) to the left hand stop.

32. Tighten the inlet camshaft screw connection on cylinder bank 5–8 to 85 ft. lbs. (110 Nm).

33. Tighten the exhaust camshaft screw connection on cylinder bank 5–8 to 85 ft. lbs. (110 Nm).

34. Install the sensor gear to cylinder bank 5–8 and hand tighten the nut.

35. Align the locating bore on the sensor gear to the positioning pin on special tool 11–6–452. Press the tool downward and align it to the cylinder head. Torque the sensor gear screw to 30 ft. lbs. (40 Nm). Remove the special tool.

36. Check for the correct seating of the dowel sleeves. Clean the sealing surfaces thoroughly, and then place a new gasket on the lower cover.

37. Trim the protruding ends of the gasket, making sure the cutting tool is level. Do not allow the pieces to fall into the engine.

38. Position the lower cover and install the mounting bolts with an even distribution of pressure. Tighten the 6mm bolts to 84 inch lbs. (10 Nm), 8mm bolts to 16 ft. lbs. (22 Nm) and 10mm bolts to 35 ft. lbs. (47 Nm).

39. Install the oil seal in the timing case cover using tool No. 11–1–220. Make sure the seal is flush with the cover.

40. Install the vibration damper hub and install the mounting bolt. Tighten the hub bolt to:
   a. Step 1: 74 ft. lbs. (100 Nm).
   b. Step 2: turn an additional 60 degrees.
   c. Step 3: turn an additional 60 degrees.
   d. Step 4: turn an additional 30 degrees.

41. Position the vibration damper pulleys and install the mounting bolts for the damper.

42. Install or connect the following:
- Water pump pulley
- Drive belt and the cooling fan. Rotate the fan counterclockwise to install.
- Intake hose between the throttle body and the air volume meter
- Battery positive cable for the alternator and install the protective tube mounting fasteners and connect the remaining wires to the alternator
- Oil filter housing and the return pipe and replace the housing cover
- Alternator and cylinder head cover
- Negative battery cable

43. Fill the engine with clean oil.

44. Start the vehicle and check for leaks, repair if necessary

Piston and Ring Positioning

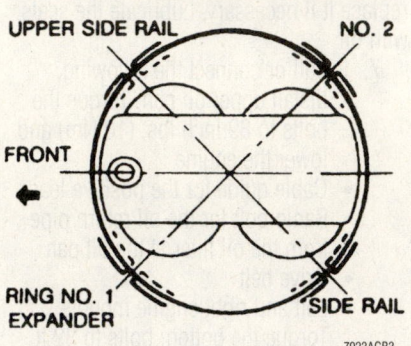

BMW engines Piston ring end-gap spacing

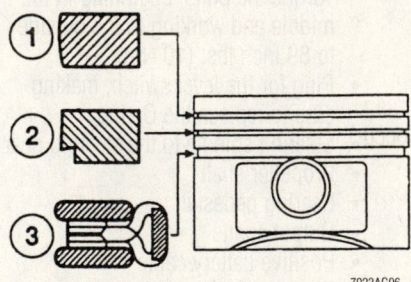

BMW engines compression and oil control ring locations

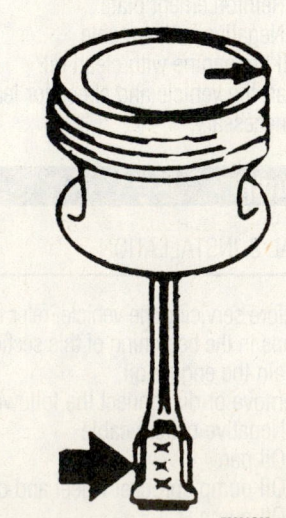

BMW engines connecting rod-to-piston positioning

FUEL SYSTEM

Fuel System Service Precautions

Safety is the most important factor when performing not only fuel system maintenance but also any type of maintenance. Failure to conduct maintenance and repairs in a safe manner may result in serious personal injury or death. Maintenance and testing of the vehicle's fuel system components can be accomplished safely and effectively by adhering to the following rules and guidelines.

1. To avoid the possibility of fire and personal injury, always disconnect the negative battery cable unless the repair or test procedure requires that battery voltage be applied.

2. Always relieve the fuel system pressure prior to disconnecting any fuel system component (injector, fuel rail, pressure regulator, etc.), fitting or fuel line connection. Exercise extreme caution whenever relieving fuel system pressure, to avoid exposing skin, face and eyes to fuel spray. Fuel under pressure may penetrate the skin or any part of the body that it contacts.

3. Always place a shop towel or cloth around the fitting or connection prior to loosening to absorb any excess fuel due to spillage. Ensure that all fuel spillage (should it occur) is quickly removed from engine surfaces. Ensure that all fuel soaked cloths or towels are deposited into a suitable waste container.

4. Always keep a dry chemical (Class B) fire extinguisher near the work area.

5. Do not allow fuel spray or fuel vapors to come into contact with a spark or open flame.

6. Always use a back-up wrench when loosening and tightening fuel line connection fittings. This will prevent unnecessary stress and torsion to fuel line piping. Always follow the proper torque specifications.

7. Always replace worn fuel fitting O-rings with new. Do not substitute fuel hose or equivalent where fuel pipe is installed.

Fuel System Pressure

RELIEVING

To relieve the pressure in the system, locate fuel pump relay located on the cowl. The relay can sometimes be distinguished by the orange color of the housing. Unplug and remove the relay, and place it in a safe location. With the fuel pump relay removed, start the engine and operate it until it stalls. Crank the engine for 10 seconds after it stalls to remove any residual pressure.

Fuel Filter

REMOVAL & INSTALLATION

1. Before servicing the vehicle, refer to the precautions in the beginning of this section.

2. Properly relieve the fuel system pressure.

3. Remove or disconnect the following:
- Negative battery cable
- Fuel pressure regulator and seal the fuel line before and after the filter with special tool 13–3–010
- Clips and fuel line from the filter
- Fuel filter

To install:
- New fuel filter
- Fuel lines onto the correct fittings. Tighten the fuel line clamps until tight, but not to the point where the fuel lines become excessively pinched or damaged, then tighten the mounting bracket until snug.
- Negative battery cable and cycle the ignition **ON** and **OFF** several times to build fuel pressure

4. Start the vehicle and check for leaks, repair if necessary.

Fuel Pump

REMOVAL & INSTALLATION

1. Before servicing the vehicle, refer to the precautions in the beginning of this section.

2. Drain the fuel tank.

3. Properly relieve the fuel system pressure.

4. Remove or disconnect the following:
- Negative battery cable
- Rear seat bench
- Rubber plug above the sender unit and fold the rubber mat back
- Metal cover
- Fuel gauge level sending unit electrical connector
- Fuel lines
- Rotary connection with special tool 16–1–020

5. Raise the fuel level sensor and expose the spiral hose.

6. Remove the fuel level sensor and fuel pump from the tank.

To install:

➡**Always use a new seal or gasket when installing the fuel pump or fuel level gauge sending unit assembly.**

7. Install or connect the following:
- Fuel pump into the fuel tank taking care not to bend or damage the fuel sending unit assembly
- New seal and torque the sealing ring using tool No. 16-1-020 as follows:
  a. Metal sealing rings: 26 ft. lbs. (35 Nm).
  b. Plastic sealing rings: 41 ft. lbs. (55 Nm).

8. Install or connect the following:
- Fuel lines
- Fuel gauge level sending unit electrical connector
- Metal cover
- Rubber plug above the sender unit
- Rear seat bench
- Negative battery cable

9. Start the vehicle and check for leaks, repair if necessary.

Fuel Injector(s)

REMOVAL & INSTALLATION

1. Before servicing the vehicle, refer to the precautions in the beginning of this section.

2. Properly relieve the fuel system pressure.

3. Remove or disconnect the following:
- Negative battery cable
- Acoustic cover
- Knock Sensor (KS) electrical connector from the cable strips
- Changeover valve electrical connector
- Camshaft (CMP) sensor electrical connector
- Left side cylinder head ignition coil cover
- Ignition coil electrical connectors
- Ignition coil cover
- Cable strip from the fuel injectors
- Vacuum accumulator lines
- Fuel line
- Both fuel injection pipe retaining brackets
- Fuel injectors from the fuel pipe

4. Check the O-rings on the fuel injectors and replace if damaged.

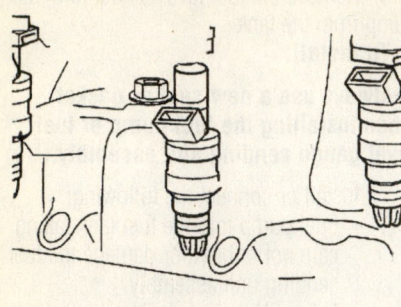

Remove the fuel injector from the injection pipe—4.4L engine

To install:

5. If the O-rings are being replaced, coat the new O-ring with petroleum jelly.

6. Install or connect the following:
- Fuel injectors to the fuel pipe
- Fuel line
- Vacuum lines to the vacuum accumulator
- Cable strip to the fuel injectors
- Ignition coil electrical connectors
- Ignition coil cover
- CMP sensor electrical connector
- Changeover valve electrical connector
- KS electrical connector
- Acoustic cover
- Negative battery cable

7. Start the vehicle and check for leaks, repair if necessary.

DRIVE TRAIN

Transmission Assembly

REMOVAL & INSTALLATION

Automatic Transmission

1. Before servicing the vehicle, refer to the precautions in the beginning of this section.

2. Drain the transmission fluid.

3. Remove or disconnect the following:
- Negative battery cable
- Exhaust system
- Front splash guard
- Reinforcement plate
- Heat shields and unclip the Oxygen (O2S) sensor
- Stabilizer bar and slide it forward
- Rear heat shield

- Front propeller shaft and unclip the vent line from the transmission
- Retaining plate and brace the clamping bush
- Bracket for the oil lines at the oil pan
- Power steering pump oil line bracket
- Oil line and banjo bolt
- Union screw on the oil return line and properly support the transmission and transfer case assembly
- O2S cable from the transmission crossmember
- Transmission crossmember
- Nuts for the center bearing after bracing the propeller shaft

➡ **Do not allow the propeller shaft to damage the CV-joints.**

- Transmission output flange by bending the propeller shaft downward at the center bearing
- Cable connector from the transmission case
- Impulse sensor electrical connector
- Torque converter retaining screws

4. Support the engine at the front housing and turn the front wheel to the right lock position.

5. Remove the remaining screws and remove the transmission and transfer case assembly.

To install:

6. Align the transmission/transfer case as an assembly.

7. Torque the transmission to engine screws as follows:
- a. M8 Hex screws: 18 ft. lbs. (24 Nm).
- b. M10 Hex screws: 33 ft. lbs. (45 Nm).
- c. M12 Hex screws: 60 ft. lbs. (82 Nm).
- d. M8 Torx bolts: 16 ft. lbs. (21 Nm).
- e. M10 Torx bolts: 31 ft. lbs. (42 Nm).
- f. M12 Torx bolts: 54 ft. lbs. (72 Nm).

8. Install or connect the following:
- Torque converter. Torque the bolts to 30 ft. lbs. (40 Nm).
- Impulse sensor electrical connector
- Transmission case cable connector
- Transmission output flange
- Center bearing. Torque the bolts to 16 ft. lbs. (21 Nm).
- Transmission crossmember. Torque the bolts to 16 ft. lbs. (21 Nm).
- O2S cable to the crossmember
- Union screw to the oil return line. Torque the screw to 21 ft. lbs. (28 Nm).
- Oil line and banjo bolt. Torque the bolt to 21 ft. lbs. (28 Nm).
- Oil line bracket for the power steering pump

- Retaining plate
- Front propeller shaft. Torque the bolts to 47 ft. lbs. (64 Nm) and clip the vent line to the transmission.
- Rear heat shield
- Stabilizer bar. Torque the bolts to 16 ft. lbs. (22 Nm).
- Front heat shields
- O2S connector
- Reinforcement plate
- Front splash guard
- Exhaust system
- Negative battery cable

9. Fill the transmission with the proper fluid to the proper level.

10. Start the vehicle and check for leaks, repair if necessary.

Transfer Case

REMOVAL & INSTALLATION

1. Before servicing the vehicle, refer to the precautions in the beginning of this section.

2. Drain the transmission fluid.

3. Remove or disconnect the following:
- Negative battery cable
- Exhaust system
- Front splash guard
- Reinforcement plate
- Heat shields and unclip the Oxygen (O2S) sensor
- Stabilizer bar and slide it forward
- Rear heat shield
- Front propeller shaft and unclip the vent line from the transmission. Properly support the transmission.
- O2S cable from the transmission crossmember
- Transmission crossmember
- O2S cable from the transfer case
- Center bearing after bracing the properller shaft. Do not allow the propeller shaft to damage the CV-joints.
- Transmission output flange by bending the propeller shaft downward at the center bearing
- Transfer case from the transmission

To install:

4. Connect the transfer case to the transmission. Torque the bolts as follows:
- a. M8 Hex screws: 18 ft. lbs. (24 Nm).
- b. M10 Hex screws: 33 ft. lbs. (45 Nm).
- c. M12 Hex screws: 60 ft. lbs. (82 Nm).
- d. M8 Torx bolts: 16 ft. lbs. (21 Nm).
- e. M10 Torx bolts: 31 ft. lbs. (42 Nm).

f. M12 Torx bolts: 54 ft. lbs. (72 Nm).

5. Install or connect the following:
- Transmission output flange
- Center bearing. Torque the bolts to 16 ft. lbs. (21 Nm).
- Transmission crossmember. Torque the bolts to 16 ft. lbs. (21 Nm).
- O_2S cable to the crossmember
- Union screw to the oil return line. Torque the screw to 21 ft. lbs. (28 Nm).
- Front propeller shaft. Torque the bolts to 47 ft. lbs. (64 Nm) and clip the vent line to the transmission.
- Rear heat shield
- Stabilizer bar. Torque the bolts to 16 ft. lbs. (22 Nm).
- Front heat shields
- O_2S connector
- Reinforcement plate
- Front splash guard
- Exhaust system
- Negative battery cable

6. Fill the transmission with the proper fluid to the proper level.

7. Start the vehicle and check for leaks, repair if necessary.

Halfshafts

REMOVAL & INSTALLATION

Front

1. Before servicing the vehicle, refer to the precautions in the beginning of this section.

2. Remove or disconnect the following:
- Negative battery cable
- Front wheel
- Reinforcement plate
- Front splash guard
- Swivel bearing
- Output shaft from the differential by pressing it out with special tool 31–5–110

To install:

3. Install or connect the following:
- New output shaft radial seal
- New snap ring on the output shaft
- Press the output shaft in by pushing it in over the resistance of the snap ring
- Swivel bearing
- Front splash guard
- Reinforcement plate
- Front wheel
- Negative battery cable

Rear

1. Before servicing the vehicle, refer to the precautions in the beginning of this section.

2. Remove or disconnect the following:
- Negative battery cable
- Rear tire and wheel assembly
- Collar nut

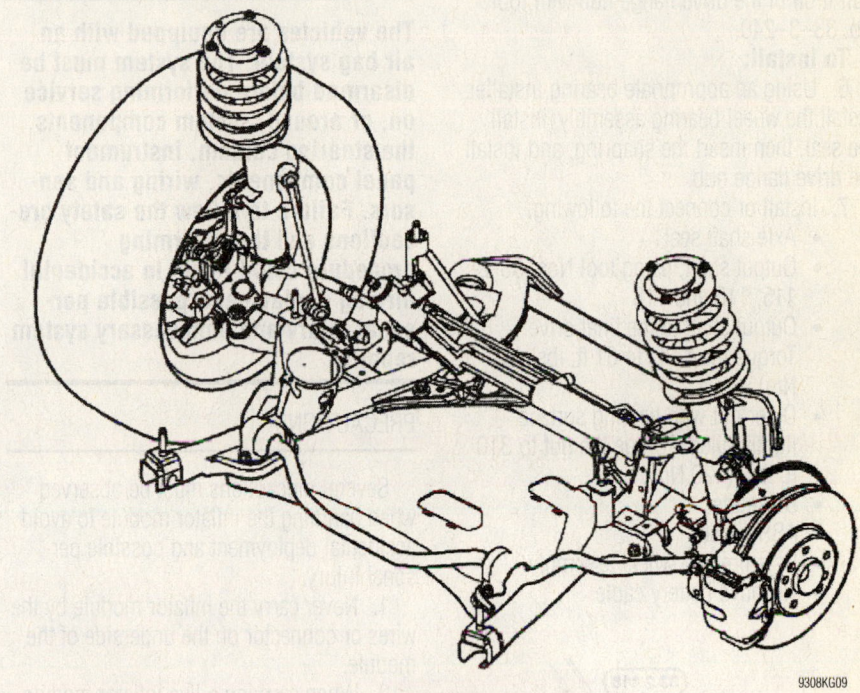

Exploded view of the front axle assembly–X5 Series

- Brake disc
- ABS sensor
- Retaining nut from the output flange. Remove the drive flange hub

➡ **The wheel bearing will be destroyed when the flange is removed. The wheel bearing must be replaced.**

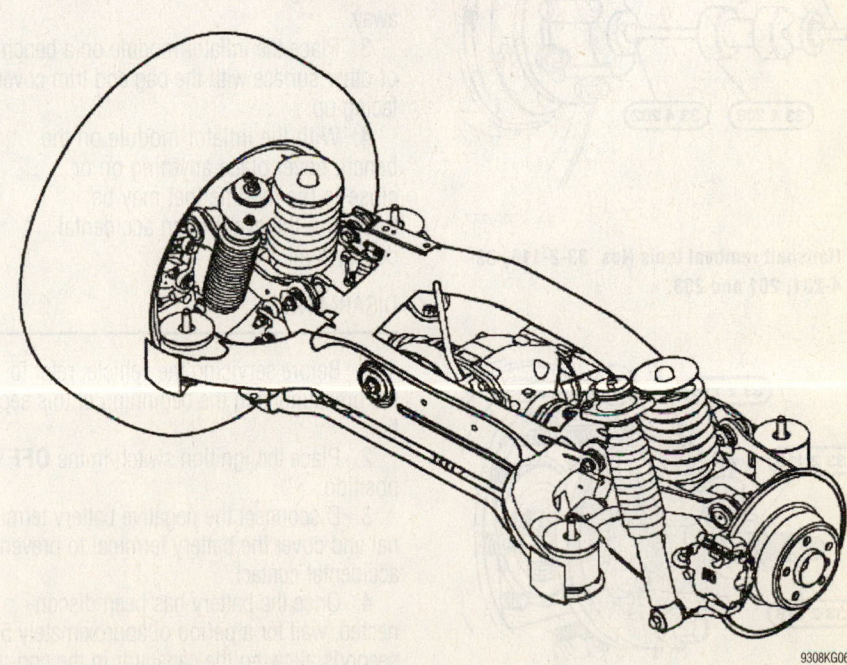

Exploded view of the rear halfshaft and suspension system–X5 Series

For complete service labor times order Nichols' Chilton Labor Guide Manual

- Halfshaft from the vehicle by removing the shaft from the final drive output flange and by pressing the halfshaft out of the drive flange hub using tool Nos. 33-2-116, 201, 202 and 203

3. Press out the drive flange hub.

4. Pull out the seal with a suitable tool.

5. If the bearing inner race is damaged, pull it off of the drive flange hub with tool No. 33–3–240.

To install:

6. Using an appropriate bearing installer, install the wheel bearing assembly, install the seal, then insert the snapring, and install the drive flange hub.

7. Install or connect the following:
- Axle shaft seal
- Output shaft, using tool Nos. 33-2-115, 116 and 118
- Output shaft to the final drive. Torque the bolts to 61 ft. lbs. (83 Nm).
- Outer nut with bearing surface lightly oiled. Torque the nut to 310 ft. lbs. (420 Nm).
- Brake disc
- ABS sensor
- Rear tire and wheel assembly
- Negative battery cable

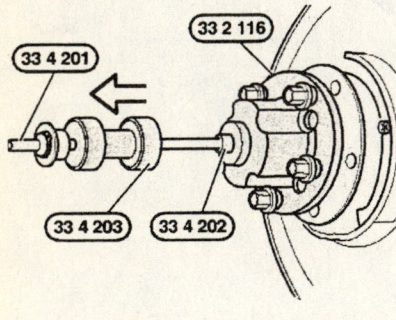

Halfshaft removal tools Nos. 33-2-116, 33-4-201, 201 and 203

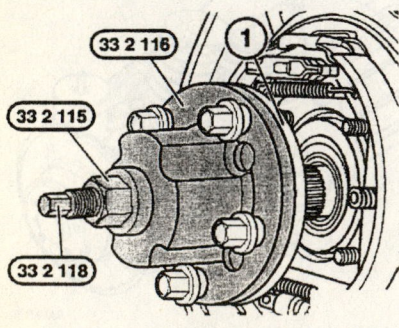

Drive flange hub tool Nos. 33-2-115, 116 and 118 used for drive flange installation

STEERING AND SUSPENSION

Air Bag

✳✳ CAUTION

The vehicles are equipped with an air bag system. The system must be disarmed before performing service on, or around, system components, the steering column, instrument panel components, wiring and sensors. Failure to follow the safety precautions and the disarming procedure could result in accidental air bag deployment, possible personal injury and unnecessary system repairs.

PRECAUTIONS

Several precautions must be observed when handling the inflator module to avoid accidental deployment and possible personal injury.

1. Never carry the inflator module by the wires or connector on the underside of the module.

2. When carrying a live inflator module, hold securely with both hands, and ensure that the bag and trim cover are pointed away.

3. Place the inflator module on a bench or other surface with the bag and trim cover facing up.

4. With the inflator module on the bench, never place anything on or close to the module that may be thrown in the event of an accidental deployment.

DISARMING

1. Before servicing the vehicle, refer to the precautions in the beginning of this section.

2. Place the ignition switch in the **OFF** position.

3. Disconnect the negative battery terminal and cover the battery terminal to prevent accidental contact.

4. Once the battery has been disconnected, wait for a period of approximately 5 seconds allowing the capacitor in the control unit to discharge. Once the capacitor is discharged, a trigger pulse cannot be generated inadvertently.

REARMING

1. Before servicing the vehicle, refer to the precautions in the beginning of this section.

2. Place the ignition switch in the **OFF** position.

3. Attach the sensors, the steering column connector and the seat belt tensioner connectors.

4. Connect the negative battery terminal.

5. Place the ignition switch in the **ON** position. Check that the SRS light illuminates for 6 seconds and extinguishes. If it illuminates in any other pattern, check the components and their connections for proper operation and recheck operation of the warning light.

Power Rack and Pinion Steering Gear

REMOVAL & INSTALLATION

1. Before servicing the vehicle, refer to the precautions in the beginning of this section.

2. Set the steering gear in the straight ahead position by aligning the marks on the steering gear and spindle.

3. Drain the power steering fluid.

4. Remove or disconnect the following:
- Negative battery cable
- Front wheels
- Reinforcement plate
- Nuts from the left and right engine support arms and raise the engine slightly
- Lower clamping screw
- Steering gear clamps
- Tie rod by pressing it off with special tool 32–3–090
- Self-locking nuts and brace the front axle support
- Banjo bolts and slide the steering gear out through the left wheel opening

To install:

5. Install the steering gear through the left side wheel opening

6. Install new sealing rings and banjo bolts. Torque the bolts as follows:
   a. M10: 7 ft. lbs. (12 Nm).
   b. M14: 25 ft. lbs. (35 Nm).
   c. M16: 29 ft. lbs. (40 Nm).
   d. M18: 34 ft. lbs. (45 Nm).

7. Install or connect the following:
- Front axle support screws. Torque the screws to 74 ft. lbs. (100 Nm).
- Self-locking nuts. Torque the nuts to 74 ft. lbs. (100 Nm).

- Tie rod. Torque the castle nut to 58 ft. lbs. (80 Nm).
- Steering gear to the spindle. Torque the fastener to 18 ft. lbs. (24 Nm).
- Steering gear clamp
- Engine support arm nuts. Torque the nuts to 60 ft. lbs. (85 Nm).
- Reinforcement plate
- Splash guard
- Both front wheels
- Negative battery cable

8. Fill and bleed the power steering system.

9. Start the vehicle and check for leaks, repair if necessary.

Strut

REMOVAL & INSTALLATION

1. Before servicing the vehicle, refer to the precautions in the beginning of this section.

2. Mark the position of the threaded pin to the wheel arch to retain the camber setting when installed.

3. Remove or disconnect the following:
- Negative battery cable
- Tire and wheel assembly
- Two of the nuts on the spring strut support bearing
- Center strut bracket nut
- Speed sensor/brake wear cable and disconnect the plug housing
- Swivel bearing and tie it aside
- Remaining nut on the spring strut support bearing
- Strut assembly

To install:
4. Install or connect the following:
- Strut assembly
- One nut to the spring strut support bearing and hand tighten at this time
- Swivel bearing. Torque the new self-locking nut to 176 ft. lbs. (250 Nm).
- Speed sensor/brake wear cable and connect the housing plug
- Center strut bracket. Torque the nut to 74 ft. lbs. (100 Nm).

5. Align the three upper spring strut support bearing nuts and match the threaded pin with the mark made during the removal procedure. When aligned properly torque the nuts to 25 ft. lbs. (34 Nm).

6. Install or connect the following:
- Tire and wheel assembly
- Negative battery cable

Shock Absorber

REMOVAL & INSTALLATION

1. Before servicing the vehicle, refer to the precautions in the beginning of this section.

2. Remove or disconnect the following:
- Fuse in the air supply system
- Negative battery cable
- Rear wheel
- Nuts and expansion rivets and luggage compartment trim
- 3 upper nuts after supporting the wheel carrier
- Shock absorber from the swinging arm and insert a bushing into the bore of the arm
- Thrust bearing after bracing the piston rod with a ring spanner
- Upper nut and remove the shock absorber

To install:
3. Install or connect the following:
- Shock absorber to the swinging arm. Torque the bolt to 41 ft. lbs. (56 Nm).
- Thrust bearing. Torque the nut to 18 ft. lbs. (25 Nm).
- Upper nuts. Torque the nuts to 41 ft. lbs. (56 Nm).
- New expansion rivets and nuts
- Luggage compartment trim
- Rear wheel
- Negative battery cable
- Fuse for the air supply system

Coil Spring

REMOVAL & INSTALLATION

Front

✳✳ CAUTION

This procedure calls for the spring to be compressed. A compressed spring has high potential energy and if released suddenly can cause severe damage and personal injury.

1. Before servicing the vehicle, refer to the precautions in the beginning of this section.

2. disconnect the negative battery cable.

3. Remove the strut from the vehicle and mount in a vise using a strut holder. This will prevent damage to the strut tube

4. Using a proper spring compressor, compress the spring until the stress on the thrust bearing is released.

5. Remove the top nut of the strut mount. Counterhold the strut rod during removal.

6. Pull the strut mount off the strut rod. Note the positioning of the spacers and washer for replacement.

7. Pull the spring off the strut and place aside in a safe area.

8. slowly release the compression of the spring.

To install:
9. Install or connect the following:
- Spring in the compressor and compress
- Spring and strut mount with all the spacers and washers in their original positions. Torque the new strut rod nut: 47 ft. lbs. (65 Nm).

10. Release the spring slowly and check that it seats in the spring holders. Install the strut in the vehicle.

11. Connect the negative battery cable.

Lower Ball Joint

REMOVAL & INSTALLATION

1. Before servicing the vehicle, refer to the precautions in the beginning of this section.

2. Remove or disconnect the following:
- Negative battery cable
- Push rod/integral link assembly and properly support the wheel carrier
- Shock absorber from the swinging arm
- Circlip

3. Using special tool 33–4–191, 192, 193 and 33–3–333 pull the ball joint out of the steering knuckle.

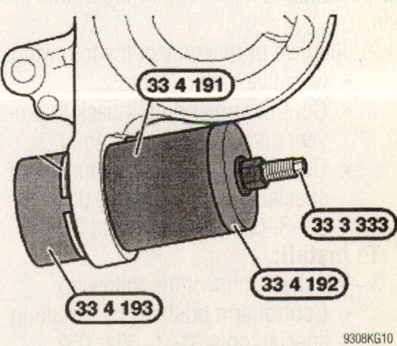

Remove the lower ball joint from the steering knuckle–X5 Series

To install:

4. Install or connect the following:
- Ball joint into the steering knuckle with special tools 33–4–191, 192, 194 and 33–3–333
- New circlip
- Shock absorber and remove the support from the wheel carrier
- Push rod/integral link
- Negative battery cable

Lower Control Arm

REMOVAL & INSTALLATION

1. Before servicing the vehicle, refer to the precautions in the beginning of this section.
2. Remove or disconnect the following:
- Negative battery cable
- Front wheel
- Control arm from the front axle support and loosen the nut from the control arm to swivel bearing
- Control arm from the swivel bearing by pressing it off with special tool 31–2–240

To install:

3. Install or connect the following:
- Lower control arm to the swivel bearing. Torque the nut to 58 ft. lbs. (80 Nm).
- Lower control arm to the front axle support. Torque the nut to 74 ft. lbs. (100 Nm) plus an additional 90 degrees.
- Front wheel
- Negative battery cable
4. Check and adjust the front end alignment as needed.

BUSHING REPLACEMENT

1. Before servicing the vehicle, refer to the precautions in the beginning of this section.
2. Remove or disconnect the following:
- Negative battery cable
- Control arm and tie it back to prevent damage to the ball joint
- Control arm bushing by installing special tools 31–1–051, 052, 33–3–051, 052, 054 and 310

To install:

3. Install or connect the following:
- Control arm bushing by installing special tools 31–1–051, 052, 33–3–051, 052, 054 and 310

- Control arm
- Negative battery cable

Upper Control Arm

REMOVAL & INSTALLATION

1. Before servicing the vehicle, refer to the precautions in the beginning of this section.
2. Remove or disconnect the following:
- Negative battery cable
- Wheel assembly
- Fuse for the air supply system, if equipped with air suspension and loosen the pipes on the distributor block
- Upper control arm from the steering knuckle
- Plastic shim and unhook the lines
- Upper control arm

To install:

3. Install or connect the following:
- Upper control arm. Torque the bolt to 74 ft. lbs. (100 Nm).
- Plastic shim and connect the lines
- Upper control arm to the steering knuckle. Torque the bolt to 122 ft. lbs. (165 Nm).
- Fuse for the air supply system and tighten the pipes on the distributor block
- Wheel assembly
- Negative battery cable

Wheel Bearings

ADJUSTMENT

Wheel bearings can not be adjusted and must be replaced as a unit and never be reused once removed.

REMOVAL & INSTALLATION

Front

➡The wheel bearings are only removed if they are worn. They cannot be removed without destroying them (due to side thrust created by the bearing puller). They cannot be disassembled, repacked or adjusted.

1. Before servicing the vehicle, refer to the precautions in the beginning of this section.

2. Remove or disconnect the following:
- Negative battery cable
- Swivel bearing and clamp it in a vise
- Drive flange by installing special tools 33–2–116, 150 and 33–4–200
- Bearing inner race from the flange
- Circlip
- Snap ring
- Bearing by installing special tools 31–2–113, 33–3–261, 262 and 266

To install:

3. Install or connect the following:
- Wheel bearing with the wider camfer facing the swivel bearing to the drive flange with special tools 33–2–261, 264, 268 and 31–2–113
- Snap ring and circlip
- inner race to the drive flange
- Drive flange to the swivel bearing by using special tool 33–3–261, 266, 268 and 31–2–113
- Swivel bearing
- Negative battery cable

Rear

1. Before servicing the vehicle, refer to the precautions in the beginning of this section.

2. Remove or disconnect the following:
- Negative battery cable
- Wheel assembly
- Collar nut
- Brake disc
- Drive flange by installing special tool 33–2–116, 33–4–201, 202 and 203
- Inner race from the drive flange
- Wheel bearing

To install:

3. Install or connect the following:
- Wheel bearing
- Inner race to the drive flange. Torque the bolts to 74 ft. lbs. (100 Nm).
- Drive flange to the axle shaft. Torque the collar nut to 310 ft. lbs. (420 Nm).
- Brake disc
- Wheel assembly
- Negative battery cable

PRECAUTIONS

Before servicing any vehicle, please be sure to read all of the following precautions, which deal with personal safety, prevention of component damage, and important points to take into consideration when servicing a motor vehicle:

• Never open, service or drain the radiator or cooling system when the engine is hot; serious burns can occur from the steam and hot coolant.

• Observe all applicable safety precautions when working around fuel. Whenever servicing the fuel system, always work in a well-ventilated area. Do not allow fuel spray or vapors to come in contact with a spark, open flame, or excessive heat (a hot drop light, for example). Keep a dry chemical fire extinguisher near the work area. Always keep fuel in a container specifically designed for fuel storage; also, always properly seal fuel containers to avoid the possibility of fire or explosion. Refer to the additional fuel system precautions later in this section.

• Fuel injection systems often remain pressurized, even after the engine has been turned **OFF**. The fuel system pressure must be relieved before disconnecting any fuel lines. Failure to do so may result in fire and/or personal injury.

• Brake fluid often contains polyglycol ethers and polyglycols. Avoid contact with the eyes and wash your hands thoroughly after handling brake fluid. If you do get brake fluid in your eyes, flush your eyes with clean, running water for 15 minutes. If eye irritation persists, or if you have taken brake fluid internally, IMMEDIATELY seek medical assistance.

• The EPA warns that prolonged contact with used engine oil may cause a number of skin disorders, including cancer! You should make every effort to minimize your exposure to used engine oil. Protective gloves should be worn when changing oil. Wash your hands and any other exposed skin areas as soon as possible after exposure to used engine oil. Soap and water, or waterless hand cleaner should be used.

• All new vehicles are now equipped with an air bag system, often referred to as a Supplemental Restraint System (SRS) or Supplemental Inflatable Restraint (SIR) system. The system must be disabled before performing service on or around system components, steering column, instrument panel components, wiring and sensors. Failure to follow safety and disabling procedures could result in accidental air bag deployment, possible personal injury and unnecessary system repairs.

• Always wear safety goggles when working with, or around, the air bag system. When carrying a non-deployed air bag, be sure the bag and trim cover are pointed away from your body. When placing a non-deployed air bag on a work surface, always face the bag and trim cover upward, away from the surface. This will reduce the motion of the module if it is accidentally deployed. Refer to the additional air bag system precautions later in this section.

• Clean, high quality brake fluid from a sealed container is essential to the safe and proper operation of the brake system. You should always buy the correct type of brake fluid for your vehicle. If the brake fluid becomes contaminated, completely flush the system with new fluid. Never reuse any brake fluid. Any brake fluid that is removed from the system should be discarded. Also, do not allow any brake fluid to come in contact with a painted surface; it will damage the paint.

• Never operate the engine without the proper amount and type of engine oil; doing so WILL result in severe engine damage.

• Timing belt maintenance is extremely important! Many models utilize an interference-type, non-freewheeling engine. If the timing belt breaks, the valves in the cylinder head may strike the pistons, causing potentially serious (also time-consuming and expensive) engine damage. Refer to the maintenance interval charts in the front of this manual for the recommended replacement interval for the timing belt, and to the timing belt section for belt replacement and inspection.

• Disconnecting the negative battery cable on some vehicles may interfere with the functions of the on-board computer system(s) and may require the computer to undergo a relearning process once the negative battery cable is reconnected.

• When servicing drum brakes, only disassemble and assemble one side at a time, leaving the remaining side intact for reference.

• Only an MVAC-trained, EPA-certified automotive technician should service the air conditioning system or its components.

ENGINE REPAIR

➡**Disconnecting the negative battery cable on some vehicles may interfere with the functions of the on board computer system. The computer may undergo a relearning process once the negative battery cable is reconnected.**

Distributor

REMOVAL

3.0L Engine

1. Before servicing the vehicle, refer to the precautions in the beginning of this section.
2. Remove or disconnect the following:
   • Negative battery cable
   • Distributor cap
   • Camshaft Position (CMP) sensor connector
3. Matchmark the distributor housing and the rotor.
4. Remove the distributor.

INSTALLATION

3.0L Engine

TIMING NOT DISTURBED

➡**The rotor will rotate counterclockwise as the gears engage.**

1. Position the rotor slightly clockwise of the matchmark made during removal.
2. Install the distributor. Ensure that the rotor moves into alignment with the matchmark.
3. Tighten the distributor hold down nut to 10 ft. lbs. (14 Nm).
4. Install or connect the following:
   • CMP sensor connector
   • Distributor cap
   • Negative battery cable

TIMING DISTURBED

1. Set the crankshaft at Top Dead Center (TDC) of the compression stroke for the No. 1 cylinder.
2. Install the distributor so that the rotor points to the No. 1 spark plug wire terminal.
3. Tighten the distributor hold down nut to 10 ft. lbs. (14 Nm).
4. Install or connect the following:

- CMP sensor connector
- Distributor cap
- Negative battery cable

Alternator

REMOVAL

2.4L Engine

1. Before servicing the vehicle, refer to the precautions in the beginning of this section.
2. Remove or disconnect the following:
   - Negative battery cable
   - Accessory drive belt
   - Alternator harness connections
   - Alternator

3.0L Engine

1. Before servicing the vehicle, refer to the precautions in the beginning of this section.
2. Remove or disconnect the following:
   - Negative battery cable
   - Wiper module
   - Accessory drive belt
   - Alternator mounting bolts
   - Alternator harness connectors
   - Alternator

3.3L and 3.8L Engines

1. Before servicing the vehicle, refer to the precautions in the beginning of this section.
2. Remove or disconnect the following:
   - Negative battery cable
   - Wiper module
   - Accessory drive belt
   - Alternator mount bracket
   - Alternator harness connectors
   - Alternator pivot bolt
   - Alternator

INSTALLATION

2.4L Engine

Install or connect the following:
- Alternator
- Alternator harness connections
- Accessory drive belt. Tighten the alternator mounting fasteners to 40 ft. lbs. (54 Nm).
- Negative battery cable

3.0L Engine

Install or connect the following:
- Alternator

- Alternator harness connectors
- Alternator mounting bolts. Tighten the bolts to 40 ft. lbs. (54 Nm).
- Accessory drive belt
- Wiper module
- Negative battery cable

3.3L and 3.8L Engines

Install or connect the following:
- Alternator
- Alternator pivot bolt
- Alternator harness connectors
- Alternator mount bracket. Tighten the alternator mounting fasteners to 40 ft. lbs. (54 Nm).
- Accessory drive belt
- Wiper module
- Negative battery cable

Ignition Timing

ADJUSTMENT

The base ignition timing cannot be adjusted. The Powertrain Control Module (PCM) regulates the ignition timing automatically.

Engine Assembly

REMOVAL & INSTALLATION

2.4L Engine

1. Before servicing the vehicle, refer to the precautions in the beginning of this section.
2. Drain the cooling system.
3. Relieve the fuel system pressure.
4. Recover the A/C refrigerant.
5. Remove or disconnect the following:
   - Negative battery cable
   - Air cleaner and hoses
   - Fuel line
   - Radiator hoses
   - Engine cooling fans
   - Transaxle cooler lines
   - Transaxle shift linkage
   - Throttle body linkage
   - Engine wiring harness
   - Heater hoses
   - Front wheels
   - Right inner splash shield
   - Power steering pump drive belt
   - Axle halfshafts
   - Exhaust front pipe

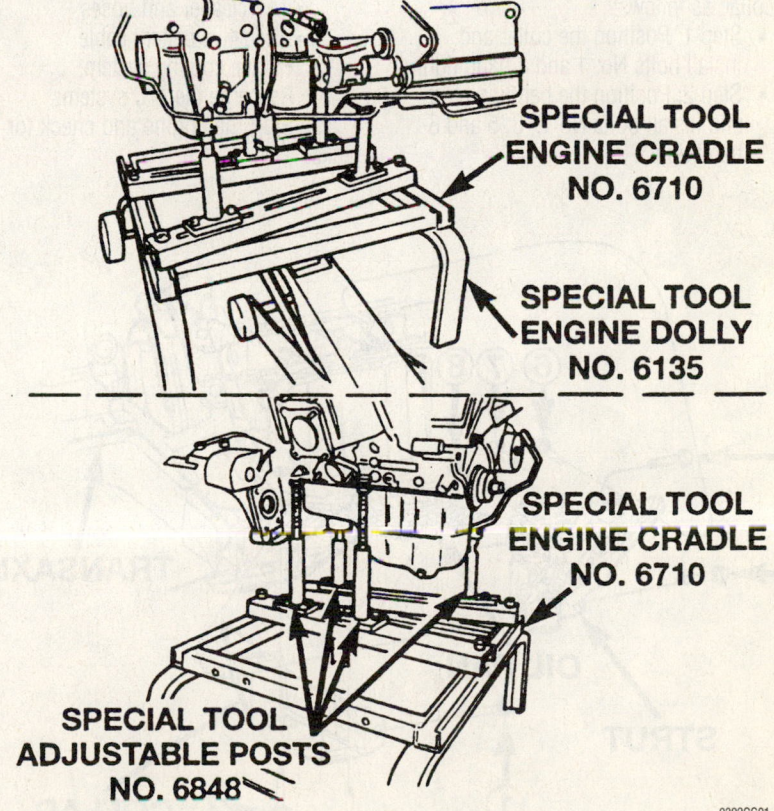

**SPECIAL TOOL
ENGINE CRADLE
NO. 6710**

**SPECIAL TOOL
ENGINE DOLLY
NO. 6135**

**SPECIAL TOOL
ENGINE CRADLE
NO. 6710**

**SPECIAL TOOL
ADJUSTABLE POSTS
NO. 6848**

9302CG01

Chrysler powertrain support tools

- Front motor mount
- Rear motor mount
- Bending strut
- Structural collar
- Torque converter
- Power steering pump
- A/C compressor lines
- Body ground straps

6. Support the powertrain from below.

7. Remove the left and right motor mounts.

8. Raise the vehicle away from the powertrain.

To install:

9. Lower the vehicle over the powertrain.

10. Install or connect the following:
- Left motor mount. Tighten the bracket bolts to 40 ft. lbs. (55 Nm) and the through bolt to 55 ft. lbs. (75 Nm).
- Right motor mount. Tighten the frame rail bolts to 50 ft. lbs. (68 Nm), the vertical fastener to 75 ft. lbs. (102 Nm) and the horizontal fastener to 111 ft. lbs. (150 Nm).
- Axle halfshafts
- Torque converter. Tighten the bolts to 50 ft. lbs. (68 Nm).

11. Install the bending struts and structural collar, as follows:
- Step 1: Position the collar and install bolts No. 1 and 4 hand tight
- Step 2: Position the bending strut and install bolts No. 2, 3, 5 and 6 hand tight

- Step 3: Tighten bolts No. 1, 2 and 3 to 75 ft. lbs. (101 Nm)
- Step 4: Install bolts No. 7 and 8
- Step 5: Tighten bolts No. 4, 5, 6, 7 and 8 to 45 ft. lbs. (61 Nm)

12. Install or connect the following:
- Body ground straps
- A/C compressor lines
- Power steering pump
- Rear motor mount. Tighten the bolts to 45 ft. lbs. (61 Nm).
- Front motor mount. Tighten the large bracket bolts to 80 ft. lbs. (108 Nm), the small bracket bolts to 40 ft. lbs. (54 Nm) and the through bolt to 45 ft. lbs. (61 Nm).
- Exhaust front pipe
- Axle halfshafts
- Power steering pump drive belt
- Right inner splash shield
- Front wheels
- Heater hoses
- Engine wiring harness
- Throttle body linkage
- Transaxle shift linkage
- Transaxle cooler lines
- Engine cooling fans
- Radiator hoses
- Fuel line
- Air cleaner and hoses
- Negative battery cable

13. Fill the cooling system.

14. Recharge the A/C system.

15. Start the engine and check for leaks.

3.0L Engine

1. Before servicing the vehicle, refer to the precautions in the beginning of this section.

2. Drain the cooling system.

3. Relieve the fuel system pressure.

4. Remove or disconnect the following:
- Battery and tray
- Air cleaner and hoses
- Heater hoses
- Engine cooling fan
- Radiator
- Transaxle shift linkage
- Throttle body linkage and vacuum lines
- Accessory drive belts
- Alternator
- A/C compressor
- Axle halfshafts
- Left and right inner splash shields
- Exhaust front pipe
- Front motor mount and bracket
- Rear transaxle mount and bracket
- Power steering pump and bracket
- Engine wiring harness
- Bending braces
- Torque converter
- Body ground straps

5. Support the powertrain from below.

6. Remove the right motor mount and the left transaxle mount through bolt.

7. Raise the vehicle away from the powertrain.

To install:

8. Lower the vehicle over the powertrain.

9. Install or connect the following:
- Right motor mount. Tighten the frame rail bolts to 50 ft. lbs. (68 Nm), the vertical fastener to 75 ft. lbs. (102 Nm) and the horizontal fastener to 111 ft. lbs. (150 Nm).
- Left transaxle mount through bolt. Tighten the bolt to 55 ft. lbs. (75 Nm).
- Body ground straps
- Torque converter. Tighten the bolts to 50 ft. lbs. (68 Nm).
- Bending braces
- Engine wiring harness
- Power steering pump and bracket
- Rear transaxle mount and bracket. Tighten the bolts to 45 ft. lbs. (61 Nm).
- Front motor mount and bracket. Tighten the large bracket bolts to 80 ft. lbs. (108 Nm), the small bracket bolts to 40 ft. lbs. (54 Nm) and the through bolt to 45 ft. lbs. (61 Nm).
- Exhaust front pipe

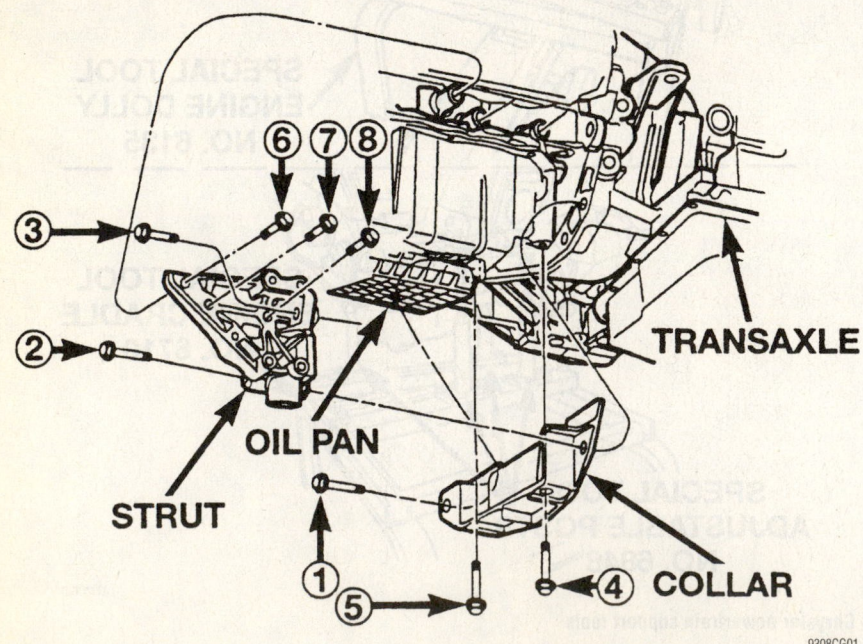

9308CG01

Structural collar and bending strut torque sequence—2.4L engine

- Left and right inner splash shields
- Axle halfshafts
- A/C compressor
- Alternator
- Accessory drive belts
- Throttle body linkage and vacuum lines
- Transaxle shift linkage
- Radiator
- Engine cooling fan
- Heater hoses
- Air cleaner and hoses
- Battery and tray
10. Fill the cooling system.
11. Start the engine and check for leaks.

3.3L and 3.8L Engines

1. Before servicing the vehicle, refer to the precautions in the beginning of this section.
2. Drain the cooling system.
3. Relieve the fuel system pressure.
4. Remove or disconnect the following:
   - Battery and tray
   - Air cleaner and hoses
   - Heater hoses
   - Engine cooling fan
   - Radiator
   - Transaxle shift linkage
   - Throttle body linkage and vacuum lines
   - Accessory drive belt
   - Alternator
   - A/C compressor
   - Axle halfshafts
   - Rear driveshaft, if equipped
   - Left and right inner splash shields
   - Exhaust front pipe
   - Front motor mount and bracket
   - Rear transaxle mount and bracket
   - Power steering pump and bracket
   - Engine wiring harness
   - Bending braces
   - Torque converter
   - Body ground straps
5. Support the powertrain from below.
6. Remove the right motor mount and the left transaxle mount through bolt.
7. Raise the vehicle away from the powertrain.
To install:
8. Lower the vehicle over the powertrain.
9. Install or connect the following:
   - Right motor mount. Tighten the frame rail bolts to 50 ft. lbs. (68 Nm), the vertical fastener to 75 ft. lbs. (102 Nm) and the horizontal fastener to 111 ft. lbs. (150 Nm).

- Left transaxle mount through bolt. Tighten the bolt to 55 ft. lbs. (75 Nm).
- Body ground straps
- Torque converter. Tighten the bolts to 55 ft. lbs. (75 Nm).
- Bending braces
- Engine wiring harness
- Power steering pump and bracket
- Rear transaxle mount and bracket. Tighten the bolts to 45 ft. lbs. (61 Nm).
- Front motor mount and bracket. Tighten the large bracket bolts to 80 ft. lbs. (108 Nm), the small bracket bolts to 40 ft. lbs. (54 Nm) and the through bolt to 45 ft. lbs. (61 Nm).
- Exhaust front pipe
- Left and right inner splash shields
- Rear driveshaft, if equipped
- Axle halfshafts
- A/C compressor
- Alternator
- Accessory drive belt
- Throttle body linkage and vacuum lines
- Transaxle shift linkage
- Radiator
- Engine cooling fan
- Heater hoses
- Air cleaner and hoses
- Battery and tray
10. Fill the cooling system.
11. Start the engine and check for leaks.

Water Pump

REMOVAL & INSTALLATION

2.4L Engine

1. Before servicing the vehicle, refer to the precautions in the beginning of this section.
2. Drain the cooling system.
3. Remove or disconnect the following:
- Negative battery cable
- Right inner splash shield
- Accessory drive belts
- Right motor mount
- Front cover
- Timing belt. Refer to the Timing Belt unit repair section.
- Timing belt idler pulley
- Camshaft sprockets
- Timing belt rear cover
- Water pump

To install:
4. Install or connect the following:
   - Water pump. Tighten the bolts to 105 inch lbs. (12 Nm).
   - Timing belt rear cover
   - Camshaft sprockets. Tighten the bolts to 75 ft. lbs. (101 Nm).
   - Timing belt idler pulley. Tighten the bolt to 45 ft. lbs. (61 Nm).
   - Timing belt
   - Front cover
   - Right motor mount. Tighten the frame rail bolts to 50 ft. lbs. (68 Nm), the vertical fastener to 75 ft. lbs. (102 Nm) and the horizontal fastener to 111 ft. lbs. (150 Nm).
   - Accessory drive belts
   - Right inner splash shield
   - Negative battery cable
5. Fill the cooling system.
6. Start the engine and check for leaks.

3.0L Engine

1. Before servicing the vehicle, refer to the precautions in the beginning of this section.
2. Drain the cooling system.
3. Remove or disconnect the following:
   - Negative battery cable
   - Right inner splash shield
   - Accessory drive belts
   - Right motor mount
   - Front cover
   - Timing belt. Refer to the Timing Belt unit repair section.
   - Water pump

To install:
4. Install or connect the following:
   - Water pump. Tighten the bolts to 20 ft. lbs. (27 Nm).
   - Timing belt
   - Front cover
   - Right motor mount. Tighten the frame rail bolts to 50 ft. lbs. (68 Nm), the vertical fastener to 75 ft. lbs. (102 Nm) and the horizontal fastener to 111 ft. lbs. (150 Nm).
   - Accessory drive belts
   - Right inner splash shield
   - Negative battery cable
5. Fill the cooling system.
6. Start the engine and check for leaks.

3.3L and 3.8L Engines

1. Before servicing the vehicle, refer to the precautions in the beginning of this section.
2. Drain the cooling system.

Timing belt service is covered in Section 4 of this manual

3. Remove or disconnect the following:
- Negative battery cable
- Accessory drive belt
- Right inner splash shield
- Water pump pulley
- Water pump

To install:

4. Install or connect the following:
- Water pump. Tighten the bolts to 105 inch lbs. (12 Nm).
- Water pump pulley. Tighten the bolts to 22 ft. lbs. (30 Nm).
- Right inner splash shield
- Accessory drive belt
- Negative battery cable

5. Fill the cooling system.
6. Start the engine and check for leaks.

Cylinder Head

REMOVAL & INSTALLATION

2.4L Engine

1. Before servicing the vehicle, refer to the precautions in the beginning of this section.
2. Drain the cooling system.
3. Relieve the fuel system pressure.
4. Remove or disconnect the following:
- Negative battery cable
- Air cleaner and hoses
- Engine control wiring harness
- Intake manifold vacuum lines
- Ground straps
- Fuel line
- Throttle linkage
- Throttle body support bracket
- Intake manifold support bracket
- Exhaust Gas Recirculation (EGR) tube
- Heater tube support bracket
- Upper radiator hose
- Heater hose
- Accessory drive belts
- Brake booster vacuum line
- Exhaust front pipe
- Power steering pump reservoir and line support bracket
- Ignition coil and spark plug wires
- Fuel injector harness connectors
- Camshaft Position (CMP) sensor connector
- Right motor mount
- Front cover
- Timing belt. Refer to the Timing Belt unit repair section.
- Camshaft sprockets
- Timing belt idler pulley
- Rear timing cover
- Valve cover

➡ **Keep all valvetrain components in order for assembly.**
- Camshafts and cam followers
- Cylinder head

To install:

5. Examine the cylinder head bolts and replace any that have stretched.

➡ **Refer to Section 1 of this manual for the cylinder head torque sequence illustration. The illustration is located after the Torque Specification Chart.**

6. Install the cylinder head and tighten the bolts in sequence, as follows:
- Step 1: 25 ft. lbs. (34 Nm)
- Step 2: 50 ft. lbs. (68 Nm)
- Step 3: 50 ft. lbs. (68 Nm)
- Step 4: Plus 90 degrees

7. Install or connect the following:
- Camshafts and cam followers
- Valve cover
- Rear timing cover
- Timing belt idler pulley. Tighten the bolt to 45 ft. lbs. (61 Nm).
- Camshaft sprockets. Tighten the bolts to 75 ft. lbs. (101 Nm).
- Timing belt
- Front cover
- Right motor mount. Tighten the frame rail bolts to 50 ft. lbs. (68 Nm), the vertical fastener to 75 ft. lbs. (102 Nm) and the horizontal fastener to 111 ft. lbs. (150 Nm).
- CMP sensor connector
- Fuel injector harness connectors
- Ignition coil and spark plug wires
- Power steering pump reservoir and line support bracket
- Exhaust front pipe
- Brake booster vacuum line
- Accessory drive belts
- Heater hose
- Upper radiator hose
- Heater tube support bracket
- EGR tube

- Intake manifold support bracket
- Throttle body support bracket
- Throttle linkage
- Fuel line
- Ground straps
- Intake manifold vacuum lines
- Engine control wiring harness
- Air cleaner and hoses
- Negative battery cable

8. Fill the cooling system.
9. Start the engine and check for leaks.

3.0L Engine

1. Before servicing the vehicle, refer to the precautions in the beginning of this section.
2. Drain the cooling system.
3. Relieve the fuel system pressure.
4. Remove or disconnect the following:
- Negative battery cable
- Right inner splash shield
- Accessory drive belts
- Alternator
- A/C compressor and bracket
- Right motor mount
- Front cover
- Timing belt. Refer to the Timing Belt unit repair section.
- Camshaft sprockets
- Rear timing cover
- Alternator bracket
- Spark plug wires
- Distributor
- Valve covers
- Intake manifold
- Exhaust front pipe
- Exhaust crossover pipe
- Exhaust manifolds
- Cylinder heads

To install:

➡ **Refer to Section 1 of this manual for the cylinder head torque sequence illustration. The illustration is located after the Torque Specification Chart.**

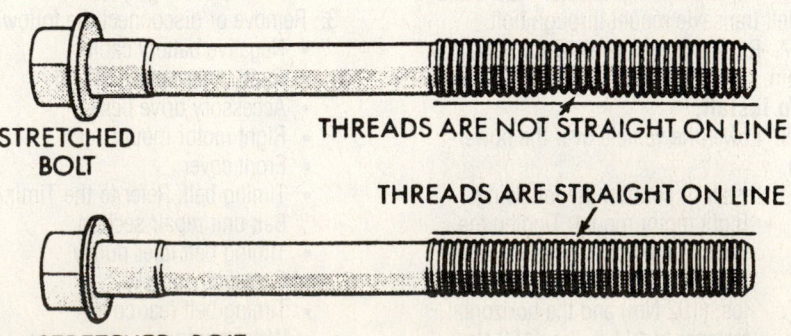

STRETCHED BOLT

THREADS ARE NOT STRAIGHT ON LINE

THREADS ARE STRAIGHT ON LINE

UNSTRETCHED BOLT

7924CG38

Check the cylinder head bolts for stretching—2.4L engine

5. Install or connect the following:
- Cylinder heads. Tighten the bolts in sequence and in several passes to 80 ft. lbs. (108 Nm).
- Exhaust manifolds
- Exhaust crossover pipe
- Exhaust front pipe
- Intake manifold
- Valve covers
- Distributor
- Spark plug wires
- Alternator bracket
- Rear timing cover
- Camshaft sprockets. Tighten the bolts to 70 ft. lbs. (95 Nm).
- Timing belt
- Front cover
- Right motor mount. Tighten the frame rail bolts to 50 ft. lbs. (68 Nm), the vertical fastener to 75 ft. lbs. (102 Nm) and the horizontal fastener to 111 ft. lbs. (150 Nm).
- A/C compressor and bracket
- Alternator
- Accessory drive belts
- Right inner splash shield
- Negative battery cable

6. Fill the cooling system.
7. Start the engine and check for leaks.

3.3L and 3.8L Engines

1. Before servicing the vehicle, refer to the precautions in the beginning of this section.
2. Drain the cooling system.
3. Relieve the fuel system pressure.
4. Remove or disconnect the following:
- Negative battery cable
- Wiper module
- Intake manifold
- Ignition coil and spark plug wires
- Heater hoses
- Bypass hose
- Engine Coolant Temperature (ECT) sensor connector
- Positive Crankcase Ventilation (PCV) valve and hose
- Evaporative Emissions (EVAP) hoses
- Valve covers
- Exhaust front pipe
- Exhaust crossover pipe
- Exhaust manifolds

➡ **Keep all valvetrain components in order for assembly**

- Rocker arm and shaft assemblies
- Pushrods
- Cylinder heads

To install:

5. Examine the cylinder head bolts and replace any that have stretched.

➡ **Refer to Section 1 of this manual for the cylinder head torque sequence illustration. The illustration is located after the Torque Specification Chart.**

6. Install the cylinder head and tighten the bolts in sequence, as follows:
- Step 1: Tighten bolts 1–8 to 45 ft. lbs. (61 Nm)
- Step 2: Tighten bolts 1–8 to 65 ft. lbs. (88 Nm)
- Step 3: Tighten bolts 1–8 to 65 ft. lbs. (88 Nm)
- Step 4: Bolts 1–8 plus 90 degrees
- Step 5: Tighten bolt 9 to 25 ft. lbs. (33 Nm)

7. Check that the torque on bolts 1–8 has exceeded 90 ft. lbs. (122 Nm). If not, replace the bolt.
8. Install or connect the following:
- Pushrods
- Rocker arm and shaft assemblies
- Exhaust manifolds
- Exhaust crossover pipe
- Exhaust front pipe
- Valve covers
- Evaporative Emissions (EVAP) hoses
- Positive Crankcase Ventilation (PCV) valve and hose
- Engine Coolant Temperature (ECT) sensor connector
- Bypass hose
- Heater hoses
- Ignition coil and spark plug wires
- Intake manifold
- Wiper module
- Negative battery cable

9. Fill the cooling system.
10. Start the engine and check for leaks.

Rocker Arms/Shafts

REMOVAL & INSTALLATION

2.4L Engine

1. Before servicing the vehicle, refer to the precautions in the beginning of this section.
2. Remove or disconnect the following:
- Negative battery cable
- Air cleaner and hoses
- Accessory drive belts
- Ignition coil and spark plug wires
- Camshaft Position (CMP) sensor connector

- Right motor mount
- Front cover
- Timing belt. Refer to the Timing Belt unit repair section.
- Camshaft sprockets
- Timing belt idler pulley
- Rear timing cover
- Valve cover

➡ **Keep all valvetrain components in order for assembly.**

- Camshafts
- Cam followers

To install:

3. Install or connect the following:
- Cam followers in their original positions
- Camshafts
- Valve cover
- Rear timing cover
- Timing belt idler pulley. Tighten the bolt to 45 ft. lbs. (61 Nm).
- Camshaft sprockets. Tighten the bolts to 75 ft. lbs. (101 Nm).
- Timing belt
- Front cover
- Right motor mount. Tighten the frame rail bolts to 50 ft. lbs. (68 Nm), the vertical fastener to 75 ft. lbs. (102 Nm) and the horizontal fastener to 111 ft. lbs. (150 Nm).
- CMP sensor connector
- Ignition coil and spark plug wires
- Accessory drive belts
- Air cleaner and hoses
- Negative battery cable

4. Start the engine and check for proper operation.

3.0L Engine

1. Before servicing the vehicle, refer to the precautions in the beginning of this section.
2. Remove or disconnect the following:
- Negative battery cable
- Air cleaner and hoses
- Valve covers

3. Install Lash Adjuster Retainer tools MD-998443.

➡ **Keep all valvetrain components in order for assembly.**

4. Remove the rocker arm and shaft assemblies.

To install:

5. Install the rocker arm and shaft assemblies in their original positions and tighten the bearing cap bolts as follows:

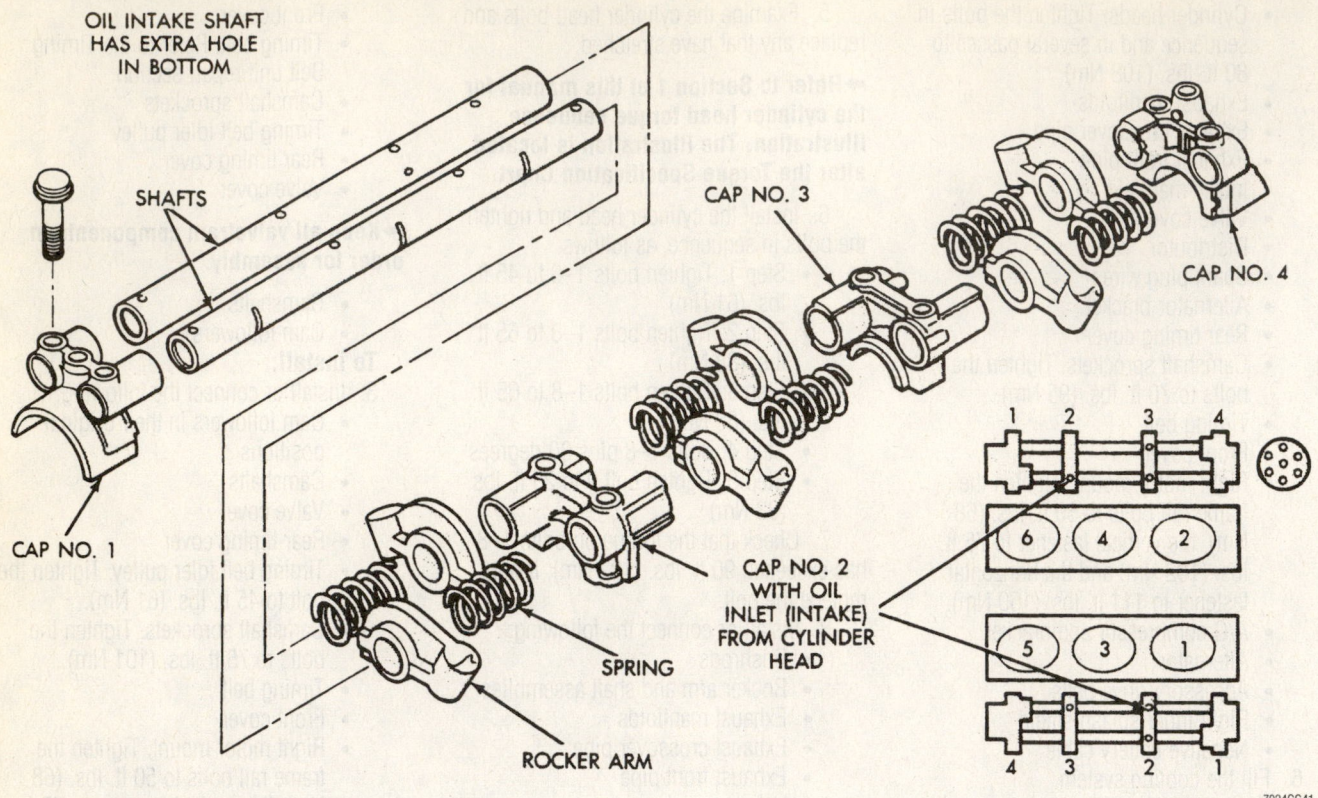

OIL INTAKE SHAFT HAS EXTRA HOLE IN BOTTOM

SHAFTS

CAP NO. 1

CAP NO. 3

CAP NO. 4

CAP NO. 2 WITH OIL INLET (INTAKE) FROM CYLINDER HEAD

SPRING

ROCKER ARM

7924CG41

Exploded view of the rocker arms and shafts—3.0L engine

- Step 1: Cap No. 3 bolts to 85 inch lbs. (10 Nm)
- Step 2: Cap No. 2 bolts to 85 inch lbs. (10 Nm)
- Step 3: Cap No. 1 bolts to 85 inch lbs. (10 Nm)
- Step 4: Cap No. 4 bolts to 85 inch lbs. (10 Nm)
- Step 5: Cap No. 3 bolts to 15 ft. lbs. (20 Nm)
- Step 6: Cap No. 2 bolts to 15 ft. lbs. (20 Nm)
- Step 7: Cap No. 1 bolts to 15 ft. lbs. (20 Nm)
- Step 8: Cap No. 4 bolts to 15 ft. lbs. (20 Nm)

6. Remove the lash adjuster retainers.
7. Install or connect the following:
- Valve covers
- Air cleaner and hoses
- Negative battery cable

8. Start the engine and check for proper operation.

3.3L and 3.8L Engines

1. Before servicing the vehicle, refer to the precautions in the beginning of this section.

2. Remove or disconnect the following:
- Negative battery cable
- Wiper module
- Upper intake manifold
- Valve covers
- Rocker arm and shaft assemblies

➡**Keep all valvetrain components in order for assembly.**

To install:

➡**Do not rotate the crankshaft during or immediately after rocker arm installa-** tion. **Wait 20 minutes for the hydraulic lash adjusters to bleed down.**

3. Install or connect the following:
- Rocker arm and shaft assemblies. Tighten the bolts to several passes to 21 ft. lbs. (28 Nm).
- Valve covers
- Upper intake manifold
- Wiper module
- Negative battery cable

4. Start the engine and check for proper operation.

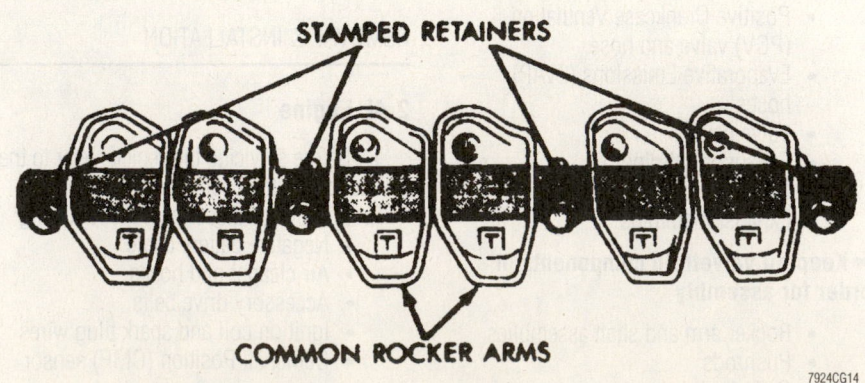

STAMPED RETAINERS

COMMON ROCKER ARMS

7924CG14

Rocker arm and shaft assembly—3.3L and 3.8L engines

Intake Manifold

REMOVAL & INSTALLATION

2.4L Engine

1. Before servicing the vehicle, refer to the precautions in the beginning of this section.
2. Drain the cooling system.
3. Relieve the fuel system pressure.
4. Remove or disconnect the following:
   - Negative battery cable
   - Air cleaner and tube
   - Throttle Position (TP) sensor connector
   - Idle Air Control (IAC) valve connector
   - Manifold Absolute Pressure (MAP) sensor connector
   - Evaporative Emissions (EVAP) canister purge solenoid vacuum line
   - Positive Crankcase Ventilation (PCV) valve and hose
   - Brake booster vacuum line
   - Cruise control vacuum reservoir line
   - Accelerator cable
   - Cruise control cable
   - Front and rear intake manifold support brackets
   - Exhaust Gas Recirculation (EGR) tube
   - Engine oil dipstick tube
   - Upper intake manifold
   - Intake Air Temperature (IAT) sensor connector
   - Fuel line
   - Upper radiator hose
   - Heater hose
   - Engine Coolant Temperature (ECT) sensor connector
   - Accessory drive belts
   - Alternator and bracket
   - Intake manifold Y-bracket
   - Fuel injector harness connectors
   - Lower intake manifold

To install:

5. Install or connect the following:
   - Lower intake manifold. Tighten the bolts in several steps to 21 ft. lbs. (28 Nm).
   - Fuel injector harness connectors
   - Intake manifold Y-bracket. Tighten the block bolts to 40 ft. lbs. (54 Nm) and the intake manifold bolts to 21 ft. lbs. (28 Nm).
   - Alternator and bracket
   - Accessory drive belts

- ECT sensor connector
- Heater hose
- Upper radiator hose
- Fuel line
- IAT sensor connector
- Upper intake manifold. Tighten the bolts in several passes to 21 ft. lbs. (28 Nm).
- Engine oil dipstick tube
- EGR tube
- Front and rear intake manifold support brackets. Tighten the bolts to 21 ft. lbs. (28 Nm).
- Cruise control cable
- Accelerator cable
- Cruise control vacuum reservoir line
- Brake booster vacuum line
- PCV valve and hose
- EVAP canister purge solenoid vacuum line
- MAP sensor connector
- IAC valve connector
- TP sensor connector
- Air cleaner and tube
- Negative battery cable

6. Fill the cooling system.
7. Start the engine and check for leaks.

3.0L Engine

1. Before servicing the vehicle, refer to the precautions in the beginning of this section.
2. Drain the cooling system.
3. Relieve the fuel system pressure.
4. Remove or disconnect the following:
   - Negative battery cable
   - Air cleaner and tube
   - Accelerator cable
   - Cruise control cable
   - Idle Air Control (IAC) valve connector
   - Throttle Position (TP) sensor connector
   - Throttle body vacuum hose harness
   - Positive Crankcase Ventilation (PCV) hose
   - Brake booster vacuum line
   - Ignition coil
   - Engine Coolant Temperature (ECT) sensor connector
   - Upper intake manifold vacuum lines
   - Fuel line
   - Upper intake manifold
   - Fuel injector harness connectors
   - Fuel supply manifold
   - Radiator hose
   - Heater hose

- Lower intake manifold

To install:

➡ Refer to Section 1 of this manual for the intake manifold torque sequence illustration. The illustration is located after the Torque Specification Chart.

5. Install or connect the following:
   - Lower intake manifold. Tighten the bolts in sequence and in several steps to 15 ft. lbs. (20 Nm).
   - Heater hose
   - Radiator hose
   - Fuel supply manifold. Tighten the bolts to 115 inch lbs. (13 Nm).
   - Fuel injector harness connectors
   - Upper intake manifold. Tighten the bolts in sequence and in several steps to 115 inch lbs. (13 Nm).
   - Fuel line
   - Upper intake manifold vacuum lines
   - ECT sensor connector
   - Ignition coil
   - Brake booster vacuum line
   - PCV hose
   - Throttle body vacuum hose harness
   - TP sensor connector
   - IAC valve connector
   - Cruise control cable
   - Accelerator cable
   - Air cleaner and tube
   - Negative battery cable

6. Fill the cooling system.
7. Start the engine and check for leaks.

3.3L and 3.8L Engines

1. Before servicing the vehicle, refer to the precautions in the beginning of this section.
2. Drain the cooling system.
3. Relieve the fuel system pressure.
4. Remove or disconnect the following:
   - Negative battery cable
   - Air cleaner and tube
   - Wiper module
   - Idle Air Control (IAC) valve connector
   - Throttle Position (TP) sensor connector
   - Exhaust Gas Recirculation (EGR) transducer connector
   - Accelerator cable
   - Cruise control cable
   - Throttle body vacuum hose harness
   - Positive Crankcase Ventilation (PCV) hose
   - Manifold Absolute Pressure (MAP) sensor connector

Refer to Section 1 for engine rebuilding specifications

- Exhaust Gas Recirculation (EGR) tube
- Upper intake manifold vacuum lines
- Upper intake manifold support bracket
- Ground strap
- Fuel line
- Spark plug wires
- Ignition coil and bracket
- Alternator and bracket
- Upper intake manifold
- Camshaft Position (CMP) sensor connector
- Engine Coolant Temperature (ECT) sensor connector
- Fuel injector harness connectors
- Fuel supply manifold
- Radiator hose
- Bypass hose
- Heater hose
- Lower intake manifold

To install:

➡ **Refer to Section 1 of this manual for the intake manifold torque sequence illustration. The illustration is located after the Torque Specification Chart.**

5. Install the lower intake manifold and tighten the bolts in sequence, as follows:
- Step 1: 10 inch lbs. (1 Nm)
- Step 2: 17 ft. lbs. (22 Nm)

6. Install or connect the following:
- Heater hose
- Bypass hose
- Radiator hose
- Fuel supply manifold. Tighten the bolts to 17 ft. lbs. (22 Nm).
- Fuel injector harness connectors
- ECT sensor connector
- CMP sensor connector
- Upper intake manifold. Tighten the bolts to 21 ft. lbs. (28 Nm).
- Alternator and bracket. Tighten the bracket bolt to 40 ft. lbs. (54 Nm).
- Ignition coil and bracket
- Spark plug wires
- Fuel line
- Ground strap
- Upper intake manifold support bracket. Tighten the bolts to 40 ft. lbs. (54 Nm).
- Upper intake manifold vacuum lines
- EGR tube
- MAP sensor connector
- PCV hose
- Throttle body vacuum hose harness
- Cruise control cable
- Accelerator cable
- EGR transducer connector
- TP sensor connector

- IAC valve connector
- Wiper module
- Air cleaner and tube
- Negative battery cable

7. Fill the cooling system.
8. Start the engine and check for leaks.

Exhaust Manifold

REMOVAL & INSTALLATION

2.4L Engine

1. Before servicing the vehicle, refer to the precautions in the beginning of this section.

2. Before servicing the vehicle, refer to the precautions in the beginning of this section.

3. Remove or disconnect the following:
- Negative battery cable
- Exhaust front pipe
- Heated Oxygen (HO$_2$S) sensor connector
- Exhaust manifold

To install:

4. Install or connect the following:
- Exhaust manifold. Tighten the fasteners in sequence to 15 ft. lbs. (20 Nm).
- HO$_2$S sensor connector
- Exhaust front pipe. Tighten the fasteners to 21 ft. lbs. (28 Nm).
- Negative battery cable

5. Start the engine and check for leaks.

3.0L Engine

1. Before servicing the vehicle, refer to the precautions in the beginning of this section.

2. Remove or disconnect the following:
- Negative battery cable
- Exhaust front pipe
- Heated Oxygen (HO$_2$S) sensor connectors
- Exhaust manifold heat shields
- Exhaust crossover pipe
- Exhaust manifolds

To install:

3. Install or connect the following:
- Exhaust manifolds. Tighten the fasteners to 15 ft. lbs. (20 Nm).
- Exhaust crossover pipe. Tighten the fasteners to 51 ft. lbs. (69 Nm).
- Exhaust manifold heat shields
- HO$_2$S sensor connectors
- Exhaust front pipe. Tighten the fasteners to 21 ft. lbs. (28 Nm).
- Negative battery cable

4. Start the engine and check for leaks.

3.3L and 3.8L Engines

1. Before servicing the vehicle, refer to the precautions in the beginning of this section.

2. Remove or disconnect the following:
- Negative battery cable
- Accessory drive belt
- Alternator
- Exhaust front pipe
- Heated Oxygen (HO$_2$S) sensor connectors

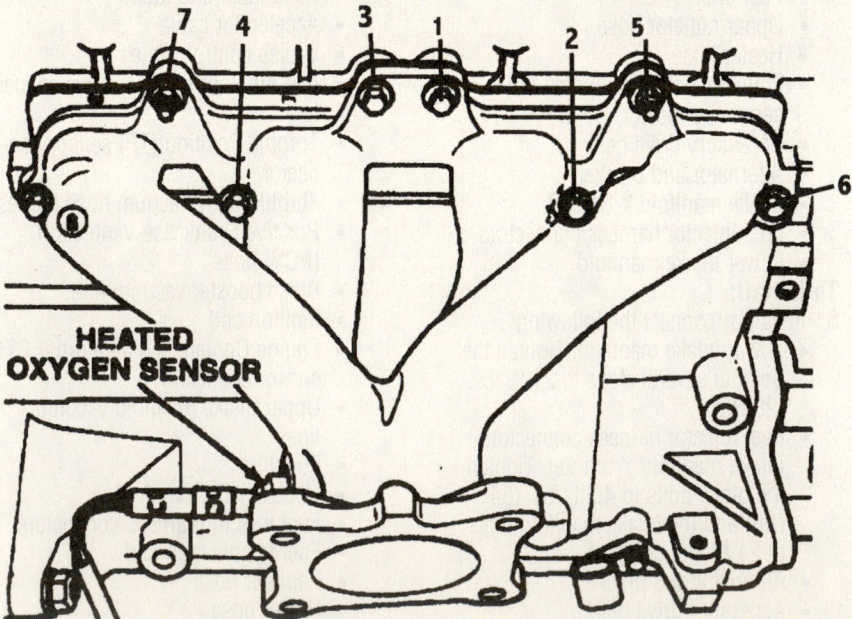

HEATED OXYGEN SENSOR

7924CG19

Exhaust manifold torque sequence—2.4L engine

- Exhaust Gas Recirculation (EGR) tube
- Heat shields
- Exhaust crossover pipe
- Alternator support strut
- Exhaust manifolds

To install:

3. Install or connect the following:
- Rear exhaust manifold. Tighten the fasteners to 17 ft. lbs. (23 Nm).
- Alternator
- Alternator support strut
- EGR tube
- Front exhaust manifold. Tighten the fasteners to 17 ft. lbs. (23 Nm).
- Exhaust crossover pipe. Tighten the fasteners to 40 ft. lbs. (54 Nm).
- Heat shields
- HO2S sensor connectors
- Exhaust front pipe. Tighten the fasteners to 21 ft. lbs. (28 Nm).
- Accessory drive belt
- Negative battery cable

4. Start the engine and check for leaks.

Front Crankshaft Seal

REMOVAL & INSTALLATION

2.4L Engine

1. Before servicing the vehicle, refer to the precautions in the beginning of this section.

2. Remove or disconnect the following:
- Negative battery cable
- Accessory drive belts
- Crankshaft pulley
- Front cover
- Timing belt. Refer to the Timing Belt unit repair section.
- Crankshaft timing sprocket
- Front crankshaft seal

To install:

3. Install the front crankshaft seal so that it is flush with the surface of the oil pump housing.

4. Install or connect the following:
- Crankshaft timing sprocket
- Timing belt
- Front cover
- Crankshaft pulley. Tighten the bolt to 105 ft. lbs. (142 Nm).
- Accessory drive belts
- Negative battery cable

5. Start the engine and check for leaks.

3.0L Engine

1. Before servicing the vehicle, refer to the precautions in the beginning of this section.

2. Remove or disconnect the following:
- Negative battery cable
- Accessory drive belts
- Crankshaft pulley
- Front cover
- Timing belt. Refer to the Timing Belt unit repair section.
- Crankshaft timing sprocket
- Front crankshaft seal

To install:

3. Install the front crankshaft seal so that it is flush with the surface of the oil pump housing.

4. Install or connect the following:
- Crankshaft timing sprocket
- Timing belt
- Front cover
- Crankshaft pulley. Tighten the bolt to 100 ft. lbs. (135 Nm).
- Accessory drive belts
- Negative battery cable

5. Start the engine and check for leaks.

Camshaft and Valve Lifters

REMOVAL & INSTALLATION

2.4L Engine

1. Before servicing the vehicle, refer to the precautions in the beginning of this section.

2. Remove or disconnect the following:
- Negative battery cable
- Air cleaner and hoses
- Accessory drive belts
- Ignition coil and spark plug wires
- Camshaft Position (CMP) sensor connector

- Right motor mount
- Front cover
- Timing belt. Refer to the Timing Belt unit repair section.
- Camshaft sprockets
- Timing belt idler pulley
- Rear timing cover
- Valve cover

➡ **Keep all valvetrain components in order for assembly.**

- Camshafts. Loosen the bearing cap bolts in the sequence shown.
- Cam followers
- Lash adjusters

To install:

3. Install or connect the following:
- Lash adjusters in their original positions
- Cam followers in their original positions
- Camshafts. Tighten the 6mm bearing cap bolts in sequence to 105 inch lbs. (12 Nm).
- Camshaft bearing end caps. Tighten the 8mm bolts to 21 ft. lbs. (28 Nm).

4. Install the valve cover and tighten the bolts in sequence, as follows:
- Step 1: 40 inch lbs. (4.5 Nm)

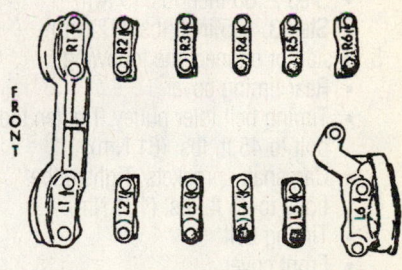

Camshaft bearing cap identification—2.4L engine

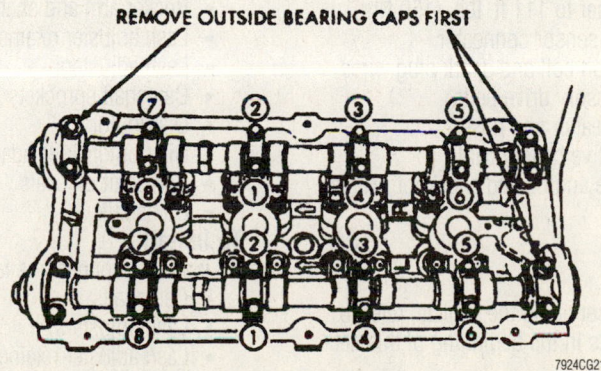

REMOVE OUTSIDE BEARING CAPS FIRST

Camshaft bearing cap loosening sequence—2.4L engine

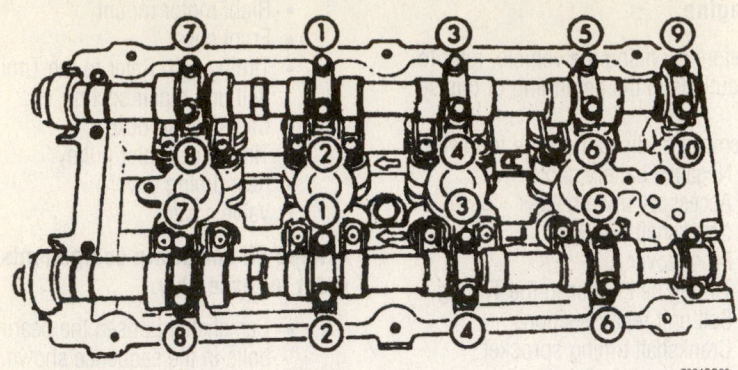

Camshaft bearing cap bolt tightening sequence—2.4L engine

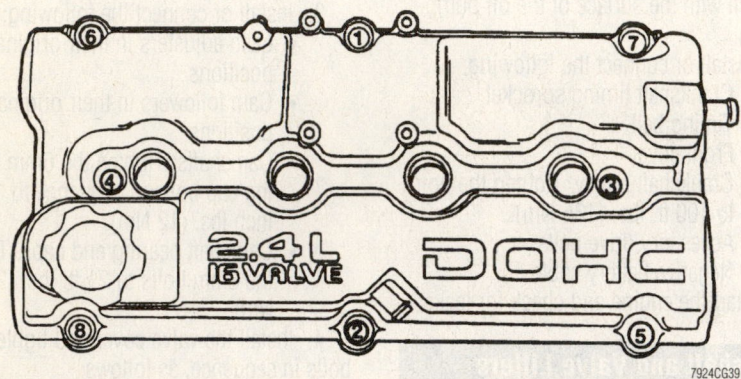

Cylinder head cover torque sequence—2.4L engine

- Step 2: 80 inch lbs. (9 Nm)
- Step 3: 105 inch lbs. (12 Nm)

5. Install or connect the following:
- Rear timing cover
- Timing belt idler pulley. Tighten the bolt to 45 ft. lbs. (61 Nm).
- Camshaft sprockets. Tighten the bolts to 75 ft. lbs. (101 Nm).
- Timing belt
- Front cover
- Right motor mount. Tighten the frame rail bolts to 50 ft. lbs. (68 Nm), the vertical fastener to 75 ft. lbs. (102 Nm) and the horizontal fastener to 111 ft. lbs. (150 Nm).
- CMP sensor connector
- Ignition coil and spark plug wires
- Accessory drive belts
- Air cleaner and hoses
- Negative battery cable

6. Start the engine and check for proper operation.

3.0L Engine

1. Before servicing the vehicle, refer to the precautions in the beginning of this section.
2. Remove or disconnect the following:

- Negative battery cable
- Air cleaner and hoses
- Accessory drive belts
- Front cover
- Timing belt. Refer to the Timing Belt unit repair section.
- Valve covers

3. Install Lash Adjuster Retainers tools MD-998443.

➡**Keep all valvetrain components in order for assembly.**

4. Remove or disconnect the following:

- Rocker arm and shaft assemblies
- Lash adjuster retainers
- Lash adjusters
- Camshaft sprockets
- Distributor
- Distributor drive adapter housing
- Camshaft oil seals
- Camshafts

To install:
5. Install or connect the following:
- Camshafts
- Lash adjusters
- Lash adjuster retainers
6. Install the rocker arm and shaft assemblies in their original positions

and tighten the bearing cap bolts, as follows:

- Step 1: Cap No. 3 bolts to 85 inch lbs. (10 Nm)
- Step 2: Cap No. 2 bolts to 85 inch lbs. (10 Nm)
- Step 3: Cap No. 1 bolts to 85 inch lbs. (10 Nm)
- Step 4: Cap No. 4 bolts to 85 inch lbs. (10 Nm)
- Step 5: Cap No. 3 bolts to 15 ft. lbs. (20 Nm)
- Step 6: Cap No. 2 bolts to 15 ft. lbs. (20 Nm)
- Step 7: Cap No. 1 bolts to 15 ft. lbs. (20 Nm)
- Step 8: Cap No. 4 bolts to 15 ft. lbs. (20 Nm)

7. Remove the lash adjuster retainers.
8. Install or connect the following:
- Camshaft oil seals
- Distributor drive adapter housing
- Distributor
- Camshaft sprockets
- Timing belt. Refer to the Timing Belt unit repair section.
- Front cover
- Accessory drive belts
- Air cleaner and hoses
- Negative battery cable

9. Start the engine and check for proper operation.

3.3L and 3.8L Engines

➡**Keep all valvetrain components in order for assembly.**

1. Before servicing the vehicle, refer to the precautions in the beginning of this section.
2. Remove the engine from the vehicle and mount it on a stand.
3. Install or connect the following:
- Valve covers
- Rocker arm and shaft assemblies
- Pushrods
- Intake manifold
- Cylinder heads
- Yoke retainer
- Aligning yokes
- Hydraulic lifters
- Oil pan
- Oil pump pickup tube
- Crankshaft pulley
- Front cover
- Timing chain and sprockets
- Camshaft thrust plate
- Camshaft

To install:
4. Install or connect the following:

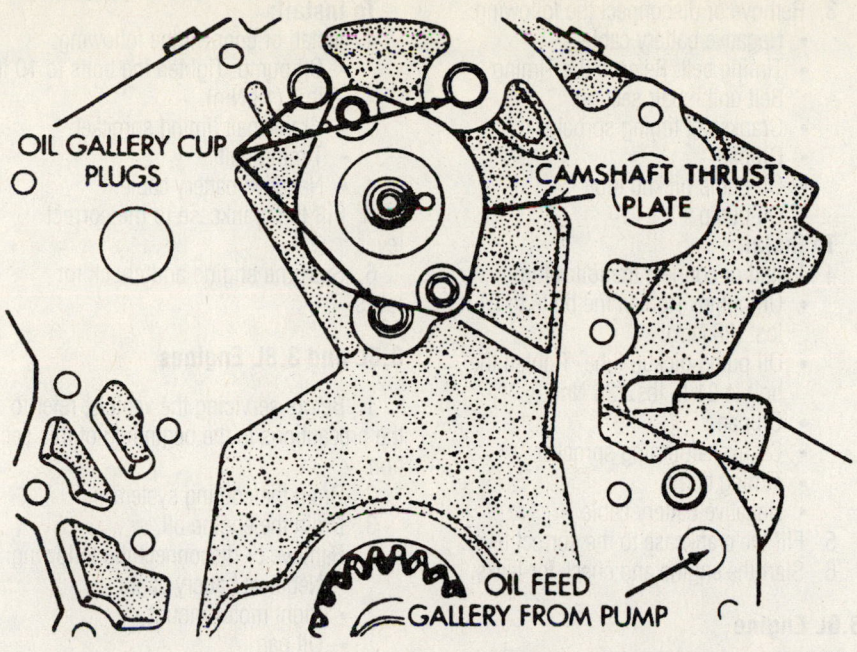

Remove the thrust plate and withdraw the camshaft from the engine—3.3L and 3.8L engines

- Camshaft
- Camshaft thrust plate. Tighten the bolts to 105 inch lbs. (12 Nm).
- Timing chain and sprockets. Tighten the camshaft sprocket bolt to 40 ft. lbs. (54 Nm).
- Front cover. Tighten the bolts to 20 ft. lbs. (27 Nm).
- Crankshaft pulley. Tighten the bolt to 40 ft. lbs. (54 Nm).
- Oil pump pickup tube
- Oil pan
- Hydraulic lifters
- Aligning yokes
- Yoke retainer. Tighten the bolts to 105 inch lbs. (12 Nm).
- Cylinder heads
- Intake manifold
- Pushrods
- Rocker arm and shaft assemblies
- Valve covers
5. Install the engine to the vehicle.

Valve Lash

ADJUSTMENT

All engines covered in this section are equipped with hydraulic lash adjusters. No adjustment is necessary.

Starter Motor

REMOVAL & INSTALLATION

1. Before servicing the vehicle, refer to the precautions in the beginning of this section.
2. Remove or disconnect the following:
   - Negative battery cable
   - Starter harness connectors
   - Starter motor
To install:
3. Install or connect the following:
   - Starter motor. Tighten the bolts to 40 ft. lbs. (54 Nm)

- Starter harness connectors. Tighten the battery cable nut to 90 inch lbs. (10 Nm).
- Negative battery cable

Oil Pan

REMOVAL & INSTALLATION

2.4L Engine

1. Before servicing the vehicle, refer to the precautions in the beginning of this section.
2. Drain the engine oil.
3. Remove or disconnect the following:
   - Negative battery cable
   - Right splash shield
   - Dust shield
   - Oil pan
To install:
4. Install or connect the following:
   - Oil pan. Tighten the bolts to 105 inch lbs. (12 Nm).
   - Dust shield
   - Right splash shield
   - Negative battery cable
5. Fill the crankcase to the correct level.
6. Start the engine and check for leaks.

3.0L Engine

1. Before servicing the vehicle, refer to the precautions in the beginning of this section.
2. Drain the engine oil.
3. Remove or disconnect the following:
   - Negative battery cable
   - Starter motor
   - Front motor mount bracket
   - Bending braces
   - Torque converter dust shield

Oil pan mounting bolt tightening sequence—3.0L engine

- Oil pan

To install:
4. Install or connect the following:
- Oil pan. Tighten the bolts in sequence to 50 inch lbs. (6 Nm).
- Torque converter dust shield
- Bending braces
- Front motor mount bracket
- Starter motor
- Negative battery cable
5. Fill the crankcase to the correct level.
6. Start the engine and check for leaks.

3.3L and 3.8L Engines

1. Before servicing the vehicle, refer to the precautions in the beginning of this section.
2. Drain the engine oil.
3. Remove or disconnect the following:
- Negative battery cable
- Engine oil dipstick
- Bending brace
- Dust cover
- Oil pan

To install:
4. Install or connect the following:
- Oil pan. Tighten the bolts to 105 inch lbs. (12 Nm).
- Dust cover
- Bending brace
- Engine oil dipstick
- Negative battery cable
5. Fill the crankcase to the correct level.
6. Start the engine and check for leaks.

Oil Pump

REMOVAL & INSTALLATION

2.4L Engine

1. Before servicing the vehicle, refer to the precautions in the beginning of this section.
2. Drain the engine oil.

3. Remove or disconnect the following:
- Negative battery cable
- Timing belt. Refer to the Timing Belt unit repair section.
- Crankshaft timing sprocket
- Oil pan
- Oil pump pickup tube
- Oil pump

To install:
4. Install or connect the following:
- Oil pump. Tighten the bolts to 21 ft. lbs. (28 Nm).
- Oil pump pickup tube. Tighten the bolt to 21 ft. lbs. (28 Nm).
- Oil pan
- Crankshaft timing sprocket
- Timing belt
- Negative battery cable
5. Fill the crankcase to the correct level.
6. Start the engine and check for leaks.

3.0L Engine

1. Before servicing the vehicle, refer to the precautions in the beginning of this section.
2. Drain the engine oil.
3. Remove or disconnect the following:
- Negative battery cable
- Timing belt. Refer to the Timing Belt unit repair section.
- Crankshaft timing sprocket
- Oil pump

➡ **The oil pump bolts vary in length. Note their locations for assembly.**

To install:
4. Install or connect the following:
- Oil pump. Tighten the bolts to 10 ft. lbs. (13 Nm).
- Crankshaft timing sprocket
- Timing belt
- Negative battery cable
5. Fill the crankcase to the correct level.
6. Start the engine and check for leaks.

3.3L and 3.8L Engines

1. Before servicing the vehicle, refer to the precautions in the beginning of this section.
2. Drain the cooling system.
3. Drain the engine oil.
4. Remove or disconnect the following:
- Negative battery cable
- Right motor mount
- Oil pan
- Oil pickup tube
- Accessory drive belt
- A/C compressor and bracket
- Crankshaft pulley
- Idler pulley
- Motor mount bracket
- Camshaft Position (CMP) sensor
- Front cover
- Oil pump

To install:
5. Install or connect the following:
- Oil pump. Tighten the cover screws to 105 inch lbs. (12 Nm).

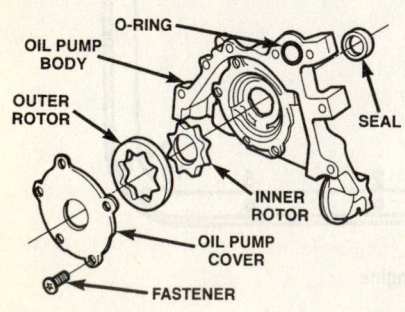

Exploded view of the oil pump—2.4L engine

7924CG25

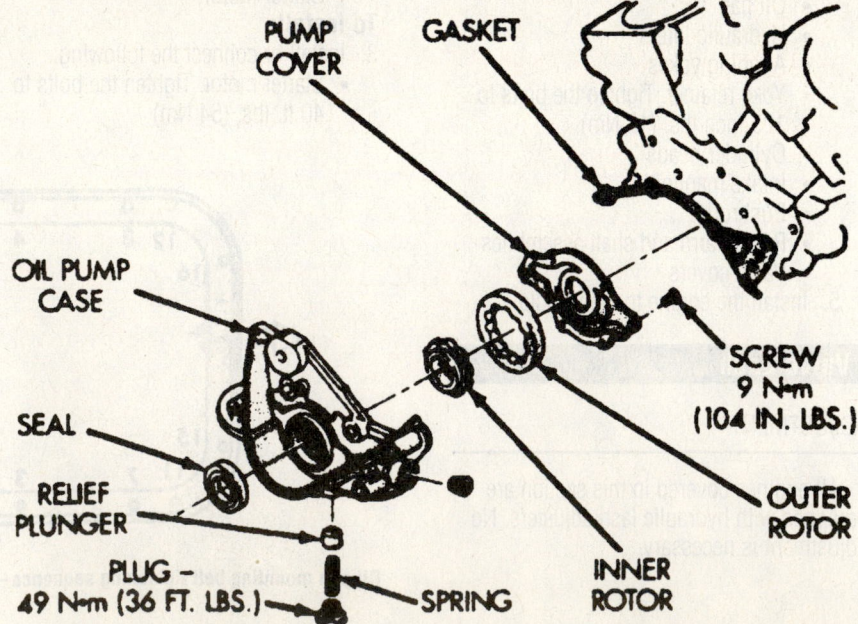

Exploded view of the oil pump assembly—3.0L engine

7924CG26

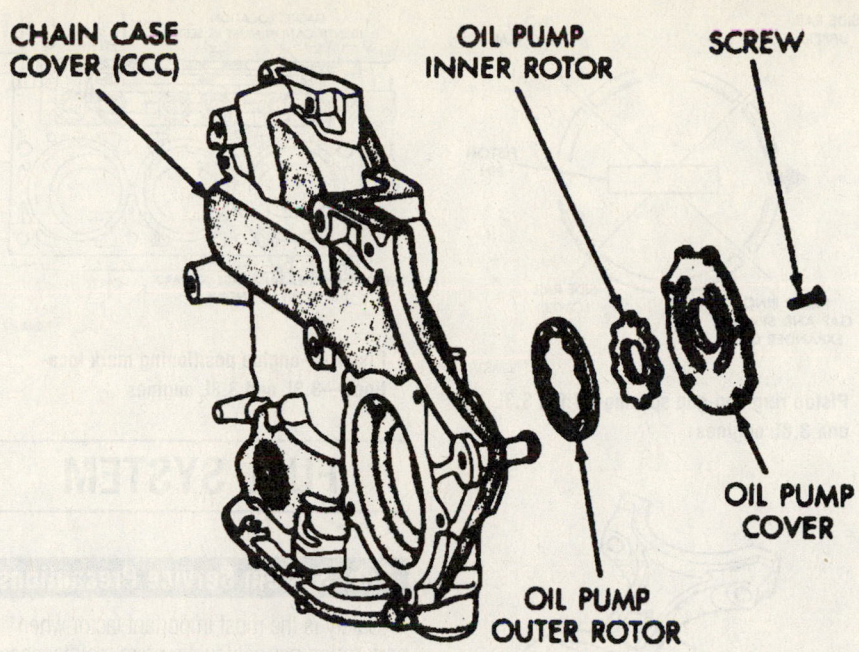

CHAIN CASE COVER (CCC)

OIL PUMP INNER ROTOR

SCREW

OIL PUMP COVER

OIL PUMP OUTER ROTOR

7924CG27

Exploded view of the oil pump assembly—3.3L and 3.8L engines

- Front cover. Tighten the bolts to 20 ft. lbs. 927 Nm).
- CMP sensor
- Motor mount bracket. Tighten the bolts to 40 ft. lbs. (54 Nm).
- Idler pulley
- Crankshaft pulley. Tighten the bolt to 40 ft. lbs. (54 Nm).
- A/C compressor and bracket
- Accessory drive belt
- Oil pickup tube. Tighten the bolt to 21 ft. lbs. (28 Nm).
- Oil pan
- Right motor mount
- Negative battery cable
6. Fill the crankcase to the correct level.
7. Fill the cooling system.
8. Start the engine and check for leaks.

Rear Main Seal

REMOVAL & INSTALLATION

1. Before servicing the vehicle, refer to the precautions at the beginning of this section.
2. Remove or disconnect the following:
   - Negative battery cable
   - Transaxle
   - Flexplate
   - Rear main seal
To install:
3. Install or connect the following:

- Rear main seal flush with the cylinder block surface
- Flexplate Tighten the bolts to 70 ft. lbs. (95 Nm).
- Transaxle
- Negative battery cable
4. Run the engine and check for leaks.

Timing Chain, Sprockets, Front Cover and Seal

REMOVAL & INSTALLATION

3.3L and 3.8L Engines

1. Before servicing the vehicle, refer to the precautions in the beginning of this section.
2. Drain the cooling system.
3. Drain the engine oil.
4. Remove or disconnect the following:

- Negative battery cable
- Right motor mount
- Oil pan
- Oil pickup tube
- Accessory drive belt
- A/C compressor and bracket
- Crankshaft pulley
- Idler pulley
- Motor mount bracket
- Camshaft Position (CMP) sensor
- Front cover
- Timing chain and sprockets
To install:
5. Align the timing chain colored links with the dots on the timing sprockets.
6. Align the timing sprocket arrows with the crankshaft and camshaft centers and install the timing chain and sprockets.

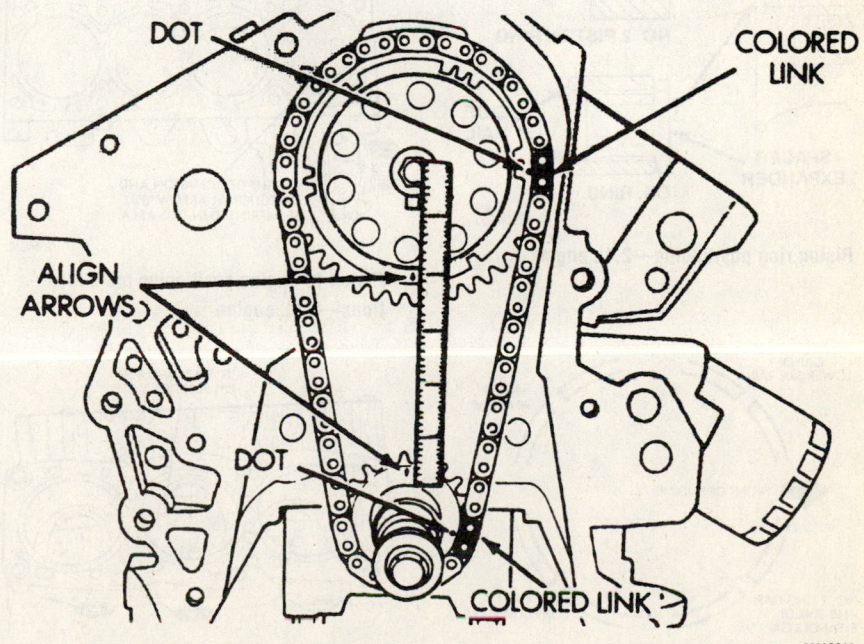

DOT

COLORED LINK

ALIGN ARROWS

DOT

COLORED LINK

9308CG02

Timing mark alignment—3.3L and 3.8L engines

Please refer to Section 8 for electric cooling fan wiring schematics

Tighten the camshaft sprocket bolt to 40 ft. lbs. (54 Nm).

7. Install or connect the following:
- Front cover. Tighten the bolts to 20 ft. lbs. 927 Nm).
- CMP sensor
- Motor mount bracket. Tighten the bolts to 40 ft. lbs. (54 Nm).
- Idler pulley
- Crankshaft pulley. Tighten the bolt to 40 ft. lbs. (54 Nm).
- A/C compressor and bracket
- Accessory drive belt
- Oil pickup tube. Tighten the bolt to 21 ft. lbs. (28 Nm).
- Oil pan
- Right motor mount
- Negative battery cable

8. Fill the crankcase to the correct level.
9. Fill the cooling system.
10. Start the engine and check for leaks.

Piston and Ring

POSITIONING

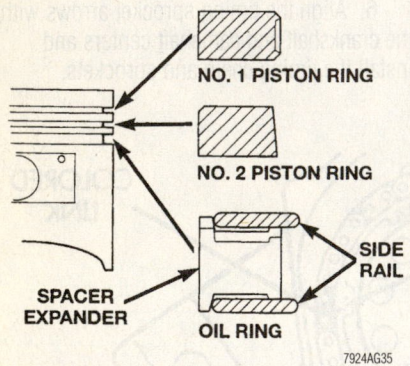

Piston ring positioning—2.4L engine

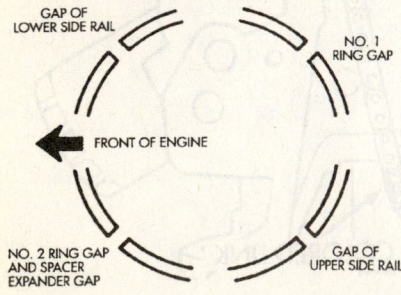

Piston ring end-gap spacing—2.4L engine

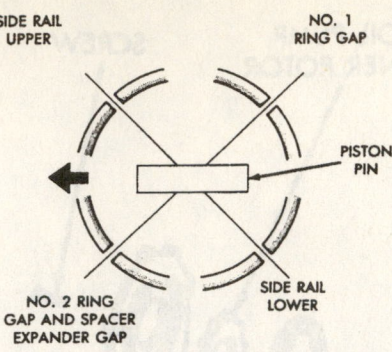

Piston ring end-gap spacing—3.0L, 3.3L and 3.8L engines

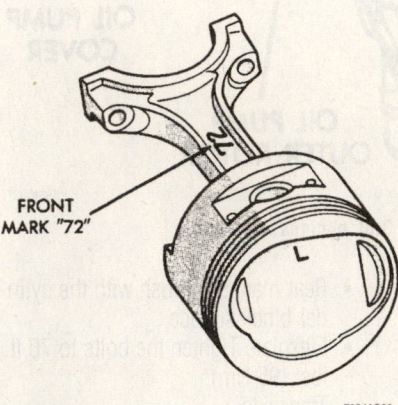

Piston and connecting rod front mark locations—3.0L, 3.3L and 3.8L engines

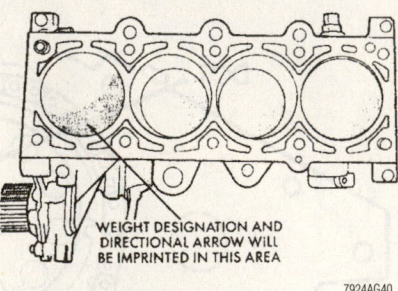

Piston-to-engine positioning mark locations—2.4L engine

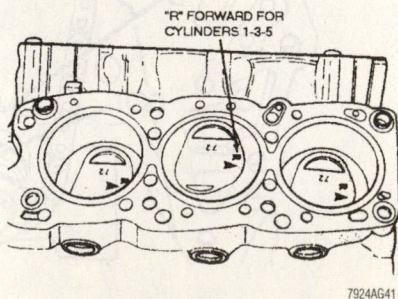

Piston-to-engine positioning mark locations—3.0L engine

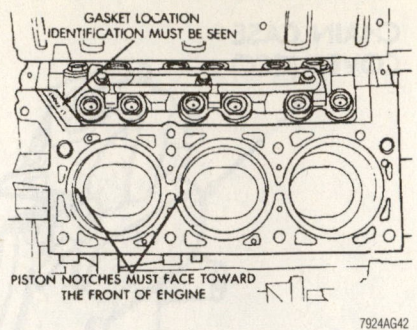

Piston-to-engine positioning mark locations—3.3L and 3.8L engines

FUEL SYSTEM

Fuel System Service Precautions

Safety is the most important factor when performing not only fuel system maintenance but any type of maintenance. Failure to conduct maintenance and repairs in a safe manner may result in serious personal injury or death. Maintenance and testing of the vehicle's fuel system components can be accomplished safely and effectively by adhering to the following rules and guidelines.

- To avoid the possibility of fire and personal injury, always disconnect the negative battery cable unless the repair or test procedure requires that battery voltage be applied.
- Always relieve the fuel system pressure prior to disconnecting any fuel system component (injector, fuel rail, pressure regulator, etc.), fitting or fuel line connection. Exercise extreme caution whenever relieving fuel system pressure to avoid exposing skin, face and eyes to fuel spray. Please be advised that fuel under pressure may penetrate the skin or any part of the body that it contacts.
- Always place a shop towel or cloth around the fitting or connection prior to loosening to absorb any excess fuel due to spillage. Ensure that all fuel spillage (should it occur) is quickly removed from engine surfaces. Ensure that all fuel soaked cloths or towels are deposited into a suitable waste container.
- Always keep a dry chemical (Class B) fire extinguisher near the work area.
- Do not allow fuel spray or fuel vapors to come into contact with a spark or open flame.
- Always use a back-up wrench when loosening and tightening fuel line connec-

tion fittings. This will prevent unnecessary stress and torsion to fuel line piping.

• Always replace worn fuel fitting O-rings with new ones. Do not substitute fuel hose or equivalent, where fuel pipe is installed.

Fuel System Pressure

RELIEVING

2.4L, 3.3L and 3.8L Engines

1. Before servicing the vehicle, refer to the preceding fuel system precautions, as well as the precautions in the beginning of this section.

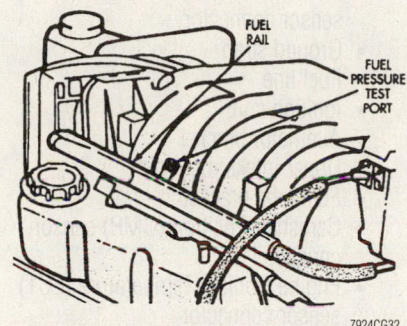

7924CG32

Fuel pressure test port—3.3L and 3.8L engines

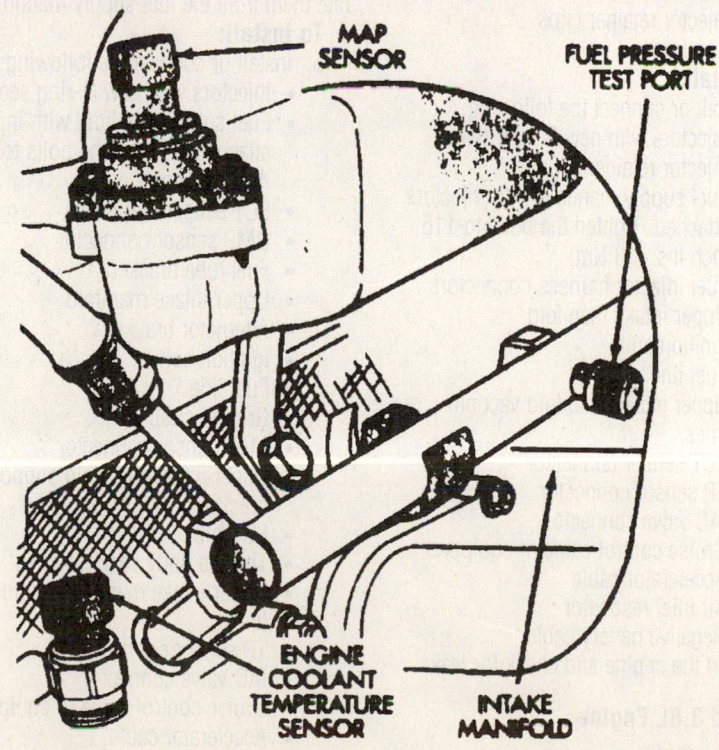

7924CG31

Fuel pressure test port—2.4L engine

2. Disconnect the negative battery cable.

3. Remove the fuel tank filler cap to release the pressure in the fuel tank.

4. Remove the cap from the fuel pressure test port on the fuel rail.

5. Place the open end of fuel pressure release hose tool C-4799-1, into an approved gasoline container. Place a shop towel under the test port.

6. Connect the other end of the hose onto the fuel pressure test port to relieve the system pressure.

7. After the fuel pressure has been released, remove the hose from the test port and install the cap.

8. When repairs are completed, connect the negative battery cable.

3.0L Engine

1. Before servicing the vehicle, refer to the preceding fuel system precautions, as well as the precautions in the beginning of this section.

2. Remove the fuel pump relay from the Power Distribution Center (PDC) located on the left side in the engine compartment.

3. Start the engine and allow it to run until it stalls.

4. Continue to start the engine until it will no longer run.

5. Turn the ignition key to the **OFF** position.

6. Disconnect any fuel injector.

7. Connect one end of a jumper wire to either injector terminal of the fuel injector harness connector. Connect the other end of the jumper wire to the positive battery terminal.

8. Connect one end of a second jumper wire to the remaining injector terminal.

9. Momentarily touch the other end of the second jumper wire to the negative battery terminal for no more than 4 seconds.

10. When repairs are completed, connect the negative battery cable.

Fuel Filter

REMOVAL & INSTALLATION

➡The fuel filter mounts to the top of the fuel tank.

1. Before servicing the vehicle, refer to the precautions in the beginning of this section.

2. Relieve the fuel system pressure.

3. Remove or disconnect the following:
   • Negative battery cable
   • Quick-connect fittings at the fuel pump module and the chassis fuel supply tube
   • Mounting bolt and the fuel filter

To install:

4. Install or connect the following:
   • Fuel filter
   • Quick-connect fittings at the fuel pump module and the chassis fuel supply tube
   • Negative battery cable

5. Start the engine and check for leaks.

Fuel Pump

REMOVAL & INSTALLATION

1. Before servicing the vehicle, refer to the precautions in the beginning of this section.

2. Relieve the fuel system pressure.

3. Drain the fuel tank.

4. Remove or disconnect the following:
   • Negative battery cable
   • Fuel tank straps. Support the fuel tank.
   • Fuel lines
   • Fuel pump module harness connector

5. Lower the tank for access and remove

the fuel pump module locking ring and the fuel pump module.

To install:

6. Install or connect the following:
   • Fuel pump module. Tighten the locking ring to 40 ft. lbs. (54 Nm).
   • Fuel pump module harness connector
   • Fuel lines
   • Fuel tank straps. Tighten the bolts to 40 ft. lbs. (54 Nm)
   • Negative battery cable
7. Start the engine and check for leaks.

Fuel Injector

REMOVAL & INSTALLATION

2.4L Engine

1. Before servicing the vehicle, refer to the precautions in the beginning of this section.
2. Relieve the fuel system pressure.
3. Remove or disconnect the following:
   • Negative battery cable
   • Air cleaner inlet hose
   • Accelerator cable
   • Cruise control cable, if equipped
   • Throttle Position (TP) sensor connector
   • Idle Air Control (IAC) valve connector
   • Upper intake manifold vacuum lines
   • Intake Air Temperature (IAT) sensor connector
   • Manifold Absolute Pressure (MAP) sensor connector
   • Fuel line
   • Intake manifold support brackets
   • Fuel injector harness connectors
   • Intake manifold
   • Fuel supply manifold with injectors attached
4. Rotate and pull the injectors to separate them from the fuel supply manifold.

To install:

5. Install or connect the following:
   • Injectors with new O-ring seals
   • Fuel supply manifold with injectors attached. Tighten the bolts to 16 ft. lbs. (22 Nm).
   • Intake manifold
   • Fuel injector harness connectors
   • Intake manifold support brackets
   • Fuel line
   • MAP sensor connector
   • IAT sensor connector
   • Upper intake manifold vacuum lines

   • IAC valve connector
   • TP sensor connector
   • Cruise control cable, if equipped
   • Accelerator cable
   • Air cleaner inlet hose
   • Negative battery cable
6. Start the engine and check for leaks.

3.0L Engine

1. Before servicing the vehicle, refer to the precautions in the beginning of this section.
2. Relieve the fuel system pressure.
3. Remove or disconnect the following:
   • Negative battery cable
   • Air inlet resonator
   • Accelerator cable
   • Cruise control cable, if equipped
   • Idle Air Control (IAC) valve connector
   • Throttle Position (TP) sensor connector
   • Engine Coolant Temperature (ECT) sensor connector
   • Upper intake manifold vacuum lines
   • Fuel line
   • Ignition coil
   • Upper intake manifold
   • Fuel injector harness connectors
   • Fuel supply manifold with injectors attached
   • Injector retainer clips
   • Injectors

To install:

4. Install or connect the following:
   • Injectors with new O-ring seals
   • Injector retainer clips
   • Fuel supply manifold with injectors attached. Tighten the bolts to 115 inch lbs. (13 Nm).
   • Fuel injector harness connectors
   • Upper intake manifold
   • Ignition coil
   • Fuel line
   • Upper intake manifold vacuum lines
   • ECT sensor connector
   • TP sensor connector
   • IAC valve connector
   • Cruise control cable, if equipped
   • Accelerator cable
   • Air inlet resonator
   • Negative battery cable
5. Start the engine and check for leaks.

3.3L and 3.8L Engines

1. Before servicing the vehicle, refer to the precautions in the beginning of this section.
2. Relieve the fuel system pressure.

3. Remove or disconnect the following:
   • Negative battery cable
   • Intake manifold cover
   • Air inlet resonator
   • Accelerator cable
   • Cruise control cable, if equipped
   • Idle Air Control (IAC) valve connector
   • Throttle Position (TP) sensor connector
   • Upper intake manifold vacuum lines
   • Throttle body vacuum lines
   • Exhaust Gas Recirculation (EGR) tube
   • Upper intake manifold support bracket
   • Manifold Absolute Pressure (MAP) sensor connector
   • Ground strap
   • Fuel line
   • Ignition coil
   • Alternator bracket
   • Upper intake manifold
   • Fuel tube bracket
   • Camshaft Position (CMP) sensor connector
   • Engine Coolant Temperature (ECT) sensor connector
   • Fuel supply manifold with injectors attached
4. Rotate and pull the injectors to separate them from the fuel supply manifold.

To install:

5. Install or connect the following:
   • Injectors with new O-ring seals
   • Fuel supply manifold with injectors attached. Tighten the bolts to 16 ft. lbs. (22 Nm).
   • ECT sensor connector
   • CMP sensor connector
   • Fuel tube bracket
   • Upper intake manifold
   • Alternator bracket
   • Ignition coil
   • Fuel line
   • Ground strap
   • MAP sensor connector
   • Upper intake manifold support bracket
   • EGR tube
   • Throttle body vacuum lines
   • Upper intake manifold vacuum lines
   • TP sensor connector
   • IAC valve connector
   • Cruise control cable, if equipped
   • Accelerator cable
   • Air inlet resonator
   • Intake manifold cover
   • Negative battery cable
6. Start the engine and check for leaks.

DRIVE TRAIN

Automatic Transaxle Assembly

REMOVAL & INSTALLATION

1. Before servicing the vehicle, refer to the precautions in the beginning of this section.

2. Attach a support fixture to the engine lifting eyes.

3. Remove or disconnect the following:
- Negative battery cable
- Air cleaner and hoses
- Shift cable
- Throttle valve cable
- Torque converter clutch harness connector
- Gear position switch connector
- Transaxle solenoid harness connectors
- Transaxle fluid dipstick tube
- Transaxle fluid cooler lines
- Vehicle Speed (VSS) sensor connector
- Front wheels
- Axle halfshafts
- Rear driveshaft, if equipped
- Exhaust front pipe
- Torque converter
- Front motor mount and bracket
- Rear motor mount. Support the transaxle.
- Left motor mount
- Starter motor
- Crankshaft Position (CKP) sensor
- Transaxle flange bolts
- Transaxle

To install:

4. Install or connect the following:
- Transaxle. Tighten the flange bolts to 70 ft. lbs. (95 Nm).
- CKP sensor
- Starter motor
- Left motor mount. Tighten the through bolt to 55 ft. lbs. (75 Nm).
- Rear motor mount. Tighten the bolts to 45 ft. lbs. (61 Nm).
- Front motor mount and bracket. Tighten the large bracket bolts to 80 ft. lbs. (108 Nm), the small bracket bolts to 40 ft. lbs. (54 Nm) and the through bolt to 45 ft. lbs. (61 Nm).
- Torque converter. Tighten the bolts to 55 ft. lbs. (75 Nm).

- Exhaust front pipe
- Rear driveshaft, if equipped
- Axle halfshafts
- Front wheels
- VSS sensor connector
- Transaxle fluid cooler lines
- Transaxle fluid dipstick tube
- Transaxle solenoid harness connectors
- Gear position switch connector
- Torque converter clutch harness connector
- Throttle valve cable
- Shift cable
- Air cleaner and hoses
- Negative battery cable

5. Start the engine and check for proper operation.

Power Transfer Unit

REMOVAL & INSTALLATION

1. Before servicing the vehicle, refer to the precautions in the beginning of this section.

2. Remove or disconnect the following:
- Right front wheel
- Right axle halfshaft
- Cradle plate
- Rear driveshaft
- Power transfer unit brackets
- Power transfer unit

To install:

3. Install or connect the following:
- Power transfer unit and brackets. Tighten the bolts to 37 ft. lbs. (50 Nm).
- Rear driveshaft
- Cradle plate. Tighten the bolts to 123 ft. lbs. (166 Nm).
- Right axle halfshaft
- Right front wheel

Halfshaft

REMOVAL & INSTALLATION

Front

1. Before servicing the vehicle, refer to the precautions in the beginning of this section.

2. Remove or disconnect the following:
- Front wheel
- Split pin
- Nut lock
- Spring washer
- Hub nut
- Brake caliper and rotor
- Outer tie rod end
- Wheel speed sensor harness, if equipped
- Lower ball joint

3. Separate the outer CV-joint stub shaft from the steering knuckle.

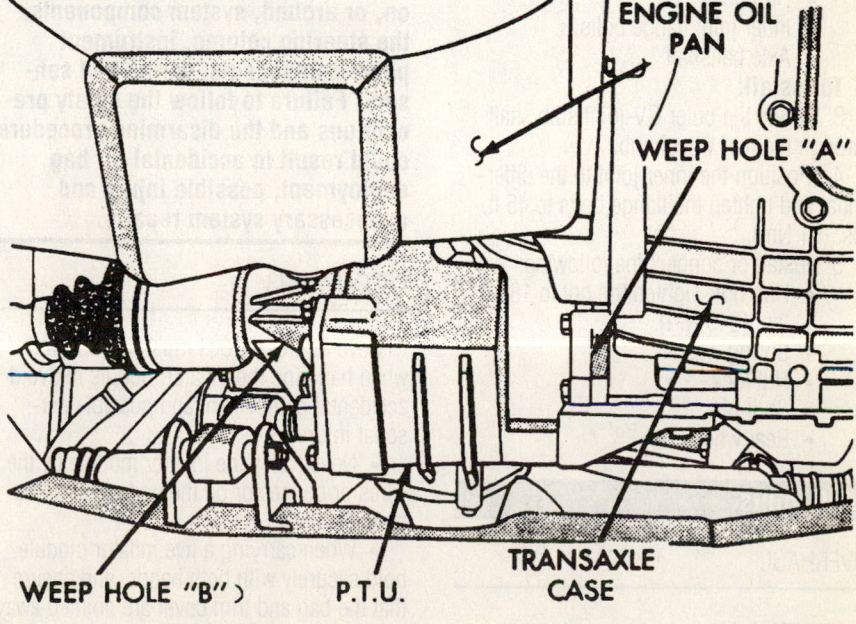

Power transfer unit and related components

4. Pry the inner tri-pot joint out of the transaxle and remove the axle halfshaft.

To install:

5. Install the axle halfshaft so that the inner joint circlip seats in the transaxle side gear.

6. Guide the outer CV-joint stub shaft through the steering knuckle hub.

7. Install or connect the following:
- Lower ball joint. Tighten the nut to 70 ft. lbs. (95 Nm).
- Wheel speed sensor harness, if equipped
- Outer tie rod end. Tighten the nut to 45 ft. lbs. (61 Nm).
- Brake caliper and rotor. Tighten the caliper bolts to 23 ft. lbs. (31 Nm).
- Hub nut. Tighten the nut to 180 ft. lbs. (245 Nm).
- Spring washer
- Nut lock
- Split pin
- Front wheel

8. Check the wheel alignment and adjust as necessary.

Rear

1. Before servicing the vehicle, refer to the precautions in the beginning of this section.

2. Remove or disconnect the following:
- Rear wheel
- Split pin
- Nut lock
- Spring washer
- Hub nut
- Inner joint flange bolts
- Axle halfshaft

To install:

3. Guide the outer CV-joint stub shaft through the rear wheel hub.

4. Position the inner joint to the differential and tighten the flange bolts to 45 ft. lbs. (61 Nm).

5. Install or connect the following:
- Hub nut. Tighten the nut to 180 ft. lbs. (245 Nm).
- Spring washer
- Nut lock
- Split pin
- Rear wheel

CV-Joints

OVERHAUL

Outer CV-Joint

The outer CV-joint and boot are serviced with the axle halfshaft as an assembly.

Inner Tri-pot Joint

1. Before servicing the vehicle, refer to the precautions in the beginning of this section.

2. Remove or disconnect the following:
- Axle halfshaft from the vehicle
- Inner tri-pot joint boot clamps
- Tri-pot joint housing
- Snapring
- Tri-pot joint

To install:

➡ **Use new snaprings, clips, and boot clamps for assembly.**

3. Install or connect the following:
- Tri-pot joint
- Snapring
- Tri-pot joint housing

4. Fill the tri-pot joint housing and boot with grease and tighten the boot clamps.

5. Install the axle halfshaft.

STEERING AND SUSPENSION

Air Bag

✹✹ CAUTION

Some vehicles are equipped with an air bag system. The system must be disarmed before performing service on, or around, system components, the steering column, instrument panel components, wiring and sensors. Failure to follow the safety precautions and the disarming procedure could result in accidental air bag deployment, possible injury and unnecessary system repairs.

PRECAUTIONS

Several precautions must be observed when handling the inflator module to avoid accidental deployment and possible personal injury.

- Never carry the inflator module by the wires or connector on the underside of the module.
- When carrying a live inflator module, hold securely with both hands, and ensure that the bag and trim cover are pointed away from your body. In the unlikely event of an accidental deployment, the bag will then deploy with minimal chance of injury.

- Place the inflator module on a bench or other surface with the bag and trim cover facing up. This will reduce the motion of the module if accidentally deployed.
- With the inflator module on the bench, never place anything on or close to the module which may be thrown in the event of an accidental deployment.

DISARMING

1. Disconnect and isolate the negative battery cable from the battery.

2. Allow the SIR system capacitor to discharge for at least two (2) minutes, before performing any repairs.

3. When repairs are completed, connect the negative battery cable.

Power Rack and Pinion Steering Gear

REMOVAL & INSTALLATION

1. Before servicing the vehicle, refer to the precautions in the beginning of this section.

2. Lock the steering wheel in the straight ahead position.

3. Remove or disconnect the following:
- Negative battery cable
- Steering column shaft coupler
- Front wheels
- Outer tie rod ends
- Anti-lock brake Hydraulic Control Unit (HCU) mounting bolts, if equipped
- Cradle plate
- Power steering fluid line bracket
- Power steering pressure and return lines
- Steering gear mounting fasteners
- Intermediate shaft coupler
- Power steering gear

To install:

4. Install or connect the following:
- Power steering gear
- Intermediate shaft coupler
- Steering gear mounting fasteners. Tighten the fasteners to 100 ft. lbs. (136 Nm).
- Power steering pressure and return lines
- Power steering fluid line bracket
- Cradle plate. Tighten the bolts to 123 ft. lbs. (166 Nm).
- Anti-lock brake HCU mounting bolts, if equipped
- Outer tie rod ends
- Front wheels

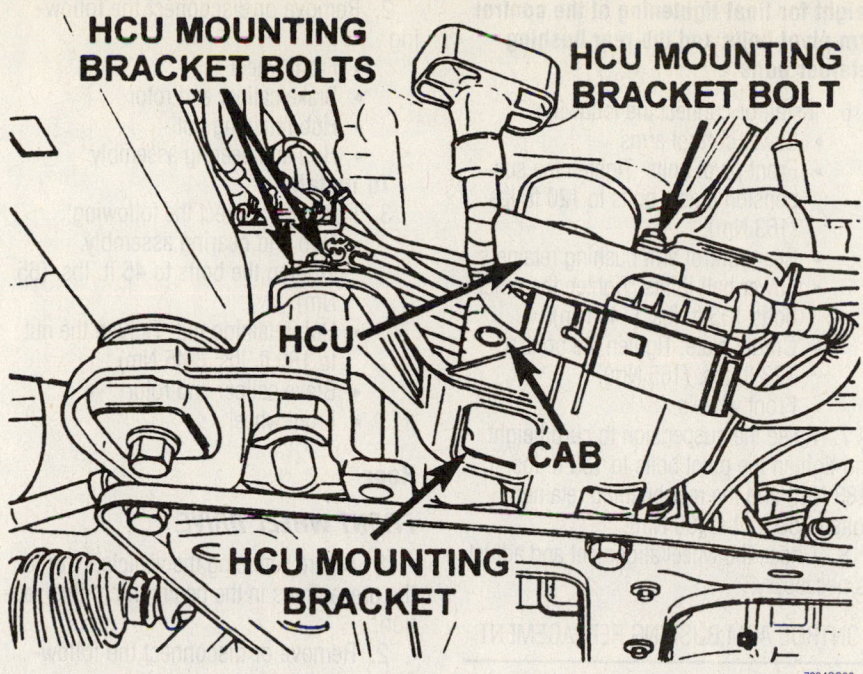

HCU MOUNTING BRACKET BOLTS

HCU MOUNTING BRACKET BOLT

HCU

CAB

HCU MOUNTING BRACKET

7924CG36

Anti-lock brake Hydraulic Control Unit (HCU) mounting

- Steering column shaft coupler. Tighten the pinch bolt to 21 ft. lbs. (28 Nm).
- Negative battery cable

5. Check the wheel alignment and adjust as necessary.

Strut

REMOVAL & INSTALLATION

1. Before servicing the vehicle, refer to the precautions in the beginning of this section.
2. Remove or disconnect the following:
   - Front wheel
   - Brake hose bracket
   - Wheel speed sensor harness bracket, if equipped
   - Stabilizer bar link
   - Steering knuckle bracket bolts
   - Upper strut mount nuts
   - Strut assembly
   To install:
3. Install or connect the following:
   - Strut assembly. Tighten the upper strut mount nuts to 21 ft. lbs. (28 Nm).
   - Steering knuckle bracket bolts. Tighten the bolts to 65 ft. lbs. (88 Nm) plus 90 degrees.

- Stabilizer bar link. Tighten the nut to 65 ft. lbs. (88 Nm).
- Wheel speed sensor harness bracket, if equipped. Tighten the bolt to 10 ft. lbs. (13 Nm).
- Brake hose bracket. Tighten the bolt to 10 ft. lbs. (13 Nm).
- Front wheel

4. Check the wheel alignment and adjust as necessary.

Shock Absorber

REMOVAL & INSTALLATION

Rear

1. Before servicing the vehicle, refer to the precautions in the beginning of this section.
2. Support the rear axle with a jackstand.
3. Remove the top and bottom shock absorber bolts.
4. Remove the shock absorber.
   To install:
5. Install the shock absorber and tighten the mounting bolts to 75 ft. lbs. (101 Nm).
6. Remove the jackstand.

Coil Spring

REMOVAL & INSTALLATION

Front

1. Before servicing the vehicle, refer to the precautions in the beginning of this section.
2. Remove the strut assembly from the vehicle.
3. Compress the coil spring and remove the piston rod nut.
4. Remove or disconnect the following:
   - Upper strut mount
   - Pivot bearing
   - Spring upper seat
   - Coil spring
   - Jounce bumper and dust shield
   - Lower spring isolator
   To install:
5. Install or connect the following:
   - Lower spring isolator
   - Jounce bumper and dust shield
   - Coil spring
   - Spring upper seat
   - Pivot bearing
   - Upper strut mount. Tighten the piston rod nut to 70 ft. lbs. (94 Nm).
6. Remove the spring compressor and install the strut assembly to the vehicle.

Leaf Springs

REMOVAL & INSTALLATION

1. Before servicing the vehicle, refer to the precautions in the beginning of this section.
2. Remove the axle halfshaft, if equipped.
3. Support the vehicle at the frame rail with jackstands.
4. Support the axle with a floor jack.
5. Remove or disconnect the following:
   - Shock absorber
   - Axle plate from the axle and spring
6. Slowly lower the axle so that the leaf spring hangs free.
7. Remove or disconnect the following:
   - Front spring mount
   - Rear spring shackle plate
   - Leaf spring
   To install:
8. Install or connect the following:
   - Leaf spring

- Rear spring shackle plate. Tighten the nuts to 45 ft. lbs. (61 Nm).
- Front spring mount. Tighten the through bolt to 115 ft. lbs. (156 Nm) and the mount bolts to 45 ft. lbs. (61 Nm).
- Axle plate. Tighten the bolts to 75 ft. lbs. (101 Nm).
- Shock absorber
- Axle halfshaft, if equipped

Lower Ball Joint

REMOVAL & INSTALLATION

1. Before servicing the vehicle, refer to the precautions in the beginning of this section.
2. Remove or disconnect the following:
   - Front wheel
   - Lower control arm
   - Ball joint seal boot
3. Remove the ball joint from the control arm with a press.

To install:
4. Install the ball joint to the control arm with a press so that the ball joint flange contacts the control arm with no visible gaps.
5. Install or connect the following:
   - Ball joint seal boot
   - Lower control arm
   - Front wheel
6. Check the wheel alignment and adjust as necessary.

Lower Control Arm

REMOVAL & INSTALLATION

1. Before servicing the vehicle, refer to the precautions in the beginning of this section.
2. Remove or disconnect the following:
   - Front wheels
   - Cradle plate
   - Lower ball joints
   - Rear control arm bushing retainers
3. Matchmark the suspension cradle and the frame rail.
4. Loosen the left suspension cradle bolts and lower the cradle to allow the pivot bolt to be removed.
5. Remove or disconnect the following:
   - Front pivot bolts
   - Lower control arms

To install:
The suspension must be at curb height for final tightening of the control arm pivot bolts and the rear bushing retainer bolts.

6. Install or connect the following:
   - Lower control arms
   - Front pivot bolts. Tighten the suspension cradle bolts to 120 ft. lbs. (163 Nm).
   - Rear control arm bushing retainers
   - Lower ball joints. Tighten the pinch bolts 105 ft. lbs. (145 Nm).
   - Cradle plate. Tighten the bolts to 123 ft. lbs. (165 Nm).
   - Front wheels
7. Raise the suspension to curb height and tighten the pivot bolts to 135 ft. lbs. (183 Nm) and the rear bushing retainer bolts to 50 ft. lbs. (68 Nm).
8. Check the wheel alignment and adjust as necessary.

CONTROL ARM BUSHING REPLACEMENT

1. Before servicing the vehicle, refer to the precautions in the beginning of this section.
2. Remove the control arm from the vehicle.
3. Press the front bushing out of the control arm.
4. Cut the rear bushing lengthwise and remove it from the control arm.

To install:
5. Press the front bushing into the control arm until the bushing flange contacts the control arm.
6. Lubricate the rear bushing with silicone spray lubricant and push it onto the control arm.
7. Install the control arm to the vehicle.

Wheel Bearings

ADJUSTMENT

The front and rear wheel bearings are designed for the life of the vehicle and require no type of adjustment or periodic maintenance. The bearing is a sealed unit with the wheel hub and can only be removed and/or replaced as an assembly.

REMOVAL & INSTALLATION

Front

1. Before servicing the vehicle, refer to the precautions in the beginning of this section.

2. Remove or disconnect the following:
   - Front wheel
   - Brake caliper and rotor
   - Hub retaining nut
   - Hub and bearing assembly

To install:
3. Install or connect the following:
   - Hub and bearing assembly. Tighten the bolts to 45 ft. lbs. (65 Nm).
   - Hub retaining nut. Tighten the nut to 180 ft. lbs. (245 Nm).
   - Brake caliper and rotor
   - Front wheel

Rear

FRONT WHEEL DRIVE

1. Before servicing the vehicle, refer to the precautions in the beginning of this section.
2. Remove or disconnect the following:
   - Rear wheel
   - Brake drum
   - Wheel speed sensor, if equipped
   - Hub and bearing assembly

To install:
3. Install or connect the following:
   - Hub and bearing assembly. Tighten the bolts to 95 ft. lbs. (129 Nm).
   - Wheel speed sensor, if equipped. Tighten the bolt to 105 inch lbs. (12 Nm).
   - Brake drum
   - Rear wheel

ALL WHEEL DRIVE

1. Before servicing the vehicle, refer to the precautions in the beginning of this section.
2. Remove or disconnect the following:
   - Rear wheel
   - Brake caliper and rotor
   - Wheel speed sensor
   - Axle halfshaft
   - Hub and bearing assembly

To install:
3. Install or connect the following:
   - Hub and bearing assembly. Tighten the bolts to 95 ft. lbs. (129 Nm).
   - Axle halfshaft
   - Wheel speed sensor
   - Brake caliper and rotor
   - Rear wheel

PRECAUTIONS

Before servicing any vehicle, please be sure to read all of the following precautions, which deal with personal safety, prevention of component damage, and important points to take into consideration when servicing a motor vehicle:

• Never open, service or drain the radiator or cooling system when the engine is hot; serious burns can occur from the steam and hot coolant.

• Observe all applicable safety precautions when working around fuel. Whenever servicing the fuel system, always work in a well-ventilated area. Do not allow fuel spray or vapors to come in contact with a spark, open flame, or excessive heat (a hot drop light, for example). Keep a dry chemical fire extinguisher near the work area. Always keep fuel in a container specifically designed for fuel storage; also, always properly seal fuel containers to avoid the possibility of fire or explosion. Refer to the additional fuel system precautions later in this section.

• Fuel injection systems often remain pressurized, even after the engine has been turned **OFF**. The fuel system pressure must be relieved before disconnecting any fuel lines. Failure to do so may result in fire and/or personal injury.

• Brake fluid often contains polyglycol ethers and polyglycols. Avoid contact with the eyes and wash your hands thoroughly after handling brake fluid. If you do get brake fluid in your eyes, flush your eyes with clean, running water for 15 minutes. If eye irritation persists, or if you have taken brake fluid internally, IMMEDIATELY seek medical assistance.

• The EPA warns that prolonged contact with used engine oil may cause a number of skin disorders, including cancer! You should make every effort to minimize your exposure to used engine oil. Protective gloves should be worn when changing oil. Wash your hands and any other exposed skin areas as soon as possible after exposure to used engine oil. Soap and water, or waterless hand cleaner should be used.

• All new vehicles are now equipped with an air bag system, often referred to as a Supplemental Restraint System (SRS) or Supplemental Inflatable Restraint (SIR) system. The system must be disabled before performing service on or around system components, steering column, instrument panel components, wiring and sensors. Failure to follow safety and disabling procedures could result in accidental air bag deployment, possible personal injury and unnecessary system repairs.

• Always wear safety goggles when working with, or around, the air bag system. When carrying a non-deployed air bag, be sure the bag and trim cover are pointed away from your body. When placing a non-deployed air bag on a work surface, always face the bag and trim cover upward, away from the surface. This will reduce the motion of the module if it is accidentally deployed. Refer to the additional air bag system precautions later in this section.

• Clean, high quality brake fluid from a sealed container is essential to the safe and proper operation of the brake system. You should always buy the correct type of brake fluid for your vehicle. If the brake fluid becomes contaminated, completely flush the system with new fluid. Never reuse any brake fluid. Any brake fluid that is removed from the system should be discarded. Also, do not allow any brake fluid to come in contact with a painted surface; it will damage the paint.

• Never operate the engine without the proper amount and type of engine oil; doing so WILL result in severe engine damage.

• Timing belt maintenance is extremely important! Many models utilize an interference-type, non-freewheeling engine. If the timing belt breaks, the valves in the cylinder head may strike the pistons, causing potentially serious (also time-consuming and expensive) engine damage. Refer to the maintenance interval charts in the front of this manual for the recommended replacement interval for the timing belt, and to the timing belt section for belt replacement and inspection.

• Disconnecting the negative battery cable on some vehicles may interfere with the functions of the on-board computer system(s) and may require the computer to undergo a relearning process once the negative battery cable is reconnected.

• When servicing drum brakes, only disassemble and assemble one side at a time, leaving the remaining side intact for reference.

• Only an MVAC-trained, EPA-certified automotive technician should service the air conditioning system or its components.

Ignition Timing

ADJUSTMENT

The ignition timing is controlled by the Powertrain Control Module (PCM) and is not adjustable.

Engine Assembly

REMOVAL & INSTALLATION

Ram Van

1. Before servicing the vehicle, refer to the precautions in the beginning of this section.
2. Drain the cooling system.
3. Recover the A/C refrigerant, if equipped.
4. Drain the engine oil.
5. Relieve the fuel system pressure.
6. Remove or disconnect the following:
   - Negative battery cable
   - Hood
   - Grille
   - Radiator support brace
   - Inside engine cover
   - Air cleaner assembly
   - Transmission oil cooler, if equipped
   - Radiator hoses
   - Heater hoses
   - Radiator and fan shroud
   - A/C condenser
   - Accessory drive belt
   - Power steering pump
   - Air injection pump
   - Intake manifold vacuum lines
   - Washer solvent bottle
   - A/C compressor, if equipped
   - Throttle linkage
   - Engine control sensor harness connectors
   - Alternator
   - Cooling fan
   - Distributor cap and spark plug wires
   - Fuel line
   - Throttle body
   - Fuel supply manifold
   - Intake manifold
   - Exhaust front pipe
   - Starter motor
   - Transmission
   - Engine mounts
   - Engine

To install:

7. Install or connect the following:

- Engine. Tighten the mount bolts to 30 ft. lbs. (41 Nm) and the nuts to 75 ft. lbs. (101 Nm).
- Transmission
- Starter motor
- Exhaust front pipe
- Intake manifold
- Fuel supply manifold
- Throttle body
- Fuel line
- Distributor cap and spark plug wires
- Cooling fan
- Alternator
- Engine control sensor harness connectors
- Throttle linkage
- A/C compressor, if equipped
- Washer solvent bottle
- Intake manifold vacuum lines
- Air injection pump
- Power steering pump
- Accessory drive belt
- A/C condenser
- Radiator and fan shroud
- Heater hoses
- Radiator hoses
- Transmission oil cooler, if equipped
- Air cleaner assembly
- Inside engine cover
- Radiator support brace
- Grille
- Hood
- Negative battery cable

8. Fill the crankcase to the correct level.
9. Fill the cooling system.
10. Start the engine and check for leaks.

Dakota, Durango and Ram Truck

1. Before servicing the vehicle, refer to the precautions in the beginning of this section.
2. Drain the cooling system.
3. Drain the engine oil.
4. Relieve the fuel system pressure.
5. Remove or disconnect the following:
   - Negative battery cable
   - Hood
   - Upper crossmember and top core support
   - Radiator hoses
   - Cooling fan and shroud
   - Radiator
   - Accelerator cable
   - Cruise control cable, if equipped
   - Transmission cable, if equipped
   - Heater hoses
   - Intake manifold vacuum lines

- Accessory drive belt
- Power steering pump
- A/C compressor, if equipped
- Engine control sensor harness connectors
- Engine block heater, if equipped
- Fuel line
- Exhaust front pipe
- Starter motor
- Torque converter, if equipped
- Transmission oil cooler lines, if equipped
- Engine mounts
- Transmission flange bolts. Support the transmission.
- Engine

✷✷ WARNING

Do not lift the engine by the intake manifold. Damage to the manifold may result.

6. Install or connect the following:
   - Engine. Tighten the engine mount bolts to 70 ft. lbs. (95 Nm).
   - Transmission flange bolts. Tighten the bolts to 40–45 ft. lbs. (54–61 Nm).
   - Transmission oil cooler lines, if equipped
   - Torque converter, if equipped. Tighten the bolts to 23 ft. lbs. (31 Nm).
   - Starter motor
   - Exhaust front pipe
   - Fuel line
   - Engine block heater, if equipped
   - Engine control sensor harness connectors
   - A/C compressor, if equipped
   - Power steering pump
   - Accessory drive belt
   - Intake manifold vacuum lines
   - Heater hoses
   - Transmission cable, if equipped
   - Cruise control cable, if equipped
   - Accelerator cable
   - Radiator
   - Cooling fan and shroud
   - Radiator hoses
   - Upper crossmember and top core support
   - Hood
   - Negative battery cable

7. Fill the crankcase to the correct level.
8. Fill the cooling system.
9. Start the engine and check for leaks.

Timing belt service is covered in Section 4 of this manual

Water Pump

REMOVAL & INSTALLATION

2.5L Engine

➡The 2.5L engine uses a reverse rotation water pump. The letter R is stamped on the impeller to identify. Engines from previous years may be equipped with forward rotation water pumps. Installation of the wrong water pump will cause engine over heating.

1. Before servicing the vehicle, refer to the precautions in the beginning of this section.
2. Drain the cooling system.
3. Remove or disconnect the following:
   • Negative battery cable
   • Accessory drive belt
   • Engine cooling fan and pulley

➡Do not store the fan clutch assembly horizontally, silicone may leak into the bearing grease and cause contamination.

   • Power steering pump
   • Lower radiator hose
   • Heater hose
   • Water pump

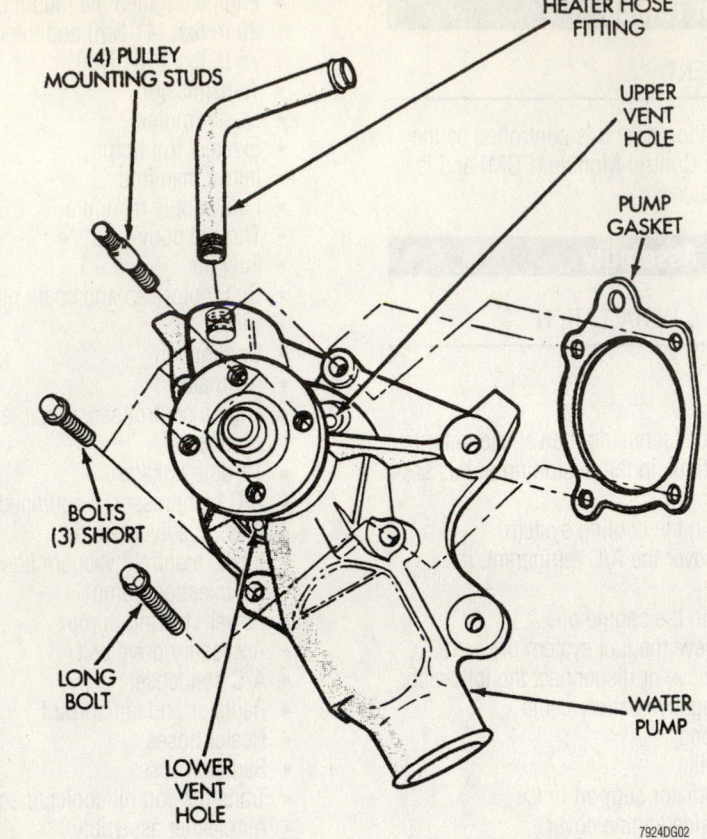

Water pump assembly—2.5L engine

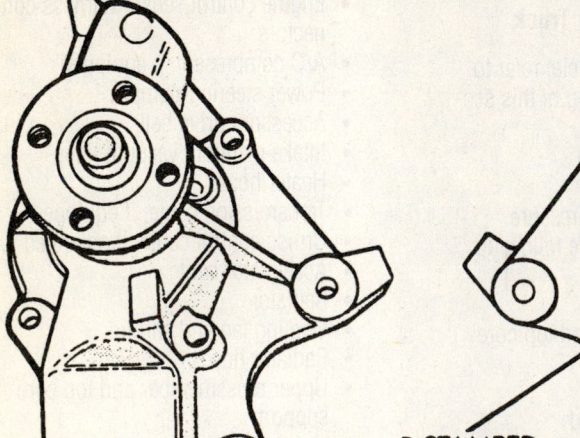

FRONT VIEW

ROTATION DIRECTION AS VIEWED

Reverse rotation water pump—2.5L engine

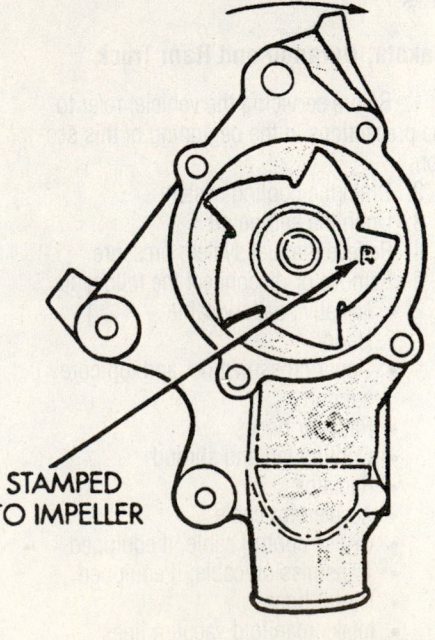

BACK VIEW

ROTATION DIRECTION AS VIEWED

R STAMPED INTO IMPELLER

➡One of the water pump bolts is longer than the others. Note the location for reassembly.

To install:

4. Install or connect the following:
   • Water pump using a new gasket. Tighten the bolts to 17 ft. lbs. (23 Nm).
   • Heater hose
   • Lower radiator hose
   • Power steering pump
   • Engine cooling fan and pulley
   • Accessory drive belt
   • Negative battery cable
5. Fill the cooling system.
6. Run the engine and check for leaks.

4.7L Engine

1. Before servicing the vehicle, refer to the precautions in the beginning of this section.
2. Drain the cooling system.
3. Remove or disconnect the following:
   • Negative battery cable
   • Engine cooling fan and shroud

➡The 4.7L engine is equipped with a fan clutch that threads directly onto the water pump shaft. This fan clutch is equipped with right-hand threads.

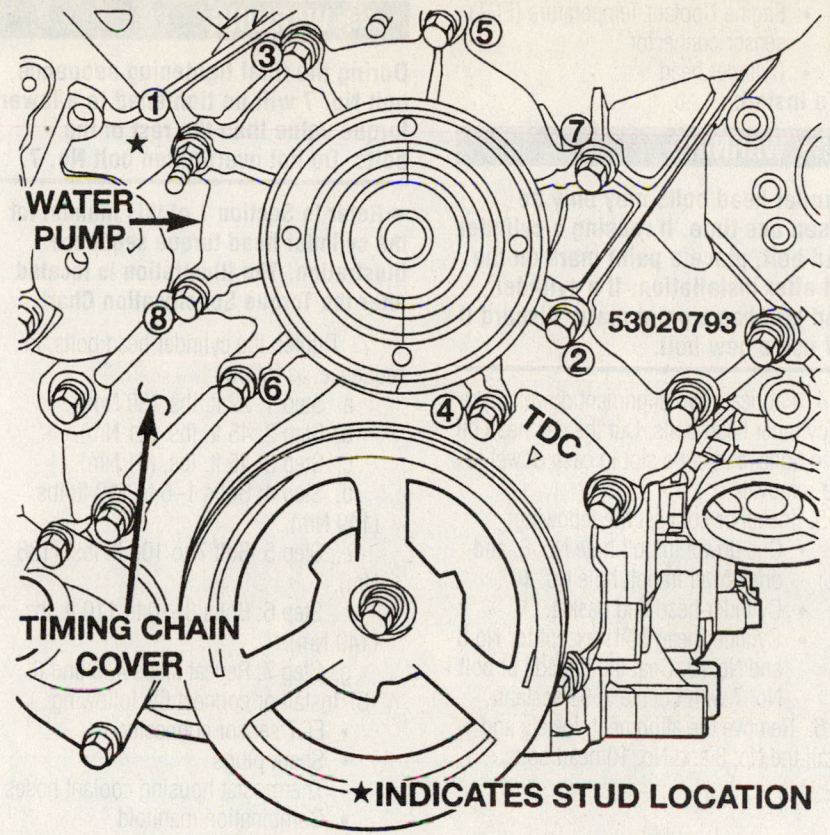

WATER PUMP

TIMING CHAIN COVER

53020793

TDC

★INDICATES STUD LOCATION

9302PG06

Water pump torque sequence—4.7L engine

➡️Do not store the fan clutch assembly horizontally, silicone may leak into the bearing grease and cause contamination.

- Accessory drive belt
- Lower radiator hose
- Water pump

To install:

4. Install the water pump using a new gasket. tighten the bolts in sequence to 40 ft. lbs. (54 Nm).

5. Install or connect the following:
- Lower radiator hose
- Accessory drive belt
- Engine cooling fan and shroud
- Negative battery cable

6. Fill the cooling system.
7. Start the engine and check for leaks.

3.9L, 5.2L and 5.9L Engines

1. Before servicing the vehicle, refer to the precautions in the beginning of this section.

2. Drain the cooling system.
3. Remove or disconnect the following:
- Negative battery cable
- Engine cooling fan and shroud

➡️Do not store the fan clutch assembly horizontally, silicone may leak into the bearing grease and cause contamination.

- Accessory drive belt
- Water pump pulley
- Lower radiator hose
- Heater hose and tube
- Bypass hose
- Water pump

To install:

4. Install or connect the following:
- Water pump, using a new gasket. Tighten the bolts to 30 ft. lbs. (40 Nm).
- Bypass hose
- Heater hose and tube. Use a new O-ring seal.
- Lower radiator hose
- Water pump pulley. Tighten the bolts to 20 ft. lbs. (27 Nm).
- Accessory drive belt
- Engine cooling fan and shroud
- Negative battery cable

5. Fill the cooling system.
6. Start the engine and check for leaks.

8.0L Engine

1. Before servicing the vehicle, refer to the precautions in the beginning of this section.

2. Drain the cooling system.
3. Remove or disconnect the following:
- Negative battery cable
- Washer solvent bottle
- Upper radiator hose

➡️The 8.0L engine is equipped with a fan clutch that threads directly onto the

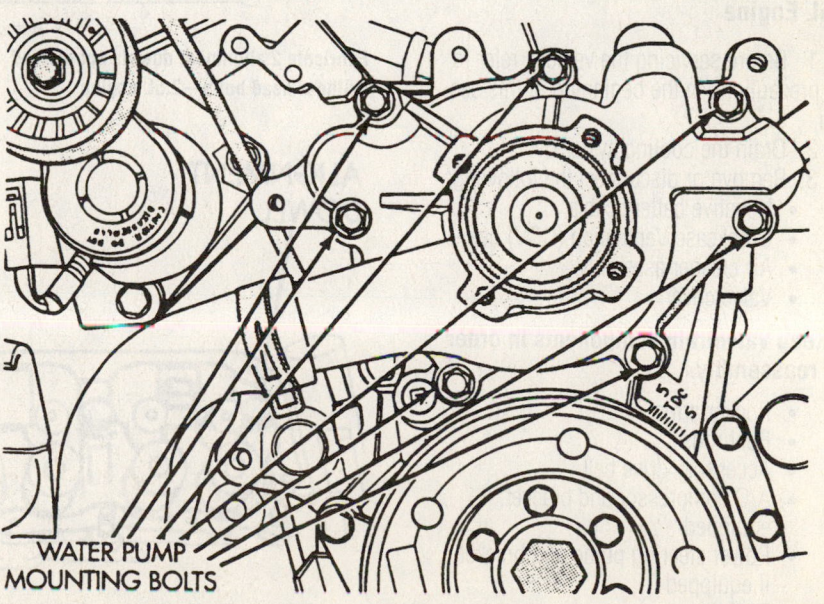

WATER PUMP MOUNTING BOLTS

7924DG03

Water pump mounting bolt locations—3.9L, 5.2L and 5.9L engines, 8.0L engine is similar

water pump shaft. This fan clutch is equipped with right-hand threads.

➡ Do not store the fan clutch assembly horizontally, silicone may leak into the bearing grease and cause contamination.

- Engine cooling fan and shroud
- Accessory drive belt
- Water pump pulley
- Lower radiator hose
- Heater hose
- Bypass hose
- Water pump

To install:

4. Install or connect the following:
   - Water pump. Use a new O-ring seal and tighten the bolts to 30 ft. lbs. (40 Nm).
   - Bypass hose
   - Heater hose
   - Lower radiator hose
   - Water pump pulley. Tighten the bolts to 16 ft. lbs. (22 Nm).
   - Accessory drive belt
   - Engine cooling fan and shroud
   - Upper radiator hose
   - Washer solvent bottle
   - Negative battery cable
5. Fill the cooling system.
6. Start the engine and check for leaks.

Cylinder Head

REMOVAL & INSTALLATION

2.5L Engine

1. Before servicing the vehicle, refer to the precautions in the beginning of this section.
2. Drain the cooling system.
3. Remove or disconnect the following:
   - Negative battery cable
   - Crankcase Ventilation (CCV) hoses
   - Air cleaner assembly
   - Valve cover

➡ Keep valvetrain components in order for reassembly.

- Rocker arms
- Pushrods
- Accessory drive belt
- A/C compressor and bracket, if equipped
- Power steering pump and bracket, if equipped
- Fuel line
- Combination manifold
- Thermostat housing coolant hoses
- Spark plugs

- Engine Coolant Temperature (ECT) sensor connector
- Cylinder head

To install:

✴ WARNING

Cylinder head bolts may only be reused one time. If reusing a cylinder head bolt, place a paint mark on the bolt after installation. If a cylinder head bolt has a paint mark, discard it and use a new bolt.

4. Fabricate two alignment dowels from old cylinder head bolts. Cut the hex head off of the bolts, and cut a slot in each dowel to ease removal.
5. Install or connect the following:
   - One dowel in bolt hole No. 8, and one dowel in bolt hole No. 10.
   - Cylinder head and gasket.
   - Cylinder head bolts except for No 8 and No 10. Coat the threads of bolt No. 7 with Loctite® 592 sealant.
6. Remove the alignment dowels and install the No. 8 and No. 10 head bolts.

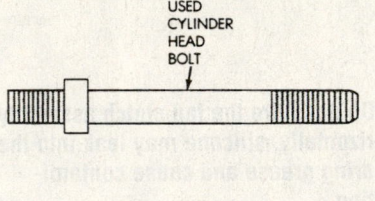
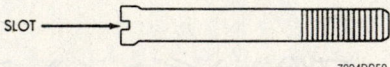

Fabricate 2 alignment dowels out of used cylinder head bolts—2.5L engine

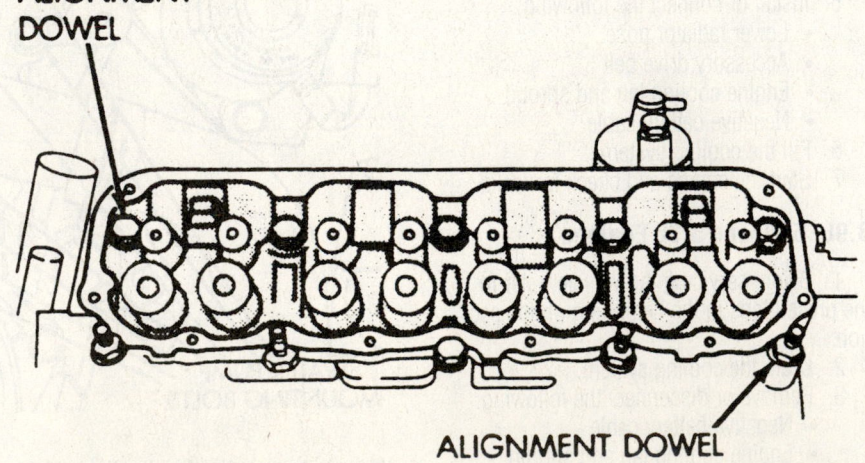

Alignment dowel locations—2.5L engine

✴ WARNING

During the final tightening sequence, bolt No. 7 will be tightened to a lower torque value than the rest of the bolts. Do not overtighten bolt No. 7.

➡ Refer to Section 1 of this manual for the cylinder head torque sequence illustration. The illustration is located after the Torque Specification Chart.

7. Tighten the cylinder head bolts, in sequence, as follows:
   a. Step 1: 22 ft. lbs. (30 Nm).
   b. Step 2: 45 ft. lbs. (61 Nm).
   c. Step 3: 45 ft. lbs. (61 Nm).
   d. Step 4: Bolts 1–6 to 110 ft. lbs. (149 Nm).
   e. Step 5: Bolt 7 to 100 ft. lbs. (136 Nm).
   f. Step 6: Bolts 8–10 to 110 ft. lbs. (149 Nm).
   g. Step 7: Repeat steps 4, 5 and 6.
8. Install or connect the following:
   - ECT sensor connector
   - Spark plugs
   - Thermostat housing coolant hoses
   - Combination manifold
   - Fuel line
   - Power steering pump and bracket, if equipped
   - A/C compressor and bracket, if equipped
   - Accessory drive belt
   - Pushrods and rocker arms in their original positions
   - Valve cover
   - Air cleaner assembly
   - CCV hoses
   - Negative battery cable

9. Fill the cooling system.
10. Start the engine and check for leaks.

3.9L Engine

1. Before servicing the vehicle, refer to the precautions in the beginning of this section.
2. Relieve the fuel pressure.
3. Drain the cooling system.
4. Remove or disconnect the following:
   - Negative battery cable
   - Accessory drive belt
   - Alternator
   - A/C compressor, if equipped
   - Alternator and A/C compressor bracket
   - Air injection pump, if equipped
   - Closed Crankcase Ventilation (CCV) system
   - Air cleaner and hose
   - Fuel line
   - Accelerator linkage
   - Cruise control cable, if equipped
   - Transmission cable, if equipped
   - Spark plug wires
   - Distributor
   - Ignition coil harness connectors
   - Engine Coolant Temperature (ECT) sensor connector
   - Heater hoses
   - Bypass hose
   - Intake manifold vacuum lines
   - Fuel injector harness connectors
   - Valve covers
   - Intake manifold
   - Exhaust front pipe
   - Exhaust manifolds

➡Keep all valvetrain components in order for assembly.

   - Rocker arms
   - Pushrods
   - Cylinder heads

To install:

❋❋ WARNING

Position the crankshaft so that no piston is at Top Dead Center (TDC) prior to installing the cylinder heads. Do not rotate the crankshaft during or immediately after rocker arm installation. Wait 5 minutes for the hydraulic lash adjusters to bleed down.

➡Refer to Section 1 of this manual for the cylinder head torque sequence illustration. The illustration is located after the Torque Specification Chart.

5. Install the cylinder heads with new gaskets. Tighten the bolts in sequence as follows:
   a. Step 1: 50 ft. lbs. (68 Nm).
   b. Step 2: 105 ft. lbs. (143 Nm).
   c. Step 3: 105 ft. lbs. (143 Nm).
6. Install or connect the following:
   - Pushrods in their original locations
   - Rocker arms in their original locations. Tighten the bolts to 21 ft. lbs. (28 Nm).
   - Exhaust manifolds
   - Exhaust front pipe
   - Intake manifold
   - Valve covers
   - Fuel injector harness connectors
   - Intake manifold vacuum lines
   - Bypass hose
   - Heater hoses
   - ECT sensor connector
   - Ignition coil harness connectors
   - Distributor
   - Spark plug wires
   - Transmission cable, if equipped
   - Cruise control cable, if equipped
   - Accelerator linkage
   - Fuel line
   - Air cleaner and hose

   - CCV system
   - Air injection pump, if equipped
   - Alternator and A/C compressor bracket
   - Alternator
   - A/C compressor
   - Accessory drive belt
   - Negative battery cable
7. Fill the cooling system.
8. Start the engine and check for leaks.

4.7L Engine

1. Before servicing the vehicle, refer to the precautions in the beginning of this section.
2. Drain the cooling system.
3. Remove or disconnect the following:
   - Negative battery cable
   - Exhaust Y-pipe
   - Intake manifold
   - Valve covers
   - Engine cooling fan and shroud
   - Accessory drive belt
   - Oil fill housing
   - Power steering pump
   - Rocker arms
4. Rotate the crankshaft so that the crankshaft timing mark aligns with the Top

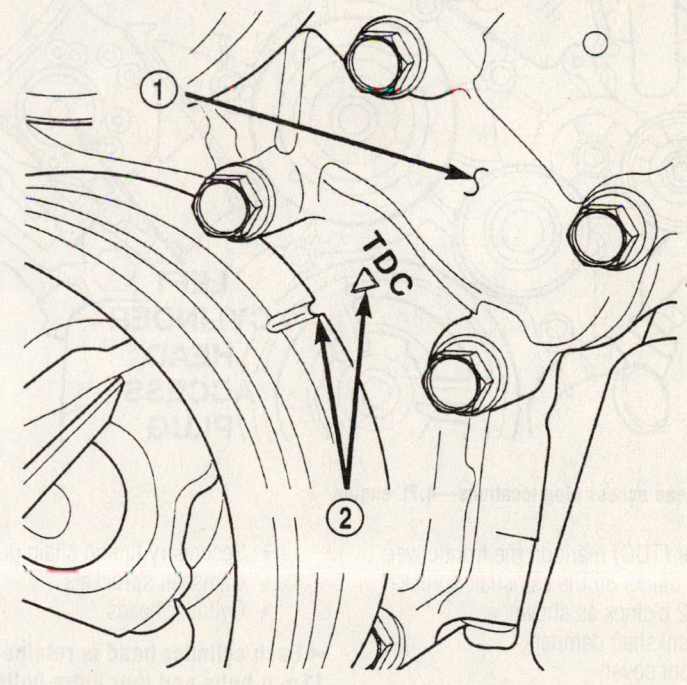

1 – TIMING CHAIN COVER
2 – CRANKSHAFT TIMING MARKS

9308PG04

Crankshaft timing marks—4.7L engine

Refer to Section 1 for engine rebuilding specifications

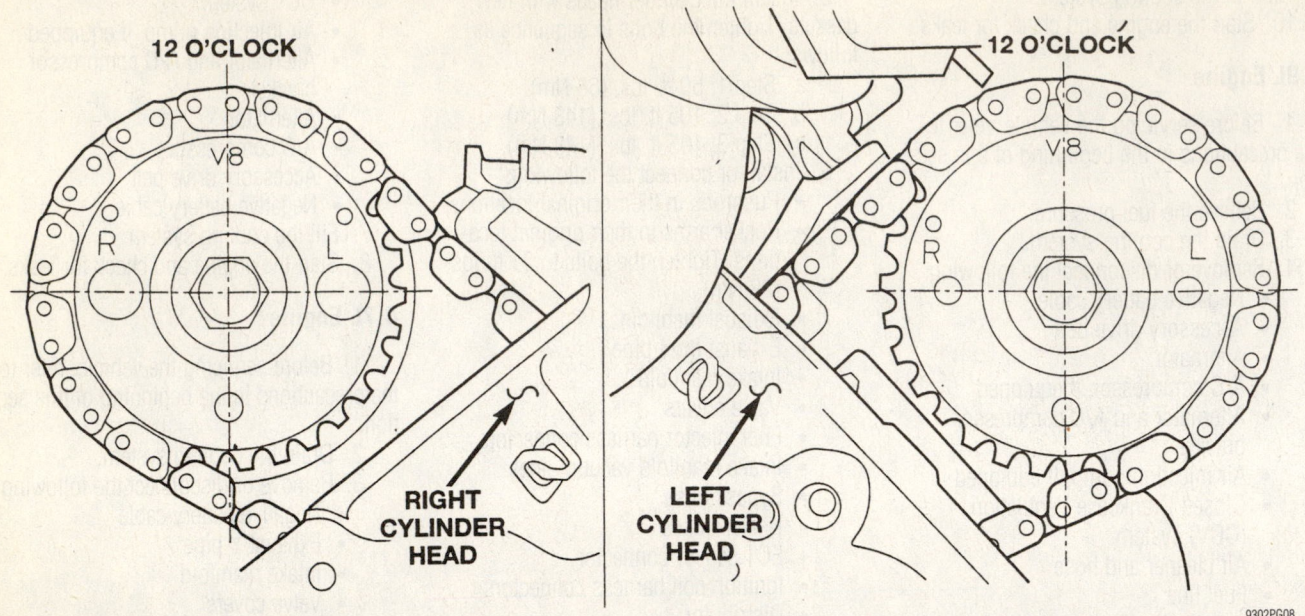

Camshaft positioning—4.7L engine

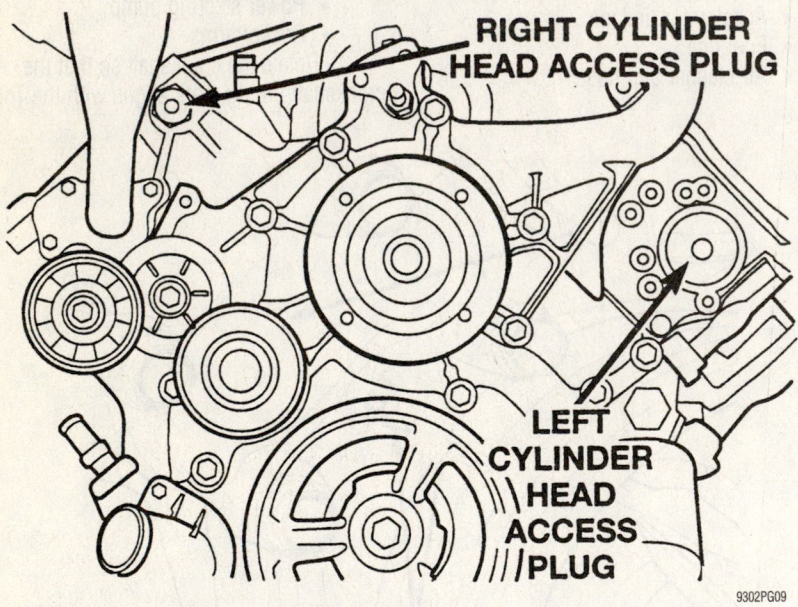

Cylinder head access plug locations—4.7L engine

Dead Center (TDC) mark on the front cover, and the **V8** marks on the camshaft sprockets are at 12 o'clock as shown.

- Crankshaft damper
- Front cover

5. Lock the secondary timing chains to the idler sprocket with Timing Chain Locking tool 8515.

6. Matchmark the secondary timing chains to the camshaft sprockets.

7. Remove or disconnect the following:

- Secondary timing chain tensioners
- Cylinder head access plugs
- Secondary timing chain guides
- Camshaft sprockets
- Cylinder heads

➡**Each cylinder head is retained by ten 11mm bolts and four 8mm bolts.**

To install:

8. Check the cylinder head bolts for signs of stretching and replace as necessary.

9. Lubricate the threads of the 11mm bolts with clean engine oil.

10. Coat the threads of the 8mm bolts with Mopar® Lock and Seal Adhesive.

➡**Refer to Section 1 of this manual for the cylinder head torque sequence illustration. The illustration is located after the Torque Specification Chart.**

11. Install the cylinder heads. Use new gaskets and tighten the bolts, in sequence, as follows:

   a. Step 1: Bolts 1–10 to 15 ft. lbs. (20 Nm).

   b. Step 2: Bolts 1–10 to 35 ft. lbs. (47 Nm).

   c. Step 3: Bolts 11–14 to 18 ft. lbs. (25 Nm).

   d. Step 4: Bolts 1–10 plus ¼ (90 degree) turn.

   e. Step 5: Bolts 11–14 to 22 ft. lbs. (30 Nm).

12. Install or connect the following:

- Camshaft sprockets. Align the secondary chain matchmarks and tighten the bolts to 90 ft. lbs. (122 Nm).
- Secondary timing chain guides
- Cylinder head access plugs
- Secondary timing chain tensioners. Refer to the timing chain procedure in this section.

13. Remove the Timing Chain Locking tool 8515.

14. Install or connect the following:

- Front cover
- Crankshaft damper. Tighten the bolt to 130 ft. lbs. (175 Nm).
- Rocker arms
- Power steering pump
- Oil fill housing
- Accessory drive belt

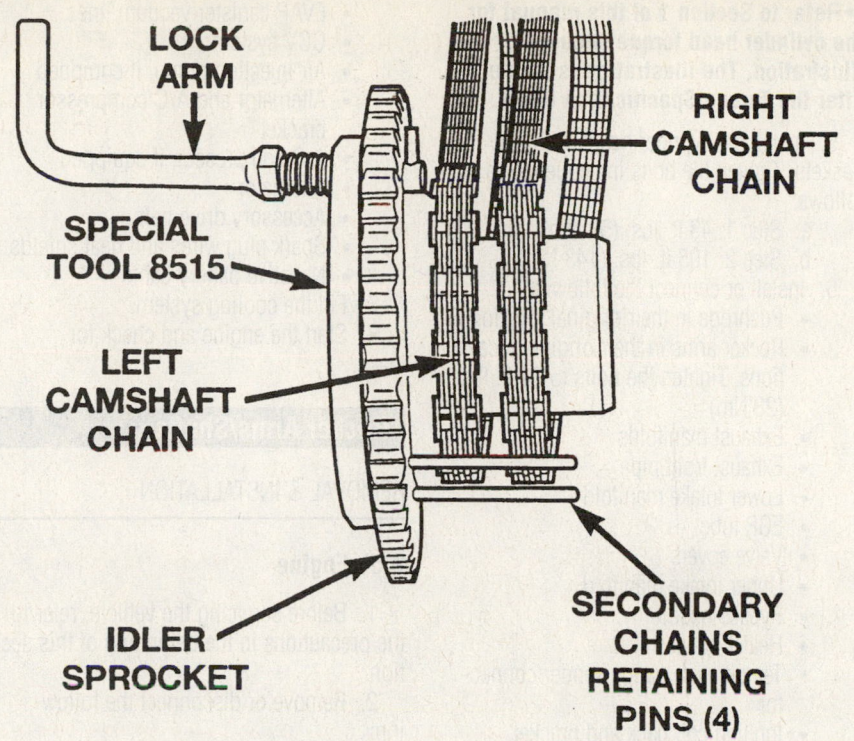

Use the special tool to lock the timing chains on the idler gear—4.7L engine

9302PG07

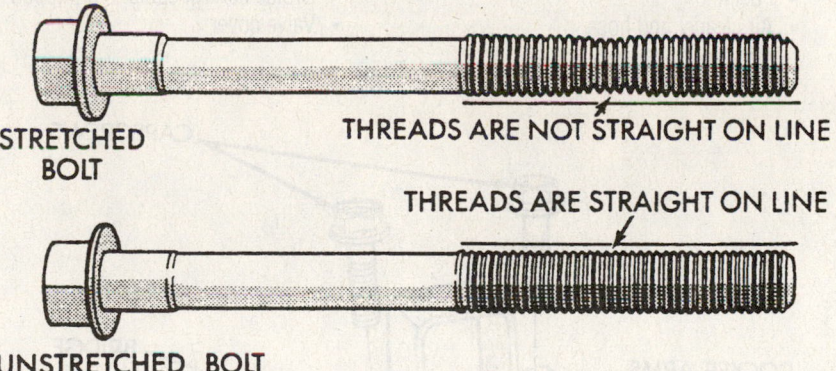

Examine the head bolts for signs of stretching—4.7L engine

9302PG10

- Distributor cap and wires
- Ignition coil wiring
- Engine Coolant Temperature (ECT) sensor connector
- Heater hoses
- Bypass hose
- Upper radiator hose
- Intake manifold
- Valve covers

➡ **Keep valvetrain components in order for reassembly.**

- Rocker arms
- Pushrods
- Exhaust manifolds
- Spark plugs
- Cylinder heads

To install:

✳✳ WARNING

Position the crankshaft so that no piston is at Top Dead Center (TDC) prior to installing the cylinder heads. Do not rotate the crankshaft during or immediately after rocker arm installation. Wait 5 minutes for the hydraulic lash adjusters to bleed down.

➡ **Refer to Section 1 of this manual for the cylinder head torque sequence illustration. The illustration is located after the Torque Specification Chart.**

4. Install the cylinder heads. Use new gaskets and tighten the bolts in sequence as follows:
    a. Step 1: 50 ft. lbs. (68 Nm).
    b. Step 2: 105 ft. lbs. (143 Nm).
    c. Step 3: 105 ft. lbs. (143 Nm).

5. Install or connect the following:
- Spark plugs
- Exhaust manifolds
- Pushrods and rocker arms in their original positions
- Valve covers
- Intake manifold
- Upper radiator hose
- Bypass hose
- Heater hoses
- ECT sensor connector
- Ignition coil wiring
- Distributor cap and wires
- Transmission cable
- Cruise control cable
- Accelerator linkage
- Fuel line
- Evaporative emissions control system
- CCV system

- Engine cooling fan and shroud
- Valve covers
- Intake manifold
- Exhaust Y-pipe
- Negative battery cable
15. Fill the cooling system.
16. Start the engine and check for leaks.

5.2L and 5.9L Engines

1. Before servicing the vehicle, refer to the precautions in the beginning of this section.
2. Drain the cooling system.
3. Remove or disconnect the following:

- Negative battery cable
- Accessory drive belt
- Alternator
- A/C compressor, if equipped
- Air injection pump, if equipped
- Air cleaner assembly
- Closed Crankcase Ventilation (CCV) system
- Evaporative emissions control system
- Fuel line
- Accelerator linkage
- Cruise control cable
- Transmission cable

- Air cleaner assembly
- A/C compressor, if equipped
- Air injection pump, if equipped
- Alternator
- Accessory drive belt
- Negative battery cable

6. Fill the cooling system.
7. Start the engine and check for leaks.

8.0L Engine

1. Before servicing the vehicle, refer to the precautions in the beginning of this section.
2. Drain the cooling system.
3. Relieve the fuel system pressure.
4. Remove or disconnect the following:

- Negative battery cable
- Spark plug wires and heat shields
- Accessory drive belt
- Alternator
- A/C compressor, if equipped
- Alternator and A/C compressor bracket
- Air injection pump, if equipped
- Closed Crankcase Ventilation (CCV) system
- Evaporative Emissions (EVAP) canister vacuum lines
- Air cleaner and hose
- Fuel line
- Accelerator linkage
- Cruise control cable, if equipped
- Transmission cable, if equipped
- Ignition coil pack and bracket
- Temperature gauge sender connector
- Heater hoses
- Bypass hose
- Upper intake manifold
- Valve covers
- Exhaust Gas Recirculation (EGR) tube
- Lower intake manifold
- Exhaust front pipe
- Exhaust manifolds

➡Keep all valvetrain components in order for assembly.

- Rocker arms
- Pushrods
- Cylinder heads

To install:

❋❋ WARNING

Position the crankshaft so that no piston is at Top Dead Center (TDC) prior to installing the cylinder heads. Do not rotate the crankshaft during or immediately after rocker arm installation. Wait 5 minutes for the hydraulic lash adjusters to bleed down.

➡**Refer to Section 1 of this manual for the cylinder head torque sequence illustration. The illustration is located after the Torque Specification Chart.**

5. Install the cylinder heads with new gaskets. Tighten the bolts in sequence as follows:

   a. Step 1: 43 ft. lbs. (58 Nm).
   b. Step 2: 105 ft. lbs. (143 Nm).

6. Install or connect the following:

- Pushrods in their original locations
- Rocker arms in their original locations. Tighten the bolts to 21 ft. lbs. (28 Nm).
- Exhaust manifolds
- Exhaust front pipe
- Lower intake manifold
- EGR tube
- Valve covers
- Upper intake manifold
- Bypass hose
- Heater hoses
- Temperature gauge sender connector
- Ignition coil pack and bracket
- Transmission cable, if equipped
- Cruise control cable, if equipped
- Accelerator linkage
- Fuel line
- Air cleaner and hose

- EVAP canister vacuum lines
- CCV system
- Air injection pump, if equipped
- Alternator and A/C compressor bracket
- A/C compressor, if equipped
- Alternator
- Accessory drive belt
- Spark plug wires and heat shields
- Negative battery cable

7. Fill the cooling system.
8. Start the engine and check for leaks.

Rocker Arms/Shafts

REMOVAL & INSTALLATION

2.5L Engine

1. Before servicing the vehicle, refer to the precautions in the beginning of this section.
2. Remove or disconnect the following:

- Negative battery cable
- Accelerator cable
- Transmission cable, if equipped
- Cruise control cable, if equipped
- Valve cover

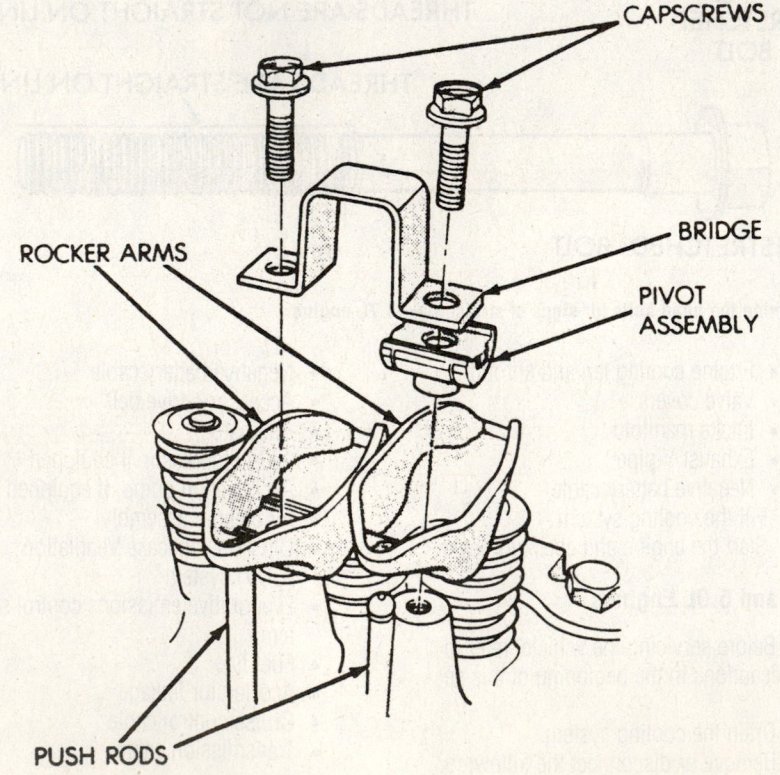

Exploded view of the rocker arm mounting—2.5L engine

7924DG54

- Rocker arm bolts, loosen them evenly to avoid damaging the alignment bridges
- Rocker arms

➡**Keep valvetrain components in order for reassembly.**

To install:

3. Install or connect the following:
- Rocker arms, pivots and bridges in their original positions. Tighten the bolts for each bridged pair one turn at a time to 21 ft. lbs. (28 Nm).
- Valve cover
- Cruise control cable, if equipped
- Transmission cable, if equipped
- Accelerator cable
- Negative battery cable

3.9L Engine

1. Before servicing the vehicle, refer to the precautions in the beginning of this section.

2. Remove or disconnect the following:
- Negative battery cable
- Valve covers
- Rocker arms

➡**Keep all valvetrain components in order for assembly.**

To install:

3. Rotate the crankshaft so that the **V6** mark on the crankshaft damper aligns with the timing mark on the front cover. The **V6** mark is located 147 degrees **AFTER** Top Dead Center (TDC).

4. Install the rocker arms in their original positions and tighten the bolts to 21 ft. lbs. (28 Nm).

✳✳ CAUTION

Do not rotate the crankshaft during or immediately after rocker arm installation. Wait 5 minutes for the hydraulic lash adjusters to bleed down.

5. Install or connect the following:
- Valve covers
- Negative battery cable

4.7L Engine

1. Before servicing the vehicle, refer to the precautions in the beginning of this section.

2. Remove or disconnect the following:

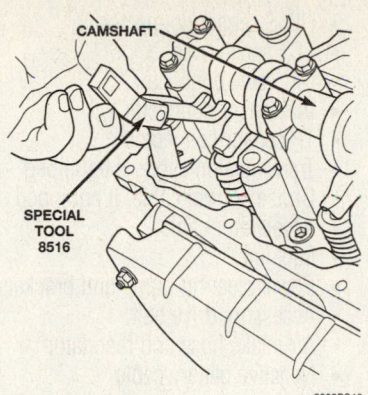

Rocker arm service—4.7L engine

- Negative battery cable
- Valve covers

3. Rotate the crankshaft so that the piston of the cylinder to be serviced is at Bottom Dead Center (BDC) and both valves are closed.

4. Use special tool 8516 to depress the valve and remove the rocker arm.

5. Repeat for each rocker arm to be serviced.

➡**Keep valvetrain components in order for reassembly.**

To install:

6. Rotate the crankshaft so that the piston of the cylinder to be serviced is at BDC.

7. Compress the valve spring and install each rocker arm in its original position.

8. Repeat for each rocker arm to be installed.

9. Install or connect the following:
- Cylinder head cover
- Negative battery cable

5.2L and 5.9L Engines

1. Before servicing the vehicle, refer to the precautions in the beginning of this section.

2. Remove or disconnect the following:
- Negative battery cable
- Valve covers
- Rocker arms

➡**Keep valvetrain components in order for reassembly.**

To install:

3. Rotate the crankshaft so that the **V8** mark on the crankshaft damper aligns with the timing mark on the front cover. The **V8** mark is located 147 degrees **AFTER** Top Dead Center (TDC).

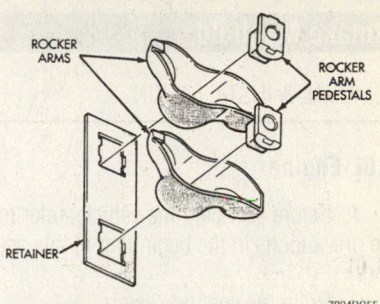

Exploded view of the rocker arm assembly—8.0L engine

4. Install the rocker arms in their original positions and tighten the bolts to 21 ft. lbs. (28 Nm).

✳✳ CAUTION

Do not rotate the crankshaft during or immediately after rocker arm installation. Wait 5 minutes for the hydraulic lash adjusters to bleed down.

5. Install or connect the following:
- Valve covers
- Negative battery cable

8.0L Engine

1. Before servicing the vehicle, refer to the precautions in the beginning of this section.

2. Remove or disconnect the following:
- Negative battery cable
- Valve covers
- Rocker arms

➡**Keep valvetrain components in order for reassembly.**

To install:

✳✳ CAUTION

When installing the rocker arms, ensure that the piston is not at Top Dead Center. Tighten the rocker arm bolts slowly. Do not rotate the crankshaft during or immediately after rocker arm installation. Wait 5 minutes for the hydraulic lash adjusters to bleed down.

3. Install or connect the following:
- Rocker arms in their original positions. Tighten the bolts to 21 ft. lbs. (28 Nm).
- Valve covers
- Negative battery cable

For complete mechanical specifications, refer to Section 1 of this manual

Intake Manifold

REMOVAL & INSTALLATION

2.5L Engine

1. Before servicing the vehicle, refer to the precautions in the beginning of this section.
2. Drain the cooling system.
3. Relieve the fuel system pressure.
4. Remove or disconnect the following:
   - Negative battery cable
   - Air intake hose and resonator
   - Accessory drive belt
   - Power steering pump and brackets
   - Fuel line
   - Accelerator cable
   - Cruise control cable, if equipped
   - Transmission cable, if equipped
   - Throttle Position (TP) sensor connector
   - Intake Air Temperature (IAT) sensor connector
   - Idle Air Control (IAC) valve connector
   - Engine Coolant Temperature (ECT) sensor connector
   - Heated Oxygen (HO2S) sensor connector
   - Fuel injector harness connectors
   - Manifold Absolute Pressure (MAP) sensor vacuum line
   - Closed Crankcase Ventilation (CCV) hose
   - Intake manifold vacuum hoses
   - Molded vacuum hose harness
5. Remove bolts 2–5. Loosen bolt No. 1 and nuts 6–7.
6. Remove the intake manifold.

To install:

➡ **Refer to Section 1 of this manual for the intake manifold torque sequence illustration. The illustration is located after the Torque Specification Chart.**

7. Install the intake manifold with a new gasket. Tighten the fasteners in sequence as follows:
   a. Step 1: Tighten bolt No. 1 to 30 ft. lbs. (41 Nm)
   b. Step 2: Tighten bolts 2–5 to 23 ft. lbs. (31 Nm)
   c. Step 3: Tighten nuts 6–7 to 17 ft. lbs. (23 Nm)
8. Install or connect the following:
   - Molded vacuum hose harness
   - Intake manifold vacuum hoses
   - CCV hose
   - MAP sensor vacuum line
   - Fuel injector harness connectors

- HO2S sensor connector
- ECT sensor connector
- IAC valve connector
- IAT sensor connector
- TP sensor connector
- Transmission cable, if equipped
- Cruise control cable, if equipped
- Accelerator cable
- Fuel line
- Power steering pump and brackets
- Accessory drive belt
- Air intake hose and resonator
- Negative battery cable

9. Fill the cooling system.
10. Start the engine and check for leaks.

3.9L Engine

1. Before servicing the vehicle, refer to the precautions in the beginning of this section.
2. Drain the cooling system.
3. Remove or disconnect the following:
   - Negative battery cable
   - Accessory drive belt
   - Alternator
   - A/C compressor
   - Alternator and A/C compressor bracket
   - Air cleaner assembly
   - Fuel line
   - Fuel supply manifold
   - Accelerator cable
   - Transmission cable
   - Cruise control cable
   - Distributor cap and wires
   - Ignition coil wiring
   - Engine Coolant Temperature (ECT) sensor connector
   - Heater hose
   - Upper radiator hose
   - Bypass hose
   - Closed Crankcase Ventilation (CCV) system
   - Evaporative emissions system
   - Intake manifold

To install:

➡ **Refer to Section 1 of this manual for the intake manifold torque sequence illustration. The illustration is located after the Torque Specification Chart.**

4. Install the intake manifold. Use a new gasket and tighten the bolts in sequence as follows:
   a. Step 1: Bolts 1–2 to 72 inch lbs. (8 Nm) using 12 inch lb. (1.4 Nm) increments.
   b. Step 2: Bolts 3–12 to 72 inch lbs. (8 Nm).
   c. Step 3: Bolts 1–12 to 72 inch lbs. (8 Nm).

   d. Step 4: Bolts 1–12 to 12 ft. lbs. (16 Nm).
   e. Step 5: Bolts 1–12 to 12 ft. lbs. (16 Nm).
5. Install or connect the following:
   - Evaporative emissions system
   - CCV system
   - Bypass hose
   - Upper radiator hose
   - Heater hose
   - ECT sensor connector
   - Ignition coil wiring
   - Distributor cap and wires
   - Cruise control cable
   - Transmission cable
   - Accelerator cable
   - Fuel supply manifold
   - Fuel line
   - Air cleaner assembly
   - Alternator and A/C compressor bracket
   - A/C compressor
   - Alternator
   - Accessory drive belt
   - Negative battery cable
6. Fill the cooling system.
7. Start the engine and check for leaks.

4.7L Engine

1. Before servicing the vehicle, refer to the precautions in the beginning of this section.
2. Drain the cooling system.
3. Remove or disconnect the following:
   - Negative battery cable
   - Air cleaner assembly
   - Accelerator cable
   - Cruise control cable
   - Manifold Absolute Pressure (MAP) sensor connector
   - Intake Air Temperature (IAT) sensor connector
   - Throttle Position (TP) sensor connector
   - Idle Air Control (IAC) valve connector
   - Engine Coolant Temperature (ECT) sensor
   - Positive Crankcase Ventilation (PCV) valve and hose
   - Canister purge vacuum line
   - Brake booster vacuum line
   - Cruise control servo hose
   - Accessory drive belt
   - Alternator
   - A/C compressor
   - Engine ground straps
   - Ignition coil towers
   - Oil dipstick tube

- Fuel line
- Fuel supply manifold
- Throttle body and mounting bracket
- Cowl seal
- Right engine lifting stud
- Intake manifold. Remove the fasteners in reverse of the tightening sequence.

To install:

➡ **Refer to Section 1 of this manual for the intake manifold torque sequence illustration. The illustration is located after the Torque Specification Chart.**

4. Install or connect the following:
   - Intake manifold using new gaskets. Tighten the bolts, in sequence, to 105 inch lbs. (12 Nm).
   - Right engine lifting stud
   - Cowl seal
   - Throttle body and mounting bracket
   - Fuel supply manifold
   - Fuel line
   - Oil dipstick tube
   - Ignition coil towers
   - Engine ground straps
   - A/C compressor
   - Alternator
   - Accessory drive belt
   - Cruise control servo hose
   - Brake booster vacuum line
   - Canister purge vacuum line
   - PCV valve and hose
   - ECT sensor
   - IAC valve connector
   - TP sensor connector
   - IAT sensor connector
   - MAP sensor connector
   - Cruise control cable
   - Accelerator cable
   - Air cleaner assembly
   - Negative battery cable
5. Fill the cooling system.
6. Start the engine and check for leaks.

5.2L and 5.9L Engines

1. Before servicing the vehicle, refer to the precautions in the beginning of this section.
2. Drain the cooling system.
3. Remove or disconnect the following:
   - Negative battery cable
   - Accessory drive belt
   - Alternator
   - A/C compressor
   - Alternator and A/C compressor bracket
   - Air cleaner assembly

- Fuel line
- Fuel supply manifold
- Accelerator cable
- Transmission cable
- Cruise control cable
- Distributor cap and wires
- Ignition coil wiring
- Engine Coolant Temperature (ECT) sensor connector
- Heater hose
- Upper radiator hose
- Bypass hose
- Closed Crankcase Ventilation (CCV) system
- Evaporative emissions system
- Intake manifold

To install:

➡ **Refer to Section 1 of this manual for the intake manifold torque sequence illustration. The illustration is located after the Torque Specification Chart.**

4. Install the intake manifold. Use a new gasket and tighten the bolts in sequence as follows:
   a. Step 1: Bolts 1–4 to 72 inch lbs. (8 Nm) using 12 inch lb. (1.4 Nm) increments.
   b. Step 2: Bolts 5–12 to 72 inch lbs. (8 Nm).
   c. Step 3: Bolts 1–12 to 72 inch lbs. (8 Nm).
   d. Step 4: Bolts 1–12 to 12 ft. lbs. (16 Nm).
   e. Step 5: Bolts 1–12 to 12 ft. lbs. (16 Nm).
5. Install or connect the following:
   - Evaporative emissions system
   - CCV system
   - Bypass hose
   - Upper radiator hose
   - Heater hose
   - ECT sensor connector
   - Ignition coil wiring
   - Distributor cap and wires
   - Cruise control cable
   - Transmission cable
   - Accelerator cable
   - Fuel supply manifold
   - Fuel line
   - Air cleaner assembly
   - Alternator and A/C compressor bracket
   - A/C compressor
   - Alternator
   - Accessory drive belt
   - Negative battery cable
6. Fill the cooling system.
7. Start the engine and check for leaks.

8.0L Engines

1. Before servicing the vehicle, refer to the precautions in the beginning of this section.
2. Drain the cooling system.
3. Relieve the fuel system pressure.
   - Negative battery cable
   - Accessory drive belt
   - Alternator and brace
   - A/C compressor and brace
   - Air cleaner housing
   - Fuel line
   - Accelerator linkage
   - cruise control cable, if equipped
   - Transmission cable, if equipped
   - Ignition coil pack and spark plug wires
   - Intake manifold vacuum lines
   - Engine control sensor harness connectors
   - Heater hoses
   - Bypass hose
   - Evaporative Emissions (EVAP) system
   - Closed Crankcase Ventilation (CCV) system
   - Throttle body
   - Upper intake manifold
   - Lower intake manifold

To install:

➡ **Refer to Section 1 of this manual for the intake manifold torque sequence illustration. The illustration is located after the Torque Specification Chart.**

4. Install or connect the following:
   - Lower intake manifold. Tighten the bolts in sequence to 40 ft. lbs. (54 Nm).
   - Upper intake manifold. Tighten the bolts in sequence to 16 ft. lbs. (22 Nm).
   - Throttle body. Tighten the bolts to 17 ft. lbs. (23 Nm).
   - CCV system
   - EVAP system
   - Bypass hose
   - Heater hoses
   - Engine control sensor harness connectors
   - Intake manifold vacuum lines
   - Ignition coil pack and spark plug wires
   - Transmission cable, if equipped
   - cruise control cable, if equipped
   - Accelerator linkage
   - Fuel line
   - Air cleaner housing
   - A/C compressor and brace

Please refer to Section 8 for electric cooling fan wiring schematics

- Alternator and brace
- Accessory drive belt
- Negative battery cable
5. Fill the cooling system.
6. Start the engine and check for leaks.

Exhaust Manifold

REMOVAL & INSTALLATION

2.5L Engine

1. Before servicing the vehicle, refer to the precautions in the beginning of this section.
2. Remove or disconnect the following:
   - Negative battery cable
   - Exhaust front pipe
   - Intake manifold
   - Exhaust manifold

To install:

➡Refer to Section 1 of this manual for the intake manifold torque sequence illustration. The illustration is located after the Torque Specification Chart.

3. Install or connect the following:
   - Exhaust manifold
   - Intake manifold
   - Exhaust front pipe
   - Negative battery cable
4. Start the engine and check for leaks.

3.9L Engine

1. Before servicing the vehicle, refer to the precautions in the beginning of this section.

2. Remove or disconnect the following:
   - Negative battery cable
   - Heated Oxygen (HO2S) sensor connectors
   - Exhaust manifold heat shields
   - Exhaust front pipe
   - Exhaust manifolds

To install:

➡If the exhaust manifold studs came out with the nuts when removing the exhaust manifolds, replace them with new studs.

3. Install or connect the following:
   - Exhaust manifolds. Tighten the fasteners to 25 ft. lbs. (34 Nm), starting with the center fasteners and working out to the ends.
   - Exhaust front pipe
   - Exhaust manifold heat shields
   - HO2S sensor connectors
   - Negative battery cable
4. Start the engine and check for leaks.

4.7L Engine

1. Before servicing the vehicle, refer to the precautions in the beginning of this section.
2. Drain the cooling system.
3. Remove or disconnect the following:
   - Battery
   - Power distribution center
   - Battery tray
   - Windshield washer fluid bottle
   - Air cleaner assembly
   - Accessory drive belt
   - A/C compressor

- A/C accumulator bracket
- Heater hoses
- Exhaust manifold heat shields
- Exhaust Y-pipe
- Starter motor
- Exhaust manifolds

To install:

4. Install or connect the following:
   - Exhaust manifolds, using new gaskets. Tighten the bolts to 18 ft. lbs. (25 Nm), starting with the inner bolts and work out to the ends.
   - Starter motor
   - Exhaust Y-pipe
   - Exhaust manifold heat shields
   - Heater hoses
   - A/C accumulator bracket
   - A/C compressor
   - Accessory drive belt
   - Air cleaner assembly
   - Windshield washer fluid bottle
   - Battery tray
   - Power distribution center
   - Battery
5. Fill the cooling system.
6. Start the engine and check for leaks.

5.2L and 5.9L Engines

1. Before servicing the vehicle, refer to the precautions in the beginning of this section.
2. Remove or disconnect the following:
   - Negative battery cable
   - Exhaust manifold heat shields
   - Exhaust Gas Recirculation (EGR) tube
   - Exhaust Y-pipe
   - Exhaust manifolds

To install:

➡If the exhaust manifold studs came out with the nuts when removing the exhaust manifolds, replace them with new studs.

3. Install or connect the following:
   - Exhaust manifolds. Tighten the fasteners to 20 ft. lbs. (27 Nm), start-

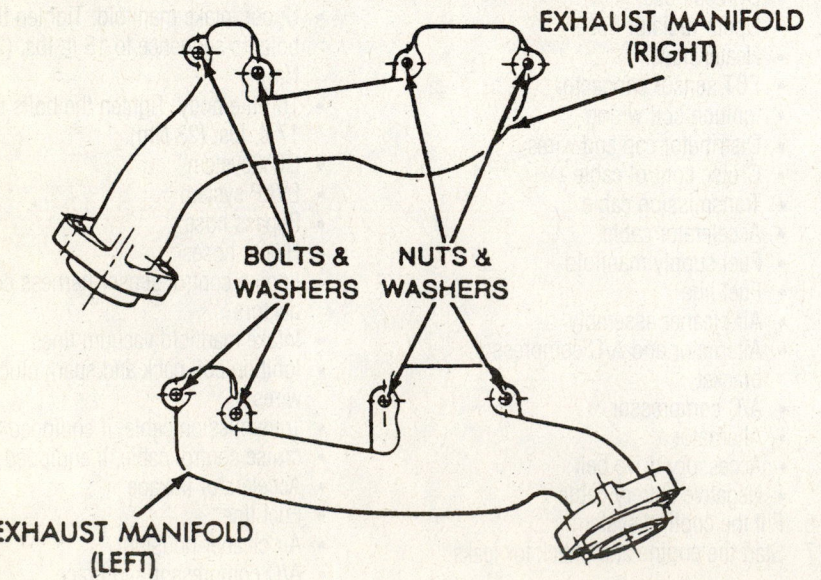

BOLTS & WASHERS   NUTS & WASHERS

EXHAUST MANIFOLD (RIGHT)

EXHAUST MANIFOLD (LEFT)

7924DG57

Stud and bolt locations—3.9L engine

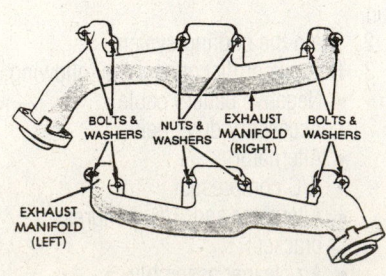

BOLTS & WASHERS   NUTS & WASHERS   EXHAUST MANIFOLD (RIGHT)   BOLTS & WASHERS

EXHAUST MANIFOLD (LEFT)

7924DG58

Exhaust manifold fastener locations—5.2L and 5.9L engines

ing with the center nuts and work out to the ends.

- Exhaust Y-pipe
- EGR tube
- Exhaust manifold heat shields
- Negative battery cable

4. Fill the cooling system.
5. Start the engine and check for leaks.

8.0L Engine

1. Before servicing the vehicle, refer to the precautions in the beginning of this section.
2. Remove or disconnect the following:
   - Negative battery cable
   - Exhaust front pipe
   - Exhaust manifold heat shields
   - Exhaust Gas Recirculation (EGR) tube
   - Oil dipstick tube bracket
   - Exhaust manifolds

To install:

3. Install or connect the following:
   - Exhaust manifolds. Tighten the fasteners to 16 ft. lbs. (22 Nm).
   - Oil dipstick tube bracket
   - EGR tube

- Exhaust manifold heat shields
- Exhaust front pipe
- Negative battery cable

4. Start the engine and check for leaks.

Camshaft and Valve Lifters

REMOVAL & INSTALLATION

2.5L Engine

1. Before servicing the vehicle, refer to the precautions in the beginning of this section.
2. Drain the cooling system.
3. Recover the A/C refrigerant, if equipped with air conditioning.
4. Remove or disconnect the following:
   - Negative battery cable
   - Grille, if necessary
   - Radiator
   - A/C condenser, if equipped
   - Distributor
   - Valve cover

➡ **Keep all valvetrain components in order for assembly.**

- Rocker arms and pushrods
- Hydraulic valve tappets
- Accessory drive belt
- Crankshaft damper
- Front cover
- Timing chain and gears
- Camshaft

To install:

➡ **If the camshaft sprocket appears to have been rubbing against the cover, check the oil pressure relief holes in the rear cam journal for debris.**

5. Lubricate the camshaft with clean engine oil.
6. Install or connect the following:
   - Camshaft
   - Timing chain and gears
   - Front cover
   - Crankshaft damper
   - Accessory drive belt
   - Hydraulic valve tappets
   - Rocker arms and pushrods
   - Valve cover
   - Distributor
   - A/C condenser, if equipped
   - Radiator
   - Grille, if removed
   - Negative battery cable
7. Fill the cooling system.
8. Recharge the A/C system, if equipped.
9. Start the engine and check for leaks.

4.7L Engine

1. Before servicing the vehicle, refer to the precautions in the beginning of this section.
2. Remove or disconnect the following:
   - Negative battery cable
   - Cylinder head covers
   - Rocker arms
   - Hydraulic lash adjusters

➡ **Keep all valvetrain components in order for assembly.**

3. Set the engine at Top Dead Center (TDC) of the compression stroke for the No. 1 cylinder.
4. Install Timing Chain Wedge 8350 to retain the chain tensioners.
5. Matchmark the timing chains to the camshaft sprockets.
6. Install Camshaft Holding Tool 6958 and Adapter Pins 8346 to the left camshaft sprocket.
7. Remove or disconnect the following:
   - Right camshaft timing sprocket and target wheel

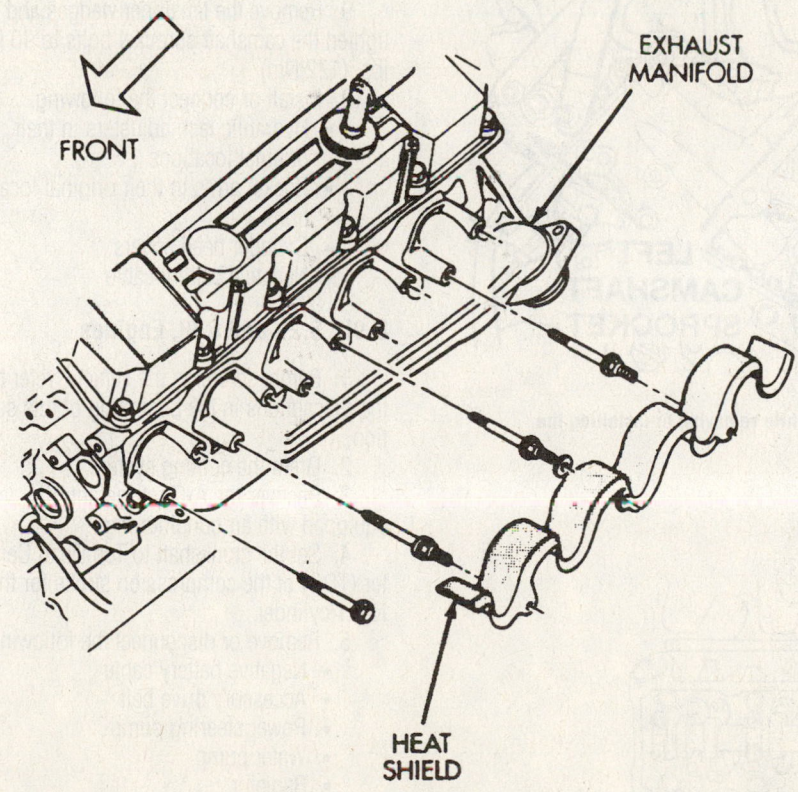

FRONT

EXHAUST MANIFOLD

HEAT SHIELD

7924DG14

Exhaust manifold fastener locations—8.0L engine

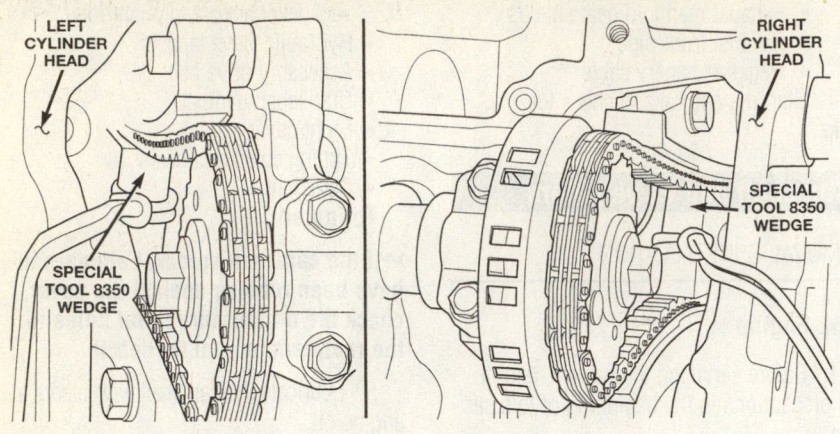

Chain Tensioner Retaining Wedges—4.7L engine

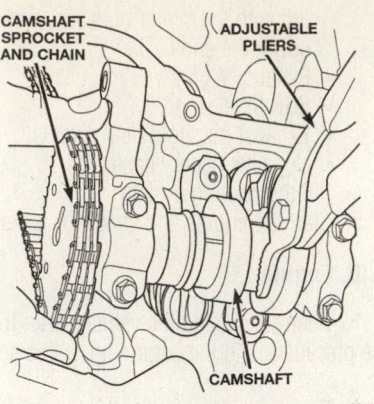

Turn the camshaft with pliers, if needed, to align the dowel in the sprocket—4.7L engine

- Left camshaft sprocket
- Camshaft bearing caps, by reversing the tightening sequence
- Camshafts

To install:

8. Install or connect the following:
   - Camshafts. Tighten the bearing cap bolts in ½ turn increments, in sequence, to 100 inch lbs. (11 Nm).
   - Target wheel to the right camshaft
   - Camshaft timing sprockets and chains, by aligning the matchmarks

9. Remove the tensioner wedges and tighten the camshaft sprocket bolts to 90 ft. lbs. (122 Nm).

10. Install or connect the following:
    - Hydraulic lash adjusters in their original locations
    - Rocker arms in their original locations
    - Cylinder head covers
    - Negative battery cable

3.9L, 5.2L and 5.9L Engines

1. Before servicing the vehicle, refer to the precautions in the beginning of this section.

2. Drain the cooling system.

3. Recover the A/C refrigerant, if equipped with air conditioning.

4. Set the crankshaft to Top Dead Center (TDC) of the compression stroke for the No. 1 cylinder.

5. Remove or disconnect the following:
   - Negative battery cable
   - Accessory drive belt
   - Power steering pump
   - Water pump
   - Radiator
   - A/C condenser
   - Grille
   - Crankshaft damper
   - Front cover

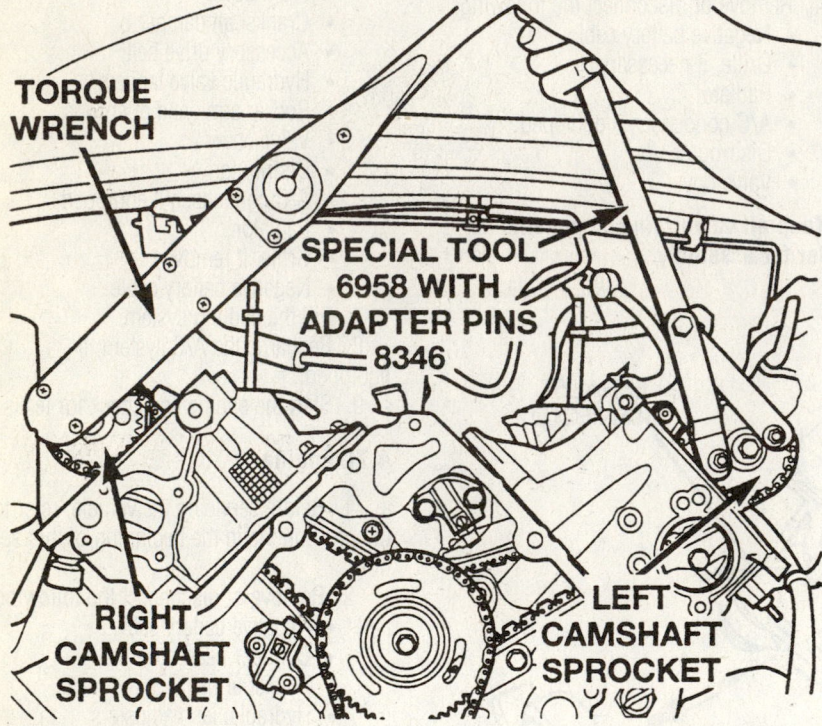

Hold the left camshaft sprocket with a spanner wrench while removing or installing the camshaft sprocket bolts—4.7L engine

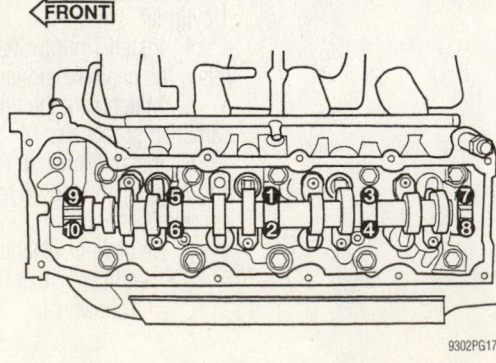

Camshaft bearing cap bolt tightening sequence—4.7L engine

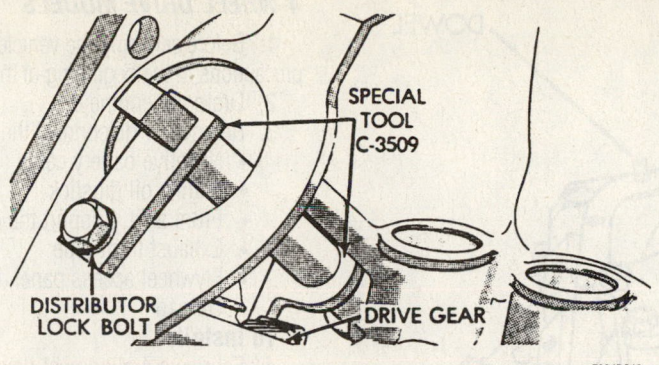

SPECIAL TOOL C-3509

DISTRIBUTOR LOCK BOLT

DRIVE GEAR

7924DG19

Camshaft holding tool C-3509—3.9L, 5.2L and 5.9L engines

- Valve covers
- Distributor
- Intake manifold

➡**Keep all valvetrain components in order for assembly.**

- Rocker arms and pushrods
- Hydraulic lifters
- Timing chain and sprockets
- Camshaft thrust plate and chain oil tab
- Camshaft

To install:
6. Install or connect the following:
- Camshaft
- Camshaft Holding Tool C-3509
- Camshaft thrust plate and chain oil tab. Tighten the bolts to 18 ft. lbs. (24 Nm).
- Timing chain and sprockets. Tighten the camshaft sprocket bolt to 50 ft. lbs. (68 Nm).
7. Remove the camshaft holding tool.
8. Install or connect the following:
- Hydraulic lifters in their original positions
- Rocker arms and pushrods in their original positions
- Intake manifold
- Distributor
- Valve covers
- Front cover
- Crankshaft damper
- Grille
- A/C condenser
- Radiator
- Water pump
- Power steering pump
- Accessory drive belt
- Negative battery cable
9. Fill the cooling system.
10. Recharge the A/C system, if equipped.
11. Start the engine and check for leaks.

8.0L Engine

1. Before servicing the vehicle, refer to the precautions in the beginning of this section.
2. Recover the A/C refrigerant, if equipped with air conditioning.
3. Drain the cooling system.
4. Relieve the fuel system pressure.
5. Remove or disconnect the following:
- Negative battery cable
- Valve covers
- Upper and lower intake manifolds

➡**Keep all valvetrain components in order for assembly.**

- Rocker arms
- Pushrods
- Cylinder heads
- Valve lifters
- Crankshaft pulley
- Front cover
- Timing chain and sprockets
- Camshaft thrust plate
- Camshaft

To install:
6. Install or connect the following:
- Camshaft
- Camshaft thrust plate
- Timing chain and sprockets. Tighten the bolt to 55 ft. lbs. (75 Nm).
- Front cover
- Crankshaft pulley
- Valve lifters
- Cylinder heads
- Pushrods
- Rocker arms
- Upper and lower intake manifolds
- Valve covers
- Negative battery cable
7. Fill the cooling system.
8. Recharge the A/C system, if equipped.
9. Start the engine and check for leaks.

Valve Lash

ADJUSTMENT

All gasoline engines covered in this section use hydraulic lifters. No maintenance or periodic adjustment is required.

Starter Motor

REMOVAL & INSTALLATION

1. Before servicing the vehicle, refer to the precautions in the beginning of this section.
2. Remove or disconnect the following:
- Negative battery cable
- Starter mounting bolts
- Starter solenoid harness connections
- Starter

To install:
3. Connect the starter solenoid wiring connectors.
4. Install the starter and tighten the bolts to the following specifications:
   a. 2.5L engine: 33 ft. lbs. (45 Nm).
   b. 4.7L engine: 40 ft. lbs. (54 Nm).
   c. 3.9L, 5.2L, 5.9L and 8.0L engines: 50 ft. lbs. (68 Nm).
5. Install the negative battery cable and check for proper operation.

Oil Pan

REMOVAL & INSTALLATION

2.5L Engine

1. Before servicing the vehicle, refer to the precautions in the beginning of this section.
2. Drain the engine oil.
3. Remove or disconnect the following:
- Negative battery cable
- Exhaust front pipe
- Starter motor
- Bell housing access cover
- Oil level sensor connector, if equipped
- Left and right motor mounts
4. Place a jack under the crankshaft damper and raise the engine for clearance.
5. Remove the oil pan.

To install:
6. Fabricate 4 alignment dowels from 1½ inch x ¼ inch bolts. Cut the heads off the bolts and cut a slot into the top of the

Timing belt service is covered in Section 4 of this manual

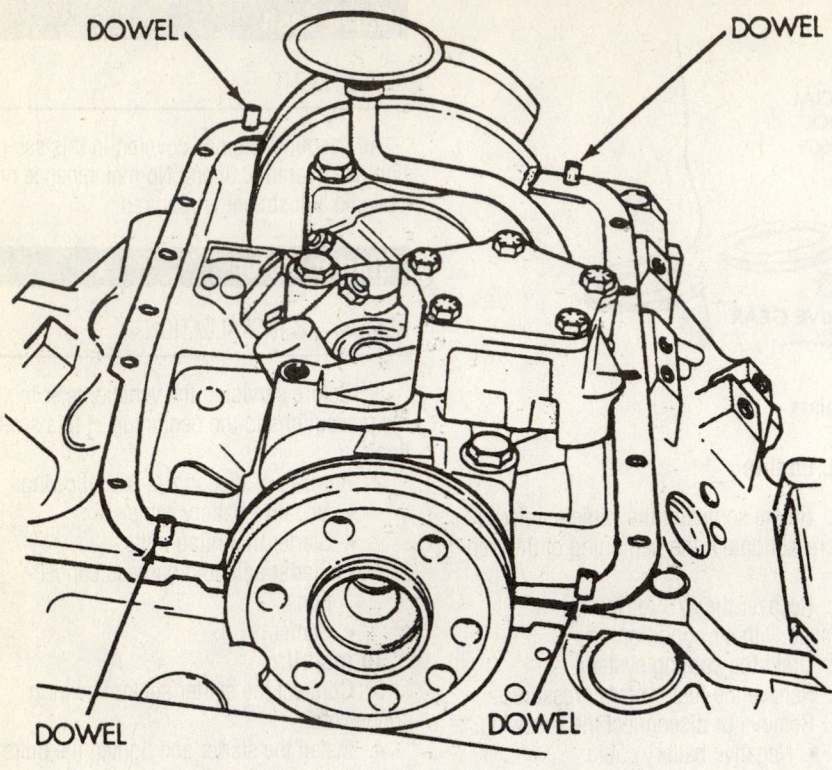

Oil pan alignment dowel placement—3.9L engine shown

7924DG62

dowel to allow installation/removal with a screwdriver.

7. Install or connect the following:
- Dowels
- Oil pan, using a new gasket. Tighten the ¼ inch bolts to 85 inch lbs. (9.5 Nm) and the ⁵⁄₁₆ inch bolts to 11 ft. lbs. (15 Nm).

8. Replace the alignment dowels with ¼ inch bolts and tighten them to 85 inch lbs. (9.5 Nm).

9. Install or connect the following:
- Left and right motor mounts
- Oil level sensor connector, if equipped
- Bell housing access cover
- Starter motor
- Exhaust front pipe
- Negative battery cable

10. Fill the crankcase.

11. Start the engine and check for leaks.

3.9L Engine

2-WHEEL DRIVE MODELS

1. Before servicing the vehicle, refer to the precautions in the beginning of this section.

2. Drain the engine oil.

3. Remove or disconnect the following:
- Negative battery cable

- Distributor cap
- Oil dipstick
- Exhaust front pipe
- Flywheel access panel, if equipped
- Left and right motor mount through bolts
- Oil pan. Raise the engine as necessary for clearance.

To install:

4. Fabricate 4 alignment dowels from 1½ inch x ¼ inch bolts. Cut the heads off the bolts and cut a slot into the top of the dowel to allow installation/removal with a screwdriver.

5. Install or connect the following:
- Alignment dowels
- Oil pan. Replace the dowels with bolts and tighten all bolts to 17 ft. lbs. (23 Nm).
- Left and right motor mount through bolts
- Flywheel access panel, if equipped
- Exhaust front pipe
- Oil dipstick
- Distributor cap
- Negative battery cable

6. Fill the crankcase to the correct level.

7. Start the engine and check for leaks.

4-WHEEL DRIVE MODELS

1. Before servicing the vehicle, refer to the precautions in the beginning of this section.

2. Drain the engine oil.

3. Remove or disconnect the following:
- Negative battery cable
- Engine oil dipstick
- Front axle. Support the engine
- Exhaust front pipe
- Flywheel access panel, if equipped
- Oil pan

To install:

4. Fabricate 4 alignment dowels from 1½ inch x ¼ inch bolts. Cut the heads off the bolts and cut a slot into the top of the dowel to allow installation/removal with a screwdriver.

5. Install or connect the following:
- Alignment dowels
- Oil pan. Replace the dowels with bolts and tighten all bolts to 17 ft. lbs. (23 Nm).
- Flywheel access panel, if equipped
- Exhaust front pipe
- Front axle
- Engine oil dipstick
- Negative battery cable

6. Fill the crankcase to the correct level.

7. Start the engine and check for leaks.

4.7L Engine

1. Before servicing the vehicle, refer to the precautions in the beginning of this section.

2. Drain the engine oil.

3. Remove or disconnect the following:
- Negative battery cable
- Structural cover
- Exhaust Y-pipe
- Starter motor
- Transmission oil cooler lines
- Oil pan
- Oil pump pickup tube
- Oil pan gasket

To install:

4. Install or connect the following:
- Oil pan gasket
- Oil pump pickup tube, using a new O-ring. Tighten the tube bolts to 20 ft. lbs. (28 Nm); tighten the O-ring end bolt first.
- Oil pan. Tighten the bolts, in sequence, to 11 ft. lbs. (15 Nm).
- Transmission oil cooler lines
- Starter motor
- Exhaust Y-pipe
- Structural cover
- Negative battery cable

5. Fill the crankcase to the proper level with engine oil.

6. Start the engine and check for leaks.

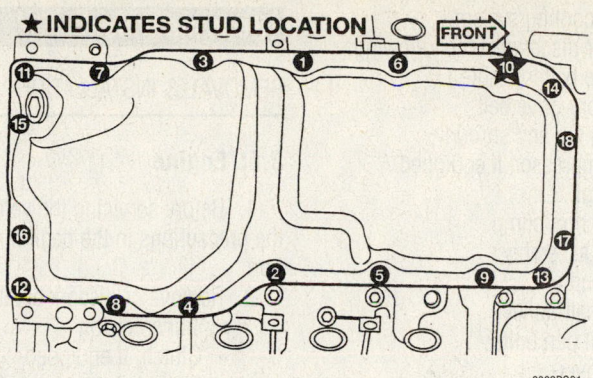

★ INDICATES STUD LOCATION

FRONT

9302PG21

Oil pan mounting bolt tightening sequence—4.7L engine

5.2L and 5.9L Engines

1. Before servicing the vehicle, refer to the precautions in the beginning of this section.
2. Drain the engine oil.
3. Remove or disconnect the following:

- Oil filter
- Starter motor
- Cooler lines
- Oil level sensor connector
- Heated Oxygen (HO2S) sensor connector
- Exhaust Y-pipe
- Oil pan

To install:

4. Install or connect the following:

- Oil pan, using a new gasket. Tighten the bolts to 18 ft. lbs. (24 Nm).
- Exhaust Y-pipe
- Heated Oxygen (HO2S) sensor connector
- Oil level sensor connector
- Cooler lines
- Starter motor
- Oil filter

5. Fill the crankcase.
6. Start the engine and check for leaks.

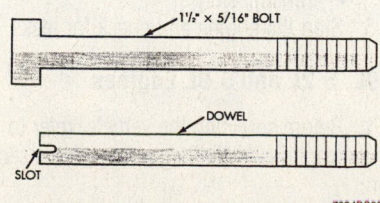

1½" × 5/16" BOLT

DOWEL

SLOT

7924DG20

Oil pan alignment dowels—3.9L, 5.2L, 5.9L and 8.0L engines

8.0L Engine

1. Before servicing the vehicle, refer to the precautions in the beginning of this section.
2. Drain the engine oil.
3. Remove or disconnect the following:

- Negative battery cable
- Engine oil dipstick
- Left transmission brace
- Oil pan

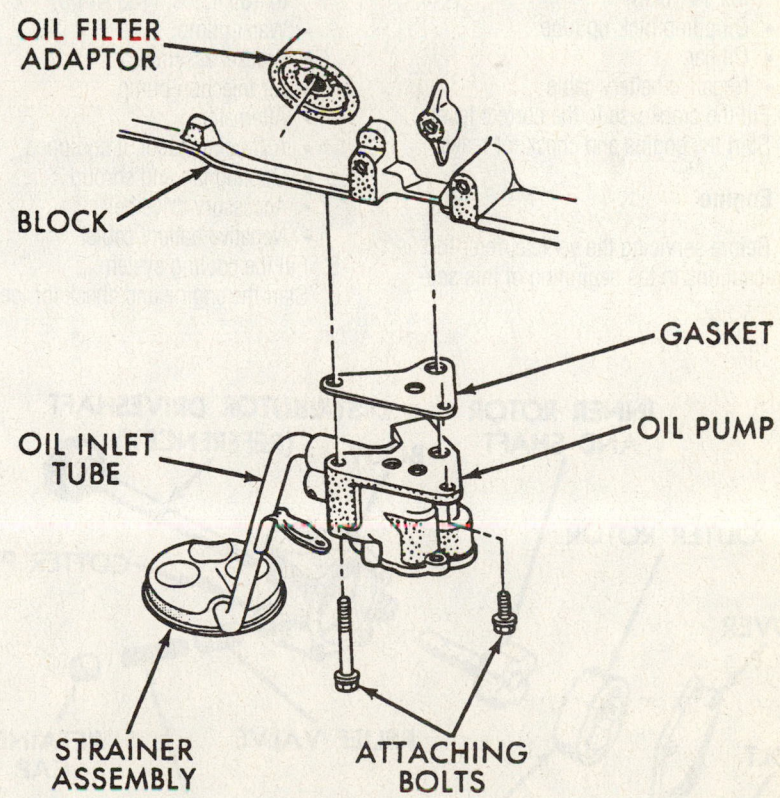

OIL FILTER ADAPTOR

BLOCK

OIL INLET TUBE

GASKET

OIL PUMP

STRAINER ASSEMBLY

ATTACHING BOLTS

7924DG22

Exploded view of the oil pump assembly—2.5L engine

To install:

4. Install or connect the following:

- Oil pan. Tighten the 5/16 bolts to 12 ft. lbs. (16 Nm) and the ¼ bolts to 96 inch lbs. (11 Nm).
- Left transmission brace
- Engine oil dipstick
- Negative battery cable

5. Fill the crankcase.
6. Start the engine and check for leaks.

Oil Pump

REMOVAL & INSTALLATION

2.5L Engine

1. Before servicing the vehicle, refer to the precautions in the beginning of this section.
2. Drain the engine oil.
3. Remove or disconnect the following:

- Negative battery cable
- Oil pan
- Oil pump and pickup tube

➡ **If the oil pump is not to be serviced, do not disturb the position of the oil** inlet tube and strainer assembly in the pump body. If the tube is moved within the pump body, a replacement tube and strainer assembly must be installed to assure an airtight seal.

To install:

4. Install or connect the following:
   - Oil pump. Tighten the mounting bolts to 17 ft. lbs. (23 Nm).
   - Oil pan
   - Negative battery cable
5. Fill the crankcase to the correct level.
6. Start the engine and check for leaks.

3.9L, 5.2L and 5.9L Engines

1. Before servicing the vehicle, refer to the precautions in the beginning of this section.
2. Drain the engine oil.
3. Remove or disconnect the following:
   - Negative battery cable
   - Oil pan
   - Oil pump pick-up tube
   - Oil pump

To install:

4. Install or connect the following:
   - Oil pump. Tighten the bolts to 30 ft. lbs. (41 Nm).
   - Oil pump pick-up tube
   - Oil pan
   - Negative battery cable
5. Fill the crankcase to the correct level.
6. Start the engine and check for leaks.

8.0L Engine

1. Before servicing the vehicle, refer to the precautions in the beginning of this section.

2. Drain the cooling system.
3. Remove or disconnect the following:
   - Negative battery cable
   - Accessory drive belt
   - Cooling fan and shroud
   - A/C compressor, if equipped
   - Alternator
   - Air injection pump
   - Bracket assembly
   - Water pump
   - Crankshaft pulley
   - Front oil pan bolts
   - Front cover
   - Oil pump pressure relief valve
   - Oil pump cover
   - Oil pump rotors

To install:

4. Install or connect the following:
   - Oil pump rotors
   - Oil pump cover. Tighten the bolts to 10 ft. lbs. (14 Nm).
   - Oil pump pressure relief valve. Tighten the plug to 15 ft. lbs. (20 Nm).
   - Front cover. Tighten the bolts to 35 ft. lbs. (47 Nm).
   - Front oil pan bolts. Tighten the bolts to 12 ft. lbs. (16 Nm).
   - Crankshaft pulley. Tighten the bolt to 135 ft. lbs. (183 Nm).
   - Water pump
   - Bracket assembly
   - Air injection pump
   - Alternator
   - A/C compressor, if equipped
   - Cooling fan and shroud
   - Accessory drive belt
   - Negative battery cable
5. Fill the cooling system.
6. Start the engine and check for leaks.

Rear Main Seal

REMOVAL & INSTALLATION

2.5L Engine

1. Before servicing the vehicle, refer to the precautions in the beginning of this section.
2. Remove or disconnect the following:
   - Transmission
   - Clutch, if equipped
   - Flywheel
   - Rear main seal

To install:

3. Install the rear main seal so that it is flush with the cylinder block.
4. Install or connect the following:
   - Flywheel. Use new bolts and tighten to 50 ft. lbs. (68 Nm) plus 60 degrees
   - Clutch, if equipped
   - Transmission
5. Start the engine and check for leaks.

4.7L Engine

1. Before servicing the vehicle, refer to the precautions in the beginning of this section.
2. Remove or disconnect the following:
   - Transmission
   - Flexplate
3. Thread Oil Seal Remover 8506 into the rear main seal as far as possible and remove the rear main seal.

To install:

4. Install or connect the following:
   - Seal Guide 8349-2 onto the crankshaft
   - Rear main seal on the seal guide
   - Rear main seal, using the Crankshaft Rear Oil Seal Installer 8349 and Driver Handle C-4171; tap it into place until the installer is flush with the cylinder block
   - Flexplate. Tighten the bolts to 45 ft. lbs. (60 Nm).
   - Transmission
5. Start the engine and check for leaks.

3.9L, 5.2L and 5.9L Engines

1. Before servicing the vehicle, refer to the precautions in the beginning of this section.
2. Drain the engine oil.
3. Remove or disconnect the following:
   - Oil pan
   - Oil pump
   - Rear main bearing cap

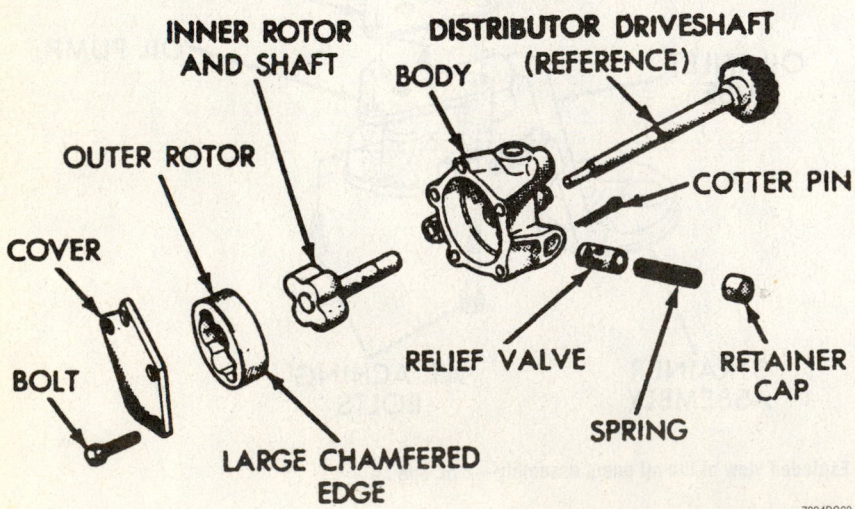

Exploded view of the oil pump assembly—3.9L, 5.2L and 5.9L engines

7924DG63

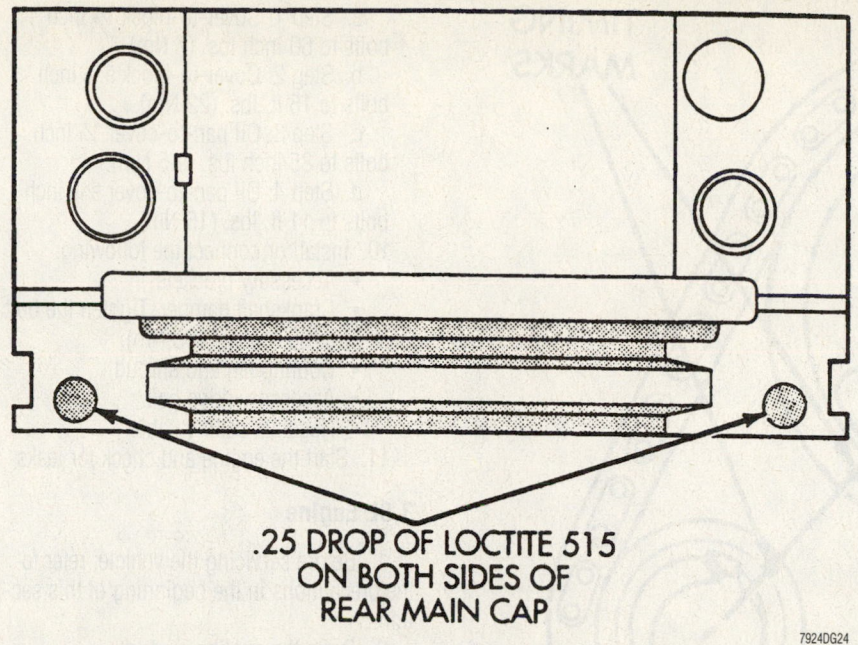

.25 DROP OF LOCTITE 515
ON BOTH SIDES OF
REAR MAIN CAP

Sealant application locations —3.9L, 5.2L and 5.9L engines

4. Loosen the other main bearing cap bolts for clearance and remove the rear main seal halfs.

To install:

5. Install or connect the following:
- New upper seal half to the cylinder block
- New lower seal half to the bearing cap

6. Apply sealant to the rear main bearing cap.

7. Install or connect the following:
- Rear main bearing cap. Tighten **all** main bearing cap bolts to 85 ft. lbs. (115 Nm).
- Oil pump and oil pan

8. Fill the engine.

9. Start the engine and check for leaks.

8.0L Engine

1. Before servicing the vehicle, refer to the precautions in the beginning of this section.

2. Remove or disconnect the following:
- Transmission
- Clutch, if equipped
- Flywheel
- Rear main seal

To install:

3. Install the rear main seal so that it is flush with the cylinder block.

4. Install or connect the following:

- Flywheel. Tighten the bolts to 55 ft. lbs. (75 Nm).
- Clutch, if equipped
- Transmission

5. Start the engine and check for leaks.

Timing Chain, Sprockets, Front Cover and Seal

REMOVAL & INSTALLATION

2.5L Engine

1. Before servicing the vehicle, refer to the precautions in the beginning of this section.

2. Remove or disconnect the following:
- Negative battery cable
- Accessory drive belt
- Cooling fan and shroud
- Crankshaft damper
- Front crankshaft seal
- Accessory brackets
- Front cover
- Oil slinger

3. Rotate the crankshaft so that the timing marks are aligned.

4. Remove the timing chain and sprockets.

To install:

5. Turn the timing chain tensioner lever to the unlock (down) position. Pull the tensioner block toward the tensioner lever to compress the spring. Hold the block and turn the tensioner lever to the lock (up) position.

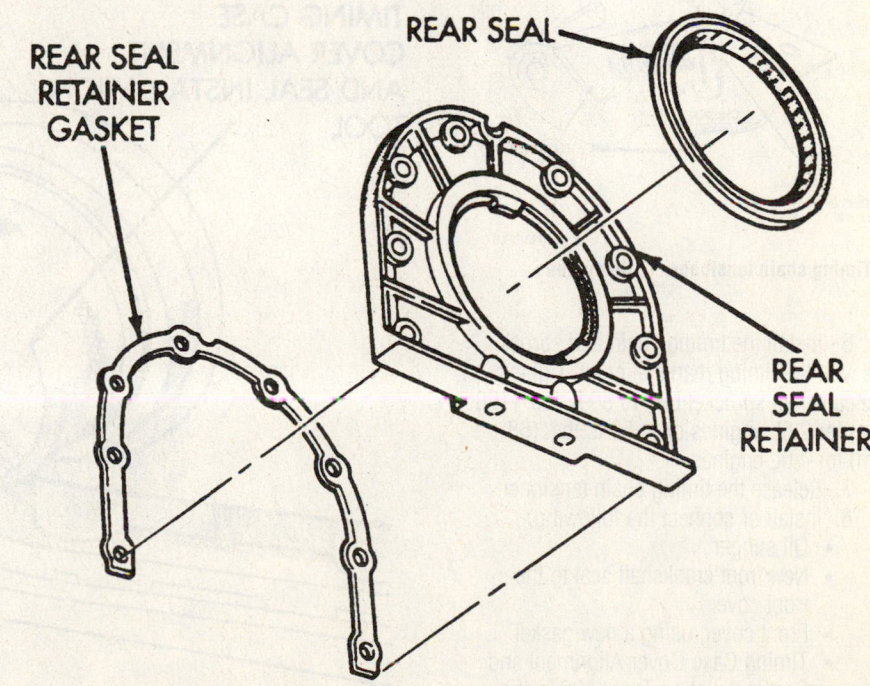

REAR SEAL RETAINER GASKET

REAR SEAL

REAR SEAL RETAINER

Exploded view of the rear oil seal and retainer—8.0L engine

Refer to Section 1 for engine rebuilding specifications

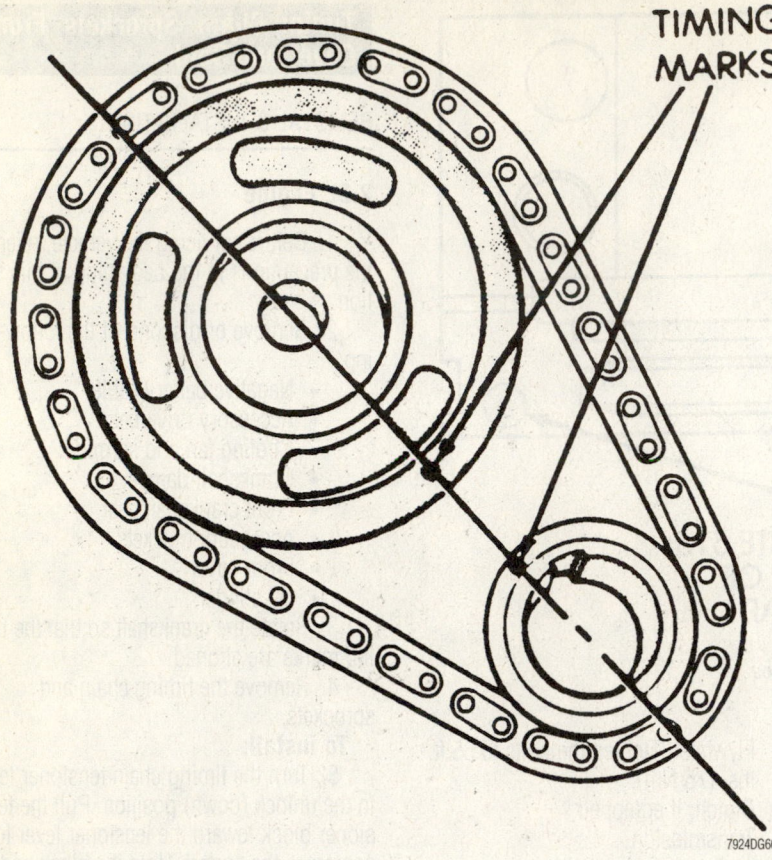

Timing mark alignment—2.5L engine

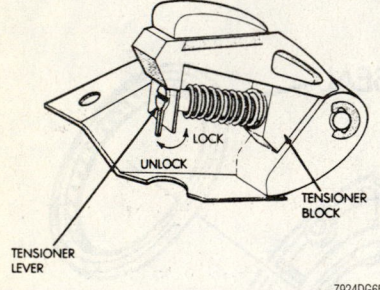

Timing chain tensioner—2.5L engines

6. Install the timing chain and sprockets with the timing marks aligned. Tighten the camshaft sprocket bolt to 80 ft. lbs. (108 Nm) for 2.5L engines or to 50 ft. lbs. (68 Nm) for 4.0L engines.

7. Release the timing chain tensioner.

8. Install or connect the following:
- Oil slinger
- New front crankshaft seal to the front cover
- Front cover, using a new gasket
- Timing Case Cover Alignment and Seal Installation Tool 6139 in the crankshaft opening to center the front cover

9. Tighten the front cover bolts as follows:

a. Step 1: Cover-to-block ¼ inch bolts to 60 inch lbs. (7 Nm).

b. Step 2: Cover-to-block ⁵⁄₁₆ inch bolts to 16 ft. lbs. (22 Nm).

c. Step 3: Oil pan-to-cover ¼ inch bolts to 85 inch lbs. (9.5 Nm).

d. Step 4: Oil pan-to-cover ⁵⁄₁₆ inch bolts to 11 ft. lbs. (15 Nm).

10. Install or connect the following:
- Accessory brackets
- Crankshaft damper. Tighten the bolt to 80 ft. lbs. (108 Nm).
- Cooling fan and shroud
- Accessory drive belt
- Negative battery cable

11. Start the engine and check for leaks.

3.9L Engine

1. Before servicing the vehicle, refer to the precautions in the beginning of this section.

2. Drain the cooling system.

3. Remove or disconnect the following:
- Negative battery cable
- Accessory drive belt
- Radiator
- Cooling fan
- Water pump
- Crankshaft pulley

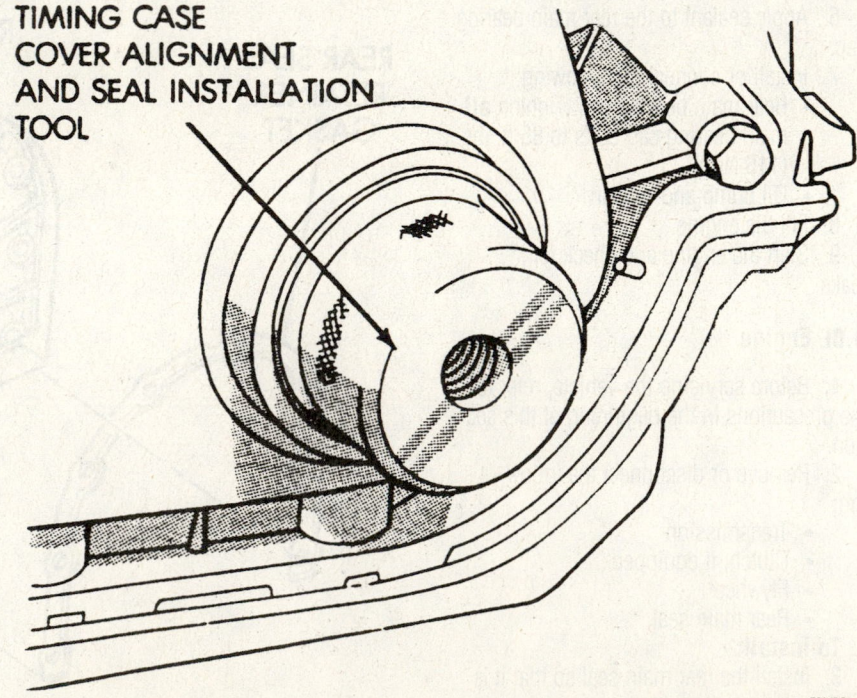

Timing Case Cover Alignment and Seal Installation Tool 6139—2.5L engine

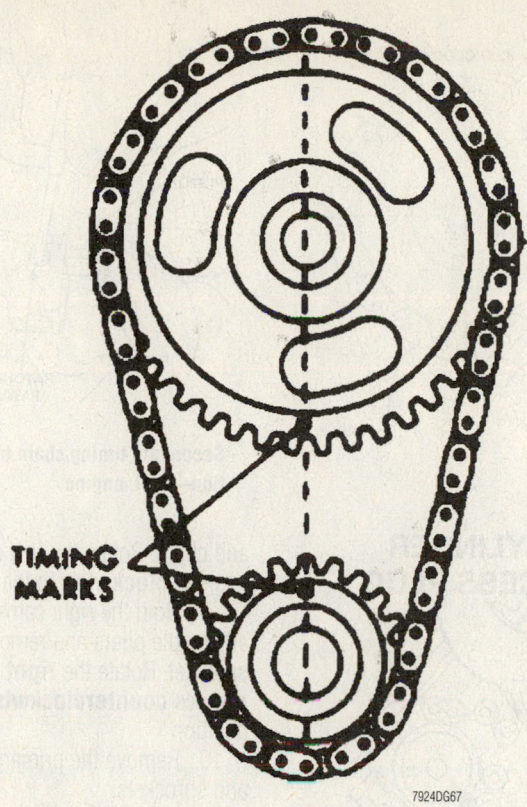

TIMING MARKS

7924DG67

Timing chain alignment marks—3.9L, 5.2L, 5.9L and 8.0L engines

- Front crankshaft seal
- Front cover
- Timing chain and gears

To install:

4. Install or connect the following:
  - Timing chain and gears. Align the timing marks and tighten the camshaft sprocket bolt to 35 ft. lbs. (47 Nm).
  - Front cover. Tighten the bolts to 30 ft. lbs. (41 Nm).
  - Front crankshaft seal
  - Crankshaft pulley. Tighten the bolt to 135 ft. lbs. (183 Nm).
  - Water pump
  - Cooling fan
  - Radiator
  - Accessory drive belt
  - Negative battery cable
5. Fill the cooling system.
6. Start the engine and check for leaks.

4.7L Engine

1. Before servicing the vehicle, refer to the precautions in the beginning of this section.
2. Drain the cooling system.
3. Remove or disconnect the following:
  - Negative battery cable

- Valve covers
- Camshaft Position (CMP) sensor
- Engine cooling fan and shroud
- Accessory drive belt
- Heater hoses
- Lower radiator hose
- Power steering pump

4. Rotate the crankshaft so that the crankshaft timing mark aligns with the Top Dead Center (TDC) mark on the front cover, and the **V8** marks on the camshaft sprockets are at 12 o'clock.

5. Remove or disconnect the following:
  - Crankshaft damper
  - Oil fill housing
  - Accessory drive belt tensioner
  - Alternator
  - A/C compressor
  - Front cover
  - Front crankshaft seal
  - Cylinder head access plugs
  - Secondary timing chain guides

6. Compress the primary timing chain tensioner and install a lockpin.

7. Remove the secondary timing chain tensioners.

8. Hold the left camshaft with adjustable pliers and remove the sprocket

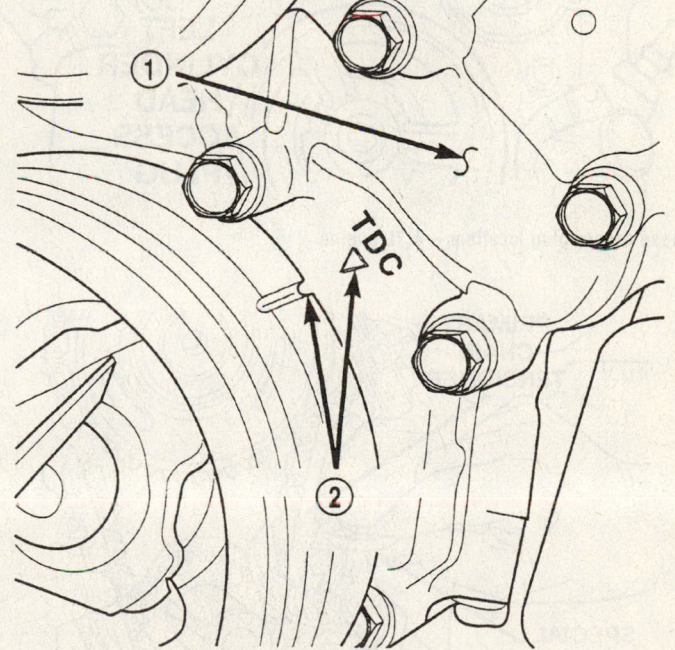

1 – TIMING CHAIN COVER
2 – CRANKSHAFT TIMING MARKS

9308PG04

Crankshaft timing marks—4.7L engine

For engine torque specifications, refer to Section 1 of this manual

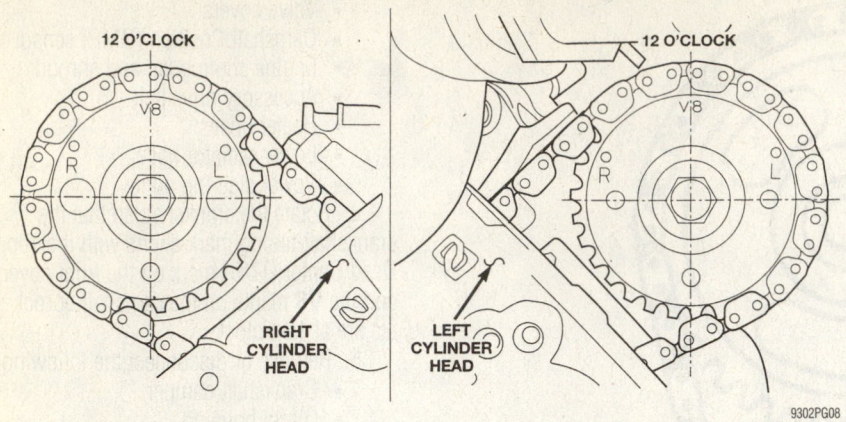

Camshaft positioning—4.7L engine

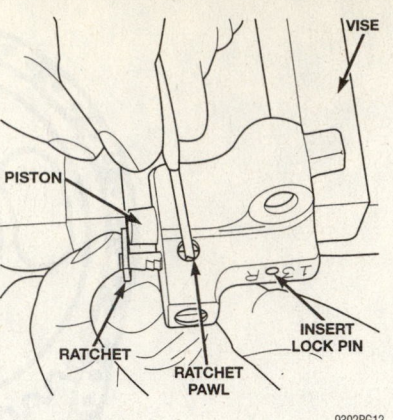

Secondary timing chain tensioner preparation—4.7L engine

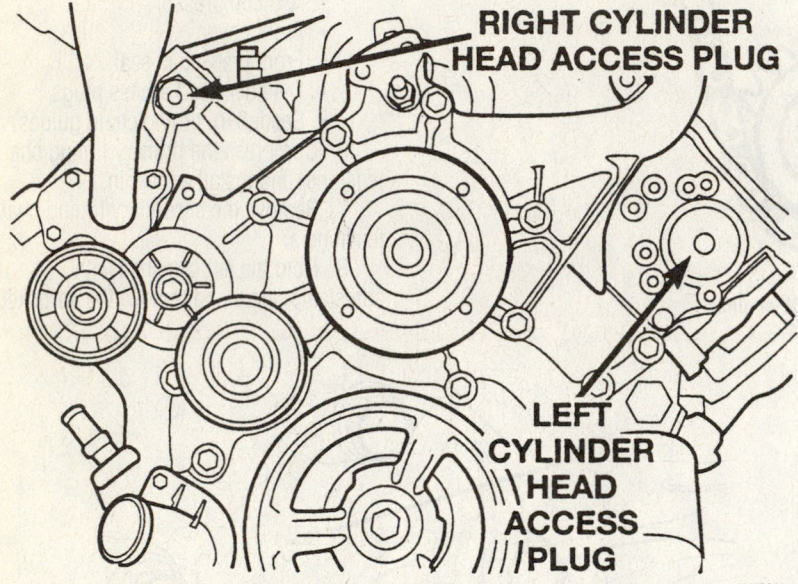

RIGHT CYLINDER HEAD ACCESS PLUG

LEFT CYLINDER HEAD ACCESS PLUG

Cylinder head access plug locations—4.7L engine

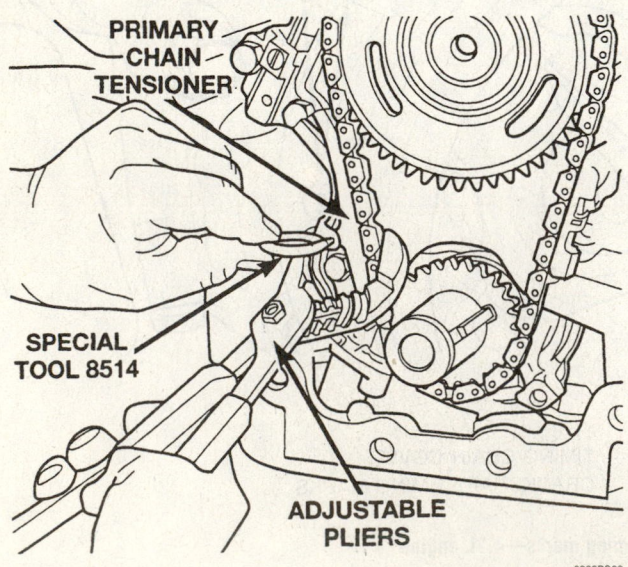

PRIMARY CHAIN TENSIONER

SPECIAL TOOL 8514

ADJUSTABLE PLIERS

Compress and lock the primary chain tensioner—4.7L engine

and chain. Rotate the **left** camshaft 15 degrees **clockwise** to the neutral position.

9. Hold the right camshaft with adjustable pliers and remove the camshaft sprocket. Rotate the **right** camshaft 45 degrees **counterclockwise** to the neutral position.

10. Remove the primary timing chain and sprockets.

To install:

11. Use a small prytool to hold the ratchet pawl and compress the secondary timing chain tensioners in a vise and install locking pins.

➡ **The black bolts fasten the guide to the engine block and the silver bolts fasten the guide to the cylinder head.**

12. Install or connect the following:
- Secondary timing chain guides. Tighten the bolts to 21 ft. lbs. (28 Nm).
- Secondary timing chains to the idler sprocket so that the double plated links on each chain are visible through the slots in the primary idler sprocket

13. Lock the secondary timing chains to the idler sprocket with Timing Chain Locking tool 8515 as shown.

14. Align the primary chain double plated links with the idler sprocket timing mark and the single plated link with the crankshaft sprocket timing mark.

15. Install the primary chain and sprockets. Tighten the idler sprocket bolt to 25 ft. lbs. (34 Nm).

16. Align the secondary chain single plated links with the timing marks on the secondary sprockets. Align the dot at the **L** mark on the left sprocket with the plated link on the left chain and the dot at the **R** mark on the right sprocket with the plated link on the right chain.

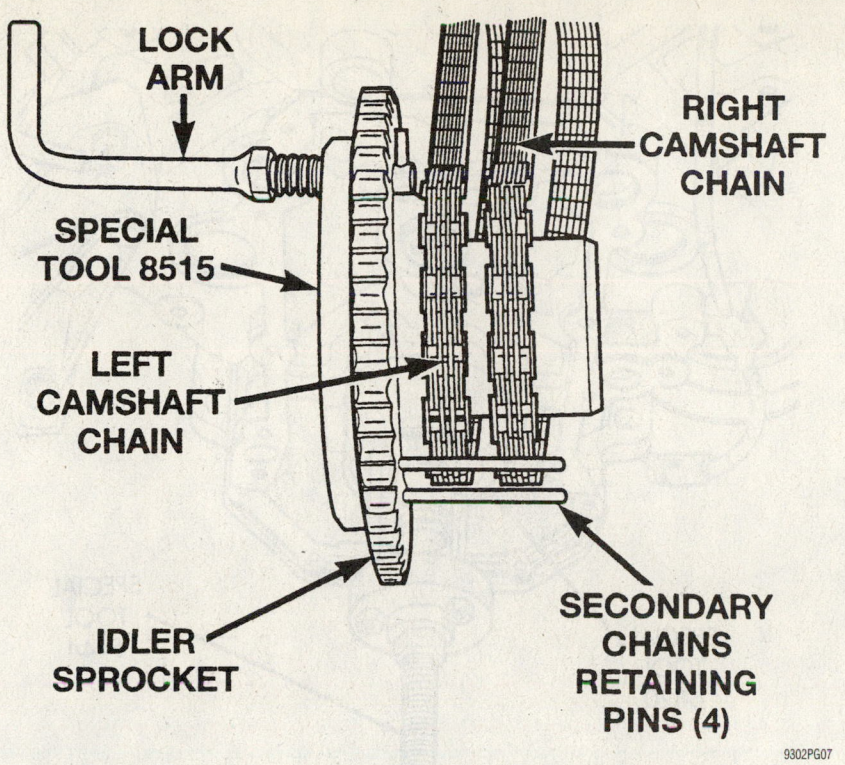

Use the Timing Chain Locking tool to lock the timing chains on the idler gear—4.7L engine

9302PG07

17. Rotate the camshafts back from the neutral position and install the camshaft sprockets.

18. Remove the secondary chain locking tool.

19. Remove the primary and secondary timing chain tensioner locking pins.

20. Hold the camshaft sprockets with a spanner wrench and tighten the retaining bolts to 90 ft. lbs. (122 Nm).

21. Install or connect the following:

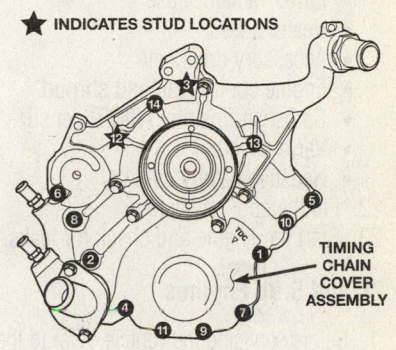

★ INDICATES STUD LOCATIONS

9302PG26

Timing chain cover bolt torque sequence—4.7L engine

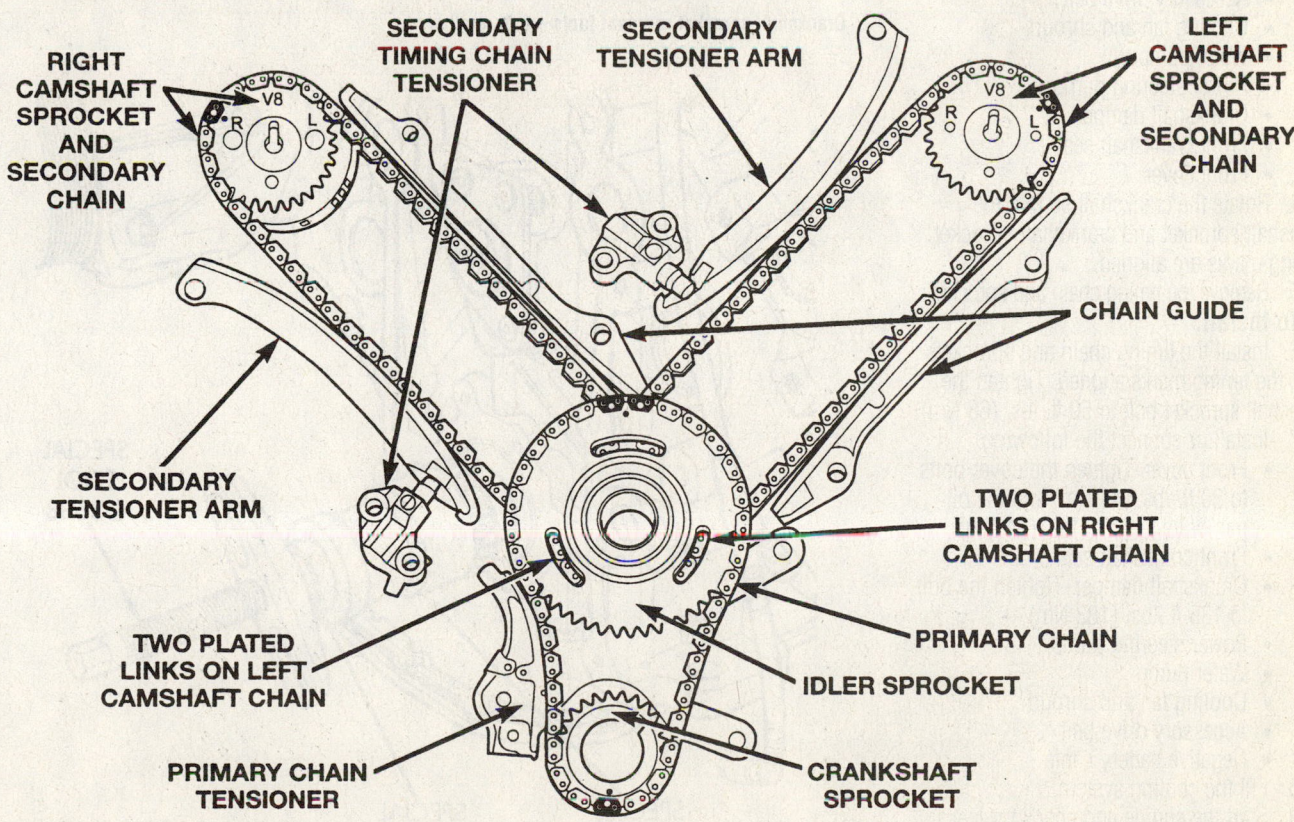

Timing chain system and alignment marks—4.7L engine

9302PG24

For complete mechanical specifications, refer to Section 1 of this manual

- Front cover. Tighten the bolts, in sequence, to 40 ft. lbs. (54 Nm).
- Front crankshaft seal
- Cylinder head access plugs
- A/C compressor
- Alternator
- Accessory drive belt tensioner. Tighten the bolt to 40 ft. lbs. (54 Nm).
- Oil fill housing
- Crankshaft damper. Tighten the bolt to 130 ft. lbs. (175 Nm).
- Power steering pump
- Lower radiator hose
- Heater hoses
- Accessory drive belt
- Engine cooling fan and shroud
- Camshaft Position (CMP) sensor
- Valve covers
- Negative battery cable

22. Fill the cooling system.
23. Start the engine and check for leaks.

5.2L and 5.9L Engines

1. Before servicing the vehicle, refer to the precautions in the beginning of this section.
2. Drain the cooling system.
3. Remove or disconnect the following:
- Negative battery cable
- Accessory drive belt
- Cooling fan and shroud
- Water pump
- Power steering pump
- Crankshaft damper
- Front crankshaft seal
- Front cover

4. Rotate the crankshaft so that the camshaft sprocket and crankshaft sprocket timing marks are aligned.
5. Remove the timing chain and sprockets.

To install:

6. Install the timing chain and sprockets with the timing marks aligned. Tighten the camshaft sprocket bolt to 50 ft. lbs. (68 Nm).
7. Install or connect the following:
- Front cover. Tighten the cover bolts to 30 ft. lbs. (41 Nm) and the oil pan bolts to 18 ft. lbs. (24 Nm).
- Front crankshaft seal
- Crankshaft damper. Tighten the bolt to 135 ft. lbs. (183 Nm).
- Power steering pump
- Water pump
- Cooling fan and shroud
- Accessory drive belt
- Negative battery cable

8. Fill the cooling system.
9. Start the engine and check for leaks.

8.0L Engine

1. Before servicing the vehicle, refer to the precautions in the beginning of this section.

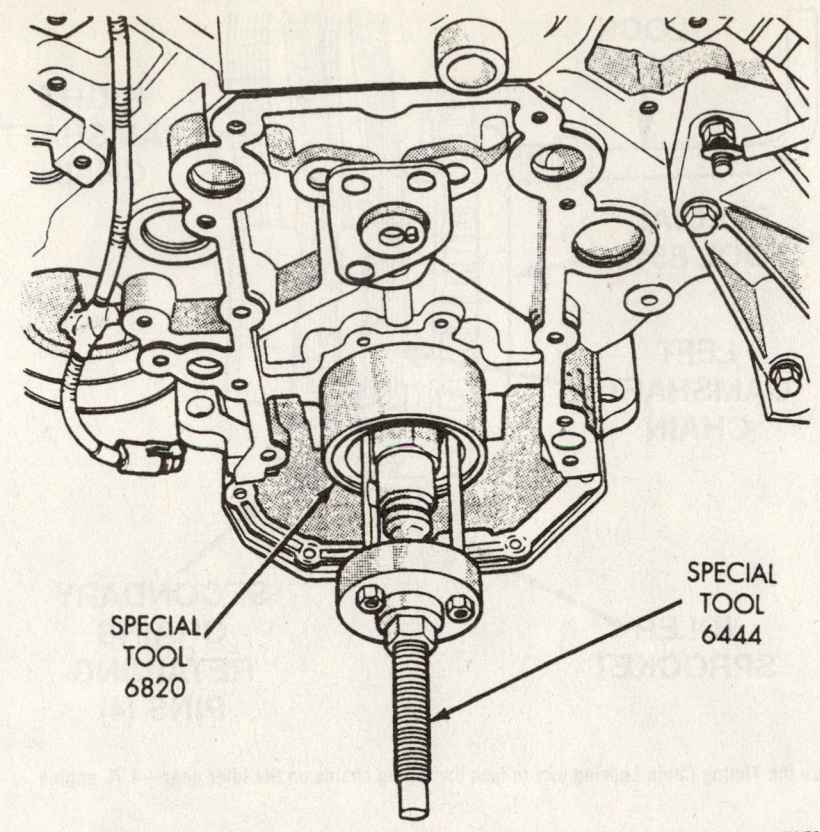

Crankshaft sprocket removal tools—8.0L engine

7924DG68

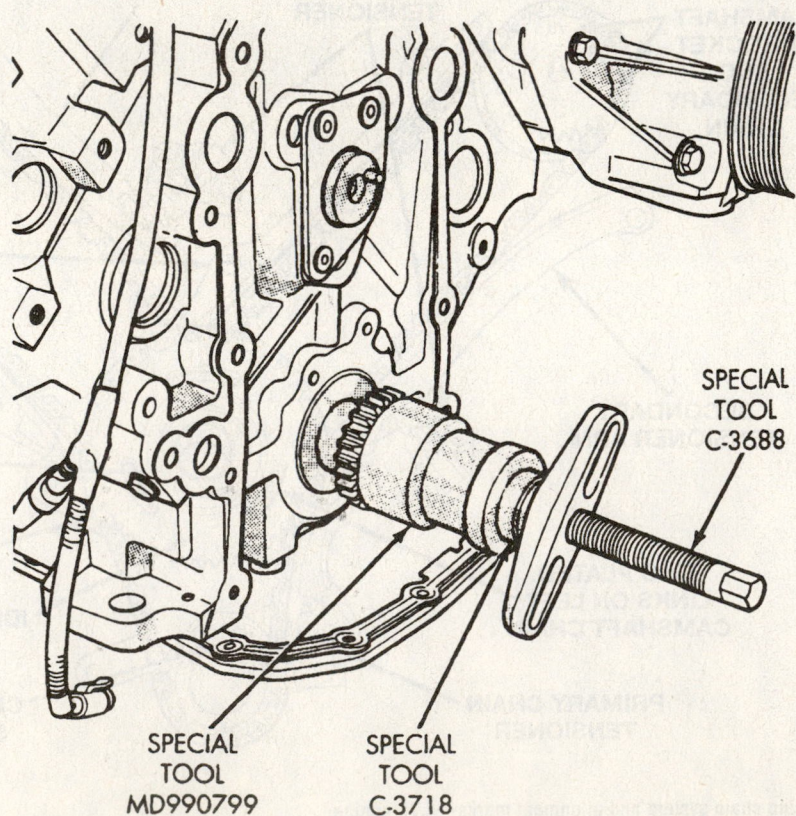

Crankshaft installation tools—8.0L engine

7924DG69

2. Drain the cooling system.
3. Remove or disconnect the following:
   - Negative battery cable
   - Accessory drive belt
   - Cooling fan and shroud
   - A/C compressor, if equipped
   - Alternator
   - Air injection pump
   - Bracket assembly
   - Water pump
   - Crankshaft pulley
   - Front crankshaft seal
   - Front oil pan bolts
   - Front cover
   - Camshaft sprocket and timing chain
4. Remove the crankshaft sprocket with Special tools 6444 and 6820.

To install:

5. Install the crankshaft sprocket with Special tools C-3688, C-3718 and MD990799.
6. Install or connect the following:
   - Timing chain and camshaft sprocket with the timing marks aligned. Tighten the bolt to 45 ft. lbs. (61 Nm).
   - Front cover. Tighten the bolts to 35 ft. lbs. (47 Nm).
   - Front oil pan bolts. Tighten the bolts to 12 ft. lbs. (16 Nm).
   - Front crankshaft seal
   - Crankshaft pulley. Tighten the bolt to 135 ft. lbs. (183 Nm).
   - Water pump
   - Bracket assembly
   - Air injection pump
   - Alternator
   - A/C compressor, if equipped
   - Cooling fan and shroud
   - Accessory drive belt
   - Negative battery cable
7. Fill the cooling system.
8. Start the engine and check for leaks.

Piston and Ring

POSITIONING

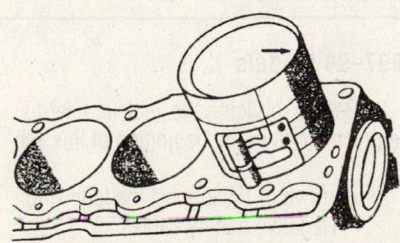

Piston to engine positioning—2.5L, 3.9L, 5.2L, 5.9L and 8.0L engines

7924AG34

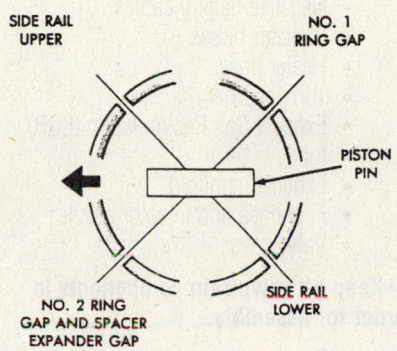

7924AG28

Piston ring end-gap spacing—2.5L, 3.9L, 5.2L, 5.9L and 8.0L engines

9302AG03

Piston ring end-gap spacing. Position raised "F" on piston towards front of engine—4.7L engine

DIESEL ENGINE REPAIR

Engine Assembly

REMOVAL & INSTALLATION

1. Before servicing the vehicle, refer to the precautions in the beginning of this section.
2. Drain the cooling system.
3. Drain the engine oil.
4. Recover the A/C refrigerant, if equipped.
5. Remove or disconnect the following:
   - Battery
   - Hood
   - Upper crossmember and top core support
   - Transmission oil cooler, if equipped
   - Accessory drive belt
   - A/C compressor
   - Washer fluid bottle
   - Coolant recovery bottle
   - A/C condenser, if equipped
   - Radiator hoses
   - Cooling fan and shroud
   - Radiator
   - Alternator
   - Heater hoses
   - Air inlet tube
   - Exhaust front pipe
   - Intercooler inlet and outlet ducts
   - Accelerator linkage
   - Cruise control cable, if equipped
   - Transmission cable, if equipped
   - Power steering hoses
   - Transmission oil cooler lines, if equipped
   - Engine control sensor harness connectors
   - Fuel lines
   - Transmission
   - Oil pan
   - Starter motor
   - Engine mounts
   - Engine

To install:

6. Install or connect the following:
   - Engine. Tighten the through bolts to 57 ft. lbs. (77 Nm).
   - Starter motor
   - Oil pan
   - Transmission
   - Fuel lines
   - Engine control sensor harness connectors
   - Transmission oil cooler lines, if equipped
   - Power steering hoses
   - Transmission cable, if equipped
   - Cruise control cable, if equipped
   - Accelerator linkage
   - Intercooler inlet and outlet ducts
   - Exhaust front pipe
   - Air inlet tube
   - Heater hoses
   - Alternator
   - Radiator
   - Cooling fan and shroud
   - Radiator hoses
   - A/C condenser, if equipped
   - Coolant recovery bottle
   - Washer fluid bottle
   - A/C compressor
   - Accessory drive belt
   - Transmission oil cooler, if equipped
   - Upper crossmember and top core support
   - Hood
   - Battery
7. Fill the cooling system.

8. Fill the crankcase to the correct level.
   • Recharge the A/C system, if equipped.
9. Start the engine and check for leaks.

Water Pump

REMOVAL & INSTALLATION

1. Before servicing the vehicle, refer to the precautions in the beginning of this section.
2. Drain the cooling system.
3. Remove or disconnect the following:
   • Negative battery cables
   • Wiring harness retainer
   • Accessory drive belt
   • Water pump

To install:

4. Install or connect the following:
   • Water pump. Tighten the bolts to 18 ft. lbs. (24 Nm).
   • Accessory drive belt
   • Wiring harness retainer
   • Negative battery cables
5. Fill the cooling system.
6. Start the engine and check for leaks.

Glow Plugs

REMOVAL & INSTALLATION

The 5.9L diesel engine uses an intake manifold air heater instead of glow plugs to preheat the air for improved starting ability. The heater element is located within the intake manifold top cover. Refer to the intake manifold removal and installation procedure to service the intake manifold air heater.

Cylinder Head

REMOVAL & INSTALLATION

1. Before servicing the vehicle, refer to the precautions in the beginning of this section.
2. Drain the cooling system.
3. Drain the engine oil.
4. Remove or disconnect the following:
   • Negative battery cables
   • Radiator hoses
   • Heater hoses
   • Turbocharger
   • Exhaust Gas Recirculation (EGR) tube
   • Exhaust manifold
   • Fuel lines and injector nozzles
   • Valve cover

➡**Keep all valvetrain components in order for assembly.**

   • Rocker levers and pedestal assemblies
   • Pushrods
   • Fuel filter and water separator assembly

➡**If the cylinder head is hot, gradually loosen the cylinder head bolts using the TIGHTENING sequence. If the engine is cold, then the loosening sequence for the head bolts is not important.**

➡**The cylinder head bolts are different sizes. Note their locations for assembly.**

   • Cylinder head bolts
   • Cylinder head

To install:

5. Install or connect the following:
   • Cylinder head
   • Pushrods
   • Rocker levers and pedestal assemblies

➡**Refer to Section 1 of this manual for the cylinder head torque sequence illustration. The illustration is located after the Torque Specification Chart.**

6. Install the cylinder head bolts and tighten them in sequence as follows:
   a. Step 1: Tighten all 12mm bolts to 66 ft. lbs. (90 Nm).
   b. Step 2: Retighten all 12mm bolts to 66 ft. lbs. (90 Nm).
   c. Step 3: Tighten bolts 4, 5, 12, 13, 20 and 21 to 89 ft. lbs. (120 Nm).
   d. Step 4: Retighten bolts 4, 5, 12, 13, 20 and 21 to 89 ft. lbs. (120 Nm).
   e. Step 5: Tighten all 12mm bolts 90 degrees.
   f. Step 6: Tighten the 8mm bolts to 18 ft. lbs. (24 Nm).
7. Install or connect the following:
   • Fuel filter and water separator assembly
   • Valve cover
   • Fuel lines and injector nozzles
   • Exhaust manifold
   • EGR tube
   • Turbocharger
   • Heater hoses
   • Radiator hoses
   • Negative battery cables
8. Fill the crankcase to the correct level.
9. Fill the cooling system.
10. Start the engine and check for leaks.

Rocker Arms/Shafts

REMOVAL & INSTALLATION

1997–98 Models

1. Before servicing the vehicle, refer to the precautions in the beginning of this section.
2. Remove or disconnect the following:
   • Negative battery cables
   • Exhaust Gas Recirculation (EGR) tube
   • Valve cover
3. Loosen the locknuts and back the adjustment screws out until they stop.

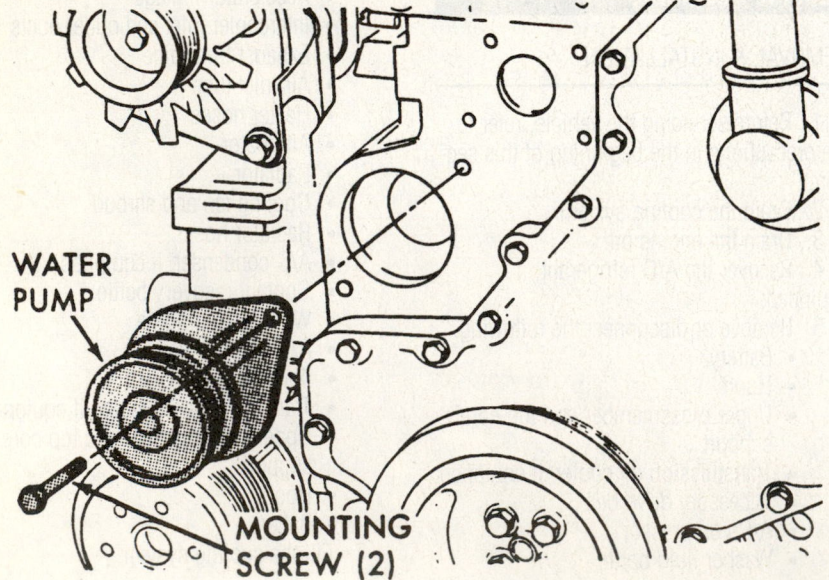

WATER PUMP

MOUNTING SCREW (2)

7924DG70

Exploded view of the water pump mounting—5.9L diesel engine

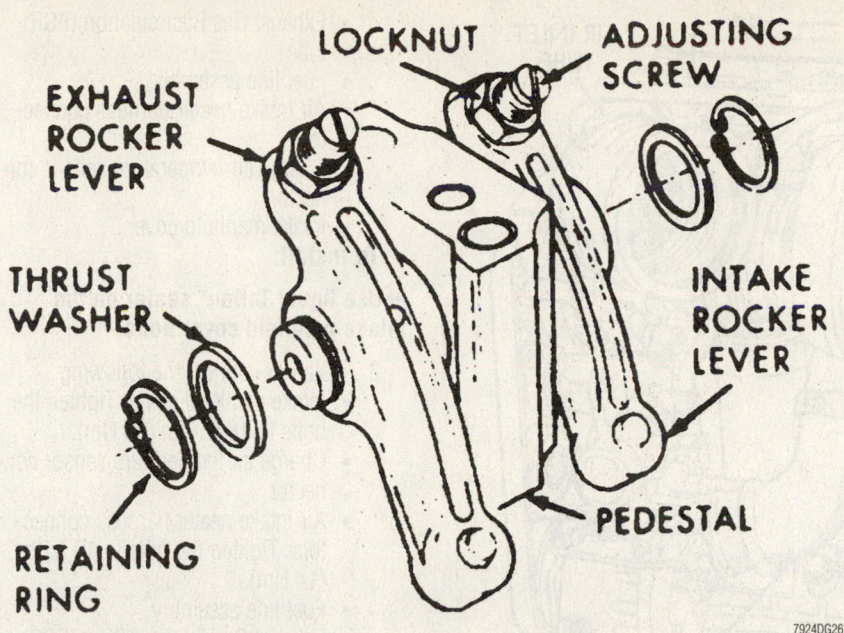

Rocker arms and related components—1997-98 5.9L diesel engine

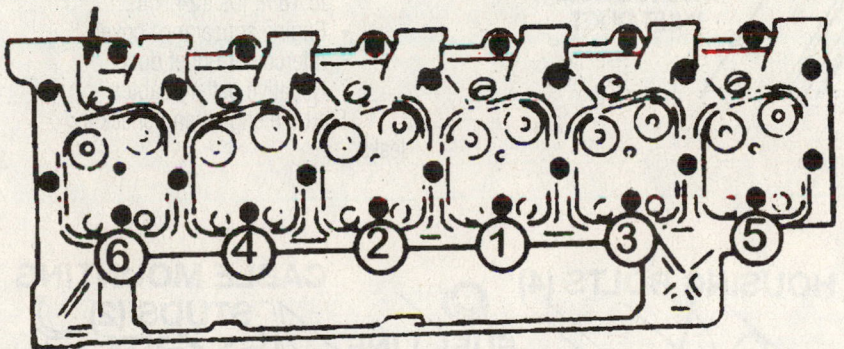

Rocker arm bolt tightening sequence—1997-98 5.9L diesel engine

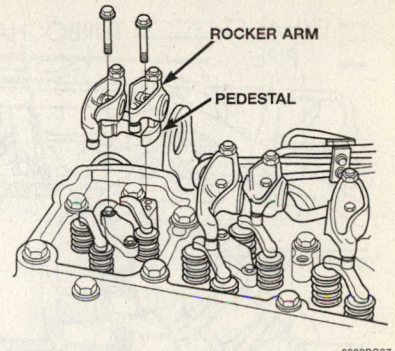

Exploded view of the rocker arm mounting—1999-01 diesel engines

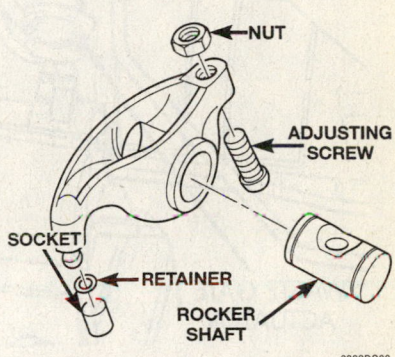

Exploded view of the rocker arm—1999-01 diesel engines

➡ **Keep all valvetrain components in order for assembly.**

4. Remove the rocker levers and pedestal assemblies.

To install:

5. Install the rocker levers and pedestal assemblies. Tighten the bolts in sequence as follows:

  a. Step 1: Tighten the 12mm bolts to 66 ft. lbs. (90 Nm).

  b. Step 2: Retighten the 12mm bolts to 66 ft. lbs. (90 Nm).

  c. Step 3: Tighten the 12mm bolts to 89 ft. lbs. (120 Nm).

  d. Step 4: Retighten the 12mm bolts to 89 ft. lbs. (120 Nm).

  e. Step 5: Tighten the 12mm bolts 90 degrees.

  f. Step 6: Tighten the 8mm bolts to 18 ft. lbs. (24 Nm).

6. Adjust the valves.
7. Install or connect the following:
  • Valve cover. Tighten the bolts to 18 ft. lbs. (24 Nm).
  • Exhaust Gas Recirculation (EGR) tube
  • Negative battery cables

1999-01 Models

1. Before servicing the vehicle, refer to the precautions in the beginning of this section.
2. Remove or disconnect the following:
  • Negative battery cables
  • Valve cover

✳✳ WARNING

The sockets may fall out of the rocker arms as the rocker arms are lifted

from the cylinder head. Do not drop the sockets into the engine.

➡ **Keep all valvetrain components in order for assembly.**

  • Rocker arms and pedestal assemblies

To install:

3. Install or connect the following:
  • Rocker arm and pedestal assemblies. Tighten the bolts to 27 ft. lbs. (36 Nm).
  • Valve cover. Tighten the bolts to 18 ft. lbs. (24 Nm).
  • Negative battery cables

Turbocharger

REMOVAL & INSTALLATION

1. Before servicing the vehicle, refer to the precautions in the beginning of this section.
2. Remove or disconnect the following:
  • Negative battery cable
  • Exhaust front pipe
  • Air inlet and outlet tubes

Timing belt service is covered in Section 4 of this manual

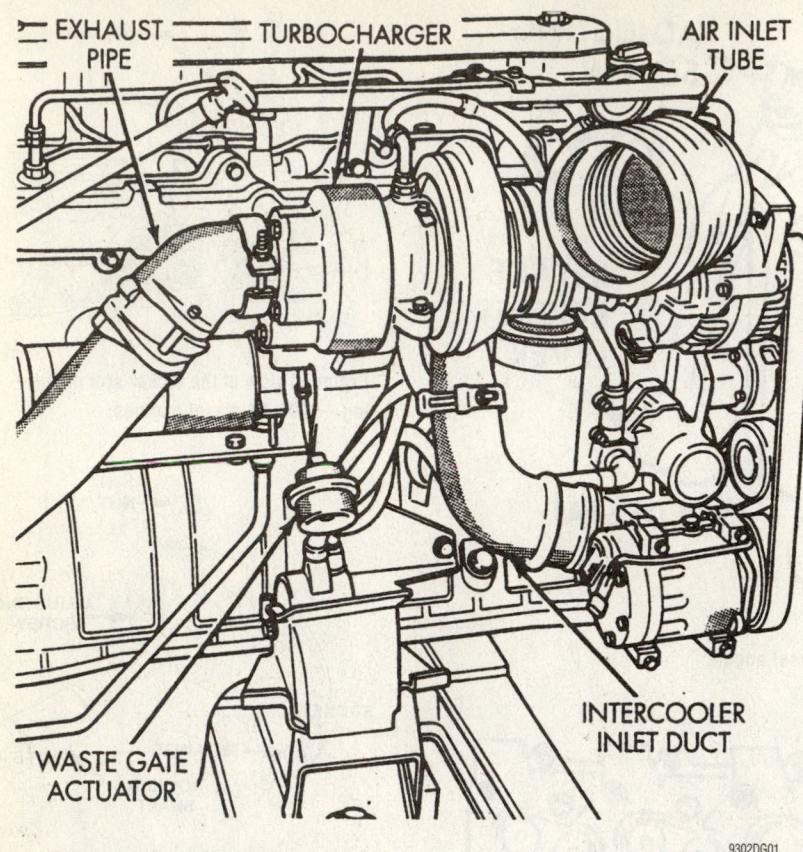

Turbocharger and related components—5.9L diesel engine

- Exhaust Gas Recirculation (EGR) tube
- Fuel line assembly
- Air intake heater harness connectors
- Charge air temperature sensor connector
- Intake manifold cover

To install:

➡**Use liquid Teflon® sealer on the intake manifold cover bolts.**

3. Install or connect the following:
   - Intake manifold cover. Tighten the bolts to 18 ft. lbs. (24 Nm).
   - Charge air temperature sensor connector
   - Air intake heater harness connectors. Tighten the nuts to 10 ft. lbs. (14 Nm).
   - Fuel line assembly
   - Exhaust Gas Recirculation (EGR) tube
   - Air inlet housing. Tighten the bolts to 18 ft. lbs. (24 Nm).
   - Engine appearance cover
   - Intercooler outlet duct
   - Negative battery cables
4. Start the engine and check for leaks.

- Oil supply and drain lines
- Turbocharger

To install:

➡**Use anti-seize compound on the turbocharger mounting studs.**

3. Install or connect the following:
   - Turbocharger. Tighten the nuts to 24 ft. lbs. (32 Nm).
   - Oil supply and drain lines
   - Air inlet and outlet tubes
   - Exhaust front pipe
   - Negative battery cable
4. Start the engine and check for leaks.

Intake Manifold

REMOVAL & INSTALLATION

1. Before servicing the vehicle, refer to the precautions in the beginning of this section.

2. Remove or disconnect the following:
   - Negative battery cables
   - Intercooler outlet duct
   - Engine appearance cover
   - Air inlet housing

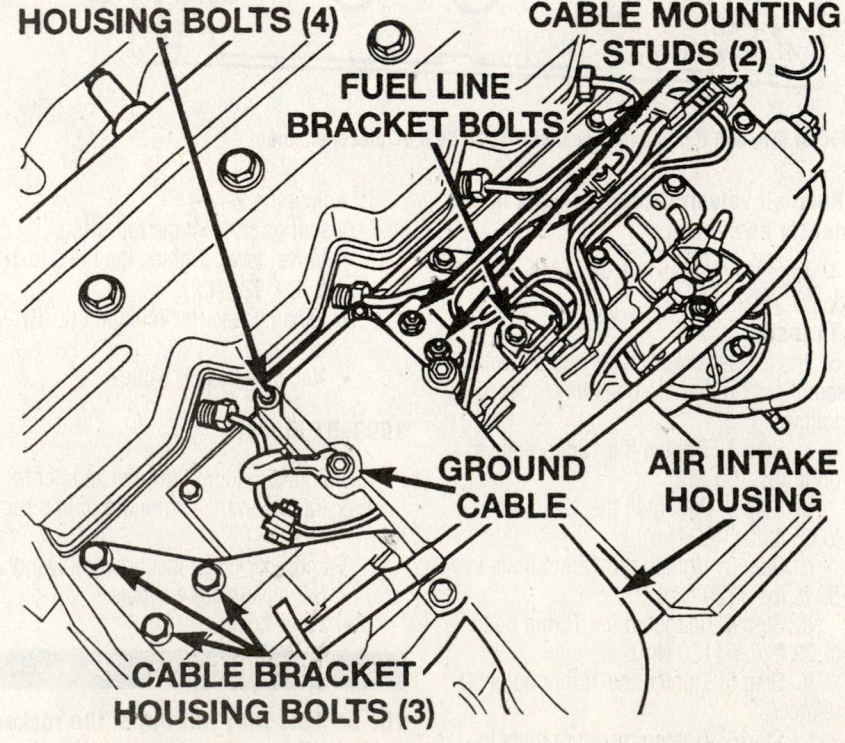

Intake air heater electrical connections—5.9L diesel engine

Exhaust Manifold

REMOVAL & INSTALLATION

1. Before servicing the vehicle, refer to the precautions in the beginning of this section.

2. Remove or disconnect the following:
- Negative battery cables
- Turbocharger
- Exhaust Gas Recirculation (EGR) tube
- Cab heater supply and return lines
- Exhaust manifold

To install:

➡ **Use anti-seize compound on the exhaust manifold bolts.**

3. Install or connect the following:
- Exhaust manifold. Tighten the bolts in sequence to 32 ft. lbs. (43 Nm).
- Cab heater supply and return lines
- EGR tube. Tighten the bolts to 18 ft. lbs. (24 Nm).
- Turbocharger
- Negative battery cables

4. Start the engine and check for leaks.

Camshaft and Valve Lifters

REMOVAL & INSTALLATION

1. Before servicing the vehicle, refer to the precautions in the beginning of this section.

2. Recover the A/C refrigerant, if equipped.

3. Drain the cooling system.

4. Remove or disconnect the following:
- Negative battery cables
- Accessory drive belt
- Cooling fan and shroud
- Radiator
- A/C condenser, if equipped
- Intercooler
- Auxiliary transmission cooler
- Upper radiator support
- Exhaust Gas Recirculation (EGR) tube
- Engine appearance cover
- Valve cover

➡ **Keep all valvetrain components in order for assembly.**

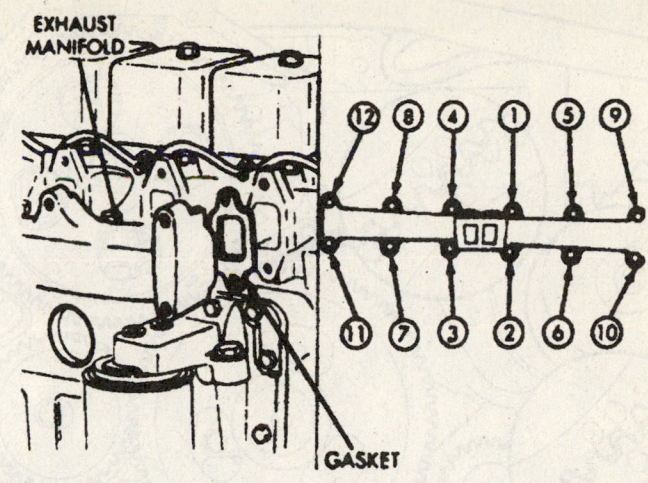

Exhaust manifold torque sequence—5.9L diesel engine

- Rocker arms
- Pushrods
- Crankshaft pulley
- Front cover
- Lift pump

5. Insert dowel tools into the tappets. Raise the dowels and secure them with rubber bands.

6. Unbolt the thrust plate and remove the camshaft.

7. Install Cummins Tappet Changing Tool 3822513 into the camshaft bore.

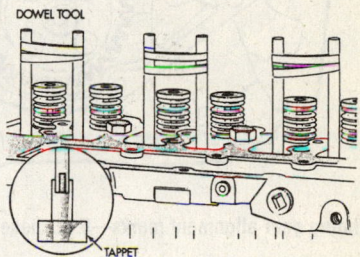

Use dowel tools and rubber bands to hold the lifters up in the bore while removing the camshaft—5.9L diesel engine

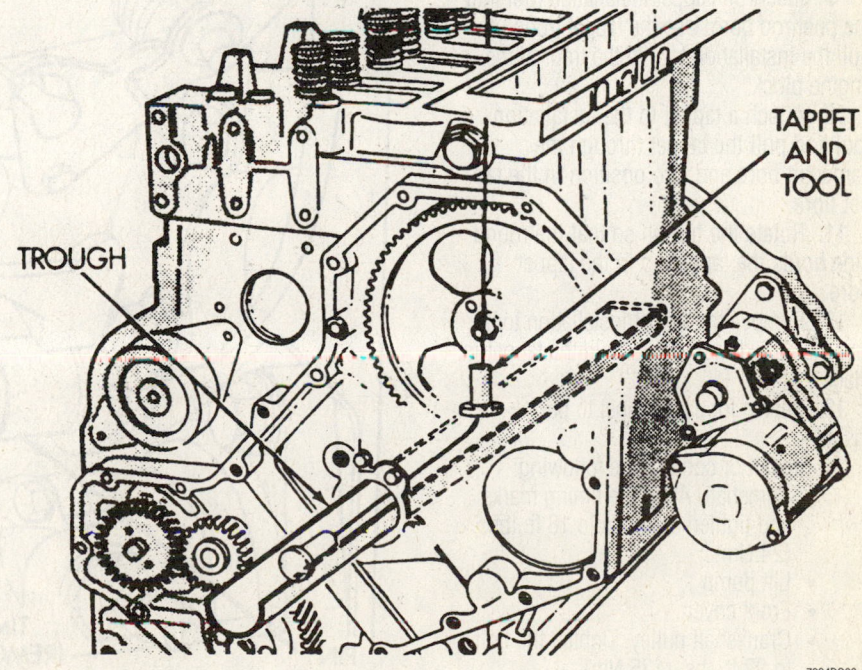

Tappet installation tools—5.9L diesel engine

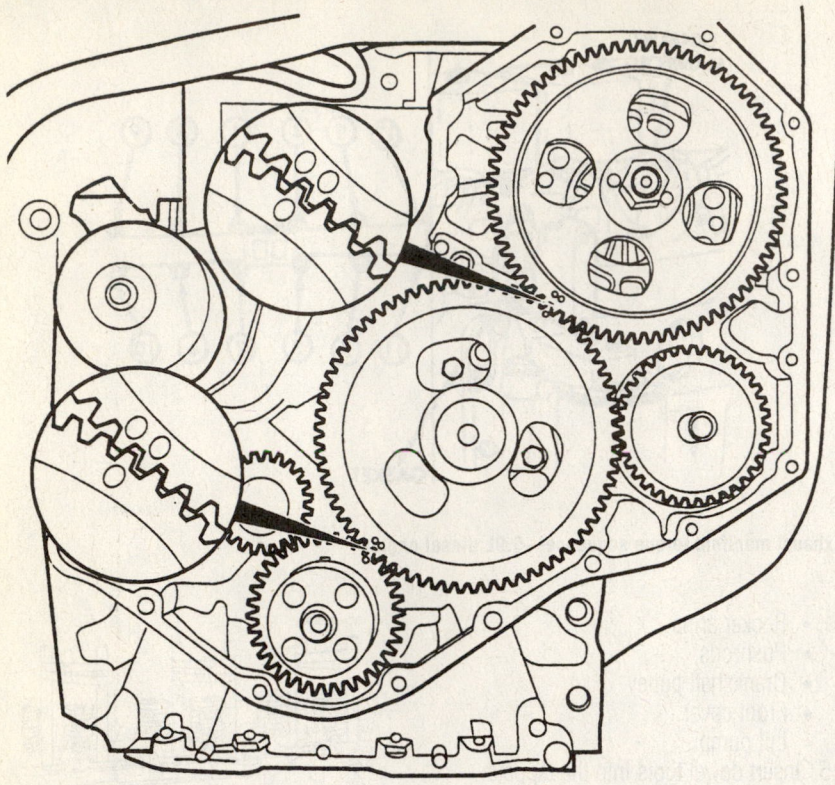

Timing gear alignment marks—5.9L diesel engine

9302DG06

8. Remove the dowel tools and remove the tappets. If the tappets are to be reused, note their locations for assembly.

To install:

9. Insert the tappet installation tool into the pushrod bore. Use the tappet trough to pull the installation tool to the front of the engine block.

10. Attach a tappet to the installation tool and pull the tappet through the camshaft bore and into position in the tappet bore.

11. Rotate the trough so that the round side holds the tappet up in the tappet bore.

12. Remove the tappet installation tool and install a dowel tool to hold the tappet in place.

13. Repeat for each tappet to be installed.

14. Install or connect the following:
- Camshaft. Align the timing marks and tighten the bolts to 18 ft. lbs. (24 Nm).
- Lift pump
- Front cover
- Crankshaft pulley. Tighten the bolt to 92 ft. lbs. (125 Nm).
- Pushrods
- Rocker arms
- Valve cover

- Engine appearance cover
- EGR tube
- Upper radiator support
- Auxiliary transmission cooler
- Intercooler
- A/C condenser, if equipped
- Radiator
- Cooling fan and shroud
- Accessory drive belt
- Negative battery cables

15. Fill the cooling system.

16. Start the engine and check for leaks.

Valve Lash

ADJUSTMENT

1997–98 Models

➡Adjust the valves with the engine cold.

➡The timing pin is used in this procedure to locate Top Dead Center (TDC). It is found at the back of the gear housing and below the injection pump. Be sure to disengage the timing pin after locating TDC.

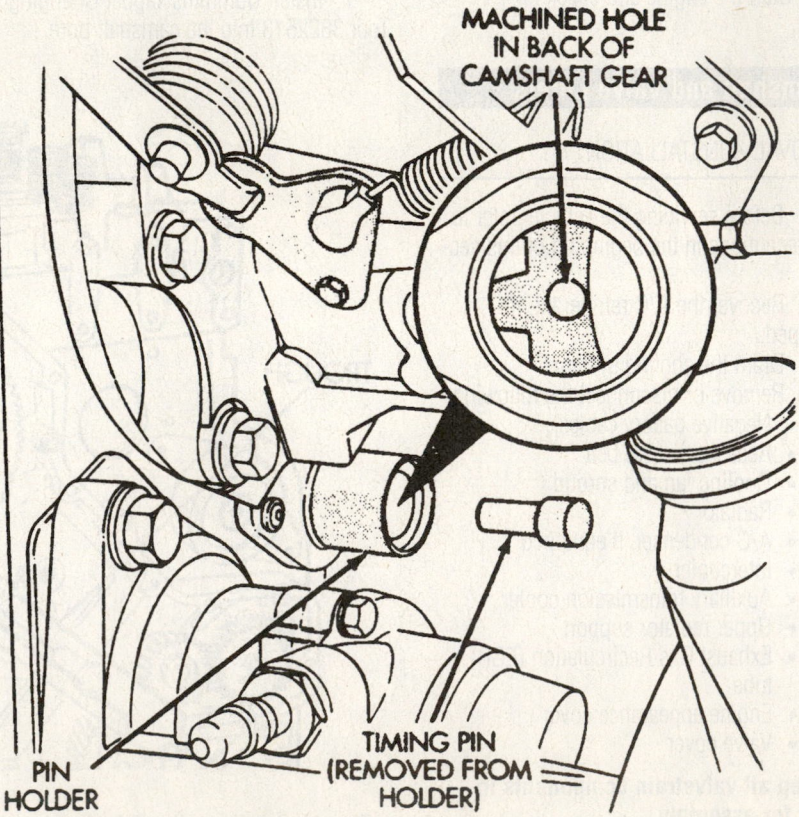

MACHINED HOLE IN BACK OF CAMSHAFT GEAR

PIN HOLDER

TIMING PIN (REMOVED FROM HOLDER)

7924DG30

Use the timing pin to locate TDC—1997–98 diesel engine

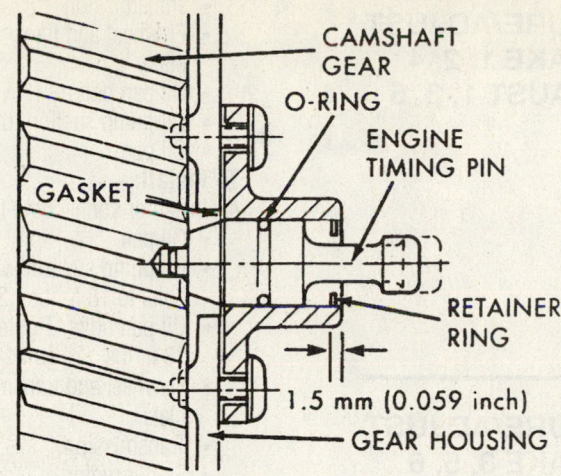

Cut away view of the timing pin entering the hole in the cam gear—1997–98 diesel engine

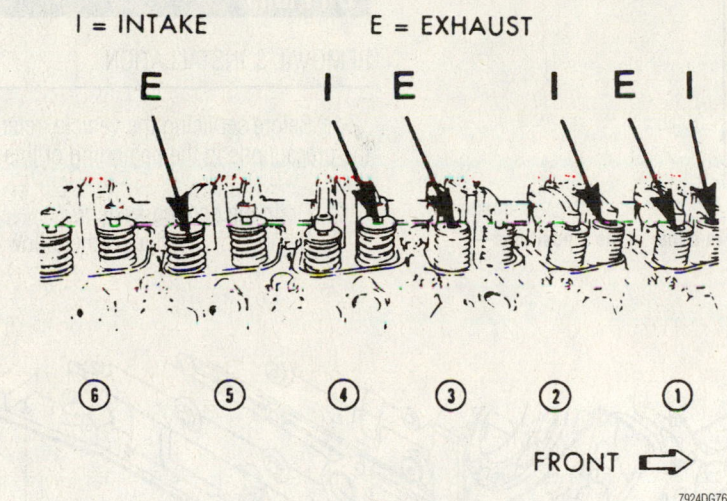

Step 1. Adjust the lash on the valves indicated—1997–98 diesel engine

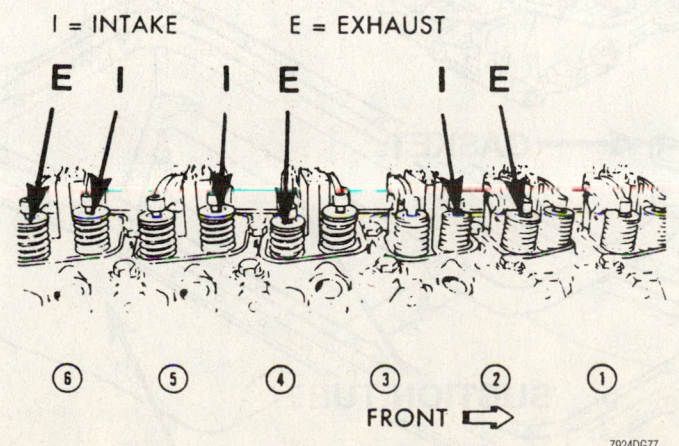

Step 2. Adjust the lash on the remaining valves not adjusted during Step 1—1997–98 diesel engine

1. Before servicing the vehicle, refer to the precautions in the beginning of this section.

2. Remove the valve cover.

3. Rotate the crankshaft so that the timing pin can be pressed into the cam gear as shown.

4. Measure and adjust the valves indicated in the illustration. The clearance for the intake valves is 0.010 inch (0.254mm). The clearance for the exhaust valves is 0.20 inch (0.508mm).

5. After adjustment, tighten the locknuts to 18 ft. lbs. (24 Nm).

6. Ensure that the timing pin is disengaged from the cam gear, then rotate the crankshaft 360 degrees and repeat the procedure for the valves in the following illustration.

7. Install the valve cover.

1999–01 Models

1. Before servicing the vehicle, refer to the precautions in the beginning of this section.

2. Remove or disconnect the following:

- Negative battery cables
- Valve cover
- Fuel pump gear access cover

3. Position the gear as shown and measure the clearance of the indicated valves. No adjustment is necessary if the lash falls within the following specifications:

   a. Intake—0.006–0.015 inch (0.152–0.381mm).

   b. Exhaust—0.015–0.030 inch (0.381–0.762mm).

4. Install or connect the following: Fuel pump access cover

- Valve cover
- Negative battery cables

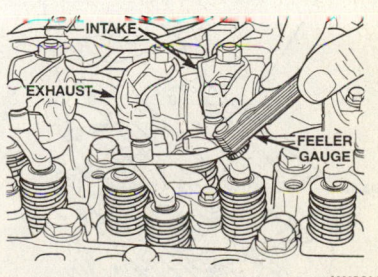

Use a feeler gauge to measure the valve lash—1999–01 diesel engine

Refer to Section 1 for engine rebuilding specifications

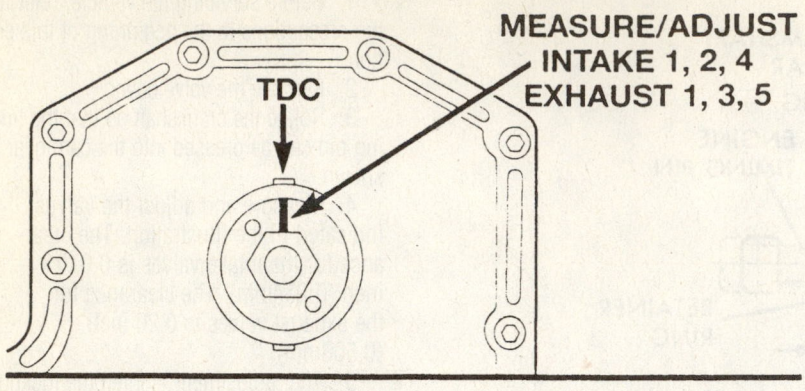

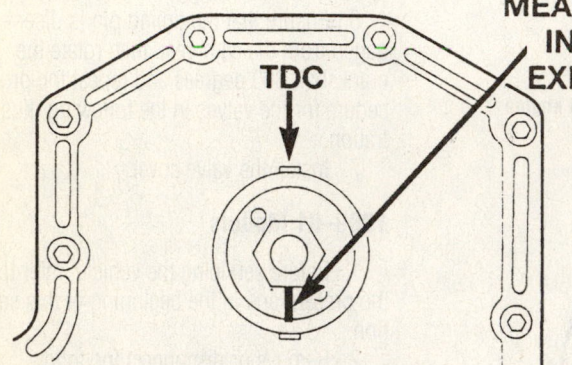

Adjust the specified valves when the mark on the pump gear is in either of the 2 positions—1999–01 diesel engines

- Transmission
- Flywheel and transmission adapter plate.
- Oil pan bolts
- Oil pump suction tube
- Oil pan

To install:

4. Install or connect the following:
   - Oil pan
   - Oil pump suction tube. Tighten the bolts to 18 ft. lbs. (24 Nm).
   - Oil pan bolts. Tighten the bolts to 18 ft. lbs. (24 Nm).
   - Flywheel and transmission adapter plate.
   - Transmission
   - Starter motor
5. Fill the crankcase to the correct level.

Oil Pump

REMOVAL & INSTALLATION

1. Before servicing the vehicle, refer to the precautions in the beginning of this section.
2. Drain the cooling system.
3. Remove or disconnect the following:

Oil Pan

REMOVAL & INSTALLATION

1. Before servicing the vehicle, refer to the precautions in the beginning of this section.
2. Drain the engine oil.
3. Remove or disconnect the following:
   - Negative battery cables
   - Starter motor

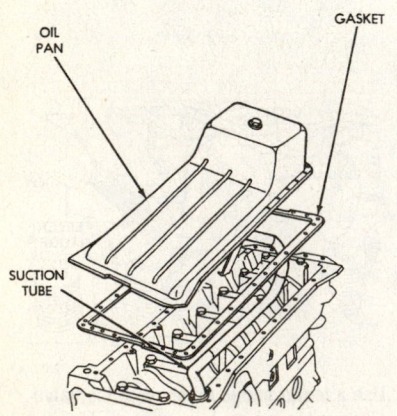

Exploded view of oil pan mounting—1997–98 diesel engine

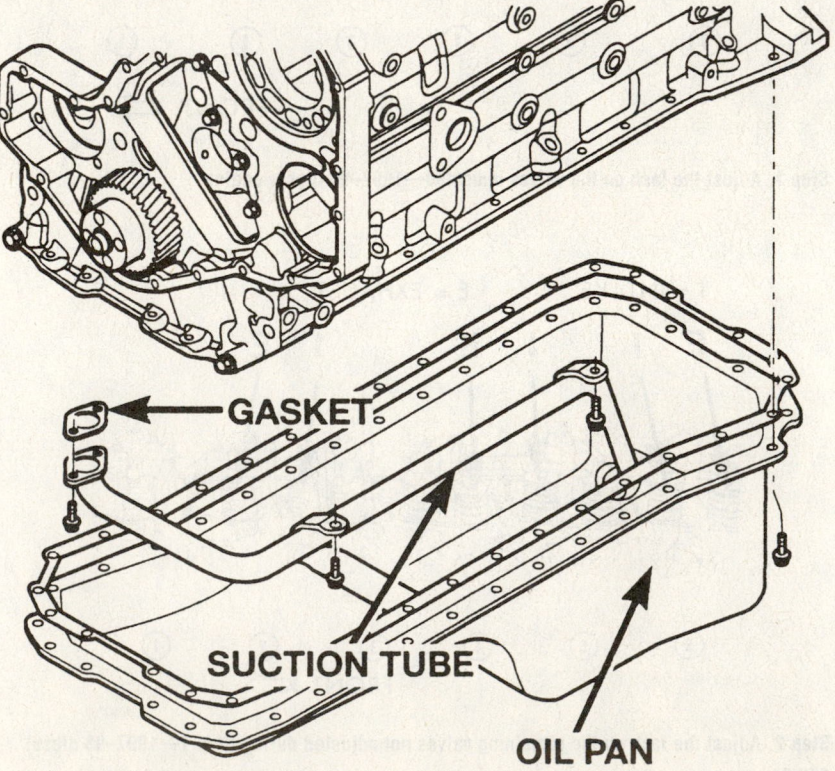

Exploded view of the oil pan mounting—1999–01 diesel engines

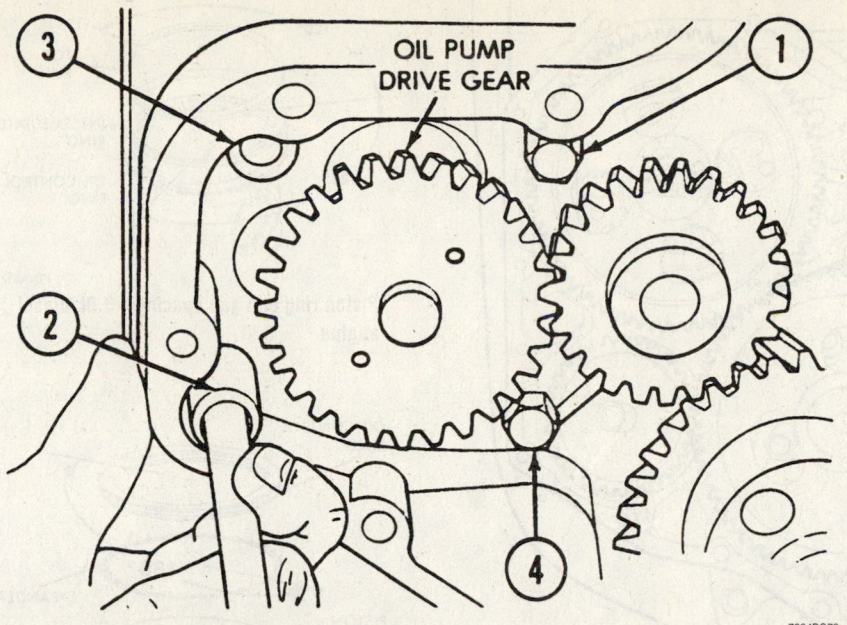

Oil pump torque sequence—5.9L diesel engine

- Negative battery cables
- Accessory drive belt
- Cooling fan and shroud
- Radiator
- Oil fill tube and adapter
- Crankshaft pulley
- Front cover
- Oil pump

To install:

➡ **When the pump is correctly installed, the flange on the pump does not touch the block; the back plate on the pump seats against the bottom of the bore.**

4. Install the oil pump. Tighten the bolts in sequence as follows:
   a. Step 1: 44 inch lbs. (5 Nm).
   b. Step 2: 18 ft. lbs. (24 Nm).
5. Install or connect the following:
   - Front cover
   - Crankshaft pulley
   - Oil fill tube and adapter
   - Radiator
   - Cooling fan and shroud
   - Accessory drive belt
   - Negative battery cables

Rear Main Seal

REMOVAL & INSTALLATION

1. Before servicing the vehicle, refer to the precautions in the beginning of this section.
2. Remove or disconnect the following:

- Negative battery cables
- Transmission
- Clutch and pressure plate, if equipped
- Flywheel
- Seal retainer housing
- Rear main seal

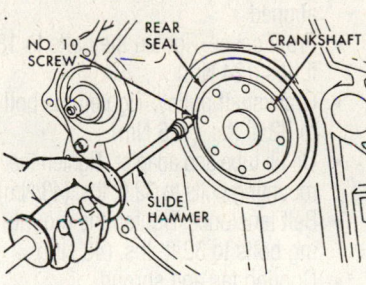

Removing the rear seal with a sheet metal screw and slide hammer—5.9L diesel engine

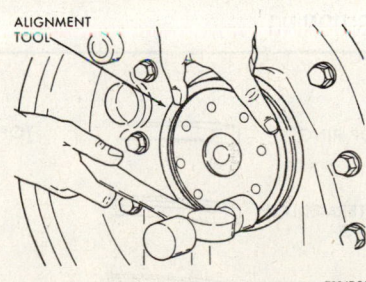

Place the alignment tool on the seal and tap the seal into place—5.9L diesel engine

To install:

3. Install or connect the following:
   - Rear main seal. Use the alignment tool supplied with the seal kit.
   - Seal retainer housing. Tighten the bolts to 84 inch lbs. (9 Nm).
   - Flywheel
   - Clutch and pressure plate, if equipped
   - Transmission
   - Negative battery cables
4. Start the engine and check for leaks.

Timing Gears, Front Cover and Seal

REMOVAL & INSTALLATION

Front Cover and Seal

1. Before servicing the vehicle, refer to the precautions in the beginning of this section.
2. Remove or disconnect the following:
   - Negative battery cables
   - Accessory drive belt
   - Cooling fan and shroud
   - Accessory drive belt tensioner
   - Oil fill tube and adapter
   - Crankshaft pulley
   - Front cover
   - Front crankshaft seal

To install:

3. Install or connect the following:
   - Front crankshaft seal
   - Front cover. Tighten the bolts to 18 ft. lbs. (24 Nm).
   - Crankshaft pulley
   - Oil fill tube and adapter. Tighten the bolts to 32 ft. lbs. (43 Nm).
   - Accessory drive belt tensioner. Tighten the bolts to 32 ft. lbs. (43 Nm).
   - Cooling fan and shroud
   - Accessory drive belt. Tighten the crankshaft pulley bolts to 92 ft. lbs. (125 Nm).
   - Negative battery cables
4. Start the engine and check for leaks.

Timing Gears

1. Before servicing the vehicle, refer to the precautions in the beginning of this section.
2. Remove or disconnect the following:
   - Negative battery cables
   - Accessory drive belt
   - Cooling fan and shroud
   - Belt tensioner

For engine torque specifications, refer to Section 1 of this manual

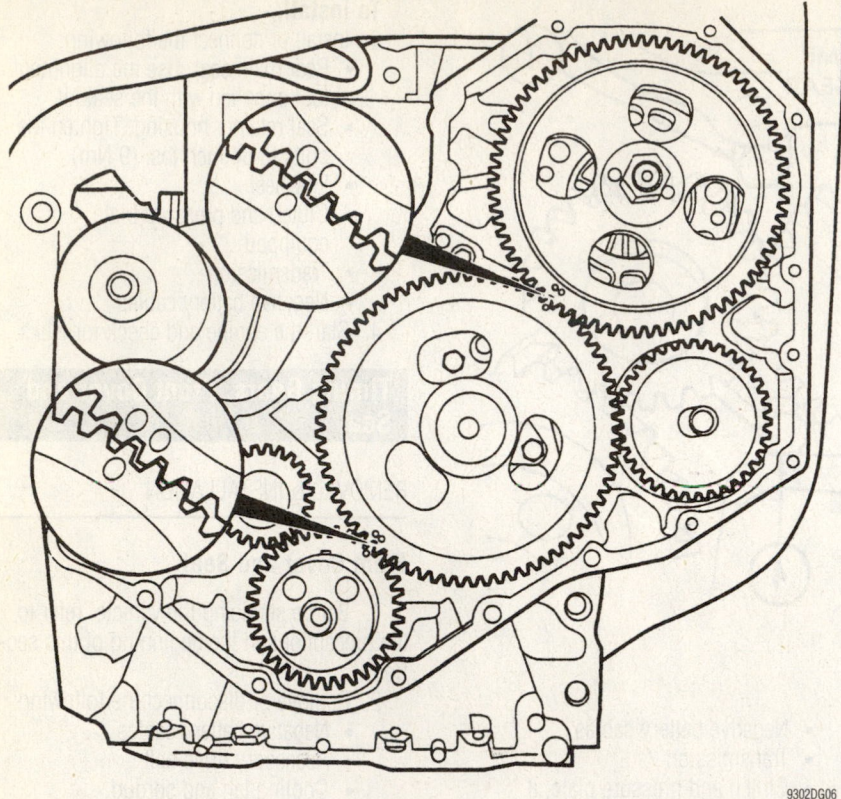

Timing gear alignment marks—5.9L diesel engine

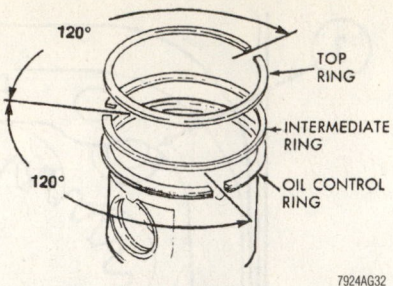

Piston ring end gap spacing—5.9L diesel engine

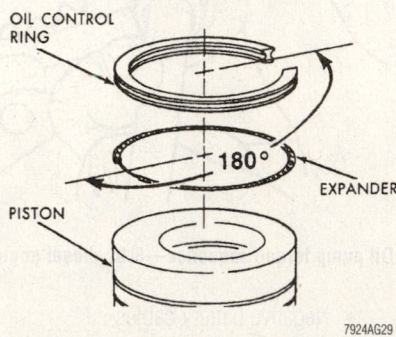

Oil control ring-to-spacer end gap spacing—5.9L diesel engine

- Oil fill tube and adapter
- Crankshaft pulley
- Front cover
- Camshaft

3. Press the camshaft out of the timing gear.

To install:

4. Install the camshaft key.

5. Heat the timing gear in an oven to 350°F (177°C) for 45 minutes.

➡**The camshaft gear will be permanently distorted if overheated. Do not exceed 350°F (177°C).**

6. Install the timing gear to the camshaft with the timing marks facing out and the gear seated on the camshaft shoulder.

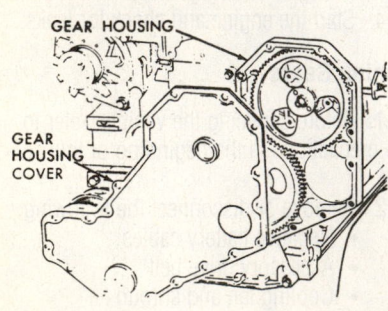

Remove the gear cover to replace the timing gears—5.9L diesel engine

7. Install or connect the following:
- Camshaft with the timing marks aligned
- Front cover. Tighten the bolts to 18 ft. lbs. (24 Nm).
- Crankshaft pulley. Tighten the bolt to 92 ft. lbs. (125 Nm).
- Oil fill tube and adapter. Tighten the mounting bolts to 32 ft. lbs. (43 Nm).
- Belt tensioner. Tighten the mounting bolts to 32 ft. lbs. (43 Nm).
- Cooling fan and shroud
- Accessory drive belt
- Negative battery cables

Piston and Ring

POSITIONING

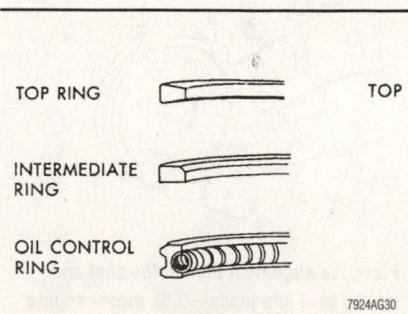

Piston ring identification—5.9L diesel engine

GASOLINE FUEL SYSTEM

Fuel System Service Precautions

Safety is the most important factor when performing not only fuel system maintenance but any type of maintenance. Failure to conduct maintenance and repairs in a safe manner may result in serious personal injury or death. Maintenance and testing of the vehicle's fuel system components can be accomplished safely and effectively by adhering to the following rules and guidelines.

- To avoid the possibility of fire and personal injury, always disconnect the negative battery cable unless the repair or test procedure requires that battery voltage be applied.
- Always relieve the fuel system pressure prior to detaching any fuel system component (injector, fuel rail, pressure regulator, etc.), fitting or fuel line connection. Exercise extreme caution whenever relieving fuel system pressure to avoid exposing skin, face and eyes to fuel spray. Please be advised that fuel under pressure may penetrate the skin or any part of the body that it contacts.
- Always place a shop towel or cloth

around the fitting or connection prior to loosening to absorb any excess fuel due to spillage. Ensure that all fuel spillage (should it occur) is quickly removed from engine surfaces. Ensure that all fuel soaked cloths or towels are deposited into a suitable waste container.

• Always keep a dry chemical (Class B) fire extinguisher near the work area.

• Do not allow fuel spray or fuel vapors to come into contact with a spark or open flame.

• Always use a back-up wrench when loosening and tightening fuel line connection fittings. This will prevent unnecessary stress and torsion to fuel line piping.

• Always replace worn fuel fitting O-rings with new. Do not substitute fuel hose or equivalent, where fuel pipe is installed.

Before servicing the vehicle, also make sure to refer to the precautions in the beginning of this section as well.

Fuel System Pressure

RELIEVING

1. Before servicing the vehicle, refer to the precautions in the beginning of this section.

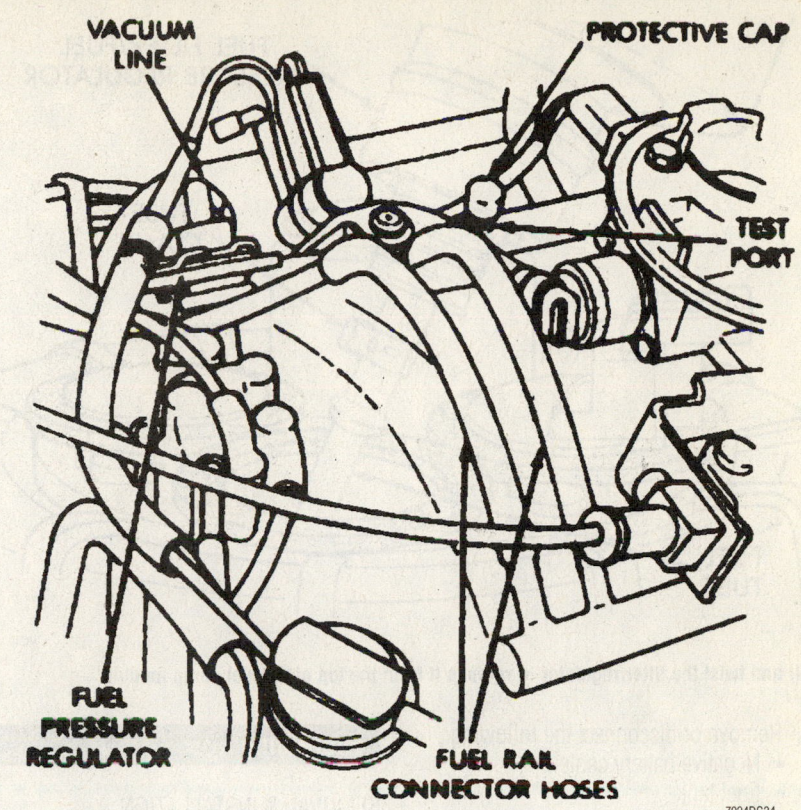

Fuel pressure test port—5.2L engine, 5.9L engine is similar

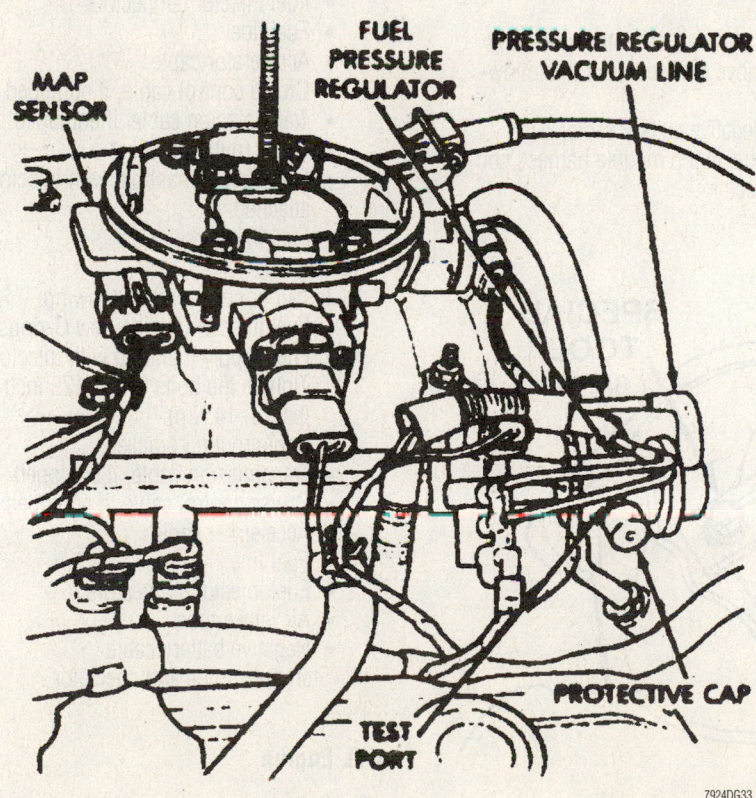

Fuel pressure test port—3.9L engine

2. Disconnect the negative battery cable.
3. Remove the fuel tank filler cap to release any fuel tank pressure.
4. Unscrew the plastic cap from the pressure test port on the fuel rail. On the 8.0L engine, the test port is found at the front of the engine.
5. Obtain a fuel pressure gauge/hose from a fuel pressure gauge tool set No. 5069, or equivalent. Remove the gauge, then place the gauge end of the hose into a suitable gasoline container.
6. Place a shop towel under the test port.
7. Screw the other end of the hose onto the fuel pressure port to relieve the pressure.
8. When the pressure has been relieved, remove the hose and cap the port.

Fuel Filter

REMOVAL & INSTALLATION

1. Before servicing the vehicle, refer to the precautions in the beginning of this section.
2. Relieve the fuel system pressure.

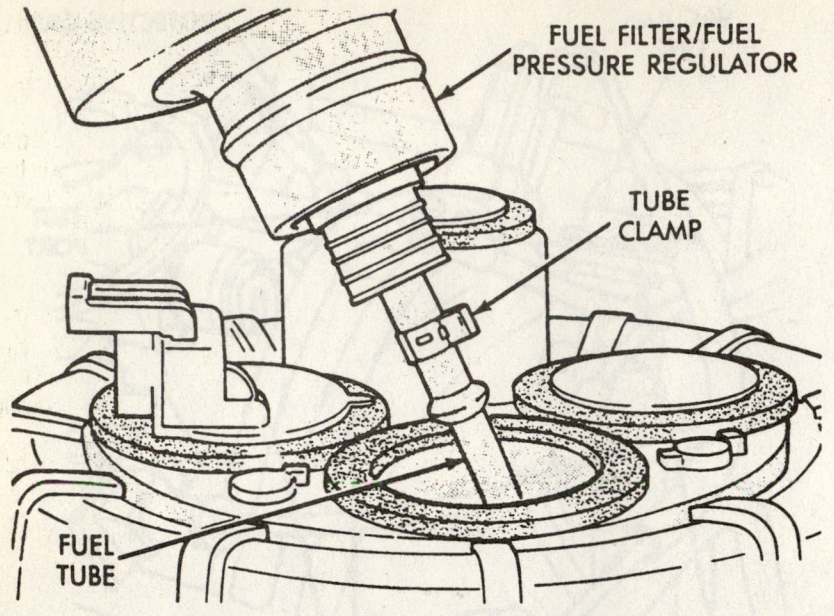

FUEL FILTER/FUEL PRESSURE REGULATOR

TUBE CLAMP

FUEL TUBE

7924DG35

Pull and twist the filter/regulator to remove it from the top of the fuel pump module

3. Remove or disconnect the following:
   • Negative battery cable
   • Fuel tank
4. Pull the filter/regulator out of the rubber grommet. Cut the hose clamp and remove the fuel line.

To install:

5. Install the filter/regulator with a new clamp and push it into the rubber grommet.
6. Install or connect the following:
   • Fuel tank
   • Negative battery cable
7. Start the engine and check for leaks.

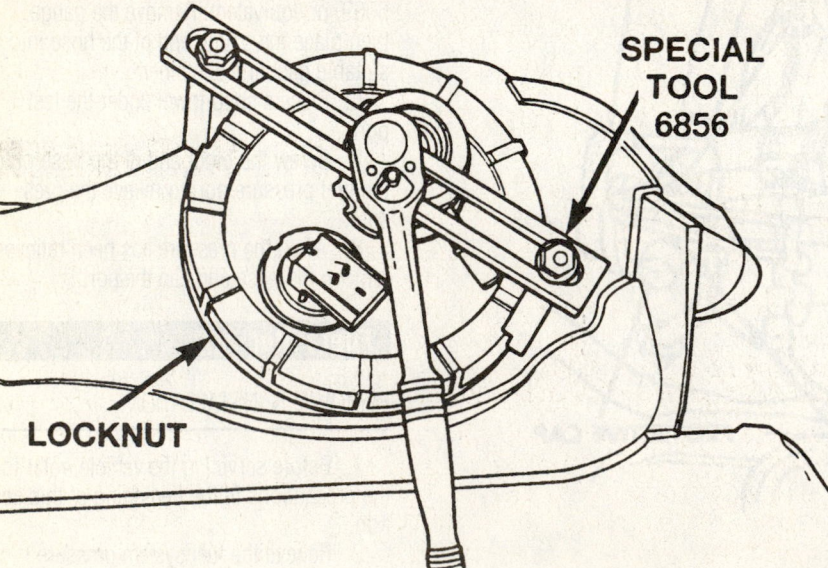

SPECIAL TOOL 6856

LOCKNUT

7924DG82

Fuel pump module locknut removal

Fuel Pump

REMOVAL & INSTALLATION

1. Before servicing the vehicle, refer to the precautions in the beginning of this section.
2. Relieve the fuel system pressure.
3. Remove or disconnect the following:

   • Negative battery cable
   • Fuel pump module harness connector

   • Fuel line
   • Fuel tank
   • Fuel pump module locknut
   • Fuel pump module

To install:

4. Install or connect the following:
   • Fuel pump module
   • Fuel pump module locknut
   • Fuel tank
   • Fuel line
   • Fuel pump module harness connector
   • Negative battery cable
5. Start the engine and check for leaks.

Fuel Injector

REMOVAL & INSTALLATION

2.5L Engine

1. Before servicing the vehicle, refer to the precautions in the beginning of this section.
2. Relieve fuel system pressure.
3. Remove or disconnect the following:

   • Negative battery cable
   • Air intake tube
   • Fuel injector connectors
   • Fuel line
   • Accelerator cable
   • Cruise control cable, if equipped
   • Transmission cable, if equipped
   • Cable routing bracket
   • Fuel supply manifold with injectors attached
   • Fuel injectors

To install:

4. Install or connect the following:
   • Fuel injectors, using new O-rings
   • Fuel supply manifold with injectors. Tighten the bolts to 75–125 inch lbs. (8–14 Nm).
   • Cable routing bracket
   • Transmission cable, if equipped
   • Cruise control cable, if equipped
   • Accelerator cable
   • Fuel line
   • Fuel injector connectors
   • Air intake tube
   • Negative battery cable
5. Start the engine and check for leaks.

4.7L Engine

1. Before servicing the vehicle, refer to the precautions in the beginning of this section.
2. Relieve fuel system pressure.

3. Remove or disconnect the following:

- Negative battery cable
- Air intake assembly
- Alternator wiring connectors
- Fuel line
- Throttle body vacuum lines and electrical connectors
- Fuel injector connectors
- Manifold Absolute Pressure (MAP) sensor connector
- Intake Air Temperature (IAT) sensor connector
- Ignition coils
- Fuel supply manifold with injectors attached
- Fuel injectors

To install:

4. Install or connect the following:

- Fuel injectors, using new O-rings
- Fuel supply manifold with injectors attached. Tighten the bolts to 20 ft. lbs. (27 Nm).
- Ignition coils
- IAT sensor connector
- MAP sensor connector
- Fuel injector connectors
- Throttle body vacuum lines and electrical connectors
- Fuel line
- Alternator wiring connectors
- Air intake assembly
- Negative battery cable

5. Start the engine and check for leaks.

3.9L, 5.2L and 5.9L Engines

1. Before servicing the vehicle, refer to the precautions in the beginning of this section.
2. Relieve fuel system pressure.
3. Remove or disconnect the following:

- Negative battery cable
- Air intake tube
- Throttle body
- A/C compressor bracket
- Fuel injector connectors
- Fuel line
- Fuel supply manifold with injectors
- Fuel injectors

To install:

4. Install or connect the following:

- Fuel injectors with new O-ring seals
- Fuel supply manifold with injectors. Tighten the bolts to 17 ft. lbs. (23 Nm).
- Fuel line

- Fuel injector connectors
- A/C compressor bracket
- Throttle body
- Air intake tube
- Negative battery cable

5. Start the engine and check for leaks.

8.0L Engine

1. Before servicing the vehicle, refer to the precautions in the beginning of this section.
2. Relieve the fuel system pressure.
3. Remove or disconnect the following:

- Negative battery cable
- Air cleaner housing and tube
- Throttle body
- Ignition coil pack and bracket
- Upper intake manifold
- Fuel injector harness connectors
- Fuel line
- Fuel supply manifold with injectors attached
- Fuel injector retainer clips
- Fuel injectors

To install:

4. Install or connect the following:

- Fuel injectors with new O-ring seals
- Fuel injector retainer clips
- Fuel supply manifold. Tighten the bolts to 11 ft. lbs. (15 Nm).
- Fuel line
- Fuel injector harness connectors
- Upper intake manifold
- Ignition coil pack and bracket
- Throttle body
- Air cleaner housing and tube
- Negative battery cable

5. Start the engine and check for leaks.

DIESEL FUEL SYSTEM

Fuel System Service Precautions

Safety is the most important factor when performing not only fuel system maintenance, but any type of maintenance. Failure to conduct maintenance and repairs in a safe manner may result in serious personal injury or death. Maintenance and testing of

the vehicle's fuel system components can be accomplished safely and effectively by adhering to the following rules and guidelines.

- To avoid the possibility of fire and personal injury, always disconnect the negative battery cable unless the repair or test procedure requires that battery voltage be applied.
- Always relieve the fuel system pressure prior to disengaging any fuel system component (injector, fuel rail, pressure regulator, etc.), fitting or fuel line connection. Exercise extreme caution whenever relieving fuel system pressure, to avoid exposing skin, face and eyes to fuel spray. Please be advised that fuel under pressure may penetrate the skin or any part of the body that it contacts.
- Always place a shop towel or cloth around the fitting or connection prior to loosening to absorb any excess fuel due to spillage. Ensure that all fuel spillage (should it occur) is quickly removed from engine surfaces. Ensure that all fuel soaked cloths or towels are deposited into a suitable waste container.
- Always keep a dry chemical (Class B) fire extinguisher near the work area.
- Do not allow fuel spray or fuel vapors to come into contact with a spark or open flame.
- Always use a back-up wrench when loosening and tightening fuel line connection fittings. This will prevent unnecessary stress and torsion to fuel line piping.
- Always replace worn fuel fitting O-rings with new. Do not substitute fuel hose or equivalent, where fuel pipe is installed.

Before servicing the vehicle, also make sure to refer to the precautions in the beginning of this section as well.

Fuel System

BLEEDING AIR

1. Loosen the low pressure bleed bolt.
2. Operate the rubber push-button primer on the fuel transfer pump. Do this until the fuel exiting the bleed screw is free of air. If the primer button feels as if it is not pumping, rotate (crank) the engine approximately 90°, then continue pumping as described.
3. Tighten the low pressure bleed screw to 72 inch lbs. (8 Nm).

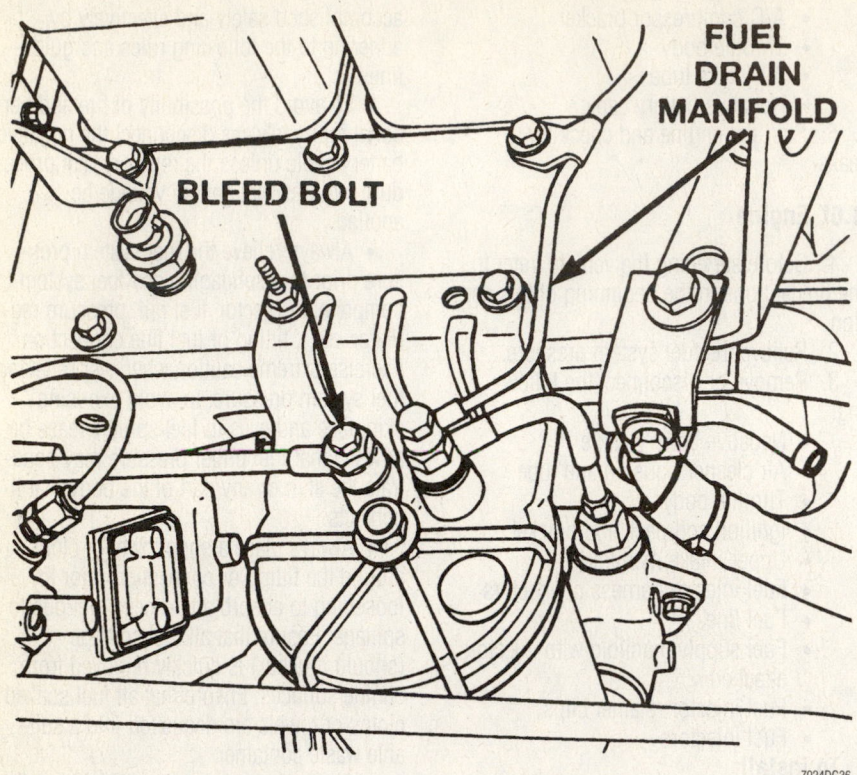

Location of the low pressure bleed bolt—5.9L diesel engine

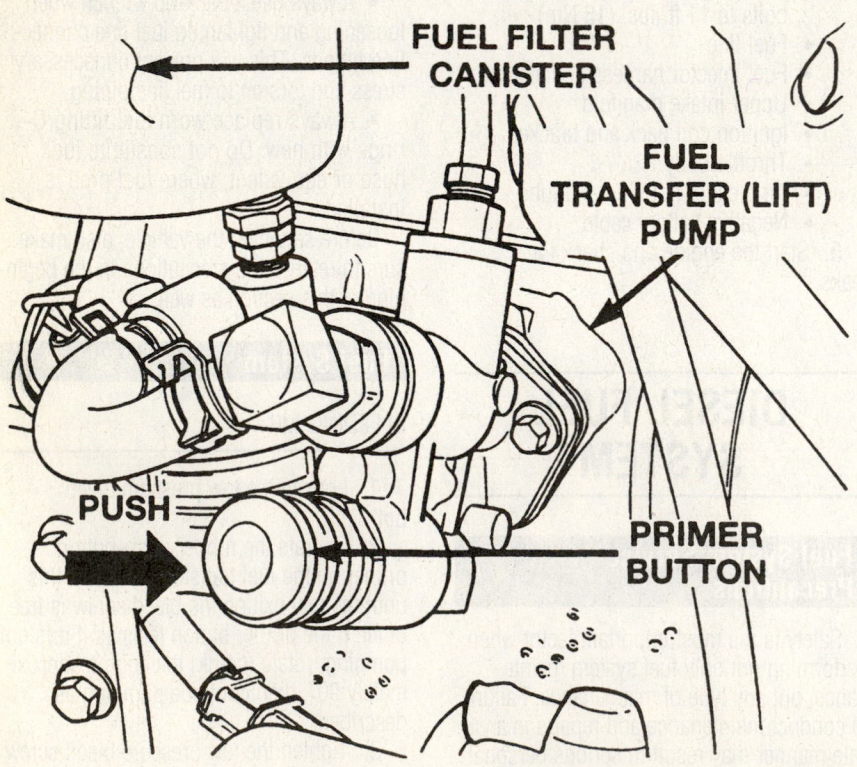

Operate the push-button primer on the fuel transfer pump until the escaping fuel is free of air

Idle Speed

ADJUSTMENT

1. Start the engine and run until normal operating temperature is reached.
2. An optical tachometer must be used to read engine speed.
3. If equipped, turn the air conditioning **ON**.
4. Turn the idle speed screw until the desired idle speed is obtained. The specification for a vehicle equipped with automatic transmission is 700 rpm. The specification for a vehicle equipped with manual transmission is 750 rpm.

Fuel Water Separator/Filter

DRAINING WATER

Filtration and separation of water from the fuel is important for trouble-free operation and long life of the fuel system. Regular maintenance, including draining moisture from the fuel/water separator filter is essential to keep water out of the fuel pump. To remove the collected water, unscrew the drain at the bottom of the Water-In-Filter (WIF) assembly located at the bottom of the filter separator.

REMOVAL & INSTALLATION

1. Before servicing the vehicle, refer to the precautions in the beginning of this section.
2. Remove or disconnect the following:
   - Negative battery cables
   - Water In Filter (WIF) sensor connector
   - Separator filter assembly

To install:
3. Install or connect the following:
   - Separator filter assembly with a new O-ring seal
   - WIF sensor connector
   - Negative battery cables
4. Bleed air from the system.
5. Start the engine and check for leaks.

Diesel Injection Pump

REMOVAL & INSTALLATION

➡The Bosch VE lever is indexed to the shaft during pump calibration. Do not remove it from the pump during removal.

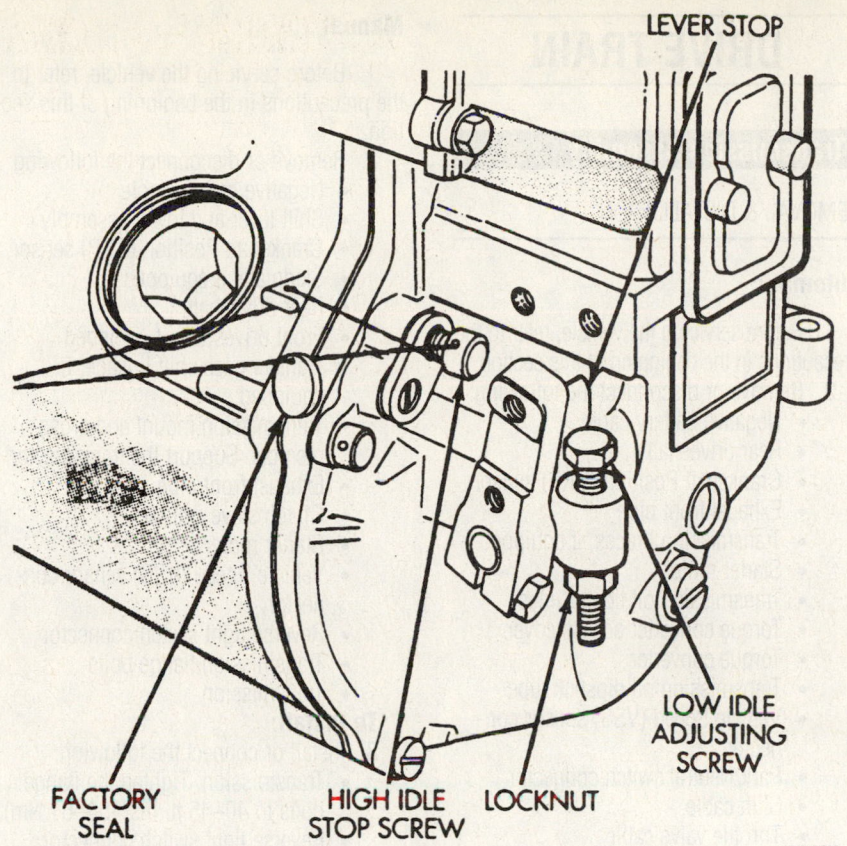

Idle speed adjusting screw location—5.9L diesel engine

LEVER STOP

LOW IDLE
ADJUSTING
SCREW

FACTORY
SEAL

HIGH IDLE
STOP SCREW

LOCKNUT

7924DG38

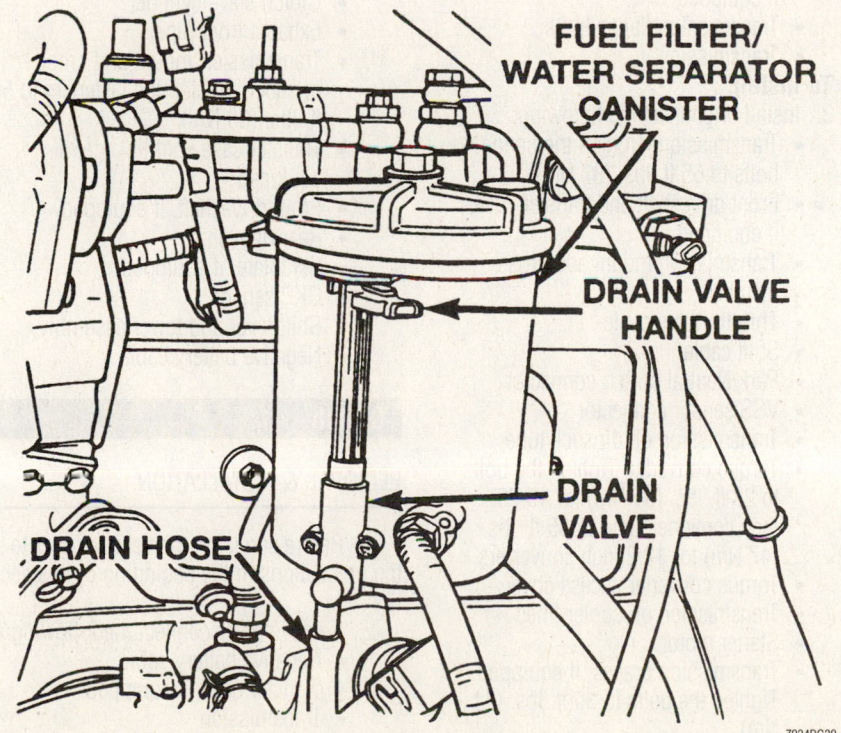

Fuel filter/water separator assembly and related components

FUEL FILTER/
WATER SEPARATOR
CANISTER

DRAIN VALVE
HANDLE

DRAIN
VALVE

DRAIN HOSE

7924DG39

1. Before servicing the vehicle, refer to the precautions in the beginning of this section.

2. Remove or disconnect the following:
   - Negative battery cables
   - Throttle linkage and bracket
   - Fuel drain manifold
   - Injection pump supply line
   - High pressure lines
   - Fuel air control tube
   - Fuel shut off valve connector
   - Pump support bracket
   - Oil fill tube and adapter

3. Place a shop towel in the gear cover opening in a position that will prevent the nut and washer from falling into the gear housing. Remove the gear retaining nut and washer.

4. Turn the engine until the keyway on the fuel pump shaft is pointing approximately in the 6 o'clock position.

5. Locate Top Dead Center (TDC) for cylinder No. 1 by turning the engine slowly while pushing in on the TDC pin. Stop turning the engine as soon as the pin engages with the gear timing hole. Disengage the pin after locating TDC and remove the turning equipment.

6. Loosen the lockscrew, remove the special washer from the injection pump and wire it to the line above it so it will not get misplaced. Retighten the lockscrew to 22 ft. lbs. (30 Nm) to lock the driveshaft.

7. Press the pump drive gear from the driveshaft.

➡ **Be careful not to drop the drive gear key into the front cover when removing or installing the pump. If it does drop in, it must be removed before proceeding.**

8. Remove the 3 mounting nuts and remove the injection pump from the vehicle.

9. Remove the gasket and clean the mounting surface.

To install:

➡ **The shaft of a new or reconditioned pump is locked so the key aligns with the drive gear keyway with cylinder No. 1 at TDC.**

10. Install the pump and finger-tighten the mounting nuts; the pump must be free to move in the slots.

11. Install the pump drive gear, washer and nut to the driveshaft. The pump will rotate slightly because of gear helix and clearance. This is acceptable providing the pump is free to move on the flange slots and the crankshaft does not move. Tighten

the nut to 11–15 ft. lbs. (15–20 Nm). Do not overtighten.

12. If installing the original pump, rotate the pump to align the original timing marks and tighten the mounting nuts to 18 ft. lbs. (24 Nm).

13. If installing a replacement pump, take up gear lash by rotating the pump counterclockwise toward the cylinder head, and tighten the mounting nuts to 18 ft. lbs. (24 Nm). Permanently mark the new injection pump flange to match the mark on the gear housing.

14. Loosen the lockscrew and install the special washer under the lockscrew; tighten to 13 ft. lbs. (18 Nm). Disengage the TDC pin.

15. Install or connect the following:
- Pump support bracket. Tighten the pump drive gear nut to 48 ft. lbs. (65 Nm).
- Oil fill tube and adapter
- Fuel shut off valve connector
- Fuel air control tube
- High pressure lines
- Injection pump supply line
- Fuel drain manifold
- Throttle linkage and bracket
- Negative battery cables

16. Bleed air from the system.

17. Start the engine and check for leaks.

Fuel Injectors

REMOVAL & INSTALLATION

1. Before servicing the vehicle, refer to the precautions in the beginning of this section.

2. Remove or disconnect the following:
- Negative battery cables
- High pressure fuel lines
- Fuel drain manifold
- Fuel injector. Hold the injector with a backing wrench while loosening the mounting nut.

To install:

3. Use a new copper washer and coat the backing nut threads with anti-seize compound.

4. Install or connect the following:
- Fuel injector. Tighten the mounting nut to 44 ft. lbs. (60 Nm).
- Fuel drain manifold. Use new copper gaskets and tighten the fitting screws to 84 inch lbs. (9 Nm).
- High pressure fuel lines
- Negative battery cables

5. Bleed the fuel system.

6. Start the engine and check for leaks.

DRIVE TRAIN

Transmission Assembly

REMOVAL & INSTALLATION

Automatic

1. Before servicing the vehicle, refer to the precautions in the beginning of this section.

2. Remove or disconnect the following:
- Negative battery cable
- Rear driveshaft
- Crankshaft Position (CKP) sensor
- Exhaust front pipe
- Transmission braces, if equipped
- Starter motor
- Transmission oil cooler lines
- Torque converter access cover
- Torque converter
- Transmission oil dipstick tube
- Vehicle Speed (VSS) sensor connector
- Park/Neutral switch connector
- Shift cable
- Throttle valve cable
- Transmission mount and crossmember. Support the transmission.
- Front driveshaft and transfer case, if equipped
- Transmission flange bolts
- Transmission

To install:

3. Install or connect the following:
- Transmission. Tighten the flange bolts to 65 ft. lbs. (87 Nm).
- Front driveshaft and transfer case, if equipped
- Transmission mount and crossmember
- Throttle valve cable
- Shift cable
- Park/Neutral switch connector
- VSS sensor connector
- Transmission oil dipstick tube
- Torque converter. Tighten the bolts to 23 ft. lbs. (31 Nm) for 10.75 inch converters and to 35 ft. lbs. (47 Nm) for 12.2 inch converters.
- Torque converter access cover
- Transmission oil cooler lines
- Starter motor
- Transmission braces, if equipped. Tighten the bolts to 30 ft. lbs. (41 Nm).
- Exhaust front pipe
- CKP sensor
- Rear driveshaft
- Negative battery cable

Manual

1. Before servicing the vehicle, refer to the precautions in the beginning of this section.

2. Remove or disconnect the following:
- Negative battery cable
- Shift lever and tower assembly
- Crankshaft Position (CKP) sensor
- Skidplate, if equipped
- Rear driveshaft
- Front driveshaft, if equipped
- Transfer case shift linkage, if equipped
- Transmission mount and crossmember. Support the transmission.
- Exhaust front pipe
- Clutch slave cylinder
- Starter motor
- Vehicle Speed (VSS) sensor connector
- Reverse light switch connector
- Transmission flange bolts
- Transmission

To install:

3. Install or connect the following:
- Transmission. Tighten the flange bolts to 40–45 ft. lbs. (54–61 Nm).
- Reverse light switch connector
- Vehicle Speed (VSS) sensor connector
- Starter motor
- Clutch slave cylinder
- Exhaust front pipe
- Transmission mount and crossmember. Tighten the fasteners to 50 ft. lbs. (68 Nm).
- Transfer case shift linkage, if equipped
- Front driveshaft, if equipped
- Rear driveshaft
- Skidplate, if equipped
- CKP sensor
- Shift lever and tower assembly
- Negative battery cable

Clutch

REMOVAL & INSTALLATION

1. Before servicing the vehicle, refer to the precautions in the beginning of this section.

2. Remove or disconnect the following:
- Negative battery cable
- Transfer case, if equipped
- Transmission
- Pressure plate. Loosen the bolts evenly in ½ turn steps.
- Clutch disc

To install:

3. Install or connect the following:

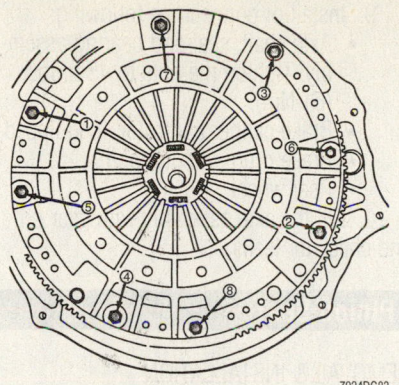

Pressure plate torque sequence

- Clutch disc and pressure plate. Tighten the pressure plate bolts evenly in ½ turns to 21 ft. lbs. (28 Nm).
- Transmission
- Transfer case, if equipped
- Negative battery cable

Hydraulic Clutch System

BLEEDING

The system is self-bleeding. Press the clutch pedal repeatedly to release air from the fluid. The air will be vented from the reservoir.

Transfer Case Assembly

REMOVAL & INSTALLATION

1. Before servicing the vehicle, refer to the precautions in the beginning of this section.
2. Shift the transfer case into **N**.
3. Remove or disconnect the following:
   - Front and rear driveshafts
   - Transmission mount and cross-member. Support the transmission.
   - Vehicle Speed (VSS) sensor connector
   - Shift linkage
   - Vent hose
   - Vacuum hose
   - Indicator switch connector
   - Transfer case attaching nuts
   - Transfer case

To install:
4. Install or connect the following:
   - Transfer case. Tighten the nuts to 26 ft. lbs. (35 Nm).
   - Indicator switch connector
   - Vacuum hose

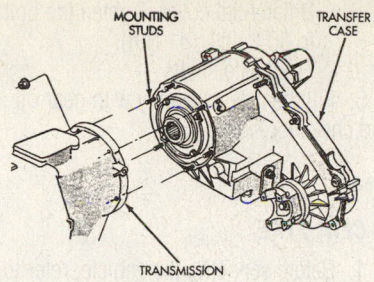

Typical transfer case mounting

- Vent hose
- Shift linkage
- VSS sensor connector
- Transmission mount and cross-member
- Front and rear driveshafts

Halfshaft

REMOVAL & INSTALLATION

1. Before servicing the vehicle, refer to the precautions in the beginning of this section.
2. Remove or disconnect the following:
   - Skid plate, if equipped
   - Front wheel
   - Split pin
   - Nut lock
   - Spring washer
   - Hub nut
   - Brake caliper and rotor
   - Wheel speed sensor, if equipped
   - Wheel bearing and hub assembly
3. Pry the inner tripod joint out of the differential and remove the axle halfshaft.

To install:
4. Install the axle halfshaft so that the snapring is felt to seat in the joint housing groove.

5. Install or connect the following:
   - Wheel bearing and hub assembly
   - Wheel speed sensor, if equipped
   - Brake caliper and rotor
   - Hub nut. Tighten the nut to 180 ft. lbs. (244 Nm).
   - Spring washer
   - Nut lock
   - Split pin
   - Front wheel
   - Skid plate, if equipped

CV-Joints

OVERHAUL

Outer CV-Joint

1. Before servicing the vehicle, refer to the precautions in the beginning of this section.
2. Remove or disconnect the following:
   - Axle halfshaft from the vehicle
   - CV-joint boot and clamps
   - Snapring
   - CV-joint

To install:
3. Install or connect the following:
   - CV-joint
   - Snapring
   - CV-joint boot and clamps
4. Fill the joint housing and boot with grease and tighten the boot clamps.
5. Install the axle halfshaft.

Inner Tripod Joint

1. Before servicing the vehicle, refer to the precautions in the beginning of this section.
2. Remove or disconnect the following:
   - Axle halfshaft from the vehicle

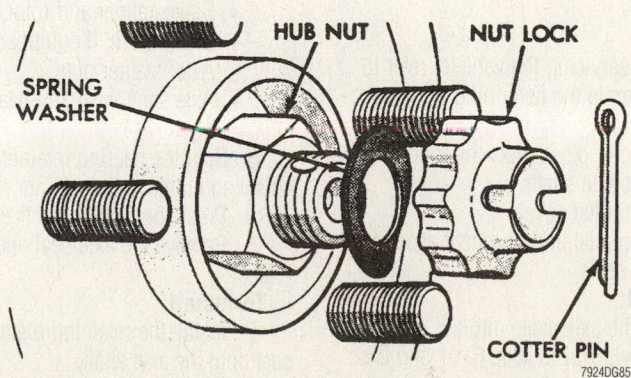

To separate the halfshaft from the hub, remove the cotter pin, nut lock and spring washer from the axle shaft

- Inner tripod joint boot clamps
- Tripod joint housing
- Snapring
- Circlip
- Tripod joint

To install:

➡ **Use new snaprings, clips, and boot clamps for assembly.**

3. Install or connect the following:
   - Tripod joint
   - Circlip
   - Snapring
   - Tripod joint housing
4. Fill the tripod joint housing and boot with grease and tighten the boot clamps.
5. Install the axle halfshaft.

Axle Shaft, Bearing and Seal

REMOVAL & INSTALLATION

Front

AXLE SHAFT

1. Before servicing the vehicle, refer to the precautions in the beginning of this section.
2. Remove or disconnect the following:
   - Front wheel
   - Brake caliper and rotor
   - Wheel speed sensor, if equipped
   - Axle hub nut
   - Wheel bearing and hub assembly
   - Axle shaft

To install:

3. Install or connect the following:
   - Axle shaft
   - Wheel bearing and hub assembly
   - Axle hub nut. Tighten the nut to 175 ft. lbs. (237 Nm).
   - Wheel speed sensor, if equipped
   - Brake caliper and rotor
   - Front wheel

SEAL

1. Before servicing the vehicle, refer to the precautions in the beginning of this section.
2. Remove or disconnect the following:
   - Front axle shafts
   - Differential cover
   - Differential and ring gear assembly
   - Axle seals

To install:

3. Press the axle seals into the differential housing with Turnbuckle 6797 and Disc set 8110.
4. Install or connect the following:
   - Differential and ring gear assembly. Tighten the bearing cap bolts to 45 ft. lbs. (61 Nm).

- Differential cover. Tighten the bolts to 30 ft. lbs. (41 Nm).
- Front axle shafts
5. Fill the axle assembly with gear oil and check for leaks.

Rear

C-CLIP TYPE

1. Before servicing the vehicle, refer to the precautions in the beginning of this section.
2. Remove or disconnect the following:
   - Rear wheel
   - Brake drum
   - Differential cover
   - Differential gear shaft retainer
   - Differential gear shaft
   - C-clip
   - Axle shaft
   - Axle seal
   - Axle bearing

To install:

3. Install or connect the following:
   - Axle bearing
   - Axle seal
   - Axle shaft
   - C-clip
   - Differential gear shaft. Use Loctite® and tighten the retainer to 14 ft. lbs. (19 Nm).
   - Differential cover. Tighten the bolts to 30 ft. lbs. (41 Nm).
   - Brake drum
   - Rear wheel
4. Fill the axle assembly with gear oil and check for leaks.

NON C-CLIP TYPE

1. Before servicing the vehicle, refer to the precautions in the beginning of this section.
2. Remove or disconnect the following:
   - Rear wheel
   - Brake caliper and rotor, if equipped
   - Brake drum, if equipped
   - Axle retainer nuts
   - Axle shaft, seal and bearing assembly
3. Split the bearing retainer with a chisel and remove the retainer ring.
4. Press the bearing off the axle shaft.
5. Remove the axle seal and retaining plate.

To install:

6. Install the retaining plate and axle seal onto the axle shaft.
7. Pack the wheel bearing with axle grease and press the bearing on to the axle shaft.
8. Press the retaining ring onto the axle shaft.

9. Install or connect the following:
   - Axle shaft, seal and bearing assembly. Tighten the nuts to 45 ft. lbs. (61 Nm).
   - Brake caliper and rotor, if equipped
   - Brake drum, if equipped
   - Rear wheel
10. Fill the axle assembly with gear oil and check for leaks.

Pinion Seal

REMOVAL & INSTALLATION

C-Clip Type

1. Before servicing the vehicle, refer to the precautions in the beginning of this section.
2. Remove or disconnect the following:
   - Wheels
   - Brake drums
   - Driveshaft
3. Check the bearing preload with an inch lb. torque wrench.
4. Remove the pinion flange and seal.

To install:

➡ **Use a new pinion nut for assembly.**

5. Install the new pinion seal and flange. Tighten the nut to 210 ft. lbs. (285 Nm).
6. Check the bearing preload. The bearing preload should be equal to the reading taken earlier, plus 5 inch lbs.
7. If the preload torque is low, tighten the pinion nut in 5 inch lb. increments until the torque value is reached. Do not exceed 350 ft. lbs. (474 Nm) pinion nut torque.
8. If the pinion bearing preload torque cannot be attained at maximum pinion nut torque, replace the collapsible spacer.
9. Install or connect the following:
   - Driveshaft
   - Brake drums
   - Wheels
10. Fill the axle assembly with gear oil and check for leaks.

Non C-Clip Type

FRONT

1. Before servicing the vehicle, refer to the precautions in the beginning of this section.
2. Remove or disconnect the following:
   - Wheels
   - Brake rotors
   - Driveshaft
3. Check the bearing preload with an inch lb. torque wrench.
4. Remove the pinion flange and seal.

To install:

➡ **Use a new pinion nut for assembly.**

5. Install the new pinion seal and flange. Tighten the nut to 160 ft. lbs. (217 Nm).

6. Check the bearing preload. The bearing preload should be equal to the reading taken earlier, plus 5 inch lbs.

7. If the preload torque is low, tighten the pinion nut in 5 inch lb. increments until the torque value is reached. Do not exceed 260 ft. lbs. (353 Nm) pinion nut torque.

8. If the pinion bearing preload torque can not be attained at maximum pinion nut torque, replace the collapsible spacer.

9. Install or connect the following:
- Driveshaft
- Brake rotors
- Wheels

10. Fill the axle assembly with gear oil and check for leaks.

REAR

1. Before servicing the vehicle, refer to the precautions in the beginning of this section.

2. Remove or disconnect the following:
- Wheels
- Brake rotors or drums
- Driveshaft

3. Check the bearing preload with an inch lb. torque wrench.

4. Remove the pinion flange and seal.

To install:

➡ **Use a new pinion nut for assembly.**

5. Install the new pinion seal and flange. Tighten the nut to 160 ft. lbs. (217 Nm).

6. Check the bearing preload. The bearing preload should be equal to the reading taken earlier, plus 5 inch lbs.

7. If the preload torque is low, tighten the pinion nut in 5 inch lb. increments until the torque value is reached. Do not exceed 260 ft. lbs. (353 Nm) pinion nut torque.

8. If the pinion bearing preload torque can not be attained at maximum pinion nut torque, remove one or more pinion preload shims.

9. Install or connect the following:
- Driveshaft
- Brake rotors or drums
- Wheels

10. Fill the axle assembly with gear oil and check for leaks.

Axle Housing Assembly

REMOVAL & INSTALLATION

Front

1. Before servicing the vehicle, refer to the precautions in the beginning of this section.

2. Remove or disconnect the following:

- Wheels
- Brake calipers and rotors
- Wheel speed sensor, if equipped
- Vent hose
- Driveshaft
- Stabilizer bar links
- Track bar
- Shock absorbers
- Tie rod ends
- Steering damper
- Upper and lower control arms
- Coil springs
- Axle housing

To install:

➡ **The weight of the vehicle must be supported by the springs when the control arm and track bar fasteners are tightened.**

3. Install or connect the following:
- Axle housing and coil springs to the vehicle
- Upper and lower control arms
- Steering damper
- Tie rod ends
- Shock absorbers
- Track bar
- Stabilizer bar links. Tighten the nuts to 70 ft. lbs. (95 Nm).
- Driveshaft
- Vent hose
- Wheel speed sensor, if equipped
- Brake calipers and rotors
- Front wheels

4. Tighten the upper control arm nuts to 55 ft. lbs. (75 Nm), the lower control arm nuts to 85 ft. lbs. (115 Nm) and the track bar bolts to 74 ft. lbs. (100 Nm).

5. Check the wheel alignment and adjust as necessary.

Rear

1. Before servicing the vehicle, refer to the precautions in the beginning of this section.

2. Remove or disconnect the following:
- Rear wheels
- Brake drums

- Parking brake cables
- Wheel speed sensors, if equipped
- Brake hose
- Vent hose
- Driveshaft
- Stabilizer bar links
- Shock absorbers
- Axle housing

To install:

3. Install or connect the following:
- Axle housing. Tighten the nuts to 52 ft. lbs. (70 Nm).
- Shock absorbers
- Stabilizer bar links. Tighten the nuts to 55 ft. lbs. (74 Nm).
- Driveshaft
- Vent hose
- Brake hose
- Wheel speed sensors, if equipped
- Parking brake cables
- Brake drums
- Rear wheels

STEERING AND SUSPENSION

Air Bag

✳✳ CAUTION

Some vehicles are equipped with an air bag system. The system must be disarmed before performing service on, or around, system components, the steering column, instrument panel components, wiring and sensors. Failure to follow the safety precautions and the disarming procedure could result in accidental air bag deployment, possible injury and unnecessary system repairs.

PRECAUTIONS

Several precautions must be observed when handling the inflator module to avoid accidental deployment and possible personal injury.

- Never carry the inflator module by the wires or connector on the underside of the module.

- When carrying a live inflator module, hold securely with both hands, and ensure that the bag and trim cover are pointed away.

• Place the inflator module on a bench or other surface with the bag and trim cover facing up.

• With the inflator module on the bench, never place anything on or close to the module which may be thrown in the event of an accidental deployment.

Before servicing the vehicle, also make sure to refer to the precautions in the beginning of this section as well.

DISARMING

1. Disconnect and isolate the negative battery cable. Wait 2 minutes for the system capacitor to discharge before performing any service.

2. When repairs are completed, connect the negative battery cable.

Recirculating Ball Power Steering Gear

REMOVAL & INSTALLATION

1. Before servicing the vehicle, refer to the precautions in the beginning of this section.

2. Remove or disconnect the following:
   • Negative battery cable
   • Power steering pressure and return lines
   • Intermediate shaft
   • Pitman arm
   • Steering gear

To install:

3. Install or connect the following:
   • Steering gear. Tighten the bolts to 100 ft. lbs. (136 Nm).
   • Pitman arm. Tighten the nut to 175 ft. lbs. (237 Nm).
   • Intermediate shaft. Tighten the pinch bolt to 36 ft. lbs. (49 Nm).
   • Power steering pressure and return lines
   • Negative battery cable

4. Fill the power steering fluid reservoir.

5. Start the engine and check for leaks.

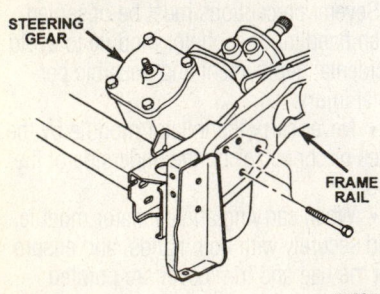

Typical recirculating ball power steering gear mounting

7924DG41

Rack and Pinion Steering Gear

REMOVAL & INSTALLATION

1. Before servicing the vehicle, refer to the precautions in the beginning of this section.

2. Remove or disconnect the following:

   • Front wheels
   • Outer tie rod ends
   • Steering shaft coupler
   • Power steering hoses
   • Steering gear

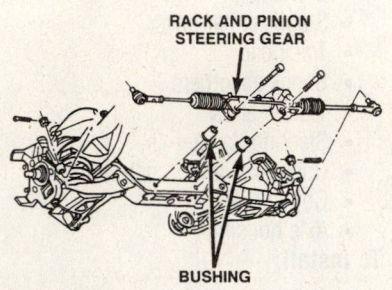

7924DG42

Rack and pinion steering gear mounting used on the 2WD Dakota and Durango models

To install:

3. Install or connect the following:
   • Steering gear. Tighten the bolts to 190 ft. lbs. (258 Nm).
   • Power steering hoses. Tighten the fittings to 25 ft. lbs. (35 Nm).
   • Steering shaft coupler. Tighten the bolt to 36 ft. lbs. (49 Nm).
   • Outer tie rod ends. Tighten the nuts to 65 ft. lbs. (88 Nm).
   • Front wheels

Shock Absorber

REMOVAL & INSTALLATION

Front

COIL SPRING SUSPENSION

1. Before servicing the vehicle, refer to the precautions in the beginning of this section.

2. Remove or disconnect the following:

   • Front wheel
   • Upper mounting bolt
   • Lower mounting bolts
   • Shock absorber

To install:

3. Install or connect the following:

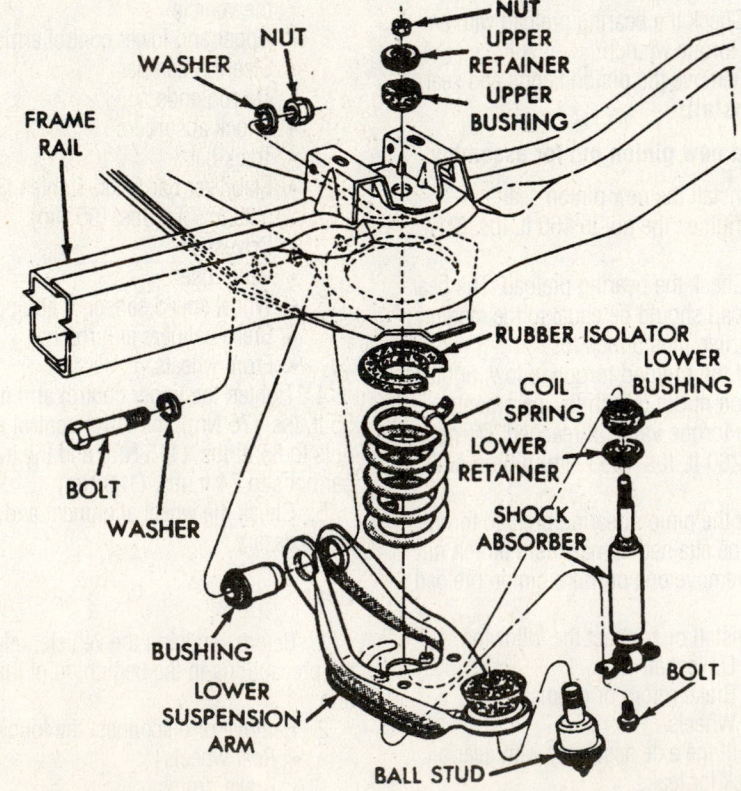

Front shock absorber mounting—Ram Van models

7924DG87

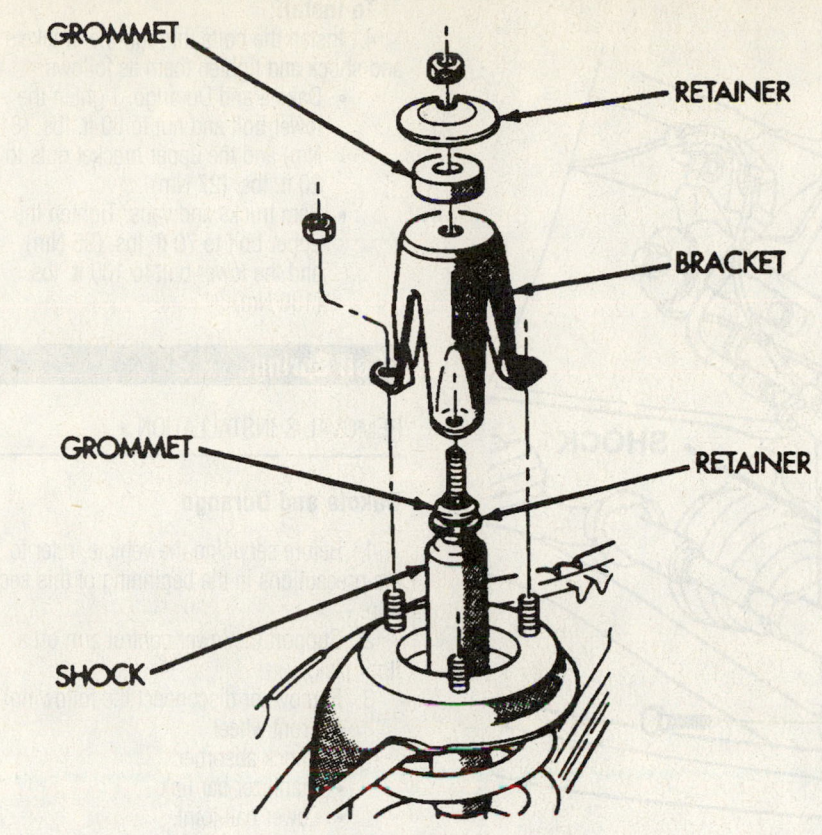

Upper shock absorber mounting—Ram Truck models

Labels: GROMMET, RETAINER, BRACKET, GROMMET, RETAINER, SHOCK

7924DG88

- Shock absorber. Tighten the upper bolt to 25 ft. lbs. (34 Nm) and the lower bolts to 15 ft. lbs. (20 Nm).
- Front wheel

LEAF SPRING SUSPENSION

1. Before servicing the vehicle, refer to the precautions in the beginning of this section.

2. Remove or disconnect the following:

- Front wheel
- Upper shock bracket
- Lower shock mount bolt
- Shock absorber

To install:

3. Install or connect the following:

- Shock absorber. Tighten the lower bolt to 50 ft. lbs. (68 Nm).
- Upper shock bracket. Tighten the fasteners to 50 ft. lbs. (68 Nm).
- Front wheel

TORSION BAR SUSPENSION

1. Before servicing the vehicle, refer to the precautions in the beginning of this section.

2. Remove or disconnect the following:

3. Install or connect the following:

- Front wheel
- Upper mount nut
- Lower mount bolt
- Shock absorber

To install:

4. Install or connect the following:

- Shock absorber. Tighten the lower bolt to 100 ft. lbs. (136 Nm) and the upper nut to 30 ft. lbs. (41 Nm).
- Front wheel

Lower shock absorber mounting—Ram Truck models

Labels: SHOCK, SPRING, SHOCK BOLT, FLAG NUT

7924DG89

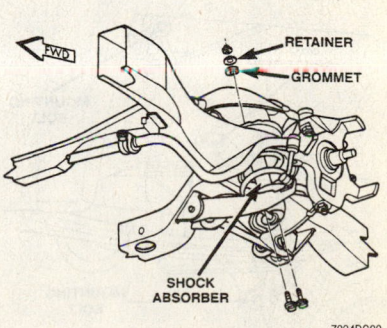

Front shock absorber mounting—2WD Dakota and Durango models

Labels: 2WD, RETAINER, GROMMET, SHOCK ABSORBER

7924DG90

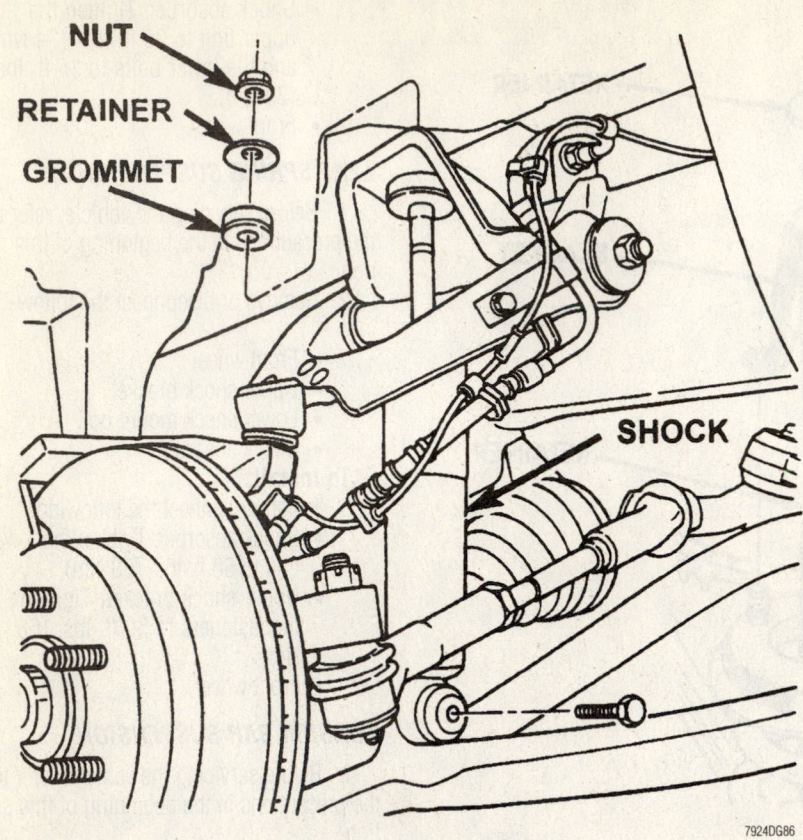

NUT
RETAINER
GROMMET
SHOCK

7924DG86

Front shock absorber mounting—4WD Dakota and Durango models

To install:

4. Install the bolts through the brackets and shock and tighten them as follows:

- Dakota and Durango: Tighten the lower bolt and nut to 60 ft. lbs. (81 Nm) and the upper bracket nuts to 20 ft. lbs. (27 Nm)
- Ram trucks and vans: Tighten the upper bolt to 70 ft. lbs. (95 Nm) and the lower bolt to 100 ft. lbs. (136 Nm)

Coil Spring

REMOVAL & INSTALLATION

Dakota and Durango

1. Before servicing the vehicle, refer to the precautions in the beginning of this section.

2. Support the lower control arm on a floor jack.

3. Remove or disconnect the following:
- Front wheel
- Shock absorber
- Stabilizer bar link
- Lower ball joint.

4. Lower the jack and remove the coil spring.

Rear

1. Before servicing the vehicle, refer to the precautions in the beginning of this section.

2. Support the axle.

3. Remove or disconnect the following:
- Upper bolt
- Lower bolt
- Shock absorber

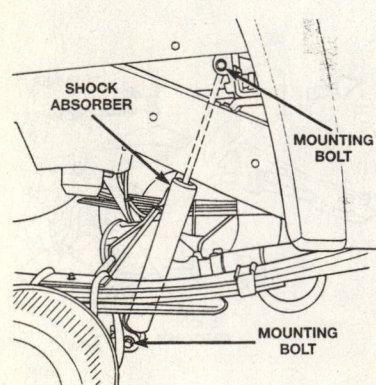

SHOCK ABSORBER
MOUNTING BOLT
MOUNTING BOLT

7924DG91

Rear shock absorber mounting—Dakota and Durango models

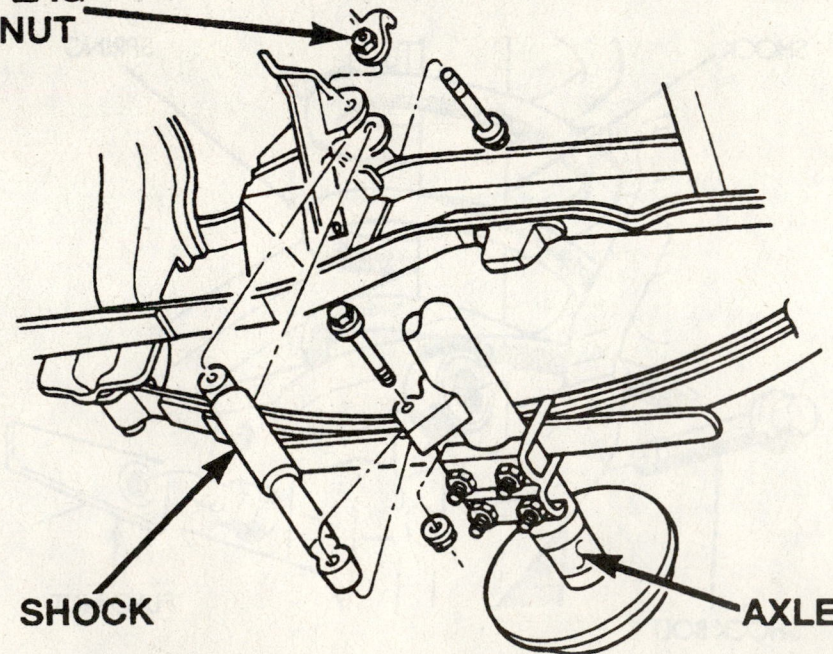

FLAG NUT
SHOCK
AXLE

7924DG92

Rear shock absorber mounting—Ram Truck and Van models

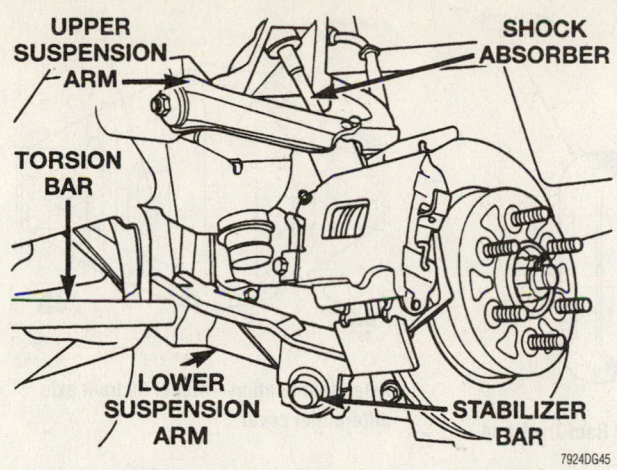

Front suspension components—4WD Dakota and Durango models

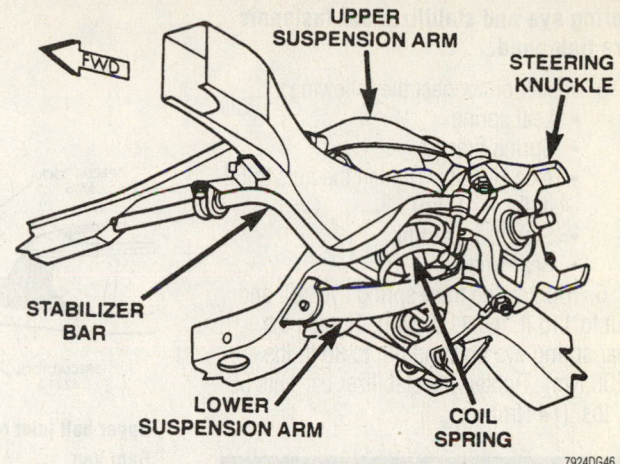

Front suspension components—2WD Dakota models

To install:

5. Install the coil spring and raise the control arm into position.

6. Install or connect the following:
- Lower ball joint. Tighten the nut to 135 ft. lbs. (183 Nm).
- Stabilizer bar link
- Shock absorber
- Front wheel

Ram Truck and Ram Van

1. Before servicing the vehicle, refer to the precautions in the beginning of this section.

2. Support the lower control arm on a floor jack.

3. Remove or disconnect the following:
- Front wheel
- Brake caliper and rotor

- Outer tie rod end
- Stabilizer bar link
- Lower ball joint
- Shock absorber

4. Lower the jack and remove the coil spring.

To install:

5. Install the coil spring and raise the control arm into position.

6. Install or connect the following:
- Shock absorber
- Lower ball joint. Tighten the nut to 95 ft. lbs. (129 Nm).
- Stabilizer bar link. Tighten the nut to 27 ft. lbs. (37 Nm).
- Outer tie rod end. Tighten the nut to 65 ft. lbs. (88 Nm).
- Brake caliper and rotor
- Front wheel

Leaf Spring

REMOVAL & INSTALLATION

1. Before servicing the vehicle, refer to the precautions in the beginning of this section.

2. Support the vehicle at the frame rails.

3. Support the rear axle with a jack.

4. Remove or disconnect the following:
- Rear wheel
- Stabilizer bar link
- Axle U-bolts
- Spring bracket
- Leaf spring

To install:

➡ **The weight of the vehicle must be supported by the springs when the**

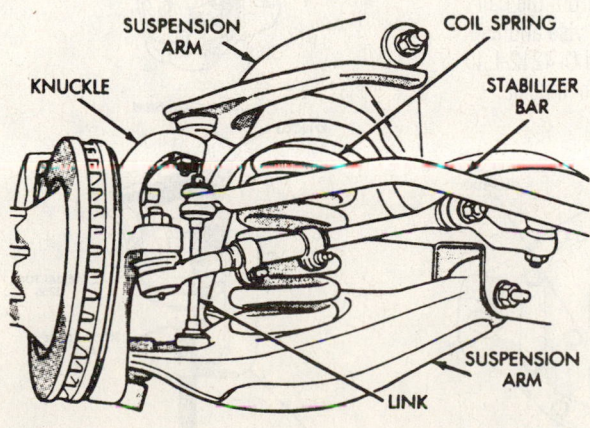

Independent front suspension components—2WD Ram Truck and Van models

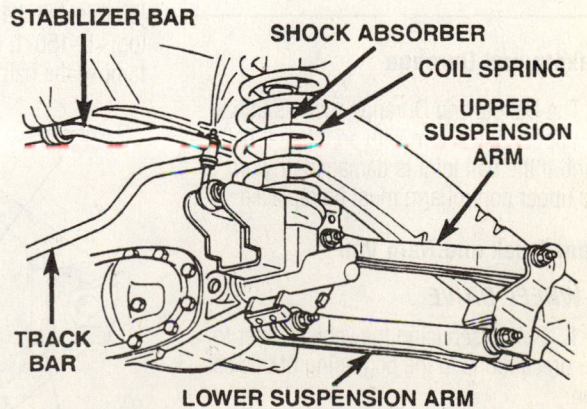

Link and coil front suspension components—4WD Ram Truck and Van models

Turn to Section 5 for brake system applications

spring eye and stabilizer bar fasteners are tightened.

5. Install or connect the following:
- Leaf spring
- Spring bracket
- Axle U-bolts. Tighten the nuts to 52 ft. lbs. (70 Nm).
- Stabilizer bar link
- Rear wheel

6. Tighten the front spring eye bolt and nut to 115 ft. lbs. (156 Nm). Tighten the rear spring eye bolt and nut to 80 ft. lbs. (108 Nm). Tighten the stabilizer bar nuts 55 ft. lbs. (74 Nm).

Torsion bar

REMOVAL & INSTALLATION

1. Before servicing the vehicle, refer to the precautions in the beginning of this section.

2. Loosen the adjustment bolt to remove spring load. Note the number of turns for installation.

3. Remove or disconnect the following:
- Adjustment bolt, swivel and bearing
- Torsion bar and anchor

4. Separate the torsion bar and anchor.

To install:

5. Assemble the torsion bar and anchor.
6. Install or connect the following:
- Torsion bar and anchor
- Adjustment bolt, swivel and bearing

7. Tighten the adjustment bolt the recorded number of turns.

Upper Ball Joint

REMOVAL & INSTALLATION

Dakota and Durango

The Dakota and Durango models utilize an upper control arm with an integral ball joint. If the ball joint is damaged or worn, the upper control arm must be replaced.

Ram Truck and Ram Van

2-WHEEL DRIVE

1. Before servicing the vehicle, refer to the precautions in the beginning of this section.
2. Support the lower control arm.
3. Remove the front wheel.
4. Remove the stud nut and separate the ball joint from the steering knuckle.
5. Unscrew the ball joint from the control arm with tool C-3561.

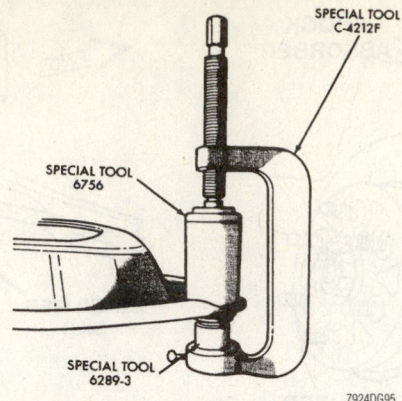

Upper ball joint removal— Ram Truck and Ram Van

To install:

6. Thread the ball joint into the upper control arm and tighten it to 125 ft. lbs. (169 Nm). Tighten the upper ball stud nut to 135 ft. lbs. (183 Nm).
7. Install the front wheel.

4-WHEEL DRIVE

1. Before servicing the vehicle, refer to the precautions in the beginning of this section.

2. Remove or disconnect the following:
- Front wheel
- Brake caliper and rotor
- Hub retainer
- Axle shaft
- Outer tie rod ends
- Upper and lower ball joint stud nuts

3. If equipped with a Model 44 front axle, use a brass drift and hammer to separate the steering knuckle from the axle tube yoke. Use tool C-4169 to remove the sleeve from the upper yoke arm.

4. Remove the snapring from the ball joint. Install the knuckle in a vise and use tools D-150-1, D-150–3 and C-4212-L to remove the ball joint from the knuckle.

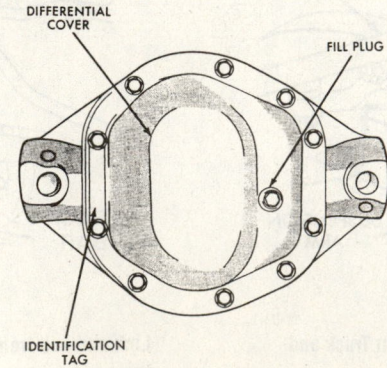

Axle identification—Model 44 front axle differential cover

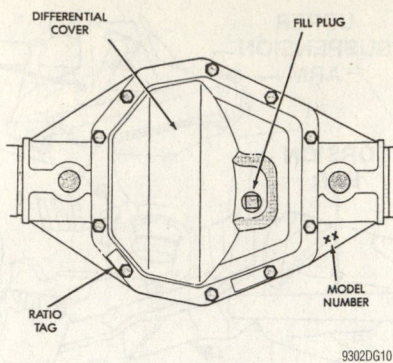

Axle identification—Model 60 front axle differential cover

5. If equipped with a Model 60 front axle, remove the bolts from the knuckle lower cap. Dislodge the cap from the steering knuckle and axle tube yoke. Remove the steering knuckle. Use tool D-192 to remove the upper socket pin from the axle tube upper arm bore. Remove the seal.

To install:

6. If equipped with a Model 44 front axle, use tools C-4212-L and C-4288 to force the upper ball joint into the steering knuckle. Install the snapring and install a new rubber boot. Thread the replacement sleeve into the upper yoke bore so that 2

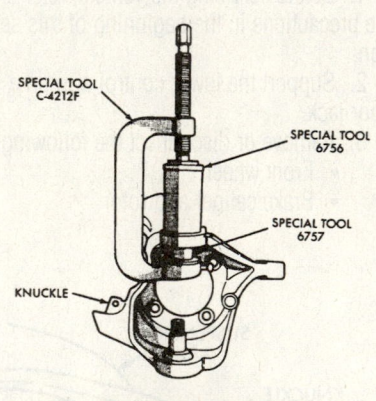

Upper Ball Stud

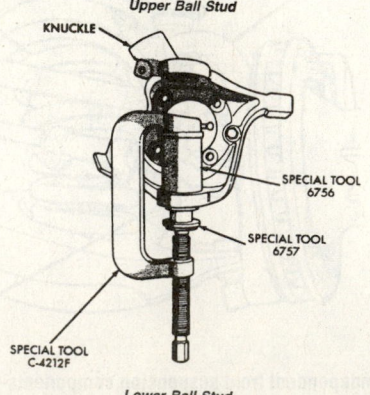

Lower Ball Stud

Typical ball joint removal using the special tools—248 FBI axle shown

threads are exposed at the top of the yoke. Position the knuckle on the axle tube yoke and install a new lower ball stud nut, then tighten to 80 ft. lbs. (108 Nm). Using the special socket, tighten the sleeve to 40 ft. lbs. (54 Nm). Install the upper ball stud nut and tighten to 100 ft. lbs. (136 Nm) and install a new cotter pin.

7. If equipped with a Model 60 front axle, use tool D-192 to install the upper socket pin in the axle tube upper arm bore. Install a new seal. Tighten to 500–600 ft. lbs. (668–813 Nm). Position the knuckle over the socket pin. Fill the lower socket cavity with grease. Install the lower cap and tighten the bolts to 80 ft. lbs. (108 Nm).

8. Install or connect the following:
   - Outer tie rod ends
   - Axle shaft
   - Hub retainer
   - Brake caliper and rotor
   - Front wheel

Lower Ball Joint

REMOVAL & INSTALLATION

Dakota and Durango

The Dakota and Durango models utilize a lower control arm with an integral ball joint. If the ball joint is damaged or worn, the upper control arm must be replaced.

Ram Truck and Ram Van

2WD MODELS

1. Before servicing the vehicle, refer to the precautions in the beginning of this section.
2. Remove or disconnect the following:
   - Front wheel

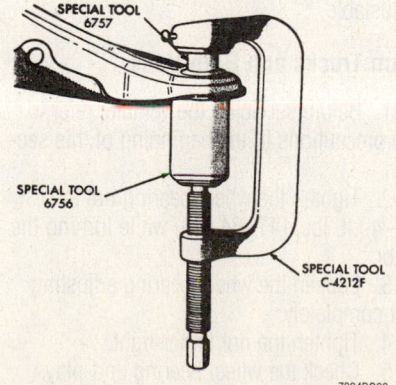

Lower ball joint removal—2WD Ram Truck and Van models

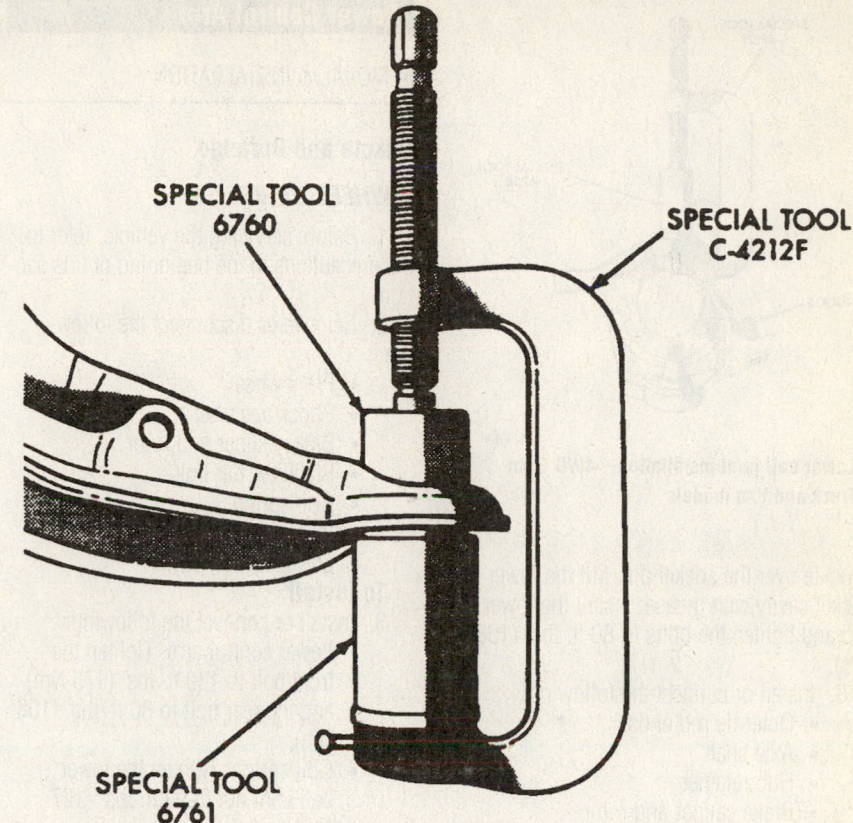

Lower ball joint installation—2WD Ram Truck and Van models

   - Shock absorber
   - Stabilizer bar link
   - Coil spring
3. Press the ball joint out of the control arm.

To install:

4. Use the remover tool to press the ball joint into the arm.
5. Install or connect the following:
   - Coil spring. Tighten $1\frac{1}{16}$ lower ball joint nuts to 135 ft. lbs. (183 Nm). Tighten $\frac{3}{4}$ nuts to 175 ft. lbs. (237 Nm).
   - Stabilizer bar link
   - Shock absorber
   - Front wheel

4WD MODELS

1. Before servicing the vehicle, refer to the precautions in the beginning of this section.
2. Remove or disconnect the following:
   - Front wheel
   - Brake caliper and rotor
   - Hub retainer
   - Axle shaft
   - Outer tie rod ends
   - Upper and lower ball joint stud nuts

3. If equipped with a Model 44 front axle, use a brass drift and hammer to separate the steering knuckle from the axle tube yoke.

4. Remove the snapring from the ball joint. Install the knuckle in a vise and use tools D-150-1, D-150–3 and C-4212-L to remove the ball joint from the knuckle.

5. If equipped with a Dana 60 front axle, use tools C-4212-L, C-4366–1 and C-4366-2 (or equivalents) to remove the lower ball joint.

To install:

6. If equipped with a Model 44 front axle, use tools C-4212-L and C-4288 to force the lower ball joint into the steering knuckle. Install the snapring and install a new rubber boot. Position the knuckle on the axle tube yoke and install a new lower ball stud nut. Tighten to 80 ft. lbs. (108 Nm). Install the upper ball stud nut and tighten to 100 ft. lbs. (136 Nm).

7. If equipped with a Model 60 front axle, use tools C-4212-L, C-4366-3 and C-4366-4 to install the seal and lower bearing cup into the axle tube yoke lower bore. Reposition the tools and install the lower bearing and seal into the bore. Position the

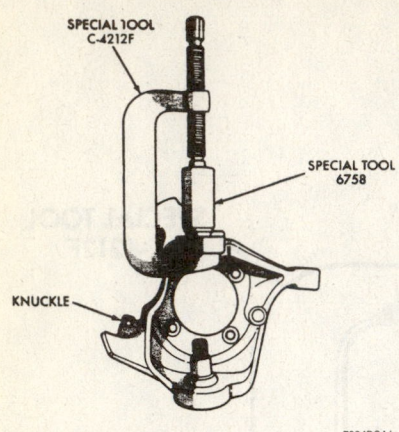

Lower ball joint installation—4WD Ram Truck and Van models

knuckle over the socket pin. Fill the lower socket cavity with grease. Install the lower cap and tighten the bolts to 80 ft. lbs. (108 Nm).

8. Install or connect the following:
  - Outer tie rod ends
  - Axle shaft
  - Hub retainer
  - Brake caliper and rotor
  - Front wheel

Upper Control Arm

REMOVAL & INSTALLATION

1. Before servicing the vehicle, refer to the precautions in the beginning of this section.
2. Support the lower control arm.
3. Remove or disconnect the following:
  - Front wheel
  - Brake hose brackets
  - Upper ball joint
  - Pivot mounting nuts
  - Upper control arm

To install:
4. Install or connect the following:
  - Upper control arm. Tighten the pivot nuts to 155 ft. lbs. (210 Nm).
  - Upper ball joint. Tighten the nut to 60 ft. lbs. (81 Nm).
  - Brake hose brackets
  - Front wheel
5. Check the wheel alignment and adjust as necessary.

CONTROL ARM BUSHING REPLACEMENT

The control arm bushings are serviced with the control arm as an assembly.

Lower Control Arm

REMOVAL & INSTALLATION

Dakota and Durango

2 WHEEL DRIVE

1. Before servicing the vehicle, refer to the precautions in the beginning of this section.
2. Remove or disconnect the following:
  - Front wheel
  - Shock absorber
  - Brake caliper and rotor
  - Stabilizer bar link
  - Coil spring
  - Inner mounting bolts
  - Lower control arm

To install:
3. Install or connect the following:
  - Lower control arm. Tighten the front bolt to 130 ft. lbs. (175 Nm) and the rear bolt to 80 ft. lbs. (108 Nm).
  - Coil spring. Tighten the lower ball joint nut to 94 ft. lbs. (127 Nm).
  - Stabilizer bar link
  - Brake caliper and rotor
  - Shock absorber
  - Front wheel

4 WHEEL DRIVE

1. Before servicing the vehicle, refer to the precautions in the beginning of this section.
2. Remove or disconnect the following:
  - Front wheel
  - Front driveshaft
  - Torsion bar
  - Shock absorber
  - Stabilizer bar
  - Lower ball joint
  - Pivot bolts
  - Lower control arm

To install:
3. Install or connect the following:
  - Lower control arm. Tighten the front pivot bolt to 80 ft. lbs. (108 Nm) and the rear bolt to 140 ft. lbs. (190 Nm).
  - Lower ball joint. Tighten the nut to 135 ft. lbs. (183 Nm).
  - Stabilizer bar
  - Shock absorber
  - Torsion bar
  - Front driveshaft
  - Front wheel

Ram Truck and Ram Van

1. Before servicing the vehicle, refer to the precautions in the beginning of this section.
2. Support the lower control arm with a floor jack.
3. Remove or disconnect the following:
4. Remove or disconnect the following:
  - Front wheel
  - Brake caliper and rotor
  - Stabilizer bar link
  - Lower ball joint
  - Coil spring
  - Crossmember nuts
  - Lower control arm

To install:
5. Install or connect the following:
  - Lower control arm. Tighten the crossmember nuts to 145 ft. lbs. (196 Nm).
  - Coil spring
  - Lower ball joint. Tighten the nut to 135 ft. lbs. (183 Nm).
  - Stabilizer bar link
  - Brake caliper and rotor
  - Front wheel

CONTROL ARM BUSHING REPLACEMENT

The control arm bushings are serviced with the control arm as an assembly.

Wheel Bearings

ADJUSTMENT

Dakota and Durango

The Dakota and Durango models utilize a hub/bearing assembly which is not adjustable.

Ram Trucks and Ram Vans

1. Before servicing the vehicle, refer to the precautions in the beginning of this section.
2. Tighten the wheel bearing nut to 30–40 ft. lbs. (41–54 Nm) while turning the rotor.
3. Loosen the wheel bearing adjusting nut completely.
4. Tighten the nut finger-tight.
5. Check the wheel bearing end-play. The specification is 0.001–0.003 inch (0.025–0.076mm).
6. Install the nut lock and cotter pin.

REMOVAL & INSTALLATION

Dakota and Durango

2 WHEEL DRIVE

1. Before servicing the vehicle, refer to the precautions in the beginning of this section.
2. Remove or disconnect the following:
   - Front wheel
   - Brake caliper and rotor
   - Spindle nut
   - Hub and bearing assembly

To install:

3. Install or connect the following:
   - Hub and bearing assembly
   - Spindle nut. Tighten the nut to 185 ft. lbs. (251 Nm).
   - Brake caliper and rotor
   - Front wheel

4 WHEEL DRIVE

1. Before servicing the vehicle, refer to the precautions in the beginning of this section.
2. Remove or disconnect the following:
   - Front wheel
   - Brake caliper and rotor

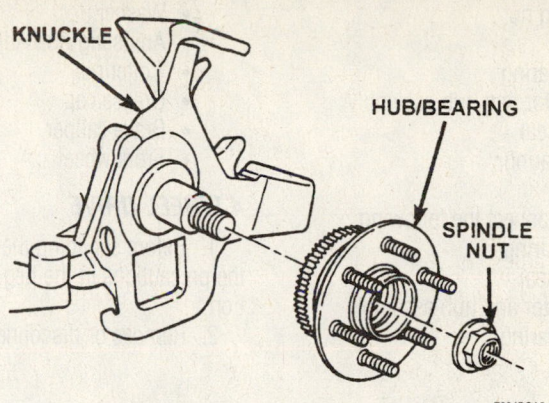

Hub/bearing assembly—Dakota and Durango 2 wheel drive

   - Hub retainer nut
   - Hub and bearing assembly

To install:

3. Install or connect the following:
   - Hub and bearing assembly. Tighten the bolts to 123 ft. lbs. (166 Nm).
   - Hub retainer nut. Tighten the nut to 173 ft. lbs. (235 Nm).
   - Brake caliper and rotor
   - Front wheel

Ram Trucks and Ram Vans

2 WHEEL DRIVE

1. Before servicing the vehicle, refer to the precautions in the beginning of this section.
2. Remove or disconnect the following:
   - Front wheel
   - Brake caliper
   - Grease cap
   - Cotter pin

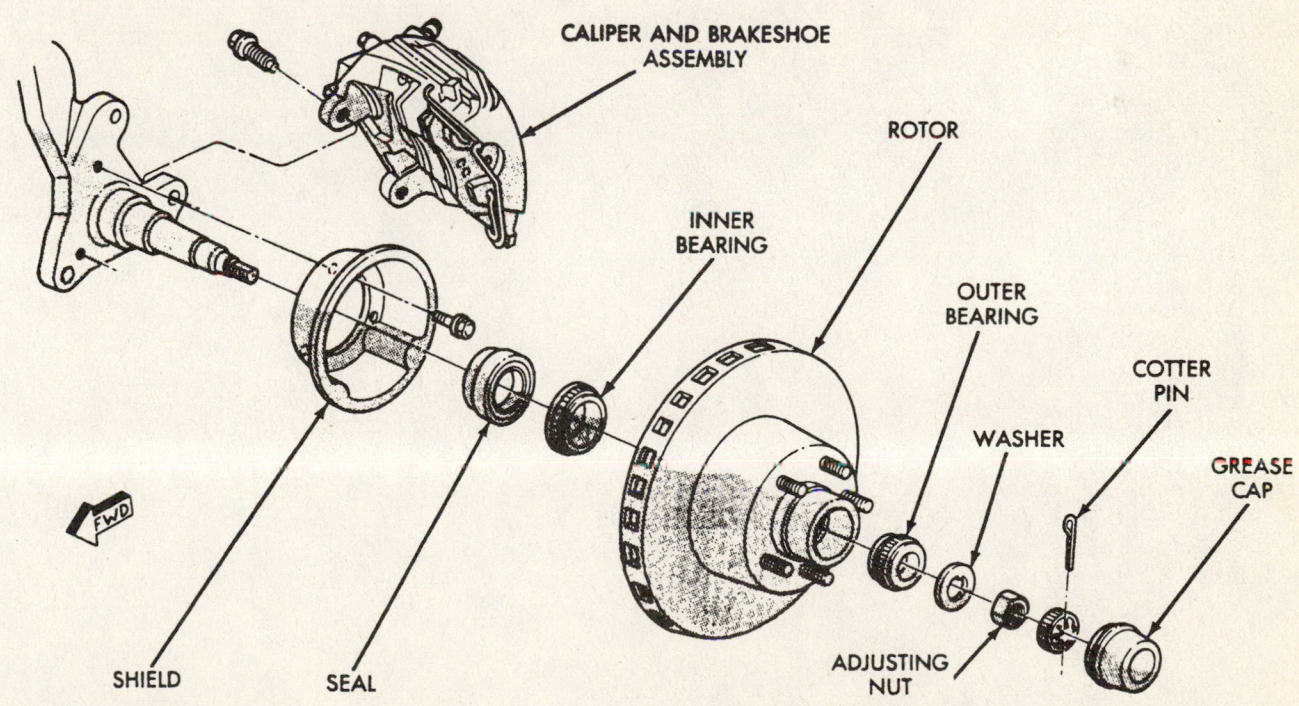

Exploded view of the front rotor, caliper and bearing mounting—except 1997–01 Dakota and Durango

- Adjusting nut
- Washer
- Outer bearing
- Brake rotor and hub assembly
- Grease seal
- Inner bearing

To install:

3. Install or connect the following:
   - Inner bearing
   - Grease seal
   - Brake rotor and hub assembly
   - Outer bearing

- Washer
- Adjusting nut. Adjust the bearings.
- Cotter pin
- Grease cap
- Brake caliper
- Front wheel

4 WHEEL DRIVE

1. Before servicing the vehicle, refer to the precautions in the beginning of this section.

2. Remove or disconnect the following:

- Front wheel
- Brake caliper and rotor
- Hub retainer nut
- Hub and bearing assembly

To install:

3. Install or connect the following:
   - Hub and bearing assembly. Tighten the bolts to 125 ft. lbs. (170 Nm).
   - Hub retainer nut. Tighten the nut to 175 ft. lbs. (237 Nm).
   - Brake caliper and rotor
   - Front wheel

FORD MOTOR CO.

Ford-Aerostar • Explorer • Explorer Sport Trac • Ranger • Mercury-Mountaineer • Mazda-B Series Pick-ups

14

PRECAUTIONS

Before servicing any vehicle, please be sure to read all of the following precautions, which deal with personal safety, prevention of component damage, and important points to take into consideration when servicing a motor vehicle:

• Never open, service or drain the radiator or cooling system when the engine is hot; serious burns can occur from the steam and hot coolant.

• Observe all applicable safety precautions when working around fuel. Whenever servicing the fuel system, always work in a well-ventilated area. Do not allow fuel spray or vapors to come in contact with a spark, open flame, or excessive heat (a hot drop light, for example). Keep a dry chemical fire extinguisher near the work area. Always keep fuel in a container specifically designed for fuel storage; also, always properly seal fuel containers to avoid the possibility of fire or explosion. Refer to the additional fuel system precautions later in this section.

• Fuel injection systems often remain pressurized, even after the engine has been turned **OFF**. The fuel system pressure must be relieved before disconnecting any fuel lines. Failure to do so may result in fire and/or personal injury.

• Brake fluid often contains polyglycol ethers and polyglycols. Avoid contact with the eyes and wash your hands thoroughly after handling brake fluid. If you do get brake fluid in your eyes, flush your eyes with clean, running water for 15 minutes. If eye irritation persists, or if you have taken brake fluid internally, IMMEDIATELY seek medical assistance.

• The EPA warns that prolonged contact with used engine oil may cause a number of skin disorders, including cancer! You should make every effort to minimize your exposure to used engine oil. Protective gloves should be worn when changing oil. Wash your hands and any other exposed skin areas as soon as possible after exposure to used engine oil. Soap and water, or waterless hand cleaner should be used.

• All new vehicles are now equipped with an air bag system, often referred to as a Supplemental Restraint System (SRS) or Supplemental Inflatable Restraint (SIR) system. The system must

be disabled before performing service on or around system components, steering column, instrument panel components, wiring and sensors. Failure to follow safety and disabling procedures could result in accidental air bag deployment, possible personal injury and unnecessary system repairs.

• Always wear safety goggles when working with, or around, the air bag system. When carrying a non-deployed air bag, be sure the bag and trim cover are pointed away from your body. When placing a non-deployed air bag on a work surface, always face the bag and trim cover upward, away from the surface. This will reduce the motion of the module if it is accidentally deployed. Refer to the additional air bag system precautions later in this section.

• Clean, high quality brake fluid from a sealed container is essential to the safe and proper operation of the brake system. You should always buy the correct type of brake fluid for your vehicle. If the brake fluid becomes contaminated, completely flush the system with new fluid. Never reuse any brake fluid. Any brake fluid that is removed from the system should be discarded. Also, do not allow any brake fluid to come in contact with a painted surface; it will damage the paint.

• Never operate the engine without the proper amount and type of engine oil; doing so WILL result in severe engine damage.

• Timing belt maintenance is extremely important! Many models utilize an interference-type, non-freewheeling engine. If the timing belt breaks, the valves in the cylinder head may strike the pistons, causing potentially serious (also time-consuming and expensive) engine damage. Refer to the maintenance interval charts in the front of this manual for the recommended replacement interval for the timing belt, and to the timing belt section for belt replacement and inspection.

• Disconnecting the negative battery cable on some vehicles may interfere with the functions of the on-board computer system(s) and may require the computer to undergo a relearning process once the negative battery cable is reconnected.

• When servicing drum brakes, only disassemble and assemble one side at a time, leaving the remaining side intact for reference.

ENGINE REPAIR

Alternator

REMOVAL

2.3L, 2.5L Engines

1. Before servicing the vehicle, refer to the precautions in the beginning of this section.

2. Remove or disconnect the following:
  • Negative battery cable
  • Drive belt
  • Electrical connections to the alternator
  • Alternator

To install:

3. Install or connect the following:
  • Alternator. Torque the bolts to 40 ft. lbs. (55 Nm).
  • Electrical connectors to the alternator
  • Drive belt
  • Negative battery cable

3.0L 4.0L and 5.0L Engines

1. Before servicing the vehicle, refer to the precautions in the beginning of this section.

2. Remove or disconnect the following:
  • Negative battery cable
  • Air cleaner outlet tube
  • Drive belt
  • Electrical connectors from the alternator
  • A/C manifold and tube bracket aside, 5.0L engine only
  • Wiring harness to alternator push pin
  • Alternator

To install:

3. Install or connect the following:
  • Alternator. Torque the bolts to 40 ft. lbs. (55 Nm).
  • Push pin for the alternator wiring harness
  • A/C manifold and tube bracket, 5.0L engine only. Torque the bolt to 106 inch lbs. (12 Nm).
  • Electrical connectors to the alternator
  • Drive belt
  • Air cleaner outlet tube
  • Negative battery cable

Ignition Timing

ADJUSTMENT

The ignition timing is preset to 10 degrees Before Top Dead Center (BTDC) and is not adjustable.

Engine Assembly

REMOVAL & INSTALLATION

Aerostar

➡ **The engine and subframe assembly on the Aerostar is removed from the bottom of the vehicle. An assortment of jacks and stands are needed to perform this procedure safely. The vehicle must be raised about 3–4ft. off the ground for clearance to remove the engine assembly.**

1. Before servicing the vehicle, refer to the precautions in the beginning of this section.
2. Relieve the fuel system pressure.
3. Drain the cooling system.
4. Drain the engine oil.
5. Remove or disconnect the following:
   - Both battery cables
   - Upper and lower radiator hoses and remove the radiator
   - Air cleaner hose assembly
   - Electrical connectors, fuel lines, throttle linkage and hoses from the engine. Label the connections as needed to aid installation
   - Drive belts
   - A/C compressor without disconnecting the lines and position it out of the way with wire, if equipped
   - Engine cover from inside the vehicle. Raise and safely support the vehicle
   - Transmission
   - Exhaust pipe and catalytic converter
   - Both front wheels
   - Engine ground straps
   - Stabilizer bar from the lower control arms. Discard the nuts
   - Brake lines at the bracket on the frame
6. Position a jack under the lower control arm and raise the arm until tension is applied to the coil spring. Install safety chains around the lower control arm and spring seat. Remove the bolt and nut retaining the spindle to the upper control arm ball joint. Slowly lower the jack to disconnect

the spindle from the ball joint. Install safety chains around the lower control arm and spring seat.

7. Position drive train removal lift 109-00002, under the crossmember and engine assembly.
8. Slowly lower the vehicle until the crossmember rests on the removal lift. Place wood blocks under the front crossmember and rear of the engine block to keep the engine and crossmember assembly level. Install safety chains around the crossmember and lift.
9. With the engine and crossmember securely supported on the lift, remove the nuts that retain the engine crossmember assembly to the frame on each side of the vehicle.
10. Carefully lower the engine assembly out of the vehicle, making sure the air conditioning compressor, wiring and hoses do not interfere. When the assembly is clear, roll the lift away from the vehicle.

To install:

11. Position the engine assembly on the crossmember. Install the retaining nuts and tighten to 71–94 ft. lbs. (96–127 Nm).
12. Roll the removal lift under the vehicle. Align the lift, engine and crossmember assembly so the mounting bolts on each side of the frame are in alignment with the holes in the crossmember.
13. Slowly lower the vehicle so the bolts are piloted in the crossmember holes. Raise the lift or lower the vehicle so the crossmember is against the frame. Install the nuts retaining the crossmember to the frame and tighten to 145–195 ft. lbs. (196–264 Nm). Raise the vehicle and remove the lift.
14. Install the transmission assembly.
15. Remove the safety chains from around the lower control arms and spring seat. Install a jack under the lower control arms. Slowly raise the control arm until the coil spring is under tension. Continue to raise the arm until the spindle is connected to the upper arm ball joint. Install a new nut and bolt and tighten to 27–37 ft. lbs. (37–50 Nm).
16. Install or connect the following:
   - Stabilizer bar with new nuts
   - Brake lines to the caliper hoses at the frame brackets
   - Both front wheels
   - Driveshaft by aligning the marks that were made during removal
   - New gaskets on the exhaust manifold and catalytic converter. Install

the exhaust pipe and catalytic converter. Torque the converter-to-muffler nuts and bolts to 18–26 ft. lbs. (25–35 Nm). Torque the exhaust pipe-to-exhaust manifold nuts to 25–34 ft. lbs. (34–46 Nm).
   - All electrical connectors, fuel lines, throttle linkage, speedometer cable and hoses to the engine
   - A/C compressor, if equipped
   - Drive belts. Place the injector harness behind the belt tension idler arm and tighten the idler arm.
   - Throttle linkage to the ball stud located on the throttle body
   - Shroud covering the throttle body
   - Fan and fan shroud
   - Both battery cables
   - Air cleaner and duct assembly
17. Bleed the brakes.
18. Fill the cooling system.
19. Fill the engine with clean oil.
20. Run the engine and check for leaks and proper operation.
21. Check and adjust the front end alignment.

2.3L Engine

1. Before servicing the vehicle, refer to the precautions in the beginning of this section.
2. Relieve the fuel system pressure.
3. Drain the cooling system.
4. Drain the engine oil.
5. Properly discharge the A/C system.
6. Remove or disconnect the following:
   - Both battery cables
   - Intake Air Temperature (IAT) sensor
   - Air cleaner outlet tube
   - Drive belt
   - Accelerator control splash shield
   - Upper and lower radiator hoses
   - Fan guard/shroud
   - Radiator overflow hoses
   - Radiator
   - Engine Coolant Temperature (ECT) sensor
   - Alternator
   - Upper and lower heater hoses
   - Ignition wires from the coils
   - Ignition coil wiring
   - Radio ignition interference capacitor wiring
   - Water pump inlet tube
   - Alternator mounting bracket
   - Acceleratgor cable
   - Both engine compartment wiring harness, 42 pin and 104 pin connectors

- Exhaust Gas Recirculation (EGR) pressure sensor
- Evaporative (EVAP) emissions purge hose
- A/C hoses
- A/C compressor manifold and tube
- Power steering pump bracket
- Heated Oxygen (HO2S) sensor
- Catalytic converter from the exhaust manifold
- Fuel supply and return hoses from the fuel injection supply manifold
- 3 transmission connector leads
- Ground cable from the left side of the engine
- Starter
- Torque converter-to-flywheel bolts, if equipped
- Engine-to-transmission from the rear support brackets
- Lower engine-to-transmission bolts and spacers, if equipped

7. Support the transmission with a floor jack.

8. Using an engine crane or hoist, lift the engine out of the vehicle. Be sure to lift the engine slowly and check often that nothing (such as wires, hoses, etc.) will cause the engine to hang up on the vehicle.

To install:

➡Lightly oil all bolts and stud threads, except those specifying special sealant, prior to installation.

9. Using the hoist or engine crane, slowly and carefully position the engine in the vehicle. Make sure the exhaust manifolds are properly aligned with the exhaust pipes.

10. Align the engine to the transmission and install 2 engine-to-transmission bolts.

➡Seat the left-hand side, front engine support insulator locating pin prior to the right-hand side, front engine support insulator.

11. Lower the engine onto the front engine support insulators.

12. Detach the engine crane or hoist from the engine.

13. Remove the floor jack from beneath the transmission fluid pan.

14. Install or connect the following:
- Torque the engine-to-transmission bolts to 38 ft. lbs. (51 Nm)
- Torque converter-to-transmission bolts. Torque the bolts to 39 ft lbs. (52 Nm).
- Starter. Torque the bolts to 20 ft. lbs. (27 Nm).
- Ground cable to the left side of the engine

- Transmission lead to fuel charging wiring
- Fuel supply and return lines
- Catalytic converter to the exhaust manifold. Torque the bolts to 25 ft. lbs. (34 Nm).
- Cable brackets
- HO2S sensor
- Starter electrical connectors
- Top engine-to-transmission bolts. Torque the bolts to 38 ft. lbs. (51 Nm).
- 42 and 104 pin engine harness connectors
- EVAP purge hose
- EGR pressure sensor
- Dash panel ground cable
- Brake booster vacuum hose
- Accelerator cable bracket. Torque the bolts to 21 ft. lbs. 28 Nm).
- Accelerator cable to the throttle body
- Upper and lower heater hoses
- Alternator mounting bracket. Torque the bolts to 40 ft. lbs. (54 Nm).
- Alternator. Torque the bolts to 40 ft. lbs. (54 Nm).
- Ignition coil electrical connectors
- Spark plug wires to the ignition coils
- Drive belt. Torque the fan clutch bolts to 16 ft. lbs. (23 Nm).
- ECT sensor
- Alternator electrical connectors
- Fan shroud on the fan blade, if equipped with A/C
- Radiator and install the fan shroud/guard
- Radiator overflow hose
- Upper and lower cooling hoses
- A/C compressor and recharge the system
- Air cleaner outlet tube
- Accelerator control splash shield
- IAT sensor
- Both battery cables

15. Fill the cooling system.

16. Fill the engine with clean oil.

17. Run the engine and check for leaks and proper operation.

18. Check and adjust the front end alignment.

2.5L, 3.0L and 4.0L Engines

1. Before servicing the vehicle, refer to the precautions in the beginning of this section.

2. Relieve the fuel system pressure.

3. Drain the cooling system.

4. Drain the engine oil.

5. Properly discharge the A/C system.

6. Remove or disconnect the following:
- Both battery cables
- Mass Air Flow (MAF) sensor
- Air cleaner outlet tube
- Drive belt
- Accelerator control splash shield
- Upper and lower radiator hoses
- Fan guard/shroud
- Radiator overflow tube
- Radiator
- Transmission cooler lines, if equipped
- Heater hoses
- Alternator electrical connectors
- Vacuum reservoir connection
- Throttle body heater hose
- A/C cycling switch
- Powertrain Control Module (PCM) connector
- Ground wire from the PCM
- Power steering cut-out switch
- Peanut fitting from the A/C condenser core
- A/C high pressure cut-out switch
- A/C manifold hose
- Accelerator and speed control cables
- Brake booster vacuum hose and tube from the intake manifold
- Vacuum reservoir line
- Fuel lines
- Power steering pressure and return hoses
- Block heater, if equipped
- Engine ground cable
- Automatic transmission harness connectors, if equipped
- Heated Oxygen (HO2S) sensor, if equipped
- Starter
- Catalytic converter
- Torque converter bolts, if equipped and properly support the transmission
- Differential pressure feedback sensor and support the engine with a floor crane
- Exhaust Gas Recirculation (EGR) transducer
- Upper transmission-to-engine bolts
- Engine from the vehicle
- Clutch/ flywheel, if equipped

To install:

7. Install or connect the following:
- Flywheel. Torque the bolts to 64 ft. lbs. (87 Nm).
- Engine. Torque the mounting bolts to 85 ft. lbs. (115 Nm).
- HO2S sensor
- Upper transmission-to-engine bolts. Torque the bolts to 38 ft. lbs. (51 Nm).
- EGR transducer and remove the

floor jack from the transmission
- Torque converter-to-engine bolts. Torque the bolts to 38 ft. lbs. (51 Nm).
- Catalytic converter
- Transmission wiring harness connectors
- Engine ground cable. Torque the bolt to 106 inch lbs. (12 Nm).
- Block heater, if equipped
- A/C high pressure cut out switch
- A/C manifold to the evaporator core
- Power steering cut-out switch
- Power steering pressure and return lines
- Engine sensor control wiring harness to the A/C compressor
- Fuel lines
- 42 pin connector
- Vacuum reservoir vacuum line
- Brake booster vacuum hose and tube
- Accelerator cable
- Ground strap. Torque the bolt to 106 inch lbs. (12 Nm).
- A/C manifold hose
- PCM ground strap. Torque the bolt to 106 inch lbs. (12 Nm).
- PCM wire harness bracket bolt. Torque the bolt to 61 inch lbs. (7 Nm).
- A/C low pressure cut-out switch
- Throttle body heater hose
- Fan clutch and water pump pulley. Torque the bolt 17 ft. lbs. (23 Nm).
- Drive belt
- Alternator electrical connectors
- Inlet and outlet heater hoses
- Fuel charging wiring
- Radiator and fan shroud
- Transmission cooler lines, if equipped
- Upper, lower and overflow hoses to the radiator
- Accelerator control splash shield. Torque the bolts to 89 inch lbs. 10 Nm).
- Drive belt
- Air cleaner outlet tube
- MAF sensor
- Both battery cables

8. Recharge the A/C system.
9. Fill the cooling system.
10. Fill the engine with clean oil.
11. Run the engine and check for leaks and proper operation.
12. Check and adjust the front end alignment.

5.0L Engine

1. Before servicing the vehicle, refer to the precautions in the beginning of this section.
2. Relieve the fuel system pressure.
3. Drain the cooling system.
4. Drain the engine oil.
5. Properly discharge the A/C system.
6. Remove or disconnect the following:
   - Battery
   - Drive belt
   - Fan shroud
   - Air cleaner outlet tube
   - A/C condenser core
   - Upper radiator hose
   - Power steering reservoir and move it aside
   - Power steering pump
   - Spark plug wire bracket from the A/C compressor
   - A/C compressor and bracket
   - Alternator
   - Wide-open A/C cut-off switch electrical connector
   - Vapor Management Valve (VMV) hose
   - Lower steering column shaft and move it aside
   - Left and right hand side vacuum connections
   - Accelerator and speed control cables
   - Accelerator cable bracket
   - Powertrain Control Module (PCM) connector
   - PCM ground connector
   - Engine bulkhead connector
   - Heater hoses
   - Transmission fill tube
   - Power steering cooler and move it aside
   - Ground cable from the engine front cover
   - Ground strap from the lower intake manifold
   - Transmission cooler lines from the retainer on the right engine mount
   - Starter
   - Transmission inspection cover
   - Torque converter nuts
   - Transmission
   - Left and right side Heated Oxygen (HO2S) sensor electrical connectors
   - Transmission bulkhead connector
   - Brake booster vacuum supply line at the left upper intake manifold
   - Low oil level sensor electrical connector
   - Oil bypass filter
   - Lower radiator hose
   - Exhaust manifolds
   - Left and right side motor mounts and install the lifting brackets to the exhaust manifold studbolts on No. 1–No. 8 cylinders
   - Engine from the vehicle
   - Flywheel, if equipped

To install:

7. Install or connect the following:
   - Flywheel. Torque the new bolts to 85 ft. lbs. (115 Nm).
   - Engine. Torque the motor mount bolts to 109 ft. lbs. (148 Nm).
   - Exhaust manifolds
   - Lower radiator hose
   - Oil bypass filter
   - Brake booster vacuum supply line to the left side upper intake connection
   - Transmission bulkhead connector
   - Left and right HO2S sensor connectors
   - Transmission
   - Torque converter bolts. Torque the bolts to 38 ft. lbs. (51 Nm).
   - Transmission inspection cover
   - Starter
   - Transmission cooler lines to the retainer by the right side motor mount
   - Battery-to-starter relay cable
   - Ground strap to the engine front cover
   - Ground strap to the rear of the lower intake manifold
   - Ground cable to the engine front cover
   - Power steering cooler
   - transmission fill tube
   - Heater hoses
   - Engine bulkhead connector. Torque the bolt to 89 inch lbs. (10 Nm).
   - PCM and body ground connectors. Torque the bolt to 89 inch lbs. (10 Nm).
   - Accelerator and speed control cables to the clip
   - Accelerator cable bracket. Torque the upper bolts to 15 ft. lbs. (20 Nm) and lower the bolt to 80 inch lbs. (9 Nm).
   - Accelerator and sped control cables to the throttle linkage
   - Accelerator control shield. Torque the bolt to 106 inch lbs. (12 Nm).
   - Left and right side vacuum connections
   - Lower power steering column shaft.

Timing belt service is covered in Section 4 of this manual

Torque the bolt to 40 ft. lbs. (55 Nm).

- VMV hose
- Fuel lines
- Wide-open A/C cutoff switch electrical connector
- Alternator and electrical connectors
- A/C compressor
- Spark plug wire bracket. Torque the nut to 89 inch lbs. (10 Nm).
- Power steering pump. Torque the bolts to 21 ft. lbs. (29 Nm).
- Power steering reservoir. Torque the bolts to 106 inch lbs. (12 Nm).
- Upper radiator hose
- Fan blade
- Drive belt
- A/C condenser core
- Air cleaner outlet tube
- Battery and cables

8. Recharge the A/C system.
9. Fill the cooling system.
10. Fill the engine with clean oil.
11. Run the engine and check for leaks and proper operation.
12. Check and adjust the front end alignment.

Water Pump

REMOVAL & INSTALLATION

2.3L and 2.5L Engines

1. Before servicing the vehicle, refer to the precautions in the beginning of this section.
2. Drain the cooling system.
3. Remove or disconnect the following:
   - Negative battery cable
   - Drive belt
   - Fan clutch and shroud
   - Water pump pulley
   - Heater hose from the water pump inlet tube
   - Lower radiator hose
   - Water pump inlet tube
   - Water pump and discard the gasket

To install:

4. Clean the mating surface with the water pump connects to the engine.
5. Install or connect the following:
   - Water pump with a new O-ring. Torque the bolts to 15 ft. lbs. (20 Nm).
   - Inlet tube. Torque the bolts to 89 inch lbs. (10 Nm).
   - Lower radiator hose
   - Water pump pulley
   - Heater hose from the water pump inlet tube

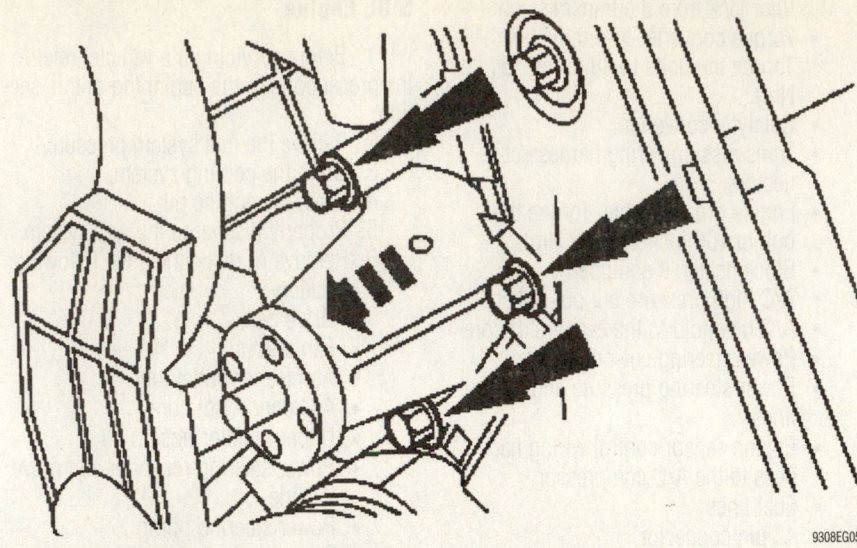

Exploded view of the water pump—2.3L and 2.5L engines

9308EG05

- Fan clutch and shroud
- Drive belt
- Negative battery cable

6. Fill the cooling system.
7. Start the vehicle and check for leaks, repair if necessary.

3.0L and 4.0L OHV Engines

1. Before servicing the vehicle, refer to the precautions in the beginning of this section.
2. Drain the cooling system.
3. Remove or disconnect the following:
   - Negative battery cable
   - Air cleaner outlet tube
   - Fan and radiator shroud
   - Water bypass tube
   - Drive belt
   - Heater hose
   - Water pump pulley
   - Lower radiator hose
   - A/C compressor and bracket assembly and move them aside
   - Water pump

To install:

4. Clean the mating surfaces where the water pump attaches to the engine.
5. Install or connect the following:
   - Water pump. Torque the bolts to 106 in lbs. (12 Nm).
   - A/C compressor mounting bracket. Torque the bolts to 44 ft. lbs. (61 Nm).
   - Water pump pulley. Torque the bolts to 20 ft. lbs. (28 Nm).
   - Drive belt
   - Heater hose
   - Lower radiator hose
   - Fan and shroud

- Air cleaner outlet tube
- Negative battery cable

6. Fill the cooling system.
7. Start the vehicle and check for leaks, repair if necessary.

4.0L SOHC and 5.0L Engines

1. Before servicing the vehicle, refer to the precautions in the beginning of this section.
2. Drain the cooling system.
3. Remove or disconnect the following:
   - Negative battery cable
   - Fan shroud
   - Fan and clutch assembly, 4.0L only
   - Drive belt
   - Idler pulley, 4.0L only
   - Water bypass hose
   - Heater hose from the water pump
   - Engine control sensor wiring and move it aside, 5.0L only
   - Lower radiator hose, 4.0L only
   - Water pump pulley
   - Water pump from the engine front cover, 5.0L only
   - Water pump inlet hose, 5.0L only
   - Water pump

To install:

4. Clean the mounting surfaces of the pump and front cover thoroughly. Remove all traces of gasket material.
5. Install or connect the following:
   - Apply adhesive gasket sealer to both sides of a new gasket and place the gasket on the pump.
   - Inlet hose to the water pump, 5.0L only. Torque the clamps to 11 ft. lbs. (15 Nm).
   - Water pump. Torque the bolts to 20 ft. lbs. (28 Nm).

- Water bypass hose, 4.0L only
- Water pump pulley. Torque the bolts to 20 ft. lbs. (28 Nm).
- Engine control sensor wiring, 5.0L only
- Lower radiator hose, 4.0L only
- Heater hose
- Drive belt idler pulley, 4.0L only. Torque the bolts to 33 ft. lbs. (45 Nm).
- Water bypass tube, 5.0L only. Torque the clamps to 11 ft. lbs. (15 Nm).
- Dive belt
- Fan and clutch assembly, 4.0L only
- Fan shroud
- Negative battery cable

6. Fill the cooling system.
7. Start the vehicle and check for leaks, repair if necessary.

Cylinder Head

REMOVAL & INSTALLATION

2.3L and 2.5L Engines

1. Before servicing the vehicle, refer to the precautions in the beginning of this section.
2. Relieve the fuel system pressure.
3. Drain the cooling system.
4. Properly discharge the A/C system.
5. Remove or disconnect the following:
- Negative battery cable
- Loosen the water pump pulley bolts
- Drive belt
- Water pump pulley
- Fan and clutch assembly
- Intake manifolds
- Ignition wires from the spark plugs
- Spark plugs
- Oil level indicator tube
- Exhaust Gas Recirculation (EGR) valve to the exhaust manifold tube
- Valve cover
- Engine control wiring from the A/C compressor
- A/C compressor mounting bracket with the power steering pump attached and move them aside
- Engine control sensor wiring from the alternator
- Lower radiator hose
- Water pump inlet tube
- Upper radiator hose
- Alternator
- Alternator mounting bracket
- Ignition wire and bracket

- Outer timing belt cover
- Timing belt
- Exhaust manifold
- Cylinder head and discard the bolts and the gasket

To install:

6. Clean the mating surface where the cylinder head attaches to the engine.
7. Install a new gasket and the cylinder head.

➡**Refer to Section 1 of this manual for the cylinder head torque sequence illustration. The illustration is located after the Torque Specification Chart.**

8. Torque the new cylinder head bolts in stages as follows:
   a. Step 1: 51 ft. lbs. (70 Nm).
   b. Step 2: An additional 51 ft. lbs. (70 Nm).
   c. Step 3: Plus and additional 90 degrees.

9. Install or connect the following:
- Exhaust manifold. Torque the bolts to 15 ft. lbs. (20 Nm) plus an additional 30 ft. lbs. (40 Nm).
- Timing belt tensioner and timing belt
- Timing belt cover
- Ignition wires and coil

10. Install the alternator bracket. Torque the bolts in 4 stages as follows:
   a. Step 1: Hand tighten bolt No. 1.
   b. Step 2: Torque bolt No. 2 to 40 ft. lbs. (55 Nm).
   c. Step 3: Torque bolt No. 3 to 40 ft. lbs. (55 Nm).
   d. Step 4: Torque bolt No. 1 to 40 ft. lbs. (55 Nm).

11. Install or connect the following:
- Water pump inlet tube with a new O-ring to the water pump. Torque the bolts to 89 inch lbs. (10 Nm).
- Lower radiator hose

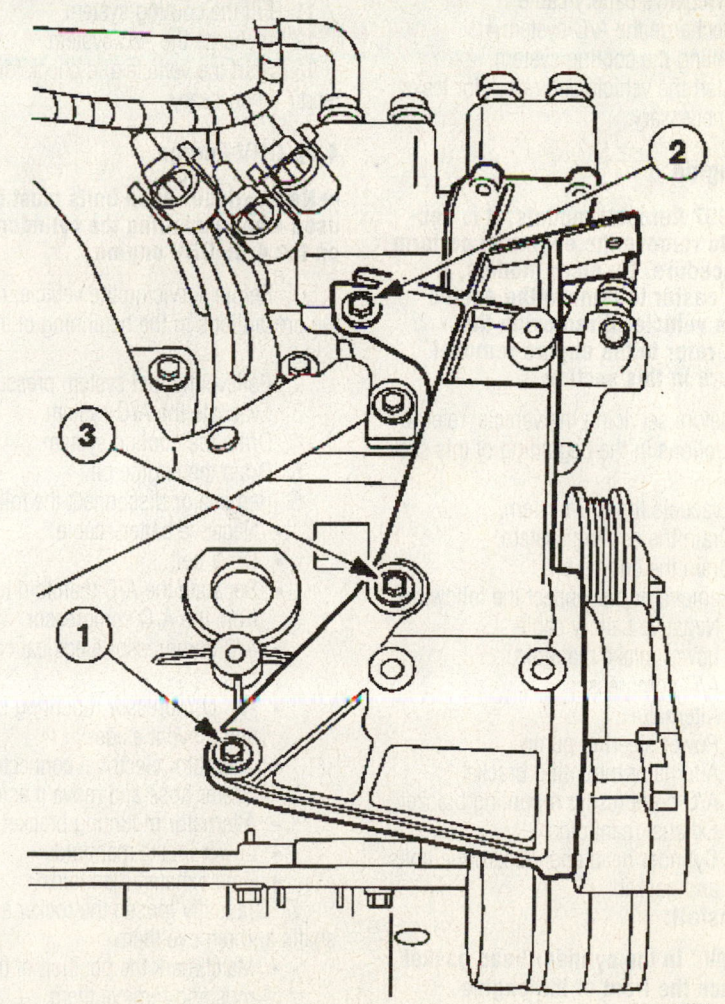

Alternator bracket bolt tightening sequence 2.3L–2.5L engines

9308EG06

- Alternator
- Upper radiator hose and heater hose
- A/C compressor mounting bracket with the power steering pump attached. Torque the bolts to 40 ft. lbs. (55 Nm).
- A/C compressor. Torque the bolts to 20 ft. lbs. (28 Nm).
- Water pump pulley and fan clutch. Hand tighten the bolts
- Drive belt. When the belt is positioned properly, torque the fan clutch bolts to 16 ft. lbs. (23 Nm).
- Fan shroud
- Sparks plugs
- Oil level indicator tube
- Engine control sensor wiring
- Upper intake manifold
- EGR valve to the exhaust manifold tube. Torque the bolts to 34 ft. lbs. (47 Nm).
- EGR transducer to the rear of the engine
- Negative battery cable

12. Recharge the A/C system.
13. Filling the cooling system.
14. Start the vehicle and check for leaks, repair if necessary.

3.0L Engine

➡On 1997 Aerostar models, it is necessary to remove the engine to perform this procedure. On other models, it may be easier to remove the engine from the vehicle. If removing the engine, refer to the engine removal procedure in this section.

1. Before servicing the vehicle, refer to the precautions in the beginning of this section.
2. Evacuate the A/C system.
3. Drain the cooling system.
4. Drain the engine oil.
5. Remove or disconnect the following:
- Negative battery cable
- Lower intake manifold
- A/C compressor
- Alternator
- Power steering pump
- Alternator mounting bracket
- A/C compressor mounting bracket
- Exhaust manifolds
- Cylinder head and discard the bolts and gasket

To install:

➡The "V" in the cylinder head gasket must face the front of the engine.

6. Clean the mating surfaces where the head attaches to the engine.
7. Install a new cylinder head gasket and the cylinder head to the engine.

➡Refer to Section 1 of this manual for the cylinder head torque sequence illustration. The illustration is located after the Torque Specification Chart.

8. Torque the new cylinder head bolts in stages as follows:
   a. Step 1: 59 ft. lbs. (80 Nm).
   b. Step 2:Loosen the bolts one full turn.
   c. Step 3:40 ft. lbs. (55 Nm).
   d. Step 4: 63 ft. lbs. (85 Nm).
9. Install or connect the following:
- Lower intake manifold
- Exhaust manifold
- A/C compressor mounting bracket. Torque the bolts to 44 ft. lbs. (66 Nm).
- Alternator mounting bracket
- Power steering pump
- Alternator
- A/C compressor
- Negative battery cable

10. Fill the engine with clean oil.
11. Fill the cooling system.
12. recharge the A/C system
13. Start the vehicle and check for leaks, repair if necessary.

4.0L OHV Engine

➡New cylinder head bolts must be used when installing the cylinder head on the 4.0L OHV engine.

1. Before servicing the vehicle, refer to the precautions in the beginning of this section.
2. Relieve the fuel system pressure.
3. Evacuate the A/C system.
4. Drain the cooling system.
5. Drain the engine oil.
6. Remove or disconnect the following:
- Negative battery cable
- Drive belt
- Separate the A/C manifold tube from the A/C compressor
- A/C compressor electrical connectors
- A/C compressor mounting bracket and move it aside
- Alternator electrical connectors
- Heater hose and move it aside
- Alternator mounting bracket
- Lower intake manifold
- Both exhaust manifolds

7. Gradually loosen the rocker arm shafts and remove them.
- Matchmark the position of the push rods and remove them
- Cylinder head and gasket

To install:

8. Clean the mating surface where the cylinder head attaches to the engine.

9. Install a new cylinder head gasket and the cylinder head to the engine.

➡Refer to Section 1 of this manual for the cylinder head torque sequence illustration. The illustration is located after the Torque Specification Chart.

10. Torque the new cylinder head bolts in sequence as follows:
   a. Step 1: 25 ft. lbs. (34 Nm).
   b. Step 2: 53 ft. lbs. (72 Nm).
   c. Step 3: Plus an additional 90 degrees.
11. Install or connect the following:
- Push rods
- Rocker arm shafts gradually. Torque the bolts to 24 ft lbs. (33 Nm) plus an additional 90 degrees
- Exhaust manifolds
- Lower intake manifold
- Alternator bracket. Torque the bolts to 35 ft. lbs. (47 Nm).
- Heater hose retaining clip
- Alternator electrical connectors
- A/C compressor mounting bracket. Torque the bolts to 35 ft. lbs. (47 Nm).
- A/C compressor electrical connectors
- A/C manifold tube to the A/C compressor
- Drive belt
- Negative battery cable

12. Fill the cooling system.
13. Fill the engine with clean oil. A filter replacement is also recommended.
14. Recharge the A/C system.

➡When the battery has been disconnected and reconnected, some abnormal drive symptoms may occur while the Powertrain Control Module (PCM) relearns its adaptive strategy. The vehicle may need to be driven about 10 miles (16 km) or more to relearn the strategy.

15. Start the engine and check for leaks.

4.0L SOHC Engine

➡If only one cylinder head is to be removed, only follow the procedures that apply. The following tools, or their equivalents are absolutely necessary to properly perform this procedure:

- Cam Chain Tensioner tool T97T-6K254-A
- Cam Gear Removal tool T97T-6256-F
- Cam Gear Torque adapter T97T-6256-G

- Camshaft Gear Positioning/Holding tool T97T-6256-B
- Camshaft Gear Positioning/Holding tool adapter T97T-6256-A
- Camshaft holding tool T97T-6256-C
- Crankshaft holding tool T97T-6303-A
- Camshaft holding tool adapter T97T-6256-D

1. Before servicing the vehicle, refer to the precautions in the beginning of this section.

2. Properly relieve the fuel system pressure.

3. Drain the cooling system.

4. Remove or disconnect the following:

- Negative battery cable
- Lower intake manifold
- Fan blade and shroud
- Valve cover
- Roller followers, if equipped
- Drive belt
- Upper radiator hose and tube
- Alternator electrical connectors
- Alternator mounting bracket
- Engine accessory bracket and move it aside
- Camshaft Position (CMP) electrical connector
- Crankshaft Position (CKP) sensor electrical connector
- Engine Coolant Temperature (ECT) sensor electrical connector
- Coil pack electrical connector
- Exhaust Gas Recirculation (EGR) valve electrical connector
- EGR valve bracket and move it aside
- Heater hoses
- Fuel injector electrical connectors
- Water bypass hose
- Thermostat housing
- Spark plug wires
- Fuel injection supply manifold
- Fuel injectors
- Crankcase vent separator spring
- Oil dipstick housing
- Exhaust manifold
- Hydraulic chain tensioner
- Cassette retaining bolt
- Camshaft sprocket
- Cylinder head and discard the gasket

To install:

5. Thoroughly clean all gasket mating surfaces. Remove all traces of old gasket material, oil, grease or dirt.

6. Insure that the rubber band is holding the right-hand chain to the cassette.

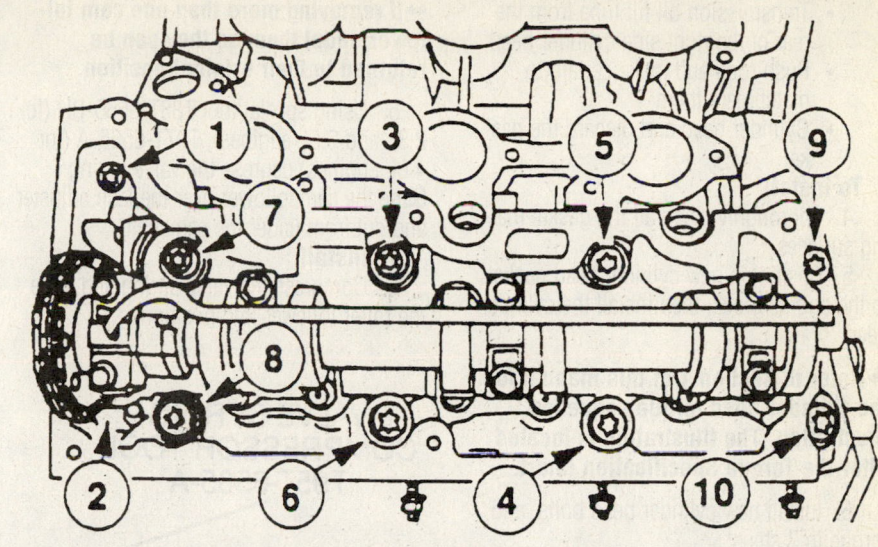

The correct cylinder head bolt loosening sequence must be used to prevent warpage—4.0L SOHC engine

7. Install a new head gasket and the cylinder head.

➡ **Refer to Section 1 of this manual for the cylinder head torque sequence illustration. The illustration is located after the Torque Specification Chart.**

8. Torque the new cylinder head bolts in sequence as follows:

  a. Step 1: 26 ft. lbs. (34 Nm).
  b. Step 2: Plus 90 degrees.
  c. Step 3: Plus an additional 90 degrees.

9. Install or connect the following:

- Camshaft sprocket in the cassette and make certain that the camshaft sprocket turns freely on the camshaft
- Cassette retaining bolt. Torque the bolt to 89 inch lbs. (10 Nm).
- Exhaust manifold
- Oil level indicator tube. Torque the bolt to 18 ft. lbs. (25 Nm).
- Crankcase vent separator and spring
- Thermostat housing. Torque the bolts to 8 ft. lbs. (11 Nm).
- Water bypass hose
- Heater hoses
- EGR bracket. Torque the bolt to 89 inch lbs. (10 Nm).
- EGR tube. Torque the nut to 30 ft. lbs. (40 Nm).
- ECT sensor electrical connector
- Electrical harness retainer. Torque the bolt to 89 inch lbs. (10 Nm).

- CKP and CMP electrical connectors
- Accessory bracket. Torque the bolts to 31 ft. lbs. (42 Nm).
- Alternator mounting bracket. Torque the bolts to 31 ft. lbs. (42 Nm).
- Alternator and electrical connectors
- Drive belt
- Fan shroud
- Roller followers
- Valve cover
- Lower intake manifold
- Negative battery cable

10. Change the engine oil and filter.

11. Refill the cooling system.

12. Start the engine and check for leaks, repair if necessary.

5.0L Engine

1. Before servicing the vehicle, refer to the precautions in the beginning of this section.

2. Drain the cooling system.

3. Remove or disconnect the following:

- Negative battery cable
- Lower intake manifold
- Valve cover
- Matchmark the rocker arms and push rods to ease installation and remove the rocker arm fulcrums
- Rocker arms and fulcrum guides
- Exhaust manifold
- A/C compressor and power steering bracket, left side cylinder head only
- Alternator electrical connectors, right side cylinder head only

- Transmission oil fill tube from the rear of the right side cylinder head
- Push rods and make certain to matchmark them
- Cylinder head and discard the gasket

To install:

4. Thoroughly clean all the gasket mating surfaces.

5. Position a new cylinder head gasket to the engine block, then install the cylinder head.

➡ **Refer to Section 1 of this manual for the cylinder head torque sequence illustration. The illustration is located after the Torque Specification Chart.**

6. Install new cylinder head bolts, and torque in 3 steps:
   a. Step 1: 30 ft. lbs. (40 Nm).
   b. Step 2: 50 ft. lbs. (68 Nm).
   c. Step 3: Plus an additional 90 degrees.
7. Install or connect the following:
   - Lubricate and install the push rods in their original positions
   - Rocker arms and fulcrum guides
   - Rocker arm fulcrums. Torque the bolts to 25 ft. lbs. (34 Nm).
   - Valve cover
   - Transmission oil fill tube. Torque the bolt to 25 ft. lbs. (34 Nm).
   - Alternator bracket, if removed. Torque the bolts to 48 ft. lbs. (65 Nm).
   - Alternator electrical connectors, if removed
   - Exhaust manifold
   - Lower intake manifold
   - Negative battery cable
8. Fill the cooling system
9. Fill the engine with clean oil and replace the filter.
10. Start the engine and check for leaks, repair if necessary.

Rocker Arms/Shafts

REMOVAL & INSTALLATION

2.3L, 2.5L and 4.0L SOHC Engines

➡ **A special tool is required to compress the valve spring.**

1. Before servicing the vehicle, refer to the precautions in the beginning of this section.
2. Disconnect the negative battery cable.
3. Remove the valve cover.
4. Rotate the camshaft so that the base circle of the cam is against the cam follower you intend to remove.

➡ **If removing more than one cam follower, label them so they can be returned to their original position.**

5. Using special tool T88T-6565-BH (for 2.3L and 2.5L engines), T97T-6565-A (for 4.0L engines) depress the valve spring. Slide the cam follower over the lash adjuster and out from under the camshaft.

To install:

6. Compress the valve spring and slide the roller follower into position.

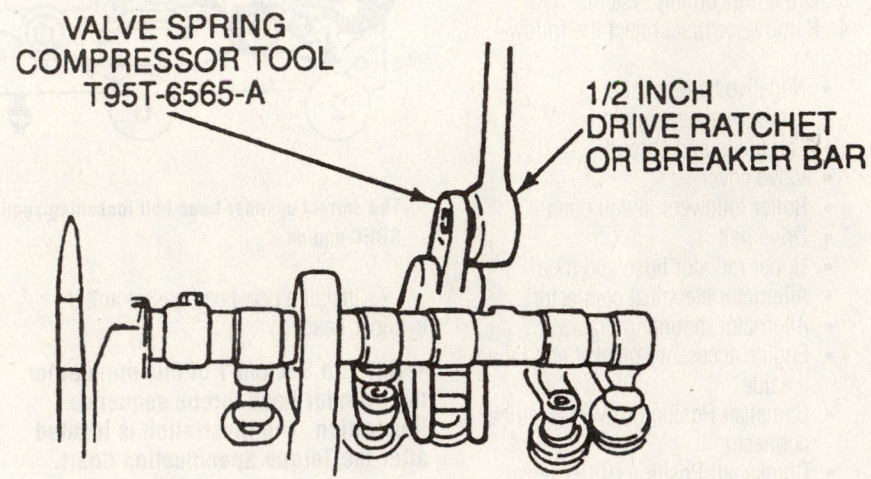

To remove the cam follower (rocker arm), use the special tool to depress the valve spring, then remove the cam follower—2.3L and 2.5L engines

7. Release the tension from the spring.
8. Install the valve cover and connect the negative battery cable.

3.0L and 5.0L Engines

1. Before servicing the vehicle, refer to the precautions in the beginning of this section.
2. Remove or disconnect the following:
   - Negative battery cable

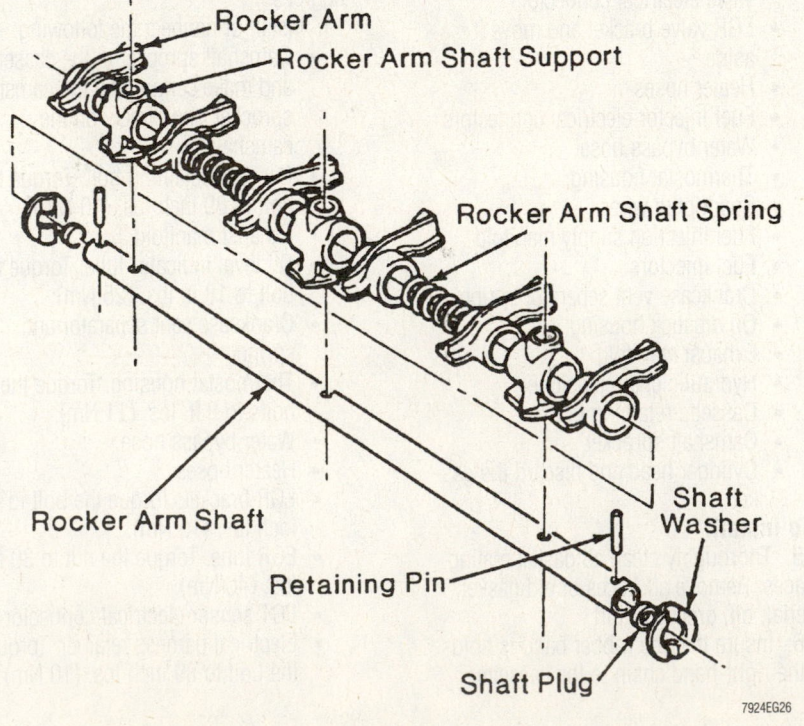

Rocker arm and shaft assembly—4.0L SOHC engine

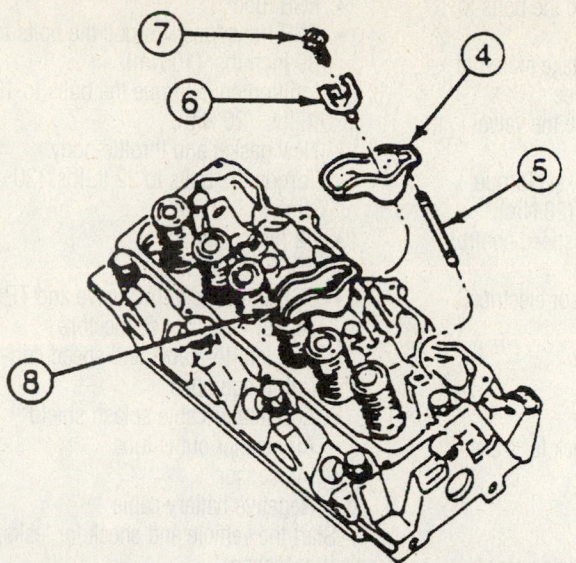

4. Rocker arm
5. Pushrod
6. Fulcrum
7. Bolt
8. Assembled rocker arm

7924EG27

Exploded view of the rocker arm assembly—3.0L engine

1. Rocker arm bolt
2. Rocker arm fulcrum
3. Rocker arm
4. Fulcrum guide
5. Threaded pedestal (Part of cylinder head)

7924EG28

Exploded view of the rocker arm assembly. Notice the fulcrum guide between the pedestals used for extra stability—5.0L engine

- Rocker arm covers
- Retaining bolt at each rocker arm

3. The rocker arm and pushrod may then be removed from the engine. Keep all rocker arms and pushrods in order so they may be installed in their original locations.

To install:

4. Lubricate the rocker arm assemblies with SAE 50W engine oil.

5. Ensure that the fulcrums are properly seated into the cylinder head (3.0L engines) or the fulcrum guide (5.0L engines). Torque the rocker arm fulcrum bolts to 19 ft. lbs. (26 Nm).

6. Install the rocker arm covers and connect the negative battery cable.

4.0L OHV Engine

1. Before servicing the vehicle, refer to the precautions in the beginning of this section.

2. Remove or disconnect the following:
- Negative battery cable
- Rocker arm covers
- Rocker arm shaft stand attaching bolts by loosening the bolts 2 turns at a time, in sequence (from the end of the shaft to the middle of the shaft)
- Rocker arm and shaft assembly

To install:

3. If equipped, loosen the valve lash adjusting screws a few turns. Apply engine

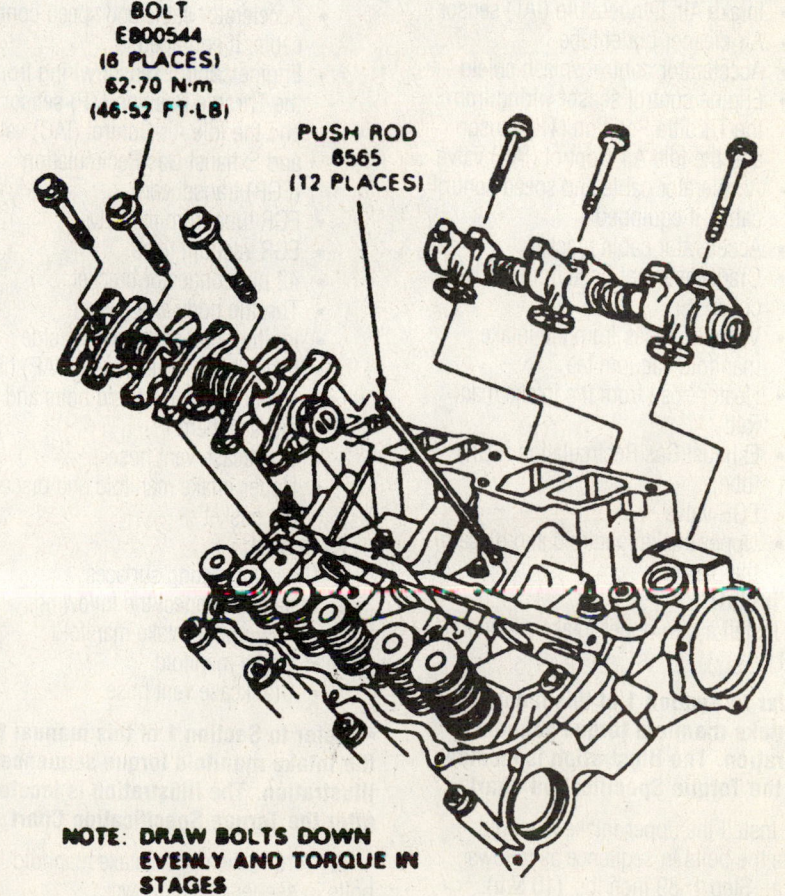

BOLT
E800544
(6 PLACES)
62-70 N·m
(46-52 FT-LB)

PUSH ROD
6565
(12 PLACES)

NOTE: DRAW BOLTS DOWN EVENLY AND TORQUE IN STAGES

7924EG29

Rocker arm and shaft assembly—4.0L OHV engine

For engine torque specifications, refer to Section 1 of this manual

oil to the assembly to provide initial lubrication.

4. Install or connect the following:
   - Rocker arm shaft assembly to the cylinder head and guide adjusting screws on to the pushrods
   - Rocker arm stand. Torque the bolts to 46–52 ft. lbs. (62–70 Nm), 2 turns at a time, in sequence (from middle of shaft to the end of the shaft).
   - Rocker arm covers
   - Negative battery cable

Intake Manifold

REMOVAL & INSTALLATION

Upper

2.3L AND 2.5L ENGINES

1. Before servicing the vehicle, refer to the precautions in the beginning of this section.
2. Remove or disconnect the following:
   - Negative battery cable
   - Intake Air Temperature (IAT) sensor
   - Air cleaner outlet tube
   - Accelerator control splash shield
   - Engine control sensor wiring from the Throttle Position (TP) sensor and the Idle Air Control (IAC) valve
   - Accelerator cable and speed control cable, if equipped
   - Accelerator cable bracket
   - Crankcase vent hose from the valve cover
   - Vacuum hoses from the intake manifold vacuum tee
   - Heater hose from the intake manifold
   - Exhaust Gas Recirculation (EGR) tube
   - EGR valve
   - Upper intake manifold and discard the gasket

To install:

3. Install a new upper intake manifold gasket.

➡ **Refer to Section 1 of this manual for the intake manifold torque sequence illustration. The illustration is located after the Torque Specification Chart.**

4. Install the upper intake manifold. Torque the bolts in sequence as follows:
   a. Step 1: 89 inch lbs. (10 Nm).
   b. Step 2: 28 ft. lbs. (38 Nm).
5. Install or connect the following:
   - EGR valve. Torque the bolts to 22 ft. lbs. (30 Nm).

   - EGR valve tube. Torque the bolts to 34 ft. lbs. (47 Nm).
   - Heater hoses to the intake manifold
   - Vacuum hoses to the tee
   - Crankcase vent hose to the valve cover
   - Accelerator cable bracket. Torque the bolts to 20 ft. lbs. (28 Nm).
   - Accelerator cable and speed control cable, if equipped
   - IAC valve and TP sensor electrical connectors
   - Air cleaner outlet tube
   - IAT sensor
   - Negative battery cable
6. Start the engine and check for leaks, repair if necessary.

3.0L ENGINE

1. Before servicing the vehicle, refer to the precautions in the beginning of this section.
2. Remove or disconnect the following:
   - Negative battery cable
   - Intake Air Temperature (IAT) sensor
   - Air cleaner outlet tube
   - Accelerator control splash shield
   - Accelerator cable and speed control cable, if equipped
   - Engine control sensor wiring from the Throttle Position (TP) sensor and the Idle Air Control (IAC) valve and Exhaust Gas Recirculation (EGR) transducer
   - EGR tube from the valve
   - EGR vacuum lines
   - 42 pin connector bracket
   - Throttle body and gasket
   - Ignition coil and move it aside
   - Evaporative Emissions (EVAP) hose
   - Upper intake manifold bolts and discard them
   - Crankcase vent hose
   - Upper intake manifold and discard the gasket

To install:

3. Clean all mating surfaces.
4. Install or connect the following:
   - New upper intake manifold
   - Intake manifold
   - Crankcase vent hose

➡ **Refer to Section 1 of this manual for the intake manifold torque sequence illustration. The illustration is located after the Torque Specification Chart.**

5. Torque the upper intake manifold bolts in sequence as follows:
   a. Step 1: 15 ft. lbs. (20 Nm).
   b. Step 2: 18 ft. lbs. (25 Nm).
6. Install or connect the following:
   - EVAP hose

   - EGR tube
   - EGR transducer. Torque the bolts to 89 inch lbs. (10 Nm).
   - Ignition coil. Torque the bolts to 15 ft. lbs. (20 Nm).
   - New gasket and throttle body. Torque the bolts to 22 ft. lbs. (30 Nm).
   - 42 pin connector
   - EGR vacuum lines
   - EGR transducer, IAC valve and TP sensor electrical connectors
   - Accelerator cable and speed control, if equipped
   - Accelerator cable splash shield
   - Air cleaner outlet tube
   - IAT sensor
   - Negative battery cable
7. Start the vehicle and check for leaks, repair if necessary.

4.0L OHV ENGINE

The intake manifold is a 4-piece assembly, consisting of the upper intake manifold, the throttle body, the fuel supply manifold, and the lower intake manifold.

1. Before servicing the vehicle, refer to the precautions in the beginning of this section.
2. Remove or disconnect the following:
   - Negative battery cable
   - Air cleaner outlet tube
   - Accelerator cable splash shield
   - Spark plug wires from the ignition coil
   - Ignition coil and radio interference capacitor electrical connectors
   - Throttle Position (TP) sensor electrical connector
   - Idle Air Control (IAC) valve electrical connector
   - Brake booster vacuum hose
   - Positive Crankcase Ventilation (PCV) hose
   - Canister purge line from the throttle body
   - Fuel line bracket
   - Upper intake manifold and discard the gasket

To install:

➡ **Refer to Section 1 of this manual for the intake manifold torque sequence illustration. The illustration is located after the Torque Specification Chart.**

3. Install or connect the following:
   - New gasket and the upper manifold. Torque the nuts to 18 ft. lbs. (25 Nm).
   - Fuel line bracket
   - Canister purge line to the throttle body

- Brake booster vacuum hose
- IAC valve electrical connector
- TP sensor electrical connector
- Ingition coil and radio interference capacitor electrical connectors
- Spark plug wires to the proper spark plug
- Accelerator cable and speed control cable, if equipped
- Accelerator cable splash shield
- Air cleaner outlet tube
- Negative battery cable

4. Start the vehicle and check for leaks, repair if necessary.

4.0L SOHC Engine

1. Before servicing the vehicle, refer to the precautions in the beginning of this section.

2. Remove or disconnect the following:
- Negative battery cable
- Air cleaner-to-intake tube
- Accelerator splash shield
- Accelerator and, if equipped with cruise control, speed control cables from the throttle control cam
- Accelerator cable retaining bracket from the upper intake manifold
- Label and disengage all vacuum and electrical connections on the intake manifold.
- Upper intake manifold attaching bolts
- Lift up on the manifold and remove both fuel Vapor Management Valve (VMV) hoses
- Upper intake manifold and discard the gasket

To install:

➡Ford does not specify a sequence for either upper or lower intake manifolds, but it is recommended that you start tightening in the middle and work your way out to the ends. Repeat the tightening sequence several times until the bolts will no longer turn at the specified torque.

3. Position the upper manifold on the lower manifold.
4. Install or connect the following:
- Attach both VMV hoses to the manifold
- Upper manifold attaching bolts. Torque the bolts to 62 inch lbs. (7 Nm).
- Attach any vacuum and electrical connections that were removed

- Accelerator cable bracket to the intake and the cable (or cables if equipped with cruise control) to the throttle cam
- Accelerator splash shield
- Air cleaner-to-intake supply tube
- Negative battery cable

5. Start the vehicle and check for leaks, repair if necessary.

5.0L Engine

UPPER

1. Before servicing the vehicle, refer to the precautions in the beginning of this section.

2. Remove or disconnect the following:
- Negative battery cable
- Air cleaner outlet tube
- Idle Air Control (IAC) valve electrical connector
- Accelerator control splash shield
- Throttle Position (TP) sensor electrical connector
- Accelerator cable and if equipped, speed control cable from the throttle linkage
- Accelerator cable bracket
- Fuel pressure regulator vacuum connection
- Pressure transducer hoses
- Upper Exhaust Gas Recirculation (EGR) valve-to-exhaust manifold tubing
- Engine Vacuum Regulator (EVR) electrical connector
- EVR vacuum connector
- EGR back pressure electrical connector
- Ignition coil bracket
- Accelerator cable from the upper intake manifold clips
- Intake cover plate
- Vacuum connections from the front of the manifold
- Vapor Management Valve (VMV) purge line
- Brake booster vacuum supply line
- Positive Crankcase Ventilation (PCV) hose
- PCV heater hoses
- Upper intake manifold and discard the gasket

To install:

3. Ensure that all of the gasket mating surfaces are clean and free of grease, oil or dirt. Also ensure that the EGR passages in the manifolds and heads are clear.
4. Apply a ¹⁄₁₆ in. (1.6mm) bead of sili-

cone sealer to the points where the cylinder block rails meet the cylinder heads.

5. Position new seals on the cylinder block and new gaskets on the cylinder heads with the gaskets interlocked with the seal tabs. Make sure the holes in the gaskets are aligned with the holes in the cylinder heads.

6. Apply a ¹⁄₁₆ in. (1.6mm) bead of sealer to the outer end of each intake manifold seal for the full width of the seal. Make sure the silicone sealer will not fall into the engine and possibly block oil passages.

7. Using guide pins to ease installation, carefully lower the intake manifold into position on the cylinder block and cylinder heads. Also, ensure that the water pump bypass hose is installed at the same time.

8. Install or connect the following:
- Intake manifold and new gasket and hand tighten the bolts
- Upper intake vacuum connections
- PCV tube and heater hoses
- Brake booster vacuum supply line
- Torque the intake manifold bolts to 18 ft. lbs. (25 Nm).
- Intake manifold cover plate. Torque the bolts to 15 ft. lbs. (20 Nm).
- Accelerator cable bracket. Torque the upper bolt to 15 ft. lbs. (20 Nm) and lower bolt to 80 inch lbs. (9 Nm).
- Accelerator cable and speed control cable to the throttle linkage, if equipped
- Ignition coils and bracket
- EVR electrical connector
- EVR vacuum connector
- EGR valve vacuum connector
- Fuel pressure regulator vacuum connector
- Upper EGR valve-to-exhaust manifold connector. Torque the fastener to 25 ft. lbs. (34 Nm).
- EGR back pressure transducer electrical connector
- TP sensor electrical connector
- IAC valve electrical connector
- Accelerator control splash shield. Torque the bolt to 89 inch lbs. (10 Nm).
- Air cleaner outlet tube
- Negative battery cable

LOWER

1. Before servicing the vehicle, refer to the precautions in the beginning of this section.

2. Drain the cooling system.
3. Remove or disconnect the following:

- Negative battery cable
- Radiator overflow hose and set it aside
- Upper intake manifold
- Water bypass hose
- Engine Coolant Temperature (ECT) electrical connector
- Wire harness retainer nut
- Heater hoses
- Positive Crankcase Ventilation (PCV) hoses
- Upper radiator hose
- Fuel injector electrical connectors
- Ground strap at the rear of the lower intake manifold
- Water temperature indicator sender electrical connector
- Camshaft Position (CMP) sensor and the camshaft synchronizer
- Bolts from the lower intake manifold
- Lower intake manifold and discard the gaskets

To install:

4. Ensure that all of the gasket mating surfaces are clean and free of grease, oil or dirt. Also ensure that the EGR passages in the manifolds and heads are clear.

5. Apply a ¹⁄₁₆ in. (1.6mm) bead of silicone sealer to the points where the cylinder block rails meet the cylinder heads.

6. Position new seals on the cylinder block and new gaskets on the cylinder heads with the gaskets interlocked with the seal tabs. Make sure the holes in the gaskets are aligned with the holes in the cylinder heads.

7. Apply a ¹⁄₁₆ in. (1.6mm) bead of sealer to the outer end of each intake manifold seal for the full width of the seal. Make sure the silicone sealer will not fall into the engine and possibly block oil passages.

➡Refer to Section 1 of this manual for the intake manifold torque sequence illustration. The illustration is located after the Torque Specification Chart.

8. Install the lower intake manifold and tighten the bolts in 2 steps as follows:
   a. 89 inch lbs. (10 Nm).
   b. 24 ft. lbs. (32 Nm).

9. Install or connect the following:
   - CMP sensor and camshaft synchronizer
   - Water temperature indicator sender electrical connector
   - Fuel injector electrical connectors
   - Fuel line
   - Water bypass hose
   - Upper radiator hose
   - Heater hoses
   - Wire harness retainer nut. Torque to

the bolt to 18 ft. lbs. (25 Nm).
   - ECT electrical connector
   - Water heater bypass hose to the heater tube
   - PCV hoses to the heater tube
   - Upper intake manifold
   - Radiator overflow hose
   - Negative battery cable

10. Fill the cooling system.

11. Start the vehicle and check for leaks, repair if necessary.

Exhaust Manifold

REMOVAL & INSTALLATION

2.3L and 2.5L Engines

1. Before servicing the vehicle, refer to the precautions in the beginning of this section.

2. Remove or disconnect the following:
   - Negative battery cable
   - Intake Air Temperature (IAT) sensor
   - Air cleaner outlet tube
   - Differential Pressure Feedback (DPFE) sensor and move it aside
   - Exhaust Gas Recirculation (EGR) transducer lines at the tube
   - Loosen and remove the EGR valve-to-exhaust manifold tube
   - Catalytic converter from the exhaust manifold
   - Rear engine lifting eye nuts
   - Exhaust manifold and discard the gasket

To install:

3. Clean the mating surfaces on the exhaust manifold and the cylinder head.

4. Install a new gasket and the exhaust manifold. Torque the bolts in sequence as follows:
   a. 16 ft. lbs. (23 Nm).
   b. 59 ft. lbs. (80 Nm).

5. Install or connect the following:
   - Rear engine lifting eye. Torque the bolts to 15 ft. lbs. (20 Nm).
   - Catalytic converter to the exhaust manifold
   - EGR valve to the exhaust manifold tube
   - EGR transducer lines
   - DPFE sensor
   - Air cleaner outlet tube
   - IAT sensor
   - Negative battery cable

6. Start the vehicle and check for leaks, repair if necessary.

3.0L Engine

LEFT SIDE

1. Before servicing the vehicle, refer to the precautions in the beginning of this section.

2. Install or connect the following:
   - Negative battery cable
   - Exhaust flange nuts
   - Exhaust Gas Recirculation (EGR) valve from the exhaust manifold tube
   - Oil lever indicator and bracket

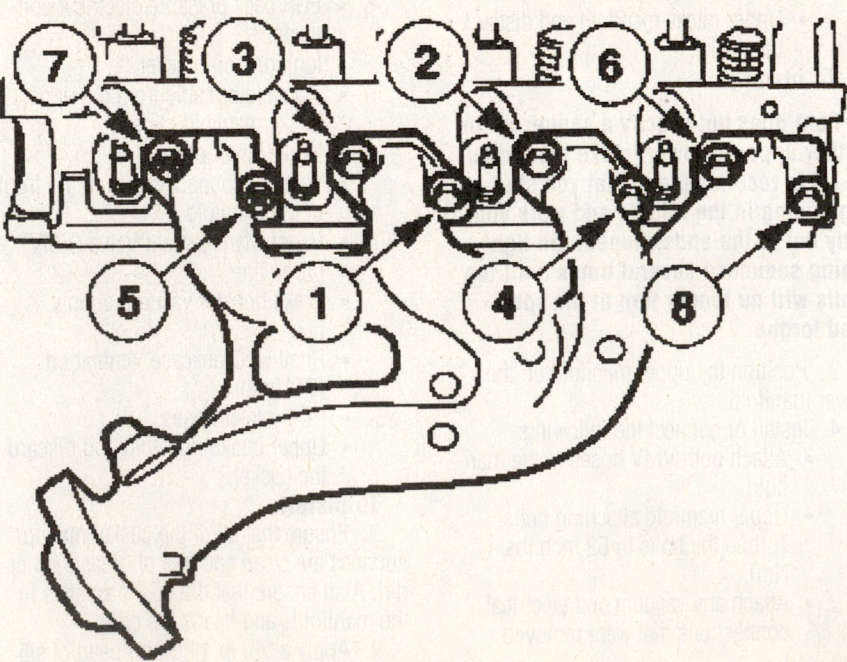

Tighten the exhaust manifold bolts in 2 stages

9308EG07

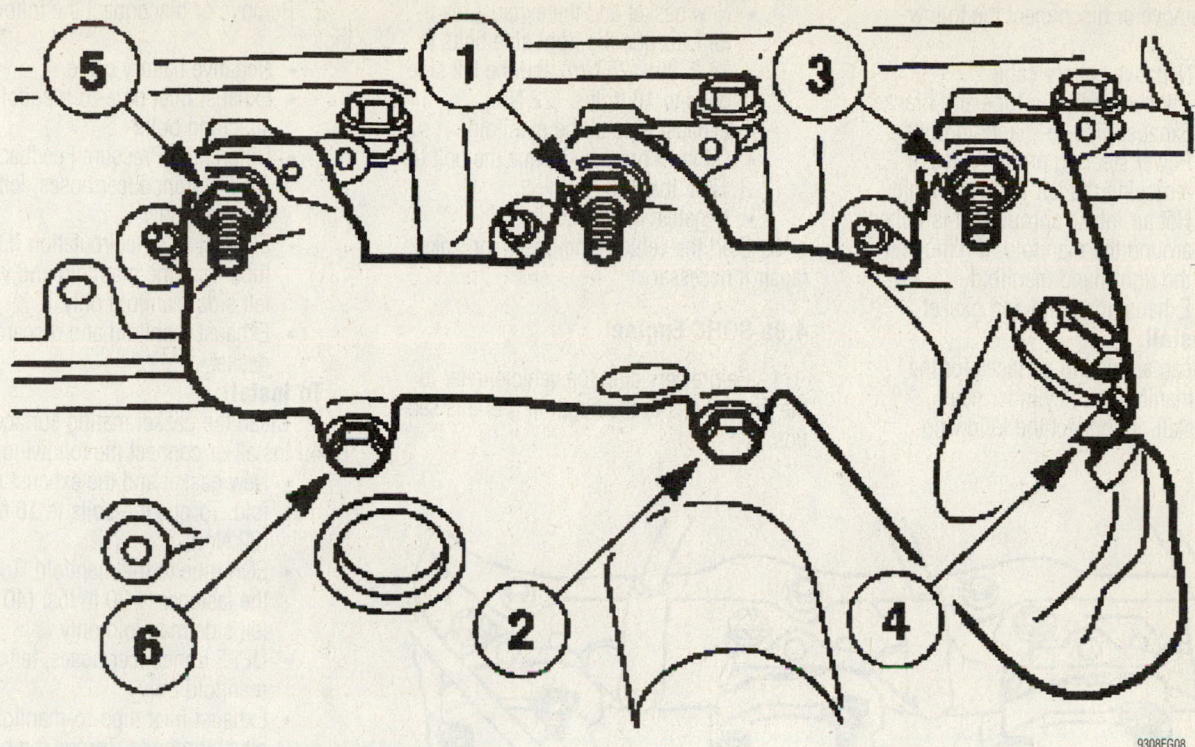

9308EG08

Tighten the exhaust manifold bolts in sequence–3.0L left side

- Exhaust manifold and discard the gasket

To install:

3. Clean the mating surfaces for the exhaust manifold and cylinder head.

4. Install a new gasket and the exhaust manifold. Torque the bolts in sequence to:
    a. 89 inch lbs. (10 Nm).
    b. 15 ft. lbs. (20 Nm).

5. Install or connect the following:
- Oil lever indicator tube and bracket. Torque the bolt to 12 ft. lbs. (16 Nm).
- EGR valve to the exhaust manifold tube. Torque the fastener to 26 ft. lbs. (35 Nm).
- Exhaust flange. Torque the nuts to 25 ft. lbs. (34 Nm).
- Negative battery cable

6. Start the vehicle and check for leaks, repair if necessary.

RIGHT SIDE

1. Before servicing the vehicle, refer to the precautions in the beginning of this section.

2. Remove or disconnect the following:
- Negative battery cable
- Exhaust manifold flange
- Ignition coil support bracket
- Exhaust manifold and discard the gasket

To install:

3. Clean the mating surfaces for the exhaust manifold and cylinder head

4. Install a new gasket and the exhaust manifold. Torque the bolts is sequence to:
    a. 89 inch lbs. (10 Nm).
    b. 18 ft. lbs. (25 Nm).

5. Install or connect the following:
- Ignition coil support bracket. Torque the bolts to 15 ft. lbs. (20 Nm).

- Exhaut flange nuts. Torque the nuts to 33 ft. lbs. (46 Nm).
- Negative battery cable

6. Start the vehicle and check for leaks, repair if necessary.

4.0L OHV Engine

1. Before servicing the vehicle, refer to the precautions in the beginning of this section.

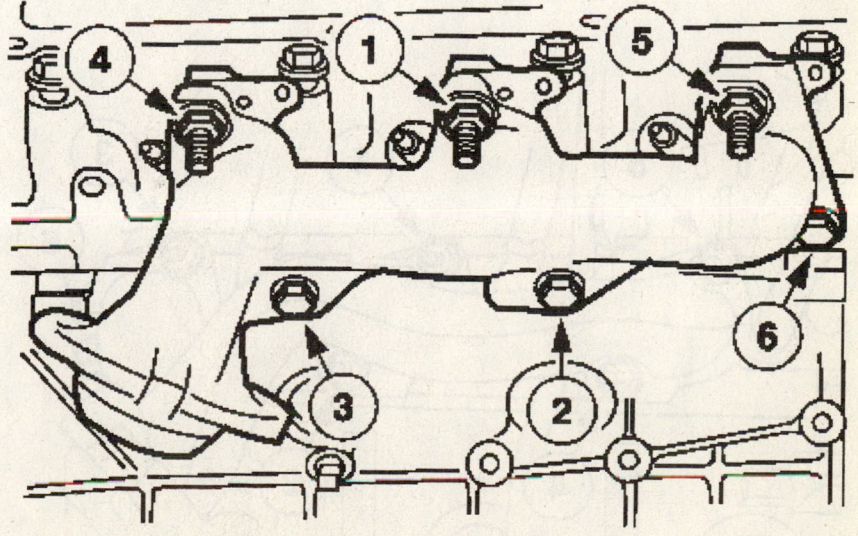

9308EG09

Tighten the right side exhaust manifold bolts in the proper sequence–3.0L

Please refer to Section 8 for electric cooling fan wiring schematics

2. Remove or disconnect the following:

- Negative battery cable
- Oil level indicator tube and bracket
- Exhaust pipe-to-manifold bolts
- Power steering pump hoses, if removing the left-hand manifold
- Hot air intake shroud that is bolted around the manifold, if removing the right-hand manifold
- Exhaust manifold and gasket

To install:

3. Clean all mating surfaces for the exhaust manifold and cylinder head.

4. Install or connect the following:

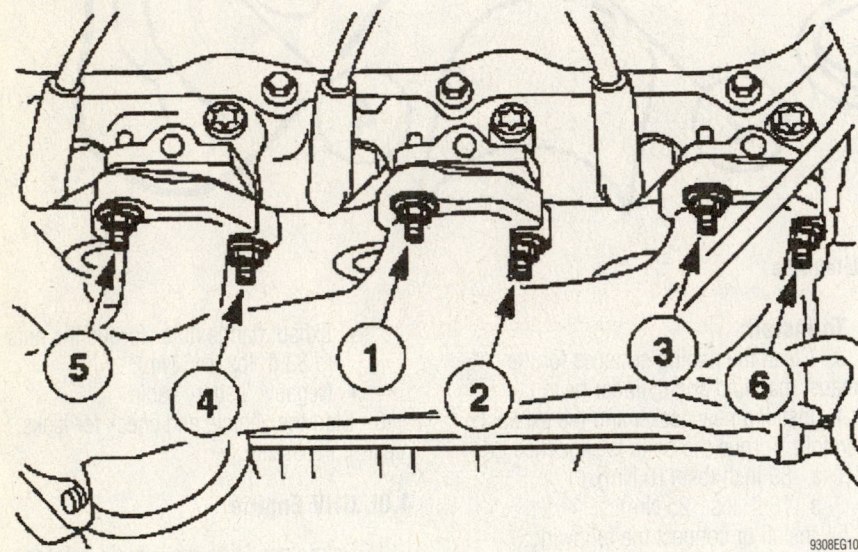

Tighten the right side exhaust manifold in sequence

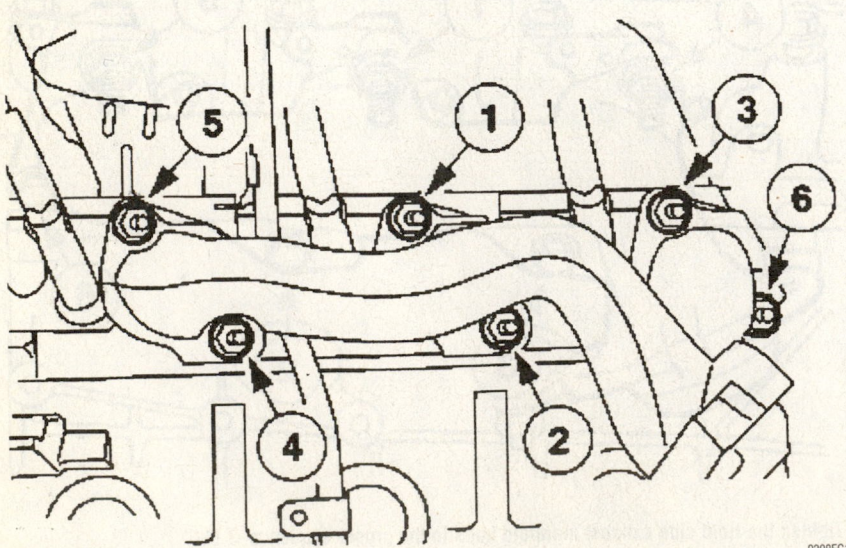

Tighten the left side exhaust manifold in sequence

- New gasket and the exhaust manifold. Torque the right side bolts to 18 ft. lbs. (25 Nm) and the left side bolts to 16 ft. lbs. (22 Nm).
- Exhaust pipe to the manifold
- Oil level bracket. Torque the bolt to 17 ft. lbs. (23 Nm).
- Negative battery cable

5. Start the vehicle and check for leaks, repair if necessary.

4.0L SOHC Engine

1. Before servicing the vehicle, refer to the precautions in the beginning of this section.

2. Remove or disconnect the following:

- Negative battery cable
- Exhaust inlet pipe-to-manifold attaching bolts
- Differential Pressure Feedback EGR (DPFE) transducer hoses, left side manifold only
- Exhaust Gas Recirculation (EGR) tube from the manifold and valve, left side manifold only
- Exhaust manifold and discard the gasket

To install:

3. Clean the gasket mating surfaces.

4. Install or connect the following:

- New gasket and the exhaust manifold. Torque the bolts to 16 ft. lbs. (22 Nm).
- EGR tube to the manifold. Torque the fastener to 30 ft. lbs. (40 Nm) left side manifold only
- DPFE transducer hoses, left side manifold only
- Exhaust inlet pipe-to-manifold attaching bolts. Torque the bolts to 30 ft. lbs. (40 Nm).
- Negative battery cable

5. Start the vehicle and check for leaks, repair if necessary.

5.0L Engine

LEFT SIDE

1. Before servicing the vehicle, refer to the precautions in the beginning of this section.

2. Discharge and recover the A/C system.

3. Remove or disconnect the following:

- Negative battery cable
- Spark plug wires and retaining brackets
- A/C manifold and tube
- Condenser to evaporator tube from the A/C condenser core
- Oil level indicator tube
- Left wheel
- Wheel well apron pin retainers
- Exhaust manifold and discard the gasket

To install:

4. Clean the gasket mating surfaces.

5. Install or connect the following:

- New gasket and the exhaust manifold. Torque the bolts to 30 ft. lbs. (40 Nm).
- Wheel well pin retainers
- Left wheel
- Oil level indicator tube. Torque the bolt to 18 ft. lbs. (25 Nm).

- Condenser to evaporator tube
- A/C manifold and tube
- Spark plug wires and brackets
- Negative battery cable

6. Recharge the A/C system.

7. Start the vehicle and check for leaks, repair if necessary.

RIGHT SIDE

1. Before servicing the vehicle, refer to the precautions in the beginning of this section.

2. Remove or disconnect the following:

- Negative battery cable
- Air cleaner outlet tube
- Drive belt tensioner
- Alternator electrical connectors
- Alternator and bracket
- Exhaust flange
- Right front wheel
- Wheel well apron pin retainers
- Exhaust Gas Recirculation (EGR) valve from the manifold tube
- Spark plug wires and retaining brackets
- Exhaust manifold heat shield
- Exhaust manifold and discard the gasket

To install:

3. Clean the gasket mating surfaces.

4. Install or connect the following:

- New gasket and the exhaust manifold. Torque the bolts to 30 ft. lbs. (40 Nm).
- Exhaust manifold heat shield. Torque the bolts to 61 inch lbs. (7 Nm).
- Spark plug wires and retaining brackets
- EGR valve to the manifold tube
- Wheel well apron pin retainers
- Right front wheel
- Exhaust flange. Torque the nuts to 26 ft. lbs. (34 Nm).

5. Install the alternator and bracket. Torque the bolts in sequence as follows:

    a. Bolts NO. 1–2 to 26 ft. lbs. (34 Nm).

    b. Bolt NO. 3 to 48 ft. lbs. (65 Nm).

    c. Torque the remaining bolt to 26 ft. lbs. (34 Nm).

6. Install or connect the following:

- Drive belt tensioner
- Air cleaner outlet tube
- Negative battery cable

7. Start the vehicle and check for leaks, repair if necessary.

Front Crankshaft Seal

REMOVAL & INSTALLATION

➡ **The 3.0L, 4.0L and 5.0L engines use timing chains; only engines using timing belts will be covered here.**

2.3L and 2.5L Engines

1. Before servicing the vehicle, refer to the precautions in the beginning of this section.

2. Remove or disconnect the following:

- Negative battery cable
- Timing belt cover
- Drive belt

3. Align the crankshaft and camshaft timing marks and remove the timing belt.

- Crankshaft pulley center bolt and slide the pulley off of the crankshaft
- Crankshaft key

✳✳ WARNING

Do not damage the crankshaft sealing surface while removing the oil seal.

- Crankshaft Seal Remover tool T74P-6700-B on the crankshaft and into the oil seal.
- Oil seal and clean the seal journal

To install:

4. Apply clean engine oil to the rubber lip of the new seal to aid installation.

5. Using Cam Bearing Adapter Tube T72C-6250, or equivalent, and crankshaft center bolt, carefully install the new oil seal until flush with the engine.

6. Install or connect the following:

- Key and crankshaft pulley, washer and bolt. Torque the bolt to 92–121 ft. lbs. (125–165 Nm).
- Timing belt
- Timing belt and cover
- Drive belt
- Negative battery cable

7. Start the vehicle and check for leaks, repair if necessary.

Camshaft and Valve Lifters

➡ **Although Ford suggests that this component is removable while the engine is installed in the vehicle, depending on the particular options with which your truck is equipped, working clearance may be extremely tight and this procedure may be much easier to perform with the engine removed. Before commencing, read**

through this procedure and make certain enough clearance, or working room, exists with the engine in the vehicle; if there is not enough space, the engine should be removed.

REMOVAL & INSTALLATION

2.3L and 2.5L Engines

1. Drain the cooling system.

2. Before servicing the vehicle, refer to the precautions in the beginning of this section.

3. Remove or disconnect the following:

- Negative battery cable
- Air cleaner
- Spark plug wires and retainers
- Vacuum lines
- Drive belts
- Alternator and bracket
- Upper radiator hose
- Radiator shroud
- Fan blades
- Water pump pulley
- Fan shroud

4. Align the engine timing marks at Top Dead Center (TDC) for No. 1 cylinder. Remove the timing belt.

- Valve covers
- Rocker arms (camshaft followers)
- Camshaft drive gear and belt guide using a suitable puller. Remove the front oil seal with Front Seal Replacer T74P-6150-A
- Camshaft retainer located on the rear mounting stand
- Front motor mount bolts
- Lower radiator hose from the radiator
- Automatic transmission cooler lines, if equipped

5. Position a piece of wood on a floor jack and raise the engine carefully as far as it will go. Place blocks of wood between the engine mounts and crossmember pedestals.

6. Remove camshaft by carefully withdrawing it toward the front of the engine. Caution should be used to prevent damage to cam bearings, lobes and journals.

7. Check the camshaft journals and lobes for wear. Inspect the cam bearings, if worn (unless the proper bearing installing tool is on hand), the cylinder head must be removed for new bearings to be installed by a machine shop.

To install:

8. Install or connect the following:

- Camshaft and lower the engine to its original position

- Transmission cooler lines, if equipped
- Lower radiator hose
- Front motor mount. Torque the bolts to 65 ft. lbs. (88 Nm).
- Camshaft retainer on the rear mounting stand
- Camshaft drive gear and belt guide
- Valve covers
- Timing belt. Make certain that the timing marks are properly aligned
- Fan shroud
- Water pump pulley
- Fan blades
- Upper radiator hose and radiator shroud
- Alternator and bracket
- Drive belts
- Vacuum lines
- Spark plugs wires and retainers
- Air cleaner
- Negative battery cable

9. Fill the cooling system.

10. Start the engine and check for leaks, repair if necessary.

3.0L Engine

1. Before servicing the vehicle, refer to the precautions in the beginning of this section.

2. Properly relieve the fuel system pressure.

3. Drain the cooling system.

4. Drain the engine oil.

5. Evacuate the A/C system.

6. Remove or disconnect the following:

- Negative battery cable
- Air cleaner hoses
- Fan, spacer and shroud
- Radiator

7. Rotate the crankshaft so that No. 1 piston is at Top Dead Center (TDC) on the compression stroke.

- A/C condenser
- Fuel lines from the fuel supply manifold
- Vacuum hoses
- Electrical wiring
- Engine front cover
- Water pump
- Alternator
- Power steering pump. Do not disconnect the hoses
- A/C compressor. Do not disconnect the hoses
- Throttle body
- Fuel injection wire harness

8. Turn the engine by hand to TDC of the power stroke on No. 1 cylinder.

- Spark plug wires from the plugs

- Distributor cap with the spark plug wires as an assembly, if equipped

9. Matchmark the rotor, distributor body and engine. Disconnect the distributor wiring harness and remove the distributor, if equipped.

- Rocker arm covers
- Intake manifold
- Loosen the rocker arm bolts enough to pivot the rocker arms out of the way and remove the pushrods. Identify them for installation
- Lifters and identify them for installation
- Crankshaft pulley/damper
- Starter
- Oil pan
- Camshaft gear attaching bolt and washer, then slide the gear off the camshaft
- Camshaft thrust plate

10. Carefully slide the camshaft out of the engine block, using caution to avoid any damage to the camshaft bearings.

To install:

11. Oil the camshaft journals and cam lobes with heavy SJ engine oil (50W). Install the spacer ring with the chamfered side toward the camshaft, then insert the camshaft key.

12. Install or connect the following:

- Camshaft using caution to avoid any damage to the camshaft bearings
- Thrust plate. Torque the screws to 84 inch lbs. (10 Nm).

13. Rotate the camshaft and crankshaft as necessary to align the timing marks. Install the camshaft gear and chain. Torque the bolt to 46 ft. lbs. (62 Nm).

14. Coat the tappets with 50W engine oil and place them in their original locations.

15. Apply 50W engine oil to both ends of the pushrods. Install the pushrods in their original locations.

16. Pivot the rocker arms into position. Torque the fulcrum bolts to 96 inch lbs. (11 Nm).

17. Rotate the engine until both timing marks are at the top of their sprockets and aligned. Torque the following fulcrum bolts to 18 ft. lbs. (24 Nm):

   a. No.1 intake.
   b. No.2 exhaust.
   c. No.4 intake.
   d. No.5 exhaust.

18. Rotate the engine until the camshaft timing mark is at the bottom of the sprocket and the crankshaft timing mark is at the top of the sprocket, and both are aligned. Torque the following fulcrum bolts to 18 ft. lbs. (24 Nm):

   a. No.1 exhaust.
   b. No.2 intake.
   c. No.3 intake and exhaust.
   d. No.4 exhaust.
   e. No.5 intake.
   f. No.6 intake and exhaust.

19. Torque all the bolts to 24 ft. lbs. (33 Nm).

20. Turn the engine by hand to 0 degrees Before Top Dead center (BTDC) of the power stroke on No. 1 cylinder.

21. Install or connect the following:

- Engine front cover and water pump assembly
- Oil pan
- Crankshaft damper/pulley and tighten the retaining bolt to 107 ft. lbs. (145 Nm).
- Intake manifold
- Starter
- Crankshaft pulley and damper
- Rocker arm covers
- Rotor and distributor cap, if equipped
- Spark plug wires
- Fuel lines to the fuel supply manifold
- Fuel injection wire harness
- Throttle body
- A/C compressor
- Power steering pump
- Alternator
- Water pump
- Engine front cover
- All electrical connectors and vacuum lines
- A/C condenser
- Radiator
- Fan, spacer and shroud
- Air cleaner hoses
- Negative battery cable

22. Recharge the A/C system.

23. Refill the cooling system.

24. Replace the oil filter and refill the engine with the specified amount of engine oil.

25. Start the engine and check the ignition timing and idle speed. Adjust if necessary. Run the engine at fast idle and check for coolant, fuel, vacuum or oil leaks.

4.0L OHV Engine

➡ **It is necessary to replace the oil pan gasket when removing and installing the engine front cover. It will also be necessary to remove the transmission to properly reseal the oil pan.**

1. Before servicing the vehicle, refer to the precautions in the beginning of this section.

2. Drain the engine oil.

3. Drain the cooling system.

4. Evacuate the A/C system.

5. Relieve fuel system pressure.

6. Remove or disconnect the following:

- Negative battery cable
- Radiator
- A/C compressor. Do not disconnect the lines
- A/C condenser
- Fan, spacer and shroud
- Air cleaner hoses
- Spark plug wires
- Ignition coil and bracket
- Crankcase pulley and damper
- Oil pump drive
- Alternator
- Fuel lines at the supply manifold
- Upper and lower intake manifold
- Rocker arm covers
- Rocker arm shafts
- Pushrods and identify them for installation
- Tappets and identify them for installation
- Oil pan
- Engine front cover
- Water pump

7. Turn the engine by hand until the timing marks align at Top dead Center (TDC) of the power stroke on No.1 piston.

8. Place the timing chain tensioner in the retracted position and install the retaining clip.

9. Check the camshaft end-play. If excessive, you'll have to replace the thrust plate.

10. Remove the camshaft gear attaching bolt and washer, then slide the gear off the camshaft.

11. Remove the camshaft thrust plate.

12. Carefully slide the camshaft out of the engine block, using caution to avoid any damage to the camshaft bearings.

To install:

13. Lubricate the camshaft using a good assembly lubricant.

14. Install or connect the following:

- Camshaft using caution to avoid any damage to the camshaft bearings
- Thrust plate. Make sure that it covers the main oil gallery. Torque the screws to 84–120 inch lbs. (9–13 Nm).

15. Rotate the camshaft and crankshaft, as necessary, to align the timing marks.

- Camshaft gear and chain. Torque the bolt to 44–50 ft. lbs. (60–68 Nm).

16. Remove the clip from the chain tensioner

- Engine front cover and water pump
- Crankshaft damper/pulley. Torque the bolt to 107 ft. lbs. (146 Nm).
- Oil pan

17. Coat the tappets with 50W engine oil and place them in their original locations.

18. Apply 50W engine oil to both ends of the pushrods. Install the pushrods in their original locations.

- Tappets
- Rocker arm shafts and covers
- Upper and lower intake manifolds
- Fuel lines to the fuel supply manifold
- Alternator and electrical connectors
- Oil pump drive
- Crankcase pulley and damper
- Ignition coil and bracket
- Spark plug wires
- Air cleaner hoses
- Fan, spacer and shroud
- A/C condenser
- A/C compressor
- Radiator
- Negative battery cable

19. Fill the cooling system.

20. Recharge the A/C system.

21. Replace the oil filter and refill the engine with clean oil.

22. Start the engine and check the ignition timing and idle speed; adjust if necessary. Run the engine at fast idle and check for coolant, fuel, vacuum or oil leaks.

4.0L SOHC Engine

1. Before servicing the vehicle, refer to the precautions in the beginning of this section.

2. Remove or disconnect the following:

- Negative battery cable for safety
- Valve cover
- Hydraulic camshaft tensioner

➡ **The right-hand camshaft sprocket bolt uses left-hand threads.**

3. For the right-hand camshaft use the Cam Gear Torque Adapter tool T97T-6256-F, to remove the camshaft sprocket bolt.

4. For the left-hand camshaft, remove the sprocket bolt.

➡ **When removing the followers, label them so that they may be returned to their original positions.**

5. Using the Valve Spring Compressor tool ST1330-A, remove the camshaft roller followers.

6. Install or connect the following:

- Camshaft bearing cap bolts and the oil rail
- Camshaft

To install:

7. Lubricate all of the moving parts with SAE 50W engine oil.

8. Install camshaft onto the cylinder head.

9. Position the oil rail and install the bearing caps and bolts. Torque the bolts in 2 steps:

Use the proper sequence to prevent damage to the camshaft both when installing and removing the bearing caps—4.0L SOHC engine

7924EG15

Timing belt service is covered in Section 4 of this manual

a. Step 1—53.5 inch lbs. (6 Nm).

b. Step 2—11–12.5 ft. lbs. (15–17 Nm).

10. Install or connect the following:
- Camshaft followers
- Camshaft sprocket bolt and hand tighten the bolt
- Camshaft Chain Tensioner T97T-6K254-A in the hole that the hydraulic chain tensioner was in

11. Turn the crankshaft one revolution clockwise until No. 1 piston is Top Dead Center (TDC).

12. Install or connect the following:
- Crankshaft Holding tool T97T-6303-A on the crankshaft to keep it from turning
- Position the timing slot on the rear of the camshaft to fit Camshaft Holding tool T97T-6256-C and install the holding tool on the rear of the head
- Camshaft Gear Holding tool T97T-6256-B and Camshaft Gear Holding tool T97T-6256-A on the front of the cylinder head to securely hold the camshaft gear
- Tighten the camshaft sprocket bolt to 63 ft. lbs. (85 Nm).

13. Remove the Camshaft Chain Tensioner tool and install the hydraulic chain tensioner, tighten the tensioner to 35–39 ft. lbs. (47–53 Nm).

14. Remove the special tools from the engine.

15. Install or connect the following:
- Valve cover
- Negative battery cable

16. Start the engine check for leaks and repair if necessary.

5.0L Engine

1. Before servicing the vehicle, refer to the precautions in the beginning of this section.

2. Remove or disconnect the following:
- Negative battery cable
- Timing chain cover
- Camshaft sprocket and chain assembly
- Upper and lower intake manifolds
- Both valve covers
- Loosen the rocker arm bolts and rotate the rocker arms to the side
- Pushrods in sequence so that they may be installed to their original positions
- Lifters
- Camshaft thrust plate bolts and the plate
- Camshaft from the engine, taking

care not to damage the bearings, lobes or journals

To install:

3. Apply SAE 50W engine oil to the camshaft lobes and journals.

4. Install or connect the following:
- Camshaft

5. Apply SAE 50W engine oil to the camshaft thrust plate. Position the thrust plate with the groove toward the block and install the retaining bolts. Torque to 10–12 ft. lbs. (13–16 Nm).

6. Apply SAE 50W engine oil to the valve tappets and install them. If reusing the old lifters, place them in their original positions.

7. Install or connect the following:
- Pushrods to their original positions
- Rocker arms
- Valve covers
- Lower and upper intake manifolds
- Camshaft sprocket and chain assembly. Ensure that the timing marks on the cam and crankshaft sprockets are aligned.
- Timing chain cover
- Negative battery cable

8. Start the engine, check for leaks and repair if necessary.

Oil Pan

REMOVAL & INSTALLATION

2.3L and 2.5L Engines

1. Before servicing the vehicle, refer to the precautions in the beginning of this section.

2. Drain the engine oil.

3. Remove or disconnect the following:
- Negative battery cable
- Engine from the vehicle and place it on a suitable engine stand
- Oil pan and discard the gasket

To install:

4. Clean the mating surface on the oil pan.

5. Install or connect the following:
- Oil pan gasket
- Apply a bead of silicone sealant to the oil pan
- Oil pan. Torque the bolts in sequence to 141 inch lbs. (16 Nm).
- Engine
- Negative battery cable

6. Fill the engine with clean oil.

7. Start the vehicle and check for leaks, repair if necessary.

3.0L Engine

2WD

1. Before servicing the vehicle, refer to the precautions in the beginning of this section.

2. Drain the engine oil.

3. Remove or disconnect the following:
- Negative battery cable
- Oil level dipstick tube
- Fan shroud. Leave the fan shroud over the fan assembly
- Motor mount nuts from the frame

✴✴ WARNING

On models equipped with distributor ignition, failure to remove the distributor will damage or break it when the engine is lifted.

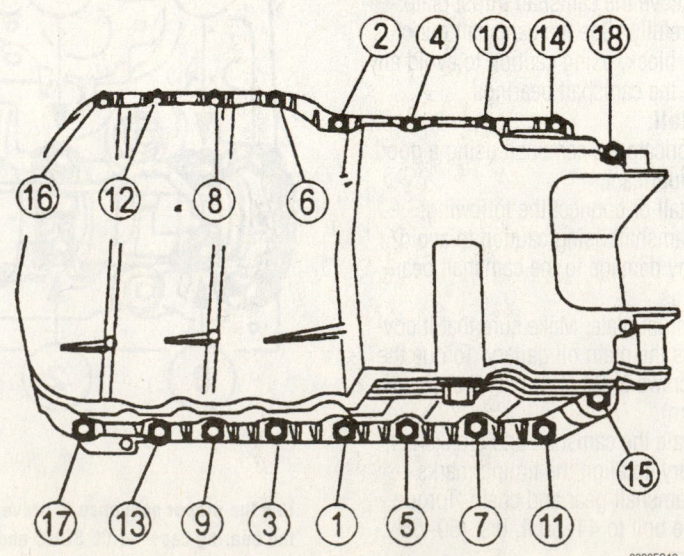

Tighten the oil pan bolts in sequence—2.3L and 2.5L engines

9308EG12

- Starter
- Transmission inspection cover
- Right hand axle I-beam. The brake caliper must be removed and secured out of the way.
- Oil pan attaching bolts, using a suitable lifting device, raise the engine about 2 in. (5cm)
- Oil pan and discard the gasket

➡ **The oil pan fits tightly between the transmission spacer plate and oil pump pick-up tube. Use care when removing the oil pan from the engine.**

4. Clean all gasket surfaces on the engine and oil pan. Remove all traces of old gasket and/or sealer.

To install:

5. Apply a ⅛ (4mm) bead of RTV sealer to the junctions of the rear main bearing cap and block, and the front cover and block. The sealer sets in 15 minutes, so work quickly!

6. Apply adhesive to the gasket surfaces and install the oil pan gasket.

7. Install or connect the following:
- Oil pan on the engine block. Torque the bolts EVENLY to 9 ft. lbs. (12 Nm) working from the center to the end position on the oil pan.
- Right hand axle I-beam
- Brake caliper
- Transmission inspection cover
- Starter
- Fan shroud
- Motor mount retaining nuts
- Oil level dipstick tube
- Negative battery cable

8. Fill the engine with clean oil.

9. Start the vehicle and check for leaks, repair if necessary.

4WD

1. Before servicing the vehicle, refer to the precautions in the beginning of this section.

2. Drain the engine oil.

3. Remove or disconnect the following:
- Negative battery cable
- Engine from the vehicle and place it on a suitable engine stand
- Oil pan and discard the gasket

To install:

4. Install or connect the following:
- New oil pan gasket and secure the gasket with trim adhesive
- Oil pan. Torque the bolts to 9 ft. lbs. (12 Nm).
- Engine
- Negative battery cable

5. Fill the engine with clean oil.

6. Start the vehicle and check for leaks, repair if necessary.

4.0L OHV Engine

➡ **Review the complete service procedure before starting this repair.**

1. Before servicing the vehicle, refer to the precautions in the beginning of this section.

2. Drain the engine oil.

3. Remove or disconnect the following:
- Negative battery cable
- Engine from the vehicle and mount the engine on a suitable engine stand with the oil pan facing up
- Oil pan attaching bolts (note location of 2 spacers) and remove the pan from the engine block
- Oil pan gasket and crankshaft rear main bearing cap wedge seal

4. Clean all gasket surfaces on the engine and oil pan. Remove all traces of old gasket and/or sealer.

To install:

5. Install or connect the following:
- New crankshaft rear main bearing cap wedge seal. The seal should fit snugly into the sides of the rear main bearing cap
- New oil pan gasket to the engine block and place the oil pan in correct position on the 4 locating studs. Torque the bolts EVENLY to 60–84 inch lbs. (7–10 Nm).
- Transmission bolts to the engine and oil pan. There are 2 spacers on the rear of the oil pan to allow proper mating of the transmission and oil pan.
- Spacers to the mounting pads on the rear of the oil pan before bolting the engine and transmission together
- Engine to the vehicle
- Negative battery cable

6. Fill the engine with clean oil.
- Start the vehicle and check for leaks, repair if necessary.

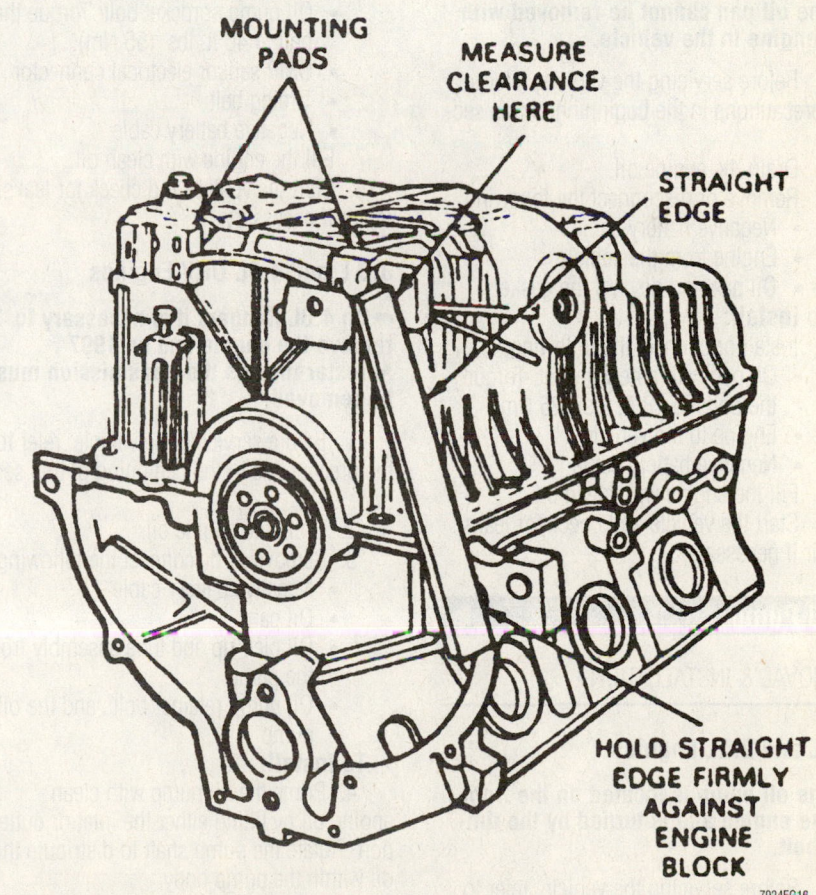

MOUNTING PADS

MEASURE CLEARANCE HERE

STRAIGHT EDGE

HOLD STRAIGHT EDGE FIRMLY AGAINST ENGINE BLOCK

7924EG16

The correct spacer must be used to extend the mounting surface of the oil pan so it is flush with the mounting surface of the engine block–4.0L OHV engine

4.0L SOHC Engine

➡ The 4.0L SOHC engine does not use an oil pan in the conventional sense. There is a separate access panel that unbolts from what would be considered the oil pan (which is now known as the ladder frame).

1. Before servicing the vehicle, refer to the precautions in the beginning of this section.
2. Drain the engine oil.
3. Remove or disconnect the following:
   • Negative battery cable
   • Oil pan and discard the gasket

To install:

4. Install or connect the following:
   • New gasket and oil pan. Torque the bolts to 80 inch lbs. (9 Nm).
   • Negative battery cable
5. Fill the engine with clean oil.
6. Start the vehicle and check for leaks, repair if necessary.

5.0L Engine

➡ The oil pan cannot be removed with the engine in the vehicle.

1. Before servicing the vehicle, refer to the precautions in the beginning of this section.
2. Drain the engine oil.
3. Remove or disconnect the following:
   • Negative battery cable
   • Engine from the vehicle
   • Oil pan and discard the gasket

To install:

4. Install or connect the following:
   • Oil pan with a new gasket. Torque the bolts to 18 ft. lbs. (25 Nm).
   • Engine to the vehicle
   • Negative battery cable
5. Fill the engine with clean oil.
6. Start the vehicle and check for leaks, repair if necessary.

Oil Pump

REMOVAL & INSTALLATION

2.3L and 2.5L Engines

➡ The oil pump is located on the front of the engine and is turned by the timing belt.

1. Before servicing the vehicle, refer to the precautions in the beginning of this section.
2. Remove or disconnect the following:
   • Negative battery cable
   • Timing belt

   • Camshaft Position (CMP) sensor electrical connector
   • Oil pump sprocket
   • CMP sensor

➡ Use a prybar or drift through one of the holes in the pump sprocket to keep it from turning while loosening the bolt.

   • 4 bolts retaining the oil pump to the engine block
   • Oil pump from the front of the engine and discard the gasket
3. Inspect the oil pump and O-rings and replace as necessary.
4. Clean all gasket mating surfaces thoroughly.

To install:

5. Prime the oil pump and with 8 ounces (236ml) of new engine oil and lubricate the O-rings.
6. Install or connect the following:
   • New gasket on the oil pump
   • Oil pump. Torque the bolts to 89 inch lbs. (10 Nm).
   • CMP sensor. Torque the bolts to 61 inch lbs. (7 Nm).
   • Oil pump sprocket bolt. Torque the bolt to 40 ft. lbs. (55 Nm).
   • CMP sensor electrical connector
   • Timing belt
   • Negative battery cable
7. Fill the engine with clean oil.
8. Start the vehicle and check for leaks, repair if necessary.

3.0 L and 4.0L OHV Engines

➡ On 4.0L Rangers it is necessary to remove the engine and on 1997 Aerostar models the transmission must be removed.

1. Before servicing the vehicle, refer to the precautions in the beginning of this section.
2. Drain the engine oil.
3. Remove or disconnect the following:
   • Negative battery cable
   • Oil pan
   • Oil pick-up and tube assembly from the pump
   • Oil pump retainer bolts and the oil pump

To install:

4. Prime the oil pump with clean engine oil by filling either the inlet or outlet port. Rotate the pump shaft to distribute the oil within the pump body.
5. Install the oil pump and tighten the mounting bolts to:
6. 3.0L: 30–40 ft. lbs. (41–54 Nm).
7. 4.0L: 13–15 ft. lbs. (18–20 Nm).

Do not force the oil pump if it does not seat readily. The oil pump driveshaft may be misaligned with the distributor or shaft assembly. If the pump is tightened down with the driveshaft misaligned, damage to the pump could occur. To align, rotate the intermediate driveshaft into a new position.

8. Install or connect the following:
   • Oil pick-up and tube assembly
   • Oil pan
9. Fill the engine with clean oil.
10. Start the vehicle and check for leaks, repair if necessary.

4.0L SOHC and 5.0L Engines

➡ The oil pump cannot be removed with the engine in the vehicle.

1. Before servicing the vehicle, refer to the precautions in the beginning of this section.
2. Drain the engine oil.
3. Remove or disconnect the following:
   • Engine from the vehicle
   • Oil pan
   • Unbolt the oil pick-up tube
4. On the 4.0L engine, perform the following:
   a. Remove the 8 ladder frame bolts that were under the oil pan.
   b. Remove the 2 rear outer ladder frame bolts.
   c. Remove the 7 left-hand and the 8 right-hand ladder frame bolts.
   d. Lift the ladder frame from the engine.
5. Remove the 2 oil pump attaching bolts and the pump.

To install:

6. Submerge the pump in clean engine oil to prime it.
7. On the 4.0L engine, do the following:
   a. Position the ladder frame on the engine.
   b. Install the 8 right-hand and 7 left-hand ladder frame bolts.
   c. Install the 2 rear outer and the 8 frame bolts under the pan.
8. Insatall the oil pump. Torque the bolts to:
   a. 4.0L: 13–15 ft. lbs. (17–21 Nm).
   b. 5.0L: 23–31 ft. lbs. (30–43 Nm).
9. Install or connect the following:
   • Oil pick-up tube
   • Oil pan
   • Engine to the vehicle
   • Negative battery cable

10. Fill the engine with clean oil.

11. Start the vehicle and check for leaks, repair if necessary.

Rear Main Seal

REMOVAL & INSTALLATION

If the crankshaft rear oil seal replacement is the only operation being performed, it can be done in the vehicle as detailed in the following procedure. If the oil seal is being replaced in conjunction with a rear main bearing replacement, the engine must be removed from the vehicle and installed on a work stand.

1. Before servicing the vehicle, refer to the precautions in the beginning of this section.

2. Remove or disconnect the following:
   - Negative battery cable
   - Starter
   - Transmission from the vehicle
   - Pressure plate and clutch disc, on vehicles with a manual transmission
   - Flywheel attaching bolts
   - Flywheel and engine rear cover plate

3. Use an awl to punch 2 holes in the crankshaft rear oil seal. Punch the holes on opposite sides of the crankshaft and just above the bearing cap to cylinder block split line. Install a sheet metal screw in each hole. Use 2 small pry bars and pry against both screws at the same time to remove the crankshaft rear oil seal. It may be necessary to place small blocks of wood against the cylinder block to provide a fulcrum point for the pry bars. Use caution throughout this procedure to avoid scratching or otherwise damaging the crankshaft oil seal surface.

To install:

4. Clean the oil seal recess in the cylinder block and main bearing cap.

5. Clean, inspect and polish the rear oil seal rubbing surface on the crankshaft. Coat a new oil seal and the crankshaft with a light film of engine oil. Start the seal in the recess with the seal lip facing forward and install it with a seal driver. Keep the tool, T82L-6701-A (4-cyl. engines) or T72C-6165 (6-cyl. engine) straight with the centerline of the crankshaft and install the seal until the tool contacts the cylinder block surface. Remove the tool and inspect the seal to be sure it was not damaged during installation.

6. On 8-cylinder engines, coat the new oil seal and crankshaft with a light film of clean engine oil. Start the seal in the recess

with the seal lip facing forward and install it with Rear Crank Seal Replacer T95P-6701-BH and Spacer T96T-6701-B.

7. Install or connect the following:
   - Engine rear cover plate. Position the flywheel on the crankshaft flange. Coat the threads of the flywheel attaching bolts with oil-resistant sealer and install the bolts. Torque the bolts in sequence across from each other to 75–85 ft. lbs. (102–115 Nm).
   - Clutch disc and the pressure plate, on vehicles with a manual transmission
   - Transmission
   - Negative battery cable

8. Check the fluid levels and top off if necessary.

9. Start the engine, check for leaks and repair if necessary.

Timing Chain, Sprockets, Front Cover and Seal

REMOVAL & INSTALLATION

3.0L and 4.0L OHC Engines

1. Before servicing the vehicle, refer to the precautions in the beginning of this section.

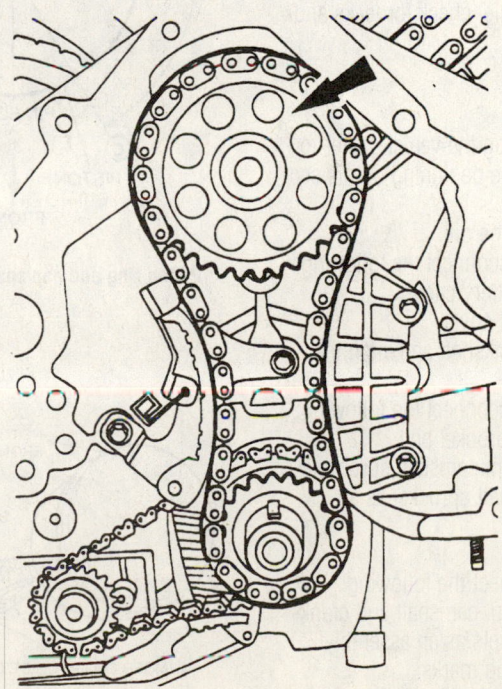

Remove the jackshaft sprocket–4.0L SOHC Engine

2. Remove or disconnect the following:
   - Negative battery cable
   - Engine front cover
   - Rotate the crankshaft and align the timing marks
   - Timing chain tensioner, 4.0L OHC engine only
   - Sprocket bolt
   - Timing chain, camshaft sprocket and crankshaft sprocket as an assembly

To install:

3. Install or connect the following:
   - Timing chain, camshaft and crankshaft sprockets as an assembly

4. Align the timing marks.

5. Install or connect the following:
   - Timing chain tensioner
   - Sprocket bolt. Torque the bolt to 51 ft. lbs. (70 Nm).
   - Engine front cover
   - Negative battery cable

4.0L OHC Engine

1. Before servicing the vehicle, refer to the precautions in the beginning of this section.

2. Drain the engine oil.

3. Remove or disconnect the following:
   - Negative battery cable
   - Engine from the vehicle
   - Oil pan

89683G51

- Engine front cover
- Cylinder heads

4. Lock the jackshaft tensioner by installing a pin.

- Jackshaft sprocket and chain assembly
- Left front cassette retaining bolt
- Cassette chain and tensioner assembly
- Rear jackshaft plug from the engine
- Right rear cassette retaining bolt and spacer
- Right rear cassette chain and tensioner
- Timing chain (s)

To install:

5. Install or connect the following:

- Timing chain(s)
- Right rear cassette chain, tensioner and sprocket
- Jackshaft sprocket and chain on the engine and remove the tensioner pin

6. Torque the jackshaft sprocket bolt in 2 stages:

   a. 32–35 ft. lbs. (43–47 Nm).

   b. Turn an additional 65 degrees.

7. Install or connect the following:

- Cylinder heads
- Front cover
- Oil pan
- Engine to the vehicle
- Negative battery cable

8. Fill the engine with clean oil.

9. Start the vehicle, check for leaks and repair if necessary.

5.0L Engine

1. Before servicing the vehicle, refer to the precautions in the beginning of this section.

2. Drain the engine oil.

3. Remove or disconnect the following:

- Negative battery cable
- Engine front cover

4. Rotate the crankshaft and align the timing marks.

5. Remove or disconnect the following:

- Camshaft sprocket bolt
- Timing chain, camshaft sprocket and crankshaft sprocket as an assembly

To install:

6. Install or connect the following:

- Timing chain, camshaft and crankshaft sprockets as an assembly

7. Align the timing marks.

- Camshaft sprocket bolt. Torque the bolt to 45 ft. lbs. (61 Nm).
- Engine front cover
- Negative battery cable

Piston and Ring

POSITIONING

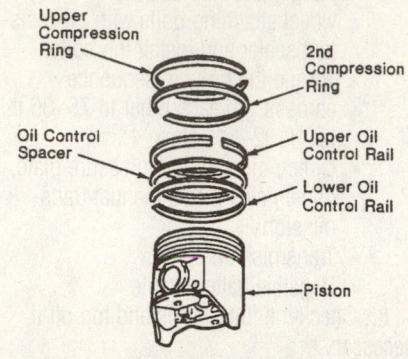

Piston ring positioning—Ford/Mazda

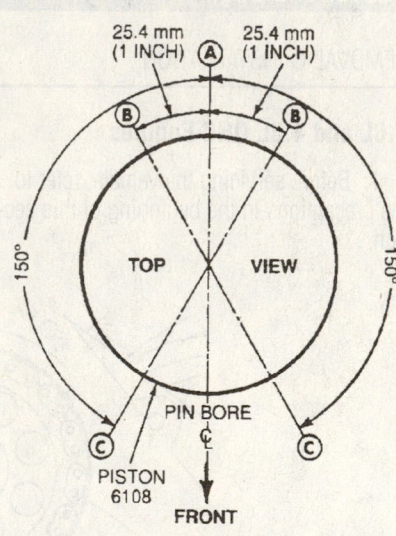

Piston ring end gap spacing—Ford/Mazda

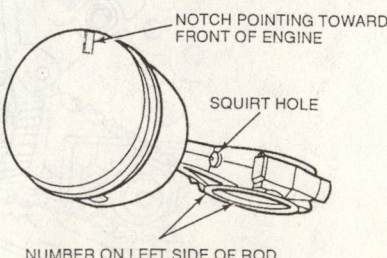

Piston and connecting rod positioning on Ford/Mazda 2.3L–2.5L engines

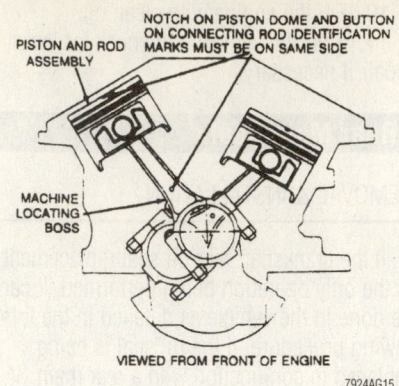

Piston and connecting rod positioning on Ford/Mazda 3.0L

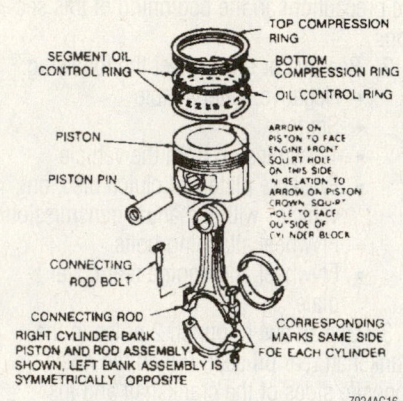

Piston and connecting rod positioning on Ford/Mazda 4.0L

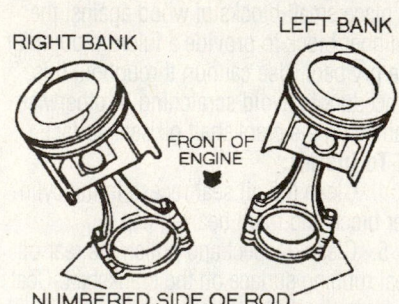

Piston and connecting rod positioning on Ford/Mazda 5.0L

FUEL SYSTEM

Fuel System Service Precautions

Safety is the most important factor when performing not only fuel system maintenance, but any type of maintenance. Failure to conduct maintenance and repairs in a safe manner may result in serious personal injury or death. Work on a vehicle's fuel system components can be accomplished safely and effectively by adhering to the following rules and guidelines.

• To avoid the possibility of fire and personal injury, always disconnect the negative battery cable unless the repair or test procedure requires that battery voltage be applied.

• Always relieve the fuel system pressure prior to disconnecting any fuel system component (injector, fuel rail, pressure regulator, etc.) fitting or fuel line connection. Exercise extreme caution whenever relieving fuel system pressure, to avoid exposing your skin, face and eyes to fuel spray. Please be advised that fuel under pressure may penetrate the skin or any part of the body that it contacts.

• Always place a shop towel or cloth around the fitting or connection prior to loosening to absorb any excess fuel due to spillage. Ensure that all fuel spillage is quickly remove from engine surfaces. Ensure that all fuel-soaked cloths or towels are deposited into a flame-proof waste container with a lid.

• Always keep a dry chemical (Class B) fire extinguisher near the work area.

• Do not allow fuel spray or fuel vapors to come into contact with a light bulb, spark or open flame.

• Always use a second wrench when loosening or tightening fuel line connection fittings. This will prevent unnecessary stress and torsion to fuel piping. Always follow the proper torque specifications.

• Always replace worn fuel fitting O-rings with new ones. Do not substitute fuel hose where rigid pipe is installed.

Relieving Fuel System Pressure

All Sequential Fuel Injection (SFI) fuel injected engines are equipped with a pressure relief valve located on the fuel supply manifold. Remove the fuel tank cap and attach fuel pressure gauge T80L-9974-B, to the valve to release the fuel pressure. Be sure to drain the fuel into a suitable container and to avoid gasoline spillage. If a pressure gauge is not available, disconnect the vacuum hose from the fuel pressure regulator and attach a hand-held vacuum pump. Apply about 25 in. Hg (84 kPa) of vacuum to the regulator to vent the fuel system pressure into the fuel tank through the fuel return hose. Note that this procedure will remove the fuel pressure from the lines, but not the fuel. Take precautions to avoid the risk of fire

and use clean rags to soak up any spilled fuel when the lines are disconnected.

An alternate method of relieving the fuel system pressure involves disconnecting the inertia switch.

Fuel Filter

REMOVAL & INSTALLATION

2.3L, 2.5L and 3.0L Engines

1. Before servicing the vehicle, refer to the precautions in the beginning of this section.

2. Properly relieve the fuel system pressure.

3. Remove or disconnect the following:
   • Negative battery cable
   • Push connect and R-clip fittings from the fuel filter
   • Fuel filter

To install:

4. Install or connect the following:
   • Fuel filter. Torque the nut to 17 ft. lbs. (23 Nm).
   • R-clip and push connect fittings
   • Negative battery cable

5. Start the vehicle, check for leaks and repair if necessary.

4.0L and 5.0L Engines

1. Before servicing the vehicle, refer to the precautions in the beginning of this section.

2. Properly relieve the fuel system pressure.

3. Remove or disconnect the following:
   • Negative battery cable
   • Fuel lines
   • Fuel filter from the support

To install:

4. Install or connect the following:
   • Fuel filter to the support
   • Fuel lines
   • Negative battery cable

5. Start the vehicle, check for leaks and repair if necessary.

Fuel Pump

REMOVAL & INSTALLATION

2.3L, 2.5L and 3.0L Engines

1. Before servicing the vehicle, refer to the precautions in the beginning of this section.

2. Properly relieve the fuel system pressure.

3. Remove or disconnect the following:
   • Negative battery cable
   • Fuel tank
   • Fuel tank pump locking retainer ring
   • Fuel pump mounting gasket and discard the gasket
   • Fuel pump

To install:

4. Install or connect the following:
   • Fuel pump and a new mounting gasket
   • Fuel tank pump locking retainer ring. Torque the ring to 66 ft. lbs. (90 Nm).
   • Fuel tank
   • Negative battery cable

5. Start the vehicle, check for leaks and repair if necessary.

4.0L and 5.0L Engines

1. Before servicing the vehicle, refer to the precautions in the beginning of this section.

2. Properly relieve the fuel system pressure.

3. Remove or disconnect the following:
   • Negative battery cable
   • Fuel tank
   • Fuel pressure transducer electrical connector
   • Fuel pump assembly

To install:

4. Install or connect the following:
   • Fuel pump and align the arrow on the flange with the dimple on the fuel tank. Torque the bolts to 80 inch lbs. (9 Nm).
   • Fuel pressure transducer electrical connector
   • Fuel tank
   • Negative battery cable

5. Start the vehicle, check for leaks and repair if necessary.

Fuel Injectors

REMOVAL & INSTALLATION

2.3L, 2.5L 4.0L and 5.0L Engines

1. Before servicing the vehicle, refer to the precautions in the beginning of this section.

2. Properly relieve the fuel system pressure.

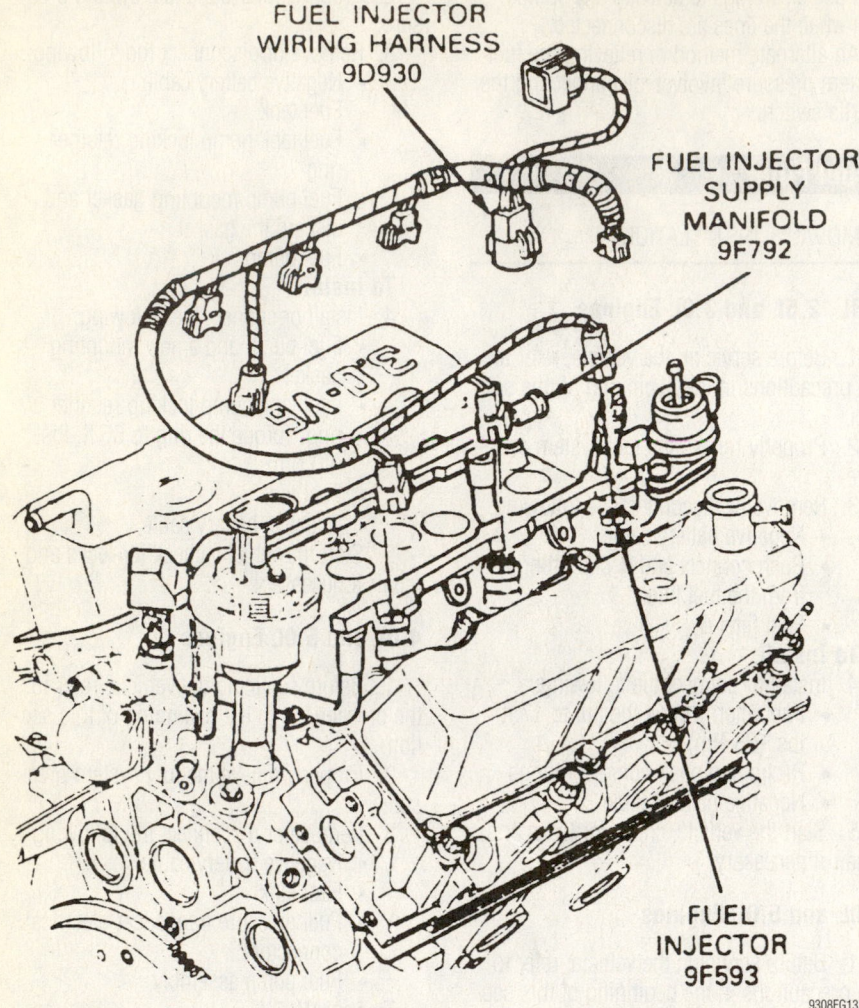

FUEL INJECTOR
WIRING HARNESS
9D930

FUEL INJECTOR
SUPPLY
MANIFOLD
9F792

FUEL
INJECTOR
9F593

9308EG13

Exploded view of the fuel injection system–2.3L engine

3. Remove or disconnect the following:
- Negative battery cable
- Fuel injection supply manifold
- Fuel injectors by gently twisting them
- Inspect the O-rings and replace as needed

To install:

4. Install or connect the following:
- Fuel injectors
- Fuel injector supply manifold
- Negative battery cable

5. Start the vehicle, check for leaks and repair if necessary.

3.0L Engine

1. Before servicing the vehicle, refer to the precautions in the beginning of this section.

2. Properly relieve the fuel system pressure.

3. Remove or disconnect the following:
- Negative battery cable
- Upper intake manifold

- Engine control sensor wiring from the fuel injectors
- Fuel lines
- Fuel injection supply manifold and injectors as an assembly
- Vacuum line
- Fuel injectors from the supply manifold
- Inspect the O-rings and replace them as needed

To install:

4. Install or connect the following:
- Fuel injectors
- Vacuum line
- Fuel injection supply manifold. Torque the bolts to 89 inch lbs. (10 Nm).
- Fuel line
- Engine control sensor wiring to the fuel injectors
- Upper intake manifold
- Negative battery cable

5. Start the vehicle, check for leaks and repair if necessary.

DRIVE TRAIN

Transmission Assembly

REMOVAL & INSTALLATION

Manual Transmission

1. Before servicing the vehicle, refer to the precautions in the beginning of this section.

2. Drain the transmission fluid.

3. Place the transmission in **Neutral**.

4. Remove or disconnect the following:
- Negative battery cable
- Gearshift lever assembly from the control housing

5. On 2WD vehicles, matchmark the driveshaft to the rear axle flange. Position a drain pan under the rear of the transmission. Remove the driveshaft-to-rear axle flange fasteners and pull the driveshaft rearward to disengage it from the transmission.
- Heated Oxygen (HO_2S) sensor
- Back-up lamp switch electrical connector
- Fan shroud
- Clutch hydraulic line at the clutch housing
- Speedometer from the transfer case/extension housing and place a wood block on a service jack and position the jack under the engine oil pan
- Transfer case on 4WD vehicles
- Starter

6. Position a transmission jack under the transmission.
- Transmission-to-engine retaining bolts and washers
- Transmission mount and damper to the crossmember
- Crossmember and lower the engine jack slightly to angle the transmission assembly. Work the clutch housing off the locating dowels and slide the clutch housing and the transmission rearward until the input shaft clears the clutch disc
- Exhaust inlet cross over pipe
- Transmission from the vehicle

To install:

7. Check that the mating surfaces of the clutch housing, engine rear and dowel holes are free of burrs, dirt and paint.

8. Place the transmission on the transmission jack. Position the transmission under the vehicle, then raise it into position. Align the input shaft splines with the clutch

disc splines and work the transmission forward onto the locating dowels.

9. Install or connect the following:
- Transmission-to-engine retaining bolts and washers. Tighten the retaining bolts to 30–41 ft. lbs. (40–55 Nm).
- Exhaust inlet cross over pipe and remove the transmission jack
- Right side transmission mount. Torque the bolt to 81 ft. lbs. (110 Nm).
- Rear crossmember. Torque the bolts to 53 ft. lbs. (72 Nm).
- Starter motor and tighten the attaching nuts
- Transfer case on 4WD vehicles. Torque the bolts to 87 ft. lbs. (119 Nm).
- Rear driveshaft
- Starter motor, back-up lamp switch connectors
- Hydraulic clutch line and bleed the system
- Speedometer cable
- Gearshift lever assembly
- Negative battery cable

10. Fill the transmission fluid to the proper level.

11. Check for proper shifting and operation of the transmission.

Automatic Transmission

1. Before servicing the vehicle, refer to the precautions in the beginning of this section.

2. Drain the transmission fluid.

3. Place the transmission in **Neutral**.

4. Remove or disconnect the following:
- Negative battery cable
- Fluid level indicator
- Fan shroud
- Transfer case on 4WD vehicles
- Rear driveshaft after matchmarking the yoke and axle flange
- Starter
- Torque converter access cover from the lower right side of the converter housing on the 3.0L engine
- Torque converter access cover from the bottom of the engine oil pan on the 2.3L and 2.5L engines
- Access cover and adapter plate bolts from the lower left side of the converter housing, on all other applications
- Flywheel-to-converter attaching nuts. Use a socket and breaker bar on the crankshaft pulley attaching bolt. Rotate the pulley clockwise as viewed from the front to gain access to each of the nuts.

➡ **On belt-driven overhead cam engines, never rotate the pulley in a counterclockwise direction as viewed from the front.**

- Shifter cable
- Transmission wire harness
- Heated Oxygen (HO2S) sensor connector
- Transmission connector
- Digital Transmission Range (TR) sensor connector
- Catalytic converter
- Speedometer cable and/or vehicle speed sensor from the transfer case (4WD) or extension housing (2WD)
- Transmission cooler lines
- Engine rear support-to-crossmember bolts and the crossmember-to-frame side support attaching nuts and bolts
- Crossmember
- Transmission mount
- Transmission upper fill tube
- Vent tube on 4WD vehicles
- Converter housing-to-engine bolts

5. Move the transmission to the rear so it disengages from the dowel pins and the converter is disengaged from the flywheel. Lower the transmission from the vehicle.

6. Remove the torque converter from the transmission, if necessary.

To install:

7. Install the converter on the transmission.

❉❉ WARNING

Before installing an automatic transmission, always check that the torque converter is fully seated into the transmission. Typically, the converter has notches or tangs on the hub that must engage the transmission fluid pump. If they are not engaged in the pump, the transmission will not mate to the engine properly, as the converter will be holding it away. Severe damage to the pump, converter or transmission casting can occur if the transmission-to-engine bolts are tightened to force the transmission to mate to the engine.

Proper installation of the converter requires full engagement of the converter hub in the pump gear. To accomplish this, the converter must be pushed and at the same time rotated through what feels like 2 notches or bumps. When fully installed, rotation of the converter will usually result in a clicking noise heard, caused by the converter surface touching the housing to case bolts.

For reference, a properly installed converter will have a distance from the converter pilot nose from face-to-converter housing outer face of $1\frac{3}{32}$–$\frac{9}{16}$ in. (10.5–14.5mm).

8. Rotate the converter so that the drive studs are in alignment with the holes in the flywheel.

9. Move the converter and transmission assembly forward into position, being careful not to damage the flywheel and converter pilot. The converter housing is piloted into position by the dowels in the rear of the engine block.

➡ **During this move, to avoid damage, do not allow the transmission to get into a nose down position as this will cause the converter to move forward and disengage from the pump gear.**

10. Install or connect the following:
- Converter housing to engine. Torque the bolts to 30–41 ft. lbs. (40–55 Nm). The 2 longer bolts are located at the dowel holes.
- Upper fluid filler tube and bracket. Torque the bolt to 41 ft. lbs. (55 Nm).
- Transfer case, 4WD vehicles
- Exhaust bracket. Torque the bolts to 64 ft. lbs. (87 Nm).
- Crossmember. Torque the bolts to 87 ft. lbs. (118 Nm).
- Transmission mount. Torque the bolts to 81 ft. lbs. (110 Nm).
- Transmission cooler lines. Torque the bolts to 23 ft. lbs. (31 Nm).
- Starter. Torque the bolts to 30 ft. lbs. (40 Nm).
- Transmission wire harness
- HO2S sensor
- Transmission connector
- TR sensor connector
- Shift cable and bracket
- Driveshaft. Torque the bolts to 95 ft. lbs. (129 Nm).
- Shroud. Torque the bolts to 71 inch lbs. (8 Nm).
- Fluid level indicator
- Negative battery cable

11. Fill the transmission to the proper level.

12. Start the vehicle and check for leaks, repair if necessary.

Clutch

REMOVAL & INSTALLATION

1. Before servicing the vehicle, refer to the precautions in the beginning of this section.
2. Remove or disconnect the following:
   - Negative battery cable
   - Clutch hydraulic system master cylinder from the clutch pedal
   - Starter
   - Hydraulic coupling at the transmission
   - Transmission from the vehicle
3. Mark the assembled position of the pressure plate in relation to the flywheel to aid during reassemble.
   - Loosen the pressure plate and cover attaching bolts evenly until the pressure plate springs are expanded
   - Pressure plate and cover assembly and the clutch disc from the flywheel
   - Pilot bearing, only if replacing

To install:

4. Position the clutch disc on the flywheel so that the Clutch Alignment Shaft tool T74P-7137-K can enter the clutch pilot bearing and align the disc.
5. When reinstalling the original pressure plate and cover assembly, align the assembly and flywheel according to the marks made during the removal operations.

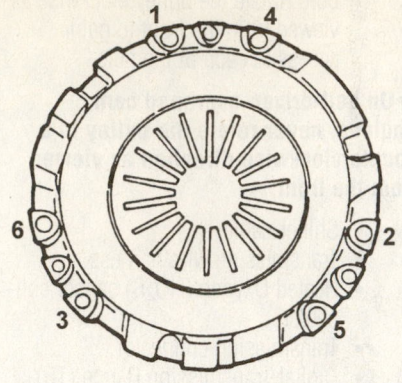

Tighten the bolts gradually in the correct sequence to avoid warping the pressure plate

6. Install or connect the following:
   - Pressure plate and cover assembly on the flywheel, align the pressure plate and disc, and install the retaining bolts that fasten the assembly to the flywheel. Torque the bolts to 15–25 ft. lbs. (21–35 Nm) in the proper sequence. Remove the clutch disc pilot tool
   - Transmission into the vehicle
   - Starter
   - Coupling by pushing the male coupling into the slave cylinder
   - Hydraulic clutch master cylinder pushrod to the clutch pedal
   - Negative battery cable
7. Bleed the hydraulic clutch system.

ADJUSTMENT

Because the clutch is hydraulically driven, there is no adjustment required.

In the event the clutch pedal develops a squeak or uneven feel when depressing, spray the pedal bushing assembly with penetrating oil and work the pedal back-and-forth.

Hydraulic Clutch System

BLEEDING

The following procedure is recommended for bleeding the clutch hydraulic system installed on the vehicle. It is recommended that the original clutch tube, with quick-connect fitting be replaced when servicing the hydraulic system, because air can be trapped in the quick-connect fitting and prevent complete bleeding of the system. The replacement tube does not include a quick-connect fitting.

1. Before servicing the vehicle, refer to the precautions in the beginning of this section.
2. Clean the dirt and grease from the dust cap.
3. Remove the cap and diaphragm and fill the reservoir to the top with approved brake fluid C6AZ-19542-AA or BA, (ESA-M6C25-A).

➡**To keep brake fluid from entering the clutch housing, route a suitable rubber tube of appropriate inside diameter from the bleed screw to a container.**

4. Loosen the bleed screw, located in the slave cylinder body, next to the inlet connection. Fluid will now begin to move from the master cylinder down the tube to the slave cylinder.

➡**The reservoir must be kept full at all times during the bleeding operation, to ensure no additional air enters the system.**

5. Observe the bleed screw outlet. When the slave cylinder is full, a steady stream of fluid will flow from the outlet port. Tighten the bleed screw.
6. Depress the clutch pedal to the floor and hold for 1–2 seconds. Release the pedal as rapidly as possible. The pedal must be released completely. Pause for 1–2 seconds. Repeat 10 times.
7. Check the fluid level in the reservoir. The fluid should be level with the step when the diaphragm is removed.
8. Hold the pedal to the floor, slightly

FLYWHEEL

TRANSMISSION

DOWEL PIN

PILOT BEARING

CLUTCH DISC

BOLT 21-32 N·m (15-24 FT·LB)

CLUTCH PLATE AND COVER

BOLT 20-27 N·m (15-20 FT·LB)

CLUTCH SLAVE CYLINDER ASSEMBLY

Clutch disc, pressure plate and bearing assembly for 2.3L, 2.5L, 3.0L and 4.0L engines—the 5.0L engine is similar

open the bleed screw to allow any additional air to escape. Close the bleed screw, then release the pedal.

9. Check the fluid in the reservoir. The hydraulic system should now be fully bled, and should actuate the clutch.

10. Check the vehicle by starting, pushing the clutch pedal to the floor and selecting reverse gear. There should be no grating of gears. If there is, and the hydraulic system still contains air; repeat the bleeding procedure.

Transfer Case Assembly

REMOVAL & INSTALLATION

1. Before servicing the vehicle, refer to the precautions in the beginning of this section.
2. Place the transmission in **Neutral**.
3. Drain the transfer case.
4. Remove or disconnect the following:
   - Negative battery cable
   - Skid plate
   - Damper, if equipped
   - Wire connector from rear of the transfer case, on electronic-shift models

- Front driveshaft from the axle input yoke
- Clamp retaining the front driveshaft boot to the transfer case, and pull the driveshaft and front boot assembly out of the transfer case front output shaft, if equipped
- Rear driveshaft from the transfer case output shaft yoke
- Speedometer driven gear from the transfer case rear cover, if equipped
- Electrical plug from the Vehicle Speed Sensor (VSS), if equipped
- Vent hose

5. On manual-shift models, perform the following:

a. Remove the shift lever retaining nut and remove the lever.

b. Remove the bolts that retains the shifter to the extension housing. Note the size and location of the bolts to aid during installation. Remove the lever assembly and bushing.

6. If equipped, remove the heat shield from the transfer case.

7. Support the transfer case with a transmission jack.

8. Install or connect the following:
   - 5 bolts (6 bolts on the AWD trans-

fer case) retaining the transfer case to the transmission and the extension housing
- Slide the transfer case rearward off the transmission output shaft and lower the transfer case from the vehicle.
- Gasket from between the transfer case and extension housing

To install:

9. Install or connect the following:
   - Heat shield onto the transfer case, if equipped

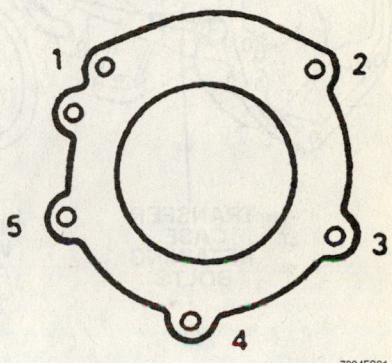

Transfer case-to-extension bolt torque sequence

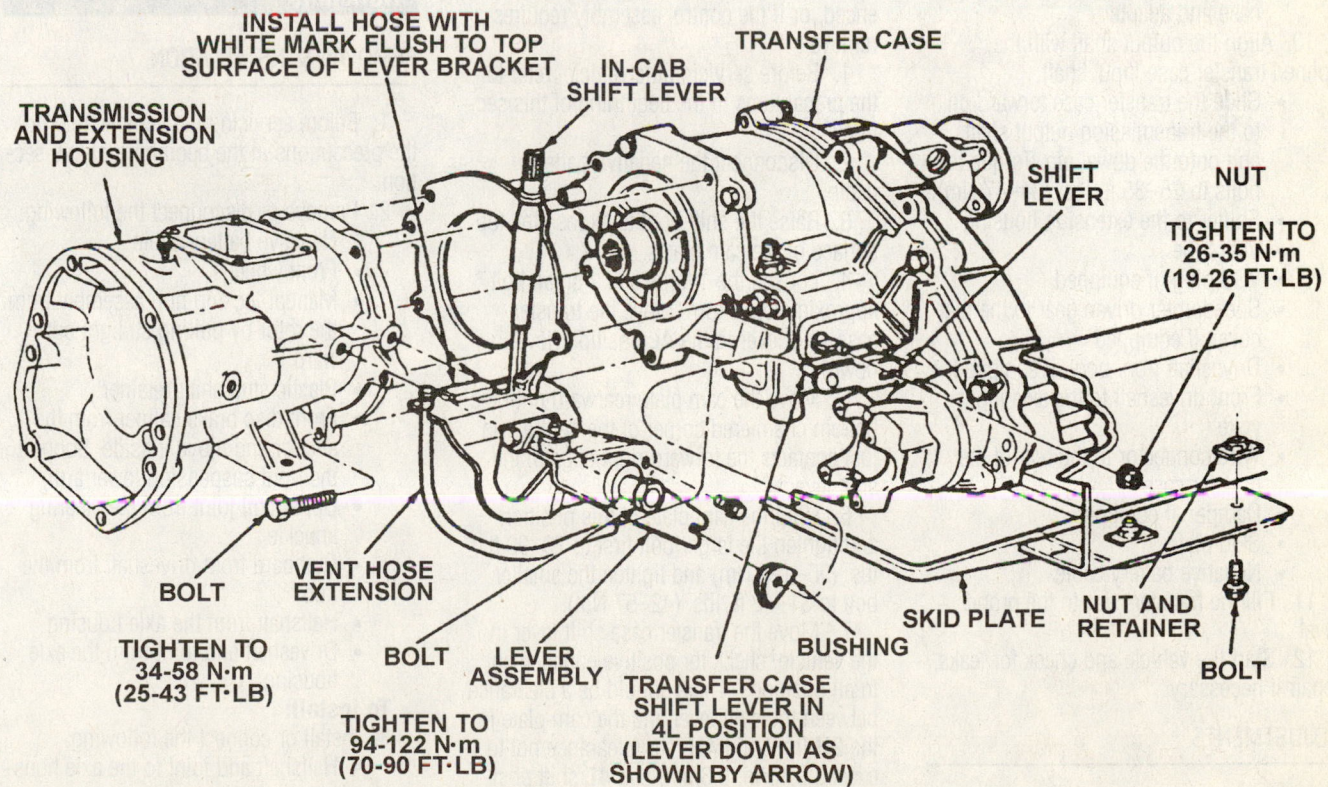

BOLT

TIGHTEN TO 34-58 N·m (25-43 FT·LB)

VENT HOSE EXTENSION

BOLT

TIGHTEN TO 94-122 N·m (70-90 FT·LB)

LEVER ASSEMBLY

TRANSFER CASE SHIFT LEVER IN 4L POSITION (LEVER DOWN AS SHOWN BY ARROW)

BUSHING

SKID PLATE

NUT AND RETAINER

BOLT

TRANSMISSION AND EXTENSION HOUSING

INSTALL HOSE WITH WHITE MARK FLUSH TO TOP SURFACE OF LEVER BRACKET

IN-CAB SHIFT LEVER

TRANSFER CASE

SHIFT LEVER

NUT

TIGHTEN TO 26-35 N·m (19-26 FT·LB)

Exploded view of the 13-54 mechanical shift transfer case-to-transmission mounting

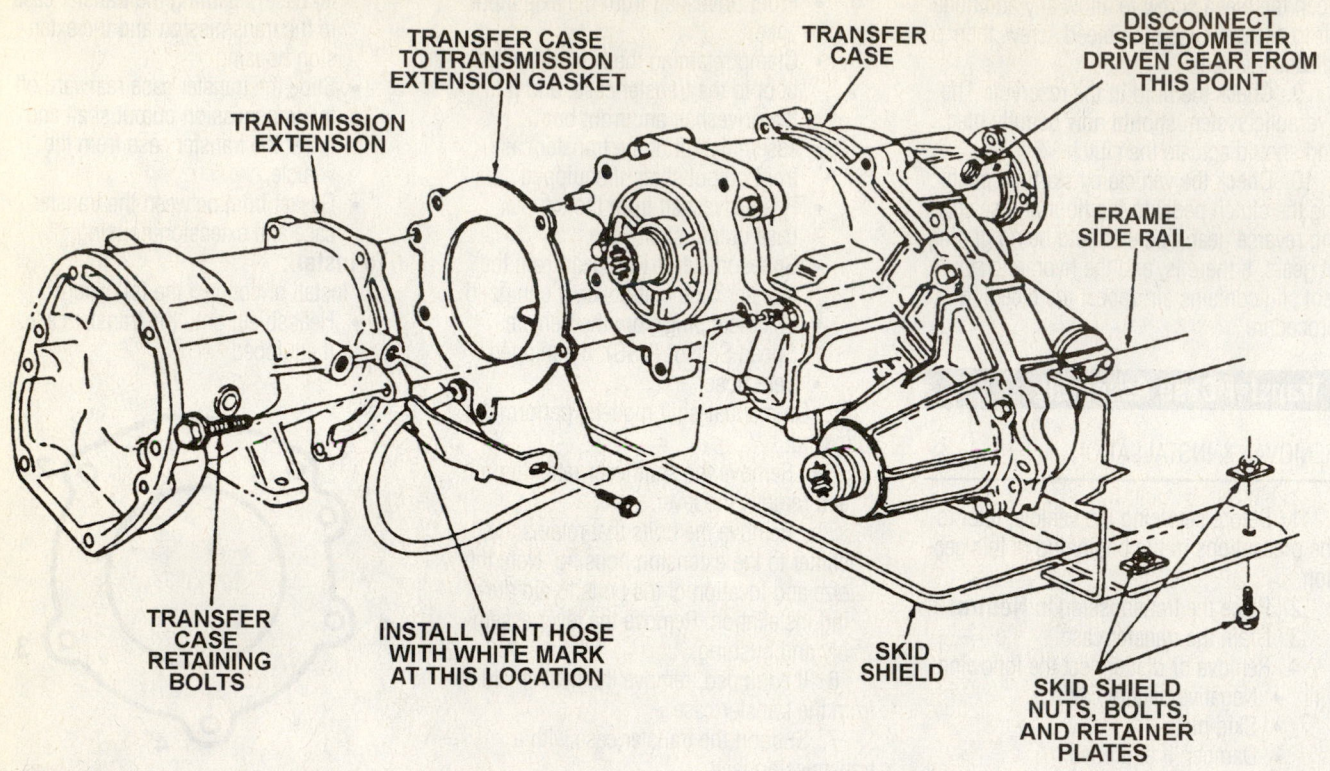

TRANSFER CASE TO TRANSMISSION EXTENSION GASKET

TRANSMISSION EXTENSION

TRANSFER CASE

DISCONNECT SPEEDOMETER DRIVEN GEAR FROM THIS POINT

FRAME SIDE RAIL

TRANSFER CASE RETAINING BOLTS

INSTALL VENT HOSE WITH WHITE MARK AT THIS LOCATION

SKID SHIELD

SKID SHIELD NUTS, BOLTS, AND RETAINER PLATES

7924EG20

Exploded view of the 13-54 electronic shift transfer case-to-transmission mounting—44-05 model is similar

- New gasket between the transfer case and adapter

10. Align the output shaft with the splined transfer case input shaft.
- Slide the transfer case forward on to the transmission output shaft and onto the dowel pin. Torque the bolts to 25–35 ft. lbs. (34–47 Nm).
- Shifter to the extension housing
- Vent tube
- VSS plug, if equipped
- Speedomter driven gear to the rear cover, if equipped
- Driveshaft front boot, if equipped
- Front driveshaft to the axle input yoke
- Wire connector to the rear of the transfer case
- Damper, if equipped
- Skid plate
- Negative battery cable

11. Fill the transfer case to the proper level.

12. Start the vehicle and check for leaks, repair if necessary.

ADJUSTMENTS

Manual Shift Models

The following procedure should be used, if a partial or incomplete engagement of the transfer case shift lever detent is experienced, or if the control assembly requires removal.

1. Before servicing the vehicle, refer to the precautions in the beginning of this section.

2. Disconnect the negative battery cable.

3. Raise the shift boot to expose the top surface of the cam plates.

4. Loosen the 1 large and 1 small bolt, approximately 1 turn. Move the transfer case shift lever to the **4L** position (lever down).

5. Move the cam plate rearward until the bottom chamfered corner of the neutral lug just contacts the forward right edge of the shift lever.

6. Hold the cam plate in this position and tighten the larger bolt first to 70–90 ft. lbs. (95–122 Nm) and tighten the smaller bolt to 31–42 ft. lbs. (42–57 Nm).

7. Move the transfer case shift lever in the vehicle, check for positive engagement in all positions. There should be a clearance between the shift lever and the cam plate in the **2H** front and **4H** rear (clearance not to exceed 0.13 in./3.3mm) and **4L** shift positions.

8. Install the shift boot assembly.

9. Connect the negative battery cable.

Halfshaft

REMOVAL & INSTALLATION

1. Before servicing the vehicle, refer to the precautions in the beginning of this section.

2. Remove or disconnect the following:
- Negative battery cable
- Front wheel
- Manual locking hub assembly from the rotor by pulling straight outward
- Plastic stub shaft retainer
- Front disc brake caliper from the anchor and move it aside. Support the front suspension lower arm.
- Upper ball joint from the steering knuckle
- Outboard front driveshaft from the hub
- Halfshaft from the axle housing
- Driveshaft and joint from the axle housing

To install:

3. Install or connect the following:
- Halfshaft and joint to the axle housing
- Outboard front driveshaft to the hub
- Upper ball joint to the steering knuckle

- Brake caliper to the anchor and remove the front suspension support
- New stub shaft retainer
- Locking hub to the brake rotor
- Front wheel
- Negative battery cable

CV-Joints

OVERHAUL

1. Before servicing the vehicle, refer to the precautions in the beginning of this section.
2. Remove or disconnect the following:
   - Negative battery cable
   - Halfshaft and place it in a vice with the inboard joint lower than the outboard joint
3. Cut the inner boot clamps with side cutters and remove the clamp from the boot.
   - Larger boot end off the joint
   - Inboard CV-joint bolts and separate the spacer and grease cap
   - Snap-ring retaining the interconnecting shaft end to the CV-joint cage
   - CV-joint and discard the washer

➡ **The outboard CV-joint is non-serviceable other than to replace the boot.**

To install:
4. Install or connect the following:
   - Slide the boot over the shaft
5. Fill the CV-joint area with grease.
   - Assemble the outer boot to the outboard CV-joint and interconnecting shaft. Make certain that the boot is seated in the grooves on the outer race and on the shaft
   - New clamps to the boot
   - New inner boot to the shaft
   - New washer to the end of the shaft
   - Assemble the inboard CV-joint to the interconnecting shaft spline until it rests on the washer
   - Snap-ring
6. Fill the CV-joint area with grease.
   - Boot into position and make certain that it is seated in the grooves on the boot adapter and the shaft
   - New clamps and tighten the clamps with crimping pliers
   - Spacer to the CV-joint end pilot. Torque the bolts to 25 ft. lbs. (34 Nm).
   - Halfshaft
   - Negative battery cable

Locking Hubs

REMOVAL & INSTALLATION

Manual Type

1. Before servicing the vehicle, refer to the precautions in the beginning of this section.
2. Remove or disconnect the following:
   - Negative battery cable
   - Front wheel
   - Manual locking hub assembly from the rotor by pulling straight outward

To install:
3. Install or connect the following:
   - Inspect the O-ring seal on the back-side of the hub assembly and, if damaged, replace it.
   - Manual locking hub to the rotor
   - Front wheel
   - Negative battery cable

Automatic Type

MOUNTAINEER AND EXPLORER

The Mountaineer and Explorer models use a locking mechanism mounted in the differential. This system is called a vacuum disconnect axle lock.

EXCEPT MOUNTAINEER AND EXPLORER

1. Before servicing the vehicle, refer to the precautions in the beginning of this section.
2. Remove or disconnect the following:
   - Negative battery cable
   - Wheel

➡ **Some gentle tapping with a soft-faced hammer may help to loosen the locking hub cover if it seems stuck.**

   - Automatic locking hub cover assembly from the rotor by pulling straight outward
3. Inspect the O-ring seal on the back-side of the hub assembly and, if damaged, replace it.
   - Snap-ring from the end of the splined axle shaft
   - Axle shaft spacer(s)

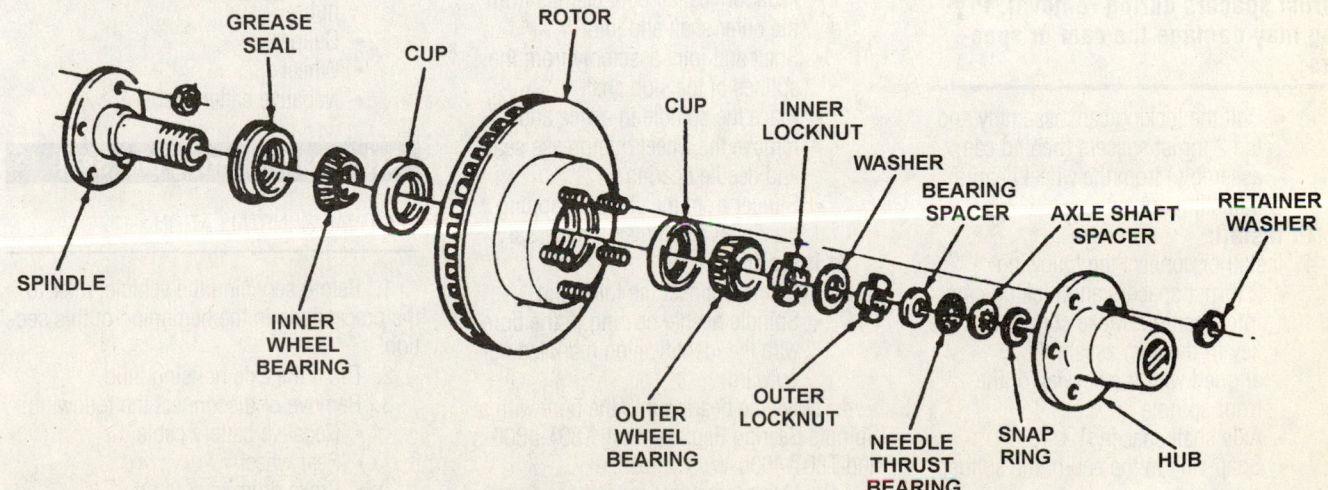

Exploded view of the manual locking hub assembly and related components

7924EG22

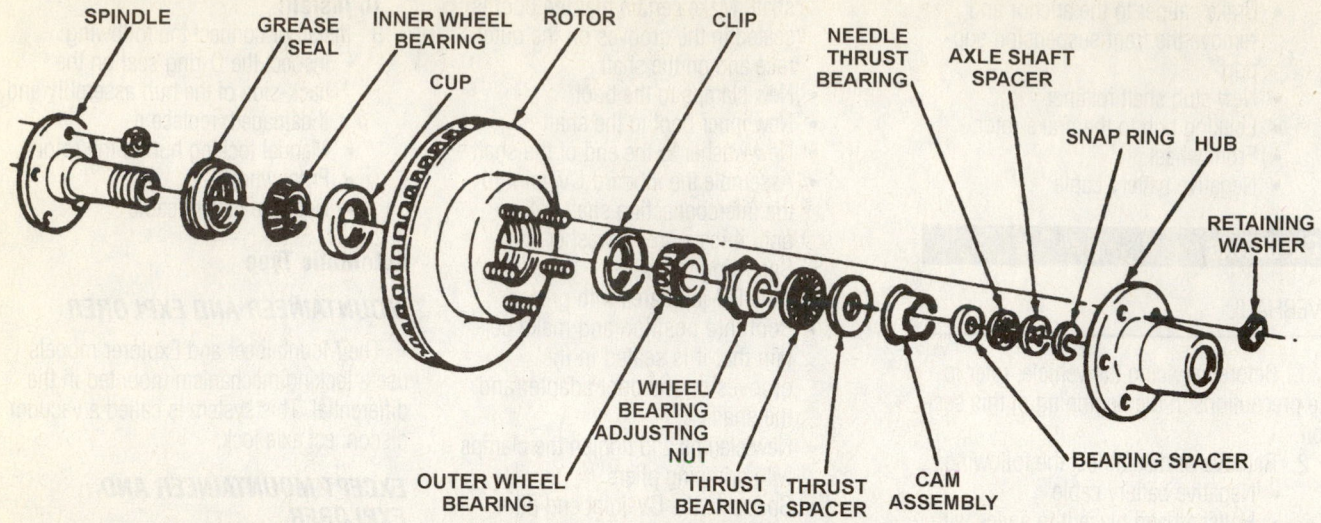

SPINDLE GREASE SEAL INNER WHEEL BEARING ROTOR CLIP NEEDLE THRUST BEARING AXLE SHAFT SPACER SNAP RING HUB RETAINING WASHER CUP WHEEL BEARING ADJUSTING NUT OUTER WHEEL BEARING THRUST BEARING THRUST SPACER CAM ASSEMBLY BEARING SPACER

7924EG23

Exploded view of the automatic locking hubs and related components—4WD except Mountaineer and Explorer models

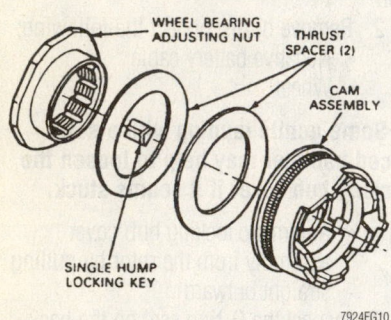

WHEEL BEARING ADJUSTING NUT THRUST SPACER (2) CAM ASSEMBLY SINGLE HUMP LOCKING KEY

7924EG10

Exploded view of the locking cam assembly—4WD except Mountaineer and Explorer models

** WARNING

Do not pry on the locking cam or thrust spacers during removal. Prying may damage the cam or spacers.

- Pull the locking cam assembly and the 2 thrust spacers (behind cam assembly) from the wheel bearing adjusting nut.

To install:
4. Install or connect the following:
- 2 thrust spacers and locking cam into position. Make certain that the key in the cam assembly is aligned with the keyway of the front spindle
- Axle shaft spacer(s)
- Snap-ring to the end of the splined axle shaft
- Locking hub cover to the rotor
- Wheel
- Negative battery cable

Spindle Bearings

REMOVAL & INSTALLATION

1. Before servicing the vehicle, refer to the precautions in the beginning of this section.
2. Remove or disconnect the following:
- Negative battery cable
- Wheel
- Brake caliper
- Locking hubs and wheel bearings
- Brake rotor
- Font wheel spindle from the steering knuckle
- Brake shield
- Shaft and joint by pulling it out of the carrier, left side only
- Front driveshaft boot clamps from the outer shaft and joint
- Shaft and joint assembly from the splines of the stub shaft
- Place the spindle in a vice and remove the wheel hub grease seal and needle bearing
- Slinger from the shaft by tapping on it with a hammer, if necessary

To install:
3. Install or connect the following:
- Spindle needle bearing in the bore with the identification mark facing outward
4. Drive the bearing into the bore with a Spindle Bearing Replacer tool, T80T-4000-s and T80T-4000-W.
- Hub grease seal in the bearing bore with lip side facing the tool and coat the lip with a high temperature lubricant

- Place the axle shaft in a press and install a new slinger, if removed
- Rubber boot and clamps on the right side of the carrier
- Slide the right shaft and joint into the slip yoke and fully engage the splines
- Slide the boot over the assembly and crimp the new clamps
- Slide the shaft and joint through the steering knuckle and engage the splines on the shaft, left side
- Brake rotor shield. Torque the bolts to 40 ft. lbs. (54 Nm).
- Brake rotor to the spindle
- Outer differential bearing into the bearing cup
- Wheel bearing, locknut, thrust bearing, snap-rings and locking hubs
- Caliper
- Wheel
- Negative battery cable

Axle Shaft, Bearing and Seal

REMOVAL & INSTALLATION

1. Before servicing the vehicle, refer to the precautions in the beginning of this section.
2. Drain the axle housing fluid.
3. Remove or disconnect the following:
- Negative battery cable
- Rear wheel
- Brake drum
- Wheel speed sensor, if equipped
- Axle housing cover
- Bearing retainer nuts

- Axle shaft and bearing
- Axle shaft inner oil seal

4. If equipped with ABS, grind a flat spot on the wheel speed sensor tone ring, then split the ring with a chisel.

5. Press the wheel bearing off the axle shaft.

6. Remove the bearing retainer and the outer oil seal.

To install:

7. Install or connect the following:
- Outer oil seal to the bearing retainer
- Bearing retainer to the axle shaft
- Bearing and retainer ring pressed onto the axle shaft
- Wheel speed sensor tone ring pressed onto the axle shaft, if equipped
- Axle shaft inner oil seal
- Axle shaft and bearing
- Bearing retainer nuts. Tighten them to 17 ft. lbs. (23 Nm).
- Wheel speed sensor, if equipped
- Brake drum
- Rear wheel
- Negative battery cable

8. Fill the rear differential to the correct level.

Pinion Seal

REMOVAL & INSTALLATION

1. Before servicing the vehicle, refer to the precautions in the beginning of this section.

2. Drain the axle housing fluid.

3. Remove or disconnect the following:
- Negative battery cable
- Rear wheels
- Driveshaft
- Brake calipers and pads or brake drum

➡ **The brake calipers and pads or brake drum must be removed so that there is no additional drag when measuring pinion bearing preload.**

4. Use an inch lb. torque wrench and measure and record the amount of torque required to maintain pinion rotation through several revolutions.

5. Remove or disconnect the following:
- Pinion flange
- Pinion seal
- Pinion bearing
- Collapsible spacer

To install:

➡ **Use a new collapsible spacer and flange nut for assembly.**

6. Install or connect the following:
- Collapsible spacer
- Pinion bearing
- Pinion seal
- Pinion flange

7. Rotate the pinion flange occasionally while tightening the flange nut to make sure the pinion bearings seat correctly.

8. Take frequent bearing preload torque readings. Tighten the flange nut to achieve the preload torque readings originally recorded.

✳✳ CAUTION

Never loosen the pinion nut to reduce bearing preload. If it is necessary to reduce bearing preload, install a new collapsible spacer and pinion nut.

9. Install or connect the following:
- Driveshaft
- Brake calipers and pads or brake drum
- Wheels
- Negative battery cable

10. Fill the differential with gear lubricant and check for leaks.

Axle Housing

REMOVAL & INSTALLATION

1. Before servicing the vehicle, refer to the precautions in the beginning of this section.

2. Drain the axle housing fluid.

3. Support the vehicle at the frame.

4. Support the rear axle with a floor jack.

5. Remove or disconnect the following:
- Negative battery cable
- Rear wheels
- Rear brake drums
- Axle shafts and matchmark the driveshaft and pinion flanges for proper installation
- Driveshaft and wire it out of the way
- Axle housing vent tube
- Brake hose junction block
- Brake drum backing plates
- Shock absorber lower bolts
- Rear axle U-bolts
- Axle housing

To install:

6. Install or connect the following:
- Axle housing
- U-bolts. Torque the bolts to 76 ft. lbs. (103 Nm).
- Shock absorber lower bolts. Torque the bolts to 50 ft. lbs. (68 Nm).
- Brake drum backing plates
- Brake hose junction block
- Axle housing vent tube
- Driveshaft
- Axle shafts using the matchmarks made during removal
- Rear Brake drums
- Rear wheels
- Negative battery cable

7. Fill the axle fluid to the proper level.

STEERING AND SUSPENSION

Air Bag

PRECAUTIONS

- Always wear safety glasses when servicing an air bag vehicle, and when handling an air bag.
- Never attempt to service the steering wheel or steering column on an air bag-equipped vehicle without first properly disarming the air bag system. The air bag system should be properly disarmed whenever ANY service procedure in this manual indicates that you should do so.
- When carrying a live air bag module, always make sure the bag and trim cover are pointed away from your body. In the unlikely event of an accidental deployment, the bag will then deploy with minimal chance of injury.
- When placing a live air bag on a bench or other surface, always face the bag and trim cover up, away from the surface. This will reduce the motion of the air bag if it is accidentally deployed.
- If you should come in contact with a deployed air bag, be advised that the air bag surface may contain deposits of sodium hydroxide, which is a product of the gas combustion and is irritating to the skin. Always wear gloves and safety glasses when handling a deployed air bag, and wash your hands with mild soap and water afterwards.

DISARMING THE SYSTEM

1. Before servicing the vehicle, refer to the precautions in the beginning of this section.

2. Disconnect the negative battery cable from the battery.

3. Disconnect the positive battery cable from the battery.

4. Wait 1 minute. This time is required for the back-up power supply in the air bag diagnostic monitor to completely drain. The system is now disarmed.

ARMING THE SYSTEM

1. Before servicing the vehicle, refer to the precautions in the beginning of this section.

2. Connect the positive battery cable.

3. Connect the negative battery cable.

4. Stand outside the vehicle and carefully turn the ignition to the **RUN** position. Be sure that no part of your body is in front of the air bag module on the steering wheel, to prevent injury in case of an accidental air bag deployment.

5. Ensure the air bag indicator light turns off after approximately 6 seconds. If the light does not illuminate at all, does not turn off, or starts to flash, test the system.

Manual Rack and Pinion Steering Gear

REMOVAL & INSTALLATION

1. Before servicing the vehicle, refer to the precautions in the beginning of this section.

2. Rotate the steering wheel from lock-to-lock (entire gear travel) and record the number of steering wheel rotations. Divide the number of steering wheel rotations by 2 to get the required number of turns to place the steering wheel in the centered (straight-ahead) position. From 1 lock position, rotate the steering wheel the required number of turns to center the steering rack.

3. Remove or disconnect the following:
- Negative battery cable
- Bolt retaining the intermediate steering column shaft to the steering gear pinion. Separate the shaft from the pinion.
- Cotter pin retaining the nut to the tie rod ends. Discard the cotter pin.
- Separate the tie rod ends from the spindle arms

4. Support the steering gear and remove the 2 nuts, bolts and washers retaining the gear to the crossmember.

- Steering gear and, if required, remove the front and rear insulators from the gear housing

To install:

5. Install or connect the following:
- Front and rear insulators in the gear housing, if removed
- Steering gear on the crossmember. Torque the nuts to 65–90 ft. lbs. (88–122 Nm).

6. With the steering gear, steering wheel and front wheels in the centered position, attach the tie rod ends to the spindle arms. Torque the nuts to 52–73 ft. lbs. (70–100 Nm). If required, advance the castle nuts to the next castellation and install new cotter pins. Do not loosen the nuts to line up the cotter pin hole.

➡**Make sure the tie rod ball studs are seated in the spindle tapers to prevent rotation while tightening the nut.**

7. Install or connect the following:
- Steering column intermediate shaft to the gear pinion. Torque the bolt to 30–42 ft. lbs. (41–57 Nm).
- Negative battery cable

8. Check and adjust the front end alignment, if necessary.

Power Rack and Pinion Steering Gear

REMOVAL & INSTALLATION

Aerostar

REAR WHEEL DRIVE MODELS

1. Before servicing the vehicle, refer to the precautions in the beginning of this section.

2. On vehicles equipped with automatic transmissions, position the transmission selector in PARK and set the hand brake.

3. For vehicles equipped with manual transmissions, put the gear shift lever in Reverse and set the hand brake.

4. Drain the steering fluid.

5. Remove or disconnect the following:
- Negative battery cable
- Both front wheels
- Lower intermediate steering column shaft retaining bolt from the steering gear
- Shaft from the steering gear
- Fitting for the power steering pressure and return lines at the rack and pinion steering gear valve housing

➡**Do not remove the right and left transfer tube fitting.**

- Cotter pin retaining the tie rod end. Discard the cotter pin.
- Tie rod end nut
- Separate the steering tie rod ends from the spindle using a Pitman arm puller T64P-3590-F

6. Support the steering gear and remove the 2 nuts, bolts, and washer assemblies retaining the steering gear to the vehicle crossmember.
- Front and rear insulators from the gear housing, if equipped
- Steering gear from the vehicle

To install:

7. If removed, install the insulators into the steering gear housing.

➡**The larger end of the inner sleeve faces the rear of the vehicle and contacts the crossmember.**

8. Push the insulators in until there is no space between the lip on the insulator and edge of the steering gear housing.

9. Position the steering gear on the crossmember. Install the nuts, bolts and washers retaining the gear to the crossmember. Tighten the nuts to 80–105 ft. lbs. (108–142 Nm).

10. Unplug the power steering fluid lines and steering gear valve housing.

11. If required, replace the TFE seal on the power steering pressure and return line quick-connect fitting. Install a new seal as follows:

a. Unscrew the tube nut, then replace the plastic seal washer.

b. To facilitate assembly of the new TFE seal, a tapered shaft may be required to stretch the washer so that it may be slipped over the tube nut threads. Recommended tools are D90P-3517-A2 and D90P-3517-A3 or their equivalents.

12. Install or connect the following:
- Pressure and return lines to the appropriate ports on the steering gear valve housing. Torque the fittings to 20–25 ft. lbs. (27–34 Nm).

➡**The fittings' design allows the hoses to swivel when properly tightened. Do not attempt to eliminate looseness by over-tightening, since this can cause damage to the fittings.**

- Tie rod ends to the spindle arms. Torque the nuts to 52–73 ft. lbs. (70–100 Nm).

➡**Make sure that the tie rod end ball studs are seated in the tapered spindle holes to prevent rotation while tightening the nut.**

- Steering column lower intermediate shaft over the steering gear input shaft spline and dust seal. Replace the pinch bolt and torque it to 30–42 ft. lbs. (41–56 Nm).
- Front wheels
- Negative battery cable

13. Refill the power steering pump reservoir with the proper fluid.

14. Purge air from the power steering system. Verify the absence of any unusual power steering noise.

15. Align the front end.

16. Make sure that the power steering system operates correctly and is not leaking.

17. Check and adjust the fluid level in the power steering pump reservoir.

ALL WHEEL DRIVE MODELS

1. Before servicing the vehicle, refer to the precautions in the beginning of this section.

2. Start the engine, then rotate the steering wheel from lock-to-lock (entire gear travel) and record the number of rotations. Divide the number of steering wheel rotations by 2 to get the required number of turns to place the steering wheel in the centered (straight-ahead) position. From one lock position, rotate the steering wheel the required number of turns to center the steering rack.

➡ **Verify that the front wheels and steering wheel are in the straight-ahead position.**

3. Drain the steering fluid.

4. On automatic transmissions, put the transmission selector in PARK and set the hand brake.

5. On manual transmissions, put the gear shift lever in Reverse and set the hand brake.

6. Remove or disconnect the following:
- Negative battery cable
- Front wheels
- Bolt retaining the lower intermediate steering column shaft to the steering gear, then disconnect the shaft from the gear
- Pressure and return lines from the steering gear valve housing. Plug the lines and ports in the steering gear valve housing to prevent the entry of dirt into the system.
- Both steering knuckles
- Both lower control arms
- Nuts from the forward edge of the crossmember lower plate assembly

- Nut from the driver side rear edge of the crossmember lower plate assembly
- Bolts from the center and passenger side rear edge of the crossmember lower plate assembly
- Lower plate

7. While supporting the steering gear, remove the 2 bolts and spacers retaining the steering gear to the crossmember.
- Power steering rack and pinion gear from the vehicle

To install:

8. Install or connect the following:
- Insulators into the steering gear housing, if removed

➡ **The larger end of the inner sleeve faces the rear of the vehicle and contacts the crossmember.**

9. Push the insulators in until there is no space between the lip on the insulator and edge of the steering gear housing.
- Steering gear on the crossmember. Install the nuts, bolts and washers retaining the gear to the crossmember. Torque the nuts to 61–82 ft. lbs. (83–111 Nm).
- Crossmember lower plate by inserting the studs on the plate through the front edge of the crossmember
- Bolts in the center and passenger's side of the crossmember lower plate assembly. Torque the nuts to 35–47 ft. lbs. (47–64 Nm).
- Nut on the stud located at the driver side rear edge of the crossmember lower plate assembly. Torque it to 22–30 ft. lbs. (30–41 Nm).
- Nuts on the studs at the forward edge of the crossmember lower plate assembly. Torque these nuts to 22–30 ft. lbs. (30–41 Nm).
- Lower control arms
- Steering knuckles

➡ **Make sure that the steering gear and front wheels are in the straight-ahead position before attaching the tie rod ends to the steering knuckles. Make sure that the tie rod end ball studs are seated in the tapered spindle holes to prevent rotation while tightening the nut.**

10. If required, replace the TFE seal on the power steering pressure and return line quick-connect fitting. Install a new seal as follows:

  a. Unscrew the tube nut, then replace the plastic seal washer.

  b. To facilitate assembly of the new TFE seal, a tapered shaft may be required to stretch the washer so that it may be slipped over the tube nut threads. Recommended tools are D90P-3517-A2 and D90P-3517-A3 or their equivalents.

11. Install or connect the following:
- Pressure and return lines to the appropriate ports on the steering gear valve housing. Torque the fittings to 20–25 ft. lbs. (27–34 Nm).

➡ **The fittings' design allows the hoses to swivel when properly tightened. Do not attempt to eliminate looseness by over-tightening, since this can cause damage to the fittings.**

- Steering column lower intermediate shaft over the steering gear input shaft spline and dust seal. Replace the pinch bolt and torque it to 30–42 ft. lbs. (41–56 Nm).
- Front wheels

12. Refill the power steering pump reservoir with the proper fluid.

13. Purge air from the power steering system. Verify the absence of any unusual power steering noise.

14. Align the front end.

15. Make sure that the power steering system operates correctly and is not leaking.

16. Check and adjust the fluid level in the power steering pump reservoir.

Except Aerostar

✳✳ WARNING

If equipped, always turn off the Automatic Ride Control (ARC) service switch before lifting the vehicle off of the ground. Failure to do so could damage the ARC system components.

1. Before servicing the vehicle, refer to the precautions in the beginning of this section.

2. Raise and safely support the front of the vehicle, block the rear wheels and apply the parking brake.

3. Start the engine then rotate the steering wheel from lock-to-lock and record the number of rotations.

4. Divide the number of rotations by 2. This gives the number of rotations to achieve true center of the steering. Turn the wheel in one direction to the full lock.

5. Turn the wheel in the opposite direction the number of turns equal to true steering (lock-to-lock number divided by 2).

✳✳ WARNING

Do not rotate the steering wheel when the shaft is disconnected from the steering gear as damage to the clock spring could occur.

6. Drain the power steering fluid reservoir.

7. Remove or disconnect the following:
- Negative battery cable
- Bolt retaining the lower steering column shaft to the steering gear input shaft
- Stabilizer bar
- Quick-connect fittings for the power steering pressure and return hoses at the steering gear housing
- Nuts securing the power steering cooler and remove the cooler
- Outer tie rod ends
- Nuts, bolts and washer assemblies retaining the steering gear housing to the front crossmember
- Steering gear from the vehicle

To install:

8. Install or connect the following:
- Position the steering gear to the front crossmember and install the nuts, bolts and washer assemblies. Torque to 94–127 ft. lbs. (128–172 Nm).
- Power steering cooler retaining bolts
- Power steering lines to the steering gear housing and torque the fittings to 20–25 ft. lbs. (27–34 Nm).
- Outer tie rod ends and ensure that the steering shaft or gear input shaft has not been rotated
- Intermediate shaft-to-steering input shaft retaining (pinch) bolt and torque the bolt to 30–42 ft. lbs. (41–56 Nm)
- Negative battery cable

9. Fill the power steering pump reservoir.

10. Bleed the air from the power steering system.

11. Ensure that there are no leaks and the fluid is maintained at the proper level.

12. Check the alignment.

Recirculating Ball Manual Steering Gear

REMOVAL & INSTALLATION

1. Before servicing the vehicle, refer to the precautions in the beginning of this section.

2. Remove or disconnect the following:
- Negative battery cable

- Flex coupling shield from the steering gear input shaft shield and slide it up the intermediate shaft
- Bolt that retains the flex coupling to the steering gear
- Steering gear input shaft shield
- Pitman arm to the sector shaft by using a Pitman Arm Puller tool T64P-3590-F. Do not hammer on the end of the puller as this can damage the steering gear.
- Bolts attaching the steering gear to the side rail
- Steering gear from the vehicle

To install:

3. Rotate the gear input shaft (wormshaft) from stop-to-stop, counting the total number of turns. Then turn back exactly half-way, placing the gear on center.

4. Install or connect the following:
- Slide the steering gear input shaft shield on the steering gear input shaft
- Flex coupling on the steering gear input shaft. Ensure that the flat on the gear input shaft is facing straight up and aligns with the flat on the flex coupling.
- Steering gear to side rail. Torque the bolts to 66 ft. lbs. (89 Nm).
- Pitman arm on the sector shaft and install the attaching washer and nut. Align the 2 blocked teeth on the Pitman arm with 4 missing teeth on the steering gear sector shaft. Torque the nut to 170–228 ft. lbs. (230–310 Nm).
- Flex coupling to steering gear input shaft attaching bolt and torque to 50–62 ft. lbs. (68–84 Nm).
- Snap the flex coupling shield to the steering gear input shield
- Negative battery cable

5. Check the system to ensure equal turns from center to each lock position.

Recirculating Ball Power Steering Gear

REMOVAL & INSTALLATION

1. Before servicing the vehicle, refer to the precautions in the beginning of this section.

2. Remove or disconnect the following:
- Negative battery cable
- Pressure and return lines from the steering gear
- Upper and lower steering gear shaft U-joint shield from the flex coupling

- Bolts that secure the flex coupling to the steering gear and to the column steering shaft assembly
- Pitman arm from the sector shaft, using tool T64P-3590-F. Remove the tool from the Pitman arm. Do not damage the seals

3. Support the steering gear, and remove the steering gear attaching bolts.

4. Work the steering gear free of the flex coupling and remove the steering gear from the vehicle.

To install:

5. Install or connect the following:
- Lower U-joint shield onto the steering gear lugs. Slide the upper U-joint shield into place on the steering shaft assembly.
- Slide the flex coupling into place on the steering shaft assembly. Turn the steering wheel so that the spokes are in the horizontal position and center the steering gear input shaft.
- Steering gear input shaft into the flex coupling and into place on the frame side rail. Torque the bolts to 50–62 ft. lbs. (68–84 Nm). Torque the flex coupling bolt 30–40 ft. lbs. (41–54 Nm).
- Pitman arm on the sector shaft. Torque the nut to 170–228 ft. lbs. (230–310 Nm).
- Pressure and the return lines to the steering gear
- Negative battery cable

6. Fill the power steering reservoir to the proper level.

Shock Absorber

REMOVAL & INSTALLATION

➡ **Low pressure gas shocks are charged with Nitrogen gas. Do not attempt to open, puncture or apply heat to them. Prior to installing a new shock absorber, hold it upright and extend it fully. Invert it and fully compress and extend it at least 3 times. This will bleed trapped air.**

1997 Aerostar

1. Before servicing the vehicle, refer to the precautions in the beginning of this section.

2. Remove or disconnect the following:
- Negative battery cable
- Hardware retaining the front shock absorber to the coil spring upper bracket

- Hardware retaining the shock absorber to the bottom of the suspension lower arm
- Shock absorber through the lower arm opening

To install:

3. Install or connect the following:
- Shock absorber to the suspension lower arm. Torque the bolt to 24 ft. lbs. (32 Nm).
- Position the shock absorber to the coil spring upper bracket. Torque the nut to 34 ft. lbs. (46 Nm).
- Negative battery cable

1997 Ranger and B-Series

1. Before servicing the vehicle, refer to the precautions in the beginning of this section.
2. Remove or disconnect the following:
- Negative battery cable
- Shock absorber from the upper spring seat
- Slide the shock absorber off the radius arm and slightly compress it by hand
- Shock absorber

To install:

3. Install or connect the following:
- Shock absorber to the radius arm. Torque the nut to 53 ft. lbs. (72 Nm).
- Shock absorber to the upper spring seat. Torque the nut to 34 ft. lbs. (46 Nm).
- Negative battery cable

Mountaineer, Explorer, 1998–01 Ranger and B-Series Models

1. Before servicing the vehicle, refer to the precautions in the beginning of this section.
2. Remove or disconnect the following:
- Negative battery cable
- Upper shock-to-frame attaching nut, washer and insulator assembly
- Lower shock-to-control arm attaching nuts
- Slightly compress the shock absorber by hand and remove it from the vehicle

To install:

3. Install or connect the following:
- Position the lower washer and insulator on the shock absorber rod and position the shock absorber to the upper frame bracket mount
- Position the upper insulator and washer on the shock absorber rod

and install the attaching nut loosely.
- Position the lower shock absorber mounting studs into the control arm and install the attaching nuts loosely.
- Torque the lower shock attaching nuts to 15–21 ft. lbs. (21–29 Nm), and the upper shock attaching bolts to 30–40 ft. lbs. (40–55 Nm).
- Negative battery cable

Coil Spring

REMOVAL & INSTALLATION

Aerostar

FRONT

1. Before servicing the vehicle, refer to the precautions in the beginning of this section.
2. Place the steering wheel and front wheels in the centered (straight-ahead) position.

➡ **Whenever the steering linkage is disconnected, the steering system must be centered prior to beginning any work.**

3. Remove or disconnect the following:
- Negative battery cable
- Front wheels
- Stabilizer bar link bolt from the lower control arm
- Bolts attaching the shock absorber to the lower arm assembly
- Upper nut and washer retaining the shock absorber and remove the shock absorber from the vehicle

4. Using spring compressor tool D78P-5310-A, install 1 plate with the pivot ball seat facing downward into the coils of the spring. Rotate the plate so that it is flush with the upper surface of the lower arm.

5. Install the other plate with the pivot ball seat facing upward into the coils of the spring, so that the nut rests in the upper plate.

6. Insert the compression rod into the opening in the lower arm, through the upper and lower plate and upper ball nut. Insert the securing pin through the upper ball nut and compression rod. This pin can only be inserted one way into the upper ball nut because of a stepped-hole design.

7. With the upper ball nut secured, turn the upper plate so that it walks up the coil until it contacts the upper spring seat, then back it off ½ turn.

8. Install the lower ball nut and thrust washer on the compression rod, then screw on the forcing nut. Tighten the forcing nut until the spring is compressed enough so that it is free in its seat.

9. Loosen the 2 lower arm pivot bolts. Remove the cotter pin and loosen, but do not remove the nut attaching the lower ball joint to the spindle. Using Pitman arm puller T64P-3590-F, loosen the lower ball joint.

10. remove the puller tool.

11. Support the lower control arm with an hydraulic jack, then remove the ball joint nut. Slowly lower the control arm and remove the coil spring.

✳✳ CAUTION

Handle the coil spring with care. A compressed coil spring has enough stored energy to be dangerous if suddenly released. Mount the spring securely in a vise and slowly loosen the spring compressor if the spring is being replaced.

12. If the coil spring is being replaced, measure the compressed length of the old spring and mark the position of the compressor plates on the old spring with chalk. Remove the spring compressor from the old spring carefully.

To install:

13. Install or connect the following:
- Spring compressor on the new spring, placing the compressor

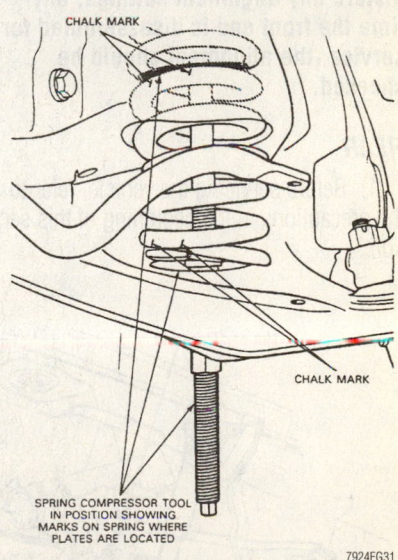

CHALK MARK

CHALK MARK

SPRING COMPRESSOR TOOL IN POSITION SHOWING MARKS ON SPRING WHERE PLATES ARE LOCATED

7924EG31

Mark the position of the spring compressor on the spring so the new spring can be mounted in the same position—Aerostar front coil spring shown

Turn to Section 5 for brake system applications

plates in the same position as marked on the old spring. Make sure the upper ball nut securing pin is installed properly, then compress the new spring to the compressed length of the old spring

- Coil spring assembly into the lower control arm

14. Place a hydraulic jack under the lower control arm and slowly raise it into position. Reconnect the ball joint and install the nut. Tighten the ball joint castle nut to 80–120 ft. lbs. (108–163 Nm) and install a new cotter pin. The nut may be tightened slightly to align the cotter pin hole, but not loosened.

15. Slowly release the spring compressor and remove it from the coil spring.

16. Install or connect the following:
- Steering center link to the Pitman arm
- Shock absorber
- Stabilizer bar link bolt to the lower control arm. Tighten the nuts to 10–12 ft. lbs. (12–16 Nm).
- Front wheels
- Negative battery cable

➡ **Control arm bushing bolts must be tightened while the vehicle is at normal ride height.**

17. Lower the vehicle to the ground and tighten the 2 lower control arm-to-frame bolts to 100–140 ft. lbs. (136–190 Nm).

➡ **Although this procedure should not disturb any alignment settings, anytime the front end is disassembled for service, the alignment should be checked.**

REAR

1. Before servicing the vehicle, refer to the precautions in the beginning of this section.

2. Raise the vehicle and support it safely with jackstands placed beneath the frame rear lift points or under the rear bumper support brackets.

3. Remove or disconnect the following:
- Negative battery cable

4. Support the rear axle assembly by placing a hydraulic floor jack under the differential housing.
- Bolt retaining the shock absorber to the axle mount on the lower control arm
- Shock absorber from the axle bracket

5. Carefully lower the rear axle until the coil springs are no longer under compression.
- Nut securing the lower retainer and spring to the control arm
- Bolt securing the upper retainer and spring to the frame
- Spring, retainers and the upper and lower insulators

To install:

6. Before installing the spring, first make sure the axle is in the lowered (spring unloaded) position. Place the lower insulator on the control arm and the upper insulator at the top of the spring.

7. Install or connect the following:
- Coil spring in position between the control arm and vehicle frame. The small diameter, tapered coils (white colored) must face upward.
- Upper retainer and bolt. Torque the bolt to 30–40 ft. lbs. (40–55 Nm).
- Lower retainer and nut. Torque the nut to 41–65 ft. lbs. (55–88 Nm).

8. Raise the axle to the normal ride position with the hydraulic floor jack.
- Shock absorber in the axle bracket, then install the bolt so the head is positioned outboard of the bracket. Torque the nut to 41–65 ft. lbs. (55–88 Nm).
- Negative battery cable

9. Remove the jackstands and lower the vehicle.

1997 Ranger and B-Series Models

2-WHEEL DRIVE VEHICLES

1. Before servicing the vehicle, refer to the precautions in the beginning of this section.

2. Raise the front of the vehicle and place jackstands under the frame and a jack under the axle.

✳✳ WARNING

The axle must not be permitted to hang by the brake hose. If the length of the brake hoses is not sufficient to provide adequate clearance for removal and installation of the spring, the disc brake caliper must be removed from the spindle. A Strut Spring Compressor T81P-5310-A, may be used to compress the spring sufficiently, so that the caliper does not have to be removed. After removal, the caliper must be placed on the frame or otherwise supported to prevent suspending the caliper from the brake hose. These precautions are absolutely necessary to prevent serious damage to the tube portion of the brake hose!

3. Remove or disconnect the following:
- Negative battery cable
- Shock absorber at the lower shock stud. Remove the nut securing the lower retainer to spring seat
- Lower retainer

4. Lower the axle as far as it will go without stretching the brake hose and tube assembly. The axle should now be unsupported without hanging by the brake hose. If not, then either remove the caliper or use Strut Spring Compressor tool, T81P-5310-A. Remove the spring.

5. If there is a lot of slack in the brake hose assembly, a pry bar can be used to lift the spring over the bolt that passes through the lower spring seat.

6. Rotate the spring so the built-in retainer on the upper spring seat is cleared.

7. Remove the coil spring.

To install:

8. Install or connect the following:
- Bolt in the axle arm and install the nut all the way down
- Spring lower seat and insulator

9. With the axle in the lowest position, install the top of the spring in the upper seat. Rotate the spring into position.

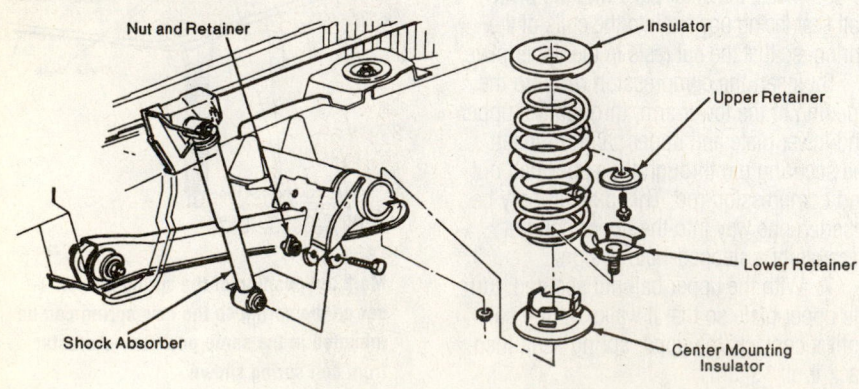

Nut and Retainer

Shock Absorber

Insulator

Upper Retainer

Lower Retainer

Center Mounting Insulator

7924EG32

Exploded view of the rear spring assembly—Aerostar

10. Lift the lower end of the spring over the bolt.

11. Raise the axle slowly until the spring is seated in the lower spring seat and install the lower retainer and nut.

12. Install or connect the following:
- Shock absorber to the lower shock stud
- Negative battery cable

4-WHEEL DRIVE VEHICLES

1. Before servicing the vehicle, refer to the precautions in the beginning of this section.

2. Raise the vehicle and install jack-stands under the frame. Position a jack beneath the spring under the axle. Raise the jack and compress the spring.

3. Remove or disconnect the following:
- Negative battery cable
- Nut retaining the shock absorber to the radius arm. Slide the shock out from the stud
- Nut that retains the spring to the axle and radius arm and remove the retainer

4. Slowly lower the axle until all spring tension is released and adequate clearance exists to remove the spring from its mounting.
- Spring by rotating the upper coil out of the tabs in the upper spring seat
- Spacer and the seat

✸✸ WARNING

The axle must be supported on the jack throughout spring removal and installation, and must not be permitted to hang by the brake hose. If the length of the brake hose is not sufficient to provide adequate clearance for removal and installation of the spring, the disc brake caliper must be removed from the spindle. After removal, the caliper must be placed on the frame or otherwise supported to prevent suspending the caliper from the brake line hose. These precautions are absolutely necessary to prevent serious damage to the tube portion of the caliper hose assembly!

- Stud from the axle assembly, if necessary

To install:

5. Install or connect the following:
- Stud on the axle. Torque the stud to

190–230 ft. lbs. (258–313 Nm), if removed
- Lower seat and spacer over the stud

6. Place the spring in position and slowly raise the front axle. Ensure springs are positioned correctly in the upper spring seats.
- Spring lower retainer over the stud and lower seat. Torque the nut to 70–100 ft. lbs. (95–136 Nm).
- Shock absorber to the lower stud and install the attaching nut. Torque the nut to 41–63 ft. lbs. (56–85 Nm).
- Negative battery cable

Leaf Springs

REMOVAL & INSTALLATION

Ranger

1. Before servicing the vehicle, refer to the precautions in the beginning of this section.

2. Remove or disconnect the following:
- Negative battery cable
- Rear wheels
- U-bolts from the rear spring plate
- Hardware from the spring to bracket at the front of the rear spring
- Upper and lower shackle bolts at the rear of the spring
- Spring and shackle from the bracket

To install:

3. Install or connect the following:
- Spring and shackle to the bracket
- Upper and lower shackle bolts at the rear of the spring. Torque the nuts to 87 ft. lbs. (118 Nm).
- U-bolts to the spring plate. Torque the nuts 87 ft. lbs. (113 Nm).
- Rear wheels
- Negative battery cable

B-Series, Explorer and Mountaineer

1. Before servicing the vehicle, refer to the precautions in the beginning of this section.

2. Turn the air suspension switch off, if equipped.

3. Remove or disconnect the following:
- Negative battery cable
- Rear wheels and support the rear axle
- Separate the rear spring from the

axle and position the spring plate aside
- Rear spring

To install:

4. Install or connect the following:
- Rear spring. Torque the dual bolts to 85 ft. lbs. (115 Nm) and the single bolt to 66 ft. lbs. (90 Nm).
- Properly position the spring plate and install the U-bolts. Torque the bolts to 87 ft. lbs. (117 Nm).
- Rear wheels and remove the rear axle support
- Negative battery cable

5. Turn the air suspension switch on, if equipped.

Torsion Bar

REMOVAL & INSTALLATION

1. Before servicing the vehicle, refer to the precautions in the beginning of this section.

2. Remove or disconnect the following:
- Negative battery cable
- Torsion bar cover plate and measure the length of the torsion bar adjustment bolt
- Relieve torsion bar tension
- Torsion bar adjustment bolt
- Torsion bar and insulator

To install:

3. Install or connect the following:
- Torsion bar in the front suspension lower arm
- Torsion bar adjuster and position the insulator

4. Preload the torsion bar and install a **NEW** adjuster bolt. Turn the bolt until it reaches the measurement made during the removal procedure.
- Torsion bar cover plate. Torque the bolts to 46 ft. lbs. (63 Nm).
- Negative battery cable

Upper Ball Joint

REMOVAL & INSTALLATION

Aerostar

➥**Ford Motor Company recommends replacement of the upper control arm and ball joint as an assembly, rather than replacement of the ball joint alone. However, aftermarket ball joints are available. The following procedure is for replacement of the ball joint only.**

1. Before servicing the vehicle, refer to the precautions in the beginning of this section.

2. Raise the vehicle and support it safely with jackstands placed under the frame lifting pads. Allow the front suspension to hang unsupported.

3. Disconnect the negative battery cable.

4. Remove the front wheels and place a hydraulic floor jack under the lower control arm and raise the jack until it just contacts the arm.

5. Drill a 1⁄8 in. (3mm) hole completely through each ball joint attaching rivet.

6. Use a chisel to cut the head off of each rivet, then drive them from the upper control arm with a suitable small drift or blunt punch.

7. Raise the lower control arm about 6 in. (15cm) with the hydraulic jack.

8. remove the pinch nut and bolt holding the ball joint stud to the spindle.

9. Loosen the ball joint stud from the spindle.

10. Remove the ball joint from the upper arm.

To install:

11. Clean all metal burrs from the upper arm and install a new ball joint, using the service part nuts and bolts to attach the ball joint to the upper arm. Do not attempt to rivet the ball joint again once it has been removed.

12. Install or connect the following:
   • Ball joint stud to the spindle. Torque the pinch bolt to 27–37 ft. lbs. (36–50 Nm).
   • Front wheels and remove the hydraulic jack
   • Negative battery cable

13. Check and adjust the front end alignment.

1997 Ranger and B-Series Models

➡**The ball joints are arranged such that, if the upper ball joint is to be removed, the lower ball joint must be removed first. Conversely, the upper ball joint must be installed first, before the lower ball joint. Failure to install the upper ball joint before the lower, will result in a lack of clearance for the installation tool.**

1. Before servicing the vehicle, refer to the precautions in the beginning of this section.

2. Remove or disconnect the following:
   • Negative battery cable
   • Front wheels
   • Steering knuckle

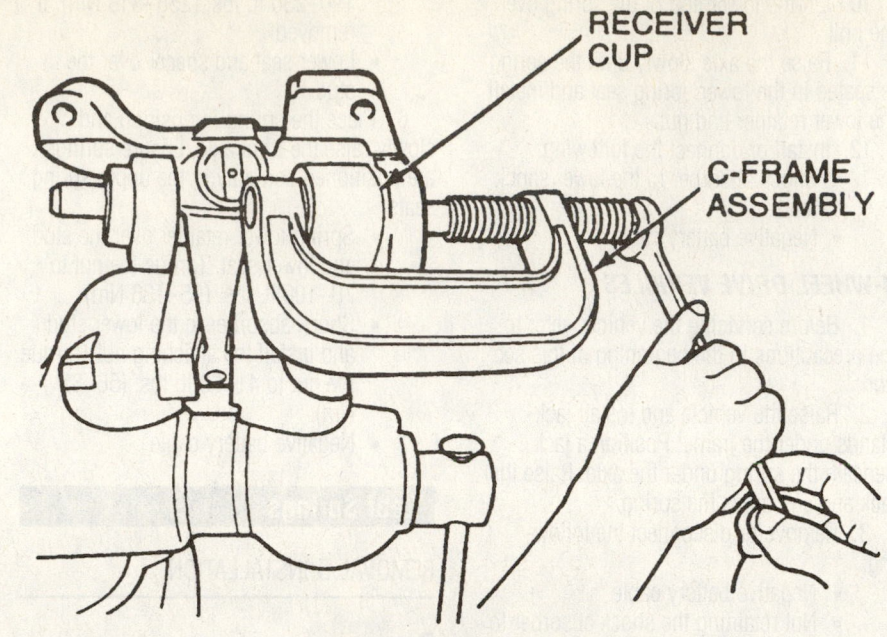

RECEIVER CUP

C-FRAME ASSEMBLY

REMOVING LOWER BALL JOINT

7924EG33

Press the ball joint out of the knuckle using the special tools—2WD Ranger shown

3. Place the knuckle in a vise and remove the snapring from the bottom ball joint socket.

4. Assemble the C-frame, T74P-4635-C, forcing screw, D79T-3010-AE and ball joint remover T83T-3050-A on the lower ball joint.

5. Turn the forcing screw clockwise until the lower ball joint is removed from the steering knuckle.

6. Repeat this procedure to remove the upper ball joint.

➡**Always remove the lower ball joint first.**

To install:

7. Clean the steering knuckle bore and insert the lower ball joint in the knuckle as straight as possible. The lower ball joint doesn't have a cotter pin hole in the stud.

8. Assemble the C-frame, T74P-4635-C, forcing screw, D790T-3010-AE, ball joint installer, T83T-3050-A and receiver cup T80T-3010-A3, to install the upper ball joint.

9. Turn the forcing screw clockwise until the upper ball joint is firmly seated.

➡**If the ball joint cannot be installed to the proper depth, realignment of the receiver cup and ball joint installer will be necessary.**

10. Install or connect the following:
   • Snapring on the lower ball joint
   • Steering knuckle
   • Front wheels
   • Negative battery cable

Mountaineer, Explorer, 1998–01 Ranger and B-Series Models

The ball joints on the Mountaineer and Explorer are integral with the control arm. If the ball joint is defective, the entire control arm must be replaced.

Lower Ball Joint

REMOVAL & INSTALLATION

Aerostar

➡**The manufacturer recommends that the lower control arm and ball joint should be replaced as an assembly.**

The lower ball joint is pressed into the lower control arm. Although Ford recommends replacing the lower arm and ball joint together, the old ball joint can also be pressed out and the new one pressed in. Refer to the lower control arm removal procedures to remove the lower control arm. Once the lower control arm is removed, the ball joint may be pressed out.

1997 Ranger and B-Series Models

Refer to the procedure for the upper ball joint outlined earlier in this section.

Mountaineer, Explorer, 1998–01Ranger and B-Series Models

The ball joints on the Mountaineer and Explorer are integral with the control arm. If the ball joint is defective, the entire control arm must be replaced.

Upper Control Arm

REMOVAL & INSTALLATION

Aerostar

1. Before servicing the vehicle, refer to the precautions in the beginning of this section.
2. Remove or disconnect the following:
   - Negative battery cable
   - Front wheels
   - Front wheel spindle
   - Retainer plate and matchmark the position of the control arm mounting brackets
   - Front mounting bracket from the flat plate
   - Front suspension upper arm mounting brackets
3. Rotate the front suspension upper arm and remove the 3 bolts retaining the brackets to the body.
   - Upper arm assembly from the vehicle

To install:

4. Install or connect the following:
   - Front suspension upper arm to the pivot arm, if removed. Torque the nuts to 100 ft. lbs. (135 Nm).
   - Flat plate to the frame. Torque the bolt to 14 ft. lbs. (19 Nm).
   - 3 long retaining bolts retaining the brackets to the frame
   - Mounting brackets to the flat plate
   - Retaining plate on the mounting bracket. When aligned properly, torque the screw to 14 ft. lbs. (19 Nm).
   - Mounting bracket bolts. Torque the bolts to 195 ft. lbs. (264 Nm).
   - Front mounting bracket to flat plate bolts. Torque the bolts to 47 ft. lbs. (64 Nm).
   - Front wheel spindle
   - Front wheels
   - negative battery cable

B-Series and Ranger

1. Before servicing the vehicle, refer to the precautions in the beginning of this section.
2. Remove or disconnect the following:
   - Negative battery cable
   - Front wheel
   - Front wheel spindle
   - Brake rotor shield and support the front suspension
   - Upper ball joint retaining nut and pinch bolt
   - Ball joint from the front spindle
   - Upper control arm

To install:

3. Install or connect the following:
   - Bushing to the joint

➡**The front suspension upper arm nut must be tightened first while the arm is held at the curb position ride height.**

   - Upper control arm. Torque the bolts to 98 ft. lbs. (133 Nm).
   - Upper ball joint to the front spindle. Torque the pinch bolt to 46 ft. lbs. (63 Nm).
   - Brake rotor shield and remove the support from the front suspension
   - Front wheel
   - Negative battery cable

4. Check and adjust the front end alignment, as needed.

UPPER CONTROL ARM BUSHING REPLACEMENT

The control arm bushings are not serviceable. If they require service, the upper or lower arm must be replaced.

Explorer and Mountaineer

1. Before servicing the vehicle, refer to the precautions in the beginning of this section.
2. Turn off the air suspension switch, if equipped.
3. Remove or disconnect the following:
   - Negative battery cable
   - Front wheel
   - Pinch bolt and nut from the spindle
   - Upper control arm

To install:

4. Install or connect the following:
   - Upper control arm. Torque the bolts to 112 ft. lbs. (153 Nm).

   - Pinch bolt and nut to the front spindle. Torque the bolt to 46 ft. lbs. (63 Nm).
   - Front wheel
   - Negative battery cable
   - Turn on the air suspension switch, if equipped.

UPPER CONTROL ARM BUSHING REPLACEMENT

The control arm bushings are not serviceable. If they require service, the upper or lower arm must be replaced.

Lower Control Arm

REMOVAL AND & INSTALLATION

Aerostar

➡**Ford Motor Company recommends replacement of the upper control arm and ball joint as an assembly, rather than replacement of the ball joint alone.**

B-Series and Ranger

1. Before servicing the vehicle, refer to the precautions in the beginning of this section.
2. Remove or disconnect the following:
   - Negative battery cable
   - Front wheel
   - Brake rotor shield
   - Shock absorber
   - Stabilizer bar link hardware
3. Using a spring compressor tool, compress the coil spring.
   - Lower ball joint from the spindle
   - Lower control arm bolts
   - Lower control arm and coil spring

To install:

4. Install or connect the following:
   - Coil spring to the lower control arm
   - Lower control arm assembly and install the lower arm adjustment cam bolt. Torque the forward nut first to 148 ft. lbs. (201 Nm) then torque the remaining bolts to 148 ft. lbs. (201 Nm).
   - Lower ball joint. Torque the castle nut to 113 ft. lbs. (153 Nm).
   - Front stabilizer bar link. Torque the nut to 21 ft. lbs. (29 Nm). Remove the coil spring compressor tool.
   - Shock absorber. Torque the nuts to 41 ft. lbs. (55 Nm).
   - Brake rotor shield
   - Front wheel
   - Negative battery cable

LOWER CONTROL ARM BUSHING REPLACEMENT

The control arm bushings are not serviceable. If they require service, the upper or lower arm must be replaced.

Explorer and Mountaineer

1. Before servicing the vehicle, refer to the precautions in the beginning of this section.
2. Turn off the air suspension switch, if equipped.
3. Remove or disconnect the following:
   - Negative battery cable
   - Front wheel
   - Brake rotor shield
   - Shock absorber
   - Torsion bar
   - Lower ball joint from the spindle
   - Lower control arm

To install:
4. Install or connect the following:
   - Lower control arm assembly to the crossmember and hand tighten the bolts at this time
   - Lower ball joint to the spindle. Torque the new castle nut to 21 ft. lbs. (29 Nm).
   - Torsion bar. Torque the bolts to 21 ft. lbs. (29 Nm). Check and adjust the ride height.
   - Shock absorber. Torque the bolts to 21 ft. lbs. (29 Nm).
   - Brake rotor shield
   - Torque the lower control arm bolts to 148 ft. lbs. (200 Nm)
   - Front wheel
   - Negative battery cable
5. Turn on the air suspension switch, if equipped.
6. Check and adjust the front end alignment as needed.

LOWER CONTROL ARM BUSHING REPLACEMENT

The control arm bushings are not serviceable. If they require service, the upper or lower arm must be replaced.

Wheel Bearings

ADJUSTMENT

Explorer, Mountaineer and AWD Aerostar

The wheel bearings on the Explorer, Mountaineer and all-wheel drive Aerostar are not adjustable. If they become loose or make noise, they must be replaced.

Ranger, B-Series Models and Aerostar

2-WHEEL DRIVE VEHICLES

1. Before servicing the vehicle, refer to the precautions in the beginning of this section.
2. Remove the grease cap from the hub and wipe the excess grease from the end of the spindle. Remove the cotter pin and retainer. Discard the cotter pin.
3. Loosen the adjusting nut 3 turns.

✳✳ WARNING

Obtain running clearance between the disc brake rotor surface and shoe linings by rocking the entire wheel assembly in and out several times in order to push the caliper and brake pads away from the rotor. An alternate method to obtain proper running clearance is to tap lightly on the caliper housing. Be sure not to tap on any other area that may damage the disc brake rotor or the brake lining surfaces. Do not pry on the phenolic caliper piston. The running clearance must be maintained throughout the adjustment procedure. If proper clearance cannot be maintained, the caliper must be removed from its mounting.

To install:
4. While rotating the wheel assembly, tighten the adjusting nut to 17–25 ft. lbs. (23–34 Nm) in order to seat the bearings. Loosen the adjusting nut a half turn. Retighten the adjusting nut 18–20 inch lbs. (2.0–2.2 Nm).
5. Place the retainer on the adjusting nut. The castellations on the retainer must be in alignment with the cotter pin holes in the spindle. Once this is accomplished install a new cotter pin and bend the ends to insure its being locked in place.
6. Check for proper wheel rotation. If correct, install the grease cap.
7. Lower the vehicle and tighten the lug nuts to 100 ft. lbs., (136 Nm) if the wheel was removed. Before driving the vehicle, pump the brake pedal several times to restore normal brake pedal travel.

✳✳ CAUTION

If the wheel was removed, retighten the wheel lug nuts to specification after about 500 miles (804km) of driving. Failure to do this could result in the wheel coming off while the vehicle is in motion causing loss of vehicle control or collision.

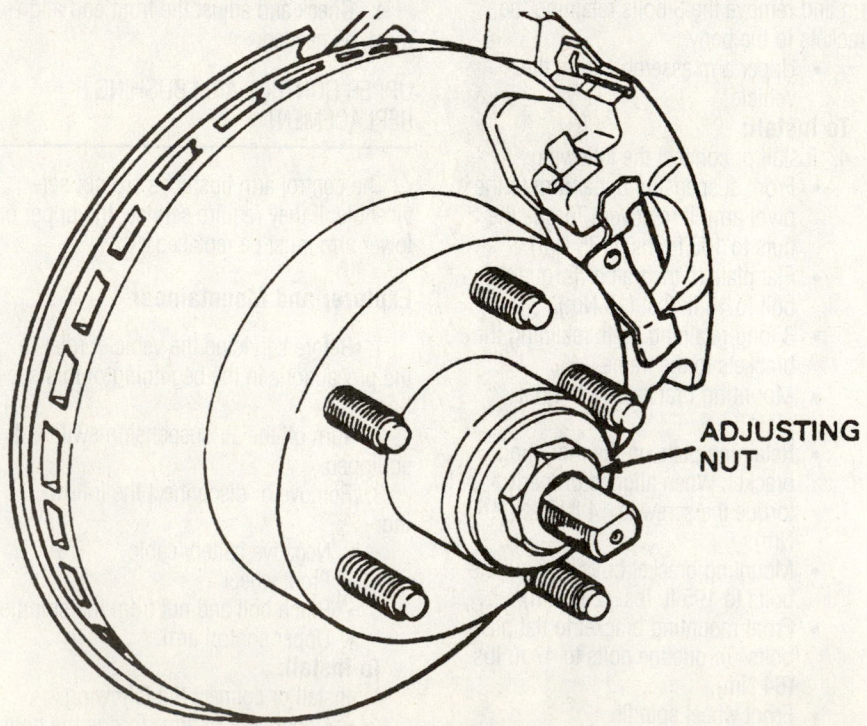

ADJUSTING NUT

7924EG34

Loosen the adjusting nut 3 turns, then rock the entire wheel assembly in-and-out to spread the brake pads before attempting to adjust the bearing—2wd vehicles

4-WHEEL DRIVE WITH MANUAL HUBS

1. Before servicing the vehicle, refer to the precautions in the beginning of this section.

2. Remove or disconnect the following:
   - Wheel assembly
   - Retainer washers from the lug nut studs and remove the manual locking hub assembly from the spindle
   - Snapring and spacer from the end of the spindle shaft
   - Outer wheel bearing locknut from the spindle using 4 prong spindle nut spanner wrench, T86T-1197-A. Make sure the tabs on the tool engage the slots in the locknut.
   - Locknut washer from the spindle
   - Loosen the inner wheel bearing locknut using 4 prong spindle nut spanner wrench, tool T86T-1197-A. Make sure that the tabs on the tool engage the slots in the locknut and that the slot in the tool is over the pin on the locknut
   - Tighten the inner locknut to 35 ft. lbs. (47 Nm) to seat the bearings.
   - Spin the rotor and back off the inner locknut ¼ turn. Install the lockwasher on the spindle. Retighten the inner locknut to 16

inch lbs. (1.8 Nm). It may be necessary to turn the inner locknut slightly so that the pin on the locknut aligns with the closest hole in the lockwasher.
   - Outer wheel bearing locknut using 4 prong spindle nut spanner wrench, tool T86T-1197-A. Torque locknut to 150 ft. lbs. (203 Nm).
   - Axle shaft spacer
   - Clip the snapring onto the end of the spindle
   - Manual hub assembly over the spindle
   - Retainer washers
   - Wheel assembly

3. Check the end-play of the wheel and tire assembly on the spindle. End-play should be 0.001–0.003 in. (0.025–0.076mm) and the maximum torque to rotate the hub should be 25 inch lbs. (2.8 Nm).

4-WHEEL DRIVE WITH AUTOMATIC HUBS

1. Before servicing the vehicle, refer to the precautions in the beginning of this section.

2. Remove or disconnect the following:
   - Wheel assembly
   - Retainer washers from the lug nut studs and remove the automatic

locking hub assembly from the spindle
   - Snapring and spacer from the end of the spindle shaft
   - Pull the locking cam assembly and the 2 plastic spacers off of the wheel bearing adjusting nut

3. Use a magnet and remove the locking key from under the adjusting nut. If required, rotate the adjusting nut slightly to relieve pressure against the locking key.

❊❊ WARNING

To prevent damage to the adjusting nut and spindle threads on vehicles equipped with automatic hubs, look into the spindle keyway under the adjusting nut and remove the separate locking key before removing the adjusting nut.

4. Loosen the wheel bearing locknut using a 2⅜ inch (60.3mm) hex socket, such as Hex Locknut Wrench T70T-4252-B.

5. Tighten the inner locknut to 35 ft. lbs. (47 Nm) to seat the bearings.

6. Spin the rotor and back off the inner locknut ¼ turn (90°). Retighten the locknut to 16 inch lbs. (1.8 Nm).

7. Align the closest lug in the bearing adjusting nut with the center of the spindle keyway slot. Advance the nut to the next if required.

To install:

8. Separate locking key in the spindle keyway under the adjusting nut.

❊❊ CAUTION

Extreme care must be taken when aligning the adjusting nut with the center of the spindle keyway slot to prevent damage to the separate locking key. The wheel and tire assembly may come off while the vehicle is in motion if the key is damaged.

9. Install or connect the following.
   - 2 plastic thrust spacers and push or press the cam assembly onto the adjusting nut by lining up the keyway in the cam assembly with the separate locking key

❊❊ WARNING

Do not damage the locking key when installing the cam assembly.

   - Axle shaft spacer

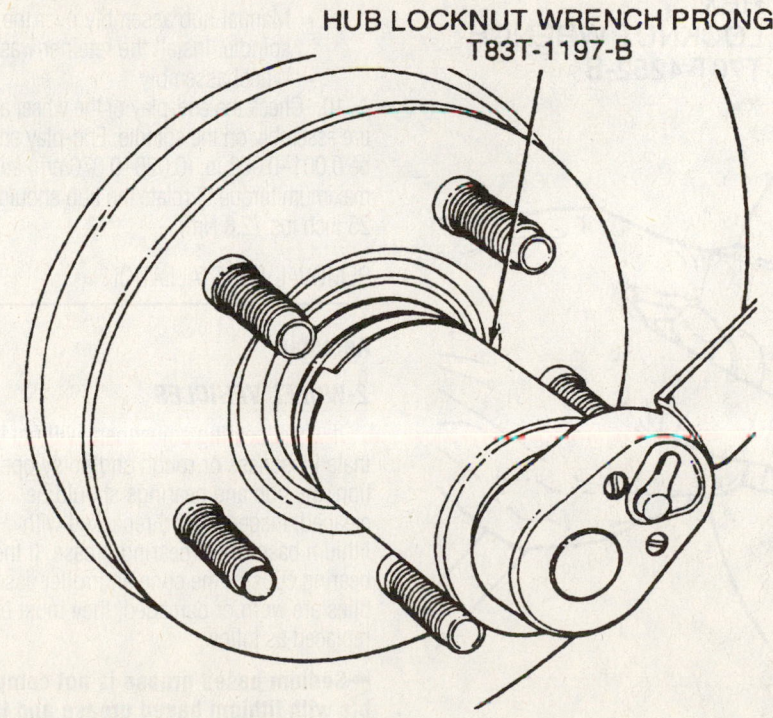

HUB LOCKNUT WRENCH PRONG
T83T-1197-B

7924EG35

Obtain the special socket to properly adjust the wheel bearing—manual locking hub shown

Turn to Section 5 for brake system applications

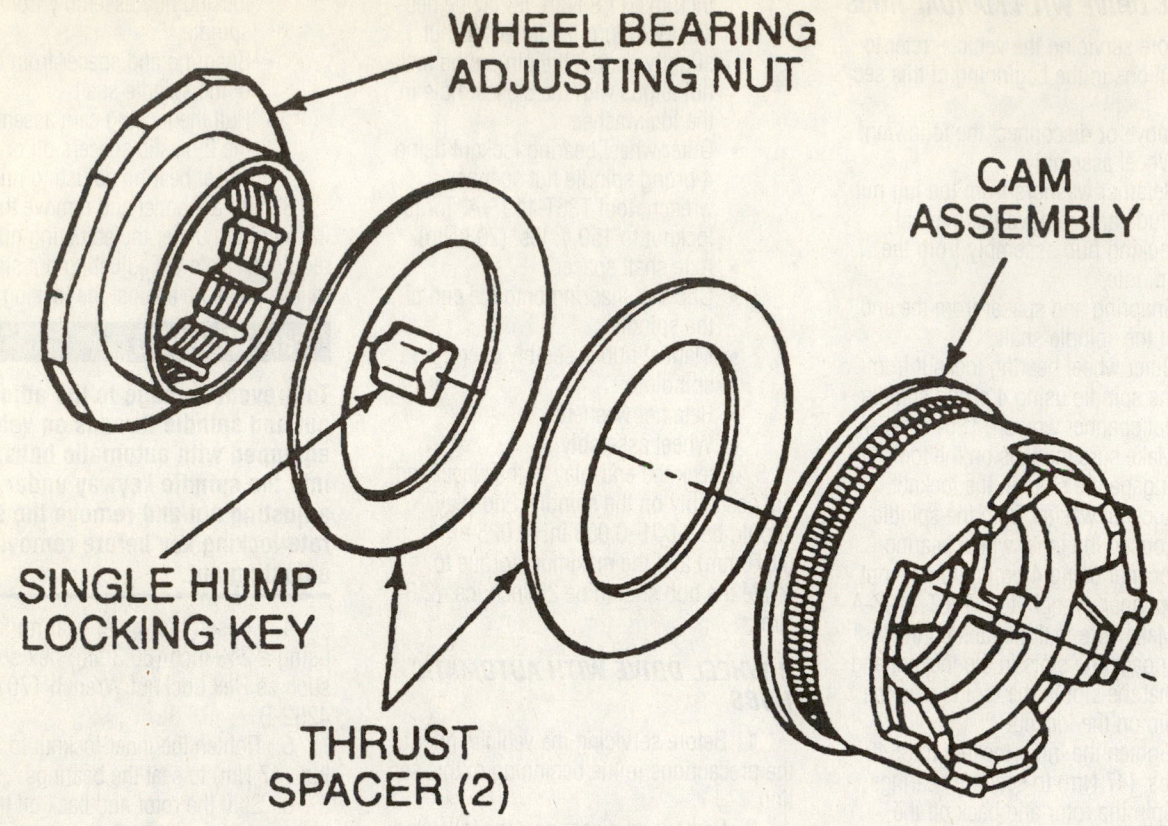

Exploded view of the wheel bearing adjusting nut and related components—automatic locking hub shown

7924EG36

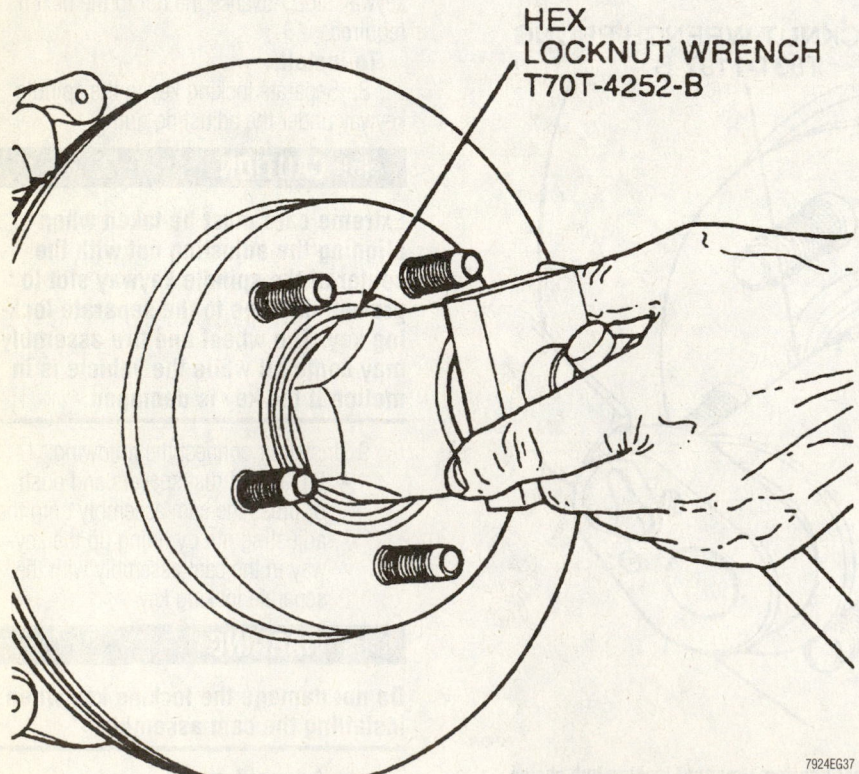

An oversize socket is needed to properly adjust the wheel bearing—automatic locking hub shown

7924EG37

- Clip the snapring onto the end of the spindle
- Manual hub assembly over the spindle. Install the retainer washers
- Wheel assembly

10. Check the end-play of the wheel and tire assembly on the spindle. End-play should be 0.001–0.003 in. (0.025–0.076mm) and the maximum torque to rotate the hub should be 25 inch lbs. (2.8 Nm).

REMOVAL & INSTALLATION

Aerostar

2-WHEEL VEHICLES

If wheel bearing adjustment will not eliminate looseness or rough and noisy operation, the hub and bearings should be cleaned, inspected and repacked with lithium base wheel bearing grease. If the bearing cups or the cone and roller assemblies are worn or damaged, they must be replaced as follows:

➡Sodium based grease is not compatible with lithium based grease and the 2 should not be mixed. Do not lubricate the front and/or rear wheel bearings without first identifying the type of grease being used. Use of incompatible

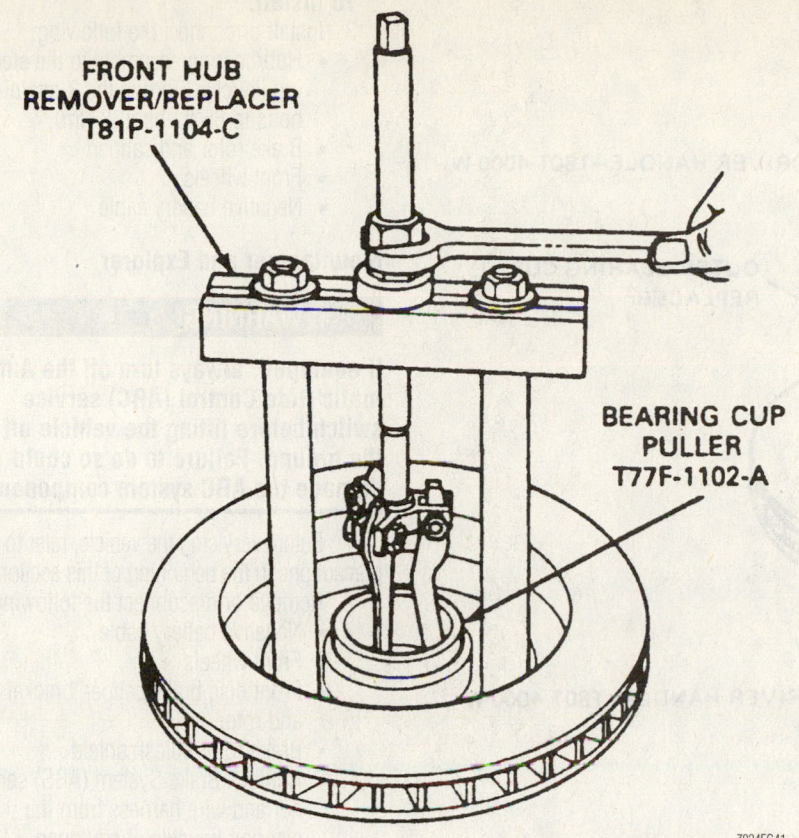

FRONT HUB REMOVER/REPLACER T81P-1104-C

BEARING CUP PULLER T77F-1102-A

7924EG41

Use an internal 3-jaw puller to remove the races (cups) from the hub assembly—2WD models

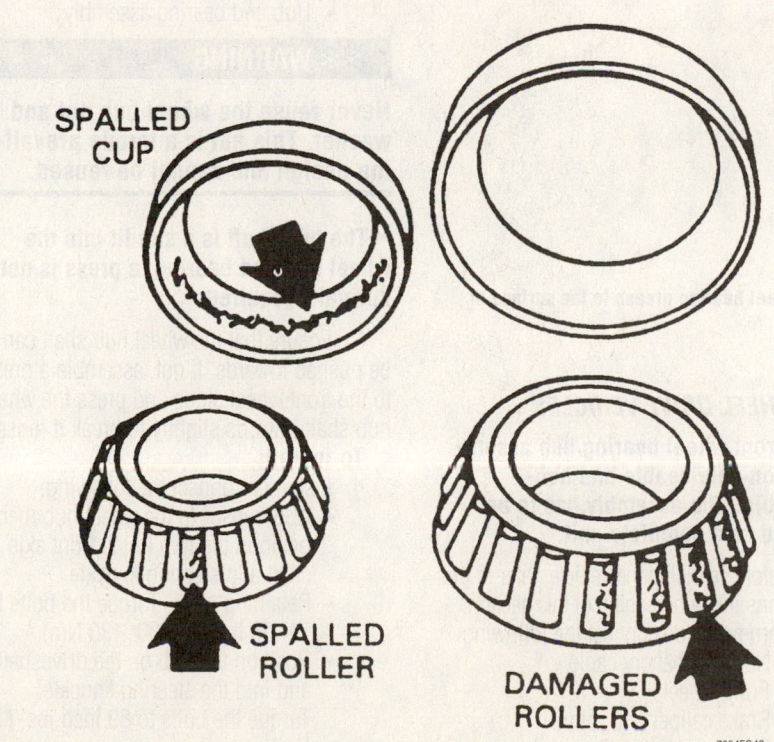

SPALLED CUP

SPALLED ROLLER

DAMAGED ROLLERS

7924EG40

Examine the bearings and races (cups) for damage and excessive wear

wheel bearing lubricant could result in premature lubricant breakdown and subsequent bearing damage.

1. Before servicing the vehicle, refer to the precautions in the beginning of this section.

2. Remove or disconnect the following:
   - Negative battery cable
   - Front wheel
   - Brake caliper from the spindle and wire it to the underbody
   - Grease cap from the hub
   - Cotter pin, castle nut and flat washer from the spindle
   - Outer bearing assembly and pull the hub and rotor assembly off the spindle

3. Place the hub and rotor on a clean workbench with the back-side facing up. Remove and discard the grease seal using a suitable seal remover or small prybar.
   - Inner bearing assembly from the hub

4. Clean the inner and outer bearing races with solvent. Inspect them for scratches, pits, scoring, excessive wear and other damage. If the cups are worn or damaged, remove them with a bearing cup puller (T77F–1102–A).

5. Wipe all old lubricant from the spindle and the inside of the hub with a clean rag. Cover the spindle and brush all loose dirt and dust from the dust shield. Remove the cover cloth carefully to prevent dirt from falling on the spindle.

To install:

6. If the inner or outer bearing cups were removed, install replacement cups using a suitable driver tool (T80T–4000–W or equivalent) and bearing cup replacer. Make sure the cups are seated properly in the hub and not cocked in the bore.

7. Thoroughly clean all old grease from the surrounding surfaces.

8. Pack the bearing and cone assemblies with suitable wheel bearing grease using a bearing packer tool. If a packer tool is not available, work as much grease as possible between the rollers and cages, then grease the cone surfaces.

9. Install or connect the following:
   - Inner bearing cone and roller assembly in the inner cup. Apply a light film of grease to the lip of a new grease seal and install the seal with an appropriate driver tool. Make sure the grease seal is properly seated
   - Hub and rotor assembly on the spindle. Keep the hub centered on

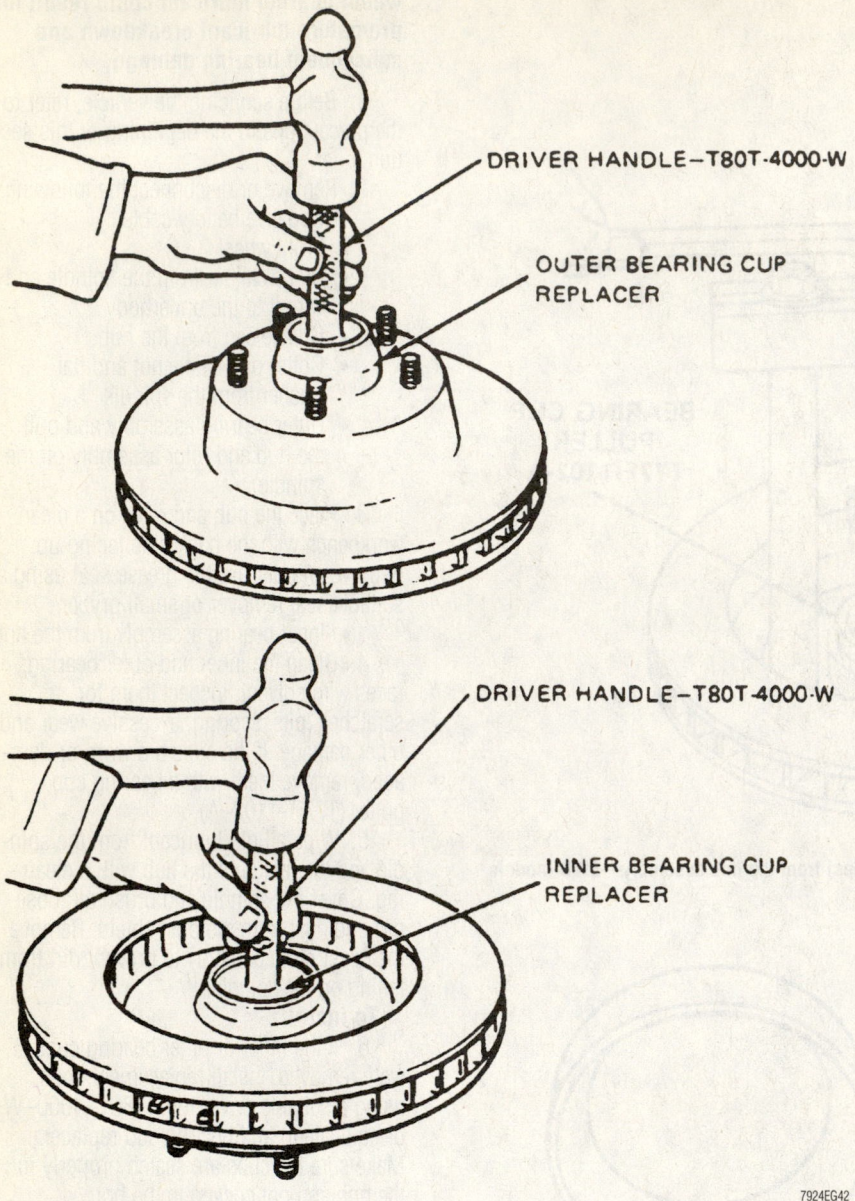

DRIVER HANDLE—T80T-4000-W

OUTER BEARING CUP REPLACER

DRIVER HANDLE—T80T-4000-W

INNER BEARING CUP REPLACER

7924EG42

Install the races using the proper size driver, then apply wheel bearing grease to the surface of the race—2WD models

the spindle to prevent damage to the retainer and the spindle threads
- Outer bearing cone and roller assembly (after being fully greased) and the flat washer on the spindle
- Adjusting nut finger-tight and adjust the wheel bearing as needed
- Caliper onto the spindle
- Front wheel
- Negative battery cable

10. Before moving the vehicle, pump the brake pedal several times to restore normal brake travel.

ALL-WHEEL DRIVE VEHICLES

➡The front wheel bearing/hub assembly is non-serviceable and non-adjustable. The assembly has to be replaced as a complete unit.

1. Before servicing the vehicle, refer to the precautions in the beginning of this section.
2. Remove or disconnect the following:
   - Negative battery cable
   - Front wheels
   - Brake caliper and rotor
   - 3 bolts retaining the hub/bearing assembly to the spindle and remove the hub/bearing assembly from the spindle

To install:
3. Install or connect the following:
   - Hub/bearing assembly to the steering knuckle. Torque the 3 retaining bolts to 65 ft. lbs. (88 Nm).
   - Brake rotor and caliper
   - Front wheels
   - Negative battery cable

Mountaineer and Explorer

> ❋❋ **WARNING**

If equipped, always turn off the Automatic Ride Control (ARC) service switch before lifting the vehicle off of the ground. Failure to do so could damage the ARC system components.

1. Before servicing the vehicle, refer to the precautions in the beginning of this section.
2. Remove or disconnect the following:
   - Negative battery cable
   - Front wheels
   - Front disc brake caliper, bracket and rotor
   - Brake rotor splash shield
   - Antilock Brake System (ABS) sensor and wire harness from the steering knuckle, if equipped
   - Front wheel hub nut and washer
   - Wheel hub/bearing to steering knuckle retaining bolts
   - Hub and bearing assembly

> ❋❋ **WARNING**

Never reuse the wheel hub nut and washer. This nut is a torque prevailing design and cannot be reused.

➡The hub shaft is a slip fit into the wheel hub and bearing; a press is not normally required.

3. Ensure that the wheel hub shaft can be pushed inwards. If not, assemble a press to the front wheel studs and press the wheel hub shaft inwards slightly to break it loose.

To install:
4. Install or connect the following:
   - ABS sensor to the wheel hub then position the hub to the front axle shaft and steering knuckle
   - Retaining bolts. Torque the bolts to 74–96 ft. lbs. (100–130 Nm).
   - Position the hub on the driveshaft and into the steering knuckle. Torque the bolts to 89 inch lbs. (10 Nm).
   - Brake rotor splash shield
   - ABS sensor. Torque the bolt to 89 inch lbs. (10 Nm).

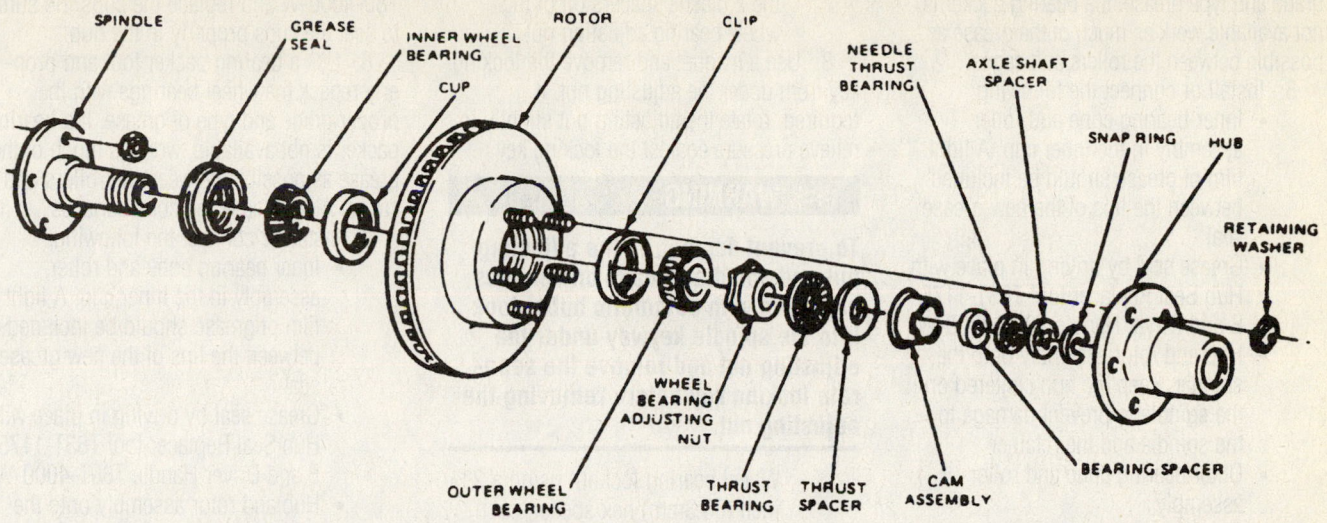

Exploded view of the wheel bearing and automatic locking hub assembly

- Hub washer and nut and tighten to 157–213 ft. lbs. (212–288 Nm)
- Front brake rotor, bracket and caliper
- Front wheels
- Negative battery cable

Ranger and B-Series Models

WITH MANUAL HUBS

1. Before servicing the vehicle, refer to the precautions in the beginning of this section.
2. Remove or disconnect the following:
   - Negative battery cable
   - Wheel
   - Retaining washers from the lug nut studs and remove the manual

locking hub assembly from the spindle
   - Snapring and spacer from the end of the spindle shaft
   - Outer wheel bearing locknut from the spindle using 4 prong spindle nut spanner wrench, T86T-1197-A
   - Locknut washer from the spindle
   - Inner wheel bearing locknut from the spindle using 4 prong spindle nut spanner wrench, T86T-1197-A
   - Outer bearing cone and roller assembly from the hub
   - Hub and rotor from the spindle
   - Grease seal using seal removal tool 1175-AC and discard
   - Inner bearing cone and roller assembly from the hub

3. Clean the inner and outer bearing assemblies in solvent. Inspect the bearings and the cones for wear and damage. Replace defective parts, as required.
4. If the cups are worn or damaged, remove them with front hub remover tool T81P-1104-C and tool T77F-1102-A.
5. Wipe the old grease from the spindle. Check the spindle for excessive wear or damage. Replace defective parts, as required.

To install:

6. If the inner and outer cups were removed, use bearing driver handle tool, T80-4000-W, and replace the cups. Be sure to seat the cups properly in the hub.
7. Use a bearing packer tool and properly repack the wheel bearings with the proper

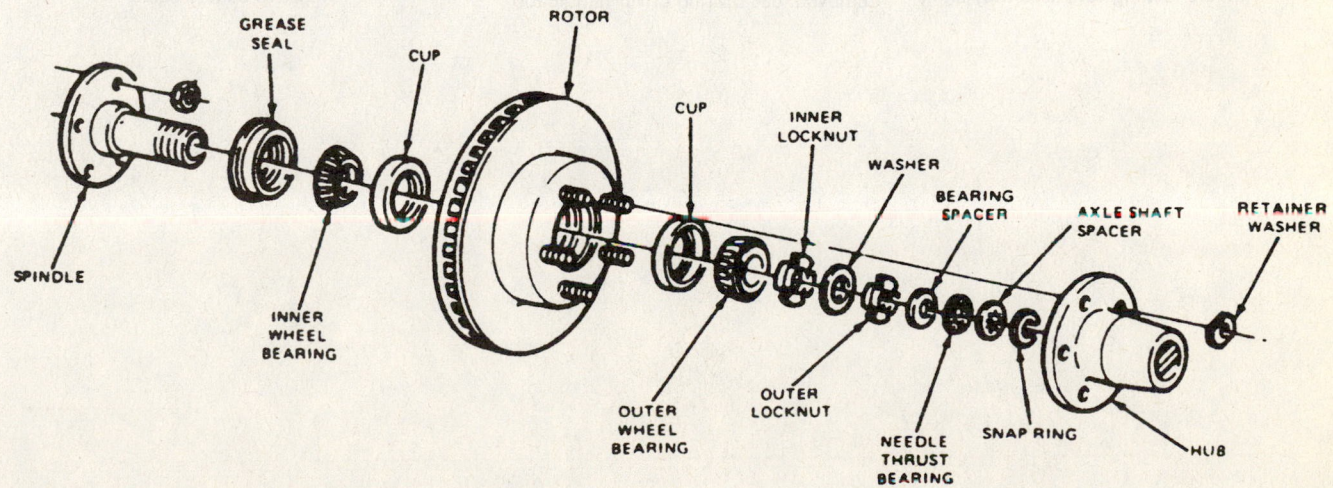

Exploded view of the wheel bearing and manual locking hub assembly

grade and type grease. If a bearing packer is not available work as much of the grease as possible between the rollers and cages.

8. Install or connect the following:
- Inner bearing cone and roller assembly in the inner cup. A light film of grease should be included between the lips of the new grease seal
- Grease seal by driving in place with Hub Seal Replacer tool T83T-1175-B and Driver Handle T80T-4000-W
- Hub and rotor assembly onto the spindle. Keep the hub centered on the spindle to prevent damage to the spindle and the retainer
- Outer bearing cone and roller assembly
- Rotor onto the spindle
- Outer wheel bearing in the rotor
- Inner adjusting nut with the pin facing out. Torque the nut to 35 ft. lbs. (47 Nm) to seat the bearings and adjust the bearing as needed
- Front wheel
- Negative battery cable

WITH AUTOMATIC LOCKING HUBS

1. Before servicing the vehicle, refer to the precautions in the beginning of this section.
2. Remove or disconnect the following:
- Negative battery cable
- Wheel assembly
- Retainer washers from the lug nut studs and remove the automatic locking hub assembly from the spindle
- Snapring and spacer from the end of the spindle shaft
- Pull the locking cam assembly and

the 2 plastic spacers off of the wheel bearing adjusting nut
3. Use a magnet and remove the locking key from under the adjusting nut. If required, rotate the adjusting nut slightly to relieve pressure against the locking key

✳✳ WARNING

To prevent damage to the adjusting nut and spindle threads on vehicles equipped with automatic hubs, look into the spindle keyway under the adjusting nut and remove the separate locking key before removing the adjusting nut.

- Wheel bearing locknut using a 2⅜ inch (60.3mm) hex socket, such as Hex Locknut Wrench T70T-4252-B
- Outer bearing cone and roller assembly from the hub
- Hub and rotor from the spindle
- Grease seal, using seal removal tool 1175-AC and discard
- Inner bearing cone and roller assembly from the hub

4. Clean the inner and outer bearing assemblies in solvent. Inspect the bearings and the cones for wear and damage. Replace defective parts, as required.
5. If the cups are worn or damaged, remove them with front hub remover tool T81P-1104-C and tool T77F-1102-A.
6. Wipe the old grease from the spindle. Check the spindle for excessive wear or damage. Replace defective parts, as required.

To install:

7. If the inner and outer cups were removed, use bearing driver handle tool

T80-4000-W and replace the cups. Be sure to seat the cups properly in the hub.

8. Use a bearing packer tool and properly repack the wheel bearings with the proper grade and type of grease. If a bearing packer is not available, work as much of the grease as possible between the rollers and cages. Also, grease the cone surfaces.
9. Install or connect the following:
- Inner bearing cone and roller assembly in the inner cup. A light film of grease should be included between the lips of the new grease seal.
- Grease seal by driving in place with Hub Seal Replacer tool T83T-1175-B and Driver Handle T80T-4000-W
- Hub and rotor assembly onto the spindle. Keep the hub centered on the spindle to prevent damage to the spindle and the retainer
- Outer bearing cone and roller assembly
- Rotor onto the spindle
- Outer wheel bearing in the rotor
- Adjusting nut. Torque the nut to 35 ft. lbs. (47 Nm) to seat the bearings. Adjust the bearing as needed.
- Thrust spacers and press the cam assembly on the locknut by aligning the key in the fixed cam with the keyway of the front spindle
- Axle shaft spacer
- Snapring on the end of the shaft
- Locking hub assembly over the front spindle
- Align the 3 hub legs to the cam pockets and install the retainer washers
- Wheel assembly
- Negative battery cable

FORD/MAZDA

Escape

PRECAUTIONS

Before servicing any vehicle, please be sure to read all of the following precautions, which deal with personal safety, prevention of component damage, and important points to take into consideration when servicing a motor vehicle:

• Never open, service or drain the radiator or cooling system when the engine is hot; serious burns can occur from the steam and hot coolant.

• Observe all applicable safety precautions when working around fuel. Whenever servicing the fuel system, always work in a well-ventilated area. Do not allow fuel spray or vapors to come in contact with a spark, open flame, or excessive heat (a hot drop light, for example). Keep a dry chemical fire extinguisher near the work area. Always keep fuel in a container specifically designed for fuel storage; also, always properly seal fuel containers to avoid the possibility of fire or explosion. Refer to the additional fuel system precautions later in this section.

• Fuel injection systems often remain pressurized, even after the engine has been turned **OFF**. The fuel system pressure must be relieved before disconnecting any fuel lines. Failure to do so may result in fire and/or personal injury.

• Brake fluid often contains polyglycol ethers and polyglycols. Avoid contact with the eyes and wash your hands thoroughly after handling brake fluid. If you do get brake fluid in your eyes, flush your eyes with clean, running water for 15 minutes. If eye irritation persists, or if you have taken brake fluid internally, IMMEDIATELY seek medical assistance.

• The EPA warns that prolonged contact with used engine oil may cause a number of skin disorders, including cancer! You should make every effort to minimize your exposure to used engine oil. Protective gloves should be worn when changing oil. Wash your hands and any other exposed skin areas as soon as possible after exposure to used engine oil. Soap and water, or waterless hand cleaner should be used.

• All new vehicles are now equipped with an air bag system, often referred to as a Supplemental Restraint System (SRS) or Supplemental Inflatable Restraint (SIR) system. The system must be disabled before performing service on or around system components, steering column, instrument panel components, wiring and sensors. Failure to follow safety and disabling procedures could result in accidental air bag deployment, possible personal injury and unnecessary system repairs.

• Always wear safety goggles when working with, or around, the air bag system. When carrying a non-deployed air bag, be sure the bag and trim cover are pointed away from your body. When placing a non-deployed air bag on a work surface, always face the bag and trim cover upward, away from the surface. This will reduce the motion of the module if it is accidentally deployed. Refer to the additional air bag system precautions later in this section.

• Clean, high quality brake fluid from a sealed container is essential to the safe and proper operation of the brake system. You should always buy the correct type of brake fluid for your vehicle. If the brake fluid becomes contaminated, completely flush the system with new fluid. Never reuse any brake fluid. Any brake fluid that is removed from the system should be discarded. Also, do not allow any brake fluid to come in contact with a painted surface; it will damage the paint.

• Never operate the engine without the proper amount and type of engine oil; doing so WILL result in severe engine damage.

• Timing belt maintenance is extremely important! Many models utilize an interference-type, non-freewheeling engine. If the timing belt breaks, the valves in the cylinder head may strike the pistons, causing potentially serious (also time-consuming and expensive) engine damage. Refer to the maintenance interval charts in the front of this manual for the recommended replacement interval for the timing belt, and to the timing belt section for belt replacement and inspection.

• Disconnecting the negative battery cable on some vehicles may interfere with the functions of the on-board computer system(s) and may require the computer to undergo a relearning process once the negative battery cable is reconnected.

• When servicing drum brakes, only disassemble and assemble one side at a time, leaving the remaining side intact for reference.

• Only an MVAC-trained, EPA-certified automotive technician should service the air conditioning system or its components.

ENGINE REPAIR

Distributor

The Escape uses a Direct Ignition System (DIS), no distributor is used.

Alternator

REMOVAL

2.0L Engine

Remove or disconnect the following:

• Negative battery cable
• Drive belt
• Alternator electrical connectors and loosen the upper alternator bolt while moving the alternator to the rear of the engine
• Alternator

3.0L Engine

Remove or disconnect the following:

• Negative battery cable
• Right side intermediate axle shaft
• Right side splash shield and retainers
• Drive belt
• Alternator electrical connectors
• Alternator

INSTALLATION

2.0L Engine

Install or connect the following:

• Alternator with the upper bolt in the alternator before installation. Torque the bolts to 18 ft. lbs. (25 Nm).
• Alternator electrical connectors
• Drive belt
• Negative battery cable

3.0L Engine

Install or connect the following:

• Alternator. Torque the bolts to 35 ft. lbs. (48 Nm).
• Alternator electrical connectors
• Drive belt
• Negative battery cable

Ignition Timing

ADJUSTMENT

Ignition timing is controlled by the Powertrain Control Module (PCM). No adjustment is necessary or possible.

Engine Assembly

REMOVAL & INSTALLATION

2.0L Engine

MANUAL TRANSMISSION

1. Before servicing the vehicle, refer to the precautions in the beginning of this section.
2. Properly recover the air conditioning system refrigerant.
3. Properly relieve the fuel system pressure.
4. Drain the cooling system.
5. Drain the engine oil.
6. Remove or disconnect the following:
   - Hood
   - Battery and battery tray
   - Air cleaner housing
   - Fuel lines
   - Throttle cable and speed control cable, if equipped
   - Exhaust Gas Recirculation (EGR) vacuum valve regulator
   - EGR electrical connectors and vacuum hoses
   - Brake booster vacuum hose
   - Powertrain Control Module (PCM) wire harness and ground
   - Wire harness connector
   - Power distribution board electrical connectors
   - Evaporative emissions (EVAP) canister vacuum lines
   - Upper radiator hose
   - Power steering line bracket
   - Upper power steering pump bolts
   - Coolant hose
   - Heater hoses
   - Speed control unit, if equipped
   - Catalytic converter
   - A/C compressor
   - Both halfshafts
   - Shifter linkages
   - Block heater electrical connector, if equipped
   - Front transmission through bolt
   - Engine-to-transmission bolts
   - Lower radiator hose
   - Power steering pump
   - Clutch slave cylinder line from the bracket and move it aside
   - Rear transmission mount
   - Left side transmission mount
   - Lower ground cable
   - Engine mount upper bracket
   - Engine and transmission as an assembly by using a proper lifting device
   - Alternator electrical connectors
   - Knock Sensor (KS) electrical connector
   - Oil pressure sender electrical connector
   - Starter electrical connector
   - Vehicle Speed Sensor (VSS) electrical connector
   - Park Neutral Position (PNP) electrical connector
   - Fuel charging wire harness electrical connector
   - PCM wire harness from the bracket
   - PCM ground wire
   - Back up lamp switch electrical connector
   - Wire harness
   - Differential Pressure Feedback (DPFEE) EGR sensor

7. Separate the engine from the transmission.
8. Lock the flywheel to the engine.
9. Clutch pressure plate and disc.
10. Flywheel and rear cover plates.

To install:

11. Install or connect the following:
   - Flywheel. Torque the bolts to 83 ft. lbs. (112 Nm).
   - Clutch disc to the flywheel
   - Pressure plate to the flywheel. Torque the bolts in the proper sequence to 18 ft. lbs. (25 Nm).
   - Transmission to the engine. Torque the bolts to 33 ft. lbs. (45 Nm).
   - Starter. Torque the bolts to 18 ft. lbs. (25 Nm).
   - Wire harness and attach it to the powertrain assembly
   - DPFEE sensor electrical connector
   - Reverse lamp switch electrical connector
   - Ground wire. Torque the bolt to 80 inch lbs. (9 Nm).
   - PCM wire harness to the bracket
   - Fuel charging wire harness electrical connector
   - PNP switch electrical connector
   - VSS electrical connector
   - KS, Oil pressure sender and starter electrical connector. Torque the fasteners to 9 ft. lbs. (12 Nm).
   - Alternator electrical connectors. Torque the fasteners to 71 inch lbs. (8 Nm).
   - Powertrain assembly in the vehicle
   - Left side transmission mount. Torque the side bolts to 41 ft. lbs. (55 Nm) and the center bolt to 66 ft. lbs. (90 Nm).
   - Engine mount upper bracket. Torque the side bolts to 72 ft. lbs. (98 Nm) and the center bolt to 57 ft. lbs. (77 Nm).
   - Ground wire. Torque the bolt to 25 ft. lbs. (34 Nm).
   - Rear transmission mount. Torque the bolts to 41 ft. lbs. (55 Nm).
   - Speed control unit, if equipped. Torque the bolts to 89 inch lbs. (10 Nm).
   - Power steering pump and hand tighten the bolts
   - Lower power steering line bracket. Torque the bolt to 89 inch lbs. (10 Nm).
   - Upper power steering line bolt. Torque the bolt to 15 ft. lbs. (20 Nm).

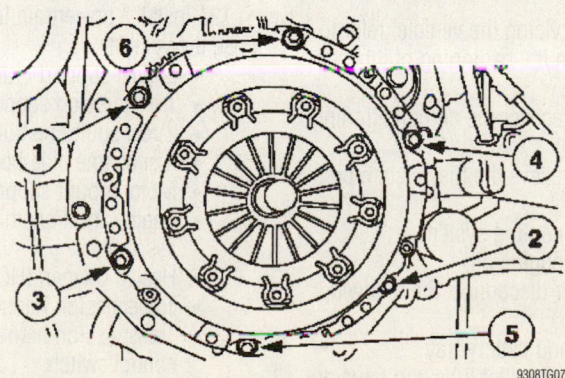

Tighten the pressure plate bolts in the proper sequence—2.0L engine

9308TG07

- Slave cylinder line and clip. Torque the bolts to 16 ft. lbs. (22 Nm).
- Power steering lines. Torque the retaining bolts to 89 inch lbs. (10 Nm). Torque the power steering pump bolts to 18 ft. lbs. (25 Nm).
- Lower radiator hose
- Engine-to-transmission bolts. Torque the bolts to 33 ft. lbs. (45 Nm).
- Front transmission through bolt. Torque the bolt to 66 ft. lbs. (90 Nm).
- Block heater electrical connector
- Shifter linkages. Torque the upper bolt to 33 ft. lbs. (45 Nm) and the lower bolt to 15 ft. lbs. (20 Nm).
- Coolant hose
- Catalytic converter
- Heater hoses
- Upper radiator hose
- EVAP canister vacuum lines
- Power distribution box electrical connector. Torque the fastener to 9 ft. lbs. (12 Nm).
- Wire harness electrical connector
- Ground wires
- PCM wire harness and ground
- Brake booster vacuum supply hose to the intake manifold
- EGR vacuum regulator valve hoses and electrical connector
- Throttle cable and speed control cable, if equipped
- Fuel lines
- Battery tray and battery
- Air cleaner
- Hood

12. Fill the engine with clean oil.
13. Fill and bleed the cooling system.
14. Recharge the A/C system.
15. Start the vehicle, check for leaks and repair if necessary.

3.0L Engine

1. Before servicing the vehicle, refer to the precautions in the beginning of this section.
2. Properly recover the air conditioning system refrigerant.
3. Properly relieve the fuel system pressure.
4. Drain the cooling system.
5. Drain the engine oil.
6. Remove or disconnect the following:
   - Hood
   - Battery and battery tray
   - Air cleaner outlet tube and housing
   - Lower radiator air deflectors
   - Fuel lines

- Water pump drive belt
- Accelerator cable and speed control cable, if equipped
- Vapor Management Valve (VMV)
- Powertrain Control Module (PCM)
- PCM ground wire
- Thermostat housing and hose assembly and move them aside
- Power distribution box electrical connector
- Power distribution box cover
- Nuts and cables from inside the power distribution box
- Transmission linkage
- Brake booster vacuum hose
- Heater hoses
- Power steering return line
- Power Steering Pressure (PSP) switch electrical connector
- Power steering supply line
- Oil level indicator
- Catalytic converter
- A/C compressor
- Both front wheels
- Intermediate drive shaft, if equipped

7. Separate both side ball joints.
8. Separate both side tie rod ends from the steering knuckles.
9. Separate both sway bar links from the strut mounts.
10. Separate the struts from the steering knuckles.
11. Remove or disconnect the following:

- Both wheel speed sensors, if equipped
- Brake calipers from the steering knuckles and properly support the struts
- Steering shaft from the rack
- Transmission line bracket bolt
- Transmission cooler lines
- Torque converter inspection cover
- Torque converter nuts
- Block heater wiring, if equipped

12. Install a powertrain lifting devise and raise the vehicle.

- Engine support bracket
- Transmission support
- 2 rear subframe bolts
- 2 subframe side bolts
- Motor mount support bolts
- Engine and transmission as an assembly
- Heated Oxygen (HO2S) sensor
- Transmission Range (TR) sensor
- Transmission harness electronic control switch
- Transmission control harness from the bracket
- Starter and wire harness

- Knock Sensor (KS) electrical connector
- Output Shaft Speed (OSS) sensor electrical connector
- HO2S sensor and Exhaust Gas Recirculation (EGR) tube from the exhaust manifold
- Alternator and electrical connectors
- Right side exhaust manifold and gasket
- Halfshaft support bracket and move it aside

13. Separate the engine from the transmission assembly

To install:

14. Install or connect the following:

- Powertrain assembly on the sub-frame
- Transmission-to-engine bolts. Torque the bolts to 30 ft. lbs. (40 Nm).
- Halfshaft bracket. Torque the bolts to 18 ft. lbs. (25 Nm).
- Right side exhaust manifold and new gasket. Torque the bolts to 15 ft. lbs. (25 Nm).
- Alternator. Torque the larger bolts to 18 ft. lbs. (25 Nm) and smaller bolt to 89 inch lbs. (10 Nm).
- EGR tube and HO2S sensor electrical connectors
- OSS sensor electrical connector
- KS jumper electrical connector
- Starter. Torque the bolts to 18 ft. lbs. (25 Nm).
- Transmission control harness to the bracket. Torque the bolt to 18 ft. lbs. (25 Nm).
- Transmission harness
- Transmission range sensor
- Powertrain assembly
- Motor mount support. Torque the bolts to 66 ft. lbs. (90 Nm).
- Subframe side nuts. Torque the nuts to 76 ft. lbs. (103 Nm). Raise the vehicle and support the power-train assembly with a lifting device.
- Transmission mount. Torque the bolts to side bolts to 66 ft. lbs. (90 Nm) and the other bolts to 76 ft. lbs. (103 Nm).
- Motor mount. Torque the bolts to side bolts to 66 ft. lbs. (90 Nm) and the other bolts to 76 ft. lbs. (103 Nm). Remove the powertrain lift.
- Block heater electrical connector, if equipped
- Torque converter. Torque the nuts to 27 ft. lbs. (37 Nm).
- Transmission cover plate and plug
- Transmission cooler lines

- Transmission cooler line bracket. Torque the bolt to 15 ft. lbs. (20 Nm).
- Steering shaft to the rack. Torque the bolt to 18 ft. lbs. (25 Nm).
- Struts to the steering knuckles. Torque the bolts to 75 ft. lbs. (102 Nm).
- Brake calipers to the steering knuckles
- Wheel speed sensors, if equipped. Torque the bolts to 89 inch lbs. (10 Nm).
- Sway bar links to the strut mount. Torque the bolts to 41 ft. lbs. (55 Nm).
- Tie rods to the steering knuckles. Torque the bolts to 41 ft. lbs. (55 Nm).
- Ball joints. Torque the bolts to 52 ft. lbs. (70 Nm).
- Intermediate drive shaft, if equipped
- Both front wheels
- A/C compressor
- Lower radiator air deflectors
- Catalytic converter
- Oil level indicator dipstick tube
- Power steering line and bracket. Torque the bolt to 13 ft. lbs. (17 Nm).
- PSP switch electrical connector
- Power steering return line
- Heater hoses
- Vacuum lines
- Transmission linkage
- Wire harness cables and nuts to the power distribution box. Torque the nuts to 89 inch lbs. (10 Nm).
- Power distribution box wire harness
- Thermostat housing and connect the hoses
- Ground wire. Torque the bolt to 89 inch lbs. (10 Nm).
- PCM electrical connector
- VMV electrical connector
- Accelerator cable and speed control cable, if equipped
- Air cleaner assembly
- Water pump drive belt
- Battery and tray

15. Fill and bleed the cooling system.
16. Fill the engine with clean oil.
17. Recharge the A/C system.
18. Inspect and top off the power steering fluid.
19. Start the vehicle, check for leaks and repair if necessary.

Water Pump

REMOVAL & INSTALLATION

2.0L Engine

1. Before servicing the vehicle, refer to the precautions in the beginning of this section.
2. Drain the cooling system.
3. Remove or disconnect the following:
   - Negative battery cable
   - Right front wheel
   - Splash shield
   - Drive belt
   - Water pump pulley
   - Water pump

To install:
4. Install or connect the following:
   - Water pump. Torque the bolts to 89 inch lbs. (10 Nm).
   - Water pump pulley. Torque the bolts to 89 inch lbs. (10 Nm).
   - Drive belt
   - Splash shield
   - Right front wheel
   - Negative battery cable
5. Refill the cooling system.
6. Start the vehicle and check for leaks, repair if necessary.

3.0L Engine

1. Before servicing the vehicle, refer to the precautions in the beginning of this section.
2. Drain the cooling system.
3. Remove or disconnect the following:
   - Negative battery cable
   - Air cleaner outlet tube
   - Water pump belt tensioner
   - Coolant hoses
   - Water pump
   - Water pump from the housing

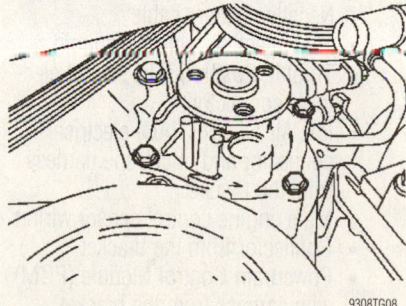

Exploded view of the water pump–2.0L engine

To install:
- Water pump to the housing. Torque the bolts to 89 inch lbs. (10 Nm).
- Water pump. Torque the bolts to 89 inch lbs. (10 Nm).
- Coolant hoses
- Water pump belt tensioner
- Air cleaner outlet tube
- Negative battery cable
4. Refill the cooling system.
5. Start the vehicle and check for leaks, repair if necessary.

Cylinder Head

REMOVAL & INSTALLATION

2.0L Engine

1. Before servicing the vehicle, refer to the precautions in the beginning of this section.
2. Properly relieve the fuel system pressure.
3. Drain the engine oil.
4. Remove or disconnect the following:
   - Negative battery cable
   - Ignition coil bracket
   - Thermostat housing
   - Positive Crankcase Ventilation (PCV) tube
   - Intake manifold
   - Exhaust manifold
   - Power steering bracket and move it aside
   - Valve tappets
   - Engine mount lower bracket
   - Engine mount upper bracket
   - Cylinder head bolts in the proper sequence and discard the gasket

To install:
5. Install a new head gasket and the cylinder head.

➡ **Refer to Section 1 of this manual for the cylinder head torque sequence illustration. The illustration is located after the Torque Specification Chart.**

6. Lubricate the cylinder head bolt threads.
7. Torque the cylinder head bolts in the proper sequence as follows:
   a. Step 1: 15 ft. lbs. (20 Nm).
   b. Step 2: 30 ft. lbs. (40 Nm).
   c. Step 3: Plus an additional 90 degrees.
8. Install or connect the following:
   - Engine mount upper bracket. Torque the 2 upper bolts to 72 ft.

Timing belt service is covered in Section 4 of this manual

lbs. (98 Nm) and the center bolt to 57 ft. lbs. (77 Nm).
- Engine mount lower bracket. Torque the bolts to 37 ft. lbs. (50 Nm).
- Valve tappets
- Power steering pump bracket. Torque the bolts to 20 ft. lbs. (28 Nm).
- Exhaust manifold
- Intake manifold
- PCV tube
- Thermostat housing
- Ignition coil bracket
- Negative battery cable

9. Fill the engine with clean oil and replace the filter.

10. Start the vehicle and check for leaks, repair if necessary.

3.0L Engine

The procedure for the left side cylinder head and right side are similar. Changes in the procedure will be noted for either side cylinder head.

1. Before servicing the vehicle, refer to the precautions in the beginning of this section.

2. Properly relieve the fuel system pressure.
- Drain the cooling system.

3. Remove or disconnect the following:
- Negative battery cable
- Camshaft
- Exhaust Gas Recirculation (EGR) tube, right side only
- Exhaust manifold
- Camshaft followers
- Hydraulic lash adjusters and matchmark them for proper installation
- Cylinder head bolts in sequence and discard them
- Cylinder head and discard the gasket

To install:

4. Install a new head gasket and the cylinder head.

➡ **Refer to Section 1 of this manual for the cylinder head torque sequence illustration. The illustration is located after the Torque Specification Chart.**

5. Lubricate the cylinder head bolt threads.

6. Torque the cylinder head bolts in the proper sequence as follows:
   a. Step 1: 30 ft. lbs. (40 Nm).
   b. Step 2: Additional 90 degrees.
   c. Step 3: Loosen the bolts one full turn.
   d. Step 4: 30 ft. lbs. (40 Nm).

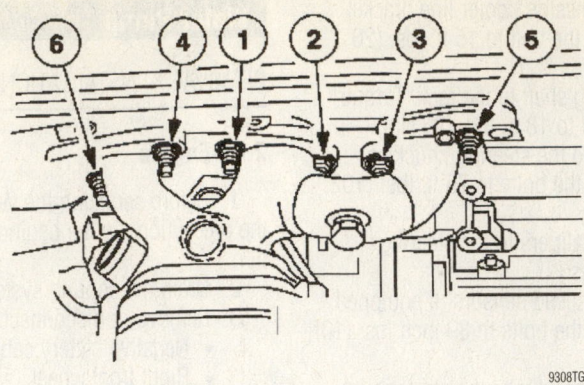

Right side exhaust manifold bolt torque sequence—3.0L engine

   e. Step 5: Plus an additional 90 degrees.
   f. Step 6: Plus an additional 90 degrees.

7. Install or connect the following:
- Hydraulic lash adjusters
- Camshaft followers
- Camshaft
- Exhaust manifold. Torque the bolts in sequence to 15 ft. lbs. (20 Nm), right side only
- EGR tube, right side only
- Coolant bypass tube
- Negative battery cable

8. Fill the coolant to the proper level.

9. Start the vehicle and check for leaks, repair if necessary.

Intake Manifold

REMOVAL & INSTALLATION

2.0L Engine

1. Before servicing the vehicle, refer to the precautions in the beginning of this section.

2. Properly relieve the fuel system pressure.

3. Remove or disconnect the following:
- Negative battery cable
- Fuel injection supply manifold
- Throttle Position (TP) sensor electrical connector
- Idle Air Control (IAC) electrical connector and unclip the harness from the bracket
- Main engine control sensor wiring
- Connector from the bracket
- Powertrain Control Module (PCM) wire harness from the bracket
- Brake booster vacuum hose
- 4 additional vacuum lines
- Positive Crankcase Ventilation (PCV) hose from the intake manifold

- Knock Sensor (KS) electrical connector
- Alternator
- Intake manifold and discard the gasket

4. Clean the mating surfaces.

To install:

➡ **Refer to Section 1 of this manual for the intake manifold torque sequence illustration. The illustration is located after the Torque Specification Chart.**

5. Install or connect the following:
- New gasket
- Intake manifold. Torque the bolts, in sequence, to 13 ft. lbs. (18 Nm).
- Alternator
- KS electrical connector
- PCV vacuum line
- 4 vacuum lines
- Brake booster vacuum supply hose
- PCM wire harness to the bracket
- Main engine control sensor wiring
- IAC valve electrical connector and attach the harness to the bracket
- TP sensor electrical connector
- Fuel injection supply manifold
- Negative battery cable

6. Start the vehicle and check for leaks, repair if necessary.

3.0L Engine

UPPER

1. Before servicing the vehicle, refer to the precautions in the beginning of this section.

2. Properly relieve the fuel system pressure.

Drain the coolant system.

3. Remove or disconnect the following:
- Negative battery cable
- Air cleaner outlet tube
- Engine appearance cover
- Throttle cable
- Speed control cable, if equipped

- Throttle cable bracket
- Throttle Position (TP) sensor electrical connector
- Idle Air Control (IAC) valve electrical connector
- Exhaust Gas Recirculation (EGR) valve vacuum hose and tube
- EGR vacuum regulator valve electrical connector and hose
- Chasis vacuum hose
- Engine vacuum hose
- Positive Crankcase Ventilation (PCV) hose
- Vapor Management Valve (VMV) vacuum hose
- Electrical connectors from the left side of the upper intake manifold
- Power Steering Pressure (PSP) sensor electrical connector
- Upper intake manifold and discard the gasket

4. Clean the mating surfaces.

To install:

➡**Refer to Section 1 of this manual for the intake manifold torque sequence illustration. The illustration is located after the Torque Specification Chart.**

5. Install or connect the following:
- New gasket
- Intake manifold. Torque the bolts, in sequence, to 89 inch lbs. (10 Nrn).
- PSP electrical connector
- Electrical connectors on the left side of the upper intake manifold
- VMV vacuum hose
- Chasis, engine and PCV hoses
- EGR valve vacuum regulator
- EGR valve vacuum hose and tube. Torque the nut to 30 ft. lbs. (40 Nm).
- TP sensor electrical connector
- IAC valve electrical connector
- Throttlle cable and speed control cable, if equipped. Torque the bracket bolts to 89 inch lbs. (10 Nm).
- Air cleaner outlet tube
- Engine appearance cover. Torque the bolts to 53 inch lbs. (6 Nm).
- Negative battery cable

6. Fill the coolant system to the proper level.

7. Start the vehicle and check for leaks, repair if necessary.

LOWER

1. Before servicing the vehicle, refer to the precautions in the beginning of this section.

2. Properly relieve the fuel system pressure.

3. Remove or disconnect the following:
- Negative battery cable
- Fuel line spring lock coupling
- Upper intake manifold
- Fuel rail
- Fuel injector electrical connectors
- Fuel pressure damper vacuum line
- Lower intake manifold
- Lower intake manifold from the fuel rail
- Fuel injectors from the manifold and discard the gasket

4. Clean the mating surfaces.

To install:

➡**Refer to Section 1 of this manual for the intake manifold torque sequence illustration. The illustration is located after the Torque Specification Chart.**

5. Inspect the fuel injector O-rings and replace if necessary.

6. Install or connect the following:
- Fuel injectors into the lower intake manifold
- Fuel rail. Torque the bolts to 89 inch lbs. (10 Nm).
- New gasket
- Intake manifold. Torque the bolts, in sequence, to 89 inch lbs. (10 Nm).
- Fuel rail electrical connectors
- Fuel injector electrical connectors
- Fuel pressure damper vacuum line
- Upper intake manifold
- Fuel line spring lock coupling
- Negative battery cable

7. Start the vehicle and check for leaks, repair if necessary.

Exhaust Manifold

REMOVAL & INSTALLATION

2.0L Engine

1. Before servicing the vehicle, refer to the precautions in the beginning of this section.

2. Remove or disconnect the following:
- Negative battery cable
- Catalytic converter
- Oil level indicator tube and bracket
- Exhaust manifold and discard the gasket

To install:

3. Clean the sealing surfaces of any old gasket material.

4. Install or connect the following:
- Exhaust manifold and new gasket. Torque the bolts to 12 ft. lbs. (16 Nm).
- Oil level indicator tube and bracket. Torque the bolt to 89 inch lbs. (10 Nm).
- Catalytic converter
- Negative battery cable

5. Start the vehicle and check for leaks, repair if necessary.

3.0L Engine

LEFT SIDE

1. Before servicing the vehicle, refer to the precautions in the beginning of this section.

2. Remove or disconnect the following:
- Negative battery cable
- Heated Oxygen (HO$_2$S) sensor and catalyst monitor
- Splash shield
- Exhaust crossover pipe
- Drive belt

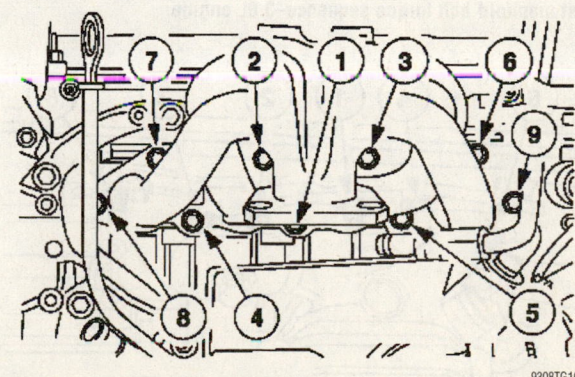

Exhaust manifold bolt torque sequence–2.0L engine

9308TG10

- A/C compressor and move it aside
- Exhaust manifold and discard the gasket

To install:

3. Clean the sealing surfaces of any old gasket material.

4. Install or connect the following:
- Exhaust manifold and new gasket. Torque the bolts to 15 ft. lbs. (20 Nm).
- A/C compressor. Torque the bolts to 18 ft. lbs. (20 Nm).
- Drive belt
- Exhaust crossover pipe. Torque the bolts to 30 ft. lbs. (40 Nm).
- Splash shield. Torque the bolts to 80 inch lbs. (9 Nm).
- Left side HO2S sensor and catalyst monitor
- Negative battery cable

5. Start the vehicle and check for leaks, repair if necessary.

RIGHT SIDE

1. Before servicing the vehicle, refer to the precautions in the beginning of this section.

2. Remove or disconnect the following:
- Negative battery cable
- Exhaust Gas Recirculation (EGR) tube

Left side exhaust manifold bolt torque sequence–3.0L engine

9308TG11

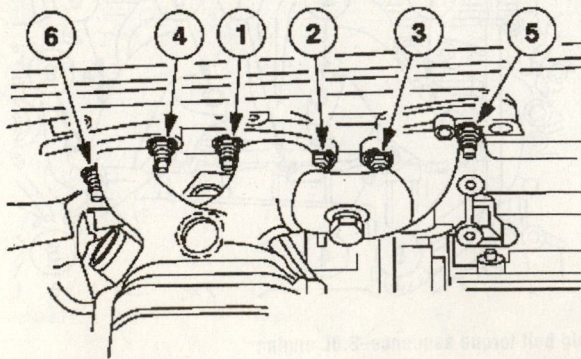

9308TG12

Right side exhaust manifold bolt torque sequence–3.0L engine

- Alternator
- Right side Heated Oxygen (HO2S) sensor
- Right side exhaust manifold and discard the gasket

To install:

3. Clean the sealing surfaces of any old gasket material.

4. Install or connect the following:
- Exhaust manifold and new gasket. Torque the bolts to 15 ft. lbs. (20 Nm).
- Right side HO2S sensor
- Alternator
- EGR tube
- Negative battery cable

5. Start the vehicle and check for leaks, repair if necessary.

Front Crankshaft Seal

REMOVAL & INSTALLATION

2.0L Engine

1. Before servicing the vehicle, refer to the precautions in the beginning of this section.

2. Remove or disconnect the following:
- Negative battery cable

- Timing belt
- Crankshaft sprocket and timing belt guide
- Crankshaft oil seal

➡**Be careful not to damage the seal surface of the cover.**

To install:

3. Install or connect the following:
- New front crankshaft oil seal
- Timing belt guide and crankshaft sprocket
- Timing belt
- Negative battery cable

4. Start the vehicle and check for leaks, repair if necessary.

3.0L Engine

1. Before servicing the vehicle, refer to the precautions in the beginning of this section.

2. Remove or disconnect the following:
- Negative battery cable
- Crankshaft pulley
- Front oil seal

To install:

3. Install or connect the following:
- New front crankshaft oil seal
- Crankshaft pulley
- Negative battery cable

4. Start the vehicle and check for leaks, repair if necessary.

Camshaft and Lifters

REMOVAL & INSTALLATION

2.0L Engine

1. Before servicing the vehicle, refer to the precautions in the beginning of this section.

2. Remove or disconnect the following:
- Negative battery cable
- Camshaft timing sprocket and verify the valve clearance
- Camshaft journal cap bolts by loosening them in several passes in the proper sequence
- Camshafts

3. Inspect the camshaft for wear and discard the oil seals

To install:

4. Install or connect the following:
- Camshaft cam followers, lubricate the bearing journals thoroughly. Torque the caps to 14 ft. lbs. (19 Nm).
- Exhaust camshaft oil seal
- Camshaft timing sprocket
- Negative battery cable

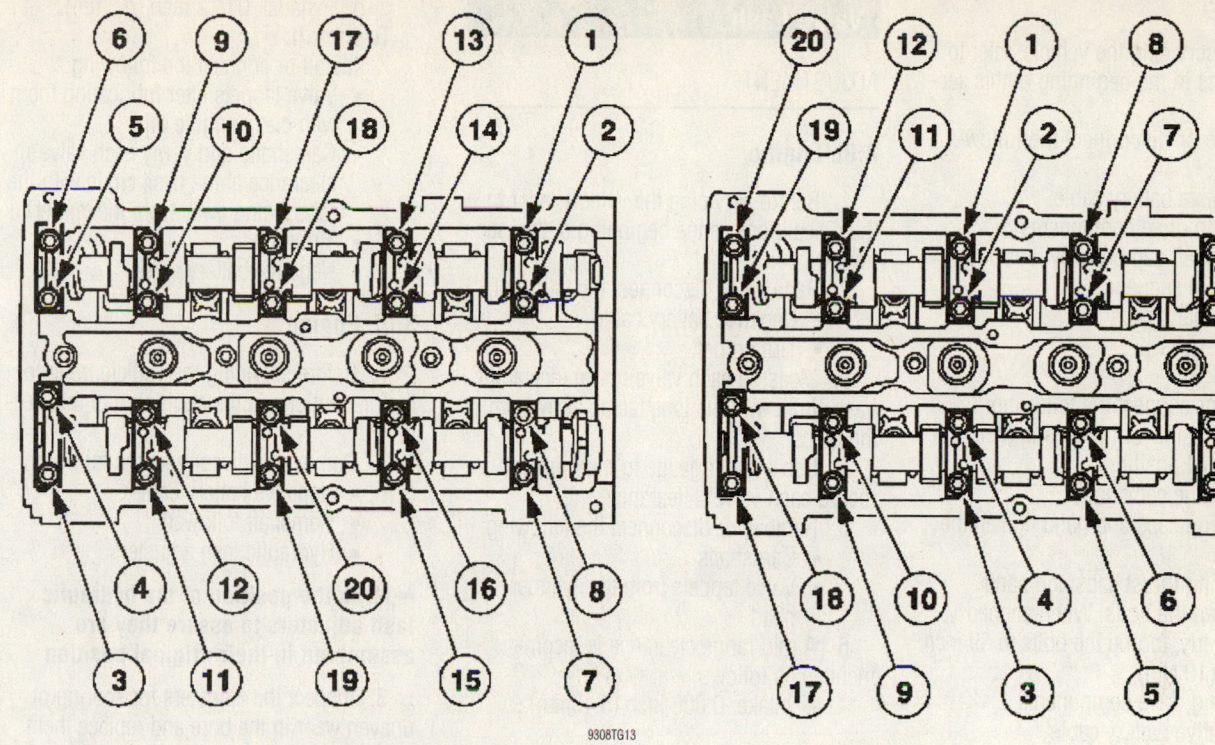

Remove the camshaft bearing caps in sequence–2.0L engine

Camshaft bearing cap tightening sequence–2.0L engine

3.0L Engine

LEFT SIDE

1. Before servicing the vehicle, refer to the precautions in the beginning of this section.

2. Remove or disconnect the following:
- Negative battery cable
- Water pump belt
- Timing drive components
- Camshaft oil seal
- Camshaft oil seal retainer
- Camshaft cap bolts by loosening them in sequence
- Camshafts

To install:

3. Install or connect the following:
- Camshaft bearing caps in their original position
- Align the camshafts
- Bearing thrust caps and hand tighten the bolts. When aligned properly, torque the bolts to 89 inch lbs. (10 Nm).
- Timing drive components
- Camshaft oil seal retainer
- Crankshaft oil seal
- Water pump drive pulley
- Water pump belt
- Negative battery cable

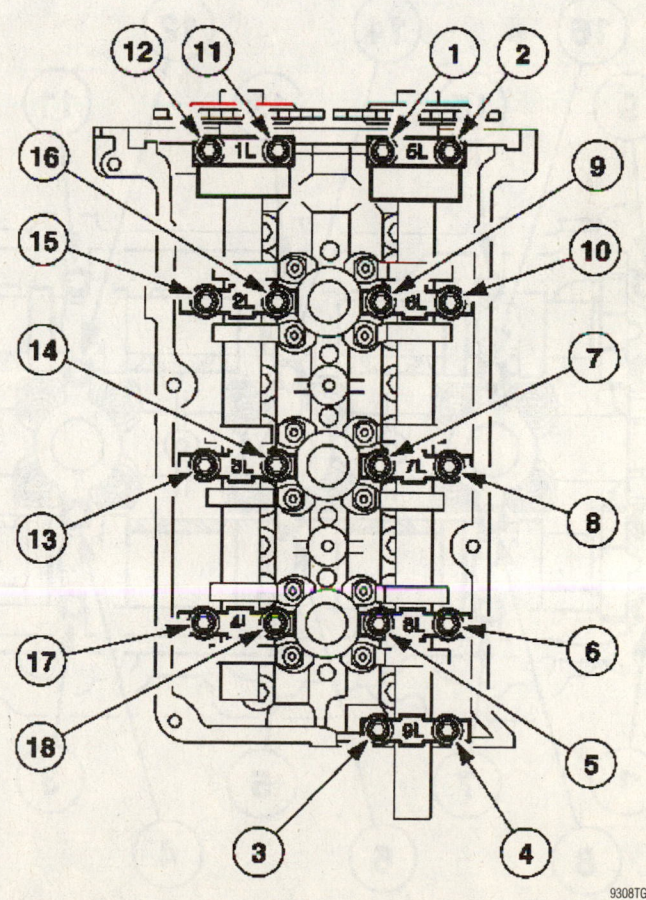

Remove and install the left side camshaft bearing caps in sequence–3.0L engine

Refer to Section 1 for engine rebuilding specifications

RIGHT SIDE

1. Before servicing the vehicle, refer to the precautions in the beginning of this section.

2. Remove or disconnect the following:
- Negative battery cable
- Timing drive components
- Camshaft cap bolts by loosening them in sequence
- Camshafts caps
- Camshafts

To install:

3. Install or connect the following:
- Camshaft bearing caps in their original position
- Align the camshafts
- Bearing caps and hand tighten the bolts
- Bearing thrust caps and hand tighten the bolts. When aligned properly, torque the bolts to 89 inch lbs. (10 Nm).
- Timing drive components
- Negative battery cable

Valve Lash

ADJUSTMENT

2.0L Engine

1. Before servicing the vehicle, refer to the precautions in the beginning of this section.

2. Remove or disconnect the following:
- Negative battery cable
- Timing belt

3. Measure each valve's clearance at the base circle with the lobe facing away from the tappet.

4. Use a feeler gauge to measure and record each valve's clearance

5. Remove or disconnect the following:
- Camshafts
- Valve tappets from the cylinder head

6. A mid range clearance is recommended as follows:
   a. Intake: 0.006 inch (0.15mm).
   b. Exhaust: 0.012 inch (0.3mm).

To install:

7. Install or connect the following:
- Valve tappets after lubricating them with clean engine oil
- Camshafts and verify each valve's clearance at the base circle with the lobe facing away from the tappet
- Timing belt
- Negative battery cable

3.0L Engine

1. Before servicing the vehicle, refer to the precautions in the beginning of this section.

2. Remove or disconnect the following:
- Negative battery cable
- Camshaft followers
- Hydraulic lash adjusters

➡**Mark the position of the hydraulic lash adjusters to assure they are assembled in their original position**

3. Inspect the adjusters for scoring or uneven wear in the bore and replace them as required.

To install:

4. Install or connect the following:
- Hydraulic lash adjusters after lubricating them with clean engine oil
- Camshaft followers
- Negative battery cable

Starter Motor

REMOVAL & INSTALLATION

2.0L Engine

1. Before servicing the vehicle, refer to the precautions in the beginning of this section.

2. Remove or disconnect the following:
- Negative battery cable
- Starter bolts
- Exhaust system, AWD vehicles only
- Halfshaft support bracket bolts
- Starter electrical connectors
- Starter

To install:

3. Install or connect the following:
- Starter. Torque bolts to 20 ft. lbs. (27 Nm).
- Starter electrical connectors
- Halfshaft support bracket. Torque the bolts to 11 ft. lbs. (15 Nm).
- Exhaust system on AWD vehicles. Torque the bolts to 18 ft. lbs. (25 Nm).
- Negative battery cable

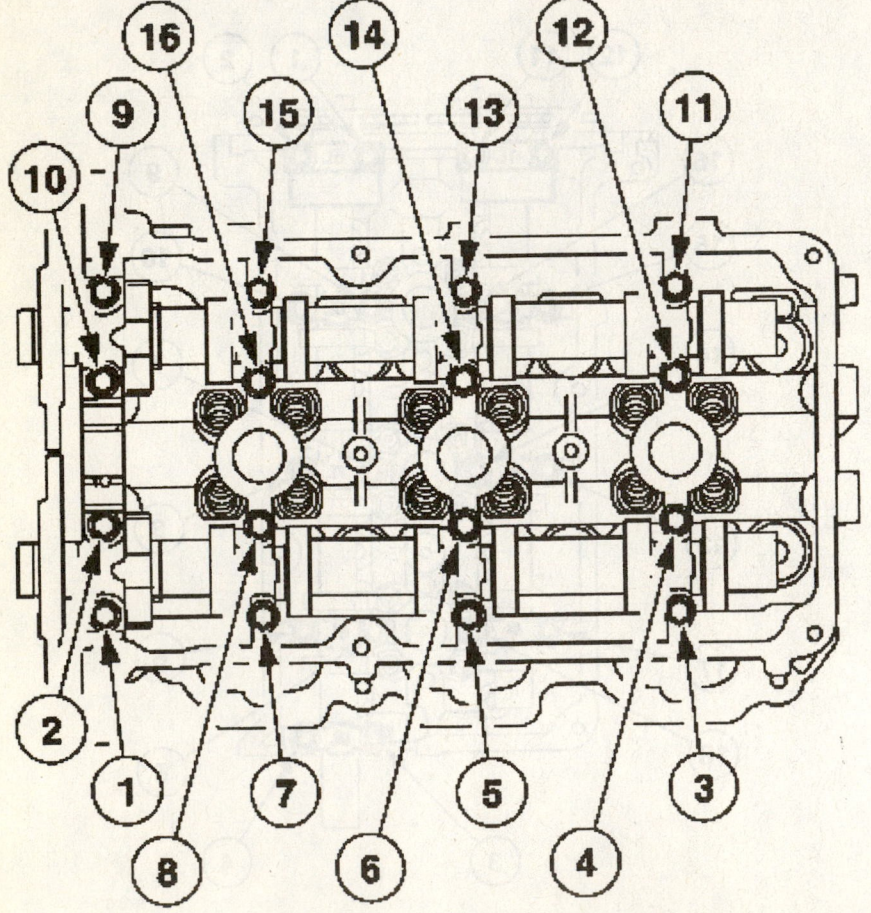

Remove and install the right side camshaft bearing caps in sequence–3.0L engine

9308TG16

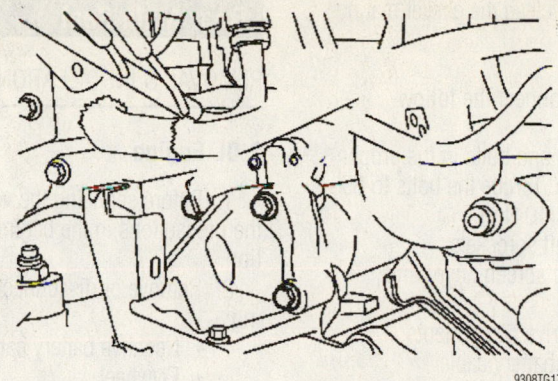

Removal of the starter motor–2.0L engine

3.0L Engine

1. Before servicing the vehicle, refer to the precautions in the beginning of this section.
2. Drain the cooling system.
3. Remove or disconnect the following:
   - Negative battery cable
   - Air cleaner outlet tube
   - Coolant hoses and move the thermostat aside
   - Starter electrical connectors
   - Starter

To install:

4. Install or connect the following:
   - Starter. Torque bolts to 20 ft. lbs. (27 Nm).
   - Starter electrical connectors and reposition the thermostat
   - Connect the 4 coolant hoses
   - Air cleaner outlet tube
   - Negative battery cable

5. Fill the cooling system to the proper level.
6. Start the vehicle and check for leaks, repair if necessary.

Oil Pan

REMOVAL & INSTALLATION

2.0L Engine

1. Before servicing the vehicle, refer to the precautions in the beginning of this section.
2. Drain the engine oil.
3. Support the powertrain assembly.
4. Remove or disconnect the following:
   - Negative battery cable
   - Catalytic converter
   - Oil pan and gasket

5. Thoroughly clean the gasket mating surfaces.

To install:

6. Apply silicone sealer to the oil pan.
7. Install a new gasket on the oil pan.
8. Oil pan. Torque the bolts in sequence to:

   a. Step 1: 53 inch lbs. (6 Nm).
   b. Step 2: 106 in lbs. (12 Nm).

9. Install or connect the following:

- Catalytic converter
- Negative battery cable

10. Fill the engine with clean oil.
11. Start the engine and check for leaks, repair if necessary.

3.0L Engine

1. Before servicing the vehicle, refer to the precautions in the beginning of this section.
2. Drain the engine oil.
3. Remove or disconnect the following:
   - Negative battery cable
   - Flexible exhaust pipe
   - Downstream catalyst monitor sensor
   - Oil pan and gasket

4. Thoroughly clean the gasket mating surfaces.

To install:

5. Apply silicone sealer to the oil pan.
6. Install or connect the following:
   - New gasket on the oil pan
   - Oil pan. Torque the bolts in sequence to 18 ft. lbs. (25 Nm).
   - Flexible exhaust pipe
   - Downstream catalyst monitor sensor
   - Negative battery cable

7. Fill the engine with clean oil.
8. Start the vehicle and check for leaks, repair if necessary.

Oil Pump

REMOVAL & INSTALLATION

2.0L Engine

1. Before servicing the vehicle, refer to the precautions in the beginning of this section.
2. Drain the engine oil.
3. Remove or disconnect the following:
   - Negative battery cable
   - Oil pan
   - Oil pump screen cover and tube
   - Oil pump and discard the gasket

4. Thoroughly clean the gasket mating surfaces.

To install:

5. Install or connect the following:
   - Oil pump screen cover and tube with a new gasket. Torque the bolts to 89 inch lbs. (10 Nm).
   - Oil pump to the oil pan
   - Oil pan
   - Negative battery cable

6. Refill the engine with clean oil.

Tighten the oil pan bolts in sequence–2.0L engine

For engine torque specifications, refer to Section 1 of this manual

7. Start the engine and check for leaks; repair if necessary.

3.0L Engine

1. Before servicing the vehicle, refer to the precautions in the beginning of this section.

2. Drain the engine oil.

3. Remove or disconnect the following:

- Negative battery cable
- Timing drive components
- Oil pump screen cover and tube
- Damper bolt and crankshaft sprockets
- Oil pump bolts in the proper sequence

4. Thoroughly clean the gasket mating surfaces.

To install:

5. Install or connect the following:

- Oil pump and bolts in the proper sequence. Torque the bolts to 89 inch lbs. (10 Nm).
- Crankshaft sprockets
- Oil pump screen cover and tube
- Timing drive components
- Negative battery cable

6. Refill the engine with clean oil.

7. Start the engine and check for leaks; repair if necessary.

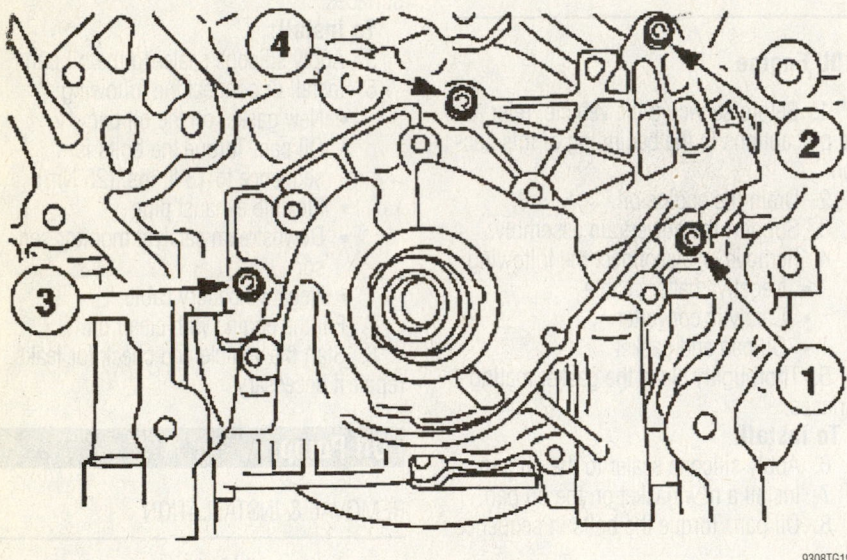

Remove the oil pump bolts in the proper sequence–3.0L engine

Install the oil pump bolts in the proper sequence–3.0L engine

Rear Main Seal

REMOVAL & INSTALLATION

2.0L Engine

1. Before servicing the vehicle, refer to the precautions in the beginning of this section.

2. Remove or disconnect the following:

- Negative battery cable
- Flywheel
- Rear main seal

To install:

3. Coat the oil seal with clean engine oil.

4. Install or connect the following:

- Crankshaft rear oil seal
- Flywheel
- Negative battery cable

3.0L Engine

1. Before servicing the vehicle, refer to the precautions in the beginning of this section.

2. Remove or disconnect the following:

- Negative battery cable
- Flexplate
- Rear main oil seal

To install:

3. Coat the oil seal with clean engine oil.

4. Install or connect the following:

- Crankshaft rear oil seal
- Flywheel
- Negative battery cable

Timing Gears, Front Cover and Seal

REMOVAL & INSTALLATION

3.0L Engine

1. Before servicing the vehicle, refer to the precautions in the beginning of this section.

2. Remove or disconnect the following:

- Negative battery cable
- Engine front cover
- Ignition pulse wheel and install a damper bolt
- Spark plugs

3. Rotate the crankshaft clockwise to position the keyway at the 11 o'clock posi-

tion and the camshafts in the correct positions. The No. 1 cylinder will be at Top Dead Center (TDC).

4. Rotate the crankshaft clockwise 120 degrees to the 3 o'clock position to locate the right side camshafts in the neutral position.

5. Remove or disconnect the following:
- Right side timing chain and tensioner
- Tensioner arm and timing chain guide

6. Rotate the crankshaft clockwise 2 times to position the keyway at the 11 o'clock position. This will position the left side camshafts in the neutral position.

7. Verify that the left side crankshafts are in the neutral position and mark the link position on the crankshaft sprocket.

8. Remove or disconnect the following:
- Left side timing chain and tensioner
- Tensioner arm and timing chain guide
- Damper bolt and crankshaft sprockets

To install:

9. Install the crankshaft sprockets.

10. Position the timing chain tensioner in a soft jaw vise. Hold the ratchet lock mechaisnt away from the ratchet stem and slowly compress the timing chain tensioner

11. If the timing marks on the chain are not visible, use a permanent marker to mark the left and right side timing chains. Mark the timing chains in the following sequence:

  a. Mark any link to use as the crankshaft timing mark.

  b. Count 29 links from the crankshaft timing mark and mark the link as the exhaust cam sprocket timing mark.

  c. Continue counting to 42 and mark the link as the intake sprocket timing mark

12. Install the guide. Torque the bolts to 18 ft. lbs. (25 Nm).

13. Install the left side timing chain and align the chain in the following sequence:

  a. Mark any link to use as the crankshaft timing mark.

  b. Count 29 links from the crankshaft timing mark and mark the link as the exhaust cam sprocket timing mark.

  c. Continue counting to 42 and mark the link as the intake sprocket timing mark

14. Install or connect the following:
- Left side timing chain and tensioner arm. Torque the bolts to 18 ft. lbs. (25 Nm).

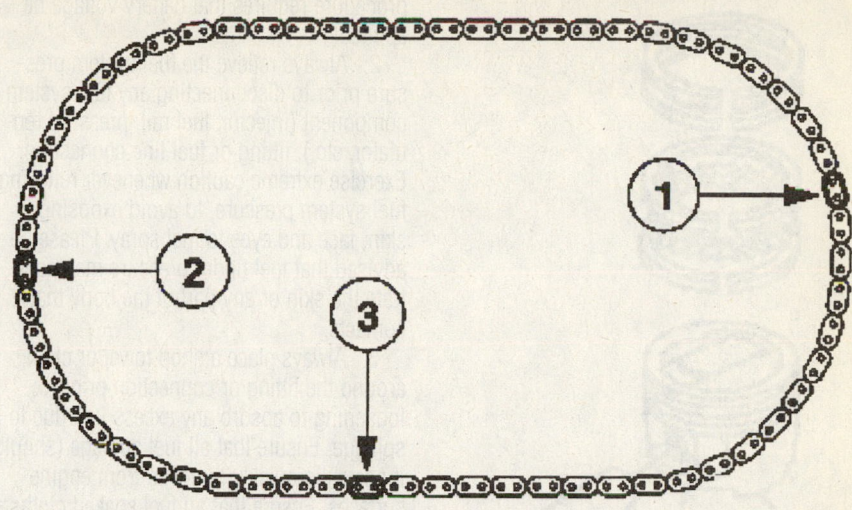

Mark the timing chain in the proper sequence–3.0L engine

- Crankshaft damper bolt and rotate the keyway to the 3 o'clock position

15. Verify that the right side camshafts are properly positioned and install the right side timing chain and guide. Torque the bolts to 18 ft. lbs. (25 Nm).

16. Make certain that the timing chain aligns with the marks on the camshaft and crankshaft sprockets

✳✳ CAUTION

Install the pulse wheel with the keyway in the slot stamped 20–25–34Y–30M (Color Blue).

17. Install or connect the following:
- Right side timing chain tensioner and arm. Torque the bolts to 18 ft. lbs. (25 Nm) and remove the damper bolt
- Ignition pulse wheel
- Spark plugs
- Engine front cover
- Negative battery cable

Piston and Ring

POSITIONING

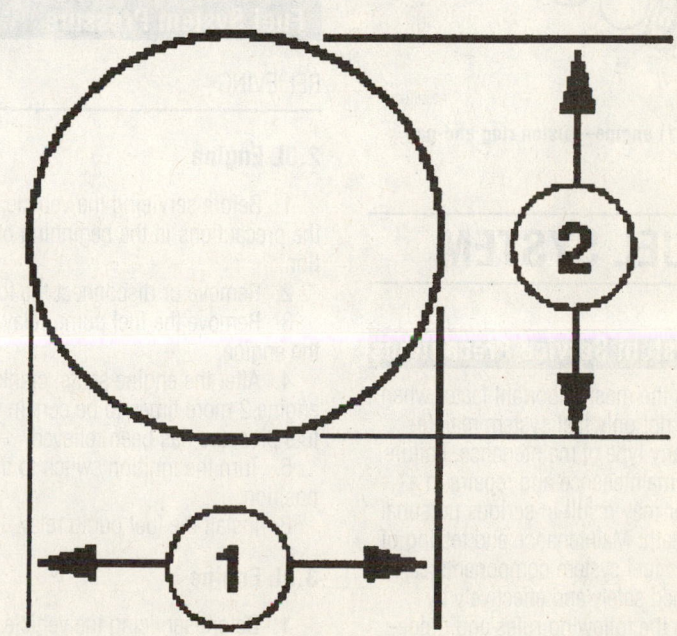

2.0L (VIN B) engine —piston ring end-gap spacing

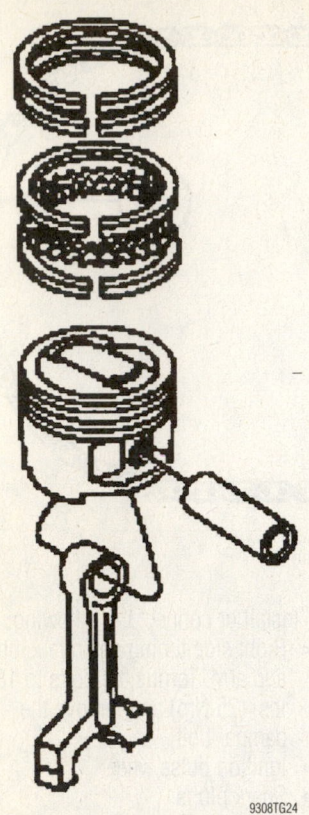

2.0L engine piston and connecting rod positioning ring end-gap spacing

9308TG24

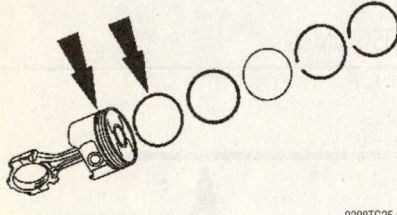

9308TG25

3.0L (VIN 1) engine—piston ring end-gap spacing

FUEL SYSTEM

Fuel System Service Precautions

Safety is the most important factor when performing not only fuel system maintenance but any type of maintenance. Failure to conduct maintenance and repairs in a safe manner may result in serious personal injury or death. Maintenance and testing of the vehicle's fuel system components can be accomplished safely and effectively by adhering to the following rules and guidelines.

1. To avoid the possibility of fire and personal injury, always disconnect the negative battery cable unless the repair or test procedure requires that battery voltage be applied.

2. Always relieve the fuel system pressure prior to disconnecting any fuel system component (injector, fuel rail, pressure regulator, etc.), fitting or fuel line connection. Exercise extreme caution whenever relieving fuel system pressure, to avoid exposing skin, face and eyes to fuel spray. Please be advised that fuel under pressure may penetrate the skin or any part of the body that it contacts.

3. Always place a shop towel or cloth around the fitting or connection prior to loosening to absorb any excess fuel due to spillage. Ensure that all fuel spillage (should it occur) is quickly removed from engine surfaces. Ensure that all fuel soaked cloths or towels are deposited into a suitable waste container.

4. Always keep a dry chemical (Class B) fire extinguisher near the work area.

5. Do not allow fuel spray or fuel vapors to come into contact with a spark or open flame.

6. Always use a backup wrench when loosening and tightening fuel line connection fittings. This will prevent unnecessary stress and torsion to fuel line piping.

7. Always replace worn fuel fitting O-rings with new. Do not substitute fuel hose or equivalent, where fuel pipe is installed.

Before servicing the vehicle, make sure to refer to the precautions in the beginning of this section as well.

Fuel System Pressure

RELIEVING

2.0L Engine

1. Before servicing the vehicle, refer to the precautions in the beginning of this section.

2. Remove or disconnect the following:

3. Remove the fuel pump relay and start the engine.

4. After the engine stalls, crank the engine 2 more times to be certain that all fuel pressure has been relieved.

5. Turn the ignition switch to the **OFF**-position.

6. Install the fuel pump relay.

3.0L Engine

1. Before servicing the vehicle, refer to the precautions in the beginning of this section.

2. Remove or disconnect the following:

3. Remove the schrader valve cap at the end of the fuel injection supply manifold and attach a fuel pressure gauge.

4. Open the manual valve slowly and drain the fuel into a suitable container.

5. Continue draining the fuel system to relieve fuel pressure.

Fuel Filter

REMOVAL & INSTALLATION

1. Before servicing the vehicle, refer to the precautions in the beginning of this section.

2. Properly relieve the fuel system pressure.

3. Remove or disconnect the following:
- Negative battery cable
- Fuel line to the fuel filter

4. Loosen the clamp and remove the filter

To install:

5. Install or connect the following:
- New clips to the fuel lines
- Fuel filter and tighten the clamp
- Fuel lines to the fuel filter
- Negative battery cable

6. Start the vehicle and check for leaks, repair if necessary.

Fuel Pump

REMOVAL & INSTALLATION

1. Before servicing the vehicle, refer to the precautions in the beginning of this section.

2. Properly relieve the fuel system pressure.

3. Remove or disconnect the following:
- Negative battery cable
- Gas cap to relieve any additional fuel pressure
- Left rear seat cushion and lift the access cover on the scuff plate
- Pin type retainers and move the carpet aside
- Screws from the fuel pump module access cover
- Fuel pump module electrical connectors
- Fuel and vapor lines from the fuel tank
- Fuel pump module and discard the gasket

To install:

4. Install or connect the following:
- New fuel pump module gasket
- Fuel pump module. Torque the module to 60 ft. lbs. (81 Nm).

- Fuel and vapor lines to the fuel tank
- Fuel pump module electrical connectors
- Fuel pump module access cover and tighten the screws securely
- Pin type retainers and reposition the carpet
- Left rear seat cushion
- Gas cap
- Negative battery cable

5. Start the engine and check for leaks, repair if necessary.

Fuel Injectors

REMOVAL & INSTALLATION

1. Before servicing the vehicle, refer to the precautions in the beginning of this section.
2. Release the fuel system pressure.
3. Remove or disconnect the following:
   - Negative battery cable
   - Fuel injection supply manifold
   - Retaining clips and gently twist the fuel injector out of the manifold
4. Check the O-rings and replace if damaged.

To install:

5. Install or connect the following:
   - Fuel injector(s) using new O-rings lubricated with clean engine oil
   - Fuel injector into the supply manifold
   - Retaining clips when the fuel injectors are seated properly
   - Fuel injection supply manifold
   - Negative battery cable
6. Start the vehicle and check for leaks, repair if necessary.

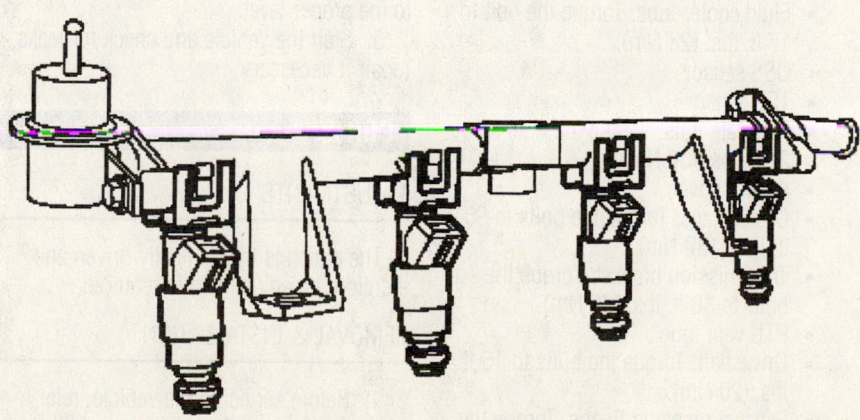

Remove the fuel injectors from the fuel supply manifold–2.0L engine

9308TG22

DRIVE TRAIN

Transmission Assembly

REMOVAL & INSTALLATION

Manual Transmission

1. Before servicing the vehicle, refer to the precautions in the beginning of this section.
2. Drain the transmission fluid.
3. Remove or disconnect the following:
   - Battery cables
   - Battery and tray
   - Mass Air Flow (MAF) sensor electrical connector
   - Accelerator cable from the air cleaner outlet tube
   - Emission management tube and hose
   - Crankcase ventilation hose
   - Air cleaner outlet tube
   - Air cleaner housing
   - Back-up lamp switch electrical connector
   - Front wire harness bracket and move it aside
   - Front wire harness bracket spacer
   - Wire harness from the rear harness bracket
   - Park Neutral Position (PNP) electrical connector
   - Rear wire harness bracket and move it aside
   - Vehicle Speed Sensor (VSS) electrical connector
   - Clutch slave cylinder line from the

bracket and move it aside while properly supporting the engine
   - Left side transmission support insulator and bracket
   - Rear transmission support insulator
   - Front transmission support insulator and bracket
   - Starter and move it aside
   - Top transmission flywheel housing bolts
   - Front transmission flywheel housing bolts
   - Transfer case, if equipped
   - Left side halfshaft
   - Rear transmission support insulator bracket
   - Shifter linkage and stabilizer bar
   - Transverse crossmember
   - Front to aft crossmeber
   - Left side splash shield and properly support the transmission
   - Remaining transmission flywheel housing bolts
   - Transmission and separate the right side halfshaft from the transmission

To install:

4. Align the right side half shaft to the transmission and position the transmission to the engine.
5. Install or connect the following:
   - Transmission flywheel housing bolts. Torque the bolts to 33 ft. lbs. (45 Nm) and remove the transmission support
   - Left side splash shield
   - Front-to-aft crossmember. Torque the bolts to 66 ft. lbs. (90 Nm).
   - Transverse crossmember. Torque the bolts to 85 ft. lbs. (115 Nm).
   - Shifter linkage. Torque the bolt to 15 ft. lbs. (20 Nm).
   - Stabilizer bar. Torque the bolt to 30 ft. lbs. (40 Nm).
   - Rear transmission support bracket. Torque the bolts to 66 ft. lbs. (90 Nm).
   - Left side halfshaft
   - Transfer case, If equipped
   - Front transmission flywheel housing bolts. Torque the bolts to 33 ft. lbs. (45 Nm).
   - Top transmission flywheel housing bolts. Torque the bolts to 33 ft. lbs. (45 Nm).
   - Starter. Torque the bolts to 33 ft. lbs. (45 Nm).
   - Front transmission support insulator and bracket. Torque the lower bolt to 66 ft. lbs. (90 Nm) and the 3 upper bolts to 41 ft. lbs. (55 Nm).

- Rear transmission support insulator bolt. Torque the bolt to 66 ft. lbs. (90 Nm).
- Left side transmission support insulator bracket. Torque the bolts to 66 ft. lbs. (90 Nm).
- Left side transmission support insulator. Torque the large bolt to 66 ft. lbs. (90 Nm) and the 3 remaining bolts to 41 ft. lbs. (55 Nm).
- Clutch slave cylinder. Torque the bolt to 15 ft. lbs. (20 Nm).
- Clutch slave cylinder line to the bracket and install the retaining clip
- VSS electrical connector
- Rear wire harness bracket. Torque the bolts to 80 inch lbs. (9 Nm).
- PNP switch electrical connector
- Wire harness to the rear bracket
- Front wire harness bracket spacer and bracket. Torque the bolt to 9 ft. lbs. (12 Nm).
- Back-up lamp switch electrical connector
- Air cleaner housing
- MAF sensor electrical connector
- Air cleaner outlet tube
- Crankcase ventilation hose
- Emission management tube and hose
- Accelerator cable to the air cleaner outlet tube
- Battery and tray
- Both battery cables

6. Fill the transmission to the proper level.

7. Start the vehicle and check for leaks, repair if necessary.

Automatic Transmission

1. Before servicing the vehicle, refer to the precautions in the beginning of this section.

2. Remove or disconnect the following:
- Battery cables
- Battery and tray
- Breather tube
- Mass Air Flow (MAF) sensor
- Intake tube and air cleaner cover
- Air cleaner assembly
- Transmission Range (TR) sensor
- Heated Oxygen (HO2S) sensors
- Transmission harness connector and bracket
- Wire harness bracket spacer and move the bracket aside
- Shift cable
- Shift cable bracket and move the bracket aside

- Starter electrical connectors
- Starter
- Electrical connectors from the valve cover and install an engine support bar
- Upper transmission retaining bolts
- Left side upper transmission mounting plate
- Rear transmission mount
- Right side engine mount bolt and slightly raise the engine
- Both front wheels and splash shields
- Right side halfshaft and intermediate shaft assembly after matchmarking them
- Cross brace
- Center exhaust pipe and rubber hanger
- Front exhaust pipe and flange
- Rear exhaust pipe flange
- Driveshaft
- PTU vent tube
- Lower transmission bracket
- Access cover
- Flexplate nuts
- Output Shaft Speed (OSS) sensor
- Turbine Shaft Speed (TSS) sensor
- Fluid cooler tube and move it aside
- Fluid cooler line and install a transmission jack
- Bolts from the PTU unit
- Transmission with the PTU unit attached

To install:

3. Install or connect the following:
- Transmission with the PTU unit. Torque the engine-to-transmission mounting bolts to 30 ft. lbs. (40 Nm).
- Fluid cooler line. Torque the fastener to 17 ft. lbs. (23 Nm) and remove the transmission jack.
- Fluid cooler tube. Torque the bolt to 17 ft. lbs. (23 Nm).
- OSS sensor
- TSS sensor
- Flexplate nuts. Torque the nuts to 27 ft. lbs. (36 Nm).
- Access cover
- Cross brace. Torque the bolts to 96 ft. lbs. (130 Nm).
- Transmission bracket. Torque the bolts to 30 ft. lbs. (40 Nm).
- PTU vent tube
- Driveshaft. Torque the bolts to 15 ft. lbs. (20 Nm).
- Exhaust pipe and flange. Torque the bolts to 21 ft. lbs. (29 Nm).
- Exhaust pipe and rubber hanger.

Torque the bolts to 21 ft. lbs. (29 Nm).
- Left side halfshaft assembly
- Right side halfshaft and intermediate shaft assembly by aligning the matchmarks
- Splash shields
- Both front wheels and lower the engine on to the right side engine mount
- Right side engine mount bolt. Torque the bolt to 89 ft. lbs. (120 Nm).
- Rear transmission mount. Torque the upper bolt to 89 ft. lbs. (120 Nm) and the lower bolts to 35 ft. lbs. (45 Nm).
- Transmission mount assemble. Torque the bolts to 30 ft. lbs. (40 Nm) and remove the engine support bar.
- Electrical connectors to the valve cover
- Starter. Torque the bolts to 20 ft. lbs. (27 Nm).
- Starter electrical connectors
- Shifter cable and bracket. Torque the bolt to 14 ft. lbs. (19 Nm) and connect the shifter cable.
- Wire harness and install the harness bracket spacer
- Wire harness bracket. Torque the bolt to 89 inch lbs. (10 Nm).
- HO2S sensor
- TR sensor and make certain it is properly aligned
- Air cleaner assembly
- Intake tube and air cleaner cover
- Breather tube
- MAF sensor
- Battery tray
- Battery and cables

4. Fill the transmission with clean fluid to the proper level.

5. Start the vehicle and check for leaks, repair if necessary

Clutch

ADJUSTMENTS

The clutch is hydraulically driven and therefore no adjustment is required.

REMOVAL & INSTALLATION

1. Before servicing the vehicle, refer to the precautions in the beginning of this section.

2. Remove or disconnect the following:

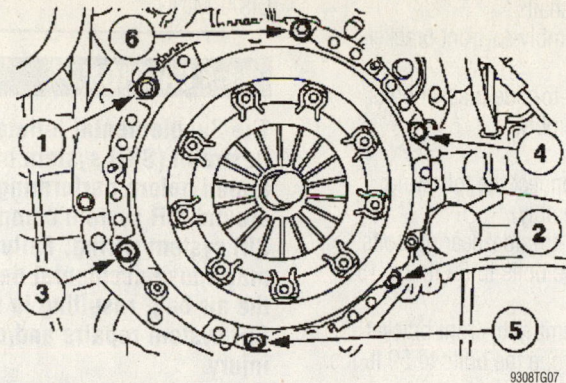

Torque the pressure plate bolts in the proper sequence

9308TG07

- Negative battery cable
- Transmission and lock the flywheel to the engine with special tool 303–103
- Pressure plate bolts by loosening them evenly
- Clutch pressure plate and disc

3. Clean the pressure plate and inspect it for burn marks, scores, flatness or ridges, replace if damaged.

4. Inspect the pressure plate diaphragm finger for wear, replace if damaged.

5. Measure the depth of the rivet heads. Minimum depth is 0.012 inch (0.3mm).

6. Inspect the clutch disc for signs of wear and replace if needed.

7. Check the clutch disc runout. Replace the disc if not with specification: 0.027 inch (0.7mm).

To install:

8. Install or connect the following:
- Clutch disc to the flywheel
- Pressure plate to the flywheel. Torque the bolts in sequence to 21 ft. lbs. (29 Nm).
- Transmission
- Negative battery cable

9. Check the transmission fluid level and top off if necessary.

Hydraulic Clutch System

BLEEDING

The following procedure is recommended for bleeding the clutch hydraulic system installed on the vehicle. It is recommended that the original clutch tube, with quick-connect fitting be replaced when servicing the hydraulic system, because air can be trapped in the quick-connect fitting and prevent complete bleeding of the system.

1. Before servicing the vehicle, refer to the precautions in the beginning of this section.

2. Clean the dirt and grease from the dust cap.

3. Remove the cap and diaphragm and fill the reservoir ¾ of the way with approved brake fluid C6AZ-19542-AB or DOT 3 equivalent fluid (ESA-M6C25-A).

4. Loosen the bleeder screw cover from the slave cylinder and attach a hose to the screw.

5. Place the hose in a container and slowly pump the clutch pedal several times.

6. With the clutch pedal depressed, loosen the bleeder screw to release the fluid and air.

7. Remove the hose and tighten the bleeder screw.

8. Repeat this procedure until all the air is removed from the hydraulic system.

Transfer Case

REMOVAL & INSTALLATION

3.0L Engine

1. Before servicing the vehicle, refer to the precautions in the beginning of this section.

Place the transmission in the NEUTRAL position.

2. Remove or disconnect the following:
- Negative battery cable
- Driveshaft
- Intermediate shaft
- Exhaust crossover pipe
- Right side exhaust manifold
- Heat shield
- Lower bracket
- Crossmember brace
- Transfer case bolts and vent tube
- Transfer case

To install:

3. Install or connect the following:
- Transfer case with a new driven gear seal. Torque the bolts to 33 ft. lbs. (45 Nm).
- Transver case vent tube
- Crossmember brace. Torque the bolts to 30 ft. lbs. (40 Nm).
- Lower bracket. Torque the bolts to 30 ft. lbs. (40 Nm).
- Exhaust manifold
- Heat shield. Torque the bolts to 10 ft. lbs. (14 Nm).
- Exhaust crossover pipe
- Intermediate shaft
- Driveshaft
- Negative battery cable

4. Check the transfer case fluid level and top off if necessary.

5. Start the vehicle and check for leaks, repair if necessary.

Halfshaft

REMOVAL & INSTALLATION

1. Before servicing the vehicle, refer to the precautions in the beginning of this section.

2. Place the transmission in the PARK position.

3. Remove or disconnect the following:
- Negative battery cable
- Front wheel
- Front brake disc
- Front axle wheel hub nut and discard the nut
- Tie rod end and separate the lower ball from the steering knuckle
- Halfshaft from the steering knuckle
- Halfshaft

To install:

4. When seated properly, the halfshaft bearing retainer circlip will snap into the differential side gear groove.

5. Position the halfshaft and joint so that the splines align with differential side gear splines. Push the halfshaft into side gear.

6. Install or connect the following:
- Halfshaft into the steering knuckle
- Lower ball joint to steering knuckle. Torque the pinch bolt to 52 ft. lbs. (70 Nm).
- Tie rod end. Torque the nut to 41 ft. lbs. (55 Nm).
- New front axle wheel hub nut. Torque the nut to 214 ft. lbs. (290 Nm).
- Front brake disc
- Front wheel
- Negative battery cable

7. Check the fluid level and adjust as needed.

CV-Joints

OVERHAUL

1. Before servicing the vehicle, refer to the precautions in the beginning of this section.
2. Remove or disconnect the following:
   - Negative battery cable
   - Halfshaft and secure it in a soft-jawed vise
   - Inboard halfshaft boot clamp
   - Boot from the inboard CV-joint housing
   - Tripod joint from the CV-joint housing and matchmark the tripod joint to the halfshaft
   - Snapring and boot from the halfshaft
   - Outboard halfshaft boot clamps
   - Outboard boot back to expose the CV-joint and matchmark the joint to the halfshaft
   - Outboard CV-joint from the halfshaft
   - Halfshaft retainer circlip and discard it
   - Boot from the halfshaft

To install:

3. Install or connect the following:
   - Outboard CV-joint and boot
   - New halfshaft bearing circlip
   - Inboard CV-joint to the halfshaft
   - Outboard halfshaft boot forward on to the ourtboard CV-joint
   - New outboard halfshaft boot clamps
   - Inboard halfshaft boot
   - Tripod joint on the halfshaft by aligning the matchmarks
   - New snapring to the tripod joint and lubricate the needle bearings while filling the housing with CV-joint grease, E43Z–19590–A
   - Inboard halfshaft boot with new clamps
   - Halfshaft
   - Negative battery cable

Axle Housing

REMOVAL & INSTALLATION

1. Before servicing the vehicle, refer to the precautions in the beginning of this section.
2. Remove or disconnect the following:
   - Negative battery cable
   - Rotary blade coupling
   - Rear halfshafts
   - Axle assembly-to-front bracket bolts
   - Rear axle-to-side bracket bolts
   - Axle assembly

To install:

3. Install or connect the following:
   - Axle assembly
   - Rear axle-to-side-bearing bolts. Torque the bolts to 59 ft. lbs. (80 Nm).
   - Axle assembly-to-front bracket bolts. Torque the bolts to 59 ft. lbs. (80 Nm).
   - Rotary blade coupling
   - Negative battery cable

STEERING AND SUSPENSION

Air Bag

✳✳ CAUTION

Some vehicles are equipped with an air bag system. The system MUST BE disabled before performing service on or around system components, steering column, instrument panel components, wiring and sensors. Failure to follow safety and disabling procedures could result in accidental air bag deployment, possible personal injury and unnecessary system repairs.

PRECAUTIONS

Several precautions must be observed when handling the inflator module to avoid accidental deployment and possible personal injury:

1. Never carry the inflator module by the wires or connector on the underside of the module.
2. When carrying a live inflator module, hold securely with both hands and ensure that the bag and trim cover are pointed away.
3. Place the inflator module on a bench or other surface with the bag and trim cover facing up.
4. With the inflator module on the bench, never place anything on or close to the module, which may be thrown in the event of an accidental deployment.

DISARMING

✳✳ CAUTION

The Supplemental Inflatable Restraint (SIR) system must be disarmed before performing service around SIR system components or SIR system wiring. Failure to do so may cause accidental deployment of the air bag, resulting in unnecessary SIR system repairs and/or personal injury.

The positive battery cable must be disconnected for a minimum of 1 minute before beginning any air bag work to de-energize the back-up power supply. It is a good idea to disengage both the positive and negative battery cables to ensure that the Air Bag system is definitely discharged.

ARMING THE SYSTEM

✳✳ WARNING

If the air bag simulators have been used, the air bag simulators must be removed and the air bags reconnected when the system is reactivated to avoid non-deployment in a collision resulting in possible personal injury.

1. Disconnect the positive battery cable.
2. Wait 1 minute, this is required for the back-up power supply in the air bag diagnostic monitor to deplete its stored energy.
3. Remove the air bag simulator from the air bag sliding contact connector at the top of the steering column. Reconnect the driver's side air bag module assembly. Position the driver's air bag module on the steering wheel and secure with the 2 bolts and washers. Tighten the bolt and washer assembly to 8–10 ft. lbs. (10–14 Nm).
4. Connect the positive battery cable.
5. Turn the ignition switch from the **OFF** to **RUN** and visually monitor the air bag warning indicator. The light will illuminate continuously for approximately 6 seconds and then turn off. If a fault occurs, the air bag indicator will either fail to light, remain lighted continuously or flash. The flashing may not occur until approximately 30 seconds after the ignition switch has been turned from **OFF** to **RUN**. This is the time needed for the air bag diagnostic monitor to complete testing the system. If the air bag indicator is inoperative, an air bag system fault exists, a tone will sound in a pattern of

5 sets of 5 beeps. If this occurs, the air bag indicator will need to be serviced before further diagnostics can be done.

Steering Gear

REMOVAL & INSTALLATION

1. Before servicing the vehicle, refer to the precautions in the beginning of this section.

2. Place the steering wheel in the straight-ahead position. Lock the steering wheel in place, using a steering wheel holder.

➡**Locking the steering wheel keeps the clockspring in alignment position.**

3. Drain the power steering fluid.
4. Remove or disconnect the following:
   - Negative battery cable
   - Rear transmission insulator
   - Rear transmission insulator bracket, if equipped with an automatic transmission
   - Both front wheels
   - Rear transmission insulator bracket, if equipped with a manual transmission
   - Tie rod end cotter pin and nut
   - Tie rod end from the steering knuckle and record the number of turns required to remove the tie rod end
   - Steering gear coupling pinch bolt
   - Power steering pressure and return lines and bracket
   - Steering gear mounting bolts
   - Steering gear and separate the steering coupling from the steering gear shaft
   - Steering gear

To install:

5. Slide the steering gear rearward to connect the steering coupling to the steering gear shaft

6. Install or connect the following:
   - Steering gear mounting bolts. Torque the bolts to 93 ft. lbs. (126 Nm).
   - Pressure and return lines and bracket. Torque the bracket bolts to 89 inch lbs. (10 Nm).
   - Power steering pressure and return lines to the steering gear. Torque the bolt to 18 ft. lbs. (25 Nm).
   - Steering gear pinch bolt and reposition the boot. Torque the bolt to 18 ft. lbs. (25 Nm).

- Tie rod end to the tie rod using the number of turns required to remove the tie rod end
- Jam nuts. Torque the nuts to 35 ft. lbs. (47 Nm).
- Tie rod end to the steering knuckle. Torque the nut to 41 ft. lbs. (57 Nm) and install a new cotter pin
- Rear transmission insulator bracket. Torque the bolts to 66 ft. lbs. (90 Nm).
- Both front wheels
- Rear transmission insulator bracket. Torque the bolts to 66 ft. lbs. (90 Nm).
- Rear transmission insulator. Torque the bolts to 66 ft. lbs. (90 Nm).
- Negative battery cable

7. Fill and bleed the power steering system.

8. Start the vehicle and check for leaks, repair if necessary.

9. Check and adjust the front end alignment.

Strut

REMOVAL & INSTALLATION

1. Before servicing the vehicle, refer to the precautions in the beginning of this section.

2. Install or connect the following:
   - Negative battery cable
   - Front wheel
   - Brake hose grommet from the bracket
   - Antilock Brake System (ABS) harness from the strut assembly and move the brake hose bracket aside
   - Stabilizer bar link nut and move the bar aside
   - Strut to steering knuckle bolts and support the strut assembly
   - Upper strut nuts
   - Strut and coil spring assembly

To install:

3. Install or connect the following:
   - Strut and spring assembly. Torque the upper nuts to 59 ft. lbs. (80 Nm).
   - Lower strut assembly to the steering knuckle. Torque the lower bolts to 85 ft. lbs. (115 Nm).
   - Stabilizer bar into position. Torque the bolts to 35 ft. lbs. (48 Nm).
   - Brake hose bracket. Torque the bolts to 14 ft. lbs. (18 Nm).
   - ABS harness to the strut assembly, if equipped

- Brake hose grommet to the bracket
- Front wheel
- Negative battery cable

Shock Absorber

REMOVAL & INSTALLATION

1. Before servicing the vehicle, refer to the precautions in the beginning of this section.

2. Remove or disconnect the following:
   - Negative battery cable
   - Rear quarter trim panel
   - Upper shock absorber nut and raise the vehicle enough to relax the suspension
   - Lower shock absorber nut
   - Shock absorber

To install:

3. Install or connect the following:
   - Shock absorber. Torque the lower nut to 85 ft. lbs. (115 Nm).
   - Upper shock absorber nut. Torque the nut to 13 ft. lbs. (18 Nm).
   - Rear quarter trim panel
   - Negative battery cable

Coil Spring

REMOVAL & INSTALLATION

Front

1. Before servicing the vehicle, refer to the precautions in the beginning of this section.

2. Install or connect the following:
   - Negative battery cable
   - Front wheel
   - Strut and spring assembly and mount the strut assembly in a holding fixture and compress the coil spring using a suitable tool
   - Strut piston rod nut

3. Coil spring by disassembling the strut in the following sequence:
   a. Step 1: Metal sheet plate.
   b. Step 2: Upper strut mount.
   c. Step 3: Thrust bearing plate.
   d. Step 4: Thrust bearing.
   e. Step 5: Upper spring seat.
   f. Step 6: Upper spring seat isolator.
   g. Step 7: Coil spring.
   h. Step 8: Dust boot.
   i. Step 9: Rubber bump stopper.
   j. Step 10: Lower spring seat.

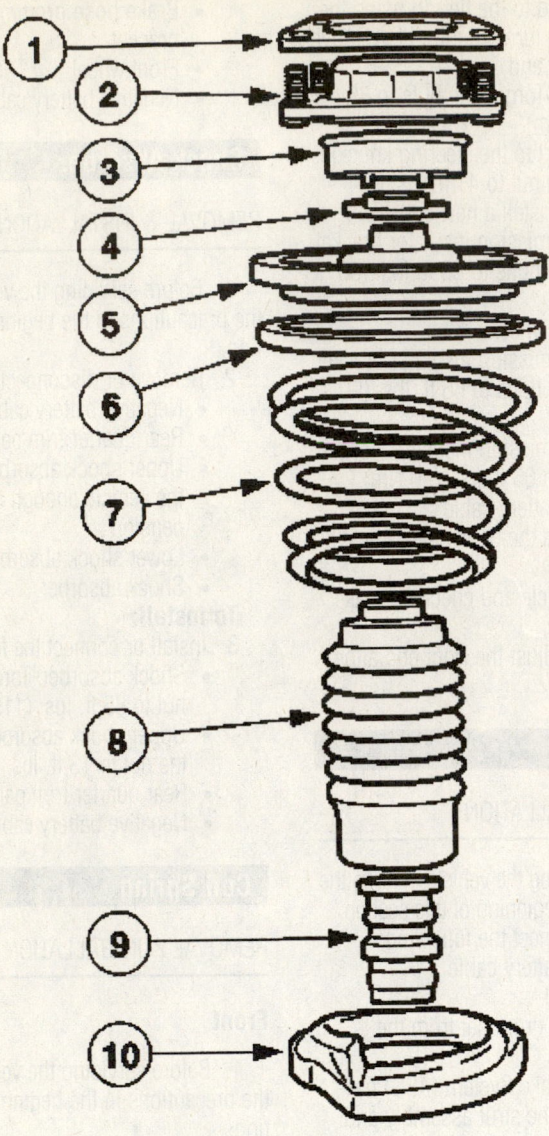

1. Metal sheet plate
2. Upper strut mount
3. Thrust bearing plate
4. Thrust bearing
5. Upper spring seat
6. Upper spring seat isolator
7. Spring
8. Dust boot
9. Rubber bump stopper
10. Lower spring seat

9308TG23

Disassemble the strut assembly in the proper sequence

To install:
- Assemble the strut assembly in the reverse order of the removal procedure
4. Install or connect the following:
   - Strut piston rod nut. Torque the nut to 76 ft. lbs. (103 Nm) and remove the assembly from the holding fixture
   - Strut and spring assembly
   - Front wheel
   - Negative battery cable

Rear

1. Before servicing the vehicle, refer to the precautions in the beginning of this section.
2. Remove or disconnect the following:
   - Wheel and install 1 lug nut to retain the brake drum
   - Brake line from the wheel cylinder
   - Brake line bracket
   - Bolts from the Antilock Braking System (ABS) sensor bracket and move the sensor aside, if equipped
   - Rear knuckle and loosen the inside upper and lower arm bolts
   - Shock absorber lower nut
   - Spring

To install:
3. Install or connect the following:
   - Spring to the shock absorber
   - Lower shock absorber nut. Torque the nut to 85 ft. lbs. (115 Nm).
   - Inside upper and lower arm bolts. Torque the bolts to 85 ft. lbs. (115 Nm).
   - ABS sensor bracket, if equipped. Torque the bolts to 80 inch lbs. (9 Nm).
   - Brake line bracket. Torque the bolt to 15 ft. lbs. (20 Nm).
   - Brake line to the wheel cylinder. Torque the fastener to 11 ft. lbs. (15 Nm) and remove the lug nut
   - Wheel
   - Negative battery cable

Upper Control Arm

REMOVAL & INSTALLATION

The upper and lower ball joints are an integral part of the control arms and are not a serviceable components. Replacement of the ball joint requires replacing the appropriate control arm.

1. Before servicing the vehicle, refer to the precautions in the beginning of this section.
2. Remove or disconnect the following:

- Negative battery cable
- Rear wheel
- Upper control arm from the knuckle while holding the ball joint stud from turning
- Upper ball joint nut
- Upper control arm
- Upper control arm inner bolt

To install:

3. Install or connect the following:
- Upper control arm inner bolt
- Upper control arm. Torque the bolts to 85 ft. lbs. (115 Nm).
- Upper ball joint nut
- Upper control arm to the knuckle. Torque the ball joint nut to 85 ft. lbs. (115 Nm).
- Rear wheel
- Negative battery cable

Lower Control Arm

REMOVAL & INSTALLATION

Front

1. Remove or disconnect the following:
- Negative battery cable
- Front wheel
- Lower ball joint from the knuckle and support the subframe
- Lower control arm

To install:

2. Install or connect the following:
- Lower control arm bolts and hand tighten them
- Pich bolt to the wheel knuckle. Torque the nut to 52 ft. lbs. (70 Nm) and remove the subframe support
- Front wheel and jounce the vehicle

3. Torque the inner lower control arm bolt to 148 ft. lbs. (200 Nm) and outer bolt 85 ft. lbs. (115 Nm).

Rear

1. Remove or disconnect the following:
- Negative battery cable
- Front wheel
- Lower ball joint from the knuckle while holding the ball joint stud from moving
- Lower ball joint nut
- Lower control arm
- Lower control arm inner bolt

To install:

2. Install or connect the following:

- Lower control arm inner bolt
- Lower control arm. Torque the bolts to 85 ft. lbs. (115 Nm).
- Lower ball joint nut
- Lower ball joint the knuckle. Torque the ball joint nut to 85 ft. lbs. (115 Nm).
- Rear wheel
- Negative battery cable

Wheel Bearings

REMOVAL & INSTALLATION

Front

1. Before servicing the vehicle, refer to the precautions in the beginning of this section.

2. Remove or disconnect the following:
- Negative battery cable
- Front wheel
- Brake disc
- Wheel hub nut
- Tie rod end cotter pin and nut
- Tie rod end from the knuckle
- Antilock Brake System (ABS) sensor bolt and move the sensor aside, if equipped
- Lower ball joint from the knuckle
- Halfshaft from the knuckle and properly support the halfshaft
- Steering knuckle

3. Press the hub from the wheel bearing and knuckle

4. Press the inner wheel bearing race from the knuckle and remove the snapring

5. Press the outer wheel bearing race from the knuckle

To install:

6. Install or connect the following:
- Wheel bearing into the steering knuckle
- Snapring
- Wheel hub into the wheel bearing by using a press
- Steering knuckle. Torque the bolts to 85 ft. lbs. (115 Nm).
- Halfshaft into the wheel hub
- Pinch bolt to knuckle. Torque the nut to 52 ft. lbs. (70 Nm).
- Ball joint stud into the knuckle
- ABS sensor. Torque the bolt to 80 inch lbs. (9 Nm), if equipped
- Tie rod end to the knuckle. Torque the nut to 41 ft. lbs. (55 Nm).
- New cotter pin to the tie rod end nut
- Wheel hub. Torque the nut to 214 ft. lbs. (290 Nm).

- Brake disc
- Front wheel
- Negative battery cable

Rear

2WD VEHICLES

1. Before servicing the vehicle, refer to the precautions in the beginning of this section.

2. Remove or disconnect the following:
- Negative battery cable
- Rear wheel
- Rear brake drum
- Wheel hub nut
- Wheel hub
- Inner wheel bearing race from the hub
- Snapring
- Wheel bearing outer race from the knuckle

To install:

3. Install or connect the following:
- Wheel bearing in to the knuckle
- Snapring
- Wheel hub into the wheel bearing
- Wheel hub nut. Torque the nut to 214 ft. lbs. (290 Nm).
- Brake drum
- Rear wheel
- Negative battery cable

4WD VEHICLES

1. Before servicing the vehicle, refer to the precautions in the beginning of this section.

2. Remove or disconnect the following:
- Negative battery cable
- Rear wheel
- Rear brake shoes
- Rear halfshaft nut and loosen the halfshaft from the hub
- Wheel hub and place it in a vise
- Inner wheel bearing race from the hub
- Antilock Brake System (ABS) sensor bracket and move the sensor aside, if equipped
- Parking brake cable from the steering knuckle
- Brake line from the wheel cylinder and support the knuckle
- Lower shock absorber nut
- Lower ball joint by holding the ball joint stud
- Upper ball joint
- Coil spring while noting the location of the insulator
- Steering knuckle cam

- Steering knuckle
- Snapring and press out the outer wheel bearing race from the knuckle

To install:

3. Install or connect the following:
   - New wheel bearing into the steering knuckle
   - Snapring to the knuckle
   - Wheel hub
   - Steering knuckle cam and hand tighten the bolt
   - Coil spring

- Shock absorber lower nut. Torque the nut to 85 ft. lbs. (115 Nm).
- Upper ball joint. Torque the nut to 85 ft. lbs. (115 Nm).
- Lower ball joint. Torque the nut to 85 ft. lbs. (115 Nm). Align the steering knuckle cam and torque the bolt to 85 ft. lbs. (115 Nm).
- Brake line to the wheel cylinder. Torque the brake line bracket bolt to 15 ft. lbs. (20 Nm) and the brake line fastener to 11 ft. lbs. (15 Nm).
- Parking brake cable to the backing plate. Torque the bolt to 16 ft. lbs. (22 Nm).
- ABS sensor bracket. Torque the bolt to 80 inch lbs. (9 Nm), if equipped
- Halfshaft nut. Torque the nut to 214 ft. lbs. (290 Nm).
- Brake shoes
- Rear wheel
- Negative battery cable

4. Fill and bleed the brake system.
5. Check and adjust the wheel alignment as needed.

PRECAUTIONS

Before servicing any vehicle, please be sure to read all of the following precautions, which deal with personal safety, prevention of component damage and important points to take into consideration when servicing a motor vehicle:

• Never open, service or drain the radiator or cooling system when the engine is hot; serious burns can occur from the steam and hot coolant.

• Observe all applicable safety precautions when working around fuel. Whenever servicing the fuel system, always work in a well-ventilated area. Do not allow fuel spray or vapors to come in contact with a spark, open flame, or excessive heat (a hot drop light, for example). Keep a dry chemical fire extinguisher near the work area. Always keep fuel in a container specifically designed for fuel storage; also, always properly seal fuel containers to avoid the possibility of fire or explosion. Refer to the additional fuel system precautions later in this section.

• Fuel injection systems often remain pressurized, even after the engine has been turned **OFF**. The fuel system pressure must be relieved before disconnecting any fuel lines. Failure to do so may result in fire and/or personal injury.

• Brake fluid often contains polyglycol ethers and polyglycols. Avoid contact with the eyes and wash your hands thoroughly after handling brake fluid. If you do get brake fluid in your eyes, flush your eyes with clean, running water for 15 minutes. If eye irritation persists, or if you have taken brake fluid internally, seek medical assistance IMMEDIATELY.

• The EPA warns that prolonged contact with used engine oil may cause a number of skin disorders, including cancer! You should make every effort to minimize your exposure to used engine oil. Protective gloves should be worn when changing oil. Wash your hands and any other exposed skin areas as soon as possible after exposure to used engine oil. Soap and water, or waterless hand cleaner should be used.

• All new vehicles are now equipped with an air bag system, often referred to as a Supplemental Restraint System (SRS) or Supplemental Inflatable Restraint (SIR) system. The system must be disabled before performing service on or around system components, steering column, instrument panel components, wiring and sensors. Failure to follow safety and disabling procedures could result in accidental air bag deployment, possible personal injury and unnecessary system repairs.

• Always wear safety goggles when working with, or around, the air bag system. When carrying a non-deployed air bag, be sure the bag and trim cover are pointed away from your body. When placing a non-deployed air bag on a work surface, always face the bag and trim cover upward, away from the surface. This will reduce the motion of the module if it is accidentally deployed. Refer to the additional air bag system precautions later in this section.

• Clean, high quality brake fluid from a sealed container is essential to the safe and proper operation of the brake system. You should always buy the correct type of brake fluid for your vehicle. If the brake fluid becomes contaminated, completely flush the system with new fluid. Never reuse any brake fluid. Any brake fluid that is removed from the system should be discarded. Also, do not allow any brake fluid to come in contact with a painted surface; it will damage the paint.

• Never operate the engine without the proper amount and type of engine oil; doing so WILL result in severe engine damage.

• Timing belt maintenance is extremely important! Many models utilize an interference-type, non-freewheeling engine. If the timing belt breaks, the valves in the cylinder head may strike the pistons, causing potentially serious (also time-consuming and expensive) engine damage. Refer to the maintenance interval charts in the front of this manual for the recommended replacement interval for the timing belt and to the timing belt section for belt replacement and inspection.

• Disconnecting the negative battery cable on some vehicles may interfere with the functions of the on-board computer system(s) and may require the computer to undergo a relearning process once the negative battery cable is reconnected.

• When servicing drum brakes, only dissemble and assemble one side at a time, leaving the remaining side intact for reference.

• Only an MVAC-trained, EPA-certified automotive technician should service the air conditioning system or its components.

GASOLINE ENGINE REPAIR

➡ **Disconnecting the negative battery cable on some vehicles may interfere with the functions of the on board computer systems and may require the computer to undergo a relearning process, once the negative battery cable is reconnected.**

Distributor

REMOVAL

1. Before servicing the vehicle, refer to the precautions in the beginning of this section.
2. Disengage the primary wiring connector from the distributor.
3. Mark the position of the cap's No. 1 terminal on the distributor base.
4. Unclip and remove the cap. Remove the adapter.
5. Remove the rotor.
6. Remove the TFI connector.
7. Matchmark the distributor base and engine for installation reference.

8. Remove the hold-down bolt and lift out the distributor.

INSTALLATION

Timing Not Disturbed

1. Before servicing the vehicle, refer to the precautions in the beginning of this section.
2. Visually inspect the distributor. The O-ring should fit tightly onto the housing and be free of cuts. The drive gear should be free of nicks, cracks or excessive wear. The distributor shaft should rotate freely, without any binding.
3. Lubricate the distributor gear teeth with a coating of engine oil meeting.
4. Align the locating boss and fully seat the distributor rotor on the distributor shaft, if removed.
5. Rotate the distributor shaft so that the distributor rotor blade points toward the marked position on the distributor base adapter.
6. Install the distributor assembly into the engine block with a slight side-to-side twist.

➡ **If the vane and vane switch assembly cannot be kept on the leading edge after installation, remove the distribu-**

tor from the cylinder block by pulling upward enough for the distributor gear to disengage the distributor gear from the camshaft gear. Rotate the distributor rotor enough so that the gear will align on the next tooth of the camshaft gear.

7. Install the distributor hold-down clamp and bolt; leave it snug.
8. On V8 engines, position the adapter base in place, then install the attaching bolts.
9. Attach the electrical connector to the distributor.
10. Install the distributor cap. On V8 engines, secure the distributor cap using the spring clips. If the spark plug wires were removed from the distributor cap, install them in their proper position, as marked during the removal procedure.
11. Connect the negative battery cable. Check the initial timing according to the proper procedure.
12. Adjust the timing, as necessary, then tighten the distributor hold-down bolt to 17–25 ft. lbs. (23–34 Nm).

Timing Disturbed

1. Disconnect the No. 1 spark plug wire and remove the No. 1 spark plug.

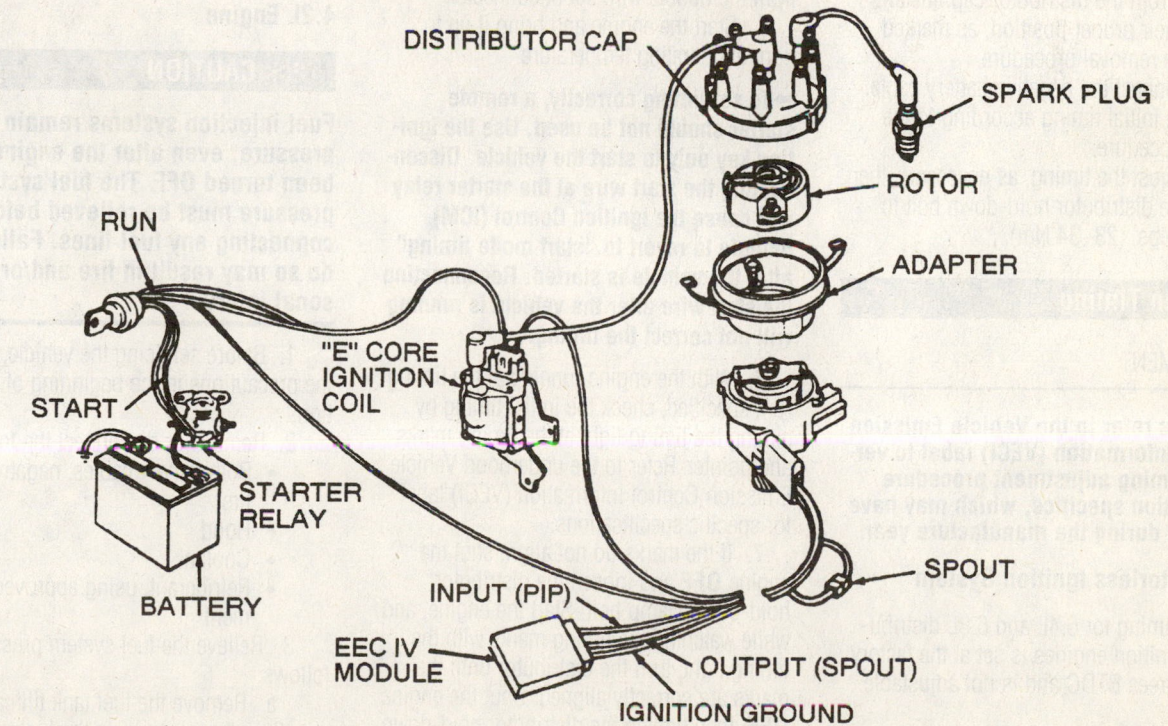

Exploded view of the TFI ignition system with universal distributor—5.0L (VIN N), 5.8L (VIN H) and 7.5L (VIN G) engines

7924FG34

2. Place a finger over the spark plug hole and crank the engine slowly until compression is felt.

3. Align the TDC mark on the crankshaft pulley with the pointer on the timing cover. This places the No. 1 cylinder at TDC on the compression stroke.

4. Turn the distributor shaft until the rotor points to the No. 1 spark plug tower on the cap.

5. Install the distributor assembly into the engine block with a slight side-to-side twist.

➡**If the vane and vane switch assembly cannot be kept on the leading edge after installation, remove the distributor from the cylinder block by pulling upward enough for the distributor gear to disengage the distributor gear from the camshaft gear. Rotate the distributor rotor enough so that the gear will align on the next tooth of the camshaft gear.**

6. Install the distributor hold-down clamp and bolt; leave it snug.

7. On V8 engines, position the adapter base in place, then install the attaching bolts.

8. Attach the electrical connector to the distributor.

9. Install the distributor cap. On V8 engines, secure the distributor cap using the spring clips. If the spark plug wires were removed from the distributor cap, install them in their proper position, as marked during the removal procedure.

10. Connect the negative battery cable. Check the initial timing according to the proper procedure.

11. Adjust the timing, as necessary, then tighten the distributor hold-down bolt to 17–25 ft. lbs. (23–34 Nm).

Ignition Timing

ADJUSTMENT

➡**Always refer to the Vehicle Emission Control Information (VECI) label to verify the timing adjustment procedure and ignition specifics, which may have changed during the manufacture year.**

Distributorless Ignition System

Base timing for 5.4L and 6.8L distributorless ignition engines is set at the factory at 10 degrees BTDC and is not adjustable.

Distributor Ignition System

1. Before servicing the vehicle, refer to the precautions in the beginning of this section.

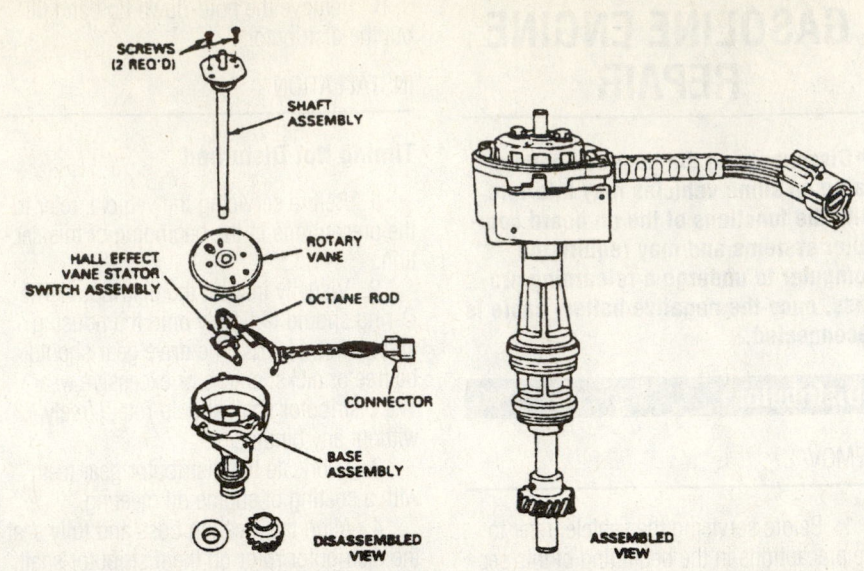

Exploded view of the closed bowl distributor used on the 5.0L, 5.8L, and 7.5L engines

7924FG35

2. Place automatic transmissions in **P** or manual transmissions in Neutral. The air conditioning and heater controls should be in the OFF position.

3. Connect a suitable inductive timing light and a tachometer according to the manufacturer's instructions.

4. Disengage the single wire inline spout connector or remove the shorting bar from the double wire spout connector.

5. Start the engine and bring it up to normal operating temperature.

➡**To set timing correctly, a remote starter should not be used. Use the ignition key only to start the vehicle. Disconnecting the start wire at the starter relay will cause the Ignition Control (ICM) module to revert to "start mode timing" after the vehicle is started. Reconnecting the start wire after the vehicle is running will not correct the timing.**

6. With the engine running at the timing rpm specified, check the initial timing by aiming the timing light at the timing marks and pointer. Refer to the underhood Vehicle Emission Control Information (VECI) label for specific specifications.

7. If the marks do not align, shut the engine **OFF** and loosen the distributor hold-down clamp bolt. Start the engine, and while watching the timing marks with the timing light, turn the distributor until the marks are correctly aligned. Shut the engine **OFF**, then tighten the distributor hold-down clamp bolt to 17–25 ft. lbs. (23–34 Nm).

8. Reattach the single wire inline spout connector or reinstall the shorting bar on the double wire spout connector. Check the

timing advance to verify the distributor is advancing beyond the initial setting.

9. Remove the timing light and tachometer.

Engine Assembly

REMOVAL & INSTALLATION

4.2L Engine

✷✷ CAUTION

Fuel injection systems remain under pressure, even after the engine has been turned OFF. The fuel system pressure must be relieved before disconnecting any fuel lines. Failure to do so may result in fire and/or personal injury.

1. Before servicing the vehicle, refer to the precautions in the beginning of this section.

2. Remove or disconnect the following:
   - Both battery cables, negative cable first
   - Hood
   - Coolant
   - Refrigerant, using approved equipment

3. Relieve the fuel system pressure as follows:

   a. Remove the fuel tank fill cap to relieve the pressure in the fuel tank.

   b. Remove the cap from the fuel pressure relief valve located on the fuel injection supply manifold.

c. Attach a fuel pressure gauge to the relief valve and drain the fuel through the drain tube into a suitable container.

d. After the fuel system pressure is relieved, remove the fuel pressure gauge and install the cap on the relief valve. Secure the fuel tank fill cap.

4. Remove or disconnect the following:

- Engine cooling fan, shroud and radiator
- Engine air cleaner outlet tube
- Accelerator and cruise control cables at the throttle body
- VMV hose
- Manifold vacuum connection
- Intake Manifold Runner Control (IMRC) vacuum connectors, fuel pressure regulator vacuum connector, IMRC solenoid vacuum connector and vacuum reservoir connector
- Exhaust Gas Recirculation (EGR) valve vacuum connector.
- The 3 power steering reservoir retaining bolts and position aside
- Air conditioning compressor manifold bolt and disconnect, then position the air conditioning lines aside.
- The 4 power steering pump retaining bolts and position the pump aside.
- Alternator electrical harness connectors. Remove the positive battery cable nut and disconnect the battery cable.
- Electrical harness connectors to the fuel injectors
- Wires at the spark plugs
- Both heater hoses
- Brake booster vacuum hose
- EGR Differential Pressure Feedback (DPFE) transducer hose
- Breather tube from the cylinder head cover
- Upper intake manifold
- Fuel supply and return lines, and remove the fuel injection supply manifold.
- Block heater cable
- Exhaust system from the exhaust manifolds and support with wire hung from the crossmember.
- Starter motor
- Transmission from the vehicle. If equipped with a manual transmission, remove the clutch assembly.
- Right-hand and left-hand engine support insulator through-bolts

5. Install a suitable engine lifting bracket and connect suitable engine lifting equipment to the lifting brackets.

6. Carefully raise the engine out of the engine compartment and position on a work stand. Remove the engine lifting equipment.

To install:

7. Install the engine lifting brackets. Support the engine using a suitable floor crane installed to the lifting equipment and remove the engine from the work stand.

8. Carefully lower the engine into the engine compartment aligning the engine support insulators.

9. Remove the engine lifting equipment and brackets.

10. Raise and safely support the vehicle.

11. Install or connect the following:

- Left-hand and right-hand engine support insulator through-bolts and tighten them to 51–67 ft. lbs. (68–92 Nm).
- Transmission, and the clutch assembly
- Starter motor
- Exhaust pipes to the exhaust manifolds and tighten to 30 ft. lbs. (41 Nm).
- Block heater
- Heater cable
- Alternator electrical harness connectors and install the positive battery cable to the retaining stud. Tighten the retaining nut to 96 inch lbs. (11 Nm).
- Fuel injectors and the fuel injection supply manifold
- New upper intake gasket and install the upper intake manifold.
- Electrical harness connectors to the fuel injectors
- Power steering pump in position and install 4 retaining bolts. Tighten the bolts to 17–20 ft. lbs. (22–28 Nm).

➡Ensure that the air conditioning manifold O-rings are in place.

- Air conditioning manifold to the compressor and install the retaining bolt. Tighten the bolt to 14–18 ft. lbs. (18–24 Nm).
- Power steering reservoir and 3 retaining bolts. Tighten the bolts to 107 inch lbs. (12 Nm).
- VMV hose
- IMRC vacuum connectors, fuel pressure regulator vacuum connector, IMRC solenoid vacuum con-

nector and vacuum reservoir connector.

- EGR valve vacuum connector
- Brake booster hose
- The 2 EGR DPFE transducer hoses
- Manifold vacuum connection
- Accelerator cable and speed control cable in position, if equipped. Tighten the speed control cable retaining bolt to 72 inch lbs. (8 Nm) and accelerator cable retaining bolt to 25 inch lbs. (3 Nm).
- Radiator, cooling fan and shroud
- Engine air cleaner outlet tube
- Engine oil
- Coolant; bleed the system
- Battery cables, negative cable last

12. Start the engine and allow to reach normal operating temperature while checking for leaks.

13. Check all fluid levels.

14. Properly evacuate and recharge the air conditioning system using approved equipment.

15. Install the hood, aligning the marks that were made during removal.

16. Road test the vehicle and check the engine and transmission for proper operation.

4.6L, 5.4L and 6.8L Engines

⁂ CAUTION

Fuel injection systems remain under pressure, even after the engine has been turned OFF. The fuel system pressure must be relieved before disconnecting any fuel lines. Failure to do so may result in fire and/or personal injury.

1. Before servicing the vehicle, refer to the precautions in the beginning of this section.

2. Remove or disconnect the following:

- Both battery cables, negative cable first
- Hood
- Coolant
- Refrigerant, using approved equipment

3. Relieve the fuel system pressure as follows:

a. Remove the fuel tank fill cap to relieve the pressure in the fuel tank.

b. Remove the cap from the fuel pressure relief valve located on the fuel injection supply manifold.

c. Attach a fuel pressure gauge to the relief valve and drain the fuel through the drain tube into a suitable container.

d. After the fuel system pressure is relieved, remove the fuel pressure gauge and install the cap on the relief valve. Secure the fuel tank fill cap.

- Engine cooling fan, shroud and radiator
- Accessory drive belt
- Engine air cleaner outlet tube
- Intake manifold assembly
- Bulkhead connector cover and disconnect the bulkhead connector.
- The 3 power steering reservoir bracket retaining bolts and move the reservoir aside.
- The 2 Differential Pressure Feedback (DPFE) transducer hoses
- Upper and lower EGR valve to exhaust manifold tube fittings and remove the tube.
- Heater water hose
- Ignition coil, radio capacitor and CMP sensor electrical harness connectors
- Both ignition coils and mounting bracket bolts and remove the coil and bracket assemblies.
- Starter motor
- The 3 lower radiator air deflector screws. Remove the 5 clips and remove the air deflector.
- Air conditioning compressor electrical harness connector
- Air conditioning manifold-to-compressor bolt and remove the manifold and tube assembly.
- The 3 air conditioning compressor retaining bolts and remove the air conditioning compressor.
- Fluid cooler hoses from the block mounted clip
- On vehicles with automatic transmissions: the inspection cover, torque converter bolts and transmission-to-engine retaining bolts.
- On vehicles with manual transmission: the transmission and the clutch assembly.
- Upper and lower power steering pump bolts and move the power steering pump aside.
- Exhaust system from the exhaust manifolds and support with wire hung from the crossmember.
- Right-hand and left-hand engine support insulator (mount) through-bolts

4. Install a suitable engine lifting bracket and connect suitable engine lifting equipment to the lifting brackets.

5. Carefully raise the engine out of the engine compartment and place on a work stand. Remove the engine lifting equipment.

To install:

6. Install the engine lifting brackets. Support the engine using a suitable floor crane installed to the lifting equipment and remove the engine from the work stand.

7. Carefully lower the engine into the engine compartment. Start the converter pilot into the flywheel and align the paint marks on the flywheel and torque converter. Be sure the studs on the torque converter align with the holes in the flywheel.

8. Fully engage the engine to the transmission and lower onto the engine support insulators.

9. Remove the engine lifting equipment and brackets.

10. Raise and safely support the vehicle.

11. Install or connect the following:
- If equipped with a manual transmission: the clutch and transmission assemblies.
- The 6 engine-to-transmission retaining bolts and tighten to 30–44 ft. lbs. (40–60 Nm).
- The engine support insulator through-bolts and tighten to 15–22 ft. lbs. (20–30 Nm).
- The 4 torque converter retaining nuts and tighten to 22–25 ft. lbs. (20–30 Nm).
- Transmission housing cover to the cylinder block
- Exhaust pipes to the exhaust manifolds and tighten to 30 ft. lbs. (41 Nm)
- Power steering pump in position on the cylinder block and install 4 retaining nuts. Tighten to 15–20 ft. lbs. (20–30 Nm).
- Starter motor
- Transmission fluid cooler hoses into the cylinder block mounted clip
- Air conditioning compressor in position and install the 3 retaining bolts. Tighten the bolts to 15–22 ft. lbs. (20–30 Nm).
- Air conditioning manifold and tube assembly on the compressor and install the retaining bolt. Tighten the bolt to 14–18 ft. lbs. (18–24 Nm).
- Air conditioning compressor clutch electrical harness connector
- Lower radiator air deflector
- Ignition coil and bracket assemblies. Tighten the retaining nuts to 15–23 ft. lbs. (20–30 Nm).
- Ignition coil, radio capacitor and CMP sensor electrical harness connectors

- Rear heater water hose and compress and slide the clamp in position.
- EGR valve to exhaust manifold tube and tighten the upper and lower fittings to 26–33 ft. lbs. (35–45 Nm).
- DPFE transducer hoses
- Power steering pump reservoir in position and install the 3 retaining bolts. Tighten the bolts to 71–107 inch lbs. (8–12 Nm).
- Engine bulkhead connector and install the retaining bolt. Tighten the bolt to 36–50 inch lbs. (4–6 Nm). Install the cover.
- Intake manifold assembly
- Accessory drive belt
- Radiator, cooling fan and shroud
- Engine air cleaner outlet tube
- Engine oil

12. Fill and bleed the engine cooling system.

13. Connect both battery cables, negative cable last.

14. Start the engine and allow to reach normal operating temperature while checking for leaks.

15. Check all fluid levels.

16. Properly evacuate and recharge the air conditioning system using approved equipment.

17. Install the hood, aligning the marks that were made during removal.

18. Road test the vehicle and check the engine and transmission for proper operation.

5.0L, 5.8L and 7.5L Engines

E-SERIES

> **✷✷ CAUTION**
>
> **Fuel injection systems remain under pressure, even after the engine has been turned OFF. The fuel system pressure must be relieved before disconnecting any fuel lines. Failure to do so may result in fire and/or personal injury.**

1. Before servicing the vehicle, refer to the precautions in the beginning of this section.

2. Remove or disconnect the following:
- Engine cover
- Coolant
- Engine oil
- Battery and alternator cables
- Air intake hoses, PCV tube and carbon canister hose

3. Properly relieve the residual fuel system pressure.

4. Remove or disconnect the following:
- Upper and lower radiator hoses
- Refrigerant, using approved equipment
- Refrigerant lines at the compressor. Cap all openings immediately.
- Automatic transmission oil cooler lines
- Engine fan shroud and lay it over the fan
- Radiator and fan, shroud, fan, spacer, pulley and belt
- Grille
- Gravel deflector
- Upper grille support bracket
- Hood lock support
- Air bag electrical connector
- Alternator
- Oil pressure sending unit lead from the sending unit
- Fuel supply and return lines at the fuel injector rails
- Accelerator linkage and speed control linkage at the throttle body
- Automatic transmission kick-down rod and remove the return spring, if so equipped.
- Power brake booster vacuum hose
- Throttle bracket from the upper intake manifold and swing it out of the way with the cables still attached.
- Heater hoses from the water pump and intake manifold or tee
- Oil fill pipe
- Temperature sending unit wire from the sending unit
- Transmission dipstick tube
- Upper intake manifold
- Fuel feed and return lines
- Distributor cap, rotor and ignition wires
- Upper bell housing-to-engine attaching bolts
- Wiring harness from the left rocker arm cover and position the wires out of the way.
- Ground strap from the cylinder block
- Air conditioning compressor clutch wire
- Starter
- Exhaust pipe from the exhaust manifolds
- Engine mounts from the brackets on the frame
- On vehicles with automatic transmissions: the converter inspection

plate and remove the torque converter-to-flywheel attaching bolts.
- Remaining bell housing-to-engine attaching bolts

5. Lower the vehicle and support the transmission with a jack.

6. Install an engine lifting device.

7. Raise the engine slightly, carefully pull it out of the transmission and lift the engine out of the engine compartment.

To install:

8. Lower the engine carefully into the transmission. Be sure that the dowels in the engine block engage the holes in the bell housing through the rear cover plate. If equipped with a manual transmission, turn the crankshaft with the transmission in gear until the input shaft splines mesh with the clutch disc splines.

9. Install or connect the following:
- The lower bell housing-to-engine attaching bolts. Tighten the bolts to 50 ft. lbs. (68 Nm).
- The engine mount nuts and washers. Tighten the nuts to 80 ft. lbs. (109 Nm).

10. Remove the engine lifting device.

11. Remove the transmission support jack.

12. Install or connect the following:
- On vehicles with automatic transmissions: the torque converter-to-flywheel attaching bolts. Tighten the bolts to 30 ft. lbs. (41 Nm).
- Converter inspection plate. Tighten the bolts to 60 inch lbs. (7 Nm).
- Exhaust pipe to the exhaust manifolds. Tighten the exhaust pipe-to-exhaust manifold nuts to 25–35 ft. lbs. (34–48 Nm).
- Starter. Tighten the mounting bolts to 20 ft. lbs. (27 Nm).
- Starter cable to the starter
- Upper intake manifold
- Transmission dipstick tube
- Fuel feed and return lines
- Upper bell housing-to-engine attaching bolts. Tighten the bolts to 50 ft. lbs. (68 Nm).
- Distributor cap, rotor and ignition wires
- Wiring harness at the left rocker arm cover
- Ground strap to the cylinder block
- Air conditioning compressor clutch wire
- Oil fill pipe
- Heater hoses at the water pump and intake manifold or tee

- Temperature sending unit wire at the sending unit
- Air bag electrical connector
- Accelerator linkage and speed control linkage at the throttle body
- Automatic transmission kick-down rod and install the return spring, if so equipped.
- Power brake booster vacuum hose
- Throttle bracket to the upper intake manifold
- Oil pressure sending unit lead to the sending unit
- Alternator
- Refrigerant lines to the compressor
- Hood lock support
- Upper grille support bracket
- Gravel deflector
- Grille
- Radiator, shroud, fan and spacer, pulley and belt
- Upper and lower radiator hoses, if so equipped, the automatic transmission oil cooler lines.
- Air intake hoses, PCV tube and carbon canister hose
- Battery and alternator cables
- Coolant
- Engine oil
- Automatic transmission fluid

13. Start the engine and check for leaks.

14. Bleed the cooling system.

15. Bring the engine to normal operating temperature and recheck all fluid levels. Top off as necessary.

16. Using approved equipment, evacuate, recharge and leak test the air conditioning system.

17. Install the engine cover.

EXCEPT E-SERIES

❄❄ CAUTION

Fuel injection systems remain under pressure, even after the engine has been turned OFF. The fuel system pressure must be relieved before disconnecting any fuel lines. Failure to do so may result in fire and/or personal injury.

1. Before servicing the vehicle, refer to the precautions in the beginning of this section.

2. Remove or disconnect the following:
- Hood
- Coolant
- Engine oil
- Battery and alternator cables

- Fuel system pressure
- Air intake hoses, PCV tube and carbon canister hose
- Upper and lower radiator hoses
- Air conditioning system, using approved equipment
- Refrigerant lines at the compressor. Cap all openings immediately.
- Automatic transmission oil cooler lines
- Power steering hoses from the power steering pump and cap the lines.
- Fan shroud and lay it over the fan
- Radiator and fan, shroud, fan, spacer, pulley and belt
- Alternator pivot and adjusting bolts. Remove the alternator.
- Oil pressure sending unit lead from the sending unit
- Fuel tank-to-pump fuel line at the fuel pump and plug the line
- Chassis fuel line at the fuel rails
- Accelerator linkage and speed control linkage at the throttle body
- Automatic transmission kick-down rod and remove the return spring, if so equipped.
- Power brake booster vacuum hose
- Throttle bracket from the upper intake manifold and swing it out of the way with the cables still attached.
- Heater hoses from the water pump and intake manifold or tee
- Temperature sending unit wire from the sending unit
- Upper bell housing-to-engine attaching bolts
- Wiring harness from the left rocker arm cover and position the wires out of the way.
- Ground strap from the cylinder block
- Air conditioning compressor clutch wire
- Starter
- Exhaust pipe from the exhaust manifolds
- Engine mounts from the brackets on the frame
- On vehicles with automatic transmissions: the converter inspection plate and remove the torque converter-to-flywheel attaching bolts.
- Remaining bell housing-to-engine attaching bolts

3. Lower the vehicle and support the transmission with a jack.

4. Install an engine lifting device.

5. Raise the engine slightly, carefully pull it out of the transmission, and lift the engine out of the engine compartment.

To install:

6. Remove the engine mount brackets from the frame and attach them to the engine mounts. Tighten the mount-to-bracket nuts just enough to hold them securely.

7. Lower the engine carefully into the transmission. Be sure that the dowel in the engine block engage the holes in the bell housing through the rear cover plate. If the engine hangs up after the transmission input shaft enters the clutch disc (manual transmission only), turn the crankshaft with the transmission in gear until the input shaft splines mesh with the clutch disc splines.

8. Install or connect the following:
- Engine mount nuts and washers. Tighten the nuts to 80 ft. lbs. (109 Nm). Tighten the bracket-to-frame bolts to 70 ft. lbs. (95 Nm).
- Lower bell housing-to-engine attaching bolts. Tighten the bolts to 50 ft. lbs. (68 Nm).
- On vehicles with automatic transmissions: the torque converter-to-flywheel attaching bolts. Tighten the bolts to 30 ft. lbs. (41 Nm).
- Converter inspection plate. Tighten the bolts to 60 inch lbs. (7 Nm).
- Exhaust pipe to the exhaust manifolds. Tighten the exhaust pipe-to-exhaust manifold nuts to 25–35 ft. lbs. (34–48 Nm).
- Starter. Tighten the mounting bolts to 20 ft. lbs. (27 Nm).
- Starter cable
- Upper bell housing-to-engine attaching bolts. Tighten the bolts to 50 ft. lbs. (68 Nm).
- Wiring harness at the left rocker arm cover
- Ground strap to the cylinder block
- Air conditioning compressor clutch wire
- Heater hoses at the water pump and intake manifold or tee
- Temperature sending unit wire at the sending unit
- Accelerator linkage and speed control linkage at the throttle body
- Automatic transmission kick-down rod and install the return spring, if so equipped.
- Power brake booster vacuum hose
- Throttle bracket to the upper intake manifold
- Fuel tank-to-pump fuel line at the fuel pump. Connect the chassis fuel line at the fuel rails.
- Oil pressure sending unit lead to the sending unit
- Alternator

- Refrigerant lines to the compressor
- Power steering hoses to the power steering pump
- Radiator and fan, shroud, fan, spacer, pulley and belt
- Upper and lower radiator hoses, if so equipped, the automatic transmission oil cooler lines
- Air cleaner, intake duct assembly, and the PCV hose
- Air intake hoses, PCV tube and carbon canister hose
- Cooling system and crankcase
- Engine oil
- Automatic transmission fluid level
- Battery and alternator cables

9. Start the engine and check for leaks.

10. Bleed the cooling system.

11. Using approved equipment, evacuate, recharge and leak test the air conditioning system.

12. Bring the engine to normal operating temperature and recheck the fluid levels. Top off as necessary.

13. Install the hood.

Water Pump

REMOVAL & INSTALLATION

1. Before servicing the vehicle, refer to the precautions in the beginning of this section.

2. Remove or disconnect the following:
- Negative battery cable
- Radiator, fan blade assembly and fan shroud
- Accessory drive belt
- Water pump pulley
- Heater hose from the water pump
- Water pump bolts and nuts. Note the locations of the bolts if different lengths.
- Water pump stud bolt, the water pump and the water pump housing gasket. Discard the water pump housing gasket.

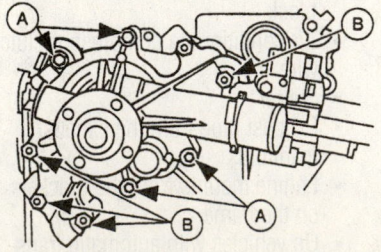

7924FG01

When removing the water pump, note the locations of the mounting bolts (A) and nuts (B)—4.2L engine

To install:

3. Before installing the water pump, be sure to completely clean the water pump mounting surfaces of all dirt, grime and old gasket material.

➡**All water pump housing bolts, nuts and studs are tightened to 15–22 ft. lbs. (20–30 Nm).**

4. Install or connect the following:
- Water pump onto the engine with a

new gasket. Install the water pump stud bolt temporarily finger-tight.
- Water pump mounting nuts and bolts temporarily finger-tight, then tighten all water pump housing fasteners to 15–22 ft. lbs. (20–30 Nm).
- Water outlet tube for the heater, if equipped
- Water pump pulley and accessory drive belt

- Fan shroud, fan blade assembly and the radiator
- Coolant
- Negative battery cable

5. Start the engine and check for any fluid leaks.

6. If necessary, bleed the cooling system.

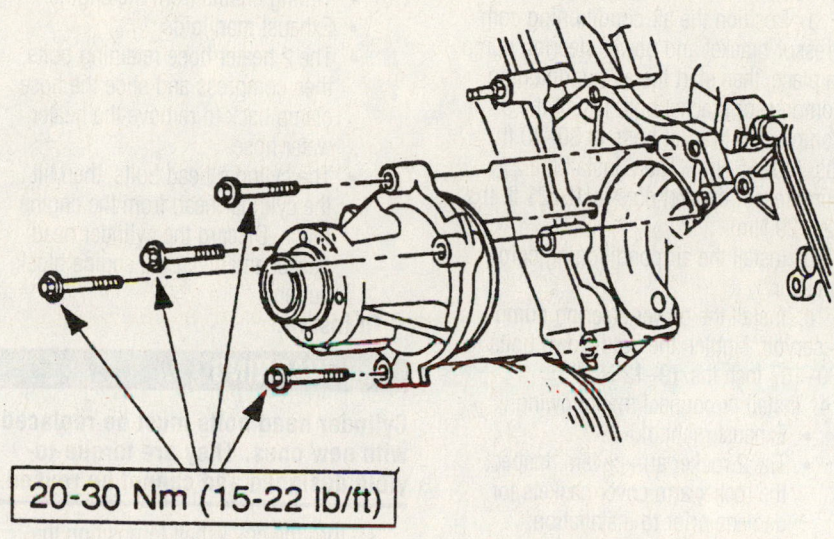

20-30 Nm (15-22 lb/ft)

7924FG02

Exploded view of the water pump mounting—4.6L, 5.4L and 6.8L engines

7924FG36

Exploded view of the cooling fan which is mounted on the water pump—7.5L engine

Cylinder Head

REMOVAL & INSTALLATION

4.2L Engine

➡**Cylinder head bolt torque sequences can be found in Section 1, following the Torque Specifications Chart.**

✷✷ CAUTION

Fuel injection systems remain under pressure, even after the engine has been turned OFF. The fuel system pressure must be relieved before disconnecting any fuel lines. Failure to do so may result in fire and/or personal injury.

1. Before servicing the vehicle, refer to the precautions in the beginning of this section.

2. Remove or disconnect the following:
- Air conditioning system, using approved equipment
- Negative battery cable
- Coolant
- Upper and lower intake manifolds and related components
- Rocker arm covers
- Exhaust manifold

3. If removing the left-hand cylinder head, perform the following:

a. Position the power steering pump reservoir aside and remove the air conditioning compressor.

b. Remove and support the air conditioning compressor bracket and power steering pump aside.

4. If removing the right-hand cylinder head, perform the following:

a. Remove the alternator.

b. Remove the idler pulley.

c. Remove the alternator bracket.

➡**If the cylinder head components, such as rocker arms, valve springs, etc., are to be reinstalled, they must be installed in the same position. Mark the components for original location.**

Refer to Section 1 for engine rebuilding specifications

5. Remove or disconnect the following:
- Rocker arms
- Pushrods. Be sure to label or mark the components removed for reinstallation in their original location.
- Cylinder head bolts. New cylinder head bolts must be used when the cylinder head is reinstalled.
- Cylinder head. Remove the cylinder head gasket and discard.

To install:

6. Clean and inspect the cylinder head for flatness.
7. Install or connect the following:
- New cylinder head gasket on the cylinder block with the small hole to the front of the engine.
- Cylinder head

✳✳ WARNING

Always use new cylinder head bolts for installation. Lubricate the cylinder head bolts with clean engine oil prior to installation. Be sure to tighten the cylinder head bolts in three (3) steps.

- New cylinder head bolts and torque the bolts following the proper tightening sequence in 3 steps to the following values:
  a. Step 1: 14 ft. lbs. (20 Nm)
  b. Step 2: 29 ft. lbs. (40 Nm)
  c. Step 3: 36 ft. lbs. (50 Nm)

✳✳ WARNING

Do not loosen all of the cylinder head bolts at one time. Each cylinder head bolt must be loosened and the final tightening performed prior to loosening the next bolt in the sequence.

8. In the same sequence as used previously, loosen the cylinder head bolt 3 turns, then tighten the cylinder head bolt to the specific value according to its length. The short bolts (A) should be tightened to 15–22 ft. lbs. (20–30 Nm) and the long bolts (B) to 30–36 ft. lbs. (40–50 Nm). Finally, tighten each cylinder head bolt, in sequence, an additional 175–185 degrees.
9. Lubricate the pushrods with clean engine oil prior to installation, then install them into their original positions.
10. Install the rocker arms. Tighten the rocker arm mounting bolts to 23–29 ft. lbs. (30–40 Nm).
11. If the valvetrain components were replaced with new components, inspect the valve clearance.

12. If installing the right-hand cylinder head, perform the following:
   a. Position the alternator bracket in place, then install the 2 long bolts to 31–39 ft. lbs. (41–54 Nm). Install the short bolt and tighten to 18–22 ft. lbs. (24–31 Nm).
   b. Install the idler pulley. Tighten the center retaining bolt to 35–46 ft. lbs. (47–63 Nm).
   c. Install the alternator.
13. If installing the left-hand cylinder head, complete the following steps:
   a. Position the air conditioning compressor bracket and power steering pump in place, then start the air conditioning compressor bracket bolt. Install the 3 compressor bracket bolts to 30–40 ft. lbs. (40–55 Nm). Then, install the 2 compressor bracket nuts to 16–21 ft. lbs. (21–29 Nm).
   b. Install the air conditioning compressor.
   c. Install the power steering pump reservoir. Tighten the hold-down bolts to 80–107 inch lbs. (9–12 Nm).
14. Install or connect the following:
- Exhaust manifold
- The 2 rocker arm covers. Inspect the rocker arm cover gaskets for damage prior to installation; replace them if necessary.
- Lower intake manifold and related components
- Upper intake manifold and related components

15. Drain the engine oil into a suitable container and replace the oil filter.
16. Fill the engine with the proper amount of engine oil.
17. Fill the cooling system.
18. Evacuate and recharge the air conditioning system using approved equipment.
19. Connect the negative battery cable.
20. Start the engine and check for any fluid or vacuum leaks.

4.6L, 5.4L and 6.8L Engines

➡ **Cylinder head bolt torque sequences can be found in Section 1, following the Torque Specifications Chart.**

✳✳ CAUTION

Fuel injection systems remain under pressure, even after the engine has been turned OFF. The fuel system pressure must be relieved before disconnecting any fuel lines. Failure to do so may result in fire and/or personal injury.

➡ **To correctly tighten the cylinder head bolts an angle torque wrench is needed.**

1. Before servicing the vehicle, refer to the precautions in the beginning of this section.
2. Remove or disconnect the following:
- Air conditioning system, using approved equipment
- Negative battery cable
- Cylinder head covers
- Intake manifold
- Timing chains from the engine
- Exhaust manifolds
- The 2 heater hose retaining bolts, then compress and slide the hose clamp back to remove the heater water hose.
- The cylinder head bolts, then lift the cylinder head from the engine block. Discard the cylinder head gasket and clean the engine block surface.

To install:

✳✳ WARNING

Cylinder head bolts must be replaced with new ones. They are torque-to-yield designed and cannot be reused.

3. Turn the crankshaft to position the keyway at the 12 o'clock position.
4. Clean and inspect the cylinder head for damage or warpage. Install the cylinder head gasket over the dowel pins. Then, install the cylinder head onto the engine block. Loosely install NEW cylinder head bolts.

➡ **Be sure to tighten the head bolts in 3 steps.**

5. Tighten the cylinder head bolts in the correct sequence using 3 steps, as follows:
   a. Step 1—27–32 ft. lbs. (37–43 Nm).
   b. Step 2—tighten an additional 85–95 degrees.
   c. Step 3—tighten another 85–95 degrees.
6. Install or connect the following:
- Heater hose
- Exhaust manifolds
- Timing chains
- Intake manifold
- Cylinder head covers
- Refrigerant
- Engine oil
- Coolant
- Negative battery cable
7. Start the engine and check for any fluid or vacuum leaks.

5.0L and 5.8L Engines

➡Cylinder head bolt torque sequences can be found in Section 1, following the Torque Specifications Chart.

✲✲ CAUTION

Fuel injection systems remain under pressure, even after the engine has been turned OFF. The fuel system pressure must be relieved before disconnecting any fuel lines. Failure to do so may result in fire and/or personal injury.

1. Before servicing the vehicle, refer to the precautions in the beginning of this section.
2. Remove or disconnect the following:
   - Coolant
   - Intake manifold and throttle body
   - Rocker arm cover(s)
3. If the right cylinder head is to be removed:
   a. Lift the tensioner and remove the drive belt.
   b. Loosen the alternator adjusting arm bolt and remove the alternator mounting bracket bolt and spacer.
   c. Swing the alternator down and out of the way.
   d. Remove the air cleaner inlet duct.
4. If the left cylinder head is being removed:
   a. For models with air conditioning, discharge the air conditioning system using approved equipment and remove the air conditioning compressor.
   b. Remove the oil dipstick and dipstick tube.
   c. Remove the cruise control bracket.
5. Disconnect the exhaust manifold(s) from the muffler inlet pipe(s).
6. Loosen the rocker arm stud nuts so the rocker arms can be rotated to the side. Remove the pushrods and identify them so they can be reinstalled in their original positions.
7. Disconnect the thermactor air supply hoses at the check valves and cover the check valve openings.
8. Remove the cylinder head bolts and lift the cylinder head from the block.
9. Remove the discard the gasket.

To install:

10. Clean the cylinder head, intake manifold, the valve cover and the head gasket surfaces.
11. A specially treated composition head gasket is used. Do not apply sealer to a composition gasket. Position the new gasket over the locating dowels on the cylinder block. Then, position the cylinder head on the block and install the attaching bolts.
12. The cylinder head bolts are tightened following the tightening sequence in progressive steps. Tighten all the bolts following the proper sequence to:

5.0L (VIN N) Engine
- Step 1: 25–35 ft. lbs. (34–47 Nm)
- Step 2: 45–55 ft. lbs. (61–75 Nm)
- Step 3: 85–95 degrees

5.8L (VIN H) Engine
- Step 1: 85 ft. lbs. (115 Nm)
- Step 2: 95 ft. lbs. (129 Nm)
- Step 3: 105–112 ft. lbs. (143–152 Nm)

13. Thoroughly clean the pushrods using compressed air to blow out the oil passage in the pushrods. Check the pushrods for straightness by rolling them on a piece of glass. Never try to straighten a pushrod; always replace it.
14. Apply Lubriplate® to the ends of the pushrods and install them in their original positions.
15. Apply Lubriplate® to the rocker arms and their fulcrum seats and install the rocker arms.
16. Adjust the valves.
17. Position a new gasket(s) on the muffler inlet pipe(s) as necessary. Connect the exhaust manifold(s) at the muffler inlet pipe(s).
18. If the right cylinder head was removed, install the alternator, and air cleaner duct. Install the drive belt. If the left cylinder head was removed, install the compressor. Install the dipstick and cruise control bracket.
19. Clean the valve rocker arm cover and the cylinder head gasket surfaces. Place the new gaskets in the covers, making sure the tabs of the gasket engage the notches provided in the cover.
20. Install the intake manifold and related parts. Install the thermactor hoses.
21. Fill and bleed the cooling system.
22. If the air conditioning was disconnected, evacuate and recharge the system using approved equipment.
23. Drain the engine oil into a suitable container and replace the oil filter.
24. Fill the engine with the proper amount of engine oil.
25. Connect the negative battery cable.
26. Start the engine and check for any fluid or vacuum leaks.

7.5L Engine

✲✲ CAUTION

Fuel injection systems remain under pressure, even after the engine has been turned OFF. The fuel system pressure must be relieved before disconnecting any fuel lines. Failure to do so may result in fire and/or personal injury.

1. Before servicing the vehicle, refer to the precautions in the beginning of this section.
2. Drain the cooling system.
3. Remove the upper and lower intake manifolds.
4. Disconnect the exhaust pipe from the exhaust manifold.
5. Loosen the air conditioning compressor drive belt, if equipped.
6. Loosen the alternator attaching bolts and remove the bolt attaching the alternator bracket to the right cylinder head.
7. Disconnect the air conditioning compressor from the engine and move it aside, out of the way. Do not discharge the air conditioning system.
8. Remove the bolts securing the power steering reservoir bracket to the left cylinder head. Position the reservoir and bracket out of the way. On motor home chassis, remove the oil filler tube.
9. Remove the valve rocker arm covers. Remove the rocker arm bolts, rocker arms, oil deflectors, fulcrums and pushrods in sequence so they can be reinstalled in their original positions.
10. Remove the cylinder head bolts and lift the head with the exhaust manifold off the engine. If necessary, pry at the forward corners of the cylinder head against the casting bosses provided on the cylinder block. Do not damage the gasket mating surfaces of the cylinder head and block by prying against them.

To install:

11. Remove all gasket material from the cylinder head and block. Clean all gasket material from the mating surfaces of the intake manifold. If the exhaust manifold was removed, clean the mating surfaces of the cylinder head and exhaust manifold. Apply a thin coat of graphite grease to the cylinder head exhaust port areas and install the exhaust manifold.
12. Position the 2 long cylinder head bolts in the 2 rear lower bolt holes of the left cylinder head. Place a long cylinder

head bolt in the rear lower bolt hole of the right cylinder head. Use rubber bands to keep the bolts in position until the cylinder heads are installed on the cylinder block.

13. Position the new cylinder head gaskets on the cylinder block dowels. Do not apply sealer to the gaskets, heads, or block.

14. Place the cylinder heads on the block while guiding the exhaust manifold studs into the exhaust pipe connections. Install the remaining cylinder head bolts. The longer bolts go in the lower row of holes.

15. Torque all the cylinder head attaching bolts in the proper sequence in 3 stages:
- 80–90 ft. lbs. (109–122 Nm).
- 100–110 ft. lbs. (136–149 Nm).
- 130–140 ft. lbs. (176–190 Nm).

➡**When this tightening procedure is used, it is not necessary to retorque the heads after extended use.**

16. Clean and inspect the oil holes in the pushrods, making sure the oil holes are open.

17. Place a dab of Lubriplate® to the ends of the pushrods before installing them and install the pushrods in their original positions.

18. Lubricate and install the valve rockers. Be sure the pushrods remain seated in their lifters.

19. Connect the exhaust pipes to the exhaust manifolds.

20. Install the upper and lower intake manifolds.

21. Install the air conditioning compressor.

22. Install the power steering reservoir.

23. Apply oil-resistant sealer to one side of the new valve cover gaskets and lay the cemented side in place in the valve cover. Install the covers.

24. Install the alternator and adjust the drive belt.

25. Adjust the air conditioning compressor drive belt tension.

26. On motor home chassis, install the oil filler tube.

27. Fill and bleed the cooling system.

28. Drain the engine oil into a suitable container and replace the oil filter.

29. Fill the engine with the proper amount of engine oil.

30. Connect the negative battery cable.

31. Start the engine and check for any fluid or vacuum leaks.

Rocker Arms

REMOVAL & INSTALLATION

4.2L Engine

➡**If removing more than 1 rocker arm, mark the components for proper location.**

1. Before servicing the vehicle, refer to the precautions in the beginning of this section.

2. Disconnect the negative battery cable.

3. Remove the lower intake manifold.

4. Remove the rocker arm cover.

5. Remove the rocker arm hold-down bolt, then remove the rocker arm from the cylinder head.

To install:

6. Position the rocker arms in place, then install the hold-down bolts. Tighten the bolts to 23–29 ft. lbs. (30–40 Nm).

7. Install the rocker arm cover and the lower intake manifold.

8. Connect the negative battery cable.

4.6L and 5.4L Engines

1. Before servicing the vehicle, refer to the precautions in the beginning of this section.

2. Disconnect the negative battery cable.

3. Remove the camshaft covers.

4. Position the piston of the cylinder being serviced at the bottom of its travel.

➡**Two different valve spring compressor tools are used for this procedure. Valve Spring Compressor (T91P-6565-A) is used on the exhaust camshaft and Valve Spring Compressor (T93P-6565-A) is used on the intake camshaft.**

5. Compress the valve spring and remove the rocker arm.

To install:

6. Position the piston of the cylinder being serviced at the bottom of its travel.

7. Apply clean engine oil to the rocker arm, valve stem tip and tappet bore.

➡**Valve tappet should have no more than ¹⁄₁₆ inch (1.5mm) of travel before installing the rocker arm.**

8. Compress the valve spring using the correct tool and install the rocker arm.

5.0L and 5.8L Engines

1. Before servicing the vehicle, refer to the precautions in the beginning of this section.

2. Remove the intake manifold.

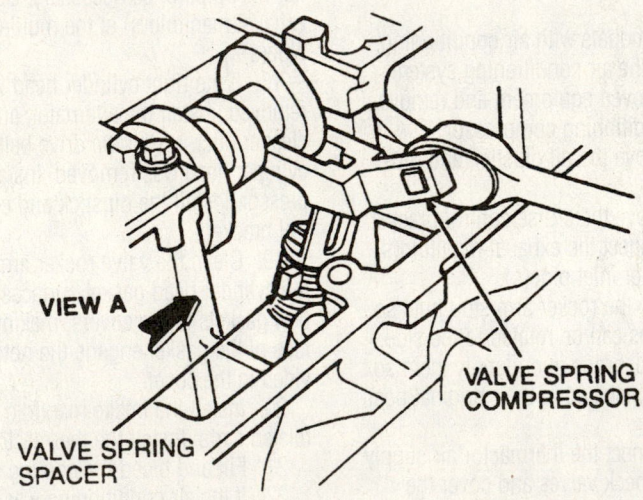

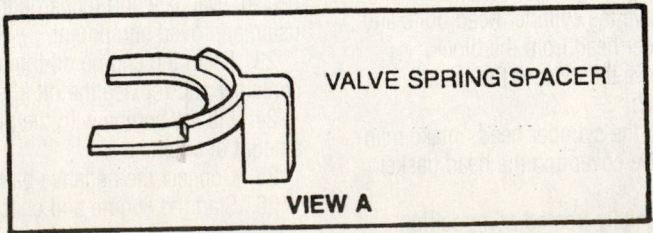

Using the proper tool, compress the valve spring and remove the rocker arm—4.6L and 5.4L engine

3. Disconnect the Thermactor air supply hose at the pump.

4. Remove the rocker arm covers.

5. Loosen the rocker arm fulcrum bolts, fulcrum seats and rocker arms; keep all parts in order for installation.

To install:

6. Apply multipurpose grease to the valve stem tips, the fulcrum seats and sockets.

7. Install the fulcrum guides, rocker arms, seats and bolts. Tighten the bolts to 18–25 ft. lbs. (25–34 Nm).

8. Install the rocker arm covers.

9. Connect the Thermactor air supply hose at the pump.

10. Install the intake manifold.

6.8L Engine

1. Before servicing the vehicle, refer to the precautions in the beginning of this section.

2. Disconnect the negative battery cable.

3. Remove the camshaft covers.

4. Position the base circle of the camshaft lobe on the rocker arm to be serviced. Also, be sure the piston is not at the top of its travel near the valve.

5. Compress the valve spring and remove the rocker arm.

To install:

6. Position the base circle of the camshaft lobe over the place where the rocker arm is to be installed.

7. Apply clean engine oil to the rocker arm, valve stem tip and tappet bore.

8. Compress the valve using the special tool and install the rocker arm.

9. Install the rocker arm covers and the remaining components.

7.5L Engine

1. Before servicing the vehicle, refer to the precautions in the beginning of this section.

2. Remove the intake manifold.

3. Remove the rocker arm covers.

4. Loosen the rocker arm fulcrum bolts, fulcrum, oil deflector, seat and rocker arms, keeping everything in order for installation.

To install:

5. Coat each end of each pushrod with multipurpose grease.

6. Coat the top of the valve stems, the rocker arms and the fulcrum seats with multipurpose grease.

7. Rotate the crankshaft by hand until No. 1 piston is at TDC of compression. The firing order marks on the damper will be aligned at TDC with the timing pointer.

8. Install the rocker arms, seats, deflectors and bolts on the following valves:
  - No. 1 intake and exhaust
  - No. 3 intake
  - No. 8 exhaust
  - No. 7 intake
  - No. 5 exhaust
  - No. 8 intake
  - No. 4 exhaust

9. Engage the rocker arms with the pushrods and tighten the rocker arm fulcrum bolts to 18–25 ft. lbs. (25–34 Nm).

10. Rotate the crankshaft 1 full turn (360 degrees) and realign the TDC mark and pointer. Install the parts and tighten the bolts on the following valves:
  - No. 2 intake and exhaust
  - No. 4 intake
  - No. 3 exhaust
  - No. 5 intake
  - No. 6 intake and exhaust
  - No. 7 exhaust

11. Install the rocker arm covers.

12. Install the intake manifold.

13. Check the valve clearance as described in this section for Valve Lash, and adjust if necessary.

Intake Manifold

REMOVAL & INSTALLATION

➡ **When the battery is disconnected and reconnected, some abnormal drive symptoms may occur while the vehicle relearns its adaptive strategy. The vehicle may need to be driven 10 miles (16 km) or more to relearn the strategy.**

4.2L Engine

➡ **Intake manifold head bolt torque sequences can be found in Section 1, following the Torque Specifications Chart.**

✳✳ CAUTION

Fuel injection systems remain under pressure, even after the engine has been turned OFF. The fuel system pressure must be relieved before disconnecting any fuel lines. Failure to do so may result in fire and/or personal injury.

1. Before servicing the vehicle, refer to the precautions in the beginning of this section.

2. Remove or disconnect the following:
  - Engine air cleaner outlet tube
  - Ignition coil electrical connector
  - Radio ignition interference capacitor electrical connector
  - Spark plug wires
  - Accelerator control splash shield
  - Accelerator cable end, if equipped, the speed control actuator cable end
  - Accelerator cable and actuator cable aside, after removing the hold-down bolts
  - Vapor Management Valve (VMV) hose

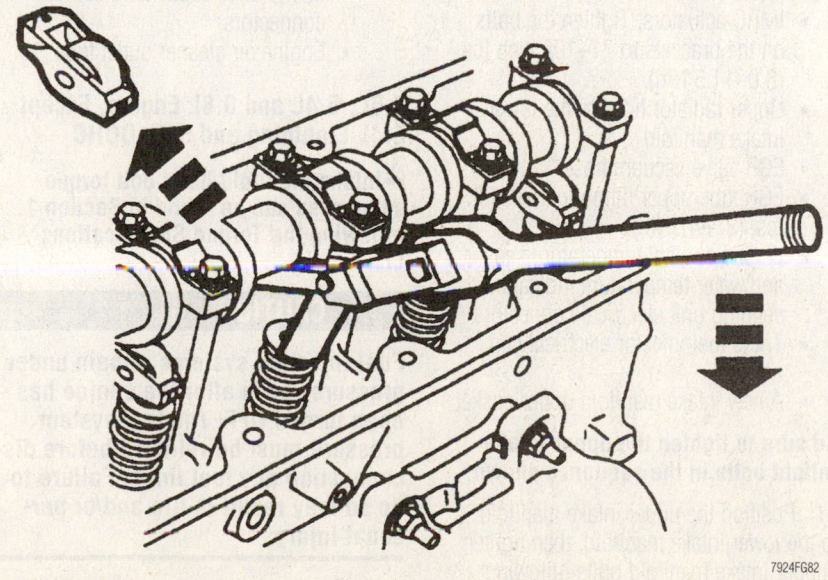

Compress the valve spring and remove the rocker arm—6.8L engine

7924FG82

- Brake booster vacuum hose
- Manifold vacuum connection
- PCV valve from the rocker arm cover
- Engine Vacuum Regulator (EVR) bracket aside
- TP sensor and IAC valve electrical connectors
- Breather from the rocker arm cover
- The 12 upper intake manifold retaining bolts, then lift the manifold off of the engine and discard the intake manifold upper gasket.
- The 6 fuel injector electrical connectors
- The engine coolant temperature sensor and the water temperature indicator sending unit electrical connectors.
- EGR valve vacuum hose
- EGR valve tube upper fitting
- Radiator hose from the lower intake manifold
- Intake Manifold Runner Control (IMRC) actuator brackets aside
- Fuel pressure regulator vacuum line
- Fuel system pressure
- Fuel lines
- Water pump bypass hose

➡**Remove the lower intake manifold with the fuel injection supply manifold and fuel injectors as one unit.**

- The 6 long bolts and the 8 short bolts, then lift the lower intake manifold off of the engine.

3. Remove and discard the lower intake manifold sealing components.

To install:

4. Clean all components of dirt, grease and old gasket material.

5. Install the lower intake manifold front and rear end seals as follows:

   a. Apply a bead of RTV sealant to the intake manifold front and rear end seal mounting points.

   b. Install the lower intake manifold front and rear end seals.

6. Install new lower intake manifold gaskets onto the cylinder heads.

➡**The lower intake manifold must be installed within 15 minutes of applying sealant.**

7. Apply a bead of RTV silicone gasket sealant to the end of the lower intake manifold end seals, where they stop on the cylinder head surface. Position the intake manifold onto the engine block and cylinder heads.

8. Install the lower intake manifold mounting bolts in the correct positions.

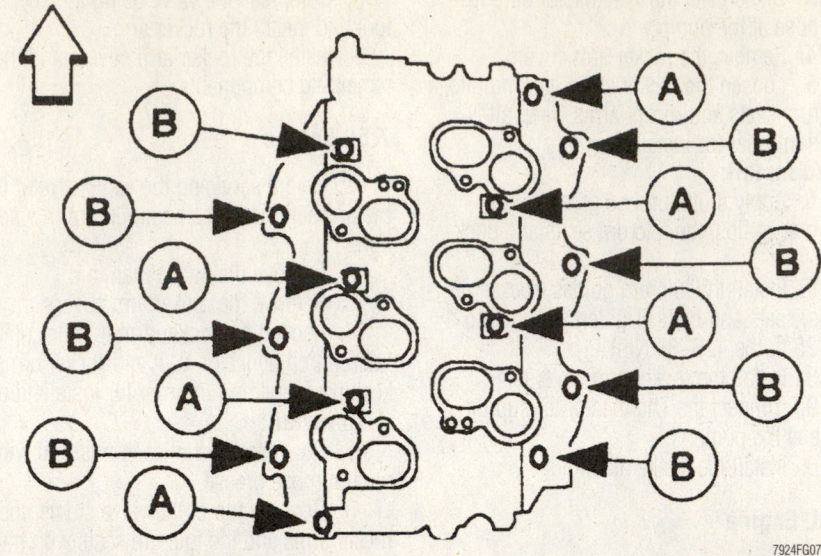

Make certain to install the long bolts (A) and the short bolts (B) in the correct lower intake manifold holes—4.2L engine

Refer to the illustration for the correct placement of the long (A) and the short (B) mounting bolts.

➡**Be sure to tighten the intake manifold bolts in 2 steps.**

9. Tighten the lower intake manifold mounting bolts following the tightening sequence:

- 44 inch lbs. (5 Nm).
- 71–101 inch lbs. (8.0–11.5 Nm).

10. Install or connect the following:

- Water bypass hose
- Fuel lines
- Fuel pressure regulator vacuum line
- IMRC actuators. Tighten the bolts on the brackets to 71–102 inch lbs. (8.0–11.5 Nm).
- Upper radiator hose to the lower intake manifold
- EGR valve vacuum hose
- EGR tube upper fitting to 25–34 ft. lbs. (37–47 Nm).
- Engine coolant temperature sensor and water temperature indicator sending unit electrical connectors
- The 6 fuel injector electrical connectors
- A new intake manifold upper gasket

➡**Be sure to tighten the upper intake manifold bolts in the sequence shown.**

11. Position the upper intake manifold onto the lower intake manifold, then tighten the upper intake manifold bolts following the tightening sequence as follows:

- 59 inch lbs. (6 Nm).
- 72–96 inch lbs. (8.0–11.5 Nm).

12. Install or connect the following:

- Breather into the rocker arm cover
- TP sensor and IAC valve electrical connectors
- EVR bracket
- Manifold vacuum connection
- PCV valve
- Brake booster vacuum hose
- Vapor Management Valve (VMV) hose
- Accelerator and speed actuator cables
- Accelerator control splash shield
- Spark plug wires
- Ignition coil and the radio ignition interference capacitor electrical connectors
- Engine air cleaner outlet tube

4.6L, 5.4L and 6.8L Engine, Except 5.4L Lightning and 5.4L DOHC

➡**Intake manifold head bolt torque sequences can be found in Section 1, following the Torque Specifications Chart.**

✱✱ CAUTION

Fuel injection systems remain under pressure, even after the engine has been turned OFF. The fuel system pressure must be relieved before disconnecting any fuel lines. Failure to do so may result in fire and/or personal injury.

1. Before servicing the vehicle, refer to the precautions in the beginning of this section.

2. Remove or disconnect the following:
   - Negative battery cable
   - Fuel system pressure
   - Coolant
   - Upper radiator hose from the intake manifold
   - Engine air cleaner outlet tube
   - Accelerator cable from the bracket and the throttle body cam
   - Speed control actuator cable from the throttle body
   - All vacuum hoses, fuel lines and electrical wires from the throttle body and intake manifold
   - Brake booster vacuum hose bracket
   - EGR valve-to-exhaust manifold tube
   - Fuel injector electrical connectors
   - On the 6.8L engine: the radio interference capacitors from the left side of the intake manifold
   - Spark plug wires, if necessary
   - Accessory drive belt
   - Alternator
   - Power steering oil reservoir bracket and set aside.
   - Heater hose from the intake manifold
   - Intake manifold bolts
   - Intake manifold from the engine, then detach the Intake Manifold Tuning Valve (IMTV) electrical connector. Remove and discard the upper intake manifold gaskets.
   - Upper-to-lower intake manifold bolts, then separate the upper intake manifold from the lower intake manifold. Discard the old gasket.

To install:

3. Position the lower intake manifold gasket and the upper intake manifold onto the lower intake manifold, then loosely install the upper-to-lower intake manifold bolts.

➡**Be sure to tighten the lower-to-upper manifold bolts in 2 steps.**

4. Tighten the 8 lower-to-upper intake manifold bolts in 2 steps following the tightening sequence as follows:
   - 18 inch lbs. (2 Nm).
   - 72–96 inch lbs. (8–12 Nm).

5. Position the 2 upper intake manifold gaskets on the cylinder heads. Set the upper intake manifold in place on the engine, then loosely install the 9 intake manifold-to-cylinder head bolts.

6. Attach the IMTV electrical connector.

➡**Check that the thermostat housing is in the correct position before the thermostat housing is installed.**

7. Install the thermostat housing and start the 2 housing bolts.

➡**Make certain to tighten the intake manifold in 2 steps.**

8. Tighten the intake manifold bolts using the sequence shown, in 2 steps.
   - 18 inch lbs. (2 Nm).
   - 15–22 ft. lbs. (20–30 Nm).

9. Install or connect the following:
   - Heater water hose
   - Power steering bracket and install the power steering pump bracket bolts to 71–107 inch lbs. (8–12 Nm).
   - All electrical connections, fuel lines, vacuum tubes and coolant hoses to the intake manifold, fuel injectors and throttle body assembly.
   - Alternator and the accessory drive belt
   - Spark plug wires
   - EGR valve-to-exhaust manifold tube. The tube fittings should be tightened to 26–33 ft. lbs. (35–45 Nm).
   - Speed actuator cable, if equipped, and the accelerator cable to the throttle body.
   - Engine air cleaner outlet tube
   - Heater hose
   - Coolant
   - Negative battery cable. Start the engine and check for fuel, vacuum or coolant leaks.

5.4L DOHC, Except Lightning

➡**Intake manifold head bolt torque sequences can be found in Section 1, following the Torque Specifications Chart.**

UPPER INTAKE MANIFOLD

1. Before servicing the vehicle, refer to the precautions in the beginning of this section.

2. Remove or disconnect the following:
   - Negative battery cable
   - Air cleaner outlet tube
   - Engine appearance cover
   - Accelerator cable, speed control cable, and the return spring
   - Bolts and position the cables and bracket out of the way

   - Evaporative emission return line
   - Positive crankcase ventilation tube from the upper intake manifold
   - PCV valve from the valve cover
   - PCV valve tube from the water heated fitting and remove the tube assembly
   - Coolant lines and plug the lines.
   - Electrical connector from the communication valve
   - Bolts and the communication valve
   - Wiring harness shield bolts and 5 clips and remove the shield
   - Balance tube from the engine
   - TP sensor and the IAC motor
   - Vacuum lines and detach the electrical connector from the EGR vacuum regulator (EVR).
   - The 2 hoses and detach the electrical connector from the differential pressure feedback EGR.
   - The bolts from the power steering reservoir bracket and position it aside.
   - The stud and position the oil fill tube aside.
   - Brake booster vacuum line
   - Vacuum line from the EGR valve
   - Bolts from the EGR adapter
   - Retaining bolts and remove the upper intake manifold.

To install:

3. Clean and inspect the sealing surfaces.

4. Install or connect the following:
   - Upper intake manifold: Tighten the bolts to 89 inch lbs. (10 Nm) and then an additional 90 degrees in the sequence shown.
   - EGR adapter with a new gasket
   - Vacuum line to the EGR valve
   - Brake booster vacuum line
   - Oil fill tube and install the stud
   - Power steering reservoir bracket and install the bolts.
   - EGR valve at the exhaust manifold
   - The 2 hoses and the electrical connector to the differential pressure feedback EGR
   - Vacuum lines and the electrical connector to the EVR
   - IAC valve and the TP sensor
   - Balance tube on the engine
   - Communication valve and the bolts
   - Wiring harness shield, the bolts and 5 clips
   - Electrical connector to the communication valve
   - Tube assembly and connect the

Please refer to Section 8 for electric cooling fan wiring schematics

PCV valve tube to the water-heated fitting.
- Coolant hoses
- PCV valve in the valve cover
- EVAP return line
- Cables and bracket and install the bolts
- Accelerator cable, speed control cable, and the return spring
- Engine appearance cover and the 3 bolts
- Engine air cleaner and outlet tube

LOWER INTAKE MANIFOLD

✳✳ CAUTION

Fuel injection systems remain under pressure, even after the engine has been turned OFF. The fuel system pressure must be relieved before disconnecting any fuel lines. Failure to do so may result in fire and/or personal injury.

1. Before servicing the vehicle, refer to the precautions in the beginning of this section.
2. Remove or disconnect the following:
   - Negative battery cable
   - Coolant
   - Upper intake manifold
   - Fuel system pressure
   - Fuel lines
   - Engine water bypass hose
   - Electrical connector from the water temperature indicator sender
   - Upper radiator hose, the heater water inlet hose and the heated PCV water fitting inlet hose.
   - The 4 bolts and the upper alternator support bracket
   - The 8 fuel injectors
   - Vacuum line from the fuel injector pressure regulator and position out of the way.
   - Lower intake manifold
   - Radio ignition interference capacitors

To install:

3. Remove and inspect the gaskets, install new gaskets if necessary.
4. Clean the sealing surfaces.
5. Install or connect the following:
   - Radio ignition interference capacitors

➡**Bolts should be hand-started, positions 7–12 first then 1–6.**

   - Lower intake manifold: Tighten the bolts to 89 inch lbs. (10 Nm) and then an additional 90 degrees in the sequence shown.

   - Water temperature indicator sensor
   - Vacuum harness and connect the vacuum line to the fuel injector pressure regulator.
   - Fuel injectors
   - Upper generator support bracket and the 4 bolts
   - Heater water inlet hose, the upper radiator hose and the water heated fitting inlet hose
   - Engine water bypass return hose
   - Fuel lines
   - Upper intake manifold
   - Coolant

5.4L Lightning

➡**Intake manifold head bolt torque sequences can be found in Section 1, following the Torque Specifications Chart.**

✳✳ CAUTION

Fuel injection systems remain under pressure, even after the engine has been turned OFF. The fuel system pressure must be relieved before disconnecting any fuel lines. Failure to do so may result in fire and/or personal injury.

1. Before servicing the vehicle, refer to the precautions in the beginning of this section.
2. Remove or disconnect the following:
   - Negative battery cable
   - Charge air cooler
   - Fuel system pressure
   - Fuel lines
   - Coolant
   - Accelerator cable bracket retaining bolts and remove the bracket.
   - Upper radiator hose from the thermostat housing

✳✳ CAUTION

Do not disconnect the PCV hose system from the intake. Installation can not be carried out with the intake in place.

   - PCV system
   - Ground strap and both radio ignition interference capacitors
   - Vacuum line
   - Charge air cooler temperature sensor connector
   - Heater hose
   - Fuel injector electrical connectors
   - Vapor management valve vacuum line

   - Vacuum line near the brake vacuum booster
   - Fuel injection supply manifold
   - Ignition coil connectors
   - Ignition coils
   - Accessory drive belt
   - Alternator bracket
   - Intake manifold

To install:

3. Position the gaskets.

✳✳ CAUTION

If the PCV system hose becomes disconnected, the intake manifold will have to be removed to reattach the hose.

4. Make sure that the PCV system hose is securely connected.
5. Install or connect the following:
   - Intake manifold
   - Thermostat outlet
   - Intake manifold bolts. Tighten the bolts in 2 stages. Stage 1: tighten to 18 inch lbs. (2 Nm). Stage 2: tighten to 19 ft. lbs. (25 Nm).
   - Alternator bracket
   - Accessory drive belt
   - Ignition coils
   - Ignition coil connectors
   - Fuel injection supply manifold and install the bolts.
   - Vacuum line near the brake vacuum booster
   - Vapor management valve vacuum line
   - Fuel injector electrical connectors
   - Heater hose
   - Charge air cooler temperature sensor
   - Vacuum line
   - Ground strap and both radio ignition interference capacitors
   - PCV system
   - Upper radiator hose
   - Accelerator cable bracket and tighten the bolts.
   - Fuel lines
   - Charge air cooler

6. Fill and bleed the engine cooling system.

5.0L, 5.8L and 7.5L Engines

➡**Intake manifold head bolt torque sequences can be found in Section 1, following the Torque Specifications Chart.**

➡**Relieve the fuel system pressure before starting any work that involves disconnecting fuel system lines.**

UPPER INTAKE MANIFOLD

⁑ CAUTION

Fuel injection systems remain under pressure, even after the engine has been turned OFF. The fuel system pressure must be relieved before disconnecting any fuel lines. Failure to do so may result in fire and/or personal injury.

1. Before servicing the vehicle, refer to the precautions in the beginning of this section.

2. Remove or disconnect the following:
- Air cleaner
- Electrical connectors at the air bypass valve, TP sensor and EGR position sensor
- Throttle linkage at the throttle ball and the transmission linkage from the throttle body. Remove the bolts that secure the bracket to the intake and position the bracket and cables out of the way.
- Upper manifold vacuum fitting connections by removing all the vacuum lines at the vacuum tree (label lines for position identification).
- Vacuum lines to the EGR valve and fuel pressure regulator
- PCV system, by disconnecting the hose from the fitting at the rear of the upper manifold.
- The 2 canister purge lines from the fittings at the throttle body
- EGR tube from the EGR valve by loosening the flange nut
- The bolt from the upper intake support bracket to upper manifold. Remove the upper manifold retaining bolts and remove the upper intake manifold and throttle body as an assembly.

3. Clean and inspect all mounting surfaces of the upper and lower intake manifolds.

To install:

4. Install or connect the following:
- New mounting gasket on the lower intake manifold
- Upper intake manifold and throttle body as an assembly.
- Upper manifold retaining bolts and install the bolt at the upper intake support bracket. Mounting bolts are tightened to 12–18 ft. lbs. (16–25 Nm).
- EGR tube at the EGR valve

- The 2 canister purge lines at the fittings at the throttle body
- PCV system hose at the fitting at the rear of the upper manifold
- Upper manifold vacuum lines at the vacuum tree
- Vacuum lines at the EGR valve and fuel pressure regulator
- Throttle bracket on the intake manifold. Attach the throttle linkage at the throttle ball and the transmission linkage at the throttle body.
- Electrical connectors at the air bypass valve, TP and EGR position sensor
- Air cleaner

LOWER INTAKE MANIFOLD

⁑ CAUTION

Fuel injection systems remain under pressure, even after the engine has been turned OFF. The fuel system pressure must be relieved before disconnecting any fuel lines. Failure to do so may result in fire and/or personal injury.

1. Before servicing the vehicle, refer to the precautions in the beginning of this section.

2. The upper manifold and throttle body must be removed first.

3. Drain the cooling system.

4. Make reference marks and remove the distributor assembly, cap and wires.

5. Remove or disconnect the following:
- Electrical connectors at the engine, coolant temperature sensor and sending unit, at the air charge temperature sensor and at the knock sensor
- Injector wiring harness from the main harness assembly
- Ground wire from the intake manifold stud. The ground wire must be installed at the same position it was removed from.
- Fuel system pressure
- Fuel supply and return lines from the fuel rails
- Upper radiator hose from the thermostat housing
- Bypass hose
- Heater outlet hose at the intake manifold
- Air cleaner mounting bracket
- Intake manifold mounting bolts and studs

➥During removal, note the location of the bolts and studs for reinstallation.

- Lower intake manifold assembly

To install:

6. Clean and inspect the mounting surfaces of the heads and manifold.

7. Apply a 1⁄16 inch (1.5mm) bead of RTV sealer to the ends of the manifold seal (the junction point of the seals and gaskets). Install the end seals and intake gaskets on the cylinder heads. The gaskets must interlock with the seal tabs.

8. Install locator bolts at opposite ends of each head and carefully lower the intake manifold into position. Install and tighten the mounting bolts and studs to 23–25 ft. lbs. (31–34 Nm).

9. Install or connect the following:
- Air cleaner mounting bracket
- Heater outlet hose at the intake manifold
- Bypass hose
- Upper radiator hose
- Fuel supply and return lines at the fuel rails
- Injector wiring harness to the main harness assembly
- Ground wire to the intake manifold stud
- Electrical connectors for the engine, coolant temperature sensor, sending unit, air charge temperature sensor and the knock sensor
- Distributor assembly, cap and wires

10. Check and adjust the ignition timing if necessary.

11. Fill the cooling system.

Exhaust Manifold

REMOVAL & INSTALLATION

4.2L Engine

1. Before servicing the vehicle, refer to the precautions in the beginning of this section.

2. Remove or disconnect the following:
- Negative battery cable
- For the right-hand manifold: the EGR valve-to-exhaust manifold tube
- For the left-hand manifold: the oil level indicator tube bracket nut, then remove the oil level indicator tube. Remove and discard the oil level indicator tube O-ring.
- Oxygen (O2S) sensor electrical connector

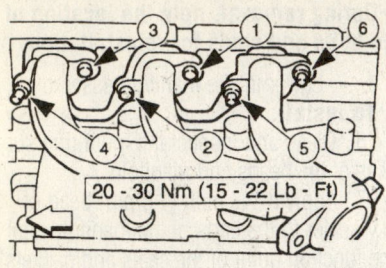

20 - 30 Nm (15 - 22 Lb - Ft)

7924FG14

Tighten the left-hand exhaust manifold bolts in the order shown—4.2L engine

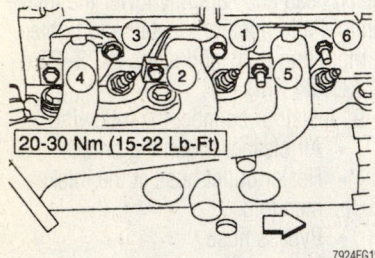

20-30 Nm (15-22 Lb-Ft)

7924FG15

Tighten the right-hand exhaust manifold bolts in the order shown—4.2L engine

- The 2 catalytic converter-to-exhaust manifold nuts, then disconnect the Y-pipe from the left-hand exhaust manifold.
- Exhaust manifold stud bolts, then remove the manifold mounting bolts
- Exhaust manifold. Remove and discard the exhaust manifold gasket.

To install:
3. Install or connect the following:
- New exhaust manifold gasket onto the engine, then install the exhaust manifold. Tighten the bolts and stud bolts in the sequence shown to 15–22 ft. lbs. (20–30 Nm).
- Y-pipe to the exhaust manifold, then install and tighten the catalytic converter nuts to 25–34 ft. lbs. (34–46 Nm).
- O_2S sensor connector, then lower the vehicle.
- Left-hand exhaust manifold: a new oil level indicator tube O-ring onto the tube. Insert the tube into the engine block and tighten the bracket retaining nut to 15–22 ft. lbs. (20–30 Nm).
- For the right-hand exhaust manifold: the EGR valve-to-exhaust manifold tube. Tighten the upper and lower fittings to 25–34 ft. lbs. (34–47 Nm).
- Negative battery cable

4.6L, 5.4 and 6.8L Engines

1. Before servicing the vehicle, refer to the precautions in the beginning of this section.
2. Remove or disconnect the following:
- Front fender splash shield
- For the left-hand exhaust manifold: the EGR valve-to-exhaust manifold tube and if equipped, the DPFE gas recirculation transducer hoses.
- On the 4.6L and 5.4L engines: the catalytic converter-to-exhaust manifold bolts
- On the 6.8L engine: the front exhaust pipe from the manifold
- The exhaust manifold mounting nuts, then remove the exhaust manifold itself. Remove and discard the old gasket.
3. Clean and inspect the exhaust manifold for damage.

To install:
4. Position a new gasket and the exhaust manifold onto the engine block.
5. Install the mounting nuts and tighten following the sequence shown.
- 4.6L and 5.4L engines: 13–16 ft. lbs. (18–22 Nm).
- 6.8L engines: 17–20 ft. lbs. (23–27 Nm).
6. On the 6.8L engine, tighten the exhaust manifold-to-front pipe fasteners to 27–34 ft. lbs. (34–46 Nm).

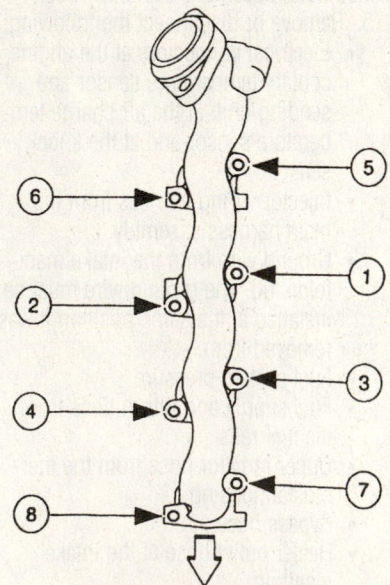

7924FG16

Tighten the exhaust manifold bolts in the sequence shown—4.6L engine shown, 5.4L engine similar

23-27 Nm (17-20 lb/ft)

7924FG85

Tighten the exhaust manifold bolts in the sequence shown—right side of 6.8L engine shown

7. On the 4.6L and 5.4L engines, attach the catalytic converter to the exhaust manifold, install the catalytic converter-to-exhaust manifold bolts and tighten to 25–34 ft. lbs. (34–46 Nm).
8. For the left-hand exhaust manifold, install the DPFE transducer hoses if equipped, and the EGR valve-to-exhaust manifold tube. Tighten the upper and lower fittings to 26–33 ft. lbs. (35–45 Nm).
9. Install the front fender splash shield.
10. Lower the vehicle to the ground.

5.0L, 5.8L and 7.5L Engines

1. Before servicing the vehicle, refer to the precautions in the beginning of this section.
2. On the 5.0L (VIN N) engine, remove the dipstick bracket.
3. Disconnect the exhaust pipe or catalytic converter from the exhaust manifold. Remove and discard the doughnut gasket.
4. Remove the exhaust manifold attaching screws and remove the manifold from the cylinder head.

To install:
5. Apply a light coat of graphite grease to the mating surface of the manifold. Install and tighten the attaching bolts, starting from the center and working alternately to both ends. Tighten to the proper torque specification.
6. Install the exhaust pipe or catalytic converter to the exhaust manifold using a new doughnut gasket.
7. If removed, install the dipstick bracket.

Camshaft and Valve Lifters

REMOVAL & INSTALLATION

4.2L Engine

1. Before servicing the vehicle, refer to the precautions in the beginning of this section.

2. Remove or disconnect the following:
- Negative battery cable
- Lower intake manifold
- Rocker arm cover
- Rocker arm hold-down bolt, then remove the rocker arm from the cylinder head.
- Pushrods
- Valve lifters by pulling them up out of their bores
- Timing chain and sprockets
- Camshaft key from the end of the camshaft, then slide the engine dynamic balance shaft drive gear off the camshaft.
- The 2 camshaft thrust plate retaining bolts (1), then remove the thrust plate (2). Remove the camshaft spacer (3), then slide the camshaft (4) out of the front of the engine block. Be cautious not to gouge or scratch the camshaft bearing journals.

To install:

3. Lubricate the camshaft with engine oil prior to installation.

4. Carefully slide the camshaft into the camshaft bore. Do not scratch the bearing surfaces.

5. Install the camshaft thrust plate with the spacer. Tighten the thrust plate mounting bolts to 72–120 inch lbs. (8–14 Nm).

6. Slide the engine dynamic balance shaft drive gear onto the camshaft. Install the camshaft key to the camshaft groove.

7. Install the timing chain and sprockets.

8. Install the valve lifters, pushrods, intake manifolds and rocker arm covers.

4.6L, 5.4L and 6.8L Engines

1. Before servicing the vehicle, refer to the precautions in the beginning of this section.

2. Remove the cylinder head covers from the engine.

3. Remove the timing chain.

✳✳ CAUTION

At no time, when the timing chains are removed and the cylinder heads are installed may the crankshaft or camshaft be rotated. Severe piston and valve damage will occur.

4. On the 6.8L engine, remove the 6 bolts securing the balance shaft to the cylinder head and remove the shaft.

5. Remove the camshaft roller lifters.

6. On VIN W engines, remove the timing chain camshaft gear by removing the gear retaining bolt.

➡**Keep the bearing caps in order so they can be installed in the same position.**

7. Remove the camshaft bearing cap bolts, then lift the camshaft bearing caps off of the cylinder head.

8. Lift the camshaft from the cylinder head.

9. Remove the rocker arms and pull the lash adjusters out of their bores. Keep all the parts in order. They must be installed in their original positions.

To install:

10. Install the lash adjusters and rocker arms in their original positions.

11. Lubricate the camshaft journals and bearing caps with SAE 5W30 engine oil. On the 6.8L engine, lubricate the balance shaft journals and bearing caps with the same lubricant.

12. Lower the camshaft onto the camshaft bearing journals.

13. Install the camshaft bearing caps, then loosely install the bearing cap bolts.

14. Tighten the camshaft bearing cap mounting bolts, in the sequence shown for the particular engine, to 71–107 inch lbs. (8–12 Nm).

15. On the 6.8L engine, align the timing marks and position the balance shaft on the journals, then install the bearing caps. Tighten the bolts in sequence to 71–106 inch lbs. (8–12 Nm).

16. On VIN W engines, install the camshaft timing chain gear by tightening the retaining bolt to 81–95 ft. lbs. (110–130 Nm).

17. Install the valve lifters.

18. Install the timing chain and sprockets, if applicable.

19. Install the cylinder head covers.

Exploded view of the camshaft retaining hardware—4.2L engine

7924FG38

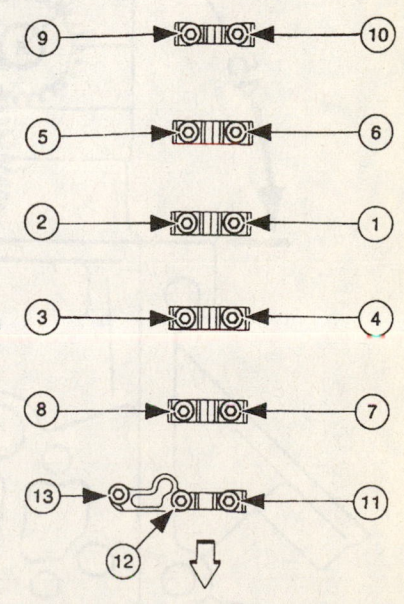

Tighten the bearing caps in the sequence shown—4.6L and 5.4L engines

7924FG18

Timing belt service is covered in Section 4 of this manual

8-12 Nm (71-106 lb/in)

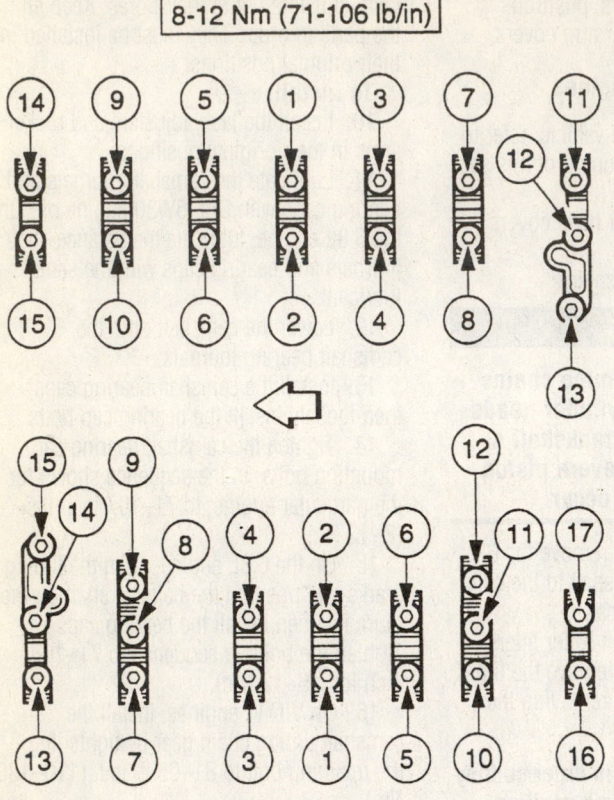

Camshaft bearing cap bolt tightening sequence—6.8L engine

8-12 Nm (71-106 lb/in)

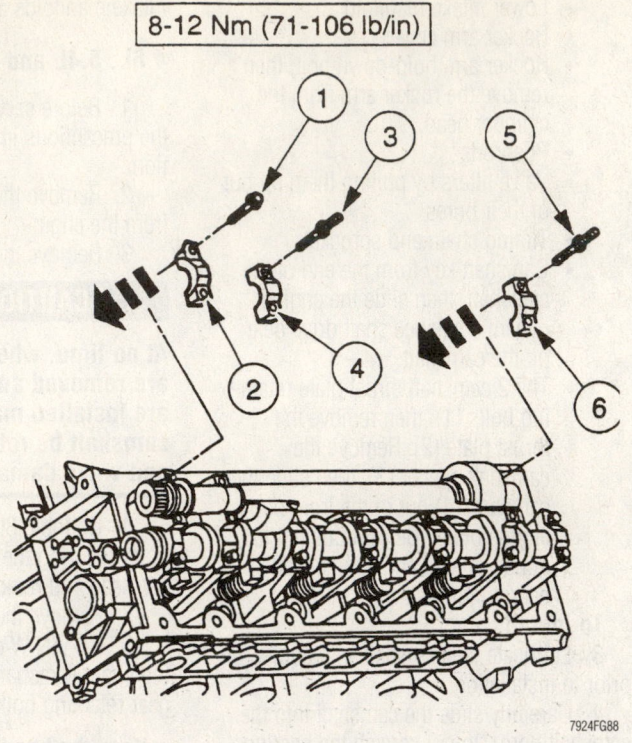

Tighten the balance shaft bearing cap bolts in the sequence shown—6.8L engine

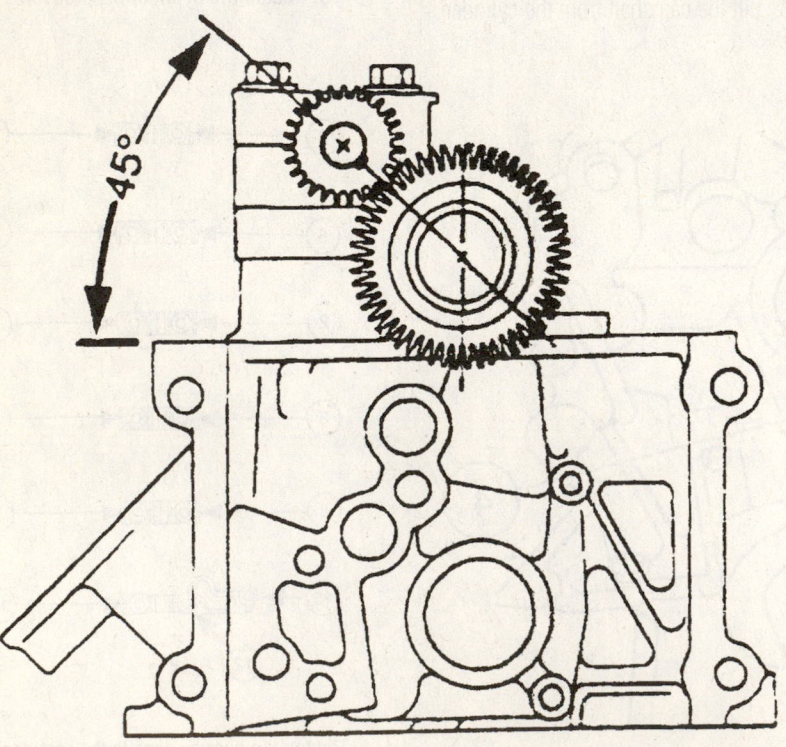

Be sure to align the balance shaft timing mark with the mark on the camshaft gear—6.8L engine

5.0L, 5.8L and 7.5L Engines

1. Before servicing the vehicle, refer to the precautions in the beginning of this section.

2. Remove the intake manifold and valley pan, if equipped.

3. Remove the rocker covers, and loosen the rockers on their pivots and remove the pushrods. The pushrods must be reinstalled in their original positions.

4. Remove the valve lifters in sequence with a magnet. They must be replaced in their original positions.

5. Remove the timing gear cover, timing chain and sprockets.

6. In addition to the radiator and air conditioning condenser, it may be necessary to remove the front grille assembly and hood lock to gain the necessary clearance to remove the camshaft out of the front of the engine.

➡A camshaft removal tool, Ford part no. T65L-6250-a and adapter 14-0314, or equivalent, is needed to remove the diesel camshaft.

To install:

7. Coat the camshaft liberally with clean engine oil before installing it. Slide

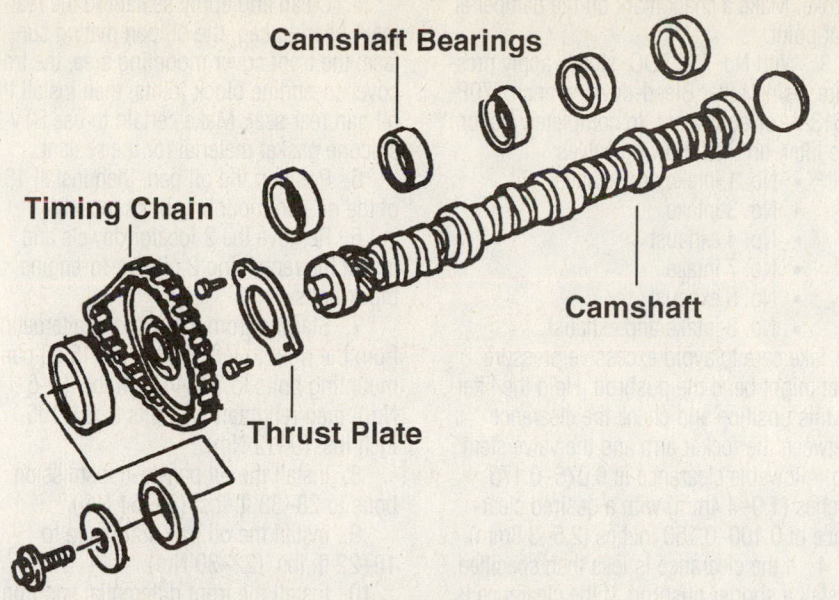

Camshaft Bearings

Timing Chain

Camshaft

Thrust Plate

Camshaft and related components—5.0L, 5.8L and 7.5L engines

the camshaft into the engine very carefully so as not to scratch the bearing bores with the camshaft lobes.

8. Install the camshaft thrust plate and tighten the attaching screws to 10–12 ft. lbs. (13–16 Nm).

9. Measure the camshaft end-play. If the end-play is more than 0.009 inch (0.228mm), replace the thrust plate.

10. Assemble the remaining components in the reverse order of removal.

11. Install the radiator, front grille, hood lock assembly and air conditioning condenser, if removed.

12. Install the timing chain and front cover.

13. Install the valve lifters. They must be replaced in their original positions.

14. Install the pushrods, the rocker arms and the rocker arm covers.

15. Install the intake manifold and valley pan, if equipped.

Valve Lash

ADJUSTMENT

4.2L, 4.6L, 5.4L and 6.8L Engines

The 4.2L, 4.6L, 5.4L and 6.8L engines do not require valve lash adjusting, because they utilize hydraulic lash components in their valve actuation systems. The 4.2L engine uses hydraulic valve lifters, whereas the 4.6L, 5.4L and 6.8L engines utilize

hydraulic lash adjusters, all of which automatically adjust the valve lash. No valve lash adjustment is necessary.

5.0L Engine

1. Before servicing the vehicle, refer to the precautions in the beginning of this section.

2. Rotate the crankshaft by hand so No. 1

piston is at TDC of the compression stroke. Make a chalk mark on the damper at that point, then, make 2 more chalk marks about 90 degrees apart in a clockwise direction.

3. With No. 1 at TDC, slowly apply pressure, using Lifter Bleed-down wrench T70P-6513-A, or equivalent, to completely bottom the lifter, on the following valves:
- No. 1 intake and exhaust
- No. 7 intake
- No. 5 exhaust
- No. 8 intake
- No. 4 exhaust

Take care to avoid excessive pressure that might bend the pushrod. Hold the lifter in this position and check the clearance between the rocker arm and the valve stem tip. Allowable clearance is 0.071–0.193 inches (1.8–4.9mm) with a desired clearance of 0.096–0.165 inches (2.4–4.2mm).

4. If the clearance is less than specified, install a shorter pushrod. If the clearance is greater than specified, install a longer pushrod.

5. Rotate the crankshaft clockwise—viewed from the front—180 degrees, until the next chalk mark is aligned with the timing pointer. Repeat the procedure for:
- No. 5 intake
- No. 2 exhaust
- No. 4 intake
- No. 6 exhaust

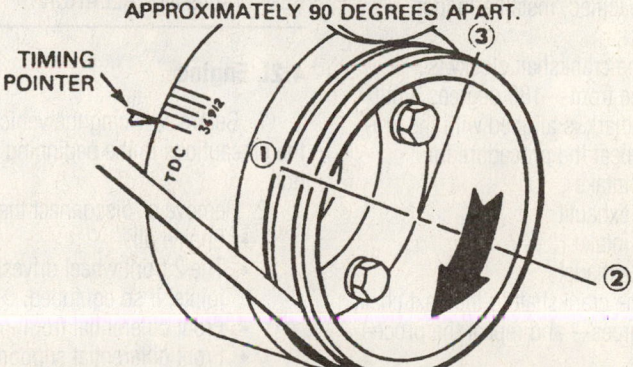

WITH NO. 1 AT TDC AT END OF COMPRESSION STROKE MAKE A CHALK MARK AT POINTS 2 AND 3 APPROXIMATELY 90 DEGREES APART.

TIMING POINTER

POSITION 1 — NO. 1 AT TDC AT END OF COMPRESSION STROKE.
POSITION 2 — ROTATE THE CRANKSHAFT 180 DEGREES (1/2 REVOLUTION) CLOCKWISE FROM POSITION 1.
POSITION 3 — ROTATE THE CRANKSHAFT 270 DEGREES (3/4 REVOLUTION) CLOCKWISE FROM POSITION 2.

Valve clearance adjustment positions on the crankshaft damper/pulley—5.0L, 5.8L and 7.5L engines

6. Rotate the crankshaft to the next chalk mark—90 degrees—and repeat the procedure for:

- No. 2 intake
- No. 7 exhaust
- No. 3 intake and exhaust
- No. 6 intake
- No. 8 exhaust

5.8L Engine

1. Before servicing the vehicle, refer to the precautions in the beginning of this section.

2. Rotate the crankshaft by hand so No. 1 piston is at TDC of the compression stroke. Make a chalk mark on the damper at that point, then, make 2 more chalk marks about 90 degrees apart in a clockwise direction.

3. With No. 1 at TDC, slowly apply pressure, using Lifter Bleed-down wrench T70P-6513-A, or equivalent, to completely bottom the lifter, on the following valves:

- No. 1 intake and exhaust
- No. 4 intake
- No. 3 exhaust
- No. 8 intake
- No. 7 exhaust

Take care to avoid excessive pressure that might bend the pushrod. Hold the lifter in this position and check the clearance between the rocker arm and the valve stem tip. Allowable clearance is 0.098–0.198 inches (2.5–5.0mm) with a desired clearance of 0.123–0.173 inches (3.1–4.4mm).

4. If the clearance is less than specified, install a shorter pushrod. If the clearance is greater than specified, install a longer pushrod.

5. Rotate the crankshaft clockwise—viewed from the front—180 degrees, until the next chalk mark is aligned with the timing pointer. Repeat the procedure for:

- No. 3 intake
- No. 2 exhaust
- No. 7 intake
- No. 6 exhaust

6. Rotate the crankshaft to the next chalk mark—90 degrees—and repeat the procedure for:

- No. 2 intake
- No. 4 exhaust
- No. 5 intake and exhaust
- No. 6 intake
- No. 8 exhaust

7.5L Engine

1. Before servicing the vehicle, refer to the precautions in the beginning of this section.

2. Rotate the crankshaft by hand so No. 1 piston is at TDC of the compression

stroke. Make a chalk mark on the damper at that point.

3. With No. 1 at TDC, slowly apply pressure, using Lifter Bleed-down wrench T70P-6513-A, or equivalent, to completely bottom the lifter, on the following valves:

- No. 1 intake and exhaust
- No. 3 intake
- No. 4 exhaust
- No. 7 intake
- No. 5 exhaust
- No. 8 intake and exhaust

Take care to avoid excessive pressure that might bend the pushrod. Hold the lifter in this position and check the clearance between the rocker arm and the valve stem tip. Allowable clearance is 0.075–0.175 inches (1.9–4.4mm) with a desired clearance of 0.100–0.150 inches (2.5–3.8mm).

4. If the clearance is less than specified, install a shorter pushrod. If the clearance is greater than specified, install a longer pushrod.

5. Rotate the crankshaft clockwise—viewed from the front—360 degrees, until the chalk mark is once again aligned with the timing pointer. Repeat the procedure for:

- No. 2 intake and exhaust
- No. 4 intake
- No. 3 exhaust
- No. 5 intake
- No. 7 exhaust
- No. 6 intake and exhaust

Oil Pan

REMOVAL & INSTALLATION

4.2L Engine

1. Before servicing the vehicle, refer to the precautions in the beginning of this section.

2. Remove or disconnect the following:

- Engine oil
- The 2 front wheel driveshafts and joints, if so equipped.
- Front differential from the vehicle
- Front differential support
- The 3 oil pan-to-transmission bolts
- The 15 oil pan-to-cylinder block mounting bolts, then lower the oil pan.

To install:

➡ **If the oil pan is not installed within 15 minutes, remove the sealer and reapply.**

3. Temporarily install 2 locator dowels in 2 of the oil pan-to-engine block corner mounting bolt holes.

4. Clean and apply sealant to the rear main bearing cap, the oil pan mating surface, the front cover mounting area, the front cover-to-engine block joints, then install the oil pan rear seal. Make certain to use RTV silicone gasket material for the sealant.

5. Position the oil pan, then install 13 of the oil pan mounting bolts loosely.

6. Remove the 2 locator dowels and install the remaining 2 oil pan-to-engine block bolts.

7. Starting from the rear and alternating from the right to left, tighten the 15 oil pan mounting bolts to 36–44 inch lbs. (4–5 Nm), then retighten the bolts to 80–106 inch lbs. (9–12 Nm).

8. Install the oil pan-to-transmission bolts to 28–38 ft. lbs. (38–51 Nm).

9. Install the oil pan drain plug to 16–22 ft. lbs. (22–30 Nm).

10. Install the front differential and front differential support.

11. Install the front driveshafts and joints.

12. Lower the vehicle to the ground.

13. Fill the engine with the correct type and amount of engine oil.

4.6L and 5.4L Engines

1. Before servicing the vehicle, refer to the precautions in the beginning of this section.

2. Raise and safely support the vehicle.

3. Remove the front axle housing from the vehicle.

4. Drain the engine oil into a suitable container.

5. Remove the 16 oil pan-to-engine block bolts.

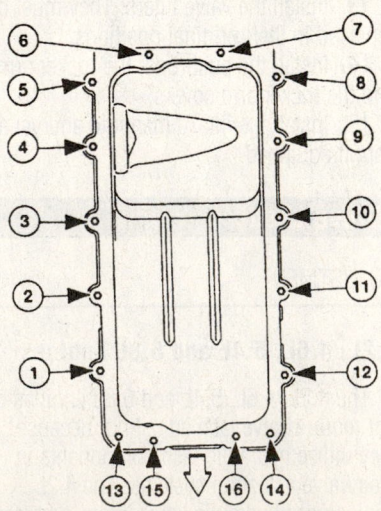

Tighten the oil pan-to-engine block bolts in 3 steps following the sequence shown—4.6L and 5.4L engines

7924FG21

6. Remove the oil pan and old oil pan gasket.

To install:

7. Clean the oil pan and engine block mating surfaces of oil and old gasket material.

8. Install the new oil pan gasket and the oil pan, then install the 16 oil pan-to-engine block bolts loosely.

➤**Be sure to tighten the oil pan bolts in 3 steps.**

9. Tighten the oil pan-to-engine bolts in the sequence shown, in the following 3 steps:

- 18 inch lbs. (2 Nm)
- 15 ft. lbs. (20 Nm)
- + 60 degrees

10. Install the oil drain plug.
11. Install the front axle housing.
12. Lower the vehicle.
13. Fill the engine with the correct amount and type of engine oil.

5.0L and 5.8L Engines

1. Before servicing the vehicle, refer to the precautions in the beginning of this section.

2. Remove or disconnect the following:

- Coolant
- Fan shroud to the radiator and position the shroud over the fan
- Upper intake manifold and throttle body
- Nuts and lockwashers attaching the engine support insulators to the chassis bracket
- Oil cooler line at the left side of the radiator
- Exhaust system

3. Raise the engine and place wood blocks under the engine supports.

4. Remove or disconnect the following:

- Engine oil
- Transmission crossmember
- Oil pan attaching bolts and lower the oil pan onto the crossmember.
- The 2 bolts attaching the oil pump pick-up tube to the oil pump
- Nut attaching the oil pump pick-up tube to the No. 3 main bearing cap stud. Lower the pick-up tube and screen into the oil pan.
- Oil pan from the vehicle

To install:

5. Clean the oil pan, inlet tube and gasket surfaces. Inspect the gasket sealing surface for damages and distortion due to over tightening of the bolts. Repair and straighten as required.

6. Install or connect the following:

- New oil pan gasket and seal to the cylinder block
- Oil pick-up tube and screen to the oil pump, and install the lower attaching bolt and gasket loosely. Install the nut on the No. 3 main bearing cap stud.
- Oil pan on the crossmember. Install the upper pick-up tube bolt. Tighten the pick-up tube bolts.
- Oil pan to the cylinder block and install the attaching bolts. Tighten to 10–12 ft. lbs. (14–16 Nm).
- Transmission crossmember

7. Raise the engine and remove the blocks under the engine supports. Bolt the engine to the supports.

8. Install or connect the following:

- Exhaust system
- Oil cooler line at the left side of the radiator
- Nuts and lockwashers attaching the engine support insulators to the chassis bracket
- Upper intake manifold and throttle body
- Fan shroud

9. Fill the crankcase.
10. Fill and bleed the cooling system.

6.8L Engine

> **❋❋ CAUTION**
>
> **Fuel injection systems remain under pressure, even after the engine has been turned OFF. The fuel system pressure must be relieved before disconnecting any fuel lines. Failure to do so may result in fire and/or personal injury.**

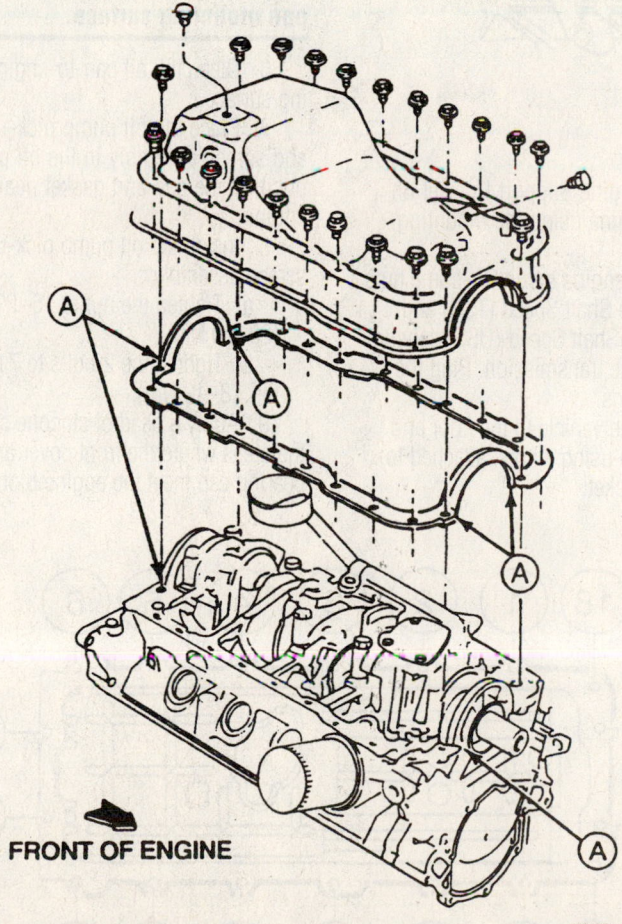

FRONT OF ENGINE

7924FG42

Exploded view of the oil pan mounting. apply RTV sealant to the areas marked "A"—5.0L and 5.8L engines

---

Refer to Section 1 for engine rebuilding specifications

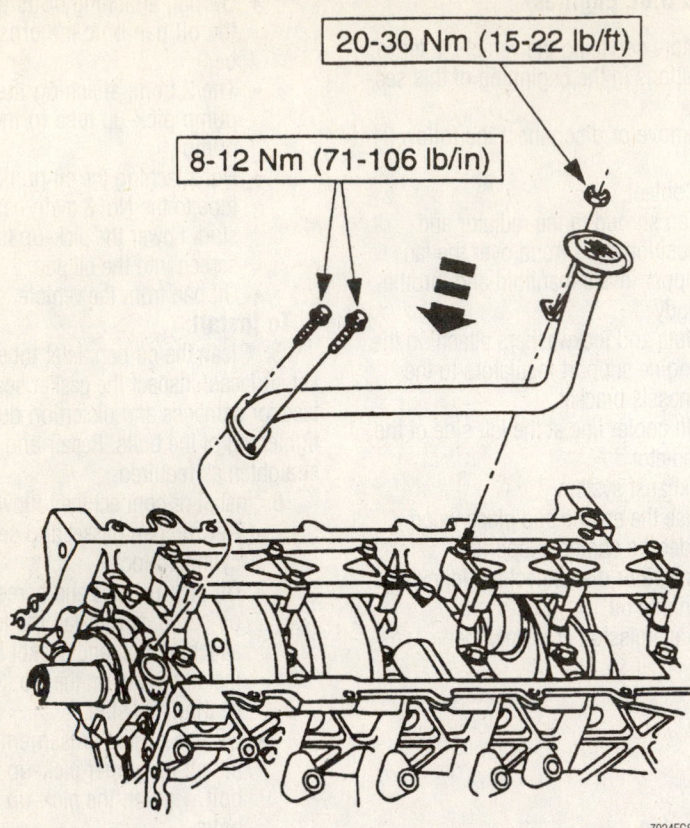

20-30 Nm (15-22 lb/ft)

8-12 Nm (71-106 lb/in)

7924FG89

Oil pump pick-up tube and screen assembly—6.8L engine

1. Before servicing the vehicle, refer to the precautions in the beginning of this section.

2. Remove or disconnect the following:
- Negative battery cable
- Fuel system pressure
- Coolant
- Upper radiator hose from the intake manifold
- Air cleaner outlet tube
- Accelerator cable from the bracket and the throttle body cam
- Speed control actuator cable from the throttle body
- All vacuum hoses, fuel lines and electrical wires from the throttle body and intake manifold
- Brake booster vacuum hose bracket
- EGR valve-to-exhaust manifold tube and disconnect the vacuum line
- Connector and vacuum line from the Engine Vacuum Regulator (EVR) solenoid
- The 4 bolts and the throttle body adapter
- Upper fan shroud mounting screws and position the shroud toward the engine.
- The alternator and install the Mod-

ular Engine Support Bracket on the engine using the mounting holes.
- Lower engine mount-to-frame nuts
- Turbine Shaft Speed (TSS) and Output Shaft Speed (OSS) sensors from the transmission. Plug the openings.

3. Lower the vehicle to the floor and raise the engine using a hoist attached to the support bracket.

4. Install an engine support fixture with a J hook to keep the engine raised, then remove the hoist.

5. Remove or disconnect the following:
- Engine oil and filter
- Dual converter Y-pipe and the flywheel inspection cover
- Driveshaft and the 2 transmission mounting nuts
- Transmission. Be sure to support the transmission along the rails of the pan to avoid damage.
- Oil pan mounting bolts and partially lower the pan.
- Oil pump pick-up tube and screen assembly and allow it to drop into the pan.
- Oil pan towards the rear of the vehicle

To install:

✻✻ WARNING

To prevent possible oil leaks, use only a plastic scraper to clean the oil pan mounting surface.

6. Clean the oil pan-to-engine mounting surface.

7. Place the oil pump pick-up tube and screen assembly in the oil pan, then position the pan and gasket near the engine.

8. Install the oil pump pick-up tube and screen assembly.

   a. Tighten the nut to 15–22 ft. lbs. (20–30 Nm).

   b. Tighten the 2 bolts to 71–106 inch lbs. (8–12 Nm).

9. Apply a bead of silicone sealant to the areas where the front cover and rear bearing cap meet the engine block.

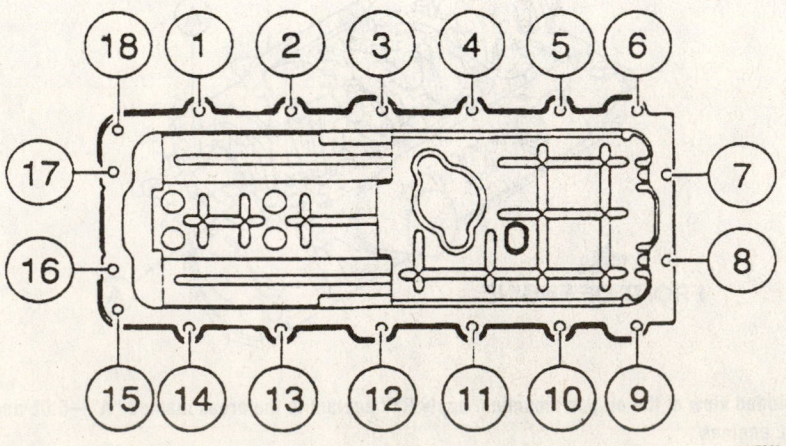

7924FG90

To prevent leaks, tighten the oil pan bolts in the order shown—6.8L engine

10. Install the oil pan. Tighten the bolts in sequence using 3 steps as follows:
- 18 inch lbs. (2 Nm)
- 15 ft. lbs. (20 Nm)
- + 60°

11. Lower the transmission and install the 2 mounting nuts. Tighten the nuts to 60–80 ft. lbs. (81–108 Nm).

12. Install the driveshaft and the TSS and OSS sensors.

13. Install the flywheel cover and dual converter Y-pipe.

14. Install the oil bypass filter.

15. Lower the vehicle and remove the engine support fixture.

16. Install the engine mounting nuts. Tighten the nuts to 66 ft. lbs. (90 Nm).

17. Remove the modular engine support bracket and install the alternator.

18. Install the fan shroud.

19. Use a new gasket and install the throttle body adapter.

20. Tighten the bolts in 2 steps:
- 71–88 inch lbs. (8–10 Nm).
- 85–95 degrees.

21. Connect the EVR solenoid harness and vacuum line.

22. Attach the vacuum line to the EGR valve.

23. Install the EGR valve-to-exhaust manifold tube. Tighten the fittings to 55 ft. lbs. (41 Nm).

24. Install the EGR transducer.

25. Install all remaining components in the reverse of the removal.

※※ WARNING

Operating the engine without the proper amount and type of engine oil will result in severe engine damage.

26. Fill the engine with SAE 5W30 oil.
27. Fill and bleed the cooling system.

7.5L Engine

※※ CAUTION

Fuel injection systems remain under pressure, even after the engine has been turned OFF. The fuel system pressure must be relieved before disconnecting any fuel lines. Failure to do so may result in fire and/or personal injury.

1. Before servicing the vehicle, refer to the precautions in the beginning of this section.

2. Remove or disconnect the following:
- Hood
- Battery ground cable
- Coolant
- Air intake tube and air cleaner assembly
- Throttle linkage at the throttle body
- Power brake vacuum line at the manifold
- Fuel system pressure
- Fuel lines at the fuel rail
- Air tubes at the throttle body
- Radiator
- Power steering pump and position it out of the way without disconnecting the lines.
- Oil dipstick tube. On motor home chassis, remove the oil filler tube.
- Front engine mount through-bolts

3. Position the air conditioner refrigerant hoses so they are clear of the firewall. If necessary, discharge the system and remove the compressor.

4. Remove or disconnect the following:
- Upper intake manifold and throttle body
- Engine oil and filter
- Exhaust pipe at the manifolds
- Transmission linkage at the transmission
- Driveshaft(s)
- Transmission fill tube

5. Raise the engine with a jack placed under the crankshaft damper and a block of wood to act as a cushion. Raise the engine until the transmission contacts the underside of the floor. Place wood blocks under the engine supports. The engine **must** remain centralized at a point at least 4 inches (102mm) above the mounts, to remove the oil pan!

6. Remove the oil pan attaching screws and lower the oil pan onto the crossmember. Remove the 2 bolts attaching the oil pump pick-up tube to the oil pump. Lower the assembly from the oil pump. Leave it on the bottom of the oil pan. Remove the oil pan and gaskets. Remove the inlet tube and screen from the oil pan.

To install:

7. Clean the gasket surfaces of the oil pan and cylinder block.

8. Apply a coating of gasket adhesive on the block mating surface and stick the one-piece silicone gasket on the block.

9. Clean the inlet tube and screen assembly and place on the pump.

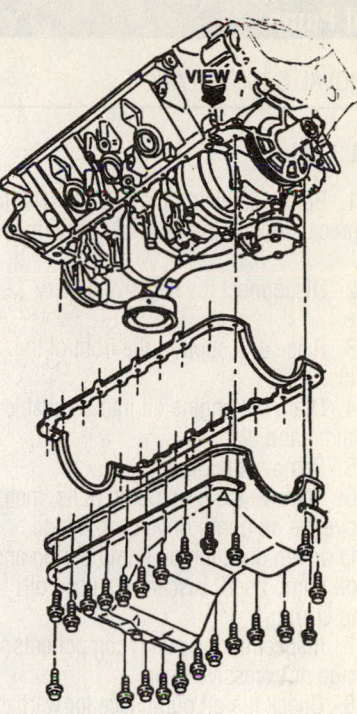

Exploded view of the oil pan mounting—7.5L engine

10. Install or connect the following:
- Oil pan against the cylinder block and install the retaining bolts. Tighten all bolts to 10 ft. lbs. (14 Nm).
- Engine and bolt it in place
- Transmission fill tube
- Driveshaft(s)
- Transmission linkage at the transmission
- Exhaust pipe at the manifolds
- Oil filter
- Upper intake manifold and throttle body
- Compressor or reposition the hoses
- Oil dipstick tube. On motor home chassis, install the oil filler tube.
- Power steering pump
- Radiator
- Air tubes at the throttle body
- Fuel lines at the fuel rail
- Power brake vacuum line at the manifold
- Throttle linkage at the throttle body
- Air intake tube and air cleaner assembly

11. Fill and bleed the cooling system.
12. Fill the crankcase.
13. Connect the battery ground cable.
14. Install the hood.

Oil Pump

REMOVAL & INSTALLATION

4.2L Engine

1. Before servicing the vehicle, refer to the precautions in the beginning of this section.

2. Disconnect the negative battery cable.

3. Raise and support the front of the vehicle.

4. Drain the engine oil into a suitable container and dispose.

5. Remove the oil filter.

6. Remove the 6 oil pump bolts, then remove the oil pump drive gear, the oil pump driven gear, the oil pump O-ring and the oil pump itself. Discard the used oil pump O-ring.

7. Inspect the oil pump components for damage or excessive wear.

8. Check the oil pump face for warpage with a flat edge ruler. The face cannot exhibit more than 0.00157 inches (0.04mm) of distortion.

9. Remove the plug over the oil pressure relief; valve.

10. Remove the oil pressure relief valve ball and spring, then clean the parts.

To install:

➡**Lubricate the parts with clean engine oil before assembly.**

11. Assemble the oil pressure relief valve ball and spring with a new plug.

12. Install the oil pump, along with a new O-ring, the oil pump driven gear and the drive gear. Install and tighten the 6 oil pump mounting bolts to the torque value specifications indicated in the illustration.

13. Apply a film of clean engine oil to the rubber O-ring on the new filter, then install the filter onto the filter mount.

14. Install the oil pan drain plug.

15. Lower the vehicle.

16. Fill the engine with the correct amount and type of new engine oil.

17. Connect the negative battery cable.

18. Start the engine and make certain that the oil light on the instrument panel extinguishes within 6–8 seconds after the engine starts.

4.6L and 5.4L Engines

1. Before servicing the vehicle, refer to the precautions in the beginning of this section.

2. Disconnect the negative battery cable.

3. Remove the timing chain.

4. Drain the engine oil into a suitable container.

5. Remove the oil pan.

6. Remove the 3 oil pump screen and cover bolts, then remove the screen and cover.

7. Remove the oil pump screen and cover spacer.

8. Remove the 4 oil pump mounting bolts, then remove the oil pump from the engine.

To install:

9. Clean and inspect the mating surfaces.

10. Install the oil pump and loosely install the 4 oil pump mounting bolts. Tighten the 4 oil pump bolts in the sequence shown to 71–106 inch lbs. (8–12 Nm).

11. Install the oil pump screen and cover spacer to 15–22 ft. lbs. (20–30 Nm).

12. Install the oil pump screen and cover, then install the 3 oil pump screen and cover bolts. Tighten the bolts near the oil pick-up screen to 15–22 ft. lbs. (20–30 Nm) and the bolts at the opposite end of the pick-up to 70–106 inch lbs. (8–12 Nm).

13. Install the timing chains, then install the oil pan.

14. Refill the engine oil with the recommended engine oil and amount.

15. Install the negative battery cable.

5.0L, 5.8L and 7.5L Engines

1. Before servicing the vehicle, refer to the precautions in the beginning of this section.

2. Disconnect the negative battery cable.

3. Drain the engine oil into a suitable container.

4. Remove the oil pan.

5. Remove the oil pump inlet tube and screen assembly.

6. Remove the oil pump attaching bolts and remove the oil pump gasket and intermediate driveshaft.

To install:

7. Before installing the oil pump, prime it by filling the inlet and outlet port with oil and rotating the shaft of the pump to distribute it.

8. Position the intermediate driveshaft into the distributor socket.

9. Position the new gasket on the pump body and insert the intermediate driveshaft into the pump body.

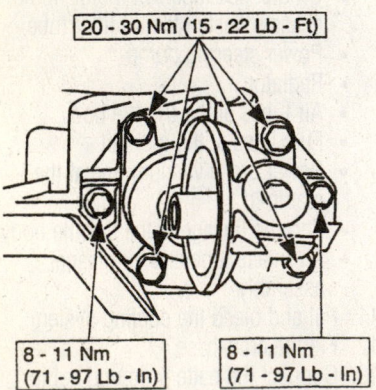

20 - 30 Nm (15 - 22 Lb - Ft)

8 - 11 Nm (71 - 97 Lb - In)

8 - 11 Nm (71 - 97 Lb - In)

7924FG22

Tighten the oil pump mounting bolts to the specifications shown—4.2L engines

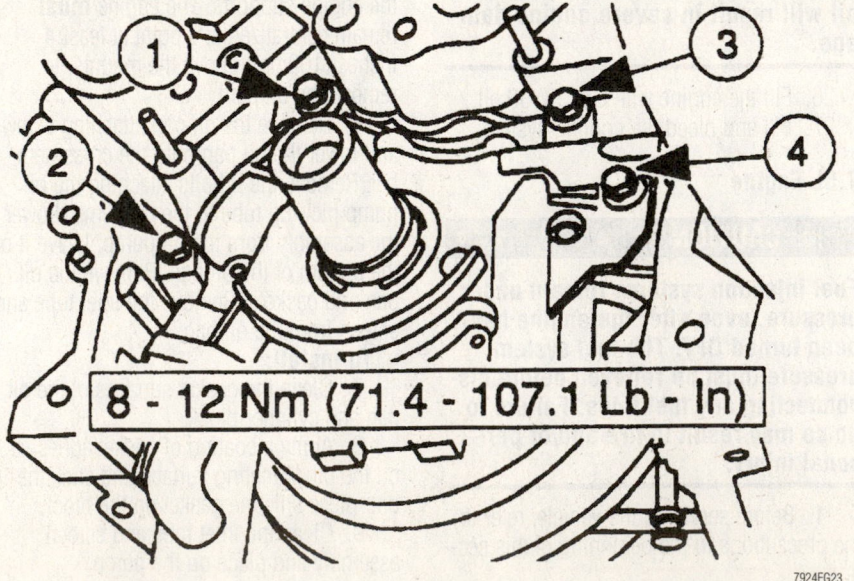

8 - 12 Nm (71.4 - 107.1 Lb - In)

7924FG23

Tighten the oil pump mounting bolts to 71–106 inch lbs. (8–12 Nm) in the sequence shown— 4.6L and 5.4L engines

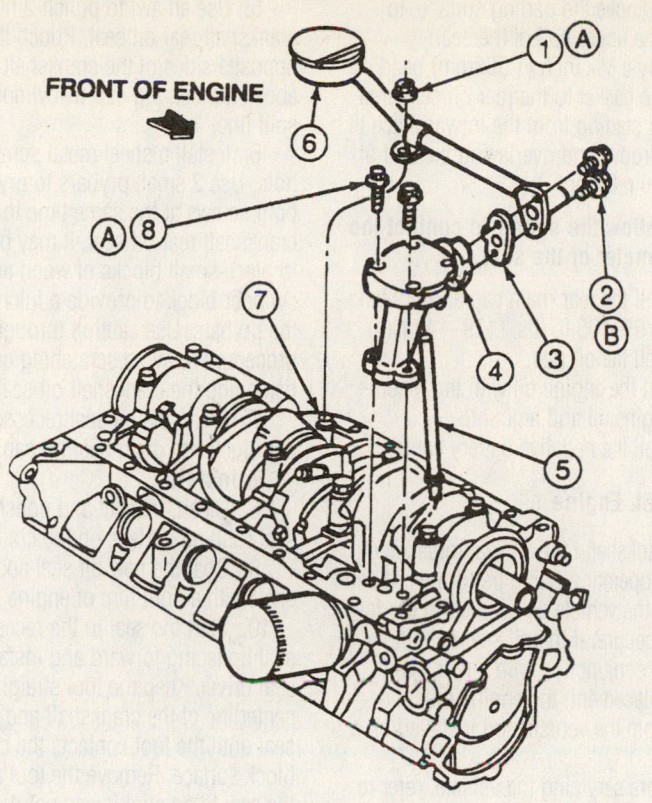

FRONT OF ENGINE

Exploded view of the oil pump mounting—5.0L engine shown, 5.8L and 7.5L engines are similar

10. Install the pump and intermediate driveshaft as an assembly. Do not force the pump if it does not seal readily. The driveshaft may be misaligned with the distributor shaft. To align it, rotate the intermediate driveshaft into a new position.

11. Install the oil pump attaching bolts and tighten them to 20–25 ft. lbs. (27–34 Nm).

12. Refill the engine oil with the recommended engine oil and amount.

13. Install the negative battery cable.

6.8L Engine

1. Before servicing the vehicle, refer to the precautions in the beginning of this section.

2. Disconnect the negative battery cable.

3. Remove the engine front cover and crankshaft sprocket.

4. Drain the engine oil into a suitable container.

5. Remove the oil pan.

6. Remove the 3 oil pump mounting bolts, then remove the oil pump from the engine.

To Install:

7. Clean and inspect the mating surfaces.

8. Install the oil pump and loosely install the oil pump mounting bolts. Tighten the bolts in the sequence shown to 71–106 inch lbs. (8–12 Nm).

9. Install the oil pan.

10. Install the crankshaft sprocket and timing chains.

11. Install the front cover.

12. Refill the engine oil with the recommended engine oil and amount.

13. Install the negative battery cable.

Rear Main Seal

REMOVAL & INSTALLATION

7.5L Engine

1. Before servicing the vehicle, refer to the precautions in the beginning of this section.

2. Disconnect the negative battery cable.

3. Raise and safely support the vehicle.

4. Drain the engine oil into a suitable container.

5. Remove the oil pan.

6. Loosen all the crankshaft main bearing cap bolts and lower the crankshaft no more than 1/32 inch (0.7938mm).

✳✳ CAUTION

Be careful that the crankshaft sealing surfaces are not damaged in this process

7. Remove the rear main bearing cap and remove the seal. On the cylinder block half of the seal, use a seal removal tool, or install a small metal screw in one end of the seal and pull on the screw to remove the seal.

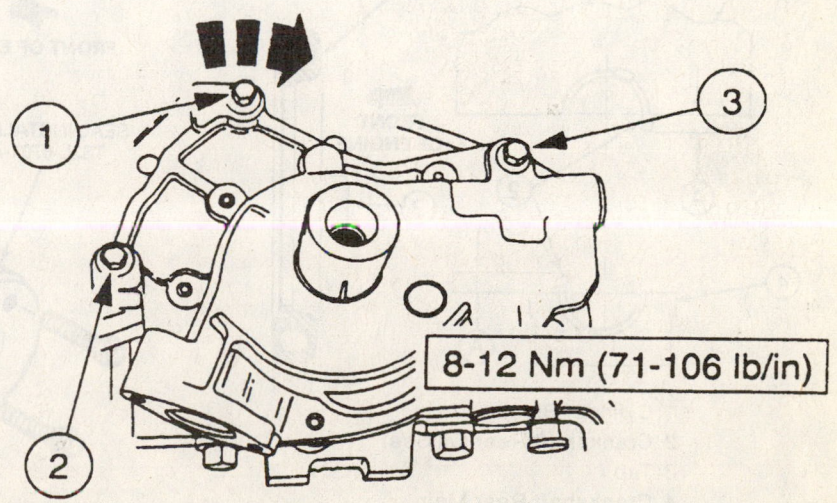

8-12 Nm (71-106 lb/in)

Be sure to tighten the oil pump mounting bolts in the sequence shown—6.8L engine

For complete mechanical specifications, refer to Section 1 of this manual

To install:

8. Clean the seal groove in the crank-shaft main bearing cap and the block using a brush and a solvent such as metal surface cleaner F4AZ-19A536-RA, or its equivalent.

9. Clean the areas where the sealer is to be applied later and dry the area thoroughly so that no solvent contacts the rear main seal.

10. Dip the seal halves in engine oil.

❊❊ CAUTION

Be sure no rubber has been removed from the outside diameter of the seal by the bottom edge of the groove. Do not allow oil to get on the sealer.

11. Install the upper half of the seal (cylinder block side) into its groove with the undercut side of the seal towards the front of the engine (with the tab side of the seal towards the rear face of the block). Rotate it on the seal journal until approximately ⅜ inch (9.525mm) protrudes below the parting surface.

12. Tighten all the crankshaft main bearing cap bolts, **EXCEPT THE REAR MAIN BEARING**, to 95–105 ft. lbs. (129–142 Nm).

13. Install the lower half of the seal in the rear crankshaft main bearing cap with the undercut side of the seal towards the front of the engine (with the tab side of the seal towards the rear face of the block). Allow the seal to protrude ⅜ inch

(9.525mm) above the parting surface, to mate with the upper half of the seal.

14. Apply a ¹⁄₁₆ inch (1.588mm) bead of RTV silicone gasket to the rear oil seal area of the block starting from the forward face of the return groove and overlaying the end of the wire seal retainer.

➡ **Do not allow the sealer to contact the inside diameter of the seal.**

15. Install the rear main cap and tighten the bolts to 95–105 ft. lbs. (129–142 Nm).

16. Install the oil pan.

17. Refill the engine oil with the recommended engine oil and amount.

18. Install the negative battery cable.

Except 7.5L Engine

If the crankshaft rear oil seal replacement is the only operation being performed, it can be done in the vehicle as detailed in the following procedure. If the oil seal is being replaced in conjunction with a rear main bearing replacement, the engine must be removed from the vehicle and installed on a work stand.

1. Before servicing the vehicle, refer to the precautions in the beginning of this section.

2. Disconnect the negative battery cable.

3. Remove the transmission from the vehicle.

4. Remove the flywheel/flexplate. If equipped, remove the crankshaft oil slinger from the crankshaft.

5. Use an awl to punch 2 holes in the crankshaft rear oil seal. Punch the holes on opposite sides of the crankshaft and just above the bearing cap-to-cylinder block split line.

6. Install a sheet metal screw in each hole. Use 2 small prybars to pry against both screws at the same time to remove the crankshaft rear oil seal. It may be necessary to place small blocks of wood against the cylinder block to provide a fulcrum point for the prybars. Use caution throughout this procedure to avoid scratching or otherwise damaging the crankshaft oil seal surface.

7. Clean the oil seal recess in the cylinder block and main bearing cap.

To install:

8. Clean, inspect and polish the rear oil seal rubbing surface on the crankshaft.

9. Coat the new oil seal and the crankshaft with a light film of engine oil.

10. Start the seal in the recess with the seal lip facing forward and install it with a seal driver. Keep the tool straight with the centerline of the crankshaft and install the seal until the tool contacts the cylinder block surface. Remove the tool and inspect the seal to be sure it was not damaged during installation.

11. If equipped, install the crankshaft oil slinger.

12. Position the flywheel on the crankshaft flange. Coat the threads of the flywheel attaching bolts with Locktite® and install the bolts. Tighten the bolts in sequence across

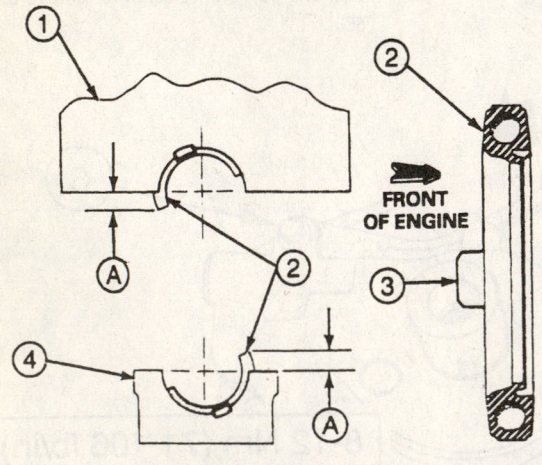

1 Cylinder Block
2 Crankshaft Rear Oil Seal
3 Tab
4 Crankshaft Rear Main Bearing Cap
5 9.53mm (3/8 Inch)

7924FG45

Rear main seal and related components—7.5L engines

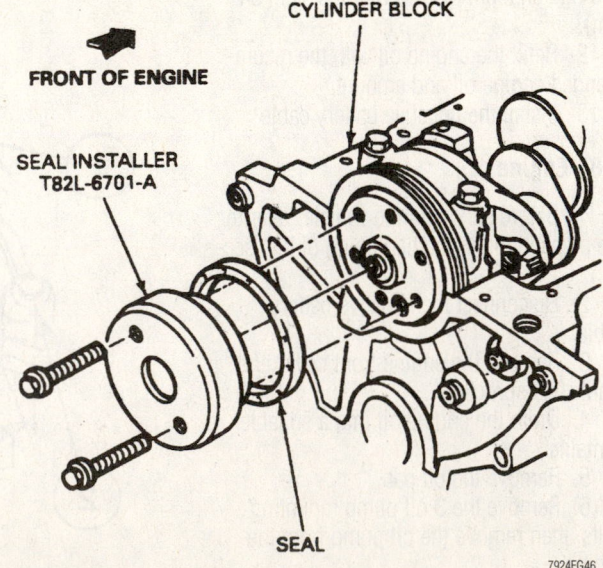

Rear main oil seal installation—5.0L and 5.8L engines

from each other to 75–85 ft. lbs. (102–115 Nm).

13. Install the transmission, following the recommended procedure.

14. Install the negative battery cable.

Piston and Ring Positioning

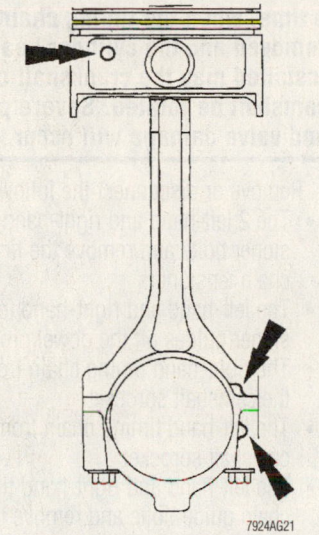

4.2L and 4.6L engines—piston and connecting rod front mark locations

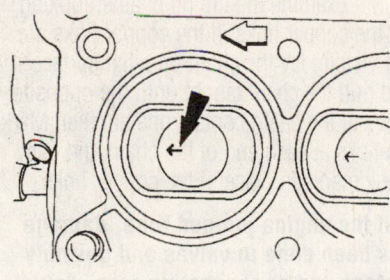

4.2L and 4.6L engines—piston-to-engine orientation

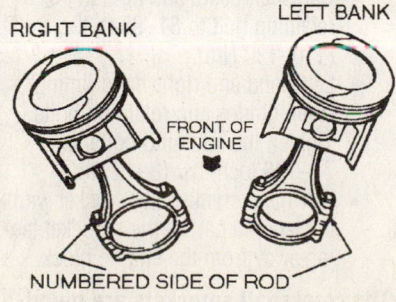

5.0L, 5.4L, 5.8L and 6.8L engines—piston and connecting rod assembly positioning

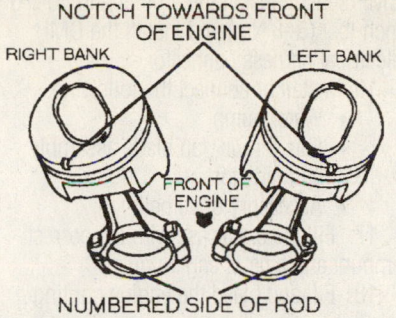

7.5L engine—piston and connecting rod assembly positioning

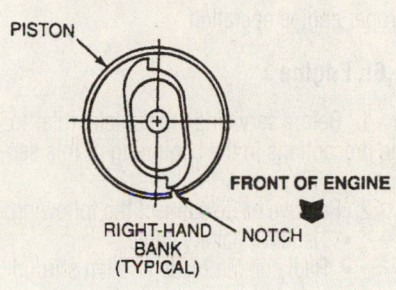

Ford 7.5L engine—piston-to-engine orientation

Timing Chain, Sprockets and Front Cover

REMOVAL & INSTALLATION

4.2L Engine

1. Before servicing the vehicle, refer to the precautions in the beginning of this section.

2. Remove or disconnect the following:
   - Negative battery cable
   - Accessory drive belt
   - Coolant
   - Radiator, fan blade assembly and fan shroud
   - Water pump
   - EGR valve vacuum hose
   - EGR tube upper fitting
   - EGR valve and adapter assembly
   - Wiring harness from the heater water outlet tube
   - Heater water outlet bolt and position the outlet tube aside
   - CMP sensor electrical harness connector and mark the position of the connector for proper installation.

3. Rotate the crankshaft until the TDC timing mark lines up with the timing mark.

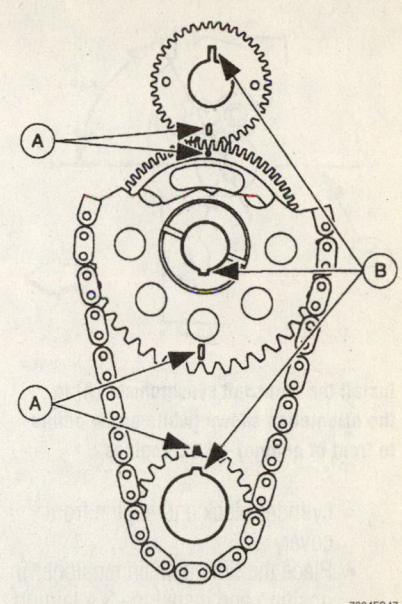

After removing the CMP drive gear, be sure the timing marks (A) and keyways (B) are aligned—4.2L engine

4. Remove or disconnect the following:
   - The 2 bolts retaining the CMP and remove the CMP from the camshaft synchronizer.
   - Camshaft synchronizer adjustment bolt and remove the camshaft synchronizer.

➡ **The oil pump drive shaft may come out with the camshaft synchronizer.**

   - Engine oil
   - Crankshaft pulley and damper
   - Engine oil pan
   - The 2 engine front cover stud bolts, front cover bolt and cap screw
   - Engine front cover and gasket off the dowels and discard the gasket.
   - CMP sensor drive gear bolt and drive gear

5. Be sure the timing marks and keyways align.

6. Compress and install a retaining pin to hold the timing chain tensioner.

7. Slide both sprockets and timing chain forward and remove as an assembly.

8. Remove the 3 bolts retaining the timing chain tensioner and remove the tensioner.

9. Check the timing chain and sprockets for excessive wear. Replace if necessary.

To install:
   - Before installation, clean and inspect all parts. Clean the gasket material from the engine oil pan,

Please refer to Section 8 for electric cooling fan wiring schematics

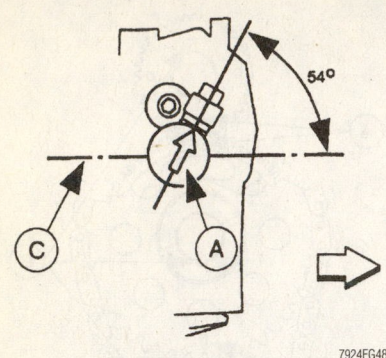

Install the camshaft synchronizer (A) in the orientation shown (white arrow points to front of engine)—4.2L engines

cylinder block and engine front cover.
- Place the timing chain tensioner in position and install the 3 retaining bolts. Tighten the bolts to 72–120 inch lbs. (8–14 Nm).
- Verify that the balance shaft timing gears are in correct alignment.
- Slide both sprockets and the timing chain onto the camshaft and crankshaft with the timing marks aligned. Install the CMP sensor drive gear and bolt. Tighten the bolt to 30–36 ft. lbs. (40–50 Nm).
- Remove the retaining pin.

10. Inspect the engine front cover seal for wear or damage and replace if necessary.

11. Install or connect the following:
- Engine front cover gasket and front cover onto the guide studs
- The 2 engine front cover stud bolts, front cover bolt and cap screw. Tighten the bolts to 15–22 ft. lbs. (20–30 Nm).
- Engine oil pan
- Crankshaft damper and pulley

❈❈ WARNING

A Synchro Positioning Tool must be used prior to installation. Failure to using this procedure will result in the fuel system being out of time, possibly causing engine damage.

12. Install Synchro Positioning Tool T89P-12200-A, or equivalent, on the camshaft synchronizer by rotating the tool until it engages the notch in the housing.

13. Install the camshaft synchronizer housing assembly so that the arrow on the tool is 54 degrees from the centerline of the engine.

14. Install the adjustment bolt and tighten to 15–22 ft. lbs. (21–30 Nm).

15. Remove the tool and position the CMP sensor. Install the 2 bolts and 40–70 inch lbs. (5–8 Nm) and install the CMP electrical harness connector.

16. Install or connect the following:
- Water pump
- Fan shroud, fan blade assembly and radiator
- Accessory drive belt

17. Fill the crankcase with the correct amount and type of engine oil.

18. Fill and bleed the engine cooling system.

19. Connect the negative battery cable.

20. Start the engine and check for coolant and oil leaks.

21. Road test the vehicle and check for proper engine operation.

4.6L Engine

1. Before servicing the vehicle, refer to the precautions in the beginning of this section.

2. Remove or disconnect the following:
- Negative battery cable
- Radiator, fan blade and fan shroud assembly
- Accessory drive belt
- Water pump pulley
- Electrical harness connectors from both ignition coils
- Both ignition coils with their brackets attached
- Left-hand and right-hand cylinder head covers
- The 2 upper power steering pump retaining bolts
- The 2 lower power steering pump retaining bolts and move the pump aside.
- CKP sensor electrical harness connector. Remove the retaining bolt and remove the CKP sensor.
- Engine oil
- The 4 oil pan-to-engine front cover retaining bolts
- Crankshaft damper retaining bolt and washer from the crankshaft
- Damper from the crankshaft
- CMP sensor retaining bolt and remove the CMP sensor
- Idler pulley bolt and remove the pulley
- The 3 belt tensioner retaining bolts and remove the tensioner
- The 8 engine front cover retaining bolts and the 7 nuts. Swing the top of the cover out off the dowel pins and remove the cover.
- Sensor ring from the crankshaft

3. Use Camshaft Positioning Tool T91P-6256-A and Camshaft Positioning Adapters T92P-6256-A or equivalents, to position the camshaft.

4. Rotate the crankshaft until both camshaft keyways are 90 degrees from the cam cover surface. Be sure the copper links line up with the dots on the camshaft sprockets.

❈❈ WARNING

At no time, when the timing chains are removed and the cylinder heads are installed may the crankshaft or the camshaft be rotated. Severe piston and valve damage will occur.

5. Remove or disconnect the following:
- The 2 left-hand and right-hand tensioner bolts and remove the timing chain tensioners
- The left-hand and right-hand tensioner guides off the dowel pins
- The right-hand timing chain from the camshaft sprocket
- The left-hand timing chain from the camshaft sprocket
- The left-hand and right-hand timing chain guide bolts and remove the timing chain guides.

6. If necessary, remove the camshaft gear bolt and remove the camshaft gear.

To install:

7. Examine the timing chains, looking for the copper links. If the copper links are not visible, lay the chain on a flat surface and pull the chain taught until the opposite sides of the chain contact one another. Mark the links at each end of the chain and use these marks in place of the copper links.

➡ **If the engine jumped time, damage has been done to valves and possibly pistons and/or connecting rods. Any damage must be corrected before installing the timing chains.**

8. Install or connect the following:
- Camshaft gears and tighten the retaining bolt to 81–95 ft. lbs. (110–130 Nm).
- Left-hand and right-hand timing chain guides and retaining bolts. Tighten the retaining bolts to 71–106 inch lbs. (8–12 Nm).
- Left-hand crankshaft sprocket with the tapered part of the sprocket facing away from the engine block.

➡ **The crankshaft sprockets are identical. They may only be installed one way, with the tapered part of the sprockets facing each other. Ensure that the keyway and timing marks on the crankshaft sprockets are aligned.**

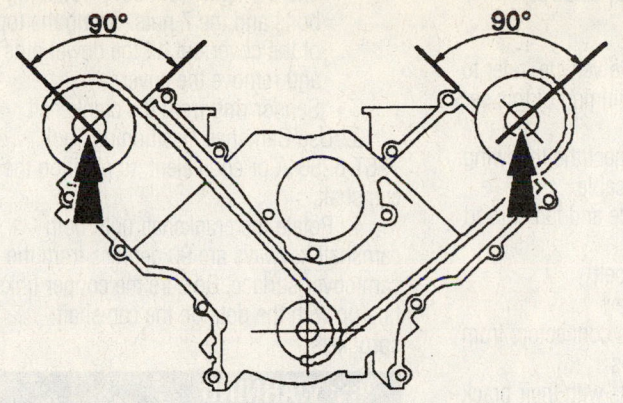

When removing the timing chains, rotate the crankshaft so that the camshaft keyways are positioned as shown—4.6L engines

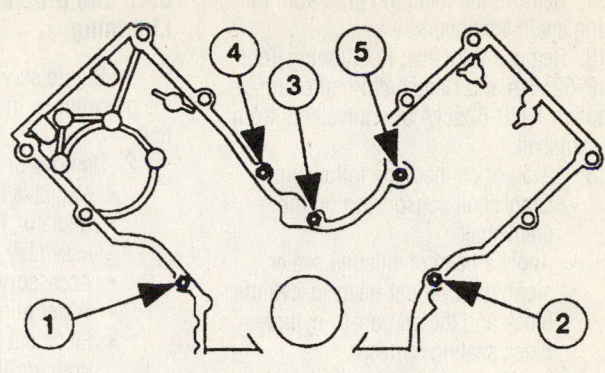

Tighten the first 5 front cover fasteners in the sequence shown—4.6L engine

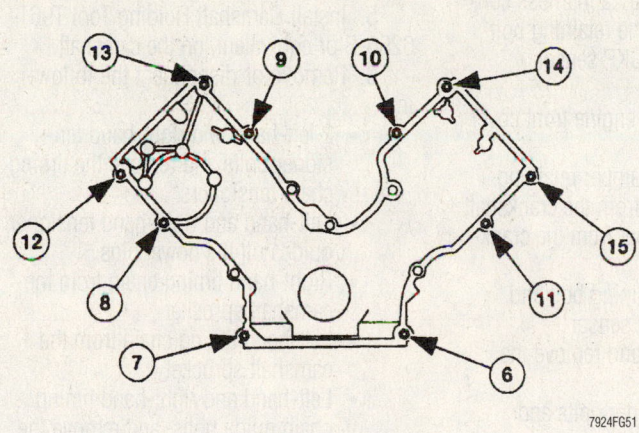

Continue tightening the remaining fasteners in the sequence shown here—4.6L engine

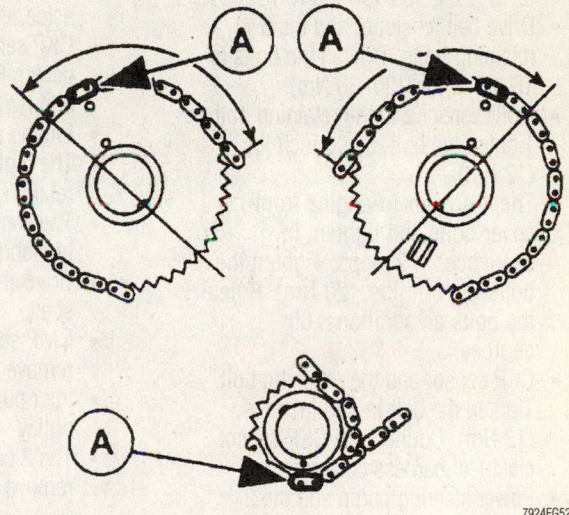

When installing the timing chains, make certain that the copper colored links (A) are aligned with the timing marks—4.6L engine

- Left-hand timing chain on the camshaft and crankshaft sprockets. Be sure the copper links of the timing chain line up with the timing marks on both sprockets.
- Right-hand crankshaft sprocket with the tapered part of the sprocket facing the left-hand crankshaft sprocket.
- Right-hand timing chain on the camshaft and crankshaft sprockets. Be sure the copper links of the timing chain line up with the timing marks on both sprockets.

9. It is necessary to bleed the timing chain tensioners before installation. Proceed as follows:

  a. Place the timing chain tensioner in a soft-jawed vise.

  b. Using a small pick or similar tool, hold the ratchet lock mechanism away from the ratchet stem and slowly compress the tensioner plunger by rotating the vise handle.

✳✳ WARNING

The tensioner must be compressed slowly or damage to the internal seals will result.

  c. Once the tensioner plunger bottoms in the tensioner bore, continue to hold the ratchet lock mechanism and push down on the ratchet stem until flush with the tensioner face.

  d. While holding the ratchet stem flush to the tensioner face, release the ratchet lock mechanism and install a paper clip or similar tool in the tensioner body to lock the tensioner in the collapsed position.

  e. The paper clip must not be removed until the timing chain, tensioner, tensioner arm and timing chain guide are completely installed on the engine.

10. Install or connect the following:
- Left-hand and right-hand timing chain tensioner guides on the dowel pins.
- Left-hand and right-hand timing chain tensioners in position and install the retaining bolts. Tighten the bolts to 15–22 ft. lbs. (20–30 Nm).

11. Remove the retaining pins from the timing chain tensioners.

12. Remove Camshaft Positioning Tool T91P-6256-A and Camshaft Positioning Adapters T92P-6256-A or equivalents from the camshaft.

13. Install or connect the following:

- Crankshaft sensor ring on the crankshaft
- Apply a bead of silicone sealer along the cylinder head-to-cylinder block and the oil pan-to-cylinder block sealing surfaces.
- Engine front cover carefully onto the dowel pins. Tighten the engine front cover bolts, in sequence, to 15–22 ft. lbs. (20–30 Nm).
- Idler pulley in position and install the retaining bolt. Tighten the bolt to 15–22 ft. lbs. (20–30 Nm).
- Drive belt tensioner and the 3 retaining bolts. Tighten the bolts to 15–22 ft. lbs. (20–30 Nm).
- CMP sensor and the retaining bolt. Tighten the bolt to 106 inch lbs. (12 Nm).
- The 4 oil pan-to-engine front cover bolts and tighten, in sequence, in 2 steps: Tighten the bolts to 15 ft. lbs. (20 Nm). Rotate the bolts an additional 60 degrees.
- CKP sensor and the retaining bolt. Tighten the bolt to 106 inch lbs. (12 Nm). Connect the CKP sensor electrical harness connector.
- Power steering pump and the 2 upper and 2 lower retaining bolts. Tighten the bolts to 15–20 ft. lbs. (20–30 Nm).
- Ignition coil and brackets on the engine front cover and install the bracket bolts. Tighten the bolts to 15–22 ft. lbs. (20–30 Nm).
- Ignition coil and capacitor electrical harness connectors
- CMP electrical harness connector
- Water pump pulley and tighten the bolts to 15–22 ft. lbs. (20–30 Nm).
- Radiator, fan blade and fan shroud assembly
- Accessory drive belt

14. Refill the engine oil with the recommended type of engine oil and the correct amount.

15. Install the negative battery cable.

16. Start the engine and check for leaks.

17. Road test the vehicle and check for proper engine operation.

5.4L and 6.8L Engines, Except Lightning

1. Before servicing the vehicle, refer to the precautions in the beginning of this section.

2. Remove or disconnect the following:

- Negative battery cable
- Radiator, fan blade and fan shroud assembly
- Accessory drive belt
- Water pump pulley
- Electrical harness connectors from both ignition coils
- Both ignition coils with their brackets attached
- The 2 upper power steering pump retaining bolts
- The 2 lower power steering pump retaining bolts and move the pump aside.
- CKP sensor electrical harness connector. Remove the retaining bolt and remove the CKP sensor.
- Engine oil
- The 4 oil pan-to-engine front cover retaining bolts
- The crankshaft damper retaining bolt and washer from the crankshaft
- Crankshaft damper from the crankshaft
- CMP sensor retaining bolt and remove the CMP sensor
- Idler pulley bolt and remove the pulley
- The 3 belt tensioner bolts and remove the tensioner

- The 8 engine front cover retaining bolts and the 7 nuts. Swing the top of the cover out off the dowel pins and remove the cover.
- Sensor ring from the crankshaft

3. Use Camshaft Positioning Tool T96T-6256-A or equivalent, to position the camshaft.

4. Rotate the crankshaft until both camshaft keyways are 90 degrees from the cam cover surface. Be sure the copper links line up with the dots on the camshaft sprockets.

✱✱ WARNING

At no time, when the timing chains are removed and the cylinder heads are installed may the crankshaft or the camshaft be rotated. Severe piston and valve damage will occur.

5. Install Camshaft Holding Tool T96T-6256-B or equivalent, on the camshaft.

6. Remove or disconnect the following:

- 2 left-hand and right-hand tensioner bolts and remove the timing chain tensioners.
- Left-hand and right-hand tensioner guides off the dowel pins
- Right-hand timing chain from the camshaft sprocket
- Left-hand timing chain from the camshaft sprocket
- Left-hand and right-hand timing chain guide bolts, and remove the timing chain guides.

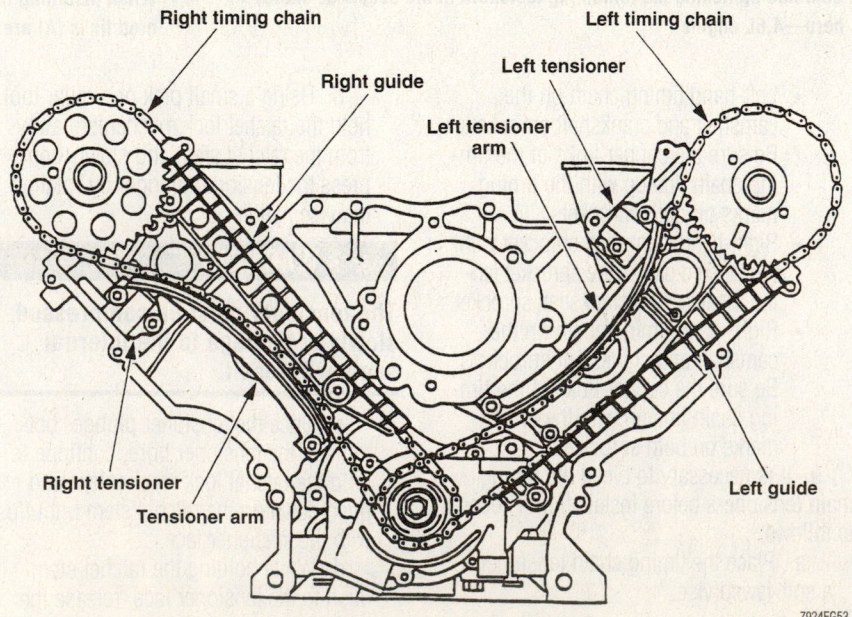

Timing chains and related components—5.4L and 6.8L engines

7924FG53

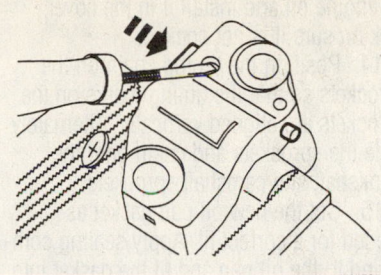

Compress the tensioner while holding the ratchet mechanism with a suitable tool—5.4L and 6.8L engines

To install:

7. Examine the timing chains, looking for the copper links. If the copper links are not visible, lay the chain on a flat surface and pull the chain taught until the opposite sides of the chain contact one another. Mark the links at each end of the chain and use these marks in place of the copper links.

➡ **If the engine jumped time, damage has been done to valves and possibly pistons and/or connecting rods. Any damage must be corrected before installing the timing chains.**

8. Install or connect the following:
- Left-hand and right-hand timing chain guides and retaining bolts. Tighten the retaining bolts to 71–106 inch lbs. (8–12 Nm).
- Left-hand crankshaft sprocket with the tapered part of the sprocket facing away from the engine block.

➡ **The crankshaft sprockets are identical. They may only be installed one way, with the tapered part of the sprockets facing each other. Ensure that the keyway and timing marks on the crankshaft sprockets are aligned.**

- Left-hand timing chain on the camshaft and crankshaft sprockets. Be sure the 1 copper link aligns

If the copper links are not visible, mark one link on one end of the chain and 2 links on the opposite end of the chain—5.4L and 6.8L engines

with the mark on the crankshaft sprocket and the 2 copper links align with the mark on the camshaft sprocket.
- Right-hand crankshaft sprocket with the tapered part of the sprocket facing the left-hand crankshaft sprocket.
- Right-hand timing chain on the camshaft and crankshaft sprockets. Be sure the copper links of the timing chain line up with the timing marks on both sprockets.

9. It is necessary to bleed the timing chain tensioners before installation. Proceed as follows:

a. Place the timing chain tensioner in a soft-jawed vise.

b. Using a small pick or similar tool, hold the ratchet lock mechanism away from the ratchet stem and slowly compress the tensioner plunger by rotating the vise handle.

✴✴ WARNING

The tensioner must be compressed slowly or damage to the internal seals will result.

c. Once the tensioner plunger bottoms in the tensioner bore, continue to hold the ratchet lock mechanism and push down on the ratchet stem until flush with the tensioner face.

d. While holding the ratchet stem flush to the tensioner face, release the ratchet lock mechanism and install a paper clip or similar tool in the tensioner body to lock the tensioner in the collapsed position.

e. The paper clip must not be removed until the timing chain, tensioner, tensioner arm and timing chain guide are completely installed on the engine.

10. Install the left-hand and right-hand timing chain tensioner guides on the dowel pins.

11. Place the left-hand and right-hand timing chain tensioners in position and install the retaining bolts. Tighten the bolts to 15–22 ft. lbs. (20–30 Nm).

12. Remove the retaining pins from the timing chain tensioners.

13. Remove Cam Holding Tool T96T-6256-B or equivalent, from the camshaft.

14. Install the crankshaft sensor ring on the crankshaft.

15. Apply silicone gasket along the

cylinder head-to-cylinder block and engine oil pan-to-cylinder block sealing surfaces.

16. Install or connect the following:
- Engine front cover carefully onto the dowel pins
- Engine front cover bolts, in sequence, in the following manner: bolts 1 through 5: 15–22 ft. lbs. (20–30 Nm); bolts 6 through 15: 29–40 ft. lbs. (40–55 Nm).
- Idler pulley in position and install the retaining bolt. Tighten the bolt to 15–22 ft. lbs. (20–30 Nm).
- Drive belt tensioner in position and install 3 retaining bolts. Tighten the bolts to 15–22 ft. lbs. (20–30 Nm).
- CMP sensor in position and install the retaining bolt. Tighten the bolt to 106 inch lbs. (12 Nm).
- Damper on the crankshaft. Ensure the crankshaft key and keyway are aligned.
- 4 front oil pan-to-engine front cover retaining bolts and tighten in sequence in 2 steps: Tighten the bolts to 15 ft. lbs. (20 Nm); Rotate the bolts an additional 60 degrees.
- CKP sensor in position and install the retaining bolt. Tighten the bolt to 106 inch lbs. (12 Nm).
- CKP sensor electrical harness connector.
- Power steering pump with 2 upper and 2 lower retaining bolts. Tighten the bolts to 15–20 ft. lbs. (20–30 Nm).
- Ignition coil and brackets on the engine front cover and install the bracket bolts. Tighten the bolts to 15–22 ft. lbs. (20–30 Nm).
- Ignition coil and capacitor electrical harness connectors
- CMP electrical harness connector
- Water pump pulley and tighten the bolts to 15–22 ft. lbs. (20–30 Nm).
- Radiator
- Negative battery cable

17. Refill the engine oil with the recommended type of engine oil and the correct amount.

18. Start the engine and check for leaks.

19. Road test the vehicle and check for proper engine operation.

5.4L Lightning

1. Before servicing the vehicle, refer to the precautions in the beginning of this section.

Timing belt service is covered in Section 4 of this manual

2. Remove or disconnect the following:
- Negative battery cable
- Drive belt
- Nuts and position the under vehicle shield aside
- Starter motor

➡ The auxiliary supercharger pulley has left-hand threads.

- Pulley and brace assembly
- Supercharger pulley adapter
- Crankshaft pulley
- Front cover oil seal

To install:

3. Clean the engine front cover seal bore, then lubricate the seal bore and the seal lip with clean engine oil.

4. Install the new front cover oil seal. Make sure the seal is installed evenly and straight.

➡ The crankshaft pulley must be installed within 4 minutes after applying the silicone.

5. Apply silicone sealant to the woodruff key slot on the crankshaft pulley.

6. Using the special tool, install the crankshaft pulley.

7. Install the bolt and washer. Tighten the bolt in 4 stages.
- 66 ft. lbs. (90 Nm)
- Loosen the bolt
- 34–39 ft. lbs. (47–53 Nm)
- + 85–90 degrees.

8. Install the supercharger pulley adapter.

➡ Coat the threads of the supercharger pulley with High Temperature Nickel Anti-Seize Lubricant F6AZ-9L494-AA.

➡ The auxiliary supercharger pulley has left-hand threads.

9. Install the pulley and brace assembly.

10. Remove the special tool.

11. Install the starter motor.

12. Position the transmission cooler line clip and install the 2 nuts and 1 bolt.

13. Position the shield and install the nut.

14. Lower the vehicle.

15. Install the drive belt.

16. Connect the negative battery cable.

5.0L and 5.8L Engines

1. Before servicing the vehicle, refer to the precautions in the beginning of this section.

2. Remove or disconnect the following:
- Negative battery cable
- Coolant

- Upper and lower radiator hoses and the transmission oil cooler lines and remove the radiator
- Heater hose from the water pump. Slide the water pump bypass hose clamp toward the water pump.

3. Loosen the alternator pivot bolt and the bolt which secures the alternator adjusting arm to the water pump. Position the alternator out of the way.

4. Remove or disconnect the following:
- Power steering pump and air conditioning compressor from their mounting brackets, if so equipped.
- Fan, spacer, pulley and drive belts
- Crankshaft pulley from the crankshaft damper. Remove the damper attaching bolt and washer and remove the damper with a puller.
- If necessary, the oil level dipstick and the bolt holding the dipstick tube to the exhaust manifold
- Oil pan-to-cylinder front cover attaching bolts. Use a sharp, thin cutting blade to cut the oil pan gasket flush with the cylinder block. Remove the front cover and water pump as an assembly.

5. Discard the front cover gasket. If necessary, properly support the cover and carefully drive the oil seal out towards the front of the cover.

6. Rotate the crankshaft counterclockwise to take up the slack on the left side of the chain.

7. Establish a reference point on the cylinder block and measure from this point to the chain.

8. Rotate the crankshaft in the opposite direction to take up the slack on the right side of the chain.

9. Force the left side of the chain out with your fingers and measure the distance between the reference point and the chain. The timing chain deflection is the difference between the 2 measurements. If the deflection exceeds ½ inch (13mm), replace the timing chain and sprockets.

10. Turn the crankshaft until the timing marks on the sprockets are aligned vertically.

11. Remove the camshaft sprocket retaining screw, if equipped, remove the fuel pump eccentric and washers.

12. Alternately slide both of the sprockets and timing chain off the crankshaft and camshaft until free of the engine.

To install:

13. Clean the front cover mating surfaces of all gasket material and/or sealer. If the front cover seal is being replaced, support the cover to prevent damage and drive out the seal. Coat the new seal with heavy

SJ engine oil and install it in the cover, making sure it is not cocked.

14. Position the timing chain on the sprockets so that the timing marks on the sprockets are aligned vertically. Alternately slide the sprockets and chain onto the crankshaft and camshaft sprockets.

15. Cut the new oil pan gasket as needed for a correct fit. Apply sealing compound to the oil pan and fit the gasket into place.

16. Apply sealing compound to the gasket surfaces on the cylinder block and back side of the front cover. Position the gasket onto the cylinder block and fit the front cover onto the engine.

17. Coat the screw threads with sealing compound and start all the screws. Center the cover by inserting an alignment tool in the oil seal.

18. Tighten the oil pan screws first to 12–18 ft. lbs. (17–24 Nm), then tighten the front cover screws to the same torque.

19. Apply Lubriplate® to the oil seal lip and to the vibration damper to prevent damage to the seal. Coat the front of the crankshaft with engine oil for damper installation.

20. Line up the damper keyway with the key on the crankshaft and push the damper onto the crankshaft. Install the bolt and washer and tighten to 80 ft. lbs. (109 Nm). Install the crankshaft pulley.

21. Install the fan, spacer, pulley and drive belts.

22. Install the bolts holding the fan shroud to the radiator, if so equipped.

23. Install the power steering pump and air conditioning compressor.

24. Install the alternator and adjust the belt tension.

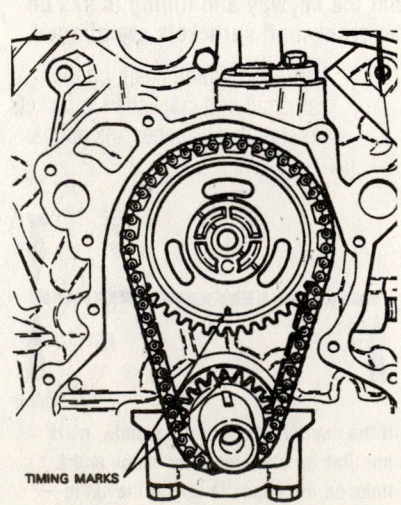

TIMING MARKS

7924FG55

Align the marks when installing the timing chain—5.0L, 5.8L and 7.5L engines

25. Connect the heater hose at the water pump.

26. Install the radiator.

27. Connect the upper and lower radiator hoses, and transmission oil cooler lines.

28. Fill the cooling system and the crankcase.

29. Connect the negative battery cable.

7.5L Engine

1. Before servicing the vehicle, refer to the precautions in the beginning of this section.

2. Remove or disconnect the following:
   - Negative battery cable
   - Coolant and engine oil
   - Radiator shroud and fan
   - Upper and lower radiator hoses, and the automatic transmission oil cooler lines, from the radiator
   - Radiator upper support and remove the radiator.
   - Drive belts with the water pump pulley. Remove the bolts attaching the compressor support to the water pump and remove the bracket (support), if equipped.
   - Crankshaft pulley from the vibration damper. Remove the bolt and washer attaching the crankshaft damper and remove the damper with a puller. Remove the woodruff key from the crankshaft.

3. Loosen the bypass hose at the water pump and disconnect the heater return tube at the water pump.

4. Remove the bolts attaching the front cover to the cylinder block. Cut the oil pan seal flush with the cylinder block face with a thin knife blade prior to separating the cover from the cylinder block. Remove the cover and water pump as an assembly. Discard the front cover gasket and oil pan seal.

5. Rotate the crankshaft counterclockwise to take up the slack on the left side of the chain.

6. Establish a reference point on the cylinder block and measure from this point to the chain.

7. Rotate the crankshaft in the opposite direction to take up the slack on the right side of the chain.

8. Force the left side of the chain out and measure the distance between the reference point and the chain. The timing chain deflection is the difference between the 2 measurements. If the deflection exceeds ½

inch (13mm), replace the timing chain and sprockets.

9. Turn the crankshaft until the timing marks on the sprockets are aligned vertically.

10. Remove the camshaft sprocket retaining screw and remove the fuel pump eccentric and washers.

11. Alternately slide both of the sprockets and timing chain off the crankshaft and camshaft until free of the engine.

To install:

12. Position the timing chain on the sprockets so the timing marks on the sprockets are aligned vertically. Alternately slide the sprockets and chain onto the crankshaft and camshaft sprockets.

13. Transfer the water pump if a new cover is going to be installed. Clean all gasket sealing surfaces on both the front cover and the cylinder block.

14. Coat the gasket surface of the oil pan with sealer. Cut and position the required sections of a new seal on the oil pan. Apply sealer to the corners.

15. Drive out the old front cover oil seal with a pin punch. Clean out the seal recess in the cover. Coat a new seal with Lubriplate® grease. Install the seal, making sure the seal spring remains in the proper position. A front cover seal tool makes installation easier.

16. Coat the gasket surfaces of the cylinder block and cover with sealer and position the new gasket on the block.

17. Position the front cover on the cylinder block. Use care not to damage the seal and gasket or misplace them.

18. Coat the front cover attaching screws with sealer and install them.

➡ **It may be necessary to force the front cover downward to compress the oil pan seal in order to install the front cover attaching bolts. Use a prybar or drift to engage the cover screw holes through the cover and pry downward.**

19. Tighten the bypass hose at the water pump.

20. Install or connect the following:
   - Heater return tube at the water pump
   - Woodruff key from the crankshaft
   - Damper
   - Crankshaft pulley on the vibration damper
   - Compressor support on the water pump and install the bracket (support), if equipped.

   - Drive belts with the water pump pulley
   - Radiator and upper support
   - Upper and lower radiator hoses and the automatic transmission oil cooler lines
   - Radiator shroud and fan

21. Fill the cooling system and crankcase.

22. Connect the negative battery cable. Tighten the fasteners to the following specifications:
   - Front cover bolts: 15–20 ft. lbs. (20–27 Nm)
   - Water pump attaching screws: 12–15 ft. lbs. (16–20 Nm)
   - Crankshaft damper: 70–90 ft. lbs. (95–122 Nm)
   - Crankshaft pulley: 35–50 ft. lbs. (47–68 Nm)
   - Oil pan bolts: 10–11 ft. lbs. (13–15.0 Nm) for the 5⁄16 inch (7.9mm) screws and to 84–108 inch lbs. (9.5–12.2 Nm) for the ¼ inch (6.3mm) screws
   - Alternator pivot bolt: 45–57 ft. lbs. (61–77 Nm)

DIESEL ENGINE REPAIR

Engine Assembly

REMOVAL & INSTALLATION

7.3L Engine

✳ CAUTION

The fuel system remains under pressure, even after the engine has been turned OFF. The fuel system pressure must be relieved before disconnecting any fuel lines. Failure to do so may result in fire and/or personal injury.

1. Before servicing the vehicle, refer to the precautions in the beginning of this section.

2. Remove or disconnect the following:
   - Hood
   - Coolant
   - Engine oil
   - Negative battery cable

- Air cleaner and intake duct assembly
- Upper grille support bracket

3. Upper air conditioning condenser mounting bracket

- Refrigerant, using approved equipment to remove the condenser
- Radiator fan shroud halves
- Fan and clutch assembly
- Radiator hoses and the transmission cooler lines, if equipped
- Condenser. Cap all openings immediately!
- Radiator
- Power steering pump and position it out of the way
- Fuel supply line heater and alternator wires at the alternator
- Oil pressure sending unit wire at the sending unit, remove the sender from the firewall and lay it on the engine.
- Accelerator cable and the speed control cable, if equipped, from the injection pump. Remove the cable bracket with the cables attached, from the intake manifold and position it out of the way.
- Transmission kickdown rod from the injection pump, if equipped
- Main wiring harness connector from the right side of the engine and the ground strap from the rear of the engine.
- Fuel system pressure
- Fuel return hose from the left rear of the engine
- The 2 upper transmission-to-engine attaching bolts
- Heater hoses
- Water temperature sender wire
- Overheat light switch wire and position the wire out of the way
- Battery ground cables from the front of the engine and the cables from the starter
- Fuel inlet line, and plug the fuel line at the fuel pump.
- Exhaust pipe at the exhaust manifold
- Engine insulators from the no. 1 crossmember
- Flywheel inspection plate and the 4 converter-to-flywheel attaching nuts, if equipped with automatic transmission

4. Support the transmission on a jack.

5. Remove the 4 lower transmission attaching bolts.

6. Attach an engine lifting sling and remove the engine from the vehicle.

To install:

7. Lower the engine into vehicle.

8. Align the converter to the flexplate and the engine dowels to the transmission.

9. Install the engine mount bolts and tighten them to 80 ft. lbs. (109 Nm).

10. Remove the engine lifting sling.

11. Install the 4 lower transmission attaching bolts. Tighten the bolts to 65 ft. lbs. (88 Nm).

12. Remove transmission jack.

13. Raise and support the front end.

14. Install or connect the following:

- If equipped with an automatic transmission, the 4 converter-to-flywheel attaching nuts. Tighten the nuts to 34 ft. lbs. (47 Nm).
- Flywheel inspection plate. Tighten the bolts to 60–90 inch lbs. (6.7–10 Nm).
- Exhaust pipe at the exhaust manifold
- Fuel inlet line
- Battery ground cables to the front of the engine
- Starter cables at the starter
- Overheat light switch wire
- Water temperature sender wire
- Heater hoses
- The 2 upper transmission-to-engine attaching bolts. Tighten the bolts to 65 ft. lbs. (88 Nm).
- Fuel return hose at the left rear of the engine
- Main wiring harness connector at the right side of the engine and the ground strap from the rear of the engine.
- Transmission kickdown rod at the injection pump, if equipped
- Accelerator cable and the speed control cable, if equipped, at the injection pump.
- Cable bracket with the cables attached, to the intake manifold
- Oil pressure sending unit
- Oil pressure sending unit wire at the sending unit
- Fuel supply line heater and alternator wires at the alternator
- Power steering pump
- Radiator
- Condenser
- Radiator hoses and the transmission cooler lines, if equipped
- Fan and clutch assembly
- Radiator fan shroud halves
- Upper grille support bracket and upper air conditioning condenser mounting bracket.

- Air cleaner and intake duct assembly

15. Refill the engine oil with the recommended type of engine oil and the correct amount.

16. Connect the negative battery cable.

17. If equipped with air conditioning, charge the system.

18. Fill the cooling system.

19. Install the hood.

Water Pump

REMOVAL & INSTALLATION

1. Disconnect both battery ground cables.

2. Drain the cooling system.

3. Remove the radiator shroud and the fan clutch and fan.

➡ **The fan clutch bolts are right-hand thread. Remove them by turning counter-clockwise.**

4. Loosen, but do not remove, the water pump pulley bolts.

5. Remove the drive belt.

6. Remove the water pump pulley bolts and remove the pulley from the pump.

7. Detach the ECT sensor connector.

8. Remove the heater hose from the water pump.

9. Remove the bolts attaching the water pump to the front cover and lift off the pump.

To install:

10. Thoroughly clean the mating surfaces of the pump and front cover.

11. Using a new gasket, position the water pump over the dowel pins and into place on the front cover.

12. Install the attaching bolts. Tighten the bolts to 15 ft. lbs. (20 Nm).

13. Connect the heater hose to the pump.

14. Attach the ECT sensor connector.

15. Install the water pump pulley and start the water pump pulley bolts.

16. Install the drive belt.

17. Install and tighten the pulley retaining bolts to 12–18 ft. lbs. (16–24 Nm).

18. Install the fan and fan shroud assembly.

19. Fill and bleed the cooling system.

20. Connect the battery ground cables.

21. Start the engine and check for leaks.

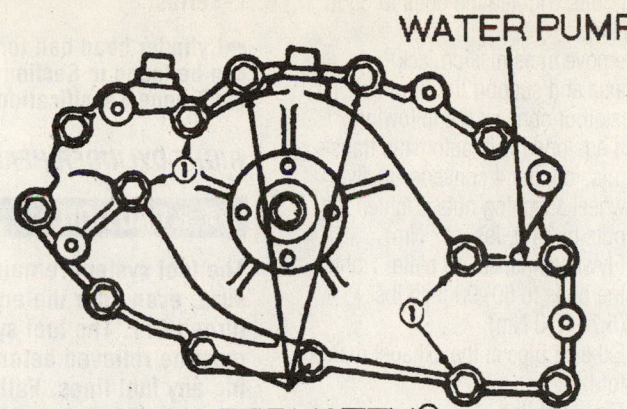

WATER PUMP

APPLY AVIATION PERMATEX®
NO. 3 OR EQUIVALENT
TO THESE BOLTS

① THESE BOLTS 2 3/4 IN. LONG
ALL OTHERS ARE 1 1/2 IN. LONG

7924FG56

Apply RTV sealant to the bolts indicated—7.3L diesel engine

Glow Plugs

REMOVAL & INSTALLATION

✳✳ CAUTION

The red-striped wiring harness carries 115v direct current. Severe electrical shock may be received. DO NOT pierce.

1. Before servicing the vehicle, refer to the precautions in the beginning of this section.
2. Disconnect the negative battery cable.
3. Remove the rocker arm cover.
4. Disconnect the glow plug electrical leads using a pair of pliers.
5. Remove the glow plugs by unscrewing them from the cylinder head with a 10mm socket and wrench.
6. Inspect the tips of the plugs for any evidence of distortion or missing tip ends; replace them if necessary.

To install:

7. Install the glow plug into the cylinder head. Tighten the glow plugs to 14 ft. lbs. (19 Nm).
8. Attach the glow plug electrical connector. Be sure that the glow plug wiring is routed to avoid moving components in the engine bay.
9. Install the rocker arm cover.

➡When the battery is disengaged and reconnected, some abnormal drive symptoms may occur while the vehicle relearns its adaptive strategy. The vehicle may need to be driven 10 miles (16 km) or more to relearn this strategy.

10. Connect the negative battery cable.

Cylinder Head

REMOVAL & INSTALLATION

F-Series

➡Cylinder head bolt torque sequences can be found in Section 1, following the Torque Specifications Chart.

✳✳ CAUTION

The fuel system remains under pressure, even after the engine has been turned OFF. The fuel system pressure must be relieved before disconnecting any fuel lines. Failure to do so may result in fire and/or personal injury.

1. Before servicing the vehicle, refer to the precautions in the beginning of this section.
2. Remove or disconnect the following:
   - Negative battery cable
   - Hood
   - Engine oil
   - Coolant
   - Air cleaner and intake duct assembly
   - Upper grille support bracket
   - Upper air conditioning condenser mounting bracket
   - Refrigerant, using approved equipment to remove the condenser

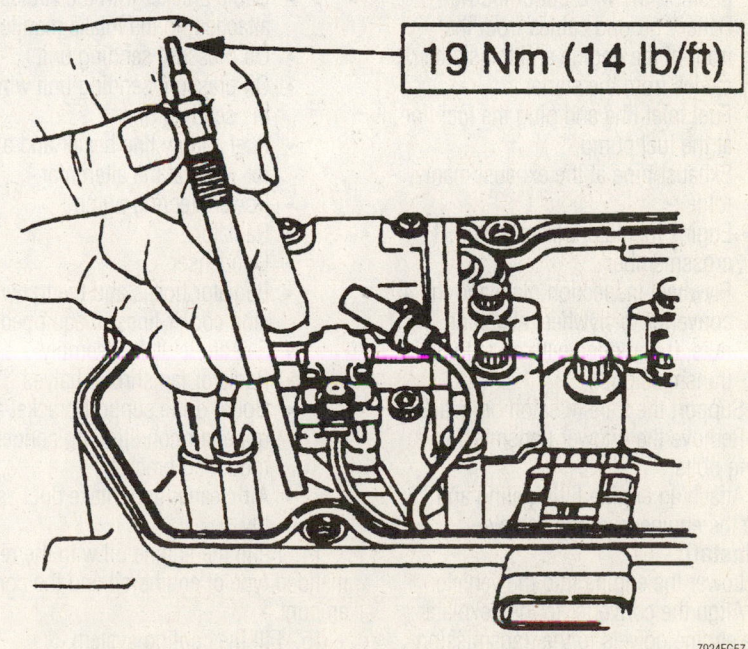

19 Nm (14 lb/ft)

7924FG57

Tighten the glow plugs to 14 ft. lbs. (19 Nm) and attach the connector—7.3L engine

Timing belt service is covered in Section 4 of this manual

- Radiator fan shroud halves
- Fan and clutch assembly
- Radiator hoses and the transmission cooler lines, if equipped
- Condenser. Cap all openings at once!
- Radiator
- Power steering pump and position it out of the way
- Fuel supply line heater and alternator wires at the alternator
- Oil pressure sending unit wire at the sending unit, remove the sender from the firewall and lay it on the engine.
- Accelerator cable and the speed control cable, if equipped, from the injection pump. Remove the cable bracket, with the cables attached, from the intake manifold and position it out of the way.
- Transmission kickdown rod from the injection pump, if equipped
- Main wiring harness connector from the right side of the engine and the ground strap from the rear of the engine.
- Fuel system pressure
- Fuel return hose from the left rear of the engine
- The 2 upper transmission-to-engine attaching bolts
- Heater hoses
- Water temperature sender wire
- Overheat light switch wire and position the wire out of the way
- Battery ground cables from the front of the engine and the starter cables from the starter
- Fuel inlet line and plug the fuel line at the fuel pump
- Exhaust pipe at the exhaust manifold
- Engine insulators from the no. 1 crossmember
- Flywheel inspection plate and the 4 converter-to-flywheel attaching nuts, if equipped with an automatic transmission.

3. Support the transmission on a jack.

4. Remove the 4 lower transmission attaching bolts.

5. Attach an engine lifting sling and remove the engine from the vehicle.

To install:

6. Lower the engine into the vehicle.

7. Align the converter to the flexplate and the engine dowels to the transmission.

8. Install the engine mount bolts and tighten them to 80 ft. lbs. (109 Nm).

9. Remove the engine lifting sling.

10. Install the 4 lower transmission attaching bolts. Tighten the bolts to 65 ft. lbs. (88 Nm).

11. Remove transmission jack.

12. Raise and support the front end.

13. Install or connect the following:
- If equipped with automatic transmission, the 4 converter-to-flywheel attaching nuts. Tighten the nuts to 34 ft. lbs. (47 Nm).
- Flywheel inspection plate. Tighten the bolts to 60–90 inch lbs. (6.7–10.0 Nm).
- Exhaust pipe at the exhaust manifold
- Fuel inlet line
- Battery ground cables to the front of the engine
- Starter cables at the starter
- Overheat light switch wire
- Water temperature sender wire
- Heater hoses
- The 2 upper transmission-to-engine attaching bolts. Tighten the bolts to 65 ft. lbs. (88 Nm).
- Fuel return hose at the left rear of the engine
- Main wiring harness connector at the right side of the engine and the ground strap from the rear of the engine.
- Transmission kickdown rod at the injection pump, if equipped
- Accelerator cable and the speed control cable, if equipped, at the injection pump
- Cable bracket with the cables attached, to the intake manifold
- Oil pressure sending unit
- Oil pressure sending unit wire at the sending unit
- Fuel supply line heater and alternator wires at the alternator
- Power steering pump
- Radiator
- Condenser
- Radiator hoses and the transmission cooler lines, if equipped
- Fan and clutch assembly
- Radiator fan shroud halves
- Upper grille support bracket and upper air conditioning condenser mounting bracket
- Air cleaner and intake duct assembly

14. Refill the engine oil with the recommended type of engine oil and the correct amount.

15. Fill the cooling system.

16. If equipped with air conditioning, charge the system.

17. Connect the negative battery cable.

18. Install the hood.

E-Series

➡Cylinder head bolt torque sequences can be found in Section 1, following the Torque Specifications Chart.

RIGHT CYLINDER HEAD

❄❄ CAUTION

The fuel system remains under pressure, even after the engine has been turned OFF. The fuel system pressure must be relieved before disconnecting any fuel lines. Failure to do so may result in fire and/or personal injury.

1. Before servicing the vehicle, refer to the precautions in the beginning of this section.

2. Remove or disconnect the following:
- Negative battery cable
- Coolant
- Engine oil
- Vacuum hose from the right intake manifold
- Both electrical harness connectors from the valve cover
- Valve cover and gasket
- Intake manifold covers
- Fuel injector electrical injectors
- Fuel lines from the heads
- Fuel supply assembly
- Heater hose
- Dipstick tube bracket retainer at the right exhaust manifold
- Rocker arms and pushrods

3. Loosen the 4 inboard fuel injector hold-down bolts.

4. Remove or disconnect the following:
- The 4 outboard fuel injector hold-down bolts, retaining screws and 4 oil deflectors

❄❄ WARNING

Remove the oil drain plugs prior to removing the injectors or oil could enter the combustion chamber, which could result in hydrostatic lock and severe engine damage.

- Oil rail drain plugs
- Fuel injectors using Injector Remover No. T94T-9000-aH1, or equivalent. Position the tool's fulcrum beneath the fuel injector hold-down plate and over the edge of the cylinder head. Install the remover screw in the threaded hole of the fuel injector plate (see illustration). Tighten the screw to lift out

the injector from its bore. Place the injector in a suitable protective sleeve such as Rotunda Injector Protective Sleeve, No. 014-00933-2 or equivalent, and set the injector in a suitable holding rack.

➡ **During removal the injector tab (located above the fuel injector) must be bent completely flat and flush with the cowl and heat shield.**

5. Use a vacuum pump, remove the oil and fuel left over in the injector bores.

6. Remove or disconnect the following:
- The 4 glow plugs
- High pressure oil pump supply line from the cylinder head
- Grille opening reinforcement, headlamp assembly, radiator, oil reservoir and fuel filter assembly.
- Exhaust back pressure line

7. Loosen the glow plug relay bracket retainers and disengage the ground wire.

8. Disconnect the fuel return line at the front of the cylinder head.

9. Loosen the cylinder head bolts.

10. Carefully lift the cylinder head out of the engine compartment and remove the head gaskets.

To install:

➡ **To prepare a good seat for the fuel injector O-rings, use a suitable injector sleeve brush to clean any debris from the bore.**

11. Carefully clean the cylinder block and head mating surfaces.

12. Position the cylinder head gasket on the engine block and carefully lower the cylinder head in place.

13. Install the cylinder head bolts and tighten in 3 steps using the sequence shown in the illustration.

➡ **Lubricate the threads and the mating surfaces of the bolt heads and washers with engine oil.**

14. Install or connect the following:
- Fuel return line to the cylinder head
- Glow plug relay bracket and ground wire, then tighten the retainers
- Exhaust back pressure line
- High pressure fuel supply line and tighten the fitting to 19 ft. lbs. (26 Nm).
- Heater hose to the cylinder head
- Manifold hoses
- Fuel supply lines to the rear of the cylinder head
- Banjo bolt through the fuel line and

into the pump. Tighten the pump to 40 ft. lbs. (55 Nm).
- Glow plugs, coated with anti-seize compound. Tighten the glow plugs to 14 ft. lbs. (19 Nm).
- Fuel injectors using special tools as follows:

a. Lubricate the injector O-rings with clean engine oil. Using new copper washers, carefully push the injectors square into the bore using hand pressure only to seat the O-rings.

b. Position the open end of Injector replacer, No. T94T-9000-aH2, or equivalent, between the fuel injector body and injector hold-down plate, while positioning the opposite end of the tool over the edge of the cylinder head.

c. Align the hole in the tool with the threaded hole in the cylinder head and install the bolt from the tool kit. Tighten the bolt to fully seat the injector, then remove the bolt and tool.

15. Install or connect the following:
- Oil rail drain plugs and tighten them to 53 inch lbs. (6 Nm).
- The 4 outboard fuel injector hold-down bolts, the 4 oil deflectors and retaining screws. Tighten them to 120 inch lbs. (12 Nm).
- The 4 inboard fuel injector hold-down bolts and tighten them to 120 inch lbs. (12 Nm).
- Oil deflectors

16. Turn the engine by hand until the timing mark is at the 11 o'clock position as viewed from the front.

17. Dip the pushrod ends in clean engine oil and install the pushrods with the copper colored ends toward the rocker arms, making sure the pushrods are fully seated in the tappet pushrod seats.

18. Install or connect the following:
- Rocker arms and posts in their original positions. Apply multipurpose grease to the valve stem tips. Install the rocker arm posts, bolts and tighten to 27 ft. lbs. (37 Nm).
- Valve cover gasket
- Wiring to the fuel injectors and glow plugs
- Valve cover, tightening the bolts to 97 inch lbs. (11 Nm).
- Both electrical harness connectors to the valve cover
- Vacuum hose to the right intake valve manifold cover

19. Refill the engine coolant with the recommended type and the correct amount.

20. Refill the engine oil with the recommended type of engine oil and the correct amount.

21. Install the engine in the van.

22. Connect the negative battery cable.

LEFT CYLINDER HEAD

❊❊ **CAUTION**

Fuel system remains under pressure, even after the engine has been turned OFF. The fuel system pressure must be relieved before disconnecting any fuel lines. Failure to do so may result in fire and/or personal injury.

1. Before servicing the vehicle, refer to the precautions in the beginning of this section.

2. Remove or disconnect the following:
- Negative battery cable
- Coolant
- Engine oil
- Wiring harness bracket
- Electrical connections from the valve cover gasket, then remove the valve cover
- Electrical connections from the fuel injectors and glow plugs
- Valve cover gasket
- Rocker arms and pushrods

➡ **Be sure to note the location of each part prior to removal, as each reinstalled part must be returned to their original location.**

- The 4 inboard fuel injector hold-down bolts

❊❊ **WARNING**

Remove the oil drain plugs prior to removing the injectors or oil could enter the combustion chamber, which could result in hydrostatic lock and severe engine damage.

- The oil rail drain plugs

❊❊ **CAUTION**

Be sure to retrieve the fuel injector copper washer, located at the tip of the injector during removal.

- The 4 outboard fuel injector hold-down bolts, retaining screws and 4 oil deflectors.
- Fuel injectors using Injector Remover No. T94T-9000-aH1, or

equivalent. Position the tool's fulcrum beneath the fuel injector hold-down plate and over the edge of the cylinder head. Install the remover screw in the threaded hole of the fuel injector plate (see illustration). Tighten the screw to lift out the injector from its bore. Place the injector in a suitable protective sleeve such as Rotunda Injector Protective Sleeve, No. 014-00933-2 or equivalent, and set the injector in a suitable holding rack.

3. Use a vacuum pump to remove the oil and fuel left over in the injector bores.

4. Remove or disconnect the following:
- The 4 glow plugs
- Fuel system pressure
- Fuel supply lines from the rear of the cylinder head
- Banjo bolt from the fuel line at the pump
- Oil line from the high pressure oil pump
- Electrical connection from the injection control pressure sensor
- High pressure oil supply line from the left cylinder head

5. Loosen the fuel line nut from the intake manifold stud, then disconnect the fuel return line from the left cylinder head.

6. Loosen the fuel return line block screws at the front of the left cylinder head.

7. Remove the fuel line retaining clamp from the intake manifold cover.

8. Loosen the cylinder head bolts.

9. Remove the oil reservoir and fuel filter.

10. Remove the cylinder head and gasket.

To install:

➡ **To prepare a good seat for the fuel injector O-rings, use a suitable injector sleeve brush to clean any debris from the bore.**

11. Carefully clean the cylinder block and head mating surfaces.

12. Position the cylinder head gasket on the engine block and carefully lower the cylinder head in place.

13. Install or connect the following:
- Cylinder head bolt and tighten in 3 steps using the sequence shown in the illustration.
- Fuel line retaining clamp to the intake manifold cover
- Fuel return line block screws at the front of the left cylinder head
- Fuel return line to the left cylinder head
- Fuel line nut at the intake manifold stud

- High pressure oil supply line to the left cylinder head
- Electrical connection to the injection control pressure sensor
- Oil line to the high pressure oil pump
- Manifold hoses
- Fuel supply line
- Banjo bolt through the fuel line into the pump and tighten the bolt to 40 ft. lbs. (55 Nm).
- Fuel supply lines at the rear of the cylinder heads
- Glow plugs, coated with anti-seize compound. Tighten the glow plugs to 14 ft. lbs. (19 Nm).
- Fuel injectors using special tools as follows:

a. Lubricate the injector O-rings with clean engine oil. Using new copper washers, carefully push the injectors square into the bore using hand pressure only to seat the O-rings.

b. Position the open end of Injector replacer, No. T94T-9000-aH2 or equivalent between the fuel injector body and injector hold-down plate, while positioning the opposite end of the tool over the edge of the cylinder head.

c. Align the hole in the tool with the threaded hole in the cylinder head and install the bolt from the tool kit. Tighten the bolt to fully seat the injector, then remove the bolt and tool.

- The 4 outboard fuel injector hold-down bolts, the 4 oil deflectors and retaining screws. Tighten them to 120 inch lbs. (12 Nm).
- Oil deflectors and tighten the bolts to 120 inch lbs. (12 Nm).
- Oil rail drain plugs and tighten them to 53 inch lbs. (6 Nm).
- The 4 inboard fuel injector hold-down bolts and tighten them to 120 inch lbs. (12 Nm).

14. Turn the engine over by hand until the timing mark is at the 11 o'clock position as viewed from the front.

15. Dip the pushrod ends in clean engine oil and install the pushrods with the copper colored ends toward the rocker arms, making sure the pushrods are fully seated in the tappet pushrod seats.

16. Install the rocker arms and posts in their original positions. Apply multipurpose grease to the valve stem tips. Install the rocker arm posts, bolts and tighten to 27 ft. lbs. (37 Nm).

17. Install the valve cover gasket.

18. Connect the wiring to the fuel injectors and glow plugs.

19. Install the valve cover, tightening the bolts to 97 inch lbs. (11 Nm).

20. Connect both electrical harness connectors to the valve cover.

21. Install the engine in the van.

22. Connect the negative battery cable.

Rocker Arms

REMOVAL & INSTALLATION

1. Before servicing the vehicle, refer to the precautions in the beginning of this section.

2. Disconnect the ground cables from both batteries.

3. Remove the valve cover attaching screws and remove both valve covers.

4. Remove the valve rocker arm post mounting bolts. Remove the rocker arms and posts in order and mark them with tape so they can be installed in their original positions.

5. If the cylinder heads are to be removed, then the pushrods can now be removed. Make a holder for the pushrods out of a piece of wood or cardboard and remove the pushrods in order. It is very important that the pushrods be reinstalled in their original order. The pushrods can remain in position if no further disassembly is required.

To install:

6. If the pushrods were removed, install them in their original locations. Make sure they are fully seated in the tappet seats.

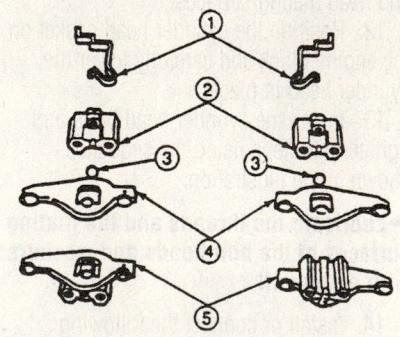

Item	Description
1	Snap Retaining Clip
2	Rocker Arm Pedestal
3	Rocker Arm Ball
4	Rocker Arm
5	Rocker Arm Assembly

7924FG58

Exploded view of the rocker arm assembly—diesel engines

➡The copper colored end of the pushrod goes toward the rocker arm.

7. Apply a polyethylene grease to the valve stem tips. Install the rocker arms and posts in their original positions.

8. Turn the engine over by hand until the valve timing mark is at the 11:00 o'clock position, as viewed from the front of the engine. Install all of the rocker arm post attaching bolts and tighten to 20 ft. lbs. (27 Nm).

9. Install new valve cover gaskets and install the valve cover.

10. Install the battery cables, start the engine and check for leaks.

Turbocharger

REMOVAL & INSTALLATION

1. Before servicing the vehicle, refer to the precautions in the beginning of this section.

2. Remove or disconnect the following:
- Negative battery cable
- The 2 air intake tube assembly bolts, clamps at the turbocharger, crankcase breather assembly, engine air cleaner and air intake tube and hoses.
- Exhaust outlet clamp from the turbocharger
- Engine charge exhaust pipe bolt from the transmission, if so equipped
- Bolts and nuts from the catalytic converter-to-engine charge exhaust pipe, if so equipped

3. Loosen 2 bolts retaining the turbocharger exhaust inlet pipe to the left exhaust manifold.

4. For automatic transmissions, remove the bolts retaining the left turbocharger exhaust inlet pipe to the turbocharger exhaust inlet adapter.

5. Loosen the 2 bolts retaining the turbocharger exhaust inlet pipe to the right exhaust manifold.

6. Remove or disconnect the following:
- Lower bolt retaining the right turbocharger exhaust inlet pipe to the turbocharger exhaust inlet adapter

7. For automatic transmissions, the upper bolts retaining the right and left turbocharger exhaust inlet pipes to the turbocharger exhaust inlet adapter.
- Right engine lift hook and bolt
- Air inlet hose clamp at the tur-

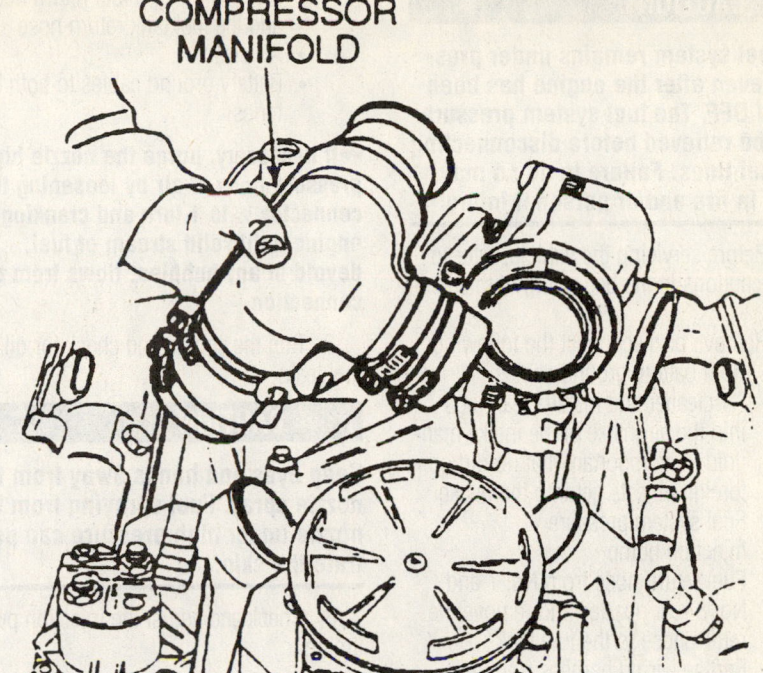

COMPRESSOR MANIFOLD

7924FG59

After loosening the clamps, the compressor manifold can be removed—diesel engines

bocharger. Disconnect the hose and lay aside.
- Compressor manifold
- The 4 bolts retaining the turbocharger pedestal assembly to the cylinder block
- Turbocharger assembly and detach all electrical connectors from it.

➡If the turbocharger is not being removed for service, install the Fuel/Oil turbo Protector Cap Set T94T-9395-AH or equivalent.

- Oil gallery O-rings

To install:

8. Install or connect the following:
- Oil gallery O-rings
- Turbocharger electrical connectors and install the turbocharger assembly.
- The 4 bolts retaining the turbocharger pedestal assembly to the engine block. Tighten the bolts to 18 ft. lbs. (25 Nm).

9. Loosely install the 4 bolts retaining the right and left turbocharger exhaust inlet pipes to the turbocharger exhaust inlet adapter.

10. Install or connect the following:
- Compressor manifold, intake manifold hoses and clamps. Be sure the compressor outlet seal is in position.

- Right engine lift hook and bolt
- The 2 right and left lower bolts (retaining the turbocharger exhaust inlet pipes to the turbocharger exhaust inlet adapter) to 36 ft. lbs. (49 Nm).
- The 4 right and left bolts and nuts (retaining the turbocharger exhaust inlet pipes to the exhaust manifolds) to 36 ft. lbs. (49 Nm).
- Catalytic converter to the engine charge exhaust pipe bolts and nuts
- The 2 right and left upper bolts (retaining the turbocharger exhaust inlet pipes to the turbocharger exhaust inlet adapter) to 36 ft. lbs. (49 Nm).
- Exhaust outlet clamp to the turbocharger
- Air intake tube and hose assembly
- Negative battery cable

Intake Manifold

REMOVAL & INSTALLATION

➡Intake manifold head bolt torque sequences can be found in Section 1, following the Torque Specifications Chart.

Refer to Section 1 for engine rebuilding specifications

✳✳ CAUTION

The fuel system remains under pressure, even after the engine has been turned OFF. The fuel system pressure must be relieved before disconnecting any fuel lines. Failure to do so may result in fire and/or personal injury.

1. Before servicing the vehicle, refer to the precautions in the beginning of this section.

2. Remove or disconnect the following:
- Both battery ground cables
- Air cleaner and install clean rags into the air intake of the intake manifold. It is important that no dirt or foreign objects get into the intake.
- Fuel system pressure
- Injection pump
- Fuel return hose from No. 7 and No. 8 rear nozzles and remove the return hose to the fuel tank.
- Engine wiring harness from the engine

➡ **The engine harness ground cables must be removed from the back of the left cylinder head.**

- Bolts attaching the intake manifold to the cylinder heads and remove the manifold.
- Crankcase Depression Regulator (CDR) valve tube grommet from the valley pan
- Bolts attaching the valley pan strap to the front of the engine block and remove the strap.
- Valley pan drain plug and remove the valley pan.

To install:

3. Apply a ⅛ inch (3mm) bead of RTV sealer to each end of the cylinder block.

➡ **The RTV sealer should be applied immediately prior to the valley pan installation.**

4. Install or connect the following:
- Valley pan drain plug, CDR valve tube and new grommet into the valley pan.
- New O-ring and new back-up ring on the CDR valve
- Valley pan strap on the front of the valley pan
- Intake manifold and tighten the bolts to 24 ft. lbs. (33 Nm) using the sequence
- Engine wiring harness and the engine ground wire located to the rear of the left cylinder head
- Injection pump

- No. 7 and No. 8 fuel return hoses and the fuel tank return hose
- Air cleaner
- Battery ground cables to both batteries

➡ **If necessary, purge the nozzle high pressure lines of air by loosening the connector ½ to 1 turn and cranking the engine until solid stream of fuel, devoid of any bubbles, flows from the connection.**

5. Run the engine and check for oil and fuel leaks.

✳✳ CAUTION

Keep eyes and hands away from the nozzle spray. Fuel spraying from the nozzle under high pressure can penetrate the skin.

6. Check and adjust the injection pump timing.

Exhaust Manifold

REMOVAL & INSTALLATION

1. Before servicing the vehicle, refer to the precautions in the beginning of this section.

2. Disconnect the ground cables from both batteries.

3. Raise the vehicle and safely support it.

4. Disconnect the muffler inlet pipe from the exhaust manifolds.

5. If removing the right manifold, lower the vehicle. When removing the left manifold, raise the vehicle and remove the manifold from underneath. Bend the tabs on the manifold attaching bolts, then remove the bolts and manifold.

To install:

6. Before installing, clean all mounting surfaces on the cylinder heads and the manifold. Apply an anti-seize compound on the manifold both threads and install the left manifold, using a new gasket and new locking tabs.

7. Tighten the bolts to 45 ft. lbs. (61 Nm) and bend the tabs over the flats on the bolt heads to prevent the bolts from loosening.

8. Raise the vehicle to install the right manifold. Install the right manifold steps 5 and 6.

9. Connect the inlet pipes to the manifold and tighten. Lower the vehicle, connect the batteries and run the engine to check for exhaust leaks.

Camshaft and Valve Lifters

REMOVAL & INSTALLATION

➡ **Ford recommends removing the diesel engine from the vehicle for camshaft removal.**

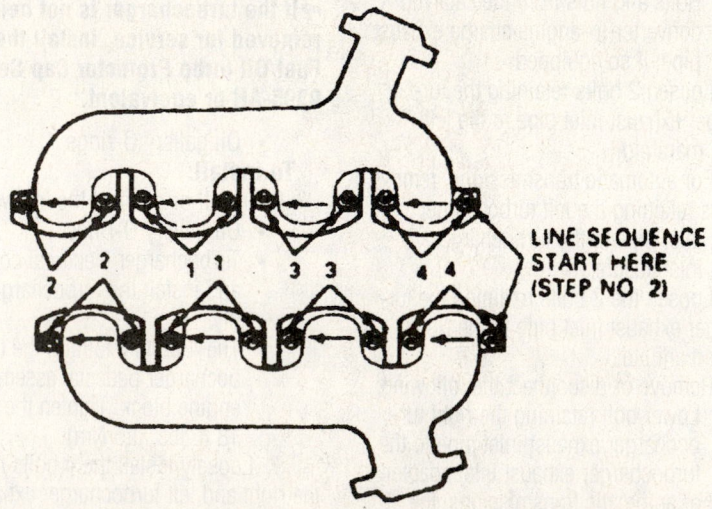

LINE SEQUENCE START HERE (STEP NO 2)

STEP 1. TIGHTEN BOLTS TO 35 FT.LB. IN NUMBERED SEQUENCE SHOWN ABOVE
STEP 2. TIGHTEN BOLTS TO 35 FT.LB. IN LINE SEQUENCE SHOWN ABOVE

7924FG26

Tighten the manifold bolts in the proper sequence—diesel engines

1. Before servicing the vehicle, refer to the precautions in the beginning of this section.

2. Remove the intake manifold and valley pan, if equipped.

3. Remove the rocker covers, and either remove the rocker arm shafts or loosen the rockers on their pivots and remove the pushrods. The pushrods must be reinstalled in their original positions.

4. Remove the valve lifters in sequence with a magnet. They must be replaced in their original positions.

5. Remove the timing gear cover, timing gear and sprockets.

➡A camshaft removal tool, Ford part no. T65L-6250-a and adapter 14-0314, or equivalents, is needed to remove the diesel camshaft.

To install:

6. liberally coat the camshaft with oil before installing it. Slide the camshaft into the engine very carefully so as not to scratch the bearing bores with the camshaft lobes. Install the camshaft thrust plate and tighten the attaching screws to 10–12 ft. lbs. (13–16 Nm). Measure the camshaft end-play. If the end-play is more than 0.009 inch (0.228mm), replace the thrust plate. Assemble the remaining components in the reverse order of removal.

7. Install the timing gear and front cover.

8. Install the valve lifters. They must be replaced in their original positions.

9. Install the pushrods, the rocker arms and the rocker arm covers.

10. Install the intake manifold and valley pan, if equipped.

Valve Lash

ADJUSTMENT

Valve lash on the 7.3L diesel engine is not adjustable.

Oil Pan

REMOVAL & INSTALLATION

1. Before servicing the vehicle, refer to the precautions in the beginning of this section.

2. Remove the engine.
3. Remove the oil pan bolts.
4. Lower the oil pan.

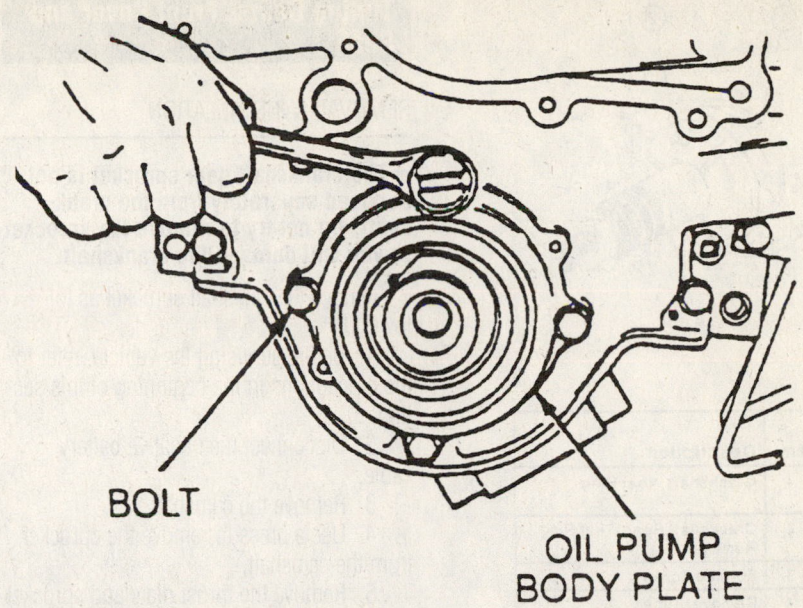

BOLT

OIL PUMP BODY PLATE

7924FG62

The oil pump is mounted on the cylinder block with 4 bolts—diesel engine

➡The oil pan is sealed to the crankcase with RTV silicone sealant in place of a gasket. It may be necessary to separate the pan from the crankcase with a utility knife. Also, the crankshaft may have to be turned to allow the pan to clear the crankshaft throws.

5. Clean the pan and crankcase mating surfaces thoroughly.

To install:

6. Apply a ⅛ in. (3mm) bead of RTV silicone sealant to the pan mating surfaces, and a ¼ in. (6mm) bead on the front and rear covers and in the corners; you have 15 minutes within which to install the pan!

7. Install the locating dowels into position.

8. Position the pan on the engine and install the pan bolts loosely.

9. Remove the dowels.

10. Tighten the pan bolts to:
- ¼ in.-20 bolts: 84 inch lbs. (10 Nm)
- 5⁄16 in.-18 bolts: 14 ft. lbs. (19 Nm)
- ⅜ in.-16 bolts: 24 ft. lbs. (33 Nm)
11. Install the engine.

Oil Pump

REMOVAL & INSTALLATION

1. Before servicing the vehicle, refer to the precautions in the beginning of this section.

2. Disconnect the negative battery cable.

3. Remove the oil pan.

4. Remove the oil pick-up tube from the pump.

5. Unbolt and remove the oil pump.

To install:

6. Assemble the pick-up tube and pump. Use a new gasket.

7. Install the oil pump and tighten the bolts to 14 ft. lbs. (19 Nm).

8. Install the oil pick up tube.

9. Install the oil pan.

10. Connect the negative battery cable.

Rear Main Seal

REMOVAL & INSTALLATION

1. Before servicing the vehicle, refer to the precautions in the beginning of this section.

2. Remove the transmission.

3. Remove the flywheel.

4. Loosen the crankshaft rear oil seal bolts and remove the seal.

5. Clean the seal mating surfaces.

6. If installing the old seal, inspect it for damage.

7. Using crankshaft wear ring removal tool T94T-6701-AH1, forcing screw T84T-7025-B, remover tube T77J-7025-B and wear ring remover sleeve T94T-6701-AH2 (refer to the illustration), or their equivalents, remove the wear ring.

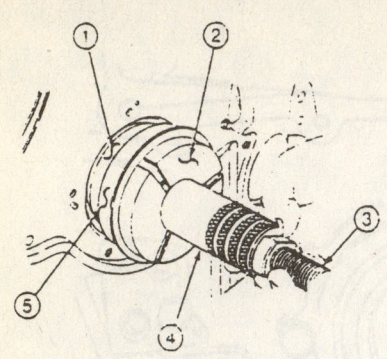

Item	Description
1	Crankshaft Wear Ring
2	Crankshaft Rear Wear Ring Remover
3	Forcing Screw
4	Remover Tube
5	Crankshaft Rear Wear Ring Remover Sleeve

7924FG61

Assemble the seal and wear ring removal tools, then remove the wear ring—diesel engine

To install:

8. Apply RTV silicone sealant to the seal retaining ring and the seal retaining bolts.

9. Using seal replacers T94T-6701-AH3 and T94T-AH4, driver sleeve T79T-6316-A4 (part of T79T-6316-A) and guide pins T94P-7000-P or their equivalents, install the wear ring and oil seal.

10. Install and tighten the seal retaining bolts.

11. Remove the installation tools and install the flywheel.

12. Install the transmission.

Piston and Ring Positioning

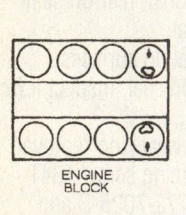 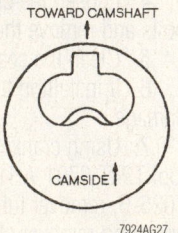

ENGINE BLOCK

TOWARD CAMSHAFT

CAMSIDE↑

7924AG27

7.3L Diesel engines—piston-to-engine orientation

Timing Gears, Front Cover and Seal

REMOVAL & INSTALLATION

➡ **The crankshaft gear sprocket is not serviced separately from the crankshaft. Do not try to remove the sprocket or you will damage the crankshaft.**

Remove the camshaft sprocket as follows:

1. Before servicing the vehicle, refer to the precautions in the beginning of this section.

2. Disconnect the negative battery cable.

3. Remove the camshaft.

4. Use a press to remove the sprocket from the camshaft.

5. Remove the thrust plate and sprocket key.

6. Inspect the camshaft and related parts for wear and damage.

To install:

7. Clean the nose of the camshaft and install the thrust plate.

8. Place the key in the keyway on the camshaft.

9. Heat the sprocket in an oven to 500°F (260°C).

10. Remove the sprocket from the oven, align the sprocket keyway with the camshaft key and install the sprocket on the camshaft until it is fully seated. Allow the camshaft assembly to cool before installation

11. Install the camshaft in the engine and align the timing marks on the gears.

12. Connect the negative battery cable.

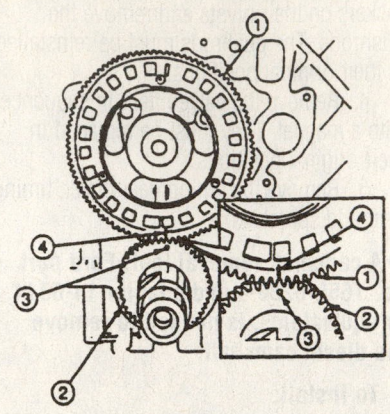

Item	Description
1	Camshaft Sprocket
2	Crankshaft Sprocket
3	Crankshaft Sprocket Timing Mark
4	Camshaft Sprocket Timing Mark

7924FG64

Be sure the timing marks are aligned as illustrated—diesel engines

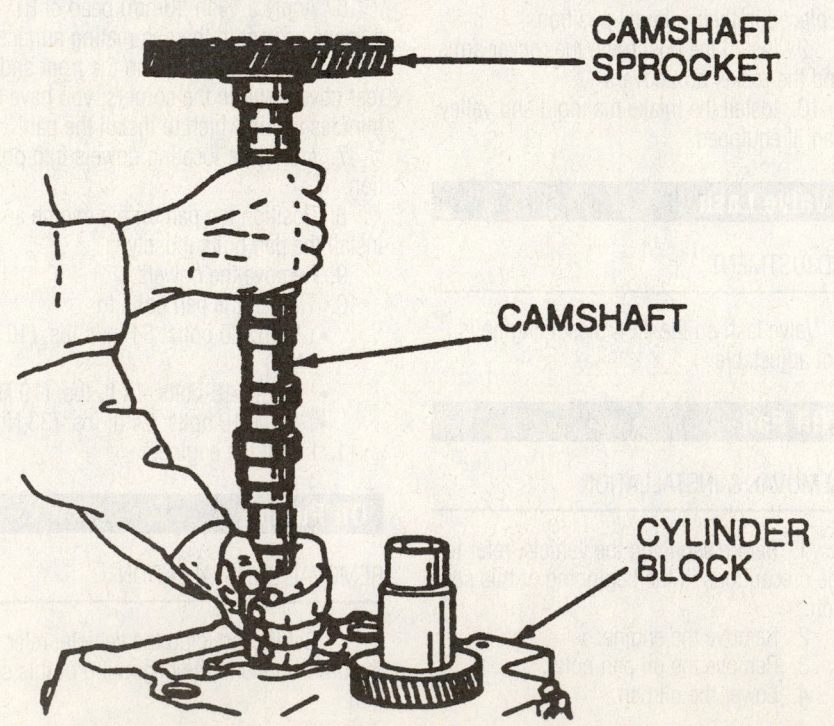

CAMSHAFT SPROCKET

CAMSHAFT

CYLINDER BLOCK

7924FG63

The camshaft gear is removed with the camshaft, then pressed off-diesel engines

GASOLINE FUEL SYSTEM

Fuel System Service Precautions

Safety is the most important factor when performing not only fuel system maintenance, but any type of maintenance. Failure to conduct maintenance and repairs in a safe manner may result in serious personal injury or death. Maintenance and testing of the vehicle's fuel system components can be accomplished safely and effectively by adhering to the following rules and guidelines.

• To avoid the possibility of fire and personal injury, always disconnect the negative battery cable unless the repair or test procedure requires that battery voltage be applied.

• Always relieve the fuel system pressure prior to disconnecting any fuel system component (injector, fuel rail, pressure regulator, etc.), fitting or fuel line connection. Exercise extreme caution whenever relieving fuel system pressure, to avoid exposing skin, face and eyes to fuel spray. Please be advised that fuel under pressure may penetrate the skin or any part of the body that it contacts.

• Always place a shop towel or cloth around the fitting or connection prior to loosening to absorb any excess fuel due to spillage. Ensure that all fuel spillage (should it occur) is quickly removed from engine surfaces. Ensure that all fuel soaked cloths or towels are deposited into a suitable waste container.

• Always keep a dry chemical (Class B) fire extinguisher near the work area.

• Do not allow fuel spray or fuel vapors to come into contact with a spark or open flame.

• Always use a back-up wrench when loosening and tightening fuel line connection fittings. This will prevent unnecessary stress and torsion to fuel line piping. Always follow the proper torque specifications.

• Always replace worn fuel fitting O-rings with new. Do not substitute fuel hose or equivalent where fuel pipe is installed.

Fuel System Pressure

RELIEVING

➡A fuel pressure gauge is needed to correctly perform this procedure.

✳✳ CAUTION

Fuel injection systems remain under pressure, even after the engine has been turned OFF. The fuel system pressure must be relieved before disconnecting any fuel lines. Failure to do so may result in fire and/or personal injury.

1. Before servicing the vehicle, refer to the precautions in the beginning of this section.
2. Disconnect the negative battery cable and remove the fuel filler cap.
3. Remove the cap from the pressure relief valve on the fuel supply manifold. Install a fuel pressure gauge to the pressure relief valve.
4. Direct the gauge drain hose into a suitable container and depress the pressure relief button.
5. Remove the gauge and replace the cap on the pressure relief valve.

➡**As an alternate method on models except 1997–01 F-150 and Expedition, disconnect the inertia switch and crank the engine for 15–20 seconds until the pressure is relieved.**

Fuel Filter

REMOVAL & INSTALLATION

➡**On newer vehicles, especially the 1997–2001 F-150 and Expedition vehicles, a fuel line disconnect tool is needed for this procedure.**

✳✳ CAUTION

Fuel injection systems remain under pressure, even after the engine has been turned OFF. The fuel system pressure must be relieved before disconnecting any fuel lines. Failure to do so may result in fire and/or personal injury.

1. Before servicing the vehicle, refer to the precautions in the beginning of this section.
2. Disconnect the negative battery cable and relieve the fuel system pressure.
3. Disconnect the fuel lines from the fuel filter. Have a drain pan handy to catch any residual fuel once the lines are separated. On newer models, disconnect the fuel lines from the filter as follows:
   a. Disconnect the safety clip from the male hose.

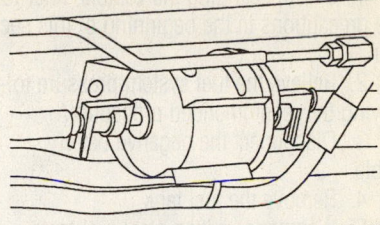

Typical fuel filter mounting along an under vehicle frame rail

7924FG65

   b. Install and push the fuel line disconnect tool into the female fitting.
   c. Separate the male and female fittings.
   d. Inspect the fuel lines for any damage after the fuel is finished draining.
4. Remove the fuel filter from the bracket and the retainer, if equipped. Note the direction of the flow arrow so the replacement filter can be installed correctly.

To install:
5. Position the fuel filter into the mounting bracket with the flow arrow pointing in the correct direction.
6. Install the fuel lines to the fuel filter. On newer models, align and push the male tube into the female fitting until a click is heard. Pull on the fitting to ensure that it is fully engaged, then install the safety clip.
7. Lower the vehicle to the ground.

➡**When the battery has been disconnected and reconnected, some abnormal drive symptoms may occur while the PCM relearns its adaptive strategy. The vehicle may need to be driven 10 miles (16 km) or more to relearn the strategy.**

8. Connect the negative battery cable.

Fuel Pump

REMOVAL & INSTALLATION

Except E-Series

1997 F-250HD, F-350 AND F-SUPER DUTY

✳✳ CAUTION

Fuel injection systems remain under pressure, even after the engine has been turned OFF. The fuel system pressure must be relieved before disconnecting any fuel lines. Failure to do so may result in fire and/or personal injury.

1. Before servicing the vehicle, refer to the precautions in the beginning of this section.

2. Relieve the fuel system pressure following the recommended procedure.

3. Disconnect the negative battery cable.

4. Remove the fuel tank.

5. If equipped with a steel fuel tank:

a. Disengage the wiring at the connector.

b. Remove all dirt from the area of the sender.

c. Disconnect the fuel lines.

d. Turn the locking ring counterclockwise to remove it. There is a wrench designed for this purpose. If the wrench is not available, loosen the locking ring by placing a wood dowel against the tabs on the locking ring and carefully hammering it loose. Never use a metal drift!

e. Lift out the fuel pump and sending unit. Discard the gasket.

❊❊ CAUTION

Use of a metal drift may result in sparks which could cause an explosion!

6. If equipped with a plastic fuel tank:

a. Disengage the wiring at the connector.

b. Remove all dirt from the area of the sender.

c. Disconnect the fuel lines.

d. Turn the locking ring counterclockwise to remove it. A band-type oil filter wrench is ideal for this purpose. Lift out the fuel pump and sending unit. Discard the gasket.

To install:

7. Place a new gasket in position in the groove in the tank.

8. Place the sending unit/fuel pump assembly in the tank, indexing the tabs with the slots in the tank. Be sure the gasket stays in place.

9. Hold the assembly in place and position the locking ring.

10. On steel tanks, turn the locking ring clockwise until the stop is against the retainer ring tab.

11. On plastic tanks, turn the retaining ring clockwise until hand-tight, then tighten it to 40–55 ft. lbs. (54–75 Nm).

12. Be sure the gasket is still in place.

13. Connect the fuel lines and wiring.

14. Install the tank.

1997–01 F-150, F-250 AND EXPEDITION AND 1998–01 F-250HD, F-350, F-450 AND NAVIGATOR

❊❊ CAUTION

Fuel injection systems remain under pressure, even after the engine has been turned OFF. The fuel system pressure must be relieved before disconnecting any fuel lines. Failure to do so may result in fire and/or personal injury.

1. Before servicing the vehicle, refer to the precautions in the beginning of this section.

2. Remove or disconnect the following:
- Negative battery cable
- Fuel pressure
- Fuel tank skid plate bolts and lower the skid plate.
- Fuel
- Fuel tank filler pipe hose from the tank
- Fuel tank filler pipe vent hose from the tank
- Fuel lines from the fuel pump
- Front fuel tank connections
- Rear EVAP hose clamp and disconnect the hose.
- Electrical connector from the fuel pump

3. Support the fuel tank with a jack.

4. Remove or disconnect the following:
- Fuel tank support strap bolts and remove the fuel tank straps.
- Fuel tank
- Fuel pump bolts
- Fuel pump

To install:

5. Install the fuel tank.

6. Tighten the fuel tank bolts to 66–91 inch lbs. (7.6–10.4 Nm).

7. Install the fuel tank.

a. Tighten the fuel tank strap bolts to 22–30 ft. lbs. (29.7–40.7 Nm).

b. Tighten the skid plate bolts to 10–13 ft. lbs. (13–17 Nm).

8. Connect the negative battery.

E-Series

❊❊ CAUTION

Fuel injection systems remain under pressure, even after the engine has been turned OFF. The fuel system pressure must be relieved before disconnecting any fuel lines. Failure to do so may result in fire and/or personal injury.

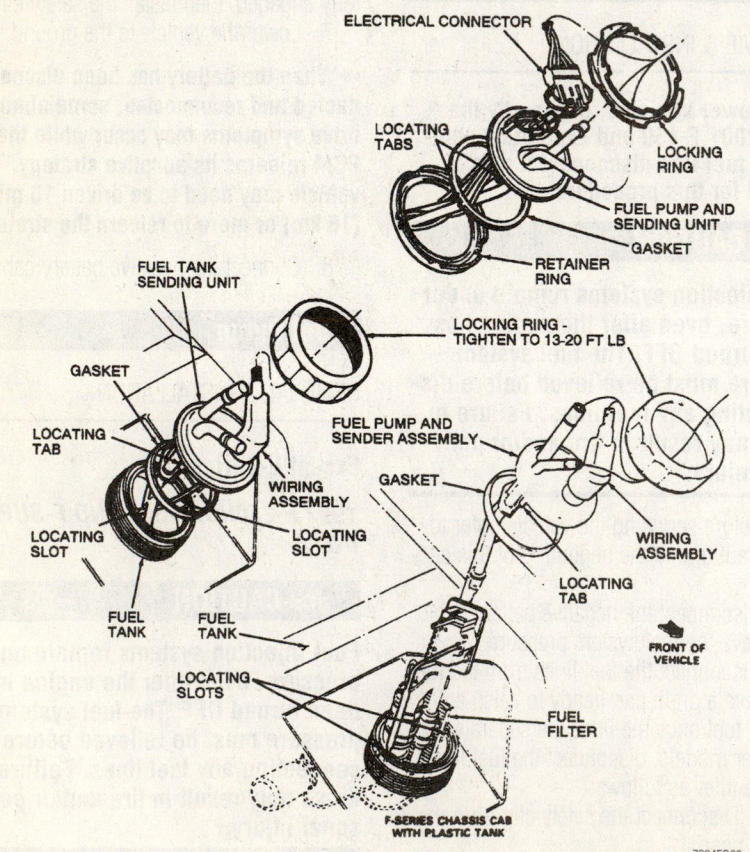

Exploded view of the in-tank fuel pump assembly—1997 F-250HD, F-350 and F-SuperDuty

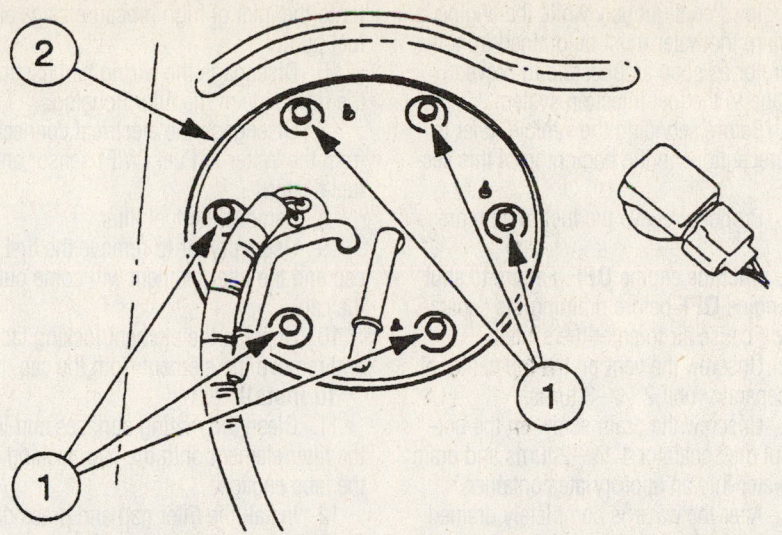

7924FG67

Remove the mounting bolts (1), then lift the fuel pump assembly (2) out of the tank—E-Series

1. Before servicing the vehicle, refer to the precautions in the beginning of this section.
2. Remove or disconnect the following:
   - Negative battery cable
   - Fuel system pressure
   - Fuel tank
   - Fuel tank filler pipe vent hose and fuel tank filler pipe from the tank
3. Support the fuel tank with a jack.
   - The 2 fuel tank support strap nuts and remove the 2 fuel tank support straps.
4. Lower the fuel tank to allow access to the electrical connections
5. Remove or disconnect the following:
   - Fuel tank connections
   - Fuel and electrical connections from the fuel pump
   - Fuel tank
   - Fuel tank screws/nuts, fuel pump and sender

To install:
6. Install or connect the following:
   - Fuel sender and fuel pump into the fuel tank. Tighten the screws/nuts.
7. Raise the fuel tank.
8. Install or connect the following:
   - Fuel and electrical connections to the fuel pump
   - Fuel tank connections
   - Fuel tank support straps and tighten the nuts to 13–17 ft. lbs. (17–23 Nm).
   - Fuel tank filler pipe vent hose and the fuel tank filler pipe to the tank
   - Negative battery cable

DIESEL FUEL SYSTEM

Fuel System Service Precautions

Safety is the most important factor when performing not only fuel system maintenance but any type of maintenance. Failure to conduct maintenance and repairs in a safe manner may result in serious personal injury or death. Maintenance and testing of the vehicle's fuel system components can be accomplished safely and effectively by adhering to the following rules and guidelines.

- To avoid the possibility of fire and personal injury, always disconnect the negative battery cable unless the repair or test procedure requires that battery voltage be applied.
- Always relieve the fuel system pressure prior to disconnecting any fuel system component (injector, fuel rail, pressure regulator, etc.), fitting or fuel line connection. Exercise extreme caution whenever relieving fuel system pressure, to avoid exposing skin, face and eyes to fuel spray. Please be advised that fuel under pressure may penetrate the skin or any part of the body that it contacts.
- Always place a shop towel or cloth around the fitting or connection prior to loosening to absorb any excess fuel due to spillage. Ensure that all fuel spillage (should it occur) is quickly removed from engine surfaces. Ensure that all fuel soaked cloths or towels are deposited into a suitable waste container.
- Always keep a dry chemical (Class B) fire extinguisher near the work area.
- Do not allow fuel spray or fuel vapors to come into contact with a spark or open flame.
- Always use a back-up wrench when loosening and tightening fuel line connection fittings. This will prevent unnecessary stress and torsion to fuel line piping. Always follow the proper torque specifications.
- Always replace worn fuel fitting O-rings with new. Do not substitute fuel hose or equivalent where fuel pipe is installed.

Fuel System Pressure

RELIEVING

✳✳ CAUTION

Before removing the fuel tank filler cap, turn the fuel tank filler cap ¼ to ¾ turn counterclockwise and wait for the tank pressure to be relieved. Personal injury may result if the fuel tank filler cap is removed without the pressure fully relieved.

1. Before servicing the vehicle, refer to the precautions in the beginning of this section.
2. Remove the fuel tank filler cap to relieve any pressure in the fuel tank.
3. When servicing the fuel lines, loosen the fuel fitting to allow any residual fuel line pressure to be relieved.

Idle Speed

ADJUSTMENT

1. Before servicing the vehicle, refer to the precautions in the beginning of this section.
2. Place the transmission in Neutral (manual transmissions) or **P** (automatic transmissions).
3. Bring the engine up to normal operating temperature.

➥**Idle speed is measured with the manual transmission in Neutral or the automatic transmission in D.**

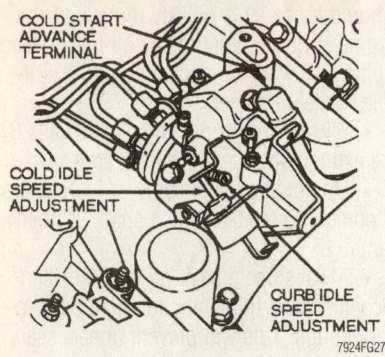

Raise or lower the curb idle speed by turning the curb idle speed adjusting screw—diesel engines

4. Ensure that the curb idle adjusting screw is against the stop. If not, correct the vehicle linkage.

5. Check curb idle speed. Curb idle speed is specified on the Vehicle Emissions Control Information (VECI) decal on the underside of the vehicle's hood. Adjust the idle speed to specification using the idle speed adjusting screw.

6. Place the transmission in Neutral (manual) or **P**. Rev the engine momentarily, then place the transmission in the specified gear and recheck the idle speed. Adjust again if necessary.

7. Remove the tachometer and close the hood.

Fuel Filter/Water Separator

DRAINING WATER

→ Drain water from the water separator manual drain valve whenever the warning light comes ON or every 5000 miles (8000km). The "Water in Fuel" light will glow when approximately 3.5 oz. (103.5ml) of water accumulates in the separator.

✳✳ CAUTION

The fuel system remains under pressure, even after the engine has been turned OFF. The fuel system pressure must be relieved before disconnecting any fuel lines. Failure to do so may result in fire and/or personal injury.

The diesel engines are equipped with a fuel/water separator in the fuel supply line. A "Water in Fuel" indicator light is provided on the instrument panel to alert the driver. The light should glow when the ignition switch is in the **start** position to indicate proper light and water sensor function. If the light glows continuously while the engine is running, the water must be drained from the separator as soon as possible to prevent damage to the fuel injection system.

1. Before servicing the vehicle, refer to the precautions in the beginning of this section.

2. Properly relieve the fuel system pressure.

3. Shut the engine **OFF**. Failure to shut the engine **OFF** before draining the separator will cause air to enter the system.

4. Unscrew the vent on the top center of the separator unit 2 ½ –3 turns.

5. Unscrew the drain screw on the bottom of the separator 1 ½ –2 turns and drain the water into an appropriate container.

6. After the water is completely drained, close the water drain finger-tight.

7. Tighten the vent until snug, then turn it an additional ¼ turn.

8. Start the engine and check the "Water in Fuel" indicator light; it should not be lit. If it is lit and continues to stay so, there is a problem somewhere else in the fuel system.

REMOVAL & INSTALLATION

✳✳ CAUTION

The fuel system remains under pressure, even after the engine has been turned OFF. The fuel system pressure must be relieved before disconnecting any fuel lines. Failure to do so may result in fire and/or personal injury.

1. Before servicing the vehicle, refer to the precautions in the beginning of this section.

2. Remove or disconnect the following:
   • Negative battery cable
   • Turbocharger assembly
   • Baffle and the air inlet crossover manifold

3. Place a suitable container under the drain hose and open the filter drain.

4. Remove or disconnect the following:
   • The 2 capscrews securing the fuel filter base to the crankcase
   • Water drain hose from the filter
   • Fuel system pressure
   • Fuel outlet hose, located between the fuel and filter housing, and the fuel return hose from the fuel pressure regulator valve.
   • The 2 fuel supply hoses that connect the regulator block to the cylinder head fuel rails

5. Loosen the clamp at the fuel pump end of the hose, which connects the fuel filter to the inlet of high pressure stage at the fuel pump.

6. Disengage the wiring harness from the right side of the filter housing.

7. Disengage the electrical connections from the Water In Fuel (WIF) sensor and the fuel heater.

8. Remove the fuel filter.

9. Use a prybar to remove the fuel filter cap and the filter element will come out with the cap.

10. Depress the element locking tabs and remove the element from the cap.

To install:

11. Clean the mating surfaces and install the filter element onto the cap, making sure the tabs engage.

12. Install the filter gap and press down firmly, but gently, to engage it.

13. Install or connect the following:
   • Wiring connections to the fuel heater and WIF sensor
   • Wiring harness to the filter housing

14. Tighten the clamp at the fuel pump end of the hose, which connects the fuel filter to the inlet of high pressure stage at the fuel pump.

15. Engage the 2 fuel supply hoses that connect the regulator block to the cylinder head fuel rails.

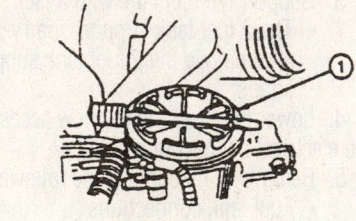

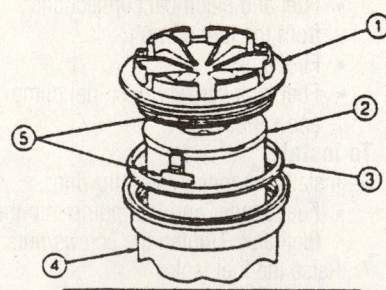

Item	Description
1	Fuel Filter Cap
2	Fuel Filter Element
3	Fuel Filter Bevel Cut Gasket
4	Fuel Filter Housing and Gland
5	Fuel Filter Element and Cap Locking Tabs

Use a prytool to remove the fuel filter cap to gain access to the filter element-diesel fuel systems

16. Install or connect the following:
- Fuel outlet hose, located between the fuel and filter housing, and the fuel return hose from the fuel pressure regulator valve.
- Water drain hose to the filter
- The 2 capscrews securing the fuel filter base to the crankcase
- Air inlet crossover manifold and baffle
- Turbocharger assembly
- Negative battery cable

Injection Pump

REMOVAL & INSTALLATION

✳✳ CAUTION

The fuel system remains under pressure, even after the engine has been turned OFF. The fuel system pressure must be relieved before disconnecting any fuel lines. Failure to do so may result in fire and/or personal injury.

1. Before servicing the vehicle, refer to the precautions in the beginning of this section.

2. Remove or disconnect the following:
- Negative battery cable
- Turbocharger assembly
- Fuel system pressure
- Fuel line banjo bolt at the pump
- Fuel line fittings at the rear of the cylinder heads
- Fuel lines
- The 3 hose clamps at the injection pump fittings
- Water drain hose at the fuel filter
- Filter and position it forward
- Injection pump retaining bolts, then lift the pump out of the crankcase bore.
- Injection pump tappet from the crankcase bore.

To install:

3. Rotate the engine so the injection pump eccentric is on the base circle.

4. Install or connect the following:
- Injection pump tappet in the base of the injection pump
- O-ring on the injection pump base
- Injection pump and tighten the bolts to 19–27 ft. lbs. (26–37 Nm).
- Fuel filter and connect the water drain hose
- The 3 fuel hoses at the front of the injection pump

- The fuel line clamps and install the fuel filter retaining bolts.
- Fuel line assembly and new seal rings at the rear of the pump.
- Fuel line fittings at the rear of the cylinder heads
- Fuel line banjo fitting at the pump. Tighten the bolt to 18 ft. lbs. (24 Nm).
- Turbocharger assembly
- Negative battery cable

DRIVE TRAIN

Transmission Assembly

REMOVAL & INSTALLATION

1. Before servicing the vehicle, refer to the precautions in the beginning of this section.

2. Remove or disconnect the following:
- Negative battery cable
- On manual transmissions, the shifter boot and lever from inside the vehicle
- On 4-wheel drive vehicles, the front driveshaft and transfer case
- All cables, connectors and fluid lines that may interfere with transmission removal. Tag them if helpful for installation.
- On automatic transmissions, the torque converter from the flexplate and disconnect the shift linkage.
- Transmission fluid

3. Position a transmission jack under the transmission and safety-chain the case to the jack.

4. Remove or disconnect the following:
- Driveshaft
- Transmission rear mount
- Crossmember
- On automatic transmissions, the transmission-to-engine block bolts
- For manual transmissions, the bolts securing the transmission to the bell housing

✳✳ CAUTION

The torque converter will fall out of the transmission if it is tilted forward. Keep a hand on it while lowering the transmission out of the vehicle.

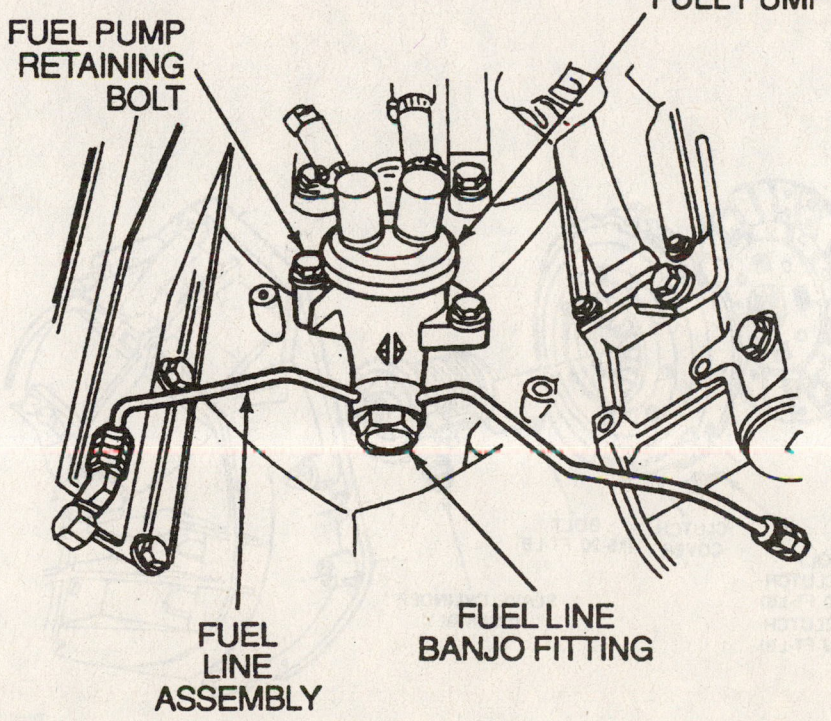

FUEL PUMP RETAINING BOLT

FUEL PUMP

FUEL LINE ASSEMBLY

FUEL LINE BANJO FITTING

7924FG28

Injection pump assembly components—diesel engines

5. Roll the transmission rearward until the input shaft clears, lower the jack and remove the transmission.

To install:

6. Carefully raise the transmission to the engine or bell housing.

7. Roll the transmission forward and into position.

8. Install or connect the following:

- On automatic transmissions tighten the bolts to 65 ft. lbs. (87 Nm) for the diesel or to 50 ft. lbs. (67 Nm) for gasoline engines. On manual transmissions, tighten the bolts to 50 ft. lbs. (64 Nm).
- Crossmember and tighten the bolts to 55 ft. lbs. (74 Nm).
- Transmission rear insulator and lower retainer. Tighten the bolts to 60 ft. lbs. (81 Nm).

9. The rest of the installation is the reverse of removal.

10. Refill all transmissions with the correct amount of Motorcraft MERCON® automatic transmission fluid.

11. Connect the negative battery cable.

Clutch

REMOVAL & INSTALLATION

1. Before servicing the vehicle, refer to the precautions in the beginning of this section.

2. Disconnect the negative battery cable.

3. Raise and safely support the vehicle.

4. On vehicles with the externally mounted slave cylinder, remove the clutch slave cylinder. On vehicles with an internally mounted slave cylinder, disengage the quick-disconnect coupling with a spring coupling tool.

5. Remove the transmission.

6. On gasoline engine models, except the 7.5L engine, remove the starter. Remove the flywheel housing attaching bolts and remove the housing. On diesel engine models and the 7.5L gasoline engine, remove the cover, then remove the release lever and bearing from the clutch housing. To remove the release lever:

a. Remove the dust boot.

b. Push the release lever forward to compress the slave cylinder.

c. Remove the slave cylinder by prying on the steel clip to free the tangs while pulling the cylinder clear.

d. Remove the release lever by pulling it outward.

7. Mark the pressure plate and cover assembly and the flywheel so that they can be reinstalled in the same relative position.

8. Loosen the pressure plate and cover attaching bolts evenly in a staggered sequence a turn at time until the pressure plate springs are relieved of their tension. Remove the attaching bolts.

9. Remove the pressure plate and cover assembly and the clutch disc from the flywheel.

10. Inspect the flywheel for wear, damage and flatness.

To install:

11. Position the clutch disc on the flywheel so that an aligning tool or spare transmission mainshaft can enter the clutch pilot bearing and align the disc.

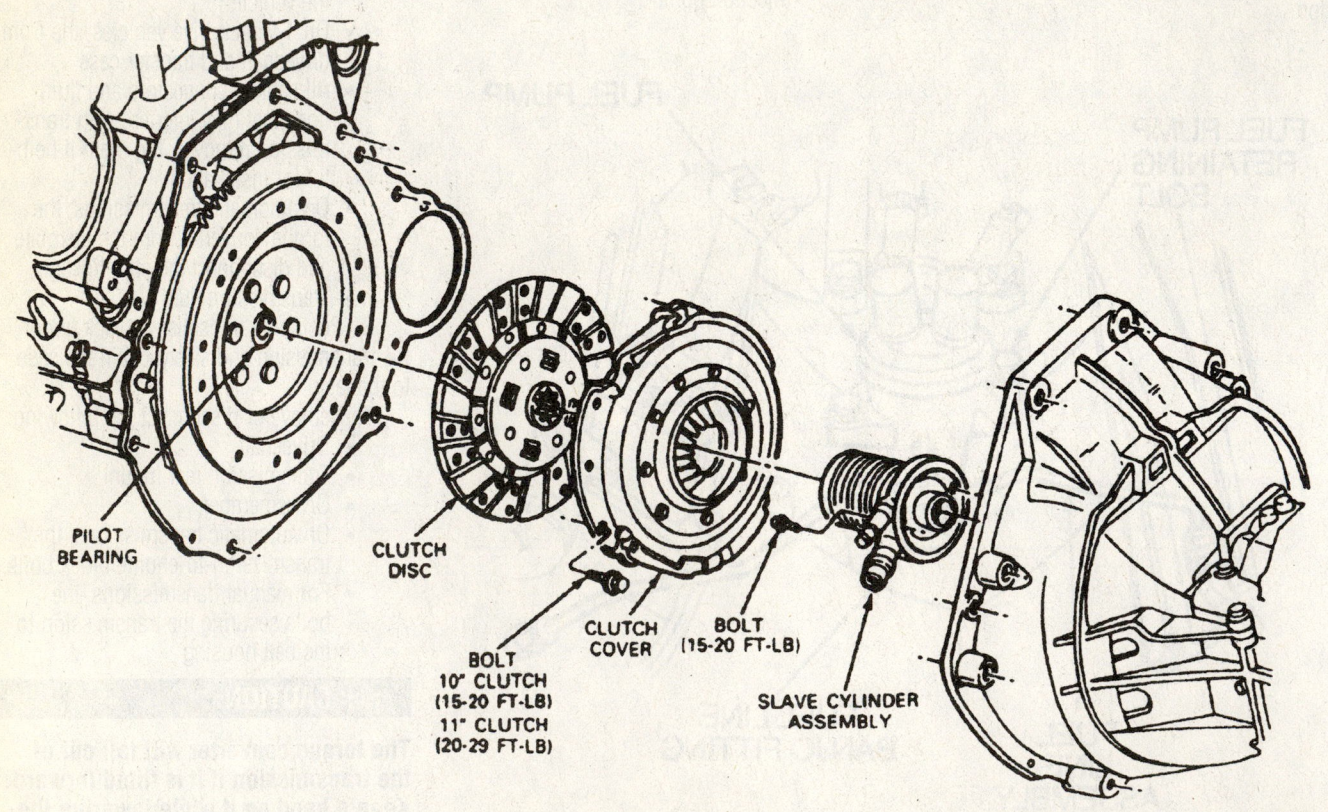

PILOT BEARING

CLUTCH DISC

CLUTCH COVER

BOLT
10" CLUTCH
(15-20 FT-LB)
11" CLUTCH
(20-29 FT-LB)

BOLT
(15-20 FT-LB)

SLAVE CYLINDER ASSEMBLY

7924FG29

Typical clutch assembly with internal slave cylinder

12. When reinstalling the original pressure plate and cover assembly, align the assembly and flywheel according to the marks made during removal. Position the pressure plate and cover assembly on the flywheel, align the pressure plate and disc, and install the retaining bolts. Tighten the bolts in an alternating sequence a few turns at a time until the proper torque is reached:

- 10 inch clutch: 15–20 ft. lbs. (20–27 Nm)
- 11 inch clutch: 20–29 ft. lbs. (27–39 Nm)

13. Remove the tool used to align the clutch disc.

14. With the clutch fully released, apply a light coat of grease on the sides of the driving lugs.

15. Position the clutch release bearing and the bearing hub on the release lever. Install the release lever on the fulcrum in the flywheel housing. Apply a light coating of grease to the release lever fingers and the fulcrum. Fill the groove of the release bearing hub with grease.

16. If the flywheel housing has been removed, position it against the rear engine cover plate and install the attaching bolts and tighten them to 40–50 ft. lbs. (54–68 Nm).

17. Install the starter motor, if removed.

18. Install the transmission.

19. Install the slave cylinder and bleed the system.

20. Connect the negative battery cable.

Hydraulic Clutch System

BLEEDING

Externally Mounted Slave Cylinder

1. Before servicing the vehicle, refer to the precautions in the beginning of this section.

2. Clean the reservoir cap and the slave cylinder connection.

3. Remove the slave cylinder from the housing.

4. Using a 3/32 inch punch, drive out the pin that holds the tube in place.

5. Remove the tube from the slave cylinder and place the end of the tube in a container.

6. Hold the slave cylinder so the connector port is at the highest point, by tipping it about 30 degrees from horizontal. Fill the cylinder with DOT 3 brake fluid through the port. It may be necessary to rock the cylinder or slightly depress the pushrod to expel all the air.

✳✳ CAUTION

Pushing too hard on the pushrod will spurt fluid from the port!

7. When all air is expelled—no more bubble are seen—install the slave cylinder.

➡ **Some fluid will be expelled during installation as the pushrod is depressed.**

8. Remove the reservoir cap. Some fluid will run out of the tube end into the container. Pour fluid into the reservoir until a steady stream of fluid runs out of the tube and the reservoir is filled. Quickly install the diaphragm and cap. The flow should stop.

9. Connect the tube and install the pin. Check the fluid level.

10. Check the clutch operation.

Internally Mounted Slave Cylinder

EXCEPT 1997–01 F-150, EXPEDITION AND NAVIGATOR MODELS

➡ **With the quick-disconnect coupling, no air should enter the system when the coupling is disengaged. However, if air should somehow enter the system, it must be bled.**

1. Before servicing the vehicle, refer to the precautions in the beginning of this section.

2. Remove the reservoir cap and diaphragm. Fill the reservoir with DOT 3 brake fluid.

3. Connect a piece of rubber tubing to the slave cylinder bleed screw. Place the other end in a container.

4. Loosen the bleed screw. Gravity will force fluid from the master cylinder to flow down to the slave cylinder, forcing air out of the bleed screw. When a steady stream—no bubbles—flows out, the system is bled. Close the bleed screw.

➡ **Check periodically to be sure the master cylinder reservoir doesn't run dry.**

5. Add fluid to fill the master cylinder reservoir.

6. Fully depress the clutch pedal. Release it as quickly as possible. Pause for 2 seconds. Repeat this procedure 10 times.

7. Check the fluid level. Refill it if necessary. It should be kept full.

8. Repeat Steps 5 and 6, 5 more times.

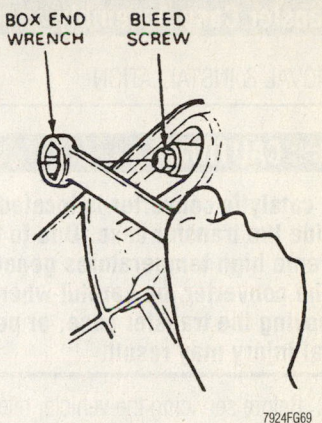

Bleed screw location for internally mounted slave cylinders

9. Install the diaphragm and cap.

10. Have an assistant hold the pedal to the floor while you crack the bleed screw—not too far—just far enough to expel any trapped air. Close the bleed screw, then release the pedal.

11. Check, and if necessary, fill the reservoir.

1997–01 F-150, EXPEDITION AND NAVIGATOR MODELS

➡ **Be sure to keep the clutch master cylinder reservoir full of brake fluid during the bleeding process to prevent air from entering the clutch master cylinder.**

1. Before servicing the vehicle, refer to the precautions in the beginning of this section.

2. Raise and safely support the front of the vehicle.

➡ **It is necessary to have the assistance of a helper to bleed this system.**

3. Fill the clutch system reservoir with DOT 3 brake fluid.

4. Have your assistant depress the clutch pedal rapidly for 5–10 strokes.

5. Wait 1–3 minutes.

6. Repeat Steps 3 and 4 3 more times.

7. Loosen the bleeder screw on the transmission for the slave cylinder.

8. Have the helper fully depress the clutch pedal and hold it down.

9. Tighten the bleeder screw.

10. The helper should now release the clutch pedal.

11. Apply pressure to the clutch pedal. If the clutch pedal travels more than 6–7 inches (15.3–17.7 cm), repeat the bleeding process.

Transfer Case Assembly

REMOVAL & INSTALLATION

⁂ CAUTION

The catalytic converter is located beside the transfer case. Due to the extreme high temperatures generated by the converter, be careful when removing the transfer case, or personal injury may result.

1. Before servicing the vehicle, refer to the precautions in the beginning of this section.
2. Remove or disconnect the following:
   - Negative battery cable
   - Fluid from the transfer case
   - 4WD indicator switch wire connector at the transfer case
   - Skid plate from the frame, if equipped
   - Front driveshaft from the front output yoke
   - Rear driveshaft from the rear output shaft yoke
   - Speedometer driven gear from the transfer case rear bearing retainer
   - Retaining rings and shift rod from the transfer case shift lever
   - Vent hose from the transfer case
   - Heat shield from the frame
3. Support the transfer case with a transmission jack.
4. Remove the bolts retaining the transfer case to the transmission adapter.
5. Lower the transfer case from the vehicle.

To install:

6. When installing place a new gasket between the transfer case and the adapter.
7. Raise the transfer case with the transmission jack so the transmission output shaft aligns with the splined transfer case input shaft. Install the bolts retaining the transfer case to the adapter.
8. Remove the transmission jack from the transfer case.

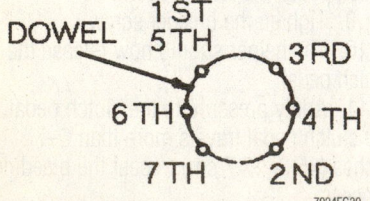

Transfer case-to-adapter bolt torque sequence—Borg-Warner model 13-45

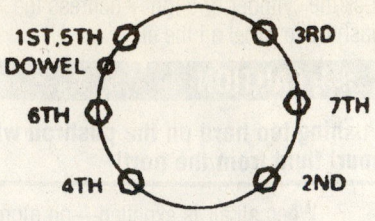

Transfer case-to-adapter bolt torque sequence—Borg-Warner 13–56 electronic and manual shift transfer case used in F-Series

9. Install or connect the following:
   - Rear driveshaft to the rear output shaft yoke. Tighten the bolts to 15 ft. lbs. (20 Nm).
   - Shift lever to the transfer case and install the retaining nut.
   - Speedometer driven gear to the transfer case
   - 4WD indicator switch wire connector at the transfer case
   - Front driveshaft to the front output yoke. Tighten the bolts to 15 ft. lbs. (20 Nm).
   - Heat shield to the frame crossmember and the mounting lug on the transfer case. Install and tighten the retaining bolts.
   - Skid plate to the frame
   - Drain plug. Remove the filler plug and install 6 pts. (2.8L) of Dexron®II transmission.
   - Connect the negative battery cable.

Halfshaft

REMOVAL & INSTALLATION

1997–01 F-150, F-250, Navigator And Expedition Models

The F-150 and F-250 series Heavy Duty and Super Duty models do not have halfshafts.

1. Before servicing the vehicle, refer to the precautions in the beginning of this section.
2. Remove or disconnect the following:
   - Front wheels
   - Front hub cotter pin, retainer and nut
3. Using a floor hydraulic jack, support the lower suspension arm.
4. Remove or disconnect the following:
   - Upper ball joint cotter pin and castle nut
   - Knuckle from the front suspension upper arm

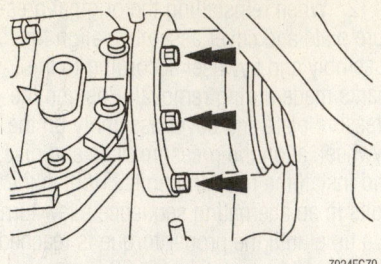

Halfshaft-to-differential mounting bolts (3 of the 6 bolts shown)—1997–01 F-150 and Expedition models

5. Lower the lower suspension arm and steering knuckle slightly to facilitate easier halfshaft removal.
6. Remove the 2 disc caliper mounting bolts, then lift the front disc caliper off of the front disc brake caliper anchor plate and position aside. Do not allow the caliper to hang by the brake hose; suspend it from the vehicle's frame with strong cord or wire.
7. Remove the 6 front halfshaft-to-differential bolts.

⁂ WARNING

Use care to avoid damaging the hub seal when removing the front halfshaft.

8. Remove the inboard end of the halfshaft from the differential case or extension axle case. Separate the front halfshaft and joints from the hub, then remove the halfshaft and joints from the vehicle.

To install:

9. Slide the halfshaft outboard end into the hub, making sure that the splines engage.
10. Situate the inboard end of the halfshaft against the front differential flange and install the 6 halfshaft-to-differential bolts. Tighten the halfshaft bolts to 51–67 ft. lbs. (68–92 Nm).
11. Install the front disc brake caliper onto the rotor and anchor plate, then install and tighten the 2 caliper mounting bolts to 21–26 ft. lbs. (28–36 Nm).
12. Lift the lower suspension arm and steering knuckle up until the upper ball joint stud is inserted into the steering knuckle. Install the upper ball joint castle nut and tighten to 57–76 ft. lbs. (77–104 Nm). Install a new cotter pin.
13. Install the hub nut onto the halfshaft and tighten the hub nut to 188–254 ft. lbs. (255–345 Nm).
14. Install the hub nut retainer and a new cotter pin.

15. Install the front wheels and tighten the lug nuts in a star-shaped sequence to 83–112 ft. lbs. (113–153 Nm).

16. Lower the vehicle to the ground.

Locking Hubs

REMOVAL & INSTALLATION

Manual

1. Before servicing the vehicle, refer to the precautions in the beginning of this section.

2. Remove or disconnect the following:
   - Wheels
   - Disc brake caliper
   - Disc brake pads and anti-rattle clips
   - Anchor plate retaining bolts and remove the anchor plate.
   - Disc brake rotor
   - Disc brake rotor shield retaining bolts and the shield
   - If equipped with 4-wheel ABS, the speed sensor retaining bolt and move the speed sensor and harness aside.
   - Hub nut cotter pin, retainer and the hub nut. Discard the cotter pin.
   - Hub assembly retaining bolts from the inside of the steering knuckle
   - Hub assembly

➡**If necessary, use a suitable puller to separate the hub assembly from the CV-joint. Use care not to over-extend the CV-joint and boot when removing the hub assembly.**

   - Grease seal from the steering knuckle

To install:

3. Install or connect the following:
   - New grease seal
   - Hub assembly to the steering knuckle and secure with the 3 retaining bolts. Tighten the bolts to 110–145 ft. lbs. (149–201 Nm).
   - CV-joint into the hub assembly
   - If equipped with 4-wheel ABS, the speed sensor and secure with 1 retaining bolt. Tighten the bolt to 60–84 inch lbs. (7–9 Nm).
   - Disc brake rotor shield and the 3 retaining bolts. Tighten the bolts to 80–107 inch lbs. (9–12 Nm).
   - Hub nut and tighten to 188–254 ft. lbs. (255–345 Nm).
   - Hub nut retainer and a new cotter pin
   - Disc brake rotor
   - Anchor plate in position and install the 2 retaining bolts. Tighten the bolts to 125–168 ft. lbs. (170–230 Nm).
   - Brake pad anti-rattle clips and install the disc brake pads.
   - Disc brake caliper
   - Wheels. Tighten the lug nuts to 83–112 ft. lbs. (113–153 Nm).

4. Lower the vehicle.

5. Pump the brake pedal several times to position the brake pads prior to moving the vehicle.

6. Road test the vehicle and check for proper operation.

Automatic

1. Before servicing the vehicle, refer to the precautions in the beginning of this section.

2. Raise and safely support the vehicle.

3. Remove the tire.

4. Remove the 3 screws and separate the cap from the body.

5. Remove the lockring seated in the groove of the hub assembly.

6. Remove the body assembly from the brake rotor/hub.

7. Remove the snapring from the groove in the stub-shaft.

8. Remove the 3 thrust washers from the stub-shaft.

9. Pull the cam assembly to remove it.

To install:

10. Align the fixed cam retaining key on the cam assembly with the keyway on the spindle. Firmly push the cam assembly on the wheel retaining nut.

11. Install the metal, plastic, then the splined washers on the stub-shaft.

12. Install the snapring in the groove of the stub-shaft. It may be necessary to push the stub-shaft outward from the back of the knuckle assembly.

✷✷ WARNING

Do not pack the hub assembly with grease. Too much grease will damage the hub assembly.

13. Rotate the moving cam assembly to the 1 o'clock position in relation to the fixed cam retaining key. Use any 1 of the 3 stops.

14. Install the body assembly onto the hub by lining up the 3 legs with the 3 pockets in the cam assembly. Be sure the assembly is in far enough to see the groove in the hub.

15. Install the large lockring in the groove on the hub. Ensure the lockring is seated completely.

16. Install the cap using the 3 screws. Tighten the screws to 35–53 inch lbs. (4–6 Nm).

17. Install the tire and lower the vehicle to the floor.

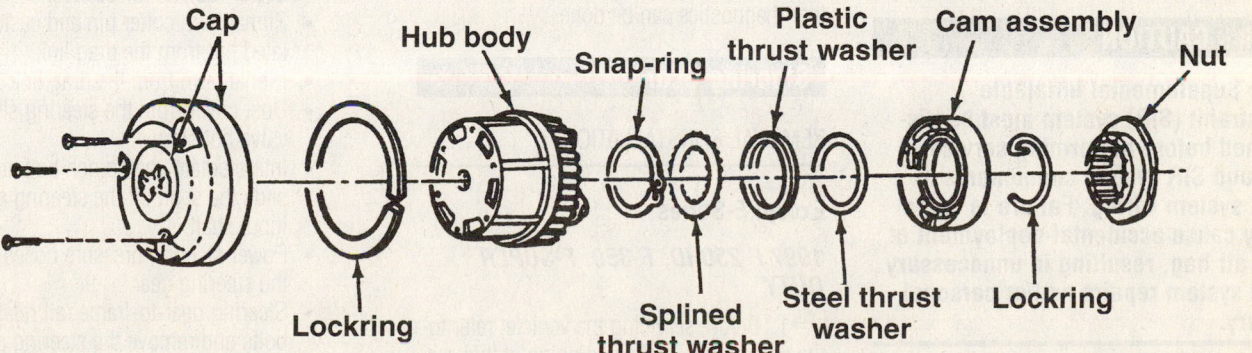

Cap — Hub body — Snap-ring — Plastic thrust washer — Cam assembly — Nut — Lockring — Splined thrust washer — Steel thrust washer — Lockring

7924FG93

Exploded view of the typical automatic locking hub assembly

Turn to Section 5 for brake system applications

STEERING AND SUSPENSION

Air Bag

❋❋ CAUTION

Some vehicles are equipped with an air bag system. The system must be disabled before performing service on or around system components, steering column, instrument panel components, wiring and sensors. Failure to follow safety and disabling procedures could result in accidental air bag deployment, possible personal injury and unnecessary system repairs.

PRECAUTIONS

Several precautions must be observed when handling the inflator module to avoid accidental deployment and possible personal injury:

• Never carry the inflator module by the wires or connector on the underside of the module.

• When carrying a live inflator module, hold securely with both hands and ensure that the bag and trim cover are pointed away.

• Place the inflator module on a bench or other surface with the bag and trim cover facing up.

• With the inflator module on the bench, never place anything on or close to the module, which may be thrown in the event of an accidental deployment.

DISARMING

❋❋ CAUTION

The Supplemental Inflatable Restraint (SIR) system must be disarmed before performing service around SIR system components or SIR system wiring. Failure to do so may cause accidental deployment of the air bag, resulting in unnecessary SIR system repairs and/or personal injury.

The positive battery cable must be disconnected for a minimum of 1 minute before beginning any air bag work to de-energize the back-up power supply. It is a good idea to disengage both the positive and negative battery cables to ensure that the Air Bag system is definitely discharged.

ARMING THE SYSTEM

❋❋ WARNING

If the air bag simulators have been used, the air bag simulators must be removed and the air bags reconnected when the system is reactivated to avoid non-deployment in a collision resulting in possible personal injury.

1. Disconnect the positive battery cable.
2. Wait 1 minute, this is required for the back-up power supply in the air bag diagnostic monitor to deplete its stored energy.
3. Remove the air bag simulator from the air bag sliding contact connector at the top of the steering column. Reconnect the driver's side air bag module assembly. Position the driver's air bag module on the steering wheel and secure with the 2 bolts and washers. Tighten the bolt and washer assembly to 8–10 ft. lbs. (10–14 Nm).
4. Connect the positive battery cable.
5. Turn the ignition switch from the **OFF** to **RUN** and visually monitor the air bag warning indicator. The light will illuminate continuously for approximately 6 seconds and then turn off. If a fault occurs, the air bag indicator will either fail to light, remain lighted continuously or flash. The flashing may not occur until approximately 30 seconds after the ignition switch has been turned from **OFF** to **RUN**. This is the time needed for the air bag diagnostic monitor to complete testing the system. If the air bag indicator is inoperative, an air bag system fault exists, a tone will sound in a pattern of 5 sets of 5 beeps. If this occurs, the air bag indicator will need to be serviced before further diagnostics can be done.

Steering Gear

REMOVAL & INSTALLATION

Except E-Series

1997 F-250HD, F-350, F-SUPER DUTY

1. Before servicing the vehicle, refer to the precautions in the beginning of this section.
2. Place the wheels in the straight-ahead position.
3. Remove or disconnect the following:

• Pressure and return lines. Cap the openings.
• Splash shield from the flex coupling
• Flex coupling at the gear
• Pitman arm from the sector shaft
• Steering gear mounting bolts
• Steering gear. It may be necessary to work it free of the flex coupling.

To install:

4. Place the splash shield on the steering gear lugs.
5. Slide the flex coupling into place on the steering shaft. Be sure the steering wheel spokes are still horizontal.
6. Center the steering gear input shaft with the indexing flat facing downward.
7. Slide the steering gear input shaft into the flex coupling and into place on the frame side rail. Install the flex coupling bolt and tighten it to 30 ft. lbs. (41 Nm).
8. Install or connect the following:

• Steering gear mounting bolts and tighten them to 65 ft. lbs. (88 Nm).
• Pitman arm. Tighten the nut to 230 ft. lbs. (312 Nm).
• Pressure, then, the return lines. Tighten the pressure line to 25 ft. lbs. (34 Nm).
• Flex coupling shield

9. Fill the steering reservoir.
10. Run the engine and turn the steering wheel lock-to-lock several times to expel air. Check for leaks.

1997–01 F-150, F-250 AND EXPEDITION AND 1998–01 F-250HD, F-350, F-450 AND NAVIGATOR.

1. Before servicing the vehicle, refer to the precautions in the beginning of this section.
2. Remove or disconnect the following:

• Skid plate
• Lower radiator air deflector
• Pitman arm cotter pin and castellated nut from the drag link
• Pitman arm from the drag link
• Dust cover from the steering shaft valve housing
• Intermediate shaft pinch bolt and slide the shaft off the steering gear input shaft.
• Power steering pressure hoses at the steering gear
• Steering gear-to-frame rail retaining bolts and remove the steering gear.

3. If replacing or servicing the steering gear, match mark the sector shaft arm to the sector shaft and remove the steering gear sector shaft arm retaining nut and lockwasher. Remove the sector shaft arm.

To install:

4. If removed, install the steering gear sector shaft arm to the sector shaft aligning the match marks made during removal. Install the retaining nut and lockwasher and tighten to 170–228 ft. lbs. (234–316 Nm).

5. Install or connect the following:

- Steering gear in position. Install the 3 retaining bolts and tighten them to 50–68 ft. lbs. (68–92 Nm).
- Power steering pressure hoses to the steering gear using new seals, if necessary.
- Intermediate shaft on the steering gear input shaft and install the shaft pinch bolt. Tighten the pinch bolt to 30–42 ft. lbs. (41–57 Nm).
- Dust cover over the steering shaft valve housing
- Pitman arm to the drag link. Install the castellated nut and tighten to 57–76 ft. lbs. (77–104 Nm). Install a new cotter pin.
- Radiator air deflector and secure with the retaining screws and push clips.

- Skid plate and secure it with the retaining bolts.

6. Lower the vehicle.

7. Fill and bleed the power steering system.

8. Road test the vehicle and check the steering system for proper operation.

E-Series

1. Before servicing the vehicle, refer to the precautions in the beginning of this section.

2. Place the wheels in the straight-ahead position.

3. Remove or disconnect the following:

- Pressure and return lines. Cap the openings.
- Splash shield from the flex coupling
- Flex coupling at the gear
- Pitman arm from the sector shaft
- Steering gear and remove the mounting bolts.
- Steering gear. It may be necessary to work it free of the flex coupling.

To install:

4. Install or connect the following:

- Splash shield on the steering gear lugs
- Flex coupling into place on the steering shaft. Be sure the steering wheel spokes are still horizontal.

5. Center the steering gear input shaft with the indexing flat facing downward.

6. Install or connect the following:

- Steering gear input shaft into the flex coupling and into place on the frame side rail. Install the flex coupling bolt and tighten it to 30 ft. lbs. (41 Nm).
- Gear mounting bolts and tighten them to 65 ft. lbs. (88 Nm).
- Pitman arm. Tighten the nut to 230 ft. lbs. (312 Nm).
- Pressure, then, the return lines. Tighten the pressure line to 25 ft. lbs. (34 Nm).
- Flex coupling shield into place.

7. Fill the steering reservoir.

8. Run the engine and turn the steering wheel lock-to-lock several times to expel air. Check for leaks.

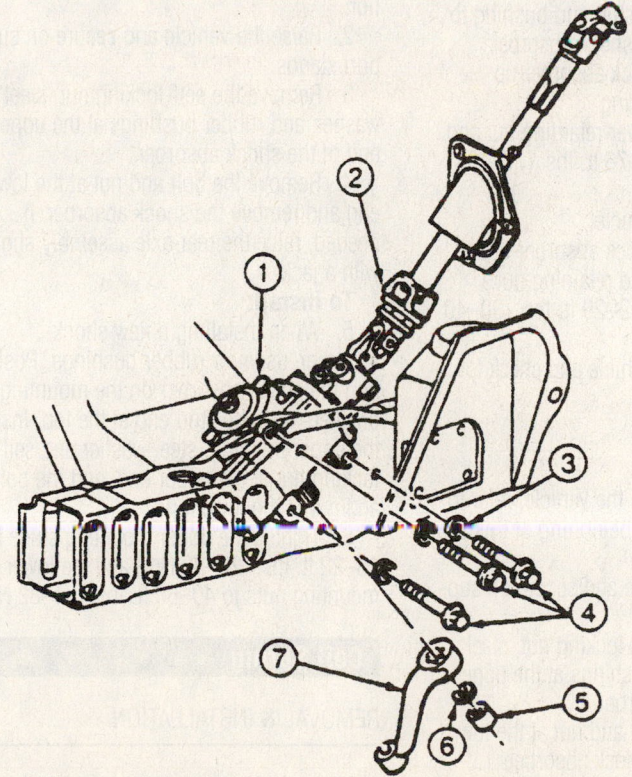

Item	Description
1	Steering Gear
2	Lower Steering Column Shaft
3	Washer
4	Bolt 73-90 N-m (54-66 Ft-Lb)
5	Nut 230-310 N-m (170-228 Ft-Lb)
6	Washer
7	Steering Gear Sector Shaft Arm

7924FG72

The steering gear is mounted on the left frame rail as show—E-Series

Front Shock Absorber

REMOVAL & INSTALLATION

Except E-Series

1997 F-250HD, F-350 AND F-SUPER DUTY

1. Before servicing the vehicle, refer to the precautions in the beginning of this section.

2. Raise the vehicle and secure on support stands.

3. Remove the self-locking nut, steel washer, and rubber bushings at the upper end of the shock absorber.

4. Remove the bolt and nut at the lower end and remove the shock absorber.

To install:

5. When installing a new shock absorber, use new rubber bushings. Position the shock absorber on the mounting brackets with the stud end at the top. Install the upper bushing, steel washer and self-locking nut at the upper end, and the bolt and nut at the lower end.

6. Tighten the upper mounting studs to 18–22 ft. lbs. (24–30 Nm) and the lower mounting nuts to 40–60 ft. lbs. (54–82 Nm).

1997–01 F-150, F-250 AND EXPEDITION; 1998–01 F-250HD, F-350, F-450 AND NAVIGATOR

1. Before servicing the vehicle, refer to the precautions in the beginning of this section.

2. If equipped with 2-wheel drive, perform the following:

a. Hold the shock absorber stem and remove the nut from the top of the shock.

b. Raise and safely support the vehicle.

c. Remove the 2 lower retaining nuts and remove the shock absorber.

3. If equipped with 4-wheel drive, perform the following:

a. Hold the shock absorber stem and remove the nut, washer and bushing from the top of the shock absorber stud.

b. Raise and support the vehicle.

c. Remove the lower retaining nut and bolt.

d. Remove the shock absorber from the vehicle.

To install:

4. On 4-wheel drive models, perform the following:

a. Install the washer and bushing to the top stem of the shock absorber.

b. Place the shock absorber up through the coil spring.

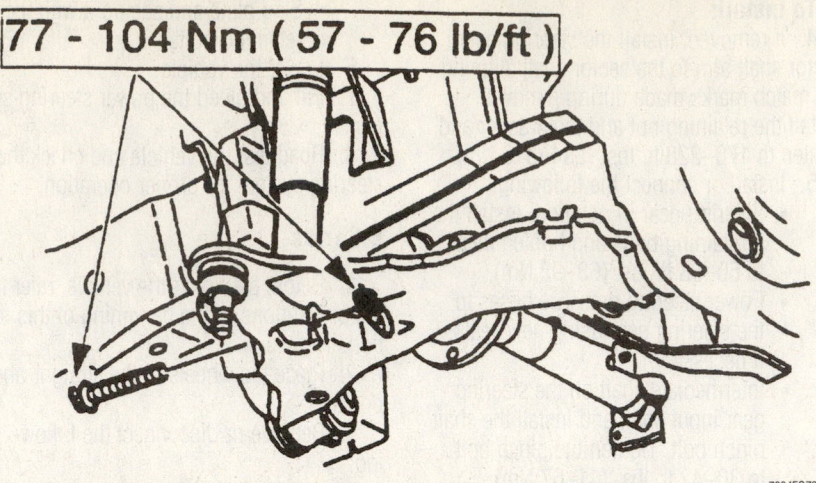

77 - 104 Nm (57 - 76 lb/ft)

7924FG73

Lower shock absorber mounting—late models with torsion bar suspension

c. Install the 2 lower retaining nuts. Tighten the nuts to 19–25 ft. lbs. (26–34 Nm).

d. Lower the vehicle.

e. Install the bushing, washer and retaining nut to the top of the shock absorber stud. Tighten the nut to 34–46 ft. lbs. (47–63 Nm).

5. On 4-wheel drive models, perform the following:

a. Install the washer and bushing to the top stem of the shock absorber.

b. Place the shock absorber up through the coil spring.

c. Install the lower retaining nut and bolt. Tighten to 57–76 ft. lbs. (77–104 Nm).

d. Lower the vehicle.

e. Install the shock absorber upper bushing, washer and retaining nut. Tighten the nut to 22–29 ft. lbs. (30–40 Nm).

6. Road test the vehicle and check for proper operation.

E-Series

1. Before servicing the vehicle, refer to the precautions in the beginning of this section.

2. Raise the vehicle and secure on support stands.

3. Remove the self-locking nut, steel washer, and rubber bushings at the upper end of the shock absorber.

4. Remove the bolt and nut at the lower end and remove the shock absorber.

To install:

5. When installing a new shock absorber, use new rubber bushings. Position the shock absorber on the mounting brackets with the stud end at the top. Install the upper bushing, steel washer and self-

locking nut at the upper end, and the bolt and nut at the lower end.

6. Tighten the upper mounting studs to 18–22 ft. lbs. (24–30 Nm) and the lower mounting nuts to 40–60 ft. lbs. (54–82 Nm).

Rear Shock Absorber

1. Before servicing the vehicle, refer to the precautions in the beginning of this section.

2. Raise the vehicle and secure on support stands.

3. Remove the self-locking nut, steel washer, and rubber bushings at the upper end of the shock absorber.

4. Remove the bolt and nut at the lower end and remove the shock absorber. If needed, raise the rear axle assembly slightly with a jack.

To install:

5. When installing a new shock absorber, use new rubber bushings. Position the shock absorber on the mounting brackets with the stud end at the top. Install the upper bushing, steel washer and self-locking nut at the upper end, and the bolt and nut at the lower end.

6. Tighten the upper mounting studs to 18–22 ft. lbs. (24–30 Nm) and the lower mounting nuts to 40–60 ft. lbs. (54–82 Nm).

Coil Spring

REMOVAL & INSTALLATION

1997 E- and F-250HD, E- and F-350 and E- and F-Super Duty.

1. Before servicing the vehicle, refer to the precautions in the beginning of this section.

2. Raise and safely support the vehicle. Place a jack under the lower control arm.

3. Remove the wheels.

4. Disconnect the shock absorber from the lower bracket.

5. Remove 1 bolt and nut and remove the rebound bracket.

6. Remove the 2 spring upper retainer attaching bolts from the top of the spring upper seat and remove the retainer.

7. Remove the nut attaching the spring lower retainer to the lower seat and axle and remove the retainer.

8. Place a safety chain through the spring to prevent it from suddenly coming loose. Slowly lower the control arm and remove the spring.

To install:

9. Place the spring in position and raise the lower control arm with a jack.

10. Position the spring lower retainer over the stud and lower seat, and install the 2 attaching bolts.

11. Position the upper retainer over the spring coil and against the spring upper seat, and install the 2 attaching bolts.

12. Tighten the upper retaining bolts to 13–18 ft. lbs. (18–24 Nm); the lower retainer attaching nuts to 70–100 ft. lbs. (95–136 Nm).

13. Connect the shock absorber to the lower bracket. Tighten the bolt and nut to 40–60 ft. lbs. (54–81 Nm). Install the rebound bracket.

14. Remove the jack and safety stands.

1997–01 F-150, F-250 and Expedition and 1998–01 F-250HD, F-350, F-450 and Navigator.

This procedure applies to 2-wheel drive vehicles only. In order to remove the coil spring, the lower control arm must also be removed.

1. Before servicing the vehicle, refer to the precautions in the beginning of this section.

2. Remove or disconnect the following:
- Wheels
- Disc brake caliper and support aside with wire
- Disc brake adapter
- Rotor
- Rotor splash shield
- Shock absorber
- Bracket supporting the brake hose
- Sway bar link retaining nut and bushing from the lower control arm. Separate the sway bar link from the lower control arm.

3. Install a coil spring compressor and compress the coil spring enough to relieve the tension of the spring between the upper and lower control arms.

4. Remove the cotter pin and castellated nut from the lower ball joint. Separate the lower ball joint from the wheel spindle.

5. Matchmark the lower control arm alignment cams for installation reference.

6. Remove the lower control arm retaining nuts and bolts.

7. Remove the lower control arm and the compressed coil spring as an assembly.

8. Loosen the coil spring compressor and remove the coil spring from the lower control arm.

9. Inspect the coil spring and replace as needed.

To install:

10. Place the coil spring correctly in the saddle of the lower control arm. Install coil spring compressor and compress the coil spring. The end of the coil spring **A**, must cover the hole designated **B** and be visible in the second hole designated as **C**, for proper installation.

11. Place the lower control arm to the frame. Install the retaining bolts, adjusting cams, and nuts.

12. Align the match marks on the adjusting cams. The forward nut must be tightened first while the control arm is held at the curb position height. Tighten the nuts to 197–241 ft. lbs. (270–330 Nm).

13. Install the lower ball joint stud into the wheel spindle. Install the castellated nut and tighten to 83–113 ft. lbs. (113–153 Nm). Install a new cotter pin.

14. Connect the sway bar link to the lower control arm. Install the bushing and retaining nut. Tighten to 15–21 ft. lbs. (21–29 Nm).

15. Remove the coil spring compressor.

16. Install the shock absorber. Tighten the lower bolts to 22 ft. lbs. (32 Nm) and the top nut to 45 ft. lbs. (61 Nm).

17. Connect the brake hose bracket.

18. Install the brake rotor splash shield. Install the 3 retaining bolts and tighten them to 90–107 inch lbs. (10–14 Nm).

19. Install the disc brake rotor and caliper assemblies.

20. Install the wheel and tire assembly.

21. Lower the vehicle.

22. Pump the brake pedal several times to position the brake pads prior to moving the vehicle.

23. Check the alignment and adjust if out of specification.

24. Road test the vehicle and check for proper operation.

Upper Ball Joint

REMOVAL & INSTALLATION

1997 F-250HD, F-350 and F-Super Duty and E-Series

✱✱ WARNING

Do not use a forked ball joint removal tool to separate the ball joints as this will damage the seal and the ball joint socket. Do not use heat to aid in removal or installation of any suspension parts or components.

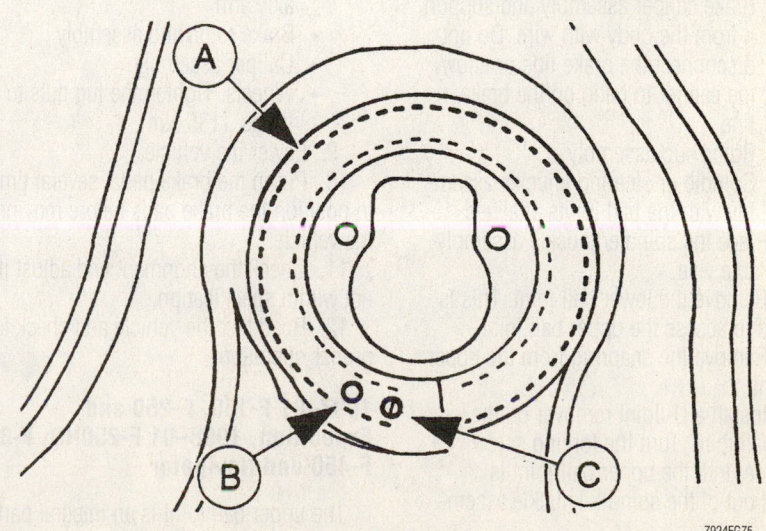

Be sure the coil spring is mounted correctly in the lower control arm

7924FG75

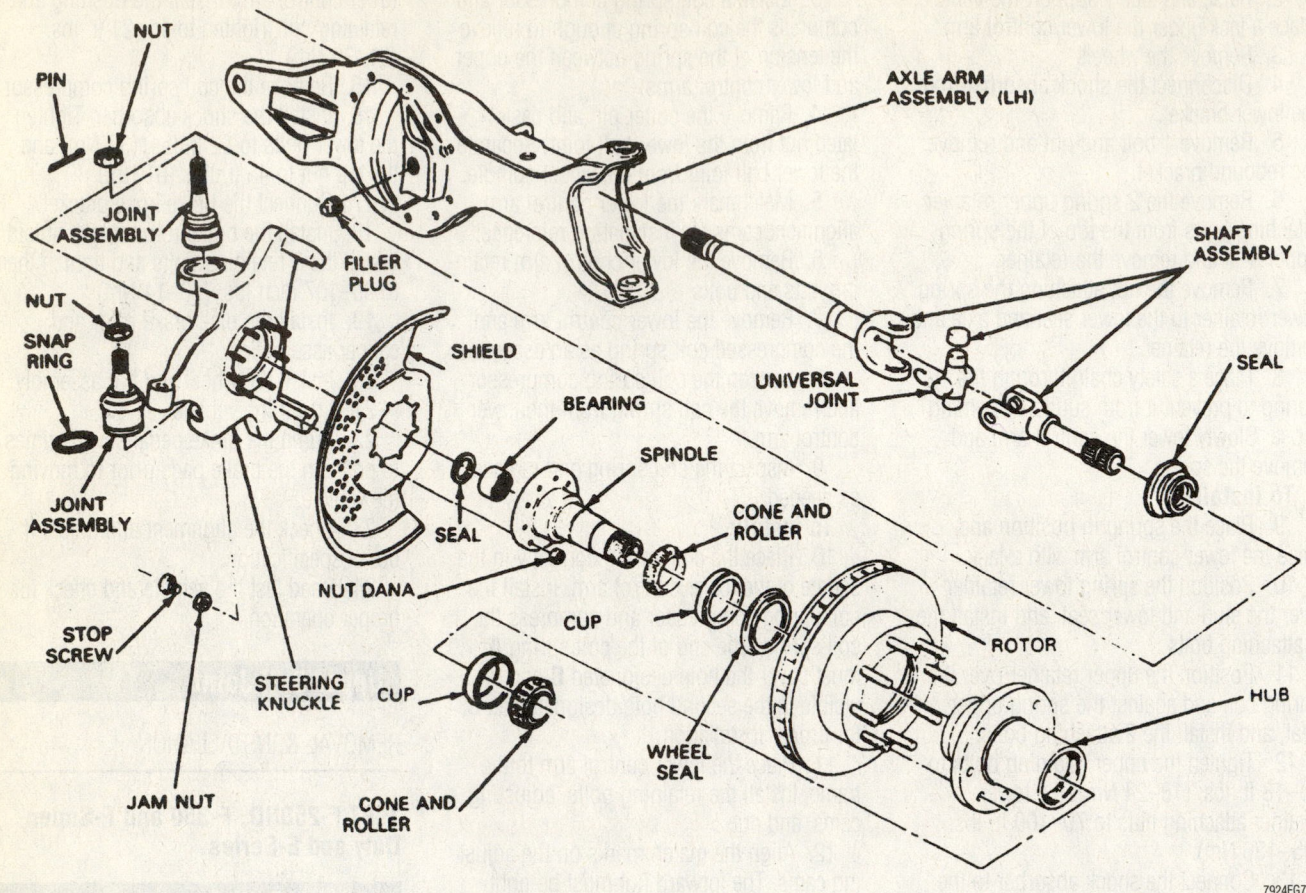

Dana models 44 and 50 axle shaft and joint assemblies—early models

1. Before servicing the vehicle, refer to the precautions in the beginning of this section.

2. Remove or disconnect the following:

- Wheels
- Brake caliper assembly and support it from the body with wire. Do not disconnect the brake line or allow the caliper to hang on the brake line.
- Rotor/hub assembly
- Spindle or steering knuckle assembly with the ball joints attached

3. Place the spindle/knuckle assembly in a suitable vise.

4. Remove the lower ball joint. This is required to access the upper ball joint.

5. Remove the snapring from the upper ball joint.

6. Install a U-Joint remover on the upper ball joint. Turn the forcing screw clockwise until the upper ball joint is pressed out of the spindle/knuckle assembly.

To install:

7. Place the new upper ball joint to the spindle/knuckle assembly and install the U-Joint tool. Turn the forcing screw clockwise until the upper ball joint is seated.

8. Install or connect the following:

- Snapring onto the upper ball joint
- Lower ball joint
- Spindle/knuckle assembly to the axle arm
- Brake rotor/hub assembly
- Caliper assembly
- Wheels. Tighten the lug nuts to 100 ft. lbs. (135 Nm).

9. Lower the vehicle.

10. Pump the brake pedal several times to position the brake pads before moving the vehicle.

11. Check the alignment and adjust if not within specification.

12. Road test the vehicle and check for proper operation.

1997–01 F-150, F-250 and Expedition, 1998–01 F-250HD, F-350, F-450 and Navigator

The upper ball joint is an integral part of the upper control arm and is not a serviceable component. Replacement of the ball joint requires replacing the upper control arm assembly.

Lower Ball Joint

REMOVAL & INSTALLATION

1997 F-250HD, F-350 and F-Super Duty and E-Series

✲✲ WARNING

Do not use a forked ball joint removal tool to separate the ball joints as this will damage the seal and the ball joint socket. Do not use heat to aid in removal or installation of any suspension parts or components.

1. Before servicing the vehicle, refer to the precautions in the beginning of this section.

2. Remove or disconnect the following:

- Wheels
- Caliper assembly and support it from the body with wire. Do not disconnect the brake line or allow the caliper to hang on the brake line.
- Brake rotor/hub assembly

- Spindle or steering knuckle assembly with the ball joints attached
- Snapring from the lower ball joint

3. Install a U-Joint remover on the lower ball joint. Turn the forcing screw clockwise until the lower ball joint is pressed out of the spindle/knuckle assembly.

To install:

4. Inspect the upper ball joint for wear. If replacing the upper ball joint, do so before installing the lower ball joint.

5. Place the new lower ball joint in the spindle/knuckle assembly and install a U-Joint remover. Turn the forcing screw clockwise until the lower ball joint is seated.

6. Install the snapring onto the lower ball joint.

7. Remove the spindle/knuckle assembly from the vise and install to the axle arm.

8. Install or connect the following:
- Brake rotor/hub assembly
- Caliper assembly
- Wheels. Tighten the lug nuts to 100 ft. lbs. (135 Nm).

9. Lower the vehicle.

10. Pump the brake pedal several times to position the brake pads before moving the vehicle.

11. Check the alignment and adjust if not within specification.

12. Road test the vehicle and check for proper operation.

1997–01 F-150, F-250 and Expedition, 1998–01 F-250HD, F-350, F-450 and Navigator

The lower ball joint is an integral part of the lower control arm and is not a serviceable component. Replacement of the ball joint requires replacing the lower control arm.

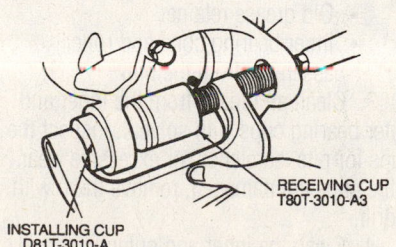

INSTALLING CUP
D81T-3010-A

RECEIVING CUP
T80T-3010-A3

7924FG77

Use the ball joint press with the proper adapters to install the new ball joint in the control arm—E-Series and early non-E-Series models

Front Wheel Bearings

ADJUSTMENT

✱✱ CAUTION

If equipped with the automatic air suspension system, the service switch near the right kick panel must be turned OFF before raising the vehicle for service.

1997 F-250HD, F-350 and F-Super Duty and E-Series.

2-WHEEL DRIVE MODELS

1. Before servicing the vehicle, refer to the precautions in the beginning of this section.

2. Raise and support the front end.

3. Remove the wheel cover.

4. Remove the grease cap from the hub. Then, remove the cotter pin and nut lock. Back off the adjusting nut.

5. Adjust the wheel bearings by tightening the adjusting nut to 17–25 ft. lbs. (23–34 Nm) with the wheel rotating to seat the bearing. Then, back off the adjusting nut ½ turn. Retighten the adjusting nut to 10–15 inch lbs. (1–1.7 Nm). Install the locknut so that the castellations are aligned

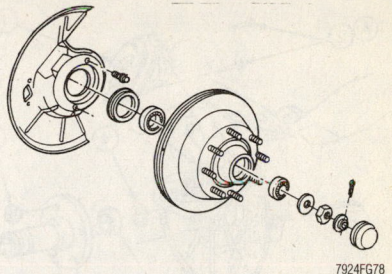

7924FG78

Exploded view of the brake rotor and wheel bearing assembly—1997 F-250HD, F-350 and F-Super Duty models

with the cotter pin hole. Install the cotter pin. Bend the ends of the cotter pin around the castellations of the locknut to prevent interference with the radio static collector in the grease cap. Install the grease cap.

6. Install the wheels.

7. Check the wheel for proper rotation, then install the grease cap. If the wheel still does not rotate properly, inspect and clean or replace the wheel bearings and cups.

8. Install the wheel cover.

4-WHEEL DRIVE MODELS

1. Before servicing the vehicle, refer to the precautions in the beginning of this section.

2. Raise and safely support the vehicle.

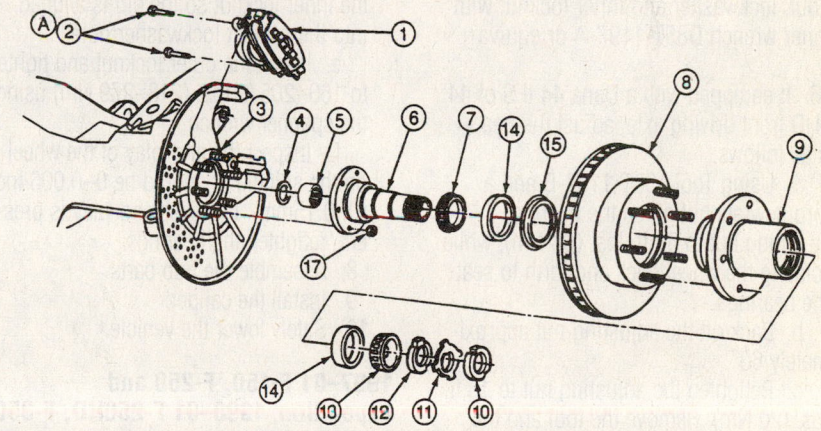

1	Disc Brake Caliper	9	Hub
2	Bolt, M8-1.25 x 65	10	Locknut
3	Front Disc Brake Rotor Shield	11	Retainer
4	Seal	12	Locknut
5	Bearing	13	Differential Bearing
6	Front Wheel Spindle	14	Differential Bearing Cup
7	Differential Bearing	15	Wheel Seal
8	Front Disc Brake Hub and Rotor	17	Dana Nut
		A	Tighten to 30-36 N·m (22-26 Lb-Ft)

7924FG79

Exploded view of the brake rotor and wheel bearing assembly—1997 F-150 with automatic locking hubs

Turn to Section 5 for brake system applications

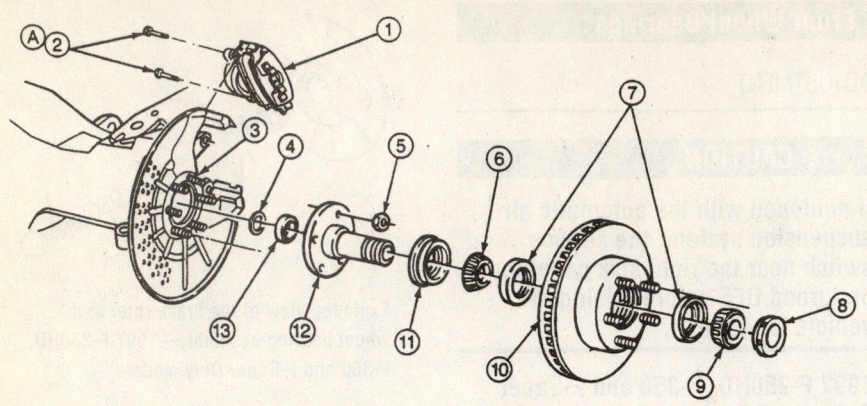

1 Disc Brake Caliper
2 Bolt, M8-1.25 x 65
3 Front Disc Brake Rotor Shield
4 Spindle Seal
5 Nut
6 Differential Bearing
7 Bearing Cups
8 Adjusting Nut
9 Differential Bearing
10 Front Disc Brake Hub and Rotor
11 Grease Seal
12 Front Wheel Spindle
13 Spindle Needle Bearing
A Tighten to 30-36 N·m (22-26 Lb-Ft)

7924FG80

Exploded view of the brake rotor and wheel bearing assembly—1997 F-150 with manual locking hubs

3. Remove the hub assemblies.

4. If equipped with Dana 44 IFS, back off the adjusting nut using spanner wrench, Tool T59T-1197-B, or equivalent.

5. If equipped with Dana 50 or Dana 60 Monobeam front axle, remove the outer locknut, lockwasher and inner locknut with spanner wrench D85T-1197-A or equivalent.

6. If equipped with a Dana 44 IFS of 44 IFS HD front driving axle, adjust the bearings as follows:

  a. Using Tool T59T-1197-B and a torque wrench, tighten the bearing adjusting nut to 50 ft. lbs. (68 Nm), while rotating the wheel back and forth to seat the bearings.

  b. Back off the adjusting nut approximately 60°.

  c. Retighten the adjusting nut to 15 ft. lbs. (20 Nm). Remove the tool and the torque wrench.

  d. Inspect the end-play of the wheel on the spindle. It should be 0–0.006 inch (0.00–0.15mm). If excess end-play is present, retighten the bearings.

7. If equipped with a Dana 50 IFS and Dana 60 Monobeam front driving axle, adjust bearings as follows:

  a. With the outer locknut and lockwasher removed, tighten the inner locknut to 50 ft. lbs. (68 Nm) while rotating the wheel back and forth to seat the bearings.

  b. Back off the adjusting nut and retighten to 31–39 ft. lbs. (42–53 Nm).

  c. While rotating the hub, back off the locknut 135–150°.

  d. Install the lockwasher so the key is positioned in the spindle groove. Rotate the inner locknut so the pin is aligned into the nearest lockwasher hole.

  e. Install the outer locknut and tighten to 160–205 ft. lbs. (218–279 Nm) using the spanner wrench.

  f. Inspect the end-play of the wheel on the spindle. It should be 0–0.006 inch (0–0.15mm). If excess end-play is present, retighten the bearings.

8. Assemble the hub parts.

9. Install the caliper.

10. Safely lower the vehicle.

1997–01 F-150, F-250 and Expedition; 1998–01 F-250HD, F-350, F-450 and Navigator.

➡ **On 4-wheel drive vehicles, the front wheel bearings are not adjustable.**

1. Before servicing the vehicle, refer to the precautions in the beginning of this section.

2. Raise and safely support the vehicle.

3. Support the front end.

4. Remove the wheel cover, if equipped.

5. Remove the grease cap.

➡ **Check the wheel bearings for sufficient grease.**

6. Remove the cotter pin and retaining washer. Back off the spindle nut. Discard the cotter pin.

7. Adjust the wheel bearings as follows:

  a. Tighten the spindle nut to 17–24 ft. lbs. (23–34 Nm) while rotating the wheel and tire assembly to seat the wheel bearings.

  b. Back off the spindle nut no less than ½ turn.

  c. Tighten the spindle nut to 17 inch lbs. (2 Nm).

8. Install the retaining washer so the castellations are aligned with the cotter pin hole. Install a new cotter pin.

9. Check the wheel and tire assembly for proper rotation, then install the grease cap. If the wheel still does not rotate properly, inspect and clean or replace the wheel bearings and cups.

10. Install the wheel cover, if equipped.

11. Lower the vehicle.

12. Road test the vehicle and check for proper operation.

REMOVAL & INSTALLATION

1997 F-250HD, F-350 and F-Super Duty, and E-Series.

2-WHEEL DRIVE

1. Before servicing the vehicle, refer to the precautions in the beginning of this section.

2. Remove or disconnect the following:
  • Wheels
  • Caliper from the disc and wire it to the underbody to prevent damage to the brake hose.
  • Grease cap, cotter pin, nut lock, adjusting nut and flat washer from the spindle
  • Outer bearing assembly from the hub
  • Hub and disc assembly off the wheel spindle
  • Old grease retainer
  • Inner bearing cone and roller assembly from the hub

3. Clean all grease from the inner and outer bearing cups with solvent. Inspect the cups for pits, scratches, or excessive wear. If the cups are damaged, remove them with a drift.

4. Clean the inner and outer cone and roller assemblies with solvent and shake them dry. If the cone and roller assemblies show excessive wear or damage, replace them with the bearing cups as a unit.

5. Clean the spindle and the inside of the hub with solvent to thoroughly remove all old grease.

6. Covering the spindle with a clean cloth, brush all loose dirt and dust from the brake assembly. Remove the cloth carefully so as to not get dirt on the spindle.

To install:

7. If the inner and/or outer bearing cups were removed, install the replacement cups on the hub. Be sure that the cups seat properly in the hub.

➡ **It is imperative that all old grease be removed from the bearings and surrounding surfaces before repacking. The new lithium-based grease is not compatible with the sodium base grease used in the past.**

8. Install the hub and disc on the wheel spindle. To prevent damage to the grease retainer and spindle threads, keep the hub centered on the spindle.

9. Install the outer bearing cone and roller assembly and the flat washer on the spindle. Install the adjusting nut.

10. Adjust the wheel bearings by tightening the adjusting nut to 17–25 ft. lbs. (23–34 Nm) with the wheel rotating to seat the bearing. Then, back off the adjusting nut ½ turn. Retighten the adjusting nut to 10–15 inch lbs. (1–1.7 Nm). Install the locknut so that the castellations are aligned with the cotter pin hole. Install the cotter pin. Bend the ends of the cotter pin around the castellations of the locknut to prevent interference with the radio static collector in the grease cap. Install the grease cap.

➡ **New bolts must be used when servicing floating caliper units. The upper bolt must be tightened first.**

11. Install the wheels.
12. Install the wheel cover.

4-WHEEL DRIVE MODELS WITH MANUAL LOCKING HUBS

1. Before servicing the vehicle, refer to the precautions in the beginning of this section.
2. Raise the vehicle and install safety stands.
3. Remove the hub assemblies.
4. On F-150 and F-250 with the Dana 44 axle: apply inward pressure on the bearing adjusting nut, using a socket made for that purpose, available at most auto parts stores, to disengage the adjusting nut locking splines, while turning it counterclockwise to remove it.
5. On F-250 HD (Dana 50 axle) and F-350, use the hub nut tool to unscrew the

outer locking nut. Then, remove the lock ring from the bearing adjusting nut. This can be done with your finger tips or a screwdriver. Use the locknut socket to remove the bearing adjusting nut.

6. Remove the caliper and suspend it out of the way.

7. Slide the hub and disc assembly off the spindle. The outer wheel bearing will slide out as the hub is removed, so be prepared to catch it.

8. Lay the hub on a clean work surface. Carefully drive the inner bearing cone and grease seal out of the hub.

To install:

9. Inspect the bearing cups for pits or cracks. If necessary, remove them with a drift. If new cups are installed, install new bearings.

10. Lubricate the bearings with multipurpose lubricant. Clean all old grease from the hub. Pack the cones and rollers. If a bearing packer is not available, work as much lubricant as possible between the rollers and the cages.

11. Drive new cups into place with a driver, making sure that they are fully seated.

12. Position the inner bearing cone and roller in the inner cup and install the grease retainer.

13. Carefully position the hub and disc assembly on the spindle.

14. Install the outer bearing cone and roller, and the adjusting nut.

15. On F-150 and F-250 LD with the Dana 44 axle:

a. Be sure the metal stamping on the adjusting nut faces inboard and the inner diameter key on the nut enters the spindle keyway.

b. Apply inward pressure on the hub nut wrench and tighten the adjusting nut to 70 ft. lbs. (95 Nm) while rotating the hub back and forth to seat the bearings.

c. Apply inward pressure on the wrench and back off the nut about 90 degrees, then retighten the nut to 15–20 ft. lbs. (20–27 Nm).

d. Remove the wrench. End-play of the hub/rotor assembly should be 0 (zero) and the torque required to rotate the hub assembly should not exceed 20 inch lbs. (2.2 Nm).

16. On the F-250 HD (Dana 50 axle) and F-350:

➡ **The adjusting nut has a small dowel on one side. This dowel faces outward to engage the locking ring.**

a. Using the hub nut socket and a torque wrench, tighten the bearing adjusting nut to 50 ft. lbs. (68 Nm), while rotating the wheel back and forth to seat the bearings.

b. Back off the adjusting nut approximately 90 degrees.

c. Install the lock ring by turning the nut to the nearest hole and inserting the dowel pin.

✳✳ CAUTION

The dowel pin must seat in a lock ring hole for proper bearing adjustment and wheel retention!

d. Install the outer locknut and tighten to 160–205 ft. lbs. (218–279 Nm). Final end-play of the wheel on the spindle should be 0–0.004 inch (0–0.15mm).

17. Assemble the hub parts.
18. Install the caliper.
19. Safety lower the vehicle.

4-WHEEL DRIVE MODELS WITH AUTOMATIC LOCKING HUBS

1. Before servicing the vehicle, refer to the precautions in the beginning of this section.
2. Raise and safely support the vehicle.
3. Remove the hub assemblies.
4. Using a socket made for that purpose, available at most auto parts stores, use the hub nut tool to unscrew the outer locking nut.
5. Remove the lockring from the bearing adjusting nut. This can be done with your finger tips or a screwdriver.
6. Use the locknut socket to remove the bearing adjusting nut.
7. Remove the caliper and suspend it out of the way.
8. Slide the hub and disc assembly off the spindle. The outer wheel bearing will slide out as the hub is removed, so be prepared to catch it.
9. Lay the hub on a clean work surface. Carefully drive the inner bearing cone and grease seal out of the hub.

To install:

10. Inspect the bearing cups for pits or cracks. If necessary, remove them with a drift. If new cups are installed, install new bearings.

11. Lubricate the bearings with multipurpose lubricant. Clean all old grease from the hub. Pack the cones and rollers. If a bearing packer is not available, work as much lubricant as possible between the rollers and the cages.

12. Drive new cups into place with a driver, making sure that they are fully seated.

13. Position the inner bearing cone and roller in the inner cup and install the grease retainer.

14. Carefully position the hub and disc assembly on the spindle.

15. Install the outer bearing cone and roller, and the adjusting nut.

➡The adjusting nut has a small dowel on one side. This dowel faces outward to engage the locking ring.

16. Using the hub nut socket and a torque wrench, tighten the bearing adjusting nut to 50 ft. lbs. (68 Nm), while rotating the wheel back and forth to seat the bearings.

17. Back off the adjusting nut approximately 90°.

18. Install the lockring by turning the nut to the nearest hole and inserting the dowel pin.

➡The dowel pin must seat in a lock-ring hole for proper bearing adjustment and wheel retention.

19. Install the outer locknut and tighten to 160–205 ft. lbs. (218–279 Nm). Final end-play of the wheel on the spindle should be 0–0.004 inch (0–0.15mm).

20. Assemble the hub parts.
21. Install the caliper.
22. Lower the vehicle.

1997–01 F-150, F-250 and Expedition and 1998–01 F-250HD, F-350, F-450 and Navigator.

2-WHEEL DRIVE

The hub is part of the disc brake rotor and cannot be serviced separately. The inner and outer wheel bearing and races are serviced individually. Be sure to have a new hub grease seal when servicing the wheel bearings.

1. Before servicing the vehicle, refer to the precautions in the beginning of this section.

2. Remove or disconnect the following:
   • Wheels
   • Caliper
   • Brake pads and anti-rattle clips
   • Anchor plate
   • Hub grease cap, cotter pin, retainer washer and the spindle nut
   • Wheel bearing retainer washer and the outer wheel bearing
   • Brake hub and rotor assembly
   • Grease seal
   • Inner wheel bearing

3. Clean and inspect the wheel bearings and races for unusual wear or damage. Replace parts as necessary.

4. Inspect the hub and brake rotor assembly. If required, the hub and brake rotor assembly must be replaced as a unit.

To install:

5. If needed, pack the wheel bearing with a suitable high temperature wheel bearing grease before assembly.

6. Install or connect the following:
   • Inner wheel bearing in the hub and brake rotor assembly
   • New grease seal
   • Hub and rotor assembly on the wheel spindle and install the outer wheel bearing.
   • Retainer washer and the spindle nut

7. Adjust the wheel bearings as follows:

   a. Tighten the spindle nut to 17–24 ft. lbs. (23–34 Nm) while rotating the wheel and tire assembly to seat the wheel bearings.

   b. Back off the spindle nut no less than ½ turn.

   c. Tighten the spindle nut to 17 inch lbs. (2 Nm).

8. Install or connect the following:
   • Retaining washer, so the castellations are aligned with the cotter pin hole. Install a new cotter pin.
   • Anchor plate, and install 2 retaining bolts. Tighten the bolts to 125–168 ft. lbs. (170–230 Nm).
   • Anti-rattle clips, and install the disc brake pads.
   • Caliper
   • Wheels. Tighten the lug nuts to 83–112 ft. lbs. (113–153 Nm).

9. Check the wheel and tire assembly for proper rotation, then install the grease cap.

10. Lower the vehicle.

11. Road test the vehicle and check for proper operation.

4-WHEEL DRIVE

The wheel bearings are of the cartridge design and are an integral part of the hub assembly. The bearings are permanently lubricated and require no maintenance or adjustments. If required, a new hub assembly must be installed.

1. Before servicing the vehicle, refer to the precautions in the beginning of this section.

2. Remove or disconnect the following:
   • Wheels
   • Caliper

   • Brake pads and anti-rattle clips
   • Anchor plate
   • Brake rotor
   • Rotor shield
   • If equipped with 4-wheel ABS, the speed sensor retaining bolt and move the speed sensor and harness aside.
   • Hub nut cotter pin, retainer and the hub nut. Discard the cotter pin.
   • The 3 hub assembly retaining bolts from the inside of the steering knuckle
   • Hub assembly

➡If necessary, use a suitable puller to separate the hub assembly from the CV-joint. Use care not to over extend the CV-joint and boot when removing the hub assembly.

   • Grease seal from the steering knuckle

To install:

3. Install or connect the following:
   • New grease seal
   • Hub assembly to the steering knuckle and secure with the 3 retaining bolts. Tighten the bolts to 110–145 ft. lbs. (149–201 Nm).
   • CV-joint into the hub assembly
   • If equipped with 4-wheel ABS, the speed sensor and secure with the retaining bolt. Tighten the bolt to 60–84 inch lbs. (7–9 Nm).
   • Brake rotor shield and the 3 retaining bolts. Tighten the bolts to 80–107 inch lbs. (9–12 Nm).
   • Hub nut and tighten to 188–254 ft. lbs. (255–345 Nm).
   • Hub nut retainer and a new cotter pin
   • Brake rotor
   • Anchor plate in position and install the 2 retaining bolts. Tighten the bolts to 125–168 ft. lbs. (170–230 Nm).
   • Anti-rattle clips and install the disc brake pads.
   • Caliper
   • Wheels. Tighten the lug nuts to 83–112 ft. lbs. (113–153 Nm).

4. Lower the vehicle.

5. Pump the brake pedal several times to position the brake pads prior to moving the vehicle.

6. Road test the vehicle and check for proper operation.

PRECAUTIONS

Before servicing any vehicle, please be sure to read all of the following precautions, which deal with personal safety, prevention of component damage, and important points to take into consideration when servicing a motor vehicle:

• Never open, service or drain the radiator or cooling system when the engine is hot; serious burns can occur from the steam and hot coolant.

• Observe all applicable safety precautions when working around fuel. Whenever servicing the fuel system, always work in a well-ventilated area. Do not allow fuel spray or vapors to come in contact with a spark, open flame, or excessive heat (a hot drop light, for example). Keep a dry chemical fire extinguisher near the work area. Always keep fuel in a container specifically designed for fuel storage; also, always properly seal fuel containers to avoid the possibility of fire or explosion. Refer to the additional fuel system precautions later in this section.

• Fuel injection systems often remain pressurized, even after the engine has been turned **OFF**. The fuel system pressure must be relieved before disconnecting any fuel lines. Failure to do so may result in fire and/or personal injury.

• Brake fluid often contains polyglycol ethers and polyglycols. Avoid contact with the eyes and wash your hands thoroughly after handling brake fluid. If you do get brake fluid in your eyes, flush your eyes with clean, running water for 15 minutes. If eye irritation persists, or if you have taken brake fluid internally, IMMEDIATELY seek medical assistance.

• The EPA warns that prolonged contact with used engine oil may cause a number of skin disorders, including cancer! You should make every effort to minimize your exposure to used engine oil. Protective gloves should be worn when changing oil. Wash your hands and any other exposed skin areas as soon as possible after exposure to used engine oil. Soap and water, or waterless hand cleaner should be used.

• All new vehicles are now equipped with an air bag system. The system must be disabled before performing service on or around system components, steering column, instrument panel components, wiring

and sensors. Failure to follow safety and disabling procedures could result in accidental air bag deployment, possible personal injury and unnecessary system repairs.

• Always wear safety goggles when working with, or around, the air bag system. When carrying a non-deployed air bag, be sure the bag and trim cover are pointed away from your body. When placing a non-deployed air bag on a work surface, always face the bag and trim cover upward, away from the surface. This will reduce the motion of the module if it is accidentally deployed. Refer to the additional air bag system precautions later in this section.

• Clean, high quality brake fluid from a sealed container is essential to the safe and proper operation of the brake system. You should always buy the correct type of brake fluid for your vehicle. If the brake fluid becomes contaminated, completely flush the system with new fluid. Never reuse any brake fluid. Any brake fluid that is removed from the system should be discarded. Also, do not allow any brake fluid to come in contact with a painted surface; it will damage the paint.

• Never operate the engine without the proper amount and type of engine oil; doing so WILL result in severe engine damage.

• Timing belt maintenance is extremely important! Many models utilize an interference-type, non-freewheeling engine. If the timing belt breaks, the valves in the cylinder head may strike the pistons, causing potentially serious (also time-consuming and expensive) engine damage. Refer to the maintenance interval charts in the front of this manual for the recommended replacement interval for the timing belt, and to the timing belt section for belt replacement and inspection.

• Disconnecting the negative battery cable on some vehicles may interfere with the functions of the on-board computer system(s) and may require the computer to undergo a relearning process once the negative battery cable is reconnected.

• When servicing drum brakes, only disassemble and assemble one side at a time, leaving the remaining side intact for reference.

• Only an MVAC-trained, EPA-certified automotive technician should service the air conditioning system or its components.

ENGINE REPAIR

Alternator

REMOVAL & INSTALLATION

3.0L Engine

1. Disconnect the negative battery cable.
2. Disconnect the alternator wiring harness.
3. Detach the alternator drive belt.
4. Loosen the alternator pivot bolt.
5. Remove the alternator brace.
6. Remove the alternator pivot bolt.
7. Remove the alternator.

To install:

8. Position the alternator on the engine.
9. Install the alternator pivot bolt and brace.
10. Tighten the alternator brace to 15–22 ft. lbs. (20–30 Nm) and the pivot bolt to 30–41 ft. lbs. (40–55 Nm).
11. Install and tension the alternator drive belt.
12. Connect the alternator wiring harness. Tighten the output terminal nut to 80–97 inch lbs. (9–11 Nm).
13. Connect the negative battery cable.

3.8L Engine

1. Disconnect the negative battery cable.
2. Disconnect the alternator wiring harness.
3. Detach the alternator drive belt.
4. Remove the three alternator attaching bolts.
5. Remove the alternator.

To install:

6. Position the alternator on the engine.
7. Install the three alternator attaching bolts. Tighten the bolts 30–41 ft. lbs. (40–55 Nm).
8. Install and tension the alternator drive belt.
9. Connect the alternator wiring harness. Tighten the output terminal nut to 80–97 inch lbs. (9–11 Nm).
10. Connect the negative battery cable.

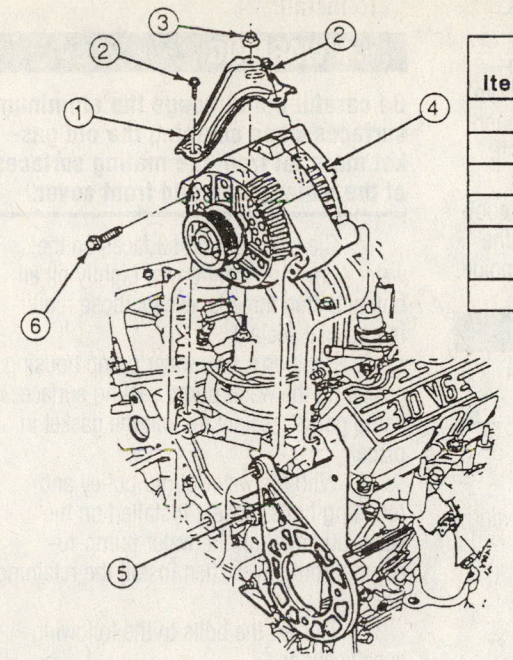

Item	Description
1	Alternator Brace
2	Bolt
3	Nut and Washer Assembly
4	Alternator
5	Power Steering Pump Support
6	Bolt

Alternator mounting—3.0L engine

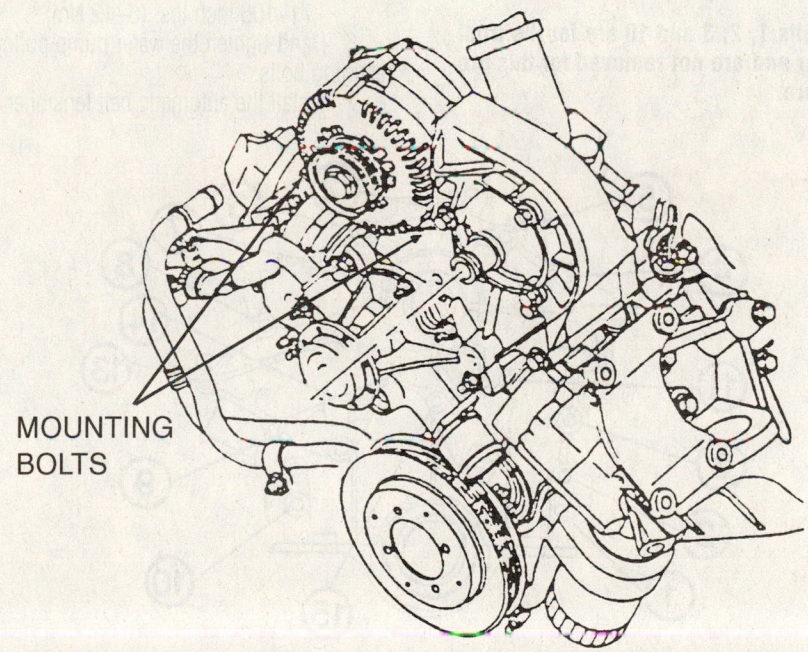

MOUNTING
BOLTS

Alternator mounting—3.8L engine

Engine Assembly

REMOVAL & INSTALLATION

1. Remove or disconnect the following:
   - Negative battery cable
   - Coolant
   - Refrigerant, into a refrigerant recovery station.
   - Cowl top vent panel
   - Wiring from the alternator
   - Air cleaner assembly
   - Upper and lower radiator hoses from the engine
   - Heater water hoses and secure to body

- Air conditioning discharge and suction hoses, then secure them to the engine. Cap the open lines to prevent moisture from entering the system.
- Accelerator cable and speed control cable from the throttle body lever
- Accelerator cable bracket from the throttle body
- Fuel supply and return lines from the fuel injection supply manifold
- All engine wiring harnesses from the engine and secure to the body
- All vacuum hoses from the engine
- Gear shift cable from the transaxle

➡️**Damage to the steering column air bag wiring can result if the steering wheel is allowed to rotate freely. The wire is wound like a watch spring and can be over-tightened and break if the steering wheel is rotated too far in either direction.**

2. Lock the steering wheel with the wheels in the straight-ahead position by turning the ignition to the **OFF** position.

3. Remove or disconnect the following:
   - Wheels
   - Engine oil
   - Transaxle cooler lines at the transaxle. Secure the lines to the radiator.
   - Heated oxygen sensor wiring harness

➡️**Do not allow the flex connector of the duel converter Y-pipe to hang unsupported or damage to the flex joint will result.**

   - Dual converter Y-pipe and support it from the body

➡️**The routing of the battery ground cable to the cylinder block is critical. It should go between the transaxle and the bracket. Take note during disassembly.**

   - Starter motor wires and secure out of the way
   - Starter motor
   - Engine rear plate and torque converter-to-flywheel nuts
   - Power steering cooler lines
   - Upper bolt from the sway bar links
   - Dust boot from the steering rack pinion support
   - Steering coupling pinch bolt from the steering column intermediate shaft at the steering gear

- Intermediate shaft from the steering gear
- Front stabilizer bar links
- Front suspension lower arms from the knuckles at the ball joint
- Tie rod ends from the knuckle
- Front axle wheel hub retainers from the halfshaft ends
- Halfshafts from the front wheel knuckle

4. Support the front subframe, engine and transaxle assembly.

5. Remove or disconnect the following:

- The 4 retaining bolts, and lower the engine transaxle and front subframe from the vehicle.
- Power steering pressure hose from the power steering pump

6. Attach an engine hoist and lift the engine slightly.

7. Remove the engine support insulators.

8. Lift the engine and transaxle assembly from the front subframe.

9. Lower the engine and transaxle.

10. Support the transaxle on a level stationary surface and separate the engine from the transaxle.

To install:

11. If removed, install the transaxle on the engine.

12. Install the engine on the subframe.

13. Install the engine support insulators.

14. Connect the power steering hose to the pump.

15. Carefully raise the engine/transaxle assembly into the vehicle.

16. Install the 4 subframe bolts.

17. The remainder of the installation is the reverse of removal.

18. Please note the following torque specifications:

- Engine-to-transaxle: 30–44 ft. lbs. (40–60 Nm)
- Torque converter nuts: 20–34 ft. lbs. (27–46 Nm)
- Subframe-to-body bolts: 57–76 ft. lbs. (77–103 Nm)
- Steering coupling pinch bolt: 25–34 ft. lbs. (34–46 Nm)
- Dual converter Y-pipe-to-exhaust manifold: 25–34 ft. lbs. (34–46 Nm)
- Flex pipe retaining bolts: 25–34 ft. lbs. (34–46 Nm)
- Accelerator cable bracket retaining bolts: 71–106 inch lbs. (8–12 Nm)
- Front engine support insulator-to-subframe (3.8L): 50–68 ft. lbs. (68–92 Nm)
- Front engine support insulator-to-

subframe (3.0L): 65–87 ft. lbs. (88–119 Nm)
- Transmission insulator-to-subframe: 65–87 ft. lbs. (88–119 Nm)
- Rear engine and transaxle support insulator-to-subframe: 56–75 ft. lbs. (76–103 Nm)

19. Refill the engine, transaxle and cooling system with the correct amount of the appropriate fluids before starting the engine.

Water Pump

REMOVAL & INSTALLATION

3.0L Engine

1. Remove or disconnect the following:
- Negative battery cable
- Coolant
- Accessory drive belt
- Water pump pulley
- Drive belt tensioner
- Lower radiator and heater hose from the water pump
- Water pump

➡ **Bolts 1, 2, 3 and 10 are for the front cover and are not removed for this procedure.**

To install:

✳✳ **WARNING**

Be careful not to gouge the aluminum surfaces when scraping the old gasket material from the mating surfaces of the water pump and front cover.

2. Clean the gasket surfaces on the water pump and front cover. Lightly oil all bolt and stud threads, except those requiring special sealant.

3. Position a new water pump housing gasket on the water pump sealing surface using gasket sealant to hold the gasket in place.

4. With the water pump pulley and retaining bolts loosely installed on the water pump, align the water pump-to-engine front cover, then install the retaining bolts.

5. Tighten the bolts to the following specifications:

- Bolt numbers 4, 5, 6, 7, 8 and 9: 15–22 ft. lbs. (20–30 Nm).
- Bolt numbers 11 through 15: 71–106 inch lbs. (8–12 Nm).

6. Hand-tighten the water pump pulley retaining bolts.

7. Install the automatic belt tensioner

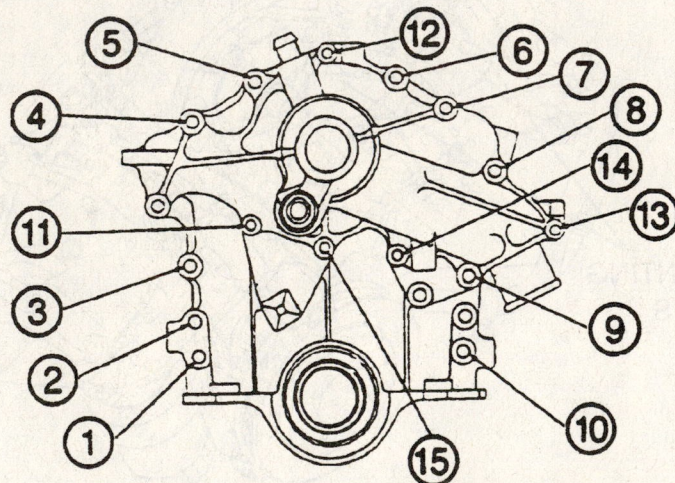

1. M8 x 1.25 x 43.5	9. M8 x 1.25 x 104.3
2. M8 x 1.25 x 43.5	10. M8 x 1.25 x 52
3. M8 x 1.25 x 70	11. M8 x 1 x 28.5
4. M8 x 1.25 x 70	12. M8 x 1 x 28.5
5. M8 x 1.25 x 42	13. M8 x 1 x 28.5
6. M8 x 1.25 x 70	14. M8 x 1 x 28.5
7. M8 x 1.25 x 70	15. M8 x 1 x 28.5
8. M8 x 1.25 x 70	

7924GG01

Water pump bolts come in different sizes, make sure the bolts go back into the correct holes— 3.0L engine

assembly. Tighten the 2 retaining nuts and bolt to 35 ft. lbs. (47 Nm).

8. Install the alternator and power steering belts. Final tighten the water pump pulley retaining bolts to 15–22 ft. lbs. (20–30 Nm).

9. Position the hose clamps between the alignment marks on both ends of the hose, then slide the hose on the connection. Tighten the hose clamps to 20–30 inch lbs. (2.3–3.4 Nm).

10. Fill and bleed the cooling system.

11. Connect the negative battery cable.

12. Start the engine and check for leaks.

3.8L Engine

1. Remove or disconnect the following:
  - Negative battery cable
  - Coolant
  - Drive belts
  - Lower radiator hose
  - Lower nut on both front engine supports
  - Alternator
  - Power steering pressure line from the pump
  - Power steering reservoir filler cap
  - Water bypass hose and oil cooler hose from the heater water outlet tube
  - Heater water outlet tube from the water pump
  - Air conditioning bracket brace

2. Raise the engine approximately 2 inches (51mm) to provide necessary clearance for water pump removal.

3. Remove the water pump pulley.

4. Remove the drive belt tensioner form the power steering pump brace.

5. Remove the power steering pump brace and place the pump and brace aside in the engine compartment.

6. Remove the water pump.

To install:

7. Clean all gasket mating surfaces thoroughly.

✳✳ WARNING

Be careful not to gouge the aluminum surfaces when scraping the old gasket material from the mating surfaces of the water pump and front cover.

8. Cover the threads of the No. 1 engine front cover stud with Teflon® tape.

9. Install or connect the following:
  - New water pump housing gasket on the water pump sealing surface using gasket sealant to hold the gasket in place.
  - Water pump and tighten the bolts to 15–22 ft. lbs. (20–30 Nm) and the nuts to 71–106 inch lbs. (8–12 Nm).
  - Power steering pump brace
  - Drive belt tensioner
  - Water pump pulley
  - Air conditioning bracket brace
  - Heater water outlet tube
  - Water bypass hose and oil cooler hose

- Power steering reservoir filler cap
- Power steering pressure line
- Alternator
- Lower nut on both front engine supports
- Lower radiator hose
- Drive belts

10. Fill and bleed the cooling system.

11. Connect the negative battery cable.

Cylinder Head

REMOVAL & INSTALLATION

➡ Cylinder head bolt torque sequences can be found in Section 1, following the Torque Specifications Chart.

3.0L Engine

1. Rotate the crankshaft to **0** TDC on the compression stroke.

2. Remove or disconnect the following:
  - Negative battery cable
  - Coolant
  - Cowl top vent panel
  - Air cleaner outlet tube from the throttle body
  - All necessary vacuum lines
  - EGR backpressure transducer from the EGR valve
  - EGR valve tube away from the valve
  - All necessary engine wiring
  - Fuel system pressure
  - Fuel line safety clips and disconnect the fuel lines

➡ The fuel injectors and fuel injection supply manifold may be removed with the lower intake manifold as an assembly.

  - Ignition wires and ignition coil pack
  - Upper radiator and heater hoses
  - Camshaft position sensor

3. If the front cylinder head is being removed, perform the following:

  a. Disconnect the alternator electrical harness.

  b. Rotate the tensioner clockwise and remove the accessory drive belt.

  c. Remove the automatic belt tensioner assembly.

  d. Remove the alternator.

  e. Remove the power steering mounting bracket retaining bolts. Leave the hoses connected and place the pump aside in a position to prevent fluid from leaking out.

  f. Remove the engine oil dipstick tube from the exhaust manifold.

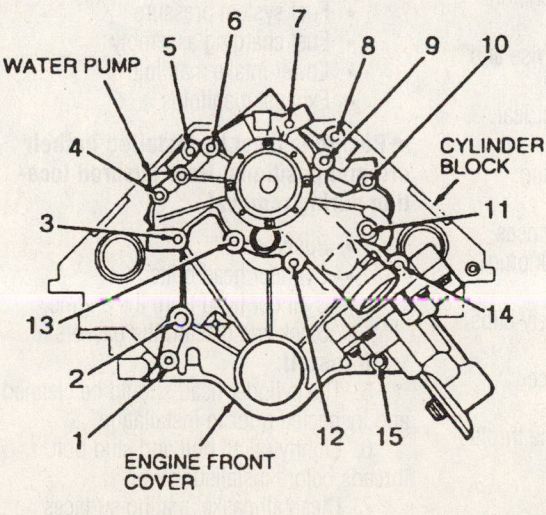

WATER PUMP
CYLINDER BLOCK
ENGINE FRONT COVER

1. M8 x 1.25 x 98
2. M8 x 1.25 x 98
3. M8 x 1.25 x 131
4. M8 x 1.25 x 131
5. M8 x 1.25 x 25
6. M8 x 1.25 x 35
7. M8 x 1.25 x 35
8. M8 x 1.25 x 25
9. M8 x 1.25 x 61.5
10. M8 x 1.25 x 141
11. M8 x 1 x 131
12. M8 x 1 x 35
13. M8 x 1 x 35
14. M8 x 1 x 105
15. M8 x 1 x 20

7924GG02

Because of their varying lengths, be sure to install the water pump bolts in the correct bolt holes—3.8L engine

Timing belt service is covered in Section 4 of this manual

4. If the rear cylinder head is being removed, perform the following:

   a. Remove the alternator belt tensioner bracket.

   b. Remove the heater supply tube retaining brackets from the exhaust manifold.

   c. Remove the vehicle speed sensor cable retaining bolt.

   d. Remove the EGR vacuum regulator sensor and bracket.

5. Remove or disconnect the following:
- Valve covers

➡ **Pushrods must be installed in their original positions. Note pushrod location during removal.**

- Pushrods
- Lower intake manifold
- Spark plugs
- Exhaust manifolds
- Cylinder head bolts
- Cylinder head from the engine block and discard the gaskets.

To install:

6. The cylinder head should be cleaned and inspected prior to installation.

7. Lightly oil all bolt and stud bolt threads before installation.

8. Clean all gasket mating surfaces thoroughly.

9. Install or connect the following:
- New head gaskets on the cylinder block, noting the **UP** position mark on the gasket face and using the dowels in the engine block for alignment. If the dowels are damaged, they must be replaced.

❊❊ WARNING

Always use new cylinder head bolts when installing the cylinder head or damage to the engine may occur.

- Cylinder head on the cylinder block. Tighten the cylinder head bolts in 2 steps following the proper torque sequence. The first step is 37 ft. lbs. (50 Nm) and the second step is 68 ft. lbs. (92 Nm).

➡ **When the cylinder head attaching bolts have been tightened using this procedure, it is not necessary to retighten the bolts after extended engine operation. The bolts can be rechecked for tightness if desired.**

- Intake manifold
- All engine wiring harnesses previously disconnected.
- Pushrods. Dip each end in engine assembly lubricant.

- Rocker arms, seats and retaining bolts. Lubricate all rocker arm components with engine assembly lubricant. Tighten the bolts to 62–132 inch lbs. (7–15 Nm).

➡ **The rocker arm seats must be fully seated in the cylinder head and the pushrods must be seated in the rocker arm sockets prior to the final tightening.**

- Final tighten all rocker arm retaining bolts to 20–28 ft. lbs. (26–38 Nm).
- Exhaust manifolds
- Spark plugs
- Valve covers

10. If the rear cylinder head is being installed, perform the following:

   a. Install the EGR vacuum regulator sensor and bracket.

   b. Install the vehicle speed sensor cable retaining bolt.

   c. Install the heater supply tube retaining brackets from the exhaust manifold.

   d. Install the alternator belt tensioner bracket.

   e. Install the engine oil dipstick tube from the exhaust manifold.

11. If the front cylinder head is being installed, perform the following:

   a. Install the power steering mounting bracket retaining bolts. Leave the hoses connected and place the pump aside in a position to prevent fluid from leaking out.

   b. Install the alternator.

   c. Install the automatic belt tensioner assembly.

   d. Rotate the tensioner clockwise and install the accessory drive belt.

   e. Connect the alternator electrical harness.

12. Install or connect the following:
- Camshaft position sensor
- Upper radiator and heater hoses
- Ignition coil pack and spark plug wires
- Fuel lines and fuel line safety clips
- EGR valve tube
- EGR backpressure transducer
- All necessary vacuum lines
- Air cleaner outlet tube to the throttle body
- Cowl top vent panel

13. Fill and bleed the cooling system.

➡ **Engine coolant is corrosive to engine bearing material. Replace the engine oil after removal of any coolant-carrying component to help prevent potential bearing damage.**

14. Change the engine oil and filter

15. Connect the negative battery cable.

16. Start the engine and check for leaks.

3.8L Engine

1. Remove or disconnect the following:
- Negative battery cable
- Coolant
- Air cleaner assembly
- Cowl top vent panel
- Accessory drive belt

2. If the front cylinder head is being removed, perform the following:

   a. Remove the oil filler cap.

   b. Remove the air conditioning compressor mounting bracket and set the air conditioning compressor aside with the refrigerant lines still connected.

   c. Remove the power steering pump and bracket. Leave the power steering hoses connected and place the pump aside in the engine compartment.

   d. Remove the alternator and mounting bracket.

3. If the rear cylinder head is being removed, perform the following:

   a. Remove the accessory drive belt tensioner.

   b. Remove the PCV valve

   c. Remove the power steering line bracket.

   d. Remove the tensioner bracket.

   e. Remove the coil pack assembly.

4. Remove or disconnect the following:
- Upper intake manifold
- Valve cover
- Fuel system pressure
- Fuel charging assembly
- Lower intake manifold
- Exhaust manifolds

➡ **Pushrods must be installed in their original positions. Note pushrod location during removal.**

- Pushrods
- Cylinder head bolts
- Cylinder head from the engine block and discard the gaskets.

To install:

5. The cylinder head should be cleaned and inspected prior to installation.

6. Lightly oil all bolt and stud bolt threads before installation.

7. Clean all gasket mating surfaces thoroughly.

8. Position new head gaskets on the cylinder block, noting the **UP** position mark on the gasket face, using the dowels in the engine block for alignment. If the dowels are damaged, they must be replaced.

✳✳ WARNING

Always use new cylinder head bolts when installing cylinder head or damage to the engine may occur.

9. Position the cylinder head on the cylinder block.

10. Lubricate the cylinder head bolts with engine oil and install. Tighten the cylinder head bolts in 3 steps following the proper torque sequence to:

- step 1: 15 ft. lbs. (20 Nm)
- step 2: 29 ft. lbs. (40 Nm)
- step 3: 37 ft. lbs. (50 Nm).

➡**Do not loosen all of the cylinder head bolts at once. Only work on 1 bolt at a time or damage to the engine may occur.**

11. In sequence, loosen each cylinder head bolt 2–3 turns and retighten in 2 steps.

- Long bolts, step 1: 29–37 ft. lbs. (40–50 Nm); step 2: tighten an additional 175–185 degrees.
- Short bolts, step 1: 15–22 ft. lbs. (20–30 Nm); second 2: tighten an additional 175–185 degrees.

12. Dip each pushrod end in engine assembly lubricant. Install the pushrods in their original positions.

13. Lubricate all rocker arm components with engine assembly lubricant.

14. For the rocker arm being installed, rotate the engine clockwise until the valve tappet rests on the heel (base circle) of the camshaft lobe.

15. Install the rocker arms, seats and bolts and tighten to 44 inch lbs. (5 Nm).

16. Perform the previous 2 steps for each rocker arm.

17. After all rocker arms have been installed, final tighten all bolts to 22–29 ft. lbs. (30–40 Nm).

18. Install or connect the following:

- Exhaust manifolds
- Lower intake manifold
- Fuel injection charging assembly
- Valve covers with new gaskets. Tighten the bolts to 71–97 inch lbs. (8–11 Nm).
- Upper intake manifold
- Spark plugs and ignition wires

19. If the front cylinder head is being installed, perform the following:

a. Install the alternator and mounting bracket.

b. Install the power steering pump and bracket.

c. Install the air conditioning compressor bracket.

d. Install the oil filler cap.

20. If the rear cylinder head is being installed, perform the following:

a. Install the coil pack assembly.

b. Install the tensioner bracket.

c. Install the power steering line bracket.

d. Install the PCV valve.

e. Install the accessory drive belt tensioner.

f. Rotate the tensioner clockwise and install the accessory drive belt.

21. Install the cowl top vent panel.

22. Install the air cleaner assembly.

23. Fill and bleed the cooling system.

24. Connect the negative battery cable.

Rocker Arms

REMOVAL & INSTALLATION

1. Remove the valve cover.

2. Remove the rocker arm retaining bolt.

➡**Rocker the arms should be installed in their original location during assembly.**

3. Remove the rocker arms. If more than 1 rocker arm is to be removed, identify each rocker arm location.

To install:

4. Lubricate the pushrods and rocker arms with engine assembly lubricant. Lubricate the retaining bolts with engine oil.

➡Prior to final tightening, the rocker arm seats must be fully seated into the cylinder head. The pushrods must be fully seated in the rocker arm and valve tappet sockets.

5. Install the rocker arms into position with the pushrods and snug the retaining bolt.

6. Rotate the crankshaft until the lifter for the rocker arm being installed, is on the base circle (heel) of the cam lobe.

7. Tighten the rocker arm retaining bolt to:

- 3.0L: 60–132 inch lbs. (7–15 Nm)
- 3.8L: 44 inch lbs. (5 Nm)

8. Finally, tighten the bolt with the camshaft in any position to 20–28 ft. lbs. (26–38 Nm).

9. Install the valve cover.

Intake Manifold

REMOVAL & INSTALLATION

➡Intake manifold torque sequences can be found in Section 1, following the Torque Specifications Chart.

3.0L Engine

1. Remove or disconnect the following:

- Negative battery cable
- Coolant
- Crankcase ventilation tube from the valve cover
- Air cleaner inlet and outlet tubes
- Fuel system pressure

ROCKER ARM SEAT AND BOLT MUST BE FULLY SEATED AFTER FINAL TORQUE

CLEARANCE SHOULD BE 2.25–4.79mm (0.09–0.19 INCH) WITH VALVE TAPPET FULLY COLLAPSED ON BASE CIRCLE OF CAMSHAFT AFTER ASSEMBLED.

7924GG17

When the lifter is fully collapsed and on the base circle of the cam, check for proper clearance between the tip of the valve and the rocker arm—3.8L engine

- Fuel line safety clips and disconnect the fuel lines
- Vacuum lines
- All electrical wiring attached to the intake manifold
- All control cables
- Radiator and heater hoses
- Alternator brace
- EGR tube and EGR valve
- Fuel charging assembly
- Ignition wires
- Ignition coil pack
- Camshaft position sensor
- Valve covers
- No. 3 intake valve pushrod

➡ **The lower intake manifold may be removed with the fuel injection supply manifold and fuel injectors in place as an assembly.**

- Lower intake manifold retaining bolts using a Torx® head socket. Use a soft-faced mallet to tap the manifold upward if it is hard to remove.
- Intake manifold

To install:

2. Thoroughly clean all gasket mating surfaces on the intake manifold and cylinder head.

❊❊ WARNING

When cleaning the cylinder head gasket surfaces, lay a clean cloth in the valve tappet area to prevent any particles from entering the oil drainback area.

3. Apply a 0.25 in. (6mm) bead of silicone rubber sealant to the intersection of the cylinder block and cylinder head at the 4 corners of the intake manifold.

4. Install the intake manifold gaskets, aligning the intake gasket locking tabs to provisions on the head. Install the front and rear intake manifold end seals and secure with retainers.

5. Install or connect the following:
- Intake manifold
- Intake bolts Nos. 1, 2, 3, and 4. Tighten by hand.
- Remaining intake bolts and tighten all bolts in sequence to 15–22 ft. lbs. (20–30 Nm). Tighten again in sequence to 20–23 ft. lbs. (26–32 Nm).
- No. 3 intake valve pushrod and rocker arm
- Valve covers
- Camshaft position sensor
- Coil pack and ignition wires
- Fuel charging assembly, and

tighten the bolts to 71–106 inch lbs. (8–12 Nm).
- EGR tube and EGR valve
- Alternator brace
- Radiator and heater hoses
- Control cables
- All electrical wiring
- Vacuum lines
- Fuel lines and install the fuel line safety clips
- Air cleaner inlet and outlet tubes
- Crankcase ventilation tube

6. Fill and bleed the engine cooling system.

7. Connect the negative battery cable.

8. Start the engine and check for leaks.

3.8L Engine

UPPER MANIFOLD

1. Remove or disconnect the following:
- Air cleaner outlet tube
- Accelerator cable and speed control actuator cable at the throttle body
- Accelerator cable bracket and position it aside
- Vacuum lines
- Necessary electrical harnesses
- Crankcase ventilation tube from the PCV valve
- Throttle body
- Idle air control valve
- Intake manifold retaining bolts, noting their positions

➡ **Keep the intake manifold bolts in order, so they can be installed in their original positions.**

- Upper intake manifold

To install:

2. Inspect the intake gasket to ensure the seals are completely installed in the manifold groove and the seals show no signs of damage.

3. Install or connect the following:
- Intake manifold and tighten the bolts to 71–106 inch lbs. (8–12 Nm) in the sequence shown.
- Idle air control valve
- Throttle body
- Crankcase ventilation tube to the PCV valve
- Electrical harnesses
- Vacuum lines
- Accelerator cable bracket and tighten the bolts to 71–106 inch lbs. (8–12 Nm).
- Accelerator cable and speed control actuator cable at the throttle body
- Air cleaner outlet tube

LOWER MANIFOLD

1. Remove or disconnect the following:
- Coolant
- Upper intake manifold
- Water bypass hose from the heater water outlet tube
- Bypass hose from the lower intake manifold

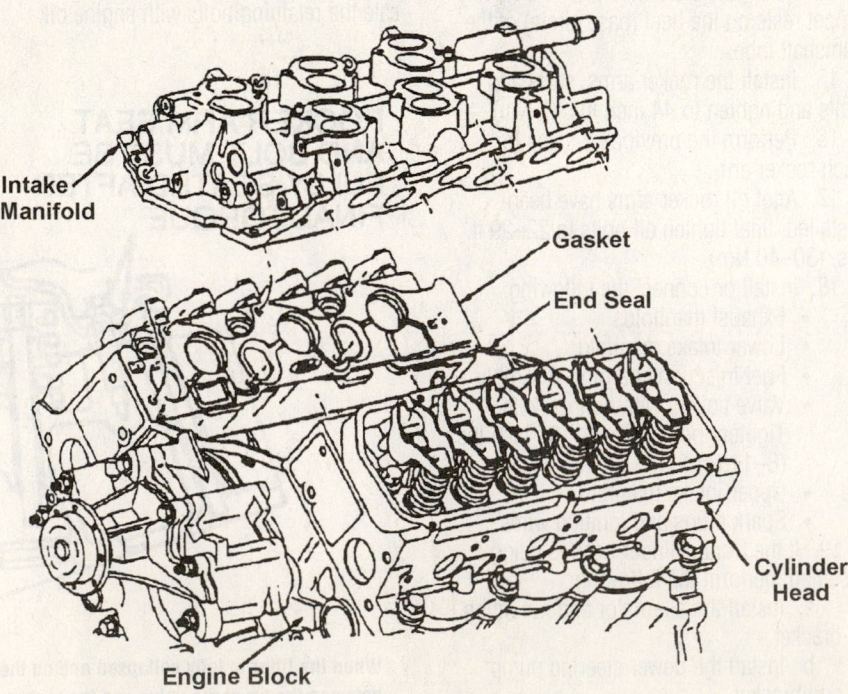

Lower intake manifold and related components—3.8L engine

7924GG07

- Fuel system pressure
- Electrical wiring harnesses
- Fuel injectors and fuel charging assembly
- Vacuum motor and bracket assemblies
- Valve assembly and linkage from the IMRC lever and bushing by using a prytool
- Tube retaining bolts
- Old bushing from the lever
- EGR valve and adapter
- Lower intake manifold retaining bolts

➡ **The lower intake manifold is sealed at each corner with sealer. To break the seal it may be necessary to pry on the front of the intake manifold with a pry-bar. If it is necessary, use care to prevent damage to the machined surfaces.**

- Lower intake manifold

To install:

2. Thoroughly clean all gasket mating surfaces.

➡ **When using silicone rubber sealer, assembly must occur within 15 minutes after sealer application. After this time, the sealer may start to set up and its sealing effectiveness may be reduced.**

3. Install or connect the following:
- New bushings into the IMRC levers
- Apply a 3mm bead of RTV silicone sealer at each corner where the cylinder head joins the engine block.
- Front and rear intake manifold seals
- Lower intake manifold into position on the cylinder block, using new gaskets.
- Apply pipe sealant to the intake bolts and install in their original locations. Tighten in sequence to 71–106 inch lbs. (8–12 Nm).
- EGR valve and adapter
- IMRC vacuum motors, and tighten the retaining bolts to 71–106 inch lbs. (8–12 Nm).
- Fuel injectors and charging assembly. Tighten retaining bolts to 71–97 inch lbs. (8–11 Nm).
- Water bypass tube to the lower intake manifold. Tighten the retaining bolts to 71–97 inch lbs. (8–11 Nm).
- Water bypass tube hose to the outlet tube and tighten the hose clamp securely.

- Electrical wiring harnesses
- Vacuum lines to the IMRC motors
- Upper radiator hose to water hose connection and tighten the hose clamp securely.
- Upper intake manifold

4. Fill and bleed the cooling system.
5. Start the engine and check for leaks.

Exhaust Manifold

REMOVAL & INSTALLATION

➡ **Spray the exhaust system fasteners with penetrating lubricant before removing them to help prevent broken studs and bolts. The use of a 6-point socket is highly recommended when removing exhaust system fasteners.**

✳✳ CAUTION

To prevent serious burns, allow the exhaust manifold to cool down before attempting to remove it.

3.0L Engine

REAR MANIFOLD

1. Disconnect the negative battery cable.
2. Remove the cowl vent panel.
3. Label and disconnect the EGR back-pressure transducer hoses.
4. Remove the EGR valve tube from the exhaust manifold.

➡ **Use a backup wrench to prevent damaging the tube.**

5. Raise and support the vehicle safely.
6. Disconnect the dual converter Y-pipe from the exhaust manifold.
7. Lower the vehicle.
8. Remove the exhaust manifold.

To install:

9. Clean all mating surfaces thoroughly.
10. Position the exhaust manifold and tighten the bolts to 15–22 ft. lbs. (20–30 Nm).
11. Raise and support the vehicle safely.
12. Connect the dual converter Y-pipe and tighten the bolts to 25–34 ft. lbs. (34–47 Nm).
13. Lower the vehicle.
14. Install the EGR valve tube and tighten the fitting to 26–48 ft. lbs. (35–65 Nm).
15. Connect the EGR backpressure transducer hoses.
16. Install the cowl vent panel.
17. Connect the negative battery cable.

18. Start the engine and check for exhaust leaks.

FRONT MANIFOLD

1. Disconnect the negative battery cable.
2. Remove the oil level indicator tube support bracket and retaining nut.
3. Remove the oil level dipstick and oil level indicator tube.
4. Raise and support the vehicle safely.
5. Disconnect the dual converter Y-pipe from the exhaust manifold.
6. Lower the vehicle.
7. Remove the exhaust manifold.

To install:

8. Clean all mating surfaces thoroughly.
9. Position exhaust manifold and tighten the bolts to 15–22 ft. lbs. (20–30 Nm).
10. Raise and support the vehicle safely.
11. Connect the dual converter Y-pipe and tighten the bolts to 25–34 ft. lbs. (34–47 Nm).
12. Lower the vehicle.
13. Install the oil level dipstick and oil level indicator tube. Tighten the nut to 11–14 ft. lbs. (15–20 Nm).
14. Connect the negative battery cable.
15. Start the engine and check for exhaust leaks.

3.8L Engine

REAR MANIFOLD

1. Disconnect the negative battery cable.
2. Remove the cowl vent panel.
3. Remove the engine air cleaner and air cleaner outlet tube.
4. Disconnect the ignition wires from the rear cylinder head and ignition coil.
5. Remove the spark plugs from the rear cylinder head.
6. Raise and support the vehicle safely on jackstands.
7. Disconnect the dual converter Y-pipe from the exhaust manifold.
8. Lower the vehicle.
9. Remove the exhaust manifold.

To install:

10. Clean all gasket mating surfaces thoroughly.

➡ **A slight warpage in the exhaust manifold may cause a misalignment between the bolt holes in the cylinder head and exhaust manifold. Elongate the holes in the exhaust manifold as necessary to correct the misalignment. Do not elongate the pilot hole.**

Refer to Section 1 for engine rebuilding specifications

11. Install a new exhaust manifold gasket and the exhaust manifold on the cylinder head. Start 2 bolts to hold the manifold in position.

12. Install the remaining bolts. Tighten the bolts beginning from the center port and working outward to 15–22 ft. lbs. (20–30 Nm).

13. Raise and support the vehicle safely.

14. Connect the dual converter Y-pipe and tighten the bolts to 25–34 ft. lbs. (34–47 Nm).

15. Lower the vehicle.

16. Install the spark plugs in the rear cylinder head.

17. Connect the ignition wires.

18. Install the engine air cleaner and air cleaner outlet tube.

19. Install the cowl vent panel.

20. Connect the negative battery cable.

21. Start the engine and check for exhaust leaks.

FRONT MANIFOLD

1. Disconnect the negative battery cable.

2. Remove the oil level indicator tube.

3. Label and disconnect the ignition wires from the front cylinder head.

4. Disconnect the EGR-to-exhaust manifold tube.

5. Raise and support the vehicle safely on jackstands.

6. Disconnect the dual converter Y-pipe from the exhaust manifold.

7. Lower the vehicle.

8. Remove the exhaust manifold.

To install:

9. Clean all gasket mating surfaces thoroughly.

➡**A slight warpage in the exhaust manifold may cause a misalignment between the bolt holes in the cylinder head and exhaust manifold. Elongate the holes in the exhaust manifold as necessary to correct the misalignment. Do not elongate the pilot hole.**

10. Install a new gasket and the exhaust manifold on the cylinder head. Start 2 bolts to hold the manifold in position.

11. Install the remaining bolts. Tighten the bolts, starting from the center port and working outward, to 15–22 ft. lbs. (20–30 Nm).

12. Raise and support the vehicle safely on jackstands.

13. Connect the dual converter Y-pipe and tighten the bolts to 25–34 ft. lbs. (34–47 Nm).

14. Lower the vehicle.

15. Connect the EGR to the exhaust manifold tube.

16. Connect the ignition wires.

17. Install the oil level indicator tube.

18. Connect the negative battery cable.

19. Start the engine and check for exhaust leaks.

Camshaft and Lifters

REMOVAL & INSTALLATION

3.0L Engine

1. Remove the engine from the vehicle.

2. Rotate the crankshaft until the No. 1 piston is at the TDC on its compression stroke and the timing marks are aligned.

3. Remove or disconnect the following:
- Throttle body
- Ignition wires
- Camshaft position sensor
- Ignition coil
- Valve covers
- No. 3 intake valve pushrod
- Alternator and mounting brackets
- Drive belt tensioner and drive belt
- Intake manifold
- Remaining pushrods
- Tappet guide plate from the valve tappets by lifting straight up
- Tappets
- Crankshaft pulley and damper

- Oil pan assembly
- Front cover assembly

4. Align the timing marks on the camshaft and crankshaft sprockets.

5. Check the camshaft end-play as follows:

   a. Push the camshaft toward the rear of the engine and install a dial indicator, so the indicator point is on the camshaft sprocket attaching screw.

   b. Zero the dial indicator. Position a small prybar between the camshaft sprocket and block.

   c. Pull the camshaft forward and release it. Camshaft end-play should be 0.007 in. (0.17mm) or less.

   d. If the camshaft end-play is not within specification, replace the thrust plate.

6. Remove or disconnect the following:
- Timing chain and sprockets
- Camshaft thrust plate

7. Carefully remove the camshaft by pulling it toward the front of the engine. Remove it slowly to avoid damaging the bearings, journals and lobes.

To install:

8. Clean and inspect all parts before installation.

9. Lubricate the camshaft lobes and journals with Molylube® or heavy engine oil.

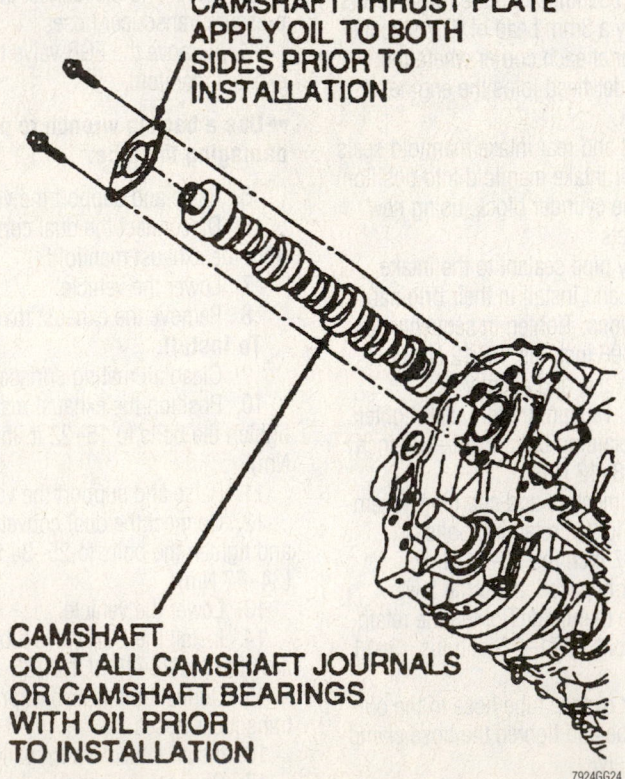

CAMSHAFT THRUST PLATE APPLY OIL TO BOTH SIDES PRIOR TO INSTALLATION

CAMSHAFT COAT ALL CAMSHAFT JOURNALS OR CAMSHAFT BEARINGS WITH OIL PRIOR TO INSTALLATION

7924GG24

The thrust plate, which holds the camshaft in position, comes in different thicknesses to allow for camshaft free-play adjustment—3.0L and 3.8L engines

10. Carefully install the camshaft.

➡**If a new camshaft is being installed, recheck camshaft end-play.**

11. Lubricate the engine thrust plate with engine assembly lubricant, then install the thrust plate. Tighten the retaining bolts to 84 inch lbs. (10 Nm).

12. Install or connect the following:
- Timing chain and sprockets

➡**Check the camshaft sprocket bolt for blockage of the drilled oil passages prior to installation, and clean if necessary.**

- Engine front cover
- Crankshaft damper and pulley
- Tappets
- Tappet guide plate with the word **UP** facing you.
- Intake manifold assembly
- Pushrods and rocker arms
- Oil pan
- Valve covers
- Alternator and brackets
- Drive belt tensioner and the drive belt
- Throttle body
- Ignition wires
- Engine into the vehicle

3.8L Engine

1. Rotate the crankshaft until the No. 1 piston is at the TDC on its compression stroke and the timing marks are aligned.

2. Remove or disconnect the following:
- Engine from the vehicle
- Valve covers
- Intake manifolds
- Pushrod
- Tappet guide plate
- Tappets
- Crankshaft pulley and damper
- Oil pan
- Engine front cover assembly

3. Check the camshaft end-play as follows:

a. Push the camshaft toward the rear of the engine and install a dial indicator, so the indicator point is on the camshaft sprocket attaching screw.

b. Zero the dial indicator. Position a small prybar between the camshaft sprocket or gear and block.

c. Pull the camshaft forward and release it. Camshaft end-play should be 0.001–0.006 in. (0.025–0.15mm).

d. If the camshaft end-play is not

within specification, replace the thrust plate upon reassembly.

4. Remove or disconnect the following:
- Remove the timing chain and sprockets.
- Remove the camshaft thrust plate.

5. Carefully remove the camshaft by pulling it toward the front of the engine. Remove it slowly to avoid damaging the bearings, journals and lobes.

To install:

6. Clean and inspect all parts before installation.

7. Lubricate the camshaft lobes and journals with Molylube® or heavy engine oil.

8. Carefully install the camshaft.

➡**If a new camshaft is being installed, recheck camshaft end-play.**

9. Lubricate the engine thrust plate with engine assembly lubricant, then install the thrust plate. Tighten the retaining bolts to 71–124 inch lbs. (8–14 Nm).

10. Install the timing chain and sprockets.

➡**Check the camshaft sprocket bolt for blockage of the drilled oil passages prior to installation, and clean if necessary.**

11. Install or connect the following:
- Install the engine front cover.
- Install the crankshaft damper and pulley.
- Lubricate and install the hydraulic tappets into their original bores.
- Align the valve tappet flats and install the tappet guide plate with the word **UP** facing you.
- Install the intake manifold assembly.
- Lubricate and install the pushrods and rocker arms.
- Install the oil pan.
- Install the valve covers.
- Install the engine assembly into the vehicle.

Starter

REMOVAL & INSTALLATION

1. Disconnect the negative battery cable.
2. Raise and support the vehicle safely.

➡**When removing the hard shell connector at terminal "S", grasp the plastic shell. Do not pull on the wire.**

3. Disconnect the starter electrical harness.

4. Remove the upper starter bolt.
5. Support the starter and remove the lower bolt.
6. Remove the starter from the vehicle.

To install:

7. Position the starter in the vehicle.
8. Install the upper and lower bolts. Tighten to 15–20 ft. lbs. (20–27 Nm).
9. Connect the starter electrical harness. Tighten the starter cable nut to 80–124 inch lbs. (9–14 Nm).

➡**When installing the hard shell connector, be careful to push it straight on and make sure it locks in position with a notable click or detent.**

10. Lower the vehicle.
11. Connect the negative battery cable.

Oil Pan

✴✴ CAUTION

The EPA warns that prolonged contact with used engine oil may cause a number of skin disorders, including cancer! You should make every effort to minimize your exposure to used engine oil. Protective gloves should be worn when changing the oil. Wash your hands and any other exposed skin areas as soon as possible after exposure to used engine oil. Soap and water, or waterless hand cleaner, should be used.

REMOVAL & INSTALLATION

3.0L Engine

1. Remove or disconnect the following:
- Negative battery cable
- Oil level dipstick
- Retainer clip at the low oil level sensor. Disconnect the wiring harness from the sensor.
- Engine oil
- Wiring harness from the oxygen sensors
- Dual converter Y-pipe
- Starter motor
- Lower engine/flywheel dust cover from the torque converter housing
- Oil pan bolts, then slowly remove the oil pan, making sure the internal pan baffle does not snag the oil pump screen cover and tube.
- Oil pan gasket

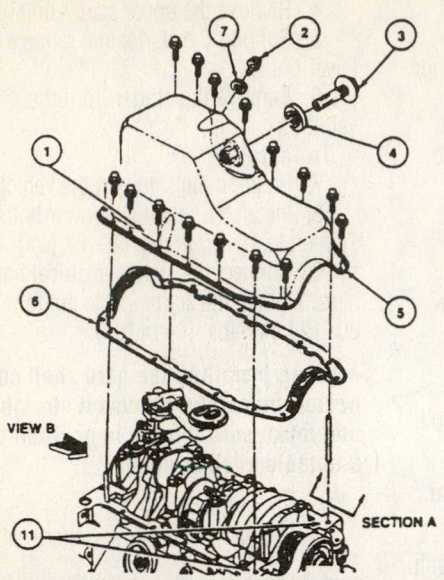

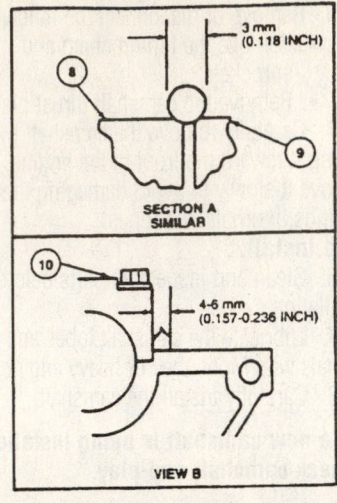

1. Bolt
2. Oil pan drain plug
3. Low oil level sensor
4. Low oil level sensor washer
5. Oil pan
6. Oil pan gasket
7. Drain plug gasket
8. Cylinder block
9. Engine front cover
10. Rear main bearing cap
11. Silicone gasket and sealant

7924GG18

Oil pan and related components. Apply silicone gasket sealant in the places shown—3.0L engine

To install:

2. Clean the gasket mating surfaces thoroughly.

➡ **When using a silicone sealer, the assembly process should occur within 15 minutes after the sealer has been applied. After this time, the sealer may start to set-up and its sealing effectiveness may be affected.**

3. Apply a 0.25 in. (6mm) thick bead of silicone sealer to the junction of the rear main bearing cap and cylinder block junction of the front cover assembly and cylinder block.

4. Position the oil pan gasket to the oil pan with sealing bends against the oil pan surface and secure with gasket adhesive.

5. Position the oil pan on the engine block and install the oil pan attaching bolts. Tighten the bolts to 96–120 inch lbs. (11–14 Nm).

6. Back off all of the bolts and retighten them.

7. Install or connect the following:
- Install the lower engine/flywheel dust cover to the torque converter housing.
- Install the starter motor.
- Install the dual converter Y-pipe.

- Connect the wiring harness to the oxygen sensors.
- Connect the low oil level sensor wiring harness and install the retainer clip.
- Lower the vehicle.
- Install the oil level dipstick.
- Connect the negative battery cable.

8. Fill the engine with oil.
9. Start the engine and check for leaks.

3.8L Engine

1. Disconnect the negative battery cable.
2. Raise and support the vehicle safely on jackstands.

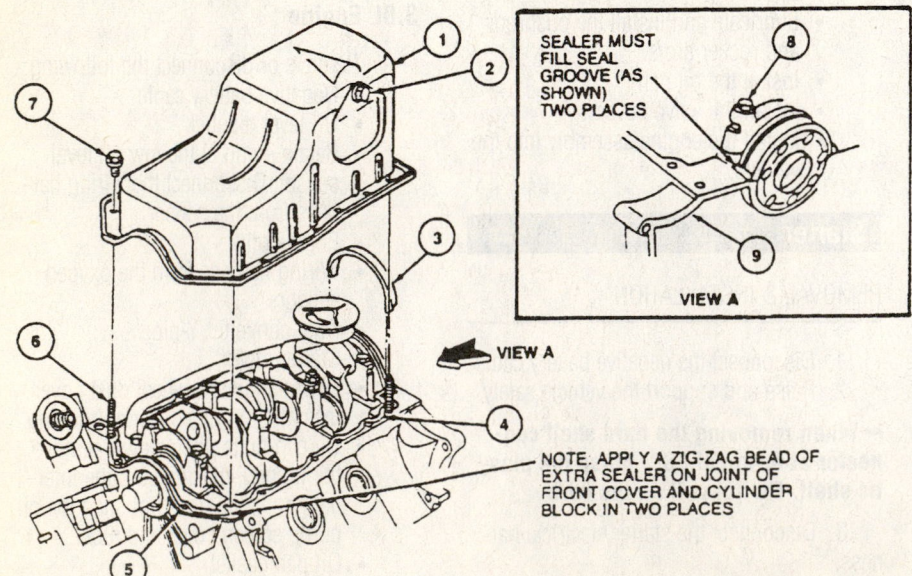

1. Oil pan
2. Oil pan drain plug
3. End seal
4. Silicone gasket and sealant
5. Engine front cover
6. Guide pin
7. Bolt
8. Rear bearing cap
9. Cylinder block

NOTE: APPLY A ZIG-ZAG BEAD OF EXTRA SEALER ON JOINT OF FRONT COVER AND CYLINDER BLOCK IN TWO PLACES

7924GG19

Exploded view of the oil pan and related components. Apply silicone gasket sealant in the places shown—3.8L engine

3. Drain the engine oil.

4. Remove the oil filter.

5. Remove the dual converter Y-pipe assembly.

6. Remove the starter motor.

7. Remove the engine rear plate/converter housing cover.

8. Remove the retaining bolts and remove the oil pan.

To install:

9. Clean the gasket mating surfaces thoroughly.

10. Trial fit the oil pan to the cylinder block. Ensure that enough clearance has been provided to allow the oil pan to be installed without sealant being scraped off when pan is positioned under the engine.

11. Apply a bead of silicone sealer to the oil pan flange. Also apply a bead of sealer to the front cover/cylinder block joint and fill the grooves on both sides of the rear main seal cap.

➡**When using silicone rubber sealer, assembly must occur within 15 minutes after sealer application. After this time, the sealer may start to harden and its sealing effectiveness may be reduced.**

12. Install the oil pan and secure to the block with the attaching screws. Tighten the screws to 80–106 inch lbs. (9–12 Nm).

13. Install a new oil filter.

14. Install the engine rear plate/converter housing cover.

15. Install the starter motor.

16. Install the Y-pipe converter assembly.

17. Lower the vehicle.

18. Fill the engine with the proper type and amount of clean oil.

19. Connect the negative battery cable.

20. Start the engine and check for leaks.

Oil Pump

REMOVAL & INSTALLATION

3.0L Engine

1. Disconnect the negative battery cable.

2. Remove the oil pan.

3. Remove the oil pump attaching bolts. Lift the oil pump from the engine.

4. If replacing the oil pump, remove the oil pump intermediate shaft.

To install:

5. Prime the oil pump by filling either the inlet or the outlet port with engine oil. Rotate the pump shaft to distribute the oil within the oil pump body cavity.

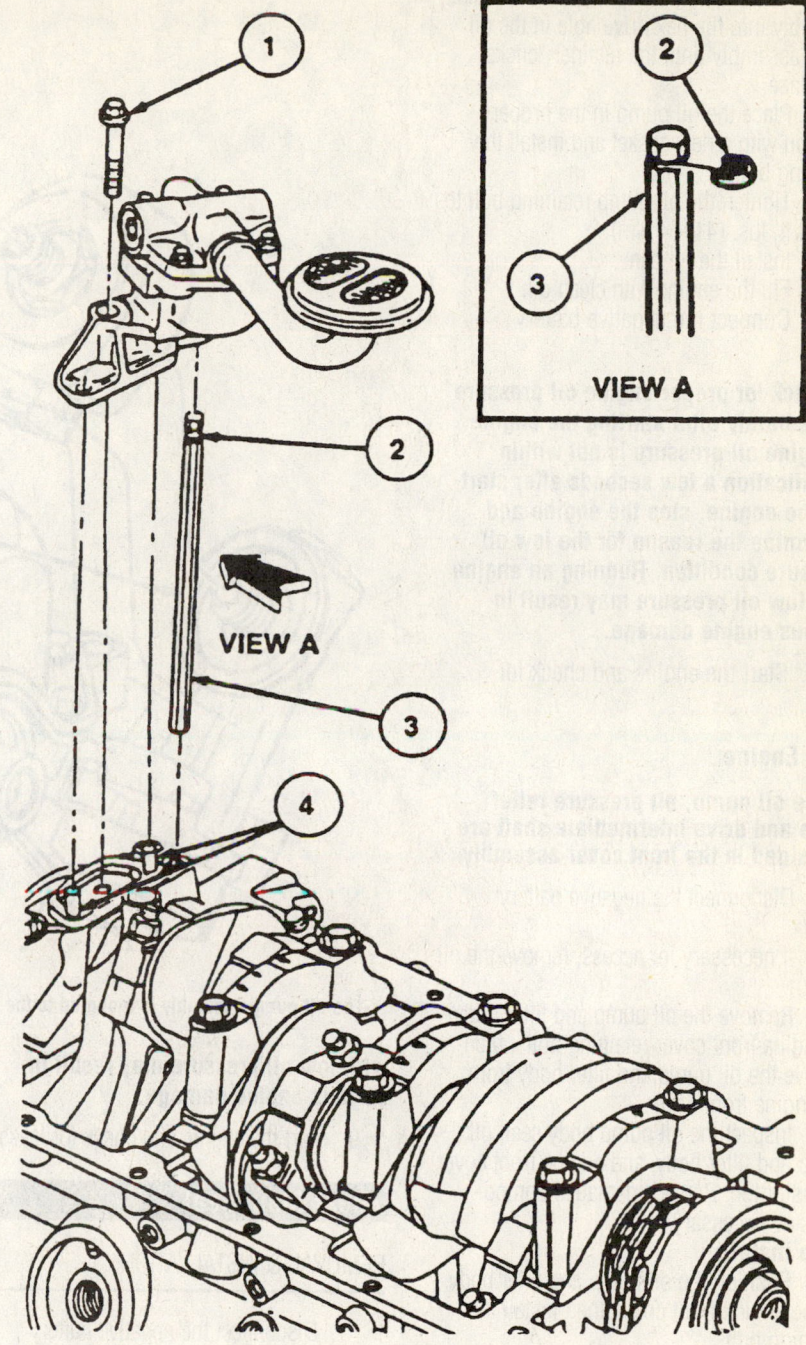

VIEW A

1	Bolt
2	Oil Pump Intermediate Shaft Retaining Ring
3	Oil Pump Intermediate Shaft
4	Dowel

7924GG20

Remove the oil pan to gain access to the oil pump assembly on the 3.0L engine

For complete mechanical specifications, refer to Section 1 of this manual

6. Insert the oil pump intermediate shaft assembly into the hex drive hole in the oil pump assembly until the retainer "clicks" into place.

7. Place the oil pump in the proper position with a new gasket and install the retaining bolt.

8. Tighten the oil pump retaining bolt to 30–40 ft. lbs. (41–54 Nm).

9. Install the oil pan.

10. Fill the engine with clean oil.

11. Connect the negative battery cable.

➡**Check for proper engine oil pressure immediately after starting the engine. If engine oil pressure is not within specification a few seconds after starting the engine, stop the engine and determine the reason for the low oil pressure condition. Running an engine with low oil pressure may result in serious engine damage.**

12. Start the engine and check for leaks.

3.8L Engine

➡**The oil pump, oil pressure relief valve and drive intermediate shaft are contained in the front cover assembly.**

1. Disconnect the negative battery cable.

2. If necessary for access, remove the oil filter.

3. Remove the oil pump and filter body-to-engine front cover retaining bolts, then remove the oil pump and filter body from the engine front cover.

4. Inspect the oil pump body seal, oil pump and filter body, and engine front cover for distortion. Replace damaged components as necessary.

To install:

5. Position the oil pump and filter body on the engine front cover, then install the retaining bolts.

6. Tighten the 4 large engine front cover retaining bolts to 17–23 ft. lbs. (23–31 Nm), then tighten the remaining retaining bolts to 71–97 inch lbs. (8–11 Nm).

7. If removed, install the oil filter.

8. Connect the negative battery cable.

➡**Check for proper engine oil pressure immediately after starting the engine. If engine oil pressure is not within specification a few seconds after starting the engine, stop the engine and determine the reason for the low oil pressure condition. Running an engine**

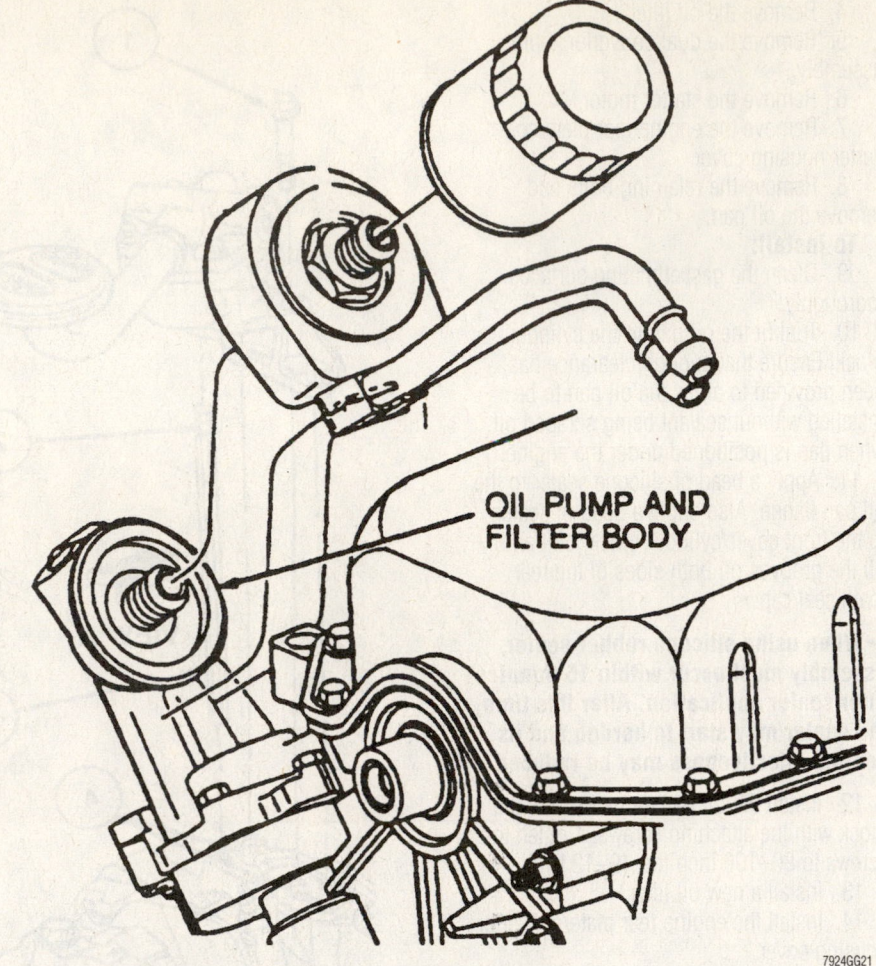

OIL PUMP AND FILTER BODY

7924GG21

The oil pump assembly is mounted to the side of the 3.8L engine

with low oil pressure may result in serious engine damage.

9. Start the engine and check for leaks.

Rear Main Seal

REMOVAL & INSTALLATION

1. Disconnect the negative battery cable.

2. Raise and support the vehicle safely on jackstands.

3. Remove the transaxle.

4. Remove the flywheel and the rear cover plate, if necessary.

5. Using a sharp awl, punch 1 hole into the crankshaft rear oil seal metal surface between the seal lip and the cylinder block.

✳✳ WARNING

Use caution when working near the crankshaft sealing surface. If the sur-

face becomes damaged, an oil leak may occur.

6. Screw in the threaded end of a crankshaft rear seal replacer tool, then use the tool to remove the seal.

To install:

7. Inspect the crankshaft seal area for any damage that may cause the seal to leak. If damage is evident, service or replace the crankshaft as necessary.

8. Coat the crankshaft seal area and the seal lip with engine oil.

9. Using a crankshaft seal replacer tool, install the seal. Tighten the bolts of the seal installer tool evenly so the seal is straight and seats without misalignment.

10. Install the flywheel.

11. Install the rear cover plate, if necessary.

12. Install the transaxle, lower the vehicle and connect the battery.

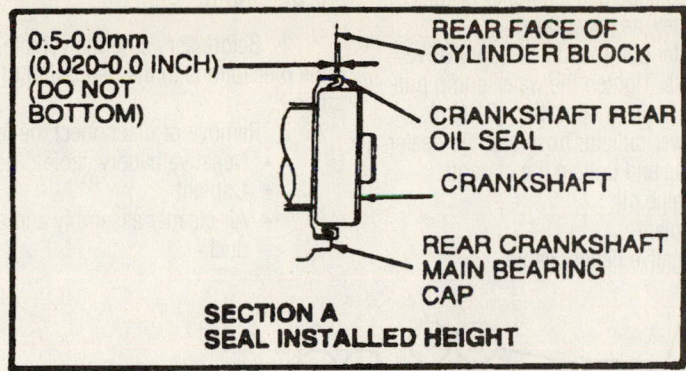

SECTION A
SEAL INSTALLED HEIGHT

0.5-0.0mm
(0.020-0.0 INCH)
(DO NOT
BOTTOM)

REAR FACE OF
CYLINDER BLOCK

CRANKSHAFT REAR
OIL SEAL

CRANKSHAFT

REAR CRANKSHAFT
MAIN BEARING
CAP

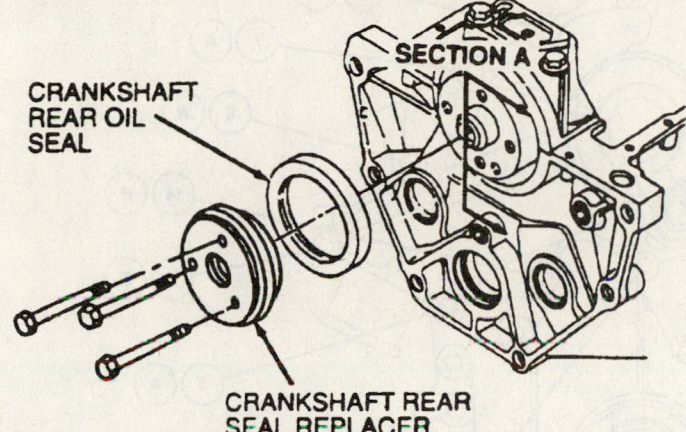

SECTION A

CRANKSHAFT
REAR OIL
SEAL

CRANKSHAFT REAR
SEAL REPLACER

7924GG08

The rear main seal must be installed with the proper tools to avoid damaging the seal or crank-

Timing Chain, Sprockets, Front Cover and Seal

REMOVAL & INSTALLATION

3.0L Engine

1. Before servicing the vehicle, refer to the precautions at the beginning of this section.

2. Remove or disconnect the following:

- Negative battery cable
- Coolant
- Accessory drive belts
- Idler pulley or automatic tensioner, as necessary
- Lower radiator hose and the heater hose from the water pump and front cover
- Crankshaft pulley and damper
- On flexible fuel vehicles, the CKP sensor
- Engine oil
- Oil pan
- If necessary, the water pump pulley bolts, then remove the pulley.

- Bolts from the timing cover to the cylinder block
- Timing cover

3. Tap the seal out of the cover with a seal driver.

4. Remove the crankshaft damper and timing chain front cover.

5. Rotate the crankshaft until the No. 1 piston is at TDC of its compression stroke and the timing marks are aligned.

6. Remove the camshaft sprocket attaching bolt and washer. Slide both sprockets and timing chain forward and remove as an assembly.

7. Check the timing chain and sprockets for excessive wear. Replace if necessary.

To install:

8. Before installation, clean and inspect all parts. Clean the gasket material and dirt from the oil pan, cylinder block and front cover.

9. Slide both sprockets and timing chain onto the camshaft and crankshaft with the timing marks aligned. Install the camshaft bolt and washer and tighten to 46 ft. lbs. (63 Nm). Apply clean engine oil to the timing chain and sprockets after installation.

➡ The camshaft bolt has a drilled oil passage in it for timing chain lubrication. Prior to installation, clean the passage and be sure it is clear. Never replace the camshaft bolt with a standard bolt.

10. Lightly oil all bolt and stud threads except bolts 1, 2 and 3 that require a suitable pipe sealant.

11. Install or connect the following:

- New seal in the timing cover
- New timing cover gasket over the cylinder block dowels
- Timing cover/water pump assembly onto the cylinder block with the water pump pulley loosely attached to the water pump hub.

12. Apply a non-hardening sealant to bolt numbers 1, 2 and 3 and hand start them along with the rest of the cover bolts. Tighten bolts 1–10 to 19 ft. lbs. (25 Nm) and bolts 11–15 to 84 inch lbs. (10 Nm).

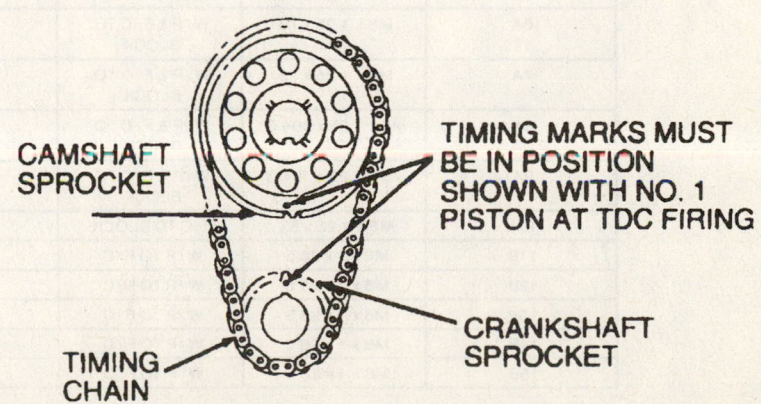

CAMSHAFT
SPROCKET

TIMING MARKS MUST
BE IN POSITION
SHOWN WITH NO. 1
PISTON AT TDC FIRING

TIMING
CHAIN

CRANKSHAFT
SPROCKET

7922KG47

Be sure the timing marks are facing each other after the chain has been installed—3.0L (OHV) engine

Please refer to Section 8 for electric cooling fan wiring schematics

13. Install or connect the following:
- Engine oil pan. Tighten the bolts to 108 inch lbs. (12 Nm).
- Water pump pulley bolts, hand-tight
- Crankshaft damper and pulley. Tighten the damper bolt to 107 ft. lbs. (145 Nm).
- On flexible fuel vehicles, the CKP sensor. Tighten the bolt to 44–61 inch lbs. (5–7 Nm).

- Automatic belt tensioner or idler pulley, as necessary
- Water pump and accessory drive belts. Tighten the water pump pulley bolts to 16 ft. lbs. (21 Nm).
- Lower radiator hose and the heater hose and tighten the clamps.
- Engine oil
- Coolant
- Negative battery cable

3.8L Engine

1. Before servicing the vehicle, refer to the precautions in the beginning of this section.
2. Remove or disconnect the following:
- Negative battery cable
- Coolant
- Air cleaner assembly and air intake duct

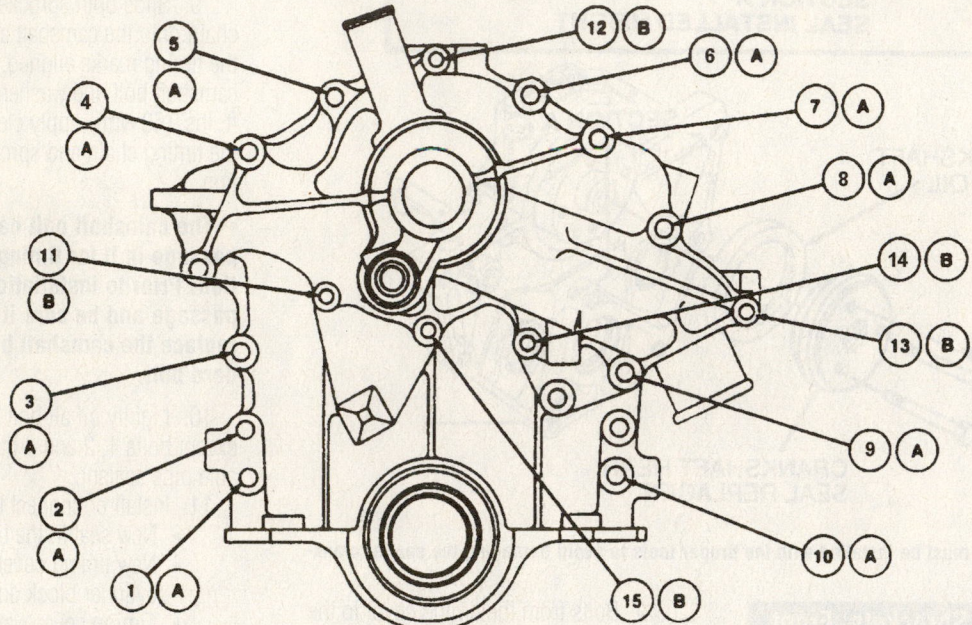

Fasteners			Torque Specifications	
Fastener And Hole No.	Size	Fastener Application	N·m	LB-FT
1A	M8 x 1.25 x 43.5	F/C TO BLOCK	20-30	15-22
2A	M8 x 1.25 x 43.5	F/C TO BLOCK	20-30	15-22
3A	M8 x 1.25 x 73	W/P & F/C TO BLOCK	20-30	15-22
4A	M8 x 1.25 x 104.3	W/P & F/C TO BLOCK	20-30	15-22
5A	M8 x 1.25 x 73	F/C TO BLOCK	20-30	15-22
6A	M8 x 1.25 x 73	W/P & F/C TO BLOCK	20-30	15-22
7A	M8 x 1.25 x 73	W/P & F/C TO BLOCK	20-30	15-22
8A	M8 x 1.25 x 104.3	W/P & F/C TO BLOCK	20-30	15-22
9A	M8 x 1.25 x 104.3	W/P & F/C TO BLOCK	20-30	15-22
10A	M8 x 1.25 x 52	F/C TO BLOCK	20-30	15-22
11B	M6 x 1 x 28.5	W/P TO F/C	8-12	71-106 (lb-in)
12B	M6 x 1 x 28.5	W/P TO F/C	8-12	71-106 (lb-in)
13B	M6 x 1 x 28.5	W/P TO F/C	8-12	71-106 (lb-in)
14B	M6 x 1 x 28.5	W/P TO F/C	8-12	71-106 (lb-in)
15B	M6 x 1 x 28.5	W/P TO F/C	8-12	71-106 (lb-in)

W/P—Water Pump
F/C—Engine Front Cover

Timing chain front cover bolt location and identification—3.0L (OHV) engine

7922KG48

- Fan/clutch assembly and shroud
- Accessory drive belt idlers, drive belts and the water pump pulley
- Power steering pump bracket retaining bolts. Leaving the hoses connected, place the pump/bracket assembly aside in a position to prevent fluid from leaking out.
- Compressor front support bracket but leave the compressor in place.
- Coolant bypass hose and heater hose at the water pump
- Upper radiator hose at the thermostat housing
- Coil wire from the distributor cap
- Cap with the secondary wires attached
- Distributor hold-down clamp and lift the distributor out of the front cover.
- Crankshaft damper and pulley

➡️**If the crankshaft pulley and vibration damper have to be separated, mark the damper and pulley so they may be reassembled in the same relative position. This is important as the damper and pulley are initially balanced as a unit. If the crankshaft damper is being replaced, check if the original damper has balance pins installed. If so, new balance pins must be installed on the new damper in the same position as the original damper. The crankshaft pulley, new or original, must also be installed in the same relative position as originally installed.**

- Oil filter
- Lower radiator hose at the water pump
- Oil pan

➡️**The front cover cannot be removed without lowering the oil pan.**

- Front cover retaining bolts. It is not necessary to separate the water pump from the front cover.

➡️**Do not overlook the cover retaining bolt located behind the oil filter adapter. The front cover will break if pried on, and all retaining bolts are not removed.**

- Front cover and water pump as an assembly. Drive the crankshaft seal out of the front cover with a suitable seal driver. Remove and discard the cover gasket.

➡️**The front cover contains the oil pump, water pump and crankshaft seal. If a new front cover is to be installed, remove the water pump and oil pump from the old front cover and install them on the new cover along with a new crankshaft seal.**

- Camshaft bolt and washer from the end of the camshaft
- Distributor drive gear, camshaft sprocket, crankshaft sprocket and timing chain

➡️**If the crankshaft sprocket is difficult to remove, pry the sprocket off the shaft using a pair of large prybars positioned on both sides of the sprocket.**

To install:

3. Clean all gasket mating surfaces. If reusing the front cover, replace the front cover oil seal.

4. If removed, install the timing chain vibration damper. Tighten the mounting bolts to 71–123 inch lbs. (8–14 Nm).

5. Rotate the crankshaft to position the No. 1 piston at TDC and the crankshaft keyway at the 12 o'clock position.

6. Lubricate the timing chain with engine oil.

7. Install or connect the following:

- Camshaft sprocket, crankshaft sprocket and timing chain. Be sure the timing marks align.
- Distributor drive gear. Install the bolt and washer assembly on the end of the camshaft and tighten to 30–37 ft. lbs. (40–50 Nm).
- New crankshaft seal in the front cover and lubricate the seal lip with engine oil.
- New gasket on the cylinder block and install the front cover using dowels for proper alignment. Install the front cover retaining bolts and tighten to 15–22 ft. lbs. (20–30 Nm).
- Oil pan
- Lower radiator hose
- Oil filter

8. Coat the crankshaft damper sealing surface with clean engine oil. Apply a small amount of silicone sealer to the crankshaft keyway.

9. Position the crankshaft pulley key in the crankshaft keyway and install the damper, using a suitable installation tool.

10. Install or connect the following:

- Damper washer and retaining bolt and tighten to 103–132 ft. lbs. (140–180 Nm).
- Crankshaft pulley and tighten the

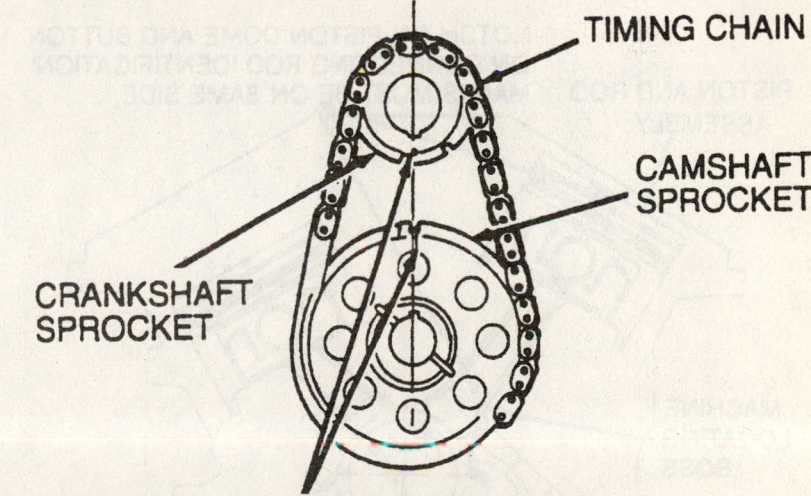

POSITIONING OF TIMING MARKS AND KEYWAYS IN CAMSHAFT AND CRANKSHAFT SPROCKETS MUST BE IN LINE AS SHOWN WITH NO. 1 PISTON AT TOP DEAD CENTER FIRING

7922QG21

The timing marks should be facing each other, when the timing chain is installed correctly—3.8L engines

retaining bolts to 20–28 ft. lbs. (26–38 Nm).
- Coolant bypass hose
- Distributor with the rotor pointing at the No. 1 distributor cap tower
- Distributor cap and coil wire
- Upper radiator hose at the thermostat housing
- Heater hose
- Compressor and mounting brackets. Tighten the retaining bolts to 30–45 ft. lbs. (41–61 Nm).
- Power steering pump and mounting bracket. Tighten the retaining bolts to 30–45 ft. lbs. (41–61 Nm).
- Water pump pulley. Position the accessory drive belts over the pulleys.
- Fan/clutch assembly and fan shroud. Cross-tighten the fan/clutch assembly retaining bolts to 12–18 ft. lbs. (16–24 Nm).

11. Fill the crankcase with the proper type and quantity of engine oil. Fill and bleed the cooling system. Connect the negative battery cable.

12. Start the engine and check for leaks. Check the ignition timing and curb idle speed and adjust, as necessary.

Piston and Ring Positioning

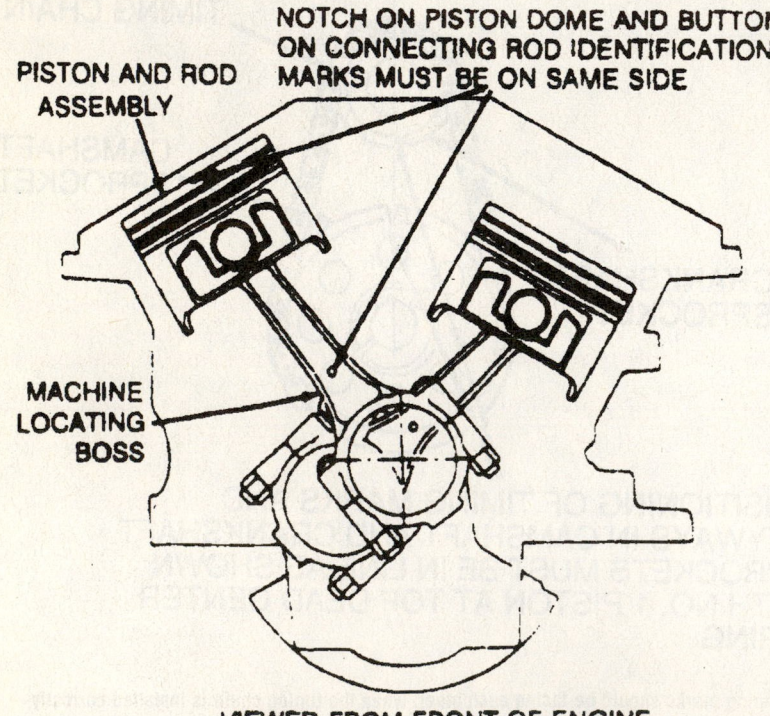

NOTCH ON PISTON DOME AND BUTTON ON CONNECTING ROD IDENTIFICATION MARKS MUST BE ON SAME SIDE

PISTON AND ROD ASSEMBLY

MACHINE LOCATING BOSS

VIEWED FROM FRONT OF ENGINE

7924AG15

3.0L and 3.8L engines—piston and connecting rod assembly positioning

FUEL SYSTEM

Fuel System Service Precautions

Safety is the most important factor when performing not only fuel system maintenance, but any type of maintenance. Failure to conduct maintenance and repairs in a safe manner may result in serious personal injury or death. Work on a vehicle's fuel system components can be accomplished safely and effectively by adhering to the following rules and guidelines.

- To avoid the possibility of fire and personal injury, always disconnect the negative battery cable unless the repair or test procedure requires that battery voltage by applied.
- Always relieve the fuel system pressure prior to disconnecting any fuel system component (injector, fuel rail, pressure regulator, etc.) fitting or fuel line connection. Exercise extreme caution whenever relieving fuel system pressure, to avoid exposing skin, face and eyes to fuel spray. Please be advised that fuel under pressure may penetrate the skin or any part of the body that it contacts.
- Always place a shop towel or rag around the fitting or connection prior to loosening to absorb any excess fuel due to spillage. Ensure that all fuel spillage is quickly remove from engine surfaces. Ensure that all fuel-soaked cloths or towels are deposited into a flame-proof waste container with a lid.
- Always keep a dry chemical (Class B) fire extinguisher near the work area.
- Do not allow fuel spray or fuel vapors to come into contact with a light bulb, spark or open flame.
- Always use a second wrench when loosening or tightening fuel line connections fittings. This will prevent unnecessary stress and torsion to fuel piping. Always follow the proper torque specifications.
- Always replace worn fuel fitting O-rings with new ones. Do not substitute fuel hose where rigid pipe is installed.

Fuel System Pressure

RELIEVING

All Sequential Electronic Fuel Injection (SEFI) engines are equipped with a pressure relief valve located on the fuel supply manifold. Remove the fuel tank cap and attach a fuel pressure gauge to the valve to release the fuel pressure. Be sure to drain the fuel into a suitable container and to avoid gasoline spillage. If a pressure gauge is not available, disconnect the vacuum hose from the fuel pressure regulator and attach a hand-held vacuum pump. Apply about 25 in. Hg (84 kPa) of vacuum to the regulator to vent the fuel system pressure into the fuel tank through the fuel return hose. Note that this procedure will remove the fuel pressure from the lines, but not the fuel. Take precautions to avoid the risk of fire and use clean rags to soak up any spilled fuel when the lines are disconnected.

Fuel Filter

REMOVAL & INSTALLATION

Although the manufacturer does not specify a replacement interval for fuel filters, we at Chilton feel the fuel filter should be replaced every 30,000 miles (48,000 km) under normal conditions or 15,000 miles (24,000 km) under severe conditions. Those intervals are industry standards.

1. Relieve the fuel system pressure.
2. Raise and support the vehicle safely on jackstands.

3. Place a rag under the fuel filter to catch any residual fuel that may leak out when the filter is removed.

4. Remove the push-connect fittings at both ends of the fuel filter.

5. Install retainer clips in each fitting.

6. Note the flow arrow direction for installation reference.

7. Remove the fuel filter by pulling it from the bracket.

To install:

8. Install the fuel filter in its bracket, ensuring proper direction of flow as noted earlier.

9. Install push-connect fittings at both ends of the fuel filter.

10. Start the engine and check the filter connections for leaks by running the tip of your finger around each connection.

11. Turn the engine off and lower the vehicle.

Fuel Pump

REMOVAL & INSTALLATION

➡**To gain access to the fuel pump, it is necessary to remove the fuel tank.**

1. Depressurize the fuel system and remove the fuel tank from the vehicle.

2. Remove any dirt that has accumulated around the fuel pump module attaching flange to prevent it from entering the tank during service.

3. Turn the fuel pump module locking ring counterclockwise using a locking ring removal tool or a brass drift, and remove the locking ring.

4. Remove the fuel pump module.

5. Remove the seal gasket and discard it.

To install:

6. Put a light coating of grease on a new seal ring to hold it in place during assembly. Install it in the fuel tank ring groove.

7. Insert the fuel pump module into the fuel tank, then secure it in place with the locking ring. Tighten the ring until secure.

8. Install the tank in the vehicle.

9. Install a minimum of 10 gallons (38L) of fuel and check for leaks.

10. Install a pressure gauge on the throttle body valve and turn the ignition **ON** for 3 seconds. Turn the key **OFF**, then repeat the key cycle 5 to 10 times until the pressure gauge shows at least 30 psi. (207 kPa).

11. Check for fuel leaks at the fittings.

12. Remove the pressure gauge.

13. Start the engine and check for fuel leaks.

Fuel Injectors

REMOVAL & INSTALLATION

1. Remove the upper intake manifold.
2. Remove the fuel injection supply manifold.

3. Carefully remove the fuel charging wiring harness connectors from the fuel injectors.

4. Pull fuel injector body up while gently rocking fuel injector from side to side.

To install:

5. Inspect fuel injector O-rings for signs of deterioration and replace as required.

➡**Never use silicone grease on fuel injectors.**

6. Lubricate O-rings with clean engine oil and install fuel injectors using a slight twisting motion.

7. Install fuel injection supply manifold.

8. Install the fuel charging wiring connectors.

9. Install the upper intake manifold.

DRIVE TRAIN

Transaxle Assembly

REMOVAL & INSTALLATION

1. Remove or disconnect the following:
- Battery and battery tray
- Hood and cowl vent
- Air cleaner assembly
- All transaxle electrical harnesses
- Transaxle shift cable from the lever by unsnapping the shift cable end from the lever ball stud
- Transaxle fluid cooler lines

➡**Leave the 2 lower engine-to-transaxle bolts in place to hold the transaxle secure against the engine block until a suitable jack can be placed under the transaxle to support it during removal.**

- Upper transaxle-to-engine bolts
- Engine electrical harness bracket
- Battery cable bracket

➡**Install engine lifting eyes to support the engine during transaxle removal.**

2. Install an engine support kit and suitably support the engine.

3. Raise and support the vehicle.

4. Remove or disconnect the following:

- Transaxle fluid
- Front wheels
- Halfshafts

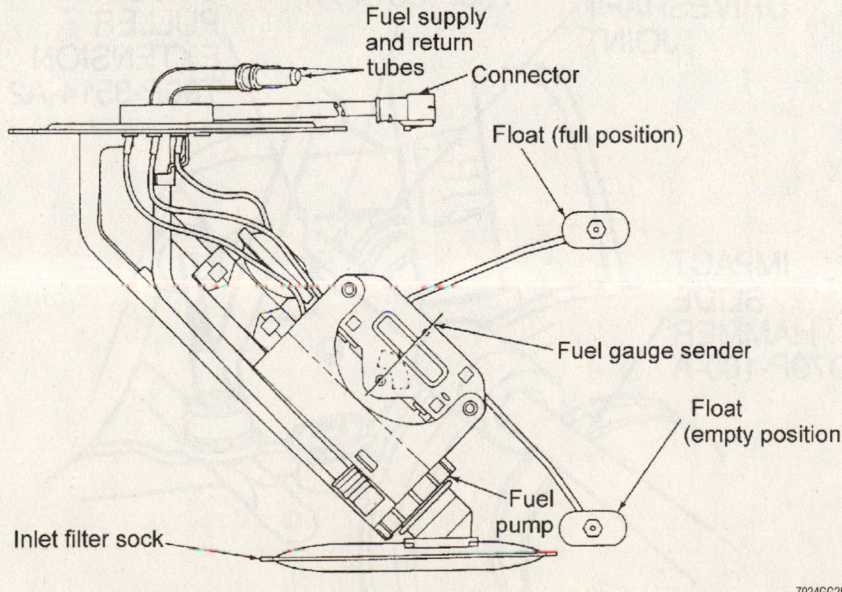

Fuel supply and return tubes — Connector
Float (full position)
Fuel gauge sender
Float (empty position)
Fuel pump
Inlet filter sock

7924GG25

In-tank electric fuel pump and related components

- Bolts retaining the rear engine support to the transaxle
- Front subframe
- Speedometer cable from the vehicle speed sensor
- Starter
- Transaxle housing cover
- The 4 flexplate-to-converter nuts

5. Support the transaxle with a suitable jack and remove the remaining transaxle-to-engine bolts.

6. Remove the engine bracket-to-transaxle bolts.

7. Separate the transaxle from the engine block by carefully moving the transaxle rearward until enough clearance exists to remove the transaxle from the engine compartment.

8. Slowly lower the transaxle from the engine compartment.

To install:

9. Place the transaxle on a suitable jack and position it in place.

10. Install or connect the following:
- Engine bracket-to-transaxle bolts, and tighten the bolts to 39–53 ft. lbs. (53–72 Nm).
- Lower transaxle-to-engine bolts, and tighten the bolts to 39–53 ft. lbs. (53–72 Nm).
- Flexplate-to-torque converter bolts, and tighten them to 20–34 ft. lbs. (27–46 Nm).
- Transaxle housing cover, and tighten the bolts to 80–106 inch lbs. (9–12 Nm).
- Starter motor, and connect the electrical harness.
- Speedometer cable
- Front subframe
- The 4 bolts retaining the rear engine support, and tighten them to 39–53 ft. lbs. (53–72 Nm).
- Both halfshafts
- Front wheels and lower the vehicle.

11. Remove the engine support kit.

12. Install or connect the following:
- Transaxle electrical harnesses
- Upper transaxle-to-engine bolts and tighten to 39–53 ft. lbs. (53–72 Nm).
- Fluid cooler-to-transaxle lines
- Transaxle shift cable to the manual lever ball stud
- Air cleaner assembly
- Cowl vent and hood
- Battery tray and battery

13. Fill the transaxle with proper amount of Mercon® fluid.

14. Connect the positive, then the negative battery cable.

Halfshafts

REMOVAL & INSTALLATION

➡ **Do not begin this removal procedure unless a new wheel hub retainer nut, a new retainer circlip and a new lower ball joint-to-front wheel knuckle retaining bolt and nut are available. Once removed, these parts must not be reused during assembly. Their torque holding ability, or retention capability, is diminished during removal.**

1. Remove or disconnect the following:
- Front wheels
- Axle hub nut. Discard the nut.
- Ball joint-to-front wheel knuckle retaining nut. Drive the bolt out of the front wheel knuckle using a punch and hammer.
- Front brake anti-lock sensor and position it out of the way.
- Ball joint from the knuckle

✳✳ WARNING

Use care to prevent damage to the CV-joint boot.

- Stabilizer bar link at the front stabilizer bar

➡ **Make sure the CV-joint puller does not contact the transaxle shaft speed sensor. Damage to the sensor will result.**

2. Install a CV-joint puller between the inboard CV-joint and the transaxle case.

3. Install a CV-joint extension into the puller and hand-tighten.

4. Using a slide hammer, remove the driveshaft from the transaxle.

✳✳ WARNING

Do not allow the halfshaft to hang unsupported. Damage to the CV-joint may result. Do not wrap wire around the joint boot. Damage to the boot may result.

5. Support the end of the halfshaft assembly by suspending it from the chassis using a length of wire.

✳✳ WARNING

Never use a hammer to separate the outboard CV-joint from the wheel hub. Damage to the outboard CV joint threads and internal components may result.

6. Separate the outboard CV-joint from the wheel hub using a front hub remover/replacer. Make sure the hub

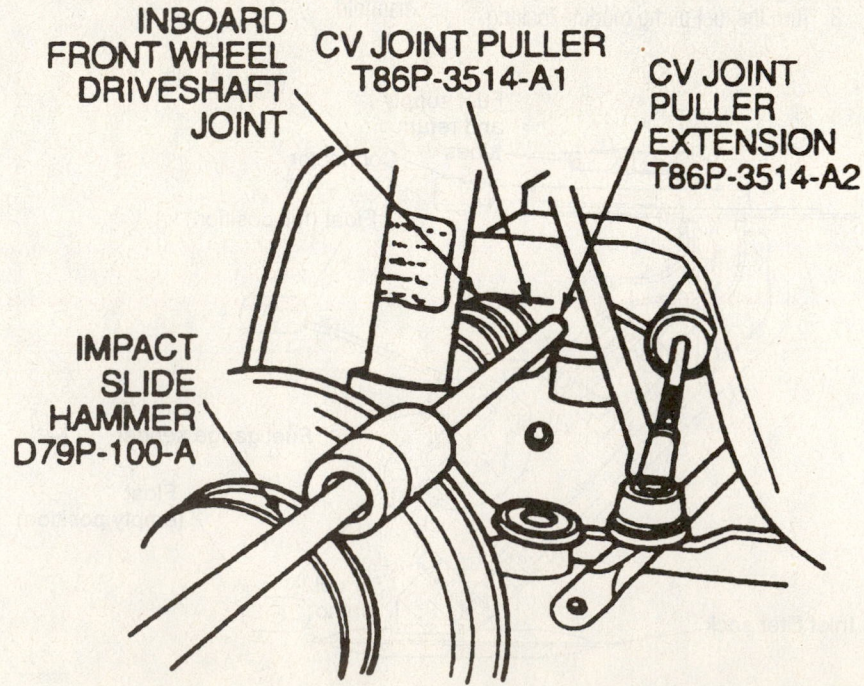

Remove the halfshaft from the transaxle using a CV-joint puller, extension and impact slide

7924GG09

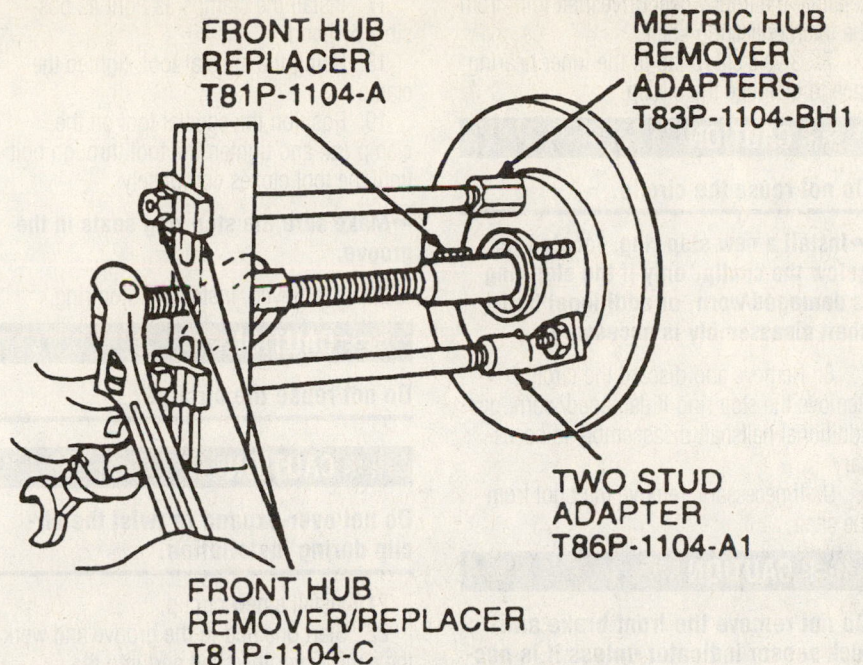

FRONT HUB
REPLACER
T81P-1104-A

METRIC HUB
REMOVER
ADAPTERS
T83P-1104-BH1

TWO STUD
ADAPTER
T86P-1104-A1

FRONT HUB
REMOVER/REPLACER
T81P-1104-C

7924GG10

The front hub adapter must be used to remove the hub without damage

remover adapter is fully threaded onto the hub stud.

✳✳ WARNING

Do not move vehicle without the outboard CV-joint properly installed as damage to the bearing may occur.

7. Remove the halfshaft assembly from the vehicle.
To install:

✳✳ WARNING

Do not reuse the retainer circlip. A new circlip must be installed each time the inboard CV-joint stub shaft is installed into the transaxle differential.

8. Install a new retainer circlip on the inboard CV-joint stub shaft by starting one end in the groove and working the retainer circlip over the inboard shaft housing end and into the groove. The will avoid over-expanding the circlip.

➡**A non-metallic mallet may be used to aid in seating the retainer circlip into the differential side gear groove. If a mallet is necessary, tap only on the outboard CV-joint shaft.**

9. Carefully align the splines of the inboard CV-joint stub shaft housing with the splines in the differential. Exerting some force, push the inboard CV-joint stub shaft housing into the differential until the retainer circlip is felt to seat in the differential side gear. Use care to prevent damage to the inboard CV-joint stub shaft and transaxle seal.

10. Carefully align the splines of the outboard CV-joint with the splines in the wheel hub and push the shaft into the wheel hub as far as possible.

11. Temporarily fasten the front disc brake rotor to the wheel hub with washers and 2 lug nuts. Insert a steel rod into the front disc brake rotor and rotate clockwise to contact the front wheel knuckle to prevent the front disc brake rotor from turning when the nut is tightened.

➡**A new front axle wheel hub retaining nut must be installed.**

12. Manually thread the front axle wheel hub retaining nut onto the outboard CV-joint stub shaft housing as far as possible.

➡**A new bolt and nut must be used to connect the front suspension arm to the knuckle.**

13. Connect the front suspension lower arm to the front wheel knuckle. Tighten the nut and bolt to 40–55 ft. lbs. (54–75 Nm).

14. Install the front brake anti-lock sensor.

15. Connect the front stabilizer bark link and tighten to 35–45 ft. lbs. (47–65 Nm).

➡**Do not use power or impact tools to tighten the hub nut.**

16. Tighten front axle wheel hub retaining nut to 157–212 ft. lbs. (213–288 Nm).

17. Install the front wheels and lower the vehicle.

18. Fill the transaxle to the proper level with Mercon® automatic transmission fluid.

CV-Joint

OVERHAUL

Inboard Joint

1. Remove the clamps.
2. Separate the front wheel driveshaft joint boot from the inboard CV joint housing.
3. Check the CV joint grease for contamination by rubbing it between two fingers. Any gritty feeling indicates contamination.

➡**Other than the front wheel driveshaft joint boot, the interconnecting shaft and inboard CV joint housing are not repairable. Install a new assembly if worn/damaged.**

4. To install a new inboard CV joint housing assembly front wheel driveshaft joint boot, remove the front wheel driveshaft joint and boot.
5. Slide the front wheel driveshaft joint boot off the interconnecting shaft.
6. Install the front wheel driveshaft joint boot.
7. Position the boot into the small boot groove.
8. Using the special tool, install the small clamp.
9. Position the special tool on the clamp ear, and tighten the tool through bolt until the tool closes completely.
10. Install the front wheel driveshaft joint boot and the joint.
11. Fill the inboard CV joint housing with 475 grams (16.75 ounces) of grease. Spread the remaining grease evenly inside the front wheel driveshaft joint boot. Use constant velocity joint grease, only.

➡**Remove all excess grease from the CV joint external surface and the front wheel driveshaft joint boot sealing surface.**

12. Seat the front wheel driveshaft joint boot in the inboard CV joint housing boot groove.

13. Set the halfshaft assembled length to specification. Halfshaft assembled length, left side: 612.6 mm (24.5 in); right side: 746.4 mm (29.85 in). Measure the entire assembly length. Push in or pull out on the inner joint as necessary to adjust the halfshaft assembled length to specification.

14. Hold the inner joint to prevent the assembled length from changing, and insert a small flat blade screwdriver between the boot and the joint to equalize the pressure.

➡**Make sure the front wheel driveshaft joint boot seats in the groove.**

15. Install the clamps as tight as possible by hand.

16. Using the special tool, tighten the clamp.

17. Position the special tool on the clamp ear, and tighten the tool through bolt until the tool closes completely.

18. Move the CV joints through their full range of travel at various angles. The joints must flex, extend and compress smoothly.

Outboard Joint

※※ CAUTION

Do not allow the vise jaws to contact the front wheel driveshaft joint boot or the clamp. Use a vise equipped with soft jaws or wood blocks.

1. Clamp the halfshaft assembly in a vise.

2. Remove the clamps.

3. Separate the front wheel driveshaft joint boot from the front wheel driveshaft joint.

4. Check the CV joint grease for contamination by rubbing it between two fingers. Any gritty feeling indicates contamination.

5. If the grease is contaminated/additional disassembly is necessary, proceed as follows.

※※ CAUTION

Do not allow the front wheel driveshaft joint to fall.

6. Using a brass drift and a hammer,

separate the front wheel driveshaft joint from the interconnecting shaft.

7. Give a sharp tap to the inner bearing race to dislodge the circlip.

※※ CAUTION

Do not reuse the circlip.

➡**Install a new stop ring, located just below the circlip, only if the stop ring is damaged/worn, or additional halfshaft disassembly is necessary.**

8. Remove and discard the circlip. Remove the stop ring if damaged/worn, or additional halfshaft disassembly is necessary.

9. If necessary, remove the boot from the shaft.

※※ CAUTION

Do not remove the front brake anti-lock sensor indicator unless it is necessary to install a new one.

10. Position the special tool on a press bed, and place the front wheel driveshaft joint on the special tool.

11. Press the damaged front brake anti-lock sensor indicator off of the front wheel driveshaft joint and discard it.

※※ CAUTION

Do not damage the front brake anti-lock sensor indicator. Tooth damage will affect brake performance.

12. If removed, position the special tool on a press bed, and place the new front brake anti-lock sensor indicator on the special tool.

13. Position the front wheel driveshaft joint in the special tool.

14. Place a steel plate across the front wheel driveshaft joint back face.

➡**Installation is complete when the front wheel driveshaft joint bottoms out in the special tool.**

15. Press the front brake anti-lock sensor indicator on the front wheel driveshaft joint.

➡**Make sure the front wheel driveshaft joint boot seats in the shaft boot groove.**

16. If removed, install the clamp and the front wheel driveshaft joint boot.

17. Install the clamps as tight as possible by hand.

18. Using the special tool, tighten the clamp.

19. Position the special tool on the clamp ear, and tighten the tool through bolt until the tool closes completely.

➡**Make sure the stop ring seats in the groove.**

20. If removed, install the stop ring.

※※ CAUTION

Do not reuse the circlip.

※※ CAUTION

Do not over-expand or twist the circlip during installation.

21. Install a new circlip.

22. Start one end in the groove and work the circlip over the shaft and into the groove. This will avoid over-expanding the circlip.

23. Fill the front wheel driveshaft joint with 180 grams (6.3 ounces) of grease. Spread the remaining grease evenly inside the front wheel driveshaft joint boot. Use constant velocity joint grease only!

➡**The front wheel driveshaft joint has seated when the circlip locks in the groove cut in the inner race.**

24. Using a non-metallic hammer, tap the front wheel driveshaft joint onto the interconnecting shaft. Make sure the front wheel driveshaft joint has locked on the interconnecting shaft by attempting to pull the joint off the shaft.

➡**Remove all excess grease from the front wheel driveshaft joint external surface and the front wheel driveshaft joint boot mating surface.**

25. Seat the front wheel driveshaft joint boot in the front wheel driveshaft joint boot groove.

26. Install the clamp as tight as possible by hand.

27. Using the special tool, tighten the clamp.

28. Position the special tool on the clamp ear, and tighten the tool through bolt until the tool closes completely.

STEERING AND SUSPENSION

Air Bag (Supplemental Restraint) System

The Supplemental Restraint System (SRS) is designed to work in conjunction with the standard 3-point safety belts to reduce injury in a head-on collision.

✳✳ CAUTION

The SRS can actually cause physical injury or death if the safety belts are not used, or if the manufacturer's warnings are not followed. The manufacturer's warnings can be found in your owner's manual, or, in some cases, on your sun visor.

The SRS is comprised of the following components:

- Driver's side air bag module
- Passenger's side air bag module
- Right-hand and left-hand primary crash front air bag sensors
- Air bag diagnostic monitor computer
- Electrical wiring

The SRS primary crash front air bag sensors are hard-wired to the air bag modules and determine when the air bags are deployed. During a frontal collision, the sensors quickly inflate the 2 air bags to reduce injury by cushioning the driver and front passenger from striking the dashboard, windshield, steering wheel and any other hard surfaces. The air bag inflates so quickly (in a fraction of a second) that in most cases it is fully inflated before you actually start to move during a collision.

Since the SRS is a complicated and essentially important system, its components are constantly being tested by a diagnostic computer. The computer illuminates the air bag indicator light on the instrument cluster for approximately 6 seconds when the ignition switch is turned to the **RUN** position when the SRS is functioning properly. After being illuminated for the 6 seconds, the indicator light should then turn off.

If the air bag light does not illuminate at all, stays on continuously, or flashes at any time, a problem has been detected by the diagnostic computer.

✳✳ CAUTION

If at any time the air bag light indicates that the computer has noted a problem, immediately diagnose the problem. A faulty SRS can cause severe physical injury or death.

SERVICE PRECAUTIONS

Whenever working around, or on, the air bag supplemental restraint system, ALWAYS adhere to the following warnings and cautions.

- Always wear safety glasses when servicing an air bag vehicle and when handling an air bag module.
- Carry a live air bag module with the bag and trim cover facing away from your body, so that an accidental deployment of the air bag will have a small chance of personal injury.
- Place an air bag module on a table or other flat surface with the bag and trim cover pointing up.
- Wear gloves, a dust mask and safety glasses whenever handling a deployed air bag module. The air bag surface may contain traces of sodium hydroxide, a byproduct of the gas that inflates the air bag and which can cause skin irritation.
- Ensure to wash your hands with mild soap and water after handling a deployed air bag.
- All air bag modules with discolored or damaged cover trim must be replaced, not repainted.
- All component replacement and wiring service must be made with the negative and positive battery cables disconnected from the battery for a minimum of 1 minute prior to attempting service or replacement.
- NEVER probe the air bag electrical terminals. Doing so could result in air bag deployment, which can cause serious physical injury.
- If the vehicle is involved in a fender-bender that results in a damaged front bumper or grille, the air bag sensors should be inspected to ensure that they were not damaged.
- If at any time, the air bag light indicates that the computer has noted a problem, immediately diagnose the problem. A faulty SRS can cause severe physical injury or death.

DISARMING THE SYSTEM

1. Disconnect the negative battery cable from the battery.
2. Disconnect the positive battery cable from the battery.
3. Wait 1 minute. This time is required for the back-up power supply in the air bag diagnostic monitor to completely drain. The system is now disarmed.

ARMING THE SYSTEM

1. Connect the positive battery cable.
2. Connect the negative battery cable.
3. Stand outside the vehicle and carefully turn the ignition to the **RUN** position. Be sure that no part of your body is in front of the air bag module on the steering wheel, to prevent injury in case of an accidental air bag deployment.
4. Ensure the air bag indicator light turns off after approximately 6 seconds. If the light does not illuminate at all, does not turn off, or starts to flash, diagnose the problem. If the light does turn off after 6 seconds and does not flash, the SRS is working properly.

Rack and Pinion Steering Gear

REMOVAL & INSTALLATION

1. Remove or disconnect the following:
   - Front wheels
   - Tie rod end cotter pins and castle nuts
   - Tie rod ends from the knuckles
   - Front stabilizer bar
2. Position the dash opening weather seal for the steering column out of the way.
3. Remove or disconnect the following:
   - Pinch bolt retaining the steering column intermediate shaft coupling
   - Steering gear retaining nuts/bolts
   - Rear subframe bolts

➡**Use wire to support exhaust components unless you are removing them completely.**

4. Support the exhaust system flex tube and remove the flex tube-to-dual converter Y-pipe attachment.
5. Lower the vehicle slightly until the rear subframe separates from the body approximately 4 inches (10cm).
6. Remove the heat shield band and fold the heat shield down.

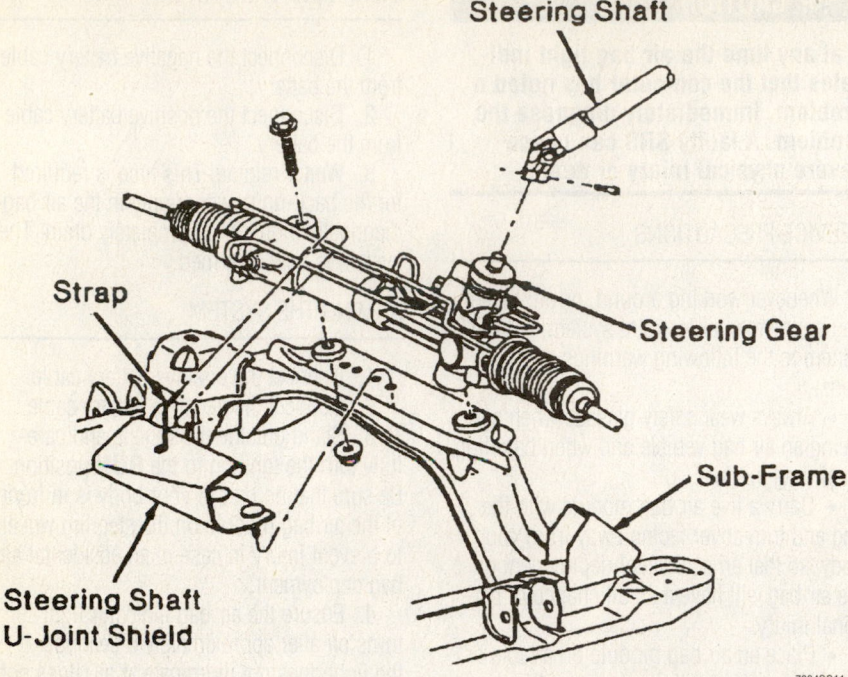

Steering Shaft

Strap

Steering Gear

Sub-Frame

Steering Shaft U-Joint Shield

7924GG11

Exploded view of the rack and pinion steering gear mounting on the front subframe of the

7. Rotate the rack and pinion assembly to clear the bolts from the front subframe, and pull toward the driver's side of the vehicle.

8. Place a drain pan under the vehicle and disconnect the power steering lines.

9. Remove the rack and pinion assembly through the driver's side of the vehicle.

To install:

10. Install new Teflon® O-rings on the power steering line fittings.

11. Place the rack and pinion retaining bolts in the gear housing.

12. Install or connect the following:
   - Rack and pinion assembly through the driver's side of the vehicle
   - Power steering lines on the rack and pinion assembly
   - Rack and pinion assembly on the subframe
   - Strap on the heat shield
   - Tie rod ends to the knuckles. Tighten the castle nuts and install the cotter pins.
   - Stabilizer bar
   - Rack and pinion assembly retaining bolts, and tighten them to 85–99 ft. lbs. (115–135 Nm).

13. Raise the vehicle until the subframe contacts the body.

14. Install or connect the following:
   - Rear subframe retaining bolts, and tighten them to 83–112 ft. lbs. (113–153 Nm).

- Exhaust system flex tube-to-dual converter Y-pipe
- Front wheels

15. Using a new pinch bolt, install the steering column intermediate shaft coupling on the rack input shaft. Tighten the pinch bolt to 25–33 ft. lbs. (34–46 Nm).

16. Position the steering column opening weather seal over the steering gear housing.

17. Lower the vehicle.

18. Fill the power steering oil reservoir.

19. Start the vehicle and check for leaks.

20. Check for proper wheel alignment and steering wheel position.

MacPherson Struts

REMOVAL & INSTALLATION

➡ **Do not begin this procedure unless a new front axle wheel hub nut, a new lower arm ball joint pinch bolt and nut, and a new tie rod and knuckle nut and cotter pin are available. Once removed, these parts must not be reused during assembly. Their torque holding ability, or retention capability, is diminished during removal.**

1. Turn the ignition switch **OFF** and place the steering column in the unlocked position.

2. Loosen but do not remove the 3 front strut-to-tower nuts.

✸✸ WARNING

Do not raise the vehicle by the lower arms.

3. Remove or disconnect the following:
   - Front wheel
   - Caliper and suspend it out of the way using a piece of wire

➡ **The hydraulic brake system will need to be bled if the brake hose is removed from the caliper.**

   - Rotor
   - Axle hub nut
   - Wheel bearing and knuckle as an assembly
   - Tie rod end from the front wheel knuckle

✸✸ WARNING

Use extreme care to not damage the ball joint boot seal.

   - Stabilizer bar link from the lower arm
   - Lower arm-to-front wheel knuckle pinch bolt and nut. Discard them.
   - Lower arm from the knuckle
   - Speed sensor bracket and speed sensor from the front wheel knuckle
   - Strut-to-front wheel knuckle pinch bolt
   - Knuckle and wheel hub assembly from the front strut
   - The 3 front strut mounting bracket-to-strut tower nuts and remove the front strut assembly from the vehicle.

To install:

4. Install or connect the following:
   - Front strut assembly and tighten the strut-to-strut tower mounting bolts hand-tight.
   - Knuckle and wheel hub assembly
   - New strut-to-wheel knuckle pinch bolt and tighten to 85–97 ft. lbs. (115–132 Nm).
   - Halfshaft into the wheel hub
   - Lower arm, ensuring that the ball stud groove is properly positioned
   - New pinch bolt and nut. Tighten to 46–52 ft. lbs. (62–71 Nm).
   - Knuckle making sure the front stabilizer bar link is properly positioned.

➡ **The words "top left-hand" and "top right-hand" are molded into the stabilizer bar link for correct assembly reference.**

- New stabilizer link nut and tighten to 66–74 ft. lbs. (90–100 Nm).
- Tie rod to the front wheel knuckle. Tighten the new tie rod castellated nut to 66–74 ft. lbs. (90–100 Nm).

- Front brake anti-lock sensor and bracket on the knuckle
- Rotor
- Wheels

5. Tighten the 3 strut mounting bracket-to-strut tower bolts to 25–30 ft. lbs. (35–40 Nm).

6. Lower the vehicle and tighten the front axle wheel hub nut to 170–202 ft. lbs. (230–275 Nm).

7. Check the wheel alignment.

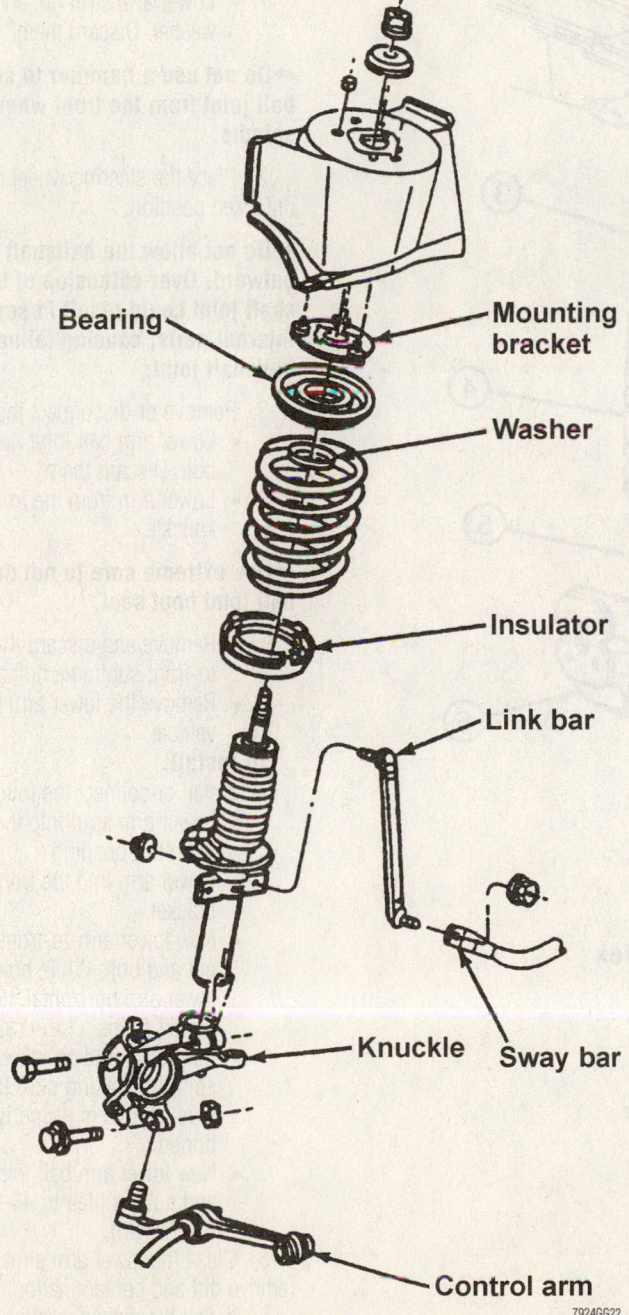

Bearing

Mounting bracket

Washer

Insulator

Link bar

Knuckle   **Sway bar**

Control arm

7924GG22

Exploded view of the MacPherson strut and related components

Shock Absorbers

REMOVAL & INSTALLATION

1. Loosen the lug nuts on the rear wheels.
2. Raise and safely support the vehicle.
3. Remove the rear wheels.
4. Position a jack under the rear axle assembly and raise it slightly to put the suspension at normal ride height.
5. Remove the lower shock absorber bolt/nut and disconnect the shock from the rear axle.
6. Lower the rear axle slightly to help aid removal of the upper shock absorber bolt/nut.
7. Remove the shock absorber.

To install:

8. Attach the shock absorber to the upper mounting bracket and install a new retaining bolt/nut.
9. Slowly raise the rear axle assembly with a jack, and guide the lower shock absorber into the bracket on the rear axle assembly. Install a new retaining bolt/nut.
10. Raise the rear suspension to normal ride height and tighten the shock absorber retaining bolts to 50–68 ft. lbs. (68–92 Nm).
11. Install the wheels.
12. Lower the vehicle.

Coil Springs

REMOVAL & INSTALLATION

1. Raise and safely support the vehicle.
2. Remove the rear wheels.

➡ **The rear axle will need to be supported when the shock absorbers are removed.**

3. Position an adjustable stand or jack under the rear axle.
4. Remove the shock absorber-to-rear axle nut and disconnect the shock from the rear axle.
5. Slowly lower the rear axle assembly until the rear spring can be removed.
6. Remove the rear spring.

To install:

7. Position the rear spring insulator on the rear axle assembly and press the insulator downward into place. Verify rear spring insulator is properly seated into correct position.

8. Slowly raise the rear axle assembly with a jack, and guide the upper rear spring insulator onto the upper spring seat on the underbody.

9. Position the shock absorber on the lower rear axle assembly and install new nuts and bolts. Tighten to 50–68 ft. lbs. (68–92 Nm).

10. Install the wheels.

11. Lower the vehicle.

Lower Ball Joint

REMOVAL & INSTALLATION

The lower ball joint and seal are an integral part of the lower control arm assembly, and can not be replaced separately. If the lower ball joint or seal is found to be defective, the lower control arm must be replaced as an assembly.

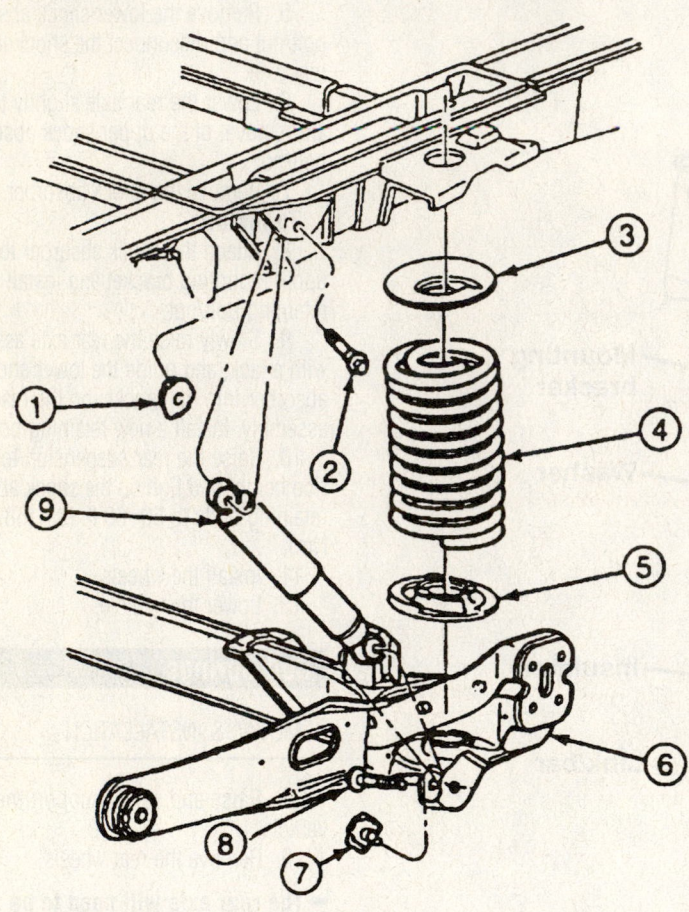

1   J-Nut
2   Bolt M12-1.75 x 66 Hex Flanged Head
3   Rear Spring Insulator (Upper)
4   Rear Spring
5   Rear Spring Insulator (Lower)
6   Axle Assembly
7   Nut
8   Bolt
9   Shock Absorber

7924GG12

Exploded view of the rear coil spring and shock absorber mounting between the axle and chassis

Lower Arm

REMOVAL & INSTALLATION

➡ **do not begin the removal procedure unless a new strut-to-lower arm nut, a new ball joint pinch bolt/nut and a new lower arm-to-front subframe bolt/nut are available.**

1. Remove or disconnect the following:
   - Wheels
   - Lower arm strut nut and dished washer. Discard them.

➡ **Do not use a hammer to separate the ball joint from the front wheel hub and spindle.**

2. Place the steering wheel in the unlocked position.

➡ **Do not allow the halfshaft to move outward. Over-extension of the halfshaft joint could result in separation of internal parts, causing failure of the halfshaft joint.**

3. Remove or disconnect the following:
   - Lower arm ball joint nut and pinch bolt. Discard them.
   - Lower arm from the front wheel knuckle

➡ **Use extreme care to not damage the ball joint boot seal.**

   - Remove and discard the lower arm-to-front subframe bolt and nut.
   - Remove the lower arm front the vehicle.

To install:

4. Install or connect the following:
   - Lower arm strut into the lower arm rear strut bushing
   - Lower arm into the front sub-frame bracket
   - New lower arm-to-front subframe nut and bolt. While holding the lower arm horizontal, tighten to 85–97 ft. lbs. (115–132 Nm).
   - Ball joint stud-to-wheel hub and spindle, making sure that the ball stud groove is properly positioned.
   - New lower arm ball joint pinch bolt and nut. Tighten to 46–52 ft. lbs. 62–71 Nm).

5. Clean the lower arm strut threads to remove dirt and contamination.

6. Install the dished washer with the dished side away from the lower arm rear strut bushing.

7. Install the front suspension lower arm strut-to-strut nut and tighten to 85–97 ft. lbs. (115–142 Nm).

8. Install the wheels.

9. Lower the vehicle.

LOWER ARM BUSHING REPLACEMENT

➡**Prior to starting this procedure, ensure that new replacement fasteners are available.**

1. Remove the lower arm from the vehicle.

2. Using a bushing remover, remove the bushing from the lower arm using a large C-clamp as a press.

To install:

3. Saturate the lower arm and new bushing in vegetable oil.

➡**Use only vegetable oil. Any mineral or petroleum based oil or brake fluid will deteriorate the rubber.**

4. Using a bushing driver, press the bushing into the lower arm using a C-clamp as a press.

5. Install the lower arm on the vehicle.

Hub and Wheel Bearing

ADJUSTMENT

Front

The front wheel bearings on the Ford Windstar are not adjustable. If the bearings become loose or make noise they must be replaced as an assembly.

Rear

1. Loosen the lug nuts on the rear wheel(s).

2. Block the front wheels, then raise and safely support the rear of the vehicle securely on jackstands.

3. Remove the rear wheel(s).

4. Remove the hub grease cap.

5. Remove the cotter pin.

6. Tighten nut to 18–23 ft. lbs. (24–31 Nm) while rotating the hub to set the end-play. Back off the nut and retighten to 18 inch lbs. (2 Nm).

7. Install a new cotter pin.

8. Install the hub grease cap.

9. Install the brake drum or disc.

10. Install the wheels

11. Lower the vehicle.

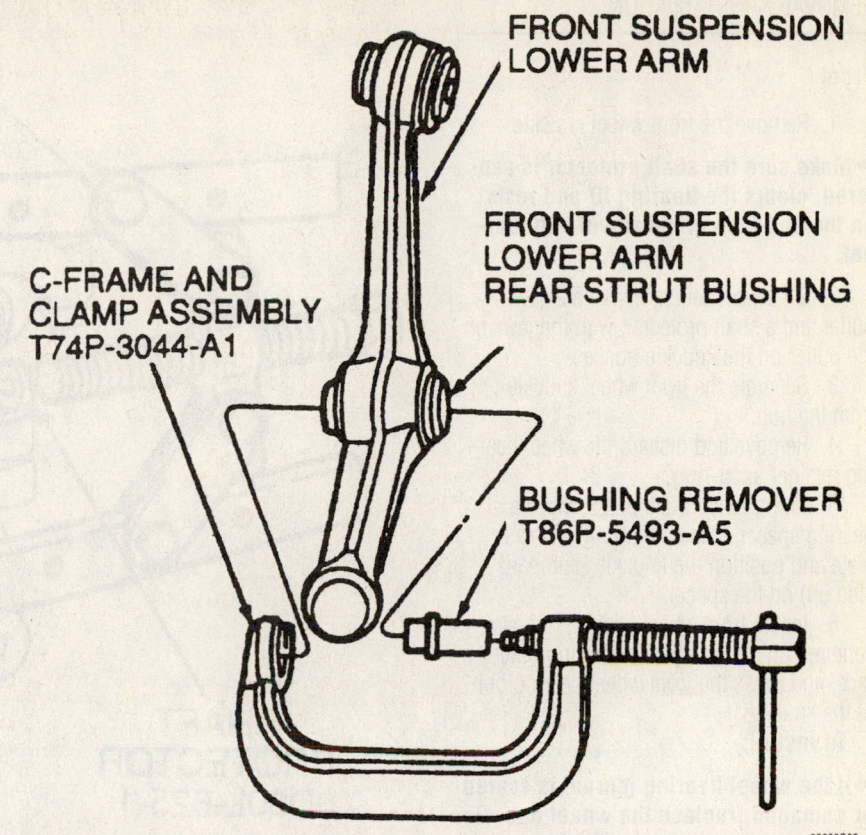

FRONT SUSPENSION LOWER ARM

FRONT SUSPENSION LOWER ARM REAR STRUT BUSHING

C-FRAME AND CLAMP ASSEMBLY T74P-3044-A1

BUSHING REMOVER T86P-5493-A5

89698G02

Removing the lower arm bushing using a C-clamp and the proper adapters

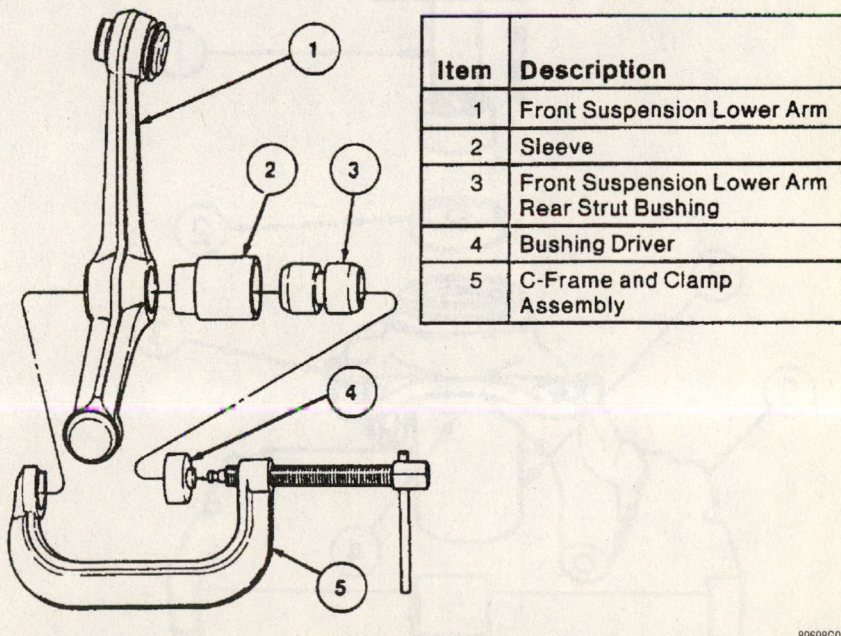

Item	Description
1	Front Suspension Lower Arm
2	Sleeve
3	Front Suspension Lower Arm Rear Strut Bushing
4	Bushing Driver
5	C-Frame and Clamp Assembly

89698G03

Installing the lower arm bushing using a C-clamp and the proper adapters

Turn to Section 5 for brake system applications

REMOVAL & INSTALLATION

Front

1. Remove the front wheel knuckle.

➡ **Make sure the shaft protector is centered, clears the bearing ID and rests on the end-face of the wheel hub journal.**

2. On a workbench, install a 2-jaw puller and a shaft protector, with the jaws of the puller on the knuckle bosses.

3. Separate the front wheel knuckle from the hub.

4. Remove and discard the wheel bearing retainer snap-ring.

5. Using a hydraulic press, place a bearing spacer, step side up, on a press plate and position the knuckle (outboard side up) on the spacer.

6. Install front wheel bearing remover centered on the front wheel bearing outer race, and press the front wheel bearing out of the knuckle.

To install:

➡ **If the wheel bearing journal is scored or damaged, replace the wheel hub. Do not attempt to service it. The front wheel bearings are of a cartridge**

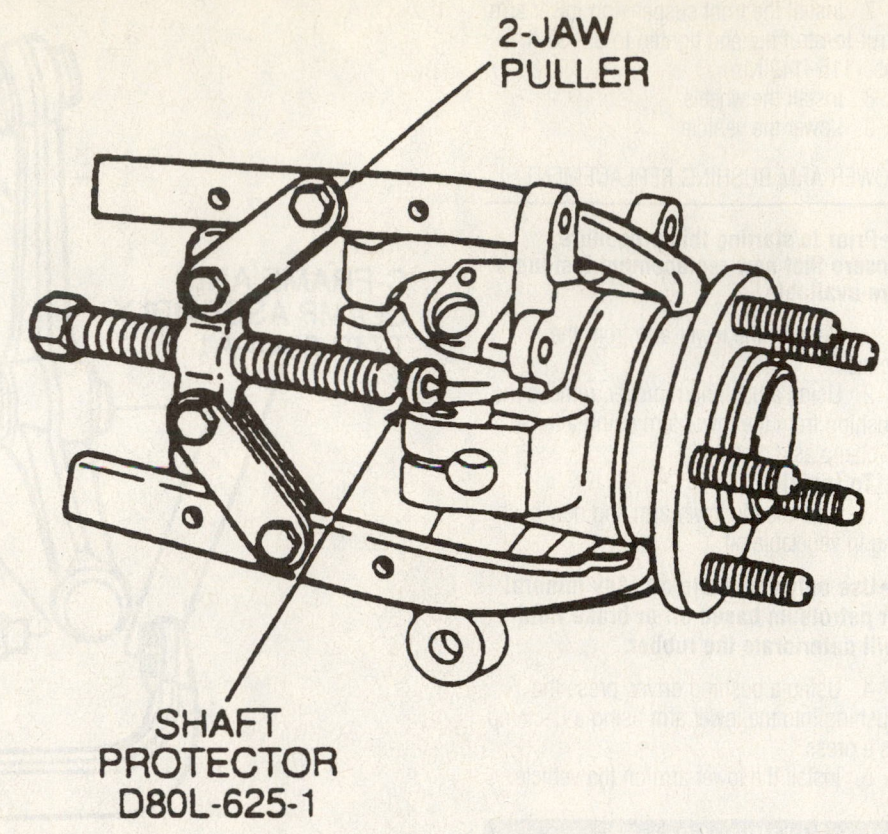

Use a 2-jaw puller to separate the knuckle from the hub

7924GG13

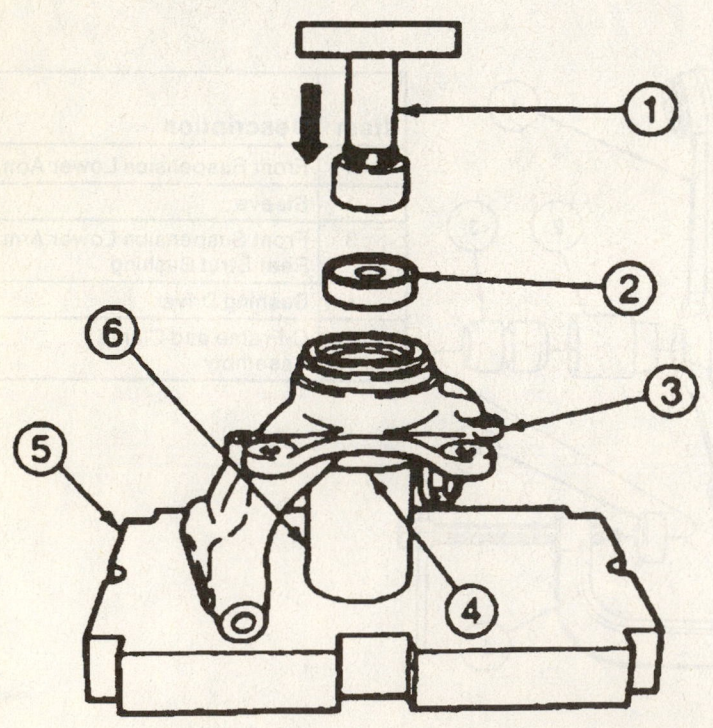

1 Arbor Press
2 Front Bearing Remover
3 Front Wheel Knuckle
4 Step Side Up
5 Press Plate
6 Front Bearing Spacer

7924GG14

Remove the wheel bearing from the knuckle using a hydraulic press and the proper adapters

design. Wheel bearings are pre-greased, sealed and require no scheduled maintenance. The front wheel bearings are preset and cannot be adjusted. If a front wheel bearing is disassembled for any reason, it must be replaced as an assembly. No individual components are available.

7. Thoroughly clean the wheel hub and bearing journal to ensure correct seating of the new wheel bearing.

8. Place the a bearing spacer, or equivalent, step side down, on a hydraulic press plate and position the front wheel knuckle (outboard side down) on the spacer.

9. Position a new wheel bearing in the inboard side of the wheel hub and spindle. Install a hub bearing replacer, with the undercut side facing the bearing, and press the wheel bearing into the knuckle.

➡Make sure the wheel bearing seats completely against the shoulder of the knuckle bore.

10. Install the new front wheel bearing retainer snap-ring into the hub and spindle groove.

11. Place a bearing spacer on the arbor press plate, and position the wheel hub on

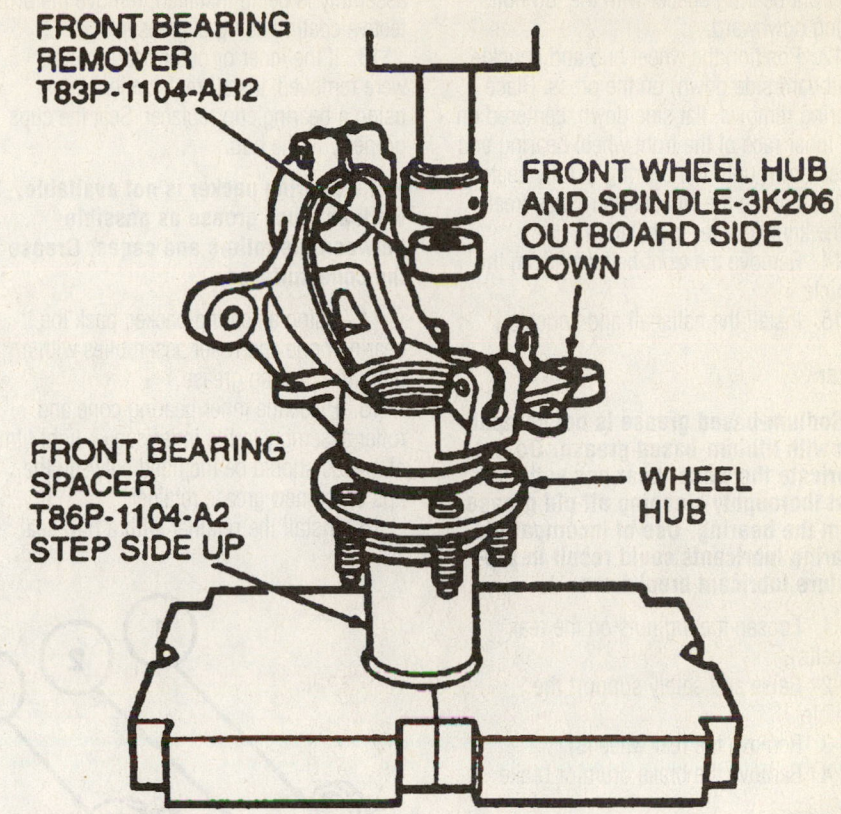

Press the knuckle and hub together using a hydraulic press, as shown

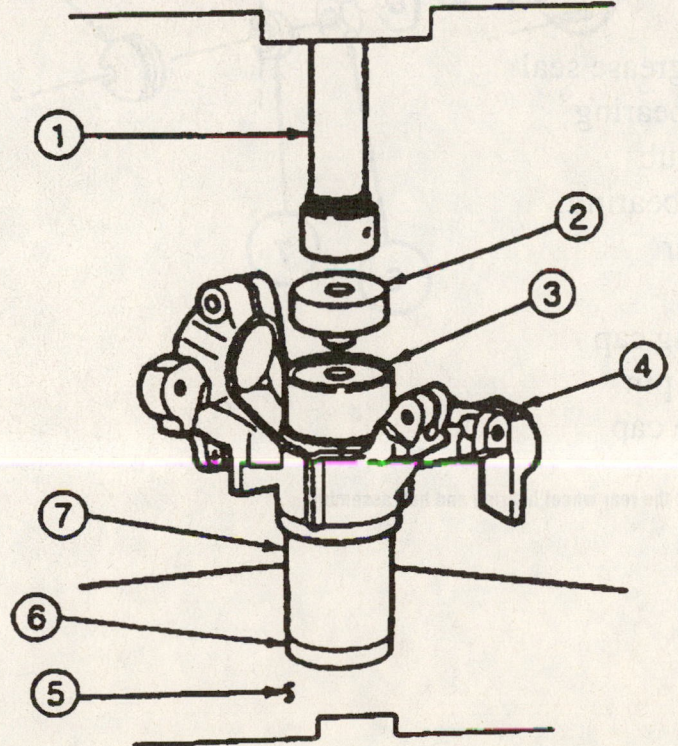

1 Arbor Press
2 Hub Bearing Replacer (Must Be Positioned with Undercut Side Facing Bearing)
3 Front Wheel Bearing
4 Front Wheel Knuckle
5 Press Plate
6 Step Side Down
7 Front Bearing Spacer

Installing the wheel bearing into the knuckle using a hydraulic press and the proper adapters

the front bearing spacer with the lug bolts facing downward.

12. Position the wheel hub and knuckle (outboard side down) on the press. Place bearing remover, flat side down, centered on the inner race of the front wheel bearing and press down until the bearing is fully seated.

13. Ensure the wheel hub rotates freely in the knuckle after installation.

14. Remove the front halfshaft from the vehicle.

15. Install the halfshaft and knuckle.

Rear

➡ **Sodium-based grease is not compatible with lithium-based grease. Do not lubricate the wheel bearings without first thoroughly cleaning all old grease from the bearing. Use of incompatible bearing lubricants could result in premature lubricant breakdown.**

1. Loosen the lug nuts on the rear wheel(s).

2. Raise and safely support the vehicle.

3. Remove the rear wheel(s).

4. Remove the brake drum or brake disc.

5. Remove the hub grease cap.

6. Remove the cotter pin retainer, adjusting nut and flat washer from the rear wheel spindle. Discard the cotter pin.

7. Remove the outer bearing and cone assembly.

8. Remove the rear hub from the rear wheel spindle.

9. Using a seal remover, remove and discard the oil seal.

10. Remove the inner bearing cone and roller assembly.

11. Clean the inner and outer bearing cups with solvent. Inspect the bearing cups for scratches, pits, excessive wear and other damage. If the bearing cups are worn or damaged, remove them using a bearing cup puller.

To install:

12. Thoroughly clean all old grease from the surrounding surfaces. If a new hub

assembly is being installed, remove the protective coating using degreaser.

13. If the inner or outer bearing cups were removed, install replacement cups using a bearing cup replacer. Seat the cups properly in the hub.

➡ **If a bearing packer is not available, work as much grease as possible between the rollers and cages. Grease the cone surfaces.**

14. Using a bearing packer, pack the bearing cone and roller assemblies with a premium bearing grease.

15. Place the inner bearing cone and roller assembly in the inner cup. A light film of grease should be included between the lips of the new grease retainer.

16. Install the retainer with a hub seal

replacer. Be sure retainer is properly seated.

➡ **Keep the hub centered on the spindle to prevent damage to the retainer and spindle threads.**

17. Install the hub assembly on the spindle.

18. Install the outer bearing cone and roller assembly on the spindle.

19. Install the flat washer and nut. Tighten the nut to 18–23 ft. lbs. (24–31 Nm) while rotating the hub to set the end-play. Back off the nut and retighten it to 18 inch lbs. (2 Nm).

20. Install a new cotter pin.

21. Install the hub grease cap.

22. Install the brake drum or disc.

23. Install the rear wheels

24. Lower the vehicle.

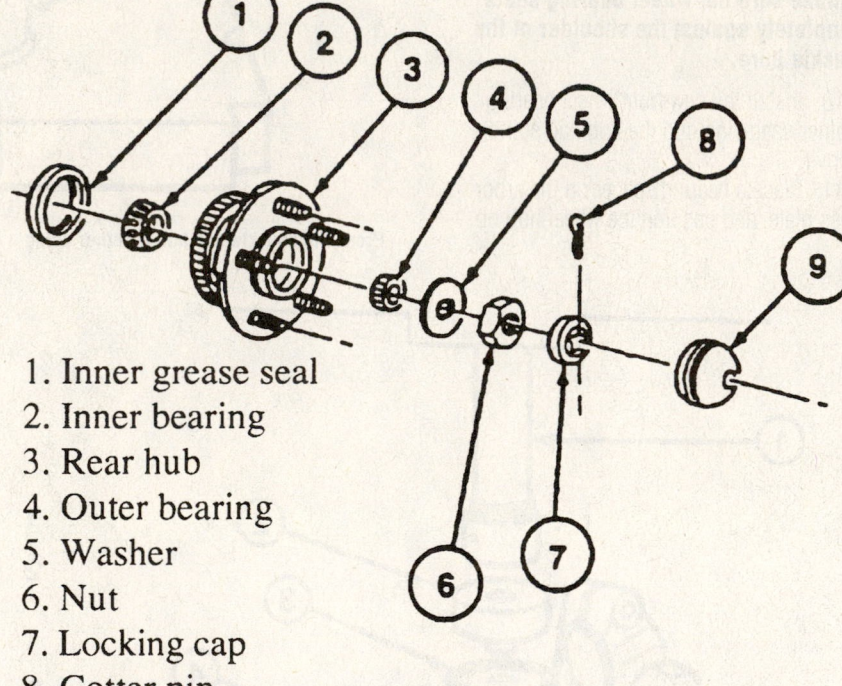

1. Inner grease seal
2. Inner bearing
3. Rear hub
4. Outer bearing
5. Washer
6. Nut
7. Locking cap
8. Cotter pin
9. Grease cap

7924GG23

Exploded view of the rear wheel bearing and hub assembly

GEO/CHEVROLET/SUZUKI

18

Tracker • Sidekick Sport • X-90 • Vitara • Grand Vitara

PRECAUTIONS

Before servicing any vehicle, please be sure to read all of the following precautions, which deal with personal safety, prevention of component damage and important points to take into consideration when servicing a motor vehicle:

• Never open, service or drain the radiator or cooling system when the engine is hot; serious burns can occur from the steam and hot coolant.

• Observe all applicable safety precautions when working around fuel. Whenever servicing the fuel system, always work in a well-ventilated area. Do not allow fuel spray or vapors to come in contact with a spark, open flame, or excessive heat (a hot drop light, for example). Keep a dry chemical fire extinguisher near the work area. Always keep fuel in a container specifically designed for fuel storage; also, always properly seal fuel containers to avoid the possibility of fire or explosion. Refer to the additional fuel system precautions later in this section.

• Fuel injection systems often remain pressurized, even after the engine has been turned **OFF**. The fuel system pressure must be relieved before disconnecting any fuel lines. Failure to do so may result in fire and/or personal injury.

• Brake fluid often contains polyglycol ethers and polyglycols. Avoid contact with the eyes and wash your hands thoroughly after handling brake fluid. If you do get brake fluid in your eyes, flush your eyes with clean, running water for 15 minutes. If eye irritation persists, or if you have taken brake fluid internally, IMMEDIATELY seek medical assistance.

• The EPA warns that prolonged contact with used engine oil may cause a number of skin disorders, including cancer. You should make every effort to minimize your exposure to used engine oil. Protective gloves should be worn when changing oil. Wash your hands and any other exposed skin areas as soon as possible after exposure to used engine oil. Soap and water, or waterless hand cleaner should be used.

• All new vehicles are now equipped with an air bag system, often referred to as a Supplemental Restraint System (SRS) or Supplemental Inflatable Restraint (SIR) system. The system must be disabled before performing service on or around system components, steering column, instrument panel components, wiring and sensors. Failure to follow safety and disabling procedures could result in accidental air bag deployment, possible personal injury, and unnecessary system repairs.

• Always wear safety goggles when working with, or around, the air bag system. When carrying a non-deployed air bag, be sure the bag and trim cover are pointed away from your body. When placing a non-deployed air bag on a work surface, always face the bag and trim cover upward, away from the surface. This will reduce the motion of the module if it is accidentally deployed. Refer to the additional air bag system precautions later in this section.

• Clean, high quality brake fluid from a sealed container is essential to the safe and proper operation of the brake system. You should always buy the correct type of brake fluid for your vehicle. If the brake fluid becomes contaminated, completely flush the system with new fluid. Never reuse any brake fluid. Any brake fluid that is removed from the system should be discarded. Also, do not allow any brake fluid to come in contact with a painted surface; it will damage the paint.

• Never operate the engine without the proper amount and type of engine oil; doing so WILL result in severe engine damage.

• Timing belt maintenance is extremely important. Many models utilize an interference-type, non-freewheeling engine. If the timing belt breaks, the valves in the cylinder head may strike the pistons, causing potentially serious (also time-consuming and expensive) engine damage. Refer to the maintenance interval charts in the front of this manual for the recommended replacement interval for the timing belt, and to the timing belt section for belt replacement and inspection.

• Disconnecting the negative battery cable on some vehicles may interfere with the functions of the on-board computer system(s) and may require the computer to undergo a relearning process once the negative battery cable is reconnected.

• When servicing drum brakes, only disassemble and assemble one side at a time, leaving the remaining side intact for reference.

ENGINE REPAIR

➡ **Disconnecting the negative battery cable on some vehicles may interfere with the functions of the on board computer system. The computer may undergo a relearning process once the negative battery cable is reconnected.**

Distributor

REMOVAL

The 1.8L, 2.0L, 2.5L and 1999–01 1.6L Engines are equipped with a Distributorless Ignition System (DIS).

1997–98 1.6L Engine

1. Before servicing the vehicle, refer to the precautions in the beginning of this section.
2. Remove or disconnect the following:
   • Negative battery cable
   • Distributor cap
   • Distributor wiring harness connector
3. Matchmark the rotor to the distributor housing and the distributor housing to the cylinder head.
4. Remove the distributor.

INSTALLATION

Timing Not Disturbed

Install or connect the following:
   • Distributor by aligning the matchmarks made during removal
   • Distributor wiring harness connector
   • Distributor cap
   • Negative battery cable

Timing Disturbed

1. Set the engine to Top Dead Center (TDC) of the compression stroke for the No. 1 cylinder.
2. Install the distributor so that rotor is aligned with the No. 1 cylinder spark plug wire tower.
3. Install or connect the following:
   • Distributor wiring harness connector
   • Distributor cap
   • Negative battery cable

Alternator

REMOVAL

1. Before servicing the vehicle, refer to the precautions in the beginning of this section.
2. Remove or disconnect the following:
   - Negative battery cable
   - Evaporative Emission (EVAP) canister
   - Accessory drive belt
   - Alternator harness connectors
   - Alternator mounting bracket
   - Alternator

INSTALLATION

Install or connect the following:
   - Alternator
   - Alternator mounting bracket. Tighten the bolts to 20 ft. lbs. (27 Nm).
   - Alternator harness connectors
   - Accessory drive belt. Tighten the alternator bolts to 24 ft. lbs. (33 Nm).
   - EVAP canister
   - Negative battery cable

Ignition Timing

ADJUSTMENT

1999–01 1.6L Engine

This engine is equipped with a Distributorless Ignition System (DIS). All timing functions are controlled by the Powertrain Control Module (PCM). No adjustment is possible.

1.8L, 2.0L, 2.5L and 1997–98 1.6L Engines

➡The 1.8L, 2.0L and 2.5L engines use a Camshaft Position (CMP) sensor that is rotated to set base timing. The procedure is the same as for the 1997–98 1.6L engine distributor.

➡Check and adjust the ignition timing with the engine at normal operating temperature, all electrical accessories OFF and transmission in P, N for automatic transmission or neutral for manual transmission.

1. Before servicing the vehicle, refer to the precautions in the beginning of this section.

2. With the engine **OFF**, connect a jumper wire between terminals **4** and **5** of the Data Link Connector (DLC) for Tracker or between terminals **D** and **E** of the DLC for all others.
3. Connect a timing light to the No. 1 spark plug wire and start the engine.
4. Ignition timing at idle should be 4–6 degrees Before Top Dead Center (BTDC).
5. Adjust the timing as necessary, then turn the engine **OFF**.
6. Remove the jumper wire from the DLC and remove the timing light.

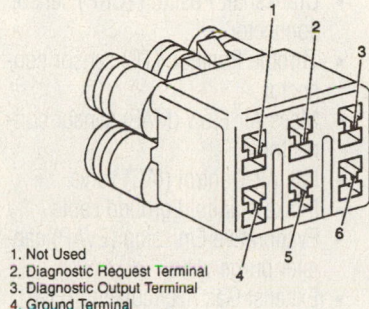

1. Not Used
2. Diagnostic Request Terminal
3. Diagnostic Output Terminal
4. Ground Terminal
5. Test Switch Terminal
6. Duty Check Terminal

7924HG01

Duty Check Data Link Connector terminal identification for ignition timing

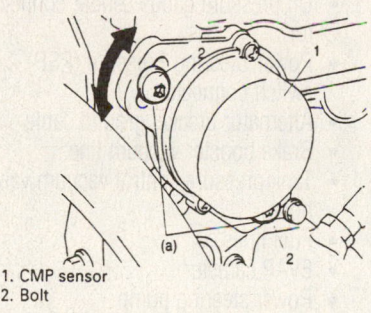

1. CMP sensor
2. Bolt

7924HG82

Camshaft position sensor—1.8L engine shown

Engine Assembly

REMOVAL & INSTALLATION

1.6L Engine

1. Before servicing the vehicle, refer to the precautions in the beginning of this section.
2. Relieve the fuel system pressure.
3. Drain the cooling system and engine oil.

4. Remove or disconnect the following:
   - Negative battery cable
   - Hood
   - Strut tower bar, if equipped
   - Cooling fan and shroud
   - Heater hoses
   - Radiator hoses
   - Bypass hose
   - Radiator
   - Air intake tube
   - Accelerator cable
   - Transmission cable, if equipped
   - Positive Crankcase Ventilation (PCV) valve and hose
   - Exhaust Gas Recirculation (EGR) valve and temperature sensor
   - EGR vacuum valve connector
   - EGR bypass valve connector
   - Idle Air Control (IAC) valve hoses and connector
   - Fuel lines
   - Main engine control wiring harness connectors at the firewall
   - Throttle Position (TP) sensor connector
   - Heated Oxygen (HO2S) sensor connectors
   - Engine Coolant Temperature (ECT) sensor connector
   - Temperature gauge sender connector
   - A/C temperature switch, if equipped
   - Injector harness connectors
   - Alternator wiring connectors
   - Manifold Absolute Pressure (MAP) sensor connector and vacuum line
   - Brake booster vacuum line
   - Evaporative Emission (EVAP) canister and hoses
   - Distributor, if equipped
   - Front skidplate, if equipped
   - Power steering hoses
   - A/C compressor, if equipped
   - Flywheel access cover
   - Torque converter, if equipped
   - Clutch cable, if equipped
   - Transmission cooler lines, if equipped
   - Exhaust front pipe
   - Starter motor
   - Transmission flange fasteners and support the transmission
   - Left and right engine mounts
   - Engine

To install:
5. Install or connect the following:
   - Engine. Tighten the mount bolts to 40 ft. lbs. (54 Nm).
   - Transmission flange fasteners. Tighten them to 62 ft. lbs. (85 Nm).

- Starter motor
- Exhaust front pipe
- Transmission cooler lines, if equipped
- Clutch cable, if equipped
- Torque converter, if equipped. Tighten the bolts to 40 ft. lbs. (54 Nm).
- Flywheel access cover
- A/C compressor, if equipped
- Power steering hoses
- Front skidplate, if equipped
- Distributor, if equipped
- EVAP canister and hoses
- Brake booster vacuum line
- MAP sensor connector and vacuum line
- Alternator wiring connectors
- Injector harness connectors
- A/C temperature switch, if equipped
- Temperature gauge sender connector
- ECT sensor connector
- HO2S sensor connectors
- TP sensor connector
- Main engine control wiring harness connectors at the firewall
- Fuel lines
- IAC valve hoses and connector
- EGR bypass valve connector
- EGR vacuum valve connector
- EGR valve and temperature sensor
- PCV valve and hose
- Transmission cable, if equipped
- Accelerator cable
- Air intake tube
- Radiator
- Bypass hose
- Radiator hoses
- Heater hoses
- Cooling fan and shroud
- Strut tower bar, if equipped
- Hood
- Negative battery cable

6. Fill the crankcase to the correct level.
7. Fill the cooling system.
8. Start the engine and check for leaks.

1.8L, 2.0L and 2.5L Engines

1. Before servicing the vehicle, refer to the precautions in the beginning of this section.
2. Relieve the fuel system pressure.
3. Drain the cooling system.
4. Drain the engine oil.
5. Remove or disconnect the following:
   - Negative battery cable
   - Hood
   - Heater hoses
   - Radiator hoses
   - Cooling fan and shroud

- Radiator overflow tank
- Radiator
- Accelerator cable
- Transmission cable, if equipped
- Strut tower bar, if equipped
- Air intake assembly
- Engine oil dipstick tube
- Transmission oil dipstick tube, if equipped
- Ignition coil covers
- Ignition coil connectors
- Injector connectors
- Camshaft Position (CMP) sensor connector
- Crankshaft Position (CKP) sensor connector
- Throttle Position (TP) sensor connector
- Mass Air Flow (MAF) sensor connector
- Idle Air Control (IAC) valve
- Intake manifold ground cable
- Evaporative Emission (EVAP) canister purge valve
- Exhaust Gas Recirculation (EGR) valve connector
- Heated Oxygen (HO2S) sensor connectors
- Engine Coolant Temperature (ECT) sensor connector
- Alternator wiring connectors
- Oil pressure gauge sender connector
- Power Steering Pressure (PSP) switch connector
- Alternator bracket ground cable
- Brake booster vacuum line
- Tank pressure control vacuum valve hose
- Fuel lines
- EVAP canister
- Power steering pump
- A/C compressor
- Steering shaft lower assembly
- Front differential housing, if equipped
- Exhaust front pipe and bracket
- Transmission oil cooler lines, if equipped
- Transmission stiffener brackets, if equipped
- Flywheel access cover
- Torque converter, if equipped
- Starter motor
- Transmission flange fasteners and support the transmission
- Left and right engine mounts
- Engine

To install:

6. Install or connect the following:
   - Engine

- Left and right engine mounts. Tighten the nuts to 36 ft. lbs. (50 Nm).
- Transmission flange fasteners. Tighten them to 58 ft. lbs. (80 Nm).
- Starter motor
- Torque converter. Tighten the bolts to 47 ft. lbs. (65 Nm).
- Flywheel access cover
- Transmission stiffener brackets. Tighten the bolts to 36 ft. lbs. (50 Nm).
- Transmission oil cooler lines, if equipped
- Exhaust front pipe and bracket
- Front differential housing, if equipped
- Steering shaft lower assembly
- A/C compressor
- Power steering pump
- EVAP canister
- Fuel lines
- Tank pressure control vacuum valve hose
- Brake booster vacuum line
- Alternator bracket ground cable
- PSP switch connector
- Oil pressure gauge sender connector
- Alternator wiring connectors
- ECT sensor connector
- HO2S sensor connectors
- EGR valve connector
- EVAP canister purge valve
- Intake manifold ground cable
- IAC valve
- MAF sensor connector
- TP sensor connector
- CKP sensor connector
- CMP sensor connector
- Injector connectors
- Ignition coil connectors
- Ignition coil covers
- Transmission oil dipstick tube, if equipped
- Engine oil dipstick tube
- Air intake assembly
- Strut tower bar, if equipped
- Transmission cable, if equipped
- Accelerator cable
- Radiator
- Radiator overflow tank
- Cooling fan and shroud
- Radiator hoses
- Heater hoses
- Hood
- Negative battery cable

7. Fill the crankcase to the correct level.
8. Fill the cooling system.
9. Start the engine and check for leaks.

Water Pump

REMOVAL & INSTALLATION

1.6L Engines

1. Before servicing the vehicle, refer to the precautions in the beginning of this section.
2. Drain the cooling system.
3. Remove or disconnect the following:
   - Negative battery cable
   - Accessory drive belts
   - Cooling fan and shroud
   - Front cover
   - Timing belt. Refer to the Timing Belt unit repair section.
   - Oil dipstick tube
   - Alternator bracket
   - Timing belt tensioner
   - Water pump

To install:

4. Install or connect the following:
   - Water pump with a new gasket. Tighten the bolts to 106 inch lbs. (12 Nm).
   - Timing belt tensioner
   - Alternator bracket
   - Oil dipstick tube. Tighten the bolt to 97 inch lbs. (11 Nm).
   - Timing belt. Refer to the Timing Belt unit repair section.
   - Front cover
   - Cooling fan and shroud
   - Accessory drive belts
   - Negative battery cable

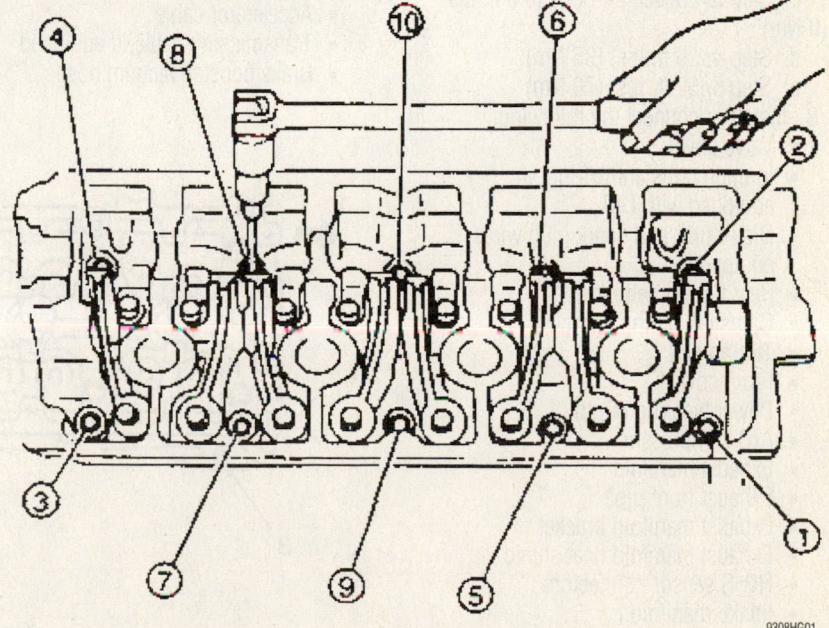

1. Water pump

7924HG04

Exploded view of the water pump mounting—1.6L engines

5. Fill the cooling system.
6. Start the engine and check for leaks.

1.8L and 2.0L Engines

1. Before servicing the vehicle, refer to the precautions in the beginning of this section.

2. Drain the cooling system.
3. Remove or disconnect the following:
   - Negative battery cable
   - Radiator hose at the thermostat housing
   - Heater outlet pipe bolt
   - Alternator belt
   - Water pump

To install:

➡**Use new water pump bolts for assembly.**

4. Install or connect the following:
   - Water pump with a new O-ring seal. Tighten the bolts to 19 ft. lbs. (27 Nm).
   - Alternator belt
   - Heater outlet pipe bolt
   - Radiator hose at the thermostat housing
   - Negative battery cable
5. Fill the cooling system.
6. Start the engine and check for leaks.

2.5L Engine

1. Before servicing the vehicle, refer to the precautions in the beginning of this section.

2. Drain the cooling system.
3. Remove or disconnect the following:
   - Negative battery cable
   - Accessory drive belts
   - Front cover
   - Water pump

To install:

4. Install or connect the following:
   - Water pump with a new O-ring seal. Tighten the bolts to 19 ft. lbs. (27 Nm).
   - Front cover
   - Accessory drive belts
   - Negative battery cable
5. Fill the cooling system.
6. Start the engine and check for leaks.

Cylinder Head

REMOVAL & INSTALLATION

1.6L Engine

1. Before servicing the vehicle, refer to the precautions in the beginning of this section.

2. Relieve the fuel system pressure.
3. Drain the cooling system.
4. Remove or disconnect the following:
   - Negative battery cable
   - Accessory drive belts
   - Air intake pipe
   - Fuel lines
   - Upper radiator hose
   - Coolant bypass hose
   - Alternator bracket
   - Intake manifold brackets
   - Intake manifold
   - Heated Oxygen (HO2S) sensor connectors

Cylinder head loosening sequence—1.6L engine

9308HG01

Timing belt service is covered in Section 4 of this manual

- Exhaust manifold heat shield
- Exhaust manifold bracket
- Exhaust front pipe
- Exhaust manifold
- A/C compressor
- Power steering pump
- Front cover
- Timing belt. Refer to the Timing Belt unit repair section.
- Camshaft timing sprocket
- Rear timing belt cover
- Distributor and spark plug wires, if equipped
- Ignition coils and wiring, if equipped with Distributorless Ignition System (DIS)
- Valve cover
- Cylinder head. Loosen the bolts in the sequence shown.

To install:

➡ Refer to Section 1 of this manual for the cylinder head torque sequence illustration. The illustration is located after the Torque Specification Chart.

5. Install the cylinder head with a new gasket.

6. For 1997–98 engines, tighten the bolts in sequence as follows:
   a. Step 1: 26 ft. lbs. (35 Nm)
   b. Step 2: 41 ft. lbs. (55 Nm)
   c. Step 3: 52 ft. lbs. (70 Nm)

7. For 1999–01 engines, tighten the bolts in sequence as follows:
   a. Step 1: 26 ft. lbs. (35 Nm)
   b. Step 2: 41 ft. lbs. (55 Nm)
   c. Step 3: Loosen all bolts to 0 ft. lbs. (0 Nm)
   d. Step 4: 26 ft. lbs. (35 Nm)
   e. Step 5: 52 ft. lbs. (70 Nm)

8. Install or connect the following:
- Valve cover
- Ignition coils and wiring, if equipped with DIS
- Distributor and spark plug wires, if equipped
- Rear timing belt cover
- Camshaft timing sprocket
- Timing belt
- Front cover
- Power steering pump
- A/C compressor
- Exhaust manifold
- Exhaust front pipe
- Exhaust manifold bracket
- Exhaust manifold heat shield
- HO2S sensor connectors
- Intake manifold
- Intake manifold brackets
- Alternator bracket
- Coolant bypass hose
- Upper radiator hose

- Fuel lines
- Air intake pipe
- Accessory drive belts
- Negative battery cable
9. Fill the cooling system.
10. Start the engine and check for leaks.

1.8L and 2.0L Engines

1. Before servicing the vehicle, refer to the precautions in the beginning of this section.
2. Relieve the fuel system pressure.
3. Drain the cooling system.
4. Drain the engine oil.
5. Remove or disconnect the following:
- Negative battery cable
- Strut tower brace
- Air intake tube
- Exhaust Gas Recirculation (EGR) valve connector
- Idle Air Control (IAC) valve connector
- Throttle Position (TP) sensor connector
- Evaporative Emission (EVAP) canister purge valve connector and hose
- Intake manifold ground cable
- Heated Oxygen (HO2S) sensor connectors
- Camshaft Position (CMP) sensor connector
- Engine Coolant Temperature (ECT) sensor connector
- Fuel injector connectors
- Ignition coils
- Accelerator cable
- Transmission cable, if equipped
- Brake booster vacuum hose

- Radiator hose
- Bypass hose
- Heater hose
- Fuel lines
- Intake manifold bracket
- Water pipe
- Valve cover
- Accessory drive belts
- Oil pan
- Front cover
- Timing chains
- Camshafts
- Exhaust front pipe
- Exhaust manifold bracket
- Cylinder head. Loosen the bolts in the sequence shown.

To install:

➡ Refer to Section 1 of this manual for the cylinder head torque sequence illustration. The illustration is located after the Torque Specification Chart.

6. Install the cylinder head with a new gasket.

7. For 1.8L engines, tighten the bolts in sequence as follows:
   a. Step 1: 38 ft. lbs. (52 Nm)
   b. Step 2: 61 ft. lbs. (84 Nm)
   c. Step 3: Loosen all bolts to 0 ft. lbs. (0 Nm)
   d. Step 4: 27 ft. lbs. (37 Nm)
   e. Step 5: 76 ft. lbs. (105 Nm)
   f. Step 6: 6mm bolt to 96 inch lbs. (8 Nm)

8. For 2.0L engines, tighten the bolts in sequence as follows:
   a. Step 1: 38 ft. lbs. (52 Nm)
   b. Step 2: 61 ft. lbs. (84 Nm)
   c. Step 3: Loosen all bolts to 0 ft. lbs. (0 Nm)

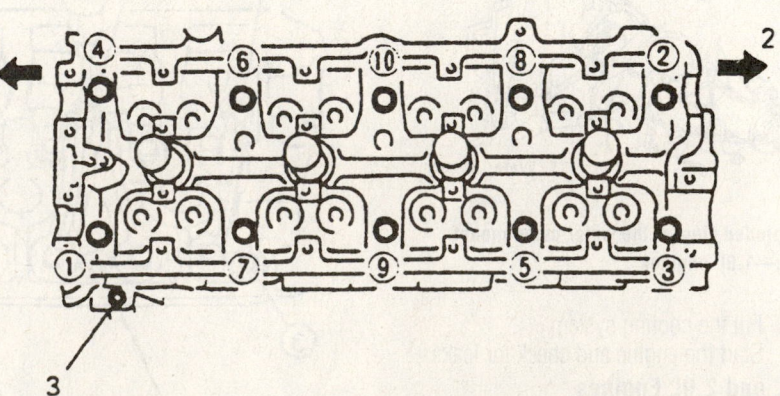

1. Crankshaft pulley side
2. Flywheel side
3. Bolt (M6)

Cylinder head loosening sequence—1.8L and 2.0L engines

7924HG09

d. Step 4: 38 ft. lbs. (52 Nm)

e. Step 5: 76 ft. lbs. (105 Nm)

f. Step 6: 6mm bolt to 96 inch lbs. (8 Nm)

9. Install or connect the following:
- Exhaust manifold bracket
- Exhaust front pipe
- Camshafts
- Timing chains
- Front cover
- Oil pan
- Accessory drive belts
- Valve cover
- Water pipe
- Intake manifold bracket
- Fuel lines
- Heater hose
- Bypass hose
- Radiator hose
- Brake booster vacuum hose
- Transmission cable, if equipped
- Accelerator cable
- Ignition coils
- Fuel injector connectors
- ECT sensor connector
- CMP sensor connector
- HO2S sensor connectors
- Intake manifold ground cable
- EVAP canister purge valve connector and hose
- TP sensor connector
- IAC valve connector
- EGR valve connector
- Air intake tube
- Strut tower brace
- Negative battery cable

10. Fill the crankcase to the correct level.
11. Fill the cooling system.
12. Start the engine and check for leaks.

2.5L Engine

1. Before servicing the vehicle, refer to the precautions in the beginning of this section.

2. Relieve the fuel system pressure.

3. Drain the cooling system and engine oil.

4. Remove or disconnect the following:
- Negative battery cable
- Intake manifold
- Ignition coil covers and ignition coils
- Valve covers
- Oil pan
- Timing chain cover and timing chains
- Camshaft Position (CMP) sensor
- Camshafts
- Exhaust manifolds

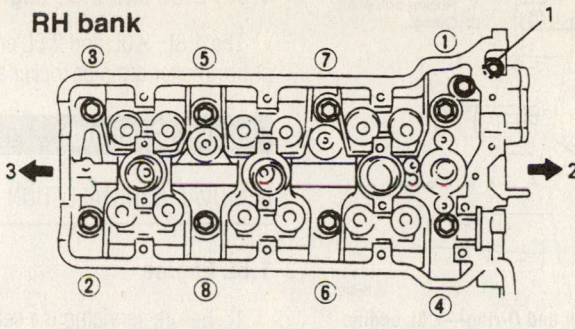

RH bank

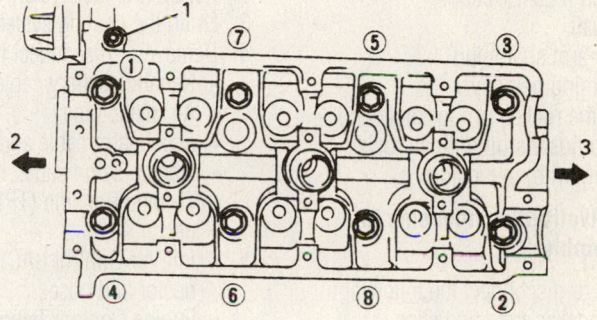

LH bank

1. Hex hole bolt
2. Timing chain side
3. Flywheel side

9302HG01

Cylinder head loosening sequence—2.5L engine

- Water outlet caps
- Cylinder heads. Loosen the bolts in the sequence shown.

To install:

➡ Refer to Section 1 of this manual for the cylinder head torque sequence illustration. The illustration is located after the Torque Specification Chart.

5. Install the cylinder heads with new gaskets. Tighten the bolts in sequence as follows:

a. Step 1: 38 ft. lbs. (52 Nm)

b. Step 2: 61 ft. lbs. (84 Nm)

c. Step 3: Loosen all bolts to 0 ft. lbs. (0 Nm)

d. Step 4: 38 ft. lbs. (52 Nm)

e. Step 5: 76 ft. lbs. (105 Nm)

f. Step 6: 6mm bolt to 96 inch lbs. (8 Nm)

6. Install or connect the following:
- Water outlet caps
- Exhaust manifolds
- Camshafts
- CMP sensor
- Timing chain cover and timing chains
- Oil pan

- Valve covers
- Ignition coil covers and ignition coils
- Intake manifold
- Negative battery cable

7. Fill the crankcase to the correct level.

8. Fill the cooling system.

9. Start the engine and check for leaks.

Rocker Arms/Shafts

REMOVAL & INSTALLATION

1.6L Engine

1. Before servicing the vehicle, refer to the precautions in the beginning of this section.

2. Drain the cooling system.

3. Remove or disconnect the following:
- Negative battery cable
- Accessory drive belts
- Cooling fan and shroud
- Radiator and hoses
- Distributor, if equipped
- Camshaft Position (CMP) sensor, if equipped
- Valve cover
- Front cover

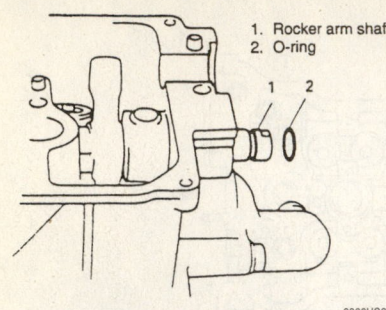

1. Rocker arm shaft
2. O-ring

9308HG02

Rocker arm shaft and O-ring—1.6L engine

- Timing belt. Refer to the Timing Belt unit repair section.
- Camshaft
- Rocker arm shaft plug
- Rear timing belt cover

4. Loosen the rocker arm locknuts and back the valve adjusters off until all rocker arms move freely with no tension.

➡**Keep all valvetrain components in order for assembly.**

5. Remove or disconnect the following:
- Intake rocker arms and clips
- Rocker arm shaft bolts

6. Push the rocker arm shaft towards the rear of the cylinder head and remove the rocker arm shaft O-ring.

7. Remove the exhaust rocker arms and springs by pulling the rocker arm shaft out of the front of the cylinder head.

To install:

8. Insert the rocker arm shaft into the front of the cylinder head, while installing the exhaust rocker arms and springs in their original positions.

9. Push the end of the rocker arm shaft out of the rear of the cylinder head and install a new O-ring.

10. Install or connect the following:
- Rocker arm shaft bolts. Tighten them to 96 inch lbs. (8 Nm).
- Intake rocker arms and clips in their original positions
- Rear timing belt cover
- Rocker arm shaft plug. Tighten it to 24 ft. lbs. (33 Nm).
- Camshaft
- Timing belt and adjust the valve clearance
- Valve cover
- Front cover
- Distributor, if equipped
- CMP sensor, if equipped
- Radiator and hoses
- Cooling fan and shroud
- Accessory drive belts
- Negative battery cable

11. Fill the cooling system.
12. Start the engine and check for leaks.

1.8L, 2.0L and 2.5L Engines

The 1.8L, 2.0L and 2.5L engines do not utilize rocker arms or rocker arm shafts.

Intake Manifold

REMOVAL & INSTALLATION

1.6L Engine

1. Before servicing the vehicle, refer to the precautions in the beginning of this section.
2. Relieve the fuel system pressure.
3. Drain the cooling system.
4. Remove or disconnect the following:
- Negative battery cable
- Air intake pipe
- Accelerator cable and bracket
- Transmission cable, if equipped
- Throttle Position (TP) sensor connector
- Idle Air Control (IAC) valve connector and hoses
- Engine Coolant Temperature (ECT) sensor connector
- Coolant temperature gauge sender connector
- A/C coolant temperature switch connector, if equipped
- Evaporative Emission (EVAP) canister purge valve connector and vacuum line
- Exhaust Gas Recirculation (EGR) temperature sensor connector
- EGR vacuum valve connector
- EGR bypass valve connector
- EGR vacuum lines
- Fuel injector connectors
- Intake manifold ground cable
- Transmission vacuum line, if equipped
- Brake booster vacuum line
- Manifold Absolute Pressure (MAP) sensor vacuum line
- Fuel lines
- Upper radiator hose
- Coolant bypass hose
- Alternator bracket
- Intake manifold brackets
- Intake manifold

To install:

5. Install or connect the following:
- Intake manifold with a new gasket. Tighten the nuts to 17 ft. lbs. (23 Nm).
- Intake manifold brackets. Tighten the fasteners to 36 ft. lbs. (50 Nm).
- Alternator bracket. Tighten the fasteners to 36 ft. lbs. (50 Nm).
- Coolant bypass hose

- Upper radiator hose
- Fuel lines
- MAP sensor vacuum line
- Brake booster vacuum line
- Transmission vacuum line, if equipped
- Intake manifold ground cable
- Fuel injector connectors
- EGR vacuum lines
- EGR bypass valve connector
- EGR vacuum valve connector
- EGR temperature sensor connector
- EVAP canister purge valve connector and vacuum line
- A/C coolant temperature switch connector, if equipped
- Coolant temperature gauge sender connector
- ECT sensor connector
- IAC valve connector and hoses
- TP sensor connector
- Transmission cable, if equipped
- Accelerator cable and bracket
- Air intake pipe
- Negative battery cable

6. Fill the cooling system.
7. Start the engine and check for leaks.

1.8L and 2.0L Engines

1. Before servicing the vehicle, refer to the precautions in the beginning of this section.
2. Relieve the fuel system pressure.
3. Drain the cooling system.
4. Remove or disconnect the following:
- Negative battery cable
- Air intake tube
- Exhaust Gas Recirculation (EGR) valve connector
- Idle Air Control (IAC) valve connector
- Throttle Position (TP) sensor connector
- Evaporative Emissions (EVAP) canister purge valve connector and hose
- Intake manifold ground cable
- Manifold Absolute Pressure (MAP) sensor connector
- Accelerator cable
- Transmission cable, if equipped
- Brake booster vacuum hose
- Positive Crankcase Ventilation (PCV) valve and hose
- Fuel pressure regulator vacuum hose
- Intake manifold vacuum hose
- Throttle body coolant hoses
- Water bypass pipe
- Fuel lines
- Fuel supply manifold with injectors attached

- Intake manifold support brackets
- Intake manifold water pipe
- Intake manifold

To install:

5. Install or connect the following:
   - Intake manifold with a new gasket. Tighten the fasteners to 17 ft. lbs. (23 Nm).
   - Intake manifold water pipe
   - Intake manifold front support bracket. Tighten the bolts to 36 ft. lbs. (50 Nm).
   - Intake manifold rear support bracket. Tighten the bolts to 18 ft. lbs. (25 Nm).
   - Fuel supply manifold with injectors attached
   - Fuel lines
   - Water bypass pipe
   - Throttle body coolant hoses
   - Intake manifold vacuum hose
   - Fuel pressure regulator vacuum hose
   - PCV valve and hose
   - Brake booster vacuum hose
   - Transmission cable, if equipped
   - Accelerator cable
   - MAP sensor connector
   - Intake manifold ground cable
   - EVAP canister purge valve connector and hose
   - TP sensor connector
   - IAC valve connector
   - EGR valve connector
   - Air intake tube
   - Negative battery cable
6. Fill the cooling system.
7. Start the engine and check for leaks.

2.5L Engine

1. Before servicing the vehicle, refer to the precautions in the beginning of this section.
2. Relieve the fuel system pressure.
3. Drain the cooling system.
4. Remove or disconnect the following:
   - Negative battery cable
   - Strut tower bar
   - Intake Air Temperature (IAT) sensor connector
   - Surge tank cover
   - Air intake assembly
   - Accelerator cable
   - Transmission cable, if equipped
   - Throttle body coolant hoses
   - Fuel injector connectors
   - Throttle Position (TP) sensor connector
   - Mass Air Flow (MAF) sensor connector

- Idle Air Control (IAC) valve connector
- Intake manifold ground cables
- Brake booster vacuum hose
- Evaporative Emissions (EVAP) canister purge valve connector and hoses
- Exhaust Gas Recirculation (EGR) valve connector
- Positive Crankcase Ventilation (PCV) valve and hose
- Heater hoses
- EGR pipe
- Fuel lines
- Throttle body and intake collector
- Intake manifold

To install:

5. Install or connect the following:
   - Intake manifold with new gaskets. Tighten the fasteners to 16 ft. lbs. (23 Nm).
   - Throttle body and intake collector with new gaskets. Tighten the fasteners to 102 inch lbs. (12 Nm).
   - Fuel lines
   - EGR pipe
   - Heater hoses
   - PCV valve and hose
   - EGR valve connector
   - EVAP canister purge valve connector and hoses
   - Brake booster vacuum hose
   - Intake manifold ground cables
   - IAC valve connector
   - MAF sensor connector
   - TP sensor connector
   - Fuel injector connectors
   - Throttle body coolant hoses
   - Transmission cable, if equipped
   - Accelerator cable
   - Air intake assembly
   - Surge tank cover
   - IAT sensor connector
   - Strut tower bar
   - Negative battery cable
6. Fill the cooling system.
7. Start the engine and check for leaks.

Exhaust Manifold

REMOVAL & INSTALLATION

1.6L, 1.8L and 2.0L Engines

1. Before servicing the vehicle, refer to the precautions in the beginning of this section.
2. Remove or disconnect the following:

- Negative battery cable
- Strut tower bar, if equipped
- Air intake assembly and bracket
- Heated Oxygen (HO2S) sensor connector
- Exhaust front pipe
- Exhaust manifold heat shield
- Exhaust manifold bracket, if equipped
- Exhaust manifold

To install:

3. Install or connect the following:
   - Exhaust manifold with a new gasket. Tighten the fasteners to 13–20 ft. lbs. (18–28 Nm).
   - Exhaust manifold bracket, if equipped. Tighten the bolts to 36–43 ft. lbs. (50–60 Nm).
   - Exhaust manifold heat shield
   - Exhaust front pipe. Tighten the fasteners to 29–43 ft. lbs. (40–60 Nm).
   - HO2S sensor connector
   - Air intake assembly and bracket
   - Strut tower bar, if equipped. Tighten the fasteners to 66 ft. lbs. (90 Nm).
   - Negative battery cable
4. Start the engine and check for leaks.

2.5L Engine

1. Before servicing the vehicle, refer to the precautions in the beginning of this section.
2. Remove or disconnect the following:
   - Negative battery cable
   - Strut tower bar
   - Air intake assembly
   - Heated Oxygen (HO2S) sensor connectors
   - Oil dipstick tube
   - Exhaust Gas Recirculation (EGR) pipe
   - Exhaust manifold heat shields
   - Evaporative Emissions (EVAP) canister
   - Front driveshaft, if equipped
   - Exhaust front pipe
   - Exhaust manifold brace
   - Exhaust manifolds

To install:

3. Install or connect the following:
   - Exhaust manifolds with new gaskets. Tighten the nuts to 21 ft. lbs. (30 Nm).
   - Exhaust manifold brace
   - Exhaust front pipe. Tighten the fasteners to 37 ft. lbs. (50 Nm).
   - Front driveshaft, if equipped
   - EVAP canister

Refer to Section 1 for engine rebuilding specifications

- Exhaust manifold heat shields
- EGR pipe
- Oil dipstick tube
- HO$_2$S sensor connectors
- Air intake assembly
- Strut tower bar
- Negative battery cable

4. Start the engine and check for leaks.

Front Crankshaft Seal

REMOVAL & INSTALLATION

1.6L Engine

1. Before servicing the vehicle, refer to the precautions in the beginning of this section.
2. Drain the cooling system.
3. Remove or disconnect the following:
   - Negative battery cable
   - Accessory drive belts
   - Cooling fan and shroud
   - Water pump pulley
   - Crankshaft pulley
   - Front cover
   - Timing belt. Refer to the Timing Belt unit repair section.
   - Crankshaft timing sprocket
   - Front crankshaft seal

To install:

4. Install or connect the following:
   - Front crankshaft seal flush with the oil pump housing
   - Crankshaft timing sprocket. Tighten the bolt to 94 ft. lbs. (128 Nm).
   - Timing belt
   - Front cover
   - Crankshaft pulley. Tighten the bolts to 12 ft. lbs. (16 Nm).
   - Water pump pulley
   - Cooling fan and shroud
   - Accessory drive belts
   - Negative battery cable
5. Start the engine and check for leaks.

Camshaft and Valve Lifters

REMOVAL & INSTALLATION

1.6L Engine

1. Before servicing the vehicle, refer to the precautions in the beginning of this section.
2. Drain the cooling system.
3. Remove or disconnect the following:
   - Negative battery cable
   - Radiator
   - Accessory drive belts
   - Crankshaft pulley
   - Front cover
   - Timing belt. Refer to the Timing Belt unit repair section.
   - Camshaft sprocket
   - Valve cover
   - Distributor and case, if equipped
   - Camshaft Position (CMP) sensor and case, if equipped
4. Loosen the rocker arm locknuts and back the valve adjusters off until all rocker arms move freely with no tension.
5. Remove or disconnect the following:
   - Camshaft bearing caps. Loosen the bolts in reverse of the tightening sequence.
   - Camshaft

To install:

6. Install or connect the following:
   - Camshaft
   - Camshaft bearing caps. Tighten the bolts in sequence to 96 inch lbs. (11 Nm).
   - CMP sensor and case, if equipped

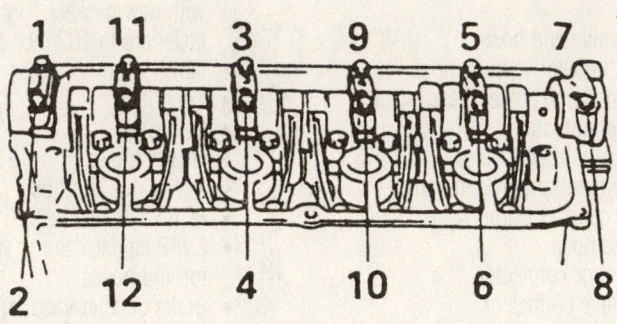

Camshaft housing torque sequence—1.6L engine

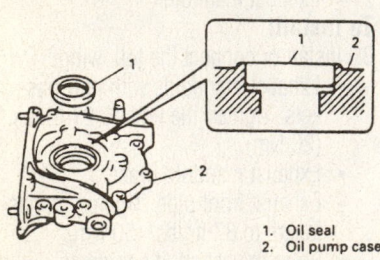

Install the new oil pump seal flush with the oil pump housing—1.6L engine

1. Oil seal
2. Oil pump case

7924HG13

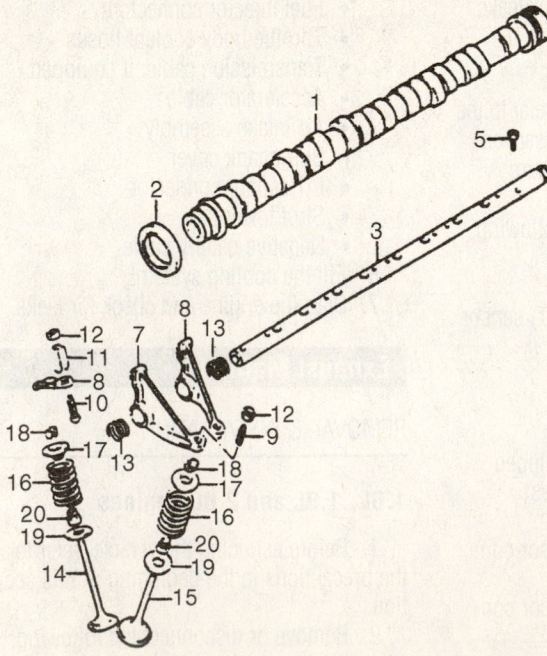

Exploded view of the valve train components—1.6L engine

1. Camshaft
2. Camshaft oil seal
3. Rocker arm shaft
4. O ring
5. Rocker shaft bolt
6. Rocker arm (IN)
7. Rocker arm No. 1 (EX)
8. Rocker arm No. 2 (EX)
9. Valve adjusting screw
10. Valve adjusting screw
11. Clip
12. Lock nut
13. Rocker arm spring
14. Intake valve
15. Exhaust valve
16. Valve spring
17. Valve spring retainer
18. Valve cotter
19. Valve spring seat
20. Valve stem seal

7924HG24

- Distributor and case, if equipped
- Camshaft sprocket. Tighten the bolt to 44 ft. lbs. (60 Nm).
- Timing belt and adjust the valve clearance
- Valve cover
- Front cover
- Crankshaft pulley. Tighten the bolts to 12 ft. lbs. (16 Nm).
- Accessory drive belts
- Radiator
- Negative battery cable

7. Fill the cooling system.
8. Start the engine and check for leaks.

1.8L and 2.0L Engines

1. Before servicing the vehicle, refer to the precautions in the beginning of this section.
2. Drain the engine oil.
3. Drain the cooling system.
4. Remove or disconnect the following:
   - Negative battery cable
   - Oil pan
   - Valve cover
   - Accessory drive belts
   - Crankshaft pulley
   - Front cover
   - Secondary timing chain
   - Camshaft Position (CMP) sensor

➡ **Keep all valvetrain components in order for installation.**

   - Camshaft bearing caps. Loosen the bolts in several steps in reverse of the tightening sequence.
   - Camshafts
   - Hydraulic lash adjusters

To install:

5. Install or connect the following:
   - Hydraulic lash adjusters in their original positions
   - Camshafts

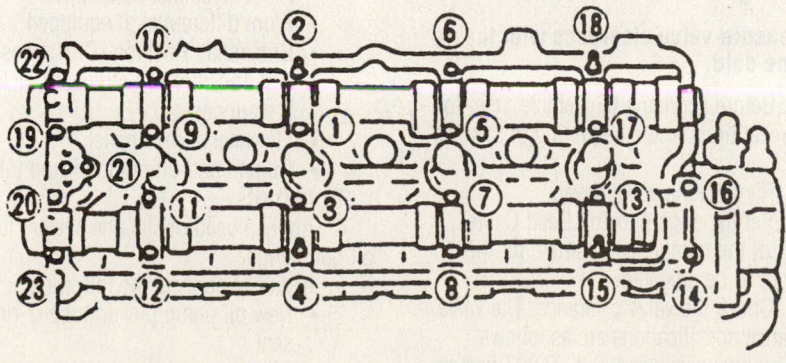

Camshaft housing torque sequence—1.8L and 2.0L engines

7924HG26

- Camshaft bearing caps in their original positions. Tighten the bolts in several steps in sequence to 96 inch lbs. (11 Nm).
- CMP sensor
- Secondary timing chain
- Front cover
- Crankshaft pulley. Tighten the bolt to 109 ft. lbs. (148 Nm).
- Accessory drive belts
- Valve cover
- Oil pan
- Negative battery cable

6. Fill the crankcase to the correct level.
7. Fill the cooling system.
8. Start the engine and check for leaks.

✳✳ WARNING

Wait ½ hour after installing the lash adjusters and camshafts before cranking or starting the engine to allow the lash adjusters to bleed down. Operating the engine before this time period may result in interference between the valves and pistons.

2.5L Engine

1. Before servicing the vehicle, refer to the precautions in the beginning of this section.
2. Drain the engine oil.
3. Drain the cooling system.
4. Remove or disconnect the following:
   - Negative battery cable
   - Intake manifold
   - Oil pan
   - Accessory drive belts
   - Water pump pulley
   - Crankshaft pulley
   - Timing chain cover
5. Align the timing marks as shown.

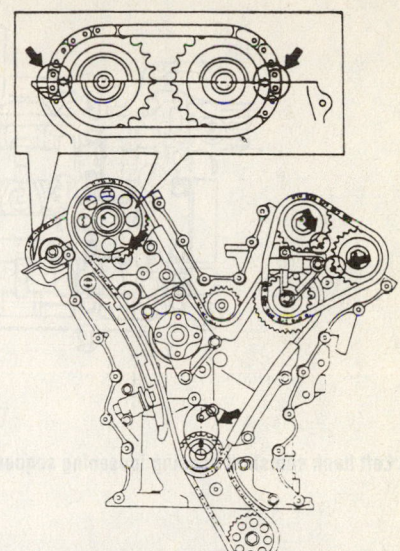

9302HG02

Timing mark alignment—2.5L engine

✳✳ WARNING

Do not allow the crankshaft or camshafts to rotate once the timing chains have been removed. Valve or piston damage could result.

6. Remove or disconnect the following:
   - Left bank secondary timing chain
   - Primary timing chain
   - Valve covers

➡ **Keep all valvetrain components in order for assembly.**

   - Right bank camshaft bearing caps. Loosen the bolts in several steps and in the sequence shown.
   - Right bank secondary timing chain, exhaust and intake camshafts as an assembly
   - Camshaft Position (CMP) sensor
   - Left bank camshaft bearing caps. Loosen the bolts in several steps and in the sequence shown.
   - Left bank camshafts
   - Hydraulic lash adjusters

To install:

7. Install or connect the following:
   - Hydraulic lash adjusters in their original positions
   - Left bank camshafts
   - Left bank camshaft bearing caps. Tighten the bolts in several steps and in reverse of the loosening sequence to 102 inch lbs. (12 Nm).
   - CMP sensor

For engine torque specifications, refer to Section 1 of this manual

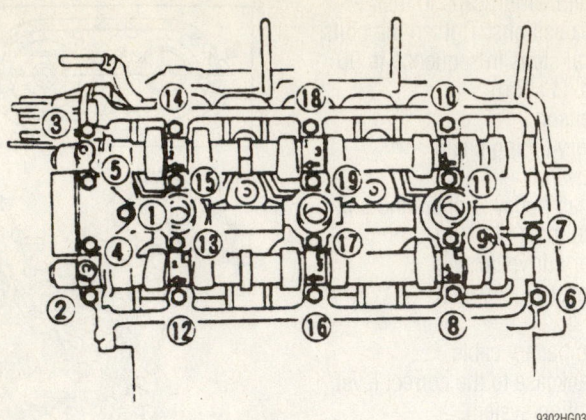

Left bank camshaft housing loosening sequence—2.5L engine

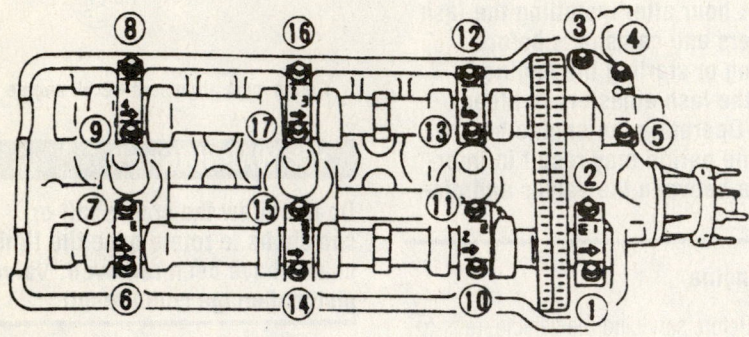

Right bank camshaft housing loosening sequence—2.5L engine

- Right bank secondary timing chain, exhaust and intake camshafts as an assembly
- Right bank camshaft bearing caps. Tighten the bolts in several steps and in reverse of the loosening sequence to 102 inch lbs. (12 Nm).

❈❈ WARNING

Wait ½ hour after installing the lash adjusters and camshafts before cranking or starting the engine to allow the lash adjusters to bleed down. Operating the engine before this time period may result in interference between the valves and pistons.

- Valve covers. Tighten the bolts to 90 inch lbs. (10.5 Nm).
- Primary timing chain
- Left bank secondary timing chain
- Timing chain cover
- Crankshaft pulley. Tighten the bolt to 109 ft. lbs. (148 Nm).
- Water pump pulley
- Accessory drive belts
- Oil pan

- Intake manifold
- Negative battery cable
8. Fill the crankcase to the correct level.
9. Fill the cooling system.
10. Start the engine and check for leaks.

Valve Lash

ADJUSTMENT

1.6L Engines

➡**Measure valve clearance with the engine cold.**

1. Before servicing the vehicle, refer to the precautions in the beginning of this section.
2. Remove the valve cover.
3. Set the engine to Top Dead Center (TDC) of the compression stroke for the cylinder to be adjusted.
4. Check the valve clearance. The valve clearance specifications are as follows:
- Intake valves: 0.005–0.007 inches (0.13–0.17mm)
- Exhaust valves: 0.005–0.007 inches (0.13–0.17mm)

5. After adjustment, tighten the locknuts to 11–14 ft. lbs. (15–19 Nm).
6. Repeat for each valve to be adjusted.

1.8L, 2.0L and 2.5L Engines

The 1.8L, 2.0L and 2.5L engines utilize automatic hydraulic lash adjusters to maintain proper valve lash at all times. Periodic valve lash inspection and adjustment is not necessary or possible.

Starter Motor

REMOVAL & INSTALLATION

1. Before servicing the vehicle, refer to the precautions in the beginning of this section.
2. Remove or disconnect the following:
- Negative battery cable
- Starter motor wiring connectors
- Starter motor

To install:
3. Install or connect the following:
- Starter motor. Tighten the bolts to 22 ft. lbs. (30 Nm).
- Starter motor wiring connectors. Tighten the solenoid nut to 11 ft. lbs. (15 Nm).
- Negative battery cable

Oil Pan

REMOVAL & INSTALLATION

1.6L Engines

1. Before servicing the vehicle, refer to the precautions in the beginning of this section.
2. Drain the engine oil.
3. Remove or disconnect the following:
- Negative battery cable
- Front skidplate, if equipped
- Front differential, if equipped
- Crankshaft Position (CKP) sensor
- Left transmission stiffener bracket, if equipped
- Flywheel access panel
- Oil pan and oil pump pickup tube

To install:
4. Apply a bead of silicone sealant to the oil pan flange.
5. Install or connect the following:
- New oil pump pickup tube O-ring seal
- Oil pan and oil pump pickup tube. Tighten the fasteners to 97 inch lbs. (11 Nm).
- Flywheel access panel

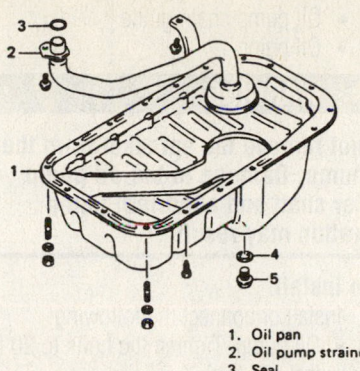

1. Oil pan
2. Oil pump strainer
3. Seal
4. Drain plug gasket
5. Drain plug

7924HG11

Exploded view of the oil pan and pump pickup mounting—1.6L engine

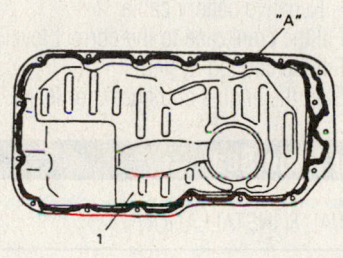

1. Oil pan
A. Sealant

7924HG79

Before installing the oil pan, apply a continuous bead of silicone sealant to the oil pan mating flange—all engines

- Left transmission stiffener bracket, if equipped
- CKP sensor
- Front differential, if equipped
- Front skidplate, if equipped. Tighten the bolts to 40 ft. lbs. (55 Nm).
- Negative battery cable

6. Fill the crankcase to the correct level.
7. Start the engine and check for leaks.

1.8L and 2.0L Engines

1. Before servicing the vehicle, refer to the precautions in the beginning of this section.
2. Drain the engine oil.
3. Remove or disconnect the following:
- Negative battery cable
- Oil dipstick tube
- Front wheels
- Front skidplate, if equipped
- Steering gear
- Front differential, if equipped
- Left transmission stiffener bracket, if equipped

- Flywheel access panel
- Exhaust front pipe
- Left and right motor mounts and raise the engine about 1 inch (25mm) for clearance
- Oil pan and oil pump pickup tube

To install:

4. Apply a bead of silicone sealant to the oil pan flange. Install new oil pump pickup tube O-ring seals.
5. Install or connect the following:
- Oil pan and oil pump pickup tube. Tighten the fasteners to 97 inch lbs. (11 Nm).
- Left and right engine mounts. Tighten the nuts to 36 ft. lbs. (50 Nm).
- Exhaust front pipe
- Flywheel access panel
- Left transmission stiffener bracket, if equipped
- Front differential, if equipped
- Steering gear
- Front skidplate, if equipped
- Front wheels
- Oil dipstick tube
- Negative battery cable
6. Fill the crankcase to the correct level.
7. Start the engine and check for leaks.

2.5L Engine

1. Before servicing the vehicle, refer to the precautions in the beginning of this section.
2. Drain the engine oil.
3. Remove or disconnect the following:
- Negative battery cable
- Oil dipstick tube
- Front wheels
- Front skidplate, if equipped
- Steering gear
- Front differential, if equipped
- Lower oil pan
- Oil pickup tube bracket
- Radiator outlet pipe
- Upper oil pan and oil pickup tube

To install:

4. Install a new O-ring to the lower crankcase.
5. Apply a bead of silicone sealant to the upper oil pan flange.
6. Install or connect the following:
- New oil pump pickup tube O-ring seals
- Upper oil pan and oil pump pickup tube and tighten the fasteners as shown
- Radiator outlet pipe
- Oil pickup tube bracket

1. O-ring

9302HG05

Lower crankcase O-ring seal

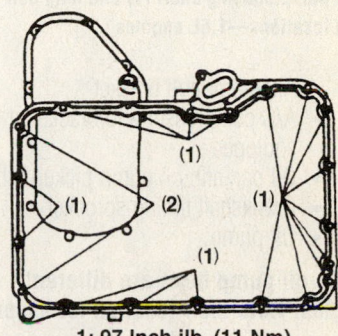

1: 97 Inch ilb. (11 Nm)
2: 20 Ft. lbs. (27 Nm)

9308HG03

Upper oil pan bolt torque values—2.5L engine

- Lower oil pan. Tighten the bolts to 97 inch lbs. (11 Nm).
- Front differential, if equipped
- Steering gear
- Front skidplate, if equipped
- Front wheels
- Oil dipstick tube
- Negative battery cable
7. Fill the crankcase to the correct level.
8. Start the engine and check for leaks.

Oil Pump

REMOVAL & INSTALLATION

1.6L Engines

1. Before servicing the vehicle, refer to the precautions in the beginning of this section.
2. Drain the engine oil.
3. Drain the cooling system.
4. Remove or disconnect the following:
- Negative battery cable
- Accessory drive belts
- Crankshaft pulley
- Front cover
- Timing belt. Refer to the Timing Belt unit repair section.

For complete mechanical specifications, refer to Section 1 of this manual

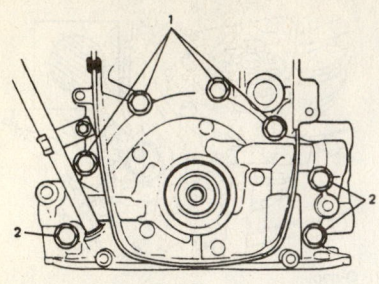

1. No. 1 bolts (short)
2. No. 2 bolts (long)

7924HG14

Oil pump housing short (1) and long bolt (2) locations—1.6L engines

- Alternator and bracket
- A/C compressor and bracket, if equipped
- Oil pan and oil pump pickup tube
- Crankshaft timing sprocket
- Oil pump

➡The oil pump bolts are different lengths. Note their location for assembly.

To install:
5. Install or connect the following:
- Oil pump with a new gasket. Tighten the bolts to 97 inch lbs. (11 Nm).
- Crankshaft timing sprocket. Tighten the bolt to 94 ft. lbs. (130 Nm).
- Oil pan and oil pump pickup tube
- A/C compressor and bracket, if equipped
- Alternator and bracket
- Timing belt
- Front cover
- Crankshaft pulley. Tighten the bolts to 12 ft. lbs. (16 Nm).

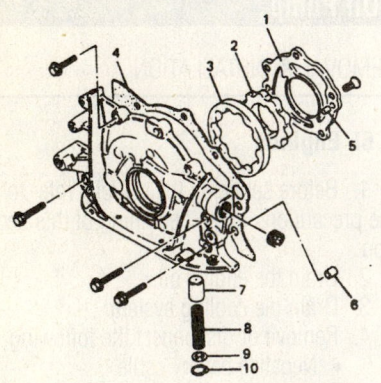

1. Rotor plate
2. Inner rotor
3. Outer rotor
4. Gasket
5. Pin
6. Pin
7. Relief valve
8. Spring
9. Retainer
10. Retainer ring

7924HG12

Exploded view of the oil pump housing—1.6L engines

- Accessory drive belts
- Negative battery cable
6. Fill the crankcase to the correct level.
7. Start the engine and check for leaks.

1.8L and 2.0L Engines

1. Before servicing the vehicle, refer to the precautions in the beginning of this section.
2. Drain the engine oil.
3. Remove or disconnect the following:
- Negative battery cable
- Oil pan and pickup tube
- Oil pump sprocket cover
- Oil pump

❄❄ WARNING

Do not remove the sprocket from the oil pump. Damage to the oil pump center shaft and abnormal pump operation may result.

To install:
4. Install or connect the following:
- Oil pump. Tighten the bolts to 20 ft. lbs. (27 Nm).
- Oil pump sprocket cover. Tighten the bolts to 108 inch lbs. (12 Nm).
- Oil pan and pickup tube
- Negative battery cable
5. Fill the crankcase to the correct level.
6. Start the engine and check for leaks.

2.5L Engine

1. Before servicing the vehicle, refer to the precautions in the beginning of this section.
2. Drain the cooling system.
3. Drain the engine oil.
4. Remove or disconnect the following:
- Negative battery cable
- Accessory drive belts
- Intake manifold
- Oil pan and oil pickup tube
- Front cover

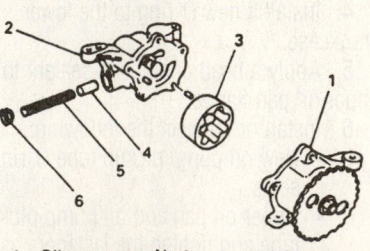

1. Oil pump case No.1
2. Oil pump case No.2
3. Outer rotor
4. Relief valve
5. Relief spring
6. Retainer

7924HG15

Exploded view of oil pump—1.8L, 2.0L and 2.5L engines

- Oil pump chain guide
- Oil pump

❄❄ WARNING

Do not remove the sprocket from the oil pump. Damage to the oil pump center shaft and abnormal pump operation may result.

To install:
5. Install or connect the following:
- Oil pump. Tighten the bolts to 20 ft. lbs. (27 Nm).
- Oil pump chain guide. Tighten the bolts to 97 inch lbs. (11 Nm).
- Front cover
- Oil pan and oil pickup tube
- Intake manifold
- Accessory drive belts
- Negative battery cable
6. Fill the crankcase to the correct level.
7. Fill the cooling system.
8. Start the engine and check for leaks.

Rear Main Seal

REMOVAL & INSTALLATION

1. Before servicing the vehicle, refer to the precautions in the beginning of this section.
2. Remove or disconnect the following:
- Negative battery cable
- Transmission
- Clutch assembly, if equipped
- Flywheel
- Rear main seal

To install:
3. Install or connect the following:
- Rear main seal flush with the cylinder block
- Flywheel. Tighten the bolts in a crossing pattern to 58 ft. lbs. (79 Nm) for 1.6L engines or to 51 ft. lbs. (69 Nm) for all other engines.
- Clutch assembly, if equipped
- Transmission
- Negative battery cable

Timing Chain, Sprockets, Front Cover and Seal

REMOVAL & INSTALLATION

1.8L and 2.0L Engines

1. Before servicing the vehicle, refer to the precautions in the beginning of this section.
2. Drain the cooling system.

3. Drain the engine oil.
4. Remove or disconnect the following:
   - Negative battery cable
   - Oil pan and pickup tube
   - Valve cover
   - Bypass pipe and hose
   - Accessory drive belts
   - Cooling fan and shroud
   - Water pump pulley
   - Alternator belt tensioner and idler pulleys
   - Upper radiator hose
   - A/C compressor and bracket, if equipped
   - Crankshaft pulley
   - Front crankshaft seal
   - Front cover
5. Rotate the crankshaft to align the timing marks as shown.

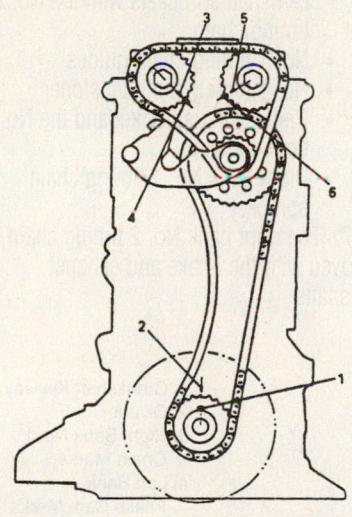

Timing mark alignment—1.8L and 2.0L engines

✳ WARNING

Do not allow the crankshaft or camshafts to rotate once the timing chains have been removed. Valve or piston damage could result.

6. Remove or disconnect the following:
   - Second timing chain tensioner
   - Camshaft sprockets and second timing chain
   - First timing chain tensioner
   - Timing chain idler sprocket and first timing chain

To install:

7. Prepare the timing chain tensioners for installation by releasing the latches,

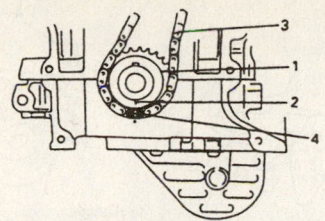

1. Crankshaft timing sprocket
2. Match mark
3. 1st timing chain
4. Yellow plate

7924HG17

Crankshaft and first timing chain alignment—1.8L and 2.0L engines

1. Idler sprocket
2. Match mark on idler sprocket
3. 1st timing chain
4. Dark blue plate

7924HG16

Idler sprocket and first timing chain alignment—1.8L and 2.0L engines

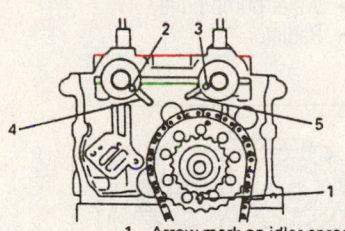

1. Arrow mark on idler sprocket
2. Knock pin of intake camshaft
3. Knock pin of exhaust camshaft
4. Timing mark of intake side
5. Timing mark of exhaust side

7924HG19

Idler sprocket and camshaft alignment—1.8L and 2.0L engines

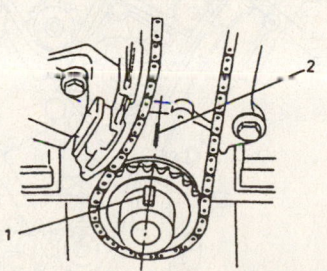

1. Crank timing sprocket key
2. Timing mark

7924HG18

Crankshaft sprocket alignment—1.8L and 2.0L engines

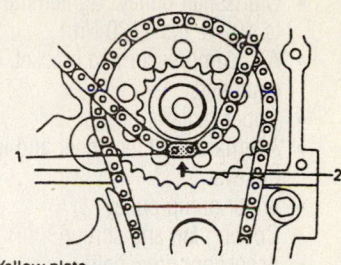

1. Yellow plate
2. Match mark of 2nd timing chain (Arrow mark)

7924HG20

Idler sprocket and second timing chain alignment—1.8L and 2.0L engines

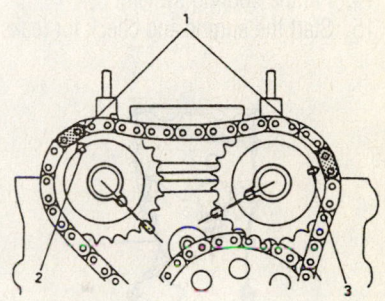

1. Dark blue
2. Arrow mark on intake camshaft timing sprocket
3. Arrow mark on exhaust camshaft timing sprocket

7924HG21

Camshaft sprocket and second timing chain alignment—1.8L and 2.0L engines

compressing the tensioner piston fully into the bore and installing retaining pins.

8. Install or connect the following:
   - Timing chain idler sprocket and first timing chain with the matchmarks and colored links aligned as shown
   - First timing chain tensioner. Tighten the bolts to 97 inch lbs. (11 Nm).
   - Camshaft sprockets and second timing chain with the matchmarks and colored links aligned as shown
   - Second timing chain tensioner. Tighten the bolts to 97 inch lbs. (11 Nm) and the nut to 33 ft. lbs. (45 Nm).
9. Tighten the camshaft sprocket bolts to 59 ft. lbs. (80 Nm).
10. Remove the timing chain tensioner retaining pins.
11. Rotate the crankshaft two complete turns and check that the timing marks align.
12. Install or connect the following:
   - Front cover. Apply sealant as shown.
   - Front crankshaft seal

Please refer to Section 8 for electric cooling fan wiring schematics

- Crankshaft pulley. Tighten the bolt to 109 ft. lbs. (130 Nm).
- A/C compressor and bracket, if equipped
- Upper radiator hose
- Alternator belt tensioner and idler pulleys
- Water pump pulley
- Cooling fan and shroud
- Accessory drive belts
- Bypass pipe and hose
- Valve cover
- Oil pan and pickup tube
- Negative battery cable

13. Fill the crankcase to the correct level.
14. Fill the cooling system.
15. Start the engine and check for leaks.

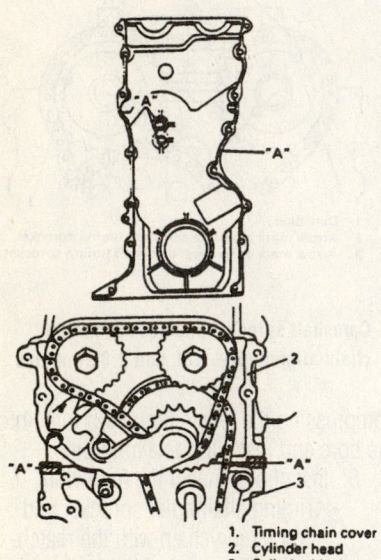

1. Timing chain cover
2. Cylinder head
3. Cylinder block

7924HG10

Prior to installing the timing chain cover on the engine block and cylinder head, apply silicone sealant to the cover as indicated (areas marked A)—1.8L, 2.0L and 2.5L engines

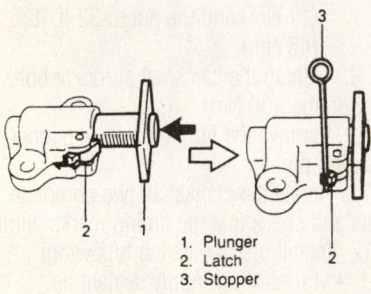

1. Plunger
2. Latch
3. Stopper

9302HG09

Preparing the No. 1 timing chain tensioner adjuster for installation—1.8L, 2.0L and 2.5L engines

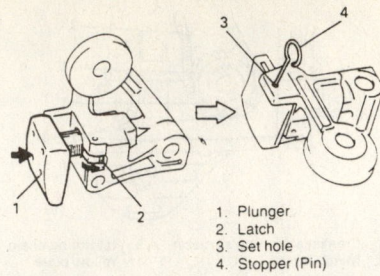

1. Plunger
2. Latch
3. Set hole
4. Stopper (Pin)

9302HG13

No. 2 timing chain tensioner—left bank tensioner shown—1.8L, 2.0L and 2.5L engines

2.5L Engine

1. Before servicing the vehicle, refer to the precautions in the beginning of this section.
2. Drain the cooling system.
3. Drain the engine oil.
4. Remove or disconnect the following:
   - Negative battery cable
   - Intake manifold
   - Ignition coils
   - Valve covers
   - Accessory drive belts
   - Cooling fan and shroud
   - Water pump pulley
   - Radiator

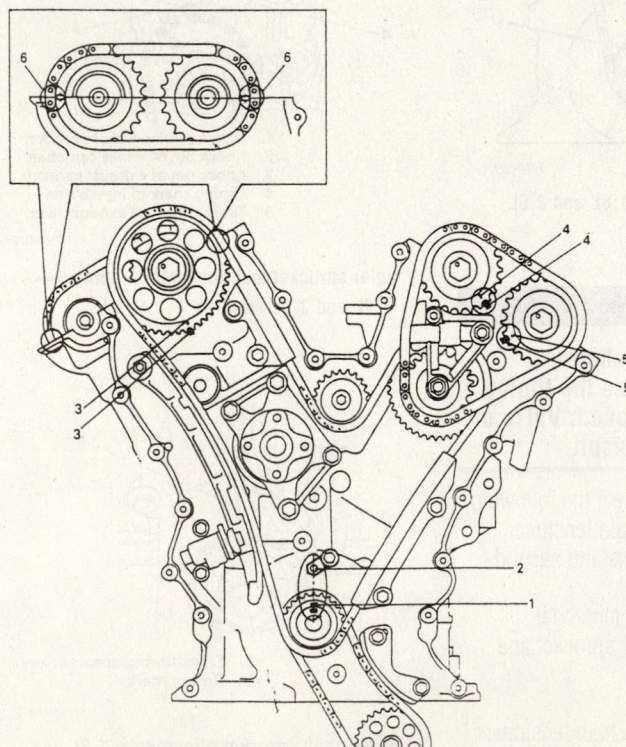

1. Crankshaft Keyway
2. Oil Jet
3. Right Bank No. 1 Chain Marks
4. Left Bank Intake Cam Marks
5. Left Bank Exhaust Cam Marks
6. Right Bank Intake and Exhaust Cam Marks

9302HG07

Timing chain alignment marks—2.5L engine

- Power steering pump and brackets
- Oil pan and pickup tube
- Crankshaft pulley
- Front crankshaft seal
- Crankshaft Position (CKP) sensor
- Front cover

5. Rotate the crankshaft so that the timing marks are aligned as shown.

❊❊ WARNING

Do not allow the crankshaft or camshafts to rotate once the timing chains have been removed. Valve or piston damage could result.

6. Remove or disconnect the following:
   - Left bank No. 2 timing chain tensioner
   - Left bank intake and exhaust camshaft sprockets with the No. 2 timing chain
   - No. 1 timing chain guides
   - No. 1 timing chain tensioner
   - Center idler sprocket and the No. 1 timing chain
   - Right bank No. 1 timing chain sprocket

7. The right bank No. 2 timing chain is removed with the intake and exhaust camshafts.

To install:

8. Prepare the timing chain tensioners for installation by releasing the latches, compressing the tensioner piston fully into the bore and installing retaining pins.

9. Align the timing chain sprocket matchmarks and colored chain links as shown during assembly.

10. Install or connect the following:

- Right bank intake and exhaust camshafts with the No. 2 timing chain

- Right bank No. 1 timing chain sprocket. Tighten the bolt to 58 ft. lbs. (80 Nm).
- Center idler sprocket and the No. 1 timing chain. Tighten the fastener to 32 ft. lbs. (45 Nm).
- No. 1 timing chain tensioner and guides. Tighten the bolts to 97 inch lbs. (11 Nm).
- Left bank intake and exhaust camshaft sprockets with the No. 2 timing chain. Tighten the bolts to 57 ft. lbs. (80 Nm).
- Left bank No. 2 timing chain ten-

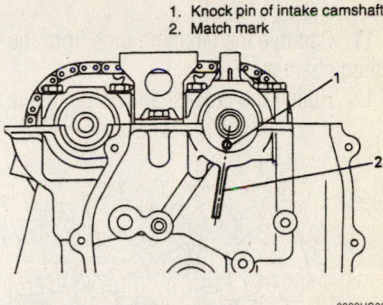

1. Knock pin of intake camshaft
2. Match mark

9302HG08

Right bank camshaft timing marks—2.5L engine

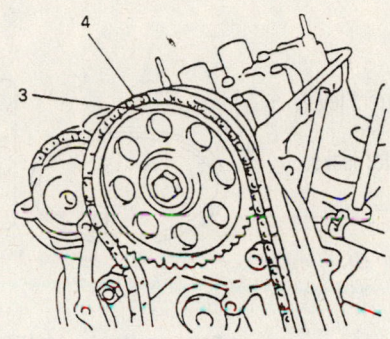

3. Match mark of RH bank 1st timing chain sprocket
4. Silver plate (LH) of 1st timing chain

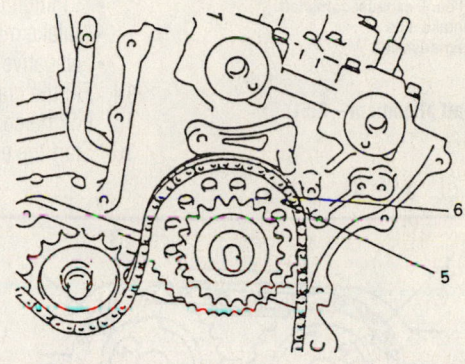

5. Match mark of idler sprocket No.2
6. Silver plate (RH) of 1st timing chain

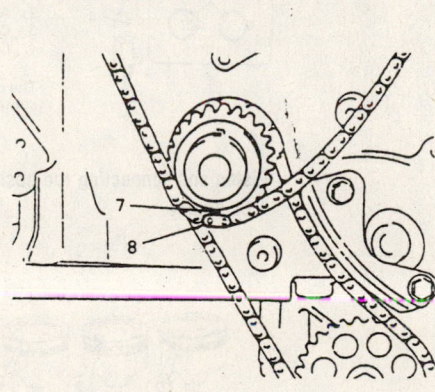

7. Match mark of crankshaft timing sprocket
8. Gold or Yellow plate of 1st timing chain

No. 1 timing chain alignment—2.5L engine

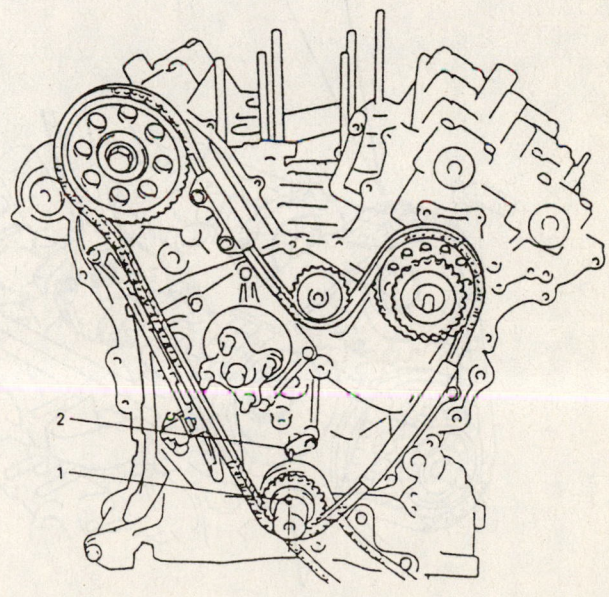

1. Crank timing pulley key
2. Oil jet

9302HG10

For complete service labor times order Nichols' Chilton Labor Guide Manual

sioner. Tighten the bolts to 97 inch lbs. (11 Nm).

11. Remove the retaining pins from the timing chain tensioners.

12. Rotate the crankshaft two complete

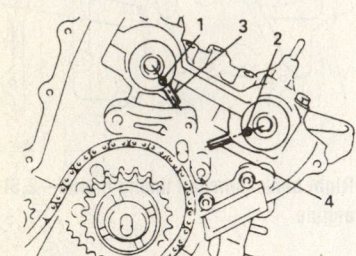

1. Knock pin of LH bank intake camshaft
2. Knock pin of LH bank exhaust camshaft
3. Match mark of intake side
4. Match mark of exhaust side

9302HG11

Left bank camshaft alignment—2.5L engine

turns and check that the timing marks align.

13. Install or connect the following:
- Front cover. Tighten the bolts to 97 inch lbs. (11 Nm).
- CKP sensor
- Front crankshaft seal
- Crankshaft pulley. Tighten the bolt to 109 ft. lbs. (148 Nm).
- Oil pan and pickup tube
- Power steering pump and brackets
- Radiator
- Water pump pulley
- Cooling fan and shroud
- Accessory drive belts
- Valve covers
- Ignition coils
- Intake manifold
- Negative battery cable

14. Fill the crankcase to the correct level.
15. Fill the cooling system.
16. Start the engine and check for leaks.

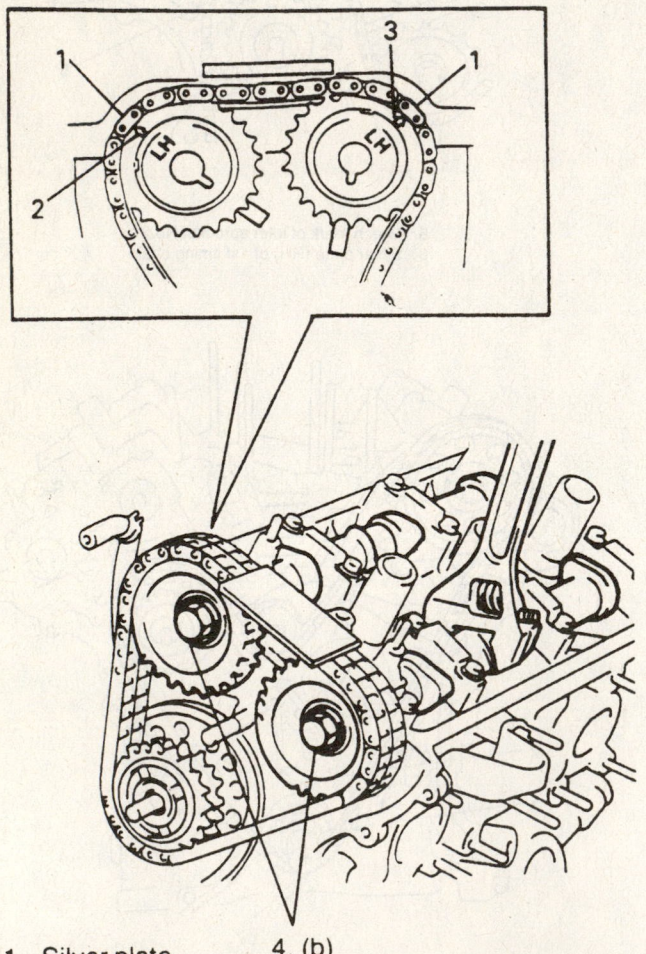

1. Silver plate
2. Arrow mark on intake camshaft timing sprocket
3. Arrow mark on exhaust camshaft timing sprocket
4. Sprocket bolt

9302HG12

Align the left bank No. 2 chain silver links—2.5L engine

Piston and Ring

POSITIONING

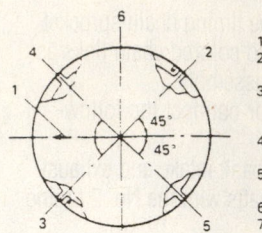

1. Arrow mark
2. 1st ring end gap
3. 2nd ring end gap and oil ring spacer gap
4. Oil ring upper rail gap
5. Oil ring lower rail gap
6. Intake side
7. Exhaust side

7924AG67

Piston ring end-gap spacing—All engines

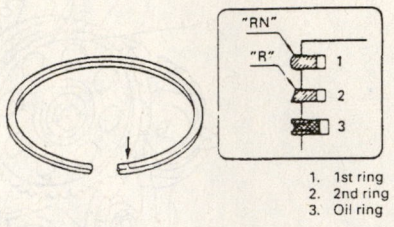

1. 1st ring
2. 2nd ring
3. Oil ring

7924AG68

Compression ring identification marks—All engines

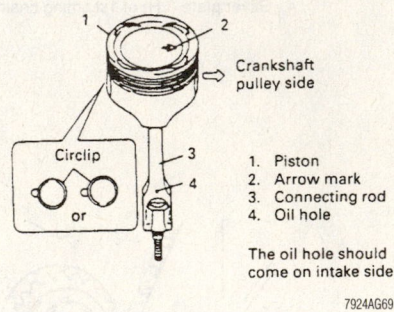

1. Piston
2. Arrow mark
3. Connecting rod
4. Oil hole

The oil hole should come on intake side

7924AG69

Piston and connecting rod positioning—1.6L engine

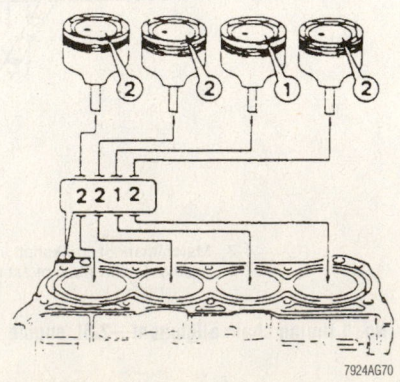

7924AG70

Piston installation—1.6L engine

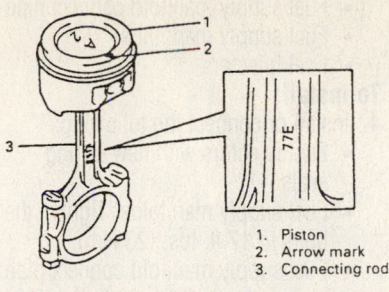

1. Piston
2. Arrow mark
3. Connecting rod

7924AG61

Piston and connecting rod positioning—1.8L, 2.0L and 2.5L engines

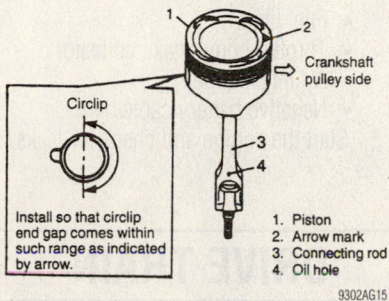

Circlip

Install so that circlip end gap comes within such range as indicated by arrow.

1. Piston
2. Arrow mark
3. Connecting rod
4. Oil hole

9302AG15

Piston pin circlip installation—2.5L engine

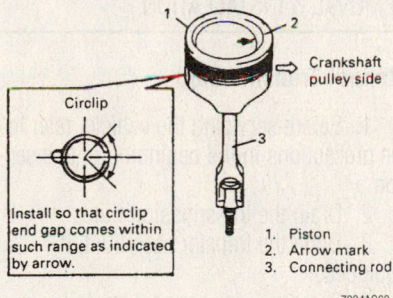

Circlip

Install so that circlip end gap comes within such range as indicated by arrow.

1. Piston
2. Arrow mark
3. Connecting rod

7924AG62

Piston pin circlip installation—1.8L and 2.0L engines

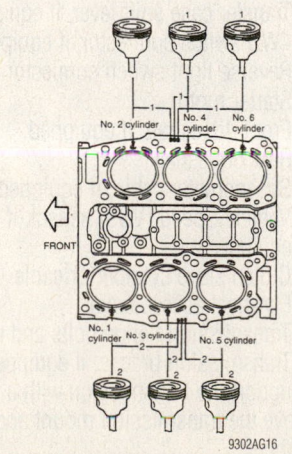

9302AG16

Piston identification—2.5L engine

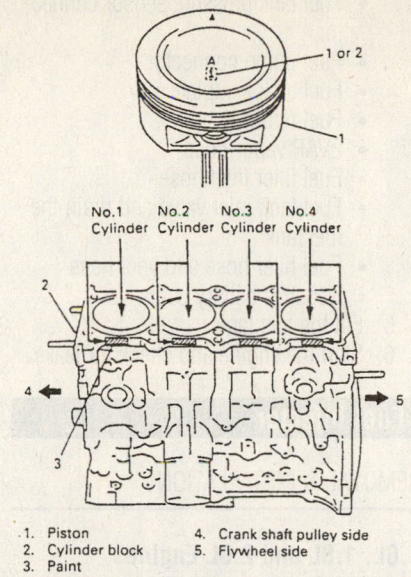

No.1 Cylinder No.2 Cylinder No.3 Cylinder No.4 Cylinder

1. Piston
2. Cylinder block
3. Paint
4. Crank shaft pulley side
5. Flywheel side

7924AG65

Piston identification—1.8L and 2.0L engines
Match pistons with "1" indicators to red cylinder paint marks
Match pistons with "2" indicators to blue cylinder paint marks

FUEL SYSTEM

Fuel System Service Precautions

Safety is the most important factor when performing not only fuel system maintenance but any type of maintenance. Failure to conduct maintenance and repairs in a safe manner may result in serious personal injury or death. Maintenance and testing of the vehicle fuel system components can be accomplished safely and effectively by adhering to the following rules and guidelines.

• To avoid the possibility of fire and personal injury, always disconnect the negative battery cable unless the repair or test procedure requires that battery voltage be applied.

• Always relieve the fuel system pressure prior to disconnecting any fuel system component (injector, fuel rail, pressure regulator, etc.), fitting or fuel line connection. Exercise extreme caution whenever relieving fuel system pressure to avoid exposing skin, face and eyes to fuel spray. Please be advised that fuel under pressure may penetrate the skin or any part of the body that it contacts.

• Always place a shop towel or cloth around the fitting or connection prior to loosening to absorb any excess fuel due to spillage. Ensure that all fuel spillage (should it occur) is quickly removed from engine surfaces. Ensure that all fuel soaked cloths or towels are deposited into a suitable waste container.

• Always keep a dry chemical (Class B) fire extinguisher near the work area.

• Do not allow fuel spray or fuel vapors to come into contact with a spark or open flame.

• Always use a backup wrench when loosening and tightening fuel line connection fittings. This will prevent unnecessary stress and torsion to fuel line piping.

• Always replace worn fuel fitting O-rings with new. Do not substitute fuel hose or equivalent, where fuel pipe is installed.

Fuel System Pressure

RELIEVING

1. Before servicing the vehicle, refer to the precautions in the beginning of this section.

2. Detach the wiring harness connector from the fuel pump relay, located under the left-hand side of the instrument panel near the ECM.

3. Start the engine and run it until it stops from lack of fuel. Crank the engine 2–3 times for a 3 second period. The fuel lines should now be depressurized.

4. After servicing, reattach the wiring harness connector to the fuel pump relay.

Fuel Filter

REMOVAL & INSTALLATION

1997 Models

1. Before servicing the vehicle, refer to the precautions in the beginning of this section.

2. Relieve fuel system pressure.

3. Remove or disconnect the following:
   • Negative battery cable
   • Fuel lines from the fuel filter
   • Fuel filter

To install:

4. Install or connect the following:
   • Fuel filter and tighten the bracket bolt. Note the fuel flow directional arrow.

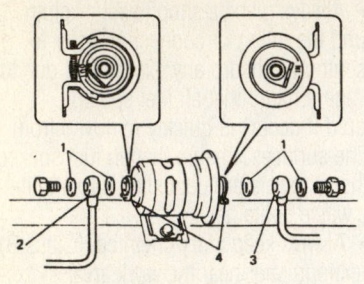

1. Gasket
2. Outlet pipe
3. Inlet pipe
4. Recess

7924HG34

Exploded view of the fuel line mounting on the fuel filter—1997 models

- Fuel lines to the fuel filter. Tighten the bolts to 25 ft. lbs. (34 Nm)
- Negative battery cable

5. Start the engine and inspect the fuel filter connections for leaks.

1998–01 Models

The fuel filter procedure is similar to the 1997 models with the exception that the 1998–01 models do not use banjo fittings at the filter. The 1998–01 models use hoses and spring clamps.

Fuel Pump

REMOVAL & INSTALLATION

1. Before servicing the vehicle, refer to the precautions in the beginning of this section.
2. Relieve the fuel system pressure.
3. Remove or disconnect the following:
- Negative battery cable
- Fuel filler hose and vent hose
- Fuel tank inlet valve and drain the fuel tank
- Fuel filter inlet hose
- Evaporative Emissions (EVAP) vapor hose
- Fuel return line
- Fuel tank skidplate
- Fuel pump connector
- Fuel tank pressure sensor connector
- Fuel tank
- Fuel pump module

To install:
4. Install or connect the following:
- Fuel pump module with a new seal. Tighten the bolts to 44 inch lbs. (5 Nm).
- Fuel tank. Tighten the strap bolts to 37 ft. lbs. (50 Nm).

- Fuel tank pressure sensor connector
- Fuel pump connector
- Fuel tank skidplate
- Fuel return line
- EVAP vapor hose
- Fuel filter inlet hose
- Fuel tank inlet valve and drain the fuel tank
- Fuel filler hose and vent hose
- Negative battery cable

5. Fill the fuel tank.
6. Start the engine and check for leaks.

Fuel Injector

REMOVAL & INSTALLATION

1.6L, 1.8L and 2.0L Engines

1. Before servicing the vehicle, refer to the precautions in the beginning of this section.
2. Relieve the fuel system pressure.
3. Remove or disconnect the following:
- Negative battery cable
- Front intake manifold bracket, if equipped
- Positive Crankcase Ventilation (PCV) valve and hose
- Fuel injector harness connectors
- Fuel line bracket
- Fuel supply manifold
- Fuel injectors

To install:
4. Install or connect the following:
- Fuel injectors with new O-ring seals
- Fuel supply manifold. Tighten the bolts to 17 ft. lbs. (23 Nm).
- Fuel line bracket
- Fuel injector harness connectors
- PCV valve and hose
- Front intake manifold bracket, if equipped
- Negative battery cable

5. Start the engine and check for leaks.

2.5L Engine

1. Before servicing the vehicle, refer to the precautions in the beginning of this section.
2. Relieve the fuel system pressure.
3. Remove or disconnect the following:
- Negative battery cable
- Air intake tube
- Throttle body intake collector
- Fuel lines
- Fuel pressure regulator vacuum line
- Fuel injector harness connectors

- Fuel supply manifold connect pipe
- Fuel supply manifolds
- Fuel injectors

To install:
4. Install or connect the following:
- Fuel injectors with new O-ring seals
- Fuel supply manifolds. Tighten the bolts to 17 ft. lbs. (23 Nm).
- Fuel supply manifold connect pipe. Tighten the bolts to 22 ft. lbs. (30 Nm).
- Fuel injector harness connectors
- Fuel pressure regulator vacuum line
- Fuel lines
- Throttle body intake collector
- Air intake tube
- Negative battery cable

5. Start the engine and check for leaks.

DRIVE TRAIN

Transmission Assembly

REMOVAL & INSTALLATION

Manual Transmission

1. Before servicing the vehicle, refer to the precautions in the beginning of this section.
2. Drain the transmission fluid.
3. Drain the transfer case fluid, if equipped.
4. Remove or disconnect the following:
- Negative battery cable
- Shift lever boots
- Gear shift lever
- Transfer case shift lever, if equipped
- 4WD switch connector, if equipped
- Reverse light switch connector
- Starter motor
- Front driveshaft, if equipped
- Rear driveshaft
- Speedometer cable, if equipped
- Vehicle Speed (VSS) sensor, if equipped
- Clutch slave cylinder or cable
- Flywheel access cover
- Transmission flange bolts and nuts
- Transmission braces, if equipped

5. Support the transmission with a jack and remove the transmission mount and crossmember.
6. Place a wooden block at the rear of the cylinder head as shown to support the engine when the transmission is removed.

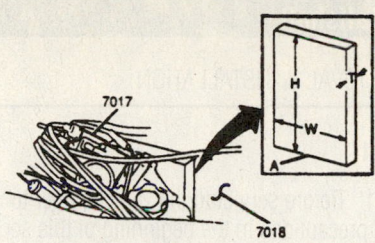

A	WOOD BLOCK
H	200 mm (8.0")
T	45 mm (1.8")
W	100–150 mm (4.0–6.0")
7017	DISTRIBUTOR CAP
7018	BULKHEAD

7924HG37

Support the engine with a wooden block between the cylinder head and the firewall—All models

7. Lower the transmission away from the vehicle.

To install:

8. Install or connect the following:

- Transmission. Tighten the flange fasteners to 62–72 ft. lbs. (85–98 Nm).
- Transmission mount and cross-member. Tighten the fasteners to 29–43 ft. lbs. (40–60 Nm).
- Transmission braces, if equipped. Tighten the bolts to 62–72 ft. lbs. (85–98 Nm).
- Flywheel access cover
- Clutch slave cylinder or cable
- VSS sensor, if equipped
- Speedometer cable, if equipped
- Rear driveshaft
- Front driveshaft, if equipped
- Starter motor
- Reverse light switch connector
- 4WD switch connector, if equipped
- Transfer case shift lever, if equipped
- Gear shift lever
- Shift lever boots
- Negative battery cable

9. Fill the transmission to the correct level.

10. Fill the transfer case, if equipped.

Automatic Transmission

1. Before servicing the vehicle, refer to the precautions in the beginning of this section.

2. Drain the transfer case oil, if equipped.

3. Remove or disconnect the following:

- Negative battery cable
- Center console and transfer case shift lever, if equipped

- Transmission dipstick tube
- Transmission wiring harness connectors
- Starter motor
- Front driveshaft, if equipped
- Rear driveshaft
- Gear select cable and bracket
- Throttle Valve (TV) cable, if equipped
- Exhaust front pipe
- Transmission oil cooler lines
- Transmission brace
- Flywheel access cover
- Torque converter
- Speedometer cable, if equipped
- Vehicle Speed (VSS) sensor connector, if equipped
- Transmission flange bolts and nuts
- Transmission braces, if equipped

4. Support the transmission with a jack and remove the transmission mount and crossmember.

5. Place a wooden block at the rear of the cylinder head as shown to support the engine when the transmission is removed.

6. Lower the transmission away from the vehicle.

To install:

7. Install or connect the following:

- Transmission. Tighten the flange fasteners to 62–72 ft. lbs. (85–98 Nm).
- Transmission mount and cross-member. Tighten the fasteners to 29–43 ft. lbs. (40–60 Nm).
- Transmission braces, if equipped. Tighten the bolts to 62–72 ft. lbs. (85–98 Nm).
- VSS sensor connector, if equipped
- Speedometer cable, if equipped
- Torque converter. Tighten the bolts to 47 ft. lbs. (65 Nm).
- Flywheel access cover
- Transmission brace
- Transmission oil cooler lines
- Exhaust front pipe
- TV cable, if equipped
- Gear select cable and bracket
- Rear driveshaft
- Front driveshaft, if equipped
- Starter motor
- Transmission wiring harness connectors
- Transmission dipstick tube
- Center console and transfer case shift lever, if equipped
- Negative battery cable

8. Fill the transmission to the correct level.

9. Fill the transfer case, if equipped.

Clutch

ADJUSTMENTS

1997–98 Models

CLUTCH PEDAL HEIGHT

The clutch pedal height should not be a periodic adjustment but may be checked after components of the mechanical clutch system have been replaced.

The proper clutch pedal height should be 0.2 in. (5mm) above the brake pedal height

If adjustment is necessary, loosen the locknut and turn the adjusting bolt until the appropriate height is reached. Once set, keep the bolt from turning and tighten the locknut to secure the adjustment.

CLUTCH PEDAL FREE-PLAY

The clutch pedal free-play should be checked from time-to-time in order to assure proper clutch operation.

The proper clutch free-play should be 0.6–1.1 in. (15–25mm).

1. Before servicing the vehicle, refer to the precautions in the beginning of this section.

2. If the free-play must be adjusted, turn the joint nut (2) located at the transmission end of the clutch cable in or out, as necessary to achieve the proper play.

3. Once the correct pedal free-play is obtained, check the free-play on the release arm (c), it should be 0.02–0.06 in. (0.5–1.5mm).

1999–01 Models

These vehicles are equipped with a hydraulic clutch system. No adjustment is necessary.

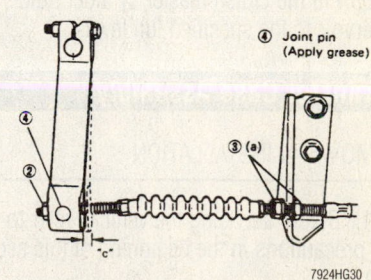

7924HG30

Pedal free-play is adjusted at the joint nut (2), while keeping the outer cable nuts (3) tightened around the center cable thread portion

REMOVAL & INSTALLATION

1. Before servicing the vehicle, refer to the precautions in the beginning of this section.
2. Remove the transmission.
3. Loosen the pressure plate mounting bolts in a 2-step crisscross sequence until the spring tension is relieved.
4. Remove the pressure plate and the clutch disc.

To install:

5. Using a clutch alignment tool, assemble the clutch disc and pressure plate onto the flywheel.
6. Tighten the pressure plate bolts in multiple passes to 17 ft. lbs. (23 Nm).
7. Install the transmission.
8. Check for proper clutch operation.

Hydraulic Clutch System

BLEEDING

1. Before servicing the vehicle, refer to the precautions in the beginning of this section.
2. Fill the master cylinder reservoir to the MAX line with clean brake fluid and keep it at least half full throughout the bleeding procedure.
3. From beneath the vehicle, remove the bleeder plug cap, then attach a clear vinyl tube to the slave cylinder bleeder plug. Insert the open end of the hose into a container.
4. Have an assistant depress the clutch pedal. Open the bleeder after the pedal is depressed.
5. Close the bleeder before releasing the clutch pedal.
6. Repeat until all air bubbles are gone from the hydraulic fluid.
7. Install the bleeder plug cap.
8. Fill the clutch master cylinder fluid reservoir to the specified full level.

Transfer Case Assembly

REMOVAL & INSTALLATION

1. Before servicing the vehicle, refer to the precautions in the beginning of this section.
2. Drain the transfer case oil.
3. Remove or disconnect the following:
   - Negative battery cable
   - Distributor or Camshaft Position (CMP) sensor, if equipped
   - Center console

   - Transmission shift lever and case, if equipped with a manual transmission
   - Transfer case shift lever
   - Front and rear driveshafts
   - Exhaust center pipe
   - Speedometer cable or Vehicle Speed (VSS) sensor, as equipped
   - Vent hose
   - 4WD switch connector
4. Support the transmission with a jack and remove the transmission mount and crossmember.
5. Place a wooden block at the rear of the cylinder head as shown to support the engine when the transfer case is removed.
6. Lower the transfer case away from the vehicle.

To install:

7. Install or connect the following:
   - Transfer case. Tighten the bolts to 30 ft. lbs. (41 Nm).
   - 4WD switch connector
   - Vent hose
   - Speedometer cable or VSS sensor, as equipped
   - Exhaust center pipe
   - Front and rear driveshafts. Tighten the bolts to 36 ft. lbs. (50 Nm).
   - Transfer case shift lever
   - Transmission shift lever and case, if equipped with a manual transmission
   - Center console
   - Distributor or CMP sensor, if equipped
   - Negative battery cable
8. Fill the transfer case.

Halfshaft

REMOVAL & INSTALLATION

Left

1. Before servicing the vehicle, refer to the precautions in the beginning of this section.
2. Remove or disconnect the following:
   - Front wheel
   - Hub drive flange or locking hub, as equipped
   - Snapring
   - Thrust washer
   - Halfshaft flange fasteners
   - Halfshaft

To install:

3. Install or connect the following:
   - Halfshaft. Tighten the flange bolts to 37 ft. lbs. (50 Nm).
   - Thrust washer
   - Snapring
   - Locking hub, if equipped. Tighten the bolts to 24 ft. lbs. (33 Nm).
   - Hub drive flange, if equipped. Tighten the bolts to 35 ft. lbs. (48 Nm).
   - Front wheel

Right

1. Before servicing the vehicle, refer to the precautions in the beginning of this section.
2. Remove or disconnect the following:
   - Front wheel
   - Hub drive flange or locking hub, as equipped

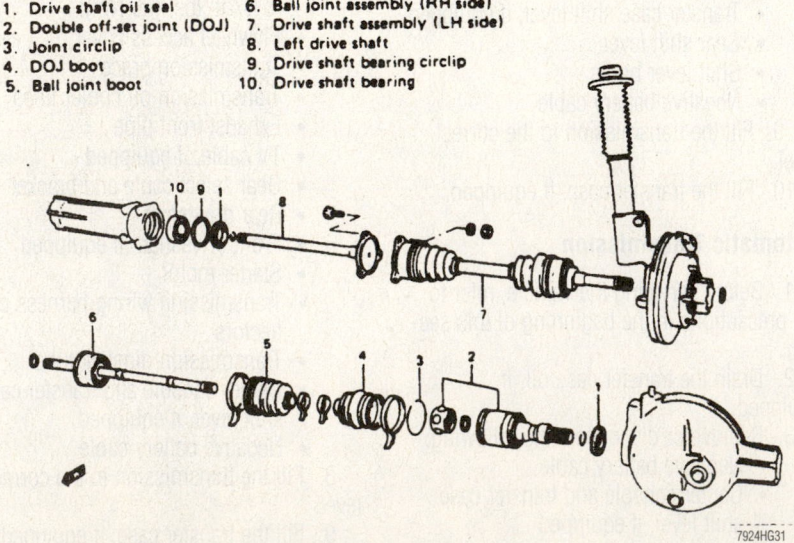

1. Drive shaft oil seal
2. Double off-set joint (DOJ)
3. Joint circlip
4. DOJ boot
5. Ball joint boot
6. Ball joint assembly (RH side)
7. Drive shaft assembly (LH side)
8. Left drive shaft
9. Drive shaft bearing circlip
10. Drive shaft bearing

Exploded view of the left- and right-hand halfshaft assemblies

7924HG31

- Snapring
- Thrust washer
- Brake caliper
- Wheel speed sensor, if equipped
- Brake rotor
- Stabilizer bar link
- Outer tie rod end
- Lower ball joint
- Strut bracket bolts
- Steering knuckle and wheel hub

3. Pry the inboard joint out of the differential and remove the halfshaft.

To install:

4. Insert the inboard joint into the differential until the circlip is felt to seat.

5. Install or connect the following:
- Steering knuckle and wheel hub
- Strut bracket bolts. Tighten them to 70 ft. lbs. (95 Nm).
- Lower ball joint. Tighten the nut to 40 ft. lbs. (55 Nm).
- Outer tie rod end. Tighten the nut to 35 ft. lbs. (48 Nm).
- Stabilizer bar link. Tighten the nut to 21 ft. lbs. (29 Nm).
- Brake rotor
- Wheel speed sensor, if equipped
- Brake caliper
- Thrust washer
- Snapring
- Locking hub, if equipped. Tighten the bolts to 24 ft. lbs. (33 Nm).
- Hub drive flange, if equipped. Tighten the bolts to 35 ft. lbs. (48 Nm).
- Front wheel

6. Check the wheel alignment and adjust as necessary.

CV-Joints

OVERHAUL

Outer CV-Joint

The outer CV-joint is serviced with the axle shaft as an assembly. The outer CV-joint boot can be serviced by removing the inner CV-joint.

Inner CV-Joint

1. Before servicing the vehicle, refer to the precautions in the beginning of this section.

2. Remove or disconnect the following:
- Halfshaft from the vehicle
- Grease boot clamps
- Outer race snapring

- Outer race
- Shaft snapring
- Inner race, cage and balls

To install:

3. Install or connect the following:
- Inner race, cage and balls
- Shaft snapring
- Outer race
- Outer race snapring

4. Fill the outer race and the grease boot with CV-joint grease and tighten the boot clamps.

5. Install the axle halfshaft.

Manual Locking Hubs

REMOVAL & INSTALLATION

1. Before servicing the vehicle, refer to the precautions in the beginning of this section.

2. Set the selector knob to the **FREE** position.

3. Remove or disconnect the following:
- Hub cover assembly
- Hub body assembly

To install:

4. Install the hub body. Tighten the bolts to 18 ft. lbs. (25 Nm).

5. Align the hub cover stopper nail with the groove in the hub body and install the hub cover. Tighten the bolts to 90 inch lbs. (10 Nm).

6. Check for proper hub operation.

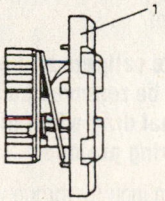

1. Cover

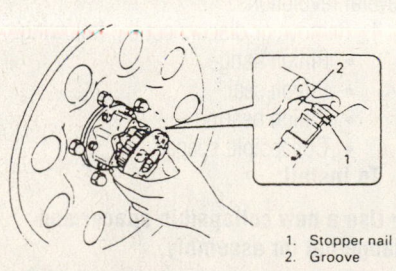

1. Stopper nail
2. Groove

9308HG06

Manual hub alignment—All models

Automatic Locking Hubs

REMOVAL & INSTALLATION

1. Before servicing the vehicle, refer to the precautions in the beginning of this section.

2. Unlock the hub by setting the transfer case in the 2H position and driving backwards at least 6.5 feet (2 meters).

3. Remove or disconnect the following:
- Hub sub assembly
- Hub brake assembly

To install:

4. Align the brake assembly key with the slot in the spindle and install the brake assembly.

5. Align the matchmark on the sub assembly with the mark on the brake assembly and install the sub assembly. Tighten the hub bolts to 24 ft. lbs. (33 Nm).

6. Check for proper hub operation.

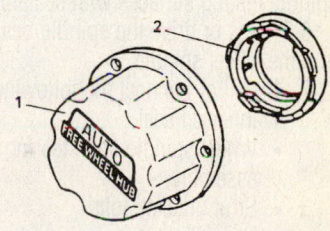

1. Free wheeling hub sub assembly
2. Free wheeling hub brake assembly

9308HG04

Automatic hub—All models

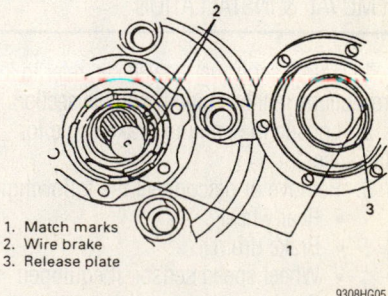

1. Match marks
2. Wire brake
3. Release plate

9308HG05

Automatic hub matchmarks—All models

Spindle Bearings

REMOVAL, PACKING & INSTALLATION

1. Before servicing the vehicle, refer to the precautions in the beginning of this section.

2. Support the control arm with a stand or floor jack.

3. Remove or disconnect the following:
   - Front wheel
   - Locking hub or drive flange, as equipped
   - Brake caliper and rotor
   - Wheel hub and bearing assembly
   - Outer tie rod end
   - Lower ball joint
   - Strut bracket bolts
   - Wheel spindle and steering knuckle assembly
   - Inner oil seal
   - Spindle bearing

To install:

4. Fill the recess in the wheel spindle with lithium grease.

5. Coat the spindle bearing and wheel spindle mating surfaces with sealant.

6. Press or drive the spindle bearing into the wheel spindle.

7. Install or connect the following:
   - Inner oil seal
   - Wheel spindle and steering knuckle assembly
   - Strut bracket bolts
   - Lower ball joint
   - Outer tie rod end
   - Wheel hub and bearing assembly
   - Brake caliper and rotor
   - Locking hub or drive flange, as equipped
   - Front wheel

Axle Shaft, Bearing and Seal

REMOVAL & INSTALLATION

1. Before servicing the vehicle, refer to the precautions in the beginning of this section.

2. Loosen the parking brake cable for clearance.

3. Remove or disconnect the following:
   - Rear wheel
   - Brake drum
   - Wheel speed sensor, if equipped
   - Bearing retainer nuts
   - Axle shaft and bearing
   - Axle shaft inner oil seal

4. If equipped with ABS, grind a flat spot on the wheel speed sensor tone ring, then split the ring with a chisel.

5. Grind flat spots on the bearing retainer and split it with a chisel.

6. Press the wheel bearing off the axle shaft.

7. Remove the bearing retainer and the outer oil seal.

To install:

8. Install or connect the following:
   - Outer oil seal to the bearing retainer
   - Bearing retainer to the axle shaft
   - Bearing and retainer ring pressed onto the axle shaft
   - Wheel speed sensor tone ring pressed onto the axle shaft, if equipped
   - Axle shaft inner oil seal
   - Axle shaft and bearing
   - Bearing retainer nuts. Tighten them to 17 ft. lbs. (23 Nm).
   - Wheel speed sensor, if equipped
   - Brake drum
   - Rear wheel

9. Fill the rear differential to the correct level.

Pinion Seal

REMOVAL & INSTALLATION

1. Before servicing the vehicle, refer to the precautions in the beginning of this section.

2. Remove or disconnect the following:
   - Driveshaft
   - Wheels
   - Brake calipers and pads or brake drum

➡ **The brake calipers and pads or brake drum must be removed so that there is no additional drag when measuring pinion bearing preload.**

3. Use an inch lb. torque wrench and measure and record the amount of torque required to maintain pinion rotation through several revolutions.

4. Remove or disconnect the following:
   - Pinion flange
   - Pinion seal
   - Pinion bearing
   - Collapsible spacer

To install:

➡ **Use a new collapsible spacer and flange nut for assembly.**

5. Install or connect the following:
   - Collapsible spacer
   - Pinion bearing
   - Pinion seal
   - Pinion flange

6. Rotate the pinion flange occasionally while tightening the flange nut to make sure the pinion bearings seat correctly.

7. Take frequent bearing preload torque readings. Tighten the flange nut to achieve the preload torque readings originally recorded.

✳✳ CAUTION

Never loosen the pinion nut to reduce bearing preload. If it is necessary to reduce bearing preload, install a new collapsible spacer and pinion nut.

8. Install or connect the following:
   - Driveshaft
   - Brake calipers and pads or brake drum
   - Wheels

9. Fill the differential with gear lubricant and check for leaks.

Axle Housing Assembly

REMOVAL & INSTALLATION

1. Before servicing the vehicle, refer to the precautions in the beginning of this section.

2. Drain the gear oil.

3. Support the vehicle at the frame with a hoist or jackstands.

4. Support the rear axle with a floor jack.

5. Remove or disconnect the following:
   - Rear wheels
   - Rear brake drums
   - Rear axle shafts
   - Load sensing proportioning valve linkage, if equipped
   - Brake fluid hose
   - Brake backing plates
   - Wheel speed sensor connector, if equipped
   - Axle vent tube
   - Rear driveshaft
   - Differential carrier assembly
   - Shock absorber lower bolts
   - Coil springs
   - Upper rods
   - Lower rods
   - Lateral rod
   - Axle housing

To install:

6. Install or connect the following:
   - Axle housing
   - Upper rods
   - Lower rods
   - Coil springs
   - Lateral rod
   - Shock absorber lower bolts

- Differential carrier assembly. Tighten the nuts to 40 ft. lbs. (55 Nm).
- Rear driveshaft
- Axle vent tube
- Wheel speed sensor connector, if equipped
- Brake backing plates
- Brake fluid hose
- Load sensing proportioning valve linkage, if equipped
- Rear axle shafts
- Rear brake drums
- Rear wheels

7. Fill the rear axle to the correct level.

8. Lower the vehicle so that the rear suspension is at curb height.

9. Tighten the upper, lower and lateral rod fasteners to 65 ft. lbs. (90 Nm).

10. Tighten the lower shock absorber fasteners to 62 ft. lbs. (85 Nm).

STEERING AND SUSPENSION

Air Bag

✳✳ CAUTION

Some vehicles are equipped with an air bag system. The system must be disarmed before performing service on, or around, system components, the steering column, instrument panel components, wiring and sensors. Failure to follow the safety precautions and the disarming procedure could result in accidental air bag deployment, possible injury and unnecessary system repairs.

PRECAUTIONS

Several precautions must be observed when handling the inflator module to avoid accidental deployment and possible personal injury.

- Never carry the inflator module by the wires or connector on the underside of the module.
- When carrying a live inflator module, hold securely with both hands and ensure

that the bag/trim cover are pointed away.

- Place the inflator module on a bench or other surface with the bag and trim cover facing up.
- With the inflator module on the bench, never place anything on or close to the module which may be thrown in the event of an accidental deployment.
- Never use air bag component parts from another vehicle.
- If there is a chance of electrical shock to any of the air bag components, remove the air bag module before servicing the vehicle.

DISARMING

1. Before servicing the vehicle, refer to the precautions in the beginning of this section.

2. Remove or disconnect the following:
- Negative battery cable
- AIR BAG fuse
- Driver air bag connector
- Glove box
- Passenger air bag connector

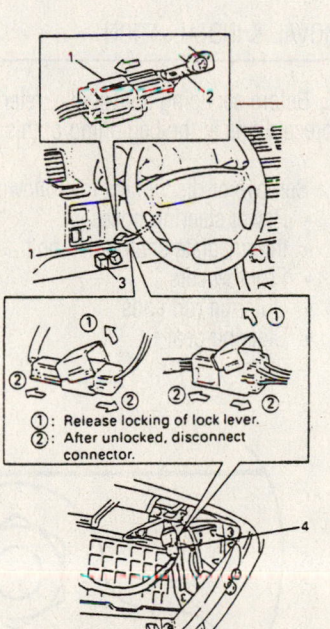

1. Yellow connector of driver air bag (inflator) module
2. Connector stay
3. Air bag fuse box
4. Yellow connector of passenger air bag (inflator) module
5. Glove box

7924HG36

Air bag component location and identification—All models

ARMING

When repairs are complete, install or connect the following:
- Passenger air bag connector
- Glove box
- Driver air bag connector
- AIR BAG fuse
- Negative battery cable

Recirculating Ball Steering Gear

REMOVAL & INSTALLATION

Manual Steering

1. Before servicing the vehicle, refer to the precautions in the beginning of this section.

2. Remove or disconnect the following:
- Skidplate, if equipped
- Intermediate shaft pinch bolt
- Pitman arm center link joint
- Steering gearbox
- Pitman arm

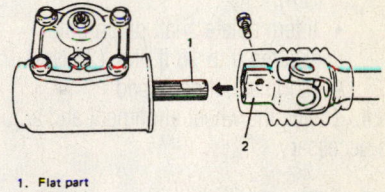

1. Flat part
2. Shaft joint

7924HG72

Remove the lower steering shaft mounting bolt and disconnect the shaft from the gearbox—1997–98 models

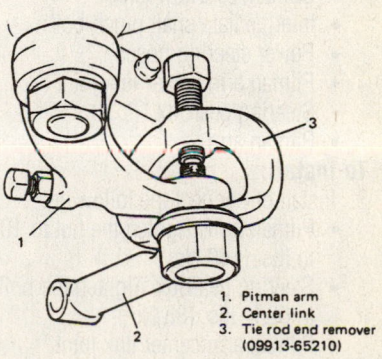

1. Pitman arm
2. Center link
3. Tie rod end remover (09913-65210)

7924HG73

Separating the center link from the Pitman arm—1997–98 models

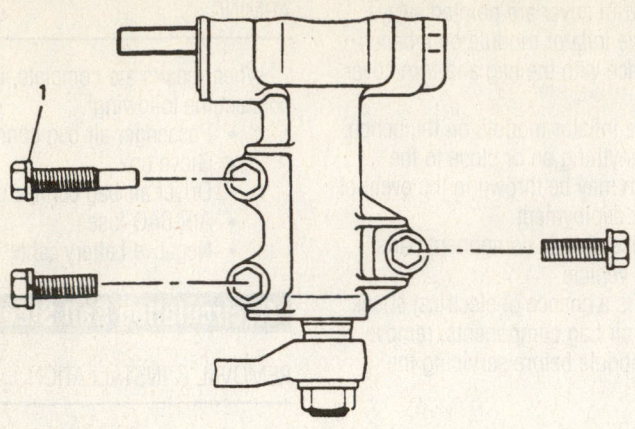

1. Guide bolt

7924HG75

When installing the steering gear box, note the position of the longer guide bolt—1997–98 models

To install:
3. Install or connect the following:
- Pitman arm. Tighten the nut to 116 ft. lbs. (160 Nm).
- Steering gearbox. Tighten the bolts to 62 ft. lbs. (85 Nm).
- Pitman arm center link joint. Tighten the nut to 37 ft. lbs. (50 Nm).
- Intermediate shaft pinch bolt. Tighten it to 18 ft. lbs. (25 Nm).
- Skidplate, if equipped
4. Check the wheel alignment and adjust as necessary.

Power Steering

1. Before servicing the vehicle, refer to the precautions in the beginning of this section.
2. Remove or disconnect the following:
- Skidplate, if equipped
- Coolant overflow tank
- Intermediate shaft pinch bolt
- Power steering hoses
- Pitman arm center link joint
- Steering gearbox
- Pitman arm

To install:
3. Install or connect the following:
- Pitman arm. Tighten the nut to 102 ft. lbs. (140 Nm).
- Steering gearbox. Tighten the bolts to 62 ft. lbs. (85 Nm).
- Pitman arm center link joint. Tighten the nut to 37 ft. lbs. (50 Nm).
- Power steering hoses
- Intermediate shaft pinch bolt. Tighten it to 18 ft. lbs. (25 Nm).
- Coolant overflow tank
- Skidplate, if equipped

4. Fill the power steering system.
5. Start the engine and check for leaks.
6. Check the wheel alignment and adjust as necessary.

Power Rack and Pinion Steering Gear

REMOVAL & INSTALLATION

1. Before servicing the vehicle, refer to the precautions in the beginning of this section.
2. Remove or disconnect the following:
- Power steering hoses
- Intermediate shaft pinch bolt
- Front wheels
- Outer tie rod ends
- Steering gear

To install:
3. Install or connect the following:
- Steering gear. Tighten the bolts to 40 ft. lbs. (55 Nm).
- Outer tie rod ends. Tighten the nuts to 32 ft. lbs. (43 Nm).
- Front wheels
- Intermediate shaft pinch bolt. Tighten it to 18 ft. lbs. (25 Nm).
- Power steering hoses
4. Fill the power steering system.
5. Start the engine and check for leaks.
6. Check the wheel alignment and adjust as necessary.

Strut

REMOVAL & INSTALLATION

1. Before servicing the vehicle, refer to the precautions in the beginning of this section.
2. Support the control arm with a stand or floor jack.
3. Remove or disconnect the following:
- Front wheel
- Brake hose bracket
- Strut bracket bolts
- Upper strut mount nuts
- Strut

To install:
4. Install or connect the following:
- Strut. Tighten the upper mount nuts to 18 ft. lbs. (25 Nm) and the bracket bolts to 70 ft. lbs. (95 Nm).
- Brake hose bracket
- Front wheel
5. Check the wheel alignment and adjust as necessary.

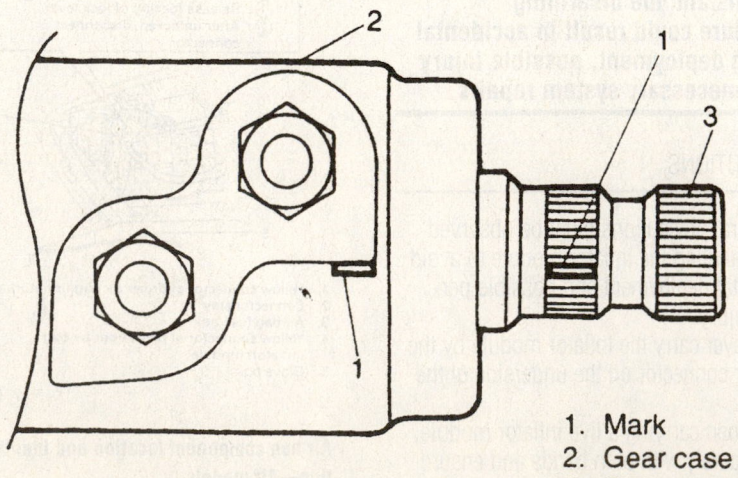

1. Mark
2. Gear case
3. Pinion shaft

9302HG14

Steering gear centering marks—1999–01 models

Shock Absorber

REMOVAL & INSTALLATION

1. Before servicing the vehicle, refer to the precautions in the beginning of this section.

2. Support the rear axle housing with a hydraulic jack or stand.

3. Remove or disconnect the following:
  - Shock absorber upper locknut and retaining nut
  - Lower shock absorber mounting nut and bolt
  - Rear shock absorber

To install:

4. Install or connect the following:
  - Rear shock absorber
  - Lower mounting nut and bolt
  - Upper retaining nut and locknut

5. Torque the upper mounting nuts to 16–25 ft. lbs. (22–35 Nm) and the lower mounting nut/bolt to 62 ft. lbs. (85 Nm).

6. Remove the jack or stand from the rear axle assembly.

Coil Spring

REMOVAL & INSTALLATION

Front

1. Before servicing the vehicle, refer to the precautions in the beginning of this section.

2. Support the vehicle at the frame with a hoist or jackstand.

3. Support the control arm with a floor jack.

4. Remove or disconnect the following:
  - Front wheel
  - Brake caliper and rotor
  - Locking hub or drive flange, if equipped
  - Axle shaft snapring and thrust washer, if equipped
  - Wheel speed sensor, if equipped
  - Stabilizer bar link
  - Lower ball joint
  - Strut bracket bolts

5. Lower the floor jack and remove the coil spring.

To install:

➡**The bottom of the spring has a larger diameter than the top.**

6. Install the coil spring onto the control arm and raise the floor jack.

7. Install or connect the following:
  - Strut bracket bolts. Tighten them to 70 ft. lbs. (95 Nm).
  - Lower ball joint. Tighten the nut to 40 ft. lbs. (55 Nm).
  - Stabilizer bar link. Tighten the nut to 21 ft. lbs. (29 Nm).
  - Wheel speed sensor, if equipped
  - Axle shaft snapring and thrust washer, if equipped
  - Locking hub or drive flange, if equipped
  - Brake caliper and rotor
  - Front wheel

8. Check the wheel alignment and adjust as necessary.

Rear

1. Before servicing the vehicle, refer to the precautions in the beginning of this section.

2. Support the vehicle at the frame with a hoist or jackstand.

3. Support the rear axle housing with a floor jack.

4. Remove or disconnect the following:
  - Rear wheels
  - Parking brake cable hanger
  - Shock absorber lower mounting bolts
  - Wheel speed sensor harness clamps, if equipped
  - Brake pipe E-ring
  - Axle vent hose

5. Lower the floor jack and remove the coil springs.

To install:

6. Install the coil springs onto the axle spring seats and raise the floor jack.

7. Install or connect the following:
  - Axle vent hose
  - Brake pipe E-ring
  - Wheel speed sensor harness clamps, if equipped
  - Shock absorber lower mounting bolts. Tighten them to 62 ft. lbs. (85 Nm).
  - Parking brake cable hanger
  - Rear wheels

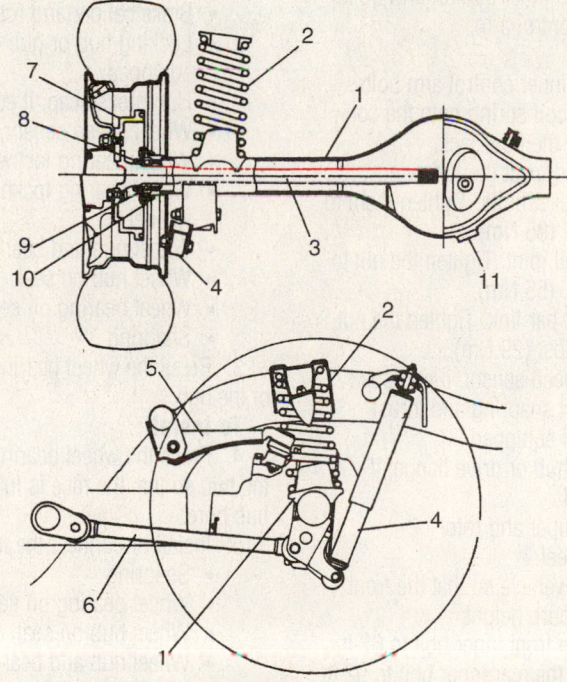

1. Rear axle housing
2. Coil spring
3. Axle shaft
4. Shock absorber
5. Upper arm
6. Trailing rod
7. Brake drum
8. Wheel bearing retainer
9. Rear wheel bearing
10. Brake back plate
11. Oil drain plug

7924HG32

Rear suspension component identification

Lower Ball Joint

REMOVAL & INSTALLATION

1997–98 Models

2 WHEEL DRIVE

1. Before servicing the vehicle, refer to the precautions in the beginning of this section.
2. Support the control arm with a floor jack.
3. Remove or disconnect the following:
   - Front wheel
   - Lower ball joint

To install:

4. Install or connect the following:
   - Lower ball joint. Tighten the control arm bolts to 62 ft. lbs. (85 Nm) and the nut to 40 ft. lbs. (55 Nm)
   - Front wheel
5. Check the wheel alignment and adjust as necessary.

4 WHEEL DRIVE

1. Before servicing the vehicle, refer to the precautions in the beginning of this section.
2. Support the control arm with a floor jack.
3. Remove or disconnect the following:
   - Front wheel
   - Brake caliper and rotor
   - Locking hub or drive flange
   - Axle shaft snapring and thrust washer
   - Wheel speed sensor, if equipped
   - Stabilizer bar link
   - Lower ball joint nut
   - Strut bracket bolts
   - Steering knuckle
   - Lower ball joint

To install:

4. Install or connect the following:
   - Lower ball joint. Tighten the control arm bolts to 62 ft. lbs. (85 Nm).
   - Steering knuckle. Tighten the ball joint nut to 40 ft. lbs. (55 Nm).
   - Strut bracket bolts. Tighten them to 70 ft. lbs. (95 Nm).
   - Stabilizer bar link
   - Wheel speed sensor, if equipped
   - Axle shaft snapring and thrust washer
   - Locking hub or drive flange
   - Brake caliper and rotor
   - Front wheel
5. Check the wheel alignment and adjust as necessary.

1999–01 Models

The lower ball joint is serviced with the lower control arm as an assembly.

Lower Control Arm

REMOVAL & INSTALLATION

1. Before servicing the vehicle, refer to the precautions in the beginning of this section.
2. Support the vehicle at the frame with a hoist or jackstand.
3. Support the control arm with a floor jack.
4. Remove or disconnect the following:
   - Front wheel
   - Brake caliper and rotor
   - Locking hub or drive flange, if equipped
   - Axle shaft snapring and thrust washer, if equipped
   - Wheel speed sensor, if equipped
   - Stabilizer bar link
   - Lower ball joint
   - Strut bracket bolts
5. Lower the floor jack and remove the coil spring.
6. Remove the inner control arm bolts and remove the control arm.

To install:

7. Install the inner control arm bolts.
8. Install the coil spring onto the control arm and raise the floor jack.
9. Install or connect the following:
   - Strut bracket bolts. Tighten them to 70 ft. lbs. (95 Nm).
   - Lower ball joint. Tighten the nut to 40 ft. lbs. (55 Nm).
   - Stabilizer bar link. Tighten the nut to 21 ft. lbs. (29 Nm).
   - Wheel speed sensor, if equipped
   - Axle shaft snapring and thrust washer, if equipped
   - Locking hub or drive flange, if equipped
   - Brake caliper and rotor
   - Front wheel
10. Lower the vehicle so that the front suspension is at curb height.
11. Tighten the front inner bolt to 62 ft. lbs. (85 Nm) and the rear inner bolt to 92 ft. lbs. (127 Nm).
12. Check the wheel alignment and adjust as necessary.

CONTROL ARM BUSHING REPLACEMENT

1. Before servicing the vehicle, refer to the precautions in the beginning of this section.
2. Remove the control arm from the vehicle.
3. Remove the control arm bushings with a hydraulic press.

To install:

4. Lubricate the control arm bushings with liquid soap.
5. Press the bushings into the control arm until the bushing flange contacts the housing edge of the control arm.
6. Install the control arm to the vehicle.
7. Check the wheel alignment and adjust as necessary.

Wheel Bearings

ADJUSTMENT

The wheel bearings are not adjustable.

REMOVAL & INSTALLATION

1. Before servicing the vehicle, refer to the precautions in the beginning of this section.
2. Remove or disconnect the following:
   - Front wheel
   - Brake caliper and rotor
   - Locking hub or hub drive flange, if equipped
   - Hub grease cap, if equipped
   - Wheel speed sensor, if equipped
   - Wheel bearing lockwasher
   - Wheel bearing locknut and inner washer
   - Wheel hub and bearing assembly
   - Wheel hub oil seal
   - Wheel bearing oil seal
   - Snapring
3. Press the wheel bearing and race out of the hub.

To install:

4. Press the wheel bearing and race into the hub so that the race is fully seated in the hub bore.
5. Install or connect the following:
   - Snapring
   - Wheel bearing oil seal
   - Wheel hub oil seal
   - Wheel hub and bearing assembly
   - Wheel bearing locknut and inner washer. Tighten the nut to 157 ft. lbs. (216 Nm).
   - Wheel bearing lockwasher. Tighten the retaining screws to 13 inch lbs. (1.5 Nm).
   - Wheel speed sensor, if equipped
   - Hub grease cap, if equipped
   - Locking hub or hub drive flange, if equipped
   - Brake caliper and rotor
   - Front wheel

General Motors Corp./Isuzu-Astro • Blazer • Bravada • Envoy •
Hombre • Jimmy • S10 • S15 • Safari • Sonoma • Xtreme

PRECAUTIONS

Before servicing any vehicle, please be sure to read all of the following precautions, which deal with personal safety, prevention of component damage, and important points to take into consideration when servicing a motor vehicle:

• Never open, service or drain the radiator or cooling system when the engine is hot; serious burns can occur from the steam and hot coolant.

• Observe all applicable safety precautions when working around fuel. Whenever servicing the fuel system, always work in a well-ventilated area. Do not allow fuel spray or vapors to come in contact with a spark, open flame, or excessive heat (a hot drop light, for example). Keep a dry chemical fire extinguisher near the work area. Always keep fuel in a container specifically designed for fuel storage; also, always properly seal fuel containers to avoid the possibility of fire or explosion. Refer to the additional fuel system precautions later in this section.

• Fuel injection systems often remain pressurized, even after the engine has been turned **OFF** . The fuel system pressure must be relieved before disconnecting any fuel lines. Failure to do so may result in fire and/or personal injury.

• Brake fluid often contains polyglycol ethers and polyglycols. Avoid contact with the eyes and wash your hands thoroughly after handling brake fluid. If you do get brake fluid in your eyes, flush your eyes with clean, running water for 15 minutes. If eye irritation persists, or if you have taken brake fluid internally, IMMEDIATELY seek medical assistance.

• The EPA warns that prolonged contact with used engine oil may cause a number of skin disorders, including cancer! You should make every effort to minimize your exposure to used engine oil. Protective gloves should be worn when changing oil. Wash your hands and any other exposed skin areas as soon as possible after exposure to used engine oil. Soap and water, or waterless hand cleaner should be used.

• All new vehicles are now equipped with an air bag system. The system must be disabled before performing service on or around system components, steering column, instrument panel components, wiring and sensors. Failure to follow safety and disabling procedures could result in accidental air bag deployment, possible personal injury and unnecessary system repairs.

• Always wear safety goggles when working with, or around, the air bag system. When carrying a non-deployed air bag, be sure the bag and trim cover are pointed away from your body. When placing a non-deployed air bag on a work surface, always face the bag and trim cover upward, away from the surface. This will reduce the motion of the module if it is accidentally deployed. Refer to the additional air bag system precautions later in this section.

• Clean, high quality brake fluid from a sealed container is essential to the safe and proper operation of the brake system. You should always buy the correct type of brake fluid for your vehicle. If the brake fluid becomes contaminated, completely flush the system with new fluid. Never reuse any brake fluid. Any brake fluid that is removed from the system should be discarded. Also, do not allow any brake fluid to come in contact with a painted surface; it will damage the paint.

• Never operate the engine without the proper amount and type of engine oil; doing so WILL result in severe engine damage.

• Timing belt maintenance is extremely important! Many models utilize an interference-type, non-freewheeling engine. If the timing belt breaks, the valves in the cylinder head may strike the pistons, causing potentially serious (also time-consuming and expensive) engine damage. Refer to the maintenance interval charts in the front of this manual for the recommended replacement interval for the timing belt, and to the timing belt section for belt replacement and inspection.

• Disconnecting the negative battery cable on some vehicles may interfere with the functions of the on-board computer system(s) and may require the computer to undergo a relearning process once the negative battery cable is reconnected.

• When servicing drum brakes, only disassemble and assemble one side at a time, leaving the remaining side intact for reference.

ENGINE REPAIR

Distributor

REMOVAL

4.3L Engines

1. Before servicing the vehicle, refer to the precautions in the beginning of this section.

2. Remove or disconnect the following:
   • Negative battery cable
   • Spark plug wires and the coil leads from the distributor
   • Electrical connector from the distributor
   • Distributor cap fasteners and the cap

3. Using a marker, matchmark the rotor-to-housing and housing-to-intake manifold positions so that they can be matched during installation.

4. Remove or disconnect the following:
   • Distributor hold-down bolt
   • Distributor from the engine

5. As the distributor is being removed from the engine the rotor will move in a counterclockwise direction about 42 degrees. This will appear as slightly more than one clock position.

6. Place a second mark on the distributor to mark the position of the rotor segment. This will help to ensure the correct rotor alignment when installing the distributor.

INSTALLATION

Engine Not Disturbed

1. If installing a new distributor, place two marks on the new distributor housing in the same position as the marks on the old distributor housing.

2. Align the rotor with the second mark made on the distributor.

3. Install the distributor in the engine making sure that the mounting hole in the distributor hold-down base is aligned over the mounting hole in the intake manifold.

4. As you are installing the distributor, watch the rotor move in a clockwise direction about 42 degrees.

5. Once the distributor is fully seated, the rotor should be aligned with the first

mark made on the distributor housing. If the rotor is not aligned with the first mark made on the housing, the distributor and camshaft teeth have meshed one or more teeth out of alignment. If this is the case, remove the distributor and reinstall it so that all the marks are aligned.

6. Install or connect the following:
- Hold-down bolt and tighten the bolt to 18 ft. lbs. (25 Nm)
- Distributor cap and engage the electrical connector to the distributor
- Spark plug wires and coil leads
- Negative battery cable

Engine Disturbed

1. Remove the No. 1 cylinder spark plug. Turn the engine using a socket wrench on the large bolt on the front of the crankshaft pulley. Place a finger near the No. 1 spark plug hole and turn the crankshaft until the piston reaches Top Dead Center (TDC). As the engine approaches TDC, you will feel air being expelled by the No. 1 cylinder. If the position is not being met, turn the engine another full turn (360 degree). Once the engine position is correct, install the spark plug.

2. Align the cast arrow in the distributor housing, the driven gear roll pin and the pre-drilled indent hole in the distributor driven gear. If the driven gear is installed correctly, the dimple will be approximately 180 degrees opposite the rotor segment when it is installed in the distributor.

➡**Installing the distributor 180° out of alignment, or locating the rotor in the wrong holes, may cause a no start condition or can cause premature engine damage and wear.**

3. Make sure the rotor is pointing to the cap hold-down mount nearest the flat side of the housing.

4. Using a long screwdriver, align the oil pump drive shaft in the engine in the mating drive tab in the distributor.

5. Install the distributor in the engine. Make sure the spark plug towers are perpendicular to the centerline of the engine.

6. When the distributor is fully seated, the rotor segment should be aligned with the pointer cast in the distributor base. The pointer will have a "6" cast into it indicating a 6 cylinder engine. If the rotor segment is not within a few degrees of the pointer, the distributor gear may be off a tooth or more. If this is the case repeat the process until the rotor aligns with the pointer.

7. Install the cap and fasten the mounting screws.

8. Tighten the distributor mounting bolt to 18 ft. lbs. (25 Nm).

9. Engage the electrical connections and the spark plug wires.

Alternator

REMOVAL

2.2L Engine

1. Before servicing the vehicle, refer to the precautions in the beginning of this section.
2. Remove or disconnect the following:
- Negative battery cable
- Passenger side wheel assembly
- Alternator brace-to-block bolt, the brace-to-intake nut and the brace-to-engine stud
- Alternator wiring
- Accessory belt
- Mounting bolts
- Alternator

4.3L Engine

1. Before servicing the vehicle, refer to the precautions in the beginning of this section.
2. Remove or disconnect the following:
- Negative battery cable
- Air inlet duct, if necessary
- Accessory belt
- Heater hose brace
- Wires
- Mounting bolts
- Alternator

INSTALLATION

2.2L Engine

Install or connect the following:
- Alternator
- Mounting bolts. Torque the left bolt to 22 ft. lbs. (30 Nm) and the right bolt to 32 ft. lbs. (43 Nm).
- Wires. Torque the battery feed wire nut to 71 inch lbs. (8 Nm).
- Alternator brace. Torque the nuts and bolts to 22 ft. lbs. (30 Nm).
- Accessory belt
- Negative battery cable

4.3L Engine

Install or connect the following:
- Alternator and loosely install the mounting bolts
- Tighten the top alternator bolt to 22 ft.

lbs. (30 Nm) and the bottom bolt to 32 ft. lbs. (43 Nm) on 1997–98 models
- Tighten the rear bolt to 37 ft. lbs. (50 Nm) and the front bolt to 18 ft. lbs. (25 Nm) on 1999–01 models
- Alternator brace, then tighten the retaining nut(s) and bolts to 22 ft. lbs. (30 Nm) on 1997–98 models
- Tighten the brace-to-alternator and brace-to-intake retainers to 18 ft. lbs. (25 Nm). Tighten the brace-to-engine stud nut to 37 ft. lbs. (50 Nm) on 1999–01 models.
- Wires and the battery feed wire nut
- Heater hose bracket
- Accessory belt
- Negative battery cable

Ignition Timing

ADJUSTMENT

The ignition timing is preset and cannot be adjusted.

Engine Assembly

REMOVAL & INSTALLATION

Astro/Safari

➡**The engine assembly on the Astro/Safari is removed from the bottom of the vehicle. A special engine lifting table is necessary to perform the following procedure.**

1. Before servicing the vehicle, refer to the precautions in the beginning of this section.
2. Disconnect the negative and positive battery cables.
3. Discharge the air conditioning refrigerant.
4. Drain the coolant.
5. Drain the crankcase.
6. Remove or disconnect the following:

- Engine cover
- Battery
- Air cleaner assembly
- Throttle cable and the cruise control cable (if equipped) from the throttle body
- Air conditioning lines at the condenser and accumulator
- Radiator
- Power steering reservoir and drain the fluid
- Lines from the Hydroboost unit
- Master cylinder from the Hydro-

boost unit and secure it to the oil fill tube

- Steering shaft from the steering gear
- Heater hoses and vacuum lines from the engine
- Fuse box and wiring harness from the bulkhead connector

➡ **The engine/transmission assembly is removed from the bottom of the vehicle. Raise the vehicle so the rear of the vehicle is slightly higher than the front. When the frame bolts are removed, the body will be lifted away from the engine/transmission assembly.**

- Driveshaft. Matchmark it for reassembly prior to removal.
- Starter and the starter opening cover
- Torque converter bolts through the starter opening
- Shift linkage from the transmission
- Exhaust pipe from the rear of the catalytic converter
- Parking brake bracket from the frame
- Rear brake line from the Brake Pressure Modulator Valve (BPMV)
- Front bumper and the power steering cooler from the front air deflector
- Supplemental Inflatable Restraint (SIR) connector
- Splash shields from the wheel openings
- Rear air conditioning lines at the rear crossmember, if equipped, leave the lines attached to the engine assembly
- Fuel lines at the filter and pull them through the crossmember
- Fuel tank electrical connector
- Transfer case vent tube, on all wheel drive models

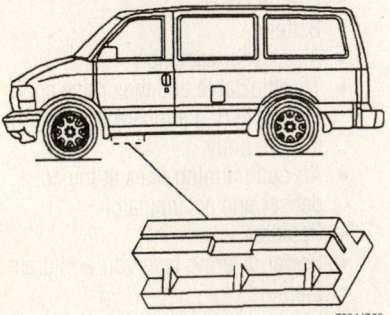

Attach the body protection pads to the pinch welds on both sides before raising the vehicle—Astro/Safari

7. Make sure all lines and connections are free between the engine/transmission assembly and the body.

8. If using a twin post lift (side lift), perform the following:

   a. Step 1: Lower the vehicle to the floor

   b. Step 2: Install the body protection lift adapter tool J 41602 pads to the pinch welds on both sides of the vehicle behind the front wheels.

   c. Step 3: Position the front lifting arms of the lift under the body protection adapters.

   d. Step 4: Be sure the rear of the vehicle will be slightly higher than the front when the lift is raised.

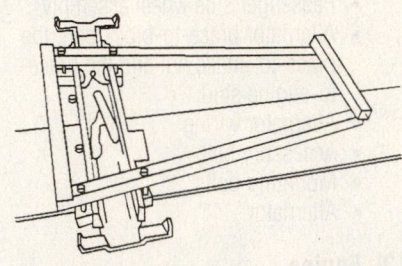

Install the engine lifting adapter to the front cylinder of the twin cylinder lift if applicable—Astro/Safari

e. Step 5: Raise the lift about halfway up.

f. Step 6: Place jackstands under the frame attached to the engine/transmission assembly and remove the frame mounting bolts.

g. Step 7: Raise the vehicle to clear the engine/transmission assembly.

9. If using a dual cylinder (1 front and 1 rear) lift do the following:

   a. Step 1: Install the body protection lift adapter tool J 41602 pads to the pinch welds on both sides of the vehicle behind the front wheels.

   b. Step 2: Install stands under the body protection lift adapters and the rear of the vehicle.

   c. Step 3: Lower the front cylinder of the lift and install the engine lifting adapter tool J 41617 to the lift.

   d. Step 4: Raise the front cylinder with the adapter attached until it touches the engine/transmission assembly.

   e. Step 5: Remove the frame bolts and lower the engine/transmission assembly from the vehicle.

10. Remove the 2 right rear and 2 left front intake manifold bolts.

11. Install the Engine Lifting Bracket tools J 41427 on the intake manifold to provide lifting points for an engine hoist. Install

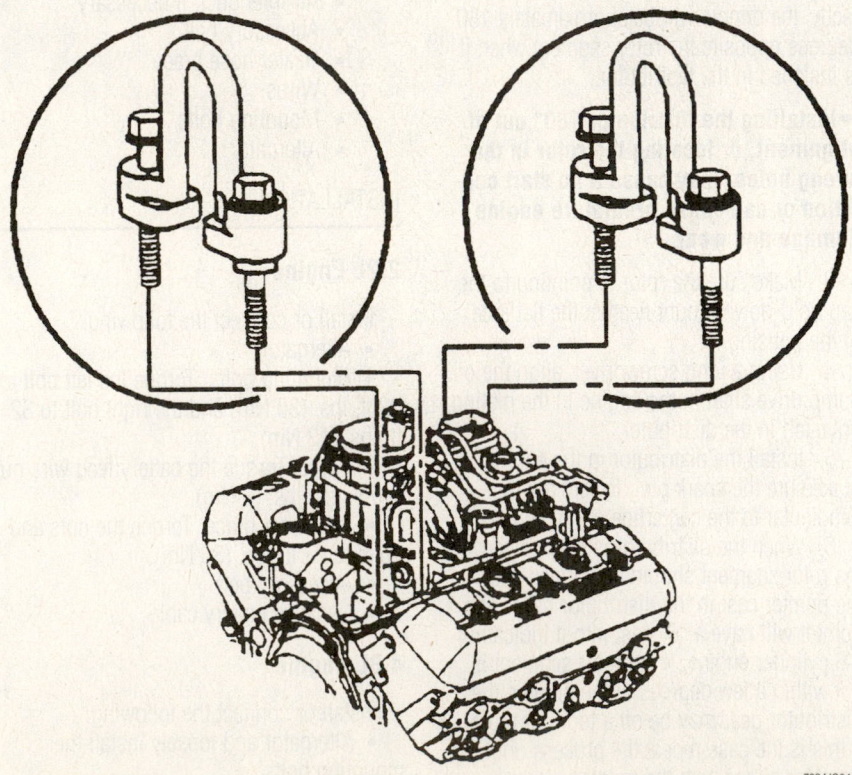

Install the engine lifting brackets at the right rear and left front of the intake manifold—Astro/Safari

the hoist and raise the engine/transmission assembly.

12. Remove or disconnect the following:
- Transmission from the engine
- Engine from the frame

To install:

13. Install or connect the following:
- Engine onto the frame and the transmission to the engine. Tighten the engine mount through-bolts to 74 ft. lbs. (100 Nm).
- Engine/transmission assembly on suitable stands or on the engine lifting adapter

14. Remove the engine lifting brackets from the intake manifold and reinstall the bolts.

15. Position the engine/transmission assembly in the vehicle. Tighten the frame bolts in the following order:

   a. Step 1: Right center bolt: 114 ft. lbs. (155 Nm)

   b. Step 2: Left center bolt: 114 ft. lbs. (155 Nm)

   c. Step 3: Right front bolt: 66 ft. lbs. (90 Nm)

   d. Step 4: Left rear bolt: 66 ft. lbs. (90 Nm)

   e. Step 5: Left front bolt: 66 ft. lbs. (90 Nm)

   f. Step 6: Right rear bolt: 66 ft. lbs. (90 Nm)

16. Remove the stands or the engine lifting adapter. If the engine lifting adapter was used, raise the vehicle and remove the stands.

17. Remove the body protection adapter from the pinch welds.

18. Install or connect the following:
- Splash shields in the wheel openings
- Steering shaft to the steering gear
- Power steering cooler
- Lines to the Hydroboost unit
- Hose to the power steering reservoir
- Wiring harness to the bulkhead and fuse box
- Heater hoses and the SIR connector
- Throttle cable and the cruise control cable (if equipped)
- Radiator and air cleaner assembly
- Master cylinder to the booster
- Rear brake line to the BMPV
- Parking brake bracket to the frame
- Fuel lines and the air conditioning lines (if equipped) at the rear crossmember
- Transfer case vent tube, on all wheel drive models

- Front bumper and transmission shift linkage
- Torque converter bolts
- Starter and driveshaft
- Exhaust pipe
- Engine cover and battery

19. Refill the power steering, engine crankcase, brake system, cooling system and transmission.

20. Discharge the air conditioning system.

21. Bleed the brake system.

22. Start the engine and check for leaks.

Except Astro/Safari

2.2L ENGINE

➡ **In certain cases on some models the A/C system will have to be evacuated because the compressor may need to be removed from the vehicle to allow clearance for engine removal. On other models you maybe able to set the compressor and lines to one side and still have enough clearance to remove the engine. In this case the system does not have to be evacuated because the lines do not have to be disconnected from the compressor. To check if your system has to be evacuated, unplug the electrical connectors from the compressor, then unbolt the compressor assembly. Unfasten any brackets holding the refrigerant lines and try to set the components aside so that you will have enough clearance for engine removal. If there is not enough clearance for engine removal you must recover the refrigerant from the A/C system with an approved recovery station before attempting to remove the engine from your vehicle. DO NOT attempt this without the proper equipment. R-134a should NOT be mixed with R-12 refrigerant and, depending on your local laws, attempting to service this system could be illegal.**

1. Disconnect the negative battery cable and properly relieve the fuel system pressure.

2. Drain the engine cooling system and the engine oil into separate drain pans.

3. Remove or disconnect the following:

- Hood
- Battery on 1997 models
- Oxygen (O_2S) sensor electrical connection
- Exhaust pipe from the manifold

➡ **On some models it may also be necessary to disconnect the catalytic converter from the exhaust pipe.**

- Braces from the engine and the transmission, if equipped
- Starter motor, on 1998–01 models
- Transmission and separate it from the engine or, if necessary, remove it from the vehicle
- Alternator rear brace by unfastening the bolt and nuts, if necessary for clearance on 1998–01 models
- Ground straps from the engine block
- Drive belt
- Water pump for clearance on 1997 models, if necessary
- A/C compressor and bracket. If possible, set the compressor and bracket to one side without disconnecting the lines.
- Hoses and transmission coolant lines engaged to the radiator
- Radiator
- Power steering pump and cap the power steering lines to avoid contamination
- Heater hoses from the heater core
- 12 volt supply from the mega fuse, if necessary
- All electrical connections and wiring harnesses
- All vacuum lines
- Throttle cable, and if equipped the cruise control cable
- Exhaust Gas Recirculation (EGR) pipe and the EGR valve, if necessary for clearance on 1998–01 models
- Fuel lines

4. Install a suitable lifting device to the engine.

5. Remove the engine mount bolts and carefully lift the engine from the vehicle. Pause several times while lifting the engine to make sure no wires or hoses have become snagged.

To install:

6. Carefully lower the engine into the vehicle and install the engine mount bolts. Remove the engine lifting device.

7. Install or connect the following:
- Fuel lines
- 12 volt supply to the mega fuse, if removed
- All vacuum lines, electrical connections and wiring harnesses
- EGR valve and pipe, if removed
- Throttle and if equipped, the cruise control cable

Timing belt service is covered in Section 4 of this manual

- Heater hoses to the heater core
- Power steering pump and attach the lines
- A/C compressor
- Radiator, all hoses and fluid cooler lines
- Water pump, if removed
- Drive belt
- Ground strap to the engine
- Alternator rear brace and tighten the bolt and nuts, if removed
- Transmission to the engine
- Starter motor, if removed
- Braces to the engine and the transmission, if equipped
- Exhaust pipe to the manifold
- Catalytic converter to the exhaust pipe, if removed
- O$_2$S sensor electrical connection
- Battery
- Hood

8. Check all powertrain fluid levels and add, as necessary. Be sure to properly fill the engine crankcase with clean engine oil.

9. Connect the battery cables and properly fill the engine cooling system.

10. Start and run the engine, then check for leaks.

4.3L ENGINES

1. Before servicing the vehicle, refer to the precautions in the beginning of this section.

2. Drain the engine cooling system
3. Drain the engine oil.
4. Remove or disconnect the following:
- Negative battery cable
- Fuel system pressure
- Vacuum reservoir and/or the underhood light from the hood, as equipped
- Outer cowl vent grilles
- Hood
- Oxygen (O$_2$S) sensor and/or wiring
- Exhaust pipes at the manifolds and loosen the hanger at the catalytic converter. This is necessary to remove the rear catalytic converter cushion mounts for removal of the exhaust assembly.
- Skid plate, if equipped
- Engine-to-transmission pencil braces
- Slave cylinder and position aside, if equipped
- Line clamp at the bell housing
- Wiring from the starter
- Starter
- Transfer case on 1998–01 models, if equipped
- Oil filter
- Engine mount through bolts

- Rear engine mount crossbar, nut and washer
- Bell housing bolts, except the upper left.
- Battery ground (negative) cable from the engine
- Front drive axle bolts and roll the axle downward, on 4WD vehicles
- Air cleaner assembly
- Upper radiator shroud
- Fan assembly
- Drive belt assembly
- Water pump pulley
- Upper radiator hose
- Air conditioning compressor, if equipped, and position aside with the lines intact
- Lower radiator hose
- Oil cooler and overflow lines from the radiator, plug the openings to prevent system contamination or excessive fluid loss.
- Radiator and lower radiator shroud
- Power steering hoses from the steering gear, then cap the openings to prevent system contamination or excessive fluid loss.
- Heater hoses from the intake manifold and the water pump
- Wiring harness and vacuum lines from the engine
- Throttle cables
- Distributor cap
- Remaining bell housing bolt
- Fuel lines and the bracket
- Ground strap(s) from the rear of the cylinder head
- Front body mount bolts, on 4WD vehicles

5. Support the transmission.

6. Install a lifting device and lift the engine.

To install:

7. Install or connect the following:
- Engine into the vehicle
- Front body mount bolts, on 4WD vehicles
- Ground strap(s) to the rear of the cylinder head
- Fuel lines and the bracket
- Upper left bell-housing bolt
- Distributor, cap and wires
- Throttle cables
- Vacuum lines and wiring harness connectors
- Heater hoses
- Power steering hoses
- Lower shroud and radiator
- Oil cooler lines to the radiator and overflow hose
- Lower radiator hose

- Air conditioning compressor to the engine, if equipped
- Upper radiator hose
- Water pump pulley
- Drive belt assembly
- Fan assembly
- Upper radiator shroud
- Air cleaner assembly
- Front drive axle, for 4WD vehicles
- Battery ground strap to the engine block
- Remaining bell housing bolts
- Engine mount through-bolts. Torque them to 49 ft. lbs. (66 Nm).
- Rear engine mount crossbar nut and washer. Tighten the nut to 33 ft. lbs. (45 Nm).
- Oil filter
- Starter motor
- Flywheel cover
- Clutch slave cylinder, if equipped
- Pencil brace and the skid plate, as equipped
- Catalytic converter Y-pipe assembly and hangers
- Hood
- Outer cowl vent grilles
- Vacuum reservoir and/or the underhood light to the hood, as equipped
- Negative battery cable

8. Check all powertrain fluid levels and add, as necessary.

9. Refill the engine crankcase.

10. Refill the engine cooling system.

11. Start and run the engine, then check for leaks.

Water Pump

REMOVAL & INSTALLATION

Astro/Safari

1. Before servicing the vehicle, refer to the precautions in the beginning of this section.

2. Disconnect the negative battery cable.
3. Drain the engine cooling system.
4. Remove or disconnect the following:
- Upper fan shroud
- Drive belt and the fan and clutch assembly
- Water pump pulley
- Hoses from the water pump, as applicable
- Water pump

➡ **On some engines, the pump retaining bolts will vary in size and thread. Be sure to note the positioning of all bolts during removal to assure proper installation.**

5. Clean gasket mounting surface.

To install:

6. Install or connect the following:
   - Water pump. Torque bolts to 33 ft. lbs. (45 Nm).
   - Coolant hoses using new clamps
   - Pulley and clutch assembly, as needed.
   - Drive belt assembly and fan shroud
   - Negative battery cable
7. Refill the cooling system
8. Run the engine and check for leaks.

Except Astro/Safari

1. Before servicing the vehicle, refer to the precautions in the beginning of this section.
2. Disconnect the negative battery cable.
3. Drain the engine cooling system.
4. Relieve the belt tension and remove the accessory drive belts or the serpentine drive belt, as applicable.
5. Remove or disconnect the following:
   - Upper fan shroud
   - Fan or fan and clutch assembly, as applicable
   - Water pump pulley
   - Coolant hose(s) from the water pump

➡ For the hoses on some engines, removal may be easier if the hose is left attached until the pump is free from the block. Once the pump is removed from the engine, the pump may be pulled (giving a better grip and greater leverage) from the tight hose connection.

   - Water pump retainers
   - Water pump from the engine

❋❋ WARNING

Note the positions of all retainers as some engines will utilize different length fasteners in different locations and/or bolts and studs in different locations.

To install:

6. Clean the gasket mounting surfaces.

➡ The water pumps on some of the earlier engines covered may have been installed using sealer only, no gasket, at the factory. If a gasket is supplied with the replacement part, it should be used. Otherwise, a 1/8 in. (3mm) bead of RTV sealer should be used around the sealing surface of the pump.

7. Apply sealant to the water pump retainer threads.
8. Install or connect the following:
   - Water pump using a new gasket. Tighten the water pump retainers to 18 ft. lbs. (25 Nm) for 2.2L engine or to 30 ft. lbs. (41 Nm) for 4.3L engine.
   - Coolant hose(s)
   - Water pump pulley

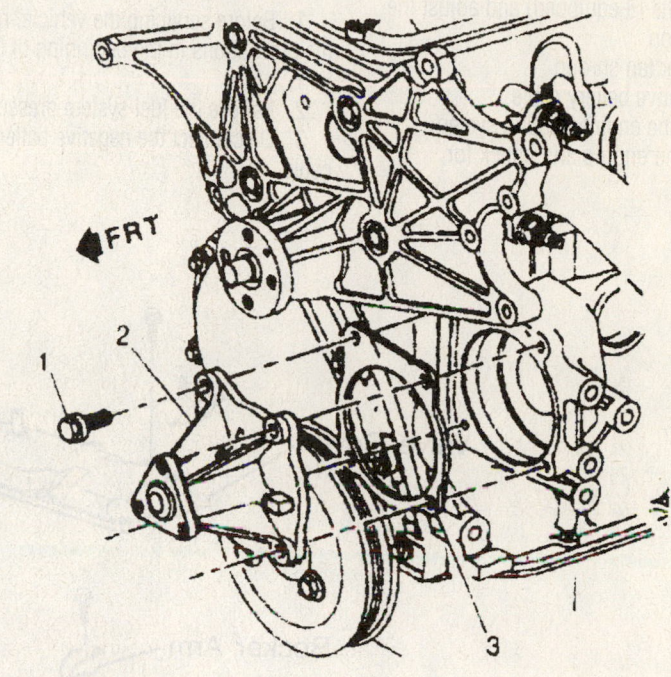

1. BOLT
2. PUMP, COOLANT
3. GASKET

7924JG05

Exploded view of the water pump mounting—2.2L engine

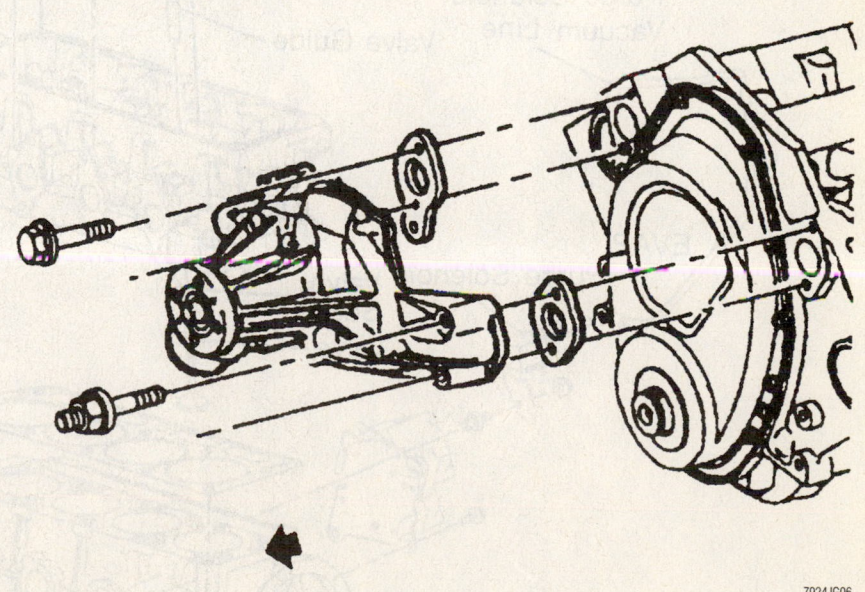

7924JG06

Exploded view of the water pump assembly mounting—4.3L engine

- Fan or fan and clutch assembly
- Serpentine drive belt (if equipped) by positioning the belt over the pulleys and carefully allow the tensioner back into contact with the belt.
- V-belts (if equipped) and adjust the tension
- Upper fan shroud
- Negative battery cable

9. Refill the engine cooling system.

10. Run the engine and check for leaks.

Cylinder Head

REMOVAL & INSTALLATION

2.2L Engine

1. Before servicing the vehicle, refer to the precautions in the beginning of this section.

2. Relieve the fuel system pressure.

3. Disconnect the negative battery cable.

4. Drain the engine cooling system.

5. Remove or disconnect the following:
- Air duct from the air inlet
- Upper radiator hose and upper fan shroud
- Radiator assembly
- Lower fan shroud
- Fan assembly
- Drive belt assembly
- Water pump pulley
- Heater hose from the intake manifold and the thermostat housing
- Thermostat housing

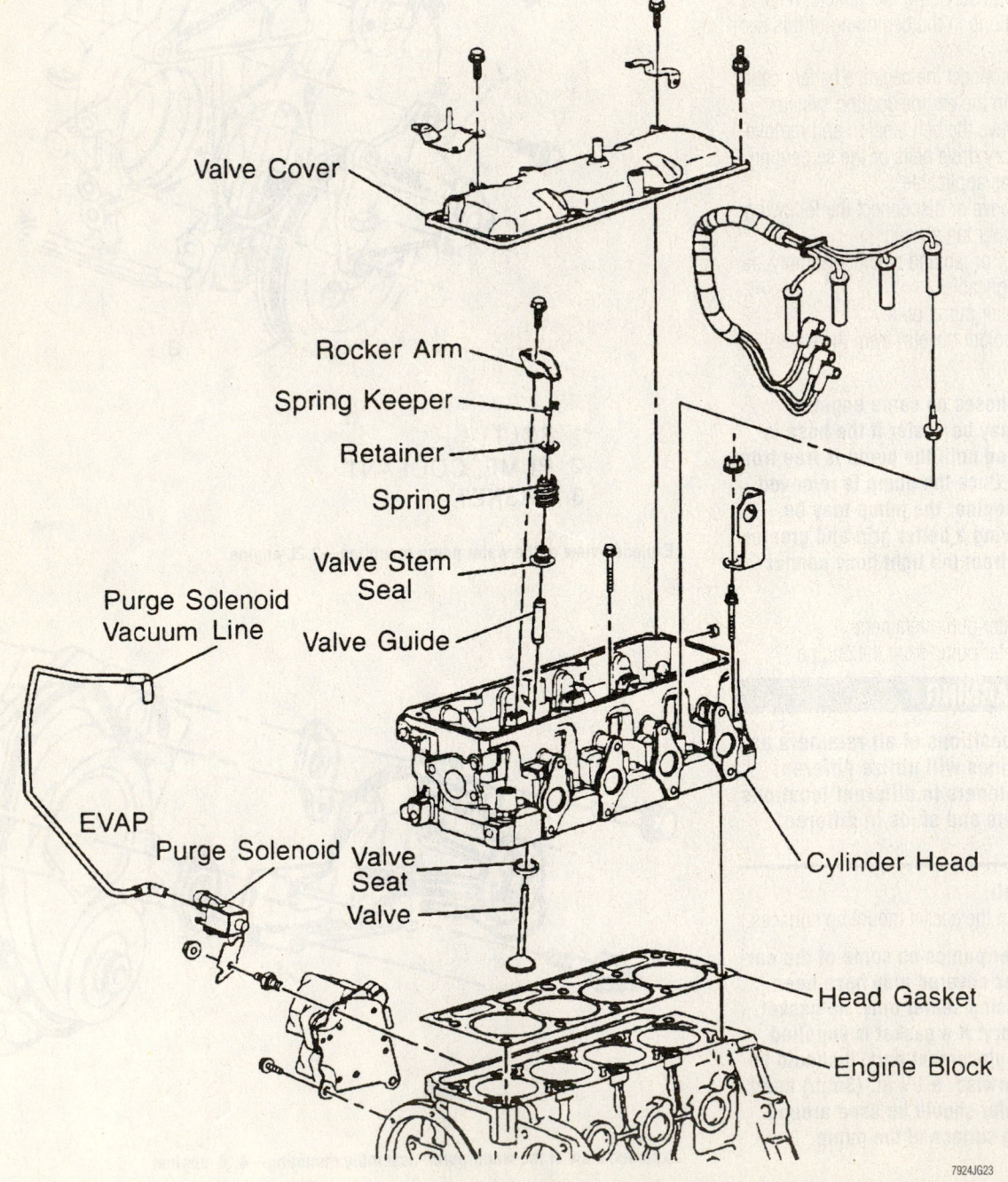

Valve Cover
Rocker Arm
Spring Keeper
Retainer
Spring
Valve Stem Seal
Valve Guide
Purge Solenoid Vacuum Line
EVAP
Purge Solenoid
Valve Seat
Valve
Cylinder Head
Head Gasket
Engine Block

Cylinder head and related components—2.2L engine

7924JG23

- Alternator support brace and the alternator wiring
- Air conditioning compressor with brackets, if equipped, move it aside without disconnecting the lines
- Accessory bracket along with the alternator and power steering pump still attached. Be careful not to damage the steering pump lines.
- Throttle cable and cable support linkage
- Heater hose from the water pump
- Oil fill tube
- Exhaust pipe
- Oxygen (O_2S) sensor
- Exhaust manifold
- Electrical wiring and the vacuum hoses from the upper intake manifold
- Upper intake manifold
- Wiring from the lower intake manifold
- Fuel lines and the spark plug wires
- Lower intake manifold
- Rocker arm cover
- Rocker arms and pushrods
- Engine lift bracket from the rear of the engine
- Cylinder head bolts and studs
- Cylinder head from the engine

To install:

6. Clean and inspect the gasket mounting surfaces.

➡**Refer to Section 1 of this manual for the cylinder head torque sequence illustration. The illustration is located after the Torque Specification Chart.**

7. Install or connect the following:
- Cylinder head using a new gasket
- Cylinder head bolt threads coated with sealer 1052080. Tighten the bolts within 15 minutes of sealer application, in sequence, to 46 ft. lbs. (63 Nm) for long bolts and to 43 ft. lbs. (58 Nm) for short bolts; then, tighten all bolts an additional 90 degree turn using a torque angle meter.
- Engine lift bracket
- Rocker arms and pushrods
- Rocker arm cover
- Lower intake manifold
- Spark plug wires and the fuel lines
- Lower intake manifold and wiring
- Upper intake manifold
- Vacuum hoses and electrical wiring to the upper intake
- Oil fill tube assembly
- Exhaust manifold

- Exhaust pipe and O_2S sensor
- Heater hose to the water pump
- Throttle cable support and throttle cable
- Accessory support bracket and components
- Air conditioning compressor, if equipped
- Power steering support brace
- Alternator support brace and wiring
- Thermostat housing and the heater hose
- Water pump pulley and drive belt assembly
- Fan assembly
- Radiator and the lower fan shroud
- Upper fan shroud and upper radiator hose
- Air inlet ductwork
- Negative battery cable

8. Refill the engine cooling system and check for leaks.

4.3L Engine

ASTRO/SAFARI

1. Before servicing the vehicle, refer to the precautions in the beginning of this section.

2. Properly relieve the fuel system pressure.

3. Remove or disconnect the following:
- Engine cover
- Negative battery cable

4. Drain the engine cooling system.

5. Remove or disconnect the following:
- Rocker arm cover
- Intake manifold
- Exhaust manifold
- Alternator and bracket
- Wiring harness clip at the rear of the cylinder head
- Coolant sensor wire
- Wiring from the spark plugs
- Spark plugs
- Pushrods by loosening the rocker arms

➡**If valvetrain components, such as the rocker arms or pushrods, are to be reused, they must be tagged or arranged to insure installation in their original locations.**

- Cylinder head bolts by loosening them in the reverse of the torque sequence
- Cylinder head

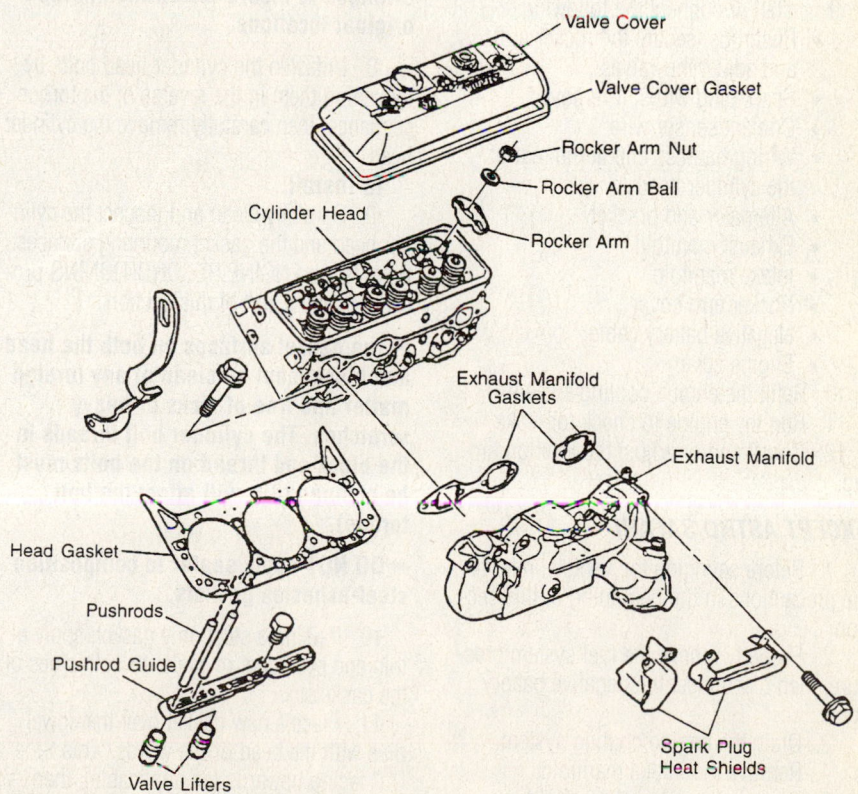

Cylinder head and related components—4.3L engine

Refer to Section 1 for engine rebuilding specifications

To install:

6. Clean and inspect the gasket mounting surfaces.

➡ **Do not apply sealer to composition steel/asbestos gaskets. If using a steel only gasket, apply a thin and even coat of sealer to both sides of the gaskets.**

7. Install or connect the following:
- New gasket over the dowel pins with the bead or the words **This Side Up** facing upwards, as applicable
- Cylinder head

➡ **Refer to Section 1 of this manual for the cylinder head torque sequence illustration. The illustration is located after the Torque Specification Chart.**

8. Coat the bolts with GM sealer 1052080, then install the bolts and tighten in sequence to 22 ft. lbs. (30 Nm). The bolts must then be tightened again in sequence in the following order:

a. Short length bolts: (11, 7, 3, 2, 6, 10) 55 degrees.

b. Medium length bolts: (12, 13) 65 degrees.

c. Long length bolts: (1, 4, 8, 5, 9) 75 degrees.

9. Install or connect the following:
- Pushrods, secure the rocker arms and adjust the valves
- Spark plug wires, if removed
- Coolant sensor wire
- Wiring harness clip at the rear of the cylinder head
- Alternator and bracket
- Exhaust manifold
- Intake manifold
- Rocker arm cover
- Negative battery cable
- Engine cover

10. Refill the engine cooling system.

11. Run the engine to check for leaks

12. Check and/or adjust the ignition timing.

EXCEPT ASTRO/SAFARI

1. Before servicing the vehicle, refer to the precautions in the beginning of this section.

2. Properly relieve the fuel system pressure, then disconnect the negative battery cable.

3. Drain the engine cooling system.

4. Remove the intake manifold.

5. Remove the exhaust manifold.

6. Remove or disconnect the following:
- Alternator and bracket, if removing the right cylinder head

- Cooling fan assembly, on 1999–01 models
- Air conditioning compressor (position it aside with the refrigerant lines attached), on 1999–01 models equipped
- Air pipe bracket and nut from the rear of the power steering pump if removing the left cylinder head on equipped 1999–01 models
- Engine accessory bracket with power steering pump (position the pump aside with the lines attached) and brackets, if removing the left cylinder head
- Wiring harness and clip from the rear of the cylinder head
- Coolant sensor wire
- Wiring from the spark plugs
- Spark plugs, if necessary
- Ground wires and if necessary, the fuel line bracket from the rear of the cylinder head, on 1999–01 models
- Rocker arm cover

7. Loosen the rocker arms and remove the pushrods.

➡ **If valve train components, such as the rocker arms or pushrods, are to be reused, they must be tagged or arranged to insure installation in their original locations.**

8. Unfasten the cylinder head bolts by loosening them in the reverse of the torque sequence, then carefully remove the cylinder head.

To install:

9. Carefully clean and inspect the cylinder head and the gasket mounting surfaces. Refer to the ENGINE RECONDITIONING procedures at the end of this section.

➡ **The gasket surfaces on both the head and block must be clean of any foreign matter and free of nicks or heavy scratches. The cylinder bolt threads in the block and thread on the bolts must be cleaned (dirt will affect the bolt torque).**

➡ **DO NOT apply sealer to composition steel-asbestos gaskets.**

10. If using a steel only gasket, apply a thin and even coat of sealer to both sides of the gaskets.

11. Place a new gasket over the dowel pins with the bead or the words "This Side Up" facing upwards (as applicable), then carefully lower the cylinder head into position over the gasket and dowels.

12. Apply a coating of 12346004 or equivalent sealer to the threads of the cylin-

der head bolts, then thread the bolts into position until finger-tight.

13. Install the bolts in sequence to 22 ft. lbs. (30 Nm). The bolts must then be tightened again in sequence in the following order:

a. Short length bolts: (11, 7, 3, 2, 6, 10) 55 degrees.

b. Medium length bolts: (12, 13) 65 degrees.

c. Long length bolts: (1, 4, 8, 5, 9) 75 degrees.

14. Install or connect the following:
- Pushrods, secure the rocker arms and adjust the valves
- Rocker arm cover
- Spark plugs, if removed
- Spark plug wires
- Attach the fuel line bracket (if removed) and ground wires to the rear of the head and tighten the bolts to 22 ft. lbs. (30 Nm) on 1999–01 models
- Air conditioning compressor and bracket, if the left cylinder head was removed
- Alternator and bracket, if the right cylinder head was removed
- Engine accessory bracket with power steering pump. if the left cylinder head was removed
- Air pipe bracket and nut to the rear of the power steering pump (if equipped), if the left cylinder head was removed on 1999–01 models. Tighten the nut to 30 ft. lbs. (41 Nm).
- A/C compressor, if the left cylinder head was removed
- Cooling fan assembly, if the left cylinder head was removed on 1999–01 models
- Wiring harness and clip to the rear of the cylinder head
- Coolant sensor wire
- Exhaust manifold
- Intake manifold
- Negative battery cable

15. Properly refill the engine cooling system.

16. Run the engine to check for leaks.

Rocker Arms

REMOVAL & INSTALLATION

2.2L Engine

1. Before servicing the vehicle, refer to the precautions in the beginning of this section.

2. Remove or disconnect the following:
- Rocker arm cover
- Rocker arm retaining nut, arm and ball.
- Pushrod, if necessary

➡**Valvetrain components, being reused, must be installed in their original positions. If removed, be sure to tag or arrange all rocker arms and pushrods to assure proper installation.**

To install:

3. Inspect the rocker arms, balls and pushrods for damage or wear and replace as necessary.

4. Check the rocker arms, balls and their mating surfaces. Be sure the surfaces are smooth and free from scoring or other damage.

5. Check the rocker arm areas that contact the valve stems and the sockets that contact the pushrods, be sure these areas are smooth and free of both damage and wear.

6. Be sure the pushrods are not bent which can be determined by rolling them on a flat surface. Check the ends of the pushrods for scoring or roughness

7. Inspect the rocker arm bolts for thread damage. Check the rocker arm bolts in the shoulder area for contact damage with the rocker arm.

8. Install or connect the following:
- Pushrods making sure they are seated within the lifters, if removed
- New rocker arms and balls by coating the friction surfaces using Dri-Slide Molykote® or equivalent pre-lube

✳✳ WARNING

When tightening a rocker arm retainer, be sure the lifter for that valve is resting on the base circle of

the camshaft and not on the lobe, otherwise the valvetrain can be damaged. Do not over-tighten the retainers.

- Rocker arms and ball. Tighten the nuts to 22 ft. lbs. (30 Nm).
- Rocker arm cover

9. Start and run the engine to check for leaks.

4.3L Engines

1. Before servicing the vehicle, refer to the precautions in the beginning of this section.

2. Remove or disconnect the following:
- Rocker arm cover(s)
- Rocker arm nut, rocker arm and ball washer

➡**If only the pushrod is to be removed, loosen the rocker arm nut, swing the rocker arm to the side and remove the pushrod.**

- Pushrod(s)

To install:

3. Inspect and replace components if worn or damaged.

4. Coat the bearing surfaces of the rocker arms and the rocker arm ball washers with Molykote® or equivalent pre-lube.

5. Install or connect the following:
- Pushrods making sure they seat properly in the lifter
- Rocker arms, ball washers and the nuts

➡**The engines are equipped with screw-in rocker arm studs with positive stop shoulders.**

- Rocker arm adjusting nuts. Tighten them against the stop shoulders to 18 ft. lbs. (24 Nm). No further adjustment is necessary or possible.

6. Install the rocker arm cover(s).

7. Start and run the engine, then check for leaks and for proper ignition timing adjustment.

Intake Manifold

REMOVAL & INSTALLATION

2.2L Engine

1997 MODELS

The intake manifold is an assembly of separate components, an upper and a lower manifold.

1. Before servicing the vehicle, refer to the precautions in the beginning of this section.

2. Properly release the fuel system pressure, if the lower manifold assembly is being removed.

3. Remove or disconnect the following:
- Negative battery cable
- Air cleaner ductwork
- Throttle cable support and cable from the manifold
- Manifold Absolute Pressure (MAP) sensor and Exhaust Gas Recirculation (EGR) solenoid valve from the upper intake manifold and engine

➡**If only the upper manifold is not being replaced, simply disengage the wiring and hoses.**

- Wiring and vacuum hoses from the upper intake manifold
- Upper intake manifold
- Fuel lines
- Spark plug wires from the Electronic Ignition (EI) coil pack
- Lower intake manifold and gasket

4. Insert clean rags into the openings in the cylinder head to prevent dirt or debris from entering the engine.

To install:

5. Clean the gasket mating surfaces. Check the EGR passage to be sure it is free of excessive carbon deposits and clean, as necessary.

➡**Refer to Section 1 of this manual for the intake manifold torque sequence illustration. The illustration is located after the Torque Specification Chart.**

6. Install or connect the following:
- Lower intake manifold using a new gasket. Torque the nuts to 24 ft. lbs. (33 Nm) using the proper sequence.

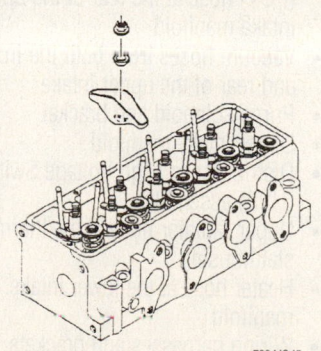

7924JG45

Exploded view of the rocker arm assembly—2.2L engine

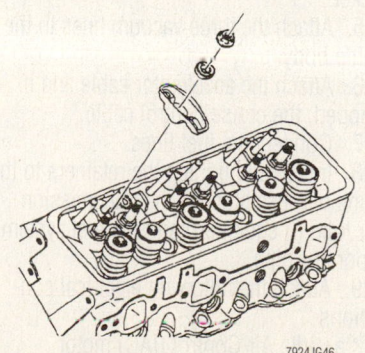

7924JG46

Exploded view of the rocker arm assembly—4.3L engine

For engine torque specifications, refer to Section 1 of this manual

- Spark plug wires to the EI coil pack
- Fuel lines
- Upper intake manifold using a new gasket. Torque the fasteners to 22 ft. lbs. (30 Nm) using the proper sequence.
- Wiring connectors and vacuum hoses to the upper intake manifold assembly
- MAP sensor and EGR solenoid valve
- Throttle cable support and cable. Torque the bracket bolts to 18 ft. lbs. (25 Nm).
- Air cleaner ductwork
- Negative battery cable.

7. Start and run the engine to check for leaks.

1998–01 MODELS

1. Disconnect the negative battery cable and remove the air cleaner resonator.

2. Tag and unplug the three vacuum hoses from the throttle body.

3. Remove the throttle cable support bracket and the throttle body assembly.

4. If necessary, remove the upper fan shroud and disconnect the vacuum brake booster hose.

5. If necessary, unfasten the EGR pipe-to-manifold bolts and the EGR pipe-to-EGR adapter bolt, then remove the EGR pipe.

6. If necessary, remove the EGR adapter.

7. Unplug the electrical connections from the following components:
   a. Idle Air Control (IAC) motor
   b. Manifold Absolute Pressure (MAP) sensor
   c. Throttle Position (TP) sensor
   d. Fuel injector harness connector

8. Remove the right fender wheelhouse extension.

9. Remove the retainers from the engine harness bracket, the transmission filler tube (if equipped) and the fuel system evaporator pipe.

10. Disconnect the fuel pipes from the fuel rail.

11. Disconnect the accelerator cable and if equipped, the cruise control cable.

12. Tag and disconnect the spark plug wires from the plugs.

13. Remove the spark plug wire harness retainer from the heater hose pipe and set aside the harness.

14. If necessary, remove the alternator rear brace by accessing the retaining nuts and bolts through the wheelhouse.

15. If equipped, remove the engine wiring harness bracket located at the rear of the cylinder head, by unfastening the

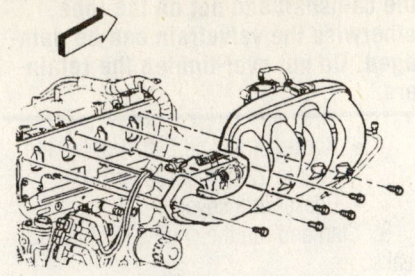

91113G02

Typical intake manifold mounting—1998–01 models

bracket-to-valve cover and bracket-to-cylinder head retainers, then slide the bracket off the bolt at the rear of the cylinder head.

16. Unfasten the intake manifold bolts.

17. Remove the fuel rail bracket.

18. Remove the intake manifold and gasket.

To install:

19. Carefully remove all traces of gasket material from the mating surfaces. Check the EGR passage to be sure it is free of excessive carbon deposits and clean, as necessary.

20. Install the lower intake manifold using a new gasket, then tighten the retaining bolts to 17 ft. lbs. (24 Nm) using the sequence illustrated.

21. If removed, install the engine wiring harness bracket. Tighten the bracket-to-valve cover bolts to 88 inch lbs. (10 Nm) and the bracket-to-cylinder head bolt to 18 ft. lbs. (25 Nm).

22. If removed, install the generator rear brace. Tighten the nuts and bolts to 18 ft. lbs. (25 Nm).

23. Install the spark plug wire harness and retainer and attach the spark plug wires to the plugs.

24. Install the throttle body assembly, if removed and the throttle cable support bracket.

25. Attach the three vacuum lines to the throttle body.

26. Attach the accelerator cable and if equipped, the cruise control cable.

27. Connect the fuel lines.

28. Install and tighten the retainers to the engine harness bracket, the transmission filler tube (if equipped) and the fuel system evaporator pipe.

29. Attach the following electrical connections:
   a. Idle Air Control (IAC) motor
   b. Manifold Absolute Pressure (MAP) sensor
   c. Throttle Position (TP) sensor
   d. Fuel injector harness connector

30. If removed, install the wheelhouse extension.

31. If removed, install the EGR adapter and tighten the retainers to 97 inch lbs. (11 Nm).

32. Install the EGR pipe to the EGR adapter and tighten the bolt to 18 ft. lbs. (25 Nm).

33. Install the EGR pipe-to-intake manifold bolts and tighten the bolts to 89 inch lbs. (10 Nm).

34. If removed, install the upper fan shroud and the brake booster hose.

35. Install the air cleaner resonator and connect the negative battery cable.

36. Start the engine and check for leaks.

4.3L Engines

➡**If only the upper intake manifold is being removed, the fuel system pressure does not need to be released. ALWAYS release the pressure before disconnecting any fuel lines.**

1. Before servicing the vehicle, refer to the precautions in the beginning of this section.

2. Remove the engine cover, if equipped

3. Properly relieve the fuel system pressure.

4. Disconnect the negative battery cable.

5. Drain the engine cooling system.

6. Remove or disconnect the following:
   - Air cleaner and air inlet duct
   - Wiring harness connectors and brackets
   - Throttle linkage from the upper intake manifold
   - Ignition coil
   - Fuel lines and bracket from the rear of the lower intake manifold
   - Brake booster vacuum hose at the upper intake manifold
   - Positive Crankcase Ventilation (PCV) hose at the rear of the upper intake manifold
   - Vacuum hoses from both the front and rear of the upper intake
   - Purge solenoid and bracket
   - Upper intake manifold
   - Distributor or High Voltage Switch (HVS) assembly
   - Upper radiator hose at the thermostat housing
   - Heater hose at the lower intake manifold
   - Wiring harnesses and brackets.
   - Automatic transmission dipstick tube
   - Exhaust Gas Recirculation (EGR) tube, clamp and tube

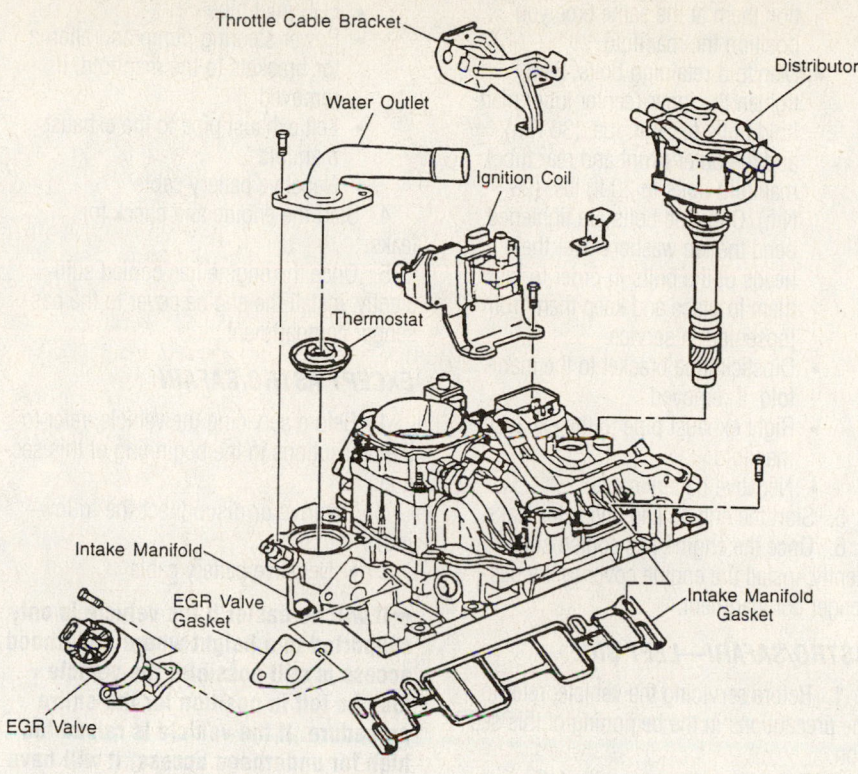

Throttle Cable Bracket

Water Outlet

Distributor

Ignition Coil

Thermostat

Intake Manifold

EGR Valve Gasket

Intake Manifold Gasket

EGR Valve

7924JG26

Intake manifold and related components—4.3L engine

- Air conditioning compressor bracket-to-lower intake manifold pencil brace
- Alternator bracket bolts near the thermostat housing
- Lower intake manifold

7. Insert clean rags into the openings in the cylinder head to prevent dirt and debris from entering the engine.

8. Clean the gasket mounting surfaces. Be sure to inspect the manifold for warpage and/or cracks. If necessary, replace it.

To install:

9. Remove the rags from the cylinder heads.

10. Position the gaskets on the cylinder head with the port blocking plates to the rear and the **this side up** stamps facing upward. Then apply a 3/16 in. (5mm) bead of RTV sealant on the front and rear of the engine block at the block-to-manifold mating surface. Extend the bead 1/2 in. (13mm) up each cylinder head to seal and retain the gaskets.

➡**Refer to Section 1 of this manual for the intake manifold torque sequence illustration. The illustration is located after the Torque Specification Chart.**

11. Install the lower intake manifold. Tighten the bolts in sequence and in 3 steps, as follows:
   a. Step 1: 26 inch lbs. (3 Nm).
   b. Step 2: 106 inch lbs. (12 Nm).
   c. Step 3: 11 ft. lbs. (15 Nm).

12. Install or connect the following:
- Alternator bracket bolt near the thermostat housing
- EGR tube, clamp and bolt
- Wiring harness to the lower manifold components, including the injector, EGR valve and ECT sensor
- Air conditioning compressor bracket-to-the lower intake manifold pencil braces
- Transmission oil dipstick tube, if necessary
- Fuel supply and return lines to the rear of the lower intake

13. Temporarily reattach the negative battery cable, then pressurize the fuel system (by cycling the ignition without starting the engine) and check for leaks.

14. Disconnect the negative battery cable.

15. Install or connect the following:
- Heater hose to the lower intake
- Upper radiator hose to the thermostat housing

- Distributor assembly and engage the wiring
- Vacuum hoses to the upper and lower intake manifold
- New upper intake manifold gasket, making sure the green sealing lines are facing upward
- Upper intake manifold being careful not to pinch the fuel injector wires between the manifolds
- Manifold retainers. Tighten them to 88 inch lbs. (10 Nm) using two passes.
- Purge solenoid and bracket
- Brake booster vacuum hose at the upper intake manifold.
- PCV hose to the rear of the upper intake manifold
- Vacuum hoses to both the front and rear of the manifold assembly
- Throttle linkage to the upper intake
- Ignition coil
- Wiring to the upper intake components including the TP sensor, IAC motor, MAP sensor and the IMTV.
- Plastic cover
- Air cleaner and air inlet duct
- Negative battery cable

16. Refill the engine cooling system.

Exhaust Manifold

REMOVAL & INSTALLATION

2.2L Engine

1. Before servicing the vehicle, refer to the precautions in the beginning of this section.

2. Remove or disconnect the following:
- Negative battery cable
- Air cleaner and duct work
- Oxygen (O2S) sensor from the manifold, if replacing it
- Drive belt
- Oil fill tube assembly
- Heater hose brace
- Power steering brace and set the pump aside
- Air conditioning pencil and rear braces. Set the compressor aside without disconnect the lines.
- Exhaust manifold nuts
- Exhaust manifold

To install:

3. Clean the exhaust manifold retainer threads and the gasket the mating surfaces.

4. Install or connect the following:

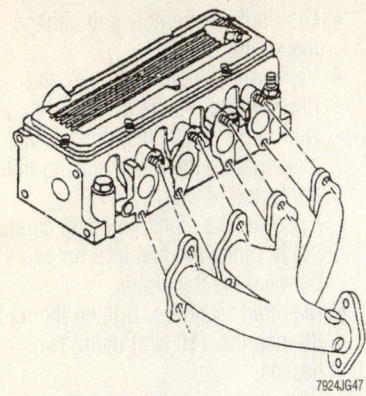

Exhaust manifold mounting—2.2L engine

- Exhaust manifold using a new gasket. Torque the nuts to 115 inch lbs. (13 Nm)
- Exhaust pipe to the manifold
- Air conditioning pencil and rear braces
- Heater hose
- Power steering and heater hose braces
- Oil fill tube assembly
- O_2S sensor. Torque it to 31 ft. lbs. (42 Nm), if necessary
- Drive belt
- Air cleaner and duct work
- Negative battery cable

4.3L Engines

ASTRO/SAFARI—RIGHT SIDE

1. Before servicing the vehicle, refer to the precautions in the beginning of this section.
2. Remove or disconnect the following:

- Negative battery cable
- Engine cover
- Right exhaust pipe from the exhaust manifold
- Dipstick tube bracket at the manifold, if necessary
- Exhaust manifold-to-engine bolts, washers and tab washers. Whenever tab washers are used, their edges should be straightened before you attempt to loosen the bolts.
- Heat shields, if equipped
- Manifold

3. Using a plastic scraper, clean the gasket mounting surfaces.

To install:

4. Install or connect the following:

- Exhaust manifold assembly using a new gasket. If heat shields were removed with the manifold as an assembly, it may be easier to posi-

tion them at the same time you position the manifold.

- Manifold retaining bolts, then tighten the inner (center tube) manifold bolts to 26 ft. lbs. (36 Nm), and the outer (front and rear tube) manifold bolts to 20 ft. lbs. (28 Nm). Once the bolts are tightened, bend the tab washers over the heads of the bolts in order to lock them in place and keep them from loosening in service.
- Dipstick tube bracket to the manifold, if removed
- Right exhaust pipe to the exhaust manifold
- Negative battery cable.

5. Start the engine and check for leaks.
6. Once the engine has cooled sufficiently, install the engine cover to the passenger compartment.

ASTRO/SAFARI—LEFT SIDE

1. Before servicing the vehicle, refer to the precautions in the beginning of this section.
2. Remove or disconnect the following:

- Negative battery cable
- Engine cover
- Right exhaust pipe from the exhaust manifold.
- Power steering pump and alternator brackets from the manifold, if necessary
- Exhaust gas Recirculation (EGR) inlet pipe
- Exhaust manifold-to-engine bolts, washers and tab washers. Whenever tab washers are used, their edges should be straightened before you attempt to loosen the bolts.
- Heat shields, if equipped
- Manifold from the engine

3. Using a plastic scraper, clean the gasket mounting surfaces.

To install:

- Exhaust manifold assembly using a new gasket. If heat shields were removed with the manifold as an assembly, it may be easier to position them at the same time you position the manifold.
- Manifold retaining bolts, then tighten the inner (center tube) manifold bolts to 26 ft. lbs. (36 Nm), and the outer (front and rear tube) manifold bolts to 20 ft. lbs. (28 Nm). Once the bolts are tightened, bend the tab washers over the heads of the bolts in order to lock them in place and keep them from loosening in service.

- EGR inlet pipe
- Power steering pump and alternator brackets to the manifold, if removed
- Left exhaust pipe to the exhaust manifold
- Negative battery cable

4. Start the engine and check for leaks.
5. Once the engine has cooled sufficiently, install the engine cover to the passenger compartment.

EXCEPT ASTRO/SAFARI

1. Before servicing the vehicle, refer to the precautions in the beginning of this section.
2. Remove or disconnect the following:

- Negative battery cable

➡ It will be easier if the vehicle is only supported to a height where underhood access is still possible, the vehicle may be left in position for the entire procedure. If the vehicle is raised too high for underhood access, it will have to lowered, raised and lowered again during the procedure.

- Exhaust pipe from the exhaust manifold. It may be necessary to remove the tires to gain access to the rear manifold bolts.
- Engine oil dipstick tube bolt, if removing the right side manifold on 1999–01 models
- Exhaust Gas Recirculation (EGR) inlet pipe from the left side manifold, if necessary.
- Engine Coolant Temperature (ECT) sensor electrical connection, on 1998–01 models
- Upper radiator support hose and nut, on 1998–01 models
- Steering intermediate shaft, if removing the left side manifold on 1999–01 models
- Wheel house extension, if removing the right side manifold on 1999–01 models
- Spark plugs wires from the plugs
- Nuts attaching the secondary air injection pipe to the manifold, on 1999–01 models
- Air injection pipe and gasket, on 1999–01 models
- Locktangs (unbend), the exhaust manifold retaining bolts, washers and tab washers
- Heat shields
- Exhaust manifold
- Old gaskets and discard

To install:

3. Using a putty knife, clean the gasket mounting surfaces. Inspect the exhaust manifold for distortion, cracks or damage; replace if necessary.

4. On 1998–01 models, apply a thread-lock such as GM 12345493 to the threads of the manifold retainers prior to installation.

5. Install or connect the following:

- Exhaust manifold to the cylinder using a new gasket, then tighten the center bolts to 11 ft. lbs. (15 Nm) and the front and rear manifold bolts to 22 ft. lbs. (30 Nm). Once the bolts are tightened, bend the tabs on the washers back over the heads of all bolts in order to lock them in position.
- Spark plug wires to the plugs
- Fender wheelhouse extension and the tire assembly, if removed on 1999–01 models
- Secondary air injection pipe with a NEW gasket to the manifold and tighten the nuts to 18 ft. lbs. (25 Nm), if removed on 1999–01 models
- EGR inlet pipe, if removed
- ECT sensor electrical connection, if removed
- Upper radiator hose support and nut, if removed
- Steering intermediate shaft., if removed on 1999–01 models (left side manifold only)
- Engine oil dipstick tube bolt to 106 inch lbs. (12 Nm), if removed
- Exhaust pipe to the manifold
- Negative battery cable

Camshaft and Valve Lifters

REMOVAL & INSTALLATION

2.2L Engine

1. Before servicing the vehicle, refer to the precautions in the beginning of this section.

2. Properly relieve the fuel system pressure.

3. Disconnect the negative battery cable.

4. Drain the engine cooling system and the engine oil.

5. Remove or disconnect the following:
- Radiator
- Rocker arm cover

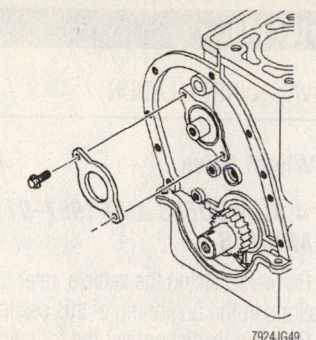

7924JG49

Remove the camshaft thrust plate and withdraw the camshaft from the engine—2.2L engine

- Cylinder head
- Anti-rotation bracket bolts and brackets
- Valve lifters
- Oil pump drive retaining bolt and the drive by lifting and twisting
- Camshaft Position (CMP) sensor, if equipped
- Crankshaft pulley and hub
- Drive belt idler pulley
- Timing cover from the engine
- Timing chain and camshaft sprocket
- Camshaft thrust plate
- Camshaft by pulling it straight out of the engine, while turning it slightly as it is withdrawn and taking care not to damage the bearings.

To install:

6. Inspect the camshaft, journals and lobes for wear and replace, if necessary.

7. If removed, use the camshaft bearing tool to install a new set of bearings.

8. Coat the camshaft lobes and journals with a high viscosity oil with zinc such as GM 12345501.

9. Install or connect the following:
- Camshaft by turning it slightly from side-to-side as it is inserted
- Thrust plate. Torque the bolts to 106 inch lbs. (12 Nm).
- Timing chain and camshaft sprocket
- Timing cover
- Serpentine drive belt idler pulley
- Crankshaft pulley and hub
- Oil pump drive by inserting while twisting. Torque the fasteners to 18 ft. lbs. (25 Nm).
- Valve lifters and the anti-rotation brackets
- Cylinder head. Torque the bolts to 46 ft. lbs. (62 Nm) plus an additional 90 degrees turn.

- Rocker arm cover
- Radiator
- Negative battery cable

10. Refill the engine cooling system.

4.3L Engines

1. Before servicing the vehicle, refer to the precautions in the beginning of this section.

2. Properly relieve the fuel system pressure.

3. Disconnect the negative battery cable.

4. Drain the engine cooling system.

5. Discharge and recover the refrigerant from the air conditioning system.

6. On Astro/Safari, remove the engine cover and engine cooling fan.

7. Remove or disconnect the following:
- Radiator
- Air conditioning condenser
- Rocker arm covers
- Intake manifold assembly
- Rocker arms, pushrods and lifters
- Crankshaft pulley and hub
- Engine front (timing) cover

8. Align the timing marks on the crankshaft and camshaft sprockets.

9. Remove or disconnect the following:
- Camshaft sprocket and timing chain
- Balance shaft drive gear, if equipped
- Camshaft thrust plate
- Camshaft by installing the sprocket bolts or longer bolts the camshaft end to act as a handle; then, remove the camshaft while turning slightly from side to side, as necessary.

➡**Take care not to damage the camshaft bearings when removing the camshaft.**

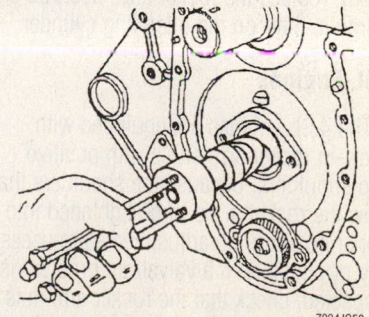

7924JG50

Thread 3 long bolts into the camshaft to use as a handle, then withdraw it from the engine

---

Please refer to Section 8 for electric cooling fan wiring schematics

To install:

10. Lubricate the camshaft journals with clean engine oil or a suitable pre-lube.

11. Install or connect the following:
- Camshaft being extremely careful not to contact the bearings with the cam lobes
- Thrust plate. Torque the bolts to 106 inch lbs. (12 Nm).
- Balance shaft drive gear, if equipped
- Timing chain and camshaft sprocket
- Engine front (timing) cover
- Crankshaft pulley and hub
- Valve lifters, pushrods and rocker arms. Adjust the valve clearance.
- Intake manifold assembly
- Rocker arm covers
- Radiator
- Negative battery cable

12. On Astro/Safari, install the engine cooling fan and engine cover.

13. Refill the engine cooling system.

Valve Lash

ADJUSTMENT

2.2L Engine

Because the rocker arm fasteners are secured and tightened, valve lash is not adjustable on the 2.2L engine. If a valve-train problem is suspected, check that the rocker arm nuts are tightened to 22 ft. lbs. (30 Nm). Be very careful not to over-tighten the rocker arm nuts. ONLY tighten the nuts when the hydraulic lifter is resting on the base circle of the camshaft and not when it is held upward on the lobe. When valve lash falls out of specification (valve tap is heard), replace the rocker arm, pushrod and hydraulic lifter on the offending cylinder.

4.3L Engines

The 4.3L engines are equipped with screw-in rocker arm studs with positive stop shoulders. Because the shoulders that allow the rocker arms to be tightened into proper position, no adjustments are necessary or possible. If a valvetrain problem is suspected, check that the rocker arm nuts are tightened to 18 ft. lbs. (24 Nm). When valve lash falls out of specification (valve tap is heard), replace the rocker arm, pushrod and hydraulic lifter on the offending cylinder.

Starter Motor

REMOVAL & INSTALLATION

Four Wheel Drive

1997 4.3L MODELS AND 1997–01 2.2L MODELS

1. Before servicing the vehicle, refer to the precautions in the beginning of this section.

2. Remove or disconnect the following:
- Negative battery cable
- Front exhaust pipe, if necessary for access
- Starter heat shield, if equipped
- Brace rod from the front of the engine and the bell housing, on 2.2L engines
- Drivers side wheel to access the starter motor wires and the starter motor attaching bracket-to-engine bolt through the opening in the wheel well, on 2.2L engines
- Wires from the starter solenoid

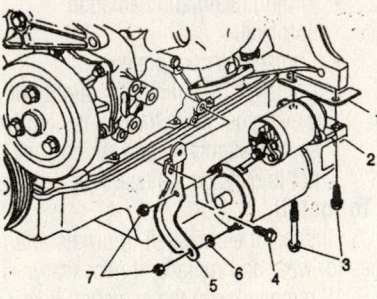

1. SHIM
2. STARTER ASSEMBLY
3. BOLT, 43 N·m (32 LBS. FT.)
4. BOLT, 43 N·m (32 LBS. FT.)
5. BRACKET, STARTER MOTOR
6. WASHER
7. NUT, 11 N·m (97 LBS. IN.)

88452G08

Starter motor and related components—2.2L engine

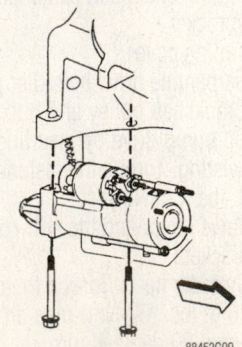

88452G09

The starter motor on later model 4.3L engines is retained by two long bolts

- Attaching bracket-to-engine mount bolt, on 2.2L engines
- Starter-to-engine block bolts. When removing the last bolt, be sure to support the starter to keep it from falling and possibly injuring you.
- Starter and shims (if equipped) from the vehicle
- Bracket (2.2L engine) or the shield (4.3L engine) from the starter assembly, if equipped

To install:

3. Install or connect the following:
- Bracket or shield to the starter, if removed. Tighten the bracket nuts to 97 inch lbs. (11 Nm) or the shield nuts to 106 inch lbs. (12 Nm).
- Starter and shims (if equipped) into position in the vehicle and thread one of the retaining bolts to hold it in position.
- Bracket-to-engine mount bolt (loosely), if equipped
- Starter mounting bolt, then tighten all mounting fasteners to 32 ft. lbs. (43 Nm)
- Wiring to the solenoid
- Brace rod and tighten the retainers, on 2.2L engines
- Front exhaust pipe and tighten the fasteners, if removed
- Starter heat shield, if equipped
- Drivers side wheel, if removed
- Negative battery cable

1998–01 4.3L MODELS

1. Before servicing the vehicle, refer to the precautions in the beginning of this section.

2. Remove or disconnect the following:
- Negative battery cable
- Wires from the starter solenoid
- Starter motor mounting bolts
- Starter motor and if equipped, the shims

To install:

3. Install or connect the following:
- Starter motor into position
- Starter motor inboard bolt but do not tighten it at this time
- Starter motor shims, if equipped
- Outboard starter motor bolt. Tighten the bolts to 32 ft. lbs. (43 Nm).
- Wires to the solenoid
- Negative battery cable

Four Wheel Drive

EXCEPT UTILITY MODELS

1. Before servicing the vehicle, refer to the precautions in the beginning of this section.

2. Remove or disconnect the following:

- Negative battery cable

➡ **In some cases it may be easier to access the starter motor bolts if you raise the vehicle and remove the wheel assembly.**

- Wheel assembly, if necessary
- Engine mounts
- Transmission mount and support the transmission assembly
- Starter-to-engine bolts and support the starter

3. Rotate the starter as necessary for access, then tag and disconnect the solenoid wiring.

4. Carefully lower the starter and shims (if equipped) from the vehicle. Note the location of any shims for installation purposes.

5. If necessary, remove the shield from the starter assembly.

To install:

6. Install or connect the following:

- Starter into position in the vehicle along with any shims (making sure they are in their original positions), then tighten the mounting bolts to 32 ft. lbs. (43 Nm).
- Shield to the starter assembly and tighten the retaining nuts to 106 inch lbs. (12 Nm), if removed
- Wiring to the solenoid
- Transmission mount and remove the supports
- Secure the engine mounts, then remove the lifting device
- Wheel assembly, if removed

7. Connect the negative battery cable.

UTILITY MODELS

1. Before servicing the vehicle, refer to the precautions in the beginning of this section.

2. Remove or disconnect the following:

- Negative battery cable
- Brush end mounting bracket, if removed
- Wiring from the starter solenoid
- Transfer case shield, if equipped
- Bolts that attach the brake pipe-to-transmission bracket to the transmission crossmember and the brackets
- Transmission crossmember bolts, (usually three on each side)
- Transmission mount bolts. Support the transmission assembly with a transmission jack and slide the

transmission crossmember out of the way.

- Bracket that attaches the transmission cooler lines to the flywheel housing, brace rod to the flywheel housing, and/or the lower flywheel housing as necessary
- Starter motor mounting bolts
- Starter and if equipped, the starter shims

To install:

3. Install or connect the following:

- Shims in their original locations (if equipped), then place the starter motor into position
- Starter motor bolts and tighten them to 33 ft. lbs. (45 Nm)
- Lower flywheel cover, if removed
- Transmission line bracket to the housing and the brace rod to the housing, if equipped
- Crossmember and tighten the retaining bolts.
- Transfer case shield, if equipped
- Solenoid wiring
- Brush end bracket and tighten the nuts to 97 inch lbs. (11 Nm), if equipped

- Negative battery cable

4. Start the vehicle to check for proper operation.

Oil Pan

REMOVAL & INSTALLATION

2.2L Engine

1. Before servicing the vehicle, refer to the precautions in the beginning of this section.

2. Remove or disconnect the following:

- Engine
- Clutch pressure plate and disc, if equipped
- Flywheel
- Oil pan retainers and the pan

To install:

3. Clean the gasket mating surfaces

4. Install or connect the following:

- New gasket and seal onto the oil pan using a thin bead of sealant at either side of the seal
- Oil pan. Torque the bolts to 89 inch. lbs. (10 Nm).
- Flywheel

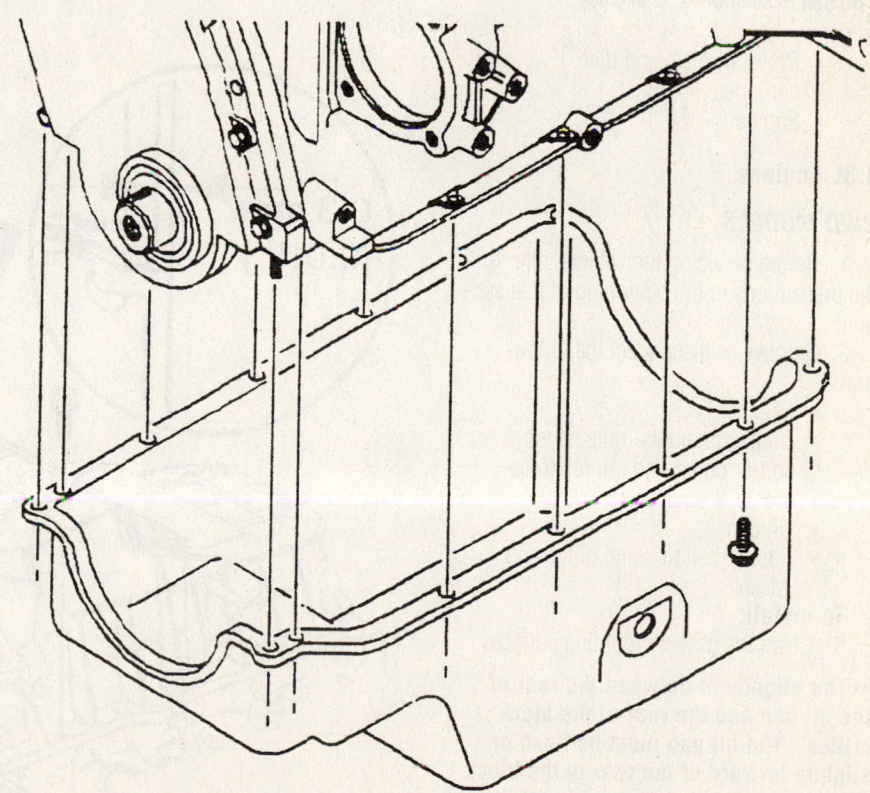

Oil pan mounting—2.2L engine

7924JG51

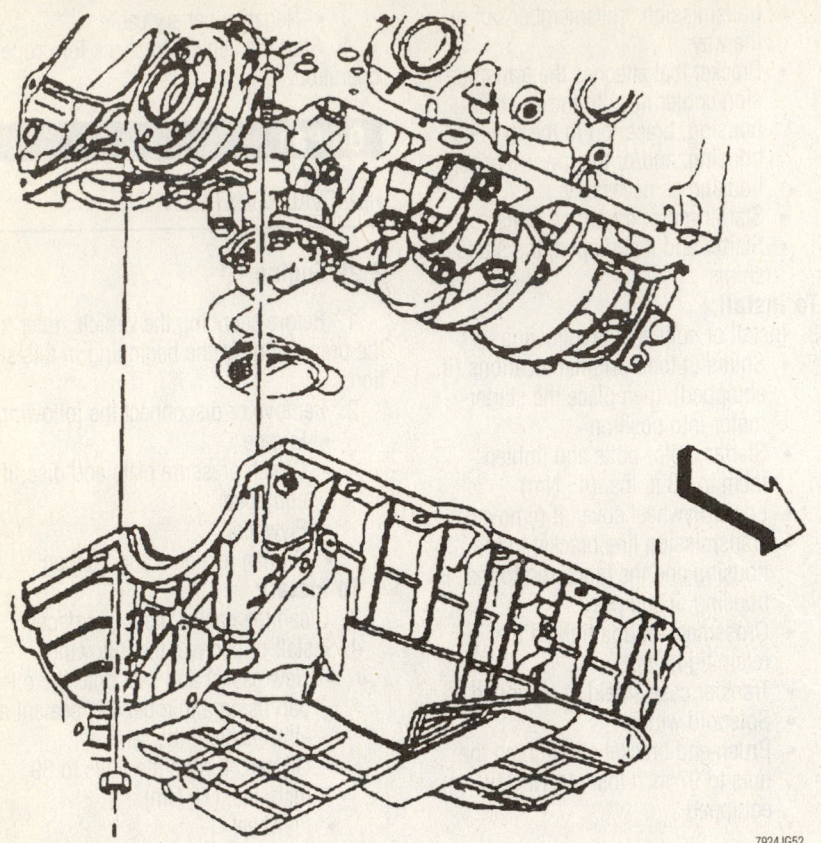

Oil pan mounting—4.3L engines

- Pressure plate and disc, if equipped
- Engine

4.3L Engines

2WD MODELS

1. Before servicing the vehicle, refer to the precautions in the beginning of this section.

2. Remove or disconnect the following:

- Engine
- Oil pan retainers (nuts, studs and/or bolts) and rail reinforcements, if equipped
- Oil pan
- Rubber bell housing plugs and gasket

To install:

3. Clean the gasket mounting surfaces.

➡The alignment between the rear of the oil pan and the rear of the block is critical. The oil pan must be flush or slightly forward of the rear of the block to allow for proper alignment with the transmission housing. Use a feeler gauge to measure the clearance between the 3 oil pan-to-transmission contact points. If the clearance exceeds

0.011 in. (0.3mm) at any of the 3 points, realign the oil pan.

4. Apply sealant to the oil pan rail where it contacts the timing cover-to-block joint (front) and the crankshaft rear seal retainer-to-block joint (rear). Continue the bead of sealant about 1 in. (25mm) in both directions from each of the 4 corners.

5. Install or connect the following:

- Rubber bell housing plugs, if equipped
- Oil pan using a new gasket

➡The alignment between the rear of the pan and rear of the block is critical. The two surfaces must be flush to allow for proper alignment with the transmission housing.

6. Use a feeler gauge to check the clearance between the oil pan-to-transmission contacts. If clearance exceeds 0.011 inch (0.3mm) at any of the three contact points, readjust the pan until the clearance is within specification.

7. Once the pan is in its correct position tighten the retainers to 18 ft. lbs. (25 Nm) using the proper sequence.

8. Install the engine into the vehicle. Refill the crankcase with fresh oil. Start the engine, establish normal operating temperatures and check for leaks.

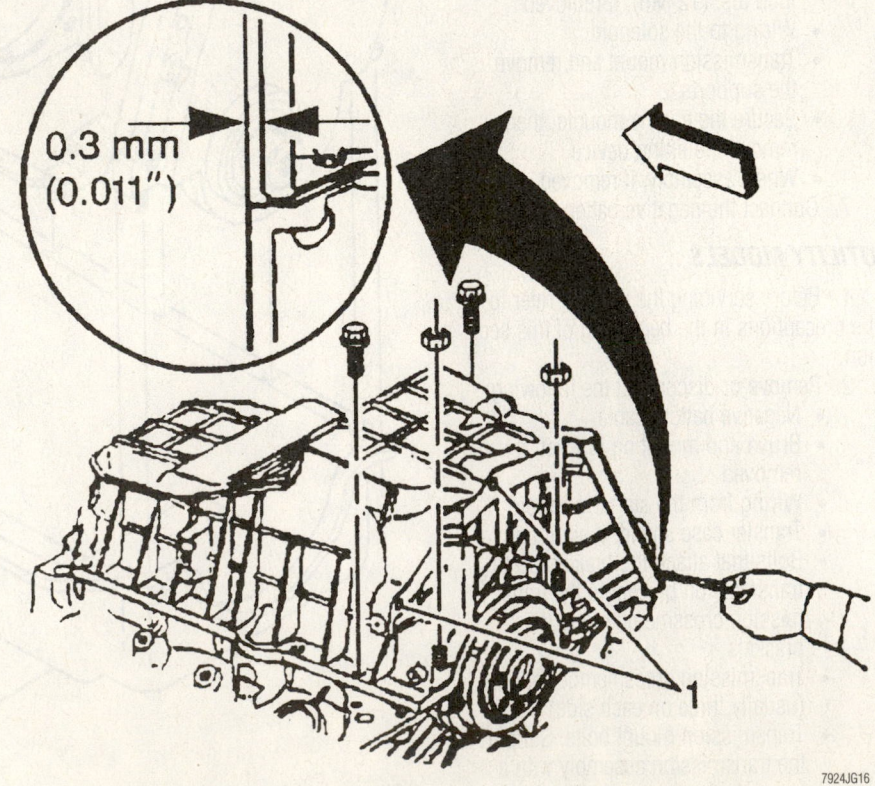

If the clearance between the 3 oil pan-to-transmission contact points exceeds 0.011 in. (0.3mm) at any of the 3 points, realign the oil pan—4.3L engine

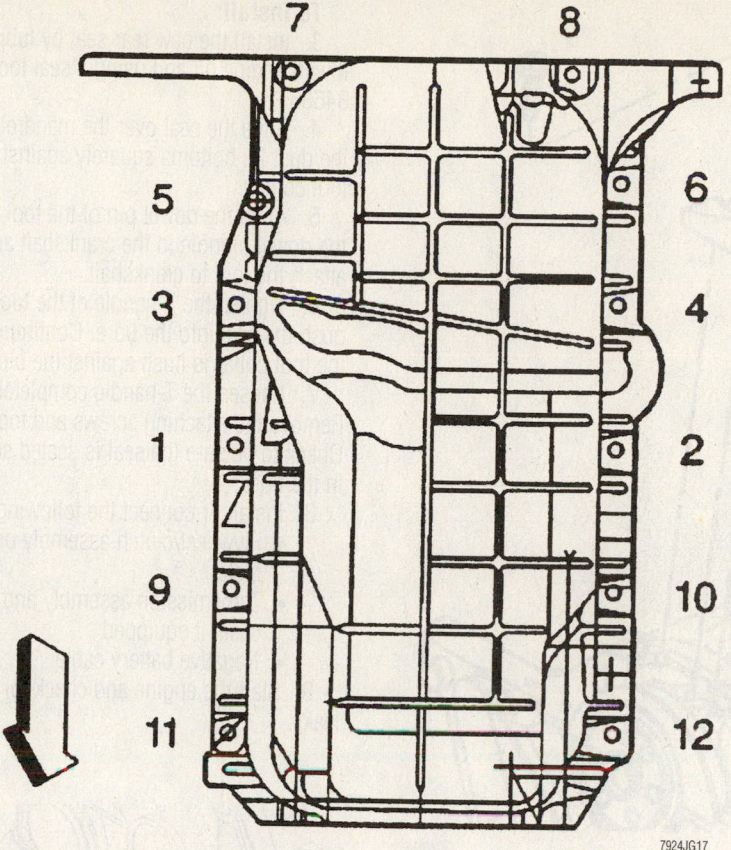

7924JG17

Tighten the bolts in sequence to prevent warping the sealing surface of the oil pan—4.3L vehicles

4WD MODELS

1. Before servicing the vehicle, refer to the precautions in the beginning of this section.

2. Disconnect the negative battery cable.

3. Drain the engine crankcase oil.

4. Remove or disconnect the following:
- Dipstick
- Drivebelt splash shield, the front axle shield and the transfer case shield
- Front skid plate and the flywheel cover
- Left and right engine mount through-bolts

5. Raise the engine using a lifting device and block in position. This may be accomplished using large wooden blocks between the motor mounts and brackets.

➡**Use extreme caution when blocking the engine in position. Get out from under the vehicle and rock the engine slightly once the blocks are in place to be sure the engine is properly supported.**

6. Remove or disconnect the following:
- Oil cooler line
- Pitman arm bolt and pitman arm
- Idler arm bolts and idler arm
- Front differential through-bolts
- Front driveshaft, if necessary
- Differential assembly by rolling it forward for clearance
- Starter motor
- Oil pan bolts, nuts and reinforcements
- Oil pan and discard the gasket

To install:

7. Clean the gasket mounting surfaces.

➡**The alignment between the rear of the oil pan and the rear of the block is critical. The oil pan must be flush or slightly forward of the rear of the block to allow for proper alignment with the transmission housing. Use a feeler gauge to measure the clearance between the 3 oil pan-to-transmission contact points. If the clearance exceeds 0.011 in. (0.3mm) at any of the 3 points, realign the oil pan.**

8. Apply sealant to the oil pan rail where it contacts the timing cover-to-block joint (front) and the crankshaft rear seal retainer-to-block joint (rear). Continue the bead of sealant about 1 in. (25mm) in both directions from each of the 4 corners.

9. Install or connect the following:
- Oil pan, using a new gasket. Tighten the retainers, in sequence, to 18 ft. lbs. (25 Nm).
- Starter motor
- Differential by rolling it back into position
- Front driveshaft
- Front differential through-bolts
- Idler arm and secure using the retaining bolts
- Pitman arm and secure using the bolts
- Transfer case shield
- Flywheel cover
- Front skid plate
- Front axle shield
- Drive belt splash shield
- Dipstick
- Negative battery cable

10. Refill the engine crankcase.

11. Start the engine and check for leaks.

Oil Pump

REMOVAL & INSTALLATION

1. Before servicing the vehicle, refer to the precautions in the beginning of this section.

2. Remove or disconnect the following:
- Oil pan
- Oil pump and the pickup tube/shaft, if equipped
- Extension shaft and retainer from the pump, if necessary for the 2.2L engine

➡**Be careful not to crack the retainer.**

To install:

3. For the 2.2L engine, if the extension shaft was removed, heat the extension shaft retainer in hot water, then install the shaft and retainer to the oil pump. Be sure the retainer does not crack during installation.

4. Ensure that the pump pickup tube is tight in the pump body. If the tube should come loose, oil pressure will be lost and oil starvation will occur. If the pickup tube is loose it should be replaced.

5. If the pump has been disassembled and is being replaced or for any reason oil has been removed, it must be primed. It can

Timing belt service is covered in Section 4 of this manual

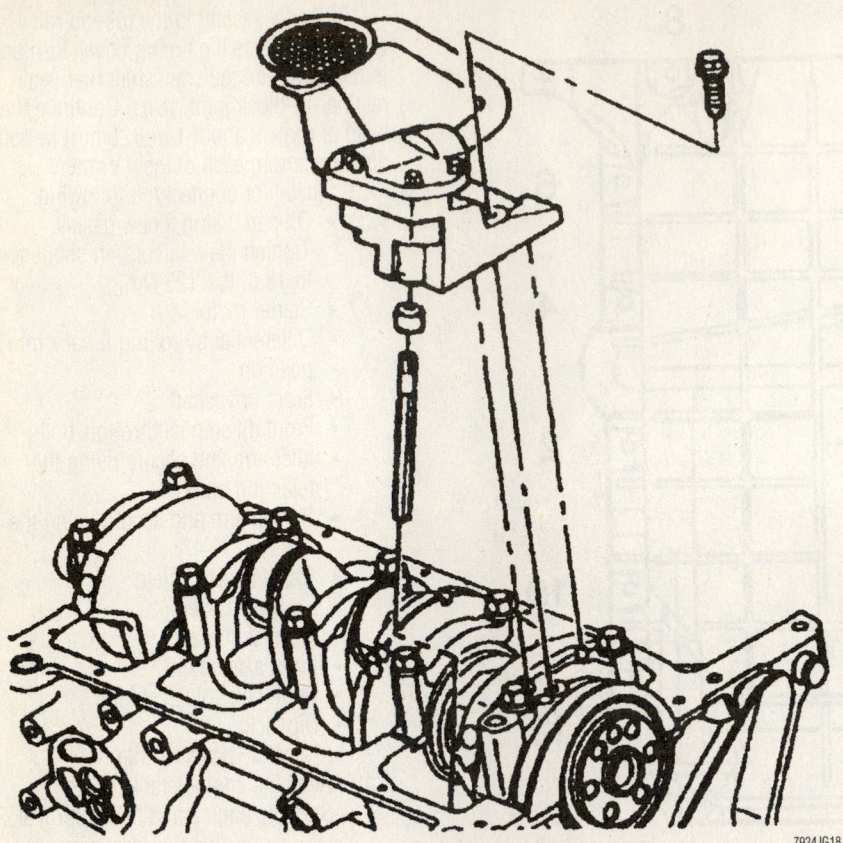

7924JG18

Exploded view of the oil pump mounting—2.2L engine

either be filled with oil before installing the cover plate and oil kept within the pump during handling or the entire pump cavity can be filled with petroleum jelly.

> ※※ **WARNING**
>
> **If the pump is not primed, the engine could be damaged upon start up.**

6. Install or connect the following:
   - Oil pump by aligning the pump shaft with the distributor drive gear as necessary. Tighten oil pump/pickup tube retainer(s) to 32 ft. lbs. (44 Nm) for the 2.2L engine or to 65 ft. lbs. (90 Nm), for the 4.3L engine.

➡ **If the oil pump does not build up oil pressure almost immediately, remove the pan and check for a loose oil pump-to-pickup tube attachment. If necessary dismantle the pump and pack the pump cavity with petroleum jelly.**

   - Oil pan
7. Refill the crankcase.
8. Disable the ignition system; crank engine for approximately 10 seconds to aid in priming the oil pump and reducing the risk of engine damage.

> ※※ **WARNING**
>
> **Running the engine without measurable oil pressure will cause extensive damage.**

Rear Main Seal

REMOVAL & INSTALLATION

2.2L Engines

Please note that the transmission assembly and transfer case, if equipped, must be removed to perform this procedure.

1. Before servicing the vehicle, refer to the precautions in the beginning of this section.
2. Remove or disconnect the following:
   - Negative battery cable
   - Transmission assembly and transfer case, if equipped
   - Flexplate, if equipped
   - Clutch assembly and flywheel, if equipped
   - Crankshaft seal by prying it from out

➡ **Be careful not to damage the crankshaft seal surface with the prying tool.**

To install:
3. Install the new rear seal by lubricating it with engine oil and using a seal tool J-34686.
4. Slide the seal over the mandrel until the dust lip bottoms squarely against the tool collar.
5. Align the dowel pin of the tool with the dowel pinhole in the crankshaft and attach the tool to crankshaft.
6. Tighten the T-handle of the tool to push the seal into the bore. Continue until the tool collar is flush against the block.
7. Loosen the T-handle completely. Remove the attaching screws and tool. Check to be sure the seal is seated squarely in the bore.
8. Install or connect the following:
   - Flywheel/clutch assembly or flexplate
   - Transmission assembly and transfer case, if equipped
   - Negative battery cable
9. Start the engine and check for leaks.

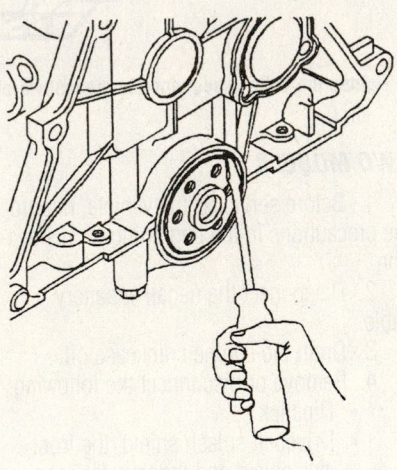

7924JG19

Carefully pry the rear main oil seal out of its bore—2.2L engine

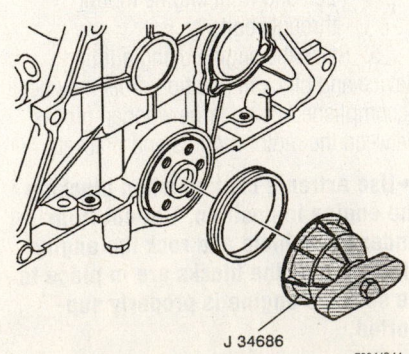

J 34686

7924JG44

Rear main oil seal installation using tool J-34686—2.2L engine

4.3L Engines

Please note that the transmission assembly and transfer case, if equipped, must be removed to perform this procedure.

1. Before servicing the vehicle, refer to the precautions in the beginning of this section.

2. Remove or disconnect the following:
   - Negative battery cable
   - Transfer case, if equipped
   - Transmission
   - Clutch assembly/flywheel or flexplate

3. Remove the crankshaft rear oil seal by inserting a suitable prying tool into the notches provided in the seal retainer and prying the seal out. Take care not to damage the crankshaft sealing surface.

To install:

4. Inspect the crankshaft for grit, rust or burrs and correct as necessary.

5. Clean the running surface of the crankshaft with a non-abrasive cleaner.

6. Install or connect the following:
   - New rear seal lubricated with engine oil and a seal installer
   - Flywheel and clutch or flexplate
   - Transmission
   - Transfer case, if equipped
   - Negative battery cable

7. Start the engine and verify no oil leaks.

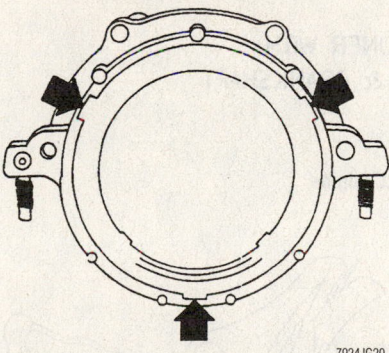

Carefully pry the rear main seal out of the retainer—4.3L engine

Timing Chain, Sprockets, Front Cover and Seal

REMOVAL & INSTALLATION

Front Cover and Seal

2.2L ENGINES

1. Before servicing the vehicle, refer to the precautions in the beginning of this section.

2. Remove or disconnect the following:
   - Negative battery cable
   - Drive belt
   - Cooling fan assembly and pulley
   - Crankshaft pulley and hub
   - Belt tensioner/idler pulley assembly
   - Front oil pan-to-front cover nuts or studs
   - Starter
   - Alternator and brackets from the engine, then position them aside
   - Oil pan bolts, loosen but do not remove
   - Crankcase (timing) front cover bolts and the cover. Make sure all bolts are removed and be careful not to force and damage the cover.
   - Old crankshaft seal from the cover using a suitable prytool. Be very careful not to distort the front cover or to score the end of the crankshaft.

To install:

3. Carefully remove all traces of gasket or sealant from the mating surfaces.

4. Lubricate the lips of a new seal with clean engine oil, then use a seal centering tool (such as J-35468) to install the seal to the front cover. Leave the tool in position in the seal until the cover is installed.

5. Apply a ⅜ in. (10mm) wide by ⁵⁄₁₆ (5mm) thick bead of RTV sealer to the oil pan at the front crankcase cover sealing surface. Then apply a ¼ in. (6mm) by ⅛ in. (3mm) thick bead of RTV to the crankcase front cover at the block sealing surface.

6. Install or connect the following:
   - Crankcase front cover to the engine using the seal tool to assure it is properly centered and prevent damage to the hub. Tighten the cover retaining bolts to 97 inch lbs. (11 Nm), then remove the seal centering tool.
   - Oil pan bolts
   - Starter
   - Alternator with brackets
   - Belt tensioner/idler pulley assembly
   - Belt assembly
   - Crankshaft pulley and hub
   - Cooling fan assembly and pulley
   - Negative battery cable

4.3L ENGINES

1. Before servicing the vehicle, refer to the precautions in the beginning of this section.

2. Remove or disconnect the following:
   - Negative battery cable
   - Drain the engine cooling system.
   - Crankshaft pulley and damper.

The outer ring (weight) of the torsional damper is bonded to the hub with rubber. The damper must be removed with a puller which acts on the inner hub only. Pulling on the outer portion of the damper will break the rubber bond or destroy the tuning of the unit.

- Water pump assembly
- Oil pan, loosen only
- Crankshaft Position (CKP) sensor, if equipped
- Front cover bolts and the reinforcements, if equipped
- Front cover from the engine

3. Pry the seal out of the front cover using a small prytool. Be very careful not to distort the front cover or to score the end of the crankshaft.

To install:

➡Anytime the front cover is removed, the cover must be replaced upon reassembly. If you reuse the old cover, oil leaks may develop.

4. Clean the gasket mating surfaces of the engine and cover of all remaining gasket or sealer material. Be careful not to score or damage the surfaces.

➡The manufacturer suggests you wait until the front cover is mounted to the engine before you install the replacement crankshaft oil seal. This assures the cover is properly supported.

5. Install or connect the following:
   - New front cover gasket to the engine or cover using gasket cement to hold it in position. Lubricate the front of the oil pan seal with engine oil to aid in reassembly.
   - Front cover to the engine. Take care while engaging the front of the oil pan seal with the bottom of the cover. On 1998–01 models, apply sealer 12346141 to the oil pan rail where it contacts the timing cover-to-block joint (front) and the crankshaft rear seal retainer-to-block joint (rear). Continue the bead of sealant about 1 in. (25mm) in both directions from each of the four corners.
   - Front cover retaining bolts and tighten to 106 inch. lbs. (12 Nm)

6. Lightly coat the lips of the replace-

ment crankshaft seal with clean engine oil, then position the seal with the open end facing inward the engine. Use a suitable seal installation driver to position the seal in the front cover.

- CKP sensor O-ring and the sensor, if equipped
- Tighten the Oil pan bolts
- Water pump
- Crankshaft damper and pulley
- Negative battery cable

7. Properly refill the engine cooling system.

8. Run the engine until normal operating temperature has been reached, then check for leaks.

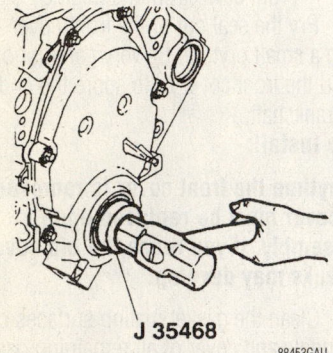

J 35468

88453GAU

Installing the crankshaft front oil seal—4.3L engines

Timing Chain and Sprockets

2.2L ENGINES

1. Before servicing the vehicle, refer to the precautions in the beginning of this section.

2. Remove or disconnect the following:

- Negative battery cable
- Crankcase (timing) front cover from the engine

3. Turn the crankshaft until the timing marks on the sprockets are in alignment. The marks should also be in alignment with the tabs on the tensioner.

- Tensioner retaining bolts
- Camshaft sprocket retaining bolts
- Camshaft sprocket and timing chain at the same time
- Tensioner assembly
- Crankshaft Position (CKP) sensor, if equipped
- Crankshaft sprocket using J-22888-20, if equipped

To install:

4. Install or connect the following:

- Crankshaft sprocket using a suitable installer such as J-5590, if

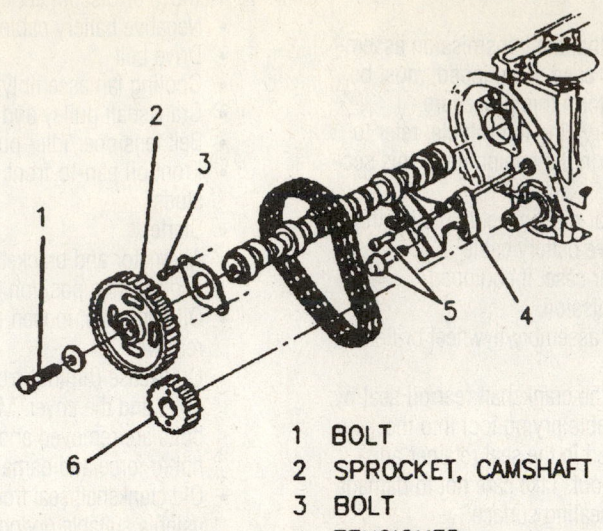

1	**BOLT**
2	**SPROCKET, CAMSHAFT**
3	**BOLT**
4	**TENSIONER**
5	**BOLTS**
6	**SPOCKET, CRANKSHAFT**

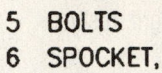

A ALIGN TABS ON TENSIONER WITH MARKS ON CAMSHAFT & CRANKSHAFT SPROCKETS.

85383289

Timing chain, sprocket and camshaft mounting—2.2L engine

removed. Make sure the sprocket is fully seated against the crankshaft.

5. Compress the tensioner spring and insert a cotter pin or nail in the hole provided to hold the tensioner in position.

- Tensioner retaining bolts
- Camshaft sprocket in the timing chain, position the chain under the crankshaft sprocket and the camshaft sprocket to the camshaft

6. Verify that the timing marks are all properly aligned, then loosely install the camshaft sprocket bolt.

- CKP sensor, if equipped
- Tighten the tensioner bolts to 18 ft. lbs. (24 Nm), then tighten the camshaft sprocket bolt to 96 ft. lbs. (130 Nm)

7. Remove the cotter pin or nail holding the tensioner in position off the chain.

- Timing cover to the engine

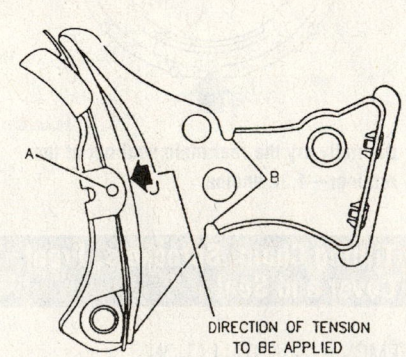

DIRECTION OF TENSION TO BE APPLIED

A INSERT PIN AFTER TENSION HAS BEEN APPLIED
B TABS, USED FOR CAMSHAFT AND CRANKSHAFT ALIGNMENT

85383290

Locking the timing chain tensioner into position for chain installation—2.2L engine

4.3L ENGINES

➡ **The following procedure requires the use of the Crankshaft Sprocket Removal tool No. J-5825-A and the Crankshaft Sprocket Installation tool No. J-5590.**

1. Before servicing the vehicle, refer to the precautions in the beginning of this section.

2. Remove the timing cover from the engine.

3. Rotate the crankshaft until the No. 4 cylinder is on the Top Dead Center (TDC) of its compression stroke and the camshaft sprocket mark aligns with the mark on the crankshaft sprocket (facing each other at a point closest together in their travel) and in line with the shaft centers.

4. Remove or disconnect the following:
   • Crankshaft Position (CKP) sensor reluctor ring, if equipped
   • Camshaft sprocket-to-camshaft nut and/or bolts
   • Camshaft sprocket (along with the timing chain). If the sprocket is difficult to remove, use a plastic mallet to bump the sprocket from the camshaft.

➡ **The camshaft sprocket (located by a dowel) is lightly pressed onto the camshaft and should come off easily. The chain comes off with the camshaft sprocket.**

5. If necessary use J-5825-A crankshaft sprocket removal tool to free the timing sprocket from the crankshaft.

6. If necessary, remove the crankshaft sprocket key.

To install:

7. Inspect the timing chain and the timing sprockets for wear or damage, replace the damaged parts as necessary.

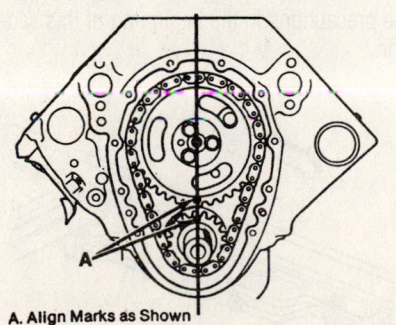

A. Align Marks as Shown

85383292

Timing mark alignment—4.3L engine

8. Using a putty knife, clean the gasket mounting surfaces. Using solvent, clean the oil and grease from the gasket mounting surfaces.

9. Install or connect the following:
   • Crankshaft sprocket key, if removed
   • Crankshaft sprocket onto the crankshaft using J-5590 crankshaft sprocket installation tool and a hammer without disturbing the position of the engine

➡ **During installation, coat the thrust surfaces lightly with Molykote• or an equivalent pre-lube.**

   • Timing chain over the camshaft sprocket. Arrange the camshaft sprocket in such a way that the timing marks will align between the shaft centers and the camshaft locating dowel will enter the dowel hole in the cam sprocket.
   • Timing chain under the crankshaft sprocket, then place the cam sprocket, with the chain still mounted over it, in position on the front of the camshaft
   • Camshaft sprocket-to-camshaft retainers to 18 ft. lbs. (25 Nm)

10. With the timing chain installed, turn the crankshaft two complete revolutions,

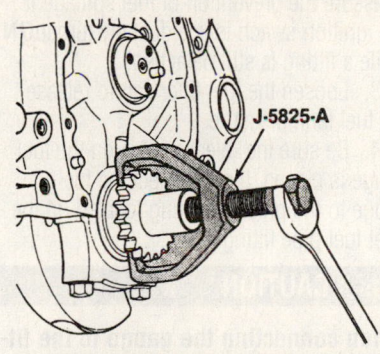

J-5825-A

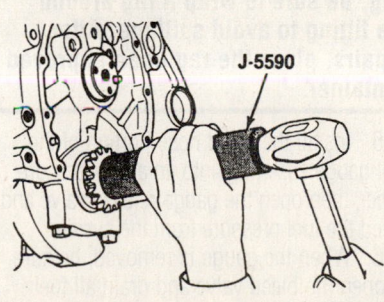

J-5590

85383293

Removal (top) and installation of the crankshaft timing gear

then check to make certain that the timing marks are in correct alignment between the shaft centers.

   • CKP sensor reluctor ring, if equipped
   • Timing cover

Piston and Ring

POSITIONING

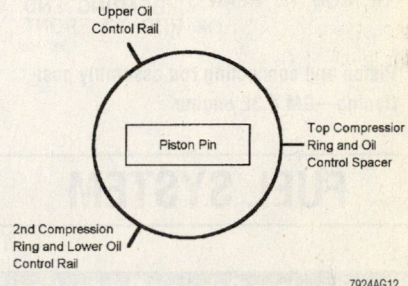

7924AG12

Piston ring end-gap spacing—GM/Isuzu 2.2L engine

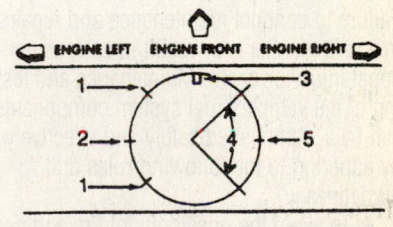

1. Oil ring rail gaps
2. 2nd Compression ring gap
3. Notch in piston
4. Oil ring spacer gap (tang in hole or slot with arc)
5. Top compression ring gap

7924AG07

Piston ring end-gap spacing—GM 4.3L engines

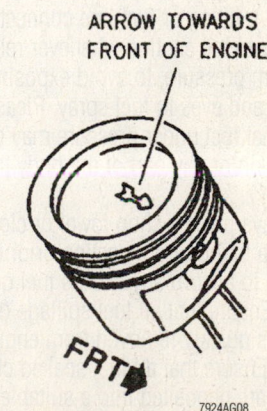

ARROW TOWARDS FRONT OF ENGINE

FRT

7924AG08

Piston/connecting rod-to-engine positioning—GM/Isuzu 2.2L engines

Refer to Section 1 for engine rebuilding specifications

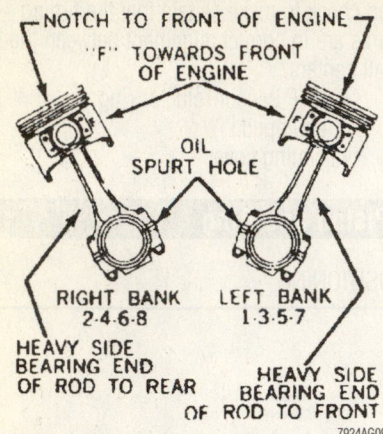

Piston and connecting rod assembly positioning—GM 4.3L engine

FUEL SYSTEM

Fuel System Service Precautions

Safety is the most important factor when performing not only fuel system maintenance but also any type of maintenance. Failure to conduct maintenance and repairs in a safe manner may result in serious personal injury or death. Maintenance and testing of the vehicle's fuel system components can be accomplished safely and effectively by adhering to the following rules and guidelines.

• To avoid the possibility of fire and personal injury, always disconnect the negative battery cable unless the repair or test procedure requires that battery voltage be applied.

• Always relieve the fuel system pressure prior to disconnecting any fuel system component (injector, fuel rail, pressure regulator, etc.), fitting or fuel line connection. Exercise extreme caution whenever relieving fuel system pressure, to avoid exposing skin, face and eyes to fuel spray. Please be advised that fuel under pressure may penetrate the skin or any part of the body that it contacts.

• Always place a shop towel or cloth around the fitting or connection prior to loosening to absorb any excess fuel due to spillage. Ensure that all fuel spillage (should it occur) is quickly removed from engine surfaces. Ensure that all fuel soaked cloths or towels are deposited into a suitable waste container.

• Always keep a dry chemical (Class B) fire extinguisher near the work area.

• Do not allow fuel spray or fuel vapors to come into contact with a spark or open flame.

• Always use a back-up wrench when loosening and tightening fuel line connection fittings. This will prevent unnecessary stress and torsion to fuel line piping. Always follow the proper torque specifications.

• Always replace worn fuel fitting O-rings with new. Do not substitute fuel hose or equivalent where fuel pipe is installed.

Fuel System Pressure

RELIEVING

Multi-Port Fuel Injection and Central Port Injection Systems

The fuel systems operate under high fuel pressures. It is very important that the pressure be properly relieved prior to servicing the system or any of its components.

A Schrader valve is provided on these fuel systems to conveniently test or release the system pressure. A fuel pressure gauge and adapter will be necessary to connect the gauge to the fitting. Most of the MFI systems utilize a service valve on one end of the fuel rail assembly.

1. Before servicing the vehicle, refer to the precautions in the beginning of this section.

2. Disconnect the negative battery cable to assure the prevention of fuel spillage if the ignition switch is accidentally turned **ON** while a fitting is still detached.

3. Loosen the fuel filler cap to release the fuel tank pressure.

4. Be sure the release valve on the fuel gauge is closed, then connect the fuel gauge to the pressure fitting located on the inlet fuel pipe fitting.

✸✸ CAUTION

When connecting the gauge to the fitting, be sure to wrap a rag around the fitting to avoid spillage. After repairs, place the rag in an approved container.

5. Install the bleed hose portion of the fuel gauge assembly into an approved container, then open the gauge release valve and bleed the fuel pressure from the system.

6. When the gauge is removed, be sure to open the bleed valve and drain all fuel from the gauge assembly.

7. When fuel service is finished, tighten the fuel filler cap and connect the negative battery cable.

Fuel Filter

REMOVAL & INSTALLATION

1997–98 4.3L ENGINES

1. Before servicing the vehicle, refer to the precautions in the beginning of this section.

2. Properly relieve the fuel system pressure.

3. Remove or disconnect the following:
• Negative battery cable
• Fuel filler cap
• Fuel lines from the filter using a back-up wrench
• Fuel filter from the retainer or mounting bolt. For most filters which are retained by band clamps, loosen the fastener(s) and remove the filter. For some filters it may be necessary to completely remove the clamp and filter assembly.

To install:
4. Install or connect the following:
• Ffilter and retaining bracket with the directional arrow facing away from the fuel tank, towards the throttle body

➡**The filter has an arrow (fuel flow direction) on the side of the case, be sure to install it correctly in the system, the with arrow facing away from the fuel tank.**

• Tighten the filter/bracket retainer(s), as applicable
• Fuel lines to the filter and tighten using a backup wrench
• Negative battery cable
• Fuel filler cap
5. Start the engine and check for leaks.

2.2L ENGINES AND 1999–01 4.3L ENGINES

1. Before servicing the vehicle, refer to the precautions in the beginning of this section.

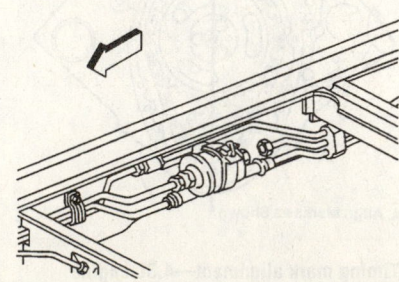

Typical fuel filter location along frame rail

2. Properly relieve the fuel system pressure.
3. Remove or disconnect the following:
   - Negative battery cable
   - Fuel filler cap
   - Quick connect fittings from the filter
   - Filter feed nut and the clamp bolt
   - Filter and the clamp from the vehicle

To install:

4. Install or connect the following:
   - Filter and clamp with the directional arrow facing away from the fuel tank, towards the throttle body

➡ **The filter has an arrow (fuel flow direction) on the side of the case, be sure to install it correctly in the system, the with arrow facing away from the fuel tank.**

   - Tighten the fuel feed nut
   - Tighten the filter clamp assembly bolt
   - Fuel quick disconnect fittings to the filter
   - Fuel filler cap
   - Negative battery cable
5. Start the engine and check for leaks.

Fuel Pump

REMOVAL & INSTALLATION

1. Before servicing the vehicle, refer to the precautions in the beginning of this section.
2. Properly relieve the fuel system pressure.
3. Drain the fuel tank.
4. Support the fuel tank.
5. Remove or disconnect the following:

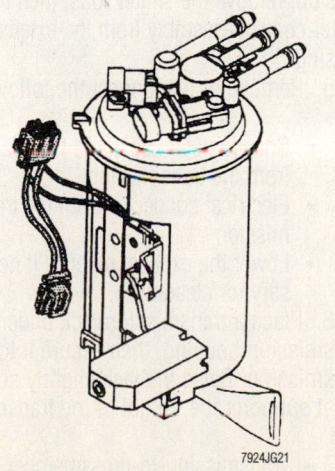

7924JG21

View of the in-tank fuel pump assembly

   - Negative battery cable
   - Filler neck from the tank
   - Shield from tank and tank straps
   - Fuel lines and vapor hose from pump
   - Electrical connection from fuel pump
   - Fuel tank
   - Fuel pump/sending unit assembly by turning the locking ring (located on top of the fuel tank) counter-clockwise using a spanner wrench
   - Fuel pump from the fuel lever sending device

To install:

6. Install or connect the following:
   - Fuel pump in tank with new seal around opening
   - Tank and connect fuel lines and vapor hose
   - Tank to the frame. Torque the fasteners to 33 ft. lbs. (45 nm).
   - Shield
   - Fuel filler neck and clamp
   - Negative battery cable
7. Refill the tank.
8. Run the engine and check for leaks.

Fuel Injector

REMOVAL & INSTALLATION

2.2L Engines

1997 Models

The bottom feed fuel injectors on the 2.2L MFI engine are installed to the lower intake manifold assembly. For access, the upper intake must first be removed.

➡ **Take care when servicing the lower intake and fuel injectors to prevent dirt or contaminants from entering the fuel system. ALL openings in the fuel lines and passages should be capped or plugged while disconnected.**

1. Before servicing the vehicle, refer to the precautions in the beginning of this section.
2. Relieve the fuel system pressure.
3. Remove or disconnect the following:
   - Negative battery cable
   - Accelerator bracket retaining bolts/nuts, then remove or reposition the bracket
   - Upper intake manifold assembly
   - Fuel return line bracket nut
   - Fuel return line retaining bracket

and position it away from the pressure regulator
   - Fuel pressure regulator assembly

➡ **DO NOT attempt to remove the injectors from their bores while lifting upward on the retaining bracket or damage may occur. DO NOT attempt to remove the bracket without first removing the pressure regulator.**

   - Fuel injector retainer bracket attaching screws, then the bracket by carefully sliding it off to clear the injector slots
   - Injector electrical connectors
   - Fuel injectors from the lower intake manifold assembly
   - Injector O-rings and discard

To install:

➡ **Because each injector is calibrated for a specific flow rate, make sure you only replace fuel injectors using an IDENTICAL part number to the old injectors.**

4. Lubricate the new O-ring seals with clean engine oil, then position them on the injectors.
5. Install or connect the following:
   - Injector assemblies into the lower manifold sockets, making sure the electrical connectors are facing inward
   - Injector bracket to the retaining slots
   - Injector electrical connectors
   - Fuel pressure regulator assembly
6. Make sure the threads of the injector retainer bracket screws are coated with a suitable threadlocking compound such as Loctite®262 or equivalent, then install and tighten them to 31 inch lbs. (3.5 Nm).
   - Upper intake manifold assembly
   - Accelerator cable bracket. Tighten the retaining nut to 22 ft. lbs. (30 Nm) and the retaining bolts to 18 ft. lbs. (25 Nm).
   - Negative battery cable
7. Pressurize the fuel system by cycling the ignition (without attempting to start the engine), then check for leaks.
8. If not done already, install the air inlet duct

1998–01 Models

1. Before servicing the vehicle, refer to the precautions in the beginning of this section.
2. Relieve the fuel system pressure.

3. Remove or disconnect the following:
- Negative battery cable
- Intake manifold, if necessary
- Fuel injector electrical connections by pushing in the wire connector clip and gently pulling on the connector
- Fuel feed inlet pipe from the rail

➡ **Use a back-up wrench on the fuel rail return fitting to prevent it from turning.**

- Fuel return pipe from the fuel pressure regulator
- Fuel pressure regulator
- Fuel rail attaching bolts and lift the fuel rail assembly from the cylinder head
- Fuel rail by moving the rail towards the front of the engine
- Fuel injector retaining clip
- Fuel injector

➡ **Because each injector is calibrated for a specific flow rate, make sure you only replace fuel injectors using an IDENTICAL part number to the old injectors.**

To install:

➡ **When installing the injector care should be taken not to tear or misalign O-rings.**

4. Lubricate the injector O-ring seals with clean engine oil and install them injector.

5. Install or connect the following:
- Upper O-ring, lower back-up O-ring and lower O-ring
- Fuel injector to the fuel rail
- Fuel injector retaining clip
- Fuel rail and insert it into the cylinder head
- Fuel rail retaining bolts and tighten to 18 ft. lbs. (25 Nm)
- Fuel pressure regulator

➡ **Use a back-up wrench on the fuel rail return fitting to prevent it from turning.**

- Return pipe to the fuel pressure regulator. Tighten the fuel pipe nut to 22 ft. lbs. (30 Nm).
- Fuel feed inlet pipe to rail

➡ **Rotate the fuel injectors as necessary to avoid stretching the wire harness.**

- Injector electrical connections
- Intake manifold, if removed
- Negative battery cable

6. Inspect for leaks as follows:
a. Turn the switch to the **ON** position for 2 seconds.

b. Turn the ignition switch **OFF** for 10 seconds.

c. Turn the ignition switch to the **ON** position and check for leaks.

4.3L Engines

1. Before servicing the vehicle, refer to the precautions in the beginning of this section.

2. Relieve the fuel system pressure. Refer to the fuel system relief procedure in this section.

3. Relieve the fuel system pressure.

4. Remove or disconnect the following:
- Negative battery cable
- Fuel meter body electrical connection and the fuel feed and return hoses from the engine fuel pipes
- Upper manifold assembly
- Poppet nozzle out of the casting socket
- Fuel meter body by releasing the locktabs

➡ **Each injector is calibrated. When replacing the fuel injectors, be sure to replace it with the correct injector.**

- Lower hold-down plate and nuts

5. While pulling the poppet nozzle tube downward, push with a small prytool down between the injector terminals and remove the injectors.

To install:

6. Lubricate the new injector O-ring seats with engine oil.

7. Install or connect the following:
- O-rings on the injector
- Fuel injector into the fuel meter body injector socket.
- Lower hold-down plate and nuts. Torque the nuts to 27 inch lbs. (3 Nm).
- Fuel meter body assembly into the intake manifold. Torque the fuel meter bracket retainer bolts to 88 inch. lbs. (10 Nm).

✳✳ CAUTION

To reduce the risk of fire or injury ensure that the poppet nozzles are properly seated and locked in their casting sockets

- Fuel meter body into the bracket and lock all the tabs in place
- Poppet nozzles into the casting sockets
- Electrical connections
- New o-ring seals on the fuel return and feed hoses.
- Fuel feed and return hoses and

tighten the fuel pipe nuts to 22 ft. lbs. (30 Nm).
- Negative battery cable

8. Turn the ignition **ON** for 2 seconds and then turn it **OFF** for 10 seconds. Again turn the ignition **ON** and check for leaks.

9. Install the manifold plenum.

DRIVE TRAIN

Manual Transmission Assembly

REMOVAL & INSTALLATION

Astro/Safari

1. Before servicing the vehicle, refer to the precautions in the beginning of this section.

- Negative battery cable
- Driveshaft from the vehicle. Match-mark the shaft prior to removal to help during installation.

2. Place a clean drain pan under the transmission, then remove the drain plug and drain the fluid from the transmission assembly. Install the drain plug to keep any remaining fluid from dripping throughout the procedure.

- Shifter control knob-to-shifter control lever nut, loosen
- Shifter control knob
- Shifter control boot-to-chassis plate and the shifter control boot

3. If removing an MH3/ML3, 5-speed transmission, unscrew the shift lever from the control lever.

4. If removing an MR2, 4-speed transmission, remove the shifter rods, then the shifter control assembly from the extension housing.

5. Remove or disconnect the following:

- Speedometer cable and the seal from the transmission
- Electrical connector from the transmission
- Lower the exhaust pipe(s), if necessary for clearance

6. Place a transmission jack under the transmission housing, then secure it to the transmission. Raise the jack slightly so that it supports the weight of the transmission.

- Transmission-to-crossmember nuts/bolts and the transmission-to-chassis braces nuts/bolts, then the braces and the crossmember

➡**If any spacers are used, make a note of them so that they may be installed in their original positions.**

7. While supporting the transmission, remove the transmission-to-bellhousing bolts; DO NOT allow it to hang on the input shaft.

8. Remove or disconnect the following:

9. Move the transmission and jack assembly rearward, then carefully lower and remove the transmission from the vehicle.

To install:

10. Place a thin coat of high temperature grease on the main drive gear splines.

11. Align the transmission's input shaft with the bellhousing and clutch assembly, then slide the transmission into the clutch.

➡**When installing the transmission, shift the transmission into High gear, then turn the output shaft to align the input shaft splines with the clutch plate.**

12. The balance of installation is the reverse of the removal procedure. Be sure to tighten all fasteners properly including:
- Transmission-to-bellhousing bolts: 50 ft. lbs. (68 Nm)
- Transmission-to-mount bolts: 40 ft. lbs. (54 Nm) for the MR2 or 33 ft. lbs. (45 Nm) for the for the MH3/ML3
- Crossmember-to-mount bolts: 26 ft. lbs. (35 Nm) for the MR2 or 18 ft. lbs. for the MH3/ML3
- Crossmember-to-chassis bolts: 37 ft. lbs. (50 Nm)
- Transmission-to-brace bolts: 26 ft. lbs. (35 Nm)
- Shifter control assembly-to-extension housing bolts: 23 ft. lbs. (31 Nm)
- Shifter rod swivel nut: 18 ft. lbs. (24 Nm)
- Shifter lever nut: 35 ft. lbs. (47 Nm)

13. Align and install the driveshaft, using the marks made during removal.

14. Remove the jackstands and carefully lower the vehicle.

15. Connect the negative battery cable.

Except Astro/Safari

1. Before servicing the vehicle, refer to the precautions in the beginning of this section.

2. Shift the transmission into 3rd or 4th gear position.

3. Remove or disconnect the following:

- Negative battery cable
- Shift lever and the if necessary, the shift housing
- Parking brake cable for clearance
- Propeller shaft
- Sid plate, if equipped
- Transfer case and shift lever, on 4WD models
- All wiring harness that would interfere with transmission removal
- Fuel line retainers from the rear crossmember
- Muffler from the catalytic converter
- Exhaust pipes from the exhaust manifold
- Catalytic converter hanger, if necessary
- Exhaust section
- Bolts and nuts attaching any transmission braces to the engine and transmission
- Hydraulic clutch quick-connect from the concentric slave cylinder following 1 of the 2 steps:

a. Use 2 small prytools at 180 degrees from each other to depress the white plastic sleeve on the quick connect to separate the clutch line from the concentric slave cylinder quick connect.

b. Use special tool J–36221 to depress the white plastic sleeve on the quick connect to separate the clutch line end from the concentric slave cylinder quick connect.

4. Remove or disconnect the following:
- Bolts securing the clutch housing cover to the transmission, if equipped
- Clutch plate and clutch cover, if necessary

5. Support the transmission with a suitable jack.
- Rear crossmember from the frame rail
- Wiring harness from the front crossmember, if equipped. Move the wiring harness away from the transmission oil pan. Lower the transmission enough to gain access to the top of the transmission.
- Fuel line retainers or wiring harness's from the top of the transmission
- Bolt, washer, and nut securing the wiring harness ground wires to the engine block
- Bolts retaining the transmission to the engine. Pull the transmission

straight back on the clutch hub splines.

6. Lower the transmission using the transmission jack.

To install:

Installation is the reverse of removal, but please note the following important steps.

7. Place a THIN coat of high-temperature grease on the main drive gear (input shaft) splines.

8. Secure the transmission to the floor jack and raise the transmission into position.

➡**On some models, it may be necessary to rotate the transmission clockwise while inserting it into the clutch hub.**

9. Slowly insert the input shaft through the clutch. Rotate the output shaft slowly to engage the splines of the input shaft into the clutch while pushing the transmission forward into place. Do not force the transmission into position, the transmission should easily fall into place once everything is properly aligned.

10. Tighten the transmission mounting bolts to 35 ft. lbs. (47 Nm).

11. Do not remove the transmission jack until the crossmembers have been installed.

12. Check the transmission fluid level and replenish as necessary.

Automatic Transmission Assembly

REMOVAL & INSTALLATION

Astro/Safari

1. Before servicing the vehicle, refer to the precautions in the beginning of this section.

2. Remove or disconnect the following:
- Negative battery cable for safety

3. Drain the transmission fluid by removing the pan.
- Shift cable from the transmission assembly, as applicable
- Driveshaft from the vehicle. Matchmark the shaft prior to removal.
- Front driveshaft on All Wheel Drive (AWD) models
- Transfer case and adapter from the transmission assembly

4. Support the transmission or transmission and transfer case (as applicable) using a suitable floor jack.
- 2 front torsion bars
- Rear transmission mount

✳✳ WARNING

DO NOT stretch or otherwise damage any cables, wires or other components when lowering the transmission in the next step.

5. Carefully lower the transmission in order to provide the necessary clearance to reach other components.

6. Remove or disconnect the following:

- Dipstick tube and seal from the transmission assembly, then cover or plug the opening to prevent dirt or contamination from entering the transmission and to minimize fluid leakage
- Speedometer harness (speed sensor) connector
- Electrical connectors and any electrical connector retaining clips from the transmission
- Oil cooler lines. Immediately cap all openings in the transmission assembly and the lines to prevent excessive fluid loss or system contamination.

➡ **On vehicles so equipped, before removal of the transmission support braces, note the brace positioning as they must be reinstalled in their original positions.**

- Starter motor assembly from the engine
- Torque converter cover, then matchmark the flexplate to the torque converter; re-aligning the marks during installation will maintain the original balance
- Torque converter-to-flywheel bolts and slide the converter back into the transmission

7. Support the rear of the engine.

- Transmission-to-engine mounting bolts. Note the location of any clips or brackets for installation purposes, then position them aside.

8. Carefully slide the transmission back off the locating pins., Once there is sufficient clearance, install a torque converter holding tool such as No. J–21366.

9. Carefully lower the transmission assembly from the vehicle.

To install:

10. Make sure the torque converter is properly seated in the transmission assembly and install a converter holding tool.

11. Support the transmission assembly (and the transfer case if it was removed with the transmission earlier AWD vehicles) on a transmission jack, then position it under the vehicle.

12. Install or connect the following:

- Transmission into position and remove the torque converter holding tool
- Transmission straight onto the locating pins while aligning the flexplate and torque converter matchmarks which were made during removal

➡ **Once in position, the torque converter must be flush onto the flexplate and must be able to rotate freely by hand.**

- Transmission assembly-to-engine retaining bolts along with any brackets or clips which were positioned aside during removal. Tighten the transmission retaining bolts to 23 ft. lbs. (32 Nm).

13. Thread the torque converter-to-flexplate screws by hand until they are finger-tight to assure proper converter seating.

- Tighten the torque converter bolts to 46 ft. lbs. (63 Nm) slowly and evenly

14. Remove the engine support.

- Converter cover. On most models the cover must be carefully hooked under the lip of the engine oil pan during installation.
- Starter motor
- Oil cooler lines to the transmission.
- Speedometer harness (speed sensor) connector
- Electrical wiring connectors to the transmission and secure any wiring clips which were removed
- Dipstick tube using a new seal

15. Carefully raise the engine and transmission assembly fully into position.

➡ **When raising the transmission into place, be sure NOT to pinch or damage any cables, wires or other components.**

- Transmission crossmember and the transmission mount, along with any other components which were removed for clearance

16 Remove the floor jack.

- Support bracket at the catalytic converter
- Transmission mount
- Transfer case and adapter, if equipped
- Driveshaft(s). On AWD vehicles, install the rear driveshaft first.
- Front torsion bars
- Shift cable

17. Refill the transmission using fresh fluid.

18. Connect the negative battery cable.

Except Astro/Safari

1. Before servicing the vehicle, refer to the precautions in the beginning of this section.

2. Remove or disconnect the following:
- Negative battery cable

3. Drain the transmission fluid.
- Driveshaft from the transmission (2WD) and transfer case, if equipped (4WD)

4. Support the transmission with a suitable transmission jack.

- Shift cable from the transmission control lever and bracket
- Nut and washer securing the transmission mount to the crossmember
- Bolts and washers securing the mount to the transmission
- Exhaust pipe from the exhaust manifold(s)
- Bolts securing the converter pan cover to the transmission, if equipped
- 3 bolts securing the torque converter to the flywheel
- Bolt, clip, and strap securing the three fuel lines and transmission vent hose to the transmission case

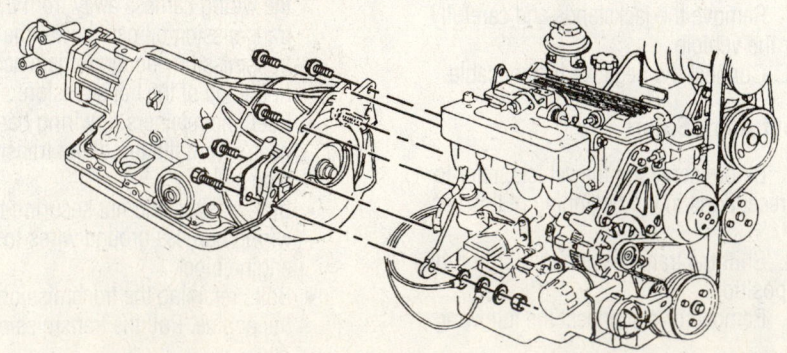

88457G33

Transmission mounting on 2.2L engines

- Bolts and nut securing the transmission to the engine
- Oil filler tube and seal from the transmission
- Transmission cooler lines from the transmission. Plug the lines and the ports in the transmission.
- Wiring harness connectors from the transmission.

5. Inspect for any other wiring, brackets etc. which may interfere with the removal of the transmission.

6. Since the transmission acts as a rear engine mount, properly support the rear of the engine with an underbody support or other suitable support before attempting to remove the transmission. Otherwise the rear of the engine may pitch downward and components on the rear of the engine and on the firewall may be damaged.

7. Remove the transmission from the engine by pulling the transmission rearward to disengage it from the locator dowel pins on the back of the block. Carefully lower the transmission from the vehicle. Use care that the torque converter does not fall out of the front of the transmission.

➡ **Use converter holding strap tool No. J-21366, to secure the torque converter to the transmission during removal and installation procedures.**

To install:

Installation is the reverse of removal, but please note the following important steps.

8. Make sure the torque converter is fully seated in the pump drive. If not, the transmission will not fit tightly to the rear of the engine block.

9. Raise the transmission into position and remove the torque converter holding strap and carefully. Slide the transmission forward until the dowel pins are engaged.

10. The torque converter should be flush with the flywheel and turn freely by hand.

11. Install the transmission–to–engine bolts. Tighten the bolts to 34 ft. lbs. (47 Nm).

12. Tighten the torque converter-to-flywheel bolts to 46 ft. lbs. (63 Nm).

13. If equipped, tighten the converter pan cover to the transmission bolts to 37 ft. lbs. (50 Nm)

14. Tighten the bolts and washers securing the transmission mount to 35 ft. lbs. (47 Nm).

15. Tighten the nut and washer securing the transmission mount to the crossmember to 38 ft. lbs. (52 Nm).

16. Refill the transmission with the proper amount and type of fluid.

17. Connect the negative battery cable. Start the vehicle and allow to warm while checking for leaks. Road test the vehicle to check for shift quality.

Clutch

REMOVAL & INSTALLATION

1. Before servicing the vehicle, refer to the precautions in the beginning of this section.

2. Remove or disconnect the following:
- Negative battery cable
- Transmission

3. Install a clutch alignment tool or a used transmission input shaft to support the clutch.

4. If the clutch assembly is going to be reused, mark the flywheel, clutch cover and a pressure plate lug for alignment when installing.

5. Remove or disconnect the following:
- Clutch cover bolts and washers
- Clutch cover assembly and the clutch plate
- Clutch alignment tool

6. Clean all parts and inspect for damage.

To install:

7. Install or connect the following:
- Clutch alignment tool, to support the clutch.
- Clutch cover by aligning the matchmarks or, if new, align the lightest part of the cover, identified by a yellow dot, with the heaviest part identified by an **X**.
- Clutch plate/clutch cover assembly to the flywheel. Tighten the bolts to

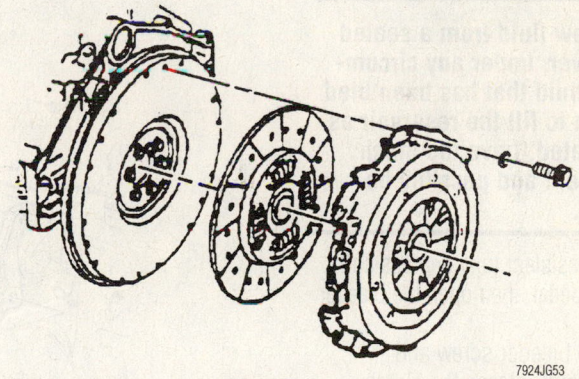

Exploded view of the clutch disc and related components

7924JG53

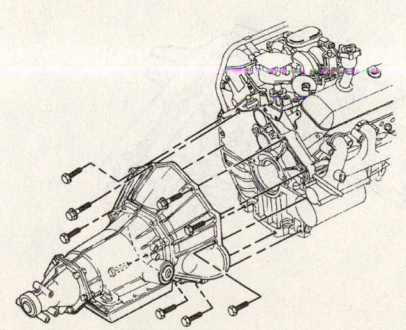

88457G34

Transmission mounting on 4.3L engines

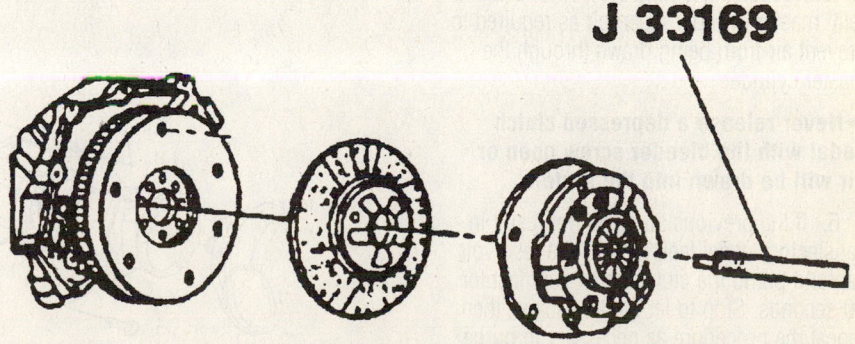

J 33169

7924JG22

Use the clutch alignment tool to center and support the clutch disc during installation

33 ft. lbs. (45 Nm) for 2.2L engines or to 29 ft. lbs. (40 Nm) for 4.3L engines.

➡**Tighten each screw 1 turn at a time to avoid warping the clutch cover.**

8. Remove the clutch alignment tool.
9. Install or connect the following:
   - Transmission
   - Negative battery cable

Hydraulic Clutch System

Bleeding air from the hydraulic clutch system is necessary whenever any part of the system has been disconnected or the fluid level (in the reservoir) has been allowed to fall so low, that air has been drawn into the master cylinder.

BLEEDING

1. Before servicing the vehicle, refer to the precautions in the beginning of this section.
2. Fill master cylinder reservoir with new brake fluid conforming to DOT 3 specifications.

✳✳ CAUTION

Always use new fluid from a sealed container. Never, under any circumstances, use fluid that has been bled from a system to fill the reservoir as it may be aerated, have too much moisture content and possibly be contaminated.

3. Have an assistant fully depress and hold the clutch pedal, then open the bleeder screw.
4. Close the bleeder screw and have your assistant release the clutch pedal.
5. Repeat the procedure until all of the air is evacuated from the system. Check and refill master cylinder reservoir as required to prevent air from being drawn through the master cylinder.

➡**Never release a depressed clutch pedal with the bleeder screw open or air will be drawn into the system.**

6. If the previous steps do not result in satisfactory pedal feel, remove the reservoir cap and pump the clutch pedal very fast for 30 seconds. Stop to let the air escape, then repeat the procedure as necessary to purge all remaining air.
7. Test the clutch for proper operation.

Transfer Case Assembly

REMOVAL & INSTALLATION

Astro/Safari

1. Before servicing the vehicle, refer to the precautions in the beginning of this section.
2. Disconnect the negative battery cable.
3. If necessary, shift the transfer case into the **4HI** position to ease linkage removal.
4. If equipped, remove the skid plate.
5. Drain the fluid from the transfer case.
6. Remove or disconnect the following:

   - Front and rear driveshafts
7. Support the transfer case
   - Breather hose
   - Electrical connections
   - Adapter-to-transfer case bolts
   - Transfer case and discard the gasket

To install:

8. Install or connect the following:
   - New transfer case-to-adapter gasket using sealer to hold it in place

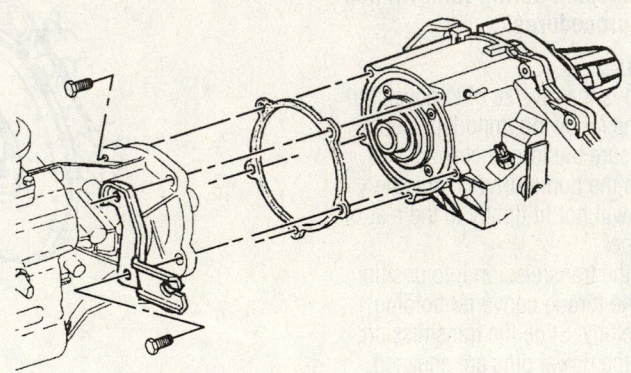

Transfer case-to-manual transmission mounting—Typical

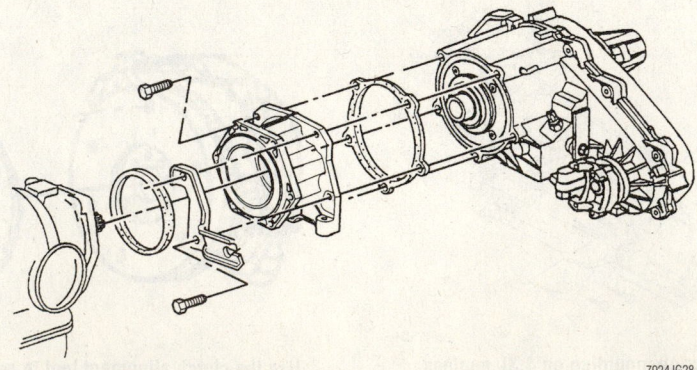

Transfer case-to-automatic transmission mounting—Typical

- Transfer case adapter to the transfer case
- Transfer case. Torque the bolts to 38 ft. lbs. (52 Nm).
9. Remove the jack from the transfer case.
10. Install or connect the following:
   - Washers and nuts. Tighten the nuts to 26 ft. lbs. (35 Nm).
   - Support brace. Tighten the bolts to 74 ft. lbs. (100 Nm).
   - Electrical connectors
   - Breather hose
   - Front and rear driveshafts.
   - Skid plate, if equipped
   - Negative battery cable
11. Fill the transfer case.

Except Astro/Safari

1. Before servicing the vehicle, refer to the precautions in the beginning of this section.
2. Disconnect the negative battery cable.
3. Shift the transfer case into the **4HI** range.
4. Drain the transfer case fluid.
5. Support the transfer case.

6. Remove or disconnect the following:
- Skid plate
- Front and rear driveshafts from the transfer case. Matchmark the shafts prior to removal.
- Vacuum lines and/or the electrical connectors, as equipped
- Transfer case shift rod/cable from the case, if applicable
- Support brace-to-transfer case bolts, if applicable
- Transfer case

7. Remove all traces of old gasket material from the mating surfaces.

To install:

8. Install or connect the following:
- New gasket using sealer to hold it in position
- Transfer case. Torque the bolts to 41 ft. lbs. (55 Nm) on 1997–98 models or 33–35 ft. lbs. (45–47 Nm) on 1999–01 models.
- Support brace bolts. Torque the bolts to 35–37 ft. lbs. (47–50 Nm), if equipped
- Shift rod to the case, if equipped
- Vacuum lines and/or electrical connections, as necessary
- Front and rear driveshafts by aligning the matchmarks

9. Refill the transfer case.

10. Install or connect the following:
- Skid plate, if equipped
- Negative battery cable

Halfshaft

REMOVAL & INSTALLATION

1. Before servicing the vehicle, refer to the precautions in the beginning of this section.

2. Unlock the steering column so the steering linkage is free to move.

3. Remove or disconnect the following:
- Negative battery cable
- Front wheels

➡ **Place a drift through the caliper into the edge of the rotor to keep the rotor from turning when the nut is removed**

- Cotter pin, retainer, nut and washer
- Brake caliper and support it with a piece of wire to avoid damaging the brake hose
- Brake rotor
- Brake line support bracket and

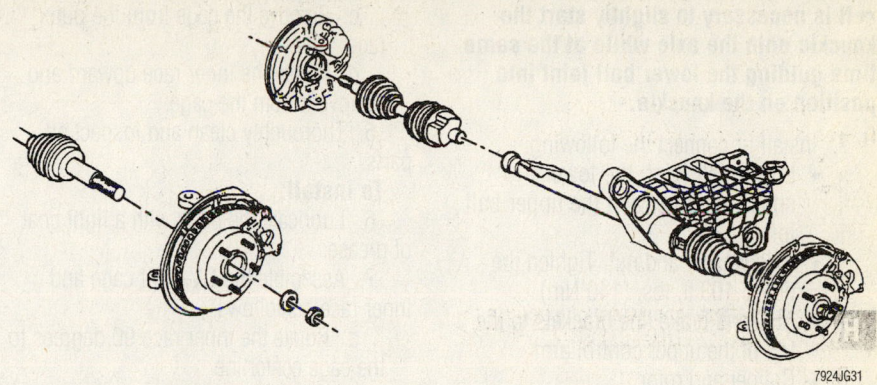

7924JG31

Halfshafts and related components

Anti-lock Brake System (ABS) wire bracket from the upper control arm

4. Place a jackstand or jack under the lower control arm.
- Axle shaft from the hub by placing a block of wood against the outer edge of the axle (to protect the threads), then strike the block of wood sharply with a hammer. Do not remove the axle at this time.
- Tie rods from the steering knuckles
- Lower shock absorber bolts
- Upper ball joint from the steering knuckle and suspend the steering knuckle on a wire
- Skid plate, if equipped
- Halfshaft-to-axle tube bolts
- Halfshaft by moving it forward and supporting it away from the frame
- Halfshaft from the hub and bearing assembly
- Halfshaft from the differential using a block of wood and a hammer

To install:

➡ **It is essential that the differential carrier and axle seals are not lubricated or damaged during installation. Prior to shaft installation, cover the shock mounting bracket, lower control arm ball stud and ALL other sharp edges with a cloth or rag to help protect the boot.**

5. Install the axle into the carrier. With both hands on the tripot housing, align the splines on the shaft with the carrier. Then center the axle into the carrier seal and push the shaft straight into the carrier until the snapring is properly seated.

➡ **Be careful when supporting the lower control arm that any components are damaged with the supporting device.**

6. Raise the lower control arm using a jackstand or jack until the full weight of the arm is supported.

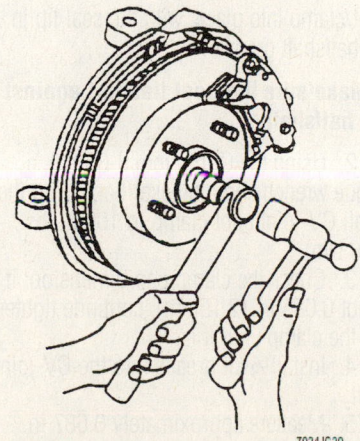

7924JG29

Tap the halfshaft out of the hub without damaging the threads

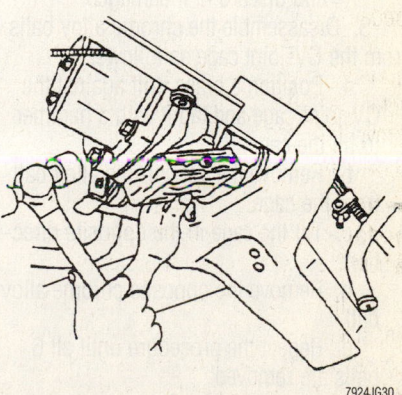

7924JG30

Using a block of wood and a mallet, disengage the halfshaft from the differential assembly

Turn to Section 5 for brake system applications

➡**It is necessary to slightly start the knuckle onto the axle while at the same time guiding the lower ball joint into position on the knuckle.**

7. Install or connect the following:
- Lower ball joint, the lower shock absorber and the upper ball joint
- Axle washer and nut. Tighten the nut to 103 ft. lbs. (140 Nm).
- ABS and brake line brackets to the top of the upper control arm
- Caliper and rotor
- Tire and wheel assembly
- Differential carrier shield

CV-Joints

OVERHAUL

Outer CV-Joint

1. Before servicing the vehicle, refer to the precautions in the beginning of this section.
2. Remove or disconnect the following:
- Front wheel
- Halfshaft and position it in a vise
- Large CV-joint boot clamp and discard it
- Small CV-joint boot clamp and discard it
- CV-joint boot and slide it back on the shaft
- Outer race from the halfshaft, by spreading the outer race-to-halfshaft retaining ring, using Snapring Pliers J-8059
- Retaining ring from the halfshaft and discard it
- CV-joint boot from the halfshaft and discard it, if damaged

3. Disassemble the chrome alloy balls from the CV-joint cage as follows:
a. Position a brass drift against the CV-joint cage and tap it with a hammer to tilt the cage.
b. Remove the 1st chrome alloy ball from the cage.
c. Tilt the cage in the opposite direction.
d. Remove the opposite chrome alloy ball.
e. Repeat the procedure until all 6 balls are removed.
4. Disassemble the CV-joint cage and inner race as follows:
a. Pivot the cage and race 90 degrees to the center line of the outer race.
b. Align the cage windows with outer race lands.

c. Remove the cage from the outer race.
d. Rotate the inner race upward and remove it from the cage.
5. Thoroughly clean and inspect all parts.

To install:
6. Lubricate the parts with a light coat of grease.
7. Assemble the CV-joint cage and inner race, as follows:
a. Rotate the inner race 90 degrees to the cage centerline.
b. Align the cage windows with inner race lands.
c. Insert the inner race into the cage by rotating the inner race downward.
d. Insert the cage/inner race into the outer race.
8. Assemble the chrome alloy balls into the CV-joint cage, as follows:
a. Position a brass drift against the CV-joint cage and tap it with a hammer to tilt the cage.
b. Insert the 1st chrome alloy ball into the cage.
c. Tilt the cage in the opposite direction.
d. Insert the opposite chrome alloy ball.
e. Repeat the procedure until all 6 balls are inserted.
9. Install ½ kit grease into the CV-joint.
10. Install or connect the following:
- Small ring clamp on the CV boot
- New retaining ring on the halfshaft
- Large ring clamp on the CV boot
- Outer race assembly onto the halfshaft until the ring engages the halfshaft groove
11. Slide the small end of the CV-joint boot/clamp into place, with the seal lip in the halfshaft groove

➡**Make sure the boot lies flat against the halfshaft.**

12. Using the Crimp tool J-35910, a torque wrench and a breaker bar, crimp the small CV-joint boot clamp to 100 ft. lbs. (136 Nm).
13. Check the clamp gap dimension; if it is not 0.085 in. (2.15mm), continue tightening the clamp until it is.
14. Install ½ kit grease into the CV-joint boot.
15. Measure approximately 0.687 in. (17.5mm) up from the bottom edge of the outer CV-joint assembly.
16. Slide the large end of the CV boot/clamp into place, with the seal lip in place over the outer race.

➡**Make sure the boot lies flat against the outer race.**

17. Using the Crimp tool J-35910, a torque wrench and a breaker bar, crimp the large CV-joint boot clamp to 130 ft. lbs. (176 Nm).
18. Check the clamp gap dimension; if it is not 0.102 in. (2.60mm), continue tightening the clamp until it is.
19. Install the halfshaft and the front wheel.

Inner (Tri-Pot) Joint

1. Before servicing the vehicle, refer to the precautions in the beginning of this section.
2. Remove or disconnect the following:
- Front wheel
- Halfshaft and place it in a vise
- Snapring from the stub shaft and discard it
- Small CV-joint boot clamp, cut and discard it
- Large CV-joint boot clamp, cut and discard it
- CV-joint boot by sliding it away from the tri-pot joint
3. Install a Stub Shaft Removal tool J-38868-A to the stub shaft snapring groove.
4. Using a slide hammer puller, press the stub shaft from the tri-pot housing.
5. Remove or disconnect the following:
- Tri-pot housing from the tri-pot spider
- Inboard spacer ring slide it rearward on the shaft using Snapring Pliers tool J-8059
- Outboard retaining ring using Snapring Pliers tool J-8059 and discard it
- Tri-pot joint spider assembly
- Inboard spacer ring and discard it
- CV-joint boot
- Trilobal tri-pot bushing from the housing
6. Thoroughly clean and inspect all parts.

To install:
7. Install or connect the following:
- New snapring onto the stub shaft
- Small boot clamp
- CV-joint boot
8. Using the Crimp tool J-35910, a torque wrench and a breaker bar, crimp the small CV-joint boot clamp to 100 ft. lbs. (136 Nm).
9. Install or connect the following:
- Inboard spacer ring slide it rearward on the shaft using Snapring Pliers tool J-8059, past the 2nd groove

- Tri-pot joint spider assembly onto the shaft until it passes the 2nd groove
- Outboard retaining ring into the axle shaft groove using Snapring Pliers tool J-8059
- Tri-pot joint spider assembly, slide it against the outboard retaining ring
- Inboard spacer ring, seat it in the groove
- ½ kit grease into the boot
- ½ kit grease into the tri-pot housing
- Trilobal tip-pot bushing flush with the tri-pot housing face
- New large seal clamp onto the CV-joint boot
- Tri-pot housing, slide it over the tri-pot joint spider assembly
- CV-joint boot/clamp, slide it into place, over the trilobal tri-pot bushing with the seal lip in the groove

➡**Make sure the boot lies flat against the trilobal bushing.**

10. Position the CV-joint boot so it measures 4.9 in. (125mm).

11. Using the Crimp tool J-35566, latch the large CV-joint boot clamp.

12. Install the halfshaft and the front wheel.

Axle Shaft, Bearing and Seal

REMOVAL & INSTALLATION

For the Axle Shaft, Bearing and Seal, Removal and Installation, please refer to Wheel Bearing procedure located in the section.

Pinion Seal

REMOVAL & INSTALLATION

1. Before servicing the vehicle, refer to the precautions in the beginning of this section.

➡**The following procedure requires the use of the Pinion Holding tool J-8614-10, the Pinion Flange Removal tool J-8614-1, J-8614-2, J-8614-3 and the Pinion Seal Installation tool J-23911.**

2. Remove or disconnect the following:
- Driveshaft from the pinion flange. Matchmark the driveshaft prior to removal.

- Driveshaft from the rear axle pinion flange and support the shaft up in body tunnel by wiring it to the exhaust pipe.

➡**If the U-joint bearings are not retained by a retainer strap, use a piece of tape to hold bearings on their journals.**

3. Mark the position of the pinion stem, flange and nut for reference.

4. Use an inch lbs. torque wrench to measure the amount of torque necessary to turn the pinion, then note this measurement as it is the combined pinion bearing, seal, carrier bearing, axle bearing and seal pre-load.

5. Remove or disconnect the following:
- Pinion flange nut and washer, using a Pinion Holding tool J-8614-10 and a Pinion Flange Removal tool J-8614-1, J-8614-2, J-8614-3, as applicable
- Pinion flange
- Pinion oil seal by driving it out of the differential with a blunt chisel; DO NOT damage the carrier

To install:

6. Examine the seal surface of pinion flange for tool marks, nicks or damage, such as a groove worn by the seal. If damaged, replace flange.

7. Examine the carrier bore and remove any burrs that might cause leaks around the O.D. of the seal.

8. Apply GM seal lubricant 1050169 to the outside diameter of the pinion flange and sealing lip of new seal.

9. Install or connect the following:
- New pinion oil seal using a seal installer tool
- Pinion flange and tighten nut to the same position as marked earlier. Tighten the nut a little at a time and turn the pinion flange several times after each tightening in order to set the rollers.

10. Measure the torque necessary to turn the pinion and compare this to the reading taken during removal. Tighten the nut additionally, as necessary to achieve the same preload as measured earlier.

➡**If fluid was lost from the differential housing during this procedure, be sure to check and add additional fluid, as necessary.**

11. Remove the support then align and secure the driveshaft assembly to the pinion flange.

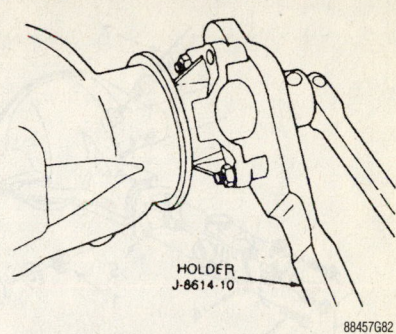

Removing the pinion nut using a pinion holding fixture tool

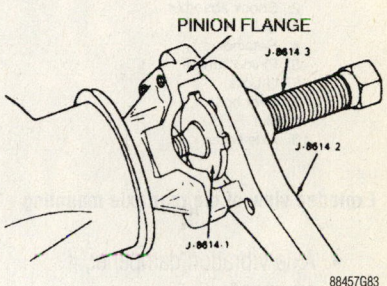

A puller and adapter should be used to withdraw the pinion from the housing

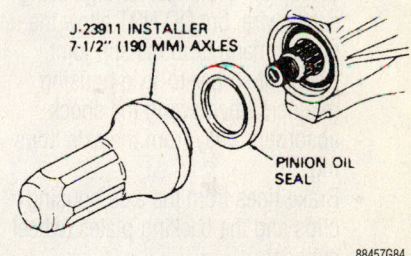

Use the appropriately sized installation tool to drive the new seal into position.

➡**The original matchmarks MUST be aligned to assure proper shaft balance and prevent vibration.**

Axle Housing

REMOVAL & INSTALLATION

1. Before servicing the vehicle, refer to the precautions in the beginning of this section.

2. Support the rear axle housing. If a floor jack is being used, take care when removing the U-bolts to keep the axle from suddenly dislodging.

3. Remove or disconnect the following:
- Rear wheels and drums for clearance and to remove some weight from the axle housing

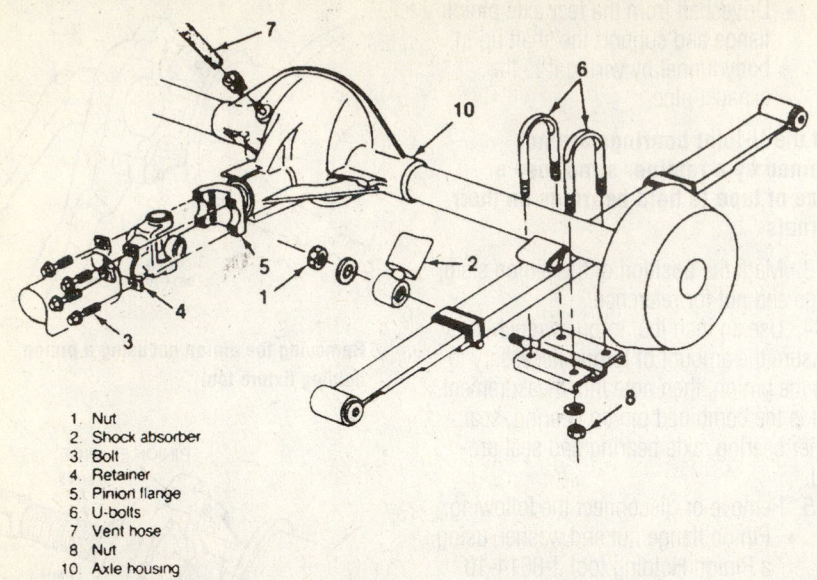

1. Nut
2. Shock absorber
3. Bolt
4. Retainer
5. Pinion flange
6. U-bolts
7. Vent hose
8. Nut
10. Axle housing

88457G85

Exploded view of the rear axle mounting

- Axle vibration dampener, if equipped
- Rear driveshaft from the pinion flange. Either remove the shaft completely from the vehicle or support it aside from the undercarriage using safety wire, but DO NOT allow the shaft to hang from the slip joint.
- Shock absorber-to-axle housing retainers, then swing the shock absorbers away from the axle housing
- Brake lines from the axle housing clips and the backing plates (wheel cylinders)

➡**When disconnecting the brake lines from the wheel cylinders, immediately plug or cap the lines to prevent system contamination or excessive fluid loss.**

- Speed sensor connectors at the junction block, if applicable
- Parking brake cable(s)
- Axle housing-to-spring U-bolt nuts, washers, U-bolts and the anchor plates
- Vent hose from the top of the axle housing
- Axle with the help of an assistant by moving it to clear the leaf spring

To install:

4. With the help of an assistant, carefully position the rear axle into the vehicle.
5. Install or connect the following:
   - Vent hose to the axle housing
6. Be sure the housing is properly positioned on the leaf spring, then loosely install the U-bolts, anchor plates, washers and nuts.

- Tighten the U-bolt nuts in a cross pattern to 18 ft. lbs. (25 Nm) to made sure everything is evenly seated. Then tighten the nuts in steps to 74 ft. lbs. (100 Nm)
- Brakes lines secure them to the axle housing
- Parking brake cable(s), if removed
- Speed sensor connectors to the junction block, if equipped
- Driveshaft assembly
- Shock absorbers to the lower mounts, then tighten the mount nuts
- Axle vibration dampener, if equipped
- Brake drums and the tire/wheel assemblies

7. Bleed the hydraulic brake system.
8. Check the fluid level in the rear axle assembly and add, as necessary. Make sure the vehicle is level when checking and adding fluid.

STEERING AND SUSPENSION

Air Bag

✳✳ CAUTION

Some vehicles are equipped with an air bag system, also known as the Supplemental Inflatable Restraint (SIR) system. **The system must be disabled before performing service on or around system components, steering column, instrument panel components, wiring and sensors. Failure to follow safety and disabling procedures could result in accidental air bag deployment, possible personal injury and unnecessary system repairs.**

PRECAUTIONS

Several precautions must be observed when handling the inflator module to avoid accidental deployment and possible personal injury.

- Never carry the inflator module by the wires or connector on the underside of the module.
- When carrying a live inflator module, hold securely with both hands, and ensure that the bag and trim cover are pointed away.
- Place the inflator module on a bench or other surface with the bag and trim cover facing up.
- With the inflator module on the bench, never place anything on or close to the module, that may be thrown in the event of an accidental deployment.

DISARMING

Astro/Safari

➡**With the AIR BAG fuse removed and the ignition switchON, the AIR BAG warning lamp will be on. This is normal and does not indicate any system malfunction.**

1. Turn the steering wheel so that the vehicle's wheels are pointing straight ahead.
2. Turn the ignition switch to **LOCK**, remove the key, then disconnect the negative battery cable.
3. Remove the AIR BAG fuse from the fuse block.
4. Remove the steering column filler panel.
5. Disengage the Connector Position Assurance (CPA) and the yellow two way connector located at the base of the steering column.
6. Connect the negative battery cable.

Except Astro/Safari

1. Turn the steering wheel so that the vehicle's wheels are pointing straight ahead.
2. Turn the ignition switch to **LOCK**, remove the key, then disconnect the negative battery cable.

3. Remove the AIR BAG fuse from the fuse block.

4. Remove the steering column filler panel or knee bolster.

5. Unplug the Connector Position Assurance (CPA) and yellow two way connector at the base of the steering column.

6. On 1998–01 models, remove the Connector Position Assurance (CPA) from the passenger yellow two way connector located behind the glove box.

7. On 1998–01 models, unplug the yellow two way connector located behind the glove box.

8. Connect the negative battery cable.

➡**With the AIR BAG fuse removed, the battery cable connected and the ignition in the ON position, the AIR BAG warning lamp will be ON. This is normal and does not indicate a system malfunction.**

ARMING

Astro/Safari

1. Disconnect the negative battery cable.
2. Turn the ignition switch to **LOCK**, then remove the key.
3. Engage the yellow SIR connector and CPA located at the base of the steering column.
4. Install the steering column filler panel.
5. Install the AIR BAG fuse to the fuse block.
6. Connect the negative battery cable.
7. Turn the ignition switch to **RUN** and make sure that the AIR BAG warning lamp flashes seven times and then shuts off. If the warning lamp does not shut off, make sure that the wiring is properly connected. If the light remains on, take the vehicle to a reputable repair facility for service.

Except Astro/Safari

1. Disconnect the negative battery cable.
2. On 1998–01 models, attach the yellow two way connector located behind the glove box.
3. On 1998–01 models, install the Connector Position Assurance (CPA) to the passenger yellow two way connector located behind the glove box.
4. Turn the ignition switch to **LOCK**, then remove the key.
5. Attach the two way connector at the base of the steering column and the Connector Position Assurance (CPA).

6. Install the steering column filler panel or knee bolster.

7. Install the AIR BAG fuse to the fuse block.

8. Connect the negative battery cable.

9. From the passenger seat, turn the ignition switch to **RUN** and make sure that the AIR BAG warning lamp flashes seven times and then shuts off. If the warning lamp does not shut off, make sure that the wiring is properly connected. If the light remains on, take the vehicle to a reputable repair facility for service.

Manual Steering Gear

REMOVAL & INSTALLATION

1. Before servicing the vehicle, refer to the precautions in the beginning of this section.
2. Remove or disconnect the following:
   • Negative battery cable
3. Raise the front of the vehicle. Turn the wheels so they are facing in the straight ahead position.
   • Retainers and the shield from the base of the intermediate shaft, if equipped
4. Matchmark the intermediate shaft-to-steering gear connection in order to assure proper installation.
   • Intermediate shaft-to-steering gear pinch bolt
   • Pitman arm from the pitman shaft. It may be easier to save this step for later as access to the pitman arm/shaft may be difficult unless the gear is loosened or removed.

➡**When separating the pitman arm from the shaft, DO NOT use a hammer or apply heat to the arm.**

   • Steering gear-to-frame mounting bolts and washers
   • Gear from the vehicle
5. If not done already and, if necessary, remove the pitman shaft from the gear at this time.
To install:
6. Install or connect the following:
   • Pitman shaft to the gear, if necessary
   • Steering gear to the frame and secure by threading the retaining bolts. On some late model vehicles, if not done already, it will be necessary to align and install the pitman arm to the shaft at this time.

   • Gear retaining bolts and tighten to 55 ft. lbs. (75 Nm)

➡**When installing the steering gear, be sure that the intermediate shaft bottoms on the worm shaft, so that the pinch bolt passes through the undercut on the worm shaft. Check and/or adjust the alignment of the pitman arm-to-pitman shaft.**

   • Intermediate shaft coupling using the pinch bolt. Tighten the bolt to 30 ft. lbs. (41 Nm).
   • Pitman arm to the shaft, if not done already
   • Coupling shield over the intermediate shaft-to-gear coupling, if equipped
   • Negative battery cable

Power Steering Gear

REMOVAL & INSTALLATION

Astro/Safari

1. Before servicing the vehicle, refer to the precautions in the beginning of this section.
2. Disconnect the negative battery cable.
3. Position a fluid catch pan under the power steering gear.
4. At the power steering gear, disconnect and plug the pressure hoses; any excess fluid will be caught by the catch pan.

➡**Be sure to cap or plug the hoses and the openings of the power steering pump to keep dirt out of the system.**

5. Remove or disconnect the following:
   • Intermediate shaft-to-steering gear bolt. Matchmark the intermediate shaft-to-power steering gear and separate the shaft from the gear.
   • Pitman arm-to-pitman shaft nut and washer, then matchmark the relationship of the arm to the shaft (this will permit proper alignment during assembly).
   • Pitman arm from the pitman shaft using J–29107 pitman arm removal tool

➡**When separating the pitman arm from the shaft, DO NOT use a hammer or apply heat to the arm.**

   • Power steering gear-to-frame bolts and washers, then carefully lower and remove the steering gear from the vehicle

To install:

6. Install or connect the following:
   - Steering gear, then tighten the gear-to-frame bolts to 55 ft. lbs. (75 Nm) for 2 wheel drive vehicles, or tighten the bolts to 100 ft. lbs. (135 Nm) for AWD vehicles
   - Pressure hoses to the power steering gear
   - Intermediate shaft-to-power steering gear bolt and tighten to 30 ft. lbs. (41 Nm)
   - Pitman arm-to-pitman shaft, then the nut and washer and tighten to 185 ft. lbs. (250 Nm)
   - Negative battery cable
7. Bleed the power steering system.

Except Astro/Safari

1. Before servicing the vehicle, refer to the precautions in the beginning of this section.

2. Position a fluid catch pan under the power steering gear.

3. Remove or disconnect the following:
   - Feed and return fluid hoses from the steering gear. Immediately cap or plug all openings to prevent sys-

tem contamination or excessive fluid loss.
   - Intermediate shaft lower coupling shield, if equipped
   - Intermediate shaft-to-steering gear bolt. Matchmark the intermediate shaft-to-power steering gear and separate the shaft from the gear.
   - Pitman arm from the gear pitman shaft
   - Power steering gear-to-frame bolts and washers, then carefully remove the steering gear from the vehicle.

To install:

4. Install or connect the following:
   - Steering gear to the vehicle and secure by finger-tightening the fasteners. For some vehicles, the pitman arm must be connected to the gear while it is still removed from the vehicle or while it is partially installed and lowered for access. If necessary, align and install the pitman arm to the shaft at this time.
   - Tighten the power steering gear-to-frame bolts to 55 ft. lbs. (75 Nm)
   - Intermediate shaft to the power steering, then secure using the pinch bolt

   - Shield over the intermediate shaft lower coupling, if equipped
   - Feed and return hoses to the power steering gear
   - Bleed the power steering system

Shock Absorbers

REMOVAL & INSTALLATION

Astro/Safari

1. Before servicing the vehicle, refer to the precautions in the beginning of this section.

2. Support the lower control arm (front) or axle assembly (rear).

3. Remove or disconnect the following:
   - Wheel
   - Inner wheel well splash shield, if removing the front shock absorber
   - Lower nut, washer and bolt
   - Upper nut, washer and bolt

➡ **Compress the front shock absorber to make removal easier.**

   - Shock absorber

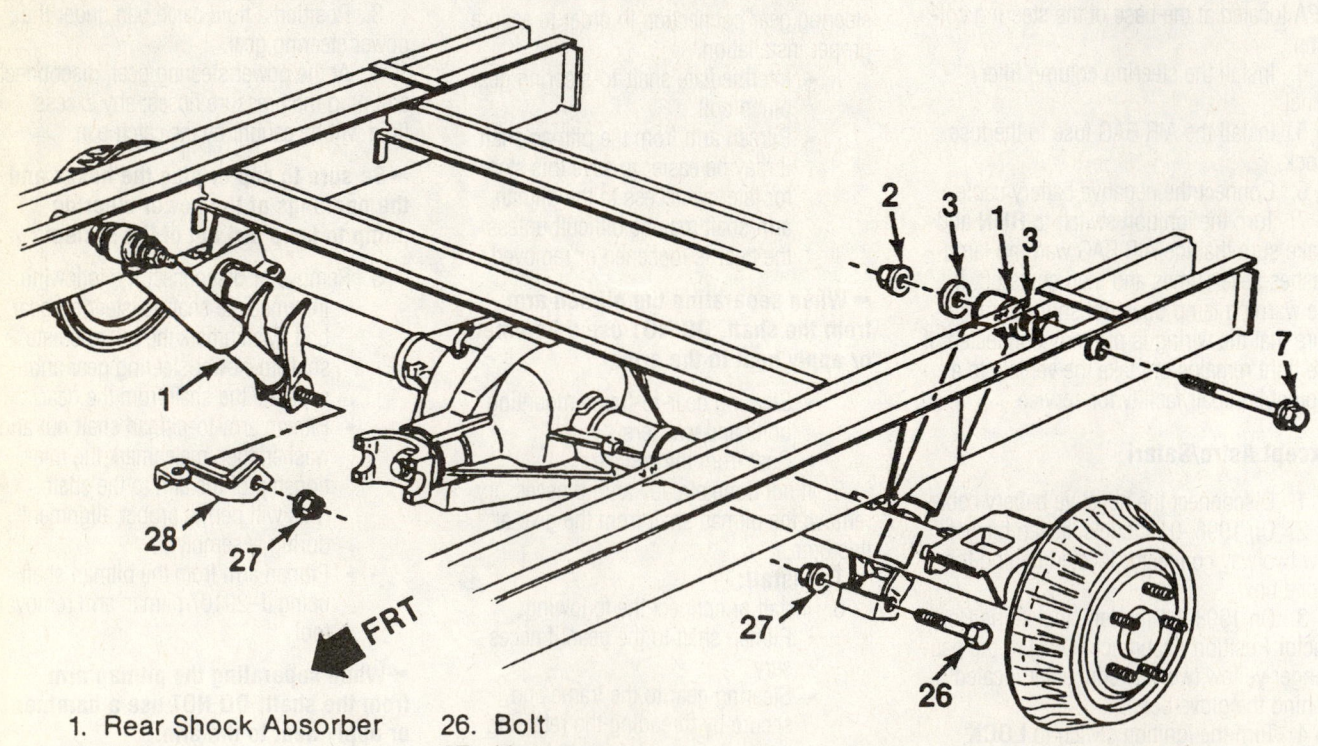

1. Rear Shock Absorber
2. Nut
3. Washer
7. Bolt
26. Bolt
27. Nut
28. Parking Brake Bracket

Rear shock absorber mounting—Astro/Safari

7924JG36

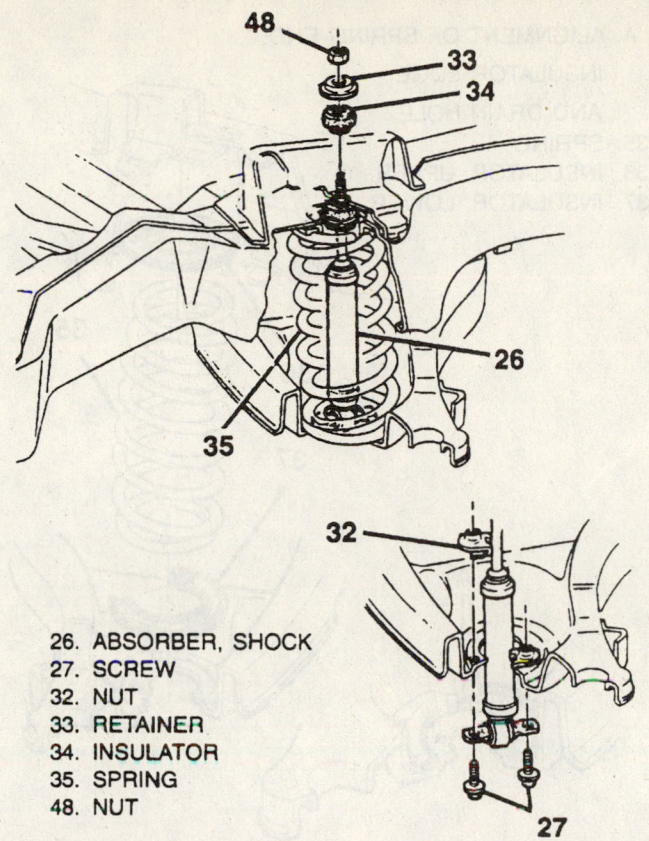

26. ABSORBER, SHOCK
27. SCREW
32. NUT
33. RETAINER
34. INSULATOR
35. SPRING
48. NUT

Front shock absorber mounting—Astro/Safari

To install:

4. Compress the front shock absorber to make installation easier.
- Shock absorber
- Lower nut. Torque the nut to 62 ft. lbs. (84 Nm).
- Upper bolt. Torque the bolts to 18 ft. lbs. (25 Nm).
- Wheel

Except Astro/Safari

FRONT

2WD MODELS

1. Before servicing the vehicle, refer to the precautions in the beginning of this section.
2. Remove or disconnect the following:
- Wheel
- Mounting nut

➡ **Hold the shock absorber stem with a wrench while backing the nut off.**

- Retaining nut and grommet
- Shock absorber-to-lower control arm bolts
- Shock absorber

- Replace the parts, as necessary.

To install:

3. Fully extend the shock absorber stem, then push it up through the lower control arm and spring so that the upper stem passes through the mounting hole in the upper control arm frame bracket.

4. Install or connect the following:
- Retaining nut and grommet on the

stem. Tighten the nut to 106 inch lbs. (12 Nm).
- Shock absorber-to-lower control arm bolts and tighten to 22 ft. lbs. (30 Nm).
- Wheel

4WD MODELS

1. Before servicing the vehicle, refer to the precautions in the beginning of this section.
2. Remove or disconnect the following:
- Wheel
- Lower nut/bolt and collapse the shock absorber
- Shock absorber upper nut and bolt
- Shock absorber

To install:

3. Install or connect the following:
- Shock absorber to the bracket. Tighten the nuts/bolts to 54 ft. lbs. (73 Nm).
- Wheel

REAR

1. Before servicing the vehicle, refer to the precautions in the beginning of this section.
2. Properly support the rear axle assembly.

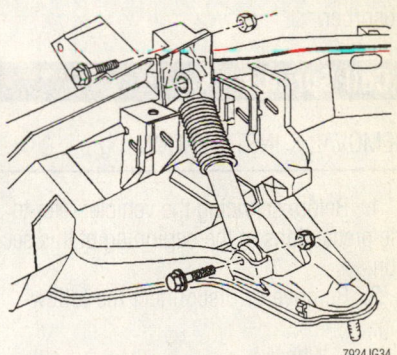

Front shock absorber mounting—4WD except Astro/Safari

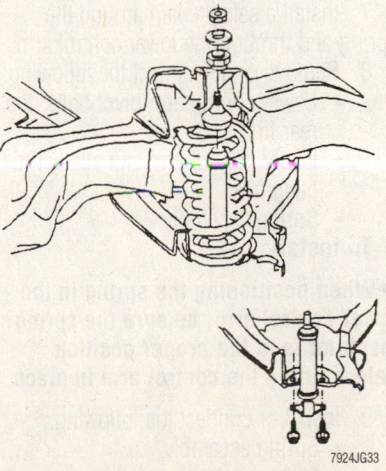

Front shock absorber mounting—2WD except Astro/Safari

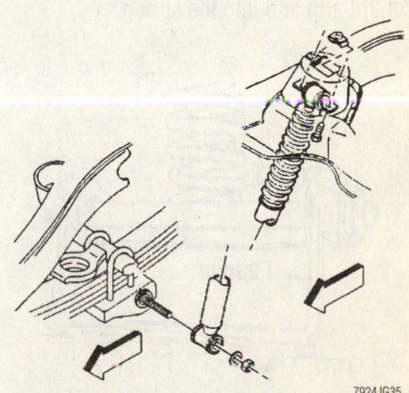

Rear shock absorber mounting—except Astro/Safari

3. Remove or disconnect the following:

- Automatic level control air lines from the shock absorber, if equipped
- Shock absorber-to-frame retainers at the top of the shock
- Shock-to-axle retainers at the bottom of the shock
- Shock absorber

To install:

4. Install the shock in the vehicle and loosely install the upper mounting fasteners to retain it

5. Align the lower-end of the shock absorber with the axle mounting, then loosely install the retainers.

6. On 1997–98 models, tighten the upper shock absorber retainers 22 ft. lbs. (30 Nm). Then tighten the lower shock absorber fastener to 62 ft. lbs. (84 Nm).

7. On 1999–01 models, tighten the upper shock retainers to 18 ft. lbs. (25 Nm). Tighten the lower shock retainers to 62 ft. lbs. (84 Nm) on pick-up and two door utility models and 74 ft. lbs. (100 Nm) on four door utility models.

8. If equipped, attach the automatic level control air lines to the shock absorber.

Coil Springs

REMOVAL & INSTALLATION

1. Before servicing the vehicle, refer to the precautions in the beginning of this section.

2. Remove or disconnect the following:

- Wheel
- Shock absorber lower bolts

3. Push the shock absorber through the control arm and into the spring.

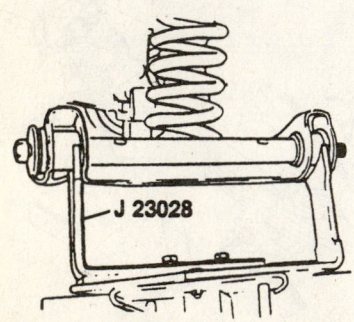

Secure tool J 23028 to a jack, then raise the jack to remove the tension on the lower control arm bolts—Astro/Safari

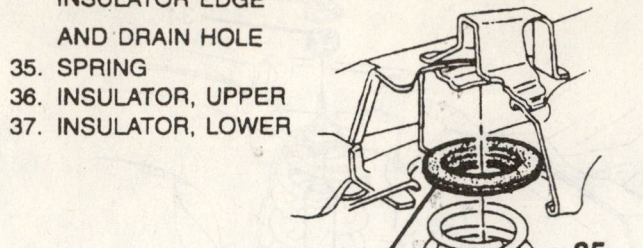

A. ALIGNMENT OF SPRING END, INSULATOR EDGE AND DRAIN HOLE
35. SPRING
36. INSULATOR, UPPER
37. INSULATOR, LOWER

7924JG39

Exploded view of the coil spring mounting—Astro/Safari

4. With the vehicle supported so the control arms hang free, install tool J-23028, onto a support and into the lower control arm bushings.

5. Remove or disconnect the following:

- Stabilizer bar from the control arm
- Stabilizer from the lower control arm

6. Raise and remove the tension on the lower control arm bolts.

7. Install a safety chain around the spring and through the lower control arm.

8. Remove or disconnect the following:

- Lower control arm pivot bolts, the rear first
- Lower control arm and allow it to hang free
- Spring assembly

To install:

➡ **When positioning the spring in the lower control arm, be sure the spring insulator is in the proper position before lifting the control arm in place.**

9. Install or connect the following:

- Spring assembly
- Lower control arm
- Lower control arm pivot bolts
- Stabilizer to the lower control arm

Leaf Springs

REMOVAL & INSTALLATION

Astro/Safari

1. Before servicing the vehicle, refer to the precautions in the beginning of this section.

➡ **When supporting the rear of the vehicle, support the axle and the body separately to relieve the load on the rear spring.**

2. Remove or disconnect the following:

- Rear wheel and tire assemblies
- Axle bumper and retainer, if necessary for access to the lower spring plate front nut
- Nuts securing the U-bolt and lower plate (attaching the spring to the axle at the center of the spring). If the vehicle is equipped with a stabilizer bar it will be necessary to remove the lower nuts, washers and clamps, then swing the stabilizer bar down to obtain clearance when lowering the axle assembly.

- U-bolt, lower plate and anchor plate, then CAREFULLY lower the axle away from the spring

✳✳ WARNING

DO NOT let the axle hang by the brake hose at any point during the procedure or the hose may be severely damaged.

- Shackle nut and bolt, then disengage the spring from the shackle, at the rear of the fiberglass spring
- Hanger nut and bolt, then the spring from the hanger, at the front of the fiberglass spring

To install:

➡ **To assure proper seating and attachment of the anchor plate over the spring end and the axle, the installation procedure must be followed closely.**

3. Install or connect the following:
   - Spring to the hanger, then loosely install the retaining nut and bolt
   - Spring to the shackle, then loosely install the retaining nut and bolt

4. CAREFULLY raise the axle until it contacts the spring.

5. Apply rubber lubricant to the isolator on the spring in order to aid installation of the anchor plate, then install the anchor plate to the top of the spring.

6. Install or connect the following:
   - Lower plate and U-bolt around the axle and through the anchor plate. If your van is equipped with a stabilizer bar it will be necessary to install the clamps, washers and nuts.
   - Nuts to the lower plate and U-bolts. Starting with the inner (lower plate side) nuts, gradually tighten the 4 nuts so the anchor plate moves uniformly, side-to-side, over the spring. Tighten the nuts to 41 ft. lbs. (56 Nm).

➡ **After tightening the fasteners to specification, there should be no gap between the anchor plate, axle tube bracket and the lower plate. A metal-to-metal contact should exist.**

7. Raise the axle so the vehicle's weight is supported by the spring. The rear suspension height should be approximately 5.3–5.7 in. (135–145mm). With the suspension at normal ride height, tighten the shackle and hanger retainers to 74 ft. lbs. (100 Nm).

- Axle bumper and tighten the nut to 33 ft. lbs. (45 Nm), if removed
- Tire and wheel assemblies

Except Astro/Safari

1. Before servicing the vehicle, refer to the precautions in the beginning of this section.

➡ **The following procedure requires the use of two sets of jackstands.**

2. Support the rear axle with jackstands, support the axle and the body separately in order to relieve the load on the rear spring.

3. Remove or disconnect the following:
   - Wheel
   - Shock absorber
   - U-bolt nuts, washers, anchor plate and bolts
   - Spare tire, if equipped
   - Rear exhaust hangers and lower the rear exhaust, if necessary
   - Shackle-to-frame bolt, washers and nut
   - Fuel tank, if necessary
   - Front bracket nut, washers and bolt
   - Spring
   - Shackle from the spring, if necessary

To install:

4. Install or connect the following:
   - Shackle to the rearward spring eye using the bolt, washers and nut, but do not fully tighten at this time.
   - Spring assembly
   - Spring to the front bracket using the bolt, washers and nut, but do not fully tighten at this time.
   - Fuel tank, if removed
   - Shackle-to-frame bolt, washers and nut, but do not fully tighten at this

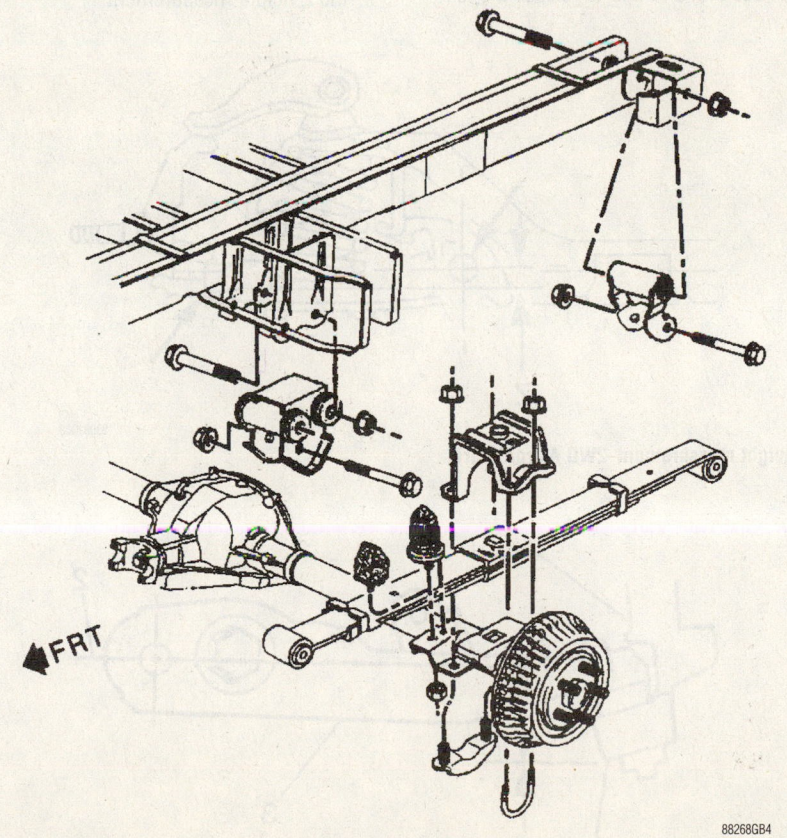

Exploded view of the leaf spring mounting—1995–96 vehicles

88268GB4

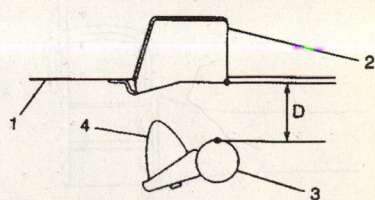

1. FRAME
2. AXLE STOP BRACKET
3. REAR AXLE (END VIEW)
4. BUMPER
5. TRIM HEIGHT 135 – 145MM (5.3 – 5.7 INCHES)

88268GB5

Measuring the rear suspension trim height

Turn to Section 5 for brake system applications

time. If used, remove the spring support.

• U-bolts, anchor plate, washers and U-bolt nuts. Torque the nuts using 2 passes of a diagonal sequence:
  a. Step 1: Torque to 18 ft. lbs. (25 Nm).
  b. Step 2: Torque to 73 ft. lbs. (100 Nm) in the sequence.

5. Position the axle to achieve an approximate gap of 6.46–6.94 in. (164–176mm) between the axle housing tube and the metal surface of the rubber frame bumper bracket. Measure from the housing between the U-bolts to the metal part of the rubber bump stop on the frame.

6. While supporting the axle in this position, tighten the front and rear spring mounting fasteners to 89 ft. lbs. (122 Nm).

7. Install or connect the following:
• Rear exhaust in position and tighten the hangers
• Spare tire
• Shock absorber

Torsion Bar

Instead of the coil spring used on the front suspension of 2WD vehicles, the 4WD vehicles are equipped with a torsion bar.

REMOVAL & INSTALLATION

Astro/Safari

1. Before servicing the vehicle, refer to the precautions in the beginning of this section.

2. Remove or disconnect the following:
• Adjustment assemblies on the torsion bar

3. Mark the adjustment bolt setting.

4. Use tool J 36202, increase the tension on the adjustment arm.

5. Remove or disconnect the following:
• Adjustment bolt and the retaining nut, then move the tool aside
• Torsion bar adjustment arm. By sliding the bar forward

6. Slide the torsion bar partially back through the crossmember.

➡ **The front end of the torsion bar are marked with a left and a right because there are different bars for both sides.**

7. Lower the front of the torsion bar down and slide it forward.

To install:

8. Lubricate the adjuster arm and the bolt. With axle grease.

9. Install or connect the following:
• Torsion bar adjuster arm. The rear face of the torsion bar should be within 1.0-2.0 mm (0.04-0.10 in) of the rear face of the adjuster arm when both are fully installed.
• Adjustment retaining nut and the adjustment bolt. Using tool J 36202, increase the tension on the torsion bar
• Retaining nut and adjustment bolt.

10. Place the adjustment bolt to the marked setting.

11. Use tool J 36202 to release the tension on the torsion bar until the load is taken up by the adjustment bolt, then remove the tool.

a. Check the Z height on rear wheel drive models as follows:

b. Lift the front bumper of the vehicle up about 38 mm (1.5 in) and then remove your hands.

c. Let the vehicle settle.

d. Repeat the previous steps twice until you have lifted the bumper 3 times.

e. Measure from the lower control arm pivot bolt center line down to the lower corner of the steering knuckle.

f. Find the average of the high measurements and the low measurements in order to determine the Z height dimension.

g. Check the Z height on rear wheel drive models as follows:

h. Lift the front bumper of the vehicle up about 38 mm (1.5 in) and then remove your hands.

i. Let the vehicle settle.

j. Repeat the previous steps twice until you have lifted the bumper 3 times.

k. Measure from the lower control arm pivot bolt center line down to the lower corner of the steering knuckle for the Z height measurement.

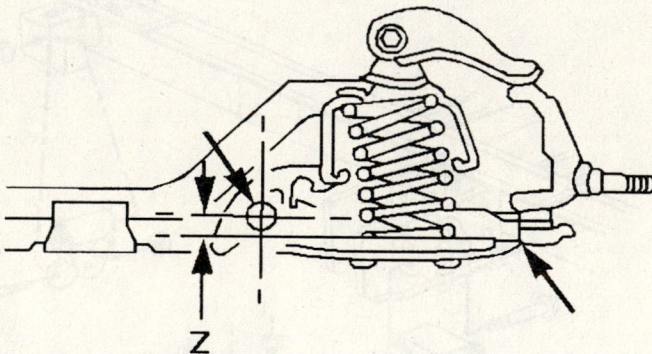

Z height measurement–2WD Astro/Safari

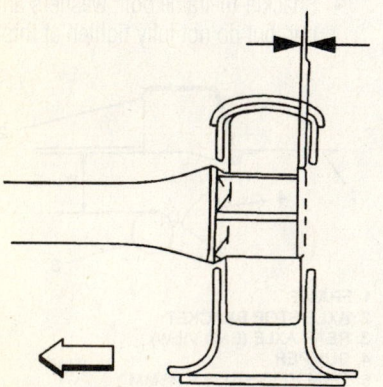

The rear face of the torsion bar should be within 1.0-2.0 mm (0.04-0.10 in) of the rear face of the adjuster arm when fully installed–Astro/Safari

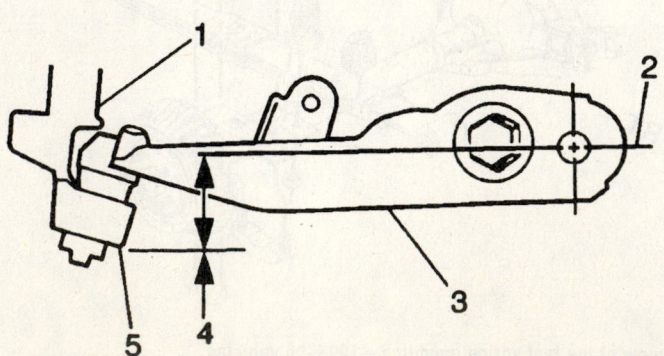

Z height measurement–4WD Astro/Safari

Except Astro/Safari

1. Before servicing the vehicle, refer to the precautions in the beginning of this section.

➡ **The following procedure requires the use of the Torsion Bar Unloader tool J-36202.**

2. Remove or disconnect the following:
- Transmission shield, if equipped
- Torsion bar unloader tool to relax the tension on the torsion bar adjusting arm screw; record the number of turns necessary to properly install the tool. Remove the adjusting screw and the unloader tool.
- Lower link mount nut from one side
- Torsion bars by disengaging them

➡ **Note the direction of the forward end and side of the torsion bar being removed**

- Lower link nut from the opposite side
- Lower link mount, upper link mount nut
- Upper link mount
- Torsion bar from the frame

To install:

3. Install or connect the following:
- Torsion bar and support
- Upper link mount. Torque the nut to 48 ft. lbs. (68 Nm).

4. Place a jack under the torsion bar to release tension.

5. Install or connect the following:
- Lower link mount bushing and nut. Torque the nut to 37 ft. lbs. (50 Nm).
- Torsion bar unloader tool. Tighten the tool against the adjusting arm the same number turns recorded earlier and remove the tool. This loads the torsion bars.
- Transmission shield, if removed

Ball Joints

REMOVAL & INSTALLATION

2WD Vehicles

UPPER

1. Before servicing the vehicle, refer to the precautions in the beginning of this section.

➡ **The following procedure requires the use of a ball joint separator tool such as J-23742 and J-9519-E ball joint remover and installer set.**

2. Raise and support the front of the vehicle safely by placing stands securely under the lower control arms. Because the vehicle's weight is used to relieve spring tension on the upper control arm, the stands must be positioned between the spring seats and the lower control arm ball joints for maximum leverage.

⁕⁕ CAUTION

With components unbolted, the stand is holding the lower control arm in place against the coil spring. Make sure the stand is firmly positioned and cannot move, or personal injury could result.

3. Remove or disconnect the following:
- Tire and wheel assembly
- Brake caliper and support it from the vehicle using a coat hanger or wire. Make sure the brake line is not stretched or damaged and that the caliper's weight is not supported by the line.
- Cotter pin and retaining nut from the upper ball joint
- Anti-lock brake sensor wire bracket, if equipped
- Upper ball joint from the steering knuckle using tool J-23742 and pull the steering knuckle free of the ball joint

➡ **After separating the steering knuckle from the upper ball joint, be sure to support the steering knuckle/hub assembly to prevent damaging the brake hose.**

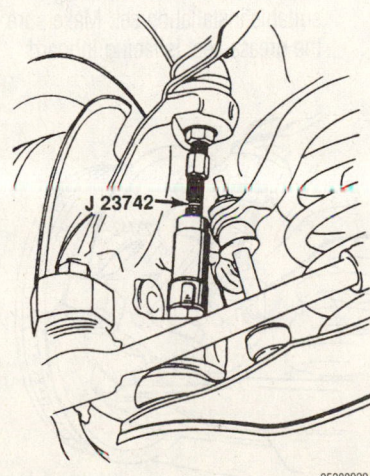
Use a ball joint separator tool to drive the upper ball joint from the steering knuckle

4. Remove the riveted upper ball joint from the upper control arm as follows:
   a. Drill a ⅛ in. (3mm) hole, about ¼ in. (6mm) deep into each rivet.
   b. Then use a ½ in. (13mm) drill bit, to drill off the rivet heads.
   c. Using a pin punch and the hammer, drive out the rivets in order to free the upper ball joint from the upper control arm assembly, then remove the upper ball joint.

5. Clean and inspect the steering knuckle hole. Replace the steering knuckle if the hole is out of round.

To install:

6. Install or connect the following:
- Ball joint in the upper control arm

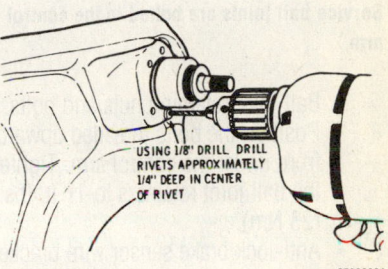
Drill a small guide hole into each ball joint rivet

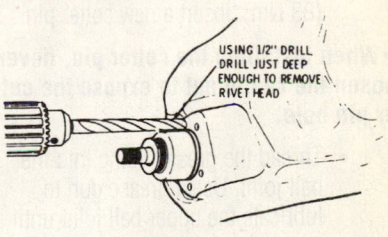
Then drill off the rivet heads

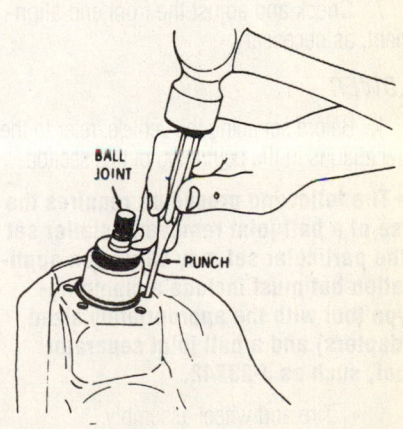
Punch the rivets out and remove the ball joint

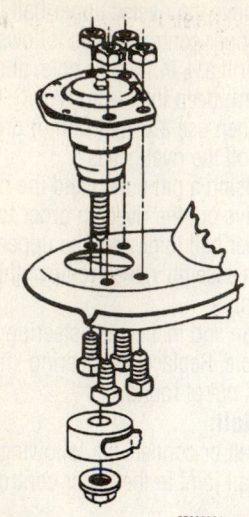

Service ball joints are bolted to the control arm

- Ball joint retaining nuts and bolts. Position the bolts threaded upward from under the control arm. Tighten the ball joint retainers to 17 ft. lbs. (23 Nm).
- Anti-lock brake sensor wire bracket, if removed
- Ball joint to the knuckle. Make sure the joint is seated, then install the stud nut and tighten to 61 ft. lbs. (83 Nm). Insert a new cotter pin.

➡ **When installing the cotter pin, never loosen the castle nut to expose the cotter pin hole.**

- Thread the grease fitting into the ball joint. Use a grease gun to lubricate the upper ball joint until grease appears at the seal.
- Brake caliper
- Tire and wheel assembly

7. Check and adjust the front end alignment, as necessary.

LOWER

1. Before servicing the vehicle, refer to the precautions in the beginning of this section.

➡ **The following procedure requires the use of a ball joint remover/installer set (the particular set may vary upon application but must include a clamping-type tool with the appropriately sized adapters) and a ball joint separator tool, such as J-23742.**

- Tire and wheel assembly

2. Position a jack under the spring seat of the lower control arm, then raise the jack to support the arm.

✱✱ CAUTION

The jack MUST remain under the lower control arm, during the removal and installation procedures, to retain the arm and spring positions. Make sure the jack is securely positioned and will not slip or release during the procedure or personal injury may result.

3. Remove or disconnect the following:
- Brake caliper and support it aside using a hanger or wire. Make sure the brake line is not stressed or damaged.
- Lower ball joint cotter pin and discard
- Ball joint stud nut
- Lower ball joint from the steering knuckle using tool J-23742

4. Carefully guide the lower control arm out of the opening in the splash shield using a putty knife. Position a block of wood between the frame and upper control arm to keep the knuckle out of the way.
- Grease fitting
- Ball joint from the control arm using the ball joint remover set along with the appropriate adapters

To install:

5. Clean the tapered hole in the steering knuckle of any dirt or foreign matter, then check the hole to see if it is out of round, deformed or otherwise damaged. If a problem is found, then knuckle must be replaced.

6. Install or connect the following:
- Press the new ball joint (with grease fitting pointing inward) until it bottoms in the control arm using a suitable installation set. Make sure the grease seal is facing inboard.

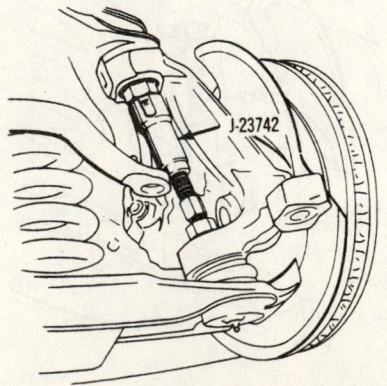

Use a ball joint separator to drive the lower joint from the knuckle

---

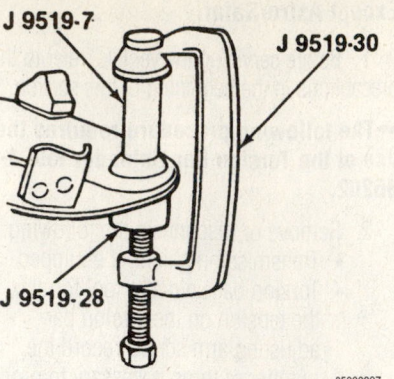

Driving the lower joint from the control arm

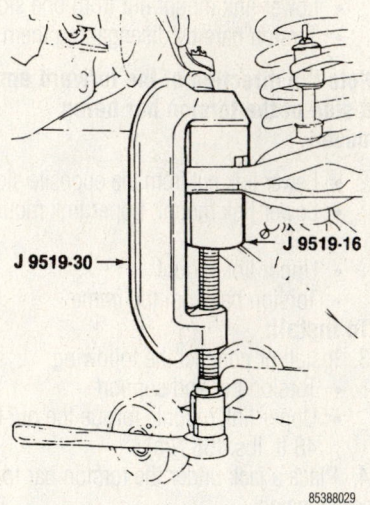

Installing a new ball joint

- Ball joint stud into the steering knuckle
- Ball joint retaining nut and tighten to 79 ft. lbs. (108 Nm)

➡ **When installing the cotter pin, never loosen the castle nut to expose the cotter pin hole.**

- Grease fitting into the ball joint, if not already installed

7. Use a grease gun to lubricate the joint until grease appears at the seal.
- Brake caliper
- Tire and wheel assembly

8. Check and adjust the front end alignment, as necessary.

4WD Vehicles

1. Before servicing the vehicle, refer to the precautions in the beginning of this section.

On 4WD vehicles both the upper and lower ball joints are removed in the same manner. Once the joint is separated from the steering knuckle the rivets are drilled and punched to free the joint from the control arm. Service joints are bolted into position with the retaining bolts threaded upward from beneath the control arm. In this manner, the joint is replaced in an almost identical fashion to the upper joints on 2WD vehicles.

2. Remove or disconnect the following:
- Tire and wheel assembly
- Wheel speed sensor wiring connector from the upper control arm, if removing the upper ball joint
- Cotter pin from the ball joint, then loosen the retaining nut

3. Position a suitable ball joint separator tool such as J-36607, then carefully loosen the joint in the steering knuckle. Remove the tool and the retaining nut, then separate the joint from the knuckle.

➡ **After separating the steering knuckle from the upper ball joint, be sure to support the steering knuckle/hub assembly to prevent damaging the brake hose.**

4. Remove the riveted ball joint from the control arm:

a. Drill a ⅛ in. (3mm) hole, about ¼ in. (6mm) deep into each rivet.

b. Then use a ½ in. (13mm) drill bit, to drill off the rivet heads.

c. Using a pin punch and the hammer, drive out the rivets in order to free the ball joint from the control arm assembly, then remove the ball joint.

To install:

5. Install or connect the following:
- Ball joint in the control arm
- Ball joint retaining nuts and bolts. Position the bolts threaded upward from under the control arm. Tighten the ball joint retainers to 17 ft. lbs. (23 Nm).
- Ball joint to the knuckle. Make sure the joint is seated, tighten the lower nut to 79 ft. lbs. (108 Nm) and the upper nut to 61 ft. lbs. (83 Nm). Install a new cotter pin.

➡ **When installing the cotter pin, never loosen the castle nut to expose the cotter pin hole, but DO NOT tighten more than an additional ⅙ turn.**

6. Use a grease gun to lubricate the upper ball joint.
- Wheel speed sensor wiring connector to the upper control arm, if the upper ball joint was removed
- Tire and wheel assembly

7. Check and adjust the front end alignment, as necessary.

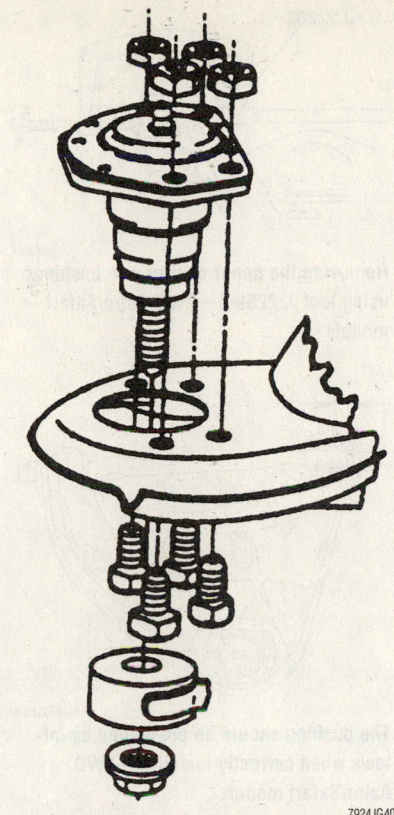

The replacement ball joint comes with nuts and bolts for installation

7924JG40

Upper Control Arm

REMOVAL & INSTALLATION

2 Wheel Drive

1. Before servicing the vehicle, refer to the precautions in the beginning of this section.

2. Remove or disconnect the following:
- Negative battery cable
- Wheel
- Wheel speed sensor harness bracket retaining bolt and nut, if equipped
- Steering knuckle from upper control arm ball joint
- Mounting nuts/bolts and shims

➡ **Make sure to note the location of the control arm shims prior to removal so that they may be installed in their original positions.**

- Upper control arm

To install:

3. Install or connect the following:
- Upper control arm

➡ **Always tighten nut on the thinner shim pack first.**

- Mounting nuts/bolts and shims. Torque the nuts to 81–85 ft. lbs. (110–115 Nm).
- Steering knuckle to upper control arm ball joint
- New cotter pin

➡ **Tighten the nut to align the hole never loosen.**

- Wheel speed sensor harness bracket retaining bolt and nut, if equipped
- Wheel

4 Wheel Drive

ASTRO/SAFARI

1. Before servicing the vehicle, refer to the precautions in the beginning of this section.

2. Support the control arm with jackstands.

3. Remove or disconnect the following:
- Tire and wheel assembly
- Brake hose bracket nut and bolt
- Speed sensor bracket nut and bolt
- Upper ball joint from the steering knuckle
- Upper control arm cam hardware nuts, cams, and bolts.
- Upper control arm

To install:

4. Install or connect the following:
- Upper control arm
- Upper control arm cam hardware bolts and the cams, making sure the bolt heads are opposed inside the bracket and that the cam lobes point down.

➡ **Tighten the nuts with the control arm at Z height**

- New upper control arm cam hardware nuts. Tighten the front nut first, then the rear nut to 103 ft. lbs. (140 Nm).
- Install the remaining components and check the wheel alignment

EXCEPT ASTRO/SAFARI

1. Before servicing the vehicle, refer to the precautions in the beginning of this section.

2. Remove or disconnect the following:
- Tire and wheel assembly
- Cotter pin from the ball joint, then loosen the retaining nut

- Steering knuckle from the upper ball joint. Be sure to support the steering knuckle/hub assembly to prevent damaging the brake hose.

➡The 4WD vehicles do not use shims to adjust the front wheel alignment. Instead, the upper control arm bolts are equipped with cams, which are rotated to achieve caster and camber adjustments. In order to preserve adjustment and ease installation, matchmark the cams to the control arm before removal. If the control arm is being replaced, transfer the alignment marks to the new component before installation.

- Front and rear nuts retaining the control arm retaining bolts to the frame
- Outer cams from the bolts
- Bolts and inner cams
- Control arm from the vehicle
- Retaining nut and the bumper from the control arm, if necessary

3. If the bushings are being replaced, use a suitable bushing service set to remove the bushings from the arm.

To install:

4. Install or connect the following:
- Bushing service set to drive the new bushings into the control arm, if removed
- Bumper and retaining nut to the control arm, if removed. Tighten the bumper retaining nut to 20 ft. lbs. (27 Nm).
- Control arm, retaining bolts (from the inside of the frame brackets facing outward) and the inner cams. The inner cams must be positioned on the bolts before they are inserted through the control arm and frame brackets.
- Outer cams over the retaining bolts, then the nuts to the ends of the bolts at the front and rear of the control arm

5. Align the cams to the reference marks made earlier, then tighten the end nuts to 85 ft. lbs. (115 Nm).
- Ball joint to the knuckle
- Tire and wheel assembly

6. Check and adjust the front end alignment, as necessary.

CONTROL ARM BUSHING REPLACEMENT

2 Wheel Drive

1. Before servicing the vehicle, refer to the precautions in the beginning of this section.
2. Remove or disconnect the following:

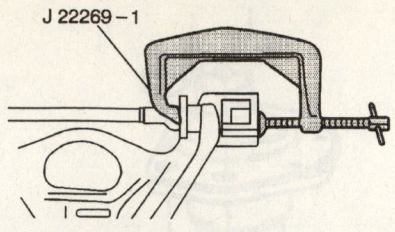

J 22269 – 1

9308JG04

Removing the upper control arm bushings using tool J22269-1—2WD Astro/Safari models

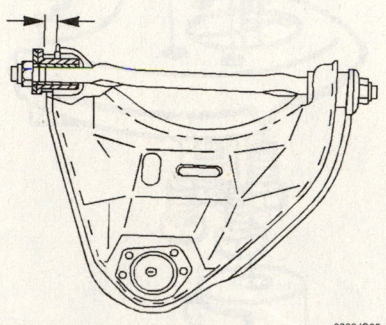

9308JG05

The bushing should be positioned as follows when correctly installed—2WD Astro/Safari models

- Upper control arm and place it in a vice
- Upper control arm shaft nuts and retainers
- Upper control arm bushings using tool J 22269-1, a slotted washer and a short piece if pipe that is slightly larger than the bushing
- Upper control arm shaft

To install:
- Upper control arm shaft
- Upper control arm bushings using tool J 22269-1, a slotted washer and a short piece if pipe that is slightly larger than the bushing

3. Tighten J 22269-1 until the bushing is positioned on the shaft and the control arm as shown in the accompanying illustration. The measurement should be 0.48-0.52 inch (12.8-13.8mm) at both sides when the properly installed.
- Upper control arm shaft nuts and retainers. Tighten to 85 ft. lbs. (115 Nm).
- Upper control arm

4 Wheel Drive

ASTRO/SAFARI

1. Before servicing the vehicle, refer to the precautions in the beginning of this section.
2. Remove or disconnect the following:

- Upper control arm
- Bushings from the arm
3. Installation is the reverse of removal

EXCEPT ASTRO/SAFARI

If the bushings require replacement, refer to the control arm removal and installation procedure for bushing replacement.

Lower Control Arm

REMOVAL & INSTALLATION

2 Wheel Drive

1. Before servicing the vehicle, refer to the precautions in the beginning of this section.
2. Remove or disconnect the following:
- Coil Spring
- Lower ball joint from the steering knuckle
- Lower control arm from the vehicle

To install:
3. Install or connect the following:
- Lower control arm
- Lower ball joint stud into the steering knuckle
- Ball joint-to-steering knuckle nut and tighten to specification
- New cotter pin to the lower ball joint stud
- Coil spring
4. Align the vehicle.

4 Wheel Drive

1. Before servicing the vehicle, refer to the precautions in the beginning of this section.

➡Tools Needed: universal tie rod separator J–24319–01, torsion bar unloader J–36202, lower control arm bushing service kit J–36618 (if the control arm bushing are being replaced) and ball joint C-clamp J–9519–23. Parts Needed: whether or not the control arm or bushing are being replaced, NEW control arm retaining nut should be used once the old ones have been loosened and removed.

2. Remove or disconnect the following:
- Front wheels
- 2 bolts from the front splash shield and pivot it in order to gain access to the tie rod
- Stabilizer bar from the control arm (keeping all of the link hardware sorted for proper installation). If necessary, completely remove the bar from the vehicle for access.
- Shock absorber

- Inner tie rod from the relay rod using a tie rod separator
- Outer halfshaft nut and washer
- Bolts from the hub and bearing kit

3. Unload the torsion bar using the unloading tool J–36202. First, mark the adjuster for installation.

- Adjustment arm. Slide the bar forward and the adapter out of the rear to remove the adjusting arm.
- Lower ball joint cotter pin, nut and ball joint from the control arm using a ball joint separator
- Nuts and bolts and lower control arm with the torsion bar assembly. Note the direction which the control arm retaining bolts are facing for installation purposes.

To install:

4. Install or connect the following:

- Torsion bar to the lower control arm and place the assembly into the vehicle. Position the front leg of the lower control arm into the crossmember before installing the rear leg into the frame bracket.
- Control arm bolts (facing in the direction as noted during removal or shown in the accompanying illustration) with NEW nuts.

➡ The control arm retainers MUST be tightened with the vehicle suspension at normal ride height. This can either be accomplished by starting the nuts now, then installing the remaining components along with the wheels and lowering the vehicle, or by moving jackstands under the ends of the lower control arms and resting the vehicle on them. If the latter solution is tried, make sure front suspension is at actual ride height compression. If you are unsure, it is best to start the nuts now and tighten them to specification once the vehicle is lowered.

- Ball joint stud in the knuckle

5. With the suspension at the correct height, tighten the control arm retaining nuts to 98 ft. lbs. (133 Nm).

➡ The lower ball joint retaining nut MUST be tightened with the vehicle suspension at normal ride height. This can either be accomplished by starting the nut now, then installing the remaining components along with the wheels and lowering the vehicle, or by moving jackstands under the ends of the lower control arms and resting the vehicle on them. If the latter solution is tried, make sure the FULL WEIGHT

of the vehicle front end is on the suspension.

6. Install or connect the following:

- Joint-to-control arm nut, then tighten the nut to 92 ft. lbs. (125 Nm) with the suspension at normal ride height and compression.
- New cotter pin to the castellated nut. Tighten the nut (but no more than an additional ⅙ turn) in order to align the cotter pin. DO NOT loosen the nut from the specified torque.
- Adjuster arm by sliding the adapter forward, over the torsion bar to install the sides of the nut. Load the torsion bar and install the adjuster bolt aligning the installation mark.
- Drive axle through the hub and bearing assembly
- Tighten the hub and bearing assembly retaining bolts
- Drive axle shaft nut and washer
- Inner tie rod end to the relay rod
- Shock absorber
- Stabilizer bar, if removed
- Stabilizer link(s) to the control arm(s)
- Splash shield
- Front wheels

7. Recheck all fasteners for proper torque and installation before road testing.

8. Refill the differential if any fluid was lost.

9. Check and adjust the front end alignment, as necessary.

CONTROL ARM BUSHING REPLACEMENT

Astro/Safari

1. Before servicing the vehicle, refer to the precautions in the beginning of this section.

2. Remove lower control arm and place it in vise.

3. Use a punch to unbend the crimps on the front bushing.

4. Use tools J 36618-2, J 9519-23 and J 36618-1 to remove the front bushing from the arm.

5. Use tools J 36618-5, J 36618-3, J 36618-2 and J 9519-23 to remove the rear bushing from the arm.

To install:

6. Install the front bushing using tools J 36618 and J 5919-23 and bend the crimps back into position to retain the bushing.

7. Install the rear bushing using tools J 36618 and J 5919-23 .

8. Install the lower control arm.

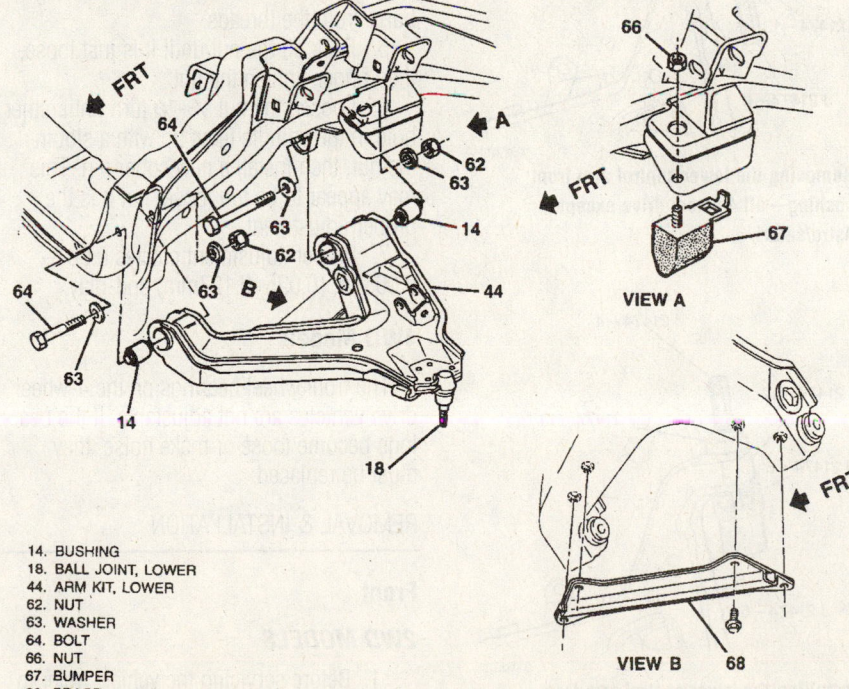

14. BUSHING
18. BALL JOINT, LOWER
44. ARM KIT, LOWER
62. NUT
63. WASHER
64. BOLT
66. NUT
67. BUMPER
68. BRACE

88268GB1

Exploded view of the lower control arm assembly mounting

VIEW A

VIEW B

Turn to Section 5 for brake system applications

2 Wheel Drive

EXCEPT ASTRO/SAFARI

1. Before servicing the vehicle, refer to the precautions in the beginning of this section.

2. Remove lower control arm and place it in vise.

3. Install tools J 22269-01, 21474-8, 12 and 13 on the rear bushing and tighten until the bushing is removed.

4. Using a blunt chisel, drive the front bushing flare flush with the rubber part of the bushing.

5. Place a wedge or a spacer between the bushing housing to keep the housing from bending while removing or installing the bushing.

6. Install tools J 21474-3, 4, 5 and 6 on the front bushing and tighten until the bushing is removed.

To install:

7. Install the front bushing into the control arm.

8. Install tools J 21474-4, 5 and

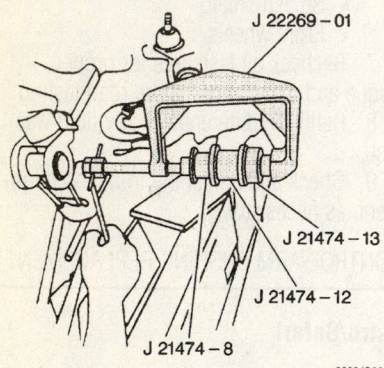

Removing the lower control arm rear bushing—all 2 wheel drive except Astro/safari

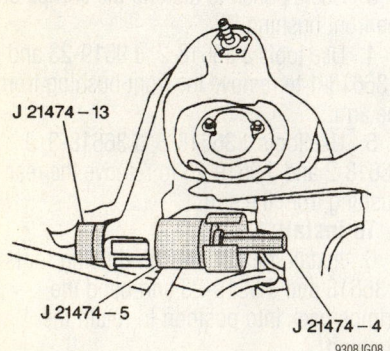

Installing the lower control arm front bushing—all 2 wheel drive except Astro/safari

13. Tighten until the bushing is fully seated.

9. Install the rear bushing into the control arm

10. Install tools J 22269-01, J 21474-2 and 13. Tighten until the bushing is fully seated.

11. Install the lower control arm.

4 Wheel Drive

EXCEPT ASTRO/SAFARI

1. Before servicing the vehicle, refer to the precautions in the beginning of this section.

2. Remove lower control arm and place it in vise.

3. Using bushing service set J 21474, remove the front and rear bushings.

To install:

4. Using bushing service set J 21474, install the front and rear bushings.

5. Install the lower control arm.

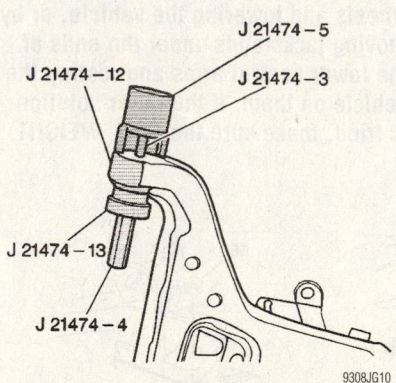

Removing the lower control arm front bushing—all 4 wheel drive except Astro/safari

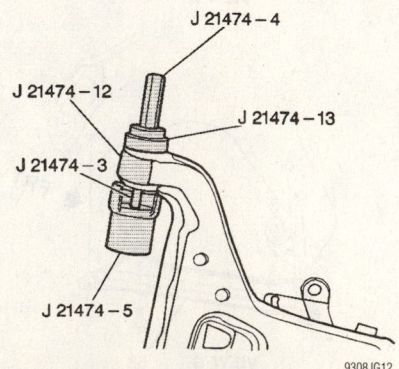

Installing the lower control arm front bushing—all 4 wheel drive except Astro/safari

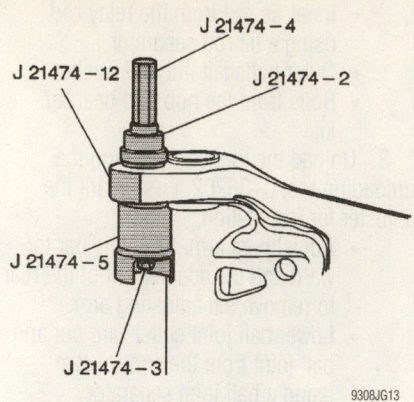

Installing the lower control arm rear bushing—all 4 wheel drive except Astro/safari

Wheel Bearings

ADJUSTMENT

2WD Models

1. Before servicing the vehicle, refer to the precautions in the beginning of this section.

2. If equipped, remove the wheel/hub cover for access, then remove the dust cap from the hub.

3. Remove the cotter pin and loosen the spindle nut.

4. Spin the wheel forward by hand and torque the nut to 12 ft. lbs. (16 Nm) in order to fully seat the bearings and remove any burrs from the threads.

5. Back off the nut until it is just loose, then finger-tighten the nut.

6. Loosen the nut ¼–½ turn until either hole in the spindle lines up with a slot in the nut, then install a new cotter pin. This may appear to be too loose, but it is the proper adjustment.

7. Proper adjustment creates 0.001–0.005 in. (0.025–0.127mm) end-play.

4WD Models

The front wheel bearings on the 4-wheel drive vehicles are not adjustable. If the bearings become loose or make noise, they must be replaced.

REMOVAL & INSTALLATION

Front

2WD MODELS

1. Before servicing the vehicle, refer to the precautions in the beginning of this section.

2. Remove or disconnect the following:

- Wheel
- Brake caliper with the pads without disconnecting the brake line
- Grease cap
- Cotter pin, spindle nut and washer
- Hub

✳✳ WARNING

Be careful not to drop the outer wheel bearing. As the hub is pulled forward, the outer wheel bearings will often fall forward and they may easily be removed at this time.

- Outer roller bearing assembly
- Inner seal by prying it out of the hub and discard it
- Inner bearing assembly

To install:

3. Clean all parts in solvent and allow to air dry, then check for excessive wear or damage. Inspect all of the parts for scoring, pitting or cracking and replace if necessary.

➡ **DO NOT remove the bearing races from the hub, unless they show signs of damage.**

4. If it is necessary to remove the wheel bearing races, use the GM front bearing race removal tool J-29117 to drive the races from the hub/disc assembly. A hammer and brass drift may also be used to drive the races from the hub, but the race removal tool is quicker.

5. If the bearing races were removed, position the replacement races in the freezer for a few minutes and then install them to the hub:

   a. Lightly lubricate the inside of the hub/disc assembly using wheel bearing grease.

   b. Using the GM seal installation tools J-8092 and J-8850, drive the inner bearing race into the hub/disc assembly until it seats. Be sure the race is properly seated against the hub shoulder and is not cocked.

➡ **When installing the bearing races, be sure to support the hub/disc assembly with GM tool J-9746-02.**

   c. Using the GM seal installation tools J-8092 and J-8457, drive the outer race into the hub/disc assembly until it seats.

6. Using a high melting point wheel bearing grease, lubricate the bearings, races and spindle; be sure to place a gob of grease (inside the hub/disc assembly) between the races to provide an ample supply of lubricant.

➡ **To lubricate each bearing, place a gob of grease in the palm of the hand, then scoop the bearing through the grease until it is well lubricated.**

7. Place the inner bearing in the hub, then apply a thin coating of grease to the sealing lip and install a new inner seal, making sure the seal flange faces the bearing cup.

➡ **Although a seal installation tool is preferable, a section of pipe with a smooth edge or a suitably sized socket may be used to drive the seal into position. Be sure the seal is flush with the outer surface of the hub assembly.**

8. Install or connect the following:
- Wheel hub over the spindle
- Outer bearing into the hub by hand
- Spindle washer and nut
- Brake caliper
- Wheel

9. Properly adjust the wheel bearings

10. Install or connect the following:
- New cotter pin
- Dust cap
- Wheel cover

4WD MODELS

1. Before servicing the vehicle, refer to the precautions in the beginning of this section.

2. Install Torsion Bar Unloading tool J 36202 on the torsion bar adjusting bolt and remove the bolt. To aid during installation, count the number of turns required to remove the bolt.

3. Remove the wheel.

4. Install an axle shaft boot seal protector to the Tri-pot axle joint.

5. Remove or disconnect the following:
- Cotter pin and retainer
- Castle nut and the thrust washer
- Brake caliper and support it aside using wire or a coat hanger

➡ **Be sure the brake line is not stretched or damaged.**

- Brake disc from the wheel hub
- Halfshaft from the hub/bearing assembly, using a Spindle Remover tool J-28733-A to prevent damage to the shaft or hub/bearing assembly
- Hub/bearing assembly from the knuckle

6. Clean and inspect the parts for nicks, scores and/or damage, then replace them as necessary.

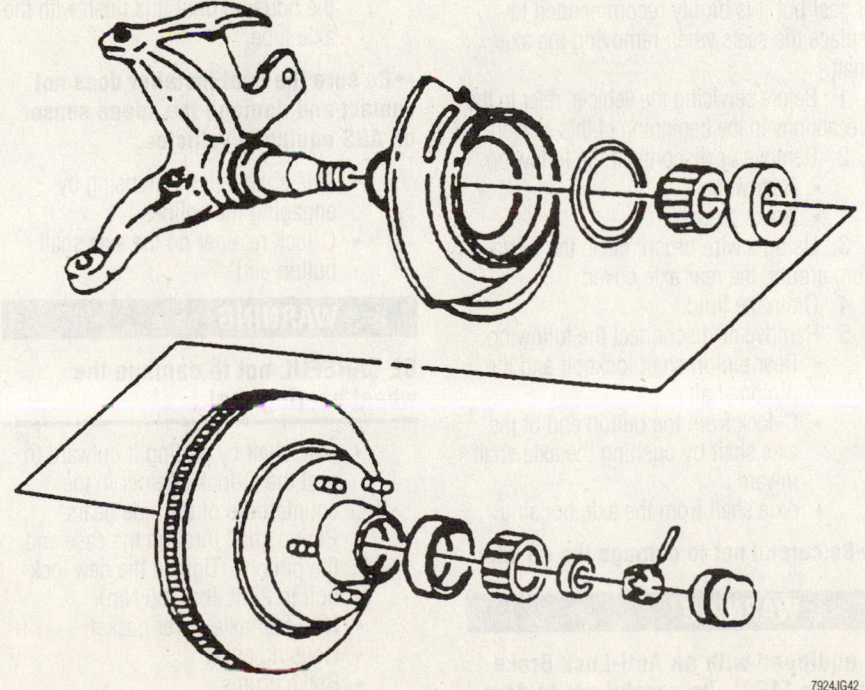

Wheel bearings, races and related components—2WD vehicles

7924JG42

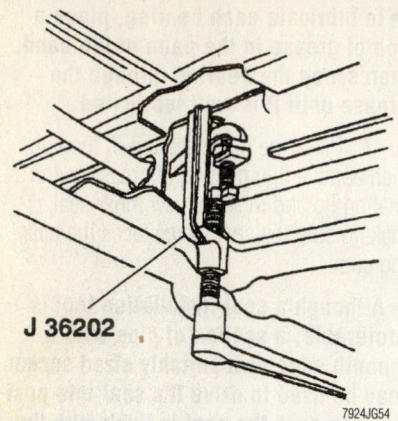

Use Torsion Bar Unloading tool J 36202 to remove the adjusting bolt and unload the torsion bar

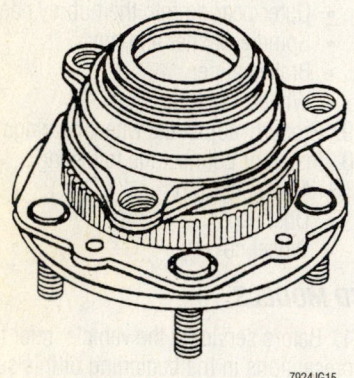

Hub and bearing assembly—4WD vehicles

To install:

7. Install or connect the following:
- Hub and bearing assembly by aligning the threaded holes. Torque the bolts to 77 ft. lbs. (105 Nm).
- Tie rod end to the steering knuckle using the retaining nut
- New cotter pin
- Brake assembly
- Halfshaft nut. Tighten the nut to 180 ft. lbs. (245 Nm).
- Retainer and a new cotter pin but DO NOT back off specification in order to insert the cotter pin.

8. Remove the torsion bar unloader tool and the drive axle boot protector.

9. Install the wheel.

10. Check and/or adjust the vehicle trim height, as necessary.

Rear

A new pinion shaft lockbolt should be installed whenever either of the axle shafts is removed.

The axle shaft and seal may be removed and replaced without disturbing the bearing

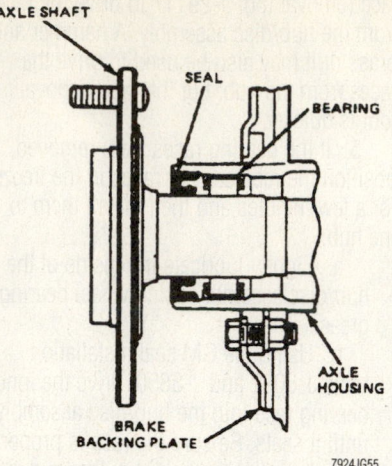

Cross-sectional view of the rear axle, bearing and seal assembly

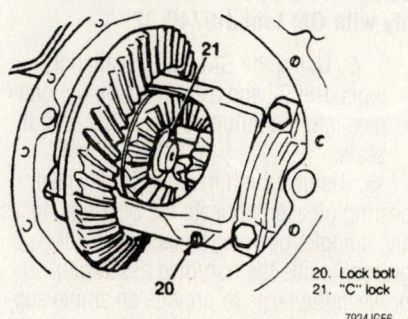

Pinion shaft lockbolt and axle C-lock locations, inside the differential

20. Lock bolt
21. "C" lock

or seal but it is highly recommended to replace the seals when removing the axle shaft.

1. Before servicing the vehicle, refer to the precautions in the beginning of this section.

2. Remove or disconnect the following:
- Rear wheels
- Brake drums

3. Using a wire brush, clean the dirt/rust from around the rear axle cover.

4. Drain the fluid.

5. Remove or disconnect the following:
- Rear pinion shaft lockbolt and the pinion shaft
- C-lock from the button end of the axle shaft by pushing the axle shaft inward
- Axle shaft from the axle housing

➡ **Be careful not to damage the oil seal.**

✳✳ WARNING

If equipped with an Anti-Lock Brake System (ABS), be careful not to damage the reflector ring on the axle shaft or the speed sensor bolted to

the backing plate, immediately adjacent to the shaft.

6. Remove or disconnect the following:
- Oil seal by prying the it from the end of the rear axle housing

✳✳ WARNING

DO NOT damage the housing oil seal surface.

- Wheel bearing using the GM Slide Hammer tool J-2619, the GM Adapter tool J-2619-4 and the GM Axle Bearing Puller tool J-22813-01

To install:

7. Clean and inspect the components for excessive wear or damage and replace them, if necessary.

8. Install or connect the following:
- New or reused bearing, coated with gear lubricant, using the Axle Shaft Bearing Installer tool J-34974 to drive the bearing in until it bottoms against the seat

✳✳ WARNING

Be sure the bearing installer does not contact and damage the speed sensor on ABS equipped vehicles.

- New seal lubricated with gear oil using the GM Axle Shaft Seal Installer tool J-33782 to seat it in the housing until it is flush with the axle tube

➡ **Be sure the seal installer does not contact and damage the speed sensor on ABS equipped vehicles.**

- Axle shaft into the housing by engaging the splines
- C-lock retainer on the axle shaft button end

✳✳ WARNING

BE CAREFUL not to damage the wheel bearing seal.

- Axle shaft by pulling it outward to seat the C-lock retainer in the counterbore of the side gears
- Pinion shaft through the case and the pinions. Tighten the new lockbolt to 27 ft. lbs. (36 Nm).
- New rear axle cover gasket
- Housing cover
- Brake drums
- Wheels

9. Refill the housing.

GENERAL MOTORS CORP.

C/K Pick-ups • Denali • Escalade • Express • G Vans •
Savana • Sierra • Silverado • Suburban • Tahoe • Yukon

20

PRECAUTIONS

Before servicing any vehicle, please be sure to read all of the following precautions, which deal with personal safety, prevention of component damage, and important points to take into consideration when servicing a motor vehicle:

• Never open, service or drain the radiator or cooling system when the engine is hot; serious burns can occur from the steam and hot coolant.

• Observe all applicable safety precautions when working around fuel. Whenever servicing the fuel system, always work in a well-ventilated area. Do not allow fuel spray or vapors to come in contact with a spark, open flame, or excessive heat (a hot drop light, for example) Keep a dry chemical fire extinguisher near the work area. Always keep fuel in a container specifically designed for fuel storage; also, always properly seal fuel containers to avoid the possibility of fire or explosion. Refer to the additional fuel system precautions later in this section.

• Fuel injection systems often remain pressurized, even after the engine has been turned **OFF**. The fuel system pressure must be relieved before disconnecting any fuel lines. Failure to do so may result in fire and/or personal injury.

• Brake fluid often contains polyglycol ethers and polyglycols. Avoid contact with the eyes and wash your hands thoroughly after handling brake fluid. If you do get brake fluid in your eyes, flush your eyes with clean, running water for 15 minutes. If eye irritation persists, or if you have taken brake fluid internally, IMMEDIATELY seek medical assistance.

• The EPA warns that prolonged contact with used engine oil may cause a number of skin disorders, including cancer! You should make every effort to minimize your exposure to used engine oil. Protective gloves should be worn when changing oil. Wash your hands and any other exposed skin areas as soon as possible after exposure to used engine oil. Soap and water, or waterless hand cleaner should be used.

• All new vehicles are now equipped with an air bag system. The system must be disabled before performing service on or around system components, steering column, instrument panel components, wiring and sensors. Failure to follow safety and disabling procedures could result in accidental air bag deployment, possible personal injury and unnecessary system repairs.

• Always wear safety goggles when working with, or around, the air bag system. When carrying a non-deployed air bag, be sure the bag and trim cover are pointed away from your body. When placing a non-deployed air bag on a work surface, always face the bag and trim cover upward, away from the surface. This will reduce the motion of the module if it is accidentally deployed. Refer to the additional air bag system precautions later in this section.

• Clean, high quality brake fluid from a sealed container is essential to the safe and proper operation of the brake system. You should always buy the correct type of brake fluid for your vehicle. If the brake fluid becomes contaminated, completely flush the system with new fluid. Never reuse any brake fluid. Any brake fluid that is removed from the system should be discarded. Also, do not allow any brake fluid to come in contact with a painted surface; it will damage the paint.

• Never operate the engine without the proper amount and type of engine oil; doing so WILL result in severe engine damage.

• Timing belt maintenance is extremely important! Many models utilize an interference-type, non-freewheeling engine. If the timing belt breaks, the valves in the cylinder head may strike the pistons, causing potentially serious (also time-consuming and expensive) engine damage. Refer to the maintenance interval charts in the front of this manual for the recommended replacement interval for the timing belt, and to the timing belt section for belt replacement and inspection.

• Disconnecting the negative battery cable on some vehicles may interfere with the functions of the on-board computer system(s) and may require the computer to undergo a relearning process once the negative battery cable is reconnected.

• When servicing drum brakes, only disassemble and assemble one side at a time, leaving the remaining side intact for reference.

GASOLINE ENGINE REPAIR

4.3L, 5.0L, 5.7L, 7.4L Distributor

REMOVAL

1. Before servicing the vehicle, refer to the precautions in the beginning of this section.
2. Remove or disconnect the following:
   • Negative battery cable
   • Spark plug wires and the coil leads from the distributor
   • Electrical connector at the base of the distributor
   • Distributor cap
3. Matchmark the rotor-to-housing and housing-to-engine block positions so that they can be matched during installation.
   • Distributor hold-down bolt
   • Distributor from the engine

INSTALLATION

Timing Not Disturbed

1. Install or connect the following:
   • Distributor, aligning the match-marks are properly alignment
   • Distributor hold-down bolt
   • Distributor cap
   • Electrical connector at the base of the distributor
   • Spark plug wires and coil leads
   • Negative battery cable

Timing Disturbed

1. Remove the No. 1 cylinder spark plug. Turn the engine using a socket wrench on the large bolt on the front of the crankshaft pulley. Place a finger near the No. 1 spark plug hole and turn the crankshaft until the piston reaches TDC. As the engine approaches TDC, you will feel air being expelled through the No. 1 cylinder spark plug hole. The timing mark on the crankshaft pulley should now be aligned with the **0** mark on the timing scale. If the position is not being met, turn the engine another full turn (360 degrees) Once the engines position is correct, install the spark plug.

➡ **Before installation, position the rotor so it points to the No. 2 terminal on the cap. As the distributor is lowered into the engine, the rotor will rotate clockwise and stop at the No. 1 terminal. This is the desired position.**

2. Turn the rotor so that it will point to the No. 1 terminal of the distributor cap when it is fully seated in the engine.
3. Install or connect the following:
   • Distributor. It may be necessary to turn the rotor a little in either direction, in order to engage the gears.

➡ **If the distributor will not seat completely in the engine, remove the distributor and align the groove on the top of the oil pump drive shaft with a long screwdriver to match the tab on the bottom of the distributor shaft. Reinstall the distributor.**

4. Tap the starter a few times to ensure that the oil pump shaft is mated to the distributor shaft.
5. Bring the engine to TDC again and check that the rotor is pointed toward the No. 1 terminal of the cap. If the marks are all aligned.
6. Install or connect the following:

• Hold-down bolt and tighten
• Cap and fasten the mounting screws
• Electrical connections and the spark plug wires

4.8L, 5.3L and 6.0L Distributor

➡ **If the Malfunction Indicator Lamp turns on, and a DTC code P1345 sets after installing the distributor, this indicates an incorrectly installed distributor. Engine damage or distributor damage may occur.**

REMOVAL

1. Turn OFF the ignition switch.
2. Remove or disconnect the following:
   • Spark plug wires from the distributor cap
   • Electrical connector from the base of the distributor
   • Two screws that hold the distributor cap to the housing. Discard the screws.
   • Distributor cap from the housing
3. Use a grease pencil in order to note the position of the rotor in relation to the distributor housing.
4. Mark the distributor housing and the intake manifold with a grease pencil.
5. Remove or disconnect the following:

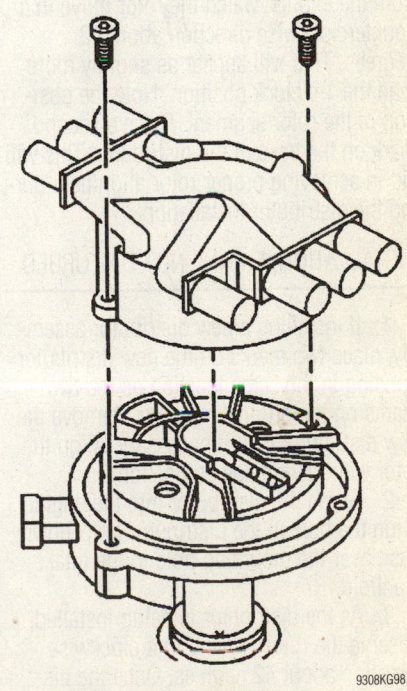

9308KG98

Distributor cap—4.8L, 5.3L, 6.0L

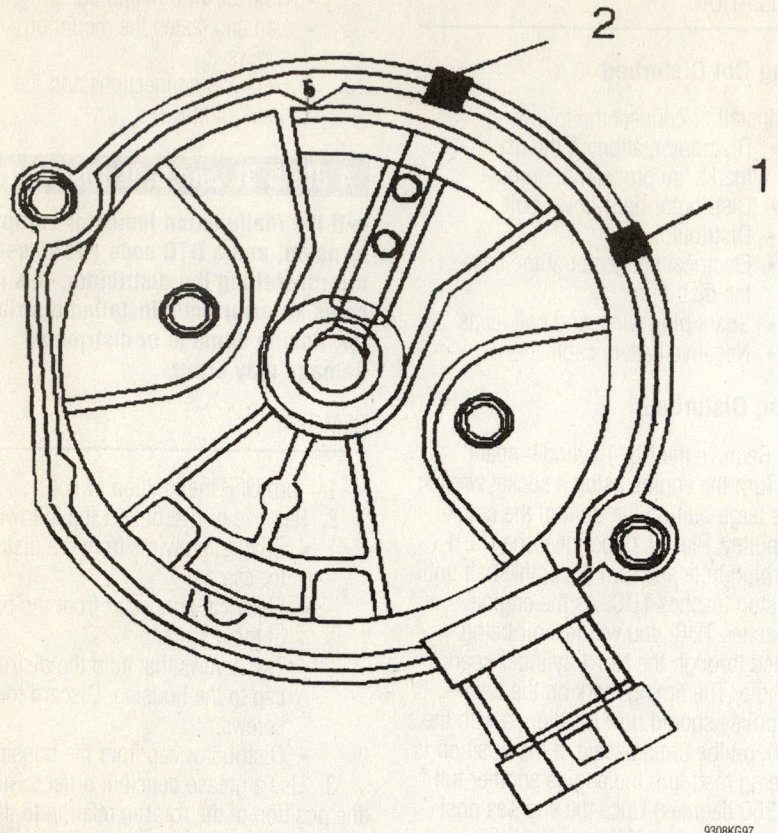

9308KG97

Distributor rotor starting point (1) and 42 degrees counterclockwise (2)—4.8L, 5.3L, 6.0L

- Mounting clamp hold-down bolt
- Distributor

6. As the distributor is being removed from the engine, watch the rotor move in a counterclockwise direction about 42 degrees. This will appear as slightly more than the 1 o'clock position. Note the position of the rotor segment. Place a second mark on the base of the distributor. This will aid in achieving proper rotor alignment during the distributor installation.

INSTALLATION, ENGINE NOT DISTURBED

1. If installing a new distributor assembly, place two marks on the new distributor housing in the same location as the two marks on the original housing. Remove the new distributor cap, if necessary. Align the rotor with mark made at location 2.

2. Guide the distributor into the engine. Align the hole in the distributor hold-down base over the mounting hole in the intake manifold.

3. As the distributor is being installed, observe the rotor moving in a clockwise direction about 42 degrees. Once the distributor is completely seated, the rotor segment should be aligned with the mark on the distributor base in location number 1. If

the rotor segment is not aligned with the number 1 mark, the driven gear teeth and the camshaft have meshed one or more teeth out of alignment.

4. Remove or disconnect the following:

5. Distributor mounting clamp bolt. Tighten the distributor clamp bolt to 25 Nm (18 ft. lbs.).

6. Distributor cap. Install two NEW distributor cap screws. Tighten the screws to 2.4 Nm (21 inch lbs.).

7. Electrical connector to the distributor

8. Spark plug wires to the distributor cap

9. Ignition coil wire.

➡**If the Malfunction Indicator lamp is turned on after installing the distributor, and a DTC P1345 is found, the distributor has been installed incorrectly.**

INSTALLATION, ENGINE DISTURBED

1. Rotate the number 1 cylinder to TDC of the compression stroke. The engine front cover has 2 alignment tabs and the crankshaft balancer has 2 alignment marks (spaced 90 degrees apart) which are used for positioning number 1 piston at top dead center (TDC). With the piston on the compression stroke and at top dead center, the

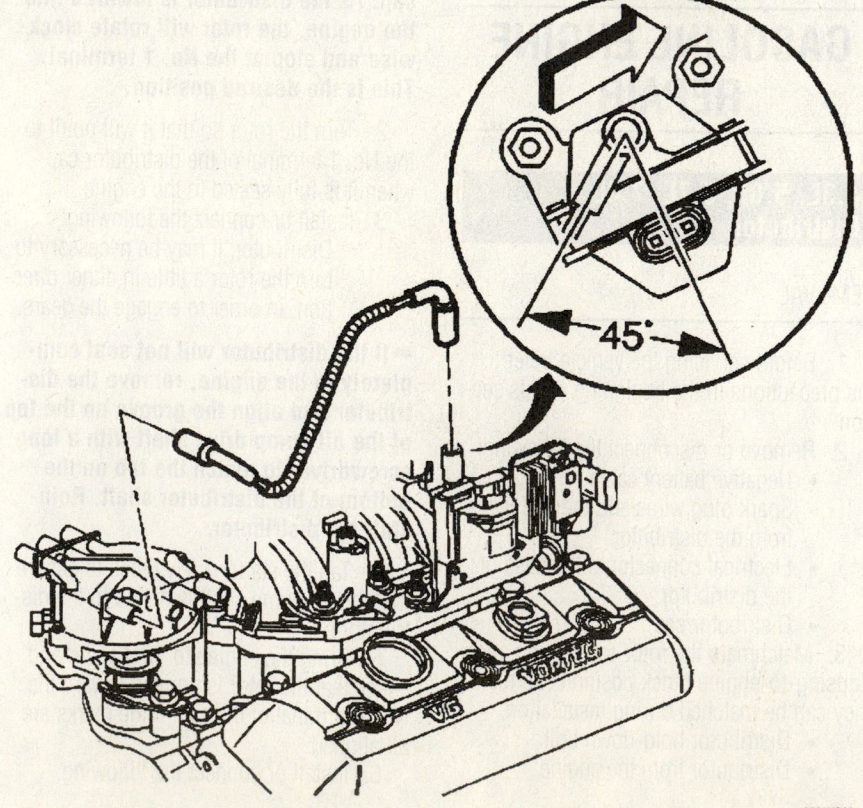

9308KG96

Distributor electrical connection—4.8L, 5.3L, 6.0L

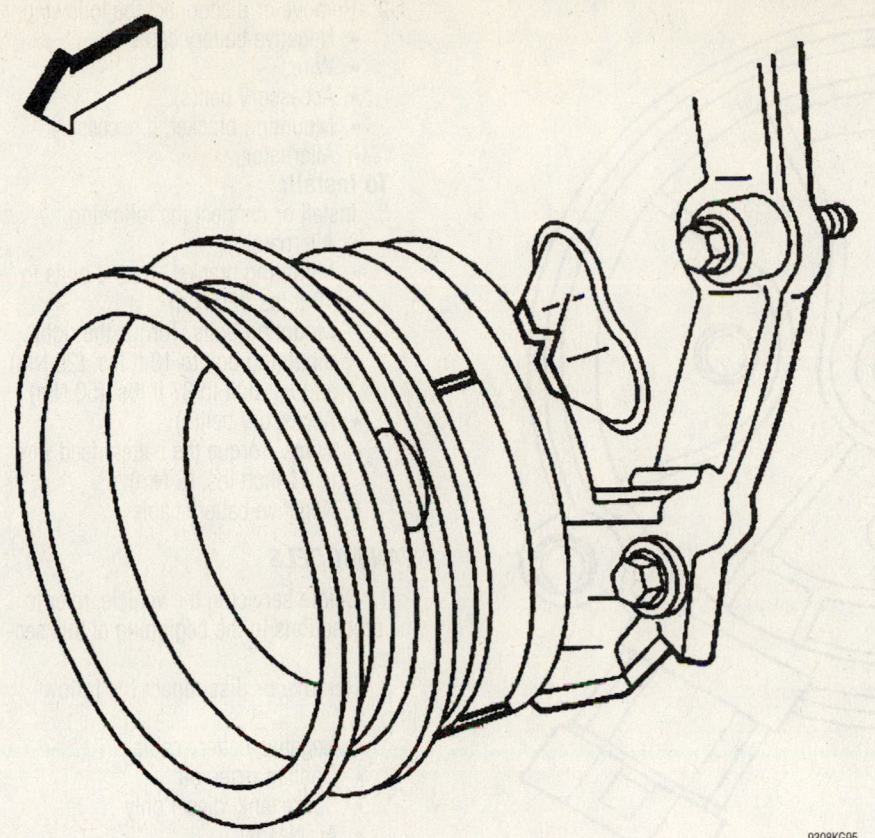

Engine at TDC compression—4.8L, 5.3L, 6.0L

9308KG95

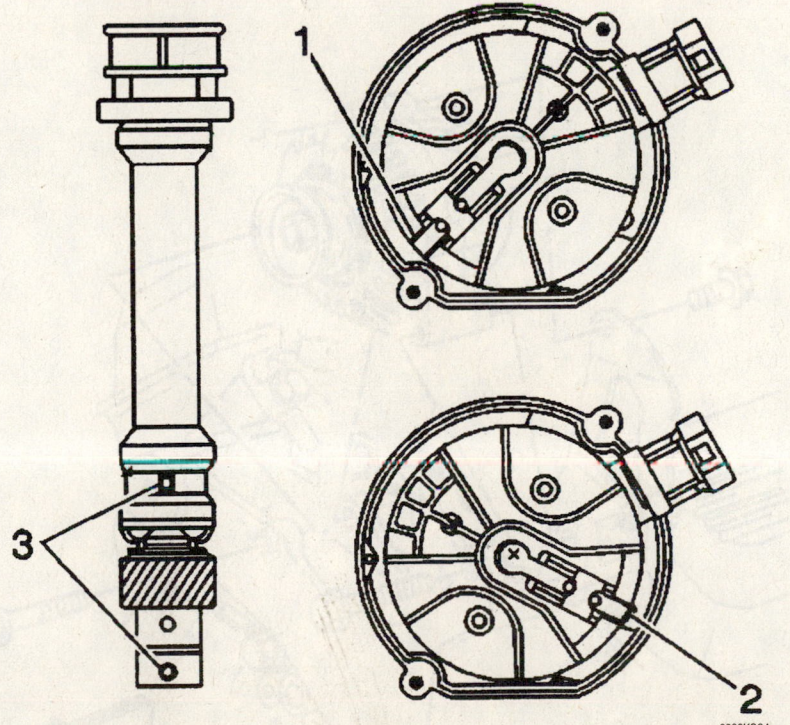

Distributor alignment. 1 is the starting point; 2 is installed; 3 are the shaft alignment marks—4.8L, 5.3L, 6.0L

9308KG94

crankshaft balancer alignment mark must align with the engine front cover tab and the crankshaft balancer alignment mark must align with the engine front cover tab.

2. Align the white paint mark on the bottom stem of the distributor with the pre-drilled indent hole in the bottom of the gear. If the driven gear is installed incorrectly, the dimple will be approximately 180 degrees opposite of the rotor segment when it is installed in the distributor.

The OBD II ignition system distributor driven gear and rotor may be installed in multiple positions. In order to avoid mistakes, mark the distributor on the following components in order to ensure the same mounting position upon reassembly:

- The distributor driven gear
- The distributor shaft
- The rotor holes

Installing the driven gear 180 degrees out of alignment, or locating the rotor in the wrong holes, will cause a no-start condition. Premature engine wear or damage may result.

3. Using a long screwdriver, align the oil pump drive shaft to the drive tab of the distributor. Guide the distributor into the engine. Ensure that the spark plug towers are perpendicular to the centerline of the engine.

Once the distributor is fully seated, the rotor segment should be aligned with the pointer cast into the distributor base.

This pointer may have a 6 cast into it, indicating that the distributor is to be used on a 6 cylinder engine or a 8 cast into it, indicating that the distributor is to be used on a 8 cylinder engine.

If the rotor segment does not come within a few degrees of the pointer, the gear mesh between the distributor and the camshaft may be off a tooth or more.

If this is the case, repeat the procedure again in order to achieve proper alignment.

➡**Use the correct fastener in the correct location. Replacement fasteners must be the correct part number for that application. Fasteners requiring replacement or fasteners requiring the use of thread locking compound or sealant are identified in the service procedure. Do not use paints, lubricants, or corrosion inhibitors on fasteners or fastener joint surfaces unless specified. These coatings affect fastener torque and joint clamping force and may damage the fastener. Use the correct tightening sequence and specifications when installing fasteners in**

Timing belt service is covered in Section 4 of this manual

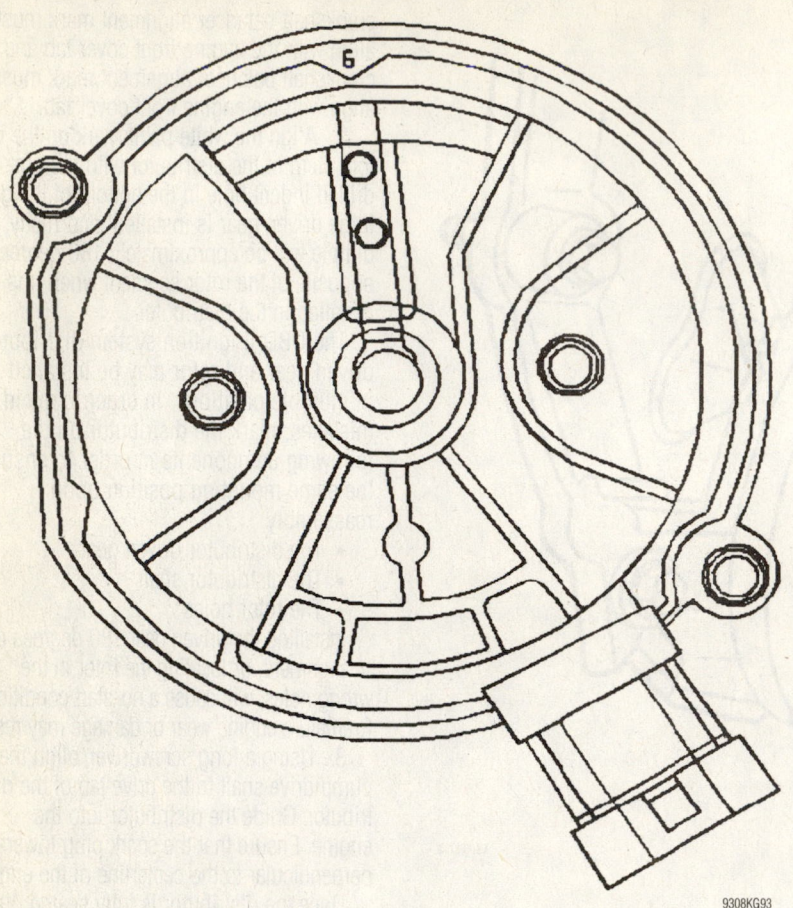

Distributor fully seated—4.8L, 5.3L, 6.0L

order to avoid damage to parts and systems.

4. Install the distributor mounting clamp bolt. Tighten the distributor clamp bolt to 25 Nm (18 ft. lbs.).

5. Install the distributor cap. Install two NEW distributor cap screws. Tighten the screws to 2.4 Nm (21 inch lbs.).

6. Install the electrical connector to the distributor.

7. Install the spark plug wires to the distributor cap.

8. Install the ignition coil wire.

➡ **If the Malfunction Indicator lamp is turned on after installing the distributor, and a DTC P1345 is found, the distributor has been installed incorrectly.**

Alternator

REMOVAL

4.3L, 5.0L, 5.7L and 7.4L Engines

EXCEPT VAN MODELS

1. Before servicing the vehicle, refer to the precautions in the beginning of this section.

2. Remove or disconnect the following:
  • Negative battery cable
  • Wires
  • Accessory belt(s)
  • Mounting bracket, if necessary
  • Alternator

To install:

3. Install or connect the following:
  • Alternator
  • Mounting bracket. Torque bolts to 18 ft lbs. (25 Nm)
  • Mounting bolts. Torque the right mounting bolt to 18 ft lbs. (25 Nm) and left bolt to 37 ft lbs. (50 Nm)
  • Accessory belt(s)
  • Wires. Torque the battery feed wire to 71 inch lbs. (8 Nm)
  • Negative battery cable

VAN MODELS

1. Before servicing the vehicle, refer to the precautions in the beginning of this section.

2. Remove or disconnect the following:
  • Negative battery cable
  • Coolant reservoir
  • Surge tank, diesel only
  • Air cleaner
  • Upper fan shroud
  • Accessory belt(s)
  • Heater hose pipe

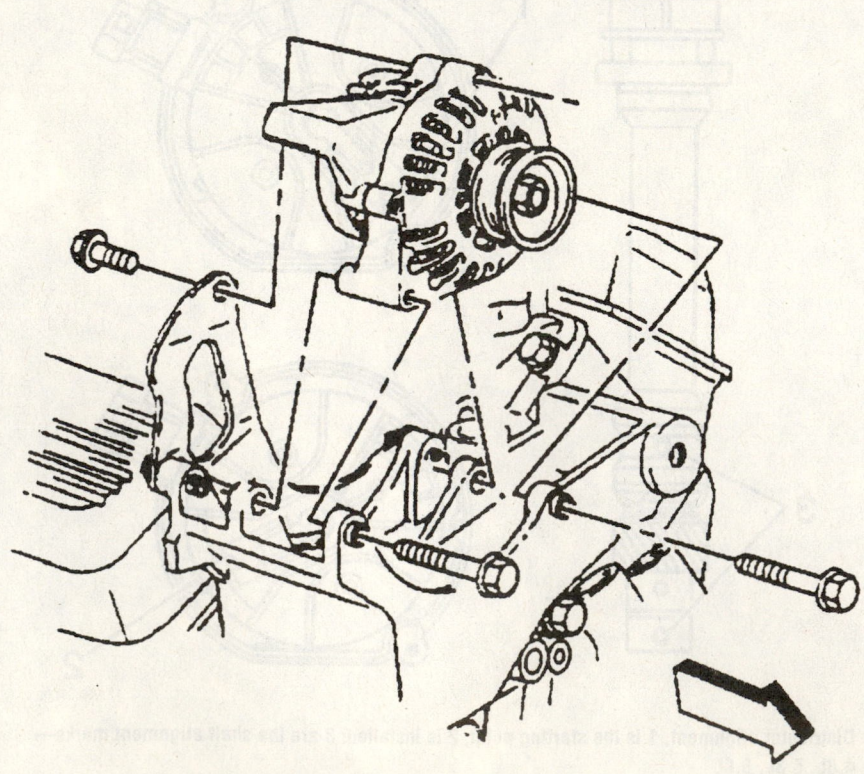

Exploded view of the alternator mounting on truck module.

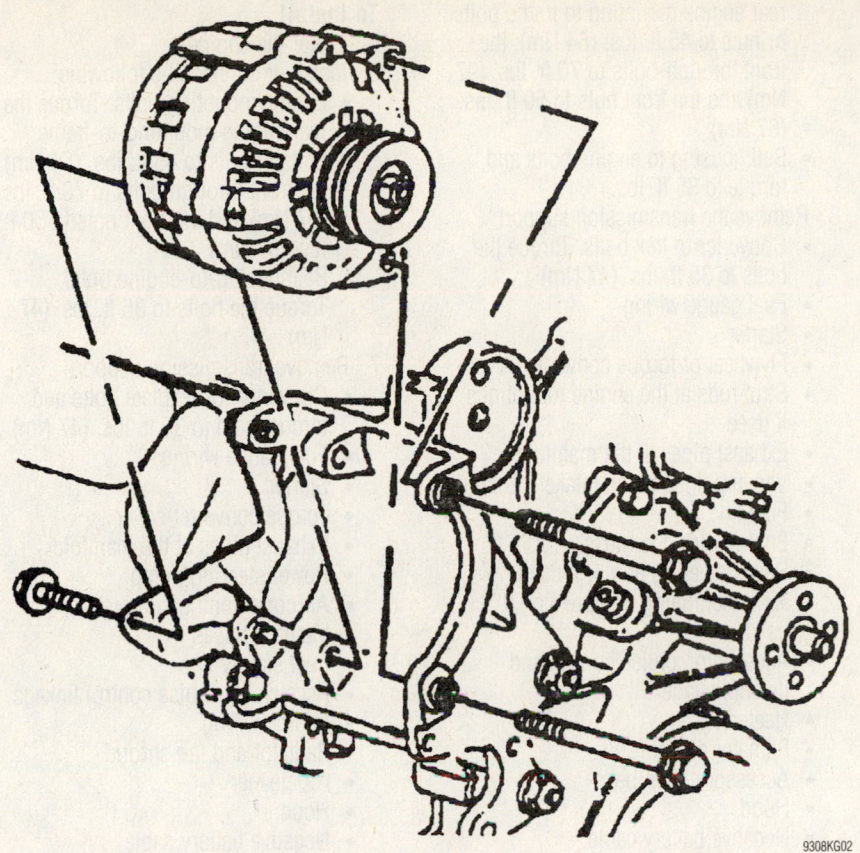

Exploded view of the alternator mounting on van module.

- Oil fill tube from bracket
- Support bracket
- Mounting bracket
- Mounting bolts
- Alternator
- Wires

To install:

3. Install or connect the following:
- Wires. Torque the battery feed wire to 15 ft lbs. (20 Nm)
- Alternator
- Mounting bolts. Torque the front mounting bolt to 37 ft lbs. (50 Nm) And rear bolt to 18 ft lbs. (25 Nm)
- Oil fill tube support bracket
- Oil fill tube to bracket
- Accessory belt(s)
- Upper fan shroud
- Air cleaner
- Coolant reservoir
- Surge tank, diesel only
- Negative battery cable

4.8L, 5.3L, 6.0L

1. Disconnect the negative battery cable.
2. Remove the accessory drive belt.
3. Disconnect the electrical connections from the generator.

4. Remove the generator mounting bolts.
5. Remove the generator.
To install:
6. Install the generator.

➡ **Use the correct fastener in the correct location. Replacement fasteners must be the correct part number for that application. Fasteners requiring replacement or fasteners requiring the use of thread locking compound or sealant are identified in the service procedure. Do not use paints, lubricants, or corrosion inhibitors on fasteners or fastener joint surfaces unless specified. These coatings affect fastener torque and joint clamping force and may damage the fastener. Use the correct tightening sequence and specifications when installing fasteners in order to avoid damage to parts and systems.**

7. Install the generator mounting bolts. Tighten the bolts to 50 Nm (37 ft. lbs.).
8. Connect the electrical connections to the generator. Tighten the B+ nut to 18 Nm (13 ft. lbs.).
9. Install the accessory drive belt.
10. Connect the negative battery cable. Tighten to bolt to 17 Nm (13 ft. lbs.).

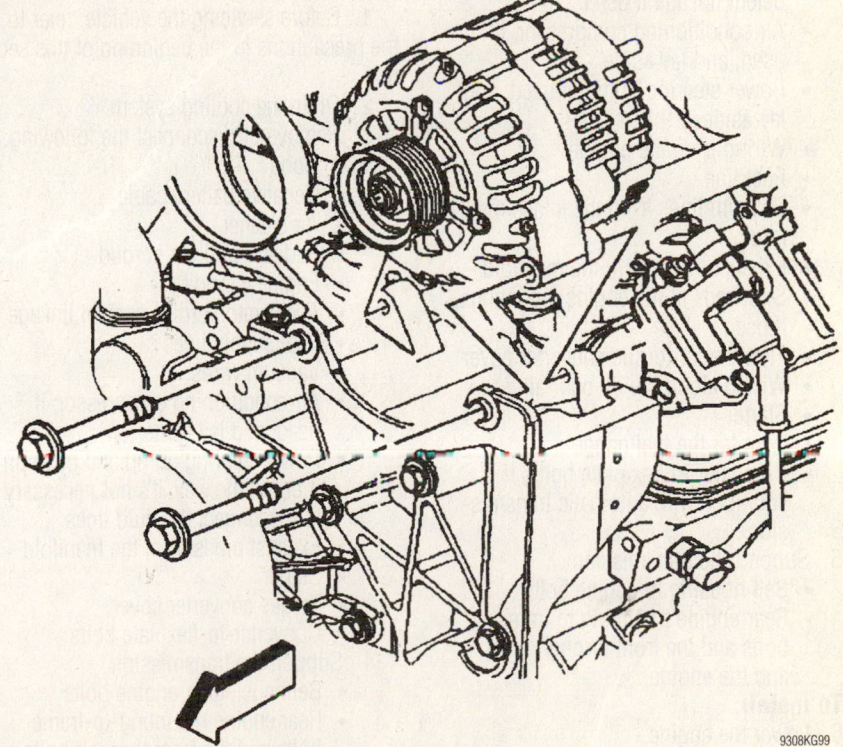

Alternator mounting—4.8L, 5.3L, 6.0L

Ignition Timing

ADJUSTMENT

Always refer to the Vehicle Emissions Control Information label in the engine compartment for base ignition timing specification and adjustment procedures.

Engine Assembly

REMOVAL & INSTALLATION

4.3L (Exc. Silverado and 2000–01 Sierra 15 Series), 5.0L, 5.7L

1. Before servicing the vehicle, refer to the precautions in the beginning of this section.
2. Drain the cooling system.
3. Drain the engine oil.
4. Remove or disconnect the following:
   - Negative battery cable
   - Hood
   - Air cleaner
   - Accessory drive belt
   - Fan
   - Water pump pulley
   - Radiator and shroud
   - Heater hoses at the engine
   - Accelerator, cruise control and detent linkage if used
   - Air conditioning compressor, if used, and lay aside
   - Power steering pump, if used, and lay aside
   - Wiring from the engine
   - Fuel line
   - Vacuum lines from the intake manifold
   - Exhaust pipes from the manifold
   - Strut rods at the engine mountings, if used
   - Flywheel or torque converter cover
   - Wiring along the oil pan rail
   - Starter
   - Wire for the fuel gauge
   - Converter to flex plate bolts, if equipped with automatic transmission
5. Support the transmission
   - Bell housing to engine bolts
   - Rear engine mounting to frame bolts and the front through bolts and the engine.

To install:

6. Lower the engine.
7. Install or connect the following:
   - Engine mounting bolts. Torque the rear engine mounting to frame bolts or nuts to 45 ft. lbs. (54 Nm), the front through-bolts to 70 ft. lbs. (97 Nm) and the front nuts to 50 ft. lbs. (67 Nm)
   - Bell housing to engine bolts and torque to 35 ft. lbs.
8. Remove the transmission support.
   - Converter to flex bolts. Torque the bolts to 35 ft. lbs. (47 Nm)
   - Fuel gauge wiring
   - Starter
   - Flywheel or torque converter cover
   - Strut rods at the engine mountings, if used
   - Exhaust pipes at the manifold
   - Vacuum lines to the intake manifold
   - Fuel line
   - Engine wiring harness
   - Power steering pump, if used
   - Air conditioning compressor, if used
   - Accelerator, cruise control and detent linkage
   - Heater hoses
   - Radiator and shroud
   - Accessory drive belts
   - Hood
   - Negative battery cable
9. Refill coolant and engine oil.

7.4L

1. Before servicing the vehicle, refer to the precautions in the beginning of this section.
2. Drain the cooling system.
3. Remove or disconnect the following:
   - Hood
   - Negative battery cable
   - Air cleaner
   - Radiator and fan shroud
   - Engine wiring
   - Accelerator, cruise control linkage
   - Fuel supply lines
   - Vacuum wires
   - Air conditioning compressor, if used, and lay aside
   - Power steering pump and position it out of the way. It's not necessary to disconnect the fluid lines.
   - Exhaust pipes from the manifold
   - Starter
   - Torque converter cover
   - Converter-to-flexplate bolts
4. Support the transmission
   - Bellhousing-to-engine bolts
   - Rear engine mounting-to-frame bolts and the front through bolts
   - Engine

To install:

5. Lower the engine.
6. Install or connect the following:
   - Engine mounting bolts. Torque the rear engine mounting-to-frame bolts or nuts to 45 ft. lbs. (54 Nm), the front through bolts to 70 ft. lbs. (97 Nm) and the front nuts to 50 ft. lbs. (67 Nm)
   - Bellhousing-to-engine bolts. Torque the bolts to 35 ft. lbs. (47 Nm)
7. Remove transmission support.
   - Converter-to-flexplate bolts and torque them to 35 ft. lbs. (47 Nm)
   - Fuel gauge wiring
   - Starter
   - Torque converter cover
   - Exhaust pipes at the manifold
   - Power steering pump
   - Air conditioning compressor
   - Vacuum hoses
   - Fuel supply line
   - Accelerator, cruise control linkage
   - Engine wiring
   - Radiator and fan shroud
   - Air cleaner
   - Hood
   - Negative battery cable
8. Refill the coolant.

4.3L Silverado and 2000–01 Sierra 15 Series

1. Remove or disconnect the following:
   - Battery negative cable
   - Coolant
   - A/C refrigerant, if equipped
   - Oil pan skid plate
   - Engine shield
   - Starter.
   - Transmission cover
   - Bolt holding the bracket for the starter cables and transmission cooler lines, if equipped
   - Nuts at the catalytic converter pipe
   - Exhaust pipes from the exhaust manifolds
   - Bolts holding the brackets to the oil pan for both battery cables
   - Crankshaft position sensor electrical connector and remove the harness from the retainer
   - Low oil level sensor electrical connector and remove the wire harness from the retainer.
   - Bolt holding the battery negative cable and a ground cable to the engine

- Torque converter to flywheel bolts, if equipped, through the starter opening
- Engine to transmission bolts

2. Move the hood hinge bolts to hold the hood in the service position.

3. Remove or disconnect the following:
- PCV hose from the air cleaner outlet duct
- Air cleaner outlet duct from the throttle body and the air cleaner assembly
- Fan shroud
- Drive belt
- Engine cooling fan
- Radiator inlet hose from the engine
- Radiator outlet hose from the engine

✳✳ CAUTION

In order to avoid possible injury or vehicle damage, always replace the accelerator control cable with a NEW cable whenever you remove the engine from the vehicle.

✳✳ WARNING

In order to avoid cruise control cable damage, position the cable out of the way while you remove or install the engine.

- Accelerator control cable
- Cruise control cable from the throttle body and the bracket on the throttle body and intake manifold, if equipped
- Engine wiring harness and clip from the accelerator control cable bracket
- Accelerator control cable bracket from the throttle body
- A/C hoses from the compressor and the accumulator, if equipped
- Secondary air injection (AIR) crossover pipe from the AIR pipe assemblies

➡**Remove the AIR pipes before engine removal. The AIR pipes can break or damage easily causing erratic engine operation.**

- AIR pipe assemblies from the left exhaust manifold, if equipped
- AIR pipe assembly from the AIR pump. Remove the AIR pipe assembly from the right exhaust manifold, if equipped.

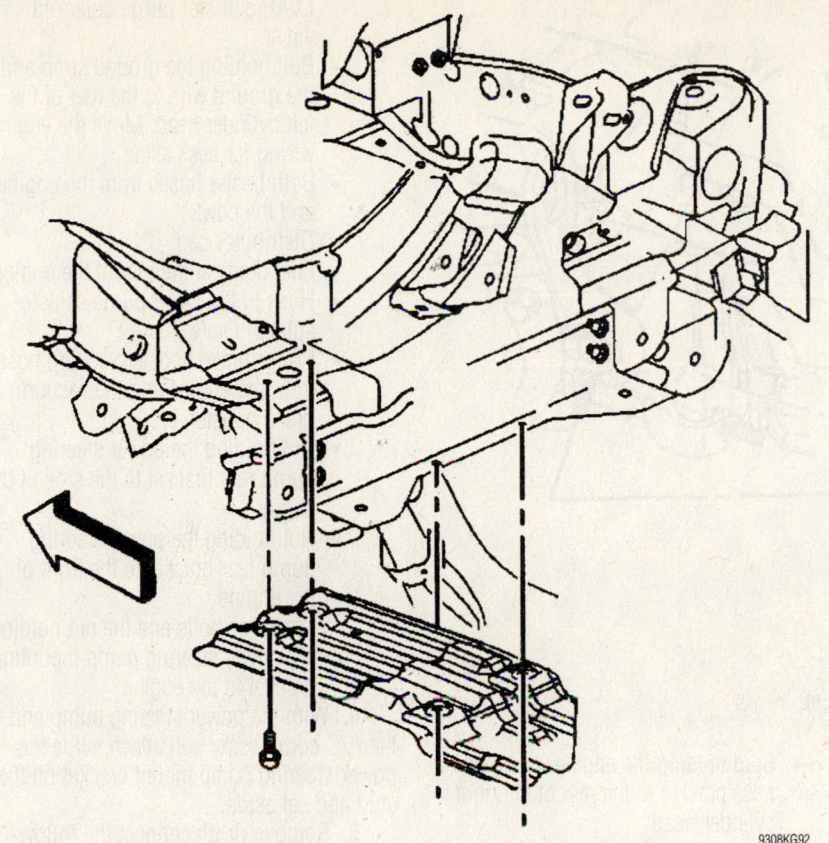

Engine shield removal—4.8L, 5.3L, 6.0L

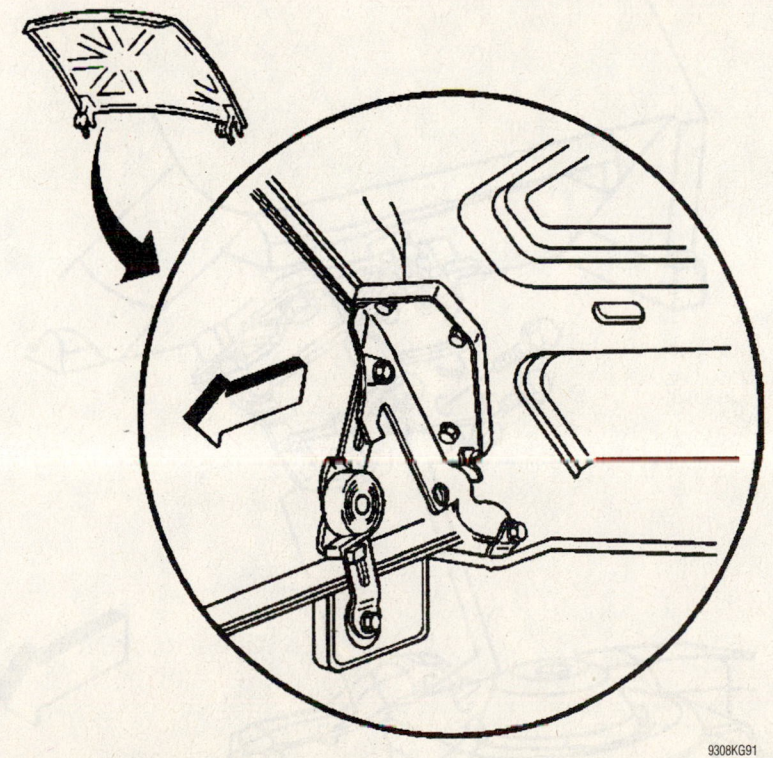

Hood in the service position—4.8L, 5.3L, 6.0L

Refer to Section 1 for engine rebuilding specifications

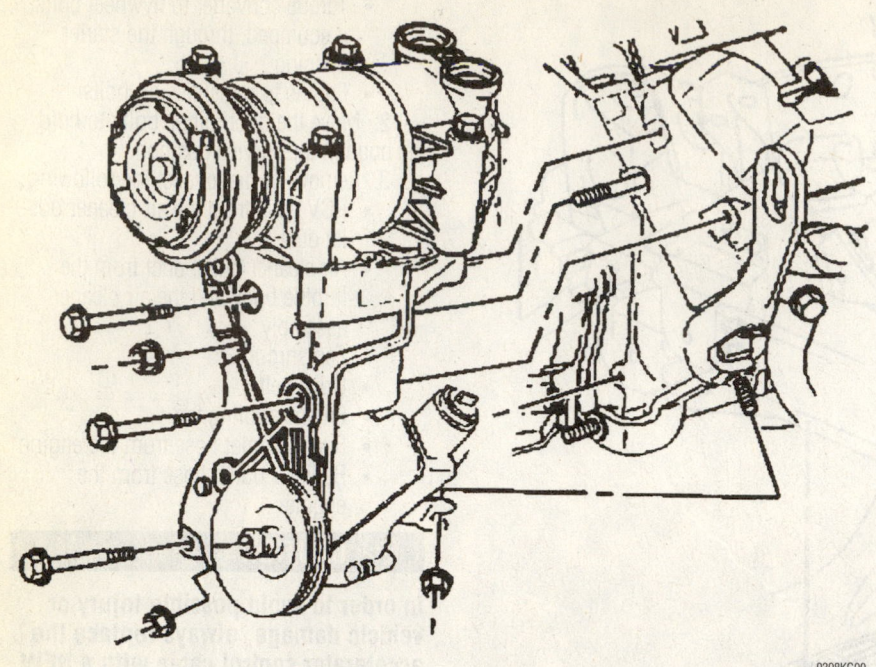

Power steering mount bracket removal—4.8L, 5.3L, 6.0L

- The A/C pressure switch, if equipped
- The A/C compressor clutch, if equipped
- The exhaust gas recirculation (EGR) valve
- The generator battery positive cable
- The fuel meter body assembly
- The idle air control (IAC) motor
- The throttle position (TP) sensor
- The engine coolant temperature (ECT) sensor
- The EVAP canister purge solenoid valve
- The manifold absolute pressure (MAP) sensor
- The ignition control module (ICM)
- The ignition coil
- The engine oil pressure gauge sensor
- The distributor
- The knock sensor (KS)
- Nuts holding the bracket for the engine wiring harness to the intake manifold studs
- Bolt holding the engine wiring harness clip to the battery positive cable junction block bracket
- Bracket for the battery positive cable junction block from the power steering pump mounting bracket
- Battery positive and negative cables
- Nut holding the ground wire to the stud at the rear of the right cylinder head

- Stud holding the engine wiring harness bracket to the rear of the right cylinder head
- Nut holding the engine wiring harness bracket to the stud for the

EVAP canister purge solenoid valve
- Bolt holding the ground strap and the ground wire to the rear of the left cylinder head. Move the engine wiring harness aside.
- Both heater hoses from the engine and the cowl
- Distributor cap
- Fuel pipes at the rear of the engine
- Hose to the EVAP purge canister solenoid valve
- Power brake booster vacuum hose from the engine and the vacuum brake booster
- Nut holding the power steering pump rear bracket to the side of the engine
- Nut holding the power steering pump rear bracket to the front of the engine
- The three bolts and the nut holding the power steering pump mounting bracket to the engine

4. With the power steering pump and the A/C compressor still attach, slide the power steering pump mount bracket off the stud and set aside.

5. Remove or disconnect the following:

- Water outlet

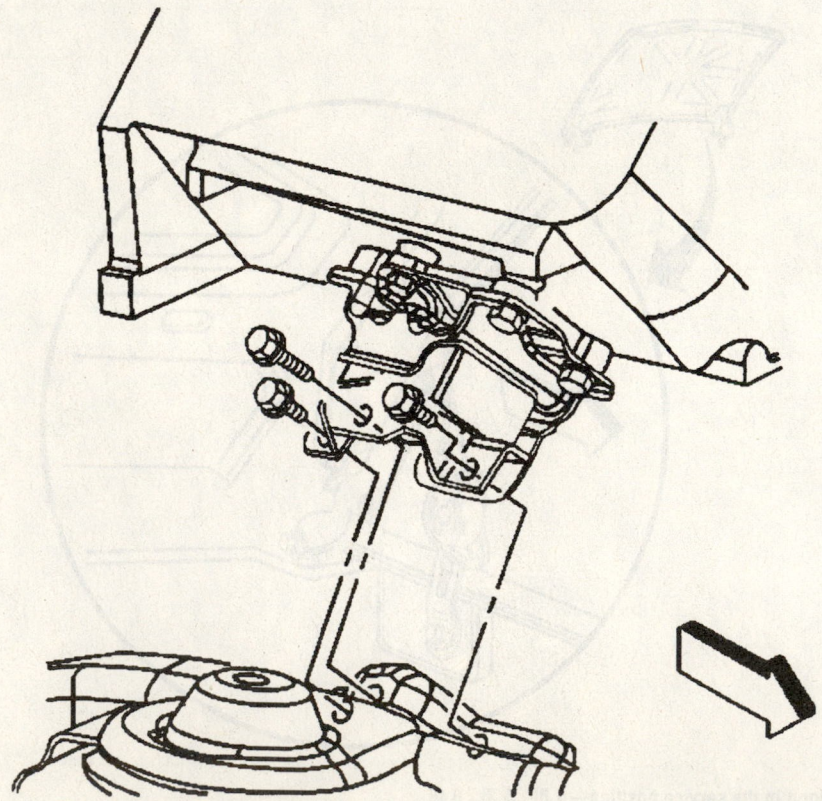

Engine mount disconnect—4.8L, 5.3L, 6.0L

- EGR valve inlet pipe from the intake and exhaust manifold

➡ **Use the correct fastener in the correct location. Replacement fasteners must be the correct part number for that application. Fasteners requiring replacement or fasteners requiring the use of thread locking compound or sealant are identified in the service procedure. Do not use paints, lubricants, or corrosion inhibitors on fasteners or fastener joint surfaces unless specified. These coatings affect fastener torque and joint clamping force and may damage the fastener. Use the correct tightening sequence and specifications when installing fasteners in order to avoid damage to parts and systems.**

6. Attach the engine crane to the left front and right rear intake manifold mounting bolts.

7. Remove the engine motor mount to frame bracket bolts.

8. Support the transmission with a suitable jack.

9. Remove the engine.

To install:

10. Install or connect the following:
    - Engine in the vehicle
    - Engine mount to frame bracket bolts. Tighten the bolts to 65 Nm (50 ft. lbs.).

11. Remove the lifting device. Apply thread lock GM P/N 12345382 or equivalent to the threads of the lower intake manifold bolts. Install the intake manifold bolts.
    a. Tighten the bolts the first pass to 3 Nm (27 inch lbs.).
    b. Tighten the bolts the second pass to 12 Nm (106 inch lbs.).
    c. Tighten the bolts the final pass to 15 Nm (11 ft. lbs.).

12. Loosely install one transmission to engine bolt. Remove the support jack from under the transmission.

13. Install the EGR valve inlet pipe to the intake and the exhaust manifold.
    a. Tighten the EGR valve inlet pipe intake nut to 25 Nm (18 ft. lbs.).
    b. Tighten the EGR valve inlet pipe exhaust nut to 30 Nm (22 ft. lbs.).
    c. Tighten the EGR valve inlet pipe clamp bolt to 25 Nm (18 ft. lbs.).

14. Install the water outlet.

15. Slide the power steering pump mounting bracket with the power steering pump and the A/C compressor on the stud.

16. Position the power steering pump rear bracket on the studs.

17. Install or connect the following:
    - Power steering pump mounting bracket three bolts and the nut
    - Nut for the power steering pump rear bracket to the front of the engine. Tighten the power steering pump mounting bracket and the power steering pump rear bracket bolts and the nuts to 41 Nm (30 ft. lbs.).
    - Fuel pipes
    - Hose to the EVAP purge canister solenoid valve
    - Vacuum brake booster hose to engine and the vacuum brake booster
    - Distributor cap
    - Both heater hoses to the engine and the cowl
    - AIR pipe assembly with new gaskets to the right exhaust manifold, if equipped. Install the AIR pipe nuts and bracket bolt. Tighten the AIR nuts to 25 Nm (18 ft. lbs.). Tighten the AIR bracket bolt to 10 Nm (88 ft. lbs.).
    - AIR pipe assembly to the AIR pump
    - AIR pipe assembly with new gaskets to the left exhaust manifold, if equipped. Install the AIR pipe nuts and bracket bolt. Tighten the AIR nuts to 25 Nm (18 ft. lbs.). Tighten the AIR bracket bolt to 10 Nm (88 ft. lbs.).
    - AIR crossover pipe to the AIR pipe assemblies
    - Position the engine wiring harness.

18. Connect the following electrical connectors:
    - The A/C pressure switch, if equipped
    - The A/C compressor clutch, if equipped
    - The exhaust gas recirculation (EGR) valve
    - The generator battery positive cable
    - The fuel meter body assembly
    - The idle air control (IAC) motor
    - The throttle position (TP) sensor
    - The engine coolant temperature (ECT) sensor
    - The EVAP canister purge solenoid valve
    - The manifold absolute pressure (MAP) sensor
    - The ignition control module (ICM)
    - The ignition coil

    - The engine oil pressure gauge sensor
    - The distributor
    - The knock sensor (KS)

19. Install the bolt holding the ground strap and the ground wire to the rear of the left cylinder head. Tighten the ground strap and ground wire bolt to 16 Nm (12 ft. lbs.).

20. Position the engine wiring harness bracket on the EVAP purge canister solenoid valve stud and install the nut.

21. Install the stud holding the wire harness bracket to the rear of the right cylinder head. Tighten the nut on the EVAP solenoid to 9 Nm (80 inch lbs.). Tighten the stud at rear of the cylinder head to 25 Nm (18 ft. lbs.).

22. Install the nut holding the ground wire on the stud at the rear of the right cylinder head. Tighten the ground wire nut to 16 Nm (12 ft. lbs.).

23. Position the battery positive and negative cables. Do not connect the negative battery cable to the battery.

24. Install or connect the following:
    - Battery positive cable junction block bracket and bolt to the power steering pump mounting bracket. Tighten the junction block bracket bolt to 25 Nm (18 ft. lbs.).
    - Bolt holding the engine wiring harness bracket to battery positive cable junction block bracket.
    - Engine wiring harness bracket on the intake manifold studs and install the nuts. Tighten the wiring harness bracket nuts to 12 Nm (106 inch lbs.). Tighten the wiring harness bracket bolt to 9 Nm (80 ft. lbs.).
    - A/C hoses to the A/C compressor and the accumulator.
    - Accelerator control cable bracket and nuts to the throttle body. Tighten the nuts to 9 Nm (80 inch lbs.).
    - Engine wire harness and clip to the accelerator control cable bracket

✳✳ CAUTION

In order to avoid possible injury or vehicle damage, always replace the accelerator control cable with a NEW cable whenever you remove the engine from the vehicle.

- NEW accelerator control cable
- Cruise control cable to the throttle body and the accelerator control

For engine torque specifications, refer to Section 1 of this manual

cable bracket, if equipped.

- Radiator inlet hose
- Radiator outlet hose
- Engine cooling fan
- Drive belt
- Upper and lower radiator shroud
- Air cleaner outlet duct to the throttle body and the air cleaner assembly
- PCV hose to the air inlet duct

25. Move the hood hinge bolts from the service position to the normal operating position.

26. Raise the vehicle.

27. Install or connect the following:
- Remaining transmission to engine bolts except for the one where the transmission cover mounts
- Torque converter to flywheel
- Transmission cover and bolts. Tighten the transmission cover to oil pan bolt to 12 Nm (106 inch lbs.). Tighten the transmission cover to transmission bolt to 47 Nm (34 ft. lbs.).
- Bolt holding the bracket for the starter cables and the transmission cooler pipes. Tighten the bracket bolt to 9 Nm (80 inch lbs.).
- Bolts holding the positive and negative battery cable brackets to the oil pan. Tighten the bracket bolts to 12 Nm (106 inch lbs.).
- Bolt for the battery negative cable and ground wire to the front of the engine. Tighten the battery negative cable and ground wire bolt to 25 Nm (18 ft. lbs.).
- CKP sensor and install the harness in the retainer
- Low oil level sensor and install the wire harness in the retainer
- Exhaust pipe to the exhaust manifolds and tighten the nuts at the catalytic converter flange
- Starter motor
- Oil pan skid plate. Tighten the oil pan skid plate bolt to 20 Nm (15 ft. lbs.).
- Engine shield

28. Lower the vehicle.
29. Install or connect the following:
30. Battery negative cable
31. Engine oil
32. Coolant
33. Recharge the A/C system.

4.8L, 5.3L and 6.0L

✳✳ CAUTION

Before servicing any electrical component, the ignition key must be in the OFF or LOCK position and all

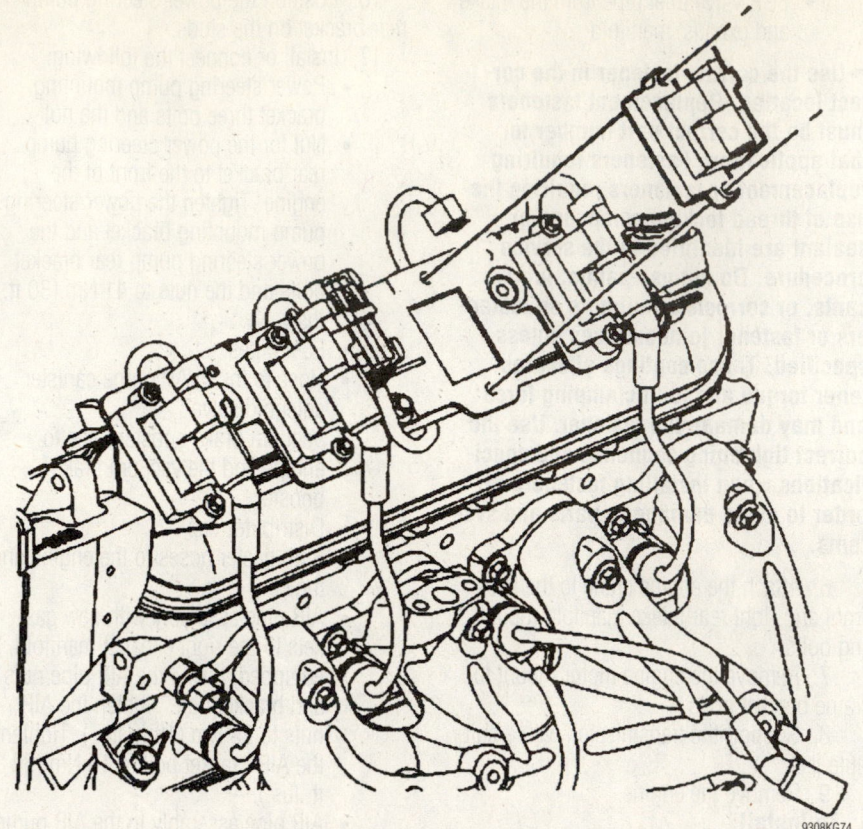

Ignition coil removal—4.8L, 5.3L, 6.0L

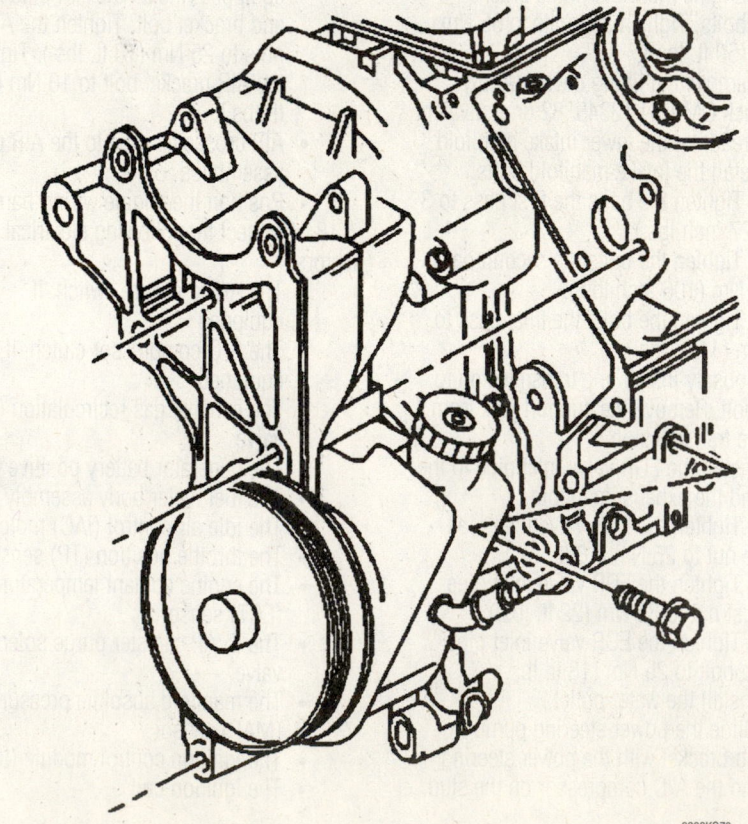

Power steering pump removal—4.8L, 5.3L, 6.0L

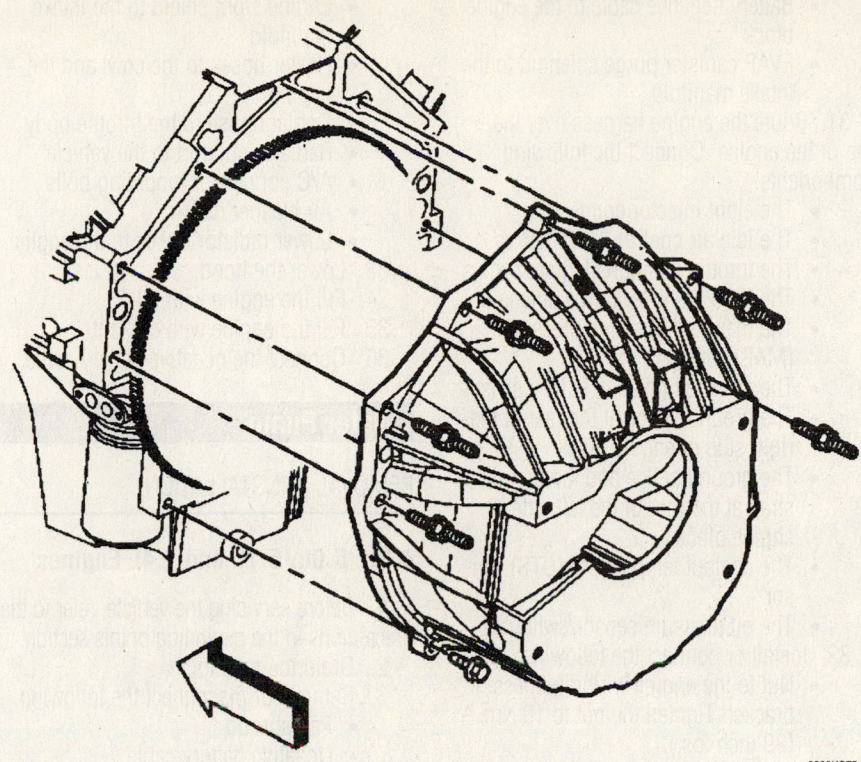

9308KG75

Bellhousing bolt removal—4.8L, 5.3L, 6.0L

electrical loads must be OFF, unless instructed otherwise in these procedures.

1. Remove or disconnect the following:
   - Battery negative cable
   - Coolant
   - A/C refrigerant

2. Raise the hood to the servicing position. Move the hood hinge bolt to hold the hood in the servicing position.

3. Remove or disconnect the following:
   - Upper and the lower radiator hoses from the engine
   - Air cleaner duct from the engine
   - A/C condenser mounting bolts
   - Radiator support from the vehicle
   - A/C compressor
   - Coolant hose from the throttle body
   - Heater hoses from the engine and the cowl
   - Engine sight shield from the intake manifold
   - Accelerator control cable mounting bracket from the intake manifold

✳✳ CAUTION

In order to avoid possible injury or vehicle damage, always replace the accelerator control cable with a NEW cable whenever you remove the engine from the vehicle. In order to avoid cruise control cable damage, position the cable out of the way while you remove or install the engine.

   - Accelerator control cable and the cruise control cable, if equipped, from the throttle shaft

4. Open the large electrical harness retainer. Remove one 10 mm nut in order to release the engine harness from the intake manifold.

5. Disconnect the following electrical connectors:
   - The eight injector connectors
   - The idle air control (IAC) motor
   - The throttle position (TP) sensor
   - The evaporative emissions (EVAP) canister purge solenoid
   - The manifold absolute pressure (MAP) sensor
   - The camshaft position (CMP) sensor
   - The ground splice at the rear of the right side of the block
   - The ground splice and the ground strap at the rear of the left side of the block
   - The coolant temperature (CTS) sensor

   - The oil pressure sensor/switch
   - The electrical connector from intake and disconnect from harness
   - Junction block bracket from alternator bracket

6. Set the electrical harness aside.

7. Remove or disconnect the following:
   - EVAP canister purge solenoid vent tube from the solenoid by squeezing the retainer, then release the tube from the solenoid
   - Battery negative cable from the engine block
   - Drive belt
   - Bolts holding the alternator mounting bracket to the cylinder head and block
   - Bolt behind the power steering pump to engine block
   - Alternator mounting bracket. Position the bracket aside.
   - Fuel pipes from the engine

8. Raise the vehicle.

9. Remove or disconnect the following:
   - Steering linkage under body shield, if equipped
   - Engine oil pan under body shield, if equipped
   - Engine oil
   - Starter motor

10. Disconnect the engine wiring harness from the following components:
    - The crankshaft position (CKP) sensor
    - The engine oil level sensor
    - The block heater, if equipped
    - The wiring harness to oil pan
    - Reposition wiring from lower engine area

11. Remove or disconnect the following:
    - Exhaust pipes from the exhaust manifolds
    - Transmission cooler pipe retainer from the right side of the engine block, if equipped
    - Torque converter shield from the engine
    - Torque converter bolts
    - Nut and the transmission oil level indicator tube from the bellhousing stud
    - Lower bellhousing studs from the engine

12. Lower the vehicle.

13. Remove or disconnect the following:
    - Remaining bellhousing bolts
    - Engine electrical harness aside
    - Ignition coil(s)

For complete mechanical specifications, refer to Section 1 of this manual

14. Install an engine crane.

15. Install a floor jack or stands to transmission for support.

16. Remove the engine mount bolts.

➡ **Use care while moving the engine assembly in order to avoid breaking the MAP sensor locating tabs. Broken MAP sensor tabs may result in decreased engine performance.**

17. Remove the engine from the vehicle.

To install:

18. Install or connect the following:
- Engine to the vehicle
- Engine mount bolts
- Upper bellhousing bolts

19. Remove transmission support apparatus.

20. Remove the lifting device.

21. Remove the lift brackets from both cylinder heads.

22. Install the ignition coil(s) and the spark plug wire(s).

23. Route the engine wiring harness to the lower right hand side of the engine.

24. Raise the vehicle.

25. Install or connect the following:
- Remaining bellhousing bolts
- Torque converter bolts
- Torque converter shield
- Transmission oil level indicator tube and nut to bellhousing stud
- A/C compressor
- Transmission cooler pipe retainer to right side of engine block
- Engine exhaust pipes to the exhaust manifolds

26. Reroute wiring to lower engine area and install bolt to oil pan.

27. Connect electrical connectors to the crankshaft position (CKP) sensor, the engine oil level sensor and the block heater, if equipped.

28. Install or connect the following:
- Starter motor
- Engine oil pan under body shield, if equipped
- Steering linkage under body shield

29. Lower the vehicle.

30. Install or connect the following:
- Fuel pipes to the engine
- Alternator mounting bracket to the cylinder head using the nuts and the bolts. Tighten the bolts to 50 Nm (37 ft. lbs.).
- Bolt at the rear of the power steering pump to the engine block. Tighten the bolt to 50 Nm (37 ft. lbs.).
- Alternator to the engine
- Drive belt

- Battery negative cable to the engine block
- EVAP canister purge solenoid to the intake manifold

31. Route the engine harness over the top of the engine. Connect the following components:
- The eight injector connectors
- The idle air control (IAC) motor
- The throttle position (TP) sensor
- The EVAP canister purge solenoid.
- The manifold absolute pressure (MAP) sensor
- The camshaft position (CMP) sensor
- The ground splice at the rear of the right side of engine block
- The ground splice and the ground strap at the rear of the left side of engine block
- The coolant temperature (CTS) sensor
- The oil pressure sensor/switch

32. Install or connect the following:
- Nut to the engine wiring harness bracket. Tighten the nut to 10 Nm (89 inch lbs.).

✵✵ CAUTION

In order to avoid possible injury or vehicle damage, always replace the accelerator control cable with a NEW cable whenever you remove the engine from the vehicle. In order to avoid cruise control cable damage, position the cable out of the way while you remove or install the engine.

- NEW accelerator control cable
- Cruise control cable, if equipped, to the throttle shaft
- Bolts for the accelerator control cable mounting bracket. Tighten the bolts to 10 Nm (89 inch lbs.).

- Engine sight shield to the intake manifold
- Heater hoses to the cowl and the engine
- Coolant hose to the throttle body
- Radiator support in the vehicle
- A/C condenser mounting bolts
- Air cleaner duct
- Lower radiator hoses to the engine

33. Lower the hood.

34. Fill the engine with oil.

35. Fill the engine with coolant.

36. Connect the negative battery cable.

Water Pump

REMOVAL & INSTALLATION

4.3L, 5.0L, 5.7L and 7.4L Engines

1. Before servicing the vehicle, refer to the precautions in the beginning of this section.

2. Drain the radiator.

3. Remove or disconnect the following:
- Fan shroud
- Negative battery cable
- Drive belt(s)
- Alternator and other accessories, if necessary
- Fan, fan clutch and pulley
- Accessory brackets that might interfere with water pump removal
- Lower radiator hose from the water pump inlet
- Heater hose from the nipple on the pump

➡ **On the 7.4L engine, remove the bypass hose.**

- Water pump assembly away from the timing cover

To install:

4. Clean all old gasket material from the timing chain cover.

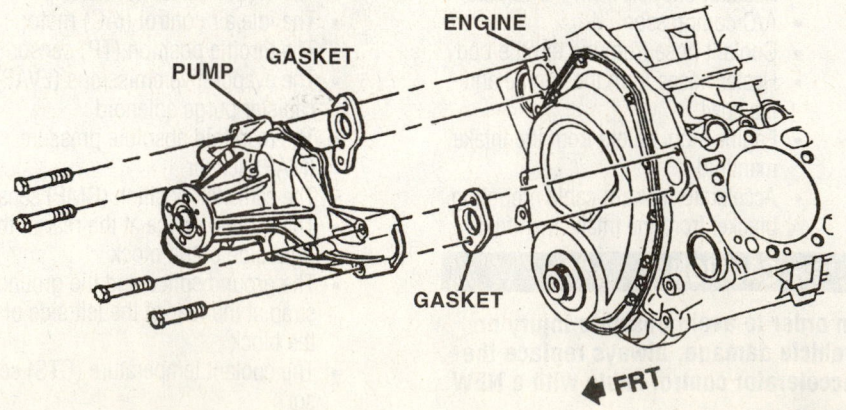

Exploded view of the water pump mounting—4.3L engine

7924KG02

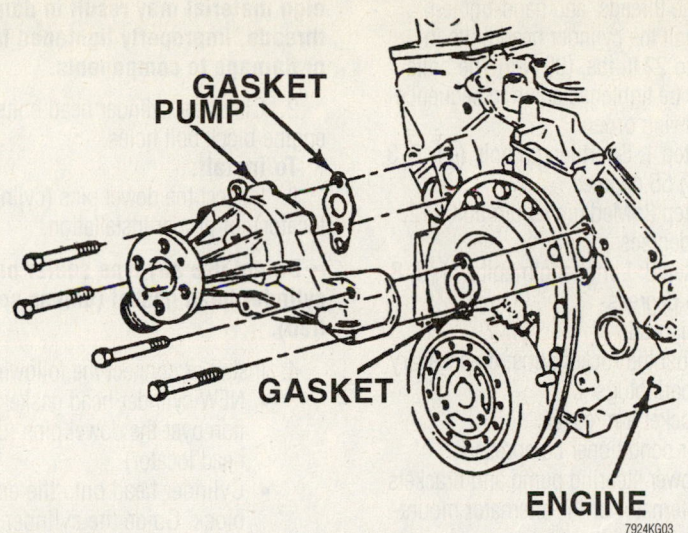

GASKET

PUMP

GASKET

ENGINE

7924KG03

Exploded view of the water pump mounting—5.0L and 5.7L engines

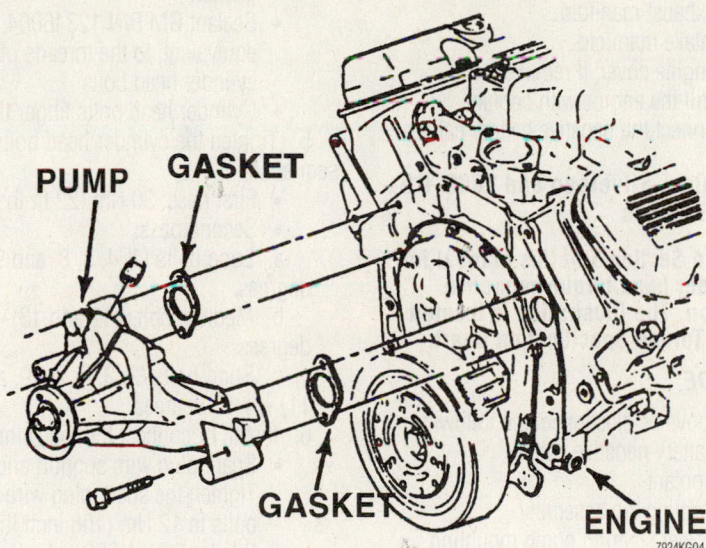

PUMP GASKET

GASKET

GASKET

ENGINE

7924KG04

Exploded view of the water pump mounting—7.4L engine

5. Install or connect the following:

- Pump assembly with a new gasket. Torque the bolts to 30 ft. lbs. (41 Nm)
- Hose between the water pump inlet and the pump
- Heater hose and the bypass hose (7.4L only)
- Fan, fan clutch and pulley
- Alternator and other accessories, if necessary
- Drive belt(s)
- Upper radiator shroud

6. Refill the cooling system.
7. Connect the battery.

4.8L, 5.3L, 6.0L

1. Remove or disconnect the following:
2. Air inlet duct
3. Coolant
4. Inlet radiator hose from the water pump
5. Upper fan shroud
6. Cooling fan and clutch assembly
7. Drive belt
8. Radiator outlet hose from the coolant pump
9. Surge tank hose
10. Heater hose
11. Water pump

To install:

➡ DO NOT use cooling system seal tabs (or similar compounds) unless otherwise instructed. The use of cooling system seal tabs (or similar compounds) may restrict coolant flow through the passages of the cooling system or the engine components. Restricted coolant flow may cause engine overheating and/or damage to the cooling system or the engine components/assembly.

12. Install or connect the following:
13. Water pump. Install the water pump bolts. Tighten the water pump bolts first pass to 15 Nm (11 ft. lbs.); tighten the bolts final pass to 30 Nm (22 ft. lbs.).
14. Water pump drive belt pulley and bolts (if applicable). Tighten the pulley bolts first pass to 10 Nm (89 inch lbs.); tighten the bolts final pass to 25 Nm (18 ft. lbs.).
15. Surge tank hose
16. Heater hose
17. Outlet radiator hose to the coolant pump
18. Drive belt
19. Cooling fan and clutch assembly

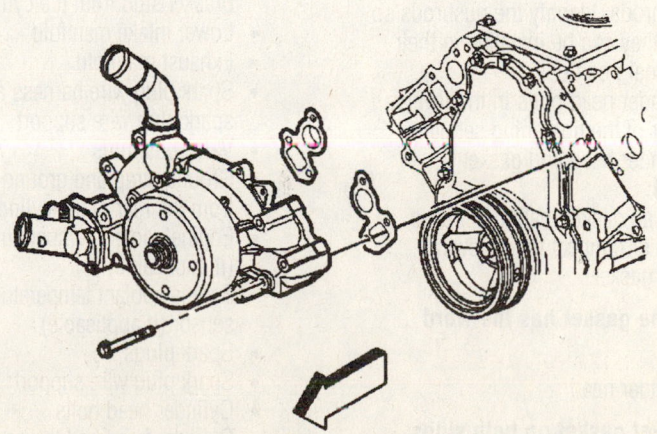

9302KG01

Exploded view of the water pump assembly—4.8L, 5.3L and 6.0L engines

Please refer to Section 8 for electric cooling fan wiring schematics

20. Upper fan shroud
21. Inlet radiator hose to the water pump
22. Air inlet duct
23. Coolant

Cylinder Head

REMOVAL & INSTALLATION

4.3L Engine, Except Silverado and 2000–01 Sierra 15 Series

1. Before servicing the vehicle, refer to the precautions in the beginning of this section.

➡**Refer to Section 1 of this manual for the cylinder head torque sequence illustration. The illustration is located after the Torque Specification Chart.**

2. Drain the coolant.
3. Remove or disconnect the following:
   - Negative battery cable
   - Engine cover, if equipped
   - Intake manifold
   - Exhaust manifold
   - Air pipe at the rear of the right cylinder head, if applicable
   - Alternator mounting bolt at the right cylinder head
   - Alternator, if necessary
   - Power steering pump and brackets from the left cylinder head and lay aside
   - Air conditioner compressor, and lay aside
   - Spark plug wires at their brackets
   - Ground strap from the right side and the coolant sensor wire from the left head
   - Cylinder cover
   - Spark plugs
   - Pushrods. Identify the pushrods so that they can be installed in their original positions.
   - Cylinder head bolts in the reverse order of the tightening sequence
   - Cylinder head and gasket

To install:
4. Clean all gasket mating surfaces.
5. Install or connect the following:
   - New gasket

➡**Be sure the gasket has the word HEAD up.**

   - Cylinder head

➡**Coat a steel gasket on both sides with sealer. If a composition gasket is used, do not use sealer.**

6. Clean the cylinder head bolts, apply sealer to the threads, and hand-tighten.

7. Install the cylinder head bolts in sequence to 22 ft. lbs. (30 Nm) The bolts must, then be tightened again in sequence in the following order:
   a. Step 1: Short length bolt: (11, 7, 3, 2, 6, 10) 55 degrees
   b. Step 2: Medium length bolt: (12, 13) 65 degrees
   c. Step 3: Long length bolts: (1, 4, 8, 5, 9) 75 degrees
   - Pushrods
8. Adjust the rocker arms, if necessary
   - Spark plugs
   - Rocker arm cover
   - Air conditioner compressor
   - Power steering pump and brackets
   - Alternator or the alternator mounting bolt at the cylinder head.
   - Air pipe at the rear of the head if removed
   - Exhaust manifold
   - Intake manifold
   - Engine cover, if removed
9. Refill the engine with coolant.
10. Connect the negative battery cable.

4.3L Engine, Silverado and 2000–01 Sierra 15 Series

➡**Refer to Section 1 of this manual for the cylinder head torque sequence illustration. The illustration is located after the Torque Specification Chart.**

LEFT SIDE

1. Remove or disconnect the following:
   - Battery negative cable
   - Coolant
   - Cooling fan assembly
   - Power steering pump mounting bracket
   - Power steering pump mounting bracket stud from the cylinder head
   - Lower intake manifold
   - Exhaust manifold
   - Spark plug wire harness and the spark plug wire support
   - Valve pushrods
   - Ground strap and ground wire bolt from the rear of the cylinder head
   - Engine coolant temperature sensor (if applicable)
   - Engine coolant temperature gauge sensor (if applicable)
   - Spark plugs
   - Spark plug wire support
   - Cylinder head bolts
   - Cylinder head and the gasket

➡**Clean all dirt, debris, and coolant from the engine block cylinder head bolt holes. Failure to remove all for-**

eign material may result in damaged threads, improperly tightened fasteners or damage to components.

2. Clean the cylinder head bolts and the engine block bolt holes.

To install:
3. Inspect the dowel pins (cylinder head locator) for proper installation.

➡**Do not use any type sealer on the cylinder head gasket (unless specified).**

4. Install or connect the following:
   - NEW cylinder head gasket in position over the dowel pins (cylinder head locator)
   - Cylinder head onto the engine block. Guide the cylinder head carefully into place over the dowel pins and the cylinder head gasket.
   - Sealant GM P/N 12346004, or equivalent, to the threads of the cylinder head bolts
   - Cylinder head bolts finger tight
5. Tighten the cylinder head bolts in sequence:
   - First pass: 30 Nm (22 ft. lbs.).
   - Second pass:
   a. Long bolts (1, 4, 5, 8, and 9)—+ 75 degrees.
   b. Medium bolts (12 and 13)—+ 65 degrees.
   c. Short bolts (2, 3, 6, 7, 10, and 11) — + 55 degrees.
6. Install or connect the following:
   - Spark plug wire support and bolts. Tighten the spark plug wire support bolts to 12 Nm (106 inch lbs.).
   - Spark plugs. USED cylinder head to 15 Nm (11 ft. lbs.); NEW cylinder head to 30 Nm (22 ft. lbs.).
7. If reusing the engine coolant temperature gauge sensor (if applicable), apply sealant GM P/N 12346004 or equivalent to the threads of the engine coolant temperature gauge sensor. Install the engine coolant temperature gauge sensor (if applicable). Tighten the engine coolant temperature gauge sensor to 20 Nm (15 ft. lbs.).
8. Install or connect the following:
   - Ground strap and the ground wire bolt. Tighten the bolt to 16 Nm (12 ft. lbs.).
   - Valve pushrods
   - Lower intake manifold
   - Exhaust manifold
   - Stud for the power steering pump mounting bracket to the cylinder head. Tighten the power steering pump mounting bracket stud to 20

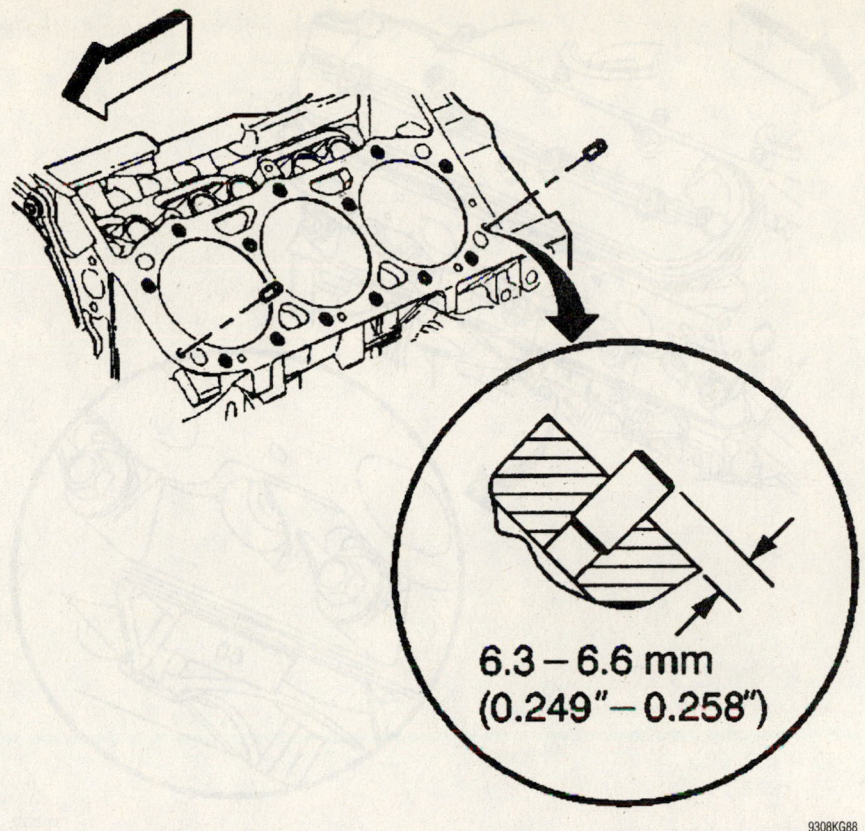

6.3 – 6.6 mm
(0.249" – 0.258")

9308KG88

Dowel pin installation—4.3L

Nm (15 ft. lbs.).
• Power steering pump mounting bracket
• Engine cooling fan assembly
• Coolant
• Battery negative cable

RIGHT SIDE

1. Remove or disconnect the following:
2. Battery negative cable
3. Coolant
4. Engine cooling fan assembly
5. Alternator mounting bracket
6. Alternator mounting bracket stud from the cylinder head
7. Lower intake manifold
8. Exhaust manifold
9. Spark plug wire harness and spark plug wire support
10. Valve pushrods
11. Cylinder head and the gasket
12. Clean the engine block and the cylinder head sealing surfaces.

To install:

13. Inspect the dowel pins (cylinder head locator) for proper installation.

➡**Do not use any type sealer on the cylinder head gasket (unless specified).**

14. Install or connect the following:
15. NEW cylinder head gasket in position over the dowel pins (cylinder head locator)
16. Cylinder head onto the engine block. Guide the cylinder head carefully into place over the dowel pins and the cylinder head gasket.
17. Sealant GM P/N 12346004 or equivalent to the threads of the cylinder head bolts
18. Cylinder head bolts finger tight
19. Tighten the cylinder head bolts in sequence:
   • First pass: 30 Nm (22 ft. lbs.).
   • Second pass:
   a. Long bolts (1, 4, 5, 8, and 9)—+ 75 degrees.
   b. Medium bolts (12 and 13)—+ 65 degrees.
   c. Short bolts (2, 3, 6, 7, 10, and 11)—+ to 55 degrees.
20. Install or connect the following:
21. Spark plug wire support and bolts. Tighten only the rear spark plug wire sup-

port bolt to 12 Nm (106 inch lbs.).
22. Front spark plug wire support bolt. The front spark plug wire support bolt is used to fasten the oil level indicator tube, and will be installed within the oil level indicator tube installation procedure.
23. Spark plugs. Tighten the spark plugs for a USED cylinder head to 15 Nm (11 ft. lbs.); NEW cylinder head to 30 Nm (22 ft. lbs.).
24. Valve pushrods
25. Lower intake manifold
26. Spark plug wire harness and the spark plug wire support. Tighten the support bolts to 12 Nm (106 inch lbs.).
27. Exhaust manifold
28. Stud for the alternator mounting bracket. Tighten the alternator mounting bracket stud to 20 Nm (15 ft. lbs.).
29. Alternator mounting bracket
30. Engine cooling fan assembly
31. Coolant
32. Battery negative cable

4.8L, 5.3L and 6.0L Engines

➡**Refer to Section 1 of this manual for the cylinder head torque sequence illustration. The illustration is located after the Torque Specification Chart.**

RIGHT SIDE

✳✳ CAUTION

Before servicing any electrical component, the ignition key must be in the OFF or LOCK position and all electrical loads must be OFF, unless instructed otherwise in these procedures.

1. Remove or disconnect the following:
   • Negative battery cable
   • Intake manifold
   • Push rods
   • Exhaust manifold(s)
   • Alternator
   • Three bolts holding the alternator mounting bracket to the cylinder head
   • The bolt behind the power steering pump
   • Alternator mounting bracket and set it aside
   • Bolt holding the oil level indicator tube to the right side cylinder head
   • Oil level indicator tube
   • Cylinder head (s) from the engine
   • Spark plugs from the cylinder head

➡The M11 cylinder head bolts are NOT reusable. Install NEW M11 cylinder head bolts during assembly.

2. Remove the cylinder head bolts.

➡After removal, place the cylinder head on two wood blocks to prevent damage.

3. Remove the gasket. Discard the gasket. Discard the M11 cylinder head bolts.

To install:

➡Do not use any type sealant on the cylinder head gasket (unless specified). The cylinder head gaskets must be installed in the proper direction and position.

4. Clean the engine block cylinder head bolt holes (if required). Thread repair tool J 42385-107 may be used to clean the threads of old threadlocking material.

5. Spray cleaner GM P/N 12346139, P/N 12377981, or equivalent into the hole.

6. Clean the cylinder head bolt holes with compressed air.

7. Check the cylinder head locating pins for proper installation.

➡When properly installed, the tab on the right cylinder head gasket will be located right of center or closer to the front of the engine.

8. Install or connect the following:
- NEW right cylinder head gasket onto the locating pins
- Cylinder head onto the locating pins and the gasket.
- NEW M11 cylinder head bolts. Apply a 5 mm (0.20 in) band of threadlock GM P/N 12345382 or equivalent to the threads of the M8 cylinder head bolts.
- M8 cylinder head bolts.

9. Tighten the cylinder head bolts:
a. M11 cylinder head bolts first pass in sequence to 30 Nm (22 ft. lbs.).
b. M11 cylinder head bolts second pass in sequence + 90 degrees.
c. M11 cylinder head bolts (1,2,3,4,5,6,7,8) + 90 degrees
d. M11 cylinder head bolts (9 and 10) + 50 degrees
e. M8 cylinder head bolts (11,12,13,14,15) to 30 Nm (22 ft. lbs.). Begin with the center bolt (11) and alternating side-to-side, work outward tightening all of the bolts.

➡The cylinder head gasket displacement can be verified by markings visible on the underside of the right gasket locating tab. Some 4.8/5.3L head gaskets

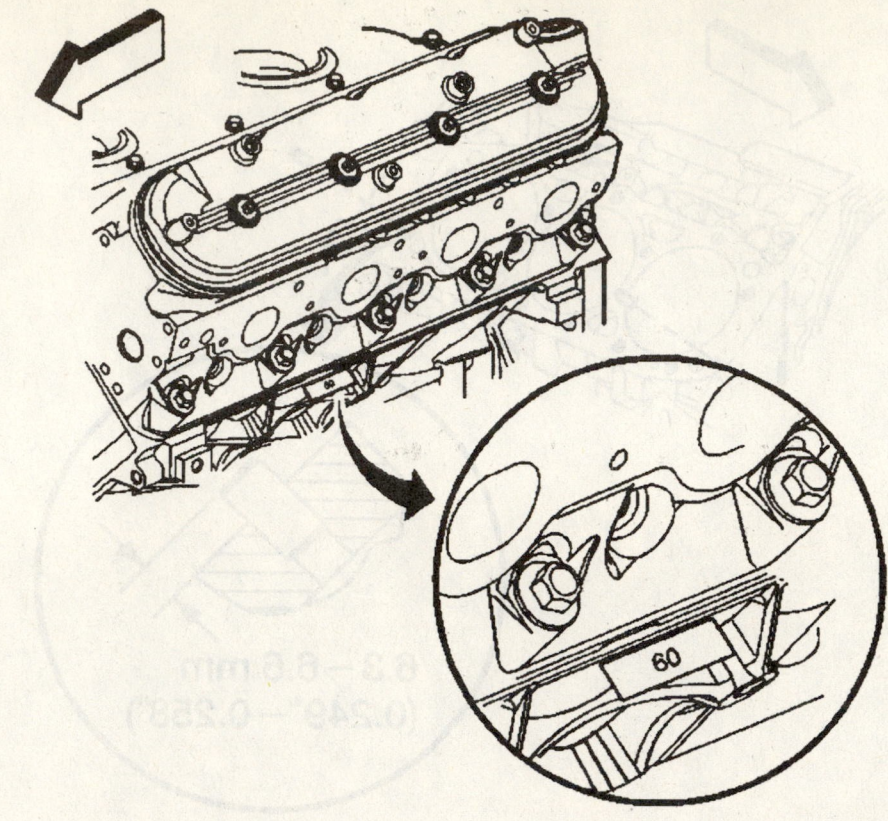

Locating tab—4.8L, 5.3L, 6.0L

9308KG57

may have 53 stamped onto the locating tab. Some 6.0L head gaskets may have 60 stamped onto the locating tab.

10. Install the alternator to the engine.
11. Install the exhaust manifold (s) to the engine.
12. Install the pushrods to the engine.
13. Install the intake manifold to the engine.
14. Connect the negative battery cable.

LEFT SIDE

✳✳ CAUTION

Before servicing any electrical component, the ignition key must be in the OFF or LOCK position and all electrical loads must be OFF, unless instructed otherwise in these procedures.

1. Remove or disconnect the following:
- Negative battery cable
- Intake manifold
- Push rods
- Exhaust manifold(s)
- Alternator
- Three bolts holding the alternator mounting bracket to the cylinder head

- The bolt behind the power steering pump
- Alternator mounting bracket and set it aside
- Bolt holding the oil level indicator tube to the right side cylinder head
- Oil level indicator tube
- Cylinder head (s) from the engine
- Spark plugs from the cylinder head

➡The M11 cylinder head bolts are NOT reusable. Install NEW M11 cylinder head bolts during assembly.

2. Remove the cylinder head bolts.

➡After removal, place the cylinder head on two wood blocks to prevent damage.

3. Remove the gasket. Discard the gasket. Discard the M11 cylinder head bolts.

To install:

➡Do not use any type sealant on the cylinder head gasket (unless specified). The cylinder head gaskets must be installed in the proper direction and position.

4. Clean the engine block cylinder head bolt holes (if required). Thread repair tool J 42385-107 may be used to clean the threads of old threadlocking material.

5. Spray cleaner GM P/N 12346139, P/N 12377981, or equivalent into the hole.

6. Clean the cylinder head bolt holes with compressed air.

7. Check the cylinder head locating pins for proper installation.

➡ **When properly installed, the tab on the left cylinder head gasket will be located left of center or closer to the front of the engine.**

8. Install or connect the following:
- NEW left cylinder head gasket onto the locating pins
- Cylinder head onto the locating pins and the gasket.
- NEW M11 cylinder head bolts. Apply a 5 mm (0.20 in) band of threadlock GM P/N 12345382 or equivalent to the threads of the M8 cylinder head bolts.
- M8 cylinder head bolts.

9. Tighten the cylinder head bolts.

a. M11 cylinder head bolts first pass in sequence to 30 Nm (22 ft. lbs.).

b. M11 cylinder head bolts second pass + 90 degrees

c. M11 cylinder head bolts (1,2,3,4,5,6,7,8) + 90 degrees

d. M11 cylinder head bolts (9 and 10) + 50 degrees

e. M8 cylinder head bolts (11,12,13,14,15) to 30 Nm (22 ft. lbs.). Begin with the center bolt (11) and alternating side-to-side, work outward tightening all of the bolts.

➡ **The cylinder head gasket displacement can be verified by markings visible on the top side of the left gasket locating tab. Some 4.8/5.3L head gaskets may have 53 stamped onto the locating tab. Some 6.0L head gaskets may have 60 stamped onto the locating tab.**

10. Install the alternator mounting bracket using the four bolts. Tighten the mounting bracket to the cylinder head bolts to 50 Nm (37 ft. lbs.).

11. Tighten the bolt at the rear of the power steering pump. Tighten the bolt to 50 Nm (37 ft. lbs.).

12. Install the exhaust manifold (s) to the engine.

13. Install the pushrods to the engine.

14. Install the intake manifold to the engine.

15. Connect the negative battery cable.

5.0L and 5.7L Engines

1. Before servicing the vehicle, refer to the precautions in the beginning of this section.

➡ **Refer to Section 1 of this manual for the cylinder head torque sequence illustration. The illustration is located after the Torque Specification Chart.**

2. Drain the coolant.

3. Remove or disconnect the following:

- Negative battery cable
- Engine cover
- Coolant recovery reservoir, if applicable
- Intake manifold
- Exhaust manifolds and position them out of the way
- Ground strap at the rear of the right AIR pipe, if equipped

4. If the van is equipped with air conditioning, remove the air conditioning compressor and the forward mounting bracket and lay the compressor aside. Do not disconnect any of the refrigerant lines.

- Exhaust Gas Recirculation (EGR) inlet tube

5. On the right side cylinder head, disconnect the fuel pipe, spark plug wires and wiring harness bracket.

- Nut and stud attaching the main accessory bracket to the cylinder head.

➡ **You may have to loosen the remaining bolts and studs in order to remove the head.**

- Coolant sensor wire
- Spark plug wire bracket
- Cylinder head covers
- Spark plugs
- Pushrods, Identify the pushrods so that they can be installed in their original positions.
- Cylinder head bolts in the reverse order of the tightening sequence
- Heads

To install:

6. Inspect the cylinder head and block mating surfaces. Clean all old gasket material.

7. Install or connect the following:
- Cylinder heads using new gaskets. Install the gaskets with the word **HEAD** up.

➡ **Coat a steel gasket on both sides with sealer. If a composition gasket is used, do not use sealer.**

8. Clean the bolts, apply sealer to the threads, and hand-tighten.

9. Install the cylinder head bolts in sequence to 22 ft. lbs. (30 Nm) The bolts must, then be tightened again in sequence in the following order:

a. Step 1: Short length bolt: (3, 4, 7, 8, 11, 12, 15, 16) 55 degrees

b. Step 2: Medium length bolt: (14, 17) 65 degrees

c. Step 3: Long length bolts: (1, 2, 5, 6, 9, 10, 13) 75 degrees

- Pushrods so that they are in their original positions
- Cylinder head covers
- Spark plugs
- Coolant sensor wire
- Spark plug wire bracket
- Main accessory bracket to the cylinder head
- EGR vent tube
- Fuel pipe
- Spark plug wires
- Wiring harness bracket
- Air conditioning compressor and forward mounting bracket
- Ground strap to the rear of the right AIR pipe
- Exhaust manifolds
- Intake manifold
- Coolant recovery reservoir, if removed
- Engine cover.

10. Connect the negative battery cable.

11. Refill the engine with coolant.

7.4L Engines

1. Before servicing the vehicle, refer to the precautions in the beginning of this section.

➡ **Refer to Section 1 of this manual for the cylinder head torque sequence illustration. The illustration is located after the Torque Specification Chart.**

2. Drain the cooling system.

3. Remove or disconnect the following:

4. Install or connect the following:
- Negative battery cable
- Engine cover
- Intake manifold
- Exhaust manifolds
- Alternator and bracket
- Air pump, if equipped
- Air conditioning compressor and the forward mounting bracket. Do not disconnect any of the refrigerant lines.

- Rocker arm cover
- Spark plugs
- Air pipes at the rear of the head, if equipped
- Ground strap at the rear of the head
- Temperature sensor wire
- Pushrods, Identify the pushrods so that they can be installed in their original positions.
- Cylinder head bolts and the heads

To install:

➡ **The cylinder head should be cleaned and inspected for warpage or damage before installation.**

5. Thoroughly clean the mating surfaces of the head and block. Clean the bolt holes thoroughly.

➡ **Coat a steel gasket on both sides with sealer. If a composition gasket is used, do not use sealer.**

6. Install or connect the following:
- Bolts, apply sealer to the threads, and hand-tighten.

7. Tighten the head bolts a little at a time in the sequence in 3 stages,
   a. Step 1: Torque the bolts to 30 ft. lbs. (40 Nm)
   b. Step 2: Then torque the bolts to 60 ft. lbs. (80 Nm)
   c. Step 3: Torque the bolts to 85 ft. lbs. (115 Nm)

8. Install or connect the following:
- New gaskets, with the word **HEAD** up
- Cylinder heads
- Intake and exhaust manifolds
- Pushrods
- Rocker arms
- Temperature sensor wire
- Ground strap at the rear of the head
- AIR pipes at the rear of the head
- Spark plugs
- Rocker arm cover
- Air conditioning compressor and the forward mounting bracket
- AIR pump
- Alternator
- Engine cover

9. Connect the battery cable and refill the cooling system.

Rocker Arms

REMOVAL & INSTALLATION

4.3L, 5.0L and 5.7L Engines

1. Before servicing the vehicle, refer to the precautions in the beginning of this section.

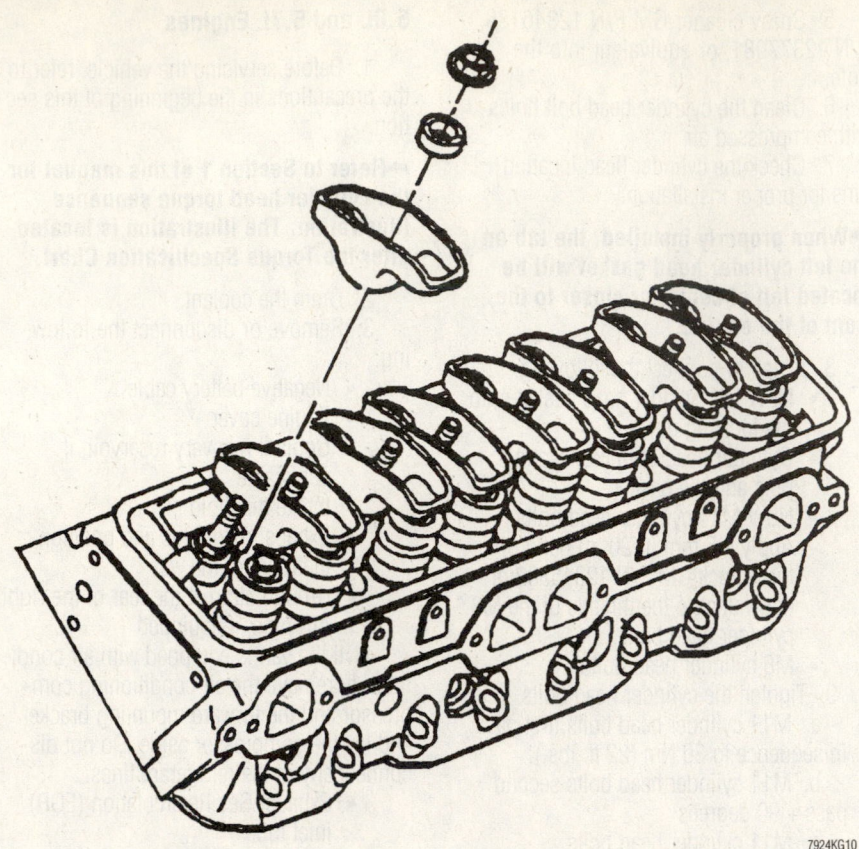

Exploded view to the rocker arm and related components—4.3L, 5.0L and 5.7L engines

2. Remove or disconnect the following:
- Engine cover
- Cylinder head cover.
- Rocker arm nut. If you are only replacing the pushrod, back the nut off until you can swing the rocker out of the way.
- Rocker arms and balls as a unit

➡ **Always remove each set of rocker arms (1 set per cylinder) as a unit.**

- Pushrods and pushrod guides

To install:

3. Install or connect the following:
- Pushrods and their guides. Be sure that they seat properly in each lifter.

4. Position a set of rocker arms (for 1 cylinder) in the proper location.

➡ **Install the rocker arms for each cylinder only when the lifters are off the cam lobe and both valves are closed.**

5. Coat the replacement rocker arm with Molykote® or its equivalent, and the rocker arm and pivot with SAE 90 gear oil, and install the pivots.
- Nuts and tighten alternately
- Engine cover

4.8L, 5.3L and 6.0L

➡ **Do not remove the ignition coils from the valve rocker arm cover unless required. Do not remove the oil fill tube from the cover unless service is required. If the oil fill tube has been removed from the cover, install a NEW tube during assembly.**

On the right side:

1. Remove or disconnect the following:
- Ignition coil bracket bolts from the rocker arm cover (if required)
- Ignition coil and bracket assembly from the cover
- Valve rocker arm cover bolts
- Valve rocker arm cover
- Gasket from the cover. Discard the gasket. The bolt grommets may be reused if not damaged.
- Oil fill cap from the oil fill tube
- Oil fill tube (if required). Discard the oil fill tube.

On the left side:

➡ **Do not remove the Positive Crankcase Ventilation (PCV) valve grommet from the cover unless service is required.**

2. Remove or disconnect the following:

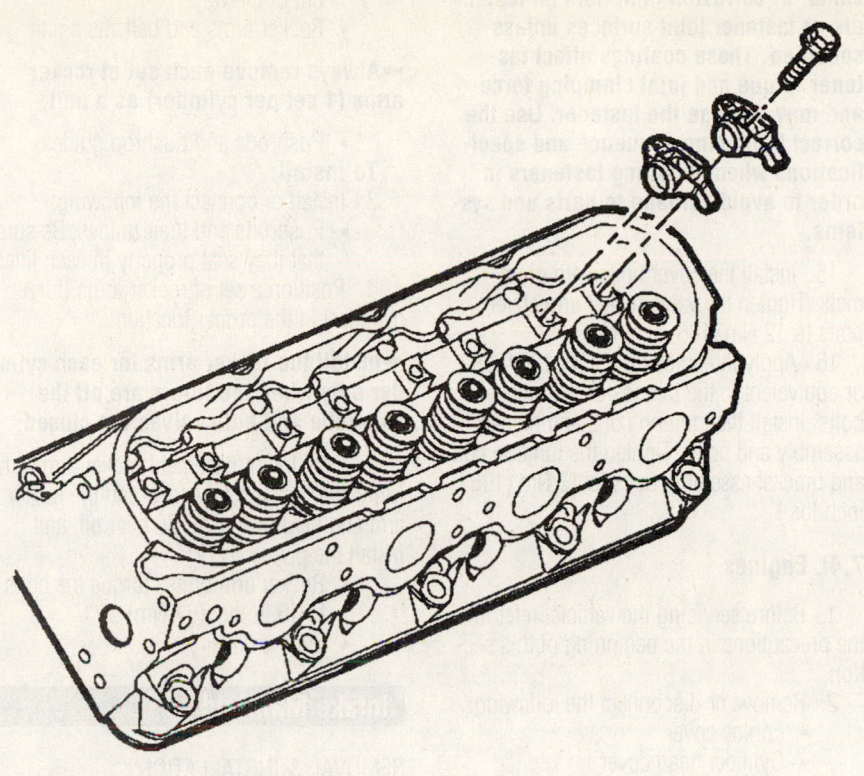

9308KG68

Rocker arm removal—4.8L, 5.3L, 6.0L

- Ignition coil bracket bolts from the rocker arm cover (if required)
- Ignition coil and bracket assembly from the cover
- Valve rocker arm cover bolts
- Valve rocker arm cover
- Gasket from the cover. Discard the gasket. The bolt grommets may be reused if not damaged.
- Valve rocker arm bolts
- Valve rocker arms
- Valve rocker arm pivot support
- Pushrods

To install:

➡**Valve lash is built in. No valve adjustment is required.**

3. Lubricate the valve rocker arms and pushrods with clean engine oil.

4. Lubricate the flange of the valve rocker arm bolts with clean engine oil.

5. Lubricate the flange or washer surface of the bolt that will contact the valve rocker arm.

6. Install or connect the following:
- Valve rocker arm pivot support

➡**Make sure that the pushrods seat properly to the valve lifter sockets.**

- Pushrods

➡**Make sure that the pushrods seat properly to the ends of the rocker arms.**

- Rocker arms and bolts. DO NOT tighten the rocker arm bolts at this time

7. Rotate the crankshaft until number one piston is at top dead center of compression stroke. In this position, cylinder number one rocker arms will be off lobe lift, and the crankshaft sprocket key will be at the 1:30 position. If viewing from the rear of the engine, the additional crankshaft pilot hole (non-threaded) will be in the 10:30 position. The engine firing order is 1, 8, 7, 2, 6, 5, 4, 3. Cylinders 1, 3, 5 and 7 are left bank. Cylinders 2, 4, 6, and 8 are right bank.

➡**Use the correct fastener in the correct location. Replacement fasteners must be the correct part number for that application. Fasteners requiring replacement or fasteners requiring the use of thread locking compound or sealant are identified in the service procedure. Do not use paints, lubricants, or corrosion inhibitors on fasteners or fastener joint surfaces unless**

specified. These coatings affect fastener torque and joint clamping force and may damage the fastener. Use the correct tightening sequence and specifications when installing fasteners in order to avoid damage to parts and systems.

8. With the engine in the number one firing position, tighten the following valve rocker arm bolts:
   a. Tighten exhaust valve rocker arm bolts 1, 2, 7, and 8 to 30 Nm (22 ft. lbs.).
   b. Tighten intake valve rocker arm bolts 1, 3, 4, and 5 to 30 Nm (22 ft. lbs.).

9. Rotate the crankshaft 360 degrees. Tighten the following valve rocker arm bolts:
   a. Tighten exhaust valve rocker arm bolts 3, 4, 5, and 6 to 30 Nm (22 ft. lbs.).
   b. Tighten intake valve rocker arm bolts 2, 6, 7, and 8 to 30 Nm (22 ft. lbs.).

On the right side:

➡**The valve rocker arm cover bolt grommets may be reused. If the oil fill tube has been removed from the valve rocker arm cover, install a NEW oil fill tube during assembly.**

10. Lubricate the O-ring seal of the NEW oil fill tube with clean engine oil.

11. Install or connect the following:
- NEW oil fill tube into the rocker arm cover and rotate the tube clockwise until locked in the proper position
- Oil fill cap into the tube and rotate clockwise until locked in the proper position
- NEW cover gasket into the valve rocker arm cover
- Valve rocker arm cover onto the cylinder head

➡**Use the correct fastener in the correct location. Replacement fasteners must be the correct part number for that application. Fasteners requiring replacement or fasteners requiring the use of thread locking compound or sealant are identified in the service procedure. Do not use paints, lubricants, or corrosion inhibitors on fasteners or fastener joint surfaces unless specified. These coatings affect fastener torque and joint clamping force and may damage the fastener. Use the correct tightening sequence and specifications when installing fasteners in order to avoid damage to parts and systems.**

12. Install the cover bolts with grommets. Tighten the valve rocker arm cover bolts to 12 Nm (106 inch lbs.).

13. Apply threadlock GM P/N 12345382 or equivalent to the threads of the bracket bolts. Install the ignition coil and bracket assembly and bolts. Tighten the ignition coil and bracket assembly studs to 12 Nm (106 inch lbs.).

On the left side:

➡ **DO NOT reuse the valve rocker arm cover gasket. The valve rocker arm cover bolt grommets may be reused. If the vapor vent grommet has been removed from the valve rocker arm cover, install a NEW vapor vent gourmet during assembly.**

14. Install or connect the following:
- NEW cover gasket (1) into the valve rocker arm cover
- Valve rocker arm cover onto the cylinder head

➡ **Use the correct fastener in the correct location. Replacement fasteners must be the correct part number for that application. Fasteners requiring replacement or fasteners requiring the use of thread locking compound or sealant are identified in the service**

procedure. Do not use paints, lubricants, or corrosion inhibitors on fasteners or fastener joint surfaces unless specified. These coatings affect fastener torque and joint clamping force and may damage the fastener. Use the correct tightening sequence and specifications when installing fasteners in order to avoid damage to parts and systems.

15. Install the cover bolts with grommets. Tighten the valve rocker arm cover bolts to 12 Nm (106 inch lbs.).

16. Apply threadlock GM P/N 12345382 or equivalent to the threads of the bracket bolts. Install the ignition coils and bracket assembly and bolts. Tighten the ignition coil and bracket assembly bolts to 12 Nm (106 inch lbs.).

7.4L Engines

1. Before servicing the vehicle, refer to the precautions in the beginning of this section.

2. Remove or disconnect the following:
- Engine cover
- Cylinder head cover
- Rocker arm bolt. If you are only replacing the pushrod, back the nut off until you can swing the rocker out of the way.
- Rocker arms and balls as a unit

➡ **Always remove each set of rocker arms (1 set per cylinder) as a unit.**

- Pushrods and pushrod guides

To install:

3. Install or connect the following:
- Pushrods and their guides, Be sure that they seat properly in each lifter.

4. Position a set of rocker arms (for 1 cylinder) in the proper location.

➡ **Install the rocker arms for each cylinder only when the lifters are off the cam lobe and both valves are closed.**

5. Coat the replacement rocker arm with Molykote® or its equivalent, and the rocker arm and pivot with SAE 90 gear oil, and install the pivots.
- Rocker arm bolts. Torque the bolts to 45 ft. lbs. (61 Nm)
- Engine cover

Intake Manifold

REMOVAL & INSTALLATION

4.3L Engine

1. Before servicing the vehicle, refer to the precautions in the beginning of this section.

➡ **Refer to Section 1 of this manual for the intake manifold torque sequence illustration. The illustration is located after the Torque Specification Chart.**

2. Relieve the fuel system pressure
3. Remove or disconnect the following:
- Negative battery cable
- Air intake duct
- Wiring harness connectors and brackets from the manifold
- Throttle linkage and bracket from the upper manifold
- Cruise control cable, if equipped
- Fuel lines at the rear of the lower intake manifold
- Brake booster vacuum hose from the upper intake manifold
- Ignition coil and bracket
- Purge solenoid and bracket
- Studs and intake manifold attaching bolts, mark for reassembly
- Upper intake manifold
- Distributor housing and rotor, mark for reassembly
- Upper radiator hose from the thermostat housing

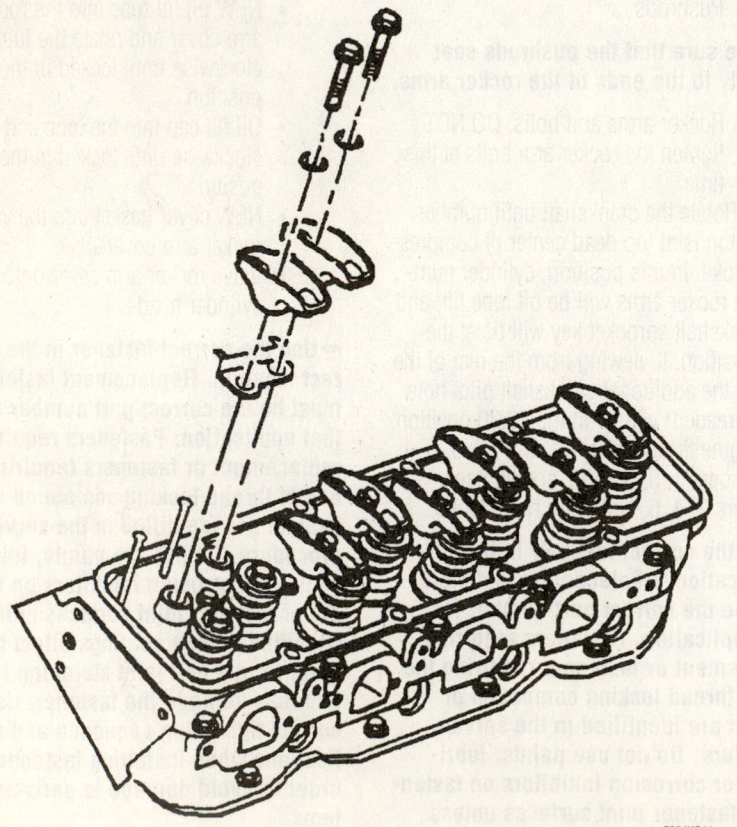

Exploded view of the rocker arms and related components—7.4L engines

7924KG11

- Heater hoses and the bypass hose from the lower intake manifold
- Exhaust Gas Recirculation (EGR) valve
- Transmission dipstick tube, if equipped
- Positive Crankcase Ventilation (PCV) valve and hoses
- Air conditioning compressor and bracket. Without disconnecting position out of the way
- Alternator bracket and bolt next to the thermostat housing. If needed
- Lower intake manifold mounting bolts and the lower manifold

To install:

4. Clean all gasket mating surfaces thoroughly.

5. Position the new gaskets on the cylinder heads with the port blocking plates at the rear and the words **THIS SIDE UP** facing up.

6. Apply a ³⁄₁₆ inch (5mm) bead of RTV to the front and rear sealing surfaces on the engine block. Extend the bead ½ inch (13mm) up each cylinder head to retain the gasket.

7. Carefully position the lower intake manifold onto the engine.

8. Apply GM 1052080 or equivalent sealer to the lower intake manifold bolts

9. Torque the bolts using 3 steps in the sequence shown,

   a. Step 1: Torque the bolt to 24 inch lbs. (3 Nm)

   b. Step 2: Then torque to 108 inch lbs. (12 Nm)

   c. Step 3: And finally torque to 11 ft. lbs. (15 Nm)

10. Install or connect the following:

- Alternator bracket and bolts near the thermostat housing, if removed
- Air conditioning compressor
- PCV valve and hose
- Transmission dipstick tube, if equipped
- EGR valve
- Upper radiator and bypass hose to the thermostat housing.
- Distributor.

11. Position the upper intake manifold gasket on the lower manifold.

❋❋ WARNING

Be careful not to pinch the injector tubes between the upper and lower manifolds.

- Upper intake manifold. Torque the

bolts and studs to 88 inch lbs. (10 Nm)

- Purge control bracket and valve
- Ignition coil
- Brake booster vacuum
- Fuel lines
- Accelerator cable
- Cruise control cable, if equipped
- Wiring harness brackets and connections
- Air intake duct
- Negative battery cable

12. Refill and bleed the cooling system.

13. Pressurize the fuel system and check for leaks.

4.8L, 5.3L and 6.0L Engines

➡ **The intake manifold, throttle body, fuel injection rail, and fuel injectors may be removed as an assembly. If not servicing the individual components, remove the manifold as a complete assembly.**

1. Remove or disconnect the following:

- PCV hose and valve
- MAP sensor, if required
- Engine coolant air bleed clamp and hose from the throttle body

- Accelerator control cable bracket and bolts, if required
- EVAP solenoid, bolt, and isolator
- Intake manifold bolts
- Intake manifold with gaskets
- Intake manifold-to-cylinder head gaskets from the manifold. Discard the intake manifold gaskets.
- Fuel rail with injectors
- Throttle body and gasket

2. Clean the intake manifold in solvent.

3. Dry the intake manifold with compressed air.

4. Inspect the throttle body studs and stud inserts for looseness or damaged threads.

5. Inspect the wire harness stud and stud insert for looseness or damaged threads.

6. Inspect the fuel rail bolt inserts for looseness or damaged threads.

7. Inspect the intake manifold vacuum passages for debris or restrictions.

8. Inspect for damaged or broken vacuum fittings, damaged MAP sensor mounting bore, or broken MAP sensor retaining tabs.

9. Inspect the composite intake manifold assembly for cracks or other damage.

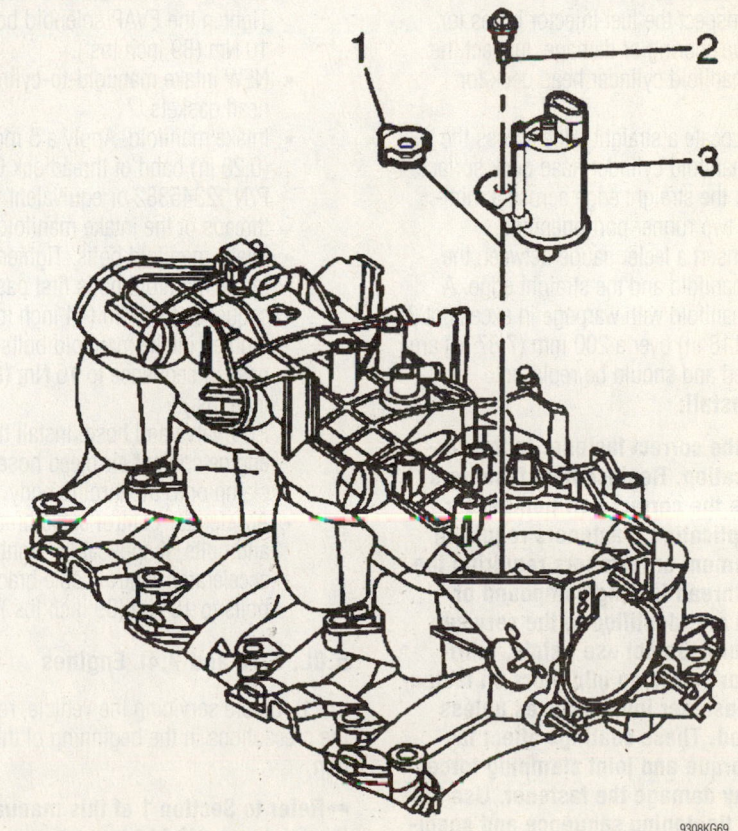

EVAP solenoid removal—4.8L, 5.3L, 6.0L

9308KG69

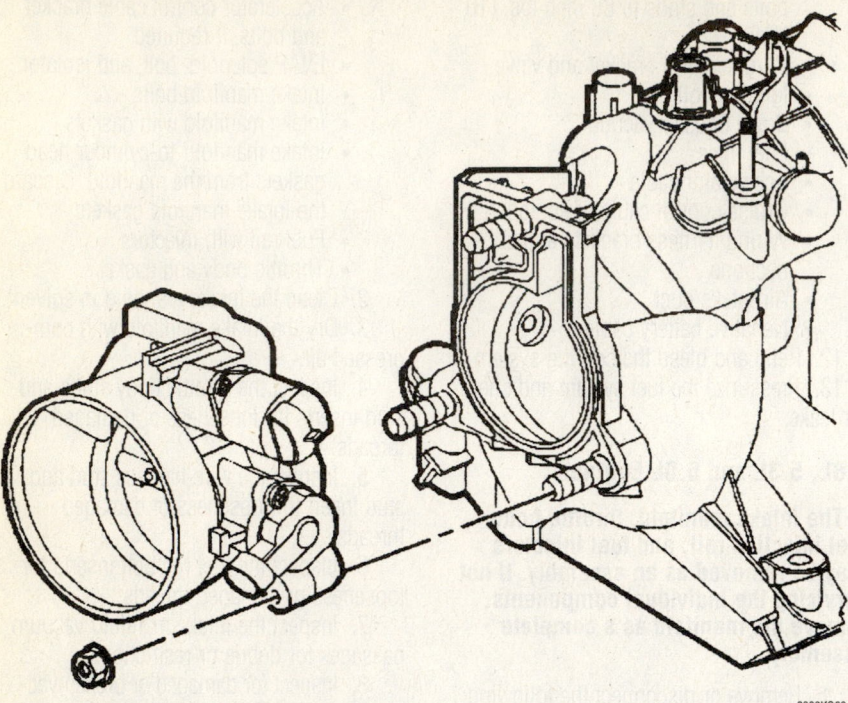

Throttle body removal—4.8L, 5.3L, 6.0L

9308KG63

10. Inspect the areas between the intake runners. Inspect all the gasket sealing surfaces for damage.

11. Inspect the fuel injector bores for excessive scoring or damage. Inspect the intake manifold cylinder head deck for warpage.

12. Locate a straight edge across the intake manifold cylinder head deck surface. Position the straight edge across a minimum of two runner port openings.

13. Insert a feeler gauge between the intake manifold and the straight edge. A intake manifold with warpage in excess of 3 mm (0.118 in) over a 200 mm (7.87 in) area is warped and should be replaced.

To install:

➥**Use the correct fastener in the correct location. Replacement fasteners must be the correct part number for that application. Fasteners requiring replacement or fasteners requiring the use of thread locking compound or sealant are identified in the service procedure. Do not use paints, lubricants, or corrosion inhibitors on fasteners or fastener joint surfaces unless specified. These coatings affect fastener torque and joint clamping force and may damage the fastener. Use the correct tightening sequence and specifications when installing fasteners in order to avoid damage to parts and systems.**

14. Install or connect the following:
- MAP sensor
- EVAP solenoid, bolt, and isolator. Tighten the EVAP solenoid bolt to 10 Nm (89 inch lbs.).
- NEW intake manifold-to-cylinder head gaskets
- Intake manifold. Apply a 5 mm (0.20 in) band of threadlock GM P/N 12345382 or equivalent to the threads of the intake manifold bolts.
- Intake manifold bolts. Tighten intake manifold bolts first pass in sequence to 5 Nm (44 inch lbs.). Tighten intake manifold bolts final pass in sequence to 10 Nm (89 inch lbs.).
- PCV valve and hose. Install the engine coolant air bleed hose and clamp onto the throttle body.
- Accelerator control cable bracket and bolts, if applicable. Tighten the accelerator control cable bracket bolts to 10 Nm (89 inch lbs.).

5.0L, 5.7L and 7.4L Engines

1. Before servicing the vehicle, refer to the precautions in the beginning of this section.

➥**Refer to Section 1 of this manual for the intake manifold torque sequence illustration. The illustration is located after the Torque Specification Chart.**

2. Remove or disconnect the following:
- Negative battery cable
- Engine cover
- Air cleaner intake duct
- Coolant reservoir
- Wiring harness connectors and brackets
- Throttle linkage and bracket from the upper intake manifold
- Cruise control cable, if equipped
- Fuel lines and the bracket from the rear of the intake manifold
- Positive Crankcase Ventilation (PCV) valve and hoses
- Ignition coil and bracket
- Purge solenoid and bracket

➥**Note the location of the manifold bolts and studs before removal for reassembly in their original positions.**

- Intake manifold bolts and studs

➥**Do not disassemble the Central Sequential Fuel Injection (CSFI) unit.**

- Upper intake manifold
3. Clean the old gasket residue from both mating surfaces.
- Distributor
- Upper radiator hose from the thermostat housing
- Heater hose from the lower intake manifold
- Coolant bypass hose
- Exhaust Gas Recirculation (EGR) valve
- Fuel pressure and return lines from the lower intake manifold
- Wiring harnesses and brackets from the lower manifold
- Left side valve cover
- Transmission oil level indicator and tube, if equipped
- EGR tube, clamp and bolt
- Positive Crankcase Ventilation (PCV) valve and hoses
- Air conditioning compressor and bracket, but do not disconnect the lines
4. Loosen the compressor mounting bracket and slide it forward, but do not remove it.
- Power brake vacuum tube
- Lower intake manifold bolts and lower intake manifold

To install:
5. Clean all gasket surfaces completely.
6. Install the intake manifold gaskets with the port blocking plates facing the rear. Factory gaskets should have the words **This Side Up** visible.
7. Apply gasket sealer to the front and rear sealing surfaces of the engine block.

Extend the sealer approximately ½ inch (13mm) onto the heads.

8. Install the lower intake manifold.

9. Apply sealer to the lower intake manifold bolts prior to installation.

10. On the 5.0L and 5.7L engines, install the bolts and torque in sequence as follows:

   a. Step 1: Torque the bolts to 71 inch lbs. (8 Nm)

   b. Step 2: Torque the bolts to 106 inch lbs. (12 Nm)

   c. Step 3: Torque the bolts to 11 ft. lbs. (15 Nm)

11. On the 7.4L engine, torque the bolts to 30 ft. lbs. (40 Nm) in the sequence shown.

12. Install or connect the following:

- Power brake vacuum tube
- PCV valve and hose
- EGR tube, clamp and bolt
- Transmission oil level indicator and tube, if equipped
- Left side valve cover
- Wiring harnesses and brackets to the lower manifold
- Fuel pressure and return lines to the lower intake manifold
- EGR valve
- Coolant bypass hose
- Heater hose to the lower intake manifold
- Upper radiator hose to the thermostat housing
- Air conditioning compressor and bracket
- Distributor
- Upper intake manifold gasket
- Upper intake manifold

❊❊ WARNING

When installing the upper intake manifold be careful not to pinch the injector wires between the upper and lower intake manifolds.

- Upper intake manifold mounting bolts/studs, torque in a crisscross pattern as follows:

   a. Step 1: Torque the bolts/studs to 44 inch lbs. (5 Nm)

   b. Step 2: Torque the bolts/studs to 83 inch lbs. (10 Nm)

- Purge solenoid and bracket
- PCV hose
- Fuel lines and the bracket at the rear of the intake manifold
- Ignition coil and bracket
- Throttle linkage and bracket to the upper intake manifold

- Throttle linkage cable
- Cruise control cable, if equipped
- Wiring harness connectors and brackets
- Air cleaner intake duct
- Coolant recovery reservoir and the engine cover
- Negative battery cable

13. Start the vehicle and verify that there are no leaks.

Exhaust Manifold

REMOVAL & INSTALLATION

4.3L Engines

1. Before servicing the vehicle, refer to the precautions in the beginning of this section.

2. Remove or disconnect the following:
- Negative battery cable
- Engine cover, if equipped
- Exhaust Gas Recirculation (EGR) valve, inlet pipe (left side manifold), if necessary
- Exhaust pipe from the exhaust manifold
- Spark plug wires from the plugs and the retaining clips
- Heat shields

3. If removing the left side manifold:

   a. Step 1: Remove the power steering/alternator rear bracket, if needed.

   b. Step 2: Check for sufficient clearance between the manifold and the intermediate steering shaft. On some models it will be necessary to disconnect the intermediate shaft from the steering gear in order to reposition the shaft for clearance.

4. If removing the right side manifold:

   a. Step 1: Remove air conditioning compressor and bracket, then position the assembly aside, if necessary. Do not disconnect the lines or allow them to become kinked or otherwise damaged.

   b. Step 2: Remove the spark plugs, dipstick tube and wiring, if necessary

5. Unbend the lock tangs.

6. Remove or disconnect the following:
- Exhaust manifold retaining bolts, washers and tab washers
- Exhaust manifold
- Old gaskets and discard

To install:

7. Clean the gasket mounting surfaces.

8. Inspect the exhaust manifold for dis-

tortion, cracks or damage; replace if necessary.

9. Install or connect the following:
- Exhaust manifold to the cylinder using a new gasket. Torque the exhaust manifold-to-cylinder head bolts to 26 ft. lbs. (36 Nm) on the center exhaust tube and to 20 ft. lbs. (28 Nm) on the front and rear exhaust tubes.

➡**Once the bolts are tightened, bend the tabs on the washers back over the heads of all bolts in order to lock them in position.**

10. On the right side install:
- Spark plugs
- Dipstick tube
- Wiring
- Air conditioning compressor and bracket assembly, if unbolted

11. If the left manifold was removed install:

- Intermediate shaft to the steering gear, if unbolted
- Power steering/alternator rear bracket
- Air cleaner along with the heat stove pipe and cold air intake pipe
- Spark plug wires to the retainer clips and plugs
- Exhaust pipe to the manifold
- Engine cover, on van models
- Negative battery cable

4.8L, 5.3L and 6.0L Engines

RIGHT SIDE

➡**Do not remove the Exhaust Gas Recirculation (EGR) valve from the pipe assembly unless service is required.**

1. Remove or disconnect the following:

2. EGR valve, gasket, and bolts

3. EGR pipe bolt from the intake manifold

4. EGR pipe bolts and gasket from the exhaust manifold

5. EGR pipe bolts from the cylinder head

6. EGR pipe assembly. With mild force, pull the EGR pipe from the intake manifold.

7. O-ring seal from the EGR pipe assembly. Discard the exhaust manifold gasket and O-ring seal.

➡**In order to properly remove the exhaust manifold, remove the AIR components when applicable.**

For engine torque specifications, refer to Section 1 of this manual

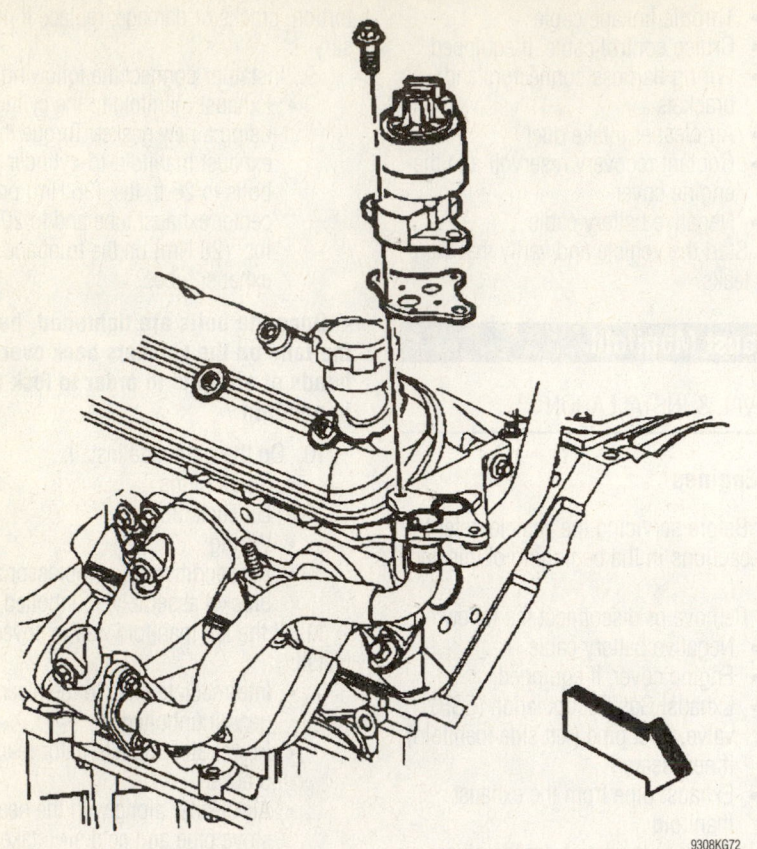

9308KG72

EGR valve removal—4.8L, 5.3L, 6.0L

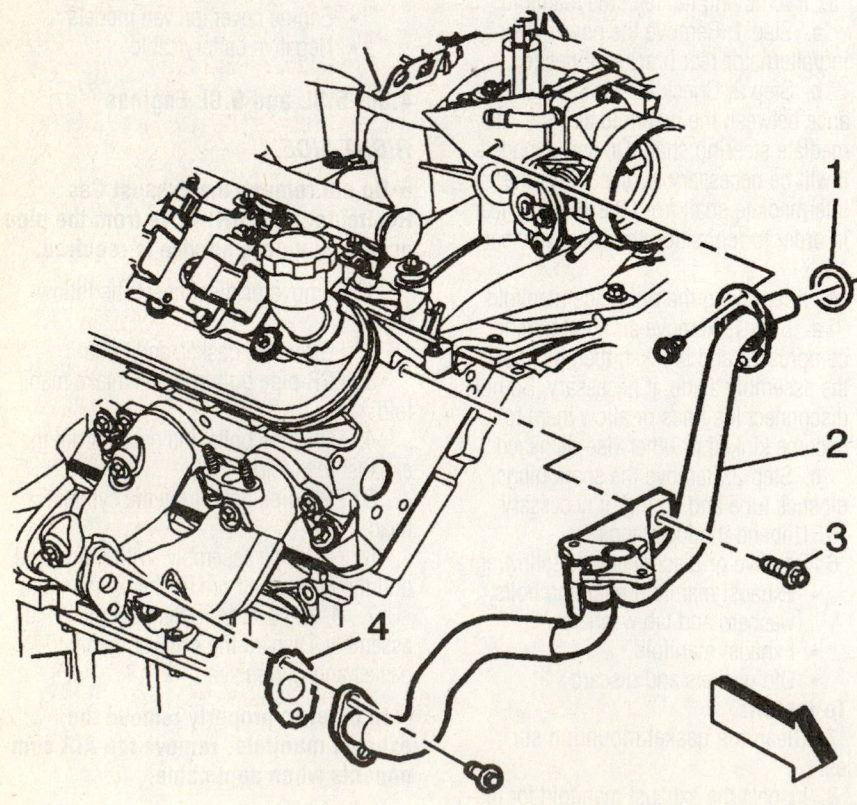

9308KG71

EGR pipe removal—4.8L, 5.3L, 6.0L

Do not remove the check valve from the Air Injection Reaction (AIR) pipe unless service is required.

8. AIR pipe (with check valve), nuts and gasket from the right exhaust manifold.
   • AIR pipe studs from the manifold (if required)
9. Spark plug wires from the spark plugs. Do not remove the spark plug wires from the ignition coils unless required.
10. Exhaust manifold, bolts, and gasket. Discard the gasket.
11. Heat shield and bolts from the manifold, if required

To install:

➡ **Do not reuse the exhaust manifold-to-cylinder head gaskets. Upon installation of the exhaust manifold, install a NEW gasket. A improperly installed gasket or leaking exhaust system may effect On-Board Diagnostics (OBD) II system performance.**

12. Clean the exhaust manifold and heat shield in solvent. Dry the exhaust manifold with compressed air. Inspect the exhaust manifold Air Injection Reaction (AIR) passages for restrictions (if applicable). Inspect the AIR flange studs and threaded bolt holes for damage. Inspect the AIR flange gasket surface for excessive scratches or gouging. Inspect the exhaust manifold-to-cylinder head gasket surface for excessive scratches or gouging. Inspect the right side manifold Exhaust Gas Recirculation (EGR) flange sealing surface for excessive scratches or gouging. Inspect the right side manifold EGR flange bolt hole threads for damage. Inspect for a loose or damaged heat shield (2). Inspect the take down studs for damaged threads.

13. Use a straight edge and a feeler gauge and measure the exhaust manifold cylinder head deck for warpage. An exhaust manifold deck with warpage in excess of 0.25 mm (0.01 in) within the two front or two rear runners or 0.5 mm (0.02 in) overall, may cause an exhaust leak and may effect OBD II system performance. Exhaust manifolds not within specifications must be replaced.

➡ **Do not reuse Exhaust Gas Recirculation (EGR) valve and pipe gaskets or seals during assembly. Install NEW gaskets and O-ring seal.**

14. Install or connect the following:
15. A 5 mm (0.2 in) wide band of threadlock GM P/N 12345493 or equivalent to the threads of the exhaust manifold bolts.
   • Exhaust manifold gasket and exhaust manifold

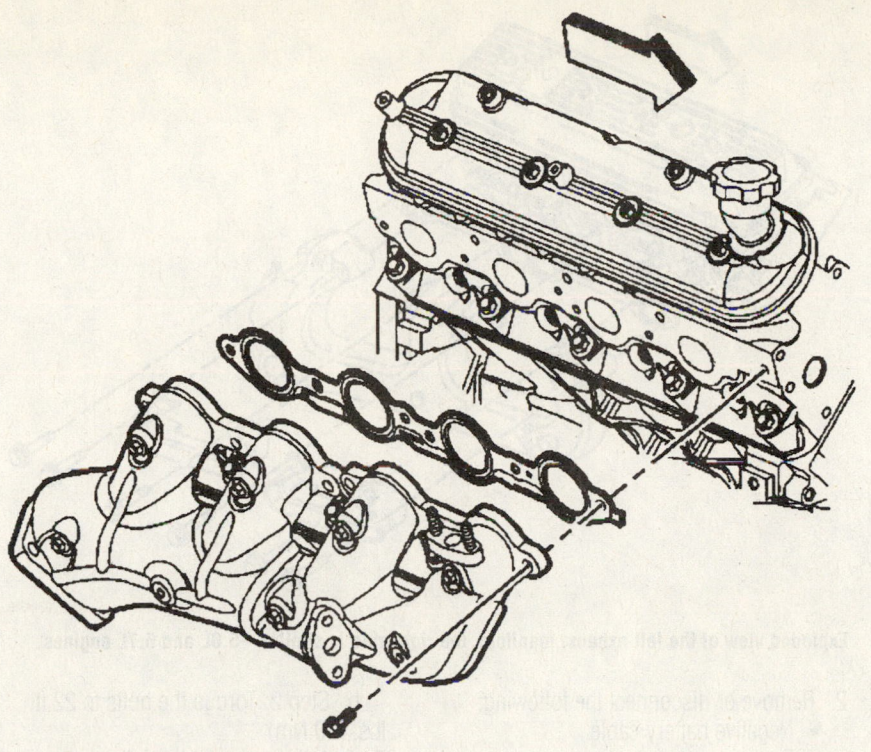

Right exhaust manifold removal—4.8L, 5.3L, 6.0L

➡ **Use the correct fastener in the correct location. Replacement fasteners must be the correct part number for that application. Fasteners requiring replacement or fasteners requiring the use of thread locking compound or sealant are identified in the service procedure. Do not use paints, lubricants, or corrosion inhibitors on fasteners or fastener joint surfaces unless specified. These coatings affect fastener torque and joint clamping force and may damage the fastener. Use the correct tightening sequence and specifications when installing fasteners in order to avoid damage to parts and systems.**

16. Install the exhaust manifold bolts:
    a. Tighten the exhaust manifold bolts first pass to 15 Nm (11 ft. lbs.). Tighten the exhaust manifold bolts beginning with the center two bolts. Alternate from side-to-side, and work toward the outside bolts.
    b. Tighten the exhaust manifold bolts final pass to 30 Nm (22 ft. lbs.). Tighten the exhaust manifold bolts beginning with the center two bolts. Alternate from side-to-side, and work toward the outside bolts.

Using a flat punch, bend over the exposed edge of the exhaust manifold gasket at the front of the right cylinder head.

17. Install or connect the following:
18. Heat shield and bolts. Tighten the heat shield bolts to 9 Nm (80 inch lbs.).
19. AIR pipe studs (if required). Tighten the studs to 5 Nm (45 inch lbs.).
20. AIR pipe (with check valve), NEW gasket and nuts (if required). Tighten the AIR pipe to exhaust manifold nuts to 25 Nm (18 ft. lbs.).
21. AIR hose assembly and clamps.
22. AIR pipe bracket-to-cylinder head bolt. Tighten the AIR pipe bracket bolt to 50 Nm (37 ft. lbs.).
23. Apply a light coating of clean engine oil to a NEW O-ring seal and install the seal onto the EGR pipe. Insert the EGR pipe into the intake manifold.
24. Start the EGR pipe to intake manifold bolt (1). Do not tighten the bolt at this time. Install the EGR pipe to cylinder head bolts. Do not tighten the bolts at this time.
25. Install a NEW EGR pipe exhaust manifold gasket and bolts:
    a. Tighten the EGR pipe to intake manifold bolt to 10 Nm (89 inch lbs.).
    b. Tighten the EGR pipe to cylinder head bolts to 50 Nm (37 ft. lbs.).

c. Tighten the EGR pipe to exhaust manifold bolts to 30 Nm (22 ft. lbs.).
26. Install the EGR valve, a NEW gasket, and bolts. Tighten the EGR valve bolts a first pass to 10 Nm (89 inch lbs.). Tighten the EGR valve bolts a second pass to 25 Nm (18 ft. lbs.).

LEFT SIDE

➡ **In order to properly remove the exhaust manifold, remove the AIR components when applicable.**

1. Remove or disconnect the following:
2. AIR center pipe bolt
3. AIR hose clamps and remove the hose assembly

➡ **Do not remove the check valve from the AIR pipe unless service is required.**

4. AIR pipe (with check valve), nuts and gasket from the left exhaust manifold
5. AIR pipe studs from the manifold (if required)
6. Spark plug wires from the spark plugs. Do not remove the spark plug wires from the ignition coils unless required.
7. Exhaust manifold, bolts, and gasket. Discard the gasket.
8. Heat shield and bolts from the manifold, if required

➡ **Do not reuse the exhaust manifold-to-cylinder head gaskets. Upon installation of the exhaust manifold, install a NEW gasket. An improperly installed gasket or leaking exhaust system may effect On-Board Diagnostics (OBD) II system performance.**

9. Clean the exhaust manifold and heat shield in solvent. Dry the exhaust manifold with compressed air. Inspect the exhaust manifold Air Injection Reaction (AIR) passages for restrictions (if applicable). Inspect the AIR flange studs and threaded bolt holes for damage. Inspect the AIR flange gasket surface for excessive scratches or gouging. Inspect the exhaust manifold-to-cylinder head gasket surface for excessive scratches or gouging. Inspect the right side manifold Exhaust Gas Recirculation (EGR) flange sealing surface for excessive scratches or gouging. Inspect the right side manifold EGR flange bolt hole threads for damage. Inspect for a loose or damaged heat shield. Inspect the take down studs for damaged threads.
10. Use a straight edge and a feeler gauge and measure the exhaust manifold cylinder head deck for warpage. An exhaust manifold deck with warpage in excess of

0.25 mm (0.01 in) within the two front or two rear runners or 0.5 mm (0.02 in) overall, may cause an exhaust leak and may effect OBD II system performance. Exhaust manifolds not within specifications must be replaced.

To install:

➡ **Do not apply sealant to the first three threads of the bolt.**

11. Apply a 5 mm (0.2 in) wide band of threadlock GM P/N 12345493 or equivalent to the threads of the exhaust manifold bolts. Install the exhaust manifold and NEW exhaust manifold gasket.

➡ **Use the correct fastener in the correct location. Replacement fasteners must be the correct part number for that application. Fasteners requiring replacement or fasteners requiring the use of thread locking compound or sealant are identified in the service procedure. Do not use paints, lubricants, or corrosion inhibitors on fasteners or fastener joint surfaces unless specified. These coatings affect fastener torque and joint clamping force and may damage the fastener. Use the correct tightening sequence and specifications when installing fasteners in order to avoid damage to parts and systems.**

12. Install the exhaust manifold bolts:
   a. Tighten the exhaust manifold bolts a first pass to 15 Nm (11 ft. lbs.). Tighten the exhaust manifold bolts beginning with the center two bolts. Alternate from side-to-side, and work toward the outside bolts.
   b. Tighten the exhaust manifold bolts a final pass to 25 Nm (18 ft. lbs.). Tighten the exhaust manifold bolts beginning with the center two bolts. Alternate from side-to-side, and work toward the outside bolts.

13. Using a flat punch, bend over the exposed edge of the exhaust manifold gasket at the rear of the left cylinder head.

14. Install the heat shield (2) and bolts (3). Tighten the heat shield bolts to 9 Nm (80 inch lbs.).

15. Install the Air Injection Reaction (AIR) pipe studs (if required). Tighten the studs to 5 Nm (45 inch lbs.).

16. Install the AIR pipe (with check valve), NEW gasket and nuts (if required). Tighten the AIR pipe to exhaust manifold nuts to 25 Nm (18 ft. lbs.).

5.0L and 5.7L Engines

1. Before servicing the vehicle, refer to the precautions in the beginning of this section.

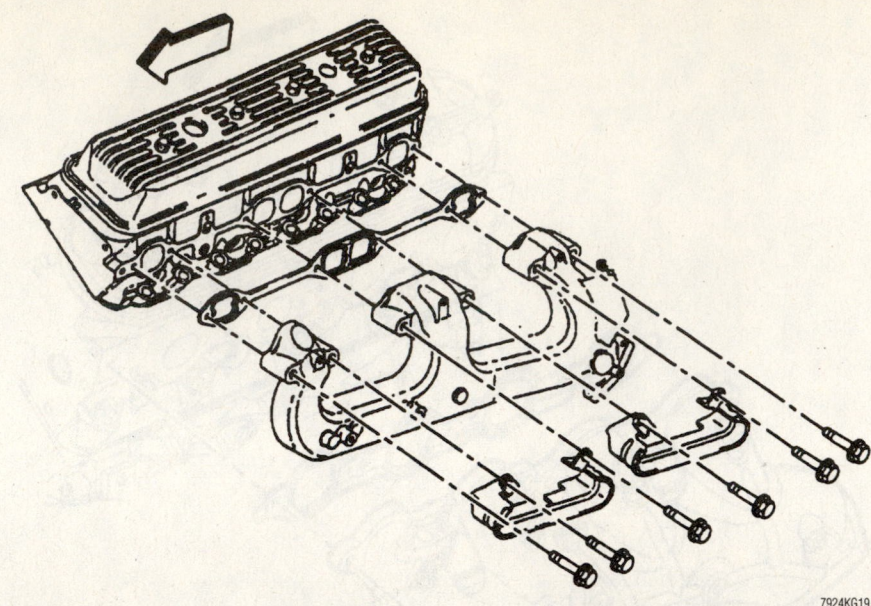

Exploded view of the left exhaust manifold, the right side is similar—5.0L and 5.7L engines

2. Remove or disconnect the following:
   - Negative battery cable
   - Engine cover
   - Air cleaner, if needed
   - Exhaust pipe at the manifold
   - Oxygen (O_2S) sensor wiring, if equipped
   - AIR hose at the check valve
   - Exhaust Gas Recirculation (EGR) valve, inlet pipe
   - Heat stove pipe and the dipstick tube bracket, if working on the right side of the engine
   - Power steering pump rear bracket at the manifold, if removing the left side manifold
   - Loosen the alternator and remove the lower bracket, if necessary
   - Air conditioner compressor rear bracket and the diverter valve and bracket. if needed

➡ **On models with air conditioning, it may be necessary to remove the compressor, do not disconnect the compressor lines.**

   - Manifold bolts and the manifold(s) Some models have lock tabs on the front and rear manifold bolts which must be removed before removing the bolts.

To install:

3. Clean gasket surfaces, and inspect manifold for cracks replace as necessary.

4. Install manifold and torque it in 2 steps.
   a. Step 1: Torque the bolts to 15 ft. lbs. (20 Nm)

   b. Step 2: Torque the bolts to 22 ft. lbs. (30 Nm)

5. Install or connect the following:
   - Alternator, if removed
   - Air conditioning compressor, if removed
   - Diverter, if removed
   - Power steering brackets, if removed
   - Dipstick tube on right side
   - EGR inlet pipe
   - Oxygen sensor connector, if equipped
   - Exhaust pipes
   - Negative battery cable

7.4L Engines

1. Before servicing the vehicle, refer to the precautions in the beginning of this section.

2. Remove or disconnect the following:
   - Negative battery cable
   - Engine cover, on van models
   - Heat stove pipe and the dipstick tube. If removing the right side manifold
   - Exhaust Gas Recirculation (EGR) valve inlet pipe
   - Oxygen (O_2S) sensor wiring, if equipped
   - AIR hose at the check valve, if applicable
   - Spark plugs and wires
   - Exhaust manifold bolts and the spark plug heat shields

➡ **Leave the front nut (left manifold) or rear nut (right manifold) in place for support.**

- Heat shield bolts from the engine mount and bell housing
- Heat shield, if equipped
- Exhaust pipe at the manifold
- Exhaust manifold

To install:

3. Clean the mating surfaces and the retainer threads.

4. Install or connect the following:
- Manifold, spark plug heat shields and nuts. Torque the nuts to 22 ft. lbs. (30 Nm), starting from the center bolts and working towards the outside.
- Exhaust pipe
- Spark plugs and wires
- AIR hose at check valve, if removed
- Oxygen sensor connector, if equipped
- EGR pipe and dipstick tube
- Negative battery cable

5. Run engine and check for leaks.

Camshaft and Valve Lifters

REMOVAL & INSTALLATION

4.3L Engines

1. Before servicing the vehicle, refer to the precautions in the beginning of this section.
2. Properly relieve the fuel system pressure.
3. Drain the engine cooling system.
4. Remove or disconnect the following:
- Negative battery cable
- Radiator
- Cooling fan
- Water pump
- Rocker arm covers from the engine
- Intake manifold assembly
- Rocker arms, pushrods and lifters
- Crankshaft pulley and hub
- Engine front cover

5. Align the timing marks on the crankshaft and camshaft sprockets.
- Camshaft sprocket and timing chain
- Balance shaft drive gear, if equipped
- Camshaft thrust plate

➡**Install the sprocket bolts or longer bolts of the same thread into the end of the camshaft as a handle.**

- Camshaft

To install:

6. Lubricate the camshaft journals with clean engine oil or a suitable pre-lube.

7. Install or connect the following:
- Camshaft
- Camshaft thrust plate
- Balance shaft drive gear, if equipped
- Timing chain and camshaft sprocket
- Engine front cover
- Crankshaft pulley and hub
- Valve lifters
- Pushrods and rocker arms, properly adjust the valve clearance
- Intake manifold assembly
- Rocker arm covers to the engine
- Radiator to the vehicle
- Negative battery cable

8. Refill the engine cooling system.

4.8L, 5.3L and 6.0L Engines

> ✴✴ **CAUTION**
>
> **Before servicing any electrical component, the ignition key must be in the OFF or LOCK position and all electrical loads must be OFF, unless instructed otherwise in these procedures.**

1. Raise the hood to the servicing position and secure it. Move the hood hinge bolt to hold the hood in the servicing position.
2. Remove or disconnect the following:
- Battery negative cable
- Coolant
- Upper and lower radiator hoses from the engine
- Air cleaner duct from the engine
- A/C condenser mounting bolts, if equipped
- Radiator support and radiator form vehicle
- Engine cooling fan
- Drive belt
- A/C drive belt, if equipped
- Engine sight shield
- Electrical wiring harness from the thermostat housing
- Water pump

3. Raise the vehicle.
4. Remove or disconnect the following:
- Starter motor
- Right side closeout cover and bolt
- Crankshaft balancer
- Engine oil pan
- Engine front cover
- Cylinder heads from the engine

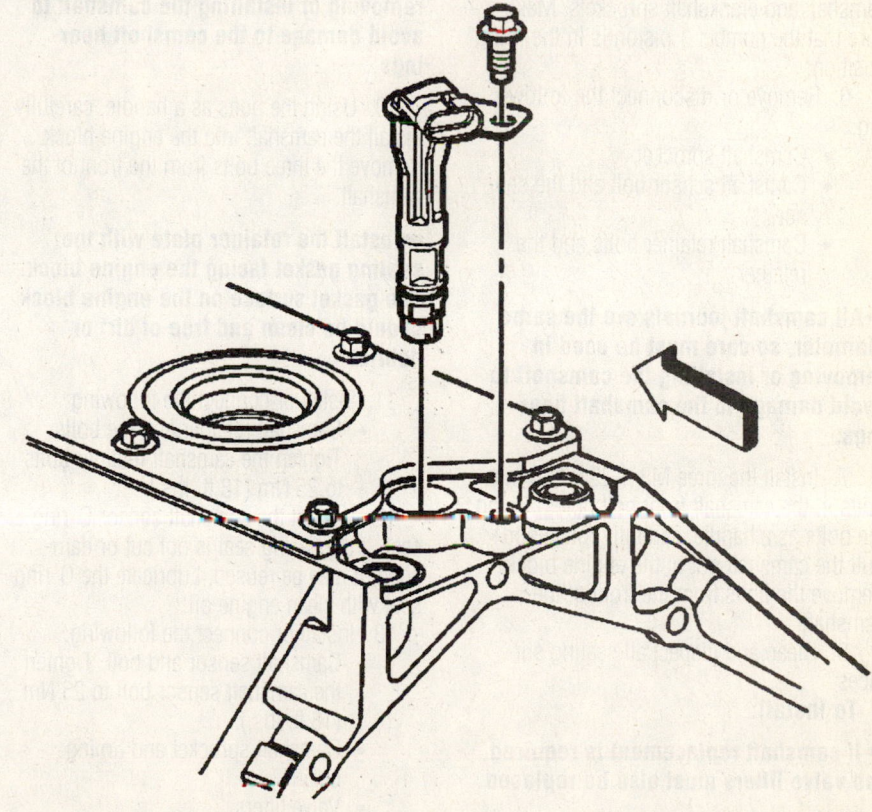

Camshaft sensor removal—4.8L, 5.3L, 6.0L

9308KG66

Please refer to Section 8 for electric cooling fan wiring schematics

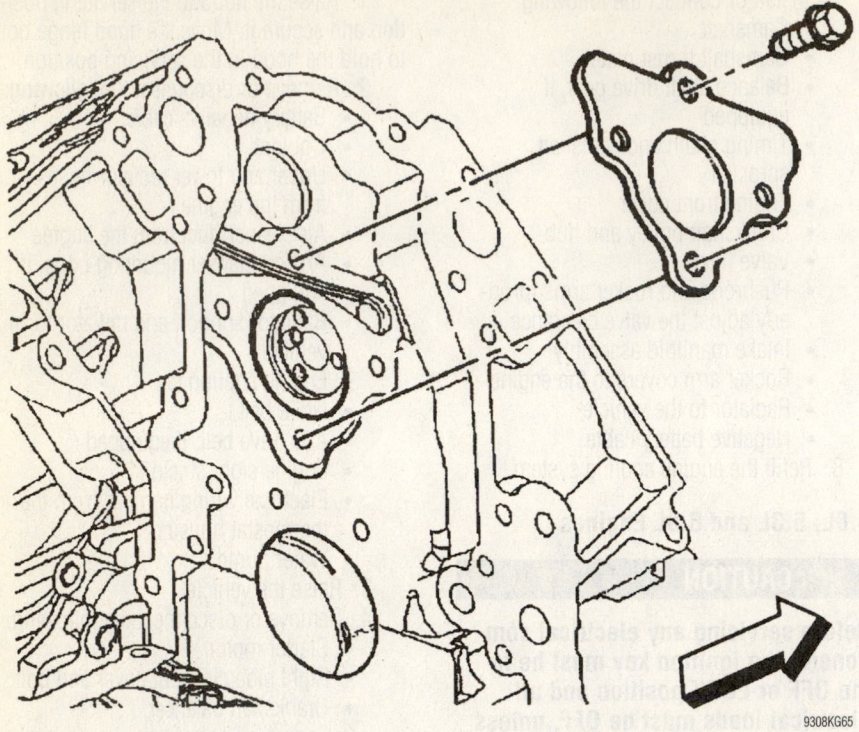

Camshaft retainer removal—4.8L, 5.3L, 6.0L

- Valve lifters from the engine

5. Align the timing marks on the camshaft and crankshaft sprockets. Make sure that the number 1 piston is in the firing position.

6. Remove or disconnect the following:

- Camshaft sprocket
- Camshaft sensor bolt and the sensor
- Camshaft retainer bolts and the retainer

➡**All camshaft journals are the same diameter, so care must be used in removing or installing the camshaft to avoid damage to the camshaft bearings.**

7. Install the three M8-1.25 x 100 mm bolts in the camshaft front bolt holes. Using the bolts as a handle, carefully rotate and pull the camshaft out of the engine block. Remove the bolts from the front of the camshaft.

8. Clean and inspect all sealing surfaces.

To install:

➡**If camshaft replacement is required, the valve lifters must also be replaced.**

9. Lubricate the camshaft journals and the bearings with clean engine oil. Install three M8-1.25 x 100 mm (M8-1.25 x 4.0 in) bolts into the camshaft front bolt holes.

➡**All camshaft journals are the same diameter, so care must be used in removing or installing the camshaft to avoid damage to the camshaft bearings.**

10. Using the bolts as a handle, carefully install the camshaft into the engine block. Remove the three bolts from the front of the camshaft.

➡**Install the retainer plate with the sealing gasket facing the engine block. The gasket surface on the engine block should be clean and free of dirt or debris.**

11. Install or connect the following:

- Camshaft retainer and the bolts. Tighten the camshaft retainer bolts to 25 Nm (18 ft. lbs.).

12. Inspect the camshaft sensor O-ring seal. If the O-ring seal is not cut or damaged, it may be reused. Lubricate the O-ring seal with clean engine oil.

13. Install or connect the following:

- Camshaft sensor and bolt. Tighten the camshaft sensor bolt to 25 Nm (18 ft. lbs.).
- Camshaft sprocket and timing chain
- Valve lifters
- Cylinder heads
- Engine front cover to the engine
- Oil pan

- Right side closeout cover
- Starter motor
- Crankshaft balancer to the crankshaft
- Water pump
- Electrical wiring harness to the thermostat housing
- A/C drive belt, if equipped
- Drive belt
- Engine sight shield
- Radiator support and radiator
- A/C condenser mounting bolts
- Engine cooling fan
- Air cleaner duct
- Battery negative cable to the battery

5.0L and 5.7L Engines

1. Before servicing the vehicle, refer to the precautions in the beginning of this section.

2. Drain the cooling system.

3. Properly relieve the fuel system pressure.

4. Remove or disconnect the following:

- Engine cover, on van models
- Air cleaner
- Grille and center support, on van models
- Air conditioning condenser and swing the condenser forward from its mounting, if equipped
- Fan, the shroud and the radiator
- Valve covers
- Water pump assembly

5. Align the timing marks and remove the torsional damper.

- Timing chain cover
- Electrical and vacuum connections at the intake manifold
- Distributor assembly, mark the distributor rotor-to-housing location

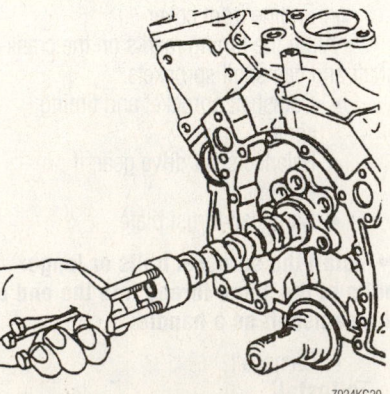

Install 2 or 3 long bolts into the camshaft to use as a handle for easy removal or installation—7.4L engine shown, other engines similar

- Intake manifold, pushrods and hydraulic lifters
- Camshaft sprocket bolts
- Camshaft sprocket and timing chain
- Crankshaft sprocket, as required
- Front engine mount through-bolts and raise the engine to gain sufficient clearance for camshaft removal, as required

6. Install 2 or 3 ⁵⁄₁₆–18 bolts 4–5 in. (102–127mm) long into the camshaft threaded holes.

- Camshaft

➡**Inspect the shaft for signs of excessive wear or damage.**

To install:

➡**Liberally coat camshaft and bearing with heavy engine oil or engine assembly lubricant.**

7. Install or connect the following:
- Camshaft, align the timing marks on the camshaft and crankshaft gears
- Engine mount through-bolts
- Camshaft sprocket and chain. Torque the bolts to 18 ft. lbs. (25 Nm).
- Hydraulic lifters and pushrods
- Distributor assembly
- Timing chain cover
- Torsional damper
- Water pump
- Valve covers
- Fan, the shroud and radiator
- Air conditioning condenser, if equipped
- Grille and center support, on van models
- Air cleaner
- Engine cover, on van models
- Negative battery cable

8. Refill the cooling system.

7.4L Engines

1. Before servicing the vehicle, refer to the precautions in the beginning of this section.
2. Drain the cooling system.
3. Properly relieve the fuel system pressure.
4. Properly discharge the air conditioning system.
5. Remove or disconnect the following:
- Negative battery cable
- Engine cover, on van models
- Air cleaner assembly

- Grille and center support section, as required
- Air conditioning compressor, condenser and auxiliary fan, if equipped
- Fan, the shroud
- Radiator
- Accessory belt, as required
- Alternator, as required
- Valve covers
- Hoses from the water pump
- Water pump

6. Align the timing marks at TDC.
- Harmonic balancer and pulley
- Engine front cover

7. Mark the distributor rotor-to-housing location.
- Distributor assembly
- Intake manifold assembly
- Lifters, pushrods, and rocker arms

8. Rotate the camshaft so the timing marks align.
- Camshaft sprocket bolts
- Camshaft sprocket and timing
- Engine mount through-bolts

9. Install 2 or 3 ⁵⁄₁₆–18 bolts in the holes in the front of the camshaft and carefully pull the camshaft from the block.

To install:

10. Liberally coat camshaft and bearing with heavy engine oil or engine assembly lubricant

11. Align the timing marks on the camshaft sprocket and crankshaft gears.

12. Install or connect the following:
- Camshaft
- Camshaft sprocket and chain. Torque the bolts to 25 ft. lbs. (34 Nm)
- Engine mount bolts
- Lifters and pushrods and adjust the valves
- Intake manifold
- Distributor using the locating marks made during removal
- Engine front cover
- Harmonic balancer and pulley
- Water pump
- Hoses at the water pump
- Valve covers
- Alternator, if removed
- Accessory belt, if removed
- Fan shroud and radiator
- Air conditioning condenser and compressor
- Grille and center support, if removed
- Air cleaner assembly
- Negative battery cable

13. Fill the cooling system with the proper type and quantity of antifreeze.

Valve Lash

ADJUSTMENT

All engines use hydraulic lifters, which require no periodic adjustment.

Starter Motor

REMOVAL & INSTALLATION

4.3L, 5.0L

1. Before servicing the vehicle, refer to the precautions in the beginning of this section.
2. Remove or disconnect the following:
- Negative battery cable
- Bracket and shield
- Wires
- Mounting bolts and shims
- Starter

To install:

3. Install or connect the following:
- Starter
- Mounting bolts and shim. Torque the bolts to 33 ft lbs. (45 Nm).
- Wires. Torque battery wire nut to 89 inch lbs. (10 Nm) and Ignition nut to 18 inch lbs. (2 Nm).
- Bracket and shield. Torque the nuts to 53 inch lbs. (6 Nm).
- Negative battery cable

5.7L, 7.4L

1. Before servicing the vehicle, refer to the precautions in the beginning of this section.
2. Remove or disconnect the following:
- Negative battery cable
- Mounting bolts and shims
- Wires
- Heat shield
- Starter

To install:

3. Install or connect the following:
- Starter
- Wires. Torque battery wire nut to 89 inch lbs. (10 Nm), and ignition nut to 18 inch lbs. (2 Nm)
- Heat shield. Torque the bolts to 53 inch lbs. (6 Nm) and the nuts to 35 inch lbs. (3 Nm)
- Mounting bolts and shim. Torque the bolts to 33 ft lbs. (45 Nm)
- Negative battery cable

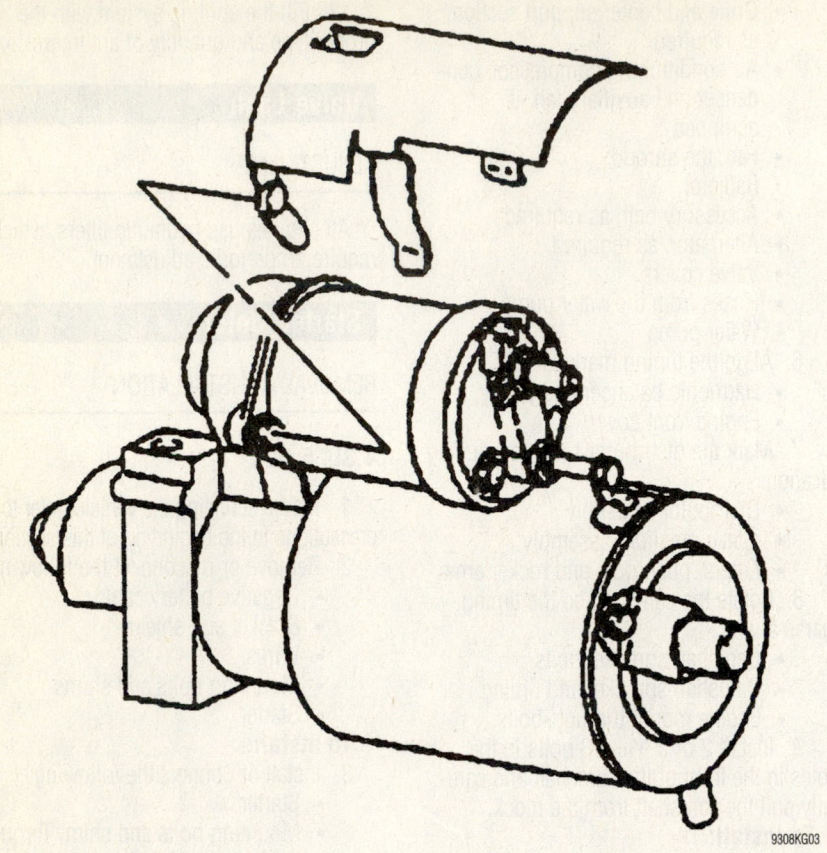

Exploded view of the starter motor.

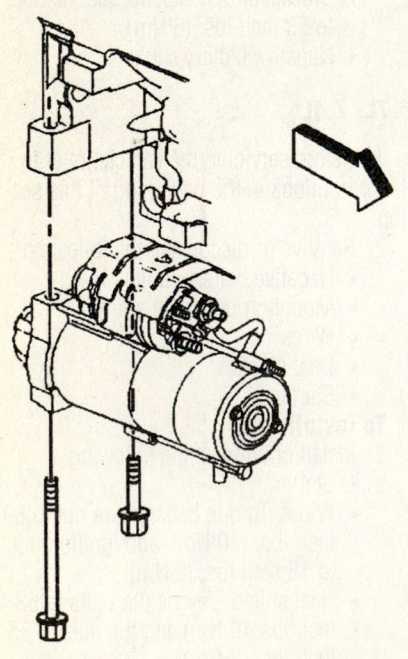

Starter removal—4.8L, 5.3L and 6.0L

4.8L, 5.3L, 6.0L

✳✳ CAUTION

Before servicing any electrical component, the ignition key must be in the OFF or LOCK position and all electrical loads must be OFF, unless instructed otherwise in these procedures.

1. Disconnect the negative battery cable.
2. Raise and support the vehicle.
3. Remove the protective shields as necessary.
4. Remove the starter solenoid shield.
5. Remove the starter to transmission close out cover bolt.
6. Disconnect the engine oil level sensor connection.
7. Remove the front axle mounting bracket through bolt nut.
8. Reposition the front axle mounting bracket through bolt until the bolt tip is flush with the support bushing. Do not remove the bolt.
9. Remove the mounting bolts from the engine block. Slide the starter forward until the starter clears the transmission. Remove the starter transmission close out cover.
10. Disconnect the positive battery cable and wiring harness from the starter. Remove the starter from the vehicle.

To install:

11. Install the starter.
12. Connect the positive battery cable to the starter. Tighten the nut to 16 Nm (12 inch lbs.).
13. Install the starter transmission close out cover. Install the mounting bolts to the engine block. Tighten the bolts to 50 Nm (37 ft. lbs.).
14. Reposition the front axle mounting bracket through bolt until the bolt is fully seated Install the front axle mounting bracket through bolt nut. Tighten the nut to 90 Nm (67 ft. lbs.).
15. Connect the engine oil level sensor connection.
16. Install the starter to transmission close out cover bolt.
17. Install the starter solenoid shield.
18. Install the protective shields as necessary.
19. Remove the safety stands.
20. Lower the vehicle.
21. Connect the negative battery cable. Tighten the bolts to 17 Nm (13 ft. lbs.).

Oil Pan

REMOVAL & INSTALLATION

4.3L Engines

1. Before servicing the vehicle, refer to the precautions in the beginning of this section.
2. Drain the engine oil.
3. Remove or disconnect the following:
   - Negative battery cable
   - Exhaust crossover pipe
   - Torque converter cover, if equipped with automatic transmission
   - Cooler lines from guides and the oil filter adapter
   - Strut rods at the flywheel/flexplate cover, if equipped
   - Strut rod at the front engine mounts, if equipped
   - Starter assembly
   - Front drive axle tube nuts and lower axle bushing bolts
   - Oil pan bolts/nuts and reinforcements
   - Oil pan and gaskets

To install:
4. Thoroughly clean all gasket surfaces
5. Install or connect the following:
   - New gasket
   - Oil pan and new gaskets
   - Oil pan bolts, nuts and reinforcements. Torque bolts to 18 ft. lbs. (25 Nm)
   - Front drive axle tube nuts and lower axle bushing bolts
   - Starter
   - Strut rod brackets at the front engine mounts
   - Strut rods at the flywheel/flexplate cover
   - Cooler lines into guides and oil filter adapter with new filter
   - Torque converter cover, if equipped with automatic transmission
   - Exhaust crossover pipe
   - Negative battery cable
6. Refill the engine with oil.

4.8L, 5.3L and 6.0L

➡ **The original oil pan gasket is retained and aligned to the oil pan by rivets. When installing a new gasket, it is not necessary to install new rivets. DO NOT reuse the oil pan gasket. When installing the oil pan, install a NEW oil pan gasket.**

Remove or disconnect the following:
   - Negative battery cable
   - Front differential if equipped with four wheel drive
   - Under body shield from the vehicle
   - Oil pan shield
   - Cross brace if equipped
   - Engine oil and filter
   - Transmission to oil pan bolts
   - Oil level sensor electrical connector
   - Two front wiring harness retainer bolts
   - Engine wiring harness retainer bolts from the engine oil pan
   - Engine oil cooler pipe to oil pan bolt
   - Transmission oil cooler pipe retainer and the bolt from the oil pan
   - Closeout covers and bolts (one each side of engine)
   - Engine mount bolts each side
   - Oil pan

To install:

➡ **The alignment of the structural oil pan is critical. The rear bolt hole locations of the oil pan provide mounting points for the transmission bellhousing.**

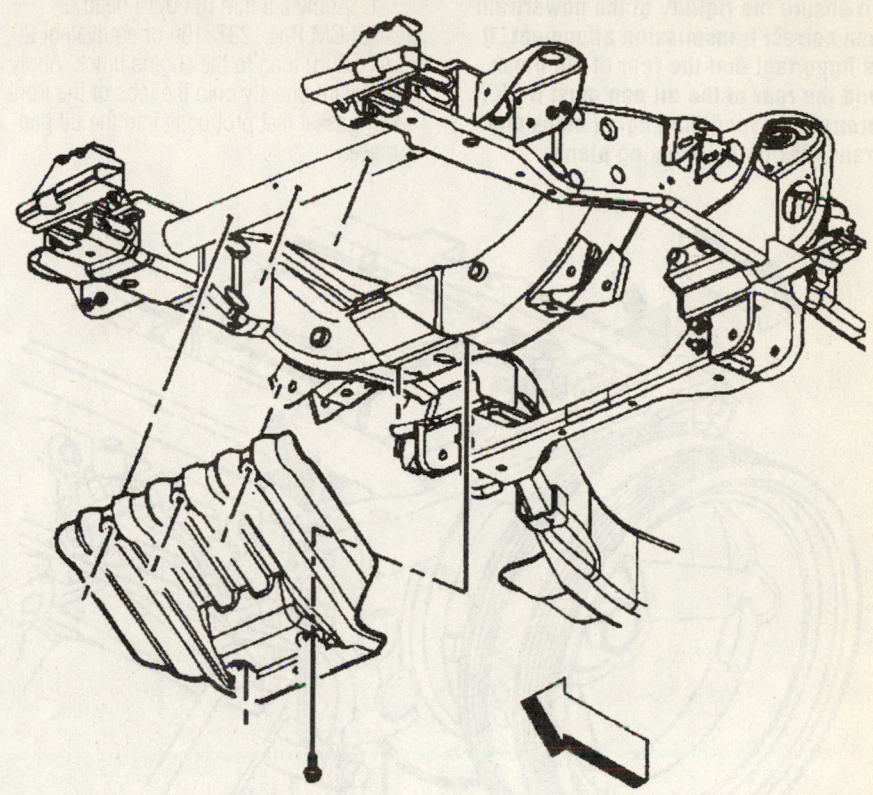

Oil pan shield—4.8L, 5.3L, 6.0L

9308KG81

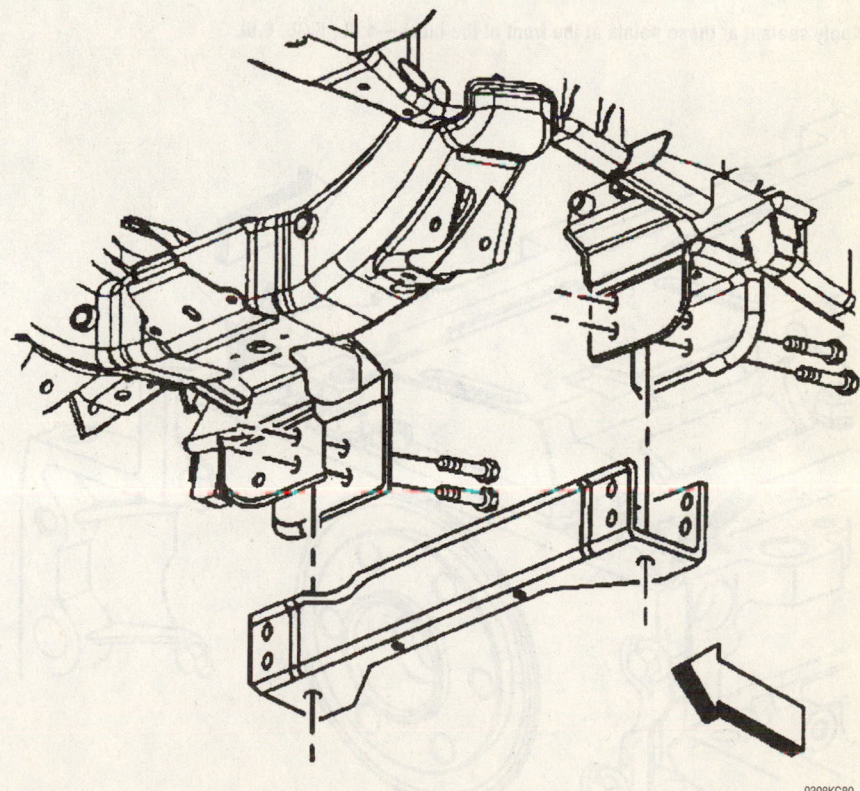

Cross brace—4.8L, 5.3L, 6.0L

9308KG80

Timing belt service is covered in Section 4 of this manual

To ensure the rigidity of the powertrain and correct transmission alignment, it is important that the rear of the block and the rear of the oil pan must NEVER protrude beyond the engine block and transmission bellhousing plane.

1. Apply a 5 mm (0.20 in) bead of sealant GM P/N 12378190 or equivalent 20 mm (0.8 in) long to the engine block. Apply the sealant directly onto the tabs of the front cover gasket that protrudes into the oil pan surface.

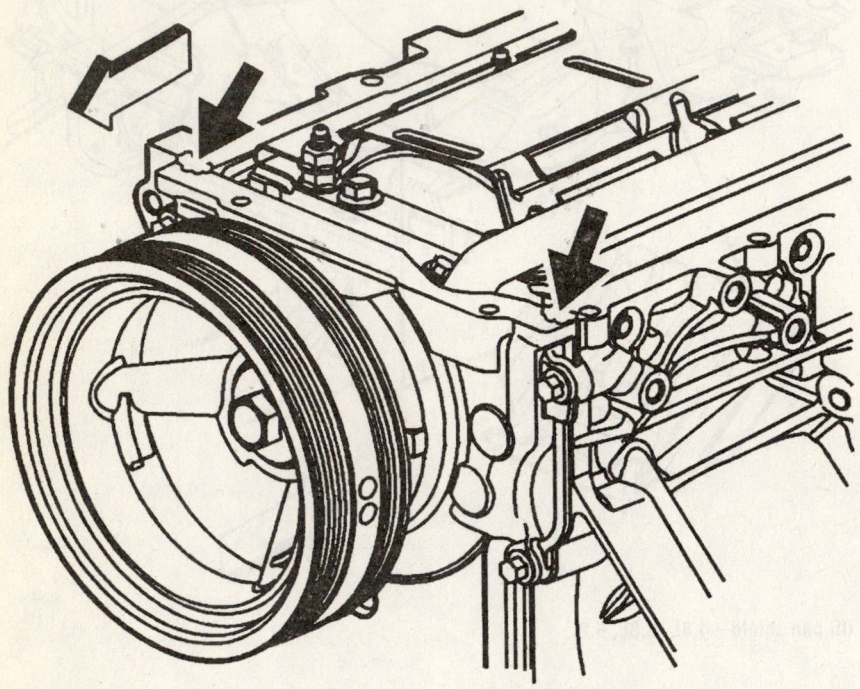

Apply sealant at these points at the front of the block—4.8L, 5.3L, 6.0L

9308KG79

2. Apply a 5 mm (0.20 in) bead of sealant GM P/N 12378190 or equivalent 20 mm (0.8 in) long to the engine block. Apply the sealant directly onto the tabs of the rear cover gasket that protrudes into the oil pan surface.

➡**Be sure to align the oil gallery passages in the oil pan and engine block properly with the oil pan gasket.**

3. Pre-assemble the oil pan gasket to the pan. Install the oil pan bolts to the pan through the gasket.

4. Install the oil pan, gasket and bolts to the engine block. Snug the oil pan bolts finger tight. Do not overtighten.

5. Install the two lower bellhousing bolts to position the oil pan correctly.

6. Snug the lower bellhousing bolt finger tight. Do not overtighten. Tighten the oil pan-to-block and oil pan-to-oil pan front cover bolts to 25 Nm (18 ft. lbs.). Tighten the oil pan-to-rear cover bolts to 12 Nm (106 inch lbs.). Tighten the bellhousing bolts to 50 Nm (37 ft. lbs.).

7. Install the transmission oil cooler pipe retainer and the bolt to the oil pan. Install the engine oil cooler pipe to oil pan bolt. Tighten the nut to 10 Nm (89 ft. lbs.).

8. Install the engine wiring harness retainer bolts to the engine oil pan.

9. Connect the oil level sensor electrical connector.

10. Install the transmission to oil pan bolts. Tighten the bolts to 55 Nm (41 ft. lbs.).

11. Install the front differential if equipped with four wheel drive.

12. Install the under body shield on the vehicle. Lower the vehicle. Fill the engine with oil and install the engine oil filter.

13. Connect the negative battery cable.

5.0L and 5.7L Engines

1. Before servicing the vehicle, refer to the precautions in the beginning of this section.

2. Drain the engine oil.

3. Remove or disconnect the following:
- Negative battery cable
- Under body protector shields
- Transmission and engine oil lines from guides
- Front driveshaft, if needed
- Front drive axles, if needed
- Exhaust crossover pipe
- Flywheel/flexplate or torque converter cover
- Oil filter and adapter
- Strut rods at the front engine mounting, if equipped

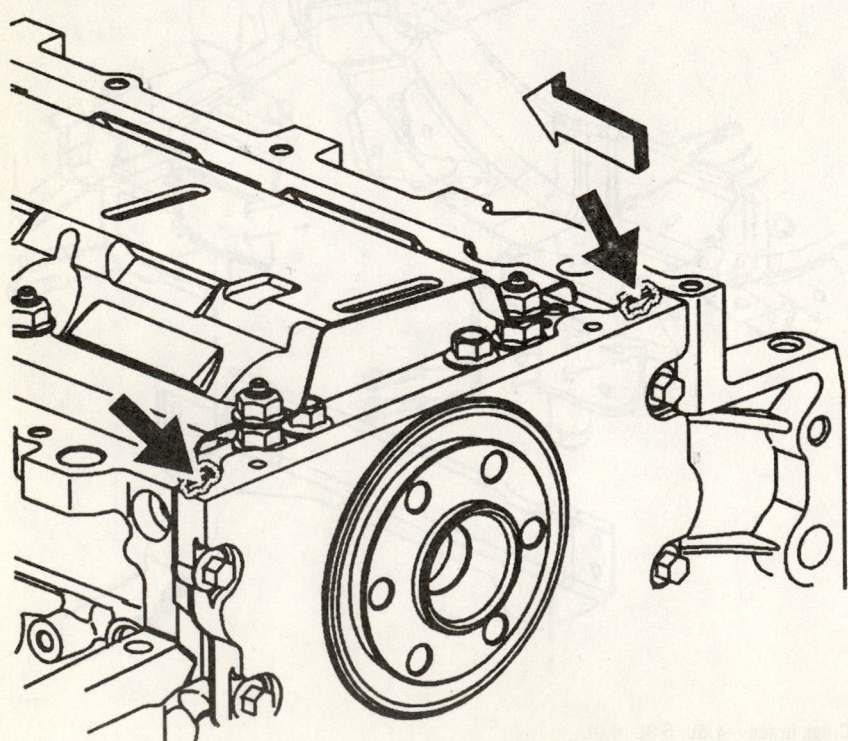

Apply sealant at these points at the rear of the block—4.8L, 5.3L, 6.0L

9308KG78

- Oil pan bolts, nuts and reinforcements
- Oil pan and gaskets

To install:

4. Thoroughly clean all gasket surfaces.
5. Install or connect the following:
   - New gasket
   - Oil pan and new gaskets
   - Oil pan bolts, nuts and reinforcements. Torque bolts to 18 ft. lbs. (25 Nm)
   - Strut rods at the front engine mounting
   - Oil filter and adapter
   - Torque converter or flywheel/flex-plate cover
   - Exhaust crossover pipe
   - Front drive axles and driveshaft, if removed
   - Transmission and engine oil lines to guides
   - Under body protectors
   - Negative battery cable
6. Fill the crankcase with oil.

7.4L Engines

➡**Removal of the transmission may be necessary on van vehicles.**

1. Before servicing the vehicle, refer to the precautions in the beginning of this section.
2. Drain the engine oil.
3. Remove or disconnect the following:
   - Negative battery cable
   - Fan shroud
   - Air cleaner
   - Distributor cap
   - Underbody protectors, if needed
   - Front driveshaft and front drive axles, if needed
   - Starter, if equipped with manual transmission
   - Torque converter or clutch housing cover
   - Oil filter and adapter
   - Oil pressure line from the side of the block
4. Support the engine
   - Engine mount through-bolts
   - Oil pan bolts
   - Oil pan and discard the gaskets

To install:

5. Clean all sealing surfaces.
6. Apply RTV gasket material to the front and rear corners of the gaskets.
7. Install or connect the following:
   - New gaskets, coat the gaskets with adhesive sealer and position them on the block
   - Rear pan seal in the pan with the seal ends mating with the gaskets.
   - Front seal on the bottom of the front cover, pressing the locating tabs into the holes in the cover.
   - Oil pan.
   - Pan bolts, clips and reinforcements. Torque the bolts to 18 ft. lbs. (25 Nm)
8. Lower the engine onto the mounts.
   - Engine mount through-bolts
   - Oil pressure line
   - Oil filter
   - Starter, if removed
   - Torque converter or clutch housing cover
   - Front drive axles and driveshaft, if removed
   - Underbody protectors, if removed
   - Distributor cap
   - Air cleaner
   - Fan shroud
   - Negative battery cable
9. Fill the crankcase with oil.

Oil Pump

REMOVAL & INSTALLATION

4.8L, 5.3L and 6.0L

1. Remove or disconnect the following:
   - Engine front cover
   - Oil pan

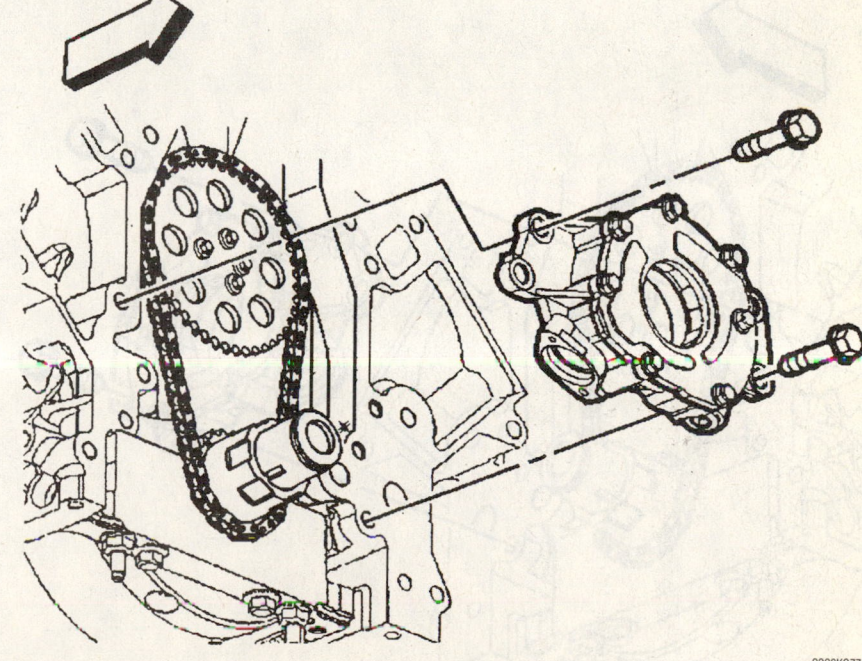

Oil pump removal—4.8L, 5.3L, 6.0L

9308KG77

- Oil pump screen bolt and nuts
- Oil pump screen with O-ring seal.
- O-ring seal from the pump screen. Discard the O-ring seal.
- Remaining crankshaft oil deflector nuts.
- Crankshaft oil deflector
- Oil pump bolts

➡**Do not allow dirt or debris to enter the oil pump assembly, cap ends as necessary.**

   - Oil pump

➡**The internal parts of the oil pump assembly are not serviced separately (excluding the spring). If the oil pump components are worn or damaged, replace the oil pump as an assembly. Do not attempt to repair the wire mesh portion of the pump and screen assembly.**

To install:

➡**Inspect the oil pump and engine block oil gallery passages. These surfaces must be clear and free of debris or restrictions.**

2. Align the splined surfaces of the crankshaft sprocket and the oil pump drive gear and install the oil pump. Install the oil pump onto the crankshaft sprocket until the pump housing contacts the face of the engine block.

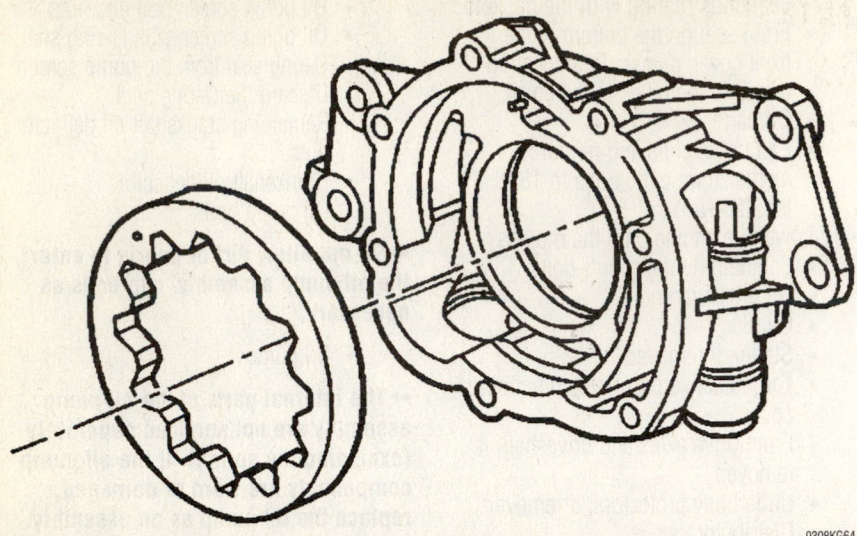

9308KG64

Oil pump disassembly—4.8L, 5.3L, 6.0L

3. Install or connect the following:
   • Oil pump bolts. Tighten the oil pump bolts to 25 Nm (18 ft. lbs.).
   • Crankshaft oil deflector.

➡**Lubricate a NEW oil pump screen O-ring seal with clean engine oil.**

   • NEW O-ring seal onto the oil pump screen.

➡**Push the oil pump screen tube completely into the oil pump prior to tightening the bolt. Do not allow the bolt to pull the tube into the pump.**

4. Align the oil pump screen mounting brackets with the correct crankshaft bearing cap studs.

5. Install the oil pump screen. Install the oil pump screen bolt and the deflector nuts. Tighten the oil pump screen bolt (4) to 12 Nm (106 inch lbs.). Tighten the crankshaft oil deflector nuts (2) to 25 Nm (18 ft. lbs.).

6. Install the engine oil pan.
7. Install the engine front cover.

4.3L, 5.0L, 5.7L and 7.4L Engines

1. Before servicing the vehicle, refer to the precautions in the beginning of this section.
2. Remove or disconnect the following:
   • Oil pan.
   • Oil pump attaching bolt, if equipped
   • Pick-up tube nut/bolt
   • Pump along with the pick-up tube and shaft, as necessary
3. Clean all sealing surfaces

To install:

4. Ensure that the pump pick-up tube is tight in the pump body. If the tube should come loose, oil pressure will be lost and oil starvation will occur. If the pick-up tube is loose it should be replaced.

5. If the pump has been disassembled and is being replaced or for any reason oil has been removed, it must be primed. It can either be filled with oil before installing the cover plate and oil kept within the pump during handling or the entire pump cavity can be filled with petroleum jelly.

➡**If the pump is not primed, the engine could be damaged before it receives adequate lubrication when the engine is started.**

6. Install or connect the following:
   • Pump, aligning the pump shaft with the oil pump drive gear as necessary. Torque oil pump/pick-up tube retainer(s) to 65 ft. lbs. (90 Nm) on all 4.3L and all V8 Engines.
   • Oil pan
7. Refill the engine crankcase
8. Disable the ignition system; crank engine for approximately 10 seconds to aid in priming the oil pump and reducing the risk of engine damage.

➡**If the oil pump does not build up oil pressure almost immediately, remove the pan and check for a loose oil pump-to-pick-up tube attachment. If necessary dismantle the pump and pack the pump cavity with petroleum jelly. Running the engine without measurable oil pressure will cause extensive damage.**

Rear Main Seal

REMOVAL & INSTALLATION

Please note that the entire transmission assembly and flywheel/flexplate must be removed to perform this procedure.

9302KG04

Exploded view of the oil pump mounting—4.8L, 5.3L and 6.0L engines

1. Remove or disconnect the following:

- Negative battery cable
- Transfer case, if equipped
- Transmission assembly
- Clutch assembly and flywheel, if equipped with manual transmission
- Flexplate, if equipped with automatic transmission
- Crankshaft rear main oil seal by inserting a suitable prying tool and prying the seal out. Take care not to damage the crankshaft sealing surface.

To install:

2. Clean the oil seal bore in the block thoroughly before installation of the new seal.

3. Inspect the crankshaft for grit, rust or burrs and correct as necessary. Also inspect the portion of the crankshaft where the oil seal makes contact, for wear due to the rubbing action of the oil seal.

4. Clean the seal running surface of the crankshaft with a non-abrasive cleaner.

5. Lubricate the inner diameter of the new seal and the outer diameter of the crankshaft with engine oil.

6. Install or connect the following:

- Rear main oil seal, using installation tool J 38841, until the tool bottoms against the block and crankshaft rear main bearing cap.
- Flywheel and clutch
- Flexplate, as required
- Transmission assembly
- Transfer case, if equipped
- Negative battery cable

7. Start the engine and verify no oil leaks.

Timing Chain, Sprockets, Front Cover and Seal

The manufacturer recommends that the front cover oil seal be replaced whenever the cover is removed.

REMOVAL & INSTALLATION

4.3L, 5.0L, 5.7L and 7.4L

1. Before servicing the vehicle, refer to the precautions in the beginning of this section.

2. Drain the cooling system.

3. Remove or disconnect the following:

- Negative battery cable
- Fan shroud assembly
- Belts, pulleys and water pump assembly
- Crankshaft pulley and damper
- Oil pan-to-front cover bolts

➡ **If equipped with a composite front cover, it must be replaced with a new one. Reusing the front cover may result in oil leaks.**

- Screws holding the timing chain cover to the block.
- Cover and gaskets.

4. Use a suitable tool to pry the old seal out of the front face of the cover.

5. Rotate the crankshaft until the timing marks on the camshaft and crankshaft sprockets are in proper alignment.

- Camshaft sprocket-to-camshaft nut and/or bolts
- Camshaft sprocket (along with the timing chain), if the sprocket is difficult to remove, use a plastic mallet to bump the sprocket from the camshaft.

➡ **The camshaft sprocket (located by a dowel) is lightly pressed onto the** camshaft and should come off easily. **The chain comes off with the camshaft sprocket.**

6. If necessary use J-5825-A, or equivalent, crankshaft sprocket removal tool to free the timing sprocket from the crankshaft.

To install:

7. Inspect the timing chain and the timing sprockets for wear or damage, replace the damaged parts as necessary.

8. Clean the gasket mounting surfaces of all remaining traces of old gasket.

➡ **During installation, coat the thrust surfaces lightly with Molykote® or equivalent pre-lube.**

9. Install or connect the following:

- Crankshaft sprocket onto the crankshaft, use tool J-5590, or equivalent, crankshaft sprocket installation tool, and a hammer, without disturbing the position of the engine.
- Timing chain, arrange the camshaft sprocket in such a way that the timing marks will align

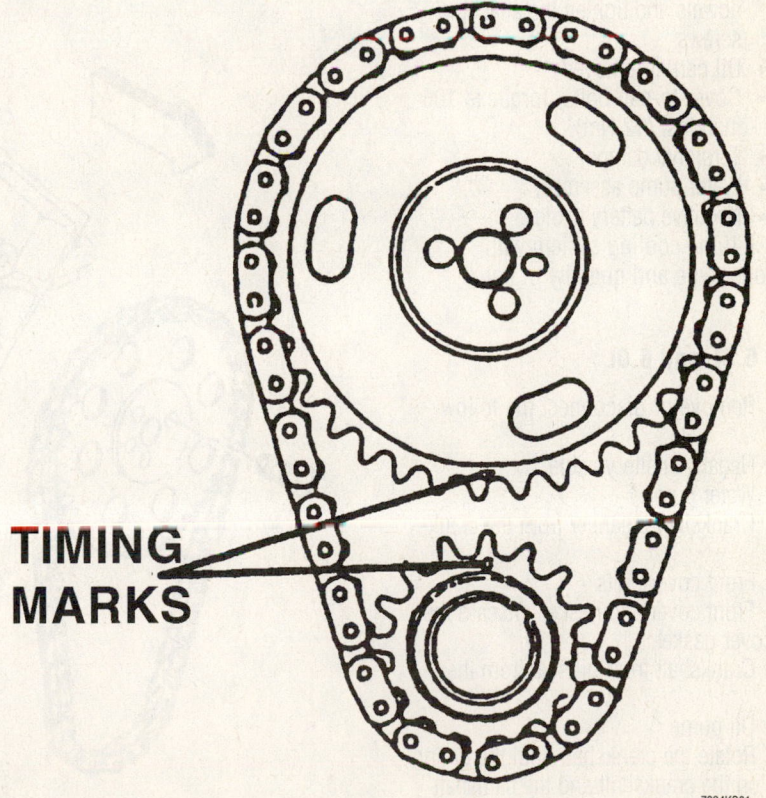

TIMING MARKS

Timing mark alignment for timing chain removal and installation—4.3L, 5.0L, 5.7L and 7.4L gasoline engines

7924KG21

Refer to Section 1 for engine rebuilding specifications

between the shaft centers and the camshaft locating dowel will enter the dowel hole in the cam sprocket.

- Cam sprocket, with the chain mounted under it in position on the front of the camshaft. Torque the camshaft sprocket-to-camshaft retainer bolts to 106 inch lbs. (12 Nm).

10. With the timing chain installed, turn the crankshaft 2 complete revolutions, then check to make certain that the timing marks are in correct alignment between the shaft centers.

➡ **Coat the lip of the new seal with oil prior to installation.**

- New seal so that the open end is toward the inside of the cover, Using seal driver J-22102, or equivalent.
- New front pan seal, cutting the tabs off.

11. Coat a new cover gasket with adhesive sealer and position it on the block.

12. Apply a ⅛ in. (3mm) bead of RTV gasket material to the front cover.

- Cover carefully onto the locating dowels and tighten the attaching screws
- Oil pan, if removed
- Cover-to-pan bolts, Torque to 106 inch lbs. (12 Nm).
- Torsional damper
- Water pump assembly
- Negative battery cable

13. Fill the cooling system with the proper type and quantity of anti-freeze.

4.8L, 5.3L and 6.0L

1. Remove or disconnect the following:
2. Negative battery cable
3. Water pump
4. Crankshaft balancer from the crankshaft
5. Front cover bolts
6. Front cover and gasket. Discard the front cover gasket.
7. Crankshaft front oil seal from the cover
8. Oil pump
9. Rotate the crankshaft until the timing marks on the crankshaft and the camshaft sprockets are aligned.

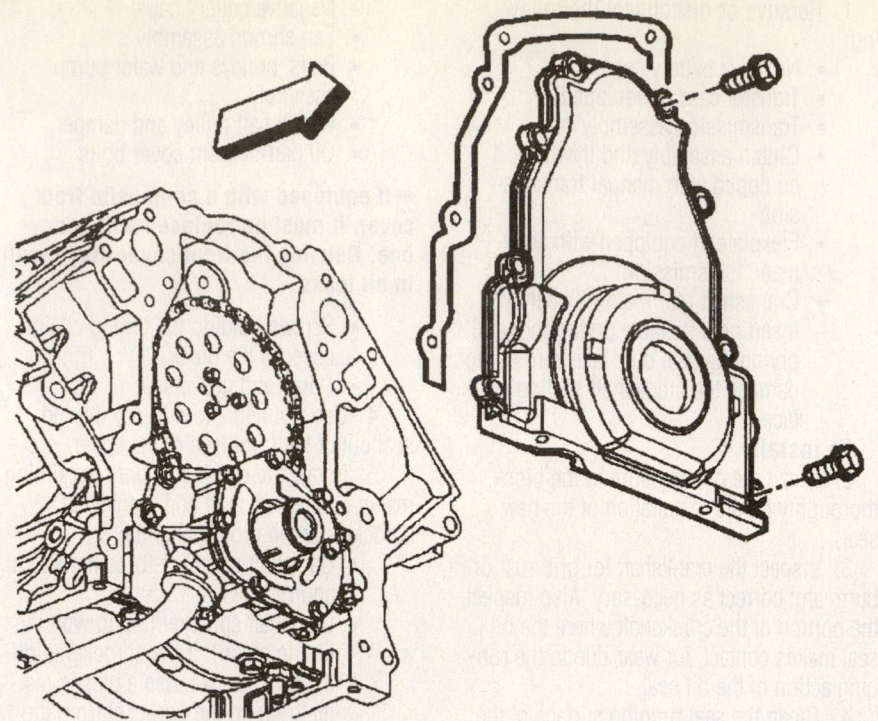

Front cover and gasket—4.8L, 5.3L, 6.0L

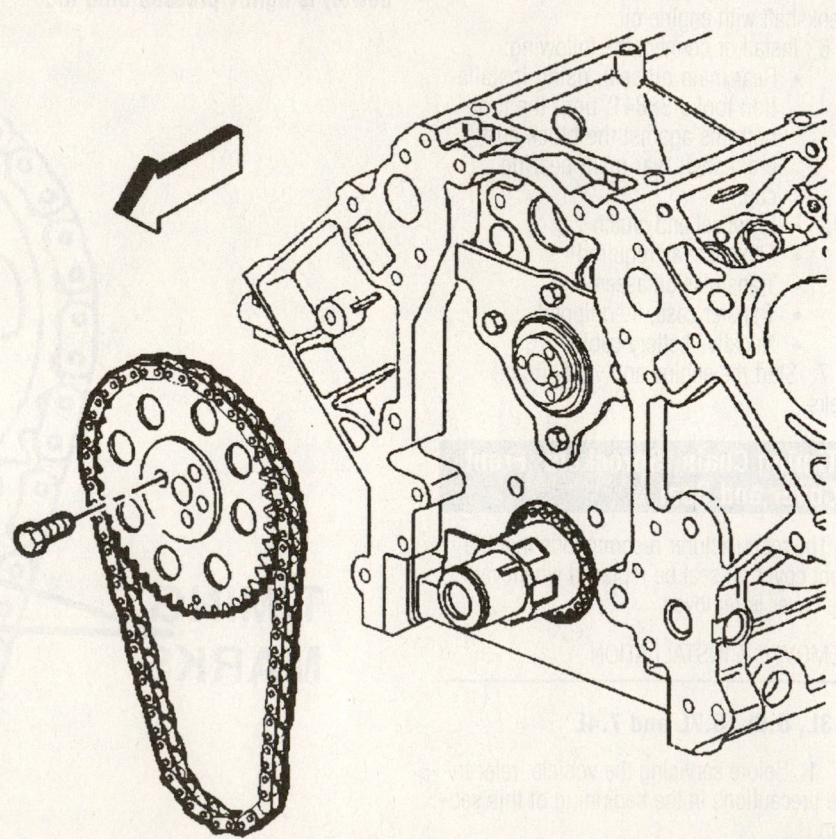

Sprocket and chain removal—4.8L, 5.3L, 6.0L

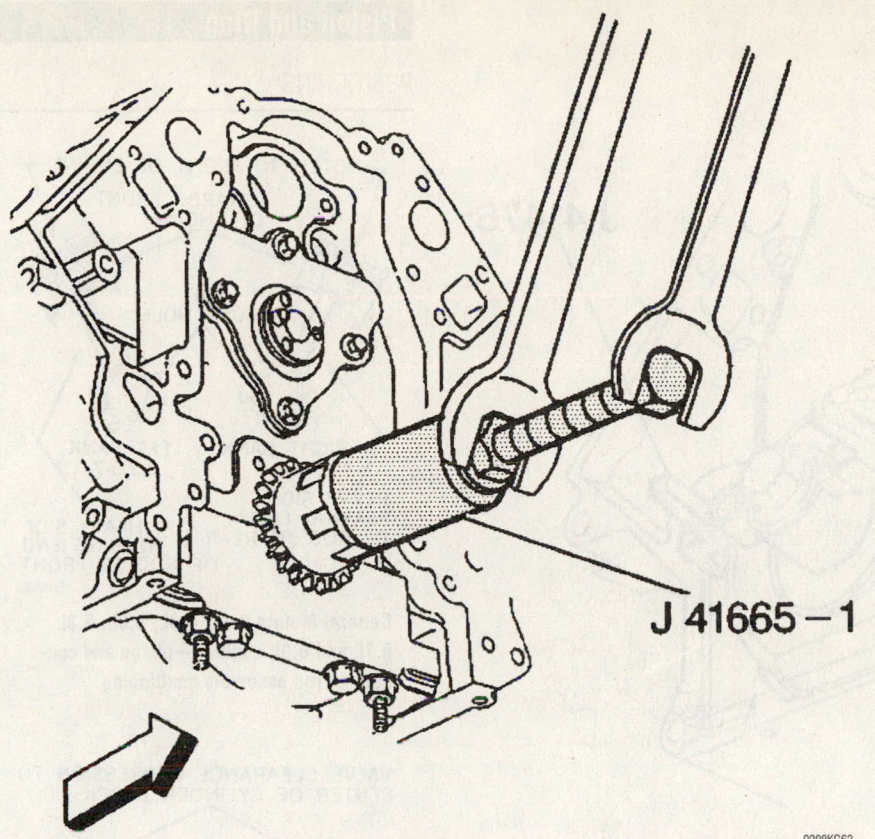

Crankshaft sprocket installation—4.8L, 5.3L, 6.0L

➡ Do not turn the crankshaft assembly after the timing chain has been removed in order to prevent damage to the piston assemblies or the valves.

10. Remove or disconnect the following:
11. Camshaft sprocket bolts
12. Camshaft sprocket and timing chain
13. Crankshaft sprocket
14. Crankshaft sprocket key

To install:

15. Install or connect the following:
16. Key into the crankshaft keyway
17. Crankshaft sprocket onto the front of the crankshaft. Align the crankshaft key with the crankshaft sprocket keyway. Rotate the crankshaft sprocket until the alignment mark is in the 12 o'clock position.
18. Camshaft sprocket and timing chain. Locate the camshaft sprocket alignment mark in the 6 o'clock position.
19. Camshaft sprocket bolts. Tighten the camshaft sprocket bolts to 35 Nm (26 ft. lbs.).

➡ Do not lubricate the oil seal sealing surface.

20. Lubricate the outer edge of the oil seal with clean engine oil. Lubricate the front cover oil seal bore with clean engine oil.

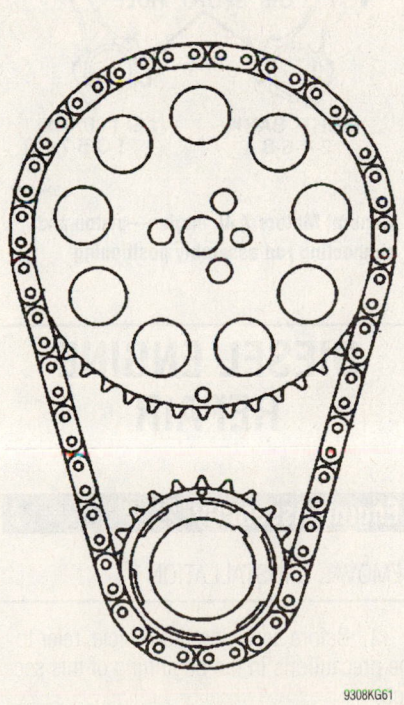

Timing mark alignment—4.8L, 5.3L, 6.0L

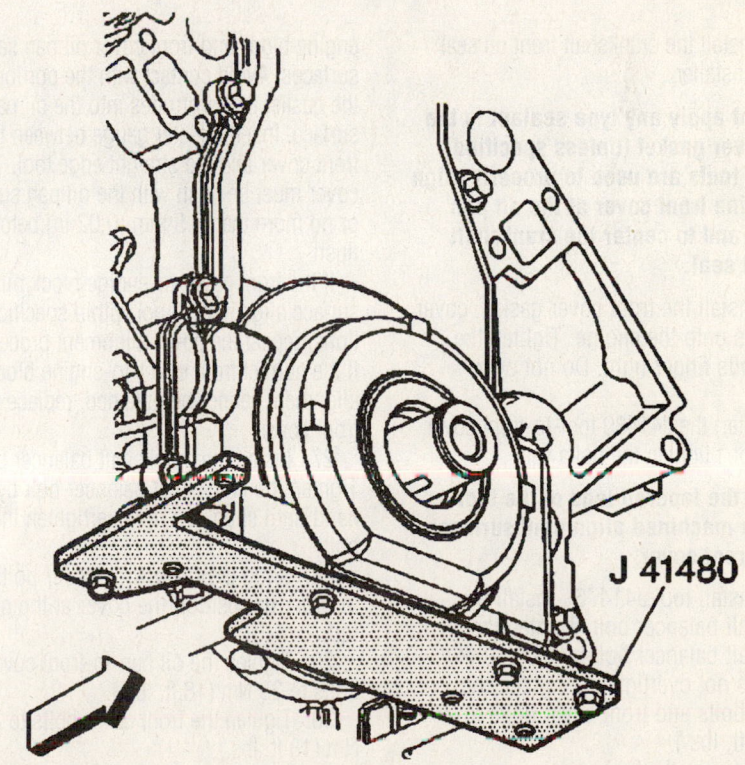

J41480 installation—4.8L, 5.3L, 6.0L

For engine torque specifications, refer to Section 1 of this manual

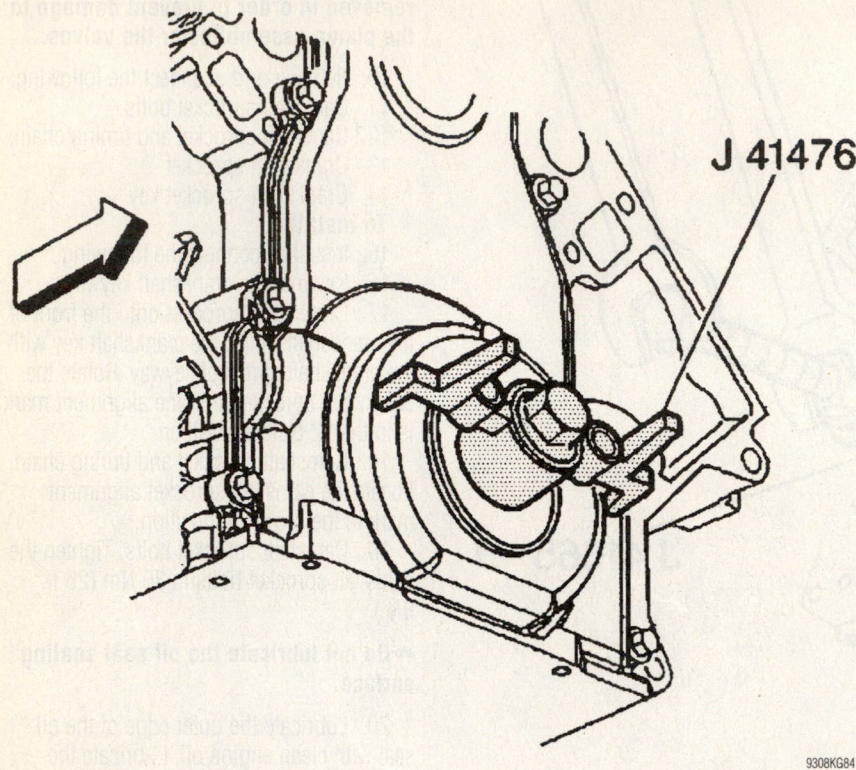

J 41476

Seal alignment tool installation—4.8L, 5.3L, 6.0L

21. Install the crankshaft front oil seal with an installer.

➡ **Do not apply any type sealant to the front cover gasket (unless specified). Special tools are used to properly align the engine front cover at the oil pan surface and to center the crankshaft front oil seal.**

22. Install the front cover gasket, cover, and bolts onto the engine. Tighten the cover bolts finger tight. Do not over-tighten.

23. Start the J41480 tool-to-front cover bolts. Don't tighten the bolts yet.

➡ **Align the tapered legs of the tool with the machined alignment surfaces on the front cover.**

24. Install tool J41476 . Install the crankshaft balancer bolt. Tighten the crankshaft balancer bolt by hand until snug. Do not overtighten. Tighten the J41480 bolts and front cover bolts to 25 Nm (18 ft. lbs.).

25. Remove the tools.

26. Place a straight edge across the engine block and front cover oil pan sealing surfaces. Avoid contact with the portion of the gasket that protrudes into the oil pan surface. Insert a feeler gauge between the front cover and the straight edge tool. The cover must be flush with the oil pan surface or no more than 0.5 mm (0.02 in) below flush.

If the front cover-to-engine block oil pan surface alignment is not within specifications, repeat the cover alignment procedure. If the correct front cover-to-engine block alignment cannot be obtained, replace the front cover.

27. Install the crankshaft balancer bolt. Tighten the crankshaft balancer bolt by hand until snug. Do not overtighten the bolt.

28. Snug the oil pan-to-cover bolts in order to position the cover at the pan rail.

29. Tighten the oil pan-to-front cover bolts to 25 Nm (18 ft. lbs.).

30. Tighten the front cover bolts to 25 Nm (18 ft. lbs.).

31. Install the water pump.

Piston and Ring

POSITIONING

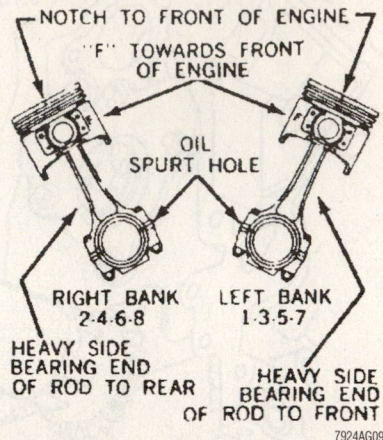

General Motors 4.3L, 4.8L, 5.0L, 5.3L, 5.7L and 6.0L engines—piston and connecting rod assembly positioning

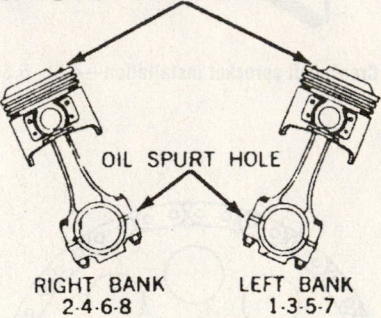

General Motors 7.4L engine—piston and connecting rod assembly positioning

DIESEL ENGINE REPAIR

Engine Assembly

REMOVAL & INSTALLATION

1. Before servicing the vehicle, refer to the precautions in the beginning of this section.

2. Drain the cooling system.

3. Discharge the air conditioning sys-

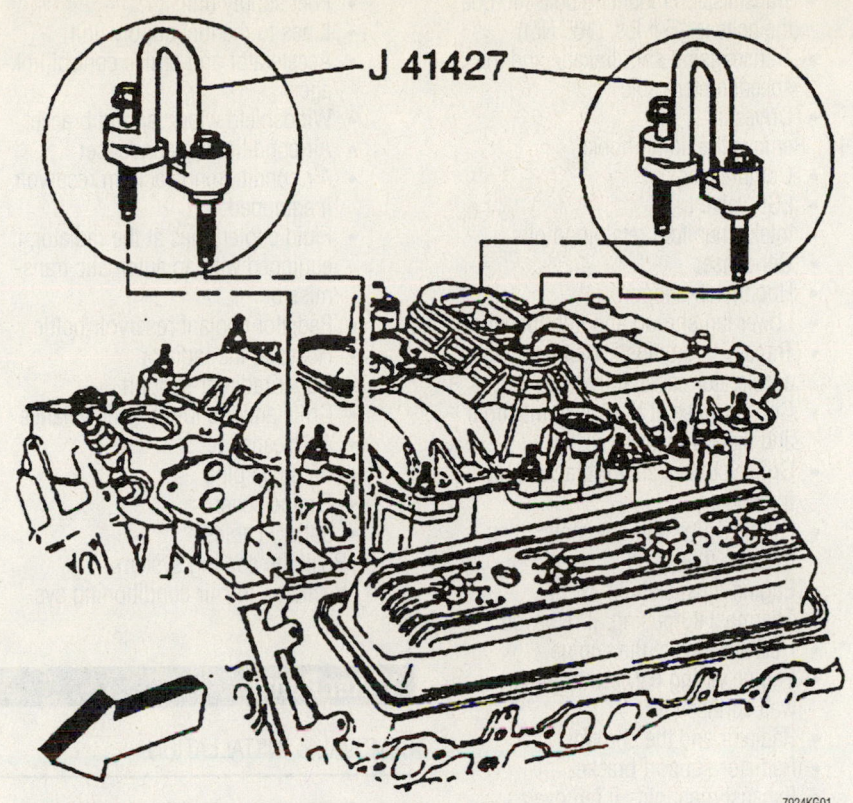

J 41427

7924KG01

For engine removal and installation, universal lift brackets should be installed in place of the proper intake manifold bolts

tem and remove the air conditioning vacuum reservoir.

4. Drain the engine oil.

5. Remove or disconnect the following:

- Battery cables
- Engine cover, if equipped
- Air cleaner
- Radiator coolant reservoir bottle
- Upper radiator support
- Grille and the lower grille valance
- Front bumper, if necessary
- Air conditioning condenser from in front of the radiator

6. If the van is equipped with an automatic transmission, remove the fluid cooler lines from the radiator.

- Radiator hoses at the radiator
- Radiator support bracket
- Radiator and the shroud
- Accelerator and cruise control linkages
- Hoses and wires at the fuel unit
- Fuel supply unit and cap the lines
- Intake manifold
- Turbocharger assembly, if equipped
- Lower intake manifold, if equipped
- Exhaust manifolds, if necessary

- Engine wiring harness from the firewall connection
- Power steering pump, it's not necessary to disconnect the hoses; just move aside
- Heater hoses at the engine
- Thermostat housing, if necessary
- Oil filler and automatic transmission tubes
- Cruise control servo, servo bracket and transducer, if equipped
- Exhaust pipes at the manifolds
- Driveshaft and plug the end of the transmission
- Transmission shift linkage and the speedometer cable
- Fuel line from the fuel tank and pump
- Transmission mounting bolts

7. Support the transmission and engine.

8. Install lifting hooks J-41427 as follows:

a. Step 1: Remove the 2 right rear lower intake manifold retainers and install lifting hook J-41427 (the one marked "right") Tighten the bolts to 11 ft. lbs. (15 Nm)

b. Step 2: Remove the air conditioning compressor and the accessory drive bracket.

c. Step 3: If equipped, disconnect the EGR tube and the 2 left lower bolts from the intake manifold.

d. Step 4: Install the lifting hook J-41427 (the one marked "left") and tighten the bolts to 11 ft. lbs. (15 Nm)

9. Remove or disconnect the following:

- Engine mount bracket-to-frame bolts
- Engine mount through-bolts

10. Raise the engine slightly and remove the engine mounts, support the engine with wood between the oil pan and the crossmember.

11. Remove the manual transmission and clutch as follows:

a. Step 1: Remove the clutch housing rear bolts.

b. Step 2: Remove the bolts attaching the clutch housing to the engine and remove the transmission and clutch as a unit.

➡ **Support the transmission as the last bolt is being removed to prevent damaging the clutch.**

c. Step 3: Remove the starter and clutch housing rear cover.

d. Step 4: Loosen the clutch mounting bolts a little at a time to prevent distorting the disc until spring pressure is released. Remove all of the bolts, the clutch disc and the pressure plate.

12. Remove the automatic transmission as follows:

a. Step 1: Lower the engine and support it on blocks.

b. Step 2: Remove the starter and converter housing cover.

c. Step 3: Remove the flexplate-to-converter attaching bolts.

d. Step 4: Support the transmission on blocks.

e. Step 5: Disconnect the detent cable.

f. Step 6: Remove the transmission-to-engine mounting bolts.

13. Attach an engine crane to the engine.

a. Step 7: Remove the blocks from the engine only and glide the engine away from the transmission.

To install:

14. Install the manual transmission and clutch as follows:

a. Step 1: Install the clutch disc and the pressure plate. Tighten the clutch mounting bolts a little at a time to prevent distorting the disc.

b. Step 2: Install the starter and clutch housing rear cover.

c. Step 3: Install the bolts attaching the clutch housing to the engine and install the transmission and clutch as a unit. Tighten the bolts to specification.

d. Step 4: Install the clutch housing rear bolts.

15. Install the automatic transmission as follows:

a. Step 1: Position the transmission.

b. Step 2: Install the transmission-to-engine mounting bolts.

c. Step 3: Connect the throttle linkage and detent cable.

d. Step 4: Install the flexplate-to-converter attaching bolts. Torque the bolts to 65 ft lbs. (90 Nm).

e. Step 5: Install the starter and converter housing cover.

16. Install or connect the following:
- Engine mount through-bolts. Torque the bolts to 50 ft lbs. (68 Nm)
- Engine mount bracket-to-frame bolts. Torque the bolts to 44 ft lbs. (59 Nm)
- Clutch cross-shaft

- Transmission mounting bolts. Torque the bolts to 75 ft lbs. (100 Nm)
- Transmission shift linkage and the speedometer cable.
- Driveshaft

17. Remove the lifting hooks.
- Compressor
- EGR valve tube
- Intake manifold retaining bolts
- Condenser
- Hood latch support
- Lower fan shroud and filler panel
- Transmission dipstick tube and the accelerator cable at the tube
- Coolant hose at the intake manifold and the PCV valve
- Cruise control servo, bracket and transducer
- Oil filler pipe and automatic transmission filler pipe
- Engine dipstick tube
- Thermostat housing, if removed
- Heater hoses at the engine
- Engine wiring harness to the firewall connection
- Radiator and the shroud
- Radiator support bracket
- Exhaust manifolds if removed
- Lower intake manifold if removed
- Intake manifold

- Fuel supply unit
- Lines to the fuel supply unit
- Accelerator and cruise control linkages
- Windshield wiper jar and bracket
- Air conditioning condenser
- Air conditioning vacuum reservoir, if equipped
- Fluid cooler lines at the radiator, if equipped with an automatic transmission
- Radiator coolant reservoir bottle
- Hoses at the radiator
- Upper radiator support
- Grille and the lower grille valance
- Air cleaner
- Air stove pipe
- Engine cover
- Battery cables

18. Refill the cooling system.
19. Recharge the air conditioning system.

Water Pump

REMOVAL & INSTALLATION

1. Before servicing the vehicle, refer to the precautions in the beginning of this section.

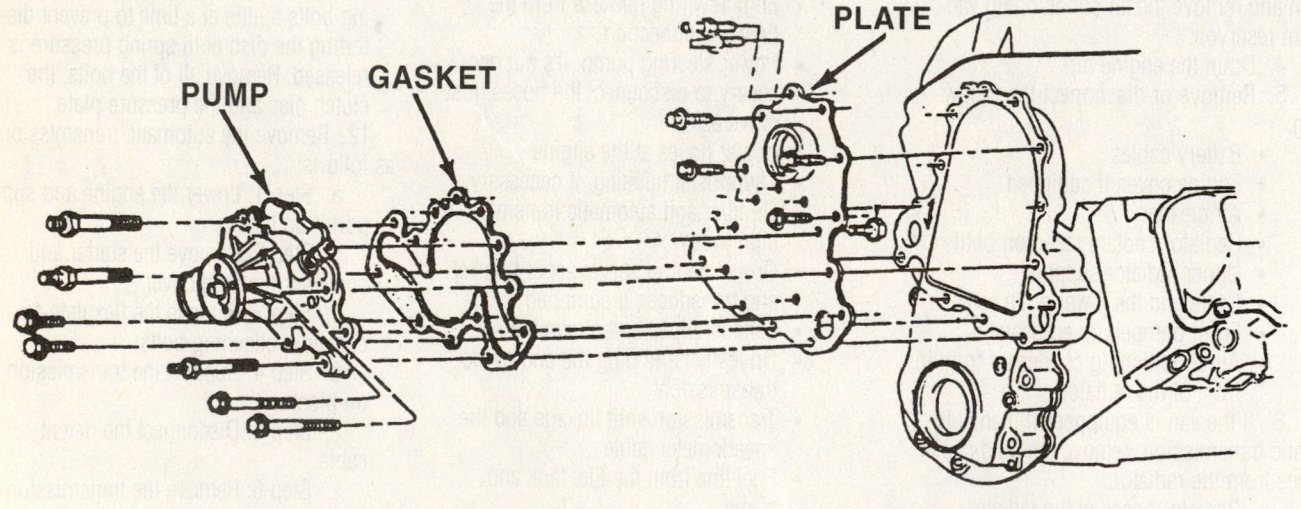

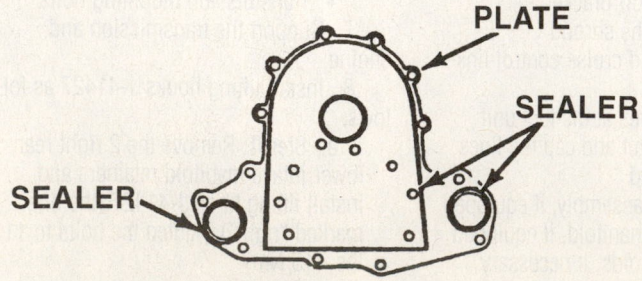

Exploded view of the water pump assembly and related components—6.5L diesel engines

7924KG05

2. Drain the engine coolant.
3. Remove or disconnect the following:
- Negative battery cables
- Fan and fan shroud
- Air conditioning hose bracket and/or the oil filler tube, as required
- Accessory drive belt(s)
- Vacuum pump mounting bracket nuts/bolt
- Vacuum pump and bracket
- Power steering pump and bracket
- Coolant hoses from the pump
- Water pump plate retaining bolts
- Pump and plate assembly from the engine

➡**Remove the bolt on the rear of the water pump plate.**

- Separate the pump and gasket from the plate

To install:

4. Install or connect the following:
- Water pump and a new gasket to the plate. Torque the retaining bolt (at the rear of the plate) to 20 ft. lbs. (28 Nm).

5. Be sure the block mating surface and the plate flanges are free of oil. Apply an anaerobic sealer GM part 1052357 or equivalent.

➡**The sealer must be wet to the touch when the bolts are tightened.**

- Water pump and plate assembly. Torque the bolts to 20 ft. lbs. (28 Nm).
- Coolant hoses to the pump assembly
- Power steering pump and bracket
- Vacuum pump and bracket, along with the bolt holding the pump and alternator
- Fan and pulley
- Accessory drive belt(s)
- Oil filler tube and/or air conditioning hose bracket nuts. If removed
- Fan shroud
- Batteries

6. Refill the radiator.

Glow Plugs

REMOVAL & INSTALLATION

1. Before servicing the vehicle, refer to the precautions in the beginning of this section.
2. Remove or disconnect the following:
- Negative battery cables

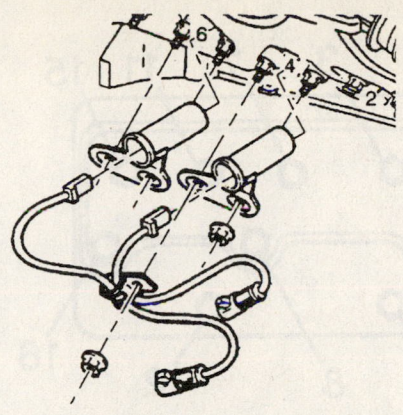

7924KG42

Exploded view of the heat shrouds and glow plug wiring—diesel engines

- Glow plug lead wires
- Plugs
- Right front tire
- Inner splash shield from the fender well.
- Lead wire from the plug at the No. 2 cylinder and the lead wires from plugs in the Nos. 4 and 6 cylinders at the harness connectors
- Heat shroud for the plug in the No. 4 and 6 cylinder. Slide the shrouds back just far enough to allow access so you can unplug the wires.
- Glow plugs in cylinders No. 2, 4 and 6.

3. Reach up under the vehicle and disconnect the lead wire at No. 8. Remove the glow plug.

➡**You may find that removing the exhaust pipe down mite make this a bit easier when working on Nos. 6 and 8.**

To install:

4. Install or connect the following:
- Glow plugs and tighten to 16 ft. lbs. (22 Nm)
- Heat shrouds and electrical connection
- Exhaust pipe, if removed
- Splash shields, if removed
- Negative battery cable

Cylinder Head

REMOVAL & INSTALLATION

1. Before servicing the vehicle, refer to the precautions in the beginning of this section.

➡**Refer to Section 1 of this manual for the cylinder head torque sequence illustration. The illustration is located after the Torque Specification Chart.**

2. Relieve the fuel system pressure.
3. Drain the coolant system.
4. Discharge the air conditioning system.
5. Remove or disconnect the following:
- Negative battery cable
- Intake manifold
- Fan upper shroud
- Compressor assembly, if equipped
- Turbocharger, if equipped
- Exhaust manifold
- Valve cover
- Rocker arm assemblies and pushrods

➡**Mark all components so they may be returned to their original location.**

- Air cleaner resonator and bracket
- Transmission and oil dipstick tube; remove the oil fill tube from the coolant crossover pipe
- Heater, radiator and bypass hoses
- Alternator upper bracket
- Alternator
- Power steering pump
- Vacuum pump
- Fuel bleeder valve at the coolant crossover pipe
- Fuel return crossover line clamp bolts from both cylinder heads
- Wire connector from the sensor in the coolant crossover pipe
- Electrical connection and brackets from cylinder head
- Coolant crossover pipe/thermostat assembly
- Head bolts and the cylinder heads

To install:

6. Clean the mating surfaces of the heads and block thoroughly.
7. Clean the head bolts thoroughly. Coat the threads of the head bolts with sealing compound GM part 1052080 or equivalent, before installation.
8. Install or connect the following:
- New gasket
- Cylinder head and bolts. Torque the bolts in the follows:
  a. Step 1: Torque the bolts to 20 ft. lbs. (25 Nm).

Timing belt service is covered in Section 4 of this manual

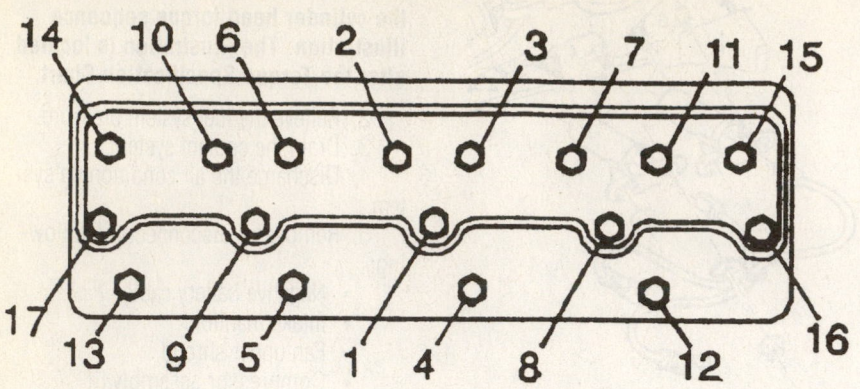

7924KG08

Tighten the cylinder head bolts according to the sequence shown for proper cylinder sealing—6.5L diesel engines

b. Step 2: Torque the bolts to 50 ft. lbs. (65 Nm).

c. Step 3: Then an additional 90 degrees (¼ turn).

- Coolant crossover pipe and thermostat
- Fuel valve
- Bypass hose
- Upper radiator hose
- Heater hoses at the head
- Transmission and oil dipstick tube
- Air cleaner resonator and bracket
- Pushrods, hardened ends facing up
- Rocker arm assemblies

9. Adjust the valves.
- Valve cover
- Alternator and upper bracket
- Exhaust manifolds. Torque bolts to 22 ft. lbs. (30 Nm)
- Upper fan shroud
- Intake manifold
- Turbocharger, if equipped
- Vacuum pump, if equipped
- Air conditioning compressor, if equipped
- Engine electrical connection
- Negative battery cable

10. Refill the cooling system with the proper type and quantity of antifreeze.

11. Evacuate and recharge the air conditioning system.

Starter Motor

REMOVAL & INSTALLATION

1. Before servicing the vehicle, refer to the precautions in the beginning of this section.

2. Remove or disconnect the following:
- Negative battery cable
- Mounting bolts/nuts and shim
- Starter
- Wires
- Heat shield and bracket

To install:

3. Install or connect the following:

- Heat shield and bracket. Torque the bolts to 13 ft lbs. (17 Nm)
- Wires. Torque battery wire nut to 89 inch lbs. (10 Nm), and Ignition nut to 18 inch lbs. (2 Nm)
- Starter
- Mounting bolts/nuts and shim. Torque the bolts to 33 ft lbs. (45 Nm) and the nut to 75 inch lbs. (8.5 Nm)
- Negative battery cable

Rocker Arms/Shaft

REMOVAL & INSTALLATION

1. Before servicing the vehicle, refer to the precautions in the beginning of this section.

2. Remove or disconnect the following:
- Engine cover

➡Rotate the engine until the mark on the crankshaft balancer is at the 2 o'clock position. Rotate the crankshaft counterclockwise 3½ in. (88mm) aligning the crankshaft balancer mark with the first lower water pump bolt, at

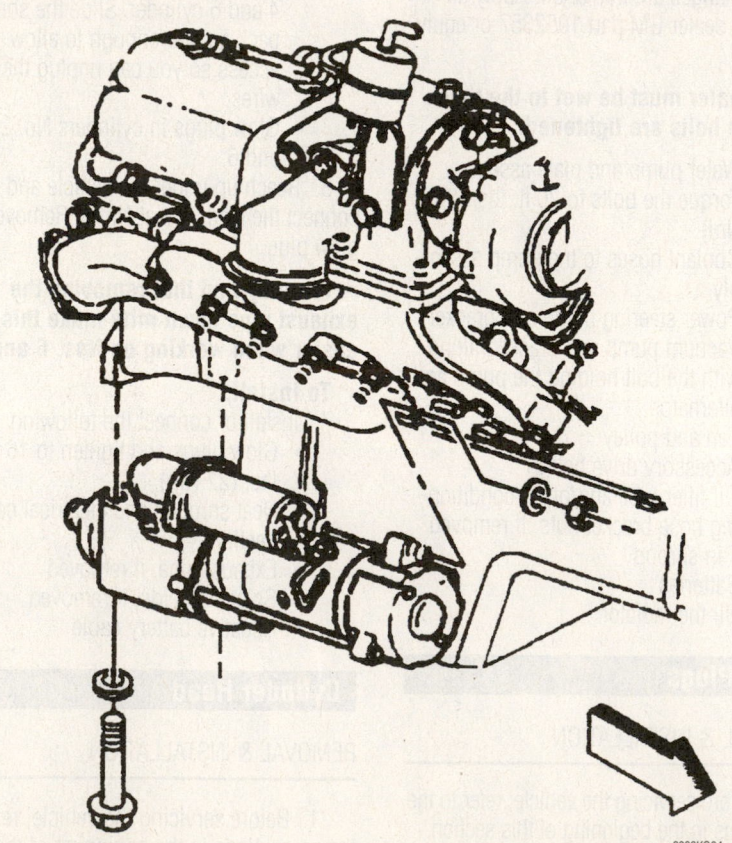

9308KG04

Exploded view of the starter motor.

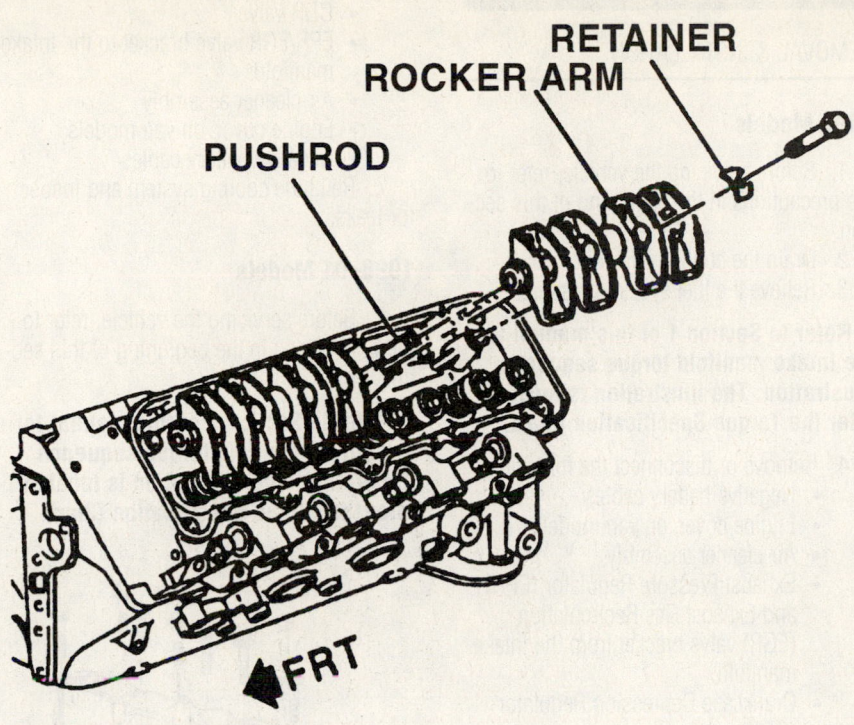

RETAINER
ROCKER ARM
PUSHROD

↖FRT

7924KG22

Rocker shaft assembly and related components—diesel engines

**about the 12:30 position. This will
ensure that no valves are close to a
piston crown**

- Cylinder head cover
- Rocker shaft assembly

➡ **The rocker assemblies are mounted
on 2 short rocker shafts per cylinder
head, with each shaft operating 4 rockers. 2 bolts secure each rocker shaft
assembly, Mark the shafts so they can
be installed in their original locations.**

• Pushrods. The pushrods MUST be
installed in the original direction! A paint
stripe usually identifies the upper end of
each rod, but if you can't see it, be sure to
mark each rod yourself.

3. Insert a small prybar into the end
of the rocker shaft bore and break off the
end of the nylon retainers. Pull off the
retainers with pliers, then slide off the
rockers.

To install:

4. Be sure first that the rocker arms and
springs go back on the shafts in the exact
order in which they were removed. It's a
good idea to coat them with engine oil.

5. Center the rockers on the corresponding holes in the shaft

6. Install or connect the following:

• New plastic retainers using a ½ in.
(13mm) drift
• Pushrods with there marked ends up
• Rocker shaft assemblies and be sure
that the ball ends of the pushrods
seat themselves in the rockers

7. Rotate the engine clockwise until the
mark on the torsional damper aligns with
the **0** on the timing tab. Rotate the engine
counterclockwise 3 ½ in. (88mm) measured
at the damper. You can estimate this by
checking that the mark on the damper is
now aligned with the FIRST lower water
pump bolt. BE CAREFUL! This ensures that
the piston is away from the valves.

• Rocker shaft bolts. Torque them to
40 ft. lbs. (55 Nm)
• Cylinder head cover
• Engine cover

Turbocharger

REMOVAL & INSTALLATION

1. Before servicing the vehicle, refer to
the precautions in the beginning of this section.

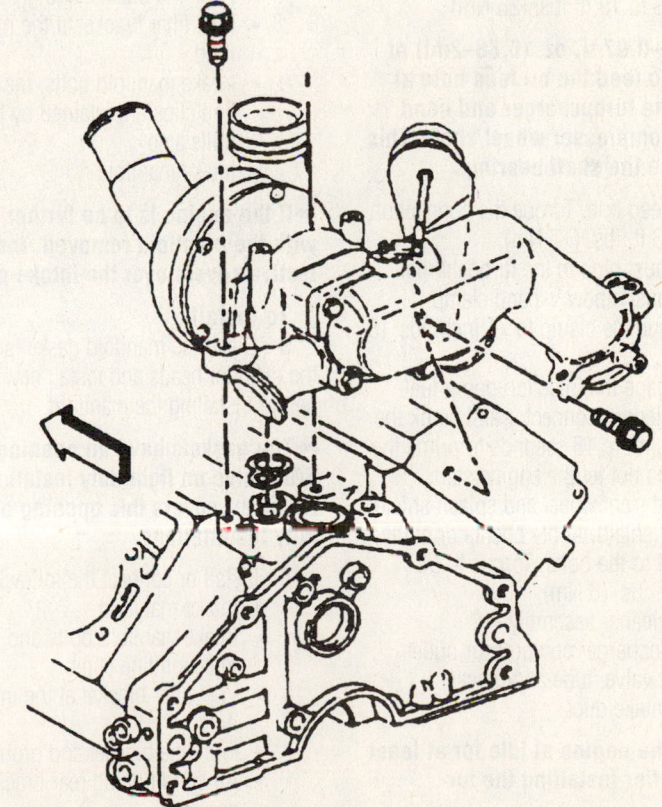

7924KG43

Turbocharger mounting—diesel engines

2. Remove or disconnect the following:
- Negative battery cable
- Air inlet duct
- Oil feed line from the top of the turbocharger
- Crankcase Depression Regulator (CDR) valve vent bracket screw
- CDR valve and vent tube
- Air cleaner assembly
- Heat shield
- Right front tire assembly and the splash shield
- Exhaust pipe-to-turbocharger exhaust outlet elbow V-band clamp
- Oil drain tube-to-turbocharger center bearing bolts
- Exhaust manifold-to-turbocharger nuts
- Turbocharger

To install:

➡**Use anti-seize compound on all threaded fasteners connected to the turbocharger**

3. Install or connect the following:
- Turbocharger to the exhaust manifold. Torque the nuts to 37 ft. lbs. (50 Nm)
- New oil drain tube flange gasket and the oil drain tube. Torque the bolts to 19 ft. lbs. (26 Nm)

➡**Use 0.03–0.07 fl. oz. (0.88–2ml) of engine oil to feed the oil feed hole at the top of the turbocharger and hand rotate the compressor wheel/shaft. This will pre-lube the shaft bearings**

- Oil feed line. Torque the connection to 13 ft. lbs. (17 Nm).
- Exhaust pipe to the turbocharger exhaust elbow V-band clamp. Torque the clamp to 71 inch. lbs. (8 Nm).

4. Disengage the injection pump fuel shutdown solenoid connector and crank the engine for no more 15 seconds to prime the oil system. Do not let the engine start.
- Right front wheel and splash shield
- Heat shield. Apply Loctite or equivalent to the bolts. Torque to 56 inch. lbs. (6 Nm)
- Air cleaner assembly
- Turbocharger compressor outlet
- CDR valve, tube and bracket
- Air intake duct

➡**Operate the engine at idle for at least 3 minutes after installing the turbocharger**

Intake Manifold

REMOVAL & INSTALLATION

1997 Models

1. Before servicing the vehicle, refer to the precautions in the beginning of this section.
2. Drain the cooling system
3. Relieve the fuel system pressure.

➡**Refer to Section 1 of this manual for the intake manifold torque sequence illustration. The illustration is located after the Torque Specification Chart.**

4. Remove or disconnect the following:
- Negative battery cables
- Engine cover, on van models
- Air cleaner assembly
- Exhaust Pressure Regulator (EPR) and Exhaust Gas Recirculation (EGR) valve bracket from the intake manifold.
- Crankcase Depression Regulator (CDR) valve
- Crankcase ventilator hose and EGR
- Air conditioning rear bracket, if equipped
- Fuel line bracket and ground strap
- Fuel filter bracket at the intake manifold
- Intake manifold bolts, the injection line clips are retained by these bolts also
- Intake manifold

➡**If the engine is to be further serviced with the manifold removed, install protective covers over the intake ports.**

To install:

5. Clean the manifold gasket surfaces on the cylinder heads and install new gaskets before installing the manifold.

➡**The gaskets have an opening for the EGR valve on light duty installations. An insert covers this opening on heavy-duty installations.**

6. Install or connect the following:
- Intake manifold
- Intake manifold bolts and fuel injection line clips
- Fuel filter bracket at the intake manifold
- Fuel line bracket and ground strap
- Air conditioning rear bracket, if equipped

- Crankcase ventilator hose and EGR
- CDR valve
- EPR/EGR valve bracket to the intake manifold.
- Air cleaner assembly
- Engine cover, on van models
- Negative battery cables

7. Refill the cooling system and inspect for leaks.

1998–01 Models

1. Before servicing the vehicle, refer to the precautions in the beginning of this section.

➡**Refer to Section 1 of this manual for the intake manifold torque sequence illustration. The illustration is located after the Torque Specification Chart.**

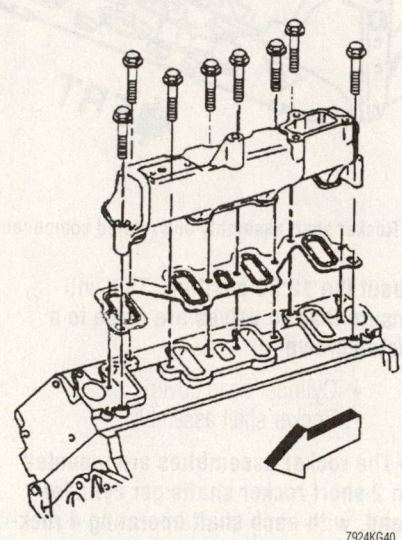

Exploded view of the side intake manifold mounting—1998–01 models

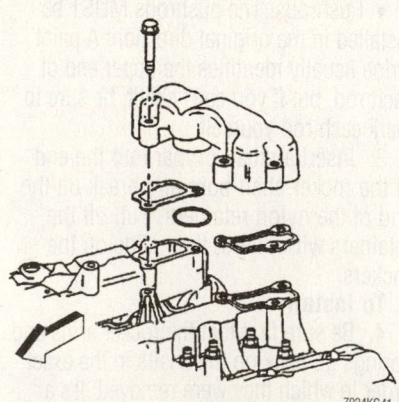

Center intake manifold mounting—1998–01 models

2. Recover air conditioning system, and reposition air conditioning lines.

3. Remove or disconnect the following:
- Negative battery cable
- Air cleaner assembly
- Fuel lines, and electrical connections
- Engine and transmission oil level tubes

✳✳ WARNING

Do not remove the center intake and side intakes as an assembly. Damage to the center intake and turbocharger may occur.

- Center intake assembly, and glow plug relay
- Side intake bolts and fuel retaining clips
- Side intakes

4. Clean all gaskets surface.

To install:

5. Install or connect the following:
- Side intakes and new gaskets. Torque the bolts to 31 ft. lbs. (42 Nm)
- Fuel lines retaining clips and electrical connection
- Center intake with new gaskets. Torque the bolts to 17 ft. lbs. (23 Nm)
- Engine oil and transmission oil level tubes
- Glow plug relay
- Air conditioning lines and recharge system
- Air cleaner assembly
- Negative battery cable

6. Recharge air conditioning system.

Exhaust Manifold

REMOVAL & INSTALLATION

1. Before servicing the vehicle, refer to the precautions in the beginning of this section.

2. Remove or disconnect the following:
- Batteries cables
- Exhaust pipe from the manifold flange
- Engine oil and transmission oil fill tubes
- Engine cover and disconnect the glow plug wires
- Glow plugs
- Turbocharger assembly, as required

- Air conditioner compressor rear bracket, as required
- Manifold bolts and the manifold

To install:

3. Install or connect the following:
- Exhaust manifold. Torque the bolts to 26 ft. lbs. (35 Nm)
- Exhaust pipe

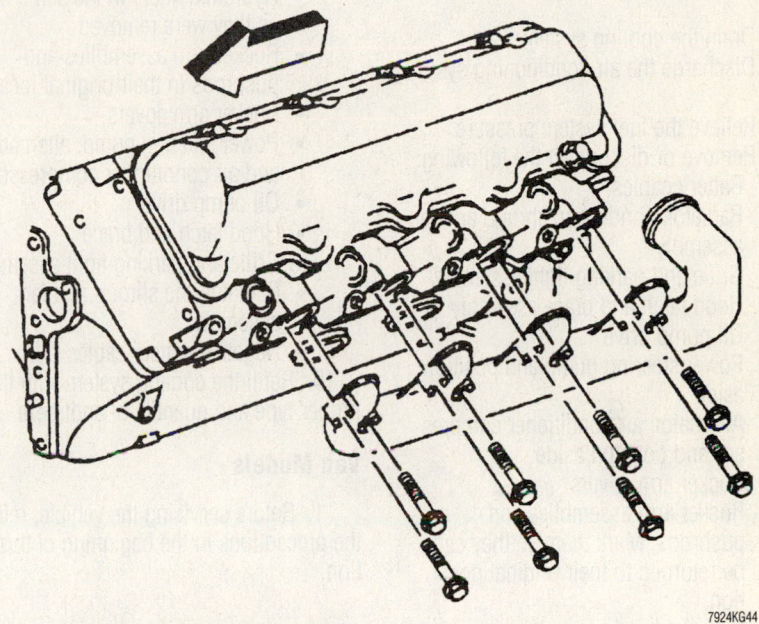

7924KG44

Exploded view of the left exhaust manifold mounting—diesel engines

- Glow plugs and electrical connection
- Engine and transmission oil fill tubes
- Air conditioning compressor bracket
- Negative battery cable

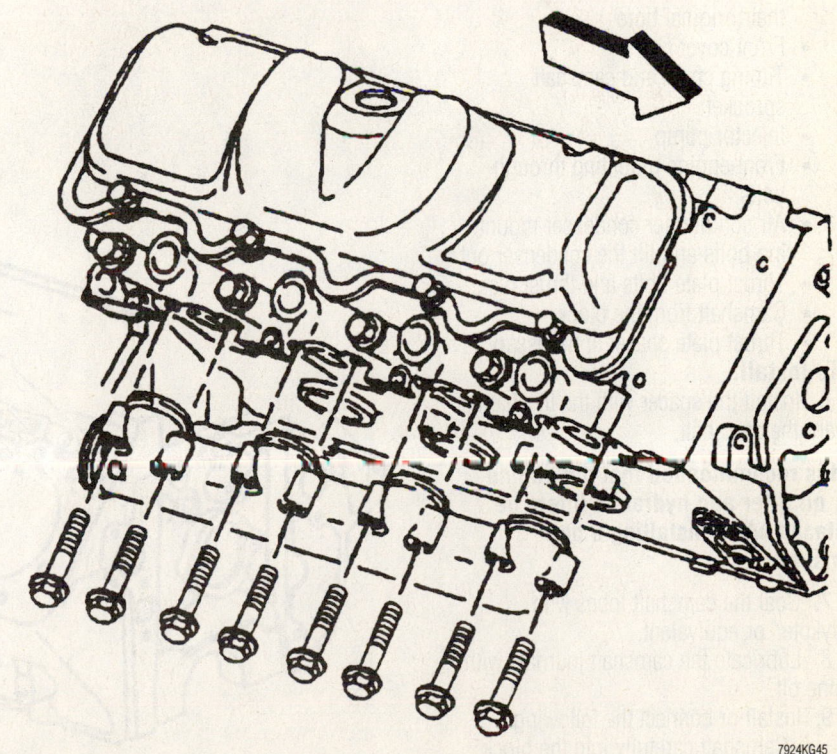

7924KG45

Exploded view of the right exhaust manifold mounting—diesel engines

Refer to Section 1 for engine rebuilding specifications

Camshaft and Valve Lifters

REMOVAL & INSTALLATION

Except Van Models

1. Before servicing the vehicle, refer to the precautions in the beginning of this section.
2. Drain the cooling system.
3. Discharge the air conditioning system.
4. Relieve the fuel system pressure.
5. Remove or disconnect the following:
   - Battery cables
   - Radiator, condenser, shroud and fan assembly
   - Grille and parking light assembly
   - Hood latch and brace assembly
   - Oil pump drive
   - Power steering pump and position aside
   - Alternator, air conditioner compressor and position aside
   - Rocker arm covers
   - Rocker arm assemblies and pushrods. Mark them so they can be returned to their original position.
   - Cylinder heads
   - Hydraulic lifters and keep them in order so they can be returned to their original bore
   - Front cover
   - Timing chain and camshaft sprocket
   - Injector pump
   - Front engine mounting through-bolts
   - Air conditioner condenser mounting bolts and lift the condenser out
   - Thrust plate bolts and thrust plate
   - Camshaft from the block
   - Thrust plate spacer, if necessary

To install:

6. Install the spacer with the ID chamfer toward the camshaft.

➡**It is recommended that the engine oil, oil filter and hydraulic lifters be replaced when installing a new camshaft.**

7. Coat the camshaft lobes with Molykote® or equivalent.
8. Lubricate the camshaft journals with engine oil.
9. Install or connect the following:
   - Camshaft carefully into the block
   - Thrust plate and bolts. Tighten to 17 ft. lbs. (23 Nm)

   - Engine mount through-bolts
   - Timing chain and sprockets, Align the timing marks
   - Air conditioner condenser, if equipped
   - Injector pump
   - Front cover
   - Cylinder head
   - Hydraulic lifters in the same bore as they were removed
   - Rocker arm assemblies and pushrods in their original locations
   - Rocker arm covers
   - Power steering pump, alternator and air conditioner compressor
   - Oil pump drive
   - Hood latch and brace
   - Grille and parking light assembly
   - Radiator, the shroud and fan assembly
   - Negative battery cables

10. Refill the cooling system with the proper type and quantity of antifreeze.

Van Models

1. Before servicing the vehicle, refer to the precautions in the beginning of this section.

2. Drain the cooling system.
3. Relieve the fuel system pressure.
4. Remove or disconnect the following:
   - Battery cables
   - Headlight bezels
   - Grille, bumper and lower valance panel
   - Hood latch
   - Coolant recovery bottle
   - Upper tie bar
   - Air conditioner compressor
   - Radiator and fan
   - Oil pump drive
   - Cylinder heads to gain clearance for lifter removal
   - Alternator lower bracket
   - Water pump
   - Torsional damper
   - Front cover
   - Injection pump
   - Rocker arm covers
   - Rocker arm assemblies and pushrods. Mark them so they can be returned to their original position.
   - Hydraulic lifters and keep them in order so they can be returned to their original bore.
   - Timing chain and camshaft sprocket

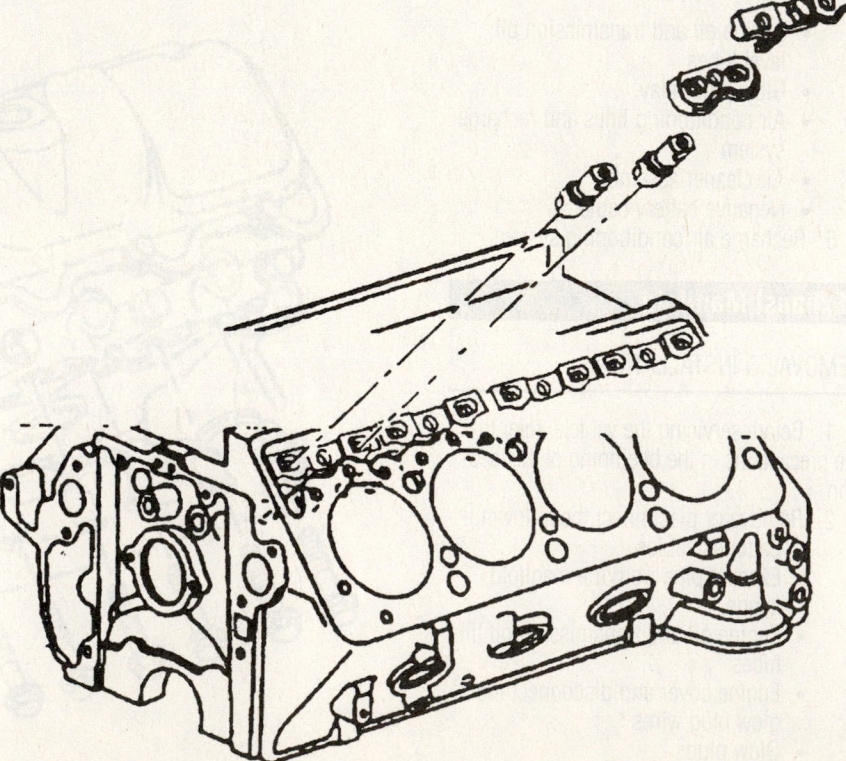

Exploded view of the lifter, guide plate and clamp—diesel engines

7924KG46

- Thrust plate bolts and thrust plate
- Camshaft from the block
- Thrust plate spacer, if necessary

To install:

5. Install the spacer with the ID chamfer toward the camshaft.

➡ **It is recommended that the engine oil, oil filter and hydraulic lifters be replaced when installing a new camshaft.**

6. Coat the camshaft lobes with Molykote®, or equivalent.

7. Lubricate the camshaft journals with engine oil.

8. Install or connect the following:

- Camshaft carefully into the block
- Thrust plate and bolts. Torque the bolts to 17 ft. lbs. (23 Nm)
- Timing chain and sprockets, align the timing marks
- Hydraulic lifters in the same bore as they were removed
- Rocker arm assemblies and pushrods in their original locations
- Rocker arm covers
- Fuel pump
- Front cover
- Torsional damper and water pump
- Alternator lower bracket
- Cylinder heads
- Oil pump drive
- Radiator and fan
- Air conditioner compressor
- Upper tie bar
- Coolant recovery bottle
- Hood latch
- Grille, bumper and lower valence panel
- Headlight bezels
- Battery cables

9. Refill the cooling system.

10. Evacuate and charge the air conditioner system.

Valve Lash

ADJUSTMENT

All engines use hydraulic lifters, which require no periodic adjustment.

Oil Pan

REMOVAL & INSTALLATION

Except Van Models

1. Before servicing the vehicle, refer to the precautions in the beginning of this section.

2. Drain the engine oil.

3. Remove or disconnect the following:

- Battery cables
- Oil dipstick
- Flywheel/flexplate cover
- Oil cooler line guides
- Front driveshaft
- Front axle, if needed
- Exhaust pipes from the manifolds
- Front engine mount through-bolts
- Oil pan bolts and the oil pan
- Oil pan rear seal

To install:

4. Clean all sealing surfaces.

5. Apply a ³⁄₁₆ in. (5mm) bead of RTV sealant to the oil pan sealing surface, inboard of the bolt holes. The sealant must be wet to the touch when the oil pan is to be installed.

6. Install or connect the following:

- Oil pan rear seal
- Oil pan to the engine. Torque all bolts except the rear 2 bolts to 84 inch lbs. (9.4 Nm) Tighten the rear bolts to 17 ft. lbs. (23 Nm).
- Engine mounting through-bolt and nut
- Front axles and front driveshaft, if removed
- Oil cooler lines in guides
- Oil dipstick
- Exhaust pipes to the manifolds
- Flywheel/flexplate cover
- Battery cables

7. Refill with the proper grade and quantity of oil.

Van Models

1. Before servicing the vehicle, refer to the precautions in the beginning of this section.

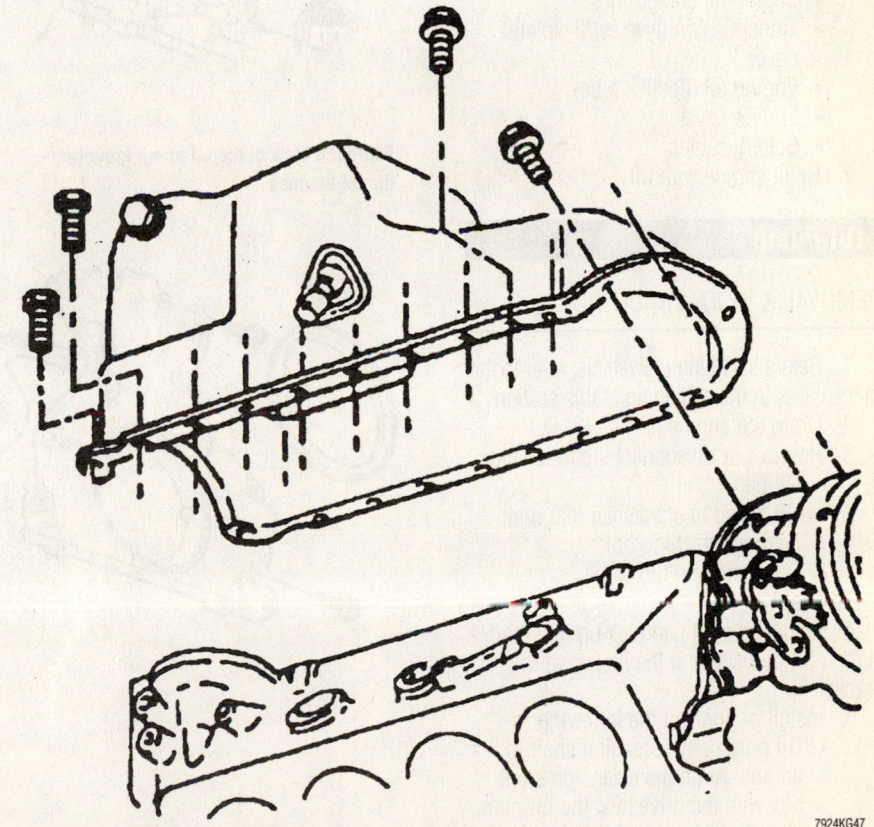

Exploded view of the oil pan mounting—diesel engines

7924KG47

2. Drain the engine oil.
3. Remove or disconnect the following:
   - Battery cables
   - Engine cover
   - Engine oil dipstick
   - Transmission flywheel/flexplate cover
   - Oil cooler lines at the block
   - Starter
   - Transmission cooler lines, battery cables and attaching clamps from the oil pan
   - Oil pan bolts
   - Oil pan and oil pan rear seal

To install:

4. Clean all sealing surfaces
5. Apply a ³⁄₁₆ in. (5mm) bead of RTV sealant to the oil pan sealing surface, inboard of the bolt holes. The sealant must be wet to the touch when the oil pan is to be installed.
6. Install or connect the following:
   - Oil pan rear seal.
   - Oil pan to the engine and the retaining bolts.
   - Starter
   - Transmission cooler lines, battery cables and attaching clamps to the oil pan
   - Engine oil cooler lines
   - Transmission flywheel/flexplate cover
   - Engine oil dipstick tube
   - Engine cover
   - Battery cables
7. Refill engine with oil.

Oil Pump

REMOVAL & INSTALLATION

1. Before servicing the vehicle, refer to the precautions in the beginning of this section.
2. Drain the engine oil
3. Remove or disconnect the following:
   - Oil pan
   - Oil pump to crankshaft rear main bearing attaching bolt
   - Oil pump and hex drive

To install:

4. Inspect the oil pan pick up tube and screen for damage and the hex drive for cracks.
5. Install or connect the following:
   - Oil pump and extension shaft to the engine. Align the extension shaft hex with the drive hex, the oil pump should push easily into place.
   - Oil pump bolt. Torque the bolt to 65 ft. lbs. (90 Nm).
   - Oil pan
6. Refill the crankcase with oil.

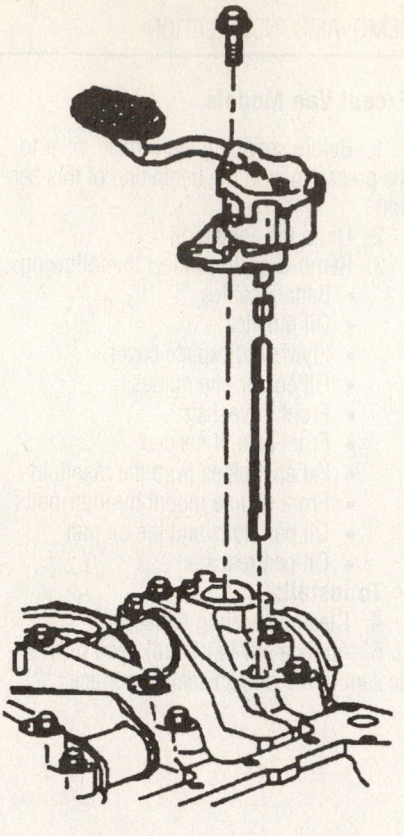

7924KG48

Exploded view of the oil pump mounting— diesel engines

Rear Main Seal

REMOVAL & INSTALLATION

Please note that the entire transmission assembly must be removed before performing this procedure. Before a new seal is installed, the Crankcase Depression Regulator (CDR) and crankcase ventilation system should be cleaned and inspected. In addition, use care removing the flywheel. Some models use a heavy, dual mass flywheel that must be handled with care.

1. Before servicing the vehicle, refer to the precautions in the beginning of this section.
2. Remove or disconnect the following:
   - Negative battery cables
   - Transfer case, if equipped
   - Transmission assembly
   - Clutch assembly and flywheel, if equipped with manual transmission
   - Flexplate, if equipped with automatic transmission
   - Crankshaft rear main oil seal by inserting a suitable prying tool and prying the seal out

To install:

3. Clean the oil seal bore in the block thoroughly before installation of the new seal.
4. Inspect the crankshaft for grit, rust or burrs and correct as necessary. Also inspect the portion of the crankshaft where the oil

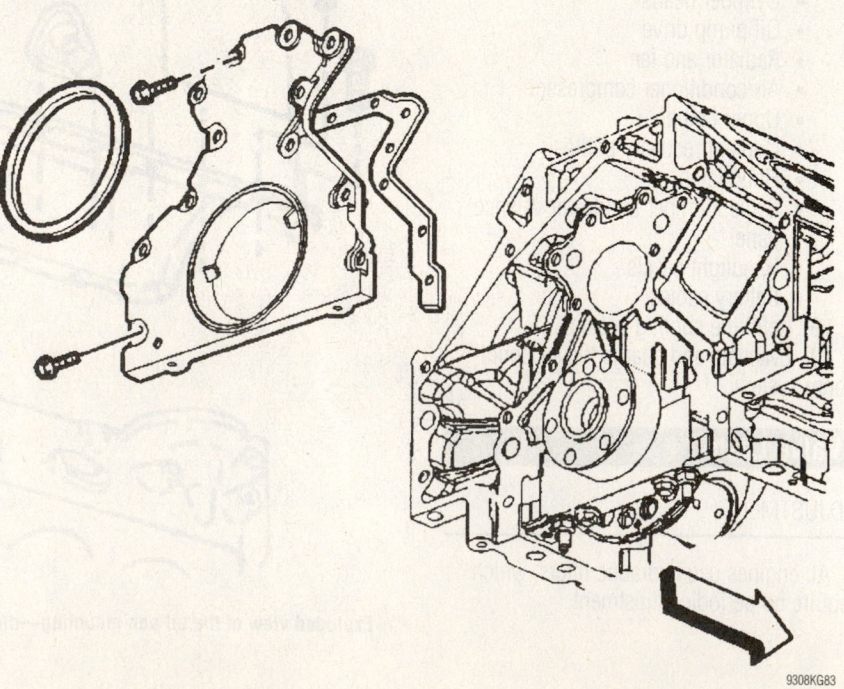

9308KG83

Rear main seal—4.8L, 5.3L, 6.0L

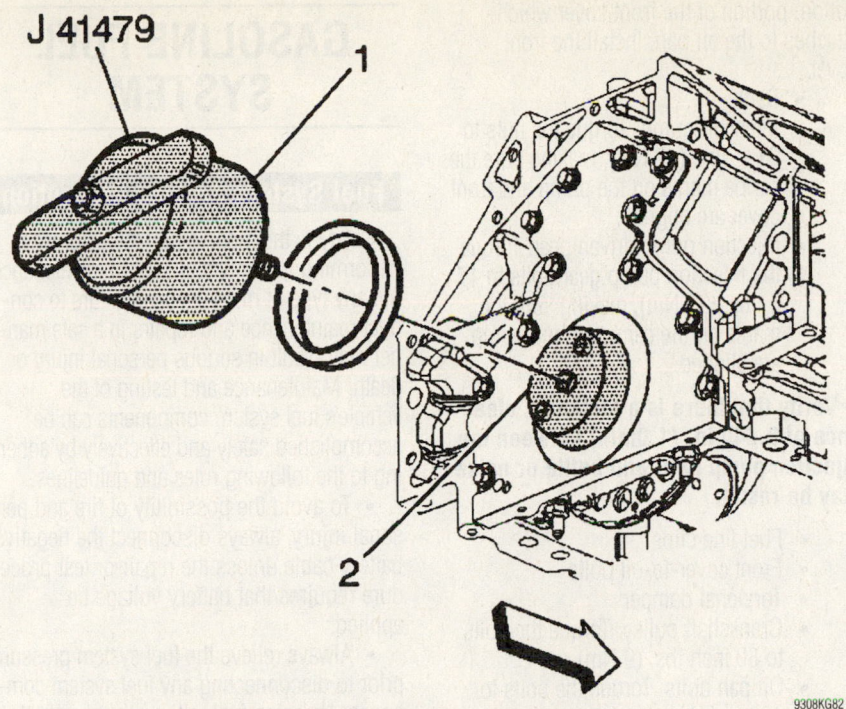

J 41479

Rear main seal installation tool—4.8L, 5.3L, 6.0L

5. Clean the running surface of the crankshaft with a non-abrasive cleaner.

6. Lubricate the inner diameter of the new seal and the outer diameter of the crankshaft with engine oil.

7. Install or connect the following:
- Rear main oil seal until. Using a J 39084 (4.3, 5.0, 5.7 and 7.4L engines) or J 41479 (4.8, 5.3 and 6.0L engines) installation tool the tool bottoms against the block and crankshaft rear main bearing cap.
- Flywheel. Use thread-locking compound on the flywheel retainer bolts. Torque the bolts to 45 ft. lbs. (60 Nm) New bolts are recommended.
- Transmission assembly
- Transfer case, if equipped
- Negative battery cables

8. Start the engine and verify no oil leaks.

seal makes contact, for wear due to the rubbing action of the oil seal.

➡ **Because of rear crankshaft wear or grooving, the new oil seal should be** seated in a new location. The J 39084 installation tool will control the seal positioning. This will provide a new surface on the crankshaft for the seal to ride on.

Timing Chain, Sprockets, Front Cover and Seal

REMOVAL & INSTALLATION

1. Before servicing the vehicle, refer to the precautions in the beginning of this section.

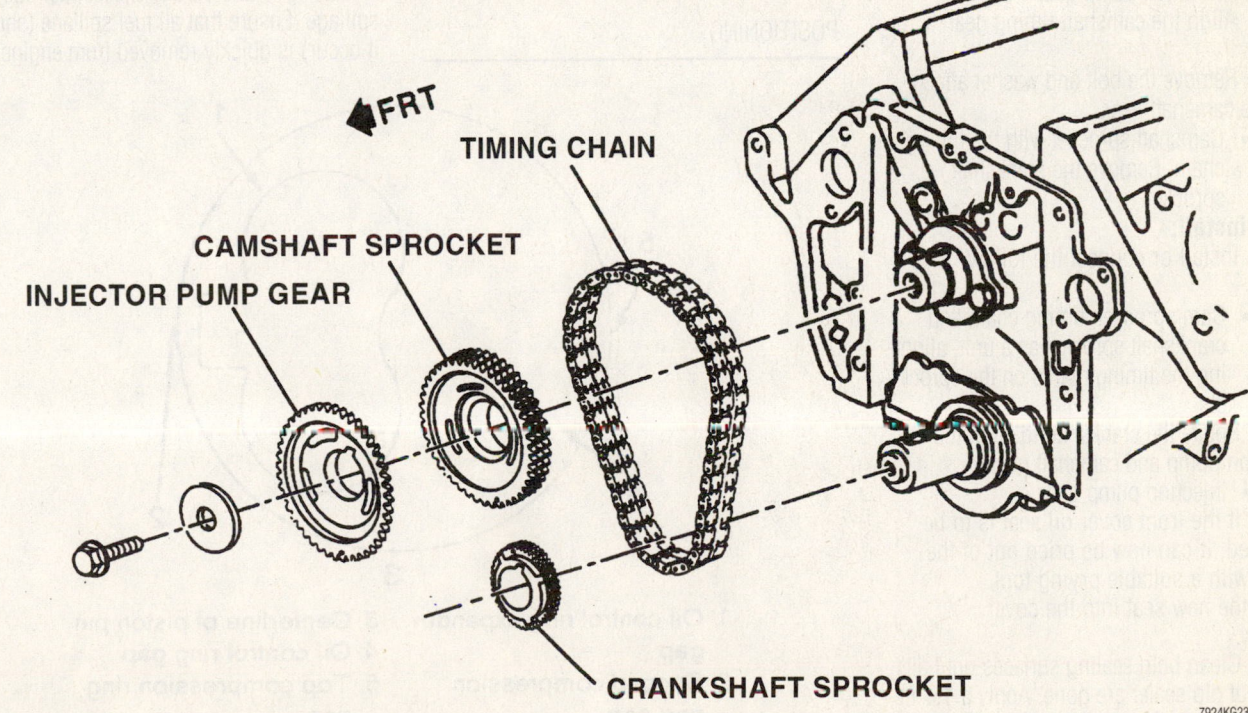

Timing chain and related components—6.5L diesel engines

For complete mechanical specifications, refer to Section 1 of this manual

2. Drain the cooling system.

3. Remove or disconnect the following:

- Negative battery cables
- Water pump and pulleys

4. Rotate the crankshaft to align the marks on the torsional damper with the **0** mark on the timing tab.

5. Scribe a mark aligning the injection pump flange and the front cover, if not already marked.

➡ **The outer ring (weight) of the torsional damper is bonded to the hub with rubber. The damper must be removed with a puller that acts on the inner hub only. Pulling on the outer portion of the damper will break the rubber bond or destroy the tuning of the unit.**

6. Remove or disconnect the following:

- Crankshaft pulley and torsional damper
- Front cover-to-oil pan bolts (4)
- 2 fuel return line clips
- Injection pump gear
- Injection pump retaining nuts from the front cover
- Crankshaft sensor
- Baffle
- Cover bolts remaining and the front cover
- Injection pump gear

7. Align the camshaft timing gear marks

8. Remove the bolt and washer attaching the camshaft gear.

- Camshaft sprocket with the timing chain. Remove the crankshaft sprocket.

To install:

9. Install or connect the following:

- Cam sprocket, timing chain and crankshaft sprocket as a unit, aligning the timing marks on the sprockets.

10. Rotate the crankshaft to align the injection pump and camshaft gears.

- Injection pump gear

11. If the front cover oil seal is to be replaced, it can now be pried out of the cover with a suitable prying tool. Press the new seal into the cover evenly.

12. Clean both sealing surfaces until all traces of old sealer are gone. Apply a ³⁄₃₂ in. (2mm) bead of GM sealant 1052357 or equivalent to the sealing surface. Apply a ³⁄₁₆ in. (5mm) bead of RTV type sealer to the

bottom portion of the front cover which attaches to the oil pan. Install the front cover.

- Baffle
- Injection pump. Torque the nuts to 31 ft. lbs. (42 Nm), making sure the scribe marks on the pump and front cover are aligned.
- Injection pump driven gear. Torque the injection pump gear bolts to 17 ft. lbs. (23 Nm), making sure the marks on the cam gear and pump are aligned.

➡ **Verify that there is a minimum clearance of 0.040 in. (1.0mm) between the injection pump gear and baffle or noise may be result.**

- Fuel line clips
- Front cover-to-oil bolts
- Torsional damper
- Crankshaft pulley. Torque the bolts to 80 inch lbs. (9 Nm).
- Oil pan bolts. Torque the bolts to 106 inch lbs. (12 Nm).
- Water pump
- Pulley assembly
- Negative battery cables

13. Refill the cooling system with the proper type and quantity of antifreeze.

14. Inspect the engine for leaks.

Piston and Ring

POSITIONING

GASOLINE FUEL SYSTEM

Fuel System Service Precautions

Safety is the most important factor when performing not only fuel system maintenance but any type of maintenance. Failure to conduct maintenance and repairs in a safe manner may result in serious personal injury or death. Maintenance and testing of the vehicle's fuel system components can be accomplished safely and effectively by adhering to the following rules and guidelines.

- To avoid the possibility of fire and personal injury, always disconnect the negative battery cable unless the repair or test procedure requires that battery voltage be applied.
- Always relieve the fuel system pressure prior to disconnecting any fuel system component (injector, fuel rail, pressure regulator, etc.), fitting or fuel line connection. Exercise extreme caution whenever relieving fuel system pressure, to avoid exposing skin, face and eyes to fuel spray. Please be advised that fuel under pressure may penetrate the skin or any part of the body that it contacts.
- Always place a shop towel or cloth around the fitting or connection prior to loosening to absorb any excess fuel due to spillage. Ensure that all fuel spillage (should it occur) is quickly removed from engine

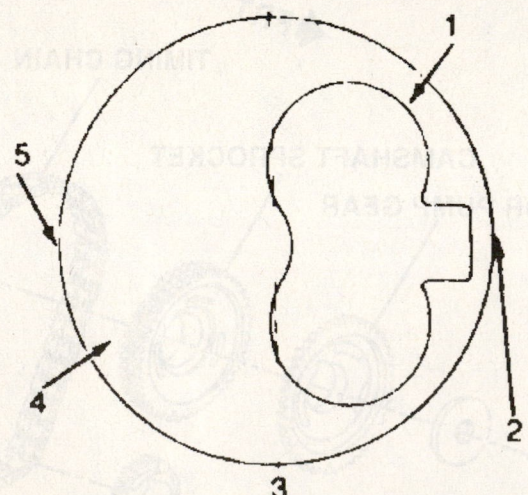

1 Oil control ring expander gap
2 Second compression ring gap
3 Centerline of piston pin
4 Oil control ring gap
5 Top compression ring gap

7924AG11

General Motors Diesel engines—piston ring end-gap spacing

surfaces. Ensure that all fuel soaked cloths or towels are deposited into a suitable waste container.

• Always keep a dry chemical (Class B) fire extinguisher near the work area.

• Do not allow fuel spray or fuel vapors to come into contact with a spark or open flame.

• Always use a back-up wrench when loosening and tightening fuel line connection fittings. This will prevent unnecessary stress and torsion to fuel line piping. Always follow the proper torque specifications.

• Always replace worn fuel fitting O-rings with new. Do not substitute fuel hose or equivalent where fuel pipe is installed.

Fuel System Pressure

RELIEVING

A Schrader valve is provided on these fuel systems, in order to conveniently test or release the system pressure. A fuel pressure gauge and adapter will be necessary to connect the gauge to the fitting. Most of the MFI systems utilize a service valve on one end of the fuel rail assembly. The CMFI system covered here uses a valve located on the inlet pipe fitting, immediately before it enters the CMFI assembly (towards the rear of the engine)

1. Before servicing the vehicle, refer to the precautions in the beginning of this section.

Except Silverado and 2000–01 Sierra 15 Series

1. Remove or disconnect the following:
   • Negative battery cable
   • Fuel filler cap to release the fuel tank pressure.
2. Be sure the release valve on the fuel gauge is closed, then connect the fuel gauge to the pressure fitting located on the inlet fuel pipe fitting.

➡ **When connecting the gauge to the fitting, be sure to wrap a rag around the fitting to avoid spillage. After repairs, place the rag in an approved container.**

   • Bleed hose portion of the fuel gauge assembly into an approved container, then open the gauge release valve and bleed the fuel pressure from the system.

To install:
3. When the gauge is removed, be sure to open the bleed valve and drain all fuel from the gauge assembly.

4. Install or connect the following:
   • Fuel filler cap
   • Negative battery cable

Silverado and 2000–01 Sierra 15 Series

1. Turn the ignition OFF.
2. Disconnect the negative battery cable.
3. Loosen the fuel filler cap in order to relieve the fuel tank vapor pressure.
4. Connect a fuel pressure gauge to the fuel pressure valve.
5. Wrap a shop towel around the fitting while connecting the gauge in order to avoid spillage.
6. Install the bleed hose of the gauge into an approved container.
7. Open the valve on the gauge to bleed the system pressure.

The fuel connections are now safe for servicing. Drain any fuel remaining in the gauge into an approved container.

Fuel Filter

REMOVAL & INSTALLATION

Except Silverado and 2000–01 Sierra 15 Series

The fuel filter is normally located along the frame rail of the vehicle. On some vehicles however, it may have been relocated to the engine compartment. When in doubt, trace a fuel line from the engine backwards or from the tank forward in order to locate the filter.

Some vehicles utilize a spin-on fuel filter located on the frame rail. This filter can be turned counterclockwise after the fuel pressure is relieved.

1. Properly relieve the fuel system pressure.

2. Remove or disconnect the following:
   • Negative battery cable
   • Fuel line connections from the filter or unscrew the filter in the case of the spin-on type
   • In line filters, remove the bolt from the filter mounting clamp, then remove the clamp and filter assembly. Separate the filter from the clamp.

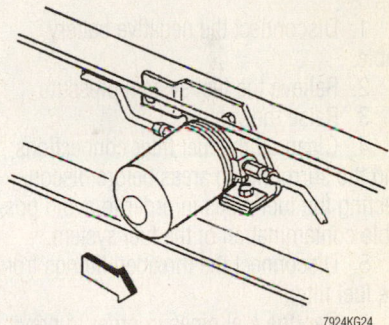

7924KG24

The spin-on fuel filter is serviced in the same manner as a spin-on oil filter

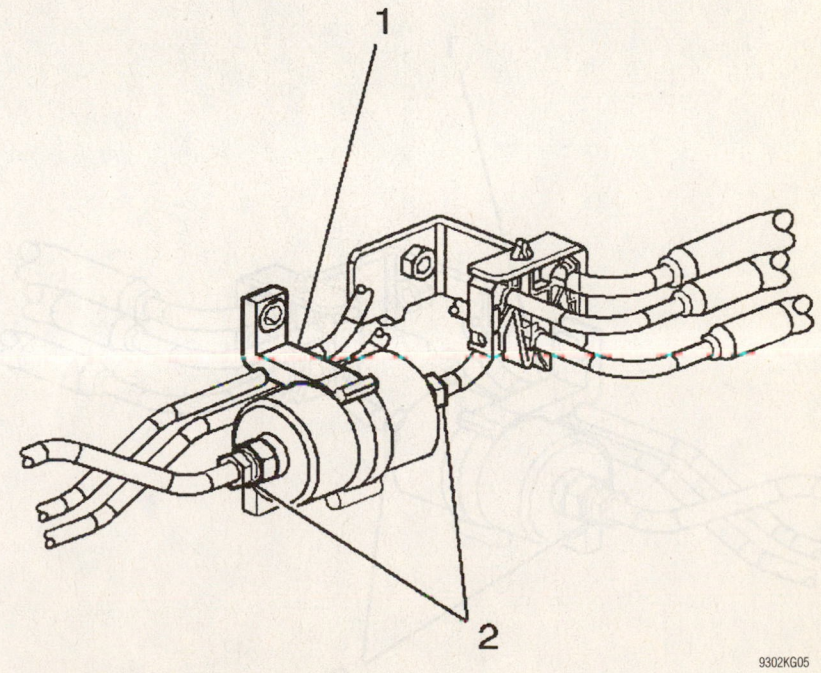

9302KG05

Typical in-line fuel filter mounting location

To install:

➡ The inline filter has an arrow (fuel flow direction) on the side of the case, be sure to install it correctly in the system, with the arrow facing away from the fuel tank.

3. Install or connect the following:
   - In line filters place filter in clamp
   - Install filter and clamp
   - Spin-on filters, lubricate the gasket before installation. Then tighten the filter an additional ¾ of a turn from the point when the gasket touches the filter adapter. Always check for leaks after a new filter is installed.

Silverado and 2000–01 Sierra 15 Series

1. Disconnect the negative battery cable.
2. Relieve the fuel system pressure.
3. Raise the vehicle.
4. Clean all the fuel filter connections and the surrounding areas before disconnecting the fuel pipes in order to avoid possible contamination of the fuel system.
5. Disconnect the threaded fittings from the fuel filter.
6. Cap the fuel pipes in order to prevent possible fuel system contamination.
7. Slide the fuel filter from the bracket.
8. Inspect the fuel pipe O-rings for cuts,

nicks, swelling, or distortion. Replace the O-rings if necessary.

To install:

9. Slide the fuel filter into the bracket. Remove the caps from the fuel pipes.
10. Connect the threaded fittings to the fuel filter. Tighten the fittings to 25 Nm (18 ft. lbs.).
11. Lower the vehicle.
12. Tighten the fuel filler cap.
13. Connect the negative battery cable.
14. Turn the ignition ON for 2 seconds.
15. Turn the ignition OFF for 10 seconds.
16. Turn the ignition ON.
17. Inspect for fuel leaks.

Fuel Pump

REMOVAL & INSTALLATION

Except Silverado and 2000–01 Sierra 15 Series

1. Before servicing the vehicle, refer to the precautions in the beginning of this section.
2. Properly relieve the fuel system pressure.
3. Drain the fuel from the vehicle.
4. Remove or disconnect the following:
   - Negative battery cable
   - Fuel tank from the vehicle
   - Locking ring (located on top of the fuel tank) counterclockwise

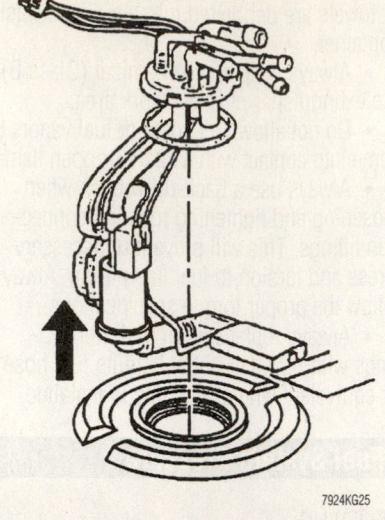

7924KG25

Lift the fuel pump assembly out of the tank after removing the locking ring

   - Lift the fuel pump assembly out of the tank

To install:
5. Install or connect the following:
   - Fuel pump and secure with locking ring
   - Fuel tank to vehicle and refill
   - Negative battery cable
6. Run engine and check for fuel leaks.

Silverado and 2000–01 Sierra 15 Series

1. Remove or disconnect the following:
   - Negative battery cable
2. Relieve the fuel system pressure.
3. Drain the fuel tank.
4. Remove or disconnect the following:
   - Fuel tank

➡ Do Not handle the fuel sender assembly by the fuel pipes. The amount of leverage generated by handling the fuel pipes could damage the joints.

   - Fuel sender assembly retaining ring using a fuel tank sending unit wrench. Remove the fuel sender assembly and the seal. Discard the seal.
   - Note the position of the fuel strainer on the fuel sender. Support the fuel sender assembly with one hand and grasp the strainer with the other hand. Pull the strainer off the fuel sender. Discard the strainer after inspection. Inspect the strainer. Replace a contaminated strainer and clean the fuel tank.
   - Fuel pump electrical connector

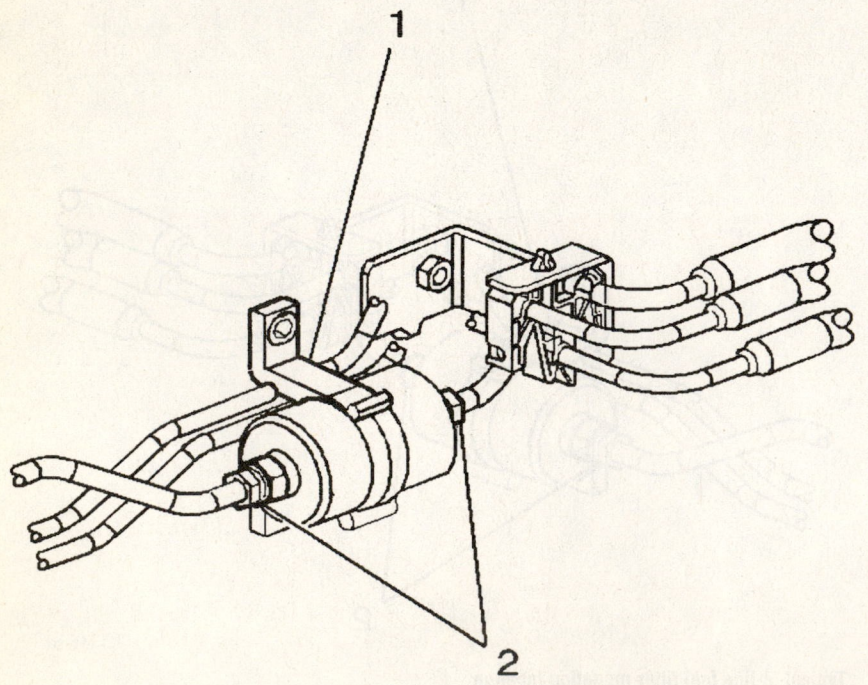

Fuel filter—4.8L, 5.3L, 6.0L

9308KG55

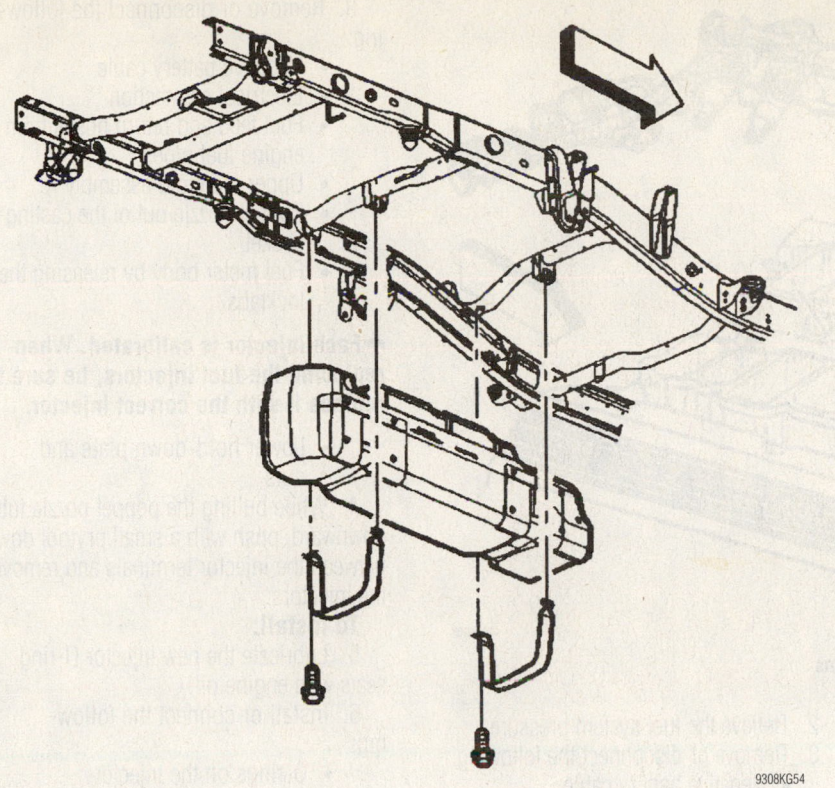

Fuel tank—Silverado

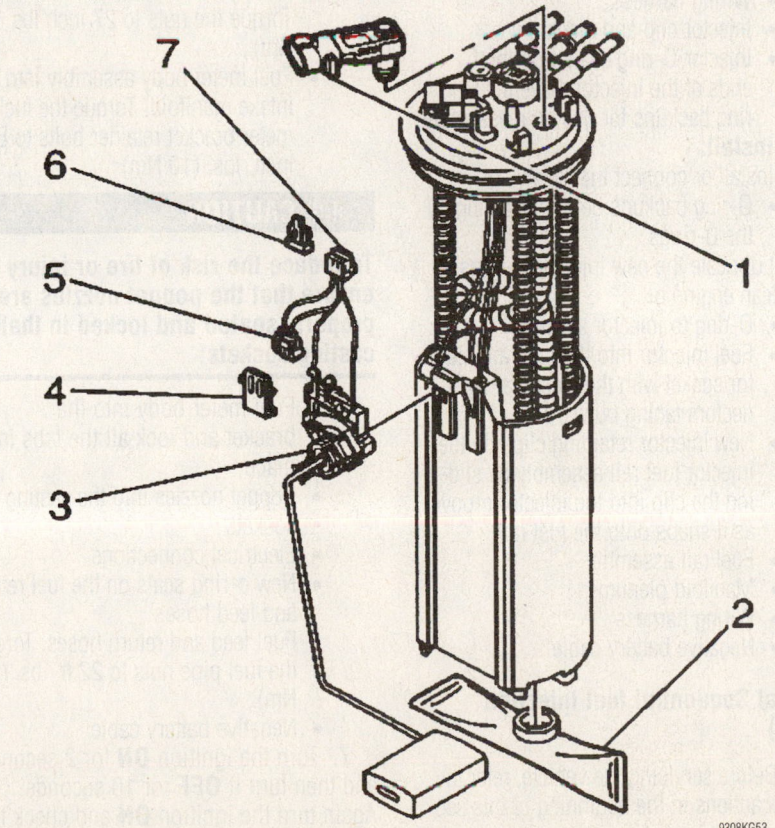

Fuel pump/sender assembly—4.8L, 5.3L, 6.0L

- Electrical connector retaining clip from the fuel level sensor
- Sensor electrical connector from under the fuel sender cover
- Fuel level sensor retaining clip

5. Squeeze the locking tangs and remove the fuel level sensor.

6. Remove the fuel pressure sensor.

To install:

7. Install or connect the following:
- Fuel pressure sensor
- Fuel level sensor
- Sensor retaining clip
- Electrical connector to the fuel level sensor
- Electrical connector retaining clip to the fuel level sensor
- Fuel pump electrical connector

➡**Always install a new fuel strainer when replacing the fuel tank fuel pump module.**

- New fuel strainer in the same position as noted during disassembly. Push the strainer on the bottom of the fuel sender until the strainer is fully seated.
- New seal on the fuel tank

➡**The fuel pump strainer must be in a horizontal position when the fuel sender is installed in the tank. When installing the fuel sender assembly, assure that the fuel pump strainer does not block full travel of the float arm.**

- Fuel sender assembly into the fuel tank
- Fuel sender assembly retaining ring
- Fuel tank. Install the fuel tank strap attaching bolts. Tighten the bolts to 40 Nm (30 ft. lbs.).

8. Refill the fuel tank. Install the fuel filler cap. Connect the negative battery cable.

9. Turn the ignition ON for 2 seconds.

10. Turn the ignition OFF for 10 seconds.

11. Turn the ignition ON.

12. Inspect for fuel leaks.

Fuel Injector

REMOVAL & INSTALLATION

4.3L, 5.0L, and 5.7L w/Multi-Port Fuel injection (MFI)

1. Before servicing the vehicle, refer to the precautions in the beginning of this section.

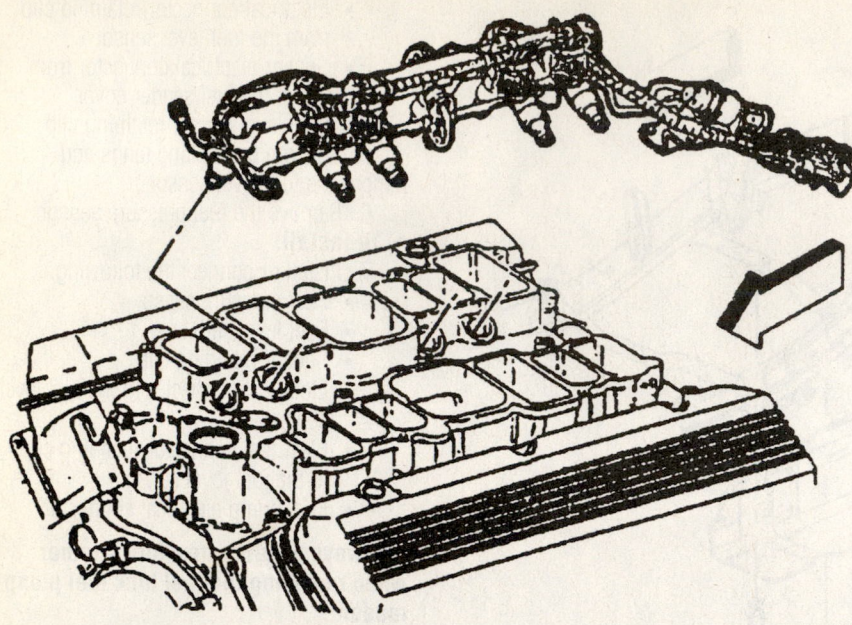

Exploded view of the fuel rail assembly—MFI systems

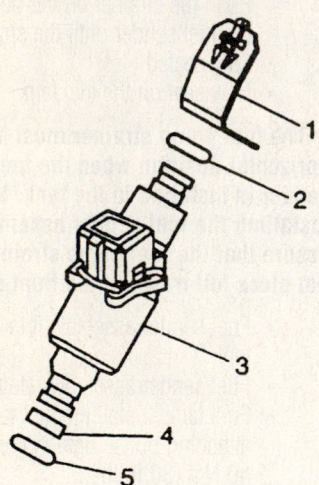

1. Clip - SFI Fuel Injector Retainer
2. O-ring - SFI Fuel Injector Upper
3. Injector Asm - SFI Fuel
4. O-ring - Backup
5. O-ring - SFI Fuel Injector Lower

9308KG06

Exploded view of the fuel injector assembly—MFI systems

➡Use care when removing the injectors to prevent damage to the electrical connector pins on the injector and the nozzle. The fuel injector is serviced as a complete assembly only. Since the injector is an electrical component, it should not be immersed in any type of cleaner.

2. Relieve the fuel system pressure.
3. Remove or disconnect the following:
   - Negative battery cable
   - Intake manifold plenum
   - Fuel rail assembly
   - Wiring harness
   - Injector clip and discard it
   - Injector O-ring seals from both ends of the injector. Save the O-ring backups for use on reassembly

To install:
4. Install or connect the following:
   - O-ring backups before installing the O-rings
5. Lubricate the new injector O-rings with clean engine oil
   - O-ring to injector assembly
   - Fuel injector into the fuel rail injector socket with the electrical connectors facing outward
   - New injector retaining clips on the injector fuel rail assembly by sliding the clip into the injector groove as it snaps onto the fuel rail
   - Fuel rail assembly
   - Manifold plenum
   - Wiring harness
   - Negative battery cable

Central Sequential fuel injection (CSFI)

1. Before servicing the vehicle, refer to the precautions in the beginning of this section.
2. Relieve the fuel system pressure.

3. Remove or disconnect the following:
   - Negative battery cable
   - Electrical connection
   - Fuel feed and return hoses from the engine fuel pipes
   - Upper manifold assembly
   - Poppet nozzle out of the casting socket
   - Fuel meter body by releasing the locktabs

➡**Each injector is calibrated. When replacing the fuel injectors, be sure to replace it with the correct injector.**

   - Lower hold-down plate and nuts

4. While pulling the poppet nozzle tube downward, push with a small prytool down between the injector terminals and remove the injectors.

To install:
5. Lubricate the new injector O-ring seats with engine oil.
6. Install or connect the following:

   - O-rings on the injector
   - Fuel injector into the fuel meter body injector socket
   - Lower hold-down plate and nuts, Torque the nuts to 27 inch lbs. (3 Nm).
   - Fuel meter body assembly into the intake manifold. Torque the fuel meter bracket retainer bolts to 88 inch. lbs. (10 Nm)

✳✳ CAUTION

To reduce the risk of fire or injury ensure that the poppet nozzles are properly seated and locked in their casting sockets

   - Fuel meter body into the bracket and lock all the tabs in place
   - Poppet nozzles into the casting sockets
   - Electrical connections
   - New o-ring seals on the fuel return and feed hoses
   - Fuel feed and return hoses. Torque the fuel pipe nuts to 22 ft. lbs. (30 Nm)
   - Negative battery cable

7. Turn the ignition **ON** for 2 seconds and then turn it **OFF** for 10 seconds. Again turn the ignition **ON** and check for leaks.

   - Manifold plenum

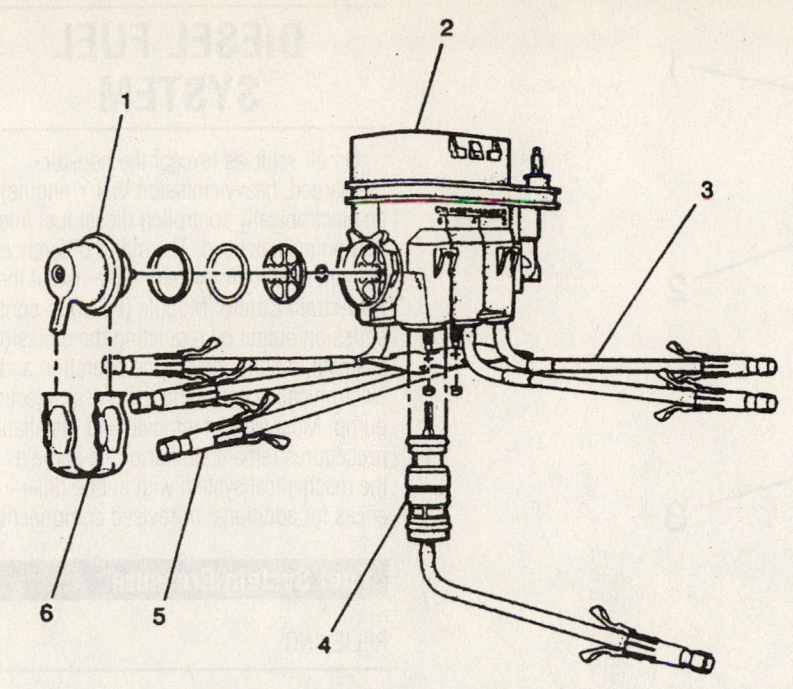

1. Regulator Assembly
2. Fuel Meter Body
3. Flexible Fuel Line
4. Injector Assembly
5. Poppet Nozzle
6. Regulator Retainer

9308KG07

Exploded view of the CSFI fuel meter body assembly

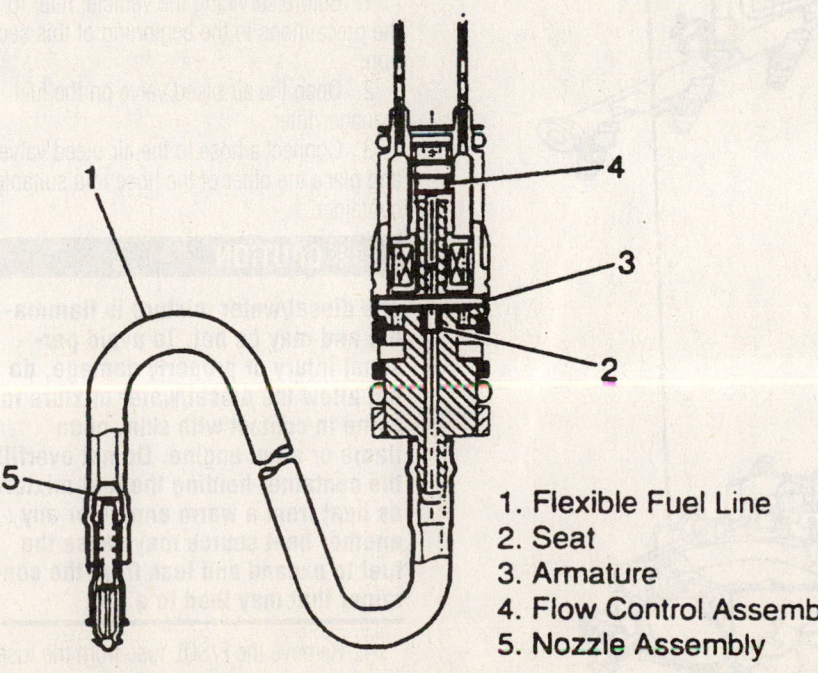

1. Flexible Fuel Line
2. Seat
3. Armature
4. Flow Control Assembly
5. Nozzle Assembly

9308KG08

Exploded view of the fuel injector assembly–CSFI systems

4.8L, 5.3L, 6.0L

1. Remove or disconnect the following:
   • Negative battery cable.
   • Engine sight shield.

➡ **Use care in removing the fuel injectors in order to prevent damage to the electrical connector pins on the injector and to prevent damage to the nozzle. Service the fuel injector as a complete assembly only. The fuel injector is an electrical component. DO NOT immerse the fuel injector in any type of cleaner.**

2. Relieve the fuel system pressure.
3. Remove or disconnect the following:
   • Fuel rail assembly.
   • Injector retainer clip. Insert the fork of a fuel injector assembly removal tool behind the injector connector between the fuel rail pod and the 3 protruding retaining clip ledges. Use a prying motion while inserting the tool in order to force the injector out of the fuel rail pod.
   • Injector retainer clip.
   • Injector O-ring seals from both ends of the injector. Discard the O-ring seals.

To install:

➡ **When ordering new fuel injectors, be sure to order the correct injector for the application being serviced. The fuel injector assembly (1) is stamped with a part number identification. A four digit build date code indicates the month, day, year, and the shift that built the injector.**

4. Lubricate the new injector O-ring seals with clean engine oil.
5. Install or connect the following:
   • New injector O-ring seals on the injector
   • New retainer clip on the injector
6. Push the fuel injector into the fuel rail injector socket with the electrical connector facing outward. The retainer clip locks on to a flange on the fuel rail injector socket.
7. Install the fuel rail assembly.
8. Tighten the fuel cap.
9. Connect the negative battery cable.
10. Turn the ignition ON for 2 seconds.
11. Turn the ignition OFF for 10 seconds.
12. Turn the ignition ON.
13. Inspect for fuel leaks.
14. Install the engine sight shield. Tighten the engine sight shield bolts to 10 Nm (89 inch lbs.)

To reset a Maintenance Indicator Lamp (MIL), turn to Section 2 of this manual

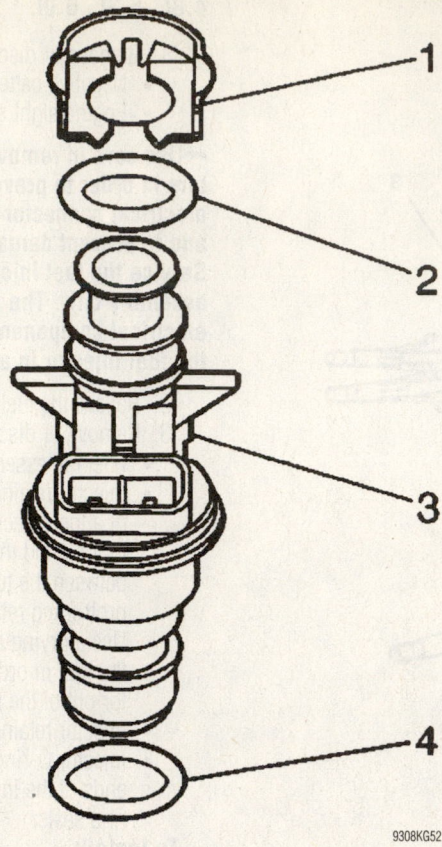

Fuel injector—4.8L, 5.3L, 6.0L

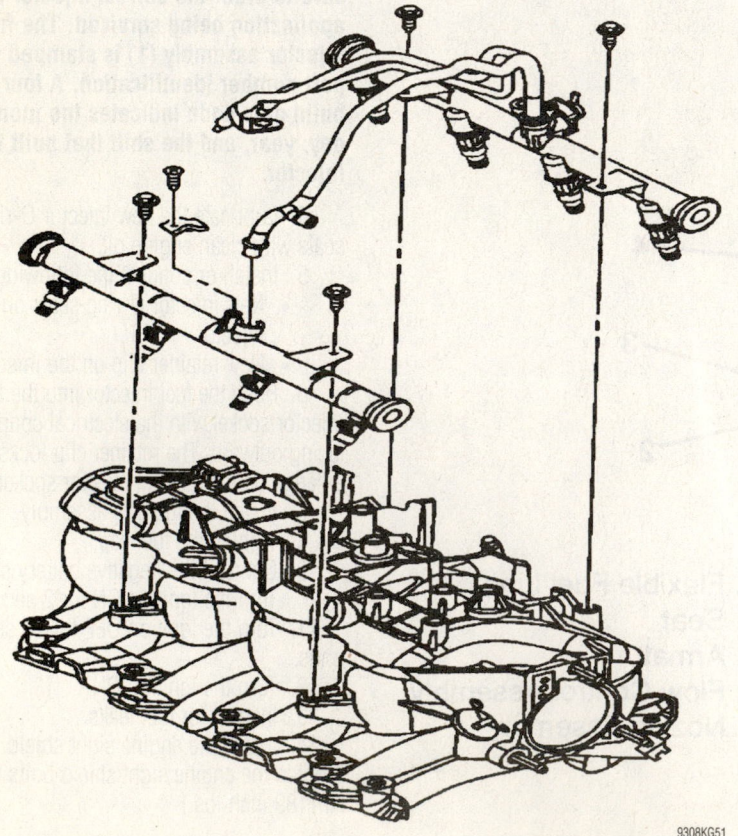

Fuel rail assembly—4.8L, 5.3L, 6.0L

DIESEL FUEL SYSTEM

On all vehicles (except the non-turbocharged, heavy emission VIN Y engine), an electronically controlled diesel fuel injection pump was used. The major difference in the new electronic system is the use of the Powertrain Control Module (PCM) to control emission output by regulating the emission systems, monitoring engine operation and electronically controlling the diesel injection pump. Most system removal and installation procedures remain similar or the same as the mechanical system with subtle differences for additional or revised components.

Fuel System Pressure

RELIEVING

Fuel system pressure can be released by wrapping a fuel fitting in a heavy shop towel and slightly loosening the fitting. NEVER perform this with any source of ignition nearby!

Fuel System Air

BLEEDING

1. Before servicing the vehicle, refer to the precautions in the beginning of this section.
2. Open the air bleed valve on the fuel manager/filter.
3. Connect a hose to the air bleed valve and place the other of the hose in a suitable container.

✳✳ CAUTION

The diesel/water mixture is flammable and may be hot. To avoid personal injury or property damage, do not allow the diesel/water mixture to come in contact with skin, open flame or a hot engine. Do not overfill the container holding the fuel mixture as heat from a warm engine or any another heat source may cause the fuel to expand and leak from the container that may lead to a fire.

4. Remove the F/SOL fuse from the fuse panel.
5. Crank the engine in short intervals of 10-to-15 seconds until clear fuel is observed at the air bleed hose (wait for 1 minute between cranking intervals)

6. Remove the hose and close the air bleed valve.

7. Install the F/SOL fuse and start the vehicle. Allow the vehicle to run at idle for 5 minutes.

8. Check for fuel leaks, and clear any Diagnostic Trouble Code's (DTC's)

Idle Speed

ADJUSTMENT

Idle speed and injection timing is controlled by the PCM. There is no provision for adjustment.

Fuel Filter

REMOVAL & INSTALLATION

1. Before servicing the vehicle, refer to the precautions in the beginning of this section.

2. Turn the ignition **OFF**. Remove the fuel tank cap to release any pressure or vacuum in the tank.

➡️**It is not necessary to drain all the fuel from the header in order to change the element since the fuel will remain in the header's cavity.**

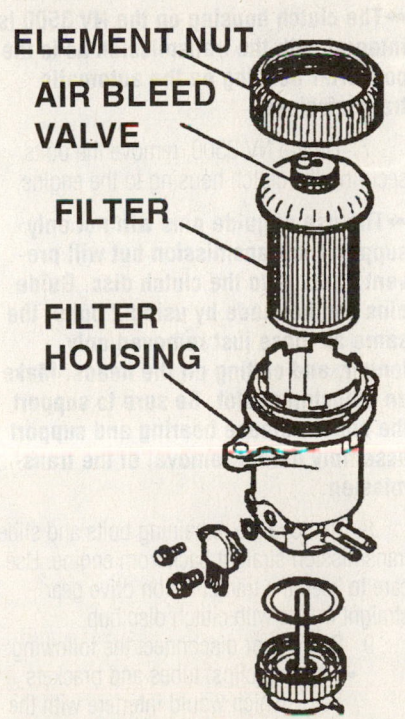

ELEMENT NUT
AIR BLEED VALVE
FILTER
FILTER HOUSING

7924KG26

Exploded view of the fuel filter assembly—6.5L diesel engines

3. Remove or disconnect the following:
- Open the air bleed valve to relieve residual pressure
- Element nut, turning it by hand to the left. If necessary, a strap wrench may be used to loosen the nut.
- Element by lifting straight up and out of the header assembly

To install:

4. Be sure the mating surface between the element assembly and the header assembly is clean.

5. Install or connect the following:
- New element by aligning the widest key slot located under the element assembly cap with the widest key in the header assembly.

6. Carefully push the element downward until the mating surfaces make contact.
- Element nut and tighten securely by hand

7. If not already done, open the air bleed valve on top of the fuel manager/filter assembly, then connect a length of hose placing the other end in a suitable container.

➡️**Be extremely cautious when handling diesel fuel. Do not expose the fuel to sparks or open flames. Also, be cautious as the fuel coming out of the drain hose could be hot.**

8. Disconnect the fuel injection pump shutdown solenoid wire.

9. Crank the engine for 10–15 seconds, then wait 1 minute for the starter motor to cool. Repeat until clear fuel is observed coming from the air bleed.

10. Close the air bleed valve, reconnect the injection pump solenoid wire and replace the fuel tank cap.

11. Start the engine, allow it to idle for 5 minutes and check the fuel manager/filter assembly for leaks.

Diesel Injection Pump

All vehicles are equipped with an electronically controlled pump. The electronic pump is driven by gears and rotates at the same speed as the camshaft. An electronic stepper motor used to control injection timing and a fuel solenoid driver used to control the fuel injection solenoid on the electronic model.

REMOVAL & INSTALLATION

1. Before servicing the vehicle, refer to the precautions in the beginning of this section.

2. Relieve the fuel system pressure.

3. Remove or disconnect the following:
- Negative battery cables
- Intake manifold
- Fuel injection and inlet lines
- Cables wires, and hoses at the injection pump
- Fuel return line at the top of the injection pump
- Fuel feed line at the injection pump, if necessary
- Oil filler tube grommet

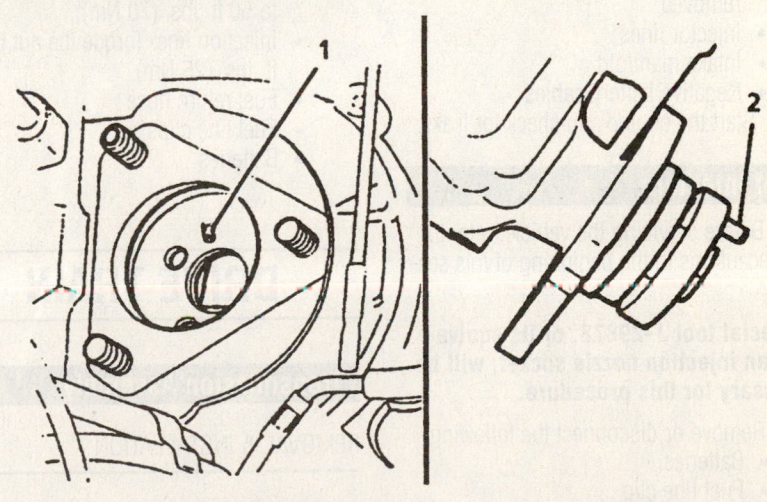

| 1 | **SLOT IN DRIVEN GEAR** | 2 | **PUMP HUB** |

7924KG27

Align the pin on the pump hub with the slot in the driven gear, NOT into the hole in the gear—diesel engines

➡️**Do not engage the starter in order to rotate the engine with the injection pump removed. The pump driven gear could jam in the front housing resulting in a sheared crankshaft or camshaft gear key and possible valvetrain damage.**

4. Scribe or paint a matchmark on the front cover and the injection pump flange.

5. Rotate the crankshaft by hand and remove the injection pump driven gear bolts, accessing the bolts through the oil filler neck hole.

6. Remove the injection pump-to-front cover attaching nuts. Remove the pump. Be sure to cap all open lines and nozzles in order to prevent system contamination and damage.

To install:

7. Align the locating pin on the pump hub with the slot in the injection pump driven gear (the SLOT not the hole in the gear) At the same time, align the timing marks.

8. Attach the injection pump to the front cover. Torque the nuts to 30 ft. lbs. (40 Nm) checking the timing marks before tightening.

9. Install or connect the following:
- Driven gear-to-injection pump bolts. Torque the bolts to 20 ft. lbs. (25 Nm).
- Grommet and oil fill tube
- Air conditioning bracket. If applicable
- Fuel feed line. Torque to 20 ft. lbs. (25 Nm).
- Fuel return line to the pump, if removed
- Cables, wires and hoses previously removed
- Injector lines
- Intake manifold
- Negative battery cables

10. Start the engine and check for leaks.

Fuel Injectors

1. Before servicing the vehicle, refer to the precautions in the beginning of this section.

➡️**Special tool J–29873, or its equivalent, an injection nozzle socket, will be necessary for this procedure.**

2. Remove or disconnect the following:
- Batteries.
- Fuel line clip
- Fuel return hose
- Fuel injection lines

3. Using GM special tool J–29873, remove the injector. Always remove the injector by turning the 30mm hex portion of the injector; turning the round portion will damage the injector. Always cap the injector

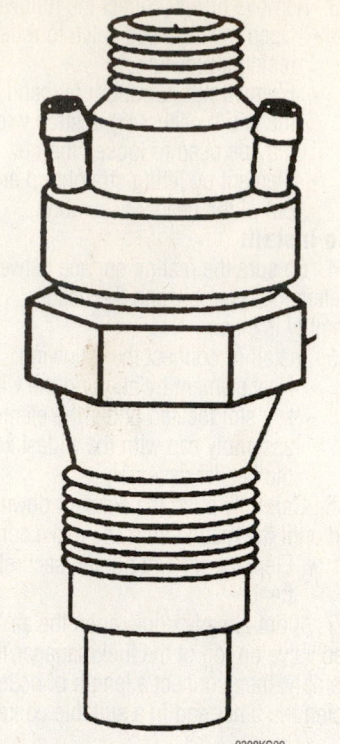

9308KG09

Exploded view of the fuel injector nozzle.

and fuel lines when disconnected, to prevent contamination.

To install:

4. Always install the injector by turning the 30mm hex portion of the injector; turning the round portion will damage the injector.

5. Install or connect the following:
- Injector with a new gasket. Torque to 50 ft. lbs. (70 Nm).
- Injection line. Torque the nut to 20 ft. lbs. (25 Nm).
- Fuel return hose
- Fuel line clips
- Batteries

DRIVE TRAIN

Transmission Assembly

REMOVAL & INSTALLATION

Manual Transmission

EXCEPT SILVERADO AND 2000–01 SIERRA SERIES 15

1. Before servicing the vehicle, refer to the precautions in the beginning of this section.

2. Drain the transmission.

3. Remove or disconnect the following:
- Negative battery cable
- Shifter boot and lever
- Exhaust pipes
- Parking brake cables
- Driveshaft, matchmark for reassembly
- Transfer case, if equipped
- Transmission to engine braces (vehicles equipped with diesel engines have only 1 brace)
- Wiring harness at the transmission

4. Support the transmission with a transmission jack.
- Nut securing the transmission mount to the cross member

5. Position a transmission jack or equivalent, under the transmission for support.
- Crossmember. Visually inspect to see if other equipment, brackets or lines, must be removed to permit removal of transmission.

➡️**Mark position of crossmember when removing to prevent incorrect installation. The tapered surface should face the rear.**

6. Except the NV 3500, remove the top 2 transmission to housing bolts and insert 2 guide pins.

➡️**The clutch housing on the NV 3500 is integral with the transmission as is the converter housing on the automatic transmissions.**

7. On the NV 3500, remove the bolts securing the clutch housing to the engine.

➡️**The use of guide pins will not only support the transmission but will prevent damage to the clutch disc. Guide pins can be made by using 2 bolts, the same as those just removed only longer, and cutting off the heads. Make an adjustment slot. Be sure to support the clutch release bearing and support assembly during removal of the transmission.**

8. Remove the remaining bolts and slide transmission straight back from engine. Use care to keep the transmission drive gear straight in line with clutch disc hub.

9. Remove or disconnect the following:
- Wiring, clips, tubes and brackets etc., which would interfere with the removal of the transmission.

➡️**Ensure that the engine is supported with a jack stand before detaching the transmission from the engine.**

- Transmission from the engine

10. Carefully lower the transmission using the transmission jack.

To install:

11. Check the area behind the torque converter for leaks. Replace the front seal, if required.

12. It is good practice to examine the area around the rear crankshaft seal, checking for leaks. If necessary, remove the flywheel and replace the seal.

13. Inspect the flywheel ring gear teeth. If damaged, replace the flywheel.

14. Perform the following steps:

   a. Step 1: Place the transmission in high gear. Lightly coat the input shaft splines with high temperature grease.

   b. Step 2: Raise the transmission into position.

   c. Step 3: On transmissions with a separate clutch housing, install the guide pins in the top 2 bolt holes if they have been removed.

   d. Step 4: Roll the transmission forward and engage the clutch splines. Keep pushing the transmission forward until it mates with the engine.

   e. Step 5: On transmissions with a separate clutch housing, remove the guide pins and install the bolts, tighten the bolts to 23 ft. lbs. (31 Nm)

   f. Step 6: On the NV 3500, install the transmission-to-engine bolts. Tighten the bolts to 35 ft. lbs. (47 Nm)

15. When satisfied that the transmission is properly seated, install and tighten the transmission-to-engine bolts and/or studs to 34 ft. lbs. (47 Nm).

16. Install or connect the following:

- Wiring, clips, tubes and brackets etc
- Shifter cable
- Starter
- Exhaust pipes
- Transmission crossmember. Torque the bolts to 56 ft. lbs. (77 Nm).
- Transmission mount on the transmission. Torque the bolts to 35 ft. lbs. (47 Nm).
- Nut and washer that secure the transmission mount to the crossmember. Torque the nut to 38 ft. lbs. (52 Nm).
- Transmission to engine brace(s) Torque the bolts to 41 ft. lbs. (55 Nm) for gasoline engines and to 51 ft. lbs. (70 Nm) for diesel engines.
- Transfer case, if equipped

17. Remove the transmission jack and engine support stands.

- Driveshaft
- Shifter lever and boot
- Negative battery cable

18. Refill the transmission with fluid.

19. Road test the vehicle and test for proper operation. Check for leaks.

SILVERADO AND 2000–01 SIERRA SERIES 15 W/NV3500

NV3500

1. Shift the transmission into 3rd or 4th speed gear.

2. Remove or disconnect the following:

- Shift lever
- Shift tower
- Transmission oil
- If equipped with a transfer case, remove the front propeller shaft.
- Rear propeller shaft.
- If equipped, remove the two transfer case shields.
- If equipped with a manual transfer case, remove the manual transfer case shift linkage.
- If equipped with a transfer case, remove the bolt securing the left side support brace to the transmission.
- If equipped with a transfer case, remove the bolt and stud securing the left side support brace to the transfer case.
- If equipped with a transfer case, remove the bolt securing the right side support brace to the transmission.
- If equipped with a transfer case, remove the bolt securing the right side support brace to the transfer case.

3. Using tool J42371, push back on the white plastic sleeve on the quick connect in order to separate the hydraulic clutch line from the concentric slave cylinder quick connect.

4. Disconnect the wiring harness and connector from the vehicle speed sensor, backup lamp switch, and transmission harness retainers.

5. If equipped with a 4.3L engine, remove the two bolts securing the clutch housing cover. Remove the transmission rear mount. Support the transmission with a transmission jack.

6. Remove or disconnect the following:

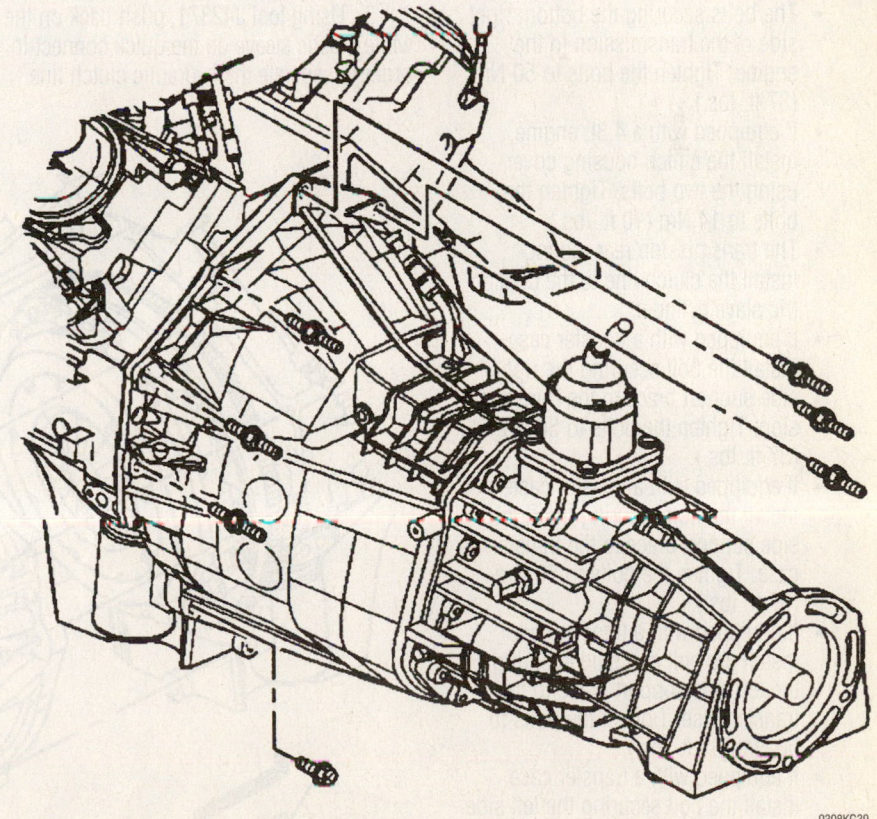

NV3500 removal—Silverado

9308KG39

- The bolts securing the bottom right side of the transmission to the engine
- The stud securing the right side of the transmission to the engine
- The bolt and six studs securing the transmission to the engine

7. Pull the transmission straight back on the clutch hub splines. Do not let the transmission hang from the clutch plate and the clutch cover.

8. Remove the transmission from the vehicle.

9. Remove the clutch plate and the clutch cover from the engine flywheel if required.

To install:

10. Install the clutch plate and the clutch cover to the engine flywheel if removed.

11. Ensure the transmission is positioned in the 3rd or 4th speed gear. Rotate the transmission clockwise onto the clutch hub splines. Install the bolt and the studs securing the transmission to the engine. Tighten the bolts to 50 Nm (37 ft. lbs.).

12. Install or connect the following:
- The stud securing the right side of the transmission to the engine. Tighten the stud to 50 Nm (37 ft. lbs.).
- The bolts securing the bottom right side of the transmission to the engine. Tighten the bolts to 50 Nm (37 ft. lbs.).
- If equipped with a 4.3L engine, install the clutch housing cover using the two bolts. Tighten the bolts to 14 Nm (10 ft. lbs.).
- The transmission rear mount. Install the clutch line to the concentric slave cylinder.
- If equipped with a transfer case, install the bolt securing the right side support brace to the transmission. Tighten the bolts to 50 Nm (37 ft. lbs.).
- If equipped with a transfer case, install the bolt securing the right side support brace to the transfer case. Tighten the bolts to 50 Nm (37 ft. lbs.).
- If equipped with a transfer case, install the bolt and stud securing the left side support brace to the transfer case. Tighten the bolts to 50 Nm (37 ft. lbs.).
- If equipped with a transfer case, install the bolt securing the left side support brace to the transmission. Tighten the bolts to 50 Nm (37 ft. lbs.).
- If equipped with a manual transfer

case, install the manual transfer case shift linkage.
- If equipped, installed the two transfer case shields.
- If equipped with a transfer case, install the front propeller shaft.
- The rear propeller shaft.
- The shift tower.

13. Fill the transmission with transmission fluid.

14. Install the shift lever.

SILVERADO AND 2000–01 SIERRA SERIES 15 W/NV4500

1. Shift the transmission into 3rd or 4th speed gear.

2. Remove or disconnect the following:
- The shift lever.
- The shift tower.
- The transmission oil.
- If equipped with a transfer case, remove the front propeller shaft.
- The rear propeller shaft.
- The two transfer case shields.
- If equipped with a manual transfer case, remove the manual transfer case shift linkage.
- The two bolts securing the right side support bracket to the transmission.

3. Using tool J42371, push back on the white plastic sleeve on the quick connect in order to separate the hydraulic clutch line

from the concentric slave cylinder quick connect.

4. Remove or disconnect the following:
- The wiring harness and connector from the vehicle speed sensor, backup lamp switch, and transmission harness retainers.
- The four bolts securing the clutch housing cover to the transmission.
- The bolt securing the left side transmission to engine cover.
- The bolt securing the right side transmission to engine cover.
- The transmission rear mount. Support the transmission with a transmission jack.
- The bolts and studs securing the transmission to the engine.

5. Pull the transmission straight back on the clutch hub splines. Do not let the transmission hang from the clutch plate and the clutch cover. Remove the transmission from the vehicle.

6. Remove the clutch plate and the clutch cover from the engine flywheel if required.

To install:

7. Install or connect the following:
- The clutch plate and the clutch cover to the engine flywheel if removed

8. Ensure the transmission is positioned in the 3rd or 4th speed gear. Rotate

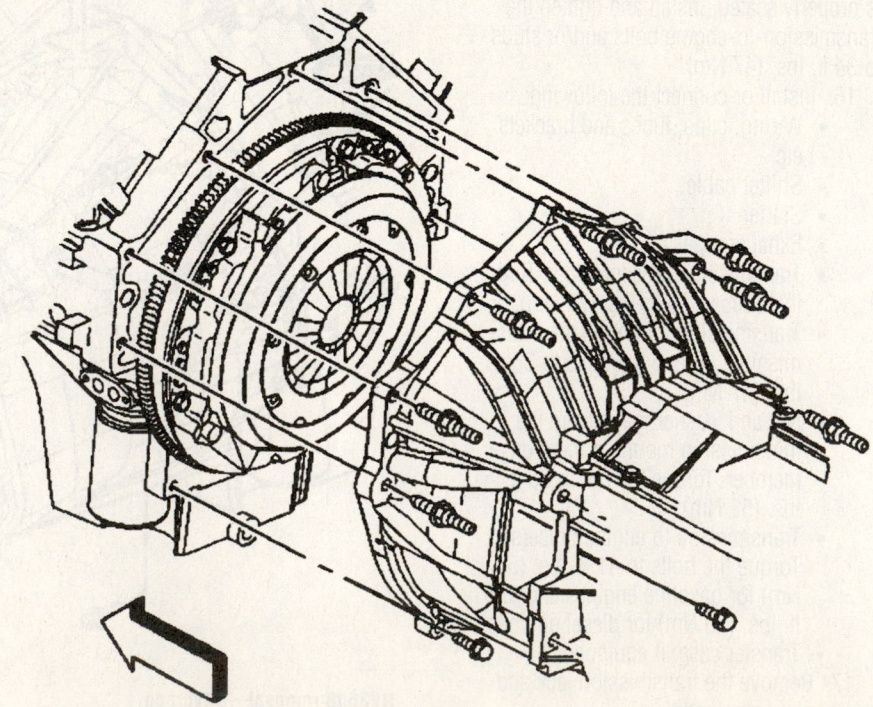

NV4500 removal—Silverado

9308KG38

the transmission clockwise onto the clutch hub splines. Install the bolt and the studs securing the transmission to the engine. Tighten the bolts to 50 Nm (37 ft. lbs.).

9. Install or connect the following:
   - The bolt securing the right side transmission to engine cover. Tighten the bolt to 14 Nm (10 ft. lbs.).
   - The bolt securing the left side transmission to engine cover. Tighten the bolt to 14 Nm (10 ft. lbs.).
   - The four bolts securing the clutch cover to the transmission. Tighten the bolt to 14 Nm (10 ft. lbs.).
   - The transmission rear mount. Install the clutch line to the concentric slave cylinder.
   - The two bolts securing the right side support bracket to the transmission. Tighten the bolts to 50 Nm (37 ft. lbs.).
   - If equipped with a manual transfer case, install the manual transfer case shift linkage.
   - If equipped, installed the two transfer case shields.
   - If equipped with a transfer case, install the front propeller shaft.
   - The rear propeller shaft.
   - The shift tower.

10. Fill the transmission with transmission fluid.

11. Install the shift lever.

Automatic Transmission

EXCEPT SILVERADO AND 2000–01 SIERRA SERIES 15

1. Before servicing the vehicle, refer to the precautions in the beginning of this section.
2. Drain the transmission.
3. Remove or disconnect the following:
   - Negative battery cable
   - Shift cable, control lever and the bracket
   - Exhaust pipes
   - Parking brake cables
   - Driveshaft, matchmark for reassembly
   - Transfer case, if equipped
   - Transmission to engine braces (vehicles equipped with diesel engines have only 1 brace)
   - Wiring harness at the transmission
4. Support the transmission with a transmission jack.

   - Nut securing the transmission mount to the cross member
5. Position a transmission jack or equivalent, under the transmission for support.
   - Crossmember. Visually inspect to see if other equipment, brackets or lines, must be removed to permit removal of transmission.

➡ **Mark position of crossmember when removing to prevent incorrect installation. The tapered surface should face the rear.**

6. Perform the following:
   a. Step 1: Remove the torque converter inspection cover.
   b. Step 2: Mark the alignment of the torque converter to the flexplate.
   c. Step 3: Remove the torque converter to flexplate bolts. Remove the dipstick tube and seal from the transmission. Plug the opening to avoid contamination.
   d. Step 4: Disconnect both transmission lines at the transmission and plug them to avoid contamination and leakage.
   e. Step 5: Position a J 21366 converter holding strap onto the transmission/torque converter to keep the torque converter from sliding off of the transmission turbine shaft.

➡ **The use of guide pins will not only support the transmission but will prevent damage to the clutch disc. Guide pins can be made by using 2 bolts, the same as those just removed only longer, and cutting off the heads. Make an adjustment slot.**

7. Remove the remaining bolts and slide transmission straight back from engine. Use care to keep the transmission drive gear straight in line with clutch disc hub.

8. Remove or disconnect the following:
   - Wiring, clips, tubes and brackets etc., which would interfere with the removal of the transmission.

➡ **Ensure that the engine is supported with a jack stand before detaching the transmission from the engine.**

   - Transmission from the engine
9. Carefully lower the transmission using the transmission jack.

To install:

10. Check the area behind the torque converter for leaks. Replace the front seal, if required.

11. It is good practice to examine the area around the rear crankshaft seal, checking for leaks. If necessary, remove the flexplate and replace the seal.

12. Inspect the flexplate ring gear teeth. If damaged, replace the flexplate.

13. Perform the following steps:
   a. Step 1: With tool J 21366 or equivalent, torque converter holding strap in place, raise the transmission into position with a transmission jack.
   b. Step 2: Remove the torque converter holding strap and slide the transmission into place. Slide the transmission straight onto the locating pins while lining up the marks on the flexplate and the torque converter. Be sure the transmission is fully seated against the rear of the engine block and the locating pins are completely engaged.

✻✻ WARNING

DO NOT attempt to draw the transmission to the block with the mounting bolts. If the transmission is not properly seated, the bolts will break the transmission case.

➡ **The torque converter must be flush with the flexplate and rotate freely by hand.**

14. When satisfied that the transmission is properly seated, install and tighten the transmission-to-engine bolts and/or studs to 34 ft. lbs. (47 Nm).

15. Perform the following steps:
   a. Step 1: Install the dipstick tube and seal.
   b. Step 2: Check the alignment marks on the torque converter and flexplate to be sure that they are properly aligned. Install the torque converter bolts. Finger-tighten the bolts to ensure proper converter seating. When the converter is properly seated, tighten the bolts to 46 ft. lbs. (63 Nm)
   c. Step 3: Install the torque converter cover. Tighten the retaining bolts to 24 ft. lbs. (33 Nm) on the 4.3L engines or 89 inch lbs. (10 Nm) on the V8 engines.

16. Install or connect the following:
   - Wiring, clips, tubes and brackets etc
   - Transmission cooling lines
   - Shifter cable
   - Starter
   - Exhaust pipes
   - Transmission crossmember. Torque the bolts to 56 ft. lbs. (77 Nm).

- Transmission mount on the transmission. Torque the bolts to 35 ft. lbs. (47 Nm).
- Nut and washer that secure the transmission mount to the crossmember. Torque the nut to 38 ft. lbs. (52 Nm).
- Transmission to engine brace(s) Torque the bolts to 41 ft. lbs. (55 Nm) for gasoline engines and to 51 ft. lbs. (70 Nm) for diesel engines.
- Transfer case, if equipped

17. Remove the transmission jack and engine support stands.
- Driveshaft
- Shifter lever and boot, on manual transmissions
- Negative battery cable

18. Refill the transmission with fluid.
19. Road test the vehicle and test for proper operation. Check for leaks.

SILVERADO AND 2000–01 SIERRA SERIES 15 W/4L60E

1. Remove or disconnect the following:
- Transmission fluid
- Transmission oil level indicator tube and seal from the transmission
- Plug the oil level indicator tube opening in the transmission.

2. Remove or disconnect the following:
- Shift cable end from the transmission shift lever ball stud

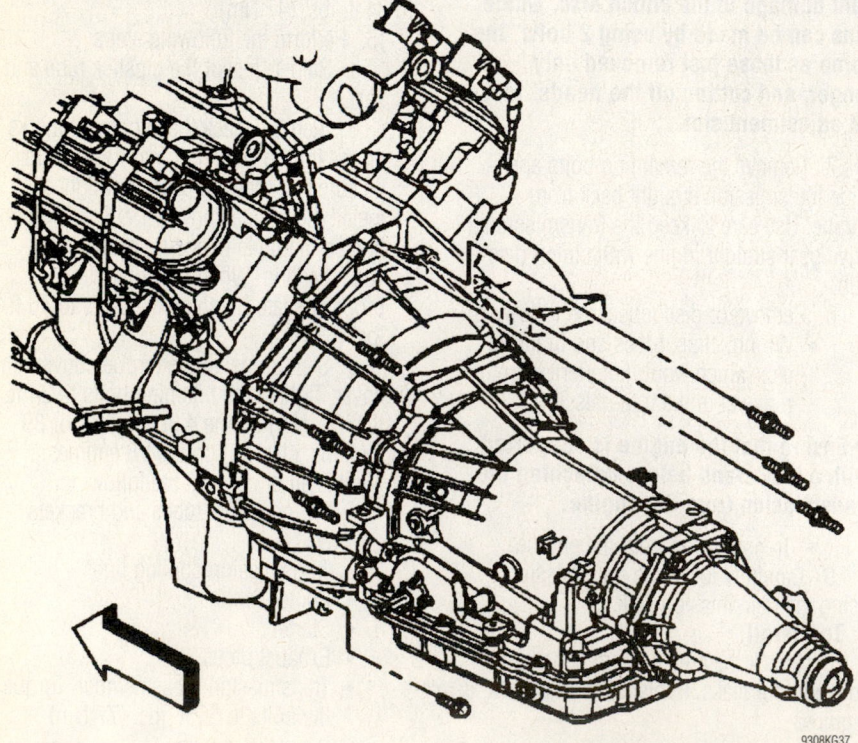

4L60E removal—Silverado

- If equipped with a transfer case, remove the front propeller shaft.
- Rear propeller shaft.

3. Plug the transmission oil cooler line connectors in the transmission case.
4. Remove or disconnect the following:
- Starter motor.

5. Support the transmission with a transmission jack.
6. Remove or disconnect the following:
- Torque converter access plug
- Flywheel to torque converter bolts
- The two bolts and nut securing the transmission rear mount to the transmission
- The two bolts securing the heat shield to the transmission
- The transmission vent hose, fuel lines, and the wiring harness from the transmission
- The stud and the bolt securing the transmission to the engine
- The six studs and one bolt securing the transmission to the engine. Install tool J21366 onto the transmission bell housing to retain the torque converter. Pull the transmission straight back.

7. The transmission from the vehicle
8. Flush the transmission oil cooler and cooling lines when you remove the transmission.

To install:

9. Install or connect the following:
- Tool J21366 onto the transmission bell housing to retain the torque converter.

10. Support the transmission with a transmission jack.
11. Raise the transmission into place and remove the tool from the transmission.
12. Slide the transmission straight onto the locating pins while lining up the marks on the flywheel and the torque converter. The torque converter must be flush onto the flywheel and rotate freely by hand.
13. Install or connect the following:
- Six studs and one bolt securing the transmission to the engine. Tighten the studs and the bolt to 50 Nm (37 ft. lbs.).
- Stud and bolt securing the transmission to the engine. Tighten the stud and the bolt to 50 Nm (37 ft. lbs.).
- Flywheel to torque converter bolts.
- Torque converter access plug.
- Transmission vent hose, fuel lines, and the wiring harness to the transmission.
- Two bolts securing the heat shield to the transmission. Tighten the bolt to 17 Nm (13 ft. lbs.).
- Two bolts and nut securing the transmission rear mount to the transmission. Tighten the bolts and nut to 25 Nm (18 ft. lbs.).

14. Remove the transmission jack from the transmission.
15. Unplug the transmission oil cooler line connectors in the transmission case.
16. Install or connect the following:
- Transmission oil cooler lines to the transmission
- If equipped with a transfer case, install the front propeller shaft.
- The rear propeller shaft
- The shift cable end to the transmission shift lever ball stud
- Unplug the oil level indicator tube opening in the transmission.

17. Install the transmission oil level indicator tube and seal to the transmission.
18. Tighten the oil pan bolts and fill the transmission with transmission fluid.
19. Lower the vehicle.

SILVERADO AND 2000–01 SIERRA SERIES 15 W/4L80E

1. Remove or disconnect the following:
- Transmission fluid
- Transmission oil level indicator tube and seal from the transmission

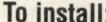

2. Plug the oil level indicator tube opening in the transmission.

3. Remove or disconnect the following:
- Shift cable from the transmission shift lever ball stud
- If 4WD vehicle, remove the propeller shaft.
- If RWD vehicle, remove the propeller shaft.
- The transmission oil cooler lines from the transmission

4. Plug the transmission oil cooler line connectors in the transmission case.

5. Remove or disconnect the following:
- Starter motor
- Support the transmission with a transmission jack.

6. Remove or disconnect the following:
- The two bolts securing the heat shield to the transmission
- The transmission vent hose, fuel lines, and the wiring harness from the transmission
- One nut and one bolt securing the transmission brace to the engine bracket and transmission
- The two bolts securing the torque converter cover to the engine

- The four bolts securing the torque converter cover to the transmission
- The six flywheel to torque converter bolts
- The two bolts and nut securing the transmission rear mount to the transmission
- The stud and the bolt on the right side securing the transmission to the engine
- The remaining six studs and the one bolt securing the transmission to the engine
- Tool J21366 onto the transmission bell housing to retain the torque converter

7. Pull the transmission straight back. Remove the transmission from the vehicle.

8. Flush the transmission oil cooler and cooling lines when you remove the transmission.

To install:

9. Install or connect the following:
- Tool J21366 onto the transmission bell housing to retain the torque converter

10. Support the transmission with a transmission jack.

11. Raise the transmission into place and remove the tool from the transmission.

12. Slide the transmission straight onto the locating pins while lining up the marks on the flywheel and the torque converter. The torque converter must be flush onto the flywheel and rotate freely by hand.

13. Install or connect the following:
- Six studs and one bolt securing the transmission to the engine. Tighten the studs and the bolt to 50 Nm (37 ft. lbs.).
- The stud and bolt on the right side securing the transmission to the engine. Tighten the stud and the bolt to 50 Nm (37 ft. lbs.).
- Six flywheel to torque converter bolts. Tighten the bolts to 60 Nm (44 ft. lbs.).
- The two bolts securing the torque converter cover to the engine. Tighten the bolt to 50 Nm (37 ft. lbs.).
- The four bolts securing the torque converter cover to the transmission. Tighten the stud and the bolt to 33 Nm (24 ft. lbs.).
- The transmission vent hose, fuel lines, and the wiring harness to the transmission.
- The two bolts securing the heat shield to the transmission. Tighten the bolt to 17 Nm (13 ft. lbs.).
- The two bolts and nut securing the transmission rear mount to the transmission. Tighten the bolts and nut to 25 Nm (18 ft. lbs.).
- The flywheel to torque converter bolts.
- One nut and one bolt securing the transmission brace to the engine bracket and transmission. Tighten the bolts and nut to 50 Nm (37 ft. lbs.).

14. Remove the transmission jack from the transmission.

15. Install or connect the following:
- Starter motor

16. Unplug the transmission oil cooler line connectors in the transmission case.

17. Connect the transmission oil cooler lines to the transmission.

18. Install or connect the following:
- The transfer case
- The rear propeller shaft
- The shift cable end to the transmission shift lever ball stud

19. Unplug the oil level indicator tube opening in the transmission.

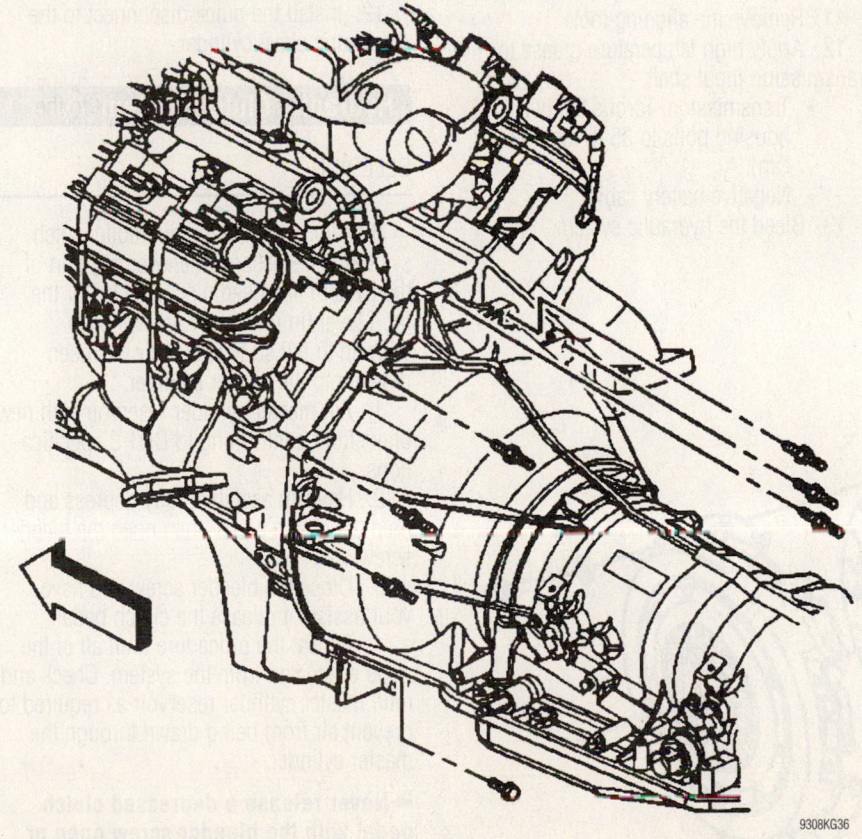

4L80E removal—Silverado

9308KG36

Turn to Section 5 for brake system applications

20. Install the transmission oil level indicator tube and seal to the transmission.

21. Tighten the oil pan bolts and fill the transmission with transmission fluid.

22. Lower the vehicle.

Clutch

ADJUSTMENTS

The hydraulic clutch system requires no periodic adjustment.

REMOVAL & INSTALLATION

Except Silverado and 2000–01 Sierra 15 Series

1. Before servicing the vehicle, refer to the precautions in the beginning of this section.

2. Remove or disconnect the following:
   - Negative battery cable
   - Slave cylinder
   - Transmission assembly

3. Install the clutch removal tool and support the clutch assembly.

➡ **Before removing the clutch from the flywheel, matchmark the flywheel, clutch cover and 1 pressure plate lug, so these parts may be assembled in their same relative positions and retain the factory balance.**

4. Loosen the clutch plate retaining bolts slowly and evenly one at a time until all pressure is released from the pressure plate assembly.

5. Remove the clutch, pressure plate and removal tool. Check the flywheel for damage, repair or replace, as required.

6. Check the clutch assembly and flywheel for signs of wear, scoring, overheating, etc. If the clutch plate, flywheel or pressure plate is oil-soaked, inspect the engine rear main seal and the transmission input shaft seal and correct leakage as required. Replace any damaged parts.

To install:

7. Assemble the pressure plate and disc assembly, as required.

➡ **The manufacturer recommends that new pressure plate bolts and washers be used.**

8. Turn the flywheel until the previously applied mark is at the bottom.

9. Install or connect the following:
   - Clutch disc, pressure plate and cover using a suitable clutch aligning tool.

10. Turn the clutch until the matchmark on the clutch cover aligns with the mark on the flywheel.
   - Attaching bolts and tighten in a crossing pattern until the spring pressure is taken up torque the bolts to 29 ft. lbs. (34 Nm).

11. Remove the aligning tool.

12. Apply high temperature grease to transmission input shaft.
   - Transmission. Torque the bell housing bolts to 35 ft. lbs. (47 Nm).
   - Negative battery cable

13. Bleed the hydraulic system.

Silverado and 2000–01 Sierra 15 Series

1. Remove or disconnect the following:
   - Transmission
   - Quick disconnect from the actuator cylinder

2. Install a clutch alignment tool.

3. Mark the flywheel and a clutch pressure plate lug for the installation alignment.

4. Remove or disconnect the following:
   - Pressure plate bolts and the washers

5. Secure the clutch pressure plate and the clutch driven plate to the flywheel.

6. Remove the clutch alignment tool.

To install:

7. Install the bolts and the washers securing the clutch pressure plate and the clutch driven plate to the flywheel.

8. Install the clutch alignment tool.

9. Align the marks made during removal or, if new align the lightest part of the clutch pressure plate identified by a yellow dot, to the heaviest part of the flywheel, identified by an "X". Tighten the clutch pressure plate to the flywheel bolts to 41 Nm (30 ft. lbs.).

10. Remove the clutch alignment tool.

11. Install the transmission.

12. Install the quick disconnect to the concentric slave cylinder.

Hydraulic Clutch System

BLEEDING

Bleeding air from the hydraulic clutch system is necessary whenever any part of the system has been disconnected or the fluid level (in the reservoir) has been allowed to fall so low, that air has been drawn into the master cylinder.

1. Fill master cylinder reservoir with new brake fluid conforming to DOT 3 specifications.

2. Have an assistant fully depress and hold the clutch pedal, then open the bleeder screw.

3. Close the bleeder screw and have your assistant release the clutch pedal.

4. Repeat the procedure until all of the air is evacuated from the system. Check and refill master cylinder reservoir as required to prevent air from being drawn through the master cylinder.

➡ **Never release a depressed clutch pedal with the bleeder screw open or air will be drawn into the system.**

5. Test the clutch for proper operation.

7924KG28

Exploded view of the typical clutch assembly

Transfer Case Assembly

REMOVAL & INSTALLATION

Except Silverado and 2000–01 Sierra 15 Series

1. Before servicing the vehicle, refer to the precautions in the beginning of this section.
2. Drain transfer case of lubricant.
3. Remove or disconnect the following:
   - Negative battery cable
   - Skid plate, if equipped
   - Vent hose clamp at the transfer case
   - Front driveshaft at the transfer case and support it aside
   - Rear driveshaft and support it aside
   - Electrical connections at the transfer case
   - Transfer case shift linkage
4. Support the transfer case with a transmission jack.
   - Transmission to transfer case bolts and spring washers
   - Transfer case assembly and gasket
5. Carefully lower the transfer case.

To install:

6. Carefully raise the transfer case into position.
7. Install or connect the following:
   - New gasket to the transmission using gasket sealer to hold it in place
   - Transfer case onto the transmission or transmission adapter. Torque the bolts to 33 ft. lbs. (45 Nm).
   - Electrical harness connectors to the transfer case connections
   - Transfer case shift linkage and make the proper adjustments
   - Front and rear driveshafts
8. Refill the transfer case with DEXRON®IIE automatic transmission fluid.
   - Skid plate, if equipped
   - Negative battery cable
9. Test drive for proper operation.

Silverado and 2000–01 Sierra 15 Series w/NVG261-NP2 2-Speed Manual Transfer Case

1. Remove or disconnect the following:
   - Transfer case shields
   - Front propeller shaft
   - Rear propeller shaft
   - Shift rod from the transfer case
   - Vent hose from the transfer case
   - Vehicle speed sensor electrical connectors
   - Any wiring harness from the transfer case
   - Support the transfer case with a transmission jack.
2. If equipped with a NV3500 manual transmission, remove the bolt securing the left side support brace to the transmission.
3. If equipped with a NV3500 manual transmission, remove the bolt and stud securing the left side support brace to the transfer case.
4. If equipped with a NV3500 manual transmission, remove the 2 bolts securing the right side support brace to the transmission and transfer case.
5. For vehicles equipped with a manual transmission, remove the 6 nuts securing the transfer case and bracket to the transmission. Remove the transfer case.
6. For vehicles equipped with a automatic transmission, remove the 6 nuts securing the transfer case and bracket to the transmission adapter. Remove the transfer case.
7. Remove and discard the gasket.

To install:

8. Install a new gasket to the transmission. Use Teflon pipe sealant GM P/N 12346004 in order to hold the gasket in place.
9. Raise and position the transfer case to the vehicle
10. For vehicles equipped with a automatic transmission, install the 6 nuts securing the transfer case and bracket to the transmission adapter. Tighten the nuts to 50 Nm (37 ft. lbs.).
11. For vehicles equipped with a manual transmission, install the 6 nuts securing the transfer case and bracket to the transmission. Tighten the nuts to 50 Nm (37 ft. lbs.).
12. If equipped with a NVG 261manual transmission, install the bolt securing the left side support brace to the transmission. Tighten the bolt to 50 Nm (37 ft. lbs.).
13. If equipped with a NVG 261 manual transmission, Install the bolt and stud securing the left side support brace to the transfer case. Tighten the bolt and stud to 50 Nm (37 ft. lbs.).
14. If equipped with a NVG 261manual transmission, install the 2 bolts securing the right side support brace to the transmission and transfer case. Tighten the bolts to 50 Nm (37 ft. lbs.).
15. Install the vent hose to the transfer case.
16. Check the transfer case oil level.

17. Connect the speed sensor electrical connectors.
18. Connect wiring harness to the transfer case.
19. Install the shift rod to the transfer case.
20. Install the rear propeller shaft.
21. Install the front propeller shaft.
22. Install the transfer case shields.
23. Lower the vehicle.

Silverado and 2000–01 Sierra 15 Series w/NVG246-NP8 2-Speed Automatic Transfer Case

1. Remove or disconnect the following:
   - Transfer case shields
   - Front propeller shaft
   - Rear propeller shaft
   - Vent hose from the transfer case
   - Vehicle speed sensor electrical connectors
   - Electrical connectors from the transfer case motor/encoder
   - Any wiring harness from the transfer case
2. Support the transfer case with a transmission jack.
3. If equipped with a NV3500 manual transmission, remove the bolt securing the left side support brace to the transmission.
4. If equipped with a NV3500 manual transmission, remove the bolt and stud securing the left side support brace to the transfer case.
5. If equipped with a NV3500 manual transmission, remove the two bolts securing the right side support brace to the transmission and transfer case.
6. For vehicles equipped with a manual transmission, remove the six nuts securing the transfer case and bracket to the transmission. Remove the transfer case.
7. For vehicles equipped with a automatic transmission, remove the six nuts securing the transfer case and bracket to the transmission adapter. Remove the transfer case.
8. Remove and discard the gasket.

To install:

9. Install a new gasket to the transmission. Use Teflon Pipe Sealant GM P/N 12346004 in order to hold the gasket in place.
10. Raise and position the transfer case to the vehicle
11. For vehicles equipped with a automatic transmission, install the six nuts securing the transfer case and bracket to the transmission adapter. Tighten the nuts to 50 Nm (37 ft. lbs.).

12. For vehicles equipped with a manual transmission, install the six nuts securing the transfer case and bracket to the transmission. Tighten the nuts to 50 Nm (37 ft. lbs.).

13. If equipped with a NV3500 manual transmission, install the bolt securing the left side support brace to the transmission. Tighten the bolt to 50 Nm (37 ft. lbs.).

14. If equipped with a NV3500 manual transmission, Install the bolt and stud securing the left side support brace to the transfer case. Tighten the bolt and stud to 50 Nm (37 ft. lbs.).

15. If equipped with a NV3500 manual transmission, install the two bolts securing the right side support brace to the transmission and transfer case. Tighten the bolts to 50 Nm (37 ft. lbs.).

16. Install or connect the following:
- Vent hose to the transfer case
- Oil
- Speed sensor electrical connectors
- Electrical connectors to the transfer case motor/encoder
- Any wiring harness to the transfer case
- Rear propeller shaft
- Front propeller shaft
- Transfer case shields

Halfshaft

REMOVAL & INSTALLATION

Silverado and 2000–01 Sierra 15 Series and 2000–01 Sierra 15 Series

1. Remove or disconnect the following:
- Wheels

2. Insert a drift or a large screwdriver through the brake caliper into one of the brake rotor vanes in order to prevent the drive axle wheel drive shaft from turning.

3. Remove or disconnect the following:
- Nut and the washer from the hub. Do not reuse the nut. A new nut must be used when installing the wheel drive shaft.
- The 6 bolts securing the wheel drive shaft inboard flange to the output shaft flange
- The drift from the rotor
- The stabilizer shaft link from the lower control arm

4. Wrap shop towels around both the inner and the outer wheel drive shaft boots in order to avoid damage to the boots during removal and installation.

5. Pull the wheel drive shaft through the lower control arm opening.

To install:

6. Wrap shop towels around both the inner and the outer wheel drive shaft boots in order to avoid damage to the boots during removal and installation.

➡**Clean the steering knuckle and the wheel drive shaft splines and threads. These areas must be dry and free of grease, dirt, and contamination.**

7. Insert the wheel drive shaft splined shank into the knuckle hub.

➡**Use only a genuine GM front wheel drive shaft nut. Installation of anything but an OEM front wheel drive shaft nut could cause damage to the vehicle.**

8. Install or connect the following:
- Washer and the new hub nut to the wheel drive shaft. Do not tighten.
- The wheel drive shaft inboard flange to the output shaft flange using the inboard flange bolts

9. Insert a drift or a large screwdriver through the brake caliper into 1 of the brake rotor vanes in order to prevent the wheel drive shaft from turning. Tighten the inboard

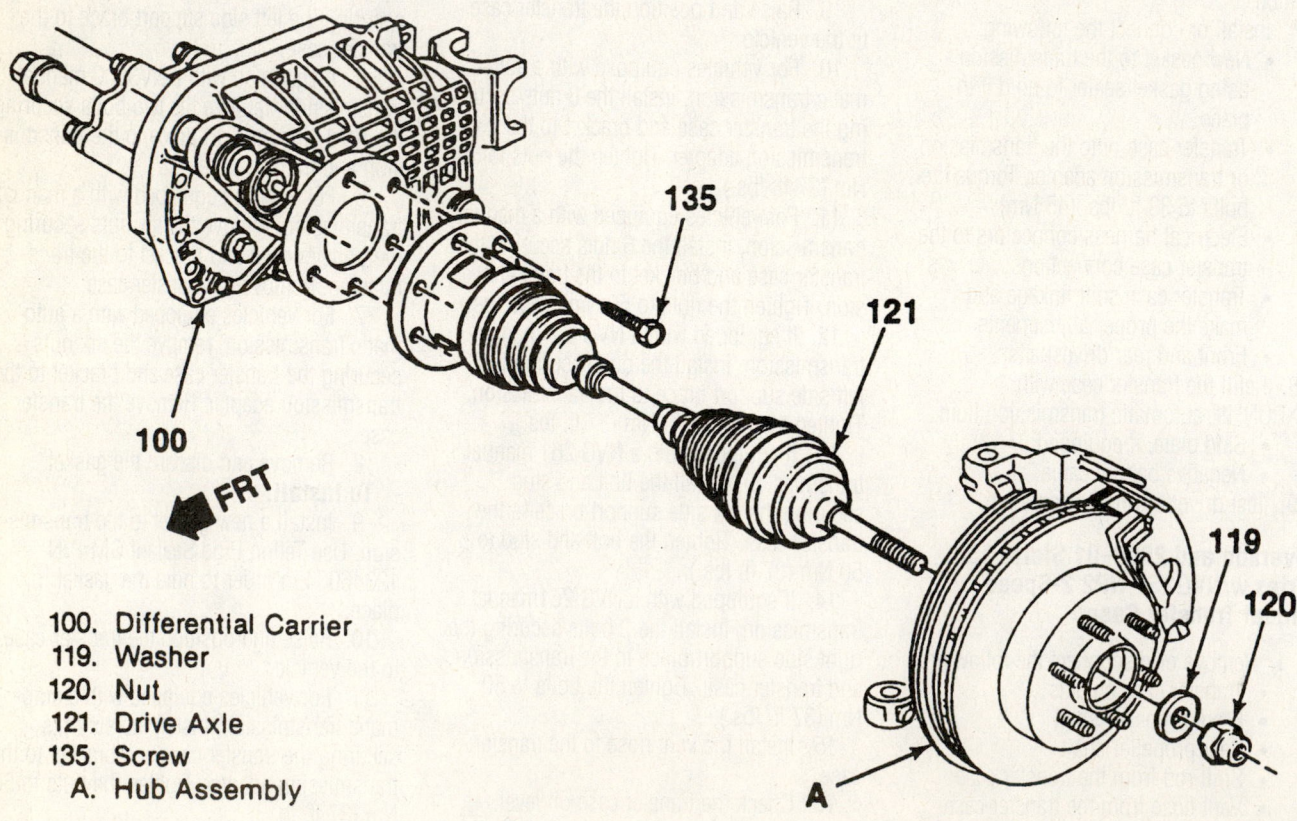

100. Differential Carrier
119. Washer
120. Nut
121. Drive Axle
135. Screw
 A. Hub Assembly

The halfshaft is mounted to the flange on the differential and through the hub assembly—4-wheel drive models

7924KG29

flange bolts to 78 Nm (58 ft. lbs.). Tighten the hub nut to 210 Nm (155 ft. lbs.).

10. Remove the drift from the rotor.
11. Install the stabilizer shaft link.
12. Install the wheel and tire assembly.

Except Silverado and 2000–01 Sierra 15 Series and 2000–01 Sierra 15 Series

1. Before servicing the vehicle, refer to the precautions in the beginning of this section.
2. Remove or disconnect the following:
   - Front wheel and tire assembly
   - Skid plate, as required. If equipped
   - Drive axle hub nut and washer
   - Brake line and wheel speed sensor support bracket from the upper control arm to allow extra travel of the control arm.
   - Left outer tie rod attaching nut and cotter pin. Separate the tie rod from the steering knuckle
3. Position the tie rod aside and push steering linkage to the opposite side of the vehicle.
   - Lower shock attaching nut and bolt; position the shock aside
   - Left stabilizer bar bracket and bushing at the frame
   - Stabilizer bar bolt, spacer and bushings at the lower control arm
4. Taking pressure off the upper control arm by placing a support below the lower control arm between the spring seat and the ball joint.
   - Upper ball joint cotter pin and loosen (do not remove) the upper ball joint attaching nut. Separate the ball joint stud from the steering knuckle. Remove the attaching nut.

➡**Cover the shock mounting bracket and lower ball joint stud with a towel to prevent the axle boot from tearing during removal and installation.**

5. Separate the axle shaft from the hub and rotor using tool J-28733 or equivalent.
   - Axle shaft inner flange bolts and shaft

To install:
6. Lubricate the axle and hub splines with an approved high temperature wheel bearing grease.
7. Install or connect the following:

- Axle shaft in the hub
- Inboard CV-joint-to-flange bolts. Torque the bolts to 60 ft. lbs. (80 Nm).
- Upper ball joint to steering knuckle. Torque the stud nut to 61 ft. lbs. (83 Nm).
- New cotter pin through the upper ball joint stud and nut, lubricate the ball joint as required.
- Left stabilizer bar bracket and bushing at the frame
- Stabilizer bar bolt, spacer and bushings at the lower control arm
- Lower shock in the mount bracket and the attaching nut and bolt
- Left tie rod end at the steering knuckle. Torque the nut to 35 ft. lbs. (47 Nm).
- New cotter pin through the tie rod stud and nut
- Brake line bracket to the control arm, ensuring the line and/or hose is not twisted or kinked
- Skid plate, as required
- Axle hub washer and nut. Insert a drift through the rotor vanes to keep the axle from turning. Toque the hub nut to 180 ft. lbs. (245 Nm)
- Wheel and tire assembly

CV-Joints

OVERHAUL

Silverado and 2000–01 Sierra 15 Series

INNER JOINT

➡**With removal of the halfshaft for any reason, the transmission sealing surface (the tripot male/female shank of the halfshaft) should be inspected for corrosion. If corrosion is evident, the surface should be cleaned with 320 grit cloth or equivalent. Transmission fluid may be used to clean off any remaining debris. The surface should be wiped dry and the halfshaft reinstalled free of any buildup.**

1. Use a hand grinder in order to cut through the swage ring.
2. Remove the tripot housing from the halfshaft. Wipe the grease off of the tripot assembly roller bearings and the tripot housing. Thoroughly degrease the tripot housing. Allow the tripot housing to dry prior to assembly.

➡**Handle the tripot spider assembly with care. Tripot balls and needle rollers may separate from the spider**

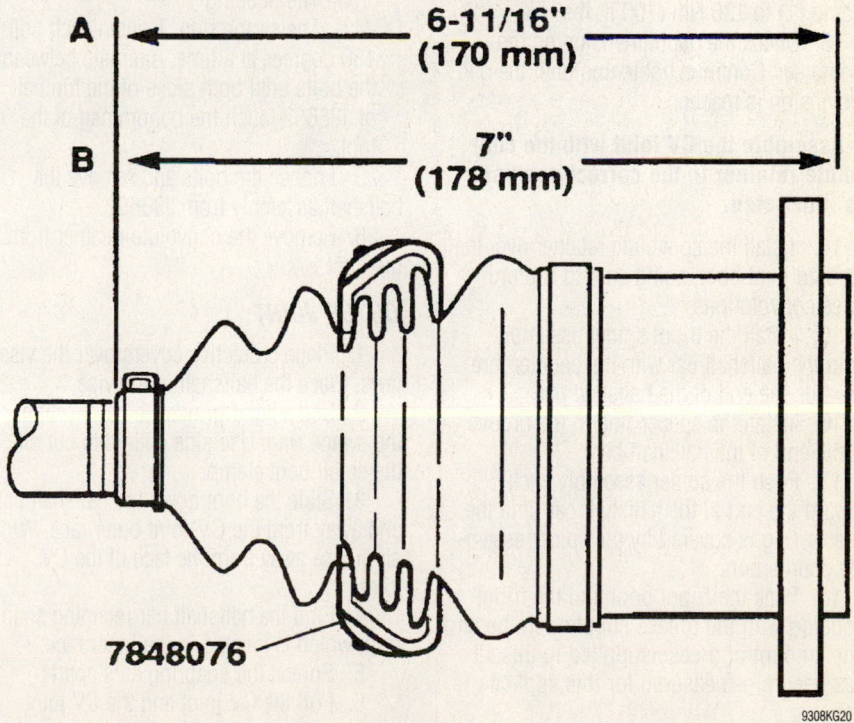

Assembled joint measurement—15 Series Silverado

9308KG20

trunnion if the tripot balls and needle rollers are not handled carefully.

3. Use side cutters to cut away the small boot clamp.

4. Compress the tripot boot up the halfshaft away from the tripot spider assembly toward the outboard (CV joint assembly) end of the halfshaft.

5. Spread the spider spacer ring with tool J8059, or equivalent.

6. Remove the following items from the halfshaft bar:

   a. The spacer ring

   b. The spider assembly

   c. The tripot boot

7. Clean the halfshaft bar. Use a wire brush in order to remove any rust in the boot mounting area (grooves).

8. Inspect the needle rollers, needle bearings, and trunnion. Check the tripot housing for unusual wear, cracks, or other damage. Replace any damaged parts.

To assemble:

9. Place the new small boot clamp onto the small end of the joint boot.

10. Compress the joint boot and small boot clamp onto the halfshaft bar.

11. Position the small end of the joint boot into the joint boot groove on the halfshaft bar.

12. Secure the small boot clamp with tool J35910, or equivalent, a breaker bar, and a torque wrench. Tighten the small boot clamp (1) to 136 Nm (100 ft. lbs.).

13. Check the gap dimension on the clamp ear. Continue tightening until the gap dimension is reached.

➡**Assemble the CV joint with the convolute retainer in the correct position, as illustrated.**

14. Install the convolute retainer over the inboard joint boot, being sure to capture three convolutions.

15. Install the tripot spider assembly onto the halfshaft bar with the counterbore towards the end of the halfshaft bar.

16. Install the spacer ring in the groove at the end of the halfshaft bar.

17. Push the spider assembly back toward the end of the halfshaft bar until the spacer ring is covered by the spider assembly counterbore.

18. Pack the tripot boot and the tripot housing with the grease supplied in the kit. The amount of grease supplied in this kit has been pre-measured for this application.

19. Reassemble the tripot housing and the tripot boot using the following procedure:

   a. Pinch the swage ring slightly by hand in order to distort it into an oval shape.

   b. Slide the distorted swage ring over the large diameter of the boot.

   c. Place the tripot housing over the spider assembly.

   d. Install the boot onto the tripot housing.

   e. Align the tripot boot with the swage ring in place, over the flat area on the tripot housing.

20. Mount tool J36652 in a vise. Install the bottom half of the split-plate swage clamp. For K15 models, use tool J36652-98. For K25 models, use tool J36652-1.

21. Check the inboard stroke position. Use measurement A for the K15 models. Use measurement B for the K25 models.

22. Position the inboard end (tripot end) of the halfshaft assembly in tool J36652. Install the top half of the proper size tool on the lower half of the tool. For K15 models, use tool J36652-98. For K25models, use tool J36652-1.

23. Align the swage ring and the swage ring clamp. Insert the bolts. Hand tighten the bolts in tool J36652 until the bolts are snug.

24. Align the following during this procedure:

   a. The tripot boot

   b. The housing

   c. The swage ring. Tighten each bolt 180 degrees at a time. Alternate between the bolts until both sides of the top half of J36652 touch the bottom half of the tool.

25. Loosen the bolts and remove the halfshaft assembly from J36652.

26. Remove the convolute retainer from the boot.

OUTER JOINT

1. Place protective covers over the vise jaws. Place the halfshaft in the vise.

2. Use a hand grinder to cut through the swage ring. Use side cutters to cut off the small boot clamp.

3. Slide the boot down the halfshaft bar and away from the CV-joint outer race. Wipe all grease away from the face of the CV joint.

4. Find the halfshaft bar retaining snap ring, which is located in the inner race.

5. Spread the snaping ears apart.

6. Pull the CV joint and the CV joint boot from the halfshaft bar. Discard the old CV joint boot.

7. Place a brass drift against the CV joint cage. Tap gently on the brass drift with a hammer in order to tilt the cage.

8. Remove the first chrome alloy ball when the CV joint cage tilts. Tilt the CV joint cage (1) in the opposite direction to remove the opposing chrome alloy ball. Repeat this process to remove all six of the balls.

9. Pivot the CV joint cage and the inner race 90 degrees to the center line of the outer race. At the same time, align the cage windows with the lands of the outer race. Lift out the cage and the inner race.

10. Remove the inner race from the cage by rotating the inner race upward. Clean the following items thoroughly with cleaning solvent. Remove all traces of old grease and any contaminates.

   a. The inner and outer race assemblies

   b. The CV joint cage

   c. The chrome alloy balls

11. Dry all the parts. Check the CV joint assembly for unusual wear, cracks, or other damage. Replace any damaged parts. Clean the halfshaft bar. Use a wire brush to remove any rust in the boot mounting area (grooves).

To assemble:

12. Inspect all of the parts for unusual wear, cracks, or other damage. Replace the CV joint assembly if necessary. Put a light coat of the recommended grease on the inner and the outer race grooves.

13. Hold the inner race at 90 degrees to the centerline of the cage. Align the lands of the inner race with the windows of the cage. Insert the inner race into the cage by rotating the inner race downward.

14. Insert the cage and inner race into the outer race.

15. Place a brass drift against the CV joint cage. Tap gently on the brass drift with a hammer in order to tilt the cage. Install the first chrome alloy ball when the CV joint cage tilts. Tilt the CV joint cage in the opposite direction to install the opposing chrome alloy ball. Repeat this process in order to install all six of the balls.

16. Pack the CV joint boot and the CV joint assembly with the grease supplied in the kit. The amount of grease supplied in this kit has been pre-measured for this application.

17. Place the new small boot clamp onto the CV joint boot.

18. Slide the CV joint boot onto the halfshaft bar.

19. Position the small end of the CV joint boot into the joint boot groove on the halfshaft bar.

20. Secure the small boot clamp, a

breaker bar, and a torque wrench. Tighten the small clamp (1) to 136 Nm (100 ft. lbs.).

21. Check the gap dimension on the clamp ear. Continue tightening until the gap dimension is reached.

22. Pinch the new swage ring slightly by hand to distort it into an oval shape. Slide the distorted swage ring over the large diameter of the boot.

➡**Be sure that the retaining ring side of the CV joint inner race faces the half-shaft bar (3) before installation.**

23. Slide the CV joint onto the halfshaft bar. The retaining snap ring inside of the inner race engages in the halfshaft bar groove with a click when the CV joint is in the proper position.

24. Pull on the CV joint to verify engagement.

25. Slide the large diameter of the CV joint boot with the large swage ring in place, over the outside edge of the CV joint outer race.

26. Clamp the CV joint boot tightly to the CV joint outer race with the large swage ring, using the following procedure:

   a. Mount tool J36652 in a vise.

   b. Install the bottom half of the split-plate swage clamp. For K15 models, use tool J36652-98.

   c. For K25 models, use tool J36652-1.

   d. Position the CV joint end (outboard end) of the halfshaft assembly in the bottom half of tool J36652.

27. Align the following during this procedure:

   a. The CV joint boot

   b. The CV joint assembly

   c. The swage ring

28. Install the top half of tool J36652 onto the lower half of the tool, over the CV joint boot and the CV joint assembly.

29. Align the swage ring and the swage ring clamp.

30. Insert the bolts into J36652. Hand tighten the bolts until the bolts are snug. Tighten each bolt 180 degrees at a time. Alternate between the bolts until both sides of the top half of the tool touch the bottom half of the tool.

31. Loosen the bolts and remove the halfshaft assembly from the tool.

Except Silverado and 2000–01 Sierra 15 Series

OUTER CV-JOINT

1. Before servicing the vehicle, refer to the precautions in the beginning of this section.

2. Remove or disconnect the following:
   - Front wheel
   - Halfshaft and position it in a vise
   - Large CV-joint boot clamp and discard it
   - Small CV-joint boot clamp and discard it
   - CV-joint boot and slide it back on the shaft
   - Outer race from the halfshaft by spreading the outer race-to-half-shaft retaining ring using Snapring Pliers J-8059
   - Retaining ring from the halfshaft and discard it
   - CV-joint boot from the halfshaft and discard it if damaged

3. Disassemble the chrome alloy balls from the CV-joint cage as follows:

   a. Position a brass drift against the CV-joint cage and tap it with a hammer to tilt the cage.

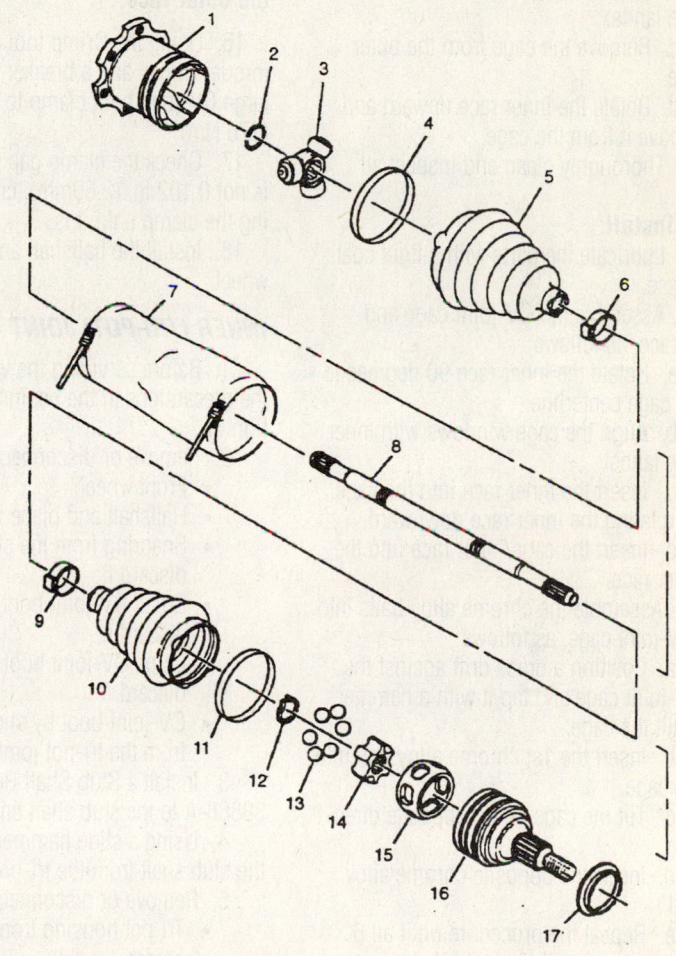

Legend
(1) Tripot Housing Assembly
(2) Spacer Ring
(3) Tripot Joint Spider Assembly
(4) Swage Ring
(5) Tripot Joint Seal
(6) Small Seal Retaining Clamp
(7) Drive Axle Seal Cover (Optional)
(8) Drive Axle Shaft
(9) CV Joint Seal
(10) Race Retaining Ring
(11) Ball
(12) CV Joint Inner Race
(13) CV Joint Cage
(14) CV Joint Outer Race
(15) Deflector Ring

9308KG10

Exploded view of the CV-Joint assembly

Turn to Section 5 for brake system applications

b. Remove the 1st chrome alloy ball from the cage.

c. Tilt the cage in the opposite direction.

d. Remove the opposite chrome alloy ball.

e. Repeat the procedure until all 6 balls are removed.

4. Disassemble the CV-joint cage and inner race as follows:

a. Pivot the cage and race 90 degrees to the center line of the outer race.

b. Align the cage windows with outer race lands.

c. Remove the cage from the outer race.

d. Rotate the inner race upward and remove it from the cage.

5. Thoroughly clean and inspect all parts.

To install:

6. Lubricate the parts with a light coat of grease.

7. Assemble the CV-joint cage and inner race, as follows:

a. Rotate the inner race 90 degrees to the cage centerline.

b. Align the cage windows with inner race lands.

c. Insert the inner race into the cage by rotating the inner race downward.

d. Insert the cage/inner race into the outer race.

8. Assemble the chrome alloy balls into the CV-joint cage, as follows:

a. Position a brass drift against the CV-joint cage and tap it with a hammer to tilt the cage.

b. Insert the 1st chrome alloy ball into the cage.

c. Tilt the cage in the opposite direction.

d. Insert the opposite chrome alloy ball.

e. Repeat the procedure until all 6 balls are inserted.

9. Install ½ of the kit grease into the CV-joint.

10. Install or connect the following:
- Small ring clamp on the CV boot
- New retaining ring on the halfshaft
- Large ring clamp on the CV boot
- Outer race assembly onto the halfshaft until the ring engages the halfshaft groove

11. Slide the small end of the CV-joint boot/clamp into place, with the seal lip in the halfshaft groove

➡**Make sure the boot lies flat against the halfshaft.**

12. Using the Crimp tool J-35910, a torque wrench and a breaker bar, crimp the small CV-joint boot clamp to 100 ft. lbs. (136 Nm).

13. Check the clamp gap dimension; if it is not 0.085 in. (2.15mm), continue tightening the clamp until it is.

14. Install ½ of the kit grease into the CV-joint boot.

15. Slide the large end of the CV boot/clamp into place, with the seal lip in place over the outer race.

➡**Make sure the boot lies flat against the outer race.**

16. Using the Crimp tool J-35910, a torque wrench and a breaker bar, crimp the large CV-joint boot clamp to 130 ft. lbs. (176 Nm).

17. Check the clamp gap dimension; if it is not 0.102 in. (2.60mm), continue tightening the clamp until it is.

18. Install the halfshaft and the front wheel.

INNER (TRI-POT) JOINT

1. Before servicing the vehicle, refer to the precautions in the beginning of this section.

2. Remove or disconnect the following:
- Front wheel
- Halfshaft and place it in a vise
- Snapring from the stub shaft and discard it
- Small CV-joint boot clamp, cut and discard it
- Large CV-joint boot clamp, cut and discard it
- CV-joint boot by sliding it away from the tri-pot joint

3. Install a Stub Shaft Removal tool J-38868-A to the stub shaft snapring groove.

4. Using a slide hammer puller, press the stub shaft from the tri-pot housing.

5. Remove or disconnect the following:
- Tri-pot housing from the tri-pot spider
- Inboard spacer ring slide it rearward on the shaft using Snapring Pliers tool J-8059
- Outboard retaining ring using Snapring Pliers tool J-8059 and discard it
- Tri-pot joint spider assembly
- Inboard spacer ring and discard it
- CV-joint boot
- Trilobal tri-pot bushing from the housing

6. Thoroughly clean and inspect all parts.

To install:

7. Install or connect the following:
- New snapring onto the stub shaft

- Small boot clamp
- CV-joint boot

8. Using the Crimp tool J-35910, a torque wrench and a breaker bar, crimp the small CV-joint boot clamp to 100 ft. lbs. (136 Nm).

9. Install or connect the following:
- Inboard spacer ring slide it rearward on the shaft using Snapring Pliers tool J-8059, past the 2nd groove
- Tri-pot joint spider assembly onto the shaft until it passes the 2nd groove
- Outboard retaining ring into the axle shaft groove using Snapring Pliers tool J-8059
- Tri-pot joint spider assembly, slide it against the outboard retaining ring
- Inboard spacer ring, seat it in the groove
- ½ of the kit grease into the boot
- ½ of the kit grease into the tri-pot housing
- Trilobal tip-pot bushing flush with the tri-pot housing face
- New large seal clamp onto the CV-joint boot
- Tri-pot housing, slide it over the tri-pot joint spider assembly
- CV-joint boot/clamp, slide it into place, over the trilobal tri-pot bushing with the seal lip in the groove

➡**Make sure the boot lies flat against the trilobal bushing.**

10. Using the Crimp tool J-35910, a torque wrench and a breaker bar, crimp the large CV-joint boot clamp to 130 ft. lbs. (176 Nm)

11. Check the clamp gap dimension; if it is not 0.102 in. (2.60mm), continue tightening the clamp until it is.

12. Install the halfshaft and the front wheel.

Manual Locking Hubs

The engagement and disengagement of the hubs is a manual operation which must be performed at each hub assembly. The hubs should be placed FULLY in either Lock or Free position or damage will result.

✱✷✱ WARNING

Do not place the transfer case in either 4-wheel mode unless the hubs are in the Lock position!

Locking hubs should be run in the Lock position periodically for a few miles to assure proper differential lubrication.

REMOVAL & INSTALLATION

1. Before servicing the vehicle, refer to the precautions in the beginning of this section.

2. Remove or disconnect the following:
   - Wheels

3. Lock the hubs. Remove the outer retaining plate, Allen head bolts and take off the plate, O-ring, and knob assembly.
   - External snapring from the axle shaft
   - Compression spring
   - Clutch cup
   - O-ring and dial screw
   - Clutch nut and seal
   - Large internal snapring from the wheel hub
   - Inner drive gear
   - Clutch ring and spring
   - Smaller internal snapring from the clutch hub body
   - Hub body

4. Clean all hub parts in a safe, non-flammable solvent and wipe them dry.

5. Inspect each component for wear or damage. Make sure that the springs are functional and stiff. Make sure that all gear teeth are intact, with no chips or burrs.

6. Make sure that the splines on the inside of the wheel hub are clean and free of dirt, chips and burrs.

7. Surface irregularities can be cleaned up with light filing or emery paper.

8. Prior to assembly, coat all parts with the same wheel bearing grease.

To install:

9. Install or connect the following:
   - Hub body
   - Smaller internal snapring in the clutch hub body
   - Clutch ring and spring
   - Inner drive gear
   - Large internal snapring in the wheel hub
   - External snapring on the axle shaft. If the snapring groove is not completely visible, reach around, inside the knuckle and push the axle shaft outwards.
   - Clutch nut and seal
   - O-ring and dial screw
   - Clutch cup
   - Compression spring

10. Place the hub dial in the Lock position.

11. Coat the hub dial assembly O-ring with wheel bearing grease and position the hub dial and retainer on the hub.

- Allen head bolts. Make sure that you used any washers that were there originally. Torque these bolts to 45 inch lbs. (5 Nm)

12. Rotate the hub dial to the free position and turn the wheel hubs to make sure that the axle is free.
   - Wheels

Automatic Locking Hubs

REMOVAL & INSTALLATION

The following procedure covers removal & installation only, for the hub assembly. The hub should be disassembled ONLY if overhaul is necessary. In that event, an overhaul kit will be required. Follow the instructions in the overhaul kit to rebuild the hub.

1. Before servicing the vehicle, refer to the precautions in the beginning of this section.

2. Remove or disconnect the following:

   - Capscrews and washer from the hub cap
   - Hub cap and spring
   - Bearing race, bearing and retainer
   - Keeper from the outer clutch housing
   - Large snapring to release the locking unit
   - Locking unit from the hub. You can make this job easier by threading 2 hub cap screws into the outer clutch housing and hold these to pull out the unit.

To install:

3. Wipe clean all parts and check for wear or damage.

4. Coat all parts with the same wheel bearing grease you've used on the bearings.

5. Install or connect the following:
   - Locking unit in the hub
   - Large snapring, pull outward on the unit to make sure the snapring is fully seated in its groove
   - Keepers
   - Bearing retainer, bearing and race. Make sure that the bearing is fully pack with grease.

6. Coat the hub cap O-ring with wheel bearing grease and install the hub cap.

   - Capscrews and washers. Tighten the screws to 45 inch lbs. (5 Nm).

Front Axle Shaft, Bearing and Seal

REMOVAL & INSTALLATION

Except Silverado and 2000–01 Sierra 15 Series

1. Before servicing the vehicle, refer to the precautions in the beginning of this section.

2. Drain the front axle.

3. Remove or disconnect the following:
   - Electrical connectors, if equipped
   - Drive axle (halfshaft)
   - Axle shaft (output shaft)
   - Axle shaft from case
   - Deflector and seal
   - Bearing

To install:

4. Install or connect the following:
   - New Bearing, square shoulder in

➡ **Lubricate the new seal with grease.**

   - New seal
   - Deflector
   - Axle shaft (output shaft)
   - Drive axle (halfshaft)
   - Electrical connectors, if equipped

5. Refill the front axle.

Silverado and 2000–01 Sierra 15 Series

1. Remove or disconnect the following:
   - Halfshaft assembly
   - Front axle fluid
   - Electrical connectors
   - Axle shaft (output shaft) tube nuts from the bracket
   - Bracket bolts from the frame. Do not remove the bracket. The bolts are removed in order to provide clearance.
   - Axle shaft (output shaft) bolts from the carrier

➡ **Keep the open end of the tube up.**

   - Axle shaft (output shaft) tube from the carrier. Ensure the spring is not lost during removal. In a vise, hold the axle shaft (output shaft) tube by the mounting flange.

2. Remove the following components:
   a. The shift shaft
   b. The damper spring
   c. The fork
   d. The clip assembly

3. Remove or disconnect the following:

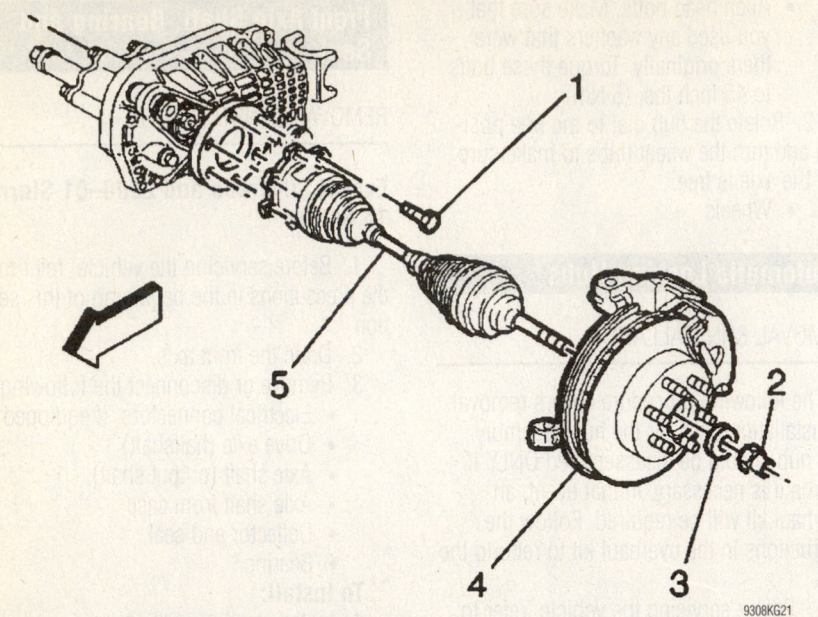

Front axle shaft removal—15 Series Silverado

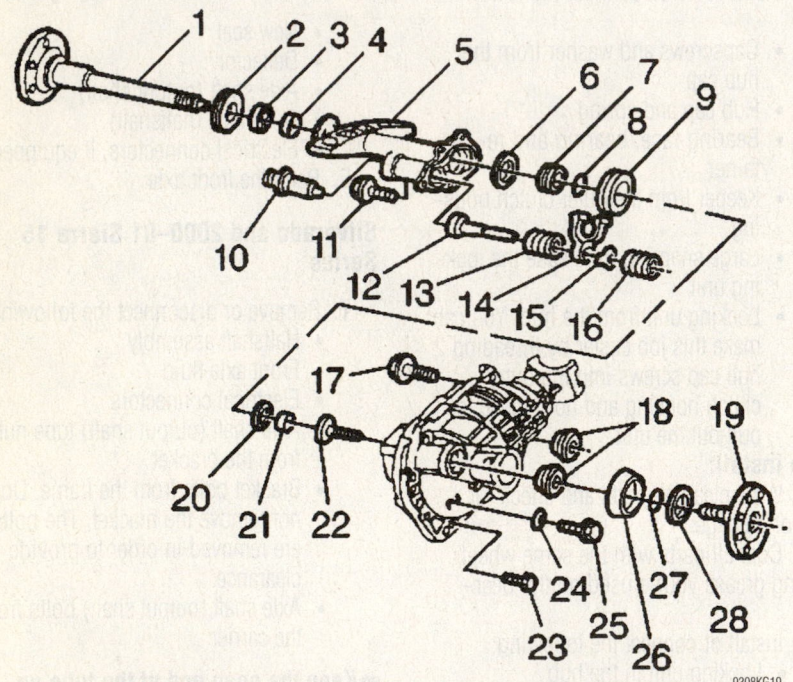

Front axle shaft exploded view—15 Series Silverado

- Sleeve
- Gear
- Thrust washer
- Axle shaft (output shaft). Tap out the axle shaft (output shaft) with a soft mallet.
- Deflector. Pry out the deflector with a screwdriver.
- Seal. Pry out the seal with a screwdriver.
- Bearing, using a slide hammer.
4. Clean the parts in suitable solvent.

Clean the gasket surfaces on the axle shaft (output shaft) tube and carrier housing.

To install:

5. Install or connect the following:
- New bearing into the axle shaft tube using a driver. Apply axle lubricant to the bearing.
- New seal using a driver. Coat the seal lips with axle lubricant.
- Deflector
- Axle shaft
- Thrust washer. Use grease in order

to hold the thrust washer in place. Ensure the tabs on the thrust washer align with the slot in the axle shaft tube.
- Gear
- Sleeve
- Shift shaft
- Damper spring
- Fork
- Clip assembly

6. Apply sealant GM P/N 12345739 or the equivalent to the carrier sealing surfaces.

7. Install or connect the following:
- Spring into the carrier case
- Axle shaft tube to the carrier
- Axle shaft (output shaft) bolts. Tighten the bolts to 40 Nm (30 ft. lbs.).
- Bracket bolts to the frame. Tighten the bolts to 90 Nm (67 ft. lbs.).
- Axle shaft (output shaft) tube nuts to the bracket. Tighten the nuts to 100 Nm (75 ft. lbs.).
- Halfshaft assembly
- Electrical connectors

8. Fill the front differential with lubricant until the level is 12mm (0.5 in) below the fill plug.

Rear Axle Shaft, Bearing and Seal

REMOVAL & INSTALLATION

Except Silverado and 2000–01 Sierra 15 Series

SEMI-FLOATING NON-LOCKING DIFFERENTIALS

1. Remove the wheels and brake drums.
2. Remove the differential cover
3. Turn the differential until you can reach the differential pinion shaft lockscrew. Remove the lockscrew and the pinion shaft.
4. Push in on the axle end. Remove the C-lock from the inner (button) end of the shaft.
5. Remove the shaft, being careful of the oil seal.
6. You can pry the oil seal out of the housing by placing the inner end of the axle shaft behind the steel case of the seal, then prying it out carefully.
7. A puller or a slide hammer is required to remove the bearing from the housing.

To install:

8. Pack the new or reused bearing with wheel bearing grease and lubricate the cavity between the seal lips with the same grease.

Remove the differential pinion shaft lockscrew

87987P14

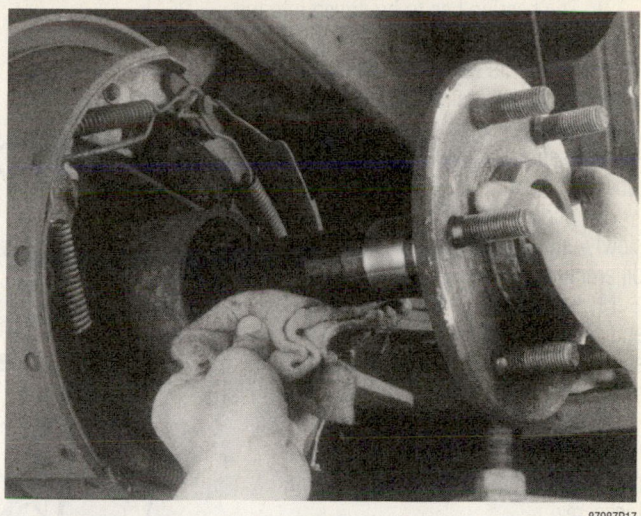

Remove the axle shaft from the vehicle

87987P17

Remove the pinion shaft

87987P15

Use a puller to remove the oil seal

87987P18

Remove the C-lock from the inner (button) end of the shaft

87987P16

Install the oil seal using a seal installer

87987P19

9. The bearing has to be driven into the housing. Don't use a drift, you might cock the bearing in its bore. Use a piece of pipe or a large socket instead. Drive only on the outer bearing race. In a similar manner, drive the seal in flush with the end of the tube.

10. Slide the shaft into place, turning it slowly until the splines are engaged with the differential. Be careful of the oil seal.

11. Install the C-lock on the inner axle end. Pull the shaft out so that the C-lock seats in the counterbore of the differential side gear.

12. Position the differential pinion shaft through the case and the pinion gears, aligning the lockscrew hole. Install the lockscrew.

13. Install the cover with a new gasket and tighten the bolts evenly in a criss-cross pattern.

14. Fill the axle with lubricant.

15. Replace the brake drums and wheels.

SEMI-FLOATING LOCKING DIFFERENTIALS

This axle uses a thrust block on the differential pinion shaft.

1. Remove the wheels and brake drums.

2. Clean off the differential cover area, loosen the cover to drain the lubricant, and remove the cover.

3. Rotate the differential case so that you can remove the lockscrew and support the pinion shaft so it can't fall into the housing. Remove the differential pinion shaft lockscrew.

4. Carefully pull the pinion shaft partway out and rotate the differential case until the shaft touches the housing at the top.

5. Use a screwdriver to position the C-lock with its open end directly inward. You can't push in the axle shaft till you do this.

6. Push the axle shaft in and remove the C-lock.

7. Remove the shaft, being careful of the oil seal.

8. You can pry the oil seal out of the housing by placing the inner end of the axle shaft behind the steel case of the seal, then prying it out carefully.

9. A puller or a slide hammer is required to remove the bearing from the housing.

To install:

10. Pack the new or reused bearing with wheel bearing grease and lubricate the cavity between the seal lips with the same grease.

11. The bearing has to be driven into the housing. Don't use a drift, you might cock

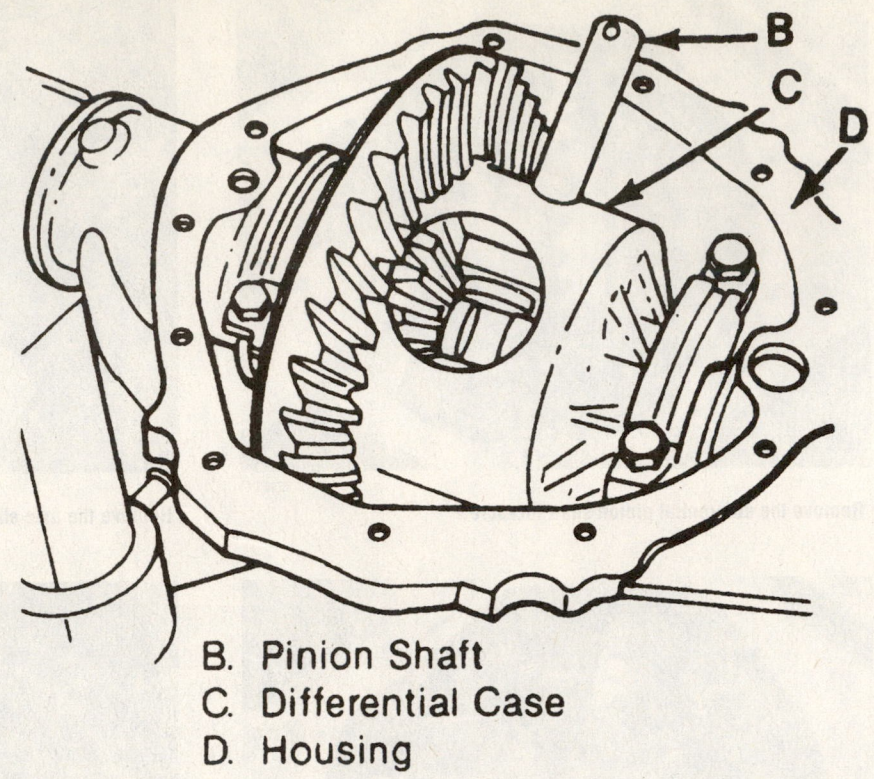

B. Pinion Shaft
C. Differential Case
D. Housing

84907357

Positioning the case for the best clearance—semi-floating axle w/locking differential

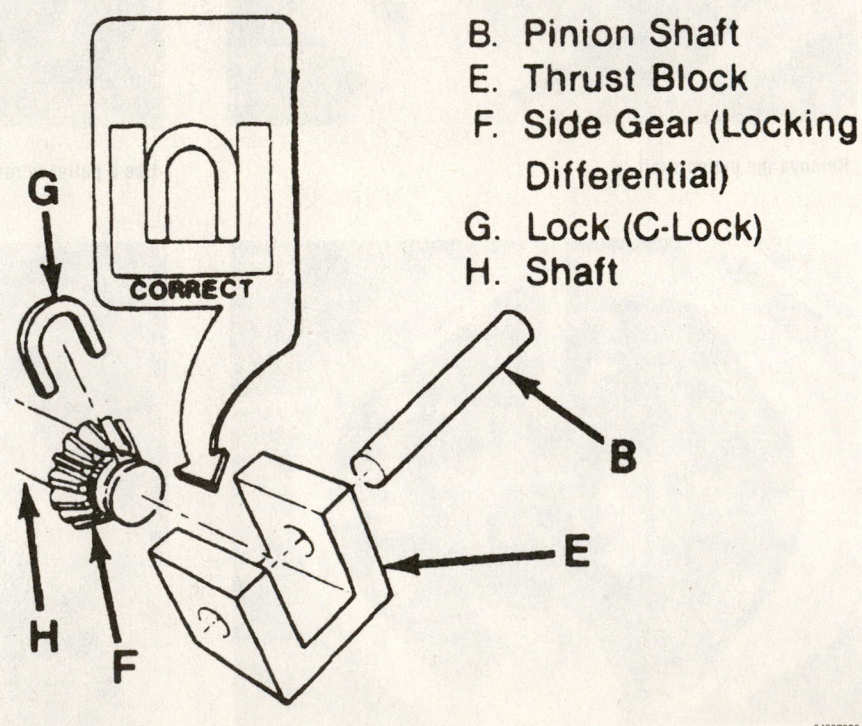

B. Pinion Shaft
E. Thrust Block
F. Side Gear (Locking Differential)
G. Lock (C-Lock)
H. Shaft

84907358

Aligning the lock—semi-floating axle w/locking differential

the bearing in its bore. Use a piece of pipe or a large socket instead. Drive only on the outer bearing race. In a similar manner, drive the seal in flush with the end of the tube.

12. Slide the shaft into place, turning it slowly until the splines are engaged with the differential. Be careful of the oil seal.

13. Keep the pinion shaft partway out of the differential case while installing the C-lock on the axle shaft. Put the C-lock on the axle shaft and carefully pull out on the axle shaft until the C-lock is clear of the thrust block.

14. Position the differential pinion shaft through the case and the pinion gears, aligning the lockscrew hole. Install the lockscrew.

15. Install the cover with a new gasket and tighten the bolts evenly in a criss-cross pattern.

16. Fill the axle with lubricant.

17. Replace the brake drums and wheels.

FULL-FLOATING AXLES

The procedures are the same for locking and non-locking axles.

The best way to remove the bearings from the wheel hub is with an arbor press. Use of a press reduces the chances of damaging the bearing races, cocking the bearing in its bore, or scoring the hub walls. A local machine shop is probably equipped with the tools to remove and install bearings and seals. However, if one is not available, the hammer and drift method outlined can be used.

1. Support the axles on jackstands.

2. Remove the wheels.

3. Remove the bolts and lock washers that attach the axle shaft flange to the hub.

4. Rap on the flange with a soft faced hammer to loosen the shaft. Grip the rib on the end of the flange with a pair of locking pliers and twist to start shaft removal. Remove the shaft from the axle tube.

5. The hub and drum assembly must be removed to remove the bearings and oil seals. You will need a large socket to remove and later adjust the bearing adjustment nut. There are also special tools available.

6. Disengage the tang of the locknut retainer from the slot or slat of the locknut, then remove the locknut from the housing tube.

7. Disengage the tang of the retainer from the slot or flat of the adjusting nut and remove the retainer from the housing tube.

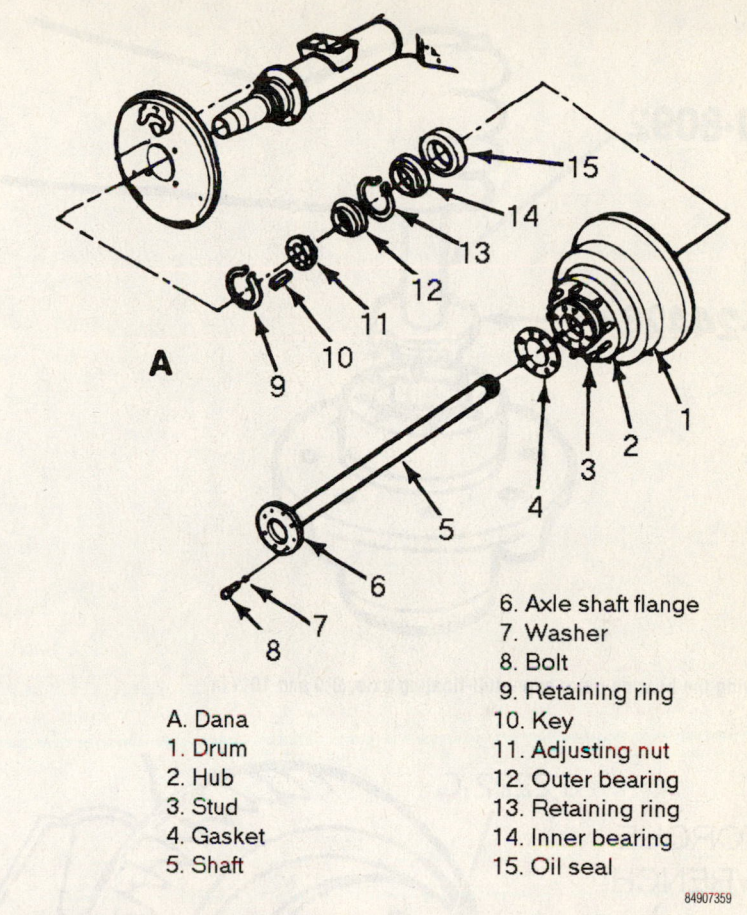

A. Dana	6. Axle shaft flange
1. Drum	7. Washer
2. Hub	8. Bolt
3. Stud	9. Retaining ring
4. Gasket	10. Key
5. Shaft	11. Adjusting nut
	12. Outer bearing
	13. Retaining ring
	14. Inner bearing
	15. Oil seal

84907359

Exploded view of the axle, hub and drum assembly—full-floating axle, 9¾ and 10½ in.

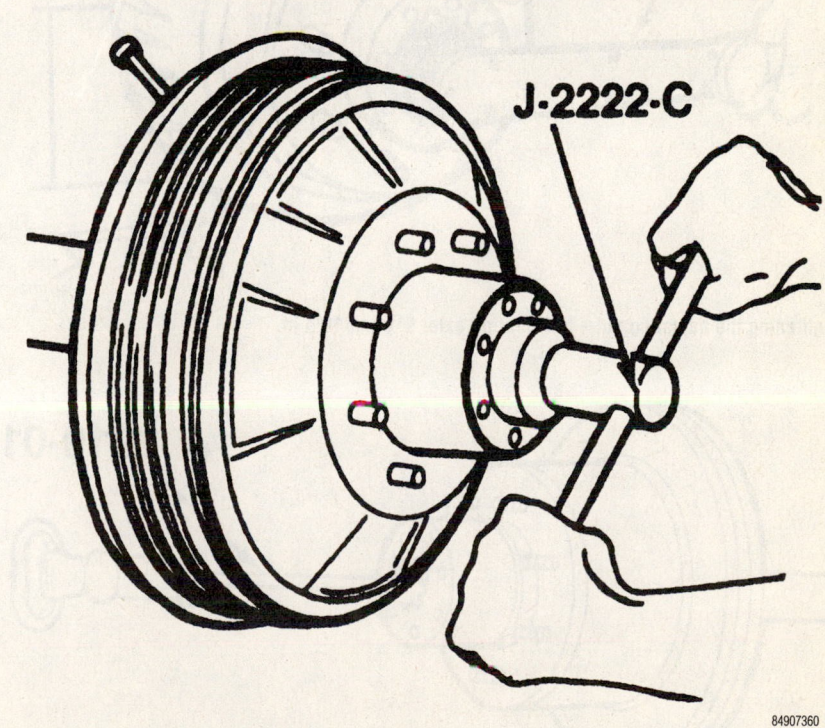

J-2222-C

84907360

Removing the bearing adjusting nut—full-floating axle, 9¾ and 10½ in.

Turn to Section 5 for brake system applications

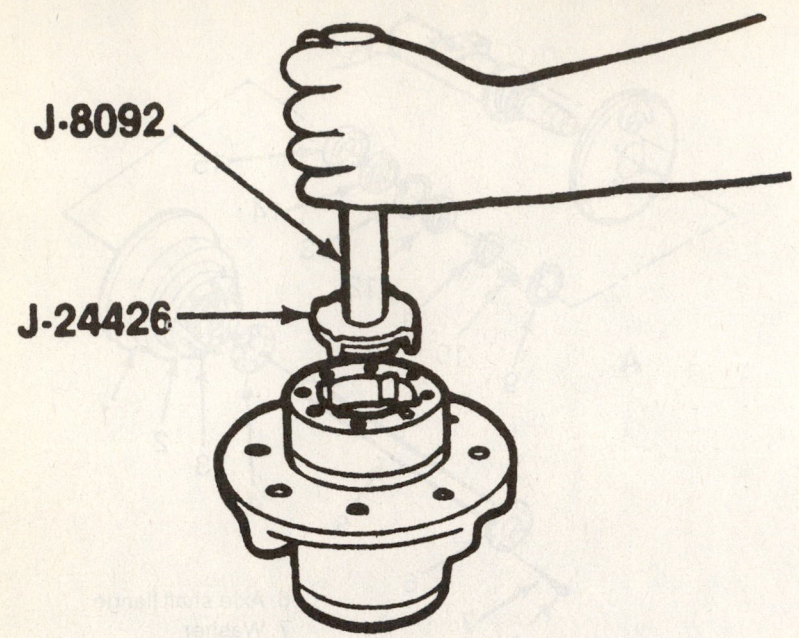

Removing the bearing outer cup—full-floating axle, 9¾ and 10½ in.

84907361

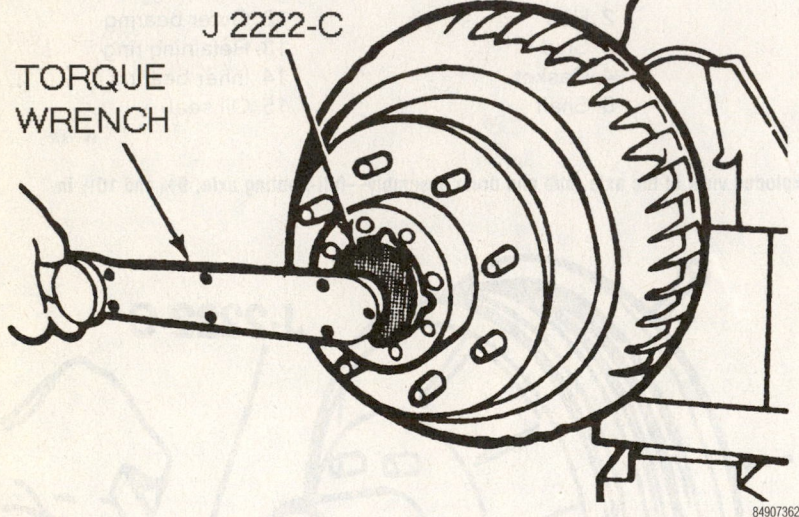

Tightening the adjusting nut—full-floating axle, 9¾ and 10½ in.

84907362

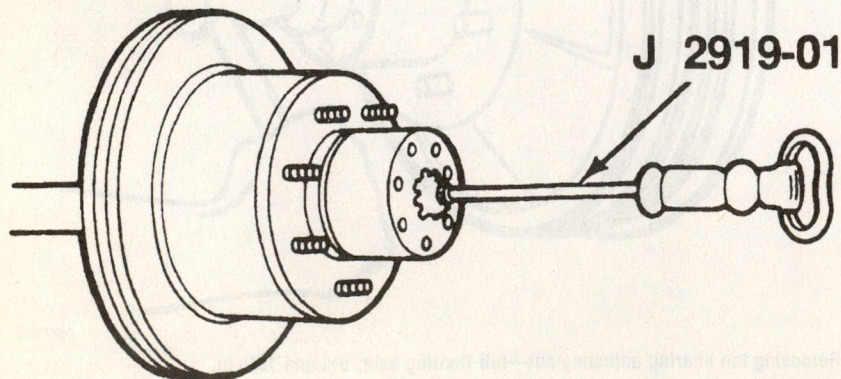

Removing the axle shaft—full-floating axle, 12 in.

84907364

8. Remove the adjusting nut from the housing tube.

9. Remove the thrust washer from the housing tube.

10. Pull the hub and drum straight off the axle housing.

11. Remove the oil seal and discard.

12. Use a hammer and a long drift to knock the inner bearing, cup, and oil seal from the hub assembly.

13. Remove the outer bearing snapring with a pair of pliers. It may be necessary to tap the bearing outer race away from the retaining ring slightly by tapping on the ring to remove the ring.

14. Drive the outer bearing from the hub with a hammer and drift.

To install:

15. Place the outer bearing into the hub. The larger outside diameter of the bearing should face the outer end of the hub. Drive the bearing into the hub using a washer that will cover both the inner and outer races of the bearing. Place a socket on top of this washer, then drive the bearing into place with a series of light taps. If available, an arbor press should be used for this job.

16. Drive the bearing past the snapring groove, and install the snapring. Then, turning the hub assembly over, drive the bearing back against the snapring. Protect the bearing by placing a washer on top of it. You can use the thrust washer that fits between the bearing and the adjusting nut for the job.

17. Place the inner bearing into the hub. The thick edge should be toward the shoulder in the hub. Press the bearing into the hub until it seats against the shoulder, using a washer and socket as outlined earlier. Make certain that the bearing is not cocked and that it is fully seated on the shoulder.

18. Pack the cavity between the oil seal lips with wheel bearing grease, and position it in the hub bore. Carefully press it into place on top of the inner bearing.

19. Pack the wheel bearings with grease, and lightly coat the inside diameter of the hub bearing contact surface and the outside diameter of the axle housing tube.

20. Make sure that the inner bearing, oil seal, axle housing oil deflector, and outer bearing are properly positioned. Install the hub and drum assembly on the axle housing, being careful so as not to damage the oil seal or dislocate other internal components.

21. Install the thrust washer so that the tang on the inside diameter of the washer is in the keyway on the axle housing.

22. Install the adjusting nut. Tighten to 50 ft. lbs. (68 Nm) while rotating the hub. Back off the nut ¼ turn and retighten to 35 ft. lbs. (47 Nm) on models with the 11 inch

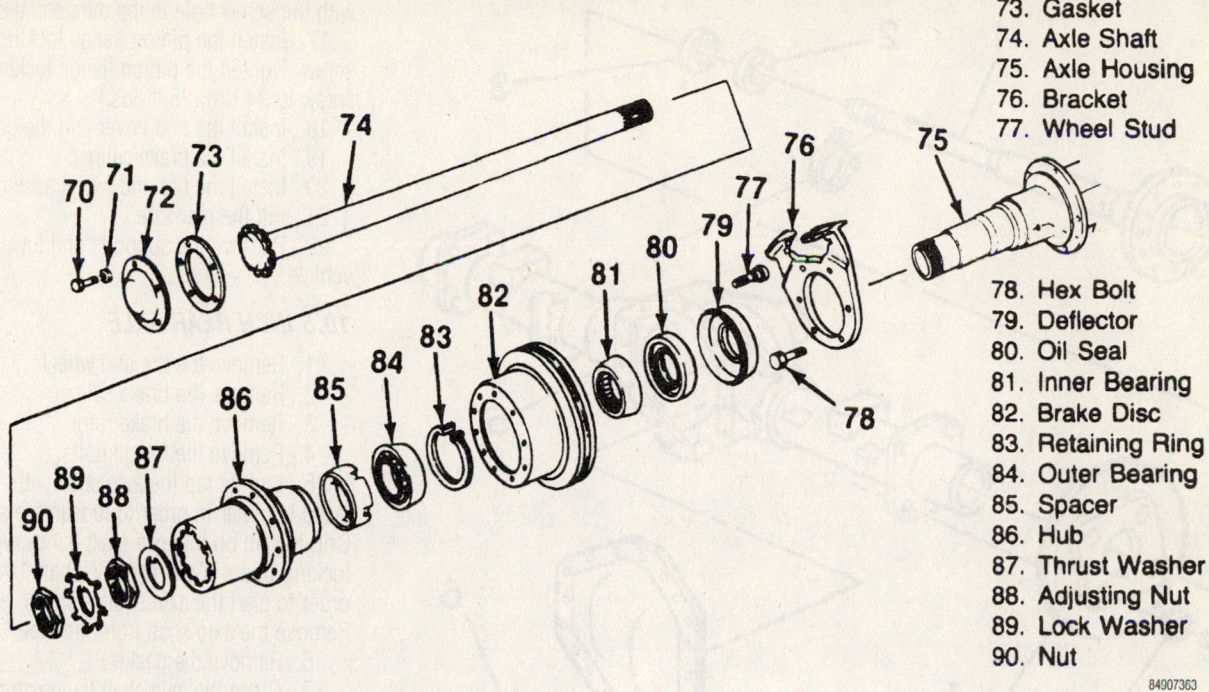

73. Gasket
74. Axle Shaft
75. Axle Housing
76. Bracket
77. Wheel Stud
78. Hex Bolt
79. Deflector
80. Oil Seal
81. Inner Bearing
82. Brake Disc
83. Retaining Ring
84. Outer Bearing
85. Spacer
86. Hub
87. Thrust Washer
88. Adjusting Nut
89. Lock Washer
90. Nut

84907363

Exploded view of the axle and hub assembly—full-floating axle, 12 in.

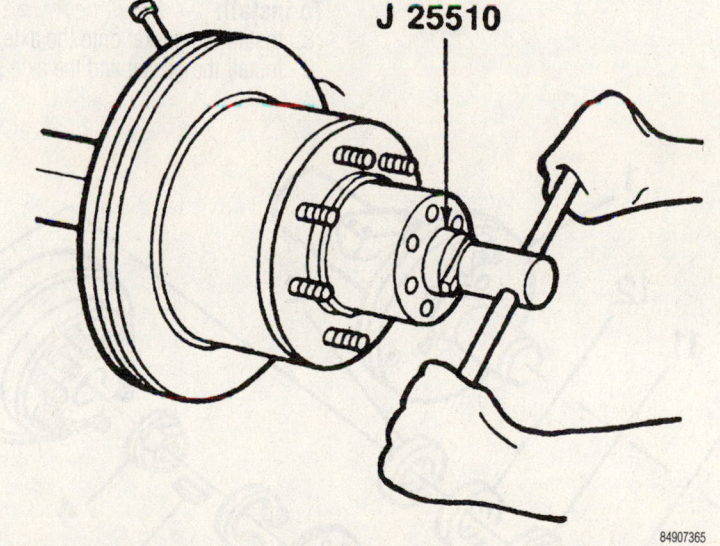

J 25510

84907365

Removing the wheel bearing nut—full-floating axle, 12 in.

ring gear and 13 ft. lbs. (17 Nm) on models with the 10 ½ inch ring gear.

23. Install the tanged retainer against the inner adjusting nut. Align the adjusting nut so that the short tang of the retainer will engage the nearest slot on the adjusting nut.

24. Install the outer locknut and tighten to 65 ft. lbs. (88 Nm). Bend the long tang of the retainer into the slot of the outer nut. This method of adjustment should provide 0.001–0.010 in. (0.0254–0.254mm) end-play.

25. Place a new gasket over the axle shaft and position the axle shaft in the housing so that the shaft splines enter the differential side gear. Position the gasket so that the holes are in alignment, and install the flange-to-hub attaching bolts. Tighten to 115 ft. lbs. (156 Nm) on models with the 10 ½ inch ring gear and tighten the axle cap bolts on models with the 11 inch ring gear to 15 ft. lbs. (20 Nm).

➡To prevent lubricant from leaking through the flange holes, apply a non-hardening sealer to the bolt threads. Use the sealer sparingly.

26. Replace the wheels.

Silverado and 2000–01 Sierra 15 Series

8.5 INCH AND 9.5 INCH REAR AXLE

1. Raise and support the vehicle on a hoist.
2. Remove the tire and wheel assembly.
3. Remove the brake caliper.
4. Remove the rear cover and the gasket.
5. Remove the pinion shaft locking screw.
6. On axles without a locking differential, remove the pinion shaft.
7. On axles with a locking differential, remove the shaft part way. Rotate the case until the pinion shaft touches the housing.
8. On axles with a locking differential, use a screwdriver, or a similar tool, in order to enter the differential case and rotate the lock until the lock aligns with the thrust block.
9. Push the flange of the axle shaft toward the differential. Remove the lock from the button end of the axle shaft.

➡When removing the axle shaft, do not rotate the shaft. Rotating the shaft will misalign the gears. Misaligning the gears will make the assembly difficult.

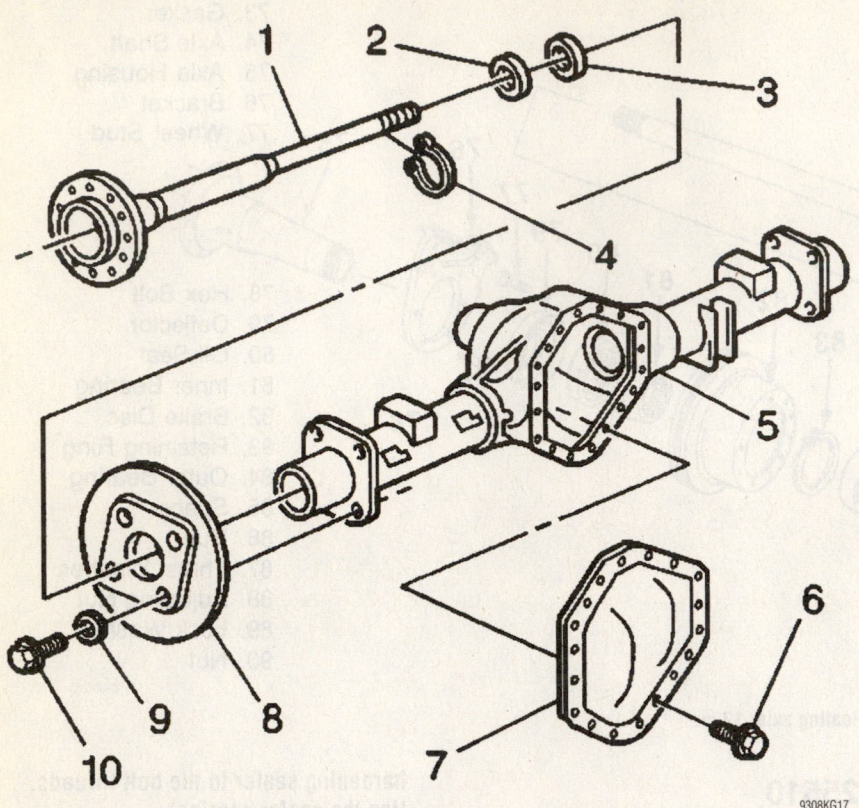

Rear axle shaft removal—8.5/9.5 inch 15 Series Silverado

10. Remove the axle shaft from the housing.

11. Inspect all the parts for damage. Replace the parts as necessary.

To install:

→ **Carefully insert the axle shaft in order to not damage the seal.**

12. Install the axle shaft into the housing. Slide the axle shaft into place allowing the splines to engage the differential side gear.

13. On axles without a locking differential, place the lock on the button end of the axle shaft.

14. On axles with a locking differential, keep the pinion shaft partially withdrawn.

15. On axles with a locking differential, place the lock on the axle shaft so that the ends are flush with the thrust block. Pull the shaft flange outward in order to seat the lock in the differential gear.

→ **Anytime you remove a differential pinion shaft locking screw, coat the screw threads with LOCTITE 242 before reinstalling the screws. The screw has an adhesive coating in order to prevent the screw from loosening in the case. Removing the screw removes the adhesive on the screw.**

16. Align the hole in the pinion shaft with the screw hole in the differential case.

17. Install the pinion flange locking screw. Tighten the pinion flange locking screw to 34 Nm (25 ft. lbs.).

18. Install the rear cover and the gasket.

19. Install the brake caliper.

20. Install the tire and wheel assembly.

21. Fill the rear axle.

22. Remove the supports and lower the vehicle.

10.5 INCH REAR AXLE

1. Remove the tire and wheel.

2. Remove the brake caliper.

3. Remove the brake rotor.

4. Remove the flange bolts.

5. Lightly rap the axle shaft with a soft-faced hammer in order to loosen the shaft. Grip the rib on the axle shaft flange with a locking pliers. Twist the axle shaft flange in order to start the axle shaft removal. Remove the axle shaft from the tube.

6. Remove the gasket.

7. Clean the axle shaft flange and the outside face of the hub assembly. Inspect all the parts. Replace the parts as necessary.

To install:

8. Install the gasket onto the axle shaft.

9. Install the gasket and the axle shaft

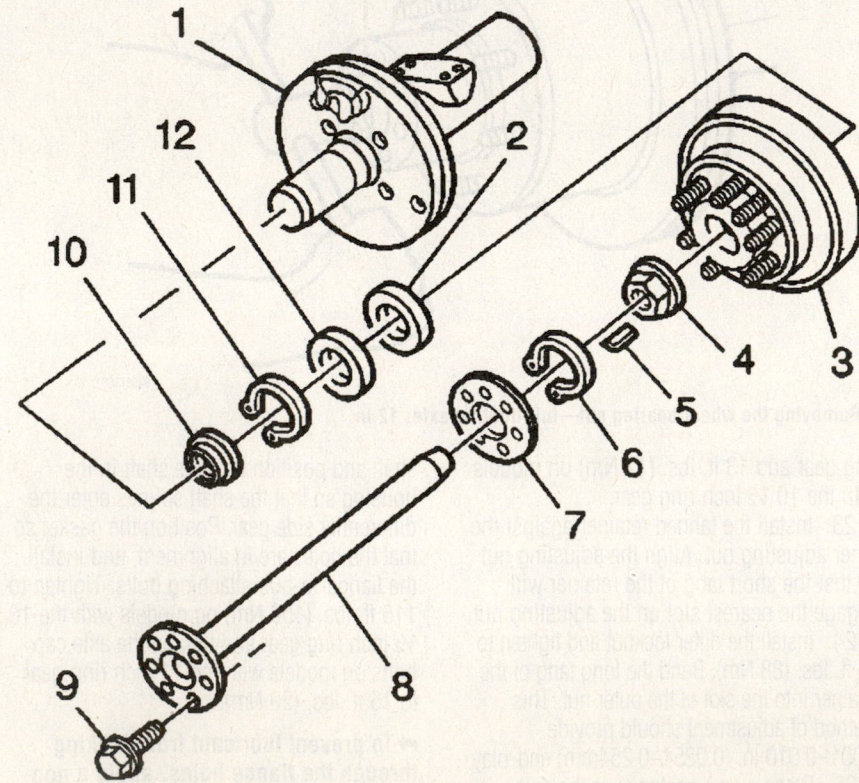

Rear axle shaft removal—10.5 inch 25 Series Silverado

into the tube. Ensure the shaft splines mesh into the differential side gear. Align the holes in the axle flange and the gasket with the holes in the hub.

10. Install the axle flange bolts. Tighten the bolts to 150 Nm (110 ft. lbs.).
11. Install the brake rotor.
12. Install the brake caliper.
13. Install the wheel and tire.

Front Drive Axle Pinion Seal

REMOVAL & INSTALLATION

Except Silverado and 2000–01 Sierra 15 Series

1. Raise and support the front end on jackstands.
2. Matchmark and disconnect the front driveshaft at the carrier.
3. Remove the wheels.
4. Dismount the calipers and wire them up, out of the way.
5. Position an inch pound torque wrench on the pinion nut. Measure the torque needed to rotate the pinion one full revolution. Record the figure.
6. Matchmark the pinion flange, shaft and nut. Count and record the number of exposed threads on the pinion shaft.
7. Hold the flange and remove the nut and washer.
8. Using a puller, remove the flange.
9. Carefully pry the seal from its bore. Be careful to avoid scratching the seal bore.
10. Remove the deflector from the flange.

   To install:
11. Clean the seal bore thoroughly.
12. Remove any burrs from the deflector staking on the flange.
13. Tap the deflector onto the flange and stake it in three places.
14. Position the new seal in the carrier bore and drive it into place until flush. Coat the seal lips with wheel bearing grease.
15. Coat the outer edge of the flange neck with wheel bearing grease and slide it onto the pinion shaft.
16. Place a new nut and washer onto the pinion shaft and tighten it to the position originally recorded. That is, the alignment marks are aligned, and the recorded number of threads are exposed on the pinion shaft.

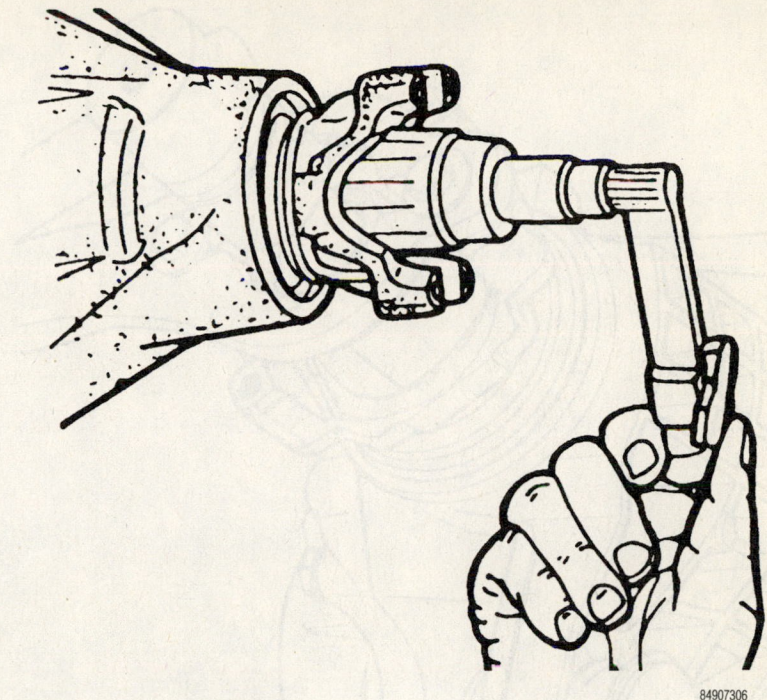

84907306

Measuring the pinion rotating torque

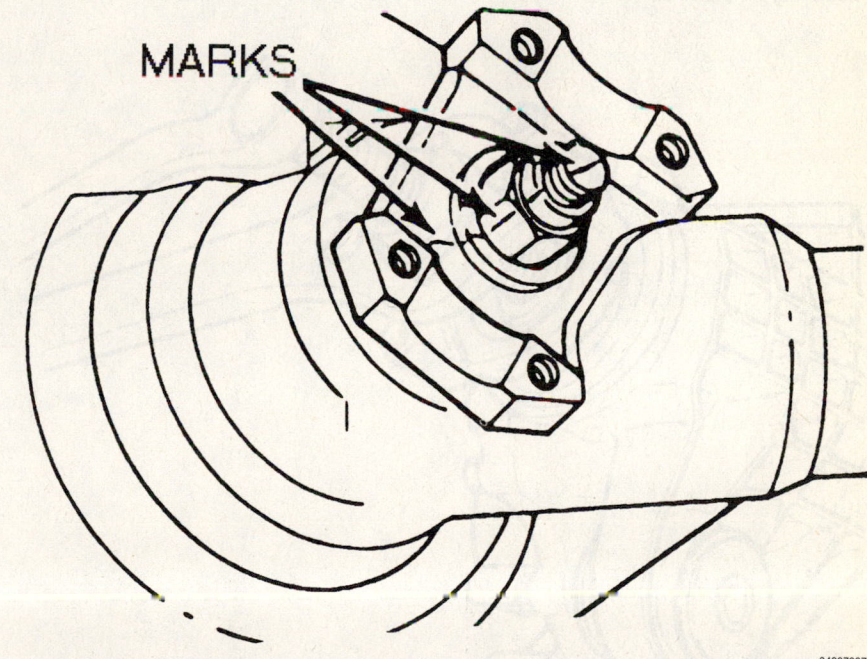

MARKS

84907307

Scribed marks

✴✴ WARNING

Never hammer the flange onto the pinion!

17. Measure the rotating torque of the pinion. Compare this to the original torque. Tighten the pinion nut, in small increments, until the rotating torque is 3 inch lbs. (0.35 Nm) GREATER than the original torque.
18. Install the driveshaft.
19. Install the calipers and install the wheels.

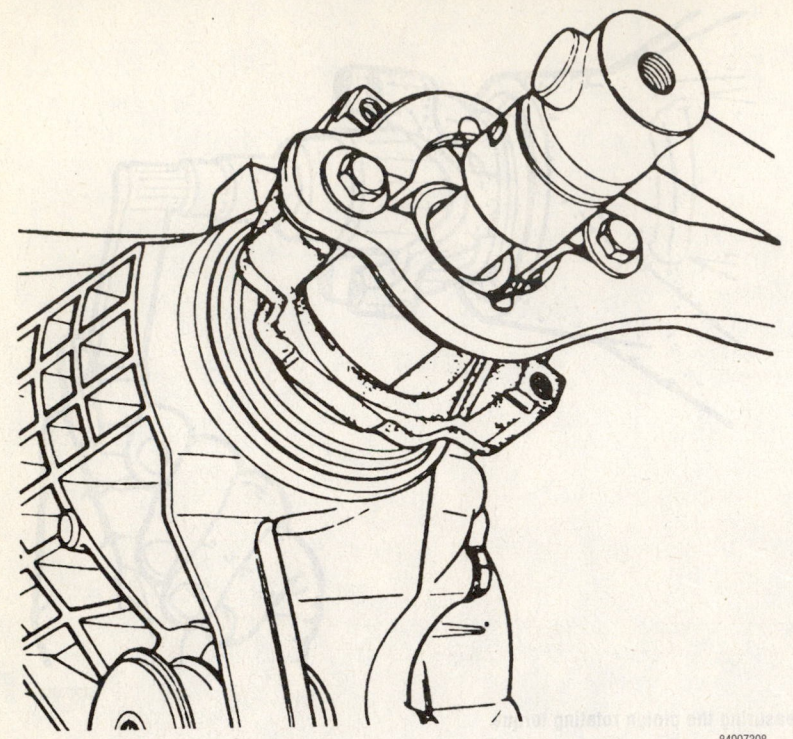

Removing the pinion nut

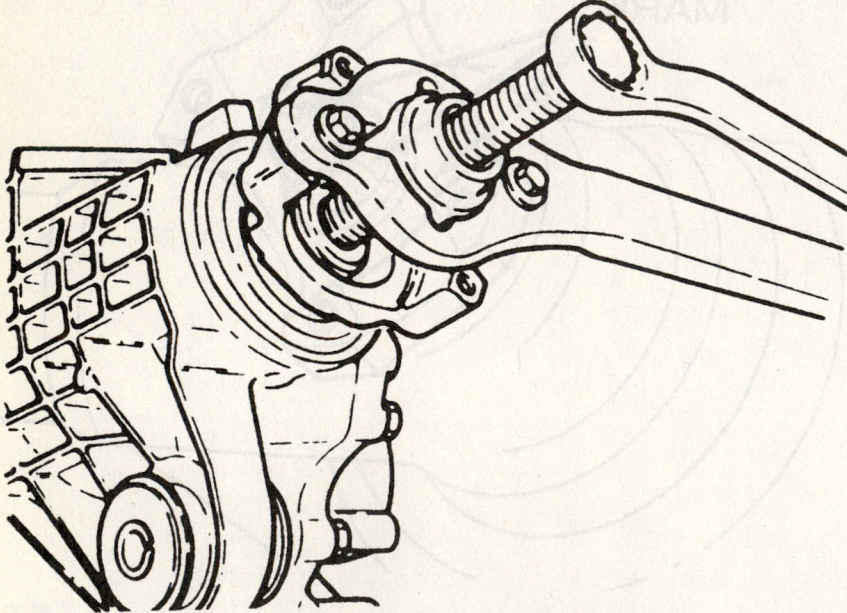

Removing the pinion flange

Silverado and 2000–01 Sierra 15 Series

1. Raise the vehicle on a hoist.
2. Remove the propeller shaft from the axle.
3. Tie the propeller shaft to a frame rail or the crossmember.
4. Measure the torque required in order to rotate the pinion. Record the torque value for reassembly.
5. Scribe a line on the pinion stem, the pinion nut and the companion flange. Record the number of exposed threads on the pinion stem.
6. Remove the nut.
7. Position tool J8614-01 on the flange so that the 4 notches on the tool face the flange.

8. Remove the flange. Use the special nut and the forcing screw.

➡**Carefully pry the seal from the bore. Do not distort or scratch the aluminum case.**

9. Remove the oil seal.
10. Inspect the pinion flange for a smooth oil seal surface. Inspect the pinion flange for worn drive splines. Replace the pinion flange if necessary.
11. Remove the dust deflector.

To install:

➡**Stake the new deflector at 3 new equally spaced positions. You must stake the new deflector in such a way that you do not damage the seal operating surface.**

12. Install and stake the dust deflector on the flange.
13. Position the oil seal in the bore. Then place the a driver over the oil seal. Strike the driver with a hammer until the seal flange seats on the axle housing surface. Drive the seal in straight, not at an angle, as this will damage the aluminum housing.

➡**Do not hammer the pinion flange/yoke onto the pinion shaft. Pinion components may be damaged if the pinion flange/yoke is hammered onto the pinion shaft.**

14. Install the flange onto the pinion using tool J8614-01. Place the washer and a new nut on the pinion threads. Tighten the nut to the original scribed position using the scribe marks and the exposed threads as reference.
15. Measure the rotating torque of the pinion. Compare the measurement with the rotating torque recorded earlier. Tighten the pinion nut by small increments until the torque required in order to rotate the pinion is 0.35 Nm (3 inch lbs.) greater than the original torque.
16. Install the propeller shaft.
17. Lower the vehicle.

Rear Drive Axle Pinion Seal

REMOVAL & INSTALLATION

Except Silverado and 2000–01 Sierra 15 Series

SEMI-FLOATING AXLES

1. Before servicing the vehicle, refer to the precautions in the beginning of this section.

2. Raise and support the truck on jackstands. It would help to have the front end slightly higher than the rear to avoid fluid loss.

3. Matchmark and remove the driveshaft.

4. Release the parking brake.

5. Remove the rear wheels. Rotate the rear wheels by hand to make sure that there is absolutely no brake drag. If there is brake drag, remove the drums.

6. Using a torque wrench on the pinion nut, record the force needed to rotate the pinion.

7. Matchmark the pinion shaft, nut and flange. Count the number of exposed threads on the pinion shaft.

8. Install a holding tool on the pinion. A very large adjustable wrench will do, or, if one is not available, put the drums back on and set the parking brake as tightly as possible.

9. Remove the pinion nut.

10. Slide the flange off of the pinion. A puller may be necessary.

11. Centerpunch the oil seal to distort it and pry it out of the bore. Be careful to avoid scratching the bore.

To install:

12. Pack the cavity between the lips of the seal with lithium-based chassis lube.

13. Position the seal in the bore and carefully drive it into place. A seal installer is VERY helpful in doing this.

14. Pack the cavity between the end of the pinion splines and the pinion flange with Permatex No.2® sealer, or equivalent non-hardening sealer.

15. Place the flange on the pinion and push it on as far as it will go.

16. Install the pinion washer and nut on the shaft and force the pinion into place by turning the nut.

✳✳ WARNING

Never hammer the flange into place!

17. Tighten the nut until the exact number of threads previously noted appear and the matchmarks align.

18. Measure the rotating torque of the pinion under the same circumstances as before. Compare the two readings. As necessary, tighten the pinion nut in VERY small increments until the torque necessary to rotate the pinion is 3 inch lbs. (0.35 Nm) higher than the originally recorded torque.

19. Install the driveshaft.

FULL-FLOATING AXLES

1. Raise and support the truck on jackstands. It would help to have the front end slightly higher than the rear to avoid fluid loss.

2. Matchmark and remove the driveshaft.

3. Matchmark the pinion shaft, nut and flange. Count the number of exposed threads on the pinion shaft.

4. Install a holding tool on the pinion. A very large adjustable wrench will do, or, if one is not available, set the parking brake as tightly as possible.

5. Remove the pinion nut.

6. Slide the flange off of the pinion. A puller may be necessary.

7. Centerpunch the oil seal to distort it and pry it out of the bore. Be careful to avoid scratching the bore.

To install:

8. Pack the cavity between the lips of the seal with lithium-based chassis lube.

9. Position the seal in the bore and carefully drive it into place. A seal installer is VERY helpful in doing this.

10. Place the flange on the pinion and push it on as far as it will go.

✳✳ WARNING

Never hammer the flange into place!

11. Install the pinion washer and nut on the shaft and force the pinion into place by turning the nut.

12. On models with the 11 inch ring gear, tighten the nut to 440–500 ft. lbs. (596–678 Nm)

13. On models with the 10 ½ inch ring gear Tighten the nut until the exact number of threads previously noted appear and the matchmarks align.

14. Install the driveshaft.

Silverado and 2000–01 Sierra 15 Series

1. Raise the vehicle on a hoist

➡Observe and accurately mark the positions of all driveline components relative to the propeller shaft and axles prior to disassembly. These components include the propeller shaft, drive axles, pinion flanges, output shafts, etc. Reassemble all components in the exact relationship the components had to each other during removal. Follow the specifications and the torque values. Follow any measurements made prior to removal.

2. Accurately mark the installed position of the rear propeller shaft. Remove the rear propeller shaft.

3. Measure the torque required to turn the pinion. Record the torque number measurement which gives the combined pinion bearing, seal, carrier bearing, axle bearing and seal preload.

4. Make and accurate alignment mark on the pinion flange. Record the number of exposed threads on the pinion stem.

5. Remove the pinion flange nut and the washer. Use a container in order to catch any lubricant.

➡Use care not to damage any of the machined surfaces.

6. Remove the pinion flange.

➡The pinion flange has an oil seal that is part of the pinion flange assembly. The pinion flange must be inspected to ensure that the seal is not damaged.

7. Pry the oil seal from the bore.

8. Thoroughly clean any foreign material from the contact area. Replace any parts as necessary.

To install:

9. Lubricate the cavity between the lips of the oil seal with wheel bearing lubricant.

10. Install the oil seal into the bore using a driver.

➡Do not hammer the pinion flange onto the pinion stem.

11. Install the pinion flange. Use the alignment marks in the installation of the pinion flange.

12. Install the washer and a new nut. Tighten the nut on the pinion stem as close as possible to the alignment marks without going past the marks. Use the alignment marks and the thread count as a reference. Tighten the nut a little at a time. Turn the pinion flange several times after each tightening in order to seat the rollers.

➡If the recorded preload torque value was less than 4 Nm (36 inch lbs.), reset the torque specification to 3-5 Nm (4-7 ft. lbs.).

13. Measure the torque required to rotate the pinion flange. Compare the measured torque with the recorded value. Continue tightening the pinion nut and measuring the torque until you achieve the recorded value.

14. Align the propeller shaft with the alignment marks. Connect the propeller shaft.

Turn to Section 5 for brake system applications

15. Install the retainers and the bolts. Tighten the bolts to 20 Nm (15 ft. lbs.).

16. Fill the rear axle.

17. Lower the vehicle.

Front Drive Axle Differential Carrier

REMOVAL & INSTALLATION

Except Silverado and 2000–01 Sierra 15 Series

1. Remove or disconnect the following:
   • Wheels
   • Skid plate
   • Fluid

2. Matchmark and remove the front driveshaft.

3. Remove or disconnect the following:
   • Right axle shaft at the tube flange
   • Left axle shaft at the carrier flange

➡ **Wire both axle shafts out of the way.**

   • Connectors at the indicator switch and actuator
   • Carrier vent hose
   • Axle tube-to-frame bolts, washers and nuts
   • Lower carrier mounting bolt
   • Right side inner tie rod end at the relay rod

➡ **Depending on the model, it may be necessary to remove the engine oil filter.**

4. Support the carrier on a floor jack

5. Remove or disconnect the following:
   • Upper carrier mounting bolt

6. Lower the carrier assembly from the truck.

To install:

7. Raise the carrier into position.

8. Install or connect the following:
   • Upper carrier mounting bolt, washers and nut. Then, install the lower carrier mounting bolt, washers and nut. Tighten the bolts to 80 ft. lbs. (110 Nm).
   • Oil filter
   • Tie rod end. Tighten the nut to 35 ft. lbs. (47 Nm).
   • Axle tube-to-frame bolts, washers and nuts. Tighten the nuts to 75 ft. lbs. (100 Nm) for 15 and 25 series; 107 ft. lbs. (145 Nm) for 35 series.
   • Vent hose
   • Wiring
   • Axle shafts at the flanges. Tighten the bolts to 59 ft. lbs. (80 Nm).
   • Driveshaft. Tighten the bolts to 15 ft. lbs. (20 Nm).
   • Gear oil
   • Wheels

9. Add any engine oil lost when the filter was removed.

Silverado and 2000–01 Sierra 15 Series

1. Remove or disconnect the following:

2. Front axle fluid

3. Front propeller shaft

4. Left and the right drive axle wheel drive shaft

5. Axle tube nuts from the bracket

6. Wiring at the axle

7. Vent hose at the axle

8. Carrier assembly lower mounting bolt and the nut

9. Idler arm from the relay rod

10. Pitman arm from the relay rod

11. Attach a transmission jack to the carrier assembly.

12. Remove the upper carrier assembly mounting bolt and the nut.

13. Remove the carrier assembly from the vehicle.

To install:

14. Install or connect the following:

15. Carrier assembly in the vehicle

16. Carrier assembly upper mounting bolt and the nut

17. Lower carrier assembly mounting bolt and the nut. Tighten the bolts to 100 Nm (75 ft. lbs.).

18. Pitman arm to the relay rod

19. Idler arm to the relay rod

20. Axle tube nuts to the bracket. Tighten the bolts to 100 Nm (75 ft. lbs.).

21. Vent hose

22. Wiring to the axle

23. Left and the right drive axle wheel drive shaft

24. Front propeller shaft to the pinion flange

25. Fill the front differential with lubricant.

Rear Drive Axle Housing

REMOVAL & INSTALLATION

Except Silverado and 2000–01 Sierra 15 Series

1. Before servicing the vehicle, refer to the precautions in the beginning of this section.

2. Drain the lubricant from the axle housing

3. Remove or disconnect the following:
   • Driveshaft
   • Wheel, the brake drum or hub and the drum assembly
   • Parking brake cable from the lever and at the brake flange plate
   • Hydraulic brake lines from the connectors
   • Shock absorbers from the axle brackets

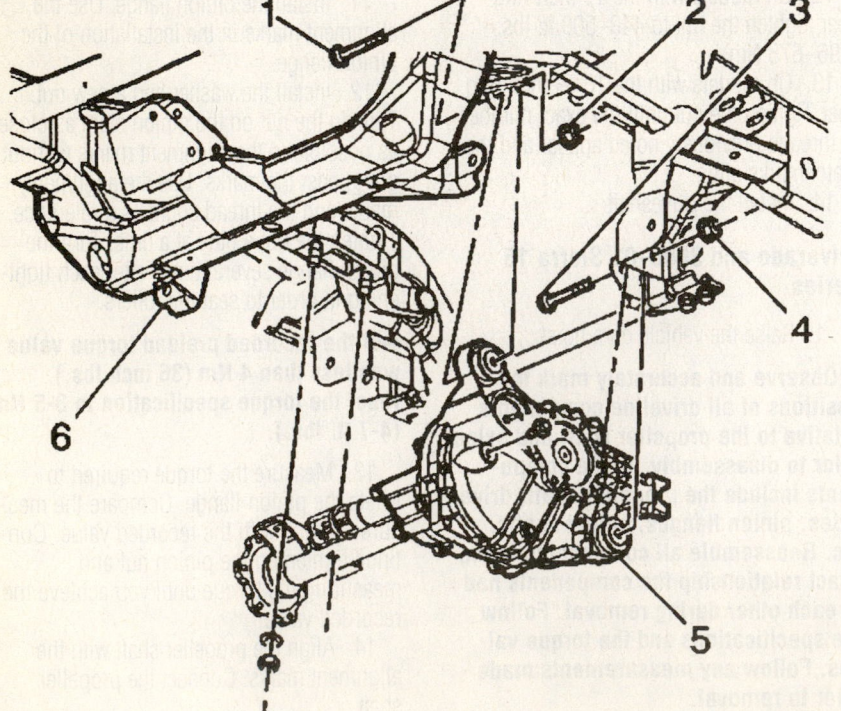

Front differential carrier removal—15 Series Silverado

9308KG18

- Vent hose from the axle vent fitting, if equipped
- Height sensing and brake proportional valve linkage, if equipped
- Stabilizer shaft, if equipped
4. Support the axle assembly with a jack.
   - U-bolts
   - Spring plates and spacers
   - Axle assembly

To install:
5. Raise the axle assembly into position.
6. Install or connect the following:
   - U-bolts
   - Spring plates and spacers
   - Nuts and washers on the U-bolts. Torque the nuts to 81 ft. lbs. (110 Nm).
   - Stabilizer shaft, if equipped
   - Height sensing and brake proportional valve linkage, if equipped
   - Vent hose at the axle vent fitting, if equipped
   - Shock absorbers at the axle brackets
   - Hydraulic brake lines
   - Parking brake cable
   - Wheels
   - Driveshaft
7. Fill the axle housing.

Silverado and 2000–01 Sierra 15 Series

1. Remove or disconnect the following:
   - Axle lubricant
   - Propeller shaft
   - Wheel assemblies
   - Parking brake cable
   - Brake calipers
   - Shock absorbers from the axle brackets
   - Vent hose from the rear axle vent fitting
   - Nuts and the washers from the U-bolts.
   - U-bolts, the spring plates and the spacers form the axle assembly.
2. Lower the axle assembly.

To install:
3. Place the rear axle assembly under the vehicle. Align the rear axle assembly with the springs. Connect the spacers, the spring plates and the U-bolts to the rear axle. Raise the rear axle assembly into position.
4. Install or connect the following:
   - Washers and nuts to the U-bolts. Tighten the nuts to 80 Nm (59 ft. lbs.). first, then to 120 Nm (89 ft. lbs.).
   - Vent hose to the rear axle vent fitting

- Shock absorbers to the rear axle
- Brake calipers
- Parking brake cable
- Wheel assemblies
- Propeller shaft
5. Fill the rear axle.
6. Bleed the brake system.
7. Remove the supports and lower the vehicle.

STEERING AND SUSPENSION

Air Bag

✳ CAUTION

Some vehicles are equipped with an air bag system. The system must be disabled before performing service on or around system components, steering column, instrument panel components, wiring and sensors. Failure to follow safety and disabling procedures could result in accidental air bag deployment, possible personal injury and unnecessary system repairs.

PRECAUTIONS

Several precautions must be observed when handling the inflator module to avoid accidental deployment and possible personal injury.
- Never carry the inflator module by the wires or connector on the underside of the module
- When carrying a live inflator module, hold securely with both hands, and ensure that the bag and trim cover are pointed away
- Place the inflator module on a bench or other surface with the bag and trim cover facing up
- With the inflator module on the bench, never place anything on or close to the module that may be thrown in the event of an accidental deployment

DISARMING

1. Turn the front wheels to the straight-ahead position.
2. Turn the ignition switch to the **LOCK** position and remove the key.

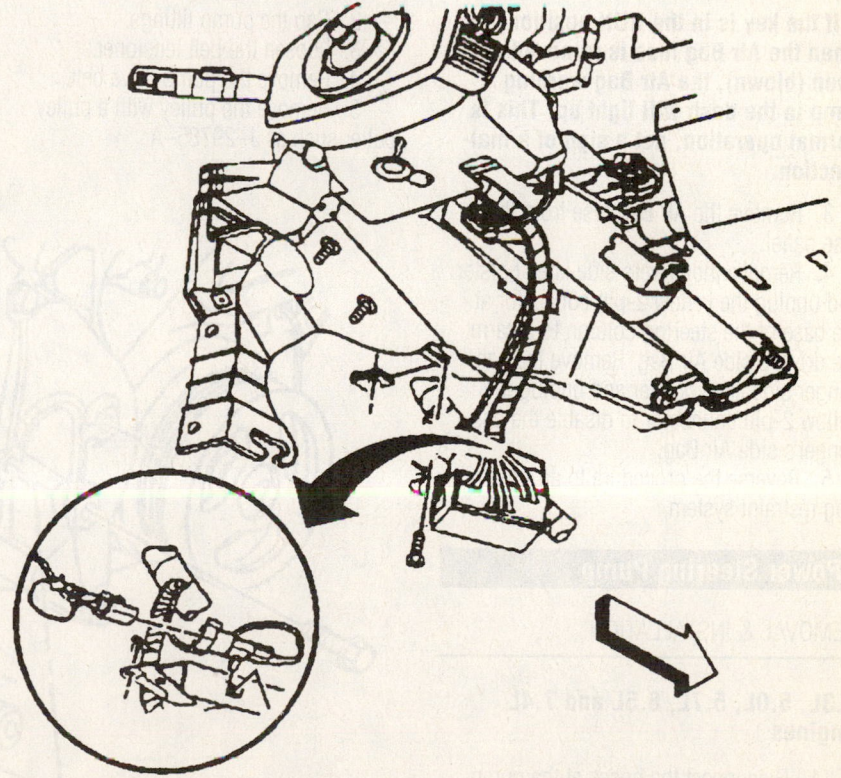

Typical air bag connector location—driver's side

7924KG30

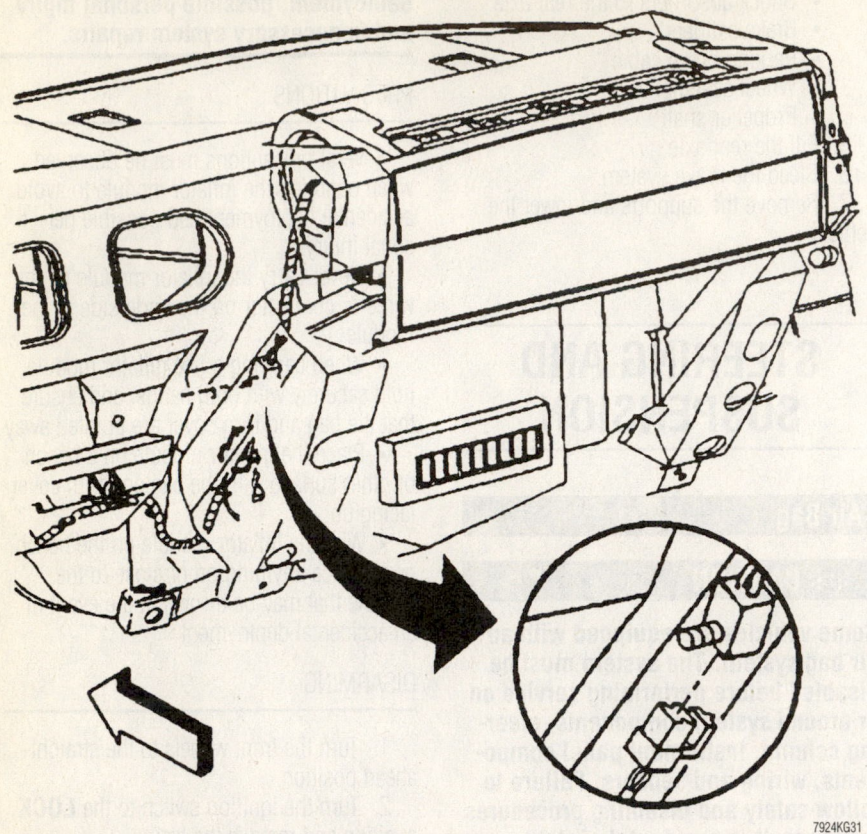

Typical air bag connector location—passenger's side

➡ **If the key is in the RUN position when the Air Bag fuse is removed or open (blown), the Air Bag warning lamp in the dash will light up. This is normal operation, not a sign of a malfunction.**

3. Remove the Air Bag fuse from the fuse panel.

4. Remove the drivers side knee bolster and unplug the yellow 2-pin connector at the base of the steering column to disarm the driver's side Air Bag. Remove the passenger side knee bolster and unplug the yellow 2-pin connector to disable the passenger's side Air Bag.

5. Reverse the procedure to arm the Air Bag restraint system.

Power Steering Pump

REMOVAL & INSTALLATION

4.3L, 5.0L, 5.7L, 6.5L and 7.4L Engines

1. Disconnect the hoses at the pump. When the hoses are disconnected, secure the ends in a raised position to prevent leakage. Cap the ends of the hoses to prevent the entrance of dirt.

2. Cap the pump fittings.
3. Loosen the belt tensioner.
4. Remove the pump drive belt.
5. Remove the pulley with a pulley puller such as J–29785–A.

6. Remove the following fasteners:
   • 6–4.3L, 8–5.0L, 8–5.7L engines: front mounting bolts
   • 8–7.4L engine: rear brace
   • 8–6.5L diesel: front brace and rear mounting nuts
7. Lift out the pump.

To install:

8. Observe the following torques:
   • 6–4.3L, 8–5.0L, 8–5.7L engines, front mounting bolts: 37 ft. lbs. (50 Nm)
   • 8–7.4L engine, rear brace nut: 61 ft. lbs. (82 Nm); rear brace bolt: 24 ft. lbs. (32 Nm); mounting bolts: 37 ft. lbs. (50 Nm)
   • 8–6.5L diesel, front brace: 30 ft. lbs. (40 Nm); rear mounting nuts: 17 ft. lbs. (23 Nm).
9. Install the pulley with J–25033–B.
10. Install the drive belt.
11. Install the hoses.
12. Fill and bleed the system.

4.8L, 5.3L and 6.0L Engines

1. Remove the upper radiator fan shroud.
2. Remove the drive belt.
3. Remove the pulley.
4. Place a drain pan under the pump. Remove the hoses from the pump.
5. Remove the bolts from the rear of the pump.
6. Remove the bolts from the front of the pump. Remove the pump from the vehicle.

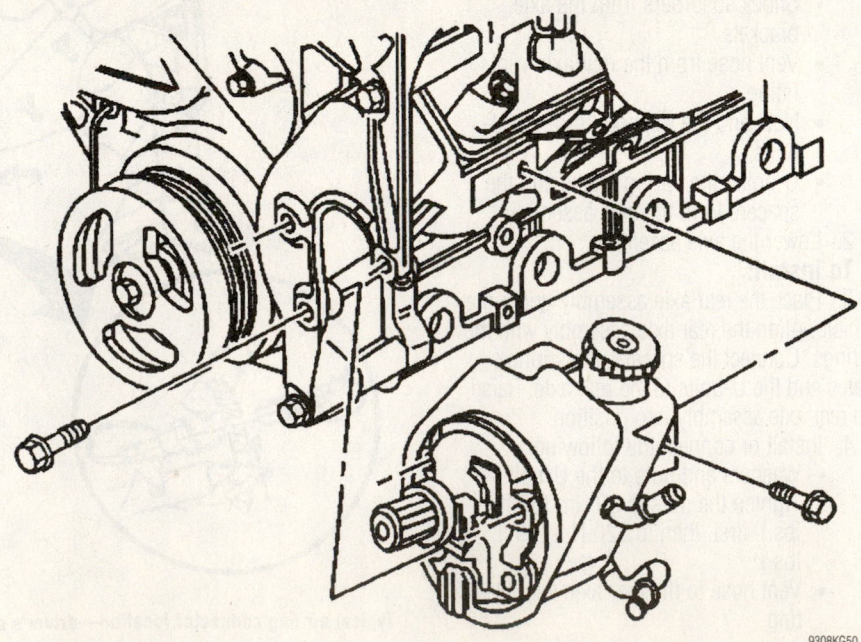

Power steering pump—4.8L, 5.3L, 6.0L

To install:

7. Install the pump.

8. Install the bolts to the front and the rear of the pump. Tighten the bolts to 50 Nm (37 ft. lbs.).

9. Install the hoses to the pump. Tighten the nut to 28 Nm (20 ft. lbs.).

10. Install the pulley. Install the pulley with 0.5 mm (0.020 in) play.

11. Install the drive belt.

12. Install the upper radiator shroud.

13. Fill and bleed the power steering system.

Recirculating Ball Power Steering Gear

REMOVAL & INSTALLATION

Except Silverado and 2000–01 Sierra 15 Series

These vehicles use a conventional power steering gear with a recirculating ball system. All tubes, hoses and fittings should be inspected for leakage at regular intervals. Fittings must be tight. Be sure the clips, clamps and supporting tubes and hoses are in place and properly secured. Inspect the hoses with the wheels in the straight-ahead position. Then, turn the wheels fully to the left and right while observing the movement of the hoses. Correct any hose contact with other parts of the vehicle that could cause chafing or wear. Power steering hoses and pipes should not be twisted, kinked or tightly bent. The hoses should have sufficient natural curvature in the routing to absorb movement and hose shortening during vehicle operation.

1. Before servicing the vehicle, refer to the precautions in the beginning of this section.

2. Set the front wheels in the straight-ahead position.

3. Place a drain pan under the steering gear and disconnect the fluid lines. Cap the openings to protect the system from contamination.

4. Remove or disconnect the following:

- Negative battery cable
- Adapter and shield from the gear and flexible coupling
- Flexible coupling clamp and steering box input shaft, matchmark for reassemble
- Flexible coupling pinch bolt
- Pitman arm to the Pitman shaft, matchmark for reassemble
- Pitman shaft nut and lockwasher
- Pitman arm from the shaft using the proper puller
- Steering gear to frame bolts
- Gear assembly

To install:

5. Install or connect the following:

- Steering gear in position, guiding the input shaft into the flexible coupling. Align the flat in the coupling with the flat on the input shaft.
- Steering gear-to-frame bolts. Torque the bolts to 100 ft. lbs. (135 Nm)
- Flexible coupling pinch bolt. Torque the pinch bolt to 22 ft. lbs. (30 Nm)

➡ **Check that the relationship of the flexible coupling to the flange is ¼–¾ in. (6–19mm) of flat.**

- Pitman arm onto the Pitman shaft, lining up the marks made at removal. Torque the nut to 215 ft. lbs. (285 Nm).
- Adapter and shield
- Fluid lines and refill the reservoir with the proper power steering fluid

6. Properly bleed the system and verify no leaks.

7. Road test the vehicle for proper steering system operation.

Silverado and 2000–01 Sierra 15 Series

1. Raise the vehicle.

2. Remove the shield.

3. Place a drain pan below the steering gear. Remove the hoses from the steering gear.

4. Disconnect the intermediate shaft from the steering gear.

5. Disconnect the Pitman arm from the relay rod.

6. Remove the steering gear frame bolts and the steering gear.

To install:

7. Place the steering gear in position.

8. Install the steering gear to the frame bolts. Tighten the bolts to 135 Nm (100 ft. lbs.).

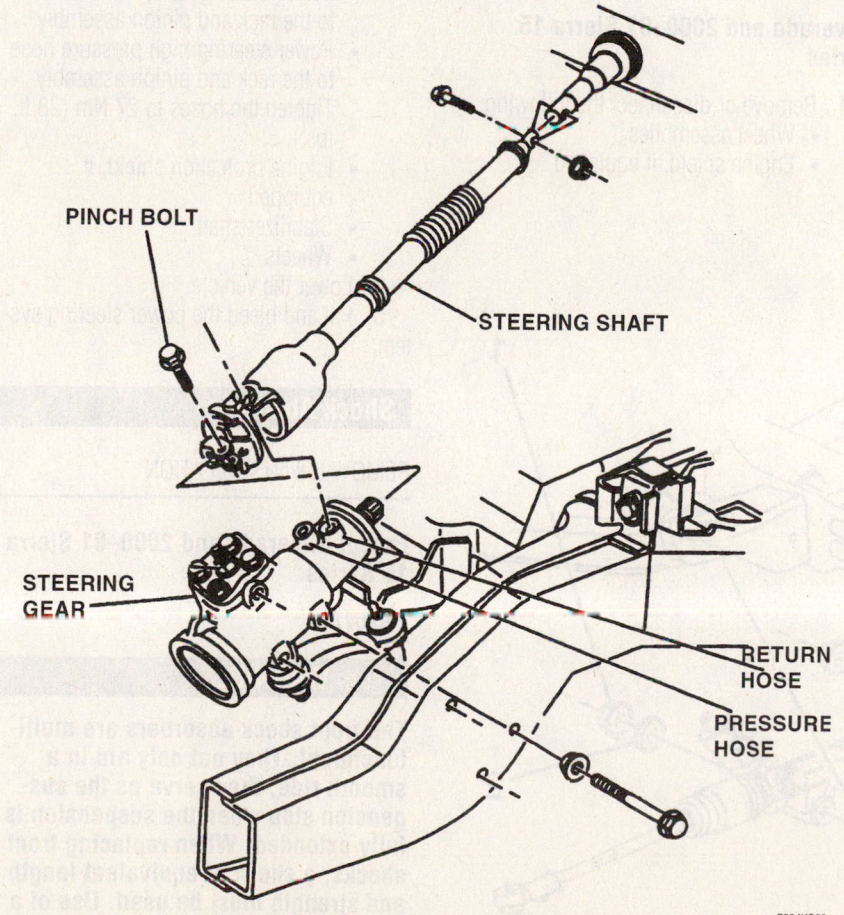

PINCH BOLT

STEERING SHAFT

STEERING GEAR

RETURN HOSE

PRESSURE HOSE

7924KG32

3 long bolts attach the power steering gear to the driver's side frame rail

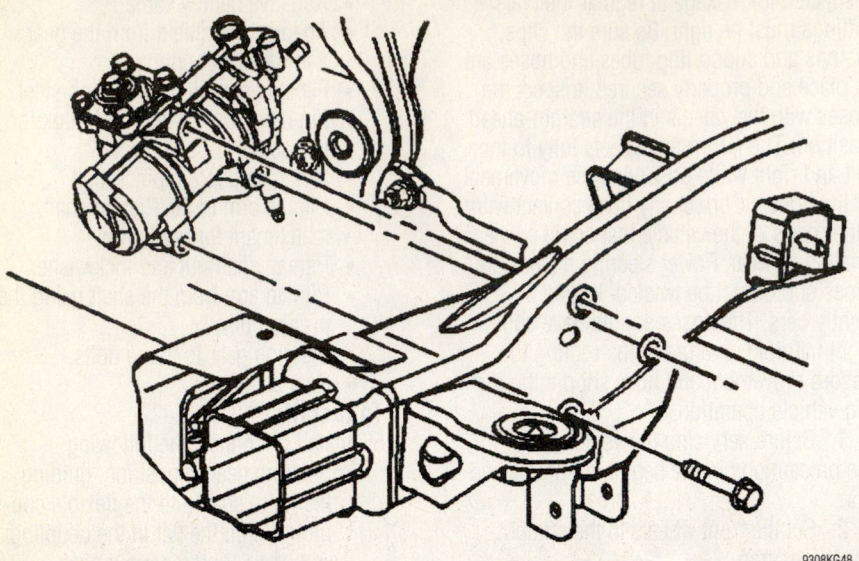

Recirculating ball gear—Silverado

9. Install the Pitman arm.
10. Install the intermediate shaft.
11. Remove the plugs and the caps from the steering gear and the hoses. Connect the hoses to the steering gear. Tighten the hose connection to 28 Nm (20 ft. lbs.).
12. Install the shield.
13. Fill and bleed the system.
14. Lower the vehicle.

Rack & Pinion Steering Gear

REMOVAL & INSTALLATION

Silverado and 2000–01 Sierra 15 Series

1. Remove or disconnect the following:
   • Wheel assemblies
   • Engine shield, if equipped
   • Stabilizer shaft
   • Power steering high pressure line from the rack and pinion assembly
   • Power steering low pressure line from the rack and pinion assembly
   • Coupler clamp bolt from the intermediate shaft
   • Intermediate shaft from the rack and pinion assembly
   • Rack and pinion assembly mounting nuts, the washers and the bolts
2. Remove the rack and pinion assembly from the vehicle.

   To install:
3. Install or connect the following:
   • Rack and pinion assembly into the vehicle
   • Rack and pinion assembly mounting bolts, the washers and the nuts. Tighten the nuts to 185 Nm (136 ft. lbs.).
   • Intermediate shaft to the rack and pinion assembly. Install the coupler clamp bolt to the intermediate shaft. Tighten the coupler clamp bolt to 45 Nm (33 ft. lbs.).
   • Power steering low pressure hose to the rack and pinion assembly.
   • Power steering high pressure hose to the rack and pinion assembly. Tighten the hoses to 27 Nm (28 ft. lbs.).
   • Engine protection shield, if equipped
   • Stabilizer shaft
   • Wheels
4. Lower the vehicle.
5. Fill and bleed the power steering system.

Shock Absorber

REMOVAL & INSTALLATION

Except Silverado and 2000–01 Sierra 15 Series

FRONT

❊❊ WARNING

The front shock absorbers are multifunctional. They not only aid in a smooth ride, they serve as the suspension stop when the suspension is fully extended. When replacing front shocks, a shock of equivalent length and strength must be used. Use of a shock that does not comply may result in suspension over travel and component failure.

Rack and pinion gear—Silverado

1. Support the front of the vehicle safely under the lower control arms.
2. Remove or disconnect the following:
   - Tire and wheel assembly
   - Upper and lower shock absorber retaining fastener(s)

➡ **Vehicles equipped with quad shocks have a spacer between them.**

   - Shock absorber

To install:
3. Install or connect the following:
   - Shock absorber
4. On 2-wheel drive vehicles. Torque the upper bolt to 12 ft. lbs. (16 Nm) and the lower bolts to 24 ft. lbs. (33 Nm)
5. On 4-wheel drive vehicles. Torque the nuts to 66 ft. lbs. (90 Nm) Be sure the bolts are inserted in the proper direction. The upper bolt head should be forward; the bottom bolt head should be rearward.

REAR

✳✳ WARNING

Original equipment shock absorbers serve additionally as suspension drop cutoffs. Replacement shock absorbers must have a built in suspension cutoff feature and must not be longer than original shocks when they are fully extended or serious vehicle or component damage could result.

1. The vehicle's weight should rest on correctly placed safety stands located under the frame. Chock the front wheels to prevent vehicle movement.
2. Support the rear axle with a floor jack.
3. If the vehicle is equipped with air lift type shocks, bleed the air from the lines and disconnect the line from the shock absorber.
4. Remove or disconnect the following:
   - Shock absorber at the top by removing the 2 mounting bolts/nuts from the frame bracket
   - Nut, washers and bolt from the bottom mount
   - Shock

To install:
5. Install or connect the following:
   - Shock
   - Upper mounting nuts/bolts. Torque the nuts/bolts to 20 ft lbs. (25 Nm).
   - Lower mounting bolt/nuts. Torque the nuts/bolts to 60 ft lbs. (80 Nm).
6. Check that no parts such as exhaust components bind on the shock absorbers.

Silverado and 2000–01 Sierra 15 Series

2WD FRONT

1. Raise and support the vehicle.
2. If equipped with selectable ride, disconnect the Real Time Damping (RTD) link rod from the sensor. Grasp the connector lock tabs. Rotate the connector tabs counter clockwise until the connector is unlocked. Disengage the connector from the tennon by firmly pulling the connector up. Hold the tennon end with a wrench while removing the nut. Remove the nut.
3. Remove the upper insulator. Do not discard the plastic pilot ring.
4. Remove the shock absorber mounting bolts at the lower control arm. Remove the shock absorber through the lower control arm from below.

To install:
5. Support the lower control arm with a suitable jack in order to align the tennon with the mounting hole if equipped with selectable ride.
6. Install the shock absorber through the lower control arm from below. Insert the tennon through the mounting hole in the upper spring pocket. Align the shock absorber with the mounting holes in the lower control arm.
7. Install the shock absorber mounting bolts to the lower control arm. Tighten the bolts to 25 Nm (18 ft. lbs.).

➡ **The upper insulators are substantially larger that the lower insulators. The upper insulator must be installed above the shock mounting bracket on the frame. The plastic pilot ring will assist the alignment of the isolators.**

8. Install the upper insulator to the shock absorber. Install the nut to the tennon end. Do not tighten the nut.
9. Connect the RTD link rod to the sensor (if equipped).
10. Remove the safety stands.
11. Lower the vehicle. Hold the tennon end with a wrench while torquing the nut. Tighten the nut to 20 Nm (15 ft. lbs.).
12. Connect the electrical connector using the following procedure:
   a. Verify that the connector is unlocked.
   b. Align the connector so that the tabs are perpendicular to the wrench flats on the tennon end.
   c. Engage the connector to the tennon by firmly pushing the connector down.

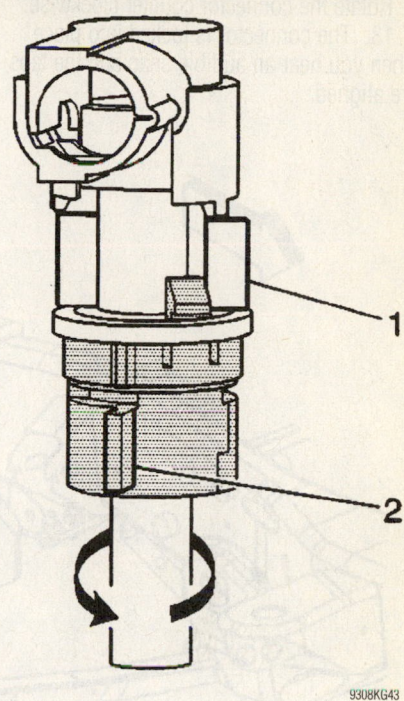

RTD connector—Silverado

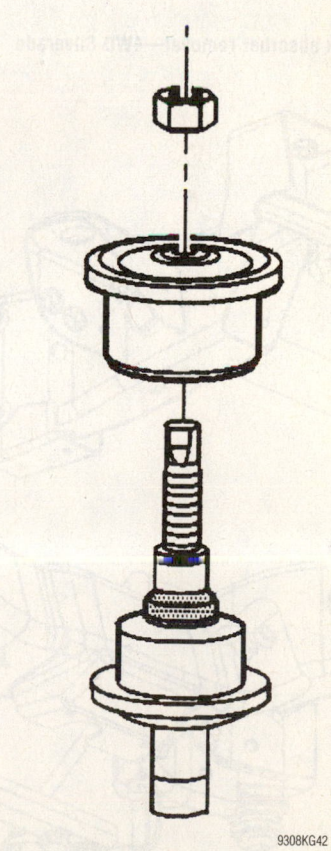

Upper shock insulator—Silverado

Turn to Section 5 for brake system applications

d. Grasp the connector lock tabs. Rotate the connector counter clockwise.

13. The connector is locked into place when you hear an audible snap and the tabs are aligned.

4WD FRONT

1. Raise and support the vehicle.
2. Disconnect the (RTD) link rod from the sensor (if equipped).
3. Disconnect the electrical connector if

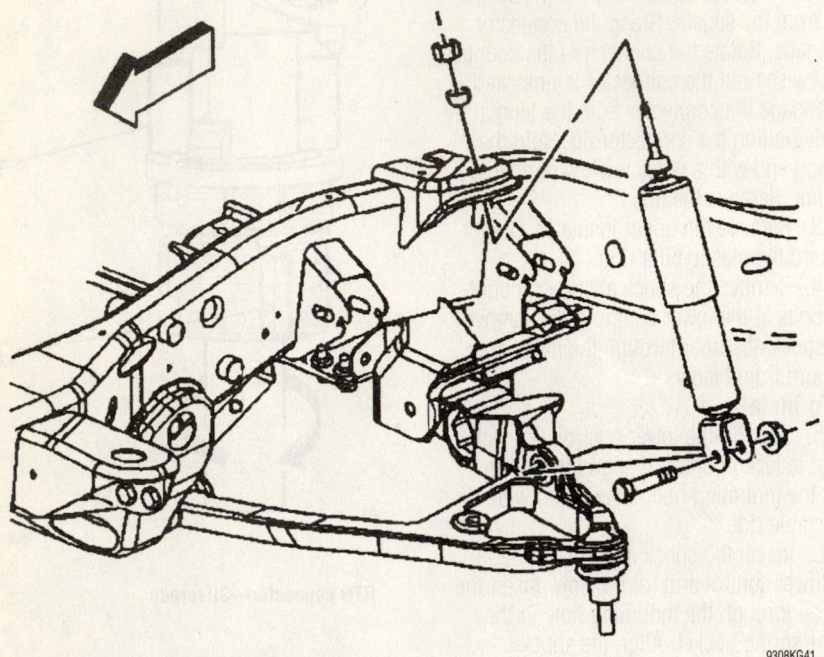

Shock absorber removal—4WD Silverado

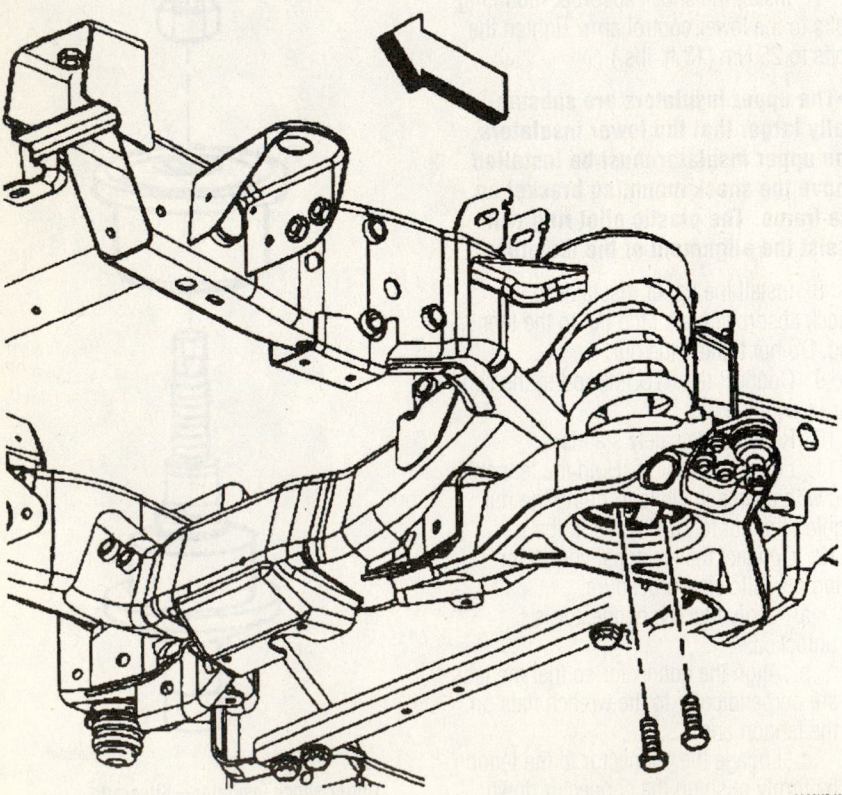

Shock absorber removal—2WD Silverado

equipped with selectable ride. Grasp the connector lock tabs. Rotate the connector tabs counter clockwise until the connector is unlocked. Disengage the connector from the tennon by firmly pulling the connector up. Hold the tennon end with a wrench while removing the nut. Remove the nut.

4. Remove the upper insulator. Do not discard the plastic pilot ring.

5. Remove the shock absorber mounting bolt at the lower control arm (15 Series). The lower shock mounting bushing is serviceable by driving the bushing out with the appropriate tool.

6. Remove the shock absorber mounting bolt at the lower control arm (25 Series).

7. Remove the shock absorber.

To install:

8. Install the shock absorber. Insert the stem through the hole in the shock bracket on the frame. Align the shock absorber with the mounting holes in the lower control arm (15 Series). Align the shock absorber with the mounting holes in the lower control arm (25 Series).

9. Install the shock absorber through bolt to the lower control arm.

10. Install the shock absorber through bolt nut. Tighten the nut to 80 Nm (59 ft. lbs.).

➡**The upper insulators are substantially larger that the lower insulators. The upper insulator must be installed above the shock mounting bracket on the frame. The plastic pilot ring will assist the alignment of the isolators.**

11. Install the upper insulator to the shock absorber. Install the nut to the tennon end. Do not tighten the nut. Connect the RTD link rod to the sensor (if equipped).

12. Remove the safety stands. Lower the vehicle. Hold the tennon end with a wrench while torquing the nut. Tighten the nut to 20 Nm (15 ft. lbs.).

13. Connect the electrical connector using the following procedure if equipped with selectable ride.

a. Verify that the connector is unlocked.

b. Align the connector so that the tabs (1) are perpendicular to the wrench flats on the tennon end.

c. Engage the connector to the tennon by firmly pushing the connector down.

d. Grasp the connector lock tabs (1, 2). Rotate the connector counter clockwise. The connector is locked into place when you hear an audible snap and the tabs are aligned.

REAR

1. Raise and support the vehicle.
2. Disconnect the electrical connector if equipped with Selectable Ride.
3. Remove the upper shock absorber nut and the bolt.
4. Remove the lower shock absorber nut and the bolt.
5. Remove the shock absorber.
6. Installation is the reverse of removal. Tighten the nuts to 95 Nm (70 ft. lbs.).
7. Connect the electrical connector if equipped with Selectable Ride. Remove the safety stands. Lower the vehicle.

Coil Springs

REMOVAL & INSTALLATION

Van Models

1. Before servicing the vehicle, refer to the precautions in the beginning of this section.
2. Support the vehicle safely under the frame rails. The control arms should hang freely.
3. Remove or disconnect the following:
   • Wheel
   • Shock absorber lower end mounting nut/bolt
   • Stabilizer bar from the lower control arm
4. Support the lower control arm and install a spring compressor on the spring or chain the spring to the control arm as a safety precaution.

➡If equipped with an air cylinder inside the spring, remove the valve core from the cylinder and expel the air by compressing the cylinder with a pry-bar. With the cylinder compressed, replace the valve core so the cylinder will stay in the compressed position. Push the cylinder as far as possible towards the top of the spring.

5. Raise the front end to remove the tension from the lower control arm the bolts securing the control arm.

➡The cross-shaft and lower control arm keeps the coil spring compressed. Use care when lowering the assembly.

6. Slowly lower the control arm until the spring can be removed. Be sure all compression is relieved from the spring.
7. If the coil spring was chained, remove the chain and spring. If a compressor was used, remove the spring and slowly release the compressor.
8. Remove the air cylinder, if equipped.

To install:

9. Install or connect the following:
   • Air cylinder so the protector plate is towards the upper control arm. The Schrader valve should protrude through the hole in the lower control arm.
   • Chain and spring or compress the spring and install the assembly
10. Slowly raise the control arm.
    • Bolts securing the control arm. Torque the nuts to 115 ft. lbs. (155 Nm).
    • Stabilizer bar to the lower control arm. Torque the nuts to 24 ft. lbs. (34 Nm).
    • Shock absorber at the lower end. Torque the nuts to 37 ft. lbs. (50 Nm).
    • Air cylinders, inflate the cylinder to 60 psi (414 kPa) if equipped
    • Wheel
11. Once the weight of the vehicle is on the wheels, reduce the air cylinder pressure to 50 psi.

SUVs and Pickups, Except Silverado and 2000–01 Sierra 15 Series

1. Before servicing the vehicle, refer to the precautions in the beginning of this section.
2. Allow the control arms to hang free.
3. Remove or disconnect the following:
   • Tire and wheel assembly
   • Shock absorber assembly
4. Install tool J-23028, or equivalent, under the lower control arm and a jack. Install a safety chain around the spring and through the lower control arm.
   • Stabilizer shaft from the lower control arm. Remove the tension on the lower control arm bolts.
   • Lower control arm rear bolt, than the other retaining bolt
   • Spring assembly

To install:

5. Install or connect the following:
   • Chain and spring. If you used spring compressors, install the spring and compressors.
6. Be sure the insulator is in place and the tape is towards the bottom of the spring. Position the gripper notch on the top coil in the frame bracket.

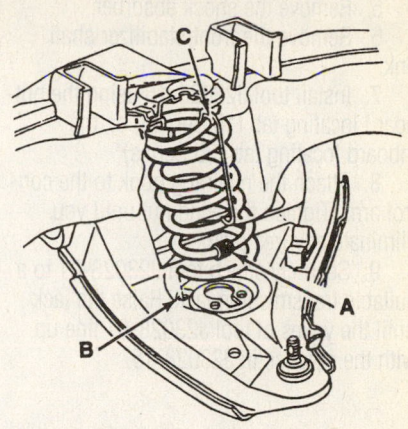

7924KG33

Position the coil spring so the bottom end of the spring covers only one drain hole—the other hole must remain open

7. Be sure one drain hole in the lower arm is covered by the bottom coil and the other is open.
8. Slowly raise the lower control arm. Guide the control arm into place with a pry-bar.
9. Install or connect the following:
   • Pivot shaft bolts, front one first. The bolts must be installed with the heads towards the front of the vehicle. Remove the safety chain or spring compressors.

➡Do not tighten the bolts yet. The bolts must be tightened with the vehicle at its proper ride height.

10. Remove the jack.
    • Stabilizer bar to the lower control arm. Torque the nuts to 24 ft lbs. (33 Nm).
    • Shock absorber
    • Wheel
11. Once the weight of the vehicle is on the wheels, bounce the vehicle 2 or 3 times by pushing down on the front bumper a couple of inches. When the vehicle settles, tighten the front nut first,, then the rear nut to 101 ft. lbs. (137 Nm).

Silverado and 2000–01 Sierra 15 Series

FRONT

1. Raise and support the vehicle.
2. Remove the engine protection shield.
3. Remove the frame cross bar (25 series only).
4. Remove the tire and wheel assembly.

5. Remove the shock absorber.

6. Remove the front stabilizer shaft link.

7. Install tool J23028-15 using the outboard locating tab (15 Series), or, the inboard locating tab (25 Series).

8. Attach the retaining hook to the control arm. Tighten the wing nut until you eliminate any free play.

9. Securely attach tool J23028-01 to a suitable transmission jack. Raise the jack until the yokes of tool J23028-01 line up with the notches in J23028-15.

10. Using the tools and the transmission jack, relieve the spring tension from the lower control arm pivot bolts.

11. Remove the lower control arm pivot bolt nuts (15 Series). Remove the rear pivot bolt. Remove the front pivot bolt.

12. Remove the lower control arm pivot bolt nuts (25 Series). Remove the rear pivot bolt. Remove the front pivot bolt.

13. Slowly lower the transmission jack in order to unload the front coil spring. It may be necessary to use a pry bar in order to guide the lower control arm out of position.

14. Remove the coil spring and the insulator.

To install:

15. Install the coil spring and the insulator to the lower control arm.

16. Raise the transmission jack in order to compress the front coil spring. It may be necessary to use a pry bar in order to guide the lower control arm into position.

17. Install the front pivot bolt (15 Series).

18. Install the rear pivot bolt.

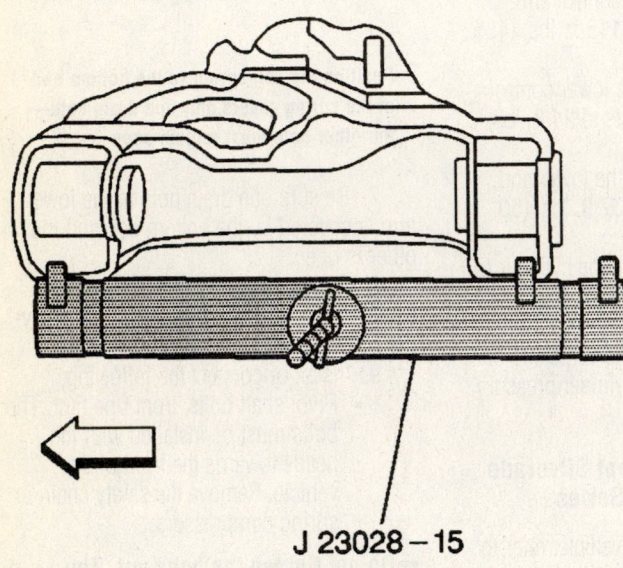

Installing J23028-15 on the 25 Series

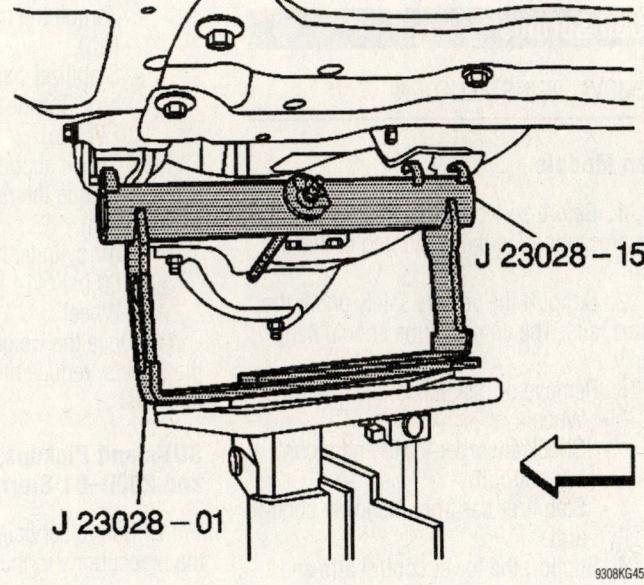

Tool attached to a jack

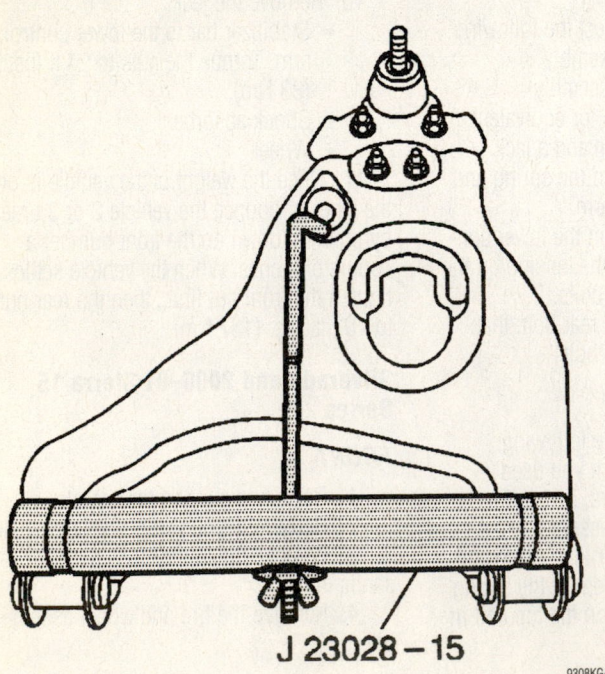

Retaining hook installation

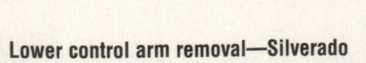

Lower control arm removal—Silverado

19. Install the lower control arm pivot nuts. Tighten the pivot bolt nuts to 145 Nm (107 ft. lbs.).

20. Install the front pivot bolt (25 Series). Install the rear pivot bolt. Install the lower control arm pivot nuts. Tighten the pivot bolt nuts to 145 Nm (107 ft. lbs.).

21. Lower the jack. Remove the tool from the control arm.

22. Install the front stabilizer shaft link.

23. Install the shock absorber.

24. Install the tire and wheel assembly.

25. Install the frame cross bar (25 series only). Tighten the nuts to 100 Nm (74 ft. lbs.).

26. Install the engine protection shield.

27. Remove the safety stands. Lower the vehicle.

REAR

1. Raise and support the vehicle.
2. Disconnect the Real Time Damping (RTD) sensor, if equipped.
3. Remove the lower shock absorber nuts and bolt from the rear axle.
4. Lower the rear axle until the springs are fully unloaded.

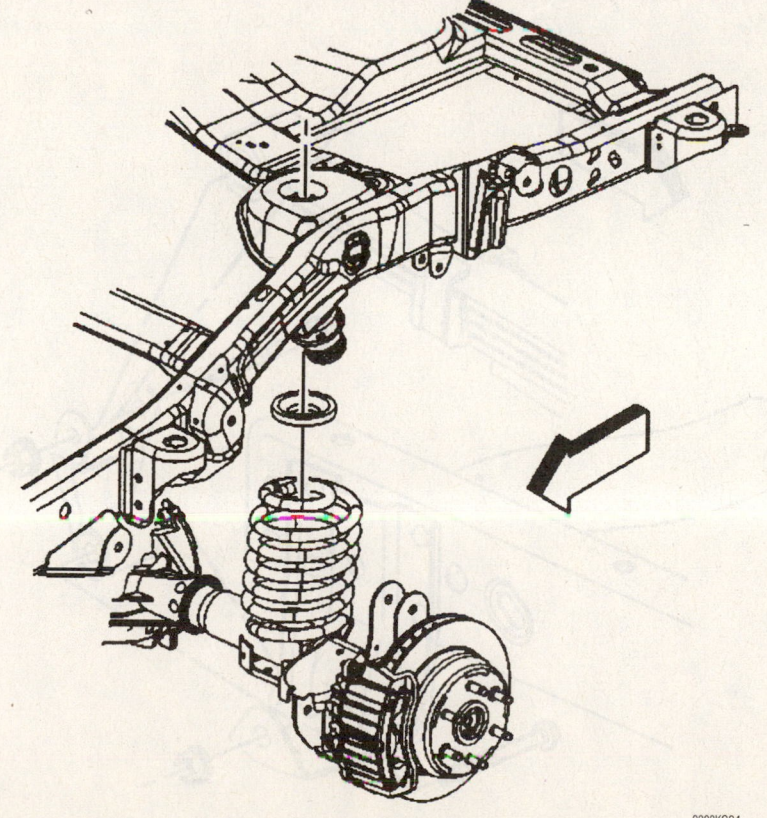

Rear coil spring removal—15 Series Silverado

9308KG24

5. Remove the spring and the upper and lower insulators.

To install:

6. Position the spring and the upper and lower insulators.

7. Install the rear spring to the rear axle.

8. Raise the rear axle. Install the lower shock absorber nuts to the rear axle.

9. Connect the RTD sensor, if equipped.

10. Remove the rear axle support. Lower the vehicle.

Leaf Springs

REMOVAL & INSTALLATION

Except Silverado and 2000–01 Sierra 15 Series

1. Before servicing the vehicle, refer to the precautions in the beginning of this section.

2. Raise the vehicle and support it so that there is no tension on the leaf spring assembly.

3. Remove or disconnect the following:
- U-bolt nuts, plates, and spacer(s)

- Anchor plate
- Spring-to-shackle retaining bolts. (Do not remove these bolts)
- Bolts which attach the shackle to the rear bracket
- Bolt which attaches the spring to the front bracket
- Spring from the vehicle

4. Inspect the spring and replace any damaged components.

To install:

➡ If the spring bushings are defective, use the following procedures for replacement. On bushings that are staked in place, the stakes must first be straightened. Using a press or vise, remove the bushing and install the new one. When a new, previously staked bushing is installed, stake it in 3 equally spaced locations.

5. Place the spring assembly onto the axle housing. Position the front and rear of the spring at the brackets. Raise the axle with a floor jack as necessary to make the alignments.

6. Install or connect the following:
- Front and rear brackets bolts loosely
- Spacers and spring plate
- New u-bolts, washers and nuts
- Anchor plate
- U-bolt nuts. Torque them in a diagonal sequence, to 17 ft. lbs. (23 Nm) When the spring is evenly seated, tighten the nuts to 81 ft. lbs. (110 Nm)
- Hanger and shackle bolts are properly installed. All bolt heads should be inboard. Don't tighten them yet.

7. Using the floor jack, raise the axle until the distance between the bottom of the rebound bumper and its contact point on the axle is 182mm plus or minus 6mm.

8. When the spring is properly positioned, tighten all the hanger and shackle nuts to 70 ft. lbs. (95 Nm)
- Leaf spring-to-shackle nuts 15/25/35 series: 70 ft. lbs. (95 Nm).
- Leaf spring-to-shackle nuts C3HD series: 157 ft. lbs. (213 Nm).
- Shackle-to-bracket nuts C3HD series: 157 ft. lbs. (213 Nm).

Silverado and 2000–01 Sierra 15 Series

1. Raise and support the vehicle.
2. Support the rear axle independently

in order to relieve the tension on the leaf springs.

3. Disconnect the Real Time Damping (RTD) sensors (25 series utilities if equipped).

4. Remove the trailer hitch if equipped.

5. Remove the fuel tank for left side applications.

6. Remove the U-bolt nuts. Remove the U-bolts. Remove the spring spacer. Remove the anchor plate.

7. Remove the shackle to the frame bracket nut and the bolt.

8. Remove the front spring bracket bolt. Remove the leaf spring assembly from the vehicle.

9. Remove the shackle from the spring.

To install:

10. Loosely assemble the spring shackle bracket to the frame. Install the shackle bolt. Install the shackle nut.

11. Install the leaf spring assembly to the vehicle.

12. Loosely assemble the spring to the front hanger bracket.

13. Install the front spring hanger bracket bolt.

14. Install the front spring hanger bracket nut.

15. Install the shackle to the spring bolt.

16. Install the shackle to the spring nut.

➡**Do not reuse the U-bolts.**

17. Install the spring spacer.
18. Install the U-bolts.
19. Install the anchor plate.
20. Install the U-bolt nuts.
21. Observe the following torques:
   - 14mm U-bolt nuts to 80 Nm (59 ft. lbs.)
   - 16mm U-bolt nuts to 120 Nm (89 ft. lbs.)
   - Front hanger bracket nut to 125 Nm(92 ft. lbs.).
   - Shackle to the frame nut to 95 Nm(70 ft. lbs.).
   - Shackle to the spring nut to 95 Nm(70 ft. lbs.).

22. Install the fuel tank for left side applications.

23. Install the trailer hitch if equipped.

24. Connect the RTD sensors (25 series utilities if equipped).

25. Remove the rear axle support.

26. Remove the safety stands. Lower the vehicle.

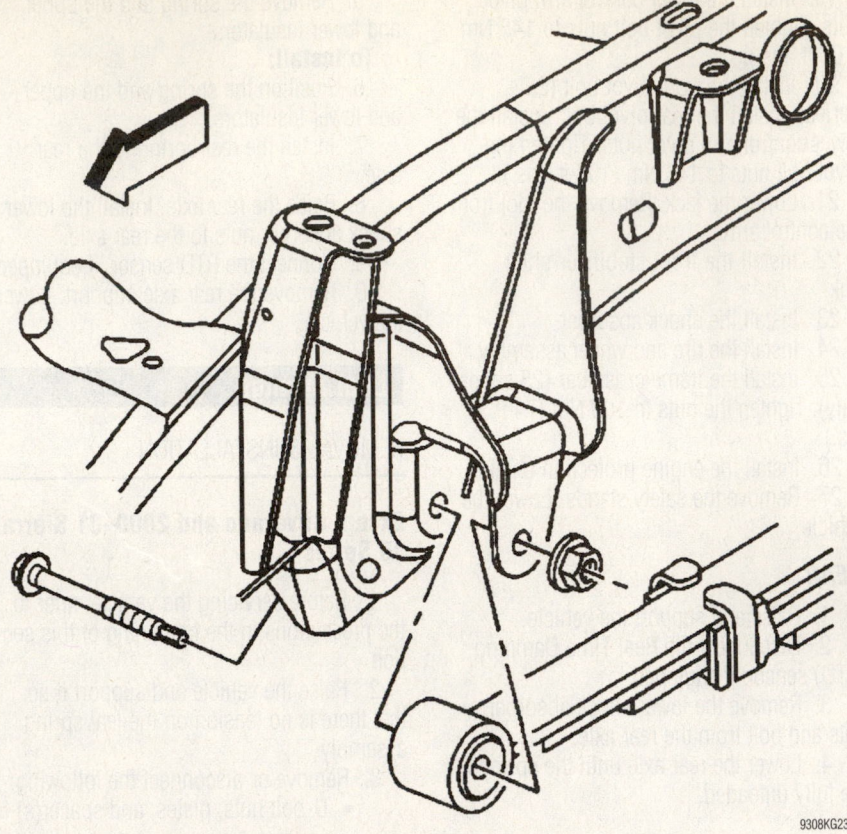

9308KG23

Rear leaf spring front shackle—Silverado

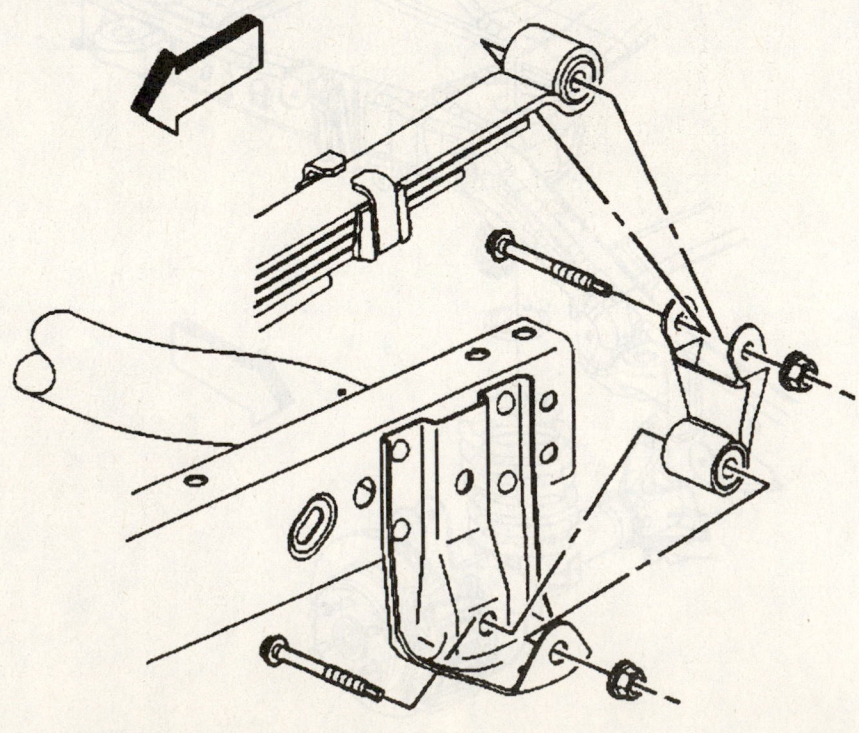

9308KG22

Rear leaf spring rear shackle—Silverado

Torsion Bars

REMOVAL & INSTALLATION

Except Silverado and 2000–01 Sierra 15 Series

1. Before servicing the vehicle, refer to the precautions in the beginning of this section.

➡**Special tool J–36202, or its equivalent, is necessary for this procedure.**

2. Remove or disconnect the following:
   • Wheels
3. Support the lower control arm with a floor jack.
4. Matchmark both torsion bar adjustment bolt positions.
5. Using tool J–36202, increase the tension on the adjusting arm.
6. Remove or disconnect the following:
   • Adjustment bolt and retaining plate
7. Move the tool aside, and slide the torsion bars forward.
   • Adjusting arms
   • Torsion bar support crossmember and slide the support crossmember rearwards
   • Torsion bars, matchmark the position. They are not interchangeable
   • Support crossmember
   • Retainer, spacer and bushing from the support crossmember

To install:

8. Install or connect the following:
   • Retainer, spacer and bushing to the support crossmember
   • Support assembly on the frame, out of the way
   • Torsion bars, sliding them forward until they are supported. Align the marks made when removed.
   • Support crossmember into position. Torque the center nut to 18 ft. lbs. (24 Nm), the edge nuts to 46 ft. lbs. (62 Nm).
   • Adjuster retaining plate and bolt on each torsion bar
9. Using tool J–36202, increase tension on both torsion bars.
10. Set the adjustment bolt to the marked position.
11. Release the tension on the torsion bar until the load is taken up by the adjustment bolt.
12. Install both wheels

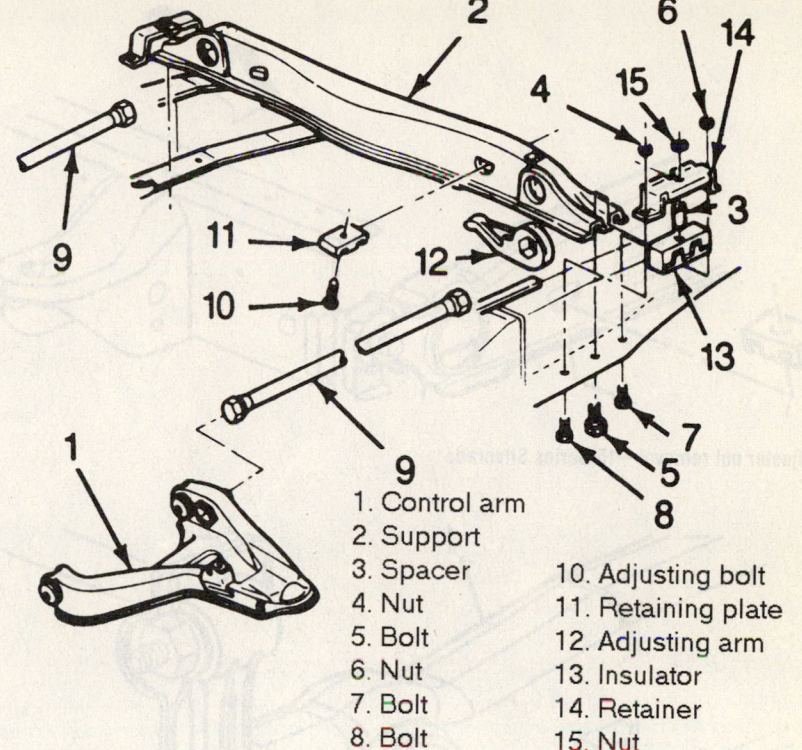

1. Control arm
2. Support
3. Spacer
4. Nut
5. Bolt
6. Nut
7. Bolt
8. Bolt
9. Torsion bar
10. Adjusting bolt
11. Retaining plate
12. Adjusting arm
13. Insulator
14. Retainer
15. Nut

84908058

Installing the torsion bar—K-Series

Silverado and 2000–01 Sierra 15 Series

➡**This procedure requires the removal of both torsion bars.**

1. Raise and support the vehicle.

2. Mark the adjustment bolt setting. Install tool J36202 to the adjustment arm and the crossmember.

3. Increase the tension on the adjustment arm until the load is removed from the adjustment bolt and the adjuster nut.

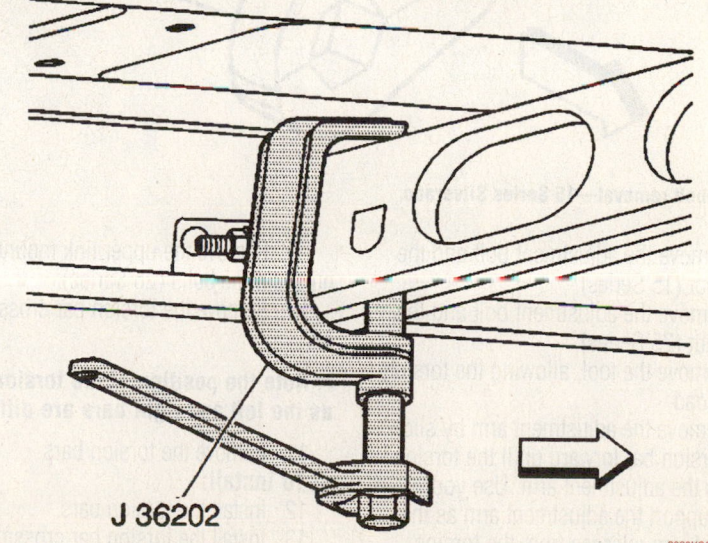

J 36202

9308KG27

Retainer installation—Silverado torsion bar

Turn to Section 5 for brake system applications

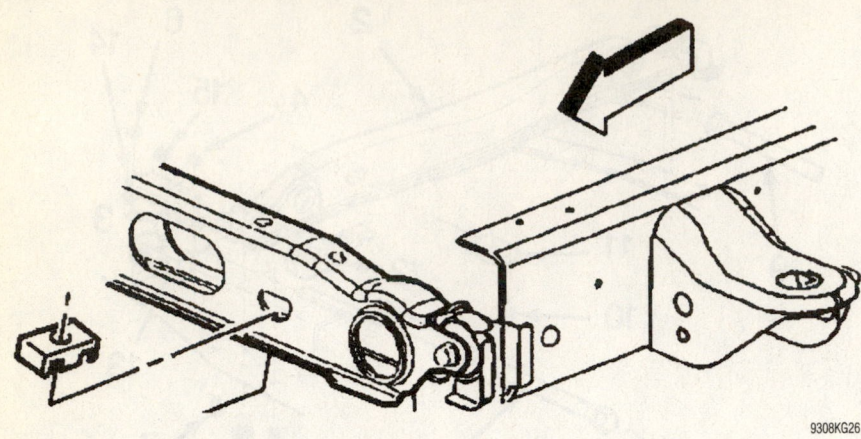

Adjuster nut removal—15 Series Silverado

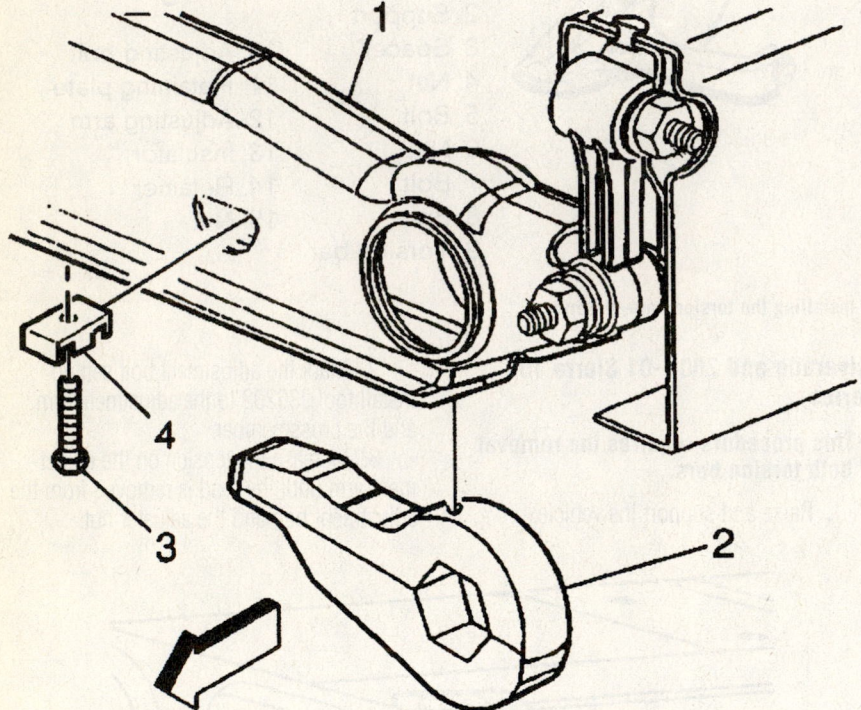

Adjuster bolt removal—15 Series Silverado

4. Remove the adjustment bolt and the adjuster nut (15 Series).

5. Remove the adjustment bolt and the adjuster nut (25 Series).

6. Remove the tool, allowing the torsion bar to unload.

7. Remove the adjustment arm by sliding the torsion bar forward until the torsion bar clears the adjustment arm. Use your hand to support the adjustment arm as the adjustment arm releases from the torsion bar.

8. Remove the torsion bar crossmember bolts from the weld nuts (15 Series).

9. Remove the upper link mounting nuts and the bolts (25 Series).

10. Remove the torsion bar crossmember.

➡**Note the position of the torsion bars as the left and right bars are different.**

11. Remove the torsion bars.
To install:

12. Install the torsion bars.

13. Install the torsion bar crossmember.

14. Install the torsion bar crossmember bolts to the weld nuts (15 Series). Tighten the bolt to 95 Nm (70 ft. lbs.).

15. Install the upper link mounting nuts and the bolts (25 Series). Tighten the nut to 95 Nm (70 ft. lbs.).

16. While supporting the adjustment arm, slide the torsion bar rearward until the torsion bar fully engages the adjustment arm. Install tool J36202 to the adjustment arm and the crossmember. Increase the tension on the adjustment arm in order to load the torsion bar.

17. Install the adjustment bolt and the adjuster nut (15 Series).

18. Install the adjustment bolt and the adjuster nut (25 Series). Remove the tool, releasing the tension on the torsion bar until the load is taken up by the adjustment bolt.

19. Remove the safety stands.

20. Lower the vehicle.

21. Measure the ride height.

22. Turn the adjustment bolt clockwise to increase the ride height and counterclockwise to decrease it.

Upper Ball Joint

REMOVAL & INSTALLATION

Silverado and 2000–01 Sierra 15 Series

1. Before servicing the vehicle, refer to the precautions in the beginning of this section.

2. Remove or disconnect the following:
   • Wheel
   • Brake hose bracket from the control arm

3. Using a ⅛ in. drill bit, drill a pilot hole through each ball joint rivet.

4. Drill out the rivets with a ½ in. drill bit. Punch out any remaining rivet material.
   • Cotter pin and nut from the ball stud

5. Support the lower control arm.
   • Stud from the knuckle. Using a ball joint separator
To install:

6. Install or connect the following:
   • New ball joint on the control arm

➡**Service replacement ball joints come with nuts and bolts to replace the rivets.**

   • Bolts and nuts. Torque the nuts to 17 ft. lbs. (23 Nm) for 15- and 25-Series, 52 ft. lbs. (70 Nm) for 35-Series.

➡**The bolts are inserted from the bottom.**

7. Start the ball stud into the knuckle. Ensure it is squarely seated. Install the ball stud nut and pull the ball stud into the knuckle with the nut. Tighten the nut after the vehicle wheels are on the ground and the suspension is loaded.
  • Wheel

8. Once the weight of the vehicle is on the wheels tighten the nut to 84 ft. lbs. (115 Nm).

Silverado and 2000–01 Sierra 15 Series

1. Raise and support the vehicle.
2. Remove the tire and wheel assembly.
3. Remove the upper control arm.
4. Using a press, remove the upper ball joint.

To install:

➡**The ball joint must be installed with the flat edges or notches in the same position as the replaced ball joint. The ball joint is directional and damage will occur if this procedure is not followed.**

5. Using a press, install the upper ball joint.
6. Install the upper control arm.
7. Install the tire and wheel assembly.
8. Remove the safety stands.
9. Lower the vehicle.
10. Verify the wheel alignment.

Lower Ball Joint

REMOVAL & INSTALLATION

Except Silverado and 2000–01 Sierra 15 Series

2-WHEEL DRIVE MODELS

1. Before servicing the vehicle, refer to the precautions in the beginning of this section.
2. Place jack under lower control arm, then raise the jack slightly.
3. Remove or disconnect the following:
  • Tire and wheel assembly
  • Brake caliper and position it to the side
  • Cotter pin and the lower ball joint retaining nut. Using the proper tool

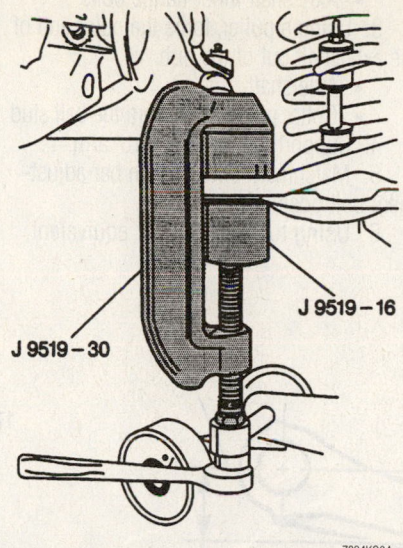

J 9519 – 30   J 9519 – 16

7924KG34

Installing the lower ball joint into the lower control arm—2-wheel drive

separate the ball joint from its mounting. Support the knuckle assembly so its weight will not damage the brake hose.
  • Ball joint out of the lower control

arm, using tool J-9519-30-D or equivalent.

To install:

4. Start the new ball joint into the control arm. Position the bleed vent in the rubber boot facing inward.
5. Install or connect the following:
  • Ball joint into the control arm until fully seated
  • Lower ball joint stud into the steering knuckle
  • Brake caliper, if removed
  • Ball stud nut. Torque the nut to 90 ft. lbs. (122 Nm) plus the additional tighten necessary to align the cotter pin hole. Do not exceed 130 ft. lbs. (175 Nm) or back the nut off to align the holes with the pin.
  • New lube fitting and lubricate the new joint.
  • Tire and wheel

4-WHEEL DRIVE MODELS

1. Before servicing the vehicle, refer to the precautions in the beginning of this section.

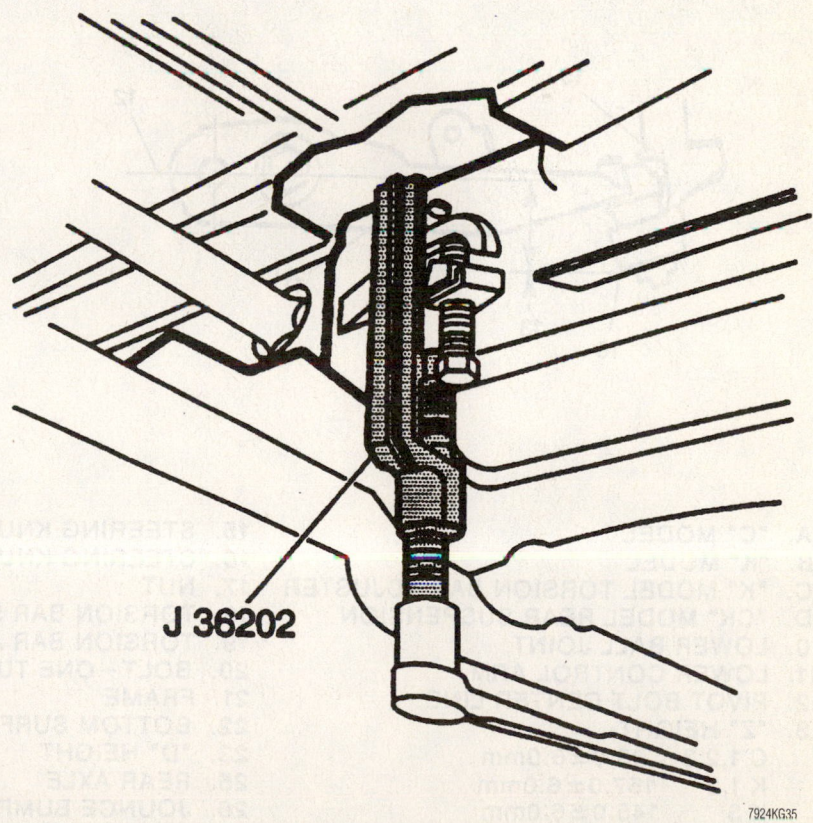

J 36202

7924KG35

A special tool is available for removing or installing the torsion bar adjusting bolt—4-wheel drive

2. Remove or disconnect the following:
- Wheel
- Splash shield from the knuckle
- Inner tie rod end from the relay rod using a ball joint separator
- Hub nut and washer. Insert a long drift or dowel through the vanes in the brake rotor to hold the rotor in place.

- Axle shaft inner flange bolts
3. Using a puller, force the outer end of the axle shaft out of the hub.
- Axle shaft.
- Cotter pin and nut from the ball stud
4. Support the lower control arm.
5. Matchmark both torsion bar adjustment bolt positions.
6. Using tool J-36202 or equivalent,

increase the tension on the adjusting arm.
7. Remove or disconnect the following:

- Adjustment bolt and retaining plate
8. Move the tool aside and slide the torsion bars forward.
- Ball joint from the knuckle. Using a screw-type forcing tool

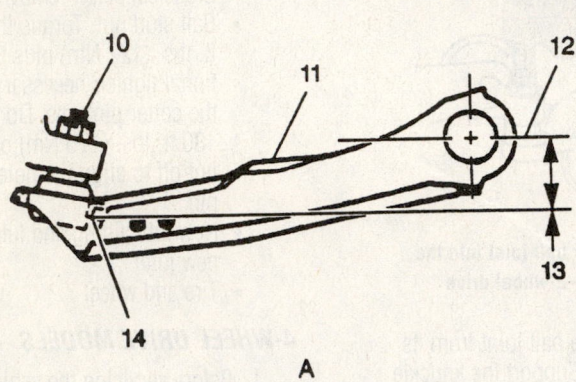

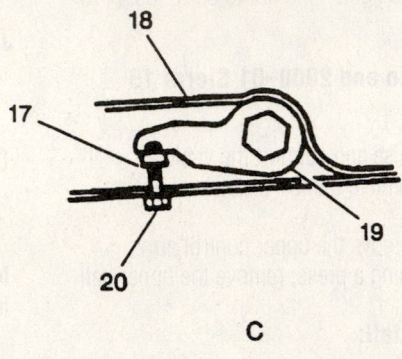

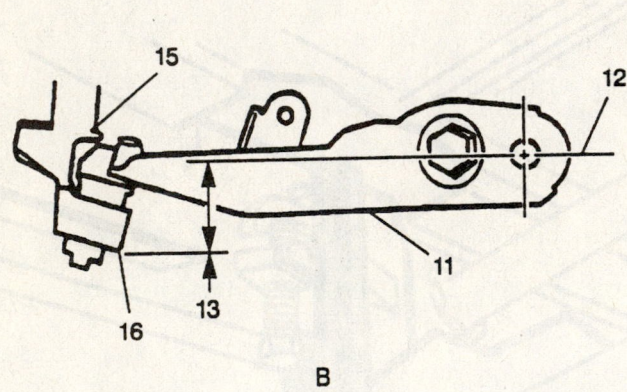

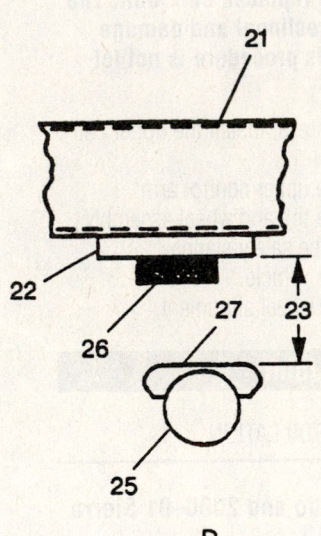

A. "C" MODEL
B. "K" MODEL
C. "K" MODEL TORSION BAR ADJUSTER
D. "CK" MODEL REAR SUSPENSION
10. LOWER BALL JOINT
11. LOWER CONTROL ARM
12. PIVOT BOLT CENTER LINE
13. "Z" HEIGHT
    C 1,2,3   95.0 ±6.0mm
    K 1,2   157.0 ±6.0mm
    K 3   145.0 ±6.0mm
14. LOWER BALL JOINT EXTRUSION

15. STEERING KNUCKLE
16. STEERING KNUCKLE LOWER CORNER
17. NUT
18. TORSION BAR SUPPORT ASM.
19. TORSION BAR ADJUSTMENT ARM
20. BOLT – ONE TURN EQUALS 6mm HEIGHT CHANGE
21. FRAME
22. BOTTOM SURFACE OF JOUNCE BRACKET
23. "D" HEIGHT
25. REAR AXLE
26. JOUNCE BUMPER
27. AXLE JOUNCE PAD

Use these specifications and diagrams to determine if the vehicle ride height is correct

7924KG36

- Lower control arm
- Lower ball joint out of control arm with tool J-9519-E or equivalent ball joint press

To install:

9. Install or connect the following:
   - New ball joint into the control arm with tool J-9519-E or equivalent
   - Lower control arm
10. Using tool J-36202 or equivalent, increase tension on both torsion bars.
   - Adjustment retainer plate and bolt on both torsion bars
11. Set the adjustment bolt to the marked position.
12. Release the tension on the torsion bar until the load is take up by the adjustment bolt and remove the tool.
   - Shaft in the hub and the washer and hub nut. Leave the drift in the rotor vanes and torque the hub nut to 175 ft. lbs. (238 Nm).
   - Flange bolts. Tighten them to 59 ft. lbs. (80 Nm), remove the drift.
   - Inner tie rod end at the steering relay rod. Torque the nut to 35 ft. lbs. (48 Nm).
   - Splash shield
   - wheel
13. Once the weight of the vehicle is on the wheels follow these steps:
   a. Step 1: Lift the front bumper about 1½ in. (38mm) and let it drop.
   b. Step 2: Repeat this procedure 2–3 more times.
   c. Step 3: Draw a line on the side of the lower control arm from the centerline of the control arm pivot shaft, dead level to the outer end of the control arm.
   d. Step 4: Measure the distance between the lowest corner of the steering knuckle and the line on the control arm, record the figure.
   e. Step 5: Push down about 1½ in. (38mm) on the front bumper and let it return. Repeat the procedure 2–3 more times.
   f. Step 6: Re-measure the distance at the control arm.
   g. Step 7: Determine the average of the 2 measurements. This is the "Z" height measurement. The "Z" height should be as specified in the chart.
   h. Step 8: If the figure is correct, tighten the control arm pivot nuts to 94 ft. lbs. (128 Nm).
   i. Step 9: If the figure is not correct, tighten the pivot bolts to 94 ft. lbs. (128

Nm) and have the front end alignment corrected.

Silverado and 2000–01 Sierra 15 Series

2WD

1. Raise and support the vehicle.
2. Remove the tire and wheel assembly.
3. Remove the front coil spring.
4. Remove the lower control arm.
5. Secure the lower control arm in a bench vice or equivalent.
6. Center punch the rivet heads.
7. Drill out the rivets.

To install:

8. Install the ball joint to the lower control arm.
9. Install the replacement bolts to the lower control arm.
10. Install the nuts to the bolts. Tighten the nuts to 70 Nm (52 ft. lbs.).
11. Remove the lower control arm from the bench vice.
12. Install the lower control arm.
13. Install the coil spring.
14. Install the tire and wheel tire assembly.
15. Remove the safety stands.
16. Lower the vehicle.
17. Verify the wheel alignment.

4WD

1. Raise and support the vehicle.
2. Remove the tire and wheel assembly.
3. Remove the lower control arm.
4. Place the lower control arm in a bench vice.
5. Using a chisel, remove the 4 securing crimps from the ball joint body (15 series only).
6. Using a press, remove the ball joint from the lower control arm.

To install:

➡**Use the outer flange of the ball joint in order to press the ball joint into place.**

7. Install the new ball joint using a press.
8. Place the lower control arm in a bench vice.
9. Using a punch, install 4 crimps to the ball joint. Use the replaced ball joint as a reference (15 series only).
10. Install the lower control arm.
11. Install the tire and wheel assembly.
12. Remove the safety stands.

13. Lower the vehicle.
14. Verify the wheel alignment.

Upper Control Arm

REMOVAL & INSTALLATION

Except Silverado and 2000–01 Sierra 15 Series

1. Before servicing the vehicle, refer to the precautions in the beginning of this section.
2. Support the lower control arm with a floor jack.
3. Remove or disconnect the following:
   - Wheel
   - Brake hose bracket from the control arm
   - Air cleaner extension (if necessary)
   - Brake hose bracket retainer and wire the hose aside
   - Cotter pin from the upper control arm ball stud and loosen the stud nut until the bottom surface of the nut is slightly below the end of the stud
   - Ball joint from the knuckle
   - Control arm to the frame brackets
   - Shims and spacers

To install:

4. Install or connect the following:
   - Control arm in position
   - Shims and spacers, bolts and new nuts. Both bolt heads **must** be inboard of the control arm brackets. Tighten the nuts finger tight for now.

➡**Do not tighten the bolts yet. The bolts must be torqued with the truck at its proper ride height.**

   - Ball joint to the knuckle. Torque the nut to 84 ft. lbs. (115 Nm).
   - Cotter pin. Never back off the nut to install the cotter pin. Always advance it. Never advance it more than ⅙ turn.
5. Lower the truck. Once the weight of the truck is on the wheels. Torque the control arm pivot nuts to 140 ft. lbs. (190 Nm)

Silverado and 2000–01 Sierra 15 Series

1. Raise and support the vehicle.
2. Remove the tire and wheel assembly.
3. Disconnect the Real Time Damping (RTD) link rod from the sensor (if equipped).

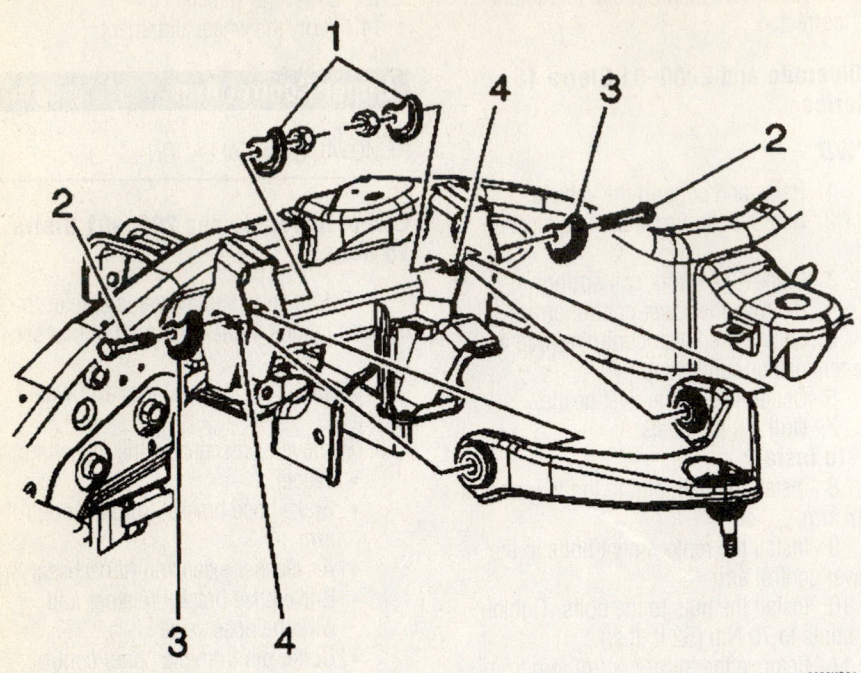

9308KG31

Upper control arm—Silverado

4. Remove the retaining bolt for the brake hose and the wheel speed sensor brackets.

5. Remove the halfshaft.

6. Remove the nut at the upper ball joint. Discard the nut.

7. Disconnect the upper control arm from the steering knuckle.

8. Remove the upper control arm nuts and the adjustment cams (15 Series RWD, 4WD, and 25 Series RWD).

9. Remove the upper control arm bolts (15 Series RWD, 4WD, and 25 Series RWD).

10. Remove the upper control arm nuts and the adjustment cams (25 Series 4WD).

11. Remove the upper control arm bolts (25 Series 4WD). Remove the upper control arm.

12. Install the upper control arm.

13. Install the upper control arm bolts (25 Series 4WD).

14. Install the upper control arm nuts and the adjustment cams (25 Series 4WD). Tighten the nuts to 190 Nm (140 ft. lbs.).

15. Install the upper control arm bolts (15 Series RWD, 4WD, and 25 Series RWD).

16. Install the upper control arm nuts and the adjustment cams (2) (15 Series RWD, 4WD, and 25 Series RWD). Tighten the nuts to 190 Nm (140 ft. lbs.).

17. Connect the upper control arm to steering knuckle.

18. Install the halfshaft.

19. Install the new nut to the upper ball joint stud. Tighten the nut to 50 Nm (37 ft. lbs.).

20. Install the retaining bolts for the brake hose and wheel speed sensor brackets. Tighten the bolts to 9 Nm (80 inch lbs.).

21. Connect the RTD link rod to the sensor (if equipped).

22. Install the tire and wheel assembly.

23. Remove the safety stands.

24. Lower the vehicle. Verify the wheel alignment.

CONTROL ARM BUSHING REPLAMENT

The control arm bushings are removed and installed using a press.

Lower Control Arm and Bushing

REMOVAL & INSTALLATION

Except Silverado and 2000–01 Sierra 15 Series

➡**Special tools J–36202, J–36618–1, J–36618–2, J–36618–3, J–36618–4, J–36618–5, and J–9519–23, or their equivalents, are necessary for this procedure.**

1. Before servicing the vehicle, refer to the precautions in the beginning of this section.

2. Remove or disconnect the following:
   • Wheel

3. Matchmark the both torsion bar adjustment bolt positions.

4. Using tool J–36202, increase the tension on the adjusting arm.
   • Adjustment bolt and retaining plate, and move the tool aside

5. Slide the torsion bars forward.
   • Adjusting arm
   • Splash shield from the knuckle, if equipped
   • Hub nut and washer. Insert a long drift or dowel through the vanes in the brake rotor to hold the rotor in place.
   • Axle shaft out of the hub
   • Brake caliper and wire it aside
   • Rotor
   • Shock absorber from control arm
   • Inner tie rod end from the relay rod

6. Support the lower control arm with a floor jack.
   • Stabilizer bar from the control arm
   • Cotter pin from the lower ball stud and loosen the nut
   • Ball joint from control arm
   • Control arm-to-frame bracket bolts, nuts and washers
   • Lower control arm and torsion bar as a unit

7. Separate the control arm and torsion bar.

   To install:

8. Install or connect the following:
   • Control arm assembly into position. Insert the front leg of the control arm into the crossmember first, then the rear leg into the frame bracket.
   • Mounting bolts, front one first. The bolts **must** be installed with the front bolt head heads towards the front of the truck and the rear bolt head towards the rear of the truck!

➡**Do not tighten the bolts yet. The bolts must be torqued with the truck at its proper ride height.**

   • Ball joint into the knuckle. Torque the nut to 94 ft. lbs. (128 Nm).
   • Adjuster arm

9. Using tool J–36202, increase tension on both torsion bars.
   • Adjustment retainer plate and bolt on both torsion bars and set to marked positions. Release the tension on the torsion bar until the

load is taken up by the adjustment bolt.

• Wheel

10. Lower the truck. Once the weight of the truck is on the wheels. Torque the bolts to 121 ft. lbs. (165 Nm).

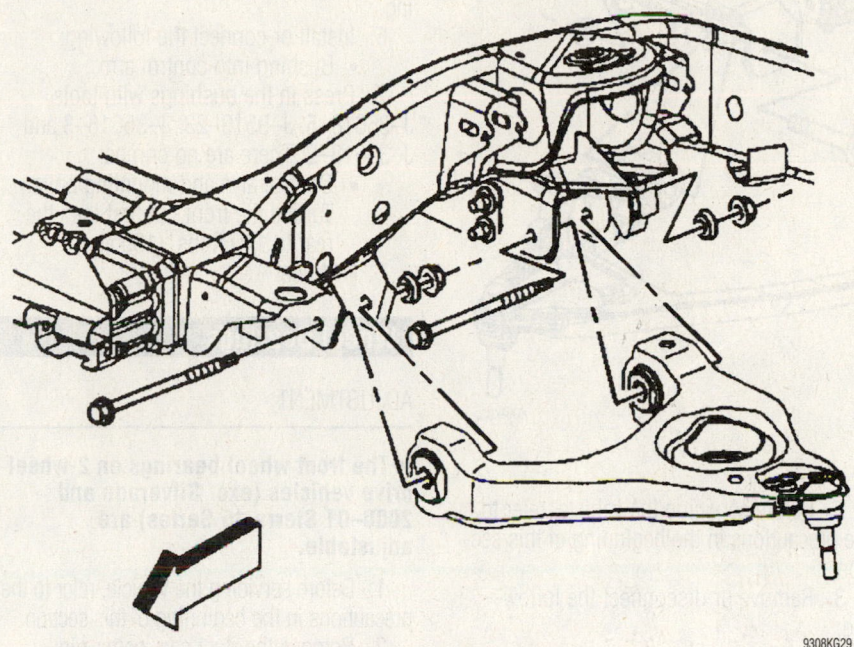

2WD lower control arm—15 Series Silverado

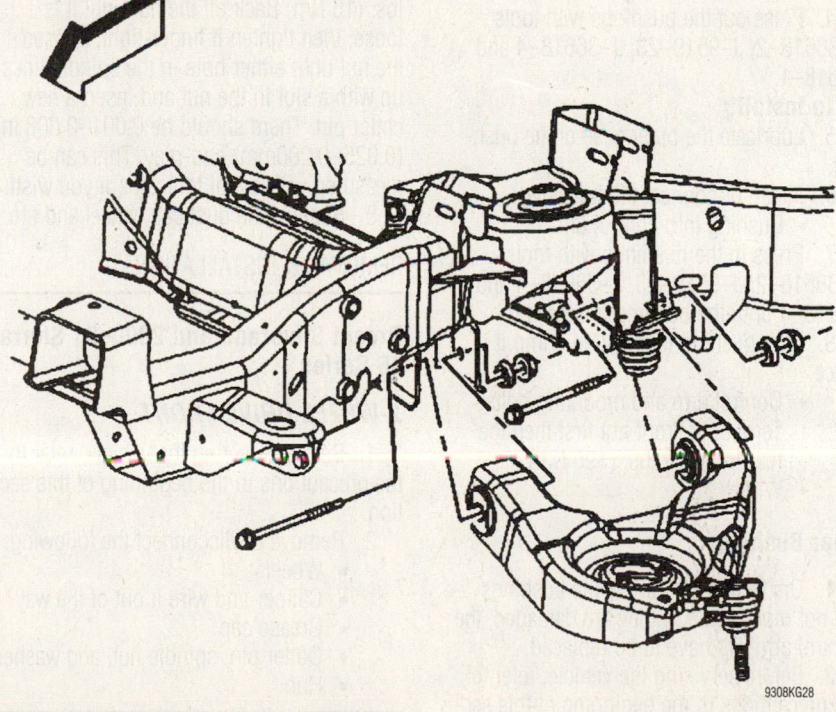

2WD lower control arm—25 Series Silverado

Silverado and 2000–01 Sierra 15 Series

2WD

1. Raise and support the vehicle.
2. Remove the tire and wheel assembly.

3. Disconnect the Real Time Damping (RTD) link rod from the sensor (if equipped).
4. Remove the shock absorber.
5. Remove the front stabilizer shaft link.
6. Remove the front coil spring.
7. Remove the lower control arm nuts and the washers (15 Series). Remove the lower control arm bolts (15 Series).
8. Remove the lower control arm nuts and washers (25 Series).
9. Remove the lower control arm bolts (25 Series).
10. Remove the lower ball joint stud nut.
11. Disconnect the lower ball joint stud from the steering knuckle.
12. Remove the lower control arm.

To install:

13. Install the lower control arm.
14. Connect the ball joint stud to the steering knuckle.
15. Install the lower ball joint stud nut. Tighten the lower ball joint stud nut to 100 Nm (74 ft. lbs.).
16. Install the front coil spring.
17. Install the lower control arm bolts (15 Series).
18. Install the lower control arm nuts and the washers (15 Series). Tighten the lower control arm nuts to 145 Nm (107 ft. lbs.).
19. Install the lower control arm bolt (25 Series). Install the lower control arm nuts and the washers (25 Series). Tighten the lower control arm nuts to 145 Nm (107 ft. lbs.).
20. Install the front stabilizer shaft link.
21. Install the shock absorber.
22. Install the tire and wheel assembly.
23. Remove the safety stands. Lower the vehicle. Verify the wheel alignment.

4WD

1. Raise and support the vehicle.
2. Remove the tire and wheel assembly.
3. Disconnect the Real Time Damping (RTD) link rod from the sensor (if equipped).
4. Remove the stabilizer shaft links from the lower control arm.
5. Remove the shock absorber nut and the bolt.
6. Remove the torsion bars.
7. Remove the halfshaft.
8. Remove the lower ball joint stud nut.
9. Disconnect the lower ball joint stud from the steering knuckle.
10. Remove the lower control arm nuts and the washers (15 Series).
11. Remove the lower control arm bolts.

Turn to Section 5 for brake system applications

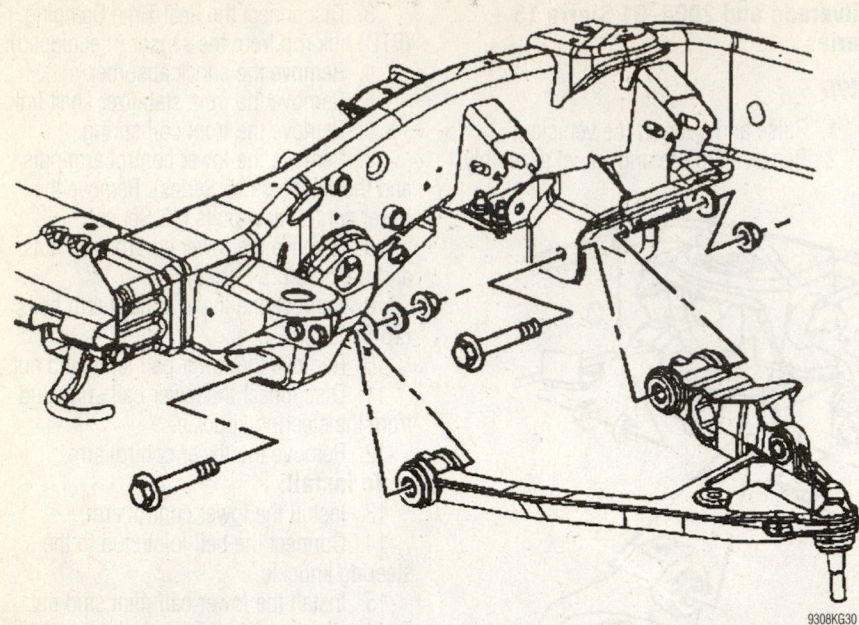

4WD lower control arm—15 Series Silverado

12. Remove the lower control arm nuts and the washers (25 Series).

13. Remove the lower control arm bolts.

14. Remove the lower control arm.

To install:

15. Install the lower control arm.

16. Install the lower control arm bolts (15 Series).

17. Install the lower control arm bolts (25 Series).

18. Install the washers with the shoulder facing the arm.

19. Install the nuts. Tighten the nuts to 145 Nm (107 ft. lbs.).

20. Install the halfshaft.

21. Connect lower ball joint stud to the steering knuckle. Install the nut to the ball joint stud. Tighten the nut to 100 Nm (74 ft. lbs.).

22. Install the torsion bars.

23. Install the shock absorber through nut and bolt.

24. Install the stabilizer shaft links to the lower control arm.

25. Connect the RTD link rod to the sensor (if equipped).

26. Install the tire and wheel assembly.

27. Remove the safety stands. Lower the vehicle. Verify the wheel alignment.

CONTROL ARM BUSHING REPLAEMENT

Front bushing

1. On 15 and 25 Series, the bushings are not replaceable. If they are damaged, the control arm will have to be replaced.

2. Before servicing the vehicle, refer to the precautions in the beginning of this section.

3. Remove or disconnect the following:

- Wheel
- Lower control arm
- Unbend the crimps with a punch on the front bushing

4. Press out the bushings with tools J–36618–2, J–9519–23, J–36618–4 and 36618–1.

To install:

5. Lubricate the outer case of the bushing.

6. Install or connect the following:

- Bushing into control arm

7. Press in the bushings with tools J–36618–2, J–9519–23, J–36618–4 and 36618–1 until the bushing is seated in.

8. After bushing is installed crimp it in place.

- Control arm and mounting bolts. Torque the front nut first then the rear to 140 ft lbs. (190 Nm)
- Wheel

Rear Bushing

1. On 15 and 25 Series, the bushings are not replaceable. If they are damaged, the control arm will have to be replaced.

2. Before servicing the vehicle, refer to the precautions in the beginning of this section.

3. Remove or disconnect the following:

- Wheel
- Lower control arm

4. Press out the bushings with tools. J–36618–5, J–9519–23, J–36618–3 and J–36618–2. There are no crimps.

To install:

5. Lubricate the outer case of the bushing.

6. Install or connect the following:

- Bushing into control arm

7. Press in the bushings with tools J–36618–5, J–9519–23, J–36618–3 and J–36618–2. There are no crimps.

- Control arm and mounting bolts. Torque the front nut first then the rear to 140 ft lbs. (190 Nm)
- Wheel

Wheel Bearings

ADJUSTMENT

➡The front wheel bearings on 2-wheel drive vehicles (exc. Silverado and 2000–01 Sierra 15 Series) are adjustable.

1. Before servicing the vehicle, refer to the precautions in the beginning of this section.

2. Remove the dust cap, cotter pin.

3. Loosen the spindle nut.

4. Spin the wheel hub by hand and tighten the nut until it is just snug—12 ft. lbs. (16 Nm) Back off the nut until it is loose, then tighten it finger-tight. Loosen the nut until either hole in the spindle lines up with a slot in the nut and insert a new cotter pin. There should be 0.001–0.008 in. (0.025–0.200mm) end-play. This can be measured with a dial indicator, if you wish.

5. Replace the dust cap, wheel and tire.

REMOVAL & INSTALLATION

Except Silverado and 2000–01 Sierra 15 Series

2-WHEEL DRIVE FRONT

1. Before servicing the vehicle, refer to the precautions in the beginning of this section.

2. Remove or disconnect the following:

- Wheel.
- Caliper and wire it out of the way
- Grease cap
- Cotter pin, spindle nut, and washer
- Hub.

✳✳ CAUTION

Do not drop the wheel bearings.

- Outer roller bearing assembly from the hub

3. The inner bearing assembly will remain in the hub and may be removed after prying out the inner seal. Discard the seal.

4. Clean all parts in a non-flammable solvent and let them air dry. Never spin-dry a bearing with compressed air! Check for excessive wear and damage.

5. If necessary for replacement, remove the bearing races from the hub using a hammer and drift. They are driven out from the inside out.

To install:

6. Install or connect the following:
- New bearing races, if required. When installing new races, ensure that they are not cocked and that they are fully seated against the hub shoulder.

7. Pack both wheel bearings using high melting point wheel bearing grease for disc brakes.
- Inner bearing in the hub and a new inner seal, making sure that the seal flange faces the bearing race.
- Wheel hub over the spindle
- Outer bearing into the hub

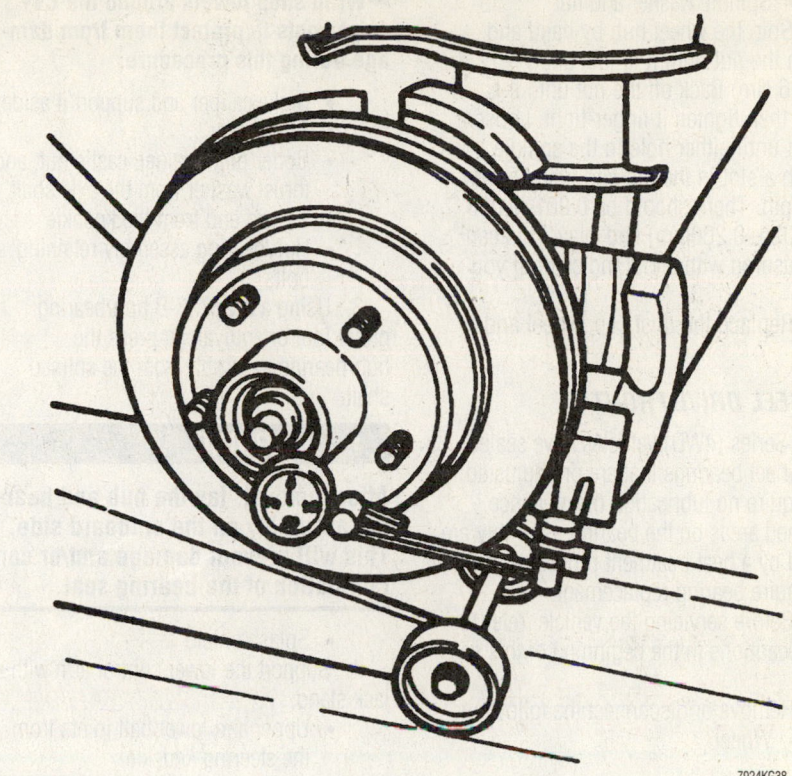

7924KG38

Use a dial indicator to measure the wheel bearing end-play—2-wheel drive vehicles

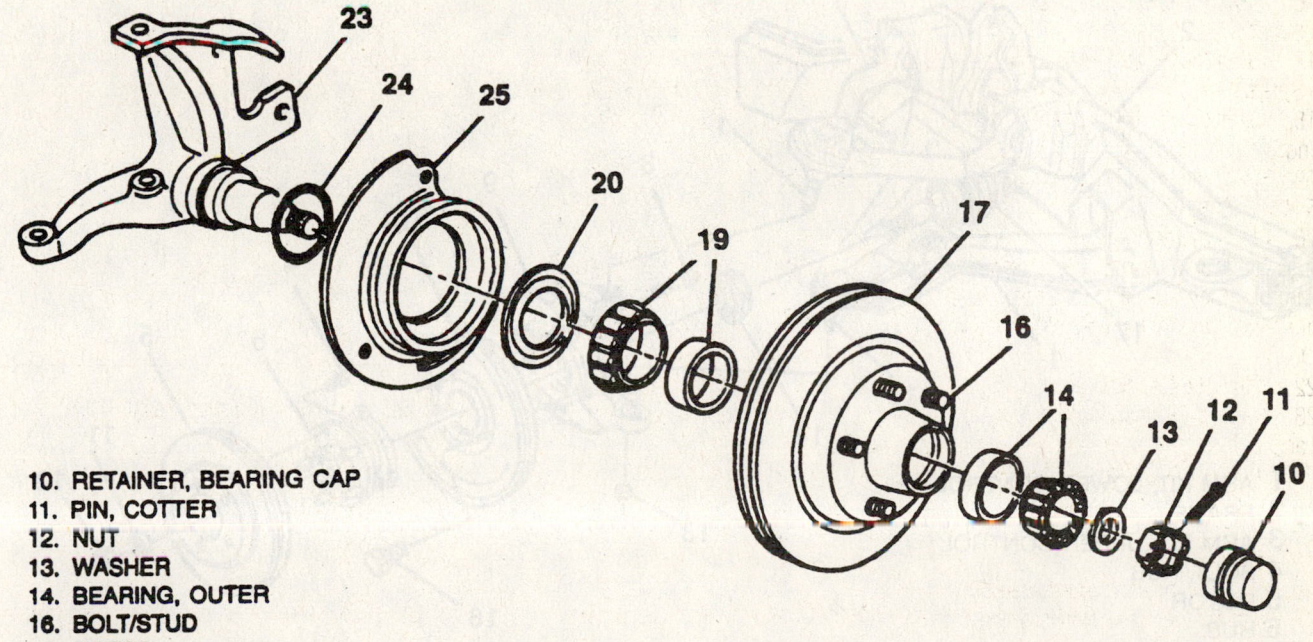

10. RETAINER, BEARING CAP
11. PIN, COTTER
12. NUT
13. WASHER
14. BEARING, OUTER
16. BOLT/STUD
17. ROTOR
19. BEARING, INNER
20. SEAL
23. KNUCKLE
24. GASKET
25. SHIELD

7924KG53

Exploded view of the front wheel bearing and related components—2-wheel drive models

- Spindle washer and nut

8. Spin the wheel hub by hand and tighten the nut until it is just snug—12 ft. lbs. (16 Nm) Back off the nut until it is loose, then tighten it finger-tight. Loosen the nut until either hole in the spindle lines up with a slot in the nut and insert a new cotter pin. There should be 0.001–0.008 in. (0.025–0.200mm) end-play. This can be measured with a dial indicator, if you wish.

9. Replace the dust cap, wheel and tire.

4-WHEEL DRIVE FRONT

"K" Series (4WD) vehicles have sealed front wheel bearings that are pre-adjusted and require no lubrication maintenance. Darkened areas on the bearing assembly are caused by a heat treatment process and do not require bearing replacement.

1. Before servicing the vehicle, refer to the precautions in the beginning of this section.

2. Remove or disconnect the following:
- Wheel

➡Wrap shop towels around the CV-Joint boots to protect them from damage during this procedure.

- Brake caliper and support it aside
- Brake rotor
- Cotter pin, retainer, castle nut, and thrust washer from the axle shaft
- Tie rod end from the knuckle
- Hub/bearing assembly retaining bolts

3. Using a J-28733-B hub/bearing puller tool or equivalent, press the hub/bearing assembly from the splined shaft.

❊❊ WARNING

After removal, lay the hub and bearing assembly on the outboard side. This will prevent damage and/or contamination of the bearing seal.

- Splash shield

4. Support the lower control arm with a jack stand.
- Upper and lower ball joints from the steering knuckle

- Steering knuckle
- Seal from the steering knuckle

To install:

5. Install or connect the following:
- New seal in the steering knuckle, using a J 36605 seal installer
- Steering knuckle on the ball joints and the retaining nuts. Torque the upper ball joint nut to 74 ft. lbs. (100 Nm) and the lower ball joint nut to 94 ft. lbs. (128 Nm) Tighten the nuts to align the holes for cotter pin insertion, but do NOT tighten more than an additional 1/6 turn.
- Splash shield
- Hub/bearing assembly over the splined shaft, making sure the splines line up correctly. Torque the bolts to 133 ft. lbs. (180 Nm)
- Tie rod end at the steering knuckle
- Thrust washer and axle nut, Torque the nut to 165 ft. lbs. (225 Nm).
- Retainer and cotter pin
- Rotor and caliper

6. Remove the shop towels from the CV-Joint boot.

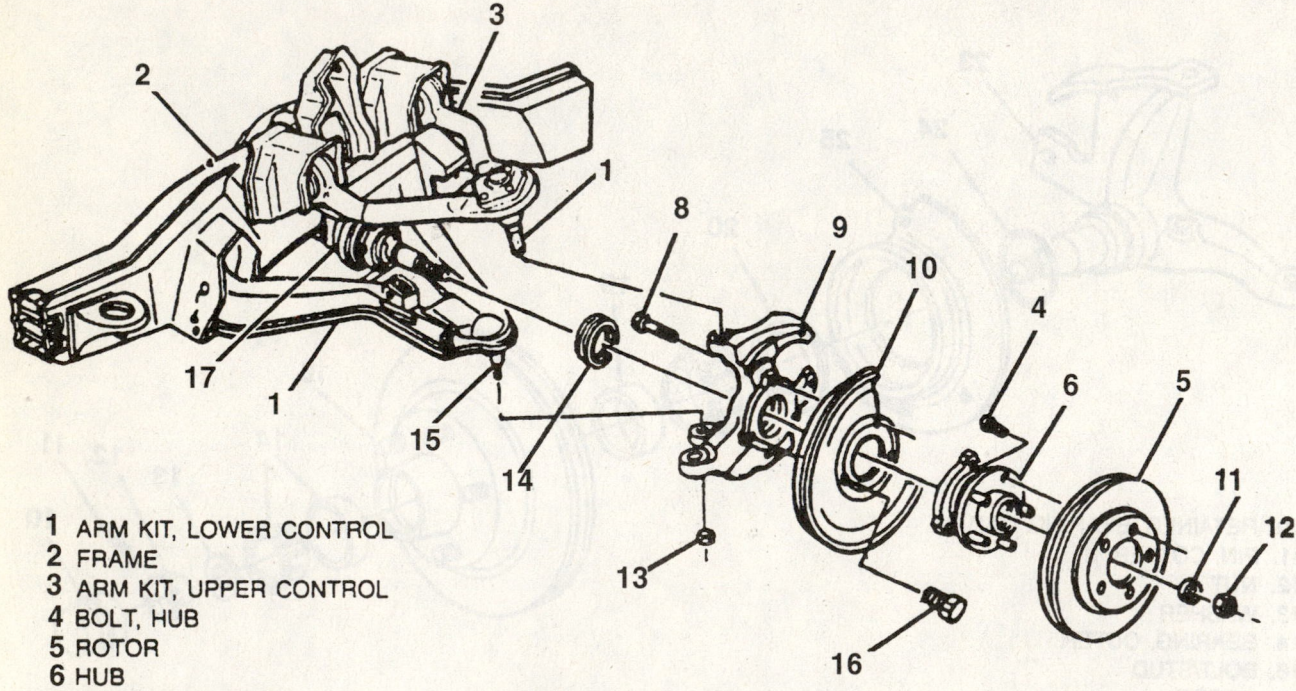

1 ARM KIT, LOWER CONTROL
2 FRAME
3 ARM KIT, UPPER CONTROL
4 BOLT, HUB
5 ROTOR
6 HUB
7 BALL JOINT, UPPER
8 BOLT
9 KNUCKLE, STEERING
10 SHIELD
11 WASHER
12 NUT
13 NUT
14 SEAL
15 BALL JOINT, LOWER
16 BOLT
17 JOINT KIT, FRONT AXLE

7924KG37

Exploded view of the front hub and knuckle assembly—4-wheel drive

- Tire and wheel assemblies

7. Check and adjust the front end alignment and road test the vehicle.

REAR

1. Before servicing the vehicle, refer to the precautions in the beginning of this section.

A new pinion shaft lockbolt should be installed whenever either of the axle shafts is removed.

➡ Axle shaft seal removal and installation uses the following special tools: the GM Axle Shaft Seal Installer tool No. J-33782 (seal driver) or equivalent and the Axle Shaft Bearing Installer tool No. J-34974 (bearing driver) or equivalent.

2. Place a catch pan under the differential, then remove the drain plug (if equipped) or rear axle cover and drain the fluid (discard the old fluid)

3. Remove or disconnect the following:
- Rear wheel assemblies
- Brake drums

4. Using a wire brush, clean the dirt/rust from around the rear axle cover.
- Rear pinion shaft lockbolt and the pinion shaft, at the differential
- C-lock from the button end of the axle shaft, push the axle shafts inward.
- Axle shaft from the axle housing. Be careful not to damage the oil seal.

✳✳ WARNING

On vehicles equipped with an Anti-Lock Brake System (ABS) be careful

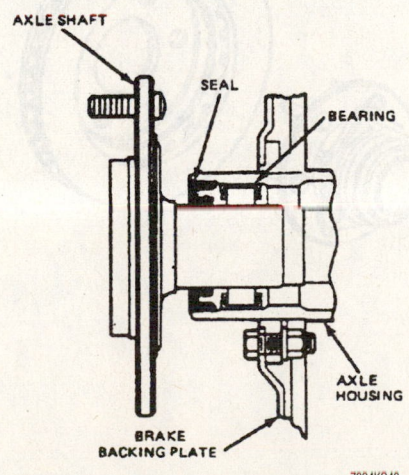

Cutaway view of the rear axle shaft and bearing assembly

not to damage the reluctor ring on the axle shaft or the speed sensor bolted to the backing plate, immediately adjacent to the shaft.

5. Clean the gasket mounting surfaces.

➡ It is recommended, when the axle shaft is removed, to replace the oil seal.

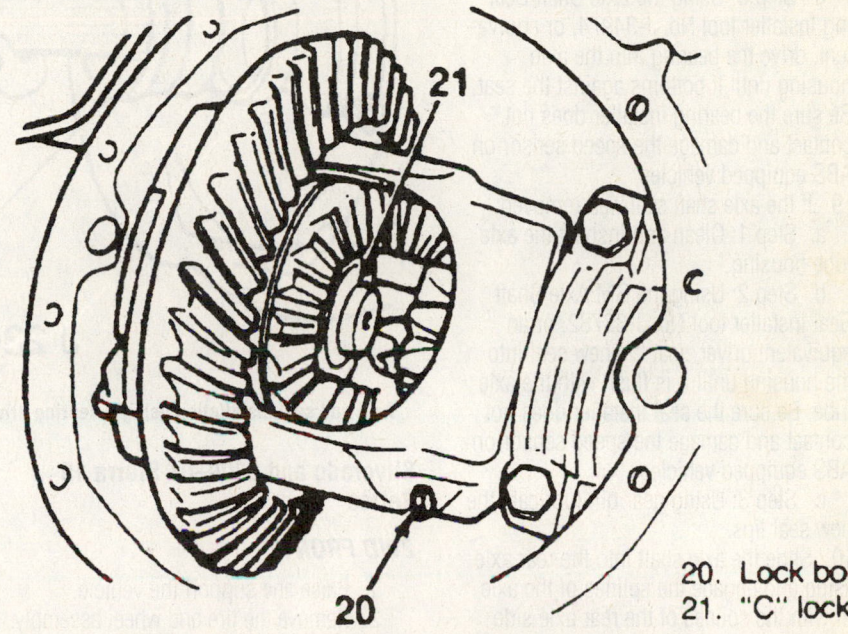

20. Lock bolt
21. "C" lock

Remove the lockbolt and pinion shaft, then push in the axle shaft and remove the C-lock

6. To replace the oil seal use a medium prybar or, better yet, an inexpensive seal removal tool, to pry the oil seal from the end of the rear axle housing. DO NOT damage the housing oil seal surface. And again, on late-model ABS equipped vehicles, STAY CLEAR OF THE SPEED SENSOR.

7. Using the slide hammer and adapter, pull the bearing out of the axle tube.

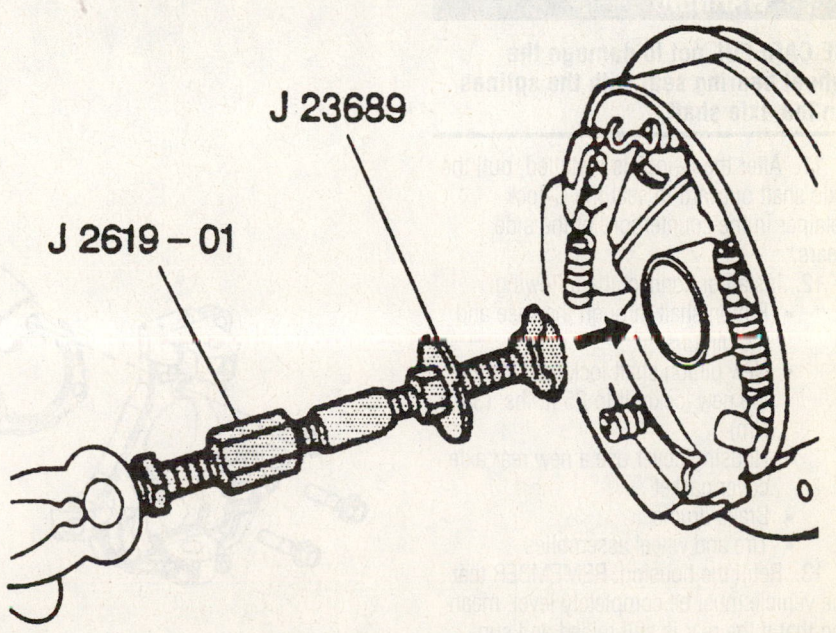

J 23689
J 2619-01

Using a slide hammer and adapters, remove the axle bearing and seal

To install:

8. If the wheel bearing was removed:

   a. Step 1: Using solvent, thoroughly clean the wheel bearing, then blow dry with compressed air. Inspect the wheel bearing for excessive wear or damage, then replace it (if necessary)

   b. Step 2: With a new or the reused bearing, thoroughly coat the bearing with gear lubricant.

   c. Step 3: Using the Axle Shaft Bearing Installer tool No. J-34974, or equivalent, drive the bearing into the axle housing until it bottoms against the seat. Be sure the bearing installer does not contact and damage the speed sensor on ABS equipped vehicles.

9. If the axle shaft seal was removed:

   a. Step 1: Clean and inspect the axle tube housing.

   b. Step 2: Using the GM Axle Shaft Seal Installer tool No. J-33782, or an equivalent driver, seat the new seal into the housing until it is flush with the axle tube. Be sure the seal installer does not contact and damage the speed sensor on ABS equipped vehicles.

   c. Step 3: Using gear oil, lubricate the new seal lips.

10. Slide the axle shaft into the rear axle housing and engage the splines of the axle shaft with the splines of the rear axle side gear, then install the C-lock retainer on the axle shaft button end.

❊❊ WARNING

BE CAREFUL not to damage the wheel bearing seal with the splines on the axle shaft.

11. After the C-lock is installed, pull the axle shaft outward to seat the C-lock retainer in the counterbore of the side gears.

12. Install or connect the following:

- Pinion shaft through the case and the pinions
- New pinion shaft lockbolt. Torque the new lockbolt to 25 ft. lbs. (34 Nm).
- Housing cover use a new rear axle cover gasket
- Brake drums
- Tire and wheel assemblies

13. Refill the housing. REMEMBER that the vehicle must be completely level, meaning that if the rear is still raised and supported, the front should also be raised.

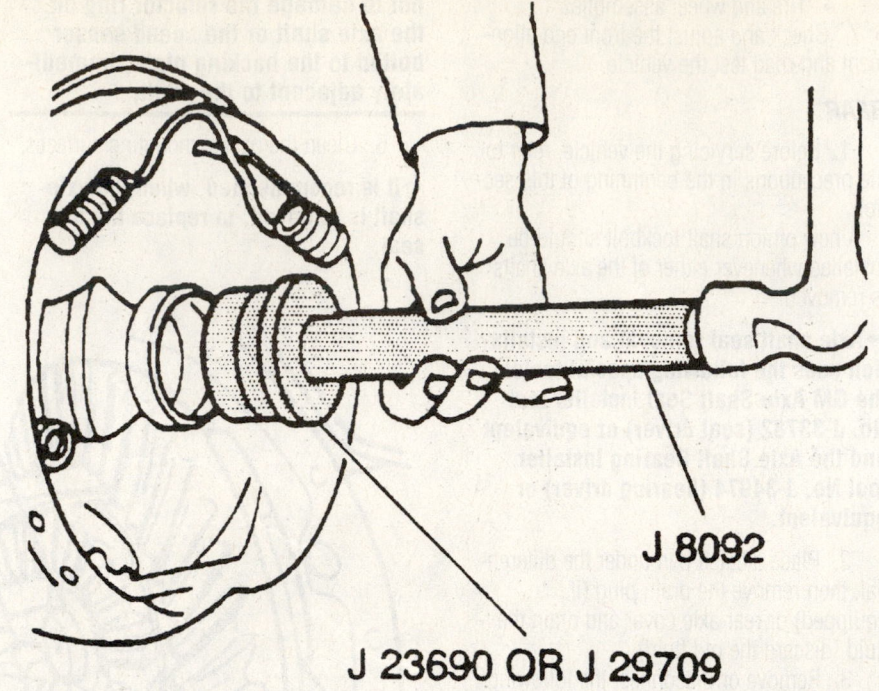

Axle and seal installation using a bearing driver

Silverado and 2000–01 Sierra 15 Series

2WD FRONT

1. Raise and support the vehicle.
2. Remove the tire and wheel assembly.
3. Remove the rotor.
4. Remove the wheel speed sensor and brake hose mounting bracket bolt from the steering knuckle.
5. Disconnect the electrical connection for the wheel speed sensor.
6. Remove the hub and bearing assembly mounting bolts (15 Series).
7. Remove the hub and bearing assembly mounting bolts (25 Series).

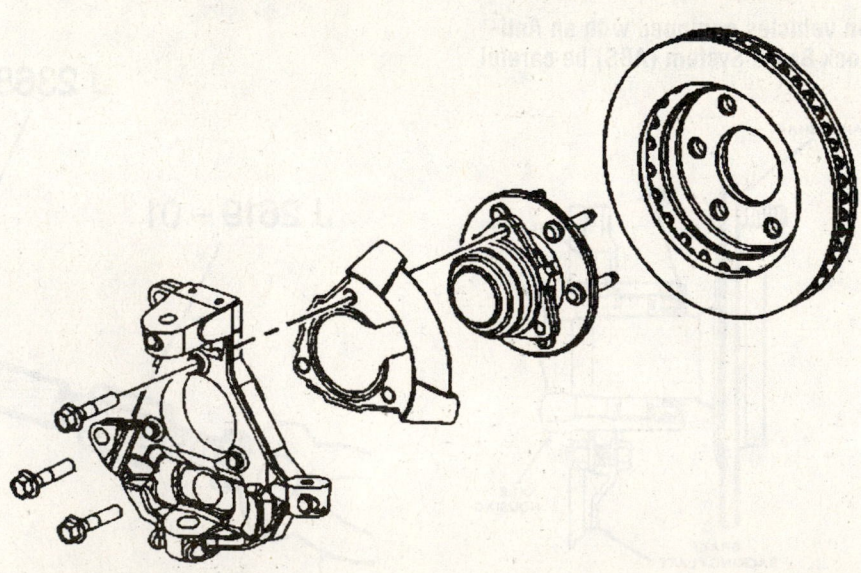

2WD front hub—15 Series Silverado

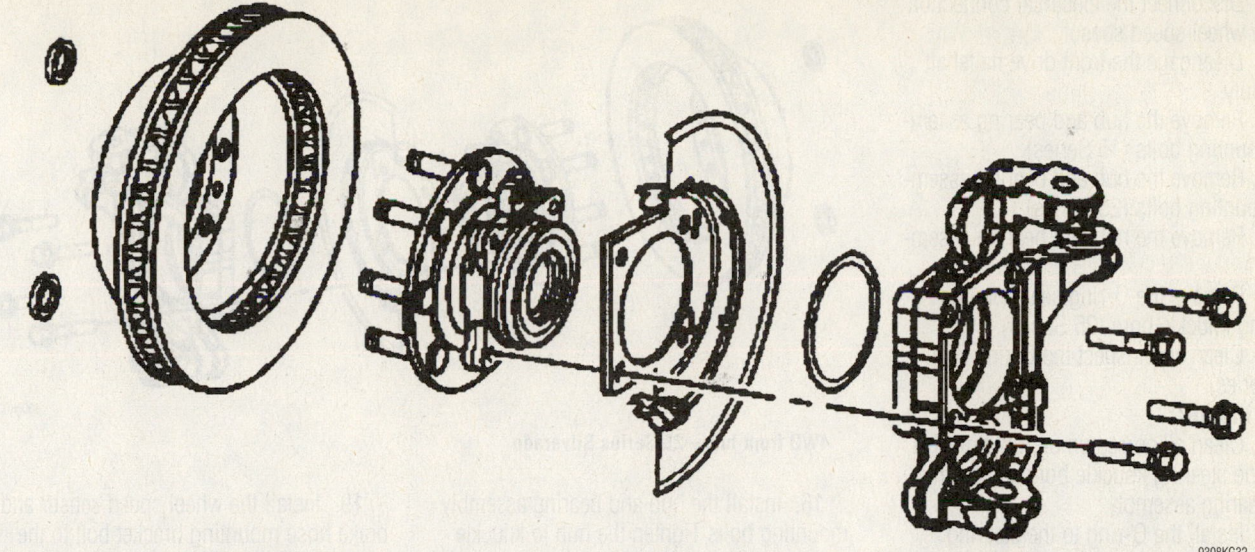

9308KG32

2WD front hub—25 Series Silverado

8. Remove the hub and bearing assembly.

9. Remove the O-ring seal from the steering knuckle bore (25 Series).

10. Clean and inspect the O-ring seal (25 Series).

To install:

11. Clean all corrosion or contaminates from the steering knuckle bore and the hub and bearing assembly.

12. Install the O-ring to the steering knuckle (25 Series).

13. Lubricate the steering knuckle bore

with wheel bearing grease or the equivalent.

14. Install the hub and bearing assembly.

15. Install the hub and bearing assembly mounting bolts (15 Series). Install the hub and bearing assembly mounting bolts (25 Series). Tighten the hub to knuckle bolts to 180 Nm (133 ft. lbs.).

16. Connect the electrical connection for the wheel speed sensor.

17. Install the wheel speed sensor and brake hose mounting bracket bolt to the steering knuckle. Tighten the bolt to 12 Nm (106 inch lbs.).

18. Install the rotor.

19. Install the tire and wheel assembly.

20. Remove the safety stands. Lower the vehicle.

4WD FRONT

1. Raise and support the vehicle.

2. Remove the tire and wheel assembly.

3. Remove the rotor.

4. Remove the wheel speed sensor and brake hose mounting bracket bolt from the steering knuckle.

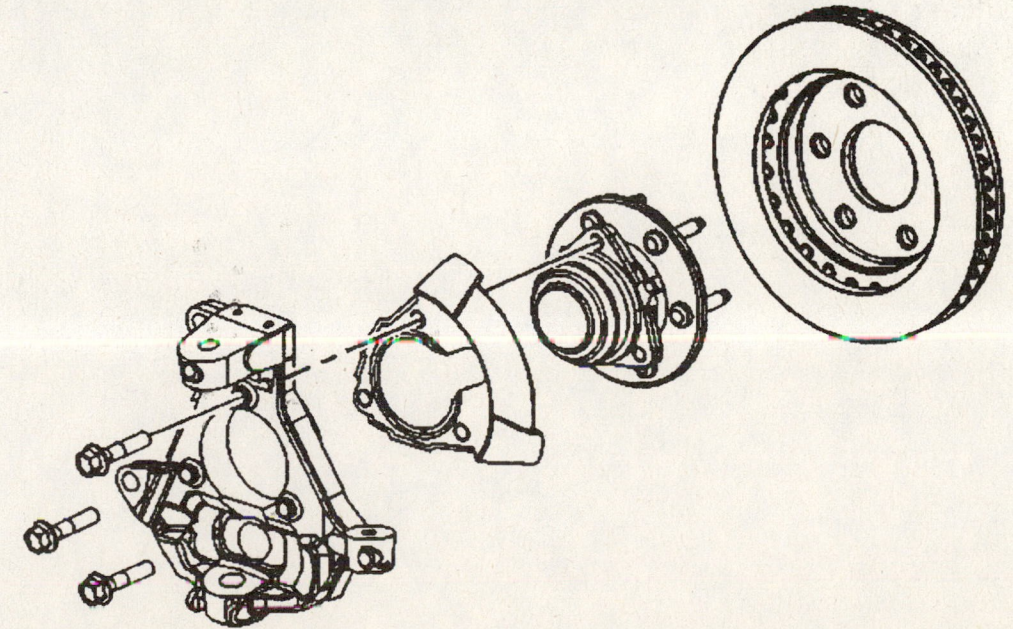

9308KG35

4WD front hub—15 Series Silverado

Turn to Section 5 for brake system applications

5. Disconnect the electrical connection for the wheel speed sensor.

6. Disengage the front drive halfshaft assembly.

7. Remove the hub and bearing assembly mounting bolts (15 Series).

8. Remove the hub and bearing assembly mounting bolts (25 Series).

9. Remove the hub and bearing assembly.

10. Remove the O-ring seal from the steering knuckle bore (25 Series).

11. Clean and inspect the O-ring seal (25 Series).

To install:

12. Clean all corrosion or contaminates from the steering knuckle bore and the hub and bearing assembly.

13. Install the O-ring to the steering knuckle (25 Series).

14. Lubricate the steering knuckle bore with wheel bearing grease or the equivalent.

15. Install the hub and bearing assembly.

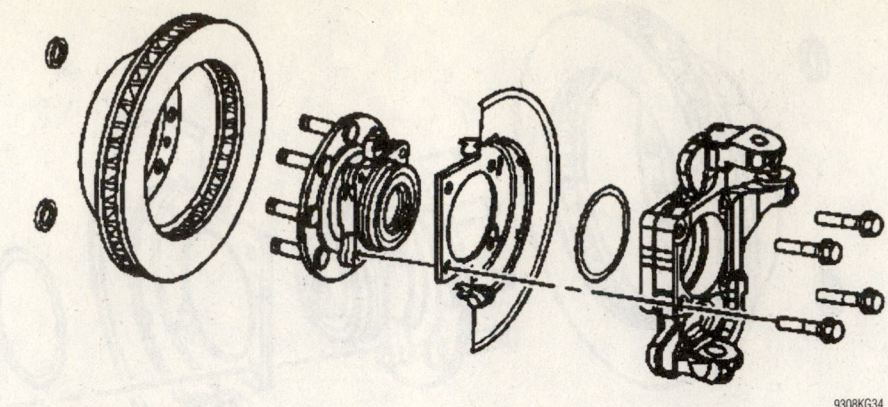

4WD front hub—25 Series Silverado

16. Install the hub and bearing assembly mounting bolts Tighten the hub to knuckle bolts to 180 Nm (133 ft. lbs.).

17. Disengage the front drive halfshaft assembly.

18. Connect the electrical connection for the wheel speed sensor.

19. Install the wheel speed sensor and brake hose mounting bracket bolt to the steering knuckle. Tighten the bolt to 12 Nm (106 inch lbs.).

20. Install the rotor.

21. Install the tire and wheel assembly.

GENERAL MOTORS CORP.

21

Chevrolet-Venture • **Oldsmobile**-Premier, Silhouette • **Pontiac**-Montana • Trans Sport

PRECAUTIONS

Before servicing any vehicle, please be sure to read all of the following precautions, which deal with personal safety, prevention of component damage, and important points to take into consideration when servicing a motor vehicle:

• Never open, service or drain the radiator or cooling system when the engine is hot; serious burns can occur from the steam and hot coolant.

• Observe all applicable safety precautions when working around fuel. Whenever servicing the fuel system, always work in a well-ventilated area. Do not allow fuel spray or vapors to come in contact with a spark, open flame or excessive heat (a hot drop light, for example). Keep a dry chemical fire extinguisher near the work area. Always keep fuel in a container specifically designed for fuel storage; also, always properly seal fuel containers to avoid the possibility of fire or explosion. Refer to the additional fuel system precautions later in this section.

• Fuel injection systems often remain pressurized, even after the engine has been turned **OFF**. The fuel system pressure must be relieved before disconnecting any fuel lines. Failure to do so may result in fire and/or personal injury.

• Brake fluid often contains polyglycol ethers and polyglycols. Avoid contact with the eyes and wash your hands thoroughly after handling brake fluid. If you do get brake fluid in your eyes, flush your eyes with clean, running water for 15 minutes. If eye irritation persists, or if you have taken brake fluid internally, IMMEDIATELY seek medical assistance.

• The EPA warns that prolonged contact with used engine oil may cause a number of skin disorders, including cancer! You should make every effort to minimize your exposure to used engine oil. Protective gloves should be worn when changing oil. Wash your hands and any other exposed skin areas as soon as possible after exposure to used engine oil. Soap and water, or waterless hand cleaner should be used.

• All new vehicles are now equipped with an air bag system, often referred to as a Supplemental Restraint System (SRS) or Supplemental Inflatable Restraint (SIR) system. The system must be disabled before performing service on or around system components, steering column, instrument panel components, wiring and sensors. Failure to follow safety and disabling procedures could result in accidental air bag deployment, possible personal injury and unnecessary system repairs.

• Always wear safety goggles when working with, or around, the air bag system. When carrying a non-deployed air bag, be sure the bag and trim cover are pointed away from your body. When placing a non-deployed air bag on a work surface, always face the bag and trim cover upward, away from the surface. This will reduce the motion of the module if it is accidentally deployed. Refer to the additional air bag system precautions later in this section.

• Clean, high quality brake fluid from a sealed container is essential to the safe and proper operation of the brake system. You should always buy the correct type of brake fluid for your vehicle. If the brake fluid becomes contaminated, completely flush the system with new fluid. Never reuse any brake fluid. Any brake fluid that is removed from the system should be discarded. Also, do not allow any brake fluid to come in contact with a painted surface; it will damage the paint.

• Never operate the engine without the proper amount and type of engine oil; doing so WILL result in severe engine damage.

• Timing belt maintenance is extremely important! Many models utilize an interference-type, non-freewheeling engine. If the timing belt breaks, the valves in the cylinder head may strike the pistons, causing potentially serious (also time-consuming and expensive) engine damage. Refer to the maintenance interval charts in the front of this manual for the recommended replacement interval for the timing belt, and to the timing belt section for belt replacement and inspection.

• Disconnecting the negative battery cable on some vehicles may interfere with the functions of the on-board computer system(s) and may require the computer to undergo a relearning process once the negative battery cable is reconnected.

• When servicing drum brakes, only disassemble and assemble one side at a time, leaving the remaining side intact for reference.

ENGINE REPAIR

Distributor

This engine utilizes a Distributorless ignition system (DIS). There is no distributor to remove and no provision for adjustment.

Alternator

REMOVAL

1. Before servicing the vehicle, refer to the precautions in the beginning of this section.
2. Remove or disconnect the following:
   • Negative battery cable
   • Wiper system module cover
   • Fuel injector sight shield
3. Rotate the engine forward.
4. Remove or disconnect the following:
   • Alternator terminal nut, lead and electrical connector
   • Serpentine belt
   • Front bolts and two rear bolts
   • Alternator from the bracket
   • Serpentine belt tensioner
   • Bracket
   • Power steering pipes from the retainer
   • Fuel pressure test port cap from the injector rail

➡**Do not disconnect the power steering pipes from the pump**

   • Power steering pump and reposition it to gain access to the alternator
   • Alternator

INSTALLATION

1. Install or connect the following:
   • Alternator
   • Power steering pump. Torque the bolts to 25 ft. lbs. (34 Nm).
   • Fuel pressure test port cap to the fuel rail
   • Power steering pipes to the retainer. Torque the fastener to 54 inch lbs. (6 Nm).
   • Alternator bracket. Torque the bolt to 37 ft. lbs. (50 Nm).
   • Serpentine belt tensioner
   • Alternator to the bracket. Torque the bolts to 37 ft. lbs. (50 Nm).

- Serpentine belt
- Alternator electrical connector, lead and nut. Torque the nut to 115 inch lbs. (13 Nm).

2. Rotate the engine to its original position.

3. Install or connect the following:
   - Fuel injector sight shield. Torque the nut to 54 inch lbs. (6 Nm).
   - Wiper system module cover
   - Negative battery cable

4. Perform a charging system test and verify the proper operation of the system.

Engine Assembly

REMOVAL & INSTALLATION

1. Before servicing the vehicle, refer to the precautions in the beginning of this section.

2. Drain the cooling system.

3. Drain the engine oil.

4. Relieve the fuel system pressure.

5. Remove or disconnect the following:
   - Negative battery cable
   - Fuel injector sight shield
   - Throttle body air inlet duct
   - Cruise control cable
   - Accelerator control cable
   - Radiator hoses from the engine
   - Heater hoses from the engine
   - Engine mount struts
   - Fuel lines from the fuel rail
   - Engine wiring harness connectors
   - Vacuum hoses
   - Brake booster vacuum hose
   - Automatic transaxle range selector cable
   - Wiring harness grounds
   - Catalytic converter three-way pipe from the right side exhaust manifold
   - Front wheels
   - Splash shields
   - Stabilizer shaft links from the lower control arms
   - Tie rod ends from the steering knuckles
   - Lower ball joints from the steering knuckles
   - Cooler lines and bracket from the transaxle
   - Axles from the transaxle and secure them to the steering knuckle/struts

✳✳ CAUTION

Failure to remove the intermediate shaft from the steering gear may result in damage to the gear or intermediate shaft and may cause a loss of steering control.

6. Remove or disconnect the following:
   - Intermediate shaft from the steering gear
   - Frame bolts and make certain that an engine stand (such as J 39580) is aligned below the engine
   - Engine to transaxle bolts and studs
   - Engine flywheel to torque converter bolts
   - Engine from the transaxle and place it on the engine stand

To install:

7. Install or connect the following:
   - Engine to the transaxle/frame and install the bolts. Torque the bolts to 133 ft. lbs. (180 Nm) for 1997 or to 55 ft. lbs. (75 Nm) for 1998–01.
   - Torque converter to flywheel bolts. Torque the bolts to 47 ft. lbs. (63 Nm).
   - New frame to body bolts. Torque them to 118 ft. lbs. (160 Nm).
   - Interdemiate shaft to the steering gear

✳✳ CAUTION

When installing the intermediate shaft be certain that the shaft is seated properly before installing the pinch bolt. If the pinch bolt is inserted into the coupling before the shaft, the mating surfaces disengage. Disengagement of the two shafts may lead to a loss of steering control.

- Pinch bolt at the intermediate shaft. Torque the bolt 35 ft. lbs. (48 Nm)
- Drive axles to the transaxle.
- Cooler lines and bracket to the transaxle. Torque the fasteners to 17 ft. lbs. (23 Nm).
- Lower ball joints to the steering knuckles. Torque to 40 ft. lbs. (55 Nm).
- Tie rod ends to the steering knuckles
- Stabilizer shaft links to the lower control arms. Torque the bolts 17 ft. lbs. (23 Nm).
- Inner fender splash shield. Torque the fasteners to 18 inch lbs. (2 Nm).
- Front wheels

- Catalytic converter pipe to the right side exhaust manifold. Torque the nuts to 25 ft. lbs. (34 Nm).
- Wiring harness grounds
- Brake booster vacuum hose
- Vacuum hoses to the engine
- Range selector cable. Torque the screw to 14 ft. lbs. (20 Nm).
- Engine wiring harness connectors
- Fuel lines to the fuel rail. Torque the fasteners to 13 ft. lbs. (17 Nm).
- Throttle body brackets and cables. Torque the fasteners to 18 ft. lbs. (25 Nm).
- Engine mount strut. Torque the bolt to 35 ft. lbs. (48 Nm).
- Heater hoses
- Radiator hoses

✳✳ CAUTION

Whenever the engine has been removed from the vehicle it is necessary to install a new accelerator control cable to avoid damage or personal injury.

- New accelerator control cable
- Cruise control cable
- Throttle body air inlet duct
- Fuel injector sight shield
- Negative battery cable

8. Fill the engine with oil.

9. Fill the engine with coolant.

10. Inspect the transmission fluid level and top off, if necessary.

11. Turn the ignition to the **ON** position several times to pressurize the fuel system.

12. Start the engine and inspect for leaks, repair if necessary.

13. Check and top off the fluid levels if required.

Water Pump

REMOVAL & INSTALLATION

1. Before servicing the vehicle, refer to the precautions in the beginning of this section.

2. Drain the coolant from the engine.

3. Remove or disconnect the following:
   - Negative battery cable
   - Serpentine drive belt guard
   - Loosen the water pump pulley bolts
   - Serpentine drive belt
   - Water pump pulley
   - Water pump
   - Water pump gasket

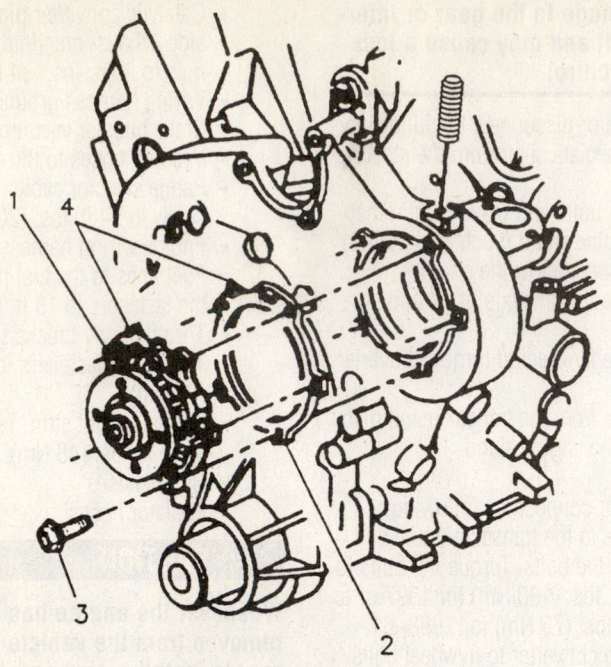

1 WATER PUMP
2 GASKET
3 10 N•m (89 LB. IN.)
4 LOCATOR — MUST BE VERTICAL

7924LG01

Water pump assembly mounting

To install:

4. Clean the gasket mounting surfaces.
5. Install or connect the following:
   - Gasket
   - Water pump. Torque the bolts to 89 inch lbs. (10 Nm).
   - Water pump pulley and hand-tighten the bolts at this time.
   - Serpentine drive belt
   - Torque the water pump pulley bolts to 18 inch lbs. (25 Nm).
   - Serpentine drive belt guard
   - Fill the cooling system
6. Start the engine and check for leaks, repair if necessary.
7. Road test the vehicle and verify there is no air in the cooling system.

Cylinder Head

REMOVAL & INSTALLATION

This engine uses aluminum cylinder heads. Use care when working with light alloy parts. Valve guides are pressed in. Roller rocker arms are located on a pedestal in a slot in the cylinder head and are retained on individual threaded bolts.

The cylinder heads are retained by torque-to-yield bolts. A torque angle meter is required for proper torque during assembly. New replacement head bolts are recommended.

Before removing the cylinder head(s) from the engine and before disassembling the valve mechanism, perform a compression test and note the results. During disassembly, be sure that the valvetrain components are kept together and identified so that they can be installed in their original locations.

Left (Front) Side

1. Before servicing the vehicle, refer to the precautions in the beginning of this section.
2. Relieve the fuel system pressure using the recommended procedure.
3. Drain the cooling system.
4. Drain the oil.
5. Remove or disconnect the following:
   - Negative battery cable
   - Upper intake manifold
   - Lower intake manifold
   - Valve rocker arms and pushrods
   - Exhaust crossover pipe
   - Thermostat bypass pipe
   - Right side engine mount strut bracket
   - Oil level indicator tube
   - Left side spark plug wires and spark plugs
   - Left side exhaust manifold
   - Left side cylinder head and gasket

To install:

6. Clean all parts well. Clean all gasket surfaces. Carefully remove all varnish soot and carbon to the bare metal. DO NOT use a motorized wire brush on any gasket surface since the soft aluminum will be damaged. If necessary, the head can be disassembled for thorough inspection and reconditioning.
7. Inspect the cylinder head for cracks. Do not attempt to weld the cylinder head. If cracked, replace it. Check the cylinder head deck, intake and exhaust manifold mating surfaces for flatness. These surfaces may be reconditioned by milling. If the surfaces are warped more than 0.005 in. (0.127mm), the surface should be milled. If more than 0.010 in. (0.251mm) of metal must be removed from the head, the head should be replaced.
8. Clean the cylinder head bolts and the bolt holes. Check the head bolts for damaged threads or stretching. New replacement head bolts are recommended.

➡ **Refer to Section 1 of this manual for the cylinder head torque sequence illustration. The illustration is located after the Torque Specification Chart.**

9. Install or connect the following:
   - New cylinder head gasket which is marked which side is **UP**
   - Cylinder head by aligning it with the dowel pins
   - New cylinder head bolts coated with a sealant (such as GM 1052080). Torque the bolts in the proper sequence (1-8) to 37 ft. lbs. (50 Nm). Using a torque angle meter turn the bolts 90 degrees in the proper sequence.
   - Left side exhaust manifold. Torque the bolts to 12 ft. lbs. (16 Nm).
   - Spark plugs. Torque the plugs 11 ft. lbs. (15 Nm).
   - Spark plug wires
   - Oil level indicator tube. Torque the fastener to 18 ft. lbs. (25 Nm).
   - Right side mount strut bracket. Torque the fastener to 37 ft. lbs. (50 Nm).
   - Thermostat bypass pipe. Torque it to 18 ft. lbs. (25 Nm).
   - Exhaust crossover pipe. Torque the fastener to 18 ft. lbs. (25 Nm).
   - Valve rocker arms and pushrods. Torque the fastener to 89 inch lbs. (10 Nm). Using a torque angle meter torque the fastener an additional 30 degrees.

- Lower intake manifold. Torque the bolts to 115 inch lbs. (13 Nm).
- Upper intake manifold. Torque the bolts to 18 ft. lbs. (25 Nm).
- Negative battery cable

10. Refill the coolant system.

11. Change the oil filter and fill the engine with clean oil.

12. Turn the ignition to the **ON** position several times to pressurize the fuel system. Start the engine and inspect for any leaks, repair if necessary. Check and top off the fluid levels if required.

Right (Rear) Side

1. Before servicing the vehicle, refer to the precautions in the beginning of this section.

2. Relieve the fuel system pressure using the recommended procedure.

3. Drain the coolant system.

4. Drain the oil from the engine.

5. Remove or disconnect the following:
- Negative battery cable
- Upper intake manifold
- Lower intake manifold
- Valve rocker arms and pushrods
- Exhaust crossover pipe
- Right side spark plug wires
- Right side exhaust manifold
- Right side cylinder head and gasket
- Right side spark plugs from the cylinder head

To install:

6. Clean all parts well. Clean all gasket surfaces. Carefully remove all varnish soot and carbon to the bare metal. DO NOT use a motorized wire brush on any gasket surface since the soft aluminum will be damaged. If necessary, the head can be disassembled for thorough inspection and reconditioning.

7. Inspect the cylinder head for cracks. Do not attempt to weld the cylinder head. If cracked, replace it. Check the cylinder head deck, intake and exhaust manifold mating surfaces for flatness. These surfaces may be reconditioned by milling. If the surfaces are "out of flat" by more than 0.005 inch, the surface should be milled. If more than 0.010 inch of metal must be removed from the head, the head should be replaced.

8. Clean the cylinder head bolts and the bolt holes. Check the head bolts for damaged threads or stretching. New replacement head bolts are recommended.

➡**Refer to Section 1 of this manual for the cylinder head torque sequence illustration. The illustration is located after the Torque Specification Chart.**

9. Install or connect the following:
- New cylinder head gasket
- Cylinder head on top of the gasket and make certain it is lined up properly with the dowel pins
- New cylinder head bolts coated with a sealant (such as GM 1052080). Torque the bolts in the proper sequence (1-8) to 37 ft. lbs. (50 Nm). Using a torque angle meter turn the bolts 90 degrees in the proper sequence.
- Right side exhaust manifold. Torque the bolts to 12 ft. lbs. (16 Nm).
- Spark plugs. Torque the plugs 11 ft. lbs. (15 Nm).
- Spark plug wires
- Exhaust crossover pipe. Torque the fastener to 18 ft. lbs. (25 Nm).
- Valve rocker arms and pushrods. Torque the fastener to 89 inch lbs. (10 Nm). Using a torque angle meter torque the fastener an additional 30 degrees.
- Lower intake manifold. Torque the bolts to 115 inch lbs. (13 Nm).
- Upper intake manifold. Torque the bolts to 18 ft. lbs. (25 Nm).
- Negative battery cable

10. Refill the coolant system.

11. Change the oil filter and fill the engine with clean oil.

12. Start the vehicle and verify no leaks, abnormal noises and correct engine operation.

13. Check the fluid levels and top off if necessary.

Rocker Arms

REMOVAL & INSTALLATION

➡**Valve train components which are to be reused must be installed in their original positions. If removed, be sure to tag or arrange all rocker arms and pushrods to assure proper installation.**

1. Before servicing the vehicle, refer to the precautions in the beginning of this section.

2. Remove or disconnect the following:
- Negative battery cable
- Rocker arm cover
- Rocker arm bolts
- Rocker arms

➡**Place the valve train parts in order to ensure they are installed in the proper**

location. **Intake pushrods are yellow and measure 5.68 inches (144.18mm). Exhaust pushrods are green and measure 6.0 inches (152.51mm). When removing the pushrods, make certain they do not fall into the lifter valley.**

- Pushrods

To install:

3. Inspect and replace components if worn or damaged. Clean all old thread locking material from the pedestal bolts.

4. Coat the bearing surface of the rocker arms, pushrods and rocker arm bolts with a prelube (such as GM 1052365). Make certain to install the components in their original position.

5. Install or connect the following:
- Intake valve pushrods which are 5.68 inches (144.18mm) long
- Exhaust valve pushrods which are 6.0 inches (152.51mm) long
- Rocker arms. Torque the bolt to 14 ft. lbs. (19 Nm) plus 30 degrees
- Rocker arm cover. Torque the bolt to 89 inch lbs. (10 Nm).
- Negative battery cable

6. Start the engine and verify the vehicle is running properly.

Intake Manifold

REMOVAL & INSTALLATION

Upper

This engine uses a 2-piece intake manifold. The upper half (often called a plenum) mounts the throttle body. The lower half of the manifold bolts to the engine and contains the fuel injectors. Please note that this engine uses a sequential multi-port fuel injection system. Injector connectors must be connected to their appropriate fuel injector assembly or engine emissions and engine performance will be seriously affected. Identify and tag for identification all wiring connectors as well as vacuum and other components as required to assure correct assembly.

1. Before servicing the vehicle, refer to the precautions in the beginning of this section.

2. Drain the engine coolant. Remove the coolant recovery bottle.

3. Relieve the fuel system pressure using the recommended procedure.

4. Remove or disconnect the following:
- Negative battery cable
- Throttle body air inlet duct

Timing belt service is covered in Section 4 of this manual

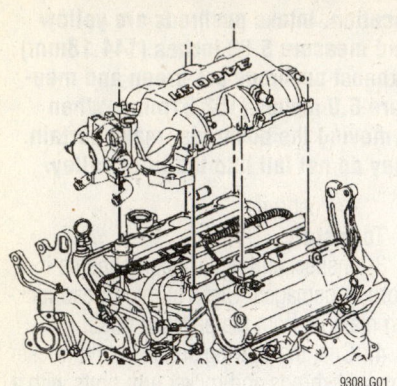

Remove upper intake manifold

- Accelerator and cruise control cables and bracket from the throttle body
- Throttle Position (TP) sensor connector from the throttle body
- Idle Air Control (IAC) valve connector from the throttle body
- Left side spark plug wires
- Left side spark plug wire harness clip and harness
- Throttle body heater hoses
- Evaporative emissions (EVAP) canister purge solenoid valve vacuum hoses
- EVAP canister purge solenoid valve
- Ignition coil bracket and coils
- Wire harness for the Manifold Air Pressure (MAP) sensor and upper intake manifold
- Emissions control vacuum harness
- Brake booster vacuum hose from the upper intake manifold
- Vacuum hose connection for the Heater Vent Air Conditioning (HVAC) source hose
- Vacuum hose connection for the fuel pressure regulator
- Exhaust Gas Recirculation (EGR) valve
- MAP sensor and bracket
- Upper intake manifold
- Upper intake manifold gasket
- Throttle body, if replacing the manifold

To install:

5. Clean all parts well. Use care in cleaning old gasket material from the machined aluminum surfaces on the plenum and manifold as sharp tools may damage sealing surfaces.

6. Clean the mating surfaces to the upper intake manifold and engine block. Remove any loose pieces of RTV sealer.

7. Install or connect the following:
- Throttle body to the upper intake manifold (if removed). Torque the

bolts to 18 ft. lbs. (25 Nm).
- Upper intake manifold gasket
- Upper intake manifold
- MAP sensor and bracket. Torque the bolt to 44 inch lbs. (5 Nm).
- Upper intake manifold bolts. Torque the bolts to 18 ft. lbs. (25 Nm).
- EGR valve. Torque the fastener to 18 ft. lbs. (25 Nm).
- HVAC vacuum source hose to the upper intake manifold
- Fuel pressure regulator vacuum hose to the upper intake manifold
- Brake booster vacuum hose
- MAP sensor and bracket. Torque the bolt to 44 inch lbs. (5 Nm).
- Emissions control vacuum harness
- Vacuum hose for the MAP sensor
- Wiring harness to the MAP sensor
- Ignition coil bracket and coils. Torque the fasteners to 18 ft. lbs. (25 Nm).
- EVAP canister purge solenoid valve
- Vacuum hoses to the EVAP canister purge solenoid valve
- Throttle body heater hose
- Left side spark plug wire harness clip
- Spark plugs wires
- TP sensor wire harness connector to the throttle body
- IAV valve wire harness connector to the throttle body
- Accelerator and cruise control cables and bracket to the throttle body. Torque the fasteners to 106 inch lbs. (12 Nm).
- Throttle body air inlet duct
- Negative battery cable

8. Fill the coolant system.

9. Fill the engine with new oil.

10. Turn the ignition to the **ON** position several times to pressurize the fuel system.

11. Start the engine and check for any leakage and repair if necessary.

12. Check and top off all fluid levels if needed.

Lower

This engine uses a 2-piece intake manifold. The upper half (often called a plenum) mounts the throttle body. The lower half of the manifold bolts to the engine and contains the fuel injectors. Please note that this engine uses a sequential multi-port fuel injection system. Injector connectors must be connected to their appropriate fuel injector assembly or engine emissions and engine performance will be seriously affected.

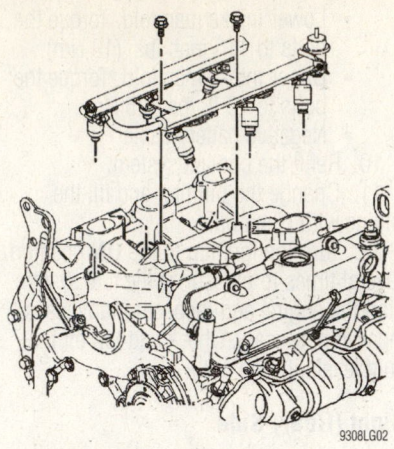

Remove the fuel injector rail

Identify and tag for identification all wiring connectors as well as vacuum and other components as required to assure correct assembly.

1. Before servicing the vehicle, refer to the precautions in the beginning of this section.

2. Drain the engine coolant.

3. Relieve the fuel system pressure using the recommended procedure.

4. Remove or disconnect the following:
- Negative battery cable
- Upper intake manifold
- Left side valve rocker arm cover
- Right side valve rocker arm cover
- Wire harness from the Engine Coolant Temperature (ECT) sensor
- Fuel injector, Manifold Absolute Pressure (MAP) and ECT wire harness
- Fuel feed and return pipe from the injector rail
- Fuel injector rail
- Power steering pump from the front cover

➡ **Do not disconnect the power steering pipes or hoses from the steering pump.**

- Heater inlet pipe with the heater hose from the lower intake manifold
- Radiator inlet hose
- Thermostat bypass hose from the manifold
- Lower intake manifold
- Pushrods after loosening the rocker arms
- Lower intake manifold gasket and seals
- ECT sensor, if replacing the manifold
- Thermostat and housing, if replacing the manifold

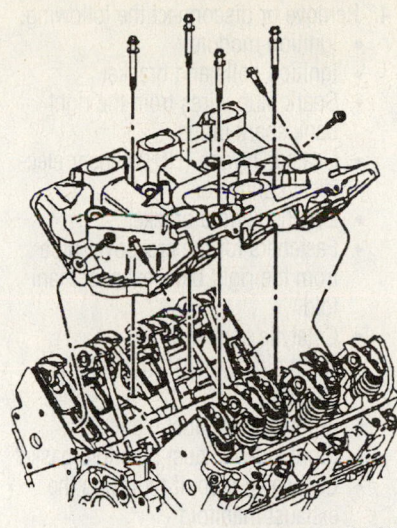

Lower intake manifold assembly

To install:

5. Clean the gasket mounting surfaces.

6. Inspect the intake manifold for cracks or damage, replace if necessary.

7. Install or connect the following:

- ECT sensor, if removed. Torque the sensor to 17 ft. lbs. (23 Nm).
- Thermostat and housing, if removed. Torque the fastener to 18 ft. Lbs. (25 Nm).
- Thin bead of RTV sealer (such as GM 12345739) on the ridge of the engine block where the lower intake manifold makes contact
- Lower intake manifold gaskets
- Pushrods and tighten the rocker arms. Torque the arms to 14 ft. lbs. (19 Nm) plus 30 degrees.
- Lower intake manifold. Torque the bolts to 115 inch lbs. (13 Nm) after applying a sealant (such as GM 12345382) to the threads of the bolts.
- Thermostat bypass hose to the lower intake manifold pipe. Torque the fastener to 18 ft. lbs. (25 Nm).
- Radiator inlet hose from the engine
- Power steering pump to the front cover
- Fuel injector rail. Torque the fastener to 89 inch lbs. (10 Nm).
- Fuel feed and return pipes to the injector rail. Torque the fasteners to 13 ft. lbs. (17 Nm).
- Wire harness for the fuel injector, MAP sensor and the ECT sensor
- Right side rocker arm cover. Torque the bolts to 89 inch lbs. (10 Nm).

- Left side rocker arm cover. Torque the bolts to 89 inch lbs. (10 Nm).
- Upper intake manifold. Torque the bolts to 18 ft. lbs. (25 Nm).
- Negative battery cable

8. Fill the coolant system.

9. Turn the ignition to the **ON** position several times to pressurize the fuel system.

10. Start the engine and check for any leakage and repair if necessary.

11. Check and top off all fluid levels if needed.

Exhaust Manifold

REMOVAL & INSTALLATION

The exhaust manifolds are conventional iron castings. The left and right manifolds are connected by a crossover pipe. Use care with the exhaust manifold-to-cylinder head fasteners. The cylinder heads are aluminum.

Left (Front) Side

1. Before servicing the vehicle, refer to the precautions in the beginning of this section.

2. Drain the cooling system.

3. Remove or disconnect the following:

- Negative battery cable
- Throttle body air inlet duct
- Right side engine mount strut bracket
- Radiator inlet hose
- Thermostat bypass pipe
- Exhaust crossover pipe heat shield
- Exhaust crossover pipe
- Left side exhaust manifold heat shield
- Left side exhaust manifold and discard the gasket

To install:

4. Clean the gasket mounting surfaces.

5. Install or connect the following:

- Left side exhaust manifold gasket
- Left side exhaust manifold. Torque the nuts to 12 ft. lbs. (16 Nm).
- Left side exhaust manifold heat shield. Torque the fasteners to 89 inch lbs. (10 Nm).
- Exhaust crossover pipe. Torque the bolts to 18 ft. lbs. (25 Nm).
- Exhaust crossover pipe heat shield. Torque the bolts to 89 inch lbs. (10 Nm).

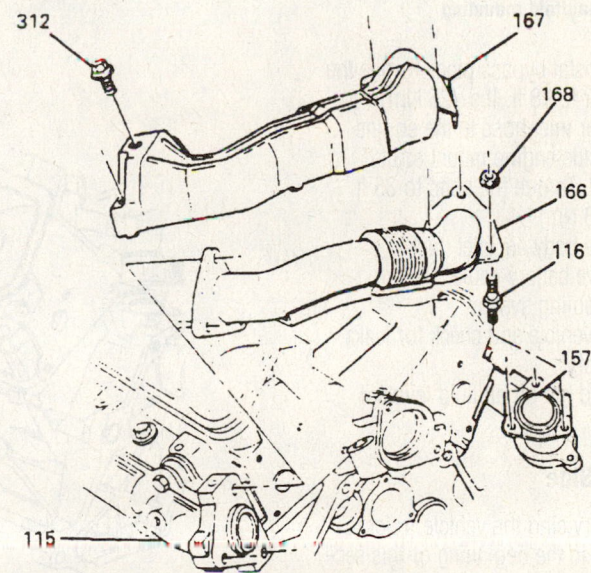

115	MANIFOLD, LEFT HAND EXHAUST
116	STUD, EXHAUST CROSSOVER
157	MANIFOLD, RIGHT HAND EXHAUST
166	CROSSOVER PIPE, EXHAUST
167	SHIELD, EXHAUST CROSSOVER UPPER HEAT
168	NUT, EXHAUST CROSSOVER
312	BOLT/SCREW, EXHAUST CROSSOVER UPPER HEAT SHIELD

Exploded view of the exhaust crossover and heat shield mounting

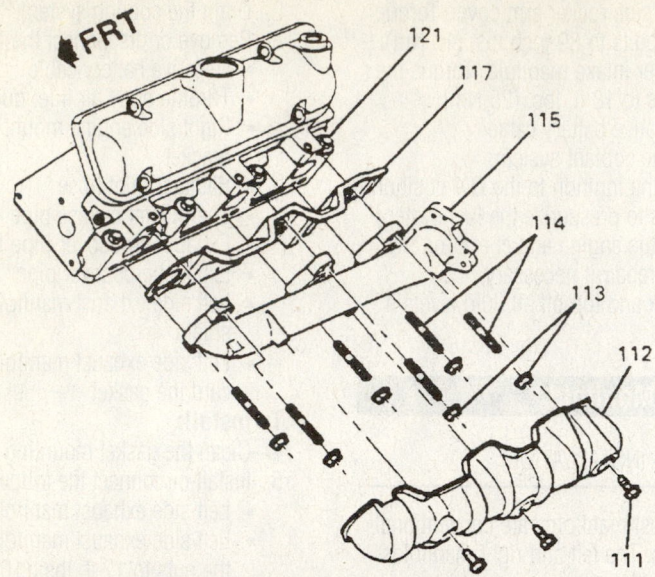

111 SCREW, LH EXHAUST MANIFOLD HEAT SHIELD
112 SHIELD LH EXHAUST MANIFOLD
113 NUT, LH EXHAUST MANIFOLD
114 STUD, LH EXHAUST MANIFOLD
115 MANIFOLD, LH EXHAUST
117 GASKET, LH EXHAUST MANIFOLD
121 HEAD, LH CYLINDER

7924LG29

Left exhaust manifold mounting

- Thermostat bypass pipe. Torque the fastener to 18 ft. lbs. (25 Nm).
- Radiator inlet hose to the engine
- Right side engine mount strut bracket. Torque the bolts to 35 ft. lbs. (48 Nm).
- Throttle body air inlet duct
- Negative battery cable

6. Fill the cooling system

7. Start the vehicle and check for leaks, repair if necessary.

8. Check and top off all fluid levels if necessary.

Right (Rear) Side

1. Before servicing the vehicle, refer to the precautions in the beginning of this section.

2. Remove or disconnect the following:
- Negative battery cable
- Windshield wiper motor cover
- Fuel injector sight shield
- Throttle body air inlet duct
- Accelerator cable bracket from the throttle body
- Manifold Absolute Pressure (MAP) sensor
- Exhaust Gas Recirculation (EGR) valve

3. Rotate the engine for access.

4. Remove or disconnect the following:
- Ignition module
- Ignition coils and bracket
- Spark plug wires from the right bank spark plugs
- Heated Oxygen (HO2) sensor electrical connector
- EVAP solenoid bracket
- Fasteners for the crossover pipe from the right bank exhaust manifold
- Catalytic converter
- Right side exhaust manifold heat shields
- Right side exhaust manifold
- Right side exhaust manifold gasket
- EGR valve pipe, if replacing the exhaust manifold
- HO2 sensor, if replacing the exhaust manifold

To install:
5. Clean the gasket mounting surfaces.
6. Install or connect the following:
- HO2 sensor, if removed. Torque the sensor to 31 ft. lbs. (42 Nm).
- EGR valve pipe, if removed. Torque the fastener to 18 ft. lbs. (25 Nm).
- Exhaust manifold gasket
- Exhaust manifold. Torque the bolts to 12 ft. lbs. (16 Nm).

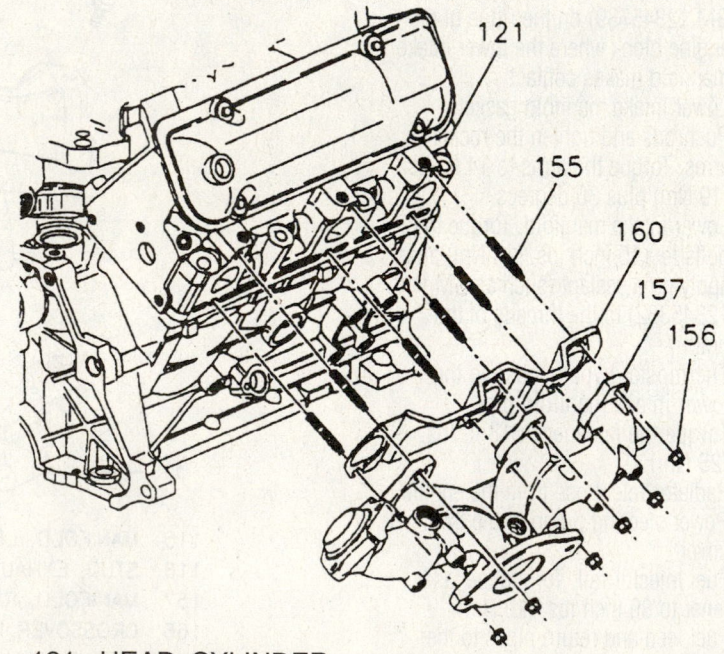

121 HEAD, CYLINDER
155 STUD, EXHAUST MANIFOLD
156 NUT, EXHAUST MANIFOLD
157 MANIFOLD RIGHT EXHAUST
160 GASKET, RIGHT EXHAUST MANIFOLD

7924LG30

Exploded view of the right exhaust manifold mounting

- Both manifold heat shields. Torque the bolts to 89 inch lbs. (10 Nm).
- Catalytic converter. Torque the fasteners to 25 ft. lbs. (34 Nm).
- Exhaust manifold crossover pipe. Torque the bolts to 18 ft. lbs. (25 Nm).
- HO_2 sensor electrical connector
- EVAP solenoid bracket
- Plug wires to the spark plugs
- Ignition module
- Ignition coils and bracket. Torque the fastener to 18 ft. lbs. (25 Nm).

7. Rotate the engine to its original position.

8. Install or connect the following:
- EGR valve to the intake manifold
- MAP sensor
- Accelerator cable bracket to the throttle body. Torque the bolt to 89 inch lbs. (10 Nm).
- Throttle body air inlet duct
- Windshield wiper motor cover
- Fuel injector sight shield
- Negative battery cable

9. Start the engine and inspect for leaks, repair if necessary.

Camshaft and Valve Lifters

REMOVAL & INSTALLATION

1. Before servicing the vehicle, refer to the precautions in the beginning of this section.

2. Relieve the fuel system pressure.

3. Remove or disconnect the following:
- Engine assembly

☀ WARNING

When removing valvetrain components they must be marked for installation in their original location. When the camshaft is being replaced, the valve lifters must also be replaced.

- Rocker arm covers
- Intake manifold
- Rocker arm bolts, balls, rocker arms and pushrods
- Lifter guide bolts and the guide
- Valve lifter(s) from the bores
- Crankshaft balancer and front cover
- Timing chain and sprockets
- Oil pump driven gear bolt and gear
- Camshaft thrust plate
- Camshaft

☀ WARNING

Avoid damaging the camshaft bearing surfaces.

To install:

4. Coat the camshaft with Prelube.

5. Install or connect the following:
- Camshaft
- Camshaft thrust plate. Tighten the bolts to 89 inch lbs. (10 Nm).
- Oil pump driven gear. Tighten the bolt to 27 ft. lbs. (36 Nm).
- Timing chain and sprocket
- Camshaft thrust button and front cover
- Crankshaft balancer

6. Lubricate the bearing surfaces with Molykote®.

➡ Installation of a new camshaft or a wear pattern on the old valve lifter will require the replacement of the camshaft and lifters together. If camshaft replacement is not necessary, be sure to install the used valve lifters in their original position.

7. Install or connect the following:
- Lifters in their original locations
- Lifter guide. Tighten the guide bolts to 89 inch lbs. (10 Nm).
- Pushrods, rocker arms, balls and bolts. Tighten the nuts to 89 inch lbs. (10 Nm) plus an additional 30 degree turn.
- Intake manifold
- Rocker arm covers
- Engine assembly
- Negative battery cable

8. Adjust the valves, as required. Start the engine and verify no oil leaks.

Valve Lash

ADJUSTMENT

Because the rocker arm fasteners are secured and tightened, valve lash is not adjustable. If a valve train problem is suspected, check that the rocker arm pedestals bolts are tightened to specification. During initial installation the bolts are coated with thread locking compound. If they are suffi-

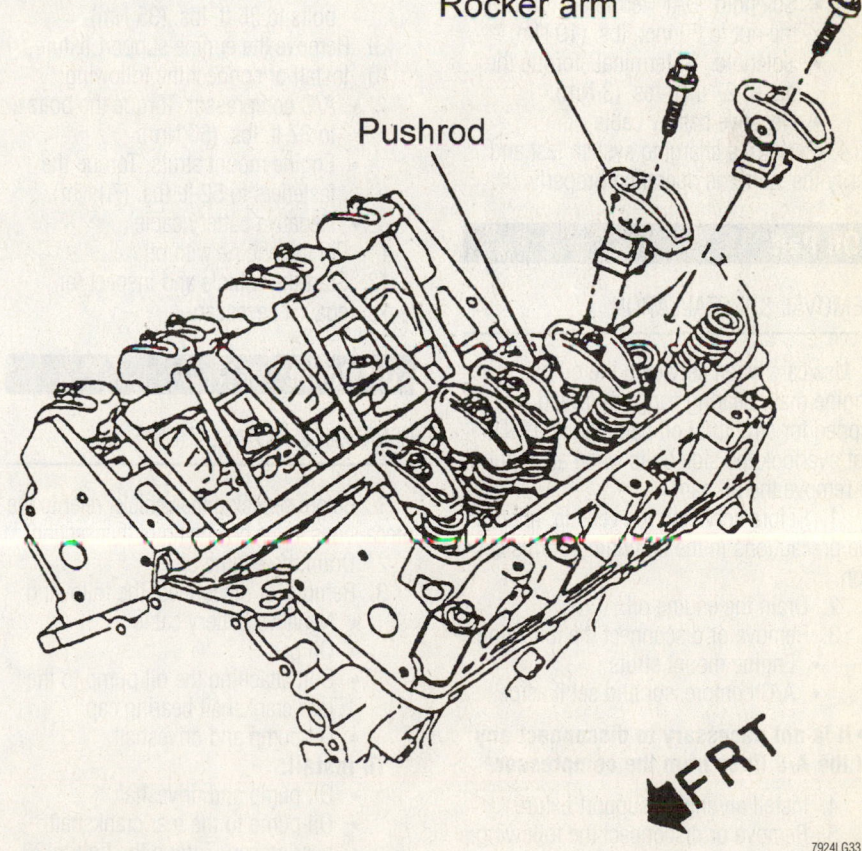

Rocker arm

Pushrod

FRT

Valve rocker arm and related components

7924LG33

Refer to Section 1 for engine rebuilding specifications

ciently loosened to cause valvetrain noise, they should be removed and thoroughly cleaned. Apply thread locking compound to the rocker arm pedestal bolts. Tighten the bolts to 14 ft. lbs. (19 Nm) plus 30 degrees.

When valve lash falls out of specification (valve tap is heard) and tightening the bolts does not solve the problem, replace the rocker arm, pushrod and hydraulic lifter on the offending cylinder.

Starter Motor

REMOVAL & INSTALLATION

1. Before servicing the vehicle, refer to the precautions in the beginning of this section.
2. Remove or disconnect the following:
   - Negative battery cable
   - Electrical connections
   - Torque converter cover
   - Starter

To install:
3. Install or connect the following:
   - Starter. Torque the bolts to 35 ft. lbs. (47 Nm).
   - Torque converter cover
   - Solenoid "BAT" terminal. Torque the nut to 89 inch lbs. (10 Nm).
   - Solenoid "S" terminal. Torque the nut to 27 inch lbs. (3 Nm).
   - Negative battery cable
4. Perform a charging system test and verify the starter is operating properly

Oil Pan

REMOVAL & INSTALLATION

Use care when servicing the oil pan. The engine main bearing caps are drilled and tapped for structural oil pan side bolts. Do not overlook the side bolts when attempting to remove the oil pan.

1. Before servicing the vehicle, refer to the precautions in the beginning of this section.
2. Drain the engine oil.
3. Remove or disconnect the following:
   - Engine mount struts
   - A/C compressor and set it aside

➡ **It is not necessary to disconnect any of the A/C lines from the compressor.**

4. Install an engine support fixture.
5. Remove or disconnect the following:
   - Catalytic converter pipe from the right side exhaust manifold
   - Oil level sensor wiring harness connector

   - Starter
   - Transaxle brace from the oil pan
   - Transaxle mount lower nuts
   - Engine mount lower nuts and raise the engine with the support fixture
   - Engine mount and bracket from the oil pan
   - Oil pan and gasket

To install:
6. Clean the gasket mounting surfaces.
7. Apply a small amount of sealer GM 1234579 on both sides of the bearing cap.
8. Install or connect the following:
   - Oil pan gasket
   - Oil pan. Tighten the bottom bolts to 18 ft. lbs. (25 Nm) and the side bolts to 37 ft. lbs. (50 Nm).
   - Engine mount and bracket to the oil pan. Torque the bolt to 43 ft. lbs. (58 Nm).
   - Lower the engine into position
   - Transaxle lower nuts. Torque the nuts to 90 inch lbs. (10 Nm).
   - Transaxle brace to the oil pan. Torque the bolts to 32 ft. lbs. (43 Nm).
   - Starter. Torque the bolts to 35 ft lbs. (47 Nm).
   - Catalytic converter pipe to the right side exhaust manifold. Torque the bolts to 26 ft. lbs. (35 Nm).
9. Remove the engine support fixture.
10. Install or connect the following:
    - A/C compressor. Torque the bolts to 37 ft. lbs. (50 Nm).
    - Engine mount struts. Torque the fasteners to 52 ft. lbs. (70 Nm).
    - Negative battery cable
11. Fill the engine with oil.
12. Start the vehicle and inspect for leaks, repair if necessary.

Oil Pump

REMOVAL & INSTALLATION

1. Before servicing the vehicle, refer to the precautions in the beginning of this section.
2. Drain the engine oil.
3. Remove or disconnect the following:
   - Negative battery cable
   - Oil pan
   - Bolt attaching the oil pump to the rear crankshaft bearing cap
   - Oil pump and driveshaft

To install:
   - Oil pump and driveshaft
   - Oil pump to the rear crankshaft bearing cap. Torque the bolt to 30 ft. lbs. (41 Nm).
   - Oil pan
   - Negative battery cable

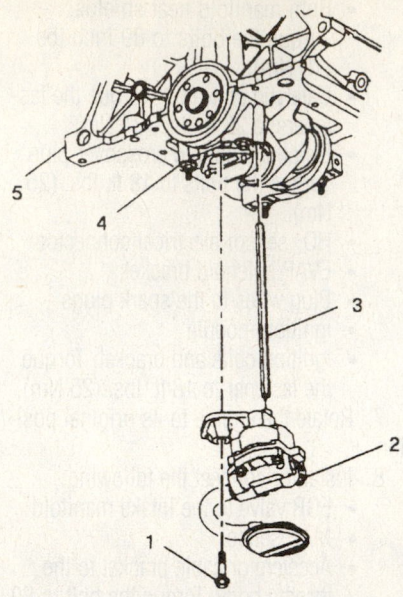

1. Oil pump bolt
2. Oil pump
3. Oil pump drive rod
4. Main bearing cap
5. Engine block

7924LG37

Exploded view of the oil pump mounting

4. Fill the engine with oil.
5. Start the vehicle and inspect for leaks, repair if necessary.

Rear Main Seal

REMOVAL & INSTALLATION

The transaxle assembly must be removed to perform this service. This requires special tooling to support the engine assembly while the transaxle and sub-frame are lowered from under the vehicle.

1. Before servicing the vehicle, refer to the precautions in the beginning of this section.
2. Remove or disconnect the following:
   - Negative battery cable
   - Transmission assembly
   - Engine flywheel
   - Oil seal

✻✻ WARNING

When removing the seal, use care so that no damage occurs to the crankshaft. Once the seal is removed, inspect the crankshaft surface for any nicks or burrs. Repair or replace crankshaft as necessary.

To install:
3. Install or connect the following:
   - New oil seal lubricated with engine

oil, using an Oil Seal Installer tool J 34686 until it is seated properly over the crankshaft
- Flywheel
- Transmission assembly
- Negative battery cable

4. Start the vehicle and check for leaks, repair if necessary.

Timing Chain, Sprockets, Front Cover and Seal

REMOVAL & INSTALLATION

1. Before servicing the vehicle, refer to the precautions in the beginning of this section.
2. Drain the engine oil.
3. Drain the coolant.
4. Remove or disconnect the following:
- Negative battery cable
- Crankshaft balancer
- Drive belt tensioner
- Power steering pump and lines. Do not disconnect the lines from the pump
- Thermostat bypass pipe from the front cover
- Radiator outlet hose from the water pump
- Water pump
- Upper and lower Crankshaft Posi-

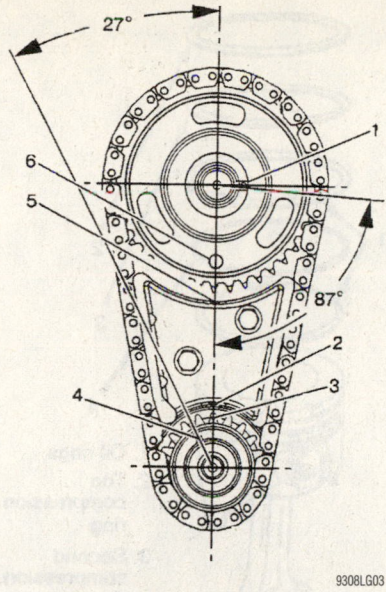

9308LG03

Crankshaft timing mark locations

tion (CKP) sensor wire harness bracket from the front cover
- CKP sensor from the front cover
- Front cover and gasket

5. Rotate the crankshaft until the timing marks are aligned in the following locations:
- Camshaft alignment pin (1)
- Timing chain damper (2) to the crankshaft sprocket (3)
- Crankshaft key (4)

- Timing chain damper (5) to the camshaft sprocket locator hole (6)
6. Remove or disconnect the following:
- Camshaft sprocket bolt
- Timing chain, timing chain sprockets and damper
- Front oil seal

To install:
7. Install or connect the following:
- New front oil seal by making certain the seal is fully seated
- Timing chain damper. Torque the bolts to 15 ft. lbs. (21 Nm).
- Timing chain to the camshaft sprocket
- Crankshaft sprocket
- Timing chain to the crankshaft sprocket by making certain the chain is fully seated
8. Align the crankshaft timing mark to the bottom mark on the damper.
9. Align the timing mark on the camshaft gear center line of the locator hole with the timing mark on the top of the damper.
10. Align the dowel in the camshaft with the dowel hole in the camshaft sprocket.
11. Install or connect the following:
- Camshaft sprocket bolt. Torque the bolt to 103 ft. lbs. (140 Nm).
- Front cover. Torque the 5 small bolts to 15 ft. lbs. (21 Nm), the 3 large bolts to 41 ft. lbs. (55 Nm)

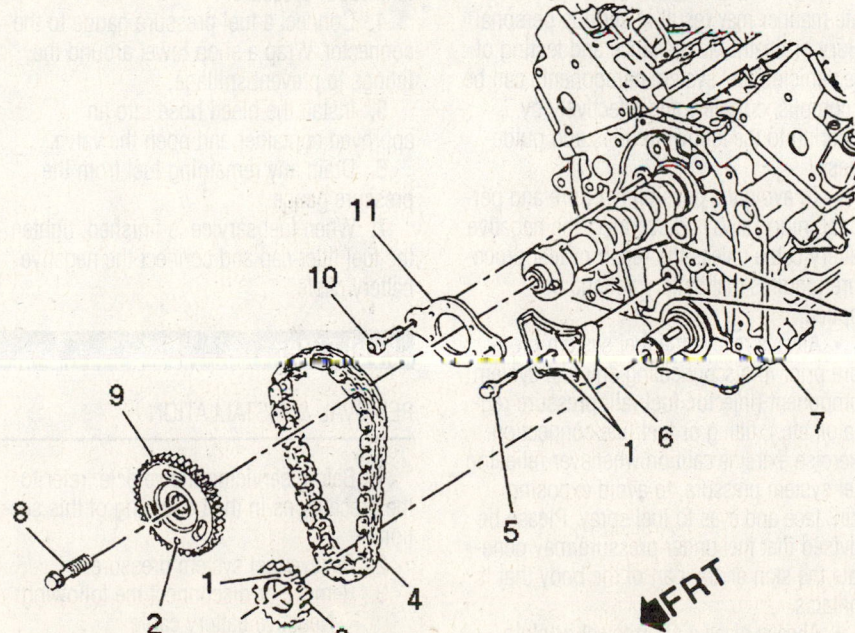

1. Timing alignment marks
2. Locator hole
3. Crankshaft sprocket
4. Timing chain
5. Timing chain dampener bolt
6. Timing chain dampener
7. Engine block
8. Camshaft sprocket bolt
9. Camshaft sprocket
10. Thrust plate bolt
11. Thrust plate

7924LG14

Exploded view of the timing chain assembly

For engine torque specifications, refer to Section 1 of this manual

and the 2 remaining bolts to 35 ft. lbs. (47 Nm).

- Water pump to the front cover. Torque the bolts to 89 inch lbs. (10 Nm).
- Water pump pulley. Torque the bolt to 18 ft. lbs. (25 Nm).
- CKP sensor to the front cover
- Upper/lower CKP wire harness brackets to the front cover
- Radiator outlet hose to the water pump
- Thermostat bypass pipe to the front cover
- Power steering pump and lines
- Drive belt tensioner
- Crankshaft balancer
- Negative battery cable

12. Fill the engine with oil.
13. Fill the coolant system.
14. Start the vehicle and verify that the engine is running properly.

Pistons and Ring

POSTIONING

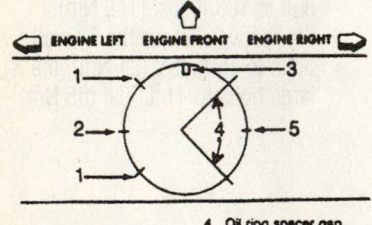

1. Oil ring rail gaps
2. 2nd Compression ring gap
3. Notch in piston
4. Oil ring spacer gap (tang in hole or slot with arc)
5. Top compression ring gap

7924AG07

Piston ring end-gap spacing—3.4L engine

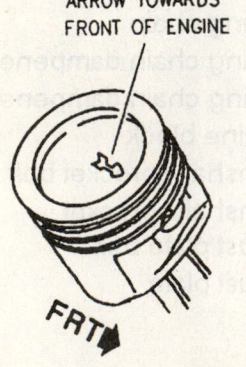

ARROW TOWARDS FRONT OF ENGINE

FRT

7922AG47

Piston positioning. Often the arrow is replaced with a notch, which must face toward the front of the engine—3.4L engine

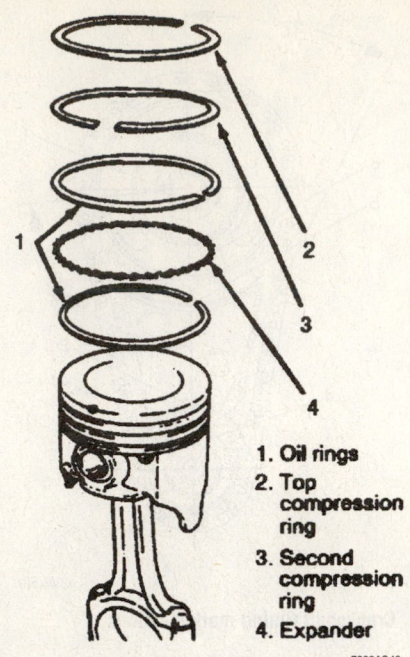

1. Oil rings
2. Top compression ring
3. Second compression ring
4. Expander

7922AG48

Piston ring positioning—3.4L engine

FUEL SYSTEM

Fuel System Service Precaution

Safety is the most important factor when performing not only fuel system maintenance but any type of maintenance. Failure to conduct maintenance and repairs in a safe manner may result in serious personal injury or death. Maintenance and testing of the vehicle's fuel system components can be accomplished safely and effectively by adhering to the following rules and guidelines.

- To avoid the possibility of fire and personal injury, always disconnect the negative battery cable unless the repair or test procedure requires that battery voltage be applied.
- Always relieve the fuel system pressure prior to disconnecting any fuel system component (injector, fuel rail, pressure regulator, etc.), fitting or fuel line connection. Exercise extreme caution whenever relieving fuel system pressure, to avoid exposing skin, face and eyes to fuel spray. Please be advised that fuel under pressure may penetrate the skin or any part of the body that it contacts.
- Always place a shop towel or cloth around the fitting or connection prior to loosening to absorb any excess fuel due to spillage. Ensure that all fuel spillage (should it occur) is quickly removed from engine surfaces. Ensure that all fuel soaked cloths or towels are deposited into a suitable waste container.
- Always keep a dry chemical (Class B) fire extinguisher near the work area.
- Do not allow fuel spray or fuel vapors to come into contact with a spark or open flame.
- Always use a back-up wrench when loosening and tightening fuel line connection fittings. This will prevent unnecessary stress and torsion to fuel line piping. Always follow the proper torque specifications.
- Always replace worn fuel fitting O-rings with new ones. Do not substitute fuel hose, or equivalent, where fuel pipe is installed.

Fuel System Pressure

RELIEVING

A Schrader valve is provided on these fuel systems to conveniently test or release the system pressure. A fuel pressure gauge and adapter will be necessary to connect the gauge to the fitting. Most of the MFI systems utilize a service valve on one end of the fuel rail assembly.

1. Before servicing the vehicle, refer to the precautions in the beginning of this section.
2. Disconnect the negative battery cable
3. Loosen the fuel filler cap to relieve tank vapor pressure.
4. Connect a fuel pressure gauge to the connector. Wrap a shop towel around the fittings to prevent spillage.
5. Install the bleed hose into an approved container and open the valve.
6. Drain any remaining fuel from the pressure gauge.
7. When fuel service is finished, tighten the fuel filler cap and connect the negative battery cable.

Fuel Filter

REMOVAL & INSTALLATION

1. Before servicing the vehicle, refer to the precautions in the beginning of this section.
2. Relieve fuel system pressure.
3. Remove or disconnect the following:
   - Negative battery cable
   - Quick connect fittings at the inlet/outlet sides of the in-pipe fuel filter
   - Fuel filter and drain any remaining fuel

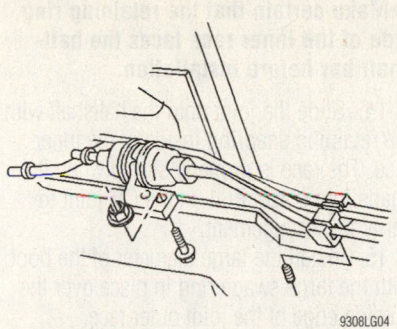

Fuel filter component identification—the fuel filter is located on the frame rail near the tank

To install:

4. Install or connect the following:
   - Fuel filter to the bracket
   - Fuel filter assembly to the side rail near the fuel tank. Torque the nut to 89 inch lbs. (10 Nm).
   - Inlet/outlet quick connectors to the fuel filter
   - Negative battery cable

5. Start the vehicle and checks for leaks, repair if necessary.

Fuel Pump

REMOVAL & INSTALLATION

1. Before servicing the vehicle, refer to the precautions in the beginning of this section.
2. Properly relieve the fuel system pressure.
3. Drain and remove the fuel tank from the vehicle
4. Remove or disconnect the following:
   - Negative battery cable
   - Quick connect fittings at the fuel pump
   - Fuel pump locking nut with a Fuel Pump Spanner Wrench J 39348
   - Fuel pump assembly from the fuel tank and discard the O-ring

To install:

5. Install or connect the following:
   - New O-ring on the fuel tank
   - Fuel pump into the fuel tank making certain not to fold or twist the strainer and that it does not interfere with the full travel of the float arm
   - Fuel pump locking nut with the scanner tool
   - Quick connect fittings at the fuel pump

- Fuel tank and fill the tank
- Negative battery cable

6. Prime the fuel system as follows:
   a. Turn the ignition switch **ON** for two seconds.
   b. Turn the ignition switch **OFF** for 10 seconds.
   c. Turn the ignition switch **ON** and checks for leaks. Repair if necessary.

Fuel Injector

REMOVAL & INSTALLATION

1. Before servicing the vehicle, refer to the precautions in the beginning of this section.
2. Relieve the fuel system pressure.
3. Remove or disconnect the following:
   - Negative battery cable
   - Upper intake manifold
   - Fuel rail
   - Fuel injector retaining clips and injectors
   - O-rings and discard them

To install:

➡**When replacing the fuel injector O-rings install the brown O-ring in the lower position. The lower O-ring uses a nylon collar to properly position it on the injector. Be sure to install the O-ring backup or the sealing O-ring may move when the injector is installed to the fuel rail. If the sealing ring is not seated properly, a vacuum leak is possible thus causing driveability complaints.**

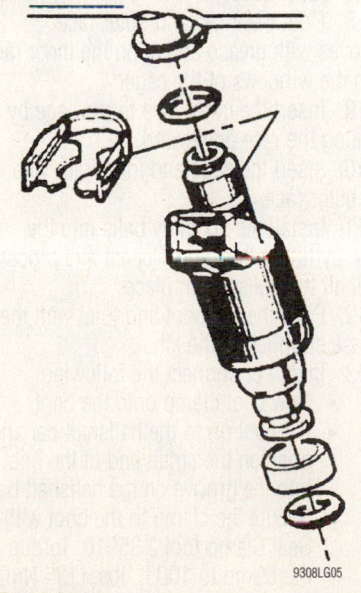

Fuel injector

4. Install or connect the following:
   - Upper O-ring to the fuel injector
   - Lower O-ring backup to the injector
   - Lower O-ring to the injector
   - Fuel injector to the fuel rail
   - Fuel rail with the retaining clips
   - Upper intake manifold
   - Negative battery cable

5. Prime the fuel system as follows:
   a. Turn the ignition switch **ON** for two seconds.
   b. Turn the ignition switch **OFF** for 10 seconds.
   c. Turn the ignition switch **ON** and checks for leaks. Repair if necessary.

DRIVE TRAIN

Transaxle Assembly

REMOVAL & INSTALLATION

The automatic transaxle can be removed only as an assembly with the engine and subframe. See the procedures under Engine Removal and Installation.

Halfshaft

REMOVAL & INSTALLATION

1. Before servicing the vehicle, refer to the precautions in the beginning of this section.
2. Remove or disconnect the following:
   - Front wheel
   - Stabilizer shaft link
   - Tie rod end from the steering knuckle
   - Lower ball joint from the steering knuckle by inserting a flat blade tool through the caliper hole and into the rotor to prevent the rotor from rotating
   - Halfshaft nut
   - Halfshaft from the wheel bearing/hub with a front hub spindle remover tool
   - Right side halfshaft from the transaxle with an axle shaft remover tool
   - Left side halfshaft by installing a flat blade tool between the lower control arm and the frame. Insert

the tip of the blade into the groove of the tri-pot joint
- Left side halfshaft

To install:

3. Install or connect the following:
- Left side halfshaft and make certain that it is fully seated
- Push the halfshaft into place and pull on the tri-pot joint and verify that the retaining ring in fully engaged

❊❊ WARNING

Do not pull on the halfshaft.

- Right side halfshaft and make certain that it is fully seated
- Push the halfshaft into place and pull on the tri-pot joint and verify that the retaining ring in fully engaged

❊❊ WARNING

Do not pull on the halfshaft.

- Halfshaft into the wheel bearing/hub by inserting a flat blade tool through the caliper and into the rotor so that the rotor does not move
- New halfshaft nut. Torque it to 118 ft. lbs. (160 Nm).
- Ball joint to the steering knuckle
- Tie rod end to the steering knuckle
- Stabilizer shaft link. Torque the nut to 17 ft. lbs. (23 Nm).
- Front wheel

4. Road test the vehicle and check for any abnormal noise.

5. Check and adjust the alignment as needed.

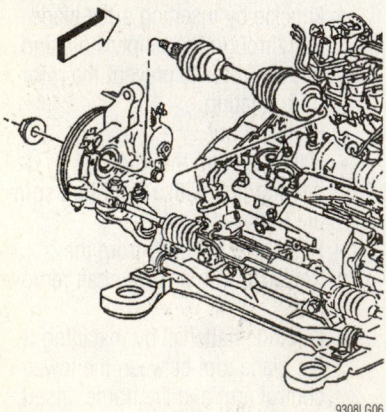

9308LG06

Install the left side halfshaft

CV-Joints

OVERHAUL

1. Before servicing the vehicle, refer to the precautions in the beginning of this section.

2. Remove or disconnect the following:
- Halfshaft
- Large seal retaining clamp from the CV-joint and discard the clamp
- Swage ring by using a hand grinder to cut through it. Do not damage the axle shaft with the grinder
- Halfshaft outboard seal from the CV-joint outer race and slide the seal away from the joint
- CV-joint and boot from the halfshaft and discard the boot

3. Place a brass drift against the CV-joint cage and gently tap on it until it tilts. Remove the chrome alloy ball. Tilt the cage in the opposite direction and remove the ball. Continue to rotate the cage until all six alloy balls have been removed.

4. Pivot the cage and inner race 90 degrees to the center line of the of the outer race. Align the cage windows with the outer race lands. Lift the cage and the inner race out of the CV-joint.

5. Remove the inner race from the cage by rotating the race upward.

6. Clean the grease and contaminates with cleaning solvent from the inner/outer races; CV-joint cage and the alloy balls.

7. Remove any rust from the boot mounting area and clean the halfshaft bar.

To assemble:

8. Coat the inner and outer race grooves with grease and align the inner race with the windows of the cage.

9. Insert the inner race to the cage by rotating the race downward.

10. Insert the cage and inner race into the outer race.

11. Install the six alloy balls into the cage by tilting the cage. Repeat this process until all the balls are in place.

12. Pack the CV boot and joint with the grease supplied in the kit.

13. Install or connect the following:
- New boot clamp onto the boot
- CV boot on to the halfshaft bar and position the small end of the boot into the groove on the halfshaft bar. Secure the clamp to the boot with a Seal Clamp tool J 35910. Torque the clamp to 100 ft. lbs. (136 Nm).
- Swage ring over the large diameter of the boot by pinching the ring into an oval shape

➥Make certain that the retaining ring side of the inner race faces the halfshaft bar before installation.

14. Slide the joint onto the halfshaft with the retaining snapring inside of the inner race. The race is properly seated when it snaps into place. Pull on the CV-joint to verify full engagement.

15. Install the large diameter of the boot with the large swage ring in place over the outside edge of the joint outer race.

16. Clamp the boot tightly to the outer race with the large swage ring by mounting Split Plate Swage Clamp tool J 36652 in a vise.

17. Position the outboard end of the halfshaft in the bottom of the tool.

18. Align the CV boot, joint and swage ring.

19. Install the top half of the tool and align the swage ring and clamp. Install the bolts to the top of the tool and tighten snugly. Tighten each bolt an additional 180 degrees. Alternate between the bolts until both sides of the top portion of the tool touch the bottom half.

20. Loosen the bolts and remove the split plate swage clamp tool.

21. Install the halfshaft.

22. Road test the vehicle and make certain there are no abnormal noises in the front end.

23. Check and adjust the alignment if necessary.

STEERING AND SUSPENSION

Air Bag

❊❊ CAUTION

All models are equipped with a Supplemental Inflatable Restraint (SIR) system. Before attempting any work on or near the steering column, ALWAYS disarm the air bag to prevent a costly and possibly dangerous accidental deployment.

PRECAUTIONS

Several precautions must be observed when handling the inflator module to avoid accidental deployment and possible personal injury.

• Never carry the inflator module by the wires or connector on the underside of the module

• When carrying a live inflator module, hold securely with both hands, and ensure that the bag and trim cover are pointed away from your body

• Place the inflator module on a bench or other surface with the bag and trim cover facing up

• With the inflator module on the bench, never place anything on or close to the module that may be thrown in the event of an accidental deployment

DISARMING

1. Turn the wheels to the straight-ahead position, then turn the ignition switch to **LOCK**.

2. Remove the instrument panel lower extension for access to the fuse block.

3. Remove the "AIR BAG" or "SIR" fuse from the block, as applicable.

4. Remove the steering column filler panel or left-hand sound insulator, as applicable, for access to the SIR wiring harness.

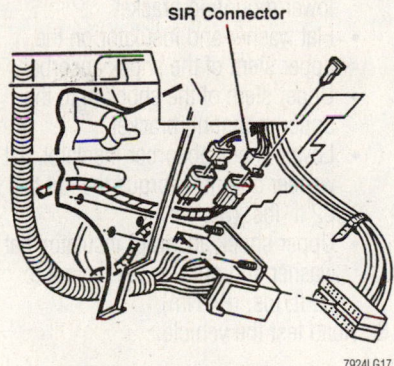

SIR Connector

7924LG17

Driver's side air bag connector location

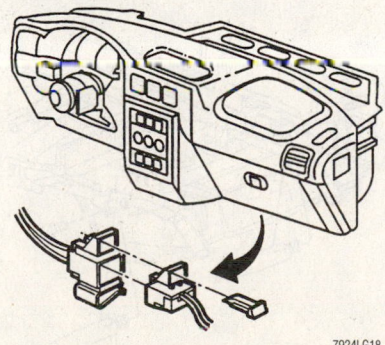

7924LG18

Passenger's side air bag connector location

5. Remove the Connector Position Assurance (CPA) device, then disengage the yellow 2-way connector at the base of the steering column.

➡ **With the fuse removed, the AIR BAG or SIR light will illuminate if the ignition switch is turned ON at any time. This is normal and does not indicate a problem when the system is disarmed.**

To enable:

6. Be sure the ignition is in the **LOCK** position.

7. Engage the yellow SIR connector, then secure using the CPA device.

8. Install the steering column filler or sound insulator panel, as applicable.

9. Install the SIR system fuse to the fuse block.

10. Turn the ignition switch to the **ON** position and verify that the AIR BAG indicator light flashes 7 times, then extinguishes. If it does not go out, troubleshoot the SIR system fault.

11. Install the instrument panel lower extension.

Power Steering Rack and Pinion

REMOVAL & INSTALLATION

1. Before servicing the vehicle, refer to the precautions in the beginning of this section.

2. Remove or disconnect the following:
   • Negative battery cable
   • Left front wheel

• Stabilizer shaft
• Tie rod ends from the steering knuckle
• Intermediate shaft from the steering gear
• Frame rear bolts and discard them. Properly support the frame
• Power steering gear heat shield
• Cooler pipe from the power steering gear
• Pressure hose from the power steering gear
• Power steering gear through the left wheel opening

To install:

3. Install or connect the following:
   • Power steering gear through the left wheel opening
   • New power steering gear bolts. Torque them to 59 ft. lbs. (80 Nm).
   • Pressure hose and cooler pipe to the power steering gear. Torque the fasteners to 20 ft. lbs. (27 Nm).
   • Heat shield. Torque the bolts to 54 inch lbs. (6 Nm).
   • Utility stand to support the frame
   • New rear frame bolts. Torque them to 118 ft. lbs. (160 Nm).

4. Remove the utility stand.

5. Install or connect the following:
   • Intermediate shaft to the steering gear. Torque the bolt to 35 ft. lbs. (47 Nm).
   • Tie rod ends to the steering knuckle
   • Stabilizer shaft. Torque the bolt to 17 ft. lbs. (23 Nm).
   • Left front wheel

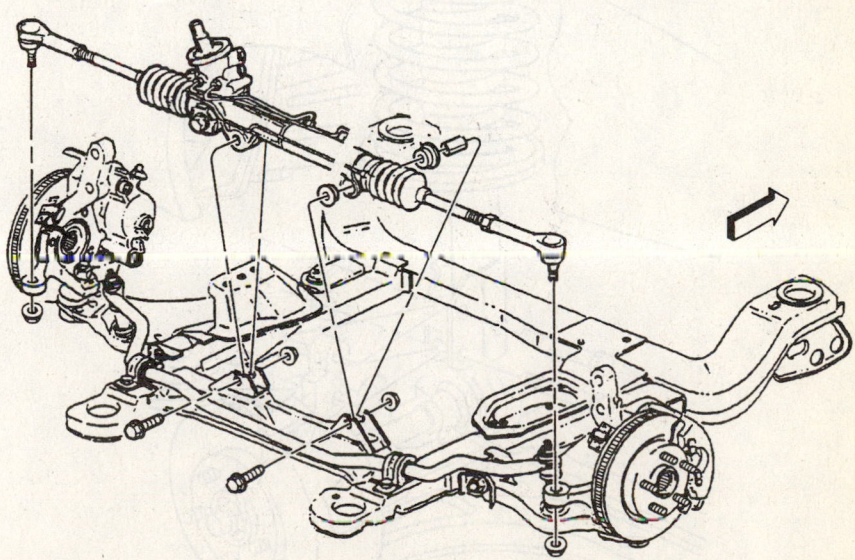

7924LG19

The rack and pinion steering gear is bolted to the rear of the subframe, as shown

6. Fill and bleed the power steering system and check for leaks.

7. Road test the vehicle and adjust the toe as necessary.

Strut

REMOVAL & INSTALLATION

❈❈ CAUTION

Do not remove the top center nut from the strut assembly. This nut should only be removed when the strut assembly is out of the vehicle, mounted in a holding fixture and the coil spring is in a compressed position using the proper coil spring compressor.

1. Before servicing the vehicle, refer to the precautions in the beginning of this section.

2. Remove or disconnect the following:
- Front wheel
- Three upper strut nuts
- Lower strut bolts after marking the position of the strut to the knuckle

➡**The strut to steering knuckle position must be marked so that the camber angle will not change. If the angle is change, the wheel alignment will also be affected.**

- Strut
- Nut from the top of the strut by placing the assembly in a Strut Compressor tool J 34013-B and Damper Rod Clamp J 34013-20. Turn the compressor forcing screw until the spring compresses slightly
- Strut mount
- Spring from the strut assembly

To install:

3. Install or connect the following:
- Spring over the strut in the proper position
- Strut mount
- Compressor screw and start turning the screw clockwise until the strut shaft threads are visible through the top of the strut. Torque the nut to 63 ft. lbs. (85 Nm).
- Strut and the upper nuts. Torque the nuts to 30 ft. lbs. (41 Nm).
- Lower strut bolts by aligning the strut to the steering knuckle. Torque the bolts 90 ft. lbs. (123 Nm).
- Front wheel

4. Road test the vehicle and check the front end alignment and adjust as needed.

Shock Absorber

REMOVAL & INSTALLATION

1. Before servicing the vehicle, refer to the precautions in the beginning of this section.

2. Set the parking brake and chock the wheels.

3. Remove or disconnect the following:
- Shock absorber at the lower bracket
- Shock absorber at the upper bracket
- Shock absorber from the brackets by compressing it slightly
- Remaining hardware from the shock absorber

To install:

4. Inspect the shock absorber, upper and lower mounting brackets and the frame mounting hole for cracks excessive wear and burrs.

5. Install or connect the following:
- Flat washer and insulator on the lower stem of the shock absorber
- Lower stem of the shock into the lower mounting bracket
- Flat washer and insulator on the upper stem of the shock absorber
- Upper stem of the shock in to the upper mounting bracket
- Lower shock absorber insulator, flat washer and nut. Torque the nut to 62 ft. lbs. (84 Nm).
- Upper shock absorber insulator, flat washer and nut. Torque the nut to 62 ft. lbs. (84 Nm).

6. Road test the vehicle.

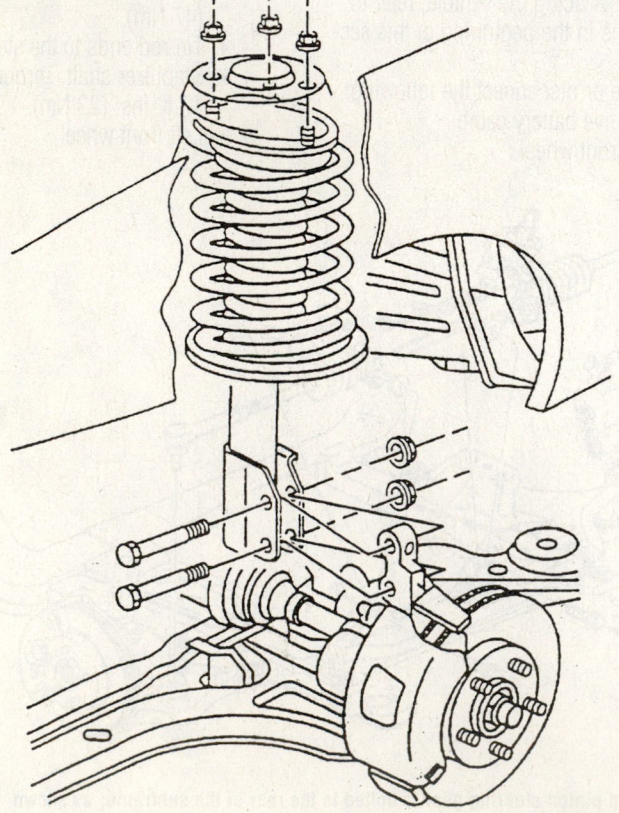

9308LG07

Strut assembly/disassembly

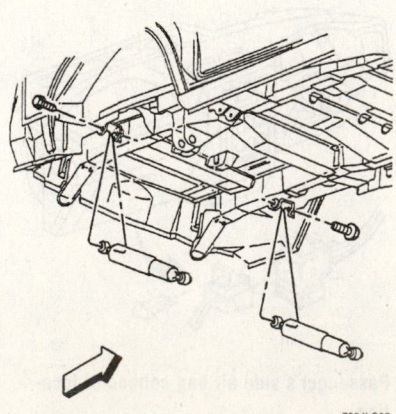

7924LG25

Rear shock absorber upper mounting

Coil Spring

REMOVAL & INSTALLATION

Front

The service procedure for the front coil springs is covered under MacPherson Strut removal and installation.

Rear

1. Before servicing the vehicle, refer to the precautions in the beginning of this section.
2. Remove or disconnect the following:
   - Brake hose bracket screw from the control arm
   - Shock absorber lower bolt while using a utility stand to support the rear axle
   - Tie rod from the rear axle
   - Spring and insulators after lowering the rear axle

To install:

3. Install or connect the following:
   - Insulators and springs on the rear axle with the paint stripe is facing rearward

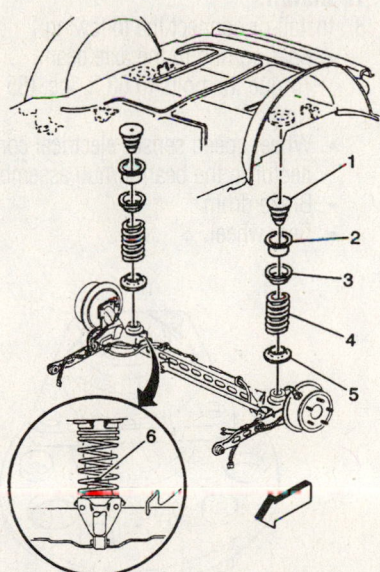

Legend

(1) Rear Suspension Jounce Bumper
(2) Rear Suspension Jounce Bumper Retainer
(3) Rear Suspension Insulator
(4) Rear Spring
(5) Rear Spring Insulator
(6) Paint Stripe

7924LG21

Exploded view of the coil spring assembly

- Rear axle tie rod after raising the rear axle into its proper position. Torque the nut to 92 ft. lbs. (125 Nm).
- Shock absorbers to the rear axle. Torque the upper and lower nuts to 63 ft. lbs. (85 Nm).
- Brake hose bracket to the control arm. Torque the bolt to 33 ft. lbs. (44 Nm).
4. Remove the axle supports.

Lower Ball Joint

REMOVAL & INSTALLATION

1. Before servicing the vehicle, refer to the precautions in the beginning of this section.
2. Remove or disconnect the following:
   - Front wheel
   - Brake caliper after properly supporting the lower control arm. Support the caliper to prevent damage to the brake line
   - Cotter pin and nut from the lower ball joint
   - Ball joint from the steering knuckle
   - Lower ball joint from the lower control arm

To install:

3. Install or connect the following:
   - New ball joint in the control arm until it bottoms on the lower part of the control arm
   - Ball joint stud into the steering knuckle. Torque the nut to 94 ft. lbs. (128 Nm).
   - New cotter pin to the ball stud by aligning the slots in the nut with the hole in the stud
   - Grease fitting and bend the ends of the cotter pin
   - Front brake caliper
   - Front wheel assembly
4. Road test the vehicle and check the front wheel alignment and adjust if necessary.

Lower Control Arm

REMOVAL & INSTALLATION

1. Before servicing the vehicle, refer to the precautions in the beginning of this section.
2. Remove or disconnect the following:

- Front wheel
- Anit-lock Brake System (ABS) wheel speed sensor connector and jumper harness
- Stabilizer shaft link
- Cotter pin from the ball joint stud and loosen the nut
- Ball Joint from the steering knuckle
- Lower control arm

To install:

3. Install or connect the following:
   - Lower control arm
   - Ball joint stud to the knuckle

➡**Align the ball stud cotter pin hole parallel to the knuckle to ease the pin installation.**

- Ball joint stud castle nut. Torque it to 40 ft. lbs. (55 Nm).
- New cotter pin
- Stabilizer shaft link. Torque the nut to 17 ft. lbs. (23 Nm).
- ABS jumper harness to the retainer clips
- ABS sensor connector
- Lower control arm nuts. Torque them to 83 ft. lbs. (113 Nm).
- Front wheel
4. Road test the vehicle and check the front end alignment, adjust if necessary.

CONTROL ARM BUSHING REPLACEMENT

1. Before servicing the vehicle, refer to the precautions in the beginning of this section.
2. Remove the lower control arm and secure it in a vise and mark the control arm along the flat edge of the bushing flange.
3. Assemble the bushing removal tool.
4. Tighten the assembly until the bushing is removed.

To install:

5. Install the bushing into the control arm by align the flat edge of the bushing to the mark in the control arm.
6. Make certain that the flat edge of the bushing is 30 degrees from the centerline of the control arm and the thin slot in the bushing is facing outboard.
7. Fully seat the bushing in the control arm.
8. Install the lower control arm.
9. Road test the vehicle and adjust the alignment, if necessary.

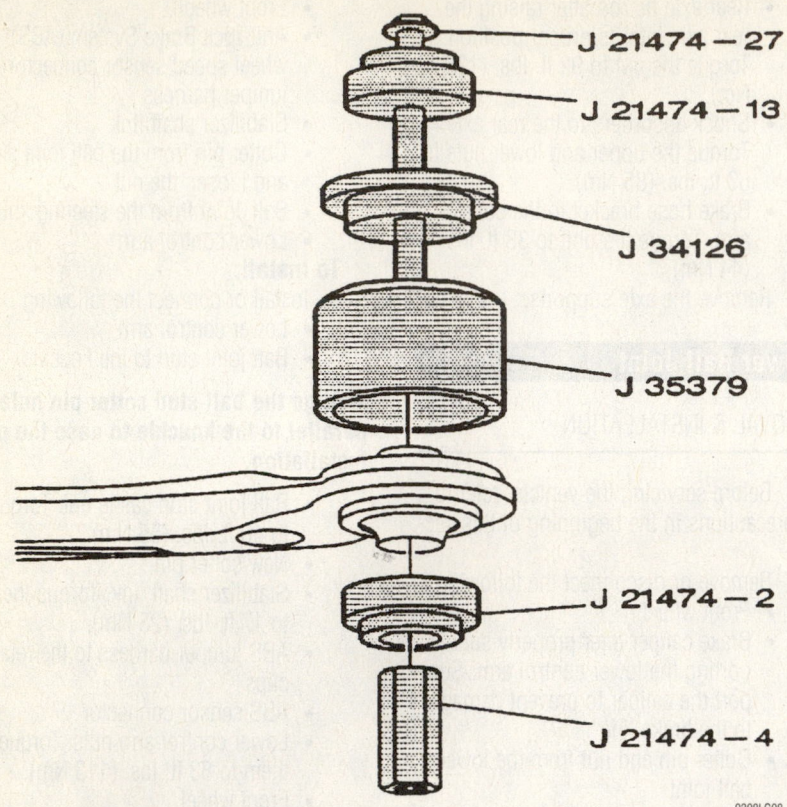

J 21474 – 27
J 21474 – 13
J 34126
J 35379
J 21474 – 2
J 21474 – 4

9308LG08

View of the lower control arm bushing

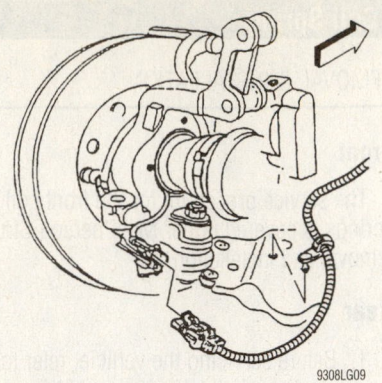

9308LG09

View of the front steering assembly

Wheel Bearings

ADJUSTMENT

Both front and rear wheel bearings are integral to the hub assembly and are not adjustable. If the bearings are found to be defective, the hub assembly must be replaced.

REMOVAL & INSTALLATION

Front

1. Before servicing the vehicle, refer to the precautions in the beginning of this section.
2. Remove or disconnect the following:
   • Front wheel
   • Wheel speed sensor electrical connector and the connector from the bracket
   • Brake caliper and bracket
   • Brake rotor
   • Halfshaft nut
3. Attach a front hub spindle removal tool to the wheel bearing/hub.

4. Push the halfshaft out of the wheel bearing hub assembly.
5. Remove or disconnect the following:
   • Wheel bearing/hub bolts and discard them
   • Wheel bearing/hub assembly

To install:
6. Install or connect the following:
   • Wheel bearing/hub assembly

✳✳ CAUTION

The wheel bearing/hub bolts must be replaced whenever they are loosened or removed.

   • New wheel bearing/hub bolts. Torque them to 96 ft. lbs. (130 Nm).
   • Halfshaft nut. Torque it to 118 ft. lbs. (160 Nm).
   • Brake rotor
   • Brake caliper. Torque the bolts to 63 ft. lbs. (85 Nm).
   • Wheel speed sensor electrical connector to the bracket
   • Wheel speed sensor electrical connector
   • Front wheel

7. Road test the vehicle and check the front alignment, adjust if necessary.

Rear

1. Before servicing the vehicle, refer to the precautions in the beginning of this section.
2. Remove or disconnect the following:
   • Rear wheel
   • Brake drum
   • Bearing/hub assembly from the axle beam
   • Wheel speed sensor
   • Bearing/hub assembly

To install:
3. Install or connect the following:
   • Bearing/hub to the axle beam. Torque the bolts to 63 ft. lbs. (85 Nm).
   • Wheel speed sensor electrical connector to the bearing/hub assembly
   • Brake drum
   • Rear wheel

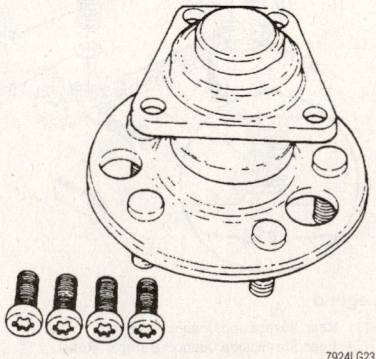

7924LG23

The rear wheel hub is mounted with 4 Torx® head bolts

PRECAUTIONS

Before servicing any vehicle, please be sure to read all of the following precautions, which deal with personal safety, prevention of component damage, and important points to take into consideration when servicing a motor vehicle:

• Never open, service or drain the radiator or cooling system when the engine is hot; serious burns can occur from the steam and hot coolant.

• Observe all applicable safety precautions when working around fuel. Whenever servicing the fuel system, always work in a well-ventilated area. Do not allow fuel spray or vapors to come in contact with a spark, open flame, or excessive heat (a hot drop light, for example). Keep a dry chemical fire extinguisher near the work area. Always keep fuel in a container specifically designed for fuel storage; also, always properly seal fuel containers to avoid the possibility of fire or explosion. Refer to the additional fuel system precautions later in this section.

• Fuel injection systems often remain pressurized, even after the engine has been turned OFF. The fuel system pressure must be relieved before disconnecting any fuel lines. Failure to do so may result in fire and/or personal injury.

• Brake fluid often contains polyglycol ethers and polyglycols. Avoid contact with the eyes and wash your hands thoroughly after handling brake fluid. If you do get brake fluid in your eyes, flush your eyes with clean, running water for 15 minutes. If eye irritation persists, or if you have taken brake fluid internally, seek medical assistance IMMEDIATELY.

• The EPA warns that prolonged contact with used engine oil may cause a number of skin disorders, including cancer. You should make every effort to minimize your exposure to used engine oil. Protective gloves should be worn when changing oil. Wash your hands and any other exposed skin areas as soon as possible after exposure to used engine oil. Soap and water, or waterless hand cleaner should be used.

• All new vehicles are now equipped with an air bag system. The system must be disabled before performing service on or around system components, steering column, instrument panel components, wiring and sensors. Failure to follow safety and disabling procedures could result in accidental air bag deployment, possible personal injury and unnecessary system repairs.

• Always wear safety goggles when working with, or around, the air bag system. When carrying a non-deployed air bag, be sure the bag and trim cover are pointed away from your body. When placing a non-deployed air bag on a work surface, always face the bag and trim cover upward, away from the surface. This will reduce the motion of the module if it is accidentally deployed. Refer to the additional air bag system precautions later in this section.

• Clean, high quality brake fluid from a sealed container is essential to the safe and proper operation of the brake system. You should always buy the correct type of brake fluid for your vehicle. If the brake fluid becomes contaminated, completely flush the system with new fluid. Never reuse any brake fluid. Any brake fluid that is removed from the system should be discarded. Also, do not allow any brake fluid to come in contact with a painted surface; it will damage the paint.

• Never operate the engine without the proper amount and type of engine oil; doing so WILL result in severe engine damage.

• Timing belt maintenance is extremely important. Many models utilize an interference-type, non-freewheeling engine. If the timing belt breaks, the valves in the cylinder head may strike the pistons, causing potentially serious (also time-consuming and expensive) engine damage. Refer to the maintenance interval charts in the front of this manual for the recommended replacement interval for the timing belt, and to the timing belt section for belt replacement and inspection.

• Disconnecting the negative battery cable on some vehicles may interfere with the functions of the on-board computer system(s) and may require the computer to undergo a relearning process once the negative battery cable is reconnected.

• When servicing drum brakes, only disassemble and assemble one side at a time, leaving the remaining side intact for reference.

• Only an MVAC-trained, EPA-certified automotive technician should service the air conditioning system or its components.

ENGINE REPAIR

➡Disconnecting the negative battery cable on some vehicles may interfere with the functions of the on board computer system. The computer may undergo a relearning process once the negative battery cable is reconnected.

Distributor

The 1999–01 Odyssey is equipped with a Distributorless Ignition System (DIS).

REMOVAL & INSTALLATION

CR-V, Oasis and 1997–98 Odyssey

1. Before servicing the vehicle, refer to the precautions in the beginning of this section.

2. Remove or disconnect the following:

• Negative battery cable
• Cruise control cable
• Air intake duct
• Distributor harness connector
• Spark plug wires
• Distributor

To install:

3. Install or connect the following:

• Distributor. Use a new O-ring seal.
• Spark plug wires
• Distributor harness connector
• Air intake duct
• Cruise control cable
• Negative battery cable

4. Set the ignition timing and tighten the mounting bolts to 13 ft. lbs. (18 Nm).

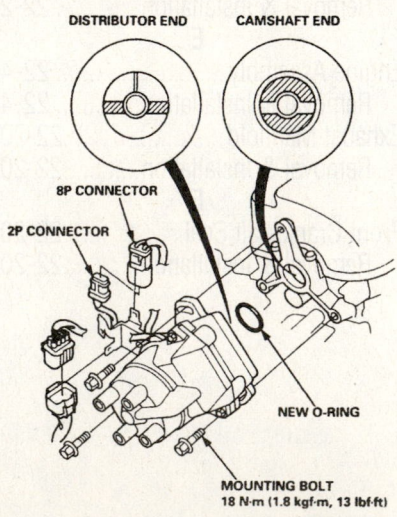

DISTRIBUTOR END   CAMSHAFT END

8P CONNECTOR
2P CONNECTOR
NEW O-RING
MOUNTING BOLT
18 N·m (1.8 kgf·m, 13 lbf·ft)

7924MG01

Exploded view of the distributor mounting—Oasis and 1997–98 Odyssey

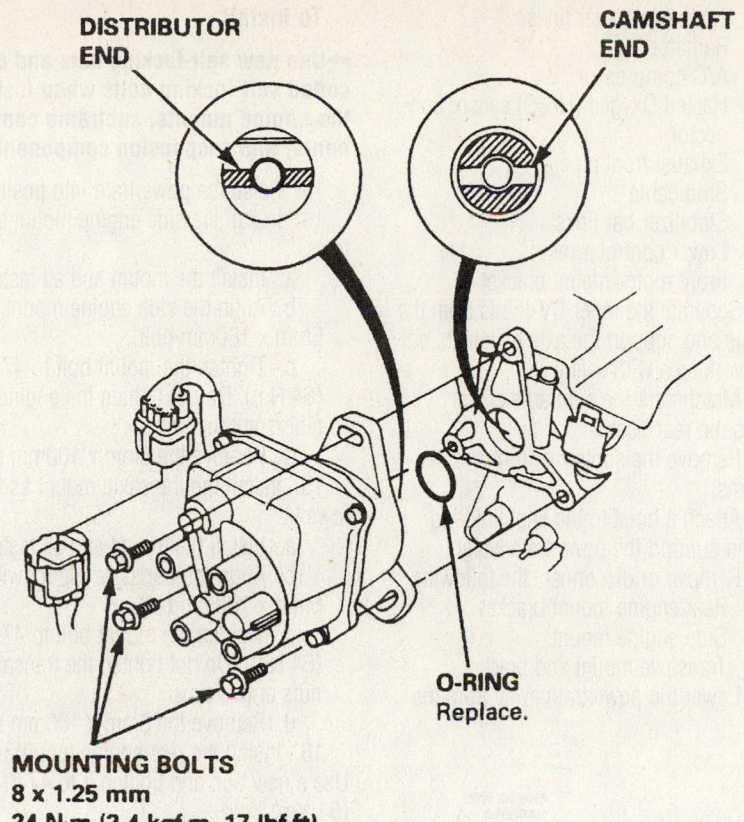

DISTRIBUTOR END

CAMSHAFT END

O-RING
Replace.

MOUNTING BOLTS
8 x 1.25 mm
24 N·m (2.4 kgf·m, 17 lbf·ft)

7924MG02

Exploded view of the distributor mounting—CR-V

Alternator

REMOVAL

Oasis and 1997–98 Odyssey

1. Before servicing the vehicle, refer to the precautions in the beginning of this section.
2. Remove or disconnect the following:
   - Negative battery cable
   - Accessory drive belts
   - Power steering pump
   - Alternator wiring harness connectors
   - Alternator

1999–01 Odyssey

1. Before servicing the vehicle, refer to the precautions in the beginning of this section.
2. Remove or disconnect the following:
   - Negative battery cable
   - Accessory drive belt
   - Alternator wiring harness connectors

   - Alternator mounting bolts
   - Wiring harness clamp
   - Alternator

CR-V

1. Before servicing the vehicle, refer to the precautions in the beginning of this section.
2. Remove or disconnect the following:
   - Negative battery cable
   - Accessory drive belts
   - Alternator wiring harness connectors
   - Alternator

INSTALLATION

Oasis and 1997–98 Odyssey

Install or connect the following:
- Alternator. Tighten the through bolt to 33 ft. lbs. (44 Nm) and the adjustment locknut to 16 ft. lbs. (22 Nm).
- Alternator wiring harness connectors. Tighten the battery terminal nut to 70 inch lbs. (8 Nm).
- Power steering pump

- Accessory drive belts
- Negative battery cable

1999–01 Odyssey

Install or connect the following:
- Alternator
- Wiring harness clamp. Tighten the bolt to 105 inch lbs. (12 Nm).
- Alternator mounting bolts. Tighten the 10mm bolt to 33 ft. lbs. (44 Nm) and the 8mm bolt to 16 ft. lbs. (22 Nm).
- Alternator wiring harness connectors. Tighten the battery terminal nut to 105 inch lbs. (12 Nm).
- Accessory drive belt
- Negative battery cable

CR-V

Install or connect the following:
- Alternator. Tighten the mounting nut to 33 ft. lbs. (44 Nm) and the adjustment locknut to 17 ft. lbs. (24 Nm).
- Alternator wiring harness connectors. Tighten the battery terminal nut to 70 inch lbs. (8 Nm).
- Accessory drive belts
- Negative battery cable

Ignition Timing

ADJUSTMENT

1999–01 Odyssey

The 1999–01 Odyssey is equipped with a Distributorless Ignition System (DIS). The ignition timing is controlled by the Powertrain Control module (PCM). No adjustment is necessary.

CR-V, Oasis and 1997–98 Odyssey

➡**Timing adjustments are made with the engine at operating temperature.**

1. Before servicing the vehicle, refer to the precautions in the beginning of this section.
2. Short the **2P** Service Check connector.
3. Connect a timing light to the No. 1 ignition wire.
4. The timing should be 13–17 degrees Before Top Dead Center (BTDC) (red timing mark on crankshaft pulley) at 650–750 rpm.
5. Adjust the timing as necessary and tighten the distributor bolts to 13 ft. lbs. (18 Nm).
6. Remove the **2P** connector jumper.

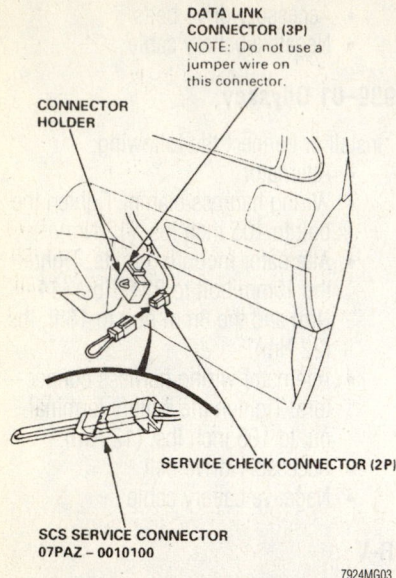

Service Check connector and shorting jumper

Engine Assembly

REMOVAL & INSTALLATION

Oasis and 1997–98 Odyssey

➡ **The engine and transaxle are removed from the vehicle as a unit.**

1. Before servicing the vehicle, refer to the precautions in the beginning of this section.
2. Drain the cooling system.
3. Drain the transaxle fluid.
4. Drain the engine oil.
5. Relieve fuel system pressure.
6. Remove or disconnect the following:
   - Hood
   - Battery and tray
   - Accessory drive belts
   - Accelerator cable
   - Cruise control cable
   - Air intake duct
   - Fuse/relay boxes
   - Left and right engine wiring harness connectors
   - Injector resistor connector
   - Brake booster vacuum line
   - Evaporative Emissions (EVAP) control canister hose
   - Fuel lines
   - Power steering hose bracket
   - Power steering pump
   - Alternator and bracket
   - Front wheels
   - Engine splash shield
   - Radiator hoses
   - Heater hoses

   - Transaxle cooler lines
   - Radiator
   - A/C compressor
   - Heated Oxygen (HO2S) sensor connector
   - Exhaust front pipe
   - Shift cable
   - Stabilizer bar links
   - Lower control arms
   - Front motor mount bracket

7. Separate the inner CV-joints from the transaxle and support the axle halfshafts out of the work area with safety wire.
8. Matchmark the subframe center beam to the rear beam.
9. Remove the subframe front and center beams.
10. Attach a hoist to the engine lifting eyes and support the powertrain weight.
11. Remove or disconnect the following:
    - Rear engine mount bracket
    - Side engine mount
    - Transaxle mount and bracket
12. Lower the powertrain away from the vehicle.

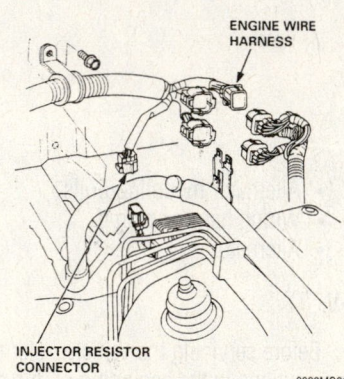

Left side engine wiring harness connectors—Oasis and 1997–98 Odyssey

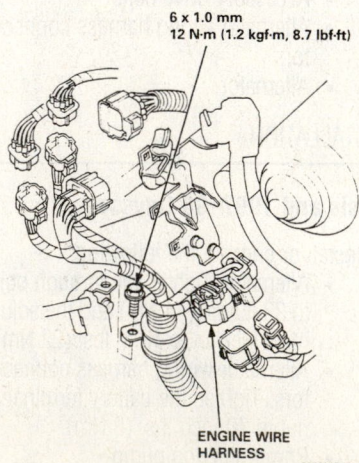

Right side engine wiring harness connectors—Oasis and 1997–98 Odyssey

To install:

➡ **Use new self-locking nuts and color-coded self-locking bolts when installing the engine mounts, subframe components, and suspension components.**

13. Raise the powertrain into position.
14. Install the side engine mount as follows:
    a. Install the mount and all fasteners.
    b. Align the side engine mount with a 6mm x 100mm bolt.
    c. Tighten the mount bolt to 47 ft. lbs. (64 Nm). Do not tighten the engine fasteners at this time.
    d. Remove the 6mm x 100mm bolt.
15. Install the transaxle mount as follows:
    a. Install the mount and all fasteners.
    b. Align the transaxle mount with a 6mm x 100mm bolt.
    c. Tighten the mount bolt to 47 ft. lbs. (64 Nm). Do not tighten the transaxle nuts at this time.
    d. Remove the 6mm x 100mm bolt.
16. Install the rear engine mount bracket. Use a new bolt and tighten it to 47 ft. lbs. (64 Nm).
17. Install the subframe front and center beams with new bolts.

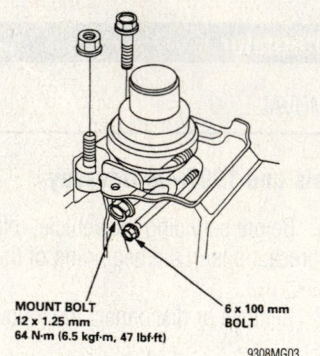

Side engine mount alignment—Oasis and 1997–98 Odyssey

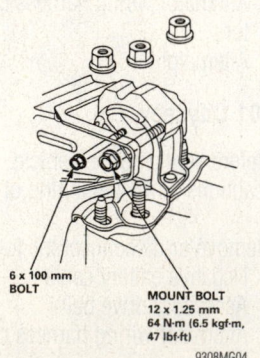

Transaxle mount alignment—Oasis and 1997–98 Odyssey

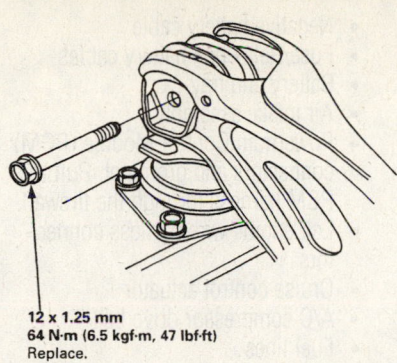

12 x 1.25 mm
64 N·m (6.5 kgf·m, 47 lbf·ft)
Replace.

9308MG05

Rear engine mount—Oasis and 1997–98 Odyssey

18. Align the matchmarks.

19. Tighten the front beam bolts to 47 ft. lbs. (64 Nm) and the center beam bolts to 37 ft. lbs. (50 Nm).

20. Install or connect the following:
- Axle halfshafts
- Lower control arms
- Stabilizer bar links
- Front motor mount bracket. Use a new through bolt and tighten it to 47 ft. lbs. (64 Nm).

21. Tighten the side engine mount fasteners to 40 ft. lbs. (54 Nm).

22. Tighten the transaxle mount nuts to 28 ft. lbs. (38 Nm).

23. Tighten the front mount bolts to 28 ft. lbs. (38 Nm).

24. Install or connect the following:
- Shift cable
- Exhaust front pipe
- HO2S sensor connector
- A/C compressor
- Radiator
- Transaxle cooler lines
- Heater hoses
- Radiator hoses
- Engine splash shield
- Front wheels
- Alternator and bracket
- Power steering pump
- Power steering hose bracket
- Fuel lines
- EVAP control canister hose
- Brake booster vacuum line
- Injector resistor connector
- Left and right engine wiring harness connectors
- Fuse/relay boxes
- Air intake duct
- Cruise control cable
- Accelerator cable
- Accessory drive belts
- Battery and tray
- Hood

25. Fill the engine crankcase to the correct level.

26. Fill the transaxle to the correct level.

27. Fill the cooling system.

28. Start the engine and check for leaks.

29. Check the wheel alignment and adjust as necessary.

1999–01 Odyssey

➡**The engine and transaxle are removed from the vehicle as a unit.**

1. Before servicing the vehicle, refer to the precautions in the beginning of this section.

2. Drain the cooling system.

3. Drain the transaxle fluid.

4. Drain the engine oil.

5. Relieve fuel system pressure.

6. Remove or disconnect the following:
- Negative battery cable
- Evaporative Emissions (EVAP) control canister hose
- Air intake duct
- Battery
- Left engine wire harness connectors
- Relay bracket
- Battery tray
- Fuel lines
- Accessory drive belts
- Accelerator cable
- Cruise control cable
- Brake booster vacuum line
- Vacuum supply hose
- Powertrain Control Module (PCM) connectors and grommet. Pull the PCM harness through the firewall.
- Fuse/Relay box battery cable
- Ground cable
- Power steering pump
- Starter cable and harness clamp
- Radiator hoses
- Heater hoses
- Bypass hose
- Transaxle oil cooler lines
- Front wheels
- Splash shield
- Heated Oxygen (HO2S) sensor connector
- Exhaust front pipe
- Stabilizer bar links
- Lower ball joints

7. Separate the inner CV-joints from the transaxle and support the axle halfshafts out of the work area with safety wire.

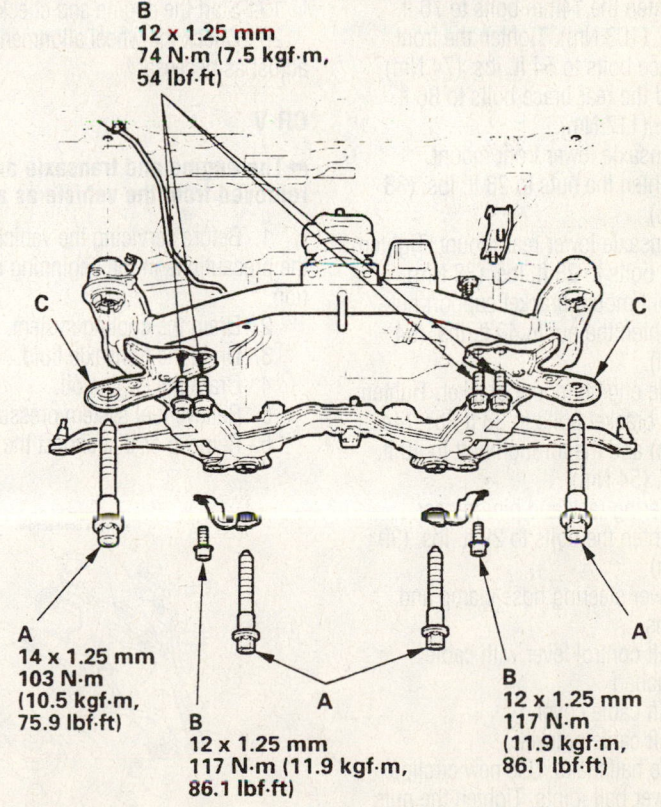

B
12 x 1.25 mm
74 N·m (7.5 kgf·m, 54 lbf·ft)

C

C

A
14 x 1.25 mm
103 N·m
(10.5 kgf·m, 75.9 lbf·ft)

B
12 x 1.25 mm
117 N·m (11.9 kgf·m, 86.1 lbf·ft)

A

B
12 x 1.25 mm
117 N·m
(11.9 kgf·m, 86.1 lbf·ft)

A

9302MG69

Sub-frame fastener locations and tightening torque—1999–01 Odyssey

Timing belt service is covered in Section 4 of this manual

8. Remove or disconnect the following:
- Shift cable bracket
- Shift cable cover
- Shift control lever with cable attached
- Power steering hose clamp and clips
- Transaxle lower front mount
- Transaxle lower rear mount
- Steering rack and pinion gear. Support the steering gear with safety wire.

9. Attach a hoist to the engine lifting eyes and support the powertrain weight.

10. Remove or disconnect the following:
- Side engine mount bracket
- Front mount bracket support nut

11. Matchmark the front subframe to the mounting points.

12. Remove or disconnect the following:
- Front subframe
- A/C compressor

13. Lower the powertrain away from the vehicle.

To install:

14. Raise the powertrain into position.

15. Install or connect the following:
- A/C compressor. Tighten the bolts to 16 ft. lbs. (22 Nm).
- Front subframe. Use new bolts and tighten the 14mm bolts to 76 ft. lbs. (103 Nm). Tighten the front brace bolts to 54 ft. lbs. (74 Nm) and the rear brace bolts to 86 ft. lbs. (117 Nm).
- Transaxle lower front mount. Tighten the nuts to 28 ft. lbs. (38 Nm).
- Transaxle lower rear mount. Tighten the bolts to 28 ft. lbs. (38 Nm).
- Front mount bracket support nut. Tighten the nut to 40 ft. lbs. (54 Nm).
- Side engine mount bracket. Tighten the bracket bolts to 33 ft. lbs. (44 Nm) and the through bolt to 40 ft. lbs. (54 Nm).
- Steering rack and pinion gear. Tighten the bolts to 29 ft. lbs. (39 Nm).
- Power steering hose clamp and clips
- Shift control lever with cable attached
- Shift cable cover
- Shift cable bracket
- Axle halfshafts. Use new circlips.
- Lower ball joints. Tighten the nuts to 43–51 ft. lbs. (59–69 Nm).
- Stabilizer bar links. Tighten the nuts to 58 ft. lbs. (78 Nm).
- Exhaust front pipe

- HO2S sensor connector
- Splash shield
- Front wheels
- Transaxle oil cooler lines
- Radiator hoses
- Heater hoses
- Bypass hose
- Starter cable and harness clamp
- Power steering pump
- Ground cable
- Fuse/Relay box battery cable
- PCM connectors and grommet
- Vacuum supply hose
- Brake booster vacuum line
- Cruise control cable
- Accelerator cable
- Accessory drive belts
- Fuel lines
- Battery tray
- Relay bracket
- Left engine wire harness connectors
- Battery
- Air intake duct
- EVAP control canister hose
- Negative battery cable

16. Fill the engine crankcase to the correct level.

17. Fill the transaxle to the correct level.

18. Fill the cooling system.

19. Start the engine and check for leaks.

20. Check the wheel alignment and adjust as necessary.

CR-V

➡️**The engine and transaxle are removed from the vehicle as a unit.**

1. Before servicing the vehicle, refer to the precautions in the beginning of this section.

2. Drain the cooling system.

3. Drain the transaxle fluid.

4. Drain the engine oil.

5. Relieve fuel system pressure.

6. Remove or disconnect the following:

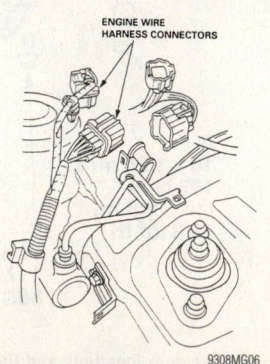

Left engine wire harness connectors— CR-V

- Negative battery cable
- Fuse/Relay box battery cables
- Battery and tray
- Air intake assembly
- Powertrain Control Module (PCM) connectors and grommet. Pull the PCM harness through the firewall.
- Left engine wire harness connectors
- Cruise control actuator
- A/C compressor drive belt
- Fuel lines
- Brake booster vacuum line
- Accelerator cable
- Power Steering Pressure (PSP) switch
- Splash shield
- Radiator hoses
- Heater hoses
- Heated Oxygen (HO2S) sensor connector
- Exhaust front pipe
- Right damper fork
- Lower ball joints

7. Separate the inner CV-joints from the transaxle and support the axle halfshafts out of the work area with safety wire.

8. If equipped with a manual transaxle, remove or disconnect the following:
- Clutch slave cylinder
- Clutch hose bracket

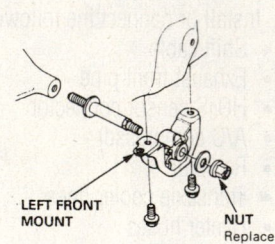

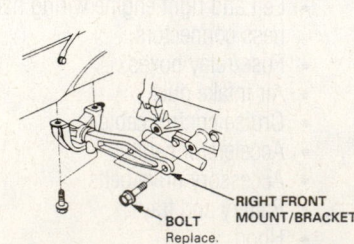

Front mounts—CR-V

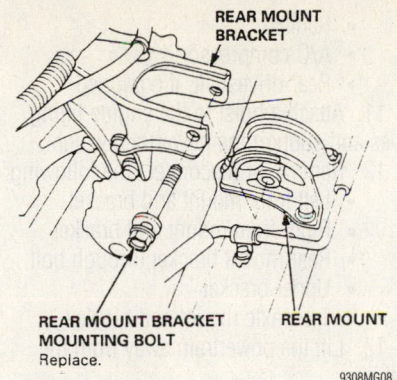

Rear mount—CR-V

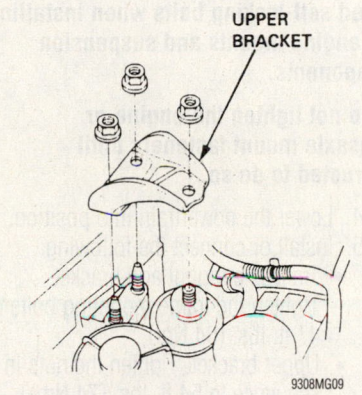

Upper bracket—CR-V

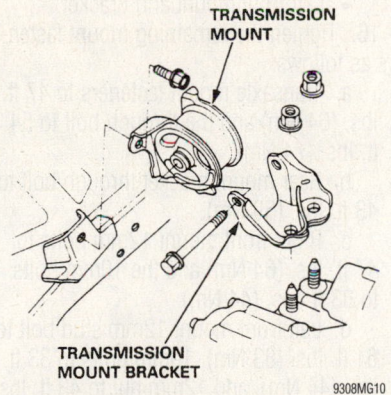

Transaxle mount—CR-V

- Transaxle ground cable
- Shift cables
9. If equipped with an automatic trans-axle, remove or disconnect the following:
  - Shift cable cover
  - Shift cable
  - Transaxle ground cable and hose clamp
  - Transaxle fluid cooler lines
10. For all vehicles, remove or disconnect the following:
  - A/C hose clamp

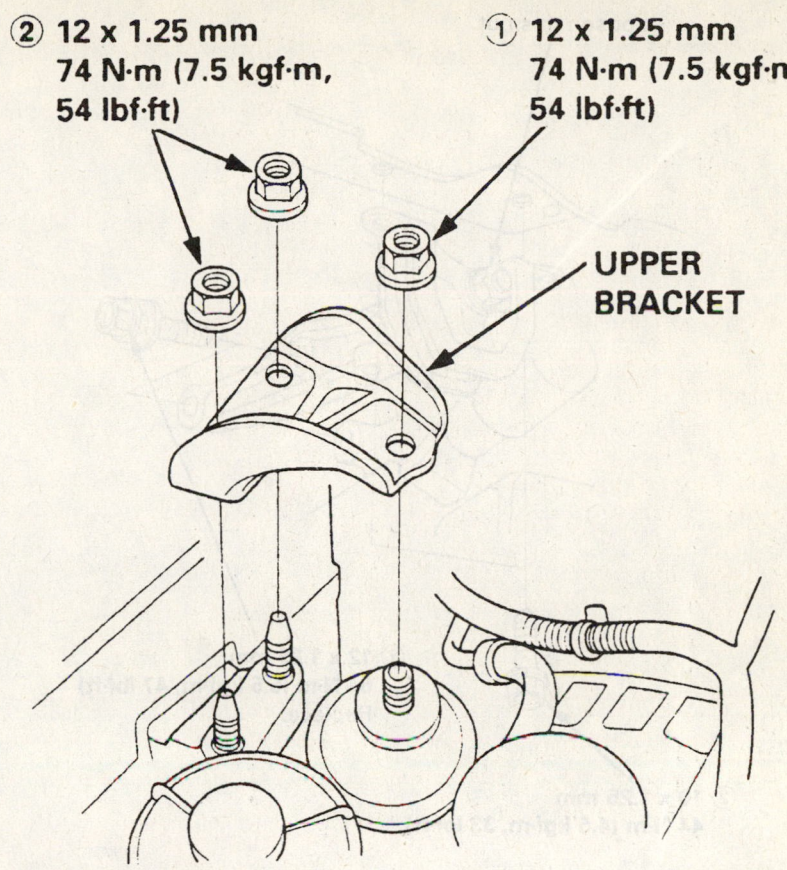

② 12 x 1.25 mm
74 N·m (7.5 kgf·m, 54 lbf·ft)

① 12 x 1.25 mm
74 N·m (7.5 kgf·m, 54 lbf·ft)

UPPER BRACKET

Upper bracket tightening sequence—CR-V

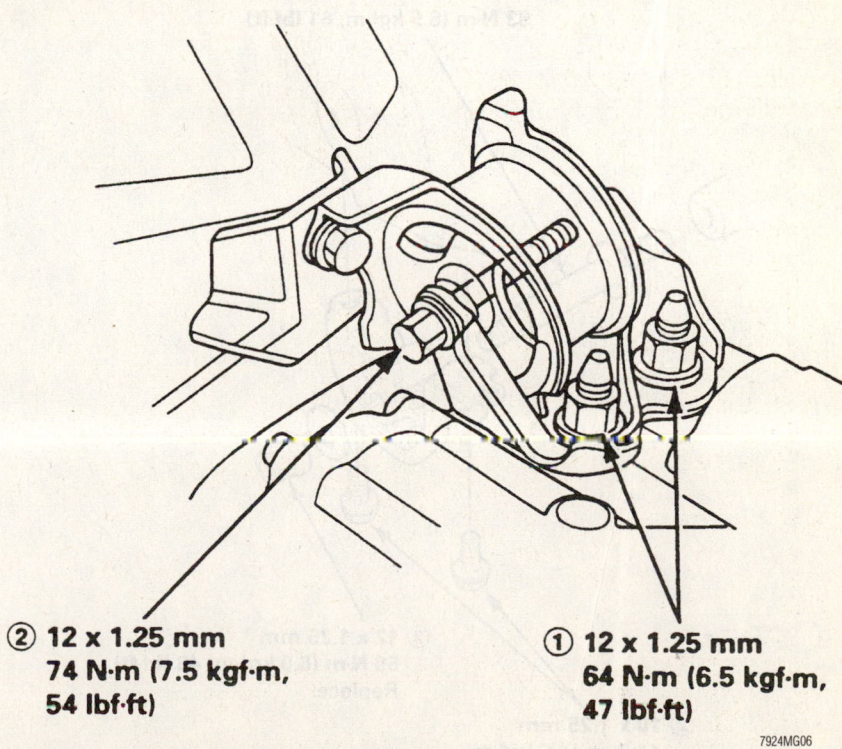

② 12 x 1.25 mm
74 N·m (7.5 kgf·m, 54 lbf·ft)

① 12 x 1.25 mm
64 N·m (6.5 kgf·m, 47 lbf·ft)

Transaxle mount fastener tightening sequence—CR-V

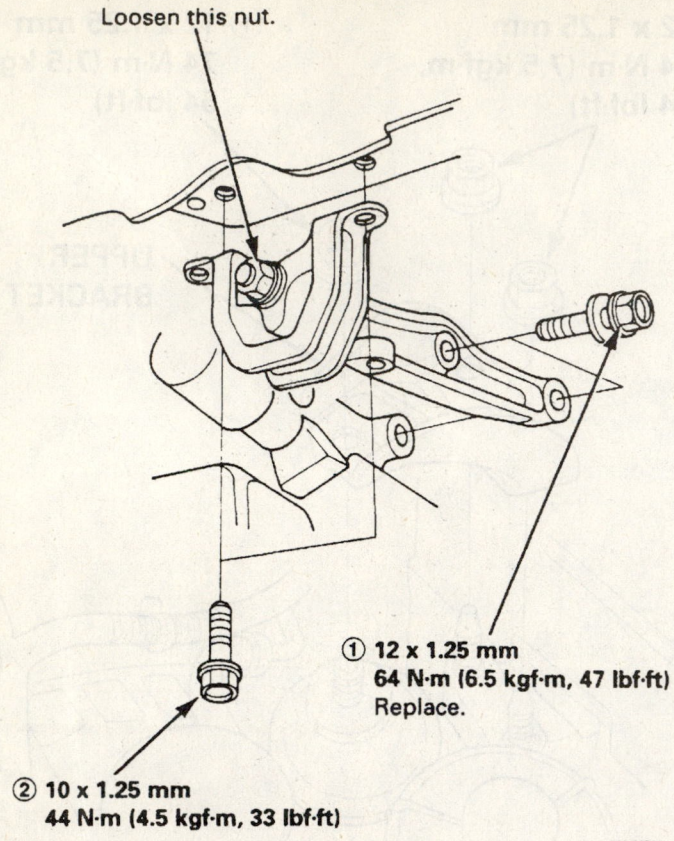

Loosen this nut.

① 12 x 1.25 mm
64 N·m (6.5 kgf·m, 47 lbf·ft)
Replace.

② 10 x 1.25 mm
44 N·m (4.5 kgf·m, 33 lbf·ft)

Right front mount tightening sequence—CR-V

7924MG08

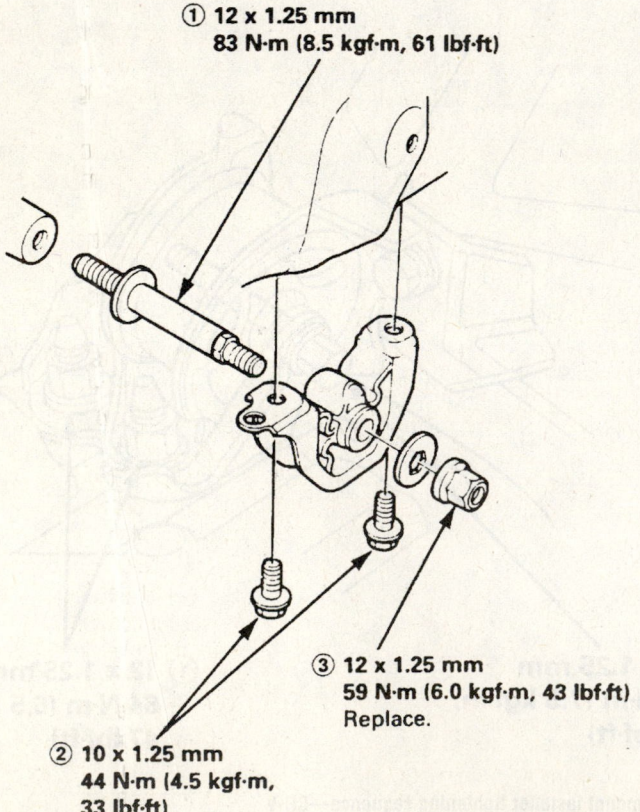

① 12 x 1.25 mm
83 N·m (8.5 kgf·m, 61 lbf·ft)

③ 12 x 1.25 mm
59 N·m (6.0 kgf·m, 43 lbf·ft)
Replace.

② 10 x 1.25 mm
44 N·m (4.5 kgf·m, 33 lbf·ft)

7924MG07

Left front mount tightening sequence—CR-V

- Radiator
- A/C compressor
- Rear driveshaft, if equipped

11. Attach a hoist to the engine lifting eyes and support the powertrain weight.

12. Remove or disconnect the following:
- Left front mount and bracket
- Right front mount and bracket
- Rear mount bracket through bolt
- Upper bracket
- Transaxle mount and bracket

13. Lift the powertrain away from the vehicle.

To install:

➡**Use new self-locking nuts and color-coded self-locking bolts when installing the engine mounts and suspension components.**

➡**Do not tighten the engine or transaxle mount fasteners until instructed to do so.**

14. Lower the powertrain into position.

15. Install or connect the following:
- Transaxle mount and bracket. Tighten the frame mounting bolts to 47 ft. lbs. (64 Nm).
- Upper bracket. Tighten the nuts in sequence to 54 ft. lbs. (74 Nm).
- Rear mount bracket through bolt
- Right front mount and bracket
- Left front mount and bracket

16. Tighten the remaining mount fasteners as follows:

a. Transaxle mount fasteners to 47 ft. lbs. (64 Nm) and the through bolt to 54 ft. lbs. (74 Nm).

b. Rear mount bracket through bolt to 43 ft. lbs. (59 Nm).

c. Right front mount 12mm bolts to 47 ft. lbs. (64 Nm) and the 10mm bolts to 33 ft. lbs. (44 Nm).

d. Left front mount 12mm stud bolt to 61 ft. lbs. (83 Nm), 10mm bolts to 33 ft. lbs. (44 Nm), and 12mm nut to 43 ft. lbs. (59 Nm).

e. Right front mount 12mm nut to 43 ft. lbs. (59 Nm).

17. Install or connect the following:
- Rear driveshaft, if equipped
- A/C compressor
- Radiator
- A/C hose clamp

18. If equipped with a manual transaxle, install or connect the following:
- Shift cables
- Transaxle ground cable
- Clutch hose bracket
- Clutch slave cylinder

19. If equipped with an automatic transaxle, install or connect the following:

- Transaxle fluid cooler lines
- Transaxle ground cable and hose clamp
- Shift cable
- Shift cable cover

20. For all vehicles, install or connect the following:

- Axle halfshafts
- Lower ball joints
- Right damper fork
- Exhaust front pipe
- HO2S sensor connector
- Heater hoses
- Radiator hoses
- Splash shield
- PSP switch
- Accelerator cable
- Brake booster vacuum line
- Fuel lines
- A/C compressor drive belt
- Cruise control actuator
- Left engine wire harness connectors
- PCM connectors and grommet
- Air intake assembly
- Battery and tray
- Fuse/Relay box battery cables
- Negative battery cable

21. Fill the engine crankcase to the correct level.
22. Fill the transaxle to the correct level.
23. Fill the cooling system.
24. Start the engine and check for leaks.
25. Check the wheel alignment and adjust as necessary.

Water Pump

REMOVAL & INSTALLATION

1. Before servicing the vehicle, refer to the precautions in the beginning of this section.
2. Drain the cooling system.
3. Remove or disconnect the following:
   - Negative battery cable
   - Accessory drive belts
   - Front cover
   - Timing belt. Refer to the Timing Belt unit repair section.
   - Timing belt tensioner, for 1999–01 Odyssey
   - Camshaft sprocket and rear timing cover, for Oasis and 1997–98 Odyssey
   - Water pump

To install:

4. Install or connect the following:
   - Water pump. Use a new O-ring seal

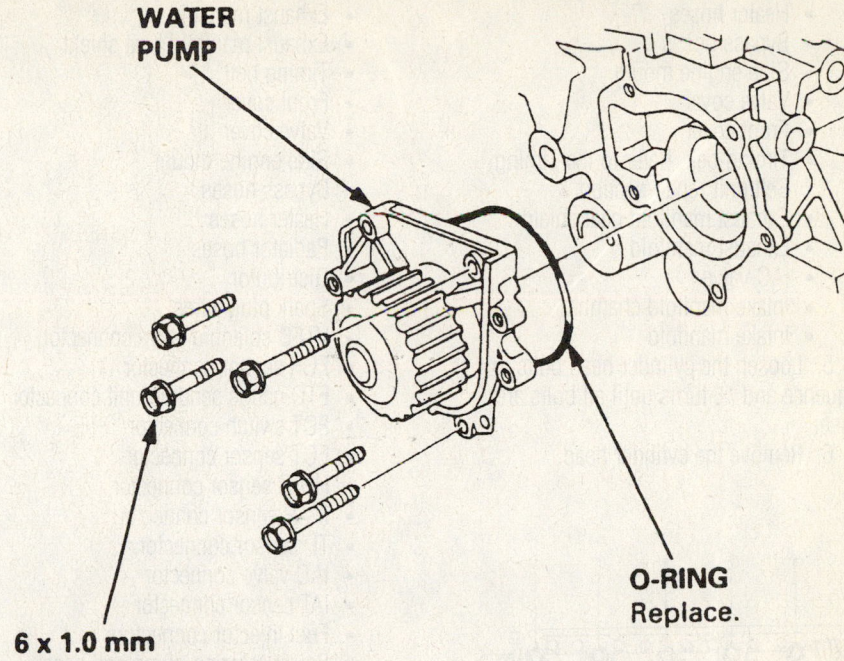

WATER PUMP

O-RING
Replace.

6 x 1.0 mm
12 N·m (1.2 kgf·m, 8.7 lbf·ft)

7924MG10

Exploded view of the water pump mounting

and tighten the bolts to 105 inch lbs. (12 Nm).
- Camshaft sprocket and rear timing cover, for Oasis and 1997–98 Odyssey
- Timing belt tensioner, for 1999–01 Odyssey
- Timing belt
- Front cover
- Accessory drive belts
- Negative battery cable

5. Fill the cooling system.
6. Start the engine and check for leaks.

Cylinder Head

REMOVAL & INSTALLATION

Oasis and 1997–98 Odyssey

1. Before servicing the vehicle, refer to the precautions in the beginning of this section.
2. Drain the cooling system.
3. Relieve fuel system pressure.
4. Remove or disconnect the following:
   - Negative battery cable
   - Air intake duct
   - Accessory drive belts
   - Accelerator cable
   - Cruise control cable
   - Brake booster vacuum line

- Evaporative Emissions (EVAP) control canister hose and vacuum hose
- Positive Crankcase Ventilation (PCV) valve and hose
- Fuel lines
- Intake manifold ground cable and vacuum line
- Power steering pump and hose bracket
- Fuel injector connectors
- Intake Air Temperature (IAT) sensor connector
- Idle Air Control (IAC) valve connector
- Throttle Position (TP) sensor connector
- Manifold Absolute Pressure (MAP) sensor connector
- Heated Oxygen (HO2S) sensor connector
- Engine Coolant Temperature (ECT) sensor connector
- ECT switch connector
- ETC gauge sending unit connector
- Exhaust Gas Recirculation (EGR) sensor connector
- Variable Valve Timing and Valve Lift Electronic Control (VTEC) solenoid valve connector
- Spark plug wires
- Distributor
- Radiator hoses

Refer to Section 1 for engine rebuilding specifications

- Heater hoses
- Bypass hoses
- Side engine mount
- Valve cover
- Front cover
- Timing belt. Refer to the Timing Belt unit repair section.
- Exhaust manifold heat shield
- Exhaust manifold
- IAC valve
- Intake manifold chamber
- Intake manifold

5. Loosen the cylinder head bolts in sequence and ⅓ turns until all bolts are loose.

6. Remove the cylinder head.

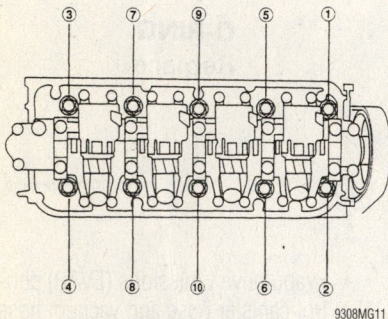

Cylinder head bolt loosening sequence—Oasis and 1997–98 Odyssey

To install:

7. Set the crankshaft to Top Dead Center (TDC) for the No. 1 cylinder.

8. Set the camshaft sprocket **UP** mark to 12 o'clock.

9. Install the cylinder head with a new gasket.

➡Refer to Section 1 of this manual for the cylinder head torque sequence illustration. The illustration is located after the Torque Specification Chart.

10. For 2.2L engine, tighten the bolts in sequence as follows:
   a. Step 1: 29 ft. lbs. (39 Nm)
   b. Step 2: 51 ft. lbs. (69 Nm)
   c. Step 3: 72 ft. lbs. (98 Nm)

11. For 2.3L engines, tighten the bolts in sequence as follows:
   a. Step 1: 22 ft. lbs. (29 Nm)
   b. Step 2: Plus 90 degrees
   c. Step 3: Plus 90 degrees
   d. Step 4: Plus 90 degrees, for new cylinder head bolts

12. Install or connect the following:
   - Intake manifold
   - Intake manifold chamber
   - IAC valve

- Exhaust manifold
- Exhaust manifold heat shield
- Timing belt
- Front cover
- Valve cover
- Side engine mount
- Bypass hoses
- Heater hoses
- Radiator hoses
- Distributor
- Spark plug wires
- VTEC solenoid valve connector
- EGR sensor connector
- ETC gauge sending unit connector
- ECT switch connector
- ECT sensor connector
- HO2S sensor connector
- MAP sensor connector
- TP sensor connector
- IAC valve connector
- IAT sensor connector
- Fuel injector connectors
- Power steering pump and hose bracket
- Intake manifold ground cable and vacuum line
- Fuel lines
- PCV valve and hose
- EVAP control canister hose and vacuum hose
- Brake booster vacuum line
- Cruise control cable
- Accelerator cable
- Accessory drive belts
- Air intake duct
- Negative battery cable

13. Fill the cooling system.

14. Start the engine and check for leaks.

1999–01 Odyssey

1. Before servicing the vehicle, refer to the precautions in the beginning of this section.

2. Drain the cooling system.

3. Relieve the fuel system pressure.

4. Remove or disconnect the following:
   - Negative battery cable
   - Evaporative Emissions (EVAP) control canister hose and vacuum hose
   - Air intake tube
   - Accessory drive belts
   - Ignition coil covers
   - Intake manifold cover
   - Accelerator cable
   - Cruise control cable
   - Fuel lines
   - Brake booster vacuum line
   - Intake manifold vacuum line
   - Positive Crankcase Ventilation (PCV) valve and hose

- Side engine mount bracket
- Power steering pump
- Power steering hose clamp
- Alternator
- Intake Air Temperature (IAT) sensor connector
- Idle Air Control (IAC) valve connector
- Throttle Position (TP) sensor connector
- Manifold Absolute Pressure (MAP) sensor connector
- Engine Coolant Temperature (ECT) sensor connector
- Radiator fan switch connectors
- ECT gauge sending unit connector
- Crankshaft Position (CKP) sensor connector
- Top Dead Center (TDC) sensor connector
- Exhaust Gas Recirculation (EGR) connector
- Variable Valve Timing and Valve Lift Electronic Control (VTEC) solenoid valve connector
- VTEC oil pressure switch connector
- Oil pressure switch connector
- Ignition coils
- Intake manifold
- Fuel injector connectors
- Fuel supply manifold
- Fuel injection air control valve vacuum lines
- Front cover
- Timing belt. Refer to the Timing Belt unit repair section.
- Radiator hoses
- Heater hoses
- Front and rear exhaust manifolds
- Coolant cross-over pipe
- Valve covers

5. Loosen the cylinder head bolts in sequence and ⅓ turns until all bolts are loose.

6. Remove the cylinder head.

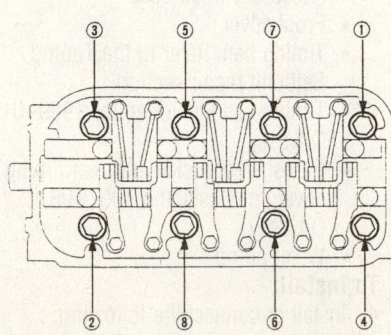

Cylinder head bolt loosening sequence—1999–01 Odyssey

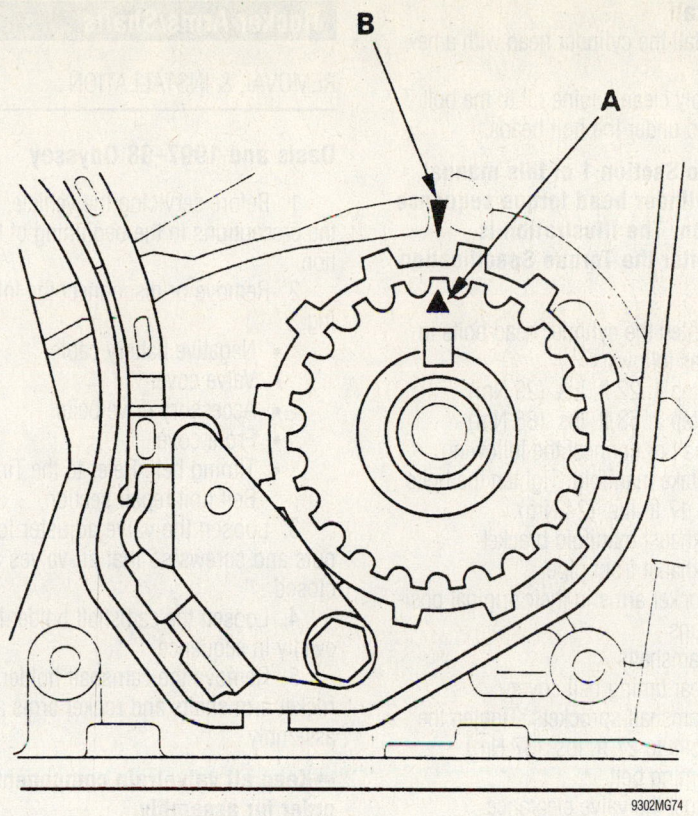

Crankshaft timing belt sprocket TDC marks. Align sprocket mark (A) with pointer (B)—1999–01 Odyssey

9302MG74

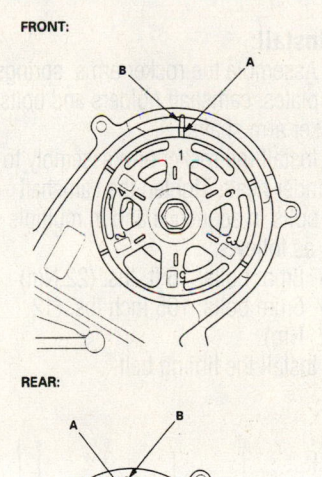

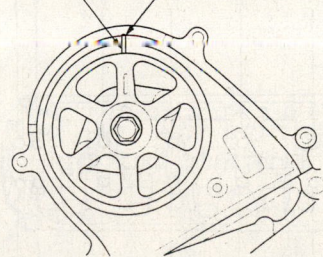

Camshaft TDC marks. Align sprocket mark (A) with the back cover pointer (B)— 1999–01 Odyssey

9302MG85

FRONT:

REAR:

To install:

7. Align the crankshaft and camshaft sprocket TDC marks as shown.

8. Install the cylinder heads with new gaskets.

9. Apply clean engine oil to the cylinder head bolt threads and flanges.

➡ **Refer to Section 1 of this manual for the cylinder head torque sequence illustration. The illustration is located after the Torque Specification Chart.**

10. Tighten the cylinder head bolts in sequence as follows:
   a. Step 1: 29 ft. lbs. (39 Nm)
   b. Step 2: 51 ft. lbs. (69 Nm)
   c. Step 3: 72 ft. lbs. (98 Nm)

11. Install or connect the following:
   • Valve covers
   • Coolant cross-over pipe
   • Front and rear exhaust manifolds
   • Heater hoses
   • Radiator hoses
   • Timing belt
   • Front cover
   • Fuel injection air control valve vacuum lines

   • Fuel supply manifold
   • Fuel injector connectors
   • Intake manifold
   • Ignition coils
   • Oil pressure switch connector
   • VTEC oil pressure switch connector
   • VTEC solenoid valve connector
   • EGR connector
   • TDC sensor connector
   • CKP sensor connector
   • ECT gauge sending unit connector
   • Radiator fan switch connectors
   • ECT sensor connector
   • MAP sensor connector
   • TP sensor connector
   • IAC valve connector
   • IAT sensor connector
   • Alternator
   • Power steering hose clamp
   • Power steering pump
   • Side engine mount bracket
   • PCV valve and hose
   • Intake manifold vacuum line
   • Brake booster vacuum line
   • Fuel lines
   • Cruise control cable
   • Accelerator cable
   • Intake manifold cover
   • Ignition coil covers
   • Accessory drive belts
   • Air intake tube
   • EVAP control canister hose and vacuum hose
   • Negative battery cable

12. Fill the cooling system.

13. Start the engine and check for leaks.

CR-V

1. Before servicing the vehicle, refer to the precautions in the beginning of this section.

2. Drain the cooling system.

3. Relieve the fuel system pressure.

4. Remove or disconnect the following:

   • Negative battery cable
   • Air intake assembly
   • Accessory drive belts
   • Power steering pump and bracket
   • Accelerator cable
   • Fuel lines
   • Evaporative Emissions (EVAP) control canister hose and vacuum hose
   • Brake booster vacuum line
   • Intake manifold vacuum line

For engine torque specifications, refer to Section 1 of this manual

- Positive Crankcase Ventilation (PCV) valve and hose
- Upper radiator hose
- Heater hose
- Bypass hoses
- Fuel injector connectors
- Engine Coolant Temperature (ECT) sensor connector
- Radiator fan switch connector
- ECT gauge sending unit connector
- Throttle Position (TP) sensor connector
- Manifold Absolute Pressure (MAP) sensor connector
- Heated Oxygen (HO2S) sensor connector
- Idle Air Control (IAC) valve connector
- Spark plug wires
- Distributor
- Cruise control actuator
- Engine side mount bracket
- Front cover
- Timing belt. Refer to the Timing Belt unit repair section.
- Camshaft sprockets
- Rear timing belt cover
- Valve cover

5. Loosen the valve adjuster locknuts and screws so that all valves are closed.

➡**Keep all valvetrain components in order for assembly.**

6. Remove or disconnect the following:

- Camshafts
- Rocker arms
- Exhaust front pipe
- Exhaust manifold bracket
- Intake manifold

7. Loosen the cylinder head bolts in sequence and ⅓ turns until all bolts are loose.

8. Remove the cylinder head.

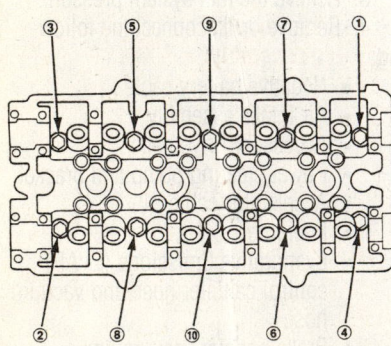

Cylinder head bolt loosening sequence—CR-V

To install:

9. Install the cylinder head with a new gasket.

10. Apply clean engine oil to the bolt threads and under the bolt heads.

➡**Refer to Section 1 of this manual for the cylinder head torque sequence illustration. The illustration is located after the Torque Specification Chart.**

11. Tighten the cylinder head bolts in sequence as follows:
   a. Step 1: 22 ft. lbs. (29 Nm)
   b. Step 2: 63 ft. lbs. (85 Nm)

12. Install or connect the following:

- Intake manifold. Tighten the bolts to 17 ft. lbs. (24 Nm).
- Exhaust manifold bracket
- Exhaust front pipe
- Rocker arms in their original positions
- Camshafts
- Rear timing belt cover
- Camshaft sprockets. Tighten the bolts to 27 ft. lbs. (37 Nm).
- Timing belt

13. Adjust the valve clearance.

14. Install or connect the following:

- Valve cover
- Front cover
- Engine side mount bracket
- Cruise control actuator
- Distributor
- Spark plug wires
- IAC valve connector
- HO2S sensor connector
- MAP sensor connector
- TP sensor connector
- ECT gauge sending unit connector
- Radiator fan switch connector
- ECT sensor connector
- Fuel injector connectors
- Bypass hoses
- Heater hose
- Upper radiator hose
- PCV valve and hose
- Intake manifold vacuum line
- Brake booster vacuum line
- EVAP control canister hose and vacuum hose
- Fuel lines
- Accelerator cable
- Power steering pump and bracket
- Accessory drive belts
- Air intake assembly
- Negative battery cable

15. Fill the cooling system.

16. Start the engine and check for leaks.

Rocker Arms/Shafts

REMOVAL & INSTALLATION

Oasis and 1997–98 Odyssey

1. Before servicing the vehicle, refer to the precautions in the beginning of this section.

2. Remove or disconnect the following:

- Negative battery cable
- Valve cover
- Accessory drive belts
- Front cover
- Timing belt. Refer to the Timing Belt unit repair section.

3. Loosen the valve adjuster locknuts and screws so that all valves are closed.

4. Loosen the camshaft holder bolts evenly in sequence.

5. Remove the camshaft holders, rocker arm shafts and rocker arms as an assembly.

➡**Keep all valvetrain components in order for assembly.**

6. Remove the camshaft holder bolts, camshaft holders, rocker arms, timing plates and springs from the rocker arm shafts.

To install:

7. Assemble the rocker arms, springs, timing plates, camshaft holders and bolts to the rocker arm shafts.

8. Install the rocker arm assembly to the cylinder head. Tighten the camshaft holder bolts in sequence and in multiple passes as follows:

- 8mm bolts: 16 ft. lbs. (22 Nm)
- 6mm bolts: 105 inch lbs. (12 Nm)

9. Install the timing belt.

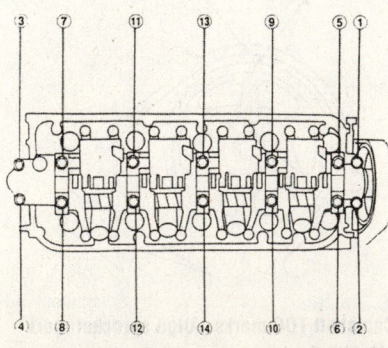

Camshaft holder loosening sequence—Oasis and 1997–98 Odyssey

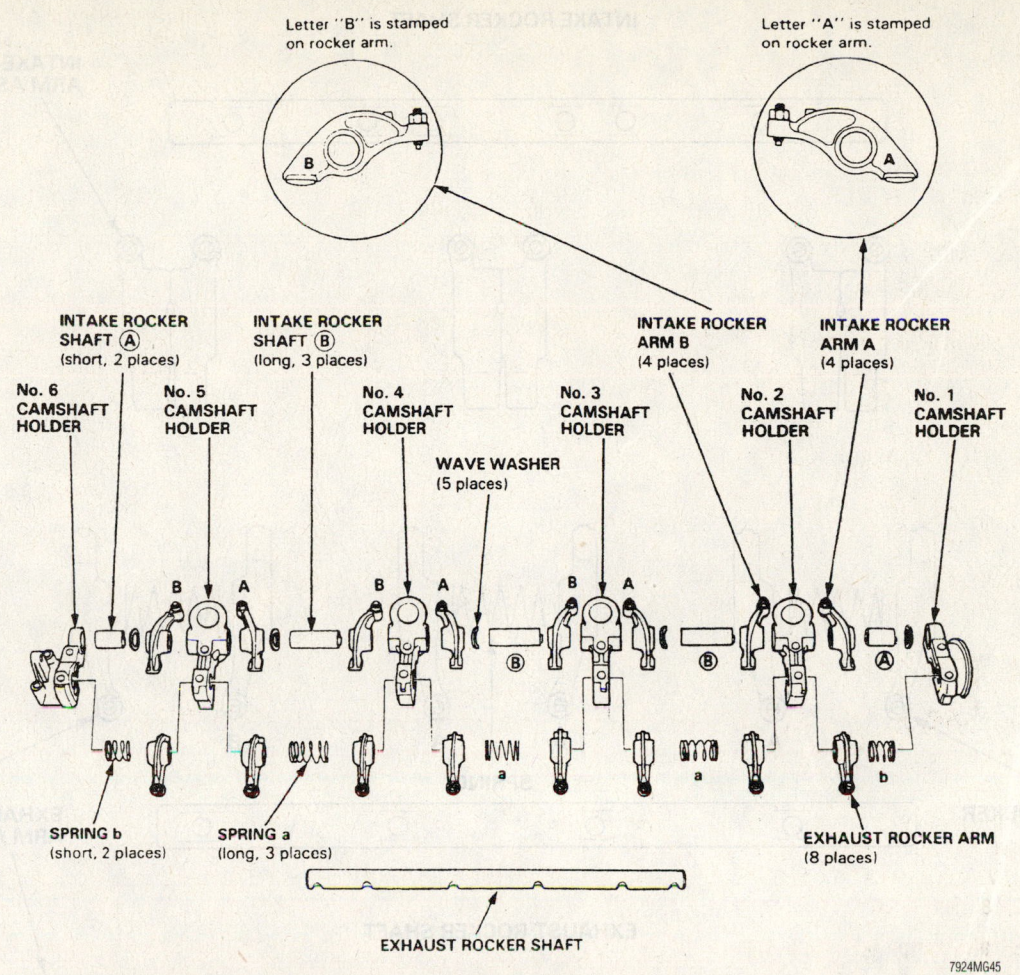

Letter "B" is stamped on rocker arm.

Letter "A" is stamped on rocker arm.

INTAKE ROCKER SHAFT (A) (short, 2 places)

INTAKE ROCKER SHAFT (B) (long, 3 places)

INTAKE ROCKER ARM B (4 places)

INTAKE ROCKER ARM A (4 places)

No. 6 CAMSHAFT HOLDER

No. 5 CAMSHAFT HOLDER

No. 4 CAMSHAFT HOLDER

No. 3 CAMSHAFT HOLDER

No. 2 CAMSHAFT HOLDER

No. 1 CAMSHAFT HOLDER

WAVE WASHER (5 places)

SPRING b (short, 2 places)

SPRING a (long, 3 places)

EXHAUST ROCKER ARM (8 places)

EXHAUST ROCKER SHAFT

Exploded view of the rocker arm and shaft components—Oasis and 1997–98 Odyssey

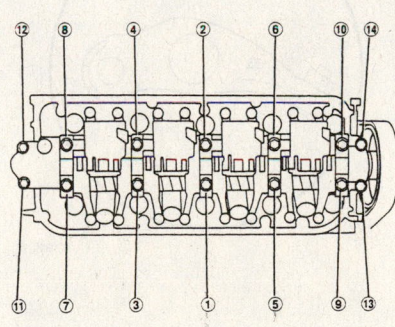

Camshaft holder torque sequence—Oasis and 1997–98 Odyssey

10. Adjust the valve clearance.
11. Install or connect the following:
- Front cover
- Accessory drive belts
- Valve cover
- Negative battery cable
12. Start the engine and check for leaks.

1999–01 Odyssey

1. Before servicing the vehicle, refer to the precautions in the beginning of this section.

2. Remove or disconnect the following:
- Negative battery cable
- Air intake tube

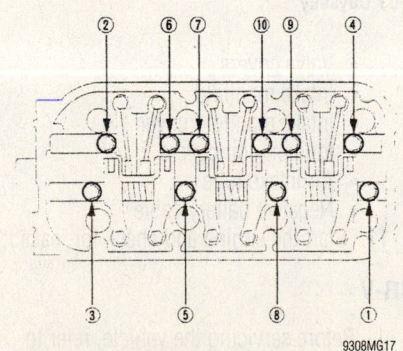

Rocker arm shaft loosening sequence— 1999–01 Odyssey

- Ignition coil covers
- Intake manifold cover
- Intake manifold
- Valve cover

3. Loosen the valve adjuster locknuts and screws so that all valves are closed.

4. Loosen the rocker arm shaft bolts evenly in sequence.

5. Remove the rocker arms and shafts from the vehicle as an assembly.

➡**Keep all valvetrain components in order for assembly.**

6. Remove the rocker arms and springs from the rocker arm shafts.

To install:

7. Assemble the rocker arms and springs to the rocker arm shafts in their original positions.

8. Install the rocker arm assemblies. Tighten the bolts in sequence and in multiple passes to 17 ft. lbs. (24 Nm).

9. Adjust the valve clearance.

10. Install or connect the following:

For complete mechanical specifications, refer to Section 1 of this manual

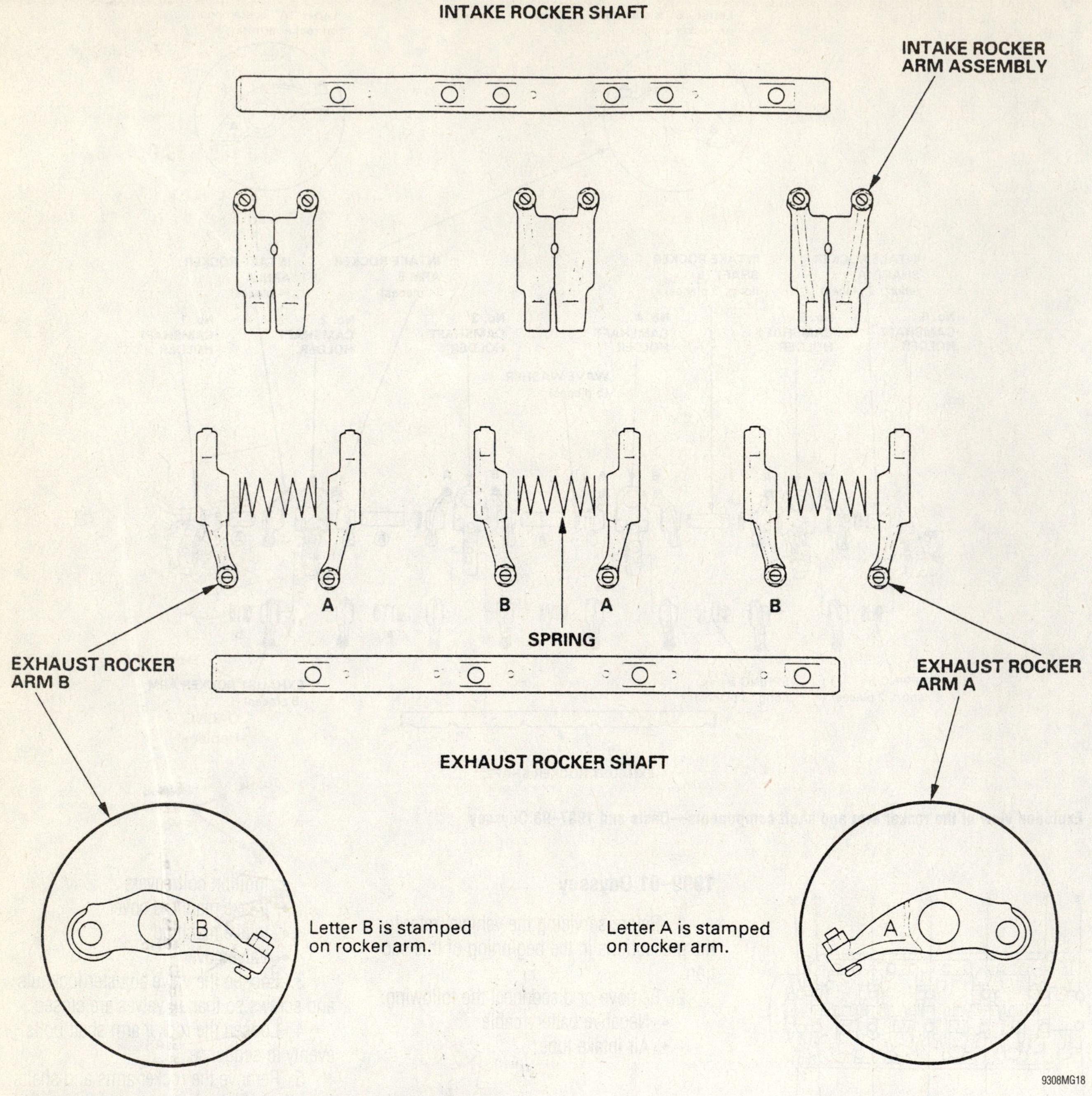

INTAKE ROCKER SHAFT

INTAKE ROCKER
ARM ASSEMBLY

EXHAUST ROCKER
ARM B

A   B   A   B

SPRING

EXHAUST ROCKER
ARM A

EXHAUST ROCKER SHAFT

Letter B is stamped
on rocker arm.

Letter A is stamped
on rocker arm.

9308MG18

Exploded view of the rocker arms and shafts—1999–01 Odyssey

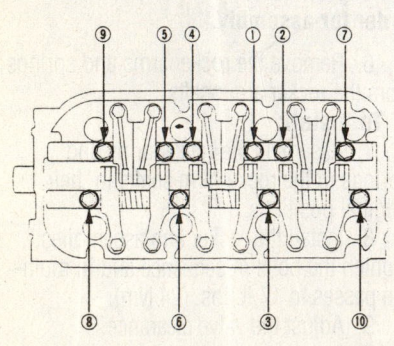

9302MG84

**Rocker shaft tightening sequence—
1999–01 Odyssey**

- Valve covers
- Intake manifold
- Intake manifold cover
- Ignition coil covers
- Air intake tube
- Negative battery cable

11. Start the engine and check for leaks.

CR-V

1. Before servicing the vehicle, refer to the precautions in the beginning of this section.

2. Remove or disconnect the following:
- Negative battery cable

- Spark plug wires
- Distributor
- Valve cover
- Accessory drive belts
- Front cover
- Timing belt. Refer to the Timing Belt unit repair section.

3. Loosen the valve adjuster locknuts and screws so that all valves are closed.

➡ **Keep all valvetrain components in order for assembly.**

4. Remove or disconnect the following:
- Camshaft sprockets
- Rear timing belt cover

- Camshafts
- Rocker arms

To install:

5. Install or connect the following:
   - Rocker arms in their original positions
   - Camshafts
   - Rear timing belt cover
   - Camshaft sprockets. Tighten the bolts to 27 ft. lbs. (37 Nm).

- Timing belt
6. Adjust the valve clearance.
7. Install or connect the following:
   - Front cover
   - Accessory drive belts
   - Valve cover
   - Distributor
   - Spark plug wires
   - Negative battery cable
8. Start the engine and check for leaks.

Intake Manifold

REMOVAL & INSTALLATION

Oasis and 1997–98 Odyssey

1. Before servicing the vehicle, refer to the precautions in the beginning of this section.

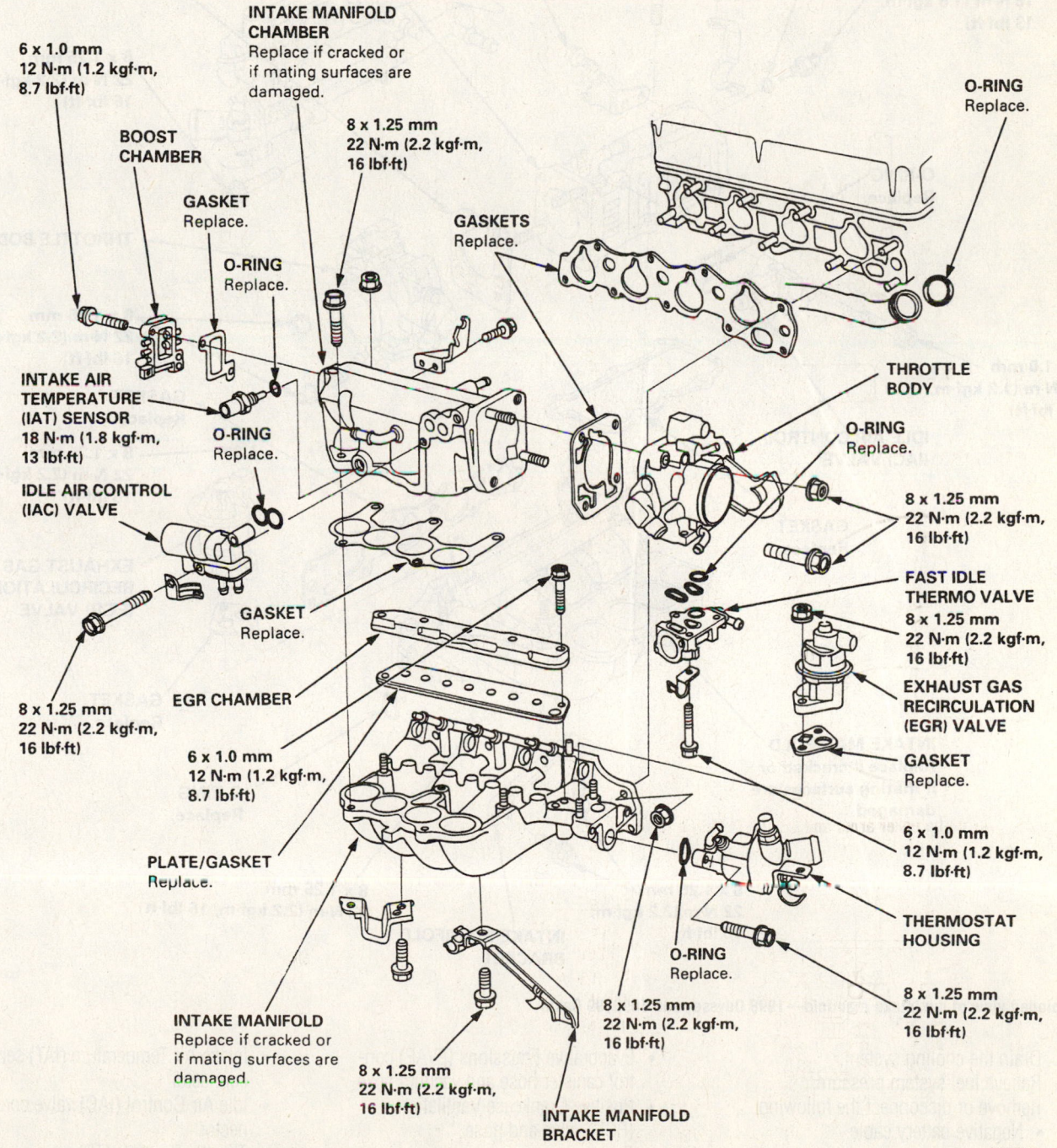

6 x 1.0 mm
12 N·m (1.2 kgf·m, 8.7 lbf·ft)

BOOST CHAMBER

INTAKE MANIFOLD CHAMBER
Replace if cracked or if mating surfaces are damaged.

GASKET
Replace.

8 x 1.25 mm
22 N·m (2.2 kgf·m, 16 lbf·ft)

O-RING
Replace.

GASKETS
Replace.

O-RING
Replace.

INTAKE AIR TEMPERATURE (IAT) SENSOR
18 N·m (1.8 kgf·m, 13 lbf·ft)

O-RING
Replace.

IDLE AIR CONTROL (IAC) VALVE

THROTTLE BODY

O-RING
Replace.

8 x 1.25 mm
22 N·m (2.2 kgf·m, 16 lbf·ft)

FAST IDLE THERMO VALVE

8 x 1.25 mm
22 N·m (2.2 kgf·m, 16 lbf·ft)

EXHAUST GAS RECIRCULATION (EGR) VALVE

GASKET
Replace.

GASKET
Replace.

EGR CHAMBER

8 x 1.25 mm
22 N·m (2.2 kgf·m, 16 lbf·ft)

6 x 1.0 mm
12 N·m (1.2 kgf·m, 8.7 lbf·ft)

6 x 1.0 mm
12 N·m (1.2 kgf·m, 8.7 lbf·ft)

PLATE/GASKET
Replace.

THERMOSTAT HOUSING

O-RING
Replace.

INTAKE MANIFOLD
Replace if cracked or if mating surfaces are damaged.

8 x 1.25 mm
22 N·m (2.2 kgf·m, 16 lbf·ft)

8 x 1.25 mm
22 N·m (2.2 kgf·m, 16 lbf·ft)

O-RING
Replace.

8 x 1.25 mm
22 N·m (2.2 kgf·m, 16 lbf·ft)

INTAKE MANIFOLD BRACKET

7924MG14

Exploded view of the intake manifold—1997 Odyssey and Oasis

Please refer to Section 8 for electric cooling fan wiring schematics

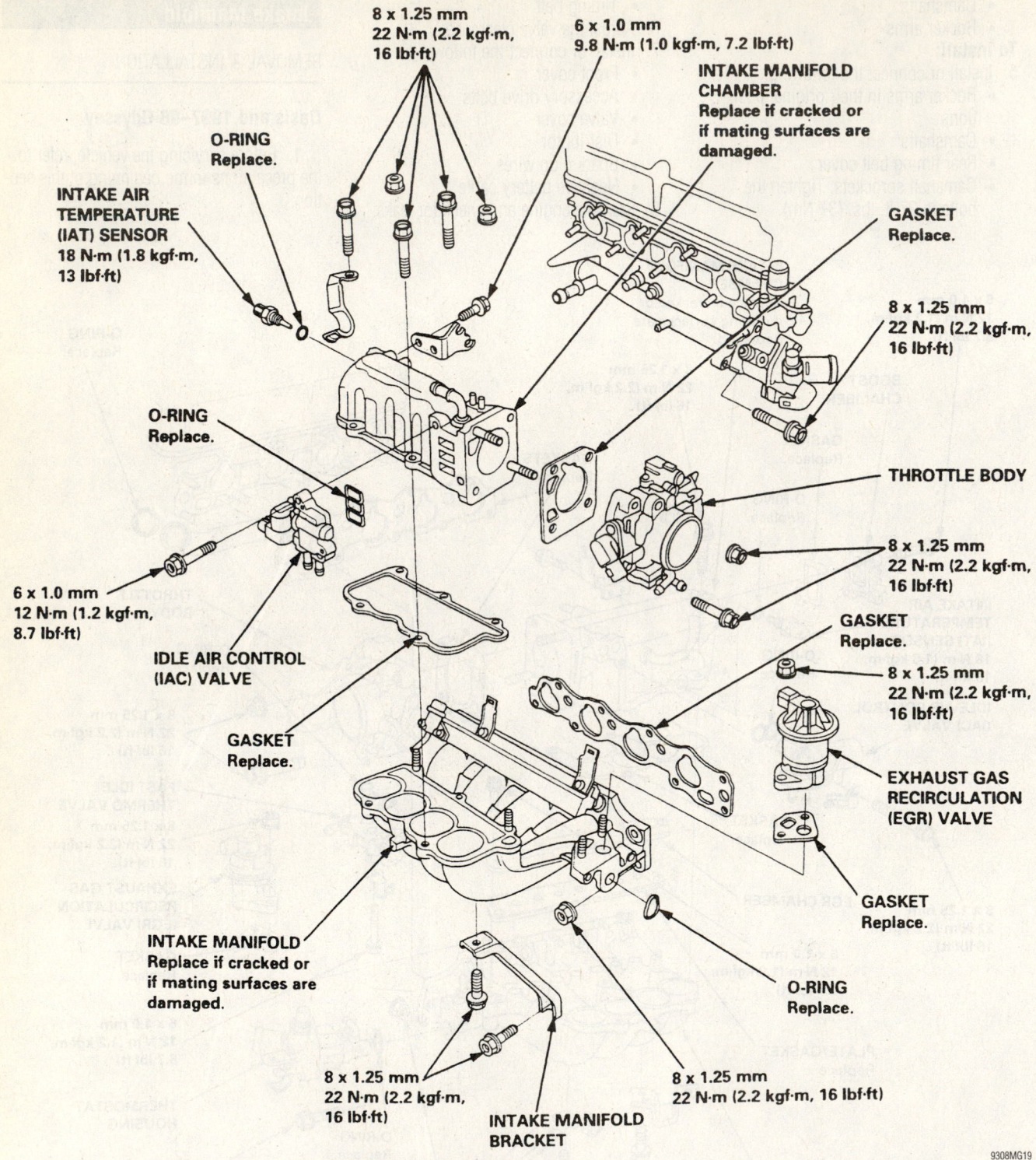

8 x 1.25 mm
22 N·m (2.2 kgf·m,
16 lbf·ft)

6 x 1.0 mm
9.8 N·m (1.0 kgf·m, 7.2 lbf·ft)

**INTAKE MANIFOLD
CHAMBER**
Replace if cracked or
if mating surfaces are
damaged.

O-RING
Replace.

**INTAKE AIR
TEMPERATURE
(IAT) SENSOR**
18 N·m (1.8 kgf·m,
13 lbf·ft)

GASKET
Replace.

8 x 1.25 mm
22 N·m (2.2 kgf·m,
16 lbf·ft)

O-RING
Replace.

THROTTLE BODY

6 x 1.0 mm
12 N·m (1.2 kgf·m,
8.7 lbf·ft)

8 x 1.25 mm
22 N·m (2.2 kgf·m,
16 lbf·ft)

**IDLE AIR CONTROL
(IAC) VALVE**

GASKET
Replace.

8 x 1.25 mm
22 N·m (2.2 kgf·m,
16 lbf·ft)

GASKET
Replace.

**EXHAUST GAS
RECIRCULATION
(EGR) VALVE**

INTAKE MANIFOLD
Replace if cracked or
if mating surfaces are
damaged.

GASKET
Replace.

O-RING
Replace.

8 x 1.25 mm
22 N·m (2.2 kgf·m,
16 lbf·ft)

8 x 1.25 mm
22 N·m (2.2 kgf·m, 16 lbf·ft)

**INTAKE MANIFOLD
BRACKET**

9308MG19

Exploded view of the intake manifold—1998 Odyssey and 1998–99 Oasis

2. Drain the cooling system.
3. Relieve fuel system pressure.
4. Remove or disconnect the following:
   - Negative battery cable
   - Air intake duct
   - Accelerator cable
   - Cruise control cable
   - Brake booster vacuum line
   - Evaporative Emissions (EVAP) control canister hose and vacuum hose
   - Positive Crankcase Ventilation (PCV) valve and hose
   - Fuel lines
   - Intake manifold ground cable and vacuum line
   - Fuel injector connectors
   - Intake Air Temperature (IAT) sensor connector
   - Idle Air Control (IAC) valve connector
   - Throttle Position (TP) sensor connector
   - Manifold Absolute Pressure (MAP) sensor connector

- Exhaust Gas Recirculation (EGR) sensor connector
- Bypass hoses
- Upper radiator hose
- Thermostat housing, for 1997 Odyssey and Oasis
- Intake manifold chamber
- Intake manifold

To install:

5. Install or connect the following:
   - Intake manifold. Use a new gasket and tighten the nuts to 16 ft. lbs. (22 Nm).
   - Intake manifold chamber. Use a new gasket and tighten the fasteners to 16 ft. lbs. (22 Nm).

- Thermostat housing, for 1997 Odyssey and Oasis
- Upper radiator hose
- Bypass hoses
- EGR sensor connector
- MAP sensor connector
- TP sensor connector
- IAC valve connector
- IAT sensor connector
- Fuel injector connectors
- Intake manifold ground cable and vacuum line
- Fuel lines
- PCV valve and hose
- EVAP control canister hose and vacuum hose

- Brake booster vacuum line
- Cruise control cable
- Accelerator cable
- Air intake duct
- Negative battery cable
6. Fill the cooling system.
7. Start the engine and check for leaks.

1999–01 Odyssey

1. Before servicing the vehicle, refer to the precautions in the beginning of this section.
2. Remove or disconnect the following:
   - Negative battery cable
   - Evaporative Emissions (EVAP) control canister hose and vacuum hose

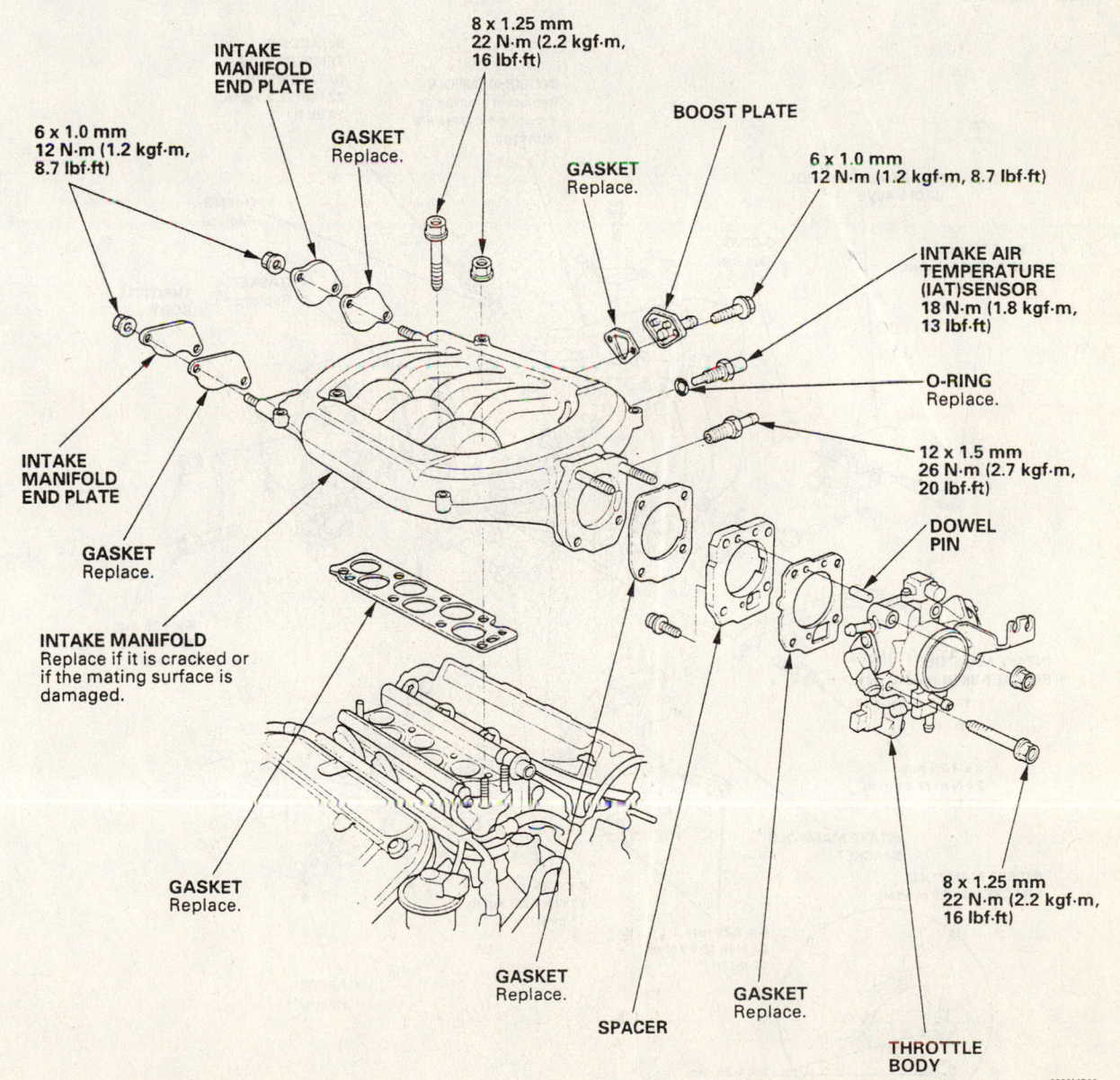

INTAKE MANIFOLD END PLATE

8 x 1.25 mm
22 N·m (2.2 kgf·m, 16 lbf·ft)

BOOST PLATE

6 x 1.0 mm
12 N·m (1.2 kgf·m, 8.7 lbf·ft)

GASKET
Replace.

GASKET
Replace.

6 x 1.0 mm
12 N·m (1.2 kgf·m, 8.7 lbf·ft)

INTAKE AIR TEMPERATURE (IAT)SENSOR
18 N·m (1.8 kgf·m, 13 lbf·ft)

O-RING
Replace.

12 x 1.5 mm
26 N·m (2.7 kgf·m, 20 lbf·ft)

INTAKE MANIFOLD END PLATE

GASKET
Replace.

DOWEL PIN

INTAKE MANIFOLD
Replace if it is cracked or if the mating surface is damaged.

GASKET
Replace.

GASKET
Replace.

8 x 1.25 mm
22 N·m (2.2 kgf·m, 16 lbf·ft)

GASKET
Replace.

SPACER

THROTTLE BODY

9308MG20

Exploded view of the intake manifold—1999–01 Odyssey

- Air intake tube
- Intake manifold cover
- Accelerator cable
- Cruise control cable
- Brake booster vacuum line
- Intake manifold vacuum line
- Positive Crankcase Ventilation (PCV) valve and hose
- Intake Air Temperature (IAT) sensor connector
- Idle Air Control (IAC) valve connector
- Throttle Position (TP) sensor connector
- Manifold Absolute Pressure (MAP) sensor connector
- Intake manifold

To install:

➡️ **Refer to Section 1 of this manual for the intake manifold torque sequence illustration. The illustration is located after the Torque Specification Chart.**

3. Install or connect the following:
   - New intake manifold gasket
   - Intake manifold. Tighten the fasteners in sequence and in several passes to 16 ft. lbs. (22 Nm).
   - MAP sensor connector
   - TP sensor connector
   - IAC valve connector
   - IAT sensor connector
   - PCV valve and hose
   - Intake manifold vacuum line

- Brake booster vacuum line
- Cruise control cable
- Accelerator cable
- Intake manifold cover
- Air intake tube
- EVAP control canister hose and vacuum hose
- Negative battery cable

4. Start the engine and check for proper operation.

CR-V

1. Before servicing the vehicle, refer to the precautions in the beginning of this section.
2. Drain the cooling system.
3. Relieve the fuel system pressure.

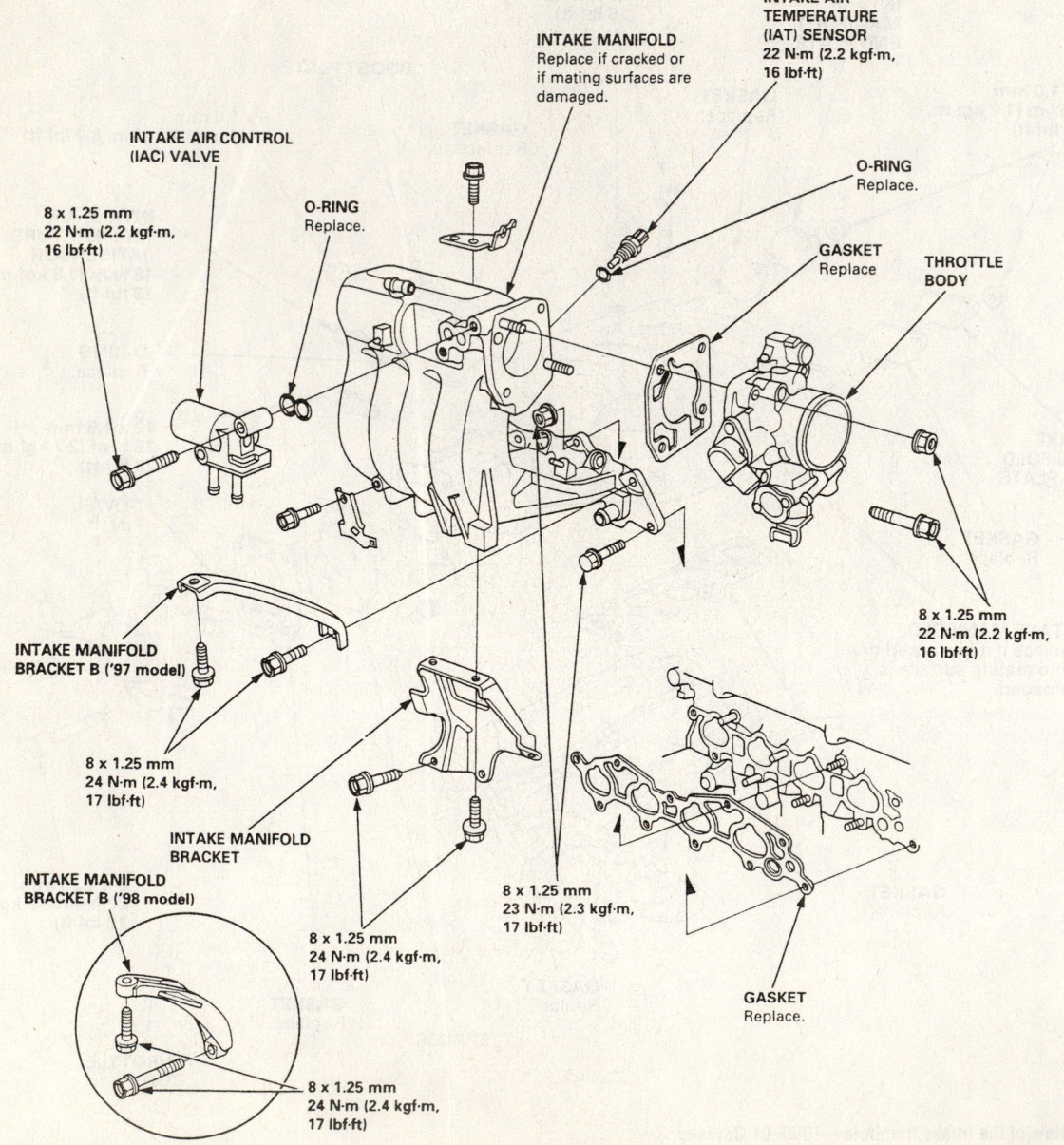

INTAKE MANIFOLD
Replace if cracked or if mating surfaces are damaged.

INTAKE AIR TEMPERATURE (IAT) SENSOR
22 N·m (2.2 kgf·m, 16 lbf·ft)

O-RING
Replace.

INTAKE AIR CONTROL (IAC) VALVE

8 x 1.25 mm
22 N·m (2.2 kgf·m, 16 lbf·ft)

O-RING
Replace.

GASKET
Replace

THROTTLE BODY

INTAKE MANIFOLD BRACKET B ('97 model)

8 x 1.25 mm
24 N·m (2.4 kgf·m, 17 lbf·ft)

INTAKE MANIFOLD BRACKET

INTAKE MANIFOLD BRACKET B ('98 model)

8 x 1.25 mm
24 N·m (2.4 kgf·m, 17 lbf·ft)

8 x 1.25 mm
23 N·m (2.3 kgf·m, 17 lbf·ft)

8 x 1.25 mm
22 N·m (2.2 kgf·m, 16 lbf·ft)

8 x 1.25 mm
24 N·m (2.4 kgf·m, 17 lbf·ft)

GASKET
Replace.

Intake manifold exploded view—1997–98 CR-V

9308MG21

4. Remove or disconnect the following:
- Negative battery cable
- Air intake assembly
- Intake manifold resonator chamber and bracket, for 1999–01 models
- Accelerator cable
- Fuel lines
- Evaporative Emissions (EVAP) control canister hose and vacuum hose

- Brake booster vacuum line
- Intake manifold vacuum line
- Positive Crankcase Ventilation (PCV) valve and hose
- Bypass hoses
- Fuel injector connectors
- Throttle Position (TP) sensor connector
- Manifold Absolute Pressure (MAP)

sensor connector
- Idle Air Control (IAC) valve connector
- Cruise control actuator
- Intake manifold brackets
- Intake manifold

To install:
5. Install or connect the following:
- New intake manifold gasket

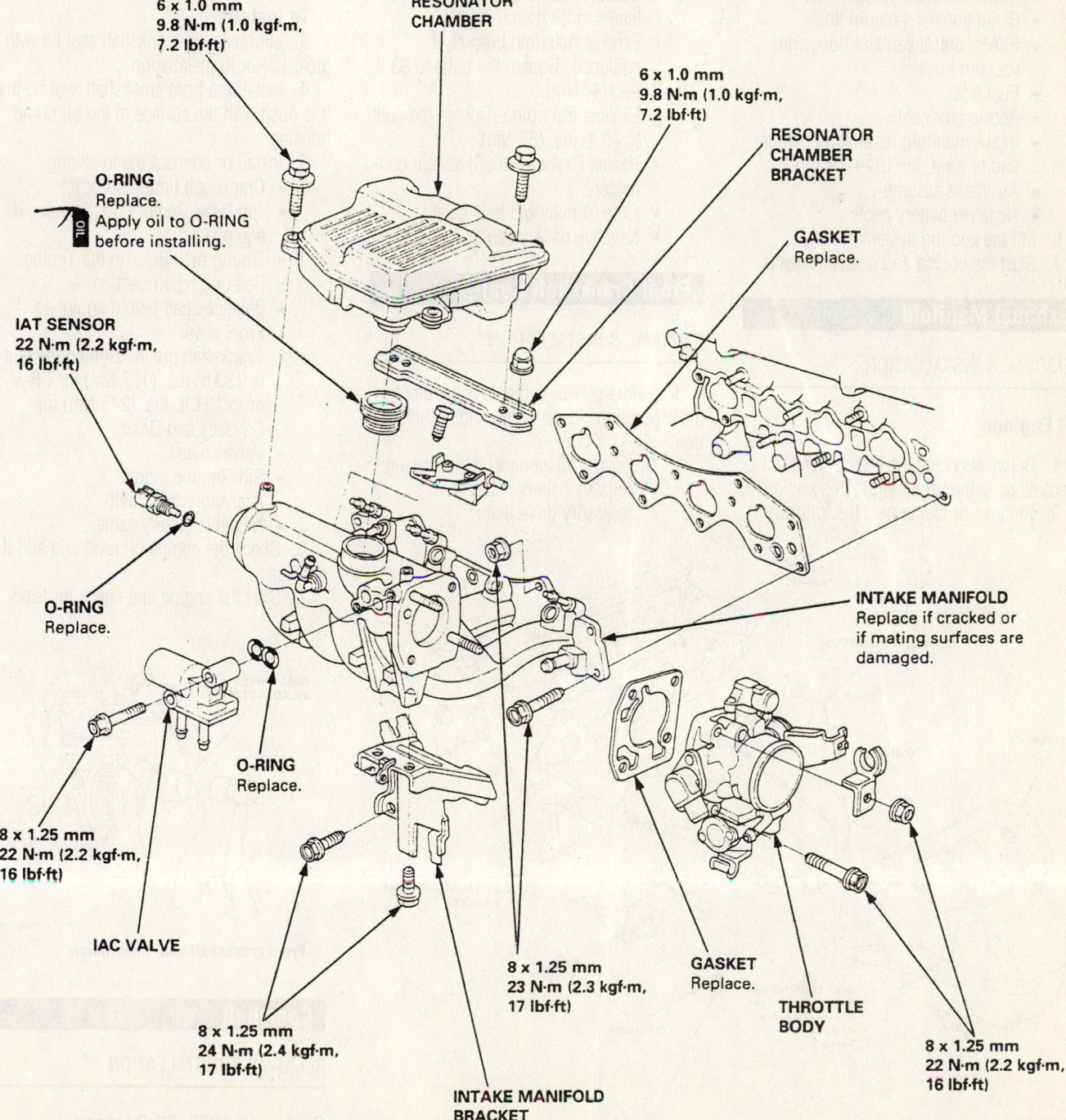

6 x 1.0 mm
9.8 N·m (1.0 kgf·m, 7.2 lbf·ft)

RESONATOR CHAMBER

6 x 1.0 mm
9.8 N·m (1.0 kgf·m, 7.2 lbf·ft)

RESONATOR CHAMBER BRACKET

O-RING
Replace.
Apply oil to O-RING before installing.

GASKET
Replace.

IAT SENSOR
22 N·m (2.2 kgf·m, 16 lbf·ft)

O-RING
Replace.

O-RING
Replace.

INTAKE MANIFOLD
Replace if cracked or if mating surfaces are damaged.

8 x 1.25 mm
22 N·m (2.2 kgf·m, 16 lbf·ft)

IAC VALVE

8 x 1.25 mm
24 N·m (2.4 kgf·m, 17 lbf·ft)

INTAKE MANIFOLD BRACKET

8 x 1.25 mm
23 N·m (2.3 kgf·m, 17 lbf·ft)

GASKET
Replace.

THROTTLE BODY

8 x 1.25 mm
22 N·m (2.2 kgf·m, 16 lbf·ft)

9308MG22

Intake manifold exploded view—1999–01 CR-V

Timing belt service is covered in Section 4 of this manual

- Intake manifold. Tighten the fasteners to 17 ft. lbs. (23 Nm).
- Intake manifold brackets
- Cruise control actuator
- IAC valve connector
- MAP sensor connector
- TP sensor connector
- Fuel injector connectors
- Bypass hoses
- PCV valve and hose
- Intake manifold vacuum line
- Brake booster vacuum line
- EVAP control canister hose and vacuum hose
- Fuel lines
- Accelerator cable
- Intake manifold resonator chamber and bracket, for 1999–01 models
- Air intake assembly
- Negative battery cable

6. Fill the cooling system.

7. Start the engine and check for leaks.

Exhaust Manifold

REMOVAL & INSTALLATION

All Engines

1. Before servicing the vehicle, refer to the precautions in the beginning of this section.

2. Remove or disconnect the following:

- Negative battery cable
- Exhaust manifold heat shield
- Heated Oxygen (HO$_2$S) sensor connector
- Exhaust front pipe
- Exhaust manifold bracket, if equipped
- Exhaust manifold

To install:

3. Install or connect the following:

- Exhaust manifold. Tighten the fasteners to 23 ft. lbs. (31 Nm).
- Exhaust manifold bracket, if equipped. Tighten the bolts to 33 ft. lbs. (44 Nm).
- Exhaust front pipe. Tighten the nuts to 40 ft. lbs. (55 Nm).
- Heated Oxygen (HO$_2$S) sensor connector
- Exhaust manifold heat shield
- Negative battery cable

Front Crankshaft Seal

REMOVAL & INSTALLATION

1. Before servicing the vehicle, refer to the precautions in the beginning of this section.

2. Remove or disconnect the following:

- Negative battery cable
- Accessory drive belts

- Side engine mount
- Valve cover
- Crankshaft pulley
- Front cover
- Balance shaft belt, if equipped
- Timing belt. Refer to the Timing Belt unit repair section.
- Top Dead Center (TDC) sensor, if equipped
- Crankshaft timing sprocket
- Front crankshaft seal

To install:

3. Lubricate the crankshaft seal lip with grease prior to installation.

4. Install the front crankshaft seal so that it is flush with the surface of the oil pump housing.

5. Install or connect the following:

- Crankshaft timing sprocket
- Top Dead Center (TDC) sensor, if equipped
- Timing belt. Refer to the Timing Belt unit repair section.
- Balance shaft belt, if equipped
- Front cover
- Crankshaft pulley. Tighten the bolt to 130 ft. lbs. (177 Nm) for CR-V or to 181 ft. lbs. (245 Nm) for Odyssey and Oasis.
- Valve cover
- Side engine mount
- Accessory drive belts
- Negative battery cable

6. Check the engine oil level and add if necessary.

7. Start the engine and check for leaks.

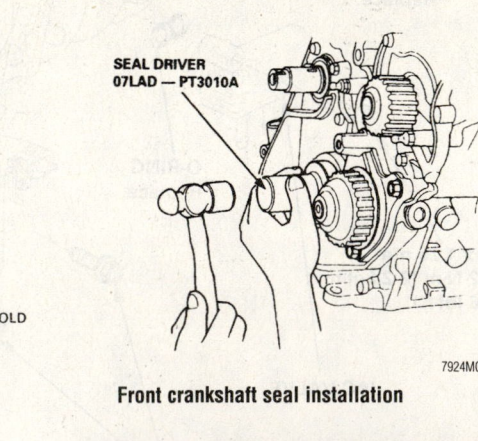

Front crankshaft seal installation

SEAL DRIVER
07LAD — PT3010A

7924MG48

Camshaft

REMOVAL & INSTALLATION

Oasis and 1997–98 Odyssey

1. Before servicing the vehicle, refer to the precautions in the beginning of this section.

2. Remove or disconnect the following:

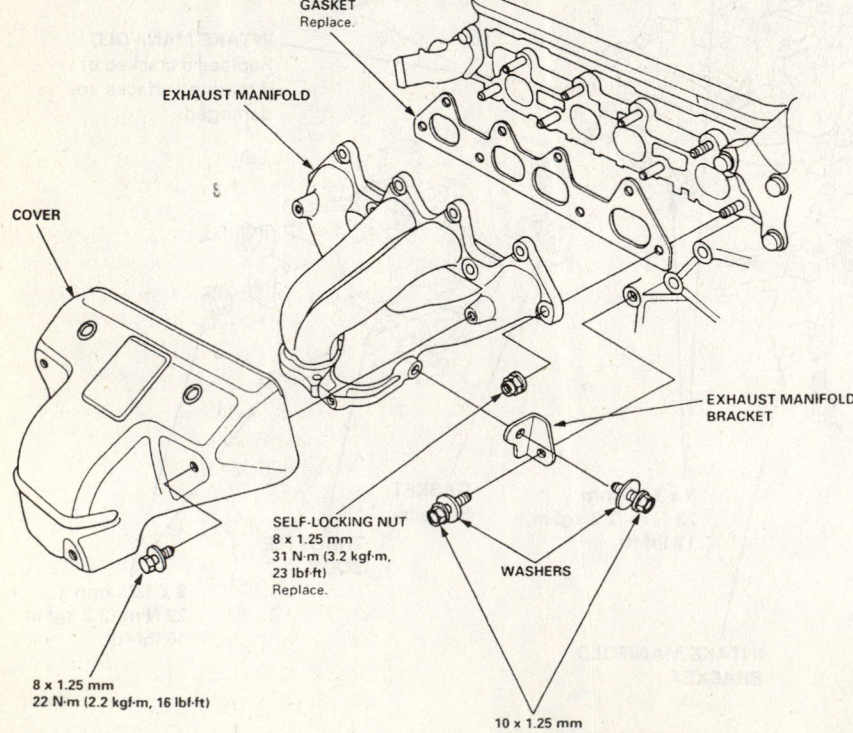

GASKET
Replace.

EXHAUST MANIFOLD

COVER

EXHAUST MANIFOLD
BRACKET

SELF-LOCKING NUT
8 x 1.25 mm
31 N·m (3.2 kgf·m, 23 lbf·ft)
Replace.

WASHERS

8 x 1.25 mm
22 N·m (2.2 kgf·m, 16 lbf·ft)

10 x 1.25 mm
44 N·m (4.5 kgf·m, 33 lbf·ft)

7924MG47

Exploded view of the exhaust manifold—2.3L engine shown

- Negative battery cable
- Valve cover
- Accessory drive belts
- Front cover
- Timing belt. Refer to the Timing Belt unit repair section.
- Camshaft sprocket
- Rear timing belt cover

3. Loosen the valve adjuster locknuts and screws so that all valves are closed.

4. Loosen the camshaft holder bolts evenly in sequence.

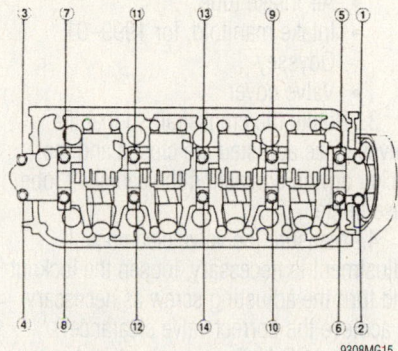

Camshaft holder loosening sequence— Oasis and 1997–98 Odyssey

5. Remove the camshaft holders, rocker arm shafts and rocker arms as an assembly.

➡**Keep all valvetrain components in order for assembly.**

6. Remove the camshaft and camshaft seal.

To install:

➡**Use new O-rings, seals and gaskets when installing the camshaft.**

7. Lubricate the camshaft lobes and

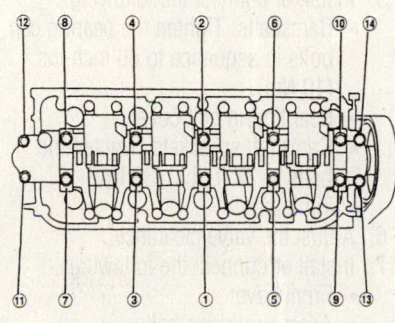

Camshaft holder torque sequence—Oasis and 1997–98 Odyssey

journals with clean engine oil and install the camshaft.

8. Install the rocker arm assembly to the cylinder head. Tighten the camshaft holder bolts in sequence and in multiple passes as follows:

- 8mm bolts: 16 ft. lbs. (22 Nm)
- 6mm bolts: 105 inch lbs. (12 Nm)

9. Install the timing belt.

10. Adjust the valve clearance.

11. Install or connect the following:

- Front cover
- Accessory drive belts
- Valve cover
- Negative battery cable

12. Start the engine and check for leaks.

1999–01 Odyssey

1. Before servicing the vehicle, refer to the precautions in the beginning of this section.

2. Remove or disconnect the following:

- Negative battery cable
- Air intake tube
- Accessory drive belts
- Front cover
- Timing belt. Refer to the Timing Belt unit repair section.
- Camshaft sprockets
- Timing belt rear covers
- Ignition coil covers
- Intake manifold cover
- Intake manifold
- Valve cover
- Rocker arms and shaft assembly
- Camshaft thrust cover
- Camshaft

To install:

➡**Use new O-rings, seals and gaskets when installing the camshaft.**

3. Install or connect the following:

- Camshaft
- Camshaft thrust cover. Tighten the bolts to 16 ft. lbs. (22 Nm).
- Rocker arms and shaft assembly
- Valve cover
- Intake manifold
- Intake manifold cover
- Ignition coil covers
- Timing belt rear covers
- Camshaft sprockets. Tighten the bolts to 67 ft. lbs. (90 Nm).
- Timing belt
- Front cover
- Accessory drive belts
- Air intake tube
- Negative battery cable

4. Start the engine and check for leaks.

Exploded view of the camshaft and valve components—Oasis and 1997–98 Odyssey

CR-V

1. Before servicing the vehicle, refer to the precautions in the beginning of this section.

2. Remove or disconnect the following:
- Negative battery cable
- Spark plug wires
- Distributor
- Valve cover
- Accessory drive belts
- Front cover
- Timing belt. Refer to the Timing Belt unit repair section.

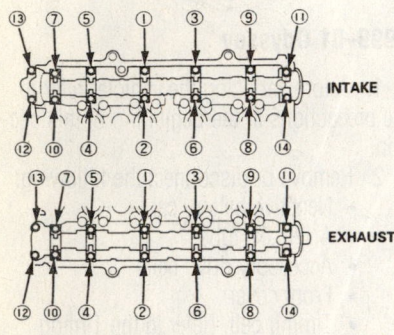

Camshaft bearing tightening sequence—CR-V

3. Loosen the valve adjuster locknuts and screws so that all valves are closed.

➡ **Keep all valvetrain components in order for assembly.**

4. Remove or disconnect the following:
- Camshaft sprockets
- Rear timing belt cover
- Camshafts

To install:

➡ **Use new O-rings, seals and gaskets when installing the camshaft.**

5. Install or connect the following:
- Camshafts. Tighten the bearing cap bolts in sequence to 86 inch lbs. (10 Nm).
- Rear timing belt cover
- Camshaft sprockets. Tighten the bolts to 27 ft. lbs. (37 Nm).
- Timing belt

6. Adjust the valve clearance.

7. Install or connect the following:
- Front cover
- Accessory drive belts
- Valve cover
- Distributor
- Spark plug wires
- Negative battery cable

8. Start the engine and check for leaks.

ADJUSTMENT

Adjust the valves only when the cylinder head temperature is less than 100°F (38°C).

1. Before servicing the vehicle, refer to the precautions in the beginning of this section.

2. Remove or disconnect the following:
- Negative battery cable
- Air intake tube
- Intake manifold, for 1999–01 Odyssey
- Valve cover

3. Rotate the crankshaft so that the valves to be adjusted are closed and the rocker arm is contacting the camshaft lobe base circle.

4. Measure the valve clearance. If adjustment is necessary, loosen the locknut and turn the adjusting screw as necessary to achieve the correct valve clearance.

5. For CR-V, the correct valve clearance is:

- Intake valves: 0.003–0.005 inches (0.08–0.12mm)
- Exhaust valves: 0.006–0.008 inches (0.16–0.20mm)

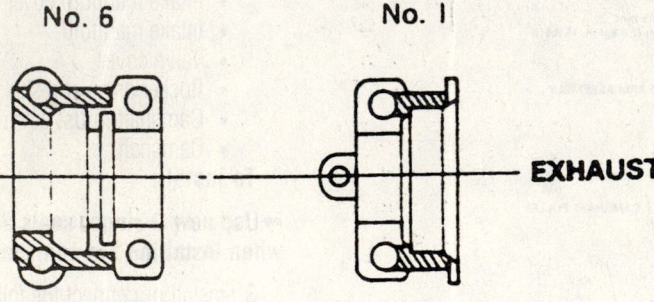

Apply liquid gasket to the shaded areas.

Apply liquid gasket to the shaded areas of the camshaft journals—CR-V

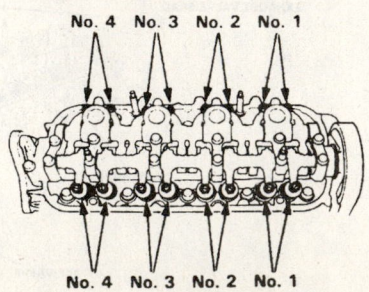

Intake and exhaust valve identification—CR-V

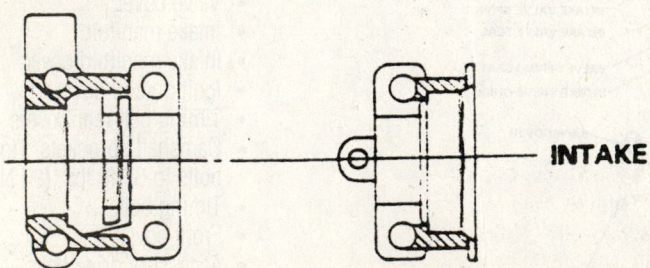

Intake and exhaust valve identification—Oasis and 1997–98 Odyssey

6. For Oasis and 1997–98 Odyssey, the correct valve clearance is:
- Intake valves: 0.009–0.011 inches (0.24–0.28mm)
- Exhaust valves: 0.011–0.013 inches (0.28–0.32mm)

7. For 1999–01 Odyssey, the correct valve clearance is:
- Intake valves: 0.008–0.009 inches (0.20–0.24mm)
- Exhaust valves: 0.011–0.013 inches (0.28–0.32mm)

8. After adjustment, tighten the locknuts to the following specifications:
- CR-V: 18 ft. lbs. (24 Nm)
- Odyssey and Oasis: 14 ft. lbs. (20 Nm)

9. Install or connect the following:
- Valve cover
- Intake manifold, for 1999–01 Odyssey
- Air intake tube
- Negative battery cable

10. Start the engine and check for proper operation.

Starter Motor

REMOVAL & INSTALLATION

Oasis and 1997–98 Odyssey

1. Before servicing the vehicle, refer to the precautions in the beginning of this section.

2. Remove or disconnect the following:
- Negative battery cable
- Lower radiator hose and engine wiring harness bracket
- Starter wiring harness connectors
- Starter motor

To install:

3. Install or connect the following:
- Starter motor. Tighten the bolts to 33 ft. lbs. (44 Nm).
- Starter wiring harness connectors. Tighten the battery cable nut to 79 inch lbs. (9 Nm).
- Lower radiator hose and engine wiring harness bracket
- Negative battery cable

1999–01 Odyssey

1. Before servicing the vehicle, refer to the precautions in the beginning of this section.

2. Remove or disconnect the following:
- Negative battery cable

- Transmission fluid cooler line clamp
- Starter wiring harness connectors
- Starter motor

To install:

3. Install or connect the following:
- Starter motor. Tighten the bolts to 33 ft. lbs. (44 Nm).
- Starter wiring harness connectors. Tighten the battery cable nut to 79 inch lbs. (9 Nm).
- Transmission fluid cooler line clamp
- Negative battery cable

CR-V

1. Before servicing the vehicle, refer to the precautions in the beginning of this section.

2. Remove or disconnect the following:
- Negative battery cable
- Starter wiring harness connectors
- Starter motor

To install:

3. Install or connect the following:
- Starter motor. Tighten the bolts to 33 ft. lbs. (44 Nm).
- Starter wiring harness connectors. Tighten the battery cable nut to 79 inch lbs. (9 Nm).
- Negative battery cable

Oil Pan

REMOVAL & INSTALLATION

1. Before servicing the vehicle, refer to the precautions in the beginning of this section.

2. Drain the engine oil.

3. Remove or disconnect the following:
- Negative battery cable
- Front splash shield
- Heated Oxygen (HO_2S) sensor connector
- Subframe center beam, for Oasis and 1997–98 Odyssey
- Exhaust front pipe
- Torque converter cover, if equipped with an automatic transaxle
- Oil pan

To install:

4. Install the oil pan. For 4 cylinder engines, use a new gasket. For the 6 cylinder engine, apply liquid gasket as shown.

5. Tighten the bolts in sequence to the following specifications:
- CR-V and 1999–01 Odyssey: 105 inch lbs. (12 Nm)

- Oasis and 1997–98 Odyssey: 10 ft. lbs. (14 Nm)

6. Install or connect the following:
- Torque converter cover, if removed
- Exhaust front pipe
- Subframe center beam, if removed
- HO_2S sensor connector
- Front splash shield
- Negative battery cable

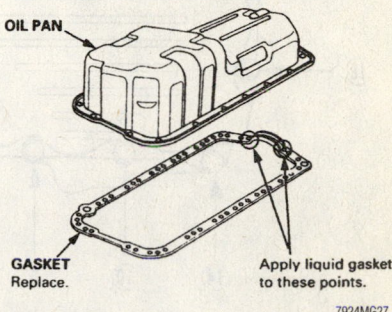

Oil pan gasket installation—all 4 cylinder engines

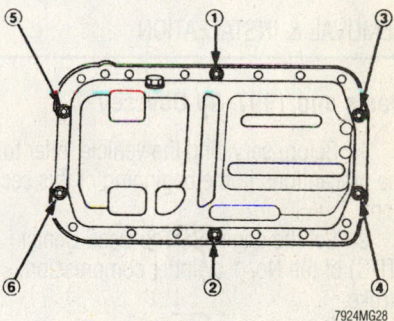

Oil pan fastener tightening sequence—all 4 cylinder engines

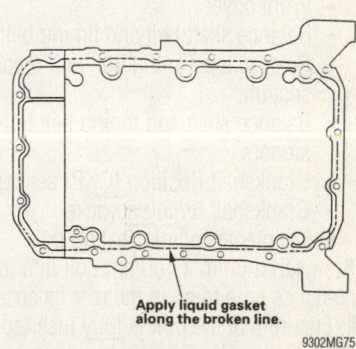

Apply liquid gasket to the inner threads of the bolt holes and the engine block along the area indicated by the broken line—1999–01 Odyssey

---

Refer to Section 1 for engine rebuilding specifications

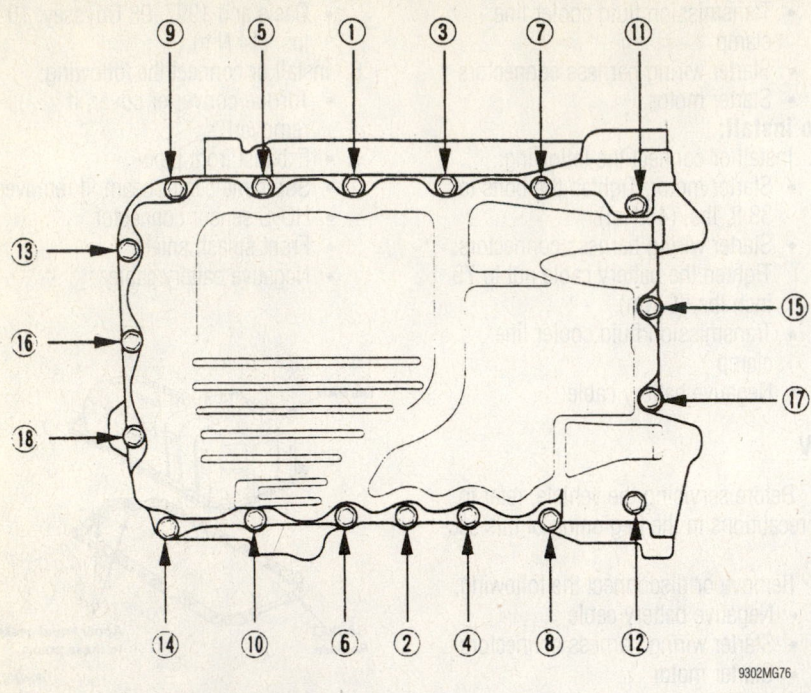

Oil pan tightening sequence—1999–01 Odyssey

9302MG76

Oil Pump

REMOVAL & INSTALLATION

Oasis and 1997–98 Odyssey

1. Before servicing the vehicle, refer to the precautions in the beginning of this section.
2. Set the engine to Top Dead Center (TDC) of the No. 1 cylinder compression stroke.
3. Drain the engine oil.
4. Remove or disconnect the following:
   - Negative battery cable
   - Accessory drive belts
   - Front cover
   - Balance shaft belt and timing belt. Refer to the Timing Belt unit repair section.
   - Balance shaft and timing belt tensioners
   - Crankshaft Position (CKP) sensor
   - Crankshaft timing sprocket
   - Maintenance hole sealing bolt
5. Insert a 6mm x 100mm bolt into the maintenance hole to align the rear balance shaft. Ensure that the bolt is fully inserted as shown.
6. Remove or disconnect the following:
   - Balance shaft gear case
   - Balance shaft sprockets
   - Oil pan
   - Oil pump pickup tube
   - Oil pump

To install:

➡ Use new gaskets and O-ring seals for assembly.

7. Apply liquid gasket to the oil pump and to the bolt hole threads.
8. Install or connect the following:
   - Oil pump. Tighten the bolts to 105 inch lbs. (12 Nm).
   - Oil pump pickup tube. Tighten the fasteners to 105 inch lbs. (12 Nm).
   - Oil pan
   - Balance shaft sprockets. Tighten the front balancer sprocket bolt to 22 ft. lbs. (29 Nm) and the rear balancer sprocket to 18 ft. lbs. (25 Nm).

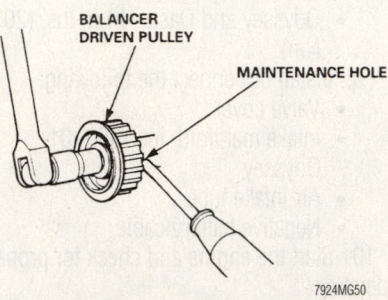

7924MG50

Hold the front balance shaft with a prytool when loosening or tightening the balance shaft sprocket bolt—Oasis and 1997–98 Odyssey

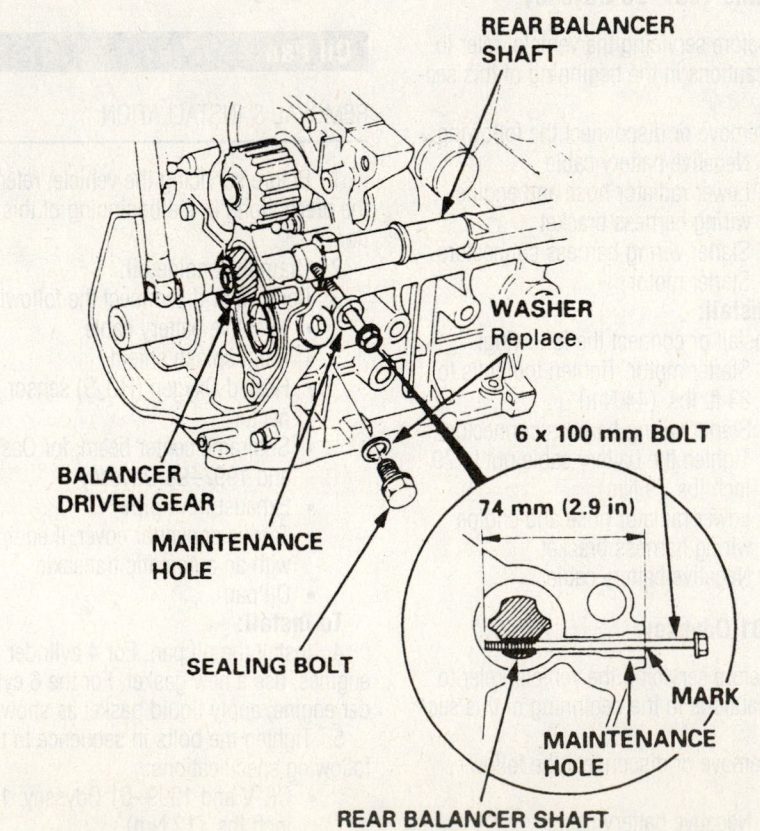

7924MG51

Rear balance shaft alignment—Oasis and 1997–98 Odyssey

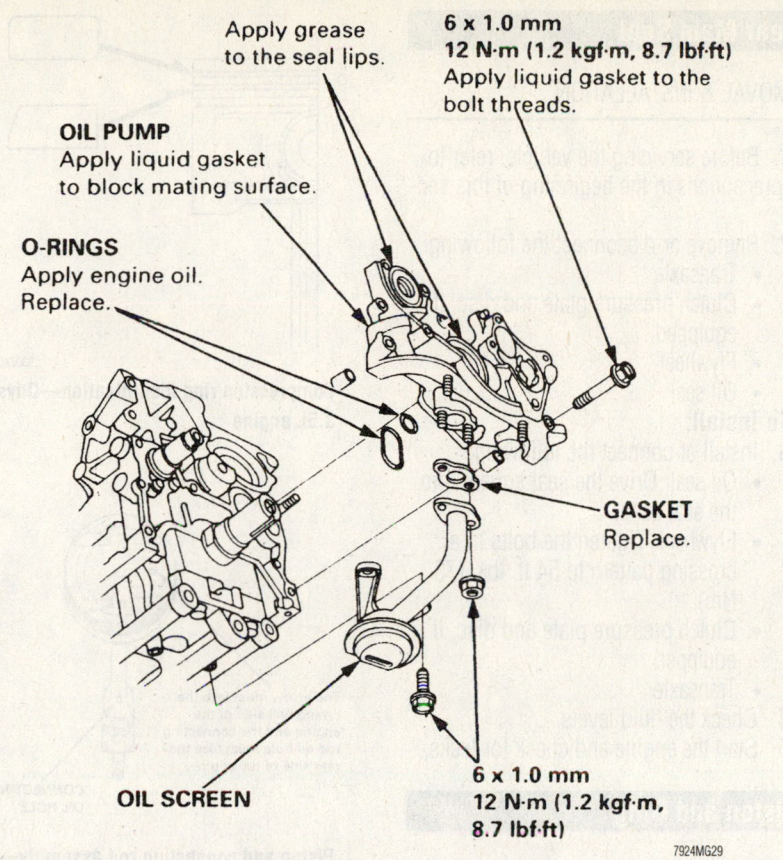

Apply grease to the seal lips.

6 x 1.0 mm
12 N·m (1.2 kgf·m, 8.7 lbf·ft)
Apply liquid gasket to the bolt threads.

OIL PUMP
Apply liquid gasket to block mating surface.

O-RINGS
Apply engine oil. Replace.

GASKET
Replace.

OIL SCREEN

6 x 1.0 mm
12 N·m (1.2 kgf·m, 8.7 lbf·ft)

7924MG29

Exploded view of the oil pump mounting—Oasis and 1997–98 Odyssey

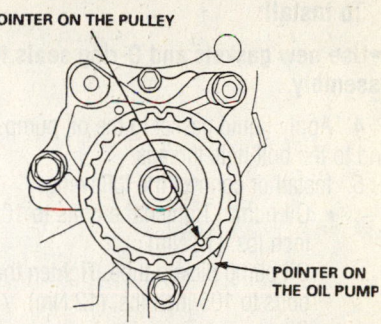

POINTER ON THE PULLEY

POINTER ON THE OIL PUMP

9308MG24

Gear case sprocket alignment after installation—Oasis and 1997–98 Odyssey

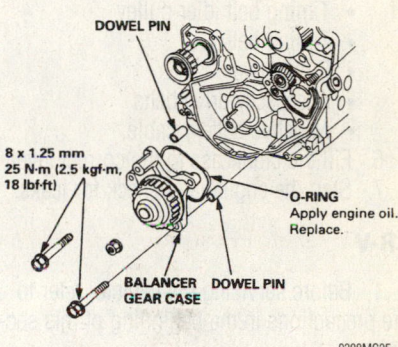

DOWEL PIN

8 x 1.25 mm
25 N·m (2.5 kgf·m, 18 lbf·ft)

O-RING
Apply engine oil. Replace.

BALANCER GEAR CASE

DOWEL PIN

9308MG25

Balance shaft gear case exploded view—Oasis and 1997–98 Odyssey

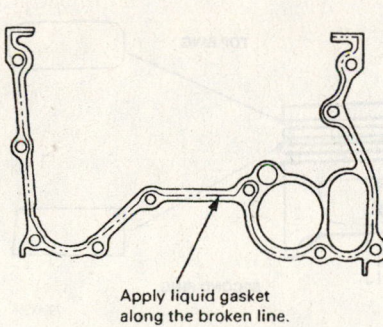

Apply liquid gasket along the broken line.

7924MG30

Apply the oil pump housing gasket sealer as indicated—Oasis and 1997–98 Odyssey

9. Install the balance shaft gear case as follows:

a. Align the rear balance shaft with a 6mm x 100mm bolt through the maintenance hole.

b. Align the notch on the sprocket flange with the pointer on the balance shaft gear case.

c. Install the gear case with a new O-ring seal. Tighten the bolts to 18 ft. lbs. (25 Nm).

d. Check that the balance shaft gear

case sprocket pointer aligns with the oil pump pointer.

10. Install or connect the following:
- Crankshaft timing sprocket
- CKP sensor
- Balance shaft and timing belt tensioners
- Balance shaft belt and timing belt
- Maintenance hole sealing bolt. Remove the 6mm x 100mm bolt

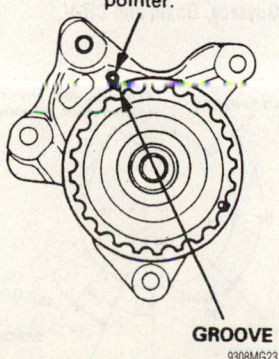

POINTER
Align the groove to pointer.

GROOVE

9308MG23

Balance shaft gear case installation alignment marks—Oasis and 1997–98 Odyssey

and tighten the sealing bolt to 22 ft. lbs. (29 Nm).
- Front cover
- Accessory drive belts
- Negative battery cable

11. Fill the crankcase to the correct level.
12. Start the engine and check for leaks.

1999–01 Odyssey

1. Before servicing the vehicle, refer to the precautions in the beginning of this section.
2. Drain the engine oil.
3. Remove or disconnect the following:
- Negative battery cable
- Accessory drive belts
- Front cover
- Timing belt. Refer to the Timing Belt unit repair section.
- Timing belt idler pulley
- Crankshaft Position (CKP) sensor
- Crankshaft timing sprocket
- Variable Valve Timing and Valve Lift Electronic Control (VTEC) solenoid valve connector
- Oil filter adapter
- Oil pan
- Oil pump pickup tube
- Oil pump

To install:

➡ **Use new gaskets and O-ring seals for assembly.**

4. Apply liquid gasket to the oil pump and to the bolt hole threads.

5. Install or connect the following:
   - Oil pump. Tighten the bolts to 105 inch lbs. (12 Nm).
   - Oil pump pickup tube. Tighten the bolts to 105 inch lbs. (12 Nm).
   - Oil pan
   - Oil filter adapter
   - VTEC solenoid valve connector
   - Crankshaft timing sprocket
   - CKP sensor
   - Timing belt idler pulley
   - Timing belt
   - Front cover
   - Accessory drive belts
   - Negative battery cable

6. Fill the crankcase to the correct level.
7. Start the engine and check for leaks.

CR-V

1. Before servicing the vehicle, refer to the precautions in the beginning of this section.

2. Drain the engine oil.

3. Remove or disconnect the following:
   - Negative battery cable
   - Accessory drive belts
   - Front cover
   - Timing belt. Refer to the Timing Belt unit repair section.
   - Crankshaft timing sprocket
   - Oil pan
   - Oil pump pickup tube
   - Oil pump

To install:

➡ **Use new gaskets and O-ring seals for assembly.**

4. Apply liquid gasket to the oil pump and to the bolt hole threads.

5. Install or connect the following:
   - Oil pump. Tighten the 8mm bolts to 17 ft. lbs. (24 Nm) and the 6mm bolts to 86 inch lbs. (10 Nm).
   - Oil pump pickup tube. Tighten the fasteners to 86 inch lbs. (10 Nm).
   - Oil pan
   - Crankshaft timing sprocket
   - Timing belt. Refer to the Timing Belt unit repair section.
   - Front cover
   - Accessory drive belts
   - Negative battery cable

6. Fill the crankcase to the correct level.
7. Start the engine and check for leaks.

Rear Main Seal

REMOVAL & INSTALLATION

1. Before servicing the vehicle, refer to the precautions in the beginning of this section.

2. Remove or disconnect the following:
   - Transaxle
   - Clutch pressure plate and disc, if equipped
   - Flywheel
   - Oil seal

To install:

3. Install or connect the following:
   - Oil seal. Drive the seal square into the seal case.
   - Flywheel. Tighten the bolts in a crossing pattern to 54 ft. lbs. (73 Nm).
   - Clutch pressure plate and disc, if equipped
   - Transaxle

4. Check the fluid levels.
5. Start the engine and check for leaks.

Piston and Ring

POSITIONING

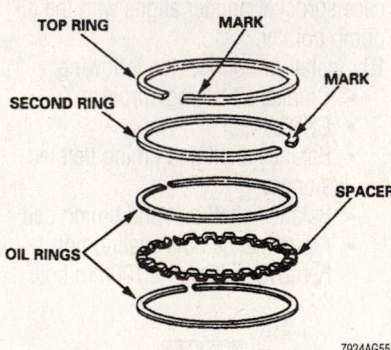

Piston ring positioning and top mark location—Odyssey, Oasis and CR-V

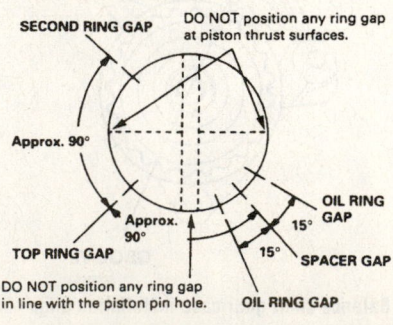

Piston ring end-gap spacing—Odyssey, Oasis and CR-V 4 cylinder engines

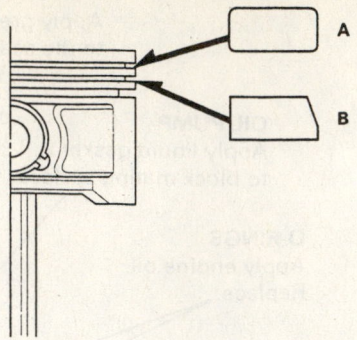

Compression ring identification—Odyssey 3.5L engine

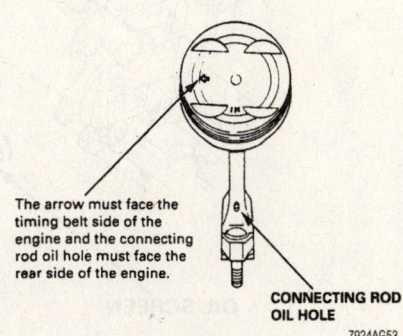

Piston and connecting rod assembly—CR-V

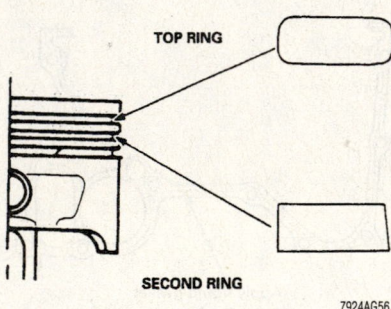

Compression ring identification—Odyssey and Oasis 4 cylinder engines

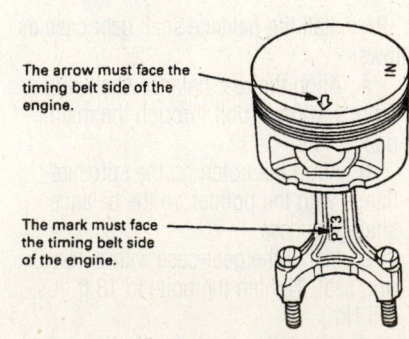

Piston and connecting rod assembly—Odyssey and Oasis 4 cylinder engines

FUEL SYSTEM

Fuel System Service Precautions

Safety is the most important factor when performing not only fuel system maintenance, but any type of maintenance. Failure to conduct maintenance and repairs in a safe manner may result in serious personal injury or death. Maintenance and testing of the vehicle's fuel system components can be accomplished safely and effectively by adhering to the following rules and guidelines:

- To avoid the possibility of fire and personal injury, always disconnect the negative battery cable unless the repair or test procedure requires that battery voltage be applied.
- Always relieve the fuel system pressure prior to disconnecting any fuel system component (injector, fuel rail, pressure regulator, etc.), fitting or fuel line connection. Exercise extreme caution whenever relieving fuel system pressure to avoid exposing skin, face and eyes to fuel spray. Please be advised that fuel under pressure may penetrate the skin or any part of the body that it contacts.
- Always place a shop towel or cloth around the fitting or connection prior to loosening to absorb any excess fuel due to spillage. Ensure that all fuel spillage (should it occur) is quickly removed from engine surfaces. Ensure that all fuel soaked cloths or towels are deposited into a suitable waste container.
- Always keep a dry chemical (Class B) fire extinguisher near the work area.
- Do not allow fuel spray or fuel vapors to come into contact with a spark or open flame.
- Always use a backup wrench when loosening and tightening fuel line connection fittings. This will prevent unnecessary stress and torsion to fuel line piping. Always follow the proper torque specifications.
- Always replace worn fuel fitting O-rings with new. Do not substitute fuel hose or equivalent, where fuel pipe is installed.

Fuel System Pressure

RELIEVING

CR-V, Oasis and 1997–98 Odyssey

1. Before servicing the vehicle, refer to the precautions in the beginning of this section.

2. Disconnect the negative battery cable.
3. Remove the fuel filler cap.
4. Hold the fuel rail inlet banjo bolt with a flare nut wrench. Hold the service bolt with a box end wrench.
5. Place a shop towel over the fitting to absorb leakage.
6. Loosen the service bolt 1 turn.
7. When repairs are complete, replace the sealing washers and tighten the service bolt to 25 ft. lbs. (33 Nm).
8. Install the fuel filler cap.
9. Connect the negative battery cable.
10. Start the engine and check for leaks.

1999–01 Odyssey

1. Before servicing the vehicle, refer to the precautions in the beginning of this section.
2. Disconnect the negative battery cable.
3. Remove the fuel filler cap.
4. Place a shop towel over the fuel pulsation damper.
5. Loosen the fuel pulsation damper 1 turn.
6. When service is completed, replace the sealing washer and tighten the pulsation damper to 16 ft. lbs. (22 Nm).

7. Replace the fuel filler cap.
8. Connect the negative battery cable.
9. Start the engine and check for leaks.

Fuel Filter

REMOVAL & INSTALLATION

CR-V, Oasis and 1997–98 Odyssey

1. Before servicing the vehicle, refer to the precautions in the beginning of this section.
2. Relieve the fuel system pressure.
3. Remove or disconnect the following:
   - Negative battery cable
   - Wire harness bracket
   - Power steering hose bracket
   - Fuel lines
   - Fuel filter

To install:
4. Install or connect the following:
   - Fuel filter
   - Fuel lines. Use new sealing washers.
   - Power steering hose bracket
   - Wire harness bracket
   - Negative battery cable
5. Start the engine and check for leaks.

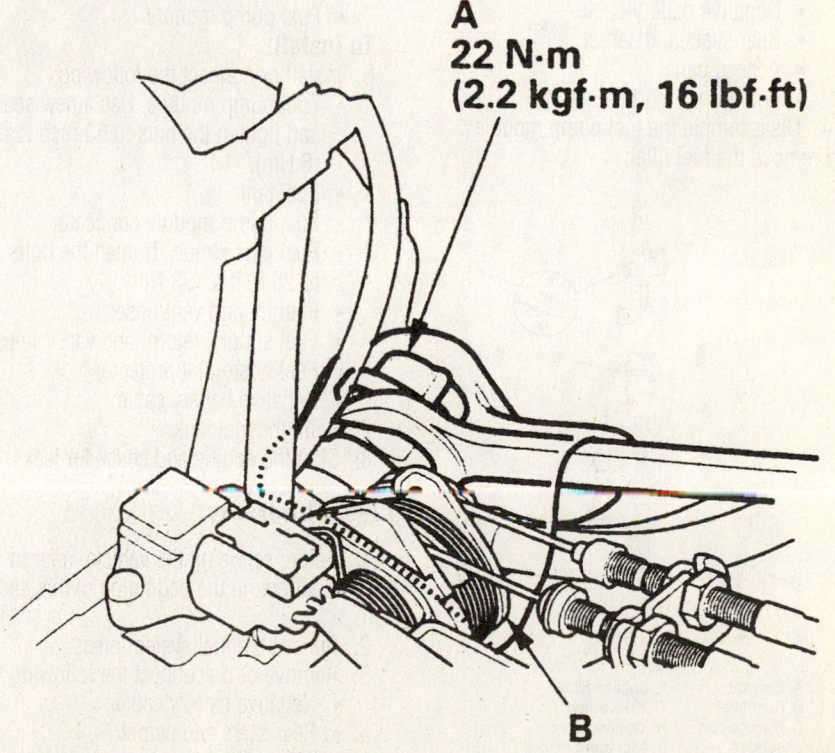

A
22 N·m
(2.2 kgf·m, 16 lbf·ft)

B

9302MG77

Use a wrench on the fuel pulsation damper (A). Place a rag over the damper (B) when relieving residual fuel pressure—1999–01 Odyssey

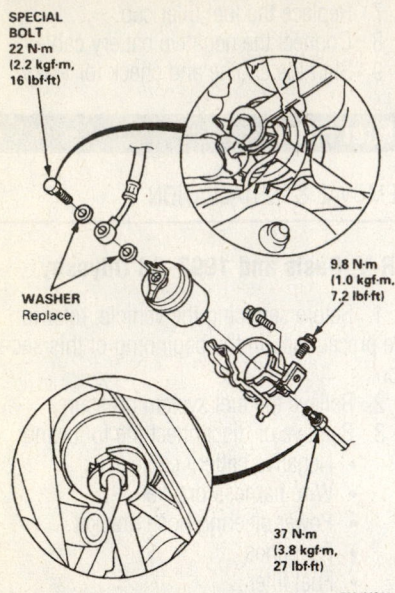

SPECIAL
BOLT
22 N·m
(2.2 kgf·m,
16 lbf·ft)

9.8 N·m
(1.0 kgf·m,
7.2 lbf·ft)

WASHER
Replace.

37 N·m
(3.8 kgf·m,
27 lbf·ft)

7924MG31

Exploded view of the fuel filter mounting—CR-V, Oasis and 1997–98 Odyssey

1999–01 Odyssey

1. Before servicing the vehicle, refer to the precautions in the beginning of this section.
2. Relieve the fuel system pressure.
3. Remove or disconnect the following:
   - Negative battery cable
   - Rear seats and carpet
   - Access panel
   - Fuel pump module
4. Disassemble the fuel pump module and remove the fuel filter.

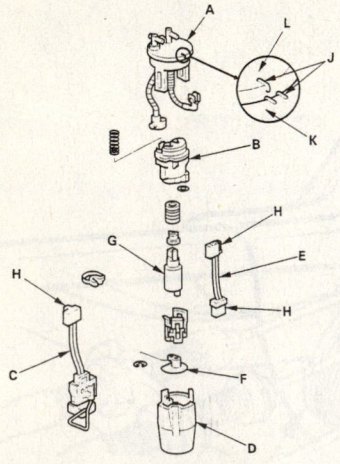

A. Bracket
B. Fuel filter
C. Fuel gauge sender
D. Case
E. Wire harness
F. Suction filter
G. Fuel pump
H. Connectors
J. Alignment marks
K. Fuel tank
L. Fuel pump module

9308MG26

Exploded view of the fuel pump module—1999–01 Odyssey

To install:

5. Install the fuel filter and assemble the fuel pump module.
6. Install or connect the following:
   - Fuel pump module
   - Access panel
   - Rear seats and carpet
   - Negative battery cable
7. Start the engine and check for leaks.

Fuel Pump

REMOVAL & INSTALLATION

Oasis and 1997–98 Odyssey

1. Before servicing the vehicle, refer to the precautions in the beginning of this section.
2. Relieve fuel system pressure.
3. Drain the fuel tank
4. Remove or disconnect the following:
   - Negative battery cable
   - Fuel hose joint protector
   - Fuel supply, return, and vapor lines
   - Fuel fill and vent hoses
5. Support the fuel tank, then remove or disconnect the following:
   - Fuel tank straps
   - Fuel pump module connector
   - Fuel tank
   - Fuel pump module

To install:

6. Install or connect the following:
   - Fuel pump module. Use a new seal and tighten the nuts to 53 inch lbs. (6 Nm).
   - Fuel tank
   - Fuel pump module connector
   - Fuel tank straps. Tighten the bolts to 28 ft. lbs. (38 Nm).
   - Fuel fill and vent hoses
   - Fuel supply, return, and vapor lines
   - Fuel hose joint protector
   - Negative battery cable
7. Refill the fuel tank.
8. Start the engine and check for leaks.

1999–01 Odyssey

1. Before servicing the vehicle, refer to the precautions in the beginning of this section.
2. Relieve the fuel system pressure.
3. Remove or disconnect the following:
   - Negative battery cable
   - Rear seats and carpet
   - Access panel
   - Fuel pump module wiring connector
   - Fuel supply and return lines
   - Fuel pump locknut
   - Fuel pump module

To install:

4. Install or connect the following:
   - Fuel pump module. Use a new seal and align the matchmarks.
   - Fuel pump locknut
   - Fuel supply and return lines
   - Fuel pump module wiring connector
   - Access panel
   - Rear seats and carpet
   - Negative battery cable
5. Start the engine and check for leaks.

CR-V

1. Before servicing the vehicle, refer to the precautions in the beginning of this section.
2. Relieve the fuel system pressure.
3. Remove or disconnect the following:
   - Negative battery cable
   - Left rear seat cushion
   - Base frame cover
   - Access panel
   - Fuel pump module wiring connector
   - Fuel supply and return lines
   - Fuel pump module

To install:

4. Install or connect the following:
   - Fuel pump module. Use a new seal and tighten the nuts to 52 inch lbs. (6 Nm).
   - Fuel supply and return lines
   - Fuel pump module wiring connector
   - Access panel
   - Base frame cover
   - Left rear seat cushion
   - Negative battery cable
5. Start the engine and check for leaks.

Fuel Injector

REMOVAL & INSTALLATION

Oasis and 1997–98 Odyssey

1. Before servicing the vehicle, refer to the precautions in the beginning of this section.
2. Relieve the fuel system pressure.
3. Remove or disconnect the following:
   - Negative battery cable
   - Exhaust Gas Recirculation (EGR) valve connector
   - Positive Crankcase Ventilation (PCV) valve and hose
   - Fuel injector connectors
   - Fuel lines
   - Fuel pressure regulator vacuum line

- Fuel supply manifold
- Fuel injectors

To install:

4. Install the fuel injectors to the fuel supply manifold with new cushion rings and O-rings.

5. Install new seal rings to the intake manifold.

6. Install or connect the following:
- Fuel supply manifold and injector assembly. Tighten the nuts to 105 inch lbs. (12 Nm).
- Fuel pressure regulator vacuum line
- Fuel lines. Tighten the supply line nut to 16 ft. lbs. (22 Nm).
- PCV valve and hose
- EGR valve connector
- Negative battery cable

7. Start the engine and check for leaks.

1999–01 Odyssey

1. Before servicing the vehicle, refer to the precautions in the beginning of this section.

2. Relieve the fuel system pressure.

3. Remove or disconnect the following:
- Negative battery cable
- Intake manifold
- Fuel lines
- Fuel injector connectors
- Fuel pressure regulator vacuum line
- Fuel supply manifold

4. Separate the fuel injectors from the fuel supply manifold.

To install:

5. Install the fuel injectors to the fuel supply manifold with new cushion rings and O-rings.

6. Install new seal rings to the intake manifold.

7. Install or connect the following:
- Fuel supply manifold and injector assembly. Tighten the bolts to 86 inch lbs. (10 Nm).
- Fuel pressure regulator vacuum line
- Fuel injector connectors
- Fuel lines
- Intake manifold
- Negative battery cable

8. Start the engine and check for leaks.

CR-V

1. Before servicing the vehicle, refer to the precautions in the beginning of this section.

2. Relieve the fuel system pressure.

3. Remove or disconnect the following:
- Negative battery cable
- Air intake resonator, for 1999–01 CR-V
- Injector connectors
- Idle Air Control (IAC) valve connector, for 1997–98 CR-V
- Evaporative Emissions (EVAP) purge control solenoid connector, for 1997–98 CR-V
- Positive Crankcase Ventilation (PCV) valve and hose
- Fuel pressure regulator vacuum line
- Fuel lines
- Fuel supply manifold
- Fuel injectors

To install:

4. Install the fuel injectors to the fuel supply manifold with new cushion rings and O-rings.

5. Install new seal rings to the intake manifold.

6. Install or connect the following:
- Fuel supply manifold and injector assembly. Tighten the nuts to 105 inch lbs. (12 Nm).
- Fuel lines
- Fuel pressure regulator vacuum line
- PCV valve and hose
- EVAP purge control solenoid connector, for 1997–98 CR-V
- IAC valve connector, for 1997–98 CR-V
- Injector connectors
- Air intake resonator, for 1999–01 CR-V
- Negative battery cable

7. Start the engine and check for leaks.

DRIVE TRAIN

Transaxle Assembly

REMOVAL & INSTALLATION

Automatic Transaxle

CR-V, OASIS AND 1997–98 ODYSSEY

1. Before servicing the vehicle, refer to the precautions in the beginning of this section.

2. Drain the transaxle.

3. Remove or disconnect the following:
- Battery
- Battery tray
- Air intake assembly
- Starter motor
- Transaxle ground cable
- Clutch pressure control solenoid valve connector
- Mainshaft speed sensor connector
- Clutch pressure switch connectors
- Shift control solenoid valve connectors
- Lockup control solenoid connector
- Countershaft speed sensor connector
- Transaxle oil cooler lines
- Gear position switch connector
- Engine splash shield
- Front wheels
- Subframe center beam
- Rear driveshaft, if equipped
- Front motor mount bracket
- Lower ball joints
- Lower damper fork bolts

4. Separate the inner CV-joints from the transaxle and intermediate shaft and support the axle halfshafts out of the work area with safety wire.

5. Remove or disconnect the following:
- Right damper fork
- Right radius rod
- Intermediate shaft
- Shift cable holder and shift cable
- Engine stiffener
- Torque converter
- Transaxle mount
- Intake manifold bracket
- Rear mount bracket
- Transaxle flange bolts
- Transaxle

To install:

➡**Use new circlips, split pins and self-locking nuts for assembly.**

6. Install or connect the following:
- Transaxle. Tighten the flange bolts to 47 ft. lbs. (64 Nm).
- Rear mount bracket. Tighten the bolts to 40 ft. lbs. (54 Nm).
- Intake manifold bracket. Tighten the bolts to 16 ft. lbs. (22 Nm).
- Transaxle mount. Tighten the stud bolt and nuts to 28 ft. lbs. (38 Nm) and the through bolt to 40 ft. lbs. (54 Nm).
- Front motor mount bracket. Tighten the bolts to 28 ft. lbs. (38 Nm).
- Torque converter. Tighten the driveplate bolts to 105 inch lbs. (12 Nm).

- Engine stiffener. Tighten the bolts to 33 ft. lbs. (44 Nm).
- Shift cable holder and shift cable
- Intermediate shaft. Tighten the bolts to 29 ft. lbs. (39 Nm).
- Axle halfshafts
- Right damper fork. Tighten the pinch bolt to 32 ft. lbs. (43 Nm).
- Right radius rod. Tighten the bolts to 76 ft. lbs. (103 Nm) and the nut to 32 ft. lbs. (43 Nm).
- Lower damper fork bolts. Tighten the nut to 47 ft. lbs. (64 Nm).
- Lower ball joints. Tighten the nut to 36–43 ft. lbs. (49–59 Nm).
- Rear driveshaft, if equipped
- Subframe center beam. Tighten the bolts to 37 ft. lbs. (50 Nm).
- Front wheels
- Engine splash shield
- Gear position switch connector
- Transaxle oil cooler lines
- Countershaft speed sensor connector
- Lockup control solenoid connector
- Shift control solenoid valve connectors
- Clutch pressure switch connectors
- Mainshaft speed sensor connector
- Clutch pressure control solenoid valve connector
- Transaxle ground cable
- Starter motor. Tighten the bolts to 33 ft. lbs. (44 Nm).
- Air intake assembly
- Battery tray
- Battery

7. Fill the transaxle to the correct level.
8. Start the engine and check for leaks.
9. Check the wheel alignment and adjust as necessary.

1999–01 ODYSSEY

1. Before servicing the vehicle, refer to the precautions in the beginning of this section.

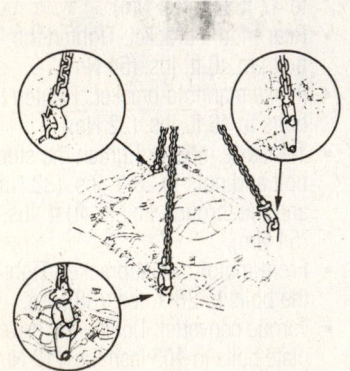

Support the engine while removing the transaxle—1999–01 Odyssey

2. Drain the transaxle.
3. Remove the engine appearance covers and install a support fixture to the engine lifting eyes.
4. Remove or disconnect the following:
- Air intake assembly
- Battery
- Battery tray
- Transaxle oil cooler lines
- Starter motor
- Transaxle ground cable
- Shift control solenoid valve connectors
- Clutch pressure switch connectors
- Mainshaft speed sensor connector
- Pressure control solenoid valve connectors
- Connector bracket
- Wiring harness cover
- Countershaft speed sensor connector
- Gear position switch connector
- Front motor mount
- Vacuum tube
- Splash shield
- Heated Oxygen (HO2S) sensor connectors
- Exhaust front pipe
- Stabilizer bar links
- Lower ball joints
- Shift cable bracket
- Shift cable cover
- Shift control lever
- Torque converter
- Power steering hose bracket
- Power steering gear and brace
- Rear engine mount
- Transaxle lower mounts

5. Matchmark the front subframe to the vehicle body.
6. Support the subframe with a jack.
7. Support the steering gear with safety wire and remove the subframe.
8. Separate the inner CV-joints from the transaxle and intermediate shaft and support the axle halfshafts out of the work area with safety wire.
9. Remove or disconnect the following:
- Intermediate shaft
- Transaxle flange bolts
- Transaxle

To install:

➡**Use new circlips, split pins and self-locking nuts for assembly.**

10. Install or connect the following:
- Transaxle. Tighten the flange bolts to 47 ft. lbs. (64 Nm).
- Intermediate shaft. Tighten the bolts to 29 ft. lbs. (39 Nm).
- Axle halfshafts

11. Raise the subframe into position and align the matchmarks. Tighten the subframe bolts to 76 ft. lbs. (103 Nm). Tighten the front subframe bracket bolts to 54 ft. lbs. (74 Nm) and the rear bracket bolts to 86 ft. lbs. (117 Nm).

12. Install or connect the following:
- Transaxle lower mounts. Tighten the nuts to 28 ft. lbs. (38 Nm).
- Rear engine mount. Tighten the bolts to 28 ft. lbs. (38 Nm).
- Power steering gear. Tighten the bolts to 29 ft. lbs. (39 Nm).
- Power steering gear brace. Tighten the bolts to 43 ft. lbs. (58 Nm).
- Power steering hose bracket
- Torque converter. Tighten the bolts to 105 inch lbs. (12 Nm).
- Shift control lever
- Shift cable cover
- Shift cable bracket
- Lower ball joints. Tighten the nuts to 43–51 ft. lbs. (59–69 Nm).
- Stabilizer bar links. Tighten the nuts to 58 ft. lbs. (78 Nm).
- Exhaust front pipe
- HO2S sensor connectors
- Splash shield
- Vacuum tube
- Front motor mount. Tighten the nut to 40 ft. lbs. (54 Nm).
- Gear position switch connector
- Countershaft speed sensor connector
- Wiring harness cover
- Connector bracket
- Pressure control solenoid valve connectors
- Mainshaft speed sensor connector
- Clutch pressure switch connectors
- Shift control solenoid valve connectors
- Transaxle ground cable
- Starter motor
- Transaxle oil cooler lines
- Battery tray
- Battery
- Air intake assembly

13. Fill the transaxle to the correct level.
14. Start the engine and check for leaks.
15. Check the wheel alignment and adjust as necessary.

Manual Transaxle

CR-V

1. Before servicing the vehicle, refer to the precautions in the beginning of this section.
2. Remove or disconnect the following:
- Negative battery cable
- Air intake assembly
- Clutch slave cylinder and hose bracket

- Starter motor
- Transaxle ground cable
- Reverse lamp switch connector
- Wire harness bracket
- Shift cables and bracket
- Vehicle Speed (VSS) sensor connector
- Splash shield
- Heated Oxygen (HO$_2$S) sensor connector
- Exhaust front pipe
- Rear driveshaft
- Lower ball joints
- Right damper fork

3. Separate the inner CV-joints from the transaxle and intermediate shaft and support the axle halfshafts out of the work area with safety wire.

4. Remove or disconnect the following:
- Intermediate shaft
- Rear engine stiffener
- Clutch housing cover
- Right front mount and bracket
- Transaxle mount and bracket
- Rear engine mounting bolts
- Transaxle flange bolts
- Transaxle

To install:

➡**Use new circlips, split pins and self-locking nuts for assembly.**

5. Install or connect the following:
- Transaxle. Tighten the flange bolts to 47 ft. lbs. (64 Nm) and the rear engine mounting bolts to 61 ft. lbs. (83 Nm).
- Transaxle mount and bracket. Tighten the bracket bolts to 47 ft. lbs. (64 Nm) and the through bolt to 54 ft. lbs. (74 Nm).
- Right front mount and bracket. Tighten the mount bolts to 33 ft. lbs. (44 Nm) and the bracket bolts to 47 ft. lbs. (64 Nm).
- Clutch housing cover. Tighten the 12mm bolts to 22 ft. lbs. (29 Nm) and the 6mm bolts to 105 inch lbs. (12 Nm).
- Rear engine stiffener. Tighten the 8mm bolts to 18 ft. lbs. (24 Nm) and the 10mm bolt to 33 ft. lbs. (44 Nm).
- Intermediate shaft. Tighten the bolts to 29 ft. lbs. (39 Nm).
- Axle halfshafts
- Right damper fork. Tighten the pinch bolt to 32 ft. lbs. (43 Nm) and the nut to 47 ft. lbs. (64 Nm).
- Lower ball joints. Tighten the nut to 36–43 ft. lbs. (49–59 Nm).

- Rear driveshaft. Tighten the bolts to 24 ft. lbs. (32 Nm).
- Exhaust front pipe
- HO$_2$S sensor connector
- Splash shield
- VSS sensor connector
- Shift cables and bracket. Tighten the bracket bolts to 20 ft. lbs. (27 Nm).
- Wire harness bracket
- Reverse lamp switch connector
- Transaxle ground cable
- Starter motor. Tighten the bolts to 32 ft. lbs. (44 Nm).
- Clutch slave cylinder and hose bracket
- Air intake assembly
- Negative battery cable

6. Fill the transaxle to the correct level.
7. Start the engine and check for leaks.
8. Check the wheel alignment and adjust as necessary.

Clutch

ADJUSTMENTS

The CR-V is equipped with a hydraulic clutch system. No adjustment is necessary.

REMOVAL & INSTALLATION

CR-V

1. Before servicing the vehicle, refer to the precautions in the beginning of this section.
2. Remove or disconnect the following:
- Negative battery cable
- Transaxle
- Pressure plate. Loosen the bolts evenly in a crossing pattern.
- Clutch disc

To install:

3. Install the clutch disc and pressure plate. Tighten the pressure plate bolts in a crossing pattern and in several steps to 19 ft. lbs. (25 Nm).

4. Install or connect the following:
- Transaxle
- Negative battery cable

Hydraulic Clutch System

BLEEDING

1. Before servicing the vehicle, refer to the precautions in the beginning of this section.

2. Attach a hose to the bleeder screw and suspend the other end in a container of clean brake fluid.
3. Open the bleeder screw.
4. Slowly pump the clutch pedal until no more air bubbles appear at the bleeder hose.
5. Tighten the bleeder screw to 70 inch lbs. (8 Nm).
6. Refill the clutch master cylinder as necessary.
7. Check for leaks and proper clutch operation.

Transfer Assembly

REMOVAL & INSTALLATION

CR-V

1. Before servicing the vehicle, refer to the precautions in the beginning of this section.
2. Drain the transaxle fluid.
3. Remove or disconnect the following:
- Negative battery cable
- Heated Oxygen (HO$_2$S) sensor connector
- Exhaust front pipe
- Rear driveshaft
- Transfer assembly and bracket

To install:

4. Install the transfer assembly and bracket with a new O-ring seal. Tighten the 10mm bolts to 33 ft. lbs. (44 Nm) and the 8mm bolts to 17 ft. lbs. (24 Nm).

5. Install or connect the following:
- Rear driveshaft. Tighten the bolts to 24 ft. lbs. (32 Nm).
- Exhaust front pipe
- HO$_2$S sensor connector
- Negative battery cable

6. Fill the transaxle to the correct level and check for leaks.

Halfshaft

REMOVAL & INSTALLATION

Oasis and 1997–98 Odyssey

1. Before servicing the vehicle, refer to the precautions in the beginning of this section.
2. Drain the transaxle.
3. Remove or disconnect the following:
- Negative battery cable
- Front wheels
- Damper fork

- Lower ball joint
- Spindle nut

4. Pry the inboard joint from the transaxle or intermediate shaft.

5. Remove the outer CV-joint stub shaft from the hub by tapping the stub shaft with a plastic hammer.

To install:

➡**Use new circlips, split pins and self-locking nuts for assembly.**

6. Install the outer CV-joint stub shaft into the hub.

7. Install the inner CV-joint to the transaxle or intermediate shaft until the circlip locks in the retaining groove.

8. Install or connect the following:
- Lower ball joint. Tighten the nut to 36–43 ft. lbs. (49–59 Nm).
- Damper fork. Tighten the pinch bolt to 32 ft. lbs. (43 Nm) and the nut to 47 ft. lbs. (64 Nm).
- Spindle nut. Tighten the nut to 181 ft. lbs. (245 Nm).
- Front wheels
- Negative battery cable

9. Fill the transaxle to the correct level and check for leaks.

1999–01 Odyssey

1. Before servicing the vehicle, refer to the precautions in the beginning of this section.

2. Drain the transaxle.

3. Remove or disconnect the following:
- Negative battery cable
- Front wheels
- Stabilizer bar link
- Lower ball joint
- Spindle nut

4. Pry the inboard joint from the transaxle or intermediate shaft.

5. Remove the outer CV-joint stub shaft from the hub by tapping the stub shaft with a plastic hammer.

To install:

➡**Use new circlips, split pins and self-locking nuts for assembly.**

6. Install the outer CV-joint stub shaft into the hub.

7. Install the inner CV-joint to the transaxle or intermediate shaft until the circlip locks in the retaining groove.

8. Install or connect the following:
- Lower ball joint. Tighten the nut to 43–51 ft. lbs. (59–69 Nm).
- Stabilizer bar link. Tighten the nut to 58 ft. lbs. (78 Nm).
- Spindle nut. Tighten the nut to 181 ft. lbs. (245 Nm).

- Front wheels
- Negative battery cable

9. Fill the transaxle to the correct level and check for leaks.

CR-V

FRONT

1. Before servicing the vehicle, refer to the precautions in the beginning of this section.

2. Drain the transaxle.

3. Remove or disconnect the following:
- Negative battery cable
- Front wheels
- Damper fork
- Lower ball joint
- Spindle nut

4. Pry the inboard joint from the transaxle or intermediate shaft.

5. Remove the outer CV-joint stub shaft from the hub by tapping the stub shaft with a plastic hammer.

To install:

➡**Use new circlips, split pins and self-locking nuts for assembly.**

6. Install the outer CV-joint stub shaft into the hub.

7. Install the inner CV-joint to the transaxle or intermediate shaft until the circlip locks in the retaining groove.

8. Install or connect the following:
- Lower ball joint. Tighten the nut to 36–43 ft. lbs. (49–59 Nm).
- Damper fork. Tighten the pinch bolt to 32 ft. lbs. (43 Nm) and the nut to 47 ft. lbs. (64 Nm).
- Spindle nut. Tighten the nut to 181 ft. lbs. (245 Nm).
- Front wheels
- Negative battery cable

9. Fill the transaxle to the correct level and check for leaks.

REAR

1. Before servicing the vehicle, refer to the precautions in the beginning of this section.

2. Drain the differential.

3. Remove or disconnect the following:
- Negative battery cable
- Rear wheels
- Spindle nut

4. Pry the inboard joint from the differential.

5. Remove the outer CV-joint stub shaft from the hub by tapping the stub shaft with a plastic hammer.

To install:

➡**Use new circlips and self-locking nuts for assembly.**

6. Install the outer CV-joint stub shaft into the hub.

7. Install the inner CV-joint to the differential until the circlip locks in the retaining groove.

8. Install or connect the following:
- Spindle nut. Tighten the nut to 134 ft. lbs. (181 Nm).
- Rear wheels
- Negative battery cable

9. Fill the differential to the correct level and check for leaks.

CV-Joint

OVERHAUL

Front

OUTBOARD JOINT

1. Before servicing the vehicle, refer to the precautions in the beginning of this section.

2. Remove or disconnect the following:
- Axle halfshaft from the vehicle and place it in a vise
- Outboard joint boot clamps and push the boot back
- Outboard joint by driving it off the axle shaft with a brass drift and hammer
- Outboard joint boot

To install:

➡**Use new circlips and boot clamps for assembly.**

3. Install the outboard joint boot and clamps to the axle shaft.

4. Fill the outboard joint with grease. Install the outboard joint to the axle shaft. Tap the stub shaft with a brass hammer to seat the circlip.

5. Fill the outboard joint boot with grease and install the boot clamps.

6. Install the axle halfshaft to the vehicle.

INBOARD JOINT

1. Before servicing the vehicle, refer to the precautions in the beginning of this section.

2. Remove or disconnect the following:
- Axle halfshaft from the vehicle.
- Inboard joint boot clamps and push the boot back
- Inboard joint housing from the axle
- Rollers from the spider
- Snapring and the spider from the axle shaft
- Inboard joint boot

To install:

➡**Use new circlips and boot clamps for assembly.**

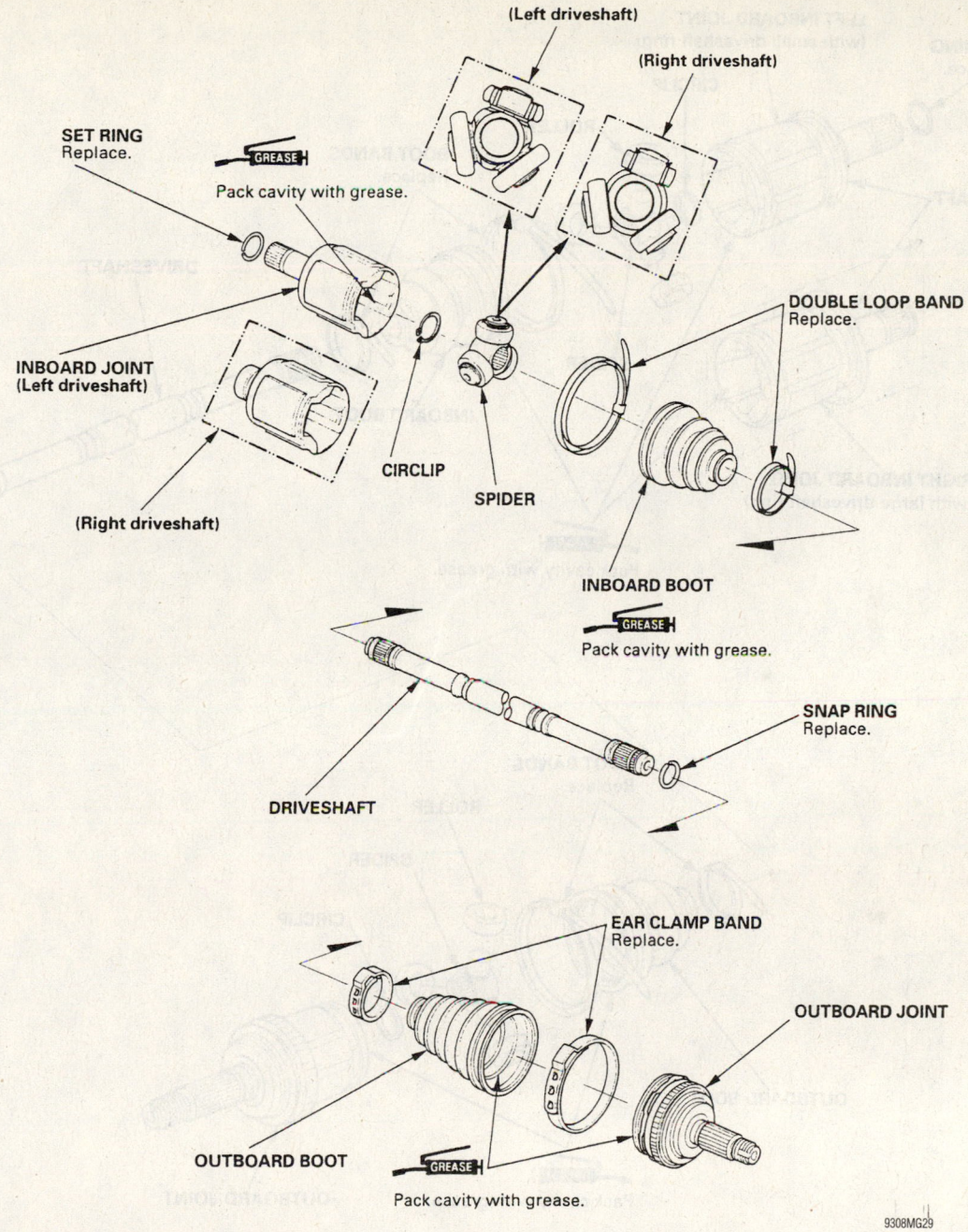

SET RING
Replace.

GREASE
Pack cavity with grease.

(Left driveshaft)

(Right driveshaft)

DOUBLE LOOP BAND
Replace.

INBOARD JOINT
(Left driveshaft)

(Right driveshaft)

CIRCLIP

SPIDER

INBOARD BOOT

GREASE
Pack cavity with grease.

SNAP RING
Replace.

DRIVESHAFT

EAR CLAMP BAND
Replace.

OUTBOARD JOINT

OUTBOARD BOOT

GREASE
Pack cavity with grease.

9308MG29

Front axle exploded view—1999–01 Odyssey shown

3. Install or connect the following:
   • Inboard joint boot and clamps to the axle shaft
   • Spider with a new snapring
   • Rollers to the spider
4. Fill the joint housing with grease and install it.
5. Fill the inboard joint boot with grease and install the boot clamps.
6. Install the axle halfshaft to the vehicle.

Rear

CR-V

1. Before servicing the vehicle, refer to the precautions in the beginning of this section.
2. Remove or disconnect the following:
   • Axle halfshaft from the vehicle
   • Joint boot clamps and push the boot back
   • Joint housing from the axle
   • Rollers from the spider

   • Snapring and the spider from the axle shaft
   • Joint boot

To install:

➡**Use new circlips and boot clamps for assembly.**

3. Install or connect the following:
   • Joint boot and clamps to the axle shaft
   • Spider with a new snapring
   • Rollers to the spider

Turn to Section 5 for brake system applications

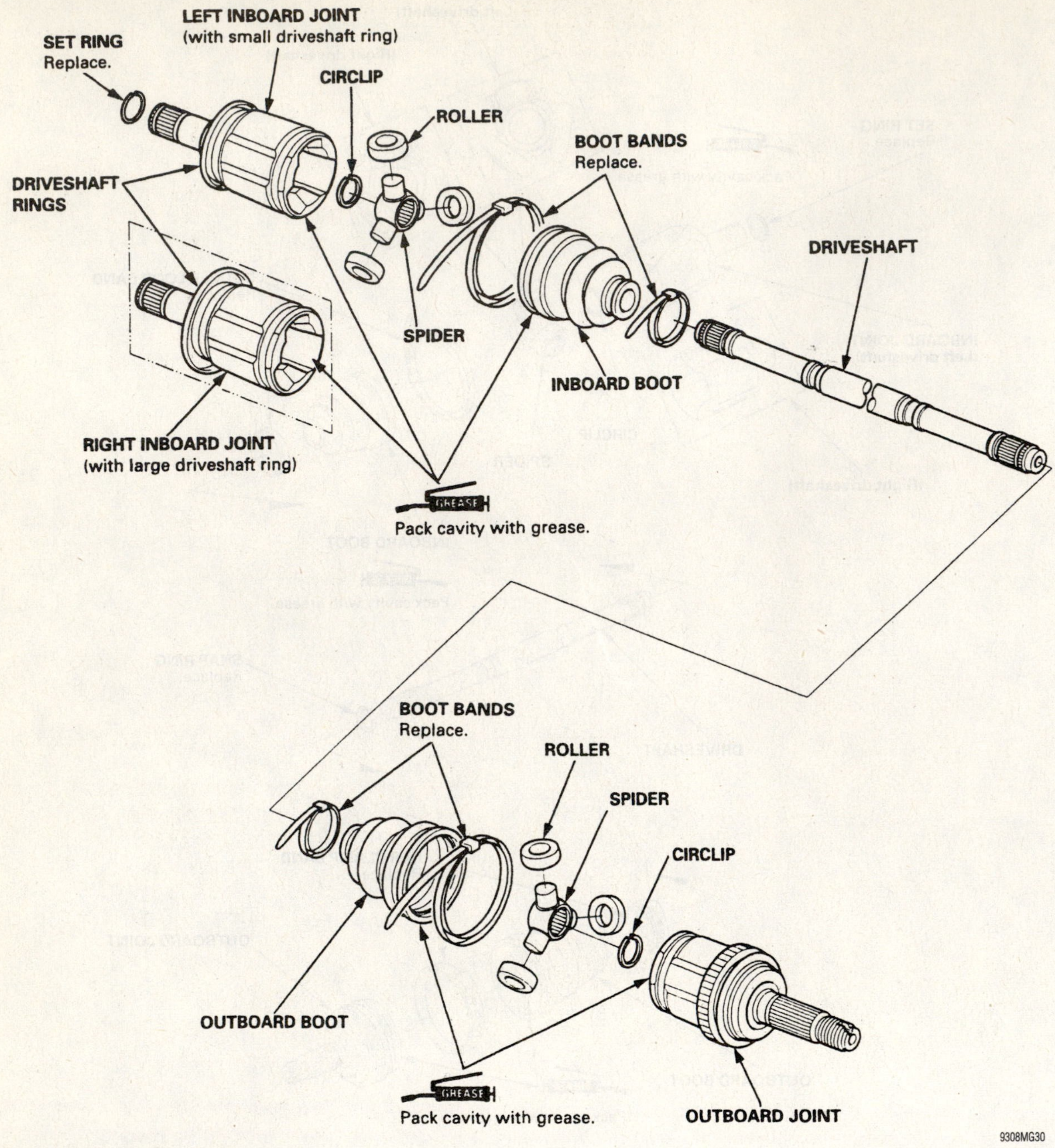

SET RING Replace.

LEFT INBOARD JOINT (with small driveshaft ring)

CIRCLIP

ROLLER

BOOT BANDS Replace.

DRIVESHAFT

DRIVESHAFT RINGS

SPIDER

INBOARD BOOT

RIGHT INBOARD JOINT (with large driveshaft ring)

GREASE
Pack cavity with grease.

BOOT BANDS Replace.

ROLLER

SPIDER

CIRCLIP

OUTBOARD BOOT

GREASE
Pack cavity with grease.

OUTBOARD JOINT

9308MG30

Exploded view of the rear axle—CR-V

4. Fill the joint housing with grease and install it.

5. Fill the joint boot with grease and install the boot clamps.

6. Install the axle halfshaft to the vehicle.

Pinion Seal

REMOVAL & INSTALLATION

CR-V

1. Before servicing the vehicle, refer to the precautions in the beginning of this section.

2. Remove or disconnect the following:
- Driveshaft
- Companion flange
- Pinion seal

To install:

➡ **Use a new locknut and O-ring for assembly.**

3. Install or connect the following:
- Pinion seal. Drive the seal square into the bore.
- Companion flange. Tighten the locknut to 87 ft. lbs. (118 Nm).
- Driveshaft. Tighten the flange bolts to 24 ft. lbs. (32 Nm).

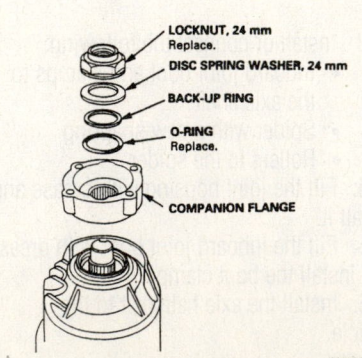

LOCKNUT, 24 mm Replace.

DISC SPRING WASHER, 24 mm

BACK-UP RING

O-RING Replace.

COMPANION FLANGE

9308MG31

Exploded view of the rear differential pinion components—CR-V

STEERING AND SUSPENSION

Air Bag

❈❈ CAUTION

Some vehicles are equipped with an air bag system. The system must be disarmed before performing service on, or around, system components, the steering column, instrument panel components, wiring and sensors. Failure to follow the safety precautions and the disarming procedure could result in accidental air bag deployment, possible injury and unnecessary system repairs.

PRECAUTIONS

Several precautions must be observed when handling the inflator module to avoid accidental deployment and possible personal injury.

- Never carry the inflator module by the wires or connector on the underside of the module.
- When carrying a live inflator module, hold securely with both hands, and ensure that the bag and trim cover are pointed away.
- Place the inflator module on a bench or other surface with the bag and trim cover facing up.
- With the inflator module on the bench, never place anything on or close to the module which may be thrown in the event of an accidental deployment.

Before servicing the vehicle, also make sure to refer to the precautions in the beginning of this section as well.

DISARMING

Disconnect and isolate the negative battery cable. Wait 3 minutes for the system capacitor to discharge before performing any service.

Power Rack and Pinion Steering Gear

REMOVAL & INSTALLATION

❈❈ WARNING

Do not permit the steering wheel to turn whenever the steering gear is disconnected from the steering column. Damage to the air bag wiring can result.

Odyssey and Oasis

1. Before servicing the vehicle, refer to the precautions in the beginning of this section.
2. Center the steering wheel and lock it in position.
3. Attach a support fixture to the engine lifting eyes.
4. Remove or disconnect the following:
   - Negative battery cable
   - Steering joint cover
   - Steering flexible joint
   - Front wheels
   - Outer tie rod ends
   - Splash shield
   - Heated Oxygen (HO$_2$S) sensor connectors
   - Exhaust front pipe
   - Power steering fluid lines
   - Rear engine mount
5. Support the front subframe with a jack.
6. Loosen the 14mm subframe bolts and remove the 12mm stiffener plate bolts.
7. Lower the subframe about 1 3/16 inches (30mm).
8. Remove or disconnect the following:
   - Right steering gear mounting bracket
   - Left steering gear mounting bolts
   - Steering gear

To install:

9. Position the steering gear in the vehicle.
10. Install or connect the following:
    - Left steering gear mounting bolts. Tighten the bolts to 43 ft. lbs. (58 Nm).

- Right steering gear mounting bracket. Tighten the bolts to 29 ft. lbs. (39 Nm).
11. Raise the subframe into position. Tighten the 14mm bolts to 76 ft. lbs. (103 Nm) and the 12mm bolts to 54 ft. lbs. (74 Nm).
12. Install or connect the following:
    - Rear engine mount
    - Power steering fluid lines
    - Exhaust front pipe
    - HO$_2$S sensor connectors
    - Splash shield
    - Outer tie rod ends
    - Front wheels. Position the wheels straight-ahead.
    - Steering flexible joint. Tighten the pinch bolts to 16 ft. lbs. (22 Nm).
    - Steering joint cover
    - Negative battery cable
13. Fill the power steering system.
14. Check the wheel alignment and adjust as necessary.

CR-V

1. Before servicing the vehicle, refer to the precautions in the beginning of this section.
2. Center the steering wheel and lock it in position.
3. Remove or disconnect the following:
   - Negative battery cable
   - Steering flexible joint
   - Front wheels
   - Outer tie rod ends
   - Heated Oxygen (HO$_2$S) sensor connector

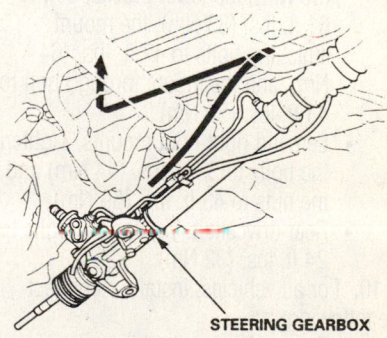

STEERING GEARBOX

9308MG27

Rack and pinion steering gear installation—CR-V

- Exhaust front pipe
- Transmission shift cable
- Power steering fluid lines

4. For 4 wheel drive vehicles, perform the following:

a. Remove the rear driveshaft.

b. Remove the right and left front mounts.

c. Remove the rear mount and bracket.

d. Tilt the engine back to lower the transfer assembly output flange about 1.57 inches (40mm).

5. For all vehicles, remove or disconnect the following:

- Stiffener plate
- Steering gear mounting brackets

6. Slide the steering gear to the right until the left end clears the subframe, then slide the gear to the left and out of the vehicle.

To install:

7. Position the steering gear in the vehicle, right end first.

8. Install or connect the following:

- Steering gear mounting brackets. Tighten the bolts to 29 ft. lbs. (39 Nm).
- Stiffener plate. Tighten the plate bolts to 28 ft. lbs. (38 Nm) and the steering bear bolt to 32 ft. lbs. (43 Nm).

➡ **Use new self-locking nuts and bolts for engine mount installation.**

9. For 4 wheel drive vehicles, install or connect the following:

- Rear mount and bracket. Tighten the upper bracket bolt to 43 ft. lbs. (59 Nm), the lower bracket bolt to 61 ft. lbs. (83 Nm), the mount attaching bolts to 47 ft. lbs. (64 Nm), and the mount through bolt to 43 ft. lbs. (59 Nm).
- Left and right front mounts. Tighten the bolts to 33 ft. lbs. (44 Nm) and the nuts to 43 ft. lbs. (59 Nm).
- Rear driveshaft. Tighten the bolts to 24 ft. lbs. (32 Nm).

10. For all vehicles, install or connect the following:

- Power steering fluid lines
- Transmission shift cable
- Exhaust front pipe
- HO$_2$S sensor connector
- Outer tie rod ends
- Front wheels. Position the wheels straight ahead.
- Steering flexible joint. Tighten the pinch bolts to 16 ft. lbs. (22 Nm).
- Negative battery cable

11. Fill the power steering system.

12. Check the wheel alignment and adjust as necessary.

Strut

REMOVAL & INSTALLATION

Front

CR-V, OASIS AND 1997–98 ODYSSEY

1. Before servicing the vehicle, refer to the precautions in the beginning of this section.

2. Remove or disconnect the following:

- Front wheel
- Brake hose retainer
- Damper fork
- Strut

To install:

➡ **Use new self-locking fasteners for assembly.**

3. Install or connect the following:

- Strut. Tighten the mounting nuts to 43 ft. lbs. (59 Nm) for CR-V or to 28 ft. lbs. (38 Nm) for Odyssey and Oasis.
- Damper fork. Tighten the pinch bolt

to 32 ft. lbs. (43 Nm) and the lower bolt to 47 ft. lbs. (64 Nm).

- Brake hose retainer
- Front wheel

1999–01 ODYSSEY

1. Before servicing the vehicle, refer to the precautions in the beginning of this section.

2. Remove or disconnect the following:

- Front wheel
- Wheel speed sensor wiring bracket
- Brake hose bracket
- Stabilizer bar link
- Strut pinch bolts
- Upper mount nuts
- Strut

To install:

3. Install or connect the following:

- Strut. Tighten the upper mount nuts to 43 ft. lbs. (59 Nm).
- Strut pinch bolts. Tighten the nuts to 116 ft. lbs. (157 Nm).
- Stabilizer bar link. Tighten the nut to 58 ft. lbs. (78 Nm).
- Brake hose bracket
- Wheel speed sensor wiring bracket
- Front wheel

4. Check the wheel alignment and adjust as necessary.

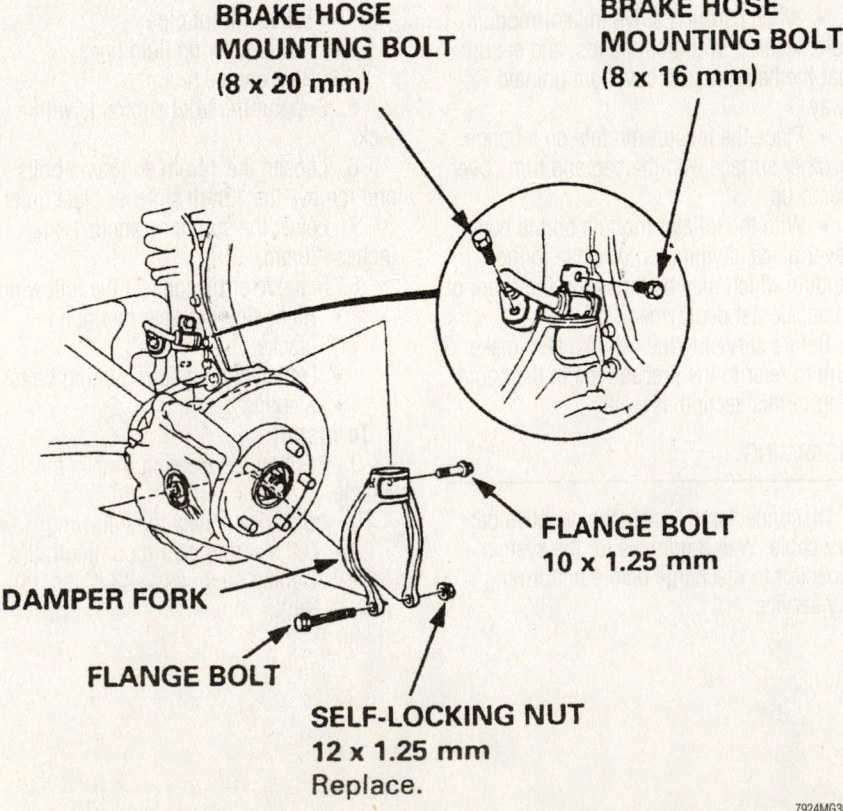

BRAKE HOSE MOUNTING BOLT (8 x 20 mm)

BRAKE HOSE MOUNTING BOLT (8 x 16 mm)

FLANGE BOLT 10 x 1.25 mm

DAMPER FORK

FLANGE BOLT

SELF-LOCKING NUT 12 x 1.25 mm Replace.

Identification of some of the front suspension components—CR-V, Oasis and 1997–98 Odyssey

7924MG36

Rear

CR-V

1. Before servicing the vehicle, refer to the precautions in the beginning of this section.

2. Support the vehicle under the lower control arm.

3. Remove or disconnect the following:
   - Rear wheel
   - Interior access panel
   - Damper cap
   - Upper strut mount nuts
   - Lower strut flange bolt
   - Strut

To install:

4. Install or connect the following:
   - Strut. Tighten the nuts to 36 ft. lbs. (49 Nm) and the bolt to 40 ft. lbs. (54 Nm).
   - Damper cap
   - Interior access panel
   - Rear wheel

Shock Absorber

REMOVAL & INSTALLATION

Rear

OASIS AND 1997–98 ODYSSEY

1. Before servicing the vehicle, refer to the precautions in the beginning of this section.

2. Support the vehicle under the lower control arm.

3. Remove or disconnect the following:
   - Rear wheel
   - Lower control arm flange bolt
   - Lower shock absorber flange bolt
   - Interior access panel
   - Upper shock absorber mount flange nuts
   - Shock absorber

To install:

4. Install or connect the following:
   - Shock absorber. Tighten the upper mount nuts to 20 ft. lbs. (30 Nm).
   - Interior access panel
   - Lower shock absorber flange bolt
   - Lower control arm flange bolt. Tighten both lower bolts to 76 ft. lbs. (103 Nm).
   - Rear wheel

1999–01 ODYSSEY

1. Before servicing the vehicle, refer to the precautions in the beginning of this section.

2. Support the vehicle under the lower control arm.

3. Remove or disconnect the following:
   - Rear wheel
   - Upper shock absorber flange bolt
   - Lower shock absorber nut
   - Shock absorber

To install:

4. Install or connect the following:
   - Shock absorber. Tighten the fasteners to 47 ft. lbs. (64 Nm).
   - Rear wheel

Coil Spring

REMOVAL & INSTALLATION

Front

1. Before servicing the vehicle, refer to the precautions in the beginning of this section.

2. Remove the strut from the vehicle and install in a strut spring compressor. Com-

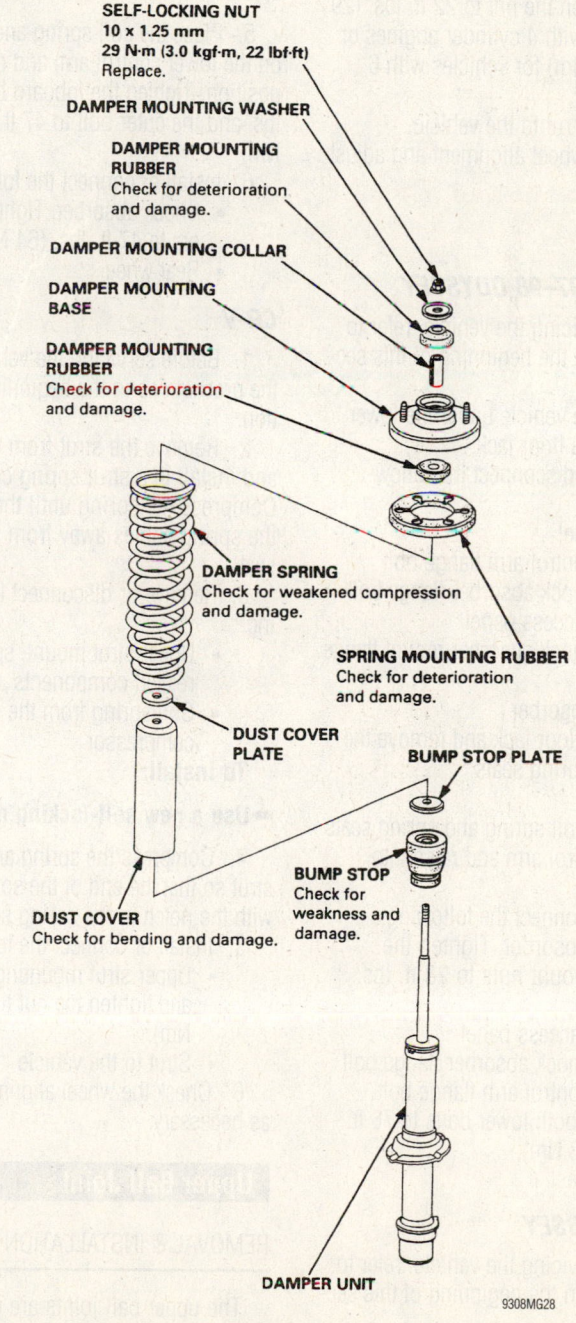

SELF-LOCKING NUT
10 x 1.25 mm
29 N·m (3.0 kgf·m, 22 lbf·ft)
Replace.

DAMPER MOUNTING WASHER

DAMPER MOUNTING RUBBER
Check for deterioration and damage.

DAMPER MOUNTING COLLAR

DAMPER MOUNTING BASE

DAMPER MOUNTING RUBBER
Check for deterioration and damage.

DAMPER SPRING
Check for weakened compression and damage.

SPRING MOUNTING RUBBER
Check for deterioration and damage.

DUST COVER PLATE

BUMP STOP PLATE

DUST COVER
Check for bending and damage.

BUMP STOP
Check for weakness and damage.

DAMPER UNIT

9308MG28

Front strut and spring exploded view—CR-V shown

press the spring until the end of the spring comes away from the spring seat.

3. Remove the upper strut mount, spring seat and related components.

4. Remove the coil spring from the strut spring compressor.

To install:

➡**Use a new self-locking nut.**

5. Compress the spring and position the strut so that the end of the spring aligns with the notch in the spring seat.

6. Install the upper strut mounting components and tighten the nut to 22 ft. lbs. (29 Nm) for vehicles with 4 cylinder engines or to 33 ft. lbs. (44 Nm) for vehicles with 6 cylinder engines.

7. Install the strut to the vehicle.

8. Check the wheel alignment and adjust as necessary.

Rear

OASIS AND 1997–98 ODYSSEY

1. Before servicing the vehicle, refer to the precautions in the beginning of this section.

2. Support the vehicle under the lower control arm with a floor jack.

3. Remove or disconnect the following:
- Rear wheel
- Lower control arm flange bolt
- Lower shock absorber flange bolt
- Interior access panel
- Upper shock absorber mount flange nuts
- Shock absorber

4. Lower the floor jack and remove the coil spring and spring seats.

To install:

5. Place the coil spring and spring seats on the lower control arm and raise into position.

6. Install or connect the following:
- Shock absorber. Tighten the upper mount nuts to 28 ft. lbs. (38 Nm).
- Interior access panel
- Lower shock absorber flange bolt
- Lower control arm flange bolt. Tighten both lower bolts to 76 ft. lbs. (103 Nm).
- Rear wheel

1999–01 ODYSSEY

1. Before servicing the vehicle, refer to the precautions in the beginning of this section.

2. Support the vehicle under the lower control arm.

3. Remove or disconnect the following:
- Rear wheel
- Upper shock absorber flange bolt
- Lower shock absorber nut
- Shock absorber
- Wheel speed sensor wiring harness
- Lower control arm bolts

4. Lower the floor jack and remove the coil spring and spring seats.

To install:

➡**Use new self-locking nuts for assembly.**

5. Place the coil spring and spring seats on the lower control arm and raise into position. Tighten the inboard bolt to 61 ft. lbs. and the outer bolt to 47 ft. lbs. (64 Nm).

6. Install or connect the following:
- Shock absorber. Tighten the fasteners to 47 ft. lbs. (64 Nm).
- Rear wheel

CR-V

1. Before servicing the vehicle, refer to the precautions in the beginning of this section.

2. Remove the strut from the vehicle and install in a strut spring compressor. Compress the spring until the end of the spring comes away from the spring seat.

3. Remove or disconnect the following:
- Upper strut mount, spring seat and related components
- Coil spring from the strut spring compressor

To install:

➡**Use a new self-locking nut.**

4. Compress the spring and position the strut so that the end of the spring aligns with the notch in the spring seat.

5. Install or connect the following:
- Upper strut mounting components and tighten the nut to 22 ft. lbs. (29 Nm).
- Strut to the vehicle

6. Check the wheel alignment and adjust as necessary.

Upper Ball Joint

REMOVAL & INSTALLATION

The upper ball joints are replaced with the upper control arms as an assembly.

Lower Ball Joint

REMOVAL & INSTALLATION

1999–01 Odyssey

The lower ball joints are replaced with the lower control arms as an assembly.

CR-V, Oasis and 1997–98 Odyssey

1. Before servicing the vehicle, refer to the precautions in the beginning of this section.

2. Remove or disconnect the following:
- Front wheel
- Spindle nut
- Brake hose bracket
- Brake caliper and rotor
- Wheel speed sensor, if equipped
- Outer tie rod end
- Upper and lower ball joints
- Steering knuckle
- Lower ball joint boot and set ring

3. Press the lower ball joint out of the steering knuckle.

To install:

➡**Use new ball joint nuts, split pins, and a new spindle nut for assembly.**

4. Press the lower ball joint into the steering knuckle.

5. Install or connect the following:
- Lower ball joint boot and set ring
- Steering knuckle. Tighten the upper ball joint nut to 29–35 ft. lbs. (39–47 Nm) and the lower ball joint nut to 36–43 ft. lbs. (49–59 Nm).
- Outer tie rod end. Tighten the nut to 32 ft. lbs. (43 Nm).
- Wheel speed sensor, if equipped
- Brake caliper and rotor. Tighten the caliper bracket bolts to 80 ft. lbs. (108 Nm).
- Brake hose bracket
- Spindle nut. Tighten the nut to 181 ft. lbs. (245 Nm).
- Front wheel

6. Check the wheel alignment and adjust as necessary.

Upper Control Arm

REMOVAL & INSTALLATION

Oasis and 1997–98 Odyssey

1. Before servicing the vehicle, refer to the precautions in the beginning of this section.

2. Support the lower control arm assembly with a floor jack.

3. Remove or disconnect the following:

- Upper ball joint
- Inner control arm flange bolts.
- Upper control arm

To install:

➡**Use new self-locking nuts for assembly.**

4. Install the upper control arm. Tighten the ball joint nut to 29–35 ft. lbs. (39–47 Nm) and the inner flange nuts to 47 ft. lbs. (64 Nm).

CR-V

1. Before servicing the vehicle, refer to the precautions in the beginning of this section.

2. Support the lower control arm assembly with a floor jack.

3. Remove or disconnect the following:

- Upper ball joint
- Inner control arm flange bolts.
- Upper control arm

To install:

➡**Use new self-locking nuts for assembly.**

4. Install the upper control arm. Tighten the ball joint nut to 29–35 ft. lbs. (39–47 Nm) and the inner flange bolts to 40 ft. lbs. (54 Nm).

CONTROL ARM BUSHING REPLACEMENT

The upper control arm bushings are serviced with the upper control arm as an assembly.

Lower Control Arm

REMOVAL & INSTALLATION

Oasis and 1997–98 Odyssey

1. Before servicing the vehicle, refer to the precautions in the beginning of this section.

2. Remove or disconnect the following:

- Front wheel
- Lower ball joint
- Radius rod flange bolts
- Damper fork lower bolt

- Stabilizer bar link
- Control arm inner flange bolt
- Lower control arm

To install:

➡**Use new self-locking nuts and split pins for assembly.**

3. Install or connect the following:

- Lower control arm. Tighten the inner flange bolt to 40 ft. lbs. (54 Nm).
- Stabilizer bar link. Tighten the nut to 14 ft. lbs. (19 Nm).
- Damper fork lower bolt. Tighten the nut to 47 ft. lbs. (64 Nm).
- Radius rod. Tighten the flange bolts to 76 ft. lbs. (103 Nm).
- Lower ball joint. Tighten the nut to 36–43 ft. lbs. (49–59 Nm).
- Front wheel

4. Check the wheel alignment and adjust as necessary.

1999–01 Odyssey

1. Before servicing the vehicle, refer to the precautions in the beginning of this section.

2. Remove or disconnect the following:

- Front wheel
- Lower ball joint
- Front inner flange bolt
- Rear inner flange bolt
- Lower control arm

To install:

➡**Use a new split pin for assembly.**

3. Install or connect the following:

- Lower control arm. Tighten the inner flange bolts to 69 ft. lbs. (93 Nm).
- Lower ball joint. Tighten the nut to 43–51 ft. lbs. (59–69 Nm).
- Front wheel

4. Check the wheel alignment and adjust as necessary.

CR-V

1. Before servicing the vehicle, refer to the precautions in the beginning of this section.

2. Remove or disconnect the following:

- Front wheel
- Lower ball joint
- Damper fork lower bolt
- Stabilizer bar link

- Front inner flange bolt
- Rear bushing bracket bolts
- Lower control arm

To install:

➡**Use new self-locking nuts and split pins for assembly.**

3. Install or connect the following:

- Lower control arm. Tighten the front flange bolt to 76 ft. lbs. (103 Nm).
- Rear bushing bracket. Tighten the bolts to 66 ft. lbs. (89 Nm).
- Stabilizer bar link. Tighten the nut to 22 ft. lbs. (29 Nm).
- Damper fork lower bolt. Tighten the nut to 47 ft. lbs. (64 Nm).
- Lower ball joint. Tighten the nut to 36–43 ft. lbs. (49–59 Nm).
- Front wheel

4. Check the wheel alignment and adjust as necessary.

CONTROL ARM BUSHING REPLACEMENT

Odyssey and Oasis

The lower control arm bushings are serviced with the lower control arm as an assembly.

CR-V

The lower control arm front inner bushing and the damper fork bushing are serviced with the control arm as an assembly.

REAR INNER BUSHING

1. Before servicing the vehicle, refer to the precautions in the beginning of this section.

2. Remove or disconnect the following:

- Front wheel
- Rear bushing bracket
- Rear bushing

To install:

➡**Use a new self-locking nut for assembly.**

3. Install or connect the following:

- Rear bushing. Tighten the nut to 61 ft. lbs. (83 Nm).
- Rear bushing bracket. Tighten the bolts to 66 ft. lbs. (89 Nm).
- Front wheel

4. Check the wheel alignment and adjust as necessary.

Wheel Bearings

ADJUSTMENT

The wheel bearings are sealed units and are not adjustable.

REMOVAL & INSTALLATION

Front

CR-V, OASIS AND 1997–98 ODYSSEY

1. Before servicing the vehicle, refer to the precautions in the beginning of this section.
2. Remove or disconnect the following:

- Front wheel
- Spindle nut
- Brake hose bracket
- Brake caliper and rotor
- Wheel speed sensor, if equipped
- Outer tie rod end
- Upper and lower ball joints
- Steering knuckle

3. Press the hub out of the wheel bearing.
4. Remove the splash guard.
5. Remove the snapring and press the wheel bearing out of the steering knuckle.
6. If necessary, press the inner bearing race off of the hub.

To install:

➡**Use new ball joint nuts, split pins, snapring and a new spindle nut for assembly.**

7. Press the bearing into the steering knuckle and install the snapring.
8. Install the splash guard.
9. Press the hub into the bearing.
10. Install or connect the following:

- Steering knuckle. Tighten the upper ball joint nut to 29–35 ft. lbs. (39–47 Nm) and the lower ball joint nut to 36–43 ft. lbs. (49–59 Nm).
- Outer tie rod end. Tighten the nut to 32 ft. lbs. (43 Nm).
- Wheel speed sensor, if equipped
- Brake caliper and rotor. Tighten the caliper bracket bolts to 80 ft. lbs. (108 Nm).
- Brake hose bracket
- Spindle nut. Tighten the nut to 181 ft. lbs. (245 Nm).
- Front wheel

11. Check the wheel alignment and adjust as necessary.

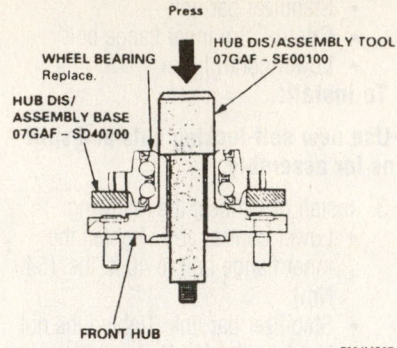

Removing the hub from the wheel bearing using the disassembly tools

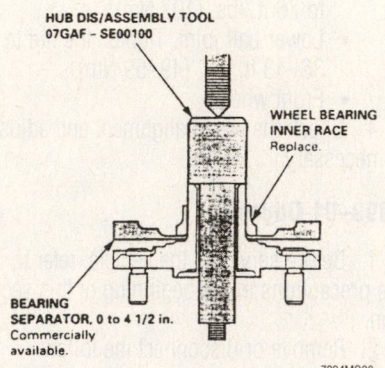

Pressing out the wheel bearing inner race

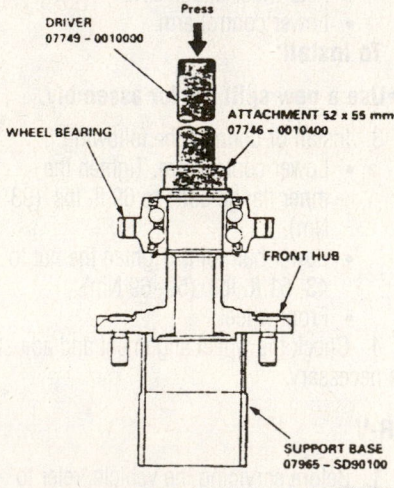

Utilizing the Hub Support Base and Driving Attachment tools to install the new wheel bearing

1999–01 ODYSSEY

1. Before servicing the vehicle, refer to the precautions in the beginning of this section.
2. Remove or disconnect the following:

- Front wheel

- Spindle nut
- Brake hose bracket
- Brake caliper and rotor
- Wheel speed sensor, if equipped
- Outer tie rod end
- Lower ball joint
- Steering knuckle

3. Press the hub out of the wheel bearing.
4. Remove the splash guard.
5. Remove the snapring and press the wheel bearing out of the steering knuckle.
6. If necessary, press the inner bearing race off of the hub.

To install:

➡**Use a new ball joint nut, split pin, snapring and spindle nut for assembly.**

7. Press the bearing into the steering knuckle and install the snapring.
8. Install the splash guard.
9. Press the hub into the bearing.
10. Install or connect the following:

- Steering knuckle. Tighten the ball joint nut to 43–51 ft. lbs. (59–69 Nm) and the damper flange bolts to 116 ft. lbs. (157 Nm).
- Outer tie rod end. Tighten the nut to 32 ft. lbs. (43 Nm).
- Wheel speed sensor, if equipped
- Brake caliper and rotor. Tighten the caliper bracket bolts to 80 ft. lbs. (108 Nm).
- Brake hose bracket
- Spindle nut. Tighten the nut to 181 ft. lbs. (245 Nm).
- Front wheel

11. Check the wheel alignment and adjust as necessary.

Rear

OASIS AND 1997–98 ODYSSEY

1. Before servicing the vehicle, refer to the precautions in the beginning of this section.
2. Remove or disconnect the following:

- Rear wheel
- Brake caliper and rotor
- Spindle cap, nut and washer
- Hub and bearing assembly

To install:

➡**Use a new spindle nut for assembly.**

3. Install or connect the following:

- Hub and bearing assembly. Tighten the spindle nut to 181 ft. lbs. (245 Nm).
- Spindle cap

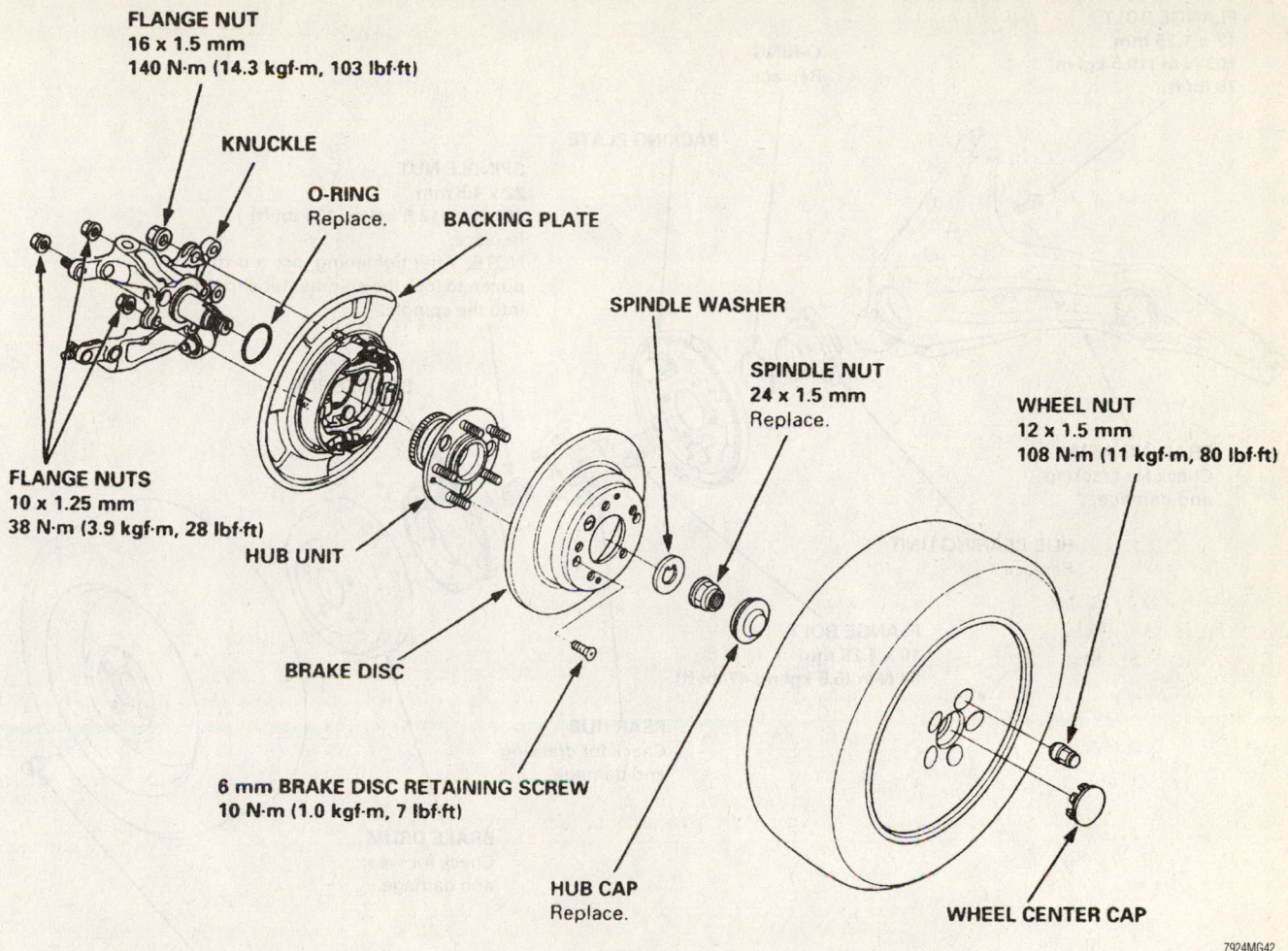

FLANGE NUT
16 x 1.5 mm
140 N·m (14.3 kgf·m, 103 lbf·ft)

KNUCKLE

O-RING
Replace.

BACKING PLATE

SPINDLE WASHER

SPINDLE NUT
24 x 1.5 mm
Replace.

WHEEL NUT
12 x 1.5 mm
108 N·m (11 kgf·m, 80 lbf·ft)

FLANGE NUTS
10 x 1.25 mm
38 N·m (3.9 kgf·m, 28 lbf·ft)

HUB UNIT

BRAKE DISC

6 mm BRAKE DISC RETAINING SCREW
10 N·m (1.0 kgf·m, 7 lbf·ft)

HUB CAP
Replace.

WHEEL CENTER CAP

7924MG42

Exploded view of the rear hub and wheel bearing components—Oasis and 1997–98 Odyssey shown

- Brake caliper and rotor. Tighten the caliper bracket bolts to 28 ft. lbs. (38 Nm).
- Rear wheel

1999–01 ODYSSEY

1. Before servicing the vehicle, refer to the precautions in the beginning of this section.
2. Remove or disconnect the following:

- Rear wheel
- Brake drum
- Spindle cap and nut
- Hub and bearing assembly

To install:

➡**Use a new spindle nut for assembly.**

3. Install or connect the following:
- Hub and bearing assembly. Tighten the spindle nut to 181 ft. lbs. (245 Nm).

- Spindle cap
- Brake drum
- Rear wheel

CR-V

1. Before servicing the vehicle, refer to the precautions in the beginning of this section.
2. Remove or disconnect the following:

- Rear wheel
- Brake drum
- Spindle nut
- Brake fluid line
- Wheel bearing flange bolts
- Hub, backing plate and bearing assembly
3. Press the hub out of the wheel bearing.
4. If necessary, press the inner bearing race off of the hub.

5. Remove the backing plate from the bearing assembly.

To install:

➡**Use a new spindle nut for assembly.**

6. Use a new O-ring and install the backing plate to the bearing assembly. Tighten the bolts to 47 ft. lbs. (64 Nm).
7. Press the hub into the bearing assembly.
8. Install or connect the following:
- Hub, backing plate and bearing assembly. Tighten the flange bolts to 76 ft. lbs. (103 Nm).
- Brake fluid line
- Spindle nut. Tighten the nut to 134 ft. lbs. (181 Nm).
- Brake drum
- Rear wheel
9. Bleed the brake system.

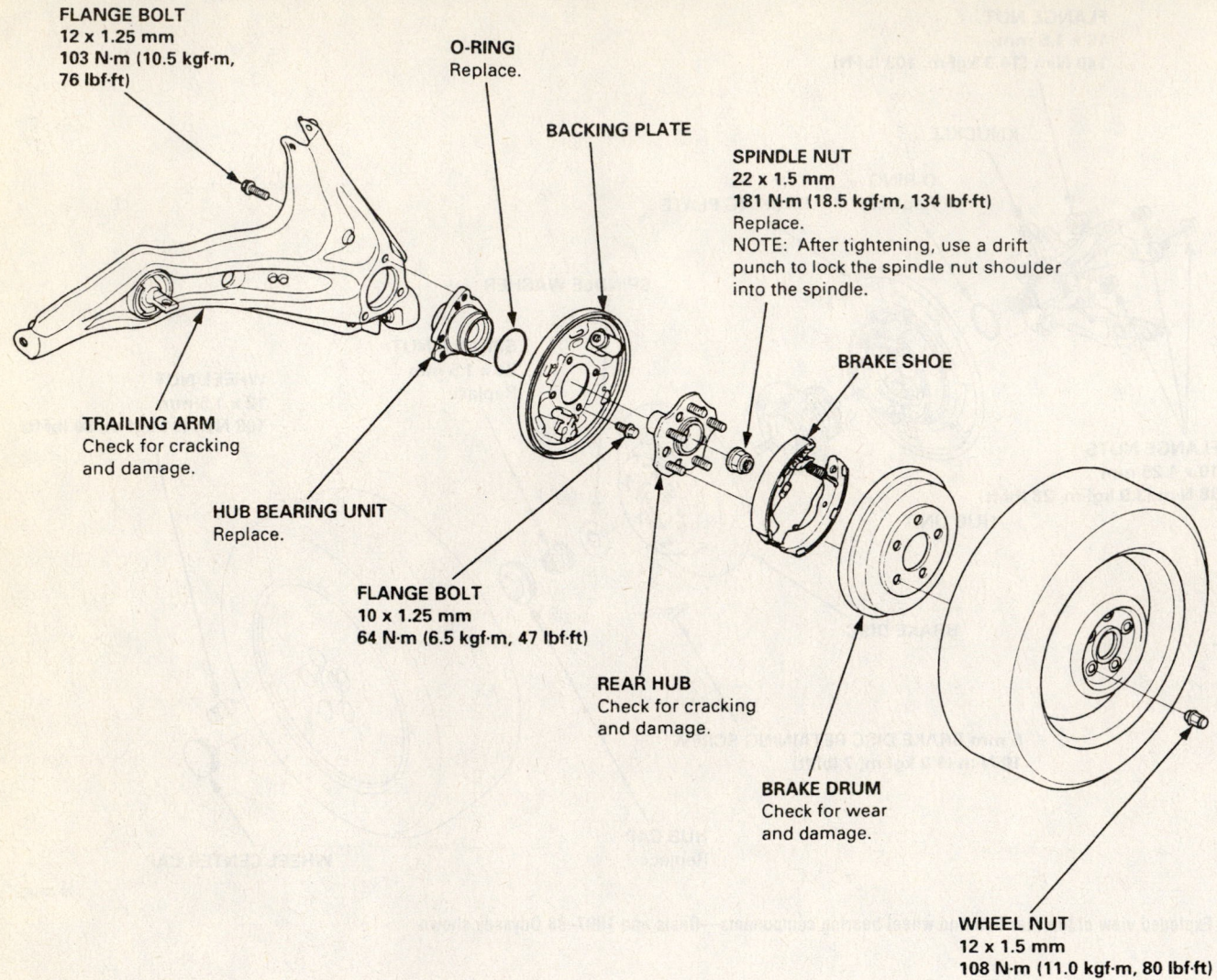

FLANGE BOLT
12 x 1.25 mm
103 N·m (10.5 kgf·m,
76 lbf·ft)

O-RING
Replace.

BACKING PLATE

SPINDLE NUT
22 x 1.5 mm
181 N·m (18.5 kgf·m, 134 lbf·ft)
Replace.
NOTE: After tightening, use a drift
punch to lock the spindle nut shoulder
into the spindle.

BRAKE SHOE

TRAILING ARM
Check for cracking
and damage.

HUB BEARING UNIT
Replace.

FLANGE BOLT
10 x 1.25 mm
64 N·m (6.5 kgf·m, 47 lbf·ft)

REAR HUB
Check for cracking
and damage.

BRAKE DRUM
Check for wear
and damage.

WHEEL NUT
12 x 1.5 mm
108 N·m (11.0 kgf·m, 80 lbf·ft)

7924MG43

Exploded view of the rear hub and wheel bearing components—CR-V

HONDA/ISUZU

Honda-Passport • **Isuzu**-Rodeo • Amigo

PRECAUTIONS

Before servicing any vehicle, please be sure to read all of the following precautions, which deal with personal safety, prevention of component damage and important points to take into consideration when servicing a motor vehicle:

• Never open, service or drain the radiator or cooling system when the engine is hot; serious burns can occur from the steam and hot coolant.

• Observe all applicable safety precautions when working around fuel. Whenever servicing the fuel system, always work in a well-ventilated area. Do not allow fuel spray or vapors to come in contact with a spark, open flame, or excessive heat (a hot drop light, for example). Keep a dry chemical fire extinguisher near the work area. Always keep fuel in a container specifically designed for fuel storage; also, always properly seal fuel containers to avoid the possibility of fire or explosion. Refer to the additional fuel system precautions later in this section.

• Fuel injection systems often remain pressurized, even after the engine has been turned **OFF**. The fuel system pressure must be relieved before disconnecting any fuel lines. Failure to do so may result in fire and/or personal injury.

• Brake fluid often contains polyglycol ethers and polyglycols. Avoid contact with the eyes and wash your hands thoroughly after handling brake fluid. If you do get brake fluid in your eyes, flush your eyes with clean, running water for 15 minutes. If eye irritation persists, or if you have taken brake fluid internally, seek medical assistance IMMEDIATELY.

• The EPA warns that prolonged contact with used engine oil may cause a number of skin disorders, including cancer. You should make every effort to minimize your exposure to used engine oil. Protective gloves should be worn when changing oil. Wash your hands and any other exposed skin areas as soon as possible after exposure to used engine oil. Soap and water, or waterless hand cleaner should be used.

• All new vehicles are now equipped with an air bag system, often referred to as a Supplemental Restraint System (SRS) or Supplemental Inflatable Restraint (SIR) sys-

tem. The system must be disabled before performing service on or around system components, steering column, instrument panel components, wiring and sensors. Failure to follow safety and disabling procedures could result in accidental air bag deployment, possible personal injury and unnecessary system repairs.

• Always wear safety goggles when working with, or around, the air bag system. When carrying a non-deployed air bag, be sure the bag and trim cover are pointed away from your body. When placing a non-deployed air bag on a work surface, always face the bag and trim cover upward, away from the surface. This will reduce the motion of the module if it is accidentally deployed. Refer to the additional air bag system precautions later in this section.

• Clean, high quality brake fluid from a sealed container is essential to the safe and proper operation of the brake system. You should always buy the correct type of brake fluid for your vehicle. If the brake fluid becomes contaminated, completely flush the system with new fluid. Never reuse any brake fluid. Any brake fluid that is removed from the system should be discarded. Also, do not allow any brake fluid to come in contact with a painted surface; it will damage the paint.

• Never operate the engine without the proper amount and type of engine oil; doing so WILL result in severe engine damage.

• Timing belt maintenance is extremely important. Many models utilize an interference-type, non-freewheeling engine. If the timing belt breaks, the valves in the cylinder head may strike the pistons, causing potentially serious (also time-consuming and expensive) engine damage. Refer to the maintenance interval charts in the front of this manual for the recommended replacement interval for the timing belt and to the timing belt section for belt replacement and inspection.

• Disconnecting the negative battery cable on some vehicles may interfere with the functions of the on-board computer system(s) and may require the computer to undergo a relearning process once the negative battery cable is reconnected.

• When servicing drum brakes, only disassemble and assemble one side at a time, leaving the remaining side intact for reference.

• Only an MVAC-trained, EPA-certified automotive technician should service the A/C system or its components.

ENGINE REPAIR

➡Disconnecting the negative battery cable on some vehicles may interfere with the functions of the on board computer system. The computer may undergo a relearning process once the negative battery cable is reconnected.

Distributor

REMOVAL

2.2L and 3.2L Engines

These engines are equipped with a Distributorless Ignition System (DIS).

2.6L Engine

➡The distributor housing has a raised ridge that aligns with a notch on the distributor mounting bracket. Locate these alignment aids before removing the distributor.

1. Before servicing the vehicle, refer to the precautions in the beginning of this section.
2. Set the engine to Top Dead Center (TDC) of the No. 4 cylinder compression stroke.
3. Remove the distributor cap and harness connectors.
4. Matchmark the rotor to the distributor housing.
5. Remove the distributor.

INSTALLATION

Timing Not Disturbed

1. Install or connect the following:
   • Distributor. Align the matchmarks made during removal.
   • Distributor harness connectors
   • Distributor cap
2. Align the distributor housing ridge with the mounting bracket notch and tighten the distributor mounting bolts to 14 ft. lbs. (19 Nm).

Timing Disturbed

1. Set the engine to TDC of the No. 4 cylinder compression stroke.
2. Align the rotor with the No. 4 tower on the distributor cap and install the distributor.
3. Install or connect the following:
   • Distributor harness connectors
   • Distributor cap
4. Align the distributor housing ridge with the mounting bracket notch and tighten the distributor mounting bolts to 14 ft. lbs. (19 Nm).

Alternator

REMOVAL

2.2L Engine

1. Before servicing the vehicle, refer to the precautions in the beginning of this section.
2. Remove or disconnect the following:
   • Negative battery cable
   • Accessory drive belt
   • Alternator harness connectors
   • Alternator

2.6L Engine

1. Before servicing the vehicle, refer to the precautions in the beginning of this section.
2. Remove or disconnect the following:
   • Negative battery cable
   • Alternator belt
   • Alternator harness connectors
   • Alternator

3.2L Engine

SOHC

1. Before servicing the vehicle, refer to the precautions in the beginning of this section.
2. Remove or disconnect the following:
   • Negative battery cable
   • Alternator belt
   • Right front wheel
   • Alternator harness connectors
   • Alternator

DOHC

1. Before servicing the vehicle, refer to the precautions in the beginning of this section.
2. Remove or disconnect the following:
   • Negative battery cable
   • Accessory drive belt
   • Alternator harness connectors
   • Alternator

INSTALLATION

2.2L Engine

Install or connect the following:
   • Alternator. Tighten the long bolt to 26 ft. lbs. (35 Nm) and the short bolt to 15 ft. lbs. (20 Nm).
   • Alternator harness connectors
   • Accessory drive belt
   • Negative battery cable

2.6L Engine

Install or connect the following:
   • Alternator
   • Alternator wiring connectors
   • Alternator belt. Tighten the adjustment bolt to 17 ft. lbs. (24 Nm) and the mounting bolt to 16 ft. lbs. (22 Nm).
   • Negative battery cable

3.2L Engine

SOHC

Install or connect the following:
   • Alternator
   • Alternator wiring connectors
   • Right front wheel
   • Alternator belt. Tighten the adjustment bolt to 17 ft. lbs. (24 Nm) and the mounting bolt to 16 ft. lbs. (22 Nm).
   • Negative battery cable

DOHC

Install or connect the following:
   • Alternator. Tighten the 10mm bolt to 30 ft. lbs. (41 Nm) and the 8mm bolt to 15 ft. lbs. 21 Nm).
   • Alternator harness connectors
   • Accessory drive belt
   • Negative battery cable

Ignition Timing

ADJUSTMENT

2.2L and 3.2L Engines

These engines are equipped with a Distributorless Ignition System (DIS). No adjustment is possible.

2.6L Engine

There is no timing adjustment. The timing signal is provided by the Crankshaft Position (CKP) sensor. The Camshaft Position (CMP) sensor in the distributor provides the injection sequence signal only.

Engine Assembly

REMOVAL & INSTALLATION

2.2L Engines

1. Before servicing the vehicle, refer to the precautions in the beginning of this section.
2. Drain the cooling system.
3. Relieve the fuel system pressure.
4. Remove or disconnect the following:
   • Battery
   • Hood
   • Accessory drive belt
   • Accelerator cable
   • Air intake assembly
   • Engine wiring harness connectors at left rear of the engine compartment
   • Brake booster vacuum line

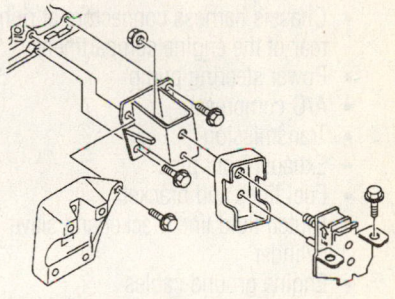

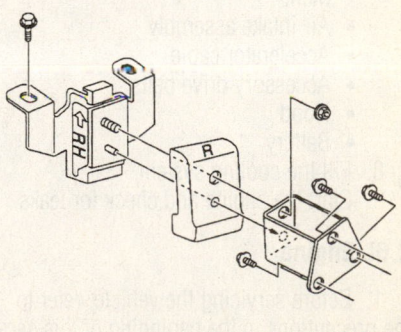

7924NG01

Left and right motor mounts—2.2L engine

- Engine ground cables
- Clutch fluid line bracket and slave cylinder
- Fuel lines and bracket
- Exhaust front pipe
- Transmission
- A/C compressor
- Power steering pump
- Chassis harness connectors at right rear of the engine compartment
- Frame ground cable
- Radiator hoses
- Heater hoses
- Cooling fan connector
- Cooling fan and shroud
- Radiator
- Left and right engine mounts

5. Lift the engine from the vehicle.

To install:

6. Position the engine in the engine compartment.

7. Install or connect the following:
- Left and right engine mounts. Tighten the fasteners to 30 ft. lbs. (41 Nm).
- Radiator
- Cooling fan and shroud
- Cooling fan connector
- Heater hoses
- Radiator hoses
- Frame ground cable
- Chassis harness connectors at right rear of the engine compartment
- Power steering pump
- A/C compressor
- Transmission
- Exhaust front pipe
- Fuel lines and bracket
- Clutch fluid line bracket and slave cylinder
- Engine ground cables
- Brake booster vacuum line
- Engine wiring harness connectors at left rear of the engine compartment
- Air intake assembly
- Accelerator cable
- Accessory drive belts
- Hood
- Battery

8. Fill the cooling system.
9. Start the engine and check for leaks.

2.6L Engine

1. Before servicing the vehicle, refer to the precautions in the beginning of this section.

2. Drain the cooling system.
3. Relieve the fuel system pressure.
4. Remove or disconnect the following:
- Battery

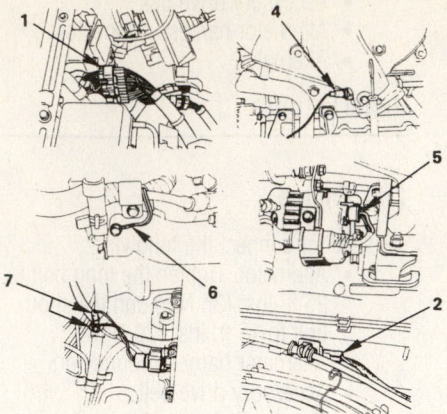
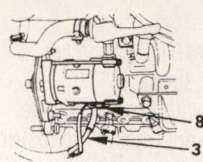

1. Engine harness connector
2. Ground cable connector
3. Negative cable connector
4. Heated oxygen sensor connector
5. Generator connector
6. Ground cables
7. Oil pressure switch connector
8. Starter motor connector

9308NG01

Wiring harness connector locations—2.6L engine

- Hood
- Accelerator cable
- Air intake assembly
- Fuel pressure regulator vacuum line
- Canister hose
- Brake booster vacuum line
- Engine wiring harness connectors at right wheel housing
- Ground cable connector at the intake manifold, starter and firewall
- Heated Oxygen (HO2S) sensor connector
- Alternator wiring connectors
- Oil pressure switch connector
- Radiator hoses
- Cooling fan and shroud
- Radiator
- Heater hoses
- A/C compressor
- Fuel lines
- Exhaust front pipe
- Starter motor
- Transmission
- Left and right engine mounts

5. Lift the engine from the vehicle.

To install:

6. Lower the engine into the vehicle.
7. Install or connect the following:
- Left and right engine mounts. Tighten the bolts to 30 ft. lbs. (41 Nm) and the nuts to 62 ft. lbs. (83 Nm).
- Transmission
- Starter motor
- Exhaust front pipe
- Fuel lines
- A/C compressor
- Heater hoses
- Radiator
- Cooling fan and shroud
- Radiator hoses
- Oil pressure switch connector
- Alternator wiring connectors

- Heated Oxygen (HO2S) sensor connector
- Ground cable connector at the intake manifold, starter and firewall
- Engine wiring harness connectors at right wheel housing
- Brake booster vacuum line
- Canister hose
- Fuel pressure regulator vacuum line
- Air intake assembly
- Accelerator cable
- Hood
- Battery

8. Fill the cooling system.
9. Start the engine and check for leaks.

3.2L Engines

1. Before servicing the vehicle, refer to the precautions in the beginning of this section.

2. Drain the cooling system.
3. Relieve the fuel system pressure.
4. Remove or disconnect the following:
- Battery
- Hood
- Accelerator cable
- Cruise control cable
- Air intake assembly
- Canister vacuum hose
- Brake booster vacuum hose
- Engine wiring harness connectors
- Front axle harness connector, if equipped
- Transmission harness connector and bracket
- Frame ground cable
- Firewall ground cable
- Starter harness connectors
- Alternator harness connectors
- Coolant overflow reservoir hose
- Radiator hoses
- Cooling fan and shroud

- Accessory drive belt
- Power steering pump
- A/C compressor
- Heated Oxygen (HO2S) sensor connectors
- Exhaust front pipes
- Heater hoses
- Fuel lines
- Transmission
- Left and right engine mounts

5. Lift the engine from the vehicle.

To install:

6. Lower the engine into the vehicle.
7. Install or connect the following:
   - Left and right engine mounts. Tighten the bolts to 30 ft. lbs. (41 Nm) and the nuts to 37 ft. lbs. (50 Nm).
   - Transmission
   - Fuel lines
   - Heater hoses
   - Exhaust front pipes
   - Heated Oxygen (HO2S) sensor connectors
   - A/C compressor
   - Power steering pump
   - Accessory drive belt
   - Cooling fan and shroud
   - Radiator hoses
   - Coolant overflow reservoir hose
   - Alternator harness connectors
   - Starter harness connectors
   - Firewall ground cable
   - Frame ground cable
   - Transmission harness connector and bracket
   - Front axle harness connector, if equipped
   - Engine wiring harness connectors
   - Brake booster vacuum hose
   - Canister vacuum hose
   - Air intake assembly
   - Cruise control cable
   - Accelerator cable
   - Hood
   - Battery

8. Fill the cooling system.
9. Start the engine and check for leaks

Water Pump

REMOVAL & INSTALLATION

2.2L Engine

1. Before servicing the vehicle, refer to the precautions in the beginning of this section.
2. Drain the cooling system.

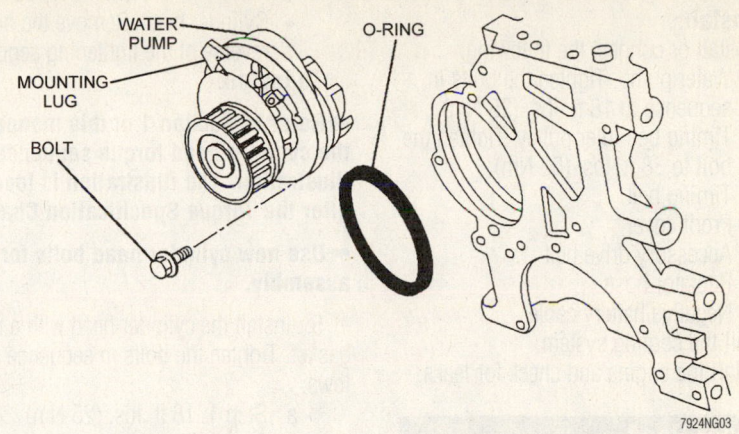

Exploded view of the water pump mounting, showing the location of the mounting lug—2.2L engine

3. Remove or disconnect the following:
   - Negative battery cable
   - Radiator hose
   - Accessory drive belt
   - Front cover
   - Timing belt. Refer to the Timing Belt unit repair section.
   - Water pump

To install:

4. Install a new O-ring and coat the water pump sealing surface with silicone grease.
5. Install or connect the following:
   - Water pump. Tighten the bolts to 18 ft. lbs. (25 Nm).
   - Timing belt
   - Front cover
   - Accessory drive belt
   - Radiator hose
   - Negative battery cable
6. Fill the cooling system.
7. Start the engine and check for leaks.

2.6L Engine

1. Before servicing the vehicle, refer to the precautions in the beginning of this section.
2. Drain the cooling system.
3. Remove or disconnect the following:
   - Negative battery cable
   - Air intake duct
   - Cooling fan and shroud
   - Accessory drive belts
   - Water pump pulley
   - Crankshaft pulley
   - Upper and lower timing belt covers
   - Water pump

To install:

4. Install or connect the following:
   - Water pump. Tighten the bolts to 14 ft. lbs. (19 Nm) and the nut to 20 ft. lbs. (25 Nm).

- Upper and lower timing belt covers
- Crankshaft pulley. Tighten the bolt to 90 ft. lbs. (122 Nm).
- Water pump pulley
- Accessory drive belts
- Cooling fan and shroud
- Air intake duct
- Negative battery cable

5. Fill the cooling system.
6. Start the engine and check for leaks.

3.2L Engines

1. Before servicing the vehicle, refer to the precautions in the beginning of this section.
2. Drain the cooling system.
3. Remove or disconnect the following:
   - Negative battery cable
   - Radiator hose
   - Accessory drive belt
   - Front cover
   - Timing belt. Refer to the Timing Belt unit repair section.
   - Timing belt idler pulley
   - Water pump

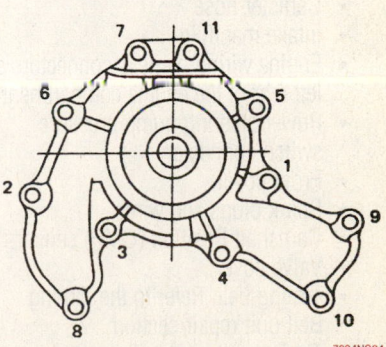

Water pump bolt tightening sequence—3.2L engines

Timing belt service is covered in Section 4 of this manual

To install:

4. Install or connect the following:
   - Water pump. Tighten the bolts in sequence to 18 ft. lbs. (25 Nm).
   - Timing belt idler pulley. Tighten the bolt to 38 ft. lbs. (52 Nm).
   - Timing belt
   - Front cover
   - Accessory drive belt
   - Radiator hose
   - Negative battery cable
5. Fill the cooling system.
6. Start the engine and check for leaks.

Cylinder Head

REMOVAL & INSTALLATION

2.2L Engine

1. Before servicing the vehicle, refer to the precautions in the beginning of this section.
2. Drain the cooling system.
3. Relieve the fuel system pressure.
4. Remove or disconnect the following:
   - Negative battery cable
   - Intake Air Temperature (IAT) sensor connector
   - Positive Crankcase Ventilation (PCV) valve and hose
   - Air intake assembly
   - Upper radiator hose
   - Accessory drive belt
   - Exhaust front pipe
   - Alternator and brackets
   - Crankshaft Position (CKP) sensor connector
   - Knock sensor connector
   - Heater hoses
   - Water bypass hose
   - Fuel lines
   - Evaporative Emissions (EVAP) valve connector
   - Canister hose
   - Intake manifold
   - Engine wiring harness connectors at left rear of the engine compartment
   - Power steering pump pressure switch connector
   - Front cover
   - Spark plugs and wires
   - Camshaft Position (CMP) sensor
   - Valve cover
   - Timing belt. Refer to the Timing Belt unit repair section.
   - Timing belt idler pulleys
   - Timing belt rear cover
   - Oil pressure switch connector
   - Camshafts

- Cylinder head. Remove the bolts in reverse of the tightening sequence.

To install:

➡ **Refer to Section 1 of this manual for the cylinder head torque sequence illustration. The illustration is located after the Torque Specification Chart.**

➡ **Use new cylinder head bolts for assembly.**

5. Install the cylinder head with a new gasket. Tighten the bolts in sequence as follows:
   a. Step 1: 18 ft. lbs. (25 Nm)
   b. Step 2: Plus 90 degrees
   c. Step 3: Plus 90 degrees
   d. Step 4: Plus 90 degrees
6. Install or connect the following:
   - Camshafts
   - Oil pressure switch connector
   - Timing belt rear cover
   - Timing belt idler pulleys. Tighten the bolts to 18 ft. lbs. (25 Nm).
   - Timing belt
   - Valve cover
   - CMP sensor
   - Spark plugs and wires
   - Front cover
   - Power steering pump pressure switch connector
   - Engine wiring harness connectors at left rear of the engine compartment
   - Intake manifold
   - Canister hose
   - EVAP valve connector
   - Fuel lines
   - Water bypass hose
   - Heater hoses
   - Knock sensor connector
   - CKP sensor connector
   - Alternator and brackets
   - Exhaust front pipe
   - Accessory drive belt

- Upper radiator hose
- Air intake assembly
- PCV valve and hose
- IAT sensor connector
- Negative battery cable
7. Fill the cooling system.
8. Start the engine and check for leaks.

2.6L Engine

1. Before servicing the vehicle, refer to the precautions in the beginning of this section.
2. Drain the cooling system.
3. Relieve the fuel system pressure.
4. Remove or disconnect the following:
   - Negative battery cable
   - Hood
   - Accessory drive belts
   - Accelerator cable
   - Positive Crankcase Ventilation (PCV) valve and hose
   - Air intake duct
   - Fuel pressure regulator vacuum line
   - Canister hose
   - Brake booster vacuum line
   - Engine wiring harness connectors at right wheel housing
   - Ground cable connector at the intake manifold, starter and firewall
   - Heated Oxygen (HO$_2$S) sensor connector
   - Alternator wiring connectors
   - Oil pressure switch connector
   - Starter motor harness connectors
   - Ignition coil connector
   - Spark plug wires
   - Distributor
   - Exhaust front pipe
   - Exhaust Gas Recirculation (EGR) gas temperature sensor connector
   - Air pump
   - EGR pipe
   - Heat shield

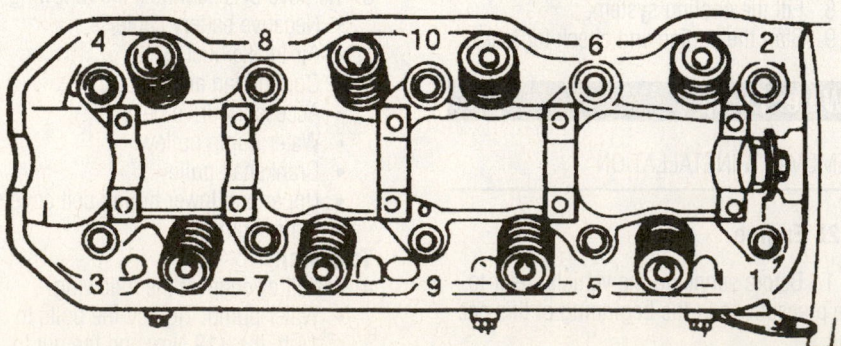

Cylinder head bolt loosening sequence—2.6L engine

7924NG07

- Exhaust manifold
- Throttle Position (TP) switch connector
- Cooling fan
- Water pump pulley
- Power steering pump
- Intake manifold
- Crankshaft pulley
- Front cover
- Timing belt. Refer to the Timing Belt unit repair section.
- Valve cover
- Rocker arms
- Camshaft
- Cylinder head

To install:

➡️**Refer to Section 1 of this manual for the cylinder head torque sequence illustration. The illustration is located after the Torque Specification Chart.**

➡️**Lubricate the cylinder head bolts with clean engine oil for assembly.**

5. Install the cylinder head with a new gasket. Tighten the bolts in sequence as follows:
    a. Step 1: 58 ft. lbs. (75 Nm)
    b. Step 2: 72 ft. lbs. (98 Nm)
6. Install or connect the following:
    - Camshaft
    - Rocker arms
    - Valve cover
    - Timing belt
    - Front cover
    - Crankshaft pulley. Tighten the bolt to 87 ft. lbs. (128 Nm).
    - Intake manifold
    - Power steering pump
    - Water pump pulley
    - Cooling fan
    - TP switch connector
    - Exhaust manifold
    - Heat shield
    - EGR pipe
    - Air pump
    - EGR gas temperature sensor connector
    - Exhaust front pipe
    - Distributor
    - Spark plug wires
    - Ignition coil connector
    - Starter motor harness connectors
    - Oil pressure switch connector
    - Alternator wiring connectors
    - HO$_2$S sensor connector
    - Ground cable connector at the intake manifold, starter and firewall
    - Engine wiring harness connectors at right wheel housing

- Brake booster vacuum line
- Canister hose
- Fuel pressure regulator vacuum line
- Air intake duct
- PCV valve and hose
- Accelerator cable
- Accessory drive belts
- Hood
- Negative battery cable
7. Fill the cooling system.
8. Start the engine and check for leaks.

3.2L Engines

SOHC

1. Before servicing the vehicle, refer to the precautions in the beginning of this section.
2. Drain the cooling system.
3. Relieve the fuel system pressure.
4. Remove or disconnect the following:
    - Negative battery cable
    - Intake manifold common chamber
    - Fuel lines
    - Fuel injector connectors
    - Intake manifold
    - Engine coolant manifold
    - Accessory drive belts
    - Power steering pump and bracket
    - Cooling fan
    - Crankshaft pulley
    - Oil cooler hose bracket
    - Front cover
    - Timing belt. Refer to the Timing Belt unit repair section.
    - Valve covers
    - Heated Oxygen (HO$_2$S) sensor connectors
    - Exhaust front pipe
    - Oil dipstick tube
    - Cylinder heads. Loosen the bolts in reverse of the tightening sequence.

To install:

➡️**Refer to Section 1 of this manual for the cylinder head torque sequence illustration. The illustration is located after the Torque Specification Chart.**

➡️**Use new cylinder head bolts for assembly.**

5. Install the cylinder heads with new gaskets. Tighten the bolts in sequence as follows:
    a. Step 1: 11mm bolts to 47 ft. lbs. (64 Nm)
    b. Step 2: 8mm bolts to 15 ft. lbs. (21 Nm)
6. Install or connect the following:

- Oil dipstick tube
- Exhaust front pipe
- HO$_2$S sensor connectors
- Valve covers
- Timing belt
- Front cover
- Oil cooler hose bracket
- Crankshaft pulley. Tighten the bolt to 127 ft. lbs. (163 Nm).
- Cooling fan
- Power steering pump and bracket
- Accessory drive belts
- Engine coolant manifold
- Intake manifold
- Fuel injector connectors
- Fuel lines
- Intake manifold common chamber
- Negative battery cable
7. Fill the cooling system.
8. Start the engine and check for leaks.

DOHC

1. Before servicing the vehicle, refer to the precautions in the beginning of this section.
2. Drain the cooling system.
3. Relieve the fuel system pressure.
4. Remove or disconnect the following:
    - Negative battery cable
    - Hood
    - Engine cover
    - Mass Air Flow (MAF) sensor connector
    - Intake Air Temperature (IAT) sensor connector
    - Positive Crankcase Ventilation (PCV) valve and hose
    - Air cleaner assembly
    - Manifold Absolute Pressure (MAP) sensor connector
    - Vacuum Switching Valve (VSV) connector and vacuum line
    - Fuel injector connectors
    - Throttle Position (TP) sensor connector
    - Idle Air Control (IAC) valve connector
    - Ignition coils
    - Brake booster vacuum line
    - Canister purge vacuum line
    - Duty solenoid valve
    - Fuel lines
    - Intake manifold
    - Radiator hoses
    - Engine coolant manifold
    - Upper fan shroud
    - Accessory drive belt and tensioner
    - Cooling fan and pulley
    - Alternator

- Idler pulley
- Power steering pump and bracket
- A/C compressor
- Crankshaft pulley
- Oil cooler hoses
- Timing belt cover
- Valve covers
- Timing belt. Refer to the Timing Belt Unit Repair Section.
- Left and right exhaust front pipes
- Oil dipstick tube
- Cylinder heads

To install:

➡ **Use new head bolts when installing the cylinder head.**

➡ **The left and right cylinder head gaskets are not interchangeable.**

➡ **Refer to Section 1 of this manual for the cylinder head torque sequence illustration. The illustration is located after the Torque Specification Chart.**

5. Install the cylinder heads with new gaskets. Tighten the bolts in sequence as follows:
   a. Step 1: 21 ft. lbs. (29 Nm)
   b. Step 2: 47 ft. lbs. (64 Nm)
6. Install or connect the following:
   - Oil dipstick tube
   - Left and right exhaust front pipes
   - Timing belt
   - Valve covers
   - Timing belt cover
   - Oil cooler hoses
   - Crankshaft pulley. Tighten the pulley bolt to 123 ft. lbs. (167 Nm).
   - A/C compressor
   - Power steering pump and bracket. Tighten the bolts to 34 ft. lbs. (46 Nm).
   - Idler pulley
   - Alternator

- Cooling fan and pulley
- Accessory drive belt and tensioner
- Upper fan shroud
- Engine coolant manifold
- Radiator hoses
- Intake manifold
- Fuel lines
- Duty solenoid valve
- Canister purge vacuum line
- Brake booster vacuum line
- Ignition coils
- IAC valve connector
- TP sensor connector
- Fuel injector connectors
- VSV connector and vacuum line
- MAP sensor connector
- Air cleaner assembly
- PCV valve and hose
- IAT sensor connector
- MAF sensor connector
- Engine cover
- Hood
- Negative battery cable
7. Fill the cooling system.
8. Start the engine and check for leaks.

Rocker Arms/Shafts

REMOVAL & INSTALLATION

➡ **The 2.2L DOHC and the 3.2L DOHC engines are not equipped with rocker arms. The camshaft lobes act directly on the valve shims.**

2.6L Engine

1. Before servicing the vehicle, refer to the precautions in the beginning of this section.
2. Remove or disconnect the following:
   - Negative battery cable
   - Valve cover
   - Accessory drive belts
   - Cooling fan
   - Water pump pulley

- Power steering pump
- Crankshaft pulley
- Front cover
- Timing belt. Refer to the Timing Belt unit repair section.
- Rocker arm assembly

➡ **Keep all valvetrain components in order for assembly.**

To install:

3. Install or connect the following:
   - Rocker arm assembly. Tighten the bolts in sequence and in several steps to 16 ft. lbs. (22 Nm).
   - Timing belt
   - Front cover
   - Crankshaft pulley
   - Power steering pump
   - Water pump pulley
   - Cooling fan
   - Accessory drive belts
   - Valve cover
   - Negative battery cable

3.2L SOHC Engine

1. Before servicing the vehicle, refer to the precautions in the beginning of this section.
2. Remove or disconnect the following:
   - Negative battery cable
   - Air cleaner assembly
   - Fuel lines
   - Upper intake manifold
   - Ignition coils
   - Valve covers
   - Upper fan shroud
   - Accessory drive belts
   - Power steering pump and bracket
   - Cooling fan and pulley
   - Crankshaft pulley
   - Oil cooler hoses
   - Timing belt cover
   - Timing belt. Refer to the Timing Belt Unit Repair Section.
   - Camshaft sprockets
   - Cylinder head front plates

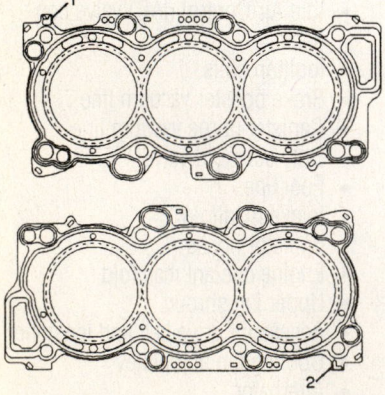

Right (1) and left (2) head gasket identification mark locations—3.2L DOHC engine

7924NG11

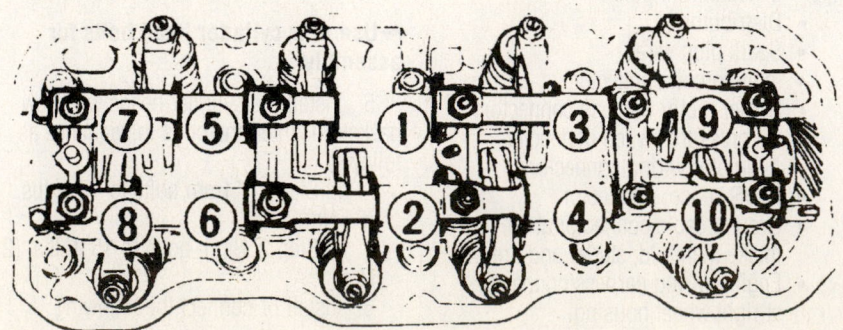

Camshaft holder mounting bolt tightening sequence—2.6L engine

7924NG13

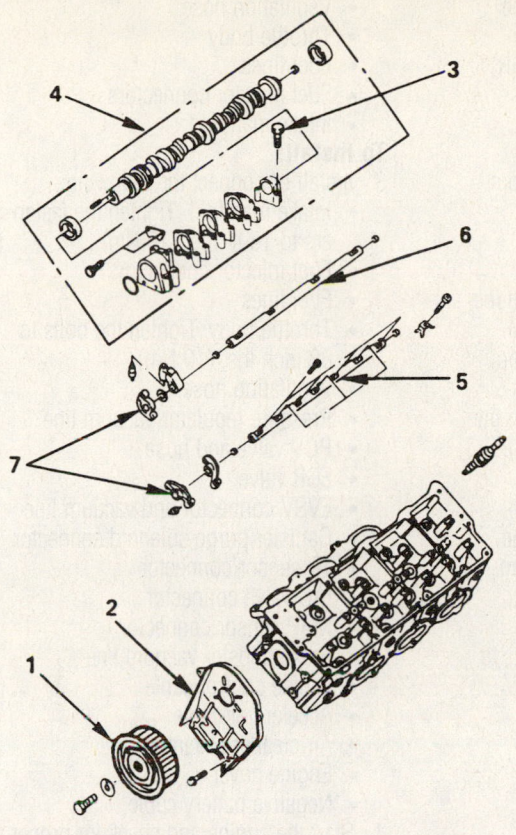

1. Camshaft timing pulley
2. Front plate
3. Camshaft bracket housing fixing bolts
4. Camshaft assembly
5. Rockershaft assembly (Exhaust side)
6. Rockershaft assembly (Intake side)
7. Rocker arm

7924BG43

Exploded view of the rocker arm/shaft assembly mounting—3.2L engines

- Camshafts
- Rocker arm shafts
- Rocker arms from the shafts

To install:
3. Install or connect the following:
- Rocker arms
- Rocker arm shafts. Tighten the bolts, in sequence, to 13 ft. lbs. (18 Nm).
- Camshafts
- Cylinder head front plates. Tighten the bolts to 12 ft. lbs. (17 Nm).
- Camshaft sprockets. Tighten the bolts to 46 ft. lbs. (64 Nm).

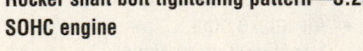

7924NG16

Rocker shaft bolt tightening pattern—3.2L SOHC engine

- Timing belt
- Timing belt cover
- Oil cooler hoses
- Crankshaft pulley. Tighten the pulley bolt to 123 ft. lbs. (167 Nm).
- Cooling fan and pulley
- Power steering pump and bracket
- Accessory drive belts
- Upper fan shroud
- Valve covers
- Ignition coils
- Upper intake manifold
- Fuel lines
- Air cleaner assembly
- Negative battery cable

Intake Manifold

REMOVAL & INSTALLATION

2.2L Engine

1. Before servicing the vehicle, refer to the precautions in the beginning of this section.
2. Drain the cooling system.
3. Relieve the fuel system pressure.
4. Remove or disconnect the following:

- Negative battery cable
- Accessory drive belt
- Positive Crankcase Ventilation (PCV) valve and hose
- Air intake duct
- Throttle body water hoses
- Throttle Position (TP) sensor connector
- Idle Air Control (IAC) valve connector
- Fuel lines
- Fuel injector connectors
- Fuel pressure regulator vacuum line
- Fuel supply manifold
- Accelerator cable
- Alternator and brackets
- Water pipe
- Intake manifold bracket
- Ignition coil and bracket
- Brake booster vacuum line
- Intake manifold

To install:
5. Install or connect the following:
- Intake manifold. Use a new gasket and tighten the bolts to 16 ft. lbs. (22 Nm).
- Brake booster vacuum line
- Ignition coil and bracket
- Intake manifold bracket. Tighten the bolts to 16 ft. lbs. (22 Nm).
- Water pipe
- Alternator and brackets. Tighten the short bolts to 14 ft. lbs. (20 Nm) and the long bolts to 25 ft. lbs. (35 Nm).
- Accelerator cable
- Fuel supply manifold
- Fuel pressure regulator vacuum line
- Fuel injector connectors
- Fuel lines
- IAC valve connector
- TP sensor connector
- Throttle body water hoses
- Air intake duct
- PCV valve and hose
- Accessory drive belt
- Negative battery cable
6. Fill the cooling system.
7. Start the engine and check for leaks.

2.6L Engine

1. Before servicing the vehicle, refer to the precautions in the beginning of this section.
2. Relieve the fuel system pressure.
3. Drain the cooling system.
4. Remove or disconnect the following:
- Negative battery cable

Refer to Section 1 for engine rebuilding specifications

- Accelerator cable
- Positive Crankcase Ventilation (PCV) valve and hose
- Air intake duct
- Exhaust Gas Recirculation (EGR) valve vacuum lines
- Fuel lines
- Throttle body water hoses
- Brake booster vacuum line
- EGR pipe
- Intake manifold common chamber
- Fuel injector connectors
- Fuel supply manifold
- Intake manifold

To install:

5. Install or connect the following:
   - Intake manifold. Tighten the fasteners to 16 ft. lbs. (22 Nm).
   - Fuel supply manifold. Tighten the bolts to 14 ft. lbs. (19 Nm).
   - Fuel injector connectors
   - Intake manifold common chamber. Tighten the bolts to 20 ft. lbs. (27 Nm).
   - EGR pipe
   - Brake booster vacuum line
   - Throttle body water hoses
   - Fuel lines
   - EGR valve vacuum lines
   - Air intake duct
   - PCV valve and hose
   - Accelerator cable
   - Negative battery cable
6. Fill the cooling system.
7. Start the engine and check for leaks.

3.2L Engine

SOHC

1. Before servicing the vehicle, refer to the precautions in the beginning of this section.
2. Remove or disconnect the following:
   - Negative battery cable
   - Air cleaner assembly
   - Accelerator cable
   - Cruise control cable
   - Brake booster vacuum line
   - Manifold Absolute Pressure (MAP) sensor connector
   - Idle Air Control (IAC) valve connector
   - Throttle Position (TP) sensor connector
   - Power switch connector
   - Electronic Vacuum Sensing Valve (EVSV) connector
   - Throttle body
   - Positive Crankcase Ventilation (PCV) valve and hose
   - Fuel pressure regulator vacuum hose

- Front axle actuator vacuum line
- Ventilation hose bracket
- Exhaust Gas Recirculation (EGR) valve assembly
- Upper intake manifold
- Fuel lines
- Fuel injector harness connectors
- Lower intake manifold

To install:

3. Install or connect the following:
   - Lower intake manifold. Tighten the fasteners to 18 ft. lbs. (25 Nm).
   - Fuel injector harness connectors
   - Fuel lines
   - Upper intake manifold. Tighten the fasteners to 18 ft. lbs. (25 Nm).
   - EGR valve assembly
   - Ventilation hose bracket
   - Front axle actuator vacuum line
   - Fuel pressure regulator vacuum hose
   - PCV valve and hose
   - Throttle body. Tighten the bolts to 10 ft. lbs. (13.5 Nm).
   - EVSV connector
   - Power switch connector
   - TP sensor connector
   - IAC valve connector
   - MAP sensor connector
   - Brake booster vacuum line
   - Cruise control cable
   - Accelerator cable
   - Air cleaner assembly
   - Negative battery cable
4. Start the engine and check for proper operation.

DOHC

1. Before servicing the vehicle, refer to the precautions in the beginning of this section.
2. Remove or disconnect the following:
   - Negative battery cable
   - Engine cover
   - Air cleaner assembly
   - Accelerator cable
   - Cruise control cable
   - Brake booster vacuum line
   - Manifold Absolute Pressure (MAP) sensor connector
   - Idle Air Control (IAC) valve connector
   - Throttle Position (TP) sensor connector
   - Canister purge solenoid connector
   - Electronic Vacuum Sensing Valve (EVSV) connector and vacuum line
   - Exhaust Gas Recirculation (EGR) valve
   - Positive Crankcase Ventilation (PCV) valve and hose
   - Pressure regulator vacuum line

- Ventilation hose
- Throttle body
- Fuel lines
- Fuel injector connectors
- Intake manifold

To install:

3. Install or connect the following:
   - Intake manifold. Tighten the fasteners to 18 ft. lbs. (25 Nm).
   - Fuel injector connectors
   - Fuel lines
   - Throttle body. Tighten the bolts to 88 inch lbs. (10 Nm).
   - Ventilation hose
   - Pressure regulator vacuum line
   - PCV valve and hose
   - EGR valve
   - EVSV connector and vacuum line
   - Canister purge solenoid connector
   - TP sensor connector
   - IAC valve connector
   - MAP sensor connector
   - Brake booster vacuum line
   - Cruise control cable
   - Accelerator cable
   - Air cleaner assembly
   - Engine cover
   - Negative battery cable
4. Start the engine and check for proper operation.

Exhaust Manifold

REMOVAL & INSTALLATION

2.2L Engine

1. Before servicing the vehicle, refer to the precautions in the beginning of this section.
2. Remove or disconnect the following:
   - Negative battery cable
   - Air intake duct
   - Exhaust front pipe
   - Exhaust manifold heat shield
   - Exhaust manifold

To install:

3. Install the exhaust manifold. Tighten the nuts in sequence as follows:
   a. Step 1: 10 ft. lbs. (14 Nm)
   b. Step 2: 14 ft. lbs. (20 Nm)
   c. Step 3: 14 ft. lbs. (20 Nm)
4. Install or connect the following:
   - Exhaust manifold heat shield. Tighten the bolts to 71 inch lbs. (8 Nm).
   - Exhaust front pipe. Tighten the bolts to 18 ft. lbs. (25 Nm).
   - Air intake duct
   - Negative battery cable
5. Start the engine and check for leaks.

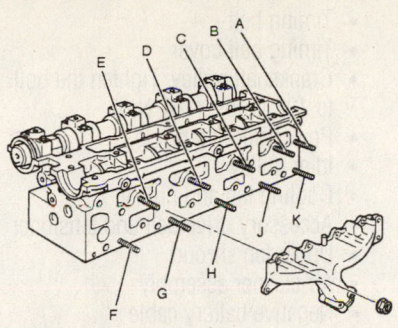

- Tightening sequence:
  Step1: J G H B D C J G B D
  Step2: A B C D E F G H J K
  Step3: A B C D E F G H J K
- Tightening torque:
  Step1: 14 N·m (10 lb ft)
  Step2: 20 N·m (14 lb ft)
  Step3: 20 N·m (14 lb ft)

7924NG17

Exhaust manifold torque sequence—2.2L engine

2.6L Engine

1. Before servicing the vehicle, refer to the precautions in the beginning of this section.
2. Remove or disconnect the following:
   - Negative battery cable
   - Air pump
   - Heated Oxygen (HO2S) sensor connector
   - Exhaust front pipe
   - Exhaust Gas Recirculation (EGR) pipe and bracket
   - Exhaust manifold heat shield
   - Exhaust manifold

To install:

3. Install or connect the following:
   - Exhaust manifold. Tighten the nuts to 33 ft. lbs. (44 Nm).
   - Exhaust manifold heat shield
   - EGR pipe and bracket. Tighten the pipe nuts to 17 ft. lbs. (24 Nm) and the bracket nuts to 49 ft. lbs. (67 Nm).
   - Exhaust front pipe
   - HO2S sensor connector
   - Air pump
   - Negative battery cable
4. Start the engine and check for leaks.

3.2L Engines

SOHC

1. Before servicing the vehicle, refer to the precautions in the beginning of this section.
2. Remove or disconnect the following:

- Negative battery cable
- Air cleaner assembly
- Exhaust Gas Recirculation (EGR) pipe
- 3rd crossmember
- Transfer case skid plate
- Heated Oxygen (HO2S) sensor connectors
- Left and right exhaust front pipes
- Heat shields
- Exhaust manifolds

To install:

➡ **Use new nuts when installing the exhaust manifolds.**

3. Install or connect the following:
   - Exhaust manifolds. Tighten the nuts to 42 ft. lbs. (57 Nm).
   - Heat shields
   - Left and right exhaust front pipes
   - HO2S sensor connectors
   - Transfer case skid plate
   - 3rd crossmember
   - EGR pipe
   - Air cleaner assembly
   - Negative battery cable
4. Start the engine and check for leaks.

DOHC

1. Before servicing the vehicle, refer to the precautions in the beginning of this section.
2. Remove or disconnect the following:
   - Negative battery cable
   - Air cleaner assembly
   - Heated Oxygen (HO2S) sensor connectors
   - Right torsion bar
   - Exhaust Gas Recirculation (EGR) pipe and bracket
   - Left and right exhaust front pipes
   - Heat shields
   - Accessory drive belt
   - A/C compressor and bracket
   - Exhaust manifolds

To install:

3. Install or connect the following:
   - Exhaust manifolds. Tighten the bolts to 42 ft. lbs. (57 Nm).
   - A/C compressor and bracket
   - Accessory drive belt
   - Heat shields
   - Left and right exhaust front pipes
   - EGR pipe and bracket
   - Right torsion bar
   - HO2S sensor connectors
   - Air cleaner assembly
   - Negative battery cable
4. Start the engine and check for leaks.

Front Crankshaft Seal

REMOVAL & INSTALLATION

2.2L and 2.6L Engines

1. Before servicing the vehicle, refer to the precautions in the beginning of this section.
2. Remove or disconnect the following:
   - Negative battery cable
   - Accessory drive belts
   - Cooling fan
   - A/C belt tensioner, if equipped
   - Water pump pulley
   - Power steering pump
   - Crankshaft pulley
   - Front cover
   - Timing belt. Refer to the Timing Belt unit repair section.
   - Crankshaft timing sprocket
   - Rear timing cover, for 2.2L engine
   - Crankshaft oil seal

To install:

3. Install or connect the following:
   - Crankshaft oil seal
   - Rear timing cover, for 2.2L engine
   - Crankshaft timing sprocket. Tighten the bolt to 90 ft. lbs. (123 Nm) for the 2.6L engine or to 94 ft. lbs. (130 Nm) plus 45 degrees for the 2.2L engine.
   - Timing belt. Refer to the Timing Belt unit repair section.
   - Front cover
   - Crankshaft pulley
   - Power steering pump
   - Water pump pulley
   - A/C belt tensioner, if equipped
   - Cooling fan
   - Accessory drive belts
   - Negative battery cable
4. Start the engine and check for leaks.

3.2L Engines

SOHC

1. Before servicing the vehicle, refer to the precautions in the beginning of this section.
2. Remove or disconnect the following:
   - Negative battery cable
   - Air cleaner assembly
   - Upper fan shroud
   - Accessory drive belts
   - Cooling fan and pulley
   - Power steering pump
   - Crankshaft pulley
   - Oil cooler lines

- Timing belt cover
- Timing belt. Refer to the Timing Belt Unit Repair Section.
- Crankshaft timing sprocket
- Oil seal

To install:

3. Install or connect the following:
- Oil seal so that it is flush with the oil pump housing
- Crankshaft timing sprocket
- Timing belt
- Timing belt cover
- Oil cooler lines
- Crankshaft pulley. Tighten the bolt to 123 ft. lbs. (167 Nm).
- Power steering pump
- Cooling fan and pulley
- Accessory drive belts
- Upper fan shroud
- Air cleaner assembly
- Negative battery cable

4. Start the engine and check for leaks.

DOHC

1. Before servicing the vehicle, refer to the precautions in the beginning of this section.

2. Remove or disconnect the following:
- Negative battery cable
- Air cleaner assembly
- Upper fan shroud
- Accessory drive belt and tensioner
- Cooling fan and pulley
- Idler pulley
- Power steering pump
- Crankshaft pulley
- Timing belt cover
- Timing belt. Refer to the Timing Belt Unit Repair Section.
- Crankshaft timing sprocket
- Oil seal

To install:

3. Install or connect the following:
- Oil seal so that it is flush with the oil pump housing
- Crankshaft timing sprocket

- Timing belt
- Timing belt cover
- Crankshaft pulley. Tighten the bolt to 123 ft. lbs. (167 Nm).
- Power steering pump
- Idler pulley
- Cooling fan and pulley
- Accessory drive belt and tensioner
- Upper fan shroud
- Air cleaner assembly
- Negative battery cable

4. Start the engine and check for leaks.

Camshaft and Valve Lifters

REMOVAL & INSTALLATION

2.2L Engine

1. Before servicing the vehicle, refer to the precautions in the beginning of this section.

2. Remove or disconnect the following:

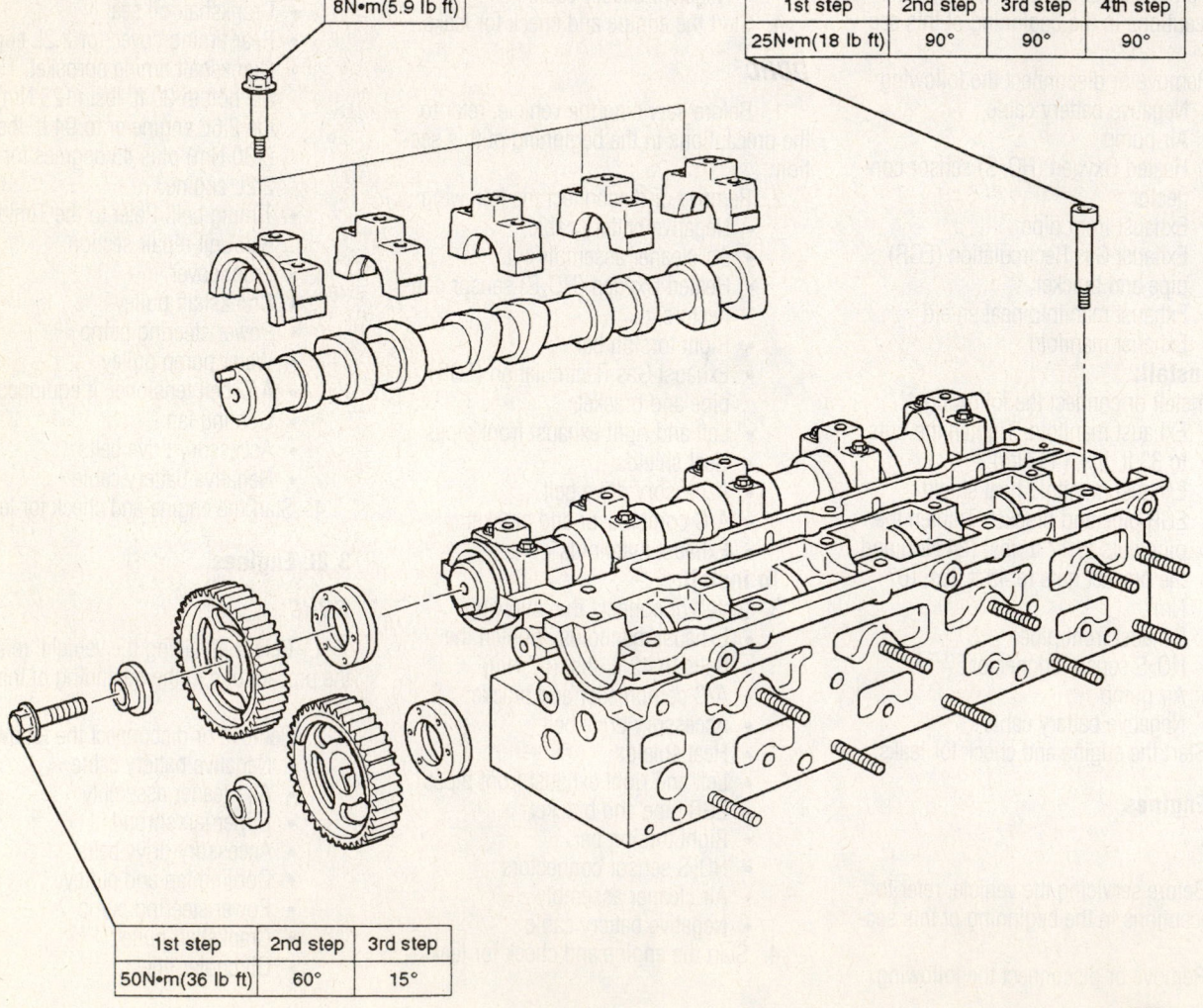

8N•m(5.9 lb ft)			

1st step	2nd step	3rd step	4th step
25N•m(18 lb ft)	90°	90°	90°

1st step	2nd step	3rd step
50N•m(36 lb ft)	60°	15°

Exploded view of the cylinder head and camshaft components—2.2L engine

7924NG41

- Negative battery cable
- Positive Crankcase Ventilation (PCV) valve and hose
- Air intake duct and bracket
- Ground cables
- Engine wiring harness connectors at left rear of the engine compartment
- Cooling fan harness connector
- Accessory drive belt
- Spark plug wire cover
- Spark plug wires
- Camshaft Position (CMP) sensor connector
- Crankshaft Position (CKP) sensor connector
- Crankshaft pulley
- Front cover
- Camshaft Position (CMP) sensor. Loosen the rear timing cover bolt for access.
- Valve cover
- Timing belt. Refer to the Timing Belt unit repair section.
- Camshaft sprockets
- Camshaft bearing caps
- Camshaft seals
- Camshafts
- Hydraulic tappets

➡ **Keep all valvetrain components in order for assembly.**

To install:
3. Install or connect the following:
- Hydraulic tappets in their original locations
- Camshafts
- Camshaft bearing caps. Tighten the bolts in sequence to 71 inch lbs. (8 Nm).
- Camshaft seals
- Camshaft sprockets
4. Tighten the camshaft sprocket bolts as follows:

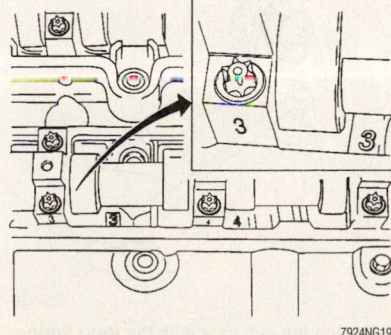

Camshaft bearing cap identification locations—2.2L engine

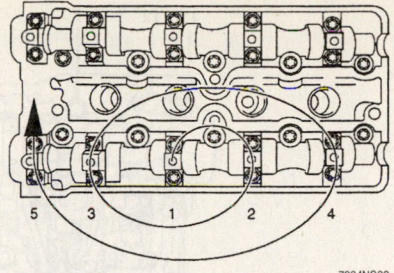

7924NG20

Camshaft bearing cap tightening sequence—2.2L engine

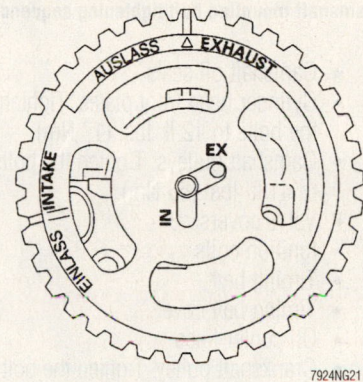

7924NG21

Guide pin location for the exhaust cam gear—2.2L engine

   a. Step 1: 36 ft. lbs. (50 Nm)
   b. Step 2: Plus 60 degrees
   c. Step 3: Plus 15 degrees
5. Install or connect the following:
- Timing belt
- Valve cover
- CMP sensor. Loosen the rear timing cover bolt for access.
- Front cover
- Crankshaft pulley. Tighten the bolts to 14 ft. lbs. (20 Nm).
- CKP sensor connector
- CMP sensor connector
- Spark plug wires
- Spark plug wire cover
- Accessory drive belt
- Cooling fan harness connector
- Engine wiring harness connectors at left rear of the engine compartment
- Ground cables
- Air intake duct and bracket
- PCV valve and hose
- Negative battery cable

2.6L Engine

1. Before servicing the vehicle, refer to the precautions in the beginning of this section.

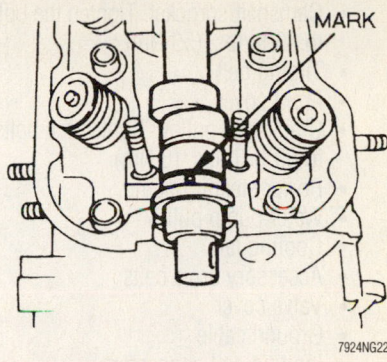

MARK

7924NG22

Camshaft installation positioning mark location—2.6L engine

2. Remove or disconnect the following:
- Negative battery cable
- Accelerator cable
- Positive Crankcase Ventilation (PCV) valve and hose
- Air intake duct
- Spark plug wires
- Ignition coil connectors
- Ground cable
- Valve cover
- Accessory drive belts
- Cooling fan
- Water pump pulley
- Power steering pump
- Crankshaft pulley
- Front cover
- Timing belt. Refer to the Timing Belt unit repair section.
- Camshaft sprocket
- Rocker arm and shaft assembly
- Camshaft seal
- Camshaft

➡ **Keep all valvetrain components in order for assembly.**

To install:
3. Install or connect the following:
- Camshaft
- Rocker arm and shaft assembly. Tighten the nuts to 16 ft. lbs. (22 Nm) and the bolt to 69 inch lbs. (8 Nm).
- Camshaft seal

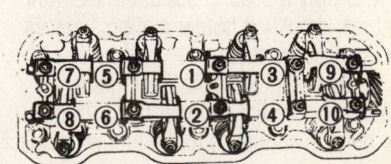

7924NG23

Camshaft bearing cap tightening sequence—2.6L engine

For complete mechanical specifications, refer to Section 1 of this manual

- Camshaft sprocket. Tighten the bolt to 43 ft. lbs. (59 Nm).
- Timing belt
- Front cover
- Crankshaft pulley. Tighten the bolts to 69 inch lbs. (8 Nm).
- Power steering pump
- Water pump pulley
- Cooling fan
- Accessory drive belts
- Valve cover
- Ground cable
- Ignition coil connectors
- Spark plug wires
- Air intake duct
- PCV valve and hose
- Accelerator cable
- Negative battery cable

3.2L Engine

SOHC

➡ **The hydraulic lifters are attached to the rocker arms. Refer to the rocker arm procedure for hydraulic lifter removal.**

1. Before servicing the vehicle, refer to the precautions in the beginning of this section.
2. Relieve the fuel pressure.
3. Remove or disconnect the following:
   - Negative battery cable
   - Upper intake manifold
   - Upper fan shroud
   - Accessory drive belts
   - Cooling fan and pulley
   - Fuel lines
   - Power steering pump
   - Crankshaft pulley
   - Oil cooler lines
   - Timing belt cover
   - Timing belt. Refer to the Timing Belt Unit Repair Section.
   - Ignition coils
   - Valve covers
   - Camshaft pulleys
   - Cylinder head front plates
   - Camshaft oil seals
   - Camshafts

To install:

4. Apply a bead of sealant to the front and rear camshaft holder mating surfaces on the cylinder head.
5. Install the camshaft and holder assembly onto the cylinder head. Tighten the bolts in sequence to the following specifications:
   - 6mm bolts: 69 inch lbs. (8 Nm)
   - 8mm bolts: 13 ft. lbs. (18 Nm)
6. Install or connect the following:

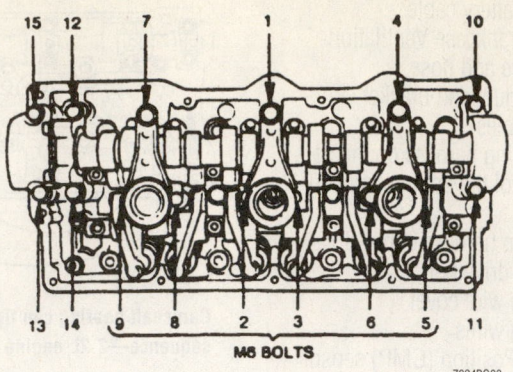

Camshaft mounting bolt tightening sequence—3.2L SOHC engines

- Camshaft oil seals
- Cylinder head front plates. Tighten the bolts to 12 ft. lbs. (17 Nm).
- Camshaft pulleys. Tighten the bolts to 41 ft. lbs. (55 Nm).
- Valve covers
- Ignition coils
- Timing belt
- Timing belt cover
- Oil cooler lines
- Crankshaft pulley. Tighten the bolt to 123 ft. lbs. (167 Nm).
- Power steering pump
- Fuel lines
- Cooling fan and pulley
- Accessory drive belts
- Upper fan shroud
- Upper intake manifold
- Negative battery cable

DOHC

1. Before servicing the vehicle, refer to the precautions in the beginning of this section.
2. Remove or disconnect the following:
   - Negative battery cable
   - Air cleaner assembly
   - Upper fan shroud
   - Accessory drive belt and tensioner
   - Cooling fan and pulley
   - Idler pulley
   - Power steering pump and move it aside
   - Crankshaft pulley
   - Timing belt cover
   - Timing belt. Refer to the Timing Belt Unit Repair Section.
   - Ignition coils
   - Valve covers
   - Camshafts
   - Valve shims and tappets

➡ **Keep the valve shims and tappets in order for installation.**

To install:

3. Install the valve tappets and shims in their original locations.
4. Using Gear Spring Lever J-42686, turn the sub gear clockwise to align the 5mm bolt holes in the sub gear and the camshaft driven gear. Tighten the 5mm bolt.
5. Install or connect the following:
   - Camshafts by aligning the timing marks as shown. Tighten the bolts in sequence to 89 inch lbs. (10 Nm).
   - Valve covers
   - Ignition coils
   - Timing belt
   - Timing belt cover
   - Crankshaft pulley. Tighten the bolt to 123 ft. lbs. (167 Nm).
   - Power steering pump
   - Idler pulley
   - Cooling fan and pulley
   - Accessory drive belt and tensioner
   - Upper fan shroud
   - Air cleaner assembly
   - Negative battery cable

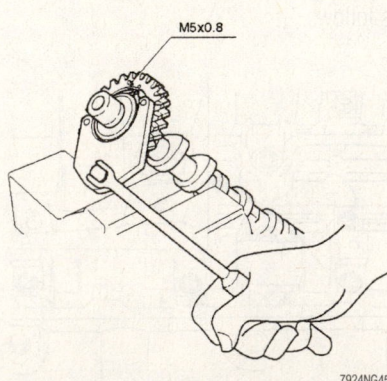

Aligning the sub gear with the Gear Spring Lever J-42686—3.2L DOHC engine

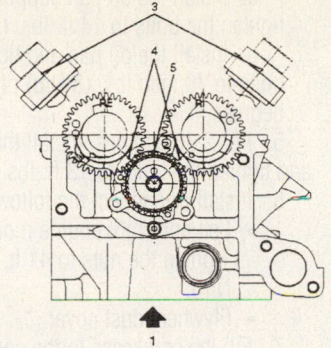
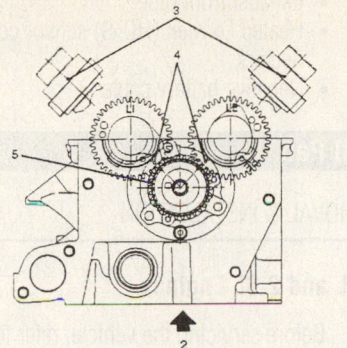

Legend
(1) Right Bank
(2) Left Bank

(3) Alignment Mark on Camshaft Drive Gear
(4) Alignment Mark on Camshaft
(5) Alignment Mark on Retainer

7924NG46

Camshaft alignment marks for the left and right cylinder heads—3.2L DOHC engine

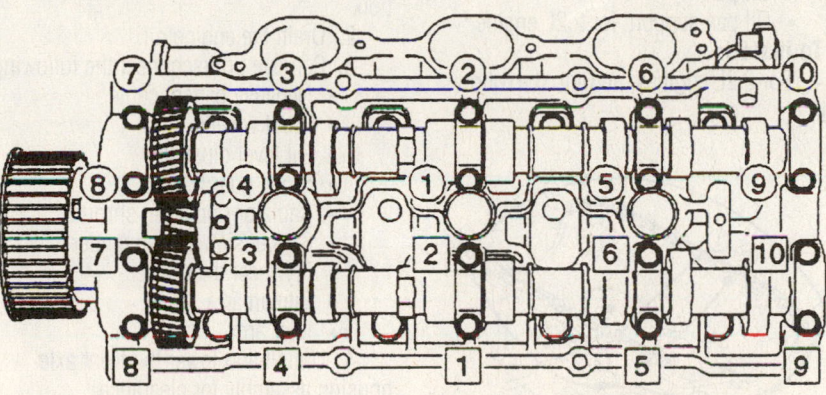

◯ : **Intake**   ☐ : **Exhaust**

7924NG47

Camshaft retaining bracket tightening sequence—3.2L DOHC engine

Valve Lash

ADJUSTMENT

2.2L Engine

The 2.2L DOHC engine is equipped with hydraulic lash adjusters. No valve adjustment is necessary.

2.6L Engine

➡ **Measure valve clearance with the engine cold.**

1. Before servicing the vehicle, refer to the precautions in the beginning of this section.
2. Remove the valve cover.

3. Set the engine to Top Dead Center (TDC) of the compression stroke for the cylinder to be adjusted.
4. Check the valve clearance. The valve clearance specifications are as follows:
- Intake valves: 0.006 inches (0.15mm)
- Exhaust valves: 0.010 inches (0.25mm)
5. After adjustment, tighten the locknuts to 113 inch lbs. (13 Nm).
6. Repeat for each valve to be adjusted.

3.2L Engines

SOHC

The 3.2L SOHC engine is equipped with hydraulic lash adjusters. No valve adjustment is necessary.

DOHC

➡ **Measure valve clearance with the engine cold.**

1. Before servicing the vehicle, refer to the precautions in the beginning of this section.
2. Remove the valve covers.
3. Check the valve clearance with the camshafts positioned as shown. Intake valve clearance should be 0.0091–0.0130 in. (0.2311–0.3302mm). Exhaust valve clearance should be 0.0098–0.0138 in. (0.2489–0.3505mm).

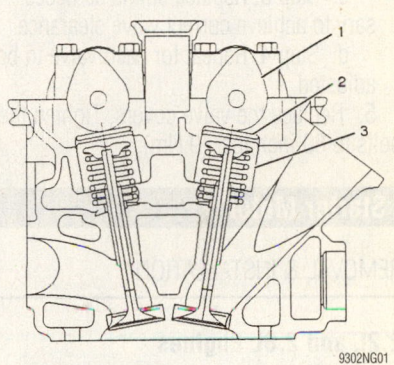

9302NG01

Cross section of the 3.2L DOHC cylinder head. Note the position of the camshaft lobe (1), adjustment shim (2) and the tappet (3)

4. If adjustment is required, replace the shims as follows:
   a. Step 1: Position special tool J-42689 on the edge of the tappet.
   b. Step 2: Rotate the crankshaft until the maximum lift portion of the camshaft lobe contacts the upper edge of the special tool and presses the tappet down to create enough clearance between the adjustment shim and the camshaft for the shim to be removed.

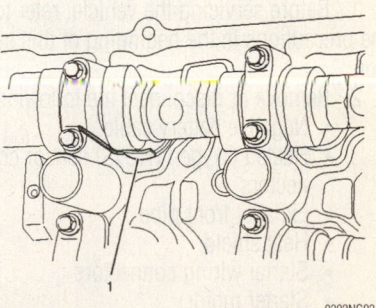

9302NG02

Insert special tool J-42689 (1) and use the camshaft to press the tappet down—3.2L DOHC engine

---

Please refer to Section 8 for electric cooling fan wiring schematics

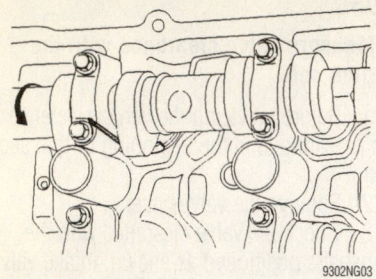

Rotate the camshaft to depress the valve with special tool J-42689—3.2L DOHC engine

c. Step 3: Replace shims as necessary to achieve correct valve clearance.

d. Step 4: Repeat for each valve to be adjusted.

5. Replace the valve covers. Tighten the bolts to 80 inch lbs. (9 Nm).

Starter Motor

REMOVAL & INSTALLATION

2.2L and 2.6L Engines

1. Before servicing the vehicle, refer to the precautions in the beginning of this section.

2. Remove or disconnect the following:
- Negative battery cable
- Starter harness connections
- Starter motor

To install:

3. Install or connect the following:
- Starter motor. Tighten the fasteners to 18 ft. lbs. (25 Nm) for the 2.2L engine or to 30 ft. lbs. (40 Nm) for the 2.6L engine.
- Starter harness connections
- Negative battery cable

3.2L Engines

1. Before servicing the vehicle, refer to the precautions in the beginning of this section.

2. Remove or disconnect the following:
- Negative battery cable
- Heated Oxygen (HO2S) sensor connectors
- Exhaust front pipe
- Heat shield
- Starter wiring connectors
- Starter motor

To install:

3. Install or connect the following:
- Starter motor. Tighten the bolts to 30 ft. lbs. (40 Nm).
- Starter wiring connectors
- Heat shield

- Exhaust front pipe
- Heated Oxygen (HO2S) sensor connectors
- Negative battery cable

Oil Pan

REMOVAL & INSTALLATION

2.2L and 2.6L Engines

1. Before servicing the vehicle, refer to the precautions in the beginning of this section.

2. Drain the engine oil.

3. Remove or disconnect the following:
- Flywheel dust cover
- Left and right engine mounts. Raise the engine for access.
- Oil pan
- Oil pan support, for 2.2L engine

To install:

4. For 2.2L engines, perform the following:

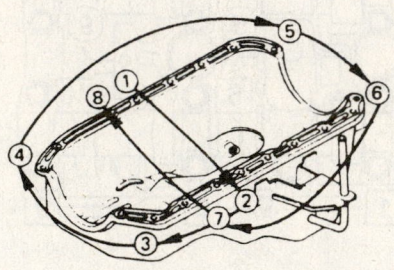

Oil pan bolt tightening sequence—2.2L and 2.6L engines

a. Install the oil pan support and tighten the bolts to 14 ft. lbs. (20 Nm).

b. Install the oil pan and tighten the bolts to 70 inch lbs. (8 Nm) plus 30 degrees.

5. For 2.6L engines, install the oil pan and tighten the bolts to 13 ft. lbs. (18 Nm).

6. Install or connect the following:
- Left and right engine mounts. Tighten the nuts to 41 ft. lbs. (55 Nm).
- Flywheel dust cover

7. Fill the crankcase to the correct level.

8. Start the engine and check for leaks.

3.2L Engines

SOHC

1. Before servicing the vehicle, refer to the precautions in the beginning of this section.

2. Drain the engine oil.

3. Remove or disconnect the following:
- Negative battery cable
- Front wheels
- Oil level dipstick
- Stone guard
- Radiator under fan shroud
- Suspension crossmember
- Flywheel dust cover
- Pitman arm
- Idler arm

4. Unbolt and lower the front axle housing assembly for clearance.

5. Remove the oil pan.

To install:

6. Apply a bead of silicone sealant to the oil pan flange and install the oil pan.

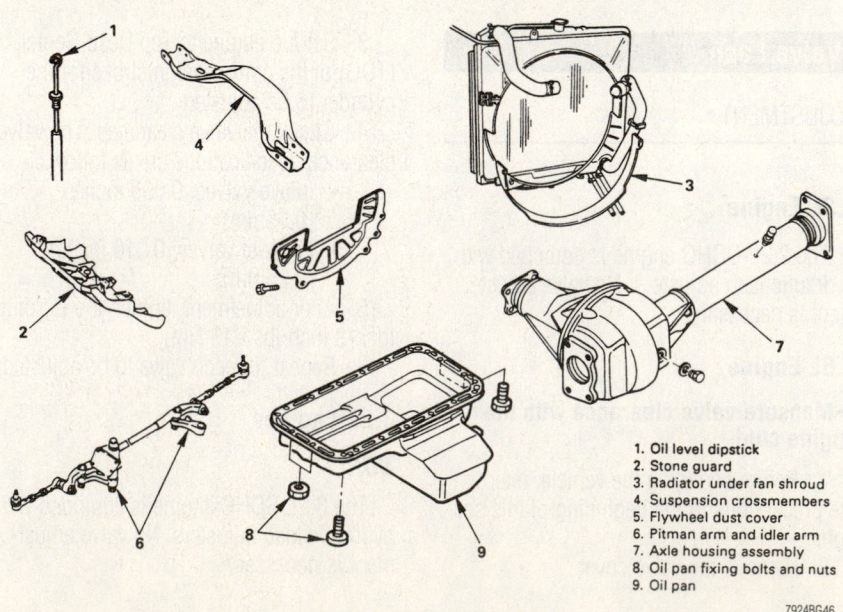

1. Oil level dipstick
2. Stone guard
3. Radiator under fan shroud
4. Suspension crossmembers
5. Flywheel dust cover
6. Pitman arm and idler arm
7. Axle housing assembly
8. Oil pan fixing bolts and nuts
9. Oil pan

Identification of the oil pan (9) and related service components

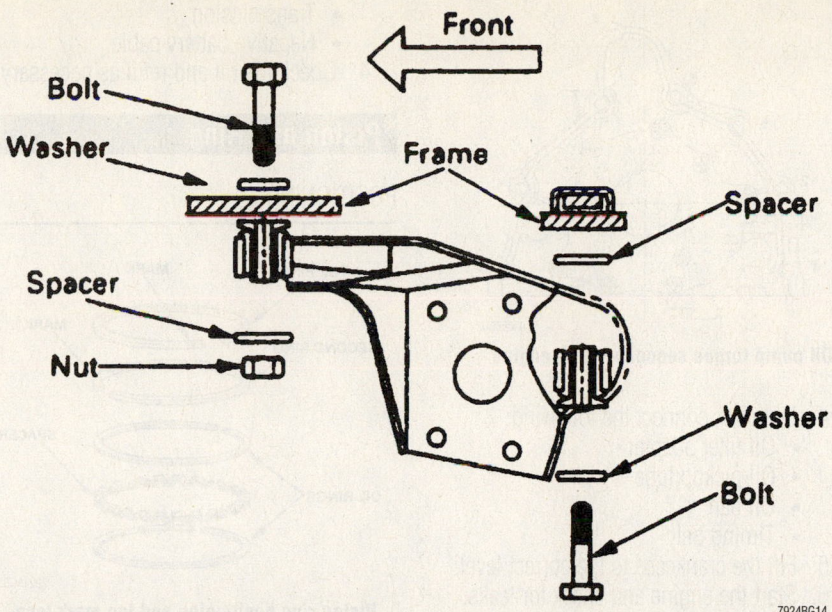

Exploded view of the axle bracket mounting bolt, spacer and nut locations

Tighten the fasteners to 89 inch lbs. (10 Nm).

7. Raise the axle housing assembly into position. Tighten the bolts to 61 ft. lbs. (82 Nm) and the nuts to 112 ft. lbs. (152 Nm).

8. Install or connect the following:
- Pitman arm. Tighten the nut to 159 ft. lbs. (216 Nm).
- Idler arm. Tighten the bolt to 33 ft. lbs. (44 Nm).
- Flywheel dust cover
- Suspension crossmember. Tighten the bolts to 58 ft. lbs. (78 Nm).
- Radiator under fan shroud
- Stone guard
- Oil level dipstick
- Front wheels
- Negative battery cable

9. Fill the crankcase with engine oil.
10. Start the engine and check for leaks.

DOHC

1. Before servicing the vehicle, refer to the precautions in the beginning of this section.
2. Drain the engine oil.
3. Remove or disconnect the following:
- Negative battery cable
- Front wheels
- Oil level dipstick
- Stone guard
- Radiator under fan shroud
- Suspension crossmember
- Flywheel dust cover
- Pitman arm
- Idler arm

4. If equipped with 4 wheel drive, unbolt and lower the front axle housing assembly for clearance.
5. Remove or disconnect the following:
- Oil pan
- Lower crankcase

To install:

6. Apply a bead of silicone sealant to the crankcase flange and install the crankcase. Tighten the fasteners in sequence to 89 inch lbs. (10 Nm).

7. Apply a bead of silicone sealant to the oil pan flange and install the oil pan. Tighten the fasteners to 89 inch lbs. (10 Nm).

8. If equipped, raise the axle housing assembly into position. Tighten the axle case bolts to 61 ft. lbs. (82 Nm) and the mounting bolts to 112 ft. lbs. (152 Nm).

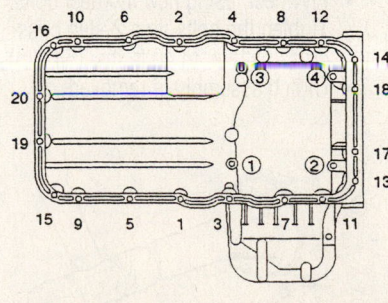

Lower crankcase torque sequence—3.2L DOHC engine

9. Install or connect the following:
- Pitman arm. Tighten the nut to 159 ft. lbs. (216 Nm).
- Idler arm. Tighten the bolt to 33 ft. lbs. (44 Nm).
- Flywheel dust cover
- Suspension crossmember. Tighten the bolts to 58 ft. lbs. (78 Nm).
- Radiator under fan shroud
- Stone guard
- Oil level dipstick
- Front wheels
- Negative battery cable

10. Fill the crankcase with engine oil.
11. Start the engine and check for leaks.

Oil Pump

REMOVAL & INSTALLATION

2.2L Engine

1. Before servicing the vehicle, refer to the precautions in the beginning of this section.
2. Drain the engine oil.
3. Remove or disconnect the following:
- Negative battery cable
- Accessory drive belts
- Cooling fan
- A/C belt tensioner, if equipped
- Water pump pulley
- Power steering pump
- Crankshaft pulley
- Front cover
- Timing belt. Refer to the Timing Belt unit repair section.
- Crankshaft timing sprocket
- Rear timing cover
- Crankshaft oil seal
- Oil pan
- Oil pump pickup tube
- Oil pump

To install:

4. Install or connect the following:
- Oil pump. Use a new gasket and tighten the bolts to 53 inch lbs. (6 Nm)
- Oil pump pickup tube. Tighten the bolts to 70 inch lbs. (8 Nm).
- Oil pan
- Crankshaft oil seal
- Rear timing cover
- Crankshaft timing sprocket. Tighten the bolt to 94 ft. lbs. (130 Nm) plus 45 degrees.
- Timing belt. Refer to the Timing Belt unit repair section.
- Front cover

- Crankshaft pulley. Tighten the bolts to 14 ft. lbs. (20 Nm).
- Power steering pump
- Water pump pulley
- A/C belt tensioner, if equipped
- Cooling fan
- Accessory drive belts
- Negative battery cable

5. Fill the crankcase to the correct level.
6. Start the engine and check for leaks.

2.6L Engine

1. Before servicing the vehicle, refer to the precautions in the beginning of this section.

2. Remove or disconnect the following:
- Negative battery cable
- Accessory drive belts
- Cooling fan
- Water pump pulley
- Power steering pump
- Crankshaft pulley
- Front cover
- Timing belt. Refer to the Timing Belt unit repair section.
- Oil pump sprocket
- Oil pump

To install:

3. Install or connect the following:
- Oil pump. Use a new seal and tighten the bolts to 14 ft. lbs. (19 Nm).
- Oil pump sprocket. Tighten the nut to 56 ft. lbs. (76 Nm).
- Timing belt
- Front cover
- Crankshaft pulley. Tighten the bolt to 87 ft. lbs. (118 Nm).
- Power steering pump
- Water pump pulley
- Cooling fan
- Accessory drive belts
- Negative battery cable

4. Start the engine and check for leaks.

3.2L Engine

1. Before servicing the vehicle, refer to the precautions in the beginning of this section.

2. Remove or disconnect the following:
- Timing belt
- Oil pan
- Oil pickup tube
- Oil filter adapter
- Oil pump

To install:

3. Apply silicone sealant to the oil pump mounting surface and install the oil pump. Tighten the bolts in sequence to 13 ft. lbs. (18 Nm) for SOHC engines or to 18 ft. lbs. (25 Nm) for DOHC engines.

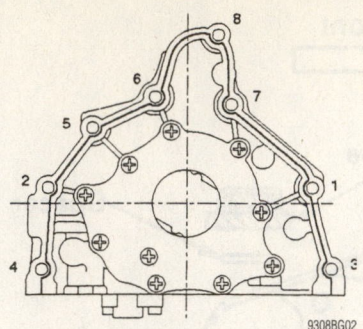

Oil pump torque sequence–3.2L engine

4. Install or connect the following:
- Oil filter adapter
- Oil pickup tube
- Oil pan
- Timing belt

5. Fill the crankcase to the correct level.
6. Start the engine and check for leaks.

Rear Main Seal

REMOVAL & INSTALLATION

1. Before servicing the vehicle, refer to the precautions in the beginning of this section.

2. Remove or disconnect the following:
- Negative battery cable
- Transmission
- Clutch assembly, if equipped with a manual transmission
- Flywheel by loosening the flywheel bolts in a 2-step crisscross sequence
- Rear main seal, using a seal puller

➡**Do not damage the crankshaft sealing surface.**

To install:

3. Install or connect the following:
- New rear main seal, by lubricating it with engine oil
- Flywheel, using new flywheel bolts. Tighten the bolts, in a 2-step crisscross pattern, to 40 ft. lbs. (54 Nm).
- Clutch assembly, if removed

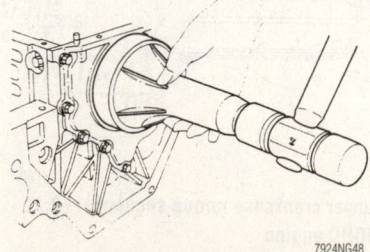

Installing a one-piece rear crankshaft oil seal

- Transmission
- Negative battery cable

4. Check the oil and refill as necessary.

Piston and Ring

POSITIONING

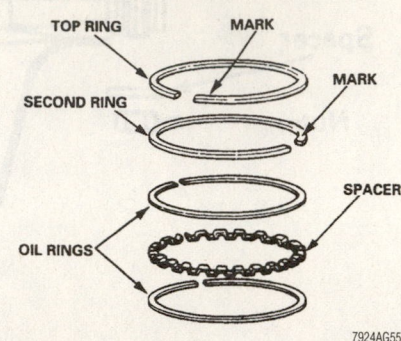

Piston ring positioning and top mark locations—all engines

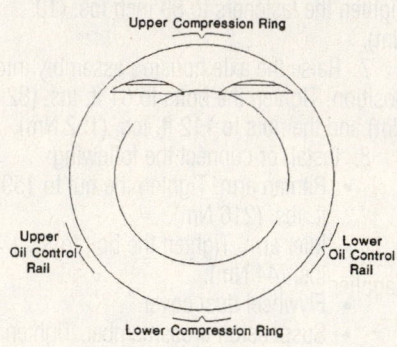

Piston ring end-gap spacing—2.2L engine

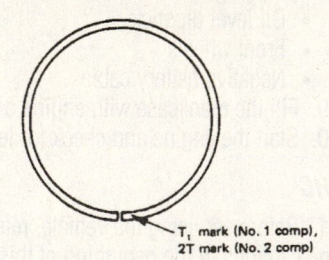

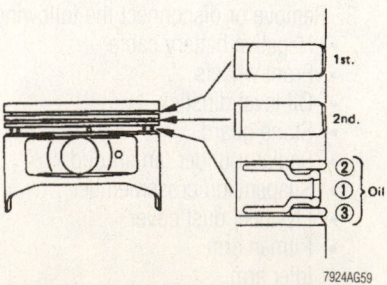

Piston ring positioning—2.6L and 3.2L engines

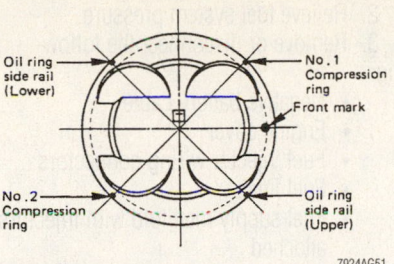

Piston ring end-gap spacing—2.6L and 3.2L engines

FUEL SYSTEM

Fuel System Service Precautions

Safety is the most important factor when performing not only fuel system maintenance but any type of maintenance. Failure to conduct maintenance and repairs in a safe manner may result in serious personal injury or death. Maintenance and testing of the vehicle's fuel system components can be accomplished safely and effectively by adhering to the following rules and guidelines:

• To avoid the possibility of fire and personal injury, always disconnect the negative battery cable unless the repair or test procedure requires that battery voltage be applied.

• Always relieve the fuel system pressure prior to disconnecting any fuel system component (injector, fuel rail, pressure regulator, etc.), fitting or fuel line connection. Exercise extreme caution whenever relieving fuel system pressure, to avoid exposing skin, face and eyes to fuel spray. Please be advised that fuel under pressure may penetrate the skin or any part of the body that it contacts.

• Always place a shop towel or cloth around the fitting or connection prior to loosening to absorb any excess fuel due to spillage. Ensure that all fuel spillage (should it occur) is quickly removed from engine surfaces. Ensure that all fuel soaked cloths or towels are deposited into a suitable waste container.

• Always keep a dry chemical (Class B) fire extinguisher near the work area.

• Do not allow fuel spray or fuel vapors to come into contact with a spark or open flame.

• Always use a backup wrench when loosening and tightening fuel line connection fittings. This will prevent unnecessary stress and torsion to fuel line piping. Always follow the proper tightening specifications.

• Always replace worn fuel fitting O-rings with new. Do not substitute fuel hose or equivalent, where fuel pipe is installed.

Fuel System Pressure

RELIEVING

1. Before servicing the vehicle, refer to the precautions in the beginning of this section.

2. Remove the fuel filler cap.

3. Remove the fuel pump relay from the underhood relay box.

4. Start the engine and let it run until it stalls, then crank the engine for an additional 30 seconds.

5. Turn the ignition switch to the **OFF** position and remove the key. Disconnect the negative battery cable.

6. When service is completed, install the fuel pump relay and connect the negative battery cable.

Fuel Filter

REMOVAL & INSTALLATION

1. Before servicing the vehicle, refer to the precautions in the beginning of this section.

2. Relieve the fuel system pressure.

3. Remove or disconnect the following:
• Fuel lines from the fuel filter
• Fuel filter

To install:

4. Install or connect the following:
• Fuel filter and tighten the bracket bolt. Note the fuel flow directional arrow.
• Fuel lines to the fuel filter
• Negative battery cable

5. Start the engine and inspect the fuel filter connections for leaks.

Fuel Pump

REMOVAL & INSTALLATION

1. Before servicing the vehicle, refer to the precautions in the beginning of this section.

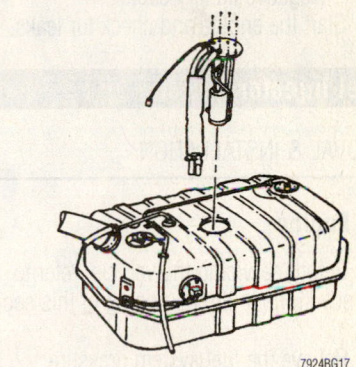

Fuel pump assembly mounting

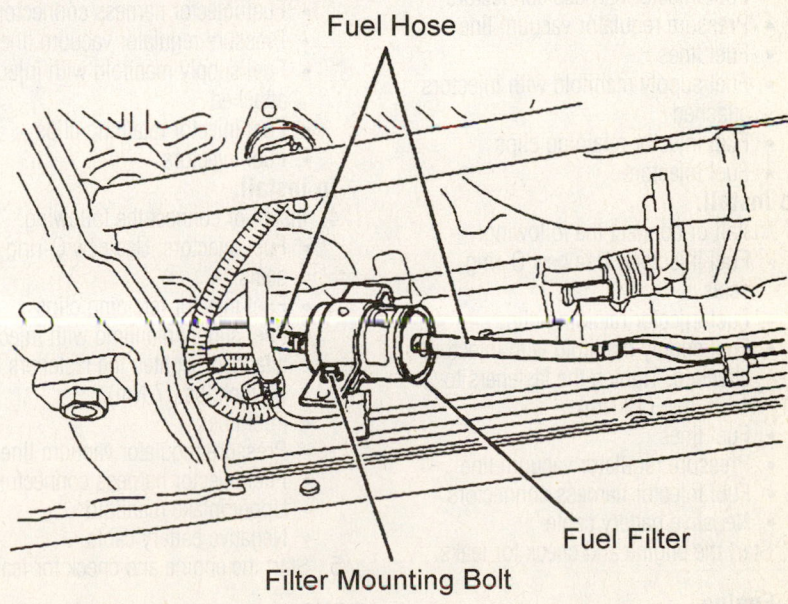

Fuel filter mounting location under the vehicle

Fuel Hose

Filter Mounting Bolt

Fuel Filter

2. Relieve fuel system pressure.
3. Drain the fuel tank.
4. Remove or disconnect the following:
   - Negative battery cable
   - Right rear inner fender liner
   - Fuel filler and vent hoses
   - Fuel tank skid plate
   - Fuel tank wiring connectors
   - Fuel supply and return lines
   - Fuel tank
   - Fuel pump assembly

To install:

5. Install or connect the following:
   - Fuel pump assembly
   - Fuel tank. Tighten the bolts to 27 ft. lbs. (36 Nm).
   - Fuel supply and return lines
   - Fuel tank wiring connectors
   - Fuel tank skid plate
   - Fuel filler and vent hoses
   - Right rear inner fender liner
   - Negative battery cable
6. Start the engine and check for leaks.

Fuel Injector

REMOVAL & INSTALLATION

2.2L Engine

1. Before servicing the vehicle, refer to the precautions in the beginning of this section.
2. Relieve the fuel system pressure.
3. Remove or disconnect the following:
   - Negative battery cable
   - Fuel injector harness connectors
   - Pressure regulator vacuum line
   - Fuel lines
   - Fuel supply manifold with injectors attached
   - Fuel injector retaining clips
   - Fuel injectors

To install:

4. Install or connect the following:
   - Fuel injectors. Use new O-ring seals.
   - Fuel injector retaining clips
   - Fuel supply manifold with injectors attached. Tighten the fasteners to 14 ft. lbs. (19 Nm).
   - Fuel lines
   - Pressure regulator vacuum line
   - Fuel injector harness connectors
   - Negative battery cable
5. Start the engine and check for leaks.

2.6L Engine

1. Before servicing the vehicle, refer to the precautions in the beginning of this section.

2. Relieve the fuel system pressure.
3. Remove or disconnect the following:
   - Negative battery cable
   - Upper intake manifold
   - Fuel lines
   - Fuel injector harness connectors
   - Pressure regulator vacuum line
   - Fuel supply manifold with injectors attached
   - Fuel injector retaining clips
   - Fuel injectors

To install:

4. Install or connect the following:
   - Fuel injectors. Use new O-ring seals.
   - Fuel injector retaining clips
   - Fuel supply manifold with injectors attached. Tighten the fasteners to 14 ft. lbs. (19 Nm).
   - Fuel lines
   - Pressure regulator vacuum line
   - Fuel injector harness connectors
   - Upper intake manifold
   - Negative battery cable
5. Start the engine and check for leaks.

3.2L Engines

SOHC

1. Before servicing the vehicle, refer to the precautions in the beginning of this section.
2. Relieve the fuel system pressure.
3. Remove or disconnect the following:
   - Negative battery cable
   - Upper intake manifold
   - Fuel lines
   - Fuel injector harness connectors
   - Pressure regulator vacuum line
   - Fuel supply manifold with injectors attached
   - Fuel injector retaining clips
   - Fuel injectors

To install:

4. Install or connect the following:
   - Fuel injectors. Use new O-ring seals.
   - Fuel injector retaining clips
   - Fuel supply manifold with injectors attached. Tighten the fasteners to 75 inch lbs. (7 Nm).
   - Fuel lines
   - Pressure regulator vacuum line
   - Fuel injector harness connectors
   - Upper intake manifold
   - Negative battery cable
5. Start the engine and check for leaks.

DOHC

1. Before servicing the vehicle, refer to the precautions in the beginning of this section.

2. Relieve fuel system pressure.
3. Remove or disconnect the following:
   - Negative battery cable
   - Engine cover
   - Fuel injector wiring connectors
   - Fuel lines
   - Fuel supply manifold with injectors attached
   - Fuel injector retaining clips
   - Fuel injectors

To install:

4. Install or connect the following:
   - Fuel injectors. Use new O-ring seals.
   - Fuel injector retaining clips
   - Fuel supply manifold with injectors attached. Tighten the bolts to 60 inch lbs. (6.5 Nm).
   - Fuel lines
   - Fuel injector wiring connectors
   - Engine cover
   - Negative battery cable
5. Start the engine and check for leaks.

DRIVE TRAIN

Transmission Assembly

REMOVAL & INSTALLATION

Manual Transmissions

2 WHEEL DRIVE

➡**The transmission flange bolts vary in length. Note their locations for assembly.**

1. Before servicing the vehicle, refer to the precautions in the beginning of this section.
2. Remove the hood.
3. Install a support fixture to the engine lifting eyes.
4. Remove or disconnect the following:
   - Negative battery cable
   - Shift lever knob
   - Rear console assembly
   - Grommet assembly
   - Shift lever
   - Clutch slave cylinder and hose bracket
   - Driveshaft
   - Fuel line heat shield
   - Vehicle Speed (VSS) sensor connector
   - Reverse light switch connector
   - Flywheel under cover

- Transmission mount and cross-member
- Transmission flange bolts
- Transmission

To install:

5. Install or connect the following:
- Transmission. Tighten the large flange bolts to 52 ft. lbs. (71 Nm) and the small bolts to 30 ft. lbs. (41 Nm).
- Crossmember. Tighten the bolts to 56 ft. lbs. (76 Nm).
- Transmission mount. Tighten the fasteners to 30 ft. lbs. (41 Nm).
- Flywheel under cover. Tighten the bolts to 69 inch lbs. (8 Nm).
- Reverse light switch connector
- Vehicle Speed (VSS) sensor connector
- Fuel line heat shield

- Driveshaft. Tighten the bolts to 37 ft. lbs. (50 Nm).
- Clutch slave cylinder and hose bracket
- Shift lever
- Grommet assembly
- Rear console assembly
- Shift lever knob
- Negative battery cable

6. Remove the engine support fixture and install the hood.

4 WHEEL DRIVE

➡ **The transmission flange bolts vary in length. Note their locations for assembly.**

1. Before servicing the vehicle, refer to the precautions in the beginning of this section.

2. Remove the hood.
3. Install a support fixture to the engine lifting eyes.

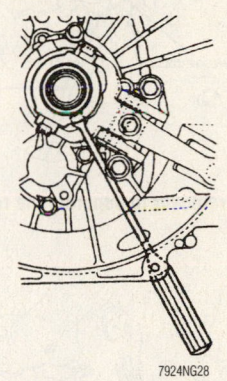

7924NG28

Insert the tool between the wedge collar and the release bearing

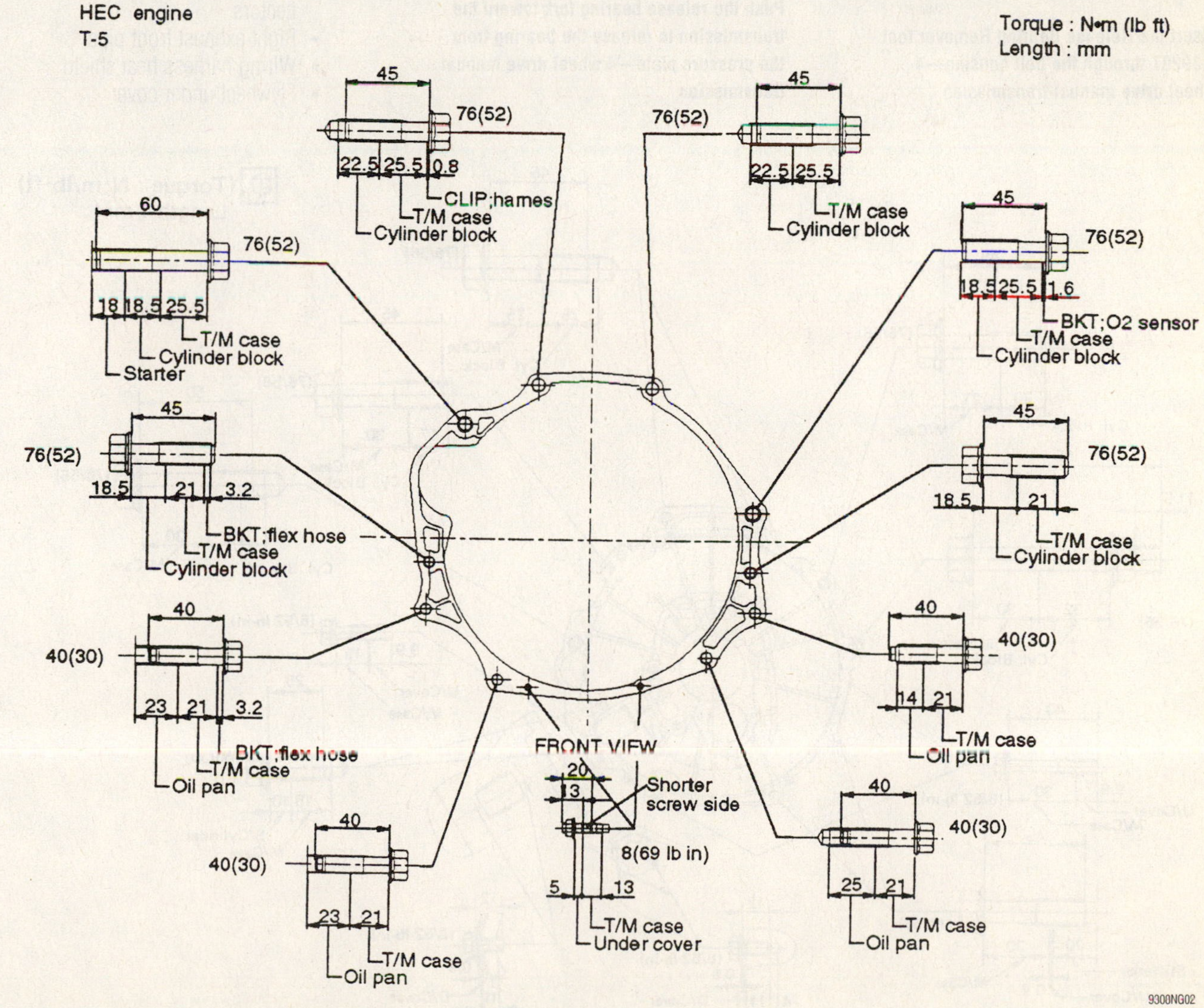

HEC engine
T-5

Torque : N•m (lb ft)
Length : mm

45
76(52)
22.5 | 25.5 | 0.8
CLIP;harnes
T/M case
Cylinder block

45
76(52)
22.5 | 25.5
T/M case
Cylinder block

60
76(52)
18 | 18.5 | 25.5
T/M case
Cylinder block
Starter

45
76(52)
18.5 | 25.5 | 1.6
BKT;O2 sensor
T/M case
Cylinder block

45
76(52)
18.5 | 21 | 3.2
BKT;flex hose
T/M case
Cylinder block

45
76(52)
18.5 | 21
T/M case
Cylinder block

40
40(30)
23 | 21 | 3.2
BKT;flex hose
T/M case
Oil pan

40
40(30)
14 | 21
T/M case
Oil pan

FRONT VIEW
20
3
Shorter screw side
8(69 lb in)
5 | 13
T/M case
Under cover

40
40(30)
23 | 21
T/M case
Oil pan

40
40(30)
25 | 21
T/M case
Oil pan

Transmission flange bolt identification and torque—2 wheel drive transmission

9300NG02

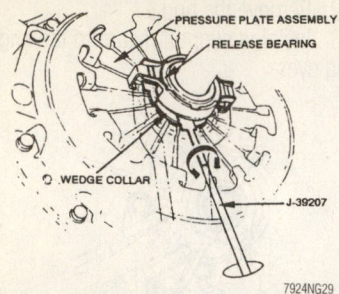

Turn the remover to separate the release bearing

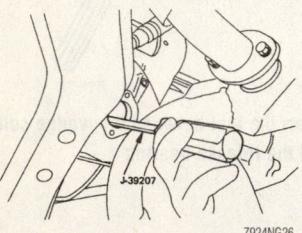

Insert the Release Bearing Remover tool J-39207 through the bell housing—4 wheel drive manual transmission

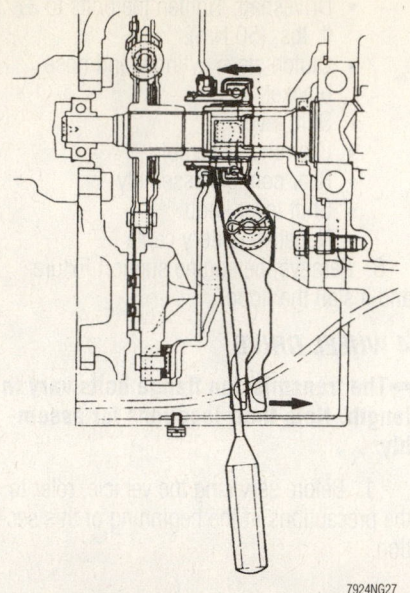

Push the release bearing fork toward the transmission to release the bearing from the pressure plate—4 wheel drive manual transmission

4. Remove or disconnect the following:
- Negative battery cable
- Shift lever knob
- Console assembly
- Grommet assembly
- Shift lever
- Transfer case control lever
- Transfer case skid plate
- Front and rear driveshafts
- Reverse lamp switch connector
- Indicator switch connectors
- Vehicle Speed (VSS) sensor connector
- 4WD actuator connector
- Transmission harness clamps
- Fuel pipe bracket
- Clutch slave cylinder and heat shield
- Transmission mount and crossmember
- Heated Oxygen (HO2S) sensor connectors
- Right exhaust front pipe
- Wiring harness heat shield
- Flywheel under cover

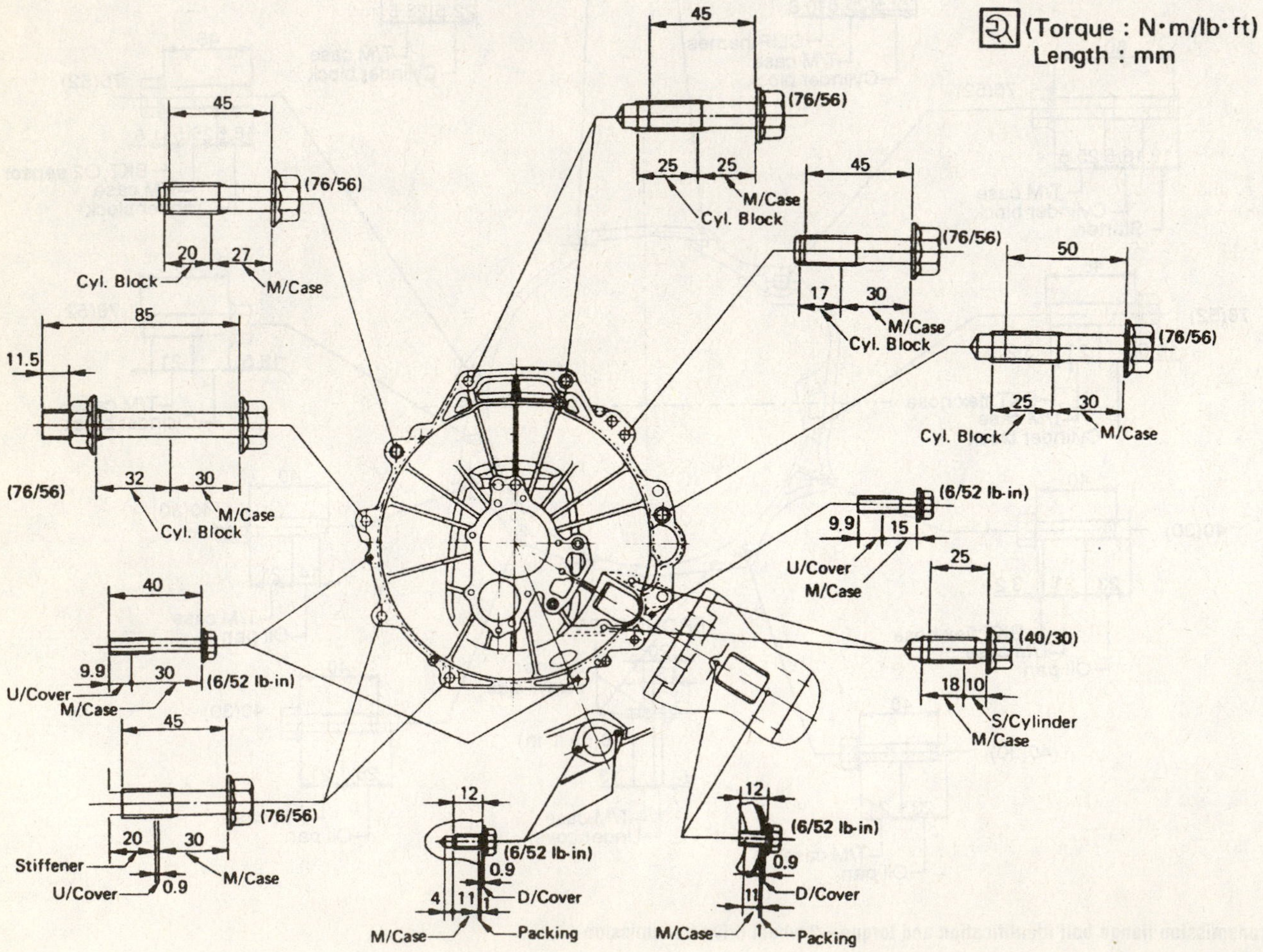

(Torque : N·m/lb·ft)
Length : mm

Transmission mounting bolt identification and torque specifications—V6 engine with 4 wheel drive transmission shown

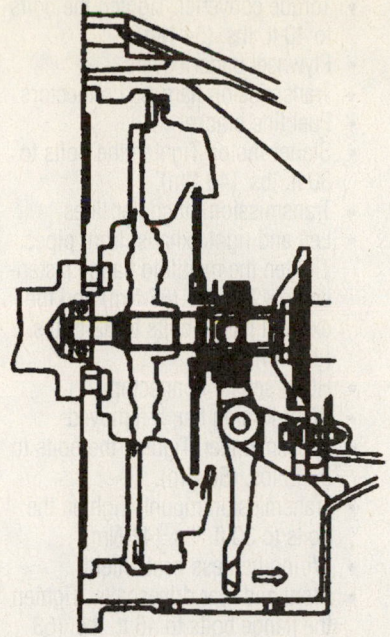

7924BG21

Push the release bearing fork toward the transmission to engage the release bearing with the pressure plate

5. Release the throw out bearing from the pressure plate as shown.

6. Remove the transmission flange bolts and remove the transmission.

To install:

7. Install the transmission. Tighten the large bolts to 56 ft. lbs. (76 Nm) and the small bolts to 52 inch lbs. (6 Nm).

8. Apply 13–18 lbs. (59–78 N) of force to the clutch fork to engage the throw out bearing to the pressure plate.

9. Install or connect the following:
- Flywheel under cover
- Wiring harness heat shield
- Right exhaust front pipe. Tighten the manifold flange fasteners to 49 ft. lbs. (67 Nm) and the exhaust flange bolts to 32 ft. lbs. (43 Nm).
- HO$_2$S sensor connectors
- Crossmember. Tighten the bolts to 37 ft. lbs. (50 Nm).
- Transmission mount. Tighten the bolts to 30 ft. lbs. (41 Nm).
- Clutch slave cylinder and heat shield
- Fuel pipe bracket
- Transmission harness clamps
- 4WD actuator connector
- VSS sensor connector
- Indicator switch connectors
- Reverse lamp switch connector

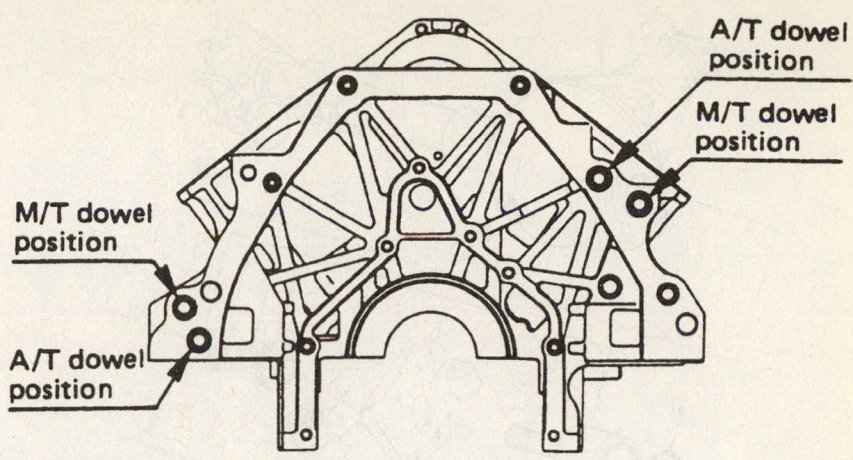

Dowel pin locations for automatic and manual transmissions—3.2L engine

7924NG02

- Front and rear driveshafts. Tighten the flange bolts to 46 ft. lbs. (63 Nm).
- Transfer case skid plate. Tighten the bolts to 27 ft. lbs. (37 Nm).
- Transfer case control lever
- Shift lever
- Grommet assembly
- Console assembly
- Shift lever knob
- Negative battery cable

10. Remove the engine support fixture and install the hood.

Automatic Transmissions

2 WHEEL DRIVE

1. Before servicing the vehicle, refer to the precautions in the beginning of this section.

2. Remove the hood.

3. Install a support fixture to the engine lifting eyes.

4. Remove or disconnect the following:
- Negative battery cable
- Front console assembly and wiring connectors
- Shift lock cable
- Shift control rod
- Selector lever assembly
- Driveshaft
- Wiring harness heat shield
- Transmission mount and crossmember
- Heated Oxygen (HO$_2$S) sensor connectors
- Left and right exhaust front pipes
- Transmission oil cooler lines
- Starter motor
- Fuel line bracket
- Transmission harness connectors

- Flywheel under covers
- Torque converter
- Transmission flange bolts
- Transmission

To install:

➡ **Use new torque converter bolts.**

5. Install or connect the following:
- Transmission. Tighten the large bolts to 56 ft. lbs. (76 Nm) and the small bolts to 69 inch lbs. (8 Nm).
- Torque converter. Tighten the bolts to 40 ft. lbs. (54 Nm).
- Flywheel under covers
- Transmission harness connectors
- Fuel line bracket
- Starter motor. Tighten the bolts to 30 ft. lbs. (40 Nm).
- Transmission oil cooler lines
- Left and right exhaust front pipes. Tighten the manifold flange fasteners to 49 ft. lbs. (67 Nm) and the exhaust flange bolts to 32 ft. lbs. (43 Nm).
- HO$_2$S sensor connectors
- Crossmember. Tighten the bolts to 37 ft. lbs. (50 Nm).
- Transmission mount. Tighten the bolts to 30 ft. lbs. (41 Nm).
- Wiring harness heat shield
- Driveshaft. Tighten the flange bolts to 46 ft. lbs. (63 Nm).
- Selector lever assembly
- Shift control rod
- Shift lock cable
- Front console assembly and wiring connectors
- Negative battery cable

6. Remove the engine support fixture and install the hood.

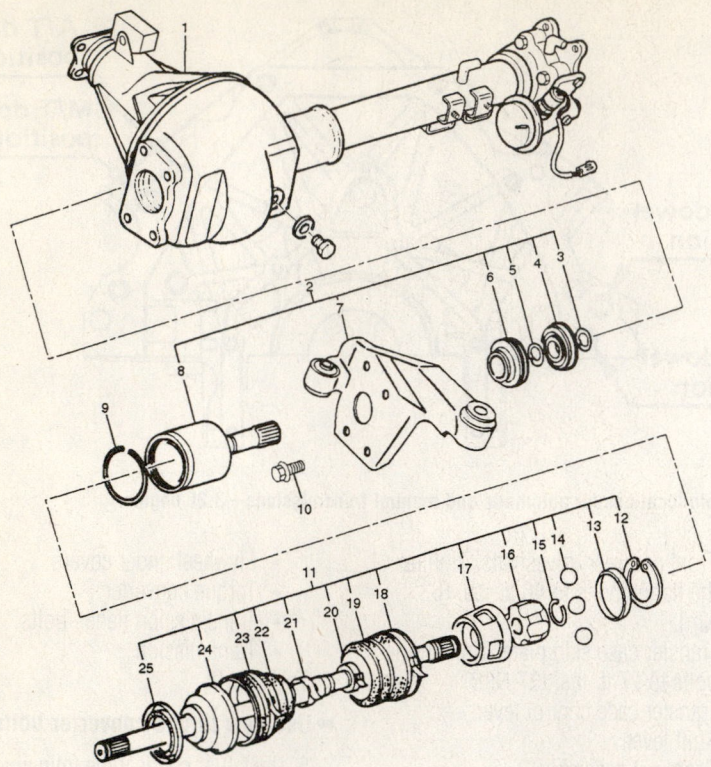

1 Axle Case and Differential	13 Spacer
2 DOJ Case Assembly	14 Ball
3 Snap Ring	15 Snap Ring
4 Bearing	16 Ball Retainer
5 Snap Ring	17 Ball Guide
6 Oil Seal	18 Band
7 Bracket	19 Bellows
8 DOJ Case	20 Band
9 Circlip	21 Band
10 Bolt	22 Band
11 Drive Shaft Joint Assembly	23 Band
12 Snap Ring	24 BJ Shaft
	25 Dust Seal

9308NG03

Automatic transmission mounting bolt locations and torque specifications

4 WHEEL DRIVE

1. Before servicing the vehicle, refer to the precautions in the beginning of this section.

2. Remove the hood.

3. Install a support fixture to the engine lifting eyes.

4. Remove or disconnect the following:
- Negative battery cable
- Transfer case shift lever knob
- Front console assembly and wiring connectors
- Shift lock cable
- Shift control rod
- Selector lever assembly
- Transfer case shift lever
- Transfer case skid plate
- Front and rear driveshafts
- Wiring harness heat shield
- Transmission mount and crossmember
- Right torsion bar, if equipped with Torque On Demand (TOD) system
- Heated Oxygen (HO2S) sensor connectors
- Left and right exhaust front pipes
- Transmission oil cooler lines
- Starter motor
- Fuel line bracket
- Transmission harness connectors
- Flywheel under covers
- Torque converter
- Transmission flange bolts
- Transmission

To install:

➡**Use new torque converter bolts.**

5. Install or connect the following:
- Transmission. Tighten the large bolts to 56 ft. lbs. (76 Nm) and the small bolts to 30 ft. lbs. (40 Nm).
- Torque converter. Tighten the bolts to 40 ft. lbs. (54 Nm).
- Flywheel under covers
- Transmission harness connectors
- Fuel line bracket
- Starter motor. Tighten the bolts to 30 ft. lbs. (40 Nm).
- Transmission oil cooler lines
- Left and right exhaust front pipes. Tighten the manifold flange fasteners to 49 ft. lbs. (67 Nm) and the exhaust flange bolts to 32 ft. lbs. (43 Nm).
- HO2S sensor connectors
- Right torsion bar, if removed
- Crossmember. Tighten the bolts to 37 ft. lbs. (50 Nm).
- Transmission mount. Tighten the bolts to 30 ft. lbs. (41 Nm).
- Wiring harness heat shield
- Front and rear driveshafts. Tighten the flange bolts to 46 ft. lbs. (63 Nm).
- Transfer case skid plate. Tighten the bolts to 27 ft. lbs. (37 Nm).
- Transfer case shift lever
- Selector lever assembly
- Shift control rod
- Shift lock cable
- Front console assembly and wiring connectors
- Transfer case shift lever knob
- Negative battery cable

6. Remove the engine support fixture and install the hood.

Clutch

ADJUSTMENTS

➡**This vehicle is equipped with a hydraulic clutch linkage. No adjustment is necessary.**

REMOVAL & INSTALLATION

1. Before servicing the vehicle, refer to the precautions in the beginning of this section.

2. Remove the transmission.

3. Loosen the pressure plate mounting bolts in a 2-step crisscross sequence until the spring tension is relieved.

4. Remove the pressure plate and the clutch disc.

To install:

5. Install a new wedge collar and wire snapring into the pressure plate.

6. Using a clutch alignment tool, assemble the clutch disc and pressure plate onto the flywheel.

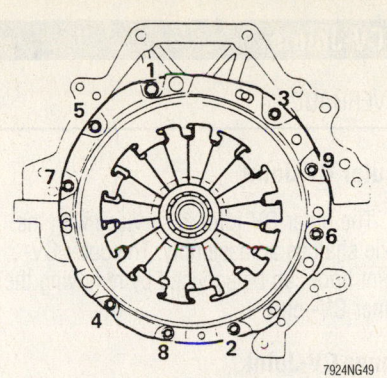

Pressure plate tightening sequence

7924NG49

7. Tighten the pressure plate bolts in sequence and in two passes to 13 ft. lbs. (8 Nm).

8. Install the transmission.

9. Road test the vehicle and check for proper clutch operation.

Hydraulic Clutch System

BLEEDING

Damping Cylinder

VEHICLES WITH 3.2L SOHC ENGINE

1. Before servicing the vehicle, refer to the precautions in the beginning of this section.

2. Have an assistant pump the clutch pedal slowly several times and hold it depressed.

3. Open the damping cylinder bleeder screw and allow air to escape.

4. Close the bleeder screw before releasing the clutch pedal.

5. Repeat until all air is purged from the damping cylinder.

6. Refill the reservoir to the full mark.

Slave Cylinder

ALL MODELS

1. Before servicing the vehicle, refer to the precautions in the beginning of this section.

2. Have an assistant pump the clutch pedal slowly several times and hold it depressed.

3. Open the slave cylinder bleeder screw and allow air to escape.

4. Close the bleeder screw before releasing the clutch pedal.

5. Repeat until all air is purged from the clutch hydraulic system.

6. Refill the reservoir to the full mark.

Transfer Case Assembly

REMOVAL & INSTALLATION

Manual Transmission

The transfer case is an integral part of the manual transmission. No separate removal procedure is available.

Automatic Transmission

1. Before servicing the vehicle, refer to the precautions in the beginning of this section.

2. Remove or disconnect the following:
   - Negative battery cable
   - Transfer case skid plate
   - Front and rear driveshafts
   - Heated Oxygen (HO2S) sensor connectors
   - Left and right exhaust front pipes
   - Transfer case control lever knob
   - Selector lever assembly
   - Transfer case control lever
   - Vehicle Speed (VSS) sensor connector
   - 4 wheel drive switch connector
   - 4 wheel drive actuator connector
   - Transfer case flange fasteners
   - Transfer case

To install:

3. Install or connect the following:
   - Transfer case. Tighten the flange fasteners to 34 ft. lbs. (46 Nm).
   - 4 wheel drive actuator connector
   - 4 wheel drive switch connector
   - VSS sensor connector
   - Transfer case control lever
   - Selector lever assembly
   - Transfer case control lever knob
   - Left and right exhaust front pipes
   - HO2S sensor connectors
   - Front and rear driveshafts. Tighten the bolts to 46 ft. lbs. (63 Nm).
   - Transfer case skid plate. Tighten the bolts to 27 ft. lbs. (37 Nm).
   - Negative battery cable

Halfshaft

REMOVAL & INSTALLATION

1. Before servicing the vehicle, refer to the precautions in the beginning of this section.

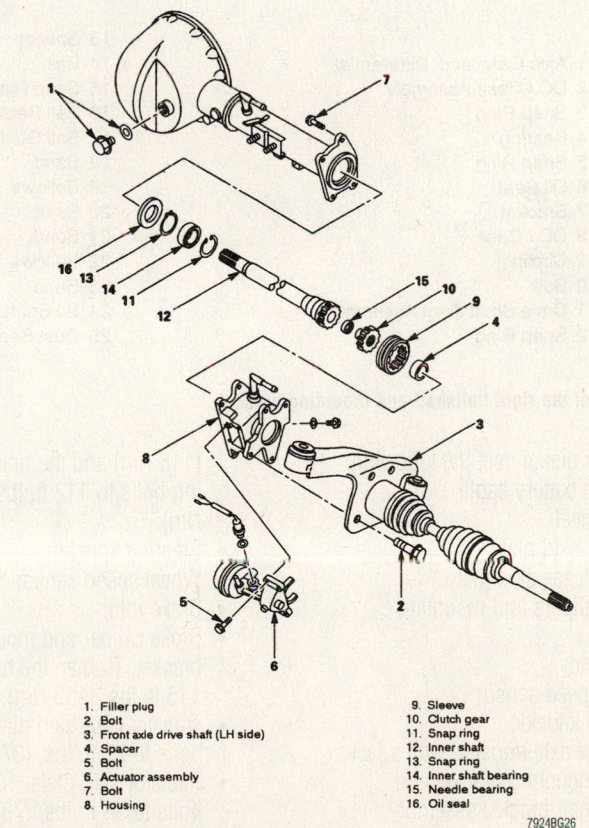

1. Filler plug
2. Bolt
3. Front axle drive shaft (LH side)
4. Spacer
5. Bolt
6. Actuator assembly
7. Bolt
8. Housing
9. Sleeve
10. Clutch gear
11. Snap ring
12. Inner shaft
13. Snap ring
14. Inner shaft bearing
15. Needle bearing
16. Oil seal

7924BG26

Exploded view of the left halfshaft, axle shaft and axle disconnect

Turn to Section 5 for brake system applications

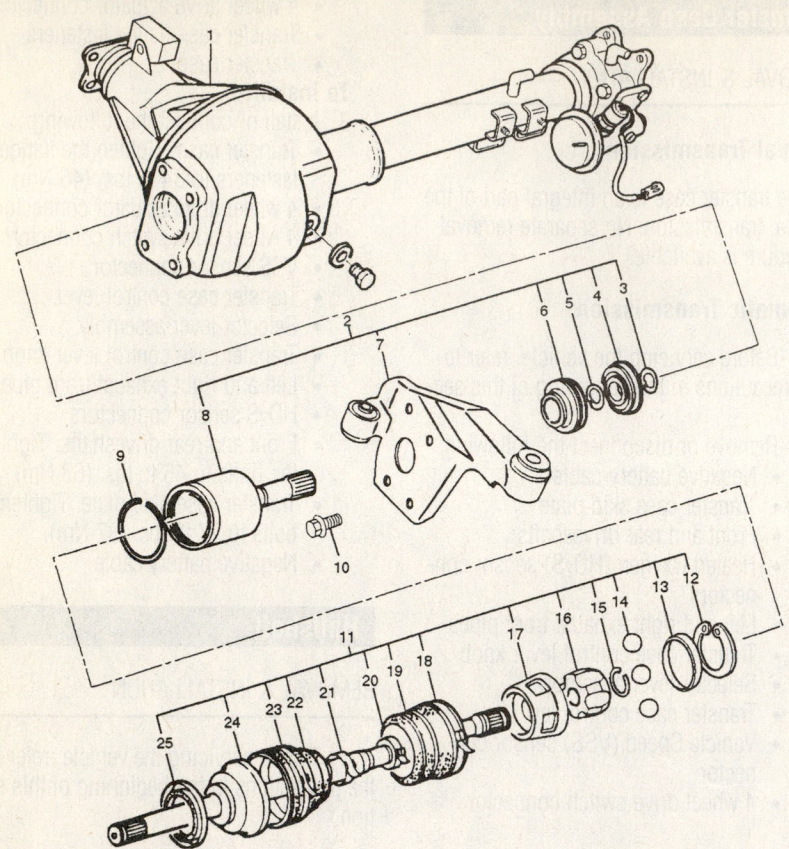

1 Axle Case and Differential
2 DOJ Case Assembly
3 Snap Ring
4 Bearing
5 Snap Ring
6 Oil Seal
7 Bracket
8 DOJ Case
9 Circlip
10 Bolt
11 Drive Shaft Joint Assembly
12 Snap Ring
13 Spacer
14 Ball
15 Snap Ring
16 Ball Retainer
17 Ball Guide
18 Band
19 Bellows
20 Band
21 Band
22 Bellows
23 Band
24 BJ Shaft
25 Dust Seal

9308BG03

Exploded view of the right halfshaft and mounting bracket

2. Remove or disconnect the following:
   • Negative battery cable
   • Front wheel
   • Radiator skid plate
   • Transfer case skid plate
   • Brake calipers and mounting bracket
   • Brake rotor
   • Wheel speed sensor
   • Steering knuckle
3. Support the axle housing with a jack. Unbolt the axle mounting bracket and remove the halfshaft/bracket assembly.
   To install:
4. Install or connect the following:
   • Axle/bracket assembly. Tighten the bracket flange bolts to 85 ft. lbs.

(116 Nm) and the bracket mounting bolts to 112 ft. lbs. (152 Nm).
   • Steering knuckle
   • Wheel speed sensor
   • Brake rotor
   • Brake caliper and mounting bracket. Tighten the bracket bolts to 115 ft. lbs. (155 Nm).
   • Transfer case skid plate. Tighten the bolts to 27 ft. lbs. (37 Nm).
   • Radiator skid plate. Tighten the bolts to 58 ft. lbs. (78 Nm).
   • Front wheel
   • Negative battery cable
5. Check the wheel alignment and adjust as necessary.

CV-Joints

OVERHAUL

Outer CV-Joint

The outer CV-joint is serviced with the axle shaft as an assembly. The outer CV-joint boot can be serviced by removing the inner CV-joint.

Inner CV-Joint

1. Before servicing the vehicle, refer to the precautions in the beginning of this section.
2. Remove or disconnect the following:
   • Halfshaft from the vehicle
   • Snapring and bearing
   • Snapring and oil seal
   • Mounting bracket
   • CV-joint boot
   • Circlip and inner joint housing
   • Snapring and spacer
   • Inner joint balls
   • Snapring and inner CV-joint

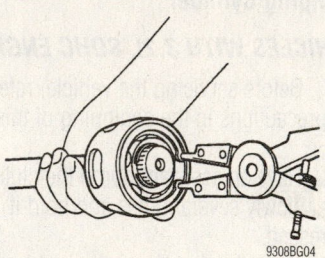

9308BG04

CV-joint spacer snapring—Inner CV-Joint

To install:
3. Install or connect the following:
   • Inner CV-joint and snapring
   • Inner joint balls
   • Spacer and snapring
   • Inner joint housing and circlip. Add 150 grams CV-joint grease.
   • CV-joint boot
   • Mounting bracket
   • Oil seal and snapring
   • Bearing and snapring
4. Install the halfshaft and mounting bracket to the vehicle.
5. Check the wheel alignment and adjust as necessary.

Axle Shaft, Bearing and Seal

REMOVAL & INSTALLATION

1. Before servicing the vehicle, refer to the precautions in the beginning of this section.

2. Remove or disconnect the following:
- Rear wheel
- Disc brake caliper and bracket
- Disc brake rotor
- Wheel speed sensor bracket
- Parking brake cable and bracket
- Parking brake shoes
- Axle shaft
- Snapring and discard it
- Bearing, press it off the axle shaft with the bearing holder and oil seal

To install:

3. Install or connect the following:
- New oil seal into the bearing housing
- Bearing housing onto the axle shaft
- Bearing, press it onto the axle shaft
- New snapring
- Axle shaft. Use new lockwashers and tighten the bearing holder nuts to 54 ft. lbs. (74 Nm).
- Parking brake shoes
- Parking brake cable and bracket
- Wheel speed sensor bracket
- Disc brake rotor
- Disc brake caliper and bracket. Tighten the bracket bolts to 76 ft. lbs. (103 Nm).
- Rear wheel

4. Check the rear axle oil level and adjust as necessary.

Pinion Seal

REMOVAL & INSTALLATION

1. Before servicing the vehicle, refer to the precautions in the beginning of this section.

2. Remove or disconnect the following:
- Driveshaft
- Wheels
- Brake calipers and pads

➡**The brake calipers and pads must be removed so that there is no additional drag when measuring pinion bearing proload.**

3. Use an inch lb. torque wrench and measure and record the amount of torque required to maintain pinion rotation through several revolutions.

4. Remove or disconnect the following:
- Pinion flange
- Pinion seal
- Pinion bearing
- Collapsible spacer

To install:

➡**Use a new collapsible spacer and flange nut for assembly.**

5. Install or connect the following:
- Collapsible spacer
- Pinion bearing
- Pinion seal
- Pinion flange

6. Rotate the pinion flange occasionally while tightening the flange nut to make sure the pinion bearings seat correctly.

7. Take frequent bearing preload torque readings. Tighten the flange nut to achieve the preload torque readings originally recorded.

✳✳ CAUTION

Never loosen the pinion nut to reduce bearing preload. If it is necessary to reduce bearing preload, install a new collapsible spacer and pinion nut.

8. Install or connect the following:
- Driveshaft
- Brake calipers and pads
- Wheels

9. Fill the differential with gear lubricant and check for leaks.

Axle Housing Assembly

REMOVAL & INSTALLATION

Front

1. Before servicing the vehicle, refer to the precautions in the beginning of this section.

2. Remove or disconnect the following:
- Negative battery cable
- Front wheels
- Radiator skid plate
- Transfer case skid plate
- Brake calipers and mounting brackets

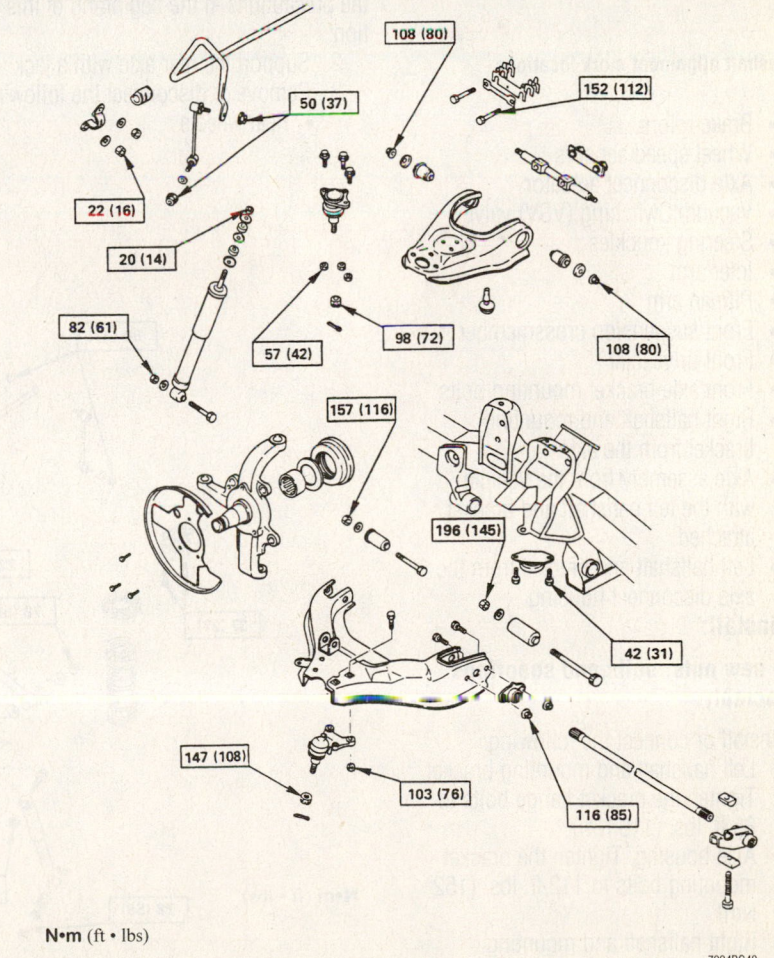

N•m (ft • lbs)

Exploded view of the front suspension, showing the tightening specifications

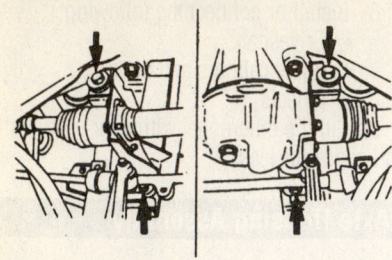

Axle assembly mounting bracket bolt locations

7924BG25

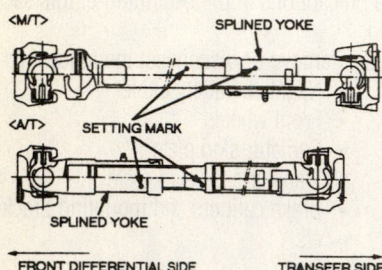

Driveshaft alignment mark locations

7924BG24

- Brake rotors
- Wheel speed sensors
- Axle disconnect actuator
- Vacuum Switching (VSV) valve
- Steering knuckles
- Idler arm
- Pitman arm
- Front suspension crossmember
- Front driveshaft
- Front axle bracket mounting bolts
- Right halfshaft and mounting bracket from the axle
- Axle assembly from the vehicle with the left halfshaft and bracket attached
- Left halfshaft and bracket from the axle disconnect housing

To install:

➡ **Use new nuts, bolts and snaprings for assembly.**

3. Install or connect the following:
- Left halfshaft and mounting bracket. Tighten the bracket flange bolts to 85 ft. lbs. (116 Nm).
- Axle housing. Tighten the bracket mounting bolts to 112 ft. lbs. (152 Nm).
- Right halfshaft and mounting bracket. Tighten the bracket flange bolts to 85 ft. lbs. (116 Nm).
- Front driveshaft. Tighten the bolts to 46 ft. lbs. (63 Nm).

- Front suspension crossmember. Tighten the bolts to 58 ft. lbs. (78 Nm).
- Pitman arm
- Idler arm
- Steering knuckles
- VSV valve
- Axle disconnect actuator
- Wheel speed sensors
- Brake rotors
- Brake calipers and mounting brackets. Tighten the bracket bolts to 115 ft. lbs. (155 Nm).
- Transfer case skid plate. Tighten the bolts to 27 ft. lbs. (37 Nm).
- Radiator skid plate. Tighten the bolts to 58 ft. lbs. (78 Nm).
- Front wheels
- Negative battery cable

4. Check the wheel alignment and adjust as necessary.

Rear

1. Before servicing the vehicle, refer to the precautions in the beginning of this section.
2. Support the rear axle with a jack.
3. Remove or disconnect the following:
- Rear wheels

- Rear driveshaft
- Parking brake cables
- Axle breather hose
- Wheel speed sensor connectors and bracket
- Brake fluid hose
- Shock absorbers
- Coil springs
- Stabilizer bar linkage
- Lateral rod
- Center link
- Trailing links
- Axle housing from the vehicle

To install:

4. Install or connect the following:
- Axle housing, raise it into position
- Trailing links
- Center link
- Lateral rod
- Stabilizer bar linkage
- Coil springs
- Shock absorbers
- Brake fluid hose
- Wheel speed sensor connectors and bracket
- Axle breather hose
- Parking brake cables
- Rear driveshaft
- Rear wheels

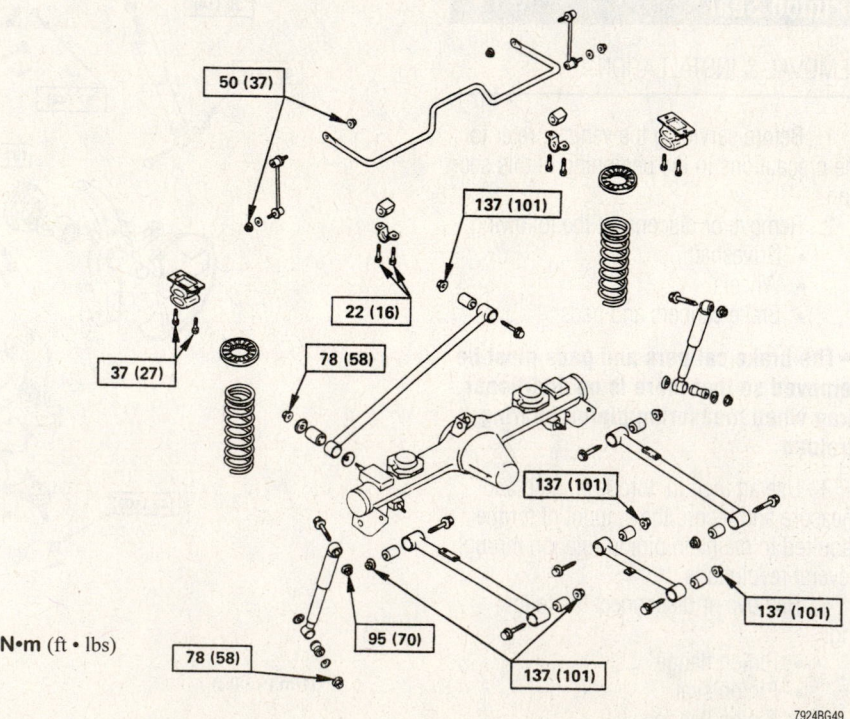

N•m (ft • lbs)

Exploded view of the rear suspension

7924BG49

STEERING AND SUSPENSION

Air Bag

❊❊ CAUTION

Some vehicles are equipped with an air bag system. The system must be disarmed before performing service on, or around, system components, the steering column, instrument panel components, wiring and sensors. Failure to follow the safety precautions and the disarming procedure could result in accidental air bag deployment, possible injury and unnecessary system repairs.

PRECAUTIONS

Several precautions must be observed when handling the inflator module to avoid accidental deployment and possible personal injury.

• Never carry the inflator module by the wires or connector on the underside of the module.

• When carrying a live inflator module, hold securely with both hands, and ensure that the bag and trim cover are pointed away from you.

• Place the inflator module on a bench or other surface with the bag and trim cover facing up.

• With the inflator module on the bench, never place anything on or close to the module which may be thrown in the event of an accidental deployment.

DISARMING

1. Before servicing the vehicle, refer to the precautions in the beginning of this section.
2. Turn the ignition switch to the **LOCK** position. Remove the key.
3. Disconnect the negative battery cable. Wait 1 minute before working around the air bags.
4. Disconnect the yellow 2-pin connector at the base of the steering column.
5. Disconnect the yellow 2-pin connector behind the glove box assembly.
6. When repairs are completed, connect the yellow 2-pin connectors.

7. Connect the negative battery cable.
8. Turn the ignition to the **ON** position, but don't start the engine. The AIR BAG warning light should turn ON and flash ON and OFF 7 times, and then turn OFF. This light sequence indicates that the SRS system is functioning normally. If the AIR BAG light doesn't come ON, or stays ON longer than 7 seconds, the system must be diagnosed.

Recirculating Ball Steering Gear

REMOVAL & INSTALLATION

1. Before servicing the vehicle, refer to the precautions in the beginning of this section.
2. Disable the air bag system.
3. Remove or disconnect the following:
   • Skid plates
   • Lower fan shroud
   • Stabilizer bar
   • Power steering pressure and return lines
   • Pitman arm
   • Steering column intermediate shaft
   • Steering gear

To install:

4. Install or connect the following:
   • Steering gear. Tighten the bolts to 33 ft. lbs. (44 Nm).
   • Steering column intermediate shaft. Tighten the pinch bolt to 18 ft. lbs. (25 Nm).
   • Pitman arm. Tighten the nut to 159 ft. lbs. (216 Nm).
   • Power steering pressure and return lines. Tighten the fittings to 33 ft. lbs. (44 Nm).
   • Stabilizer bar
   • Lower fan shroud
   • Skid plates
5. Fill the power steering fluid reservoir.
6. Check the wheel alignment and adjust as necessary.

Shock Absorber

REMOVAL & INSTALLATION

Front

1. Before servicing the vehicle, refer to the precautions in the beginning of this section.

2. Support the lower control arm with a jackstand.
3. Remove or disconnect the following:
   • Front wheels
   • Upper shock retaining nut and rubber bushing
   • Suspension bump stops
   • Shock absorber

To install:

4. Install or connect the following:
   • Shock absorber. Tighten the lower bolt to 60–61 ft. lbs. (82–84 Nm).
   • Bump stop. Tighten the bolts to 30 ft. lbs. (41 Nm).
   • Upper shock retaining nut and rubber bushing. Tighten the nut to 14–15 ft. lbs. (19–20 Nm).
   • Front wheels

Rear

1. Before servicing the vehicle, refer to the precautions in the beginning of this section.
2. Support the rear axle with jackstands.
3. Remove the rear shock absorbers.

To install:

4. Install the rear shock absorbers. Tighten the upper bolt to 70 ft. lbs. (95 Nm). Tighten the lower bolt to 58 ft. lbs. (78 Nm).
5. Remove the jackstands.

Coil Spring

REMOVAL & INSTALLATION

1. Before servicing the vehicle, refer to the precautions in the beginning of this section.
2. Support the vehicle under the frame.
3. Support the rear axle with a jack.
4. Remove or disconnect the following:
   • Rear wheels
   • Stabilizer bar links
   • Parking brake cable brackets
   • Shock absorbers
5. Lower the rear axle with the jack to release the coil spring tension. Remove the coil springs and insulators.

To install:

6. Place the coil springs on the axle assembly and the insulators on top of the springs.
7. Raise the axle assembly into position.
8. Install or connect the following:
   • Shock absorbers
   • Parking brake cable brackets

- Stabilizer bar links. Tighten the nuts to 37 ft. lbs. (50 Nm).
- Rear wheels

Torsion Bar

REMOVAL & INSTALLATION

1. Before servicing the vehicle, refer to the precautions in the beginning of this section.

2. Matchmark the adjusting bolt and end piece, then remove the bolt, end piece, and seat.

3. Matchmark the height control arm to the torsion bar, then remove the height control arm.

4. Matchmark the torsion bar to the lower control arm, then remove the torsion bar.

To install:

5. Apply grease to the torsion bar splines.

6. Apply grease to the contact points of the height control arm, adjusting bolt end piece and seat.

7. Align the matchmarks and install the torsion bar.

8. Align the matchmarks and install the height control arm.

9. Install the adjusting bolt, seat and end piece.

10. Tighten the adjusting bolt to align the matchmarks.

(1) Adjust Bolt, End Piece and Seat
(2) Height Control Arm
(3) Torsion Bar

Exploded view of the torsion bar assembly

Upper Ball Joint

REMOVAL & INSTALLATION

1. Before servicing the vehicle, refer to the precautions in the beginning of this section.

2. Support the lower control arm with a floor jack.

3. Remove or disconnect the following:

- Front wheel

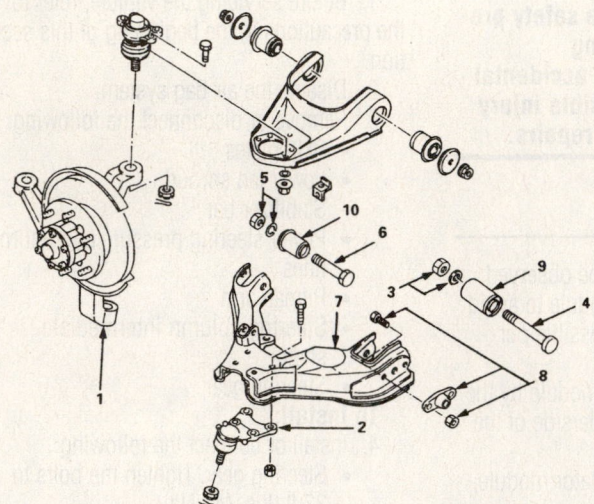

Exploded view of the control arm and ball joint components

1. Knuckle
2. Lower end
3. Nut and washer, rear
4. Bolt, rear
5. Nut and washer, front
6. Bolt, front
7. Lower control arm assembly
8. Torsion bar arm bracket
9. Bushing, rear
10. Bushing, front

7924BG34

- Wheel speed sensor
- Upper ball joint

To install:

➡ **Use new nuts, bolts and split pins for assembly.**

4. Install or connect the following:
- Upper ball joint. Tighten the mounting bolts to 42 ft. lbs. (57 Nm) and the nut to 72 ft. lbs. (96 Nm).
- Wheel speed sensor
- Front wheel

Lower Ball Joint

REMOVAL & INSTALLATION

1. Before servicing the vehicle, refer to the precautions in the beginning of this section.

2. Support the lower control arm with a jackstand.

3. Remove or disconnect the following:
- Front wheel
- Disc brake caliper and support
- Brake rotor and backing plate
- Wheel speed sensor
- Outer tie rod end
- Upper ball joint
- Steering knuckle
- Lower ball joint

To install:

➡ **Use new nuts, bolts and split pins for assembly.**

4. Install or connect the following:
- Lower ball joint. Tighten the

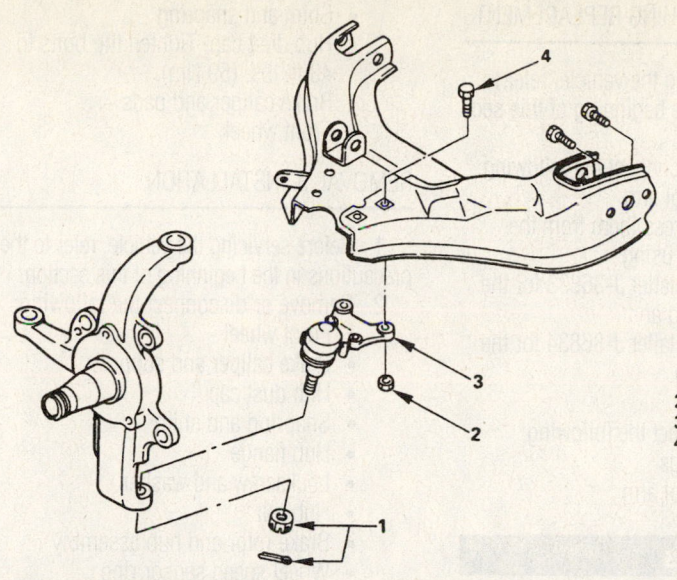

1. Nut and cotter pin
2. Nut
3. Lower ball joint
4. Bolt

7924BG35

Exploded view of the lower ball joint mounting and related components

mounting bolts to 76 ft. lbs. (103 Nm).
- Steering knuckle. Tighten the lower ball joint nut to 108 ft. lbs. (147 Nm).
- Upper ball joint. Tighten the nut to 72 ft. lbs. (96 Nm).
- Outer tie rod end. Tighten the nut to 72 ft. lbs. (98 Nm).
- Wheel speed sensor
- Brake rotor and backing plate
- Disc brake caliper and support. Tighten the support bolts to 115 ft. lbs. (155 Nm).
- Front wheel

5. Check the wheel alignment and adjust as necessary.

Upper Control Arm

REMOVAL & INSTALLATION

1. Before servicing the vehicle, refer to the precautions in the beginning of this section.
2. Support the lower control arm with a jackstand.
3. Remove or disconnect the following:
- Front wheel
- Wheel speed sensor
- Brake caliper
- Upper ball joint
- Upper control arm

➡ **Note the alignment shim location for assembly.**

To install:
4. Install or connect the following:
- Upper control arm
- Alignment shims in their original locations. Tighten the bolts to 112 ft. lbs. (152 Nm).
- Upper ball joint. Tighten the nut to 72 ft. lbs. (98 Nm).
- Brake caliper
- Wheel speed sensor
- Front wheel

5. Check the wheel alignment and adjust as necessary.

CONTROL ARM BUSHING REPLACEMENT

1. Before servicing the vehicle, refer to the precautions in the beginning of this section.
2. Remove the upper control arm.
3. Remove the nuts and washers from the fulcrum pin.
4. Press the bushings out of the control arm.

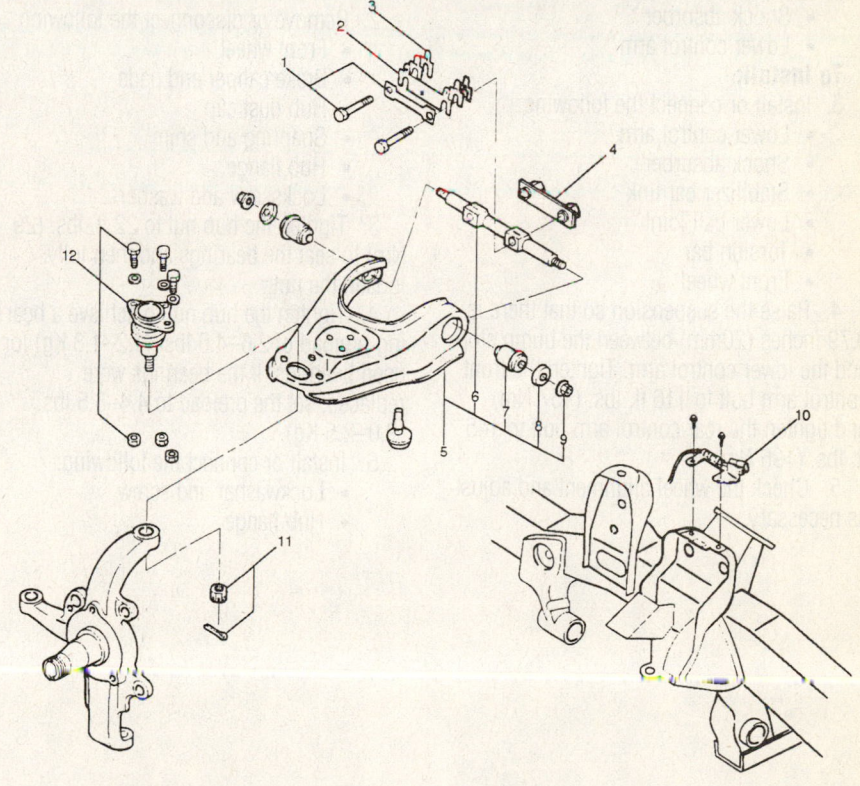

1	Bolt and Plate	7 Bushing
2	Camber Shims	8 Plate
3	Caster Shims	9 Nut
4	Nut Assembly	10 Speed Sensor Cable
5	Upper Control Arm Assembly	11 Nut and Cotter Pin
6	Fulcrum Pin	12 Upper Ball Joint

9308BG06

Upper control arm and related parts

To install:

5. Press the bushings into the control arm.

6. Install the fulcrum pin washers and nuts.

7. Install the upper control arm.

8. Raise the suspension so that there is 0.79 inches (20mm) between the bump stop and the lower control arm. Tighten the fulcrum pin nuts to 80 ft. lbs. (108 Nm).

9. Check the wheel alignment and adjust as necessary.

Lower Control Arm

REMOVAL & INSTALLATION

1. Before servicing the vehicle, refer to the precautions in the beginning of this section.

2. Remove or disconnect the following:
   • Front wheel
   • Torsion bar
   • Lower ball joint
   • Stabilizer bar link
   • Shock absorber
   • Lower control arm

To install:

3. Install or connect the following:
   • Lower control arm
   • Shock absorber
   • Stabilizer bar link
   • Lower ball joint
   • Torsion bar
   • Front wheel

4. Raise the suspension so that there is 0.79 inches (20mm) between the bump stop and the lower control arm. Tighten the front control arm bolt to 116 ft. lbs. (157 Nm) and tighten the rear control arm bolt to 145 ft. lbs. (196 Nm).

5. Check the wheel alignment and adjust as necessary.

CONTROL ARM BUSHING REPLACEMENT

1. Before servicing the vehicle, refer to the precautions in the beginning of this section.

2. Remove or disconnect the following:
   • Lower control arm
   • Bushings, press them from the control arm, using Remover/Installer J-36833 for the front bushing and Remover/Installer J-36834 for the rear bushing.

To install:

3. Install or connect the following:
   • New bushings
   • Lower control arm

Wheel Bearings

ADJUSTMENT

1. Before servicing the vehicle, refer to the precautions in the beginning of this section.

2. Remove or disconnect the following:
   • Front wheel
   • Brake caliper and pads
   • Hub dust cap
   • Snapring and shim
   • Hub flange
   • Lockscrew and washer

3. Tighten the hub nut to 22 ft. lbs. (29 Nm) to seat the bearings and then fully loosen the nut.

4. Tighten the hub nut to achieve a bearing preload of 2.6–4.0 lbs. (1.2–1.8 Kg) for used bearings. If the bearings were replaced, set the preload to 4.4–5.5 lbs. (2.0–2.5 Kg).

5. Install or connect the following:
   • Lockwasher and screw
   • Hub flange

   • Shim and snapring
   • Hub dust cap. Tighten the bolts to 43 ft. lbs. (59 Nm).
   • Brake caliper and pads
   • Front wheel

REMOVAL & INSTALLATION

1. Before servicing the vehicle, refer to the precautions in the beginning of this section.

2. Remove or disconnect the following:
   • Front wheel
   • Brake caliper and support
   • Hub dust cap
   • Snapring and shim
   • Hub flange
   • Lockscrew and washer
   • Hub nut
   • Brake rotor and hub assembly
   • Wheel speed sensor ring
   • Outer bearing
   • Grease seal
   • Inner bearing

To install:

3. Clean and inspect the bearings. Replace if necessary.

4. Apply clean wheel bearing grease to the inner and outer bearings.

5. Apply grease in the hub.

6. Install the wheel bearings into the hub along with a new grease seal.

7. Install or connect the following:
   • Wheel speed sensor ring. Tighten the bolts to 13 ft. lbs. (18 Nm).
   • Brake rotor and hub assembly
   • Hub nut. Set the bearing preload.
   • Lockscrew and washer
   • Hub flange
   • Snapring and shim
   • Hub dust cap
   • Brake caliper and support. Tighten the support bolts to 115 ft. lbs. (155 Nm).
   • Front wheel

JEEP

Cherokee • Grand Cherokee • Wrangler

24

PRECAUTIONS

Before servicing any vehicle, please be sure to read all of the following precautions, which deal with personal safety, prevention of component damage, and important points to take into consideration when servicing a motor vehicle:

• Never open, service or drain the radiator or cooling system when the engine is hot; serious burns can occur from the steam and hot coolant.

• Observe all applicable safety precautions when working around fuel. Whenever servicing the fuel system, always work in a well-ventilated area. Do not allow fuel spray or vapors to come in contact with a spark, open flame, or excessive heat (a hot drop light, for example). Keep a dry chemical fire extinguisher near the work area. Always keep fuel in a container specifically designed for fuel storage; also, always properly seal fuel containers to avoid the possibility of fire or explosion. Refer to the additional fuel system precautions later in this section.

• Fuel injection systems often remain pressurized, even after the engine has been turned **OFF**. The fuel system pressure must be relieved before disconnecting any fuel lines. Failure to do so may result in fire and/or personal injury.

• Brake fluid often contains polyglycol ethers and polyglycols. Avoid contact with the eyes and wash your hands thoroughly after handling brake fluid. If you do get brake fluid in your eyes, flush your eyes with clean, running water for 15 minutes. If eye irritation persists, or if you have taken brake fluid internally, IMMEDIATELY seek medical assistance.

• The EPA warns that prolonged contact with used engine oil may cause a number of skin disorders, including cancer. You should make every effort to minimize your exposure to used engine oil. Protective gloves should be worn when changing oil. Wash your hands and any other exposed skin areas as soon as possible after exposure to used engine oil. Soap and water, or waterless hand cleaner should be used.

• All new vehicles are now equipped with an air bag system, often referred to as a Supplemental Restraint System (SRS) or Supplemental Inflatable Restraint (SIR) system. The system must be disabled before performing service on or around system components, steering column, instrument panel components, wiring and sensors. Failure to follow safety and disabling procedures could result in accidental air bag deployment, possible personal injury and unnecessary system repairs.

• Always wear safety goggles when working with, or around, the air bag system. When carrying a non-deployed air bag, be sure the bag and trim cover are pointed away from your body. When placing a non-deployed air bag on a work surface, always face the bag and trim cover upward, away from the surface. This will reduce the motion of the module if it is accidentally deployed. Refer to the additional air bag system precautions later in this section.

• Clean, high quality brake fluid from a sealed container is essential to the safe and proper operation of the brake system. You should always buy the correct type of brake fluid for your vehicle. If the brake fluid becomes contaminated, completely flush the system with new fluid. Never reuse any brake fluid. Any brake fluid that is removed from the system should be discarded. Also, do not allow any brake fluid to come in contact with a painted surface; it will damage the paint.

• Never operate the engine without the proper amount and type of engine oil; doing so WILL result in severe engine damage.

• Timing belt maintenance is extremely important. Many models utilize an interference-type, non-freewheeling engine. If the timing belt breaks, the valves in the cylinder head may strike the pistons, causing potentially serious (also time-consuming and expensive) engine damage. Refer to the maintenance interval charts in the front of this manual for the recommended replacement interval for the timing belt, and to the timing belt section for belt replacement and inspection.

• Disconnecting the negative battery cable on some vehicles may interfere with the functions of the on-board computer system(s) and may require the computer to undergo a relearning process once the negative battery cable is reconnected.

• When servicing drum brakes, only disassemble and assemble one side at a time, leaving the remaining side intact for reference.

• Only an MVAC-trained, EPA-certified automotive technician should service the air conditioning system or its components.

ENGINE REPAIR

➡ **Disconnecting the negative battery cable on some vehicles may interfere with the functions of the on board computer system. The computer may undergo a relearning process once the negative battery cable is reconnected.**

Distributor

REMOVAL

2.5L and 4.0L Engines

1. Before servicing the vehicle, refer to the precautions in the beginning of this section.
2. Remove or disconnect the following:
   • Negative battery cable
   • Distributor cap
   • Camshaft Position (CMP) sensor connector
3. Matchmark the distributor housing and the rotor.
4. Remove the distributor.

5.2L and 5.9L Engines

1. Before servicing the vehicle, refer to the precautions in the beginning of this section.
2. Remove or disconnect the following:
   • Negative battery cable
   • Air cleaner tube
   • Distributor cap
   • Camshaft Position (CMP) sensor connector
3. Matchmark the distributor housing and the rotor.
4. Matchmark the distributor housing and the intake manifold.
5. Remove the distributor.

INSTALLATION

Timing Not Disturbed

2.5L AND 4.0L ENGINES

1. Before servicing the vehicle, refer to the precautions in the beginning of this section.

➡ **The rotor will rotate clockwise as the gears engage.**

2. Position the rotor slightly counterclockwise of the matchmark made during removal.

3. Install the distributor. Ensure that the rotor moves into alignment with the match-mark.

4. Align the locating fork with the clamp bolt hole. Install the clamp and bolt. Tighten the bolt to 17 ft. lbs. (23 Nm).

5. Install or connect the following:
- CMP sensor connector
- Distributor cap
- Air cleaner tube
- Negative battery cable

5.2L AND 5.9L ENGINES

1. Before servicing the vehicle, refer to the precautions in the beginning of this section.

➡ **The rotor will rotate clockwise as the gears engage.**

2. Position the rotor slightly counter-clockwise of the matchmark made during removal.

3. Install the distributor.

4. Align the distributor housing and intake manifold matchmarks and check that the distributor housing matchmark and rotor are also aligned.

5. Install or connect the following:
- Distributor housing clamp and bolt. Tighten the bolt to 17 ft. lbs. (23 Nm).
- CMP sensor connector
- Distributor cap
- Air cleaner tube
- Negative battery cable

Timing Disturbed

2.5L AND 4.0L ENGINES

1. Before servicing the vehicle, refer to the precautions in the beginning of this section.

2. Set the engine at Top Dead Center (TDC) of the No. 1 cylinder compression stroke.

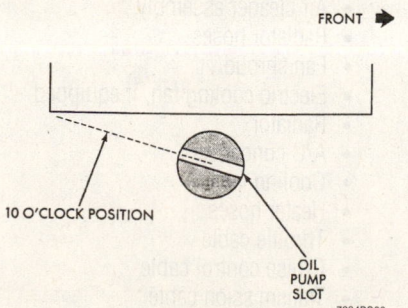

Slot in the oil pump gear at 10 o'clock position—2.5L engine

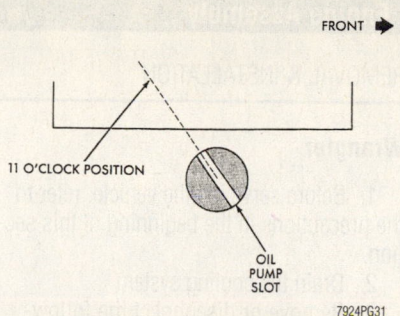

Slot in the oil pump gear at 11 o'clock position—4.0L engine

3. Position the slot in the oil pump drive gear as shown.

4. Locate the alignment holes in the plastic ring and align the correct hole with the mating hole in the distributor housing as shown. Install a locking pin.

➡ **The distributor will rotate clockwise as the gears engage.**

5. Position the base mounting slot at the 1 o'clock position and install the distributor.

6. Check that the centerline of the mounting slot aligns with the centerline of the clamp bolt hole.

7. Install the clamp and bolt. Tighten the bolt to 17 ft. lbs. (23 Nm).

8. Remove the locking pin.

9. Install or connect the following:
- CMP sensor connector
- Distributor cap
- Air cleaner tube
- Negative battery cable

5.2L AND 5.9L ENGINES

1. Before servicing the vehicle, refer to the precautions in the beginning of this section.

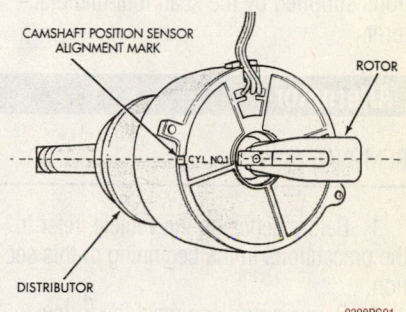

Distributor rotor alignment—5.2L and 5.9L engines

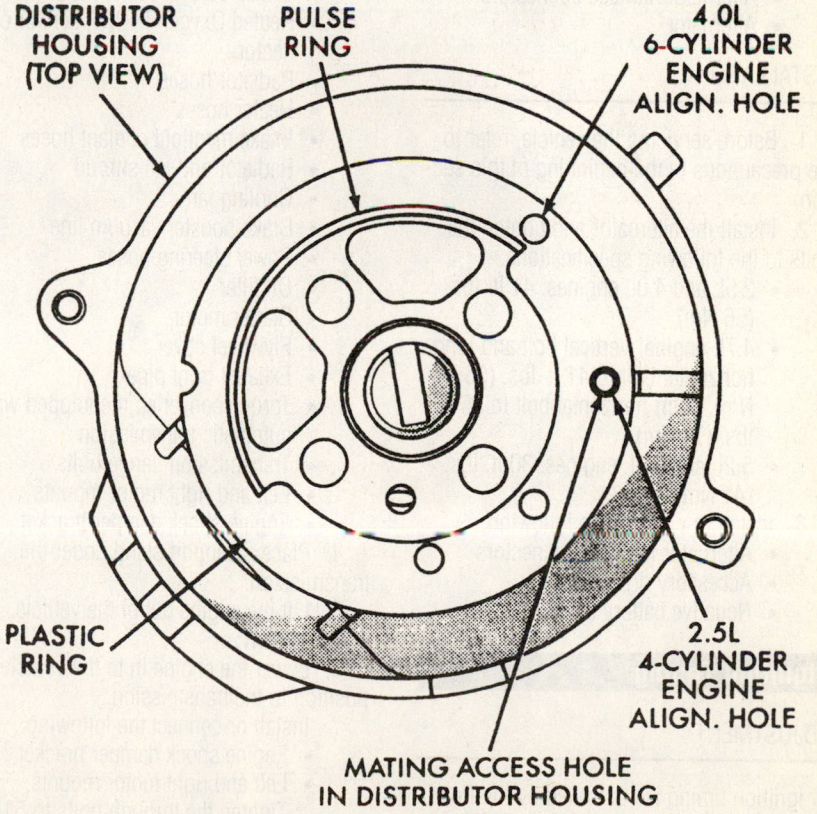

Distributor pin alignment holes—2.5L and 4.0L engines

2. Set the engine at Top Dead Center (TDC) of the No. 1 cylinder compression stroke.

3. Install the distributor, clamp and bolt.

4. Rotate the distributor so that the rotor aligns with the No. 1 cylinder mark on the Camshaft Position (CMP) sensor. Tighten the clamp bolt to 17 ft. lbs. (23 Nm).

5. Install or connect the following:
- CMP sensor connector
- Distributor cap
- Air cleaner tube
- Negative battery cable

6. The final distributor position must be set with a scan tool. Follow the instructions supplied by the scan tool manufacturer.

Alternator

REMOVAL

1. Before servicing the vehicle, refer to the precautions in the beginning of this section.

2. Remove or disconnect the following:
- Negative battery cable
- Accessory drive belt
- Alternator harness connectors
- Alternator

INSTALLATION

1. Before servicing the vehicle, refer to the precautions in the beginning of this section.

2. Install the alternator and tighten the bolts to the following specifications:
- 2.5L and 4.0L engines: 41 ft. lbs. (56 Nm)
- 4.7L engine: Vertical bolt and long horizontal bolt to 41 ft. lbs. (56 Nm), short horizontal bolt to 55 ft. lbs. (74 Nm)
- 5.2L and 5.9L engines: 30 ft. lbs. (41 Nm)

3. Install or connect the following:
- Alternator harness connectors
- Accessory drive belt
- Negative battery cable

Ignition Timing

ADJUSTMENT

Ignition timing is controlled by the Powertrain Control Module (PCM). No adjustment is possible.

Engine Assembly

REMOVAL & INSTALLATION

Wrangler

1. Before servicing the vehicle, refer to the precautions in the beginning of this section.

2. Drain the cooling system.

3. Remove or disconnect the following:
- Battery
- Accessory drive belt
- Alternator wiring connectors
- A/C compressor, if equipped
- Ignition coil wiring connector
- Camshaft Position (CMP) sensor connector
- Oil pressure sender connector
- Starter solenoid connectors
- Fuel injection wiring connectors
- Fuel line and bracket
- Engine ground strap
- Air cleaner assembly
- Canister purge vacuum hose
- Idle Air Control (IAC) valve connector
- Throttle cable
- Cruise control cable, if equipped
- Heated Oxygen (HO$_2$S) sensor connector
- Radiator hoses
- Heater hoses
- Intake manifold coolant hoses
- Radiator and fan shroud
- Cooling fan
- Brake booster vacuum line
- Power steering hoses
- Oil filter
- Starter motor
- Flywheel cover
- Exhaust front pipe
- Torque converter, if equipped with automatic transmission
- Transmission flange bolts
- Left and right motor mounts
- Engine shock damper bracket

4. Place a support stand under the transmission.

5. Lift the engine out of the vehicle.

To install:

6. Lower the engine in to the vehicle and position to the transmission.

7. Install or connect the following:
- Engine shock damper bracket
- Left and right motor mounts. Tighten the through bolts to 51 ft. lbs. (69 Nm).
- Transmission flange bolts. Tighten the bolts to 28 ft. lbs. (38 Nm).
- Torque converter, if equipped with automatic transmission. Tighten the bolts to 40 ft. lbs. (54 Nm).
- Exhaust front pipe
- Flywheel cover
- Starter motor. Tighten the bolts to 33 ft. lbs. (45 Nm).
- Oil filter
- Power steering hoses
- Brake booster vacuum line
- Cooling fan
- Radiator and fan shroud
- Intake manifold coolant hoses
- Heater hoses
- Radiator hoses
- HO$_2$S sensor connector
- Cruise control cable, if equipped
- Throttle cable
- IAC valve connector
- Canister purge vacuum hose
- Air cleaner assembly
- Engine ground strap
- Fuel line and bracket
- Fuel injection wiring connectors
- Starter solenoid connectors
- Oil pressure sender connector
- CMP sensor connector
- Ignition coil wiring connector
- A/C compressor, if equipped
- Alternator wiring connectors
- Accessory drive belt
- Battery

8. Fill the cooling system.

9. Run the engine and check for leaks.

Cherokee

1. Before servicing the vehicle, refer to the precautions in the beginning of this section.

2. Drain the cooling system.

3. Recover the A/C refrigerant.

4. Remove or disconnect the following:
- Battery
- Hood
- Air cleaner assembly
- Radiator hoses
- Fan shroud
- Electric cooling fan, if equipped
- Radiator
- A/C condenser
- Cooling fan
- Heater hoses
- Throttle cable
- Cruise control cable
- Transmission cable
- Camshaft Position (CMP) sensor connector

- Ignition coil wiring connector
- Oil pressure sender connector
- Body ground cable
- Starter solenoid connectors
- Fuel injection wiring harness
- Fuel line and bracket
- A/C compressor suction/discharge hose assembly
- Brake booster vacuum line
- Power steering hoses
- Intake manifold vacuum lines
- Crankshaft Position (CKP) sensor connector
- Oil filter
- Starter motor
- Heated Oxygen (HO2S) sensor connector
- Exhaust front pipe
- Flywheel housing access cover
- Torque converter, if equipped with automatic transmission
- Transmission flange bolts
- Left and right motor mounts

5. Support the transmission and lift the engine out of the vehicle.

To install:

6. Lower the engine in to the vehicle and position to the transmission.

7. Install or connect the following:
- Left and right motor mounts. Tighten the through bolts to 51 ft. lbs. (69 Nm).
- Transmission flange bolts. Tighten the bolts to 30 ft. lbs. (41 Nm).
- Torque converter, if equipped with automatic transmission. Tighten the bolts to 23 ft. lbs. (31 Nm).
- Flywheel housing access cover
- Exhaust front pipe
- HO2S sensor connector
- Starter motor. Tighten the bolts to 33 ft. lbs. (45 Nm).
- Oil filter
- CKP sensor connector
- Intake manifold vacuum lines
- Power steering hoses
- Brake booster vacuum line
- A/C compressor suction/discharge hose assembly
- Fuel line and bracket
- Fuel injection wiring harness
- Starter solenoid connectors
- Body ground cable
- Oil pressure sender connector
- Ignition coil wiring connector
- CMP sensor connector
- Transmission cable
- Cruise control cable
- Throttle cable

- Heater hoses
- Cooling fan
- A/C condenser
- Radiator
- Electric cooling fan, if equipped
- Fan shroud
- Radiator hoses
- Air cleaner assembly
- Hood
- Battery

8. Fill the cooling system.

9. Start the engine and check for leaks.

10. If equipped, recharge the air conditioning system.

Grand Cherokee

4.0L ENGINE

1. Before servicing the vehicle, refer to the precautions in the beginning of this section.

2. Drain the cooling system.

3. Recover the A/C refrigerant.

4. Remove or disconnect the following:
- Negative battery cable
- Hood
- Radiator hoses
- Upper radiator support
- Cooling fan and shroud
- Radiator
- A/C condenser
- Heater hoses
- Accelerator cable
- Cruise control cable
- Transmission cable
- Body ground cable
- Power steering pressure switch connector
- Engine Coolant Temperature (ECT) sensor connector
- Intake Air Temperature (IAT) sensor
- Fuel injector connectors
- Throttle Position (TP) sensor connector
- Manifold Absolute Pressure (MAP) sensor connector
- Crankshaft Position (CKP) sensor connector
- Heated Oxygen (HO2S) sensor connector
- Camshaft Position (CMP) sensor connector
- Ignition coil wiring connector
- Oil pressure sender connector
- Fuel line and bracket
- Air cleaner assembly
- Brake booster vacuum line
- Power steering hoses
- Starter motor

- Exhaust front pipe
- Flywheel cover
- Torque converter
- Transmission flange bolts
- Left and right motor mounts

5. Place a support stand under the transmission.

6. Lift the engine out of the vehicle.

To install:

7. Lower the engine in to the vehicle and position to the transmission.

8. Install or connect the following:
- Left and right motor mounts. Tighten the through bolts to 51 ft. lbs. (69 Nm).
- Transmission flange bolts. Tighten the bolts to 30 ft. lbs. (41 Nm).
- Torque converter. Tighten the bolts to 23 ft. lbs. (31 Nm).
- Flywheel cover
- Exhaust front pipe
- Starter motor. Tighten the bolts to 33 ft. lbs. (45 Nm).
- Power steering hoses
- Brake booster vacuum line
- Air cleaner assembly
- Fuel line and bracket
- Oil pressure sender connector
- Ignition coil wiring connector
- CMP sensor connector
- HO2S sensor connector
- CKP sensor connector
- MAP sensor connector
- TP sensor connector
- Fuel injector connectors
- IAT sensor
- ECT sensor connector
- Power steering pressure switch connector
- Body ground cable
- Transmission cable
- Cruise control cable
- Accelerator cable
- Heater hoses
- A/C condenser
- Radiator
- Cooling fan and shroud
- Upper radiator support
- Radiator hoses
- Hood
- Negative battery cable

9. Fill the cooling system.

10. Recharge the A/C system.

11. Start the engine and check for leaks.

4.7L ENGINE

1. Before servicing the vehicle, refer to the precautions in the beginning of this section.

Timing belt service is covered in Section 4 of this manual

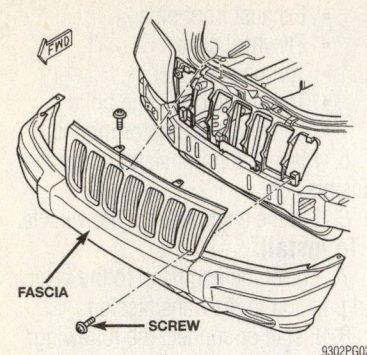

FASCIA

SCREW

9302PG02

**Exploded view of the front fascia panel—
1999–01 Grand Cherokee**

2. Drain the cooling system.
3. Recover the A/C refrigerant.
4. Remove or disconnect the following:
   • Negative battery cable
   • Front fascia
   • Left and right inner fender liners
   • Headlamp mounting module
   • Air intake resonator
   • Accelerator cable
   • Cruise control cable
   • Crankcase breather tubes
   • Accessory drive belt
   • A/C compressor
   • Cooling fan assemblies
   • Radiator hoses
   • Transmission oil cooler lines
   • Radiator
   • A/C condenser
   • Alternator

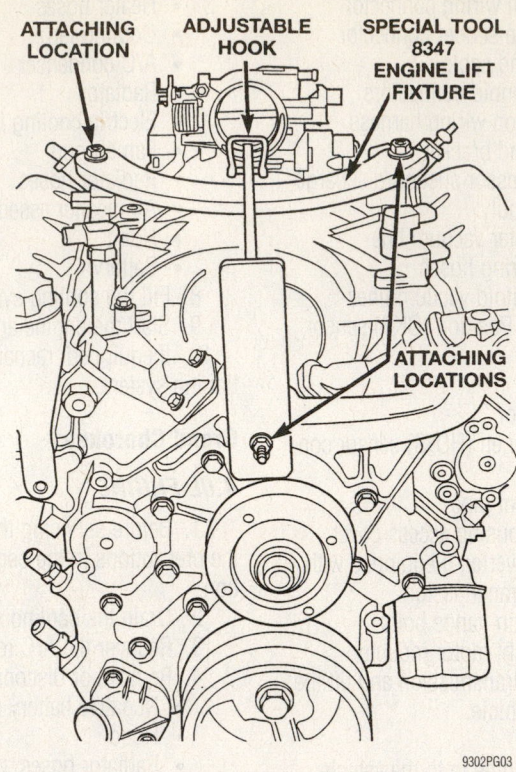

ATTACHING
LOCATION

ADJUSTABLE
HOOK

SPECIAL TOOL
8347
ENGINE LIFT
FIXTURE

ATTACHING
LOCATIONS

9302PG03

Engine Lifting Fixture—4.7L engine

• Heater hoses
• Throttle Position (TP) sensor connector
• Intake Air Temperature (IAT) sensor connector

• Fuel injector harness connectors
• Engine Coolant Temperature (ECT) sensor connector
• Idle Air Control (IAC) valve connector

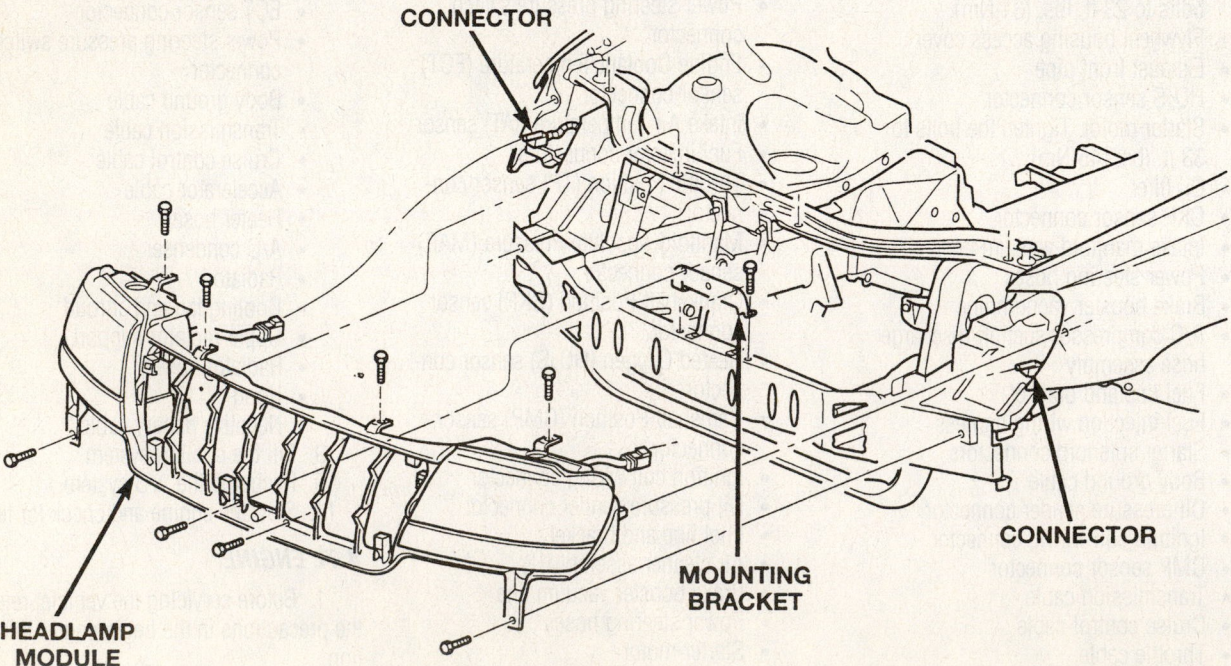

CONNECTOR

HEADLAMP
MODULE

MOUNTING
BRACKET

CONNECTOR

9302PG01

Exploded view of the headlamp module assembly—1999–01 Grand Cherokee

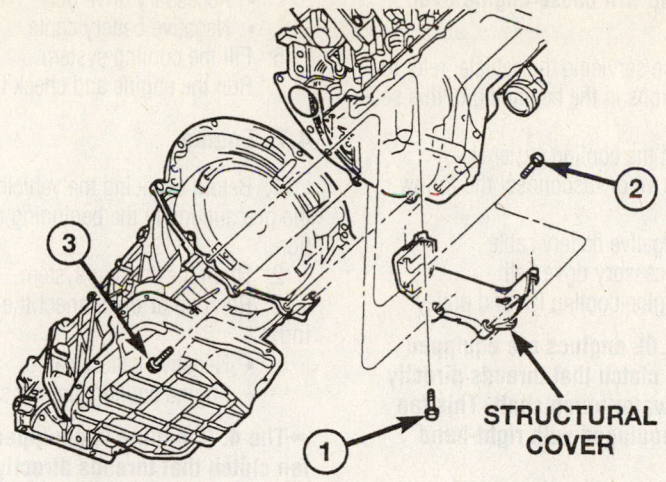

SEQUENCE	ITEM	TORQUE
1	BOLT (Qty 4)	54 N·m (40 ft. lbs.)
2	BOLT (Qty 2)	54 N·m (40 ft. lbs.)
3	BOLT (Qty 2)	54 N·m (40 ft. lbs.)

9308PG02

Structural cover torque sequence—4.7L engine

- Manifold Absolute Pressure (MAP) sensor connector
- Ignition coils
- Fuel line
- Power steering pump
- Oil fill tube
- Oil dipstick tube
- Heated Oxygen (HO2S) sensor connectors
- Engine oil filter
- Exhaust crossover pipe
- Structural cover
- Rubber splash shield
- Starter motor
- Crankshaft Position (CKP) sensor connector
- Camshaft Position (CMP) sensor connector
- Torque converter
- Engine ground straps
- Left and right motor mounts
- Transmission flange bolts

5. Install Engine Lifting Fixture 8347 as shown.
6. Place a support stand under the transmission.
7. Lift the engine out of the vehicle.

To install:
8. Lower the engine in to the vehicle and position to the transmission.
9. Remove the engine lifting fixture.
10. Install or connect the following:
- Transmission flange bolts. Tighten the bolts to 50 ft. lbs. (68 Nm).
- Left and right motor mounts. Tighten the bolts to 45 ft. lbs. (61 Nm).
- Engine ground straps
- Torque converter. Tighten the bolts to 23 ft. lbs. (31 Nm).
- CMP sensor connector
- CKP sensor connector
- Starter motor
- Rubber splash shield
11. Install the structural cover as follows:
a. Install all the bolts finger-tight.
b. Hold the cover tightly against the transmission and the engine.
c. Tighten the bolts in sequence to 40 ft. lbs. (54 Nm).
12. Install or connect the following:
- Exhaust crossover pipe
- Engine oil filter
- HO2S sensor connectors

- Oil dipstick tube
- Oil fill tube
- Power steering pump
- Fuel line
- Ignition coils
- MAP sensor connector
- IAC valve connector
- ECT sensor connector
- Fuel injector harness connectors
- IAT sensor connector
- TP sensor connector
- Heater hoses
- Alternator
- A/C condenser
- Radiator
- Transmission oil cooler lines
- Radiator hoses
- Cooling fan assemblies
- A/C compressor
- Accessory drive belt
- Crankcase breather tubes
- Cruise control cable
- Accelerator cable
- Air intake resonator
- Headlamp mounting module
- Left and right inner fender liners
- Front fascia
- Negative battery cable
13. Fill the cooling system.
14. Recharge the A/C system.
15. Run the engine and check for leaks.

5.2L AND 5.9L ENGINES

1. Before servicing the vehicle, refer to the precautions in the beginning of this section.
2. Drain the cooling system.
3. Recover the A/C refrigerant.
4. Remove or disconnect the following:
- Battery
- Hood
- Air cleaner assembly
- Radiator hoses
- Heater hoses
- Radiator and fan shroud
- Accessory drive belt
- Distributor cap and spark plug wires
- Vacuum lines
- Engine control wiring harness connectors
- Accelerator linkage
- Fuel line
- Throttle body
- Oil pressure sender connector
- A/C hoses
- Power steering hoses
- Starter motor
- Alternator

- Heated Oxygen (HO2S) sensor connectors
- Exhaust Y-pipe
- Torque converter cover
- Torque converter
- Left and right motor mounts
- Transmission flange bolts

5. Place a support stand under the transmission.

6. Lift the engine out of the vehicle.

To install:

7. Lower the engine in to the vehicle and position to the transmission.

8. Install or connect the following:
- Transmission flange bolts. Tighten the bolts to 30 ft. lbs. (41 Nm).
- Left and right motor mounts. Tighten the through bolts to 60 ft. lbs. (81 Nm).
- Torque converter. Tighten the bolts to 23 ft. lbs. (31 Nm).
- Torque converter cover
- Exhaust Y-pipe
- HO2S sensor connectors
- Alternator
- Starter motor
- Power steering hoses
- A/C hoses
- Oil pressure sender connector
- Throttle body
- Fuel line
- Accelerator linkage
- Engine control wiring harness connectors
- Vacuum lines
- Distributor cap and spark plug wires
- Accessory drive belt
- Radiator and fan shroud
- Heater hoses
- Radiator hoses
- Air cleaner assembly
- Hood
- Battery

9. Fill the cooling system.
10. Recharge the A/C system.
11. Run the engine and check for leaks.

Water Pump

REMOVAL & INSTALLATION

2.5L and 4.0L Engines

➡**The 2.5L and 4.0L engines covered use a reverse rotation water pump. The letter R is stamped on the impeller to identify. Engines from previous years may be equipped with forward rotation water pumps. Installation of the wrong water pump will cause engine over heating.**

1. Before servicing the vehicle, refer to the precautions in the beginning of this section.

2. Drain the cooling system.

3. Remove or disconnect the following:

- Negative battery cable
- Accessory drive belt
- Engine cooling fan and pulley

➡**Some 4.0L engines are equipped with a fan clutch that threads directly on to the water pump shaft. This fan clutch is equipped with right-hand threads.**

➡**Do not store the fan clutch assembly horizontally, silicone may leak into the bearing grease and cause contamination.**

- Power steering pump
- Lower radiator hose
- Heater hose
- Water pump

➡**One of the water pump bolts is longer than the others. Note the location for reassembly.**

To install:

4. Install the water pump with a new gasket. Tighten the bolts to 17 ft. lbs. (23 Nm).

5. Remove or disconnect the following:
- Heater hose
- Lower radiator hose
- Power steering pump
- Engine cooling fan and pulley

- Accessory drive belt
- Negative battery cable

6. Fill the cooling system.
7. Run the engine and check for leaks.

4.7L Engine

1. Before servicing the vehicle, refer to the precautions in the beginning of this section.

2. Drain the cooling system.

3. Remove or disconnect the following:

- Negative battery cable
- Engine cooling fan and shroud

➡**The 4.7L engine is equipped with a fan clutch that threads directly onto the water pump shaft. This fan clutch is equipped with right-hand threads.**

➡**Do not store the fan clutch assembly horizontally, silicone may leak into the bearing grease and cause contamination.**

- Accessory drive belt
- Lower radiator hose
- Water pump

To install:

4. Install the water pump using a new gasket. Tighten the bolts in sequence to 30 ft. lbs. (40 Nm).

5. Install or connect the following:
- Lower radiator hose
- Accessory drive belt
- Engine cooling fan and shroud
- Negative battery cable

6. Fill the cooling system.
7. Start the engine and check for leaks.

FRONT VIEW

ROTATION DIRECTION AS VIEWED

BACK VIEW

ROTATION DIRECTION AS VIEWED

R STAMPED INTO IMPELLER

7924PG02

Reverse rotation water pump—2.5L and 4.0L engines

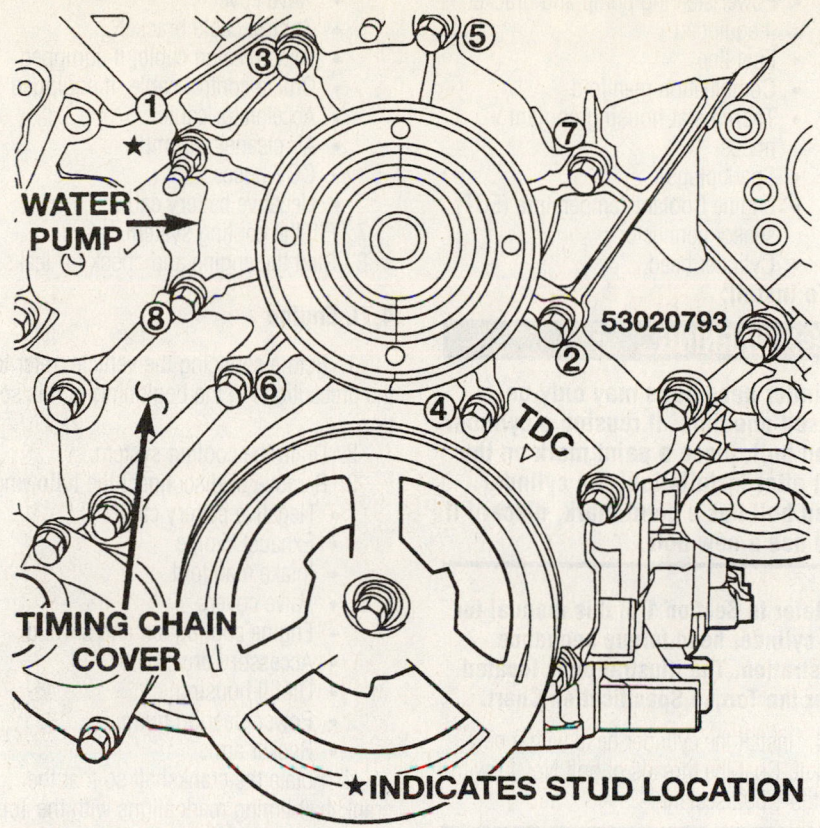

WATER PUMP

53020793

TDC

TIMING CHAIN COVER

★INDICATES STUD LOCATION

9302PG06

Water pump torque sequence—4.7L engine

5.2L and 5.9L Engines

1. Before servicing the vehicle, refer to the precautions in the beginning of this section.
2. Drain the cooling system.
3. Remove or disconnect the following:
   - Negative battery cable
   - Engine cooling fan and shroud

➡**Do not store the fan clutch assembly horizontally, silicone may leak into the bearing grease and cause contamination.**

   - Accessory drive belt
   - Water pump pulley
   - Lower radiator hose
   - Heater hose and tube
   - Bypass hose
   - Water pump

To install:

4. Install or connect the following:
   - Water pump, using a new gasket. Tighten the bolts to 30 ft. lbs. (40 Nm).
   - Bypass hose
   - Heater hose and tube. Use a new O-ring seal.

   - Lower radiator hose
   - Water pump pulley. Tighten the bolts to 20 ft. lbs. (27 Nm).
   - Accessory drive belt
   - Engine cooling fan and shroud
   - Negative battery cable
5. Fill the cooling system.
6. Start the engine and check for leaks.

Cylinder Head

REMOVAL & INSTALLATION

2.5L Engine

1. Before servicing the vehicle, refer to the precautions in the beginning of this section.
2. Drain the cooling system.
3. Remove or disconnect the following:
   - Negative battery cable
   - Crankcase Ventilation (CCV) hoses
   - Air cleaner assembly
   - Valve cover

➡**Keep valvetrain components in order for reassembly.**

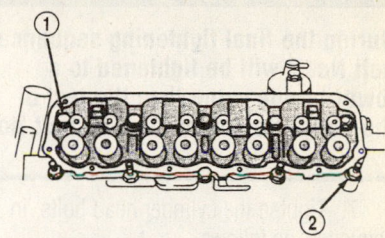

1 – ALIGNMENT DOWEL
2 – ALIGNMENT DOWEL

9308PG03

Alignment dowel locations—2.5L engine

   - Rocker arms
   - Pushrods
   - Accessory drive belt
   - A/C compressor and bracket, if equipped
   - Power steering pump and bracket, if equipped
   - Fuel line
   - Combination manifold
   - Thermostat housing coolant hoses
   - Spark plugs
   - Engine Coolant Temperature (ECT) sensor connector
   - Cylinder head

To install:

✱✱ WARNING

Cylinder head bolts may only be reused one time. If reusing a cylinder head bolt, place a paint mark on the bolt after installation. If a cylinder head bolt has a paint mark, discard it and use a new bolt.

4. Fabricate two alignment dowels from old cylinder head bolts. Cut the hex head off of the bolts, and cut a slot in each dowel to ease removal.

➡**Refer to Section 1 of this manual for the cylinder head torque sequence illustration. The illustration is located after the Torque Specification Chart.**

5. Install or connect the following:
   - One dowel in bolt hole No. 8, and one dowel in bolt hole No. 10.
   - Cylinder head and gasket.
   - Cylinder head bolts except for No 8 and No 10. Coat the threads of bolt No. 7 with Loctite® 592 sealant.
6. Remove the alignment dowels and install the No. 8 and No. 10 head bolts.

Refer to Section 1 for engine rebuilding specifications

✳✳ WARNING

During the final tightening sequence, bolt No. 7 will be tightened to a lower torque value than the rest of the bolts. Do not overtighten bolt No. 7.

7. Tighten the cylinder head bolts, in sequence, as follows.
   a. Step 1: 22 ft. lbs. (30 Nm)
   b. Step 2: 45 ft. lbs. (61 Nm)
   c. Step 3: 45 ft. lbs. (61 Nm)
   d. Step 4: Bolts 1–6 to 110 ft. lbs. (149 Nm)
   e. Step 5: Bolt 7 to 100 ft. lbs. (136 Nm)
   f. Step 6: Bolts 8–10 to 110 ft. lbs. (149 Nm)
   g. Step 7: Repeat steps 4, 5 and 6
8. Install or connect the following:
   - ECT sensor connector
   - Spark plugs
   - Thermostat housing coolant hoses
   - Combination manifold
   - Fuel line
   - Power steering pump and bracket, if equipped
   - A/C compressor and bracket, if equipped
   - Accessory drive belt
   - Pushrods and rocker arms in their original positions
   - Valve cover
   - Air cleaner assembly
   - CCV hoses
   - Negative battery cable
9. Fill the cooling system.
10. Start the engine and check for leaks.

4.0L Engines

1. Before servicing the vehicle, refer to the precautions in the beginning of this section.
2. Drain the cooling system.
3. Remove or disconnect the following:
   - Negative battery cable
   - Crankcase Ventilation (CCV) hoses
   - Air cleaner assembly
   - Accelerator cable
   - Cruise control cable, if equipped
   - Transmission cable, if equipped
   - Control cable bracket
   - Valve cover

➡ **Keep valvetrain components in order for reassembly.**

   - Rocker arms
   - Pushrods
   - Accessory drive belt
   - A/C compressor and bracket, if equipped
   - Power steering pump and bracket, if equipped
   - Fuel line
   - Combination manifold
   - Thermostat housing coolant hoses
   - Spark plugs
   - Engine Coolant Temperature (ECT) sensor connector
   - Cylinder head

To install:

✳✳ WARNING

Cylinder head bolts may only be reused one time. If reusing a cylinder head bolt, place a paint mark on the bolt after installation. If a cylinder head bolt has a paint mark, discard it and use a new bolt.

➡ **Refer to Section 1 of this manual for the cylinder head torque sequence illustration. The illustration is located after the Torque Specification Chart.**

4. Install the cylinder head with a new gasket. Coat the threads of bolt No. 11 with Loctite® 592 sealant.

✳✳ CAUTION

During the final tightening sequence, bolt No. 11 will be tightened to a lower torque value than the rest of the bolts. Do not overtighten bolt No. 11.

5. Tighten the cylinder head bolts, in sequence, as follows:
   a. Step 1: 22 ft. lbs. (30 Nm)
   b. Step 2: 45 ft. lbs. (61 Nm)
   c. Step 3: 45 ft. lbs. (61 Nm)
   d. Step 4: Bolts 1–10 to 110 ft. lbs. (149 Nm)
   e. Step 5: Bolt 11 to 100 ft. lbs. (136 Nm)
   f. Step 6: Bolts 12–14 to 110 ft. lbs. (149 Nm)
   g. Step 7: Repeat steps 4, 5 and 6
6. Install or connect the following:
   - ECT sensor connector
   - Spark plugs
   - Thermostat housing coolant hoses
   - Combination manifold
   - Fuel line
   - Power steering pump and bracket, if equipped
   - A/C compressor and bracket, if equipped
   - Accessory drive belt
   - Pushrods and rocker arms in their original positions

   - Valve cover
   - Control cable bracket
   - Transmission cable, if equipped
   - Cruise control cable, if equipped
   - Accelerator cable
   - Air cleaner assembly
   - CCV hoses
   - Negative battery cable
7. Fill the cooling system.
8. Start the engine and check for leaks.

4.7L Engine

1. Before servicing the vehicle, refer to the precautions in the beginning of this section.
2. Drain the cooling system.
3. Remove or disconnect the following:
   - Negative battery cable
   - Exhaust Y-pipe
   - Intake manifold
   - Valve covers
   - Engine cooling fan and shroud
   - Accessory drive belt
   - Oil fill housing
   - Power steering pump
   - Rocker arms
4. Rotate the crankshaft so that the crankshaft timing mark aligns with the Top Dead Center (TDC) mark on the front cover, and the **V8** marks on the camshaft sprockets are at 12 o'clock as shown.
5. Remove or disconnect the following:
   - Crankshaft damper
   - Front cover
6. Lock the secondary timing chains to the idler sprocket with Timing Chain Locking tool 8515.
7. Matchmark the secondary timing chains to the camshaft sprockets.
8. Remove or disconnect the following:
   - Secondary timing chain tensioners
   - Cylinder head access plugs
   - Secondary timing chain guides

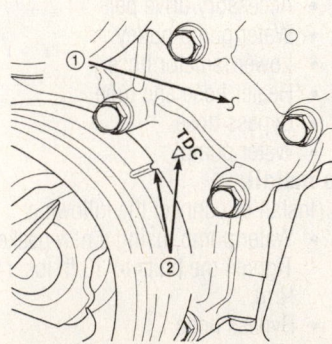

1 – TIMING CHAIN COVER
2 – CRANKSHAFT TIMING MARKS

9308PG04

Crankshaft timing marks—4.7 engine

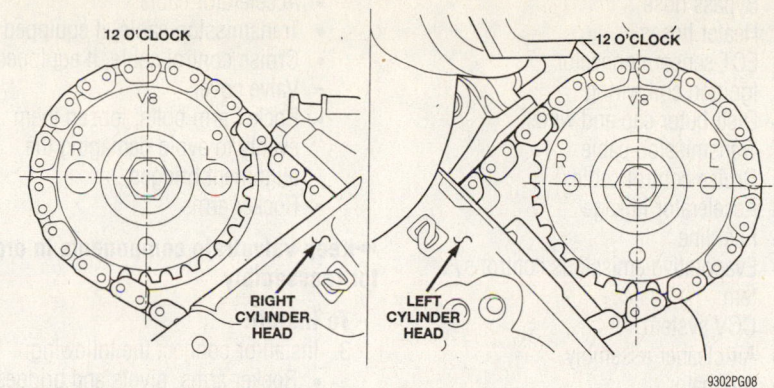

Camshaft positioning—4.7L engine

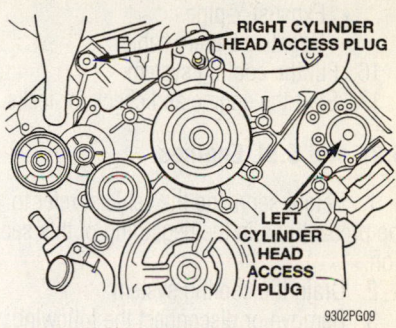

Cylinder head access plug locations—4.7L engine

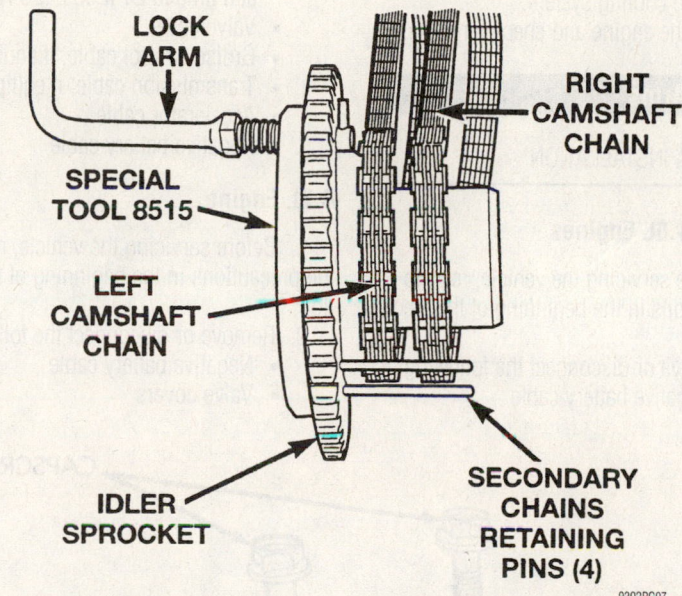

Use the special tool to lock the timing chains on the idler gear—4.7L engine

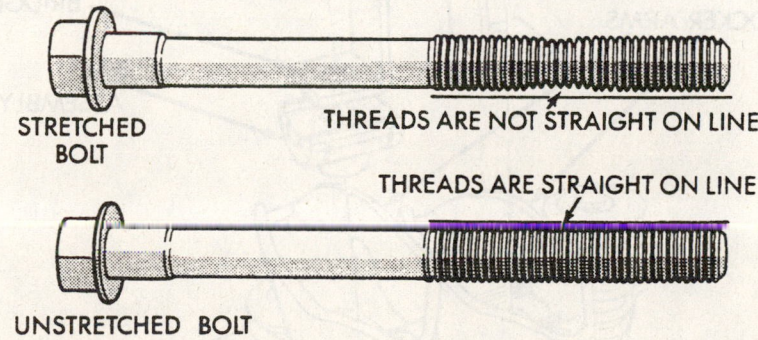

Examine the head bolts for signs of stretching—4.7L engine

- Camshaft sprockets
- Cylinder heads

➡ **Each cylinder head is retained by ten 11mm bolts and four 8mm bolts.**

To install:

9. Check the cylinder head bolts for signs of stretching and replace as necessary.

10. Lubricate the threads of the 11mm bolts with clean engine oil.

11. Coat the threads of the 8mm bolts with Mopar• Lock and Seal Adhesive.

➡ **Refer to Section 1 of this manual for the cylinder head torque sequence illustration. The illustration is located after the Torque Specification Chart.**

12. Install the cylinder heads. Use new gaskets and tighten the bolts, in sequence, as follows:

   a. Step 1: Bolts 1–10 to 15 ft. lbs. (20 Nm)

   b. Step 2: Bolts 1–10 to 35 ft. lbs. (47 Nm)

   c. Step 3: Bolts 11–14 to 18 ft. lbs. (25 Nm)

   d. Step 4: Bolts 1–10 plus ¼ (90 degree) turn

   e. Step 5: Bolts 11–14 to 22 ft. lbs. (30 Nm)

13. Install or connect the following:
- Camshaft sprockets. Align the secondary chain matchmarks and tighten the bolts to 90 ft. lbs. (122 Nm).
- Secondary timing chain guides
- Cylinder head access plugs
- Secondary timing chain tensioners. Refer to the timing chain procedure in this section.

14. Remove the Timing Chain Locking tool 8515.

15. Install or connect the following:
- Front cover
- Crankshaft damper. Tighten the bolt to 130 ft. lbs. (175 Nm).
- Rocker arms
- Power steering pump
- Oil fill housing
- Accessory drive belt
- Engine cooling fan and shroud
- Valve covers

For engine torque specifications, refer to Section 1 of this manual

- Intake manifold
- Exhaust Y-pipe
- Negative battery cable
16. Fill the cooling system.
17. Start the engine and check for leaks.

5.2L and 5.9L Engines

1. Before servicing the vehicle, refer to the precautions in the beginning of this section.
2. Drain the cooling system.
3. Remove or disconnect the following:
- Negative battery cable
- Accessory drive belt
- Alternator
- Air cleaner assembly
- Closed Crankcase Ventilation (CCV) system
- Evaporative emissions control system
- Fuel line
- Accelerator linkage
- Cruise control cable
- Transmission cable
- Distributor cap and wires
- Ignition coil wiring
- Engine Coolant Temperature (ECT) sensor connector
- Heater hoses
- Bypass hose
- Upper radiator hose
- Intake manifold
- Valve covers

➡ **Keep valvetrain components in order for reassembly.**

- Rocker arms
- Pushrods
- Exhaust manifolds
- Spark plugs
- Cylinder heads

To install:

➡ **Refer to Section 1 of this manual for the cylinder head torque sequence illustration. The illustration is located after the Torque Specification Chart.**

4. Install the cylinder heads. Use new gaskets and tighten the bolts in sequence as follows:
   a. Step 1: 50 ft. lbs. (68 Nm)
   b. Step 2: 105 ft. lbs. (143 Nm)
   c. Step 3: 105 ft. lbs. (143 Nm)
5. Install or connect the following:
- Spark plugs
- Exhaust manifolds
- Pushrods and rocker arms in their original positions
- Valve covers
- Intake manifold
- Upper radiator hose

- Bypass hose
- Heater hoses
- ECT sensor connector
- Ignition coil wiring
- Distributor cap and wires
- Transmission cable
- Cruise control cable
- Accelerator linkage
- Fuel line
- Evaporative emissions control system
- CCV system
- Air cleaner assembly
- Alternator
- Accessory drive belt
- Negative battery cable
6. Fill the cooling system.
7. Start the engine and check for leaks.

Rocker Arms

REMOVAL & INSTALLATION

2.5L and 4.0L Engines

1. Before servicing the vehicle, refer to the precautions in the beginning of this section.
2. Remove or disconnect the following:
- Negative battery cable

- Accelerator cable
- Transmission cable, if equipped
- Cruise control cable, if equipped
- Valve cover
- Rocker arm bolts, loosen them evenly to avoid damaging the alignment bridges
- Rocker arms

➡ **Keep valvetrain components in order for reassembly.**

To install:

3. Install or connect the following:
- Rocker arms, pivots and bridges in their original positions. Tighten the bolts for each bridged pair one turn at a time to 21 ft. lbs. (28 Nm).
- Valve cover
- Cruise control cable, if equipped
- Transmission cable, if equipped
- Accelerator cable
- Negative battery cable

4.7L Engine

1. Before servicing the vehicle, refer to the precautions in the beginning of this section.
2. Remove or disconnect the following:
- Negative battery cable
- Valve covers

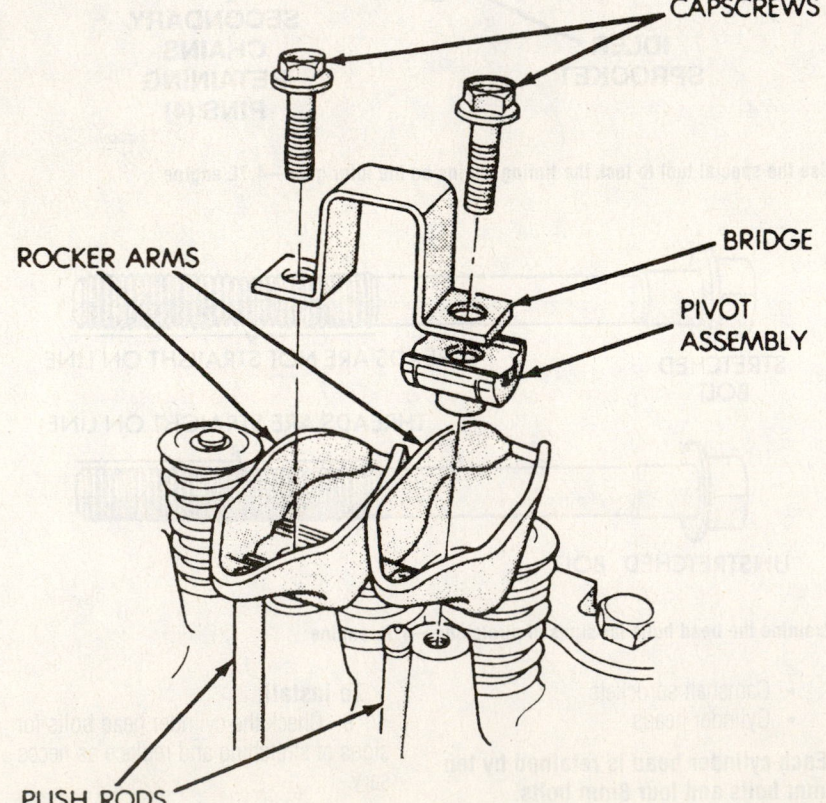

CAPSCREWS

ROCKER ARMS

BRIDGE

PIVOT ASSEMBLY

PUSH RODS

7924PG07

Exploded view of the rocker arm assembly—2.5L and 4.0L engines

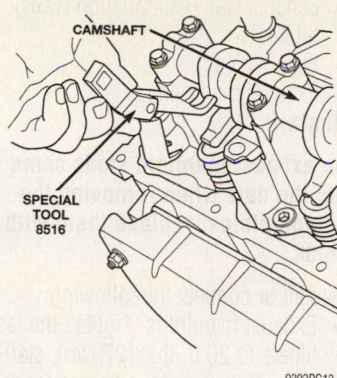

Rocker arm service—4.7L engine

9302PG13

3. Rotate the crankshaft so that the piston of the cylinder to be serviced is at Bottom Dead Center (BDC) and both valves are closed.

4. Use special tool 8516 to depress the valve and remove the rocker arm.

5. Repeat for each rocker arm to be serviced.

➡️**Keep valvetrain components in order for reassembly.**

To install:

6. Rotate the crankshaft so that the piston of the cylinder to be serviced is at BDC.

7. Compress the valve spring and install each rocker arm in its original position.

8. Repeat for each rocker arm to be installed.

9. Install or connect the following:
   • Cylinder head cover
   • Negative battery cable

5.2L and 5.9L Engines

1. Before servicing the vehicle, refer to the precautions in the beginning of this section.

2. Remove or disconnect the following:

   • Negative battery cable
   • Valve covers
   • Rocker arms

➡️**Keep valvetrain components in order for reassembly.**

To install:

3. Rotate the crankshaft so that the **V8** mark on the crankshaft damper aligns with the timing mark on the front cover. The **V8** mark is located 147 degrees **AFTER** Top Dead Center (TDC).

4. Install the rocker arms in their original positions and tighten the bolts to 21 ft. lbs. (28 Nm).

✴✴ CAUTION

Do not rotate the crankshaft during or immediately after rocker arm installation. Wait 5 minutes for the hydraulic lash adjusters to bleed down.

---

5. Install or connect the following:
   • Valve covers
   • Negative battery cable

Intake Manifold

REMOVAL & INSTALLATION

4.7L Engine

1. Before servicing the vehicle, refer to the precautions in the beginning of this section.

2. Drain the cooling system.

3. Remove or disconnect the following:
   • Negative battery cable
   • Air cleaner assembly
   • Accelerator cable
   • Cruise control cable
   • Manifold Absolute Pressure (MAP) sensor connector
   • Intake Air Temperature (IAT) sensor connector
   • Throttle Position (TP) sensor connector
   • Idle Air Control (IAC) valve connector
   • Engine Coolant Temperature (ECT) sensor
   • Positive Crankcase Ventilation (PCV) valve and hose
   • Canister purge vacuum line
   • Brake booster vacuum line
   • Cruise control servo hose
   • Accessory drive belt
   • Alternator
   • A/C compressor
   • Engine ground straps
   • Ignition coil towers
   • Oil dipstick tube
   • Fuel line
   • Fuel supply manifold
   • Throttle body and mounting bracket
   • Cowl seal
   • Right engine lifting stud
   • Intake manifold. Remove the fasteners in reverse of the tightening sequence.

To install:

➡️**Refer to Section 1 of this manual for the intake manifold torque sequence**

---

illustration. The illustration is located after the Torque Specification Chart.

4. Install or connect the following:
   • Intake manifold using new gaskets. Tighten the bolts, in sequence, to 105 inch lbs. (12 Nm).
   • Right engine lifting stud
   • Cowl seal
   • Throttle body and mounting bracket
   • Fuel supply manifold
   • Fuel line
   • Oil dipstick tube
   • Ignition coil towers
   • Engine ground straps
   • A/C compressor
   • Alternator
   • Accessory drive belt
   • Cruise control servo hose
   • Brake booster vacuum line
   • Canister purge vacuum line
   • PCV valve and hose
   • ECT sensor
   • IAC valve connector
   • TP sensor connector
   • IAT sensor connector
   • MAP sensor connector
   • Cruise control cable
   • Accelerator cable
   • Air cleaner assembly
   • Negative battery cable

5. Fill the cooling system.

6. Start the engine and check for leaks.

5.2L and 5.9L Engines

1. Before servicing the vehicle, refer to the precautions in the beginning of this section.

2. Drain the cooling system.

3. Remove or disconnect the following:
   • Negative battery cable
   • Accessory drive belt
   • Alternator
   • Air cleaner assembly
   • Fuel line
   • Fuel supply manifold
   • Accelerator cable
   • Transmission cable
   • Cruise control cable
   • Distributor cap and wires
   • Ignition coil wiring
   • Engine Coolant Temperature (ECT) sensor connector
   • Heater hose
   • Upper radiator hose
   • Bypass hose
   • Closed Crankcase Ventilation (CCV) system
   • Evaporative emissions system

For complete mechanical specifications, refer to Section 1 of this manual

- A/C compressor
- Manifold support bracket
- Intake manifold

To install:

➡ **Refer to Section 1 of this manual for the intake manifold torque sequence illustration. The illustration is located after the Torque Specification Chart.**

4. Install the intake manifold. Use a new gasket and tighten the bolts in sequence as follows:

  a. Step 1: Bolts 1–4 to 72 inch lbs. (8 Nm) using 12 inch lb. (1.4 Nm) increments

  b. Step 2: Bolts 5–12 to 72 inch lbs. (8 Nm)

  c. Step 3: Bolts 1–12 to 72 inch lbs. (8 Nm)

  d. Step 4: Bolts 1–12 to 12 ft. lbs. (16 Nm)

  e. Step 5: Bolts 1–12 to 12 ft. lbs. (16 Nm)

5. Install or connect the following:
- Manifold support bracket
- A/C compressor
- Evaporative emissions system
- CCV system
- Bypass hose
- Upper radiator hose
- Heater hose
- ECT sensor connector
- Ignition coil wiring
- Distributor cap and wires
- Cruise control cable
- Transmission cable
- Accelerator cable
- Fuel supply manifold
- Fuel line
- Air cleaner assembly
- Alternator
- Accessory drive belt
- Negative battery cable

6. Fill the cooling system.
7. Start the engine and check for leaks.

Exhaust Manifold

REMOVAL & INSTALLATION

4.7L Engine

1. Before servicing the vehicle, refer to the precautions in the beginning of this section.
2. Drain the cooling system.
3. Remove or disconnect the following:
- Battery
- Power distribution center
- Battery tray
- Windshield washer fluid bottle

- Air cleaner assembly
- Accessory drive belt
- A/C compressor
- A/C accumulator bracket
- Heater hoses
- Exhaust manifold heat shields
- Exhaust Y-pipe
- Starter motor
- Exhaust manifolds

To install:
- Exhaust manifolds, using new gaskets. Tighten the bolts to 18 ft. lbs. (25 Nm), starting with the inner bolts and work out to the ends.

4. Install or connect the following:
- Starter motor
- Exhaust Y-pipe
- Exhaust manifold heat shields
- Heater hoses
- A/C accumulator bracket
- A/C compressor
- Accessory drive belt
- Air cleaner assembly
- Windshield washer fluid bottle
- Battery tray
- Power distribution center
- Battery

5. Fill the cooling system.
6. Start the engine and check for leaks.

5.2L and 5.9L Engines

1. Before servicing the vehicle, refer to the precautions in the beginning of this section.
2. Remove or disconnect the following:
- Negative battery cable
- Exhaust manifold heat shields

- Exhaust Gas Recirculation (EGR) tube
- Exhaust Y-pipe
- Exhaust manifolds

To install:

➡ **If the exhaust manifold studs came out with the nuts when removing the exhaust manifolds, replace them with new studs.**

3. Install or connect the following:
- Exhaust manifolds. Tighten the fasteners to 20 ft. lbs. (27 Nm), starting with the center nuts and work out to the ends.
- Exhaust Y-pipe
- EGR tube
- Exhaust manifold heat shields
- Negative battery cable

4. Fill the cooling system.
5. Start the engine and check for leaks.

Combination Manifold

REMOVAL & INSTALLATION

2.5L Engine

1. Before servicing the vehicle, refer to the precautions in the beginning of this section.
2. Remove or disconnect the following:
- Negative battery cable
- Air intake hose
- Accessory drive belt
- Power steering pump and brackets, if equipped

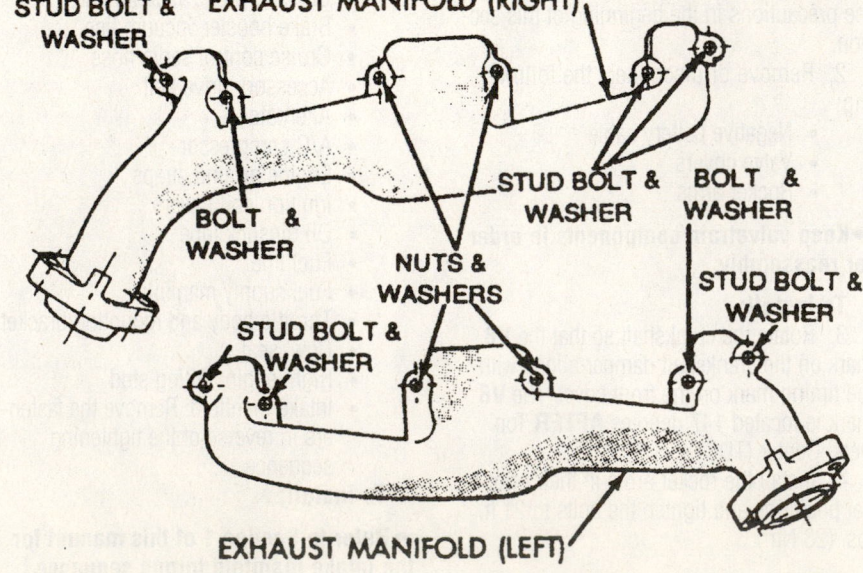

Exhaust manifold fastener locations—5.2L and 5.9L engines

- Fuel line
- Accelerator cable
- Cruise control cable, if equipped
- Transmission cable, if equipped
- Throttle Position (TP) sensor connector
- Idle Air Control (IAC) valve connector
- Engine Coolant Temperature (ECT) sensor connector
- Intake Air Temperature (IAT) sensor connector
- Heated Oxygen (HO$_2$S) sensor connector
- Fuel injector connectors
- Closed Crankcase Ventilation (CCV) system
- Manifold Absolute Pressure (MAP) sensor vacuum line
- Brake booster vacuum line
- Exhaust front pipe
- Intake manifold
- Exhaust manifold

To install:

3. Install or connect the following:
   - New gasket over the locating dowels
   - Exhaust manifold to the studs and tighten the nuts finger-tight

➡**Refer to Section 1 of this manual for the combination manifold torque sequence illustration. The illustration is located after the Torque Specification Chart.**

4. Install the intake manifold. Tighten the fasteners in sequence as follows:
   a. Step 1: Bolt 1 to 30 ft. lbs. (41 Nm)
   b. Step 2: Fasteners 2–7 to 23 ft. lbs. (31 Nm)
5. Install or connect the following:
   - Exhaust front pipe
   - Brake booster vacuum line
   - MAP sensor vacuum line
   - CCV system
   - Fuel injector connectors
   - HO$_2$S sensor connector
   - IAT sensor connector
   - ECT sensor connector
   - IAC valve connector
   - TP sensor connector
   - Transmission cable, if equipped
   - Cruise control cable, if equipped
   - Accelerator cable
   - Fuel line
   - Power steering pump and brackets, if equipped
   - Accessory drive belt
   - Air intake hose

- Negative battery cable
6. Fill the cooling system.
7. Start the engine and check for leaks.

4.0L Engine

1. Before servicing the vehicle, refer to the precautions in the beginning of this section.
2. Drain the cooling system.
3. Remove or disconnect the following:
   - Negative battery cable
   - Air cleaner assembly
   - Accessory drive belt
   - Power steering pump and brackets, if equipped
   - Fuel line
   - Fuel injector connectors
   - Fuel supply manifold and injectors
   - Accelerator cable
   - Cruise control cable, if equipped
   - Transmission cable, if equipped
   - Throttle Position (TP) sensor connector
   - Idle Air Control (IAC) valve connector
   - Engine Coolant Temperature (ECT) sensor connector
   - Intake Air Temperature (IAT) sensor connector
   - Heated Oxygen (HO$_2$S) sensor connector
   - Closed Crankcase Ventilation (CCV) system
   - Manifold Absolute Pressure (MAP) sensor vacuum line
   - Brake booster vacuum line
   - Exhaust front pipe
   - Intake and exhaust manifolds

To install:

4. Install or connect the following:
   - New gasket over the locating dowels
   - Exhaust manifold to the studs and tighten the nuts finger-tight

➡**Refer to Section 1 of this manual for the combination manifold torque sequence illustration. The illustration is located after the Torque Specification Chart.**

5. Install the intake manifold. Tighten the fasteners in sequence as follows:
   a. Step 1: Fasteners 1–5 to 24 ft. lbs. (33 Nm)
   b. Step 2: Fasteners 6 and 7 to 23 ft. lbs. (31 Nm)
   c. Step 3: Fasteners 8–11 to 24 ft. lbs. (33 Nm)
6. Install or connect the following:

- Exhaust front pipe
- Brake booster vacuum line
- MAP sensor vacuum line
- CCV system
- HO$_2$S sensor connector
- IAT sensor connector
- ECT sensor connector
- IAC valve connector
- TP sensor connector
- Transmission cable, if equipped
- Cruise control cable, if equipped
- Accelerator cable
- Fuel supply manifold and injectors
- Fuel injector connectors
- Fuel line
- Power steering pump and brackets, if equipped
- Accessory drive belt
- Air cleaner assembly
- Negative battery cable
7. Fill the cooling system.
8. Start the engine and check for leaks.

Camshaft and Valve Lifters

REMOVAL & INSTALLATION

2.5L Engine

1. Before servicing the vehicle, refer to the precautions in the beginning of this section.
2. Drain the cooling system.
3. Recover the A/C refrigerant, if equipped with air conditioning.
4. Remove or disconnect the following:
   - Negative battery cable
   - Grille, if necessary
   - Radiator
   - A/C condenser, if equipped
   - Distributor
   - Valve cover

➡**Keep all valvetrain components in order for assembly.**

- Rocker arms and pushrods
- Hydraulic valve tappets
- Accessory drive belt
- Crankshaft damper
- Front cover
- Timing chain and gears
- Camshaft

To install:

➡**If the camshaft sprocket appears to have been rubbing against the cover, check the oil pressure relief holes in the rear cam journal for debris.**

5. Lubricate the camshaft with clean engine oil.

Please refer to Section 8 for electric cooling fan wiring schematics

6. Install or connect the following:
- Camshaft
- Timing chain and gears
- Front cover
- Crankshaft damper
- Accessory drive belt
- Hydraulic valve tappets
- Rocker arms and pushrods
- Valve cover
- Distributor
- A/C condenser, if equipped
- Radiator
- Grille, if removed
- Negative battery cable

7. Fill the cooling system.
8. Recharge the A/C system, if equipped.
9. Start the engine and check for leaks.

4.0L Engine

1. Before servicing the vehicle, refer to the precautions in the beginning of this section.
2. Drain the cooling system.
3. Recover the A/C refrigerant, if equipped with air conditioning.
4. Remove or disconnect the following:
- Negative battery cable
- Grille, if necessary
- Radiator
- A/C condenser, if equipped
- Distributor or camshaft sensor housing
- Valve cover

➡ **Keep all valvetrain components in order for assembly.**

- Rocker arms and pushrods
- Cylinder head
- Hydraulic valve tappets
- Accessory drive belt
- Crankshaft damper
- Front cover
- Timing chain and gears
- Thrust plate
- Camshaft

To install:

5. Lubricate the camshaft with clean engine oil.
6. Install or connect the following:
- Camshaft
- Thrust plate. Tighten the bolts to 18 ft. lbs. (24 Nm).
- Timing chain and gears
- Front cover
- Crankshaft damper
- Accessory drive belt
- Hydraulic valve tappets
- Cylinder head
- Rocker arms and pushrods
- Valve cover

- Distributor or camshaft sensor housing
- A/C condenser, if equipped
- Radiator
- Grille, if removed
- Negative battery cable

7. Fill the cooling system.
8. Recharge the A/C system, if equipped.
9. Start the engine and check for leaks.

4.7L Engine

1. Before servicing the vehicle, refer to the precautions in the beginning of this section.

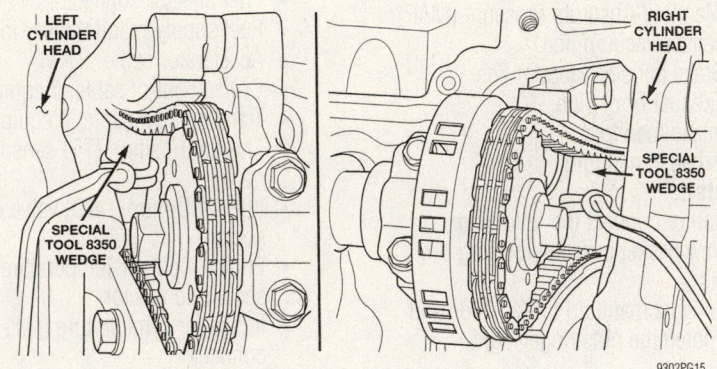

Chain Tensioner Retaining Wedges—4.7L engine

2. Remove or disconnect the following:
- Negative battery cable
- Cylinder head covers
- Rocker arms
- Hydraulic lash adjusters

➡ **Keep all valvetrain components in order for assembly.**

3. Set the engine at Top Dead Center (TDC) of the compression stroke for the No. 1 cylinder.
4. Install Timing Chain Wedge 8350 to retain the chain tensioners.
5. Matchmark the timing chains to the camshaft sprockets.
6. Install Camshaft Holding Tool 6958

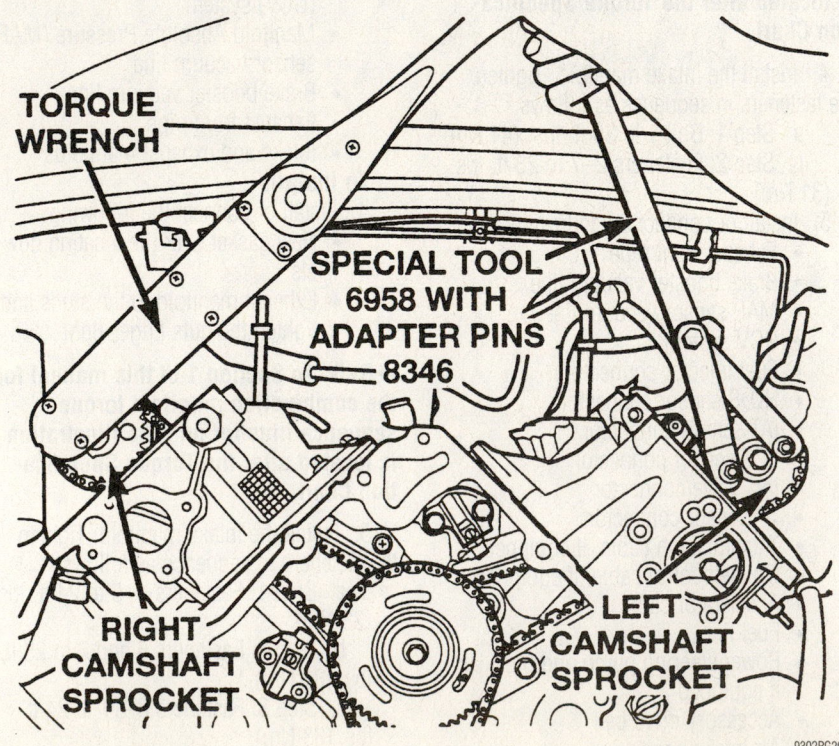

Hold the left camshaft sprocket with a spanner wrench while removing or installing the camshaft sprocket bolts—4.7L engine

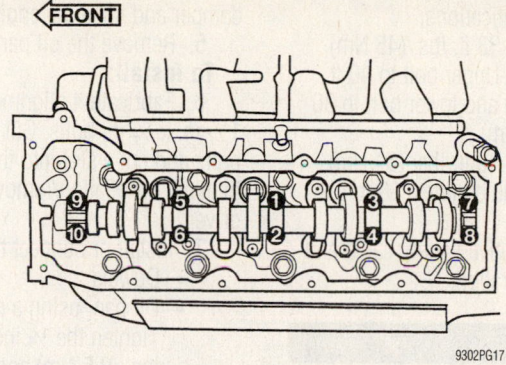

Camshaft bearing cap bolt tightening sequence—4.7L engine

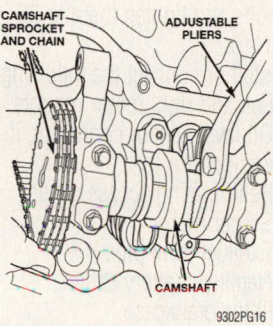

Turn the camshaft with pliers, if needed, to align the dowel in the sprocket—4.7L engine

and Adapter Pins 8346 to the left camshaft sprocket.

7. Remove or disconnect the following:
- Right camshaft timing sprocket and target wheel
- Left camshaft sprocket
- Camshaft bearing caps, by reversing the tightening sequence
- Camshafts

To install:

8. Install or connect the following:
- Camshafts. Tighten the bearing cap bolts in ½ turn increments, in sequence, to 100 inch lbs. (11 Nm).
- Target wheel to the right camshaft
- Camshaft timing sprockets and chains, by aligning the matchmarks

9. Remove the tensioner wedges and tighten the camshaft sprocket bolts to 90 ft. lbs. (122 Nm).

10. Install or connect the following:
- Hydraulic lash adjusters in their original locations
- Rocker arms in their original locations
- Cylinder head covers
- Negative battery cable

5.2L and 5.9L Engines

1. Before servicing the vehicle, refer to the precautions in the beginning of this section.

2. Drain the cooling system.

3. Recover the A/C refrigerant.

4. Set the crankshaft to Top Dead Center (TDC) of the compression stroke for the No. 1 cylinder.

5. Remove or disconnect the following:
- Negative battery cable
- Accessory drive belt

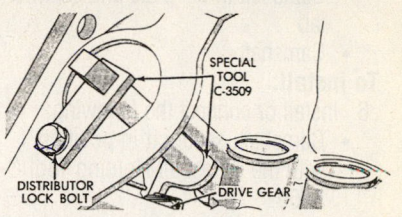

Camshaft holding tool C-3509—5.2L and 5.9L engines

- Power steering pump
- Water pump
- Radiator
- A/C condenser
- Grille
- Crankshaft damper
- Front cover
- Valve covers
- Distributor
- Intake manifold

➡**Keep all valvetrain components in order for assembly.**

- Rocker arms and pushrods
- Hydraulic lifters
- Timing chain and sprockets

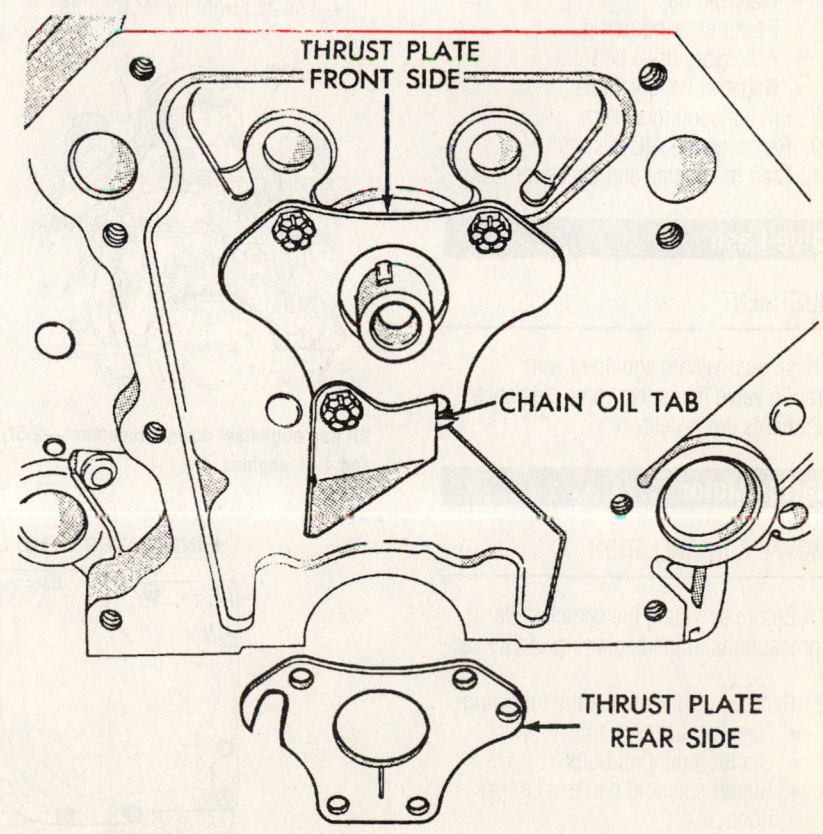

Thrust plate position—5.2L and 5.9L engines

For complete service labor times order Nichols' Chilton Labor Guide Manual

- Camshaft thrust plate and chain oil tab
- Camshaft

To install:

6. Install or connect the following:
- Camshaft, secure it in position with the Camshaft Holding Tool C-3509
- Camshaft thrust plate and chain oil tab. Tighten the bolts to 18 ft. lbs. (24 Nm).
- Timing chain and sprockets, by aligning the timing marks. Tighten the camshaft sprocket bolt to 50 ft. lbs. (68 Nm).

7. Remove the camshaft holding tool.
8. Install or connect the following:
- Hydraulic lifters in their original positions
- Rocker arms and pushrods in their original positions
- Intake manifold
- Distributor
- Valve covers
- Front cover
- Crankshaft damper
- Grille
- A/C condenser
- Radiator
- Water pump
- Power steering pump
- Accessory drive belt
- Negative battery cable

9. Fill the cooling system.
10. Recharge the A/C system.
11. Start the engine and check for leaks.

Valve Lash

ADJUSTMENT

These engines are equipped with hydraulic valve lifters. No valve clearance adjustments are necessary.

Starter Motor

REMOVAL & INSTALLATION

1. Before servicing the vehicle, refer to the precautions in the beginning of this section.
2. Remove or disconnect the following:
- Negative battery cable
- Starter mounting bolts
- Starter solenoid harness connections
- Starter

To install:

3. Connect the starter solenoid wiring connectors.

4. Install the starter and tighten the bolts to the following specifications:
- 2.5L engine: 33 ft. lbs. (45 Nm)
- 4.0L engine: Upper bolt to 40 ft. lbs. (54 Nm) and lower bolt to 30 ft. lbs. (41 Nm)
- 4.7L engine: 40 ft. lbs. (54 Nm)
- 5.2L and 5.9L engines: 50 ft. lbs. (68 Nm)

5. Install the negative battery cable and check for proper operation.

Oil Pan

REMOVAL & INSTALLATION

2.5L and 4.0L Engines

1. Before servicing the vehicle, refer to the precautions in the beginning of this section.
2. Drain the engine oil.
3. Remove or disconnect the following:
- Negative battery cable
- Exhaust front pipe
- Starter motor
- Bell housing access cover
- Oil level sensor connector, if equipped
- Left and right motor mounts

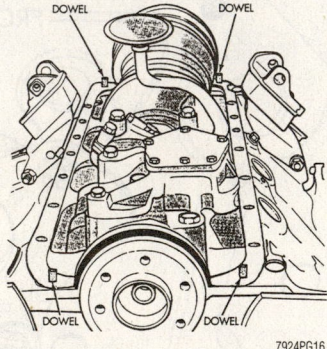

Oil pan alignment dowel placement—2.5L and 4.0L engines

4. Place a jack under the crankshaft damper and raise the engine for clearance.
5. Remove the oil pan.

To install:

6. Fabricate 4 alignment dowels from 1½ in. x ¼ in. bolts. Cut the heads off the bolts and cut a slot into the top of the dowel to allow installation/removal with a screwdriver.
7. Install or connect the following:
- Dowels
- Oil pan, using a new gasket. Tighten the ¼ inch bolts to 85 inch lbs. (9.5 Nm) and the ⁵⁄₁₆ inch bolts to 11 ft. lbs. (15 Nm).

8. Replace the alignment dowels with ¼ inch bolts and tighten them to 85 inch lbs. (9.5 Nm).
9. Install or connect the following:
- Left and right motor mounts
- Oil level sensor connector, if equipped
- Bell housing access cover
- Starter motor
- Exhaust front pipe
- Negative battery cable

10. Fill the crankcase.
11. Start the engine and check for leaks.

4.7L Engine

1. Before servicing the vehicle, refer to the precautions in the beginning of this section.
2. Drain the engine oil.
3. Remove or disconnect the following:
- Negative battery cable
- Structural cover
- Exhaust Y-pipe
- Starter motor
- Transmission oil cooler lines
- Oil pan
- Oil pump pickup tube
- Oil pan gasket

To install:

4. Install or connect the following:

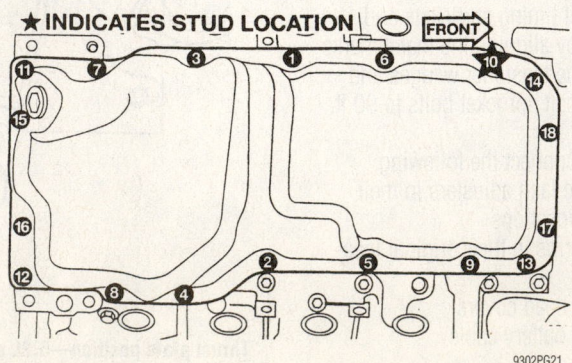

Oil pan mounting bolt tightening sequence—4.7L engine

- Oil pan gasket
- Oil pump pickup tube, using a new O-ring. Tighten the tube bolts to 20 ft. lbs. (28 Nm); tighten the O-ring end bolt first.
- Oil pan. Tighten the bolts, in sequence, to 11 ft. lbs. (15 Nm).
- Transmission oil cooler lines
- Starter motor
- Exhaust Y-pipe
- Structural cover
- Negative battery cable

5. Fill the crankcase to the proper level with engine oil.

6. Start the engine and check for leaks.

5.2L and 5.9L Engines

1. Before servicing the vehicle, refer to the precautions in the beginning of this section.

2. Drain the engine oil.

3. Remove or disconnect the following:
- Oil filter
- Starter motor
- Cooler lines
- Oil level sensor connector
- Heated Oxygen (HO2S) sensor connector
- Exhaust Y-pipe
- Oil pan

To install:

4. Install or connect the following:
- Oil pan, using a new gasket. Tighten the bolts to 18 ft. lbs. (24 Nm).
- Exhaust Y-pipe
- Heated Oxygen (HO2S) sensor connector
- Oil level sensor connector
- Cooler lines
- Starter motor
- Oil filter

5. Fill the crankcase.

6. Start the engine and check for leaks.

Oil Pump

REMOVAL & INSTALLATION

2.5L and 4.0L Engines

1. Before servicing the vehicle, refer to the precautions in the beginning of this section.

2. Drain the engine oil.

3. Remove or disconnect the following:
- Negative battery cable
- Oil pan

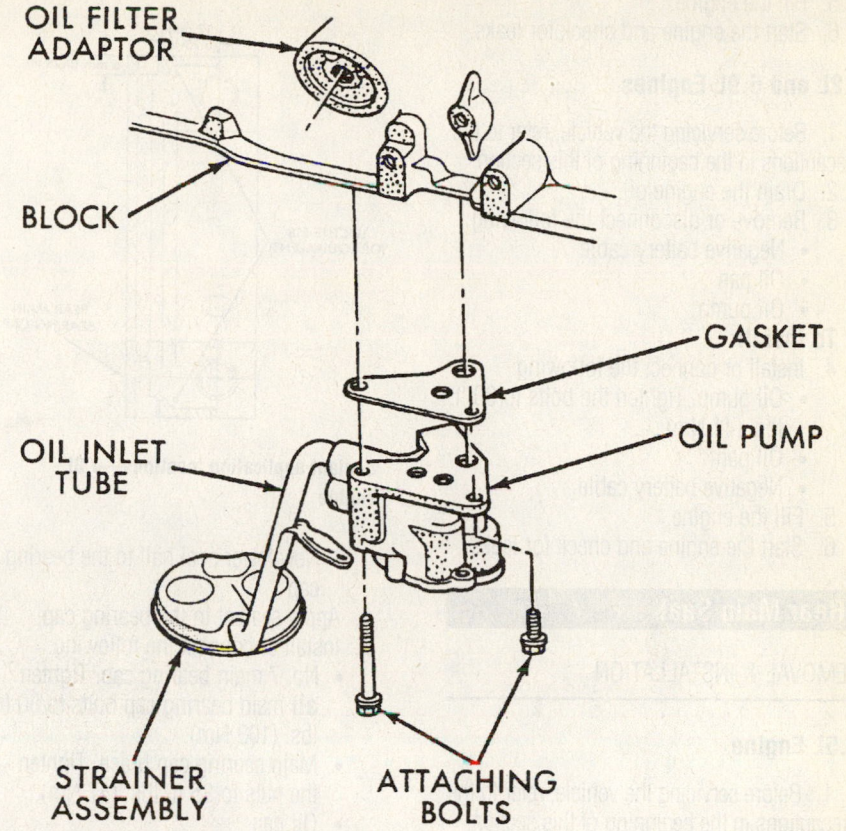

Exploded view of the oil pump assembly—2.5L and 4.0L engine

- Oil pump and pickup tube

➡ **If the oil pump is not to be serviced, do not disturb the position of the oil inlet tube and strainer assembly in the pump body. If the tube is moved within the pump body, a replacement tube and strainer assembly must be installed to assure an airtight seal.**

To install:

4. Install or connect the following:
- Oil pump. Tighten the mounting bolts to 17 ft. lbs. (23 Nm).
- Oil pan
- Negative battery cable

5. Fill the engine with the proper type and quantity of oil.

6. Start the engine and check for leaks.

4.7L Engine

1. Before servicing the vehicle, refer to the precautions in the beginning of this section.

2. Drain the engine oil.

3. Remove or disconnect the following:
- Valve covers
- Front cover
- Timing chains and sprockets

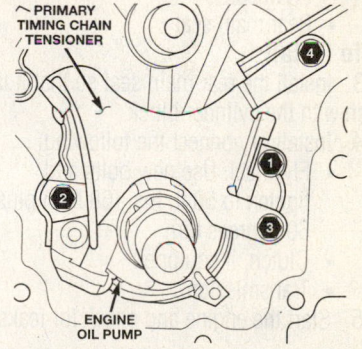

Oil pump and chain tensioner torque sequence—4.7L engine

- Oil pan and pickup tube
- Oil pump and primary timing chain tensioner

To install:

4. Install or connect the following:
- Oil pump and primary timing chain tensioner. Tighten the bolts in sequence to 21 ft. lbs. (28 Nm).
- Oil pan and pickup tube
- Timing chains and sprockets
- Front cover
- Valve covers

Timing belt service is covered in Section 4 of this manual

5. Fill the engine.
6. Start the engine and check for leaks.

5.2L and 5.9L Engines

1. Before servicing the vehicle, refer to the precautions in the beginning of this section.
2. Drain the engine oil.
3. Remove or disconnect the following:
   - Negative battery cable
   - Oil pan
   - Oil pump

To install:

4. Install or connect the following:
   - Oil pump. Tighten the bolts to 30 ft. lbs. (41 Nm).
   - Oil pan
   - Negative battery cable
5. Fill the engine.
6. Start the engine and check for leaks.

Rear Main Seal

REMOVAL & INSTALLATION

2.5L Engine

1. Before servicing the vehicle, refer to the precautions in the beginning of this section.
2. Remove or disconnect the following:
   - Transmission
   - Clutch, if equipped
   - Flywheel
   - Rear main seal

To install:

3. Install the rear main seal so that it is flush with the cylinder block.
4. Install or connect the following:
   - Flywheel. Use new bolts and tighten to 50 ft. lbs. (68 Nm) plus a 60 degrees turn
   - Clutch, if equipped
   - Transmission
5. Start the engine and check for leaks.

4.0L Engine

1. Before servicing the vehicle, refer to the precautions in the beginning of this section.
2. Drain the engine oil.
3. Remove or disconnect the following:
   - Negative battery cable
   - Oil pan
   - Main bearing cap brace
   - No. 7 main bearing cap
4. Loosen the other main bearing cap bolts for clearance and remove the rear main seal halves.

To install:

5. Install or connect the following:
   - New upper seal half to the cylinder block

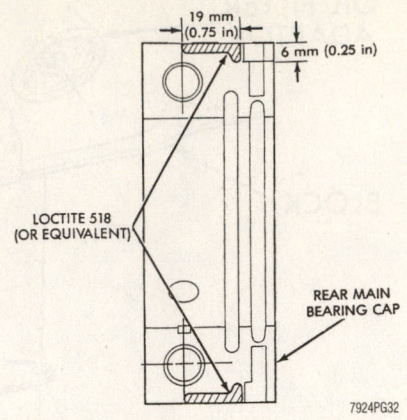

Sealant application locations—4.0L engine

   - New lower seal half to the bearing cap
6. Apply sealant to the bearing cap.
7. Install or connect the following:
   - No. 7 main bearing cap. Tighten **all** main bearing cap bolts to 80 ft. lbs. (108 Nm).
   - Main bearing cap brace. Tighten the nuts to 35 ft. lbs. (47 Nm).
   - Oil pan
   - Negative battery cable
8. Fill the engine.
9. Start the engine and check for leaks.

4.7L Engine

1. Before servicing the vehicle, refer to the precautions in the beginning of this section.
2. Remove or disconnect the following:

   - Transmission
   - Flexplate
3. Thread Oil Seal Remover 8506 into the rear main seal as far as possible and remove the rear main seal.

To install:

4. Install or connect the following:
   - Seal Guide 8349-2 onto the crankshaft
   - Rear main seal on the seal guide
   - Rear main seal, using the Crankshaft Rear Oil Seal Installer 8349 and Driver Handle C-4171; tap it into place until the installer is flush with the cylinder block
   - Flexplate. Tighten the bolts to 45 ft. lbs. (60 Nm).
   - Transmission
5. Start the engine and check for leaks.

5.2L and 5.9L Engines

1. Before servicing the vehicle, refer to the precautions in the beginning of this section.
2. Drain the engine oil.
3. Remove or disconnect the following:
   - Oil pan
   - Oil pump
   - Rear main bearing cap
4. Loosen the other main bearing cap bolts for clearance and remove the rear main seal halves.

To install:

5. Install or connect the following:
   - New upper seal half to the cylinder block
   - New lower seal half to the bearing cap

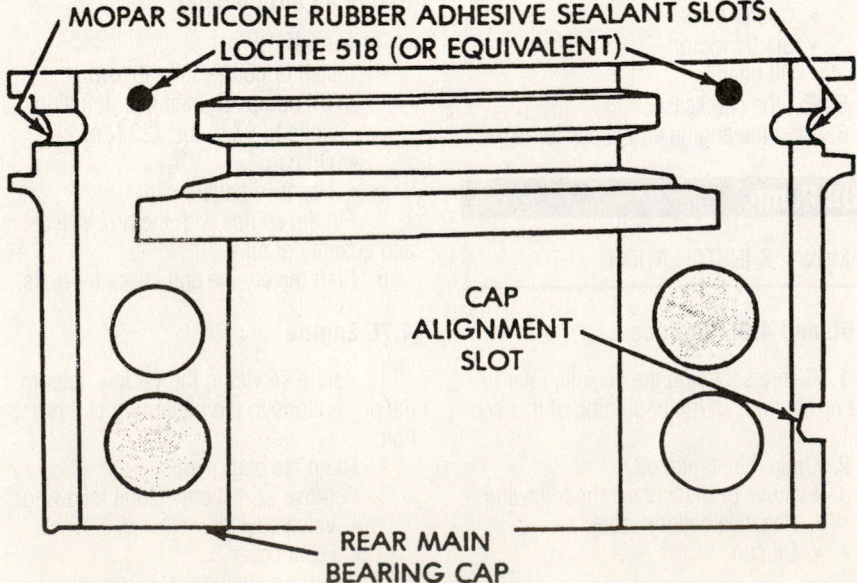

Sealant application locations —5.2L and 5.9L engines

6. Apply sealant to the rear main bearing cap.

7. Install or connect the following:
- Rear main bearing cap. Tighten **all** main bearing cap bolts to 85 ft. lbs. (115 Nm).
- Oil pump and oil pan

8. Fill the engine.

9. Start the engine and check for leaks.

Timing Chain, Sprockets, Front Cover and Seal

REMOVAL & INSTALLATION

2.5L and 4.0L Engines

1. Before servicing the vehicle, refer to the precautions in the beginning of this section.

2. Remove or disconnect the following:
- Negative battery cable
- Accessory drive belt
- Cooling fan and shroud
- Crankshaft damper
- Front crankshaft seal
- Accessory brackets
- Front cover

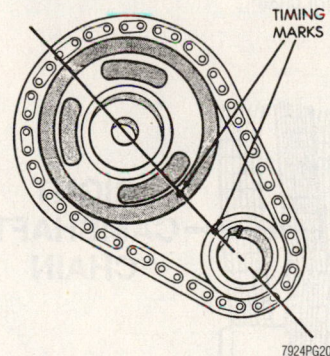

TIMING MARKS

7924PG20

Timing chain alignment marks—2.5L and 4.0L engines

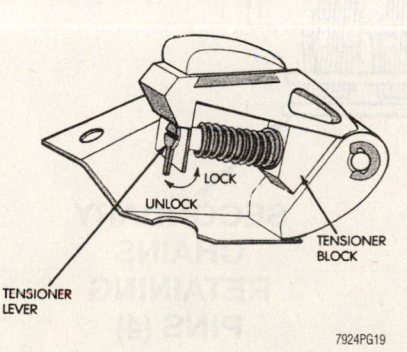

LOCK
UNLOCK
TENSIONER BLOCK
TENSIONER LEVER

7924PG19

Timing chain tensioner—2.5L engines

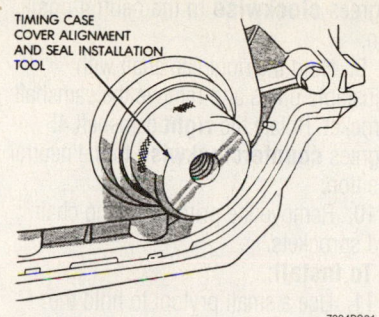

TIMING CASE COVER ALIGNMENT AND SEAL INSTALLATION TOOL

7924PG21

Timing Case Cover Alignment and Seal Installation Tool 6139—2.5L and 4.0L engines

- Oil slinger

3. Rotate the crankshaft so that the timing marks are aligned.

4. Remove the timing chain and sprockets.

To install:

5. For 2.5L engines, turn the timing chain tensioner lever to the unlock (down) position. Pull the tensioner block toward the tensioner lever to compress the spring. Hold the block and turn the tensioner lever to the lock (up) position.

6. Install the timing chain and sprockets with the timing marks aligned. Tighten the camshaft sprocket bolt to 80 ft. lbs. (108 Nm) for 2.5L engines or to 50 ft. lbs. (68 Nm) for 4.0L engines.

7. For 2.5L engines, release the timing chain tensioner.

8. Install or connect the following:
- Oil slinger
- New front crankshaft seal to the front cover
- Front cover, using a new gasket
- Timing Case Cover Alignment and Seal Installation Tool 6139 in the crankshaft opening to center the front cover

9. Tighten the front cover bolts as follows:

a. Step 1: Cover-to-block ¼ inch bolts to 60 inch lbs. (7 Nm)

b. Step 2: Cover-to-block 5⁄16 inch bolts to 16 ft. lbs. (22 Nm)

c. Step 3: Oil pan-to-cover ¼ inch bolts to 85 inch lbs. (9.5 Nm)

d. Step 4: Oil pan-to-cover 5⁄16 inch bolts to 11 ft. lbs. (15 Nm)

10. Install or connect the following:
- Accessory brackets
- Crankshaft damper. Tighten the bolt to 80 ft. lbs. (108 Nm).
- Cooling fan and shroud
- Accessory drive belt
- Negative battery cable

11. Start the engine and check for leaks.

4.7L Engine

1. Before servicing the vehicle, refer to the precautions in the beginning of this section.

2. Drain the cooling system.

3. Remove or disconnect the following:

- Negative battery cable
- Valve covers

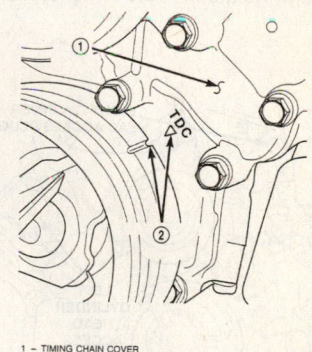

TDC

1 – TIMING CHAIN COVER
2 – CRANKSHAFT TIMING MARKS

9308PG04

Crankshaft timing marks—4.7L engine

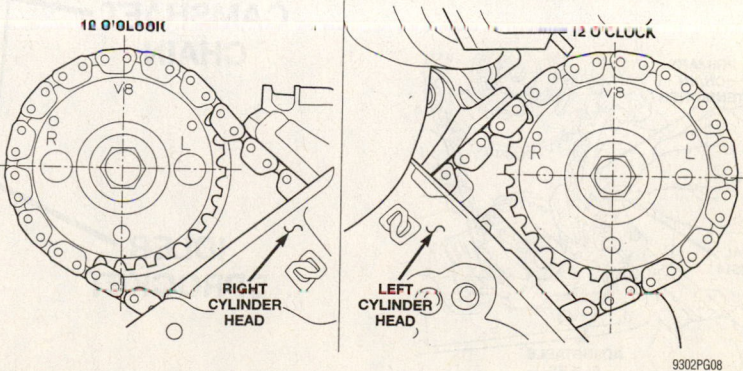

12 O'CLOCK **12 O'CLOCK**

V8 **V8**

R **L** **R** **L**

RIGHT CYLINDER HEAD **LEFT CYLINDER HEAD**

9302PG08

Camshaft positioning—4.7L engine

- Camshaft Position (CMP) sensor
- Engine cooling fan and shroud
- Accessory drive belt
- Heater hoses
- Lower radiator hose
- Power steering pump

4. Rotate the crankshaft so that the crankshaft timing mark aligns with the Top Dead Center (TDC) mark on the front cover, and the **V8** marks on the camshaft sprockets are at 12 o'clock.

5. Remove or disconnect the following:

- Crankshaft damper
- Oil fill housing
- Accessory drive belt tensioner
- Alternator
- A/C compressor
- Front cover
- Front crankshaft seal
- Cylinder head access plugs
- Secondary timing chain guides

6. Compress the primary timing chain tensioner and install a lockpin.

7. Remove the secondary timing chain tensioners.

8. Hold the left camshaft with adjustable pliers and remove the sprocket and chain. Rotate the **left** camshaft 15 degrees **clockwise** to the neutral position.

9. Hold the right camshaft with adjustable pliers and remove the camshaft sprocket. Rotate the **right** camshaft 45 degrees **counterclockwise** to the neutral position.

10. Remove the primary timing chain and sprockets.

To install:

11. Use a small prytool to hold the ratchet pawl and compress the secondary timing chain tensioners in a vise and install locking pins.

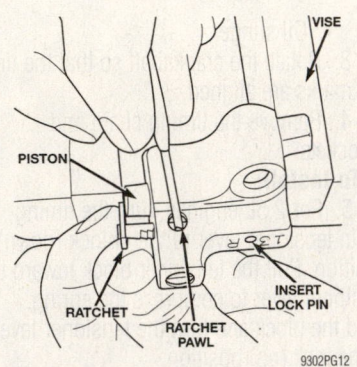

Secondary timing chain tensioner preparation—4.7L engine

➡ The black bolts fasten the guide to the engine block and the silver bolts fasten the guide to the cylinder head.

12. Install or connect the following:

- Secondary timing chain guides. Tighten the bolts to 21 ft. lbs. (28 Nm).
- Secondary timing chains to the idler sprocket so that the double plated links on each chain are visible through the slots in the primary idler sprocket

13. Lock the secondary timing chains to the idler sprocket with Timing Chain Locking tool 8515 as shown.

14. Align the primary chain double plated links with the idler sprocket timing mark and the single plated link with the crankshaft sprocket timing mark.

15. Install the primary chain and sprockets. Tighten the idler sprocket bolt to 25 ft. lbs. (34 Nm).

16. Align the secondary chain single plated links with the timing marks on the secondary sprockets. Align the dot at the **L** mark on the left sprocket with the plated link on the left chain and the dot at the **R** mark on the right sprocket with the plated link on the right chain.

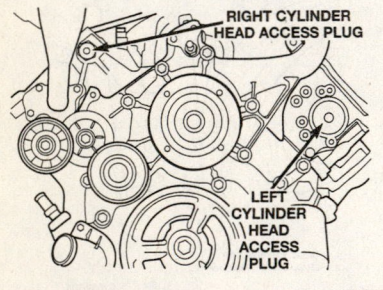

Cylinder head access plug locations—4.7L engine

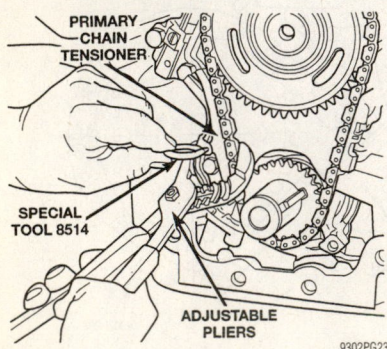

Compress and lock the primary chain tensioner—4.7L engine

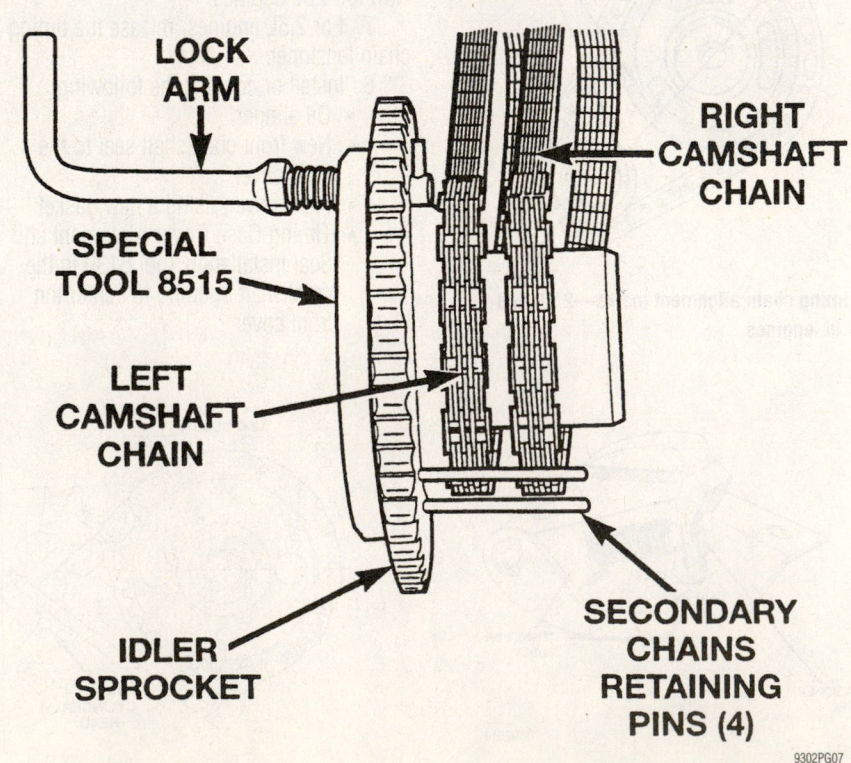

Use the Timing Chain Locking tool to lock the timing chains on the idler gear—4.7L engine

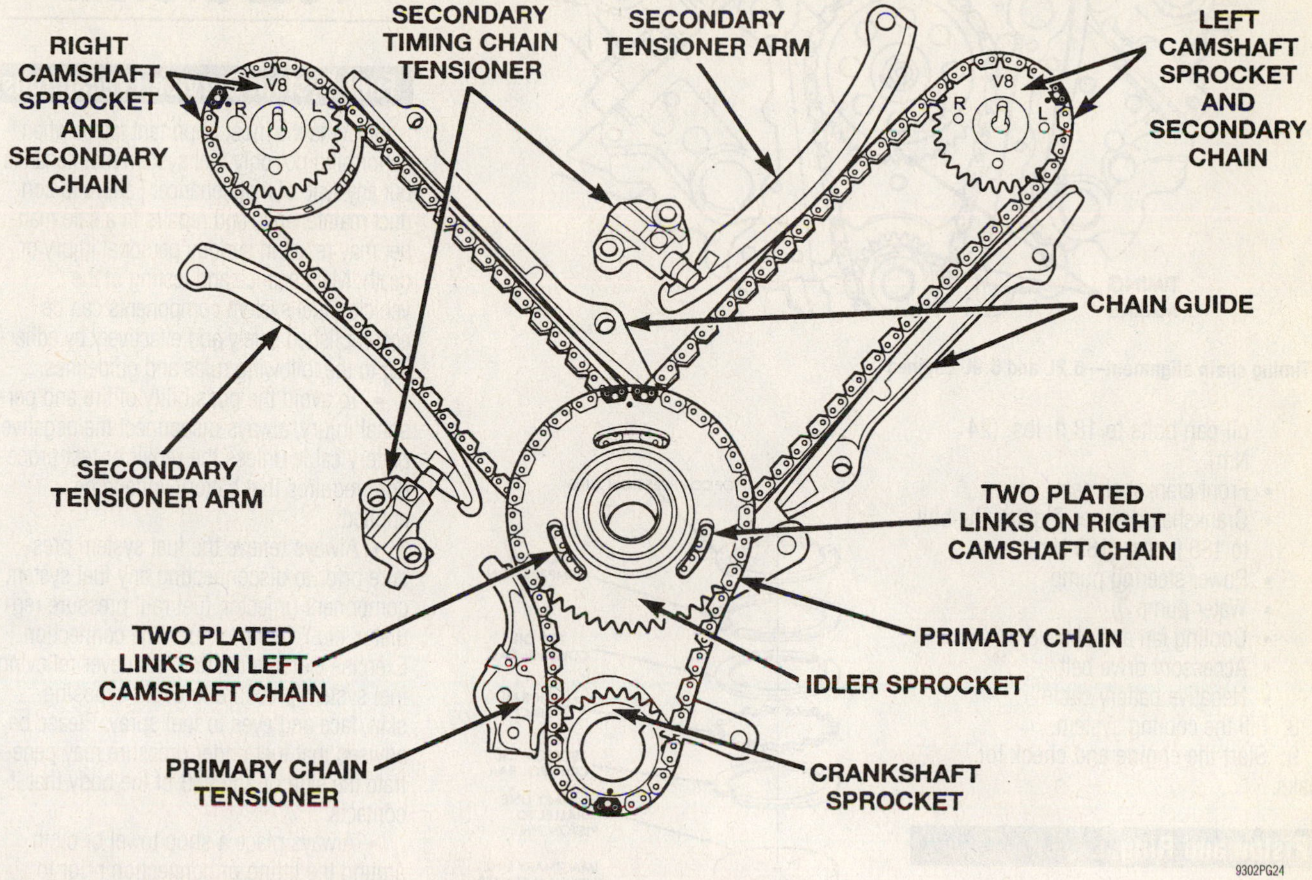

RIGHT CAMSHAFT SPROCKET AND SECONDARY CHAIN

SECONDARY TIMING CHAIN TENSIONER

SECONDARY TENSIONER ARM

LEFT CAMSHAFT SPROCKET AND SECONDARY CHAIN

CHAIN GUIDE

SECONDARY TENSIONER ARM

TWO PLATED LINKS ON RIGHT CAMSHAFT CHAIN

PRIMARY CHAIN

TWO PLATED LINKS ON LEFT CAMSHAFT CHAIN

IDLER SPROCKET

PRIMARY CHAIN TENSIONER

CRANKSHAFT SPROCKET

9302PG24

Timing chain system and alignment marks—4.7L engine

17. Rotate the camshafts back from the neutral position and install the camshaft sprockets.

18. Remove the secondary chain locking tool.

19. Remove the primary and secondary timing chain tensioner locking pins.

20. Hold the camshaft sprockets with a spanner wrench and tighten the retaining bolts to 90 ft. lbs. (122 Nm).

21. Install or connect the following:
- Front cover. Tighten the bolts, in sequence, to 40 ft. lbs. (54 Nm).
- Front crankshaft seal
- Cylinder head access plugs
- A/C compressor
- Alternator
- Accessory drive belt tensioner. Tighten the bolt to 40 ft. lbs. (54 Nm).
- Oil fill housing
- Crankshaft damper. Tighten the bolt to 130 ft. lbs. (175 Nm).
- Power steering pump
- Lower radiator hose
- Heater hoses
- Accessory drive belt
- Engine cooling fan and shroud
- Camshaft Position (CMP) sensor
- Valve covers
- Negative battery cable

22. Fill the cooling system.

23. Start the engine and check for leaks.

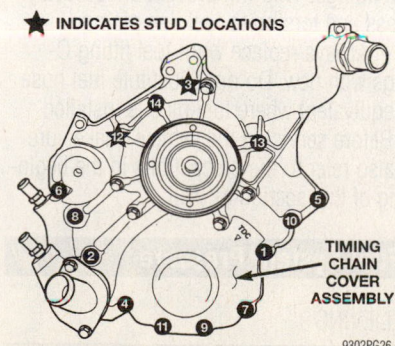

★ INDICATES STUD LOCATIONS

TIMING CHAIN COVER ASSEMBLY

9302PG26

Timing chain cover bolt torque sequence—4.7L engine

5.2L and 5.9L Engines

1. Before servicing the vehicle, refer to the precautions in the beginning of this section.

2. Drain the cooling system.

3. Remove or disconnect the following:
- Negative battery cable
- Accessory drive belt
- Cooling fan and shroud
- Water pump
- Power steering pump
- Crankshaft damper
- Front crankshaft seal
- Front cover

4. Rotate the crankshaft so that the camshaft sprocket and crankshaft sprocket timing marks are aligned.

5. Remove the timing chain and sprockets.

To install:

6. Install the timing chain and sprockets with the timing marks aligned. Tighten the camshaft sprocket bolt to 50 ft. lbs. (68 Nm).

7. Install or connect the following:
- Front cover. Tighten the cover bolts to 30 ft. lbs. (41 Nm) and the

Refer to Section 1 for engine rebuilding specifications

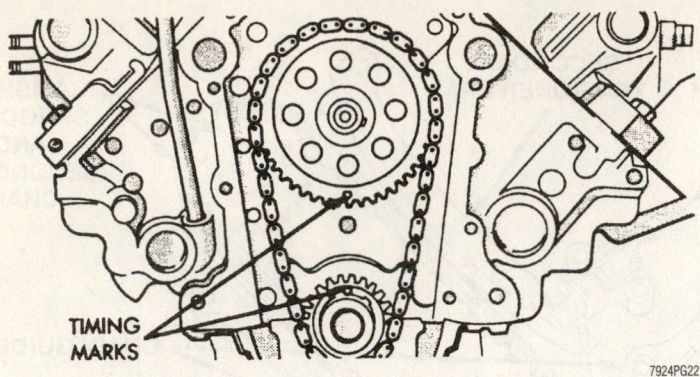

TIMING MARKS

7924PG22

Timing chain alignment—5.2L and 5.9L engines

oil pan bolts to 18 ft. lbs. (24 Nm).

- Front crankshaft seal
- Crankshaft damper. Tighten the bolt to 135 ft. lbs. (183 Nm).
- Power steering pump
- Water pump
- Cooling fan and shroud
- Accessory drive belt
- Negative battery cable

8. Fill the cooling system.
9. Start the engine and check for leaks.

Piston and Ring

POSITIONING

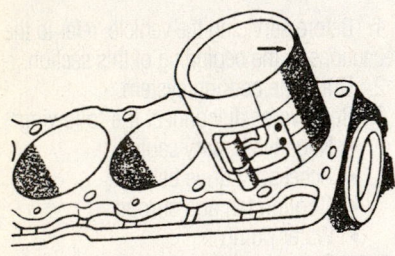

7924AG34

Piston to engine positioning—2.5L, 4.0L, 5.2L, and 5.9L engines

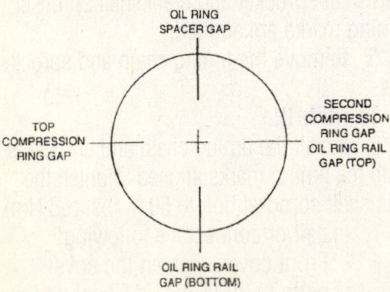

OIL RING SPACER GAP

TOP COMPRESSION RING GAP

SECOND COMPRESSION RING GAP OIL RING RAIL GAP (TOP)

OIL RING RAIL GAP (BOTTOM)

7924AG28

Piston ring end-gap spacing—2.5L, 5.2L, and 5.9L engines

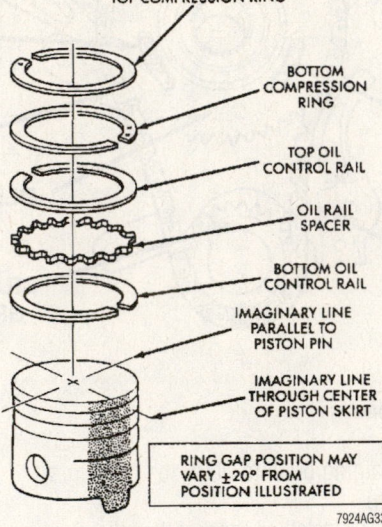

TOP COMPRESSION RING

BOTTOM COMPRESSION RING

TOP OIL CONTROL RAIL

OIL RAIL SPACER

BOTTOM OIL CONTROL RAIL

IMAGINARY LINE PARALLEL TO PISTON PIN

IMAGINARY LINE THROUGH CENTER OF PISTON SKIRT

RING GAP POSITION MAY VARY ±20° FROM POSITION ILLUSTRATED

7924AG33

Piston ring end-gap spacing—4.0L engine

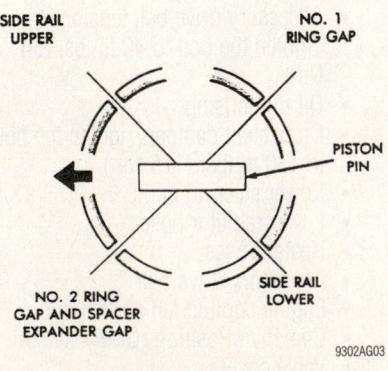

SIDE RAIL UPPER

NO. 1 RING GAP

PISTON PIN

NO. 2 RING GAP AND SPACER EXPANDER GAP

SIDE RAIL LOWER

9302AG03

Piston ring end-gap spacing—4.7L engine
Position raised "F" on piston towards front of engine

FUEL SYSTEM

Fuel System Service Precautions

Safety is the most important factor when performing not only fuel system maintenance but any type of maintenance. Failure to conduct maintenance and repairs in a safe manner may result in serious personal injury or death. Maintenance and testing of the vehicle's fuel system components can be accomplished safely and effectively by adhering to the following rules and guidelines.

- To avoid the possibility of fire and personal injury, always disconnect the negative battery cable unless the repair or test procedure requires that battery voltage be applied.
- Always relieve the fuel system pressure prior to disconnecting any fuel system component (injector, fuel rail, pressure regulator, etc.), fitting or fuel line connection. Exercise extreme caution whenever relieving fuel system pressure to avoid exposing skin, face and eyes to fuel spray. Please be advised that fuel under pressure may penetrate the skin or any part of the body that it contacts.
- Always place a shop towel or cloth around the fitting or connection prior to loosening to absorb any excess fuel due to spillage. Ensure that all fuel spillage (should it occur) is quickly removed from engine surfaces. Ensure that all fuel soaked cloths or towels are deposited into a suitable waste container.
- Always keep a dry chemical (Class B) fire extinguisher near the work area.
- Do not allow fuel spray or fuel vapors to come into contact with a spark or open flame.
- Always use a back-up wrench when loosening and tightening fuel line connection fittings. This will prevent unnecessary stress and torsion to fuel line piping.
- Always replace worn fuel fitting O-rings with new. Do not substitute fuel hose or equivalent where fuel pipe is installed.

Before servicing the vehicle, make sure to also refer to the precautions in the beginning of this section as well.

Fuel System Pressure

RELIEVING

1. Before servicing the vehicle, refer to the precautions in the beginning of this section.

2. Remove the fuel pump relay.

3. Start the engine and allow it to run until it stalls.

4. Attempt restarting the engine until it no longer runs.

5. Turn the ignition key to the **OFF** position.

6. Disconnect the negative battery cable.

7. After repairs are complete, replace the relay and connect the negative battery cable.

Fuel Filter

REMOVAL & INSTALLATION

1997–98 Models

1. Before servicing the vehicle, refer to the precautions in the beginning of this section.

2. Relieve the fuel system pressure.

3. Remove or disconnect the following:
   • Negative battery cable
   • Fuel tank
   • Retaining clamp and filter/regulator

To install:

4. Install or connect the following:
   • New O-rings on the filter/regulator
   • New gasket to the top of the fuel pump module

5. Press the filter/regulator into the top of the module until it snaps into position (a positive click must be felt or heard).

6. The arrow on top of the fuel pump module must be pointing towards the front of the vehicle. Rotate the filter/regulator until the fuel supply tube is pointed at the 10 o'clock position.

7. Install or connect the following:
   • New retainer clamp to the top of the filter/regulator
   • Fuel tank
   • Negative battery cable

8. Start the engine and check for leaks.

1999–01 Models

1. Before servicing the vehicle, refer to the precautions in the beginning of this section.

2. Relieve the fuel system pressure.

3. Remove or disconnect the following:
   • Negative battery cable
   • Fuel lines and both filter/regulator mounting bolts
   • Fuel filter

To install:

4. Install or connect the following:
   • New O-rings, lubricated with engine oil

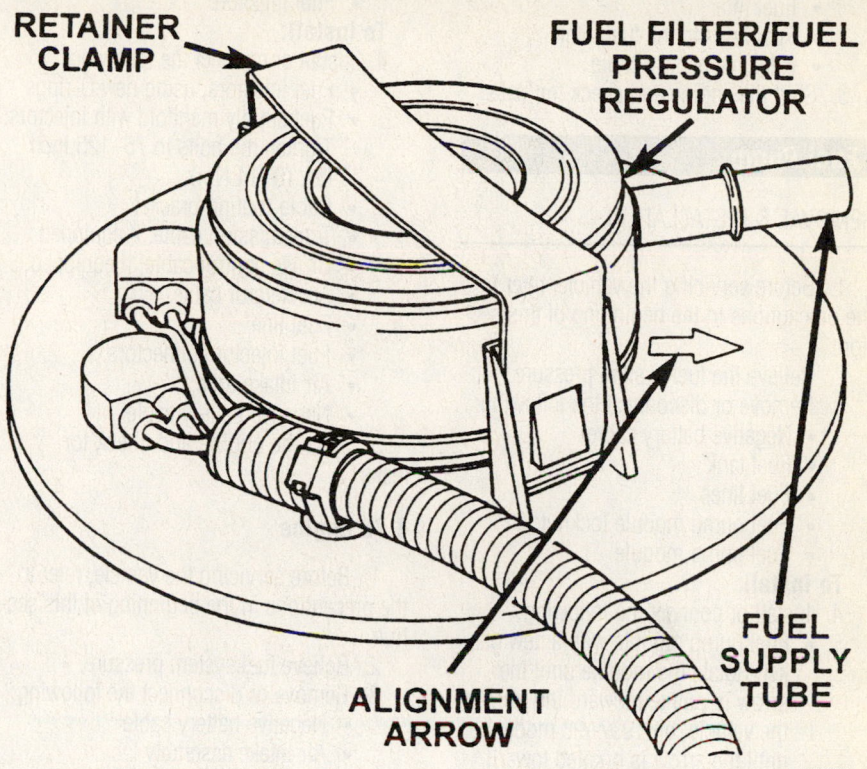

The fuel filter/pressure regulator is located on top of the fuel pump module—1997–98 models

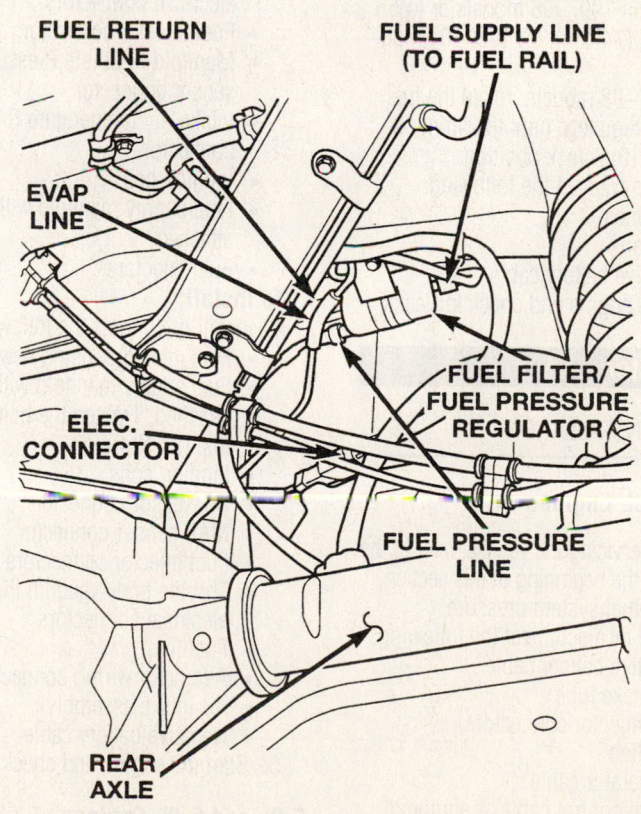

Fuel filter/pressure regulator location—1999–01 models

For complete service labor times order Nichols' Chilton Labor Guide Manual

- Fuel filter
- Fuel lines to the fuel filter
- Negative battery cable

5. Start the engine and check for leaks.

Fuel Pump

REMOVAL & INSTALLATION

1. Before servicing the vehicle, refer to the precautions in the beginning of this section.
2. Relieve the fuel system pressure.
3. Remove or disconnect the following:
   - Negative battery cable
   - Fuel tank
   - Fuel lines
   - Fuel pump module locknut
   - Fuel pump module

To install:

4. Install or connect the following:
   - Fuel pump module with a new gasket. Rotate the module until the arrow is pointed toward the front of the vehicle, on 1997–98 models or until the arrow is pointed toward the rear of the vehicle, on 1999–01 models.
   - Locknut. Tighten it to 25 ft. lbs. (34 Nm), on 1997–98 models or to 55 ft. lbs. (74 Nm), on 1999–01 models.
5. On 1997–98 models, rotate the fuel filter/pressure regulator until the fitting is pointed to the 10 o'clock position.
6. Install or connect the following:
   - Fuel lines
   - Fuel tank
   - Negative battery cable
7. Start the engine and check for leaks.

Fuel Injector

REMOVAL & INSTALLATION

2.5L and 4.0L Engines

1. Before servicing the vehicle, refer to the precautions in the beginning of this section.
2. Relieve fuel system pressure.
3. Remove or disconnect the following:
   - Negative battery cable
   - Air intake tube
   - Fuel injector connectors
   - Fuel line
   - Accelerator cable
   - Cruise control cable, if equipped
   - Transmission cable, if equipped
   - Cable routing bracket
   - Fuel supply manifold with injectors attached

- Fuel injectors

To install:

4. Install or connect the following:
   - Fuel injectors, using new O-rings
   - Fuel supply manifold with injectors. Tighten the bolts to 75–125 inch lbs. (8–14 Nm).
   - Cable routing bracket
   - Transmission cable, if equipped
   - Cruise control cable, if equipped
   - Accelerator cable
   - Fuel line
   - Fuel injector connectors
   - Air intake tube
   - Negative battery cable
5. Start the engine and check for leaks.

4.7L Engine

1. Before servicing the vehicle, refer to the precautions in the beginning of this section.
2. Relieve fuel system pressure.
3. Remove or disconnect the following:
   - Negative battery cable
   - Air intake assembly
   - Alternator wiring connectors
   - Fuel line
   - Throttle body vacuum lines and electrical connectors
   - Fuel injector connectors
   - Manifold Absolute Pressure (MAP) sensor connector
   - Intake Air Temperature (IAT) sensor connector
   - Ignition coils
   - Fuel supply manifold with injectors attached
   - Fuel injectors

To install:

4. Install or connect the following:
   - Fuel injectors, using new O-rings
   - Fuel supply manifold with injectors attached. Tighten the bolts to 20 ft. lbs. (27 Nm).
   - Ignition coils
   - IAT sensor connector
   - MAP sensor connector
   - Fuel injector connectors
   - Throttle body vacuum lines and electrical connectors
   - Fuel line
   - Alternator wiring connectors
   - Air intake assembly
   - Negative battery cable
5. Start the engine and check for leaks.

5.2L and 5.9L Engines

1. Before servicing the vehicle, refer to the precautions in the beginning of this section.

2. Relieve fuel system pressure.
3. Remove or disconnect the following:
   - Negative battery cable
   - Air intake tube
   - Throttle body
   - A/C compressor bracket
   - Fuel injector connectors
   - Fuel line
   - Fuel supply manifold with injectors
   - Fuel injectors

To install:

4. Install or connect the following:
   - Fuel injectors, using new O-rings
   - Fuel supply manifold with injectors. Tighten the bolts to 17 ft. lbs. (23 Nm).
   - Fuel line
   - Fuel injector connectors
   - A/C compressor bracket
   - Throttle body
   - Air intake tube
   - Negative battery cable
5. Start the engine and check for leaks.

DRIVE TRAIN

Transmission Assembly

REMOVAL & INSTALLATION

Automatic

1. Before servicing the vehicle, refer to the precautions in the beginning of this section.
2. Remove or disconnect the following:
   - Negative battery cable
   - Rear driveshaft
   - Crankshaft Position (CKP) sensor
   - Exhaust front pipe
   - Transmission braces, if equipped
   - Starter motor
   - Transmission oil cooler lines
   - Torque converter access cover
   - Torque converter
   - Transmission oil dipstick tube
   - Vehicle Speed (VSS) sensor connector
   - Park/Neutral switch connector
   - Shift cable
   - Throttle valve cable
   - Transmission mount and crossmember
   - Front driveshaft and transfer case, if equipped
   - Transmission flange bolts
   - Transmission

To install:
3. Install or connect the following:
- Transmission. Tighten the flange bolts to 65 ft. lbs. (87 Nm).
- Front driveshaft and transfer case, if equipped
- Transmission mount and cross-member
- Throttle valve cable
- Shift cable
- Park/Neutral switch connector
- VSS sensor connector
- Transmission oil dipstick tube
- Torque converter. Tighten the bolts to 23 ft. lbs. (31 Nm).
- Torque converter access cover
- Transmission oil cooler lines
- Starter motor
- Transmission braces, if equipped. Tighten the bolts to 30 ft. lbs. (41 Nm).
- Exhaust front pipe
- CKP sensor
- Rear driveshaft
- Negative battery cable

Manual

1. Before servicing the vehicle, refer to the precautions in the beginning of this section.
2. Remove or disconnect the following:
- Negative battery cable
- Transmission mount and cross-member
- Exhaust front pipe
- Clutch slave cylinder
- Vehicle Speed (VSS) sensor connector
- Rear driveshaft
- Front driveshaft and transfer case, if equipped
- Crankshaft Position (CKP) sensor
- Shift lever
- Reverse light switch connector
- Transmission flange bolts
- Transmission

To install:
3. Install or connect the following:
- Transmission. Tighten the ⅜ inch bolts to 27 ft. lbs. (37 Nm), the ⁷⁄₁₆ inch bolts to 43 ft. lbs. (58 Nm), and the 12mm bolts to 55 ft. lbs. (75 Nm).
- Reverse light switch connector
- Shift lever
- CKP sensor
- Front driveshaft and transfer case, if equipped
- Rear driveshaft

- VSS sensor connector
- Clutch slave cylinder
- Exhaust front pipe
- Transmission mount and cross-member
- Negative battery cable

Clutch

REMOVAL & INSTALLATION

1. Before servicing the vehicle, refer to the precautions in the beginning of this section.
2. Remove or disconnect the following:
- Negative battery cable
- Transfer case, if equipped
- Transmission
- Pressure plate. Loosen the bolts evenly in ½ turn steps.
- Clutch disk

To install:
3. Install or connect the following:
- Clutch disk and pressure plate. Tighten the pressure plate bolts evenly in ½ turns to 23 ft. lbs. (31 Nm) for 2.5L engines or to 40 ft. lbs. (54 Nm) for 4.0L engines.
- Transmission
- Transfer case, if equipped
- Negative battery cable

Hydraulic Clutch System

BLEEDING

➡ **The clutch master cylinder, slave cylinder and fluid line are serviced only as an assembly. Bleeding is not possible.**

Transfer Case Assembly

REMOVAL & INSTALLATION

1. Before servicing the vehicle, refer to the precautions in the beginning of this section.
2. Shift the transfer case into **N**.
3. Remove or disconnect the following:
- Front and rear driveshafts
- Transmission mount and cross-member. Support the transmission with a jackstand.
- Vehicle Speed (VSS) sensor connector
- Shift linkage
- Vent hose

- Vacuum hose
- Indicator switch connector
- Transfer case attaching nuts
- Transfer case

To install:
4. Install or connect the following:
- Transfer case. Tighten the nuts to 26 ft. lbs. (35 Nm).
- Indicator switch connector
- Vacuum hose
- Vent hose
- Shift linkage
- VSS sensor connector
- Transmission mount and cross-member
- Front and rear driveshafts

CV-Joints

Some Grand Cherokees have front drive-shafts that are equipped with CV-joints. The front driveshaft and CV-joints are serviced only as an assembly.

Some Grand Cherokees have front axle shafts that are equipped with CV-joints. CV-joint boot replacement is the only service possible with these axle shafts.

Axle Shaft, Bearing and Seal

REMOVAL & INSTALLATION

Front

AXLE SHAFT

1. Before servicing the vehicle, refer to the precautions in the beginning of this section.
2. Remove or disconnect the following:
- Front wheel
- Brake caliper and rotor
- Wheel speed sensor, if equipped
- Axle hub nut
- Wheel bearing and hub assembly
- Axle shaft

To install:
3. Install or connect the following:
- Axle shaft
- Wheel bearing and hub assembly
- Axle hub nut. Tighten the nut to 175 ft. lbs. (237 Nm).
- Wheel speed sensor, if equipped
- Brake caliper and rotor
- Front wheel

SEAL

1. Before servicing the vehicle, refer to the precautions in the beginning of this section.

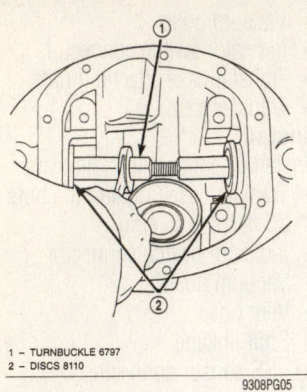

1 – TURNBUCKLE 6797
2 – DISCS 8110

9308PG05

Axle seal installation

2. Remove or disconnect the following:
- Front axle shafts
- Differential cover
- Differential and ring gear assembly
- Axle seals

To install:

3. Press the axle seals into the differential housing with Turnbuckle 6797 and Disc set 8110.

4. Install or connect the following:
- Differential and ring gear assembly. Tighten the bearing cap bolts to 45 ft. lbs. (61 Nm).
- Differential cover. Tighten the bolts to 30 ft. lbs. (41 Nm).
- Front axle shafts

5. Fill the axle assembly with gear oil and check for leaks.

Rear

C-CLIP TYPE

1. Before servicing the vehicle, refer to the precautions in the beginning of this section.

2. Remove or disconnect the following:
- Rear wheel
- Brake drum
- Differential cover
- Differential gear shaft retainer
- Differential gear shaft
- C-clip

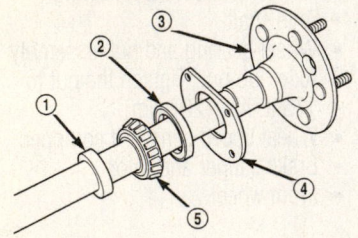

1 – RETAINING RING
2 – SEAL
3 – AXLE
4 – RETAINING PLATE
5 – AXLE BEARING

9308PG06

Rear axle seal and bearing components

- Axle shaft
- Axle seal
- Axle bearing

To install:

3. Install or connect the following:
- Axle bearing
- Axle seal
- Axle shaft
- C-clip
- Differential gear shaft. Use Loctite• and tighten the retainer to 14 ft. lbs. (19 Nm).
- Differential cover. Tighten the bolts to 30 ft. lbs. (41 Nm).
- Brake drum
- Rear wheel

4. Fill the axle assembly with gear oil and check for leaks.

NON C-CLIP TYPE

1. Before servicing the vehicle, refer to the precautions in the beginning of this section.

2. Remove or disconnect the following:
- Rear wheel
- Brake caliper and rotor, if equipped
- Brake drum, if equipped
- Axle retainer nuts
- Axle shaft, seal and bearing assembly

3. Split the bearing retainer with a chisel and remove the retainer ring.

4. Press the bearing off the axle shaft.

5. Remove the axle seal and retaining plate.

To install:

6. Install the retaining plate and axle seal onto the axle shaft.

7. Pack the wheel bearing with axle grease and press the bearing on to the axle shaft.

8. Press the retaining ring onto the axle shaft.

9. Install or connect the following:
- Axle shaft, seal and bearing assembly. Tighten the nuts to 45 ft. lbs. (61 Nm).
- Brake caliper and rotor, if equipped
- Brake drum, if equipped
- Rear wheel

10. Fill the axle assembly with gear oil and check for leaks.

Pinion Seal

REMOVAL & INSTALLATION

C-Clip Type

1. Before servicing the vehicle, refer to the precautions in the beginning of this section.

2. Remove or disconnect the following:
- Wheels
- Brake drums
- Driveshaft

3. Check the bearing preload with an inch lb. torque wrench.

4. Remove the pinion flange and seal.

To install:

➡ **Use a new pinion nut for assembly.**

5. Install the new pinion seal and flange. Tighten the nut to 200 ft. lbs. (271 Nm).

6. Check the bearing preload. The bearing preload should be equal to the reading taken earlier, plus 5 inch lbs.

7. If the preload torque is low, tighten the pinion nut in 5 inch lb. increments until the torque value is reached. Do not exceed 350 ft. lbs. (474 Nm) pinion nut torque.

8. If the pinion bearing preload torque cannot be attained at maximum pinion nut torque, replace the collapsible spacer.

9. Install or connect the following:
- Driveshaft
- Brake drums
- Wheels

10. Fill the axle assembly with gear oil and check for leaks.

Non C-Clip Type

FRONT

1. Before servicing the vehicle, refer to the precautions in the beginning of this section.

2. Remove or disconnect the following:
- Wheels
- Brake rotors
- Driveshaft

3. Check the bearing preload with an inch lb. torque wrench.

4. Remove the pinion flange and seal.

To install:

➡ **Use a new pinion nut for assembly.**

5. Install the new pinion seal and flange. Tighten the nut to 160 ft. lbs. (217 Nm).

6. Check the bearing preload. The bearing preload should be equal to the reading taken earlier, plus 5 inch lbs.

7. If the preload torque is low, tighten the pinion nut in 5 inch lb. increments until the torque value is reached. Do not exceed 260 ft. lbs. (353 Nm) pinion nut torque.

8. If the pinion bearing preload torque can not be attained at maximum pinion nut torque, replace the collapsible spacer.

9. Install or connect the following:
- Driveshaft
- Brake rotors
- Wheels

10. Fill the axle assembly with gear oil and check for leaks.

REAR

1. Before servicing the vehicle, refer to the precautions in the beginning of this section.

2. Remove or disconnect the following:
- Wheels
- Brake rotors or drums
- Driveshaft

3. Check the bearing preload with an inch lb. torque wrench.

4. Remove the pinion flange and seal.

To install:

➡ **Use a new pinion nut for assembly.**

5. Install the new pinion seal and flange. Tighten the nut to 160 ft. lbs. (217 Nm).

6. Check the bearing preload. The bearing preload should be equal to the reading taken earlier, plus 5 inch lbs.

7. If the preload torque is low, tighten the pinion nut in 5 inch lb. increments until the torque value is reached. Do not exceed 260 ft. lbs. (353 Nm) pinion nut torque.

8. If the pinion bearing preload torque can not be attained at maximum pinion nut torque, remove one or more pinion preload shims.

9. Install or connect the following:
- Driveshaft
- Brake rotors or drums
- Wheels

10. Fill the axle assembly with gear oil and check for leaks.

Axle Housing Assembly

REMOVAL & INSTALLATION

Front

1. Before servicing the vehicle, refer to the precautions in the beginning of this section.

2. Remove or disconnect the following:
- Wheels
- Brake calipers and rotors
- Wheel speed sensor, if equipped
- Vent hose
- Driveshaft
- Stabilizer bar links
- Track bar
- Shock absorbers
- Tie rod ends
- Steering damper
- Upper and lower control arms

- Coil springs
- Axle housing

To install:

➡ **The weight of the vehicle must be supported by the springs when the control arm and track bar fasteners are tightened.**

3. Install or connect the following:
- Axle housing and coil springs to the vehicle
- Upper and lower control arms
- Steering damper
- Tie rod ends
- Shock absorbers
- Track bar
- Stabilizer bar links. Tighten the nuts to 70 ft. lbs. (95 Nm).
- Driveshaft
- Vent hose
- Wheel speed sensor, if equipped
- Brake calipers and rotors
- Front wheels

4. Tighten the upper control arm nuts to 55 ft. lbs. (75 Nm), the lower control arm nuts to 85 ft. lbs. (115 Nm) and the track bar bolts to 74 ft. lbs. (100 Nm).

5. Check the wheel alignment and adjust as necessary.

Rear

CHEROKEE

1. Before servicing the vehicle, refer to the precautions in the beginning of this section.

2. Remove or disconnect the following:
- Rear wheels
- Brake drums
- Parking brake cables
- Wheel speed sensors, if equipped
- Brake hose
- Vent hose
- Driveshaft
- Stabilizer bar links
- Shock absorbers
- Axle housing

To install:

3. Install or connect the following:
- Axle housing. Tighten the nuts to 52 ft. lbs. (70 Nm).
- Shock absorbers
- Stabilizer bar links. Tighten the nuts to 55 ft. lbs. (74 Nm).
- Driveshaft
- Vent hose
- Brake hose
- Wheel speed sensors, if equipped
- Parking brake cables
- Brake drums
- Rear wheels

WRANGLER AND 1997–98 GRAND CHEROKEE

1. Before servicing the vehicle, refer to the precautions in the beginning of this section.

2. Remove or disconnect the following:
- Rear wheels
- Brake rotors or drums
- Parking brake cables
- Wheel speed sensors, if equipped
- Brake hose
- Vent hose
- Driveshaft
- Stabilizer bar links
- Shock absorbers
- Track bar
- Upper and lower control arms
- Coil springs
- Axle housing

To install:

➡ **The weight of the vehicle must be supported by the springs when the control arm and track bar fasteners are tightened.**

3. Install or connect the following:
- Axle housing and coil springs to the vehicle
- Upper and lower control arms
- Track bar
- Shock absorbers
- Stabilizer bar links. Tighten the nuts to 40 ft. lbs. (54 Nm).
- Driveshaft
- Vent hose
- Brake hose
- Wheel speed sensors, if equipped
- Parking brake cables
- Brake rotors or drums
- Rear wheels

4. Tighten the upper control arm bolts to 55 ft. lbs. (75 Nm), the lower control arm bolts to 130 ft. lbs. (177 Nm) and the track bar bolts to 74 ft. lbs. (100 Nm).

1999–01 GRAND CHEROKEE

1. Before servicing the vehicle, refer to the precautions in the beginning of this section.

2. Remove or disconnect the following:
- Rear wheels
- Brake rotors
- Parking brake cables
- Wheel speed sensors, if equipped
- Brake hose
- Vent hose
- Driveshaft
- Stabilizer bar links
- Shock absorbers

- Track bar
- Upper and lower control arms
- Coil springs
- Axle housing

To install:

➡ **The weight of the vehicle must be supported by the springs when the control arm and track bar fasteners are tightened.**

3. Install or connect the following:
- Axle housing and coil springs to the vehicle
- Upper and lower control arms. Tighten the upper control arm ball joint nut to 90 ft. lbs. (122 Nm).
- Track bar
- Shock absorbers
- Stabilizer bar links. Tighten the nuts to 40 ft. lbs. (54 Nm).
- Driveshaft
- Vent hose
- Brake hose
- Wheel speed sensors, if equipped
- Parking brake cables
- Brake rotors
- Rear wheels

4. Tighten the lower control arm bolts to 130 ft. lbs. (177 Nm) and the track bar bolts to 74 ft. lbs. (100 Nm).

STEERING AND SUSPENSION

Air Bag

✳✳ CAUTION

Some vehicles are equipped with an air bag system. The system must be disarmed before performing service on, or around, system components, the steering column, instrument panel components, wiring and sensors. Failure to follow the safety precautions and the disarming procedure could result in accidental air bag deployment, possible injury and unnecessary system repairs.

PRECAUTIONS

Several precautions must be observed when handling the inflator module to avoid accidental deployment and possible personal injury.

- Never carry the inflator module by the wires or connector on the underside of the module.
- When carrying a live inflator module, hold securely with both hands, and ensure that the bag and trim cover are pointed away.
- Place the inflator module on a bench or other surface with the bag and trim cover facing up.
- With the inflator module on the bench, never place anything on or close to the module which may be thrown in the event of an accidental deployment.

Before servicing the vehicle, also make sure to refer to the precautions in the beginning of this section as well.

DISARMING

Disconnect and isolate the negative battery cable. Wait 2 minutes for the system capacitor to discharge before performing any service.

ARMING

To arm the system, connect the negative battery cable.

Recirculating Ball Power Steering Gear

REMOVAL & INSTALLATION

1. Before servicing the vehicle, refer to the precautions in the beginning of this section.
2. Remove or disconnect the following:

- Negative battery cable
- Power steering pressure and return lines
- Intermediate shaft
- Pitman arm
- Steering gear

To install:

3. Install or connect the following:
- Steering gear. Tighten the bolts to 70 ft. lbs. (95 Nm).
- Pitman arm. Tighten the nut to 185 ft. lbs. (251 Nm).
- Intermediate shaft. Tighten the pinch bolt to 36 ft. lbs. (49 Nm).
- Power steering pressure and return lines
- Negative battery cable

4. Fill the power steering fluid reservoir.
5. Start the engine and check for leaks.

Shock Absorber

REMOVAL & INSTALLATION

Front

1. Before servicing the vehicle, refer to the precautions in the beginning of this section.
2. Remove or disconnect the following:
- Upper nut, washer and grommet from the upper stud
- Lower fasteners
- Shock absorber

To install:

3. Install or connect the following:
- Shock absorber. Tighten the lower fasteners to 21 ft. lbs. (28 Nm).
- Upper grommet, washer, and nut to the stud. Tighten it to 17 ft. lbs. (23 Nm).

Rear

1. Before servicing the vehicle, refer to the precautions in the beginning of this section.
2. Remove or disconnect the following:

- Upper locknut and washer from the frame bracket stud, on the Grand Cherokee
- Upper mounting bolts, on the Wrangler and Cherokee
- Lower bolt, nut and washers from the axle shaft tube bracket
- Shock absorber

To install:

3. Place the shock absorber upper end in position and tighten the fasteners to the following specifications:
- Wrangler: 23 ft. lbs. (31 Nm)
- Cherokee: 17 ft. lbs. (23 Nm)
- 1997–98 Grand Cherokee: 52 ft. lbs. (70 Nm)
- 1999–01 Grand Cherokee: 80 ft. lbs. (108 Nm)

4. Place the shock absorber lower end in position and tighten the fasteners to the following specifications:
- Wrangler: 74 ft. lbs. (100 Nm)
- Cherokee: 46 ft. lbs. (62 Nm)
- 1997–98 Grand Cherokee: 68 ft. lbs. (92 Nm)
- 1999–01 Grand Cherokee: 85 ft. lbs. (115 Nm)

Coil Spring

REMOVAL & INSTALLATION

Front

1. Before servicing the vehicle, refer to the precautions in the beginning of this section.
2. Remove or disconnect the following:
   - Front wheels
   - Front driveshaft, if equipped
   - Lower suspension arm
   - Stabilizer bar links
   - Track bar
   - Drag link
   - Brake hose brackets
   - Spring retainers
   - Coil springs

To install:
3. Install or connect the following:
   - Coil springs
   - Spring retainers
   - Brake hose brackets
   - Drag link
   - Track bar. Tighten the bolt to 35 ft. lbs. (47 Nm).
   - Stabilizer bar links. Tighten the bolts to 70 ft. lbs. (95 Nm).
   - Lower suspension arm. Tighten the bolt to 133 ft. lbs. (180 Nm).
   - Front driveshaft, if equipped
   - Front wheels

Rear

1. Before servicing the vehicle, refer to the precautions in the beginning of this section.
2. Remove or disconnect the following:
   - Rear wheels
   - Sway bar links
   - Shock absorbers
   - Track bar
   - Spring retainers
   - Coil springs

To install:
3. Install or connect the following:
   - Coil springs
   - Spring retainers
   - Track bar
   - Shock absorbers
   - Sway bar links
   - Rear wheels

Leaf Springs

REMOVAL & INSTALLATION

Cherokee

1. Before servicing the vehicle, refer to the precautions in the beginning of this section.
2. Support the vehicle at the frame rails.
3. Support the rear axle with a jack.

4. Remove or disconnect the following:
   - Rear wheel
   - Stabilizer bar link
   - Axle U-bolts
   - Spring bracket
   - Leaf spring

To install:

➡ **The weight of the vehicle must be supported by the springs when the spring eye and stabilizer bar fasteners are tightened.**

5. Install or connect the following:
   - Leaf spring
   - Spring bracket
   - Axle U-bolts. Tighten the nuts to 52 ft. lbs. (70 Nm).
   - Stabilizer bar link
   - Rear wheel
6. Tighten the front spring eye bolt and nut to 115 ft. lbs. (156 Nm). Tighten the rear spring eye bolt and nut to 80 ft. lbs. (108 Nm). Tighten the stabilizer bar nuts 55 ft. lbs. (74 Nm).

Upper Ball Joint

REMOVAL & INSTALLATION

1. Before servicing the vehicle, refer to the precautions in the beginning of this section.

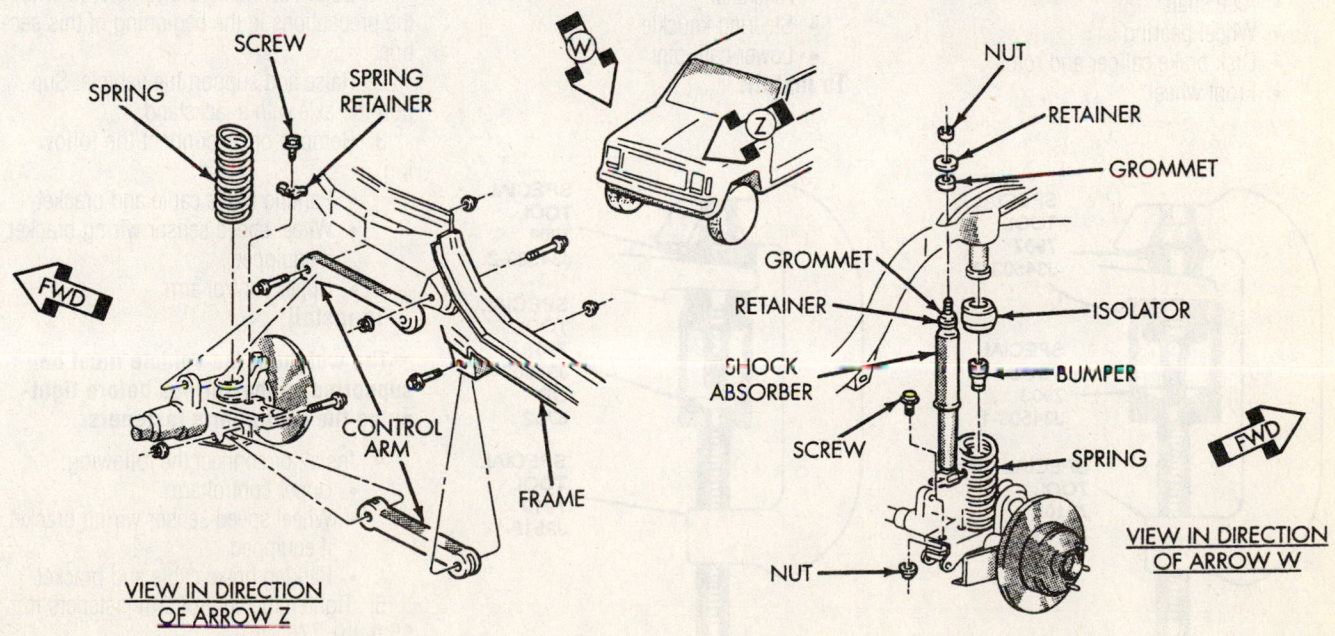

VIEW IN DIRECTION OF ARROW Z

VIEW IN DIRECTION OF ARROW W

Exploded view of the front suspension—Cherokee

7924PG25

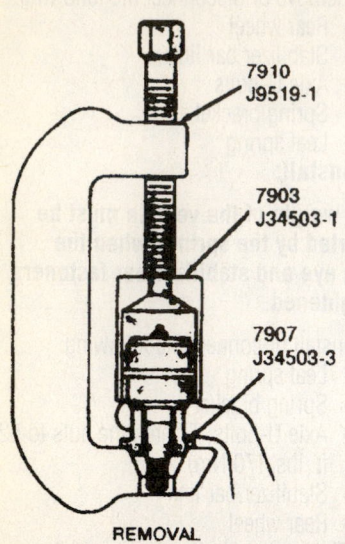

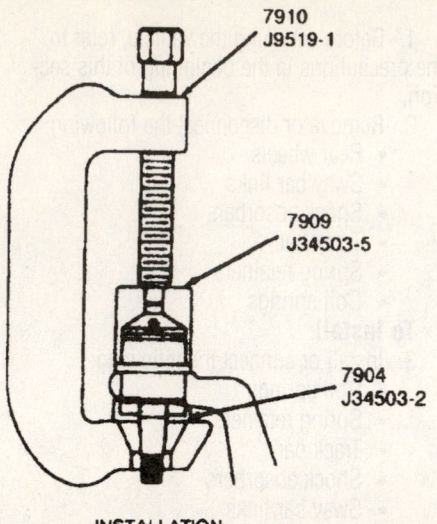

REMOVAL

INSTALLATION

7924PG26

Upper ball joint removal and installation

2. Remove or disconnect the following:
- Front wheel
- Disk brake caliper and rotor
- Wheel bearing
- Axle shaft
- Steering knuckle
- Upper ball joint

To install:

3. Install or connect the following:
- Upper ball joint
- Steering knuckle. Tighten the nuts to 100 ft. lbs. (135 Nm).
- Axle shaft
- Wheel bearing
- Disk brake caliper and rotor
- Front wheel

Lower Ball Joint

REMOVAL & INSTALLATION

1. Before servicing the vehicle, refer to the precautions in the beginning of this section.

2. Remove or disconnect the following:
- Front wheel
- Disk brake caliper and rotor
- Wheel bearing
- Axle shaft
- Steering knuckle
- Lower ball joint

To install:

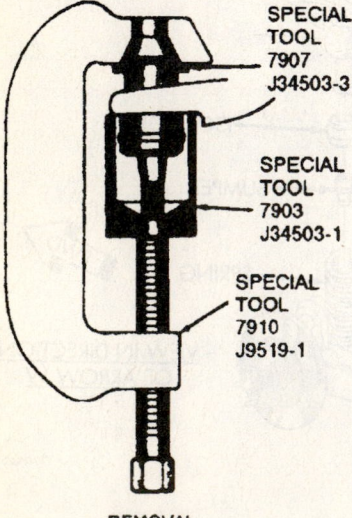

REMOVAL

Lower ball joint removal and installation

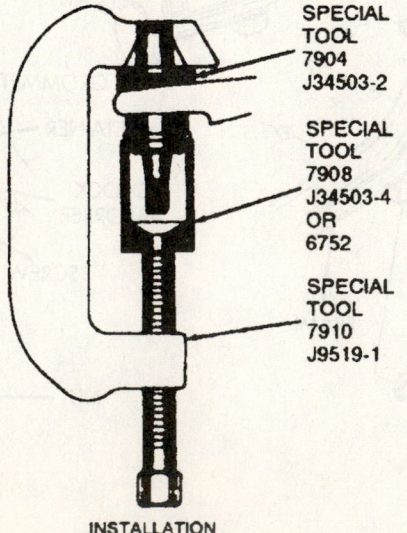

INSTALLATION

7924PG27

3. Install or connect the following:
- Lower ball joint
- Steering knuckle. Tighten the nuts to 100 ft. lbs. (135 Nm).
- Axle shaft
- Wheel bearing
- Disk brake caliper and rotor
- Front wheel

Upper Control Arm

REMOVAL & INSTALLATION

Front

1. Before servicing the vehicle, refer to the precautions in the beginning of this section.

2. Support the axle with a jackstand.

3. Unbolt and remove the upper control arm.

To install:

➡ **The weight of the vehicle must be supported by the springs before tightening the control arm fasteners.**

4. Install the control arms.

5. Tighten the axle fastener to 55 ft. lbs. (75 Nm) and the frame fastener to 66 ft. lbs. (90 Nm).

Rear

EXCEPT 1999–01 GRAND CHEROKEE

1. Before servicing the vehicle, refer to the precautions in the beginning of this section.

2. Raise and support the vehicle. Support the axle with a jackstand.

3. Remove or disconnect the following:
- Parking brake cable and bracket
- Wheel speed sensor wiring bracket, if equipped
- Upper control arm

To install:

➡ **The weight of the vehicle must be supported by the springs before tightening the control arm fasteners.**

4. Install or connect the following:
- Upper control arm
- Wheel speed sensor wiring bracket, if equipped
- Parking brake cable and bracket

5. Tighten the control arm fasteners to 55 ft. lbs. (75 Nm).

1999–01 GRAND CHEROKEE

1. Before servicing the vehicle, refer to the precautions in the beginning of this section.

2. Support the axle with a jackstand.

3. Remove or disconnect the following:

- Parking brake cable brackets
- Brake hose brackets
- Axle ball joint
- Upper control arm

To install:

➡**Use a new axle ball joint nut.**

4. Install or connect the following:

- Upper control arm. Tighten the frame bracket bolts to 74 ft. lbs. (100 Nm) and the axle ball joint nut to 105 ft. lbs. (142 Nm).
- Brake hose brackets
- Parking brake cable brackets

CONTROL ARM BUSHING REPLACEMENT

The upper control arm bushings are serviced with the control arms as complete assemblies, with the exception of the front upper axle bushing, which may be replaced after removing the upper control arm.

Front Upper Control Arm Axle Bushing

1. Before servicing the vehicle, refer to the precautions in the beginning of this section.

2. Remove the upper control arm.

3. Press the old bushing out of the axle housing.

4. Press the new bushing into the axle housing.

5. Install the upper control arm.

Lower Control Arms

REMOVAL & INSTALLATION

Front

1. Before servicing the vehicle, refer to the precautions in the beginning of this section.

2. Support the axle with a jackstand.

3. Remove or disconnect the following:

- Wheel speed sensor wiring, if equipped
- Lower control arm

To install:

➡**The weight of the vehicle must be supported by the springs before tightening the control arm fasteners.**

4. Install or connect the following:

- Lower control arm

- Wheel speed sensor wiring, if equipped

5. Tighten the control arm bolts to the following specifications:

- Wrangler and 1997–98 Grand Cherokee: Axle fastener to 85 ft. lbs. (115 Nm) and frame bracket fastener to 130 ft. lbs. (176 Nm).
- Cherokee: Both fasteners to 85 ft. lbs. (115 Nm).
- 1999–01 Grand Cherokee: Frame bracket bolt to 115 ft. lbs. (156 Nm) and axle bracket nut to 120 ft. lbs. (163 Nm).

Rear

1. Before servicing the vehicle, refer to the precautions in the beginning of this section.

2. Support the axle with a jackstand.

3. Unbolt and remove the lower control arm.

To install:

➡**The weight of the vehicle must be supported by the springs before tightening the control arm fasteners.**

4. Install the lower control arm.

5. Tighten the lower control arm fasteners to the following specifications:

- Wrangler and 1997–98 Grand Cherokee: Both fasteners to 130 ft. lbs. (177 Nm)
- 1999–01 Grand Cherokee: Frame bracket nut to 115 ft. lbs. (156 Nm) and axle bracket nut to 120 ft. lbs. (163 Nm)

CONTROL ARM BUSHING REPLACEMENT

The lower control arm bushings are serviced with the control arms as complete assemblies.

Wheel Bearings

ADJUSTMENT

Front

2-WHEEL DRIVE

1. Before servicing the vehicle, refer to the precautions in the beginning of this section.

2. Remove or disconnect the following:

- Front wheel, grease cap, cotter pin and nut cap

- Wheel bearing nut, loosen it

3. While turning the rotor, tighten the nut to 25 ft. lbs. (34 Nm) to seat the bearings.

4. Back the nut off ½ turn.

5. While turning the rotor, tighten the nut to 19 inch lbs. (2 Nm).

6. Install or connect the following:

- Nut cap, new cotter pin and the grease cap
- Wheel

4-WHEEL DRIVE

The front wheel bearings are not adjustable.

Rear

The rear axle bearing is not adjustable.

REMOVAL & INSTALLATION

Front

2WD MODELS

1. Before servicing the vehicle, refer to the precautions in the beginning of this section.

2. Remove or disconnect the following:

- Front wheel
- Brake caliper
- Grease cap
- Split pin
- Nut retainer
- Nut and washer
- Outer bearing
- Brake rotor and hub assembly
- Grease seal
- Inner bearing

To install:

➡**Use new grease seals and split pins.**

3. Pack the wheel bearings and the inside of the hub with high temperature wheel bearing grease. Add grease to the hub until it is flush with the inside diameter of the bearing cup.

4. Install or connect the following:

- Inner bearing
- Grease seal
- Brake rotor and hub assembly
- Outer bearing
- Nut and washer
- Nut retainer
- Split pin
- Grease cap
- Brake caliper
- Front wheel

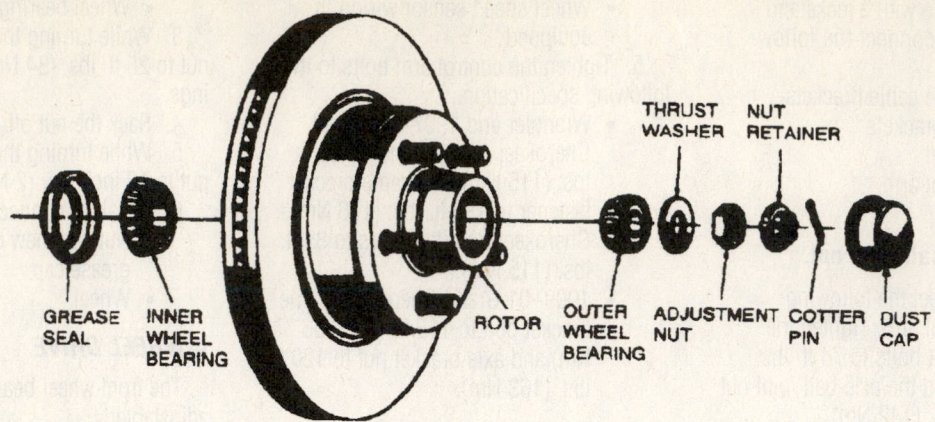

Exploded view of the front wheel bearings—2WD models

4WD MODELS

1. Before servicing the vehicle, refer to the precautions in the beginning of this section.

2. Remove or disconnect the following:
   • Front wheel
   • Brake caliper and rotor

• Axle stub shaft nut
• Hub and wheel bearing assembly
• Brake dust shield

To install:

3. Install or connect the following:
   • Brake dust shield and the hub assembly over the axle stub shaft.

Tighten the hub bolts to 75 ft. lbs. (102 Nm).
• Axle stub shaft nut. Tighten the nut to 175 ft. lbs. (237 Nm).
• Brake caliper and rotor
• Front wheel

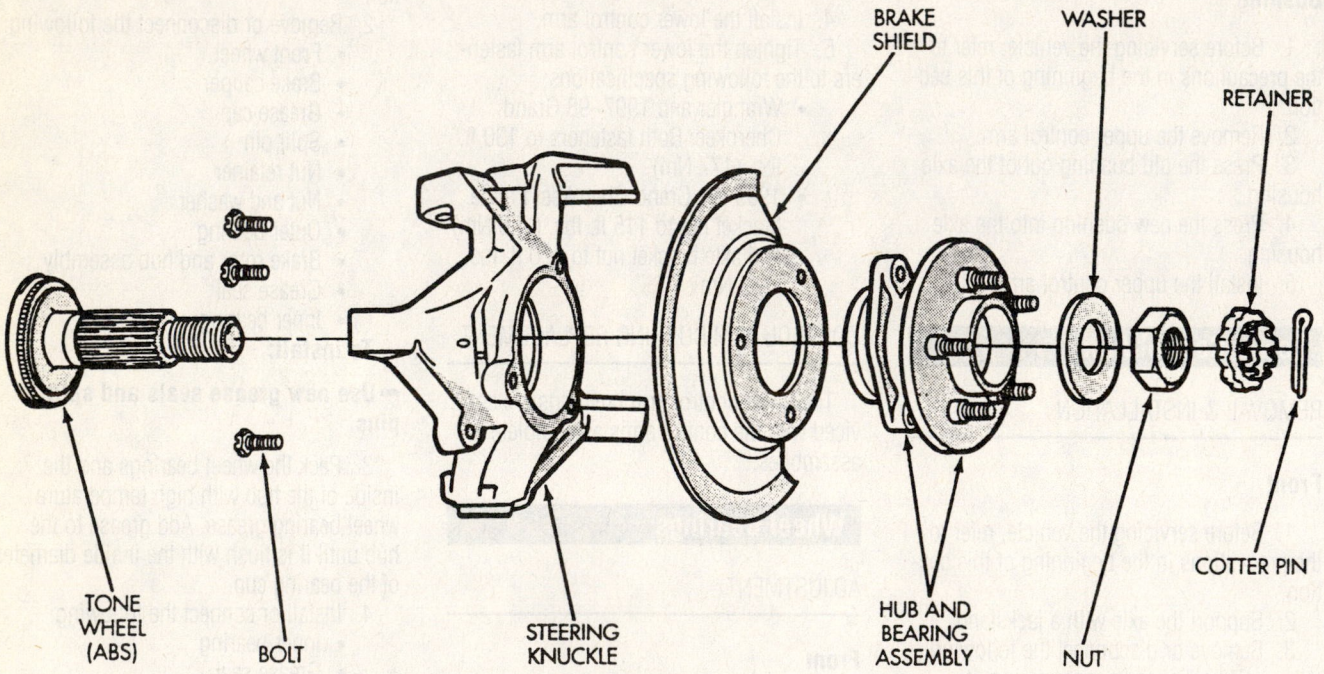

Exploded view of the hub assembly—4WD models

25

KIA

Kia-Sportage

PRECAUTIONS

Before servicing any vehicle, please be sure to read all of the following precautions, which deal with personal safety, prevention of component damage, and important points to take into consideration when servicing a motor vehicle:

• Never open, service or drain the radiator or cooling system when the engine is hot; serious burns can occur from the steam and hot coolant.

• Observe all applicable safety precautions when working around fuel. Whenever servicing the fuel system, always work in a well-ventilated area. Do not allow fuel spray or vapors to come in contact with a spark, open flame, or excessive heat (a hot drop light, for example). Keep a dry chemical fire extinguisher near the work area. Always keep fuel in a container specifically designed for fuel storage; also, always properly seal fuel containers to avoid the possibility of fire or explosion. Refer to the additional fuel system precautions later in this section.

• Fuel injection systems often remain pressurized, even after the engine has been turned **OFF**. The fuel system pressure must be relieved before disconnecting any fuel lines. Failure to do so may result in fire and/or personal injury.

• Brake fluid often contains polyglycol ethers and polyglycols. Avoid contact with the eyes and wash your hands thoroughly after handling brake fluid. If you do get brake fluid in your eyes, flush your eyes with clean, running water for 15 minutes. If eye irritation persists, or if you have taken brake fluid internally, IMMEDIATELY seek medical assistance.

• The EPA warns that prolonged contact with used engine oil may cause a number of skin disorders, including cancer! You should make every effort to minimize your exposure to used engine oil. Protective gloves should be worn when changing oil. Wash your hands and any other exposed skin areas as soon as possible after exposure to used engine oil. Soap and water, or waterless hand cleaner should be used.

• All new vehicles are now equipped with an air bag system, often referred to as a Supplemental Restraint System (SRS) or Supplemental Inflatable Restraint (SIR) system. The system must be disabled before performing service on or around system components, steering column, instrument panel components, wiring and sensors. Failure to follow safety and disabling procedures could result in accidental air bag deployment, possible personal injury and unnecessary system repairs.

• Always wear safety goggles when working with, or around, the air bag system. When carrying a non-deployed air bag, be sure the bag and trim cover are pointed away from your body. When placing a non-deployed air bag on a work surface, always face the bag and trim cover upward, away from the surface. This will reduce the motion of the module if it is accidentally deployed. Refer to the additional air bag system precautions later in this section.

• Clean, high quality brake fluid from a sealed container is essential to the safe and proper operation of the brake system. You should always buy the correct type of brake fluid for your vehicle. If the brake fluid becomes contaminated, completely flush the system with new fluid. Never reuse any brake fluid. Any brake fluid that is removed from the system should be discarded. Also, do not allow any brake fluid to come in contact with a painted surface; it will damage the paint.

• Never operate the engine without the proper amount and type of engine oil; doing so WILL result in severe engine damage.

• Timing belt maintenance is extremely important! Many models utilize an interference-type, non-freewheeling engine. If the timing belt breaks, the valves in the cylinder head may strike the pistons, causing potentially serious (also time-consuming and expensive) engine damage. Refer to the maintenance interval charts in the front of this manual for the recommended replacement interval for the timing belt, and to the timing belt section for belt replacement and inspection.

• Disconnecting the negative battery cable on some vehicles may interfere with the functions of the on-board computer system(s) and may require the computer to undergo a relearning process once the negative battery cable is reconnected.

• When servicing drum brakes, only disassemble and assemble one side at a time, leaving the remaining side intact for reference.

• Only an MVAC-trained, EPA-certified automotive technician should service the A/C system or its components.

ENGINE REPAIR

Alternator

REMOVAL & INSTALLATION

1. Before servicing the vehicle, refer to the precautions in the beginning of this section.

2. Remove or disconnect the following:

• Negative battery cable
• Air cleaner inlet pipe front bolts
• Top hose from the resonance chamber
• Air cleaner inlet pipe
• Alternator electrical connectors
• Loosen the pivot and tensioner mounting bolts, do mot remove them
• Drive belt from the alternator pulley
• Drive belt tensioner
• Alternator pivot bolt
• Loosen the bolt at the base of the adjusting bracket and rotate the bracket up
• Alternator

To install:

3. Install or connect the following:

• Alternator
• Pivot bolt and hand tighten
• Rotate the bracket down on top of the alternator
• Belt tensioner on the adjustment bracket
• Tensioner mounting bolt and hand tighten it
• Drive belt
• Torque the tensioner bolt to 19 ft. lbs. (26 Nm).
• Torque the pivot bolt to 38 ft. lbs. (51 Nm).
• Alternator electrical connectors
• Air cleaner inlet pipe and tighten the clamp
• Hose to the resonance chamber
• Air inlet pipe bolts and tighten
• Negative battery cable

Ignition Timing

ADJUSTMENT

The 2.0L engine in the Sportage is equipped with a distributorless ignition system. The ignition timing is controlled by the

Powertrain Control Module (PCM) through the input of engine control system sensors. The ignition timing is set at 4 degrees BTDC for vehicles equipped with manual or automatic transmissions. The ignition timing cannot be adjusted.

Engine Assembly

REMOVAL & INSTALLATION

1. Before servicing the vehicle, refer to the precautions in the beginning of this section.
2. Properly relieve the fuel system pressure.
3. Drain the cooling system.
4. Drain the engine oil.
5. Drain the transmission fluid.
6. Remove or disconnect the following:

- Both battery cables
- Windshield washer hose from the hood
- Hood
- 2 air duct mounting bolts from the top of the radiator. Loosen the clamp at the air intake housing and remove the duct
- Accelerator cable by pulling the throttle back and rotating the cable until it aligns with the slot in the pulley
- Transmission control cable
- Resonance chamber mounting bolt, chamber bolt and air silencer
- Idle Air Control (IAC) air hose, breather hose and vacuum line from the air intake tube
- Manifold Air Flow (MAF) sensor connector
- Loosen the air inlet hose clamp from the MAF sensor
- 3 bolts from the air intake tube to the throttle body
- Air intake hose and tube as an assembly
- Upper radiator hose
- Clutch fan nuts
- Cooling fan shroud bolts
- Fan and shroud at the same time
- Alternator drive belt
- Fan pulley
- Alternator electrical connectors
- Exhaust Gas Recirculation (EGR) solenoid valve connector on the intake manifold in front of the dynamic chamber
- Both heater hoses from the pipes

- Engine-to-body ground wire from the intake manifold and the harness bracket
- Brake booster vacuum hose from the dynamic chamber
- Fuel lines and fuel pressure regulator from the rear of the dynamic chamber
- Vacuum hose from the bottom of the EGR valve
- Purge solenoid valve vacuum hose from dynamic chamber
- Vacuum hoses from the top of the charcoal canister and slide the charcoal canister up and out of the bracket
- Lower radiator hose
- Cooling lines from the radiator, if equipped with an automatic transmission
- Radiator and raise and safely support the vehicle
- Lower splash panel
- Drive belt
- A/C pulley assembly
- A/C compressor mounting bolts and move the A/C compressor out of the way
- Power steering drive belt
- Intake manifold support bracket
- Starter wiring harness
- Starter
- Front exhaust pipe from the exhaust manifold
- Bracket bolt from the front exhaust pipe
- Exhaust-to-clutch (manual transmission) or converter (automatic transmission) housing bolts and the bracket
- Clutch housing (manual transmission) or converter (automatic transmission) housing bolts.
- Drive plate-to-torque converter bolts, if equipped

7. Support the transmission from underneath the vehicle.
8. Connect the engine hoist to the engine assembly.

- Left and right side engine mounting bolts

9. Lift the engine up and forward slightly to provide access to three electrical connectors on the rear of the cylinder head.

- Electrical connectors from the Camshaft Position (CMP) sensor, coil and condenser on the rear of the cylinder head
- Engine from the vehicle

To install:

10. Lower the engine enough to connect the three electrical connectors to the CMP sensor, coil and condenser on the rear of the cylinder head.
11. Position the engine to the transmission. Install the transmission bolts and tighten the bolts. Torque according to bolt size:

- 14mm bolts to 80 ft. lbs. (108 Nm)
- 10mm bolts to 28 ft. lbs. (38 Nm)
- 6mm bolts to 60 inch lbs. (7 Nm)
- Right and left side engine mounting bolts. Torque the bolts to 38 ft. lbs. (52 Nm).

12. Disconnect the engine hoist from the engine assembly.
13. Raise and safely support the vehicle.

- Drive plate-to-torque converter bolts, if equipped
- Connect the front exhaust pipe to the exhaust manifold. Torque the flange bolts to 24 ft. lbs. (31 Nm).
- Front exhaust pipe. Torque the bolts to 20 ft. lbs. (27 Nm).
- Starter
- Connect the starter wiring harness
- Intake manifold support bracket bolts and the bracket.

14. Install the power steering pump lock and mounting bolts. Install the power steering drive belt. Torque the bolts to 30 ft. lbs. (42 Nm).

- A/C compressor mounting bolts. Torque the bolts to 18 ft. lbs. (24 Nm).
- A/C belt pulley assembly and drive belt. Install the two A/C idler pulley bracket bolts and torque to 24 ft. lbs. (32 Nm).
- Lower splash panel
- Radiator
- Cooling lines to the radiator, if equipped
- Lower radiator hose
- Slide the charcoal canister in the bracket
- Vacuum hoses to the top of the charcoal canister
- Engine-to-body ground wire to the intake manifold and the harness bracket
- Brake booster vacuum hose to the dynamic chamber
- Fuel lines and fuel pressure regulator to the rear of the dynamic chamber
- Vacuum hose to the bottom of the EGR valve

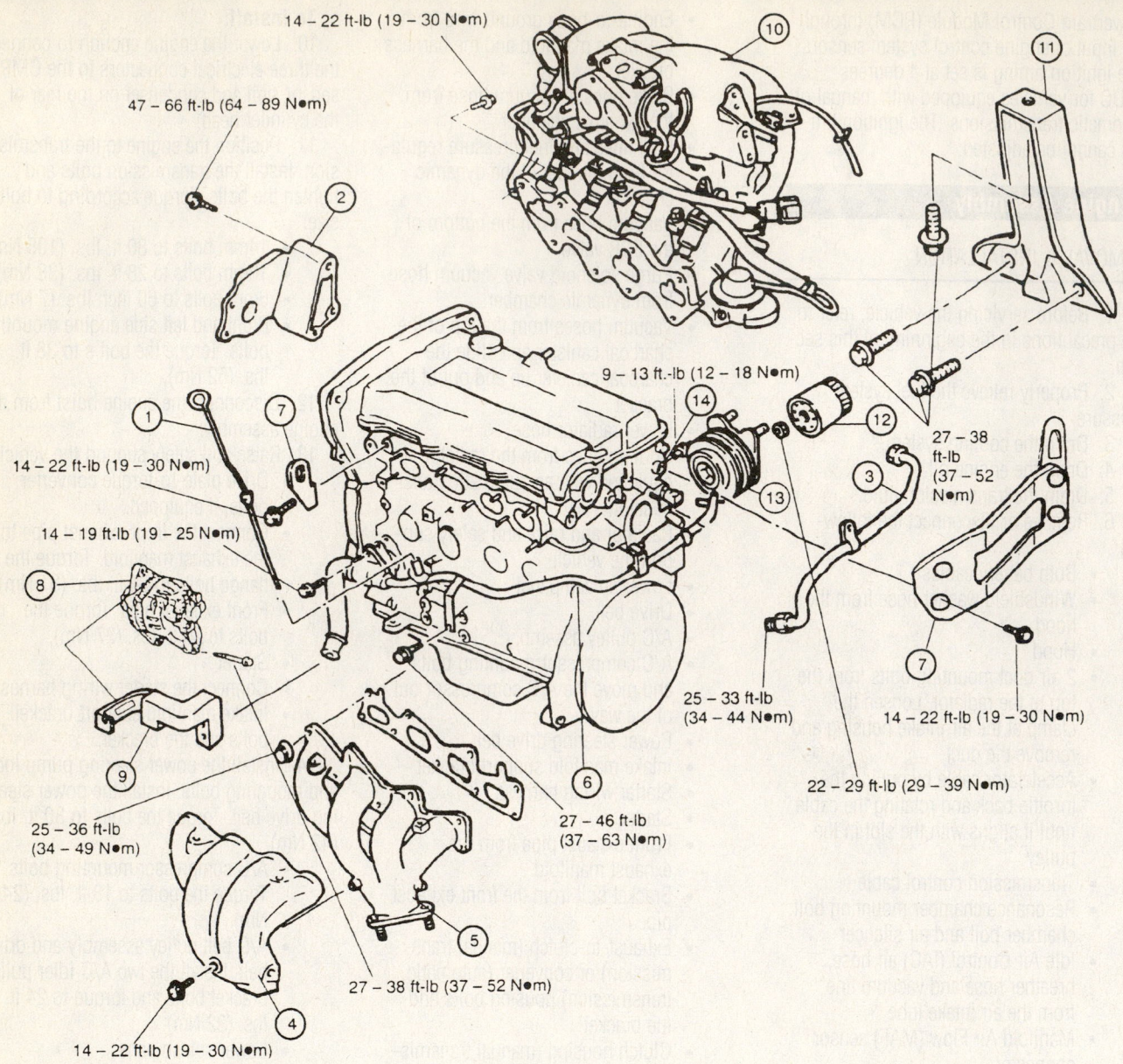

14 – 22 ft-lb (19 – 30 N•m)

47 – 66 ft-lb (64 – 89 N•m)

14 – 22 ft-lb (19 – 30 N•m)

14 – 19 ft-lb (19 – 25 N•m)

9 – 13 ft.-lb (12 – 18 N•m)

27 – 38 ft-lb (37 – 52 N•m)

25 – 33 ft-lb (34 – 44 N•m)

14 – 22 ft-lb (19 – 30 N•m)

22 – 29 ft-lb (29 – 39 N•m)

25 – 36 ft-lb (34 – 49 N•m)

27 – 46 ft-lb (37 – 63 N•m)

27 – 38 ft-lb (37 – 52 N•m)

14 – 22 ft-lb (19 – 30 N•m)

1. Oil Level Gauge
2. Thermo-Modulated Fan Bracket
3. EGR Pipe
4. Exhaust Manifold Heat Shield
5. Exhaust Manifold
6. Coolant Inlet Pipe and Bypass Pipe
7. Engine Hanger
8. Generator
9. Generator Strap and Bracket
10. Intake Manifold Assembly
11. Intake Manifold Support Bracket
12. Oil Filter
13. Oil Cooler
14. Oil Pressure Switch

7924QG36

Exploded view of some peripheral engine component mountings

- Purge solenoid valve vacuum hose to dynamic chamber
- EGR solenoid valve connector on the intake manifold in front of the dynamic chamber
- Heater hoses
- Electrical terminal connectors to the alternator
- Fan pulley

- Alternator drive belt. Torque the adjusting bolt 16 ft. lbs. (22 Nm) and the mounting bolt to 32 ft. lbs. (45 Nm).
- Fan and shroud as an assembly. Torque the five cooling fan shroud bolts to 72 inch lbs. (8 Nm)
- Clutch fan nuts. Torque the nuts to 27 ft. lbs. (37 Nm).

- Upper radiator hose
- Air intake hose and tube as an assembly
- Air intake tube to the throttle body and tighten the air inlet hose clamp to the MAF sensor
- MAF sensor electrical connector
- Resonance chamber mounting bolt, chamber bolt and air silencer

- IAC air hose, breather hose and vacuum line to the air intake tube
- Accelerator cable by pulling the throttle back and rotating the cable until it aligns with the slot in the pulley
- Transmission control cable
- Air duct mounting bolts to the top of the radiator. Torque the clamp at the air intake housing
- Hood
- Windshield washer hose to the hood

15. Fill the engine with clean engine oil.
16. Connect the battery cables.
17. Fill the cooling system.
18. Fill the transmission fluid.
19. Recharge the A/C system.
20. Start the vehicle. Check for leaks, repair if necessary.
21. Road test the vehicle to check engine performance.

Water Pump

REMOVAL & INSTALLATION

1. Before servicing the vehicle, refer to the precautions in the beginning of this section.
2. Drain the cooling system.

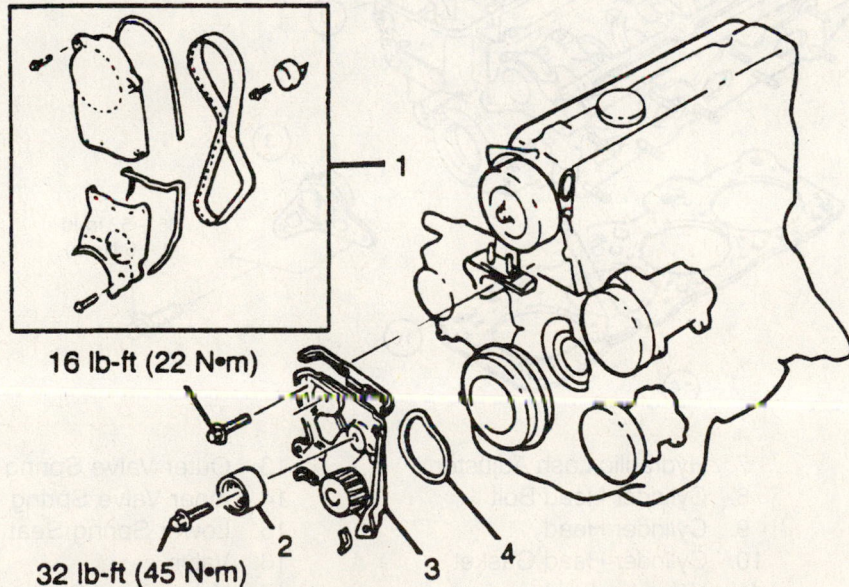

16 lb-ft (22 N•m)

32 lb-ft (45 N•m)

| 1 | TIMING BELT COVERS, GASKETS AND TIMING BELT | 3 | COOLANT PUMP |
| 2 | IDLER PULLEY | 4 | GASKET |

7924QG01

Exploded view of the water pump mounting

3. Remove or disconnect the following:

- Negative battery cable
- Lower splash shield
- Upper and lower radiator hoses
- Coolant reservoir tank hose
- Fresh air duct
- Fan and shroud
- Loosen the alternator mounting and adjusting bolts
- Alternator belt
- Fan pulley and bracket
- Upper and lower timing belt covers and turn the crankshaft until No. 1 cylinder is at Top Dead Center (TDC).
- Loosen the tensioner lockbolt and pry the tensioner away from the belt
- Timing belt
- Loosen the tensioner bolt
- Water pump
- Tensioners from the water pump

To install:

4. Clean the surface of any old gasket material.
5. Install or connect the following:

- Tensioners on the water pump
- Water pump and gasket. Torque the bolts to 19 ft. lbs. 25 Nm).
- Timing belt
- Loosen the tensioner lockbolt and allow the tensioner to rest against the belt. Torque the tensioner lockbolt to 32 ft. lbs. (43 Nm).
- Upper and lower timing belt covers
- Fan bracket assembly and fan pulley
- Drive belt
- Cooling fan and shroud
- Position the radiator and torque the bracket bolts to 89 inch lbs. (10 Nm).
- Torque the shroud bolts to 89 inch lbs. (10 Nm) and torque the alternator adjusting and mounting bolts
- Position the fresh air duct over the radiator and tighten the retaining bolt 89 inch lbs. (10 Nm)
- Radiator hoses and tighten the clamps
- Lower splash shield
- Negative battery cable

6. Fill the cooling system.
7. Start the vehicle and bring the engine to operating temperature. Check for leaks and repair if necessary.

Cylinder Head

REMOVAL & INSTALLATION

1. Before servicing the vehicle, refer to the precautions in the beginning of this section.
2. Properly relieve the fuel system pressure.
3. Drain the cooling system.
4. Remove or disconnect the following:

- Negative battery cable
- Brake booster vacuum hose from the dynamic chamber
- Fuel line from the pressure regulator and the return line from the rear of the dynamic chamber
- Ground wire from the intake manifold
- Purge solenoid valve vacuum hose
- Upper radiator hose
- Intake manifold support bracket
- Converter flange inlet pipe
- Timing belt
- Cylinder head cover
- Cylinder head with the intake and exhaust manifolds attached
- 3 wire harness connectors at the rear of the cylinder head

Timing belt service is covered in Section 4 of this manual

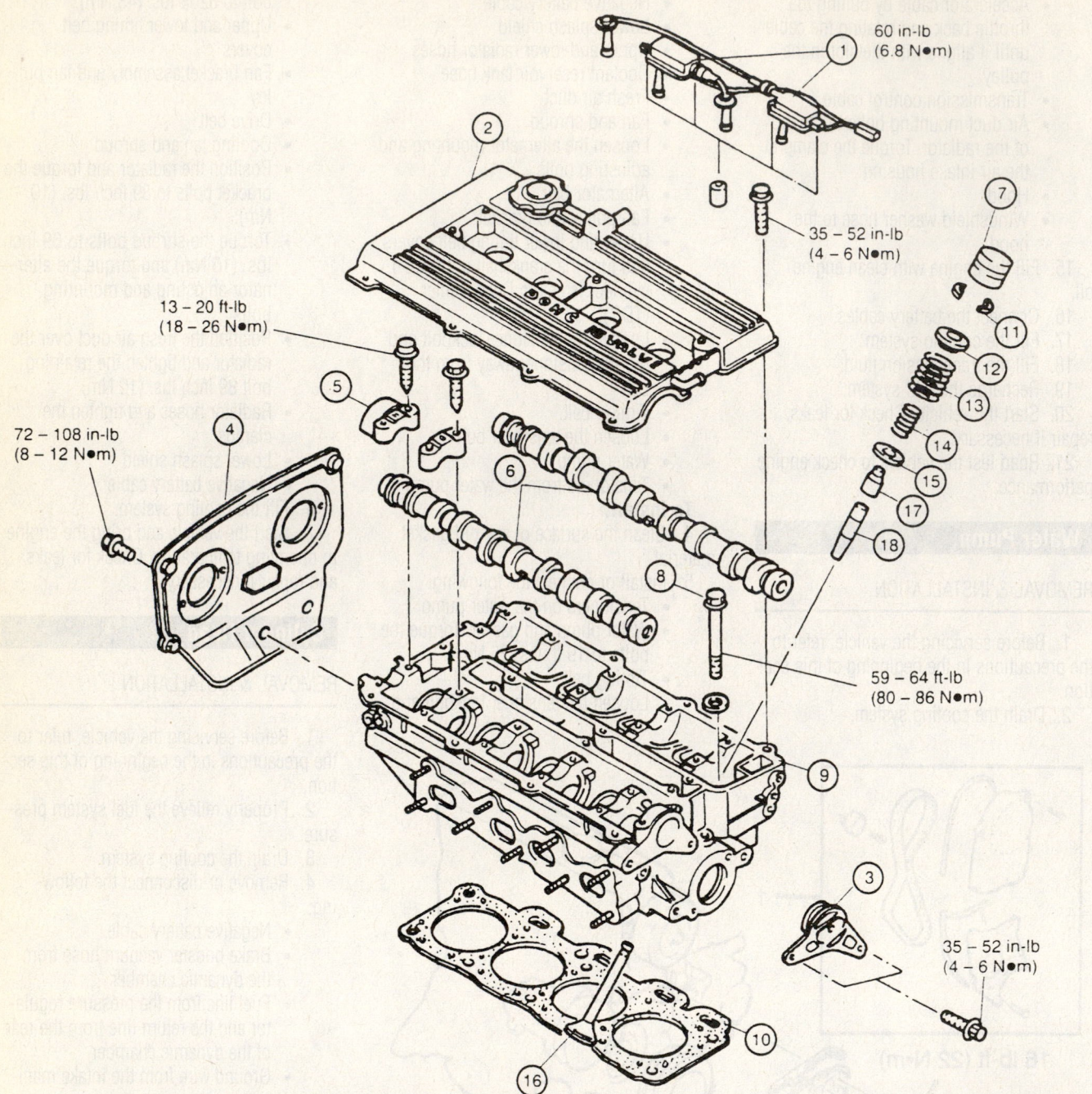

60 in-lb (6.8 N•m)

35 – 52 in-lb (4 – 6 N•m)

13 – 20 ft-lb (18 – 26 N•m)

72 – 108 in-lb (8 – 12 N•m)

59 – 64 ft-lb (80 – 86 N•m)

35 – 52 in-lb (4 – 6 N•m)

1. Ignition Coils and High Tension Leads
2. Cylinder Head Cover
3. Camshaft Position Sensor
4. Seal Plate
5. Camshaft Caps
6. Camshafts

7. Hydraulic Lash Adjuster
8. Cylinder Head Bolt
9. Cylinder Head
10. Cylinder Head Gasket
11. Valve Locks
12. Upper Spring Seat

13. Outer Valve Spring
14. Inner Valve Spring
15. Lower Spring Seat
16. Valve
17. Valve Stem Seal
18. Valve Guide

7924QG37

Exploded view of the cylinder head assembly

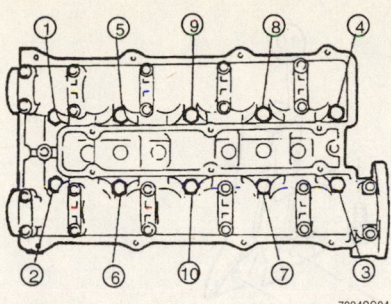

Cylinder head removal sequence

7924QG04

To install:

5. Place the new head gasket on the engine block.

6. Install or connect the following:
- Cylinder head with the intake and exhaust manifolds attached
- 3 wiring connectors at the rear of the cylinder head
- Cylinder head bolts in the proper sequence. Torque the bolts to 64 ft. lbs. (87 Nm).
- Cylinder head cover
- Timing belt
- Converter inlet pipe flange nuts. Torque the nuts to 24 ft. lbs. (33 Nm).
- Upper radiator hose
- Vacuum hose from the intake manifold to the charcoal canister
- Purge solenoid vacuum hose
- Ground wire and harness bracket to the intake manifold. Torque the bolts to 18 ft. lbs. (25 Nm).
- Fuel line to the pressure regulator and the return line to the fuel rail
- Brake booster vacuum hose
- Negative battery cable

7. Properly fill the cooling system.

8. Start the engine and check for leaks, repair if necessary.

Intake Manifold

REMOVAL & INSTALLATION

1. Before servicing the vehicle, refer to the precautions in the beginning of this section.

2. Properly relieve the fuel system pressure.

3. Drain the coolant.

4. Remove or disconnect the following:
- Negative battery cable
- Accelerator cable bracket bolts from the valve cover

- Air intake tube to cylinder head cover bolts
- Air intake tube to throttle body bolts
- Loosen the clamp attaching the air tube to the Mass Air Flow (MAF) sensor
- Idle Air Control (IAC) valve, breather hose and vacuum line from the air intake tube
- Air intake tube
- Positive Crankcase Ventilation hose (PCV) from the dynamic chamber
- Purge solenoid valve vacuum hose from the dynamic chamber
- Throttle Position (TP) sensor electrical connector
- IAC valve electrical connector
- Heater hoses
- Engine-to-body ground strap from the intake manifold and the harness bracket below it
- Brake booster vacuum line
- Vacuum hose from the fuel pressure regulator hose
- Dynamic chamber support bracket bolts
- Fuel injector electrical connectors
- Fuel pressure and return lines
- Intake manifold support bracket
- Oil filter
- Intake manifold bolts
- Bypass pipe from the heater hose
- Intake manifold and discard the gasket

To install:

5. Install or connect the following:

- Intake manifold with a new gasket to the cylinder head
- Heater hose to the bypass pipe
- Bolts and nuts attaching the intake manifold to the cylinder head. Torque the bolts to 14–22 ft. lbs. (19–30 Nm).
- New oil filter
- Intake manifold support bracket. Torque the bolts to 27–38 ft. lbs. (37–52 Nm).
- Fuel lines
- Fuel injector electrical connectors
- Engine to body ground wire. Torque the bolt to 18 ft. lbs. (25 Nm).
- Dynamic chamber support bracket. Torque the bolts to 18 ft. lbs. (25 Nm).
- Purge solenoid valve vacuum hose to the dynamic chamber
- Vacuum hose to the fuel pressure regulator
- Coolant hoses to the throttle body
- IAC valve electrical connector
- Brake booster vacuum hose
- Heater hoses
- TP sensor electrical connector
- Air intake tube and hose to the throttle body. Torque the bolts to 16 ft. lbs. (22 Nm).
- PCV hose to the dynamic chamber
- Accelerator cable to the throttle body pulley
- Accelerator cable bracket. Torque the bolts to 10 ft. lbs. (15 Nm).
- Air intake hose to the MAF sensor

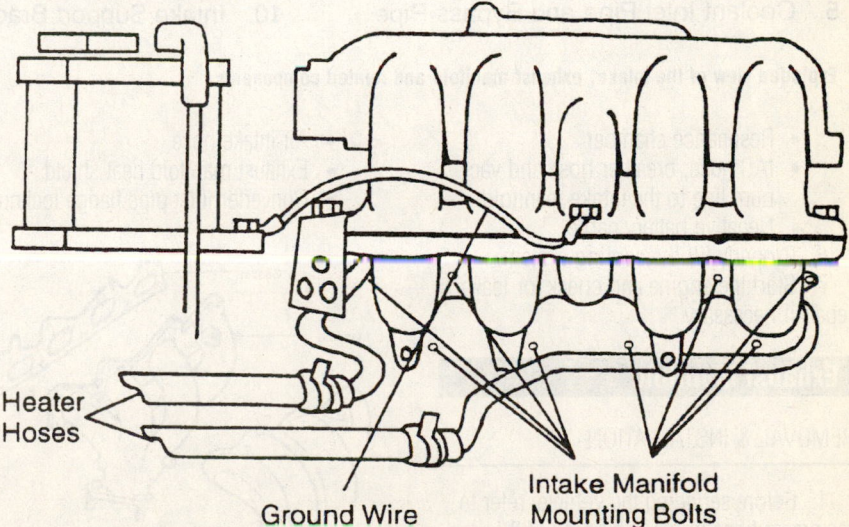

Intake manifold mounting bolt locations. Be sure to connect the ground cable

7924QG12

Please visit our web site at www.chiltonsonline.com

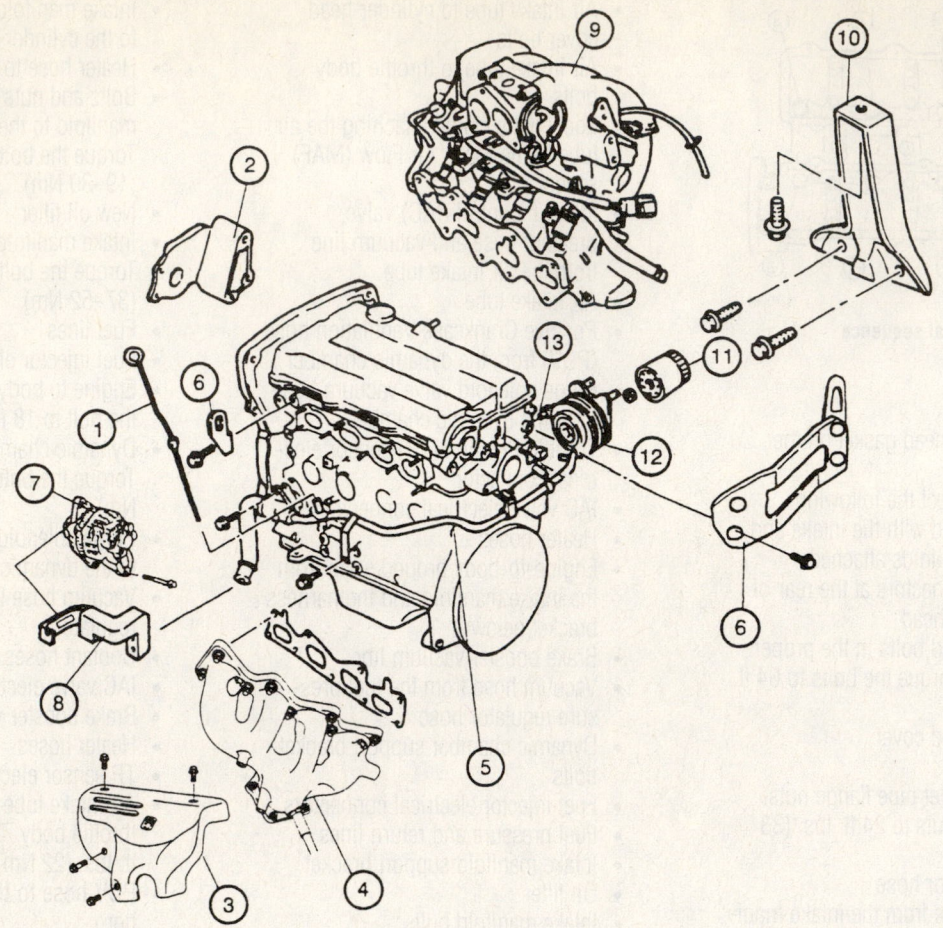

1. Oil Level Gauge
2. Thermo-Modulated Fan Bracket
3. Exhaust Manifold Heat Shield
4. Exhaust Manifold
5. Coolant Inlet Pipe and Bypass Pipe
6. Engine Hanger
7. Generator
8. Generator Strap and Bracket
9. Intake Manifold Assembly
10. Intake Support Bracket
11. Oil Filter
12. Oil Cooler
13. Oil Pressure Switch

9308QG01

Exploded view of the intake, exhaust manifold and related components

- Resonance chamber
- IAC hose, breather hose and vacuum line to the intake manifold
- Negative battery cable
6. Properly fill the cooling system.
7. Start the engine and check for leaks, repair if necessary.

Exhaust Manifold

REMOVAL & INSTALLATION

1. Before servicing the vehicle, refer to the precautions in the beginning of this section.
2. Remove or disconnect the following:
- Negative battery cable

- Air intake hose
- Exhaust manifold heat shield
- Converter inlet pipe flange locknuts

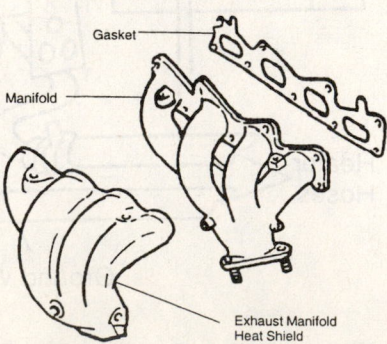

Gasket

Manifold

Exhaust Manifold
Heat Shield

7924QG14

Exploded view of the exhaust manifold assembly

- Exhaust manifold and discard the gasket
3. Clean the mating surfaces.
To install:
4. Install or connect the following:
- Exhaust manifold with a new gasket. Torque the bolts to 31 ft. lbs. (42 Nm).
- New flange gasket and install the converter inlet pipe. Torque the bolts to 24 ft. lbs. (33 Nm).
- Exhaust manifold heat shield. Torque the bolts to 18 ft. lbs. (25 Nm).
- Air intake hose
- Negative battery cable
5. Start the vehicle and check for leaks, repair if necessary.

Front Crankshaft Seal

REMOVAL & INSTALLATION

1. Before servicing the vehicle, refer to the precautions in the beginning of this section.
2. Remove or disconnect the following:
   - Negative battery cable
   - Engine under cover
   - Timing belt
   - Timing belt pulley lock bolt
   - Timing belt pulley
   - Pulley woodruff key
   - Oil seal by carefully cutting it out of the oil pump housing

To install:

3. Lubricate the lip of the new seal with clean engine oil.
4. Install or connect the following:
   - New oil seal into the oil pump housing by hand
   - Press the oil seal into pump until it is flush with the edge of the oil pump body
   - Timing belt pulley
   - Pulley woodruff key
   - Pulley lock bolt. Torque the bolt to 18 ft. lbs. (25 Nm).
   - Timing belt
   - Engine under cover. Torque the bolts to 18 ft. lbs. (25 Nm).
   - Negative battery cable
5. Start the engine and check for leaks, repair if necessary.

Camshaft

REMOVAL & INSTALLATION

1. Before servicing the vehicle, refer to the precautions in the beginning of this section.
2. Properly relieve the fuel system pressure.
3. Drain the coolant into a suitable container.
4. Remove or disconnect the following:
   - Negative battery cable
   - Upper timing belt cover
   - Timing belt from the camshaft pulley
   - Camshaft pulleys
   - Camshaft cap bolts in the proper sequence
   - Camshaft caps
   - Camshafts

To install:

5. Install or connect the following:

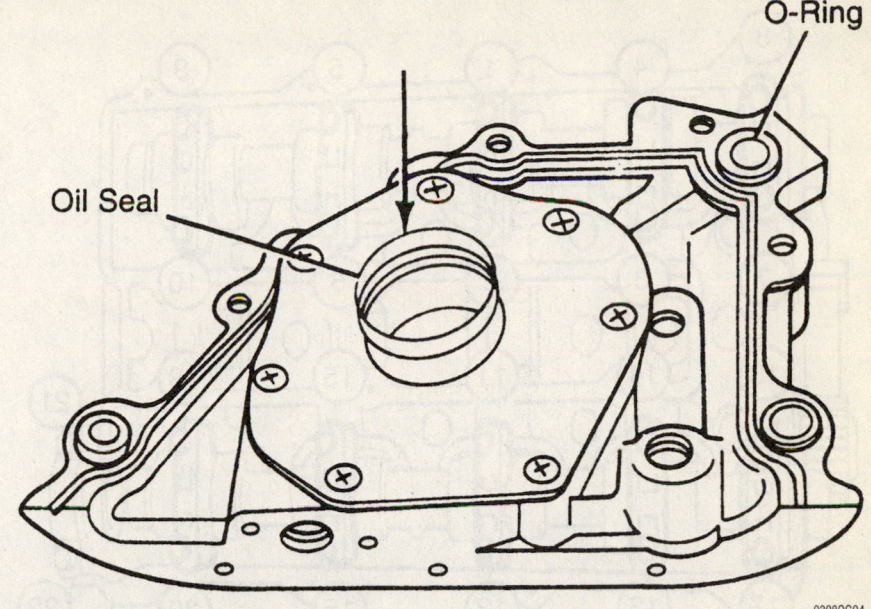

Install the oil seal into the oil pump housing

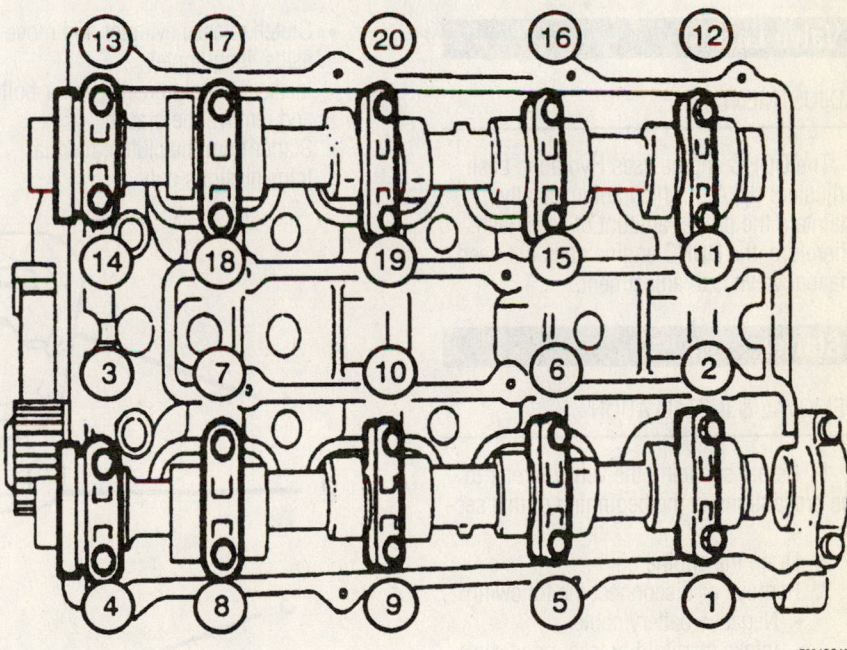

Camshaft cap bolt removal sequence

- Camshafts into the cylinder head. The exhaust camshaft has a steel dowel pin at the rear for the camshaft position sensor
- Clean engine oil to the journals and bearings
- Camshaft oil seal
- Silicone sealant to the front

camshaft cap and the camshaft position sensor mounting cap
- Camshaft caps in the proper sequence. Torque the bolts in three steps to 20 ft. lbs. (26 Nm).
- Camshaft pulleys
- Timing belt
- Timing belt cover
- Negative battery cable

Refer to Section 1 for engine rebuilding specifications

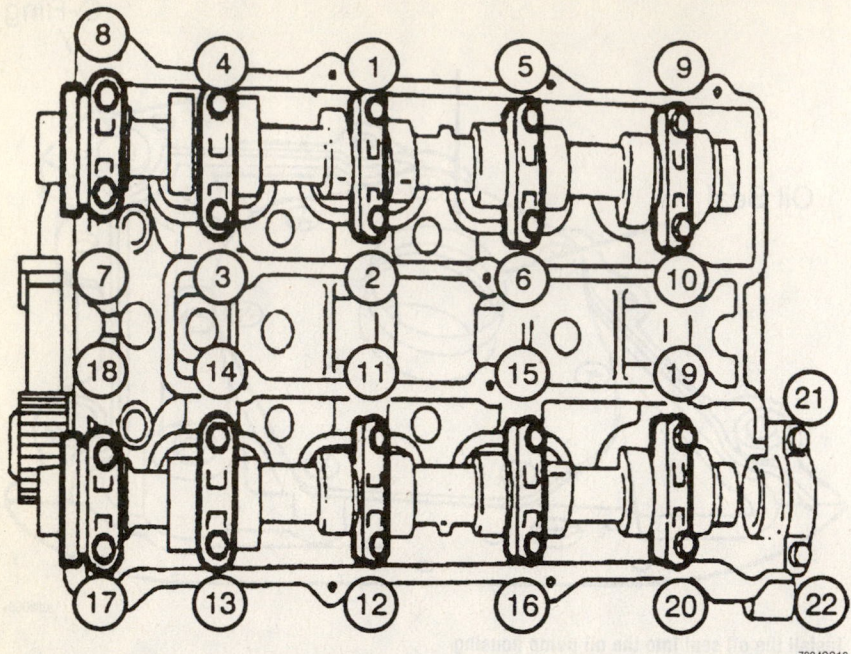

Camshaft journal bolt tightening sequence

Valve Lash

ADJUSTMENT

The DOHC engine uses Hydraulic Lash Adjusters (HLA's), which automatically maintain the proper amount of valve lash. Therefore, the DOHC engine does not need manual valve lash adjustment.

Starter

REMOVAL & INSTALLATION

1. Before servicing the vehicle, refer to the precautions in the beginning of this section.
2. Drain the engine oil.
3. Remove or disconnect the following:
   - Negative battery cable
   - Intake manifold bracket upper bolts

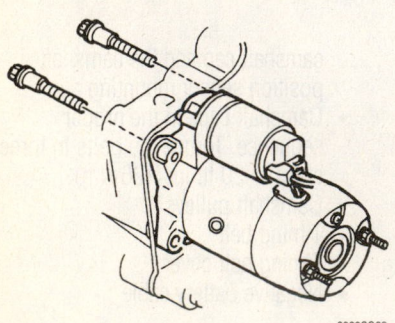

Exploded view of the starter

- Clutch release cylinder and move it aside, if equipped
- Intake manifold bracket lower bolts and remove the bracket
- Starter from the clutch, manual transmissions only
- Starter from the torque converter, automatic transmissions only
- Starter electrical connectors
- Move the transmission wire harness aside
- Starter

To install:

4. Install or connect the following:
   - Starter to the engine well
   - Starter electrical connectors
   - Lower intake manifold bracket and install the upper bolts
   - Starter into position. When aligned properly torque the bolts to 40 ft. lbs. (54 Nm).
   - Torque the intake manifold bracket bolts to 40 ft. lbs. (54 Nm).
   - Properly position the clutch release cylinder, if equipped. Torque the bolts to 40 ft. lbs. (54 Nm).
   - Torque the intake manifold bracket upper bolts to 40 ft. lbs. (54 Nm).
   - Negative battery cable

Oil Pan

REMOVAL & INSTALLATION

1. Before servicing the vehicle, refer to the precautions in the beginning of this section.

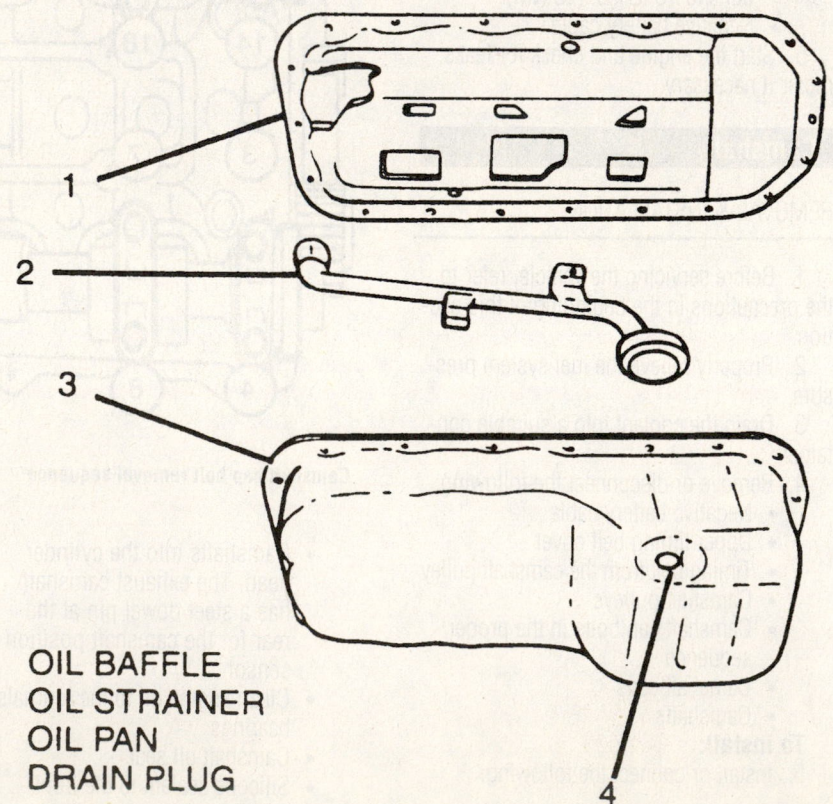

1. OIL BAFFLE
2. OIL STRAINER
3. OIL PAN
4. DRAIN PLUG

Exploded view of the oil pan assembly mounting

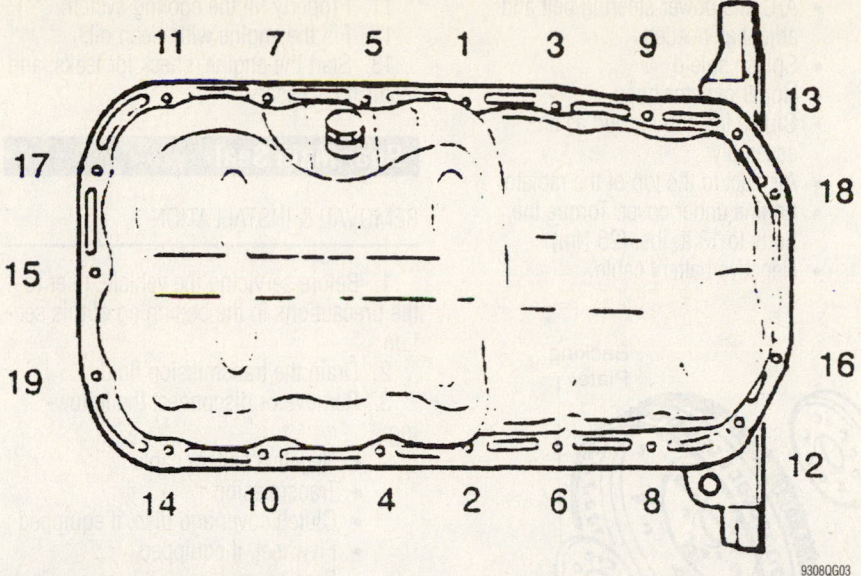

11 7 5 1 3 9

13

17

18

15

19

16

12

14 10 4 2 6 8

9308QG03

Tighten the oil pan bolts in sequence

2. Drain the engine oil.

3. Remove or disconnect the following:

- Negative battery cable
- 2 Top intake manifold bracket bolts
- Front 3 axle housing mounting bolts, 4WD only
- Left front bushing from the axle housing mount and lower the front axle housing
- Both gusset plates from the engine
- Transmission under cover
- Engine under cover
- Oil pan mounting bolts and using a scrapper tool separate the oil pan
- Oil pan
- Oil strainer assembly
- Oil baffle

To install:

4. Clean the engine block, oil pan and baffle pan surfaces of any gasket material.

5. Apply a continuous bead of Loctite Ultra Blue 587® silicone sealant around the baffle pan.

6. Install or connect the following:

- Oil baffle. Torque the bolt to 84 inch lbs., (9.5 Nm).
- Oil strainer. Torque the bolts to 84 inch lbs. (9.5 Nm).

7. Apply a continuous bead of Loctite Ultra Blue 587® silicone sealant around the oil pan.

- Oil pan. Torque the bolts to 84 inch lbs. (9.5 Nm).
- Transmission under cover. Torque the bolts to 84 inch lbs. (9.5 Nm).

- Gusset plates to the engine. Torque the bolts to 33 ft. lbs. (45 Nm).
- Engine under cover
- Front axle housing into position. When properly aligned, torque the bolts to 48 ft. lbs. (65 Nm).
- Intake manifold bracket bolts. Torque the bolts to 34 ft. lbs. (65 Nm).
- Negative battery cable

8. Fill the engine with clean oil.

9. Start the vehicle and check for leaks, repair if necessary.

Oil Pump

REMOVAL & INSTALLATION

➡**The oil pump is externally-mounted, but still requires the removal of the oil pan to disconnect the oil pump strainer.**

1. Before servicing the vehicle, refer to the precautions in the beginning of this section.

2. Properly relieve the fuel system pressure.

3. Drain the engine oil.

4. Drain the cooling system.

5. Remove or disconnect the following:

- Negative battery cable
- Alternator belt
- Fresh air duct from the radiator
- Upper radiator hose
- Clutch fan and shroud
- Splash guard
- Loosen the A/C drive belt

- Power steering belt
- Timing belt covers
- Lower timing belt pulley and lock bolt and place a support under the front axle
- Axle attaching bolts and lower the axle enough to gain access to the oil pan
- Transmission under cover
- Oil pan
- Oil pump

To install:

6. Clean the engine block, oil pan and baffle pan surfaces of any gasket material.

7. Apply a continuous bead of silicone sealant around the oil pump.

➡**Do not allow sealant to get in the oil passages when applying sealant to the contact surface.**

8. Install or connect the following:

- New O-ring and mount the oil pump to the engine. Torque the "A" bolts to 16 ft. lbs. (22 Nm) and the "B" bolts to 33 ft. lbs. (45 Nm).

9. Remove the upper and lower A/C compressor mounting bolts.

10. Loosen the A/C compressor bracket.

- Power steering pump bracket and hand tighten the bolts
- A/C compressor bracket
- A/C compressor. Torque the mounting bolts to 17 ft. lbs. (23 Nm).
- Torque the power steering pump bracket bolts to 24 ft. lbs. (33 Nm).
- Power steering pump. Torque the bolts to 43 ft. lbs. (58 Nm).
- Timing belt gear on the crankshaft. Torque the large crank bolt to 119 ft. lbs. (162 Nm).
- Oil baffle after applying sealant to the mating surface. Torque the bolt to 84 inch lbs. (9.5 Nm).
- Oil strainer. Torque the bolts to 84 inch lbs. (9.5 Nm).

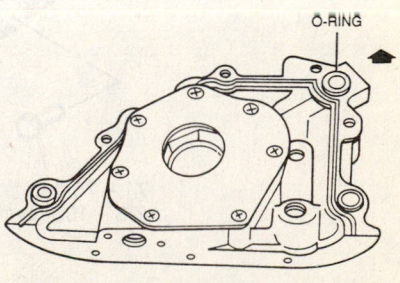

O-RING

7924QG19

Be sure the oil pump O-ring is in the proper location prior to installation

For engine torque specifications, refer to Section 1 of this manual

- Oil pan
- Transmission under cover. Torque the bolts to 84 inch lbs. (9.5 Nm).
- Both gusset plates. Torque the bolts to 33 ft. lbs. (45 Nm).
- Raise the front axle into position. When aligned properly, torque the bolts to 123 ft. lbs. (167 Nm).
- Timing belt and cover
- Alternator belt

- A/C and power steering belt and adjust as needed
- Splash shield
- Upper radiator hose
- Clutch fan and shroud as an assembly
- Air duct to the top of the radiator
- Engine under cover. Torque the bolts to 18 ft. lbs. (25 Nm).
- Negative battery cable

11. Properly fill the cooling system.
12. Fill the engine with clean oil.
13. Start the engine, check for leaks, and repair if necessary.

Rear Main Seal

REMOVAL & INSTALLATION

1. Before servicing the vehicle, refer to the precautions in the beginning of this section.
2. Drain the transmission fluid.
3. Remove or disconnect the following:

- Negative battery cable
- Transmission
- Clutch cover and disc, if equipped
- Flywheel, if equipped
- Rear cover
- Rear main oil seal

To install:
4. Coat the new seal with clean oil and press the seal into the cover.
5. Install or connect the following:

- Rear cover
- Flywheel onto the crankshaft. While holding the flywheel torque the bolts in sequence:
a. Step 1: 30 ft. lbs. (41 Nm).
b. Step 2: 60 ft. lbs. (81 Nm).
c. Step 3: 73 ft. lbs. (99 Nm).
- Clutch disc and cover. Torque the bolts to 16 ft. lbs. (22 Nm).
- Transmission
- Negative battery cable

6. Fill the transmission to the proper level.
7. Start the vehicle and check for leaks, repair if necessary.

Piston and Ring

POSITIONING

Drive Plate Adapter

Drive Plate

Backing Plate

71 – 76 ft-lb (96 – 103 N•m)

A/T

Separator Plate

6 – 9 ft-lb (8 – 12 N•m)

14 – 22 ft-lb (19 – 30 N•m)

Rear Cover

Flywheel (M/T)

Clutch Disc (M/T)

71 – 76 ft-lb (96 – 103 N•m)

Clutch Cover (M/T)

16 – 24 ft-lb (22 – 32 N•m)

M/T

7924QG38

Exploded view of the rear main seal and related components

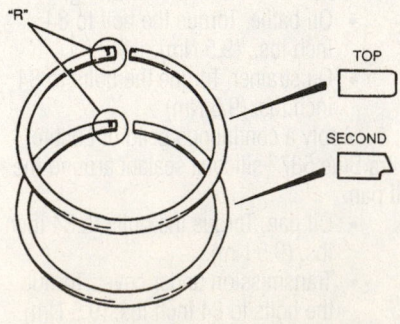

"R"

TOP

SECOND

7924AG04

Kia 2.0L engine—compression ring positioning mark locations

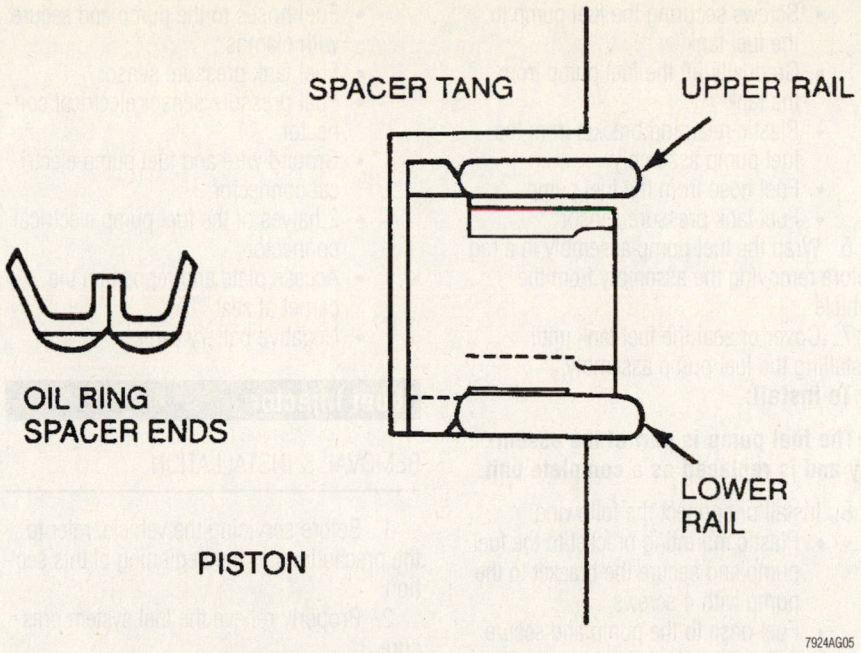

Kia 2.0L engine—oil control ring rail and spacer positioning

7924AG05

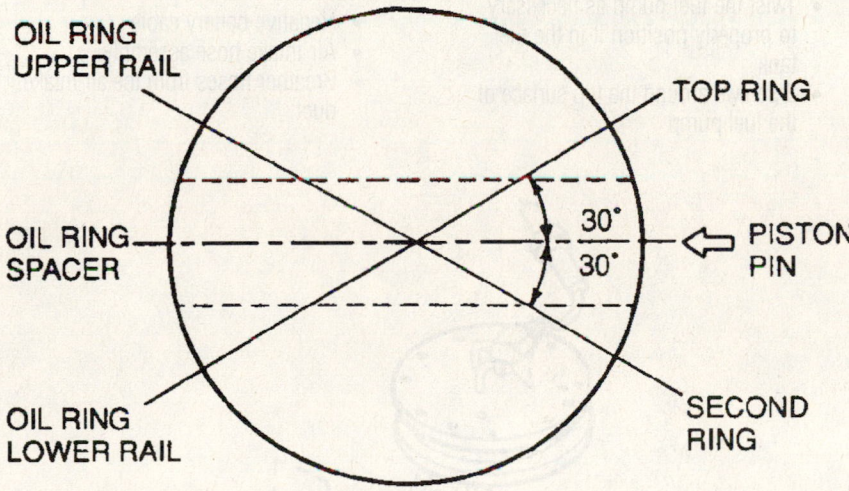

Kia 2.0L engine—piston ring end-gap spacing

7924AG06

FUEL SYSTEM

Fuel System Service Precautions

Safety is the most important factor when performing not only fuel system maintenance but any type of maintenance. Failure to conduct maintenance and repairs in a safe manner may result in serious personal injury or death. Maintenance and testing of the vehicle's fuel system components can be accomplished safely and effectively by adhering to the following rules and guidelines.

• To avoid the possibility of fire and personal injury, always disconnect the negative battery cable unless the repair or test procedure requires that battery voltage be applied.

• Always relieve the fuel system pressure prior to disconnecting any fuel system component (injector, fuel rail, pressure regulator, etc.), fitting or fuel line connection. Exercise extreme caution whenever relieving fuel system pressure to avoid exposing skin, face and eyes to fuel spray. Please be advised that fuel under pressure may penetrate the skin or any part of the body that it contacts.

• Always place a shop towel or cloth around the fitting or connection prior to loosening to absorb any excess fuel due to spillage. Ensure that all fuel spillage (should it occur) is quickly removed from engine surfaces. Ensure that all fuel soaked cloths or towels are deposited into a suitable waste container.

• Always keep a dry chemical (Class B) fire extinguisher near the work area.

• Do not allow fuel spray or fuel vapors to come into contact with a spark or open flame.

• Always use a back-up wrench when loosening and tightening fuel line connection fittings. This will prevent unnecessary stress and torsion to fuel line piping.

• Always replace worn fuel fitting O-rings with new. Do not substitute fuel hose or equivalent where fuel pipe is installed.

Fuel System Pressure

RELIEVING

1. Before servicing the vehicle, refer to the precautions in the beginning of this section.

2. Disconnect the fuel pump harness connector located behind the rear seat.

3. Start the engine and allow the engine to run out of fuel.

4. Once the engine has stalled, turn the key to the **OFF** position and connect the electrical connector.

5. Disconnect the negative battery cable so pressure cannot build up until work has been completed.

Fuel Filter

REMOVAL & INSTALLATION

1. Before servicing the vehicle, refer to the precautions in the beginning of this section.

2. Properly relieve the fuel system pressure.

3. Remove or disconnect the following:
   • Negative battery cable
   • Fuel pump connector
   • Fuel hoses from the fuel filter
   • Fuel filter from the bracket
To install:
4. Install or connect the following:

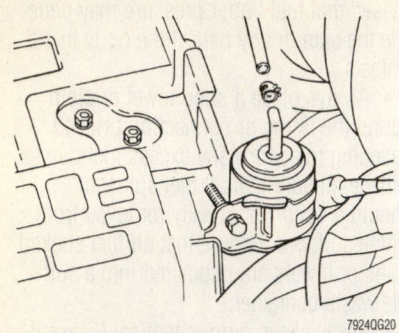

Fuel filter underhood mounting location

- Fuel filter in the bracket
- Fuel filter. Torque the bolts to 95 ft. lbs. (129 Nm).
- Fuel hoses on the filter and make certain that the hoses are seated properly
- Fuel pump connector
- Negative battery cable

5. Start the engine and check for fuel leaks, repair if necessary.

Fuel Pump

REMOVAL & INSTALLATION

1. Before servicing the vehicle, refer to the precautions in the beginning of this section.

2. Properly relieve the fuel system pressure.

3. Release the catch for the back seat and tilt the seat out of the way.

4. Move the carpet behind the seat that covers the fuel pump access panel.

5. Remove or disconnect the following:

- Negative battery cable
- Fuel pump electrical connectors
- Bolt securing the ground wire
- Fuel pump access panel
- Hose clamps connecting the fuel hoses to the fuel pump
- Hoses from the fuel pump

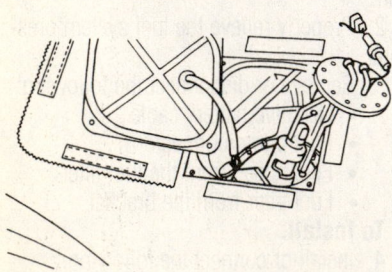

Removing the fuel pump through the access panel

- Screws securing the fuel pump to the fuel tank
- Gradually lift the fuel pump from the tank
- Plastic retaining bracket from the fuel pump assembly
- Fuel hose from the fuel pump
- Fuel tank pressure sensor

6. Wrap the fuel pump assembly in a rag before removing the assembly from the vehicle.

7. Cover or seal the fuel tank until installing the fuel pump assembly.

To install:

➡**The fuel pump is part of the assembly and is replaced as a complete unit.**

8. Install or connect the following:

- Plastic mounting bracket to the fuel pump and secure the bracket to the pump with 4 screws
- Fuel hose to the pump and secure with a new clamp
- Fuel pump into the access port on top of the fuel tank
- Twist the fuel pump as necessary to properly position it in the fuel tank
- 8 screws around the top surface of the fuel pump

- Fuel hoses to the pump and secure with clamps
- Fuel tank pressure sensor
- Fuel pressure sensor electrical connector
- Ground wire and fuel pump electrical connector
- 2 halves of the fuel pump electrical connector
- Access plate and reposition the carpet at seat
- Negative battery cable

Fuel Injector

REMOVAL & INSTALLATION

1. Before servicing the vehicle, refer to the precautions in the beginning of this section.

2. Properly relieve the fuel system pressure.

3. Drain the cooling system.

4. Remove or disconnect the following:

- Negative battery cable
- Air intake hose assembly
- Breather hoses from the air intake duct

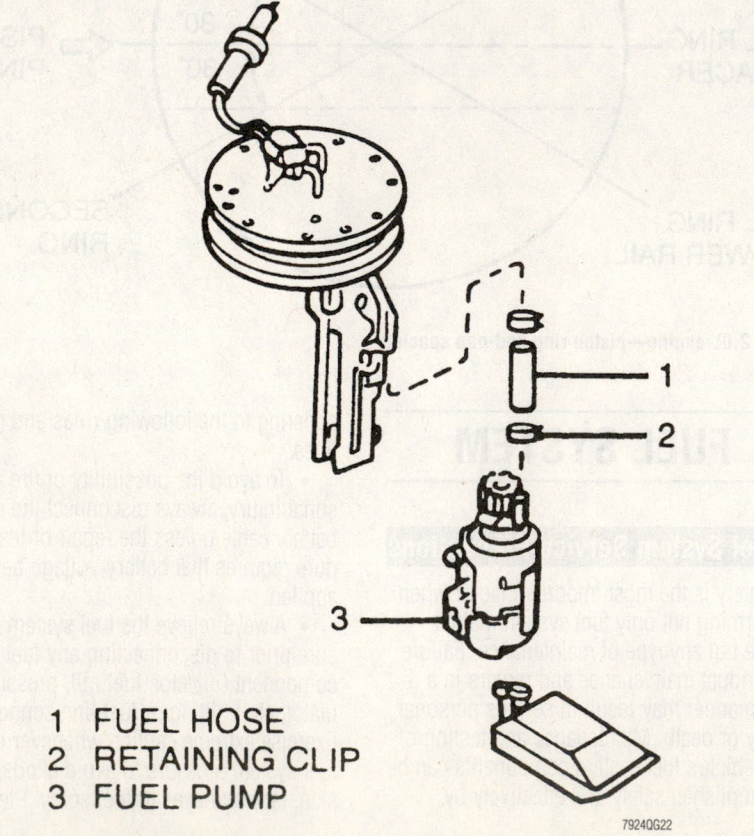

1 FUEL HOSE
2 RETAINING CLIP
3 FUEL PUMP

Exploded view of the fuel pump assembly

- Mass Air Flow (MAF) sensor electrical connector
- Air intake hose bracket
- Accelerator cable
- Vacuum hose from the intake manifold to the vacuum pipe
- Throttle Position (TP) sensor and Idle Air Control (IAC) valve electrical connectors
- Coolant hoses from the throttle body
- Clamp and hoses from the IAC valve
- Brake booster vacuum hose from the dynamic chamber
- Cruise control vacuum hose, if equipped
- Bracket from the dynamic chamber
- Manifold bracket
- heater inlet hose
- Dynamic chamber
- Fuel hose from the pressure regulator
- Fuel injector rail clips
- Fuel rail
- Fuel injector insulators
- Pressure regulator
- Fuel injectors

To install:

5. Install or connect the following:
- Fuel injectors to the fuel rail
- New insulators
- New injector clips
- Fuel rail
- Clamps and air hose to the fuel rail
- Fuel hose to the pressure regulator
- Dynamic chamber with a new gasket. Torque the bolts to 16 ft. lbs. (22 Nm).
- IAC valve bracket bottom bolt
- IAC valve and TP sensor electrical connectors
- Heater inlet hose
- Cruise control hose, if equipped
- Vacuum hose to the pressure regulator
- Air hose and clamp to the air rail
- IAC valve vacuum hose
- Manifold bracket bolts
- Coolant hoses to the throttle body
- Vacuum hose to the vacuum pipe
- MAF sensor bracket
- MAF sensor electrical connector
- Accelerator cable
- Breather hoses
- Negative battery cable

6. Fill the cooling system.
7. Start the vehicle and check for leaks, repair if necessary.

DRIVE TRAIN

Transmission Assembly

REMOVAL & INSTALLATION

Manual

➡**The removal of the manual transmission is virtually the same for 4WD and 2WD vehicles.**

1. Before servicing the vehicle, refer to the precautions in the beginning of this section.
2. Drain the transmission fluid.
3. Drain the transfer case.
4. Remove or disconnect the following:
- Negative battery cable
- Rear portion of the center console
- Shift lever and transfer lever knobs
- Slide the boot cover over the shifters and remove the center console
- Shift lever
- Transfer lever
- Front driveshaft by removing the bolts at the front differential and the bolts at the transfer case, if equipped
- Bolts from the rear differential flange and the center support. Pull the driveshaft out of the tail shaft housing, if equipped with a 4 x 4
- Bolts from the rear differential flange and center support. Pull the driveshaft out of the tail shaft housing, if equipped with a 4 x 2
- Back-up light electrical connector and the Vehicle Speed Sensor (VSS) electrical connectors and move the wire harness aside
- Crankshaft Position (CKP) sensor from the transmission housing
- Clutch release cylinder and move it aside
- Front exhaust pipe bracket
- Front lower transmission housing bolts
- Transfer case side mount, if equipped and properly support the transmission
- Transmission crossmember transmission mount bolts
- Starter from the front housing
- Transmission and transfer case, if equipped

To install:

5. Install or connect the following:
- Transmission into position at the rear of the engine

- Wire harness along the right side of the transmission and route the VSS wire over the transmission to the rear of the control rod extension
- Transmission to engine 14mm mounting bolts. Torque the bolts to 80 ft. lbs. (108 Nm).
- Transmission to engine 10mm mounting bolts. Torque the bolts to 29 ft. lbs. (39 Nm).
- Transmission to engine 6mm mounting bolts. Torque the bolts to 5 ft. lbs. (7 Nm).
- Exhaust pipe to the bracket. Torque the bolts to 20 ft. lbs. (27 Nm).
- Starter and ground wire. Torque the bolts to 29 ft. lbs. (39 Nm).
- Transmission crossmember mount. Torque the bolts to 80 ft. lbs. (108 Nm).
- Crossmember to the chassis. Torque the bolts to 32 ft. lbs. (44 Nm).
- CKP sensor. Torque the bolt to 5 ft. lbs. (7 Nm).
- 4WD indicator switch connector
- Back-up light electrical connector
- VSS electrical connector
- Clutch release cylinder. Torque the bolts to 29 ft. lbs. (39 Nm).
- Driveshaft to the rear differential flange, 4 x 4 only
- Forward end of the driveshaft into the extension housing and attach the center support to the chassis
- Shaft to the rear differential flange. Torque the bolts to 27 ft. lbs. (36 Nm).
- Front driveshaft at the transfer case and install the bolts to the front differential, 4 x 4 only
- Transfer case side mount, if equipped. Torque the bolts to 38 ft. lbs. (52 Nm).
- Transfer case side mount to the chassis. Torque the bolts to 38 ft. lbs. (52 Nm).
- Shift lever assembly. Torque the shift lever bracket bolts to 18 ft lbs. (25 Nm).
- Transfer lever assembly, if equipped. Torque the bolts to 18 ft. lbs. (25 Nm).
- Dust cover plate over the shifter lever handles. Torque the bolts to 15 ft. lbs. (20 Nm).
- Front console
- Shifter lever knobs
- Negative battery cable
- Fill the transfer case.

6. Fill the transmission assembly.

7. Start the vehicle and check for leaks, repair if necessary.

Automatic

1. Before servicing the vehicle, refer to the precautions in the beginning of this section.
2. Drain the transmission fluid.
3. Drain the cooling system.
4. Remove or disconnect the following:
   - Negative battery cable
   - Automatic transmission control cable from the throttle body
5. Slide the front seats forward and remove the 2 rear shift console mounting screws and set the parking brake.
   - Rear console and slide the front seats rearward
   - Front console mounting screws and untie the shifter boot draw strings
   - Loosen the transfer case lock nut and remove the transfer case shifter lever knob
   - Power/economy switch electrical connector
   - Front console and shift the transfer lever to the 4L position
   - transfer shift lever cover plate
   - transfer case shift lever assembly and place the transmission in the park position
   - Selector lever nuts
   - Split pin from the shift selector lever
   - Shift selector rod and spring washers
   - Electrical connectors from the base of the selector lever

➡ There is a fifth wire connection (Park Position). This wire is hard-wired, do not disconnect it.

   - Selector lever assembly
   - Control cable from the throttle linkage and slide the cable from the bellcrank
   - Upper dipstick tube from the lower dipstick tube
   - Input/Turbine speed sensor from the top rear of the transmission
   - Shift solenoids from the lower left side of the transmission
   - Vehicle Speed Sensor (VSS) from the center of the transfer case
   - Input speed sensor electrical connectors
   - Matchmark the front and rear driveshafts. Remove the attaching bolts from both flanges and remove the driveshafts
   - Oil cooler pipes at the transmission
   - Starter

- Transfer case mounting bolts
- Transfer case nuts from the crossmember and support the transmission
- Crossmember
- Transmission to engine mounting bolts
- Front lower splash shield
- Left side lower gusset
- Torque converter inspection cover
- Torque converter to drive plate bolts
- Slide the transmission away from the engine and lower the transmission slightly

- Crankshaft Position (CKP) sensor attaching bolt and sensor
- 4WD, 4WD LOW indicator switches and the VSS from the transfer case
6. Lower the transmission. Be sure all wiring is clear and disconnected. Be sure the throttle cables come out without binding or attaching to anything.

To install:

7. Install or connect the following:
   - Transmission into position to attach the sensor and indicator switch wiring. Be sure the throttle cables are guided into the engine com-

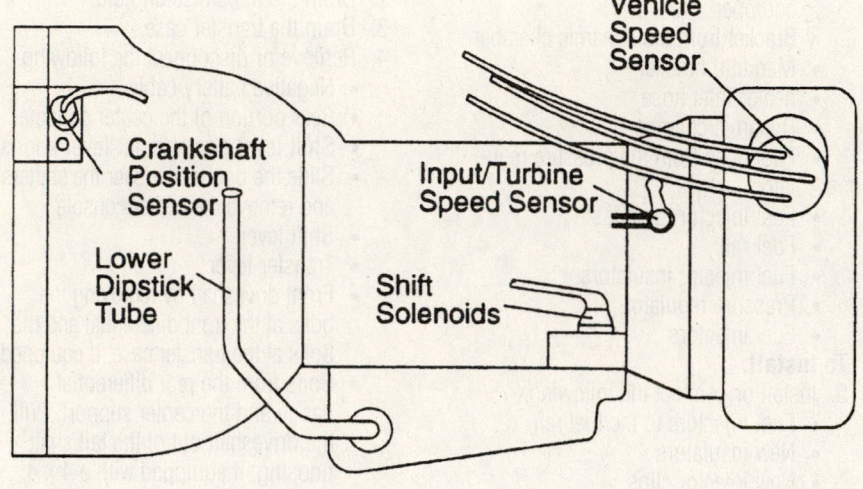

Automatic transmission wiring connections

7924QG23

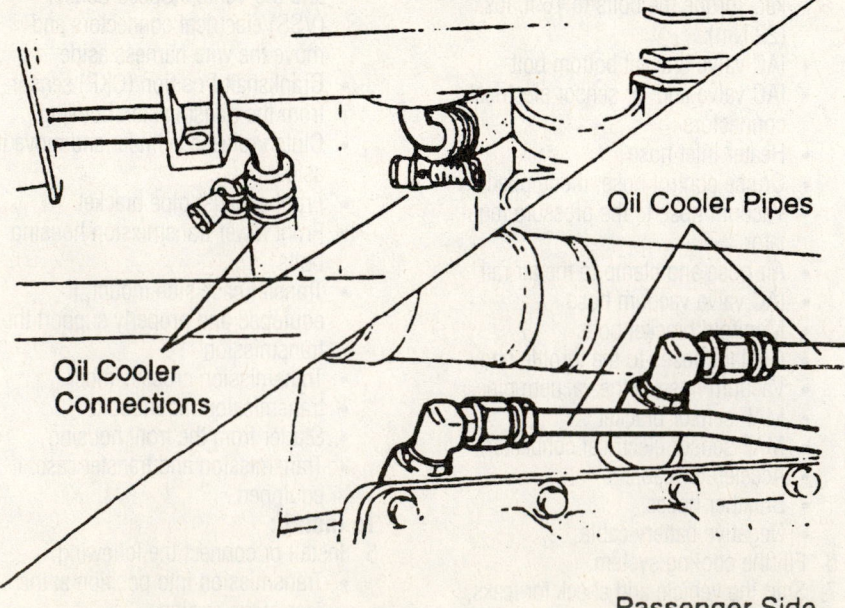

Exploded view of the oil cooler pipe connections

7924QG24

partment without binding or attaching to anything.

- 4WD, 4WD LOW indicator switches and the VSS to the transfer case
- Input/turbine speed sensor and CKP sensor. Torque the bolt to 12 ft. lbs. (16 Nm).
- Raise the transmission and position it to the engine. Install the upper housing bolts. Torque the bolts in the following sequence:

8. 10mm bolts to 38–60 ft. lbs. (57–81 Nm).

9. 12mm bolts to 51–65 ft. lbs. (69–88 Nm).

- Exhaust hanger and bracket. Torque the bolts to 38–60 ft. lbs. (57–81 Nm).
- Oil cooler pipe to the lower engine mount. Torque the bolt to 60 ft. lbs. (81 Nm).
- Crossmember. Torque the bolts to 23–34 ft. lbs. (31–46 Nm).
- Two transfer case mounting bolts located at the right center of the transfer case. Torque the bolts to 23–34 ft. lbs. (31–46 Nm).
- Four transfer case nuts to the crossmember. Torque the nuts to 23–34 ft. lbs. (31–46 Nm).
- Torque converter-to-drive plate bolts. Torque the bolts to 12–20 ft. lbs. (16–27 Nm).
- Torque converter inspection cover. Torque the bolts to 41–62 inch lbs. (5–7 Nm).
- Front splash guard. Torque the bolts to 41–62 inch lbs. (5–7 Nm).
- Starter. Torque bolts to 27–40 ft. lbs. (37–54 Nm).
- Left side lower gusset. Torque the bolts to 38–60 ft. lbs. (57–81 Nm).
- Right side lower gusset in 3 steps:

a. Install the bottom mounting bolts, but do not tighten.

b. Install the top bolt to the intake manifold support bracket and manifold. Tighten to 27–40 ft. lbs. (37–54 Nm).

c. Secure the manifold intake bracket by tightening the two attaching bolts to 38–60 ft. lbs. (57–81 Nm).

- Oil cooler pipes at the transmission. Torque the lines to 42–62 inch lbs. (5–7 Nm).
- Two oil cooling tube clamps to the lines
- Driveshafts with the matchmarks aligned. Torque the bolts to the differential flanges to 20–22 ft. lbs. (27–30 Nm) and the transfer case flange bolts to 36–43 ft. lbs. (49–59 Nm).
- Undercover splash shield. Torque the bolts to 42–62 inch lbs. (5–7 Nm).
- Upper dipstick tube to the lower tube and lower the vehicle

10. Provide automatic transmission control cable slack by gently pulling the cable to the left until the cable pin has rotated sufficiently to line the automatic transmission control cable up with the slot in the rear of the throttle body bellcrank.

11. Slide the automatic transmission control cable and cable pin into the bellcrank.

12. Tighten the locknut.

- Throttle kickdown cable to the mounting bracket
- Automatic transmission control cable to the throttle body
- Air silencer
- Shifter lever assembly to the transfer case. Torque the bolts to 72–102 inch lbs. (22–28 Nm).
- Four wiring connectors under the shift selector lever
- Shift selector lever, do not exert any force when installing the shift selector lever
- Four shift selector lever nuts. Tighten to 72–102 inch lbs. (22–28 Nm).
- Shift rod and washers to the selector lever and install the split pin to the shift selector lever
- Power/Economy switch wiring connector
- Rear console
- Front console and tie the shift boot draw strings
- Negative battery cable

13. Fill the transmission to the proper level.

14. Fill the cooling system.

15. Start the vehicle, check for leaks, and repair if necessary.

Clutch

ADJUSTMENT

Clutch Pedal Height

1. Before servicing the vehicle, refer to the precautions in the beginning of this section.

2. Pull back the carpet to measure the distance from the firewall to the top of the pedal. The standard height is 9.84 in. (250 mm).

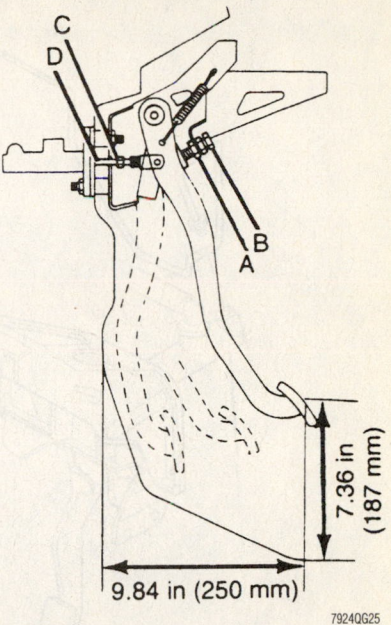

7.36 in (187 mm)

9.84 in (250 mm)

7924QG25

Clutch pedal height and free-play adjustment points

3. If adjustment is required, loosen the locknut and turn the stopper bolt.

4. After adjustment is made tighten the locknut to 12 ft. lbs. (16 Nm).

Clutch Pedal Free-Play

1. Before servicing the vehicle, refer to the precautions in the beginning of this section.

2. Depress the clutch pedal gently by hand and measure the amount of free-play (distance the pedal travels before resistance is felt). The proper amount of free-play is 0.5 in. (12.7mm). If the free-play is not within the proper specifications, continue with the procedure.

3. Measure from the floor pan to the middle point of the clutch pedal when the pedal is in the fully released position. The proper clutch pedal height is 7.25 in. (184mm).

4. If the pedal height is incorrect, loosen locknut (A) and turn the pedal adjusting bolt (B) until the proper height is achieved, then retighten the locknut.

5. Remeasure the free-play. If it is still out of specification, loosen the clutch pushrod locknut (C) and turn the pushrod (D) until the proper free-play is achieved. Tighten locknut (C) securely.

REMOVAL & INSTALLATION

1. Before servicing the vehicle, refer to the precautions in the beginning of this section.

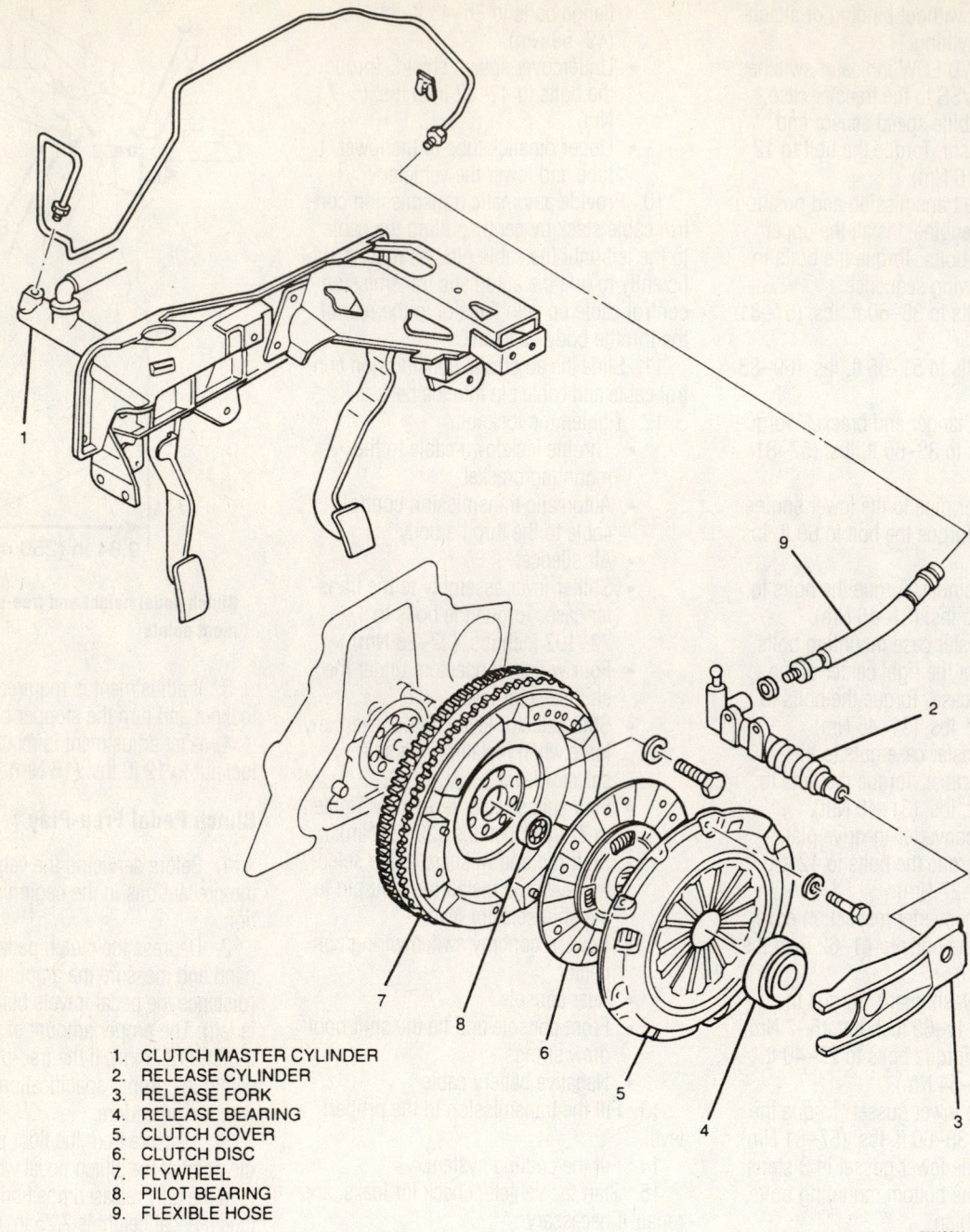

1. CLUTCH MASTER CYLINDER
2. RELEASE CYLINDER
3. RELEASE FORK
4. RELEASE BEARING
5. CLUTCH COVER
6. CLUTCH DISC
7. FLYWHEEL
8. PILOT BEARING
9. FLEXIBLE HOSE

7924QG26

Exploded view of the clutch assembly

2. Remove or disconnect the following:
- Transmission
- Pressure plate bolts and remove the clutch plate and disc

To install:

3. Install or connect the following:
- Clutch disc and plate using a centering tool
- Clutch cover. Torque the bolts to 73 ft. lbs. (99 Nm) and remove the centering tool
- Check the release bearing condition

and lubricate or replace as necessary
- Transmission

Hydraulic Clutch System

BLEEDING

1. Before servicing the vehicle, refer to the precautions in the beginning of this section.

2. With an assistant in the vehicle, raise and safely support the vehicle.

3. Have your assistant pump the clutch pedal three times and hold the pedal to the floor.

4. Open the bleeder valve on the clutch slave cylinder until the air is purged from the cylinder.

5. Tighten the bleeder valve.

6. Have your assistant release the clutch pedal.

7. Fill the clutch master cylinder if below minimum.

8. Repeat Steps 2 through 6 until no air exits from the bleeder valve.

9. Lower the vehicle.

10. Fill the clutch master cylinder fluid reservoir.

Transfer Case Assembly

REMOVAL & INSTALLATION

1. Before servicing the vehicle, refer to the precautions in the beginning of this section.

2. Drain the transfer case.

3. Remove or disconnect the following:
   - Negative battery cable
   - Two rear console mounting screws. Slide the console forward to clear the parking brake handle and set aside
   - Three mounting screws from the front console. Untie the shift boot draw strings and open the boot
   - Loosen the transfer case shift lever locknut and remove the lever knob
   - Pull the console up to access the Power/Economy switch wiring connector. Unplug the connector and remove the console

4. Shift the transfer lever to the 4L position.
   - Cover plate

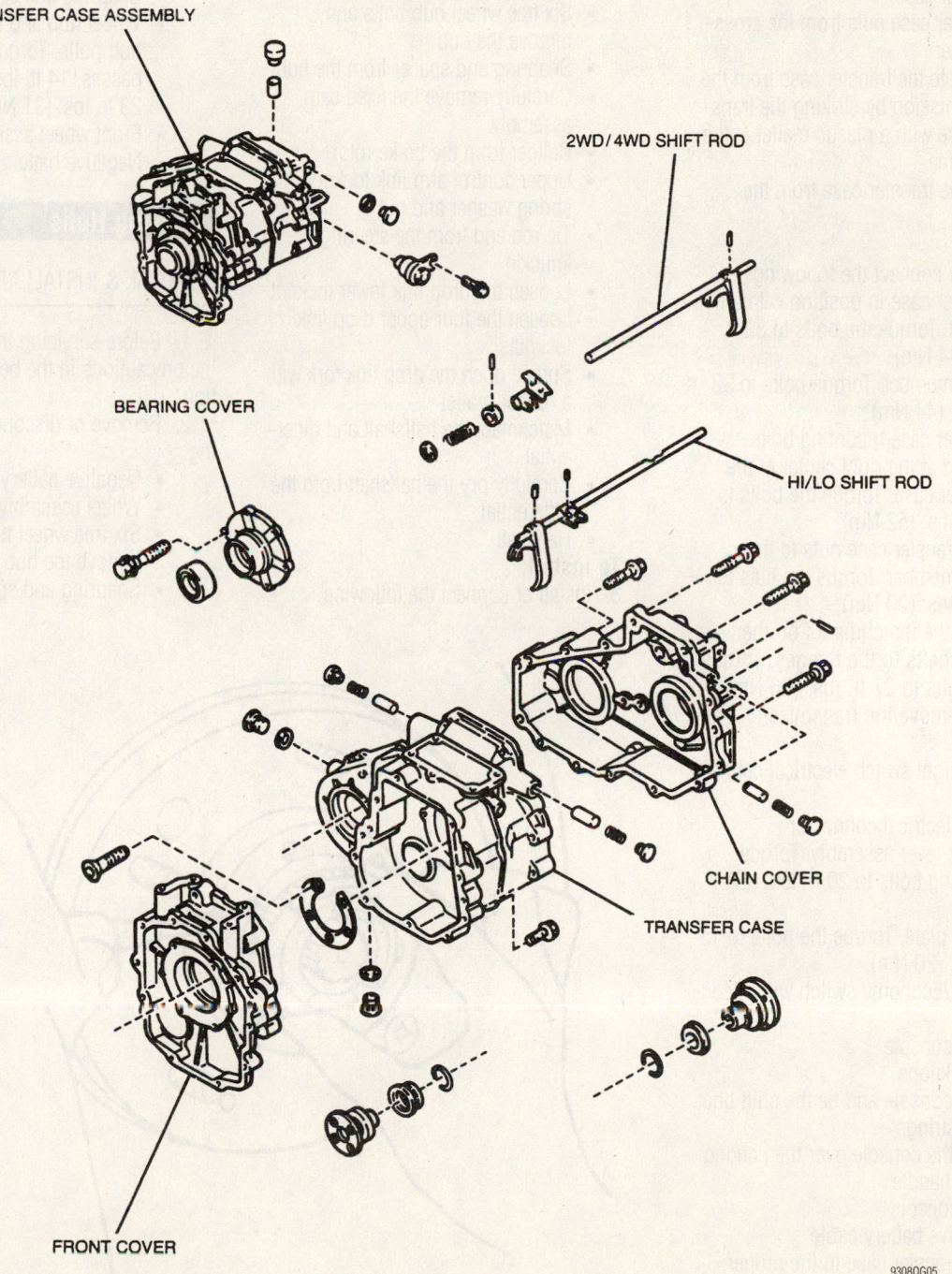

Exploded view of the transfer case assembly

TRANSFER CASE ASSEMBLY

2WD / 4WD SHIFT ROD

BEARING COVER

HI/LO SHIFT ROD

CHAIN COVER

TRANSFER CASE

FRONT COVER

9308QG05

Turn to Section 5 for brake system applications

- Retaining bolts from the transfer case and lift the shifter lever assembly straight out and properly support the transmission
- Matchmark the driveshafts at the flanges and remove the driveshafts
- Crossmember bolts
- 4WD light switch connector
- Transfer case mounting bolts located at the right center of the transfer case
- Transfer case nuts from the crossmember
- Separate the transfer case from the transmission by striking the transfer case with a plastic mallet at the seal area

5. Lower the transfer case from the vehicle.

To install:

6. Install or connect the following:
- Transfer case in position with a new gasket. Torque the bolts to 32 ft. lbs. (44 Nm).
- Crossmember. Torque bolts to 32 ft. lbs. (44 Nm).
- Transfer case mounting bolts located at the right center of the transfer case. Torque the bolts to 38 ft. lbs. (52 Nm).
- Four transfer case nuts to the crossmember. Torque the nuts to 15 ft. lbs. (20 Nm).
- Align the matchmarks on the driveshafts to the flanges. Torque the bolts to 27 ft. lbs. (36 Nm) and remove the transmission support
- 4WD light switch electrical connector
- VSS electrical connector
- Shifter lever assembly. Torque retaining bolts to 20 ft. lbs. (27 Nm).
- Cover plate. Torque the bolts to 15 ft. lbs. (20 Nm).
- Power/Economy switch wiring connector
- Front console
- Lever knobs
- Front console and tie the shift boot draw strings
- Slide the console over the parking brake handle
- Rear console
- Negative battery cable

7. Fill the transfer case to the proper level

8. Start the vehicle and check for leaks, repair if necessary.

Halfshaft

REMOVAL & INSTALLATION

1. Before servicing the vehicle, refer to the precautions in the beginning of this section.

2. Remove or disconnect the following:
- Negative battery cable
- Both front wheels
- Six free wheel hub bolts and remove the hub
- Snapring and spacer from the hub
- Carefully remove the fixed cam assembly
- Caliper from the brake rotor
- Upper control arm link lockbolt, spring washer and nut
- Tie rod end from the steering knuckle
- Loosen the drop link lower locknut
- Loosen the four upper drop link locknuts
- Spread open the drop link fork with a rubber mallet
- Matchmark the halfshaft and differential.
- Carefully pry the halfshaft from the differential
- Halfshaft

To install:

3. Install or connect the following:
- Halfshaft with the matchmarks aligned with the differential
- Torque the upper and lower drop link nuts to 36 ft. lbs. (49 Nm).
- Tie rod end to the steering knuckle. Torque the locknut to 27 ft. lbs. (36 Nm) and install a new cotter pin
- Upper control arm link lockbolt, spring washer and nut. Torque the bolt to 36 ft. lbs. (49 Nm).
- Fixed cam assembly
- Snapring and spacer in the hub
- Wheel hub and the six free wheel hub bolts. Torque the bolts in two passes, 14 ft. lbs. (17 Nm), then to 23 ft. lbs. (31 Nm).
- Front wheel assemblies
- Negative battery cable

Locking Hubs

REMOVAL & INSTALLATION

1. Before servicing the vehicle, refer to the precautions in the beginning of this section.

2. Remove or disconnect the following:
- Negative battery cable
- Wheel assembly
- Six free wheel hub bolts and remove the hub
- Snapring and spacer from the hub

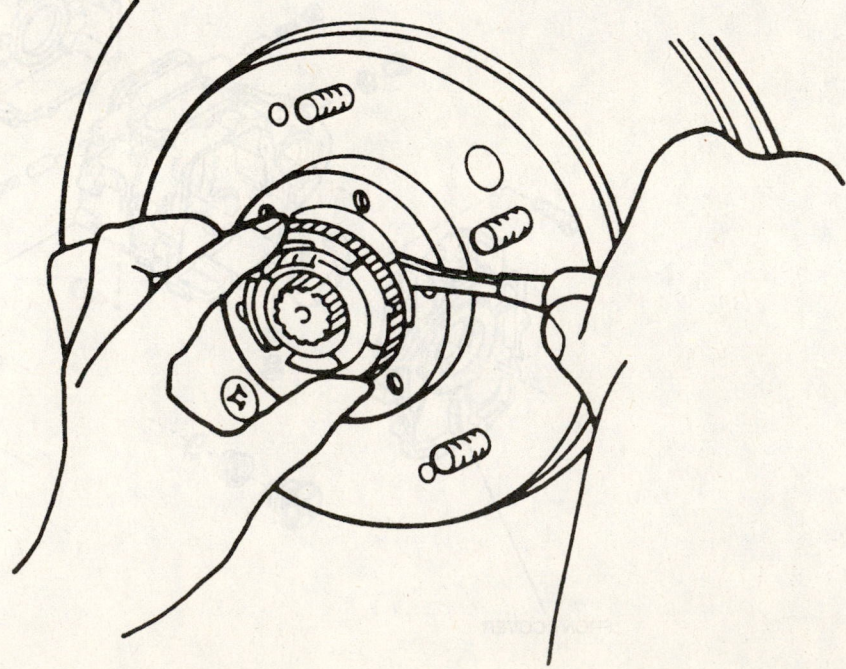

Removing the 4WD fixed cam assembly

7924QG27

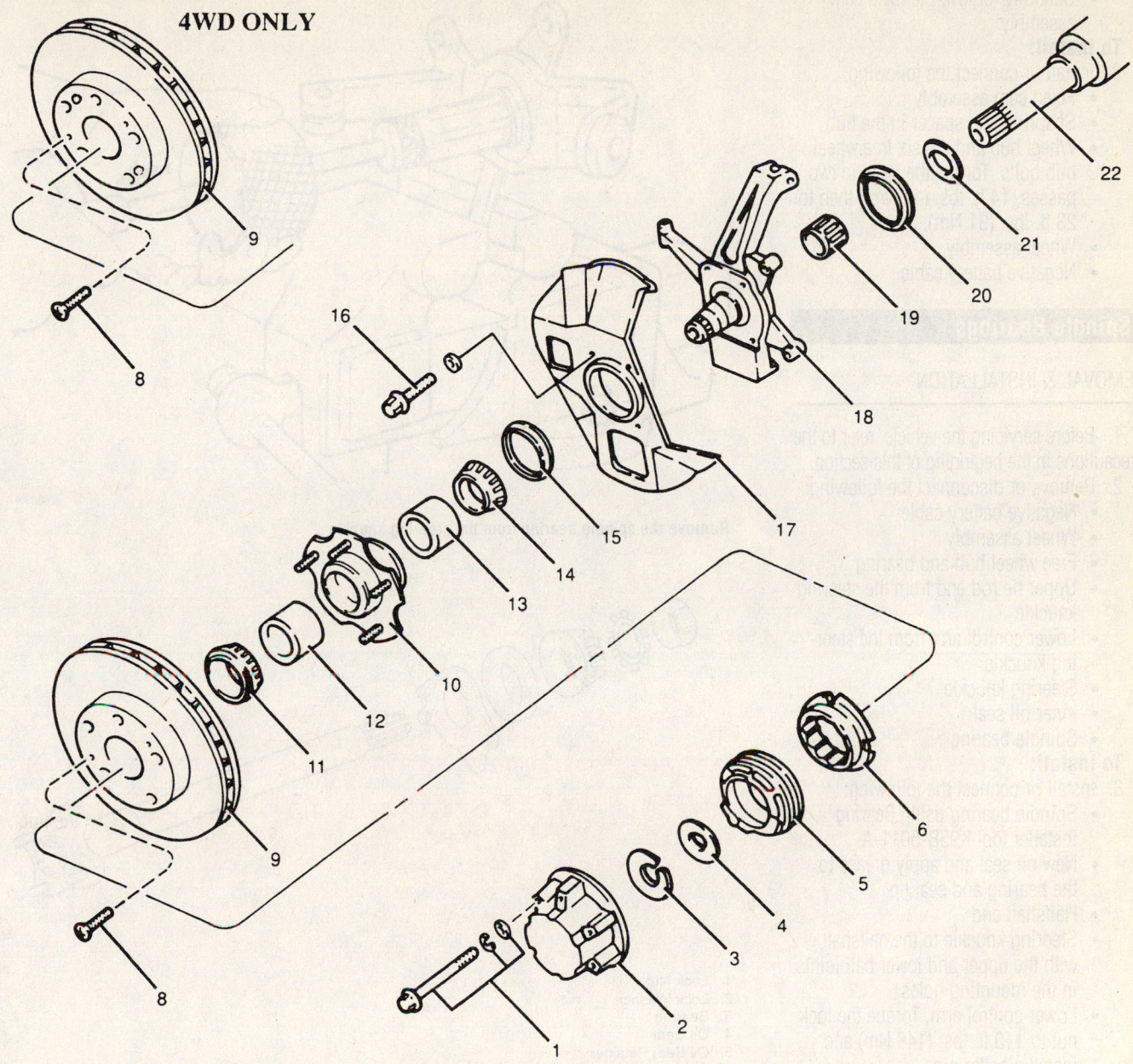

4WD ONLY

Exploded view of the 4WD locking hub assembly

1	BOLT/WASHER	9	ROTOR	16	BOLT & SPRING WASHER
2	FREE WHEEL HUB BODY	10	WHEEL HUB	17	DUST COVER
3	SNAP RING	11	INNER BEARING INNER RACE	18	KNUCKLE
4	SPACER	12	INNER BEARING OUTER RACE	19	NEEDLE BEARING
5	FIXED CAM ASSEMBLY	13	OUTER BEARING OUTER RACE	20	OIL SEAL
6	LOCK NUT	14	OUTER BEARING INNER RACE	21	SPACER
8	SCREW	15	OIL SEAL	22	DRIVE SHAFT (LH)

79240G28

- Carefully remove the fixed cam assembly

To install:

3. Install or connect the following:
- Fixed cam assembly
- Snapring and spacer in the hub
- Wheel hub and the six free wheel hub bolts. Torque the bolts in two passes, 14 ft. lbs. (17 Nm), then to 23 ft. lbs. (31 Nm).
- Wheel assembly
- Negative battery cable

Spindle Bearings

REMOVAL & INSTALLATION

1. Before servicing the vehicle, refer to the precautions in the beginning of this section.
2. Remove or disconnect the following:
- Negative battery cable
- Wheel assembly
- Free wheel hub and bearing
- Upper tie rod end from the steering knuckle
- Lower control arm from the steering knuckle
- Steering knuckle
- Inner oil seal
- Spindle bearing

To install:

3. Install or connect the following:
- Spindle bearing using Bearing Installer tool K95B-5011-A
- New oil seal and apply grease to the bearing and seal lip
- Halfshaft end
- Steering knuckle to the halfshaft with the upper and lower ball joints in the mounting holes
- Lower control arm. Torque the lock nut to 110 ft. lbs. (148 Nm) and install a cotter pin
- Tie rod end to the steering knuckle. Torque the nut to 27 ft. lbs. (36 Nm) and install a cotter pin
- Upper control arm. Torque the lock bolt to 36 ft. lbs. (49 Nm).
- Free wheel hub and bearing assembly
- Front wheel
- Negative battery cable

Axle Shaft Bearing and Seal

REMOVAL & INSTALLATION

1. Before servicing the vehicle, refer to the precautions in the beginning of this section.

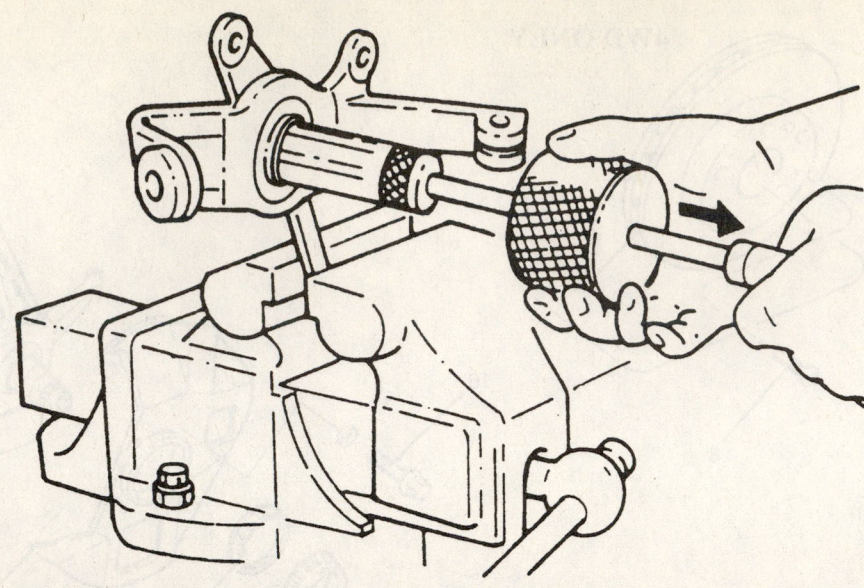

Remove the spindle bearing from the steering knuckle

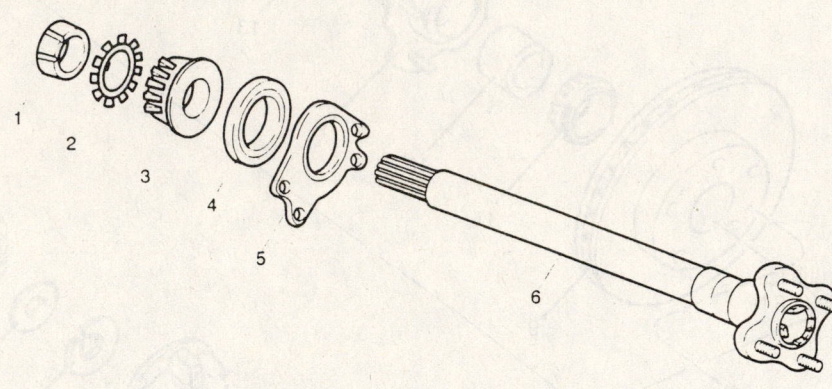

1. Lock Nut
2. Lock Washer
3. Bearing
4. Oil Seal
5. Oil Seal Retainer
6. Axle Shaft

Exploded view of the axle shaft, bearing and seal

2. Remove or disconnect the following:
- Negative battery cable
- Wheel assembly
- Rear wheel
- Brake drum
- Wheel speed sensor, if equipped
- Bearing retaining nuts
- Axle shaft and bearing

To install:

3. Install or connect the following:
- Oil seal retainer, oil seal and wheel bearing to the axle shaft. Torque the new lock nut to 220 ft. lbs. (300 Nm).

➡**Turn the right side halfshaft lock nut clockwise and the left side halfshaft lock nut counterclockwise.**

- Axle shaft assembly into the axle housing. Torque the nuts to 74 ft. lbs. (100 Nm).
- Wheel speed sensor, if equipped
- Brake drum
- Rear wheel assembly
- Negative battery cable

4. Check the fluid level and top off if necessary.

Pinion Seal

REMOVAL & INSTALLATION

1. Before servicing the vehicle, refer to the precautions in the beginning of this section.
2. Drain the gear oil.
3. Remove or disconnect the following:
   - Negative battery cable
   - Wheel assemblies
   - Brake drums
   - Driveshaft

➡ **Use an inch lb. (Nm) torque wrench , measure and record the amount of torque required to maintain rotation of the pinion.**

   - Pinion flange
   - Pinion seal

To install:

4. Install or connect the following:
   - New pinion seal lightly coated with clean gear oil
   - Pinion flange
5. Rotate the pinion flange occasionally while tightening the flange nut and make certain that the pinion bearings are seated properly.
6. Take several bearing preload torque readings. Tighten the flange nut to achieve the preload torque reading. The maximum torque reading should not exceed 14 inch lbs. (1.6 Nm).
   - Driveshaft after aligning the match-marks
   - Brake drums
   - Wheel assemblies
   - Negative battery cable
7. Fill the gear oil to the proper level.
8. Start the vehicle and check for leaks, repair if necessary.

Axle Housing

REMOVAL & INSTALLATION

1. Before servicing the vehicle, refer to the precautions in the beginning of this section.
2. Drain the gear oil.
3. Remove or disconnect the following:
   - Negative battery cable
   - Rear wheels
   - Brake drums
   - Oil seal retainer flange
   - Axle shaft assemblies
   - Brake hose
   - Brake backing plates
   - Wheel speed sensor electrical connector, if equipped
   - Shock absorbers
   - Coil springs
   - Differential carrier

To install:

4. Install or connect the following:
   - Differential carrier. Torque the small bolts to 18 ft. lbs. (25 Nm) and the larger bolts to 38 ft. lbs. (51 Nm).
   - Coil springs to the axle housing and place the housing in position
   - Shock absorbers. Torque the bolts to 66 ft. lbs. (90 Nm).
   - Wheel speed sensor electrical connector, if equipped
   - Brake backing plates
   - Axle shafts when properly aligned
   - Oil seal retainer flange
   - Brake drums
   - Rear wheels
   - Negative battery cable
5. Fill the differential with clean oil to the proper level.
6. Start the vehicle and check for leaks, repair if necessary.

STEERING AND SUSPENSION

Air Bag

PRECAUTIONS

Several precautions must be observed when handling the inflator module to avoid accidental deployment and possible personal injury.

1. Never carry the inflator module by the wires or connector on the underside of the module.
2. When carrying a live inflator module, hold securely with both hands, and ensure that the bag and trim cover are pointed away from you.
3. Place the inflator module on a bench or other surface with the bag and trim cover facing up.
4. With the inflator module on the bench, never place anything on or close to the module which may be thrown in the event of an accidental deployment.

DISARMING

1. Before servicing the vehicle, refer to the precautions in the beginning of this section.
2. Turn the ignition switch to the **LOCK** position.
3. Disconnect the negative battery cable.
4. Wait 10 minutes for the back-up power to discharge.

ARMING

Assuming the system components (air bag control module, sensors, air bag, etc.) are installed correctly and are in good working order, the system is armed whenever the battery positive and negative battery cables are connected.

If you have disarmed the air bag system for any reason, to rearm, be sure no one is in the vehicle (as an added safety measure), then connect the negative battery cable.

Power Steering Gear

ADJUSTMENT

1. Before servicing the vehicle, refer to the precautions in the beginning of this section.
2. Place the steering gear in a vise with protective jaws.
3. Place a torque wrench on the Pitman arm end of the shaft.
4. Loosen the locknut on the adjusting bolt.
5. Slowly turn the adjusting bolt to until the breakaway torque is 65 ft. lbs. (88 Nm).
6. Hold the adjusting bolt in position and tighten the locknut to 25 ft. lbs. (34 Nm).

REMOVAL & INSTALLATION

1. Before servicing the vehicle, refer to the precautions in the beginning of this section.
2. Center the steering wheel.
3. Drain the power steering fluid.
4. Remove or disconnect the following:
   - Negative battery cable
   - Left front wheel
   - Pitman arm-to-centerlink attaching nut

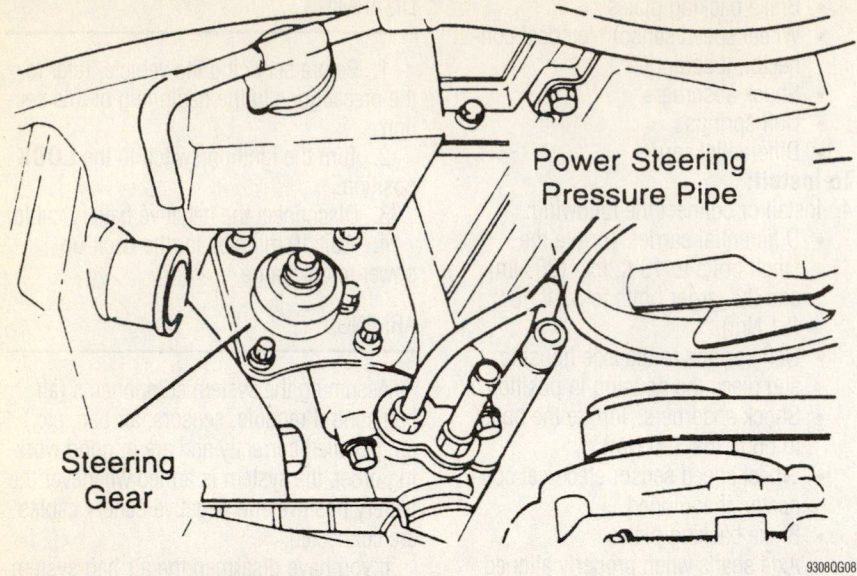

Power Steering Pressure Pipe

Steering Gear

9308QG08

Exploded view of the steering gear

- Separate the Pitman arm from the centerlink with a ball joint puller
- Power steering hoses
- Coolant recovery tank and the power steering reserve tank
- Set bolt from the intermediate shaft
- Intermediate shaft from the steering gear
- Steering gear-to-frame bolts
- Steering gear

To install:

5. Install or connect the following:
- Position the steering gear to the frame. Torque the bolts to 159 ft. lbs. (215 Nm).
- Pitman arm to the centerlink. Torque the bolt to 36 ft. lbs. (49 Nm) and install a new cotter pin
- Intermediate shaft to the steering gear shaft. Torque the set bolt o 25 ft. lbs. (34 Nm).
- Power steering hoses/lines. Torque the fasteners to 29 ft. lbs. (34 Nm).
- Power steering reserve tank over the bracket and press until full engagement is reached
- Coolant recovery tank
- Left front wheel
- Negative battery cable

6. Fill the power steering fluid to the proper level and bleed the system.

7. Start the vehicle and check for leaks, repair if necessary.

8. Road test the vehicle to check that the steering wheel is straight.

Shock Absorber

REMOVAL & INSTALLATION

Front

The front shock absorber and coil spring are removed as a single unit.

1. Before servicing the vehicle, refer to the precautions in the beginning of this section.

2. Remove or disconnect the following:
- Negative battery cable
- Both front wheels
- Upper shock absorber mounting block nuts
- Stabilizer bar
- Drop link nut and allow the drop link to remain in place
- Both halves of the front fork

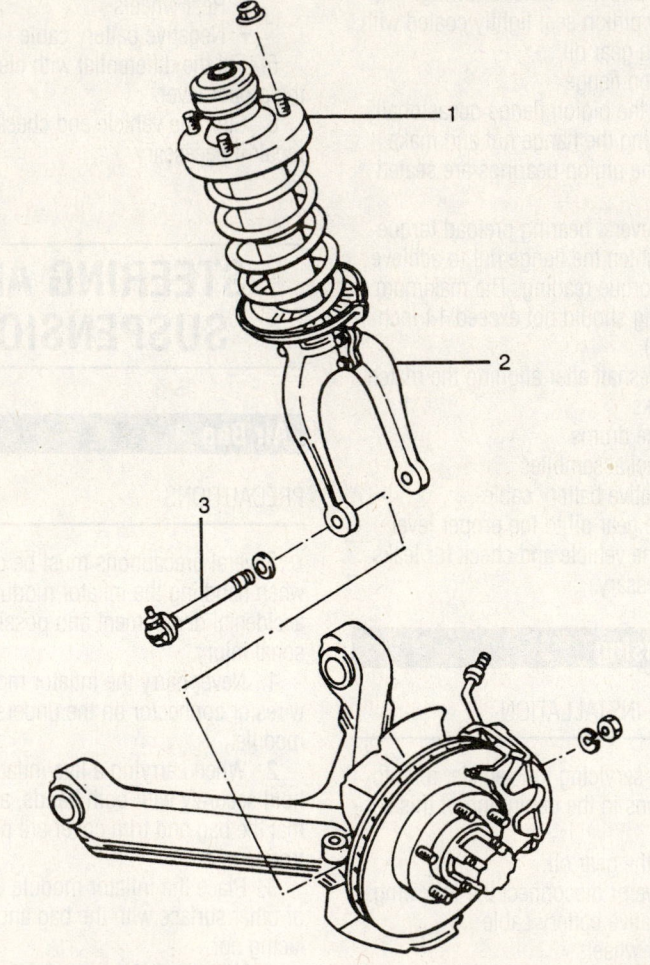

1 Front Shock Absorber & Coil Spring Assembly
2 Front Fork
3 Drop Link

9308QG09

Exploded view of the front shock absorber assembly

- Drop link
- Shock absorber and coil spring as an assembly

To install:

3. Install or connect the following:
- Coil spring to the shock absorber and position the assembly to the upper mounting block
- Upper mounting block nuts and hand tighten them
- Both front forks . Torque the bolts to 36 ft. lbs. (48 Nm).
- Drop link. Torque the nut to 145 ft. lbs. (197 Nm).
- Stabilizer bar to the drop link. Torque the nut to 36 ft. lbs. (48 Nm).
- Front wheels and torque the mounting block nuts to 18 ft. lbs. (25 Nm).
- Negative battery cable

Rear

1. Before servicing the vehicle, refer to the precautions in the beginning of this section.
2. Remove or disconnect the following:
- Negative battery cable
- Rear wheels
- Raise the rear axle with a floor jack to relax the shock absorbers and support the rear axle when the shock absorber is removed.
- Rear safety nut, upper nut and washer
- Upper rubber plate
- Lower bolt from the shock absorber
- Lower the rear axle housing
- Shock absorber
3. Remove the lower mounting bolt and remove the shock absorber.

To install:

4. Install or connect the following:
- Bottom washer and rubber cushion on the top of the shock absorber. Position the shock absorber on the vehicle
- Lower bolt
- Rubber cushion, washer and nut. Tighten to 53 ft. lbs. (72 Nm)
- Safety nut. Torque the lower bolt to 62 ft. lbs. (84 Nm).
- Rear wheels
- Negative battery cable

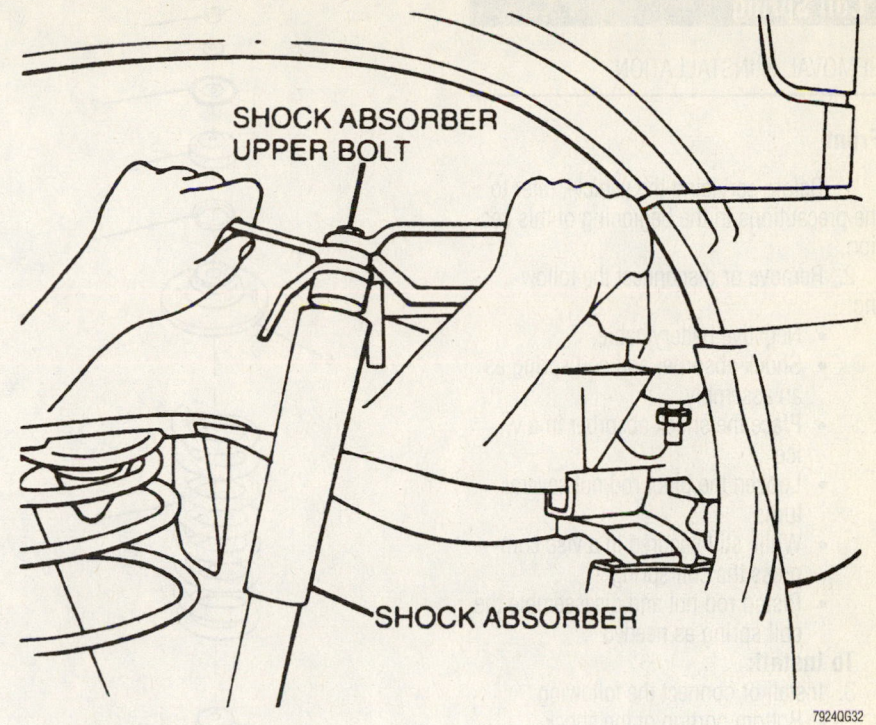

Upper shock absorber mounting nut

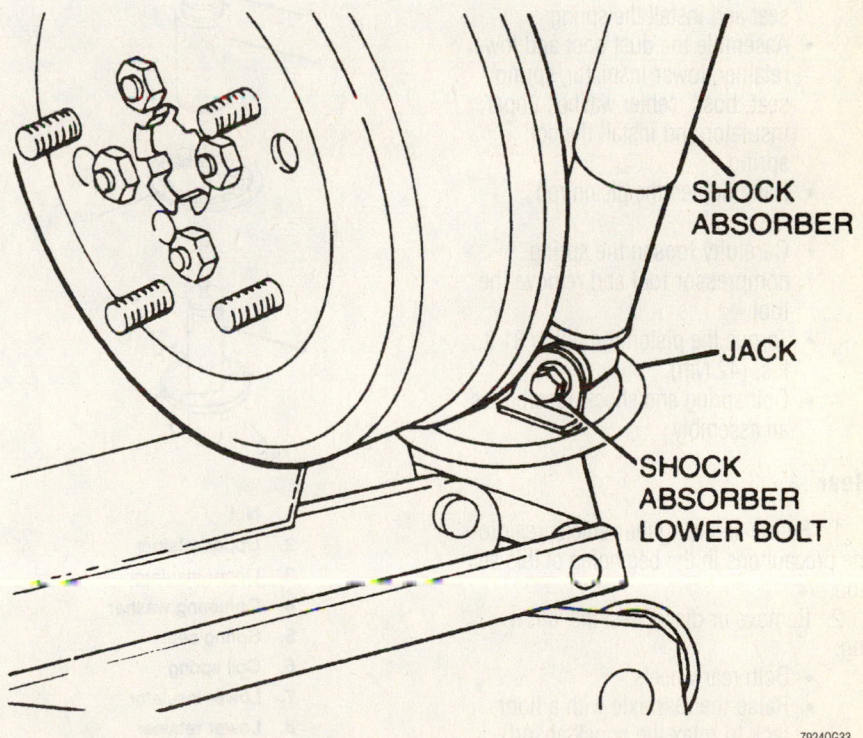

Lower shock absorber mounting bolt

Coil Spring

REMOVAL & INSTALLATION

Front

1. Before servicing the vehicle, refer to the precautions in the beginning of this section.
2. Remove or disconnect the following:
   - Negative battery cable
   - Shock absorber and coil spring as an assembly
   - Place the shock absorber in a v ice
   - Loosen the pivot rod nut several turns
   - While still secured in a vise compress the coil spring
   - Piston rod nut and disassemble the coil spring as needed

To install:

3. Install or connect the following:
   - Bottom portion of the shock absorber in a vice and compress the coil spring
   - End of the coil spring to the rubber seat and install the spring
   - Assemble the dust boot and lower retainer, lower insulator, spring seat, boss, center washer, upper insulator and install the coil spring
   - Hand tighten the piston rod nut.
   - Carefully loosen the spring compressor tool and remove the tool
   - Torque the piston rod nut to 31 ft. lbs. (42 Nm).
   - Coil spring and shock absorber as an assembly

Rear

1. Before servicing the vehicle, refer to the precautions in the beginning of this section.
2. Remove or disconnect the following:
   - Both rear wheels
   - Raise the rear axle with a floor jack to relax the shock absorbers and support the rear axle when the shock absorber is removed.

➡**For easier installation, complete one side at a time.**

   - Lower mounting bolt, then the shock absorber

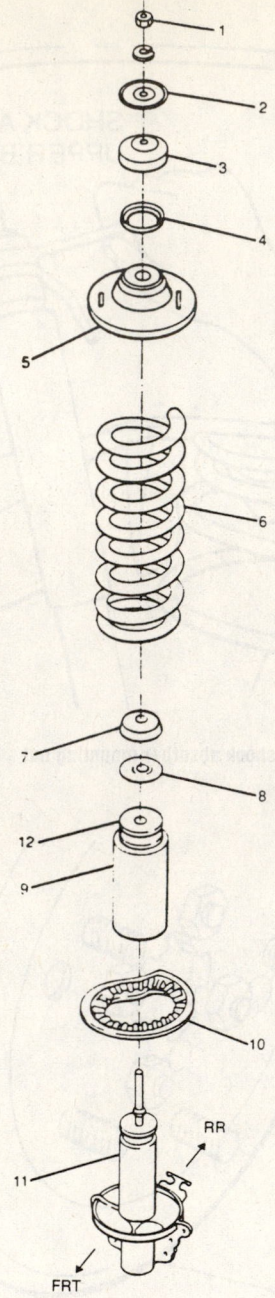

1. Nut
2. Upper retainer
3. Upper insulator
4. Centering washer
5. Spring seat
6. Coil spring
7. Lower insulator
8. Lower retainer
9. Dust boot
10. Rubber seat
11. Shock absorber
12. Front jounce stop

9308QG10

Exploded view of the front shock absorber and coil spring assembly

   - Lower the floor jack until the coil spring is fully expanded
   - Coil spring
   - Inspect the upper and lower rubber spring seats and jounce stop for wear or damage, replace if necessary

To install:

3. Install or connect the following:
   - Position the spring in the upper and lower saddles
   - Raise the floor jack and connect the lower shock absorber bolt. Torque the bolt to 62 ft. lbs. (84 Nm).
   - Rear wheels

Upper Ball Joint

REMOVAL & INSTALLATION

The upper ball joint is an integral part of the upper control arm. If the ball joint is worn, replacement of the upper control arm is necessary.

Lower Ball Joint

REMOVAL & INSTALLATION

1. Before servicing the vehicle, refer to the precautions in the beginning of this section.
2. Remove or disconnect the following:
   - Negative battery cable
   - Front wheel assembly
   - Cotter pin and lower ball joint nut
   - Separate the lower ball joint from the spindle with a puller tool by prying down on the spindle to separate it from the lower ball joint
   - Lower ball joint attaching bolts
   - Lower ball joint

To install:

3. Install or connect the following:
   - Position the lower ball joint and install the attaching nuts and bolts. Torque the fasteners to 36 ft. lbs. (48 Nm).
   - Pry down and guide the spindle onto the lower ball joint. Torque the nut 87 ft. lbs. (118 Nm) and install a new cotter pin
   - Front wheel assembly.
   - Negative battery cable

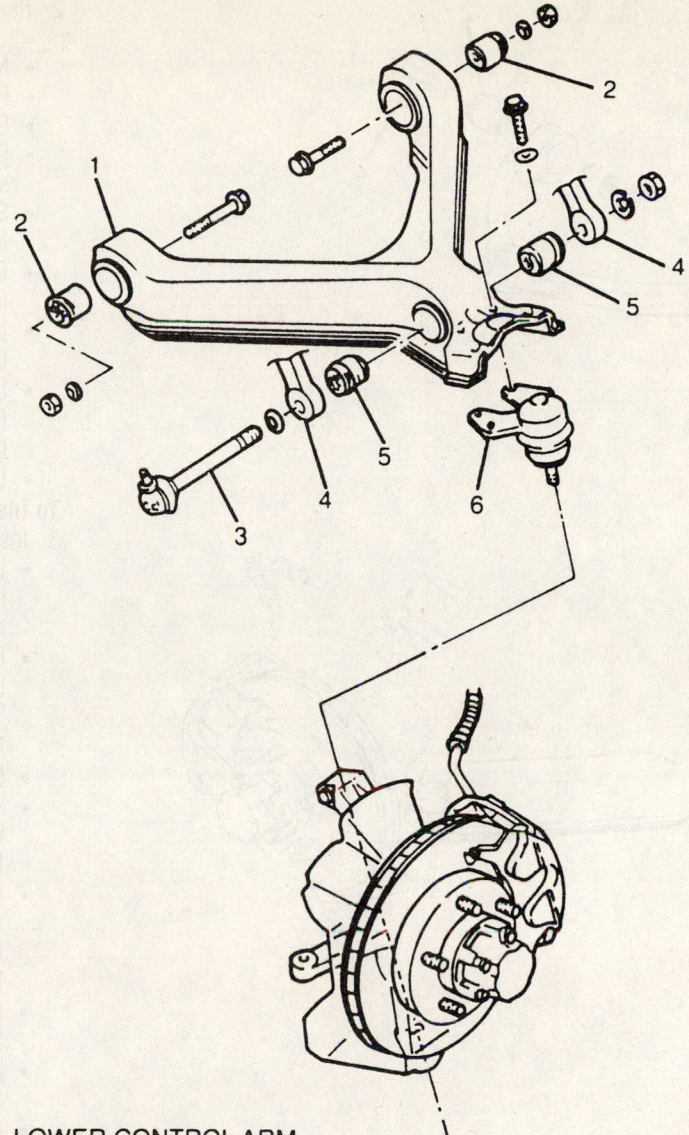

1 LOWER CONTROL ARM
2 LOWER CONTROL ARM BUSHING
3 DROP LINK
4 FRONT FORK
5 DROP LINK BUSHING
6 LOWER CONTROL ARM BALL JOINT

7924QG34

Exploded view of the lower control arm and ball joint assembly

Upper Control Arm

REMOVAL & INSTALLATION

1. Before servicing the vehicle, refer to the precautions in the beginning of this section.
2. Remove or disconnect the following:
   - Negative battery cable
   - Front wheel assembly
   - Bolt securing the upper ball joint to the steering knuckle

→Note the matchmark setting on the upper control arm mounting bolts before removal.

   - Upper control arm mounting bolts
   - Upper control arm from the vehicle.

To install:
3. Install or connect the following:
   - Position the upper control arms in the frame mounting. Hand tighten the bolts
   - Position the ball joint in the spindle. Torque the through bolt to 36 ft. lbs. (48 Nm).

→Be sure the slot in the ball joint aligns with the through-bolt during installation.

   - Align the upper control arm bolts to the previous settings. Torque bolts to 62 ft. lbs. (108 Nm).
   - Front wheel assembly

Turn to Section 5 for brake system applications

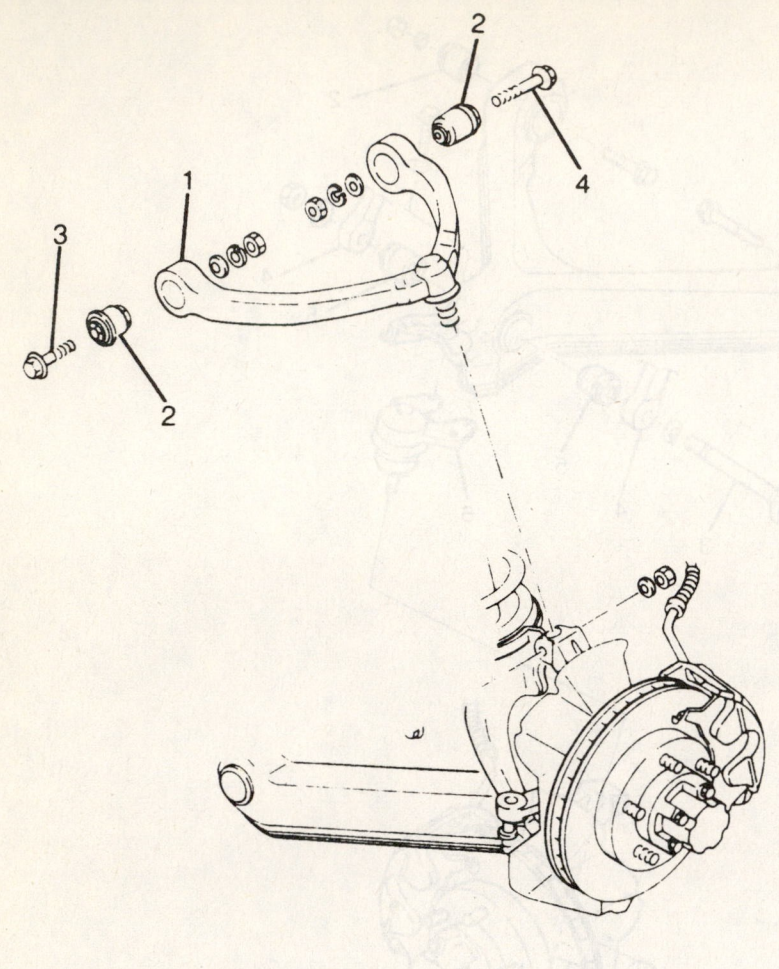

1 UPPER CONTROL ARM
2 UPPER CONTROL ARM BUSHING
3 FRONT SPINDLE
4 REAR SPINDLE

7924QG31

Exploded view of the upper control arm assembly

4. Check and adjust the alignment, if necessary.

UPPER CONTROL ARM BUSHING REPLACEMENT

1. Before servicing the vehicle, refer to the precautions in the beginning of this section.
2. Remove or disconnect the following:
   - Upper control arm assembly
   - Secure the control arm in a vise
   - Using a standard press, remove the bushing

To install:
3. Install or connect the following:
   - Lubricate the new bushing and press it into the upper control arm
   - Upper control arm to the vehicle
4. Check the wheel alignment and adjust if necessary.

Lower Control Arm

REMOVAL & INSTALLATION

1. Before servicing the vehicle, refer to the precautions in the beginning of this section.

2. Remove or disconnect the following:
   - Negative battery cable
   - Front wheel assembly
   - Stabilizer bar
   - Driveshaft from the differential and steering knuckle
   - Shock absorber and coil spring from the front half of the fork
   - Cotter pin and castle nut from the lower control arm ball joint
   - Lower control arm ball joint from the steering knuckle
   - Lower control arm bushing bolts from the front frame crossmember brackets
   - Lower control arm

To install:
3. Install or connect the following:
   - Lower control arm to the front frame crossmember brackets and hand tighten the bushing bolts
   - Lower control arm ball joint and bolt to the steering knuckle. Torque the bolt to 87 ft. lbs. (118 Nm).
   - New cotter pin and castle nut
   - Torque the lower control arm bushing bolts to 206 ft. lbs. (280 Nm).
   - Front fork halves to the shock absorber and coil spring and position the lower portion over the lower control arm drop link holes
   - Drop link. Torque the nut to 145 ft. lbs. (197 Nm).
   - Driveshaft to the front differential and steering knuckle
   - Stabilizer bar
   - Front wheel assembly
   - Negative battery cable
4. Check and adjust the front wheel alignment if necessary.

LOWER CONTROL ARM BUSHING REPLACEMENT

1. Before servicing the vehicle, refer to the precautions in the beginning of this section.

2. Remove or disconnect the following:
   - Lower control arm assembly
   - Secure the control arm in a vise
   - Using a standard press, remove the bushing

To install:
3. Install or connect the following:
   - Lubricate the new bushing and press it into the lower control arm
   - lower control arm to the vehicle
4. Check the wheel alignment and adjust if necessary.

Wheel Bearings

ADJUSTMENT

Front

1. Remove or disconnect the following:
2. Before servicing the vehicle, refer to the precautions in the beginning of this section.
   - Negative battery cable
   - Front wheel
   - Brake caliper from the rotor and hang it out of the way
3. Attach a dial indicator to the axle hub and measure the bearing play
4. If the play exceeds.004 inch (.10mm), check and adjust locknut torque. The bolts should be tightened to 23 ft. lbs. (31 Nm).

Rear

The rear wheel bearings are not adjustable.

REMOVAL & INSTALLATION

Front

1. Before servicing the vehicle, refer to the precautions in the beginning of this section.

2. Remove or disconnect the following:
   - Negative battery cable
   - Front wheel
   - Free wheel hub body
   - Brake caliper
   - Brake rotor
   - Wheel bearing and using a screw driver, pry out the oil seal
   - Inner and outer bearings
   - Using a drift punch, remove the inner and outer bearing race

To install:
3. Pack the new bearings with grease.
4. Install or connect the following:
   - Inner bearing and race and a new oil seal
   - Outer bearing and race and secure the dust cover with four screws
   - Apply grease to the new bearings and the lip of the oil seal
   - Hub assembly in the steering knuckle
   - Screw the locknut against the hub assembly until there is 10 inch lbs. (1.3 Nm) of preload on the hub
   - Brake rotor and retaining screws
   - Attach a run-out gauge to check the rotor run-out. The run-out

should not exceed 0.004 inch (0.10mm)
   - Brake caliper
   - Free wheel hub fixed cam key with the locknut groove and push the on the fixed cam assembly
   - Axle retainer snap ring
   - Apply a light coat of sealant on the free wheel hub body. Install the body on the hub. Torque the bolts in 2 passes. Tighten the bolts on the first pass to 18 ft. lbs. (25 Nm). Tighten the bolts on the second pass to 23 ft. lbs. (31 Nm).
   - Negative battery cable

Rear

1. Before servicing the vehicle, refer to the precautions in the beginning of this section.
2. Remove or disconnect the following:
   - Negative battery cable
   - Rear wheels
   - Brake drum
   - Oil seal retainer flange

➡**The axle shafts are different from side-to-side, mark the to ensure they are returned to the proper side.**

1. Bearing Collar
2. Bearing
3. Axle Shaft
4. Rib Ring
5. Oil Seal
6. Oil Seal Retainer

Rear axle bearing component identification

7924QG35

- Using a slide hammer, remove the axle shaft assembly
- Using a hydraulic press, remove the bearing collar and bearing from the axle
- oil seal from the differential

To install:

3. Install or connect the following:

- Using the appropriate seal driver, install the new axle seal into the differential

➡ **The left-hand axle is 25.5 inches (647mm) long, and the right-hand axle is 27.4 inches (697mm) long.**

- Using a hydraulic press, install the

new wheel bearing and retainer collar to the axle shaft
- Axle shaft into the carrier. Torque the nuts to 75 ft. lbs. (100 Nm).
- Brake drum and rear wheels
- Negative battery cable

LAND ROVER

Defender 90 • Discovery • Discovery Series II • Range Rover

PRECAUTIONS

Before servicing any vehicle, please be sure to read all of the following precautions, which deal with personal safety, prevention of component damage, and important points to take into consideration when servicing a motor vehicle:

• Never open, service or drain the radiator or cooling system when the engine is hot; serious burns can occur from the steam and hot coolant.

• Observe all applicable safety precautions when working around fuel. Whenever servicing the fuel system, always work in a well-ventilated area. Do not allow fuel spray or vapors to come in contact with a spark, open flame, or excessive heat (a hot drop light, for example). Keep a dry chemical fire extinguisher near the work area. Always keep fuel in a container specifically designed for fuel storage; also, always properly seal fuel containers to avoid the possibility of fire or explosion. Refer to the additional fuel system precautions later in this section.

• Fuel injection systems often remain pressurized, even after the engine has been turned **OFF**. The fuel system pressure must be relieved before disconnecting any fuel lines. Failure to do so may result in fire and/or personal injury.

• Brake fluid often contains polyglycol ethers and polyglycols. Avoid contact with the eyes and wash your hands thoroughly after handling brake fluid. If you do get brake fluid in your eyes, flush your eyes with clean, running water for 15 minutes. If eye irritation persists, or if you have taken brake fluid internally, IMMEDIATELY seek medical assistance.

• The EPA warns that prolonged contact with used engine oil may cause a number of skin disorders, including cancer! You should make every effort to minimize your exposure to used engine oil. Protective gloves should be worn when changing oil. Wash your hands and any other exposed skin areas as soon as possible after exposure to used engine oil. Soap and water, or waterless hand cleaner should be used.

• All new vehicles are now equipped with an air bag system. The system must be disabled before performing service on or around system components, steering column, instrument panel components, wiring

and sensors. Failure to follow safety and disabling procedures could result in accidental air bag deployment, possible personal injury and unnecessary system repairs.

• Always wear safety goggles when working with, or around, the air bag system. When carrying a non-deployed air bag, be sure the bag and trim cover are pointed away from your body. When placing a non-deployed air bag on a work surface, always face the bag and trim cover upward, away from the surface. This will reduce the motion of the module if it is accidentally deployed. Refer to the additional air bag system precautions later in this section.

• Clean, high quality brake fluid from a sealed container is essential to the safe and proper operation of the brake system. You should always buy the correct type of brake fluid for your vehicle. If the brake fluid becomes contaminated, completely flush the system with new fluid. Never reuse any brake fluid. Any brake fluid that is removed from the system should be discarded. Also, do not allow any brake fluid to come in contact with a painted surface; it will damage the paint.

• Never operate the engine without the proper amount and type of engine oil; doing so WILL result in severe engine damage.

• Timing belt maintenance is extremely important! Many models utilize an interference-type, non-freewheeling engine. If the timing belt breaks, the valves in the cylinder head may strike the pistons, causing potentially serious (also time-consuming and expensive) engine damage. Refer to the maintenance interval charts in the front of this manual for the recommended replacement interval for the timing belt, and to the timing belt section for belt replacement and inspection.

• Disconnecting the negative battery cable on some vehicles may interfere with the functions of the on-board computer system(s) and may require the computer to undergo a relearning process once the negative battery cable is reconnected.

• When servicing drum brakes, only disassemble and assemble one side at a time, leaving the remaining side intact for reference.

• Only an MVAC-trained, EPA-certified automotive technician should service the air conditioning system or its components.

ENGINE REPAIR

Distributor

The vehicles covered in this section are equipped with DIS.

Alternator

REMOVAL & INSTALLATION

4.0L and 4.6L

1. Before servicing the vehicle, refer to the precautions in the beginning of this section.
2. Disconnect the battery ground cable.
3. Remove the drive belt.
4. Remove the 2 mounting bolts.
5. Lift the alternator from the bracket and disconnect the wires.
6. Installation is the reverse of removal. If the pulley was removed, tighten the pulley bolt to 30 ft. lbs. (40 Nm). Torque the mounting bolts to 18 ft. lbs. (25 Nm).

Ignition Timing

➡The ignition timing is not adjustable. It is controlled by the PCM.

Engine Assembly

REMOVAL & INSTALLATION

Range Rover

The engine and transmission are removed and installed, as an assembly, from the vehicle.

1. Before servicing the vehicle, refer to the precautions in the beginning of this section.
2. Remove or disconnect the following:

• Battery
• Fuel system pressure
• Coolant
• ECM located next to the battery
• Wiring harness from the starter and alternator
• Fuel supply and return lines from the fuel rail, then plug the openings to prevent contaminants from entering.
• Purge valve

- Intake hose/air flow meter assembly
- Throttle and cruise control cables from the throttle linkage
- All coolant hoses related to engine/transmission service
- Battery tray
- The 2 fuse box mounting bolts and pivot the fuse box aside.
- Engine wiring harness connector from the base of the fuse box
- Ground cable from the valance stud
- The 2 engine wiring harness connectors from the main harness
- Hood struts from the body locations. Raise the hood in the vertical position and stabilize.

3. Properly discharge the air conditioning system.

4. Remove or disconnect the following:

- Cooling fan and viscous coupling
- Grille
- Hood release cable strap from the upper radiator support
- Radiator upper support (35 and 36)
- Left and right radiator air deflectors
- Washer bottle filler neck
- Engine and transmission oil coolers
- Coolant hoses from the radiator and thermostat housing
- The 2 fog lamp breather hoses from the clips on either side of the radiator
- Power steering fluid
- Transmission oil temperature sensor connector
- Refrigerant lines from the air conditioning condenser
- The 2 nuts and bolts securing the radiator mountings to chassis

5. With the aid of an assistant, raise the radiator assembly for access to the condenser cooling fan connectors.

6. Remove or disconnect the following:

- The 2 condenser cooling fan connectors
- Radiator/condenser/oil cooler assembly
- Window switch pack
- Handbrake and cable clevis pin (61)
- Transmission fluid
- Transfer case fluid
- Engine oil
- Exhaust pipes from the manifolds
- Hand brake cable from the grommet in tunnel (65)
- Rear driveshaft shaft guard
- Driveshafts

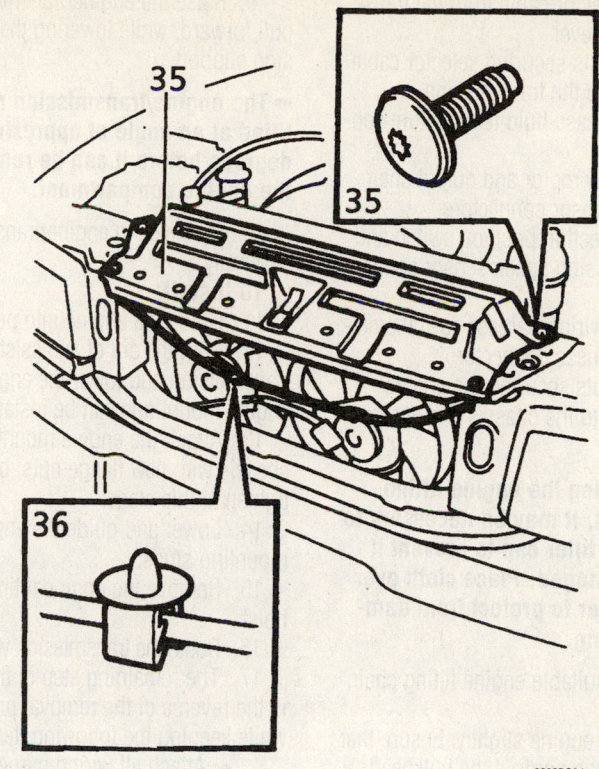

9302RG04

When removing the upper radiator support, be sure the hood release cable is not attached—

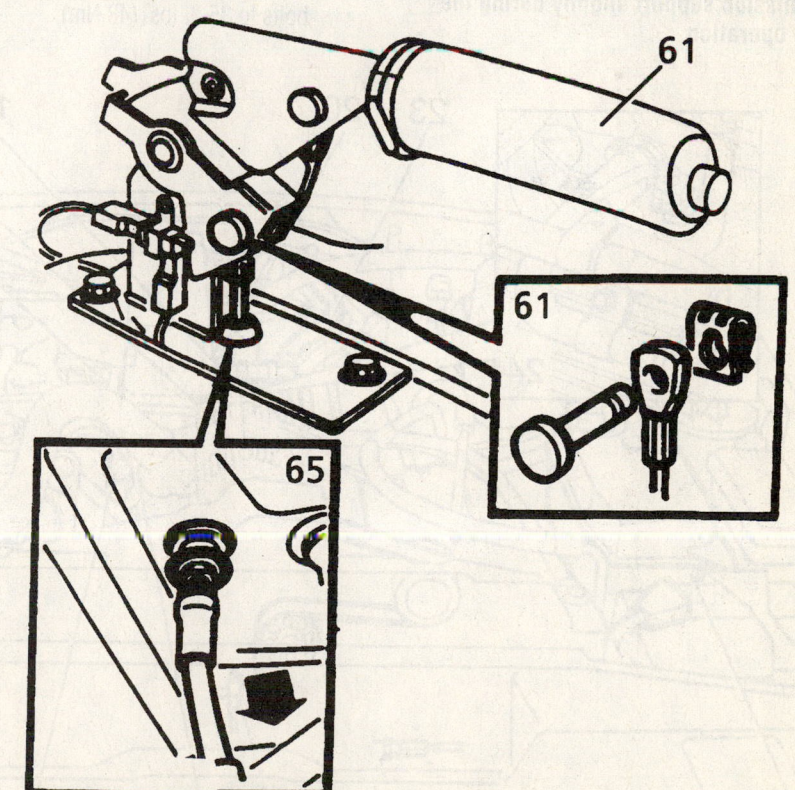

9302RG05

Exploded view of the handbrake lever components—Range Rover

For complete service labor times order Nichols' Chilton Labor Guide Manual

- Gear selector cable from the transmission lever
- The 2 bolts securing selector cable bracket to the transmission
- Transfer case fluid temperature sensor
- High/Low motor and output shaft speed sensor connectors
- Gear selection position switch and transmission speed sensor connectors
- Engine wiring harness-to-transmission harness connector
- The 4 nuts securing the engine mounts to the chassis and engine brackets

➡**When attaching the engine lifting chain and hoist, it may be necessary to remove the oil filler cap to prevent it from being damaged. Place cloth over plenum chamber to protect from damage during lifting.**

7. Install a suitable engine lifting chain and hoist.

8. Raise the engine slightly. Ensure that lifting bracket does not foul the bulkhead. Remove both engine mountings.

➡**It may be necessary to lower the transmission support slightly during the above operation.**

9. Raise the engine/transmission and pull forward, while lowering the transmission support.

➡**The engine/transmission must be tilted at an angle of approximately 45 degrees before it can be removed from the engine compartment.**

10. Remove the engine/transmission assembly.

To install:

11. Guide the engine into position.

12. With the aid of an assistant, raise the transmission and lower the engine until the engine mountings can be installed.

13. Attach the engine mounts to the chassis with new flange nuts, but do not tighten at this stage.

14. Lower and guide the engine onto the mounting studs.

15. Remove the engine lifting chain and hoist.

16. Route the transmission wiring harness.

17. The remaining step of the installation is the reverse of the removal procedure while keeping the following items in mind:

- Attach all wiring harness and electrical connectors.
- Align the driveshaft matchmarks and tighten the mounting nuts and bolts to 35 ft. lbs. (48 Nm).

- Attach all cables to the transmission.
- Tighten the engine mounting nuts to 33 ft. lbs. (45 Nm).
- Connect the handbrake cable and associated components.
- Install and connect the radiator/condenser/oil cooler assembly, using new sealing rings.
- Tighten the fittings on the air conditioning compressor to 17 ft. lbs. (23 Nm) and condenser to 11 ft. lbs. (15 Nm).
- Tighten the fittings for the power steering lines 12 ft. lbs. (16 Nm).
- Tighten the oil cooler lines to 22 ft. lbs. (30 Nm).

18. Evacuate and recharge the air conditioning system.

19. Connect the fuel supply and return lines to the fuel rail and tighten to 12 ft. lbs. (16 Nm).

20. Check and correct the fluid levels in the engine, transmission and transfer case.

21. Install and connect the battery.

22. Start the engine. Check for fuel, coolant and oil leaks.

Defender 90 and 1997–98 Discovery

1. Before servicing the vehicle, refer to the precautions in the beginning of this section.

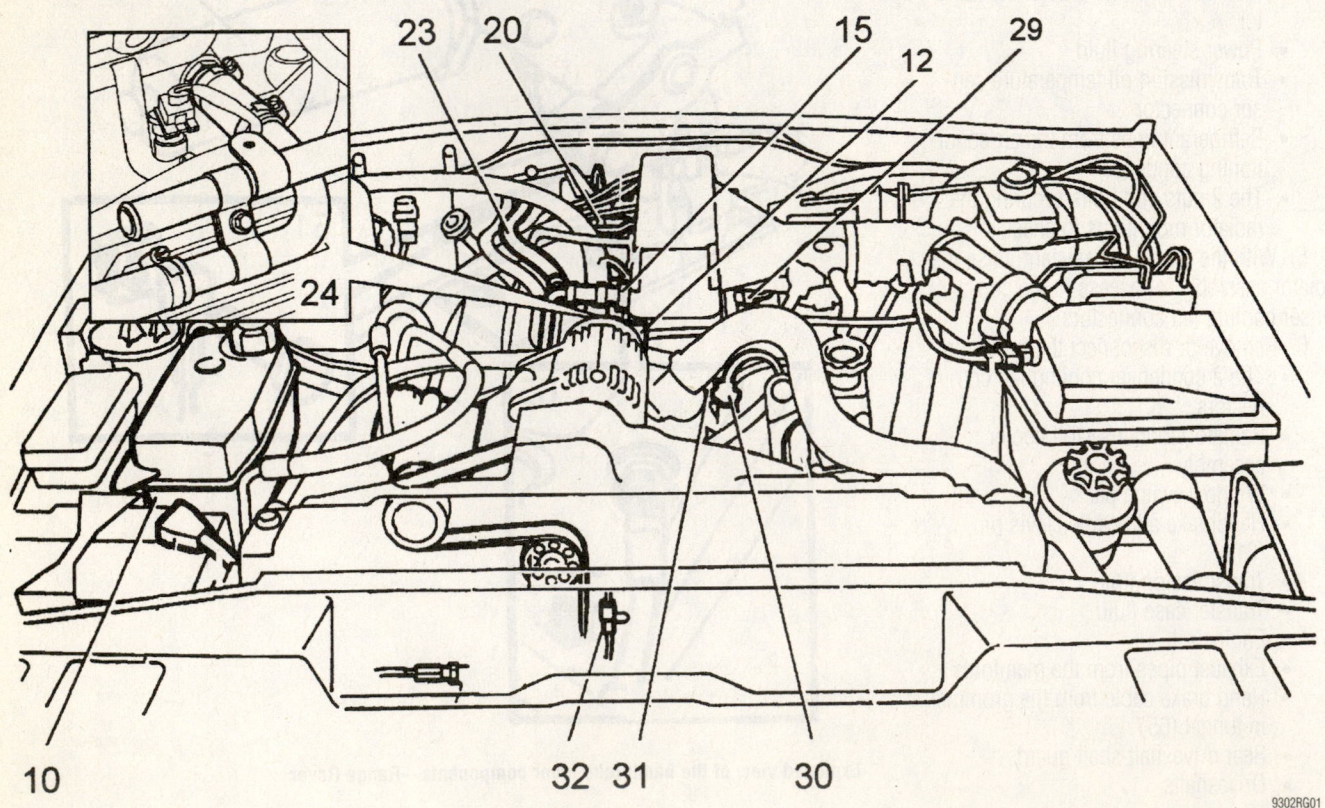

Underhood engine component identification—1997–98 Discovery

2. Disconnect the negative battery cable.

3. Properly relieve the fuel system pressure.

4. Remove or disconnect the following:
- Hood
- Coolant
- Radiator
- Intake plenum chamber
- MAF sensor
- Coolant expansion tank (10)
- Servo vacuum hose from ram housing
- Electrical connections at the alternator (12)
- Purge hose from ram pipe housing (15)
- Fuel supply and return lines (20)
- Heater hoses (23 and 24)
- Leads from spark plugs
- Ignition coils
- Fuel temperature sensor connector (29)
- Coolant sensor connector (30)
- Temperature gauge sender (31)
- Camshaft Position (CKP) sensor (32)
- Oil pressure switch
- IAT sensor connector (34)
- Any remaining wiring harnesses or connectors that would interfere with the engine removal.
- Bolts securing gearbox breather pipes to engine lifting bracket
- Accessory drive belt
- Air conditioning compressor, and position it aside leaving the hoses attached.
- Power steering hoses and plug the openings in the steering box and pump.
- Left and right engine mounting nuts

5. Position the lifting chains and attach the hooks to the engine lifting eyes, then

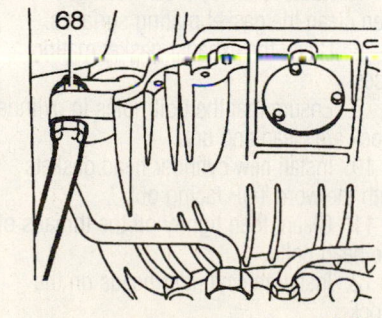

Transmission-to-transfer case tie bar location—1997–98 Discovery

raise the engine sufficiently to remove the engine mounts.

6. Lower the engine until it just rests on the engine mounting brackets.

7. Remove or disconnect the following:
- Front exhaust pipe/catalytic converter from the manifold
- Bell housing bottom cover
- Transfer case-to-transmission tie bar (68)
- Bell housing access cover

8. Matchmark the driveplate-to-torque converter relationship.

9. Remove or disconnect the following:
- The 4 torque converter-to-driveplate bolts
- CKP sensor/shield
- Starter motor heat shield and disconnect the solenoid
- Right and left knock sensor connectors
- Handbrake cable heat shield
- Top oil cooler pipe connection from the transmission
- Bolt securing the oil cooler pipe bracket to the sump and note the position of the spacer.
- Engine-to-transmission mounting bolts
- Engine ground cable from the top starter bolt
- Nut securing the kick-down cable clip to the left cylinder head

10. Insert a suitable wooden block in the access plate hole to retain the torque converter.

11. Support the transmission with a jack.

12. Install a suitable engine sling and hoist.

13. Raise the engine and transmission, then separate the engine from the transmission.

14. With the aid of an assistant, raise the engine, move aside all pipes and wires. Move the engine clear of the vehicle.

To install:

15. Clean the engine/gearbox mating faces and the dowel and dowel holes.

16. With the aid of an assistant, lower and guide the engine into the engine compartment ensuring no wires or pipes become trapped.

17. Position the clip securing the kick-down cable to the left cylinder head.

18. Install the engine ground cable and tighten the top starter bolt to 33 ft. lbs. (45 Nm).

19. With assistance, lower the engine and engage the engine with transmission.

20. Install the engine-to-transmission mounting bolts and tighten to 34 ft. lbs. (46 Nm).

21. Lower the jack supporting the transmission.

22. Lower the engine onto its mounting brackets.

23. The remaining step of installation is the reverse of the removal procedure while keeping in mind the following items:
- Align the torque converter-to-driveplate matchmarks and tighten the bolts to 33 ft. lbs. (45 Nm).
- Tighten the cover plate bolts to 33 ft. lbs. (45 Nm).
- Connect all coolant hoses.
- Attach all electrical connectors.
- Install the tie bar, align to the transmission and tighten the bolts to 18 ft. lbs. (25 Nm), then the nuts to 33 ft. lbs. (45 Nm).
- Install the engine mounts and tighten to 41 ft. lbs. (55 Nm).

24. Install the hood.

25. Reconnect battery negative lead.

26. Drain the engine oil and refill.

27. Start the engine. Check for fuel, coolant and oil leaks.

1999–01 Discovery Series II

1. Before servicing the vehicle, refer to the precautions in the beginning of this section.

2. Remove or disconnect the following:
- Negative battery cable
- Coolant
- Fuel system pressure
- Engine oil and filter
- Radiator hoses
- Radiator
- Upper intake manifold and ignition coil assemblies
- Fuel supply and return lines from the fuel rail
- Auxiliary drive belt
- The 3 bolts securing the Active Cornering Enhancement (ACE) pump, then position it aside leaving the hoses attached.
- The 4 bolts securing the air conditioning compressor, and position it aside leaving the hoses attached.
- Power steering hoses from the pump
- Coolant hoses at the water pump and rail
- Bolt securing the coolant rail and position the rail aside

Timing belt service is covered in Section 4 of this manual

- Engine ground and power supply cables
- Starter wiring harness
- The 2 engine wiring harness connectors from the fuse box
- EVAP solenoid connector
- Nut mounting the engine harness ground-to-body and detach the engine harness-to-main harness connector.
- Right side interior kick panel
- The 5 connectors attaching the engine harness to the ECM

3. Release the engine wiring harness, pull it into the engine bay and coil on top of engine.

4. Raise and safely support the vehicle.

5. Remove the 3 bolts securing the oil cooler lines to the engine block.

6. Detach the engine oil cooler lines and tie the lines aside.

7. Disconnect the front exhaust pipes from the manifolds.

8. Remove the torque converter access plug, matchmark the torque converter-to-driveplate relationship, then remove the 4 bolts securing the torque converter to the driveplate.

9. Remove the 12 engine-to-transmission mounting bolts.

10. Attach suitable lifting equipment to the engine.

11. Remove the 4 nuts securing the engine mounts, raise the engine and remove the engine mounts.

12. Support the transmission on a jack.

13. Separate the engine from the transmission dowels.

14. With the aid of an assistant, remove the engine from the engine bay.

To install:

15. Clean the mating faces of the engine and transmission, dowel and dowel holes.

16. With the aid of an assistant, position the engine in the engine bay, align to gearbox and locate on dowels.

17. Install the engine-to-transmission bolts and tighten to 37 ft. lbs. (50 Nm).

18. Install the engine mounts and tighten the fasteners to 63 ft. lbs. (85 Nm).

19. Remove the engine lifting equipment.

20. Align the torque converter to the driveplate, install the bolts and tighten to 37 ft. lbs. (50 Nm).

21. Install or connect the following:
- Torque converter access plug
- Front exhaust pipes to the manifolds
- All electrical connectors and replace any ties.
- Power steering hoses and check the fluid level

- Coolant hoses
- Radiator
- Coolant
- Air conditioning compressor mounting bolts to 16 ft. lbs. (22 Nm)
- ACE pump mounting bolts to 16 ft. lbs. (22 Nm)
- Accessory drive belt
- Fuel supply and return lines to the fuel rail
- Ignition coils
- Spark plug wires
- Upper intake manifold
- Oil filter
- Engine oil
- Transmission fluid level
- Negative battery cable

Water Pump

REMOVAL & INSTALLATION

1. Before servicing the vehicle, refer to the precautions in the beginning of this section.

2. Disconnect the negative battery cable.

3. Drain and recycle the engine coolant.

4. Remove the accessory drive belt.

5. Remove the 3 bolts securing the pulley to the coolant pump, and remove the pulley.

6. Release the clip and disconnect the feed hose from the coolant pump.

7. Remove the 9 bolts securing the coolant pump, remove the pump and discard the gasket.

To install:

8. Clean the coolant pump and mating face.

9. Install new gasket and coolant pump to the cylinder block.

10. Install the mounting bolts and tighten to 16 ft. lbs. (22 Nm).

11. Connect the feed hose to the coolant pump, and secure with clip.

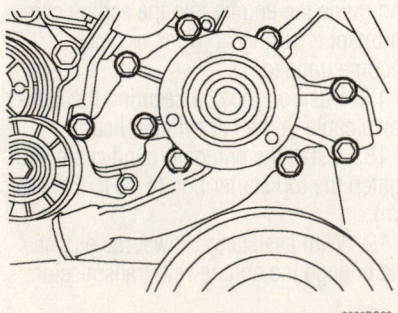

9302RG03

Water pump mounting bolt location

12. Ensure the mating faces of coolant pump pulley and flange are clean.

13. Install the pulley, and tighten the bolts to 16 ft. lbs. (22 Nm).

14. Install the auxiliary drive belt.

15. Connect the negative battery cable.

Cylinder Head

REMOVAL & INSTALLATION

➡ **The cylinder head bolt torque sequence can be found in Section 1, following the Torque Specifications Chart.**

1. Before servicing the vehicle, refer to the precautions in the beginning of this section.

2. Remove or disconnect the following:
- Negative battery cable
- Coolant
- Intake manifold
- Alternator
- Air conditioning compressor and position it aside leaving the hoses attached.
- Rocker arm cover
- Rocker shafts and pushrods
- Front exhaust pipes from the manifolds
- Exhaust manifolds
- Air cleaner and intake air duct assembly

3. On the left cylinder head, remove the ground cable attached to the left-hand cylinder head.

4. On the right cylinder head, remove the breather pipe from the engine lifting bracket.

5. Loosen the cylinder head bolts, reversing the tightening sequence.

6. Lift the cylinder head off the engine block.

To install:

7. Remove the cylinder head gaskets, then clean the gasket mating surfaces.

8. Clean the exhaust gasket mating faces.

9. Ensure that the bolt holes in cylinder block are clean and dry.

10. Install new cylinder head gaskets with the word TOP facing out.

11. Clean, then lightly oil the threads of the head bolts.

12. Install the cylinder heads on the block.

13. Install the cylinder head bolts in the positions as illustrated.
- 96mm long bolts: 2, 4, 6, 7, 8, 9, 10
- 66mm long bolts: 1, 3, 5

➡**There are no bolts fitted in the 4 lower holes in each cylinder head.**

14. Tighten the cylinder head bolts progressively in sequence, as shown, as follows:

- 15 ft. lbs. (20 Nm)
- + ¼ turn (90°)
- + ¼ (90°)

15. The remaining steps are the reverse of the removal procedure.

16. Connect the negative battery cable.

17. Fill and bleed the cooling system. Run the engine and check for leaks.

Rocker Arms/Shafts

REMOVAL & INSTALLATION

1. Before servicing the vehicle, refer to the precautions in the beginning of this section.

2. Disconnect the negative battery cable.

3. Relieve fuel system pressure.

4. Drain the cooling system.

5. Remove the rocker arm covers.

6. Remove the 4 rocker arm shaft

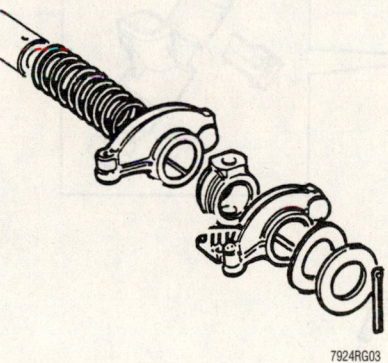

Exploded view of the rocker arm shaft components

7924RG03

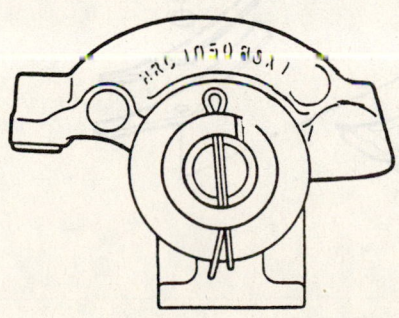

The end notches of the rocker shaft must face up

7924RG04

bolts and lift off the rocker arm shaft assemblies.

7. Remove the cotter pin from either end of the shaft and slide the components from the shaft, keeping them in order for reassembly.

8. Inspect the parts for wear or damage, and replace any suspect parts. Discard any weak springs.

To install:

9. Reassemble the shaft and components. Note the position of the oil feed holes. Use new cotter pin(s).

10. Position the rocker shaft assembly on the head. Be sure that the shaft is installed with the notches at each end on the upper side. Be sure that each rocker ball stud engages its respective pushrod.

11. Install the bolts and tighten them, gradually, to 28 ft. lbs. (38 Nm), starting with the 2 inner, then the 2 outer bolts.

Intake Manifold

REMOVAL & INSTALLATION

1. Before servicing the vehicle, refer to the precautions in the beginning of this section.

2. Remove or disconnect the following:

- Negative battery cable
- Coolant
- Fuel system pressure
- Alternator
- Air intake hose from the plenum chamber
- Throttle and cruise control cables from the throttle linkage and mounting brackets
- Breather hose from the plenum chamber
- Purge hose from plenum chamber
- TP sensor
- Stepper motor electrical connector
- The 6 bolts securing the plenum chamber to the ram housing
- Coolant hoses attached to the plenum chamber and intake manifold
- Plenum chamber assembly
- Breather hoses, as necessary
- ECT and temperature gauge sensors
- The 8 fuel injector connectors
- Fuel temperature sensor connector
- Fuel supply and return lines
- The 6 nuts securing fuel rail and ignition coil bracket to the inlet manifold

3. Lift the fuel rail slightly to remove the ignition coil bracket from the inlet manifold studs and place aside.

4. Using the sequence shown, remove the 12 bolts securing the intake manifold to the cylinder heads, then remove the manifold.

5. Remove the bolts and clamps securing the manifold gasket to the cylinder block.

6. Remove the inlet manifold gasket and discard.

7. Remove the gasket seals and discard.

To install:

8. Clean all gasket mating faces.

9. Apply a thin bead of Loctite® Superflex (black) sealant to the 4 notches between cylinder head and block.

10. Install a new gasket seals. Be sure the ends engage correctly in the notches.

11. Install a new inlet manifold gasket and tighten the manifold gasket clamps to 6 inch lbs. (0.7 Nm).

12. With the aid of an assistant, hold the harness and ignition coils aside, position the inlet manifold assembly.

➡**Tighten the manifold bolts in the reverse order of removal.**

13. Install the inlet manifold bolts and tighten as follows:

- 84 inch lbs. (10 Nm).
- 37 ft. lbs. (50 Nm).

14. Tighten the gasket clamp bolts to 13 ft. lbs. (17 Nm).

15. Install or connect the following:

- Ignition coil bracket on the inlet manifold studs, and tighten the mounting bolts to 72 inch lbs. (8 Nm).
- Fuel lines
- Connectors to the fuel injectors and fuel temperature sensor
- ECT sensor and temperature gauge sensor
- Breather hoses as removed

16. Clean the mating faces of the plenum chamber.

17. Connect any coolant hoses that were removed.

18. Apply a thin, uniform coating of Loctite® 577 sealant to the mating face of the plenum chamber.

19. Install or connect the following:

- Plenum chamber to the ram housing and tighten to 18 ft. lbs. (24 Nm)

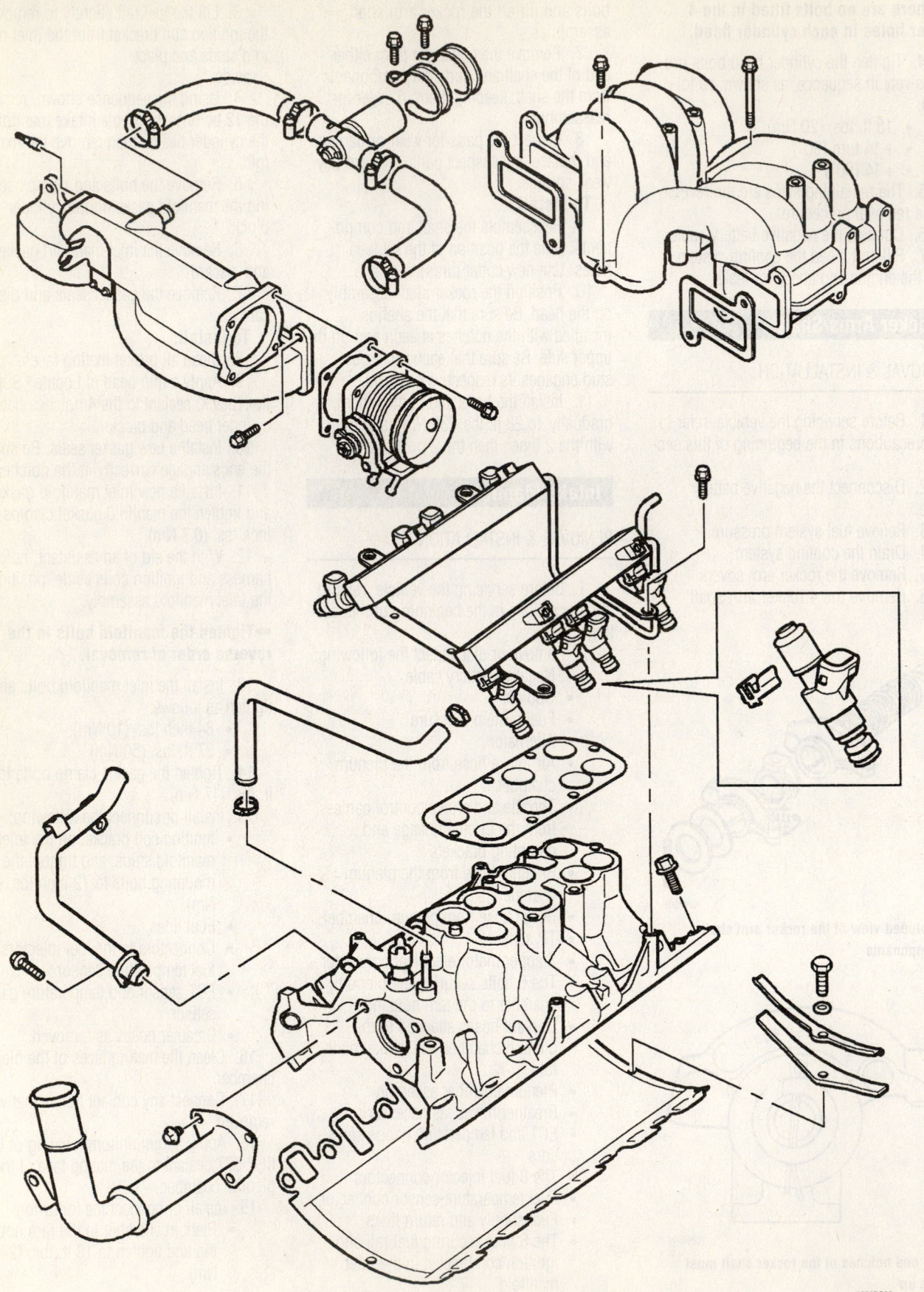

Intake manifold components

9308RG93

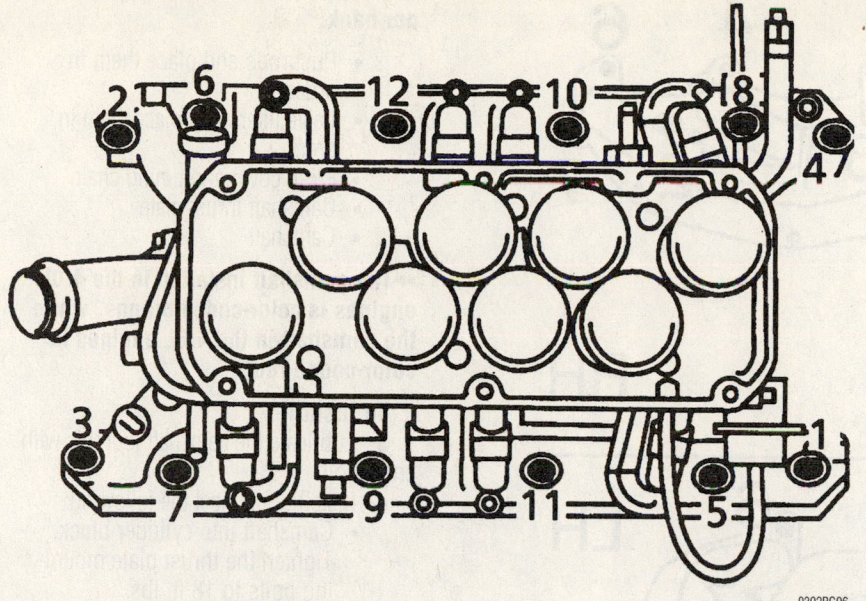

Intake manifold bolt removal sequence

- Stepper motor and TP sensor connectors
- Purge hose to the plenum chamber
- Breather hose to the plenum chamber
- Throttle and cruise control cables
- Air intake hose to the plenum chamber and secure with clip
- Coolant
- Alternator
- Negative battery cable

Exhaust Manifold

REMOVAL & INSTALLATION

Defender 90 and Discovery

1. Before servicing the vehicle, refer to the precautions in the beginning of this section.

2. Disconnect the negative battery cable.

3. Remove the exhaust manifold-to-exhaust pipe retaining nuts.

4. Remove the 8 manifold bolts. Remove the exhaust manifold and discard the gasket.

To install:

5. Clean all mating surfaces.

6. Place the exhaust manifold in position on the cylinder head along with a new gasket. Install the exhaust manifold bolts and tighten to 15 ft. lbs. (20 Nm).

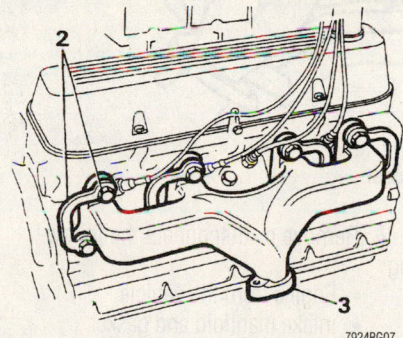

View of one of the exhaust manifolds (3), showing the mounting bolt locktabs (2)— Defender 90 and Discovery models

7. Install the exhaust pipe to the exhaust manifold, and tighten the exhaust pipe retaining nuts to 25–34 ft. lbs. (34–47 Nm).

8. Lower the vehicle.

9. Connect the negative battery cable.

10. Start the engine and check for exhaust leaks.

11. Road test the vehicle and check for proper engine operation.

Range Rover

1. Before servicing the vehicle, refer to the precautions in the beginning of this section.

2. Remove or disconnect the following:
- Negative battery cable
- Front exhaust pipes from the exhaust manifolds

3. Lower the vehicle.

4. For the left manifold, perform the following:

a. Release the intake hose from the plenum chamber.

b. Release the harness from the intake hose clip.

c. Remove the air flow meter.

d. Disconnect the purge valve (11) and position the valve aside.

5. For the right manifold, perform the following:

a. Disconnect the spark plug wires and position them out of the way.

b. Unscrew the right shock absorber top mounting bolt to provide additional clearance for the removal of the heat shield.

6. Remove or disconnect the following:
- The 8 bolts (for the right manifold) or 7 bolts (for the left manifold) securing the outer heat shield to the manifold.
- The 8 exhaust manifold-to-cylinder head mounting bolts, then remove manifolds.

To install:

7. Ensure all gasket mating surfaces are clean.

8. Install or connect the following:
- Manifolds using new gaskets. Tighten the bolts 40 ft. lbs. (55 Nm), in the sequence as shown.
- Heat shields and tighten the mounting bolts to 72 inch lbs. (8 Nm).
- Purge valve on the shock absorber turret
- Air flow meter
- Right shock absorber top mounting bolt to 63 ft. lbs. (85 Nm).
- Spark plug wires
- Front exhaust pipes to the manifolds and tighten the mounting nuts to 37 ft. lbs. (50 Nm).
- Negative battery cable

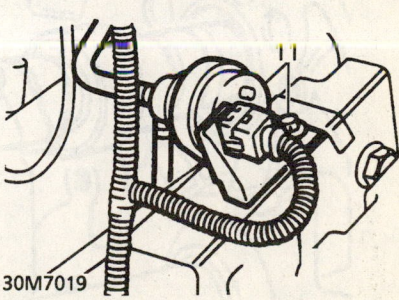

Purge valve mounting bolt location— Range Rover

Refer to Section 1 for engine rebuilding specifications

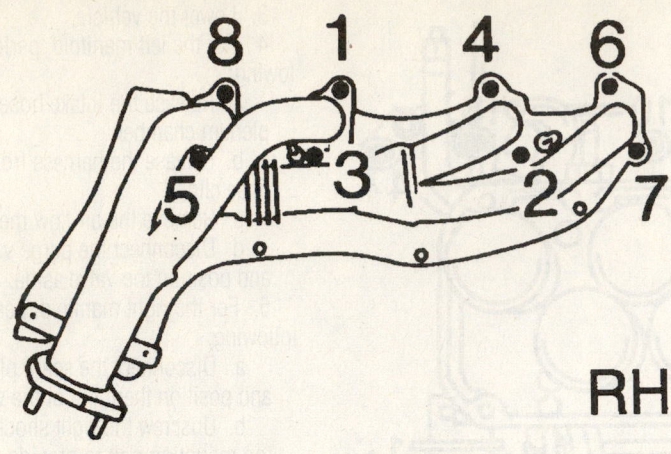

RH

LH

30M7022A

Exhaust manifold torque sequence—Range Rover model

Camshaft and Valve Lifters

REMOVAL & INSTALLATION

1. Before servicing the vehicle, refer to the precautions in the beginning of this section.

2. Remove or disconnect the following:

- Engine from the vehicle
- Intake manifold and gasket
- Both rocker arm shaft assemblies

➡**Identify each rocker shaft assembly**

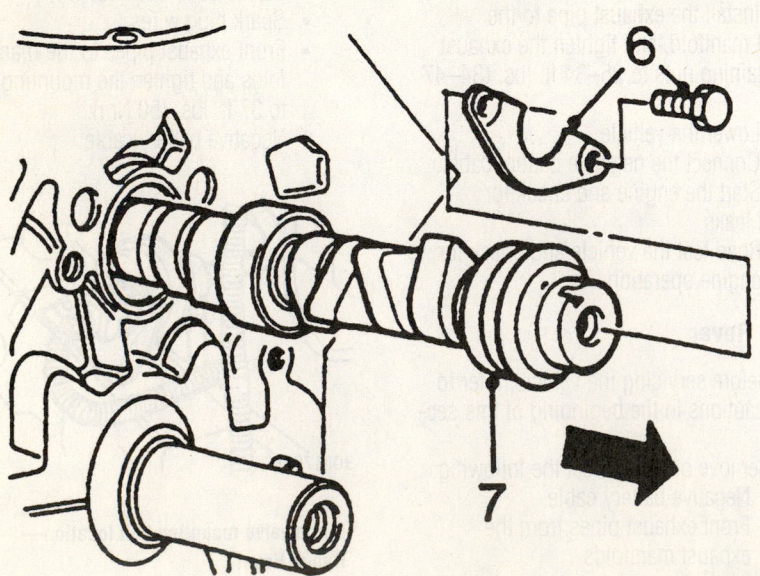

Exploded view of the camshaft (7) and thrust plate (6) mounting

to ensure installation on original cylinder bank.

- Pushrods and place them in order
- Valve lifters and place them in order
- Front cover and timing chain
- Camshaft thrust plate
- Camshaft

➡**The camshaft installed in the 4.0L engines is color-coded orange, while the camshaft in the 4.6L engines is color-coded red.**

To install:

3. Lubricate the camshaft journals with engine oil.

4. Install or connect the following:

- Camshaft into cylinder block. Tighten the thrust plate mounting bolts to 18 ft. lbs. (25 Nm).
- Timing chain and front cover

5. Soak the lifters in engine oil. Before installing each lifter, pump the inner sleeve of the lifter several times using a pushrod to prime the lifter; this will reduce lifter noise when the engine is first started.

6. Lubricate the lifter bores with engine oil, then install the lifters.

➡**Some lifter noise may still be heard on initial start-up. If necessary, run the engine at 2500 rpm for a few minutes until the noise clears.**

7. Install or connect the following:

- Pushrods
- Rocker arm shaft assemblies
- Intake manifold
- Engine

Starter Motor

REMOVAL & INSTALLATION

1. Before servicing the vehicle, refer to the precautions in the beginning of this section.

2. Disconnect the battery ground cable.

3. Remove the right side transmission sound shield.

4. Disconnect the wiring from the solenoid.

5. Remove the 2 starter mounting bolts.

6. Installation is the reverse of removal. Torque the mounting bolts to 33 ft. lbs. (45 Nm).

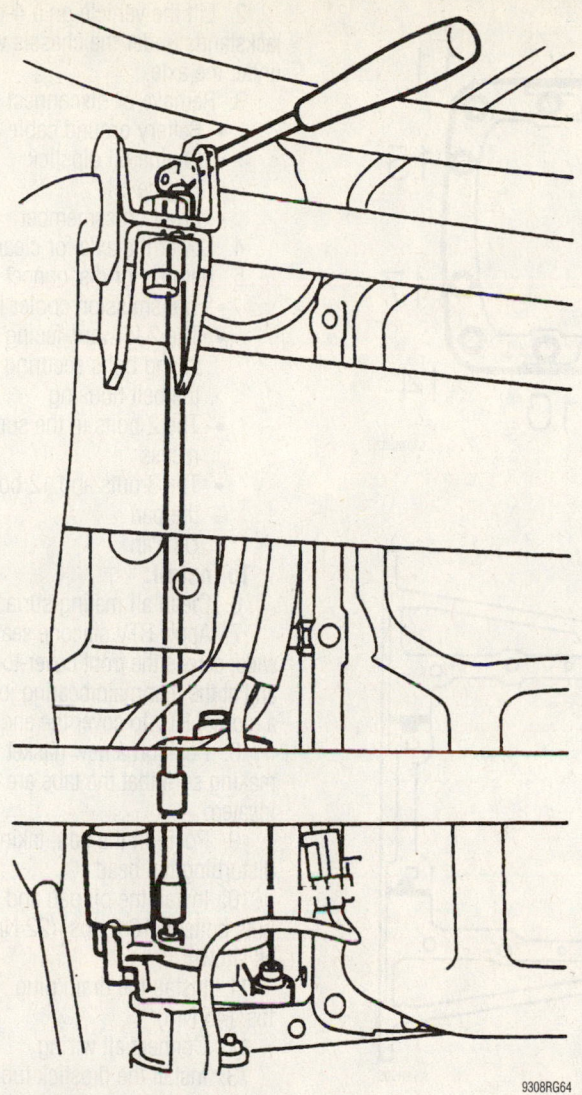

Here's how you reach the starter mounting bolts

9308RG64

Oil Pan

REMOVAL & INSTALLATION

Range Rover

1. Before servicing the vehicle, refer to the precautions in the beginning of this section.

2. Lift the vehicle on a 4-post lift, or, on jackstands under the chassis with a jack under the axle.

3. Remove or disconnect the following:
- Battery ground cable
- Engine acoustic cover
- Transmission acoustic cover
- Engine oil dipstick
- Engine oil

4. Position a support under the front crossmember.

5. Lower the axle for clearance.
6. Remove or disconnect the following:
- O_2 sensor connectors
- The 3 nuts and 14 bolts securing the pan
- Oil Pan

To install:

7. Clean all mating surfaces.

8. Apply RTV Hylosil 101 or 106, or equivalent sealant, to the oil pan. Using the illustration, the bead width and length should be:
- Width at A, B, C and D: 12mm
- Width at remaining areas: 5mm
- Length at A and B: 32mm
- Length at remaining areas: 19mm

➡**Do not spread the bead. Install the pan immediately!**

9. Position the pan, taking care to avoid disturbing the bead.

10. Install the oil pan and tighten the nuts bolts to 17 ft. lbs. (23 Nm) in sequence as shown.

11. Install the drain plug. Torque to 33 ft. lbs. (45 Nm).

12. Connect the sensors.

13. Install the dipstick tube to the rocker cover.

14. Install the covers.

15. Fill the engine with oil, start the engine and check for leaks.

Defender and Discovery

1. Before servicing the vehicle, refer to the precautions in the beginning of this section.

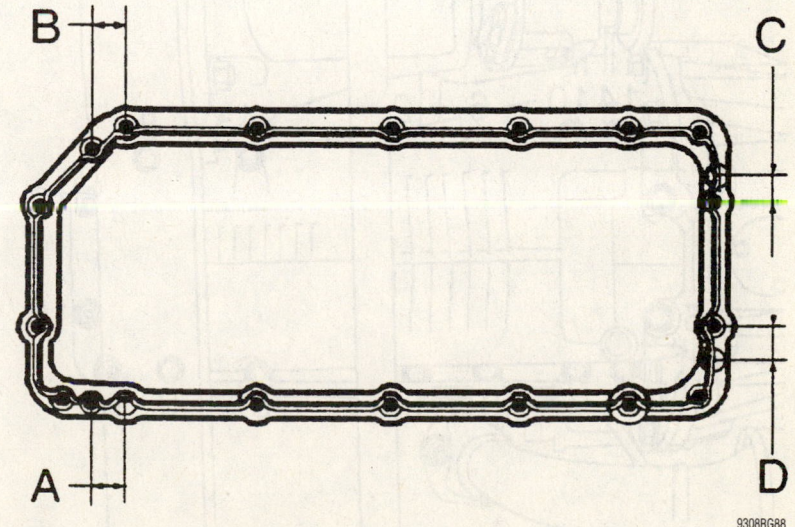

Sealant bead application—Range Rover

9308RG88

For engine torque specifications, refer to Section 1 of this manual

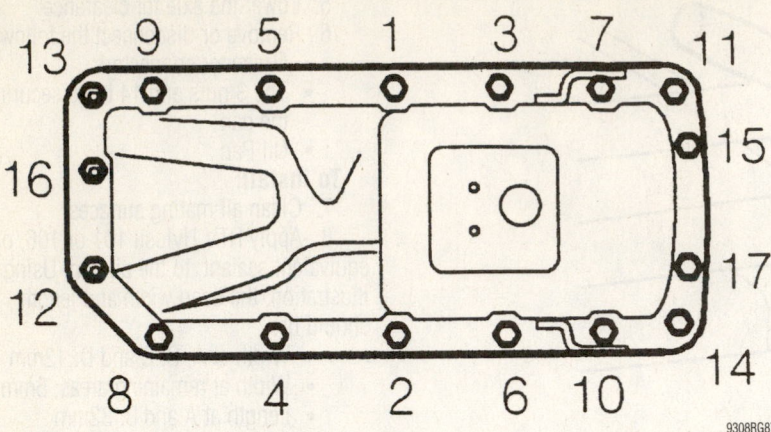

Oil pan fastener torque sequence—Range Rover

9308RG87

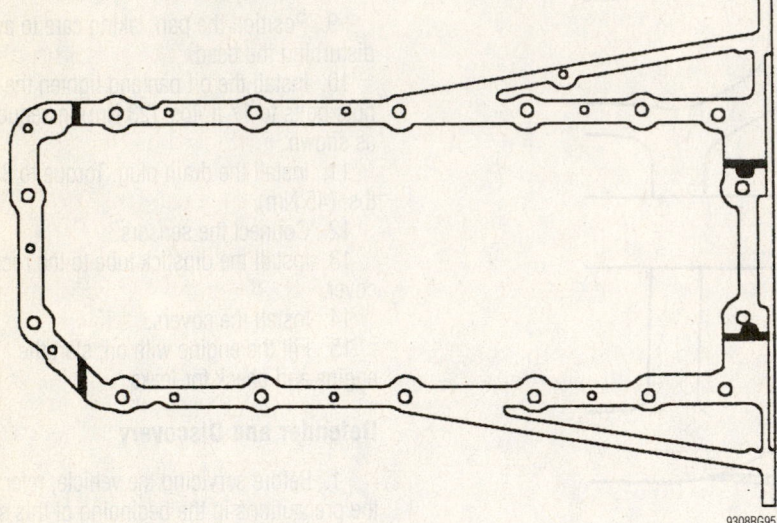

Oil pan sealant application—Discovery and Defender 90

9308RG95

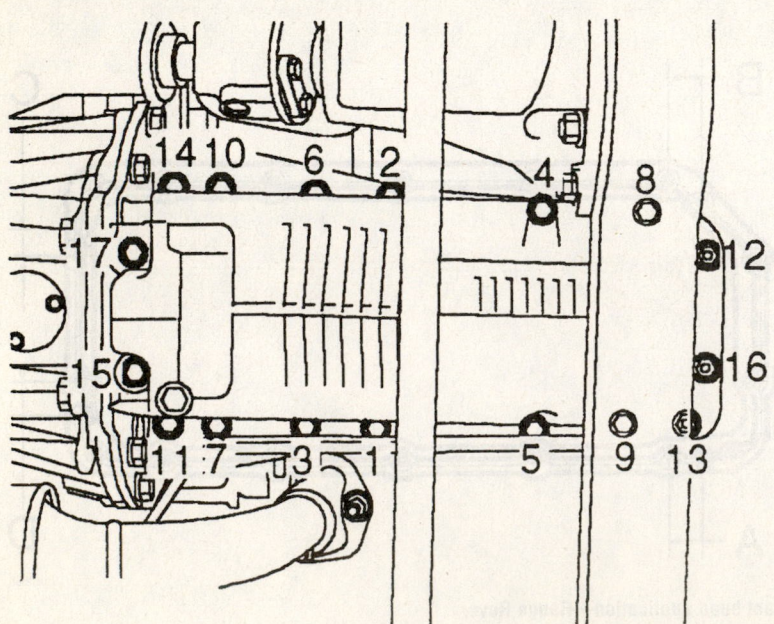

Oil pan fastener torque sequence—Discovery and Defender 90

9308RG94

2. Lift the vehicle on a 4-post lift, or, on jackstands under the chassis with a jack under the axle.

3. Remove or disconnect the following:
   • Battery ground cable
   • Engine oil dipstick
   • Engine oil
   • Front crossmember

4. Lower the axle for clearance.

5. Remove or disconnect the following:
   • Transmission cooler lines
   • The 2 forward-facing and 4 rear-facing bolts securing the oil pan to the bell housing
   • The 2 bolts in the sump oil pan recess
   • The 3 nuts and 12 bolts securing the pan
   • Oil Pan

To install:

6. Clean all mating surfaces.

7. Apply RTV silicone sealant, 5mm wide, across the front cover-to-block joint and at the rear main bearing joint. Also, apply a glob of RTV to cover the ends of the seal.

8. Position a new gasket on the pan, making sure that the tabs are correctly located.

9. Position the pan, taking care to avoid disturbing the bead.

10. Install the oil pan and tighten the nuts bolts to 16 ft. lbs. (22 Nm) in sequence as shown.

11. Install the drain plug. Torque to 33 ft. lbs. (45 Nm).

12. Connect all wiring.

13. Install the dipstick tube to the rocker cover.

14. Install the crossmember. Torque the bolts to 18 ft. lbs. (25 Nm).

15. Fill the engine with oil, start the engine and check for leaks.

Oil Pump

REMOVAL & INSTALLATION

1. Before servicing the vehicle, refer to the precautions in the beginning of this section.

2. Remove or disconnect the following:
   • Coolant
   • Oil pan
   • Oil filter
   • Oil pump pick-up tube
   • Crankshaft pulley
   • Drive belt
   • Front cover
   • Remove the timing chain and gears.
   • Remove the 7 bolts/screws mounting the oil pump cover plate.
   • Matchmark the inner and outer oil

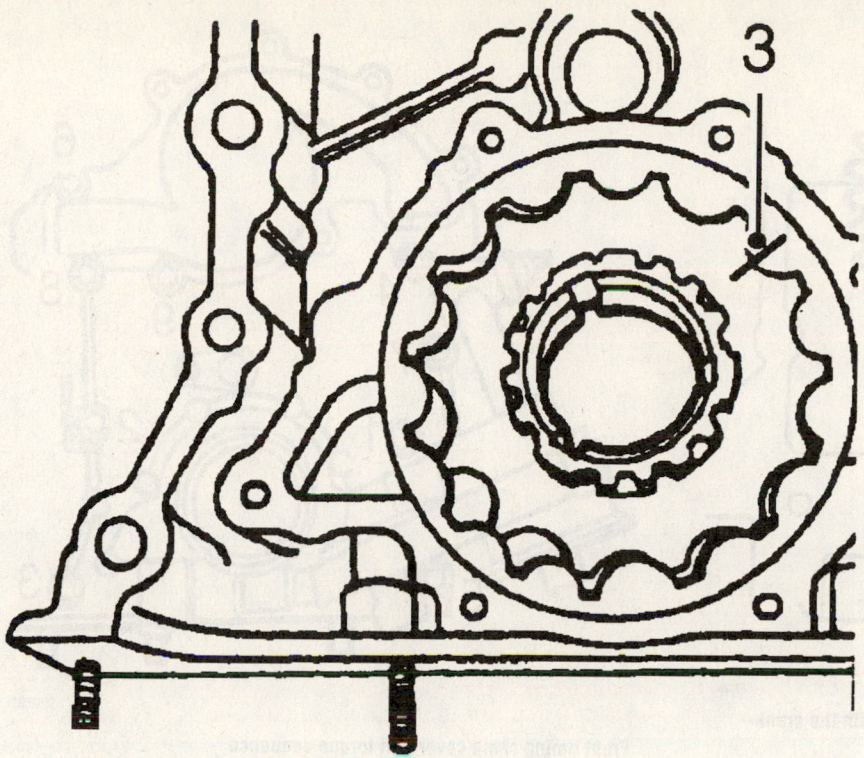

9302RG09

Place matchmarks on the rotors (3) before removing

pump rotors, then remove the rotors and oil pump drive gear as an assembly.

To install:

3. Lubricate the rotors, oil pump drive gear, cover plate and housing with engine oil.

4. Align the rotor matchmarks, then install the oil pump drive gear and rotors as an assembly.

5. Apply Loctite® 222 to the mounting bolts/screws for the oil pump cover plate, then install the plate and tighten the bolts to 72 inch lbs. (8 Nm) and the screws to 36 inch lbs. (4 Nm).

6. Install the timing chain and gears.

7. Connect the oil pump pick-up tube and install the oil pan.

8. Install a new oil filter and fill the engine with oil.

9. Start the vehicle and check for leaks.

Rear Main Seal

REMOVAL & INSTALLATION

1. Before servicing the vehicle, refer to the precautions in the beginning of this section.

2. Remove the transmission and driveplate.

3. Using a suitable seal removal tool, remove the oil seal from the engine block.

To install:

4. Be sure both the seal location and running surface on the crankshaft are clean.

5. Lubricate the lip of the seal with engine oil.

6. Install the crankshaft seal over the end of the crankshaft.

7. Using a suitable seal installer, install the seal until it is flush with the end of the engine block.

8. Install the driveplate and tighten the mounting bolts to 63 ft. lbs. (85 Nm).

9. Install the transmission.

Timing Chain, Sprockets, Front Cover and Seal

REMOVAL & INSTALLATION

Front Cover with Seal

➡**For seal replacement, see the next procedure.**

1. Before servicing the vehicle, refer to the precautions in the beginning of this section.

2. Remove or disconnect the following:
- Negative battery cable
- Coolant
- Oil pan
- Oil pick up strainer
- Crankshaft pulley and drive belt tensioner
- Hose from the water pump
- Oil cooler hoses from the front cover, then plug the hoses and connections to prevent dirt from entering.
- Oil pressure switch and CMP sensor electrical connectors
- Timing cover mounting bolts, then remove the cover.

3. Clean the gasket mating surfaces and drive out the crankshaft seal.

4. Clean the timing gears and turn the crankshaft until the timing mark on the crankshaft and camshaft face each other (camshaft at 6 o'clock and crankshaft at twelve o'clock).

5. Remove the camshaft timing gear mounting bolt.

6. Remove the timing gears and chain as an assembly.

To install:

7. Assemble the timing chain and gears on a work bench, with the timing marks aligned.

8. Install the timing chain and gear assembly onto the engine with the timing marks facing outwards.

9. Install the camshaft timing gear mounting bolt and tighten to 37 ft. lbs. (50 Nm).

10. Lubricate the new timing cover oil seal with Shell Retinax LX, or equivalent grease, ensuring that the space between seal lips is filled with grease.

11. Install or connect the following:
- Seal with a suitable seal driver
- Front cover with a new gasket and tighten the cover bolts, in the sequence shown, to 16 ft. lbs. (22 Nm).
- Oil pressure switch and CMP sensor electrical connectors
- Plugs from the oil cooler hoses
- Oil cooler hoses using new O-ring seals and tighten to 11 ft. lbs. (15 Nm)
- Drive belt tensioner and tighten the bolt to 37 ft. lbs. (50 Nm)
- Hose to the water pump
- Oil filter
- Crankshaft pulley and tighten the bolt 200 ft. lbs. (270 Nm).

For complete mechanical specifications, refer to Section 1 of this manual

9302RG10

Be sure to align the cam gear (3) timing mark (4) with the crankshaft gear (2), as shown

9302RG11

Front timing chain cover bolt torque sequence

- Oil pump with a new O-ring and tighten the mounting bolt to 72 inch lbs. (8 Nm).
- Oil pan
- Engine oil
- Coolant
- Negative battery cable

Seal Replacement Only

1. Before servicing the vehicle, refer to the precautions in the beginning of this section.

2. Remove or disconnect the following:

- Battery ground cable
- Cooling fan
- Water pump pulley bolts
- Drive belt
- Engine under-cover

3. Install a holding tool, such as LRT-12-080, on the pulley

4. Remove the pulley bolt and pulley.

5. Using a seal remover, such as LRT-12-088, remove the seal.

To install:

6. Clean all sealing surfaces.

7. Coat the outer edge of the seal with engine oil.

8. Using an installer, such as LRT-12-089, install the seal.

9. Coat the seal lip with engine oil.

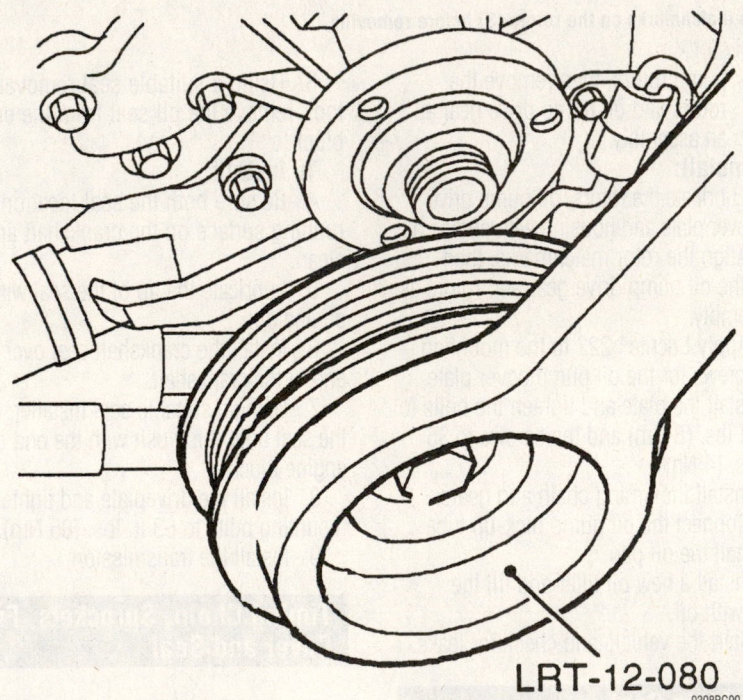

LRT-12-080

9308RG90

Crankshaft pulley holding tool

10. Install the holding tool, position the pulley on the crankshaft and install the bolt. Torque the bolt to 200 ft. lbs. (270 Nm).

11. The remainder of installation is the reverse of removal.

Piston and Ring Positioning

Before servicing the vehicle, refer to the precautions in the beginning of this section.

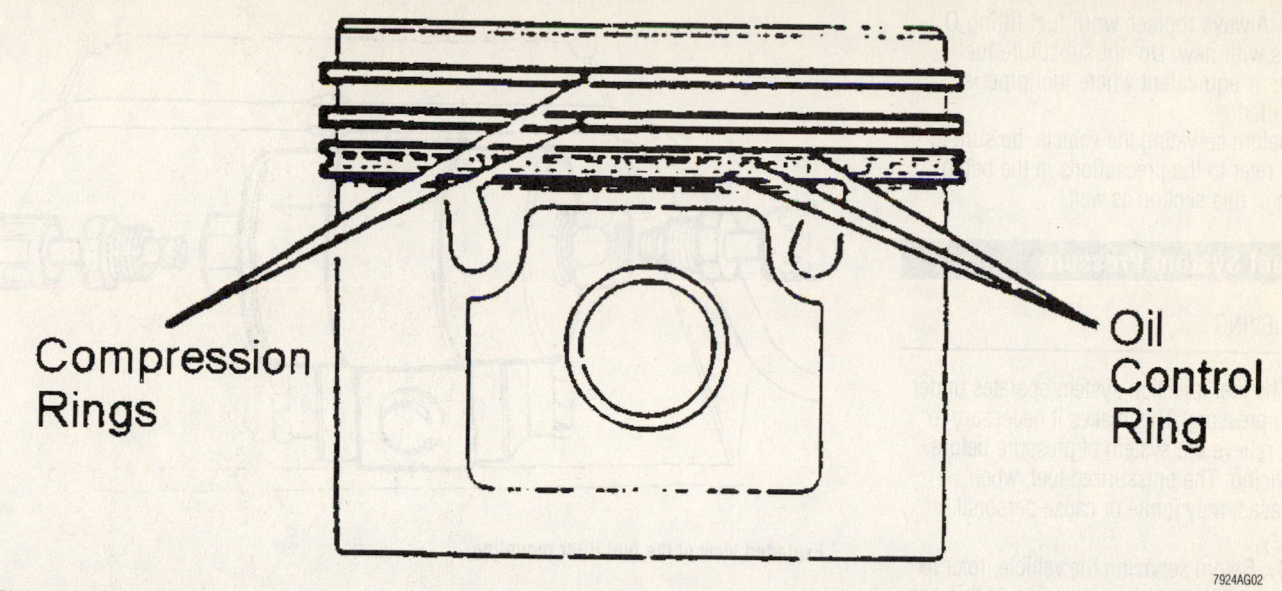

Compression Rings

Oil Control Ring

Piston ring positioning

2nd Compression Ring

Upper Oil Rail

Oil Ring Spacer

a

a

Lower Oil Rail

Piston Pin

Upper Compression Ring

a = 1 in. (25mm)

7924AG01

Piston ring end-gap spacing

Front Mark

7924AG03

Connecting rod front mark location

FUEL SYSTEM

Fuel System Service Precautions

Safety is the most important factor when performing not only fuel system maintenance but any type of maintenance. Failure to conduct maintenance and repairs in a safe manner may result in serious personal injury or death. Maintenance and testing of the vehicle's fuel system components can be accomplished safely and effectively by adhering to the following rules and guidelines.

• To avoid the possibility of fire and personal injury, always disconnect the negative battery cable unless the repair or test procedure requires that battery voltage be applied.

• Always relieve the fuel system pressure prior to disconnecting any fuel system component (injector, fuel rail, pressure regulator, etc.), fitting or fuel line connection. Exercise extreme caution whenever relieving fuel system pressure, to avoid exposing skin, face and eyes to fuel spray. Please be advised that fuel under pressure may penetrate the skin or any part of the body that it contacts.

• Always place a shop towel or cloth around the fitting or connection prior to loosening to absorb any excess fuel due to spillage. Ensure that all fuel spillage (should it occur) is quickly removed from engine surfaces. Ensure that all fuel soaked cloths or towels are deposited into a suitable waste container.

• Always keep a dry chemical (Class B) fire extinguisher near the work area.

• Do not allow fuel spray or fuel vapors to come into contact with a spark or open flame.

• Always use a back-up wrench when loosening and tightening fuel line connection fittings. This will prevent unnecessary stress and torsion to fuel line piping.

• Always replace worn fuel fitting O-rings with new. Do not substitute fuel hose or equivalent where fuel pipe is installed.

Before servicing the vehicle, be sure to also refer to the precautions in the beginning of this section as well.

Fuel System Pressure

RELIEVING

The fuel injection system operates under high pressure. This makes it necessary to first relieve the system of pressure before servicing. The pressurized fuel, when released, may ignite or cause personal injury.

1. Before servicing the vehicle, refer to the precautions in the beginning of this section.

2. Disconnect the power to the fuel pump by removing the relay or the fuel pump fuse. Check the list on the fuse box lid to be sure. The fuse can be removed to stop the fuel pump from running. With the engine operating at idle, wait until the engine stalls from fuel starvation.

3. Switch the ignition **OFF** and remove the negative battery cable.

4. Carefully loosen the fuel line on the control pressure regulator or component to be serviced.

5. Wrap a clean rag around the connection, while loosening, to catch any fuel.

6. After service is complete, discard the fuel soaked rag in the proper manner and reconnect negative battery cable, relay or fuses.

Fuel Filter

REMOVAL & INSTALLATION

1. Before servicing the vehicle, refer to the precautions in the beginning of this section.

2. Disconnect the negative battery cable and relieve the fuel system pressure.

3. Raise and support the vehicle safely.

4. Remove the bracket cover over the filter, if equipped.

5. Place a pan under the filter. Using 2 wrenches, disconnect the fuel lines from the filter.

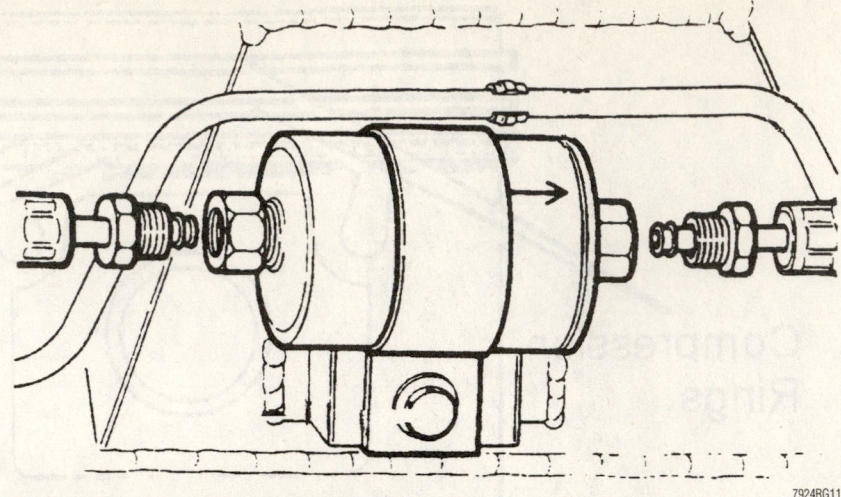

Exploded view of the fuel filter mounting

6. Remove the fuel filter from the bracket and retainer, if equipped.
Note the direction of the flow arrow so the replacement filter can be installed correctly.

To install:

7. Install the fuel filter into the bracket making sure the flow direction is correct. Tighten the clamp to 15–25 inch lbs. (2–3 Nm).

8. Connect the fuel lines, using new O-rings. Tighten the fittings to 15 ft. lbs. (20 Nm).

9. Lower the vehicle.

10. Start the engine and check for leaks.

Fuel Pump

REMOVAL & INSTALLATION

1. Before servicing the vehicle, refer to the precautions in the beginning of this section.

2. Relieve the fuel system pressure.

3. Remove or disconnect the following:

- Negative battery cable
- Fuel from the tank
- Fuel filler tube from the tank
- Feed pipe at the rear of the filter
- Return line

4. Support the fuel tank with a jack.

5. Remove the 3 nuts and 2 bolts securing the fuel tank cradle-to-the floor pan.

6. Lower the tank about 6 inches (150mm) and unplug the wiring connectors.

7. Remove the tank/cradle assembly.

8. Remove the tank from the cradle.

9. Remove any dirt that has accumulated around the fuel pump flange so it will not enter the fuel tank during removal and installation.

10. Disconnect the breather hose from the pressure sensor.

11. Disconnect the hoses from the pump.

12. Using a locking ring tool, such as LRT 19-009, unscrew the retaining ring from the pump flange.

➡**A lifting ring is provided to pull the unit out. Don't pull on any other parts!**

13. Remove the fuel pump and discard the seal ring. Separate the fuel pump from the sending unit, if required.

To install:

14. Clean the fuel pump mounting flange and tank mounting surface.

15. Apply a light coating of sealer on a new seal ring.

16. Install the fuel pump on the sending unit, if removed. Install the fuel pump assembly in the tank and tighten it to 26 ft. lbs. (35 Nm).

17. Install the fuel tank in the vehicle, tighten the mounting bolts to 33 ft. lbs. (45 Nm), and be sure to connect the fuel tank vent hose and filler neck.

18. Lower the vehicle and fill the fuel tank with at least 10 gallons of fuel. Connect the negative battery cable. Turn the ignition key to **RUN** for 3 seconds repeatedly, 5–10 times, to pressurize the system. Check for leaks.

19. Start the engine and check for leaks.

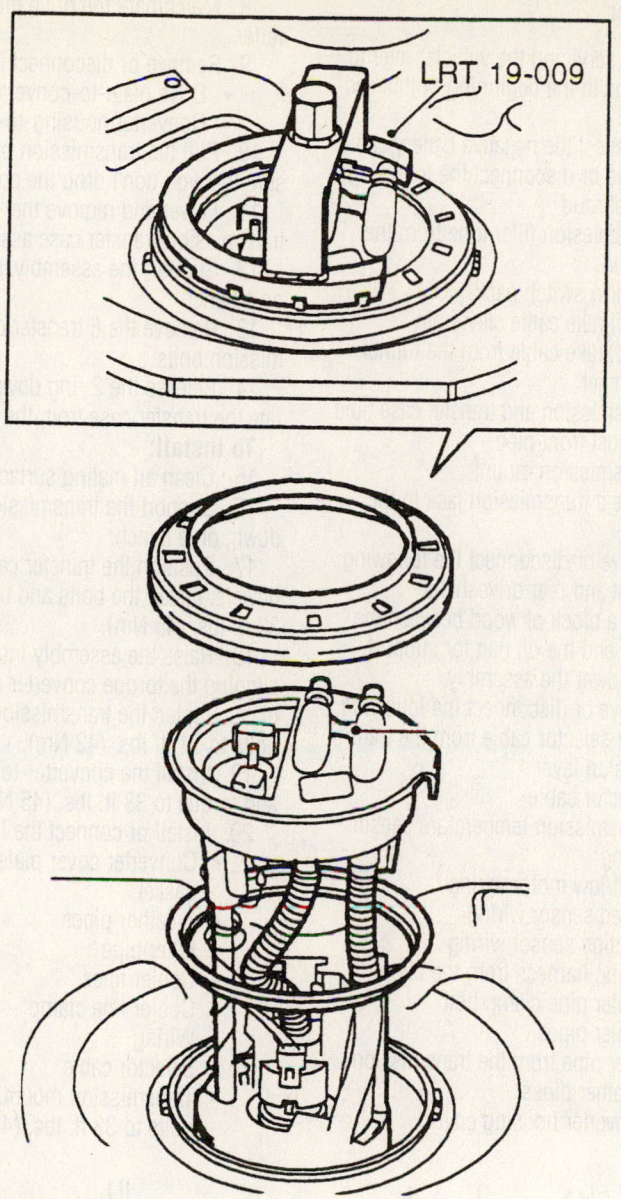

LRT 19-009

9308RG86

Fuel pump mounting

Fuel Rail and Injectors

REMOVAL & INSTALLATION

1. Before servicing the vehicle, refer to the precautions in the beginning of this section.
2. Remove or disconnect the following:
   - Battery ground cable
   - Fuel system pressure
   - Throttle cable
   - Cruise control cable
   - Harness clip from the throttle linkage bracket
   - Breather hose form the plenum
   - IAC connector

   - TPS connector
   - Plenum chamber
   - Purge hose
   - Crankcase breather hose
   - Pressure regulator vacuum hose
   - Ram housing from the intake manifold

➡ **It may be necessary to pry on the housing to break the seal. If so, use a small block of wood as a pry point between the manifold and ram housing. NEVER pry on the fuel rail!**

   - The 8 injector plugs
   - Fuel temperature sensor connection
   - Fuel feed hose form the fuel rail

   - Fuel return hose from the pressure regulator

➡ **Advanced EVAPS vehicles have a threaded connector.**

   - Fuel rail and ignition coil bracket from the manifold
   - Coil bracket
   - Fuel rail and injectors
   - Injector retaining clips and injectors
   - Two O-rings from each injector

To install:
3. Install or connect the following:
   - New O-rings coated with silicone grease
   - Injectors and clips on the rail
   - Fuel rail and injectors on the manifold
   - Ignition coil and bracket
   - Return hose
   - Fuel feed line. Torque the union to 12 ft. lbs. (16 Nm).
   - All injector wiring
   - Ram housing. Use Loctite 577, or equivalent, as a sealant. Torque the bolts to 18 ft. lbs. (24 Nm).
   - All vacuum hoses
   - All remaining wiring
   - Plenum chamber. Use Loctite 577, or equivalent, as a sealant. Torque the bolts to 18 ft. lbs. (24 Nm).
   - Coolant hoses
   - All remaining hoses and wires
   - Battery ground

DRIVE TRAIN

Transmission Assembly

REMOVAL & INSTALLATION

Defender 90 and Discovery

1. Before servicing the vehicle, refer to the precautions in the beginning of this section.
2. Remove or disconnect the following:
   - Negative battery cable
   - Fan shroud from the radiator
   - Transmission breather pipes from the right cylinder head at the rear and the dipstick
   - Kickdown cable from the throttle linkage
   - Shift boot knob and boot from the center console

- Fluid from the transmission and the transfer case
- Exhaust system, from the manifolds back
- Speedometer from the transfer case
- Driveshafts at the transmission and transfer case and support them out of the way.
- Transmission oil cooler lines and secure them out of the way.
- Transmission shift cable and the wiring harness from the transmission

3. Secure a transmission jack to the transmission.

4. Remove or disconnect the following:
- Transmission crossmember
- Transfer case side mounts and mounting brackets
- Parking brake cable from the lever
- Driveplate inspection cover and matchmark the torque converter to the driveplate.
- Torque converter bolts and the fill tube from the transmission
- Bell housing to engine bolts

5. Pull the transmission rearward, slightly, secure the torque converter to the transmission.

6. Remove the transmission from the vehicle.

To install:

7. Install or connect the following:
- Transmission to the vehicle
- Bell housing-to-engine bolts and tighten to 31 ft. lbs. (42 Nm)

8. Align the matchmarks for the torque converter to the driveplate.

9. Apply Loctite® to the torque converter bolts and tighten to 29 ft. lbs. (39 Nm).

10. Install or connect the following:
- Fill tube to the transmission
- Driveplate inspection cover
- Parking brake cable to the lever
- Transfer case side mounts and tighten the bolts to 33 ft. lbs. (45 Nm).
- Transmission crossmember
- Transmission shift cable and the wiring harness to the transmission
- Transmission oil cooler lines
- Driveshafts at the transmission and transfer case
- Speedometer to the transfer case
- Exhaust system
- Transmission and transfer case with Dexron®II ATF
- Shift boot and knob
- Kickdown cable to the throttle linkage
- Transmission breather pipes to the right cylinder head at the rear
- Fan shroud to the radiator
- Negative battery cable

Range Rover

1. Before servicing the vehicle, refer to the precautions in the beginning of this section.

2. Disconnect the negative battery cable.

3. Remove or disconnect the following:
- Fan shroud
- Transmission filler tube from the engine
- Window switch pack
- Handbrake cable clevis pin
- Handbrake cable from the tunnel grommet
- Transmission and transfer case fluid
- Exhaust front pipe
- Transmission mount

4. Secure a transmission jack to the transmission.

5. Remove or disconnect the following:
- Front and rear driveshafts

6. Place a block of wood between the axle housing and the oil pan for support, and slightly lower the assembly.

7. Remove or disconnect the following:
- Gear selector cable from the transmission lever
- Selector cable
- Transmission temperature sensor wiring
- High/low motor wiring
- Speed sensor wiring
- Position sensor wiring
- Wiring harness from the clips
- Cooler pipe clamp bolt
- Cooler pipes
- Filler pipe from the transmission
- Breather pipes
- Converter housing cover

8. Matchmark the drive plate and converter.

9. Remove or disconnect the following:
- Drive plate-to-converter bolts
- Converter housing-to-engine bolts

10. Pull the transmission back, making sure that you don't drop the converter.

11. Lower and remove the transmission/transfer case assembly.

12. Support the assembly, nose down, on a bench.

13. Remove the 6 transfer case-to-transmission bolts.

14. Release the 2 ring dowels and separate the transfer case from the transmission.

To install:

15. Clean all mating surfaces.

16. Support the transmission, nose down, on a bench.

17. Position the transfer case and ring dowels. Install the bolts and tighten them to 33 ft. lbs. (45 Nm).

18. Raise the assembly into position, aligning the torque converter and drive plate. Tighten the transmission-to-engine bolts to 31 ft. lbs. (42 Nm).

19. Install the converter-to-flexplate bolts and torque to 33 ft. lbs. (45 Nm).

20. Install or connect the following:
- Converter cover plate, with a new gasket
- Breather pipes
- Filler pipe
- Cooler lines
- Cooler line clamp
- Wiring
- Selector cable
- Transmission mount. Torque the bolts to 33 ft. lbs. (45 Nm).

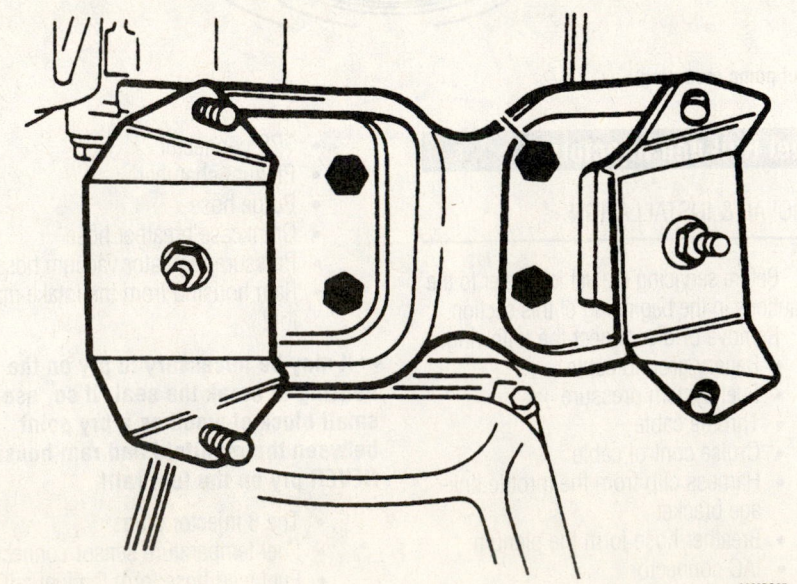

Transmission rear mount—Range Rover

9308RG85

Transfer Case Assembly

REMOVAL & INSTALLATION

Defender 90 and Discovery

1. Before servicing the vehicle, refer to the precautions in the beginning of this section.

2. Remove or disconnect the following:
- Negative battery cable
- Radiator fan shroud
- Transfer case shift knob and boot
- Transfer case fluid
- Heat shield from the front exhaust pipe
- Catalytic converter assembly
- Crossmember from under the transfer case

7924RG19

Remove the fan shroud to prevent the fan from damaging it—Defender 90 and Discovery models

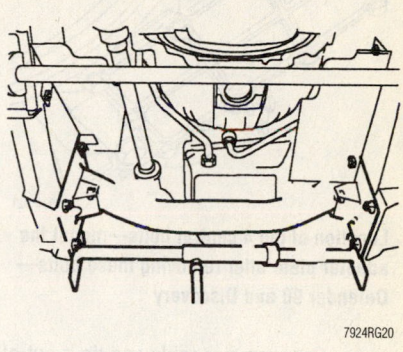

7924RG20

Be sure to support the transmission before removing the crossmember bolts—Defender 90 and Discovery models

ARC WELD

Ø·35 Ø9
·18 4·7

Ø19
Ø·75

·18 4·7

2·16
55

·35 9·5 ·37
9

72
2·83

203·2
8·0

72

2·63 2·63
67 67

14·3
·56

165·1
6·5

32° 30'

139·7
5·5

4·7
·18

241·3
9·5

47·6
1·87

38·1
1·5

38·1
1·5

31·7
1·25

Ø 11·1
·43

228·6
9

MATERIAL: STEEL PLATE

✶ = TO BE DRILLED TO FIT TRANSMISSION JACK BEING USED

FRONT

7924RG22

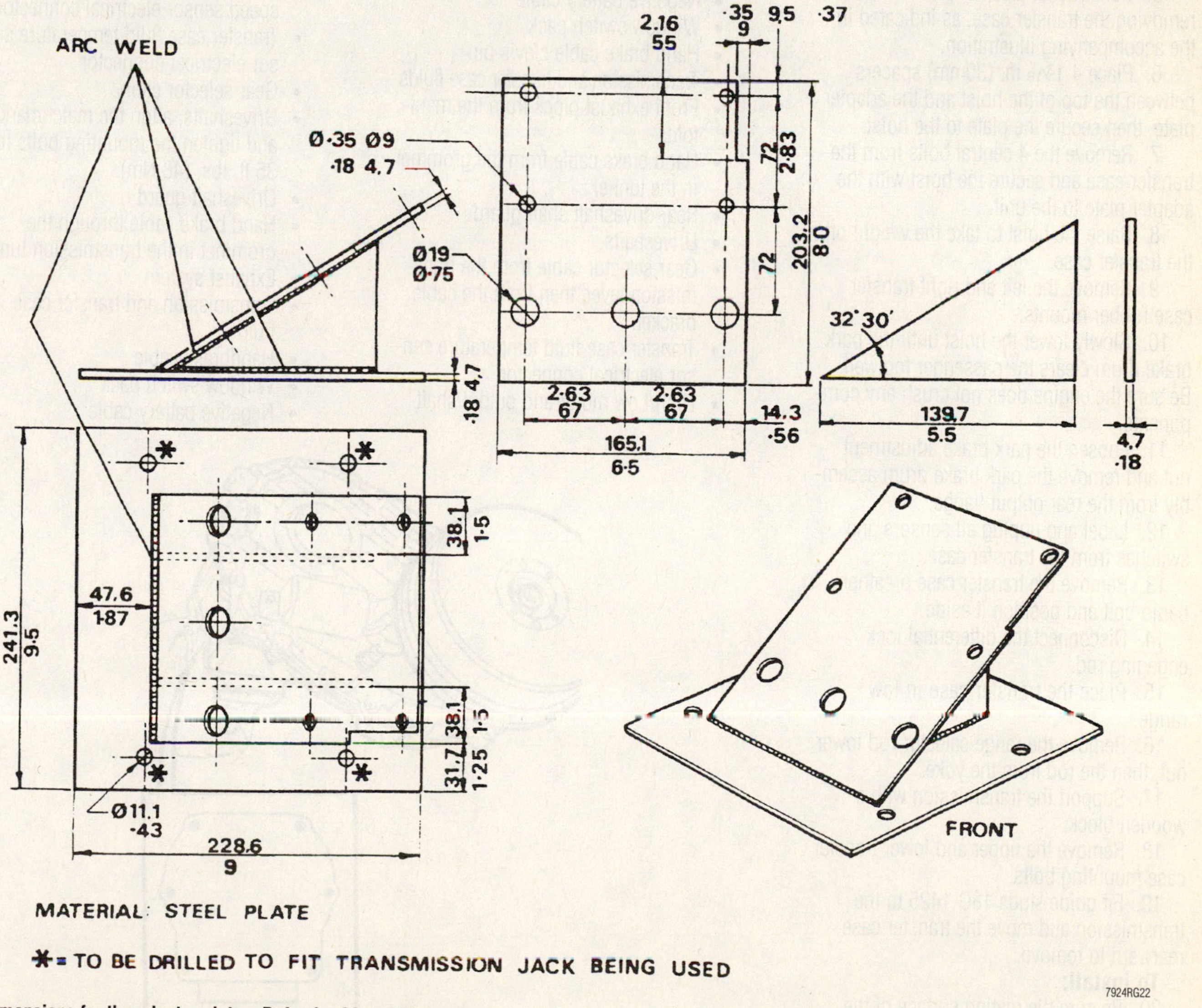

Dimensions for the adapter plate—Defender 90 and Discovery

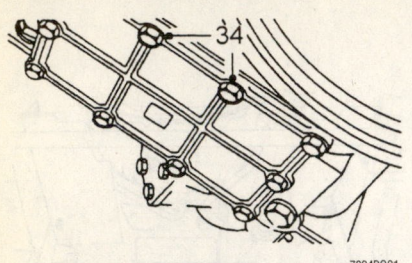

7924RG21

Location of the 4 central bolts—mount the adapter plate after removing these bolts— Defender 90 and Discovery

- Speedometer cable and tie it out of the way

3. Matchmark the front and rear driveshafts-to-flanges relation.

4. Disconnect the front and rear driveshafts and tie them out of the way.

5. Construct an adapter plate for removing the transfer case, as indicated in the accompanying illustration.

6. Place 4 1³⁄₁₆ in. (30mm) spacers between the top of the hoist and the adapter plate, then secure the plate to the hoist.

7. Remove the 4 central bolts from the transfer case and secure the hoist with the adapter plate to the unit.

8. Raise the hoist to take the weight off the transfer case.

9. Remove the left and right transfer case rubber mounts.

10. Slowly lower the hoist until the park brake drum clears the passenger footwell. Be sure the engine does not crush any components.

11. Loosen the park brake adjustment nut and remove the park brake drum assembly from the rear output flange.

12. Label and unplug all sensors and switches from the transfer case.

13. Remove the transfer case breather banjo bolt and position it aside.

14. Disconnect the differential lock engaging rod.

15. Place the transfer case in low range.

16. Remove the range selector rod lower nut, then the rod from the yoke.

17. Support the transmission with a wooden block.

18. Remove the upper and lower transfer case mounting bolts.

19. Fit guide studs 18G 1425 to the transmission and move the transfer case rearward to remove.

To install:

20. Be sure the mating surface of the transmission and transfer case is free from dirt and debris.

21. Raise the transfer case until it is located over the guide studs 18G 1425, then slide it forward onto the transmission.

22. Remove the guide studs and bolt the transfer case to the transmission.

23. Complete the installation procedure in the reverse order of the removal procedure, noting the following items:

- After removing the adapter plate, clean the 4 bottom cover bolts and coat them with Loctite ® 290, then tighten to 19 ft. lbs. (25 Nm).
- Fill the transfer case with 90W oil.
- Check and adjust the park brake cable.

Range Rover

1. Before servicing the vehicle, refer to the precautions in the beginning of this section.

2. Remove or disconnect the following:
- Negative battery cable
- Window switch pack
- Hand brake cable clevis pin
- Transmission and transfer case fluids
- Front exhaust pipes from the manifolds
- Hand brake cable from the grommet in the tunnel
- Rear driveshaft shaft guard
- Driveshafts
- Gear selector cable from the transmission lever, then from the cable bracket.
- Transfer case fluid temperature sensor electrical connector
- High/Low motor and output shaft speed sensor electrical connectors

3. Attach a suitable transmission jack to the transfer case.

4. Remove the 6 transfer case-to-transmission mounting bolts.

5. Lower the transfer case form the vehicle.

6. Using a suitable seal removal tool, remove the transmission output seal.

To install:

7. Install a new transmission output seal, using a suitable seal installer.

8. Ensure transfer case and transmission mating faces are clean.

9. Lubricate the input shaft with transmission fluid.

10. Install the transfer case and tighten the mounting bolts to 33 ft. lbs. (45 Nm).

11. Remove the transmission jack.

12. Install or connect the following:
- High/Low motor and output shaft speed sensor electrical connectors
- Transfer case fluid temperature sensor electrical connector
- Gear selector cable
- Driveshafts, align the matchmarks and tighten the mounting bolts to 35 ft. lbs. (48 Nm).
- Driveshaft guard
- Hand brake cable through the grommet in the transmission tunnel
- Exhaust system
- Transmission and transfer case fluid
- Handbrake cable
- Window switch pack
- Negative battery cable

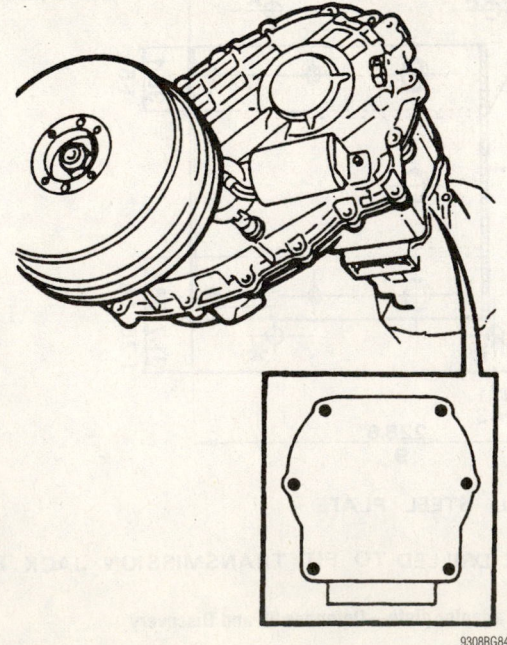

9308RG84

Transfer case bolt locations—Range Rover

Front Axle Swivel Hubs

REMOVAL & INSTALLATION

Range Rover

❊❊ CAUTION

Before beginning, depressurize the air suspension.

1. Before servicing the vehicle, refer to the precautions in the beginning of this section.
2. Remove or disconnect the following:
   - Drive hub
   - Axle shaft
   - Track rod from the swivel hub
   - Drag link from the swivel hub
   - Swivel hub. Use a forcing tool, such as the one illustrated. If the joint pin turns in its socket, use a 6mm Allen wrench to hold it.
   - Adjusting collar from the hub

To install:

3. Install or connect the following:
   - New adjusting collar into the hub. Install the collar until a 4mm gap exists between the shoulder of the collar and the top of the hub.
   - Hub onto the axle. Install the upper nut, only. Torque the nut to 81 ft. lbs. (110 Nm).
4. Clean the seal surface in the axle.
5. Turn the clamp screw of tool LRT-54-006/1 fully counterclockwise. Make sure that the clamp toggle rotates freely. Position the tool in the axle with the **TOP** mark upwards.
6. Make sure that the tool is located squarely on the sealing surface. Use a plastic or brass mallet to tap the end of the screw. This will ensure that the tool is properly positioned.
7. Install and tighten the lower nut, until the ball stud is squarely seated in the joint but the collar can still turn. Adjust the height of the collar until the tool is a slide-fit in the hub.
8. Remove the tool. Tighten the collar 1¼ turn while tightening the lower nut to 100 ft. lbs. (135 Nm). The hub should turn smoothly and evenly. If not, repeat the assembly procedure.
9. Install or connect the following:
   - Drag link. Torque the nut to 59 ft. lbs. (80 Nm).
   - Track rod. Torque the nut to 59 ft. lbs. (80 Nm).
   - Axle shaft
   - Drive hub

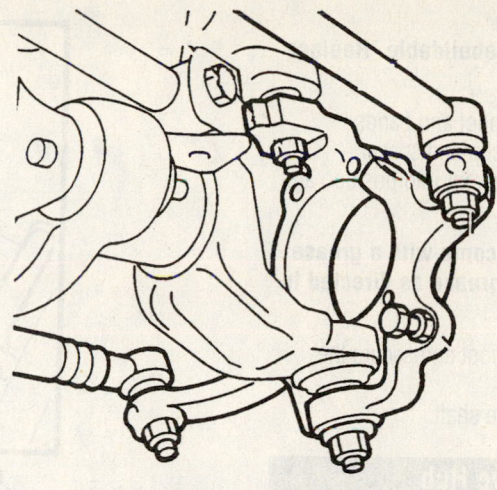

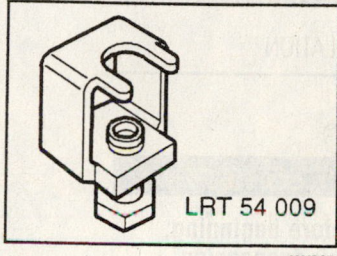

Front axle swivel hub. The inset shows the ball stud removal tool

Front Axle Shaft CV-Joints

REMOVAL & INSTALLATION

Defender 90 and Discovery

1. Before servicing the vehicle, refer to the precautions in the beginning of this section.

2. Remove or disconnect the following:
   - Axle shaft
   - Bands from the boot and pull back the boot to expose the joint.
3. Using a drift against the inner part of the joint, drive the joint from the shaft.
4. Remove and discard the circlip.
5. Remove the spacer.
6. Remove the boot.

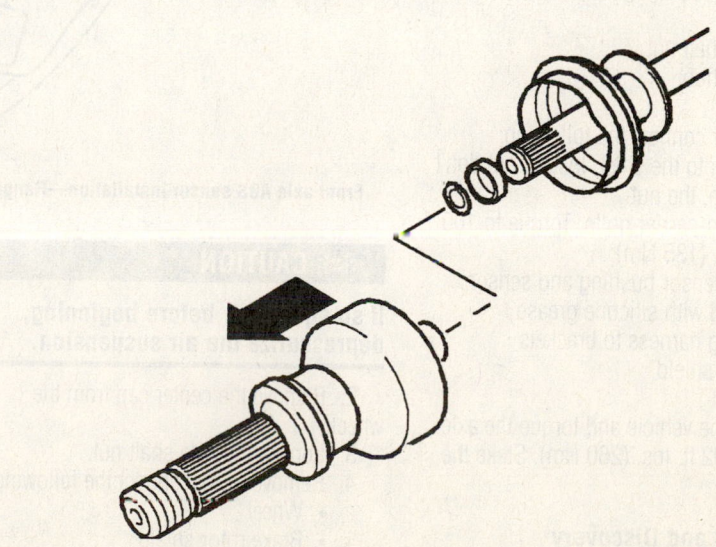

Front axle shaft CV-joint

Turn to Section 5 for brake system applications

To install:

➡ **The joint is not rebuildable. Replace it and the boot.**

7. Install a new boot and bands.
8. Install the circlip and spacer.
9. Place the new joint into position and press it into place.

➡ **A new joint will come with a grease packet. Apply the grease as directed in the kit.**

10. Position the boot and secure the bands.
11. Install the axle shaft.

Front Axle Drive Hub

REMOVAL & INSTALLATION

Range Rover

✳✳ CAUTION

If so equipped, before beginning, depressurize the air suspension.

1. Before servicing the vehicle, refer to the precautions in the beginning of this section.
2. Remove the center cap from the wheel.
3. Loosen the axle shaft nut.
4. Remove or disconnect the following:
   • Wheel
   • Brake rotor shield
   • ABS sensor harness from the brackets
   • Sensor from the hub
   • Sensor bushing
   • 4 bolts securing the hub to the carrier
   • Axle shaft nut
   • Drive hub

To install:

5. Install or connect the following:
   • Hub onto the shaft. Install, but don't tighten, the nut.
   • Hub-to-carrier bolts. Torque to 100 ft. lbs. (135 Nm).
   • ABS sensor bushing and sensor, coated with silicone grease
   • Wiring harness to brackets
   • Rotor shield
   • Wheel

6. Lower the vehicle and torque the axle shaft nut to 192 ft. lbs. (260 Nm). Stake the nut.

Defender 90 and Discovery

1. Before servicing the vehicle, refer to the precautions in the beginning of this section.

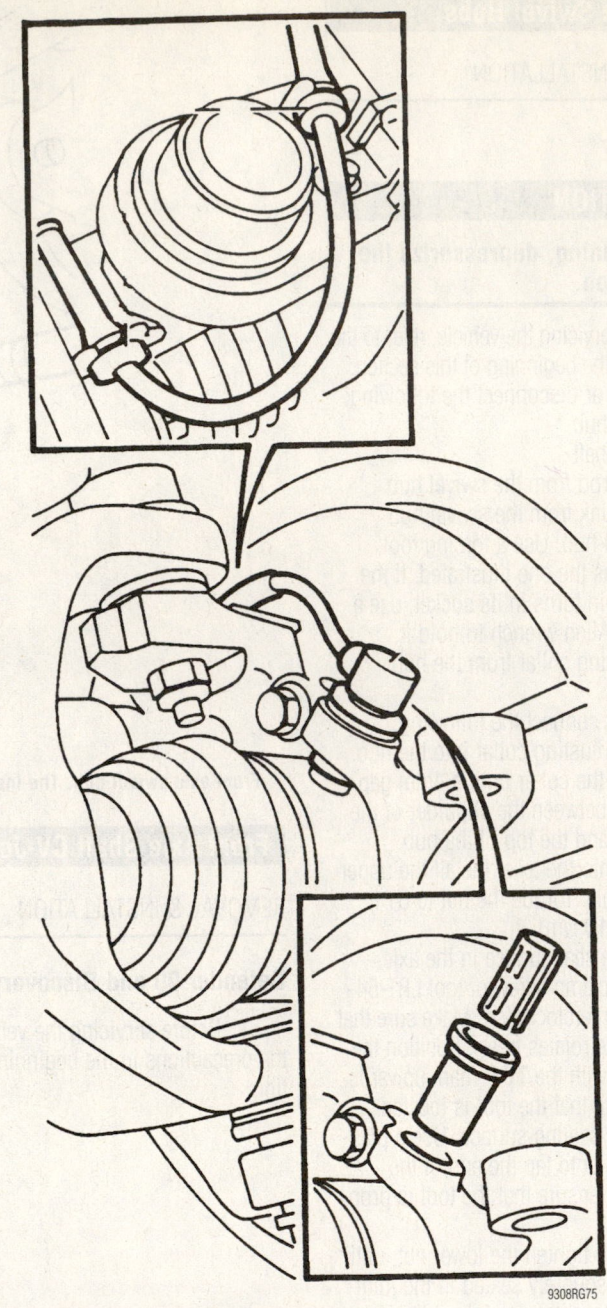

Front axle ABS sensor installation—Range Rover

9308RG75

✳✳ CAUTION

If so equipped, before beginning, depressurize the air suspension.

2. Remove the center cap from the wheel.
3. Loosen the axle shaft nut.
4. Remove or disconnect the following:
   • Wheel
   • Brake rotor shield
   • Brake rotor
   • ABS sensor harness from the brackets
   • Sensor from the hub
   • Sensor bushing
   • 4 bolts securing the hub to the carrier
   • Axle shaft nut
   • Drive hub

To install:

5. Apply anti-seize compound to the mating surfaces of the hub and knuckle.
6. Install or connect the following:
   • Hub onto the shaft. Install, but don't tighten, the nut.
   • Hub-to-carrier bolts. Torque to 74 ft. lbs. (100 Nm).

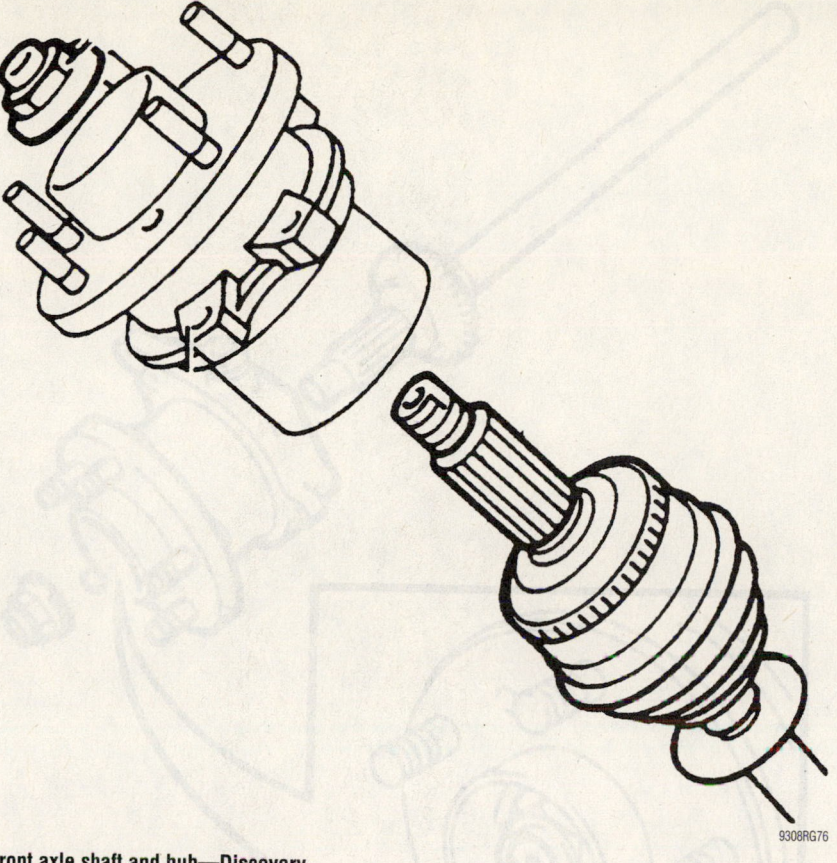

Front axle shaft and hub—Discovery

- ABS sensor bushing and sensor, coated with silicone grease
- Wiring harness to brackets
- Rotor
- Rotor shield
- Wheel

7. Lower the vehicle and torque the axle shaft nut to 360 ft. lbs. (490 Nm). Stake the nut.

Front Axle Shaft and Seal

REMOVAL & INSTALLATION

Range Rover

1. Before servicing the vehicle, refer to the precautions in the beginning of this section.

✻✻ CAUTION

Before beginning, depressurize the air suspension.

➡**If you're not separating the hub and shaft, don't loosen the axle shaft nut.**

2. Remove the center cap from the wheel.
3. Loosen the axle shaft nut.
4. Remove or disconnect the following:
   - Wheel
   - Brake rotor shield
   - ABS sensor harness from the brackets
   - Sensor from the hub
   - Sensor bushing
   - 4 bolts securing the hub to the carrier
   - Axle shaft nut, if loosened
   - Drive hub and axle shaft
   - Seal from the axle tube

To install:

5. Clean all surfaces.
6. Lubricate the new seal lip and running surface with silicone grease. Drive a new seal into place.
7. Install or connect the following:
   - Axle shaft into the axle tube
   - Hub onto the shaft. Install, but don't tighten, the nut.
   - Hub-to-carrier bolts. Torque to 100 ft. lbs. (135 Nm).

- ABS sensor bushing and sensor, coated with silicone grease
- Wiring harness to brackets
- Rotor shield
- Wheel

8. Lower the vehicle and torque the axle shaft nut to 192 ft. lbs. (260 Nm). Stake the nut.

Defender 90 and Discovery

1. Before servicing the vehicle, refer to the precautions in the beginning of this section.

✻✻ CAUTION

If so equipped, before beginning, depressurize the air suspension.

2. Remove the center cap from the wheel.
3. Loosen the axle shaft nut.
4. Remove or disconnect the following:
   - Wheel
   - Brake rotor shield
   - Brake rotor
   - ABS sensor harness from the brackets
   - Sensor from the hub
   - Sensor bushing
   - 4 bolts securing the hub to the carrier
   - Axle shaft nut
   - Drive hub
   - Axle shaft
   - Oil Seal

To install:

5. Clean all mating surfaces thoroughly.
6. Apply gear oil to the new seal's lip and outer edge.
7. Drive the new seal into place.
8. Slide the axle shaft into place.
9. Apply anti-seize compound to the mating surfaces of the hub and knuckle.
10. Install or connect the following:
    - Hub onto the shaft. Install, but don't tighten, the nut.
    - Hub-to-carrier bolts. Torque to 74 ft. lbs. (100 Nm).
    - ABS sensor bushing and sensor, coated with silicone grease
    - Wiring harness to brackets
    - Rotor
    - Rotor shield
    - Wheel

11. Lower the vehicle and torque the axle shaft nut to 360 ft. lbs. (490 Nm). Stake the nut.

Rear Axle Shaft and Bearing

REMOVAL & INSTALLATION

Range Rover

1. Before servicing the vehicle, refer to the precautions in the beginning of this section.

> ※ **CAUTION**
>
> **Before beginning, depressurize the air suspension.**

➡ **If you're not separating the hub and shaft, don't loosen the axle shaft nut.**

2. Remove the center cap from the wheel.

3. Loosen the axle shaft nut.

4. Remove or disconnect the following:
   • Wheel
   • Brake rotor shield
   • 2 bolts and remove the backstrap from the hub.
   • Sensor from the hub
   • Sensor bushing
   • 6 bolts securing the hub to the axle carrier
   • Drive hub and axle shaft
   • Axle shaft nut, if loosened
   • Seal from the axle tube

To install:

5. Clean all splines and surfaces.

6. Lubricate the new seal lip and running surface with silicone grease. Drive a new seal into place.

7. Install or connect the following:
   • Axle shaft into the axle tube
   • Hub onto the shaft. Install, but don't tighten, the nut.
   • Hub-to-carrier bolts. Torque to 48 ft. lbs. (65 Nm).
   • ABS sensor bushing and sensor, coated with silicone grease
   • Rotor shield
   • Wheel

8. Lower the vehicle and torque the axle shaft nut to 192 ft. lbs. (260 Nm). Stake the nut.

Defender 90 and Discovery

1. Before servicing the vehicle, refer to the precautions in the beginning of this section.

> ※ **CAUTION**
>
> **If so equipped, before beginning, depressurize the air suspension.**

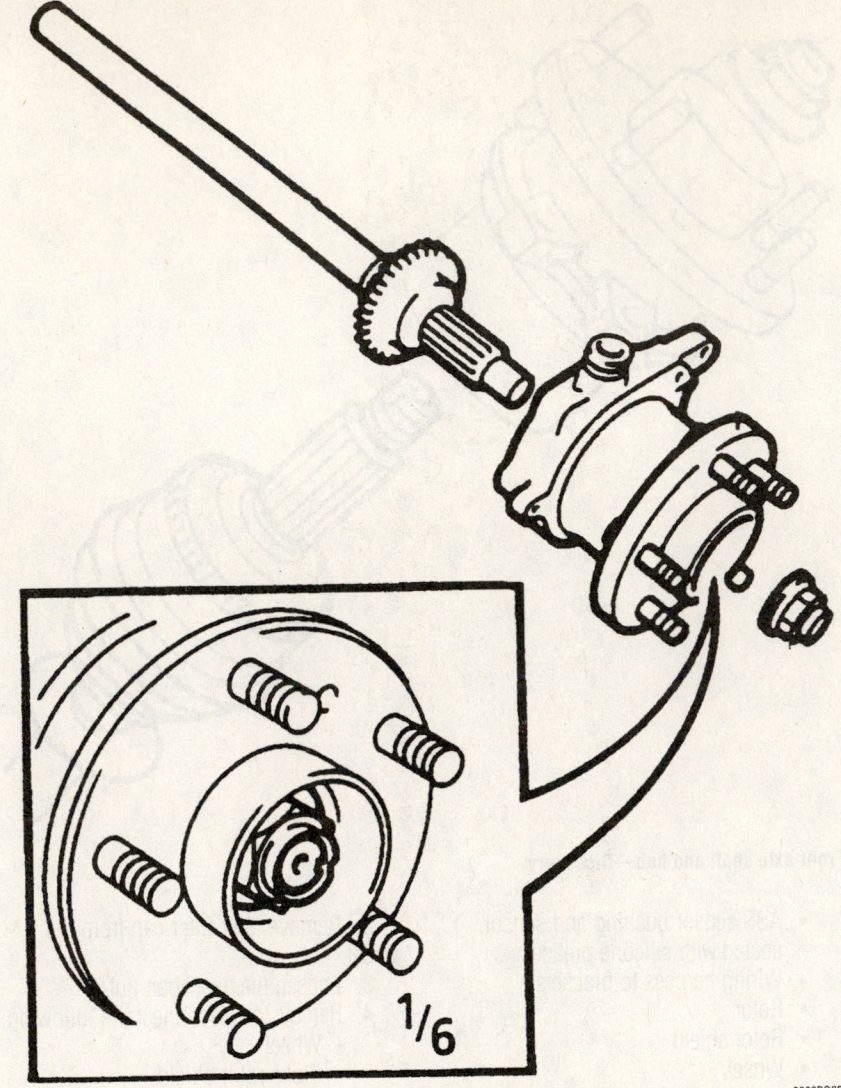

Rear axle shaft and hub/bearing assembly—Range Rover

2. Remove the center cap from the wheel.

3. Loosen the axle shaft nut.

4. Remove or disconnect the following:
   • Wheel
   • Brake rotor shield
   • Brake rotor
   • ABS sensor harness from the brackets
   • Sensor from the hub
   • Sensor bushing
   • 4 bolts securing the hub to the carrier
   • Axle shaft nut
   • Hub/bearing assembly
   • Axle shaft
   • Oil Seal

To install:

5. Clean all mating surfaces thoroughly.

6. Apply gear oil to the new seal's lip and outer edge.

7. Drive the new seal into place.

8. Slide the axle shaft into place.

9. Apply anti-seize compound to the mating surfaces of the hub and knuckle.

10. Install or connect the following:
   • Hub onto the shaft. Install, but don't tighten, the nut.
   • Hub-to-axle carrier bolts. Torque to 74 ft. lbs. (100 Nm).
   • ABS sensor bushing and sensor, coated with silicone grease
   • Wiring harness to brackets
   • Rotor
   • Rotor shield
   • Wheel

11. Lower the vehicle and torque the axle shaft nut to 360 ft. lbs. (490 Nm). Stake the nut.

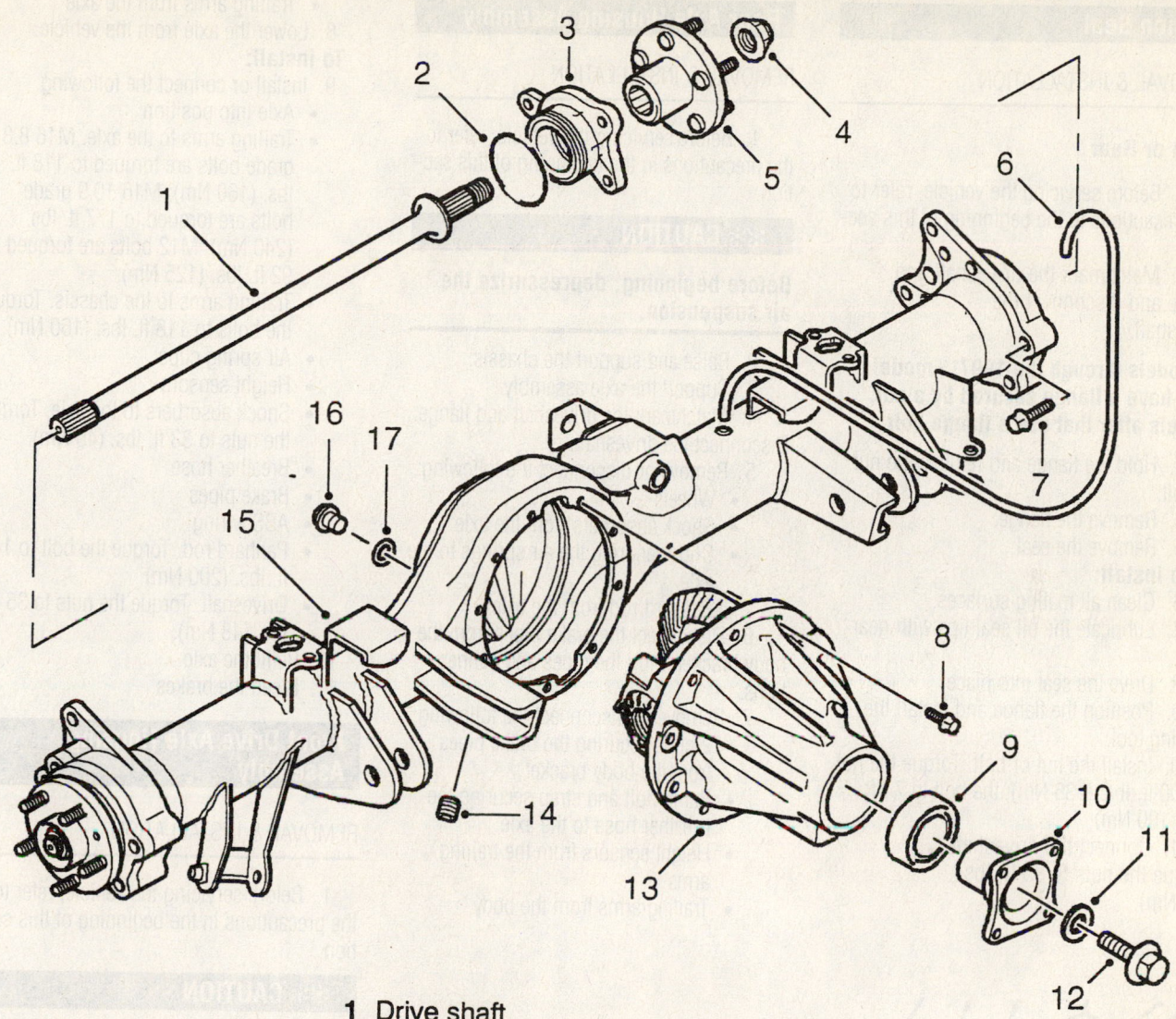

1 Drive shaft
2 'O' ring
3 Hub bearing
4 Stake nut
5 Hub flange
6 Breather tube
7 Bolt
8 Bolt
9 Oil seal
10 Drive flange
11 Washer
12 Bolt
13 Differential unit
14 Drain plug
15 Axle casing
16 Oil level plug
17 'O' ring

9308RG92

Rear axle components

Pinion Seal

REMOVAL & INSTALLATION

Front or Rear

1. Before servicing the vehicle, refer to the precautions in the beginning of this section.

2. Matchmark the driveshaft and flange and disconnect the driveshaft.

➡ **Models through the 1997½ model year have a flange secured by a nut. Models after that use a flange bolt.**

3. Hold the flange and remove the nut or bolt.

4. Remove the flange.

5. Remove the seal.

To install:

6. Clean all mating surfaces.

7. Lubricate the oil seal lips with gear oil.

8. Drive the seal into place.

9. Position the flange and install the holding tool.

10. Install the nut or bolt. Torque the nut to 100 ft. lbs. (135 Nm); the bolt to 74 ft. lbs. (100 Nm).

11. Connect the driveshaft. Torque the nuts to 35 ft. lbs. (48 Nm).

Rear Axle Housing Assembly

REMOVAL & INSTALLATION

1. Before servicing the vehicle, refer to the precautions in the beginning of this section.

❊❊ CAUTION

Before beginning, depressurize the air suspension.

2. Raise and support the chassis.

3. Support the axle assembly.

4. Matchmark the driveshaft and flange. Disconnect the driveshaft.

5. Remove or disconnect the following:
- Wheels
- Shock absorbers from the axle
- Clips securing the air springs to the axle
- Panhard rod from the axle

6. Disconnect the brake pipes from the body bracket. Plug the pipes and connections.

7. Remove or disconnect the following:
- 2 clips securing the brake pipes from the body bracket
- Banjo bolt and strap securing the breather hose to the axle
- Height sensors from the trailing arms
- Trailing arms from the body

- Trailing arms from the axle

8. Lower the axle from the vehicle.

To install:

9. Install or connect the following:
- Axle into position
- Trailing arms to the axle. M16 8.8 grade bolts are torqued to 118 ft. lbs. (160 Nm); M16 10.9 grade bolts are torqued to 177 ft. lbs. (240 Nm); M12 bolts are torqued to 92 ft. lbs. (125 Nm).
- Trailing arms to the chassis. Torque the bolts to 118 ft. lbs. (160 Nm).
- Air spring clips
- Height sensors
- Shock absorbers to the axle. Torque the nuts to 33 ft. lbs. (45 Nm).
- Breather hose
- Brake pipes
- ABS wiring
- Panhard rod. Torque the bolt to 148 ft. lbs. (200 Nm).
- Driveshaft. Torque the nuts to 35 ft. lbs. (48 Nm).

10. Refill the axle.

11. Bleed the brakes.

Front Drive Axle Housing Assembly

REMOVAL & INSTALLATION

1. Before servicing the vehicle, refer to the precautions in the beginning of this section.

❊❊ CAUTION

Before beginning, depressurize the air suspension.

2. Remove or disconnect the following:
- Brake pads
- Caliper. Tie it out of the way.
- ABS sensors
- Brake hoses from the knuckles
- Drag link from the knuckle
- Panhard rod from the axle
- Sway bar
- Track rod
- Axle oil
- Driveshaft
- Height sensors
- Breather hose

3. Support the axle

4. Remove or disconnect the following:
- Air spring retaining clips
- Air springs from the axle
- Shock absorbers from the axle
- Radius arms-to-chassis nuts

9308RG83

Pinion seal and flange

5. Move the axle forward and release the radius arms from the chassis brackets.

6. Remove the axle/radius arms assembly.

7. Remove the radius arms from the axle.

To install:

8. Clean all mating surfaces.

9. Install or connect the following:

- Radius arms to the axle. Torque the nuts to 92 ft. lbs. (125 Nm).
- Axle into position. Locate the radius arms, with bushings, into the chassis brackets. Tighten the nuts to 118 ft. lbs. (160 Nm).
- Shock absorbers. Torque the nuts to 33 ft. lbs. (45 Nm).
- Air springs
- Air spring retaining pins and bolts. Torque the bolts to 15 ft. lbs. (20 Nm).
- Breather hose
- Height sensors
- Driveshaft. Torque the nuts to 35 ft. lbs. (48 Nm).
- Track rod. Torque the nuts to 59 ft. lbs. (80 Nm).
- Sway bar

- Panhard rod. Torque the bolt to 148 ft. lbs. (200 Nm).
- Drag link. Torque the nut to 59 ft. lbs. (80 Nm).
- ABS sensors, coated with silicone grease
- Brake hoses
- Calipers. Torque the bolts to 162 ft. lbs. (220 Nm).
- Brake pads
- Axle fluid

STEERING AND SUSPENSION

Air Suspension

DEPRESSURIZING

The air suspension is pressurized up to 150 psi (1034 kPa). Before beginning work on suspension or steering components, the system should be depressurized. A special

tool called a TestBook is required to depressurize the system properly and safely. The tool is self-guiding. Depressurizing will lower the suspension to the bump stops. Before beginning any work, make sure that all air springs are deflated. A spring that remains inflated is due to a stuck solenoid valve. In that case, it will be necessary to disconnect the pipe at that air spring.

PIPE DISCONNECT

Before servicing the vehicle, refer to the precautions in the beginning of this section.

If it is necessary to disconnect a pipe:

a. **Wear hand, ear and eye protection. Wrap a cloth around the connection.**

b. Clean the connection with a stiff wire brush.

c. Peel back the boot.

d. Apply equal downward pressure on the collet flange at "A", as shown.

e. Pull the pipe firmly through the center of the collet.

f. To connect the pipe, push it firmly through the 2 O-rings until it contacts the base of the housing. Gently pull back on the pipe. Some slight movement will be noticed.

g. Reposition the boot.

When the job is done, run the engine to repressurize the system. The system must be

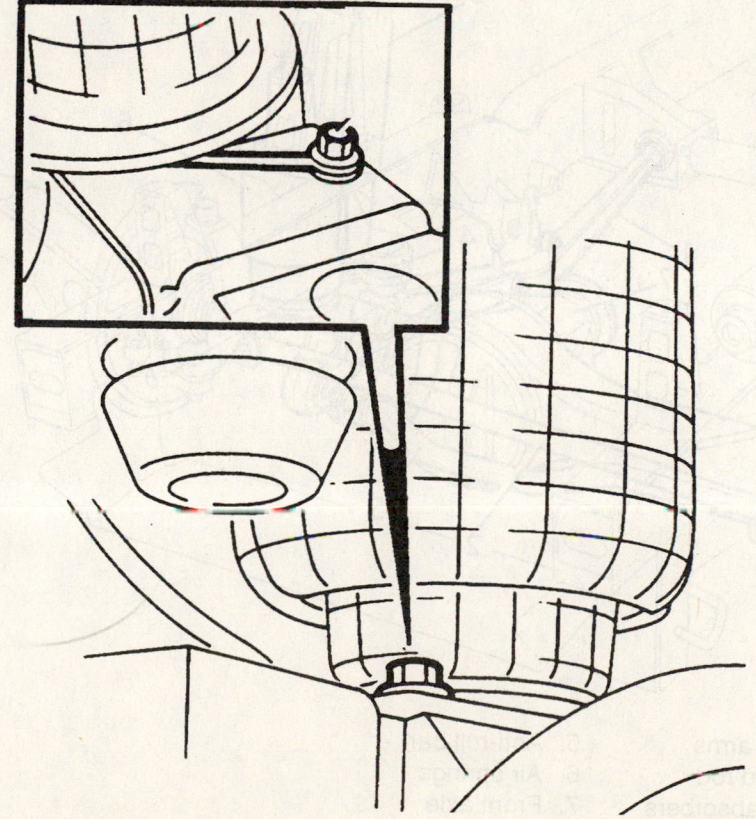

Lower air spring mounting bolt

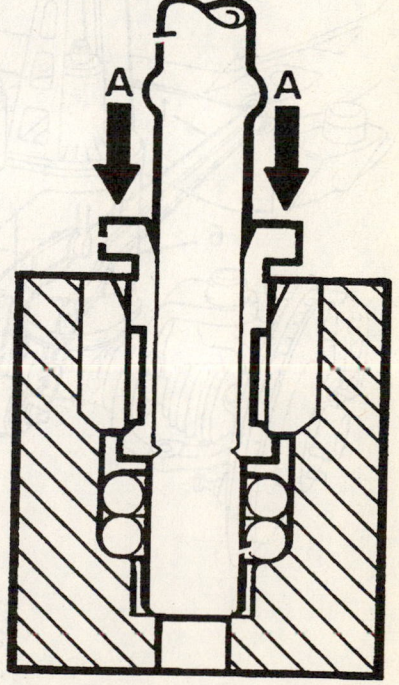

Air pipe disconnection

recalibrated using the TestBook tool. Recalibration must be done on a floor surface that is level and smooth in all directions.

Air Bag

✳✳ CAUTION

Some vehicles may be equipped with an air bag system. The system must be disabled before performing service on or around system components, steering column, instrument panel components, wiring and sensors. Failure to follow safety and disabling procedures could result in accidental air bag deployment, possible personal injury and unnecessary system repairs.

PRECAUTIONS

Several precautions must be observed when handling the inflator module to avoid accidental deployment and possible personal injury.

• Never carry the inflator module by the wires or connector on the underside of the module.

• When carrying a live inflator module, hold securely with both hands, and ensure that the bag and trim cover are pointed away.

• Place the inflator module on a bench or other surface with the bag and trim cover facing up.

• With the inflator module on the bench, never place anything on or close to the module which may be thrown in the event of an accidental deployment.

Before servicing the vehicle, be sure to also refer to the precautions in the beginning of this section as well.

DISARMING

1. Before servicing the vehicle, refer to the precautions in the beginning of this section.

2. Remove the key from the ignition.

3. Disconnect the negative battery cable first, then the positive cable.

4. Wait 20 minutes for the back-up power to discharge.

ARMING

1. After performing the required service, rearm the SRS by reconnecting the battery.

2. Start the vehicle and the SRS service light should go OFF after 5 seconds.

Power Steering Pump

REMOVAL & INSTALLATION

1. Before servicing the vehicle, refer to the precautions in the beginning of this section.

2. Remove the drive belt.

3. Remove the 3 pulley bolts.

4. Disconnect the return hose.

5. Disconnect the high pressure hose.

6. Remove the 4 bolts securing the pump/compressor bracket to the engine.

7. Remove the 3 bolts securing the mounting plate to the pump.

8. Remove the pump.

9. Installation is the reverse of removal. Tighten as follows:

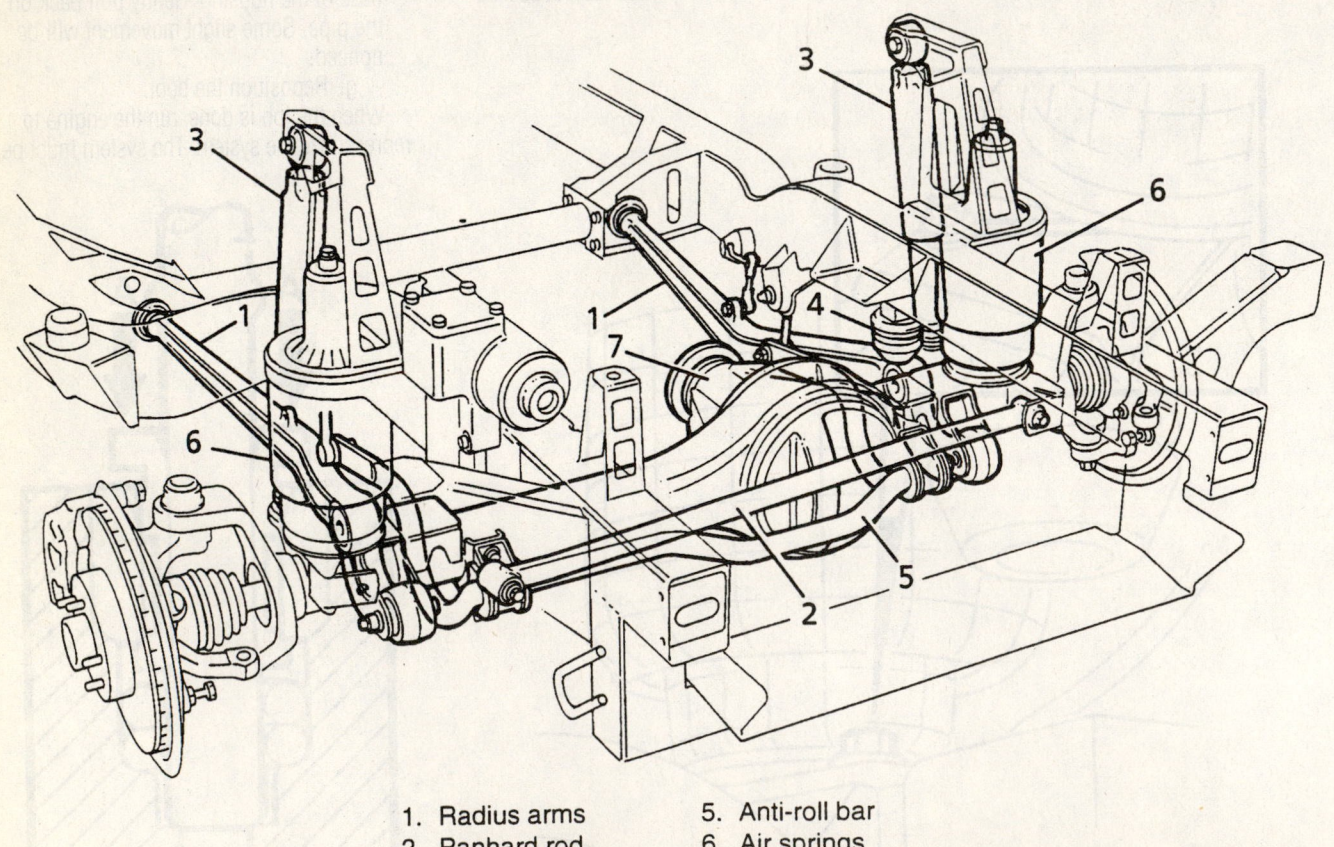

1. Radius arms
2. Panhard rod
3. Shock absorbers
4. Bump stops
5. Anti-roll bar
6. Air springs
7. Front axle

Range Rover front suspension

9308RG79

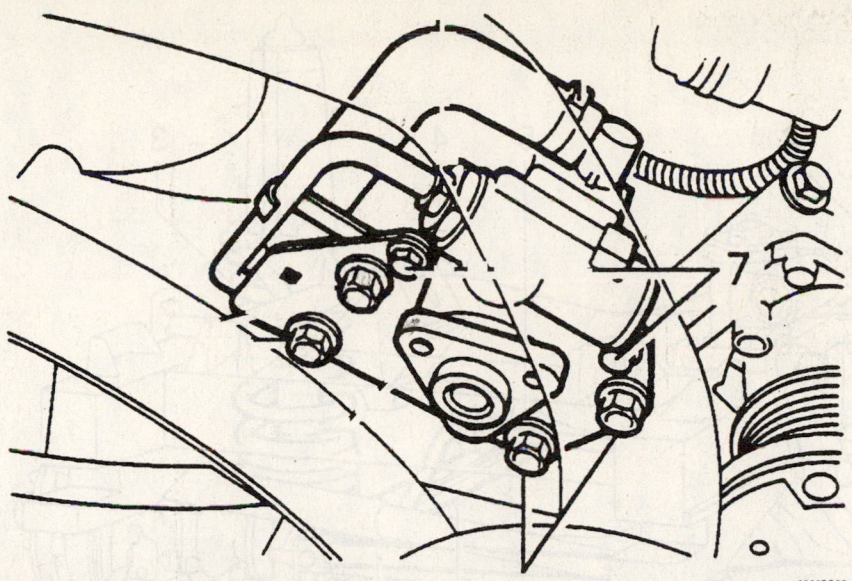

9308RG80

Power steering pump/compressor mounting bracket

- Lift bracket to the pump: 13 ft. lbs. (18 Nm).
- Bracket to the engine: 30 ft. lbs. (40 Nm).
- Pump mounting bolts: 13 ft. lbs. (18 Nm).
- High pressure fitting: 12 ft. lbs. (16 Nm).

Power Steering Gear

REMOVAL & INSTALLATION

1. Before servicing the vehicle, refer to the precautions in the beginning of this section.
2. Disconnect the negative battery cable.
3. Drain the fluid from the power steering fluid reservoir.
4. Clean the steering box to prevent dirt from entering when the hoses are removed.
5. Disconnect the feed and return lines from the steering box.
6. Raise and safely support the vehicle.
7. Remove the under tray
8. Disconnect the drag link from the drop arm.
9. Remove the universal joint connecting the steering column to the steering box.

10. Remove the power steering box mounting bolts, then remove the box from the vehicle.

To install:

11. Install the steering box and tighten the mounting bolts as follows:
    - Defender 90 and Discovery: 66 ft. lbs. (90 Nm)
    - Range Rover: 92 ft. lbs. (125 Nm)
12. Connect the universal joint and tighten the pinch bolts 18 ft. lbs. (25 Nm).
13. Connect the drag link to the drop arm and tighten the retaining nut as follows:
    - Defender 90 and Discovery: 30 ft. lbs. (40 Nm)
    - Range Rover: 59 ft. lbs. (80 Nm)
14. Lower the vehicle.
15. Connect the hydraulic hoses to the steering box and tighten the 16mm thread to 37 ft. lbs. (50 Nm) and the 14mm thread to 22 ft. lbs. (30 Nm).
16. Fill the power steering fluid reservoir.
17. With engine running, test steering system for leaks by holding steering in both full lock directions.
18. Ensure steering wheel is correctly aligned when wheels are positioned straight ahead.
19. If necessary, reposition the steering wheel.
20. Road test vehicle.

Shock Absorbers

REMOVAL & INSTALLATION

Front

RANGE ROVER

✸✸ CAUTION

Be sure to support the axle when the shock is removed, otherwise the pressurized air spring could fail and cause component damage and possible personal injury. It is possible to remove the shock absorber without depressurizing air springs, BUT the distance between the axle and chassis must be held as if the shock absorber was still fitted. This is achieved by supporting the vehicle on supports, with a jack under the axle.

1. Before servicing the vehicle, refer to the precautions in the beginning of this section.
2. Raise and safely support the vehicle.
3. Support the front axle on a jack.
4. Remove front wheel.

✸✸ WARNING

Do not lower axle when shock absorber is removed. This may result in air spring damage.

5. Remove the lower shock absorber retaining nut.
6. Remove the upper shock absorber retaining bolt.
7. Remove the shock absorber.

To install:

8. Install the shock absorber.
9. Install the upper mounting bolt and tighten to 92 ft. lbs. (125 Nm).
10. Install the lower mounting bolt and tighten to 33 ft. lbs. (45 Nm).
11. Install the front wheel and tighten the lug nuts to 80 ft. lbs. (108 Nm).
12. Remove the jack supporting the axle.
13. Remove the supports and lower vehicle.

DEFENDER 90 AND DISCOVERY

1. Before servicing the vehicle, refer to the precautions in the beginning of this section.

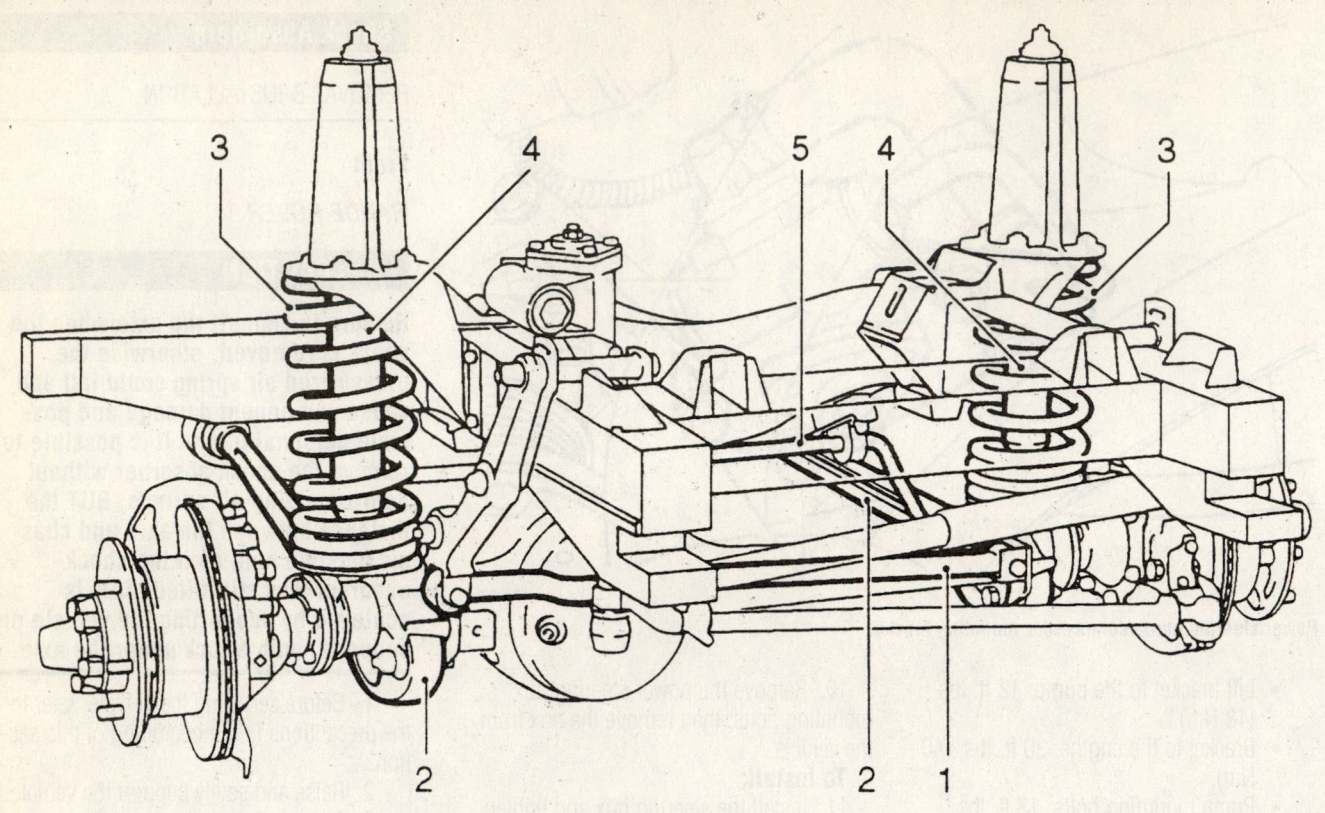

Front suspension

1. Panhard rod
2. Radius arms
3. Coil springs
4. Shock absorber
5. Anti-roll [sway] bar

Front suspension component identification—Defender 90

9302RG21

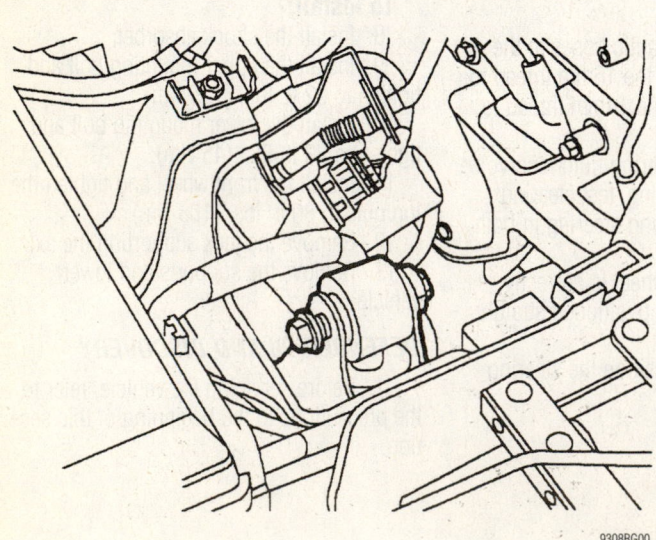

View of the upper front shock absorber bolt—Discovery

9308RG00

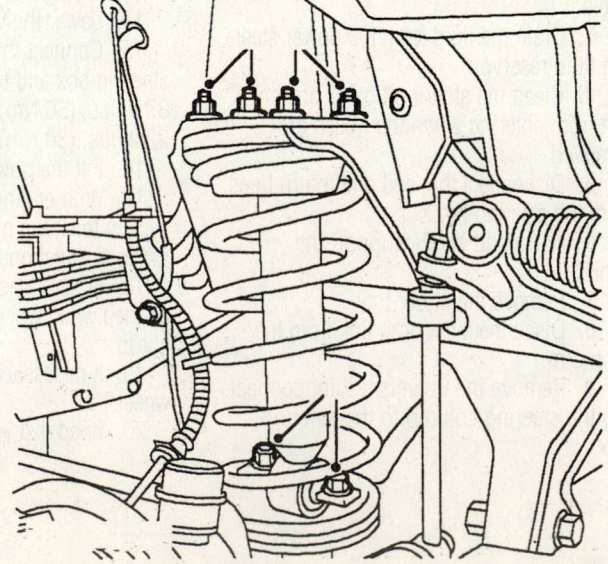

View of the lower front shock absorber attachments—Discovery

9308RG99

2. Raise and support the front end securely.

3. Remove the wheel.

4. On the right side, remove the coolant reservoir.

5. Support the weight of the axle with a jack.

6. Loosen the upper bolt securing the shock to the tower.

7. Remove the 4 nuts securing the shock tower to the chassis.

8. Remove the 2 lower shock absorber bolts.

9. On ACE equipped models, remove the ACE pipe clamp bolt and clamp.

10. Raise the tower and remove the upper bolt.

11. Compress the shock and remove the assembly.

12. Installation is the reverse of removal. Observe the following torques:

- Lower shock bolts: 92 ft. lbs. (125 Nm).
- Tower to chassis nuts: 17 ft. lbs. (23 Nm).
- Upper bolt: 92 ft. lbs. (125 Nm).

Rear

RANGE ROVER

> **❊❊ CAUTION**
>
> **Be sure to support the axle when the shock is removed. Otherwise, the pressurized air spring could fail and cause component damage and possible personal injury. It is possible to remove the shock absorber without depressurizing air springs, BUT the distance between the axle and chassis must be held as if the shock absorber was still fitted. This is achieved by supporting the vehicle with supports and a jack under the axle.**

1. Before servicing the vehicle, refer to the precautions in the beginning of this section.

2. Raise and safely support the vehicle.

3. Support the axle on a jack.

4. Remove the rear wheels.

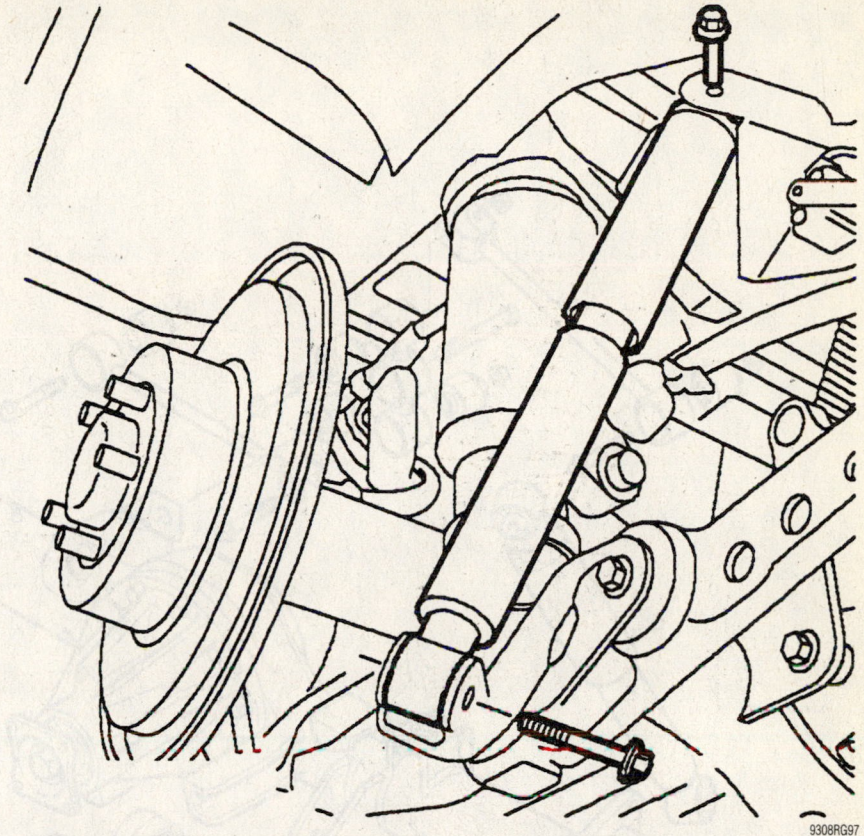

Rear shock absorber mounting—Range Rover

> **❊❊ WARNING**
>
> **Do not lower axle when shock absorber is removed. This may result in air spring damage.**

5. Remove the lower shock absorber retaining nut.

6. Remove the upper shock absorber retaining bolt.

7. Remove the shock absorber.

To install:

8. Install the shock absorber.

9. Install the upper mounting bolt and tighten to 92 ft. lbs. (125 Nm).

10. Install the lower mounting bolt and tighten to 33 ft. lbs. (45 Nm).

11. Install the rear wheel and tighten the lug nuts to 80 ft. lbs. (108 Nm).

12. Remove the jack supporting the axle.

13. Remove the supports and lower vehicle.

DEFENDER 90 AND DISCOVERY

1. Before servicing the vehicle, refer to the precautions in the beginning of this section.

2. Raise and safely support the vehicle.

3. Place a jack under the rear axle and raise it slightly to take the load off the shock absorbers.

4. Remove the shock absorber lower attaching nut, then pull the lower end free of the mounting bracket on the axle housing.

5. Remove the upper attaching nut and remove the shock absorber.

To install:

6. Install the shock absorber onto the upper bracket and screw on the attaching nut. Don't tighten it yet.

7. Swing the shock absorber down and position in the lower mounting bracket. Attach the lower mounting nut.

8. Tighten the upper and lower attaching bolts to 92 ft. lbs. (125 Nm).

Turn to Section 5 for brake system applications

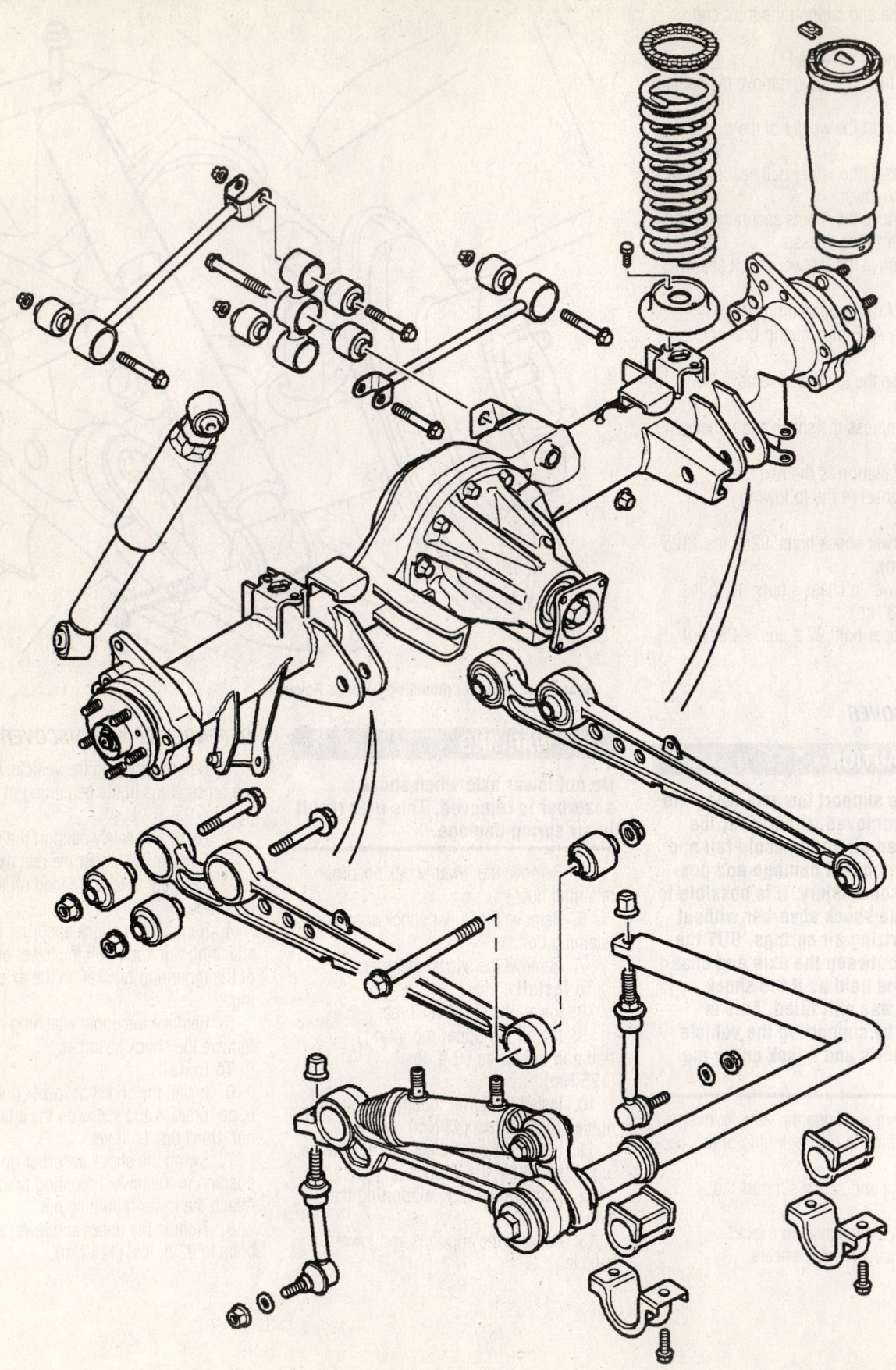

Rear suspension components—Discovery

9308RG98

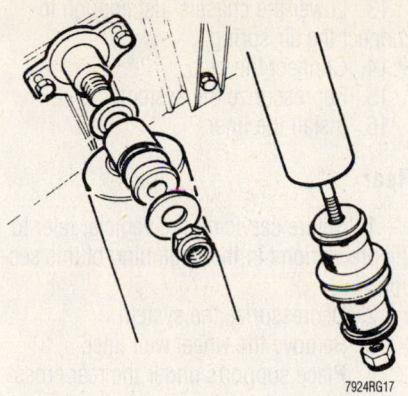

Exploded view of the upper and lower mountings for the rear shock absorber

Coil Springs

REMOVAL & INSTALLATION

The Defender 90 and Discovery models are equipped with a coil spring suspension. The Range Rover and Discovery Series II models are equipped with an air spring suspension.

Front

1. Before servicing the vehicle, refer to the precautions in the beginning of this section.

2. Raise and safely support the vehicle.
3. Disconnect the sway bar end links.
4. Remove the shock absorber-to-axle bolts.
5. Slowly lower the axle to relieve the spring tension. DO NOT STRETCH THE BRAKE HOSE!
6. Remove the spring.

To install:

7. Install the spring in the upper seat.
8. Raise the axle until the spring is seated in the lower spring seat.
9. Connect the end links.
10. Install the shock absorber.

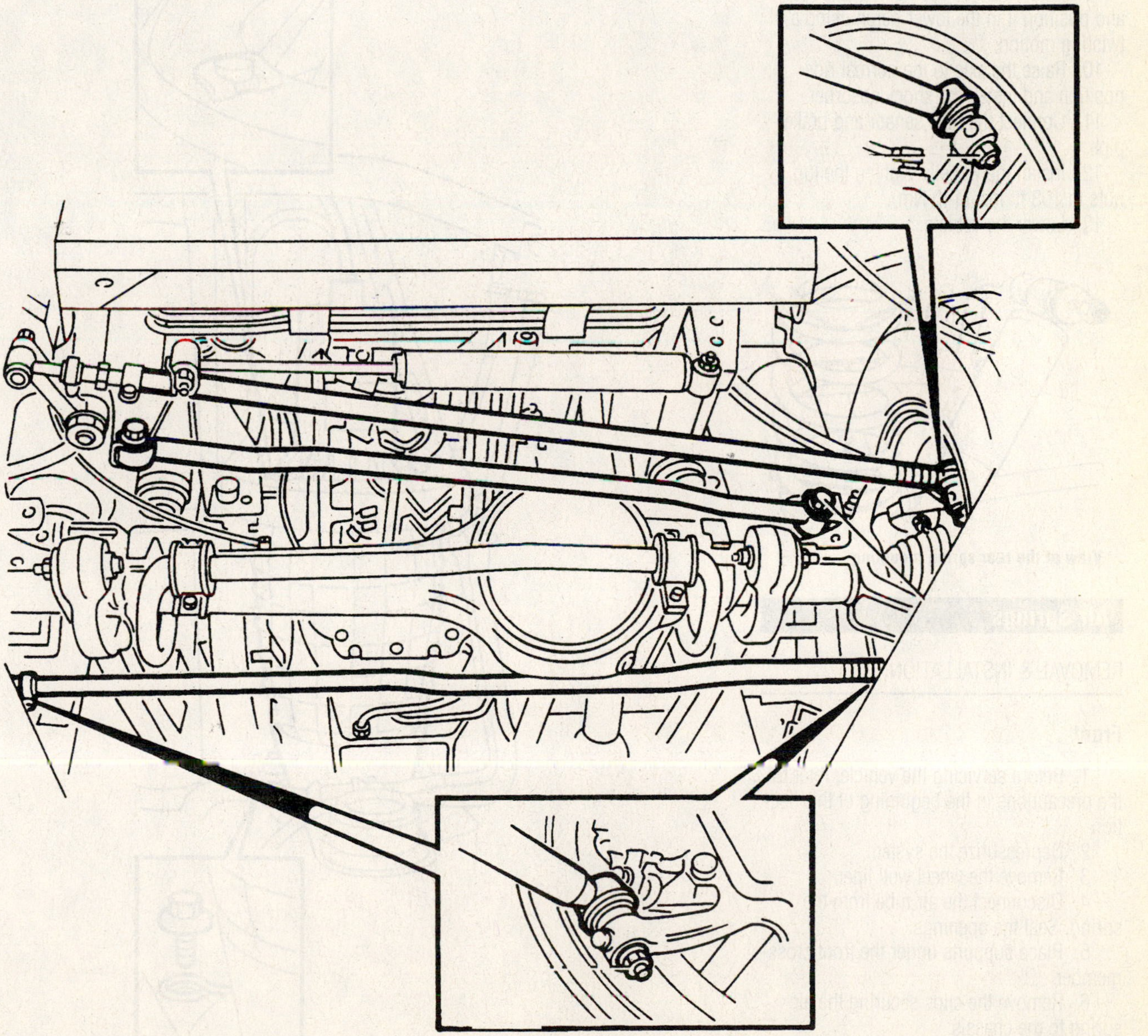

Range Rover steering linkage

Rear

1. Before servicing the vehicle, refer to the precautions in the beginning of this section.

2. Raise and safely support the vehicle.

3. Remove the wheels.

4. Support the axle on a jack.

5. Disconnect the shock absorber from the axle bracket.

6. Unclip the brake pipe from its bracket.

7. Disconnect the ABS sensor.

8. Lower the rear axle until the coil springs are no longer under compression. DO NOT STRETCH THE BRAKE LINE!

To install:

9. Install the coil spring, top end first, and position it in the lower perch using a twisting motion.

10. Raise the axle to the normal ride position and install the shock absorber.

11. Connect the ABS sensor and brake pipe.

12. Install the wheels. Tighten the lug nuts to 103 ft. lbs. (140 Nm).

13. Lower the vehicle.

View of the rear spring mounting

Air Springs

REMOVAL & INSTALLATION

Front

1. Before servicing the vehicle, refer to the precautions in the beginning of this section.

2. Depressurize the system.

3. Remove the wheel well liner.

4. Disconnect the air tube from the spring. Seal the openings.

5. Place supports under the front cross-member.

6. Remove the clips securing the air spring to the chassis.

7. Remove the bolt securing the air spring to the axle.

8. Remove the pin.

9. Raise the chassis slightly with a jack to provide clearance.

10. Remove the spring.

✲✲ WARNING

Keep the chassis supported until the system is repressurized. Never allow the chassis to rest on a deflated spring.

To install:

11. Clean the mating surfaces of the chassis, axle and spring.

12. Place the air spring on the axle and install the pin and bolt.

13. Lower the chassis just enough to connect the air spring.

14. Connect the pipe.

15. Repressurize the system.

16. Install the liner.

Rear

1. Before servicing the vehicle, refer to the precautions in the beginning of this section.

2. Depressurize the system.

3. Remove the wheel well liner.

4. Place supports under the rear cross-member.

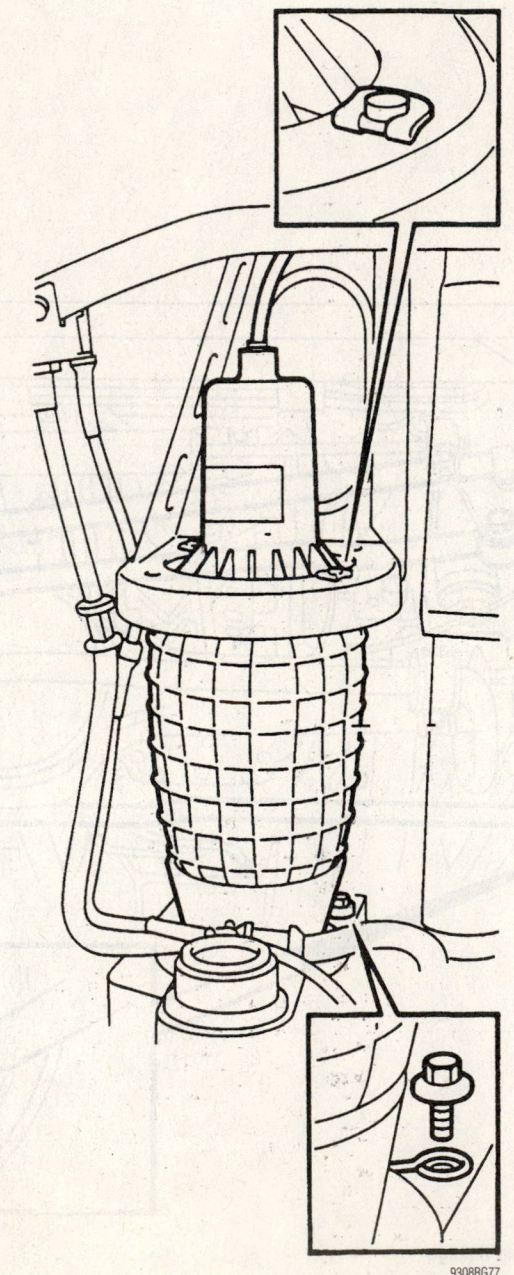

Front air spring mounting

5. Remove the clips securing the air spring to the chassis.

6. Remove the bolt securing the air spring to the axle.

7. Raise the chassis slightly with a jack to provide clearance.

8. Move the air spring away from the chassis.

9. Disconnect the air tube from the spring. Seal the openings.

10. Remove the spring.

✳✳ WARNING

Keep the chassis supported until the system is repressurized. Never allow the chassis to rest on a deflated **spring.**

To install:

11. Clean the mating surfaces of the chassis, axle and spring.

12. Connect the pipe.

13. Connect the spring to the chassis.

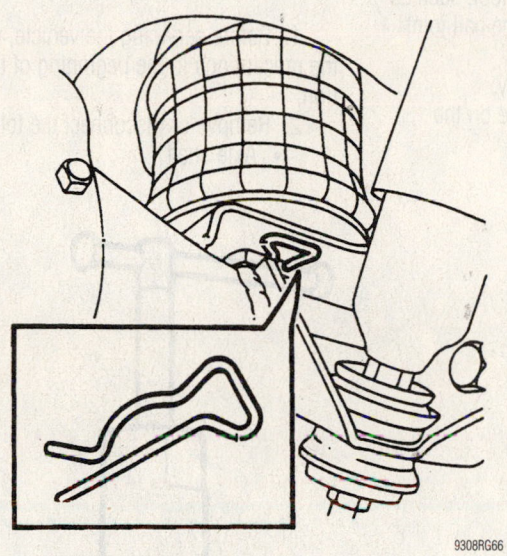

9308RG66

Rear air spring lower mounting clip

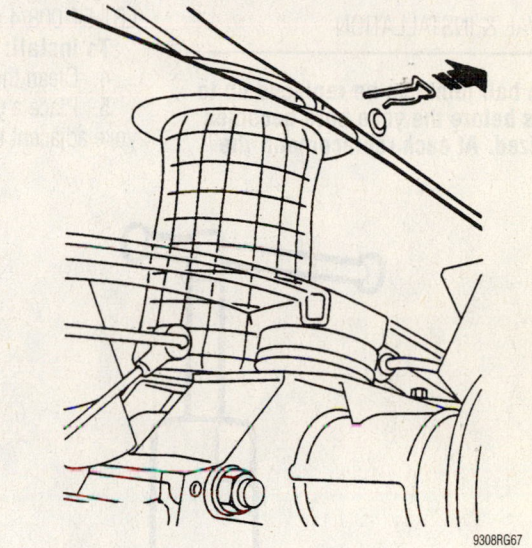

9308RG67

Rear air spring upper mounting clip

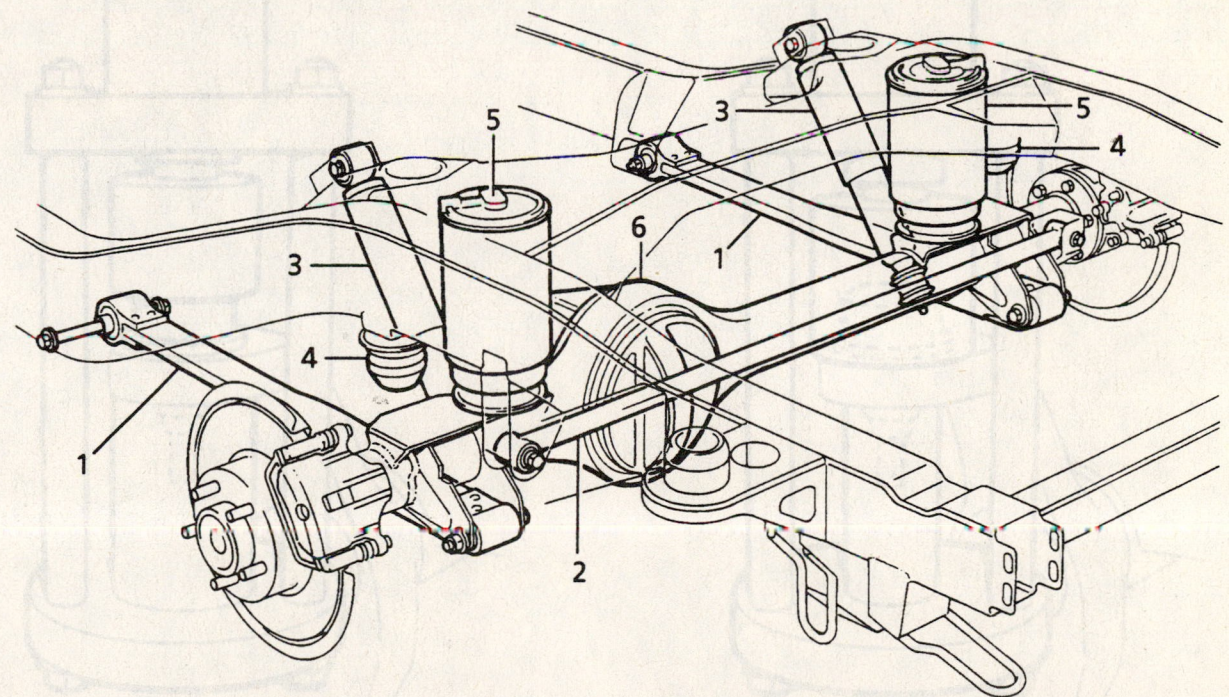

1. Radius arms
2. Panhard rod
3. Shock absorbers
4. Bump stops
5. Air springs
6. Rear axle

9308RG68

Rear air suspension

14. Lower the chassis just enough to connect the air spring to the axle.

15. Place the air spring on the axle and install the clip.

16. Repressurize the system.

17. Install the liner.

Upper Ball Joint

REMOVAL & INSTALLATION

➡**Each ball joint can be replaced up to 3 times before the yoke bore becomes over-sized. At each replacement, the yoke should be marked. Factory-trained technicians mark the yoke with yellow paint at each replacement.**

Range Rover

1. Before servicing the vehicle, refer to the precautions in the beginning of this section.

2. Remove the swivel hub.

3. Using a ball joint forcing tool, such as LRT-54-008/4 and /5, remove the ball joint.

To install:

4. Clean the yoke thoroughly.

5. Place a yellow paint stripe on the yoke adjacent to the bore.

6. Place a forcing tool, such as LRT-54-008-8, on the yoke.

7. Place base LRT-54-008/7 on the yoke. Position the ball joint and align the tool.

8. Press the ball joint into the yoke.

9. Install the swivel.

Defender 90 and Discovery

1. Before servicing the vehicle, refer to the precautions in the beginning of this section.

2. Remove or disconnect the following:
   • Axle shaft

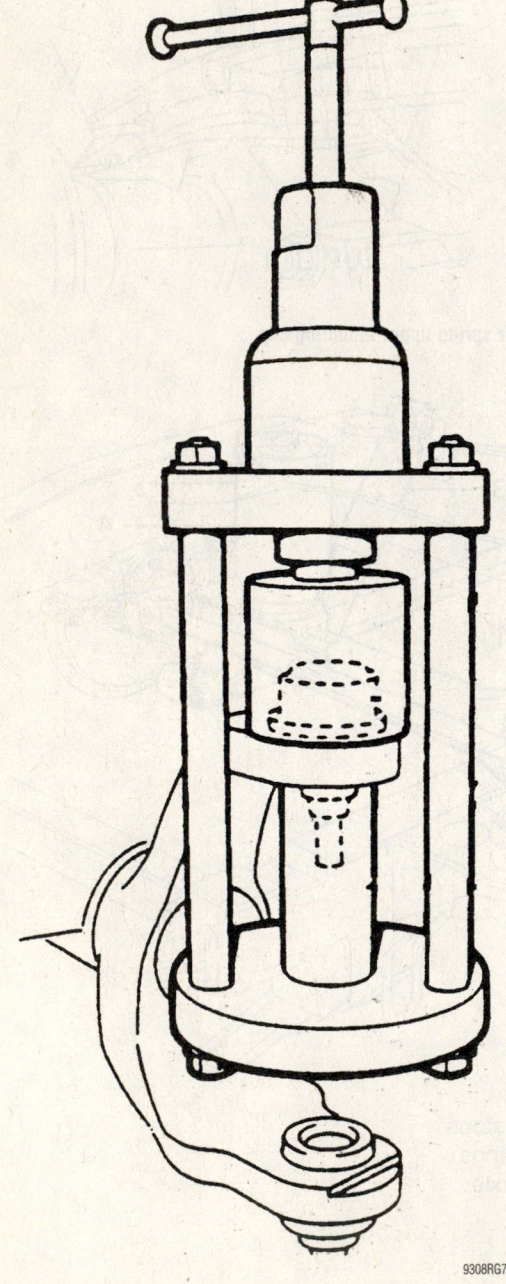

Upper ball joint removal—Range Rover

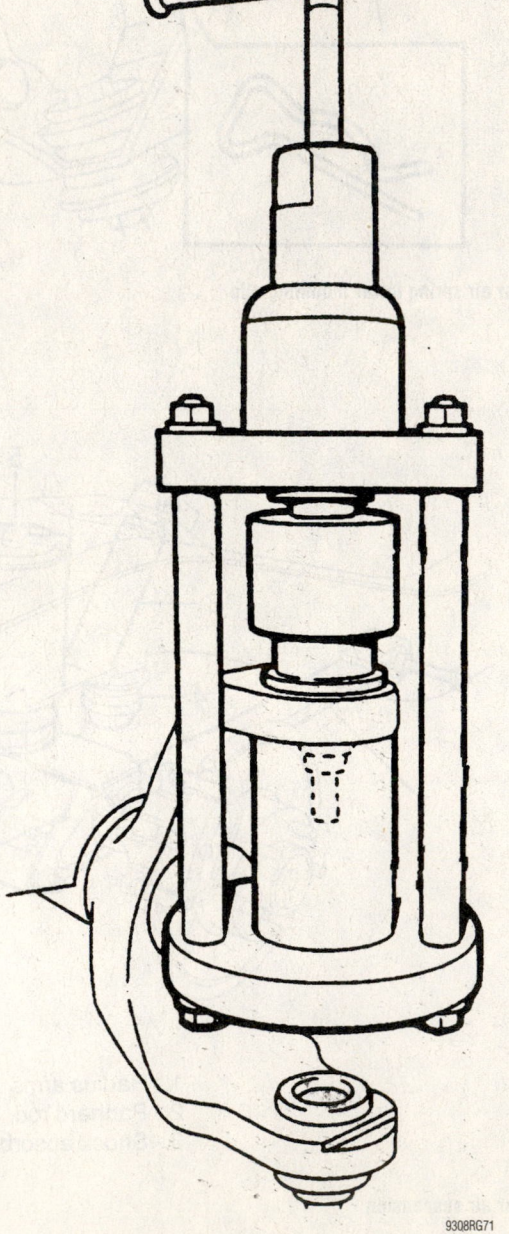

Upper ball joint installation—Range Rover

- Mud shield
- Track rod
- Drag link
- Ball joint nuts
- Break loose the knuckle

3. Using forcing tools, such as LRT-54-008 and 008/4 and /5, force the joint from the yoke.

To install:

4. Clean the yoke thoroughly.

5. Place a yellow paint stripe on the yoke adjacent to the bore.

6. Place a forcing tool, such as LRT-54-008-8, on the yoke.

7. Place base LRT-54-008/7 on the yoke. Position the ball joint and align the tool.

8. Press the ball joint into the yoke.

9. Position the knuckle on the ball studs. Torque the upper nut to 81 ft. lbs. (110 Nm); the lower nut to 100 ft. lbs. (135 Nm).

10. Connect the track rod and drag link. Torque the nuts to 59 ft. lbs. (81 Nm).

11. The remainder of assembly is the reverse of disassembly.

Lower Ball Joint

REMOVAL & INSTALLATION

➡Each ball joint can be replaced up to 3 times before the yoke bore becomes

over-sized. At each replacement, the yoke should be marked. Factory-trained technicians mark the yoke with yellow paint at each replacement.

Range Rover

❋❋ CAUTION

Each ball joint can be replaced up to 3 times before the axle yoke bore becomes oversize. Before commencing work, clean the surrounding area of the joint to be renewed and check for yellow paint marks. If more than 2 marks are found, the axle case must be renewed.

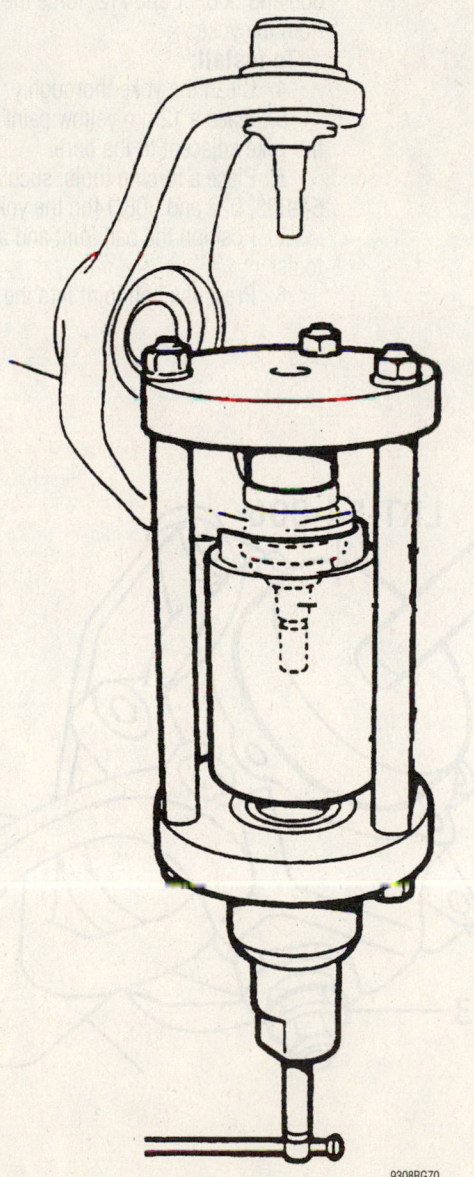

9308RG70

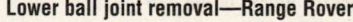

Lower ball joint removal—Range Rover

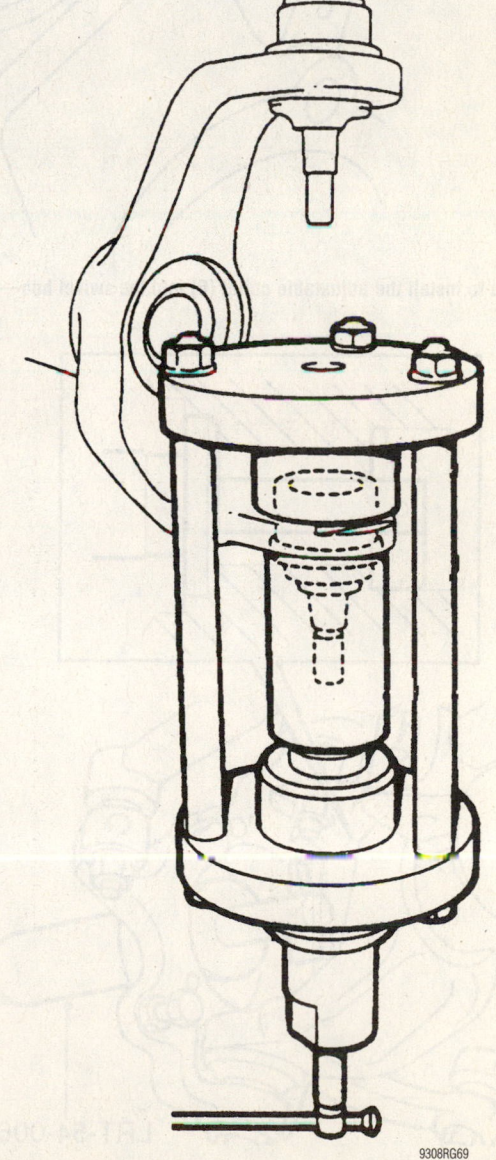

9308RG69

Lower ball joint installation—Range Rover

Turn to Section 5 for brake system applications

1. Before servicing the vehicle, refer to the precautions in the beginning of this section.

2. Remove the swivel hub.

3. Assemble the ball joint press tools LRT-54-008/10 and /11 as shown, then press the joint out of the axle yoke.

➡**When the ram lead screw reaches the end of the stroke, retract the lead screw, screw the ram into the base tool and repeat the operation the until joint is free from the axle.**

4. Remove the screw and collect the adapter from the base tool.

To install:

5. Clean the joint location and the surrounding area of the axle yoke, then make a 12mm wide yellow paint stripe on the axle yoke, adjacent to joint location.

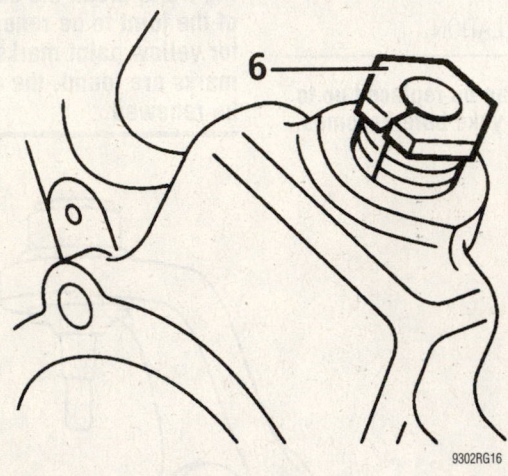

Be sure to install the adjustable collet (6) into the swivel hub—Range Rover

6. Align the tool assembly and press the joint into the axle yoke.

7. Remove the tools from the axle yoke.

8. Install the swivel hub onto the axle.

Defender 90 and Discovery

1. Before servicing the vehicle, refer to the precautions in the beginning of this section.

2. Remove or disconnect the following:
- Axle shaft
- Mud shield
- Track rod
- Drag link
- Ball joint nuts
- Break loose the knuckle

3. Using forcing tools, such as LRT-54-008 and 008/11 and /12, force the joint from the yoke.

To install:

4. Clean the yoke thoroughly.

5. Place a 12mm yellow paint stripe on the yoke adjacent to the bore.

6. Place a forcing tools, such as LRT-54-008, 022 and 008/14on the yoke.

7. Position the ball joint and align the tools.

8. Press the ball joint into the yoke.

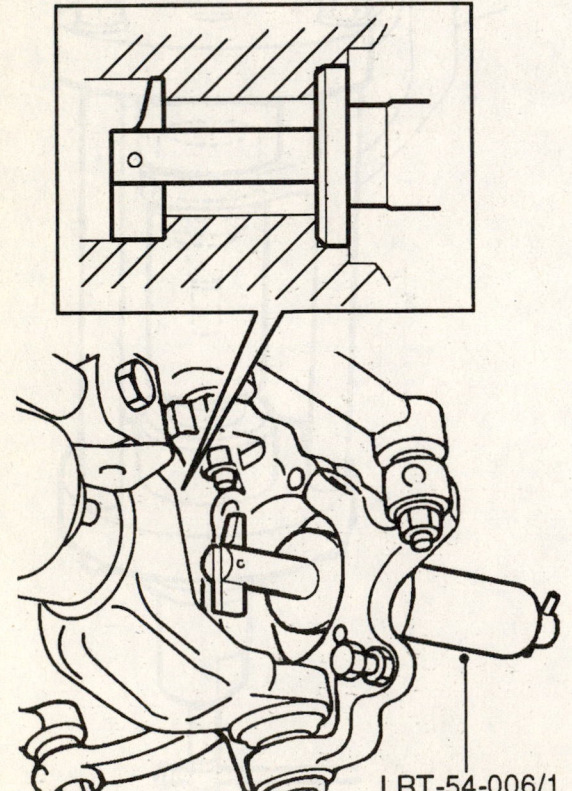

Install the tool into the axle casing with the TOP mark facing out upwards—Range Rover

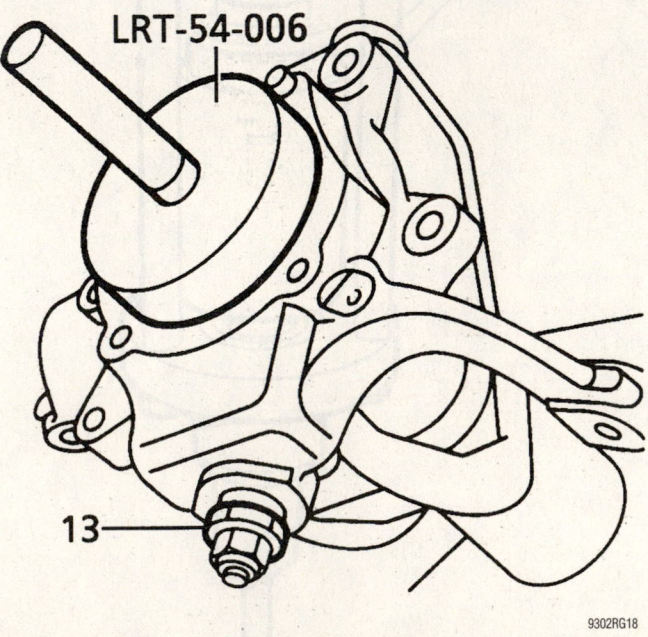

Using tool LTR-54-006/2 to adjust the height of the hub—Range Rover

9. Position the knuckle on the ball studs. Torque the upper nut to 81 ft. lbs. (110 Nm); the lower nut to 100 ft. lbs. (135 Nm).

10. Connect the track rod and drag link. Torque the nuts to 59 ft. lbs. (81 Nm).

11. The remainder of assembly is the reverse of disassembly.

Wheel Bearings

ADJUSTMENT

The front and rear wheel bearings are not adjustable.

REMOVAL & INSTALLATION

Front

1. Before servicing the vehicle, refer to the precautions in the beginning of this section.

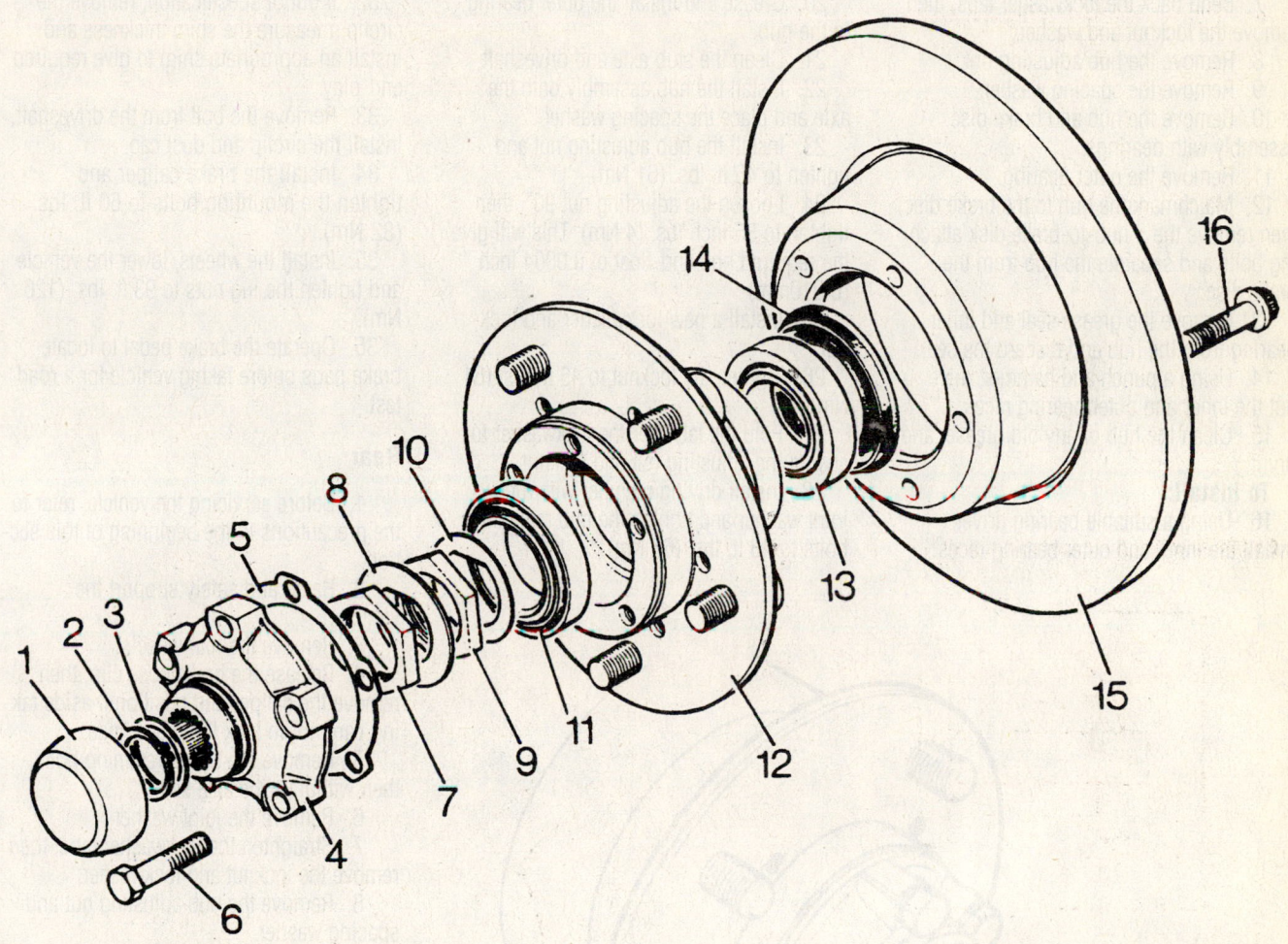

HUB COMPONENTS

1. Dust cap.
2. Drive shaft circlip.
3. Drive shaft shim.
4. Drive member.
5. Drive member joint washer.
6. Drive member retaining bolt.
7. Lock nut.
8. Lock washer.
9. Hub adjusting nut.
10. Spacing washer.
11. Outer bearing.
12. Hub.
13. Inner bearing.
14. Grease seal.
15. Brake disc.
16. Disc retaining bolt.

9302RG19

Exploded view of the front hub and related components—Discovery

2. Raise and safely support the vehicle and remove the front wheels.

3. Unbolt the brake caliper and position it aside, leaving the hose attached.

4. Remove the dust cap.

5. Remove the circlip and shim from driveshaft.

6. Remove the 5 bolts, then remove the driving member and joint washer.

7. Bend back the lockwasher tabs, then remove the locknut and washer.

8. Remove the hub adjusting nut.

9. Remove the spacing washer.

10. Remove the hub and brake disc assembly with bearings.

11. Remove the outer bearing.

12. Matchmark the hub to the brake disc, then remove the 5 hub-to-brake disk attaching bolts and separate the hub from the brake disc.

13. Remove the grease seal and inner bearing from the hub and discard the seal.

14. Using a punch and hammer, drive out the inner and outer bearing races.

15. Clean the hub of any old grease, and dry it.

To install:

16. Using a suitable bearing driver, install the inner and outer bearing races.

17. Pack the hub inner bearing with grease and install.

18. Using a suitable seal driver, install the seal until it is flush with the rear face of the hub. Apply grease between the seal lips.

19. Align the brake disc-to-hub match-marks, apply Loctite® 270 to the mounting bolts and tighten to 54 ft. lbs. (73 Nm).

20. Grease and install the outer bearing to the hub.

21. Clean the stub axle and driveshaft

22. Install the hub assembly onto the axle and place the spacing washer .

23. Install the hub adjusting nut and tighten to 45 ft. lbs. (61 Nm).

24. Loosen the adjusting nut 90°, then tighten to 35 inch lbs. (4 Nm). This will give the required hub end-float of 0.0004 inch (0.010mm)

25. Install a new lockwasher and lock-nut.

26. Tighten the locknut to 45 ft. lbs. (61 Nm).

27. Fold the tab over the lockwasher to secure the adjusting nut and locknut.

28. Install driving member with a new joint washer and tighten the hub retaining bolts to 48 ft. lbs. (65 Nm).

29. Install the original driveshaft shim and secure the shim with a circlip.

30. Check the driveshaft end-play by mounting a dial gauge as shown.

31. Install a suitable bolt to the threaded end of the driveshaft. Move the driveshaft in and out noting the dial gauge reading. The end-play should be between 0.0032–0.0098 inch (0.08–0.25 mm).

32. If out of specification, remove the circlip, measure the shim thickness and install an appropriate shim to give required end-play.

33. Remove the bolt from the driveshaft, install the circlip and dust cap.

34. Install the brake caliper and tighten the mounting bolts to 60 ft. lbs. (82 Nm).

35. Install the wheels, lower the vehicle and tighten the lug nuts to 93 ft. lbs. (126 Nm).

36. Operate the brake pedal to locate brake pads before taking vehicle for a road test.

Rear

1. Before servicing the vehicle, refer to the precautions in the beginning of this section.

2. Raise and safely support the vehicle.

3. Remove the rear wheels.

4. Release the brake hose clip, then remove the caliper and position it aside taking care not to kink the brake hose.

5. Remove the 5 axle retaining bolts, then withdraw the axle shaft.

6. Remove the joint washer.

7. Straighten the lockwasher tabs, then remove the locknut and lockwasher.

8. Remove the hub adjusting nut and spacing washer.

9. Remove the hub and brake rotor as an assembly.

10. Remove the outer bearing.

11. remove the 5 Nyloc® nuts, then the ABS tone ring.

12. Matchmark the hub to the rotor for reassembly.

13. Remove the 5 bolts and separate the hub from the brake rotor.

14. Remove the grease seal with the appropriate seal puller, then the inner bearing.

15. Remove the inner and outer bearing races.

16. Clean the hub of any old grease and dry.

To install:

17. Install the inner and outer races.

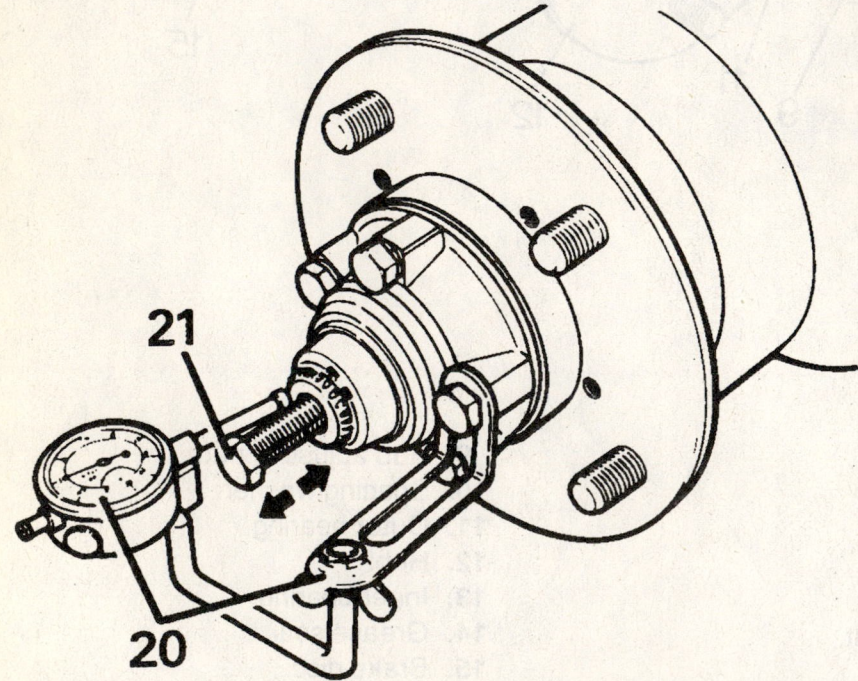

9302RG20

Install the dial indicator and bracket (20), then push and pull on bolt (21) to check the end-play—Discovery

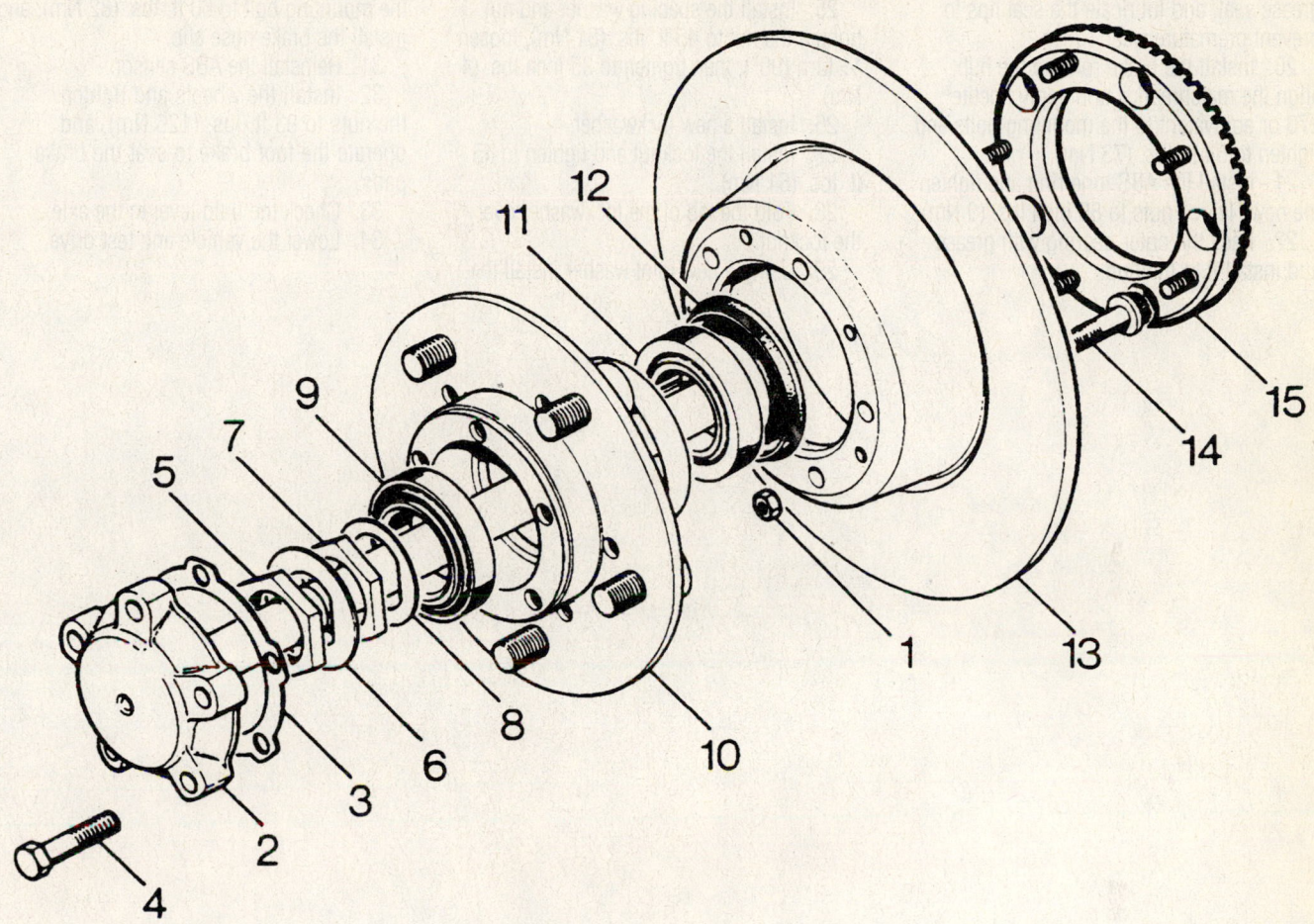

1. Sensor ring retaining nut ABS.
2. Axle shaft.
3. Axle shaft joint washer.
4. Axle shaft retaining bolt (five off).
5. Lock nut.
6. Lock washer.
7. Hub adjusting nut.
8. Spacing washer.
9. Outer bearing.
10. Hub.
11. Inner bearing.
12. Grease seal.
13. Brake disc.
14. Disc retaining bolt (five off).
15. Sensor ring ABS.

Exploded view of the rear hub components—Defender 90

7924RG23

18. Pack the inner bearing with grease and install it to the hub.

19. Using a seal driver, install the inner grease seal, and lubricate the seal lips to prevent premature wear.

20. Install the brake rotor to the hub, align the matchmarks, and apply Loctite® 270 or equivalent to the mounting bolts and tighten to 54 ft. lbs. (73 Nm).

21. Install the ABS tone ring and tighten the new Nyloc® nuts to 80 inch lbs. (9 Nm).

22. Pack the outer bearing with grease and install it to the hub.

23. Retract the ABS sensor slightly.

24. Install the hub and brake rotor assembly.

25. Install the spacing washer and nut. tighten the nut to 45 ft. lbs. (61 Nm), loosen ½ turn (90°), then tighten to 35 inch lbs. (4 Nm).

26. Install a new lockwasher.

27. Install the locknut and tighten to 45 ft. lbs. (61 Nm).

28. Fold the tab of the lockwasher over the locknut.

29. Using a new joint washer install the axle shaft to the hub, and tighten the 5 bolts to 48 ft. lbs. (65 Nm).

30. Install the brake caliper and tighten the mounting bolt to 60 ft. lbs. (82 Nm), and install the brake hose clip.

31. Reinstall the ABS sensor.

32. Install the wheels and tighten the nuts to 93 ft. lbs. (126 Nm), and operate the foot brake to seat the brake pads.

33. Check the fluid level in the axle.

34. Lower the vehicle and test drive.

TOYOTA AND LEXUS

27

Toyota-Land Cruiser • **Lexus**-LX450 • LX470

PRECAUTIONS

Before servicing any vehicle, please be sure to read all of the following precautions, which deal with personal safety, prevention of component damage, and important points to take into consideration when servicing a motor vehicle:

• Never open, service or drain the radiator or cooling system when the engine is hot; serious burns can occur from the steam and hot coolant.

• Observe all applicable safety precautions when working around fuel. Whenever servicing the fuel system, always work in a well-ventilated area. Do not allow fuel spray or vapors to come in contact with a spark, open flame, or excessive heat (a hot drop light, for example). Keep a dry chemical fire extinguisher near the work area. Always keep fuel in a container specifically designed for fuel storage; also, always properly seal fuel containers to avoid the possibility of fire or explosion. Refer to the additional fuel system precautions later in this section.

• Fuel injection systems often remain pressurized, even after the engine has been turned **OFF**. The fuel system pressure must be relieved before disconnecting any fuel lines. Failure to do so may result in fire and/or personal injury.

• Brake fluid often contains polyglycol ethers and polyglycols. Avoid contact with the eyes and wash your hands thoroughly after handling brake fluid. If you do get brake fluid in your eyes, flush your eyes with clean, running water for 15 minutes. If eye irritation persists, or if you have taken brake fluid internally, IMMEDIATELY seek medical assistance.

• The EPA warns that prolonged contact with used engine oil may cause a number of skin disorders, including cancer. You should make every effort to minimize your exposure to used engine oil. Protective gloves should be worn when changing oil. Wash your hands and any other exposed skin areas as soon as possible after exposure to used engine oil. Soap and water, or waterless hand cleaner should be used.

• All new vehicles are now equipped with an air bag system. The system must be disabled before performing service on or around system components, steering column, instrument panel components, wiring and sensors. Failure to follow safety and disabling procedures could result in accidental air bag deployment, possible personal injury and unnecessary system repairs.

• Always wear safety goggles when working with, or around, the air bag system. When carrying a non-deployed air bag, be sure the bag and trim cover are pointed away from your body. When placing a non-deployed air bag on a work surface, always face the bag and trim cover upward, away from the surface. This will reduce the motion of the module if it is accidentally deployed. Refer to the additional air bag system precautions later in this section.

• NEVER disconnect the negative battery cable with the ignition **ON** or the engine running. Removing power from the computer control module with the ignition **ON** may destroy the module.

• Clean, high quality brake fluid from a sealed container is essential to the safe and proper operation of the brake system. You should always buy the correct type of brake fluid for your vehicle. If the brake fluid becomes contaminated, completely flush the system with new fluid. Never reuse any brake fluid. Any brake fluid that is removed from the system should be discarded. Also, do not allow any brake fluid to come in contact with a painted surface; it will damage the paint.

• Never operate the engine without the proper amount and type of engine oil; doing so WILL result in severe engine damage.

• Timing belt maintenance is extremely important. Many models utilize an interference-type, non-freewheeling engine. If the timing belt breaks, the valves in the cylinder head may strike the pistons, causing potentially serious (also time-consuming and expensive) engine damage. Refer to the maintenance interval charts in the front of this manual for the recommended replacement interval for the timing belt, and to the timing belt section for belt replacement and inspection.

• Disconnecting the negative battery cable on some vehicles may interfere with the functions of the on-board computer system(s) and may require the computer to undergo a relearning process once the negative battery cable is reconnected.

• When servicing drum brakes, only disassemble and assemble one side at a time, leaving the remaining side intact for reference.

• Only an MVAC-trained, EPA-certified automotive technician should service the air conditioning system or its components.

ENGINE REPAIR

➡ **Disconnecting the negative battery cable on some vehicles may interfere with the functions of the on board computer system. The computer may undergo a relearning process once the negative battery cable is reconnected.**

Distributor

REMOVAL

1. Before servicing the vehicle, refer to the precautions in the beginning of this section.
2. Remove or disconnect the following:
   • Negative battery cable
   • Distributor cap
   • Distributor wiring harness connector
3. Matchmark the rotor to the distributor housing and the distributor housing to the cylinder head.
4. Remove the distributor.

INSTALLATION

Timing Not Disturbed

1. Install or connect the following:
   • Distributor by aligning the matchmarks made during removal
   • Distributor wiring harness connector
   • Distributor cap
   • Negative battery cable
2. Check the ignition timing and adjust as necessary.

Timing Disturbed

1. Set the engine to Top Dead Center (TDC) of the compression stroke for the No. 1 cylinder.

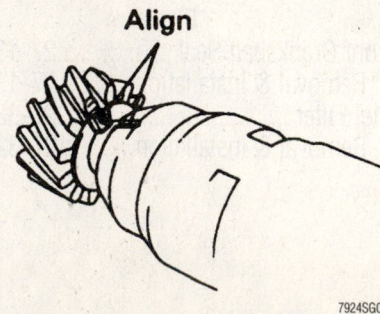

7924SG01

Distributor gear alignment—4.5L (1FZ-FE) engine

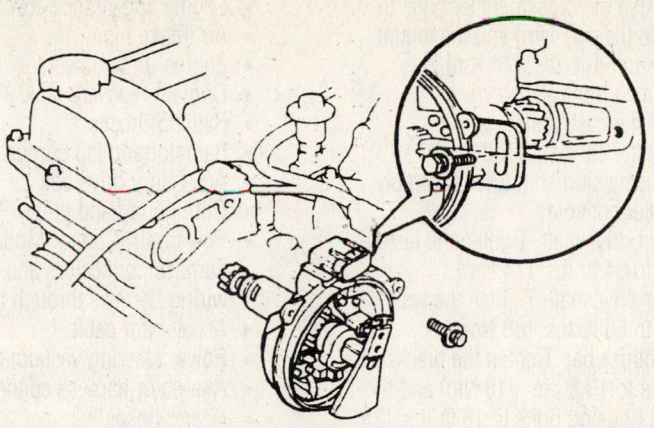

Distributor housing alignment—4.5L (1FZ-FE) engine

2. Align the protrusion on the distributor gear with the groove in the distributor housing as shown.

3. Install or connect the following:
- Distributor with the mounting bolt centered in the mounting flange slot. Tighten the bolt to 13 ft. lbs. (18 Nm).
- Distributor wiring harness connector
- Distributor cap
- Negative battery cable

4. Check the ignition timing and adjust as necessary.

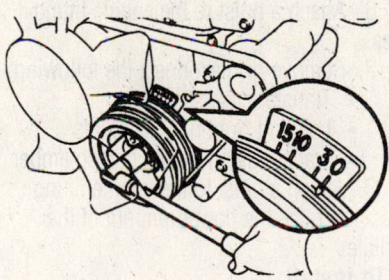

Align the groove on the crankshaft pulley with the timing mark "0" on the timing chain cover—4.5L (1FZ-FE) engine

Alternator

REMOVAL

1997 Models

1. Before servicing the vehicle, refer to the precautions in the beginning of this section.

2. Remove or disconnect the following:

- Battery and tray
- Power steering reservoir
- Accessory drive belts
- Alternator harness connectors
- Alternator

1998—01 Models

1. Before servicing the vehicle, refer to the precautions in the beginning of this section.

2. Drain the cooling system.

3. Remove or disconnect the following:
- Negative battery cable
- Accessory drive belt
- Engine under cover
- Radiator
- Power steering pump pulley
- Alternator harness connectors
- Alternator

INSTALLATION

1997 Models

Install or connect the following:
- Alternator
- Alternator harness connectors
- Accessory drive belts. Tighten the lockbolt to 15 ft. lbs. (21 Nm) and the pivot bolt to 43 ft. lbs. (58 Nm).
- Power steering reservoir
- Battery and tray

1998—01 Models

1. Install or connect the following:
- Alternator. Tighten the fasteners to 29 ft. lbs. (39 Nm).
- Alternator harness connectors
- Power steering pump pulley
- Radiator
- Engine under cover

- Accessory drive belt
- Negative battery cable

2. Fill the cooling system.

3. Start the engine and check for leaks.

Ignition Timing

ADJUSTMENT

4.5L (1FZ-FE) Engine

➡**Check and adjust the ignition timing with the engine at normal operating temperature, all electrical accessories OFF and transmission in Neutral.**

1. Before servicing the vehicle, refer to the precautions in the beginning of this section.

2. Connect the timing light to the engine.

3. Check the idle speed. Idle speed should be 600–700 rpm.

4. Connect terminals TE1 and E1 of the No. 1 Data Link Connector (DLC1) with a jumper wire.

5. Set the base timing to 3 degrees Before Top Dead Center (BTDC).

6. Remove the jumper wire.

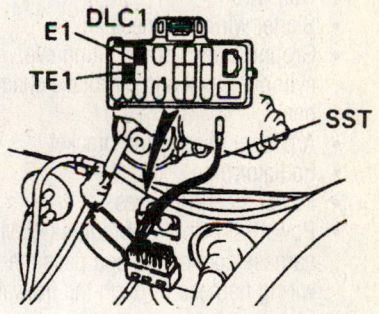

Connect a jumper wire to terminals TE1 and E1 of DLC1—4.5L (1FZ-FE) engine

4.7L (2UZ-FE) Engine

The 4.7L engine is equipped with a Distributorless Ignition System (DIS). No timing adjustment is possible.

Engine Assembly

REMOVAL & INSTALLATION

4.5L (1FZ-FE) Engine

1. Before servicing the vehicle, refer to the precautions in the beginning of this section.

2. Relieve the fuel system pressure.
3. Drain the cooling system.
4. Drain the engine oil.
5. Remove or disconnect the following:
   - Battery and tray
   - Hood
   - Radiator grille
   - Radiator hoses
   - Radiator
   - Air intake assembly
   - Oil cooler hose
   - Accelerator cable
   - Cruise control cable
   - Heater hoses
   - Heater control valve
   - Engine control wiring harness and ground strap at the cowl panel
   - Brake booster vacuum hose
   - Evaporative Emissions (EVAP) vacuum hose
   - Fuel lines
   - Heated Oxygen (HO2S) sensor connectors
   - No. 1 Data Link Connector (DLC1) clamp
   - Oil pressure gauge connectors
   - Alternator connectors
   - Intake manifold harness connector
   - Coil wire
   - Starter wiring harness
   - Ground cables at the lifting eye, cylinder block and air intake chamber
   - A/C compressor and bracket
   - Radiator pipe
   - Power steering hoses
   - Powertrain Control Module (PCM) harness connectors and pass the wiring harness through the firewall
   - Stabilizer bar
   - Front and rear driveshafts
   - Center console
   - Transmission shift lever assembly
   - Transfer case shift rod
   - Transfer case shift lever
   - Exhaust front pipe
   - Transmission mount crossmember and support the transmission
   - Left and right motor mounts

6. Attach a hoist to the engine lifting eyes and raise the powertrain out of the vehicle.

To install:

7. Lower the powertrain into the vehicle.
8. Install or connect the following:
   - Left and right motor mounts. Tighten the nuts to 54 ft. lbs. (74 Nm).
   - Transmission mount crossmember.

Tighten the crossmember bolts to 45 ft. lbs. (61 Nm) and the mount nuts to 54 ft. lbs. (74 Nm).
   - Exhaust front pipe
   - Transfer case shift lever
   - Transfer case shift rod
   - Transmission shift lever assembly
   - Center console
   - Front driveshaft. Tighten the fasteners to 54 ft. lbs. (74 Nm).
   - Rear driveshaft. Tighten the fasteners to 65 ft. lbs. (88 Nm).
   - Stabilizer bar. Tighten the bracket bolts to 13 ft. lbs. (18 Nm) and the axle housing bolts to 18 ft. lbs. (25 Nm).
   - PCM harness connectors
   - Power steering hoses
   - Radiator pipe
   - A/C compressor and bracket
   - Ground cables at the lifting eye, cylinder block and air intake chamber
   - Starter wiring harness
   - Coil wire
   - Intake manifold harness connector
   - Alternator connectors
   - Oil pressure gauge connectors
   - DLC1 clamp
   - HO2S sensor connectors
   - Fuel lines
   - EVAP vacuum hose
   - Brake booster vacuum hose
   - Engine control wiring harness and ground strap at the cowl panel
   - Heater control valve
   - Heater hoses
   - Cruise control cable
   - Accelerator cable
   - Oil cooler hose
   - Air intake assembly
   - Radiator
   - Radiator hoses
   - Radiator grille
   - Hood
   - Battery and tray

9. Fill the crankcase to the correct level.
10. Fill the cooling system.
11. Start the engine and check for leaks.

4.7L (2UZ-FE) Engine

1. Before servicing the vehicle, refer to the precautions in the beginning of this section.
2. Relieve the fuel system pressure.
3. Drain the cooling system.
4. Drain the engine oil.
5. Remove or disconnect the following:
   - Battery and tray
   - Hood

   - Engine appearance cover
   - Air intake pipe
   - Engine under covers
   - Coolant recovery tank
   - Radiator hoses
   - Radiator and fan shroud
   - Accessory drive belt
   - Cooling fan and pulley
   - Powertrain Control Module (PCM) harness connectors and pass the wiring harness through the firewall
   - Accelerator cable
   - Power steering vacuum hoses
   - Alternator harness connectors
   - Heater hoses
   - Engine control wiring harness and grommet at the firewall
   - Ground cable connector
   - Fuel lines
   - Evaporative Emissions (EVAP) canister hoses
   - Wire clamp at right inner fender
   - Negative battery cable at the relay box and right inner fender
   - Positive battery cable
   - Center console
   - Transmission shift lever assembly
   - Transfer case shift lever and rod
   - Exhaust front pipes
   - Stabilizer bar
   - Front and rear driveshafts
   - A/C compressor
   - Power steering pump

6. Attach a hoist to the engine lifting eyes.

7. Remove or disconnect the following:
   - Transfer case skid plate
   - Left and right motor mounts
   - Transmission mount crossmember

8. Attach a hoist to the engine lifting eyes and raise the powertrain out of the vehicle.

To install:

9. Lower the powertrain into the vehicle.

10. Install or connect the following:
   - Transmission mount crossmember. Tighten the bolts to 37 ft. lbs. (50 Nm) and the nuts to 55 ft. lbs. (74 Nm).
   - Transfer case skid plate
   - Left and right motor mounts. Tighten the fasteners to 22 ft. lbs. (30 Nm).
   - Power steering pump. Tighten the bolts to 13 ft. lbs. (17 Nm).
   - A/C compressor. Tighten the bolts to 36 ft. lbs. (49 Nm).
   - Front driveshaft. Tighten the fasteners to 59 ft. lbs. (80 Nm).

- Rear driveshaft. Tighten the fasteners to 78 ft. lbs. (106 Nm).
- Stabilizer bar. Tighten the bracket bolts to 13 ft. lbs. (18 Nm) and the link nuts to 18 ft. lbs. (25 Nm).
- Exhaust front pipes
- Transfer case shift lever and rod
- Transmission shift lever assembly
- Center console
- Positive battery cable
- Negative battery cable at the relay box and right inner fender
- Wire clamp at right inner fender
- EVAP canister hoses
- Fuel lines
- Ground cable connector
- Engine control wiring harness and grommet at the firewall
- Heater hoses
- Alternator harness connectors
- Power steering vacuum hoses
- Accelerator cable
- PCM harness connectors
- Cooling fan and pulley
- Accessory drive belt
- Radiator and fan shroud
- Radiator hoses
- Coolant recovery tank
- Engine under covers
- Air intake pipe
- Engine appearance cover
- Hood
- Battery and tray

11. Fill the crankcase to the correct level.
12. Fill the cooling system.
13. Start the engine and check for leaks.

Water Pump

REMOVAL & INSTALLATION

4.5L (1FZ-FE) Engine

1. Before servicing the vehicle, refer to the precautions in the beginning of this section.
2. Drain the cooling system.
3. Remove or disconnect the following:
   - Negative battery cable
   - Accessory drive belts
   - Radiator hose
   - Bypass hose
   - Cooling fan and shroud
   - Water pump pulley
   - Water pump

To install:
4. Install or connect the following:
   - Water pump. Use a new gasket and

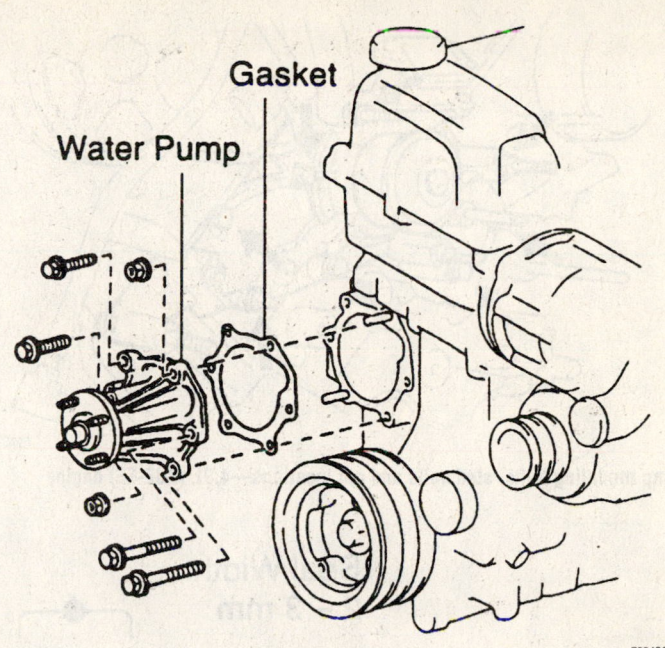

Exploded view of the water pump mounting—4.5L (1FZ-FE) engine

tighten the bolts to 15 ft. lbs. (21 Nm).
   - Water pump pulley
   - Cooling fan and shroud
   - Bypass hose
   - Radiator hose
   - Accessory drive belts
   - Negative battery cable
5. Fill the cooling system.
6. Start the engine and check for leaks.

4.7L (2UZ-FE) Engine

1. Before servicing the vehicle, refer to the precautions in the beginning of this section.
2. Drain the cooling system.

3. Remove or disconnect the following:
   - Negative battery cable
   - Timing belt. Refer to the Timing Belt unit repair section.
   - No. 2 idler pulley
   - Radiator hose
   - Bypass hose
   - Water inlet housing assembly
   - Water pump

To install:
4. Install or connect the following:
   - Water pump. Use a new gasket and tighten the bolts to 15 ft. lbs. (21 Nm). Tighten the stud bolt and nut to 13 ft. lbs. (18 Nm).

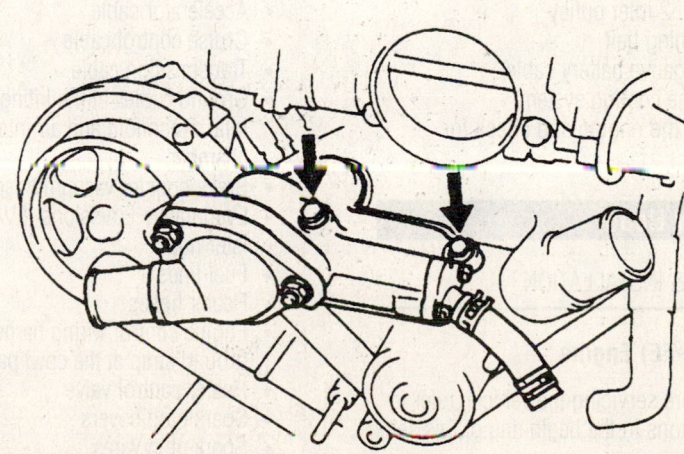

Water inlet housing attaching bolts—4.7L (2UZ-FE) engine

Timing belt service is covered in Section 4 of this manual

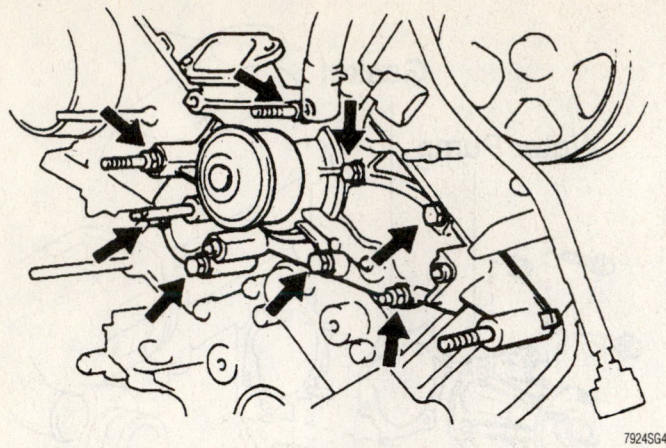

Water pump mounting bolts, stud bolts and nut locations—4.7L (2UZ-FE) engine

7924SG41

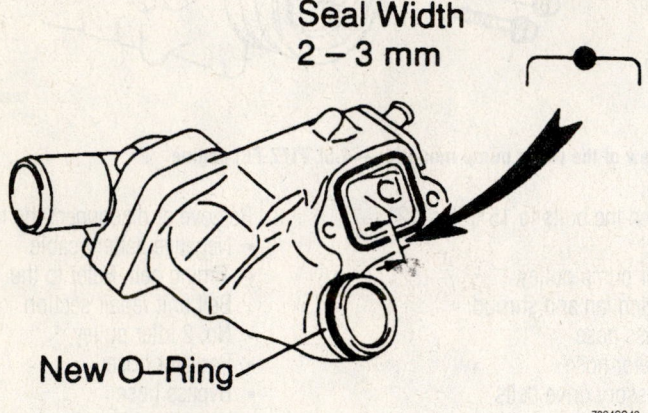

Seal Width
2 – 3 mm

New O–Ring

7924SG42

Water inlet housing sealant application—4.7L (2UZ-FE) engine

- Water inlet housing assembly. Use a new O-ring and apply sealant as shown. Tighten the bolts to 13 ft. lbs. (18 Nm).
- Bypass hose
- Radiator hose
- No. 2 idler pulley
- Timing belt
- Negative battery cable

5. Fill the cooling system.

6. Start the engine and check for leaks.

Cylinder Head

REMOVAL & INSTALLATION

4.5L (1FZ-FE) Engine

1. Before servicing the vehicle, refer to the precautions in the beginning of this section.

2. Set the engine to Top Dead Center (TDC) of the No. 1 cylinder compression stroke.

3. Relieve the fuel system pressure.
4. Drain the cooling system.
5. Remove or disconnect the following:

- Battery and tray
- Air intake tube
- Accelerator cable
- Cruise control cable
- Transmission cable
- Ground cables at the lifting eye, intake manifold and air intake chamber
- Brake booster vacuum hose
- Evaporative Emissions (EVAP) canister hose
- Fuel lines
- Heater hoses
- Engine control wiring harness and ground strap at the cowl panel
- Heater control valve
- Spark plug covers
- Spark plug wires
- Distributor
- Power steering reservoir
- Radiator hose

- Bypass hose
- Alternator
- Throttle body
- Oil dipstick tube
- Transmission dipstick tube
- Intake manifold bracket
- Engine Coolant Temperature (ECT) sensor connector
- ECT cut switch connector
- ECT gauge sender connector
- Knock sensor connectors
- Crankshaft Position (CKP) sensor connector
- Engine control wiring harness brackets
- Oil level sender connector
- Transmission harness connectors
- Starter motor connector
- Ground cable
- Heated Oxygen (HO2S) sensor connectors
- Park/Neutral Position (PNP) switch connector
- Positive Crankcase Ventilation (PCV) valve and hose
- EVAP valve connector
- Fuel injector connectors
- Exhaust Gas Recirculation (EGR) temperature sensor connector
- Water bypass pipe
- Exhaust front pipe
- Exhaust manifold heat shields
- Exhaust manifolds
- Water bypass outlet
- Valve cover
- Timing chain tensioner
- Camshaft timing chain sprocket
- Camshafts
- Two timing cover bolts at the front of the cylinder head

6. Loosen the cylinder head bolts in the sequence shown and remove the cylinder head with the intake manifold attached.

To install:

➡**Refer to Section 1 of this manual for the cylinder head torque sequence illustration. The illustration is located after the Torque Specification Chart.**

7. Install the cylinder head with a new gasket. Tighten the bolts in sequence as follows:

  a. Step 1: 29 ft. lbs. (39 Nm)
  b. Step 2: Plus 90 degrees
  c. Step 3: Plus 90 degrees
  d. Step 4: Timing cover bolts to 15 ft. lbs. (21 Nm)

8. Install or connect the following:

- Camshafts

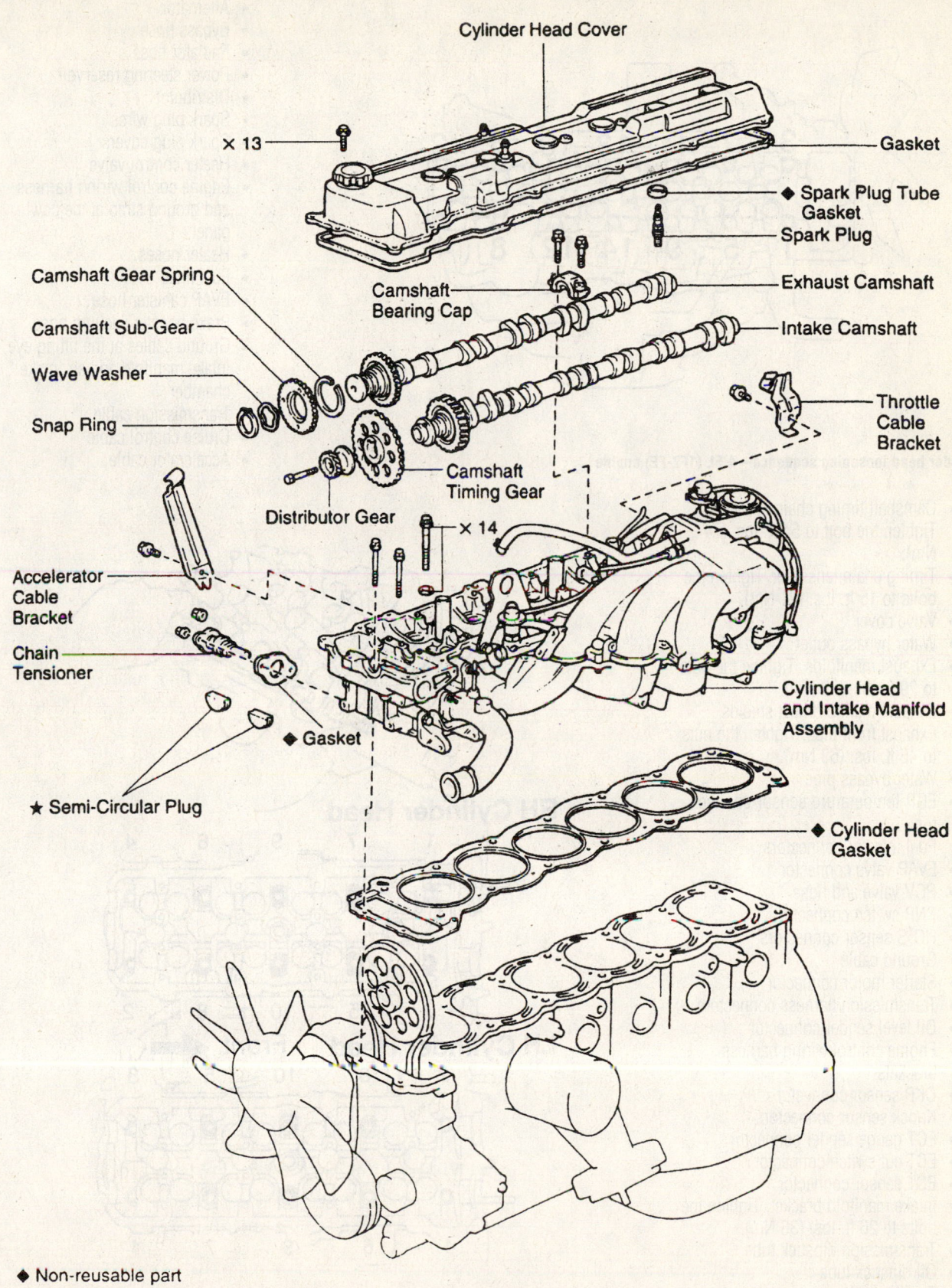

Cylinder Head Cover

Gasket

× 13

◆ Spark Plug Tube Gasket

Spark Plug

Camshaft Gear Spring

Camshaft Sub-Gear

Wave Washer

Snap Ring

Camshaft Bearing Cap

Exhaust Camshaft

Intake Camshaft

Throttle Cable Bracket

Camshaft Timing Gear

Distributor Gear

× 14

Accelerator Cable Bracket

Chain Tensioner

◆ Gasket

Cylinder Head and Intake Manifold Assembly

◆ Cylinder Head Gasket

★ Semi-Circular Plug

◆ Non-reusable part

7924SG18

Exploded view of the cylinder head and related components—4.5L (1FZ-FE) engine

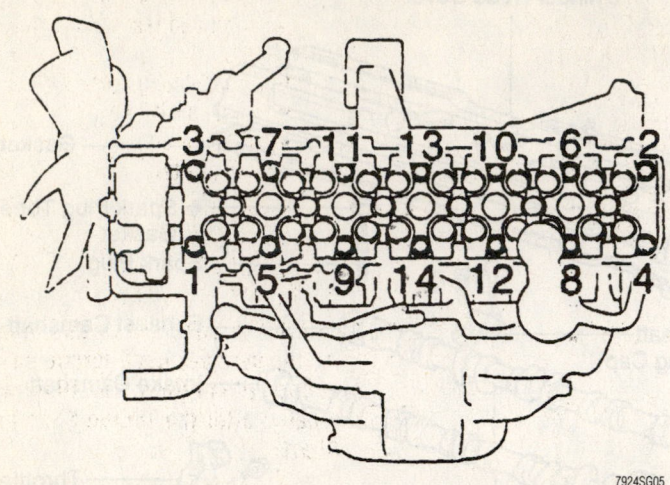

Cylinder head loosening sequence—4.5L (1FZ-FE) engine

7924SG05

- Alternator
- Bypass hose
- Radiator hose
- Power steering reservoir
- Distributor
- Spark plug wires
- Spark plug covers
- Heater control valve
- Engine control wiring harness and ground strap at the cowl panel
- Heater hoses
- Fuel lines
- EVAP canister hose
- Brake booster vacuum hose
- Ground cables at the lifting eye, intake manifold and air intake chamber
- Transmission cable
- Cruise control cable
- Accelerator cable

- Camshaft timing chain sprocket. Tighten the bolt to 54 ft. lbs. (74 Nm).
- Timing chain tensioner. Tighten the bolts to 15 ft. lbs. (21 Nm).
- Valve cover
- Water bypass outlet
- Exhaust manifolds. Tighten the nuts to 29 ft. lbs. (39 Nm).
- Exhaust manifold heat shields
- Exhaust front pipe. Tighten the nuts to 46 ft. lbs. (63 Nm).
- Water bypass pipe
- EGR temperature sensor connector
- Fuel injector connectors
- EVAP valve connector
- PCV valve and hose
- PNP switch connector
- HO2S sensor connectors
- Ground cable
- Starter motor connector
- Transmission harness connectors
- Oil level sender connector
- Engine control wiring harness brackets
- CKP sensor connector
- Knock sensor connectors
- ECT gauge sender connector
- ECT cut switch connector
- ECT sensor connector
- Intake manifold bracket. Tighten the bolts to 26 ft. lbs. (36 Nm).
- Transmission dipstick tube
- Oil dipstick tube
- Throttle body

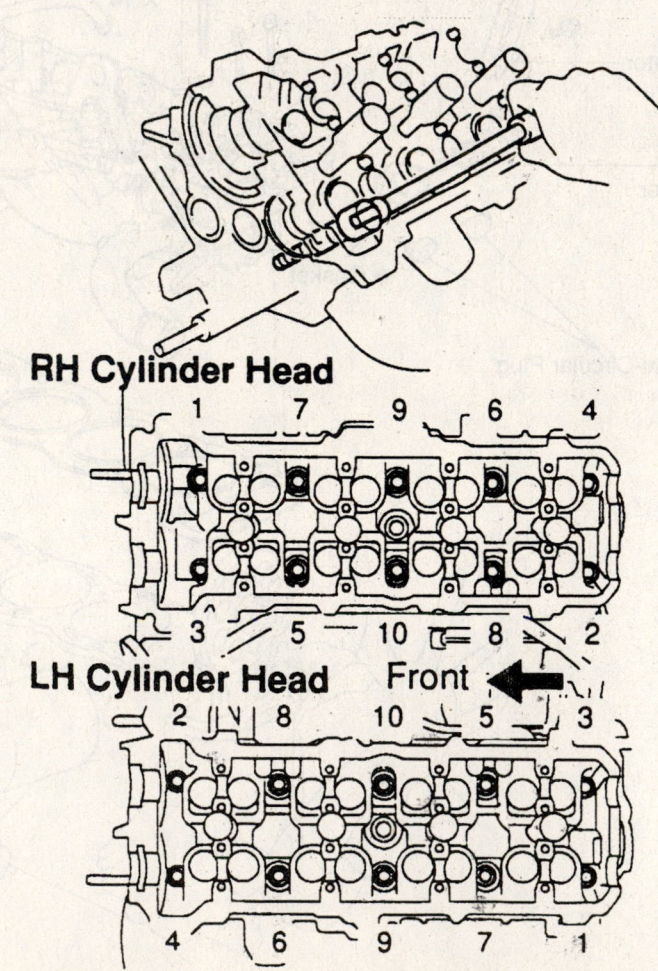

Cylinder head loosening sequence—4.7L (2UZ-FE) engine

7924SG43

RH Cylinder Head

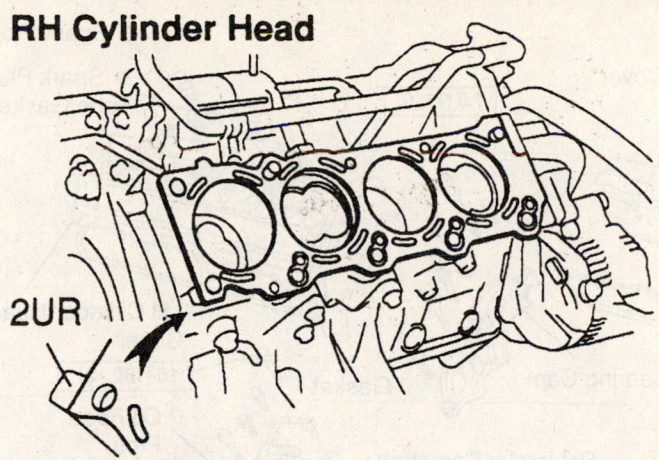

2UR

LH Cylinder Head

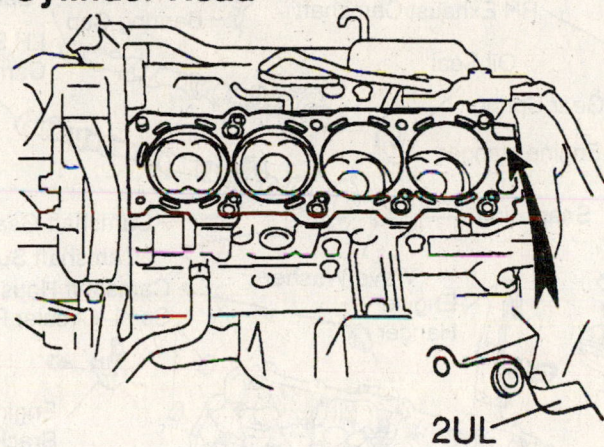

2UL

7924SG47

Cylinder head gasket identification—4.7L (2UZ-FE) engine

- Air intake tube
- Battery and tray
9. Fill the cooling system.
10. Start the engine and check for leaks.

4.7L (2UZ-FE) Engine

1. Before servicing the vehicle, refer to the precautions in the beginning of this section.
2. Drain the cooling system.
3. Relieve the fuel system pressure.
4. Remove or disconnect the following:

- Battery and tray
- Engine appearance cover
- Engine under covers
- Air intake assembly
- Accessory drive belt
- A/C compressor and bracket
- Cooling fan and bracket
- Radiator
- Idler pulley
- Front covers
- Timing belt. Refer to the Timing Belt unit repair section.
- Camshaft sprockets
- Camshaft Position (CMP) sensor
- Power steering pump
- Exhaust front pipes
- Transmission dipstick tube
- Ignition coils
- Rear timing belt covers
- Fuel lines

- Intake manifold
- Water inlet housing assembly
- Front and rear water bypass joints
- Engine lifting eyes
- Oil dipstick tube
- Valve covers
- Camshafts
- Cylinder heads with the exhaust manifolds attached. Loosen the bolts in the sequence shown.

To install:

➡ Refer to Section 1 of this manual for the cylinder head torque sequence illustration. The illustration is located after the Torque Specification Chart.

5. Install the cylinder heads with new gaskets. Tighten the bolts in sequence as follows:
   a. Step 1: 24 ft. lbs. (32 Nm)
   b. Step 2: Plus 180 degrees
6. Install or connect the following:

- Camshafts
- Valve covers
- Oil dipstick tube
- Engine lifting eyes
- Front and rear water bypass joints
- Water inlet housing assembly
- Intake manifold
- Fuel lines
- Rear timing belt covers
- Ignition coils
- Transmission dipstick tube
- Exhaust front pipes
- Power steering pump
- CMP sensor
- Camshaft sprockets
- Timing belt
- Front covers
- Idler pulley
- Radiator
- Cooling fan and bracket
- A/C compressor and bracket
- Accessory drive belt
- Air intake assembly
- Engine under covers
- Engine appearance cover
- Battery and tray

7. Fill the cooling system.
8. Start the engine and check for leaks.

Refer to Section 1 for engine rebuilding specifications

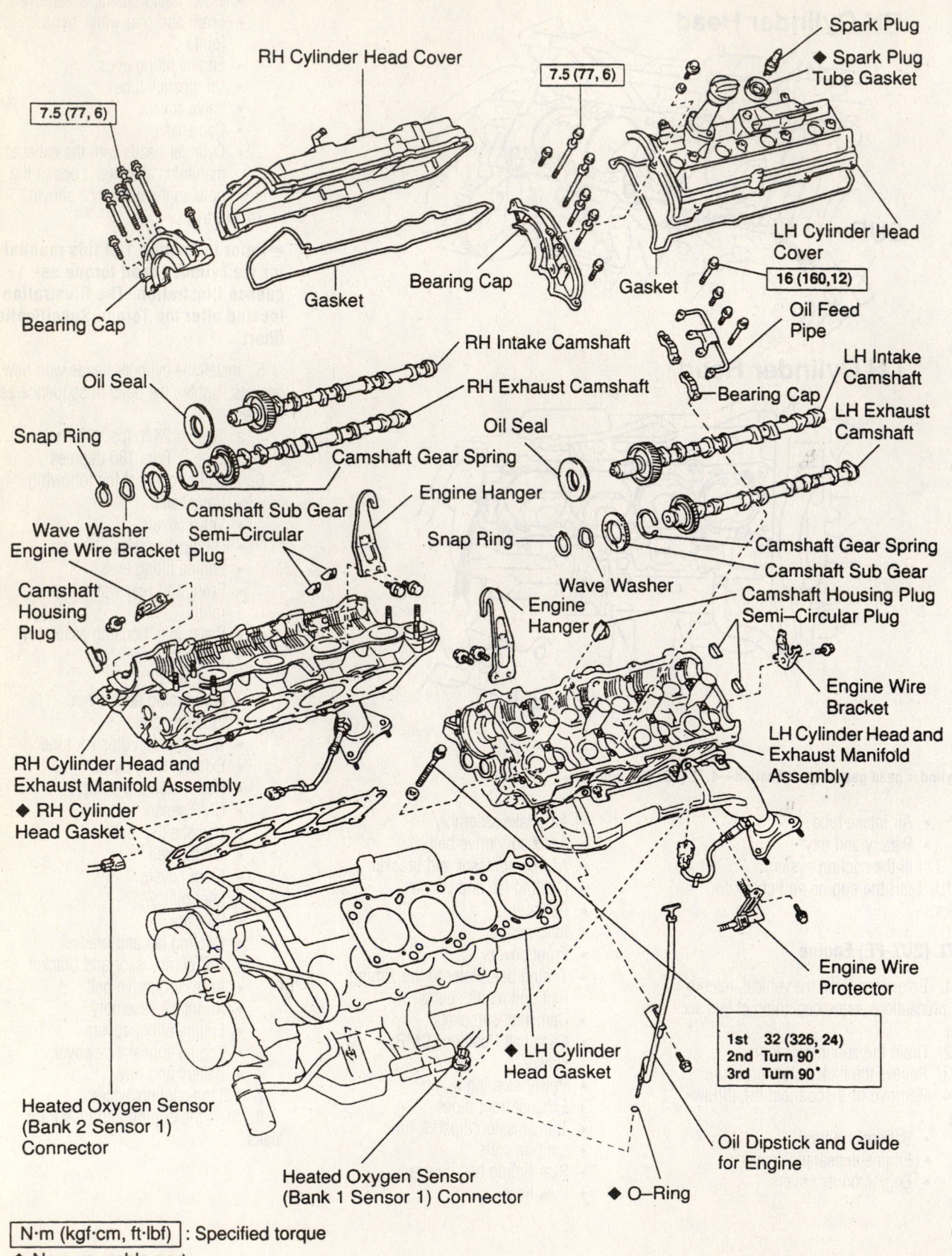

RH Cylinder Head Cover

7.5 (77, 6)

7.5 (77, 6)

Spark Plug

Spark Plug Tube Gasket

Gasket

Bearing Cap

Gasket

LH Cylinder Head Cover

16 (160, 12)

Bearing Cap

Oil Feed Pipe

Bearing Cap

Oil Seal

RH Intake Camshaft

RH Exhaust Camshaft

Oil Seal

LH Intake Camshaft

LH Exhaust Camshaft

Snap Ring

Camshaft Gear Spring

Camshaft Sub Gear

Engine Hanger

Semi–Circular Plug

Snap Ring

Wave Washer

Camshaft Gear Spring

Camshaft Sub Gear

Wave Washer
Engine Wire Bracket

Wave Washer
Engine Hanger

Camshaft Housing Plug
Semi–Circular Plug

Camshaft Housing Plug

Engine Wire Bracket

RH Cylinder Head and Exhaust Manifold Assembly

◆ RH Cylinder Head Gasket

LH Cylinder Head and Exhaust Manifold Assembly

Heated Oxygen Sensor (Bank 2 Sensor 1) Connector

◆ LH Cylinder Head Gasket

Heated Oxygen Sensor (Bank 1 Sensor 1) Connector

◆ O–Ring

Oil Dipstick and Guide for Engine

Engine Wire Protector

1st	32 (326, 24)
2nd	Turn 90°
3rd	Turn 90°

N·m (kgf·cm, ft·lbf) : Specified torque

◆ Non–reusable part

Exploded view of the cylinder head mounting—4.7L (2UZ–FE) engine

7924SG49

Intake Manifold

REMOVAL & INSTALLATION

4.5L (1FZ-FE) Engine

1. Before servicing the vehicle, refer to the precautions in the beginning of this section.
2. Relieve the fuel system pressure.
3. Drain the cooling system.
4. Remove or disconnect the following:
   - Battery and tray
   - Air intake tube
   - Alternator and bracket
   - Accelerator cable
   - Cruise control cable
   - Transmission cable
   - Positive Crankcase Ventilation (PCV) valve and hose
   - Exhaust Gas Recirculation (EGR) valve and vacuum modulator
   - Heater inlet pipe
   - Fuel pressure regulator vacuum hose
   - Water bypass hose
   - Evaporative Emissions (EVAP) hose
   - Brake booster vacuum line
   - Throttle Position (TP) sensor connector
   - Idle Air Control (IAC) valve connector
   - Engine Coolant Temperature (ECT) sensor connector
   - ECT cut switch connector
   - ECT gauge sender connector
   - Fuel injector connectors
   - EVAP valve connector
   - EGR temperature sensor connector
   - Power steering reservoir
   - Fuel lines
   - Thermal vacuum valve hoses
   - Intake manifold bracket
   - Intake manifold

To install:

5. Install or connect the following:
   - Intake manifold. Tighten the fasteners to 15 ft. lbs. (21 Nm).
   - Intake manifold bracket. Tighten the bolts to 26 ft. lbs. (36 Nm).
   - Thermal vacuum valve hoses
   - Fuel lines
   - Power steering reservoir
   - EGR temperature sensor connector
   - EVAP valve connector
   - Fuel injector connectors
   - ECT sensor connector
   - ECT cut switch connector
   - ECT gauge sender connector

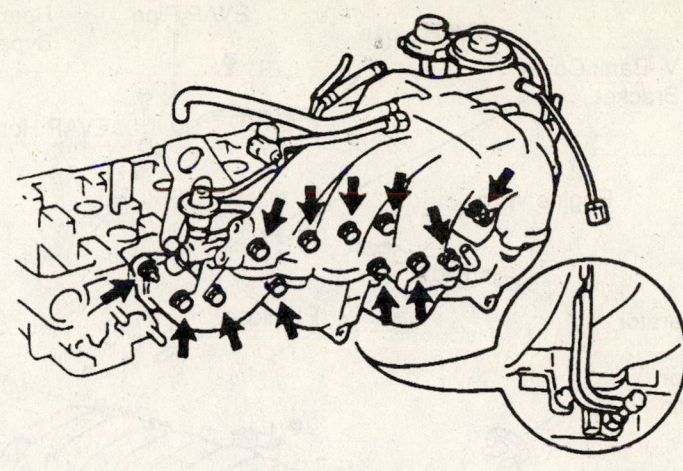

Intake manifold mounting bolts—4.5L (1Fz-FE) engine

   - IAC valve connector
   - TP sensor connector
   - Brake booster vacuum line
   - EVAP hose
   - Water bypass hose
   - Fuel pressure regulator vacuum hose
   - Heater inlet pipe
   - EGR valve and vacuum modulator
   - PCV valve and hose
   - Transmission cable
   - Cruise control cable
   - Accelerator cable
   - Alternator and bracket
   - Air intake tube
   - Battery and tray
6. Fill the cooling system.
7. Start the engine and check for leaks.

4.7L (2UZ-FE) Engine

1. Before servicing the vehicle, refer to the precautions in the beginning of this section.
2. Drain the cooling system.
3. Relieve the fuel system pressure.
4. Remove or disconnect the following:
   - Negative battery cable
   - Engine appearance cover
   - Accelerator cable
   - Throttle Position (TP) sensor connector
   - Accelerator pedal position sensor
   - Throttle motor connector
   - Evaporative Emissions (EVAP) vacuum switching valve connector
   - Fuel injector connectors
   - Engine Coolant Temperature (ECT) sensor connector

   - ETC gauge sender connector
   - Heated Oxygen (HO2S) sensor connectors
   - Fuel pressure regulator vacuum hose
   - Positive Crankcase Ventilation (PCV) valve and hose
   - EVAP hoses
   - Power steering vacuum hoses
   - Water bypass hose
   - Engine control wiring harness clamps
   - Cylinder head ground cables
   - Intake manifold wire harness protector
   - EVAP pipe
   - Engine appearance cover brackets
   - Intake manifold

To install:

5. Install or connect the following:
   - Intake manifold. Tighten the fasteners to 13 ft. lbs. (18 Nm).
   - Engine appearance cover brackets
   - EVAP pipe
   - Intake manifold wire harness protector
   - Cylinder head ground cables
   - Engine control wiring harness clamps
   - Water bypass hose
   - Power steering vacuum hoses
   - EVAP hoses
   - PCV valve and hose
   - Fuel pressure regulator vacuum hose
   - HO2S sensor connectors
   - ETC gauge sender connector
   - ECT sensor connector
   - Fuel injector connectors

For engine torque specifications, refer to Section 1 of this manual

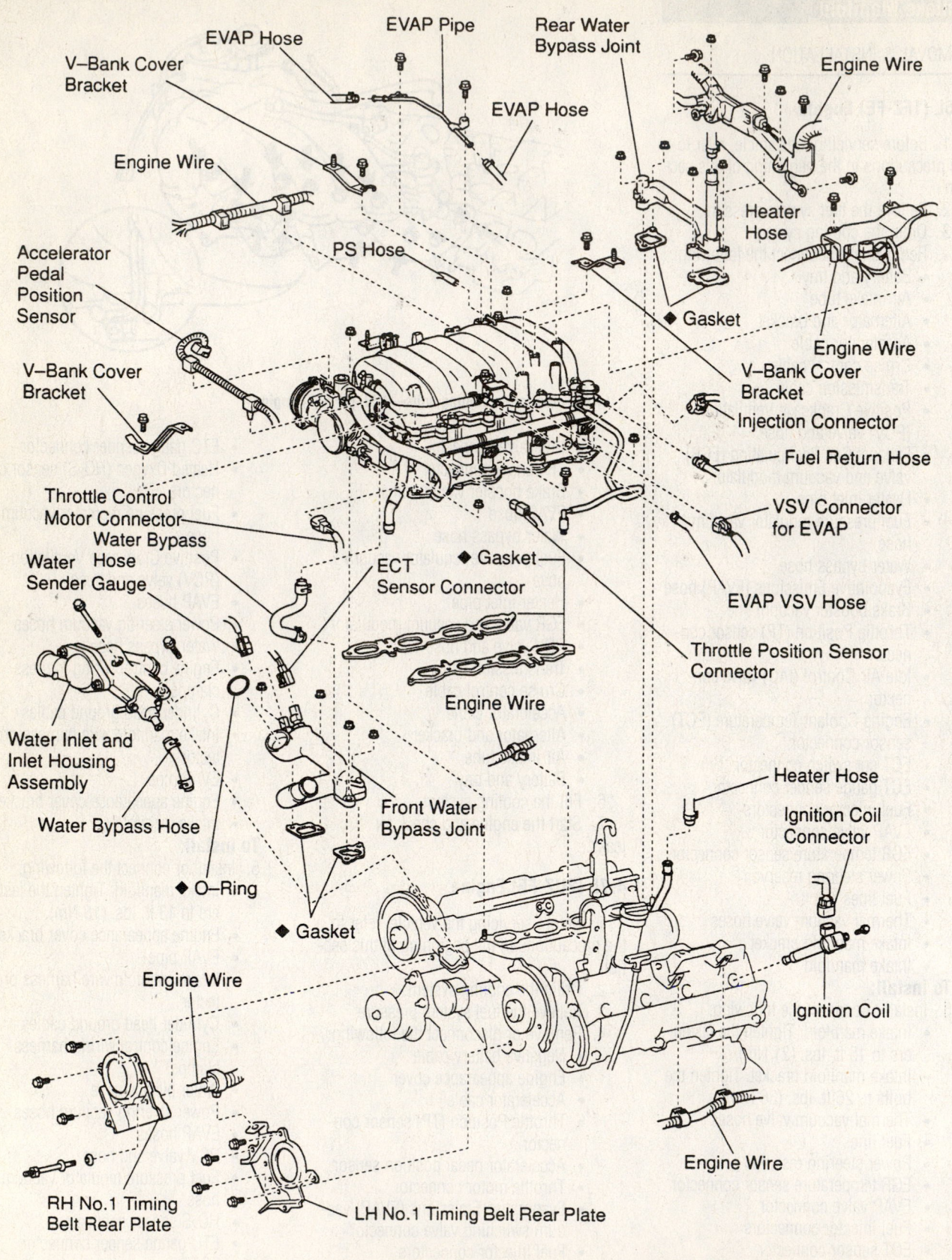

EVAP Hose

EVAP Pipe

Rear Water
Bypass Joint

Engine Wire

V–Bank Cover
Bracket

EVAP Hose

Engine Wire

Heater
Hose

Accelerator
Pedal
Position
Sensor

PS Hose

Gasket

Engine Wire

V–Bank Cover
Bracket

V–Bank Cover
Bracket

Injection Connector

Throttle Control
Motor Connector

Fuel Return Hose

Water Bypass
Hose

Water
Sender Gauge

ECT
Sensor Connector

Gasket

VSV Connector
for EVAP

EVAP VSV Hose

Throttle Position Sensor
Connector

Water Inlet and
Inlet Housing
Assembly

Engine Wire

Water Bypass Hose

Front Water
Bypass Joint

Heater Hose

Ignition Coil
Connector

O–Ring

Gasket

Engine Wire

Ignition Coil

Engine Wire

Engine Wire

RH No.1 Timing
Belt Rear Plate

LH No.1 Timing Belt Rear Plate

◆ Non–reusable part

Exploded of the intake manifold mounting—4.7L (2UZ-FE) engine

7924SG50

- EVAP vacuum switching valve connector
- Throttle motor connector
- Accelerator pedal position sensor
- TP sensor connector
- Accelerator cable
- Engine appearance cover
- Negative battery cable

6. Fill the cooling system.
7. Start the engine and check for leaks.

Exhaust Manifold

REMOVAL & INSTALLATION

4.5L (1FZ-FE) Engine

1. Before servicing the vehicle, refer to the precautions in the beginning of this section.
2. Remove or disconnect the following:
   - Negative battery cable
   - Heated Oxygen (HO$_2$S) sensor connectors
   - Exhaust manifold heat shields
   - Exhaust front pipe
   - Exhaust manifolds

To install:

➡ **Use new exhaust manifold nuts for assembly.**

3. Install or connect the following:
   - Exhaust manifolds. Tighten the nuts to 29 ft. lbs. (39 Nm).
   - Exhaust front pipe. Tighten the nuts to 46 ft. lbs. (62 Nm).
   - Exhaust manifold heat shields

- HO$_2$S sensor connectors
- Negative battery cable

4. Start the engine and check for leaks.

4.7L (2UZ-FE) Engine

1. Before servicing the vehicle, refer to the precautions in the beginning of this section.
2. Attach a hoist to the engine lifting eyes.
3. Remove or disconnect the following:
   - Negative battery cable
   - Heated Oxygen (HO$_2$S) sensor connectors
   - Exhaust manifold heat shield
   - Exhaust front pipe
   - Motor mount
   - Motor mount bracket
   - Exhaust manifold

To install:

➡ **Use new exhaust manifold nuts for assembly.**

4. Install or connect the following:
   - Exhaust manifold. Tighten the nuts to 32 ft. lbs. (44 Nm).
   - Motor mount bracket. Tighten the bolts to 27 ft. lbs. (36 Nm).
   - Motor mount. Tighten the fasteners to 22 ft. lbs. (30 Nm).
   - Exhaust front pipe. Tighten the nuts to 46 ft. lbs. (62 Nm).
   - Exhaust manifold heat shield
   - HO$_2$S sensor connectors
   - Negative battery cable

5. Start the engine and check for leaks.

Front Crankshaft Seal

REMOVAL & INSTALLATION

4.7L (2UZ-FE) Engine

1. Before servicing the vehicle, refer to the precautions in the beginning of this section.
2. Drain the cooling system.
3. Remove or disconnect the following:
   - Negative battery cable
   - Engine under cover
   - Engine appearance cover
   - Air intake assembly
   - Accessory drive belt
   - Cooling fan and pulley
   - Radiator
   - Drive belt idler pulley
   - Camshaft Position (CMP) sensor connector
   - Upper timing covers
   - Oil cooler pipe
   - Center timing cover
   - A/C compressor
   - Cooling fan bracket
   - Crankshaft pulley
   - Lower timing cover
   - Timing belt. Refer to the Timing Belt unit repair section.
   - Crankshaft timing sprocket
   - Front crankshaft seal

To install:

4. Install the oil seal so that it is flush with the oil pump housing.
5. Install or connect the following:
   - Crankshaft timing sprocket
   - Timing belt
   - Lower timing cover
   - Crankshaft pulley. Tighten the bolt to 181 ft. lbs. (245 Nm).
   - Cooling fan bracket. Tighten the 12mm bolts to 12 ft. lbs. (16 Nm) and the 14mm bolts to 24 ft. lbs. (32 Nm).
   - A/C compressor
   - Center timing cover
   - Oil cooler pipe
   - Upper timing covers
   - CMP sensor connector
   - Drive belt idler pulley. Tighten the bolt to 27 ft. lbs. (37 Nm).
   - Radiator
   - Cooling fan and pulley. Tighten the nuts to 16 ft. lbs. (21 Nm).
   - Accessory drive belt
   - Air intake assembly
   - Engine appearance cover

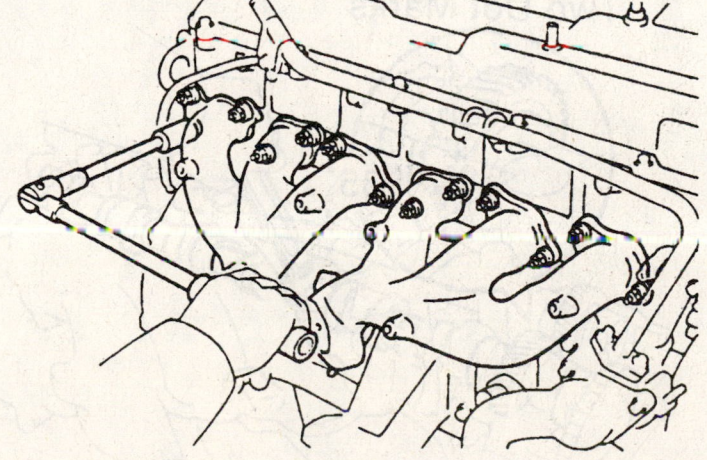

7924SG09

Exhaust manifold mounting bolts—4.5L (1FZ-FE) engine

For complete mechanical specifications, refer to Section 1 of this manual

- Engine under cover
- Negative battery cable

6. Fill the cooling system.
7. Start the engine and check for leaks.

Camshaft and Valve Lifters

REMOVAL & INSTALLATION

4.5L (1FZ-FE) Engine

1. Before servicing the vehicle, refer to the precautions in the beginning of this section.

2. Drain the cooling system.

3. Remove or disconnect the following:

- Battery and tray
- Air intake hose
- Accelerator cable
- Cruise control cable
- Transmission cable
- Water bypass hose
- Evaporative Emissions (EVAP) hoses
- Idle Air Control (IAC) valve connector
- Throttle Position (TP) sensor connector
- Throttle body
- Spark plug wire covers
- Spark plug wires
- Distributor
- Valve cover

4. Rotate the crankshaft to align the camshaft timing marks as shown.

5. Matchmark the timing chain to the camshaft timing sprocket.

6. Remove or disconnect the following:

- Timing chain tensioner
- Camshaft timing sprocket

7. Rotate the camshafts as necessary to access the exhaust camshaft sub-gear service bolt hole and install a 6mm x 1.0mm bolt.

8. Rotate the camshafts to align the 2 dot timing marks at a **35** degree angle as shown.

➡**Keep all valvetrain components in order for assembly.**

9. Remove the exhaust camshaft as follows:

  a. Step 1: Remove the No. 1 bearing cap. Loosen the bolts evenly in several passes.

  b. Step 2: Remove the No. 2, No. 3, No. 5 and No. 7 bearing caps. Loosen the bolts evenly in several passes.

  c. Step 3: Remove the No. 4 and No. 6 bearing caps. Loosen the bolts evenly

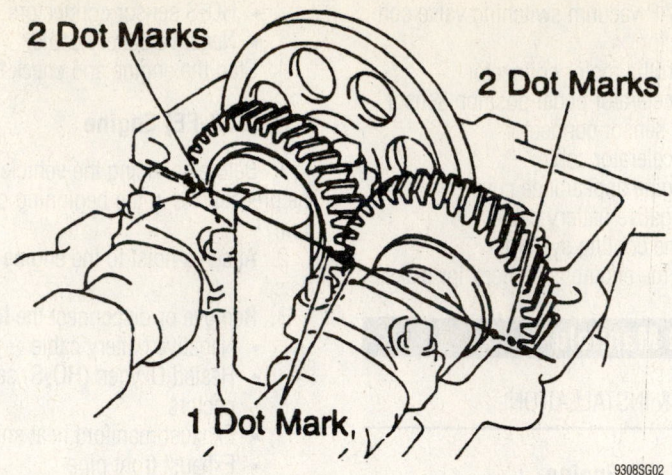

Camshaft timing marks—4.5L (1FZ-FE) engine

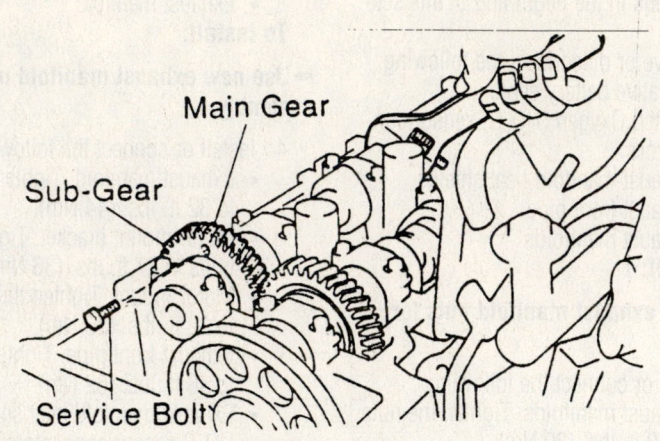

Secure the exhaust camshaft sub-gear to the main gear with a service bolt—4.5L (1FZ-FE) engine

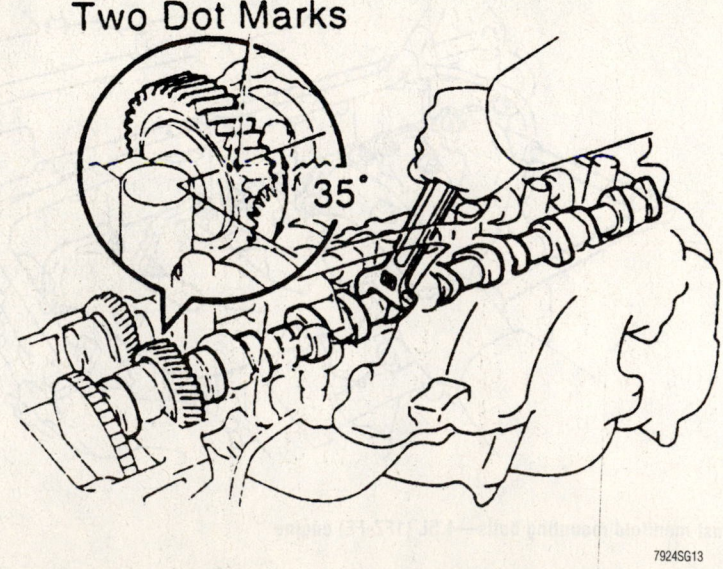

Set the timing mark (2 dot marks) of the camshaft driven gear at approximately 35 degrees—4.5L (1FZ-FE) engine

in several passes so that the exhaust camshaft is lifted straight and level.

d. Step 4: Remove the exhaust camshaft.

10. Rotate the intake camshaft so that the 2 dot timing mark is at a **25** degree angle as shown.

11. Remove the intake camshaft as follows:

a. Step 1: Remove the No. 1 bearing cap. Loosen the bolts evenly in several passes.

b. Step 2: Remove the No. 3, No. 4, No. 6 and No. 7 bearing caps. Loosen the bolts evenly in several passes.

c. Step 3: Remove the No. 2 and No. 5 bearing caps. Loosen the bolts evenly in several passes so that the intake camshaft is lifted straight and level.

d. Step 4: Remove the intake camshaft.

12. Remove the valve lifters and shims.

To install:

13. Install the valve lifters and shims in their original positions.

14. Install the intake camshaft with the No. 1 and No. 4 cam lobes positioned as shown.

15. Install the intake camshaft bearing caps as follows:

a. Step 1: Install the No. 2 and No. 5 bearing caps. Tighten the bolts evenly in several passes until the bearing caps contact the cylinder head.

b. Step 2: Install the No. 3, No. 4, No. 6 and No. 7 bearing caps. Tighten the bolts evenly in several passes until the bearing caps contact the cylinder head.

c. Step 3: Install the No. 1 bearing cap. The bearing cap should contact the cylinder head with no gaps.

d. Step 4: Tighten the intake camshaft bearing cap bolts in sequence and in several passes to 12 ft. lbs. (16 Nm).

16. Rotate the intake camshaft so that the 2 dot timing mark is at a **35** degree angle.

17. Align the exhaust camshaft 2 dot timing mark with the intake camshaft 2 dot mark and engage the gears.

18. Roll the exhaust camshaft down onto the cylinder head while keeping the timing gears engaged.

19. Install the exhaust camshaft bearing caps as follows:

a. Step 1: Install the No. 4 and No. 6 bearing caps. Tighten the bolts evenly in several passes until the bearing caps contact the cylinder head.

b. Step 2: Install the No. 2, No. 3,

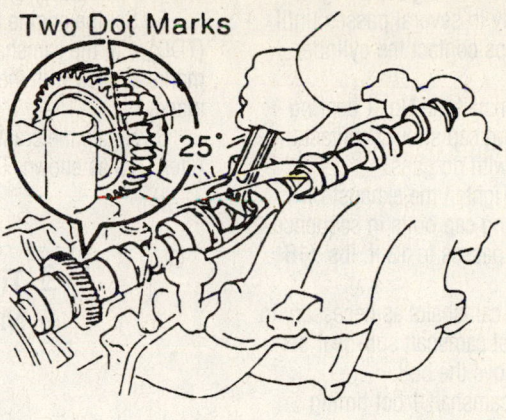

Set the timing mark (2 dot marks) of the camshaft driven gear at approximately 25 degrees—4.5L (1FZ-FE) engine

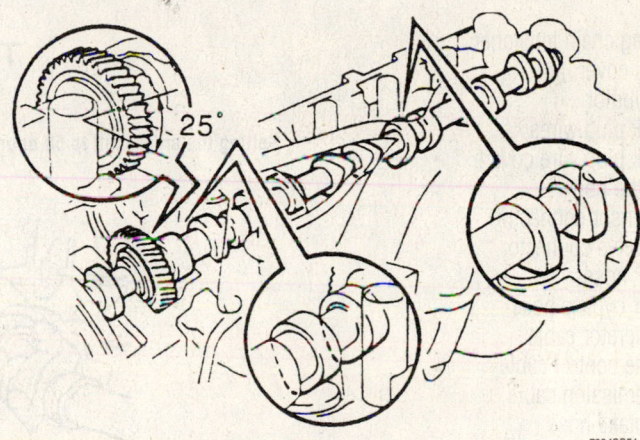

Intake camshaft with No. 1 and No. 4 cam lobes down—4.5L (1FZ-FE) engine

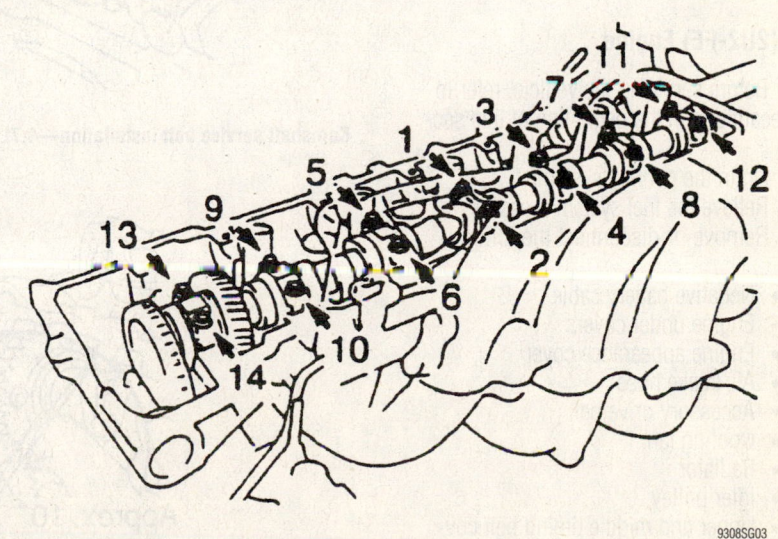

Camshaft bearing cap torque sequence—4.5L (1FZ-FE) engine

Please refer to Section 8 for electric cooling fan wiring schematics

No. 5 and No. 7 bearing caps. Tighten the bolts evenly in several passes until the bearing caps contact the cylinder head.

c. Step 3: Install the No. 1 bearing cap. The bearing cap should contact the cylinder head with no gaps.

d. Step 4: Tighten the exhaust camshaft bearing cap bolts in sequence and in several passes to 12 ft. lbs. (16 Nm).

20. Rotate the camshafts as necessary to access the exhaust camshaft sub-gear service bolt and remove the bolt.

21. Align the camshaft 1 dot timing marks.

22. Install or connect the following:
- Camshaft timing sprocket and chain with the matchmarks aligned. Tighten the bolt to 54 ft. lbs. (74 Nm).
- Timing chain tensioner
- Valve cover
- Distributor
- Spark plug wires
- Spark plug wire covers
- Throttle body
- TP sensor connector
- IAC valve connector
- EVAP hoses
- Water bypass hose
- Accelerator cable
- Cruise control cable
- Transmission cable
- Air intake hose
- Battery and tray

23. Fill the cooling system.

24. Start the engine and check for leaks.

4.7L (2UZ-FE) Engine

1. Before servicing the vehicle, refer to the precautions in the beginning of this section.

2. Drain the cooling system.

3. Relieve the fuel system pressure.

4. Remove or disconnect the following:
- Negative battery cable
- Engine under covers
- Engine appearance cover
- Air intake hose
- Accessory drive belt
- Cooling fan
- Radiator
- Idler pulley
- Upper and middle timing belt covers
- A/C compressor
- Cooling fan bracket
- Alternator

- Accessory drive belt tensioner

5. Set the engine to Top Dead Center (TDC) with the camshaft sprocket timing marks aligned with the rear cover timing marks.

6. Rotate the crankshaft to 50 degrees After TDC as shown. The crankshaft pulley timing mark should align with the center of the No. 2 idler pulley bolt.

7. Remove or disconnect the following:
- Crankshaft pulley
- Lower timing cover
- Timing belt. Refer to the Timing Belt unit repair section.

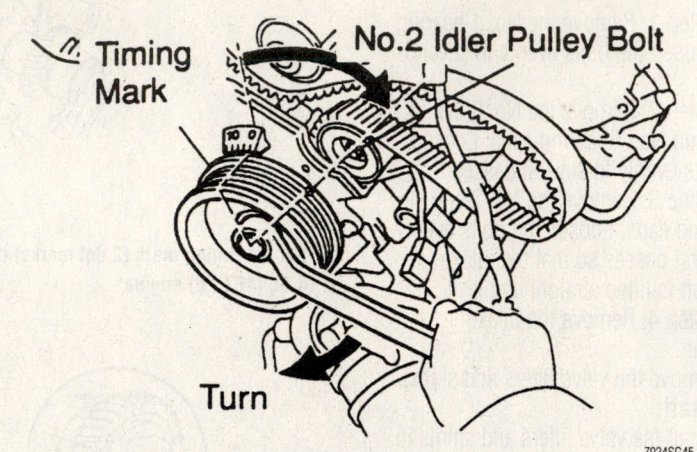

Setting the crankshaft to 50 degrees ATDC—4.7L (2UZ-FE) engine

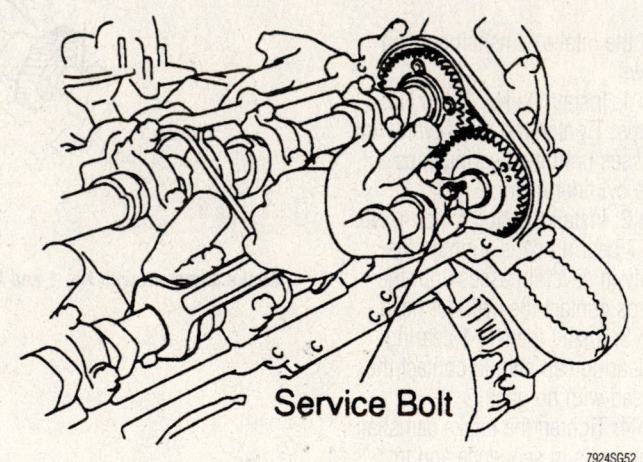

Camshaft service bolt installation—4.7L (2UZ-FE) engine

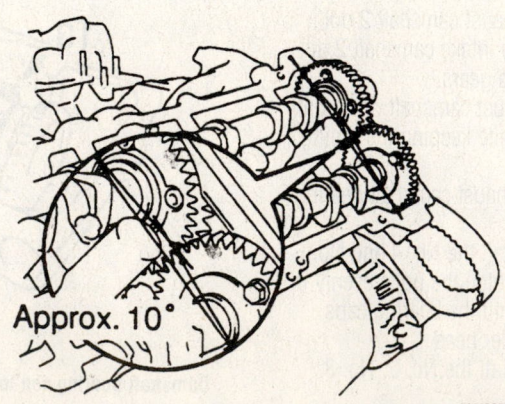

Right bank camshaft timing mark (1 dot marks) alignment—4.7L (2UZ-FE) engine

- Camshaft timing sprockets
- Camshaft Position (CMP) sensor
- Ignition coils
- Valve cover
- Timing belt rear covers

8. Rotate the right bank camshafts as necessary to access the exhaust camshaft sub-gear service bolt hole and install a 6mm x 1.0mm bolt.

➡ **Keep all valvetrain components in order for assembly.**

9. Align the right bank camshaft 1 dot timing marks to a **10** degree angle as shown.

10. Loosen the bearing cap bolts in sequence and in several passes.

11. Remove the right bank camshafts.

12. Rotate the left bank camshafts as necessary to access the exhaust camshaft sub-gear service bolt hole and install a 6mm x 1.0mm bolt.

13. Align the left bank camshaft 2 dot timing marks as shown.

14. Loosen the bearing cap bolts in sequence and in several passes.

15. Remove the left bank camshafts.

16. Remove the valve lifters and shims.

To install:

17. Ensure that the crankshaft is at 50 degrees After TDC.

18. Install or connect the following:
- Valve lifters and shims in their original positions
- Right bank camshafts with the 1 dot timing marks at 10 degrees
- Left bank camshafts with the 2 dot timing marks aligned
- Left and right bank camshaft bearing caps in their original positions. Apply sealant to the front bearing caps as shown.

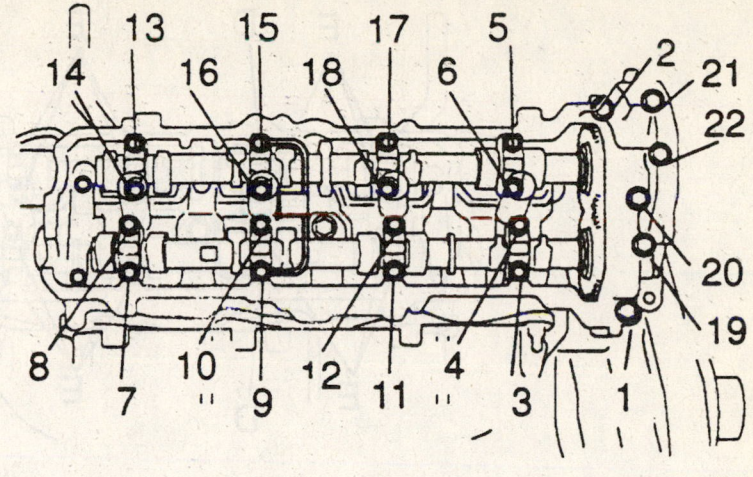

Right bank camshaft bearing cap loosening sequence—4.7L (2UZ-FE) engine

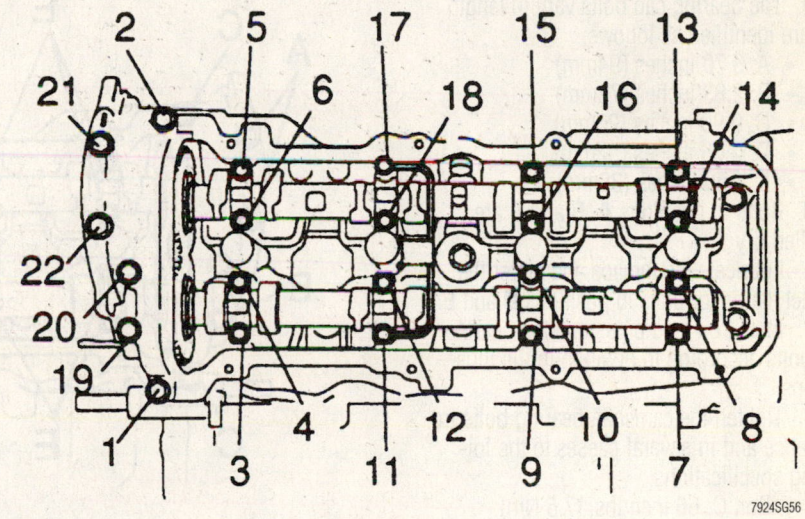

Left bank camshaft bearing cap loosening sequence—4.7L (2UZ-FE) engine

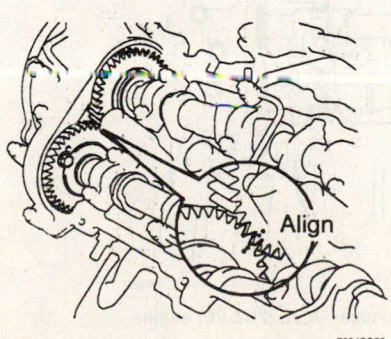

Left bank camshaft timing mark (2 dot marks) alignment—4.7L (2UZ-FE) engine

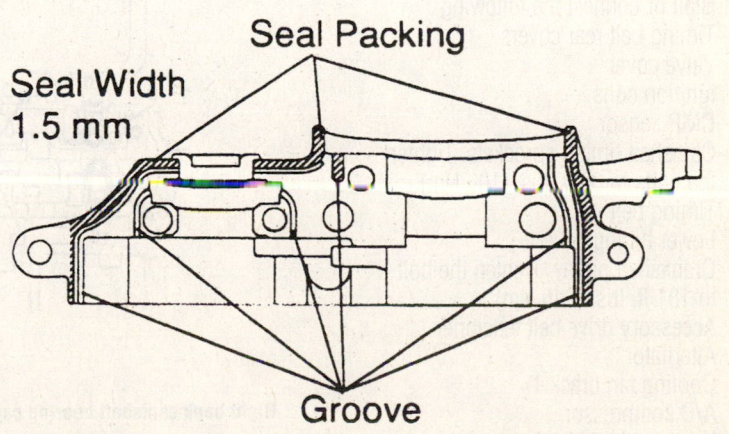

Apply a 1.5mm bead of sealant to the front bearing caps—4.7L (2UZ-FE) engine

For complete service labor times order Nichols' Chilton Labor Guide Manual

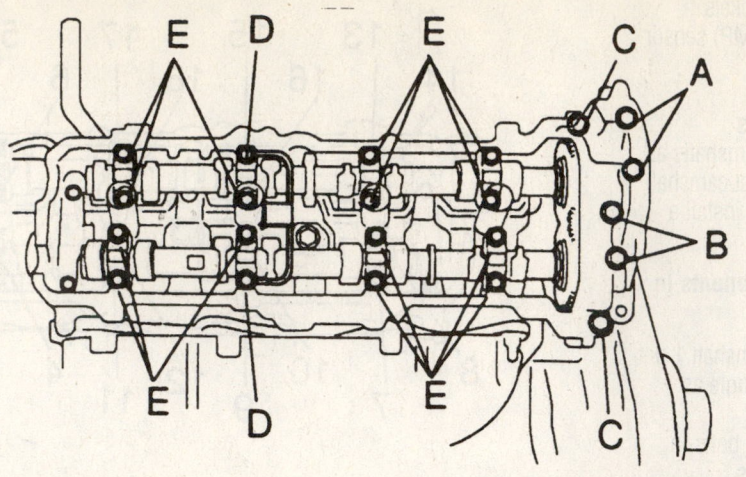

Right bank bearing cap bolt location—4.7L (2UZ-FE) engine

- Camshaft oil seals

19. The bearing cap bolts vary in length and are identified as follows:
   - A: 3.70 inches (94mm)
   - B: 2.83 inches (72mm)
   - C: 0.98 inches (25mm)
   - D: 2.05 inches (52mm)
   - E: 1.50 inches (38mm)

20. Bolts in positions **A**, **B** and **C** are installed dry.

21. Lubricate the threads and under the contact flange for bolts in positions **D** and **E**.

22. Install oil feed pipes and the bearing cap bolts according to position in the illustrations.

23. Tighten the camshaft bearing bolts in sequence and in several passes to the following specifications:
   - Bolt C: 66 inch lbs. (7.5 Nm)
   - All others: 12 ft. lbs. (16 Nm)

24. Remove the service bolts from the exhaust camshaft gears.

25. Install or connect the following:
   - Timing belt rear covers
   - Valve cover
   - Ignition coils
   - CMP sensor
   - Camshaft timing sprockets. Tighten the bolts to 80 ft. lbs. (108 Nm).
   - Timing belt
   - Lower timing cover
   - Crankshaft pulley. Tighten the bolt to 181 ft. lbs. (245 Nm).
   - Accessory drive belt tensioner
   - Alternator
   - Cooling fan bracket
   - A/C compressor
   - Upper and middle timing belt covers
   - Idler pulley. Tighten the bolt to 27 ft. lbs. (37 Nm).
   - Radiator
   - Cooling fan

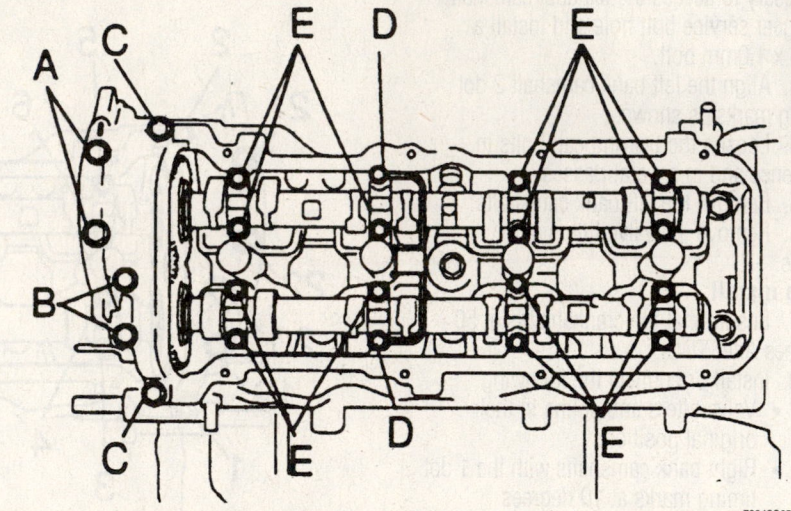

Left camshaft bearing cap bolt locations—4.7L (2UZ-FE) engine

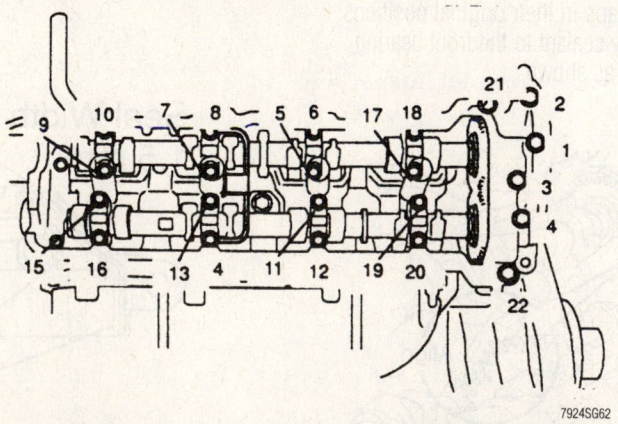

Right bank camshaft bearing cap bolt torque sequence—4.7L (2UZ-FE) engine

- Accessory drive belt
- Air intake hose
- Engine appearance cover
- Engine under covers
- Negative battery cable

26. Fill the cooling system.

27. Start the engine and check for leaks.

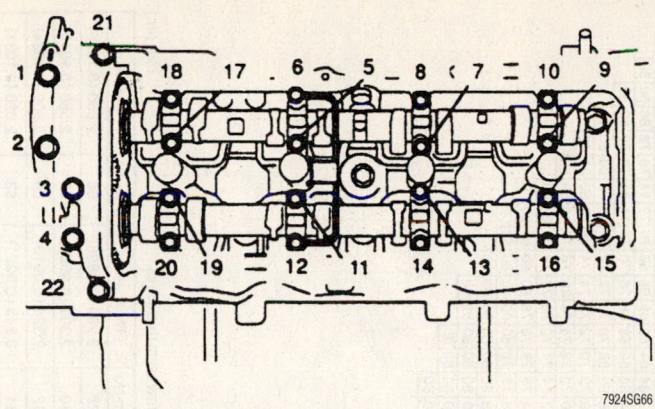

Left bank camshaft bearing cap bolt torque sequence—4.7L (2UZ-FE) engine

Valve Lash

ADJUSTMENT

4.5L (1FZ-FE) Engine

➡**Measure valve clearance with the engine cold.**

1. Before servicing the vehicle, refer to the precautions in the beginning of this section.
2. Drain the cooling system.
3. Remove or disconnect the following:

- Negative battery cable
- Air intake hose
- Accelerator cable
- Cruise control cable
- Transmission cable
- Water bypass hose
- Evaporative Emissions (EVAP) hoses
- Idle Air Control (IAC) valve connector
- Throttle Position (TP) sensor connector
- Throttle body
- Spark plug wire covers
- Spark plug wires
- Valve cover

4. Set the engine to the top of the compression stroke with the valves closed for the cylinder to be measured.
5. Check the valve clearance. The valve clearance specifications are as follows:

- Intake: 0.006–0.010 in. (0.15–0.25mm)
- Exhaust: 0.010–0.014 in. (0.25–0.35mm)

6. If adjustment is necessary, compress the valve spring with Special Service Tool

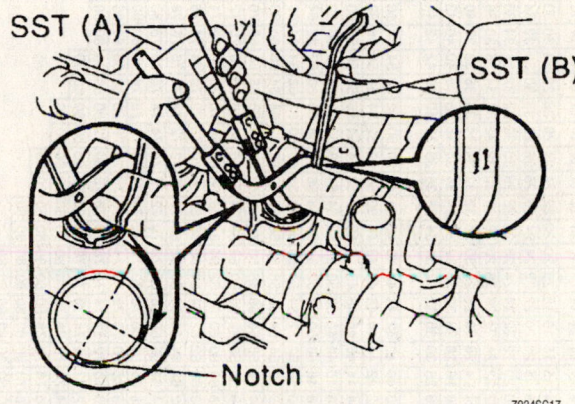

Removing and replacing valve adjustment shims—4.5L (1FZ-FE) engine

(SST) **A** and insert SST **B** to hold the valve in the open position.
7. Remove the shim and measure it.
8. Find a replacement shim in the Adjusting Shim Selection charts.
9. Remove the valve shim service tools.
10. Repeat for each valve to be adjusted.
11. Install or connect the following:

- Valve cover
- Spark plug wires
- Spark plug wire covers
- Throttle body
- TP sensor connector
- IAC valve connector
- EVAP hoses
- Water bypass hose
- Transmission cable
- Cruise control cable
- Accelerator cable
- Air intake hose
- Negative battery cable

12. Fill the cooling system.

13. Start the engine and check for leaks.

4.7L (2UZ-FE) Engine

➡**Measure valve clearance with the engine cold.**

1. Before servicing the vehicle, refer to the precautions in the beginning of this section.
2. Drain the cooling system.
3. Remove or disconnect the following:
- Negative battery cable
- Ignition coils
- Valve covers

4. Set the engine to the top of the compression stroke with the valves closed for the cylinder to be measured.
5. Check the valve clearance. The valve clearance specifications are as follows:

- Intake: 0.006–0.010 in. (0.15–0.25mm)
- Exhaust: 0.010–0.014 in. (0.25–0.35mm)

Timing belt service is covered in Section 4 of this manual

Intake valve clearance shim selection chart—4.5L (1FZ-FE) engine

Intake valve clearance (Cold):
0.15 – 0.25 mm (0.006 – 0.010 in.)

EXAMPLE:
The 2.300 mm (0.0906 in.) shim is installed, and the measured clearance is 0.440 mm (0.0173 in.). Replace the 2.300 mm (0.0906 in.) shim with a No. 54 shim.

New shim thickness — mm (in.)

Shim No.	Thickness	Shim No.	Thickness	Shim No.	Thickness
00	2.000 (0.0787)	28	2.280 (0.0898)	56	2.560 (0.1008)
02	2.020 (0.0795)	30	2.300 (0.0906)	58	2.580 (0.1016)
04	2.040 (0.0803)	32	2.320 (0.0913)	60	2.600 (0.1024)
06	2.060 (0.0811)	34	2.340 (0.0921)	62	2.620 (0.1031)
08	2.080 (0.0819)	36	2.360 (0.0929)	64	2.640 (0.1039)
10	2.100 (0.0827)	38	2.380 (0.0937)	66	2.660 (0.1047)
12	2.120 (0.0835)	40	2.400 (0.0945)	68	2.680 (0.1055)
14	2.140 (0.0843)	42	2.420 (0.0953)	70	2.700 (0.1063)
16	2.160 (0.0850)	44	2.440 (0.0961)	72	2.720 (0.1071)
18	2.180 (0.0858)	46	2.460 (0.0969)	74	2.740 (0.1079)
20	2.200 (0.0866)	48	2.480 (0.0976)	76	2.760 (0.1087)
22	2.220 (0.0874)	50	2.500 (0.0984)	78	2.780 (0.1094)
24	2.240 (0.0882)	52	2.520 (0.0992)	80	2.800 (0.1102)
26	2.260 (0.0890)	54	2.540 (0.1000)		

7924SG67

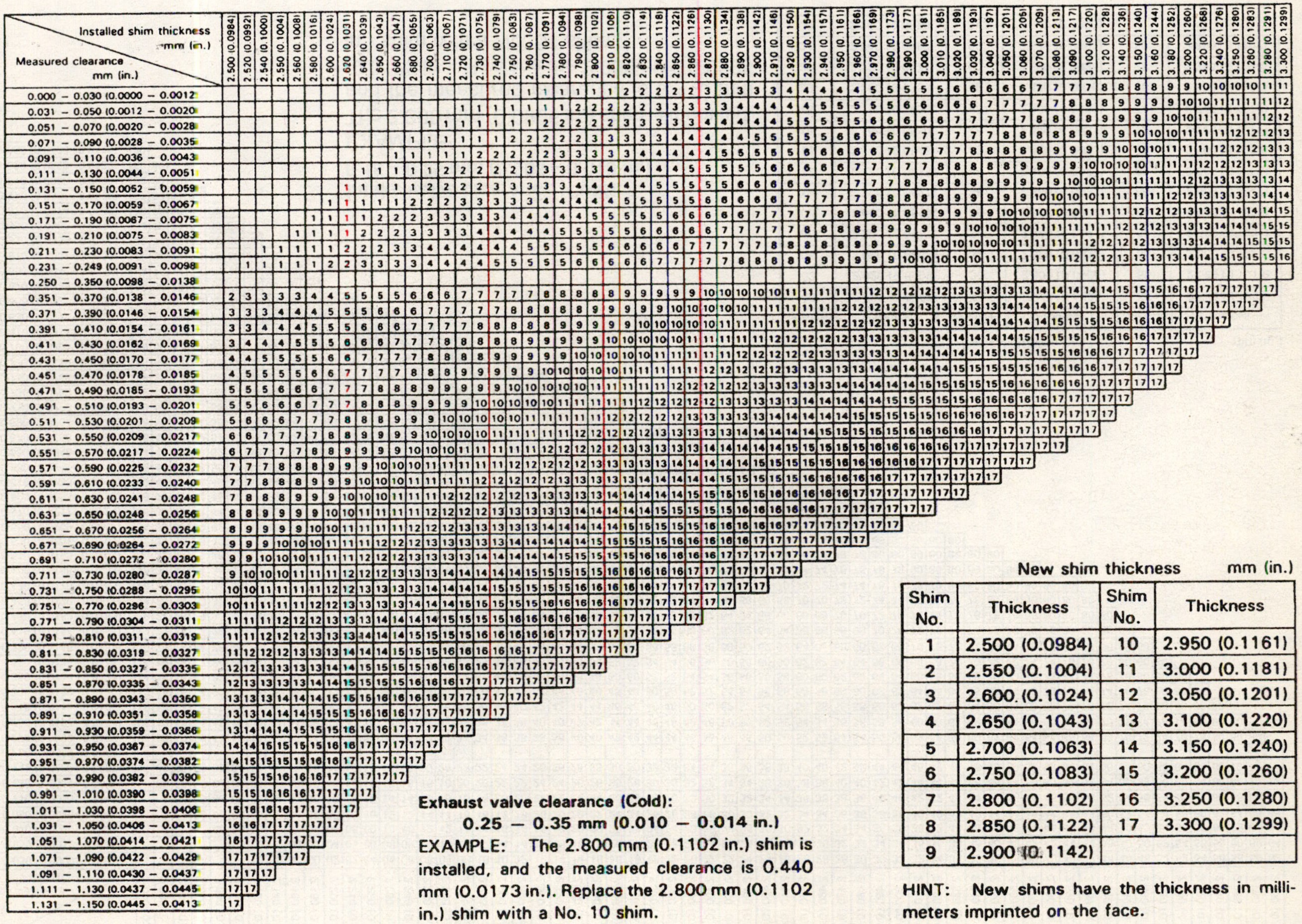

New shim thickness

Shim No.	Thickness mm (in.)	Shim No.	Thickness mm (in.)
1	2.500 (0.0984)	10	2.950 (0.1161)
2	2.550 (0.1004)	11	3.000 (0.1181)
3	2.600 (0.1024)	12	3.050 (0.1201)
4	2.650 (0.1043)	13	3.100 (0.1220)
5	2.700 (0.1063)	14	3.150 (0.1240)
6	2.750 (0.1083)	15	3.200 (0.1260)
7	2.800 (0.1102)	16	3.250 (0.1280)
8	2.850 (0.1122)	17	3.300 (0.1299)
9	2.900 (0.1142)		

HINT: New shims have the thickness in millimeters imprinted on the face.

Exhaust valve clearance (Cold):
0.25 — 0.35 mm (0.010 — 0.014 in.)

EXAMPLE: The 2.800 mm (0.1102 in.) shim is installed, and the measured clearance is 0.440 mm (0.0173 in.). Replace the 2.800 mm (0.1102 in.) shim with a No. 10 shim.

Exhaust valve clearance shim selection chart—4.5L (1FZ-FE) engine

7924SG68

Please visit our web site at www.chiltononline.com

New shim thickness

Shim No.	Thickness mm (in.)	Shim No.	Thickness mm (in.)	Shim No.	Thickness mm (in.)
00	2.000 (0.0787)	28	2.280 (0.0898)	56	2.560 (0.1008)
02	2.020 (0.0795)	30	2.300 (0.0906)	58	2.580 (0.1016)
04	2.040 (0.0803)	32	2.320 (0.0913)	60	2.600 (0.1024)
06	2.060 (0.0811)	34	2.340 (0.0921)	62	2.620 (0.1031)
08	2.080 (0.0819)	36	2.360 (0.0929)	64	2.640 (0.1039)
10	2.100 (0.0827)	38	2.380 (0.0937)	66	2.660 (0.1047)
12	2.120 (0.0835)	40	2.400 (0.0945)	68	2.680 (0.1055)
14	2.140 (0.0843)	42	2.420 (0.0953)	70	2.700 (0.1063)
16	2.160 (0.0850)	44	2.440 (0.0961)	72	2.720 (0.1071)
18	2.180 (0.0858)	46	2.460 (0.0969)	74	2.740 (0.1079)
20	2.200 (0.0866)	48	2.480 (0.0976)	76	2.760 (0.1087)
22	2.220 (0.0874)	50	2.500 (0.0984)	78	2.780 (0.1094)
24	2.240 (0.0882)	52	2.520 (0.0992)	80	2.800 (0.1102)
26	2.260 (0.0890)	54	2.540 (0.1000)		

Intake valve clearance (Cold):
0.15 – 0.25 mm (0.006 – 0.010 in.).

EXAMPLE:

The 2.300 mm (0.0906 in.) shim is installed, and the measured clearance is 0.440 mm (0.0173 in.). Replace the 2.300 mm (0.0906 in.) shim with a No. 54 shim.

Intake valve clearance shim selection chart—4.7L (2UZ-FE) engine

7924SG71

New shim thickness

mm (in.)

Shim No.	Thickness	Shim No.	Thickness	Shim No.	Thickness
00	2.000 (0.0787)	28	2.280 (0.0898)	56	2.560 (0.1008)
02	2.020 (0.0795)	30	2.300 (0.0906)	58	2.580 (0.1016)
04	2.040 (0.0803)	32	2.320 (0.0913)	60	2.600 (0.1024)
06	2.060 (0.0811)	34	2.340 (0.0921)	62	2.620 (0.1031)
08	2.080 (0.0819)	36	2.360 (0.0929)	64	2.640 (0.1039)
10	2.100 (0.0827)	38	2.380 (0.0937)	66	2.660 (0.1047)
12	2.120 (0.0835)	40	2.400 (0.0945)	68	2.680 (0.1055)
14	2.140 (0.0843)	42	2.420 (0.0953)	70	2.700 (0.1063)
16	2.160 (0.0850)	44	2.440 (0.0961)	72	2.720 (0.1071)
18	2.180 (0.0858)	46	2.460 (0.0969)	74	2.740 (0.1079)
20	2.200 (0.0866)	48	2.480 (0.0976)	76	2.760 (0.1087)
22	2.220 (0.0874)	50	2.500 (0.0984)	78	2.780 (0.1094)
24	2.240 (0.0882)	52	2.520 (0.0992)	80	2.800 (0.1102)
26	2.260 (0.0890)	54	2.540 (0.1000)		

Exhaust valve clearance (Cold):
0.25 – 0.35 mm (0.010 – 0.014 in.)

EXAMPLE:
The 2.300 mm (0.0906 in.) shim is installed, and the measured clearance is 0.440 mm (0.0173 in.). Replace the 2.300 mm (0.0906 in.) shim with a No. 44 shim.

Exhaust valve clearance shim selection chart—4.7L (2UZ-FE) engine

Installed shim thickness — mm (in.): 2.000 (0.0787) through 2.800 (0.1102)

Measured clearance — mm (in.):

Measured clearance mm (in.)
0.000–0.030 (0.0000–0.0012)
0.031–0.050 (0.0012–0.0020)
0.051–0.070 (0.0020–0.0028)
0.071–0.090 (0.0028–0.0035)
0.091–0.110 (0.0036–0.0043)
0.111–0.130 (0.0044–0.0051)
0.131–0.150 (0.0052–0.0059)
0.151–0.170 (0.0059–0.0067)
0.171–0.190 (0.0067–0.0075)
0.191–0.210 (0.0075–0.0083)
0.211–0.230 (0.0083–0.0091)
0.231–0.249 (0.0091–0.0098)
0.250–0.350 (0.0098–0.0138)
0.351–0.370 (0.0138–0.0146)
0.371–0.390 (0.0146–0.0154)
0.391–0.410 (0.0154–0.0161)
0.411–0.430 (0.0162–0.0169)
0.431–0.450 (0.0170–0.0177)
0.451–0.470 (0.0178–0.0185)
0.471–0.490 (0.0185–0.0193)
0.491–0.510 (0.0193–0.0201)
0.511–0.530 (0.0201–0.0209)
0.531–0.550 (0.0209–0.0217)
0.551–0.570 (0.0217–0.0224)
0.571–0.590 (0.0225–0.0232)
0.591–0.610 (0.0233–0.0240)
0.611–0.630 (0.0241–0.0248)
0.631–0.650 (0.0248–0.0256)
0.651–0.670 (0.0256–0.0264)
0.671–0.690 (0.0264–0.0272)
0.691–0.710 (0.0272–0.0280)
0.711–0.730 (0.0280–0.0287)
0.731–0.750 (0.0288–0.0295)
0.751–0.770 (0.0296–0.0303)
0.771–0.790 (0.0304–0.0311)
0.791–0.810 (0.0311–0.0319)
0.811–0.830 (0.0319–0.0327)
0.831–0.850 (0.0327–0.0335)
0.851–0.870 (0.0335–0.0343)
0.871–0.890 (0.0343–0.0350)
0.891–0.910 (0.0351–0.0358)
0.911–0.930 (0.0359–0.0366)
0.931–0.950 (0.0367–0.0374)
0.951–0.970 (0.0374–0.0382)
0.971–0.990 (0.0382–0.0390)
0.991–1.010 (0.0390–0.0398)
1.011–1.030 (0.0398–0.0406)
1.031–1.050 (0.0406–0.0413)
1.051–1.070 (0.0414–0.0421)
1.071–1.090 (0.0422–0.0429)
1.091–1.110 (0.0430–0.0437)
1.111–1.130 (0.0437–0.0445)
1.131–1.150 (0.0445–0.0453)

7924SG72

Refer to Section 1 for engine rebuilding specifications

6. Record the measurements for each valve.

7. When all valve clearances have been measured, remove the camshafts.

8. Remove the valve shims and measure them. Note this measurement along with the clearance measurement recorded earlier.

9. Using the valve clearance and shim thickness measurements, find replacement shims in the Adjusting Shim Selection charts.

10. Install or connect the following:
   - Replacement valve shims
   - Camshafts
   - Valve covers
   - Ignition coils
   - Negative battery cable

11. Fill the cooling system.

12. Start the engine and check for leaks.

Starter Motor

REMOVAL & INSTALLATION

4.5L (1FZ-FE) Engine

1. Before servicing the vehicle, refer to the precautions in the beginning of this section.

2. Remove or disconnect the following:
   - Negative battery cable
   - Starter wiring connectors
   - Starter motor

To install:

3. Install or connect the following:
   - Starter motor. Tighten the bolts to 29 ft. lbs. (39 Nm).
   - Starter wiring connectors. Tighten the cable nut to 86 inch lbs. (10 Nm).
   - Negative battery cable

4.7L (2UZ-FE) Engine

1. Before servicing the vehicle, refer to the precautions in the beginning of this section.

2. Drain the cooling system.

3. Relieve the fuel system pressure.

4. Remove or disconnect the following:
   - Negative battery cable
   - Engine appearance cover
   - Air intake tube
   - Intake manifold
   - Starter motor mounting bolts
   - Starter wiring connectors
   - Starter motor

To install:

5. Install or connect the following:
   - Starter motor
   - Starter wiring connectors. Tighten the cable nut to 86 inch lbs. (10 Nm).
   - Starter motor mounting bolts. Tighten the bolts to 29 ft. lbs. (39 Nm).
   - Intake manifold
   - Air intake tube
   - Engine appearance cover
   - Negative battery cable

6. Fill the cooling system.

7. Start the engine and check for leaks.

Oil Pan

REMOVAL & INSTALLATION

4.5L (1FZ-FE) Engine

1. Before servicing the vehicle, refer to the precautions in the beginning of this section.

2. Drain the engine oil.

3. Remove or disconnect the following:

   - Negative battery cable
   - Engine under covers
   - Oil cooler pipe bracket
   - Oil level sensor

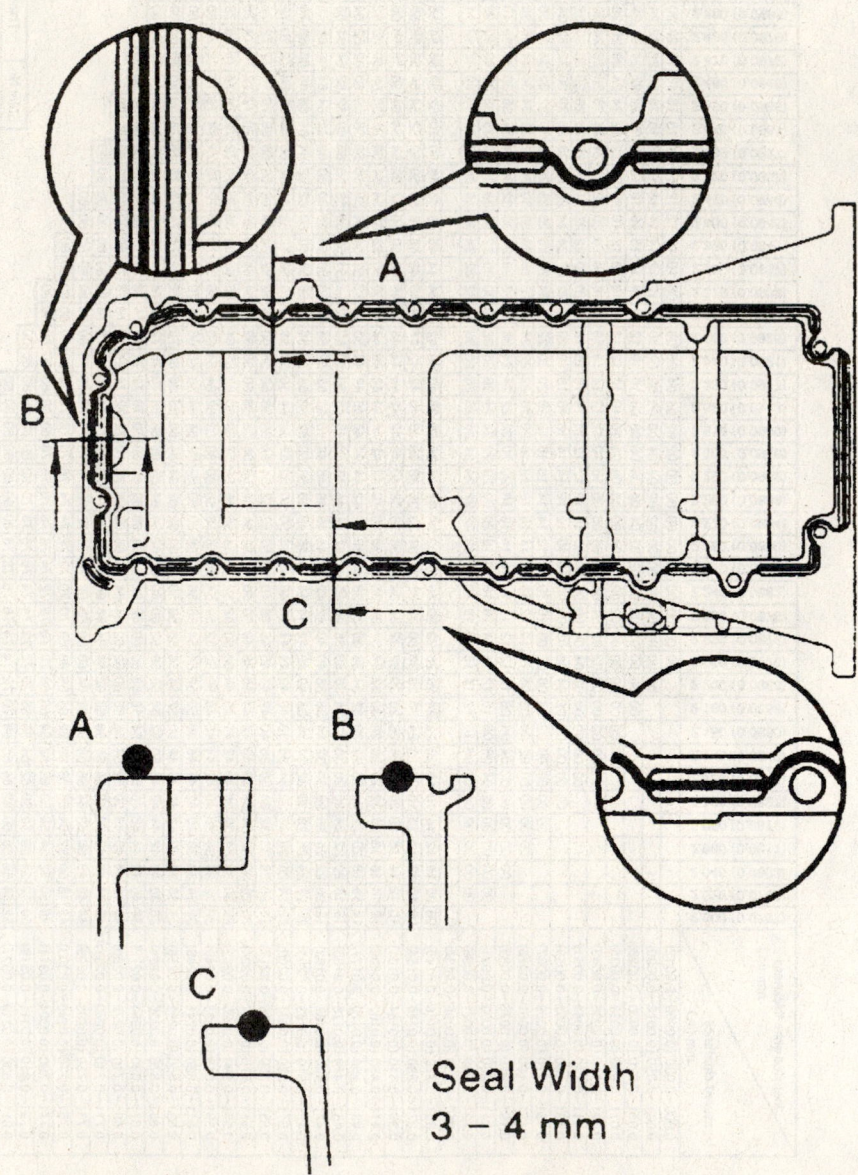

Upper oil pan sealant application—4.5L (1FZ-FE) engine

7924SG19

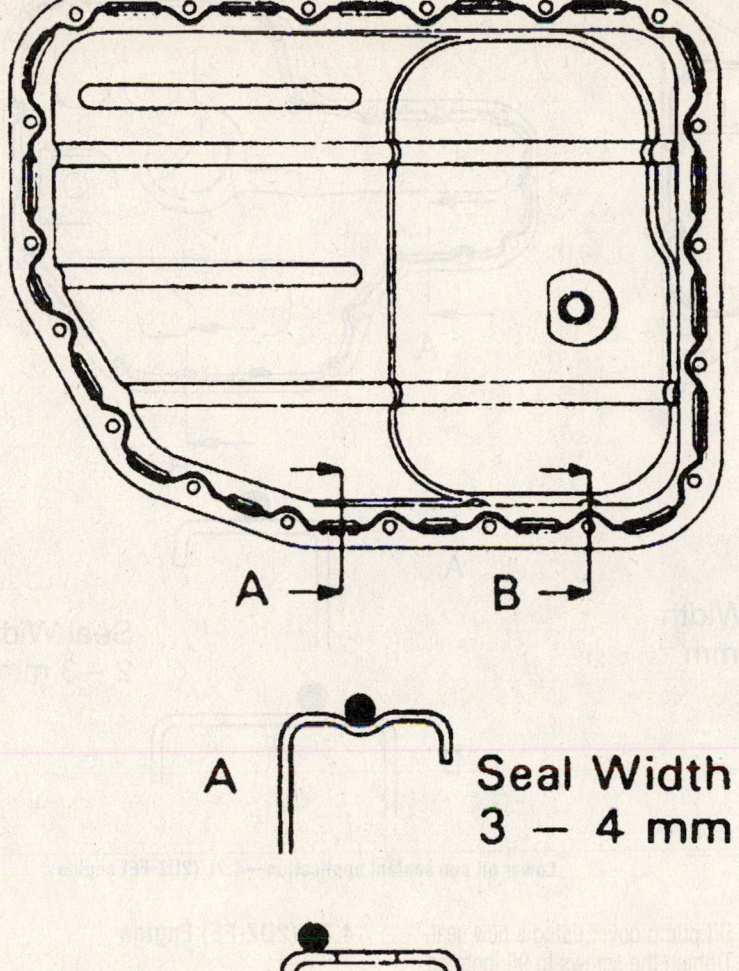

A Seal Width 3 — 4 mm

B Seal Width 2 — 3 mm

7924SG20

Lower oil pan sealant application—4.5L (1FZ-FE) engine

- Lower oil pan
- Upper oil pan

To install:

4. Apply silicone sealant to the upper oil pan as shown.

5. Install the upper oil pan and tighten the fasteners to the following specifications:
- 12mm: 14 ft. lbs. (20 Nm)
- 14mm: 32 ft. lbs. (44 Nm)
- Transmission housing bolts: 53 ft. lbs. (72 Nm)

6. Apply silicone sealant to the lower oil pan as shown.

7. Install or connect the following:
- Lower oil pan. Tighten the fasteners to 78 inch lbs. (8.8 Nm).

- Oil level sensor
- Oil cooler pipe bracket
- Engine under covers
- Negative battery cable

8. Fill the crankcase to the correct level.

9. Start the engine and check for leaks.

4.7L (2UZ-FE) Engine

1. Before servicing the vehicle, refer to the precautions in the beginning of this section.

2. Remove the engine from the vehicle and mount it on a stand.

3. Remove or disconnect the following:

- Oil dipstick tube
- Lower oil pan
- Oil pan baffle
- Upper oil pan

To install:

4. The upper oil pan bolts are different lengths and are identified as follows:
- A: 0.79 inch (20mm) w/10mm head
- B: 0.98 inch (25mm) w/12mm head
- C: 2.36 inch (60mm) w/12mm head
- D: 1.38 inch (35mm) w/10mm head

5. Apply silicone sealant to the upper oil pan as shown.

6. Install the upper oil pan and tighten the fasteners in several passes to the following specifications:
- 10mm: 66 inch lbs. (7.5 Nm)
- 12mm: 21 ft. lbs. (28 Nm)

7. Install or connect the following:

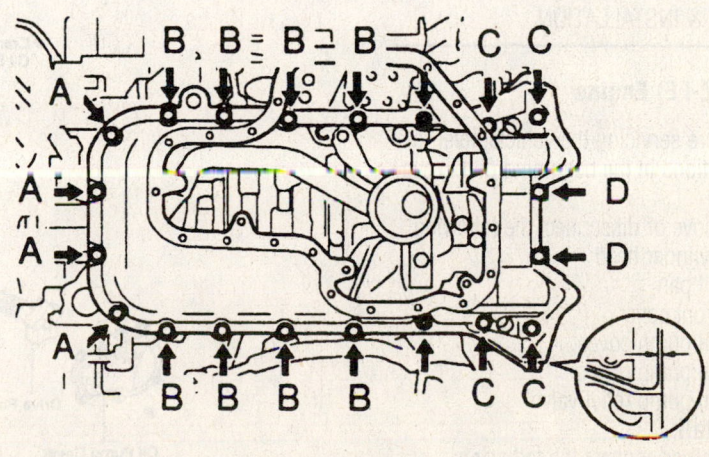

7924SG75

Upper oil pan bolt location—4.7L (2UZ-FE) engine

For engine torque specifications, refer to Section 1 of this manual

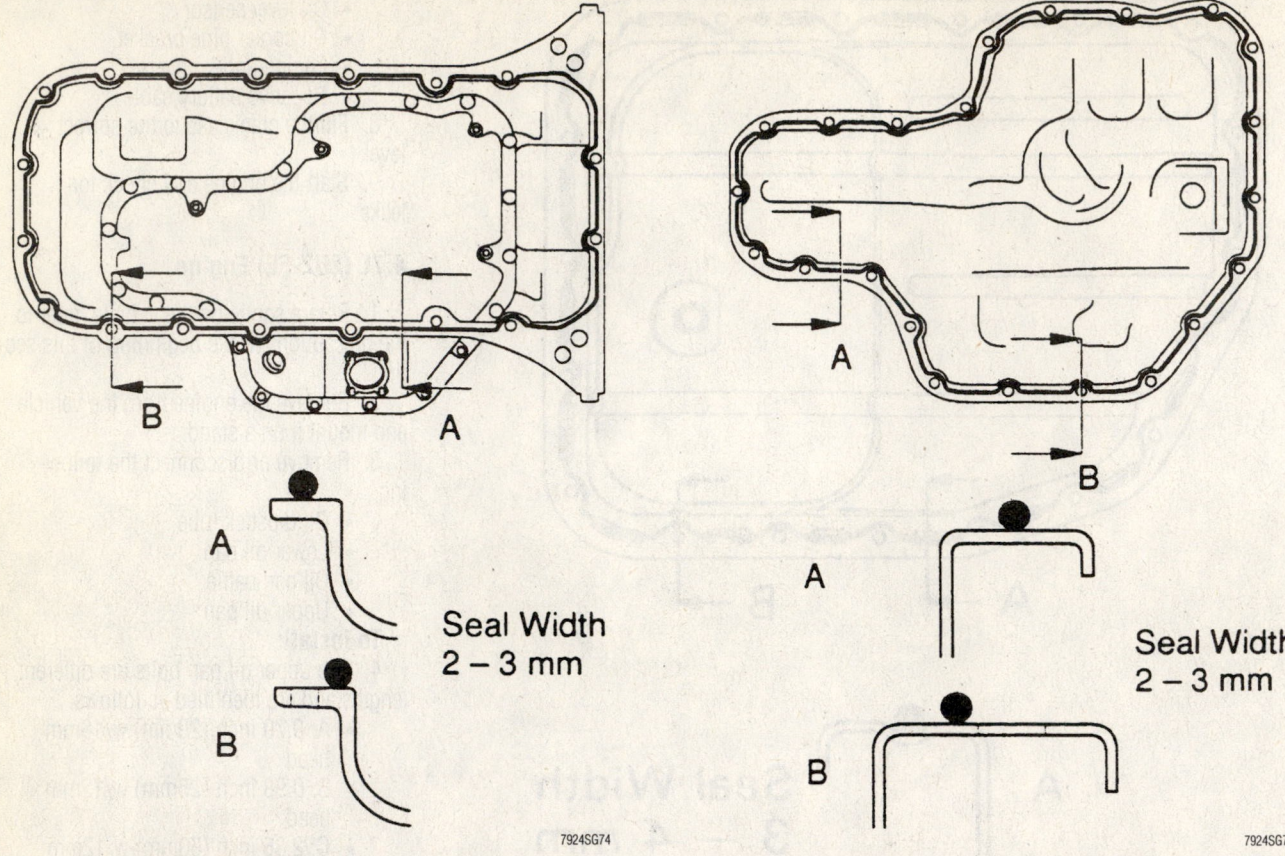

Upper oil pan sealant application—4.7L (2UZ-FE) engine

Lower oil pan sealant application—4.7L (2UZ-FE) engine

- Oil pan baffle. Tighten the fasteners to 66 inch lbs. (7.5 Nm).
- Lower oil pan. Tighten the fasteners in several passes to 66 inch lbs. (7.5 Nm).
- Oil dipstick tube
8. Install the engine.

Oil Pump

REMOVAL & INSTALLATION

4.5L (1FZ-FE) Engine

1. Before servicing the vehicle, refer to the precautions in the beginning of this section.
2. Remove or disconnect the following:
   - Cylinder head
   - Oil pan
   - Front cover
   - Oil pump cover
   - Oil pump rotors
   - Oil pump relief valve

To install:

3. Install or connect the following:
   - Oil pump relief valve. Tighten the plug to 36 ft. lbs. (49 Nm).
   - Oil pump rotors

- Oil pump cover using a new seal. Tighten the screws to 96 inch lbs. (10 Nm).
- Front cover
- Oil pan
- Cylinder head

4.7L (2UZ-FE) Engine

1. Before servicing the vehicle, refer to the precautions in the beginning of this section.
2. Remove the engine from the vehicle and mount it on a stand.

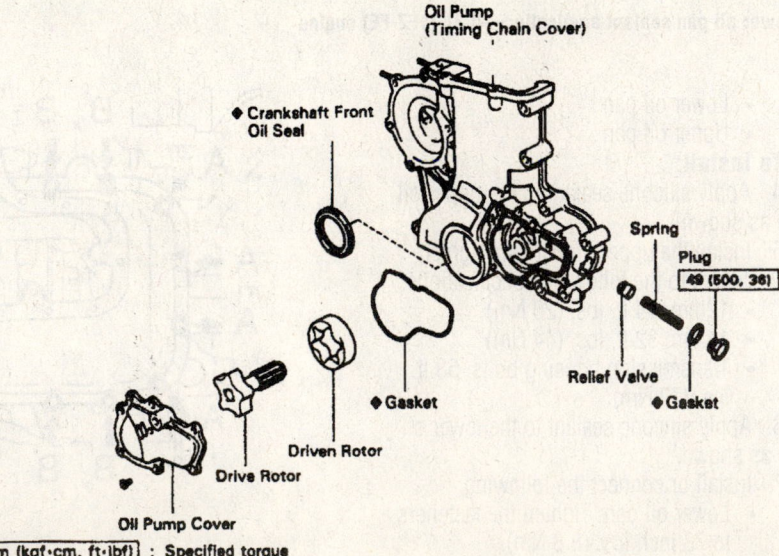

Exploded view of the oil pump components—4.5L (1FZ-FE) engine

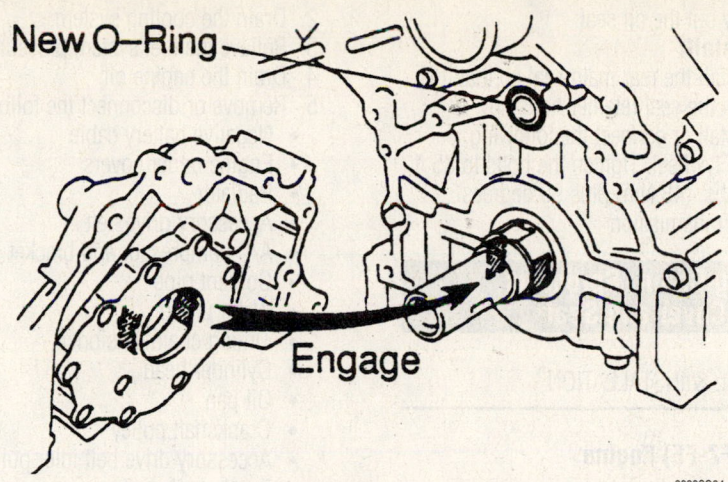

New O-Ring

Engage

9308SG04

Location of the O-ring seal—4.7L (2UZ-FE) engine

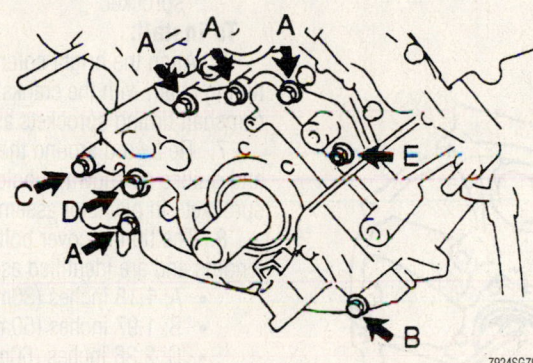

7924SG79

Oil pump bolt location—4.7L (2UZ-FE) engine

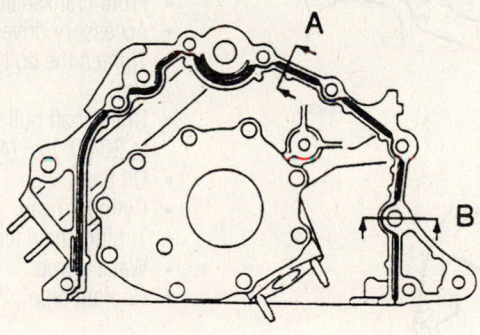

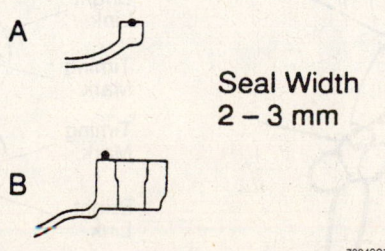

Seal Width
2 – 3 mm

7924SG78

Oil pump housing sealant application—4.7L (2UZ-FE) engine

3. Remove or disconnect the following:
  - Front cover
  - Timing belt. Refer to the Timing Belt unit repair section.
  - Timing belt idler pulleys
  - Crankshaft timing sprocket
  - Oil dipstick tube
  - Oil filter and bracket
  - Crankshaft Position (CKP) sensor
  - Oil pan and baffle
  - Oil pump pickup tube
  - Oil pump

To install:

4. The upper oil pan bolts are different lengths and are identified as follows:
  - A: 1.38 inch (35mm) w/12mm head
  - B: 1.97 inch (50mm) w/12mm head
  - C: 4.17 inch (106mm) w/12mm head
  - D: 1.57 inch (40mm) w/14mm head
  - E: 1.18 inch (30mm) w/6mm hex head

5. Install a new O-ring on the engine block.

6. Apply silicone sealant to the oil pump housing as shown.

7. Install the oil pump. Tighten the bolts in several passes to the following specifications:
  - 12mm: 11 ft. lbs. (15.5 Nm)
  - 14mm: 22 ft. lbs. (30.5 Nm)
  - 6mm Hex: 11 ft. lbs. (15.5 Nm)

8. Install or connect the following:
  - Oil pump pickup tube. Tighten the bolts to 66 inch lbs. (7.5 Nm).
  - Oil pan and baffle
  - CKP sensor
  - Oil filter and bracket. Tighten the bolts to 13 ft. lbs. (18 Nm).
  - Oil dipstick tube
  - Crankshaft timing sprocket
  - Timing belt idler pulleys
  - Timing belt
  - Front cover

9. Install the engine.

Rear Main Seal

REMOVAL & INSTALLATION

4.5L (1FZ-FE) Engine

1. Before servicing the vehicle, refer to the precautions in the beginning of this section.

2. Remove the transmission and flywheel from the vehicle.

For complete mechanical specifications, refer to Section 1 of this manual

3. Cut off the rubber lip portion of the seal with a sharp knife.

4. Pry out the oil seal.

To install:

5. Install the rear main seal so that it is flush with the seal retainer housing.

6. Install or connect the following:
- Flywheel. Tighten the bolts to 74 ft. lbs. (100 Nm).
- Transmission

4.7L (2UZ-FE) Engine

1. Before servicing the vehicle, refer to the precautions in the beginning of this section.

2. Remove the transmission and flywheel from the vehicle.

3. Cut off the rubber lip portion of the seal with a sharp knife.

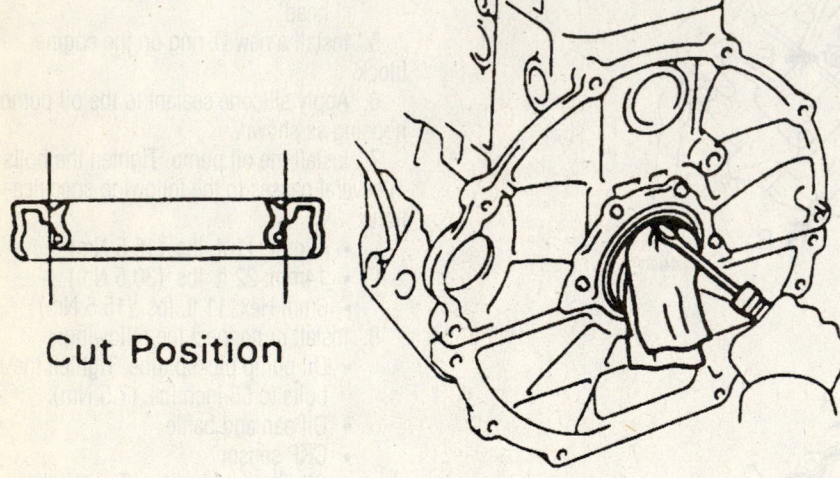

Cut Position

Rear main seal removal—4.5L (1FZ-FE) engine shown

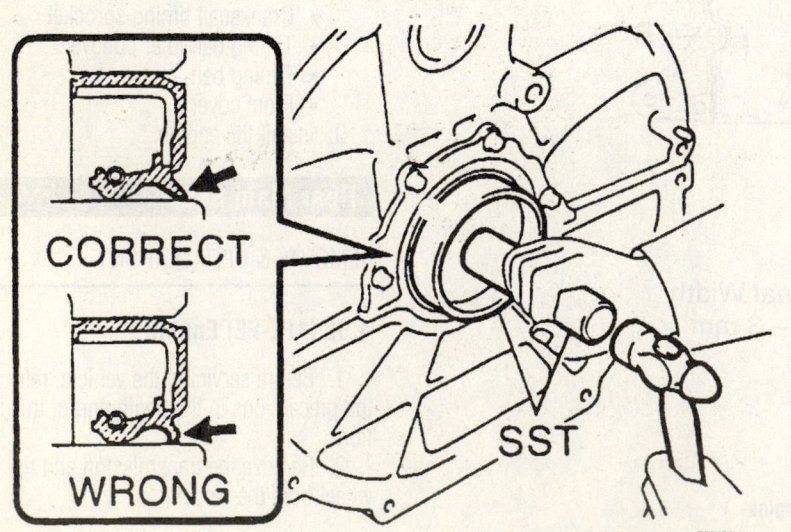

CORRECT

WRONG

SST

Rear main seal installation—4.5L (1FZ-FE) engine shown

4. Pry out the oil seal.

To install:

5. Install the rear main seal so that it is flush with the seal retainer housing.

6. Install or connect the following:
- Flywheel. Tighten the bolts to 35 ft. lbs. (48 Nm) plus 90 degrees.
- Transmission

Timing Chain, Sprockets, Front Cover and Seal

REMOVAL & INSTALLATION

4.5L (1FZ-FE) Engine

1. Before servicing the vehicle, refer to the precautions in the beginning of this section.

2. Drain the cooling system.

3. Relieve the fuel system pressure.

4. Drain the engine oil.

5. Remove or disconnect the following:
- Negative battery cable
- Engine under covers
- Radiator
- Accessory drive belt
- A/C compressor and bracket
- Coolant pipe
- Water pump
- Timing chain tensioner
- Cylinder head
- Oil pan
- Crankshaft pulley
- Accessory drive belt idler pulley
- Front crankshaft seal
- Front cover
- Timing chain and camshaft sprocket

To install:

6. Align the bright colored links of the timing chain with the crankshaft and camshaft timing sprockets as shown.

7. Tie a cord around the timing chain and guides as shown to hold the chain and sprockets in place for assembly.

8. The timing cover bolts are different lengths and are identified as follows:
- A: 1.18 inches (30mm)
- B: 1.97 inches (50mm)
- C: 2.38 inches (60mm)

9. Install or connect the following:
- Front cover. Tighten the bolts to 15 ft. lbs. (21 Nm).
- Front crankshaft seal
- Accessory drive belt idler pulley. Tighten the bolt to 32 ft. lbs. (43 Nm).
- Crankshaft pulley. Tighten the bolt to 304 ft. lbs. (412 Nm).
- Oil pan
- Cylinder head
- Timing chain tensioner
- Water pump
- Coolant pipe

Bright Link

Timing Mark

Timing Mark

Bright Link

Timing mark alignment—4.5L (1FZ-FE) engine

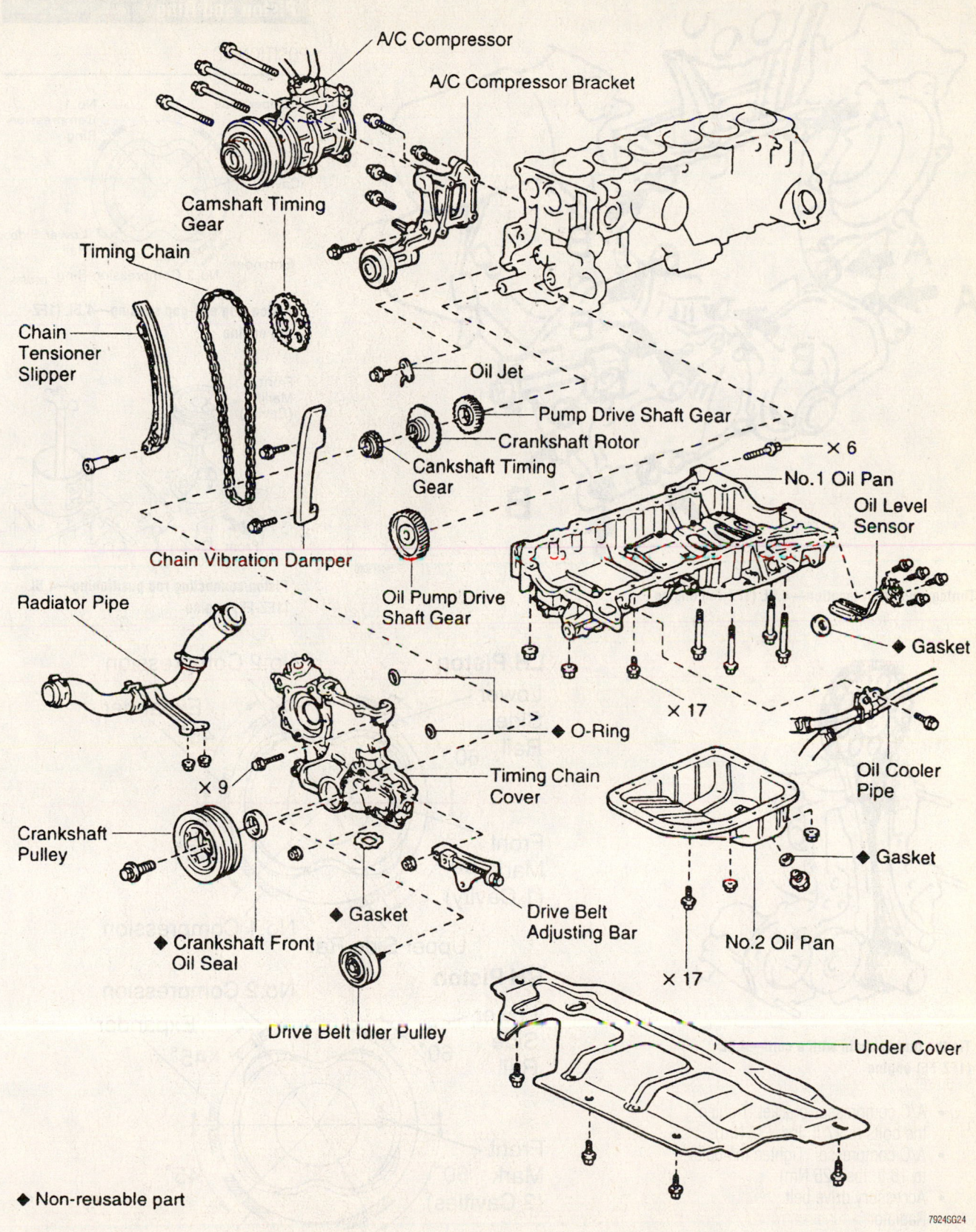

A/C Compressor

A/C Compressor Bracket

Camshaft Timing Gear

Timing Chain

Chain Tensioner Slipper

Oil Jet

Pump Drive Shaft Gear

Crankshaft Rotor

Cankshaft Timing Gear

Chain Vibration Damper

Oil Pump Drive Shaft Gear

× 6

No.1 Oil Pan

Oil Level Sensor

◆ Gasket

Radiator Pipe

× 17

◆ O-Ring

Timing Chain Cover

Oil Cooler Pipe

◆ Gasket

Crankshaft Pulley

× 9

◆ Gasket

◆ Crankshaft Front Oil Seal

Drive Belt Adjusting Bar

No.2 Oil Pan

× 17

Drive Belt Idler Pulley

Under Cover

◆ Non-reusable part

7924GG24

Exploded view of the timing chain, timing cover, oil pump and related components—4.5L (1FZ-FE) engine

Please refer to Section 8 for electric cooling fan wiring schematics

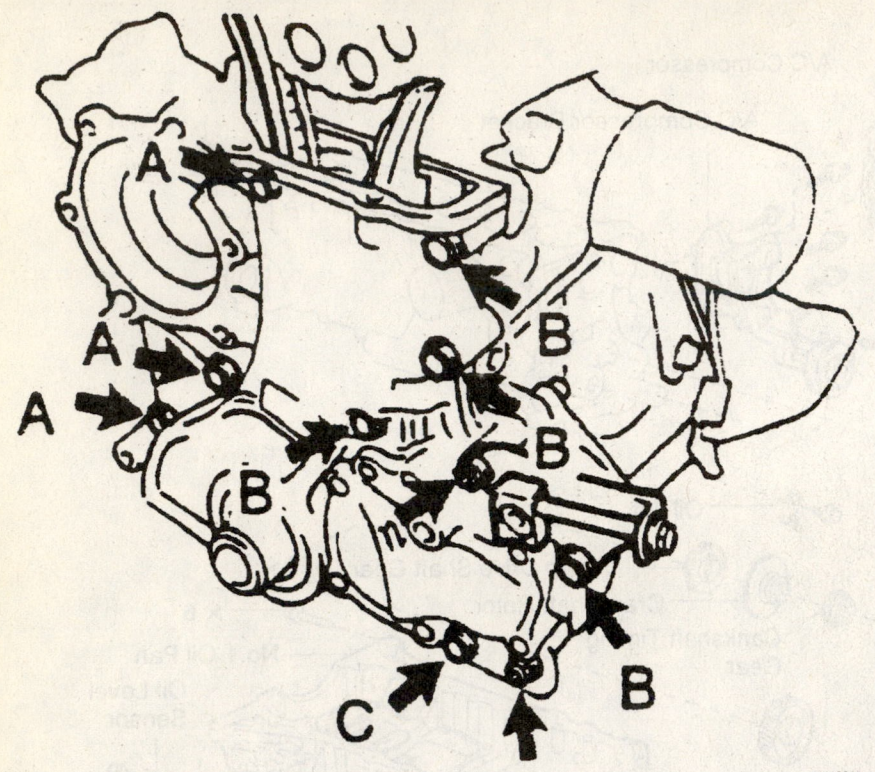

Timing cover bolt location—4.5L (1FZ-FE) engine

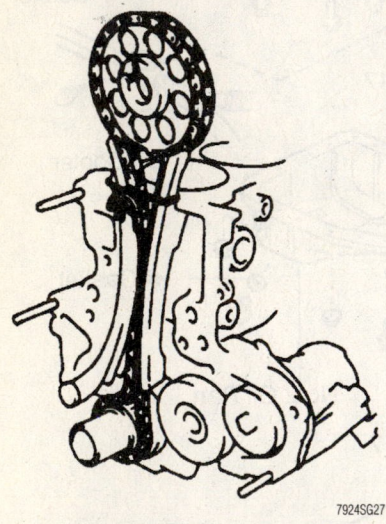

Tie the timing chain with a cord—4.5L (1FZ-FE) engine

- A/C compressor bracket. Tighten the bolts to 27 ft. lbs. (37 Nm).
- A/C compressor. Tighten the bolts to 18 ft. lbs. (25 Nm).
- Accessory drive belt
- Radiator
- Engine under covers
- Negative battery cable

10. Fill the cooling system.
11. Fill the crankcase to the correct level.
12. Start the engine and check for leaks.

Piston and Ring

POSITIONING

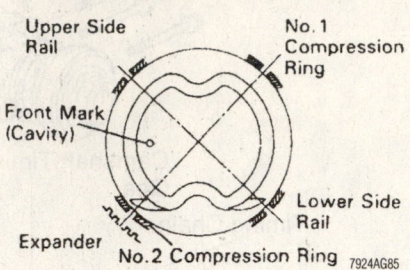

Piston ring end-gap spacing—4.5L (1FZ-FE) engine

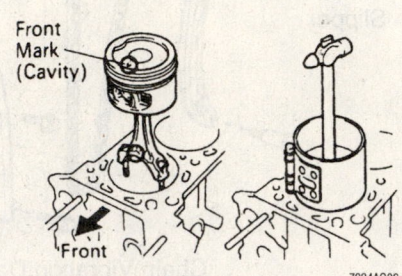

Piston/connecting rod positioning—4.5L (1FZ-FE) engine

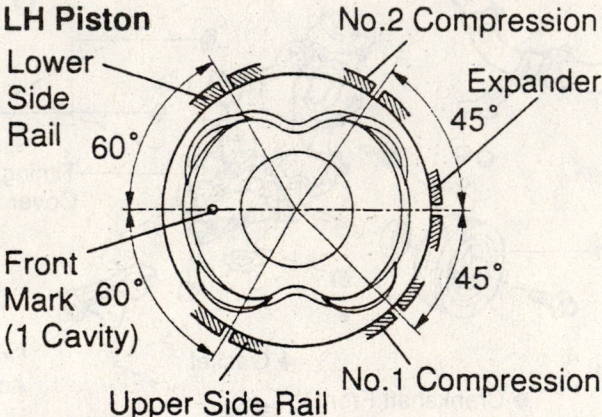

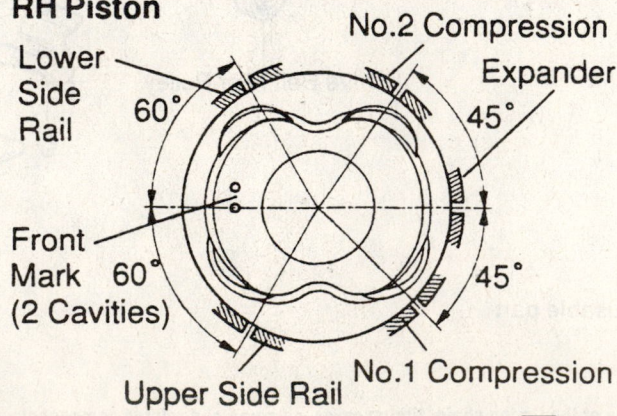

Piston ring positioning—4.7L (2UZ-FE) engine

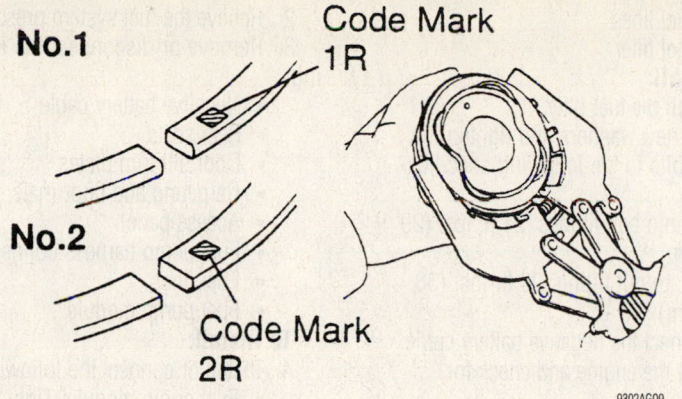

Piston ring identification—4.7L (2UZ-FE) engine

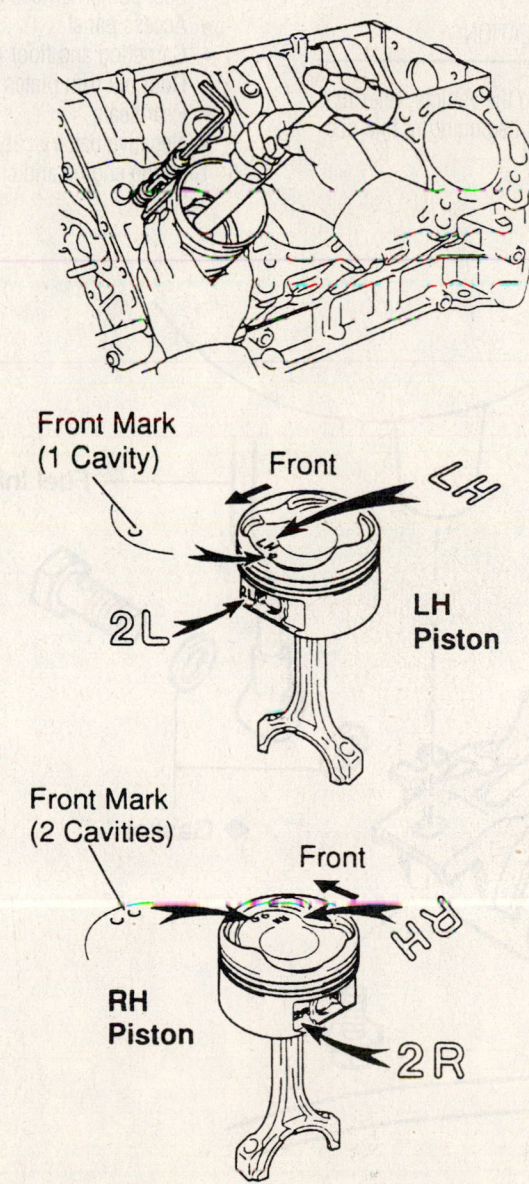

Piston positioning—4.7L (2UZ-FE) engine

FUEL SYSTEM

Fuel System Service Precautions

Safety is the most important factor when performing not only fuel system maintenance but any type of maintenance. Failure to conduct maintenance and repairs in a safe manner may result in serious personal injury or death. Maintenance and testing of the vehicle's fuel system components can be accomplished safely and effectively by adhering to the following rules and guidelines.

• To avoid the possibility of fire and personal injury, always disconnect the negative battery cable unless the repair or test procedure requires that battery voltage be applied.

• Always relieve the fuel system pressure prior to disconnecting any fuel system component (injector, fuel rail, pressure regulator, etc.), fitting or fuel line connection. Exercise extreme caution whenever relieving fuel system pressure, to avoid exposing skin, face and eyes to fuel spray. Please be advised that fuel under pressure may penetrate the skin or any part of the body that it contacts.

• Always place a shop towel or cloth around the fitting or connection prior to loosening to absorb any excess fuel due to spillage. Ensure that all fuel spillage (should it occur) is quickly removed from engine surfaces. Ensure that all fuel soaked cloths or towels are deposited into a suitable waste container.

• Always keep a dry chemical (Class B) fire extinguisher near the work area.

• Do not allow fuel spray or fuel vapors to come into contact with a spark or open flame.

• Always use a back-up wrench when loosening and tightening fuel line connection fittings. This will prevent unnecessary stress and torsion to fuel line piping.

• Always replace worn fuel fitting O-rings with new. Do not substitute fuel hose or equivalent, where fuel pipe is installed.

Fuel System Pressure

RELIEVING

1. Before servicing the vehicle, refer to the precautions in the beginning of this section.

2. Disconnect the fuel pump connector near the fuel tank.

3. Start the engine and allow it to run until it stalls. Crank the engine for a few seconds to relieve additional fuel pressure.

4. Disconnect the negative battery cable.

5. When repairs are complete, connect the negative battery cable.

Fuel Filter

REMOVAL & INSTALLATION

1. Before servicing the vehicle, refer to the precautions in the beginning of this section.

2. Relieve the fuel system pressure.

3. Remove or disconnect the following:

- Negative battery cable

- Fuel lines
- Fuel filter

To install:

4. Install the fuel filter.

5. Use new washers and tighten the fuel line bolts to the following specifications:

- Banjo bolt fittings: 21 ft. lbs. (29 Nm)
- Flare nut fitting: 28 ft. lbs. (38 Nm)

6. Connect the negative battery cable.

7. Start the engine and check for leaks.

Fuel Pump

REMOVAL & INSTALLATION

1. Before servicing the vehicle, refer to the precautions in the beginning of this section.

2. Relieve the fuel system pressure.

3. Remove or disconnect the following:

- Negative battery cable
- Rear seats
- Door sill trim plates
- Carpeting and floor mats
- Access panel
- Fuel pump harness connector
- Fuel lines
- Fuel pump module

To install:

4. Install or connect the following:

- Fuel pump module. Tighten the bolts to 35 inch lbs. (4 Nm).
- Fuel lines
- Fuel pump harness connector
- Access panel
- Carpeting and floor mats
- Door sill trim plates
- Rear seats
- Negative battery cable

5. Start the engine and check for leaks.

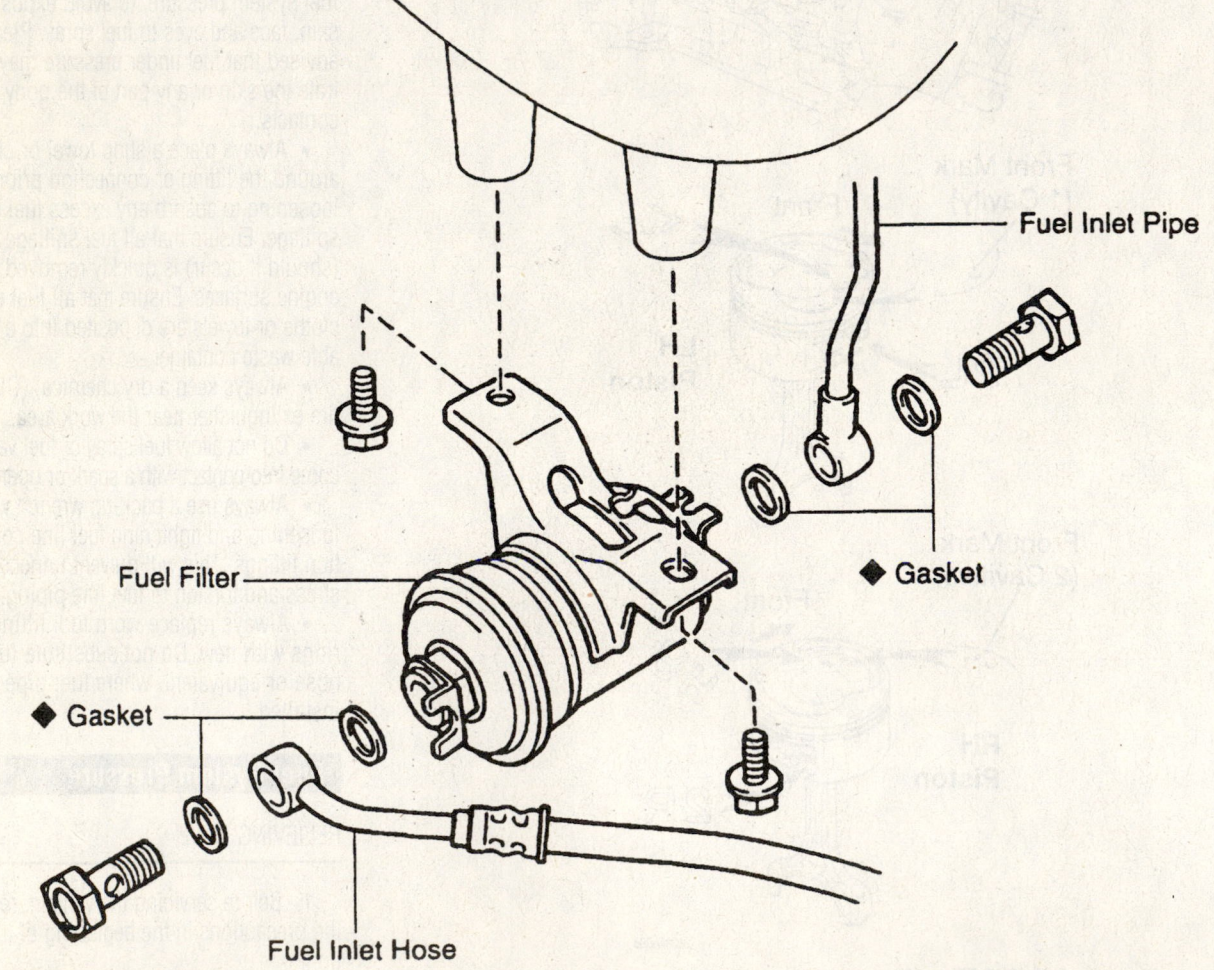

Fuel Inlet Pipe

◆ Gasket

Fuel Filter

◆ Gasket

Fuel Inlet Hose

◆ Non-reusable part

Always use new gaskets when replacing the fuel filter

7924SG28

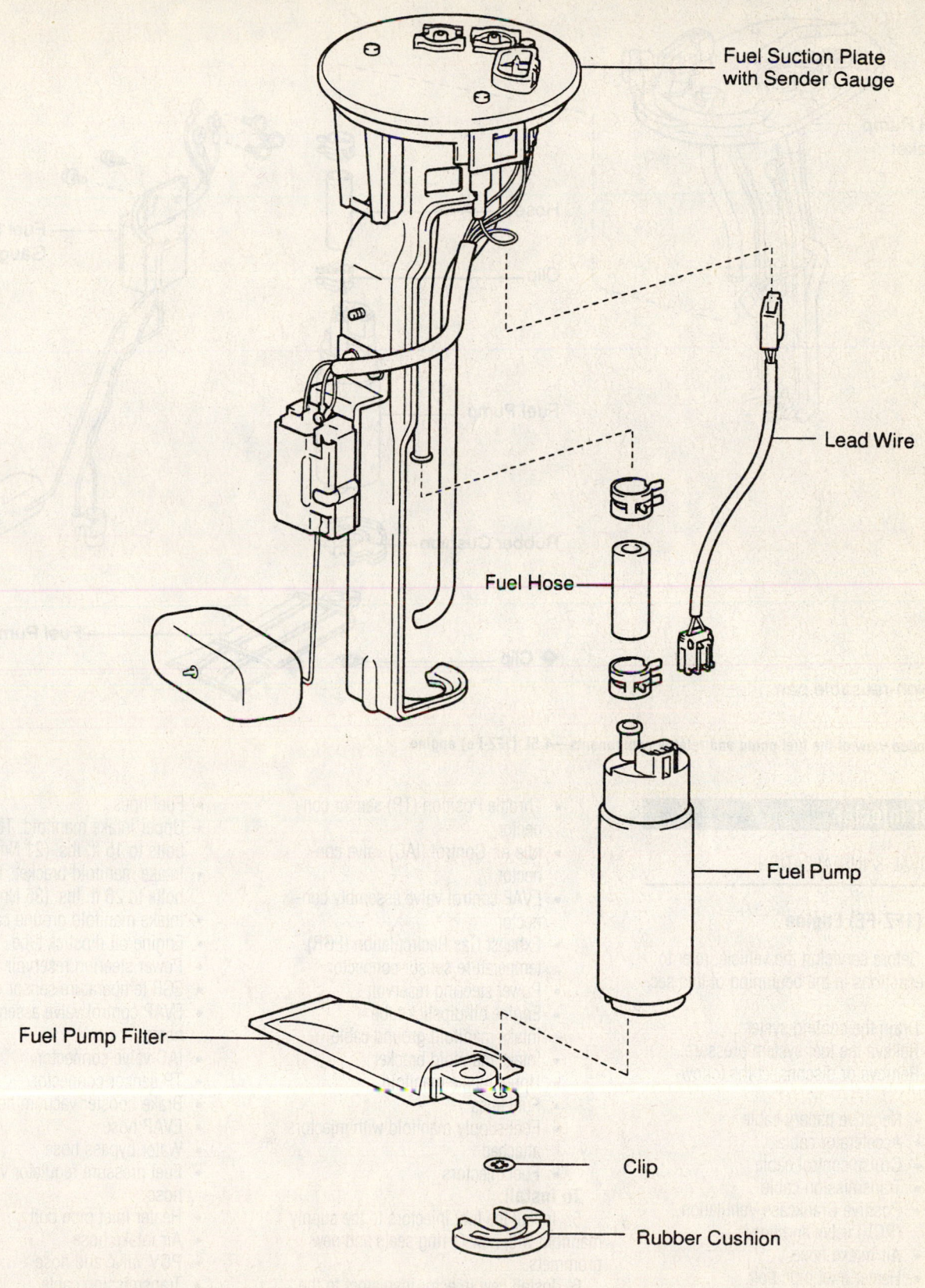

Fuel Suction Plate
with Sender Gauge

Lead Wire

Fuel Hose

Fuel Pump

Fuel Pump Filter

Clip

Rubber Cushion

◆ Non—reusable part

7924SG81

Exploded view of the fuel pump and related components—4.7L (2UZ-Fe) engine

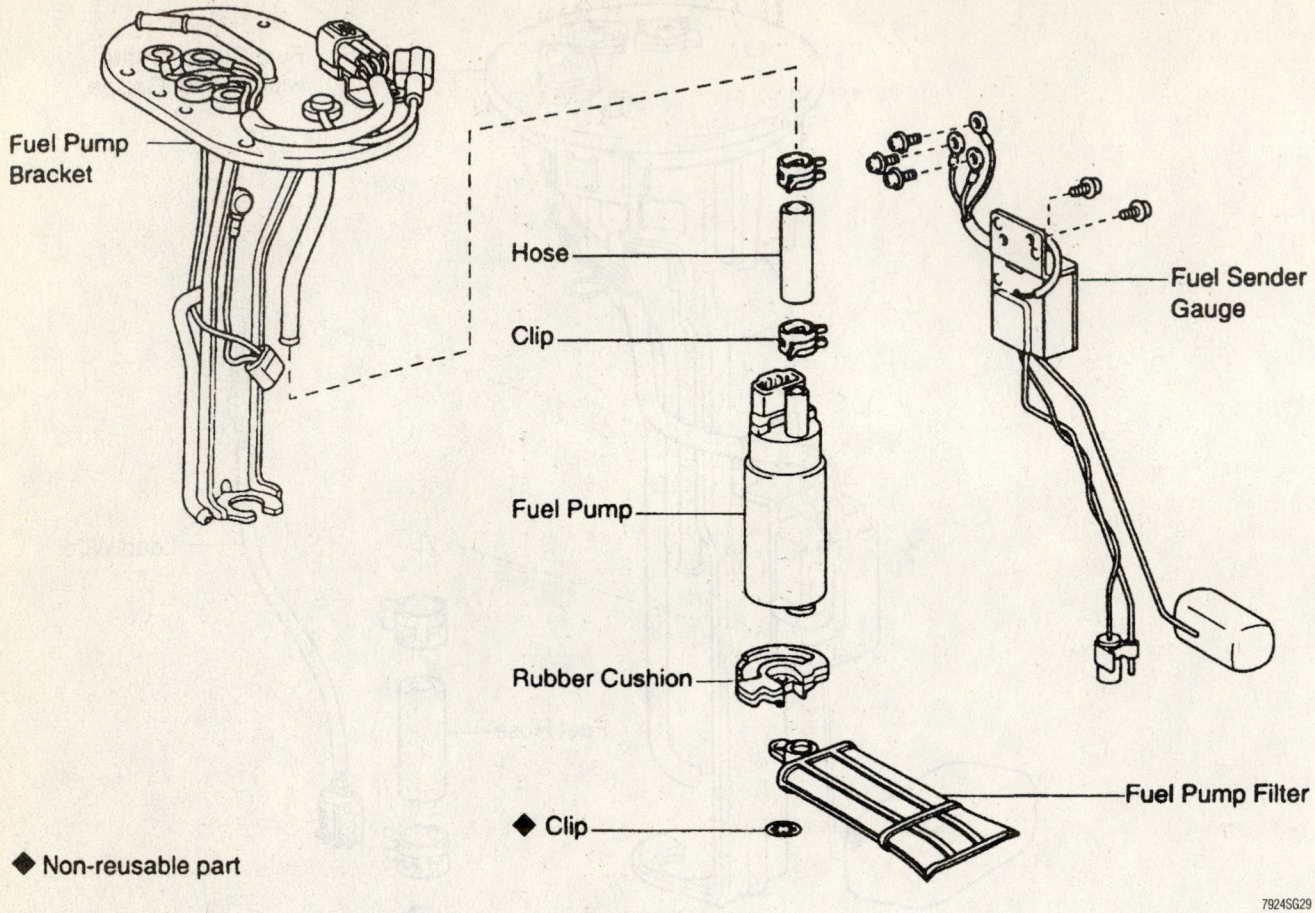

Fuel Pump Bracket

Hose

Clip

Fuel Pump

Rubber Cushion

◆ Clip

Fuel Sender Gauge

Fuel Pump Filter

◆ Non-reusable part

7924SG29

Exploded view of the fuel pump and related components—4.5L (1FZ-Fe) engine

Fuel Injector

REMOVAL & INSTALLATION

4.5L (1FZ-FE) Engine

1. Before servicing the vehicle, refer to the precautions in the beginning of this section.
2. Drain the cooling system.
3. Relieve the fuel system pressure.
4. Remove or disconnect the following:

- Negative battery cable
- Accelerator cable
- Cruise control cable
- Transmission cable
- Positive Crankcase Ventilation (PCV) valve and hose
- Air intake hose
- Heater inlet pipe bolt
- Fuel pressure regulator vacuum hose
- Water bypass hose
- Evaporative Emissions (EVAP) hose
- Brake booster vacuum hose
- Throttle Position (TP) sensor connector
- Idle Air Control (IAC) valve connector
- EVAP control valve assembly connector
- Exhaust Gas Recirculation (EGR) temperature sensor connector
- Power steering reservoir
- Engine oil dipstick tube
- Intake manifold ground cable
- Intake manifold bracket
- Upper intake manifold
- Fuel lines
- Fuel supply manifold with injectors attached
- Fuel injectors

To install:

5. Install the fuel injectors to the supply manifold with new O-ring seals and new grommets.

6. Install new injector insulators to the lower intake manifold.

7. Install or connect the following:

- Fuel supply manifold with injectors attached. Tighten the bolts to 15 ft. lbs. (21 Nm).
- Fuel lines
- Upper intake manifold. Tighten the bolts to 15 ft. lbs. (21 Nm).
- Intake manifold bracket. Tighten the bolts to 26 ft. lbs. (36 Nm).
- Intake manifold ground cable
- Engine oil dipstick tube
- Power steering reservoir
- EGR temperature sensor connector
- EVAP control valve assembly connector
- IAC valve connector
- TP sensor connector
- Brake booster vacuum hose
- EVAP hose
- Water bypass hose
- Fuel pressure regulator vacuum hose
- Heater inlet pipe bolt
- Air intake hose
- PCV valve and hose
- Transmission cable
- Cruise control cable
- Accelerator cable
- Negative battery cable

8. Fill the cooling system.
9. Start the engine and check for leaks.

4.7L (2UZ-FE) Engine

1. Before servicing the vehicle, refer to the precautions in the beginning of this section.

2. Relieve the fuel system pressure.

3. Remove or disconnect the following:

- Negative battery cable
- Engine appearance cover
- Air intake tube
- Fuel lines
- Fuel pulsation damper
- Fuel pressure regulator vacuum line
- Accelerator cable and bracket
- Positive Crankcase Ventilation (PCV) valve and hose
- Evaporative Emissions (EVAP) vacuum switching valve
- Engine appearance cover brackets
- Fuel injector harness connectors
- Engine harness protector
- Fuel supply manifold crossover pipe
- Fuel supply manifolds with injectors attached
- Fuel injectors

To install:

4. Install the fuel injectors to the supply manifold with new O-ring seals and new grommets.

5. Install new injector insulators to the intake manifold.

6. Install or connect the following:

- Fuel supply manifolds with injectors attached. Tighten the bolts to 66 inch lbs. (7.5 Nm).
- Fuel supply manifold crossover pipe. Tighten the bolts to 29 ft. lbs. (39 Nm).
- Engine harness protector
- Fuel injector harness connectors
- Engine appearance cover brackets
- EVAP vacuum switching valve
- PCV valve and hose
- Accelerator cable and bracket
- Fuel pressure regulator vacuum line
- Fuel pulsation damper
- Fuel lines
- Air intake tube
- Engine appearance cover
- Negative battery cable

7. Start the engine and check for leaks.

DRIVE TRAIN

Transmission Assembly

REMOVAL & INSTALLATION

1997 Models

1. Before servicing the vehicle, refer to the precautions in the beginning of this section.

2. Remove or disconnect the following:

- Battery and tray
- Cooling fan shroud
- Throttle valve cable
- Center console
- Gear select lever
- Transfer case lever
- Vehicle Speed (VSS) sensor connectors
- Park/Neutral Position (PNP) switch connector
- Solenoid harness connector
- Transmission fluid temperature sensor connector
- Center differential lock indicator switch connector
- L4 solenoid valve position switch connector
- Transfer case vent hose
- Front and rear driveshafts
- Transmission dipstick tube
- Transmission oil cooler lines
- Stabilizer bar brackets
- Engine under cover
- Torque converter
- Exhaust front pipe
- Starter motor
- Transmission mount crossmember. Support the transmission with a jack.
- Transmission oil cooler line bracket
- Transmission wiring harness
- Transmission flange bolts
- Transmission

To install:

3. Install or connect the following:

- Transmission. Tighten the flange bolts to 53 ft. lbs. (72 Nm).
- Transmission wiring harness
- Transmission oil cooler line bracket
- Transmission mount crossmember.

Tighten the bolts to 45 ft. lbs. (61 Nm) and the nuts to 54 ft. lbs. (74 Nm).

- Starter motor. Tighten the bolts to 29 ft. lbs. (39 Nm).
- Exhaust front pipe
- Torque converter. Tighten the bolts to 40 ft. lbs. (55 Nm).
- Engine under cover
- Stabilizer bar brackets. Tighten the bolts to 13 ft. lbs. (18 Nm).
- Transmission oil cooler lines
- Transmission dipstick tube
- Front driveshaft. Tighten the fasteners to 54 ft. lbs. (74 Nm).
- Rear driveshaft. Tighten the fasteners to 65 ft. lbs. (88 Nm).
- Transfer case vent hose
- L4 solenoid valve position switch connector
- Center differential lock indicator switch connector
- Transmission fluid temperature sensor connector
- Solenoid harness connector
- PNP switch connector
- VSS sensor connectors
- Transfer case lever
- Gear select lever
- Center console
- Throttle valve cable
- Cooling fan shroud
- Battery and tray

4. Check the transmission and transfer case fluid levels and adjust as necessary.

1998–01 Models

1. Before servicing the vehicle, refer to the precautions in the beginning of this section.

2. Remove or disconnect the following:

- Battery and tray
- Air intake assembly
- Cooling fan and shroud
- Coolant recovery reservoir
- Transmission dipstick tube
- Center console
- Transmission gear select lever and rod
- Transfer case shift lever and rod
- Engine under covers
- Exhaust front pipes
- Front and rear driveshafts
- Vehicle Speed (VSS) sensor connectors

- Overdrive clutch speed sensor connector
- Solenoid harness connector
- Transmission fluid temperature sensor connector
- Park/Neutral Position (PNP) switch connector
- Center differential lock indicator switch connector
- L4 solenoid valve position switch connector
- Motor actuator connector
- Torque converter
- Transmission oil cooler lines
- Transmission mount crossmember. Support the transmission with a jack.
- Transmission flange bolts
- Transmission

To install:

3. Install or connect the following:
- Transmission. Tighten the flange bolts to 53 ft. lbs. (72 Nm).
- Transmission mount crossmember. Tighten the bolts to 37 ft. lbs. (50 Nm) and the nuts to 54 ft. lbs. (74 Nm).
- Transmission oil cooler lines
- Torque converter. Tighten the bolts to 35 ft. lbs. (48 Nm).
- Motor actuator connector
- L4 solenoid valve position switch connector
- Center differential lock indicator switch connector
- PNP switch connector
- Transmission fluid temperature sensor connector
- Solenoid harness connector
- Overdrive clutch speed sensor connector
- VSS sensor connectors
- Front driveshaft. Tighten the fasteners to 59 ft. lbs. (80 Nm).
- Rear driveshaft. Tighten the fasteners to 78 ft. lbs. (106 Nm).
- Exhaust front pipes
- Engine under covers
- Transfer case shift lever and rod
- Transmission gear select lever and rod
- Center console
- Transmission dipstick tube
- Coolant recovery reservoir
- Cooling fan and shroud
- Air intake assembly
- Battery and tray

4. Check the transmission and transfer case fluid levels and adjust as necessary.

Transfer Case Assembly

REMOVAL & INSTALLATION

1997 Models

1. Before servicing the vehicle, refer to the precautions in the beginning of this section.
2. Drain the transfer case oil.
3. Remove or disconnect the following:

- Front and rear driveshafts
- Transfer case shift lever rod
- Ground cable
- Transmission mount crossmember. Support the transmission with a jack.
- Transfer case vent hose
- Vehicle Speed (VSS) sensor connector
- Center differential lock indicator switch connector
- Transfer case adapter bolts
- Transfer case

To install:
4. Install or connect the following:
- Transfer case. Tighten the adapter bolts to 51 ft. lbs. (69 Nm).
- Center differential lock indicator switch connector
- VSS sensor connector
- Transfer case vent hose
- Transmission mount crossmember. Tighten the bolts to 45 ft. lbs. (61 Nm) and the nuts to 54 ft. lbs. (74 Nm).
- Ground cable
- Transfer case shift lever rod
- Front driveshaft. Tighten the fasteners to 54 ft. lbs. (74 Nm).
- Rear driveshaft. Tighten the fasteners to 65 ft. lbs. (88 Nm).

5. Fill the transfer case to the correct level.

1998–01 Models

1. Before servicing the vehicle, refer to the precautions in the beginning of this section.
2. Drain the transfer case oil.
3. Remove or disconnect the following:

- Transfer case protector
- Front and rear driveshafts
- Transfer case shift lever rod
- Ground cable
- Transmission mount crossmember. Support the transmission with a jack.

- Transfer case vent hose
- Vehicle Speed (VSS) sensor connector
- Center differential lock indicator switch connector
- Motor actuator connectors
- Transfer case adapter bolts
- Transfer case

To install:
4. Install or connect the following:
- Transfer case. Tighten the adapter bolts to 51 ft. lbs. (69 Nm).
- Motor actuator connectors
- Center differential lock indicator switch connector
- VSS sensor connector
- Transfer case vent hose
- Transmission mount crossmember. Tighten the bolts to 37 ft. lbs. (50 Nm) and the nuts to 54 ft. lbs. (74 Nm).
- Ground cable
- Transfer case shift lever rod
- Front driveshaft. Tighten the fasteners to 59 ft. lbs. (80 Nm).
- Rear driveshaft. Tighten the fasteners to 78 ft. lbs. (106 Nm).
- Transfer case protector

5. Fill the transfer case to the correct level.

Halfshaft

REMOVAL & INSTALLATION

1998–01 Models

1. Before servicing the vehicle, refer to the precautions in the beginning of this section.
2. Remove or disconnect the following:

- Front wheel
- Brake caliper
- Grease cap
- Snapring
- Wheel speed sensor and wire harness
- Steering knuckle arm
- Lower ball joint
- Upper ball joint
- Steering knuckle
- Axle halfshaft

To install:

➡ **Use new split pins, snaprings and circlips for assembly.**

3. Install or connect the following:
- Axle halfshaft
- Steering knuckle

LH side:

RH side:

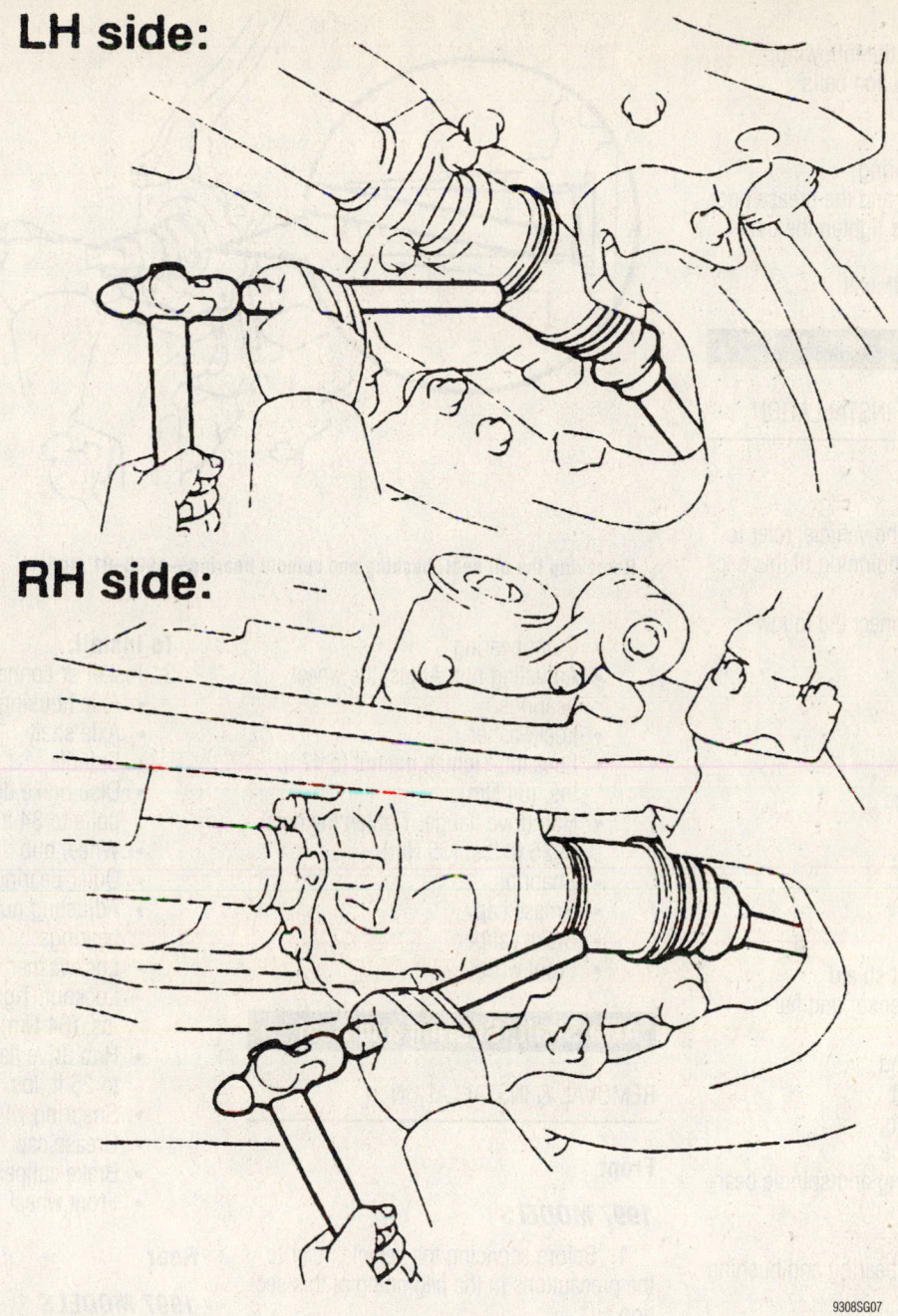

9308SG07

Axle halfshaft removal—1998–01 models

- Upper ball joint. Tighten the nut to 81 ft. lbs. (110 Nm).
- Lower ball joint. Tighten the nut to 117 ft. lbs. (159 Nm).
- Steering knuckle arm. Tighten the bolts to 108 ft. lbs. (147 Nm).
- Wheel speed sensor and wire harness
- Snapring
- Grease cap
- Brake caliper
- Front wheel

CV-Joints

OVERHAUL

1998–01 Models

OUTER CV-JOINT

The outer CV-joint is serviced with the axle shaft as an assembly. The outer CV-joint boot can be serviced by removing the inner CV-joint.

INNER CV-JOINT

1. Before servicing the vehicle, refer to the precautions in the beginning of this section.

2. Remove or disconnect the following:

- Halfshaft from the vehicle
- Grease boot clamps
- Outer race snapring
- Outer race
- Shaft snapring
- Inner race, cage and balls

Please visit our web site at www.chiltononline.com

To install:

3. Install or connect the following:
- Inner race, cage and balls
- Shaft snapring
- Outer race
- Outer race snapring

4. Fill the outer race and the grease boot with CV-joint grease and tighten the boot clamps.

5. Install the axle halfshaft.

Spindle Bearings

REMOVAL, PACKING & INSTALLATION

1998–01 Models

1. Before servicing the vehicle, refer to the precautions in the beginning of this section.

2. Remove or disconnect the following:
- Front wheel
- Brake caliper
- Grease cap
- Snapring
- Hub drive flange
- Locknut
- Lockwasher
- Adjusting nut
- Outer bearing
- Wheel hub
- Disc brake dust shield
- Wheel speed sensor and harness
- Outer tie rod end
- Upper ball joint
- Lower ball joint
- Steering knuckle
- Oil seal, bushing and spindle bearing

To install:

3. Coat the spindle bearing and bushing with lithium grease.

4. Fill the spindle cavity with lithium grease.

5. Press the spindle bearing and bushing into the spindle.

6. Install or connect the following:
- Oil seal
- Steering knuckle
- Upper ball joint. Tighten the nut to 81 ft. lbs. (110 Nm).
- Lower ball joint. Tighten the nut to 117 ft. lbs. (159 Nm).
- Outer tie rod end. Tighten the nut to 91 ft. lbs. (122 Nm).
- Wheel speed sensor and harness
- Disc brake dust shield. Tighten the bolts to 13 ft. lbs. (18 Nm).
- Wheel hub

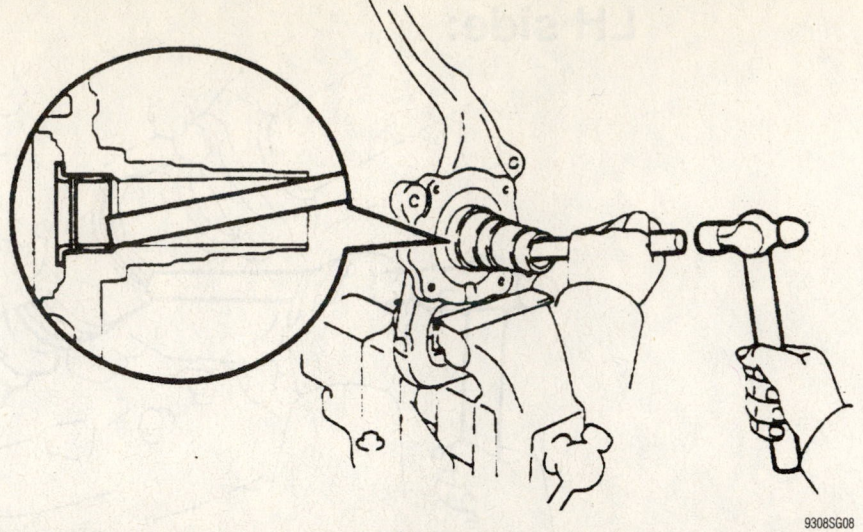

Removing the oil seal, bushing and spindle bearing—1998–01 models

- Outer bearing
- Adjusting nut. Adjust the wheel bearings.
- Lockwasher
- Locknut. Tighten the nut to 47 ft. lbs. (64 Nm).
- Hub drive flange. Tighten the nuts to 26 ft. lbs. (35 Nm).
- Snapring
- Grease cap
- Brake caliper
- Front wheel

Axle Shaft, Bearing and Seal

REMOVAL & INSTALLATION

Front

1997 MODELS

1. Before servicing the vehicle, refer to the precautions in the beginning of this section.

2. Remove or disconnect the following:
- Front wheel
- Brake caliper
- Grease cap
- Snapring
- Hub drive flange
- Locknut
- Lockwasher
- Adjusting nut
- Outer bearing
- Wheel hub
- Disc brake dust shield
- Spindle
- Axle shaft
- Axle housing oil seal

To install:

3. Install or connect the following:
- Axle housing oil seal
- Axle shaft
- Spindle
- Disc brake dust shield. Tighten the bolts to 34 ft. lbs. (47 Nm).
- Wheel hub
- Outer bearing
- Adjusting nut. Adjust the wheel bearings.
- Lockwasher
- Locknut. Tighten the nut to 47 ft. lbs. (64 Nm).
- Hub drive flange. Tighten the nuts to 26 ft. lbs. (35 Nm).
- Snapring
- Grease cap
- Brake caliper
- Front wheel

Rear

1997 MODELS

1. Before servicing the vehicle, refer to the precautions in the beginning of this section.

2. Remove or disconnect the following:
- Rear wheel
- Axle shaft
- Brake caliper and rotor
- Wheel speed sensor
- Axle bearing locknut screws
- Locknut and lockplate
- Outer bearing
- Axle hub
- Oil seal and inner bearing

To install:

3. Pack the wheel bearings with grease.

4. Fill the hub cavity with grease.

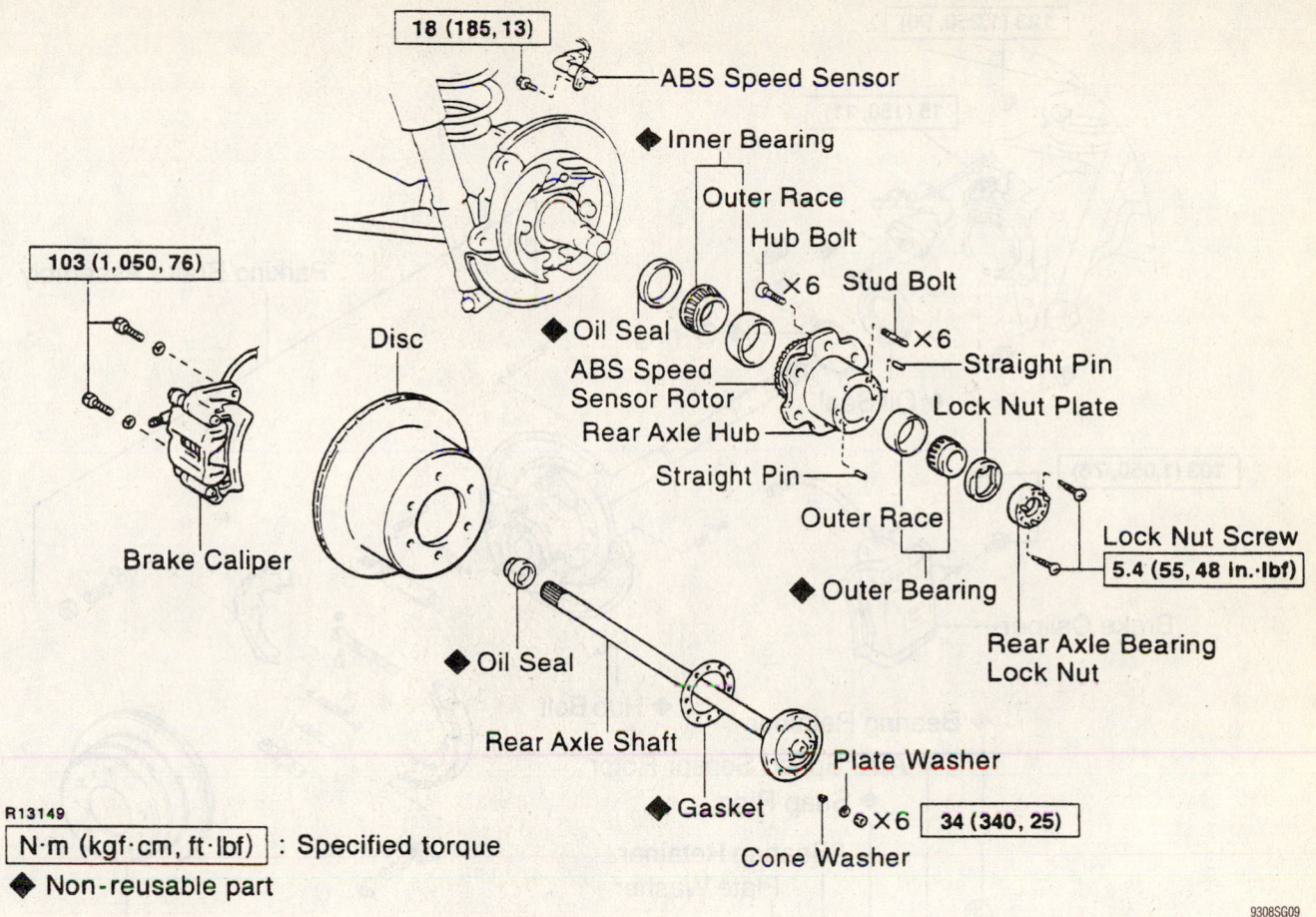

18 (185, 13) — ABS Speed Sensor

103 (1,050, 76)

◆ Inner Bearing

Outer Race
Hub Bolt
×6
Stud Bolt
×6
Straight Pin

◆ Oil Seal

ABS Speed
Sensor Rotor
Rear Axle Hub
Straight Pin
Outer Race

Lock Nut Plate

Lock Nut Screw
5.4 (55, 48 in.·lbf)

◆ Outer Bearing

Rear Axle Bearing
Lock Nut

Disc

Brake Caliper

◆ Oil Seal

Rear Axle Shaft

◆ Gasket

Plate Washer
×6
Cone Washer
34 (340, 25)

R13149

N·m (kgf·cm, ft·lbf) : Specified torque

◆ Non-reusable part

9308SG09

Rear axle exploded view—1997 models

5. Install or connect the following:
- Inner bearing
- Oil seal
- Axle hub
- Outer bearing
- Lockplate
- Locknut

6. Adjust the wheel bearings as follows:
  a. Step 1: Tighten the locknut to 43 ft. lbs. (59 Nm).
  b. Step 2: Spin the hub through several rotations.
  c. Step 3: Tighten the locknut to 43 ft. lbs. (59 Nm).
  d. Step 4: Loosen the locknut so that it can be turned by hand.
  e. Step 5: Check the bearing preload with a spring gauge and tighten the locknut until the bearing preload measures 5.7–12.8 lbs. (26–57 N).

7. Install or connect the following:
- Axle bearing locknut screws
- Wheel speed sensor. Tighten the bolts to 13 ft. lbs. (18 Nm).

- Brake caliper and rotor
- Axle shaft. Tighten the nuts to 25 ft. lbs. (34 Nm).
- Rear wheel

1998–01 MODELS

1. Before servicing the vehicle, refer to the precautions in the beginning of this section.

2. Remove or disconnect the following:
- Rear wheel
- Drake caliper and rotor
- Parking brake shoes and hardware
- Bearing case nuts
- Axle shaft and bearing assembly

3. Separate the backing plate from the bearing case by removing the serrated bolts.

4. Grind a flat spot on the wheel speed sensor rotor and retainer, then split them with a hammer and chisel.

5. Remove the axle snapring.

6. Press the axle bearing case, bearing and retainer off of the axle.

7. Press the axle bearing from the bearing case.

8. Remove or disconnect the following:
- Backing plate
- Axle housing oil seal
- Bearing case oil seal

To install:

9. Press the wheel bearing into the bearing case.

10. Install the bearing case to the backing plate with the serrated bolts.

11. Install or connect the following:
- Bearing case oil seal
- Axle housing oil seal
- Axle shaft to backing plate and bearing assembly
- Bearing retainer
- Axle snapring
- Wheel speed sensor rotor and retainer
- Axle shaft and bearing assembly to

Turn to Section 5 for brake system applications

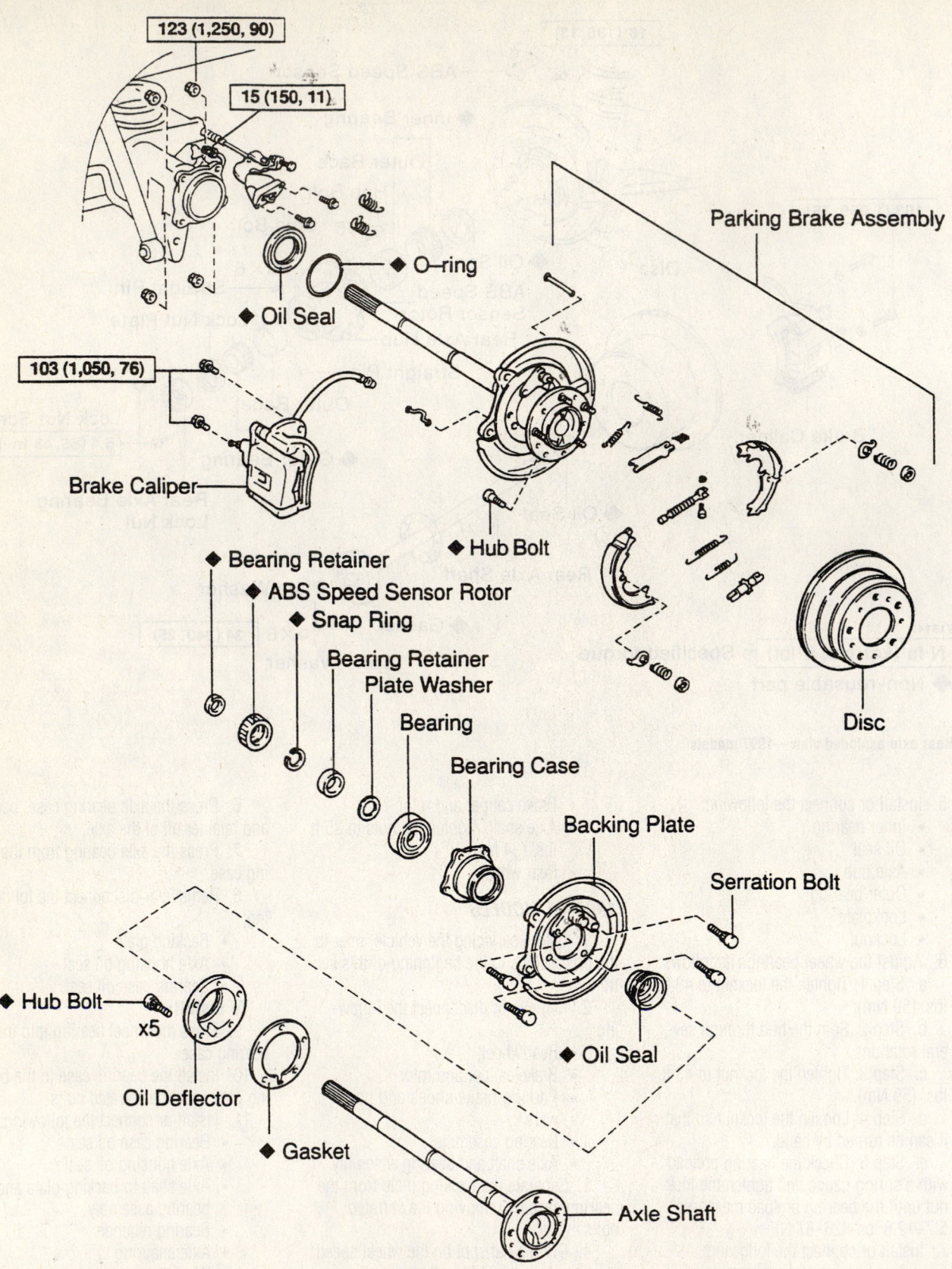

123 (1,250, 90)

15 (150, 11)

Parking Brake Assembly

◆ O-ring

◆ Oil Seal

103 (1,050, 76)

Brake Caliper

◆ Hub Bolt

◆ Bearing Retainer

◆ ABS Speed Sensor Rotor

◆ Snap Ring

Bearing Retainer
Plate Washer

Bearing

Bearing Case

Backing Plate

Serration Bolt

Disc

◆ Hub Bolt
x5

Oil Deflector

◆ Gasket

◆ Oil Seal

Axle Shaft

N·m (kgf·cm, ft·lbf) : Specified torque
◆ Non-reusable part

Rear axle exploded view—1998—01 models

9308SG11

the axle housing. Tighten the nuts to 91 ft. lbs. (123 Nm).
- Parking brake shoes and hardware
- Brake caliper and rotor
- Rear wheel

Pinion Seal

REMOVAL & INSTALLATION

Front

1997 MODELS

1. Before servicing the vehicle, refer to the precautions in the beginning of this section.
2. Remove or disconnect the following:

- Driveshaft
- Front wheels
- Front brake calipers

➡The front brake calipers must be removed so that there is no additional drag when measuring pinion bearing preload.

3. Use an inch lb. torque wrench and measure the amount of torque required to maintain pinion rotation through several revolutions.
4. Remove or disconnect the following:

- Pinion flange
- Oil seal
- Oil slinger
- Pinion bearing and race
- Oil storage ring
- Collapsible spacer

To install:

➡Use a new collapsible spacer and flange nut for assembly.

5. Install or connect the following:

- Collapsible spacer
- Oil storage ring
- Pinion bearing and race
- Pinion seal
- Pinion flange. Tighten the nut to 145 ft. lbs. (196 Nm).

6. Rotate the pinion flange occasionally while tightening the flange nut to make sure the pinion bearings seat correctly.
7. Take frequent bearing preload torque readings. Tighten the flange nut to achieve the preload torque readings originally recorded. Do not exceed 253 ft. lbs. (343 Nm) torque when tightening the pinion flange nut.

✳✳ CAUTION

Never loosen the pinion nut to reduce bearing preload. If it is necessary to reduce bearing preload, install a new collapsible spacer and pinion nut.

8. Install or connect the following:

- Front brake calipers
- Front wheels
- Driveshaft. Tighten the fasteners to 54 ft. lbs. (74 Nm).

9. Fill the differential with gear lubricant and check for leaks.

1998–01 MODELS

1. Before servicing the vehicle, refer to the precautions in the beginning of this section.
2. Remove or disconnect the following:

- Driveshaft
- Front wheels
- Front brake calipers

➡The front brake calipers must be removed so that there is no additional drag when measuring pinion bearing preload.

3. Use an inch lb. torque wrench and measure the amount of torque required to maintain pinion rotation through several revolutions.
4. Remove or disconnect the following:

- Pinion flange
- Oil seal
- Oil slinger
- Pinion bearing and race
- Oil storage ring
- Collapsible spacer

To install:

➡Use a new collapsible spacer and flange nut for assembly.

5. Install or connect the following:

- Collapsible spacer
- Oil storage ring
- Pinion bearing and race
- Pinion seal
- Pinion flange. Tighten the nut to 80 ft. lbs. (108 Nm).

6. Rotate the pinion flange occasionally while tightening the flange nut to make sure the pinion bearings seat correctly.
7. Take frequent bearing preload torque readings. Tighten the flange nut to achieve the preload torque readings originally recorded. Do not exceed 249 ft. lbs. (338 Nm) torque when tightening the pinion flange nut.

✳✳ CAUTION

Never loosen the pinion nut to reduce bearing preload. If it is necessary to reduce bearing preload, install a new collapsible spacer and pinion nut.

8. Install or connect the following:

- Front brake calipers
- Front wheels
- Driveshaft. Tighten the fasteners to 59 ft. lbs. (80 Nm).

9. Fill the differential with gear lubricant and check for leaks.

Rear

ALL MODELS

1. Before servicing the vehicle, refer to the precautions in the beginning of this section.
2. Remove or disconnect the following:

- Driveshaft
- Rear wheels
- Rear brake calipers

➡The rear brake calipers must be removed so that there is no additional drag when measuring pinion bearing preload.

3. Use an inch lb. torque wrench and measure the amount of torque required to maintain pinion rotation through several revolutions.
4. Remove or disconnect the following:

- Pinion flange
- Oil seal
- Oil slinger
- Pinion bearing and race
- Collapsible spacer

To install:

➡Use a new collapsible spacer and flange nut for assembly.

5. Install or connect the following:

- Collapsible spacer
- Pinion bearing and race
- Pinion seal
- Pinion flange. Tighten the nut to 181 ft. lbs. (245 Nm).

6. Rotate the pinion flange occasionally while tightening the flange nut to make sure the pinion bearings seat correctly.
7. Take frequent bearing preload torque readings. Tighten the flange nut to achieve the preload torque readings originally recorded. Do not exceed 326 ft. lbs. (441 Nm) torque when tightening the pinion flange nut.

✳✳ CAUTION

Never loosen the pinion nut to reduce bearing preload. If it is necessary to reduce bearing preload, install a new collapsible spacer and pinion nut.

8. Install or connect the following:
   - Rear brake calipers
   - Rear wheels
   - Driveshaft. Tighten the fasteners to 65 ft. lbs. (88 Nm) for 1997 models or to 78 ft. lbs. (106 Nm) for 1998–01 models.
9. Fill the differential with gear lubricant and check for leaks.

Axle Housing Assembly

REMOVAL & INSTALLATION

Front

1997 MODELS

1. Before servicing the vehicle, refer to the precautions in the beginning of this section.
2. Support the vehicle at the frame.
3. Support the axle housing with a floor jack.
4. Remove or disconnect the following:
   - Front wheels
   - Driveshaft
   - Shock absorbers
   - Stabilizer bar
5. Lower the floor jack.
6. Install a spring compressor. Compress the coil springs and remove them from the vehicle.
7. Remove or disconnect the following:
   - Lateral control rod
   - Brake calipers
   - Outer tie rod ends
   - Leading arm fasteners
   - Axle housing assembly

To install:

8. Install or connect the following:
   - Axle housing assembly. Tighten the leading arm fasteners to 127 ft. lbs. (171 Nm).
   - Outer tie rod ends. Tighten the nuts to 67 ft. lbs. (91 Nm).
   - Brake calipers
   - Lateral control rod. Tighten the bolts to 127 ft. lbs. (171 Nm).
   - Coil springs
   - Stabilizer bar. Tighten the fasteners to 19 ft. lbs. (25 Nm).
   - Shock absorbers

   - Driveshaft. Tighten the fasteners to 54 ft. lbs. (74 Nm).
   - Front wheels
9. Check the wheel alignment and adjust as necessary.

1998–01 MODELS

1. Before servicing the vehicle, refer to the precautions in the beginning of this section.
2. Support the vehicle at the frame.
3. Support the axle housing with a floor jack.
   - Axle halfshafts
   - Driveshaft
   - Vent hose
   - No. 3 frame crossmember
   - Front and rear differential support bolts
   - Axle housing assembly

To install:

4. Install or connect the following:
   - Axle housing assembly. Tighten the support bolts to 137 ft. lbs. (186 Nm).
   - No. 3 frame crossmember. Tighten the frame fasteners to 50 ft. lbs. (68 Nm) and the support bolt to 137 ft. lbs. (186 Nm).
   - Vent hose
   - Driveshaft. Tighten the fasteners to 59 ft. lbs. (80 Nm).
   - Axle halfshafts

Rear

1. Before servicing the vehicle, refer to the precautions in the beginning of this section.
2. Support the vehicle at the frame.
3. Support the axle with a floor jack.
4. Remove or disconnect the following:
   - Rear wheels
   - Shock absorbers
   - Stabilizer bar brackets
   - Lateral control rod
   - Coil springs
   - Flexible brake hoses
   - Brake calipers and rotors
   - Parking brake cables
   - Wheel speed sensor harness
   - Upper trailing arm bolts
   - Lower trailing arm bolts
   - Axle housing assembly

To install:

5. Install or connect the following:
   - Axle housing assembly. Tighten the trailing arm fasteners to 110 ft. lbs. (150 Nm).
   - Wheel speed sensor harness
   - Parking brake cables

   - Brake calipers and rotors
   - Flexible brake hoses
   - Coil springs
   - Lateral control rod. Tighten the bolt to 110 ft. lbs. (150 Nm).
   - Stabilizer bar brackets
   - Shock absorbers
   - Rear wheels

STEERING AND SUSPENSION

Air Bag

✳✳ CAUTION

Some vehicles are equipped with an air bag system. The system must be disarmed before performing service on, or around, system components, the steering column, instrument panel components, wiring and sensors. Failure to follow the safety precautions and the disarming procedure could result in accidental air bag deployment, possible injury and unnecessary system repairs.

PRECAUTIONS

Several precautions must be observed when handling the inflator module to avoid accidental deployment and possible personal injury.
- Never carry the inflator module by the wires or connector on the underside of the module.
- When carrying a live inflator module, hold securely with both hands and ensure that the bag and trim cover are pointed away.
- Place the inflator module on a bench or other surface with the bag and trim cover facing up.
- With the inflator module on the bench, never place anything on or close to the module which may be thrown in the event of an accidental deployment.

DISARMING

To avoid personal injury when working on vehicles equipped with an air bag, the negative battery cable must be disconnected and at least 90 seconds must elapse before working on the system. Failure to do so may result in deployment of the air bag.

Power Worm and Sector Steering Gear

REMOVAL & INSTALLATION

1997 Models

1. Before servicing the vehicle, refer to the precautions in the beginning of this section.

2. Matchmark the intermediate shaft to the steering gear input shaft.

3. Matchmark the Pitman arm to the steering gear output shaft.

4. Remove or disconnect the following:

- Negative battery cable
- Left front wheel
- Link joint protector
- Pitman arm
- Power steering hoses
- Intermediate steering shaft
- Power steering gear

To install:

5. Install or connect the following:

- Power steering gear. Tighten the bolts to 105 ft. lbs. (142 Nm).
- Intermediate steering shaft. Tighten the pinch bolts to 18 ft. lbs. (25 Nm).
- Power steering hoses
- Pitman arm. Tighten the nut to 130 ft. lbs. (177 Nm).
- Link joint protector. Tighten the bolts to 108 inch lbs. (12 Nm).
- Left front wheel
- Negative battery cable

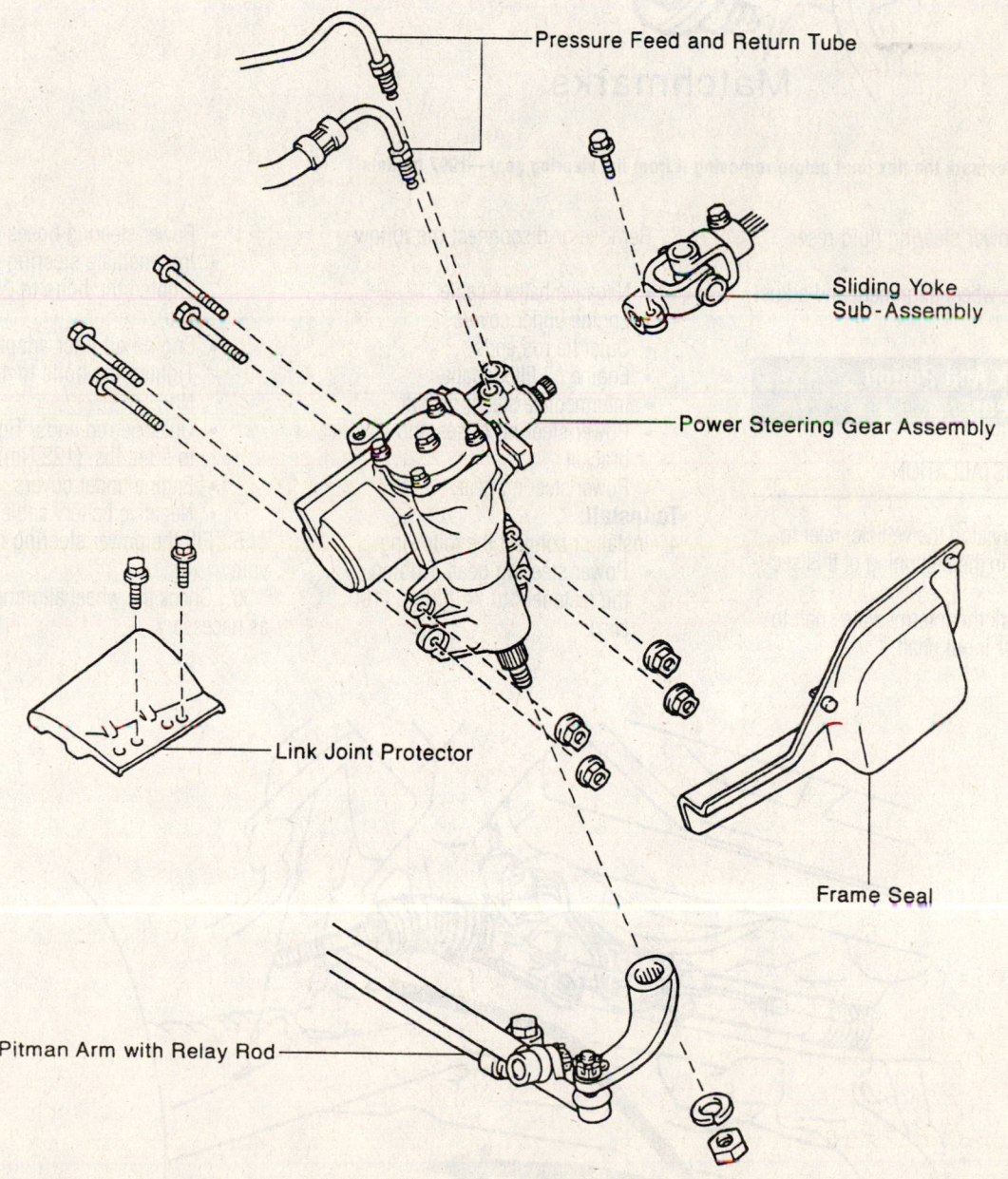

Pressure Feed and Return Tube

Sliding Yoke Sub-Assembly

Power Steering Gear Assembly

Link Joint Protector

Frame Seal

Pitman Arm with Relay Rod

7924SG91

Exploded view of the power worm and sector steering gear mounting—1997 models

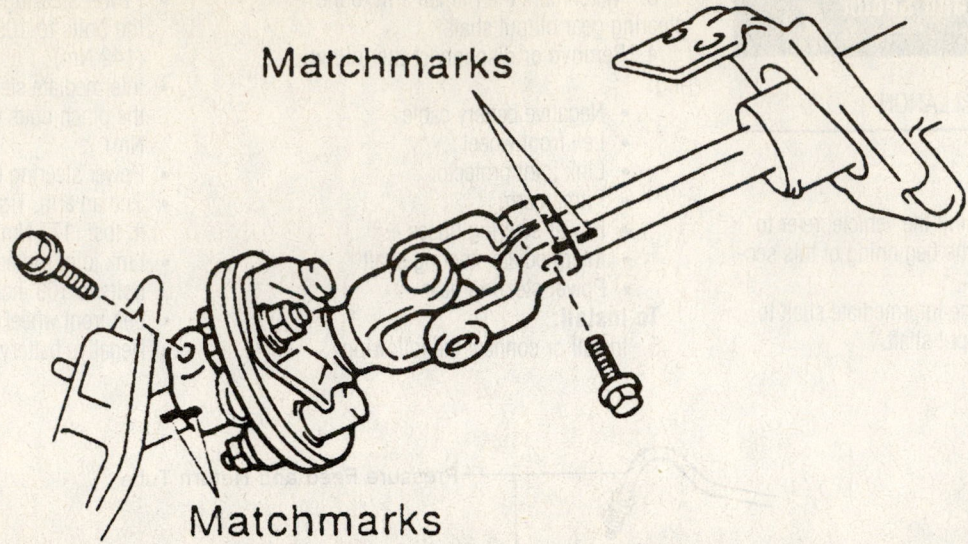

Be sure to matchmark the flex joint before removing it from the steering gear—1997 models

6. Fill the power steering fluid reservoir.

7. Check the wheel alignment and adjust as necessary.

Power Rack And Pinion Steering Gear

REMOVAL & INSTALLATION

1. Before servicing the vehicle, refer to the precautions in the beginning of this section.

2. Matchmark the intermediate shaft to the steering gear input shaft.

3. Remove or disconnect the following:

- Negative battery cable
- Engine under covers
- Outer tie rod ends
- Engine oil filter adapter
- Intermediate steering shaft
- Power steering hoses and bracket
- Power steering gear

To install:

4. Install or connect the following:

- Power steering gear. Tighten the fasteners to 74 ft. lbs. (100 Nm).
- Power steering hoses and bracket
- Intermediate steering shaft. Tighten the bolts to 25 ft. lbs. (34 Nm).
- Engine oil filter adapter. Tighten the bolts to 13 ft. lbs. (18 Nm).
- Outer tie rod ends. Tighten the nuts to 90 ft. lbs. (122 Nm).
- Engine under covers
- Negative battery cable

5. Fill the power steering fluid reservoir.

6. Check the wheel alignment and adjust as necessary.

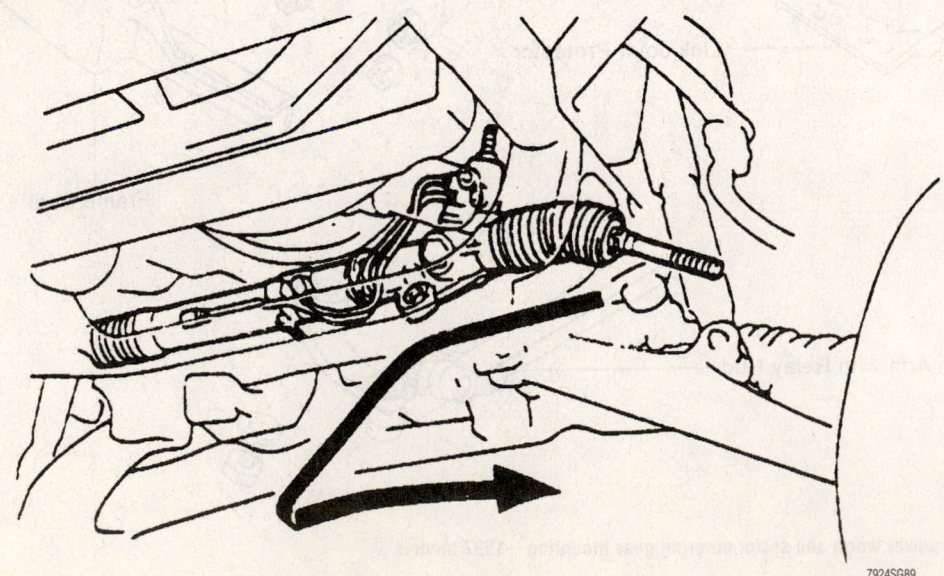

Power rack and pinion steering gear removal—1998–01 models

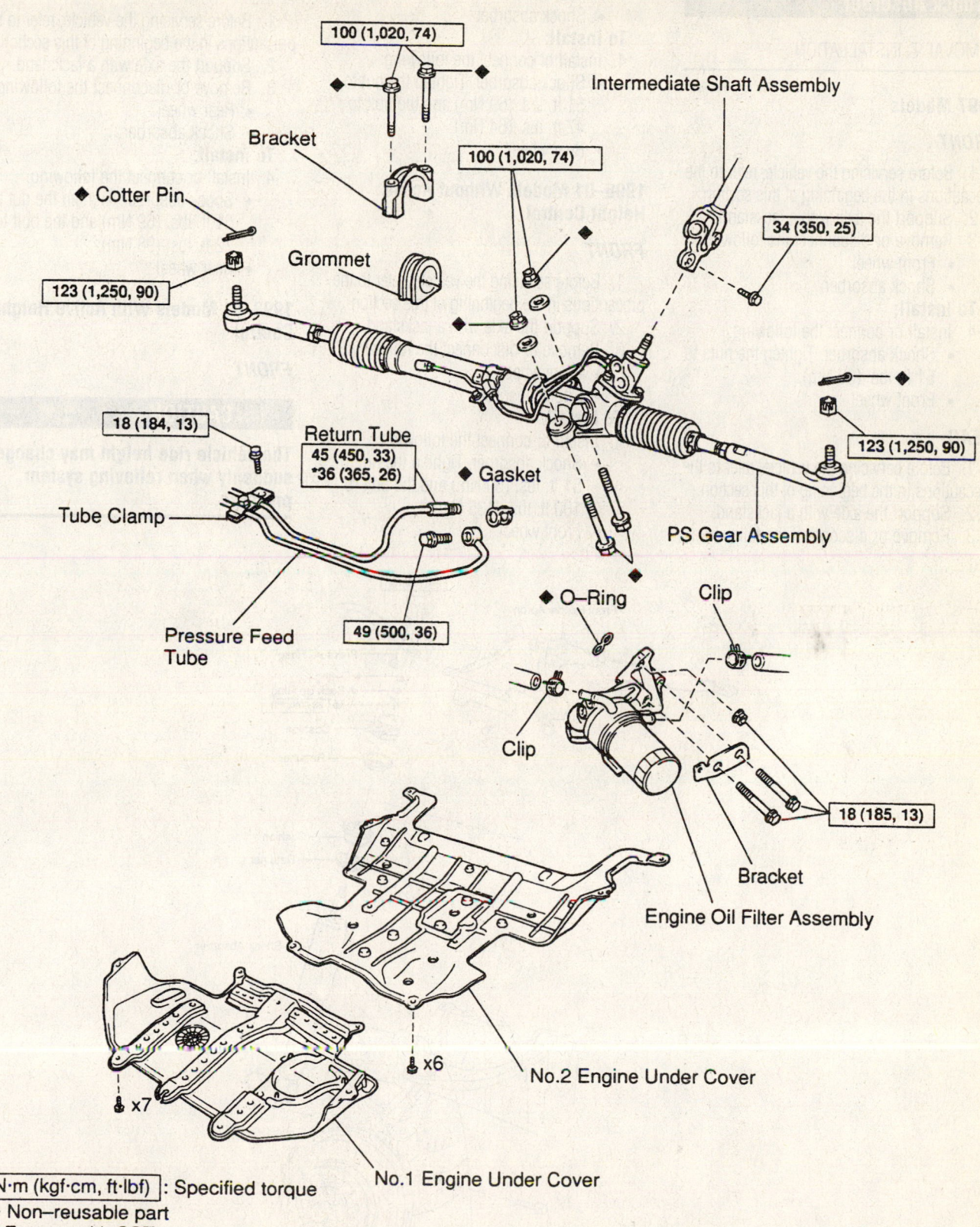

100 (1,020, 74)

Intermediate Shaft Assembly

Bracket

100 (1,020, 74)

◆ Cotter Pin

34 (350, 25)

Grommet

123 (1,250, 90)

123 (1,250, 90)

18 (184, 13)

Return Tube
45 (450, 33)
*36 (365, 26)

◆ Gasket

Tube Clamp

PS Gear Assembly

Pressure Feed
Tube

49 (500, 36)

◆ O−Ring

Clip

Clip

18 (185, 13)

Bracket

Engine Oil Filter Assembly

No.2 Engine Under Cover

x6

x7

No.1 Engine Under Cover

N·m (kgf·cm, ft·lbf) : Specified torque
◆ Non−reusable part
* For use with SST

Exploded view of the rack and pinion steering gear mounting—1998–01 models

7924SG90

Shock Absorber

REMOVAL & INSTALLATION

1997 Models

FRONT

1. Before servicing the vehicle, refer to the precautions in the beginning of this section.
2. Support the axle with a jackstand.
3. Remove or disconnect the following:
   • Front wheel
   • Shock absorber

To install:

4. Install or connect the following:
   • Shock absorber. Tighten the nuts to 51 ft. lbs. (69 Nm).
   • Front wheel

REAR

1. Before servicing the vehicle, refer to the precautions in the beginning of this section.
2. Support the axle with a jackstand.
3. Remove or disconnect the following:
   • Rear wheel
   • Shock absorber

To install:

4. Install or connect the following:
   • Shock absorber. Tighten the nut to 51 ft. lbs. (69 Nm) and the bolt to 47 ft. lbs. (64 Nm).
   • Rear wheel

1998–01 Models Without Active Height Control

FRONT

1. Before servicing the vehicle, refer to the precautions in the beginning of this section.
2. Support the axle with a jackstand.
3. Remove or disconnect the following:
   • Front wheel
   • Shock absorber

To install:

4. Install or connect the following:
   • Shock absorber. Tighten the nut to 51 ft. lbs. (69 Nm) and the bolt to 100 ft. lbs. (135 Nm).
   • Front wheel

REAR

1. Before servicing the vehicle, refer to the precautions in the beginning of this section.
2. Support the axle with a jackstand.
3. Remove or disconnect the following:
   • Rear wheel
   • Shock absorber

To install:

4. Install or connect the following:
   • Shock absorber. Tighten the nut to 51 ft. lbs. (69 Nm) and the bolt to 72 ft. lbs. (98 Nm).
   • Rear wheel

1998–01 Models With Active Height Control

FRONT

✷✷ CAUTION

The vehicle ride height may change suddenly when relieving system pressure.

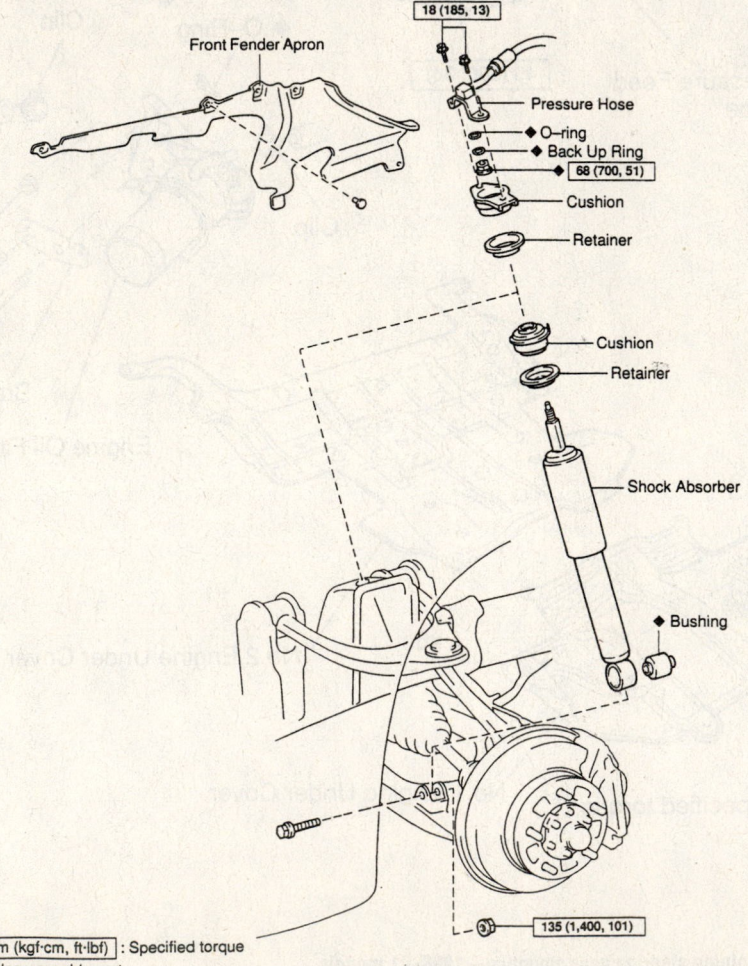

18 (185, 13)

Front Fender Apron

Pressure Hose
♦ O-ring
♦ Back Up Ring
♦ 68 (700, 51)
Cushion
Retainer

Cushion
Retainer

Shock Absorber

♦ Bushing

N·m (kgf·cm, ft·lbf) : Specified torque
♦ Non-reusable part

135 (1,400, 101)

7924SG86

Exploded view of the front shock absorber mounting—1998–01 models with Active Height Control (AHC)

1. Before servicing the vehicle, refer to the precautions in the beginning of this section.

2. Relieve the Active Height Control (AHC) hydraulic pressure as follows:

   a. Connect a hose to the control actuator bleed screw and place the other end in a container.

   b. Open the bleed screw.

   c. When the fluid pressure has dropped and oil stops flowing, close the bleed screw.

3. Remove or disconnect the following:

- Front wheel
- Inner fender liner
- Lower shock absorber mounting bolt
- AHC pressure hose
- Upper shock absorber mounting nut
- Shock absorber

To install:

4. Install or connect the following:

- Shock absorber. Tighten the upper nut to 51 ft. lbs. (68 Nm) and the lower bolt to 101 ft. lbs. (135 Nm).
- AHC pressure hose with new O-ring seals. Tighten the bolts to 13 ft. lbs. (18 Nm).
- Inner fender liner
- Front wheel

➡**Do not let the AHC reservoir run empty during this procedure.**

5. Bleed the AHC system as follows:

   a. Fill the AHC system reservoir with AHC fluid 08886-01805.

   b. Start the engine and push **N** on the vehicle height select switch.

   c. When the AHC pump stops, turn the engine **OFF**.

   d. Open the bleed screw and allow any air in the system to escape.

   e. Repeat until no air is expelled from the bleed screw.

   f. Fill the AHC reservoir to the correct level.

REAR

✷✷ CAUTION

The vehicle ride height may change suddenly when relieving system pressure.

1. Before servicing the vehicle, refer to the precautions in the beginning of this section.

2. Support the rear axle with a jack or stands.

3. Relieve the Active Height Control (AHC) hydraulic pressure as follows:

   a. Connect a hose to the control actuator bleed screw and place the other end in a container.

   b. Open the bleed screw.

   c. When the fluid pressure has dropped and oil stops flowing, close the bleed screw.

4. Remove or disconnect the following:

- Rear wheel
- Lower shock absorber mounting bolt
- AHC pressure hose
- Upper shock absorber mounting nut
- Shock absorber

To install:

5. Install or connect the following:

- Shock absorber. Tighten the upper nut to 51 ft. lbs. (68 Nm) and the lower bolt to 72 ft. lbs. (98 Nm).
- AHC pressure hose with new O-ring seals. Tighten the bolts to 13 ft. lbs. (18 Nm).
- Rear wheel

➡**Do not let the AHC reservoir run empty during this procedure.**

6. Bleed the AHC system as follows:

   a. Fill the AHC system reservoir with AHC fluid 08886-01805.

   b. Start the engine and push **N** on the vehicle height select switch.

   c. When the AHC pump stops, turn the engine **OFF**.

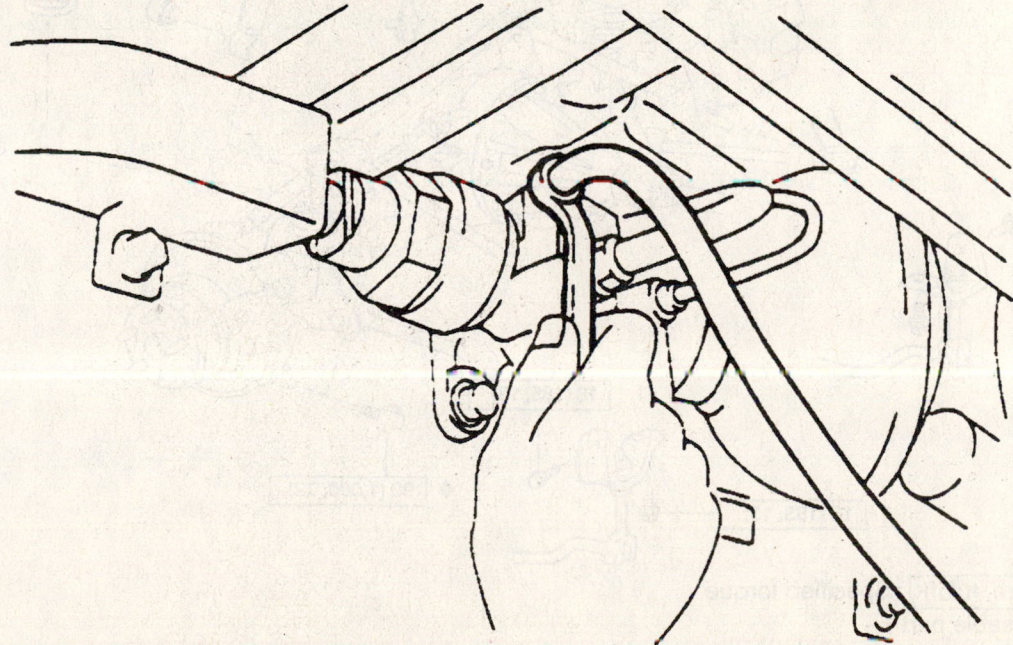

7924SG84

Relieving system pressure—1998–01 models with Active Height Control (AHC)

Turn to Section 5 for brake system applications

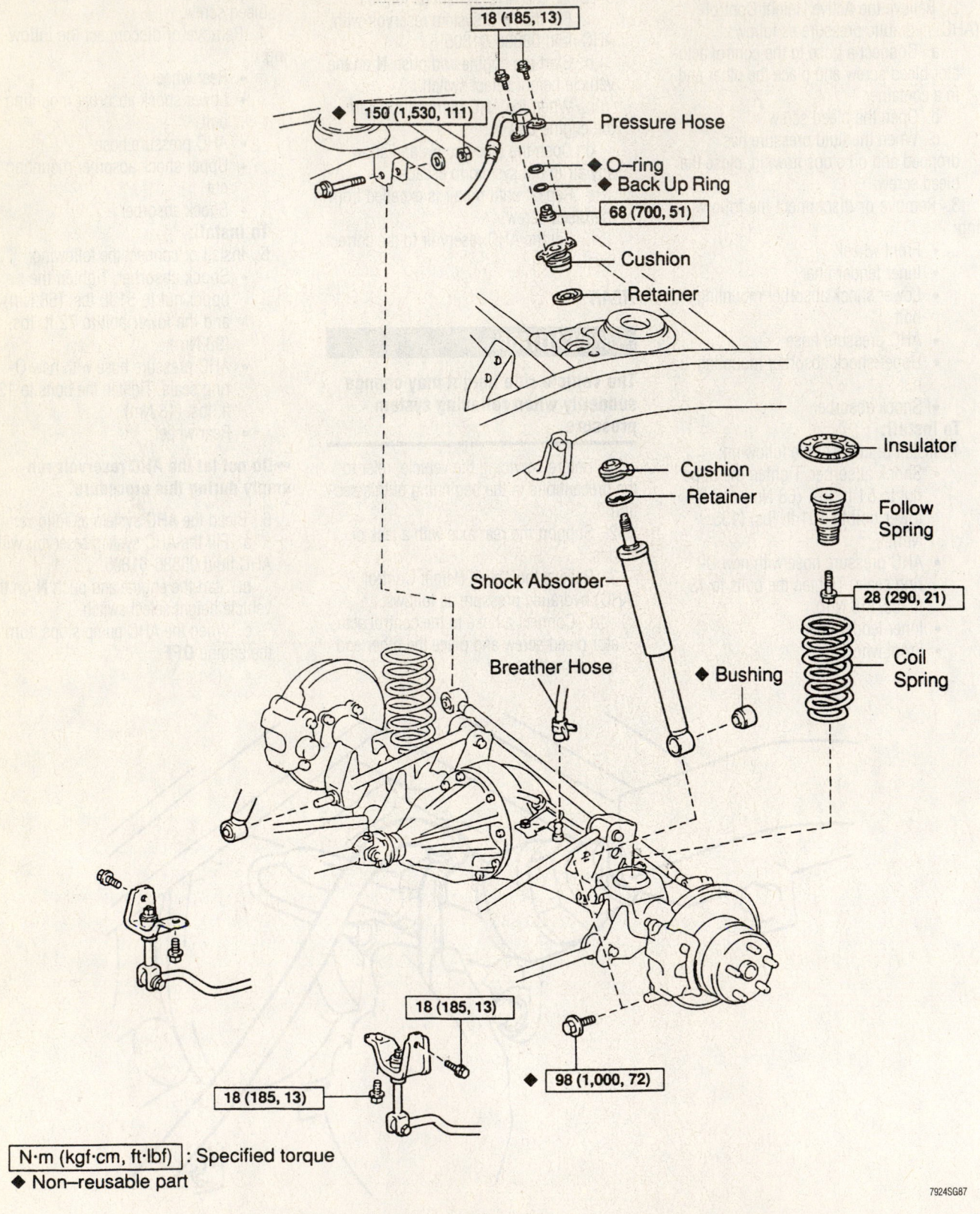

18 (185, 13)

150 (1,530, 111)

Pressure Hose

◆ O-ring

◆ Back Up Ring

68 (700, 51)

Cushion

Retainer

Cushion

Retainer

Shock Absorber

Breather Hose

◆ Bushing

Insulator

Follow Spring

28 (290, 21)

Coil Spring

18 (185, 13)

18 (185, 13)

98 (1,000, 72)

N·m (kgf·cm, ft·lbf) : Specified torque

◆ Non–reusable part

7924SG87

Exploded view of the rear shock absorber mounting—1998–01 models with Active Height Control (AHC)

d. Open the bleed screw and allow any air in the system to escape.

e. Repeat until no air is expelled from the bleed screw.

f. Fill the AHC reservoir to the correct level.

Coil Spring

REMOVAL & INSTALLATION

Front

1997 MODELS

1. Before servicing the vehicle, refer to the precautions in the beginning of this section.
2. Support the vehicle at the frame.
3. Support the axle with a floor jack.
4. Remove or disconnect the following:
   • Front wheel
   • Shock absorber
   • Stabilizer bar
5. Lower the floor jack.
6. Install a spring compressor. Compress the coil spring and remove it from the vehicle.

To install:

7. With the coil spring compressed, align the end with the lower seat and install the coil spring.
8. Remove the spring compressor.
9. Install or connect the following:
   • Stabilizer bar
   • Shock absorber
   • Front wheel

Rear

ALL MODELS

1. Before servicing the vehicle, refer to the precautions in the beginning of this section.
2. Support the vehicle at the frame.
3. Support the axle with a floor jack.
4. Remove or disconnect the following:
   • Rear wheel
   • Shock absorber
   • Stabilizer bar brackets
   • Lateral control rod
   • Coil spring

To install:

5. Install or connect the following:
   • Coil spring
   • Lateral control rod. Tighten the axle housing bolt to 181 ft. lbs. (245 Nm).

• Stabilizer bar brackets. Tighten the bolts to 13 ft. lbs. (18 Nm)
• Shock absorber
• Rear wheel

Torsion Bars

REMOVAL & INSTALLATION

1998—01 Models

1. Before servicing the vehicle, refer to the precautions in the beginning of this section.
2. Remove or disconnect the following:

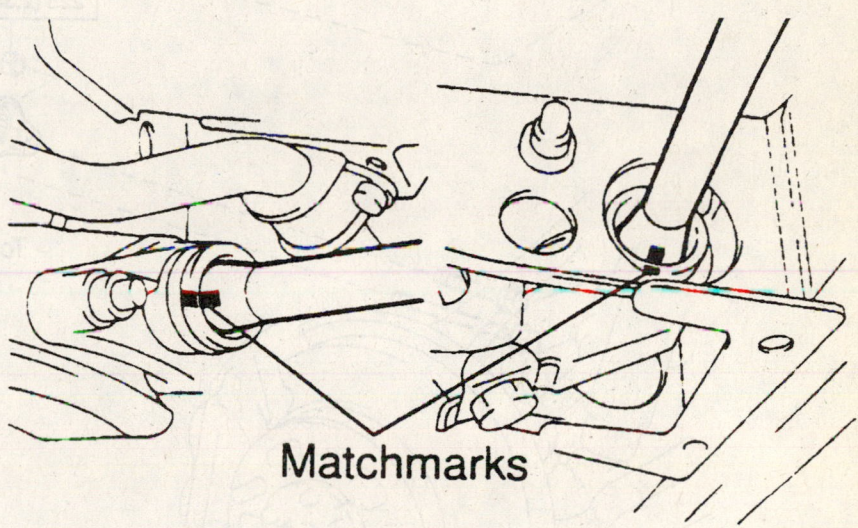

Matchmarks

9302SG03

Matchmark the torsion bar to the anchor arm and torque arm—1998–01 models

• Front wheel
• Engine under cover

3. Measure dimension **A** as shown between the adjustment bolt head and the frame.
4. Loosen the adjusting bolt until all spring tension is relieved.
5. Measure dimension **B** as shown between the adjustment bolt head and the frame.
6. Remove or disconnect the following:
   • Adjustment bolt, swivel and seat
   • Torsion bar and anchor arm. Separate the anchor arm from the torsion bar.
   • Torque arm

Front:

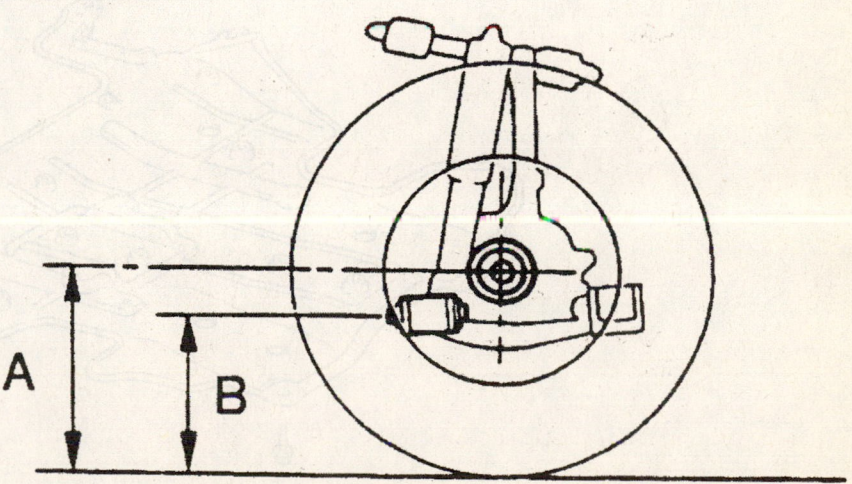

9308SG12

Ride height measurements A and B—1998–01 models

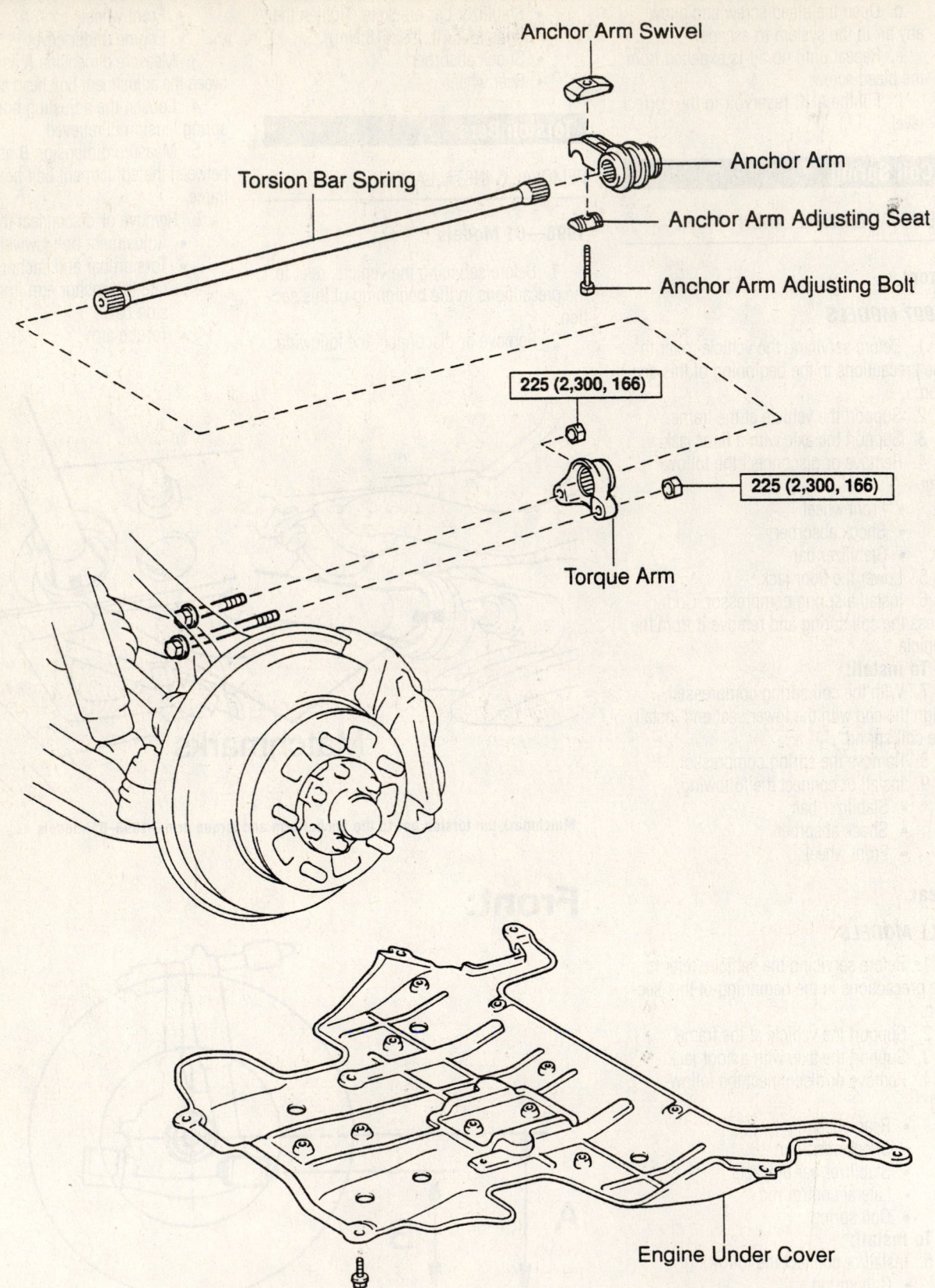

Anchor Arm Swivel

Anchor Arm

Torsion Bar Spring

Anchor Arm Adjusting Seat

Anchor Arm Adjusting Bolt

225 (2,300, 166)

225 (2,300, 166)

Torque Arm

Engine Under Cover

N·m (kgf·cm, ft·lbf) : Specified torque

9308SG10

Torsion bar mounting exploded view—1998–01 models

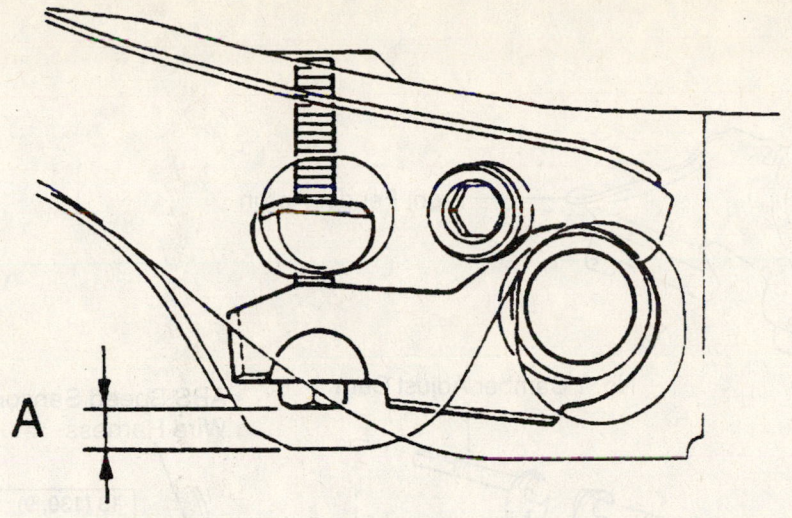

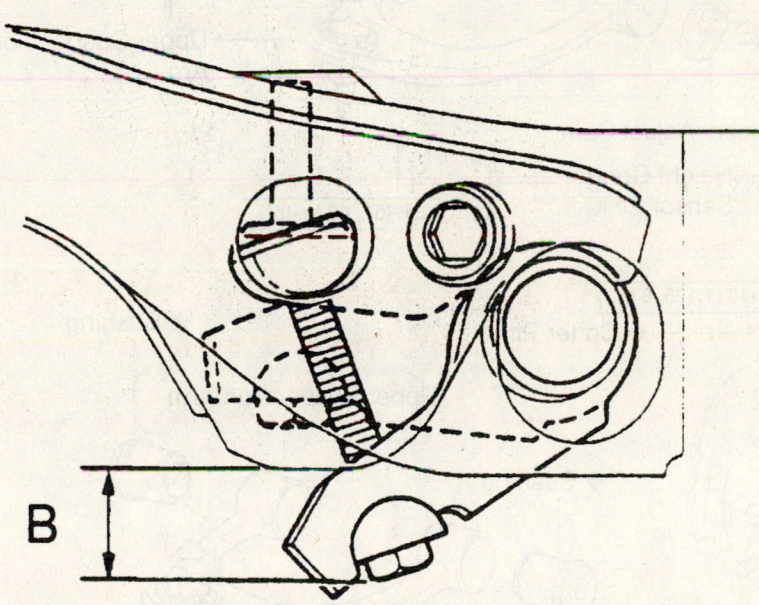

9302SG04

Reference measurements A and B—1998–01 models

face and check the vehicle curb height as follows:

  a. Step 1: Measure dimension **A** between the spindle center and the ground.

  b. Step 2: Measure dimension **B** between the lower control arm front bolt center and the ground.

  c. Step 3: Turn the adjusting bolt so that **A** minus **B** is equal to 2.795 inches (71mm).

Upper Ball Joint

REMOVAL & INSTALLATION

  the upper ball joint is serviced with the upper control arm as an assembly.

Lower Ball Joint

REMOVAL & INSTALLATION

  the lower ball joint is serviced with the lower control arm as an assembly.

Upper Control Arm

REMOVAL & INSTALLATION

1998–01 Models

  1. Before servicing the vehicle, refer to the precautions in the beginning of this section.

  2. Remove or disconnect the following:

- Front wheel
- Inner fender liner
- Wheel speed sensor harness
- Upper ball joint
- Adjustment cam bolts
- Upper control arm

To install:

  3. Install or connect the following:

- Upper control arm. Tighten the adjustment cam bolts to 72 ft. lbs. (98 Nm).
- Upper ball joint. Tighten the nut to 81 ft. lbs. (110 Nm).
- Wheel speed sensor harness. Tighten the bolts to 10 ft. lbs. (13 Nm).
- Inner fender liner
- Front wheel

  4. Check the wheel alignment and adjust as necessary.

To install:

  7. Install or connect the following:

- Torque arm. Tighten the fasteners to 166 ft. lbs. (225 Nm).
- Torsion bar and anchor arm. Align the matchmarks.
- Adjustment bolt, swivel and seat

  8. Check that dimension **B** is close to the measurement made at disassembly.

  9. If installing a new torsion bar, tighten the adjustment bolt until dimension **A** is as follows:

- Left torsion bar: 0.315–0.984 inches (8–25mm)
- Right torsion bar: 0.079–0.709 inches (2–18mm)

  10. If installing the original torsion bar, tighten the adjustment bolt until dimension **A** is close to the measurement made at disassembly.

  11. Install or connect the following:

- Engine under cover
- Front wheel

  12. Place the vehicle on a flat, level sur-

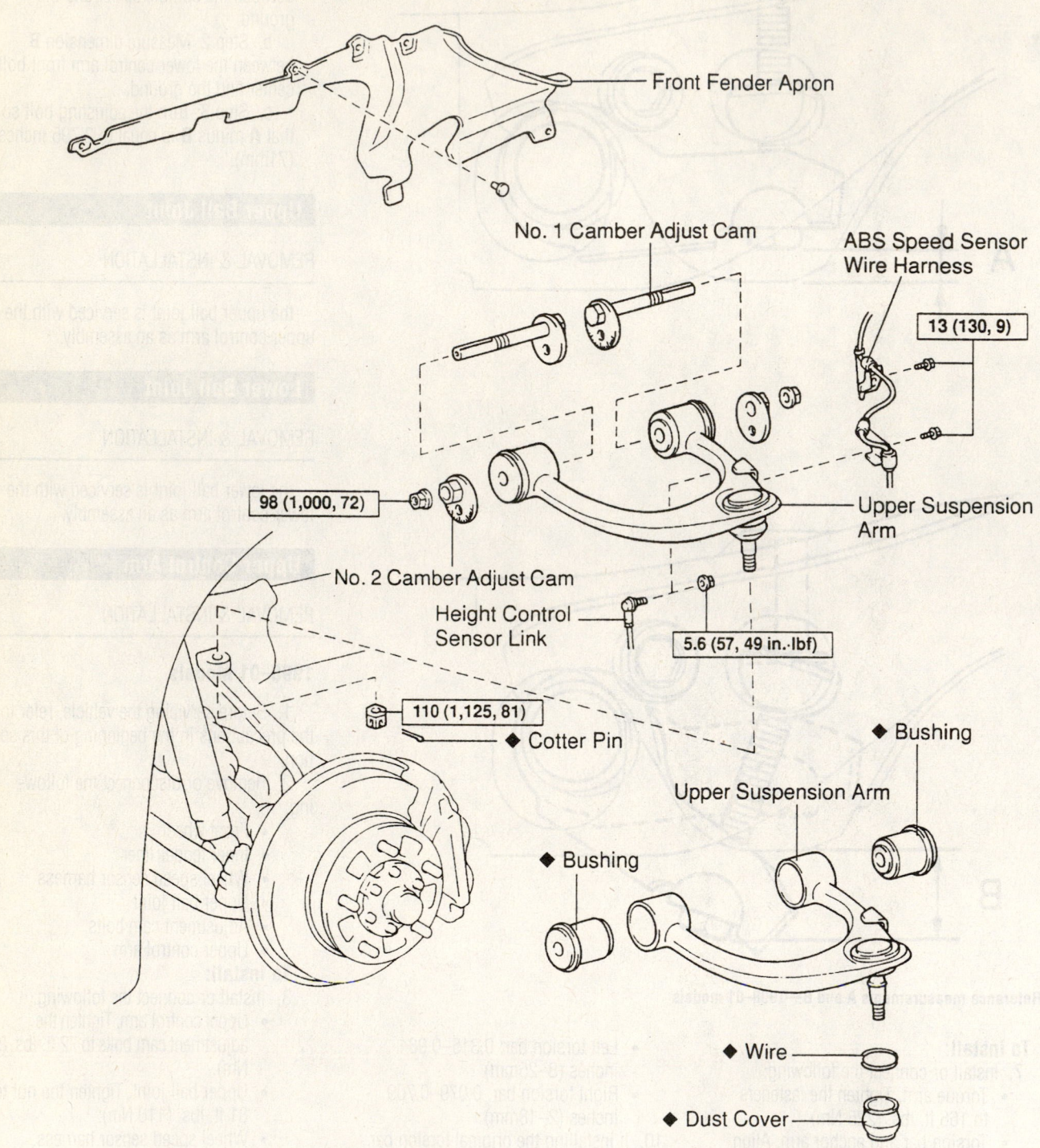

Front Fender Apron

No. 1 Camber Adjust Cam

ABS Speed Sensor Wire Harness

13 (130, 9)

Upper Suspension Arm

98 (1,000, 72)

No. 2 Camber Adjust Cam

Height Control Sensor Link

5.6 (57, 49 in.·lbf)

110 (1,125, 81)

◆ Cotter Pin

◆ Bushing

Upper Suspension Arm

◆ Bushing

◆ Wire

◆ Dust Cover

N·m (kgf·cm, ft·lbf) : Specified torque

◆ Non–reusable part

9302SG01

Exploded view of the upper control arm and related components

CONTROL ARM BUSHING REPLACEMENT

1. Before servicing the vehicle, refer to the precautions in the beginning of this section.

2. Remove the control arm from the vehicle.

3. Remove the control arm bushings with a hydraulic press.

To install:

4. Lubricate the control arm bushings with liquid soap.

5. Press the bushings into the control arm until the bushing flange contacts the housing edge of the control arm.

6. Install the control arm to the vehicle.

7. Check the wheel alignment and adjust as necessary.

Lower Control Arm

REMOVAL & INSTALLATION

1998–01 Models

1. Before servicing the vehicle, refer to the precautions in the beginning of this section.

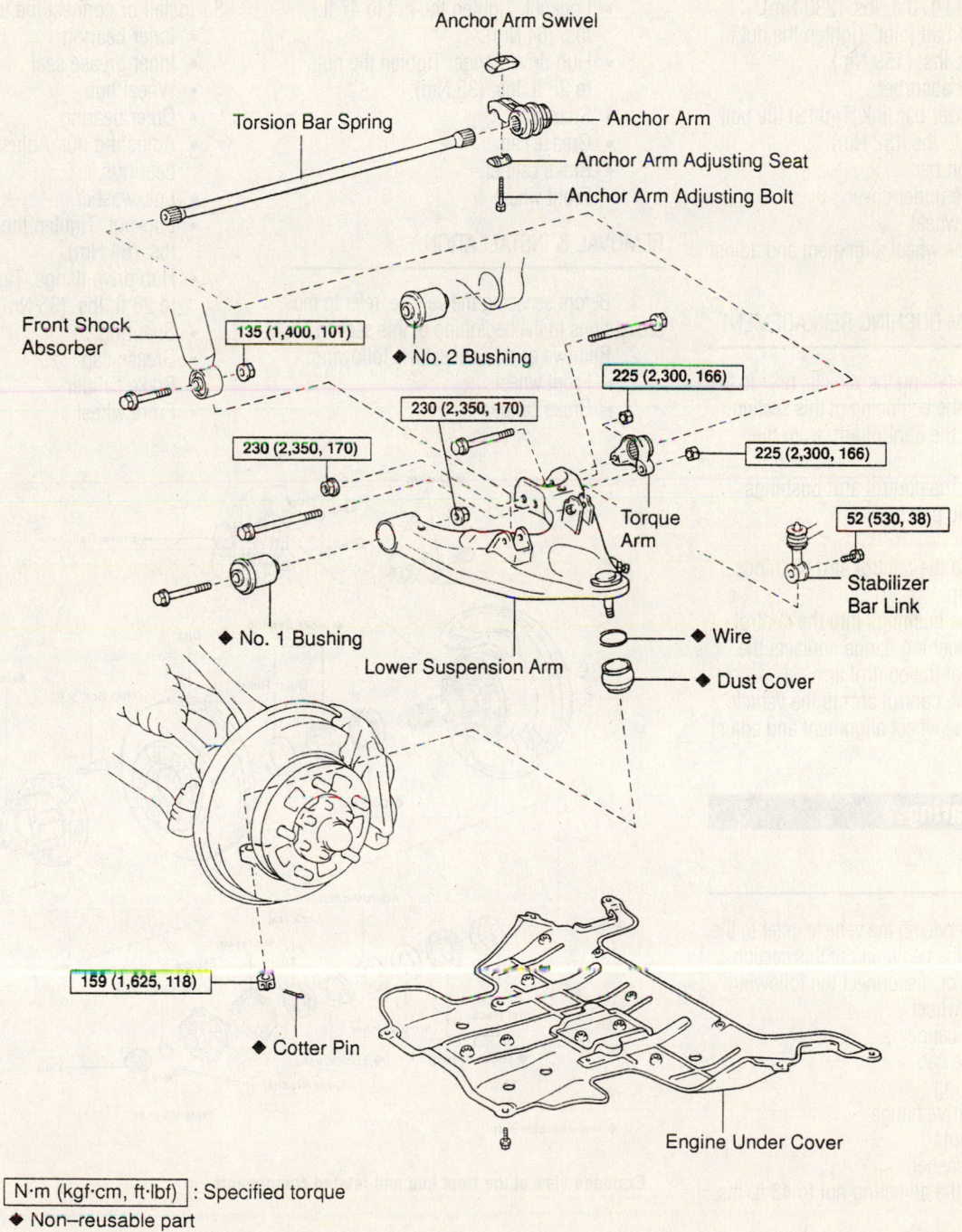

Exploded view of the lower control arm and related components

N·m (kgf·cm, ft·lbf) : Specified torque

◆ Non–reusable part

Anchor Arm Swivel

Torsion Bar Spring

Anchor Arm

Anchor Arm Adjusting Seat

Anchor Arm Adjusting Bolt

Front Shock Absorber

135 (1,400, 101)

◆ No. 2 Bushing

225 (2,300, 166)

230 (2,350, 170)

230 (2,350, 170)

225 (2,300, 166)

Torque Arm

52 (530, 38)

Stabilizer Bar Link

◆ No. 1 Bushing

Lower Suspension Arm

◆ Wire

◆ Dust Cover

159 (1,625, 118)

◆ Cotter Pin

Engine Under Cover

9302SG02

Turn to Section 5 for brake system applications

2. Remove or disconnect the following:
- Front wheel
- Engine under cover
- Torsion bar
- Stabilizer bar link
- Shock absorber
- Lower ball joint
- Lower control arm

To install:

3. Install or connect the following:
- Lower control arm. Tighten the bolts to 170 ft. lbs. (230 Nm).
- Lower ball joint. Tighten the nut to 117 ft. lbs. (159 Nm).
- Shock absorber
- Stabilizer bar link. Tighten the bolt to 38 ft. lbs. (52 Nm).
- Torsion bar
- Engine under cover
- Front wheel

4. Check the wheel alignment and adjust as necessary.

CONTROL ARM BUSHING REPLACEMENT

1. Before servicing the vehicle, refer to the precautions in the beginning of this section.
2. Remove the control arm from the vehicle.
3. Remove the control arm bushings with a hydraulic press.

To install:

4. Lubricate the control arm bushings with liquid soap.
5. Press the bushings into the control arm until the bushing flange contacts the housing edge of the control arm.
6. Install the control arm to the vehicle.
7. Check the wheel alignment and adjust as necessary.

Wheel Bearing

ADJUSTMENT

1. Before servicing the vehicle, refer to the precautions in the beginning of this section.
2. Remove or disconnect the following:
- Front wheel
- Brake caliper
- Grease cap
- Snapring
- Hub drive flange
- Locknut
- Lockwasher

3. Tighten the adjusting nut to 43 ft. lbs.

(59 Nm) while rotating the hub to seat the bearings.

4. Loosen the adjusting nut.
5. Tighten the adjusting nut to 48 inch lbs. (5.4 Nm) and check that the bearing has no play.
6. Check the bearing preload with a spring tension gauge. The preload should be 6.4–12.6 lbs. (28–56 N).
7. Install or connect the following:
- Lockwasher
- Locknut. Tighten the nut to 47 ft. lbs. (64 Nm).
- Hub drive flange. Tighten the nuts to 26 ft. lbs. (35 Nm).
- Snapring
- Grease cap
- Brake caliper
- Front wheel

REMOVAL & INSTALLATION

1. Before servicing the vehicle, refer to the precautions in the beginning of this section.
2. Remove or disconnect the following:
- Front wheel
- Brake caliper

- Grease cap
- Snapring
- Hub drive flange
- Locknut
- Lockwasher
- Adjusting nut
- Outer bearing
- Wheel hub
- Inner grease seal
- Inner bearing

To install:

3. Install or connect the following:
- Inner bearing
- Inner grease seal
- Wheel hub
- Outer bearing
- Adjusting nut. Adjust the wheel bearings.
- Lockwasher
- Locknut. Tighten the nut to 47 ft. lbs. (64 Nm).
- Hub drive flange. Tighten the nuts to 26 ft. lbs. (35 Nm).
- Snapring
- Grease cap
- Brake caliper
- Front wheel

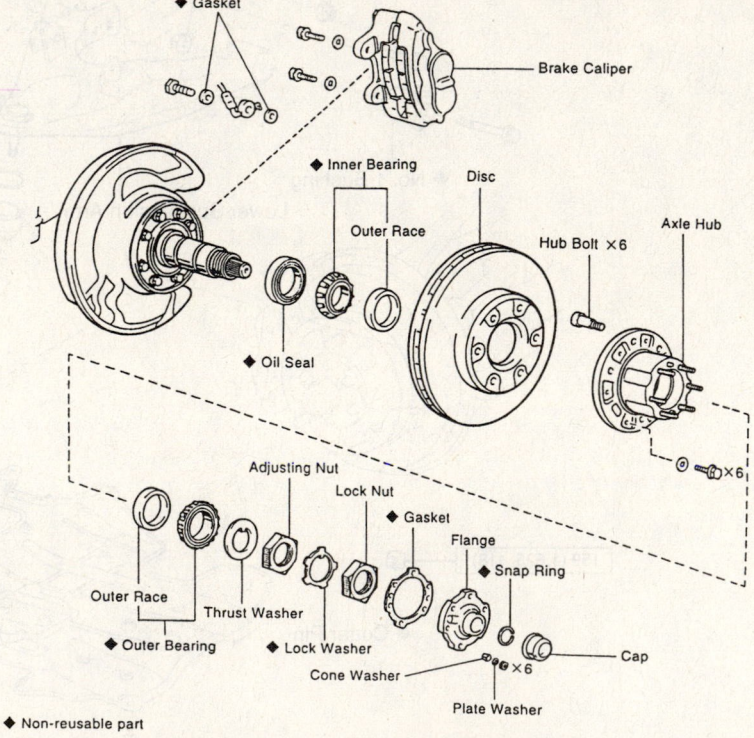

Exploded view of the front hub and related components

7924SG31

MAZDA

MPV

PRECAUTIONS

Before servicing any vehicle, please be sure to read all of the following precautions, which deal with personal safety, prevention of component damage, and important points to take into consideration when servicing a motor vehicle:

• Never open, service or drain the radiator or cooling system when the engine is hot; serious burns can occur from the steam and hot coolant.

• Observe all applicable safety precautions when working around fuel. Whenever servicing the fuel system, always work in a well-ventilated area. Do not allow fuel spray or vapors to come in contact with a spark, open flame, or excessive heat (a hot drop light, for example). Keep a dry chemical fire extinguisher near the work area. Always keep fuel in a container specifically designed for fuel storage; also, always properly seal fuel containers to avoid the possibility of fire or explosion. Refer to the additional fuel system precautions later in this section.

• Fuel injection systems often remain pressurized, even after the engine has been turned **OFF**. The fuel system pressure must be relieved before disconnecting any fuel lines. Failure to do so may result in fire and/or personal injury.

• Brake fluid often contains polyglycol ethers and polyglycols. Avoid contact with the eyes and wash your hands thoroughly after handling brake fluid. If you do get brake fluid in your eyes, flush your eyes with clean, running water for 15 minutes. If eye irritation persists, or if you have taken brake fluid internally, IMMEDIATELY seek medical assistance.

• The EPA warns that prolonged contact with used engine oil may cause a number of skin disorders, including cancer! You should make every effort to minimize your exposure to used engine oil. Protective gloves should be worn when changing oil. Wash your hands and any other exposed skin areas as soon as possible after exposure to used engine oil. Soap and water, or waterless hand cleaner should be used.

• All new vehicles are now equipped with an air bag system. The system must be disabled before performing service on or around system components, steering column, instrument panel components, wiring and sensors. Failure to follow safety and disabling procedures could result in accidental air bag deployment, possible personal injury and unnecessary system repairs.

• Always wear safety goggles when working with, or around, the air bag system. When carrying a non-deployed air bag, be sure the bag and trim cover are pointed away from your body. When placing a non-deployed air bag on a work surface, always face the bag and trim cover upward, away from the surface. This will reduce the motion of the module if it is accidentally deployed. Refer to the additional air bag system precautions later in this section.

• Clean, high quality brake fluid from a sealed container is essential to the safe and proper operation of the brake system. You should always buy the correct type of brake fluid for your vehicle. If the brake fluid becomes contaminated, completely flush the system with new fluid. Never reuse any brake fluid. Any brake fluid that is removed from the system should be discarded. Also, do not allow any brake fluid to come in contact with a painted surface; it will damage the paint.

• Never operate the engine without the proper amount and type of engine oil; doing so WILL result in severe engine damage.

• Timing belt maintenance is extremely important! Many models utilize an interference-type, non-freewheeling engine. If the timing belt breaks, the valves in the cylinder head may strike the pistons, causing potentially serious (also time-consuming and expensive) engine damage. Refer to the maintenance interval charts in the front of this manual for the recommended replacement interval for the timing belt, and to the timing belt section for belt replacement and inspection.

• Disconnecting the negative battery cable on some vehicles may interfere with the functions of the on-board computer system(s) and may require the computer to undergo a relearning process once the negative battery cable is reconnected.

• When servicing drum brakes, only disassemble and assemble one side at a time, leaving the remaining side intact for reference.

ENGINE REPAIR

➡ **Disconnecting the negative battery cable on some vehicles may interfere with the functions of the on board computer system. The computer may undergo a relearning process once the negative battery cable is reconnected.**

Distributor

REMOVAL

3.0L Engine

1. Before servicing the vehicle, refer to the precautions in the beginning of this section.

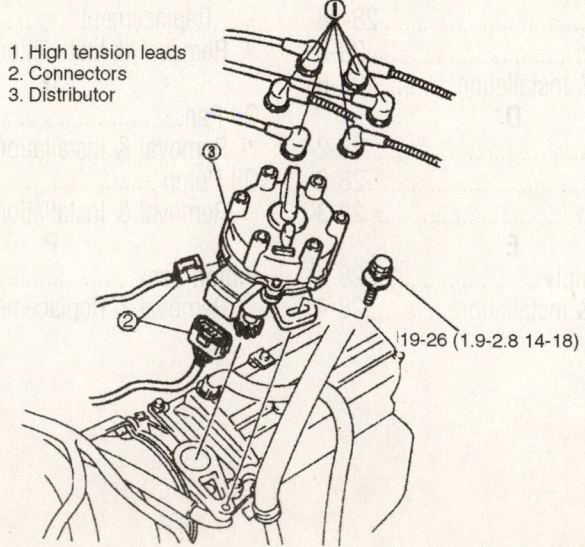

1. High tension leads
2. Connectors
3. Distributor

19-26 (1.9-2.8 14-18)

Distributor assembly—3.0L engine

7924TG02

2. Remove or disconnect the following:
- Negative battery cable
- Distributor cap
- Distributor wiring harness connector

3. Matchmark the rotor to the distributor housing, and matchmark the distributor housing to the cylinder head.

4. Remove the distributor.

INSTALLATION

Timing Not Disturbed

1. Install or connect the following:
- Distributor by aligning the matchmarks made during removal
- Distributor wiring harness connector
- Distributor cap
- Negative battery cable

2. Check the ignition timing and adjust as necessary.

Timing Disturbed

1. Set the engine to Top Dead Center (TDC) of the compression stroke for the No. 1 cylinder.

2. Align the matchmark on the drive gear with the matchmark on the distributor housing as shown.

3. Install the distributor with the mounting bolt centered in the mounting flange slot.

4. Install or connect the following:
- Distributor wiring harness connector
- Distributor cap
- Negative battery cable

5. Check the ignition timing and adjust as necessary.

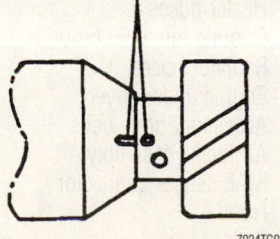

MATCHING MARKS

7924TG03

Distributor gear and housing matchmarks—3.0L engine

Alternator

REMOVAL

2.5L Engine

1. Before servicing the vehicle, refer to the precautions in the beginning of this section.

2. Remove or disconnect the following:
- Negative battery cable
- Accessory drive belt
- Subframe transverse section
- Exhaust front pipe
- Right axle halfshaft and center shaft assembly
- Alternator harness connectors
- Center shaft support bracket
- Alternator

3.0L Engine

1. Before servicing the vehicle, refer to the precautions in the beginning of this section.

2. Remove or disconnect the following:
- Negative battery cable
- Accessory drive belts
- Power steering pulley
- Alternator harness connectors
- Alternator

INSTALLATION

2.5L Engine

1. Install or connect the following:
- Alternator. Tighten the bolts to 29–41 ft. lbs. (40–50 Nm).
- Center shaft support bracket. Tighten the bolts to 32–45 ft. lbs. (43–61 Nm).
- Alternator harness connectors. Tighten the battery terminal nut to 87–130 inch lbs. (10–15 Nm).
- Right axle halfshaft and center shaft assembly
- Exhaust front pipe
- Subframe transverse section. Tighten the bolts to 69–96 ft. lbs. (94–131 Nm).
- Accessory drive belt
- Negative battery cable

3.0L Engine

1. Install or connect the following:
- Alternator
- Alternator harness connectors. Tighten the battery terminal nut to 44–60 inch lbs. (5–7 Nm).

- Power steering pulley. Tighten the nut to 29–43 ft. lbs. (40–58 Nm).
- Accessory drive belts. Tighten the alternator lockbolt to 14–18 ft. lbs. (19–25 Nm) and the pivot bolt to 28–38 ft. lbs. (38–51 Nm).
- Negative battery cable

Ignition Timing

ADJUSTMENT

2.5L Engine

This engine is equipped with a Distributorless Ignition System (DIS). No adjustment is necessary.

3.0L Engine

➡ **Ignition timing is set with the engine at operating temperature, transmission in P and all electrical loads OFF.**

1. Before servicing the vehicle, refer to the precautions in the beginning of this section.

2. Connect a timing light to the No. 1 cylinder spark plug wire.

3. Connect terminals TEN and GND of the underhood Data Link Connector (DLC) with a jumper wire.

4. Check the idle speed. Idle speed should be 500–900 rpm.

5. Set the base timing to 10–12 degrees Before Top Dead Center (BTDC).

6. Tighten the distributor bolts to 14–18 ft. lbs. (19–25 Nm).

7. Remove the jumper wire.

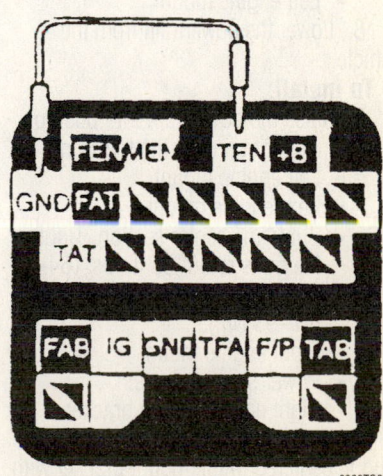

9308TG01

Underhood Data Link Connector and timing jumper—3.0L engine

Engine Assembly

REMOVAL & INSTALLATION

2.5L Engine

1. Before servicing the vehicle, refer to the precautions in the beginning of this section.
2. Drain the cooling system.
3. Drain the engine oil.
4. Drain the transaxle.
5. Relieve the fuel system pressure.
6. Install a support fixture to the engine lifting eyes.
7. Remove or disconnect the following:
   - Battery and tray
   - Inner fender liners
   - Axle halfshafts
   - Air intake assembly
   - Accelerator cable and bracket
   - Gear select cable
   - Transaxle dipstick tube
   - Cruise control actuator
   - Radiator
   - Fuel line
   - Brake booster vacuum line
   - Powertrain Control Module (PCM) connector. Pull the harness through the firewall into the engine compartment.
   - Exhaust front pipe
   - Accessory drive belt
   - Alternator and bracket
   - Right engine mount bracket
   - Power steering hoses
   - Front engine mount
   - Subframe center section
   - Rear engine mount
   - Left engine mount
8. Lower the powertrain from the vehicle.

To install:

9. Raise the powertrain into position.
10. Install or connect the following:
    - Left engine mount
    - Rear engine mount
    - Subframe center section. Tighten the bolts to 48–65 ft. lbs. (64–89 Nm) and the nut to 50–67 ft. lbs. (67–93 Nm).
    - Front engine mount
    - Power steering hoses
    - Right engine mount bracket
11. Check that the right engine mount stud is centered in the mount bracket with no tension applied to the stud by the bracket.

12. Tighten the engine mount fasteners as follows:
    a. Step 1: Left and rear engine mount through bolts to 63–86 ft. lbs. (85–116 Nm)
    b. Step 2: Front engine mount nuts to 50–67 ft. lbs. (67–93 Nm)
    c. Right engine mount bracket nuts to 56–76 ft. lbs. (75–104 Nm)
13. Install or connect the following:
    - Alternator and bracket
    - Accessory drive belt
    - Exhaust front pipe
    - PCM connector. Pull the harness through the firewall into the passenger compartment.
    - Brake booster vacuum line
    - Fuel line
    - Radiator
    - Cruise control actuator
    - Transaxle dipstick tube
    - Gear select cable
    - Accelerator cable and bracket
    - Air intake assembly
    - Axle halfshafts
    - Inner fender liners
    - Battery and tray
14. Fill the crankcase and transaxle to the correct level.
15. Fill the cooling system.
16. Start the engine and check for leaks.

3.0L Engine

1. Before servicing the vehicle, refer to the precautions in the beginning of this section.
2. Drain the cooling system.
3. Relieve the fuel system pressure.
4. Remove or disconnect the following:
   - Battery
   - Hood
   - Mass Air Flow (MAF) sensor connector
   - Air intake assembly
   - Accessory drive belts
   - Engine under cover
   - Radiator hoses
   - Radiator
   - Cooling fan and shroud
   - Heater hoses
   - Accelerator cable
   - Cruise control cable
   - Evaporative Emissions (EVAP) canister hose
   - Brake booster vacuum hose
   - Fuel lines
   - Alternator

   - Power steering pump
   - A/C compressor
   - Engine control wiring harness connectors
   - Cowl ground cable
   - A/C pipe bracket
   - Exhaust front pipe
   - Radiator grille
   - Upper radiator support
   - Starter motor
   - Torque converter
   - Transmission flange bolts
   - Left and right motor mount nuts
5. Attach a hoist to the engine lifting eyes and raise the engine out of the vehicle.

To install:

6. Lower the engine into the vehicle.
7. Install or connect the following:
   - Left and right motor mount nuts. Tighten the nuts to 24–33 ft. lbs. (32–46 Nm).
   - Transmission flange bolts. Tighten the bolts to 28–38 ft. lbs. (38–51 Nm).
   - Torque converter. Tighten the bolts to 27–39 ft. lbs. (37–53 Nm).
   - Starter motor
   - Upper radiator support
   - Radiator grille
   - Exhaust front pipe. Tighten the nuts to 26–36 ft. lbs. (35–49 Nm) and the bracket bolt to 16–20 ft. lbs. (21–27 Nm).
   - A/C pipe bracket
   - Cowl ground cable
   - Engine control wiring harness connectors
   - A/C compressor
   - Power steering pump
   - Alternator
   - Fuel lines
   - Brake booster vacuum hose
   - EVAP canister hose
   - Accelerator cable
   - Cruise control cable
   - Heater hoses
   - Cooling fan and shroud
   - Radiator hoses
   - Engine under cover
   - Accessory drive belts
   - Air intake assembly
   - MAF sensor connector
   - Hood
   - Battery
8. Fill the cooling system.
9. Start the engine and check for leaks.

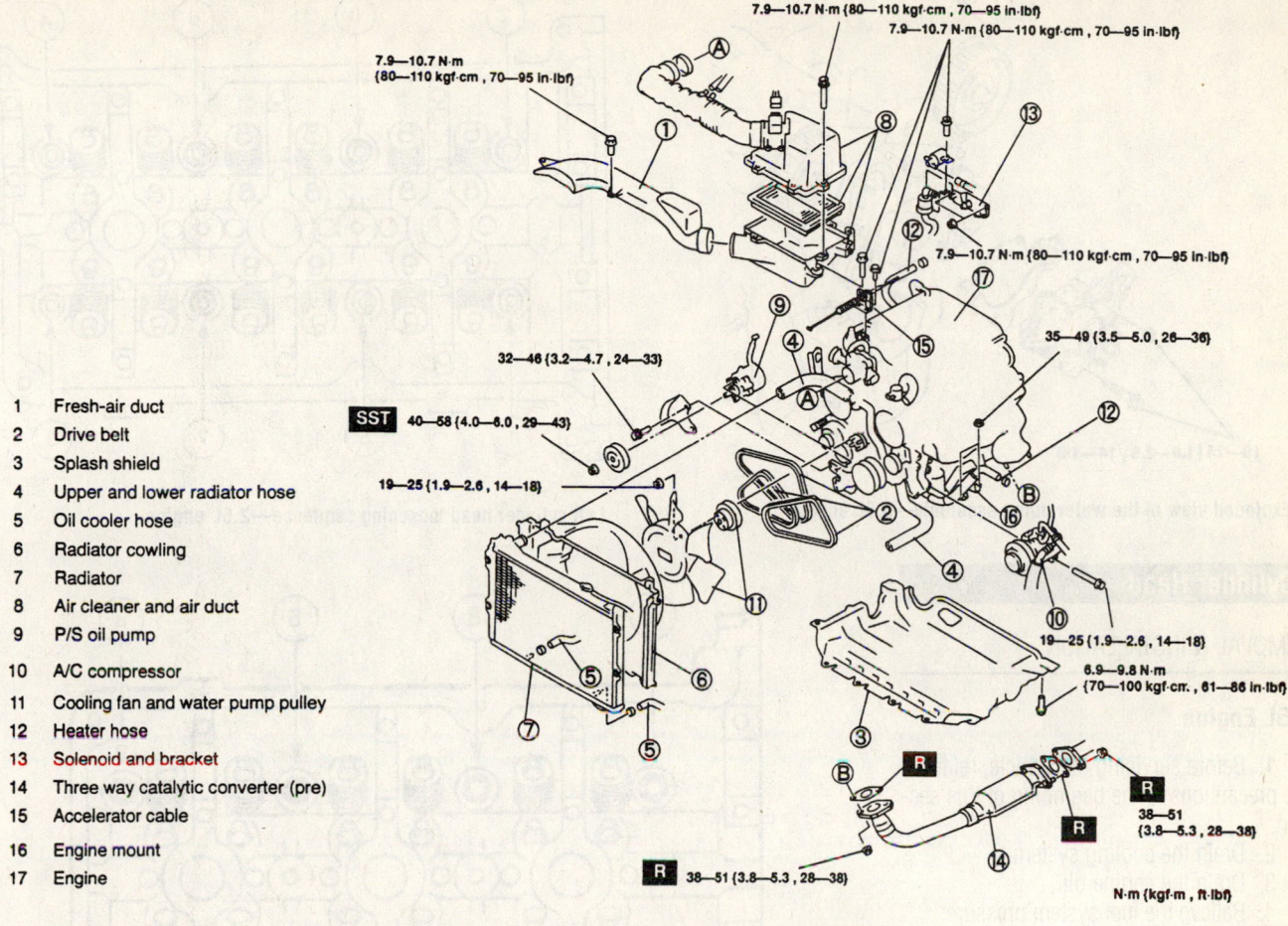

7.9—10.7 N·m {80—110 kgf·cm , 70—95 in·lbf}

7.9—10.7 N·m {80—110 kgf·cm , 70—95 in·lbf}

7.9—10.7 N·m {80—110 kgf·cm , 70—95 in·lbf}

7.9—10.7 N·m {80—110 kgf·cm, 70—95 in·lbf}

35—49 {3.5—5.0 , 26—36}

32—46 {3.2—4.7 , 24—33}

SST 40—58 {4.0—6.0 , 29—43}

19—25 {1.9—2.6 , 14—18}

19—25 {1.9—2.6 , 14—18}

6.9—9.8 N·m
{70—100 kgf·cm , 61—86 in·lbf}

38—51
{3.8—5.3 , 28—38}

38—51 {3.8—5.3 , 28—38}

N·m {kgf·m , ft·lbf}

7924TG04

1	Fresh-air duct
2	Drive belt
3	Splash shield
4	Upper and lower radiator hose
5	Oil cooler hose
6	Radiator cowling
7	Radiator
8	Air cleaner and air duct
9	P/S oil pump
10	A/C compressor
11	Cooling fan and water pump pulley
12	Heater hose
13	Solenoid and bracket
14	Three way catalytic converter (pre)
15	Accelerator cable
16	Engine mount
17	Engine

Exploded view and tightening specifications for engine installation—3.0L engine

Water Pump

REMOVAL & INSTALLATION

2.5L Engine

1. Before servicing the vehicle, refer to the precautions in the beginning of this section.
2. Drain the cooling system.
3. Remove or disconnect the following:
   • Battery and tray
   • Water pump drive belt
   • Water pump drive pulley
   • Thermostat housing
   • Water pump belt tensioner
   • Oil cooler hose
   • Water outlet pipe
   • Water pump

To install:
4. Install or connect the following:
   • Water pump. Tighten the bolts to

89 inch lbs. (10 Nm) plus 90 degrees.
   • Water outlet pipe
   • Oil cooler hose
   • Water pump belt tensioner
   • Thermostat housing
   • Water pump drive pulley
   • Water pump drive belt
   • Battery and tray
5. Fill the cooling system.
6. Start the engine and check for leaks.

3.0L Engine

1. Before servicing the vehicle, refer to the precautions in the beginning of this section.
2. Drain the cooling system.
3. Remove or disconnect the following:
   • Negative battery cable
   • Air intake assembly

   • Upper radiator hose
   • Accessory drive belts
   • Cooling fan and shroud
   • Front cover
   • Timing belt. Refer to the Timing Belt unit repair section.
   • Water pump

To install:
4. Install or connect the following:
   • Water pump. Tighten the fasteners to 14–18 ft. lbs. (19 –25 Nm).
   • Timing belt
   • Front cover
   • Cooling fan and shroud
   • Accessory drive belts
   • Upper radiator hose
   • Air intake assembly
   • Negative battery cable
5. Fill the cooling system.
6. Start the engine and check for leaks.

Timing belt service is covered in Section 4 of this manual

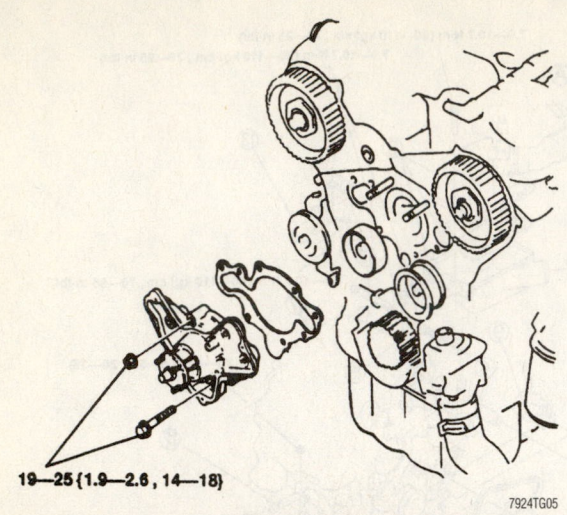

19—25 {1.9—2.6 , 14—18}

Exploded view of the water pump assembly—3.0L engine

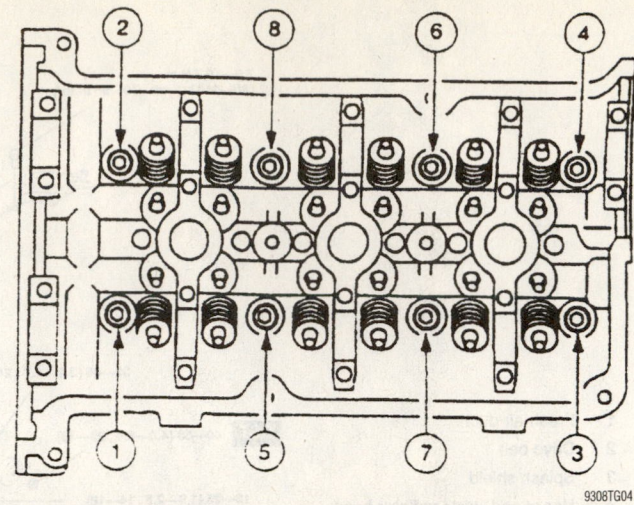

Left cylinder head loosening sequence—2.5L engine

Cylinder Head

REMOVAL & INSTALLATION

2.5L Engine

1. Before servicing the vehicle, refer to the precautions in the beginning of this section.
2. Drain the cooling system.
3. Drain the engine oil.
4. Relieve the fuel system pressure.
5. Remove or disconnect the following:
   - Battery and tray
   - Accessory drive belt
   - Water pump and drive pulley
   - Intake manifold
   - Power steering pump
   - Intake Manifold Runner Control (IMRC) actuator
   - Spark plug wires
   - Ignition coil
   - Heated Oxygen (HO$_2$S) sensor connectors
   - Exhaust front pipe
   - Exhaust Gas Recirculation (EGR) pipe
   - Exhaust manifolds
   - Oil pan
   - Alternator
   - A/C compressor
   - Valve covers
   - Front cover
   - Timing chains
   - Camshafts
   - Cylinder heads. Loosen the bolts in several passes and in the sequence shown.

To install:

➡**The cylinder head bolts are a torque-to-yield design and must be replaced.**

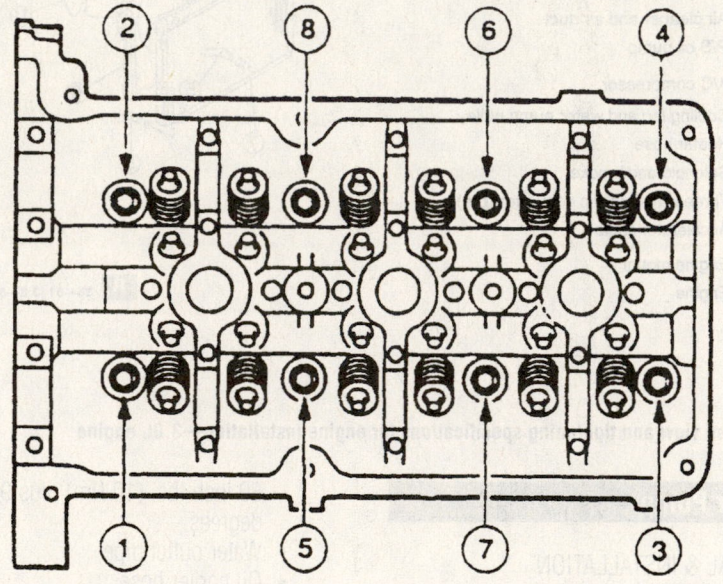

Right cylinder head loosening sequence—2.5L engine

➡**Refer to Section 1 of this manual for the cylinder head torque sequence illustration. The illustration is located after the Torque Specification Chart.**

6. Install the cylinder heads with new gaskets. Tighten the bolts in sequence as follows:
   a. Step 1: 28–31 ft. lbs. (37–43 Nm)
   b. Step 2: Plus 90 degrees
   c. Step 3: Loosen one full turn
   d. Step 4: 28–31 ft. lbs. (37–43 Nm)
   e. Step 5: Plus 90 degrees
   f. Step 6: Plus 90 degrees
7. Install or connect the following:
   - Camshafts
   - Timing chains
   - Front cover
   - Valve covers
   - A/C compressor
   - Alternator
   - Oil pan
   - Exhaust manifolds
   - EGR pipe
   - Exhaust front pipe
   - HO$_2$S sensor connectors
   - Ignition coil
   - Spark plug wires
   - IMRC actuator
   - Power steering pump
   - Intake manifold
   - Water pump and drive pulley
   - Accessory drive belt
   - Battery and tray
8. Fill the crankcase to the correct level.
9. Fill the cooling system.
10. Start the engine and check for leaks.

3.0L Engine

1. Before servicing the vehicle, refer to the precautions in the beginning of this section.
2. Drain the cooling system.
3. Relieve the fuel system pressure.
4. Remove or disconnect the following:
   - Negative battery cable
   - Air intake assembly
   - Spark plug wires
   - Distributor
   - Accessory drive belts
   - Cooling fan and shroud
   - Upper radiator hose
   - Front cover
   - Timing belt. Refer to the Timing Belt unit repair section.
   - Intake manifold
   - Exhaust manifolds

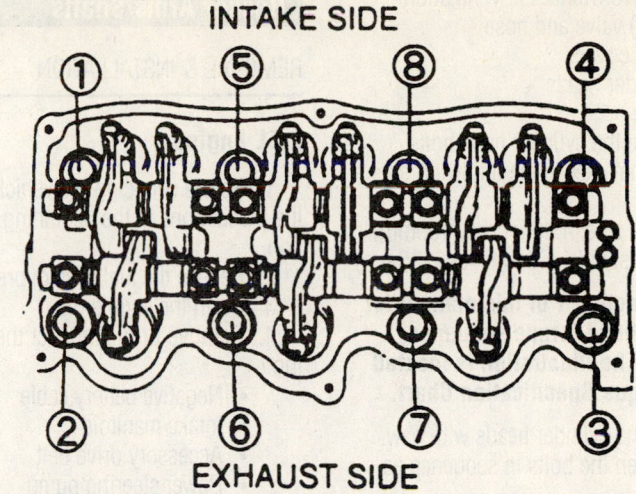

INTAKE SIDE

EXHAUST SIDE

7924TG09

Cylinder head bolt removal sequence—3.0L engine

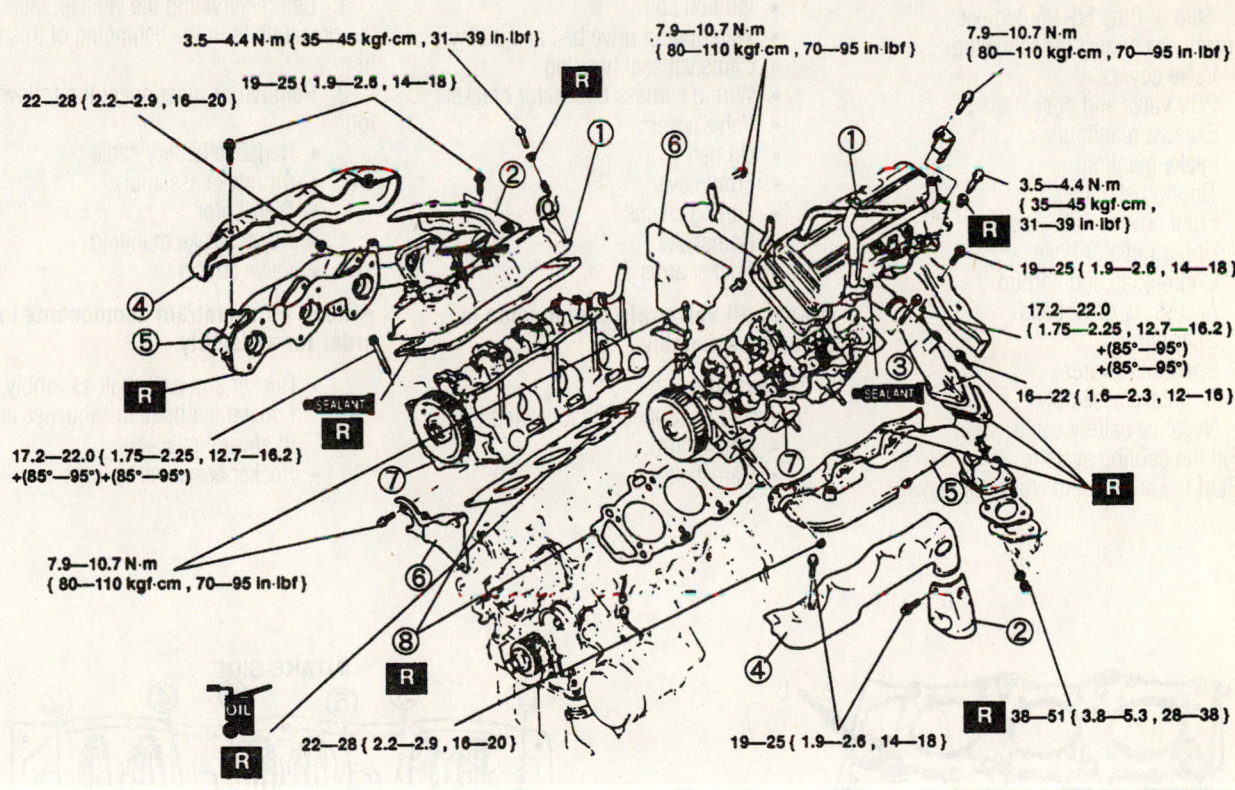

3.5—4.4 N·m { 35—45 kgf·cm , 31—39 in·lbf }

19—25 { 1.9—2.6 , 14—18 }

22—28 { 2.2—2.9 , 16—20 }

7.9—10.7 N·m { 80—110 kgf·cm , 70—95 in·lbf }

7.9—10.7 N·m { 80—110 kgf·cm , 70—95 in·lbf }

3.5—4.4 N·m { 35—45 kgf·cm , 31—39 in·lbf }

19—25 { 1.9—2.6 , 14—18 }

17.2—22.0 { 1.75—2.25, 12.7—16.2 } +(85°—95°) +(85°—95°)

16—22 { 1.6—2.3 , 12—16 }

17.2—22.0 { 1.75—2.25 , 12.7—16.2 } +(85°—95°)+(85°—95°)

7.9—10.7 N·m { 80—110 kgf·cm , 70—95 in·lbf }

22—28 { 2.2—2.9 , 16—20 }

19—25 { 1.9—2.6 , 14—18 }

38—51 { 3.8—5.3 , 28—38 }

N·m { kgf·m , ft·lbf }

R = replace

1	Cylinder head cover ☞ Installation Note	6	Seal plate
2	Center exhaust pipe insulator	7	Cylinder head
3	Center exhaust pipe	8	Cylinder head gasket
4	Exhaust manifold insulator		
5	Exhaust manifold		

7924TG06

Exploded view of the cylinder head components—3.0L engine

- Positive Crankcase Ventilation (PCV) valve and hose
- Valve covers
- Cylinder heads

To install:

5. Measure the cylinder head bolts. Replace any that exceed the following specifications:

- Intake side: 4.29 inches (109mm)
- Exhaust side: 5.47 inches (139mm)

➡ **Refer to Section 1 of this manual for the cylinder head torque sequence illustration. The illustration is located after the Torque Specification Chart.**

6. Install the cylinder heads with new gaskets. Tighten the bolts in sequence as follows:

    a. Step 1: 13–16 ft. lbs. (17–22 Nm)

    b. Step 2: Plus 85–95 degrees

    c. Step 3: Plus 85–95 degrees

7. Install or connect the following:

- Valve covers
- PCV valve and hose
- Exhaust manifolds
- Intake manifold
- Timing belt
- Front cover
- Upper radiator hose
- Cooling fan and shroud
- Accessory drive belts
- Distributor
- Spark plug wires
- Air intake assembly
- Negative battery cable

8. Fill the cooling system.
9. Start the engine and check for leaks.

Rocker Arms/Shafts

REMOVAL & INSTALLATION

2.5L Engine

1. Before servicing the vehicle, refer to the precautions in the beginning of this section.
2. Relieve the fuel system pressure.
3. Drain the engine oil.
4. Remove or disconnect the following:

- Negative battery cable
- Intake manifold
- Accessory drive belt
- Power steering pump
- Intake Manifold Runner Control (IMRC) actuator
- Spark plug wires
- Ignition coil
- Water pump drive belt and pulley
- Camshaft seal housing
- Wiring harness connector bracket
- Valve covers
- Oil pan
- Front cover
- Timing chains
- Camshafts
- Rocker arms

➡ **Keep all valvetrain components in order for assembly.**

To install:

5. Install or connect the following:
- Rocker arms
- Camshafts

- Timing chains
- Front cover
- Oil pan
- Valve covers
- Wiring harness connector bracket
- Camshaft seal housing
- Water pump drive belt and pulley
- Ignition coil
- Spark plug wires
- Intake Manifold Runner Control (IMRC) actuator
- Power steering pump
- Accessory drive belt
- Intake manifold
- Negative battery cable

6. Fill the crankcase to the correct level.
7. Start the engine and check for leaks.

3.0L Engine

1. Before servicing the vehicle, refer to the precautions in the beginning of this section.
2. Remove or disconnect the following:

- Negative battery cable
- Air intake assembly
- Distributor
- Upper intake manifold
- Valve covers

➡ **Keep all valvetrain components in order for assembly.**

- Rocker arm and shaft assembly. Loosen the bolts in sequence and in several passes.
- Rocker arms and springs

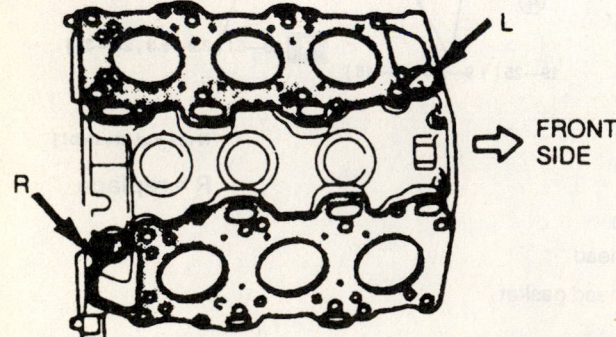

Head gasket positioning—3.0L engine

7924TG07

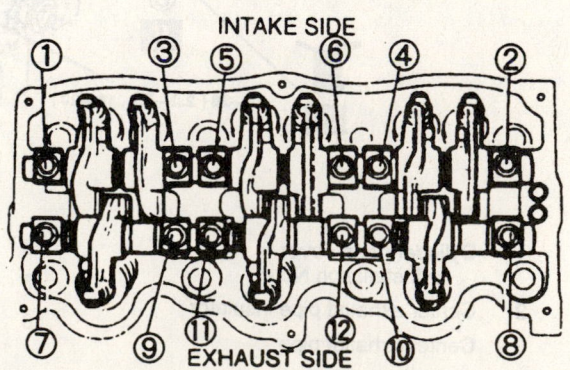

Rocker arm shaft bolt removal sequence—3.0L engine

7924TG10

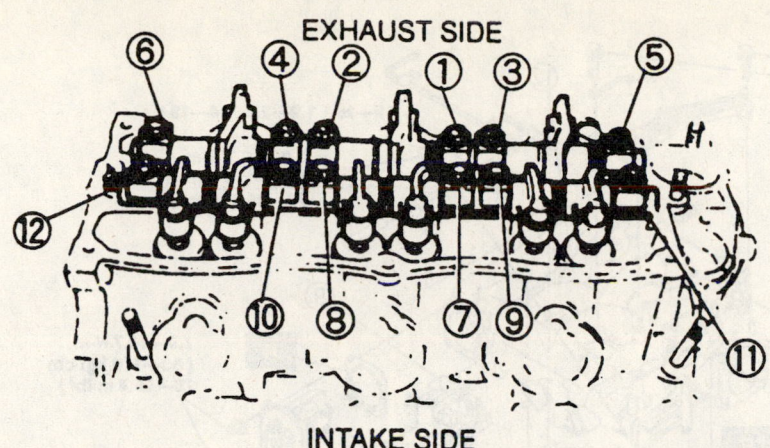

EXHAUST SIDE

INTAKE SIDE

7924TG11

Rocker arm/shaft retaining bolt tightening sequence—3.0L engine

To install:

3. Install the rocker arms and springs in their original positions on the rocker arm shafts.

4. Install or connect the following:
- Rocker arm and shaft assembly. Tighten the bolts in sequence and in several passes to 14–19 ft. lbs. (19–26 Nm).
- Valve covers
- Upper intake manifold
- Distributor
- Air intake assembly
- Negative battery cable

5. Start the engine and check for leaks.

Intake Manifold

REMOVAL & INSTALLATION

2.5L Engine

1. Before servicing the vehicle, refer to the precautions in the beginning of this section.

2. Relieve the fuel system pressure.

3. Remove or disconnect the following:
- Negative battery cable
- Air cleaner housing and fresh air duct
- Mass Air Flow (MAF) sensor
- Throttle body intake hose
- Accelerator cable and bracket
- Intake Manifold Runner Control (IMRC) cable at the IMRC housing
- Throttle body
- Exhaust Gas Recirculation (EGR) valve
- Idle Air Control (IAC) valve

- Pressure Regulator Control (PRC) solenoid
- Intake manifold
- Fuel lines
- Fuel pressure regulator vacuum line
- Fuel supply manifold
- IMRC housing

To install:

➡ Refer to Section 1 of this manual for the intake manifold torque sequence illustration. The illustration is located after the Torque Specification Chart.

4. Install or connect the following:
- IMRC housing. Tighten the bolts in sequence to 72–105 inch lbs. (8–12 Nm).
- Fuel supply manifold. Tighten the bolts to 72–105 inch lbs. (8–12 Nm).
- Fuel pressure regulator vacuum line
- Fuel lines
- Intake manifold. Tighten the bolts in sequence to 72–105 inch lbs. (8–12 Nm).
- PRC solenoid. Tighten the bolt to 45–61 inch lbs. (5–7 Nm).
- IAC valve. Tighten the bolts to 72–105 inch lbs. (8–12 Nm).
- EGR valve
- Throttle body. Tighten the bolts to 72–105 inch lbs. (8–12 Nm).
- IMRC cable
- Accelerator cable and bracket. Tighten the bolt to 71–94 inch lbs. (8–11 Nm).
- Throttle body intake hose
- MAF sensor

- Air cleaner housing and fresh air duct
- Negative battery cable

5. Start the engine and check for leaks.

3.0L Engine

1. Before servicing the vehicle, refer to the precautions in the beginning of this section.

2. Drain the cooling system.

3. Relieve the fuel system pressure.

4. Remove or disconnect the following:
- Negative battery cable
- Fresh air duct
- Air intake hose
- Air cleaner assembly
- Mass Air Flow (MAF) sensor
- Accelerator cable
- Cruise control cable
- Idle Air Control (IAC) valve connector and hoses
- Bypass air solenoid valve connector, if equipped
- Vacuum solenoid valve connectors
- Upper radiator hose
- Heater hose
- Bypass hose
- Intake manifold vacuum lines
- Upper intake manifold
- Fuel lines
- Fuel supply manifold
- Lower intake manifold

To install:

➡ Refer to Section 1 of this manual for the intake manifold torque sequence illustration. The illustration is located after the Torque Specification Chart.

5. Install the lower intake manifold with new gaskets. Install the washers with the white paint marks facing **UP**. Tighten the nuts to 14–18 ft. lbs. (19–25 Nm).

6. Install or connect the following:
- Fuel supply manifold. Tighten the nuts to 14–18 ft. lbs. (19–25 Nm).
- Fuel lines
- Upper intake manifold. Tighten the bolts to 70–95 inch lbs. (8–11 Nm).
- Intake manifold vacuum lines
- Bypass hose
- Heater hose
- Upper radiator hose
- Vacuum solenoid valve connectors
- Bypass air solenoid valve connector, if equipped
- IAC valve connector and hoses
- Accelerator cable
- Cruise control cable

Refer to Section 1 for engine rebuilding specifications

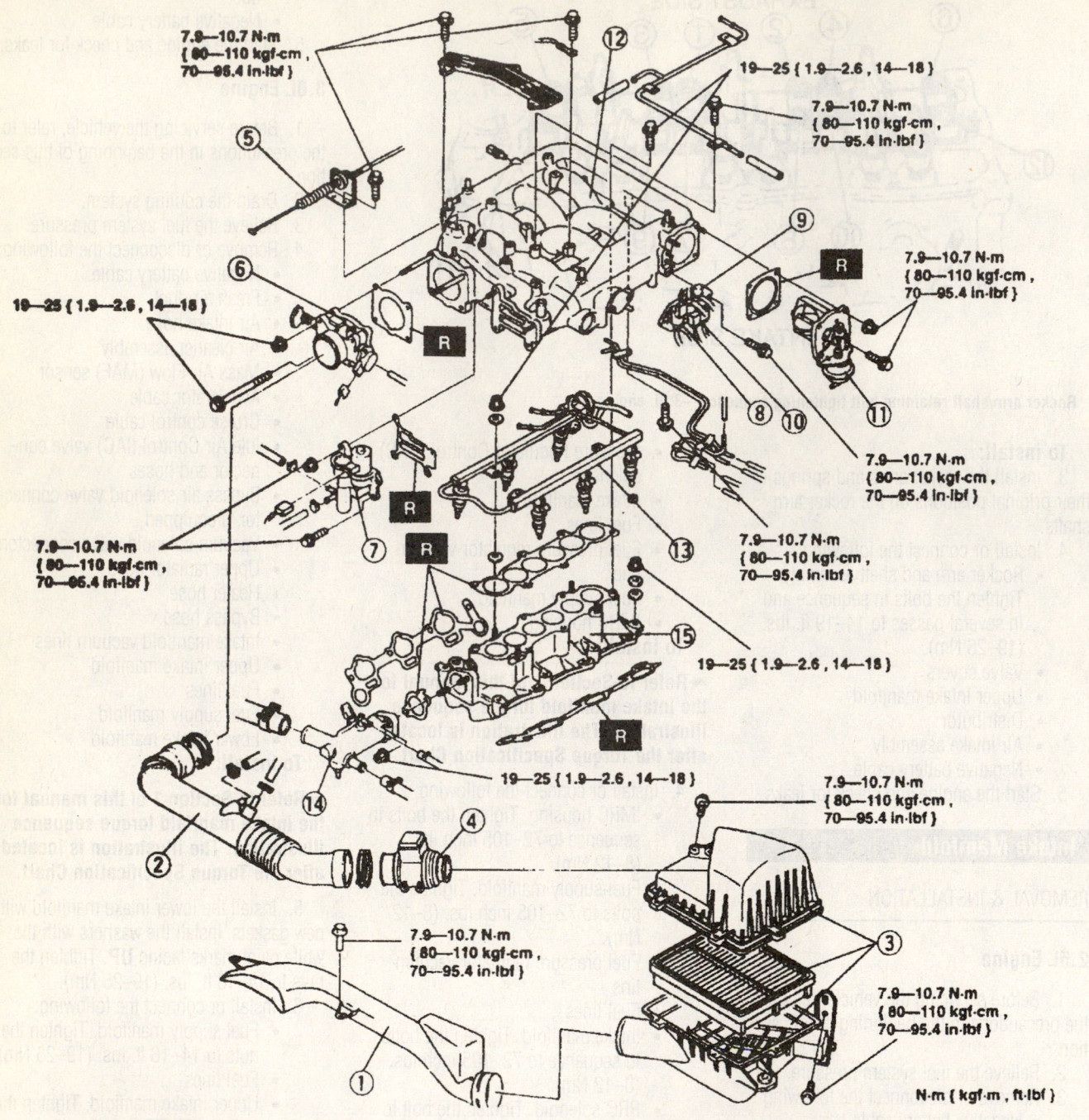

7.9—10.7 N·m
{ 80—110 kgf-cm ,
70—95.4 in-lbf }

19—25 { 1.9—2.6 , 14—18 }

7.9—10.7 N·m
{ 80—110 kgf-cm ,
70—95.4 in-lbf }

7.9—10.7 N·m
{ 80—110 kgf-cm ,
70—95.4 in-lbf }

19—25 { 1.9—2.6 , 14—18 }

7.9—10.7 N·m
{ 80—110 kgf-cm ,
70—95.4 in-lbf }

7.9—10.7 N·m
{ 80—110 kgf-cm ,
70—95.4 in-lbf }

7.9—10.7 N·m
{ 80—110 kgf-cm ,
70—95.4 in-lbf }

19—25 { 1.9—2.6 , 14—18 }

19—25 { 1.9—2.6 , 14—18 }

7.9—10.7 N·m
{ 80—110 kgf-cm ,
70—95.4 in-lbf }

7.9—10.7 N·m
{ 80—110 kgf-cm ,
70—95.4 in-lbf }

N·m { kgf·m , ft-lbf }

1. Fresh-air duct
2. Air intake hose
3. Air cleaner
4. Mass air flow sensor
5. Accelerator cable
6. Throttle body
7. BAC valve
8. VRIS solenoid valve
9. PRC solenoid valve No.1
10. PRC solenoid valve No.2
11. VRIS shutter valve actuator
12. Dynamic chamber
13. Fuel distributor
14. Water outlet pipe
15. Intake manifold

7924TG13

Exploded view of the intake air system—3.0L engine

- MAF sensor
- Air cleaner assembly
- Air intake hose
- Fresh air duct
- Negative battery cable
7. Fill the cooling system.
8. Start the engine and check for leaks.

Exhaust Manifold

REMOVAL & INSTALLATION

2.5L Engine

1. Before servicing the vehicle, refer to the precautions in the beginning of this section.
2. Remove or disconnect the following:
   - Negative battery cable
   - Subframe transverse section
   - Heated Oxygen (HO$_2$S) sensor connectors
   - Exhaust front pipe
   - Exhaust Gas Recirculation (EGR) pipe
   - Exhaust manifolds

To install:
3. Install or connect the following:
   - Exhaust manifolds. Tighten the nuts in sequence to 14 ft. lbs. (20 Nm).
   - EGR pipe

Left exhaust manifold torque sequence–2.5L engine

   - Exhaust front pipe
   - HO$_2$S sensor connectors
   - Subframe transverse section. Tighten the bolts to 69–96 ft. lbs. (94–131 Nm).
   - Negative battery cable
4. Start the engine and check for leaks.

Right exhaust manifold torque sequence–2.5L engine

3.0L Engine

1. Before servicing the vehicle, refer to the precautions in the beginning of this section.
2. Remove or disconnect the following:
   - Negative battery cable
   - Engine under cover
   - Heated Oxygen (HO$_2$S) sensor connectors
   - Exhaust front pipe
   - Exhaust manifold heat shields
   - Cross over pipe
   - Exhaust manifolds

To install:

➡**Use new fasteners and gaskets for assembly.**

3. Install or connect the following:
   - Exhaust manifolds. Tighten the fasteners to 16–20 ft. lbs. (22–28 Nm).
   - Cross over pipe. Tighten the bolts to 12–16 ft. lbs. (16–22 Nm).
   - Exhaust manifold heat shields. Tighten the bolts to 14–18 ft. lbs. (19–25 Nm).
   - Exhaust front pipe. Tighten the nuts to 28–38 ft. lbs. (38–51 Nm).
   - HO$_2$S sensor connectors
   - Engine under cover
   - Negative battery cable
4. Start the engine and check for leaks.

For engine torque specifications, refer to Section 1 of this manual

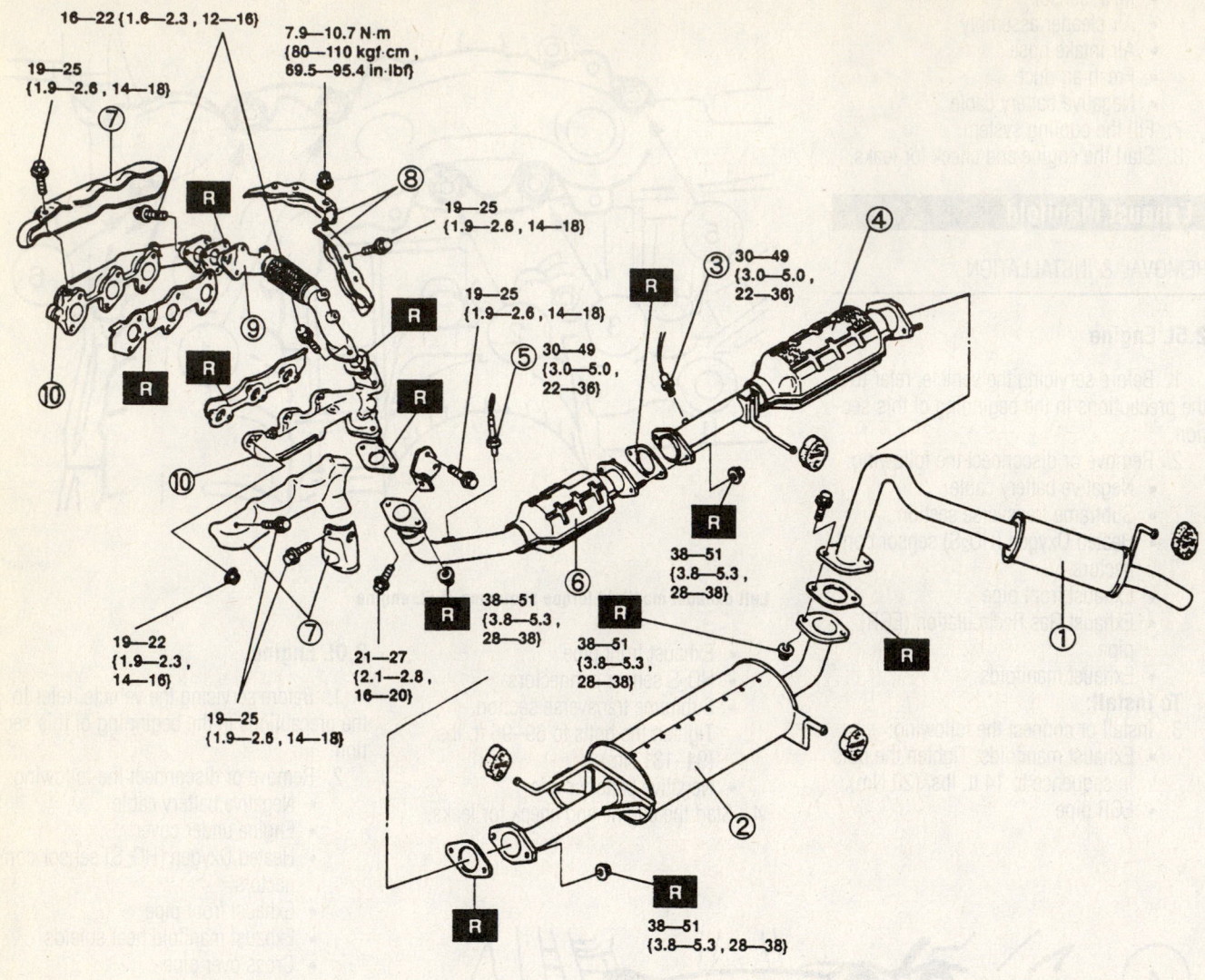

16—22 {1.6—2.3 , 12—16}

19—25
{1.9—2.6 , 14—18}

7.9—10.7 N·m
{80—110 kgf·cm ,
69.5—95.4 in·lbf}

19—25
{1.9—2.6 , 14—18}

19—25
{1.9—2.6 , 14—18}

30—49
{3.0—5.0 ,
22—36}

30—49
{3.0—5.0 ,
22—36}

38—51
{3.8—5.3 ,
28—38}

19—22
{1.9—2.3 ,
14—16}

21—27
{2.1—2.8 ,
16—20}

38—51
{3.8—5.3 ,
28—38}

38—51
{3.8—5.3 ,
28—38}

19—25
{1.9—2.6 , 14—18}

38—51
{3.8—5.3 , 28—38}

N·m {kgf·m , ft·lbf}

7924TG15

Exploded view of the exhaust system—3.0L engine

Front Crankshaft Seal

REMOVAL & INSTALLATION

2.5L Engine

Refer to the Timing Chain, Sprockets, Front Cover and Seal procedure in this section.

3.0L Engine

1. Before servicing the vehicle, refer to the precautions in the beginning of this section.
2. Remove or disconnect the following:
   - Negative battery cable
   - Accessory drive belts
   - Crankshaft pulley
   - Front cover
   - Timing belt. Refer to the Timing Belt unit repair section.
   - Crankshaft timing sprocket
   - Front crankshaft seal

To install:

3. Install or connect the following:
   - Front crankshaft seal flush with the oil pump housing
   - Crankshaft timing sprocket
   - Timing belt
   - Front cover
   - Crankshaft pulley. Tighten the bolt to 116–122 ft. lbs. (157–166 Nm).
   - Accessory drive belts
   - Negative battery cable
4. Start the engine and check for leaks.

Camshaft and Valve Lifters

REMOVAL & INSTALLATION

2.5L Engine

1. Before servicing the vehicle, refer to the precautions in the beginning of this section.
2. Relieve the fuel system pressure.
3. Drain the engine oil.
4. Remove or disconnect the following:
   - Negative battery cable
   - Intake manifold
   - Accessory drive belt
   - Power steering pump
   - Intake Manifold Runner Control (IMRC) actuator

- Spark plug wires
- Ignition coil
- Exhaust front pipe
- Oil pan
- Alternator and bracket
- A/C compressor
- Water pump belt and drive pulley
- Camshaft oil seal housing
- Wiring harness connector bracket
- Valve covers
- Front cover
- Timing chains

➡**Keep all valvetrain components in order for assembly**

➡**Remove the camshaft thrust bearing caps before loosening any of the other bearing cap bolts.**

- Camshaft thrust bearing caps. Loosen the bolts evenly in several passes.
- Remaining camshaft bearing caps. Loosen the bolts evenly in several passes.
- Camshafts
- Rocker arms
- Hydraulic lifters

To install:

⚠ **WARNING**

The crankshaft keyway must be at the 11 o'clock position before reassembly. Failure to do so may lead to engine damage.

5. Rotate the crankshaft so that the keyway is at the 11 o'clock position for installation of the camshafts.
6. Install or connect the following:
   - Hydraulic lifters
   - Rocker arms.
   - Camshafts. Align the sprocket timing marks.

➡**Do not install the camshaft journal thrust caps until the rocker arms and timing chains have been installed and the camshaft journal caps are secured into position.**

- All camshaft journal caps except the thrust caps.
- Timing chains. Tighten the camshaft journal cap bolts in reverse of the loosening order and

in several steps to 71–106 inch lbs. (8–12 Nm).
- Thrust caps. Tighten the bolts to 71–106 inch lbs. (8–12 Nm).
- Front cover
- Valve covers
- Wiring harness connector bracket
- Camshaft oil seal housing
- Water pump belt and drive pulley
- A/C compressor
- Alternator and bracket
- Oil pan
- Exhaust front pipe
- Ignition coil
- Spark plug wires
- IMRC actuator
- Power steering pump
- Accessory drive belt
- Intake manifold
- Negative battery cable

7. Fill the crankcase to the correct level.
8. Fill the cooling system.
9. Start the engine and check for leaks.

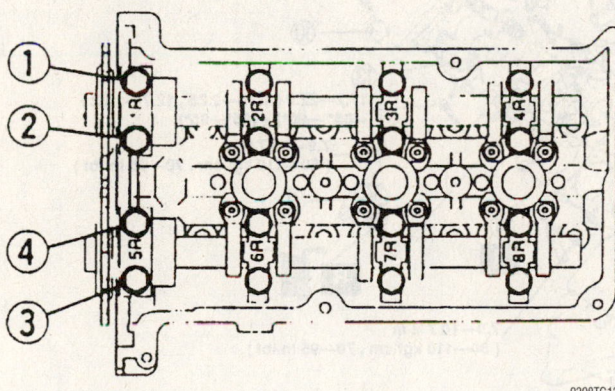

Right bank camshaft thrust cap loosening sequence—2.5L engine

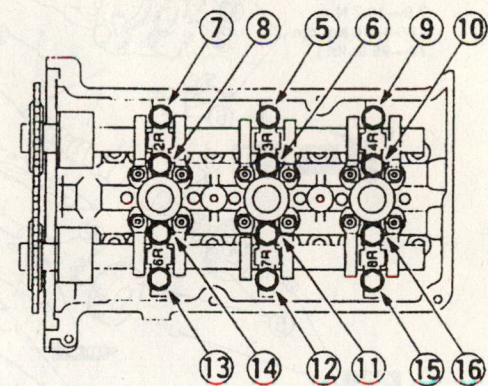

Right bank camshaft bearing cap loosening sequence—2.5L engine

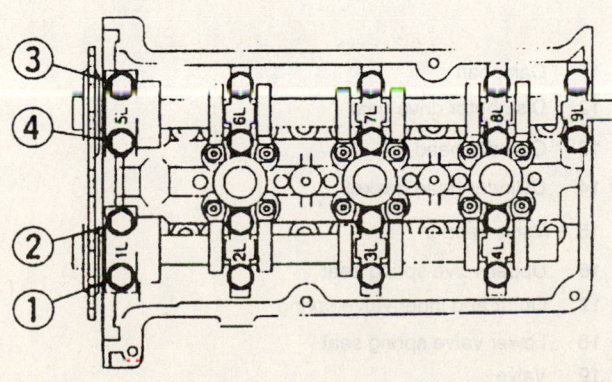

Left bank camshaft thrust cap loosening sequence—2.5L engine

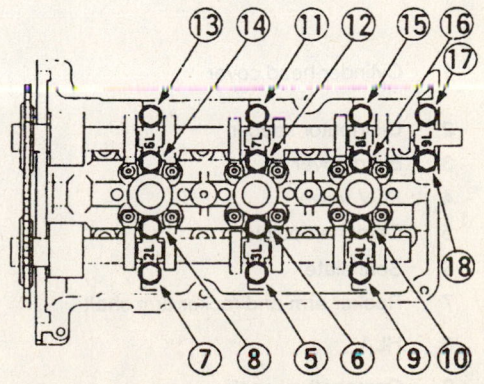

Left bank camshaft bearing cap loosening sequence—2.5L engine

For complete mechanical specifications, refer to Section 1 of this manual

3.0L Engine

VALVE LIFTERS

➡ **Keep all valvetrain components in order for assembly.**

1. Before servicing the vehicle, refer to the precautions in the beginning of this section.

2. Remove the rocker arms from the vehicle.

3. Remove the hydraulic lash adjusters from the rocker arms.

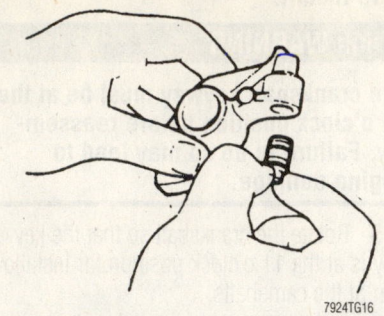

Hydraulic lash adjuster—3.0L engine

To install:

4. Inspect the hydraulic lash adjuster O-rings and replace if damaged.

5. Fill the rocker arm oil reservoir with clean engine oil.

6. Install the hydraulic lash adjusters to the rocker arms in their original positions.

7. Install the rocker arms to the vehicle.

CAMSHAFTS

1. Before servicing the vehicle, refer to the precautions in the beginning of this section.

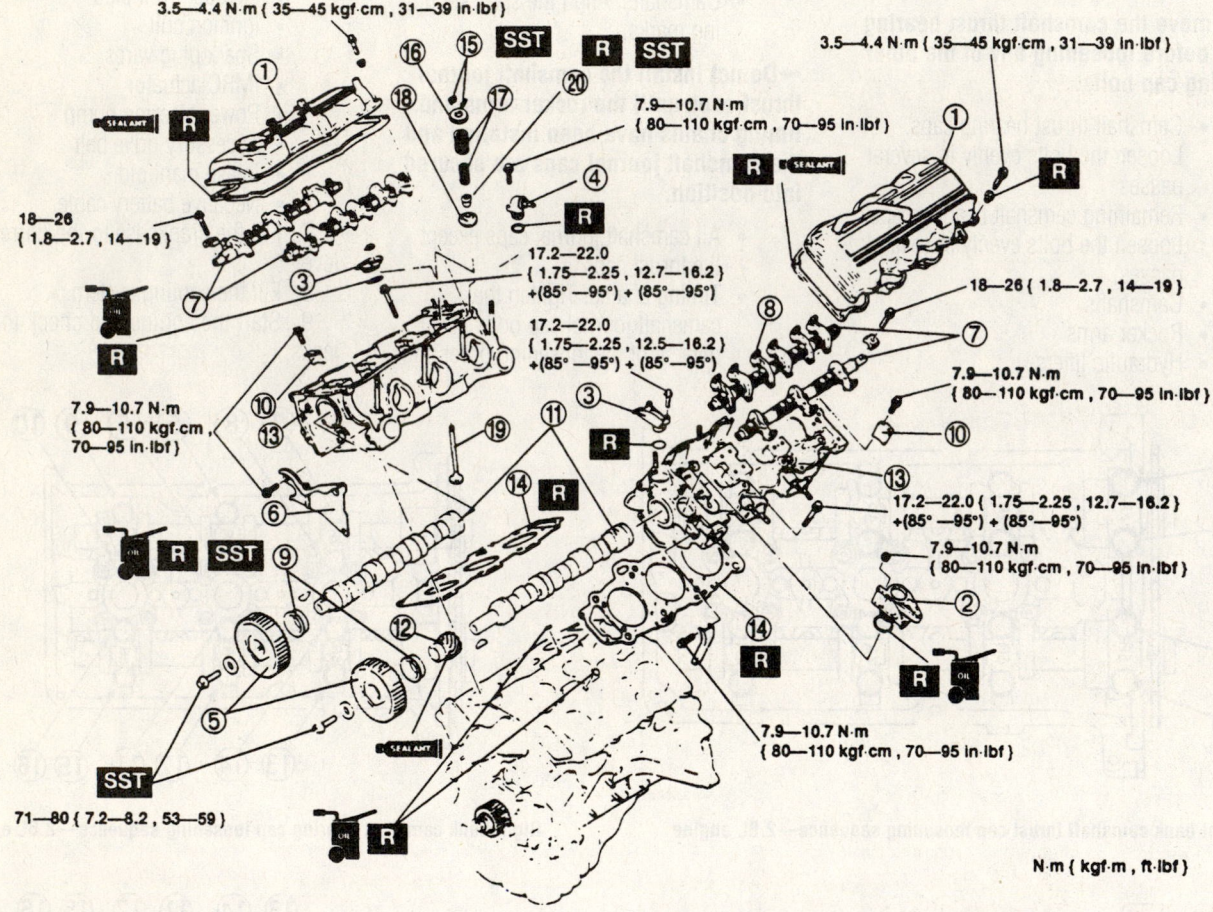

N·m { kgf·m , ft·lbf }

1	Cylinder head cover	11	Camshaft
2	Distributor spacer	12	Distributor drive gear
3	Blind cover	13	Cylinder head
4	PCV valve	14	Cylinder head gasket
5	Camshaft pulley	15	Valve keeper
6	Seal plate	16	Upper valve spring seat
7	Rocker arm and rocker arm shaft	17	Outer and inner valve spring
8	HLA	18	Lower valve spring seat
9	Camshaft oil seal	19	Valve
10	Thrust plate	20	Valve seal

Exploded view of cylinder head components—3.0L engine

2. Remove or disconnect the following:
- Negative battery cable
- Accessory drive belts
- Front cover
- Timing belt. Refer to the Timing Belt unit repair section.
- Distributor
- Distributor spacer
- Valve covers
- Rocker arms and shafts
- Camshaft sprockets
- Camshaft seal plates and seals
- Camshaft thrust plates
- Camshafts

To install:

3. Install or connect the following:
- Camshafts
- Camshaft thrust plates. Tighten the bolts to 70–95 inch lbs. (8–11 Nm).
- Camshaft seal plates and seals. Tighten the bolts to 70–95 inch lbs. (8–11 Nm).
- Camshaft sprockets. Tighten the bolts to 52–59 ft. lbs. (71–80 Nm).
- Rocker arms and shafts
- Valve covers
- Distributor spacer
- Distributor
- Timing belt
- Front cover
- Accessory drive belts
- Negative battery cable
4. Start the engine and check for leaks.

Valve Lash

ADJUSTMENT

The engines covered in this section are equipped with hydraulic lash adjusters. Valve clearance adjustments are not possible.

Starter Motor

REMOVAL & INSTALLATION

2.5L Engine

1. Before servicing the vehicle, refer to the precautions in the beginning of this section.
2. Remove or disconnect the following:
- Battery and tray
- Air intake assembly
- Gear select cable
- Starter harness connectors
- Starter motor

To install:

3. Install or connect the following:
- Starter motor. Tighten the bolts to 28–38 ft. lbs. (38–51 Nm).
- Starter harness connectors. Tighten the battery cable nut to 87–104 inch lbs. (10–12 Nm).
- Gear select cable
- Air intake assembly
- Battery and tray

3.0L Engine

2 WHEEL DRIVE

1. Before servicing the vehicle, refer to the precautions in the beginning of this section.
2. Remove or disconnect the following:
- Negative battery cable
- Starter harness connectors
- Starter motor

To install:

3. Install or connect the following:
- Starter motor. Tighten the bolts to 24–33 ft. lbs. (32–46 Nm).
- Starter harness connectors. Tighten the battery cable nut to 87–104 inch lbs. (10–12 Nm).
- Negative battery cable

4 WHEEL DRIVE

1. Before servicing the vehicle, refer to the precautions in the beginning of this section.
2. Remove or disconnect the following:
- Negative battery cable
- Alternator
- Engine under covers
- Power steering pump
- Front driveshaft
- Wiring harness bracket
- Transmission oil cooler pipe brackets
- Starter harness connectors
- Fuel and brake pipe cover
- Starter motor

To install:

3. Install or connect the following:
- Starter motor. Tighten the bolts to 28–38 ft. lbs. (38–51 Nm).
- Fuel and brake pipe cover
- Starter harness connectors. Tighten the battery cable nut to 87–104 inch lbs. (10–12 Nm).
- Transmission oil cooler pipe brackets
- Wiring harness bracket
- Front driveshaft
- Power steering pump
- Engine under covers

- Alternator
- Negative battery cable

Oil Pan

REMOVAL & INSTALLATION

1997–98 MPV

2 WHEEL DRIVE

1. Before servicing the vehicle, refer to the precautions in the beginning of this section.
2. Drain the engine oil.
3. Remove or disconnect the following:
- Negative battery cable
- Engine under cover
- Transmission brackets
- Oil pan

To install:

4. Install or connect the following:
- Oil pan. Tighten the bolts to 61–86 inch lbs. (7–10 Nm).
- Transmission brackets. Tighten the bolts to 28–38 ft. lbs. (38–51 Nm).
- Engine under cover
- Negative battery cable
5. Fill the crankcase to the correct level.
6. Start the engine and check for leaks.

4 WHEEL DRIVE

1. Before servicing the vehicle, refer to the precautions in the beginning of this section.
2. Drain the engine oil.
3. Attach a support fixture to the engine lifting eyes.
4. Remove or disconnect the following:
- Negative battery cable
- Air intake duct
- Cooling fan shroud
- Motor mounts
- Lower transmission mount. Support the transmission.
- Oil cooler hose and pipe
- Stabilizer bar brackets
- Transmission brackets
- Oil pan

To install:

5. Install or connect the following:
- Oil pan. Tighten the bolts to 61–86 inch lbs. (7–10 Nm).
- Transmission brackets. Tighten the bolts to 28–38 ft. lbs. (38–51 Nm).
- Stabilizer bar brackets. Tighten the bolts to 14–18 ft. lbs. (19–25 Nm).
- Oil cooler hose and pipe
- Lower transmission mount. Tighten the bolts to 32–44 ft. lbs. (44–60

Please refer to Section 8 for electric cooling fan wiring schematics

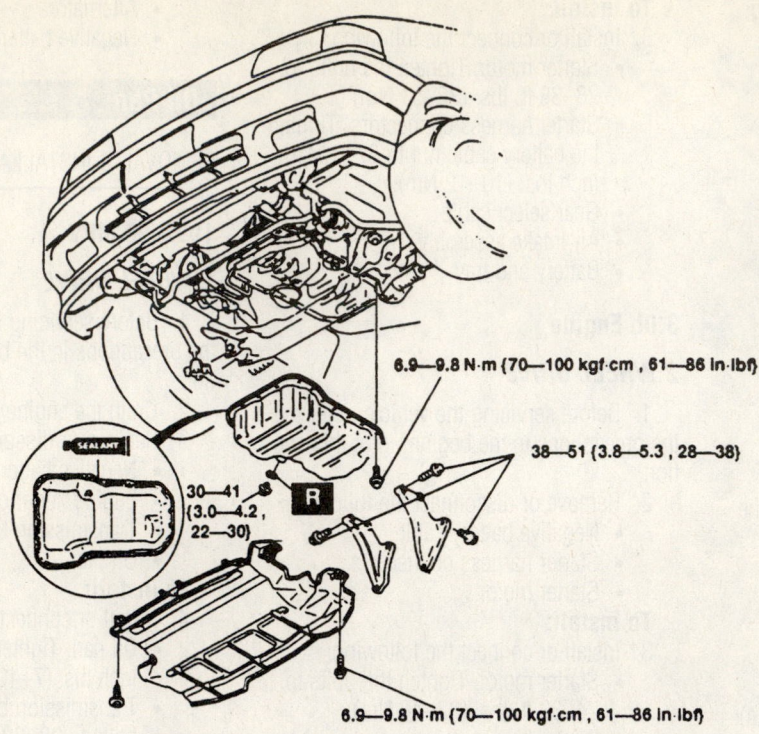

6.9—9.8 N·m {70—100 kgf·cm , 61—86 in·lbf}

38—51 {3.8—5.3 , 28—38}

30—41 {3.0—4.2 , 22—30}

R

6.9—9.8 N·m {70—100 kgf·cm , 61—86 in·lbf}

N·m {kgf·m , ft·lbf}

7924TG18

Exploded view of oil pan mounting—1997–98 2WD vehicles

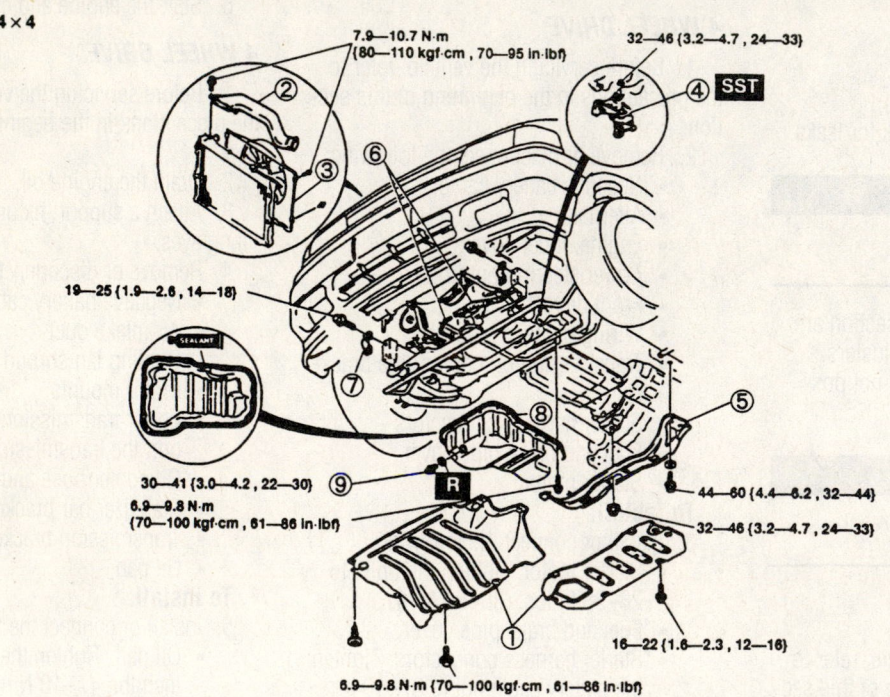

4 × 4

7.9—10.7 N·m {80—110 kgf·cm , 70—95 in·lbf}

32—46 {3.2—4.7 , 24—33}

SST

19—25 {1.9—2.6 , 14—18}

30—41 {3.0—4.2 , 22—30}

R

6.9—9.8 N·m {70—100 kgf·cm , 61—86 in·lbf}

44—60 {4.4—6.2 , 32—44}

32—46 {3.2—4.7 , 24—33}

16—22 {1.6—2.3 , 12—16}

6.9—9.8 N·m {70—100 kgf·cm , 61—86 in·lbf}

N·m {kgf·m , ft·lbf}

1 Splash shield	6 Oil cooler hose and pipe
2 Fresh-air duct	7 Stabilizer bracket
3 Fan cowling	8 Oil pan
4 Engine mount	9 Drain plug
5 Transmission lower mount	

7924TG19

Exploded view of oil pan mounting—1997–98 4WD vehicles

Nm) and the nut to 24–33 ft. lbs. (32–46 Nm).

- Motor mounts. Tighten the nuts to 24–33 ft. lbs. (32–46 Nm).
- Cooling fan shroud
- Air intake duct
- Negative battery cable

6. Fill the crankcase to the correct level.
7. Start the engine and check for leaks.

2000–01 MPV

1. Before servicing the vehicle, refer to the precautions in the beginning of this section.
2. Drain the engine oil.
3. Remove or disconnect the following:
   - Negative battery cable
   - Subframe transverse section
   - Exhaust front pipe
   - Flywheel access panel
   - Transaxle housing bolts
   - Oil pan bolts. Loosen the bolts in reverse of the tightening sequence and in several steps.
   - Oil pan

To install:

4. Apply a bead of silicone sealer to the gasket area where the pan meets the parting lines of the lower cylinder block and the front engine cover.
5. Install or connect the following:
   - Oil pan. Use a new gasket, tighten the pan bolts in several passes to 15–22 ft. lbs. (20–30 Nm), then tighten the transaxle case bolts to 28–38 ft. lbs. (38–51 Nm).
   - Flywheel access panel

- Exhaust front pipe
- Subframe transverse section. Tighten the bolts to 69–96 ft. lbs. (94–131 Nm).
- Negative battery cable

6. Fill the crankcase to the correct level.
7. Start the engine and check for leaks.

Oil Pump

REMOVAL & INSTALLATION

2.5L Engine

1. Before servicing the vehicle, refer to the precautions in the beginning of this section.
2. Drain the engine oil.
3. Remove or disconnect the following:
   - Negative battery cable
   - Oil pan
   - Timing chains
   - Oil pump pick up tube
   - Oil pump. Loosen the bolts in reverse of the tightening sequence.

To install:

4. Install or connect the following:
   - Oil pump. Tighten the bolts in sequence to 71–106 inch lbs. (8–12 Nm).
   - Oil pump pick up tube. Tighten the bolts to 71–106 inch lbs. (8–12 Nm) and the nut to 44 inch lbs. (5 Nm) plus 45 degrees.
   - Timing chains
   - Oil pan
   - Negative battery cable

5. Fill the crankcase to the correct level.
6. Start the engine and check for leaks.

3.0L Engine

1. Before servicing the vehicle, refer to the precautions in the beginning of this section.
2. Drain the cooling system.
3. Drain the engine oil.
4. Remove or disconnect the following:
   - Negative battery cable
   - Accessory drive belts
   - Crankshaft pulley
   - Front cover
   - Timing belt. Refer to the Timing Belt unit repair section.
   - Crankshaft timing sprocket
   - Front crankshaft seal
   - Thermostat housing
   - Oil pan
   - Oil pump pick up tube
   - Oil pump

To install:

5. Install or connect the following:
   - Oil pump. Tighten the bolts to 14–18 ft. lbs. (19–25 Nm).
   - Oil pump pick up tube. Tighten the bolts to 70–95 inch lbs. (8–11 Nm).
   - Oil pan
   - Thermostat housing. Tighten the bolts to 14–18 ft. lbs. (19–25 Nm).
   - Front crankshaft seal
   - Crankshaft timing sprocket
   - Timing belt
   - Front cover
   - Crankshaft pulley. Tighten the bolt to 116–122 ft. lbs. (157–166 Nm).

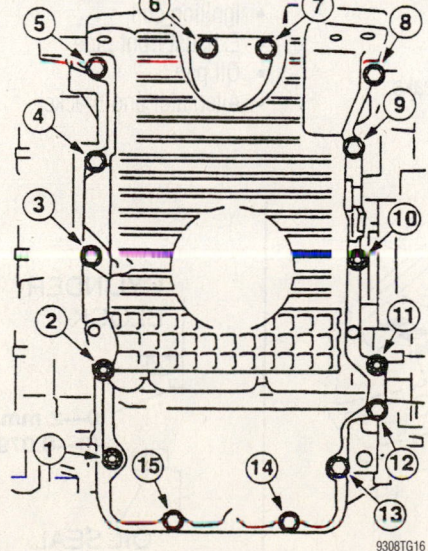

Oil pan torque sequence—2.5L Engine

9308TG16

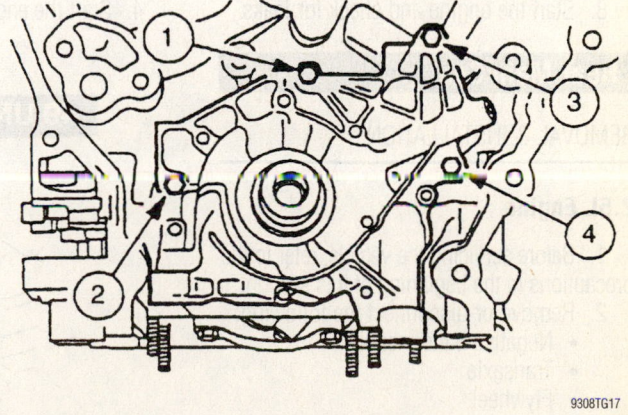

Oil pump torque sequence—2.5L engine

9308TG17

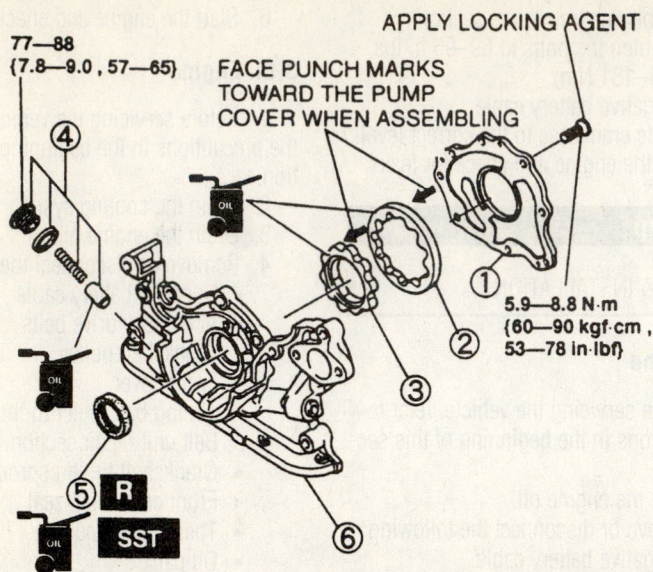

APPLY LOCKING AGENT

FACE PUNCH MARKS TOWARD THE PUMP COVER WHEN ASSEMBLING

77—88
{7.8—9.0 , 57—65}

5.9—8.8 N·m
{60—90 kgf·cm ,
53—78 in·lbf}

R
SST

N·m {kgf·m , ft·lbf}

7924TG20

1	Pump cover
2	Outer rotor
3	Inner rotor
4	Pressure relief valve
5	Oil seal
6	Oil pump body

Exploded view of the oil pump and related components—3.0L engine

- Accessory drive belts
- Negative battery cable
6. Fill the crankcase to the correct level.
7. Fill the cooling system.
8. Start the engine and check for leaks.

Rear Main Seal

REMOVAL & INSTALLATION

2.5L Engine

1. Before servicing the vehicle, refer to the precautions in the beginning of this section.
2. Remove or disconnect the following:
   - Negative battery cable
   - Transaxle
   - Flywheel
   - Oil seal
To install:
3. Install or connect the following:
   - Oil seal. Press the seal in evenly with Special Service Tools 49 UN01 070 and 303-384 as shown.

- Flywheel. Tighten the bolts to 54–64 ft. lbs. (73–87 Nm).
- Transaxle
- Negative battery cable
4. Start the engine and check for leaks.

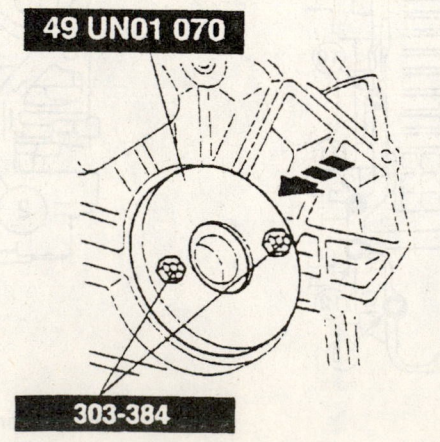

49 UN01 070

303-384

Rear main seal installation—2.5L engine

3.0L Engine

1. Before servicing the vehicle, refer to the precautions in the beginning of this section.
2. Remove or disconnect the following:
   - Negative battery cable
   - Transmission
   - Flywheel
   - Rear main seal
To install:
3. Install or connect the following:
   - Rear main seal flush with the seal housing
   - Flywheel. Tighten the bolts to 76–81 ft. lbs. (103–109 Nm).
   - Transmission
   - Negative battery cable
4. Start the engine and check for leaks.

Timing Chain, Sprockets, Front Cover and Seal

REMOVAL & INSTALLATION

2.5L Engine

1. Before servicing the vehicle, refer to the precautions in the beginning of this section.
2. Relieve the fuel system pressure.
3. Drain the engine oil.
4. Remove or disconnect the following:
   - Negative battery cable
   - Intake manifold
   - Accessory drive belt
   - Intake Manifold Runner Control (IMRC) actuator
   - Spark plug wires
   - Ignition coil
   - Exhaust front pipe
   - Oil pan
   - Alternator and bracket

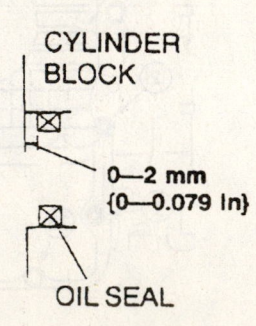

CYLINDER BLOCK

0—2 mm
{0—0.079 in}

OIL SEAL

9308TG18

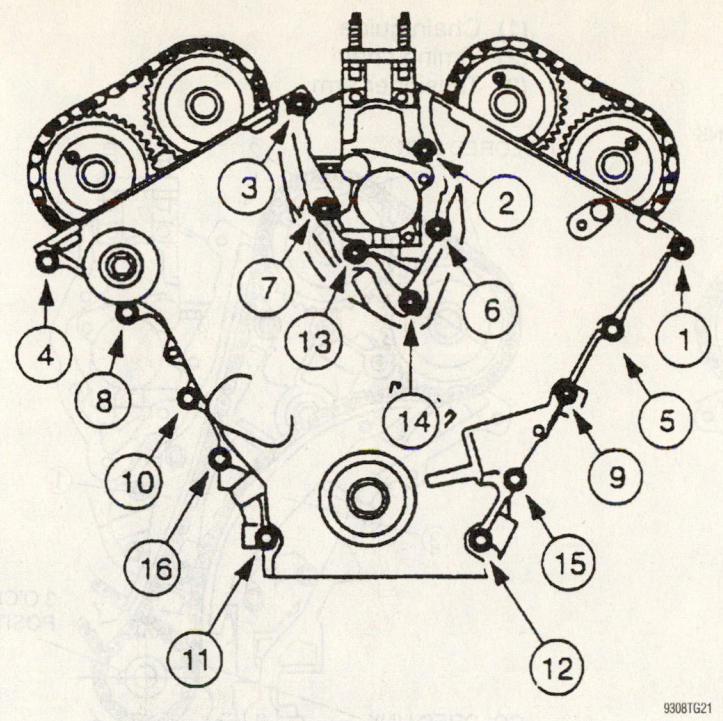

Front cover bolt removal sequence—2.5L engine

- A/C compressor
- Wiring harness connector bracket
- Water pump drive belt and pulley
- Camshaft oil seal housing
- Valve covers
- Right motor mount and bracket
- Crankshaft pulley
- Front crankshaft seal
- Front cover. Loosen the bolts in the sequence shown.
- Crankshaft Position (CKP) sensor pulse wheel

5. Rotate the crankshaft so that the keyway is at the 11 o'clock position to locate the crankshaft at TDC for No. 1 cylinder.

6. Verify that the alignment arrows on the camshafts are aligned. If not, rotate the crankshaft 1 complete revolution and recheck.

7. Rotate the crankshaft so that the keyway is at the 3 o'clock position. This positions the right cylinder head camshafts to the neutral position.

➡ **Keep all valvetrain components in order for assembly.**

8. Remove or disconnect the following:
- Right timing chain tensioner
- Right timing chain tensioner arm
- Right timing chain and crankshaft timing sprocket
- Right bank camshafts

9. Rotate the crankshaft 1 and ⅔ turns and set the crankshaft keyway at the 11 o'clock position. This places the left bank camshafts in the neutral position.

10. Remove or disconnect the following:
- Left timing chain tensioner
- Left timing chain tensioner arm
- Left timing chain and crankshaft timing sprocket

To install:

11. Prepare the timing chain tensioners for installation as follows:

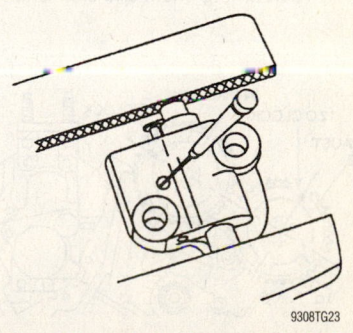

Using a thin prytool, release and hold the timing chain tensioner ratchet/pawl mechanism—2.5L engine

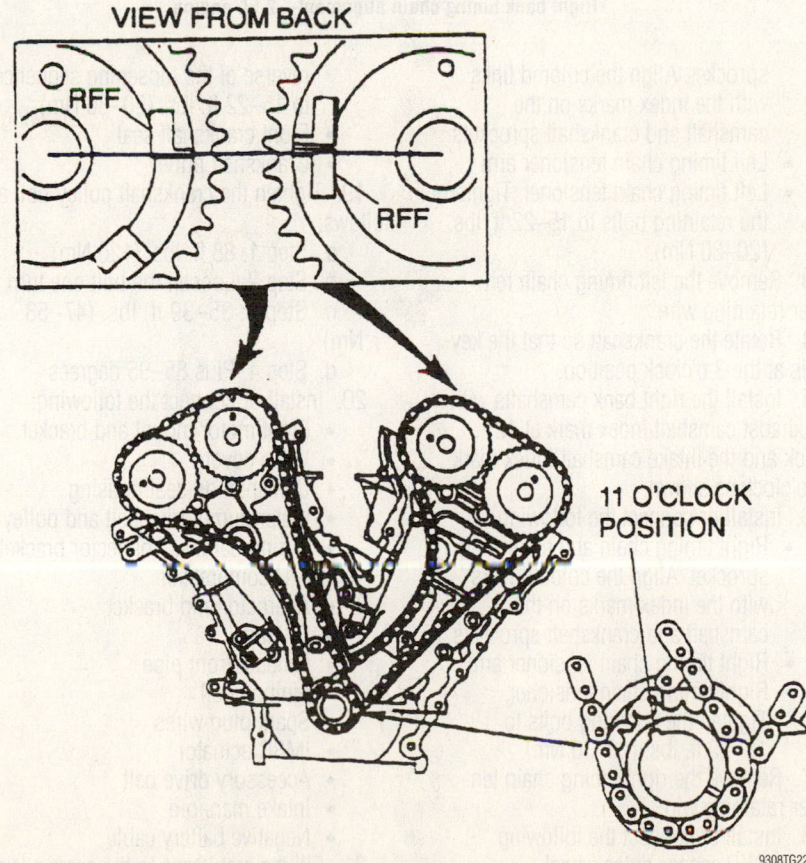

Camshaft alignment with the crankshaft in the 11 o'clock position—2.5L engine

(1) Timing chain crankshaft sprocket
(2) Chain guide
(3) Timing chain
(4) Tensioner arm

(1) Chain guide
(2) Timing chain
(3) Tensioner arm

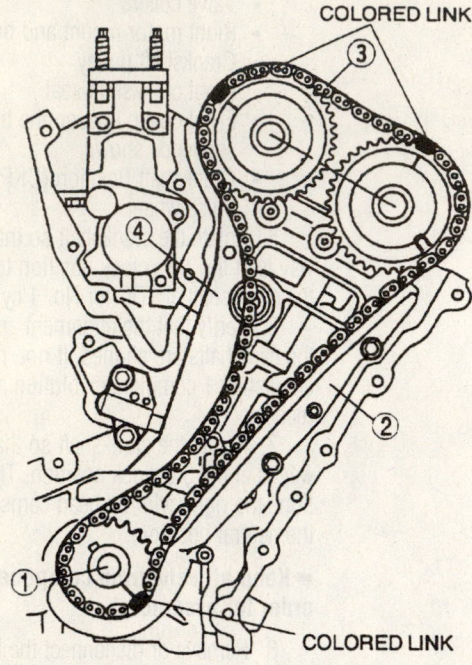

Left bank timing chain alignment—2.5L engine

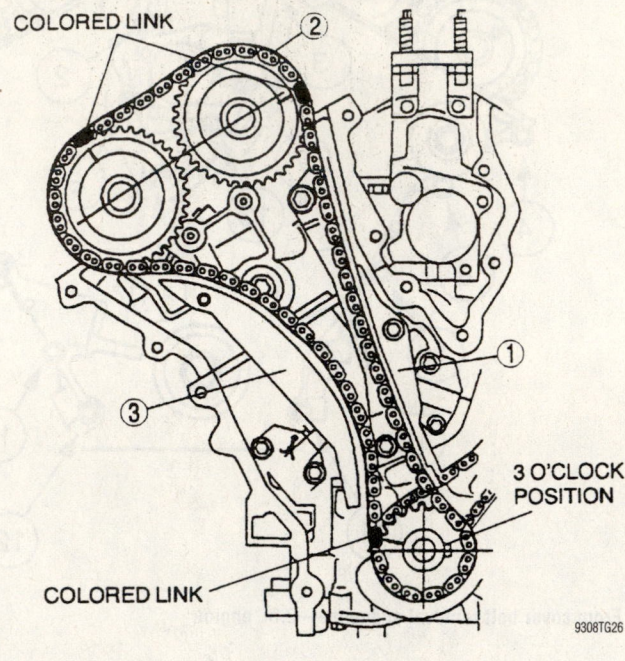

Right bank timing chain alignment—2.5L engine

a. Place the left chain tensioner in a vise.

b. Using a small prytool, release and hold the timing chain tensioner ratchet/pawl mechanism through the access hole in the timing chain tensioner.

c. Slowly compress the tensioner.

d. Lock the piston with a 1.5mm wire or paperclip.

e. Repeat for the right chain tensioner.

➡**Be sure that the crankshaft keyway is still at the 11 o'clock position.**

12. Install or connect the following:
  • Left timing chain and crankshaft

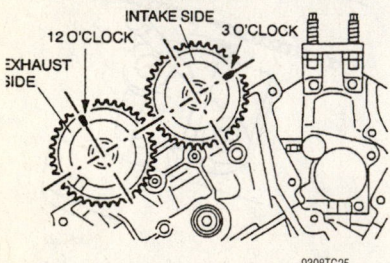

Right bank camshaft positioning—2.5L engine

sprocket. Align the colored links with the index marks on the camshaft and crankshaft sprockets.
  • Left timing chain tensioner arm
  • Left timing chain tensioner. Tighten the retaining bolts to 15–22 ft. lbs. (20–30 Nm).

13. Remove the left timing chain tensioner retaining wire.

14. Rotate the crankshaft so that the keyway is at the 3 o'clock position.

15. Install the right bank camshafts with the exhaust camshaft index mark at 12 o'clock and the intake camshaft index mark at 3 o'clock as shown.

16. Install or connect the following:
  • Right timing chain and crankshaft sprocket. Align the colored links with the index marks on the camshaft and crankshaft sprockets.
  • Right timing chain tensioner arm
  • Right timing chain tensioner. Tighten the retaining bolts to 15–22 ft. lbs. (20–30 Nm).

17. Remove the right timing chain tensioner retaining wire.

18. Install or connect the following:
  • CKP sensor pulse wheel
  • Front cover. Tighten the bolts in the

reverse of the loosening sequence to 15–22 ft. lbs. (20–30 Nm).
  • Front crankshaft seal
  • Crankshaft pulley

19. Tighten the crankshaft pulley bolt as follows:
  a. Step 1: 88 ft. lbs. (120 Nm)
  b. Step 2: Loosen the bolt one turn
  c. Step 3: 35–39 ft. lbs. (47–53 Nm)
  d. Step 4: Plus 85–95 degrees

20. Install or connect the following:
  • Right motor mount and bracket
  • Valve covers
  • Camshaft oil seal housing
  • Water pump drive belt and pulley
  • Wiring harness connector bracket
  • A/C compressor
  • Alternator and bracket
  • Oil pan
  • Exhaust front pipe
  • Ignition coil
  • Spark plug wires
  • IMRC actuator
  • Accessory drive belt
  • Intake manifold
  • Negative battery cable

21. Fill the crankcase to the correct level.

22. Start the engine and check for leaks.

Piston and Ring

POSITIONING

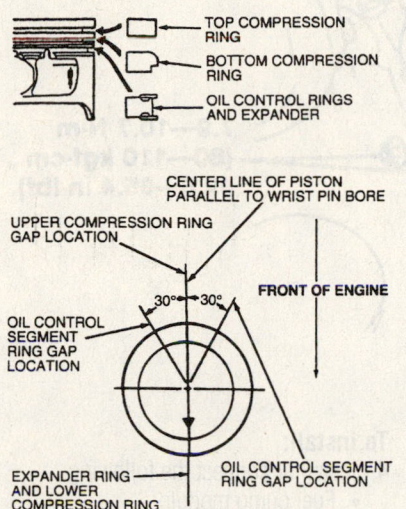

2.5L engine—piston ring positioning, end-gap spacing, and piston positioning. The small directional arrow must face the front of the engine.

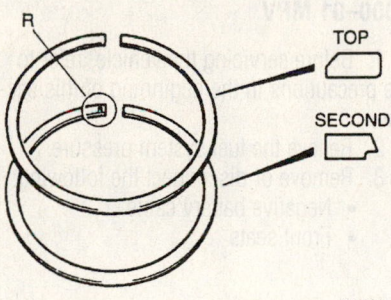

Compression ring identification—3.0L engine

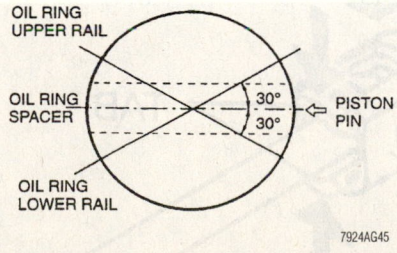

Piston ring end gap spacing—3.0L engine

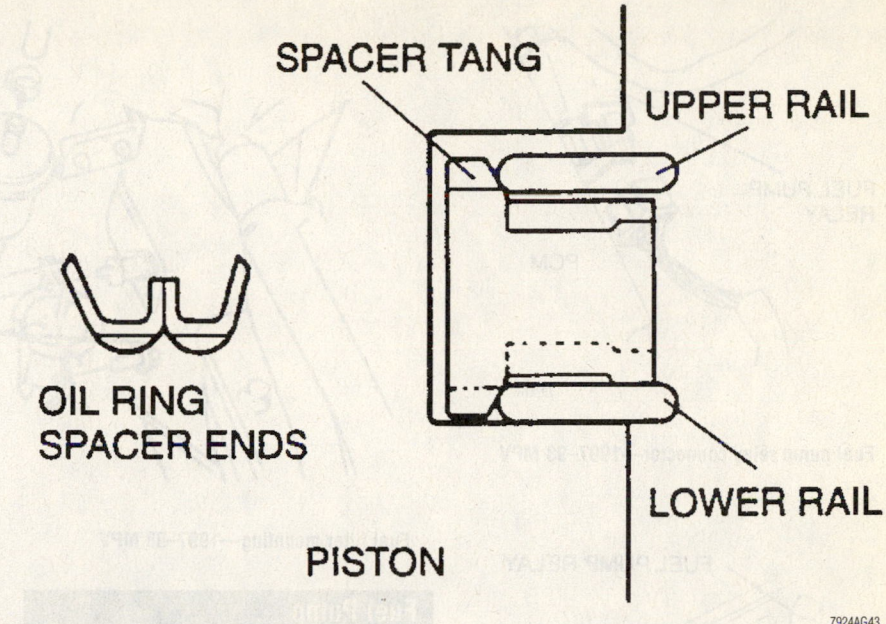

Oil control ring positioning—3.0L engine

FUEL SYSTEM

Fuel System Service Precautions

Safety is the most important factor when performing not only fuel system maintenance but any type of maintenance. Failure to conduct maintenance and repairs in a safe manner may result in serious personal injury or death. Maintenance and testing of the vehicle's fuel system components can be accomplished safely and effectively by adhering to the following rules and guidelines.

• To avoid the possibility of fire and personal injury, always disconnect the negative battery cable unless the repair or test procedure requires that battery voltage be applied.

• Always relieve the fuel system pressure prior to disconnecting any fuel system component (injector, fuel rail, pressure regulator, etc.), fitting or fuel line connection. Exercise extreme caution whenever relieving fuel system pressure, to avoid exposing skin, face and eyes to fuel spray. Please be advised that fuel under pressure may penetrate the skin or any part of the body that it contacts.

• Always place a shop towel or cloth around the fitting or connection prior to loosening to absorb any excess fuel due to spillage. Ensure that all fuel spillage

(should it occur) is quickly removed from engine surfaces. Ensure that all fuel soaked cloths or towels are deposited into a suitable waste container.

• Always keep a dry chemical (Class B) fire extinguisher near the work area.

• Do not allow fuel spray or fuel vapors to come into contact with a spark or open flame.

• Always use a back-up wrench when loosening and tightening fuel line connection fittings. This will prevent unnecessary stress and torsion to fuel line piping. Always follow the proper tighten specifications.

• Always replace worn fuel fitting O-rings with new. Do not substitute fuel hose or equivalent, where fuel pipe is installed.

Fuel System Pressure

RELIEVING

1. Before servicing the vehicle, refer to the precautions in the beginning of this section.

2. Disconnect the fuel pump relay, located at the ECM.

3. Start the engine.

4. After the engine stalls, crank the engine several times.

5. Turn the ignition switch **OFF**.

6. When repairs are complete, connect the fuel pump relay.

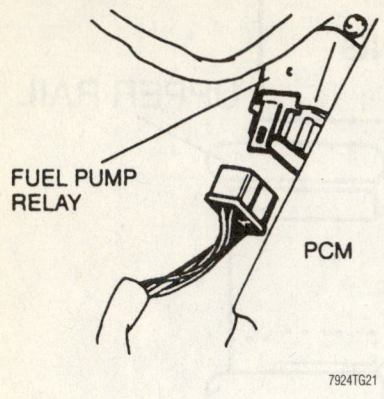

FUEL PUMP
RELAY

PCM

7924TG21

Fuel pump relay connector—1997–98 MPV

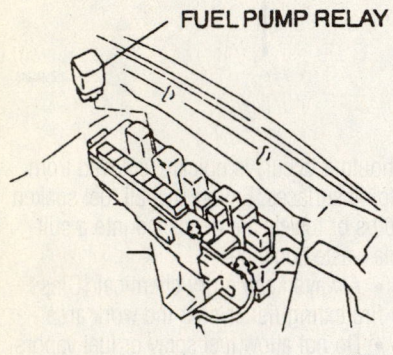

FUEL PUMP RELAY

9308TG19

Fuel pump relay—2000–01 MPV

Fuel Filter

REMOVAL & INSTALLATION

1997–98 MPV

1. Before servicing the vehicle, refer to the precautions in the beginning of this section.
2. Relieve the fuel system pressure.
3. Remove or disconnect the following:
   - Negative battery cable
   - Fuel line clamps
   - Fuel lines
   - Fuel filter

To install:

4. Install or connect the following:
   - Fuel filter. Tighten the bracket nut to 70–95 inch lbs. (8–11 Nm).
   - Fuel lines
   - Fuel line clamps
   - Negative battery cable
5. Start the engine and check for leaks.

2000–01 MPV

The fuel filter is located in the fuel tank as part of the fuel pump module.

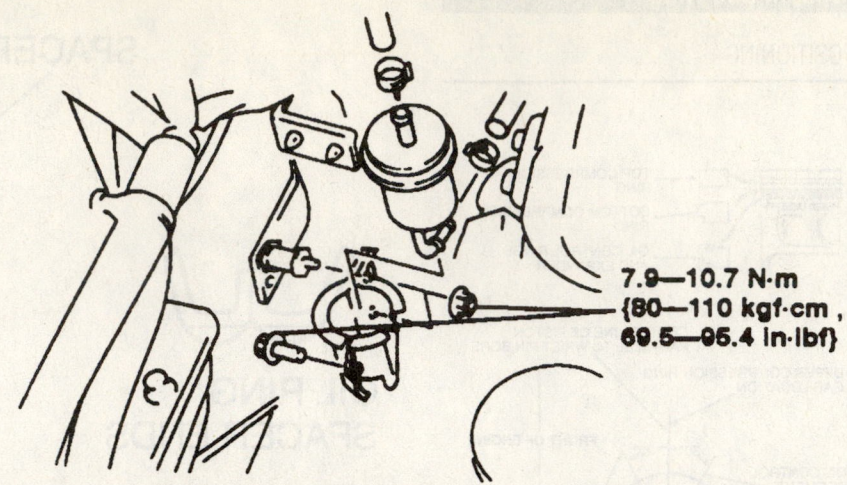

7.9—10.7 N·m
{80—110 kgf·cm ,
69.5—95.4 in·lbf}

7924TG22

Fuel filter mounting—1997–98 MPV

Fuel Pump

REMOVAL & INSTALLATION

1997–98 MPV

1. Before servicing the vehicle, refer to the precautions in the beginning of this section.
2. Relieve the fuel system pressure.
3. Remove or disconnect the following:
   - Negative battery cable
   - Rear seat
   - Floor mat
   - Access panel
   - Fuel pump harness connector
   - Fuel lines
   - Fuel pump module

To install:

4. Install or connect the following:
   - Fuel pump module
   - Fuel lines
   - Fuel pump harness connector
   - Access panel
   - Floor mat
   - Rear seat
   - Negative battery cable
5. Start the engine and check for leaks.

2000–01 MPV

1. Before servicing the vehicle, refer to the precautions in the beginning of this section.
2. Relieve the fuel system pressure.
3. Remove or disconnect the following:
   - Negative battery cable
   - Front seats

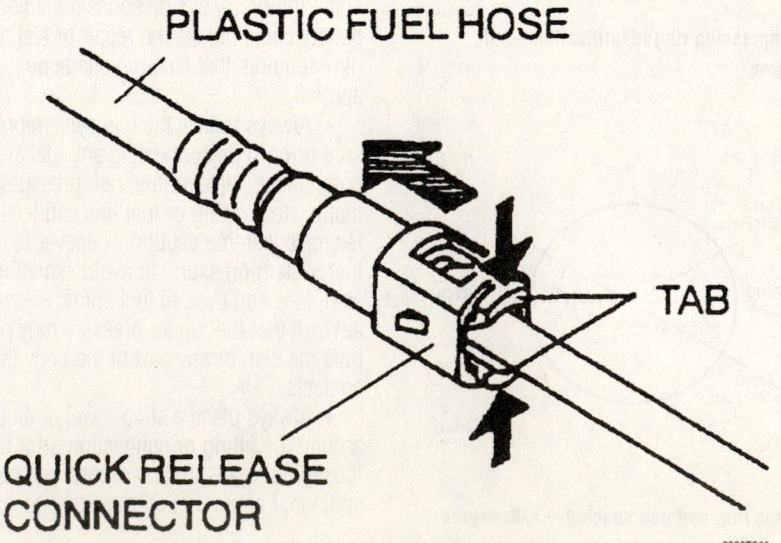

PLASTIC FUEL HOSE

TAB

QUICK RELEASE
CONNECTOR

9308TG20

Fuel hose quick release connector—2000–01 MPV

- Center console
- Door sill plates
- Parking brake lever
- Carpet
- Access panel
- Fuel lines
- Fuel pump module harness connector
- Fuel pump module

To install:

4. Install or connect the following:
- Fuel pump module
- Fuel pump module harness connector
- Fuel lines
- Access panel
- Carpet
- Parking brake lever
- Door sill plates
- Center console
- Front seats
- Negative battery cable

5. Start the engine and check for leaks.

Fuel Injector

REMOVAL & INSTALLATION

2.5L Engine

1. Before servicing the vehicle, refer to the precautions in the beginning of this section.
2. Relieve the fuel system pressure.
3. Remove or disconnect the following:

- Negative battery cable
- Air cleaner housing and fresh air duct
- Mass Air Flow (MAF) sensor
- Intake manifold
- Fuel injector harness connectors
- Fuel lines
- Pressure regulator vacuum hose
- Fuel supply manifold with injectors attached
- Fuel injectors

To install:

4. Install or connect the following:
- Fuel injectors with new O-ring seals
- Fuel supply manifold with injectors attached. Tighten the bolts to 72–101 inch lbs. (8–11 Nm).
- Pressure regulator vacuum hose
- Fuel lines
- Fuel injector harness connectors
- Intake manifold
- MAF sensor

- Air cleaner housing and fresh air duct
- Negative battery cable

5. Start the engine and check for leaks.

3.0L Engine

1. Before servicing the vehicle, refer to the precautions in the beginning of this section.
2. Drain the cooling system.
3. Relieve the fuel system pressure.
4. Remove or disconnect the following:

- Negative battery cable
- Fresh air duct
- Air intake hose
- Air cleaner assembly
- Mass Air Flow (MAF) sensor
- Accelerator cable
- Cruise control cable
- Idle Air Control (IAC) valve connector and hoses
- Bypass air solenoid valve connector, if equipped
- Vacuum solenoid valve connectors
- Upper radiator hose
- Heater hose
- Bypass hose
- Intake manifold vacuum lines
- Upper intake manifold
- Fuel lines
- Fuel supply manifold with injectors attached
- Fuel injectors

To install:

5. Install or connect the following:
- Fuel injectors with new O-ring seals
- Fuel supply manifold. Tighten the nuts to 14–18 ft. lbs. (19–25 Nm).
- Fuel lines
- Upper intake manifold with injectors attached. Tighten the bolts to 70–95 inch lbs. (8–11 Nm).
- Intake manifold vacuum lines
- Bypass hose
- Heater hose
- Upper radiator hose
- Vacuum solenoid valve connectors
- Bypass air solenoid valve connector, if equipped
- IAC valve connector and hoses
- Accelerator cable
- Cruise control cable
- MAF sensor
- Air cleaner assembly
- Air intake hose
- Fresh air duct
- Negative battery cable

6. Fill the cooling system.
7. Start the engine and check for leaks.

DRIVE TRAIN

Automatic Transmission Assembly

REMOVAL & INSTALLATION

1997–98 MPV

1. Before servicing the vehicle, refer to the precautions in the beginning of this section.
2. Drain the transmission fluid.
3. Drain the transfer case, if equipped.
4. Remove or disconnect the following:

- Negative battery cable
- Speedometer cable
- Gear select cable
- Transmission oil dipstick tube
- Exhaust front pipe
- Flywheel access cover
- Torque converter
- Starter motor
- Exhaust pipe bracket
- Front driveshaft, if equipped
- Rear driveshaft
- Transmission mount and crossmember. Support the transmission.
- Transmission oil cooler lines
- Transmission support brackets
- Transmission flange bolts
- Transmission

To install:

5. Install or connect the following:
- Transmission. Tighten the flange bolts to 28–38 ft. lbs. (38–51 Nm).
- Transmission support brackets. Tighten the bolts to 28–38 ft. lbs. (38–51 Nm).
- Transmission oil cooler lines. Tighten the bolts to 18–26 ft. lbs. (24–35 Nm).
- Transmission mount and crossmember. Tighten the bolts to 32–44 ft. lbs. (44–60 Nm) and the nuts to 24–33 ft. lbs. (32–46 Nm).
- Exhaust pipe bracket
- Front driveshaft, if equipped
- Rear driveshaft
- Starter motor
- Torque converter. Tighten the bolts to 27–39 ft. lbs. (37–53 Nm).
- Flywheel access cover
- Exhaust front pipe
- Transmission oil dipstick tube
- Gear select cable
- Speedometer cable
- Negative battery cable

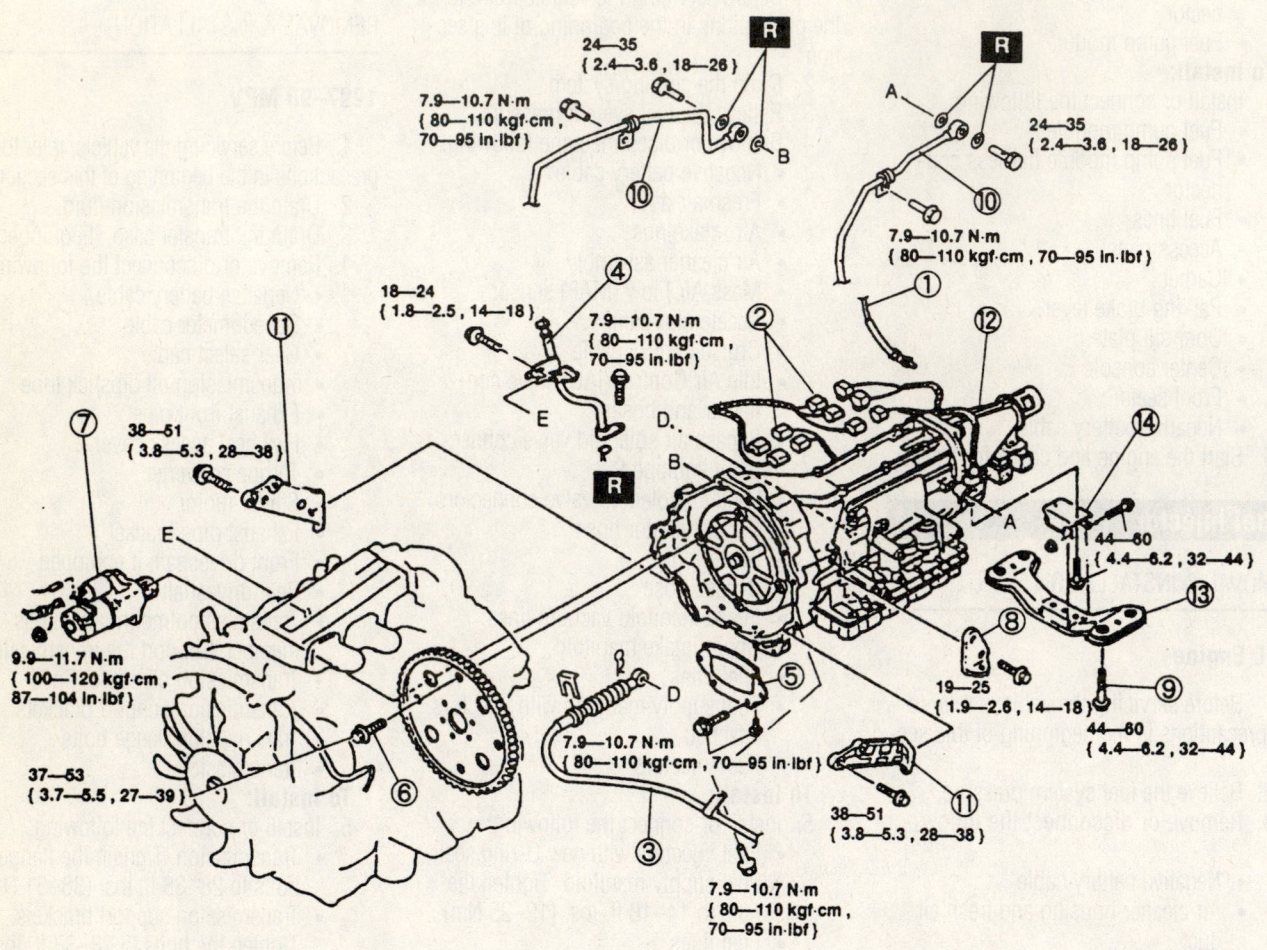

24—35
{ 2.4—3.6 , 18—26 }

7.9—10.7 N·m
{ 80—110 kgf·cm,
70—95 in·lbf }

A

24—35
{ 2.4—3.6 , 18—26 }

7.9—10.7 N·m
{ 80—110 kgf·cm, 70—95 in·lbf }

18—24
{ 1.8—2.5 , 14—18 }

7.9—10.7 N·m
{ 80—110 kgf·cm,
70—95 in·lbf }

38—51
{ 3.8—5.3 , 28—38 }

44—60
{ 4.4—6.2 , 32—44 }

9.9—11.7 N·m
{ 100—120 kgf·cm,
87—104 in·lbf }

19—25
{ 1.9—2.6 , 14—18 }

37—53
{ 3.7—5.5 , 27—39 }

44—60
{ 4.4—6.2 , 32—44 }

7.9—10.7 N·m
{ 80—110 kgf·cm, 70—95 in·lbf }

38—51
{ 3.8—5.3 , 28—38 }

7.9—10.7 N·m
{ 80—110 kgf·cm,
70—95 in·lbf }

N·m { kgf·m , ft·lbf }

UMU51328

1	Speedometer cable	
2	Connector	
3	Selector cable	
4	Filler tube	
5	Undercover	
6	Torque converter mounting bolt	
7	Starter	
8	Exhaust pipe bracket	
9	Transmission mount mounting bolt	
10	Oil pipe	
11	Gusset plate	
12	Transmission	
13	Transmission lower mount	
14	Transmission upper mount	

7924TG24

Exploded view of the transmission mounting—1997–98 2WD vehicles

(4WD)

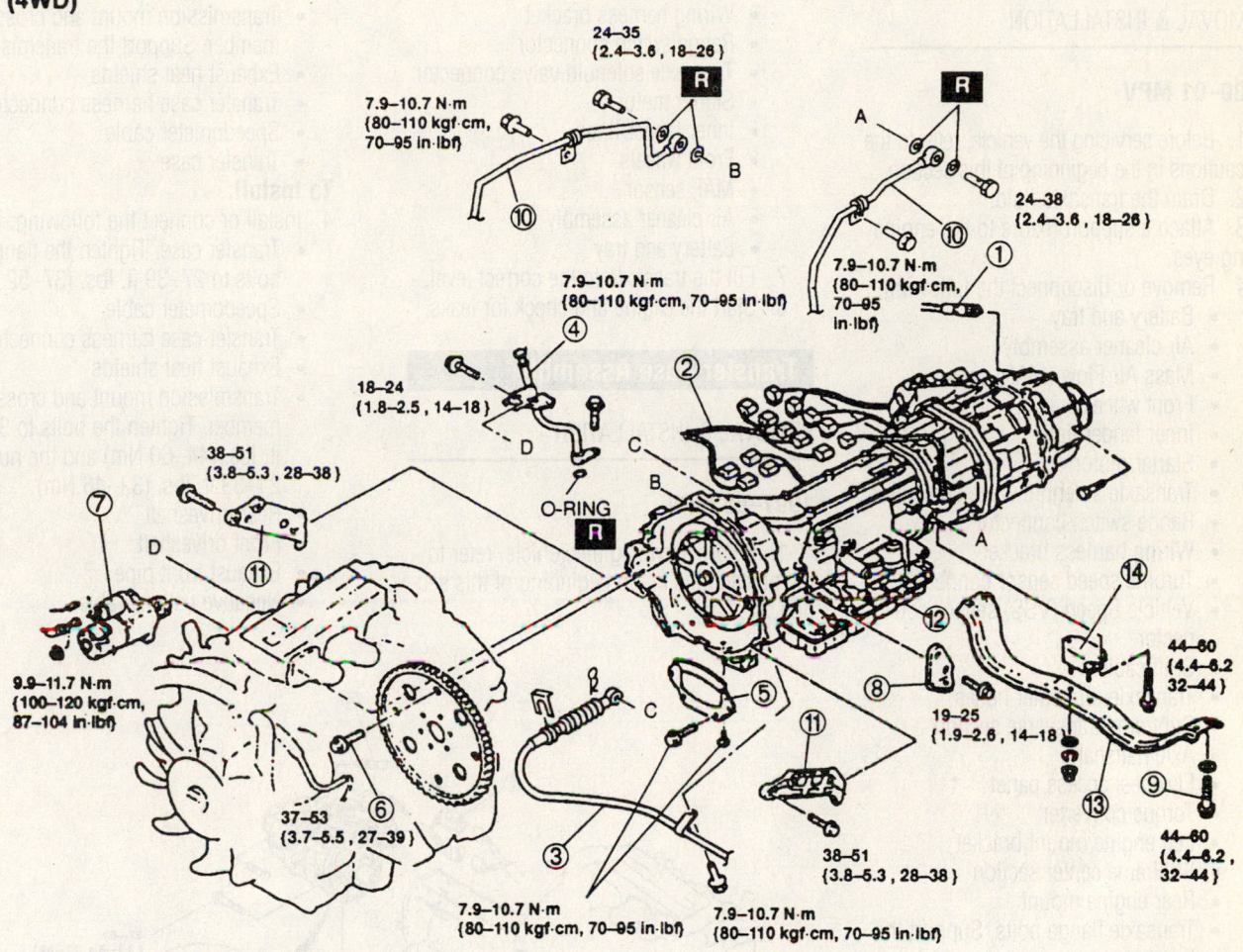

24–35
(2.4–3.6 , 18–26)

R

R

A

7.9–10.7 N·m
{80–110 kgf·cm,
70–95 in·lbf}

24–38
(2.4–3.6 , 18–26)

B

10

10

7.9–10.7 N·m
{80–110 kgf·cm,
70–95
in·lbf}

7.9–10.7 N·m
{80–110 kgf·cm, 70–95 in·lbf}

4

1

2

18–24
{1.8–2.5 , 14–18 }

D

C

B

38–51
(3.8–5.3 , 28–38)

O-RING

R

A

14

11

7

44–60
{4.4–6.2 ,
32–44 }

D

12

9.9–11.7 N·m
{100–120 kgf·cm,
87–104 in·lbf}

C

5

8

19–25
{1.9–2.6 , 14–18 }

13

9

37–53
{3.7–5.5 , 27–39 }

6

11

44–60
{4.4–6.2 ,
32–44 }

3

38–51
{3.8–5.3 , 28–38 }

7.9–10.7 N·m
{80–110 kgf·cm, 70–95 in·lbf}

7.9–10.7 N·m
{80–110 kgf·cm, 70–95 in·lbf}

N·m {kgf·m, ft·lbf}

1	Speedometer cable	9	Transmission mount mounting bolt
2	Connector	10	Oil pipe
3	Selector cable	11	Gusset plate
4	Filler tube	12	Transmission
5	Undercover	13	Transmission lower mount
6	Torque converter mounting bolt	14	Transmission upper mount
7	Starter		
8	Exhaust pipe bracket		

Exploded view of the transmission mounting—1997–98 4WD vehicles

7924TG25

6. Fill the transmission to the correct level.
7. Fill the transfer case, if equipped.
8. Start the engine and check for leaks.

Automatic Transaxle Assembly

REMOVAL & INSTALLATION

2000–01 MPV

1. Before servicing the vehicle, refer to the precautions in the beginning of this section.
2. Drain the transaxle fluid.
3. Attach a support fixture to the engine lifting eyes.
4. Remove or disconnect the following:
   - Battery and tray
   - Air cleaner assembly
   - Mass Air Flow (MAF) sensor
   - Front wheels
   - Inner fender liner
   - Starter motor
   - Transaxle solenoid valve connector
   - Range switch connector
   - Wiring harness bracket
   - Turbine speed sensor connector
   - Vehicle Speed (VSS) sensor connector
   - Shift cable
   - Transaxle oil cooler hoses
   - Subframe transverse section
   - Axle halfshafts
   - Flywheel access panel
   - Torque converter
   - Left engine mount bracket
   - Subframe center section
   - Rear engine mount
   - Transaxle flange bolts. Support the transaxle.
5. Lower the transaxle from the vehicle.

To install:

6. Install or connect the following:
   - Transaxle. Tighten the flange bolts to 28–38 ft. lbs. (38–51 Nm).
   - Rear engine mount. Tighten the bracket bolts to 50–68 ft. lbs. (67–93 Nm) and the through bolt to 63–86 ft. lbs. (86–116 Nm).
   - Subframe center section. Tighten the bolts to 48–65 ft. lbs. (64–89 Nm) and the nuts to 50–67 ft. lbs. (67–93 Nm).
   - Left engine mount bracket. Tighten the bracket fasteners to 50–68 ft. lbs. (67–93 Nm) and the through bolt to 63–86 ft. lbs. (86–116 Nm).
   - Torque converter. Tighten the nuts to 26–36 ft. lbs. (35–49 Nm).
   - Flywheel access panel
   - Axle halfshafts
   - Subframe transverse section.

Tighten the bolts to 69–97 ft. lbs. (94–131 Nm).
   - Transaxle oil cooler hoses
   - Shift cable
   - VSS sensor connector
   - Turbine speed sensor connector
   - Wiring harness bracket
   - Range switch connector
   - Transaxle solenoid valve connector
   - Starter motor
   - Inner fender liner
   - Front wheels
   - MAF sensor
   - Air cleaner assembly
   - Battery and tray
7. Fill the transaxle to the correct level.
8. Start the engine and check for leaks.

Transfer Case Assembly

REMOVAL & INSTALLATION

1997–98 MPV

1. Before servicing the vehicle, refer to the precautions in the beginning of this section.

2. Drain the transfer case.
3. Remove or disconnect the following:
   - Negative battery cable
   - Exhaust front pipe
   - Front driveshaft
   - Rear driveshaft
   - Transmission mount and cross-member. Support the transmission.
   - Exhaust heat shields
   - Transfer case harness connectors
   - Speedometer cable
   - Transfer case

To install:

4. Install or connect the following:
   - Transfer case. Tighten the flange bolts to 27–39 ft. lbs. (37–52 Nm).
   - Speedometer cable
   - Transfer case harness connectors
   - Exhaust heat shields
   - Transmission mount and cross-member. Tighten the bolts to 32–44 ft. lbs. (44–60 Nm) and the nuts to 24–33 ft. lbs. (32–46 Nm).
   - Rear driveshaft
   - Front driveshaft
   - Exhaust front pipe
   - Negative battery cable

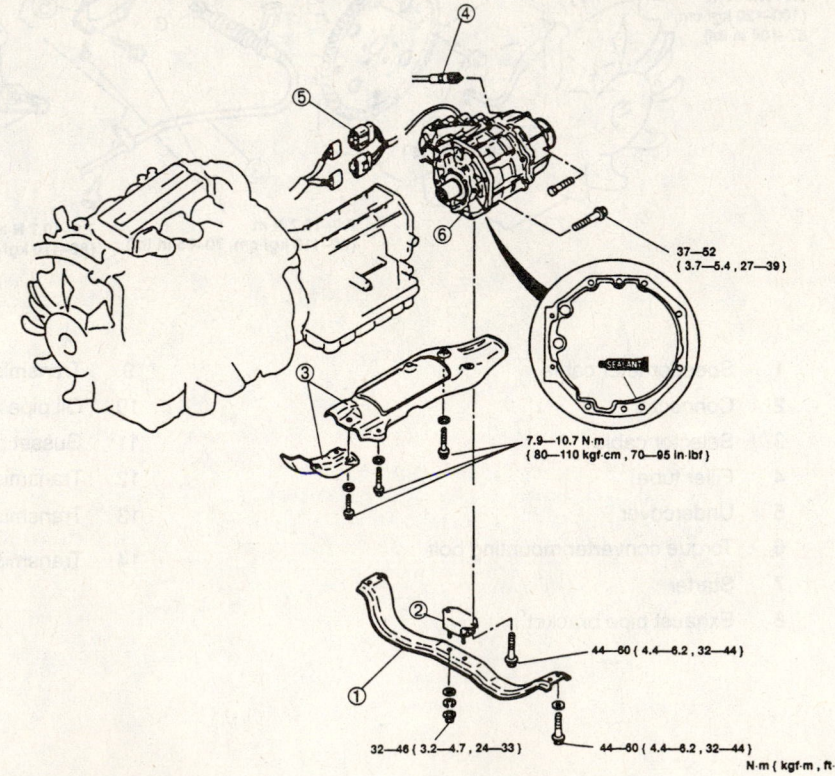

1	Transmission lower mount	4	Speedometer cable
2	Transmission upper mount	5	Connectors
3	Heat insulator	6	Transfer case

Exploded view of the transfer case and related components—1997–98 4WD vehicles

7924TG26

5. Fill the transfer case tot he correct level.

Halfshaft

REMOVAL & INSTALLATION

1997–98 MPV

1. Before servicing the vehicle, refer to the precautions in the beginning of this section.
2. Remove or disconnect the following:
   - Front wheel
   - Hub retainer nut
   - Outer tie rod end
   - Lower ball joint
   - Engine under cover
3. Separate the inner joint from the differential housing with a prybar.

4. Separate the stub shaft from the hub and remove the axle halfshaft from the vehicle.

To install:

➡**Use new circlips, split pins and locknuts for assembly.**

5. Install the inner joint to the differential so that the circlip is seated.
6. Guide the stub shaft into the hub.
7. Install or connect the following:
   - Engine under cover
   - Lower ball joint. Tighten the horizontal bolt to 95–126 ft. lbs. (128–171 Nm) and the vertical bolts to 76–101 ft. lbs. (102–137 Nm).
   - Outer tie rod end. Tighten the nut to 44–57 ft. lbs. (59–78 Nm).
   - Hub retainer nut. Tighten the lock-

nut to 174–231 ft. lbs. (236–313 Nm).
   - Front wheel

2000–01 MPV

LEFT

1. Before servicing the vehicle, refer to the precautions in the beginning of this section.
2. Drain the transaxle fluid.
3. Remove or disconnect the following:
   - Front wheel
   - Wheel speed sensor
   - Hub locknut
   - Outer tie rod end
   - Lower ball joint
   - Stabilizer bar link
4. Separate the stub shaft from the hub and pry the inner joint from the transaxle.

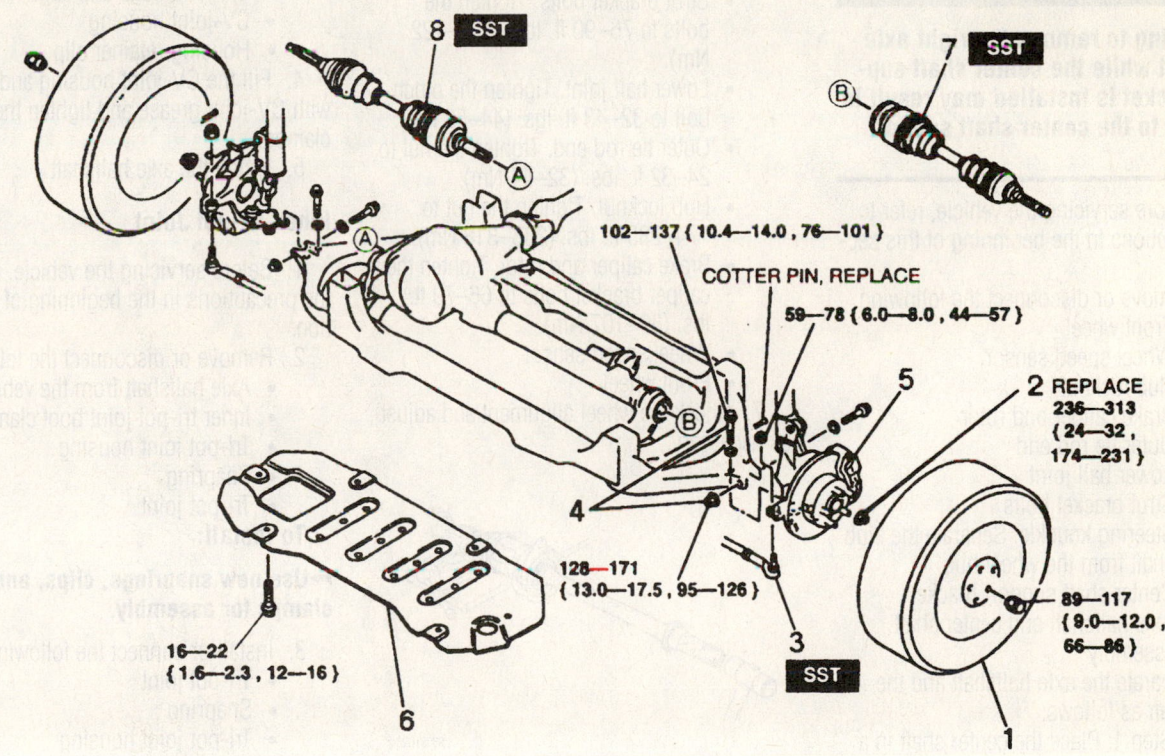

102–137 { 10.4–14.0 , 76–101 }

COTTER PIN, REPLACE

59–78 { 6.0–8.0 , 44–57 }

2 REPLACE
236–313
{ 24–32 ,
174–231 }

128—171
{ 13.0–17.5 , 95–126 }

89—117
{ 9.0–12.0 ,
66—86 }

16—22
{ 1.6—2.3 , 12—16 }

N·m { kgf·m , ft·lbf }

1. Wheel and tire
2. Locknut
3. Tie rod end
4. Ball joint bolt and nut
5. Front axle
6. Engine undercover
7. Left drive shaft
8. Right drive shaft

Exploded view of the halfshaft and related components—1997–98 4WD vehicles

7924TG27

Turn to Section 5 for brake system applications

To install:

➡ **Use a new circlip, split pin and locknut for assembly.**

5. Insert the stub shaft into the wheel hub.

6. Lubricate the oil seal with transaxle fluid, then push the axle halfshaft into the transaxle. Pull on the inner joint to confirm that the circlip is seated.

7. Install or connect the following:
- Stabilizer bar link
- Lower ball joint. Tighten the pinch bolt to 32–43 ft. lbs. (44–58 Nm).
- Outer tie rod end. Tighten the nut to 24–32 ft. lbs. (32–44 Nm).
- Hub locknut. Tighten the nut to 174–235 ft. lbs. (236–318 Nm).
- Wheel speed sensor
- Front wheel

RIGHT

> ✳✳ **WARNING**
>
> **Attempting to remove the right axle halfshaft while the center shaft support bracket is installed may result in damage to the center shaft support bracket.**

1. Before servicing the vehicle, refer to the precautions in the beginning of this section.

2. Remove or disconnect the following:
- Front wheel
- Wheel speed sensor
- Hub locknut
- Brake caliper and rotor
- Outer tie rod end
- Lower ball joint
- Strut bracket bolts
- Steering knuckle. Separate the stub shaft from the wheel hub.
- Center shaft support bracket
- Axle halfshaft and center shaft assembly

3. Separate the axle halfshaft and the center shaft as follows:

a. Step 1: Place the center shaft in a vise

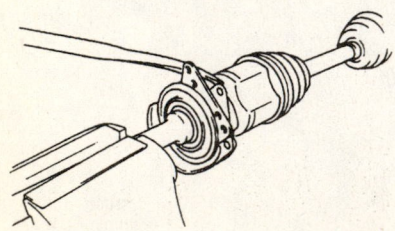

Separating the axle halfshaft from the center shaft—2000–01 MPV

b. Step 2: Insert a pry tool between the center shaft and the axle halfshaft

c. Step 3: Tap on the pry tool to separate the axle halfshaft from the center shaft

To install:

➡ **Use a new split pin, locknut, and new circlips for assembly.**

4. Place the axle halfshaft in a vise and install the center shaft by tapping it with a plastic hammer as shown.

5. Lubricate the oil seal with transaxle fluid, then push the center shaft into the transaxle. Pull on the inner joint to confirm that the circlip is seated.

6. Install or connect the following:
- Center shaft support bracket. Tighten the nuts to 16–22 ft. lbs. (22–30 Nm).
- Steering knuckle. Guide the stub shaft into the wheel hub.
- Strut bracket bolts. Tighten the bolts to 76–90 ft. lbs. (103–122 Nm).
- Lower ball joint. Tighten the pinch bolt to 32–43 ft. lbs. (44–58 Nm).
- Outer tie rod end. Tighten the nut to 24–32 ft. lbs. (32–44 Nm).
- Hub locknut. Tighten the nut to 174–235 ft. lbs. (236–318 Nm).
- Brake caliper and rotor. Tighten the caliper bracket bolts to 66–79 ft. lbs. (89–107 Nm).
- Wheel speed sensor
- Front wheel

7. Check the wheel alignment and adjust as necessary.

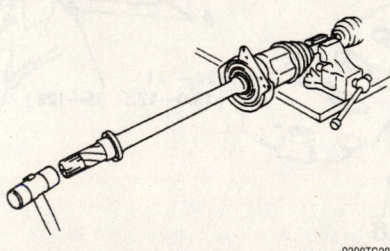

Installing the center shaft—2000–01 MPV

CV-Joint

OVERHAUL

Outer CV-Joint

The outer CV-joint is serviced with the axle halfshaft as an assembly. The outer CV-joint boot may be serviced by removing the inner joint.

Inner CV-Joint

1. Before servicing the vehicle, refer to the precautions in the beginning of this section.

2. Remove or disconnect the following:
- Axle halfshaft from the vehicle
- Inner CV-joint boot clamps
- Housing retainer clip
- CV-joint housing
- CV-joint balls and cage
- Snapring
- CV-joint inner race
- CV-joint boot

To install:

➡ **Use new snaprings, clips, and boot clamps for assembly.**

3. Install or connect the following:
- CV-joint boot
- CV-joint inner race
- Snapring
- CV-joint balls and cage
- CV-joint housing
- Housing retainer clip

4. Fill the CV-joint housing and boot with CV-joint grease and tighten the boot clamps.

5. Install the axle halfshaft.

Inner Tri-pot Joint

1. Before servicing the vehicle, refer to the precautions in the beginning of this section.

2. Remove or disconnect the following:
- Axle halfshaft from the vehicle
- Inner tri-pot joint boot clamps
- Tri-pot joint housing
- Snapring
- Tri-pot joint

To install:

➡ **Use new snaprings, clips, and boot clamps for assembly.**

3. Install or connect the following:
- Tri-pot joint
- Snapring
- Tri-pot joint housing

4. Fill the tri-pot joint housing and boot with grease and tighten the boot clamps.

5. Install the axle halfshaft.

Axle Shaft, Bearing and Seal

REMOVAL & INSTALLATION

1997–98 MPV

1. Before servicing the vehicle, refer to the precautions in the beginning of this section.

2. Remove or disconnect the following:
- Rear wheel
- Brake caliper and rotor
- Parking brake shoes and cable
- Axle shaft, backing plate and bearing assembly
- Snapring

3. Grind a flat spot on the bearing collar and break it with a hammer and chisel.

4. Grind a flat spot on the wheel speed sensor rotor and break it with a hammer and chisel.

5. Press the wheel bearing assembly off the axle shaft.

6. Remove the oil seal from the axle housing.

To install:

7. Install or connect the following:
- Oil seal
- Wheel bearing
- Wheel speed sensor rotor
- Bearing collar
- Snapring
- Axle shaft, backing plate and bearing assembly. Tighten the nuts to 40–49 ft. lbs. (54–67 Nm).
- Parking brake shoes and cable
- Brake caliper and rotor
- Rear wheel

Pinion Seal

REMOVAL & REPLACEMENT

1997–98 MPV

1. Before servicing the vehicle, refer to the precautions in the beginning of this section.

2. Drain the differential gear lubricant.

3. Remove or disconnect the following:
- Driveshaft
- Wheels
- Brake calipers

➡**The brake calipers must be removed so that there is no additional drag when measuring pinion bearing preload.**

4. Use an inch lb. torque wrench and measure the amount of torque required to maintain pinion rotation through several revolutions.

5. Remove the pinion flange and remove the seal.

To install:

6. Install or connect the following:
- Pinion seal and flange
- New pinion flange nut

7. Rotate the pinion flange occasionally while tightening the flange nut to make sure the pinion bearings seat correctly.

8. Take frequent bearing preload torque readings.

9. Tighten the pinion nut to achieve the bearing preload torque measured before disassembly.

✴✴ CAUTION

Never loosen the pinion nut to reduce bearing preload. If it is necessary to reduce bearing preload, install a new collapsible spacer and pinion nut.

10. Install or connect the following:
- Driveshaft
- Brake calipers
- Wheels

11. Fill the differential with gear lubricant and check for leaks.

Axle Housing Assembly

REMOVAL & INSTALLATION

1997–98 MPV

1. Before servicing the vehicle, refer to the precautions in the beginning of this section.

2. Support the vehicle at the frame and support the axle with a jack.

3. Remove or disconnect the following:
- Rear wheels
- Height sensor link
- Stabilizer bar
- Shock absorbers
- Coil springs
- Brake hose
- Wheel speed sensors
- Lateral rod
- Upper link bolts
- Lower link bolts
- Axle housing

To install:

4. Install or connect the following:
- Axle housing. Tighten the link bolts to 102–126 ft. lbs. (138–171 Nm).
- Lateral rod. Tighten the nut to 108–126 ft. lbs. (147–171 Nm).
- Wheel speed sensors
- Brake hose
- Coil springs
- Shock absorbers
- Stabilizer bar. Tighten the bracket bolts to 26–37 ft. lbs. (35–50 Nm)

and the links to 14–18 ft. lbs. (19–25 Nm).
- Height sensor link
- Rear wheels

STEERING AND SUSPENSION

Air Bag

✴✴ CAUTION

Some vehicles are equipped with an air bag system. The system must be disarmed before performing service on, or around, system components, the steering column, instrument panel components, wiring and sensors. Failure to follow the safety precautions and the disarming procedure could result in accidental air bag deployment, possible injury and unnecessary system repairs.

PRECAUTIONS

Several precautions must be observed when handling the inflator module to avoid accidental deployment and possible personal injury.
- Never carry the inflator module by the wires or connector on the underside of the module.
- When carrying a live inflator module, hold securely with both hands, and ensure that the bag and trim cover are pointed away.
- Place the inflator module on a bench or other surface with the bag and trim cover facing up.
- With the inflator module on the bench, never place anything on or close to the module which may be thrown in the event of an accidental deployment.

DISARMING

1. Turn the ignition switch to the **LOCK** position.

2. Disconnect the negative battery cable and wait at least 1 minute to allow the back-up power supply to deplete its stored power.

3. When repairs are complete, connect the negative battery cable.

Power Rack and Pinion Steering Gear

REMOVAL & INSTALLATION

1997–98 MPV

2 WHEEL DRIVE

1. Before servicing the vehicle, refer to the precautions in the beginning of this section.
2. Remove or disconnect the following:
   - Negative battery cable
   - Engine under cover
   - Outer tie rod ends

- Intermediate shaft
- Power steering hoses
- Steering gear brackets with the steering gear attached
- Steering gear brackets from the steering gear

To install:

3. Install or connect the following:
   - Steering gear brackets to the steering gear. Tighten the bolts to 55–68 ft. lbs. (74–93 Nm).
   - Steering gear brackets with the steering gear attached. Tighten the bolts to 47–68 ft. lbs. (63–93 Nm).
   - Power steering hoses

- Intermediate shaft. Tighten the pinch bolt to 14–19 ft. lbs. (18–26 Nm).
- Outer tie rod ends. Tighten the nuts to 44–57 ft. lbs. (59–78 Nm).
- Engine under cover
- Negative battery cable

4. Fill the power steering reservoir.
5. Check the wheel alignment and adjust as necessary.

4 WHEEL DRIVE

1. Before servicing the vehicle, refer to the precautions in the beginning of this section.

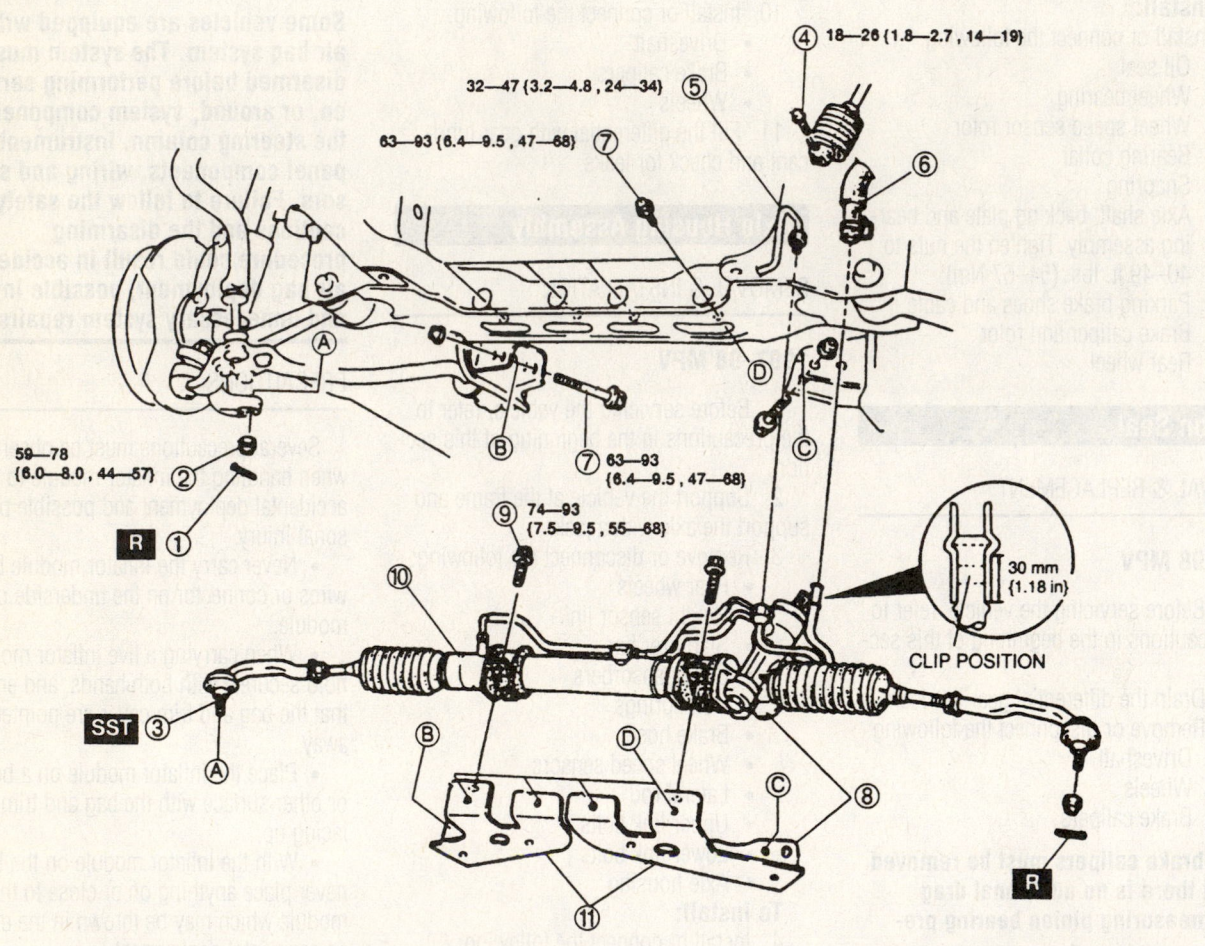

4 18—26 {1.8—2.7 , 14—19}

32—47 {3.2—4.8 , 24—34} 5

63—93 {6.4—9.5 , 47—68} 7

6

30 mm {1.18 in}

CLIP POSITION

59—78 {6.0—8.0 , 44—57} 2

R 1

SST 3

A

B

7 63—93 {6.4—9.5 , 47—68}

9 74—93 {7.5—9.5 , 55—68}

10

11

C

D

8

R

N·m {kgf·m , ft·lbf}

1	Cotter pin
2	Nut
3	Tie-rod end ball joint
4	Fixing bolt (intermediate shaft/pinion shaft)
5	Pressure pipe
6	Return hose

7	Steering bracket mounting bolt
8	Steering gear, linkage, and steering bracket
9	Mounting bracket bolt
10	Steering gear and linkage
11	Steering brackets

Exploded view of the rack and pinion mounting—1997–98 2WD vehicles

7924TG29

2. Remove or disconnect the following:
- Negative battery cable
- Engine under cover
- Outer tie rod ends
- Power steering hoses and pipes
- Intermediate shaft and steering column
- Front driveshaft
- Front differential housing bolts
- Steering gear

To install:
3. Install or connect the following:
- Steering gear. Tighten the bolts to 55–68 ft. lbs. (74–93 Nm).
- Front differential housing bolts. Tighten the bolts to 49–72 ft. lbs. (67–97 Nm).

- Front driveshaft. Tighten the flange bolts to 37–43 ft. lbs. (50–58 Nm).
- Intermediate shaft and steering column. Tighten the pinch bolt to 14–19 ft. lbs. (18–26 Nm) and the steering column fasteners to 12–16 ft. lbs. (16–22 Nm).
- Power steering hoses and pipes
- Outer tie rod ends. Tighten the nuts to 44–57 ft. lbs. (59–78 Nm).
- Engine under cover
- Negative battery cable
4. Fill the power steering reservoir.
5. Check the wheel alignment and adjust as necessary.

2000–01 MPV

1. Before servicing the vehicle, refer to the precautions in the beginning of this section.
2. Attach a support fixture to the engine lifting eyes.
3. Remove or disconnect the following:
- Front wheels
- Wheel speed sensors
- Steering shaft pinch bolt
- Outer tie rod ends
- Subframe transverse section
- Subframe center section
- Power steering pressure and return lines
- Steering gear

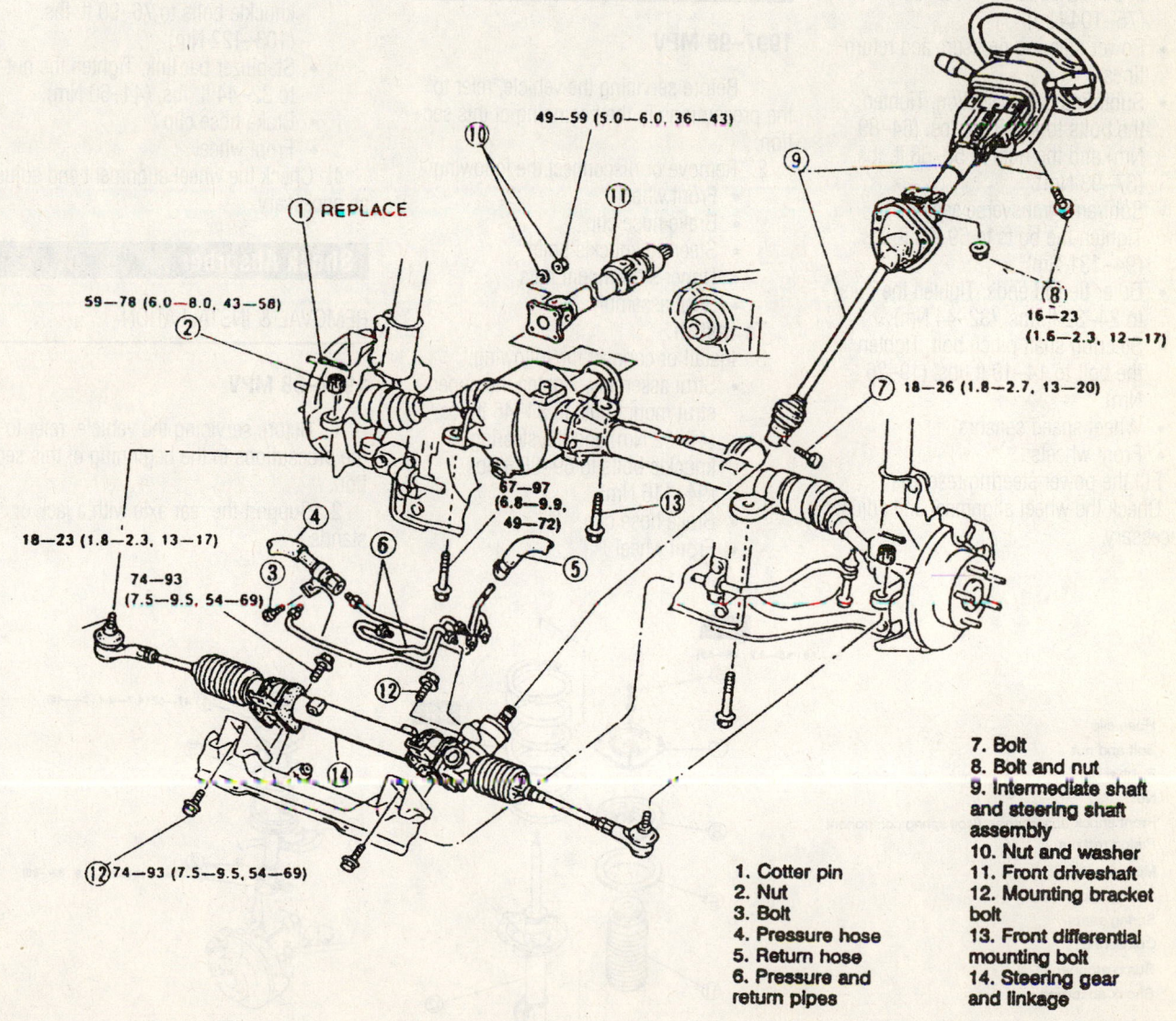

1. Cotter pin
2. Nut
3. Bolt
4. Pressure hose
5. Return hose
6. Pressure and return pipes
7. Bolt
8. Bolt and nut
9. Intermediate shaft and steering shaft assembly
10. Nut and washer
11. Front driveshaft
12. Mounting bracket bolt
13. Front differential mounting bolt
14. Steering gear and linkage

7924TG30

Exploded view of the rack and pinion mounting—1997–98 4WD vehicles

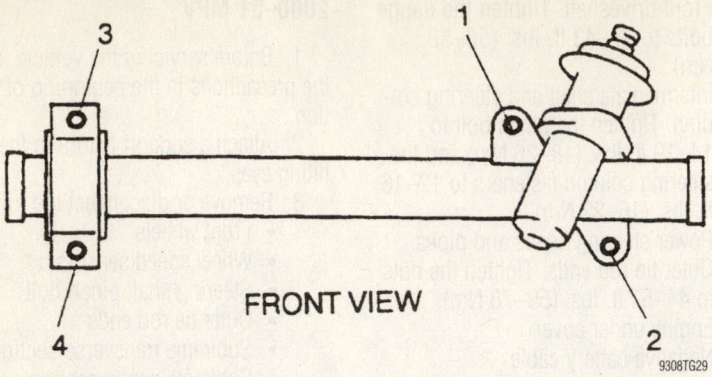

FRONT VIEW

9308TG29

Steering gear torque sequence—2000–01 MPV

To install:

4. Install or connect the following:
- Steering gear. Tighten the fasteners in sequence to 55–77 ft. lbs. (75–104 Nm).
- Power steering pressure and return lines
- Subframe center section. Tighten the bolts to 48–65 ft. lbs. (64–89 Nm) and the nuts to 50–68 ft. lbs. (67–93 Nm).
- Subframe transverse section. Tighten the bolts to 69–96 ft. lbs. (94–131 Nm).
- Outer tie rod ends. Tighten the nuts to 24–32 ft. lbs. (32–44 Nm).
- Steering shaft pinch bolt. Tighten the bolt to 14–19 ft. lbs. (19–26 Nm).
- Wheel speed sensors
- Front wheels

5. Fill the power steering reservoir.

6. Check the wheel alignment and adjust as necessary.

Strut

REMOVAL & INSTALLATION

1997–98 MPV

1. Before servicing the vehicle, refer to the precautions in the beginning of this section.

2. Remove or disconnect the following:
- Front wheel
- Brake hose clip
- Steering knuckle bolts
- Upper strut mount nuts
- Strut assembly

To install:

3. Install or connect the following:
- Strut assembly. Tighten the upper strut mount nuts to 34–46 ft. lbs. (47–62 Nm) and the steering knuckle bolts to 69–86 ft. lbs. (94–116 Nm).
- Brake hose clip
- Front wheel

4. Check the wheel alignment and adjust as necessary.

2000–01 MPV

1. Before servicing the vehicle, refer to the precautions in the beginning of this section.

2. Remove or disconnect the following:
- Front wheel
- Brake hose clip
- Stabilizer bar link
- Steering knuckle bolts
- Upper strut mount nuts
- Strut assembly

To install:

3. Install or connect the following:
- Strut assembly. Tighten the upper strut mount nuts to 34–46 ft. lbs. (47–62 Nm) and the steering knuckle bolts to 76–90 ft. lbs. (103–122 Nm).
- Stabilizer bar link. Tighten the nut to 32–44 ft. lbs. (44–60 Nm).
- Brake hose clip
- Front wheel

4. Check the wheel alignment and adjust as necessary.

Shock Absorber

REMOVAL & INSTALLATION

1997–98 MPV

1. Before servicing the vehicle, refer to the precautions in the beginning of this section.

2. Support the rear axle with a jack or stands.

1	Hose clip
2	Bolt and nut
3	Rubber cap
4	Nut
5	Front shock absorber and coil spring component
6	Piston rod nut
7	Mounting block
8	Spring upper seat
9	Spring seat
10	Coil spring
11	Bump stopper
12	Shock absorber

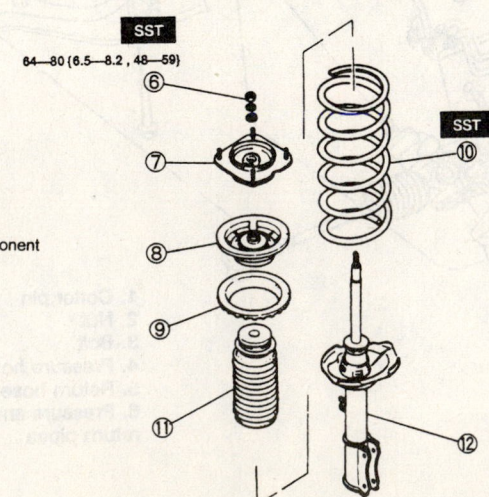

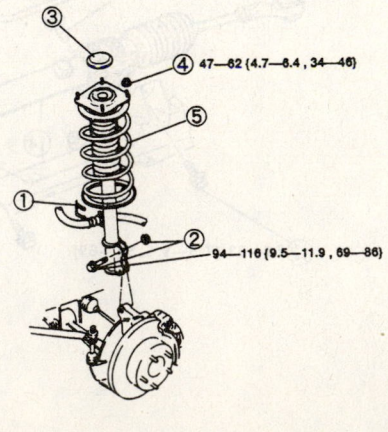

N·m (kgf·m , ft·lbf)

7924TG31

Exploded view of the strut assembly—1997–98 MPV

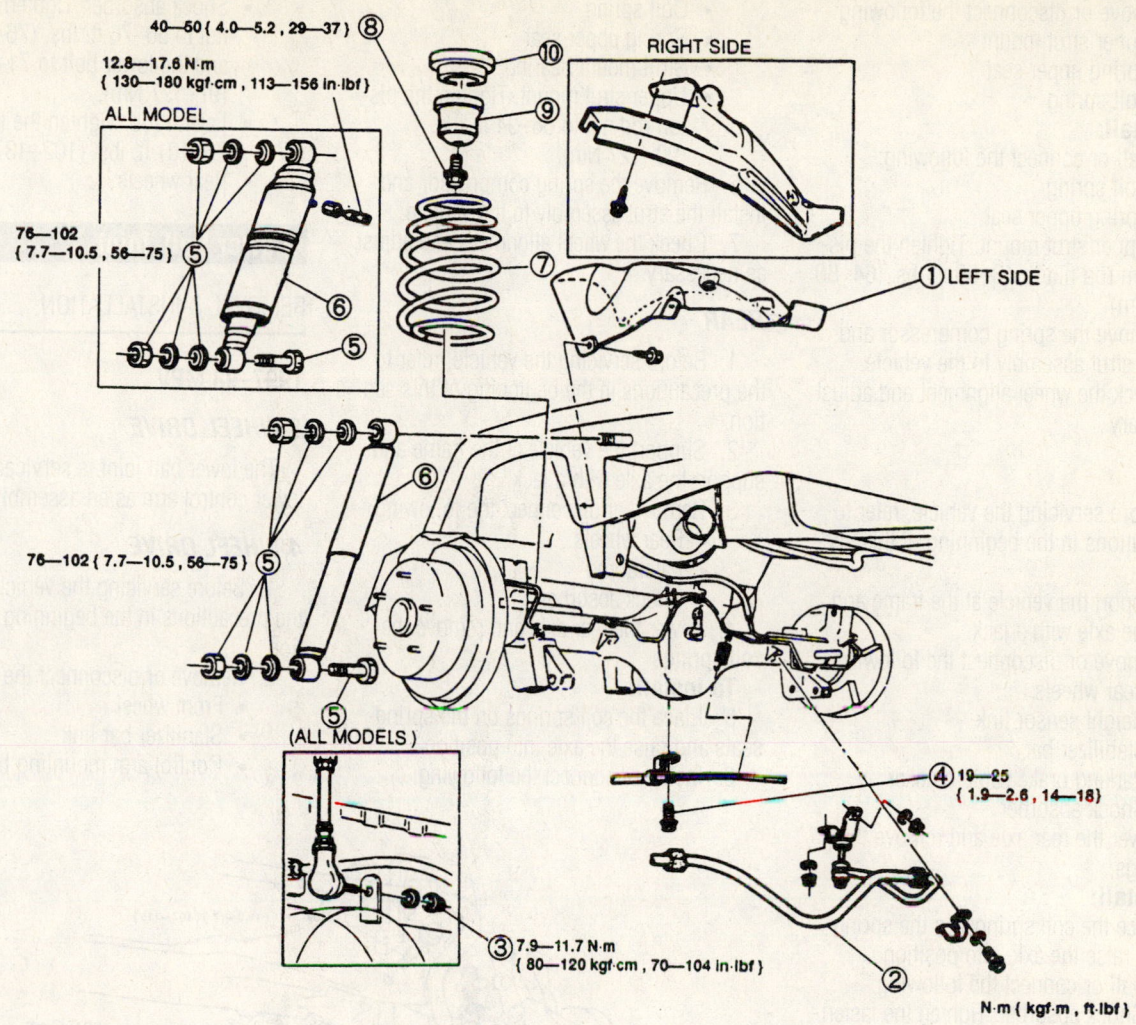

40—50 { 4.0—5.2 , 29—37 } ⑧

12.8—17.6 N·m
{ 130—180 kgf·cm , 113—156 in·lbf }

ALL MODEL

76—102
{ 7.7—10.5 , 56—75 } ⑤

⑥

⑤

RIGHT SIDE

⑩

⑨

⑦

① LEFT SIDE

76—102 { 7.7—10.5 , 56—75 } ⑤

⑥

⑤

(ALL MODELS)

④ 19—25
{ 1.9—2.6 , 14—18 }

②

N·m (kgf·m , ft·lbf)

③ 7.9—11.7 N·m
{ 80—120 kgf·cm , 70—104 in·lbf }

1	Splash shield	6	Shock absorber
2	Stabilizer	7	Coil spring
3	Nut (ALL model)	8	Bolt
4	Bolt	9	Bump stopper
5	Bolt, nut, and washer	10	Spring seat

7924TG32

Exploded view of the rear coil spring, shock absorber and related component mounting—1997–98 vehicles

3. Remove or disconnect the following:
- Rear wheel
- Splash shield
- Shock absorber

To install:

4. Install or connect the following:
- Shock absorber. Tighten the fasteners to 56–75 ft. lbs. (76–102 Nm).
- Splash shield
- Rear wheel

2000–01 MPV

1. Before servicing the vehicle, refer to the precautions in the beginning of this section.

2. Support the rear axle with a jack or stands.

3. Remove or disconnect the following:
- Rear wheel
- Shock absorber

To install:

4. Install or connect the following:
- Shock absorber. Tighten the upper nut to 56–76 ft. lbs. (76–102 Nm) and the lower bolt to 71–94 ft. lbs. (97–127 Nm).
- Rear wheel

Coil Spring

REMOVAL & INSTALLATION

1997–89 MPV

FRONT

1. Before servicing the vehicle, refer to the precautions in the beginning of this section.

2. Remove the strut assembly from the vehicle.

3. Compress the coil spring and remove the piston rod nut.

Turn to Section 5 for brake system applications

4. Remove or disconnect the following:
- Upper strut mount
- Spring upper seat
- Coil spring

To install:

5. Install or connect the following:
- Coil spring
- Spring upper seat
- Upper strut mount. Tighten the piston rod nut to 48–59 ft. lbs. (64–80 Nm).

6. Remove the spring compressor and install the strut assembly to the vehicle.

7. Check the wheel alignment and adjust as necessary.

REAR

1. Before servicing the vehicle, refer to the precautions in the beginning of this section.

2. Support the vehicle at the frame and support the axle with a jack.

3. Remove or disconnect the following:
- Rear wheels
- Height sensor link
- Stabilizer bar
- Parking brake cable bracket
- Shock absorber

4. Lower the rear axle and remove the coil springs.

To install:

5. Place the coil springs on the spring seats and raise the axle into position.

6. Install or connect the following:
- Shock absorber. Tighten the fasteners to 56–75 ft. lbs. (76–102 Nm).
- Parking brake cable bracket. Tighten the bolt to 14–18 ft. lbs. (19–25 Nm).
- Stabilizer bar. Tighten the fasteners to 14–18 ft. lbs. (19–25 Nm).
- Height sensor link. Tighten the nut to 70–104 inch lbs. (8–12 Nm).
- Rear wheels

2000–01 MPV

FRONT

1. Before servicing the vehicle, refer to the precautions in the beginning of this section.

2. Remove the strut assembly from the vehicle.

3. Compress the coil spring and remove the piston rod nut.

4. Remove or disconnect the following:
- Upper strut mount
- Strut mount bearing
- Spring upper seat
- Coil spring

To install:

5. Install or connect the following:

- Coil spring
- Spring upper seat
- Strut mount bearing
- Upper strut mount. Tighten the piston rod nut to 66–94 ft. lbs. (90–127 Nm).

6. Remove the spring compressor and install the strut assembly to the vehicle.

7. Check the wheel alignment and adjust as necessary.

REAR

1. Before servicing the vehicle, refer to the precautions in the beginning of this section.

2. Support the vehicle at the frame and support the axle with a jack.

3. Remove or disconnect the following:
- Rear wheels
- Lateral rod
- Shock absorber

4. Lower the rear axle and remove the coil springs.

To install:

5. Place the coil springs on the spring seats and raise the axle into position.

6. Install or connect the following:

- Shock absorber. Tighten the upper nut to 56–76 ft. lbs. (76–102 Nm) and the lower bolt to 71–94 ft. lbs. (97–127 Nm).
- Lateral rod. Tighten the fastener to 76–101 ft. lbs. (102–137 Nm).
- Rear wheels

Lower Ball Joint

REMOVAL & INSTALLATION

1997–98 MPV

2 WHEEL DRIVE

The lower ball joint is serviced with the lower control arm as an assembly.

4 WHEEL DRIVE

1. Before servicing the vehicle, refer to the precautions in the beginning of this section.

2. Remove or disconnect the following:
- Front wheel
- Stabilizer bar link
- Control arm mounting bolts

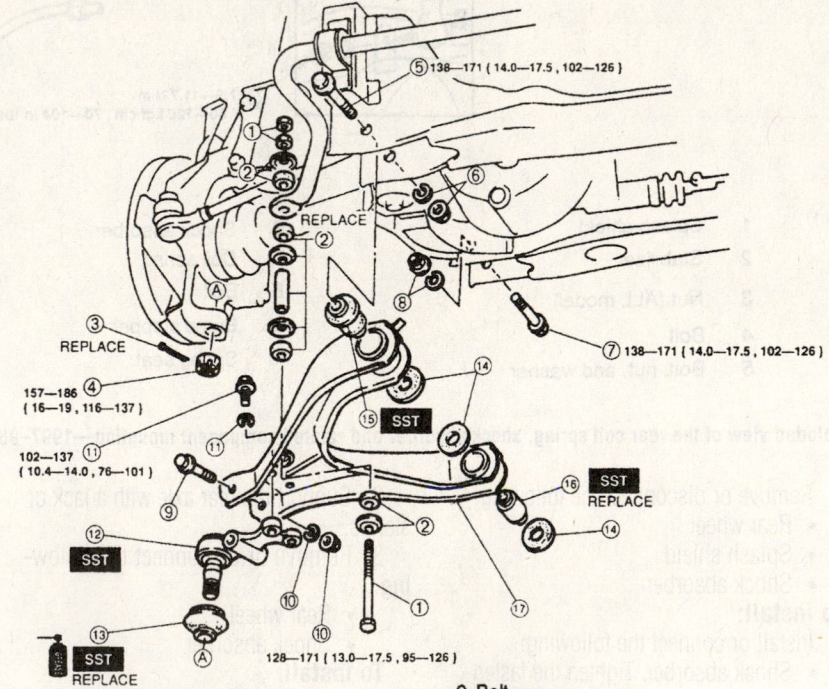

1. Stabilizer bolt and nuts
2. Retainer,bushing and spacer
3. Cotter pin
4. Nut
5. Bolt
6. Nut and washer
7. Bolt
8. Nut and washer
9. Bolt
10. Nut and washer
11. Bolt and washer
12. Lower arm ball joint
13. Dust boot
14. Rubber washer
15. Bushing(front)
16. Bushing(rear)
17. Lower arm

N·m { kgf·m , ft·lbf }

7924TG33

Exploded view of the ball joint and lower control arm assembly—1997-98 4WD MPV

- Steering knuckle nut
- Ball joint

To install:

3. Install or connect the following:
- Ball joint. Tighten the horizontal bolt to 95–126 ft. lbs. (128–171 Nm) and the vertical bolts to 76–101 ft. lbs. (102–137 Nm).
- Steering knuckle nut. Tighten the nut to 98–119 ft. lbs. (133–161 Nm).
- Stabilizer bar link. Tighten the link nut until the link bolt extends 0.20–0.28 inches (5–7mm) above the nut.
- Front wheel

4. Check the wheel alignment and adjust as necessary.

2000–01 MPV

The lower ball joint is serviced with the lower control arm as an assembly.

Lower Control Arm

REMOVAL & INSTALLATION

1997–98 MPV

2 WHEEL DRIVE

1. Before servicing the vehicle, refer to the precautions in the beginning of this section.

2. Remove or disconnect the following:
- Front wheel
- Stabilizer bar link
- Radius arm
- Lower ball joint
- Lower control arm

To install:

3. Install or connect the following:
- Lower control arm. Tighten the inner bolt to 108–126 ft. lbs. (147–171 Nm).

- Lower ball joint. Tighten the nut to 87–115 ft. lbs. (118–156 Nm).
- Radius arm. Tighten the bolts to 76–92 ft. lbs. (103–125 Nm).
- Stabilizer bar link. Tighten the link nut until the link bolt extends 0.35–0.43 inches (9–11mm) above the nut.
- Front wheel

4. Check the wheel alignment and adjust as necessary.

4 WHEEL DRIVE

1. Before servicing the vehicle, refer to the precautions in the beginning of this section.

2. Remove or disconnect the following:
- Front wheel
- Stabilizer bar link
- Lower ball joint
- Inner control arm fasteners
- Lower control arm

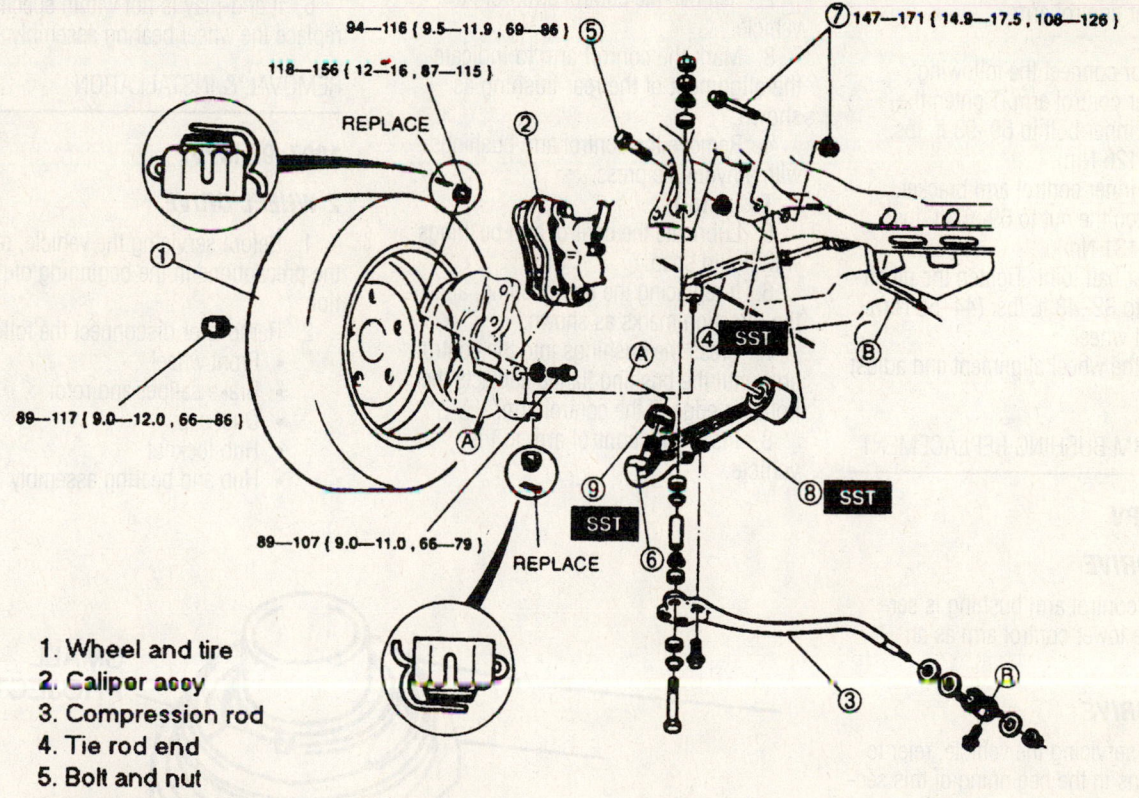

1. Wheel and tire
2. Caliper assy
3. Compression rod
4. Tie rod end
5. Bolt and nut
6. Lower arm ball joint
7. Bolt and nut
8. Lower arm
9. Dust boot

N·m { kgf·m , ft·lbf }

7924TG34

Exploded view of the ball joint and lower control arm assembly—1997–98 2WD MPV

To install:

3. Install or connect the following:
- Lower control arm. Tighten the inner bolts to 102–126 ft. lbs. (138–171 Nm).
- Lower ball joint. Tighten the nut to 97–119 ft. lbs. (133–161 Nm).
- Stabilizer bar link. Tighten the link nut until the link bolt extends 0.20–0.28 inches (5–7mm) above the nut.
- Front wheel

4. Check the wheel alignment and adjust as necessary.

2000–01 MPV

1. Before servicing the vehicle, refer to the precautions in the beginning of this section.
2. Remove or disconnect the following:
- Front wheel
- Lower ball joint
- Front inner control arm bolt
- Rear inner control arm bracket
- Lower control arm

To install:

3. Install or connect the following:
- Lower control arm. Tighten the front inner bolt to 69–93 ft. lbs. (94–126 Nm).
- Rear inner control arm bracket. Tighten the nut to 69–97 ft. lbs. (94–131 Nm).
- Lower ball joint. Tighten the pinch bolt to 32–43 ft. lbs. (44–58 Nm).
- Front wheel

4. Check the wheel alignment and adjust as necessary.

CONTROL ARM BUSHING REPLACEMENT

1997–98 MPV

2 WHEEL DRIVE

The lower control arm bushing is serviced with the lower control arm as an assembly.

4 WHEEL DRIVE

1. Before servicing the vehicle, refer to the precautions in the beginning of this section.
2. Remove the control arm from the vehicle.
3. Remove the control arm bushings with a hydraulic press.

To install:

4. Lubricate the control arm bushings with liquid soap.
5. If replacing the rear bushing, align the direction marks as shown.

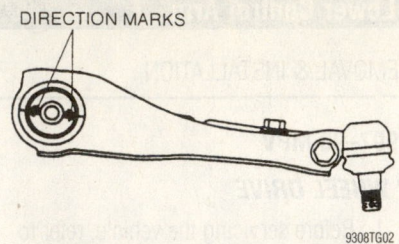

Rear bushing direction mark—1997–98 4 wheel drive MPV

6. Press the bushings into the control arm until the bushing flange contacts the housing edge of the control arm.
7. Install the control arm to the vehicle.
8. Check the wheel alignment and adjust as necessary.

2000–01 MPV

1. Before servicing the vehicle, refer to the precautions in the beginning of this section.
2. Remove the control arm from the vehicle.
3. Mark the control arm to indicate the alignment of the rear bushing as shown.
4. Remove the control arm bushings with a hydraulic press.

To install:

5. Lubricate the control arm bushings with liquid soap.
6. If replacing the rear bushing, align the direction marks as shown.
7. Press the bushings into the control arm until the bushing flange contacts the housing edge of the control arm.
8. Install the control arm to the vehicle.

9. Check the wheel alignment and adjust as necessary.

Wheel Bearing

ADJUSTMENT

All Models

1. Before servicing the vehicle, refer to the precautions in the beginning of this section.
2. Remove or disconnect the following:
- Front wheel
- Brake caliper and rotor
3. Position a dial indicator gauge against the wheel hub. Push and pull the wheel hub in and out and measure the end-play of the wheel bearing.
4. End-play should not exceed 0.002 in. (0.05mm).
5. If end-play is excessive, replace the hub retainer locknut and tighten it to specification. Recheck the end-play.
6. If end-play is not within specification, replace the wheel bearing assembly.

REMOVAL & INSTALLATION

1997–98 MPV

2 WHEEL DRIVE

1. Before servicing the vehicle, refer to the precautions in the beginning of this section.
2. Remove or disconnect the following:
- Front wheel
- Brake caliper and rotor
- Dust cap
- Hub locknut
- Hub and bearing assembly

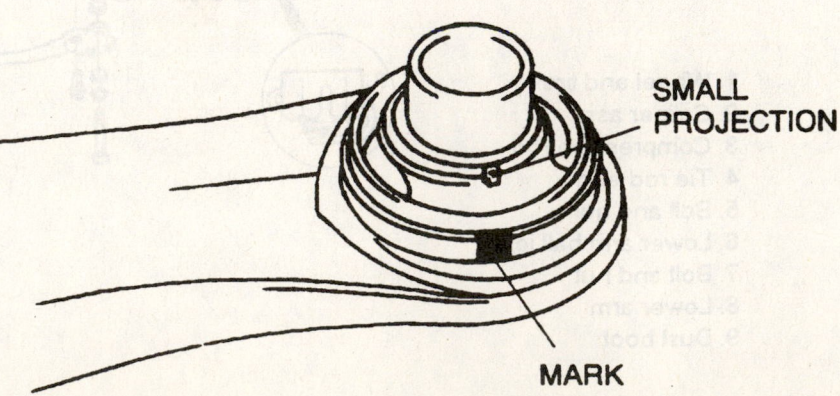

Rear bushing alignment marks—2000–01 MPV

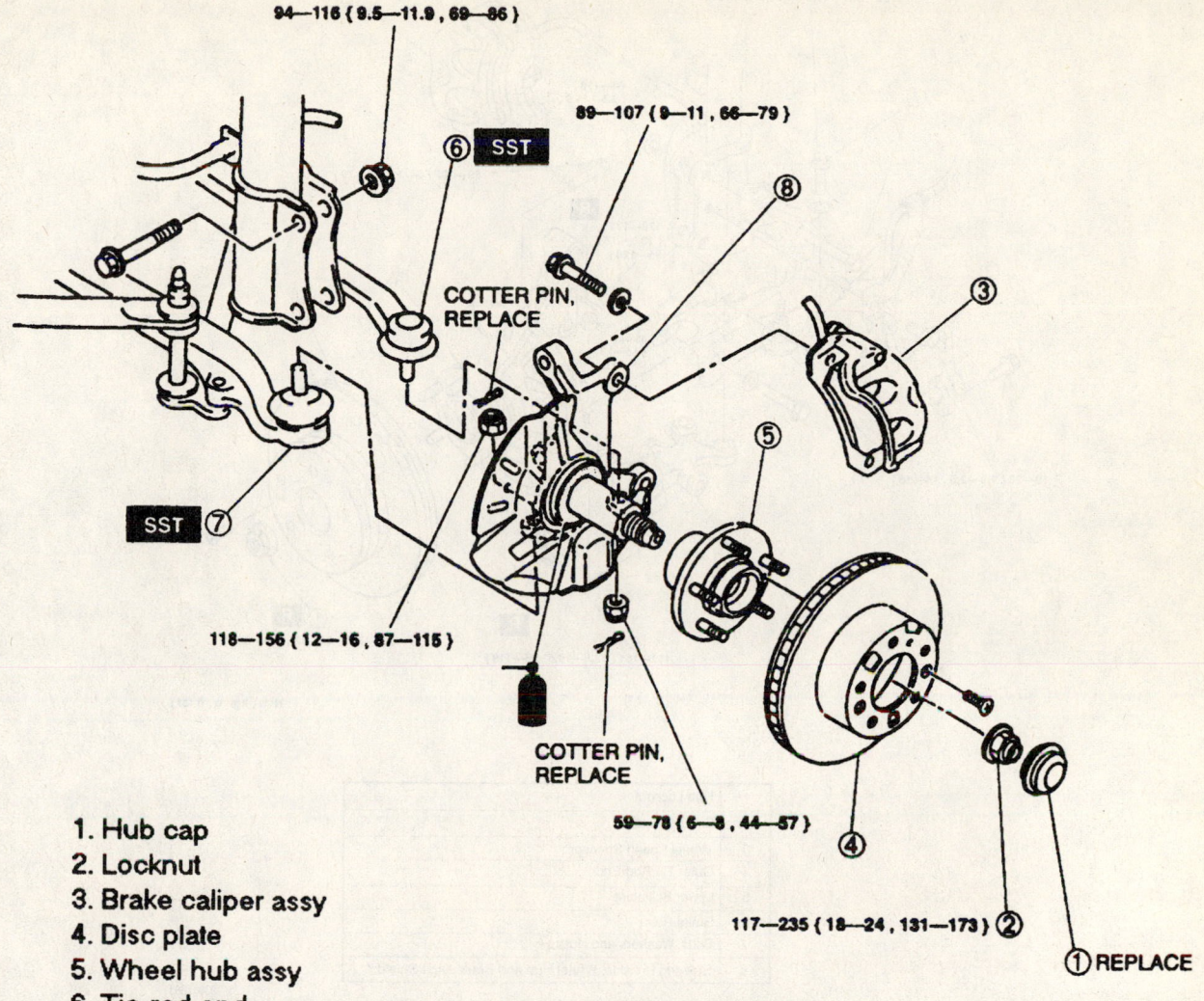

94—116 { 9.5—11.9 , 69—86 }

89—107 { 9—11 , 66—79 }

⑥ SST

COTTER PIN,
REPLACE

SST ⑦

③

⑧

⑤

118—156 { 12—16 , 87—115 }

COTTER PIN,
REPLACE

59—78 { 6—8 , 44—57 }

④

117—235 { 18—24 , 131—173 } ②

① REPLACE

1. Hub cap
2. Locknut
3. Brake caliper assy
4. Disc plate
5. Wheel hub assy
6. Tie-rod end
7. Lower arm
8. Knuckle spindle and dust cover

N·m { kgf·m , ft·lbf }

7924TG35

Exploded view of the front hub and related components—1997–98 2WD MPV

To install:

➡**Use a new locknut for assembly.**

3. Install or connect the following:
   - Hub and bearing assembly. Tighten the locknut to 131–173 ft. lbs. (117–235 Nm).
   - Dust cap
   - Brake caliper and rotor
   - Front wheel

4 WHEEL DRIVE

1. Before servicing the vehicle, refer to the precautions in the beginning of this section.

2. Remove or disconnect the following:
   - Front wheel
   - Brake caliper and rotor
   - Wheel speed sensor
   - Outer tie rod end
   - Lower ball joint
   - Hub retainer locknut
   - Strut bracket bolts
   - Steering knuckle
   - Inner oil seal
   - Hub
   - Outer oil seal
   - Snapring
   - Wheel bearing cartridge

To install:

➡**Use new locknuts, split pins and oil seals for assembly.**

3. Install or connect the following:
   - Wheel bearing cartridge
   - Snapring
   - Outer oil seal
   - Hub
   - Inner oil seal
   - Steering knuckle. Tighten the strut bracket bolts to 69–86 ft. lbs. (94–116 Nm).
   - Hub retainer locknut. Tighten the nut to 174–231 ft. lbs. (236–313 Nm).

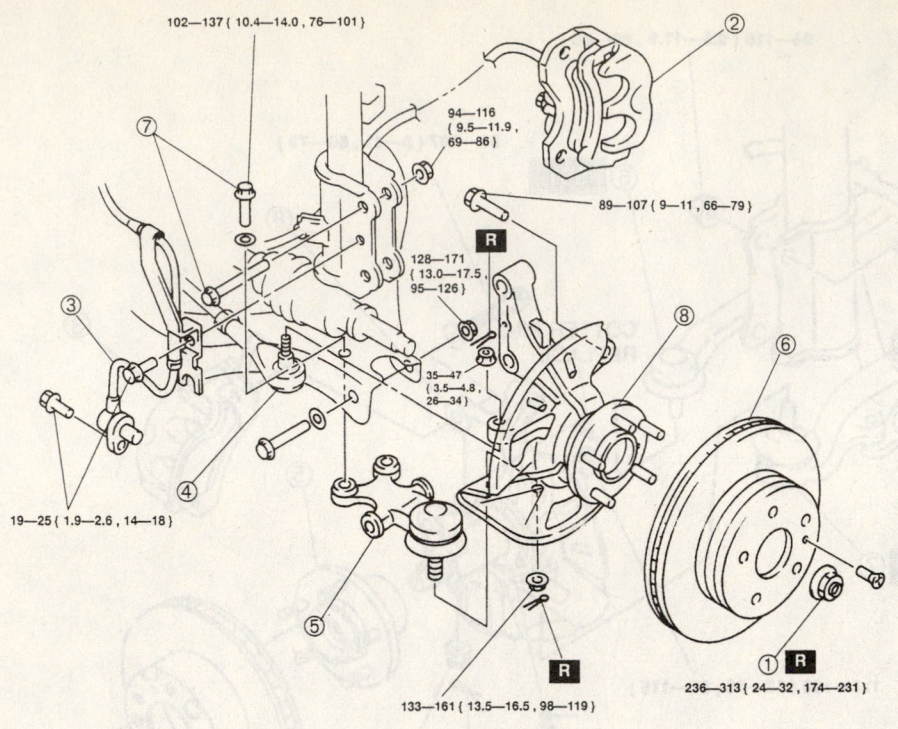

102–137 { 10.4–14.0 , 76–101 }

94–116 { 9.5–11.9 , 69–86 }

89–107 { 9–11 , 66–79 }

128–171 { 13.0–17.5 , 95–126 }

35–47 { 3.5–4.8 , 26–34 }

19–25 { 1.9–2.6 , 14–18 }

133–161 { 13.5–16.5 , 98–119 }

236–313 { 24–32 , 174–231 }

N·m { kgf·m , ft·lbf }

1	Hub Locknut
2	Brake Caliper
3	Wheel Speed Spensor
4	Outer Tie Rod End
5	Lower Ball Joint
6	Brake Rotor
7	Bolts, Washers and Nuts
8	Steering Knuckle, Wheel Hub and Brake Dust Shield

9308TG03

Exploded view of the front hub and related components—1997–98 4WD MPV

- Lower ball joint. Tighten the nut to 98–119 ft. lbs. (133–161 Nm).
- Outer tie rod end. Tighten the nut to 26–34 ft. lbs. (35–47 Nm).
- Wheel speed sensor. Tighten the bolt to 14–18 ft. lbs. (19–25 Nm).
- Brake caliper and rotor
- Front wheel

2000–01 MPV

FRONT

1. Before servicing the vehicle, refer to the precautions in the beginning of this section.
2. Remove or disconnect the following:
   - Front wheel
   - Brake caliper and rotor
   - Wheel speed sensor
   - Outer tie rod end
   - Lower ball joint
   - Hub retainer locknut
   - Strut bracket bolts

- Steering knuckle
- Inner oil seal
- Hub
- Snapring
- Wheel bearing cartridge

To install:

➡ **Use new locknuts, split pins and oil seals for assembly.**

3. Install or connect the following:
   - Wheel bearing cartridge
   - Snapring
   - Hub
   - Inner oil seal
   - Steering knuckle. Tighten the strut bracket bolts to 76–90 ft. lbs. (103–122 Nm).
   - Hub retainer locknut. Tighten the nut to 174–235 ft. lbs. (236–318 Nm).
   - Lower ball joint. Tighten the pinch bolt to 32–43 ft. lbs. (44–58 Nm).
   - Outer tie rod end. Tighten the nut to 24–32 ft. lbs. (32–44 Nm).

- Wheel speed sensor. Tighten the bolt to 14–18 ft. lbs. (19–25 Nm).
- Brake caliper and rotor
- Front wheel

REAR

1. Before servicing the vehicle, refer to the precautions in the beginning of this section.
2. Remove or disconnect the following:
   - Rear wheel
   - Brake drum
   - Dust cap
   - Hub retaining lock nut
   - Wheel bearing and hub assembly

To install:

3. Install or connect the following:
   - Wheel bearing and hub assembly. Tighten the locknut to 131–173 ft. lbs. (177–235 Nm).
   - Dust cap
   - Brake drum
   - Rear wheel

MERCEDES-BENZ

Mercedes-Benz-ML320 • ML430

PRECAUTIONS

Before servicing any vehicle, please be sure to read all of the following precautions, which deal with personal safety, prevention of component damage, and important points to take into consideration when servicing a motor vehicle:

• Never open, service or drain the radiator or cooling system when the engine is hot; serious burns can occur from the steam and hot coolant.

• Observe all applicable safety precautions when working around fuel. Whenever servicing the fuel system, always work in a well-ventilated area. Do not allow fuel spray or vapors to come in contact with a spark, open flame or excessive heat (a hot drop light, for example). Keep a dry chemical fire extinguisher near the work area. Always keep fuel in a container specifically designed for fuel storage; also, always

properly seal fuel containers to avoid the possibility of fire or explosion. Refer to the additional fuel system precautions later in this section.

• Fuel injection systems often remain pressurized, even after the engine has been turned **OFF**. The fuel system pressure must be relieved before disconnecting any fuel lines. Failure to do so may result in fire and/or personal injury.

• Brake fluid often contains polyglycol ethers and polyglycols. Avoid contact with the eyes and wash your hands thoroughly after handling brake fluid. If you do get brake fluid in your eyes, flush your eyes with clean, running water for 15 minutes. If eye irritation persists, or if you have taken brake fluid internally, IMMEDIATELY seek medical assistance.

• The EPA warns that prolonged contact with used engine oil may cause a number of skin disorders, including cancer. You should make every effort to minimize your

exposure to used engine oil. Protective gloves should be worn when changing oil. Wash your hands and any other exposed skin areas as soon as possible after exposure to used engine oil. Soap and water, or waterless hand cleaner should be used.

• All new vehicles are now equipped with an air bag system. The system must be disabled before performing service on or around system components, steering column, instrument panel components, wiring and sensors. Failure to follow safety and disabling procedures could result in accidental air bag deployment, possible personal injury, and unnecessary system repairs.

• Always wear safety goggles when working with, or around, the air bag system. When carrying a non-deployed air bag, be sure the bag and trim cover are pointed away from your body. When placing a non-deployed air bag on a work surface, always face the bag and trim cover upward, away from the surface. This will reduce the motion of the module if it is accidentally deployed. Refer to the additional air bag system precautions later in this section.

• Clean, high quality brake fluid from a sealed container is essential to the safe and proper operation of the brake system. You should always buy the correct type of brake fluid for your vehicle. If the brake fluid becomes contaminated, completely flush the system with new fluid. Never reuse any brake fluid. Any brake fluid that is removed from the system should be discarded. Also, do not allow any brake fluid to come in contact with a painted surface; it will damage the paint.

• Never operate the engine without the proper amount and type of engine oil; doing so will result in severe engine damage.

• Timing belt maintenance is extremely important. Many models utilize an interference-type, non-freewheeling engine. If the timing belt breaks, the valves in the cylinder head may strike the pistons, causing potentially serious (also time-consuming and expensive) engine damage. Refer to the maintenance interval charts in the front of this manual for the recommended replacement interval for the timing belt, and to the timing belt section for belt replacement and inspection.

• Disconnecting the negative battery cable on some vehicles may interfere with the functions of the on-board computer system(s) and may require the computer to undergo a relearning process once the negative battery cable is reconnected.

• When servicing drum brakes, only disassemble and assemble one side at a time, leaving the remaining side intact for reference.

ENGINE REPAIR

➡**Disconnecting the negative battery cable on some vehicles may interfere with the functions of the on board computer systems and may require the computer to undergo a relearning process, once the negative battery cable is reconnected.**

Ignition Timing

ADJUSTMENT

The ignition timing is controlled by the Electronic Control Module (ECM) and is not adjustable.

Engine Assembly

REMOVAL & INSTALLATION

1. Before servicing the vehicle, refer to the precautions in the beginning of this section.

2. Verify that the rear engine lifting eyes are correct. The left lifting eye is marked with a star and code number 04, and the right lifting eye is marked with a star and code number 02.

3. Remove or disconnect the following:

• Negative battery cable
• Engine undercover
• Engine cooling fan and clutch, then the fan shroud

➡**The fan clutch is equipped with right-hand thread.**

4. Place a guard plate behind the radiator/condenser to protect it from damage during removal and installation.

• Air cleaner housing
• Resonance pipe and body
• Coolant hoses from the water pump and thermostat housing
• Coolant expansion tank
• Transmission dipstick tube from the cylinder head cover
• Brake booster vacuum hose from the rear of the intake manifold

5. Drain the power steering fluid from the pump.

• Hoses from the power steering pump, then plug the openings
• Vacuum hose at the purge control valve

6. Relieve the fuel system pressure.

• Fuel pipe
• Heater hose from the rear of the cylinder head
• Engine wiring harness

7. Lock the automatic belt tensioner by rotating the tensioner counterclockwise until a 5mm drift or pin fits through the tensioner.

• Serpentine belt
• Air conditioning compressor and position it aside, leaving the hoses attached
• Exhaust system from the manifolds
• Cable for the park lock interlock

8. Matchmark the torque converter-to-ring gear.

• Torque converter bolts
• Left and right Oxygen (O2S) sensors electrical connections
• Sarter

• Engine-to-transmission mounting bolts. Leave the 2 upper bolts attached at this time.
• Motor mounts from the front suspension support
• Generator wiring harness
• Air conditioning compressor electrical connector
• Engine ground cable at the power steering pump

9. Attach the engine hoist to the lifting eyes, then raise the engine and support the transmission.

➡**Be sure that the engine does not touch the body at the rear.**

10. Remove the 2 remaining engine-to-transmission mounting bolts.

11. Slowly pull the engine out to the front and lift it out.

To install:

12. Install or connect the following:

• Engine into the vehicle
• Engine to the transmission
• Upper 2 mounting bolts
• Engine ground cable to the power steering pump
• Motor mount bolts and tighten to 26 ft. lbs. (35 Nm)

13. Remove the engine hoist from the lifting eyes.

• Remaining engine-to-transmission mounting bolts
• Air conditioning compressor electrical connector
• Generator wiring harness
• Starter
• Left and right O2S sensors

14. Align the torque converter-to-ring gear matchmarks and tighten the bolts to 31 ft. lbs. (42 Nm).

• Cable for the park lock interlock
• Exhaust system to the manifolds and tighten the mounting nuts to 15 ft. lbs. (20 Nm)
• Air conditioning compressor
• Serpentine belt and remove the locking pin
• Engine wiring harness
• Coolant hoses to the water pump, cylinder head and thermostat housing
• Fuel pipe
• Vacuum hose to the purge control valve
• Power steering hoses to the pump and fill the reservoir
• Brake booster vacuum hose to the intake manifold
• Transmission dipstick tube to the cylinder head cover
• Coolant expansion tank

- Resonance pipe and body, then the air cleaner housing
15. Remove the radiator/condenser guard plate.
    - Fan shroud and fan
    - Engine undercover
16. Fill the engine with coolant and oil.
17. Connect the negative battery cable.
18. Read fault memory, encode the radio and normalize the power windows.

Water Pump

REMOVAL & INSTALLATION

1. Before servicing the vehicle, refer to the precautions in the beginning of this section.
2. Remove or disconnect the following:
    - Negative battery cable
    - Engine cooling fan and clutch, then the fan shroud

➡️ **The fan clutch is equipped with right-hand thread.**

3. Drain the engine coolant.
    - Engine cover
4. Lock the automatic belt tensioner by

rotating the tensioner counterclockwise until a 5mm drift or pin fits through the tensioner.
    - Serpentine belt
    - Coolant hoses from the water pump
    - Belt pulley
    - Water pump mounting bolts
    - Water pump
5. Clean and dry the gasket mating surface for the water pump.

To install:

6. Install or connect the following:
    - Water pump and gasket. Tighten the M6 bolts to 88 inch lbs. (10 Nm) and the M8 bolts to 177 inch lbs. (20 Nm).
    - Water pump belt pulley and tighten the mounting bolts to 88 inch lbs. (10 Nm)
    - Coolant hoses to the water pump
    - Serpentine belt and remove the locking pin
    - Engine cover
    - Fan shroud and fan
7. Fill the engine with coolant.
8. Connect the negative battery cable.
9. Read fault memory, encode the radio and normalize the power windows.
10. Start the vehicle and check for leaks.

Cylinder Head

REMOVAL & INSTALLATION

1. Before servicing the vehicle, refer to the precautions in the beginning of this section.
2. Remove or disconnect the following:
    - Negative battery cable
3. Drain and recycle the engine coolant.
    - Engine cooling fan and clutch
    - Fan shroud

➡️ **The fan clutch is equipped with right-hand thread.**

4. Place a guard plate behind the radiator/condenser to protect it from damage during removal and installation.
    - Engine cover
    - Air cleaner housing, resonance pipe and body
5. Properly relieve the fuel system pressure.
    - Fuel line
    - Ignition coils
    - Cylinder head covers

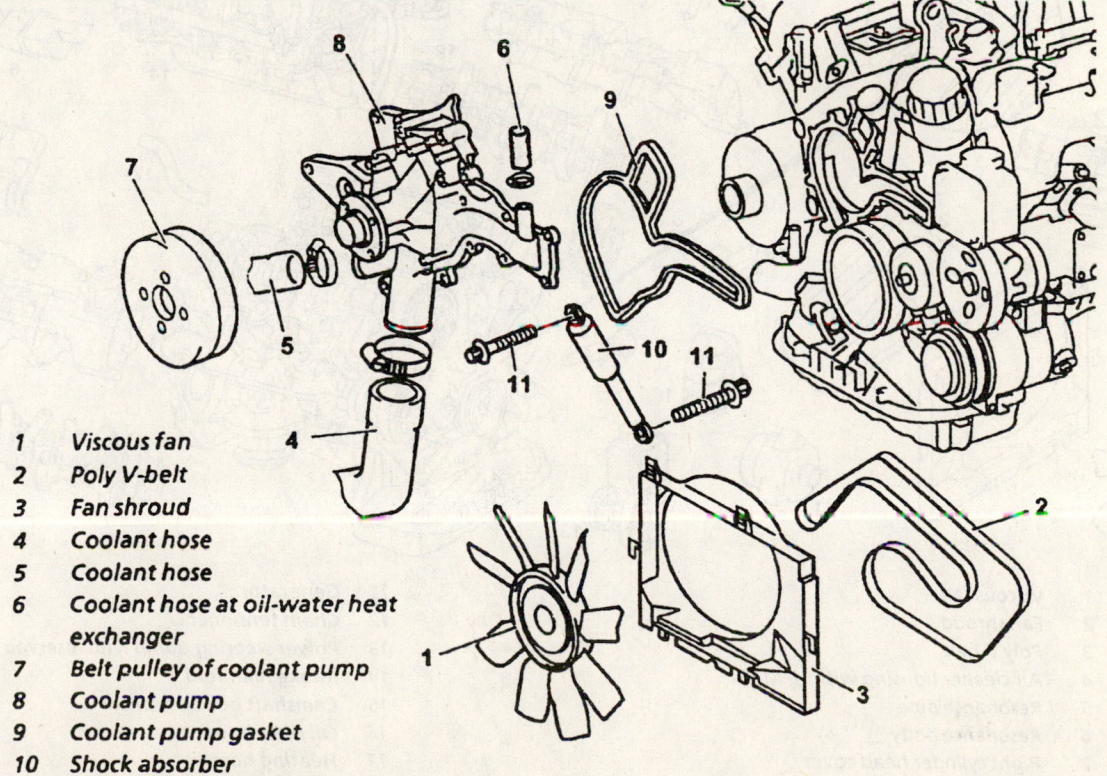

1   Viscous fan
2   Poly V-belt
3   Fan shroud
4   Coolant hose
5   Coolant hose
6   Coolant hose at oil-water heat exchanger
7   Belt pulley of coolant pump
8   Coolant pump
9   Coolant pump gasket
10 Shock absorber
11 Bolts of shock absorber

7924Z101

Exploded view of the water pump mounting and related components

➡The intake manifold system must not be disassembled.

- Intake manifold
- Vacuum switchover valve
- Camshaft Position (CMP) sensor

6. Lock the automatic belt tensioner by rotating the tensioner counterclockwise until a 5mm drift or pin fits through the tensioner.

- Serpentine belt
- Power steering pump and position it aside leaving the hoses attached
- Heater hose at the firewall
- Exhaust system from the exhaust manifolds

7. Rotate the engine clockwise to position the crankshaft 40 degrees after top dead center.

✳ WARNING

The engine must not be rotated backwards.

8. Lock the camshafts using the Camshaft Locking tools 112 589 00 32 00 and 112 589 01 32 00.

9. Remove or disconnect the following:
- Generator, then the timing chain tensioner
- Camshaft gears and attach them to the chain with a cable tie
- Camshaft bearing bridges
- Timing case-to-cylinder head bolts

10. Loosen and remove the cylinder head bolts in stages following the illustrated sequence.
- Cylinder head off the engine block
- All gasket material from the sealing surfaces of the cylinder head and engine block. Be careful not to gouge or scratch the surface of the aluminum head. Be sure the cylinder head locating dowels are positioned in the engine block. Clean and dry the head bolt holes using compressed air.

11. Measure the length of the cylinder head bolt shafts, new bolt length is 5.57 inches (141.5mm) and the maximum permissible length is 5.69 inches (144.5mm). Replace bolts that measure greater than the maximum permissible length.

To install:

➡Refer to Section 1 of this manual for the cylinder head torque sequence illustration. The illustration is located after the Torque Specification Chart.

12. Clean the head bolt threads, then apply clean engine oil to the thread and head contact surfaces.

13. Install the cylinder head to the engine block and tighten the head bolts according to sequence as follows:
   a. Step 1. 15 ft. lbs. (20 Nm).
   b. Step 2. 37 ft. lbs. (50 Nm).
   c. Step 3. 60–70 degrees.
   d. Step 4. additional 60–70 degrees.

14. Install or connect the following:
- Timing case-to-cylinder head bolts and tighten to 15 ft. lbs. (20 Nm)
- Camshaft bearing bridges

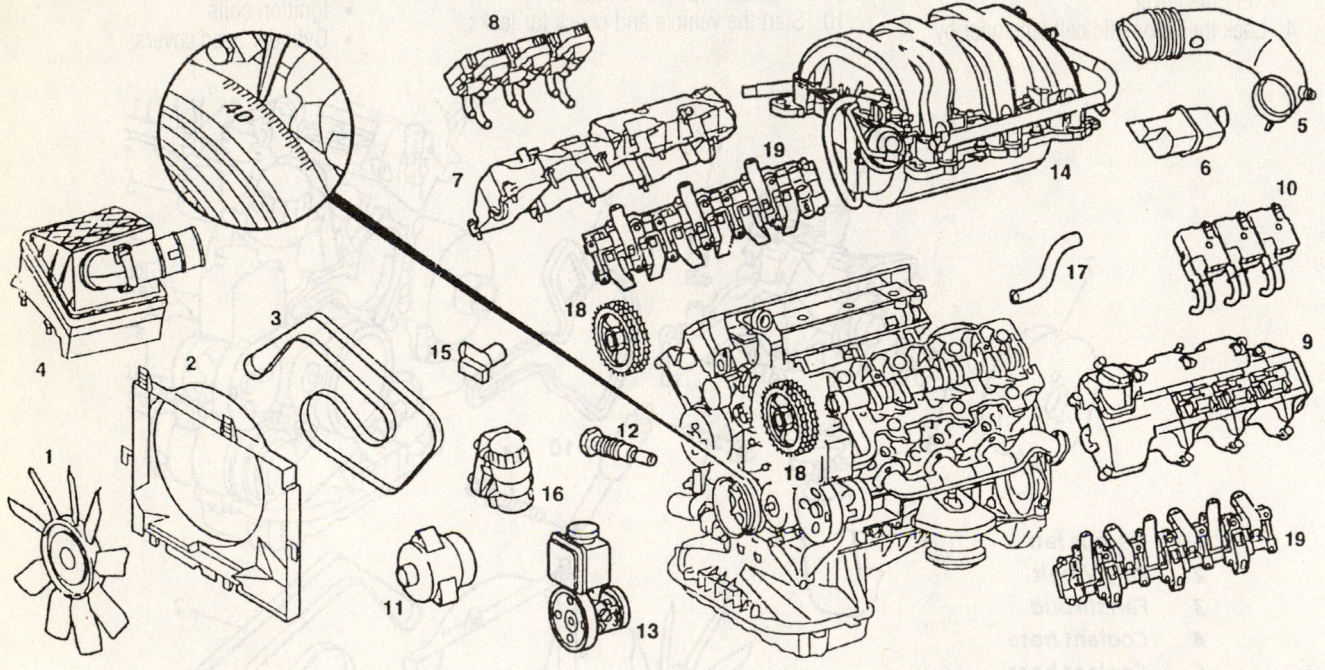

1 Viscous fan	11 Generator
2 Fan shroud	12 Chain tensioner
3 Poly V-belt	13 Power steering pump with reservoir
4 Air cleaner housing with HFM-SFI	14 Intake manifold
5 Resonance pipe	15 Camshaft position sensor
6 Resonance body	16 Oil filter housing
7 Right cylinder head cover	17 Heating hose
8 Right ignition coils	18 Camshaft gears
9 Left cylinder head cover	19 Camshaft bearing bridges
10 Left ignition coils	

Exploded view of the cylinder head accessory components—3.2L engine shown

79242Z102

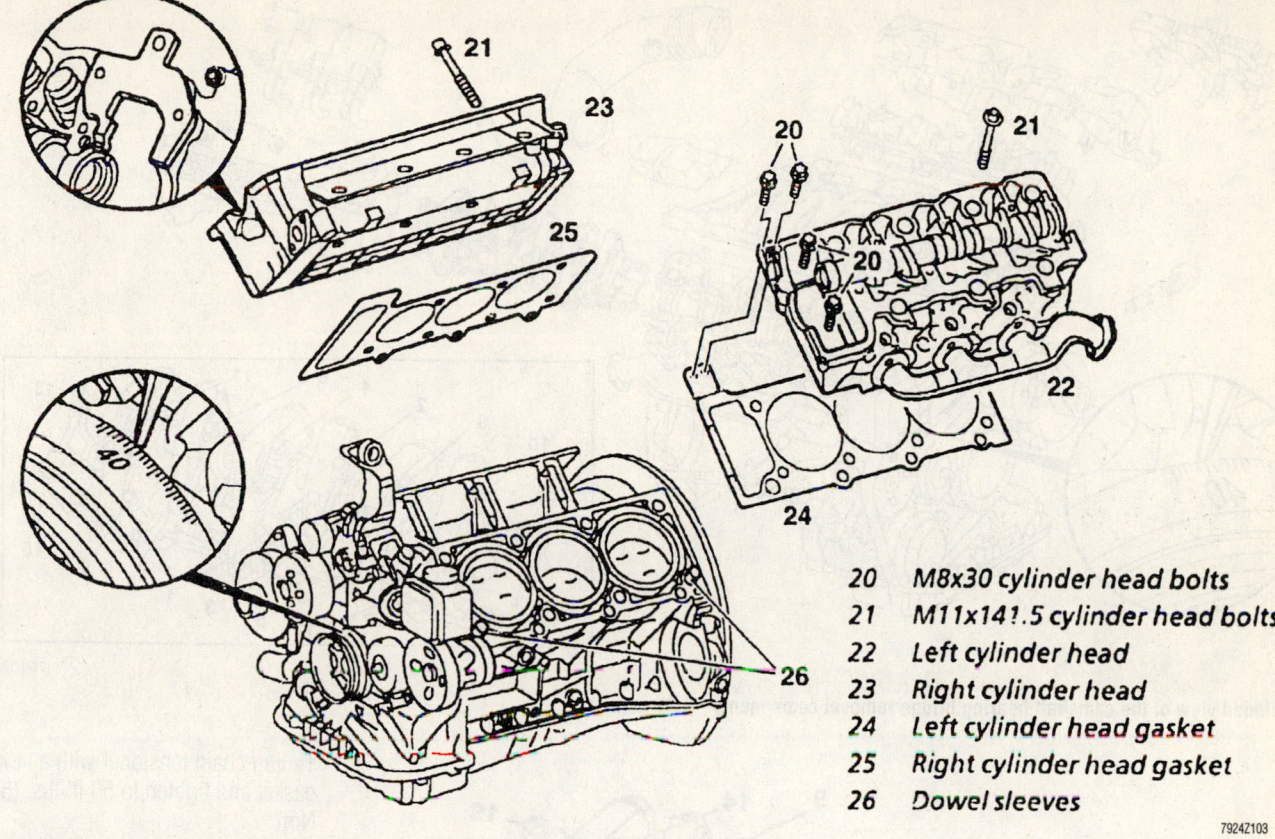

20 M8x30 cylinder head bolts
21 M11x141.5 cylinder head bolts
22 Left cylinder head
23 Right cylinder head
24 Left cylinder head gasket
25 Right cylinder head gasket
26 Dowel sleeves

Exploded view of the cylinder head removal—3.2L engine shown

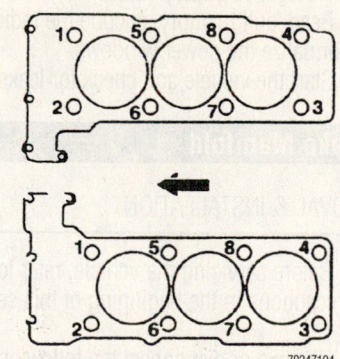

Cylinder head bolt removal sequence—
3.2L Engine

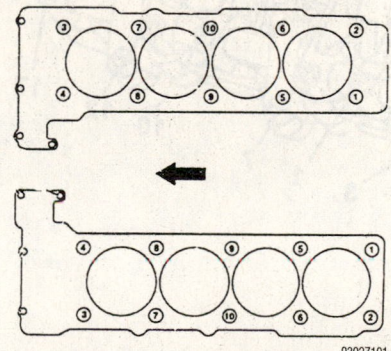

Cylinder head bolt removal sequence—
4.3L Engine

- Camshaft gear and tighten the mounting bolt to 37 ft. lbs. (50 Nm) plus an additional 90 degrees. Check the basic camshaft position and adjust if necessary.
- Timing chain tensioner with a new gasket and tighten to 59 ft. lbs. (80 Nm)
- Generator

15. Remove the camshaft locking plates.
- Exhaust system to the manifolds

and tighten the mounting nuts to 15 ft. lbs. (20 Nm)
- Heater hose to the cylinder head
- Power steering pump
- Serpentine belt and remove the locking pin
- CMP sensor
- Vacuum switchover valve
- Intake manifold
- Cylinder head covers and tighten the bolts to 88 inch lbs. (10 Nm)
- Ignition coils and tighten the

mounting bolts to 70 inch lbs. (8 Nm)
- Fuel pipe
- Air cleaner housing, resonance pipe and body
- Engine cover

16. Remove the guard plate from the radiator/condenser.
- Fan shroud, then the cooling fan

17. Fill the engine with coolant.
18. Connect the negative battery cable.
19. Read fault memory, encode the radio and normalize the power windows.
20. Start the vehicle and check for leaks.

Rocker Arms/Shafts

The rocker arm/shaft is part of the camshaft bearing cap assembly and is called the camshaft bearing bridge. This procedure is for removing and installing the camshaft bearing bridge.

REMOVAL & INSTALLATION

1. Before servicing the vehicle, refer to the precautions in the beginning of this section.

Timing belt service is covered in Section 4 of this manual

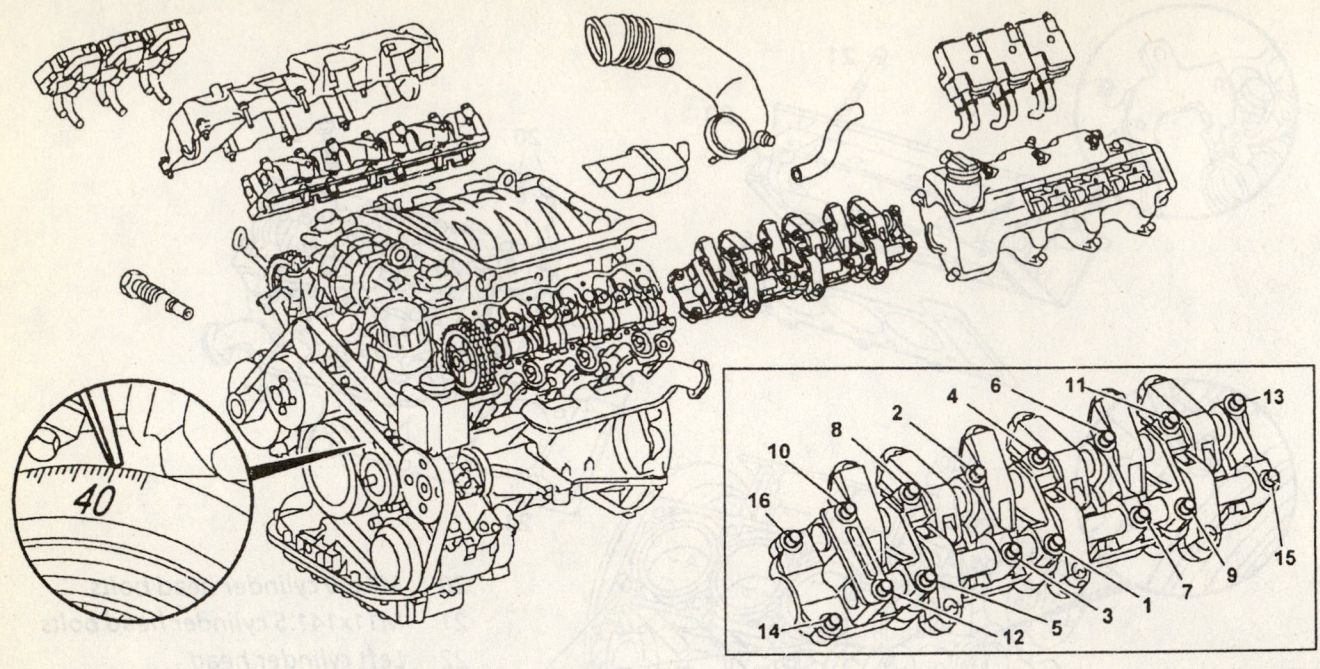

Exploded view of the camshaft bearing bridge removal components—3.2L engine

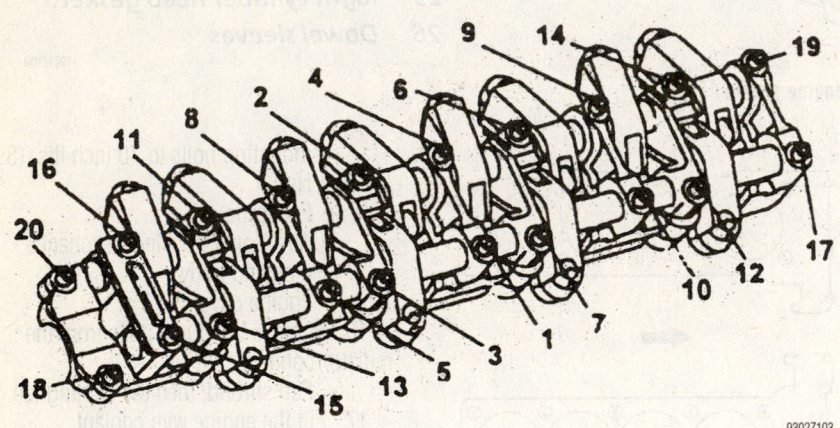

Camshaft bearing bridge—4.3L Engine

2. Remove or disconnect the following:
   - Negative battery cable
   - Cylinder head cover

3. Rotate the engine clockwise to position the crankshaft 40 degrees after Top Dead Center (TDC).

✢✢ WARNING

The engine must not be rotated backwards.

   - Generator
   - Timing chain tensioner

4. Cable tie the timing chain to the camshaft sprocket.
   - Camshaft bearing bridge bolts in the reverse order of installation,

starting at 16 for the 3.2L engine, and 20 for the 4.3L engine

➡**The camshaft bearing bridge must not be disassembled. If damage exists at the valve gear or at the top half of the camshaft bearing journal, the complete cylinder head should be replaced.**

To install:

5. Lubricate the camshaft bearing journals.

6. Install or connect the following:
   - Camshaft bearing bridge and tighten the bolts to 11 ft. lbs. (15 Nm) in sequence as illustrated

7. Remove the cable ties from the camshaft sprockets.

   - Timing chain tensioner with a new gasket and tighten to 59 ft. lbs. (80 Nm)
   - Cylinder head covers and tighten the bolts to 88 inch lbs. (10 Nm)
   - Negative battery cable

8. Read fault memory, encode the radio and normalize the power windows.

9. Start the vehicle and check for leaks.

Intake Manifold

REMOVAL & INSTALLATION

1. Before servicing the vehicle, refer to the precautions in the beginning of this section.

2. Remove or disconnect the following:
   - Negative battery cable
   - Cylinder head cover
   - Mass Air Flow (MAF) sensor with the intake pipe

3. Properly relieve the fuel system pressure.

   - Fuel rail with the injectors
   - Vacuum lines from the intake manifold
   - All electrical connections to the intake manifold
   - Exhaust Gas Recirculation (EGR) valve
   - Combination valve
   - Intake manifold mounting bolts
   - Intake manifold and gaskets

4. Place clean shop rags into the intake

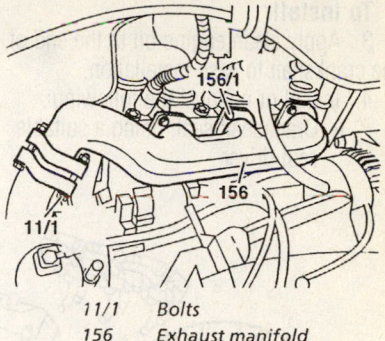

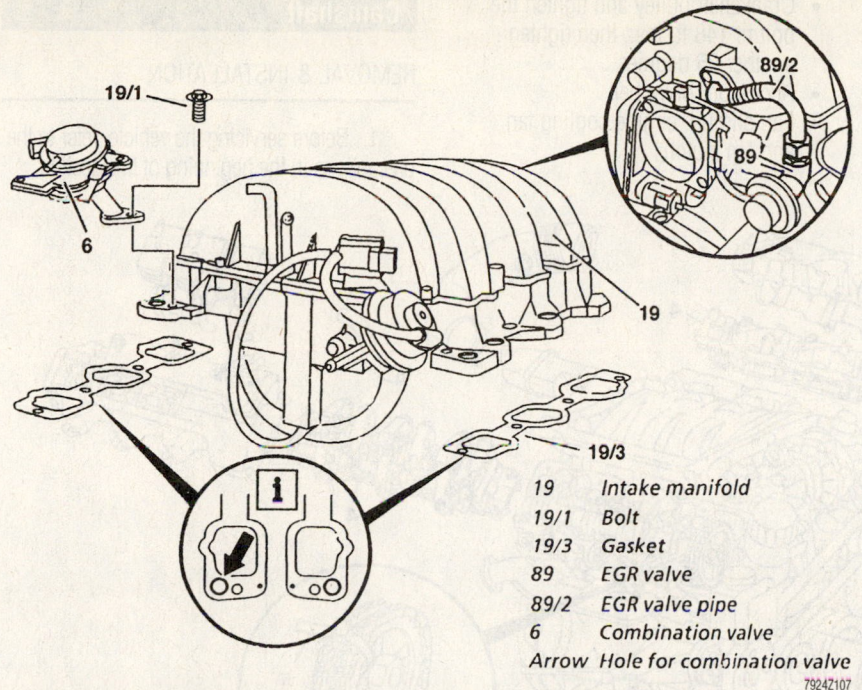

19 Intake manifold
19/1 Bolt
19/3 Gasket
89 EGR valve
89/2 EGR valve pipe
6 Combination valve
Arrow Hole for combination valve

7924Z107

Exploded view of the intake manifold and related components—3.2L engine shown

11/1 Bolts
156 Exhaust manifold
156/1 Nuts
156/5 Gasket

7924Z109

Component view of the right-hand exhaust manifold—3.2L engine shown

passages to prevent dirt from entering. Clean the gasket mating surfaces.

To install:

5. Install the new gaskets and verify the secondary air injection passage opening in the gasket.

6. Remove the shop rags from the intake passages.

7. Install or connect the following:
- Intake manifold to the engine and tighten the mounting bolts to 15 ft. lbs. (20 Nm)
- Combination valve and tighten the bolts to 15 ft. lbs. (20 Nm)
- EGR valve
- Electrical connections to the intake manifold
- Vacuum lines to the manifold
- Fuel rail with the injectors
- MAF sensor with the air intake pipe
- Cylinder head cover and tighten the bolts to 00 inch lbs. (10 Nm)
- Negative battery cable

8. Read fault memory, encode the radio and normalize the power windows.

9. Start the vehicle and check for leaks.

Exhaust Manifold

REMOVAL & INSTALLATION

1. Before servicing the vehicle, refer to the precautions in the beginning of this section.

2. Remove or disconnect the following:
- Negative battery cable
- Front wheels
- Plastic inner fender liners
- Exhaust manifold heat shields

➡**If the bolts are difficult to remove or the threads show signs of damage, replace the rivet nuts in the manifold.**

- Exhaust system-to-manifold flanged connection mounting bolts
- Front exhaust pipe at the transmission exhaust bracket

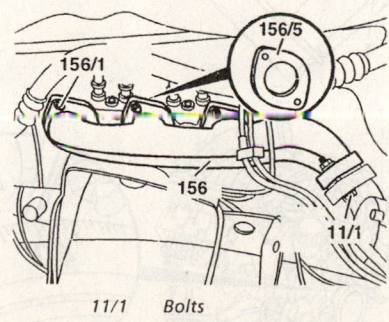

11/1 Bolts
156 Exhaust manifold
156/1 Nuts
156/5 Gasket

7924Z108

Component view of the left-hand exhaust manifold—3.2L engine shown

- Exhaust manifold-to-cylinder head mounting bolts
- Exhaust manifold

3. Clean the gasket mating surfaces.

To install:

4. Install or connect the following:
- Exhaust manifold using new gaskets and nuts. Tighten the nuts to 12 ft. lbs. (16 Nm).
- Front exhaust pipe to the transmission exhaust bracket
- Exhaust system to the manifolds and tighten the mounting bolts to 15 ft. lbs. (20 Nm)
- Exhaust manifold heat shields
- Plastic inner fender liners
- Front wheels and tighten the lug bolts to 110 ft. lbs. (150 Nm)
- Negative battery cable

5. Read fault memory, encode the radio and normalize the power windows.

6. Start the vehicle and check for leaks.

Front Crankshaft Seal

REMOVAL & INSTALLATION

1. Before servicing the vehicle, refer to the precautions in the beginning of this section.

2. Remove or disconnect the following:
- Engine cooling fan and clutch
- Fan shroud

➡**The fan clutch is equipped with right-hand thread.**

- Accessory drive belt
- Crankshaft pulley
- Crankshaft seal

To install:

3. Apply clean engine oil to the end of the crankshaft to ease installation.

4. Install or connect the following:
- Crankshaft seal, using a suitable seal driver

- Crankshaft pulley and tighten the bolt to 148 ft. lbs., then tighten another 95 degrees
- Accessory drive belt
- Fan shroud, engine cooling fan, and fan clutch

Camshaft

REMOVAL & INSTALLATION

1. Before servicing the vehicle, refer to the precautions in the beginning of this section.

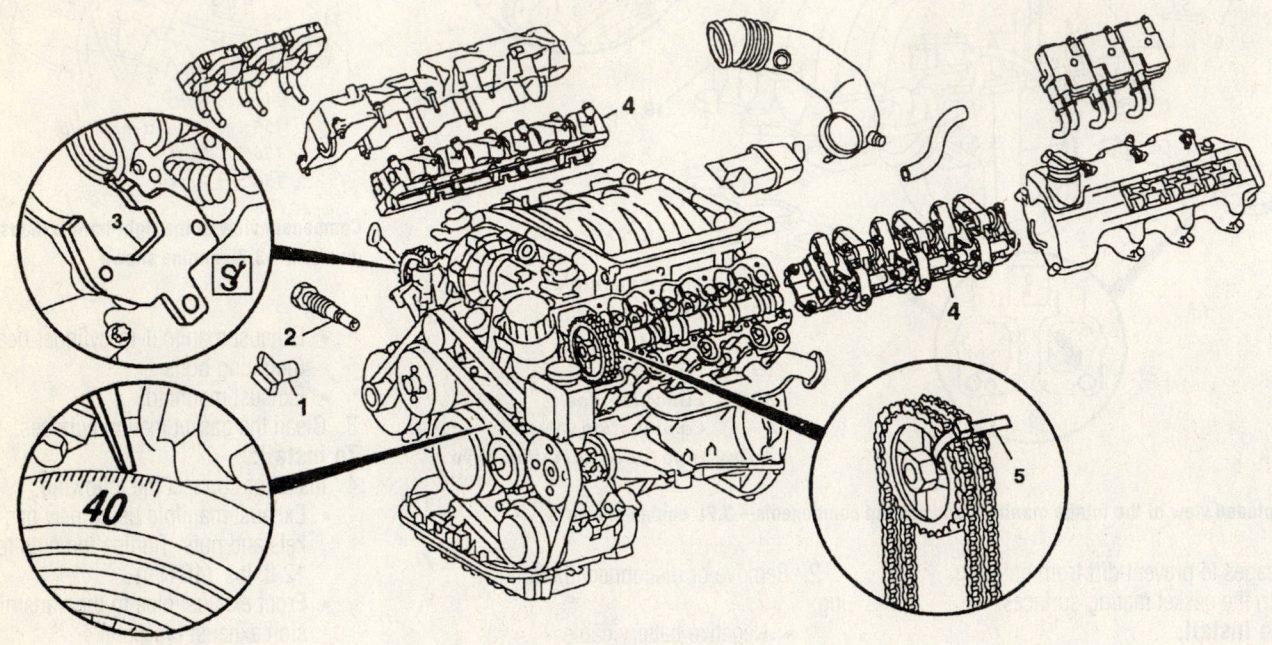

1	Camshaft Hall sensor	3	Fixing plate of right camshaft 40°
2	Chain tensioner		after first ignition TDC
		4	Camshaft bearing bridge
		5	Cable strap

7924Z110

Exploded view of the camshaft removal and related components—3.2L engine shown

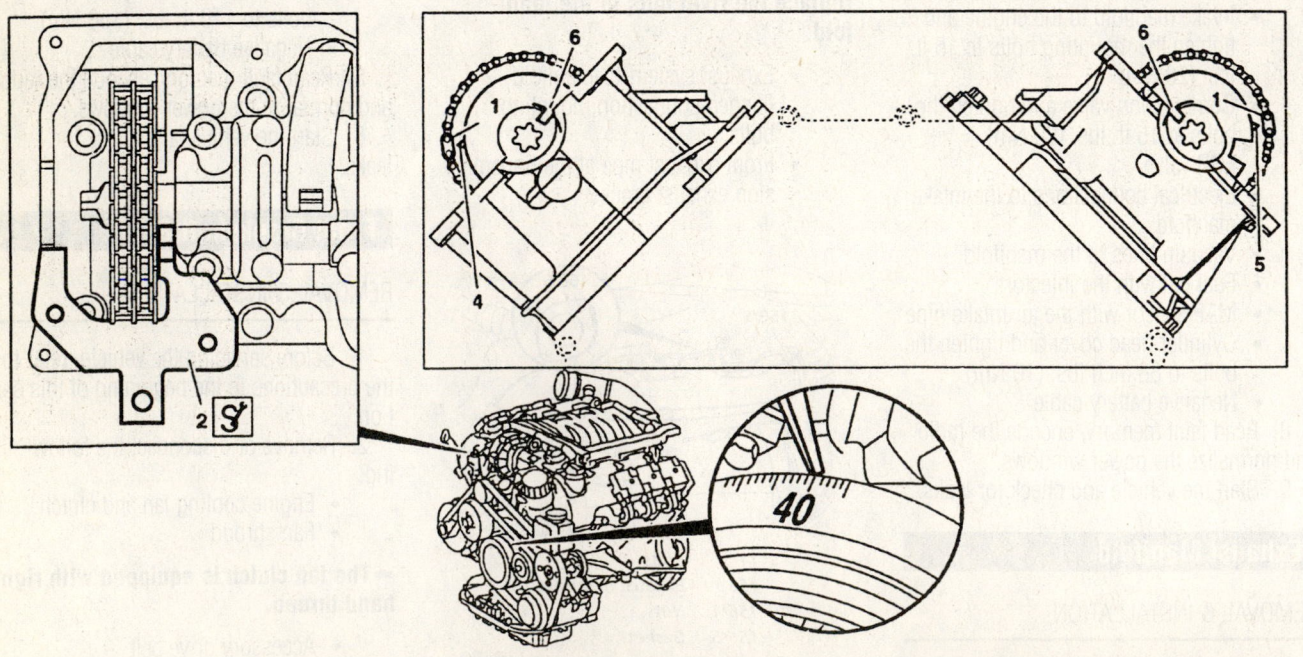

1.	Copper plate	5.	Marking on left camshaft sprocket
2.	Fixing plate for right camshaft	6.	Groove in camshaft
4.	Marking on right camshaft sprocket		

7924Z111

Be sure the camshafts are at their basic positions before installing the cam sprockets—3.2L engine shown

2. Remove or disconnect the following:
• Negative battery cable
• Cylinder head cover
3. Rotate the engine clockwise to position the crankshaft 40 degrees After Top Dead Center (ATDC).

✸✸ WARNING

The engine must not be rotated backwards.

• Generator
• Timing chain tensioner
4. Cable tie the timing chain to the camshaft sprocket.
• Camshaft Position (CMP) sensor
5. Lock the camshafts using the Camshaft Locking tools 112 589 00 32 00 and 112 589 01 32 00.
• Camshaft gears
• Camshaft bearing bridge
• Camshaft from the cylinder head
To install:

➡**Be sure to install the correct camshaft for the corresponding cylinder head.**

6. Apply clean engine oil to the camshaft contact surfaces.
7. Install or connect the following:
• Camshaft
• Camshaft bearing bridge

➡**The camshafts can be rotated 40 degrees ATDC of the No. 1 cylinder without the valves touching the pistons.**

8. Position the camshaft so that the groove points centered towards the contact surface of the cylinder head cover, then attach the camshaft fixing plate. Repeat this step for the other camshaft.
• Camshaft sprockets and tighten the attaching bolt to 37 ft. lbs. (50 Nm) plus 90–100 degrees
9. Remove the camshaft locking tools and the cable ties from the timing chain.
• CMP sensor and tighten the mounting bolt to 70 inch lbs. (8 Nm)
• Timing chain tensioner with a new gasket and tighten to 59 ft. lbs. (80 Nm)
• Cylinder head cover
• Negative battery cable
10. Read fault memory, encode the radio and normalize the power windows.

Valve Lash

ADJUSTMENT

These vehicles are equipped with Hydraulic Lash Adjusters (HLA's), which do not require periodic adjustment.

Oil Pan

REMOVAL & INSTALLATION

1. Before servicing the vehicle, refer to the precautions in the beginning of this section.
2. Disconnect the negative battery cable.
3. Drain the cooling system and engine oil.
4. Remove or disconnect the following:
• Engine cover
• Engine cooling fan, fan clutch, and fan shroud

➡**The fan clutch is equipped with right-hand thread.**

5. Attach a guard plate to protect the radiator.
• Intake resonator and pipe
• Upper and lower coolant hoses
• Engine ground cable from the frame
• Motor mounts at the front suspension supports
6. Attach an engine hoist and raise the engine. Be sure that the engine does not contact the firewall.
• Lower oil pan

➡**The upper pan bolts are different lengths and diameters. Note their locations for installation.**

• Upper pan toward the front of the vehicle. Rotate the crankshaft as necessary for clearance.
To install:
7. Clean the sealing surfaces and apply a bead of silicone sealant.

➡**The pan must be installed within ten minutes after the sealant is applied.**

8. Install or connect the following:
• Upper pan. Tighten the 6mm bolts to 90 inch lbs. (10 Nm), and the 8mm bolts to 15 ft. lbs. (20 Nm).
9. In the same manner, apply a bead of silicone sealant and install the lower oil pan. Tighten the bolts to 90 inch lbs. (10 Nm).

10. Install or connect the following:
• Motor mounts and remove the engine hoist
• Engine ground cable
• Upper and lower coolant hoses
• Intake resonator and pipe
11. Remove the radiator guard plate.
• Fan shroud, engine cooling fan, and fan clutch
• Engine cover
12. Fill the cooling system and crankcase to the correct levels.
13. Connect the negative battery cable.
14. Read fault memory, encode the radio and normalize the power windows.

Oil Pump

REMOVAL & INSTALLATION

1. Before servicing the vehicle, refer to the precautions in the beginning of this section.
2. Remove the lower oil pan. Refer to the oil pan procedure in this section.
3. Push the chain tensioner back and remove the pump drive chain.
4. Unbolt and remove the oil pump.
To install:
5. Fill the oil pump with clean engine oil and install it to the engine. Tighten the bolts to 15 ft. lbs. (20 Nm).
6. Install the pump drive chain.
7. Install the lower oil pan. Refer to oil pan procedure in this section.

Timing Chain, Sprockets, Tensioner and Front Cover

REMOVAL & INSTALLATION

1. Before servicing the vehicle, refer to the precautions in the beginning of this section.
2. Disconnect the negative battery cable.
3. Drain the cooling system and engine oil.
4. Remove or disconnect the following:
• Engine cover
• Engine cooling fan, fan clutch, and fan shroud

➡**The fan clutch is equipped with right-hand thread.**

• Upper and lower coolant hoses
• Accessory drive belt and tensioner
• Oil pan
• Cylinder head covers

Refer to Section 1 for engine rebuilding specifications

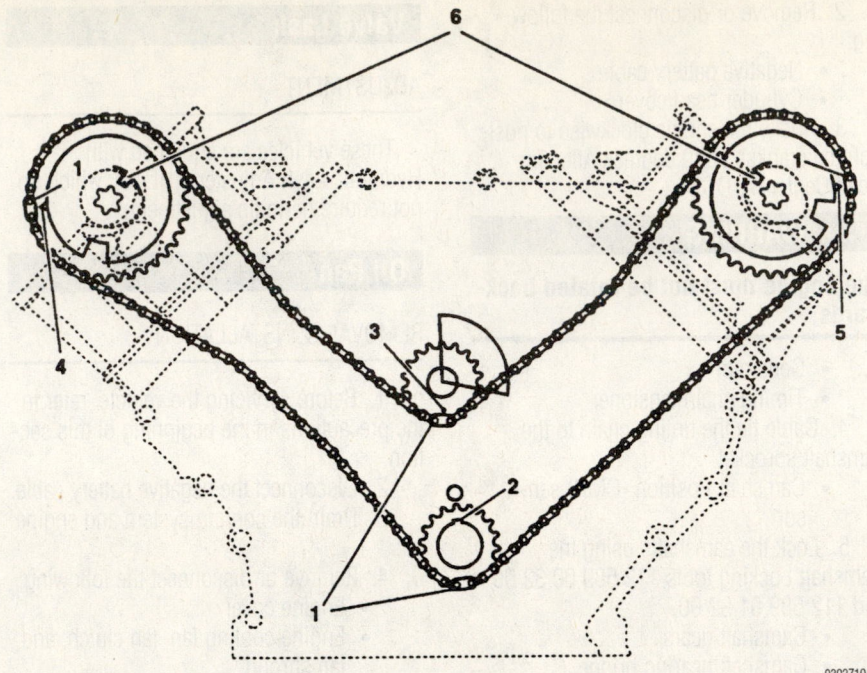

1 Copper-plated link
2 Groove in crankshaft
3 Mark on balance shaft sprocket
4 Mark on right camshaft gear
5 Mark on left camshaft gear
6 Groove in camshaft

Camshaft timing marks

✳✳ WARNING

The engine must not be rotated backwards.

5. Rotate the crankshaft clockwise to align the crankshaft timing marks at 40° After Top Dead Center (ATDC). Insure that the grooves in the camshafts (6 in the illustration) align with the cylinder head cover mating surface on the intake side of the cylinder heads.

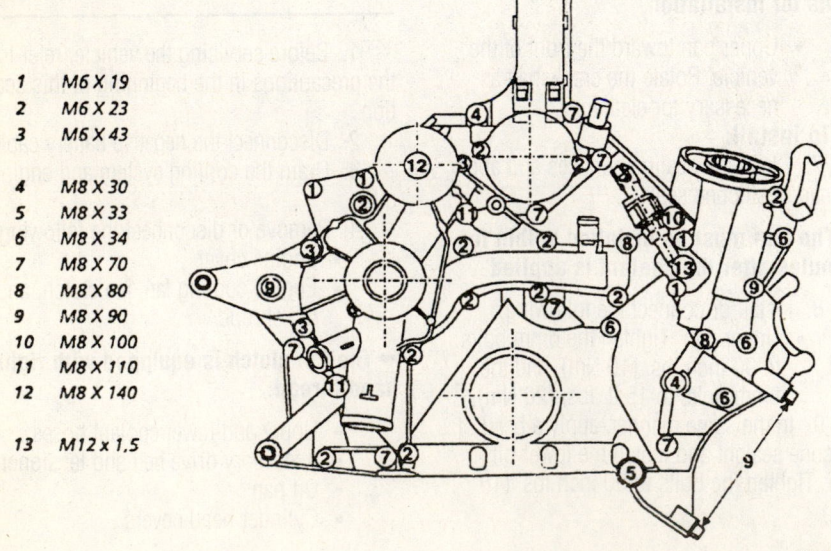

1	M6 X 19
2	M6 X 23
3	M6 X 43
4	M8 X 30
5	M8 X 33
6	M8 X 34
7	M8 X 70
8	M8 X 80
9	M8 X 90
10	M8 X 100
11	M8 X 110
12	M8 X 140
13	M12 x 1.5

Timing cover bolt placement

6. Remove or disconnect the following:

- Air conditioning compressor and power steering pump and position them to the side. Do not remove the air conditioning or power steering hoses.
- Generator
- Timing chain tensioner
- Crankshaft pulley
- Air pump, if equipped
- Coolant Temperature (CTS) sensor

➡**The timing chain cover bolts are different lengths and diameters. Note their locations for installation.**

- Timing chain cover

7. Lock the camshafts using the Camshaft Locking tools 112 589 00 32 00 and 112 589 01 32 00.

- Camshaft sprockets bolts
- Timing chain

To install:

8. Align the copper plated links of the timing chain with the marks on the camshaft sprockets, the crankshaft sprocket, and the balancer sprocket for the 3.2L engine. The 4.3L engine uses an idler sprocket in place of the balance shaft.

9. Install or connect the following:

- Camshaft sprockets along with the timing chain. Tighten the attaching bolts to 37 ft. lbs. (50 Nm) plus 90–100 degrees.

10. Clean the sealing surfaces and apply a bead of silicone sealant to the timing chain cover.

➡**The cover must be installed within ten minutes after the sealant is applied.**

- Timing cover. Refer to the illustration for bolt placement. Tighten the bolts to 15 ft. lbs. (20 Nm).
- CTS sensor
- Timing chain tensioner
- Generator
- Crankshaft pulley and tighten the bolt to 148 ft. lbs., then tighten another 95 degrees

- Air pump, if equipped
- Air conditioning compressor and the power steering pump
- Cylinder head covers
- Oil pan
- Accessory drive belt and tensioner
- Upper and lower coolant hoses
- Fan shroud, cooling fan, and fan clutch
11. Fill the cooling system and the crankcase to the correct levels.
- Engine cover
- Negative battery cable
12. Read fault memory, encode the radio and normalize the power windows.

FUEL SYSTEM

Fuel System Service Precautions

Safety is the most important factor when performing not only fuel system maintenance but any type of maintenance. Failure to conduct maintenance and repairs in a safe manner may result in serious personal injury or death. Maintenance and testing of the fuel system components can be accomplished safely and effectively by adhering to the following rules and guidelines.

- To avoid the possibility of fire and personal injury, always disconnect the negative battery cable unless the repair or test procedure requires that battery voltage be applied.
- Always relieve the fuel system pressure prior to disconnecting any fuel system component (injector, fuel rail, pressure regulator, etc.), fitting or fuel line connection. Exercise extreme caution whenever relieving fuel system pressure, to avoid exposing skin, face and eyes to fuel spray. Please be advised that fuel under pressure may penetrate the skin or any part of the body that it contacts.
- Always place a shop towel or cloth around the fitting or connection prior to loosening to absorb any excess fuel due to spillage. Ensure that all fuel spillage (should it occur) is quickly removed from engine surfaces. Ensure that all fuel soaked cloths or towels are deposited into a suitable waste container.
- Always keep a dry chemical (Class B) fire extinguisher near the work area.
- Do not allow fuel spray or fuel vapors

to come into contact with a spark or open flame.

- Always use a back-up wrench when loosening and tightening fuel line connection fittings. This will prevent unnecessary stress and torsion to fuel line piping. Always follow the proper torque specifications.
- Always replace worn fuel fitting O-rings with new ones. Do not substitute fuel hose or equivalent, where fuel pipe is installed.

Fuel System Pressure

RELIEVING

1. Before servicing the vehicle, refer to the precautions in the beginning of this section.
2. Locate the electric fuel pump fuse and remove it from the fuse box.

➡ **If the fuel pump fuse cannot be located, disconnect the vehicle wiring harness from the pump itself and perform the procedure.**

3. Start the engine and allow it to idle until the engine stalls from lack of fuel.
4. Crank the engine over for an additional 15–20 seconds.
5. Reinstall the pump fuse when repairs are completed.

Fuel Filter

REMOVAL & INSTALLATION

1. Before servicing the vehicle, refer to the precautions in the beginning of this section.
2. Relieve the fuel system pressure.
3. Remove or disconnect the following:
- Negative battery cable
4. Relieve the pressure in the fuel tank by opening, then tightening the filler cap.
- Left rear wheel
- Plastic inner fender liner

➡ **The fuel lines must not be kinked.**

- Fuel pipes from the fuel filter, by compressing the locking catches
- Breather hose from the filter assembly
- Filter securing clip
- Filter/pressure regulator

To install:
5. Install or connect the following:
- New fuel filter/pressure regulator into the housing and tighten the securing clip to 27 inch lbs. (3 Nm)
- Breather hose to the filter assembly
- Fuel lines to the filter assembly
- Plastic inner fender liner

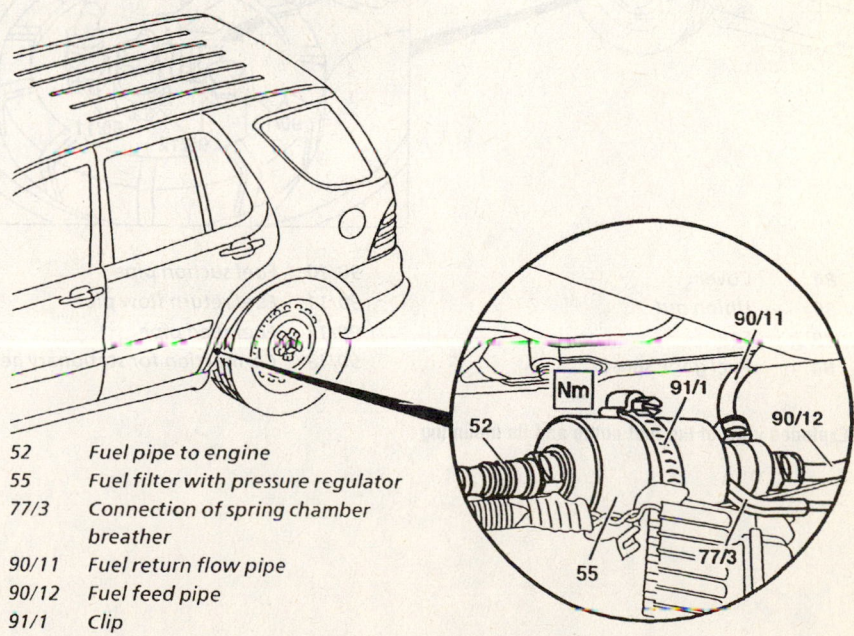

52	Fuel pipe to engine
55	Fuel filter with pressure regulator
77/3	Connection of spring chamber breather
90/11	Fuel return flow pipe
90/12	Fuel feed pipe
91/1	Clip

7924Z112

View of the fuel filter mounting location and component identification

- Left rear wheel and tighten the lug bolts to 110 ft. lbs. (150 Nm)
- Negative battery cable

6. Read fault memory, encode the radio and normalize the power windows.

7. Start the vehicle and check for leaks.

Fuel Pump

REMOVAL & INSTALLATION

1. Before servicing the vehicle, refer to the precautions in the beginning of this section.

2. Relieve the fuel system pressure.

3. Disconnect the negative battery cable.

4. Empty the fuel tank into a suitable container.

5. Raise the left rear seat approximately 20 inches (50 cm).

6. Lift the carpeting to gain access to the fuel pump cover.

7. Remove or disconnect the following:

- Fuel pump cover
- Fuel pump electrical connector

➡**Be sure not to kink the fuel pipes.**

- Supply and return fuel pipes clips and the pipes
- Union nut mounting the fuel pump-to-the tank
- Fuel pump from the tank

To install:

➡**Lightly oil the fuel pump sealing O-ring to simplify the installation.**

8. Install or connect the following:

- Fuel pump into the tank using a new union nut and O-ring. Tighten the union nut to 50 ft. lbs. (65 Nm).
- Supply and return lines to the fuel pump
- Fuel pump electrical connector
- Fuel pump access cover and the rear seat

9. Fill the fuel tank.

- Negative battery cable

10. Read fault memory, encode the radio and normalize the power windows.

11. Start the vehicle and check for leaks.

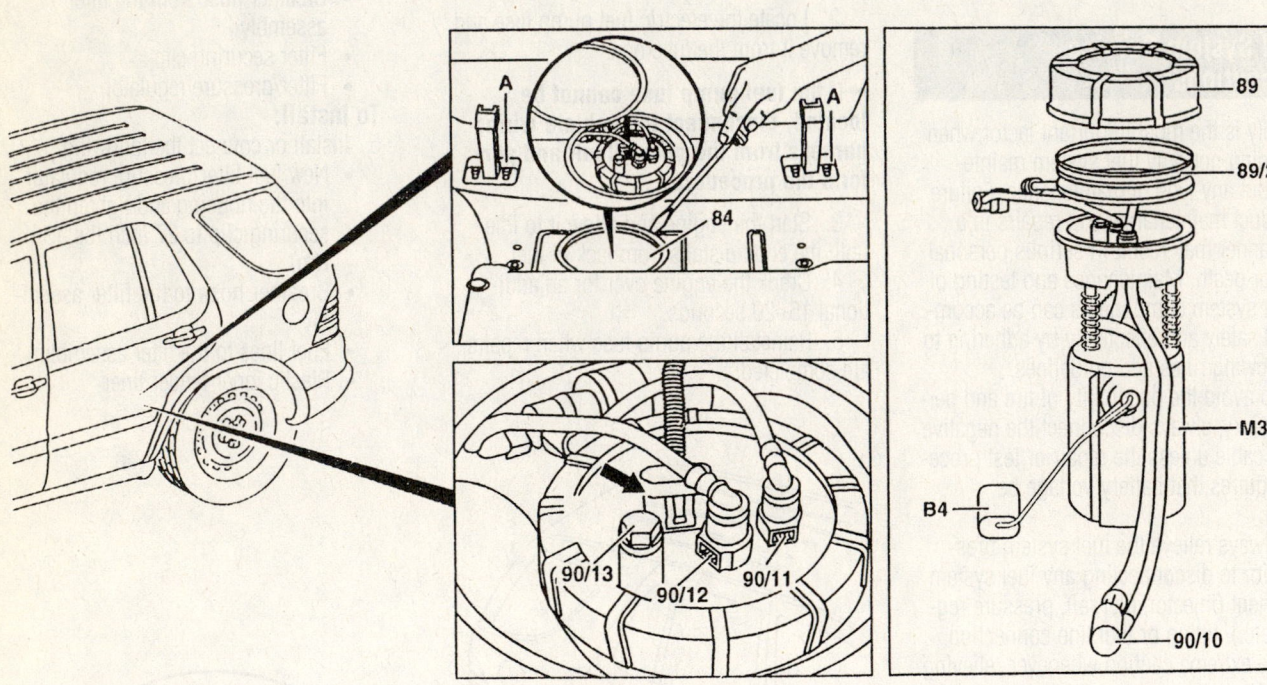

84	Cover	
89	Union nut	
89/2	Seal	
B4	Fuel gage sensor	
90/10	Fuel suction pipe	
90/11	Fuel return flow pipe	
90/12	Fuel feed pipe	
90/13	Connection for stationary heater	
Arrow	Connector for fuel pump	
A	Seat mounting brackets	
M3	Fuel pump	

7924Z113

Exploded view of the fuel pump and its mounting

30

PRECAUTIONS

Before servicing any vehicle, please be sure to read all of the following precautions, which deal with personal safety, prevention of component damage, and important points to take into consideration when servicing a motor vehicle:

• Never open, service or drain the radiator or cooling system when the engine is hot; serious burns can occur from the steam and hot coolant.

• Observe all applicable safety precautions when working around fuel. Whenever servicing the fuel system, always work in a well-ventilated area. Do not allow fuel spray or vapors to come in contact with a spark, open flame, or excessive heat (a hot drop light, for example). Keep a dry chemical fire extinguisher near the work area. Always keep fuel in a container specifically designed for fuel storage; also, always properly seal fuel containers to avoid the possibility of fire or explosion. Refer to the additional fuel system precautions later in this section.

• Fuel injection systems often remain pressurized, even after the engine has been turned **OFF**. The fuel system pressure must be relieved before disconnecting any fuel lines. Failure to do so may result in fire and/or personal injury.

• Brake fluid often contains polyglycol ethers and polyglycols. Avoid contact with the eyes and wash your hands thoroughly after handling brake fluid. If you do get brake fluid in your eyes, flush your eyes with clean, running water for 15 minutes. If eye irritation persists, or if you have taken brake fluid internally, IMMEDIATELY seek medical assistance.

• The EPA warns that prolonged contact with used engine oil may cause a number of skin disorders, including cancer! You should make every effort to minimize your exposure to used engine oil. Protective gloves should be worn when changing oil. Wash your hands and any other exposed skin areas as soon as possible after exposure to used engine oil. Soap and water, or waterless hand cleaner should be used.

• All new vehicles are now equipped with an air bag system. The system must be disabled before performing service on or around system components, steering column, instrument panel components, wiring and sensors. Failure to follow safety and disabling procedures could result in accidental air bag deployment, possible personal injury and unnecessary system repairs.

• Always wear safety goggles when working with, or around, the air bag system. When carrying a non-deployed air bag, be sure the bag and trim cover are pointed away from your body. When placing a non-deployed air bag on a work surface, always face the bag and trim cover upward, away from the surface. This will reduce the motion of the module if it is accidentally deployed. Refer to the additional air bag system precautions later in this section.

• Clean, high quality brake fluid from a sealed container is essential to the safe and proper operation of the brake system. You should always buy the correct type of brake fluid for your vehicle. If the brake fluid becomes contaminated, completely flush the system with new fluid. Never reuse any brake fluid. Any brake fluid that is removed from the system should be discarded. Also, do not allow any brake fluid to come in contact with a painted surface; it will damage the paint.

• Never operate the engine without the proper amount and type of engine oil; doing so WILL result in severe engine damage.

• Timing belt maintenance is extremely important! Many models utilize an interference-type, non-freewheeling engine. If the timing belt breaks, the valves in the cylinder head may strike the pistons, causing potentially serious (also time-consuming and expensive) engine damage. Refer to the maintenance interval charts in the front of this manual for the recommended replacement interval for the timing belt, and to the timing belt section for belt replacement and inspection.

• Disconnecting the negative battery cable on some vehicles may interfere with the functions of the on-board computer system(s) and may require the computer to undergo a relearning process once the negative battery cable is reconnected.

• When servicing drum brakes, only disassemble and assemble one side at a time, leaving the remaining side intact for reference.

ENGINE REPAIR

➡**Disconnecting the negative battery cable on some vehicles may interfere with the functions of the on board computer systems and may require the**

computer to undergo a relearning process, once the negative battery cable is reconnected.

Distributor

REMOVAL

1. Remove or disconnect the following:
   • Negative battery cable
   • Distributor pick-up lead wires and vacuum hose(s), if equipped.
   • Distributor cap retaining clips or screws and lift off the distributor cap with all ignition wires connected. Remove the coil wire if necessary.
2. Matchmark the rotor and distributor housing and matchmark the distributor housing and engine.

➡**Do not crank the engine during this procedure. If the engine is cranked, the matchmark must be disregarded.**

   • Retaining nut and remove the distributor from the engine.

INSTALLATION

Timing Not Disturbed

1. Position a new distributor housing O-ring.
2. Install the distributor in the engine so the rotor is aligned with the matchmark on the housing and the housing is aligned with the matchmark on the engine. Be sure the distributor is fully seated and the distributor shaft is fully engaged.
3. Install or connect the following:
   • Retaining nut finger-tight only. Connect the vacuum hose(s), if removed.
   • Distributor pick-up electrical harness
   • Distributor cap and secure
   • Negative battery cable
4. Check and adjust the ignition timing. Torque the retaining nut to 115 ft. lbs. (13 Nm).

Timing Disturbed

1. Install a new distributor housing O-ring
2. Rotate the engine so No. 1 piston is on TDC of compression stroke and the timing mark on the vibration damper is aligned with **T** on the timing indicator.
3. Position the distributor so the rotor is

aligned with the No. 1 ignition wire on the distributor cap. Take note that the distributor shaft is fully engaged and the housing is fully seated.

➡**Some distributor caps may contain runners inside the cap. If so, be sure the rotor is pointing to where the No. 1 runner originates inside the cap and not where the No. 1 ignition wire plugs into the cap.**

4. Install or connect the following:
• Retaining nut finger-tight only. Connect the vacuum hose(s), if removed.
• Distributor electrical harness
• Distributor cap and secure
• Negative battery cable
5. Check and adjust the ignition timing. Torque the retaining nut to 115 ft. lbs. (13 Nm).

Alternator

REMOVAL

1. Before servicing the vehicle, refer to the precautions in the beginning of this section.

2. Remove or disconnect the following:
• Negative battery cable
• Under cover

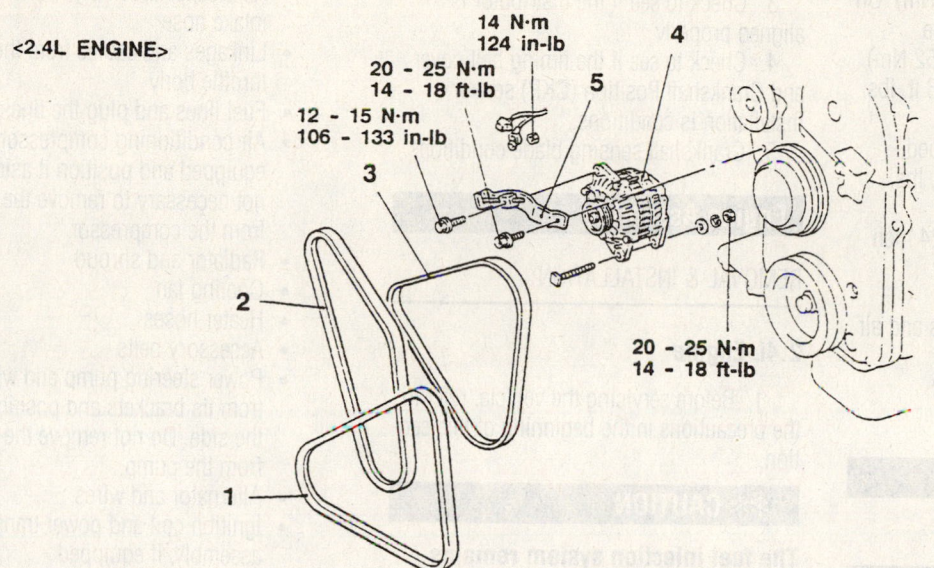

<2.4L ENGINE>

14 N·m
124 in-lb
20 – 25 N·m
14 – 18 ft-lb
12 – 15 N·m
106 – 133 in-lb

20 – 25 N·m
14 – 18 ft-lb

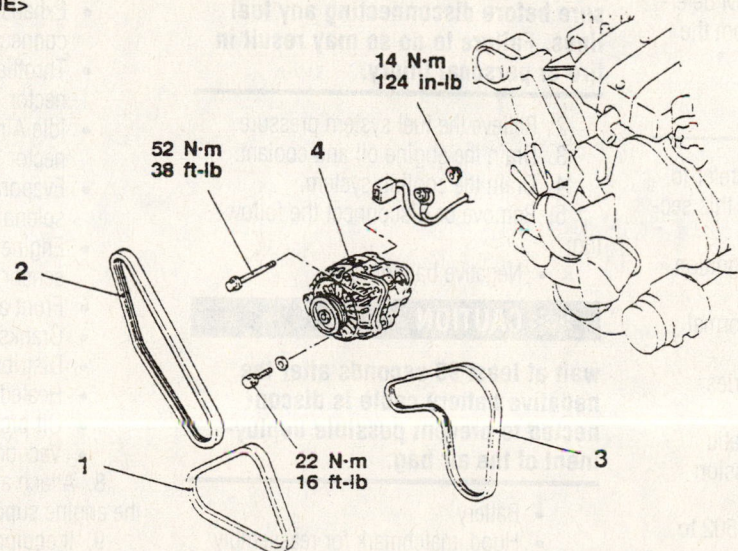

<3.0L, 3.5L ENGINE>

14 N·m
124 in-lb
52 N·m
38 ft-lb

22 N·m
16 ft-lb

01V0067

1. DRIVE BELT (FOR A/C)
2. DRIVE BELT
   (FOR POWER STEERING)
3. DRIVE BELT (FOR GENERATOR)

4. GENERATOR
5. GENERATOR BRACE ASSEMBLY
   <2.4L ENGINE>

9308UG02

Alternator mounting and related components

- Air cleaner assembly, ducts and air intake hose
- Drive belt(s)
- Wires
- Mounting bracket, if equipped
- Alternator

To install:

3. Install or connect the following:

- Alternator. On the 2.4L torque the through-bolt to 14–18 ft. lbs. (20–25 Nm) and the bracket bolt to 106–133 inch lbs. (12–15 Nm). On the 3.0L and 3.5L torque the through-bolt to 38 ft. lbs. (52 Nm) and the mounting bolt to 16 ft. lbs. (22 Nm).
- Mounting bracket, if equipped. Torque the bolt to 14–18 ft. lbs. (20–25 Nm).
- Wires. Torque the nut to 124 inch lbs. (14 Nm).
- Drive belt(s)
- Air cleaner assembly, ducts and air intake hose
- Under cover
- Negative battery cable

Ignition Timing

ADJUSTMENT

The ignition timing is controlled by the ECM and is not adjustable. The ECM determines the timing based on input from the crankshaft position sensor.

TIMING CHECK

1. Before servicing the vehicle, refer to the precautions in the beginning of this section.

Before attempting to adjust the ignition timing, be sure of the following:

- The engine should be at normal operating temperature.
- The lights and all accessories should be OFF.
- If equipped with an automatic transmission, the transmission should be in **P** or **N**.
- Connect scan tool MB991502 to the data link connector
- Set up the timing light.
- Start the engine and run at idle.
- Verify that the idle speed is 600–800 rpm.
- Select scan tool MB991502 actuator test "item number 17."
- Check that basic timing is within standard, it should be 3–7° BTDC.
- Press the clear key on the scan

tool, select forced drive stop mode and cancel the actuator test.

✳✳ CAUTION

If the actuator test is not canceled, the forced drive will continue for 27 minutes. Driving in this state could lead to engine failure.

2. If the base timing is out of specification:

3. Check to see if the distributor is aligned properly

4. Check to see if the timing belt cover and Crankshaft Position (CKP) sensor installation is conditions.

5. Crankshaft sensing blade conditions.

Engine Assembly

REMOVAL & INSTALLATION

2.4L Engine

1. Before servicing the vehicle, refer to the precautions in the beginning of this section.

✳✳ CAUTION

The fuel injection system remains under pressure after the engine has been OFF. Properly relieve fuel pressure before disconnecting any fuel lines. Failure to do so may result in fire or personal injury.

2. Relieve the fuel system pressure.
3. Drain the engine oil and coolant.
4. Drain the cooling system.
5. Remove or disconnect the following:

- Negative battery cable

✳✳ CAUTION

wait at least 90 seconds after the negative battery cable is disconnected to prevent possible deployment of the air bag.

- Battery
- Hood, matchmark for reassembly
- Oil dipstick
- Engine undercover
- Lower radiator hose
- Starter
- Exhaust pipe from the exhaust manifold
- Transfer case from vehicle, if equipped with 4WD
- Transmission, if equipped with a manual transmission

6. If equipped with an automatic transmission and 2wd:
   a. Remove the inspection plate.
   b. Matchmark the flexplate and converter. Remove the torque converter bolts and move the torque converter back as far as it will go.
   c. Remove the lower bell housing bolts.

7. Remove or disconnect the following:

- Air cleaner assembly, ducts and air intake hose
- Linkages and cables from the throttle body
- Fuel lines and plug the lines
- Air conditioning compressor, if equipped and position it aside. It is not necessary to remove the lines from the compressor.
- Radiator and shroud
- Cooling fan
- Heater hoses
- Accessory belts
- Power steering pump and wires from its brackets and position it to the side. Do not remove the hoses from the pump.
- Alternator and wires
- Ignition coil and power transistor assembly, if equipped
- Manifold Differential Pressure (MDP) sensor connector
- Exhaust Gas Recirculation (EGR) connector
- Throttle Position (TP) sensor connector
- Idle Air Control (IAC) motor connector
- Evaporative Emission (EVAP) purge solenoid
- Engine Coolant Temperature (ECT) sensor and gauge connectors
- Front and injector wiring harness
- Crankshaft position (CKP) sensor
- Distributor signal generator
- Heated oxygen (O2s) sensor
- Oil pressure switch connector
- Vacuum hoses

8. Attach an engine removal device to the engine support eyes on the engine.

9. If equipped with an automatic transmission, support the transmission with a floor jack. Remove the remaining bell housing bolts.

10. Remove the engine mount nuts and remove the engine from the vehicle.

to install:

11. Lower the engine into position
12. Install or connect the following:

- Engine mount nuts. Torque the nuts to 14–22 ft. Lbs. (30–40 nm).

- Bell housing bolts. Torque the bolts to 54 ft. Lbs. (74 nm).

13. Remove the engine removal device and the transmission support.

14. Install or connect the following:
   - Transfer case, if equipped
   - Manual transmission, if equipped

15. If equipped with an automatic transmission, align the torque converter and flexplate and install the bolts. Torque the bolts to 25–30 ft. Lbs. (34–41 nm) 1997–98 and 33–38 ft. Lbs. (45–52 nm).

16. Install or connect the following:
   - Inspection plate
   - Starter
   - Exhaust pipe to the exhaust manifold using new gaskets
   - Lower radiator hose
   - Heater hoses
   - Alternator
   - Power steering pump and all brackets
   - Air conditioning compressor
   - Linkages and cables to the throttle body
   - Ignition coil and power transistor assembly
   - Manifold differential pressure (MDP) sensor connector
   - Exhaust Gas Recirculation (EGR) connector
   - Throttle Position (TP) sensor connector
   - Idle Air Control (IAC) motor connector
   - Magnetic clutch and refrigerant temperature switch connector
   - Evaporative Emission (EVAP) purge solenoid
   - Engine Coolant Temperature (ECT) sensor and gauge connectors
   - Front and injector wiring harness
   - Crankshaft Position (CKP) sensor
   - Distributor signal generator
   - Heated oxygen (O2s) sensor
   - Oil pressure switch connector
   - Vacuum hoses
   - Radiator and shroud
   - Cooling fan
   - Accessory belts
   - Engine undercover
   - Air cleaner assembly, ducts and air intake hose
   - Oil dipstick
   - Battery and cables
   - Hood

17. Fill the engine with the specified amount of oil and fill the radiator with coolant.

18. Inspect the fuel system for leaks.
19. Check the automatic transmission fluid level, if equipped.
20. Recheck all engine adjustments.

3.0L and 3.5L Engines

1. Before servicing the vehicle, refer to the precautions in the beginning of this section.
2. Relieve the fuel system pressure.

✳✳ CAUTION

The fuel injection system remains under pressure after the engine has been OFF. Properly relieve fuel pressure before disconnecting any fuel lines. Failure to do so may result in fire or personal injury.

3. Drain the engine oil.
4. Drain the cooling system.
5. Remove or disconnect the following:

   - Battery
   - Hood, matchmark for reassembly
   - Oil dipstick
   - Engine undercover
   - Starter
   - Exhaust pipe from the exhaust manifolds
   - Transfer case, if equipped with 4WD
   - Transmission, if equipped with a manual transmission

6. If equipped with an automatic transmission and 2WD:
   a. Remove the inspection plate.
   b. Matchmark the flexplate to the converter; remove the torque converter bolts and move the torque converter back as far as it will go.
   c. Remove the lower bell housing bolts.

7. Remove or disconnect the following:
   - Air cleaner assembly, ducts and air intake hose
   - Linkages and cables from the throttle body
   - Fuel lines and plug the lines
   - Air conditioning compressor, if equipped and position it aside. It is not necessary to remove the lines from the compressor.
   - Radiator, shroud
   - Cooling fan
   - Heater hoses
   - Accessory belts
   - Power steering pump and wires from its brackets and position it to

the side. Do not remove the hoses from the pump.
   - Alternator and wires
   - Ignition coil and power transistor assembly, if equipped
   - MDP sensor connector
   - EGR connector
   - TP sensor connector
   - IAC motor connector
   - Magnetic clutch and refrigerant temperature switch connector
   - EVAP Purge Solenoid
   - ECT sensor and gauge connectors
   - Front and injector wiring harness
   - CMP sensor
   - CKP sensor
   - Distributor signal Generator
   - Compactor connector
   - Left and right heated O2S sensor
   - Oil pressure switch connector
   - Vacuum hoses

8. Attach an engine removal device to the engine support eyes on the engine.
9. If equipped with an automatic transmission, support the transmission with a floor jack. Remove the remaining bell housing bolts.
10. Remove the engine mount nuts and remove the engine from the vehicle.

To install:

11. Lower the engine into position and install the engine mount nuts. Tighten the nuts to 20 ft. lbs. (27 Nm), on the Montero, tighten to 33 ft. lbs. (44 Nm).
12. Install or connect the following:
   - Bell housing bolts

13. Remove the engine removal device and the transmission support.

14. Install or connect the following:
   - Transfer case, if equipped
   - Manual transmission, if equipped
   - Automatic transmission, if equipped align the torque converter and flexplate and the bolts.
   - Inspection plate
   - Starter motor
   - Exhaust pipe to the exhaust manifolds using new gaskets
   - Lower radiator hose
   - Heater hoses
   - Alternator and wires
   - Power steering pump and brackets
   - Air conditioning compressor
   - Linkages and cables to the carburetor or throttle body
   - Ignition coil and power transistor assembly, if equipped
   - MDP sensor connector
   - EGR connector

Timing belt service is covered in Section 4 of this manual

- TP sensor connector
- IAC motor connector
- Magnetic clutch and refrigerant temperature switch connector
- EVAP Purge Solenoid
- ECT sensor and gauge connectors
- Front and injector wiring harness
- CMP sensor
- CKP sensor
- Distributor signal Generator
- Compactor connector
- Left and right heated O_2S sensor
- Oil pressure switch connector
- Vacuum hoses
- Air cleaner assembly, ducts and air intake hose
- Accessory belts
- Radiator, shroud and upper hose
- Cooling fan
- Battery
- Oil dipstick
- Hood

15. Refill the engine with the specified amount of oil.
16. Refill the radiator with coolant.
17. Check fuel system for leaks.
18. Check the automatic transmission fluid level, if equipped.
19. Recheck all engine adjustments.

Water Pump

REMOVAL & INSTALLATION

1. Before servicing the vehicle, refer to the precautions in the beginning of this section.
2. If necessary, properly release the fuel pressure.
3. Drain the cooling system.
4. Remove or disconnect the following:
   - Negative battery cable

❋❋ CAUTION

Wait at least 90 seconds after the negative battery cable is disconnected to prevent possible deployment of the air bag.

- Upper radiator shroud
- Accessory belts
- Air conditioning compressor tensioner pulley, if equipped
- Cooling fan and clutch assembly and the water pump pulley
- Thermostat and housing on 3.0L, 3.5L engines
- Water outlet, gasket and houses
- Radiator hoses from the water pump

- Crankshaft pulley(s)
- Timing belt covers. If the same timing belt will be reused, mark the direction of the timing belt's rotation, for installation in the same direction. Be sure the engine is positioned so the No. 1 cylinder is at the TDC of its compression stroke and the sprockets timing marks are aligned with the engine's timing mark indicators.
- Timing belt
- Water pump bolts are different lengths, note their positions before removing.
- Water pump from the block
- Water pipe connection and O-ring

To install:
5. Clean and dry the mating surfaces of the block and water pump
6. Install or connect the following:
   - New O-ring on the water pipe connection, wet the new O-ring with water to aid in installation
   - Water pump, with a new gasket, Torque the bolts to 106–133 inch lbs. (12–15 Nm) on 2.4L engine, 17 ft. lbs. (23 Nm) on 3.0L 24-valve and 3.5L engines

1. **Alternator brace**
2. **Water pump**
3. **Gasket**
4. **O-ring**

12–15 Nm
9–10 ft.lbs.

20–27 Nm
15–19 ft.lbs.

12–15 Nm
9–10 ft.lbs.

12–15 Nm
9–10 ft.lbs.

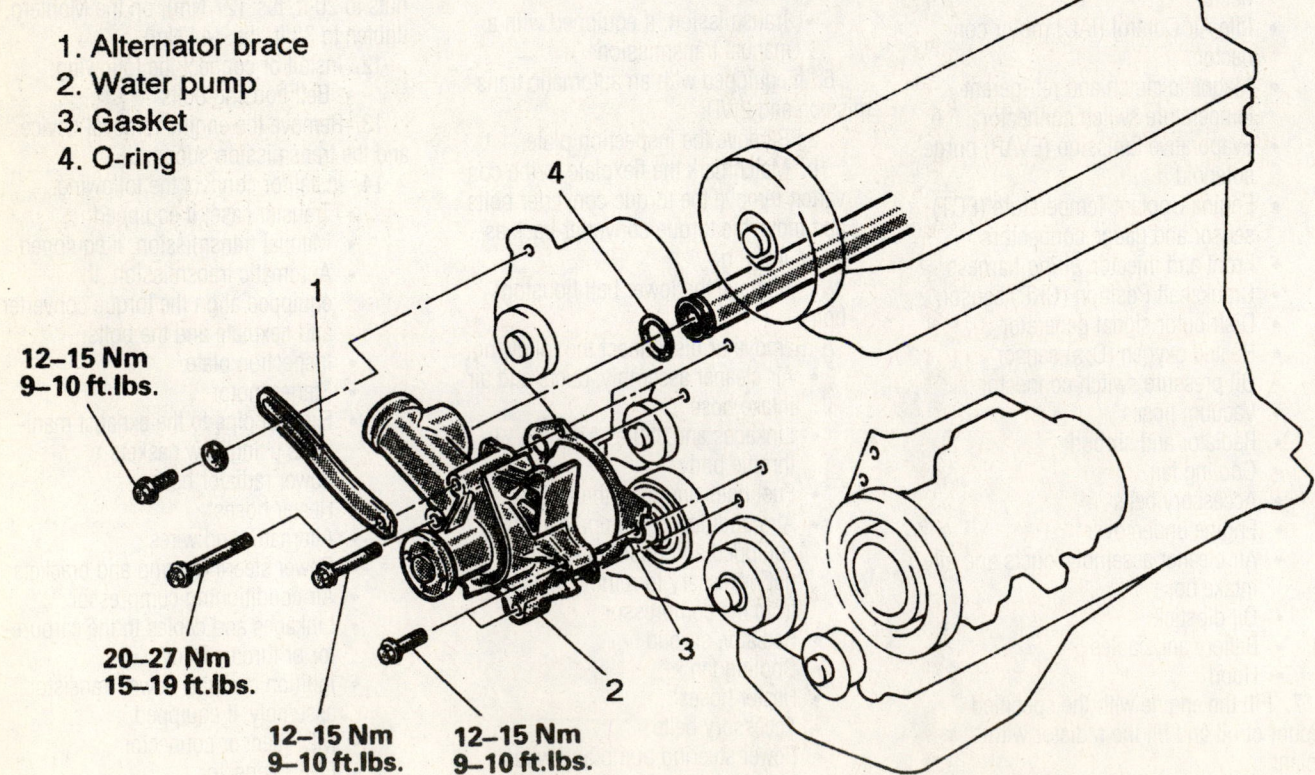

Water pump and related components—2.4L engine

7924UG06

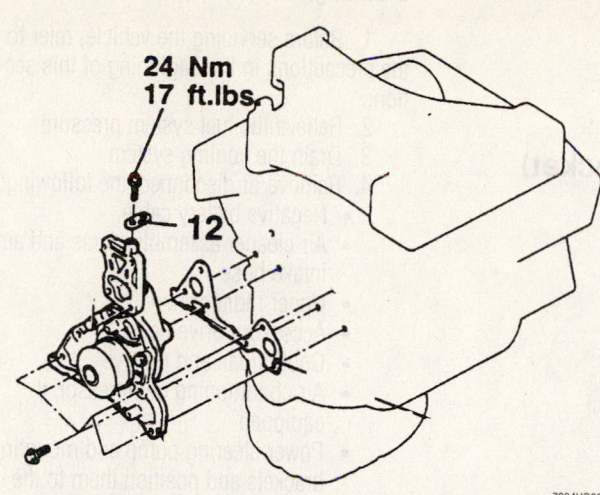

24 Nm
17 ft.lbs.

12

Water pump mounting—3.0L engine

7924UG08

24 Nm
17 ft.lbs.

13
14 N
17 N
16 N
15

24 Nm
17 ft.lbs.

Water pump and related components—3.5L engine

7924UG09

- Alternator bracket bolt to 17 ft. lbs. (23 Nm)
- Timing belt(s) and covers
- Crankshaft pulley(s)
- Thermostat and housing on 3.0L, 3.5L engines. Torque the bolts to 12–14 ft. lbs. (17–20 Nm).
- Radiator hose to the water pump
- Water outlet, new gasket and houses. Torque the bolts to 12–14 ft. lbs. (17–20 Nm).
- Water pump pulley
- Cooling fan and clutch assembly
- Air conditioning compressor tensioner pulley, if equipped
- Accessory belts
- Upper radiator shroud
- Thermostat and housing on 3.0L, 3.5L engines
- Negative battery cable

7. Refill the radiator with coolant. This cooling system has a self-bleeding thermostat, so system bleeding is not required.

8. Run the vehicle until the thermostat opens and fill the overflow tank. Check for leaks.

9. Once the vehicle has cooled, recheck the coolant level.

Cylinder Head

REMOVAL & INSTALLATION

2.4L Engine

1. Before servicing the vehicle, refer to the precautions in the beginning of this section.

2. Drain the cooling system.

✱✱ CAUTION

Some models covered by this manual may be equipped with an air bag. Whenever working near any of the Supplement Restraint System (SRS) components, such as the impact sensors, the air bag module, steering column and instrument panel, disable the SRS.

3. Properly relieve the fuel system pressure.

4. Remove or disconnect the following:
- Negative battery cable
- Air cleaner assembly, ducts and air intake hose
- Accelerator, and if equipped, kickdown cable
- Upper radiator hose
- Heater hoses
- Fuel lines and plug
- Power steering, if equipped unbolt the power steering pump from its brackets and position it to the side. Do not disconnect the power steering lines.
- Timing belt upper cover and valve cover
- Manifold Differential Pressure (MDP) sensor connector
- Exhaust Gas Recirculation (EGR) connector
- Throttle Position (TP) sensor connector
- Idle Air Control (IAC) motor connector
- Magnetic clutch and refrigerant temperature switch connector

- Evaporative Emission (EVAP) Purge Solenoid
- Engine Coolant Temperature (ECT) sensor and gauge connectors
- Front and injector wiring harness
- Camshaft Position (CMP) sensor
- Crankshaft Position (CKP) sensor
- Compactor connector
- Oil pressure switch connector
- Vacuum hoses
- Oil dipstick

5. Rotate the crankshaft clockwise and align the timing mark on the camshaft sprocket with the timing mark on the cylinder head.

6. Remove or disconnect the following:
- Camshaft bolt
- Sprocket from the camshaft (with the timing belt attached) and allow it to rest on the lower cover. Secure the belt to the sprocket so that they do not become disengaged.

✱✱ WARNING

Do not rotate the crankshaft after the camshaft sprocket is removed from the camshaft. Secure the sprocket and timing belt so there is no slack in the belt. Be sure the sprocket does not become disengaged from the timing belt. If the engine is disturbed or the timing belt moved, the camshaft timing will have to be reset.

- Spark plug wires
- Distributor cap and wires

7. Mark the position of the rotor and distributor housing in relation to the cylinder head and remove the distributor.

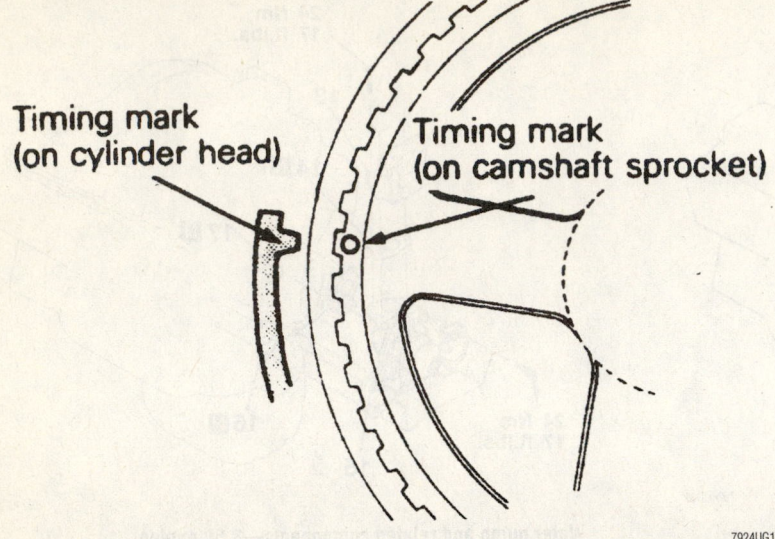

Timing mark (on cylinder head)

Timing mark (on camshaft sprocket)

7924UG10

Align the camshaft sprocket timing mark with the timing mark on the cylinder head—2.4L engines

8. Remove or disconnect the following:
- Exhaust pipe from the exhaust manifold
- Cylinder head bolts, starting from the outside and working inward
- Cylinder head from the engine
- Intake and exhaust manifolds from the cylinder head, if necessary

To install:

➡Refer to Section 1 of this manual for the cylinder head torque sequence illustration. The illustration is located after the Torque Specification Chart.

9. Clean the cylinder head gasket mating surfaces.
10. Install or connect the following:
- Intake and exhaust manifolds to the cylinder head, if removed
- New head gasket to the block and position the cylinder head assembly with all head bolts and washers.
11. Tighten the bolts in the following sequence:
    a. Step 1: Torque the bolts in sequence to 58 ft. lbs. (78 Nm).
    b. Step 2: Loosen all bolts in sequence to 0 ft. lbs.
    c. Step 3: Torque the bolts in sequence to 14 ft. lbs. (20 Nm).
    d. Step 4: Turn the bolts an additional 90 degrees.
    e. Step 5: Turn an additional 90 degrees.
12. Install or connect the following:
- Camshaft sprocket to the camshaft. Torque bolt to 65 ft. lbs. (88 Nm).
- Distributor, aligning the marks made during removal
- Distributor cap and spark plug wires
- Power steering pump and adjust the belt tension
- Heater hoses and upper radiator hose
- Valve cover. Torque the bolts to 30 ft. lbs. (34 Nm).
- Upper timing belt cover. Torque the bolts to 95 inch lbs. (11 Nm).
- Fuel lines
- Accelerator and kickdown cable, if equipped
- MDP sensor connector
- EGR connector
- TP sensor connector
- IAC motor connector
- Magnetic clutch and refrigerant temperature switch connector
- EVAP Purge Solenoid
- ECT sensor and gauge connectors
- Front and injector wiring harness
- CMP sensor
- CKP sensor
- Compactor connector
- Oil pressure switch connector
- Oil dipstick
- Air cleaner assembly, ducts and air intake hose
- Negative battery cable
13. Refill the cooling system.
14. Start the engine and check for leaks. Check the ignition timing.

3.0L Engines

1. Before servicing the vehicle, refer to the precautions in the beginning of this section.
2. Relieve the fuel system pressure.
3. Drain the cooling system.
4. Remove or disconnect the following:
- Negative battery cable
- Air cleaner assembly, ducts and air intake hose
- Upper radiator hose
- Accessory drive belts
- Cooling fan and pulleys
- Air conditioning compressor, if equipped
- Power steering pump and mounting brackets and position them to the side, without disconnecting the lines.
- Timing belt covers
5. Remove the timing belt as follows:
    a. Rotate the crankshaft and bring the No. 1 piston to Top Dead Center (TDC) on the compression stroke. Align the camshaft and crankshaft sprocket timing marks.
    b. Mark the timing belt in the direction of rotation for reinstallation purposes.
    c. Loosen the timing belt tensioner bolt and turn the tensioner counterclockwise.

✳✳ WARNING

Do not rotate the crankshaft or camshaft sprockets after the timing belt has been removed.

6. Remove or disconnect the following:
- Timing belt
- Fuel lines and plug
- Wiring connectors, vacuum lines and hoses from the air intake plenum, intake manifold and cylinder head.
- Air intake plenum
- Intake manifold
- Exhaust manifold
- Camshaft sprocket bolt and camshaft sprocket, if necessary
- Alternator bracket and/or timing belt rear cover
- Oil dipstick, on left side only
- Crankshaft position (CKP) sensor on left side only
- Spark plug wires from the spark plugs
- Valve cover
- Cylinder head bolts starting from the outside and working inward
- Cylinder head from the engine

To install:

➡**Refer to Section 1 of this manual for the cylinder head torque sequence illustration. The illustration is located after the Torque Specification Chart.**

7. Clean the gasket mounting surfaces.

8. Install or connect the following:
• New cylinder head gasket
• Cylinder head on the engine. Torque the cylinder head bolts in sequence using 3 even steps, to 80 ft. lbs. (108 Nm).
• Exhaust manifold
• Intake manifold and air intake plenum
• Fuel lines
• Wiring connectors, vacuum lines and hoses to the air intake plenum, intake manifold and cylinder head
• Valve cover
• Spark plug wires
• CKP sensor, if removed
• Oil dipstick, if removed
• Alternator bracket and/or timing belt rear cover
• Camshaft sprocket bolt and camshaft sprocket, if necessary

9. Be sure the camshaft and crankshaft sprocket timing marks are aligned.

10. Turn the timing belt tensioner to the extreme counter-clockwise position and temporarily tighten the bolt.

11. Install the timing belt in the original rotation direction. Loosen the timing belt tensioner bolt and allow the spring force of the tensioner to tension the belt.

12. Turn the crankshaft 2 turns in the normal direction of rotation and check the timing mark alignment.

13. If the timing is correct, tighten the tensioner bolt to 21 ft. lbs. (30 Nm). If the timing is incorrect, repeat the belt installation procedure.

14. Install or connect the following:
• Timing belt covers
• Alternator, alternator cover and alternator stay, if removed
• Air conditioning compressor
• Power steering pump with the brackets
• Pulleys. Torque the crankshaft pulley bolt to 134 ft. lbs. (181 Nm).
• Cooling fan
• Accessory drive belts
• Air cleaner assembly, ducts and air intake hose
• Upper radiator hose

• Negative battery
15. Refill the cooling system.
16. Start the engine and check for leaks. Check the ignition timing.

3.5L Engine

1. Before servicing the vehicle, refer to the precautions in the beginning of this section.

✳✳ CAUTION

The fuel injection system remains under pressure after the engine has been OFF. Properly relieve fuel pressure before disconnecting any fuel lines. Failure to do so may result in fire or personal injury.

2. Relieve fuel system pressure.
3. Drain the cooling system.
4. Remove or disconnect the following:
• Negative battery cable

✳✳ CAUTION

Work must be started after 90 seconds from the time the ignition switch is turned to the LOCK position and the negative battery cable is disconnected.

• Air intake hoses
• Air intake plenum and intake manifold
• Exhaust manifold
• Engine under cover
• Radiator and shroud
• Alternator
• Cooling fan
• Timing belt
• Breather hose
• Oil dipstick
• Camshaft Position (CMP) sensor
• Spark plug cable center cover and remove the spark plug cables
• Valve cover
• Intake camshaft sprocket
• Rear timing belt cover
• Ignition coil
• Water hoses from the thermostat housing and the housing
• Water inlet from the front head and discard O-ring
• Water passage

5. Loosen the cylinder head mounting bolts in 3 steps, starting from the outside and working inward. Lift off the cylinder head assembly and remove the head gasket.

To install:

➡**Refer to Section 1 of this manual for the cylinder head torque sequence illustration. The illustration is located after the Torque Specification Chart.**

6. Thoroughly clean and dry the mating surfaces of the head and block. Check the cylinder head for cracks, damage or engine coolant leakage. Remove scale, sealing compound and carbon. Clean oil passages thoroughly. Check the head for flatness. End to end, the head should be within 0.0012 in. (0.030mm), normally with 0.008 in. (0.203mm) the maximum allowed out of true. The total thickness allowed to be removed from the head and block is 0.008 in. (0.203mm) maximum.

7. Place a new head gasket on the cylinder block with the identification marks in the front top (upward) position. Do not use sealer on the gasket.

8. Install or connect the following:
• Cylinder head on the block. Be sure the head bolt washers are installed with the chamfered edge upward. Using 3 even steps, torque the head bolts in sequence, to 76–83 ft. lbs. (105–115 Nm).
• New O-ring and the water inlet to the front head
• New gaskets, thermostat housing and connect the hoses
• Water passage and new gaskets
• Ignition coil and center rear timing belt cover
• Intake camshaft sprocket. Use hex flange on camshaft to secure and tighten the retaining bolt to 65 ft. lbs. (90 Nm).
• New gasket and the valve cover. Torque the bolts to 84 inch lbs. (10 Nm).
• Spark plug cables and the center cover
• Oil dipstick
• CMP sensor
• Breather hose
• Radiator and shroud
• Timing belt
• Cooling fan
• Alternator
• Engine under cover
• Intake manifold and new gasket. Torque the nuts to 16 ft. lbs. (21 Nm).
• Air intake plenum and new gaskets. Torque the bolts to 13 ft. lbs. (18 Nm).

Refer to Section 1 for engine rebuilding specifications

- Exhaust manifold and new gaskets. Torque the nuts to 22 ft. lbs. (29 Nm).
- Air intake hoses
- Negative battery cable

9. Change the engine oil and oil filter.

10. Refill the system with coolant.

11. Run the vehicle until the thermostat opens.

12. Once the vehicle has cooled, recheck the coolant level.

Rocker Arms/Shafts

REMOVAL & INSTALLATION

2.4L Engines

1. Before servicing the vehicle, refer to the precautions in the beginning of this section.

2. Remove or disconnect the following:
- Breather hose
- Positive Crankcase Ventilation (PCV) hose
- Valve cover

➡Install the special clips MB 998443-01 to hold the auto-adjusters in place.

- Rocker arms and rocker arm shafts
- Rocker shaft springs

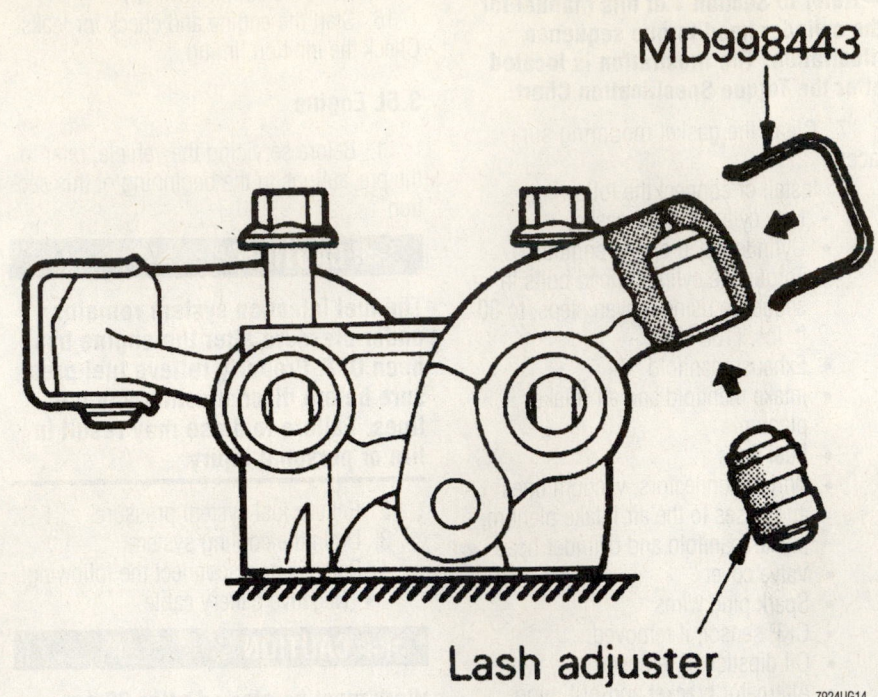

Insert the Lash Adjuster Holder tool MD998443 to prevent the lash adjuster from falling out—2.4L engines

1. Bearing cap No. 4
2. Rocker arm (B)
3. Spring
4. Rocker arm (A)
5. Spring
6. Bearing cap No. 3
7. Rocker arm (B)
8. Spring
9. Rocker arm (A)
10. Spring
11. Bearing cap No. 2
12. Rocker arm (B)
13. Spring
14. Rocker arm (A)
15. Spring
16. Rocker arm shaft (B)
17. Rocker arm shaft (A)
18. Bearing cap No. 1

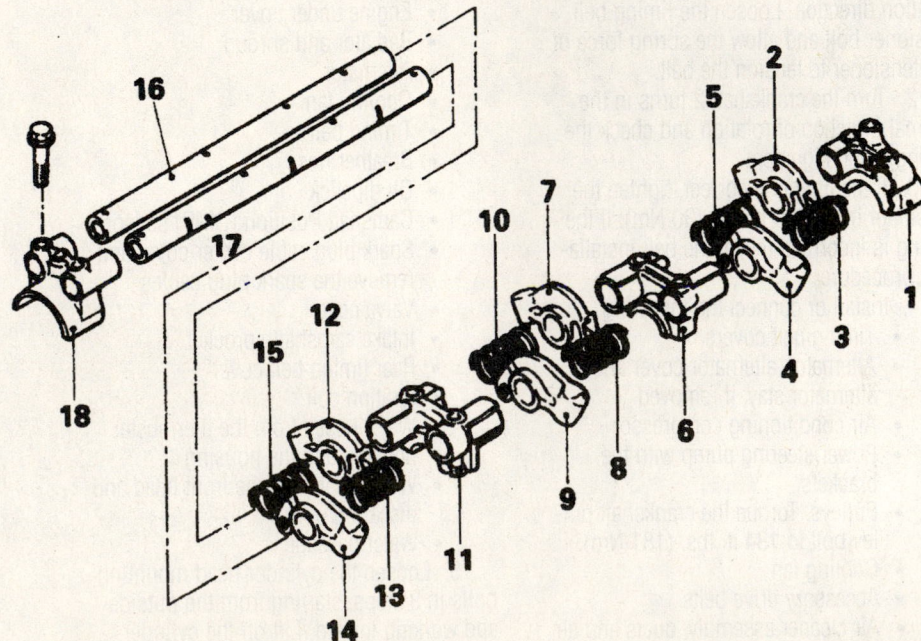

Exploded view of the rocker arms and shafts—3.0L engine

➡Take care during removal that no oil, grease or dirt comes into contact with the timing belt.

To install:

3. Disassemble the rocker assembly, checking each component for wear, scoring, or plugged oil passages. Check the roller for correct and smooth rotation. Inspect the inner diameter of each rocker for any scoring or enlargement. If wear is found inside the rocker, replace it and inspect the shaft for damage.

4. Before reassembly, coat the contact faces liberally with clean motor oil. Observe the numbers on the bearing caps so that they are replaced in the correct location. Reassemble the rocker shafts into the front bearing cap so that the notches face outward. As you continue to assemble the springs, rockers and bearing caps, remember that the arrows on the bearing caps must point in the same direction as the arrow on the head. This is particularly important if the rockers have been removed from both heads.

5. Install or connect the following:
- Rocker arms and rocker arm shafts, Torque the bolts to 23 ft. lbs. (31 Nm).
- Valve cover Torque the bolts to 30 inch lbs. (3.4 Nm).
- PCV hose
- Breather hose

3.0L Engines

1. Before servicing the vehicle, refer to the precautions in the beginning of this section.

2. Remove or disconnect the following:
- Negative battery cable

✳✳ CAUTION

Work must be started after 90 seconds from the time the ignition switch is turned to the LOCK position and the negative battery cable is disconnected.

- Valve cover
- Auto lash adjuster retainers SST MD998443 on the rocker arms
- Rocker arms, rocker shafts and bearing caps, as an assembly

To install:

3. Inspect the bearing journals on the camshaft and the cylinder head.

4. Lubricate the camshaft journals and camshaft with clean engine oil.

5. Install the rocker arms, rocker arm shaft and the rocker shaft spring as follows:

a. Temporarily tighten the rocker shaft with the bolts so that the intake valve rocker arms do not push on the valves.

b. Insert the rocker shaft spring from above and mount it at right angles to the plug guide.

c. Before installing the exhaust rocker arms and the rocker arm shaft, mount the rocker shaft spring.

d. Remove tool SST MD998443 used to hold the lash adjuster in position.

e. Check to ensure that the flat side of the rocker shaft is perpendicular to the cylinder head, and facing the valves.

f. Gradually tighten the bearing caps in 2 or 3 steps. In the final step, tighten to 23 ft. lbs. (31 Nm).

6. Install or connect the following:
- Valve cover and new gasket. Torque the bolt to 2–3 ft. lbs. (3–4 Nm).
- Negative battery cable

7. Start the engine and check for leaks and proper operation.

3.5L Engine

1. Before servicing the vehicle, refer to the precautions in the beginning of this section.

2. Relieve the fuel system pressure.

3. Remove or disconnect the following:
- Negative battery cable
- Valve cover and the semi-circular packing.
- Crankshaft Position (CKP) sensor, matchmark for reassembly
- Camshaft Position (CMP) sensor, if equipped

➡Install auto lash adjuster retainers SST MD998443 on the rocker arms

- Rocker arms and shafts
- Lash adjusters

4. Check the camshaft journals for wear or damage. Check the cam lobes for damage. Also, check the cylinder head oil holes for clogging.

To install:

➡Lubricate the valve train components with clean engine oil.

5. Bleed and install the lash adjusters to the to the original bores in the cylinder head.

6. Install or connect the following:
- Rocker arms and shafts. Torque the bolts to 23 ft. lbs. (31 Nm).
- Camshaft position sensor, if removed. Torque the mounting bolts to 78 inch lbs. (9 Nm).

- Camshaft Position (CMP) sensor, if equipped
- Valve cover and the semi-circular packing. Torque the bolts to 2.5 ft. lbs. (3.5 Nm).
- Negative battery cable

7. Run vehicle and check for leaks.

Intake Manifold

REMOVAL & INSTALLATION

2.4L Engine

1. Before servicing the vehicle, refer to the precautions in the beginning of this section.

2. Drain the engine coolant.

3. Relieve the fuel pressure.

4. Remove or disconnect the following:
- Negative battery cable

✳✳ CAUTION

Wait at least 90 seconds after the negative battery cable is disconnected to prevent possible deployment of the air bag.

- Upper radiator hose from the thermostat housing
- Air intake hoses, breather hose and the air intake pipe
- Wires, hoses and linkages from the throttle body
- Ignition coil
- Brake booster hose and vacuum hose cluster from the air intake plenum
- Air intake plenum from the intake manifold
- Fuel lines, keep the line covered or plugged
- Fuel rail assembly with injectors intact
- Heater hose from the manifold
- Engine Coolant Temperature (ECT) sensor
- Water outlet fitting
- Distributor, matchmark for reassembly
- Intake manifold from the cylinder head and engine
- Manifold Differential Pressure (MDP) sensor, if equipped

5. Clean and dry the mating surfaces of the manifold and cylinder head.

To install:

6. Install or connect the following:
- New gasket and the intake manifold to the head. Starting from the middle

For engine torque specifications, refer to Section 1 of this manual

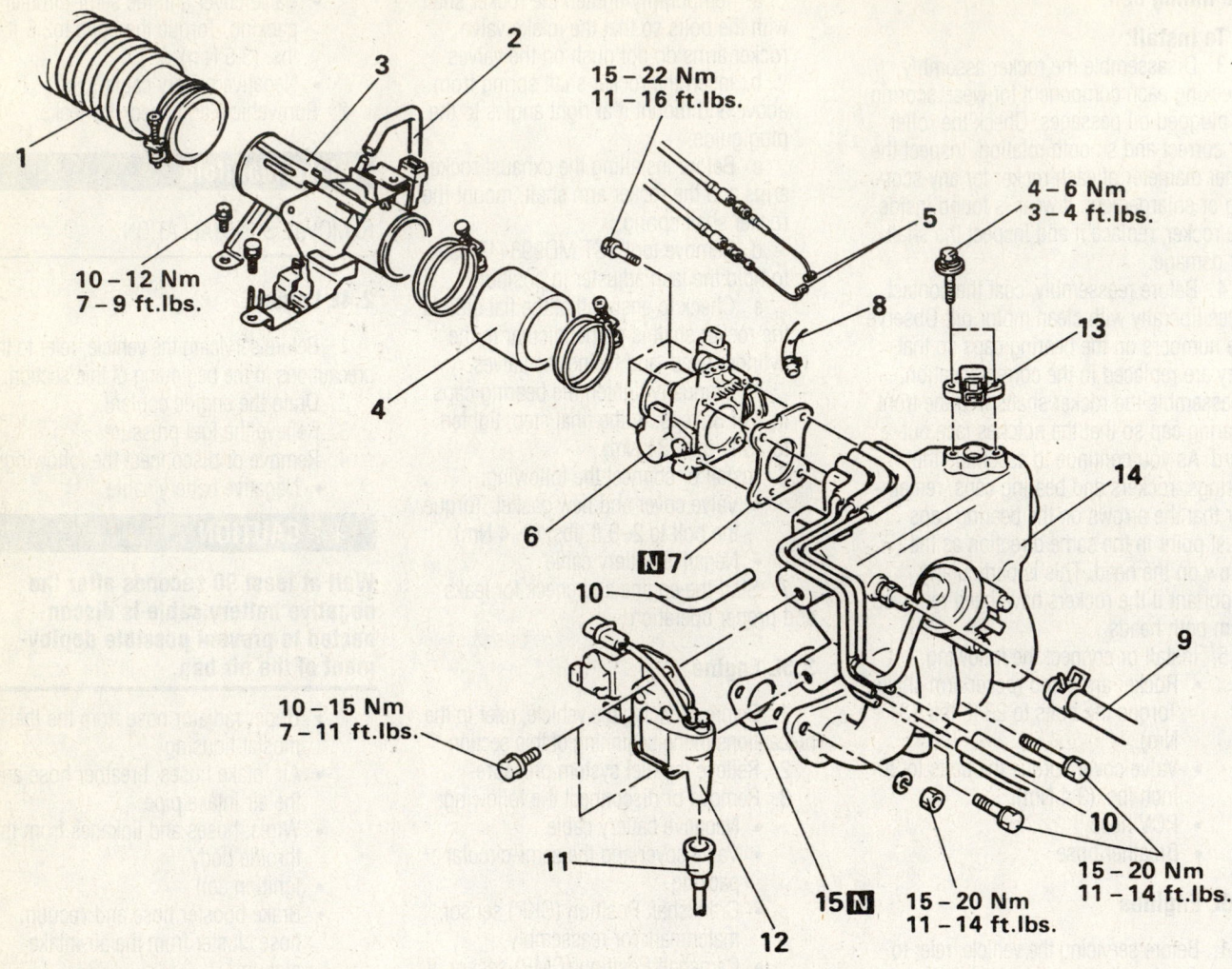

15 – 22 Nm
11 – 16 ft.lbs.

10 – 12 Nm
7 – 9 ft.lbs.

4 – 6 Nm
3 – 4 ft.lbs.

10 – 15 Nm
7 – 11 ft.lbs.

15 – 20 Nm
11 – 14 ft.lbs.

15 – 20 Nm
11 – 14 ft.lbs.

1. Air intake hose
2. Breather hose
3. Air intake pipe
4. Air hose
5. Accelerator cable and kick down plate
6. Throttle body
7. Gasket
8. Water hose
9. Brake booster vacuum hose
10. Vacuum hose connection
11. High tension cable
12. Ignition coil
13. Manifold difference pressure sensor
    <1996 models>
14. Intake manifold plenum assembly
15. Intake manifold plenum gasket

7924UG39

Exploded view of the intake plenum chamber and related components—2.4L engine shown

and working outward, tighten the
retaining nuts to 14 ft. lbs. (19 Nm).
• ECT sensor
• Water outlet fitting. Torque the bolts
  to 14 ft. lbs. (19 Nm).
• Distributor with matchmarks
  aligned
• Fuel rail assembly to the manifold
  using a new O-ring

• Fuel lines
• Heater hose to the manifold
• Air intake plenum with a new gasket. Tighten the retaining bolts to
  12 ft. lbs. (16 Nm).
• Vacuum hoses cluster, brake
  booster hose and all wires, hoses
  and linkages to the throttle body
• Ignition coil

• Air intake hoses, breather hose and
  the air intake pipe
• Manifold Differential Pressure
  (MDP) sensor, if equipped
• Upper radiator hose
• Negative battery cable
7. Refill the radiator with coolant.
8. Check the system for leaks.

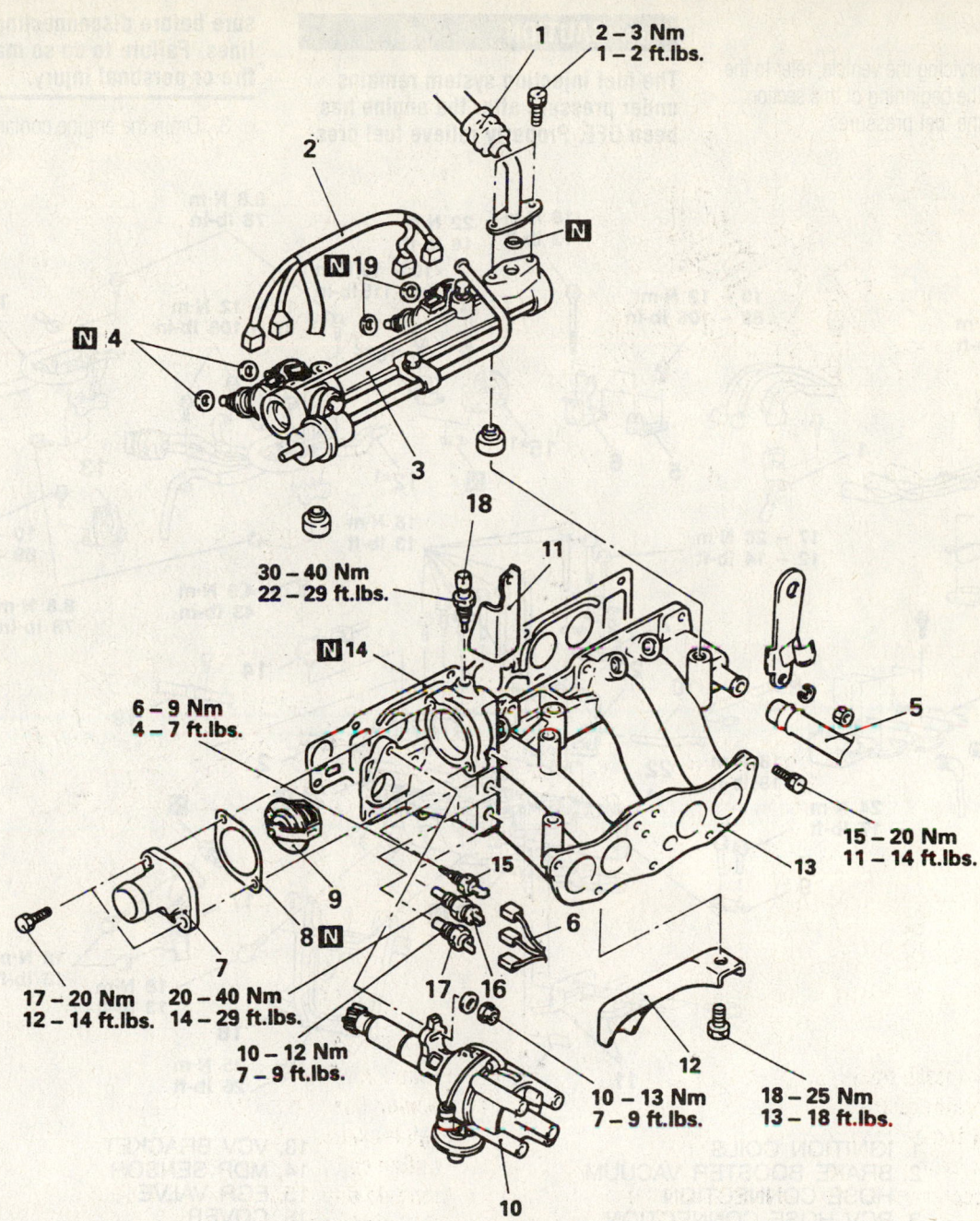

2 – 3 Nm
1 – 2 ft.lbs.

30 – 40 Nm
22 – 29 ft.lbs.

6 – 9 Nm
4 – 7 ft.lbs.

15 – 20 Nm
11 – 14 ft.lbs.

17 – 20 Nm
12 – 14 ft.lbs.

20 – 40 Nm
14 – 29 ft.lbs.

10 – 12 Nm
7 – 9 ft.lbs.

10 – 13 Nm
7 – 9 ft.lbs.

18 – 25 Nm
13 – 18 ft.lbs.

1. High pressure fuel hose connection
2. Fuel injector harness connector
3. Fuel rail
4. Insulator
5. Heater hose
6. Wiring harness connector
7. Water outlet fitting
8. Water outlet fitting gasket
9. Thermostat
10. Distributor
11. Intake manifold plenum stay
12. Intake manifold stay
13. Intake manifold
14. Intake manifold gasket
15. Thermal switch <A/T>
16. Engine coolant temperature sensor
17. Engine coolant temperature gauge unit
18. Air conditioning engine coolant temperature switch <A/C>

7924UG40

Exploded view of the intake manifold and related components—2.4L engine shown

For complete mechanical specifications, refer to Section 1 of this manual

3.0L Engine

1. Before servicing the vehicle, refer to the precautions in the beginning of this section.
2. Relieve the fuel pressure.

✳✳ CAUTION

The fuel injection system remains under pressure after the engine has been OFF. Properly relieve fuel pressure before disconnecting any fuel lines. Failure to do so may result in fire or personal injury.

3. Drain the engine coolant.

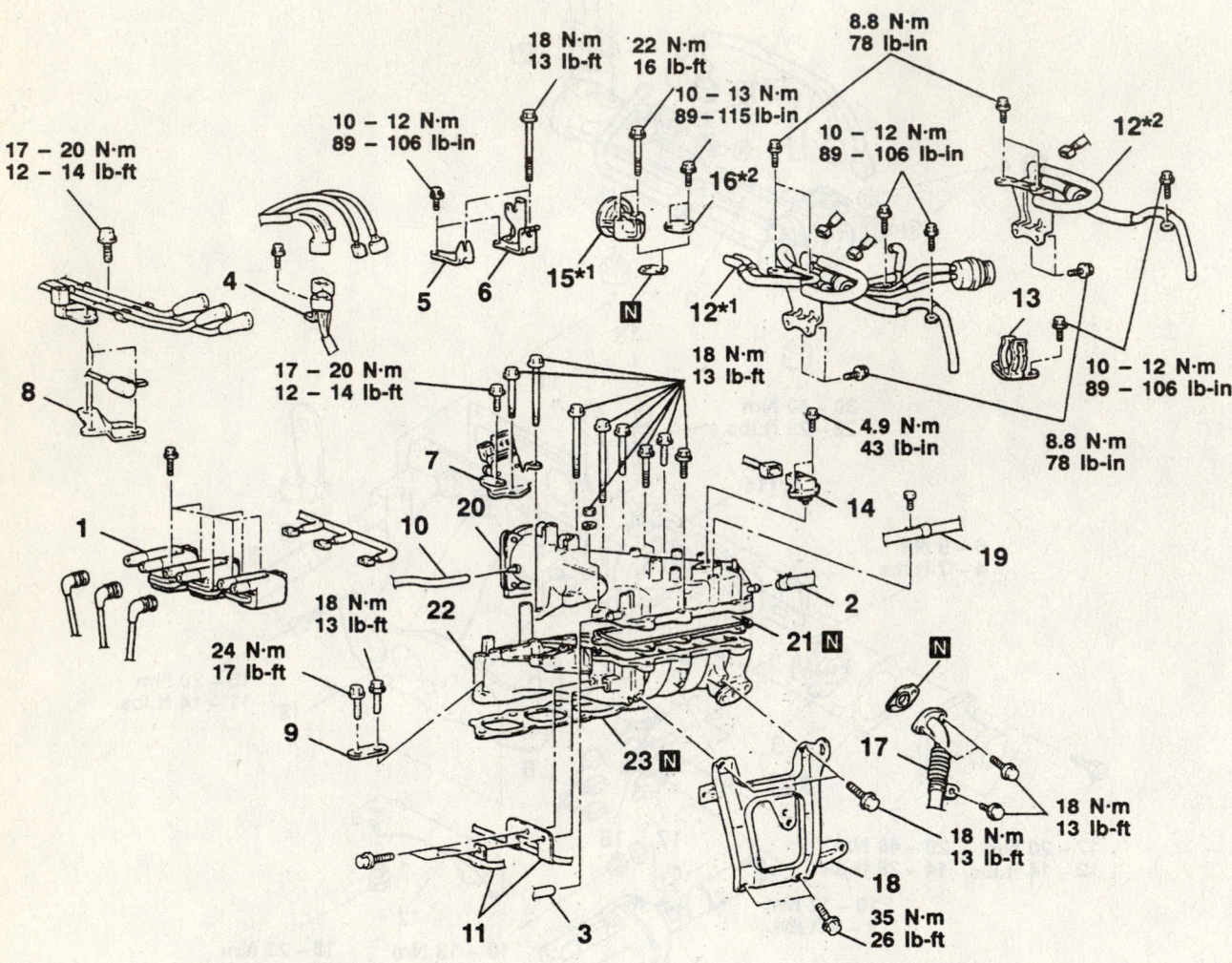

1. IGNITION COILS
2. BRAKE BOOSTER VACUUM HOSE CONNECTION
3. PCV HOSE CONNECTION
4. CRANKSHAFT POSITION SENSOR AND CAM POSITION SENSOR CONNECTOR
5. ACCELERATOR CABLE BRACKET <M/T>
6. THROTTLE CABLE BRACKET <A/T>
7. IGNITION POWER TRANSISTOR
8. WATER OUTLET FITTING BRACKET
9. WATER PUMP STAY
10. VACUUM HOSE CONNECTION
11. FUEL PIPE CONNECTION
12. SOLENOID VALVE AND VACUUM HOSE ASSEMBLY

13. VCV BRACKET
14. MDP SENSOR
15. EGR VALVE
16. COVER
17. EGR PIPE CONNECTION
18. INTAKE MANIFOLD PLENUM STAY
19. THROTTLE CABLE CONNECTION
20. AIR INTAKE FITTING
21. AIR INTAKE FITTING GASKET
22. UPPER INTAKE MANIFOLD
23. INTAKE MANIFOLD PLENUM GASKET

NOTE
*1: Vehicles for Federal
*2: Vehicles for California

Exploded view of the upper intake manifold and related components—3.0L 24-valve engine shown

7924UG41

4. Remove or disconnect the following:
- Negative battery cable

❊❊ CAUTION

Work must be started after 90 seconds from the time the ignition switch is turned to the LOCK position and the negative battery cable is disconnected.

- Air intake hose from the throttle body
- Positive Crankcase Ventilation (PCV) hose
- Exhaust Gas Recirculation (EGR) valve
- Manifold Differential Pressure (MDP) sensor

- Vacuum hoses from the throttle body and air intake plenum
- Accelerator cable and the throttle control cable
- Coolant hoses
- Engine oil filler neck bracket from the air intake plenum
- EGR tube from the air intake plenum
- Plenum brackets
- Air intake plenum assembly from the intake manifold and remove. Note the position of the mounting bolts as they are removed.
- Fuel hose from the fuel rail
- Fuel return line and vacuum hose from the fuel pressure regulator

- Electrical connectors from the injectors
- Fuel rail and injectors
- Intake manifold

5. Remove the gaskets and thoroughly clean and dry the mating surfaces of the manifold and heads.

To install:

6. Install or connect the following:
- Intake manifold. Torque the nuts to 16 ft. lbs. (21 Nm) start from the center and working outward.

7. Connect the hoses and connect the wires to the coolant switches.
- Fuel rail assembly and connect the fuel hoses
- New gasket and the air intake

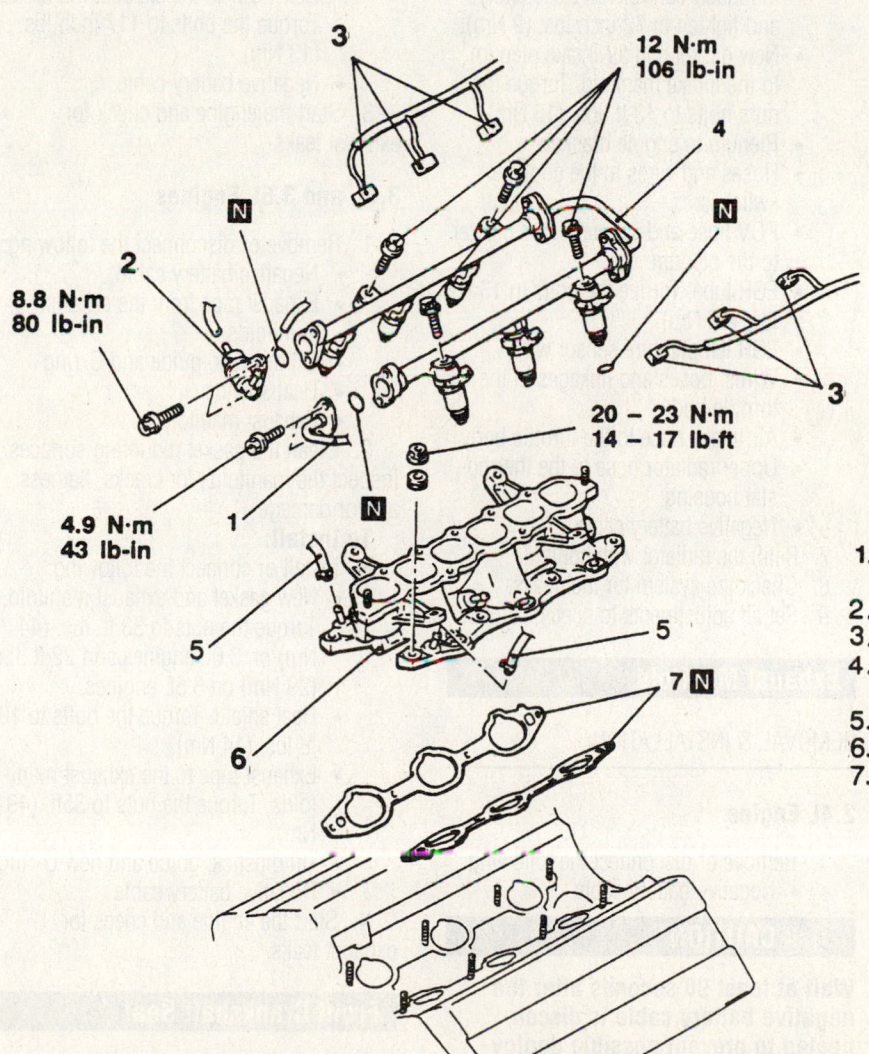

12 N·m
106 lb-in

8.8 N·m
80 lb-in

20 – 23 N·m
14 – 17 lb-ft

4.9 N·m
43 lb-in

1. HIGH-PRESSURE FUEL HOSE CONNECTION
2. FUEL PRESSURE REGULATOR
3. INJECTOR CONNECTOR
4. FUEL RAIL (WITH INJECTORS)
5. WATER HOSE CONNECTION
6. INTAKE MANIFOLD
7. INTAKE MANIFOLD GASKET

7924UG42

Exploded view of the lower intake manifold and related components—3.0L 24-valve engine shown

Please refer to Section 8 for electric cooling fan wiring schematics

plenum to the intake manifold. Torque the nuts/bolts to 13 ft. lbs. (17 Nm).
- Plenum brackets
- PCV hose and vacuum hose cluster to the plenum
- EGR tube
- EGR temperature sensor wire
- Wires, hoses and linkages to the throttle body
- Air intake hose to the throttle body
- Upper radiator hose to the thermostat housing
- Negative battery cable

8. Refill the radiator with coolant.
9. Check fuel system for leaks.

3.5L Engines

1. Before servicing the vehicle, refer to the precautions in the beginning of this section.

> **✴✴ CAUTION**
>
> **The fuel injection system remains under pressure after the engine has been OFF. Properly relieve fuel pressure before disconnecting any fuel lines. Failure to do so may result in fire or personal injury.**

2. Relieve the fuel pressure.
3. Partially drain the cooling system.
4. Remove or disconnect the following:
   - Negative battery cable

> **✴✴ CAUTION**
>
> **Wait at least 90 seconds after the negative battery cable is disconnected to prevent possible deployment of the air bag.**

- Air intake hose from the throttle body
- Electrical connectors and vacuum hoses from the throttle body and air intake plenum
- Accelerator cable and the throttle control cable
- Coolant hoses
- Positive Crankcase Ventilation (PCV) hose
- Exhaust Gas Recirculation (EGR) temperature sensor connector
- EGR tube from the air intake plenum
- Intake manifold plenum cover
- Intake manifold plenum stay brackets
- Air intake plenum assembly from the intake manifold and remove. Note the position of the mounting bolts as they are removed

- Induction control valve assembly
- Fuel hose from the fuel rail
- Fuel return line and vacuum hose from the fuel pressure regulator
- Electrical connectors from the injectors
- Fuel rail and injectors
- Intake manifold

5. Remove the gaskets and thoroughly clean and dry the mating surfaces of the manifold and heads.

To install:

6. Install or connect the following:
   - Intake manifold. Tighten the nuts to 16 ft. lbs. (21 Nm). Start from the center and work outward.
   - Fuel rail assembly and connect the fuel hoses
   - Induction control valve assembly and tighten to 72 inch lbs. (9 Nm).
   - New gasket and air intake plenum to the intake manifold. Torque the nuts/bolts to 13 ft. lbs. (18 Nm).
   - Plenum to engine brackets
   - Hoses and wires to the coolant switches
   - PCV hose and vacuum hose cluster to the plenum
   - EGR tube. Torque the bolts to 13 ft. lbs. (18 Nm).
   - EGR temperature sensor wire
   - Wires, hoses and linkages to the throttle body
   - Air intake hose to the throttle body
   - Upper radiator hose to the thermostat housing
   - Negative battery cable

7. Refill the radiator with coolant.
8. Check the system for fuel leaks.
9. Set all adjustments to specifications.

Exhaust Manifold

REMOVAL & INSTALLATION

2.4L Engine

1. Remove or disconnect the following:
   - Negative battery cable

> **✴✴ CAUTION**
>
> **Wait at least 90 seconds after the negative battery cable is disconnected to prevent possible deployment of the air bag.**

- Heat cowl from the exhaust manifold
- Aspirator valve assembly, if equipped
- Oil dipstick and guide

- Oxygen (O$_2$S) sensor connector and ground cable, if equipped
- Exhaust pipe from the manifold
- Exhaust manifold and gasket from the engine

To install:

2. Install or connect the following:
   - Exhaust manifold. Torque the M8 mounting nuts to 22 ft. lbs. (29 Nm) and the M10 mounting bolts 36 ft. lbs. (49 Nm). starting from the middle and working outward.
   - O$_2$S sensor connector and ground cable, if equipped
   - Exhaust pipe to the manifold. Torque the nuts to 35ft. (49 Nm).
   - Aspirator valve assembly, if removed
   - Heat cowl to the exhaust manifold. Torque the bolts to 117 inch lbs. (13 Nm).
   - Negative battery cable

3. Start the engine and check for exhaust leaks.

3.0L and 3.5L Engines

1. Remove or disconnect the following:
   - Negative battery cable
   - Exhaust pipe from the exhaust manifolds
   - Oil dipstick, guide and O-ring
   - Heat shields
   - Exhaust manifolds

2. Clean the gasket mounting surfaces. Inspect the manifolds for cracks, flatness and/or damage.

To install:

3. Install or connect the following:
   - New gasket and exhaust manifold. Torque the nuts to 33 ft. lbs. (44 Nm) on 3.0L engines and 22 ft. lbs. (29 Nm) on 3.5L engines.
   - Heat shield, Torque the bolts to 10 ft. lbs. (14 Nm).
   - Exhaust pipe to the exhaust manifolds. Torque the nuts to 35ft. (49 Nm).
   - Oil dipstick, guide and new O-ring
   - Negative battery cable

4. Start the engine and check for exhaust leaks.

Front Crankshaft Seal

REMOVAL & INSTALLATION

2.4L Engines

1. Before servicing the vehicle, refer to the precautions in the beginning of this section.

2. Drain the crankcase.

3. Drain and recycle the engine coolant.

4. Remove or disconnect the following:
- Negative battery cable

✳✳ CAUTION

Wait at least 90 seconds after the negative battery cable is disconnected to prevent possible deployment of the air bag.

- Fan shroud
- Radiator and cooling fan
- Accessory drive belts
- Air conditioner tension pulley, if equipped
- Ignition coil, if equipped
- Crankshaft pulley and the timing belt front covers

5. Reinstall the crankshaft pulley bolt and use it to rotate the engine clockwise until the timing marks are aligned.

6. Remove or disconnect the following:
- Timing belt and belt tension
- Crankshaft sprocket
- Crankshaft sensor blade
- Inner timing belt and inner crankshaft sprocket
- Crankshaft seal without scratching the crankshaft

To install:

7. Place the seal guide over the crankshaft and coat it with engine oil.

8. Slide the seal over the guide until it touches the front case assembly, then use the appropriate seal driver to install the seal. Remove the seal guide.

9. Install or connect the following:
- Inner crankshaft sprocket
- Inner timing belt and belt tension
- Crankshaft sensor blade

10. Install the flange and the timing belt sprocket on the crankshaft.

11. Install or connect the following:
- Timing belt. Adjust the belt tension
- Timing belt front covers and the crankshaft pulleys
- Ignition coil, if equipped
- Air conditioner belt tension pulley if equipped
- Accessory drive belts
- Radiator, cooling fan and fan shroud
- Negative battery cable

12. Refill the crankcase.

13. Refill the cooling system.

14. Start the engine and check for leaks.

3.0L and 3.5L Engines

1. Before servicing the vehicle, refer to the precautions in the beginning of this section.

2. Drain the crankcase.

3. Drain and recycle the engine coolant.

4. Remove or disconnect the following:
- Negative battery cable

✳✳ CAUTION

Wait at least 90 seconds after the negative battery cable is disconnected to prevent possible deployment of the air bag.

- Cooling fan
- Accessory drive belts
- Alternator
- Engine undercover, if equipped
- Power steering oil pump assembly
- Air conditioner compressor and bracket, if equipped
- Timing indicator bracket
- Accessory mount Assembly
- Crankshaft pulley
- Timing belt covers and the timing belt
- Crankshaft sprocket

5. Cut out a portion in the crankshaft oil seal lip and pry out the oil seal with a flat prying tool, being careful not to damage the crankshaft.

To install:

6. Coat the lip of the new seal with oil and install the seal using the proper seal driver.

7. Install or connect the following:
- Crankshaft sprocket and the timing belt
- Timing belt covers
- Crankshaft pulley. Torque the bolt to 134 ft. lbs. (181Nm).
- Accessory mount Assembly. Torque the bolts to 33 ft. lbs. (44 Nm).
- Timing indicator bracket. Torque the bolts to 97 inch lbs. (11 Nm).
- Air conditioner compressor and bracket, if equipped
- Power steering oil pump assembly
- Engine undercover, if equipped
- Alternator
- Accessory drive belts
- Cooling fan
- Negative battery cable

8. Refill the crankcase.

9. Refill the cooling system.

10. Start the engine and check for proper operation.

Camshaft and Valve Lifters

REMOVAL & INSTALLATION

2.4L Engine

1. Before servicing the vehicle, refer to the precautions in the beginning of this section.

2. Drain and recycle the engine coolant.

3. Drain and recycle the engine crankcase.

4. Remove or disconnect the following:
- Negative battery cable

✳✳ CAUTION

Wait at least 90 seconds after the negative battery cable is disconnected to prevent possible deployment of the air bag.

- Positive Crankcase Valve (PCV) hose
- Valve cover and the upper timing belt cover

5. Rotate the crankshaft clockwise and align the camshaft sprocket timing mark with the timing mark on the cylinder head.

6. Remove or disconnect the following:
- Distributor, matchmark for reassembly

7. Install auto lash adjuster retainer MD998443 to each rocker arm to hold the auto lash adjusters in place

8. Remove or disconnect the following:
- Rocker arm and shafts

✳✳ WARNING

Do not rotate the crankshaft after the sprocket is removed from the camshaft. Be sure there is no slack in the timing belt. Be sure the timing belt does not disengage from the sprocket. If the crankshaft is rotated or the timing belt position is disturbed, timing belt and sprocket alignment will have to be set.

- Thrust cage and o-ring
- Camshaft and the front seal from the engine

To install:

9. Install or connect the following:
- Front seal
- Camshaft, lubricate with engine oil
- Thrust cage and o-ring. Torque the bolts to 13 ft. lbs. (18 Nm).
- Rocker arm and shafts. Torque the bolts to 23 ft. lbs. (31 Nm).

10. Remove the auto lash adjuster retainer MD998443 from each rocker arm.

11. Install or connect the following:
- Valve cover and upper timing belt cover
- Positive Crankcase Valve (PCV) hose
- Distributor, aligning the mark made during removal
- Negative battery cable

12. Start the engine and check for leaks.

3.0L, 3.5L Engines

1. Before servicing the vehicle, refer to the precautions in the beginning of this section.

2. Relieve the fuel system pressure.

3. Drain and recycle the engine coolant.

4. Drain and recycle the engine crankcase.

5. Remove or disconnect the following:
- Negative battery cable

✳✳ CAUTION

Work must be started after 90 seconds from the time the ignition switch is turned to the LOCK position and the negative battery cable is disconnected.

- Intake manifold plenum
- Valve cover
- Timing belt
- Sprocket from the camshaft

6. Install auto lash adjuster retainers SST MD998443 on the rocker arms.

7. Remove or disconnect the following:
- Distributor and the distributor extension, if equipped
- Rocker arms, rocker shafts and bearing caps, as an assembly
- Thrust cage and o-ring
- Camshaft from the cylinder head

8. Inspect the bearing journals on the camshaft and the cylinder head.

To install:

9. Lubricate the camshaft journals and camshaft with clean engine oil

10. Install or connect the following:
- Camshaft in the cylinder head.
- Thrust cage and o-ring. Torque the bolts to 109 inch lbs. (12 Nm).
- Rocker arms, rocker arm shaft and the rocker shaft spring.

11. Temporarily tighten the rocker shaft with the bolts positioned so that the intake valve rocker arms do not push the valves.

12. Install or connect the following:
- Rocker shaft spring from above and mount it at right angles to the plug guide.

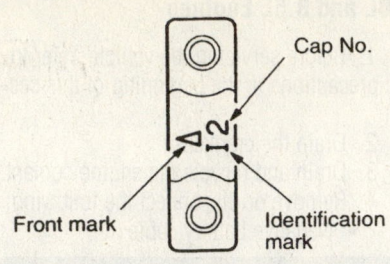

Cap No.

Front mark

Identification mark

7924UG16

The camshaft bearing caps have identification marks on them—3.5L engine

13. Before installing the exhaust rocker arms and the rocker arm shaft, mount the rocker shaft spring.

14. Remove the SST used to hold the lash adjuster in position.

15. Check to ensure that the flat side of the rocker shaft is perpendicular to the cylinder head, and facing the valves.

16. Gradually tighten the bearing caps in 2 or 3 steps. In the final step tighten to 23 ft. lbs. (31 Nm).

17. Install or connect the following:
- Distributor, if removed
- Sprockets. Torque the bolts to 65 ft. lbs. (88 Nm).
- Timing belt and timing belt cover
- Valve cover. Torque the bolts to 26 inch lbs. (3.4 Nm).
- Intake manifold plenum
- Negative battery cable

18. Start the engine and check for leaks and proper operation.

19. Refill the coolant and crankcase.

Starter Motor

REMOVAL & INSTALLATION

1. Before servicing the vehicle, refer to the precautions in the beginning of this section.

2. Remove or disconnect the following:
- Negative battery cable
- Engine under cover, if equipped
- Front engine mount heat protector

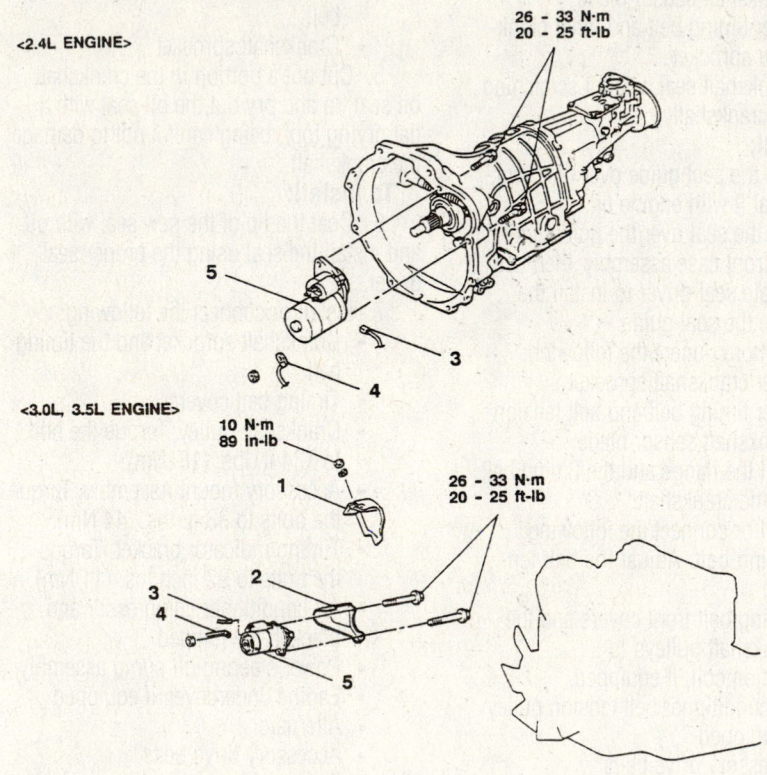

<2.4L ENGINE>

26 - 33 N·m
20 - 25 ft-lb

5

3

4

<3.0L, 3.5L ENGINE>

10 N·m
89 in-lb

1

26 - 33 N·m
20 - 25 ft-lb

2

3

4

5

1. FRONT ENGINE MOUNT HEAT PROTECTOR <RH> (REFER TO GROUP 32. ENGINE MOUNTING)

2. STARTER COVER
3. STARTER CONNECTOR
4. BATTERY CABLE
5. STARTER ASSEMBLY

9308UG03

Starter motor mounting

- Starter cover
- Wires
- Starter motor

To install:

3. Install or connect the following:
- Starter motor and cover. Torque the bolts to 20–25 ft. lbs. (26–33 Nm).
- Wires
- Front engine mount heat protector. Torque the nut to 89 inch lbs. (10 Nm).
- Engine under cover, if equipped
- Negative battery cable

Oil Pan

REMOVAL & INSTALLATION

2.4L engine

1. Before servicing the vehicle, refer to the precautions in the beginning of this section.
2. Drain the engine oil.
3. Remove or disconnect the following:
- Negative battery
- Engine under cover
- Bell housing cover
- Oil pan

To install:

4. Before installing, thoroughly clean the oil pan and cylinder block mating surfaces.
5. Apply liquid gasket around the surface of the oil pan.

➡**Assemble the oil pan to the cylinder block within 15 minutes after applying the liquid gasket.**

6. Install or connect the following:
- Oil pan. Torque the bolts to 61 inch lbs. (6.9 Nm).
- Bell housing cover. Torque the bolts to 78 inch lbs. (8.8 Nm).
- Engine under cover
- Negative battery cable

3.0L engines

1. Before servicing the vehicle, refer to the precautions in the beginning of this section.
2. Drain the engine oil.
3. Remove or disconnect the following:
- Negative battery
- Engine under cover
- Alternator and belt
- Stabilizer bar
- Front exhaust pipe
- Actuator assembly and heat protector

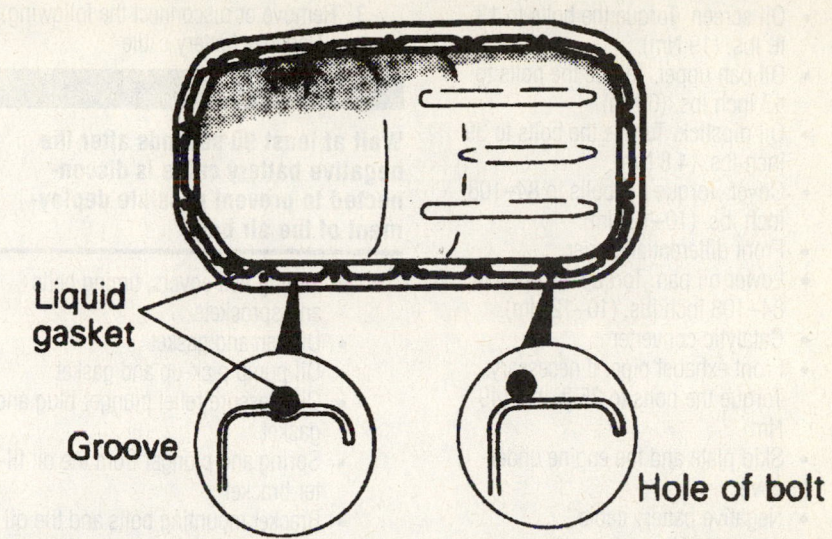

Apply a bead of sealant around the oil pan flange as shown—all engines are similar

- Oil dipstick
- Crossmember assembly
- Automatic transmission oil dipstick assembly
- Exhaust pipe support bracket
- Transmission stay
- Oil pan, lower
- Oil screen and baffle plate
- Oil pan upper

To install:

4. Before installing, thoroughly clean the oil pan and cylinder block mating surfaces.
5. Apply liquid gasket around the surface of the oil pan.

➡**Assemble the oil pan to the cylinder block within 15 minutes after applying the liquid gasket.**

6. Install or connect the following:
- Oil pan upper. Torque the bolts to 53 inch lbs. (6.0 Nm).
- Oil screen and baffle plate. Torque the bolts to 14 ft. lbs. (19 Nm).
- Oil pan, lower. Torque the bolts to 53 inch lbs. (6.0 Nm).
- Transmission stay. Torque the bolts to 26 ft. lbs. (35 Nm).
- Exhaust pipe support bracket. Torque the bolts to 35 ft. lbs. (49 Nm).
- Automatic transmission oil dipstick assembly. Torque the bolts to 33 ft. lbs. (44 Nm).
- Crossmember assembly. Torque the bolts to 80 ft. lbs. (108 Nm).
- Oil dipstick. Torque the bolts to 35 ft. lbs. (48 Nm).

- Actuator assembly and heat protector
- Front exhaust pipe
- Stabilizer bar
- Alternator and belt
- Engine under cover
- Negative battery

3.5L engines

1. Before servicing the vehicle, refer to the precautions in the beginning of this section.
2. Drain the engine oil.
3. Remove or disconnect the following:
- Negative battery cable
- Skid plate and the engine undercover
- Front exhaust pipe, if necessary
- Catalytic converter
- Lower oil pan
- Front differential carrier
- Cover
- Oil dipstick
- Oil pan upper
- Oil screen

To install:

4. Before installing, thoroughly clean the oil pan and cylinder block mating surfaces.
5. Apply liquid gasket around the surface of the oil pan.

➡**Assemble the oil pan to the cylinder block within 15 minutes after applying the liquid gasket.**

Timing belt service is covered in Section 4 of this manual

6. Install or connect the following:
- Oil screen. Torque the bolts to 13 ft. lbs. (19 Nm).
- Oil pan upper. Torque the bolts to 48 inch lbs. (6 Nm).
- Oil dipstick. Torque the bolts to 39 inch lbs. (4.8 Nm).
- Cover. Torque the bolts to 84–108 inch lbs. (10–12 Nm).
- Front differential carrier
- Lower oil pan. Torque the bolts to 84–108 inch lbs. (10–12 Nm).
- Catalytic converter
- Front exhaust pipe, if necessary. Torque the bolts to 35 ft. lbs. (49 Nm).
- Skid plate and the engine under-cover
- Negative battery cable

Oil Pump

REMOVAL & INSTALLATION

2.4L Engine

1. Before servicing the vehicle, refer to the precautions in the beginning of this section.

2. Drain the oil and remove the oil filter.
3. Remove or disconnect the following:
- Negative battery cable

✲✲ CAUTION

Wait at least 90 seconds after the negative battery cable is disconnected to prevent possible deployment of the air bag.

- Timing belt covers, timing belts and sprockets
- Oil pan and gasket
- Oil pump pick-up and gasket
- Oil pressure relief plunger plug and gasket
- Spring and plunger from the oil filter bracket
- Bracket mounting bolts and the oil filter mount and gasket
- Plug cap and gasket that covers the oil pump driven gear shaft. Using special tool MD998162 this is located on the right side of the front case, just above the protruding drive gear shaft.
- Retaining bolt from the oil pump driven gear located behind the plug removed earlier

- Front case mounting bolts and the case from the block
- Case gasket from the block

To install:

4. Prime the pump by pouring fresh oil into the pump intake and turning the drive-shaft until oil comes out of the pressure port. Repeat this a few times until no air bubbles are present. Replace all seals on the case assembly.

5. Install a special seal guide to the crankshaft, MD998285, so the smaller diameter faces outward. Coat the outer diameter of the seal with clean engine oil.

6. Install or connect the following:
- New front case gasket and the front case by carefully positioning the crankshaft seal over the seal guide and lining up all bolt holes. Torque the bolts to 17 ft. lbs. (23 Nm).

7. Remove the plug from the left side of the block. Hold the left side silent shaft by inserting a tool in the plug hole and tighten the driven gear bolt to 26 ft. lbs. (35 Nm)
- New O-ring and the plug cover
- Oil filter mounting bracket gasket
- Mounting bracket and bolts tightening the oil filter mounting bracket bolts to 12 ft. lbs. (16 Nm).

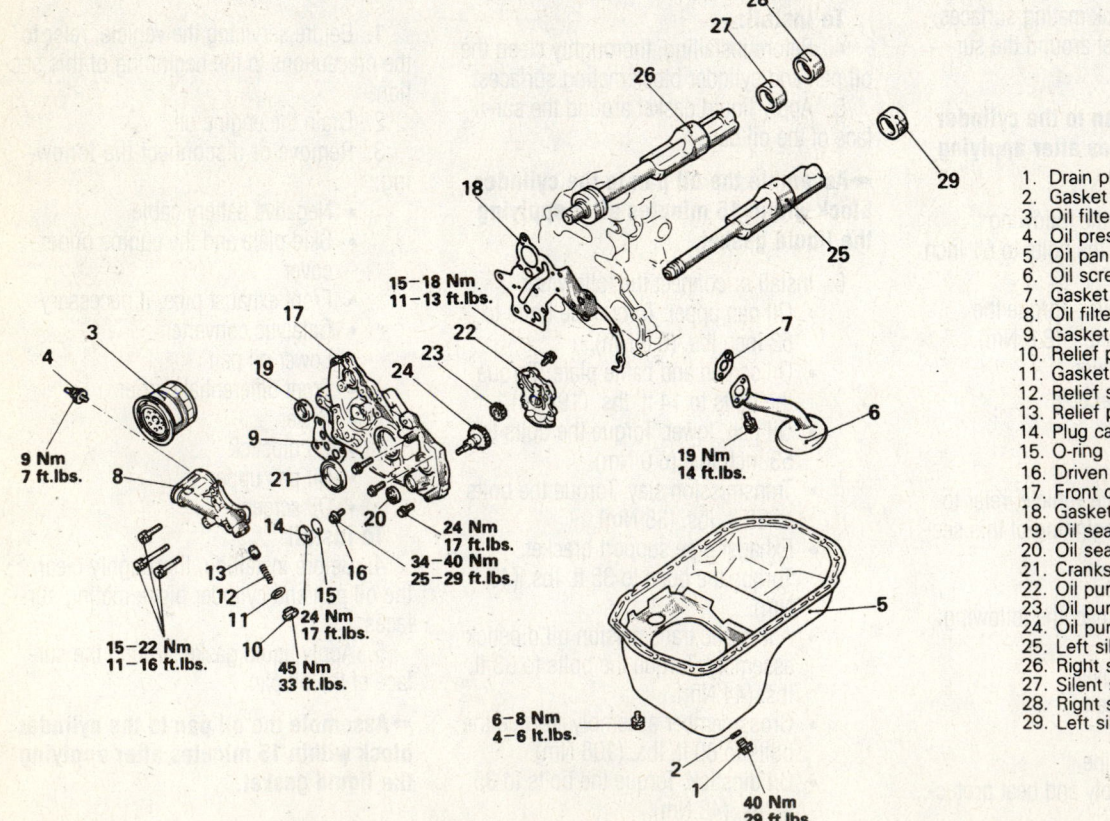

15–18 Nm
11–13 ft.lbs.

9 Nm
7 ft.lbs.

15–22 Nm
11–16 ft.lbs.

24 Nm
17 ft.lbs.

34–40 Nm
25–29 ft.lbs.

24 Nm
17 ft.lbs.

45 Nm
33 ft.lbs.

19 Nm
14 ft.lbs.

6–8 Nm
4–6 ft.lbs.

40 Nm
29 ft.lbs.

1. Drain plug
2. Gasket
3. Oil filter
4. Oil pressure switch
5. Oil pan
6. Oil screen
7. Gasket
8. Oil filter bracket
9. Gasket
10. Relief plug
11. Gasket
12. Relief spring
13. Relief plunger
14. Plug cap
15. O-ring
16. Driven gear bolt
17. Front case
18. Gasket
19. Oil seal
20. Oil seal
21. Crankshaft front oil seal
22. Oil pump cover
23. Oil pump driven gear
24. Oil pump drive gear
25. Left silent shaft
26. Right silent shaft
27. Silent shaft front bearing
28. Right silent shaft rear bearing
29. Left silent shaft rear bearing

Exploded view of the oil pump, oil pan and related components—2.4L engine shown; other engines are similar

8. Clean or replace the oil pick-up screen and install with a new gasket.

9. Install or connect the following:
- Oil pan using a new gasket
- Timing sprockets, belts and covers
- Negative battery cable

10. Refill the engine with the proper amount of engine oil.

11. Start the engine and check for proper oil pressure. Check for leaks.

3.0L and 3.5L Engines

1. Before servicing the vehicle, refer to the precautions in the beginning of this section.

2. Drain the engine oil.

3. Remove or disconnect the following:
- Negative battery cable
- Timing belt
- Oil pressure switch

- Oil dipstick
- Oil pans from the engine
- Oil baffle and screen
- Oil pump mounting bolts and the pump from the front of the engine

➡ Note the position of each oil pump case retaining bolts to facilitate installation. The bolts are of different length.

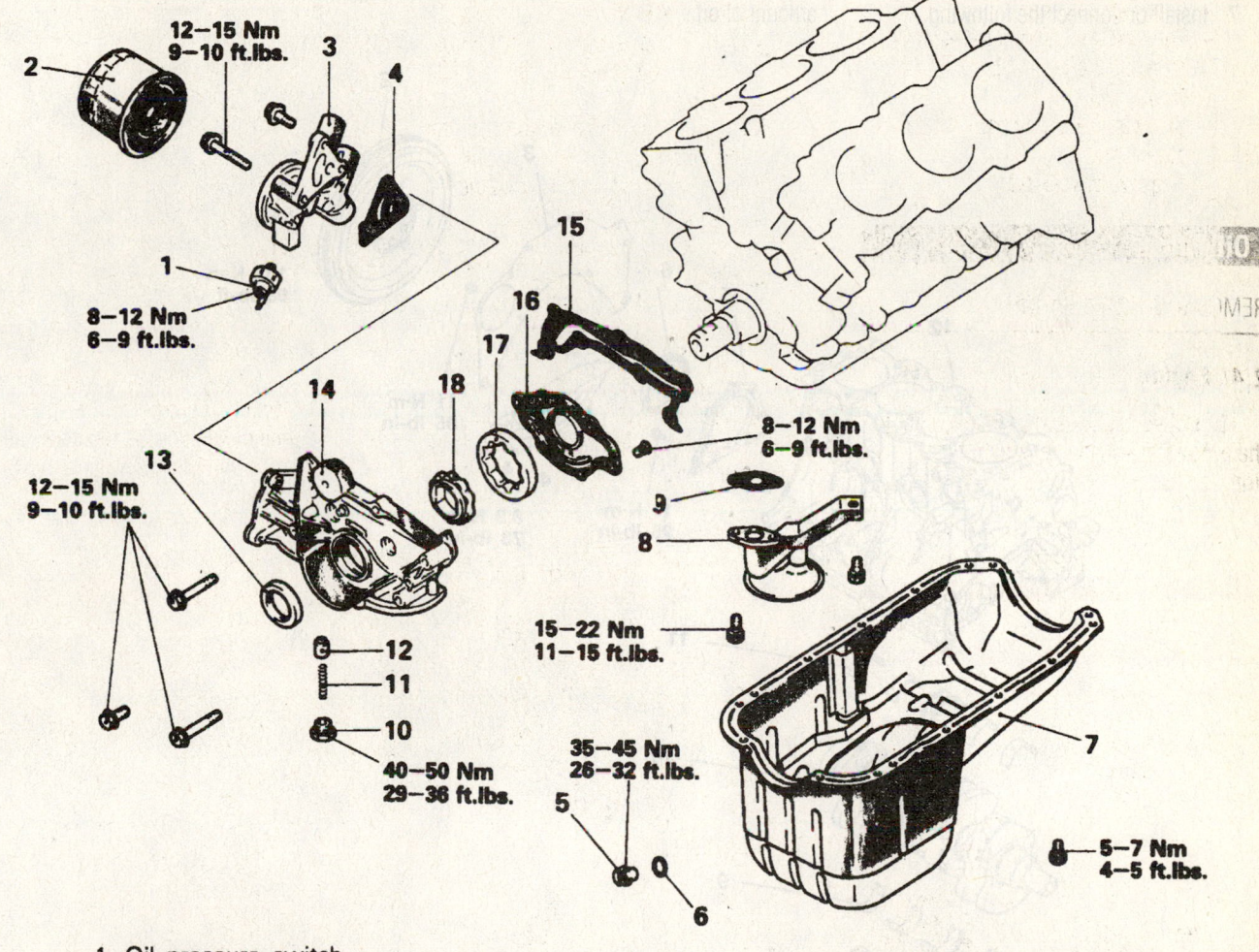

1. Oil pressure switch
2. Oil filter
3. Oil filter bracket
4. Oil filter bracket gasket
5. Drain plug
6. Drain plug gasket
7. Oil pan
8. Oil screen
9. Oil screen gasket
10. Plug
11. Relief spring
12. Relief plunger
13. Crankshaft front oil seal
14. Oil pump case
15. Oil pump gasket
16. Oil pump cover
17. Oil pump outer rotor
18. Oil pump inner rotor

Exploded view of the oil pump, oil pan and related components—2.4L engine shown; other engines are similar

7924UG19

To install:

4. Clean the gasket mounting surfaces of the pump and engine block.

5. Prime the pump by pouring fresh oil into the inlet and turning the rotors or by packing pump with petroleum jelly. Using a new gasket, install the oil pump on the engine and tighten all bolts to 10 ft. lbs. (14 Nm).

6. Clean out the oil pick-up or replace as required. Replace the oil pick-up gasket ring and install the pick-up to the pump.

7. Install or connect the following:

- Oil filter and the bracket. Torque the bolts to 17 ft. lbs. (23 Nm).
- Oil baffle and screen. Torque the bolts to 13 ft. lbs. (18 Nm).
- Oil pans. Torque the engines to 52 inch lbs. (5.9 Nm).
- Oil pressure switch. Torque the switch to 87 inch lbs. (9.8 Nm).
- Timing belt
- Dipstick
- Negative battery cable

8. Refill the engine with the proper amount of oil.

9. Start the engine and check for proper oil pressure. Check for leaks.

Rear Main Seal

REMOVAL & INSTALLATION

2.4L Engine

1. Before servicing the vehicle, refer to the precautions in the beginning of this section.

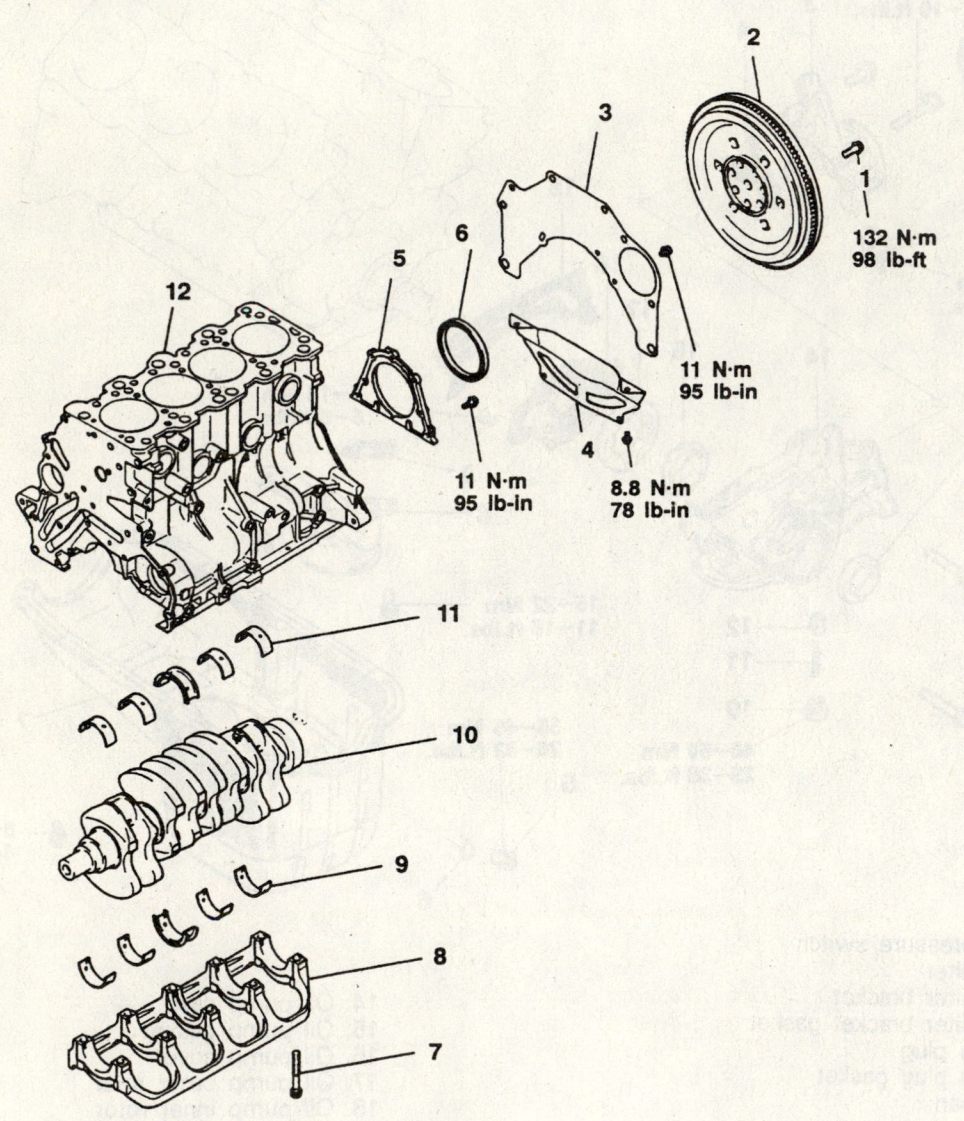

1. FLYWHEEL BOLT
2. FLYWHEEL
3. REAR PLATE
4. BELL HOUSING COVER
5. OIL SEAL CASE
6. OIL SEAL
7. BEARING CAP BOLT
8. BEARING CAP
9. CRANKSHAFT BEARING (LOWER)
10. CRANKSHAFT
11. CRANKSHAFT BEARING (UPPER)
12. CYLINDER BLOCK

Exploded view of the crankshaft, rear main seal, and related components—2.4L engines

7924UG20

2. Remove or disconnect the following:
- Transmission and clutch assembly, if equipped.
- Flywheel or the driveplate and the adapter plate, if equipped. Match-mark for reassembly.
- Oil seal

➡**Take care not to gouge or damage the metal surrounding the seal. Inspect the sealing surface at the rear of the crankshaft. If a deep groove is worn into the surface, the crankshaft will**

have to be replaced. Lubricate the sealing surface with clean engine oil.

To install:

3. Using a seal installer of the correct size, install the new seal into the bore of rear oil seal case. Make certain that the flat side of the seal will face outward when the case is installed on the engine. The inside of the seal must be flush with the inside surface of the seal case.

4. Install or connect the following:
- Rear plate and bell housing cover

- Flywheel or drive plate, observing the matchmarks made earlier
- Transmission and related components as necessary

3.0L and 3.5L Engines

1. Before servicing the vehicle, refer to the precautions in the beginning of this section.

2. Remove or disconnect the following:
- Transmission and clutch assembly, if so equipped.

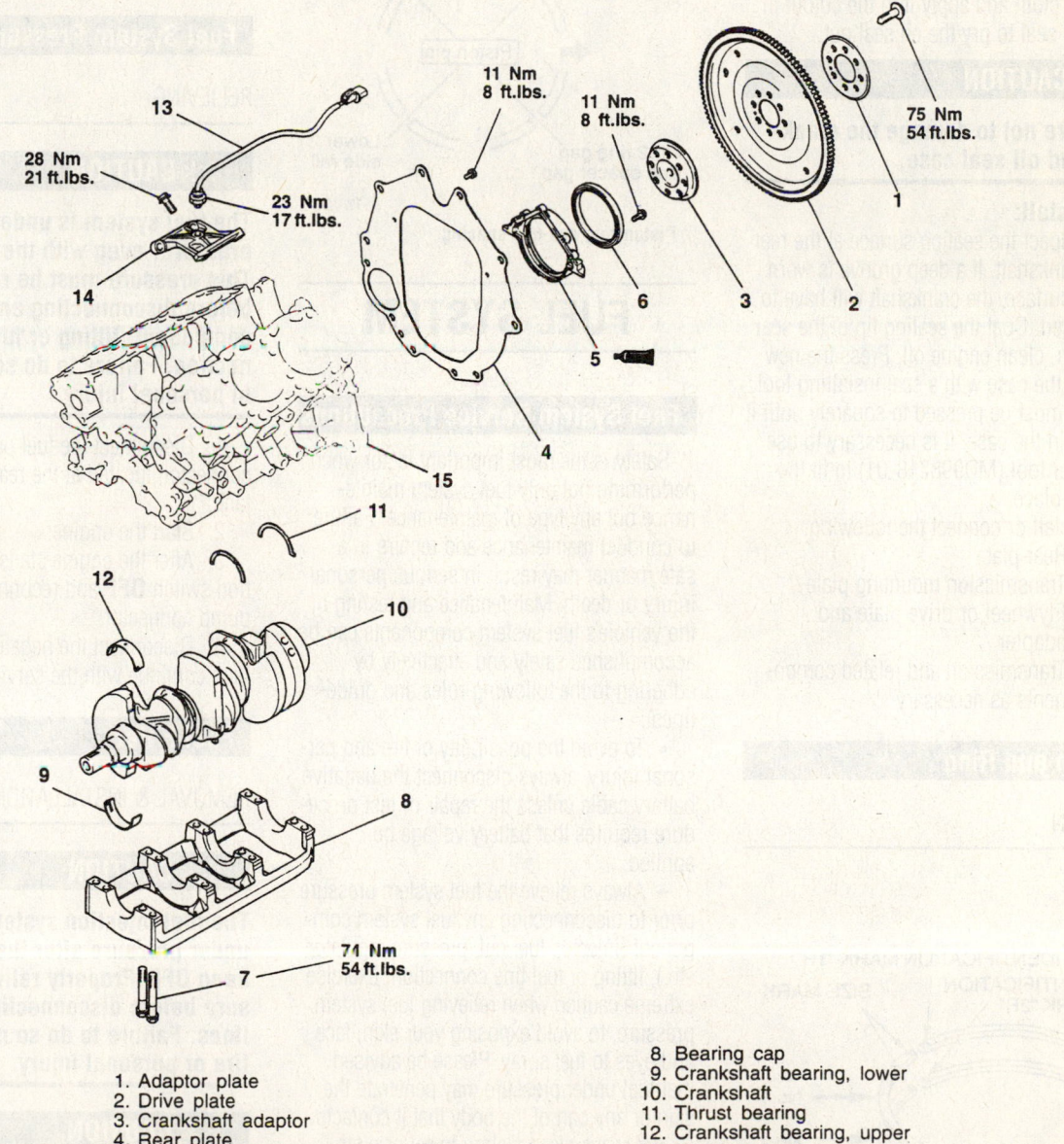

1. Adaptor plate
2. Drive plate
3. Crankshaft adaptor
4. Rear plate
5. Oil seal case
6. Crankshaft rear oil seal
7. Bearing cap bolt
8. Bearing cap
9. Crankshaft bearing, lower
10. Crankshaft
11. Thrust bearing
12. Crankshaft bearing, upper
13. Knock sensor
14. Knock sensor bracket
15. Cylinder block

7924UG22

Exploded view of the crankshaft, rear main seal and related components—3.5L engine shown; 3.0L engine is similar

Refer to Section 1 for engine rebuilding specifications

- Flywheel or driveplate and adapter plate, matchmark for reassembly. For the 3.0L engines, use the Mitsubishi tools (MB990767-01 and MIT308239) to hold the crankshaft and flywheel stationary while loosening the flywheel bolts. For the 3.5L engine, use Mitsubishi tool (MD998781) to hold the flywheel in position.
3. Remove the rear oil seal as follows:
   a. Cut out a portion in the crankshaft oil seal lip.
   b. Cover the tip of a small prytool with a cloth and apply it to the cutout in the oil seal to pry the oil seal out.

❊❊ CAUTION

Take care not to damage the crankshaft and oil seal case.

To install:

4. Inspect the sealing surface at the rear of the crankshaft. If a deep groove is worn into the surface, the crankshaft will have to be replaced. Coat the sealing lip of the seal with fresh, clean engine oil. Press the new seal into the case with a seal installing tool. The seal must be pressed in squarely until it bottoms in the case. It is necessary to use the proper tool (MD998718-01) to fit the seal into place.
5. Install or connect the following:
   - Rear plate
   - Transmission mounting plate
   - Flywheel or drive plate and adapter
   - Transmission and related components as necessary

Piston and Ring

POSITION

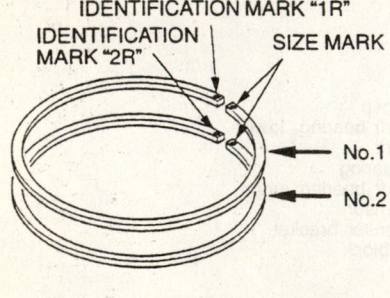

Piston ring identification

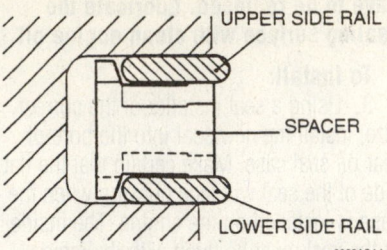

Oil ring identification

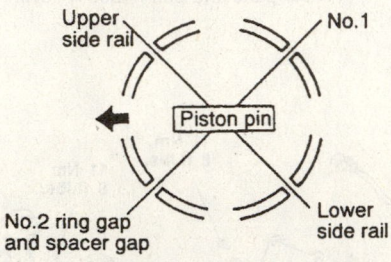

Piston ring end-gap spacing

FUEL SYSTEM

Fuel System Service Precautions

Safety is the most important factor when performing not only fuel system maintenance but any type of maintenance. Failure to conduct maintenance and repairs in a safe manner may result in serious personal injury or death. Maintenance and testing of the vehicle's fuel system components can be accomplished safely and effectively by adhering to the following rules and guidelines.

- To avoid the possibility of fire and personal injury, always disconnect the negative battery cable unless the repair or test procedure requires that battery voltage be applied.
- Always relieve the fuel system pressure prior to disconnecting any fuel system component (injector, fuel rail, pressure regulator, etc.), fitting or fuel line connection. Exercise extreme caution when relieving fuel system pressure, to avoid exposing your skin, face and eyes to fuel spray. Please be advised that fuel under pressure may penetrate the skin or any part of the body that it contacts.
- Always place a shop towel or cloth around the fitting or connection prior to loosening to absorb any excess fuel due to spillage. Ensure that all fuel spillage (should it occur) is quickly removed from engine surfaces. Ensure that all fuel soaked cloths or towels are deposited into a suitable waste container.

- Always keep a dry chemical (Class B) fire extinguisher near the work area.
- Do not allow fuel spray or fuel vapors to come into contact with a spark or open flame.
- Always use a back-up wrench when loosening and tightening fuel line connection fittings. This will prevent unnecessary stress and torsion to fuel line piping. Always follow the proper torque specifications.
- Always replace worn fuel fitting O-rings with new. Do not substitute fuel hose where fuel pipe is installed.

Fuel System Pressure

RELIEVING

❊❊ CAUTION

The fuel system is under constant pressure, even with the engine off. This pressure must be relieved before disconnecting any fuel system component, fitting or fuel line connection. Failure to do so may result in personal injury.

1. Disconnect the fuel pump electrical connector, located at the rear side of the fuel tank.
2. Start the engine.
3. After the engine stalls, turn the ignition switch **OFF** and reconnect the fuel pump connector.
4. Disconnect the negative battery cable, then continue with the service procedure.

Fuel Filter

REMOVAL & INSTALLATION

❊❊ CAUTION

The fuel injection system remains under pressure after the engine has been OFF. Properly relieve fuel pressure before disconnecting any fuel lines. Failure to do so may result in fire or personal injury.

❊❊ CAUTION

Do not allow fuel spray or fuel vapors to come in contact with a spark or open flame. Keep a dry chemical fire extinguisher nearby. Never store fuel in an open container due to risk of fire or explosion.

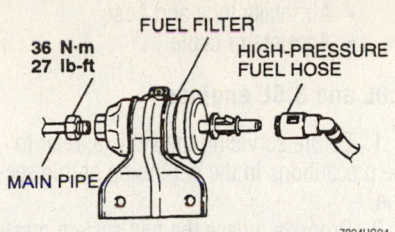

Fuel filter removal—Montero Sport shown

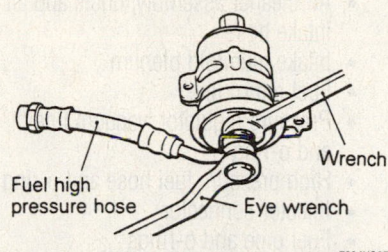

Always use a back-up wrench when removing or installing fuel lines to the filter

1. Relieve the fuel system pressure.
2. Before servicing the vehicle, refer to the precautions in the beginning of this section.
3. Disconnet the negative battery cable.
4. Remove the fuel filter protector if equipped.
5. Using a back-up wrench disconnect the fuel line(s) from the filter. If the filter uses a push-on type connector, press the retainer to release the connection.
6. Remove the filter from the mounting bracket.

To install:
7. Position the filter to the mounting bracket in the proper direction.
8. Connect the fuel lines to the filter. Use a back-up wrench to hold the fuel filter. Torque the banjo bolt(s) to 18–25 ft. lbs. (25–35 Nm) or the line fitting to 27 ft. lbs. (36 Nm).
9. Install the fuel filter protector if equipped.
10. Connect the negative battery cable.
11. Start the engine and check for leaks.

Fuel Pump

REMOVAL & INSTALLATION

Montero

➡The manufacturer recommends draining of the fuel tank.

1. Before servicing the vehicle, refer to the precautions in the beginning of this section.
2. Relieve the fuel system pressure.
3. Remove or disconnect the following:
   • Negative battery cable

☀ CAUTION

The fuel injection system remains under pressure after the engine has been OFF. Properly relieve fuel pressure before disconnecting any fuel lines. Failure to do so may result in fire or personal injury. Do not allow fuel spray or fuel vapors to come in contact with a spark or open flame. Keep a dry chemical fire extinguisher nearby. Never store fuel in an open container due to risk of fire or explosion.

   • Rear floor carpeting
   • Fuel pump cover
   • Fuel pump connector and the fuel hoses
   • Fuel pump assembly

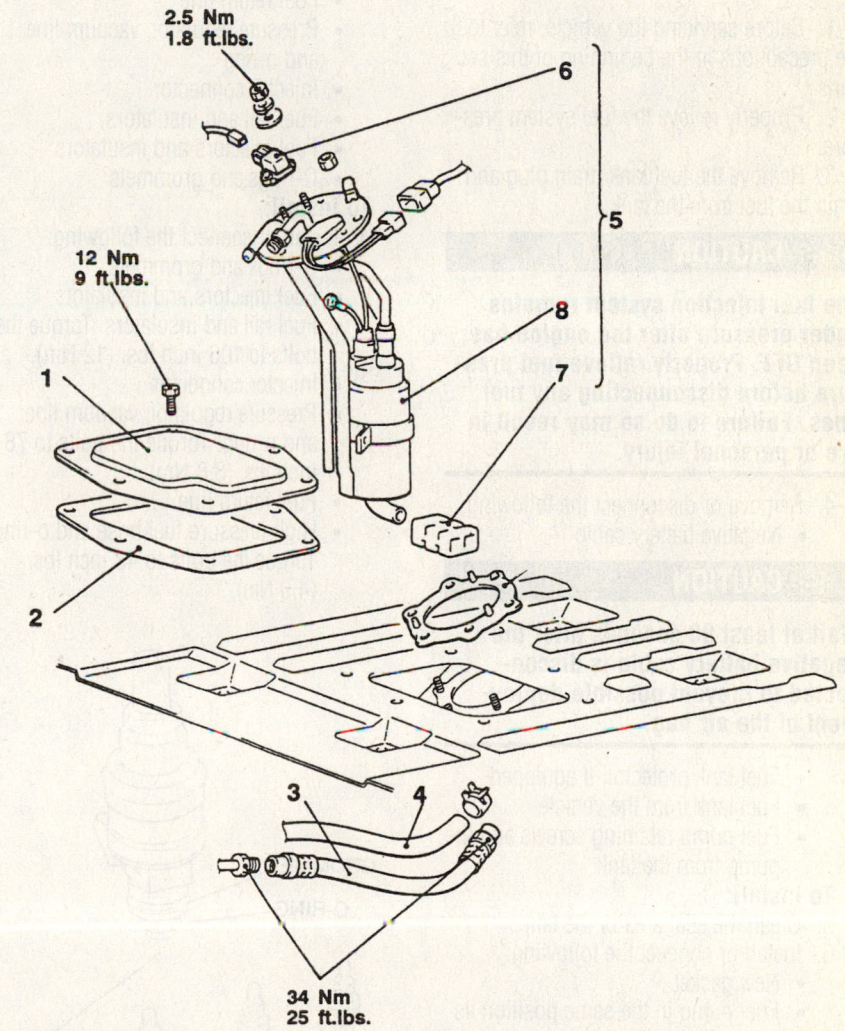

1. Floor cover
2. Packing
3. High-pressure fuel hose
4. Fuel return hose connection
5. Fuel pump and filter assembly
6. Fuel tank differential pressure sensor
7. Filter
8. Fuel pump assembly

The fuel pump on the Montero is removed through the rear floor pan

To install:

4. Install or connect the following:
   - Fuel pump assembly into the fuel tank. Torque the nuts to 24 inch lbs. (2.5 Nm).
   - Fuel lines and the fuel pump connector.
   - Fuel pump cover. Torque the bolts to 108 inch lbs. (12 Nm).
   - Rear floor carpeting.
   - Negative battery cable
5. Refill the fuel tank, if drained
6. Start the vehicle; check for leaks and proper operation.

Montero Sport

1. Before servicing the vehicle, refer to the precautions in the beginning of this section.
2. Properly relieve the fuel system pressure.
3. Remove the fuel tank drain plug and drain the fuel from the tank.

❊❊ CAUTION

The fuel injection system remains under pressure after the engine has been OFF. Properly relieve fuel pressure before disconnecting any fuel lines. Failure to do so may result in fire or personal injury.

4. Remove or disconnect the following:
   - Negative battery cable

❊❊ CAUTION

Wait at least 90 seconds after the negative battery cable is disconnected to prevent possible deployment of the air bag.

   - Fuel tank protector, if equipped
   - Fuel tank from the vehicle
   - Fuel pump retaining screws and the pump from the tank

To install:

5. Clean the seal area of the tank.
6. Install or connect the following:
   - New gasket
   - Fuel pump in the same position as originally installed.
   - Fuel pump retaining screws, Torque the nuts to 22 inch lbs. (2.5 Nm).
   - Fuel tank. Torque the bolts to 20 ft. lbs. (27 Nm).
   - Fuel tank drain plug and the fuel tank protector, if equipped
   - Negative battery cable
7. Refill the fuel tank and install the cap.
8. Check fuel system for leaks.

Fuel Injector

REMOVAL & INSTALLATION

2.4L engines

1. Before servicing the vehicle, refer to the precautions in the beginning of this section.
2. Properly relieve the fuel system pressure.
3. Remove or disconnect the following:
   - Accelerator cable
   - Air intake tube and hose
   - High pressure fuel hose and o-ring
   - Fuel return line
   - Pressure regulator, vacuum line and o-ring
   - Injector connector
   - Fuel rail and insulators
   - Fuel injectors and insulators
   - O-rings and grommets

To install:
4. Install or connect the following:
   - O-rings and grommets
   - Fuel injectors and insulators
   - Fuel rail and insulators. Torque the bolts to 106 inch lbs. (12 Nm).
   - Injector connector
   - Pressure regulator, vacuum line and o-ring. Torque the bolts to 78 inch lbs. (8.8 Nm).
   - Fuel return line
   - High pressure fuel hose and o-ring. Torque the bolts to 43 inch lbs. (4.9 Nm).

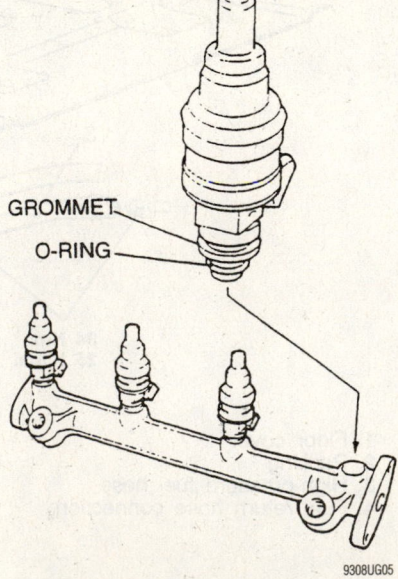

GROMMET
O-RING

9308UG05

Exploded view of fuel injector and rail on 2.4L engines other engines are similar

   - Air intake tube and hose
   - Accelerator cable

3.0L and 3.5L engines

1. Before servicing the vehicle, refer to the precautions in the beginning of this section.
2. Properly relieve the fuel system pressure.
3. Remove or disconnect the following:
   - Air cleaner assembly, ducts and air intake hose
   - Intake manifold plenum
   - Fuel return line
   - Pressure regulator, vacuum line and o-ring
   - High pressure fuel hose and o-ring
   - Injector connector
   - Fuel pipe and o-rings
   - Fuel rails and insulators
   - Fuel injectors and insulators
   - O-rings and grommets

To install:
4. Install or connect the following:
   - O-rings and grommets
   - Fuel injectors and insulators
   - Fuel rail and insulators. Torque the bolts to 106 inch lbs. (12 Nm).
   - Injector connector
   - High pressure fuel hose and o-ring. Torque the bolts to 43 inch lbs. (4.9 Nm).
   - Pressure regulator, vacuum line and o-ring. Torque the bolts to 78 inch lbs. (8.8 Nm).
   - Fuel return line
   - Intake manifold plenum
   - Air cleaner assembly, ducts and air intake hose

DRIVE TRAIN

Transmission Assembly

REMOVAL & INSTALLATION

1. Before servicing the vehicle, refer to the precautions in the beginning of this section.
2. Drain the transmission fluid.
3. Remove or disconnect the following:
   - Negative battery cable
   - Transmission and transfer case shift lever assembly. On manual transmissions
   - Transfer case protector, if equipped

- Front exhaust pipe from the 2 exhaust manifolds, then disconnect it from the intermediate pipe/catalytic converter (make certain to retain the bolts and nuts for reassembly).
- Rear driveshaft at both the rear axle and the transfer case flanges. Matchmark for reassembly.
- Front driveshaft from the front axle, by sliding it forward, plug the transfer case to prevent residual fluid leakage. On 4-wheel drive vehicles
- Dust seal from the rear extension housing.
- Ground cables
- 4WD indicator light switch connector
- Pulse generator connector
- Speed Sensor Connector
- Oxygen (O₂S) sensor connector
- Back-up light switch connector
- HI/LO detection switch connector
- Center differential lock detection switch connection.

There may be others depending on the particular year, model and engine with which the vehicle came equipped.

4. Remove or disconnect the following:
- Speedometer cable out of the transmission

5. On manual transmissions:

6. Remove or disconnect the following:
- Clutch cylinder heat protector
- Clutch release cylinder (with the clutch hose connected to it) from the transmission. Suspend it from the body by using a piece of wire or a similarly safe method.
- Starter motor and the heat shield

7. On automatic transmissions:

8. Remove or disconnect the following:
- Bolts attaching the torque converter to the flexplate
- Dipstick
- Fluid cooling lines
- Shift linkage at the transmission

9. Place a floor jack and a block of wood below the engine oil pan.

10. Lift the floor jack under the engine just until the weight of the engine is taken onto the jack—the engine should only barely be lifted by the jack.

11. Use a transmission jack or second floor jack to place under the transmission. Don't support the transmission yet, only lift the jack until it is slightly below the transmission.

12. Remove or disconnect the following:
- Left-hand and right-hand side transmission stays from the front of the transmission, if equipped
- Bell housing lower cover
- Transfer case mounting bracket, if equipped

13. Lift the floor jack up until the transmission is being slightly supported by it.

14. Remove or disconnect the following:
- Transmission-to-crossmember bolts. Lift the jack about ¼ in. (6mm) off of the crossmember support.
- Crossmember from the vehicle
- Transmission mounting blots. Pull the transmission away from the engine and lower it from the vehicle.

To install:

15. Lift the transmission and transfer assembly into position with the floor jack.

16. On the engine side, there are 2 centering locations. Be sure that the transmission mounting bolt holes are aligned with them before mounting the transmission and transfer assembly to the engine. Lowering the rear of the engine SLIGHTLY may help align the 2 assemblies.

17. Install or connect the following:
- Transmission assembly onto the engine making sure the aligning areas stay aligned. Torque the bolts to 54 ft. lbs. (75 Nm).

18. Lift the transmission/transfer assembly with the floor jack. Since the engine is now attached to the transmission, it also will rise slightly. Adjust its jack to keep only slight support.

19. Install or connect the following:
- Crossmember in place and secure with the mounting bolts. Torque the bolts to 47 ft. lbs. (65 Nm).
- Transmission and transfer case assembly onto the crossmember
- Crossmember-to-transmission bolts. Torque the bolts to 15–18 ft. lbs. (20–24 Nm) on Montero sport and to 36 ft. lbs. (49 Nm) on Montero.
- Mounting bracket back onto the transfer case, if equipped
- Bell housing lower cover
- Left-hand and right-hand side transmission stays
- Starter motor and heat shield
- Clutch release cylinder
- Speedometer cable into the transmission and secure it there with the retaining ring.

- Center differential lock detection switch connection
- HI/LO detection switch connector
- Back-up light switch connector
- O₂S sensor connector
- Speed Sensor Connector
- Pulse generator connector
- 4WD indicator light switch connector
- Ground cables
- Flexplate-to-torque converter bolts. Torque the bolts to 25–30 ft. lbs. (35–42 Nm). On automatic transmissions
- Dipstick tube
- Shift linkage
- Fluid cooler lines. Torque the line fittings to 32 ft. lbs. (44 Nm). On automatic transmissions

20. Tap the dust seal guard back onto the rear extension housing with a rubber or plastic mallet.

21. Install or connect the following:
- Front driveshaft into the transfer case, then attach it to the front differential
- Rear driveshaft, make certain that the matchmarks line up.
- Front exhaust pipe to the catalytic converter and the exhaust manifolds
- Transfer case protector, if equipped
- Transmission and transfer case shift lever assembly. On manual transmissions
- Negative battery cable to the battery

22. Refill the transmission and transfer case with oil.

23. Start the vehicle and check for any leaks.

Clutch

REMOVAL & INSTALLATION

1. Before servicing the vehicle, refer to the precautions in the beginning of this section.

2. Remove or disconnect the following:
- Negative battery cable
- Transmission assembly

3. Insert a suitable tool in the flywheel pilot bearing hole to keep the clutch disc from falling off. Loosen the clutch cover retainer bolts gradually in a crisscross fashion.

4. Remove or disconnect the following:
- Clutch cover and disc

1. Clutch cover assembly
2. Clutch disc
3. Return clip
4. Clutch release bearing
5. Release fork
6. Fulcrum
7. Release fork boot

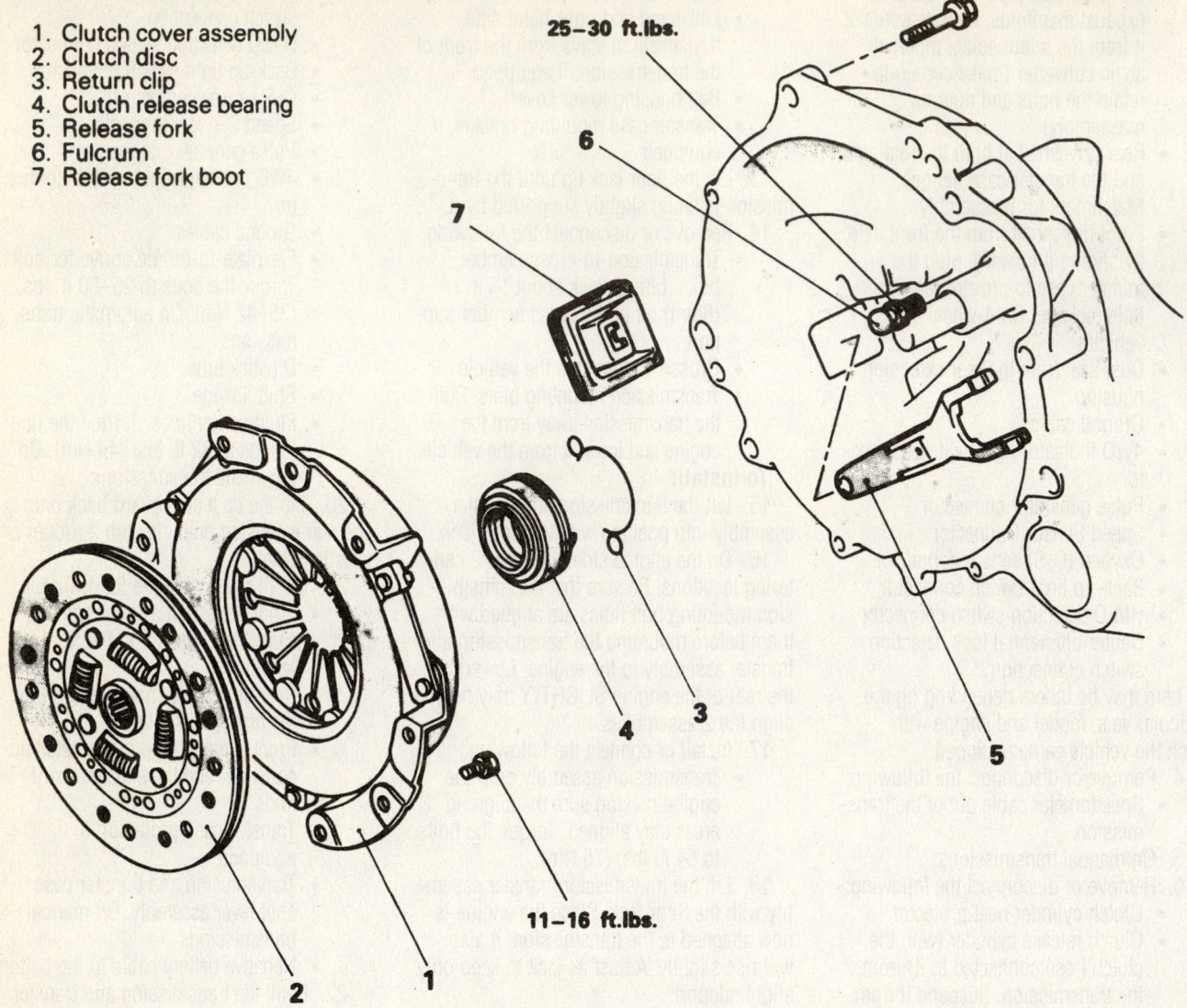

25-30 ft.lbs.

11-16 ft.lbs.

Exploded view of the typical clutch assembly components

7924UG29

5. Check the release bearing for scorching, damage or strange noise. Replace, if necessary.

6. Inspect the flywheel surface for heat cracks or scoring. Reface or replace the flywheel as required.

To install:

7. Apply high temperature grease to the clutch disc splines, input shaft, contact points of the release fork and inside diameter of the release bearing.

➡**Do not allow oil or grease to contact the clutch facing and pressure plate.**

8. Install or connect the following:
   • Flywheel, align using a suitable tool

➡**When installing the clutch disc, be sure that the surface having the manufacturer's stamped mark is on the pressure plate side.**

   • Clutch cover with the dowel pin holes in alignment with the dowel pins in the flywheel and tighten the bolt gradually in a crisscross fashion. Torque the bolts to 14 ft. lbs. (19 Nm).
   • Transmission assembly
   • Negative battery cable
9. Road test the vehicle for proper operation.

Hydraulic Clutch System

BLEEDING

❊❊ WARNING

When bleeding, keep the facial area well away from the slave cylinder and protect all painted surfaces from

fluid contact. Brake fluid will damage painted surfaces and could cause physical injury.

1. Fill the clutch master cylinder with fresh DOT 3 brake fluid.
2. Have a helper sit in the vehicle.
3. Remove the bleeder screw cap.
4. If the system is empty, the most efficient way to get fluid down to the cylinder is:
   a. Loosen the bleeder about ½ – ¾ turn
   b. Place a finger firmly over the bleeder
   c. Have a helper pump the brakes slowly until fluid pressure is felt at the bleeder
   d. Once fluid is at the bleeder, close it before the pedal is released.

➥ **If the pedal is pumped rapidly, the fluid will churn and create small air bubbles, which are difficult and time consuming to remove from the system. These air bubbles will eventually congregate and will result in a spongy pedal.**

5. Once fluid has been pumped to the slave cylinder:
- Open the bleeder screw
- Have a helper depress the clutch pedal
- Lock the bleeder and have the helper release the pedal
- Wait 15 seconds and repeat the procedure (including the 15 second wait) until no air bubbles flow from the bleeder.

Remember to close the bleeder before the pedal is released. If the bleeder is left open when the pedal is released, air will be induced into the system.

6. If a helper is not available, connect a small hose to the bleeder, submerge the other end in a clean container of fresh brake fluid placed in a position that is visible from the driver's seat. Pump the pedal until no air comes out of the tube.

Transfer Case Assembly

REMOVAL & INSTALLATION

The transfer case is removed from the vehicle along with the transmission. Refer to the Transmission Removal and Installation procedure for information.

Halfshaft

REMOVAL & INSTALLATION

Outer Axle Shafts

1. Before servicing the vehicle, refer to the precautions in the beginning of this section.
2. Remove or disconnect the following:
- Negative battery cable
- Undercover
- Wheels
- Hub cover dust cap
- Snapring from the inside of the hub and the shim
- Front brake caliper assembly and support with mechanics wire
- Speed sensor, if equipped with ABS
- Tie rod from the steering knuckle assembly

- Upper and lower ball joints from the steering knuckle assembly
- Front hub/knuckle assembly with the inner and outer bearings intact
3. On the left side, pull the halfshaft from the differential carrier.
4. For the right side, remove the fasteners and the halfshaft from the vehicle.

To install:
5. Install or connect the following:
- New circlip, on the left side halfshaft
- Inner shaft. Torque the nuts to 36–43 ft. lbs. (49–59 Nm), on the right side halfshaft
- Front hub/knuckle and bearing assembly
- Upper ball joint to the knuckle. Torque the nut to 54 ft. lbs. (74 Nm).
- Lower ball joint to knuckle. Torque the nut to 108 ft. lbs. (147 Nm).
- New cotter pins
- Tie rod end to the steering knuckle. Torque the nut to 33 ft. lbs. (44 Nm) and a new cotter pin.
- Speed sensor, if removed
- Front brake assembly
- Shim and snapring to the axle shaft. Install the front hub dust cover
- Wheels and the undercover
- Negative battery cable

Inner Axle Shafts

1. Before servicing the vehicle, refer to the precautions in the beginning of this section.
2. Remove or disconnect the following:
- Negative battery cable
- Undercover
- Right side wheel
- Right outer halfshaft
- Lower shock absorber mounting bolts
- Inner shaft from housing, using a slide hammer with tool MB990241

To install:
3. Install or connect the following:
- New circlip on the inner halfshaft
- Inner shaft into the housing, drive the axle into position.
- Lower shock absorber mounting bolts. Torque the bolts to 65–76 ft. lbs. (88–103 Nm).
- Right halfshaft assembly
- Undercover
- Wheel
- Negative battery cable

CV-Joints

OVERHAUL

1. Before servicing the vehicle, refer to the precautions in the beginning of this section.
2. Remove or disconnect the following:
- Front wheel
- Driveshaft from the car
- Small and larger band
- Circlip
- Double Offset Joint (DOJ) outer race
- Dust cover
- Circlip
- Balls from the cage
- Cage from the inner race. Turn the cage so that the projections of the inner race align with the recesses of the cage.
- Snapring from the shaft
- DOJ inner race
- Slide the boot off
- Birfield Joint (BJ) small and larger bands
- BJ boot
- BJ assembly

To install:
3. Check the shaft and splines for damage or wear. Inspect the cage, race and balls for any sign of corrosion, wear, cracking or damage. Clean all the parts thoroughly and air dry them completely before installation. Any remaining cleaning solvent can dissolve the lubricating grease.

4. Tool MB991561 can be used to crimp the bands in place.

5. Install or connect the following:
- BJ assembly
- BJ boot, slid the small end of the boot until only one shaft groove cone be seen.
- BJ small band, crimp the band. Fill the BJ boot with 4.6 oz (130 g) of grease.
- BJ larger band, crimp the band
- DOJ small band and boot, fill the boot with grease
- DOJ cage onto the driveshaft so that the smaller diameter side is installed first.
- Circlip
- DOJ inner race and new snap ring, apply grease to the inner race
- Balls into the cage, grease to the ball areas of the cage and race
- Outer race, fill the outer race about ⅓ full of grease.

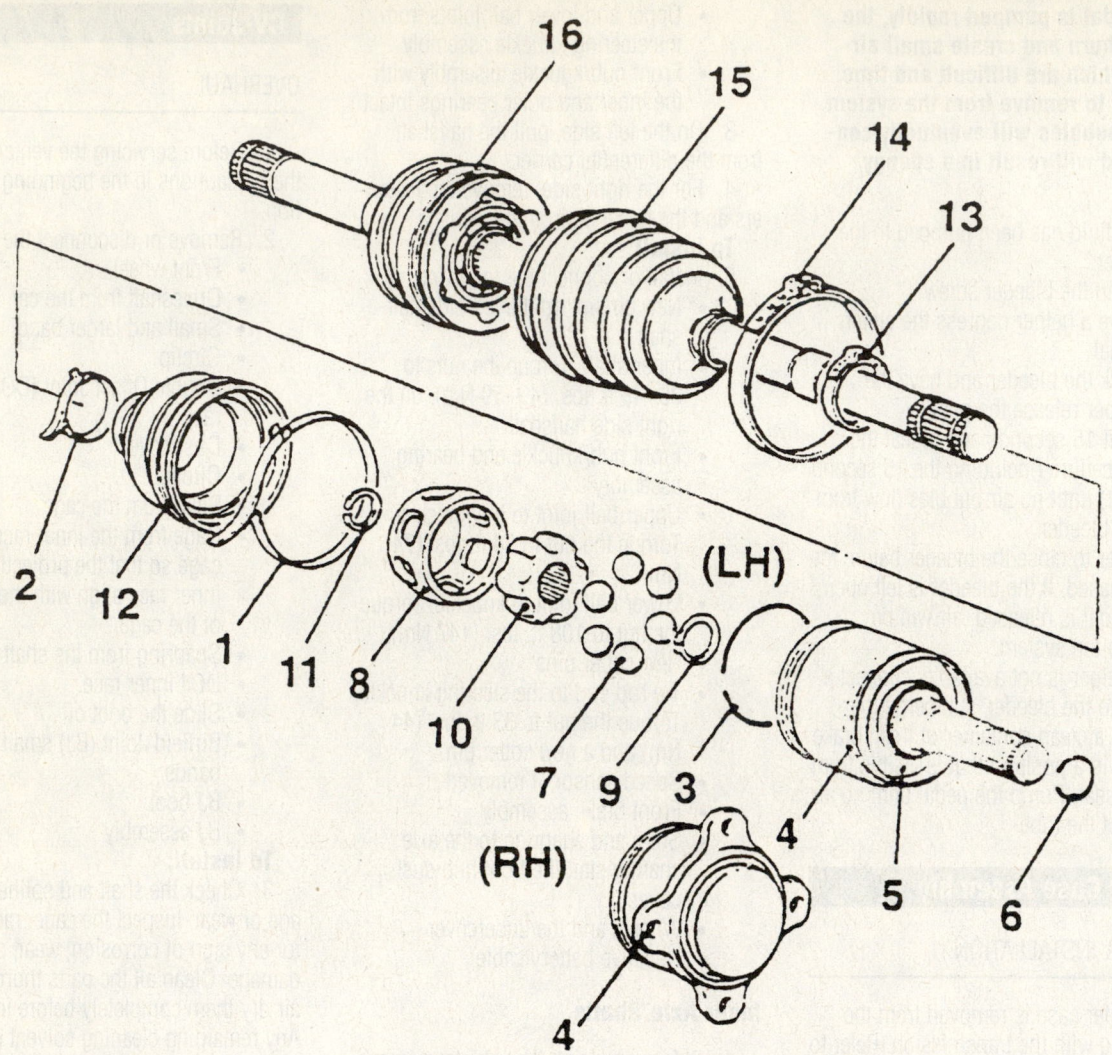

(LH)

(RH)

1. D.O.J. boot band (large)
2. D.O.J. boot band (small)
3. Circlip
4. D.O.J. outer race
5. Dust cover
6. Circlip
7. Ball
8. D.O.J. cage
9. Snap ring
10. D.O.J. inner race
11. Circlip
12. D.O.J. boot
13. B.J. boot band (small)
14. B.J. boot band (large)
15. B.J. boot
16. B.J. assembly

9308UG06

CV-Joint, exploded view

- Dust cover
- Circlip
- Large boot band, release the air from the boot then crimp
- Driveshaft into the car

Automatic Locking Hubs

REMOVAL & INSTALLATION

1. Place the locking hub in the free position. To do this, shift the transfer shift lever to the 2H position, then move the vehicle 4–7 ft. (1–2 m) backwards.
2. Before servicing the vehicle, refer to the precautions in the beginning of this section.
3. Remove or disconnect the following:
   - Front wheels of the vehicle
   - Hub cover
   - Snapring from the axle shaft

- Shim
- Drive flange
- Front brake assembly
- Speed sensor, if equipped
- Lock washer
- Lock nut
- Front hub assembly

To install:

4. Install or connect the following:
   - Front hub assembly
   - Lock nut. Torque the nut as follows:
   a. Step 1: Torque the nut to 119 ft. lbs. (162 Nm).
   b. Step 2: Loosen to 0 ft. lbs. (0 Nm).
   c. Step 3: Torque the nut to 18 ft lbs. (25 Nm).
   d. Step 4: Loosen the nut 30–40 degrees.
5. Install or connect the following:
   - Lock washer
   - Speed sensor, if equipped

- Front brake assembly. Torque the bolts to 65 ft. lbs. (88 Nm).
- Drive flange. Torque the bolts to 36–43 ft. lbs. (49–59 Nm).
- Shim
- Snapring to the axle shaft
- Hub cover
- Front wheels of the vehicle

Axle shaft, Bearing and Seal

REMOVAL & INSTALLATION

Front

1. Before servicing the vehicle, refer to the precautions in the beginning of this section.
2. Remove or disconnect the following:
   - Wheel assembly
   - Brake caliber

Removal steps

1. Cover
   Adjustment of drive shaft end play
2. Snap ring
3. Shim
4. Front brake assembly

5. Bolts
6. Automatic free-wheeling hub assembly
7. Shim
8. Lock washer
9. Lock nut
10. Front hub assembly

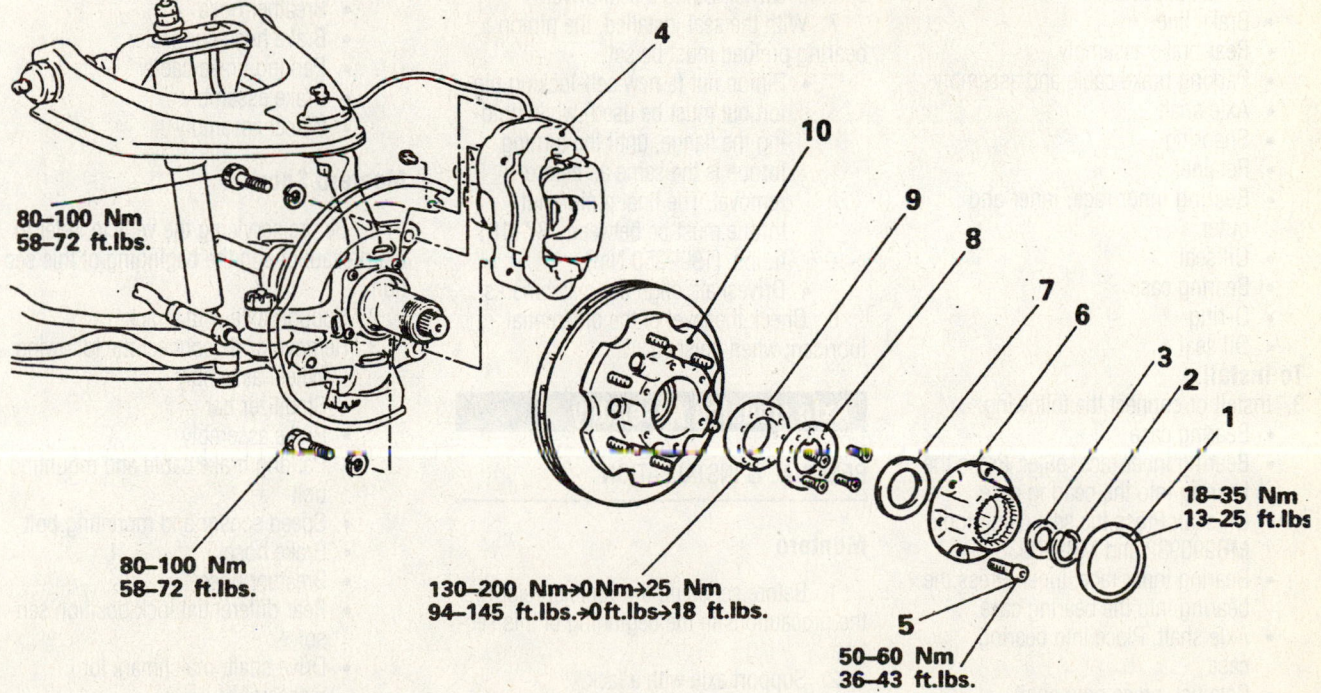

80–100 Nm
58–72 ft.lbs.

80–100 Nm
58–72 ft.lbs.

130–200 Nm→0Nm→25 Nm
94–145 ft.lbs.→0ft.lbs.→18 ft.lbs.

50–60 Nm
36–43 ft.lbs.

18–35 Nm
13–25 ft.lbs

7924UG45B

Axle hub and locking hub removal and installation—automatic hubs

Turn to Section 5 for brake system applications

- Hub and knuckle assembly
- Drive shaft
- Shock absorber lower mounting nut/bolt
- Inner shaft
- Dust cover
- Bearing, press the bearing off
- Seal

To install:

3. Install or connect the following:
- Seal, press the seal on with tool MB990938 and MB990955 until it is flush
- Dust cover, use a steel pipe to fit the cover onto the shaft
- Bearing, Press the bearing onto the inner shaft
- Inner shaft
- Drive shaft. Torque the nuts to 36–43 ft. lbs. (49–59 Nm).
- Shock absorber lower mounting nut/bolt
- Hub and knuckle assembly
- Brake caliber
- Wheel assembly

Rear

1. Before servicing the vehicle, refer to the precautions in the beginning of this section.

2. Remove or disconnect the following:
- Wheel assembly
- Brake line
- Rear brake assembly
- Parking brake cable and assembly
- Axle shaft
- Snapring
- Retainer
- Bearing inner race, inner and outer
- Oil seal
- Bearing case
- O-ring
- Oil seal

To install:

3. Install or connect the following:
- Bearing case
- Bearing inner race, outer. Press the bearing into the bearing case.
- Oil seal. Press the seal using tools MB990932 and MB990938.
- Bearing inner race, inner. Press the bearing into the bearing case.
- Axle shaft, Place into bearing case
- Retainer, press onto shaft
- Snapring
- Oil seal and O-ring into axle shaft
4. Axle shaft assembly into axle.
- Parking brake cable end
- Parking brake cable attaching bolt

- Rear brake assembly
- Brake line
- Wheel assembly

Pinion Seal

REMOVAL & INSTALLATION

1. Before servicing the vehicle, refer to the precautions in the beginning of this section.
2. Remove or disconnect the following:
- Driveshaft, matchmark for reassembly
3. Check the turning torque of the pinion before proceeding. It should be 2.6–4.5 inch lbs. (0.4–0.5 Nm). This is the torque that must be reached during installation of the pinion nut.
- Pinion nut and washer using a suitable pinion flange holding tool
- Companion flange from the drive pinion
4. Pry the pinion seal out of the differential carrier.

To install:

5. Clean and inspect the sealing surface of the housing.
6. Install or connect the following:
- New seal into the housing until the flange on the seal is flush with the carrier. Using a seal driver.
7. With the seal installed, the pinion bearing preload must be set.
- Pinion nut (a new self-locking pinion nut must be used) while holding the flange, until the turning torque is the same as before removal. The final pinion nut torque must be between 137–181 ft. lbs. (190–250 Nm).
- Driveshaft, align the matchmarks
8. Check the level of the differential lubricant when finished.

Axle Housing Assembly

REMOVAL & INSTALLATION

Montero

1. Before servicing the vehicle, refer to the precautions in the beginning of this section.
2. Support axle with a jack.
3. Remove or disconnect the following:
- Wheel assembly
- Brake assembly
- Parking brake cable
- Brake hose connector

- Breather hose
- Spring support for load sensing proportioning valve
- Rear differential lock position harness connector
- Speed sensor
- Drive shaft, matchmark for reassembly
- Stabilizer bar
- Lower arm
- Lateral rod
- Lower shock absorber mounting bolt
- Axle assembly

To install:

4. Install or connect the following:
- Axle assembly
- Lower shock absorber mounting bolt. Torque the bolts to 159–181 ft. lbs. (216–245 Nm).
- Lateral rod. Torque the bolts to 159–181 ft. lbs. (216–245 Nm).
- Lower arm
- Stabilizer bar mounting bolt. Torque the bolts to 25 ft. lbs. (34 Nm).
- Drive shaft, align matchmark
- Speed sensor
- Rear differential lock position harness connector
- Spring support for load sensing proportioning valve
- Breather hose
- Brake hose connector
- Parking brake cable
- Brake assembly
- Wheel assembly

Montero Sport

1. Before servicing the vehicle, refer to the precautions in the beginning of this section.
2. Support axle with a jack.
3. Remove or disconnect the following:
- Wheel assembly
- Stabilizer bar
- Brake assembly
- Parking brake cable and mounting bolt
- Speed sensor and mounting bolt
- Brake hose
- Breather hose
- Rear differential lock position sensor
- Drive shaft, matchmark for reassembly
- Shock absorber
- U-bolt and seat
- Bump stopper
- Shackle assembly
- Axle assembly

To install:
4. Install or connect the following:
- Axle assembly
- Shackle assembly
- Bump stopper
- U-bolt and seat
- Shock absorber. Torque the bolt to 16 ft. lbs. (22 Nm).
- Drive shaft, matchmark for reassembly
- Rear differential lock position sensor
- Breather hose
- Brake hose. Torque the tube to 11 ft. lbs. (15 Nm).
- Speed sensor and mounting bolt
- Parking brake cable and mounting bolt
- Brake assembly
- Stabilizer bar. Torque the mounting bolt to 26 ft lbs. (35 Nm).
- Wheel assembly

STEERING AND SUSPENSION

Air Bag

❋❋ CAUTION

Some vehicles are equipped with an air bag system. The system must be disabled before performing service on or around system components, steering column, instrument panel components, wiring and sensors. Failure to follow safety and disabling procedures could result in accidental air bag deployment, possible personal injury and unnecessary system repairs.

PRECAUTIONS

Several precautions must be observed when handling the inflator module to avoid accidental deployment and possible personal injury.
- Never carry the inflator module by the wires or connector on the underside of the module.
- When carrying a live inflator module, hold securely with both hands, and ensure that the bag and trim cover are pointed away.

- Place the inflator module on a bench or other surface with the bag and trim cover facing up.
- With the inflator module on the bench, never place anything on or close to the module that may be thrown in the event of an accidental deployment.

DISARMING

To avoid personal injury when working on vehicles equipped with an air bag, the negative battery cable must be disconnected and at least 60 seconds must elapse before working on the system. Failure to do so may result in deployment of the air bag.

Recirculating Ball Power Steering Gear

REMOVAL & INSTALLATION

1. On vehicles equipped with a supplemental restraint system (SRS), turn the front wheel to the straight ahead position and remove the ignition key to prevent the steering wheel from turning.

2. Drain the power steering fluid.
3. Remove or disconnect the following:
- Negative battery cable
- Pinch bolt securing the steering shaft to the steering gear
- Pitman arm from the relay rod
- Fluid lines from the steering gear
- Mounting bolts securing the gear to the frame rail and steering gear

To install:
4. Install or connect the following:
- Steering gear on the frame rail. Torque the nuts to 40–47 ft. lbs. (54–64 Nm).
- Fluid lines to the steering gear use a new O-rings. Torque the fittings to 11 ft. lbs. (15 Nm).
- Relay rod on the Pitman arm. Torque the nut to 33 ft. lbs. (44 Nm).
- Steering shaft on the steering gear. Torque the bolt to 13 ft. lbs. (18 Nm).
- Negative battery cable
5. Refill and bleed the power steering system.

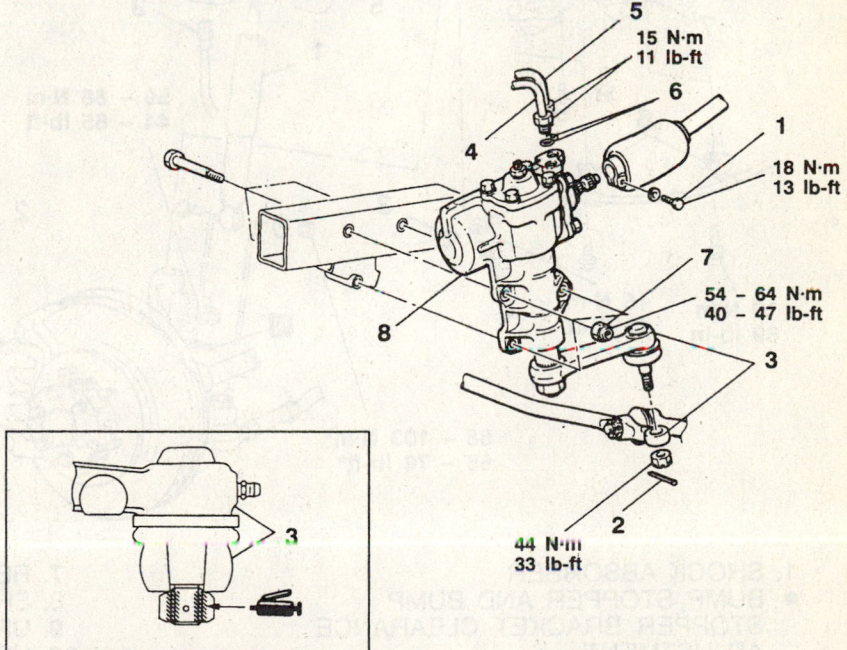

1. CONNECTING BOLT FOR STEERING GEAR BOX AND STEERING SHAFT
2. COTTER PIN
3. CONNECTION FOR PITMAN ARM AND RELAY ROD

4. PRESSURE TUBE
5. RETURN TUBE
6. O-RING
7. SELF-LOCKING NUT
8. POWER STEERING GEAR BOX

Exploded view of a typical power steering gear mounting

7924UG33

Shock Absorber

REMOVAL & INSTALLATION

Front

1. Before servicing the vehicle, refer to the precautions in the beginning of this section.

2. Remove the upper shock mounting nut, washer and bushing.

3. Remove the lower mounting bolts.

4. Remove the shock absorber.

To install:

➡ If the shock absorber has a white paint mark on the lower end, be sure the mark faces the outside of the vehicle when installed.

5. Install the shock absorber. Torque the lower nut to 65–76 ft. lbs. (88–103 Nm) and the upper nut to 11 ft. lbs. (15 Nm).

6. Test drive the vehicle and check the alignment.

Rear

1. Before servicing the vehicle, refer to the precautions in the beginning of this section.

2. Support the rear axle assembly with a hydraulic floor jack, so that the shock absorber may be removed.

3. Remove the upper and lower mounting nuts and bolts that attach the shock to the frame and bracket.

4. Remove the shock absorber from the vehicle.

To install:

5. Install the shock absorber. Torque the lower bolt to 159–181 ft. lbs. (216–245 Nm) on the Montero and 16 ft. lbs. (22 Nm) on the Montero sport.

6. Install the upper mounting nut. Tighten the nut to 11 ft. lbs. (15 Nm) on the Montero and 16 ft. lbs. (22 Nm) on the Montero Sport.

7. Remove the floor jack from under the axle assembly.

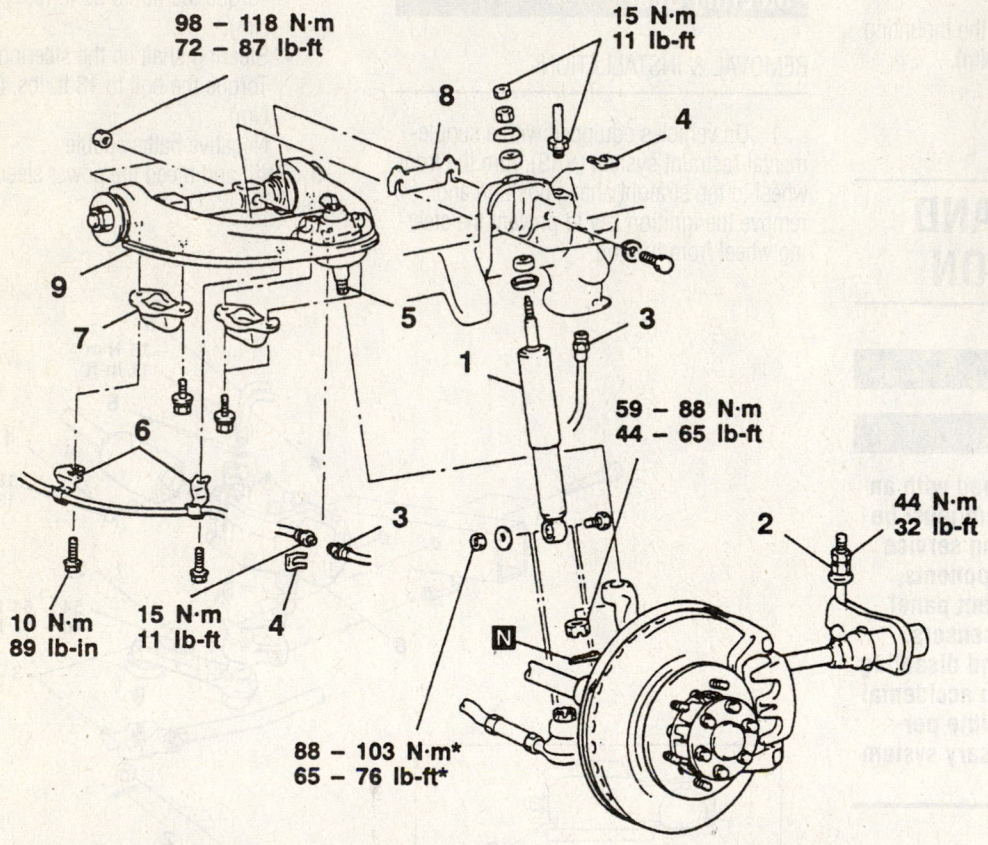

98 – 118 N·m
72 – 87 lb-ft

15 N·m
11 lb-ft

59 – 88 N·m
44 – 65 lb-ft

44 N·m
32 lb-ft

10 N·m
89 lb-in

15 N·m
11 lb-ft

88 – 103 N·m*
65 – 76 lb-ft*

1. SHOCK ABSORBER
● BUMP STOPPER AND BUMP STOPPER BRACKET CLEARANCE ADJUSTMENT
2. REAR ANCHOR ARM ADJUSTING NUT
3. BRAKE HOSE CONNECTION
4. HOSE CLIP
5. UPPER ARM BALL JOINT CONNECTION
6. SPEED SENSOR BRACKET <VEHICLES WITH ABS>

7. REBOUND STOPPER
8. SHIMS
9. UPPER ARM
10. UPPER ARM BALL JOINT ASSEMBLY

Caution
*: Indicates parts which should be temporarily tightened, and then fully tightened with the vehicle on the ground in an unladen condition.

Common shock absorber and upper control arm components

7924UG34

Coil Spring

REMOVAL & INSTALLATION

Rear

MONTERO

1. Before servicing the vehicle, refer to the precautions in the beginning of this section.

2. Remove the parking brake cable attaching bolt.

3. Support the weight of the axle.

4. Remove the bolt that attaches the lateral rod to the body.

5. Remove the lower shock mounting bolts.

6. Lower the axle and remove the coil springs with their seats.

To install:

7. Place the spring on the axle.

8. Install the lower shock mounting bolts. Torque the bolt to 159–181 ft. lbs. (216–245 Nm).

9. Remove the jack.

10. Install the lateral rod bolt. Torque the bolt to 170 ft. lbs. (230 Nm).

11. Install the parking brake cable.

12. Test drive the vehicle and check the alignment.

Leaf Springs

REMOVAL & INSTALLATION

1. Before servicing the vehicle, refer to the precautions in the beginning of this section.

2. Remove or disconnect the following:

- Parking brake cable
- Rear speed sensor
- Shock absorber
- U-bolt and seat
- Bumper stopper
- Shackle plate and assembly
- Rubber bushings
- Leaf spring

To install:

3. Install or connect the following:

- Rubber bushing
- Shackle plate and assembly. Torque the front nut to 145 ft. lbs. (196 Nm) and the rear nuts to 38 ft. lbs. (52 Nm).
- Bumper stopper
- U-bolt and seat. Torque the nuts to 72–87 (98–118).

- Shock absorber. Torque the mounting bolts to 16 ft. lbs. (22 Nm).
- Rear speed sensor
- Parking brake cable

Torsion Bars

REMOVAL & INSTALLATION

1. Before servicing the vehicle, refer to the precautions in the beginning of this section.

2. Support the lower arm with a jack.

3. Remove or disconnect the following:

- Heat protector, right side only
- Bump stopper
- Anchor adjustment nut and arm assembly
- Anchor collar
- Torsion bar
- Dust covers
- Heat covers, right side only

To install:

4. Install or connect the following:

- Heat covers, right side only
- Dust covers
- Torsion bar
- Anchor collar
- Anchor adjustment nut and arm

assembly. Torque the nut to 32 ft. lbs. (44 Nm).

- Heat protector, right side only

Upper Ball Joint

REMOVAL & INSTALLATION

Montero and Montero Sport

1. Before servicing the vehicle, refer to the precautions in the beginning of this section.

2. Remove the front wheel.

3. Support the lower control arm.

4. Remove the upper ball joint from the steering knuckle.

5. Remove the ball joint from the upper control arm.

To install:

6. Install the ball joint in the upper control arm. Tighten the bolts to 18 ft. lbs. (25 Nm)

7. Install the ball joint stud to the steering knuckle. Torque the nut to 54 ft. lbs. (74 Nm).

8. Install a new cotter pin.

9. Install the front wheel.

10. Grease the upper ball joint and all other suspension components with a grease fitting.

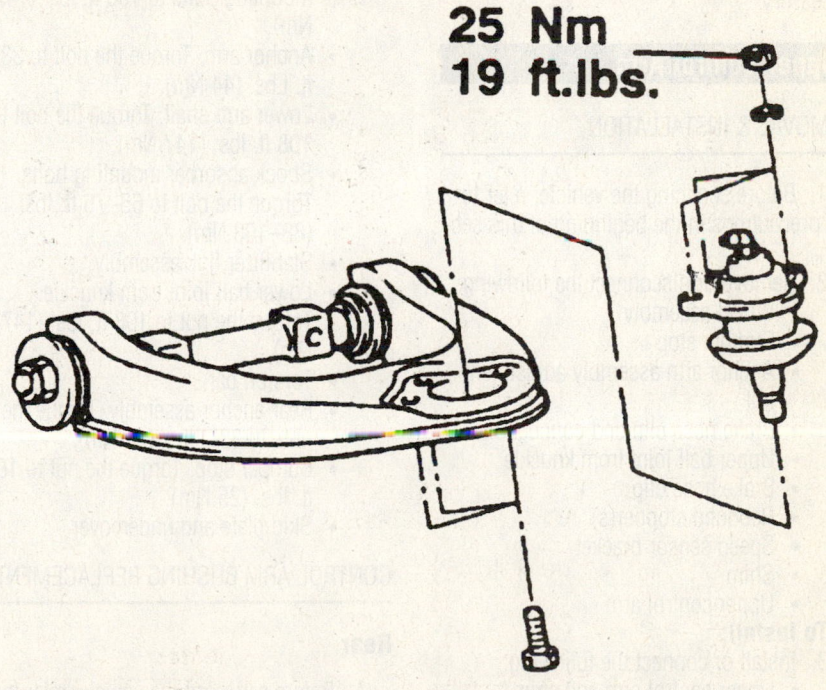

25 Nm
19 ft.lbs.

7924UG36

Exploded view of the upper ball joint and related components—Montero shown

Lower Ball Joint

REMOVAL & INSTALLATION

Montero and Montero Sport

1. Before servicing the vehicle, refer to the precautions in the beginning of this section.

2. Apply upward pressure to the lower control arm with a jack or an adjustable stand.

✳✳ CAUTION

Do not disconnect the lower ball joint stud from the steering knuckle unless the lower control arm has a stand or a jack under it.

3. Remove the ball joint stud nut/stud from the steering knuckle.

4. Remove the ball joint retaining nuts/bolts and the ball joint from the arm

To install:

5. Install the lower ball joint on the control arm. Torque the ball joint retaining nuts/bolts to 60 ft. lbs. (81 Nm).

6. Install the ball stud to the knuckle. Torque the nut to 108 ft. lbs. (147 Nm) and a new cotter pin.

7. Lubricate the ball joint with a grease gun.

8. Check and adjust the alignment if necessary.

Upper Control Arm

REMOVAL & INSTALLATION

1. Before servicing the vehicle, refer to the precautions in the beginning of this section.

2. Remove or disconnect the following:
   - Wheel assembly
   - Bumper stop
   - Anchor arm assembly adjustment nut
   - Brake hose clip and connection
   - Upper ball joint from knuckle
   - Brake hose clip
   - Rebound stopper(s)
   - Speed sensor bracket
   - Shim
   - Upper control arm

To install:

3. Install or connect the following:
   - Upper control arm and shim. Torque the nuts to 80 ft. lbs. (108 Nm).
   - Speed sensor bracket
   - Rebound stopper(s)

- Brake hose clip
- Upper ball joint from knuckle. Torque the nut to 54 ft. lbs. (74 Nm).
- New cotter pin
- Brake hose clip and connection
- Anchor arm assembly adjustment nut. Torque the nuts to 33 ft. lbs. (44 Nm).
- Bumper stop
- Wheel assembly

Lower Control Arm

REMOVAL & INSTALLATION

1. Before servicing the vehicle, refer to the precautions in the beginning of this section.

2. Remove or disconnect the following:
   - Skid plate and undercover
   - Bumper stop
   - Rear anchor assembly
   - Torsion bar
   - Lower ball joint from knuckle
   - Stabilizer link assembly
   - Shock absorber mounting bolts
   - Lower arm shaft
   - Anchor arm
   - Lower control arm

To install:

3. Install or connect the following:
   - Lower control arm. Torque the mounting bolts to 108 ft. lbs. (147 Nm).
   - Anchor arm. Torque the bolt to 33 ft. Lbs. (44 Nm).
   - Lower arm shaft. Torque the bolt to 108 ft. lbs. (147 Nm).
   - Shock absorber mounting bolts. Torque the bolt to 65–76 ft. lbs. (88–103 Nm).
   - Stabilizer link assembly
   - Lower ball joint from knuckle. Torque the nut to 108 ft. lbs. (147 Nm).
   - Torsion bar
   - Rear anchor assembly. Torque the nuts to 33ft. lbs. (44 Nm).
   - Bumper stop. Torque the nut to 18 ft. lbs. (25 Nm).
   - Skid plate and undercover

CONTROL ARM BUSHING REPLACEMENT

Rear

1. Before servicing the vehicle, refer to the precautions in the beginning of this section.

2. Remove the wheel.

3. Remove the lower control arm.

4. Using tool MB991522 press out the bushing

To install:

5. Position the bushing with the larger end facing the front of the vehicle.

6. Using tool MB991522 press the bushing into the bracket.

7. Install the lower control arm.

8. Install the wheel.

Front

1. Before servicing the vehicle, refer to the precautions in the beginning of this section.

2. Remove the wheel.

3. Remove the lower control arm and place in a vise.

4. Using tool MB990883 remove the bushing

To install:

5. Position the bushing with the larger end facing the front of the vehicle.

➡ Coat the bushing with a soap solution and take care not to twist.

6. Using tool MB991522, press the bushing into the bracket.

7. Install the lower control arm.

8. Install the wheel.

Wheel Bearings

ADJUSTMENT

Front

1. Tighten the wheel bearing nut to 119 ft. lbs. (162 Nm) while turning the rotor.

2. Loosen the wheel bearing adjusting nut completely.

3. Tighten the nut to 18 ft. lbs. (25 Nm), then loosen the nut approximately 30˚.

4. Using a dial indicator, check the wheel bearing end-play. The specification is 0.002 in. (0.05mm).

5. Install the locknut.

Rear

The rear wheel bearings are not adjustable. If the bearings are noisy or become loose, they must be replaced.

REMOVAL & INSTALLATION

Front

MONTERO AND MONTERO SPORT WITH 2WD

1. Before servicing the vehicle, refer to the precautions in the beginning of this section.

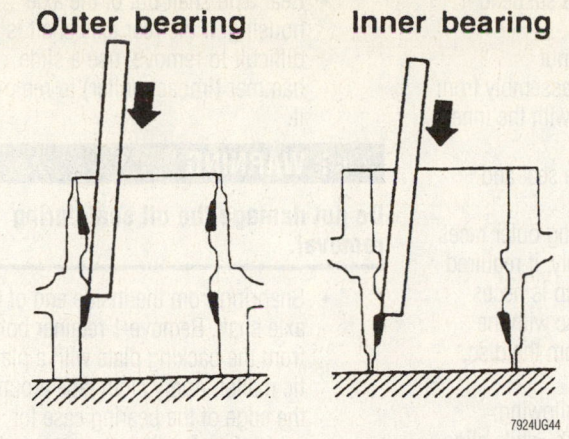

Outer bearing   **Inner bearing**

7924UG44

The bearing races can be removed from the hub using a drlft and hammer

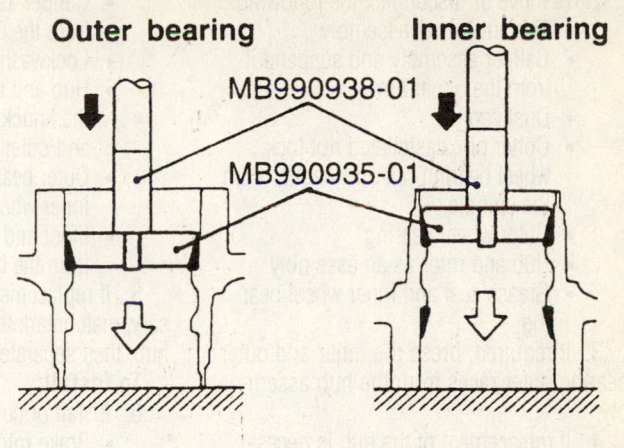

Outer bearing   **Inner bearing**

MB990938-01

MB990935-01

7924UG45A

Install the new races into the hub using the proper size driver

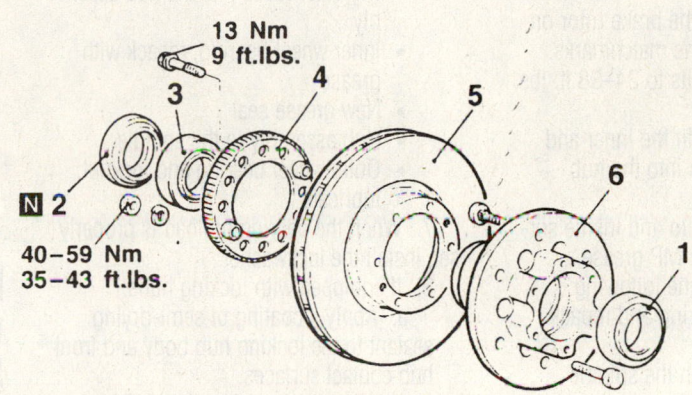

13 Nm
9 ft.lbs.

2

40–59 Nm
35–43 ft.lbs.

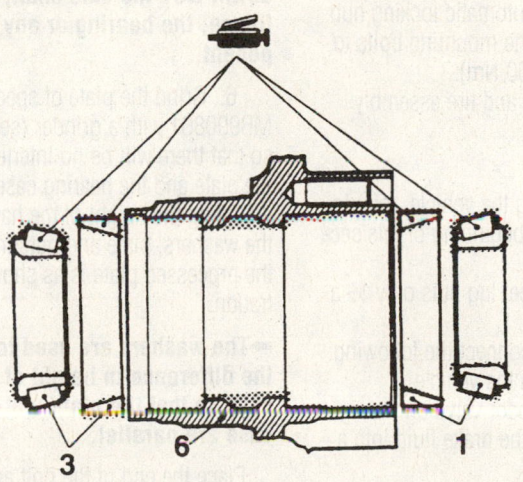

7924UG43

1. Outer bearing
2. Oil seal
3. Inner bearing

4. Rotor
5. Brake disc
6. Front hub

Exploded view of the hub and wheel bearing assembly—Montero

Turn to Section 5 for brake system applications

2. Remove or disconnect the following:
- Tire and wheel assembly
- Caliper assembly and suspend it from the upper arm
- Dust cap
- Cotter pin, castellated nut lock, wheel bearing nut and washer from the spindle
- Outer wheel bearing
- Hub and rotor as an assembly
- Grease seal and inner wheel bearing

3. If required, press the inner and outer bearing outer races from the hub assembly.

4. If replacement of the hub is necessary, matchmark the brake disc with the hub, then separate the hub from the disc.

To install:

5. If removed, place the brake rotor on the hub, while aligning the matchmarks. Tighten the mounting bolts to 34–38 ft. lbs. (47–52 Nm).

6. If removed, press-fit the inner and outer bearing outer races into the hub assembly.

7. Lubricate the seal lip and inside surface of the front hub with MP grease.

8. Install or connect the following:
- Inner wheel bearing and repack
- New grease seal
- Hub assembly on the spindle
- Outer wheel bearing, washer and nut, lubricate. When the bearing preload is properly set, install the nut lock and a new cotter pin.
- Grease cap
- Caliper assembly
- Tire and wheel assembly

MONTERO AND MONTERO SPORT WITH 4WD

1. Before servicing the vehicle, refer to the precautions in the beginning of this section.

2. Remove or disconnect the following:
- Tire and wheel assembly

3. If equipped with locking hub:

a. Place the locking hub in the free position.

➡**A free position can be obtained by shifting the transfer shift lever to the 2H position, then moving the vehicle in reverse for approximately 3–6 ft. (1–2 m).**

b. Remove the hub cover.

c. Remove the snapring from the axle shaft.

d. Remove the bolts and remove the automatic locking hub.

4. Remove or disconnect the following:

- Caliper assembly and suspend it from the upper arm.
- Lockwasher and locknut
- Hub and rotor as an assembly from the knuckle together with the inner and outer bearings
- Outer bearing, grease seal and inner wheel bearing
- Inner and outer bearing outer races from the hub assembly, if required

5. If replacement of the hub is necessary, matchmark the brake disc with the hub, then separate the hub from the disc.

To install:

6. Install or connect the following:
- Brake rotor on the hub, while aligning the matchmarks, if removed
- Press-fit the inner and outer bearing outer races into the hub assembly
- Inner wheel bearing, repack with grease
- New grease seal
- Hub assembly to the spindle
- Outer wheel bearing and locknut, lubricate

7. When the bearing preload is properly set, install the lockwasher.

8. If equipped with locking hubs:

a. Apply a coating of semi-drying sealant to the locking hub body and front hub contact surfaces.

b. Align the key of the brake **B** and the keyway of the knuckle spindle and loosely install the automatic locking hub assembly. Tighten the mounting bolts to 36–43 ft. lbs. (50–60 Nm).

9. Install the wheel and tire assembly

Rear

1. Before servicing the vehicle, refer to the precautions in the beginning of this section.

2. Loosen the wheel lug nuts only ½ a turn.

3. Remove or disconnect the following:
- Wheel(s) from the vehicle

4. Loosen the bleeder valve on the right rear caliper and drain the brake fluid into a container.

5. Remove or disconnect the following:
- Rear brake hose from the hard line on the frame
- Rear brake caliper
- Rear disc off of the rear axle
- Parking cable attaching bolt and cable end from the brake assembly
- Parking brake assembly from the end of the axle
- Speed sensor, on vehicles with Anti-lock Brakes (ABS)

- Rear axle shaft out of the axle housing. If the rear axle shaft is difficult to remove, use a slide hammer (impact puller) to remove it.

✳✳ WARNING

Do not damage the oil seal during removal.

- Snapring from the inside end of the axle shaft. Remove 1 retainer bolt from the backing plate with a plastic mallet. Apply cloth tape around the edge of the bearing case for protection. Position the axle shaft in a vise or with a similar method. Using a grinder, grind down the retainer flat, on one side, until the thickness of the retainer is only 0.04–0.08 in. (1–2mm). That is that the retainer is ground down toward the axle shaft, not toward the flange. Cut, with a chisel, the place where the retainer ring has been shaven down and remove the retainer.

✳✳ CAUTION

Be careful not to damage the bearing case and the axle shaft.

➡**Only the retainer ring is to be ground down, NOT the axle shaft, the axle flange, the bearing or any other component.**

6. Grind the plate of special tool MB990861 with a grinder (see illustration) so that there will be no interference between the plate and the bearing case. While adjusting the height of the hanger, secure the washers, plate and nuts in order so that the processed plate is as shown in the illustration.

➡**The washers are used to eliminate the difference in height of the bearing case so that the plate and the bearing case are parallel.**

Place the end of the bolt against the center of the axle shaft, then tighten the nuts to remove the axle shaft from the bearing case assembly.

➡**The hanger and plate must be placed so that they are parallel.**

7. Remove the bearing inner race and the bearing outer race. To remove the races, install the tool MB990560 and use a press to remove the bearing race from the axle shaft.

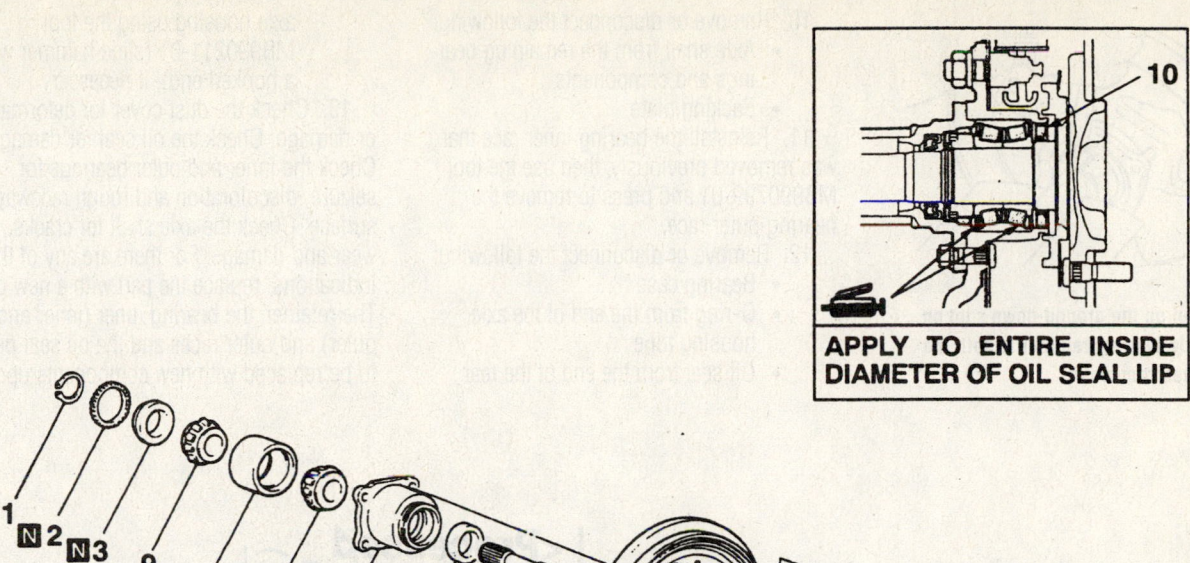

APPLY TO ENTIRE INSIDE
DIAMETER OF OIL SEAL LIP

DISASSEMBLY STEPS
1. SNAP RING
2. ABS ROTOR
3. RETAINER
4. AXLE SHAFT
5. BEARING CASE
6. BACKING PLATE
7. OUTER BEARING INNER RACE
8. DUST COVER
9. INNER BEARING INNER RACE
10. OIL SEAL
11. BEARING OUTER RACE

ASSEMBLY STEPS
11. BEARING OUTER RACE
9. INNER BEARING INNER RACE
7. OUTER BEARING INNER RACE
10. OIL SEAL
8. DUST COVER
6. BACKING PLATE
5. BEARING CASE
4. AXLE SHAFT
3. RETAINER
2. ABS ROTOR
1. SNAP RING

7924UG48

Exploded view of the typical rear axle shaft, bearings and races

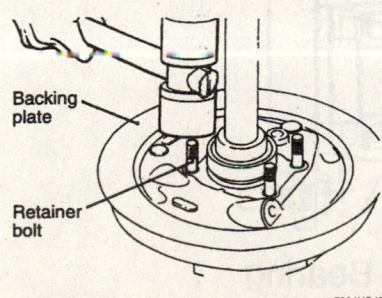

7924UG49

Remove one of the rear axle studs before attempting to grind down the retainer

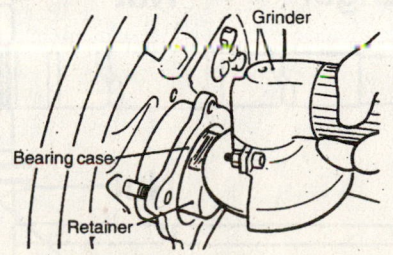

7924UG50

Using a grinder, grind the retainer, on one side, down to 1–2mm (0.04–0.08 in.) thickness

8. Remove the oil seal and the dust cover on vehicles without ABS.

9. On vehicles without ABS, insert an iron plate of approximately 0.04 in. (1mm) thickness between the rotor assembly and the axle shaft, then use a press to remove the rotor assembly.

❉❉ WARNING

In order not to bend the rotor assembly plate, place the support in contact with the axle shaft when using the press.

For complete service labor times order Nichols' Chilton Labor Guide Manual

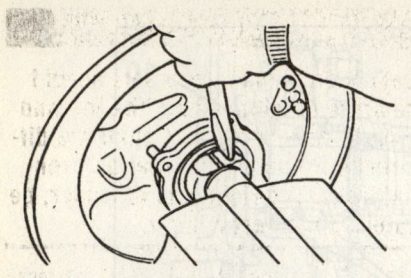

Use a chisel on the ground-down spot on the rear axle bearing retainer to split the retainer, then remove it

10. Remove or disconnect the following:
   - Axle shaft from the remaining bearings and components
   - Backing plate
11. Reinstall the bearing inner race that was removed previously, then use the tool MB990799-01 and press to remove the bearing outer race.
12. Remove or disconnect the following:
   - Bearing case
   - O-ring from the end of the axle housing tube
   - Oil seal from the end of the rear

axle housing using the tool MB990211-01 (slide hammer with a hooked end), if necessary
13. Check the dust cover for deformation or damage. Check the oil seal for damage. Check the inner and outer bearings for seizure, discoloration and rough raceway surface. Check the axle shaft for cracks, wear and damage. For there are any of these indications, replace the part with a new one. The retainer, the bearing inner (inner and outer) and outer races and the oil seal need to be replaced with new components upon

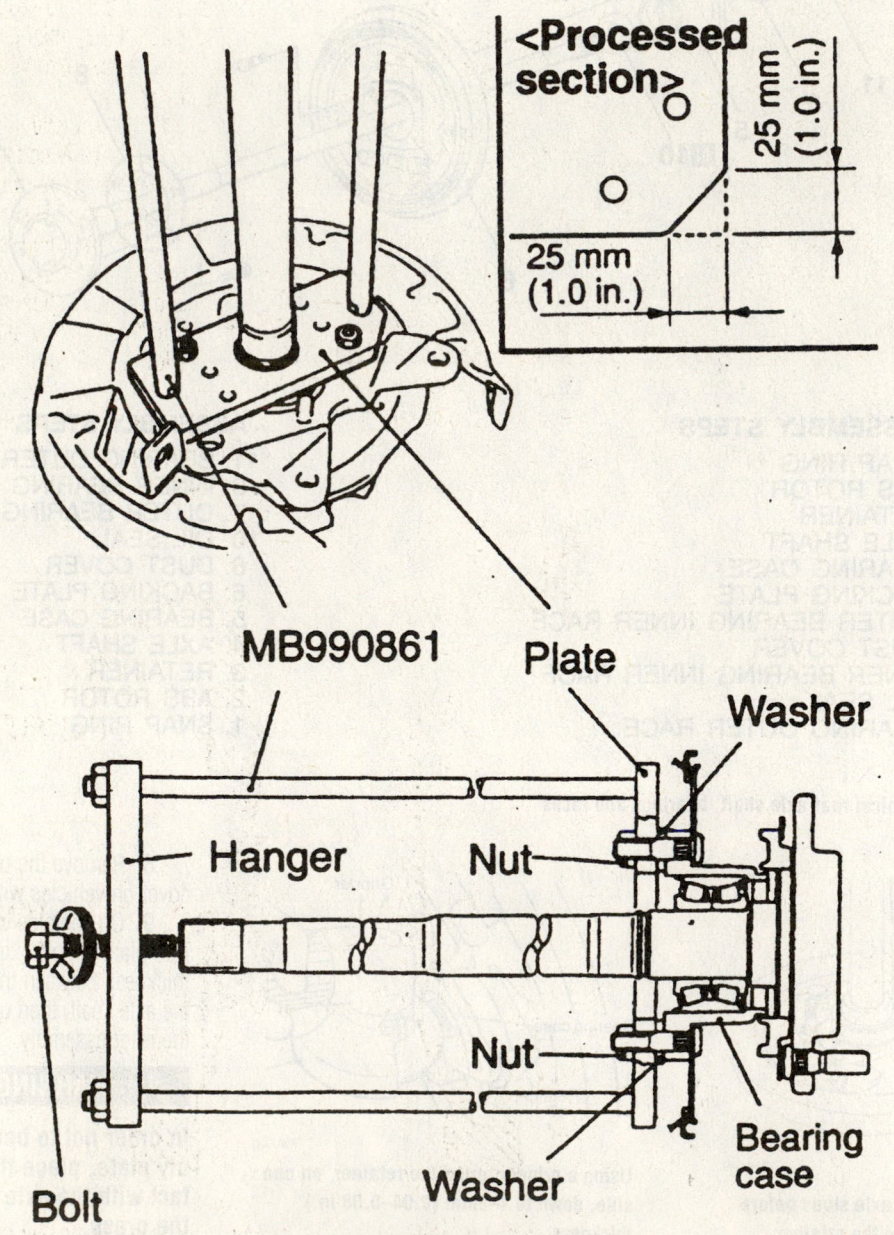

Use the special tool MB990861 to remove the rear axle shaft from the bearing case

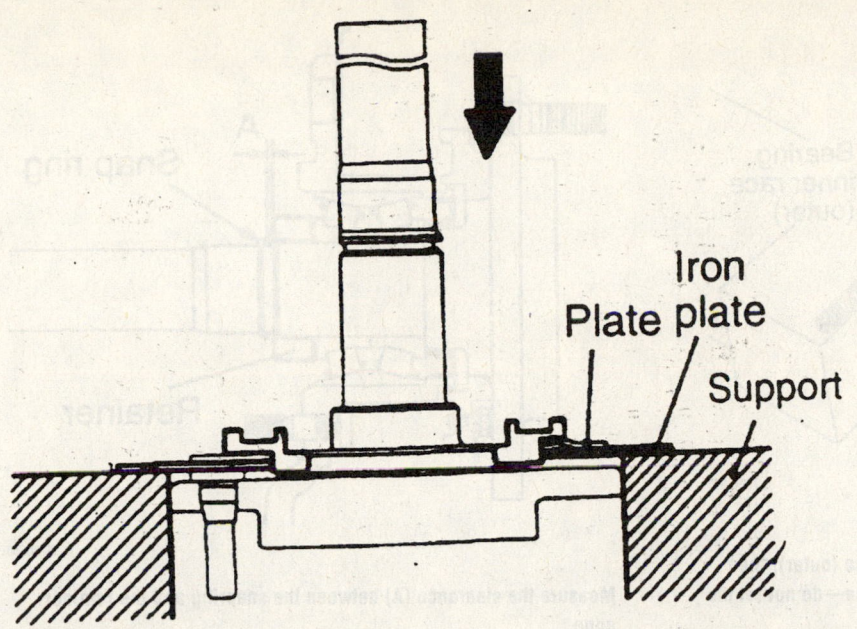

Use an iron plate and supports to remove the rotor assembly

reassembly. After all of this work, it is probably a good idea to replace the bearings and the axle housing tube oil seals.

To install:

14. Install or connect the following:
   - New oil seal into the end of the rear axle housing using the tools MB990932-01 and MB990938-01, if necessary.
   - New O-ring into the axle tube

15. Apply multi-purpose grease to the external surface of the bearing out race. Press-fit the bearing outer race into the bearing case by using the tool MB990890-01.

16. Install or connect the following:
   - Speed sensor bracket to the back of the backing plate
   - Rotor assembly to the axle shaft by press-fitting (plastic mallet will also work) it on using the special tool MB991388
   - Backing plate onto the axle shaft
   - Dust cover to the backing plate if the vehicle is equipped with ABS.
   - Bearing inner race (outer) to the bearing case
   - Oil seal to the front end of the bearing case. To do this, apply multi-purpose grease to the outside of the oil seal. Use the special tools MB990936-01 and MB990938-01 to press-fit the oil seal until it is flush with the end of the bearing case. Apply multi-purpose grease

to the lip of the oil seal.
   - Axle shaft through the bearing inner race, the bearing case and the second bearing inner race in that order. Use the special tool MB990799 to press-fit the bearing inner race to the axle shaft.

17. Use the tool MB990799-01 to press-fit the retainer onto the axle shaft, while checking that the press-fitting force is at the following values:
   - Initial press-fitting force: 11,016 lbs. (5000 kg) or more.
   - Final press-fitting force: 22,031–24,280 lbs. (98,000–108,000 N).

18. If the initial press-fitting force is less than the standard value, replace the axle shaft.

19. After installing the snapring, measure the clearance between the snapring and the retainer with a thickness gauge, and check that it is within the standard values. The standard value is 0.0065 in. (0.166mm) or less. If the clearance exceeds the standard value, change the snapring so that the clearance is at the standard value. Use the following adjusting snapring thicknesses:
   - 0.0854 in. (2.17mm): no color.
   - 0.0791 in. (2.01mm): yellow.
   - 0.0728 in. (1.85mm): blue.

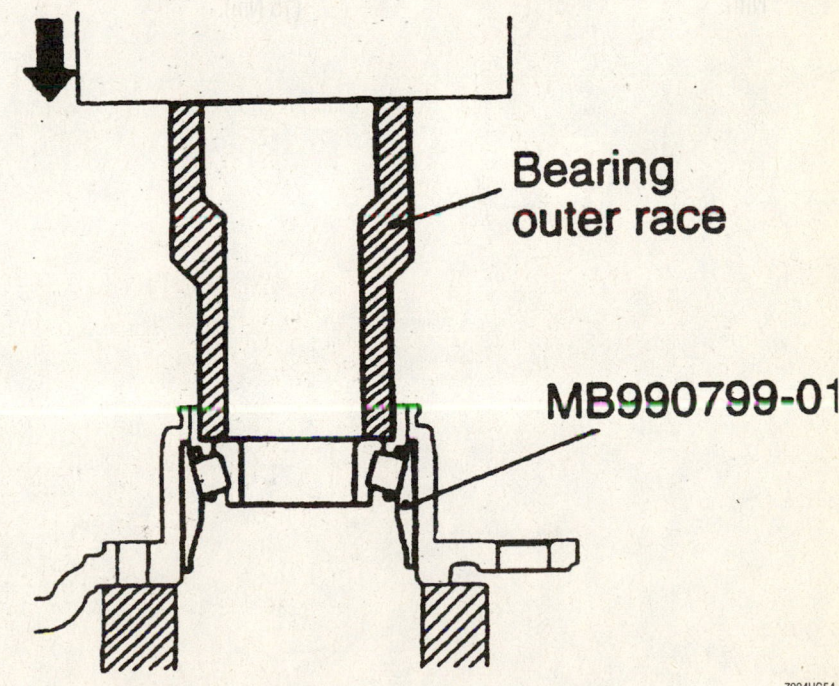

Use the tool MB990799-01 to install and remove the rear axle bearing races

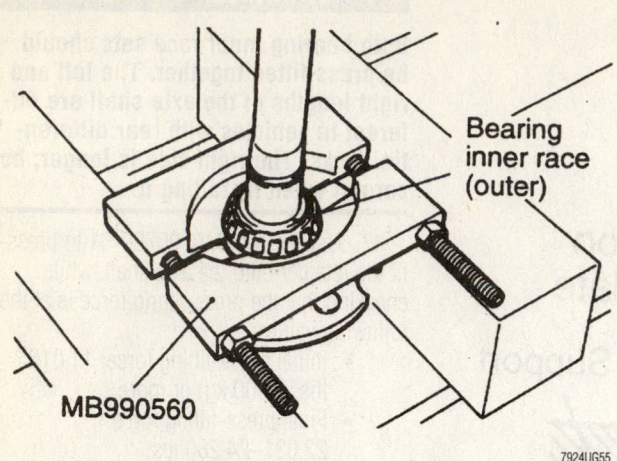

Bearing inner race (outer)

MB990560

7924UG55

Use the MB990560 tool to hold the bearing inner race (outer), then use a plastic hammer to drive the axle out of the race—do not let the axle fall onto a hard floor

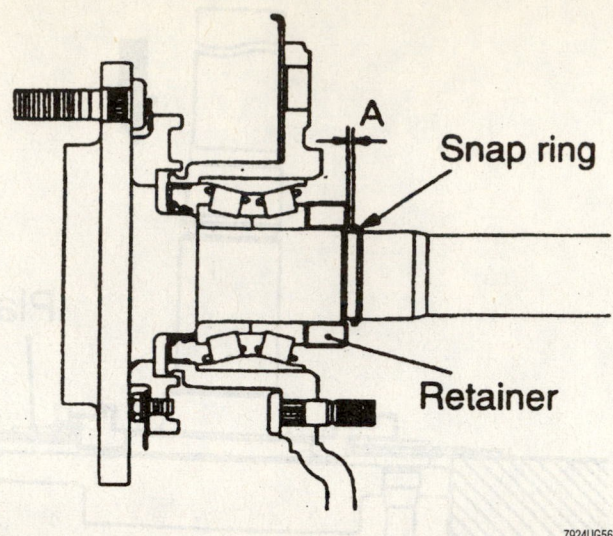

Snap ring

Retainer

7924UG56

Measure the clearance (A) between the snapring and the retainer edge

- 0.0665 in. (1.69mm): purple.
- 0.0602 in. (1.53mm): red.
20. Install or connect the following:
- Axle assembly into the axle housing. Be sure that the grooves on the end of the axle shaft line up in the differential. Use a plastic or rubber mallet to help drive the axle shaft into the differential unit. Tighten the 4 retaining bolts for the axle shafts to 36–43 ft. lbs. (49–59 Nm).

- Speed sensor
- Parking brake assembly components to the axle flange.
- Parking brake cable to the parking brake assembly, then secure it in place with the cable bracket.
- Brake rotor onto the axle shaft, and the brake caliper. Torque the caliper bolts to 65 ft. lbs. (88 Nm).
- Brake hose to the frame brake line. Torque the flare nut to 11 ft. lbs. (15 Nm).

- Wheels. Torque the lug nuts as tight as possible with the vehicle not on the ground.
21. Bleed the brake system.
22. Lower the vehicle until the wheels are touching the ground, then finish tightening the lug nuts. Lower the vehicle the rest of the way to the ground.
23. Road test the vehicle and check for leaks.

NISSAN AND INFINITI

Nissan-Pathfinder • Pick-up • Frontier • Xterra • **Infiniti-**QX4

PRECAUTIONS

Before servicing any vehicle, please be sure to read all of the following precautions, which deal with personal safety, prevention of component damage, and important points to take into consideration when servicing a motor vehicle:

• Never open, service or drain the radiator or cooling system when the engine is hot; serious burns can occur from the steam and hot coolant.

• Observe all applicable safety precautions when working around fuel. Whenever servicing the fuel system, always work in a well-ventilated area. Do not allow fuel spray or vapors to come in contact with a spark, open flame, or excessive heat (a hot drop light, for example). Keep a dry chemical fire extinguisher near the work area. Always keep fuel in a container specifically designed for fuel storage; also, always properly seal fuel containers to avoid the possibility of fire or explosion. Refer to the additional fuel system precautions later in this section.

• Fuel injection systems often remain pressurized, even after the engine has been turned **OFF**. The fuel system pressure must be relieved before disconnecting any fuel lines. Failure to do so may result in fire and/or personal injury.

• Brake fluid often contains polyglycol ethers and polyglycols. Avoid contact with the eyes and wash your hands thoroughly after handling brake fluid. If you do get brake fluid in your eyes, flush your eyes with clean, running water for 15 minutes. If eye irritation persists, or if you have taken brake fluid internally, IMMEDIATELY seek medical assistance.

• The EPA warns that prolonged contact with used engine oil may cause a number of skin disorders, including cancer! You should make every effort to minimize your exposure to used engine oil. Protective gloves should be worn when changing oil. Wash your hands and any other exposed skin areas as soon as possible after exposure to used engine oil. Soap and water, or waterless hand cleaner should be used.

• All new vehicles are now equipped with an air bag system. The system must be disabled before performing service on or around system components, steering column, instrument panel components, wiring and sensors. Failure to follow safety and disabling procedures could result in accidental air bag deployment, possible per-

sonal injury and unnecessary system repairs.

• Always wear safety goggles when working with, or around, the air bag system. When carrying a non-deployed air bag, be sure the bag and trim cover are pointed away from your body. When placing a non-deployed air bag on a work surface, always face the bag and trim cover upward, away from the surface. This will reduce the motion of the module if it is accidentally deployed. Refer to the additional air bag system precautions later in this section.

• Clean, high quality brake fluid from a sealed container is essential to the safe and proper operation of the brake system. You should always buy the correct type of brake fluid for your vehicle. If the brake fluid becomes contaminated, completely flush the system with new fluid. Never reuse any brake fluid. Any brake fluid that is removed from the system should be discarded. Also, do not allow any brake fluid to come in contact with a painted surface; it will damage the paint.

• Never operate the engine without the proper amount and type of engine oil; doing so WILL result in severe engine damage.

• Timing belt maintenance is extremely important! Many models utilize an interference-type, non-freewheeling engine. If the timing belt breaks, the valves in the cylinder head may strike the pistons, causing potentially serious (also time-consuming and expensive) engine damage. Refer to the maintenance interval charts in the front of this manual for the recommended replacement interval for the timing belt, and to the timing belt section for belt replacement and inspection.

• Disconnecting the negative battery cable on some vehicles may interfere with the functions of the on-board computer system(s) and may require the computer to undergo a relearning process once the negative battery cable is reconnected.

• When servicing drum brakes, only disassemble and assemble one side at a time, leaving the remaining side intact for reference.

ENGINE REPAIR

➡ **Disconnecting the negative battery cable on some vehicles may interfere with the functions of the on board computer system. The computer may**

undergo a relearning process once the negative battery cable is reconnected.

Distributor

REMOVAL

1. Before servicing the vehicle, refer to the precautions in the beginning of this section.

2. Remove or disconnect the following:
   • Negative battery cable
   • Distributor cap
   • Distributor wiring harness connector

3. Matchmark the rotor to the distributor housing and the distributor housing to the cylinder head.

4. Remove the distributor.

INSTALLATION

Timing Not Disturbed

1. Install or connect the following:
   • Distributor by aligning the matchmarks made during removal
   • Distributor wiring harness connector
   • Distributor cap
   • Negative battery cable

2. Check the ignition timing and adjust, as necessary.

Timing Disturbed

2.4L ENGINE

1. Set the engine to Top Dead Center (TDC) of the compression stroke for the No. 1 cylinder.

2. Install the distributor so that the distributor shaft engages the oil pump driveshaft.

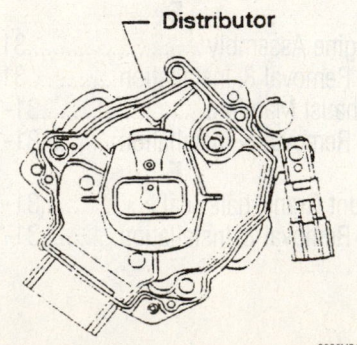

9308VG01

Distributor rotor alignment with the engine at Top Dead Center (TDC)—2.4L engine

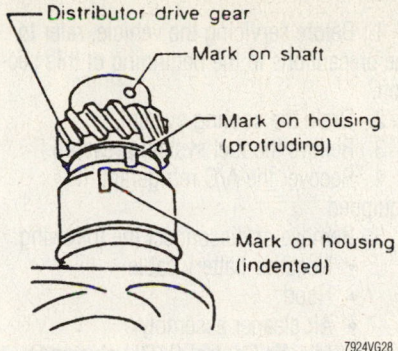

Distributor shaft alignment—3.3L engine

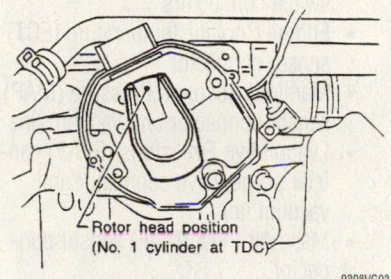

Distributor rotor alignment—3.3L engine

3. Check that the distributor rotor is aligned, as shown.

4. Install or connect the following:
- Distributor cap
- Distributor harness connector

5. Check the ignition timing and adjust, as necessary.

3.3L ENGINE

1. Set the engine to Top Dead Center (TDC) of the compression stroke for the No. 1 cylinder.

2. Align the index mark on the distributor shaft with the protrusion on the distributor housing.

3. Install the distributor and check that the distributor rotor is aligned.

4. Install or connect the following:
- Distributor cap
- Distributor harness connector

5. Check the ignition timing and adjust, as necessary.

Alternator

REMOVAL

2.4L Engine

1. Before servicing the vehicle, refer to the precautions in the beginning of this section.

2. Remove or disconnect the following:
- Negative battery cable
- Engine under cover
- Right splash shield
- Alternator harness connectors
- Alternator belt
- Alternator

3.3L Engine

1. Before servicing the vehicle, refer to the precautions in the beginning of this section.

2. Remove or disconnect the following:
- Negative battery cable
- Alternator harness connectors
- Engine under cover
- Alternator belt
- Alternator

INSTALLATION

2.4L Engine

1. Install or connect the following:
- Alternator
- Alternator belt. Tighten the adjustment bolt to 12–14 ft. lbs. (16–19 Nm) and the pivot bolt to 32–38 ft. lbs. (44–52 Nm).
- Alternator harness connectors
- Right splash shield
- Engine under cover
- Negative battery cable

3.3L Engine

1. Install or connect the following:
- Alternator
- Alternator belt. Tighten the adjustment bolt to 12–14 ft. lbs. (16–19 Nm) and the pivot bolts to 16–22 ft. lbs. (22–30 Nm).
- Engine under cover
- Alternator harness connectors
- Negative battery cable

Ignition Timing

ADJUSTMENT

➡**Ignition timing is set with the engine at operating temperature, transmission in Neutral and all electrical accessories OFF.**

1. Before servicing the vehicle, refer to the precautions in the beginning of this section.

2. Attach a timing light to the No. 1 spark plug wire.

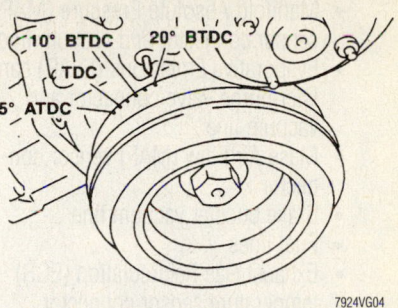

Timing indicator—3.3L engine shown

3. Start the engine and allow it to reach normal operating temperature.

4. Check that the idle speed is less than 1000 rpm.

5. Run the engine at 2000 rpm for 2 minutes.

6. Rev the engine to 3000 rpm 2–3 times and allow it to idle for 1 minute.

7. Check for the presence of Diagnostic Trouble Codes (DTC) and service as necessary.

8. Run the engine at 2000 rpm for 2 minutes.

9. Stop the engine and disconnect the Throttle Position (TP) sensor.

10. Start the engine and rev it to 3000 rpm 2–3 times and allow it to idle.

11. Set the base timing to 8–12 degrees Before Top Dead Center (BTDC).

12. Tighten the distributor lockbolt to 83–113 inch lbs. (9–13 Nm).

13. Set the base idle speed to 700–800 rpm.

14. Stop the engine and connect the TP sensor.

Engine Assembly

REMOVAL & INSTALLATION

2.4L Engine

1. Before servicing the vehicle, refer to the precautions in the beginning of this section.

2. Drain the cooling system.

3. Relieve the fuel system pressure.

4. Remove or disconnect the following:
- Negative battery cable
- Hood
- Air cleaner assembly
- Idle Air Control (IAC) valve and solenoid connectors
- Throttle Position (TP) sensor and switch connectors
- Engine Coolant Temperature (ECT) sensor connector

- Manifold Absolute Pressure (MAP) sensor connector and vacuum line
- Evaporative Emissions (EVAP) canister purge valve connector and vacuum line
- Mass Air Flow (MAF) sensor connector
- Brake booster vacuum line
- Fuel lines
- Exhaust Gas Recirculation (EGR) temperature sensor connector
- Throttle cable
- Accessory drive belts
- Radiator and hoses
- Heater hoses
- Exhaust manifold heat shield
- Heated Oxygen (HO$_2$S) sensor connectors
- Exhaust front pipe
- A/C compressor, if equipped
- Power steering pump, if equipped
- Crankshaft Position (CKP) sensor
- Starter motor
- Transmission
- Left and right engine mounts
- Engine

To install:

5. Install or connect the following:
- Engine. Tighten the engine mount nuts to 30–38 ft. lbs. (41–52 Nm).

- Transmission
- Starter motor
- CKP sensor
- Power steering pump, if equipped
- A/C compressor, if equipped
- Exhaust front pipe
- HO$_2$S sensor connectors
- Exhaust manifold heat shield
- Heater hoses
- Radiator and hoses
- Accessory drive belts
- Throttle cable
- EGR temperature sensor connector
- Fuel lines
- Brake booster vacuum line
- MAF sensor connector
- EVAP canister purge valve connector and vacuum line
- MAP sensor connector and vacuum line
- ECT sensor connector
- TP sensor and switch connectors
- IAC valve and solenoid connectors
- Air cleaner assembly
- Hood
- Negative battery cable

6. Fill the cooling system.
7. Start the engine and check for leaks.

3.3L Engine

1. Before servicing the vehicle, refer to the precautions in the beginning of this section.
2. Drain the cooling system.
3. Relieve the fuel system pressure.
4. Recover the A/C refrigerant, if equipped.
5. Remove or disconnect the following:
- Negative battery cable
- Hood
- Air cleaner assembly
- Idle Air Control (IAC) valve and solenoid connectors
- Throttle Position (TP) sensor and switch connectors
- Engine Coolant Temperature (ECT) sensor connector
- Manifold Absolute Pressure (MAP) sensor connector and vacuum line
- Evaporative Emissions (EVAP) canister purge valve connector and vacuum line
- Mass Air Flow (MAF) sensor connector
- Brake booster vacuum line
- Fuel lines
- Exhaust Gas Recirculation (EGR) temperature sensor connector

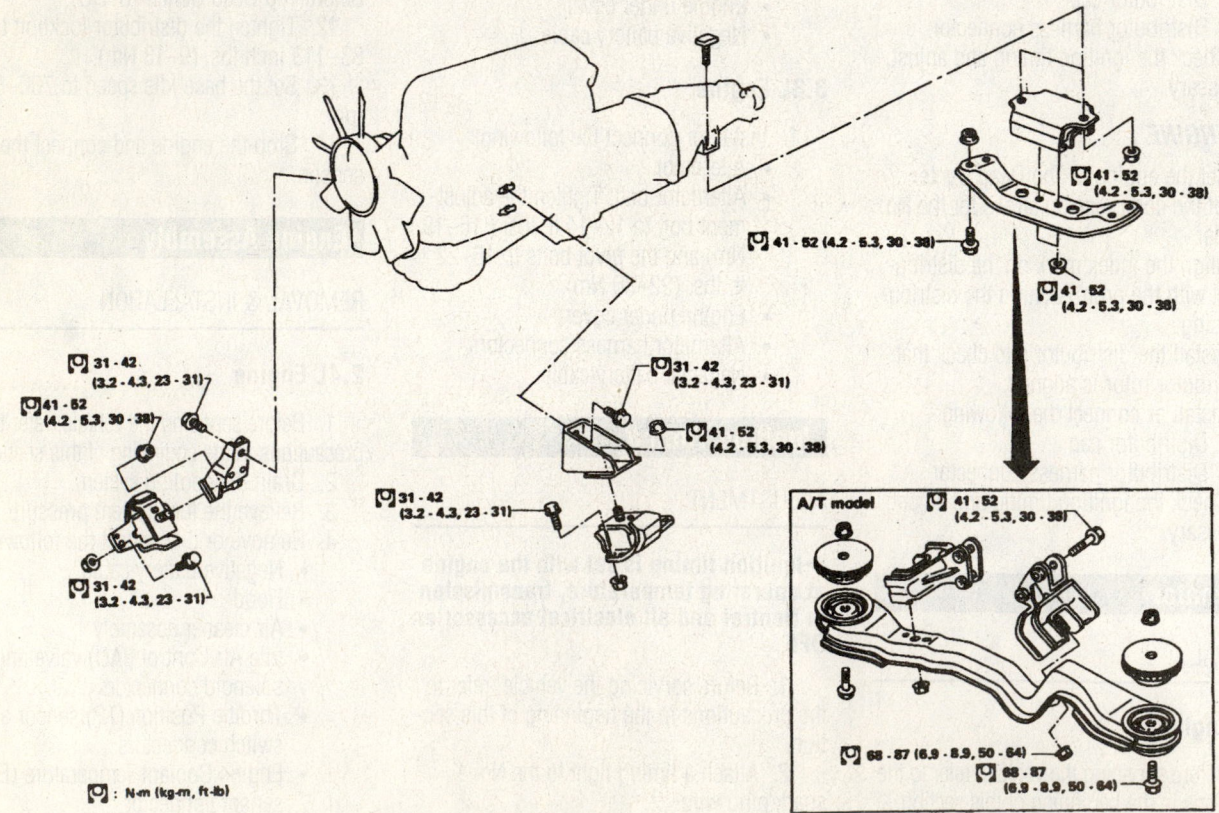

Engine and transmission mounts—2.4L engine

7924VG05

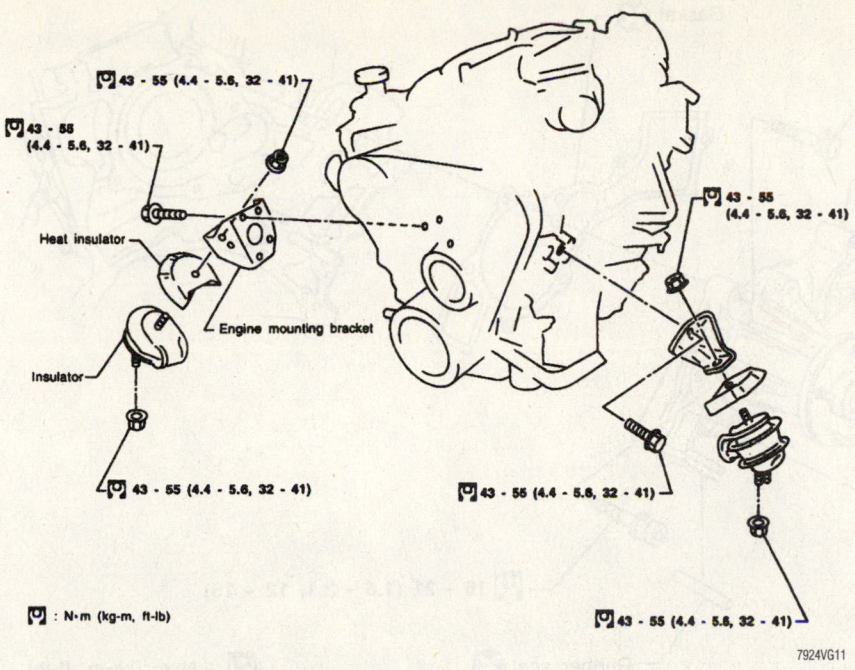

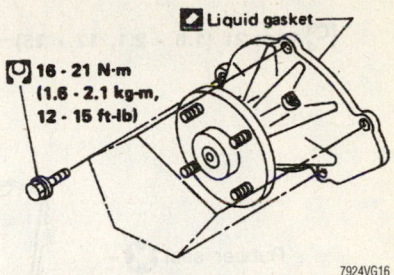

Water pump assembly—2.4L engine

Diameter of liquid gasket:
2.0 - 3.0 mm (0.079 - 0.118 in)

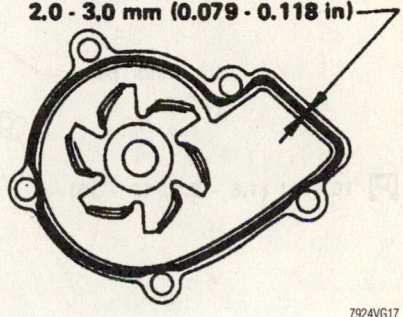

Liquid gasket application—2.4L engine

Engine mounts and related components—3.3L engine

- Throttle cable
- Accessory drive belts
- Cooling fan and shroud
- Radiator and hoses
- Engine under cover
- A/C compressor manifold
- Power steering pump
- Heated Oxygen (HO$_2$S) sensor connectors
- Exhaust front pipes
- Crankshaft Position (CKP) sensor
- Starter motor
- Transmission
- Left and right engine mounts
- Engine

➡**When removing the engine mounts, do not loosen the 4 mount cover nuts. The mount is fluid filled and will not function if the fluid leaks out.**

To install:

6. Install or connect the following:
   - Engine. Tighten the engine mount nuts to 43–58 ft. lbs. (59–78 Nm).
   - Transmission
   - Starter motor
   - CKP sensor
   - Exhaust front pipes
   - HO$_2$S sensor connectors
   - Power steering pump
   - A/C compressor manifold
   - Engine under cover
   - Radiator and hoses
   - Cooling fan and shroud

- Accessory drive belts
- Throttle cable
- EGR temperature sensor connector
- Fuel lines
- Brake booster vacuum line
- MAF sensor connector
- EVAP canister purge valve connector and vacuum line
- MAP sensor connector and vacuum line
- ECT sensor connector
- TP sensor and switch connectors
- IAC valve and solenoid connectors
- Air cleaner assembly
- Hood
- Negative battery cable

7. Fill the cooling system.
8. Recharge the A/C system, if equipped.
9. Start the engine and check for leaks.

Water Pump

REMOVAL & INSTALLATION

2.4L Engine

1. Before servicing the vehicle, refer to the precautions in the beginning of this section.
2. Drain the cooling system.
3. Remove or disconnect the following:
   - Negative battery cable

To install:

4. Install or connect the following:
   - Water pump. Apply sealant and tighten the bolts to 12–15 ft. lbs. (16–21 Nm).
   - Cooling fan
   - Accessory drive belts
   - Negative battery cable
5. Fill the cooling system.
6. Start the engine and check for leaks.

3.3L Engine

1. Before servicing the vehicle, refer to the precautions in the beginning of this section.
2. Drain the cooling system.
3. Remove or disconnect the following:
   - Negative battery cable
   - Accessory drive belts
   - Radiator hoses
   - Cooling fan and shroud
   - Water pump pulley
   - Front cover
   - Timing belt. Refer to the Timing Belt unit repair section.
   - Water pump

To install:

4. Install or connect the following:

Timing belt service is covered in Section 4 of this manual

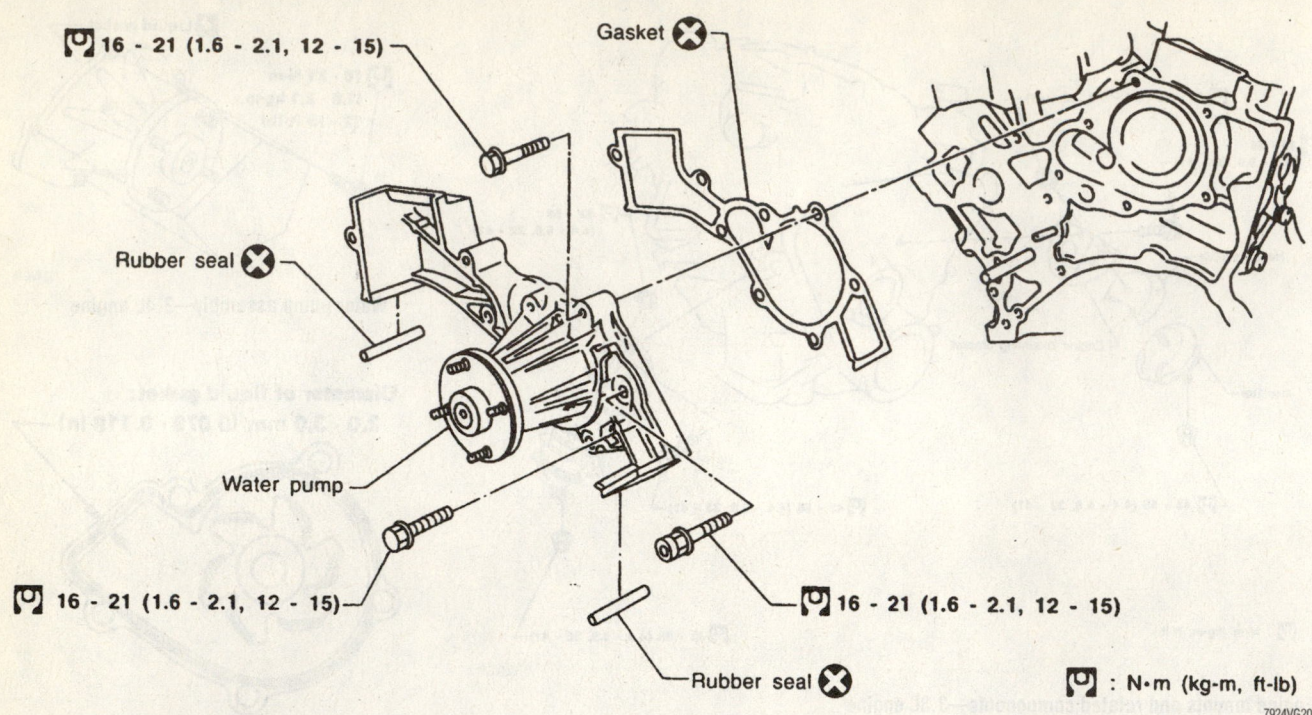

Exploded view of the water pump assembly—3.3L engine

- Water pump. Tighten the bolts to 12–15 ft. lbs. (16–21 Nm).
- Timing belt
- Front cover
- Water pump pulley
- Cooling fan and shroud
- Radiator hoses
- Accessory drive belts
- Negative battery cable
5. Fill the cooling system.
6. Start the engine and check for leaks.

Cylinder Head

REMOVAL & INSTALLATION

2.4L Engine

SOHC

1. Before servicing the vehicle, refer to the precautions in the beginning of this section.
2. Drain the cooling system.
3. Relieve the fuel system pressure.
4. Remove or disconnect the following:
- Negative battery cable
- Air cleaner assembly
- Accessory drive belts
- Power steering pump and bracket
- Idler pulley
- Exhaust Gas Recirculation (EGR) tube
- Intake manifold
- Exhaust manifold

- Valve cover
5. Wedge the timing chain in place to prevent the chain tensioner from expanding.
6. Remove or disconnect the following:
- Camshaft sprocket
- Cylinder head front cover bolts
- Cylinder head. Loosen the bolts in several passes and in sequence.

To install:

➡ **Refer to Section 1 of this manual for the cylinder head torque sequence illustration. The illustration is located after the Torque Specification Chart.**

7. Install the cylinder head with a new gasket. Tighten the bolts in sequence as follows:
- a. Step 1: 22 ft. lbs. (30 Nm)
- b. Step 2: 58 ft. lbs. (78 Nm)
- c. Step 3: Loosen all bolts completely

- d. Step 4: 22 ft. lbs. (30 Nm)
- e. Step 5: Plus 80–85 degrees **OR** 54–61 ft. lbs. (74–83 Nm)
8. Install or connect the following:
- Cylinder head front cover bolts
- Camshaft sprocket and timing chain. Tighten the sprocket bolt to 101–116 ft. lbs. (137–157 Nm).
- Valve cover. Tighten bolts 4 and 3 to 26 inch lbs. (3 Nm), then tighten all bolts in sequence to 61–95 inch lbs. (7–11 Nm).
- Exhaust manifold
- Intake manifold
- Exhaust Gas Recirculation (EGR) tube
- Idler pulley
- Power steering pump and bracket
- Accessory drive belts
- Air cleaner assembly
- Negative battery cable

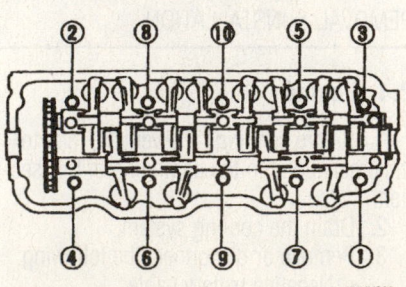

Cylinder head loosening sequence—2.4L SOHC engine

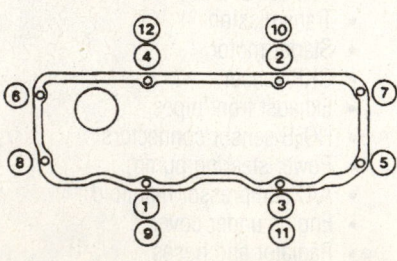

Valve cover torque sequence—2.4L SOHC engine

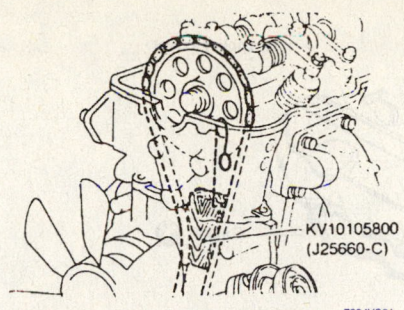

KV10105800
(J25660-C)

7924VG21

Wedge the chain in place so that it will not fall down into the front cover—2.4L SOHC engine shown

9. Fill the cooling system.
10. Start the engine and check for leaks.

DOHC

1. Before servicing the vehicle, refer to the precautions in the beginning of this section.
2. Drain the cooling system.
3. Relieve the fuel system pressure.
4. Remove or disconnect the following:
   - Negative battery cable
   - Air cleaner assembly
   - Spark plug wires
   - Radiator hoses
   - Accessory drive belts
   - Fuel lines
   - Intake manifold
   - Exhaust manifold
   - Valve cover. Remove the bolts in the sequence shown.
   - Camshaft sprocket cover
   - Camshaft sprockets and upper timing chain
5. Wedge the lower timing chain in place to prevent the chain tensioner from expanding.
6. Remove or disconnect the following:
   - Timing chain idler sprocket
   - Camshafts
   - Cylinder head. Loosen the bolts in

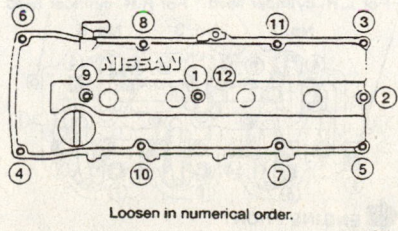

Loosen in numerical order.

9308VG06

Valve cover loosening sequence—2.4L DOHC engine

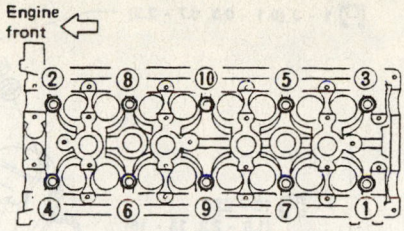

Engine front

Loosen in numerical order.

9308VG04

Cylinder head loosening sequence—2.4L DOHC engine

several passes and in sequence as shown.

To install:

➡ **Refer to Section 1 of this manual for the cylinder head torque sequence illustration. The illustration is located after the Torque Specification Chart.**

7. Install the cylinder head with a new gasket. Tighten the bolts in sequence as follows:
   a. Step 1: 22 ft. lbs. (30 Nm)
   b. Step 2: 59 ft. lbs. (79 Nm)
   c. Step 3: Loosen all bolts completely
   d. Step 4: 18–25 ft. lbs. (25–34 Nm)
   e. Step 5: Plus 86–91 degrees
8. Install or connect the following:
   - Camshafts
   - Timing chain idler sprocket and lower timing chain. Remove the wedge and tighten the bolt to 48–61 ft. lbs. (66–83 Nm).
   - Camshaft sprockets and upper timing chain. Tighten the bolts to 123–130 ft. lbs. (167–177 Nm).
   - Camshaft sprocket cover
   - Valve cover. Tighten the bolts in sequence to 69–95 ft. lbs. (8–11 Nm).
   - Exhaust manifold
   - Intake manifold
   - Fuel lines
   - Accessory drive belts
   - Radiator hoses

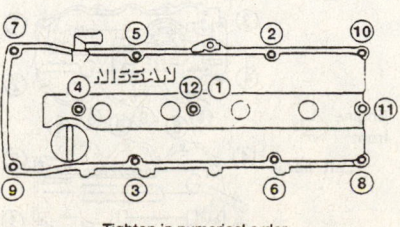

Tighten in numerical order.

9308VG07

Valve cover torque sequence—2.4L DOHC engine

- Spark plug wires
- Air cleaner assembly
- Negative battery cable
9. Fill the cooling system.
10. Start the engine and check for leaks.

3.3L Engine

1997 ENGINES

1. Before servicing the vehicle, refer to the precautions in the beginning of this section.
2. Drain the cooling system.
3. Relieve the fuel system pressure.
4. Remove or disconnect the following:
   - Negative battery cable
   - Accessory drive belts
   - Front cover
   - Timing belt. Refer to the Timing Belt unit repair section.
   - Upper intake manifold
   - Lower intake manifold
   - Camshaft sprockets
   - Rear timing cover
   - Distributor
   - Exhaust front pipes
   - A/C compressor
   - Alternator
   - Power steering pump
   - Accessory brackets
   - Valve covers. Loosen the bolts in several passes and in sequence.
   - Cylinder heads with the exhaust manifolds attached. Loosen the bolts in several passes and in sequence.

➡ **The cylinder head bolts vary in length. Note the bolt locations for assembly.**

To install:

➡ **Refer to Section 1 of this manual for the cylinder head torque sequence illustration. The illustration is located after the Torque Specification Chart.**

5. Install the cylinder heads with new gaskets. Tighten the bolts in sequence as follows:
   a. Step 1: 22 ft. lbs. (29 Nm)
   b. Step 2: 43 ft. lbs. (59 Nm)
   c. Step 3: Loosen all bolts completely
   d. Step 4: 22 ft. lbs. (29 Nm)
   e. Step 5: Plus 60–65 degrees **OR** 40–47 ft. lbs. (54–64 Nm)
   f. Step 6: Sub-bolts to 80–105 inch lbs. (9–12 Nm)
6. Install or connect the following:
   - Valve covers

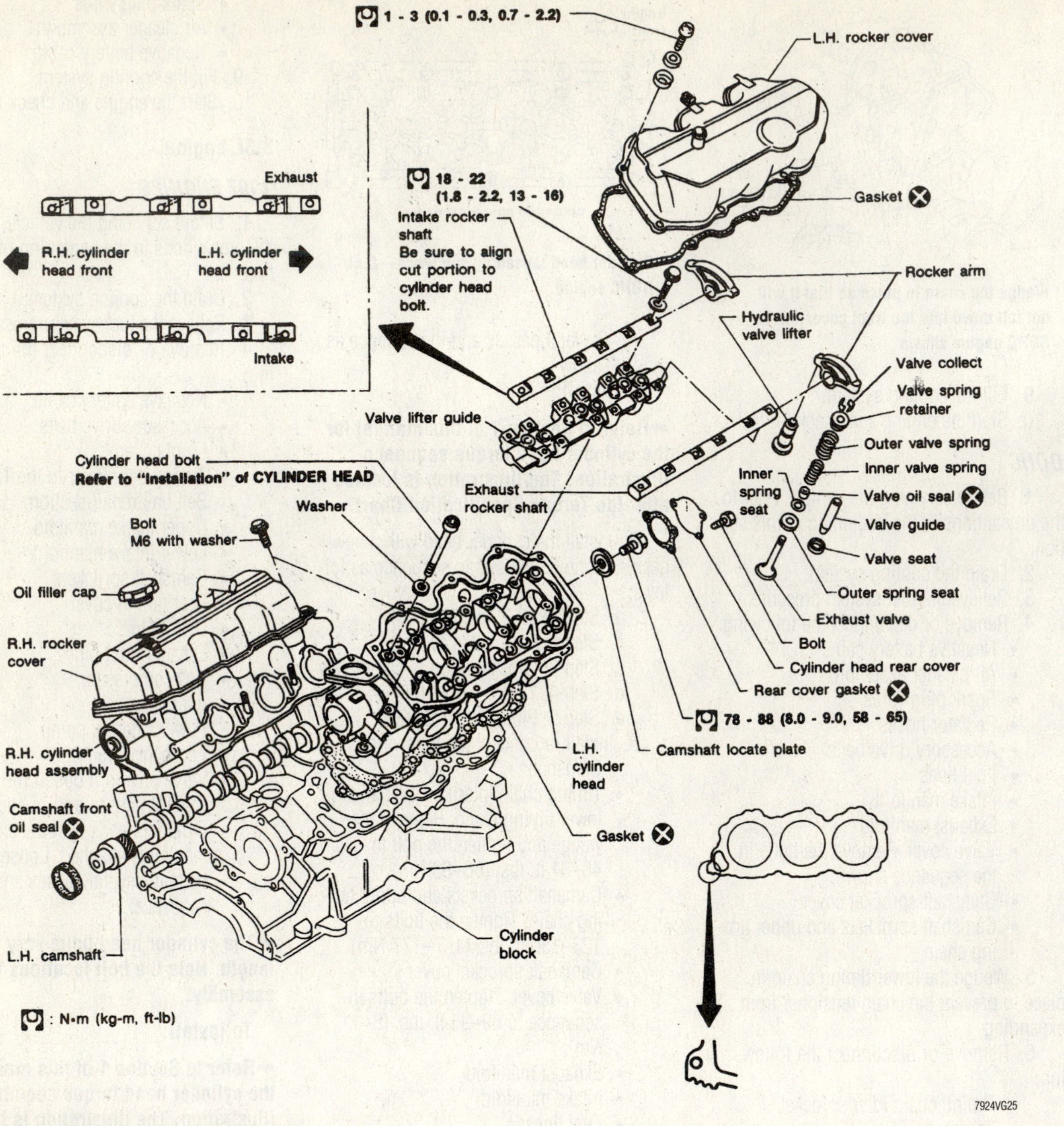

⌷ 1 - 3 (0.1 - 0.3, 0.7 - 2.2)

L.H. rocker cover

Exhaust

R.H. cylinder head front

L.H. cylinder head front

Intake

⌷ 18 - 22
(1.8 - 2.2, 13 - 16)

Intake rocker shaft
Be sure to align cut portion to cylinder head bolt.

Gasket ⊗

Valve lifter guide

Rocker arm

Hydraulic valve lifter

Valve collect

Valve spring retainer

Outer valve spring

Inner valve spring

Valve oil seal ⊗

Valve guide

Valve seat

Inner spring seat

Exhaust rocker shaft

Cylinder head bolt
Refer to "Installation" of CYLINDER HEAD

Washer

Bolt
M6 with washer

Oil filler cap

R.H. rocker cover

R.H. cylinder head assembly

Camshaft front oil seal ⊗

L.H. camshaft

Outer spring seat

Exhaust valve

Bolt

Cylinder head rear cover

Rear cover gasket ⊗

⌷ 78 - 88 (8.0 - 9.0, 58 - 65)

L.H. cylinder head

Camshaft locate plate

Gasket ⊗

Cylinder block

⌷ : N•m (kg-m, ft-lb)

Exploded view of the cylinder head assembly—3.3L engine

- Accessory brackets
- Power steering pump
- Alternator
- A/C compressor
- Exhaust front pipes
- Distributor
- Rear timing cover
- Camshaft sprockets
- Lower intake manifold
- Upper intake manifold
- Timing belt
- Front cover
- Accessory drive belts
- Negative battery cable

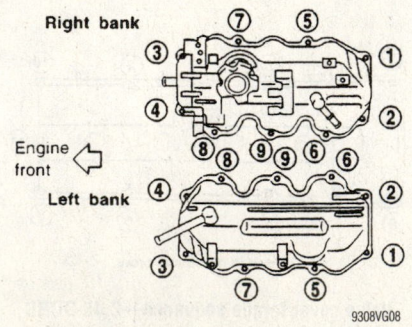

Right bank

Engine front

Left bank

9308VG08

Valve cover loosening sequence—3.3L engine

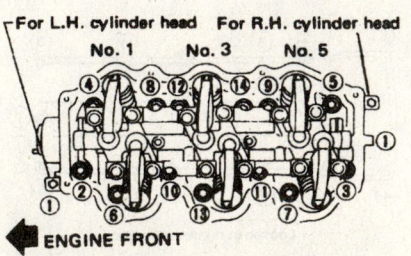

For L.H. cylinder head   For R.H. cylinder head
No. 1   No. 3   No. 5

ENGINE FRONT

7924VG26

Cylinder head loosening sequence—note the location of the sub-bolts in the No. 1 position—3.3L engine

7924VG25

7. Fill the cooling system.
8. Start the engine and check for leaks.

1998–01 ENGINES

1. Before servicing the vehicle, refer to the precautions in the beginning of this section.
2. Drain the cooling system.
3. Relieve the fuel system pressure.
4. Remove or disconnect the following:
   - Negative battery cable
   - Accessory drive belts
   - Front cover
   - Timing belt. Refer to the Timing Belt unit repair section.
   - Upper intake manifold
   - Lower intake manifold
   - Camshaft sprockets
   - Rear timing cover
   - Distributor
   - Exhaust front pipes
   - A/C compressor
   - Alternator
   - Power steering pump
   - Accessory brackets
   - Valve covers. Loosen the bolts in several passes and in sequence.
   - Cylinder heads with the exhaust manifolds attached. Loosen the bolts in several passes and in sequence.

➡ **The cylinder head bolts vary in length. Note the bolt locations for assembly.**

To install:

➡ **Refer to Section 1 of this manual for the cylinder head torque sequence illustration. The illustration is located after the Torque Specification Chart.**

5. Install the cylinder heads and the lower intake manifold at the same time. Tighten the bolts in sequence as follows:
   a. Step 1: Tighten the cylinder head bolts to 22 ft. lbs. (29 Nm)
   b. Step 2: Tighten the cylinder head bolts to 43 ft. lbs. (59 Nm)
   c. Step 3: Loosen all cylinder head bolts completely
   d. Step 4: Tighten the cylinder head bolts to 84 inch lbs. (10 Nm)
   e. Step 5: Tighten the intake manifold fasteners to 35 inch lbs. (4 Nm)
   f. Step 6: Tighten the intake manifold fasteners to 13 ft. lbs. (18 Nm)
   g. Step 7: Tighten the intake manifold fasteners to 12–14 ft. lbs. (16–20 Nm)
   h. Step 8: Loosen all intake fasteners completely

   i. Step 9: Tighten the cylinder head bolts to 22 ft. lbs. (29 Nm)
   j. Step 10: Tighten the cylinder head bolts 60–65 degrees **OR** tighten to 40–47 ft. lbs. (54–64 Nm)
   k. Step 11: Tighten the cylinder head sub-bolts to 80–105 inch lbs. (9–12 Nm)
   l. Step 12: Tighten the intake manifold fasteners to 35 inch lbs. (4 Nm)
   m. Step 13: Tighten the intake manifold fasteners to 78 inch lbs. (9 Nm)
   n. Step 14: Tighten the intake manifold fasteners to 70–84 inch lbs. (6–7 Nm)
6. Install or connect the following:
   - Valve covers
   - Accessory brackets
   - Power steering pump
   - Alternator
   - A/C compressor
   - Exhaust front pipes
   - Distributor
   - Rear timing cover
   - Camshaft sprockets
   - Upper intake manifold
   - Timing belt
   - Front cover
   - Accessory drive belts
   - Negative battery cable
7. Fill the cooling system.
8. Start the engine and check for leaks.

Rocker Arms/Shafts

REMOVAL & INSTALLATION

2.4L Engine

SOHC ENGINE

1. Before servicing the vehicle, refer to the precautions in the beginning of this section.
2. Remove or disconnect the following:
   - Negative battery cable
   - Air cleaner assembly
   - Valve cover
3. Wedge the timing chain in place to prevent the chain tensioner from expanding.
4. Remove or disconnect the following:
   - Camshaft timing sprocket and timing chain
   - Rocker arm and shaft assemblies. Loosen the bolts in the sequence shown.
   - Rocker arms from the shafts

➡ **Keep all valvetrain components in order for assembly.**

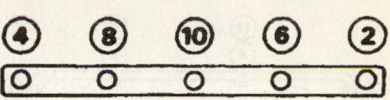

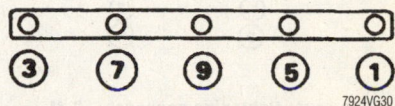

7924VG30

Rocker arm shaft loosening sequence— 2.4L SOHC engine

➡ **When the rocker arms are removed, stand them straight up or soak them in clean engine oil.**

To install:

5. Lubricate all contact points with clean engine oil and assemble the rocker arms to the shafts in their original positions.
6. Install or connect the following:
   - Rocker arm and shaft assemblies. Tighten the bolts in several passes and in reverse of the loosening sequence to 27–30 ft. lbs. (37–41 Nm).

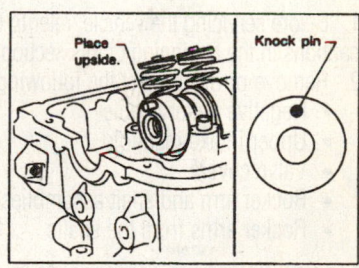

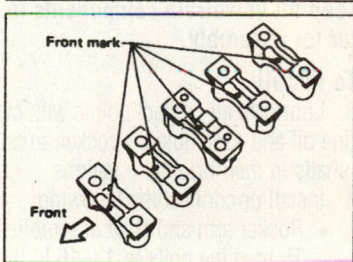

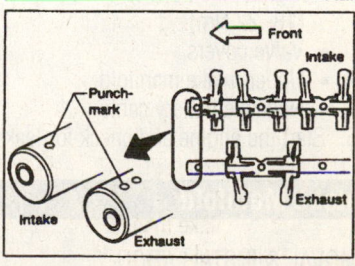

7924VG31

Rocker arm shaft identification marks— 2.4L SOHC engine

Refer to Section 1 for engine rebuilding specifications

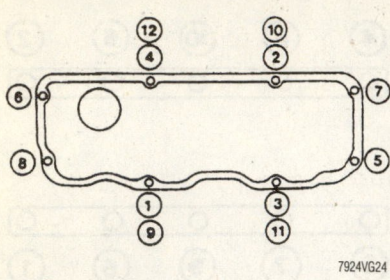

Valve cover tightening sequence—2.4L SOHC engine

- Camshaft timing sprocket and timing chain. Remove the wedge.
- Valve cover. Tighten bolts 4 and 3 to 26 inch lbs. (3 Nm), then tighten all bolts in sequence to 61–95 inch lbs. (7–11 Nm).
- Air cleaner assembly
- Negative battery cable

7. Start the engine and check for leaks.

DOHC ENGINE

This engine is not equipped with rocker arms. The camshafts act directly on the valve lifters.

3.3L Engine

1. Before servicing the vehicle, refer to the precautions in the beginning of this section.
2. Remove or disconnect the following:
   - Negative battery cable
   - Upper intake manifold
   - Valve covers
   - Rocker arm and shaft assemblies
   - Rocker arms from the shafts

➡**Keep all valvetrain components in order for assembly.**

To install:

3. Lubricate all contact points with clean engine oil and assemble the rocker arms to the shafts in their original positions.
4. Install or connect the following:
   - Rocker arm and shaft assemblies. Tighten the bolts to 13–16 ft. lbs. (18–22 Nm).
   - Valve covers
   - Upper intake manifold
   - Negative battery cable
5. Start the engine and check for leaks.

Intake Manifold

REMOVAL & INSTALLATION

2.4L Engine

1. Before servicing the vehicle, refer to the precautions in the beginning of this section.

2. Drain the cooling system.
3. Relieve the fuel system pressure.
4. Remove or disconnect the following:
   - Negative battery cable
   - Air cleaner assembly
   - Coolant hoses
   - Fuel lines
   - Accelerator cable
   - Cruise control cable, if equipped
   - Positive Crankcase Ventilation (PCV) valve and hose
   - Exhaust Gas Recirculation (EGR) tube
   - EGR temperature sensor connector
   - Idle Air Control (IAC) valve and solenoid connectors
   - Throttle Position (TP) sensor and switch connectors
   - Engine Coolant Temperature (ECT) sensor connector
   - Manifold Absolute Pressure (MAP) sensor connector and vacuum line
   - Evaporative Emissions (EVAP) canister purge valve vacuum line
   - Brake booster vacuum line
   - Fuel injector connectors
   - Intake manifold bracket
   - Intake manifold. Loosen the fasteners in reverse of the torque sequence.

To install:

➡**Refer to Section 1 of this manual for the intake manifold torque sequence illustration. The illustration is located after the Torque Specification Chart.**

5. Install or connect the following:
   - Intake manifold. Tighten the bolts to 12–14 ft. lbs. (16–19 Nm).
   - Intake manifold bracket. Tighten the bolts to 24–28 ft. lbs. (32–38 Nm).
   - Fuel injector connectors
   - Brake booster vacuum line
   - EVAP canister purge valve vacuum line
   - MAP sensor connector and vacuum line
   - ECT sensor connector
   - TP sensor and switch connectors
   - IAC valve and solenoid connectors
   - EGR temperature sensor connector
   - EGR tube
   - PCV valve and hose
   - Cruise control cable, if equipped
   - Accelerator cable
   - Fuel lines
   - Coolant hoses
   - Air cleaner assembly
   - Negative battery cable
6. Fill the cooling system.
7. Start the engine and check for leaks.

3.3L Engine

1. Before servicing the vehicle, refer to the precautions in the beginning of this section.
2. Drain the cooling system.
3. Relieve the fuel system pressure.
4. Remove or disconnect the following:
   - Negative battery cable
   - Air intake duct
   - Accelerator cable
   - Cruise control cable
   - Idle Air Control (IAC) valve connector
   - Throttle Position (TP) sensor and switch connectors
   - Ignition coil and power transistor connectors
   - Exhaust Gas Recirculation (EGR) Solenoid valve connector
   - EGR temperature sensor connector
   - Radiator hoses
   - Heater hoses
   - Positive Crankcase Ventilation (PCV) valve and hose
   - Evaporative Emissions (EVAP) canister vacuum and purge hoses
   - Brake booster vacuum hose
   - Fuel pressure regulator vacuum hose
   - EGR tube
   - Spark plug wires
   - Distributor
   - Left bank injector connectors
   - Thermal transmitter
   - Upper intake manifold ground cable
   - Breather pipe
   - Upper intake manifold
   - Fuel lines
   - Right bank injector connectors
   - Fuel supply manifold
   - Engine Coolant Temperature (ECT) sensor connector
   - Lower intake manifold. Loosen the fasteners in the sequence shown.

To install:

➡**Refer to Section 1 of this manual for the intake manifold torque sequence illustration. The illustration is located after the Torque Specification Chart.**

5. Install the lower intake manifold with a new gasket.
6. For 1997 engines, tighten the fasteners as follows:
   a. Step 1: Tighten all bolts to 26–43 inch lbs. (3–5 Nm)
   b. Step 2: Tighten all nuts to 26–43 inch lbs. (3–5 Nm)

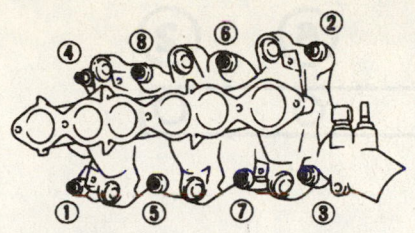

Loosen bolts in
numerical order.

7924VG32

**Intake manifold loosening sequence—
3.3L engine**

c. Step 3: Tighten all bolts to 13–16
ft. lbs. (18–22 Nm).

d. Step 4: Tighten all nuts to 13–16 ft.
lbs. (18–22 Nm).

7. For 1998–01 engines, tighten the
fasteners in sequence as follows:

a. Step 1: 35 inch lbs. (4 Nm)

b. Step 2: 78 inch lbs. (9 Nm)

c. Step 3: 70–84 inch lbs. (8–10
Nm)

8. Install or connect the following:
- ECT sensor connector
- Fuel supply manifold
- Right bank injector connectors
- Fuel lines
- Upper intake manifold
- Breather pipe
- Upper intake manifold ground
  cable
- Thermal transmitter
- Left bank injector connectors
- Distributor
- Spark plug wires
- EGR tube
- Fuel pressure regulator vacuum
  hose
- Brake booster vacuum hose
- EVAP canister vacuum and purge
  hoses
- PCV valve and hose
- Heater hoses
- Radiator hoses
- EGR temperature sensor connec-
  tor
- EGR Solenoid valve connector
- Ignition coil and power transistor
  connectors
- TP sensor and switch connectors
- IAC valve connector
- Cruise control cable
- Accelerator cable
- Air intake duct
- Negative battery cable

9. Fill the cooling system.
10. Start the engine and check for leaks.

Exhaust Manifold

REMOVAL & INSTALLATION

2.4L Engine

1. Before servicing the vehicle, refer to
the precautions in the beginning of this section.

2. Remove or disconnect the following:
- Negative battery cable
- Heated Oxygen (HO₂S) sensor con-
  nector
- Exhaust manifold heat shield
- Exhaust Gas Recirculation (EGR)
  tube
- Exhaust front pipe
- Exhaust manifold. Loosen the nuts
  in reverse of the torque sequence.

To install:

3. Install or connect the following:
- Exhaust manifold. Tighten the nuts
  in sequence to 12–15 ft. lbs.
  (16–21 Nm) for SOHC engines or
  to 28–35 ft. lbs. (37–48 Nm) for
  DOHC engines.
- Exhaust front pipe. Tighten the fas-
  teners to 32–37 ft. lbs. (43–50
  Nm).
- EGR tube. Tighten the flange fit-
  tings to 29–36 ft. lbs. (39–49 Nm).
- Exhaust manifold heat shield.
  Tighten the bolts to 45–57 inch lbs.
  (5–7 Nm).
- HO₂S sensor connector
- Negative battery cable

4. Start the engine and check for leaks.

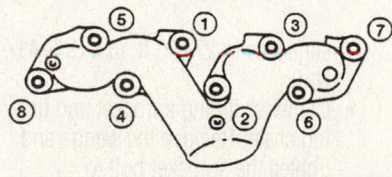

9308VG09

**Exhaust manifold torque sequence—2.4L
engine**

3.3L Engine

1. Before servicing the vehicle, refer to
the precautions in the beginning of this section.

2. Remove or disconnect the following:
- Negative battery cable
- Exhaust manifold heat shields
- Exhaust Gas Recirculation (EGR)
  tube

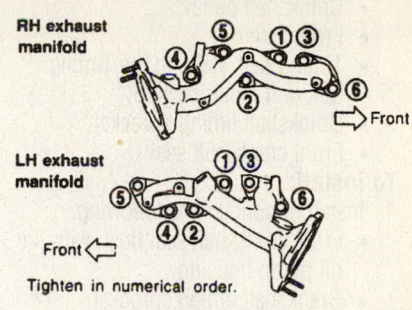

RH exhaust
manifold

Front

LH exhaust
manifold

Front

Tighten in numerical order.

7924VG36

**Exhaust manifold torque sequence—3.3L
engine**

- Heated Oxygen (HO₂S) sensor connectors
- Exhaust front pipes
- Exhaust manifolds with catalytic
  converters attached. Loosen the
  nuts in the reverse of the torque
  sequence.

To install:

3. Install or connect the following:
- Exhaust manifolds with catalytic
  converters attached. Tighten the
  nuts in sequence to 21–25 ft. lbs.
  (28–33 Nm).
- Exhaust front pipes. Tighten the
  bolts to 21–25 ft. lbs. (28–33 Nm).
- Heated Oxygen (HO₂S) sensor connectors
- EGR tube. Tighten the flange fittings to 29–36 ft. lbs. (39–49 Nm).
- Exhaust manifold heat shields.
  Tighten the bolts to 84–96 inch lbs.
  (9–11 Nm)
- Negative battery cable

4. Start the engine and check for leaks.

Front Crankshaft Seal

REMOVAL & INSTALLATION

2.4L Engine

Refer to the Timing Chain, Sprockets,
Front Cover and Seal procedure in this section.

3.3L Engine

1. Before servicing the vehicle, refer to
the precautions in the beginning of this section.

2. Drain the cooling system.

3. Remove or disconnect the following:
- Negative battery cable
- Accessory drive belts
- Radiator hoses

For engine torque specifications, refer to Section 1 of this manual

- Crankshaft pulley
- Front cover
- Timing belt. Refer to the Timing Belt unit repair section.
- Crankshaft timing sprocket
- Front crankshaft seal

To install:

4. Install or connect the following:
- Front crankshaft seal flush with the oil pump housing
- Crankshaft timing sprocket
- Timing belt
- Front cover. Tighten the bolts to 26–43 inch lbs. (3–5 Nm).
- Crankshaft pulley. Tighten the bolt to 141–156 ft. lbs. (191–211 Nm).
- Radiator hoses
- Accessory drive belts
- Negative battery cable

5. Fill the cooling system.
6. Start the engine and check for leaks.

Camshaft and Valve Lifters

REMOVAL & INSTALLATION

2.4L Engine

SOHC

1. Before servicing the vehicle, refer to the precautions in the beginning of this section.
2. Remove or disconnect the following:
- Negative battery cable
- Air cleaner assembly
- Valve cover

3. Wedge the timing chain in place to prevent the chain tensioner from expanding.
4. Remove or disconnect the following:
- Camshaft timing sprocket and timing chain
- Rocker arm and shaft assemblies. Loosen the bolts in the sequence shown.
- Hydraulic lifters
- Camshaft

➡**Keep all valvetrain components in order for assembly.**

➡**When the rocker arms are removed, stand them straight up or soak them in clean engine oil.**

To install:

5. Install or connect the following:
- Camshaft
- Hydraulic lifters in their original positions
- Rocker arm and shaft assemblies. Tighten the bolts in several passes and in reverse of the loosening

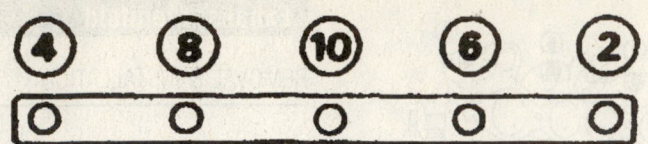

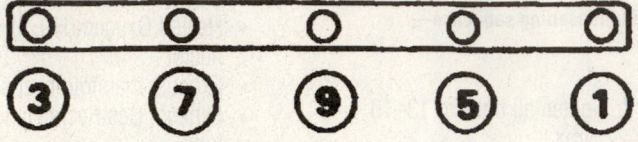

Rocker arm shaft loosening sequence—2.4L SOHC engine

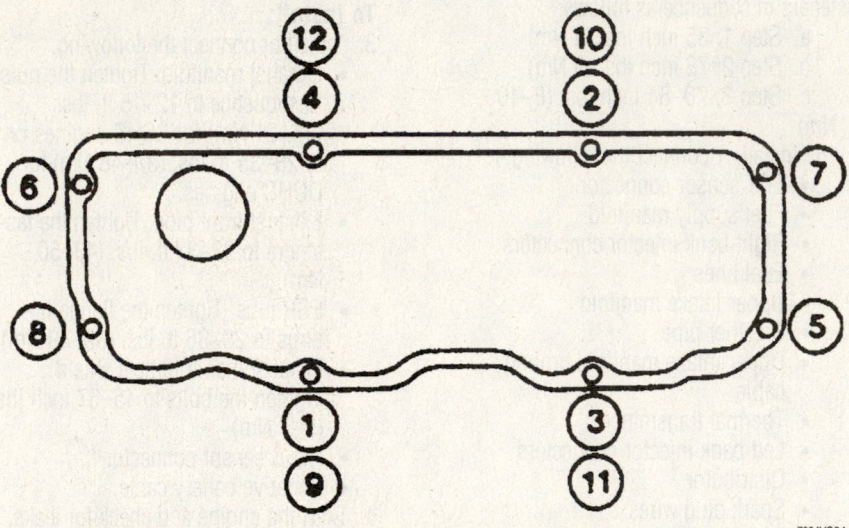

Valve cover tightening sequence—2.4L SOHC engine

sequence to 27–30 ft. lbs. (37–41 Nm).
- Camshaft timing sprocket and timing chain. Remove the wedge and tighten the sprocket bolt to 101–116 ft. lbs. (137–157 Nm).
- Valve cover. Tighten bolts 4 and 3 to 26 inch lbs. (3 Nm), then tighten all bolts in sequence to 61–95 inch lbs. (7–11 Nm).
- Air cleaner assembly
- Negative battery cable

6. Start the engine and check for leaks.

DOHC

1. Before servicing the vehicle, refer to the precautions in the beginning of this section.
2. Remove or disconnect the following:
- Negative battery cable
- Air cleaner assembly

- Spark plug wires
- Valve cover. Remove the bolts in the sequence shown.
- Camshaft sprocket cover
- Camshaft sprockets and upper timing chain

➡**Keep all valvetrain components in order for assembly.**

- Camshaft bearing caps. Loosen the bolts in several passes in reverse of the torque sequence.
- Camshafts
- Valve lifters and shims

To install:

3. Install or connect the following:
- Valve lifters and shims in their original positions
- Camshafts

4. Install the bearing caps. Tighten the bolts in sequence as follows:

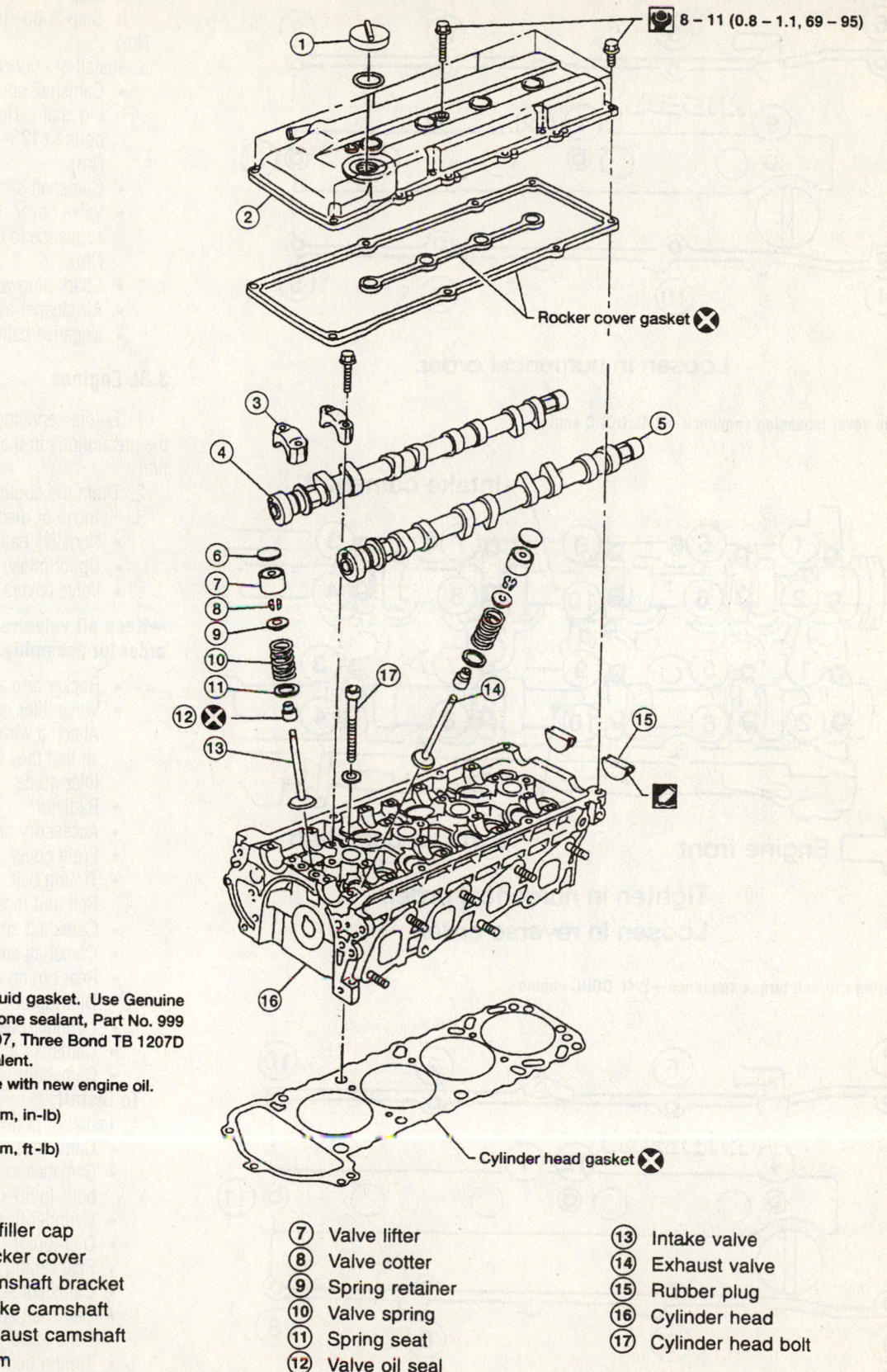

8 – 11 (0.8 – 1.1, 69 – 95)

Rocker cover gasket ⊗

Cylinder head gasket ⊗

✎ : Apply liquid gasket. Use Genuine RTV silicone sealant, Part No. 999 MP-A7007, Three Bond TB 1207D or equivalent.

▢ : Lubricate with new engine oil.

🔧 : N·m (kg-m, in-lb)

🔧 : N·m (kg-m, ft-lb)

① Oil filler cap
② Rocker cover
③ Camshaft bracket
④ Intake camshaft
⑤ Exhaust camshaft
⑥ Shim
⑦ Valve lifter
⑧ Valve cotter
⑨ Spring retainer
⑩ Valve spring
⑪ Spring seat
⑫ Valve oil seal
⑬ Intake valve
⑭ Exhaust valve
⑮ Rubber plug
⑯ Cylinder head
⑰ Cylinder head bolt

Exploded view of the camshafts and related components—2.4L DOHC engine

7924VG53

For complete mechanical specifications, refer to Section 1 of this manual

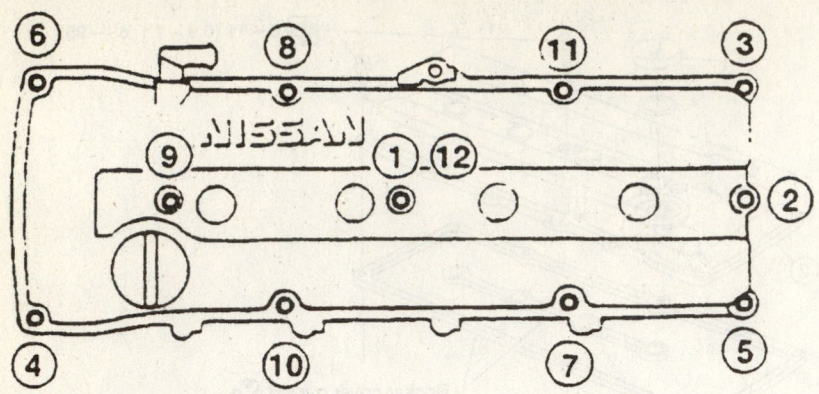

Loosen in numerical order.

9308VG06

Valve cover loosening sequence—2.4L DOHC engine

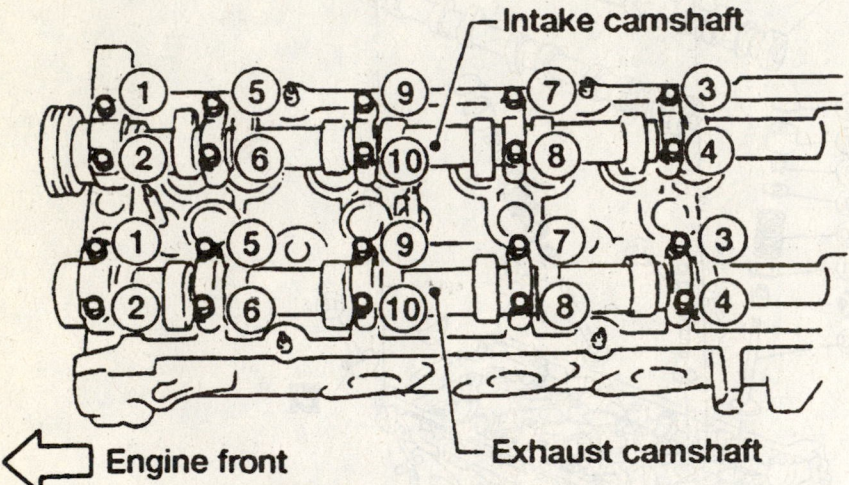

Tighten in numerical order.
Loosen in reverse order.

7924VG51

Bearing cap bolt torque sequence—2.4L DOHC engine

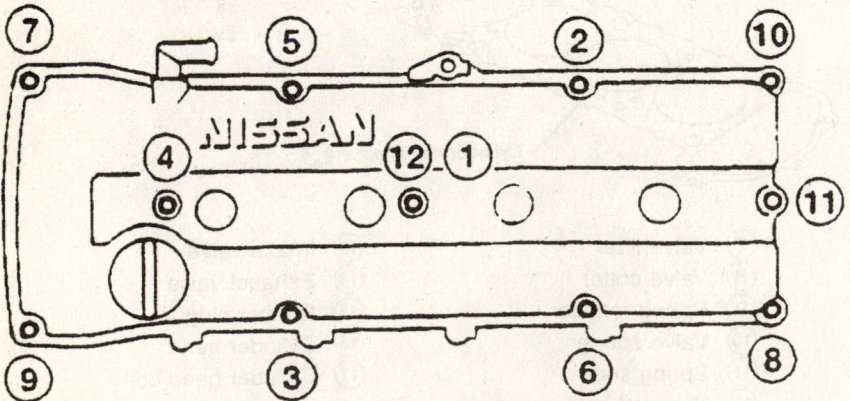

Tighten in numerical order.

9308VG07

Valve cover torque sequence—2.4L DOHC engine

a. Step 1: 17 inch lbs. (2 Nm)
b. Step 2: 80–104 inch lbs. (9–12 Nm)
5. Install or connect the following:
  • Camshaft sprockets and upper timing chain. Tighten the sprocket bolts to 123–130 ft. lbs. (167–177 Nm).
  • Camshaft sprocket cover
  • Valve cover. Tighten the bolts in sequence to 69–95 inch lbs. (8–11 Nm).
  • Spark plug wires
  • Air cleaner assembly
  • Negative battery cable

3.3L Engines

1. Before servicing the vehicle, refer to the precautions in the beginning of this section.
2. Drain the cooling system.
3. Remove or disconnect the following:
  • Negative battery cable
  • Upper intake manifold
  • Valve covers

➡ **Keep all valvetrain components in order for assembly.**

  • Rocker arm and shaft assemblies
  • Valve lifter guide and valve lifters. Attach a wire to the top of the lifters so that they will not drop from the lifter guide.
  • Radiator
  • Accessory drive belts
  • Front cover
  • Timing belt. Refer to the Timing Belt unit repair section.
  • Camshaft sprockets
  • Camshaft seals
  • Rear timing cover
  • Distributor
  • Cylinder head rear covers
  • Camshaft locating plates
  • Camshafts

To install:
4. Install or connect the following:
  • Camshafts
  • Camshaft locating plates. Tighten the bolts to 58–65 ft. lbs. (78–88 Nm).
  • Cylinder head rear covers
  • Distributor
  • Rear timing cover
  • Camshaft seals
  • Camshaft sprockets. Tighten the bolts to 58–65 ft. lbs. (78–88 Nm).
  • Timing belt
  • Front cover
  • Accessory drive belts
  • Radiator
  • Valve lifter guide and valve lifters

- Rocker arm and shaft assemblies. Tighten the bolts to 13–16 ft. lbs. (18–22 Nm).
- Valve covers
- Upper intake manifold
- Negative battery cable

5. Fill the cooling system.

6. Start the engine and check for leaks.

Valve Lash

ADJUSTMENT

2.4L SOHC and 3.3L Engines

These engines are equipped with hydraulic valve lifters that do not require periodic adjustment.

2.4L DOHC Engine

➡**Measure valve clearance with the engine warm.**

1. Before servicing the vehicle, refer to the precautions in the beginning of this section.

2. Remove the valve cover.

3. Set the engine to the top of the compression stroke with the valves closed for the cylinder to be measured.

4. Check the valve clearance. The valve clearance specifications are as follows:

- Intake: 0.012–0.015 in. (0.31–0.39mm)
- Exhaust: 0.013–0.016 in. (0.33–0.41mm)

5. If adjustment is necessary, compress the valve spring with Tool **A** and insert Tool **B** to hold the valve in the open position as shown.

6. Replace the shims as necessary to achieve the correct valve clearance.

7. Repeat for each valve to be adjusted.

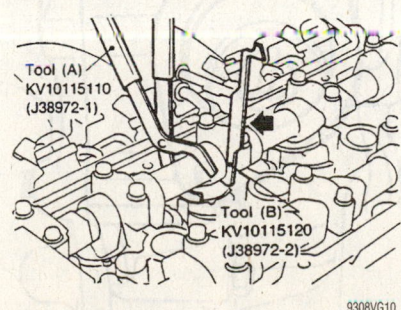

Valve adjustment tools (A) and (B)—2.4L DOHC engine

Starter Motor

REMOVAL & INSTALLATION

1. Before servicing the vehicle, refer to the precautions in the beginning of this section.

2. Remove or disconnect the following:
- Negative battery cable
- Engine under cover
- Starter harness connectors
- Starter motor

To install:

3. Install or connect the following:
- Starter motor. Tighten the bolts to 22–27 ft. lbs. (30–36 Nm).
- Starter harness connectors
- Engine under cover
- Negative battery cable

Oil Pan

REMOVAL & INSTALLATION

2.4L Engine

1. Before servicing the vehicle, refer to the precautions in the beginning of this section.

2. Drain the engine oil.

3. Remove or disconnect the following:
- Negative battery cable
- Engine under cover
- Stabilizer bar
- Oil pan. Loosen the bolts in the sequence shown.

To install:

4. Apply a continuous bead of sealant 0.138–0.177 in. (3.5–4.5mm) to the oil pan mating surface.

5. Install or connect the following:
- Oil pan. Tighten the bolts in sequence to 60–72 inch lbs. (7–8 Nm).
- Stabilizer bar. Tighten the bracket

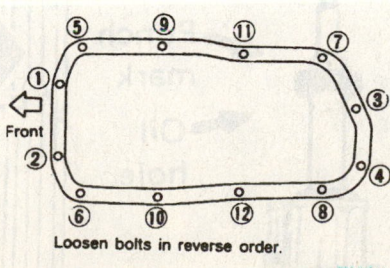

Oil pan bolt removal sequence—2.4L engine

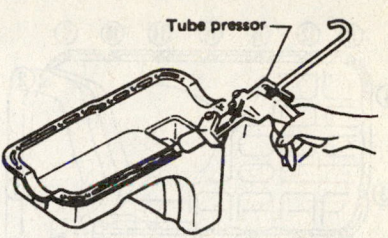

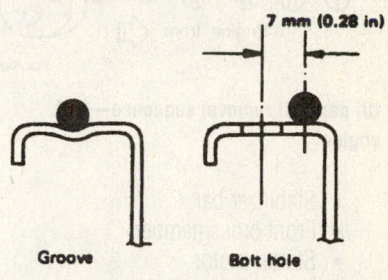

Oil pan sealant application—2.4L engine shown

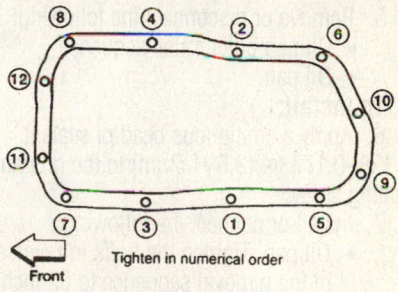

Oil pan bolt installation sequence—2.4L engine

bolts to 38–45 ft. lbs. (51–61 Nm) and the link nuts to 12–16 ft. lbs. (16–22 Nm).
- Engine under cover
- Negative battery cable

➡**Wait 30 minutes after installation of the oil pan to allow the sealant to cure before adding oil.**

6. Fill the crankcase to the correct level.

7. Start the engine and check for leaks.

3.3L Engine

2WD MODELS

1. Before servicing the vehicle, refer to the precautions in the beginning of this section.

2. Drain the engine oil.

3. Remove or disconnect the following:
- Negative battery cable
- Engine under cover

Please refer to Section 8 for electric cooling fan wiring schematics

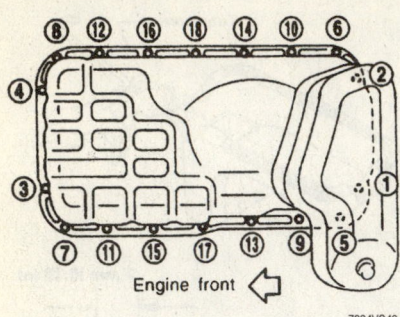

Oil pan bolt removal sequence—3.3L engine

7924VG42

- Stabilizer bar
- Front crossmember
- Starter motor
- Transmission mount
- Left and right motor mounts
- Power steering gear

4. Raise and support the engine for clearance.

5. Remove or disconnect the following:
- Oil pan bolts in the sequence
- Oil pan

To install:

6. Apply a continuous bead of sealant 0.138–0.177 in. (3.5–4.5mm) to the oil pan mating surface.

7. Install or connect the following:
- Oil pan. Tighten the bolts in reverse of the removal sequence to 62 inch lbs. (7 Nm).
- Power steering gear
- Left and right motor mounts
- Transmission mount
- Starter motor
- Front crossmember
- Stabilizer bar
- Engine under cover
- Negative battery cable

➡ **Wait 30 minutes after installation of the oil pan to allow the sealant to cure before adding oil.**

8. Fill the crankcase to the correct level.
9. Start the engine and check for leaks.

4WD MODELS

1. Before servicing the vehicle, refer to the precautions in the beginning of this section.

2. Drain the engine oil.

3. Remove or disconnect the following:
- Negative battery cable
- Engine under cover
- Stabilizer bar brackets
- Front driveshaft
- Axle halfshafts
- Front suspension crossmember

- Front differential and mounting bracket
- Starter motor
- Transmission mount
- Left and right motor mounts
- Power steering gear
- Relay rod

4. Raise and support the engine for clearance.

5. Remove or disconnect the following:
- Oil pan bolts in the sequence
- Oil pan

To install:

6. Apply a continuous bead of sealant 0.138–0.177 in. (3.5–4.5mm) to the oil pan mating surface.

7. Install or connect the following:
- Oil pan. Tighten the bolts in reverse of the removal sequence to 62 inch lbs. (7 Nm).
- Relay rod
- Power steering gear
- Left and right motor mounts
- Transmission mount
- Starter motor
- Front differential and mounting bracket
- Front suspension crossmember
- Axle halfshafts
- Front driveshaft
- Stabilizer bar brackets
- Engine under cover
- Negative battery cable

➡ **Wait 30 minutes after installation of the oil pan to allow the sealant to cure before adding oil.**

8. Fill the crankcase to the correct level.
9. Start the engine and check for leaks.

Oil Pump

REMOVAL & INSTALLATION

2.4L Engine

1. Before servicing the vehicle, refer to the precautions in the beginning of this section.

2. Set the engine to Top Dead Center (TDC) of the compression stroke for the No. 1 cylinder.

3. Remove or disconnect the following:
- Distributor cap
- Distributor
- Engine under cover
- Stabilizer bar
- Oil pump and drive spindle

To install:

4. Fill the pump housing with engine oil, then align the punch mark on the spindle with the hole in the oil pump as shown.

5. Install or connect the following:
- Oil pump and drive spindle. Tighten the mounting bolts to 96–132 inch lbs. (11–15 Nm).
- Stabilizer bar
- Engine under cover
- Distributor
- Distributor cap

6. Start the engine and check for leaks.
7. Check the ignition timing and adjust, as necessary.

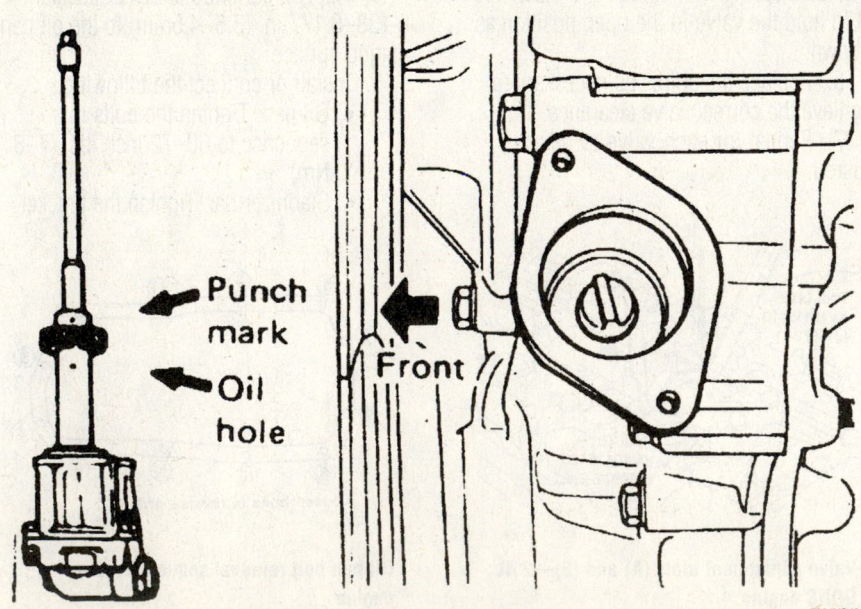

Align the punch mark with the oil hole before oil pump installation—2.4L engine

7924VG43

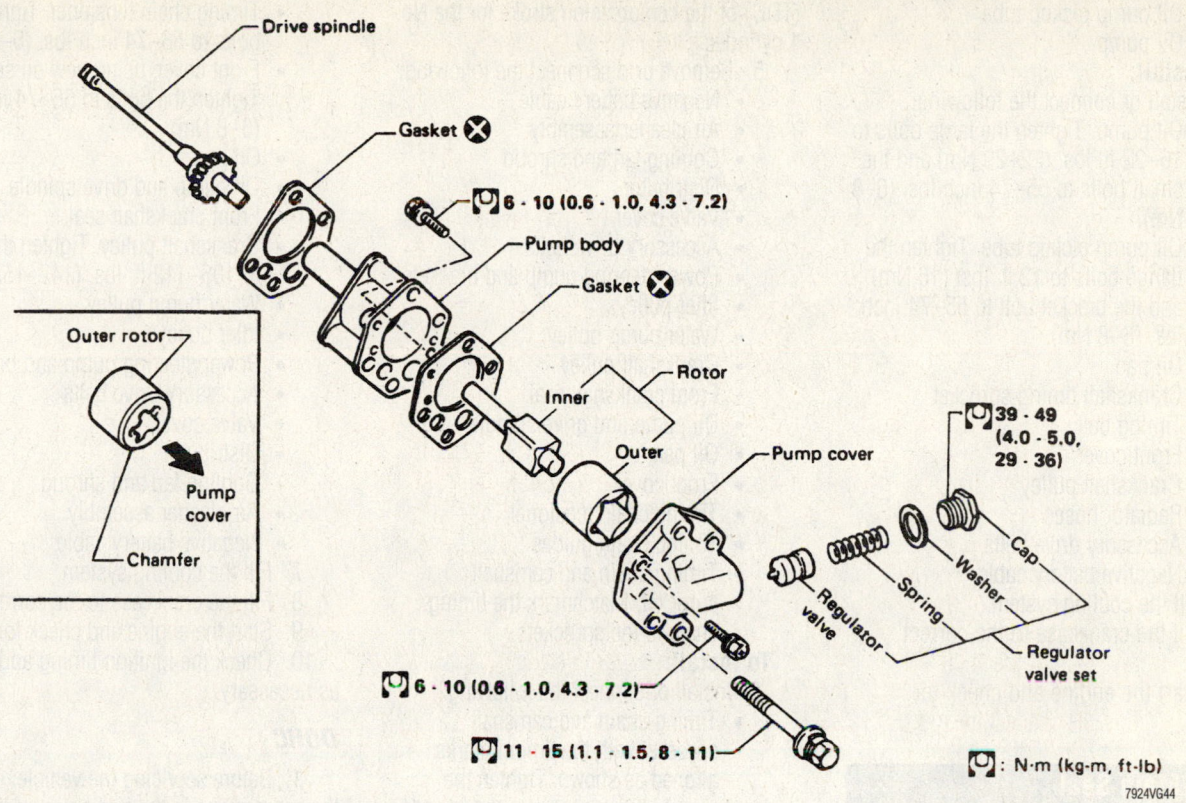

Exploded view of oil pump assembly—2.4L engine

3.3L Engine

1. Before servicing the vehicle, refer to the precautions in the beginning of this section.
2. Drain the engine oil.
3. Drain the cooling system.

4. Remove or disconnect the following:
   - Negative battery cable
   - Accessory drive belts
   - Radiator hoses
   - Crankshaft pulley
   - Front cover
   - Timing belt. Refer to the Timing Belt unit repair section.
   - Crankshaft timing sprocket
   - Oil pan

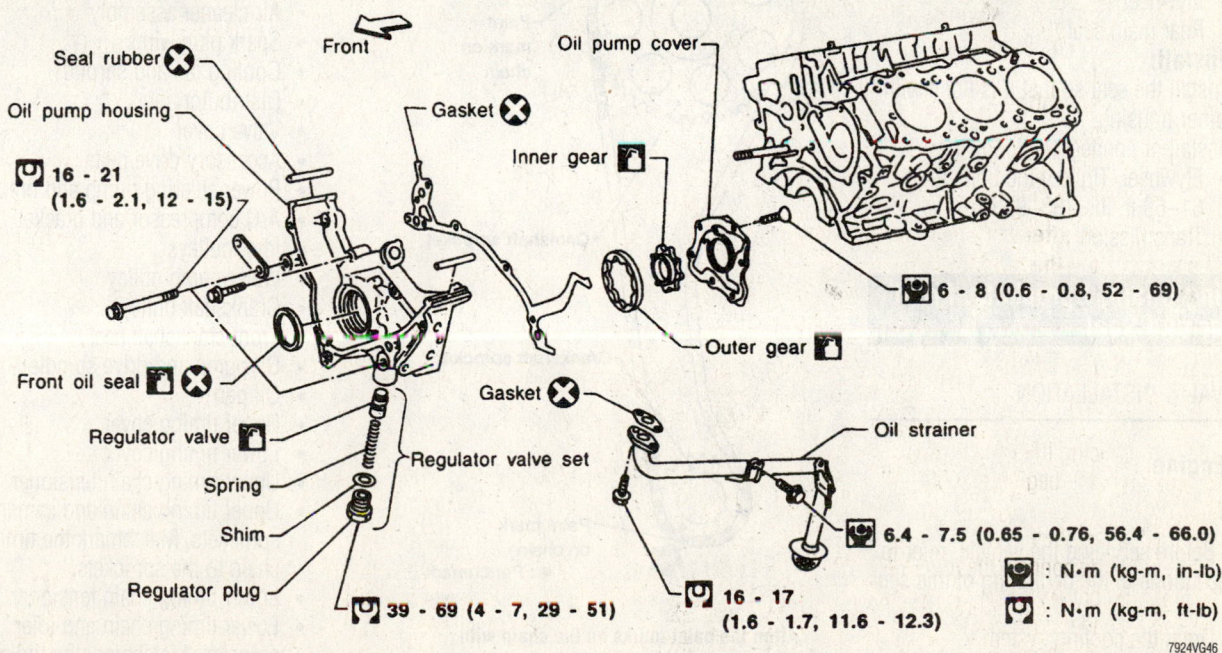

Oil pump assembly exploded view—3.3L engine

For complete service labor times order Nichols' Chilton Labor Guide Manual

- Oil pump pickup tube
- Oil pump

To install:

5. Install or connect the following:
- Oil pump. Tighten the large bolts to 16–22 ft. lbs. (22–29 Nm) and the small bolts to 55–74 inch lbs. (6–8 Nm).
- Oil pump pickup tube. Tighten the flange bolts to 12 ft. lbs. (16 Nm) and the bracket bolt to 55–74 inch lbs. (6–8 Nm).
- Oil pan
- Crankshaft timing sprocket
- Timing belt
- Front cover
- Crankshaft pulley
- Radiator hoses
- Accessory drive belts
- Negative battery cable

6. Fill the cooling system.
7. Fill the crankcase to the correct level.
8. Start the engine and check for leaks.

Rear Main Seal

REMOVAL & INSTALLATION

1. Before servicing the vehicle, refer to the precautions in the beginning of this section.
2. Remove or disconnect the following:
- Transmission
- Flywheel
- Rear main seal

To install:

3. Install the seal so that it is flush with the retainer housing.
4. Install or connect the following:
- Flywheel. Tighten the bolts to 61–69 ft. lbs. (83–93 Nm).
- Transmission

Timing Chain, Sprockets, Front Cover and Seal

REMOVAL & INSTALLATION

2.4L Engine

SOHC

1. Before servicing the vehicle, refer to the precautions in the beginning of this section.
2. Drain the cooling system.
3. Drain the engine oil.
4. Set the engine to Top Dead Center

(TDC) of the compression stroke for the No. 1 cylinder.

5. Remove or disconnect the following:
- Negative battery cable
- Air cleaner assembly
- Cooling fan and shroud
- Distributor
- Valve cover
- Accessory drive belts
- Power steering pump and brackets
- Idler pulleys
- Water pump pulley
- Crankshaft pulley
- Front crankshaft seal
- Oil pump and drive spindle
- Oil pan
- Front cover
- Timing chain tensioner
- Timing chain guides
- Timing chain and camshaft sprocket. Matchmark the timing chain to the sprockets.

To install:

6. Install or connect the following:
- Timing chain and camshaft sprocket with the timing marks aligned as shown. Tighten the camshaft sprocket bolt to 101–116 ft. lbs. (137–157 Nm).
- Timing chain guides. Tighten the bolts to 14 ft. lbs. (19 Nm).

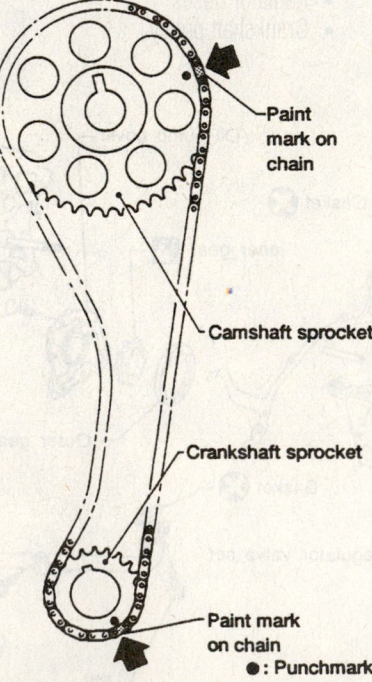

Paint mark on chain

Camshaft sprocket

Crankshaft sprocket

Paint mark on chain
● : Punchmark

7924VG48

Align the paint marks on the chain with the marks on the sprockets—2.4L SOHC engine

- Timing chain tensioner. Tighten the bolts to 56–74 inch lbs. (6–8 Nm).
- Front cover, using new oil seals. Tighten the bolts to 56–74 inch lbs. (6–8 Nm).
- Oil pan
- Oil pump and drive spindle
- Front crankshaft seal
- Crankshaft pulley. Tighten the bolt to 105–112 ft. lbs. (142–152 Nm).
- Water pump pulley
- Idler pulleys
- Power steering pump and brackets
- Accessory drive belts
- Valve cover
- Distributor
- Cooling fan and shroud
- Air cleaner assembly
- Negative battery cable

7. Fill the cooling system.
8. Fill the crankcase to the correct level.
9. Start the engine and check for leaks.
10. Check the ignition timing and adjust, as necessary.

DOHC

1. Before servicing the vehicle, refer to the precautions in the beginning of this section.
2. Drain the cooling system.
3. Drain the engine oil.
4. Set the engine to Top Dead Center (TDC) of the compression stroke for the No. 1 cylinder.

5. Remove or disconnect the following:
- Negative battery cable
- Air cleaner assembly
- Spark plug wires
- Cooling fan and shroud
- Distributor
- Valve cover
- Accessory drive belts
- Power steering pump and brackets
- A/C compressor and bracket
- Idler pulleys
- Water pump pulley
- Crankshaft pulley
- Front crankshaft seal
- Oil pump and drive spindle
- Oil pan
- Upper timing cover
- Lower timing cover
- Upper timing chain tensioner
- Upper timing chain and camshaft sprockets. Matchmark the timing chain to the sprockets.
- Lower timing chain tensioner
- Lower timing chain and idler sprocket. Matchmark the timing chain to the sprockets.

To install:

6. Install or connect the following:

- Lower timing chain and idler sprocket with the timing marks aligned as shown. Tighten the idler sprocket bolt to 48–61 ft. lbs. (66–83 Nm).
- Lower timing chain tensioner. Tighten the bolts to 56–66 inch lbs. (6.5–7.5 Nm).

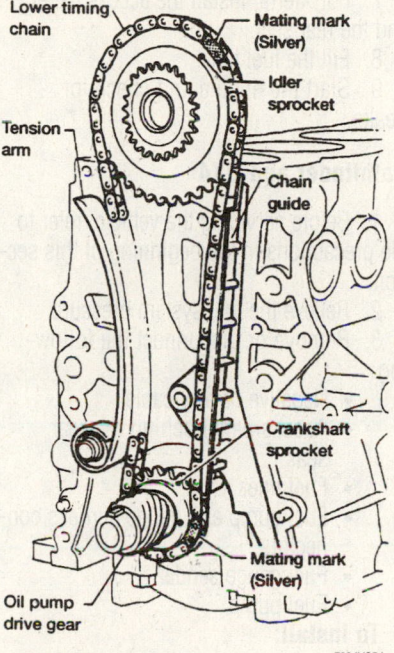

Lower timing chain alignment—2.4L DOHC engine

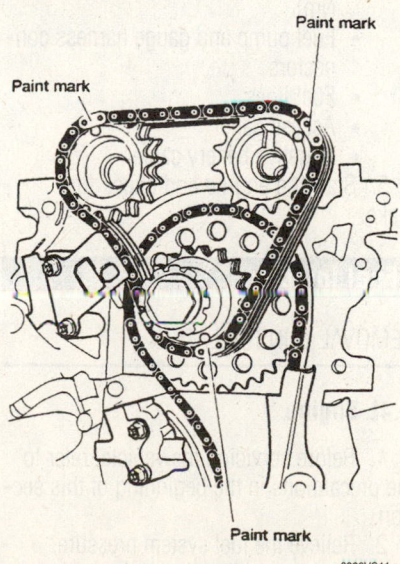

Upper timing chain alignment—2.4L DOHC engine

- Upper timing chain and camshaft sprockets with the timing marks aligned as shown. Tighten the camshaft sprocket bolts to 123–130 ft. lbs. (167–177 Nm).
- Upper timing chain tensioner. Tighten the bolts to 56–66 inch lbs. (6.5–7.5 Nm).
- Lower timing cover. Tighten the large bolts to 12–14 ft. lbs. (16–19 Nm) and the small bolts to 56–66 inch lbs. (6.5–7.5 Nm).
- Upper timing cover. Tighten the large bolts to 12–14 ft. lbs. (16–19 Nm) and the small bolts to 56–66 inch lbs. (6.5–7.5 Nm).
- Oil pan
- Oil pump and drive spindle
- Front crankshaft seal
- Crankshaft pulley. Tighten the bolt to 105–112 ft. lbs. (142–152 Nm).
- Water pump pulley
- Idler pulleys
- A/C compressor and bracket
- Power steering pump and brackets
- Accessory drive belts
- Valve cover
- Distributor
- Cooling fan and shroud
- Spark plug wires
- Air cleaner assembly
- Negative battery cable

7. Fill the cooling system.

8. Fill the crankcase to the correct level.

9. Start the engine and check for leaks.

10. Check the ignition timing and adjust, as necessary.

Piston and Ring

POSITIONING

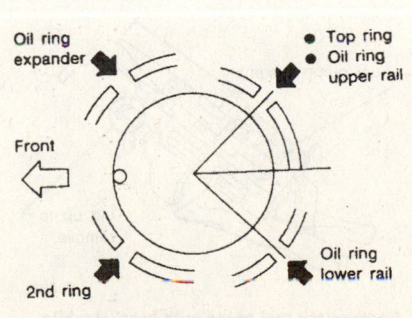

Piston ring end-gap spacing

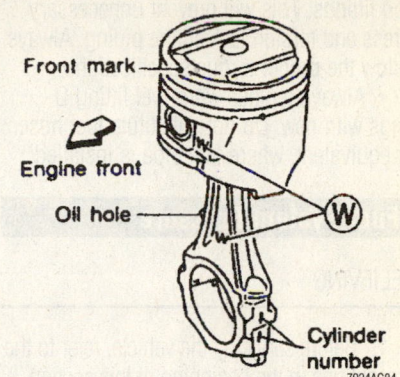

Piston and connecting rod positioning

FUEL SYSTEM

Fuel System Service Precautions

Safety is the most important factor when performing not only fuel system maintenance but any type of maintenance. Failure to conduct maintenance and repairs in a safe manner may result in serious personal injury or death. Maintenance and testing of the vehicle's fuel system components can be accomplished safely and effectively by adhering to the following rules and guidelines.

- To avoid the possibility of fire and personal injury, always disconnect the negative battery cable unless the repair or test procedure requires that battery voltage be applied.
- Always relieve the fuel system pressure prior to disconnecting any fuel system component (injector, fuel rail, pressure regulator, etc.), fitting or fuel line connection. Exercise extreme caution whenever relieving fuel system pressure, to avoid exposing skin, face and eyes to fuel spray. Please be advised that fuel under pressure may penetrate the skin or any part of the body that it contacts.
- Always place a shop towel or cloth around the fitting or connection prior to loosening to absorb any excess fuel due to spillage. Ensure that all fuel spillage (should it occur) is quickly removed from engine surfaces. Ensure that all fuel soaked cloths or towels are deposited into a suitable waste container.
- Always keep a dry chemical (Class B) fire extinguisher near the work area.
- Do not allow fuel spray or fuel vapors to come into contact with a spark or open flame.
- Always use a back-up wrench when loosening and tightening fuel line connec-

tion fittings. This will prevent unnecessary stress and torsion to fuel line piping. Always follow the proper torque specifications.

• Always replace worn fuel fitting O-rings with new. Do not substitute fuel hose or equivalent, where fuel pipe is installed.

Fuel System Pressure

RELIEVING

1. Before servicing the vehicle, refer to the precautions in the beginning of this section.
2. Remove the fuel pump fuse from the panel.
3. Start the engine and allow it to run until it stalls. Crank the engine for a few seconds to relieve additional fuel pressure.
4. Disconnect the negative battery cable.
5. When repairs are complete, replace the fuel pump fuse and connect the negative battery cable.

Fuel Filter

REMOVAL & INSTALLATION

➡The fuel filter is located under the hood in the right side of the engine compartment on 1997 Pick-Up, and under the vehicle near the fuel tank for all others.

1. Before servicing the vehicle, refer to the precautions in the beginning of this section.
2. Relieve the fuel system pressure.
3. Remove or disconnect the following:

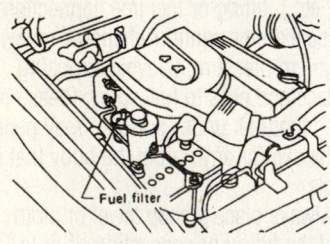

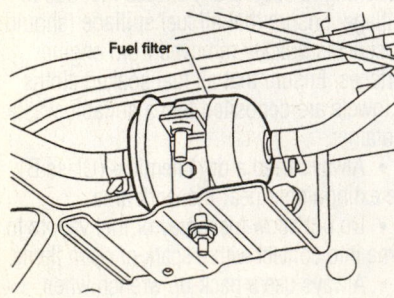

Typical fuel filter locations

7924VG56

- Fuel filter shield, if equipped
- Fuel lines
- Fuel filter from the bracket

To install:

4. Install or connect the following:
- Fuel filter to the bracket
- Fuel lines
- Fuel filter shield, if equipped
5. Start the engine and check for leaks.

Fuel Pump

REMOVAL & INSTALLATION

Pick-Up, Frontier and Xterra

1. Before servicing the vehicle, refer to the precautions in the beginning of this section.
2. Relieve the fuel system pressure.
3. For Xterra, remove the rear seat and the access panel.
4. Drain the fuel tank.
5. Remove or disconnect the following:

- Negative battery cable
- Fuel pump module harness connectors
- Filler hose shield
- Fuel pressure and return lines
- Filler hose
- Vent hose
- Evaporative Emissions (EVAP) hose
- Fuel tank skid plate
- Fuel tank
- Fuel level sender
- Fuel pump

To install:

6. Install or connect the following:
- Fuel pump
- Fuel level sender. Tighten the screws to 17–23 inch lbs. (2.0–2.5 Nm).
- Fuel tank. Tighten the bolts to 27–36 ft. lbs. (37–49 Nm).

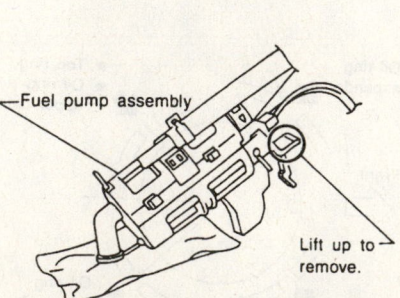

←Fuel pump assembly

Lift up to remove.

7924VG58

Remove the fuel pump with bracket while lifting the pawl of the pump bracket upward—All except Pick-Up

- Fuel tank skid plate. Tighten the bolts to 27–36 ft. lbs. (37–49 Nm).
- EVAP hose
- Vent hose
- Filler hose
- Fuel pressure and return lines
- Filler hose shield
- Fuel pump module harness connectors
- Negative battery cable

7. For Xterra, install the access panel and the rear seat.
8. Fill the fuel tank.
9. Start the engine and check for leaks.

Pathfinder and QX4

1. Before servicing the vehicle, refer to the precautions in the beginning of this section.
2. Relieve the fuel system pressure.
3. Remove or disconnect the following:

- Negative battery cable
- Access panel behind the rear seat
- Fuel lines
- Fuel pump and gauge harness connectors
- Fuel gauge sender
- Fuel pump

To install:

4. Install or connect the following:
- Fuel pump
- Fuel gauge sender. Tighten the screws to 17–23 inch lbs. (2.0–2.5 Nm).
- Fuel pump and gauge harness connectors
- Fuel lines
- Access panel
- Negative battery cable
5. Start the engine and check for leaks.

Fuel Injectors

REMOVAL & INSTALLATION

2.4L Engine

1. Before servicing the vehicle, refer to the precautions in the beginning of this section.
2. Relieve the fuel system pressure.
3. Remove or disconnect the following:

- Negative battery cable

- Air cleaner assembly
- Fuel lines
- Fuel pressure regulator vacuum line
- Fuel injector connectors
- Fuel supply manifold with the injectors attached
- Fuel injector caps
- Fuel injectors

To install:

➡ **Use new insulators and O-ring seals for assembly.**

4. Install or connect the following:
   - Fuel injectors
   - Fuel injector caps. Tighten the screws to 26–34 inch lbs. (3–4 Nm).
   - Fuel supply manifold with the injectors attached. Tighten the bolts to 96–132 inch lbs. (11–15 Nm).
   - Fuel injector connectors
   - Fuel pressure regulator vacuum line
   - Fuel lines
   - Air cleaner assembly
   - Negative battery cable

5. Start the engine and check for leaks.

3.3L Engine

1. Before servicing the vehicle, refer to the precautions in the beginning of this section.
2. Drain the cooling system.
3. Relieve the fuel system pressure.
4. Remove or disconnect the following:
   - Negative battery cable
   - Air intake duct
   - Accelerator cable
   - Cruise control cable
   - Idle Air Control (IAC) valve connector
   - Throttle Position (TP) sensor and switch connectors
   - Ignition coil and power transistor connectors
   - Exhaust Gas Recirculation (EGR) Solenoid valve connector
   - EGR temperature sensor connector
   - Radiator hoses
   - Heater hoses
   - Positive Crankcase Ventilation (PCV) valve and hose
   - Evaporative Emissions (EVAP) canister vacuum and purge hoses

- Brake booster vacuum hose
- Fuel pressure regulator vacuum hose
- EGR tube
- Left bank injector connectors
- Thermal transmitter
- Upper intake manifold ground cable
- Breather pipe
- Upper intake manifold
- Fuel lines
- Right bank injector connectors
- Fuel supply manifold with the injectors attached
- Fuel injector caps
- Fuel injectors

To install:

➡ **Use new insulators and O-ring seals for assembly.**

5. Install or connect the following:
   - Fuel injectors
   - Fuel injector caps. Tighten the screws to 26–34 inch lbs. (3–4 Nm).
   - Fuel supply manifold with the injectors attached. Tighten the bolts to 96–132 inch lbs. (11–15 Nm).
   - Right bank injector connectors
   - Fuel lines
   - Upper intake manifold
   - Breather pipe
   - Upper intake manifold ground cable
   - Thermal transmitter
   - Left bank injector connectors
   - EGR tube
   - Fuel pressure regulator vacuum hose
   - Brake booster vacuum hose
   - EVAP canister vacuum and purge hoses
   - PCV valve and hose
   - Heater hoses
   - Radiator hoses
   - EGR temperature sensor connector
   - EGR Solenoid valve connector
   - Ignition coil and power transistor connectors
   - TP sensor and switch connectors
   - IAC valve connector
   - Cruise control cable
   - Accelerator cable
   - Air intake duct
   - Negative battery cable

6. Fill the cooling system.
7. Start the engine and check for leaks.

DRIVE TRAIN

Manual Transmission

REMOVAL & INSTALLATION

2 Wheel Drive

1. Before servicing the vehicle, refer to the precautions in the beginning of this section.
2. Remove or disconnect the following:
   - Negative battery cable
   - Shift lever
   - Crankshaft Position (CKP) sensor
   - Clutch slave cylinder
   - Vehicle Speed (VSS) sensor connector
   - Back-up lamp switch connector
   - Park/Neutral Position (PNP) switch connector
   - Rear Heated Oxygen (HO2S) sensor connector
   - Starter motor
   - Driveshaft
   - Exhaust mounting bracket
   - Transmission mount and crossmember. Support the transmission.
   - Transmission flange bolts
   - Transmission

➡ **The transmission flange bolts vary in length. Note their positions for assembly.**

To install:

3. Apply sealant to the transmission flange, engine block and engine rear plate as shown.
4. Install or connect the following:
   - Transmission. Tighten the large bolts to 29–36 ft. lbs. (39–49 Nm) and the small bolts to 12–16 ft. lbs. (16–22 Nm).
   - Transmission mount and crossmember. Tighten the mount and crossmember fasteners to 30–38 ft. lbs. (41–52 Nm).
   - Exhaust mounting bracket
   - Driveshaft
   - Starter motor
   - HO2S sensor connector
   - PNP switch connector
   - Back-up lamp switch connector
   - VSS sensor connector
   - Clutch slave cylinder
   - CKP sensor
   - Shift lever
   - Negative battery cable

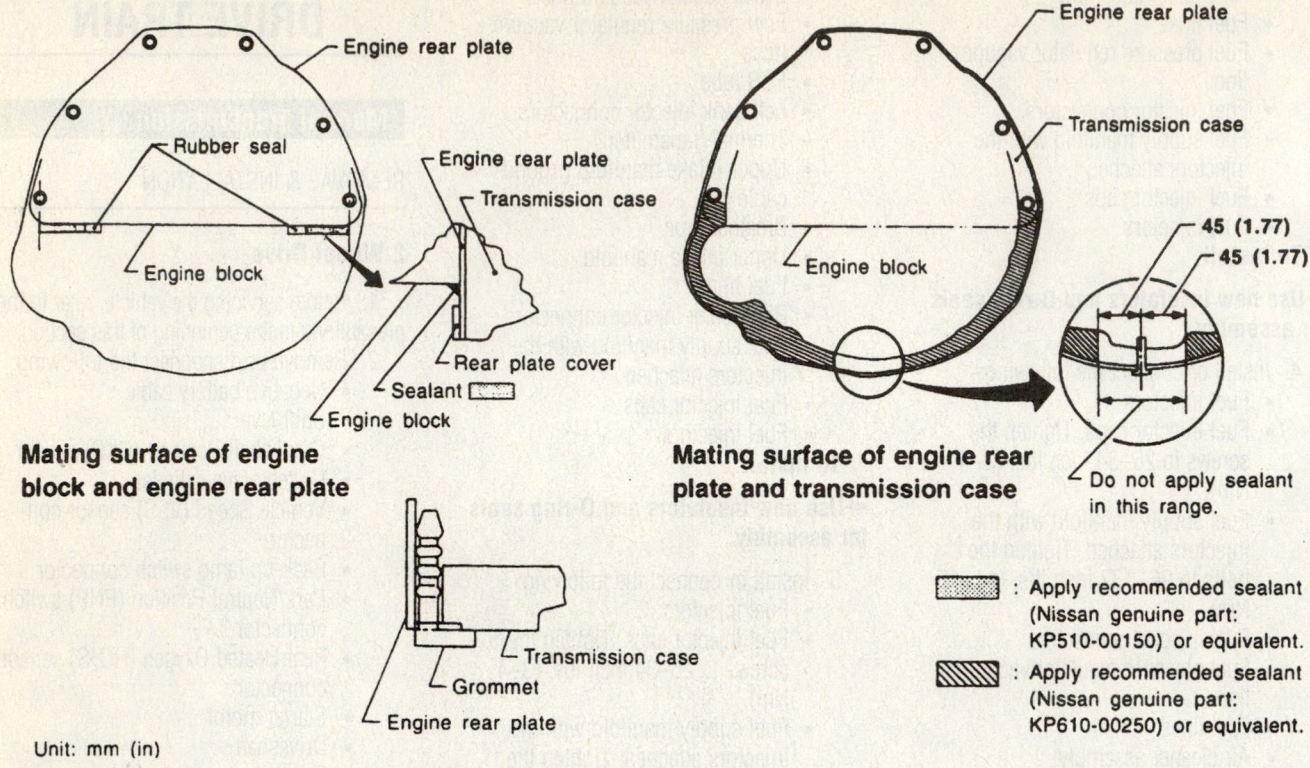

Mating surface of engine block and engine rear plate

Mating surface of engine rear plate and transmission case

Unit: mm (in)

: Apply recommended sealant (Nissan genuine part: KP510-00150) or equivalent.

: Apply recommended sealant (Nissan genuine part: KP610-00250) or equivalent.

7924VG61

Apply sealant to the indicated areas between the engine block, transmission and engine rear plate—4 Wheel Drive shown

4 Wheel Drive

EXCEPT PATHFINDER

1. Before servicing the vehicle, refer to the precautions in the beginning of this section.

2. Remove or disconnect the following:

- Negative battery cable
- Shift lever
- Transfer case select lever
- Crankshaft Position (CKP) sensor
- Clutch slave cylinder
- Vehicle Speed (VSS) sensor connector
- Back-up lamp switch connector
- Park/Neutral Position (PNP) switch connector
- Rear Heated Oxygen (HO$_2$S) sensor connector
- Starter motor
- Front and rear driveshafts
- Exhaust front pipes
- Exhaust center pipe
- Torsion bars and mounts
- Rear torsion bar cross mount
- Transmission mount and crossmember. Support the transmission.

- Transmission flange bolts
- Transmission

➡**The transmission flange bolts vary in length. Note their positions for assembly.**

To install:

3. Apply sealant to the transmission flange, engine block, and engine rear plate as shown.

4. Install or connect the following:

- Transmission. Tighten the large bolts to 29–36 ft. lbs. (39–49 Nm) and the small bolts to 22–29 ft. lbs. (29–39 Nm).
- Transmission mount and crossmember. Tighten the mount and crossmember fasteners to 30–38 ft. lbs. (41–52 Nm).
- Rear torsion bar cross mount
- Torsion bars and mounts
- Exhaust center pipe
- Exhaust front pipes
- Front and rear driveshafts
- Starter motor
- HO$_2$S sensor connector
- PNP switch connector
- Back-up lamp switch connector
- VSS sensor connector
- Clutch slave cylinder

- CKP sensor
- Transfer case select lever
- Shift lever
- Negative battery cable

PATHFINDER

1. Before servicing the vehicle, refer to the precautions in the beginning of this section.

2. Remove or disconnect the following:

- Negative battery cable
- Shift lever
- Transfer case select lever
- Crankshaft Position (CKP) sensor
- Clutch slave cylinder
- Vehicle Speed (VSS) sensor connector
- Back-up lamp switch connector
- Park/Neutral Position (PNP) switch connector
- Rear Heated Oxygen (HO$_2$S) sensor connector
- Starter motor
- Front and rear driveshafts
- Exhaust front pipes
- Exhaust center pipe
- Transmission mount and crossmember. Support the transmission.

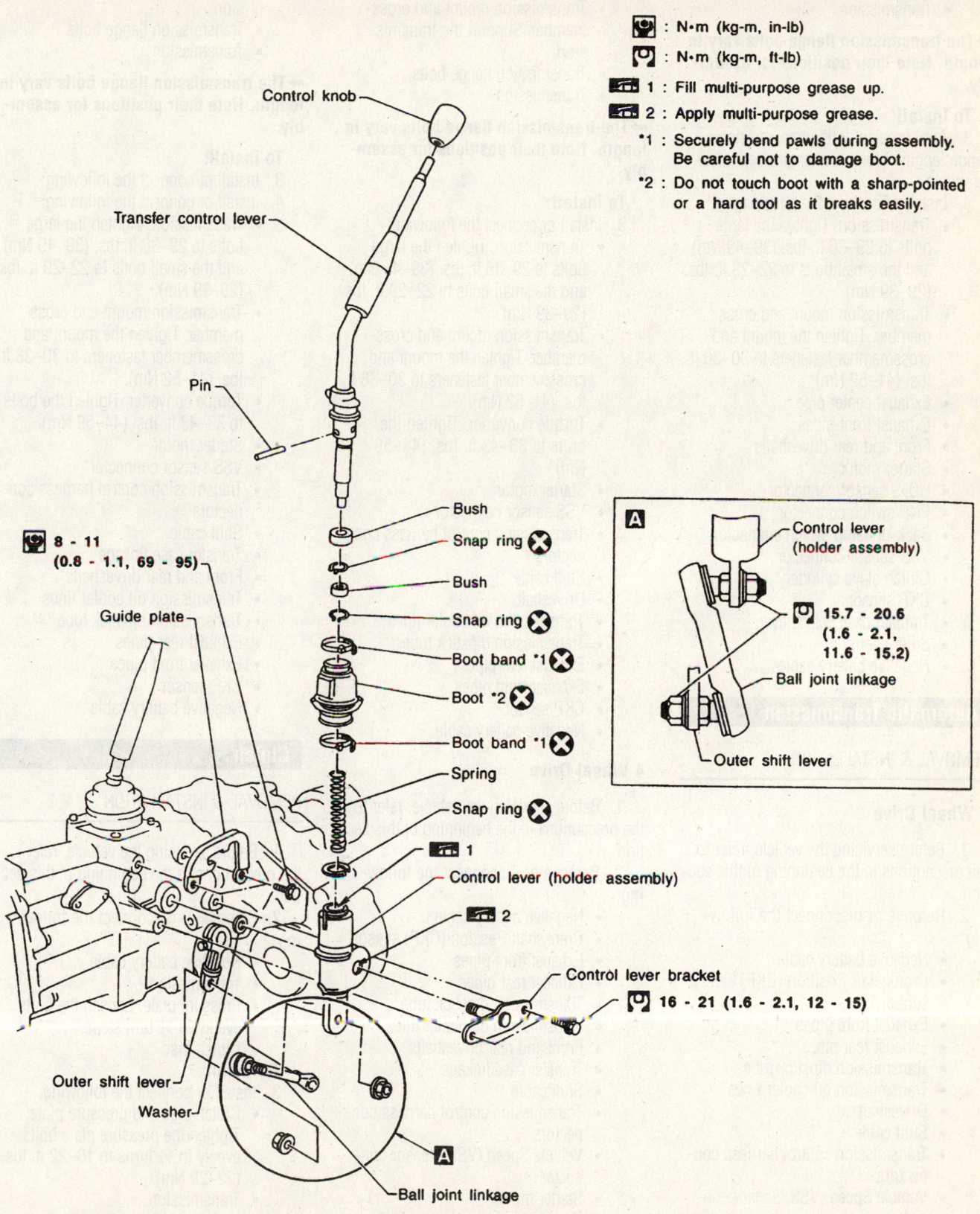

: N•m (kg-m, in-lb)

: N•m (kg-m, ft-lb)

1 : Fill multi-purpose grease up.

2 : Apply multi-purpose grease.

*1 : Securely bend pawls during assembly.
Be careful not to damage boot.

*2 : Do not touch boot with a sharp-pointed
or a hard tool as it breaks easily.

Control knob

Transfer control lever

Pin

8 - 11
(0.8 - 1.1, 69 - 95)

Guide plate

Bush
Snap ring ✗
Bush
Snap ring ✗
Boot band *1 ✗
Boot *2 ✗
Boot band *1 ✗
Spring
Snap ring ✗

1

Control lever (holder assembly)

2

Outer shift lever
Washer

Ball joint linkage

A
Control lever
(holder assembly)

15.7 - 20.6
(1.6 - 2.1,
11.6 - 15.2)

Ball joint linkage

Outer shift lever

Control lever bracket

16 - 21 (1.6 - 2.1, 12 - 15)

A

Exploded view of the transfer case shifter lever and related components—Pathfinder 4WD

7924VG60

- Transmission flange bolts
- Transmission

➡ **The transmission flange bolts vary in length. Note their positions for assembly.**

To install:

3. Apply sealant to the transmission flange, engine block, and engine rear plate as shown.

4. Install or connect the following:
- Transmission. Tighten the large bolts to 29–36 ft. lbs. (39–49 Nm) and the small bolts to 22–29 ft. lbs. (29–39 Nm).
- Transmission mount and crossmember. Tighten the mount and crossmember fasteners to 30–38 ft. lbs. (41–52 Nm).
- Exhaust center pipe
- Exhaust front pipes
- Front and rear driveshafts
- Starter motor
- HO$_2$S sensor connector
- PNP switch connector
- Back-up lamp switch connector
- VSS sensor connector
- Clutch slave cylinder
- CKP sensor
- Transfer case select lever
- Shift lever
- Negative battery cable

Automatic Transmission

REMOVAL & INSTALLATION

2 Wheel Drive

1. Before servicing the vehicle, refer to the precautions in the beginning of this section.

2. Remove or disconnect the following:
- Negative battery cable
- Crankshaft Position (CKP) sensor
- Exhaust front pipes
- Exhaust rear pipes
- Transmission dipstick tube
- Transmission oil cooler lines
- Driveshaft
- Shift cable
- Transmission control harness connectors
- Vehicle Speed (VSS) sensor connector
- Starter motor

- Torque converter
- Transmission mount and crossmember. Support the transmission.
- Transmission flange bolts
- Transmission

➡ **The transmission flange bolts vary in length. Note their positions for assembly.**

To install:

3. Install or connect the following:
- Transmission. Tighten the large bolts to 29–36 ft. lbs. (39–49 Nm) and the small bolts to 22–29 ft. lbs. (29–39 Nm).
- Transmission mount and crossmember. Tighten the mount and crossmember fasteners to 30–38 ft. lbs. (41–52 Nm).
- Torque converter. Tighten the bolts to 33–43 ft. lbs. (44–59 Nm).
- Starter motor
- VSS sensor connector
- Transmission control harness connectors
- Shift cable
- Driveshaft
- Transmission oil cooler lines
- Transmission dipstick tube
- Exhaust rear pipes
- Exhaust front pipes
- CKP sensor
- Negative battery cable

4 Wheel Drive

1. Before servicing the vehicle, refer to the precautions in the beginning of this section.

2. Remove or disconnect the following:
- Negative battery cable
- Crankshaft Position (CKP) sensor
- Exhaust front pipes
- Exhaust rear pipes
- Transmission dipstick tube
- Transmission oil cooler lines
- Front and rear driveshafts
- Transfer case linkage
- Shift cable
- Transmission control harness connectors
- Vehicle Speed (VSS) sensor connector
- Starter motor
- Torque converter
- Transmission mount and cross-

member. Support the transmission.
- Transmission flange bolts
- Transmission

➡ **The transmission flange bolts vary in length. Note their positions for assembly.**

To install:

3. Install or connect the following:

4. Install or connect the following:
- Transmission. Tighten the large bolts to 29–36 ft. lbs. (39–49 Nm) and the small bolts to 22–29 ft. lbs. (29–39 Nm).
- Transmission mount and crossmember. Tighten the mount and crossmember fasteners to 30–38 ft. lbs. (41–52 Nm).
- Torque converter. Tighten the bolts to 33–43 ft. lbs. (44–59 Nm).
- Starter motor
- VSS sensor connector
- Transmission control harness connectors
- Shift cable
- Transfer case linkage
- Front and rear driveshafts
- Transmission oil cooler lines
- Transmission dipstick tube
- Exhaust rear pipes
- Exhaust front pipes
- CKP sensor
- Negative battery cable

Clutch

REMOVAL & INSTALLATION

1. Before servicing the vehicle, refer to the precautions in the beginning of this section.

2. Remove or disconnect the following:
- Negative battery cable
- Transmission
- Pressure plate. Loosen the bolts evenly in ½ turn steps.
- Clutch disc

To install:

3. Install or connect the following:
- Clutch disc and pressure plate. Tighten the pressure plate bolts evenly in ½ turns to 16–22 ft. lbs. (22–29 Nm).
- Transmission
- Negative battery cable

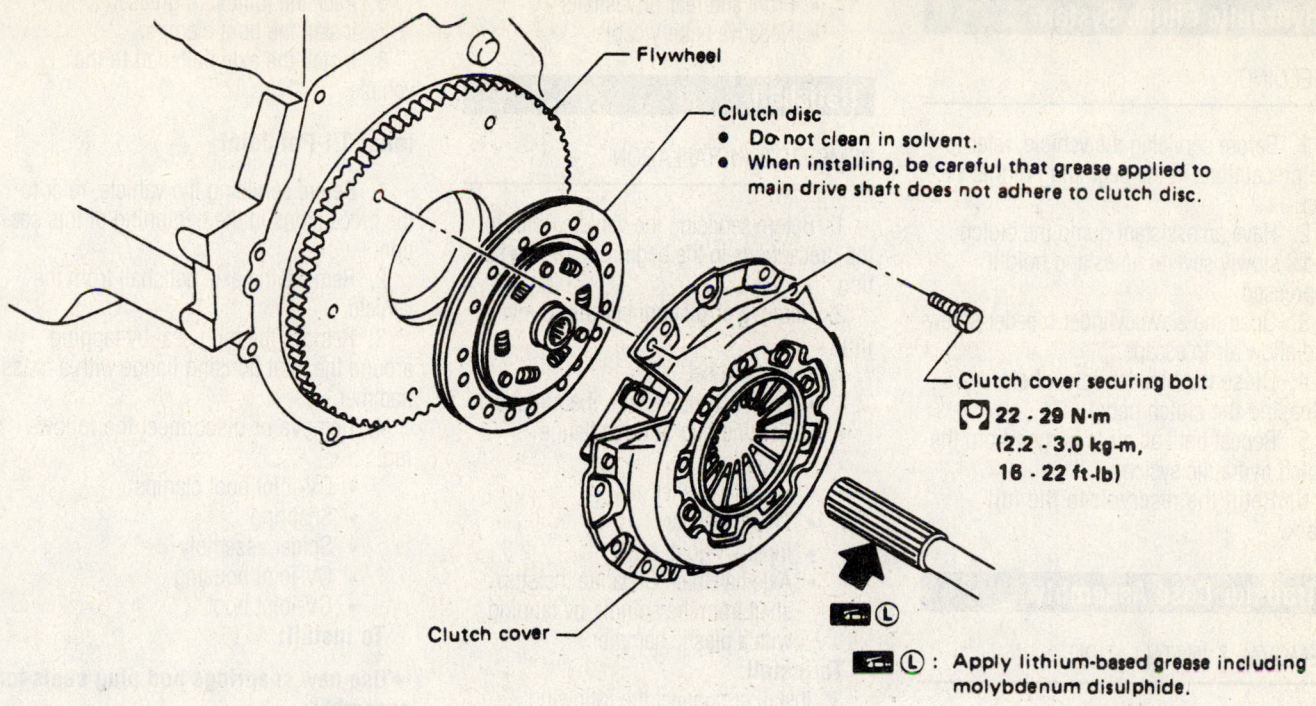

Flywheel

Clutch disc
- Do not clean in solvent.
- When installing, be careful that grease applied to main drive shaft does not adhere to clutch disc.

Clutch cover securing bolt
22 - 29 N·m
(2.2 - 3.0 kg-m,
16 - 22 ft-lb)

Clutch cover

L : Apply lithium-based grease including molybdenum disulphide.

7924VG63

Exploded view of the pressure plate and clutch disc and related components—all models

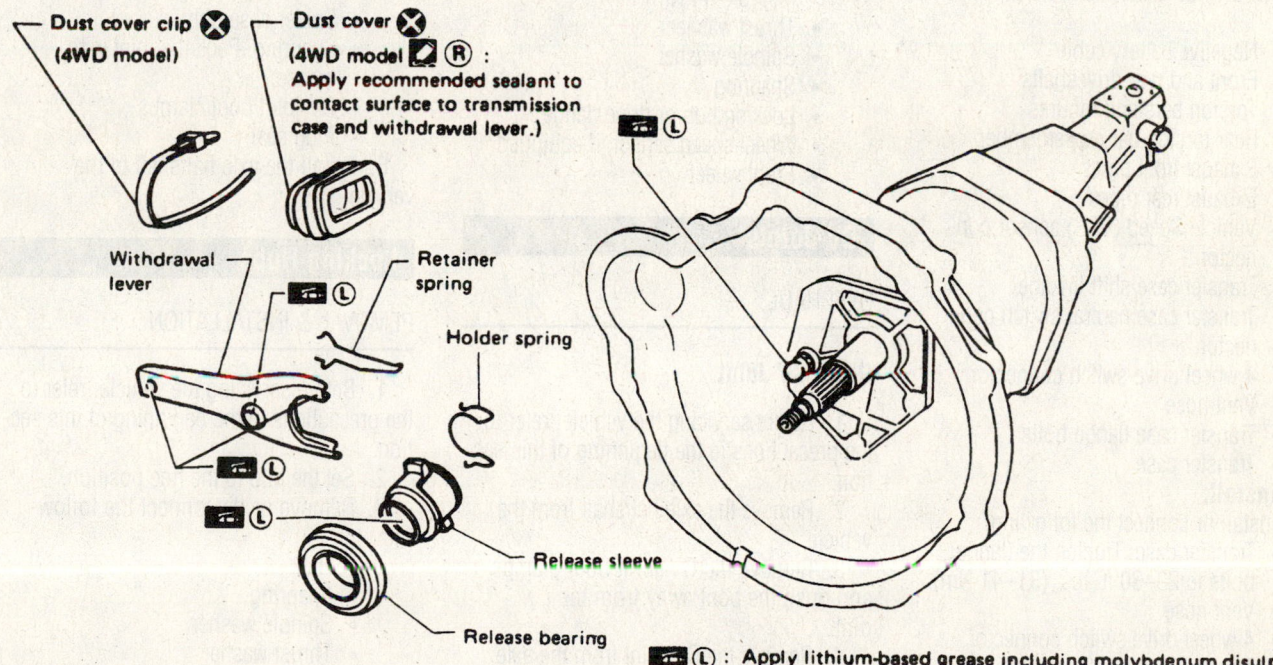

Dust cover clip ⊗ (4WD model)

Dust cover ⊗ (4WD model) ®: Apply recommended sealant to contact surface to transmission case and withdrawal lever.)

Withdrawal lever

Retainer spring

Holder spring

Release sleeve

Release bearing

L : Apply lithium-based grease including molybdenum disulphide

7924VG64

Clutch release mechanism exploded view—all models

Turn to Section 5 for brake system applications

Hydraulic Clutch System

BLEEDING

1. Before servicing the vehicle, refer to the precautions in the beginning of this section.

2. Have an assistant pump the clutch pedal slowly several times and hold it depressed.

3. Open the slave cylinder bleeder screw and allow air to escape.

4. Close the bleeder screw before releasing the clutch pedal.

5. Repeat until all air is purged from the clutch hydraulic system.

6. Refill the reservoir to the full mark.

Transfer Case Assembly

REMOVAL & INSTALLATION

1. Before servicing the vehicle, refer to the precautions in the beginning of this section.

2. Remove or disconnect the following:

- Negative battery cable
- Front and rear driveshafts
- Torsion bars and mounts
- Rear torsion bar crossmember
- Exhaust front pipes
- Exhaust rear pipes
- Vehicle Speed (VSS) sensor connector
- Transfer case shift linkage
- Transfer case neutral switch connector
- 4 wheel drive switch connector
- Vent hose
- Transfer case flange bolts
- Transfer case

To install:

3. Install or connect the following:

- Transfer case. Tighten the flange bolts to 23–30 ft. lbs. (31–41 Nm).
- Vent hose
- 4 wheel drive switch connector
- Transfer case neutral switch connector
- Transfer case shift linkage
- VSS sensor connector
- Exhaust rear pipes
- Exhaust front pipes
- Rear torsion bar crossmember
- Torsion bars and mounts

- Front and rear driveshafts
- Negative battery cable

Halfshaft

REMOVAL & INSTALLATION

1. Before servicing the vehicle, refer to the precautions in the beginning of this section.

2. Remove or disconnect the following:

- Front wheel
- Wheel speed sensor, if equipped
- Locking hub or drive flange
- Snapring
- Spindle washer
- Thrust washer
- Inner CV-joint bolts
- Axle halfshaft. Separate the stub shaft from the spindle by tapping with a plastic hammer.

To install:

3. Install or connect the following:

- Axle halfshaft. Guide the stub shaft into the spindle and tighten the inner CV-joint bolts to 25–33 ft. lbs. (34–44 Nm).
- Thrust washer
- Spindle washer
- Snapring
- Locking hub or drive flange
- Wheel speed sensor, if equipped
- Front wheel

CV-Joints

OVERHAUL

Outer CV-Joint

1. Before servicing the vehicle, refer to the precautions in the beginning of this section.

2. Remove the axle halfshaft from the vehicle.

3. Remove the CV-joint boot clamps and push the boot away from the joint.

4. Remove the CV-joint from the axle shaft by tapping it with a brass hammer.

To install:

➡**Use new circlips and boot clamps for assembly.**

5. Install the CV-joint to the axle shaft by tapping it with a brass hammer.

6. Pack the joint with grease.

7. Install the boot clamps.

8. Install the axle halfshaft to the vehicle.

Inner Tri-Pot Joint

1. Before servicing the vehicle, refer to the precautions in the beginning of this section.

2. Remove the axle halfshaft from the vehicle.

3. Remove the plug seal by tapping around the joint housing flange with a brass hammer.

4. Remove or disconnect the following:

- CV-joint boot clamps
- Snapring
- Spider assembly
- CV-joint housing
- CV-joint boot

To install:

➡**Use new snaprings and plug seals for assembly.**

5. Install or connect the following:

- CV-joint boot
- CV-joint housing
- Spider assembly
- Snapring. Pack the joint with grease.
- CV-joint boot clamps
- Plug seal

6. Install the axle halfshaft to the vehicle.

Locking Hubs

REMOVAL & INSTALLATION

1. Before servicing the vehicle, refer to the precautions in the beginning of this section.

2. Set the hub to the free position.

3. Remove or disconnect the following:

- Hub
- Snapring
- Spindle washer
- Thrust washer

To install:

4. Install or connect the following:

- Thrust washer
- Spindle washer
- Snapring
- Hub. tighten the bolts to 18–25 ft. lbs. (25–34 Nm).

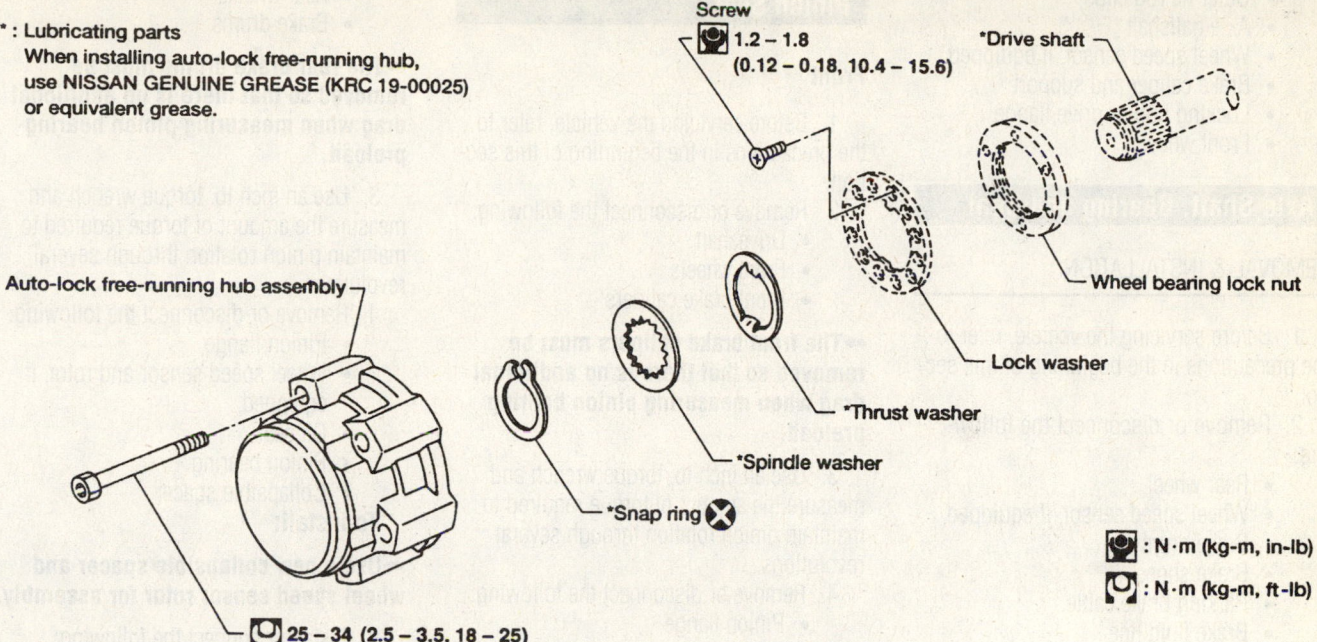

*: Lubricating parts
When installing auto-lock free-running hub,
use NISSAN GENUINE GREASE (KRC 19-00025)
or equivalent grease.

Screw
1.2 – 1.8
(0.12 – 0.18, 10.4 – 15.6)

*Drive shaft

Wheel bearing lock nut

Lock washer

*Thrust washer

*Spindle washer

*Snap ring

Auto-lock free-running hub assembly

25 – 34 (2.5 – 3.5, 18 – 25)

: N·m (kg-m, in-lb)

: N·m (kg-m, ft-lb)

7924VG73

Exploded view of the Auto-lock free running hub assembly—Pathfinder and QX4 shown

SEC. 400
*: Lubricating parts
When installing manual-lock free-running hub,
use multi-purpose grease.

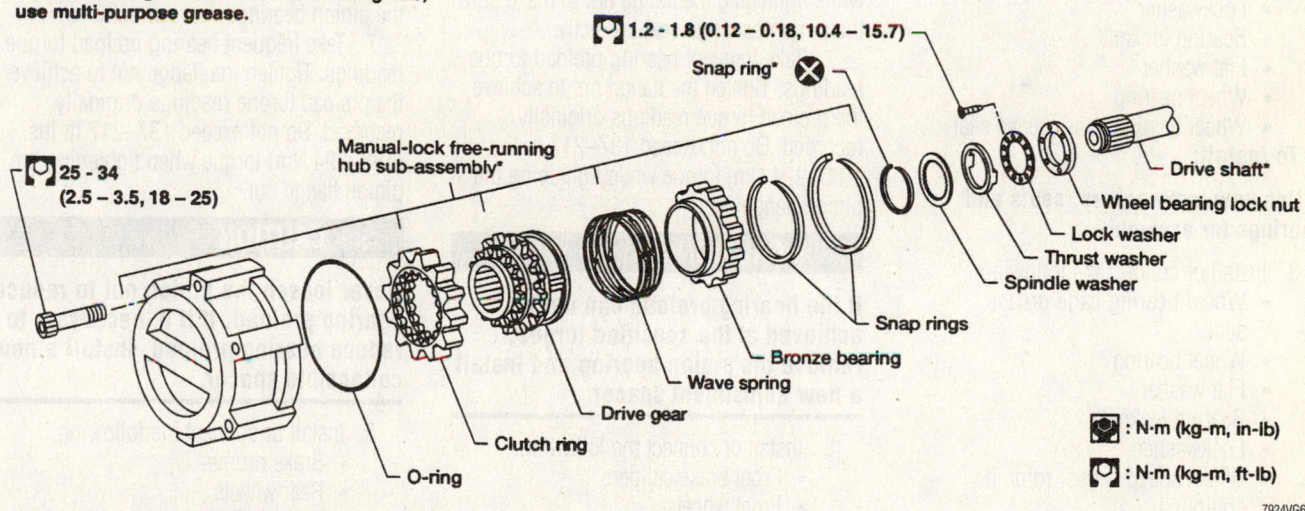

1.2 - 1.8 (0.12 – 0.18, 10.4 – 15.7)

Snap ring*

Drive shaft*

Wheel bearing lock nut

Lock washer

Thrust washer

Spindle washer

Snap rings

Bronze bearing

Wave spring

Drive gear

Clutch ring

O-ring

Manual-lock free-running
hub sub-assembly*

25 – 34
(2.5 – 3.5, 18 – 25)

: N·m (kg-m, in-lb)

: N·m (kg-m, ft-lb)

7924VG65

Exploded view of the Manual-lock free running hub assembly—Pathfinder shown

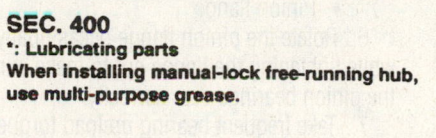

Spindle Bearings

REMOVAL, PACKING AND INSTALLATION

1. Before servicing the vehicle, refer to the precautions in the beginning of this section.
2. Remove or disconnect the following:
   - Front wheel
   - Locking hub or drive flange

   - Brake caliper and support
   - Wheel speed sensor, if equipped
   - Axle halfshaft
   - Outer tie rod ends
   - Upper ball joint or steering knuckle bracket bolts
   - Lower ball joint
   - Steering knuckle
   - Inner seal
   - Thrust washer

   - Spindle bearing

To install:
3. Install or connect the following:
   - Spindle bearing. Coat the bearing with multi-purpose grease.
   - Thrust washer
   - Inner seal
   - Steering knuckle
   - Lower ball joint
   - Upper ball joint or steering knuckle bracket bolts

For complete service labor times order Nichols' Chilton Labor Guide Manual

- Outer tie rod ends
- Axle halfshaft
- Wheel speed sensor, if equipped
- Brake caliper and support
- Locking hub or drive flange
- Front wheel

Axle Shaft, Bearing and Seal

REMOVAL & INSTALLATION

1. Before servicing the vehicle, refer to the precautions in the beginning of this section.
2. Remove or disconnect the following:

- Rear wheel
- Wheel speed sensor, if equipped
- Brake drum
- Brake shoes
- Parking brake cable
- Brake fluid line
- Bearing cage and backing plate bolts
- Axle shaft assembly
- Axle seal
- Wheel speed sensor rotor, if equipped
- Lockwasher
- Bearing locknut
- Flat washer
- Wheel bearing
- Wheel bearing cage grease seal

To install:

➡**Use new lockwashers, seals and bearings for assembly.**

3. Install or connect the following:

- Wheel bearing cage grease seal
- Wheel bearing
- Flat washer
- Bearing locknut
- Lockwasher
- Wheel speed sensor rotor, if equipped
- Axle seal
- Axle shaft assembly
- Bearing cage and backing plate bolts
- Brake fluid line
- Parking brake cable
- Brake shoes
- Brake drum
- Wheel speed sensor, if equipped
- Rear wheel

4. Bleed the rear brakes and check the rear axle lubricant level.

Pinion Seal

Front

1. Before servicing the vehicle, refer to the precautions in the beginning of this section.
2. Remove or disconnect the following:

- Driveshaft
- Front wheels
- Front brake calipers

➡**The front brake calipers must be removed so that there is no additional drag when measuring pinion bearing preload.**

3. Use an inch lb. torque wrench and measure the amount of torque required to maintain pinion rotation through several revolutions.
4. Remove or disconnect the following:

- Pinion flange
- Oil seal

To install:

5. Install or connect the following:

- Pinion seal
- Pinion flange

6. Rotate the pinion flange occasionally while tightening the flange nut to make sure the pinion bearings seat correctly.
7. Take frequent bearing preload torque readings. Tighten the flange nut to achieve the preload torque readings originally recorded. Do not exceed 137–217 ft. lbs. (186–294 Nm) torque when tightening the pinion flange nut.

✳✳ CAUTION

If the bearing preload can not be achieved at the specified torque, remove the pinion bearing and install a new adjustment spacer.

8. Install or connect the following:

- Front brake calipers
- Front wheels
- Driveshaft. Tighten the fasteners to 29–33 ft. lbs. (39–44 Nm).

9. Fill the differential with gear lubricant and check for leaks.

Rear

2 WHEEL DRIVE

1. Before servicing the vehicle, refer to the precautions in the beginning of this section.
2. Remove or disconnect the following:

- Driveshaft

- Rear wheels
- Brake drums

➡**The rear brake drums must be removed so that there is no additional drag when measuring pinion bearing preload.**

3. Use an inch lb. torque wrench and measure the amount of torque required to maintain pinion rotation through several revolutions.
4. Remove or disconnect the following:

- Pinion flange
- Wheel speed sensor and rotor, if equipped
- Oil seal
- Pinion bearing
- Collapsible spacer

To install:

➡**Use a new collapsible spacer and wheel speed sensor rotor for assembly.**

5. Install or connect the following:

- Collapsible spacer
- Pinion bearing
- Pinion seal
- Pinion flange

6. Rotate the pinion flange occasionally while tightening the flange nut to make sure the pinion bearings seat correctly.
7. Take frequent bearing preload torque readings. Tighten the flange nut to achieve the preload torque readings originally recorded. Do not exceed 137–217 ft. lbs. (186–294 Nm) torque when tightening the pinion flange nut.

✳✳ CAUTION

Never loosen the pinion nut to reduce bearing preload. If it is necessary to reduce bearing preload, install a new collapsible spacer.

8. Install or connect the following:

- Brake drums
- Rear wheels
- Driveshaft. Tighten the fasteners to 58–65 ft. lbs. (78–88 Nm).

9. Fill the differential with gear lubricant and check for leaks.

4 WHEEL DRIVE

1. Before servicing the vehicle, refer to the precautions in the beginning of this section.
2. Remove or disconnect the following:

- Driveshaft
- Rear wheels
- Brake drums

➡ **The rear brake drums must be removed so that there is no additional drag when measuring pinion bearing preload.**

3. Use an inch lb. torque wrench and measure the amount of torque required to maintain pinion rotation through several revolutions.

4. Remove or disconnect the following:
- Pinion flange
- Oil seal

To install:

5. Install or connect the following:
- Pinion seal
- Pinion flange

6. Rotate the pinion flange occasionally while tightening the flange nut to make sure the pinion bearings seat correctly.

7. Take frequent bearing preload torque readings. Tighten the flange nut to achieve the preload torque readings originally recorded. Do not exceed 137–217 ft. lbs. (186–294 Nm) torque when tightening the pinion flange nut.

❊❊ CAUTION

If the bearing preload can not be achieved at the specified torque, remove the pinion bearing and install a new adjustment spacer.

8. Install or connect the following:
- Brake drums
- Rear wheels
- Driveshaft. Tighten the fasteners to 58–65 ft. lbs. (78–88 Nm).

9. Fill the differential with gear lubricant and check for leaks.

Axle Housing Assembly

REMOVAL & INSTALLATION

Except Pathfinder and QX4

1. Before servicing the vehicle, refer to the precautions in the beginning of this section.

2. Remove or disconnect the following:
- Rear wheels
- Stabilizer bar
- Parking brake cable
- Brake fluid hose
- Axle vent tube
- Driveshaft
- Wheel speed sensor harness, if equipped
- Shock absorbers

- Spring shackles
- Axle assembly

To install:

➡ **Use new fasteners for assembly.**

3. Install or connect the following:
- Axle assembly. Tighten the U-bolts to 72–80 ft. lbs. (98–108 Nm).
- Spring shackles. Tighten the nuts to 58–72 ft. lbs. (78–98 Nm).
- Shock absorbers. Tighten the nuts to 30–37 ft. lbs. (40–50 Nm).
- Wheel speed sensor harness, if equipped
- Driveshaft. Tighten the fasteners to 58–65 ft. lbs. (78–88 Nm).
- Axle vent tube
- Brake fluid hose
- Parking brake cable
- Stabilizer bar. Tighten the bracket bolts to 32–41 ft. lbs. (43–55 Nm) and the link nuts to 30–35 ft. lbs. (41–47 Nm).
- Rear wheels

4. Bleed the rear brakes and check the rear axle lubricant level.

Pathfinder and QX4

1. Before servicing the vehicle, refer to the precautions in the beginning of this section.

2. Remove or disconnect the following:
- Rear wheels
- Stabilizer bar brackets
- Parking brake cable
- Brake fluid hose
- Axle vent tube
- Driveshaft
- Wheel speed sensor harness
- Shock absorbers
- Coil springs
- Upper links
- Lower links
- Lateral rod link
- Axle assembly

To install:

➡ **Use new fasteners for assembly.**

3. Install or connect the following:
- Axle assembly
- Lateral rod link. Tighten the nut to 80–94 ft. lbs. (108–127 Nm).
- Lower links. Tighten the bolts to 103–116 ft. lbs. (140–157 Nm).
- Upper links. Tighten the bolts to 103–116 ft. lbs. (140–157 Nm).
- Coil springs
- Shock absorbers. Tighten the bolts to 49–65 ft. lbs. (67–88 Nm).
- Wheel speed sensor harness

- Driveshaft. Tighten the fasteners to 58–65 ft. lbs. (78–88 Nm).
- Axle vent tube
- Brake fluid hose
- Parking brake cable
- Stabilizer bar brackets. Tighten the bolts to 19–24 ft. lbs. (25–32 Nm).
- Rear wheels

STEERING AND SUSPENSION

Air Bag

❊❊ CAUTION

Some vehicles are equipped with an air bag system. The system must be disarmed before performing service on, or around, system components, the steering column, instrument panel components, wiring and sensors. Failure to follow the safety precautions and the disarming procedure could result in accidental air bag deployment, possible injury and unnecessary system repairs.

PRECAUTIONS

Several precautions must be observed when handling the inflator module to avoid accidental deployment and possible personal injury.

- Never carry the inflator module by the wires or connector on the underside of the module.
- When carrying a live inflator module, hold securely with both hands, and ensure that the bag and trim cover are pointed away.
- Place the inflator module on a bench or other surface with the bag and trim cover facing up.
- With the inflator module on the bench, never place anything on or close to the module which may be thrown in the event of an accidental deployment.

DISARMING

To disarm the **SRS** system turn the ignition switch to the **OFF** position. Then, disconnect both battery cables starting with the negative cable first and wait at least 3 minutes after the cables are disconnected.

To rearm the **SRS** system, turn the ignition switch to the **OFF** position. Connect both battery cables starting with the positive cable first.

Recirculating Ball Power Steering Gear

REMOVAL & INSTALLATION

1. Before servicing the vehicle, refer to the precautions in the beginning of this section.
2. Remove or disconnect the following:
   • Pitman arm
   • Steering column intermediate shaft
   • Power steering hoses
   • Steering gear

To install:

3. Install or connect the following:
   • Steering gear. Tighten the bolts to 62–71 ft. lbs. (84–96 Nm).
   • Power steering hoses. Tighten the banjo fittings to 29–38 ft. lbs. (39–51 Nm).
   • Steering column intermediate shaft. Tighten the pinch bolt to 17–22 ft. lbs. (24–29 Nm).
   • Pitman arm. Tighten the nut to 174–195 ft. lbs. (235–265 Nm).
4. Check the wheel alignment and adjust, as necessary.

Strut

REMOVAL & INSTALLATION

Front

PATHFINDER AND QX4

1. Before servicing the vehicle, refer to the precautions in the beginning of this section.
2. Remove or disconnect the following:
   • Front wheel
   • Stabilizer bar link
   • Steering knuckle bracket bolts
   • Upper strut mount nuts
   • Strut

To install:

➡**Use new nuts and bolts for assembly.**

3. Install or connect the following:
   • Strut. Tighten the upper strut mount nuts to 29–40 ft. lbs. (39–54 Nm) and the knuckle bracket bolts to 111–122 ft. lbs. (151–165 Nm).
   • Stabilizer bar link. Tighten the nut to 61–76 ft. lbs. (83–103 Nm).

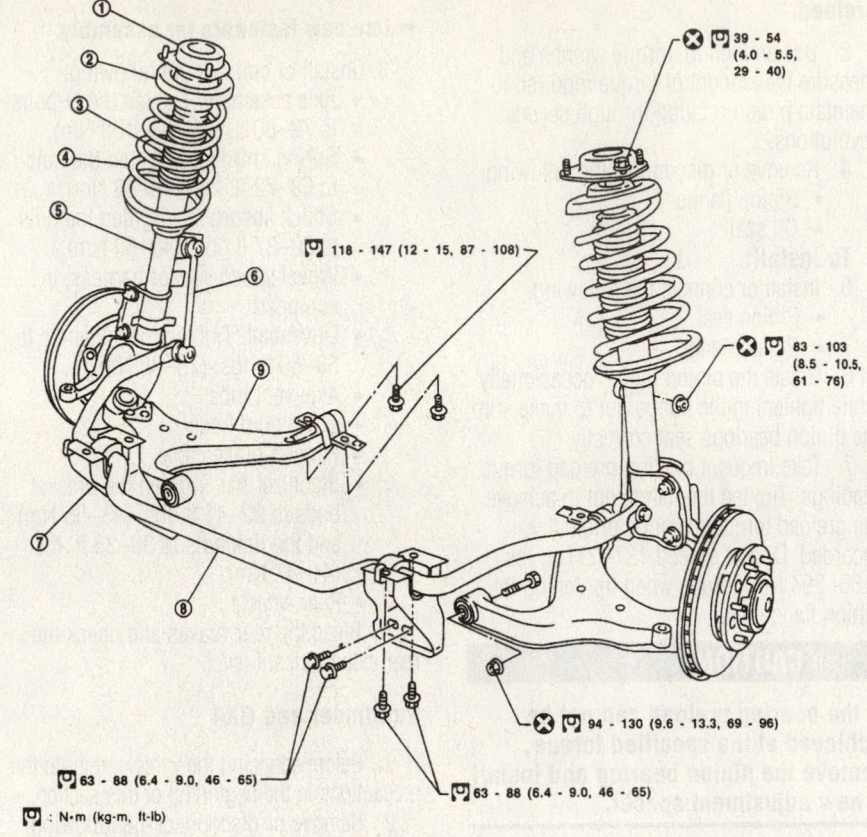

When installing rubber parts, final tightening must be carried out under unladen condition* with tires on ground. Fuel, radiator coolant and engine oil full.
Spare tire, jack, hand tools and mats in designated positions.

① Strut mounting insulator
② Spring upper seat
③ Bound bumper
④ Coil spring
⑤ Strut assembly
⑥ Stabilizer connecting rod
⑦ Bracket
⑧ Stabilizer bar
⑨ Transverse link

⊗ 🔧 39 - 54 (4.0 - 5.5, 29 - 40)
🔧 118 - 147 (12 - 15, 87 - 108)
⊗ 🔧 83 - 103 (8.5 - 10.5, 61 - 76)
⊗ 🔧 94 - 130 (9.6 - 13.3, 69 - 96)
🔧 63 - 88 (6.4 - 9.0, 46 - 65)
🔧 63 - 88 (6.4 - 9.0, 46 - 65)
🔧 : N·m (kg-m, ft-lb)

7924VG66

Exploded view of the front suspension—2WD Pathfinder shown

   • Front wheel
4. Check the wheel alignment and adjust, as necessary.

Shock Absorber

REMOVAL & INSTALLATION

Front

EXCEPT PATHFINDER AND QX4

1. Before servicing the vehicle, refer to the precautions in the beginning of this section.
2. Support the lower control arm.
3. Remove or disconnect the following:
   • Front wheel
   • Lower shock absorber mounting bolt
   • Upper shock absorber mounting nut
   • Shock absorber

To install:

4. Install or connect the following:
   • Shock absorber
   • Upper shock absorber mounting nut. Tighten the nut to 12–16 ft. lbs. (16–22 Nm).
   • Lower shock absorber mounting bolt. Tighten the bolt to 87–106 ft. lbs. (118–147 Nm).
   • Front wheel

Rear

PATHFINDER AND QX4

1. Before servicing the vehicle, refer to the precautions in the beginning of this section.
2. Support the rear axle.
3. Remove or disconnect the following:
   • Lower shock absorber bolt
   • Upper shock absorber bolt
   • Shock absorber

To install:

➡**Use new fasteners for assembly.**

4. Install the shock absorber and tighten the bolts to 49–65 ft. lbs. (67–88 Nm).

PICK-UP, FRONTIER AND XTERRA

1. Before servicing the vehicle, refer to the precautions in the beginning of this section.
2. Remove or disconnect the following:
   • Upper and lower shock absorber nuts
   • Shock absorber

To install:

➡**Use new nuts for assembly.**

3. Install the shock absorber and tighten the nuts to 30–37 ft. lbs. (40–50 Nm).

Coil Spring

REMOVAL & INSTALLATION

Pathfinder and QX4

FRONT

1. Before servicing the vehicle, refer to the precautions in the beginning of this section.

2. Remove the strut assembly.
3. Compress the coil spring and remove the piston rod nut.
4. Remove or disconnect the following:
   • Upper strut mount
   • Strut mount bracket
   • Upper strut bearing
   • Spring upper seat
   • Coil spring

To install:

➡**Use new fasteners for assembly.**

5. Install or connect the following:
   • Coil spring
   • Spring upper seat
   • Upper strut bearing
   • Strut mount bracket
   • Upper strut mount. Tighten the piston rod nut to 43–58 ft. lbs. (59–78 Nm).
6. Remove the spring compressor and install the strut assembly to the vehicle.
7. Check the wheel alignment and adjust, as necessary.

REAR

1. Before servicing the vehicle, refer to the precautions in the beginning of this section.

2. Support the vehicle at the frame.
3. Support the axle with a floor jack.
4. Remove or disconnect the following:
   • Rear wheels
   • Shock absorbers
   • Stabilizer bar links
   • Lateral control rod
   • Coil springs

To install:

➡**Use new fasteners for assembly.**

5. Install or connect the following:
   • Coil springs
   • Lateral control rod. Tighten the nut to 80–94 ft. lbs. (108–127 Nm).
   • Stabilizer bar links. Tighten the nuts to 30–35 ft. lbs. (41–47 Nm).
   • Shock absorbers
   • Rear wheels

Leaf Springs

REMOVAL & INSTALLATION

1. Before servicing the vehicle, refer to the precautions in the beginning of this section.

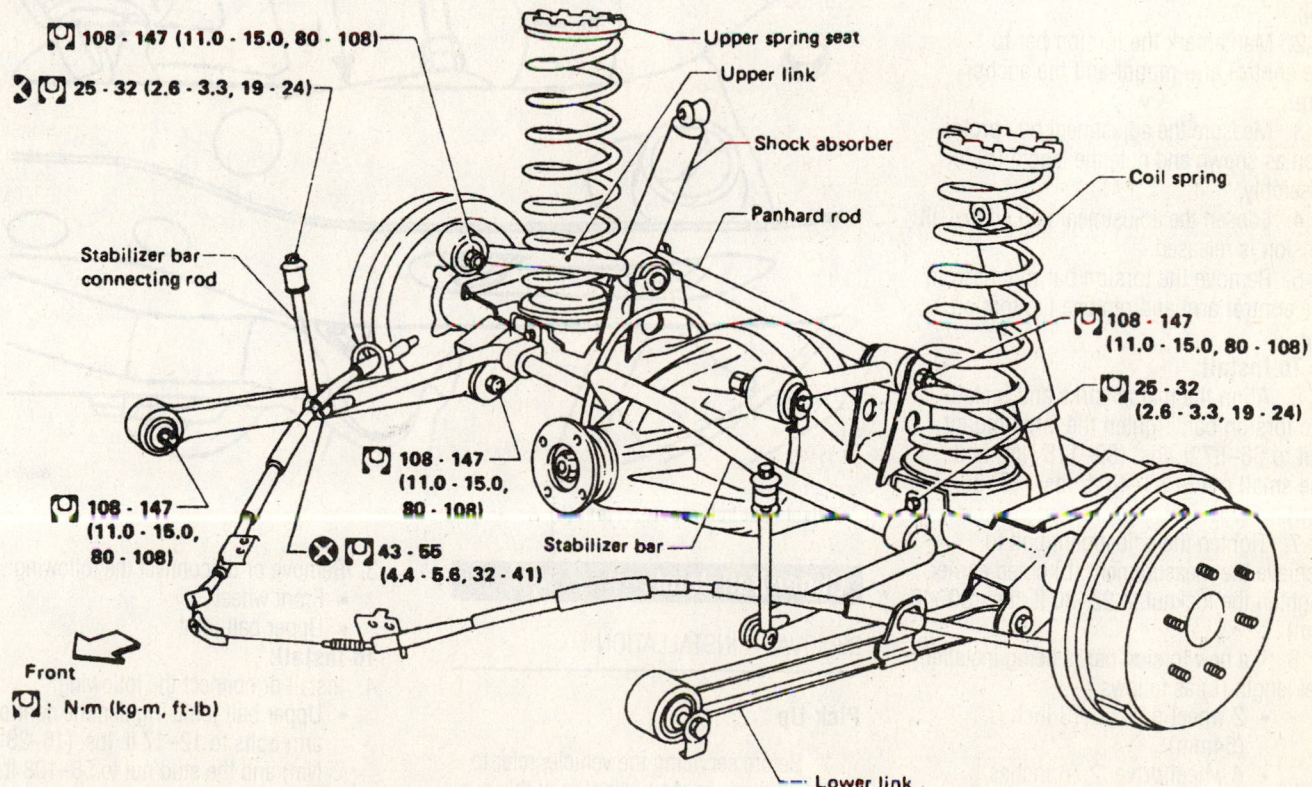

108 - 147 (11.0 - 15.0, 80 - 108)

25 - 32 (2.6 - 3.3, 19 - 24)

Stabilizer bar connecting rod

108 - 147 (11.0 - 15.0, 80 - 108)

108 - 147 (11.0 - 15.0, 80 - 108)

43 - 55 (4.4 - 5.6, 32 - 41)

Upper spring seat

Upper link

Shock absorber

Panhard rod

Coil spring

108 - 147 (11.0 - 15.0, 80 - 108)

25 - 32 (2.6 - 3.3, 19 - 24)

Stabilizer bar

Lower link

Front

: N·m (kg-m, ft-lb)

Rear suspension component identification—Pathfinder

7924VG69

2. Support the vehicle at the frame.

3. Support the axle with a floor jack.

4. Remove or disconnect the following:

- Rear wheels
- Shock absorbers
- Axle U-bolts and spring pad
- Spring shackle
- Front mount bolt
- Leaf spring

To install:

➡ **Use new fasteners for assembly.**

5. Install or connect the following:

- Leaf spring. Tighten the front mount bolt to 86–108 ft. lbs. (117–147 Nm).
- Spring shackle. Tighten the nuts to 58–72 ft. lbs. (78–98 Nm).
- Axle U-bolts and spring pad. Tighten the nuts to 72–80 ft. lbs. (98–108 Nm).
- Shock absorbers
- Rear wheels

Torsion Bar

1. Before servicing the vehicle, refer to the precautions in the beginning of this section.

2. Matchmark the torsion bar to the control arm mount and the anchor arm.

3. Measure the adjustment bolt protrusion as shown and note the length (L) for assembly.

4. Loosen the adjustment bolt so that all tension is released.

5. Remove the torsion bar mount from the control arm and remove the torsion bar.

To install:

6. Align the matchmarks and install the torsion bar. Tighten the large mount nut to 66–87 ft. lbs. (89–118 Nm) and the small nut to 33–44 ft. lbs. (45–60 Nm).

7. Tighten the adjustment bolt to achieve the measurement (L) noted earlier. Tighten the locknut to 22–30 ft. lbs. (30–40 Nm).

8. If a new torsion bar is being installed, set length (L) as follows:

- 2 wheel drive: 2.13 inches (54mm)
- 4 wheel drive: 2.76 inches (70mm)

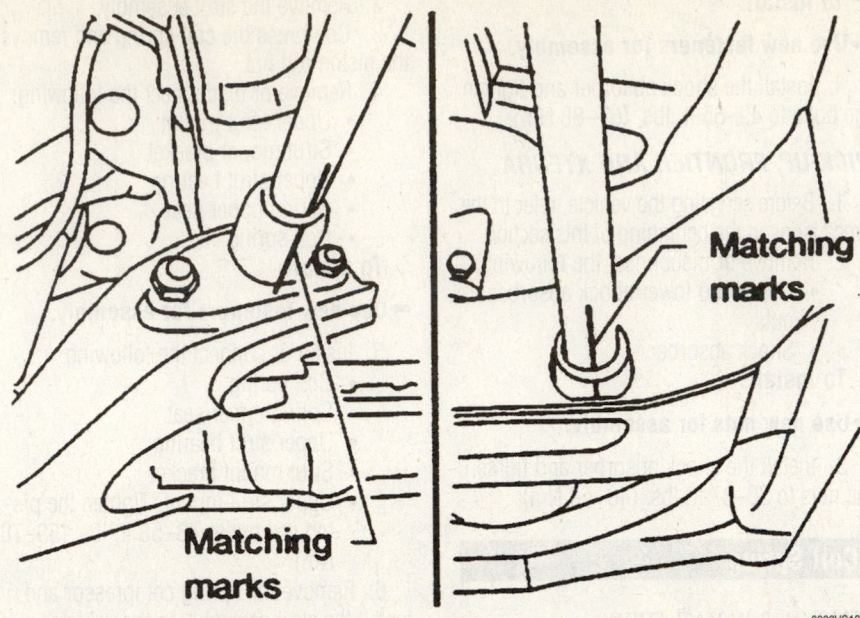

Torsion bar matchmarks

9308VG12

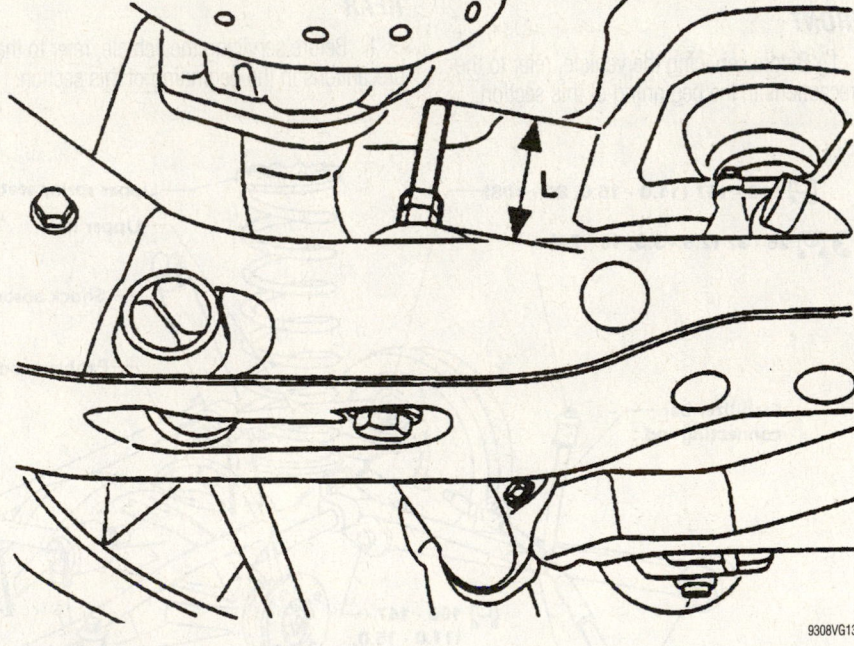

Adjustment bolt measurement (L)

9308VG13

Upper Ball Joint

REMOVAL & INSTALLATION

Pick-Up

1. Before servicing the vehicle, refer to the precautions in the beginning of this section.

2. Support the lower control arm.

3. Remove or disconnect the following:

- Front wheel
- Upper ball joint

To install:

4. Install or connect the following:

- Upper ball joint. Tighten the control arm bolts to 12–17 ft. lbs. (16–23 Nm) and the stud nut to 58–108 ft. lbs. (78–147 Nm).
- Front wheel

Frontier and Xterra

The upper ball joint is serviced with the upper control arm as an assembly.

Lower Ball Joint

REMOVAL & INSTALLATION

Pick-Up

2 WHEEL DRIVE

The lower ball joint is serviced with the lower control arm as an assembly.

4 WHEEL DRIVE

1. Before servicing the vehicle, refer to the precautions in the beginning of this section.
2. Support the lower control arm.
3. Remove or disconnect the following:
   - Front wheel
   - Lower ball joint
To install:
4. Install or connect the following:
   - Lower ball joint. Tighten the control arm bolts to 35–45 ft. lbs. (47–61 Nm) and the stud nut to 87–141 ft. lbs. (118–191 Nm).
   - Front wheel

Frontier and Xterra

The lower ball joint is serviced with the lower control arm as an assembly.

Pathfinder and QX4

1. Before servicing the vehicle, refer to the precautions in the beginning of this section.
2. Support the lower control arm.
3. Remove or disconnect the following:
   - Front wheel
   - Lower ball joint
To install:
4. Install or connect the following:
   - Lower ball joint. Tighten the control arm bolts to 76–94 ft. lbs. (103–127 Nm) and the stud nut to 87–123 ft. lbs. (118–167 Nm).
   - Front wheel

Upper Control Arm

REMOVAL & INSTALLATION

1. Before servicing the vehicle, refer to the precautions in the beginning of this section.
2. Support the lower control arm.
3. Remove or disconnect the following:
   - Front wheel
   - Shock absorber
   - Upper ball joint
   - Control arm mounting bolts
   - Upper control arm
To install:
4. Install or connect the following:
   - Upper control arm. Tighten the mounting bolts to 72–87 ft. lbs. (98–118 Nm).
   - Upper ball joint. Tighten the nut to 58–108 ft. lbs. (78–147 Nm).
   - Shock absorber
   - Front wheel
5. Check the wheel alignment and adjust, as necessary.

CONTROL ARM BUSHING REPLACEMENT

1. Before servicing the vehicle, refer to the precautions in the beginning of this section.
2. Remove the control arm from the vehicle.
3. Remove the control arm bushing with a press.
To install:
4. Lubricate the control arm bushings with liquid soap.
5. Install the bushings with a press.
6. Install the control arm to the vehicle.
7. Check the wheel alignment and adjust, as necessary.

Lower Control Arm

REMOVAL & INSTALLATION

Except Pathfinder and QX4

1. Before servicing the vehicle, refer to the precautions in the beginning of this section.
2. Remove or disconnect the following:
   - Front wheel

- Torsion bar
- Shock absorber
- Stabilizer bar link
- Axle halfshaft, if equipped
- Lower ball joint
- Control arm mounting bolts
- Lower control arm
To install:
3. Install or connect the following:
   - Lower control arm. Tighten the mount bolts to 80–105 ft. lbs. (108–142 Nm).
   - Lower ball joint. Tighten the nut to 87–141 ft. lbs. (118–191 Nm).
   - Axle halfshaft, if equipped
   - Stabilizer bar link
   - Shock absorber
   - Torsion bar
   - Front wheel
4. Check the wheel alignment and adjust, as necessary.

CONTROL ARM BUSHING REPLACEMENT

1. Before servicing the vehicle, refer to the precautions in the beginning of this section.
2. Remove the control arm from the vehicle.
3. Remove the control arm bushing with a press.
To install:
4. Lubricate the control arm bushings with liquid soap.
5. Install the bushings with a press.
6. Install the control arm to the vehicle.
7. Check the wheel alignment and adjust, as necessary.

Wheel Bearings

ADJUSTMENT

2 Wheel Drive

➡ **Use a new split pin for assembly.**

1. Before servicing the vehicle, refer to the precautions in the beginning of this section.
2. Remove or disconnect the following:
   - Dust cap
   - Split pin
   - Spindle nut cap
3. Tighten the spindle nut to 25–29 ft. lbs. (34–39 Nm).

Turn to Section 5 for brake system applications

4. Spin the hub several times to fully seat the bearings.

5. Retighten the spindle nut to 25–29 ft. lbs. (34–39 Nm).

6. Loosen the spindle nut 45–60 degrees and install the spindle nut cap and split pin.

7. Install the dust cap.

4 Wheel Drive

1. Before servicing the vehicle, refer to the precautions in the beginning of this section.

2. Remove or disconnect the following:

- Locking hub or driveplate
- Snapring
- Spindle washer
- Thrust washer
- Lockwasher

3. Tighten the wheel bearing locknut to 58–72 ft. lbs. (78–98 Nm).

4. Loosen the locknut fully.

5. Tighten the wheel bearing locknut to 4–13 inch lbs. (0.5–1.5 Nm).

6. Spin the hub several times to fully seat the bearings.

7. Retighten the wheel bearing locknut to 4–13 inch lbs. (0.5–1.5 Nm).

8. Install or connect the following:

- Lockwasher. Tighten the retaining screw to 10–16 inch lbs. (1–2 Nm).
- Thrust washer
- Spindle washer

- Snapring
- Locking hub or driveplate

REMOVAL & INSTALLATION

2 Wheel Drive

1. Before servicing the vehicle, refer to the precautions in the beginning of this section.

2. Remove or disconnect the following:

- Front wheel
- Brake caliper and support
- Dust cap
- Split pin
- Spindle nut cap
- Spindle nut
- Bearing washer
- Outer bearing
- Hub and brake rotor assembly
- Inner grease seal
- Inner wheel bearing

To install:

3. Install or connect the following:

- Inner wheel bearing
- Inner grease seal
- Hub and brake rotor assembly
- Outer bearing
- Bearing washer
- Spindle nut. Adjust the wheel bearings.
- Spindle nut cap
- Split pin
- Dust cap
- Brake caliper and support
- Front wheel

4 Wheel Drive

1. Before servicing the vehicle, refer to the precautions in the beginning of this section.

2. Remove or disconnect the following:

- Front wheel
- Brake caliper and support
- Locking hub or driveplate
- Snapring
- Spindle washer
- Thrust washer
- Lockwasher
- Wheel bearing locknut
- Outer bearing
- Hub and brake rotor assembly
- Inner grease seal
- Inner wheel bearing

To install:

3. Install or connect the following:

- Inner wheel bearing
- Inner wheel bearing
- Inner grease seal
- Hub and brake rotor assembly
- Outer bearing
- Wheel bearing locknut. Adjust the wheel bearings.
- Lockwasher
- Thrust washer
- Spindle washer
- Snapring
- Locking hub or driveplate
- Brake caliper and support
- Front wheel

MERCURY AND NISSAN

Mercury-Villager • Nissan-Quest

32

PRECAUTIONS

Before servicing any vehicle, please be sure to read all of the following precautions, which deal with personal safety, prevention of component damage, and important points to take into consideration when servicing a motor vehicle:

• Never open, service or drain the radiator or cooling system when the engine is hot; serious burns can occur from the steam and hot coolant.

• Observe all applicable safety precautions when working around fuel. Whenever servicing the fuel system, always work in a well-ventilated area. Do not allow fuel spray or vapors to come in contact with a spark, open flame, or excessive heat (a hot drop light, for example). Keep a dry chemical fire extinguisher near the work area. Always keep fuel in a container specifically designed for fuel storage; also, always properly seal fuel containers to avoid the possibility of fire or explosion. Refer to the additional fuel system precautions later in this section.

• Fuel injection systems often remain pressurized, even after the engine has been turned **OFF**. The fuel system pressure must be relieved before disconnecting any fuel lines. Failure to do so may result in fire and/or personal injury.

• Brake fluid often contains polyglycol ethers and polyglycols. Avoid contact with the eyes and wash your hands thoroughly after handling brake fluid. If you do get brake fluid in your eyes, flush your eyes with clean, running water for 15 minutes. If eye irritation persists, or if you have taken brake fluid internally, IMMEDIATELY seek medical assistance.

• The EPA warns that prolonged contact with used engine oil may cause a number of skin disorders, including cancer! You should make every effort to minimize your exposure to used engine oil. Protective gloves should be worn when changing oil. Wash your hands and any other exposed skin areas as soon as possible after exposure to used engine oil. Soap and water, or waterless hand cleaner should be used.

• All new vehicles are now equipped with an air bag system. The system must be disabled before performing service on or around system components, steering column, instrument panel components, wiring and sensors. Failure to follow safety and disabling procedures could result in accidental air bag deployment, possible personal injury and unnecessary system repairs.

• Always wear safety goggles when working with, or around, the air bag system. When carrying a non-deployed air bag, be sure the bag and trim cover are pointed away from your body. When placing a non-deployed air bag on a work surface, always face the bag and trim cover upward, away from the surface. This will reduce the motion of the module if it is accidentally deployed. Refer to the additional air bag system precautions later in this section.

• Clean, high quality brake fluid from a sealed container is essential to the safe and proper operation of the brake system. You should always buy the correct type of brake fluid for your vehicle. If the brake fluid becomes contaminated, completely flush the system with new fluid. Never reuse any brake fluid. Any brake fluid that is removed from the system should be discarded. Also, do not allow any brake fluid to come in contact with a painted surface; it will damage the paint.

• Never operate the engine without the proper amount and type of engine oil; doing so WILL result in severe engine damage.

• Timing belt maintenance is extremely important! Many models utilize an interference-type, non-freewheeling engine. If the timing belt breaks, the valves in the cylinder head may strike the pistons, causing potentially serious (also time-consuming and expensive) engine damage. Refer to the maintenance interval charts in the front of this manual for the recommended replacement interval for the timing belt, and to the timing belt section for belt replacement and inspection.

• Disconnecting the negative battery cable on some vehicles may interfere with the functions of the on-board computer system(s) and may require the computer to undergo a relearning process once the negative battery cable is reconnected.

• When servicing drum brakes, only disassemble and assemble one side at a time, leaving the remaining side intact for reference.

• Only an MVAC-trained, EPA-certified automotive technician should service the air conditioning system or its components.

ENGINE REPAIR

Distributor

REMOVAL

1. Before servicing the vehicle, refer to the precautions in the beginning of this section.
2. Remove or disconnect the following:
   • Negative battery cable
   • Distributor cap
   • Distributor wiring harness connector
3. Matchmark the rotor to the distributor housing and the distributor housing to the cylinder head.
4. Remove the distributor.

INSTALLATION

Timing Not Disturbed

1. Install or connect the following:
   • Distributor by aligning the matchmarks made during removal
   • Distributor wiring harness connector
   • Distributor cap
   • Negative battery cable
2. Check the ignition timing and adjust, as necessary.

Timing Disturbed

1. Set the engine to Top Dead Center (TDC) of the compression stroke for the No. 1 cylinder.
2. Align the index mark on the distribu-

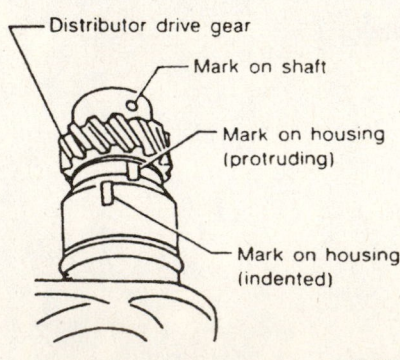

Distributor drive gear
Mark on shaft
Mark on housing (protruding)
Mark on housing (indented)

7924VG28

Distributor shaft alignment

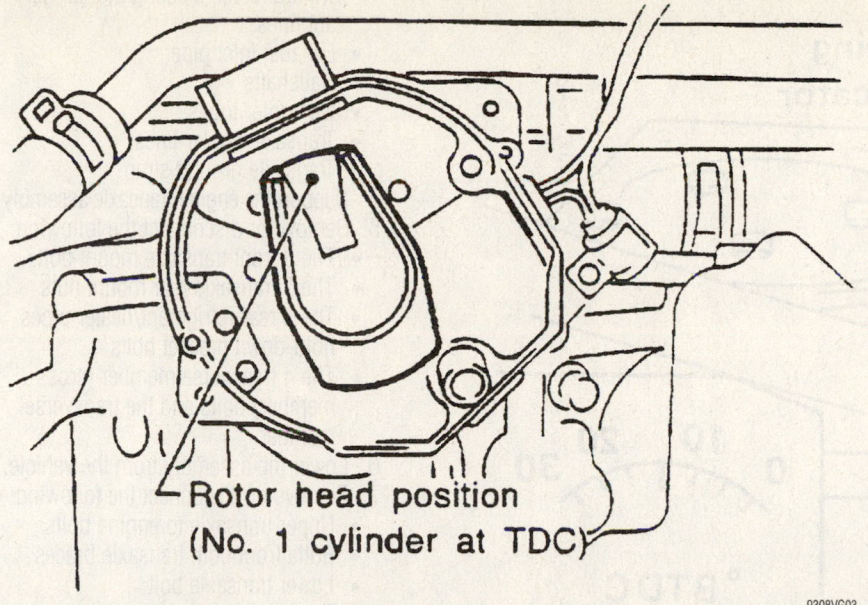

Rotor head position
(No. 1 cylinder at TDC)

Distributor rotor alignment

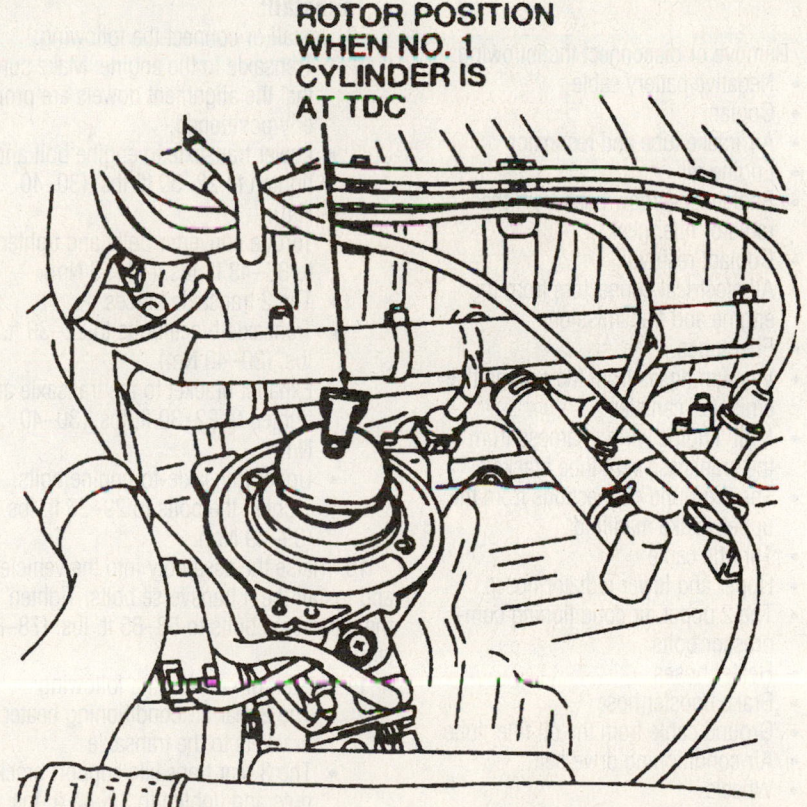

ROTOR POSITION
WHEN NO. 1
CYLINDER IS
AT TDC

Note the position of the rotor when the No. 1 piston is at TDC on the compression stroke

tor shaft with the protrusion on the distributor housing.

3. Install the distributor and check that the distributor rotor is aligned.

4. Install or connect the following:

- Distributor cap
- Distributor harness connector

5. Check the ignition timing and adjust, as necessary.

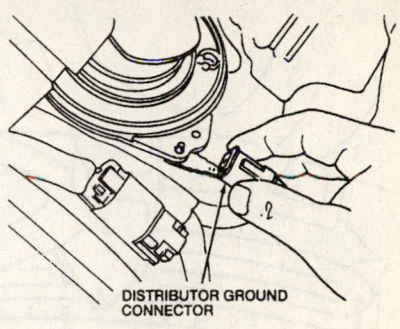

DISTRIBUTOR GROUND
CONNECTOR

Disengage the distributor ground connector when removing the distributor

Alternator

REMOVAL

1. Before servicing the vehicle, refer to the precautions in the beginning of this section.

2. Remove or disconnect the following:

- Negative battery cable
- Alternator harness connectors
- Engine under cover
- Alternator belt
- Alternator

INSTALLATION

Install or connect the following:

- Alternator
- Alternator belt. Tighten the adjustment bolt to 12–14 ft. lbs. (16–19 Nm) and the pivot bolts to 16–22 ft. lbs. (22–30 Nm).
- Engine under cover
- Alternator harness connectors
- Negative battery cable

Ignition Timing

ADJUSTMENT

1. Before servicing the vehicle, refer to the precautions in the beginning of this section.

2. Apply the parking brake and be sure that the vehicle is in PARK.

3. Start and run the engine until it reaches normal operating temperature.

4. Be sure the throttle is not touching the fast idle cam and the engine speed is below 1,000 rpm.

5. Turn off all electrical loads.

6. Run the engine at about 2000 rpm for 2 minutes under no-load.

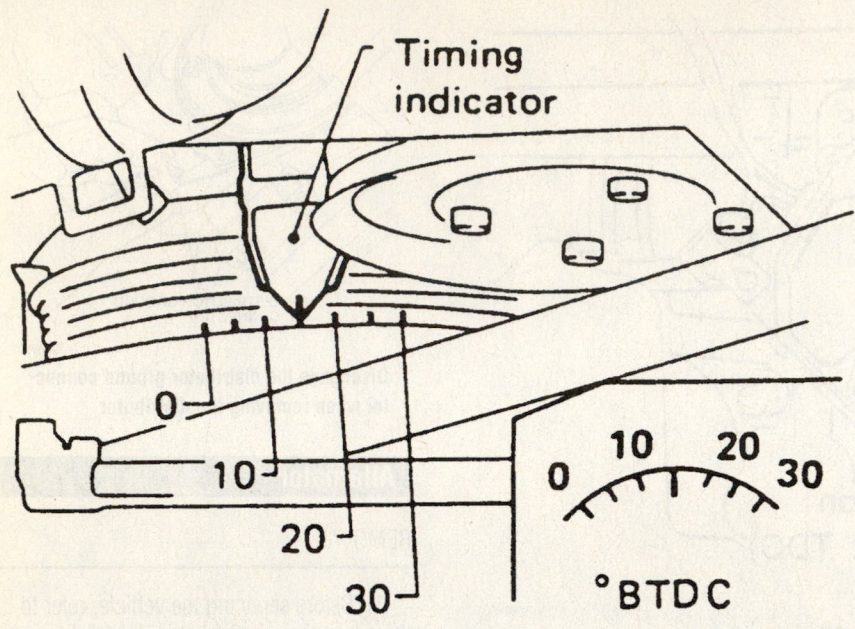

Adjust the timing so the pointer on the engine indicates 15° before top dead center (3 notches from TDC) on the crankshaft pulley.

7. Check for trouble codes and make necessary repairs if needed.

8. Turn **OFF** the engine and disconnect the TPS.

9. Start the engine

10. Rev the engine 2 or 3 times to 2,000–3,000 rpm and return the engine to idle speed.

11. Connect a timing light to the No. 1 cylinder spark plug wire at the distributor end and check the ignition timing. Be sure that the timing pointer is pointing to the 15° BTDC mark on the crankshaft pulley.

➡**Each notch on the crankshaft pulley represents 5°.**

12. If the timing is not within the specification, loosen the distributor mounting bolt and adjust the distributor until the timing is at the proper specification.

13. Tighten the distributor mounting bolt to 10–12 ft. lbs., (14–17 Nm).

14. Stop the engine and connect the TPS.

Engine Assembly

REMOVAL & INSTALLATION

The engine is removed with the transaxle attached. The engine and transaxle are lowered from the vehicle as an assembly.

1. Before servicing the vehicle, refer to the precautions in the beginning of this section.

2. Properly relieve the fuel system pressure.

3. Remove or disconnect the following:
- Negative battery cable
- Coolant
- Air intake tube and resonator
- Engine oil
- Radiator overflow hose from the radiator filler neck
- Coolant reservoir
- All electrical connectors from the engine and transmission
- Fuel tubes
- Vacuum hoses from the evaporative emission canister
- Main engine wiring harness from the crankcase vent tube brackets
- The 2 ground connections from the upper intake manifold
- Throttle cable
- Upper and lower radiator hoses
- The 2 upper air conditioning compressor bolts
- Heater hoses
- Brake booster hose
- Ground cable from the oil filler tube
- Air conditioning drive belt
- Wheels
- Inner and outer engine and transmission splash shields
- Shift cable nut from the Transmission Range (TR) switch
- Shift cable locking pin from the shift cable bracket
- Accessory drive belts
- Power steering pump
- The 2 lower compressor bolts and position the compressor aside

without disconnecting the refrigerant lines.
- Exhaust inlet pipe
- Halfshafts
- Oil cooler tubes
- Transaxle cooler lines
- Transaxle ground strap

4. Support the engine/transaxle assembly

5. Remove or disconnect the following:
- The 3 front transaxle mount bolts
- The 3 transaxle rear mount nuts
- The 2 rear refrigerant/heater pipes hold-down bracket bolts
- The 4 transverse member (crossmember) bolts and the transverse member

6. Lower the assembly from the vehicle.

7. Remove or disconnect the following:
- Upper transaxle to engine bolts
- Bolts from both transaxle braces
- Lower transaxle bolt
- Torque converter bolts

8. Separate the transaxle from the engine.

To install:

9. Install or connect the following:
- Transaxle to the engine. Make sure that the alignment dowels are properly positioned.
- Lower transaxle to engine bolt and tighten to 22–30 ft. lbs. (30–40 Nm).
- Torque converter bolts and tighten to 33–43 ft. lbs. (44–59 Nm).
- The 2 transaxle braces
- Transaxle brace bolts to 22–30 ft. lbs. (30–40 Nm)
- Exhaust bracket to the transaxle and tighten to 22–30 ft. lbs. (30–40 Nm)
- Upper transaxle-to-engine bolts. Tighten the bolts to 29–36 ft. lbs. (39–49 Nm).

10. Raise the assembly into the vehicle and install the 4 transverse bolts. Tighten the transverse bolts to 58–65 ft. lbs. (78–88 Nm).

11. Install or connect the following:
- The 2 rear air conditioning heater brackets to the transaxle
- The 3 rear transaxle support bracket nuts and tighten to 32–42 ft. lbs. (43–55 Nm).
- The 3 front transaxle mount bolts and tighten to 30–38 ft. lbs. (41–52 Nm).

12. Remove the engine lift.

13. Install or connect the following:
- Transaxle ground strap
- Transaxle cooler lines
- Oil cooler lines to the proper connections

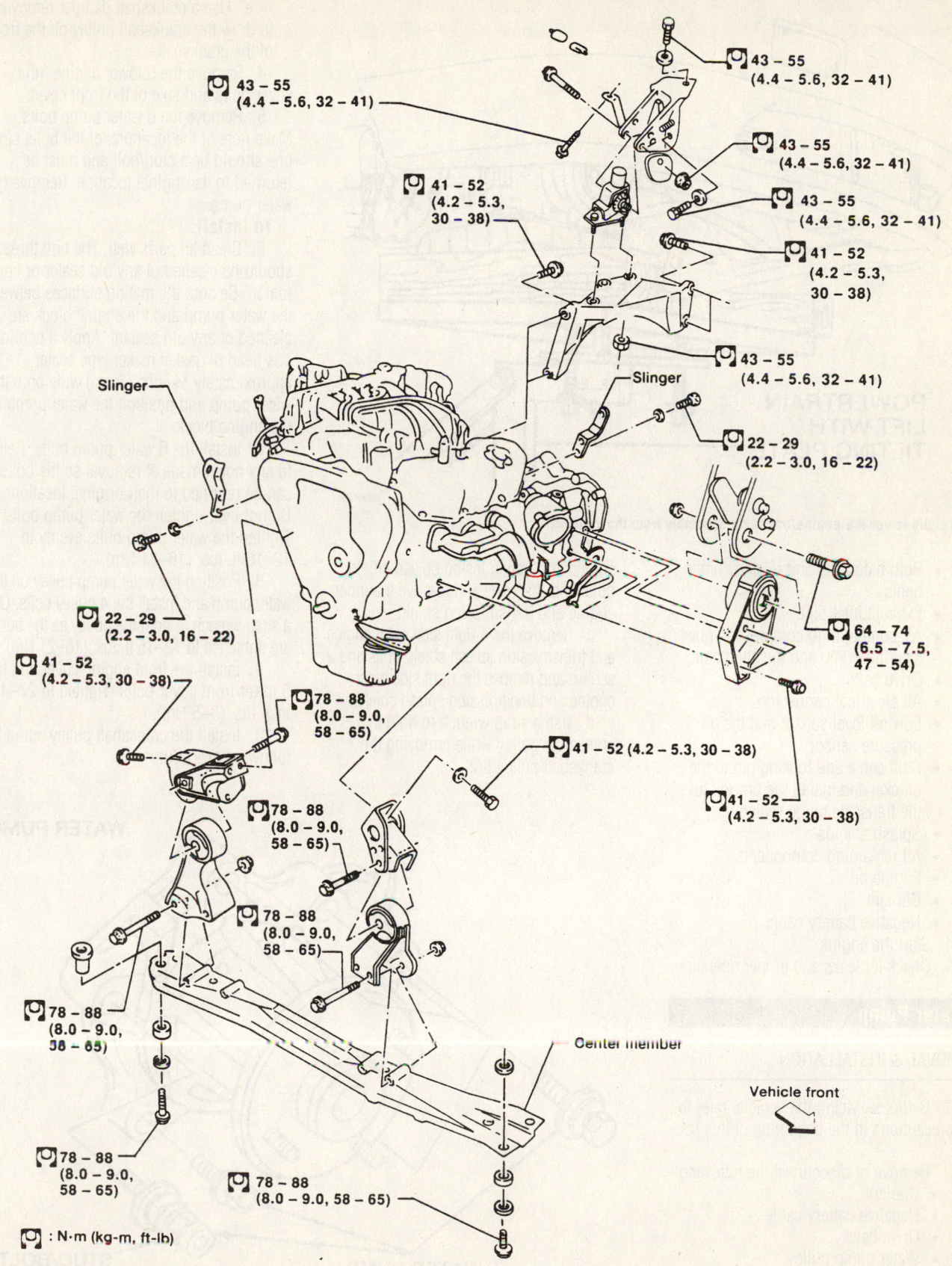

43 – 55
(4.4 – 5.6, 32 – 41)

43 – 55
(4.4 – 5.6, 32 – 41)

43 – 55
(4.4 – 5.6, 32 – 41)

43 – 55
(4.4 – 5.6, 32 – 41)

41 – 52
(4.2 – 5.3,
30 – 38)

41 – 52
(4.2 – 5.3,
30 – 38)

43 – 55
(4.4 – 5.6, 32 – 41)

22 – 29
(2.2 – 3.0, 16 – 22)

Slinger

Slinger

22 – 29
(2.2 – 3.0, 16 – 22)

64 – 74
(6.5 – 7.5,
47 – 54)

41 – 52
(4.2 – 5.3, 30 – 38)

78 – 88
(8.0 – 9.0,
58 – 65)

41 – 52 (4.2 – 5.3, 30 – 38)

41 – 52
(4.2 – 5.3, 30 – 38)

78 – 88
(8.0 – 9.0,
58 – 65)

78 – 88
(8.0 – 9.0,
58 – 65)

78 – 88
(8.0 – 9.0,
58 – 65)

Center member

Vehicle front

78 – 88
(8.0 – 9.0,
58 – 65)

78 – 88
(8.0 – 9.0, 58 – 65)

: N·m (kg-m, ft-lb)

Engine mounting components

9302WG01

Timing belt service is covered in Section 4 of this manual

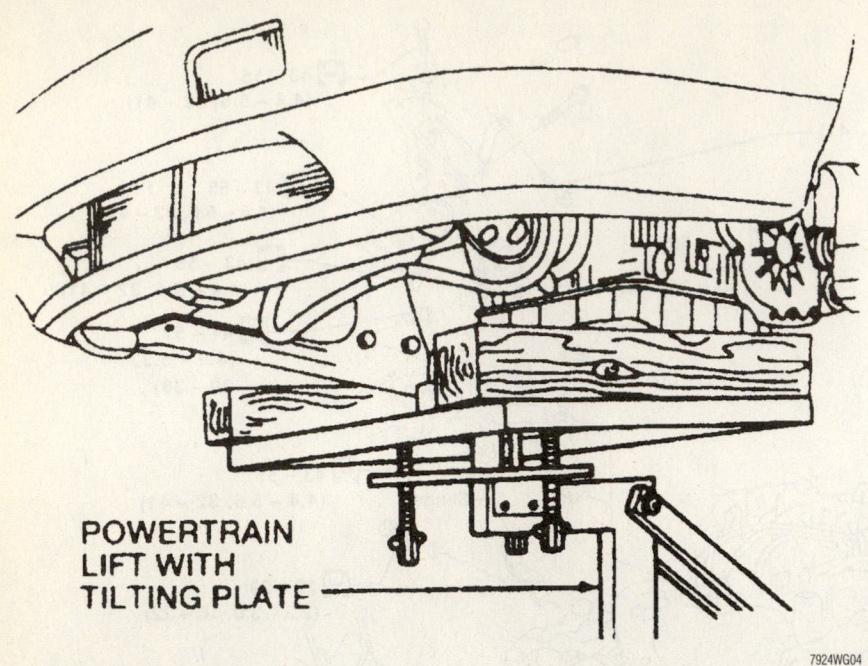

**POWERTRAIN
LIFT WITH
TILTING PLATE**

7924WG04

Carefully lower the engine/transaxle assembly from the vehicle.

- Both halfshafts and related components
- Exhaust inlet pipe
- Air conditioning compressor, power steering pump and the alternator
- Drive belts
- All electrical connectors
- Low oil level sensor and the oil pressure sensor
- Shift cable and locking pin to the bracket and install the bracket to the transaxle range switch.
- Splash shields
- All remaining components
- Engine oil
- Coolant
- Negative battery cable

14. Start the engine.
15. Check for leaks and proper operation.

Water Pump

REMOVAL & INSTALLATION

1. Before servicing the vehicle, refer to the precautions in the beginning of this section.

2. Remove or disconnect the following:
- Coolant
- Negative battery cable
- Drive belts
- Water pump pulley

3. Remove the crankshaft pulley using the following procedure:
a. Raise and safely support the vehicle.
b. Remove the 5 right side inner engine and transmission splash shield bolts and 2 screws and remove the inner engine and transmission shield.

c. Remove the 4 right side outer engine and transmission splash shield bolts and 2 screws and remove the right side outer engine and transmission splash shields.

d. Use a strap wrench to hold the crankshaft pulley while removing the crankshaft pulley bolt.

e. Use a crankshaft damper remover to draw the crankshaft pulley off the front of the crankshaft.

4. Remove the 5 lower engine front cover bolts and take of the front cover.

5. Remove the 6 water pump bolts. Make note of the locations of the bolts since one should be a stud/bolt and must be returned to its original location. Remove the water pump.

To install:

6. Clean all parts well. The bolt threads should be cleaned of any old sealer or corrosion. Be sure the mating surfaces between the water pump and the engine block are cleaned of any old sealant. Apply a continuous bead of gasket maker type sealer approximately ⅛ inch (3mm) wide onto the water pump and position the water pump on the engine block.

7. Install the 6 water pump bolts. Refer to any notes made at removal so the bolts can be returned to their original locations. Do not over-tighten the water pump bolts. Tighten the water pump bolts evenly to 12–15 ft. lbs. (16–21 Nm).

8. Position the water pump pulley on the water pump and install the 4 pulley bolts. Use a strap wrench to hold the pulley as the bolts are tightened to 12–15 ft. lbs. (16–21 Nm).

9. Install the front engine cover and the 5 lower front cover bolts. Tighten to 27–44 inch lbs. (3–5 Nm).

10. Install the crankshaft pulley using the following procedure:

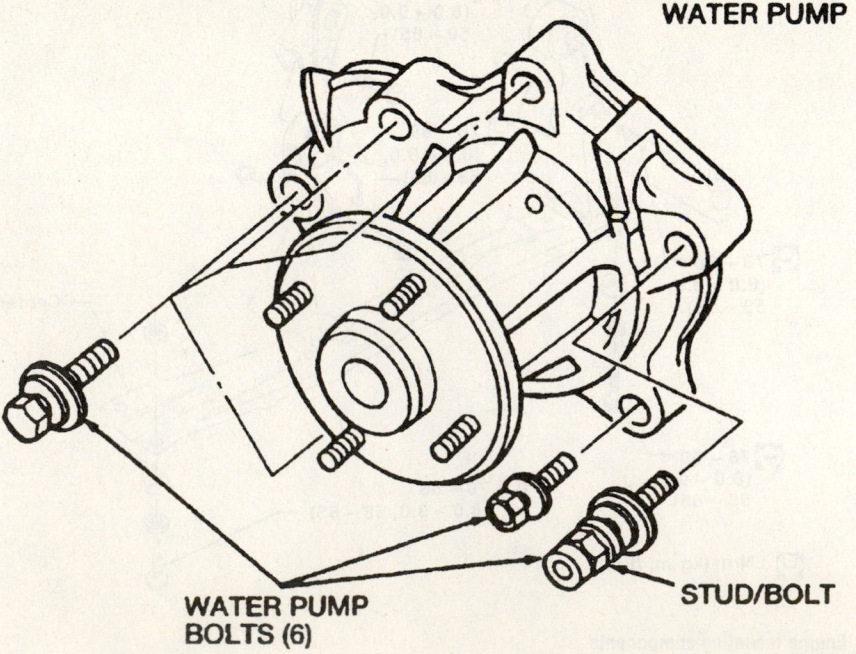

WATER PUMP

**WATER PUMP
BOLTS (6)**

STUD/BOLT

7924WG05

Water pump mounting. Note the location of the stud/bolt

a. Install the crankshaft pulley and pulley bolt.

b. Hold the pulley with a strap wrench. Tighten the crankshaft pulley bolt to 90–98 ft. lbs. (123–132 Nm).

c. Install the inner and outer engine and transmission splash shields.

11. Install the drive belts.

12. Connect the negative battery cable.

13. Refill the cooling system.

14. Start the engine and check for leaks.

Cylinder Head

REMOVAL & INSTALLATION

➡ **The cylinder head bolt torque sequences are found in Section 1, following the Torque Specifications Chart.**

The factory specifies that the cylinder head bolts ARE NOT to be reused. Obtain the proper replacement parts before beginning this procedure. Check carefully that all bolts are removed before attempting to remove a cylinder head. A tab, part of the head, contains 1 lightly tightened head bolt that is external to the valve cover. Do not overlook this "hidden" bolt or the head will be damaged.

1. Before servicing the vehicle, refer to the precautions in the beginning of this section.

2. Properly relieve the fuel system pressure.

3. Remove or disconnect the following:
- Coolant
- Negative battery cable
- Air intake tube
- Timing belt
- Upper intake manifold (plenum)
- Spark plug wires
- Ignition coil to distributor high tension wires
- Distributor
- EGR solenoid
- MAF sensor
- VSS
- Valve body wiring harness
- TR switch
- air conditioning clutch pulley
- Power transistor
- air conditioning cut-off switch
- Fuel injectors
- Ignition coil
- Water temperature indicator sender unit.
- ECT sensor.
- Main wiring harness bracket from the water hose connection

- Fuel tube bracket bolt from the EGR valve bracket
- The 4 Allen-head fuel injection supply manifold (fuel rail) and position the fuel rail and injectors aside.
- Upper heater water hose

4. Using 2 steps, remove the 4 Allen-head intake manifold to cylinder head bolts and the 4 nuts. Work from the outer fasteners, inward. Remove the lower intake manifold from the vehicle. Discard the gaskets.

5. If removing the front cylinder head, remove the 9 valve cover screws, take off the cover and discard the gasket.

6. Use Camshaft Pulley Holding Tool T92P-6312-AH, or equivalent, to hold the camshaft sprocket, while removing the sprocket retaining bolt. Remove the camshaft sprocket and the 4 seal plate bolts and seal plate.

7. If removing the front cylinder head, remove the oil level indicator (dipstick) bolts and take off the dipstick tube bracket.

8. If removing the front cylinder head, remove the 3 exhaust manifold to inlet pipe nuts. Remove and discard the gasket.

9. Remove the front exhaust manifold to mounting bracket bolt.

10. If removing the front cylinder head, remove the 2 lower air conditioning compressor bolts, if equipped.

11. If removing the front cylinder head, and if equipped with air conditioning, loosen the 2 upper air conditioning compressor bolts and move the air conditioning compressor out of he way. Secure with wire. Note that the upper air conditioning compressor bolts are too long to remove from the compressor. Remove them once the compressor is moved aside.

12. If removing the front cylinder head, remove the 2 upper alternator regulator mounting bracket bolts. Remove the 2 coolant crossover tube bracket bolts.

13. If removing the rear cylinder head, remove the 6 rear exhaust manifold nuts working from the center, outward. Remove the manifold and discard the gasket. Remove the 9 rear valve cover screws, lift off the valve cover and discard the gasket.

14. The cylinder head bolts must be removed in sequence, working from the out-

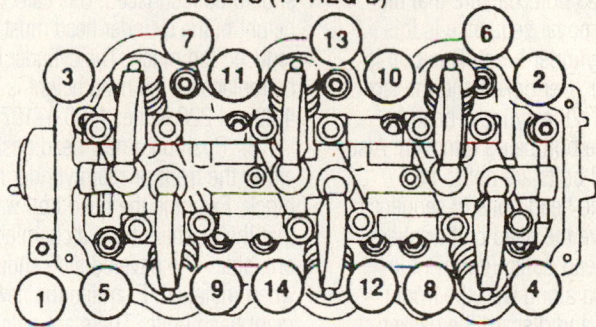

LOOSENING SEQUENCE
FRONT CYLINDER HEAD
BOLTS (14 REQ'D)

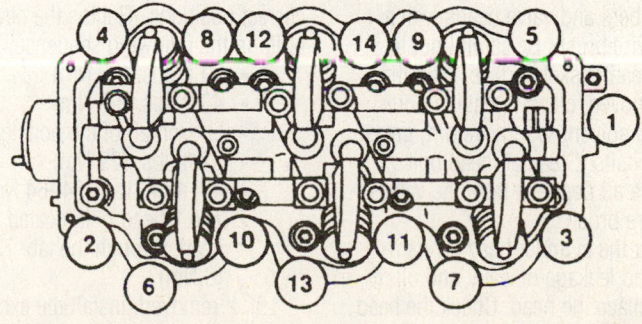

LOOSENING SEQUENCE

REAR CYLINDER HEAD
BOLTS (14 REQ'D)

7924WG06

Remove the cylinder head bolts and nuts in the proper sequence to avoid warping the head. Don't forget the hidden bolt outside of the valve cover area.

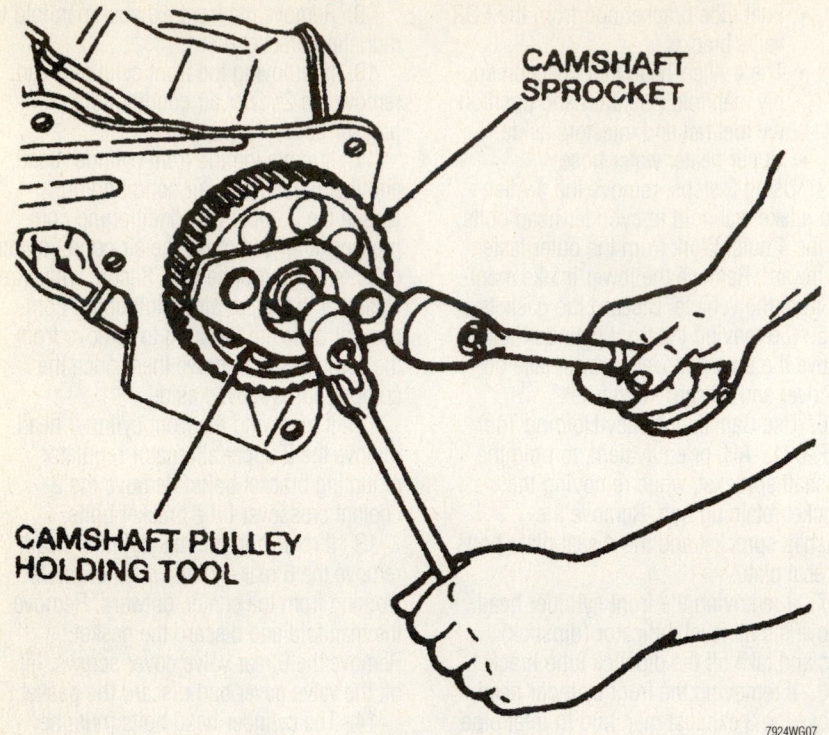

CAMSHAFT SPROCKET

CAMSHAFT PULLEY HOLDING TOOL

7924WG07

Hold the camshaft sprocket while removing the sprocket retaining bolt

side, inward. Please note that there is a "tab" on one end of each cylinder head. This tab contains a head bolt. Be sure that the first bolt in the removal sequence is this bolt outside the cylinder head. This bolt is easily forgotten or overlooked and the tab can be broken off if the cylinder head is moved prior to the bolt being removed. Also note that the head bolts are not to be reused. Loosen the head bolts in sequence, in 2 steps. Remove the head bolt washers and discard the head bolts. Remove the front cylinder head along with the front exhaust manifold and discard the gasket.

To install:

15. Clean all parts well. With the intake and exhaust valves in place to protect the valve seats, remove deposits from the combustion chambers and valve heads with a scraper and wire brush. Be careful not to damage the head gasket surface. After the valves are removed, clean the guide bores. Use a suitable solvent to remove dirt, grease and other deposits. Clean all head bolt holes. Remove all deposits from the valves with a fine wire brush.

16. Inspect the cylinder head for damage, cracks and leakage of water and oil. If necessary, replace the head. Check the head gasket surface for burrs and nicks. If the head is cracked, it must be replaced.

17. Using a straightedge and a feeler gauge, check the head for flatness. Measure lengthwise and across the head. Maximum distortion is 0.004 inch (0.10mm). If the head distortion exceeds this specification, the head should be resurfaced. Use care. The overall height of the cylinder head must not be reduced too much. The cylinder head must be replaced if the head height is not within 4.205–4.220 inches (106.8–107.2mm) tall.

18. Position a new head gasket and either the front or rear cylinder head on the block. Examine the head bolt washers. Note that the washers have a chamfer or bevel on one side. The beveled side should face "up" when installed. Examine the new replacement head bolts. There are different lengths. The head bolts in positions 4, 5, 12 and 13 are 5.00 inches (127mm) long and the rest are 4.17 inches (106mm) long. Be sure the new cylinder head bolts are installed in the correct positions. Tighten the new head bolts in the following sequence:
- 22 ft. lbs. (29 Nm)
- 43 ft. lbs. (59 Nm)
- Loosen all of the bolts completely
- 22 ft. lbs. (29 Nm)
- 40–47 ft. lbs. (54–64 Nm)
- The 1 head bolt located outside the head, through the tab: 72 inch lbs. (8 Nm)

19. If removed, install the exhaust manifold using a new gasket. Tighten the nuts from the center, outward to 13–16 ft. lbs. (18–22 Nm).

20. If installing the front cylinder head, position the coolant crossover tube on the bracket on the cylinder head and install the bolt. Install the 2 upper alternator regulator mounting bracket bolts and tighten securely.

21. If installing the front cylinder head and if equipped with air conditioning, position the air conditioning compressor on the alternator regulator mounting bracket and install the upper compressor bolts. Tighten to 33–44 ft. lbs. (45–60 Nm).

22. Raise and safely support the vehicle.

23. If installing the front cylinder head and if equipped with air conditioning, install the 2 lower compressor bolts. Tighten to 33–44 ft. lbs. (45–60 Nm).

24. Install a new gasket between the front exhaust manifold and rear manifold crossover tube, install the 2 nuts and 1 bolt. Install the front exhaust manifold mounting bracket bolt and tighten securely. Install a new gasket and position the exhaust inlet pipe onto the manifold. Tighten the nuts to 32–40 ft. lbs. (44–54 Nm).

25. Lower the vehicle.

26. If installing the front cylinder head, install the dipstick tube and bracket and secure.

27. Position the rear engine front cover install the 4 seal plate bolts. Do not over-torque. Tighten to 27–44 inch lbs. (3–5 Nm).

28. Using the Camshaft Pulley Holding Tool or equivalent, install the camshaft sprocket bolt and tighten to 58–65 ft. lbs. (78–88 Nm).

29. Using new gasket(s), install the valve cover(s), front or rear, as required. Install the 9 bolts. Do not over-torque. Tighten to just 9–26 inch lbs. (1–3 Nm).

30. Install new lower intake manifold gaskets on the cylinder heads and lay the manifold in lace. Install the 4 Allen-head bolts and 4 manifold nuts. Tighten in sequence, working from the center, outward as follows:
- 27–44 inch lbs. (3–5 Nm).
- 12–14 ft. lbs. (16–20 Nm).
- Again to 12–14 ft. lbs. (16–20 Nm).

31. Connect the upper water hose.

32. Position the fuel injectors into their respective ports and install the fuel rail bolts. Tighten evenly to 17–20 ft. lbs. (24–27 Nm).

33. Connect the water bypass hose to the intake manifold.

34. Bolt the fuel tube bracket back onto the EGR valve bracket.

35. Attach the main wiring harness bracket to the intake manifold water hose connection.

36. Connect the electrical connectors removed at disassembly.

37. Install the distributor using the recommended procedure.

38. Connect the spark plug wires using the identification made at removal.

39. Install the upper intake manifold (plenum) using the recommended intake manifold procedure.

40. Install the timing belt using the recommended procedure.

41. Install the air cleaner and intake tubes as required.

42. Connect the negative battery cable.

43. Fill the cooling system. An oil and filter change is recommended.

44. Start the vehicle and check for leaks. Check the ignition timing and adjust as required.

Rocker Arms/Shafts

REMOVAL & INSTALLATION

1. Before servicing the vehicle, refer to the precautions in the beginning of this section.

2. Remove or disconnect the following:

- Negative battery cable
- Upper intake manifold
- Valve covers
- Rocker arm and shaft assemblies
- Rocker arms from the shafts

➡ **Keep all valvetrain components in order for assembly.**

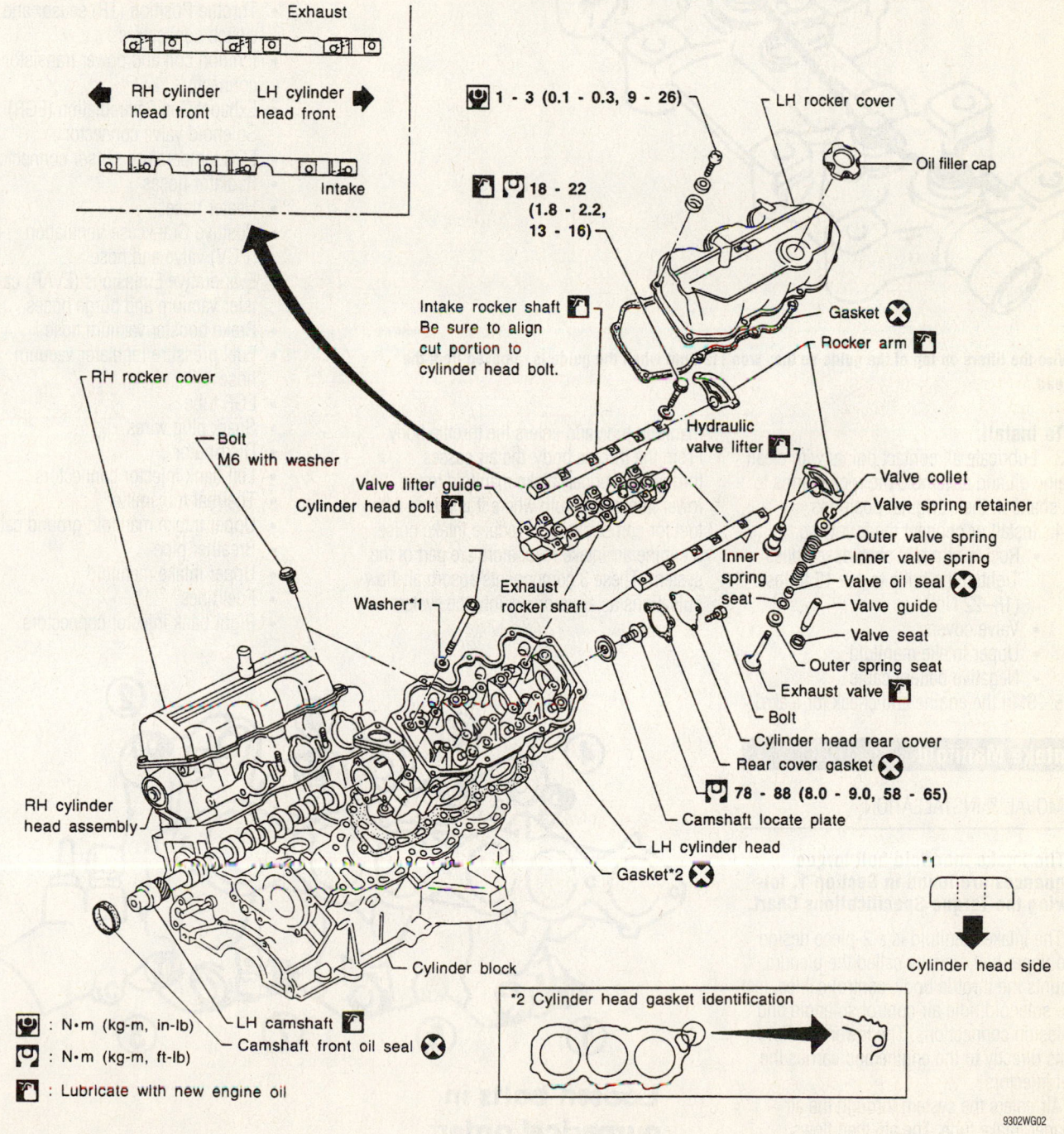

Rocker arm and shaft components

9302WG02

Refer to Section 1 for engine rebuilding specifications

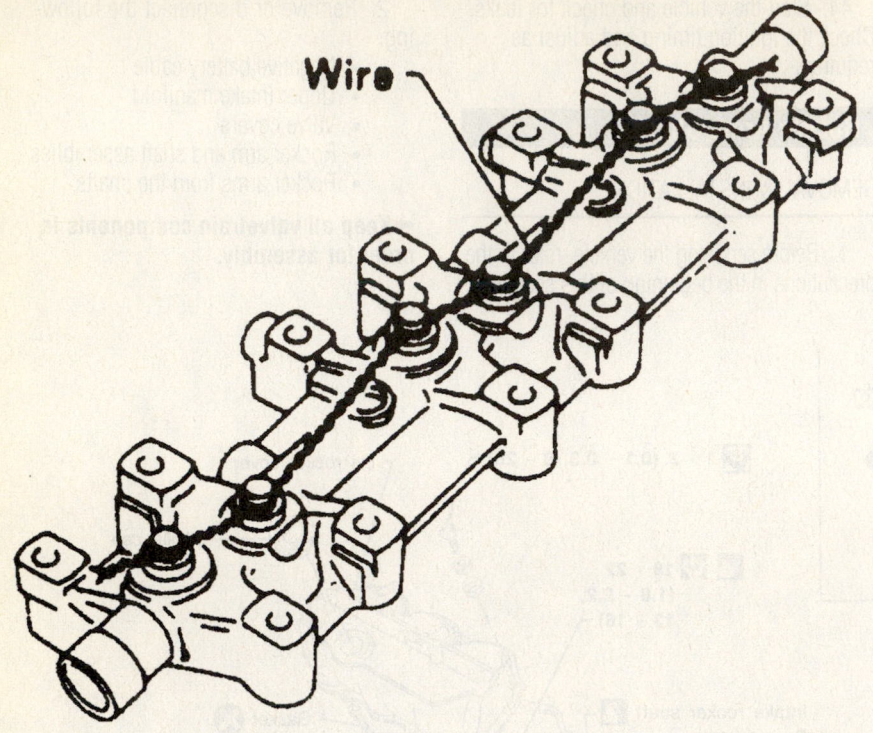

Wire

7924WG09

Wire the lifters on top of the guide so they won't fall out when the guide is removed from the head.

To install:

3. Lubricate all contact points with clean engine oil and assemble the rocker arms to the shafts in their original positions.

4. Install or connect the following:
- Rocker arm and shaft assemblies. Tighten the bolts to 13–16 ft. lbs. (18–22 Nm).
- Valve covers
- Upper intake manifold
- Negative battery cable

5. Start the engine and check for leaks.

Intake Manifold

REMOVAL & INSTALLATION

➡**The intake manifold bolt torque sequences are found in Section 1, following the Torque Specifications Chart.**

The intake manifold is a 2-piece design. The upper half, usually called the plenum, mounts the throttle body, control cables, fast idle solenoid, idle air control solenoid and emission connections. The lower manifold bolts directly to the engine and carries the fuel injectors.

Air enters the system through the air cleaner intake tube. The air, then flows through the dry element air cleaner and is metered by the MAF sensor. The metered air passes through the air cleaner to intake manifold tube and enters the throttle body. From the throttle body, the air passes through the upper intake manifold to the lower intake manifold where it is mixed with fuel for combustion. To reduce intake noise, 3 engine air intake resonators are part of the system. These 3 components absorb air-flow pulsations as air is drawn into the system.

1. Before servicing the vehicle, refer to the precautions in the beginning of this section.
2. Drain the cooling system.
3. Relieve the fuel system pressure.
4. Remove or disconnect the following:
- Negative battery cable
- Air intake duct
- Accelerator cable
- Cruise control cable
- Idle Air Control (IAC) valve connector
- Throttle Position (TP) sensor and switch connectors
- Ignition coil and power transistor connectors
- Exhaust Gas Recirculation (EGR) Solenoid valve connector
- EGR temperature sensor connector
- Radiator hoses
- Heater hoses
- Positive Crankcase Ventilation (PCV) valve and hose
- Evaporative Emissions (EVAP) canister vacuum and purge hoses
- Brake booster vacuum hose
- Fuel pressure regulator vacuum hose
- EGR tube
- Spark plug wires
- Distributor
- Left bank injector connectors
- Thermal transmitter
- Upper intake manifold ground cable
- Breather pipe
- Upper intake manifold
- Fuel lines
- Right bank injector connectors

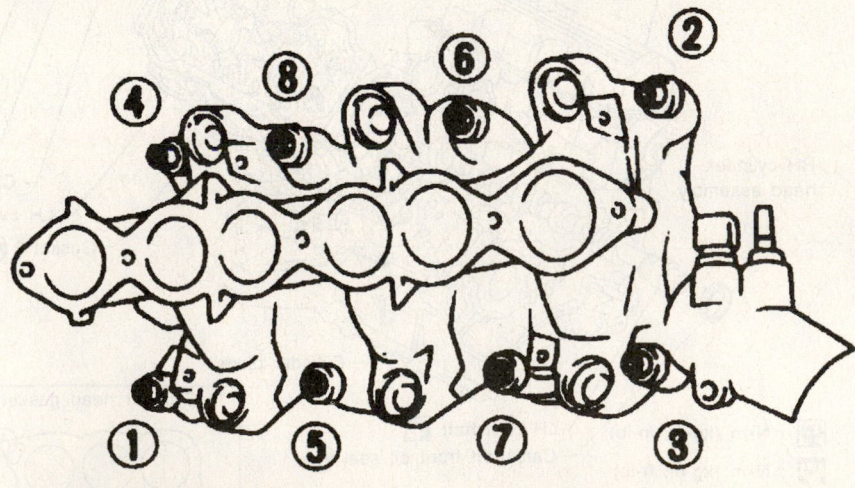

Loosen bolts in numerical order.

7924VG32

Intake manifold loosening sequence—3.3L engine

- Fuel supply manifold
- Engine Coolant Temperature (ECT) sensor connector
- Lower intake manifold. Loosen the fasteners in the sequence shown.

To install:

➡ Refer to Section 1 of this manual for the intake manifold torque sequence illustration. The illustration is located after the Torque Specification Chart.

5. Install the lower intake manifold with a new gasket.

6. For 1997 engines, tighten the fasteners as follows:

   a. Step 1: Tighten all bolts to 26–43 inch lbs. (3–5 Nm)

   b. Step 2: Tighten all nuts to 26–43 inch lbs. (3–5 Nm)

   c. Step 3: Tighten all bolts to 13–16 ft. lbs. (18–22 Nm)

   d. Step 4: Tighten all nuts to 13–16 ft. lbs. (18–22 Nm)

7. For 1998–01 engines, tighten the fasteners in sequence as follows:

   a. Step 1: 35 inch lbs. (4 Nm)

   b. Step 2: 78 inch lbs. (9 Nm)

   c. Step 3: 70–84 inch lbs. (8–10 Nm)

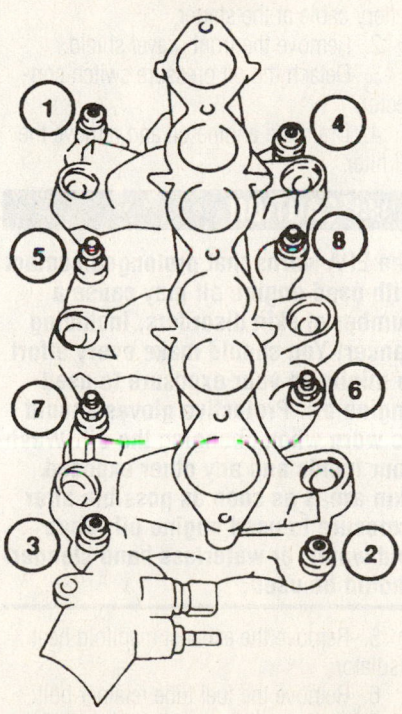

LOOSENING SEQUENCE

7924WG10

Gradually loosen the lower manifold bolts in 2 steps using the proper sequence.

8. Install or connect the following:
- ECT sensor connector
- Fuel supply manifold
- Right bank injector connectors
- Fuel lines
- Upper intake manifold
- Breather pipe
- Upper intake manifold ground cable
- Thermal transmitter
- Left bank injector connectors
- Distributor
- Spark plug wires
- EGR tube
- Fuel pressure regulator vacuum hose
- Brake booster vacuum hose
- EVAP canister vacuum and purge hoses
- PCV valve and hose
- Heater hoses
- Radiator hoses
- EGR temperature sensor connector
- EGR Solenoid valve connector
- Ignition coil and power transistor connectors
- TP sensor and switch connectors
- IAC valve connector
- Cruise control cable
- Accelerator cable
- Air intake duct
- Negative battery cable

9. Fill the cooling system.

10. Start the engine and check for leaks.

Exhaust Manifold

REMOVAL & INSTALLATION

Rear (right-hand) Exhaust Manifold

1. Before servicing the vehicle, refer to the precautions in the beginning of this section.

2. Disconnect the negative battery cable.

3. Disconnect the radiator overflow hose from the radiator.

4. Slide the radiator coolant-recovery reservoir off of the bracket and remove the reservoir.

5. Remove the air cleaner intake tube and the engine air intake resonator.

6. Remove the 6 rear (right-hand) exhaust manifold crossover tube heat-shield bolts and remove the heat shields.

7. Remove the 2 nuts and the 1 bolt securing the rear (right-hand) exhaust manifold tube to the front (left-hand) exhaust manifold. Discard the gasket.

8. Remove the transmission fluid level indicator tube heat shield.

9. Disengage the following electrical connectors:

   a. The idle switch.

   b. The throttle position sensor.

   c. The exhaust gas recirculation control solenoid.

10. Raise and safely support the vehicle.

11. Remove the exhaust gas recirculation valve to back-pressure transducer valve tube nut and position it out of the way.

12. Remove the 2 EGR valve to exhaust manifold tube nuts and remove the EGR valve to exhaust manifold tube.

13. Remove the 6 rear exhaust manifold nuts in the reverse order of the tightening sequence.

14. Safely lower the vehicle, remove the exhaust manifold and discard the exhaust manifold gasket.

To install:

15. Raise and safely support the vehicle.

16. Be sure that both the exhaust manifold and the cylinder head mating surfaces are clean of any old gasket material.

17. Position the rear (right-hand) exhaust manifold gasket onto the exhaust manifold mounting studs.

18. Lower the vehicle safely.

19. Place the rear (right-hand) exhaust manifold onto the studs.

20. Safely raise the vehicle and install the 6 rear (right-hand) exhaust manifold nuts. Tighten the nuts in sequence to 13–16 ft. lbs. (18–22 Nm).

21. Install the EGR valve to exhaust manifold tube and install the 2 EGR valve to exhaust manifold tube nuts. Tighten the EGR valve to exhaust manifold tube nuts.

22. Position the EGR valve to the back-pressure transducer valve tube nut into place. Tighten the EGR valve to the BPT valve tube nut.

23. Lower the vehicle carefully.

24. Reconnect the following electrical connectors:

   a. The exhaust gas recirculation solenoid.

   b. The throttle position sensor.

   c. The idle switch.

25. Install the transmission fluid level indicator tube heat shield.

26. Install a new gasket between the front (left-hand) exhaust manifold and the rear exhaust manifold crossover tube.

27. Install the 2 nuts and the 1 bolt securing the rear (right-hand) exhaust manifold crossover tube to the front (left-hand)

exhaust manifold. Tighten the rear exhaust manifold crossover tube-to-front (left-hand) exhaust manifold nuts and bolt.

28. Reinstall the rear (right-hand) exhaust manifold crossover tube heat shield with the 6 mounting bolts.

29. Tighten the rear (right-hand) exhaust manifold crossover tube bolts.

30. Install the air cleaner intake tube and the engine air intake resonator.

31. Install the radiator coolant recovery reservoir and reconnect the radiator overflow hose to the radiator.

32. Reconnect the negative battery cable, start the engine and check for leaks and proper operation.

Front (left-hand) Exhaust Manifold

1. Before servicing the vehicle, refer to the precautions in the beginning of this section.

2. Disconnect the negative battery cable and wait at least 90 seconds before performing any work. This allows time for the SRS or air bag system to deplete its back up energy supply.

3. Remove the 2 nuts and the 1 bolt securing the front (left-hand) exhaust manifold to the rear (right-hand) exhaust manifold crossover tube. Discard the gasket.

4. Remove the transmission fluid level indicator tube heat shield.

5. Loosen the 6 front (left-hand) exhaust manifold nuts in 2 steps in the reverse order of the tightening sequence. Do not remove the 3 lower front (left-hand) exhaust manifold nuts.

6. Remove the front (left-hand) exhaust manifold-to-mounting bracket bolt.

7. Raise and safely support the vehicle.

8. Disengage the heated oxygen sensor electrical connector.

9. Remove the 3 front (left-hand) exhaust manifold-to-inlet pipe nuts.

10. Remove the exhaust system flex tube bracket bolt.

11. Remove the left-hand inner engine and transmission splash shield bolts and screws and remove the left-hand inner engine and transmission splash shield.

12. Remove the 3 lower exhaust manifold nuts.

13. Remove the front (left-hand) exhaust manifold and discard the exhaust manifold gasket.

To install:

14. Be sure that both the exhaust manifold and the cylinder head mating surfaces are clean of any old gasket material.

15. Position a new front exhaust manifold gasket in place and install the front (left-hand) exhaust manifold. Install the 3 lower exhaust manifold mounting nuts. Do not tighten the nuts at this time.

16. Install the left-hand inner engine and transmission splash shield with their mounting bolts and screws.

17. Reinstall the exhaust system flex tube bracket bolt.

18. Install the 3 exhaust manifold-to-exhaust inlet pipe nuts.

19. Reconnect the heated oxygen sensor electrical connector.

20. Lower the vehicle.

21. Install the front (left-hand) exhaust manifold-to-mounting bracket bolt.

22. Install the 3 upper exhaust manifold mounting bolts and tighten all 6 exhaust manifold mounting bolts in sequence. Tighten the bolts to 13–16 ft. lbs. (18–22 Nm).

23. Install the transmission fluid level indicator tube heat shield.

24. Install the 2 nuts and the 1 bolt securing the front (left-hand) exhaust manifold to the rear (right-hand) exhaust manifold crossover tube.

25. Reconnect the negative battery cable, start the engine, check for leaks and road test for proper operation.

Starter

REMOVAL & INSTALLATION

1. Disconnect the negative battery cable at the battery, then disconnect the positive battery cable at the starter.

2. Remove the front gravel shield.

3. Detach the oil pressure switch connector.

4. Drain the engine oil and remove the oil filter.

✳✳ CAUTION

The EPA warns that prolonged contact with used engine oil may cause a number of skin disorders, including cancer! You should make every effort to minimize your exposure to used engine oil. Protective gloves should be worn when changing the oil. Wash your hands and any other exposed skin areas as soon as possible after exposure to used engine oil. Soap and water, or waterless hand cleaner should be used.

5. Remove the exhaust manifold heat insulator.

6. Remove the fuel tube retainer bolt.

7. Unfasten the remaining electrical connections at the starter solenoid.

8. Remove the two nuts holding the starter to the bell housing, then pull the starter toward the front of the vehicle and out.

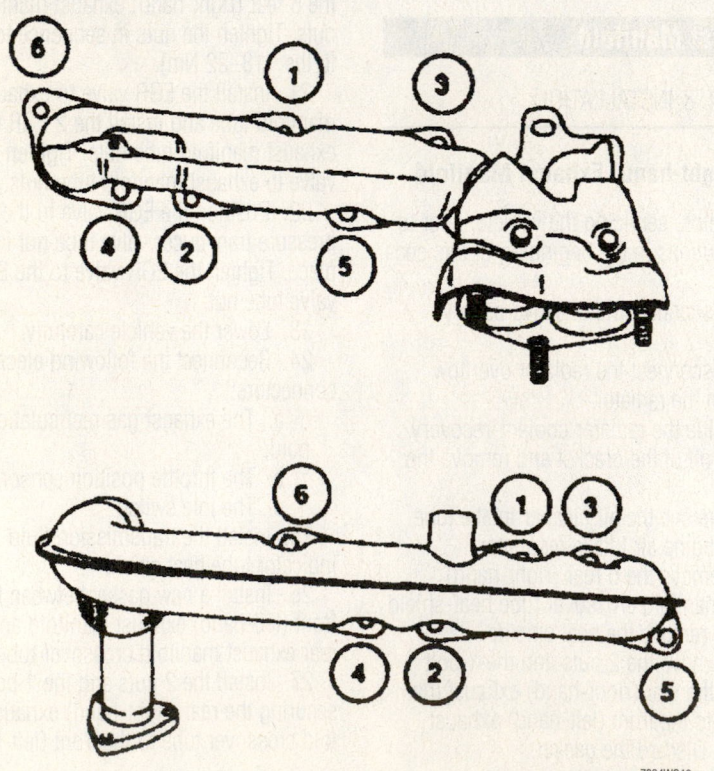

7924WG12

To avoid warping the exhaust manifolds, use this sequence when tightening the bolts

To install:

9. Insert the starter into the bell housing, being sure that the starter drive is not jammed against the flywheel.

10. Tighten the attaching nuts and secure all electrical connections to the starter assembly.

11. Install all remaining components in reverse order of removal.

12. Reconnect the battery cables. If applicable, refill and check the oil level. Check the starter assembly for proper operation.

Front Crankshaft Seal

REMOVAL & INSTALLATION

1. Before servicing the vehicle, refer to the precautions in the beginning of this section.
2. Drain the cooling system.
3. Remove or disconnect the following:
   - Negative battery cable
   - Accessory drive belts
   - Radiator hoses
   - Crankshaft pulley

- Front cover
- Timing belt
- Crankshaft timing sprocket
- Front crankshaft seal

To install:

4. Install or connect the following:
   - Front crankshaft seal flush with the oil pump housing
   - Crankshaft timing sprocket
   - Timing belt
   - Front cover. Tighten the bolts to 26–43 inch lbs. (3–5 Nm).
   - Crankshaft pulley. Tighten the bolt to 141–156 ft. lbs. (191–211 Nm).
   - Radiator hoses
   - Accessory drive belts
   - Negative battery cable
5. Fill the cooling system.
6. Start the engine and check for leaks.

Camshaft And Valve Lifters

REMOVAL & INSTALLATION

1. Before servicing the vehicle, refer to the precautions in the beginning of this section.

2. Drain the cooling system.
3. Remove or disconnect the following:
   - Negative battery cable
   - Upper intake manifold
   - Valve covers

➡**Keep all valvetrain components in order for assembly.**

- Rocker arm and shaft assemblies
- Valve lifter guide and valve lifters. Attach a wire to the top of the lifters so that they will not drop from the lifter guide.
- Radiator
- Accessory drive belts
- Front cover
- Timing belt. Refer to the Timing Belt unit repair section.
- Camshaft sprockets
- Camshaft seals
- Rear timing cover
- Distributor
- Cylinder head rear covers
- Camshaft locating plates
- Camshafts

To install:

4. Install or connect the following:
   - Camshafts

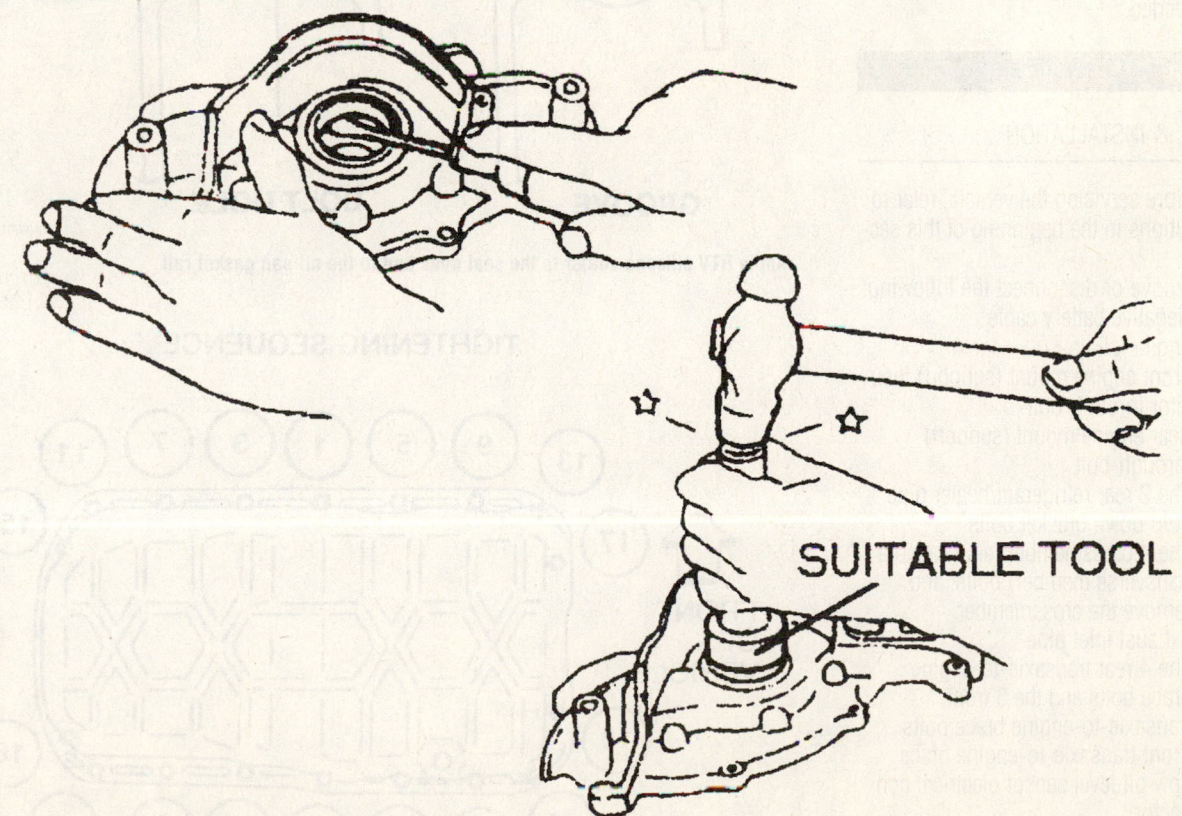

SUITABLE TOOL

Removing and installing the front crankshaft oil seal

7924WG13

For complete mechanical specifications, refer to Section 1 of this manual

- Camshaft locating plates. Tighten the bolts to 58–65 ft. lbs. (78–88 Nm).
- Cylinder head rear covers
- Distributor
- Rear timing cover
- Camshaft seals
- Camshaft sprockets. Tighten the bolts to 58–65 ft. lbs. (78–88 Nm).
- Timing belt
- Front cover
- Accessory drive belts
- Radiator
- Valve lifter guide and valve lifters
- Rocker arm and shaft assemblies. Tighten the bolts to 13–16 ft. lbs. (18–22 Nm).
- Valve covers
- Upper intake manifold
- Negative battery cable

5. Fill the cooling system.
6. Start the engine and check for leaks.

Valve Lash

ADJUSTMENT

The engines covered in this section use hydraulic valve lifters that automatically adjust the valve lash. No periodic adjustment is needed.

Oil Pan

REMOVAL & INSTALLATION

1. Before servicing the vehicle, refer to the precautions in the beginning of this section.
2. Remove or disconnect the following:
- Negative battery cable
- Engine oil
- Front engine mount (support) insulator through-bolt
- Rear engine mount (support) through-bolt
- The 2 rear refrigerant/heater pipe hold down bracket bolts
- The 4 crossmember (also called a transverse member) bolts, and remove the crossmember.
- Exhaust inlet pipe
- The 4 rear transaxle-to-engine brace bolts and the 5 front transaxle-to-engine brace bolts
- Front transaxle-to-engine brace
- Low oil level sensor electrical connector
- The 18 oil pan bolts in the reverse order of the tightening sequence, working from the outside, towards the center bolts.

- Oil pan and discard the seals

To install:

3. Clean all parts well. Be sure that all old sealing material is removed from the oil pan and engine mating surfaces.
4. Position new oil pan seals. Apply Loctite® Ultra Gray 599 Silicone Sealer, or equivalent, to the ends of the oil pan seals.

5. Apply a bead of Loctite® Ultra Gray 599 Silicone Sealer or equivalent to the oil pan gasket rail inboard of the bolt holes.
6. Install or connect the following:
- Oil pan on the engine block. Tighten the 18 oil pan bolts in sequence, working from the inside, towards the outer bolts. Do not

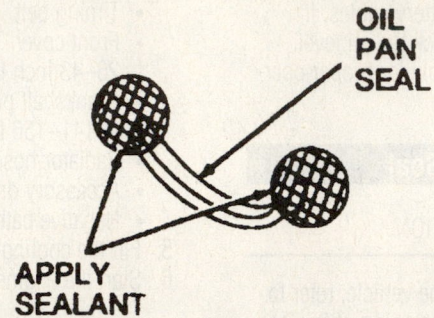

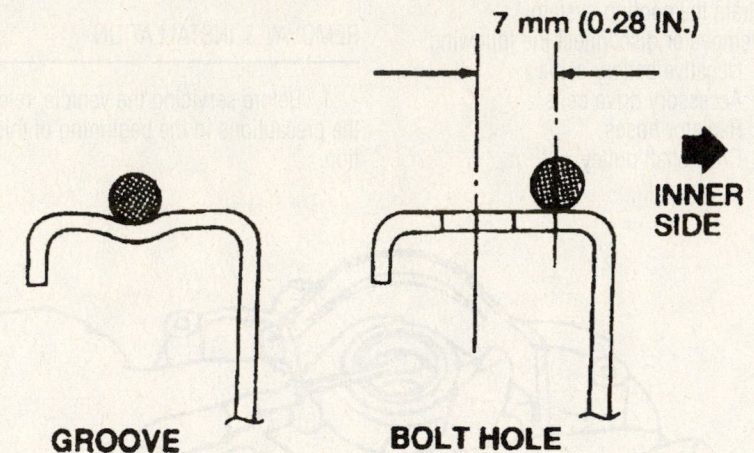

Apply RTV silicone sealer to the seal ends and to the oil pan gasket rail

7924WG14

TIGHTENING SEQUENCE

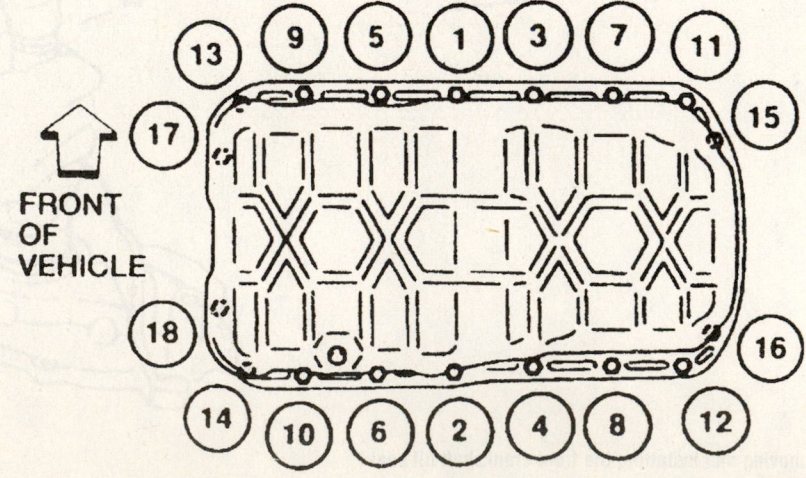

Tighten the 18 oil pan bolts in sequence, working from the inside, towards the outer bolts

7924WG15

over-tighten. Tighten to 62–70 inch lbs. (7–8 Nm).
- Low oil level sensor electrical connector.
- Front and rear transaxle braces. Tighten all bolts to 22–30 ft. lbs. (30–40 Nm).
- Exhaust inlet pipe
- Crossmember and tighten the bolts to 58–65 ft. lbs. (78–88 Nm).
- Both engine support through-bolts and tighten to 58–65 ft. lbs. (78–88 Nm).

7. Remove the support jack from under the crankshaft pulley.

8. Lower the vehicle.

9. Fill the engine with the specified engine oil to the required level.

10. Connect the negative battery cable. Start the engine and check for leaks.

Oil Pump

REMOVAL & INSTALLATION

1. Before servicing the vehicle, refer to the precautions in the beginning of this section.

2. Drain the engine oil.

3. Drain the cooling system.

4. Remove or disconnect the following:
- Negative battery cable
- Accessory drive belts
- Radiator hoses
- Crankshaft pulley
- Front cover
- Timing belt. Refer to the Timing Belt unit repair section.
- Crankshaft timing sprocket
- Oil pan
- Oil pump pickup tube
- Oil pump

To install:

5. Install or connect the following:
- Oil pump. Tighten the large bolts to 16–22 ft. lbs. (22–29 Nm) and the small bolts to 55–74 inch lbs. (6–8 Nm).
- Oil pump pickup tube. Tighten the flange bolts to 12 ft. lbs. (16 Nm) and the bracket bolt to 55–74 inch lbs. (6–8 Nm).

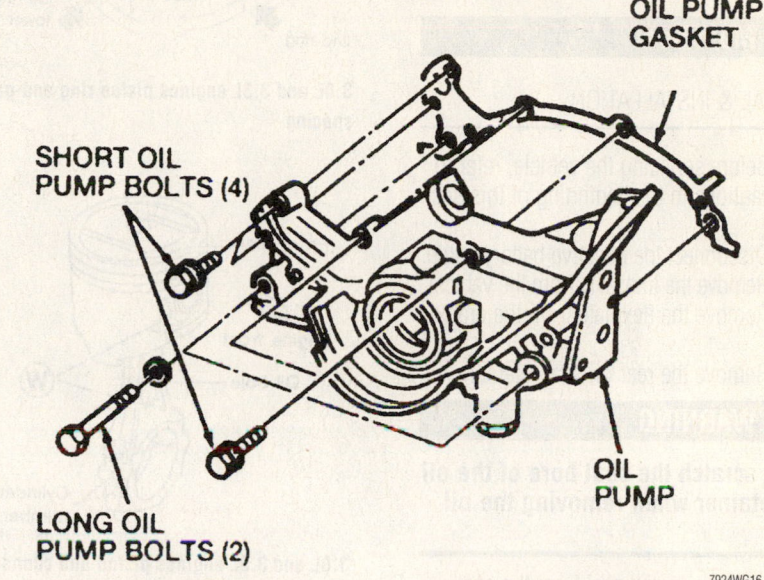

OIL PUMP GASKET

SHORT OIL PUMP BOLTS (4)

OIL PUMP

LONG OIL PUMP BOLTS (2)

7924WG16

The oil pump is mounted on the front of the engine and driven by the crankshaft.

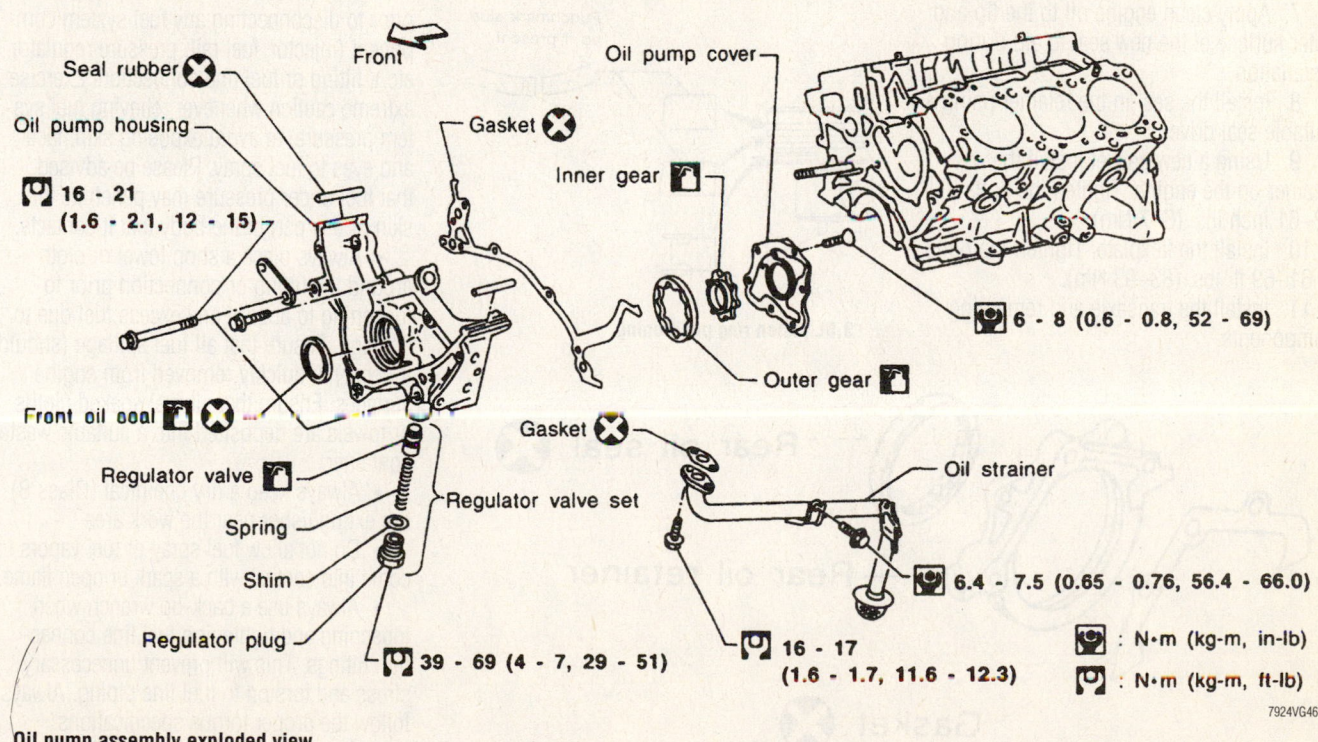

Oil pump assembly exploded view

Please refer to Section 8 for electric cooling fan wiring schematics

- Oil pan
- Crankshaft timing sprocket
- Timing belt
- Front cover
- Crankshaft pulley
- Radiator hoses
- Accessory drive belts
- Negative battery cable

6. Fill the cooling system.
7. Fill the crankcase to the correct level.
8. Start the engine and check for leaks.

Rear Main Seal

REMOVAL & INSTALLATION

1. Before servicing the vehicle, refer to the precautions in the beginning of this section.
2. Disconnect the negative battery cable.
3. Remove the transaxle from the vehicle.
4. Remove the flexplate from the crankshaft.
5. Remove the rear oil seal retainer.

✳✳ WARNING

Do not scratch the seal bore of the oil seal retainer when removing the oil seal.

6. Remove the oil seal from the seal retainer.

   To install:
7. Apply clean engine oil to the lip and outer surface of the new seal to aid during installation.
8. Install the seal in the retainer using a suitable seal driver.
9. Using a new gasket install the retainer on the engine. Tighten the bolts to 52–61 inch lbs. (6–7 Nm).
10. Install the flexplate. Tighten the bolts to 61–69 ft. lbs. (83–93 Nm).
11. Install the transaxle and remaining components.

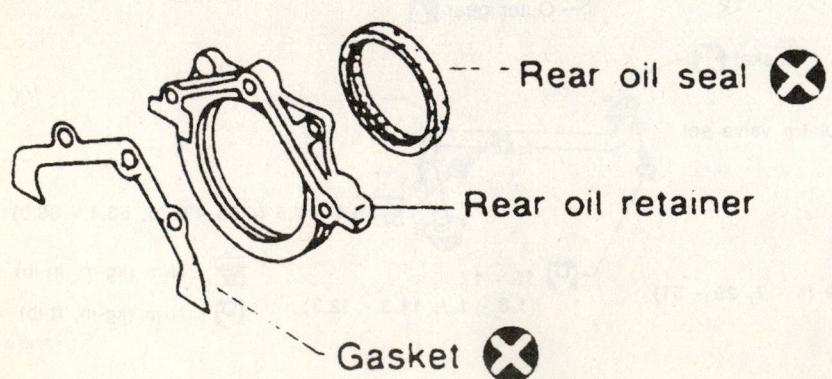

Exploded view of the oil seal, retainer and gasket

Piston and Ring Positioning

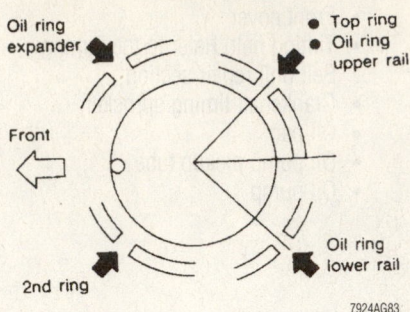

3.0L and 3.3L engines piston ring end-gap spacing

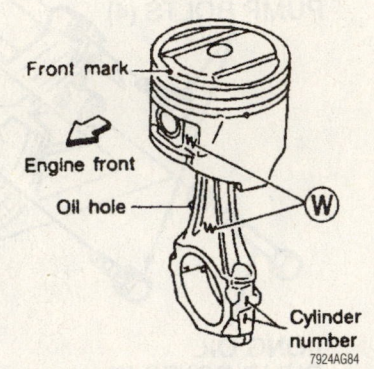

3.0L and 3.3L engines piston and connecting rod assembly positioning

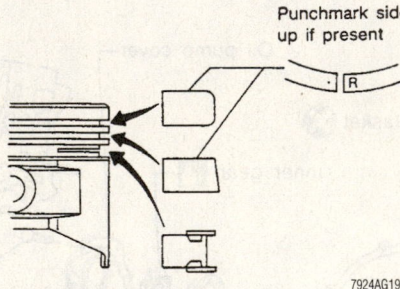

3.0L piston ring positioning

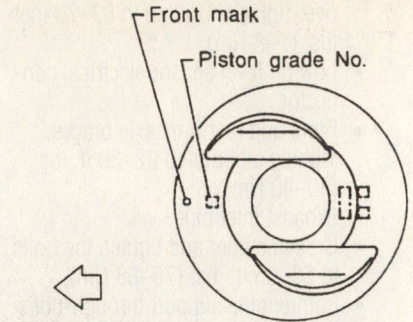

3.3L engine piston positioning

FUEL SYSTEM

Fuel System Service Precautions

Safety is the most important factor when performing not only fuel system maintenance but any type of maintenance. Failure to conduct maintenance and repairs in a safe manner may result in serious personal injury or death. Maintenance and testing of the vehicle's fuel system components can be accomplished safely and effectively by adhering to the following rules and guidelines.

- To avoid the possibility of fire and personal injury, always disconnect the negative battery cable unless the repair or test procedure requires that battery voltage be applied.
- Always relieve the fuel system pressure prior to disconnecting any fuel system component (injector, fuel rail, pressure regulator, etc.), fitting or fuel line connection. Exercise extreme caution whenever relieving fuel system pressure, to avoid exposing skin, face and eyes to fuel spray. Please be advised that fuel under pressure may penetrate the skin or any part of the body that it contacts.
- Always place a shop towel or cloth around the fitting or connection prior to loosening to absorb any excess fuel due to spillage. Ensure that all fuel spillage (should it occur) is quickly removed from engine surfaces. Ensure that all fuel soaked cloths or towels are deposited into a suitable waste container.
- Always keep a dry chemical (Class B) fire extinguisher near the work area.
- Do not allow fuel spray or fuel vapors to come into contact with a spark or open flame.
- Always use a back-up wrench when loosening and tightening fuel line connection fittings. This will prevent unnecessary stress and torsion to fuel line piping. Always follow the proper torque specifications.
- Always replace worn fuel fitting O-rings with new. Do not substitute fuel hose or equivalent, where fuel pipe is installed.

Fuel System Pressure

RELIEVING

1. Before servicing the vehicle, refer to the precautions in the beginning of this section.

2. Remove the left side engine compartment relay panel cover.

3. Locate and remove the fuel pump relay from the relay panel.

4. Start the engine.

5. Allow the engine to run until it stalls from fuel starvation. After the engine stalls, crank the engine over 2 more times to ensure all pressure has been released.

6. Turn the ignition switch to the **OFF** position and install the fuel pump relay.

7. Most service work that follows fuel pressure relief also requires that the negative battery cable (ground) be disconnected before service work begins. This also prevents accidental fuel pump energizing that could pressurize the system.

Fuel Filter

REMOVAL & INSTALLATION

1. Before servicing the vehicle, refer to the precautions in the beginning of this section.

2. Relieve the fuel system pressure using the recommended procedure.

3. Disconnect the negative battery cable.

4. Raise and safely support the vehicle.

5. Remove the fuel hose clamps.

6. Disconnect and plug the hoses to prevent leakage.

7. Remove the fuel filter from the bracket.

To install:

8. Install the fuel filter into the bracket with the arrow facing up, in the direction of the fuel travel to the engine.

9. Reconnect the fuel hoses.

10. Install and tighten the hose clamps. Verify that the clamps are properly tightened. System operating pressure is approximately 36 psi (248 kPa) and fuel will leak is connections are not properly made.

11. Lower the vehicle.

12. Reconnect the negative battery cable.

13. Check for leaks.

Fuel Pump

REMOVAL & INSTALLATION

1. Before servicing the vehicle, refer to the precautions in the beginning of this section.

2. Properly relieve the fuel system pressure.

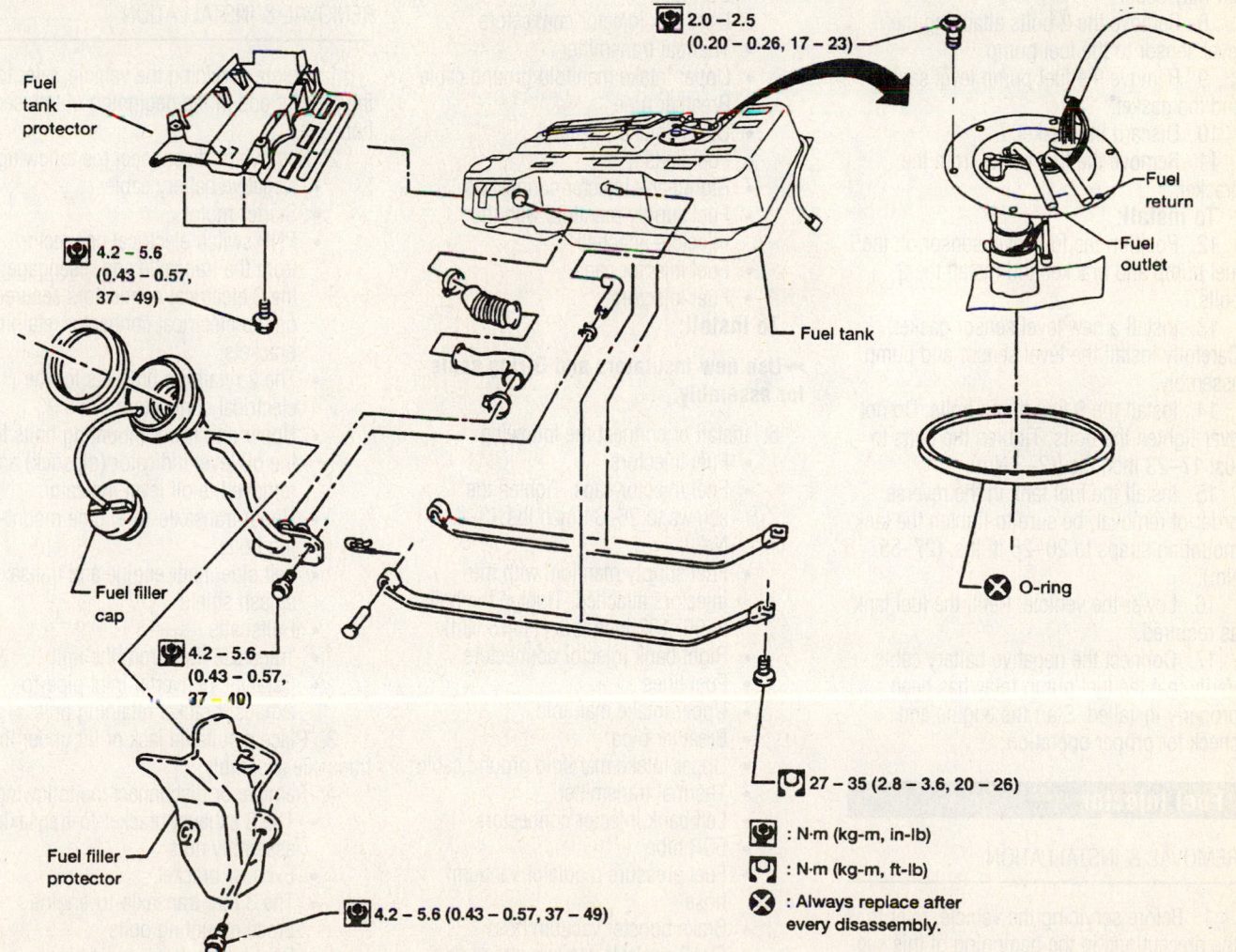

Fuel tank and related components

3. Disconnect the negative battery cable.

4. Raise and safely support the vehicle.

5. Remove the fuel tank as follows:

   a. Drain the fuel from the tank.

   b. Remove the filler protector.

   c. Disconnect the filler tube.

   d. Detach any electrical connectors related to the fuel pump and fuel level sending unit.

   e. Detach the fuel line quick connectors.

   f. Safely support the fuel tank.

   g. Remove the tank mounting straps, then lower the tank out of the vehicle.

6. Remove the 6 fuel pump bolts.

7. Lift the fuel pump out of the fuel tank. Use care. The fuel level sensor and fuel pump and bracket must be tipped to remove it from the fuel tank. Do not lift the fuel sensor and pump assembly straight out of the fuel tank or damage to the level sensor may occur.

8. Remove the 2 bolts attaching the level sensor to the fuel pump.

9. Remove the fuel pump level sensor and the gasket.

10. Discard the gasket.

11. Remove the fuel pump from the bracket.

To install:

12. Position the fuel level sensor on the fuel pump and bracket and install the 2 bolts.

13. Install a new level sensor gasket. Carefully install the level sensor and pump assembly.

14. Install the 6 fuel pump bolts. Do not over-tighten the bolts. Tighten the bolts to just 17–23 inch lbs. (2–3 Nm).

15. Install the fuel tank in the reverse order of removal, be sure to tighten the tank mounting straps to 20–26 ft. lbs. (27–35 Nm).

16. Lower the vehicle. Refill the fuel tank as required.

17. Connect the negative battery cable. Verify that the fuel pump relay has been properly installed. Start the engine and check for proper operation.

Fuel Injector

REMOVAL & INSTALLATION

1. Before servicing the vehicle, refer to the precautions in the beginning of this section.

2. Drain the cooling system.

3. Relieve the fuel system pressure.

4. Remove or disconnect the following:
   - Negative battery cable
   - Air intake duct
   - Accelerator cable
   - Cruise control cable
   - Idle Air Control (IAC) valve connector
   - Throttle Position (TP) sensor and switch connectors
   - Ignition coil and power transistor connectors
   - Exhaust Gas Recirculation (EGR) Solenoid valve connector
   - EGR temperature sensor connector
   - Radiator hoses
   - Heater hoses
   - Positive Crankcase Ventilation (PCV) valve and hose
   - Evaporative Emissions (EVAP) canister vacuum and purge hoses
   - Brake booster vacuum hose
   - Fuel pressure regulator vacuum hose
   - EGR tube
   - Left bank injector connectors
   - Thermal transmitter
   - Upper intake manifold ground cable
   - Breather pipe
   - Upper intake manifold
   - Fuel lines
   - Right bank injector connectors
   - Fuel supply manifold with the injectors attached
   - Fuel injector caps
   - Fuel injectors

To install:

➡ **Use new insulators and O-ring seals for assembly.**

5. Install or connect the following:
   - Fuel injectors
   - Fuel injector caps. Tighten the screws to 26–34 inch lbs. (3–4 Nm).
   - Fuel supply manifold with the injectors attached. Tighten the bolts to 96–132 inch lbs. (11–15 Nm).
   - Right bank injector connectors
   - Fuel lines
   - Upper intake manifold
   - Breather pipe
   - Upper intake manifold ground cable
   - Thermal transmitter
   - Left bank injector connectors
   - EGR tube
   - Fuel pressure regulator vacuum hose
   - Brake booster vacuum hose
   - EVAP canister vacuum and purge hoses
   - PCV valve and hose
   - Heater hoses
   - Radiator hoses
   - EGR temperature sensor connector
   - EGR Solenoid valve connector
   - Ignition coil and power transistor connectors
   - TP sensor and switch connectors
   - IAC valve connector
   - Cruise control cable
   - Accelerator cable
   - Air intake duct
   - Negative battery cable

6. Fill the cooling system.

7. Start the engine and check for leaks.

DRIVE TRAIN

Automatic Transaxle Assembly

REMOVAL & INSTALLATION

1. Before servicing the vehicle, refer to the precautions in the beginning of this section.

2. Remove or disconnect the following:
   - Negative battery cable
   - Starter motor
   - PNP switch electrical connector from the transaxle and disengage the 2 electrical connectors secured on the electrical connector retaining brackets.
   - The 2 retaining brackets for the electrical connectors
   - Upper and lower mounting bolts for the oil level indicator (dipstick) and remove the oil level indicator.
   - Upper transaxle-to-engine mounting bolts
   - Left side inner engine and transaxle splash shield
   - Halfshafts
   - Transaxle fluid from the unit
   - Catalytic converter inlet pipe-to-exhaust bracket retaining bolt

3. Place a suitable jack or lift under the transaxle assembly.

4. Remove or disconnect the following:
   - The 2 exhaust bracket-to-transaxle assembly nuts
   - Exhaust bracket
   - The 3 rear transaxle-to-engine brace mounting bolts
   - Rear transaxle-to-engine brace
   - The 4 front transaxle-to-engine brace mounting bolts

1   Rear Transaxle Support Insulator Through Bolt
2   Rear Transaxle Support Bracket Brace
3   Rear Transaxle Support Bracket Bolt (3 Req'd)
4   Rear Transaxle Support Bracket
5   Rear Transaxle Support Insulator Through Bolt Nut
6   Rear Transaxle Support Insulator
7   Rear Transaxle Support Insulator Bracket Bolts (4 Req'd)
8   Rear Transaxle Support Insulator Bracket
9   Rear Transaxle Support Insulator Nut (3 Req'd)
10 Front Transaxle Support Insulator Through Bolt Nut
11 Front Transaxle Support Bracket
12 Front Transaxle Support Insulator Through Bolt
13 Front Transaxle Support Insulator Bolt (3 Req'd)
14 Front Transaxle Support Insulator
15 Front Engine Support Insulator Through Bolt
16 Front Engine Support Bracket Bolt
17 Front Engine Support Bracket
18 Front Engine Support Insulator
19 Engine Insulator Mounting Bolt Nut (4 Req'd)
20 Transverse Member
21 Transverse Member Nuts (4 Req'd)
22 Transverse Member Bolts (4 Req'd)
23 Engine Insulator Mounting Bolt, Front (2 Req'd)
24 Engine Insulator Mounting Bolt, Rear (2 Req'd)
25 Rear Engine Support Insulator Through Bolt
26 Rear Engine Support Bracket Bolt (2 Req'd)
27 Rear Engine Support Bracket
28 Rear Engine Support Insulator Through Bolt Nut
29 Rear Transaxle Support Insulator
30 Front Engine Support Insulator Through Bolt Nut
A   Tighten to 43-55 N·m (32-41 Lb-Ft)
B   Tighten to 41-52 N·m (30-38 Lb-Ft)
C   Tighten to 64-74 N·m (47-54 Lb-Ft)
D   Tighten to 78-88 N·m (58-65 Lb-Ft)

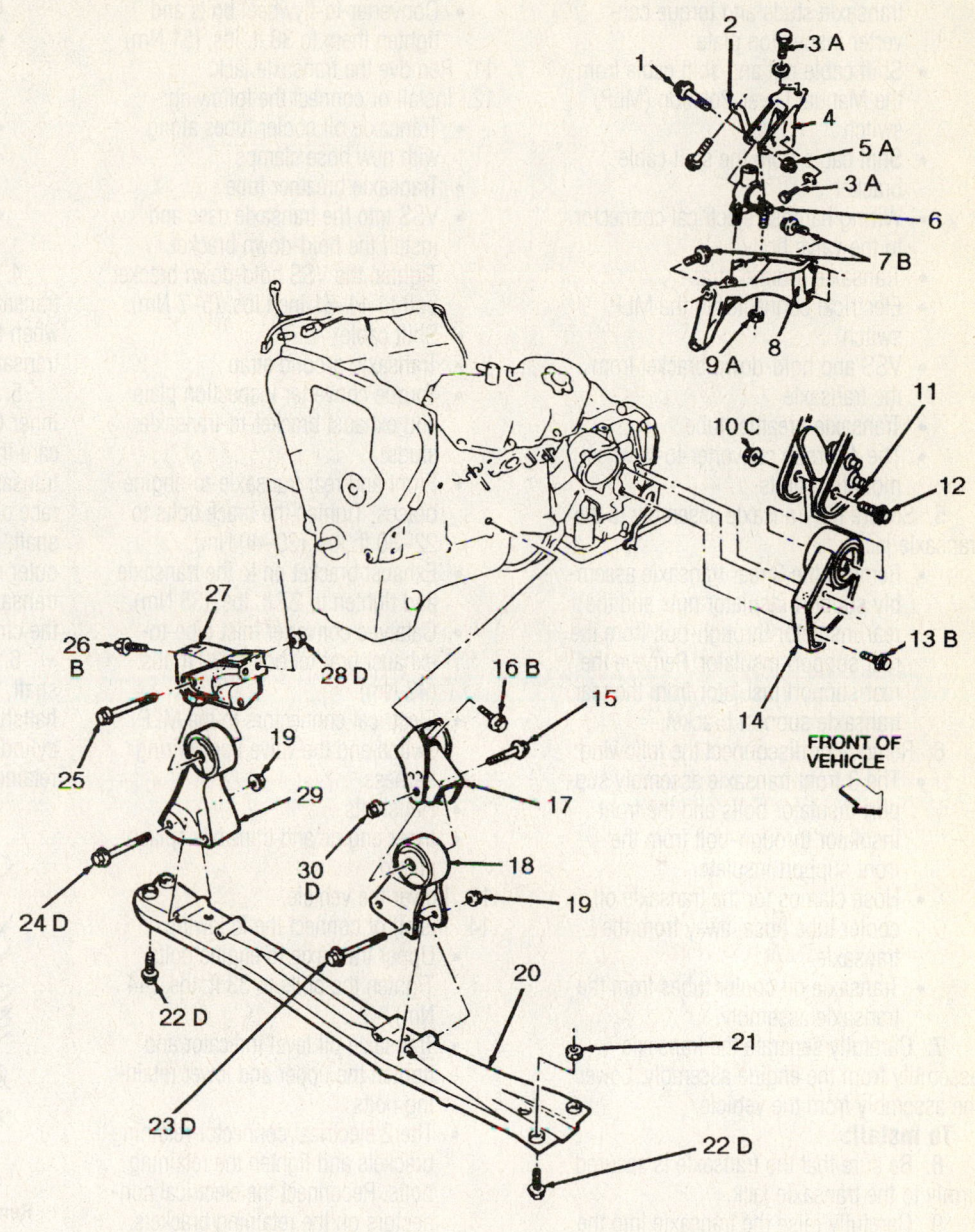

FRONT OF VEHICLE

Exploded view of the engine and transaxle mounting

7924WG24

- Front transaxle-to-engine brace
- Transaxle-to-engine mounting bolt
- The 2 exhaust system bracket-to-transaxle studs and torque converter inspection plate
- Shift cable nut and shift cable from the Manual Lever Position (MLP) switch
- Shift cable from the shift cable bracket
- Wiring harness electrical connector to the valve body
- Transaxle ground strap
- Electrical connector to the MLP switch
- VSS and hold-down bracket from the transaxle
- Transaxle breather tube
- The 4 torque converter-to-flywheel mounting bolts

5. Secure the transaxle assembly to the transaxle jack.

- Remove the 3 rear transaxle assembly support insulator nuts and the rear insulator through-bolt from the rear support insulator. Remove the rear support insulator from the rear transaxle support bracket.

6. Remove or disconnect the following:

- The 3 front transaxle assembly support insulator bolts and the front insulator through-bolt from the front support insulator
- Hose clamps for the transaxle oil cooler tube hose, away from the transaxle
- Transaxle oil cooler tubes from the transaxle assembly

7. Carefully separate the transaxle assembly from the engine assembly. Lower the assembly from the vehicle.

To install:

8. Be sure that the transaxle is secured firmly to the transaxle jack.

9. Carefully raise the transaxle into the vehicle and align the transaxle to the engine assembly, making sure that the alignment dowels are positioned properly.

10. Install or connect the following:

- Lower transaxle-to-engine bolt and tighten to 22–30 ft. lbs. (30–40 Nm).
- Rear transaxle support insulator and tighten the 3 insulator mounting nuts to 32–41 ft. lbs. (43–55 Nm).
- Rear transaxle support insulator through-bolt to 32–41 ft. lbs. (43–55 Nm).
- Front transaxle support insulator and tighten the 3 insulator mounting nuts to 30–38 ft. lbs. (41–52 Nm).

- Front transaxle support insulator through-bolt to 47–54 ft. lbs. (64–74 Nm).
- Converter-to-flywheel bolts and tighten them to 38 ft. lbs. (51 Nm)

11. Remove the transaxle jack.

12. Install or connect the following:

- Transaxle oil cooler tubes along with new hose clamps
- Transaxle breather tube
- VSS into the transaxle case and install the hold-down bracket. Tighten the VSS hold-down bracket bolt to 44–61 inch lbs. (5–7 Nm).
- Shift cable
- Transaxle ground strap
- Torque converter inspection plate and exhaust bracket-to-transaxle studs.
- Front and rear transaxle-to-engine braces. Tighten the brace bolts to 22–30 ft. lbs. (30–40 Nm).
- Exhaust bracket on to the transaxle and tighten to 27 ft. lbs. (35 Nm).
- Catalytic converter inlet pipe-to-exhaust bracket bolt to 32 ft. lbs. (43 Nm).
- Electrical connectors to the MLP switch and the valve body wiring harness
- Halfshafts
- Inner engine and transaxle splash shield

13. Lower the vehicle.

14. Install or connect the following:

- Upper transaxle to engine bolts. Tighten the bolts to 33 ft. lbs. (44 Nm).
- Transaxle oil level indicator and tighten the upper and lower retaining bolts
- The 2 electrical connector retaining brackets and tighten the retaining bolts. Reconnect the electrical connectors on the retaining brackets.
- Electrical connector to the PNP switch
- Starter motor
- Negative battery cable
- Transaxle fluid

15. Start the engine.

16. Check for leaks and proper operation.

Halfshaft

REMOVAL & INSTALLATION

1. Before servicing the vehicle, refer to the precautions in the beginning of this section.

2. Raise and safely support the vehicle.

3. Remove or disconnect the following:

- Wheel
- Fender splash shield
- Cotter pin, nut retainer, and the hub retainer washers from the front hub assembly
- Lower ball joint
- Sway bar from the lower control arm at the sway bar link nut
- Halfshaft and CV-Joint from the wheel hub

4. Position a drain pan under the transaxle since some fluid may run out when the inner joint is disengaged from the transaxle.

5. A prybar is used to separate the inner CV-Joint from the transaxle. Use great care that the prybar does not damage the transaxle case, differential oil seal, outer race or boot. If removing the left side halfshaft, position prybars on both sides of the outer race, between the outer race and the transaxle case. Gently pry outward to unseat the circlip.

6. When removing the right side halfshaft, it is not be necessary to remove the halfshaft bearing retainer bracket from the cylinder block. Remove the 3 bearing retainer bolts and pull the right side half-

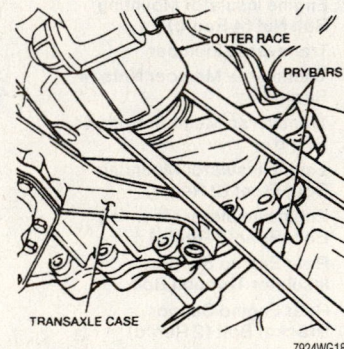

Removing the left side halfshaft by gently prying with 2 prybars to unseat the circlip

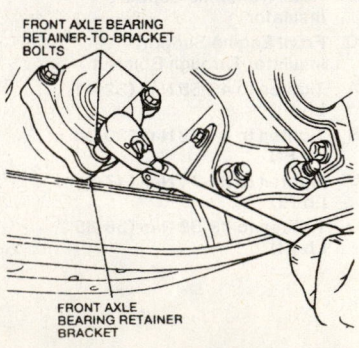

Right side halfshaft bearing retainer bracket

shaft CV-Joint with the bearing retainer from the differential side gear.

7. Support the halfshafts and remove them from the vehicle. Use care not to damage the boots. Place the halfshafts on a flat, protected work area.

To install:

※※ CAUTION

Do not reuse the circlip used on the left side halfshaft.

8. To prevent over-expanding the circlip, install the circlip carefully, starting one end in the shaft groove, then working the circlip over the CV-Joint splined end. Always use a new circlip. No circlip is used on the right side halfshaft.

9. Inspect the CV-Joint boots. If service is required, replace the CV-Joint boots.

10. Inspect the differential oil seals. If damaged, the factory recommends using a hook-type puller and slide hammer arrangement to remove the seals. A seal driver is used to install the replacement differential oil seals.

11. If installing the left side halfshaft and CV-Joint assembly, position the CV-Joint so the splines are aligned with the differential side gear splines, then push the halfshaft joint into the differential case. As the circlip locks into the differential side gear groove, a click will be felt.

12. If installing the right side halfshaft and CV-Joint assembly, simply push the CV-Joint into the differential side gear. Position the bearing retainer onto the bearing retainer bracket that should still be on the cylinder block. Install the 3 bolts and tighten to 10–14 ft. lbs. (14–19 Nm).

13. Install or connect the following:
- Halfshaft
- Lower ball joint and tighten the lower ball joint stud nut to 52–63 ft. lbs. (71–86 Nm). Secure the nut with a new cotter pin.
- Sway bar link to the lower control arm and tighten the link nut to 12–16 ft. lbs. (16–22 Nm).
- Wheel outer bearing retainer, washer and axle nut. Tighten the hub nut to

174–231 ft. lbs. (235–314 Nm). Install the nut retainer and secure with a new cotter pin.
- Splash shield
- Wheel. Tighten the lug nuts to 72–87 ft. lbs. (98–118 Nm).

14. Lower the vehicle.

15. Check the transaxle fluid level.

16. Road test the vehicle to verify correct operation and no noise or vibration.

CV-Joint

OVERHAUL

Inner

1. Remove the boot bands.

2. Matchmark the slide joint housing and inner race, prior to separating the joint assembly.

3. Pry off the snapring and remove the ball cage, inner race and balls as a unit.

4. Remove the snapring and withdraw the boot.

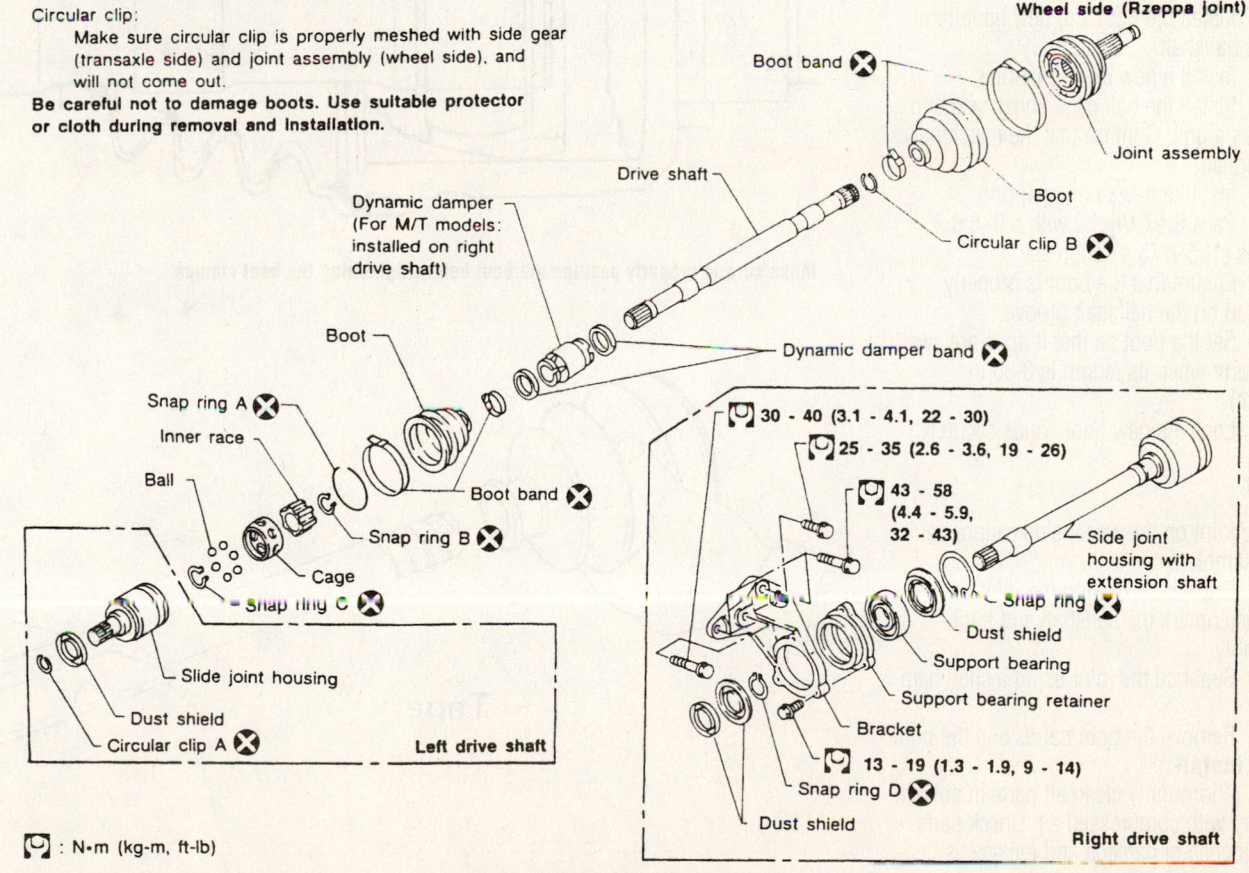

Circular clip:
  Make sure circular clip is properly meshed with side gear (transaxle side) and joint assembly (wheel side), and will not come out.

Be careful not to damage boots. Use suitable protector or cloth during removal and installation.

Wheel side (Rzeppa joint)

Boot band ⊗
Joint assembly
Boot
Circular clip B ⊗

Drive shaft

Dynamic damper (For M/T models: installed on right drive shaft)

Boot

Dynamic damper band ⊗

Snap ring A ⊗
Inner race
Ball
Boot band ⊗
Snap ring B ⊗
Cage
Snap ring C ⊗

Slide joint housing
Dust shield
Circular clip A ⊗

Left drive shaft

30 - 40 (3.1 - 4.1, 22 - 30)
25 - 35 (2.6 - 3.6, 19 - 26)
43 - 58 (4.4 - 5.9, 32 - 43)

Side joint housing with extension shaft
Snap ring ⊗
Dust shield
Support bearing
Support bearing retainer
Bracket
13 - 19 (1.3 - 1.9, 9 - 14)
Snap ring D ⊗
Dust shield

Right drive shaft

⌷ : N•m (kg-m, ft-lb)

Transaxle side (Double offset joint)

89617G09

Exploded view of the halfshafts and related components

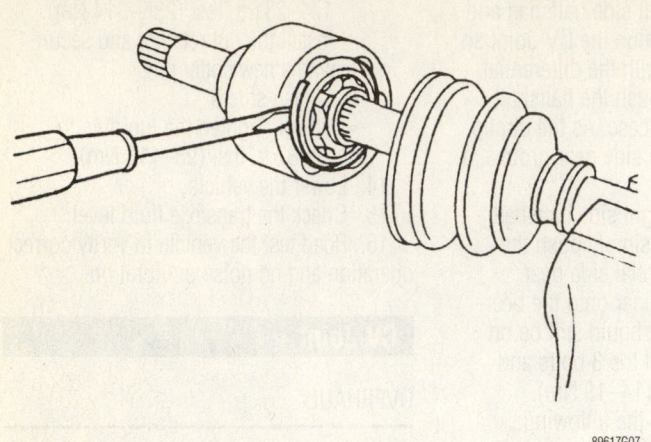

89617G07

The inner CV joint uses a large C-clip to retain the ball and cage assembly in the outer housing

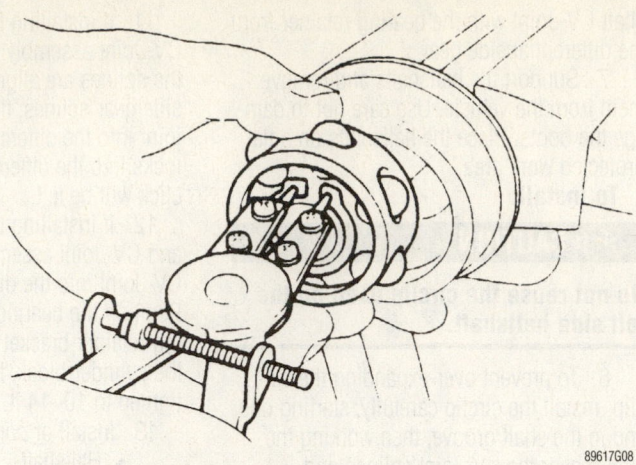

89617G08

After the outer housing is removed, the ball and cage assembly can slide from the shaft by removing the C-clip

To install:

➡ **Cover the halfshaft serrations with tape, so as not to damage the boot.**

5. Thoroughly clean all parts in solvent and dry with compressed air. Check parts for evidence of damage and replace as necessary.

6. Install the boot and new boot band on the halfshaft.

7. Install a new inner snapring.

8. Install the ball cage, inner race and balls as a unit. Confirm that the matchmarks are aligned.

9. Install a new outer snapring.

10. Pack the CV joint with 5.0–6.0 ounces (165–175 g) of grease.

11. Ensure that the boot is properly installed on the halfshaft groove.

12. Set the boot so that it does not swell or deform when its length is 3.86 in. (98mm).

13. Lock the new boot bands securely.

Outer

The joint on the wheel side cannot be disassembled.

1. Prior to separating the joint assembly, matchmark the halfshaft and joint assembly.

2. Separate the joint using a slide hammer.

3. Remove the boot bands and the boot.

To install:

4. Thoroughly clean all parts in solvent and dry with compressed air. Check parts for evidence of damage and replace as necessary.

➡ **Cover the halfshaft serrations with tape, so as not to damage the boot.**

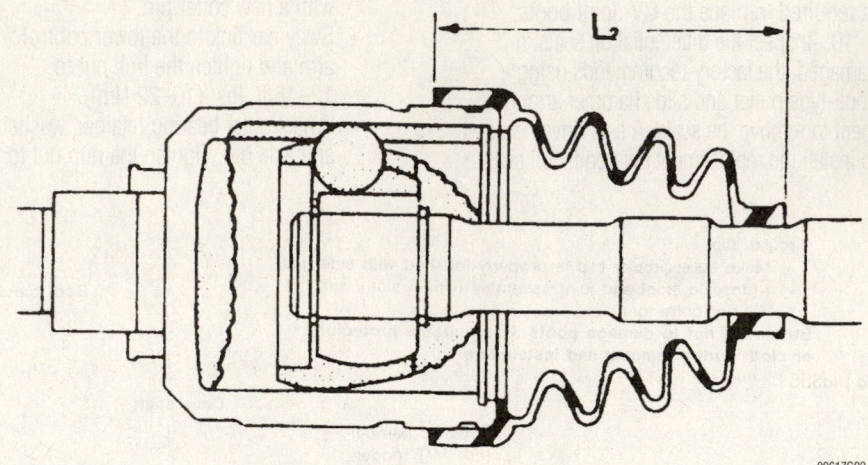

89617G02

Make sure to properly position the boot before tightening the boot clamps

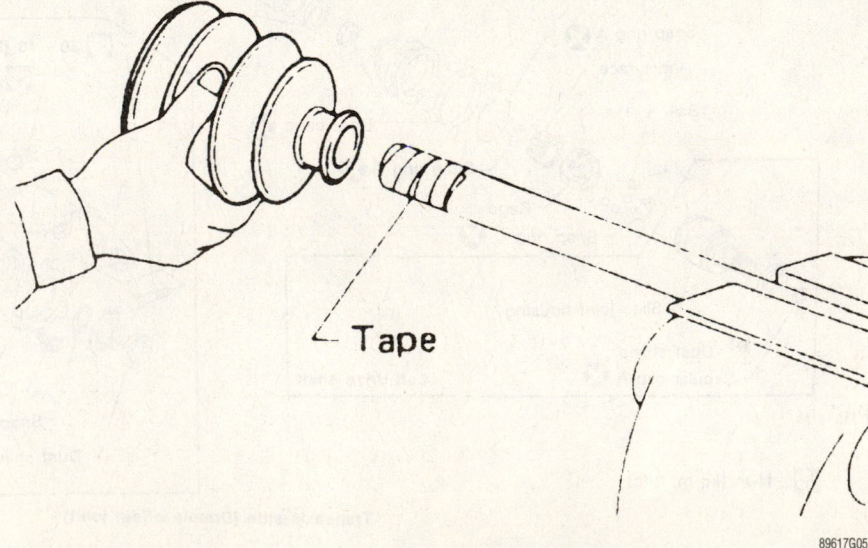

Tape

89617G05

Use vinyl tape and wrap the end of the shaft to protect the boot during installation

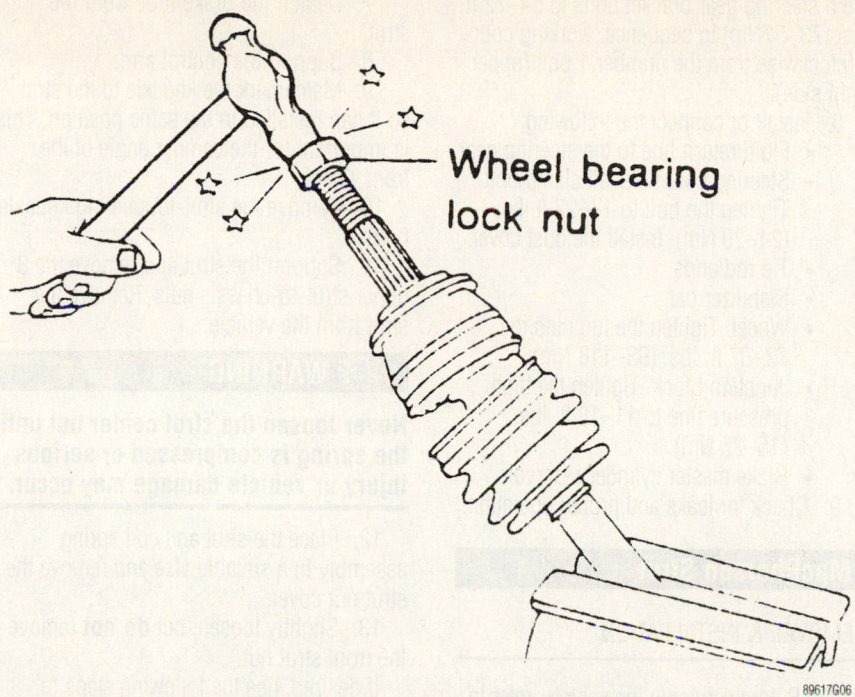

Wheel bearing lock nut

89617G06

Use an old nut to protect the threads when tapping the outer CV joint onto the shaft

5. Install the boot and small boot band on the halfshaft.

6. Set the joint assembly onto the halfshaft and align the matchmarks.

7. Attach the joint assembly to the halfshaft by lightly tapping the serrated end with a plastic hammer.

➡**Using a metal hammer may damage the threads on the end of the joint.**

8. Pack the CV joint with 4.76–5.11 ounces (135–145 g) of grease.

9. Ensure that the boot is properly installed on the halfshaft groove.

10. Set the boot so that it does not swell or deform when its length is 3.82 in. (97mm).

11. Lock the new boot bands securely.

STEERING AND SUSPENSION

Air Bag

PRECAUTIONS

Several precautions must be observed when handling the inflator module to avoid accidental deployment and possible personal injury.

• Never carry the inflator module by the wires or connector on the underside of the module.

• When carrying a live inflator module, hold securely with both hands, and ensure that the bag and trim cover are pointed away.

• Place the inflator module on a bench or other surface with the bag and trim cover facing up.

• With the inflator module on the bench, never place anything on or close to the module which may be thrown in the event of an accidental deployment.

DISARMING

※ CAUTION

To avoid rendering the Supplemental Restraint System (SRS) inoporativo, which could lead to personal injury or death in the event of a severe frontal collision, extreme caution must be taken when servicing the electrical related systems.

➡**All SRS electrical wiring harnesses and connectors are covered with YELLOW outer insulation. Do not use electrical test equipment on any circuit related to the SRS (air bag) sensors. When installing SRS components,** always install with the arrow marks facing the front of the vehicle.

Disarming

To disarm the SRS system turn the ignition switch to the **OFF** position. Then, disconnect the both battery cables starting with the negative cable first and wait at least 10 minutes after the cables are disconnected. Be sure to insulate the battery terminal ends.

Arming

To arm the SRS system turn the ignition switch to **OFF** position. Connect the both battery cables starting with the positive cable first.

➡**The SRS or air bag system is equipped with a self-diagnostic operation. After turning the ignition key to the ON or START position, the AIR BAG warning lamp will illuminate for 7 seconds. After 7 seconds, the AIR BAG lamp will extinguish if no malfunction is detected. If the AIR BAG lamp does not extinguish after 7 seconds, check the SRS self-diagnostic system for a malfunction.**

Power Steering Pump

REMOVAL & INSTALLATION

1. Disconnect the battery ground cable.
2. Remove the pulley.
3. Disconnect the hoses.
4. Remove the 3 front mounting bolts.
5. Remove the rear mounting bolt.
6. Remove the pump.
7. Installation is the reverse of removal. Torque the bolts to 11–15 ft. lbs. (15–20 Nm).

Power Rack and Pinion

REMOVAL & INSTALLATION

The power steering gear is held in position by 2 steering gear brackets and insulators. Note that the housing may move slightly when the steering wheel is turned. If the housing moves more than 0.080 inch (2mm), replace the steering gear insulators. If one or both of the brackets move, check the torque of the bracket bolts. The correct torque for these bolts is 54–72 ft. lbs. (73–97 Nm).

1. Before servicing the vehicle, refer to the precautions in the beginning of this section.

2. Place a drain pan under the steering rack.

3. Remove or disconnect the following:

- Brake master cylinder remote reservoir bracket screws. Position the reservoir out of the way and secure with wire.
- Junction block/high pressure line from the steering rack. Position the junction block and line out of the way.
- Both front wheels
- Front sway bar
- Tie rod ends from the steering knuckles
- Lower steering column shaft clamp bolt
- Power steering fluid return hose and position out of the way.
- The 5 steering rack clamp bracket bolts

4. Lower the steering rack from the vehicle.

To install:

5. Carefully slide the steering gear rack and pinion assembly in place from the left side of the vehicle. Position the input shaft so it is just below the lower steering column shaft clamp.

6. Raise the steering gear until the plastic aligning tab on the input shaft enters the clamp bolt gap on the lower column shaft. Do not install the clamp bolt yet.

7. Examine the steering gear brackets. They should be marked UP with arrows pointing to one end of the bracket. Be sure the brackets are installed correctly. Tighten

the 5 steering gear bracket bolts to 54–72 ft. lbs. (73–97Nm) in sequence, working counterclockwise from the number 1 bolt (upper right side).

8. Install or connect the following:

- Fluid return line to the steering gear
- Steering column shaft clamp bolt. Tighten the bolt to 17–22 ft lbs. (24–29 Nm). Install the dust cover.
- Tie rod ends
- Stabilizer bar
- Wheel. Tighten the lug nuts to 72–87 ft. lbs. (98–118 Nm).
- Junction block. Tighten the high-pressure line to 11–18 ft. lbs. (15–25 Nm).
- Brake master cylinder reservoir

9. Check for leaks and proper operation.

MacPherson Strut

REMOVAL & INSTALLATION

1. Before servicing the vehicle, refer to the precautions in the beginning of this section.

2. Disconnect the negative battery cable.

3. Matchmark the front strut upper mounting bracket and the chassis strut tower.

4. Raise and safely support the vehicle.

5. Remove the front wheel.

6. If equipped, remove the 2 front brake anti-lock sensor cable bracket bolts and position the anti-lock sensor cable out of the way.

7. Detach the brake tube from the strut.

8. Support the control arm.

9. Matchmark the knuckle to the strut so it can installed in the same position. This is important for the camber angle of the front wheel.

10. Remove the strut-to-steering knuckle bolts.

11. Support the strut and remove the 3 upper strut-to-chassis nuts. Remove the strut from the vehicle.

✼✼ WARNING

Never loosen the strut center nut until the spring is compressed or serious injury or vehicle damage may occur.

12. Place the strut and coil spring assembly in a suitable vise and remove the strut nut cover.

13. Slightly loosen, but **do not** remove the front strut nut.

If desired, use the following steps to remove the coil spring from the strut.

14. Using an approved coil spring compressor, compress the coil spring.

15. Remove the strut assembly top nut.

16. Remove the following components from the strut assembly:

- The upper mounting bracket.
- The strut bearing.
- The bearing seat.
- The upper coil spring seat and dust boot.
- The coil spring.

17. Slowly release the tension of the coil spring compressor and remove the coil spring from the compressor tool.

18. Remove the coil spring insulator and slide the jounce bumper off of the strut assembly.

To install:

19. Slide the jounce bumper onto the strut assembly and install the coil spring insulator.

20. Carefully compress the coil spring with an approved coil spring compressor.

21. Reinstall the following components to the strut assembly:

- The coil spring.

➡**Install the coil spring to the strut assembly with the end of the spring in the lower coil spring seat indentation.**

- The upper coil spring seat and dust boot.
- The bearing seat and the bearing.
- The upper mounting bracket.

22. Install and tighten the strut assembly

7924WG20

Tighten the power steering rack mounting bolts in the sequence shown

When installing rubber parts, final tightening must be carried out under unladen condition* with tires on ground.
*: Fuel, radiator coolant and engine oil full. Spare tire, jack, hand tools and mats in designated positions.

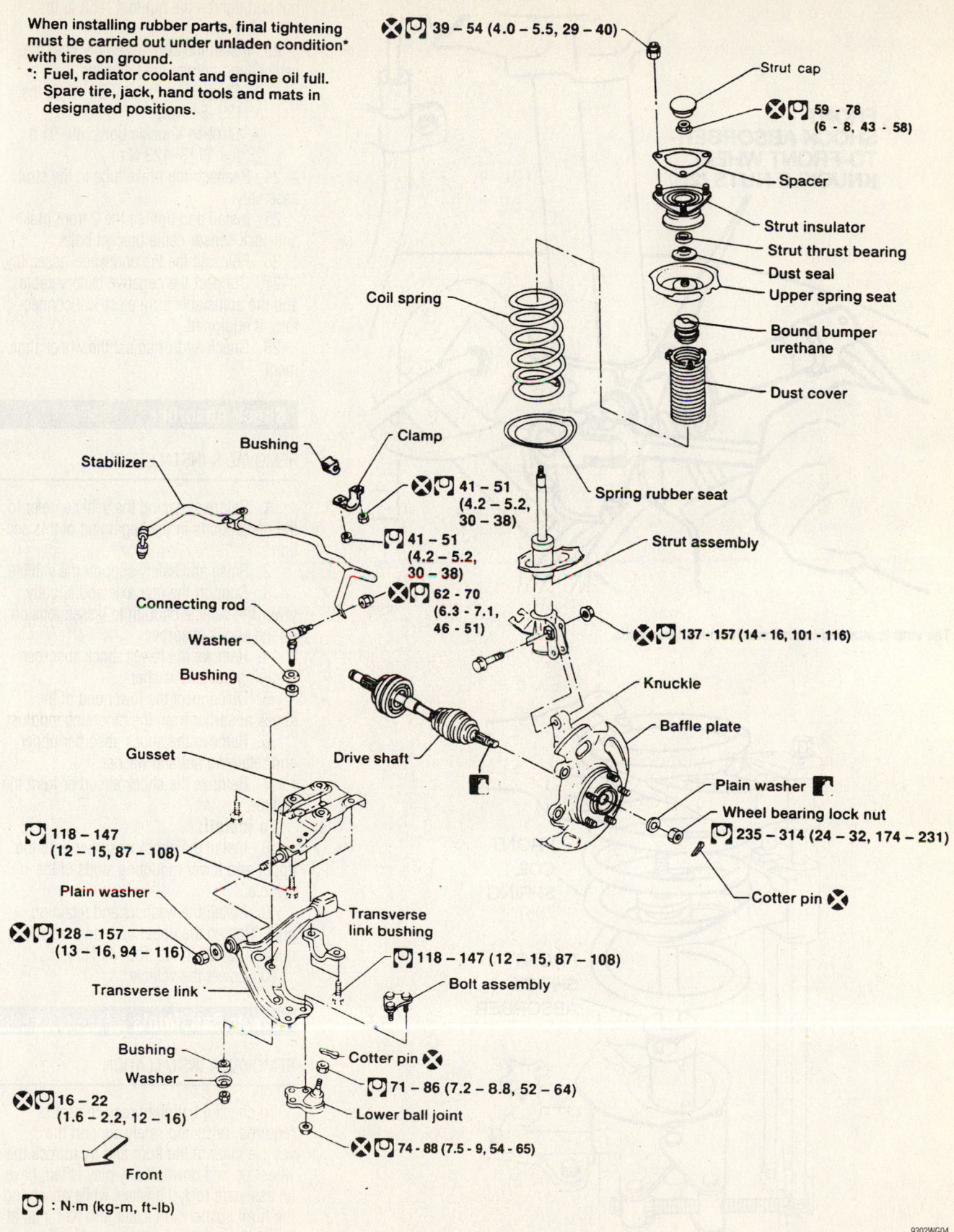

⊗ ⊡ 39 – 54 (4.0 – 5.5, 29 – 40)

Strut cap

⊗ ⊡ 59 - 78 (6 - 8, 43 - 58)

Spacer

Strut insulator

Strut thrust bearing

Dust seal

Upper spring seat

Bound bumper urethane

Dust cover

Coil spring

Spring rubber seat

Bushing

Clamp

⊗ ⊡ 41 – 51 (4.2 – 5.2, 30 – 38)

Stabilizer

⊡ 41 – 51 (4.2 – 5.2, 30 – 38)

Strut assembly

Connecting rod

⊗ ⊡ 62 – 70 (6.3 – 7.1, 46 - 51)

Washer

Bushing

⊗ ⊡ 137 - 157 (14 - 16, 101 - 116)

Knuckle

Baffle plate

Drive shaft

Gusset

⊡ 118 – 147 (12 – 15, 87 – 108)

Plain washer ▐

Wheel bearing lock nut
⊡ 235 – 314 (24 – 32, 174 – 231)

Plain washer

⊗ ⊡ 128 – 157 (13 – 16, 94 – 116)

Transverse link bushing

⊡ 118 – 147 (12 – 15, 87 – 108)

Cotter pin ⊗

Transverse link

Bolt assembly

Bushing

Washer

Cotter pin ⊗

⊗ ⊡ 16 – 22 (1.6 – 2.2, 12 – 16)

⊡ 71 – 86 (7.2 – 8.8, 52 – 64)

Lower ball joint

⊗ ⊡ 74 - 88 (7.5 - 9, 54 - 65)

Front

⊡ : N·m (kg-m, ft-lb)

9302WG04

Coil spring and strut assembly

Please visit our web site at www.chiltononline.com

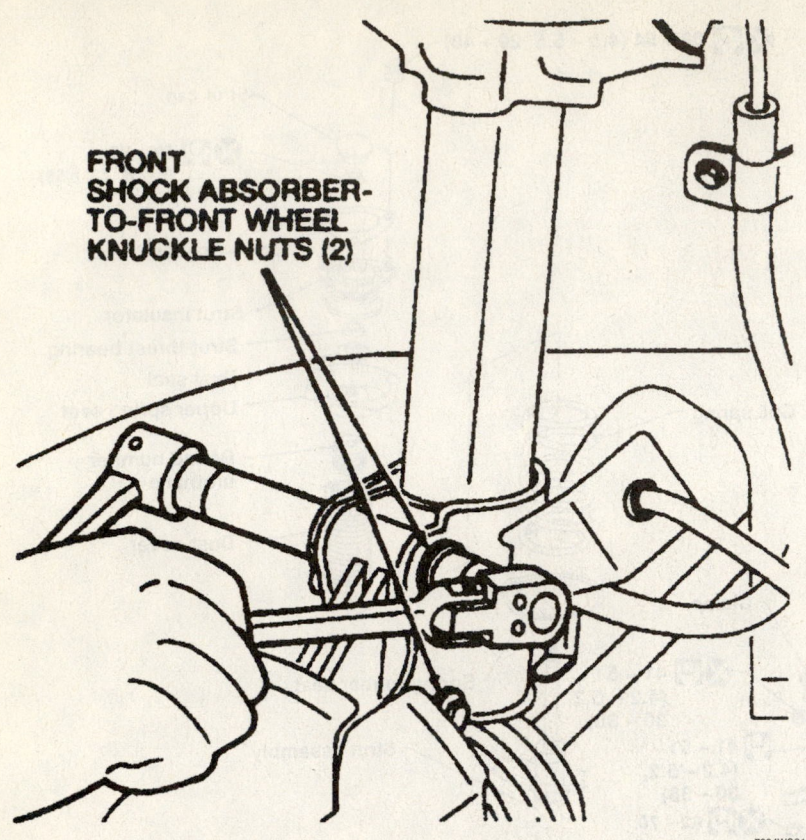

FRONT
SHOCK ABSORBER-
TO-FRONT WHEEL
KNUCKLE NUTS (2)

7924WG21

The strut is attached to the knuckle with 2 large bolts

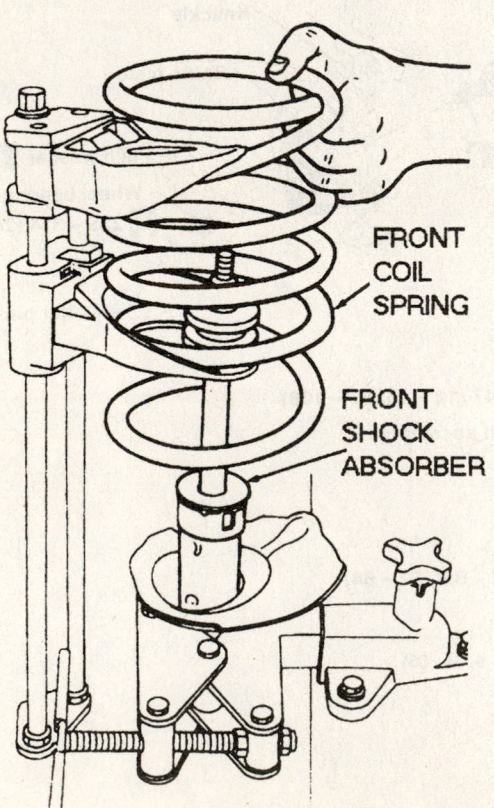

FRONT
COIL
SPRING

FRONT
SHOCK
ABSORBER

7924WG22

Compress the coil spring in a good spring compressor

nut and tighten the nut to 43–58 ft. lbs. (59–78 Nm).

23. Install the strut assembly onto the vehicle and tighten the following:
- Strut-to-body nuts: 29–40 ft. lbs. (39–54 Nm)
- Strut-to-knuckle bolts: 89–91 ft. lbs. (113–123 Nm)

24. Reattach the brake tube to the strut assembly.

25. Install and tighten the 2 front brake anti-lock sensor cable bracket bolts.

26. Reinstall the tire and wheel assembly.

27. Connect the negative battery cable and the adjustable strut electrical connectors, if equipped.

28. Check and/or adjust the wheel alignment.

Shock Absorber

REMOVAL & INSTALLATION

1. Before servicing the vehicle, refer to the precautions in the beginning of this section.

2. Raise and safely support the vehicle.

3. Support the rear axle and slightly lower the vehicle enough to lessen tension on the shock absorber.

4. Remove the lower shock absorber retaining nut and washer.

5. Disconnect the lower end of the shock absorber from the mounting stud.

6. Remove the shock absorber upper end retaining nut and washer.

7. Remove the shock absorber from the vehicle.

To install:

8. Install the shock absorber onto the upper and lower mounting studs of the vehicle.

9. Install the washers and retaining nuts. Tighten the upper and lower retaining nuts to 22–30 ft. lbs. (30–41 Nm).

10. Lower the vehicle.

Lower Ball Joints

REMOVAL & INSTALLATION

To check if ball joint replacement is required, raise and safely support the vehicle clear of the floor and try to rock the wheel up and down. If any play is felt, have an assistant rock the wheel while observing the front suspension lower arm ball joint at the bottom of the steering knuckle. If any movement is seen, the ball joint should be replaced. If not, any wheel play indicates wheel bearing wear.

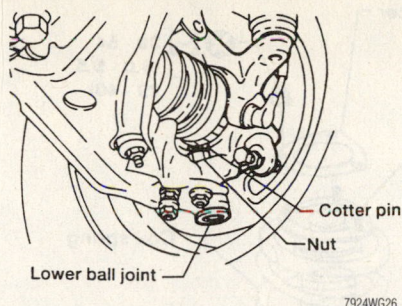

Loosen the nut on the lower ball joint stud

1. Before servicing the vehicle, refer to the precautions in the beginning of this section.

2. Raise and safely support the vehicle.

3. Remove the tire and wheel.

4. Remove and discard the ball joint cotter pin. Loosen the ball joint attaching nut from the steering knuckle. Because of tight clearance, the nut likely cannot be removed until the ball joint stud is loosened and lower slightly.

5. Strike the front knuckle with a hammer while pulling down on the lower control arm. There should now be enough clearance to allow removal of the ball joint stud nut. Separate the ball joint from the steering knuckle.

6. Remove the 3 bolts attaching the ball joint to the control arm.

7. Remove the ball joint from the control arm.

To install:

8. Install the ball joint to the control arm and install the attaching bolts.

9. Tighten the bolts to 56–80 ft. lbs. (76–109 Nm).

10. Install the ball joint into the steering knuckle, just enough to get the nut started on the stud. Then, push the ball joint stud fully in place. Tighten the nut to 52–63 ft. lbs. (71–86 Nm). Secure the nut with a new cotter pin.

11. Install the tire and wheel.

12. Lower the vehicle.

13. A front end alignment check is recommended.

Lower Control Arm

REMOVAL & INSTALLATION

1. Remove the wheel.

2. Disconnect the ball joint.

3. Disconnect the stabilizer bar from the control arm.

4. Remove the 2 rear arm bolts and the mounting bracket.

5. Remove the lower arm nut.

6. Pull the rear of the arm down and gently pry the arm forward and off the gusset.

7. Installation is the reverse of removal. Observe the following torques:

- Stabilizer bar-to-lower arm: 12–16 ft. lbs. (16–22 Nm)
- Lower arm rear bolts: 87–108 ft. lbs. (118–147 Nm)
- Lower arm nuts: 94–115 ft. lbs. (128–156 Nm)
- Ball stud nut: 56–80 ft. lbs. (76–109 Nm)

BUSHING REPLACEMENT

The bushings are press-fit types. Support the arm in a press, using the proper adapters. Ford tool numbers are: T93P-5493-A, T75L-1165-B and -DA.

Wheel Bearings

ADJUSTMENT

The wheel bearings on the Mercury Villager/Nissan Quest are not adjustable. If the bearings become loose or make noise, they must be replaced using the following procedure.

REMOVAL & INSTALLATION

Front

1. Before servicing the vehicle, refer to the precautions in the beginning of this section.

2. Raise and safely support the vehicle.

3. Remove the wheel and tire.

4. Remove the brake caliper assembly. DO NOT disconnect the brake hose. Hang the caliper on a piece of wire from a near by support such as the strut.

5. Remove the brake rotor.

6. Remove and discard the cotter pin from the end of the outboard CV-Joint stub shaft. Remove the hub nut retainer, washer and the hub nut. There should be another washer under the hub nut that acts as a front wheel bearing outer bearing retainer.

7. Disengage the lower ball joint stud from the steering knuckle using the following procedure.

a. Remove and discard the cotter pin from the front lower ball joint.

b. Loosen the lower ball joint nut until it contacts the front halfshaft joint.

c. Strike the front knuckle with a hammer while pulling down on the lower control arm until the ball joint stud separates from the knuckle.

d. Remove the ball joint nut.

e. Disengage the lower ball joint stud from the steering knuckle.

8. Disengage the outer tie rod end stud from the steering knuckle using the following procedure.

a. Remove and discard the cotter pin from the outer tie rod end stud.

b. Remove the outer tie rod end retaining nut.

c. Use a tie rod end puller to carefully press the tie rod end from the steering knuckle.

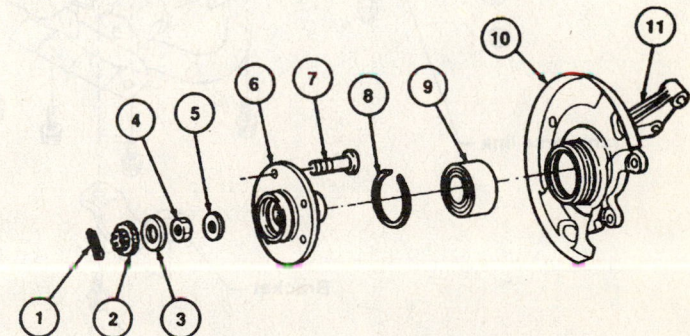

1. Cotter pin
2. Nut retainer
3. Insulator
4. Front axle wheel hub retainer
5. Front wheel outer bearing retainer washer
6. Wheel hub
7. Wheel hub bolt
8. Snap ring
9. Front wheel bearing
10. Front disc brake rotor shield
11. Front wheel knuckle

Exploded view of the knuckle, hub and bearing

Turn to Section 5 for brake system applications

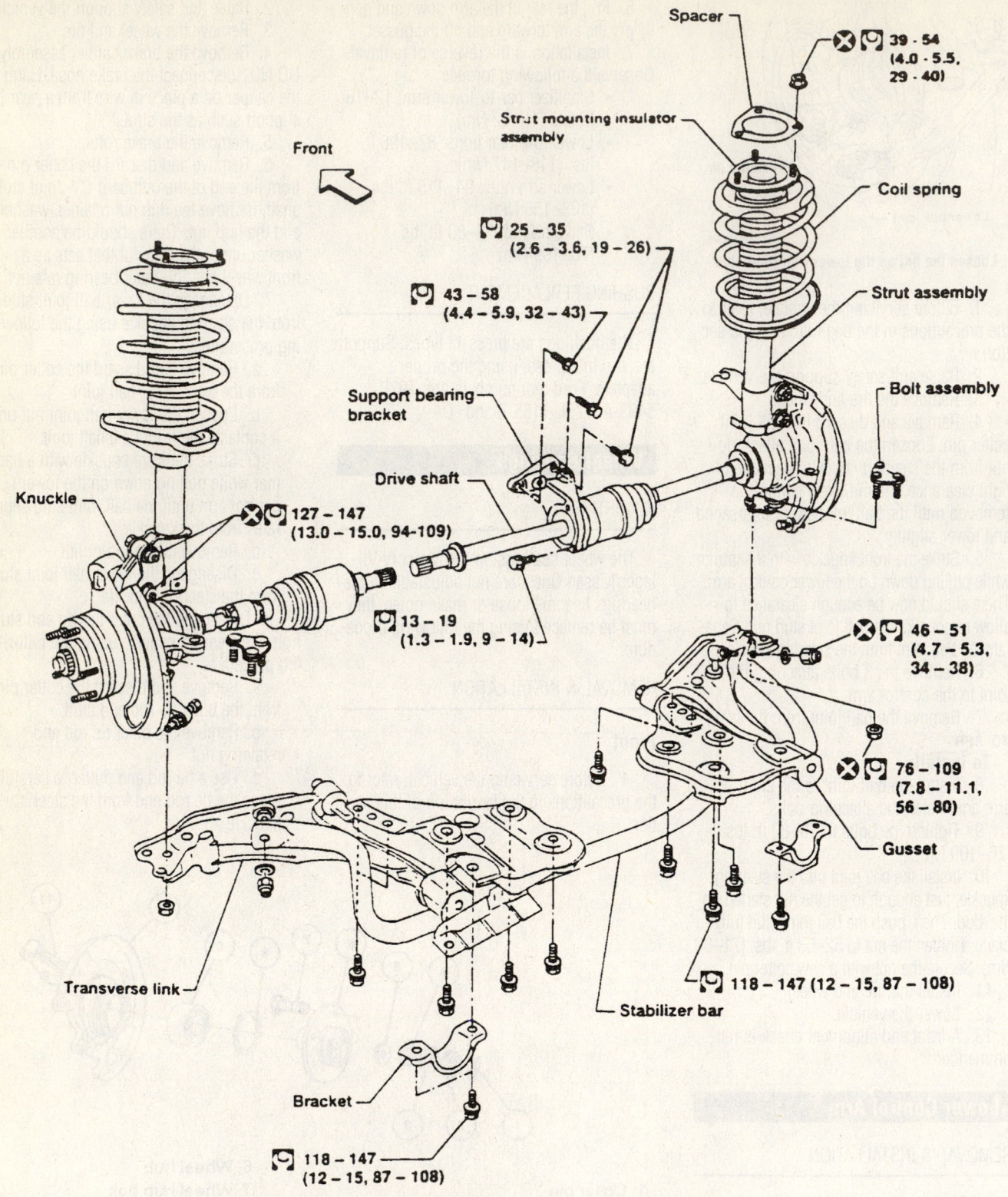

Front

Spacer

⊗ ⃞ 39 – 54
(4.0 – 5.5,
29 – 40)

Strut mounting insulator assembly

Coil spring

⃞ 25 – 35
(2.6 – 3.6, 19 – 26)

⃞ 43 – 58
(4.4 – 5.9, 32 – 43)

Strut assembly

Support bearing bracket

Bolt assembly

Drive shaft

Knuckle

⊗ ⃞ 127 – 147
(13.0 – 15.0, 94-109)

⃞ 13 – 19
(1.3 – 1.9, 9 – 14)

⊗ ⃞ 46 – 51
(4.7 – 5.3,
34 – 38)

⊗ ⃞ 76 – 109
(7.8 – 11.1,
56 – 80)

Gusset

⃞ 118 – 147 (12 – 15, 87 – 108)

Transverse link

Stabilizer bar

Bracket

⃞ 118 – 147
(12 – 15, 87 – 108)

When installing rubber parts, final tightening
must be carried out under unladen condition*
with tires on ground.
*: Fuel, radiator coolant and engine oil full.
Spare tire, jack, hand tools and mats in
designated positions.

⃞ : N·m (kg-m, ft-lb)

Exploded view of the front suspension and drive axles

7924WG25

9. Remove the front ABS sensor bolt.

10. Remove the 2 front strut-to-front knuckle nuts and remove the 2 bolts. Disengage the strut from the steering knuckle.

11. Use a 2-jaw puller to separate the front halfshaft outboard CV-Joint stub shaft from the knuckle/bearing assembly.

12. Remove the front wheel hub, knuckle and wheel bearing assembly from the vehicle.

13. If the knuckle is being replaced with a service part, change over the steering stop bolt and jam nut from the old knuckle to the replacement part.

14. To remove the front wheel bearing, jig up a puller to bear against the front wheel bearing inner race and pull the race from the hub/knuckle assembly.

15. Use a shop press to press out damaged wheel studs and also to press out the outer bearing race.

16. Use a shop press to press out the inner bearing race.

To install:

17. If the front wheel bearings were removed, assemble the ABS sensing ring, if removed and the disc brake dust shield under the steering knuckle. Use a shop press to push in new front wheel bearing inner and outer races. Support the knuckle and press the front wheel bearing into the knuckle and install the snap ring retainer. Support the bearing assemblies and press the hub onto the knuckle and wheel bearing assembly.

18. Install the hub, knuckle and bearings as an assembly. Position the assembly on the halfshaft outer CV-Joint stub axle end. Guide the knuckle into the front strut and install the 2 knuckle-to-strut bolts and nuts. Tighten the nuts to 83–91 ft. lbs. (113–123 Nm).

19. Install the ABS sensor bolt. Do not over-tighten. Tighten to just 16–21 inch lbs. (1.8–2.4 Nm).

20. Install the outer tie rod end to the steering knuckle. Tighten the nut to 22–29 ft. lbs. (29–39 Nm). If the cotter pin holes do not align, tighten the nut slightly until they do. Never loosen the nut to align the holes. Secure the nut with a new cotter pin.

21. Start the lower ball joint stud to the steering knuckle and partially install the nut, then push the ball joint stud fully in place. Tighten the ball joint stud nut to 52–63 ft. lbs. (71–86 Nm). Secure the nut with a new cotter pin.

22. Install the front wheel outer bearing retaining washer and the hub retainer nut. Tighten to 174–231 ft. lbs. (235–314 Nm). Install the nut retainer, insulator and a new cotter pin.

23. Install the front brake rotor and install the disc brake caliper.

24. If removed, install the steering stop bolt.

25. Install the tire and wheel assembly. Tighten the lug nuts to 72–87 ft. lbs. (98 to 118 Nm).

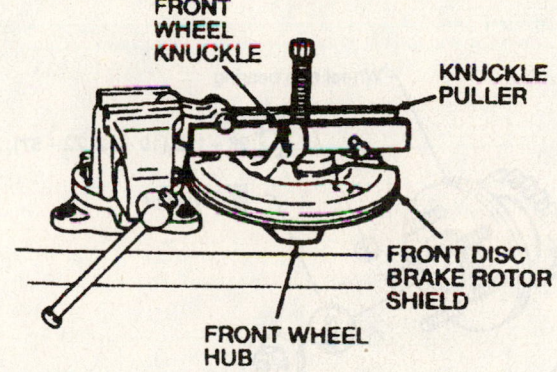

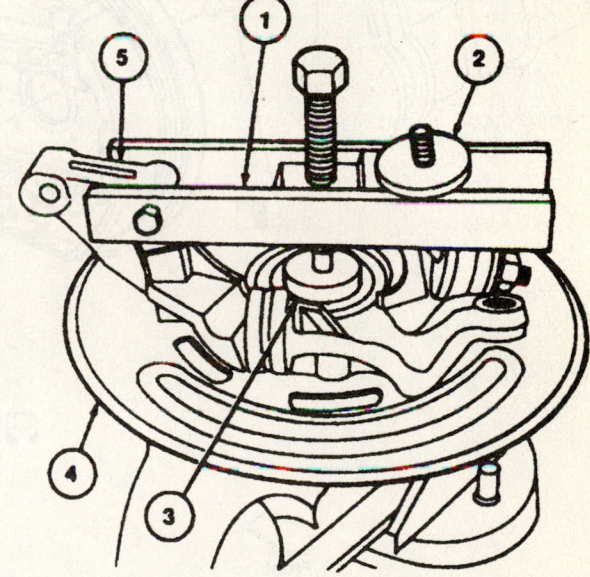

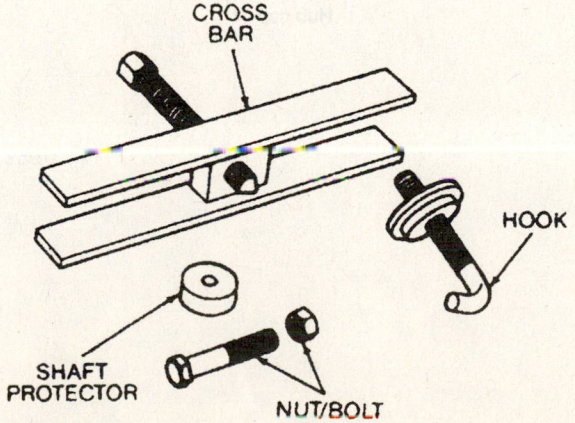

Example of a puller set up to bear against the front wheel bearing inner race

1. Knuckle puller
2. Knuckle puller adapter
3. Step plate adapter
4. Front disc brake rotor shield
5. Front wheel knuckle

7924WG27

For complete service labor times order Nichols' Chilton Labor Guide Manual

26. Lower the vehicle. Pump the brake pedal slowly to seat the front brake pads. Do not move the vehicle until a firm pedal is obtained.

27. A front end alignment is recommended.

Rear

1. Before servicing the vehicle, refer to the precautions in the beginning of this section.

2. Raise and safely support the vehicle.

3. Remove the rear wheel(s).

4. Remove the brake drum.

5. Remove the grease cap for the hub.

6. Remove and discard the cotter pin.

7. Remove the wheel bearing nut and washer.

8. Remove the rear wheel hub and bearing assembly.

To install:

9. Install the rear wheel hub and bearing assembly onto the vehicle.

10. Install the rear wheel bearing washer and nut and tighten the bearing nut to 159–210 ft. lbs. (216–284 Nm). Install a new cotter pin.

11. Install the wheel hub grease cap. Install the brake drum.

12. Install the rear wheel(s) and lug nuts. Tighten the lug nuts, in a star sequence, to 72–87 ft. lbs. (98–118 Nm).

13. Lower the vehicle.

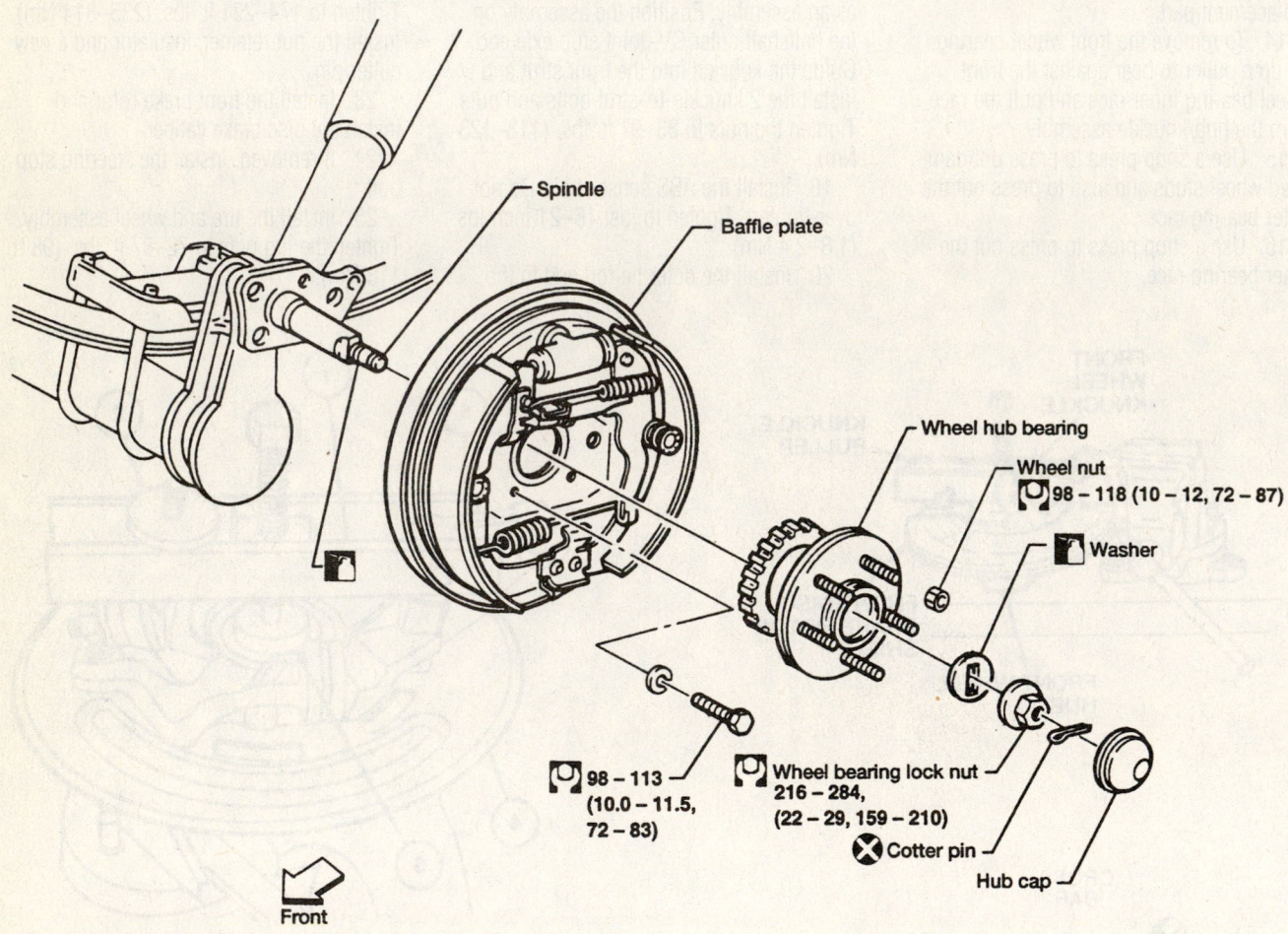

Spindle

Baffle plate

Wheel hub bearing

Wheel nut
98 – 118 (10 – 12, 72 – 87)

Washer

98 – 113
(10.0 – 11.5, 72 – 83)

Wheel bearing lock nut
216 – 284,
(22 – 29, 159 – 210)

Cotter pin

Hub cap

Front

: N·m (kg-m, ft-lb)

Rear hub assembly

9302WG05

SUBARU

Subaru-Forester

PRECAUTIONS

Before servicing any vehicle, please be sure to read all of the following precautions, which deal with personal safety, prevention of component damage, and important points to take into consideration when servicing a motor vehicle:

• Never open, service or drain the radiator or cooling system when the engine is hot; serious burns can occur from the steam and hot coolant.

• Observe all applicable safety precautions when working around fuel. Whenever servicing the fuel system, always work in a well-ventilated area. Do not allow fuel spray or vapors to come in contact with a spark, open flame, or excessive heat (a hot drop light, for example). Keep a dry chemical fire extinguisher near the work area. Always keep fuel in a container specifically designed for fuel storage; also, always properly seal fuel containers to avoid the possibility of fire or explosion. Refer to the additional fuel system precautions later in this section.

• Fuel injection systems often remain pressurized, even after the engine has been turned **OFF**. The fuel system pressure must be relieved before disconnecting any fuel lines. Failure to do so may result in fire and/or personal injury.

• Brake fluid often contains polyglycol ethers and polyglycols. Avoid contact with the eyes and wash your hands thoroughly after handling brake fluid. If you do get brake fluid in your eyes, flush your eyes with clean, running water for 15 minutes. If eye irritation persists, or if you have taken brake fluid internally, IMMEDIATELY seek medical assistance.

• The EPA warns that prolonged contact with used engine oil may cause a number of skin disorders, including cancer. You should make every effort to minimize your exposure to used engine oil. Protective gloves should be worn when changing oil. Wash your hands and any other exposed skin areas as soon as possible after exposure to used engine oil. Soap and water, or waterless hand cleaner should be used.

• All new vehicles are now equipped with an air bag system. The system must be disabled before performing service on or around system components, steering column, instrument panel components, wiring and sensors. Failure to follow safety and disabling procedures could result in accidental air bag deployment, possible personal injury, and unnecessary system repairs.

• Always wear safety goggles when working with, or around, the air bag system. When carrying a non-deployed air bag, be sure the bag and trim cover are pointed away from your body. When placing a non-deployed air bag on a work surface, always face the bag and trim cover upward, away from the surface. This will reduce the motion of the module if it is accidentally deployed. Refer to the additional air bag system precautions later in this section.

• Clean, high quality brake fluid from a sealed container is essential to the safe and proper operation of the brake system. You should always buy the correct type of brake fluid for your vehicle. If the brake fluid becomes contaminated, completely flush the system with new fluid. Never reuse any brake fluid. Any brake fluid that is removed from the system should be discarded. Also, do not allow any brake fluid to come in contact with a painted surface; it will damage the paint.

• Never operate the engine without the proper amount and type of engine oil; doing so WILL result in severe engine damage.

• Timing belt maintenance is extremely important. Many models utilize an interference-type, non-freewheeling engine. If the timing belt breaks, the valves in the cylinder head may strike the pistons, causing potentially serious (also time-consuming and expensive) engine damage. Refer to the maintenance interval charts in the front of this manual for the recommended replacement interval for the timing belt, and to the timing belt section for belt replacement and inspection.

• Disconnecting the negative battery cable on some vehicles may interfere with the functions of the on-board computer system(s) and may require the computer to undergo a relearning process once the negative battery cable is reconnected.

• When servicing drum brakes, only disassemble and assemble one side at a time, leaving the remaining side intact for reference.

ENGINE REPAIR

➡**Disconnecting the negative battery cable on some vehicles may interfere with the functions of the on board computer systems and may require the computer to undergo a relearning process, once the negative battery cable is reconnected.**

Distributor

The Forester is equipped with a distributorless ignition system.

Alternator

REMOVAL

1. Before servicing the vehicle, refer to the precautions in the beginning of this section.

2. Remove or disconnect the following:
• Negative battery Cable
• Wires
• Belt cover
• Drive belt
• Mounting bolts
• Alternator

INSTALLATION

Install or connect the following:
• Alternator
• Mounting bolts
• Drive belt. Adjust the tension to 0.276–0.354 in. (7–9mm) for new or 0.354–0.433 in. (9–11mm) for used. Torque the slider bolt to 4–6 ft. lbs. (6–10 Nm) and the lockbolt to 16.5 ft. lbs. (19.5 Nm).
• Belt cover
• Wires
• Negative battery Cable

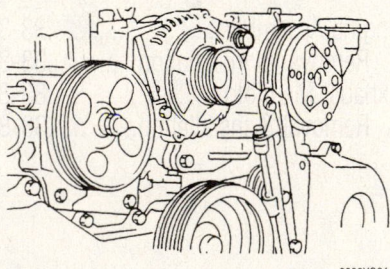

9308XG01

View of alternator mounting

Ignition Timing

ADJUSTMENT

The ignition timing is controlled by the engine control computer and is not adjustable. To check the ignition timing proceed as follows:

1. Before servicing the vehicle, refer to the precautions in the beginning of this section.

2. Warm up the engine, then turn the ignition **OFF**.

3. Connect a timing light to the No. 1 spark plug wire according to the manufactures directions.

4. Start the engine. With the vehicle at idle check the timing.

5. The timing should be 7–23 degrees BTDC at 700 RPM.

6. If the timing is not correct, there could be a problem in the ignition control system.

Engine Assembly

REMOVAL & INSTALLATION

✳✳ CAUTION

The fuel injection system remains under pressure after the engine has been turned OFF. Properly relieve fuel pressure before disconnecting any fuel lines. Failure to do so may result in fire or personal injury.

1. Before servicing the vehicle, refer to the precautions in the beginning of this section.

2. Relieve the fuel system pressure.

3. Drain the engine oil and coolant.

4. Discharge and recover the air conditioning system.

5. Remove or disconnect the following:
- Negative battery cables and battery
- Engine undercover
- Radiator hoses and fan motor harness
- Radiator
- Air conditioning compressor and cap the lines
- Air intake duct
- Air cleaner element and upper cover
- Evaporative Emissions (EVAP) canister and bracket
- Front Oxygen (O₂S) sensor

6. If equipped with California emissions specifications, disconnect the rear O₂S sensor.

7. Remove or disconnect the following:
- Engine ground terminal
- Crankshaft Position (CKP) sensor connector
- Camshaft Position (CMP) sensor connector
- Knock Sensor (KS) connector
- Alternator connector and terminal
- Air conditioning compressor connectors, if equipped
- Accelerator cable
- Cruise control cable, if equipped
- Brake booster hose
- Heater inlet and outlet hoses
- Alternator drive belt
- Wires from the spark plugs on the left side of the engine
- Power steering pump line bracket
- Power steering pump, leaving the lines connected and position it aside
- Exhaust Y-pipe
- Lower starter nuts
- Lower engine-to-transmission nuts
- Front engine mount-to-crossmember nuts
- Starter

8. If equipped with an automatic transmission, perform the following:

a. Remove the torque converter service hole plug.

b. Matchmark the torque converter-to-driveplate.

c. Rotate the engine to remove the torque converter-to-driveplate bolts as they become accessible.

9. Remove or disconnect the following:
- Flywheel cover, if equipped with a manual transmission
- Pitching stopper
- Fuel delivery, return and evaporation hoses

10. Support the engine with a suitable lifting device attached to the engine lifting eyes.

11. Slightly raise the engine.

12. Raise the transmission with a floor jack.

13. If equipped with a manual transmission, pull the engine forward then up and out of the vehicle to clear the transmission mainshaft.

14. If equipped with an automatic transmission, pull the engine forward then up and out of the vehicle.

To Install:

15. If equipped with a manual transmission, apply a small amount of grease to the splines of the mainshaft.

16. Position the engine in the engine compartment and align it with the transmission.

17. Install the engine. Torque the upper bolts to 34–40 ft. lbs. (44–54 Nm).

18. Remove the lifting device and floor jack.

19. Install or connect the following:
- Pitching stopper. Torque the bolts to 49 ft. lbs. (67 Nm) on the body side and 40 ft. lbs. (54 Nm) on the bracket side.
- Flywheel cover, if equipped with a manual transmission

20. If equipped with an automatic transmission, perform the following:

a. Align the matchmarks, install the torque converter-to-driveplate bolts while rotating the engine and tighten to 20 ft. lbs. (26 Nm).

b. Install the service hole cover.

21. Install or connect the following:
- EVAP canister and bracket
- Power steering pump. Tighten the retainer bolts to 22–36 ft. lbs. (29–47 Nm).
- Accessory drive belt
- Starter. Torque the bolts to 34–40 ft. lbs. (44–52 Nm).
- Lower engine-to-transmission nuts. Tighten them to 34–40 ft. lbs. (44–52 Nm).
- Lower engine mounting nuts. Tighten them to 61 ft. lbs. (83 Nm) in the inner most elliptical hole in the front crossmember so the clearance is 0.16–0.24 in. (4–6mm).
- Exhaust Y-pipe with new gaskets and nuts
- Brake booster hose
- Heater inlet and outlet hoses
- Accelerator cable
- Cruise control cable, if equipped
- Engine harness connectors
- Engine ground terminal
- CKP sensor connector
- CMP sensor connector
- Knock sensor connector
- Alternator connector and terminal
- Air conditioning compressor connectors, if equipped

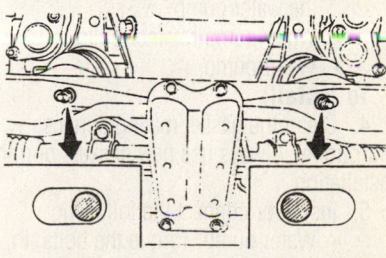

7924XG25

Be sure to tighten the front cushion rubber mounting bolts in the innermost elliptical hole in the front crossmember

- Front O$_2$S sensor, and if removed, the rear O$_2$S sensor.
- Air cleaner element and cover
- Air conditioning lines with new O-rings, if equipped. Torque the bolts to 23 ft. lbs. (31 Nm).
- Radiator
- Engine undercover
- Negative battery cable

22. Fill the crankcase to the proper level with clean engine oil.

23. Fill and bleed the cooling system.

24. Charge the air conditioning system using an approved recovery/recycling machine.

25. If equipped, check the automatic transmission fluid level and add Dexron®II if necessary.

26. Start the engine and allow it to reach normal operating temperature. Check for leaks.

Water Pump

REMOVAL & INSTALLATION

1. Before servicing the vehicle, refer to the precautions in the beginning of this section.

2. Drain the coolant into a suitable container.

3. Remove or disconnect the following:

- Negative battery cable
- Engine undercover
- Radiator outlet hose
- Radiator fan motor assembly
- Water pipe bypass pipe retaining bolt
- Accessory drive belts
- Timing belt and tensioner
- Camshaft Position (CMP) sensor
- Left side camshaft pulleys and left side rear timing belt cover
- Tensioner bracket
- Radiator hose and heater hose from the water pump
- Water pump retainer bolts
- Water pump

To install:

4. Clean the gasket mating surfaces thoroughly. Always use new gaskets during installation.

5. Install or connect the following:

- Water pump. Torque the bolts, in sequence, to 84–120 inch lbs. (10–14 Nm). After tightening the bolts once, retighten to the same specification again.
- Radiator hose and heater hose to the water pump

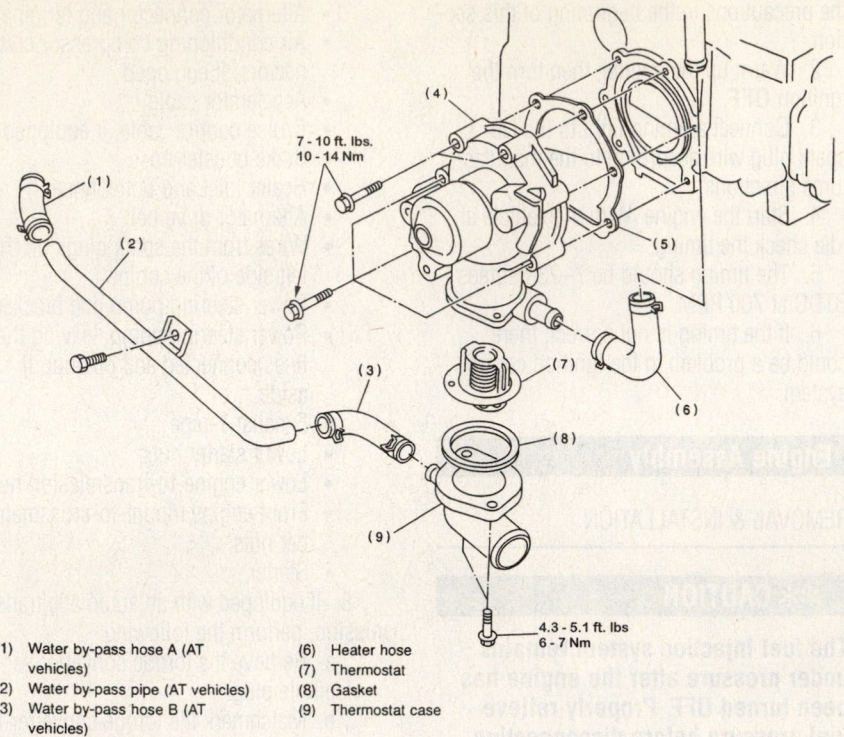

7 - 10 ft. lbs.
10 - 14 Nm

4.3 - 5.1 ft. lbs
6 - 7 Nm

(1)	Water by-pass hose A (AT vehicles)	(6)	Heater hose
(2)	Water by-pass pipe (AT vehicles)	(7)	Thermostat
(3)	Water by-pass hose B (AT vehicles)	(8)	Gasket
(4)	Water pump ASSY	(9)	Thermostat case
(5)	Gasket		

7924XG01

Exploded view of the water pump mounting and related components

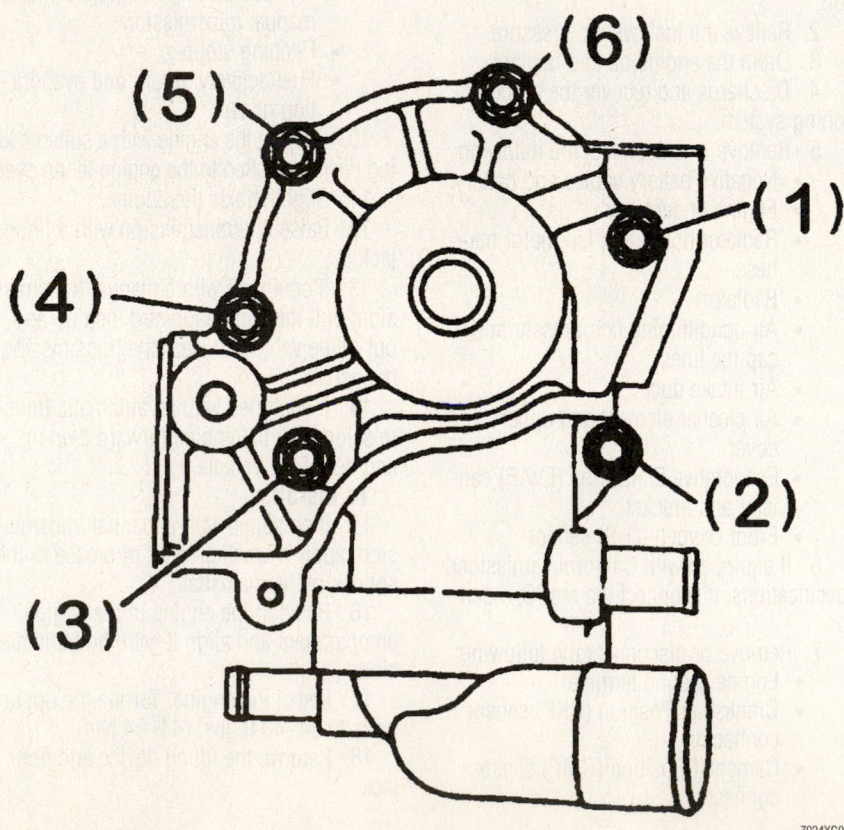

Water pump bolt tightening sequence

7924XG02

- Left side rear timing belt cover, left side camshaft pulleys and tensioner bracket
- CMP sensor
- Timing belt and tensioner
- Accessory drive belts
- Water pipe bypass pipe retaining bolt
- Radiator fan motor assembly
- Radiator outlet hose
- Engine undercover
- Negative battery cable

6. Fill the system with coolant.

7. Start the engine and allow it to reach operating temperature.

8. Check for leaks.

Cylinder Head

REMOVAL & INSTALLATION

1. Before servicing the vehicle, refer to the precautions in the beginning of this section.

2. Properly relieve the fuel system pressure.

3. Remove or disconnect the following:
- Negative battery cable
- Oxygen (O₂S) sensor. If equipped with California emissions, disconnect the rear O₂S sensor.
- Engine undercover
- Exhaust Y-pipe and lower it just enough to clear the studs in the heads. Do not allow the Y-pipe to hang without support.
- Accessory drive belts
- Engine accessories and brackets from the side of the engine the cylinder head is being removed
- Connector bracket attaching bolt, if necessary

4. On the left cylinder head, remove the CMP sensor.

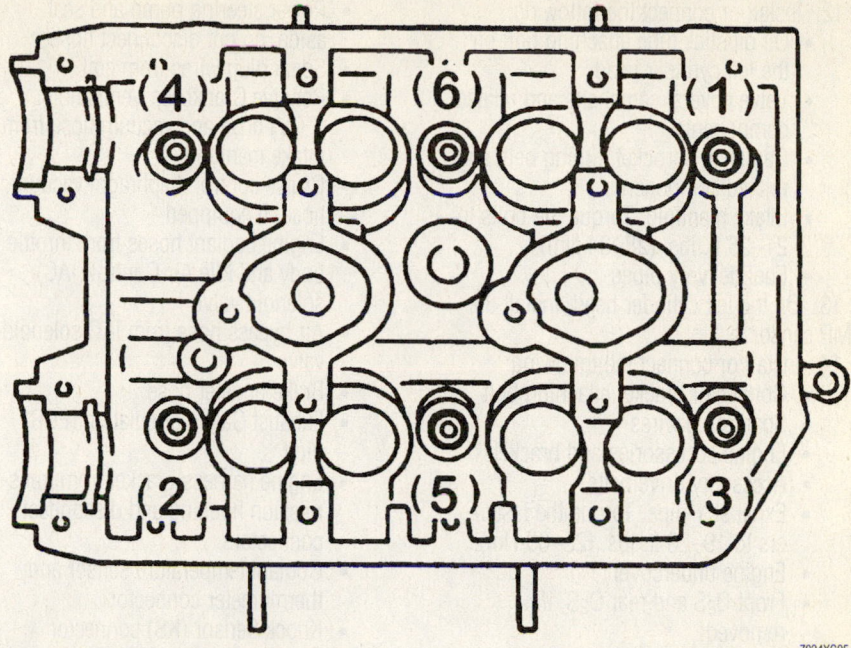

Cylinder head bolt loosening sequence

7924XG05

5. Remove or disconnect the following:
- Fuel pipes
- Intake manifold and gasket
- Timing belt, camshaft sprockets, and related components
- Valve covers, camshafts and related components
- Oil dipstick tube attaching bolt on the left cylinder head
- Cylinder head bolts in the proper sequence. Leave bolts 1 and 3 installed loosely to prevent the cylinder head from falling.

6. Separate the cylinder head from the block. Use a plastic-faced hammer, if needed.

7. Remove bolts 1 and 3. Remove the cylinder head and gasket.

8. Clean all gasket material from both mating surfaces.

To install:

9. Inspect the cylinder head for warpage. Warpage should not exceed 0.0020 in. (0.05mm).

10. Install the cylinder head(s) on the block using new gaskets. Secure in place with the mounting bolts. Coat each bolts with clean engine oil, and hand-tighten.

➥**Refer to Section 1 of this manual for the cylinder head torque sequence illustration. The illustration is located after the Torque Specification Chart.**

11. Tighten the cylinder head bolts as follows:
   a. Step 1: Torque the bolt to 22 ft. lbs. (29 Nm)
   b. Step 2: Torque the bolt to 51 ft. lbs. (69 Nm)
   c. Step 3: Loosen all bolts by 180 degrees, then loosen an additional 180 degrees.
   d. Step 4: Bolts 1 and 2: 25 ft. lbs. (24 Nm)
   e. Step 5: Bolts 3, 4, 5 and 6: 11 ft. lbs. (15 Nm).
   f. Step 6: All bolts: turn an additional 80–90 degrees.
   g. Step 7: All bolts: turn an additional 80–90 degrees.

❋❋ WARNING

Do not exceed 180 degrees total tightening.

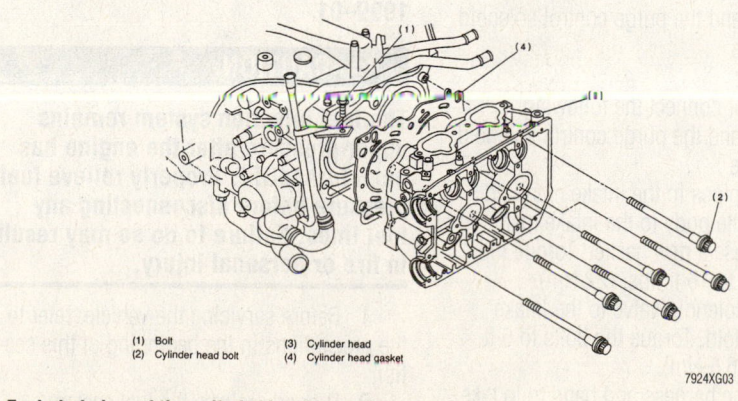

(1) Bolt
(2) Cylinder head bolt
(3) Cylinder head
(4) Cylinder head gasket

7924XG03

Exploded view of the cylinder head mounting

Timing belt service is covered in Section 4 of this manual

12. Install or connect the following:
- Oil dipstick tube attaching bolt on the left cylinder head
- Valve covers, camshafts and related components
- Camshaft sprocket, timing belt, and related components
- Intake manifold. Torque the bolts to 21–25 ft. lbs. (28–34 Nm).
- Fuel delivery pipes

13. On the left cylinder head, install the CMP sensor

14. Install or connect the following:
- Connector bracket attaching bolt
- Spark plug wires
- Engine accessories and brackets
- Accessory drive belts
- Exhaust Y-pipe. Torque the fasteners to 19–26 ft. lbs. (25–35 Nm).
- Engine undercover
- Front O2S and rear O2S, if removed.
- Negative battery cable

15. Start the engine and allow it to reach operating temperature.

16. Check for leaks.

Intake Manifold

REMOVAL & INSTALLATION

1998

✳✳ CAUTION

The fuel injection system remains under pressure after the engine has been turnedOFF. Properly relieve fuel pressure before disconnecting any fuel lines. Failure to do so may result in fire or personal injury.

1. Before servicing the vehicle, refer to the precautions in the beginning of this section.

2. Properly relieve the fuel system pressure.

3. Drain the cooling system.

4. Remove or disconnect the following:
- Negative battery cable
- Mass Air Flow (MAF) sensor connector
- Air intake duct, air cleaner upper cover and the air cleaner element
- Accelerator cable and the cruise control cable, if equipped
- V-belt covers
- Power steering v-belt
- Power steering hose brackets from intake manifold

- Power steering pump and seat aside, do not disconnect hoses
- Spark plug wires from coil
- Positive Crankcase Ventilation (PCV) hose and vacuum hose from intake manifold
- Cruise control diaphragm vacuum hose, if equipped
- Engine coolant hoses from throttle body and Idle Air Control (IAC) solenoid valve
- Air bypass hose from IAC solenoid valve
- Brake booster hose
- Exhaust Gas Recirculation (EGR) pipe
- Engine harness bracket from transmission housing and disconnect connectors
- Coolant temperature sensor and thermometer connector
- Knock Sensor (KS) connector
- Camshaft Position (CMP) sensor connector
- Crankshaft Position (CKP) sensor connector
- Oil pressure switch connector
- Fuel hoses from fuel pipes
- Intake manifold
- Ground cable from the intake manifold
- Throttle Position (TP) sensor
- Ignition coil
- Fuel injectors
- Idle Air Control (IAC) solenoid valve
- Purge control solenoid valve
- Exhaust Gas Recirculation (EGR) solenoid valve
- Engine harness and band from intake manifold
- IAC solenoid valve from the intake manifold
- Throttle body from the intake manifold and discard the gasket
- Fuel pipes from intake manifold
- EGR and the purge control solenoid valves

To install:

5. Install or connect the following:
- EGR and the purge control solenoid valves
- Fuel pipes to the intake manifold
- Throttle body to the intake manifold and use a new gasket. Torque the bolts to 16 ft. lbs. (22 Nm).
- IAC solenoid valve to the intake manifold. Torque the bolts to 5 ft. lbs. (6.5 Nm).
- Engine harness and band to in take manifold
- EGR and the purge control solenoid valves

- TP sensor
- IAC solenoid valve
- Purge control solenoid valve
- Harness band
- Ground cable from the intake manifold
- Intake manifold. Torque the bolts to 18 ft. lbs. (25 Nm).
- Fuel hoses
- Oil pressure switch connector
- CKP sensor connector
- CMP sensor connector
- KS connector
- Coolant temperature sensor and thermometer connector
- Engine harness bracket to transmission housing and connect connectors
- EGR pipe. Torque to 25 ft. lbs. (34 Nm).
- Brake booster hose
- Engine coolant hoses to throttle body and IAC solenoid valve
- Brake booster hose
- Air bypass hose and coolant hose to IAC solenoid valve
- Engine coolant hoses to the throttle body and IAC solenoid valve
- Cruise control diaphragm vacuum hose, if equipped
- PCV hose and vacuum hose to intake manifold
- Spark plug wires to coil
- Power steering pump. Torque the bolts to 15 ft. lbs. (20 Nm).
- Power steering hose brackets to intake manifold
- Power steering V-belt
- V-belt covers
- Accelerator cable and the cruise control cable, if equipped
- Air intake duct, air cleaner upper cover and the air cleaner element
- Negative battery cable

1999–01

✳✳ CAUTION

The fuel injection system remains under pressure after the engine has been turnedOFF. Properly relieve fuel pressure before disconnecting any fuel lines. Failure to do so may result in fire or personal injury.

1. Before servicing the vehicle, refer to the precautions in the beginning of this section.

2. Properly relieve the fuel system pressure.

3. Drain the cooling system.

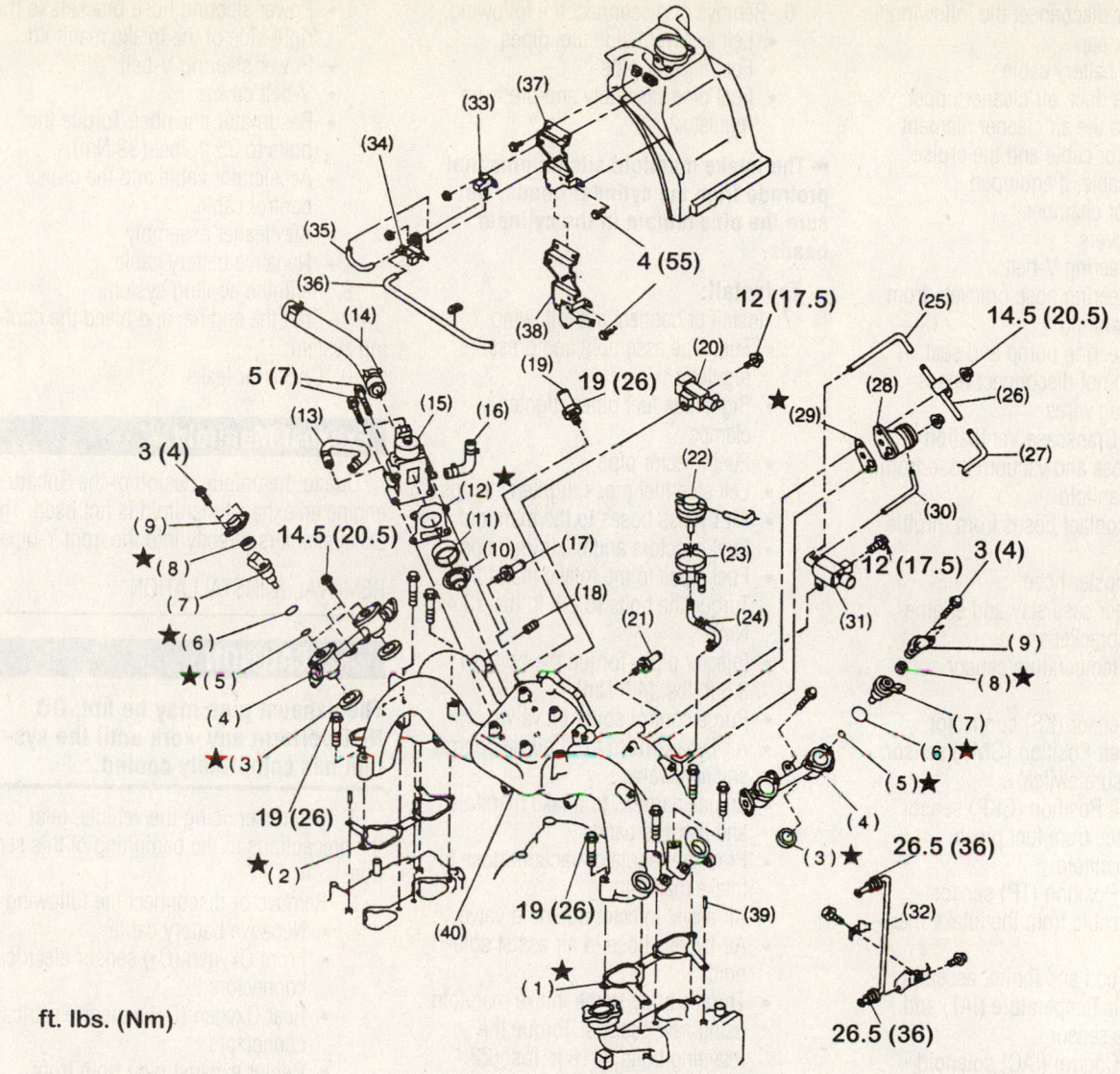

ft. lbs. (Nm)

(1) Intake manifold gasket LH
(2) Intake manifold gasket RH
(3) Fuel injector pipe insulator
(4) Fuel injector pipe
(5) O-ring A
(6) O-ring B
(7) Fuel injector
(8) Insulator
(9) Fuel injector cap
(10) Plate
(11) Sealing
(12) Gasket
(13) Engine coolant hose B
(14) Air by-pass hose
(15) Idle air control solenoid valve
(16) Engine coolant hose A

(17) Nipple (Equipped cruise control model)
(18) Plug
(19) PCV valve
(20) Purge control solenoid valve
(21) Nipple
(22) BPT
(23) BPT holder bracket
(24) Back pressure hose
(25) EGR vacuum hose A
(26) EGR vacuum pipe
(27) EGR vacuum hose C
(28) EGR valve
(29) Gasket
(30) EGR vacuum hose B
(31) EGR solenoid valve
(32) EGR pipe

(33) Pressure sensor
(34) Pressure sources switching solenoid valve
(35) Vacuum hose A
(36) Vacuum hose B
(37) Bracket (Except Canada spec. vehicles)
(38) Bracket (For Canada spec. vehicles)
(39) Collar
(40) Intake manifold

7924XG06

Exploded view of the intake manifold

4. Remove or disconnect the following:
- Fuel filler cap
- Negative battery cable
- Air intake duct, air cleaner upper cover and the air cleaner element
- Accelerator cable and the cruise control cable, if equipped
- Resonator chamber
- V-belt covers
- Power steering V-belt
- Power steering hose brackets from intake manifold
- Power steering pump and seat aside, do not disconnect hoses
- Spark plug wires
- Positive Crankcase Ventilation (PCV) hose and vacuum hose from intake manifold
- Engine coolant hoses from throttle body
- Brake booster hose
- Air cleaner case stay and engine harness bracket
- Coolant temperature sensor connector
- Knock Sensor (KS) connector
- Crankshaft Position (CMP) sensor
- Oil pressure switch
- Camshaft Position (CKP) sensor
- Fuel hoses from fuel pipes
- Intake manifold
- Throttle Position (TP) sensor
- Ground cable from the intake manifold
- Ignition coil and igniter assembly
- Intake Air Temperature (IAT) and pressure sensor
- Idle Air Control (IAC) solenoid valve
- Throttle Position (TP) sensor and air control solenoid
- Air bypass from throttle body
- Throttle body from the intake manifold and discard the gasket
- Air bypass hose from air assist solenoid
- Air assist injector solenoid valve
- Pressure regulator vacuum hose from intake manifold
- Fuel injectors
- Purge control solenoid valve
- Air bypass hose from purge control solenoid valve
- Harness bands
- Engine harness from intake manifold
- Purge control solenoid valve
- Injector pipe
- Fuel pipes from the intake manifold
- Fuel injectors and securing clips
- Air bypass hoses from the manifold

5. Loosen the right and left fuel hose to injector clamps.

6. Remove or disconnect the following:
- Left and right side fuel pipes
- Fuel injector pipe
- Fuel pipe assembly and pressure regulator

➡ The intake manifold sits on pins that protrude from the cylinder heads. Be sure the pins remain in the cylinder heads.

To install:

7. Install or connect the following:
- Fuel pipe assembly and pressure regulator
- Right side fuel pipes, tighten clamps
- Fuel injector pipe
- Left side fuel pipes, tighten clamps
- Air bypass hoses to the manifold
- Fuel injectors and securing clips
- Fuel pipes to the intake manifold. Torque the bolts to 2.5 ft. lbs. (3.4 Nm).
- Injector pipe. Torque the bolts to 3.6 ft. lbs. (4.9 Nm).
- Purge control solenoid valve
- Air bypass hose from purge control solenoid valve
- Engine harness to intake manifold and harness bands
- Pressure regulator vacuum hose to intake manifold
- Air assist injector solenoid valve
- Air bypass hose to air assist solenoid
- Throttle body to the intake manifold using new gaskets. Torque the retaining bolts to 16 ft. lbs. (22 Nm).
- TP sensor and air control solenoid
- Air bypass hoses to the manifold
- IAC solenoid valve to the intake manifold using a new gasket. Tighten the retaining bolts to 60 inch lbs. (7 Nm).
- IAT and pressure sensor use new O-ring. Torque the bolts to 1.4 ft. lbs. (2.0 Nm).
- Ignition coil and ignitor assembly
- Ground cable from the intake manifold
- Air cleaner case stay and engine harness bracket
- Brake booster hose
- Engine coolant hoses to the throttle body.
- PCV hose and vacuum hose to intake manifold
- Spark plug wires
- Power steering pump to intake manifold. Torque the bolts to 15 ft. lbs. (20 Nm).

- Power steering hose brackets to the right side of the intake manifold
- Power steering V-belt
- V-belt covers
- Resonator chamber. Torque the bolts to 25 ft. lbs. (33 Nm).
- Accelerator cable and the cruise control cable
- Air cleaner assembly
- Negative battery cable

8. Refill the cooling system.

9. Start the engine, and bleed the cooling system.

10. Check for leaks.

Exhaust Manifold

Due to the unique design of the Subaru engine an exhaust manifold is not used. The exhaust enters directly into the front Y-pipe.

REMOVAL & INSTALLATION

✳✳ CAUTION

The exhaust pipe may be hot; DO NOT perform any work until the system has completely cooled.

1. Before servicing the vehicle, refer to the precautions in the beginning of this section.

2. Remove or disconnect the following:
- Negative battery cable
- Front Oxygen (O_2) sensor electrical connectors
- Rear Oxygen (O_2) sensor electrical connectors
- Center exhaust pipe from front exhaust pipe
- Nuts that secure the exhaust pipe to the cylinder head
- Front pipe-to-front catalytic converter mounting nuts

3. Discard the gaskets.

To install:

4. Clean all gasket surfaces completely.

5. Install or connect the following:
- Catalytic converter to front exhaust pipe using new gasket. Torque the bolts to 22 ft. lbs. (30 Nm).
- Exhaust pipe to the cylinder head using new gaskets. Torque the mounting nuts to 22 ft. lbs. (30 Nm).
- Exhaust pipe to the center pipe using new gaskets. Torque the mounting nuts to 26 ft. lbs. (35 Nm).
- Rear O_2 sensors electrical connectors

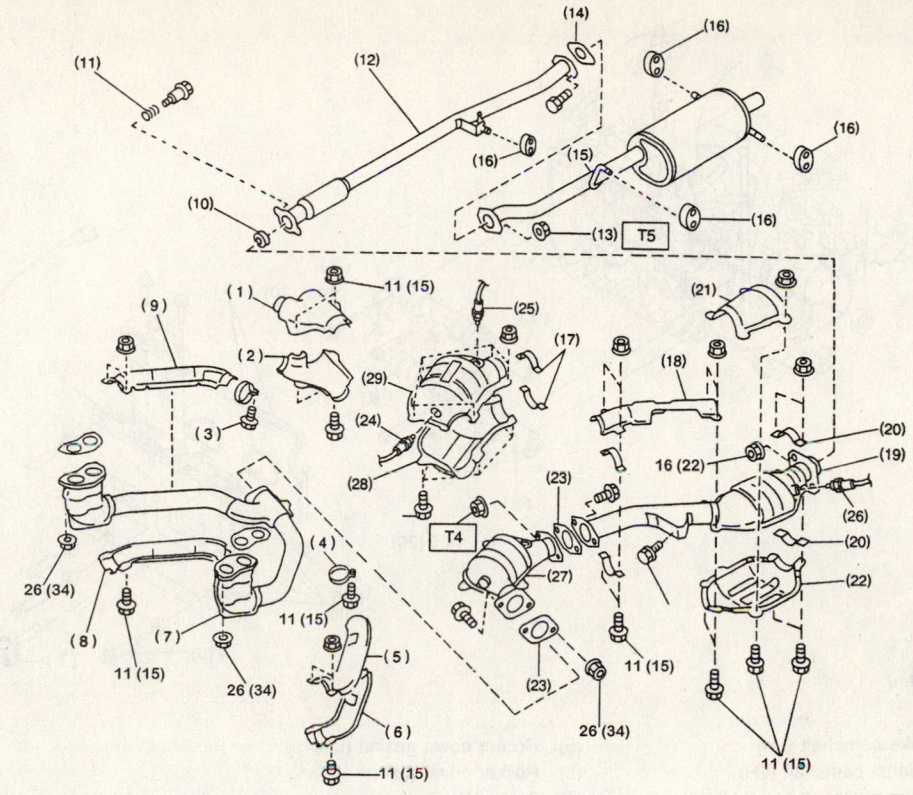

ft. lbs. (Nm)

(1) Upper front exhaust pipe cover CTR	(12) Rear exhaust pipe	(26) Rear oxygen sensor (Except California spec. vehicles)
(2) Lower front exhaust pipe cover CTR	(13) Self-locking nut	(27) Front catalytic converter
	(14) Gasket	(28) Lower front catalytic converter cover
(3) Band RH	(15) Muffler	
(4) Band LH	(16) Cushion rubber	(29) Upper front catalytic converter cover
(5) Upper front exhaust pipe cover LH	(17) Clamp	
	(18) Upper center exhaust pipe cover	
(6) Lower front exhaust pipe cover LH	(19) Center exhaust pipe	
(7) Front exhaust pipe	(20) Clamp B	
(8) Lower front exhaust pipe cover RH	(21) Upper rear catalytic converter cover	
(9) Upper front exhaust pipe cover RH	(22) Lower rear catalytic converter cover	
(10) Gasket	(23) Gasket	
(11) Spring	(24) Front oxygen sensor	
	(25) Rear oxygen sensor (California spec. vehicles)	

7924XG07

Exploded view of the exhaust system and related components

- Front O_2 sensors electrical connectors
- Negative battery cable

6. Start the engine and check for exhaust leaks.

Front Crankshaft Seal

REMOVAL & INSTALLATION

The front crankshaft seal is mounted in the oil pump. The removal and installation is covered in the oil pump procedure.

Camshaft and Valve Lifters

REMOVAL & INSTALLATION

1998

1. Before servicing the vehicle, refer to the precautions in the beginning of this section.
2. Remove or disconnect the following:
- Negative battery cable
- Timing belt covers
- Timing belt

- Camshaft sprockets
- Spark plug wires

3. On the left cylinder head, remove the Camshaft Position (CMP) sensor.

4. Remove the valve covers and gaskets.

5. Loosen the intake camshaft cap bolts in sequence, in small increments.

➤Be sure to keep the intake and exhaust bearing caps and camshafts in proper order for assembly. Also note the positioning and location of the camshafts for reinstallation.

Refer to Section 1 for engine rebuilding specifications

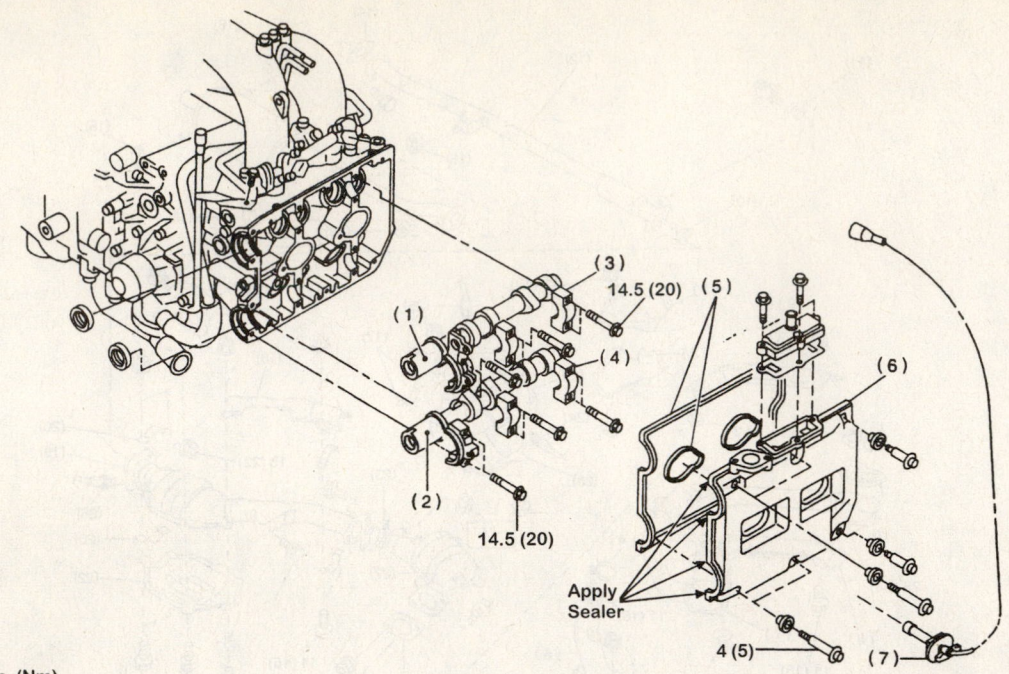

ft. lbs. (Nm)

(1) Intake camshaft (LH)
(2) Exhaust camshaft (LH)
(3) Intake camshaft cap (LH)
(4) Exhaust camshaft cap (LH)

(5) Rocker cover gasket (LH)
(6) Rocker cover (LH)
(7) Spark plug cord

7924XG08

Exploded view of the camshaft mounting

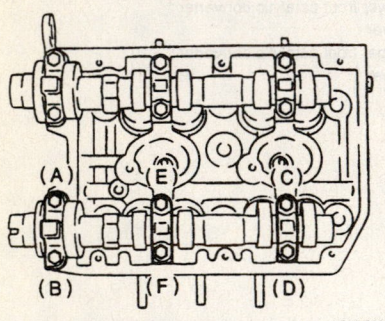

7924XG09

Camshaft bearing cap removal sequence—exhaust camshaft shown, intake camshaft is the same

6. Remove or disconnect the following:
   • Intake camshaft bearing caps, then the camshaft

➡ **When removing the exhaust camshaft, the valve lifter and valve shim may fall out. Have an assistant help keep the lifters and shims in the proper order.**

   • Exhaust camshaft cap bolts, loosen them, in sequence, in small increments
   • Exhaust camshaft bearing caps
   • Camshafts

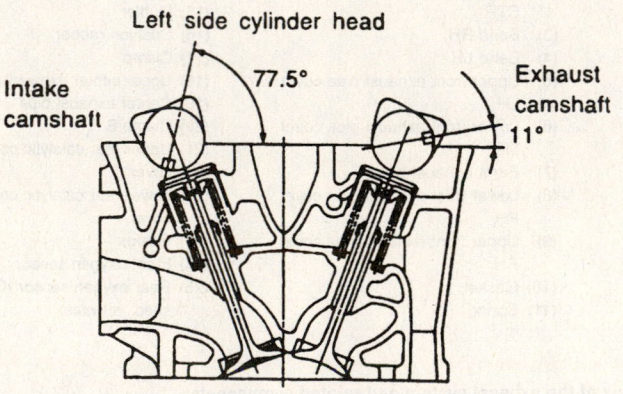

Left side cylinder head

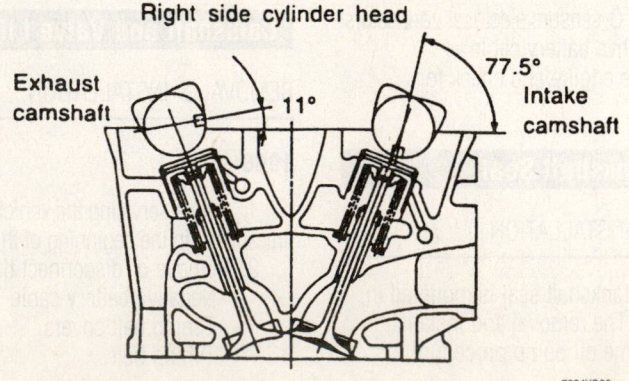

Right side cylinder head

7924XG26

Cutaway view of the camshaft positioning

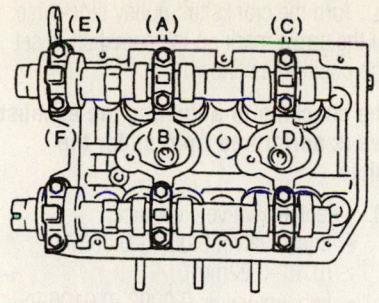

Camshaft bearing cap tightening sequence—intake camshaft shown, exhaust camshaft order is the same

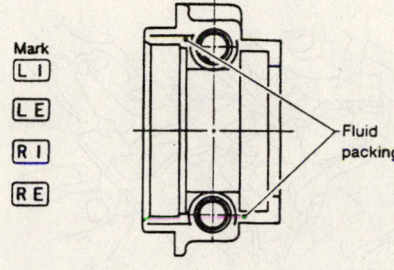

Apply the fluid packing as shown to prevent oil leaks

To install:

➡**Lubricate the camshaft bearings prior to camshaft installation.**

7. Install the camshafts so the base circle (non-lobe portion) of the camshafts are in contact with the lash adjusters. This will position the lobes of the camshafts away from the valves.

➡**The left camshaft will need to be rotated for timing belt alignment.**

8. Apply Three Bond® 1215 fluid packing to the front bearing cap mating surfaces.
9. Install or connect the following:
- Bearing caps. Torque the caps in sequence in 2 progressive steps to 14 ft. lbs. (20 Nm).
- New oil seals in the cylinder heads using a seal installation tool.

✱✱ WARNING

Only rotate camshafts the specified amount. If the camshafts are rotated beyond the specified amount, the valves will contact each other and cause severe internal damage.

10. For correct timing belt alignment, rotate the left-hand intake camshaft 80

degrees clockwise and the left-hand exhaust camshaft 45 degrees counterclockwise.

11. If new camshafts were installed, check and adjust the valve lash.
12. Install or connect the following:
- Valve covers using a new gasket be sure to apply liquid sealant to the front edges of the gasket at the camshaft opening. Torque the bolts to 3.6 ft. lbs. (5 Nm).
- CMP sensor, if removed
- Spark plug wires
- Camshaft sprockets. Torque the retaining bolts to 58 ft. lbs. (78 Nm). Be sure to secure the sprockets when tightening the bolts.

➡**Check the timing sprockets for proper alignment**

- Timing belt
- Negative battery cable

13. Check the fluid levels and start the engine.
14. Allow the engine to reach operating temperature and check for leaks

1999–01

1. Before servicing the vehicle, refer to the precautions in the beginning of this section.
2. Remove or disconnect the following:
- Negative battery cable
- Timing belt covers
- Timing belt
- Camshaft sprockets
- Spark plug wires

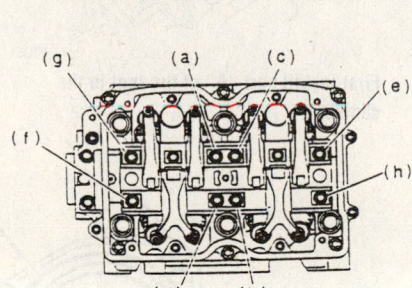

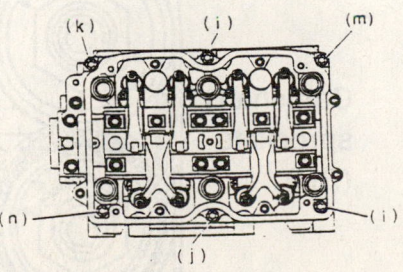

Camshaft cap tightening sequence

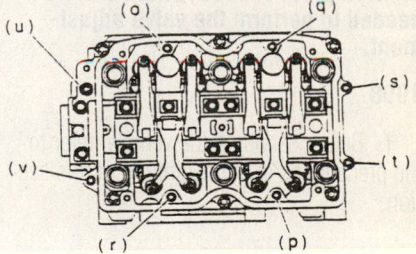

Camshaft cap removal sequence

- Oil level gauge guide and Camshaft Position (CMP) sensor support
- Positive Crankcase Ventilation (PCV) hose
- Valve cover
- Rocker arm assembly

3. Remove the camshaft cap as follows:
   a. Bolts "A" through "B" in alphabetical sequence
   b. Loosen bolts "C" through "J" equally all the way in alphabetical sequence
   c. Bolts "K" through "P" in alphabetical sequence using tool 499497000
4. Remove or disconnect the following:
- Camshaft
- Oil seal, if necessary
- Plug from the rear side of the camshaft

To install:

➡**Lubricate the camshaft bearings prior to camshaft installation.**

5. Install or connect the following:
- Camshaft

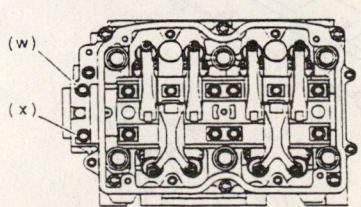

- Camshaft cap. Apply liquid gasket on the edge of the cam cap mating surface 0.12 inch (3mm) thick

6. Temporarily tighten bolts "G" through "J" in alphabetical sequence

7. Install the valve rocker assembly. Torque the bolts "A" through "H" to 18 ft. lbs. (25 Nm).

8. Torque bolts "I" through "N" to 13 ft. lbs. (25 Nm) in alphabetical sequence using tool 499497000

9. Torque bolts "O" through "X" to 7.2 ft. lbs. (10 Nm) in alphabetical sequence

10. Install or connect the following:
- Oil seal to the camshaft using tool 499597000 oil seal guide and 49958700 oil seal installer
- Plug to the rear side of the camshaft using tool 499587700 oil seal installer
- Valve cover
- Oil level gauge guide and CMP sensor support
- PCV house
- Spark plug wires
- Camshaft sprockets. Torque the bolts to 58 ft. lbs. (78 Nm).
- Timing belt
- Timing belt covers. Torque the bolts to 3.6 ft. lbs. (5 Nm).
- Negative battery cable

Valve Lash

ADJUSTMENT

➡The valve adjustment should be performed while the engine is cold. A Shim Replace Kit 498187100 will be needed to perform the valve adjustment.

1998

1. Before servicing the vehicle, refer to the precautions in the beginning of this section.

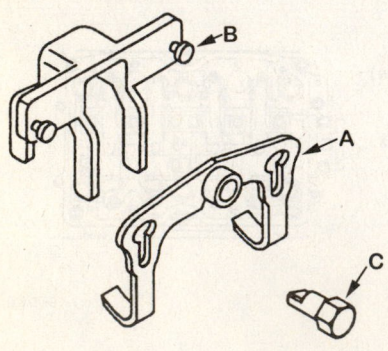

Exploded view of the shim replace kit

2. Remove or disconnect the following:
- Battery cables and tray
- Upper and center timing belt cover mounting bolts
- Engine undercover
- Timing belt cover lower mounting bolts, then the covers
- Mass Air Flow (MAF) sensor, and the air intake duct with the air cleaner assembly
- Blowby hose
- Spark plug wires
- Washer tank, motor and connectors
- Valve cover

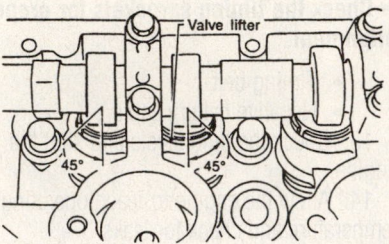

Position the lifter notch as shown, to remove the shim

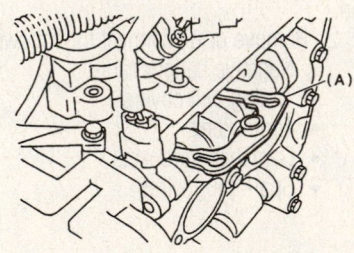

First install part "A" of the tool to the camshaft . . .

3. Turn the crankshaft pulley clockwise until the arrow mark on the camshaft is set to the position as shown.

➡the checking or adjusting the exhaust valve is performed from under the vehicle.

4. Check the valve clearance:
- Intake valve: 0.0071–0.0087 in. (0.18–0.22mm).
- Exhaust valve: 0.0090–0.0106 in. (0.23–0.27mm).

5. If any valve needs adjustment, perform the following, while referring to the accompanying illustrations:

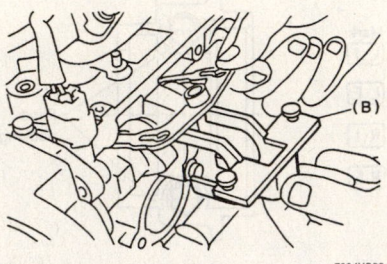

. . . then part "B" under part "A" as shown

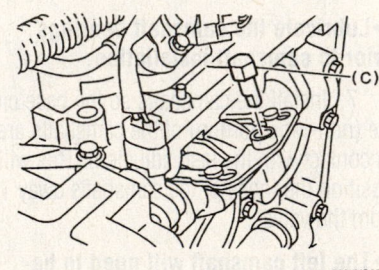

Turn part "C" until the adjusting shim can be removed

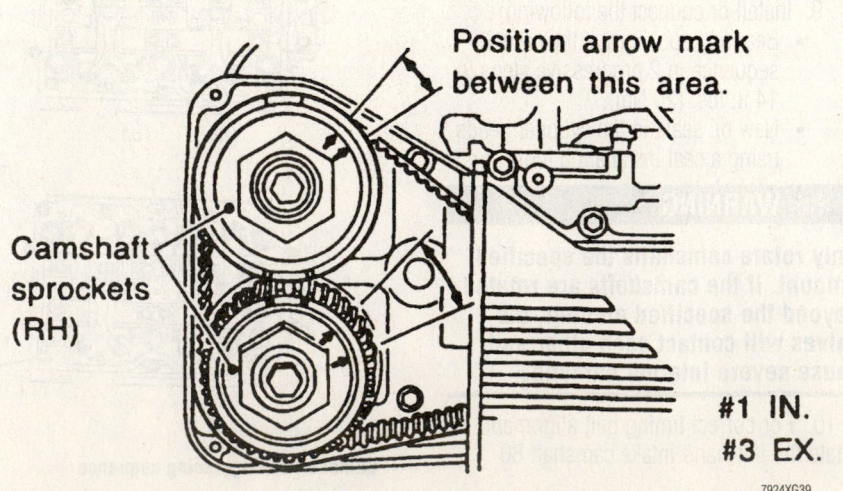

Position the camshaft as shown to adjust No. 1 intake valve and No. 3 exhaust valve

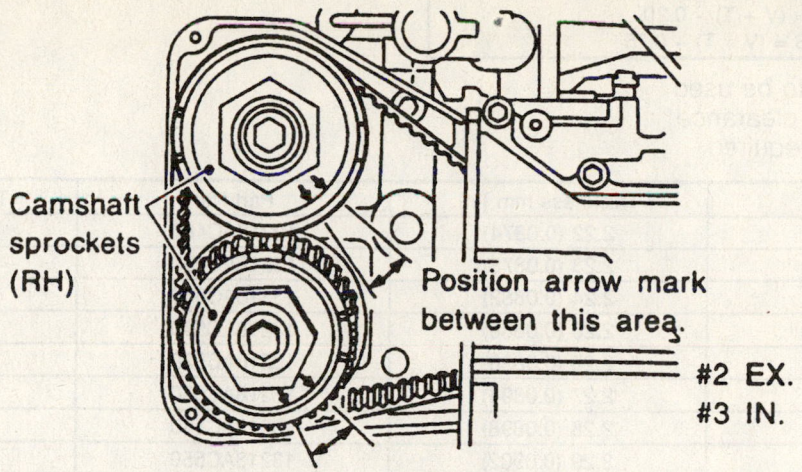

Position the camshaft as shown to adjust No. 3 intake valve and No. 2 exhaust valve

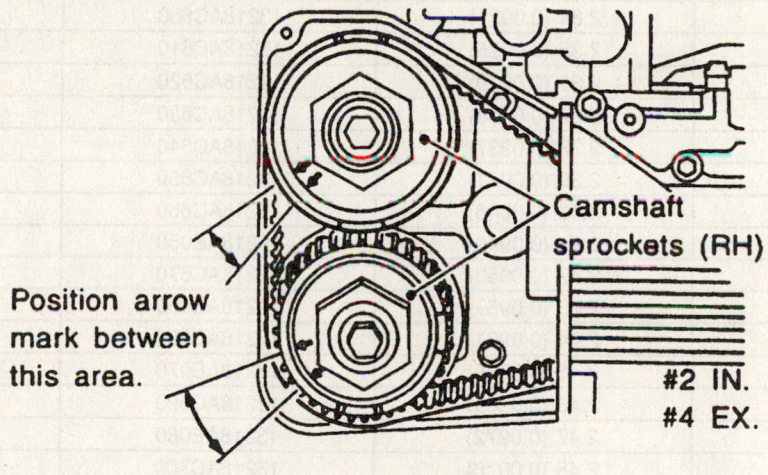

Position the camshaft as shown to adjust No. 2 intake valve and No. 4 exhaust valve

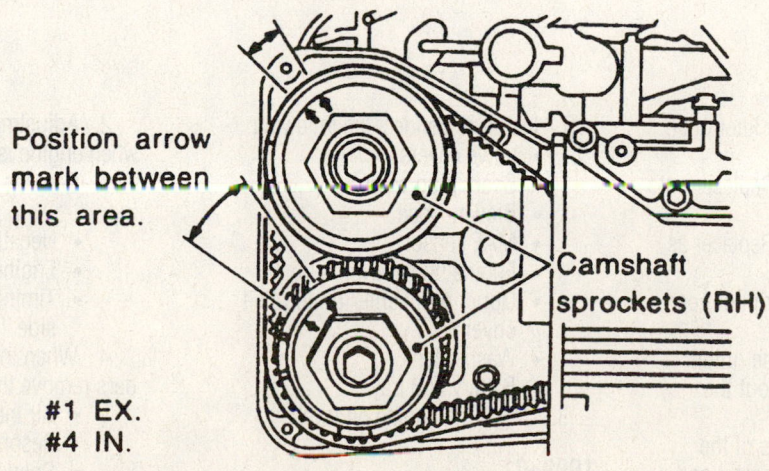

Position the camshaft as shown to adjust No. 4 intake valve and No. 1 exhaust valve

For complete mechanical specifications, refer to Section 1 of this manual

Intake valve (mm): S = (V + T) – 0.20
Exhaust valve (mm): S = (V + T) – 0.25

S: Shim thickness to be used
V: Measured valve clearance
T: Shim thickness required

Part No.	Thickness mm (in)	Part No.	Thickness mm (in)
13218AC230	2.22 (0.0874)	13218AC480	2.52 (0.0992)
13218AE000	2.23 (0.0878)	13218AC490	2.53 (0.0996)
13218AC240	2.24 (0.0882)	13218AC500	2.54 (0.1000)
13218AE010	2.25 (0.0886)	13218AC510	2.55 (0.1004)
13218AC250	2.26 (0.0890)	13218AC520	2.56 (0.1008)
13218AE020	2.27 (0.0894)	13218AC530	2.57 (0.1012)
13218AC260	2.28 (0.0898)	13218AC540	2.58 (0.1016)
13218AE030	2.29 (0.0902)	13218AC550	2.59 (0.1020)
13218AC270	2.30 (0.0906)	13218AC560	2.60 (0.1024)
13218AE040	2.31 (0.0909)	13218AC570	2.61 (0.1028)
13218AC280	2.32 (0.0913)	13218AC580	2.62 (0.1031)
13218AC290	2.33 (0.0917)	13218AC590	2.63 (0.1035)
13218AC300	2.34 (0.0921)	13218AC600	2.64 (0.1039)
13218AC310	2.35 (0.0925)	13218AC610	2.65 (0.1043)
13218AC320	2.36 (0.0929)	13218AC620	2.66 (0.1047)
13218AC330	2.37 (0.0933)	13218AC630	2.67 (0.1051)
13218AC340	2.38 (0.0937)	13218AC640	2.68 (0.1055)
13218AC350	2.39 (0.0941)	13218AC650	2.69 (0.1059)
13218AC360	2.40 (0.0945)	13218AC660	2.70 (0.1063)
13218AC370	2.41 (0.0949)	13218AE050	2.71 (0.1067)
13218AC380	2.42 (0.0953)	13218AC670	2.72 (0.1071)
13218AC390	2.43 (0.0957)	13218AE060	2.73 (0.1075)
13218AC400	2.44 (0.0961)	13218AC680	2.74 (0.1079)
13218AC410	2.45 (0.0965)	13218AE070	2.75 (0.1083)
13218AC420	2.46 (0.0969)	13218AC690	2.76 (0.1087)
13218AC430	2.47 (0.0972)	13218AE080	2.77 (0.1091)
13218AC440	2.48 (0.0976)	13218AC700	2.78 (0.1094)
13218AC450	2.49 (0.0980)	13218AE090	2.79 (0.1098)
13218AC460	2.50 (0.0984)	13218AC710	2.80 (0.1102)
13218AC470	2.51 (0.0988)	13218AE100	2.81 (0.1106)

7924XG38

Valve adjusting shim chart

a. Rotate the notch of the lifter outward by 45 degrees.

b. Install part "A" of the Replacer onto the camshaft.

c. Install part "B" of the Replacer as shown.

d. Install part "C" and turn until part "B" pushes the lifter away.

e. Insert tweezers into the notch of the valve lifter, and take out the shim.

f. Measure the thickness of the shim, then using the chart select and install a new shim and recheck the clearance.

6. Remove the adjusting tools.

7. Install or connect the following:
   • Valve covers
   • Spark plug wires
   • Blowby hose
   • MAF sensor
   • Engine undercover
   • Upper and center timing belt cover
   • Washer tank
   • Battery and tray
8. Check the engine oil level.

1999–01

1. Before servicing the vehicle, refer to the precautions in the beginning of this section.

2. Adjustment should be performed when engine is cold.

3. Remove or disconnect the following:
   • Negative battery cable
   • Engine coolant reservoir tank
   • Timing belt cover on the left hand side

4. When inspecting Nos. 1 and 3 cylinders remove the following:
   • Air intake duct as a unit
   • Resonator chamber
   • Spark plug wires from Nos. 1 and 3 cylinders
   • Blowby house from valve cover
   • Engine undercover

- Timing belt cover on the right hand side
- Valve cover on the right hand side

5. When inspecting Nos. 2 and 4 cylinders remove the following:
- Battery and battery tray
- Window washer motor connectors front and rear
- Rear gate glass washer hose from the washer motor
- Washer tank mounting bolts and secure out of the way
- Spark plug wires from Nos. 2 and 4 cylinders
- Blow by house from valve cover
- Timing belt cover on the right hand side
- Valve cover on the left hand side

6. Set No. 1 cylinder to Top Dead Center (TDC).

➡ **When arrow mark on the left hand side comes exactly to the top, No. 1 cylinder piston is brought to TDC of the compression stroke.**

7. Check the valve clearance:
- Intake valve: 0.0071–0.0087 in. (0.18–0.22mm).
- Exhaust valve: 0.0090–0.0106 in. (0.23–0.27mm).

8. If any valve needs adjustment, perform the following:
   a. Loosen the valve rocker nut and screw.
   b. Place a thickness gage in at as horizontal a direction as possible with respect to the vale stem and face.
   c. Adjust the screw until proper clearance is obtained.
   d. Tighten the rocker nut after adjusted.

9. Install or connect the following:

- Valve covers left and right
- Timing belt covers
- Blowby houses to valve covers
- Spark plug wires
- Washer tank
- Rear gate glass washer hose to the washer motor
- Washer motor connectors
- Battery and battery tray
- Engine undercover
- Resonator chamber
- Air intake duct unit
- Engine coolant reservoir tank

Starter

REMOVAL & INSTALLATION

1. Before servicing the vehicle, refer to the precautions in the beginning of this section.

2. Remove or disconnect the following:

- Negative battery
- Air intake duct and assembly
- Wires
- Starter

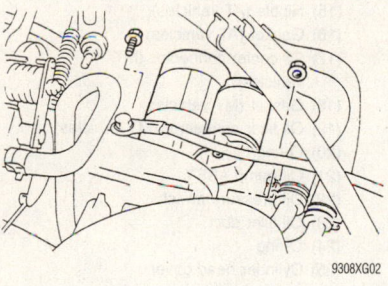

9308XG02

View of the starter mounting

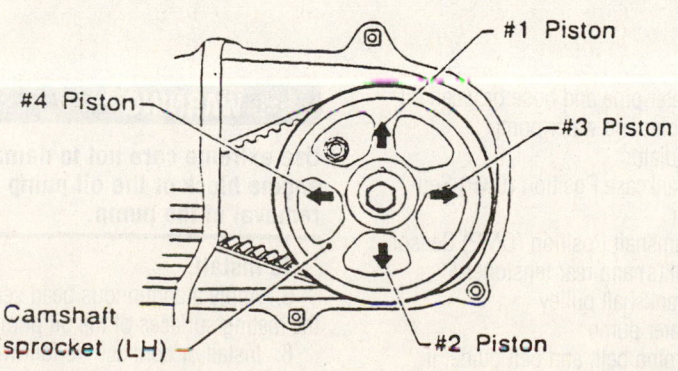

9308XG05

Position the camshaft for adjustment to valves

To install:

3. Install or connect the following:
- Starter. Torque the mounting bolts to 37 ft. lbs. (50 Nm).
- Wires
- Air intake duct and assembly
- Negative battery

Oil Pan

REMOVAL & INSTALLATION

1. Before servicing the vehicle, refer to the precautions in the beginning of this section.

2. Drain the oil from the engine.

3. Remove or disconnect the following:
- Air intake duct
- Oxygen (O_2S) sensor connectors
- Pitching stopper
- Upper radiator brackets
- Engine undercover
- Rear O_2S sensor connector, if equipped
- Exhaust front Y-pipe and center pipe
- Nuts which secure the front engine mounts to the front crossmember

4. Support the engine with a suitable lifting device and lift the engine slightly.

5. Remove the oil pan.

6. Clean all gasket material from both mating surfaces.

To install:

7. Install the drain plug with a new gasket. Torque the bolt to 33–36 ft. lbs. (43–47 Nm).

8. Apply a continuous bead of sealer to a new oil pan gasket.

9. Install the oil pan assembly. Torque the bolts to 36–48 inch lbs. (4–5 Nm).

10. Lower the engine onto the front crossmember.

11. Install or connect the following:
- Front engine mount nuts. Torque the nuts to 69 ft. lbs. (51 Nm).
- Exhaust front Y-pipe with new gaskets. Torque the nuts that secure the pipe to the engine to 23 ft. lbs. (30 Nm).
- O_2S sensor connectors
- Pitching stopper. Torque the front bolt to 36 ft. lbs. (49 Nm) and the rear bolt to 42 ft. lbs. (57 Nm).
- Upper radiator brackets
- Air intake duct
- Engine undercover

12. Refill the engine to the proper level with the recommended oil and run the engine.

13. Check for leaks.

Please refer to Section 8 for electric cooling fan wiring schematics

T1: 3.6 ft. lbs. (5Nm)   T5: 32.5 ft. lbs. (44Nm)
T2: 3.6 ft. lbs. (5Nm)
T3: 4.7 ft. lbs. (6.4Nm)
T4: 7 ft. lbs. (10Nm)

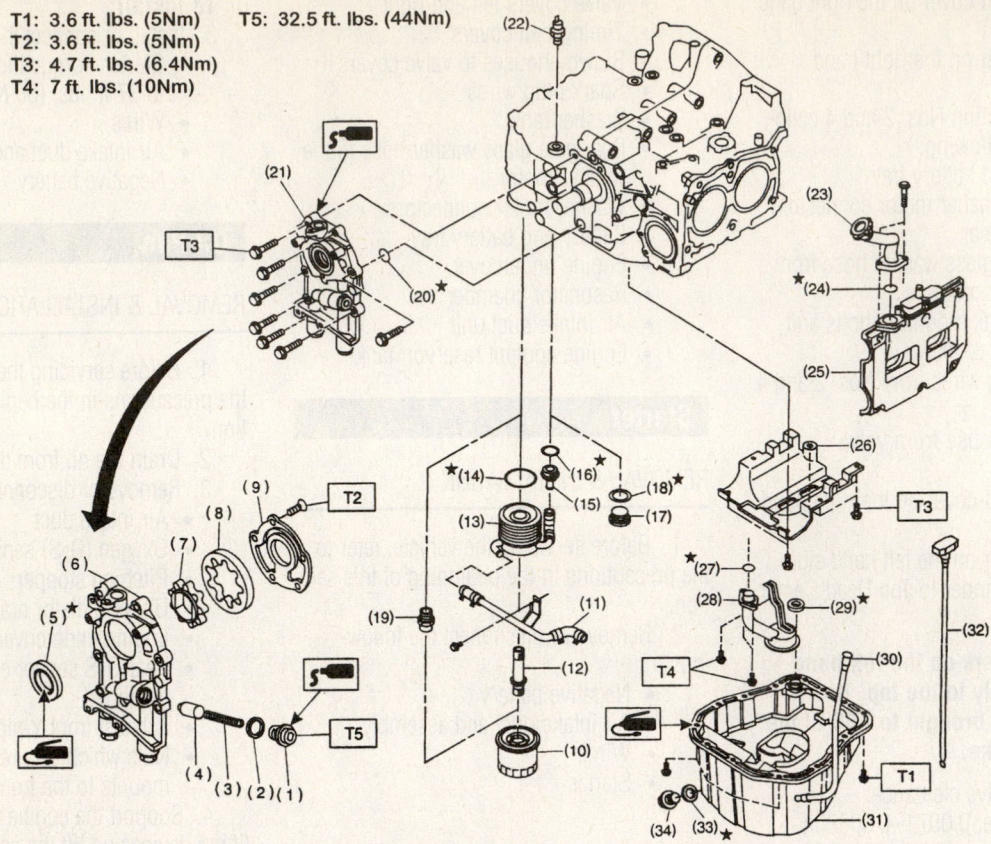

(1) Plug
(2) Washer
(3) Relief valve spring
(4) Relief valve
(5) Oil seal
(6) Oil pump case
(7) Inner rotor
(8) Outer rotor
(9) Oil pump cover
(10) Oil filter
(11) Oil cooler pipe and hose ASSY
     (AT vehicles)
(12) Connector (AT vehicles)
(13) Oil cooler (AT vehicles)
(14) O-ring (AT vehicles)

(15) Nipple (AT vehicles)
(16) Gasket (AT vehicles)
(17) Oil cooler connector (MT
     vehicles)
(18) Gasket (MT vehicles)
(19) Oil filter connector (MT vehicles)
(20) O-ring
(21) Oil pump ASSY
(22) Oil pressure switch
(23) Oil filler duct
(24) O-ring
(25) Cylinder head cover
(26) Baffle plate
(27) O-ring
(28) Oil strainer

(29) Gasket
(30) Oil level gauge guide
(31) Oil pan
(32) Oil level gauge
(33) Metal gasket
(34) Drain plug

7924XG28

Oil pan and lubrication components

Oil Pump

REMOVAL & INSTALLATION

1. Before servicing the vehicle, refer to the precautions in the beginning of this section.
2. Drain the cooling system.
3. Drain the engine oil into a separate container.
4. Remove or disconnect the following:
   - Negative battery cable
   - Engine undercover

- Water pipe and hose between oil cooler and water pump
- Radiator
- Crankcase Position (CKP) Sensor
- Camshaft Position (CMP) Sensor
- Belt(s) and rear tensioner
- Crankshaft pulley
- Water pump
- Timing belt, and belt guide, if equipped
- Oil pump mounting bolts and carefully pry the pump from the engine block

✳✳ WARNING

Use extreme care not to damage the engine block or the oil pump during removal of the pump.

To install:
5. Apply a continuous bead sealant to the mating surfaces of the oil pump.
6. Install or connect the following:
   - New front seal to the oil pump coat the inside of the seal with engine oil
   - New O-ring to the oil pump

- Oil pump. Torque the bolts to 56 inch lbs. (6.4 Nm).
- Timing belt, and belt guide, if equipped
- Water pump
- Crankshaft pulley
- Belt(s) and rear tensioner
- Camshaft Position (CMP) Sensor
- Crankcase Position (CKP) Sensor
- Radiator
- Engine coolant pipe
- Engine undercover
- Negative battery cable

7. Refill the cooling system.
8. Refill the engine to the proper level with the recommended oil.

Rear Main Seal

REMOVAL & INSTALLATION

1. Before servicing the vehicle, refer to the precautions in the beginning of this section.
2. Remove or disconnect the following:
   - Engine from the vehicle
   - Clutch assembly/flywheel, if equipped with manual transmission
   - Torque converter flexplate from the crankshaft, if equipped with an automatic transmission
3. Using a seal removal tool, pry the oil seal from the housing.
   To install:
4. Utilizing the appropriate seal installer
5. Install or connect the following:
   - New oil seal and press it into the housing using the appropriate driver
   - Clutch assembly/flywheel, if equipped
   - Flywheel/flexplate and tighten the bolts to 53 ft. lbs. (72 Nm), if equipped
   - Engine into the vehicle

Piston and Ring

POSITIONING

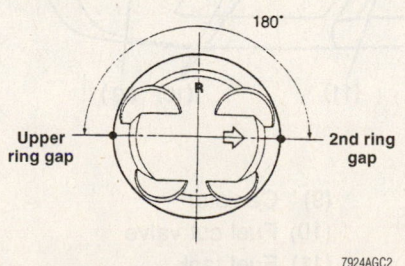

Compression ring end-gap spacing—2.5L engine

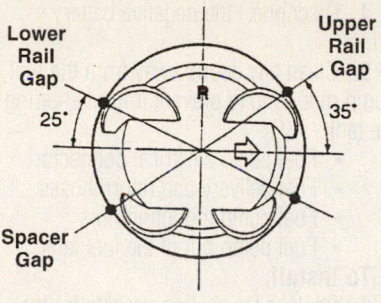

Upper, spacer and lower oil ring end-gap spacing—2.5L engine

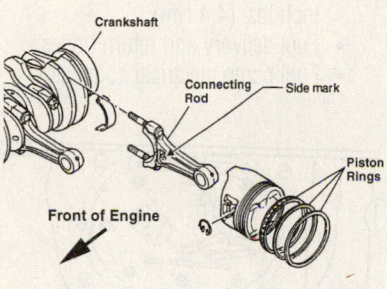

Piston and connecting rod assembly positioning—2.5L engine

FUEL SYSTEM

Fuel System Service Precautions

Safety is the most important factor when performing not only fuel system maintenance but any type of maintenance. Failure to conduct maintenance and repairs in a safe manner may result in serious personal injury or death. Maintenance and testing of the vehicle's fuel system components can be accomplished safely and effectively by adhering to the following rules and guidelines.

- To avoid the possibility of fire and personal injury, always disconnect the negative battery cable unless the repair or test procedure requires that battery voltage be applied.
- Always relieve the fuel system pressure prior to disconnecting any fuel system component (injector, fuel rail, pressure regulator, etc.), fitting or fuel line connection. Exercise extreme caution whenever relieving fuel system pressure, to avoid exposing skin, face and eyes to fuel spray. Please be advised that fuel under pressure may penetrate the skin or any part of the body that it contacts.

- Always place a shop towel or cloth around the fitting or connection prior to loosening to absorb any excess fuel due to spillage. Ensure that all fuel spillage (should it occur) is quickly removed from engine surfaces. Ensure that all fuel soaked cloths or towels are deposited into a suitable waste container.
- Always keep a dry chemical (Class B) fire extinguisher near the work area.
- Do not allow fuel spray or fuel vapors to come into contact with a spark or open flame.
- Always use a backup wrench when loosening and tightening fuel line connection fittings. This will prevent unnecessary stress and torsion to fuel line piping. Always follow the proper torque specifications.
- Always replace worn fuel fitting O-rings with new. Do not substitute fuel hose or equivalent, where fuel pipe is installed.

Fuel System Pressure

RELIEVING

➡**This procedure must be performed prior to servicing any component of the fuel injection system.**

1. Before servicing the vehicle, refer to the precautions in the beginning of this section.
2. Disconnect the fuel pump harness at the fuel pump, under the rear seat access panel.
3. Crank the engine for 5 seconds or more to relieve the fuel pressure. If the engine starts during this time, allow it to run until it stalls.
4. Connect the fuel pump harness after repairs are completed.

Fuel Filter

REMOVAL & INSTALLATION

1. Before servicing the vehicle, refer to the precautions in the beginning of this section.
2. Locate the fuel filter in the engine compartment on the left inside fender.
3. Properly relieve the fuel system pressure.
4. Remove or disconnect the following:
   - Negative battery cable
   - Fuel delivery hoses from the fuel filter
   - Fuel filter from its holder

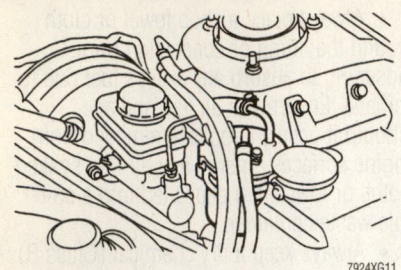

View of fuel filter mounting

7924XG11

To install:

5. Install or connect the following:
- Fuel filter into its mounting bracket
- Fuel delivery hoses and tighten the hose clamps
- Negative battery cable

Fuel Pump

REMOVAL & INSTALLATION

1. Before servicing the vehicle, refer to the precautions in the beginning of this section.

2. Remove the rear seat cushion and access panel.

3. Properly relieve the fuel system pressure.

4. Disconnect the negative battery cable.

5. Clean any debris away from the fuel pump mounting to prevent it from entering the tank.
- Fuel pump electrical connector
- Fuel delivery and return hoses
- Fuel pump mounting nuts
- Fuel pump out of the fuel tank

To install:

6. Replace the sealing gaskets for the fuel pump.

7. Install or connect the following:
- Fuel pump into the tank. Torque the mounting nuts in sequence to 39 inch lbs. (4.4 Nm).
- Fuel delivery and return hoses
- Fuel pump electrical connector

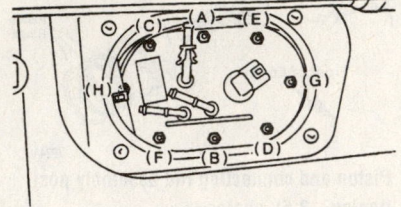

7924XG13

Fuel pump mounting nut tightening sequence

- Fuel filler cap
- Negative battery cable

8. Start the vehicle and check for leaks.

9. Install the fuel pump access cover and rear seat cushion.

Fuel Injector

REMOVAL & INSTALLATION

1998

1. Before servicing the vehicle, refer to the precautions in the beginning of this section.

2. Properly relieve the fuel system pressure.

3. Remove or disconnect the following:
- Negative battery cable
- Electrical connector from injector
- Fuel injector from fuel rail

To install:

4. Replace old O-rings and insulator with new.

5. Install or connect the following:
- Fuel injector from fuel rail. Torque the mounting bolts to 2.5 ft. lbs. (3.4 Nm).
- Electrical connector to injector
- Negative battery cable

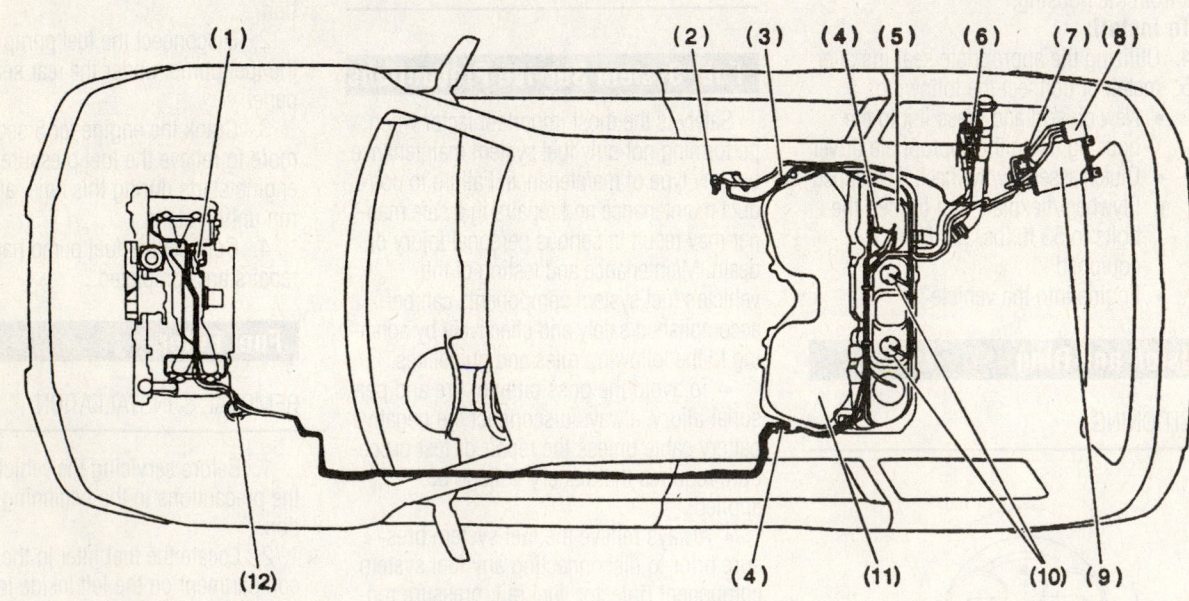

(1) Purge control solenoid valve	(5) Fuel pump
(2) Roll over valve	(6) Fuel tank pressure sensor
(3) Pressure control solenoid	(7) Vent control solenoid valve
(4) Quick connector	(8) Air filter
(9) Canister	
(10) Fuel cut valve	
(11) Fuel tank	
(12) Fuel filter	

Fuel system component locations

7924XG12

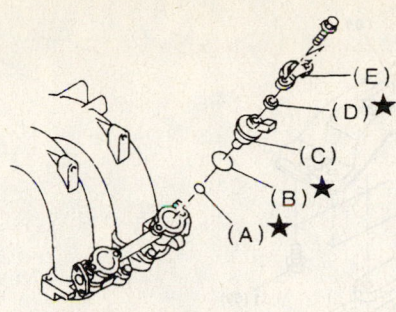

(A) O-ring B
(B) O-ring A
(C) Fuel injector
(D) Insulator
(E) Fuel injector cup

9308XG04

View of fuel injector removal—1998 models

1999–01

1. Before servicing the vehicle, refer to the precautions in the beginning of this section.

2. Properly relieve the fuel system pressure.

3. Remove or disconnect the following:

- Negative battery cable
- Air duct and cleaner assembly
- Resonator chamber
- Spark plug wires No. 1 and 3
- V-belt covers
- Power steering pump belt
- Power steering pipe bracket from manifold
- Power steering pump and seat aside
- Wires from fuel injector
- Injector pipe from intake manifold
- Fuel injector

9308XG03

View of fuel injector removal on 1999–01 models

To install:

4. Install or connect the following:

- Fuel injector
- Injector pipe to intake manifold
- Wires to fuel injector
- Power steering pump
- Power steering pipe bracket to manifold
- Power steering pump belt
- V-belt covers
- Spark plug wires No. 1 and 3
- Resonator camber
- Air duct and cleaner assembly
- Negative battery cable

DRIVE TRAIN

Transmission Assembly

REMOVAL & INSTALLATION

1. Before servicing the vehicle, refer to the precautions in the beginning of this section.

2. On automatic transmission vehicles, drain the automatic transmission fluid and the front differential.

3. Remove or disconnect the following:

- Negative battery cable
- Air intake and chamber, then the chamber stays
- Air cleaner case stay
- Front and rear Oxygen (O_2S) sensor connectors, if equipped
- Transmission harness connector, if equipped with an automatic transmission
- Transmission ground terminal
- Neutral position switch connector, if equipped with a manual transmission
- Backup light switch connector, if equipped with a manual transmission
- 2 Vehicle Speed (VSS) sensor connectors
- Starter
- Pitching stopper

4. On automatic transmission vehicles, remove the timing hole inspection plug. Matchmark the torque converter-to-driveplate and remove the 4 bolts which hold torque converter to driveplate.

5. Remove or disconnect the following:

- Automatic transmission fluid dipstick and tube

- Clutch slave cylinder, on manual transmission vehicles

6. Install engine support assembly ST 41099AA020. (Also available as part no. 927670000).

7. Remove or disconnect the following:

- Bolt securing the right upper side of the transmission to the engine
- Engine undercover
- Front Y-pipe

8. Disconnect connector from rear O_2S sensor

9. Remove or disconnect the following:

- Center exhaust pipe from rear pipe and hanger bolt
- Rear exhaust pipe and heat shield cover
- Hanger bracket from the right side of the transmission
- Transmission cooler lines
- Rear driveshaft, matchmark for reassembly
- Center bearing bracket

➡ **Plug the opening at the rear of the extension housing to prevent oil from flowing out.**

- Shifter stay and rod from the transmission, on manual transmission
- Gear shift cable from the transmission select lever, on automatic transmission
- Swaybar from the transverse link
- Parking brake cable bracket from the transverse link and bolt holding the transverse link to the crossmember on each side, lower the transverse link
- Lower ball joint from knuckle
- Spring pin and separate the halfshaft from the transmission on each side

➡ **Use a small punch to remove the spring pin. Discard old spring pin and always install a new pin.**

10. Disconnect the halfshaft from transmission on each side. Be sure to remove the axle shaft from the transmission by pushing the rear of the tire outward.

11. Remove the engine-to-transmission mounting nuts

12. Support the transmission with a jack.

➡ **Do not place jack under the transmission oil pan, otherwise the oil pan may be damaged.**

13. Remove or disconnect the following:

- Rear transmission crossmember
- Transmission

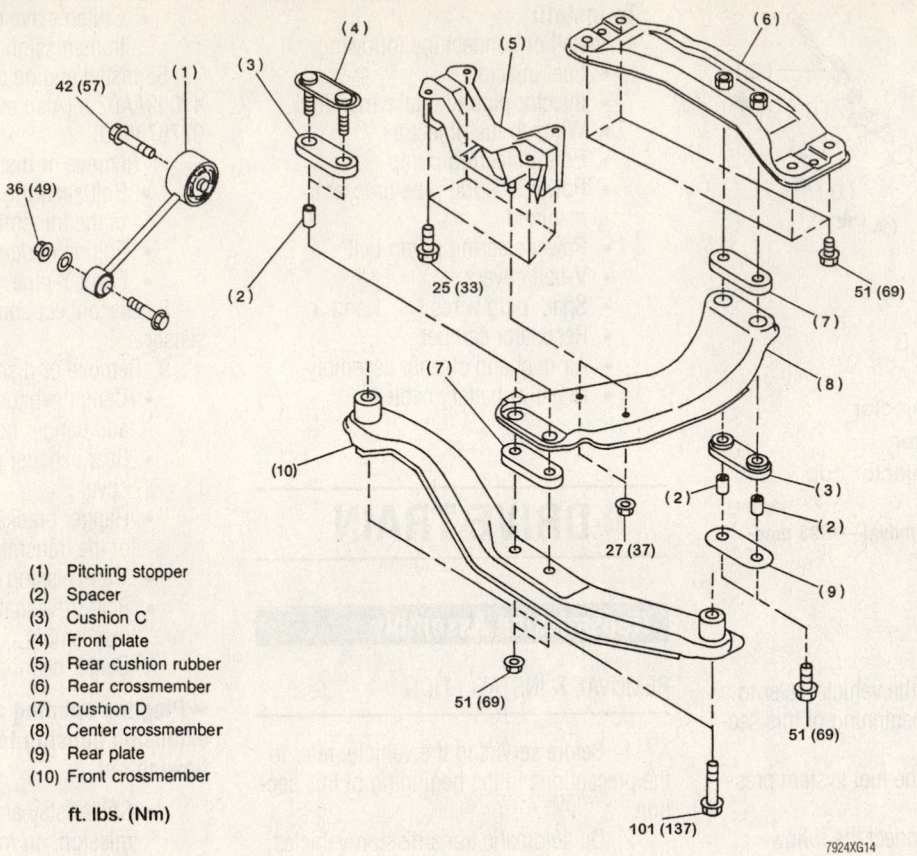

(1) Pitching stopper
(2) Spacer
(3) Cushion C
(4) Front plate
(5) Rear cushion rubber
(6) Rear crossmember
(7) Cushion D
(8) Center crossmember
(9) Rear plate
(10) Front crossmember

ft. lbs. (Nm)

7924XG14

Exploded view of the manual transmission mounting

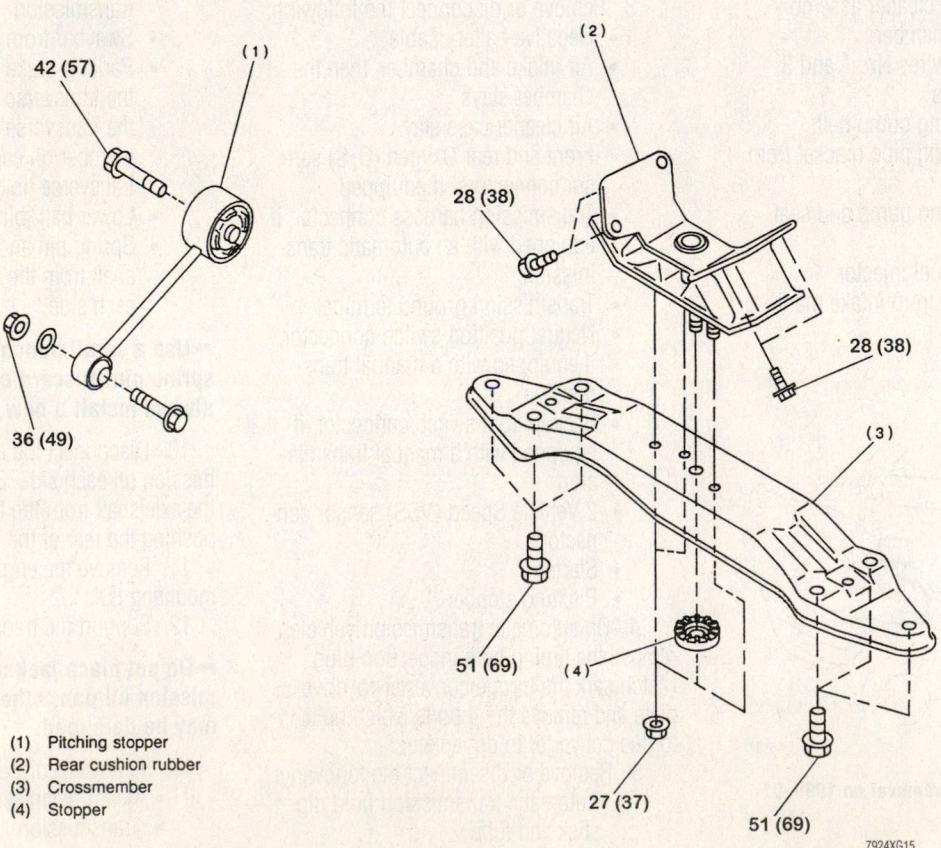

(1) Pitching stopper
(2) Rear cushion rubber
(3) Crossmember
(4) Stopper

7924XG15

Exploded view of the automatic transmission mounting

To install:

14. Install or connect the following:
- Special tool 498277200 to torque converter clutch case
- Transmission to the engine
- Transmission crossmember. Torque the front nuts/bolts to 51 ft. lbs. (69 Nm) and the rear nuts to 101 ft. lbs. (137 Nm), on manual transmissions
- Transmission crossmember. Torque the inner nuts/bolts to 25 ft. lbs. (34 Nm) and the rear nuts to 51 ft. lbs. (69 Nm), on automatic transmissions

15. Remove the transmission jack.
16. Install or connect the following:
- Transmission-to-engine mounting nuts. Torque the nuts/bolts to 37 ft. lbs. (50 Nm).
- Torque converter-to-driveplate bolts on automatic transmission vehicles. Torque the bolts to 18 ft. lbs. (25 Nm).
- Clutch slave cylinder on manual transmission vehicles. Torque the mounting bolts to 27 ft. lbs. (37 Nm).

17. Remove special tool 927670000.
18. Install or connect the following:
- Pitching stopper
- Halfshaft to transmission and spring pin into place

➡**Always use new spring pin. Be sure to align the axle shaft and shaft from the transmission at chamfered holes and install shaft splines correctly.**

- Lower ball joint to knuckle
- Sway bar to the crossmember. Torque the clamp bolts to 18 ft. lbs. (25 Nm).
- Shift control rod, shifter stay to the transmission and the spring, on manual transmission vehicles
- Gear shift cable to the select lever, on automatic transmission vehicles
- Fluid cooler lines
- Driveshaft. Tighten the bolts to 23 ft. lbs. (31 Nm).
- Center bearing bracket. Torque the bolt to 38 ft. lbs. (52 Nm).
- Heat shield cover, if removed
- Center exhaust pipe from rear pipe and hanger bolt
- Rear exhaust pipe and heat shield cover
- Hanger bracket from the right side of the transmission
- Y-pipe with new gaskets and nuts

- Rear O2S sensor connector
- Automatic transmission fluid dipstick tube
- Transmission connector bracket
- Starter. Torque the mounting bolts to 37 ft. lbs. (50 Nm).
- Front and rear O2S sensor connectors
- Transmission harness connector, on automatic transmission vehicles
- Transmission ground terminal
- Neutral position switch connector, on manual transmission vehicles
- Backup light switch connector, on manual transmission vehicles
- 2 VSS connectors
- Air intake and chamber, and the camber stays
- Negative battery cable

19. On automatic transmission vehicles, fill the automatic transmission fluid with Dexron®II or III or equivalent.
20. On manual transmission vehicles, check and fill the transmission with 75W-90 gear oil.
21. Road test the vehicle.

Clutch

ADJUSTMENT

This vehicle is equipped with a hydraulic clutch that is self-adjusting, therefore no adjustment is possible or necessary.

REMOVAL & INSTALLATION

✳✳ CAUTION

The clutch driven disc may contain asbestos, which has been determined to be a cancer-causing agent. Never clean clutch surfaces with compressed air. Avoid inhaling any dust from any clutch surface. When cleaning clutch surfaces, use a commercially available brake cleaning fluid.

1. Before servicing the vehicle, refer to the precautions in the beginning of this section.
2. Remove or disconnect the following:
- Negative battery cable
- Transmission

✳✳ WARNING

Removing the bolts on one side of the pressure plate will warp the pressure plate, rendering it useless.

3. Gradually unscrew the six 6mm bolts that hold the pressure plate assembly on the flywheel. Loosen the bolts only 1 turn at a time, working around the pressure plate. Do not unscrew all the bolts on one side at one time.

4. Remove or disconnect the following:
- Clutch plate and disc
- 2 retaining springs, the throwout bearing and the release fork

➡**Do not disassemble either the clutch cover or disc. Inspect the parts for wear or damage and replace any parts as necessary. Replace the clutch disc if there is any oil or grease on the facing. Do not wash or attempt to lubricate the throwout bearing, because it is sealed and permanently lubricated. If it requires replacement, the bearing may be removed and a new one installed in the holder by means of a press.**

To install:

5. Fit the release fork boot on the front of the transmission housing.
6. Install or connect the following:
- Release fork
- Throwout bearing assembly and secure it with the 2 springs

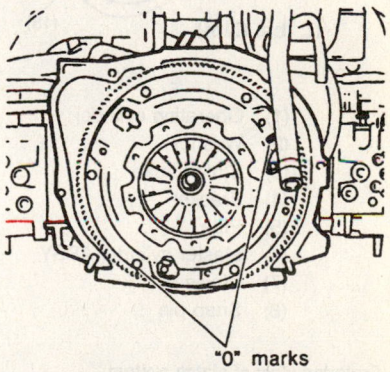

"O" marks

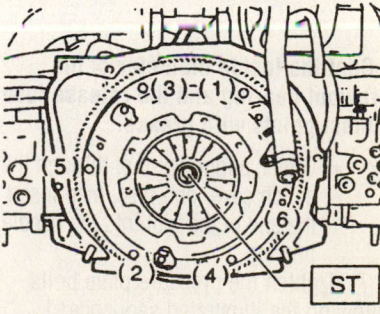

7924XG16

Clutch cover alignment and tightening sequence

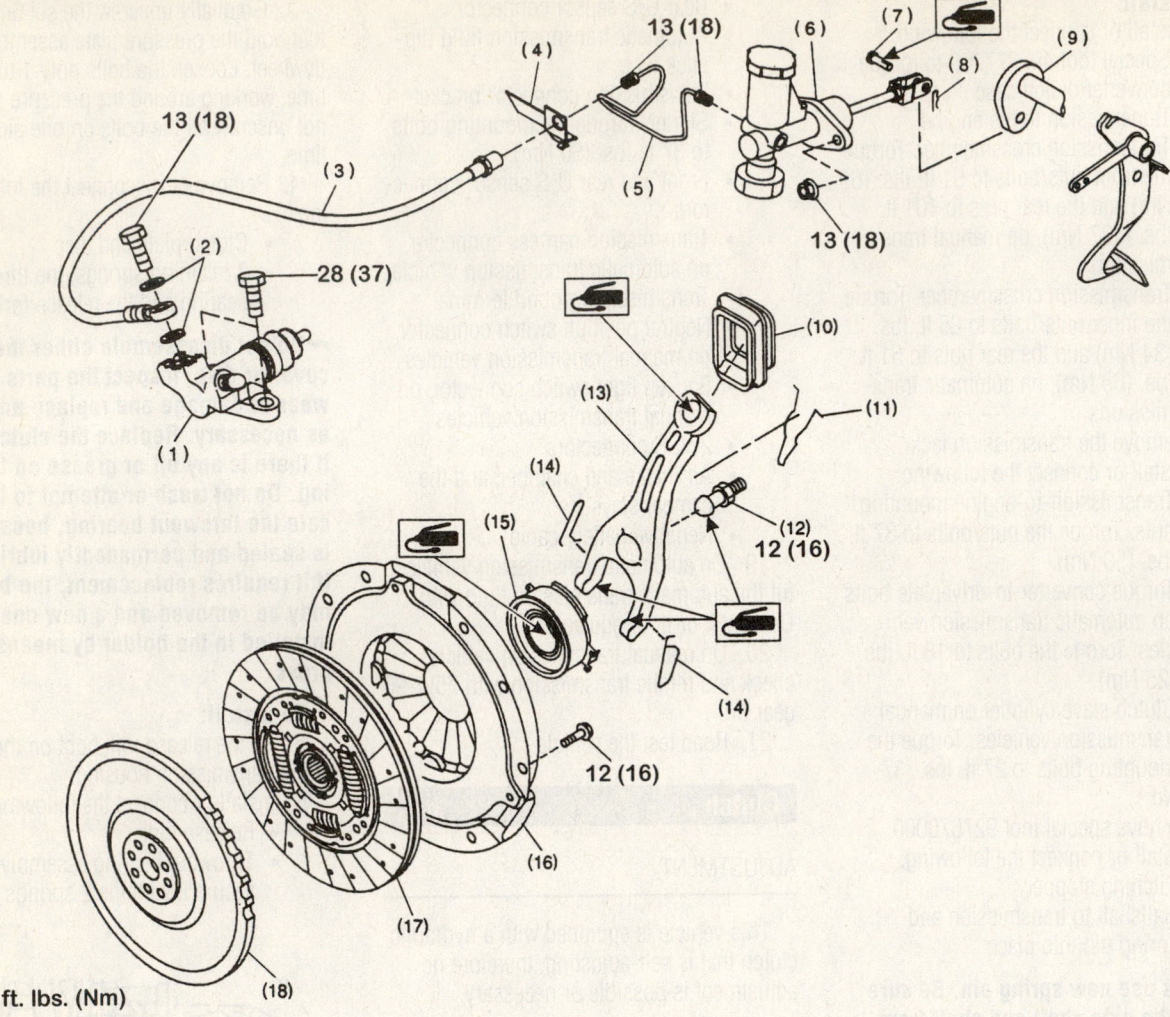

13 (18)

(3)

13 (18)

(2)

28 (37)

(1)

13 (18)

(4)

(5)

13 (18)

(6)

(7)

(8)

(9)

(10)

(13)

(11)

(14)

(12)

12 (16)

(15)

(14)

12 (16)

(16)

(17)

(18)

ft. lbs. (Nm)

7924XG17

(1) Operating cylinder
(2) Washer
(3) Clutch hose
(4) Bracket
(5) Pipe
(6) Master cylinder ASSY
(7) Clevis pin
(8) Snap pin

(9) Lever
(10) Clutch release lever sealing
(11) Retainer spring
(12) Pivot
(13) Release lever
(14) Clip
(15) Release bearing
(16) Clutch cover

(17) Clutch disc
(18) Flywheel

Exploded view of clutch system

➡Coat the inside diameter of the throwout bearing and the release lever contact points with grease.

• Clutch alignment tool through the clutch cover and disc, then insert the end of the tool into the needle bearing

7. Tighten the pressure plate bolts following the illustrated sequence, 1 turn at a time, until the proper torque is reached. Tighten to 12 ft. lbs. (16 Nm).

✳✳ WARNING

When installing the clutch pressure plate assembly, be sure that the O marks on the flywheel and the clutch pressure plate assembly are at least 120 degrees apart. These marks indicate the direction of residual unbalance. Also, be sure that the clutch disc is installed properly, noting the FRONT and REAR markings.

8. Install the transmission.

Hydraulic Clutch System

BLEEDING

➡To properly bleed the system, it must be bled at the slave cylinder and at the damper. Each of these has an air bleeder on it.

1. Before servicing the vehicle, refer to the precautions in the beginning of this section.

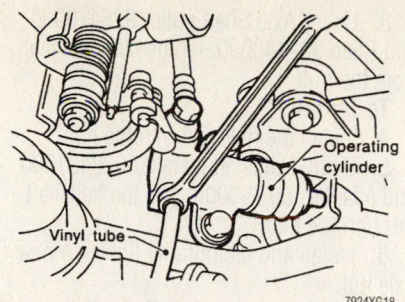

Bleeding the hydraulic clutch at the slave cylinder

2. Connect a vinyl tube to the air bleeder on the damper and put the other end in a jar with clean clutch fluid.

➡ **Do not let the fluid level fall too low**

in the master cylinder. Do not release the pedal with the bleeder open.

3. With the help of an assistant depressing the clutch pedal, slowly open the bleeder valve. Close the bleeder valve and release the pedal. Repeat this process until no air bubbles appear in the jar.

4. Move the tube to the bleeder on the slave cylinder and repeat the process. Check the operation of the clutch after the bleed procedure is complete.

Transfer Case Assembly

REMOVAL & INSTALLATION

The transfer case is an integral part of the transmission.

Halfshafts

REMOVAL & INSTALLATION

Front

1. Before servicing the vehicle, refer to the precautions in the beginning of this section.

2. Remove or disconnect the following:
   - Negative battery cable
   - Wheel
   - Axle nut
   - Stabilizer link from transverse link
   - Transverse link from housing
   - Halfshaft-to-transmission roll pin and discard it
   - Halfshaft from the transmission

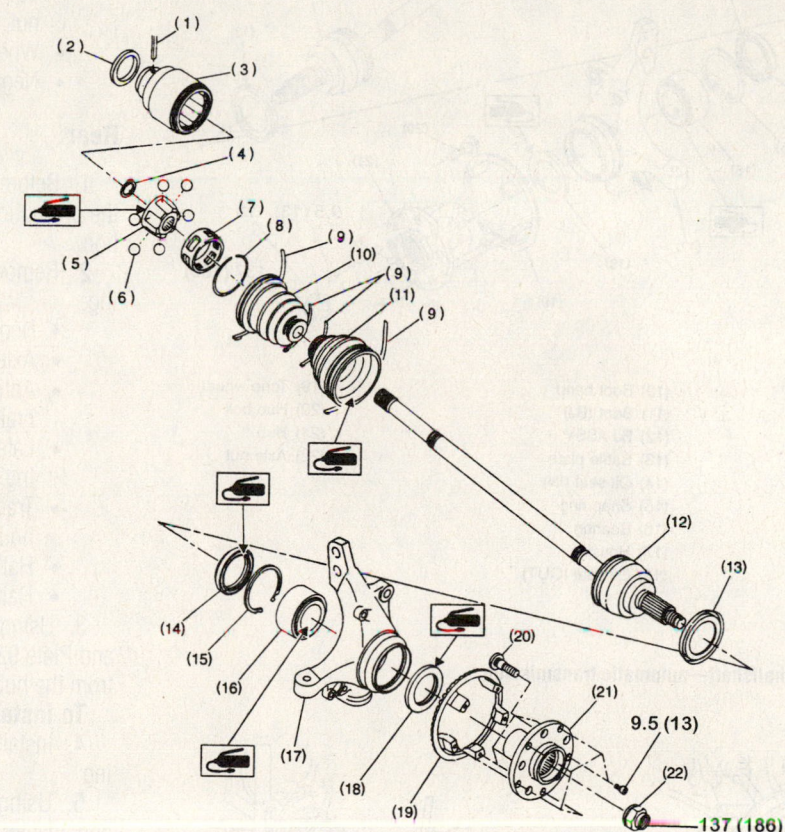

ft. lbs. (Nm)

(1) Spring pin	(10) Boot (DOJ)	(19) Tone wheel
(2) Baffle plate (DOJ)	(11) Boot (BJ)	(20) Hub bolt
(3) Outer race (DOJ)	(12) BJ ASSY	(21) Hub
(4) Snap ring	(13) Baffle plate	(22) Axle nut
(5) Inner race (DOJ)	(14) Oil seal (IN)	
(6) Ball	(15) Snap ring	
(7) Cage	(16) Bearing	
(8) Circlip	(17) Housing	
(9) Boot band	(18) Oil seal (OUT)	

Exploded view of the front halfshaft—manual transmission

Turn to Section 5 for brake system applications

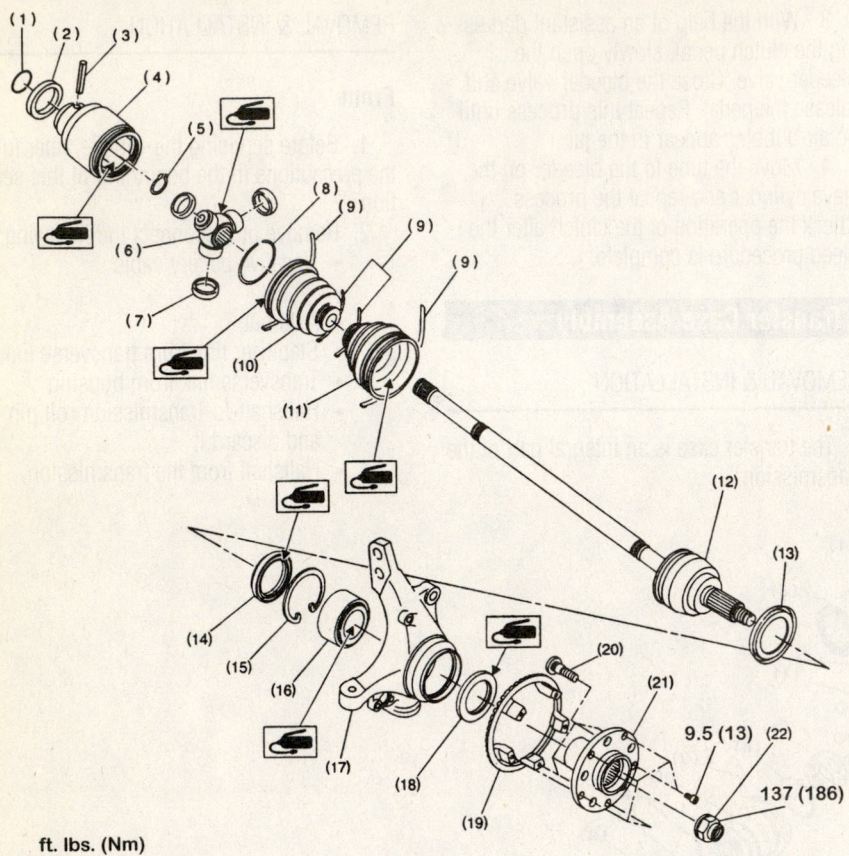

ft. lbs. (Nm)

(1)	O-ring	(10)	Boot band
(2)	Baffle plate (FTJ)	(11)	Boot (BJ)
(3)	Spring pin	(12)	BJ ASSY
(4)	Outer race (FTJ)	(13)	Baffle plate
(5)	Snap ring	(14)	Oil seal (IN)
(6)	Trunnion	(15)	Snap ring
(7)	Free ring	(16)	Bearing
(8)	Circlip	(17)	Housing
(9)	Boot band	(18)	Oil seal (OUT)

(19)	Tone wheel
(20)	Hub bolt
(21)	Hub
(22)	Axle nut

7924XG20

Exploded view of the front halfshaft—automatic transmission

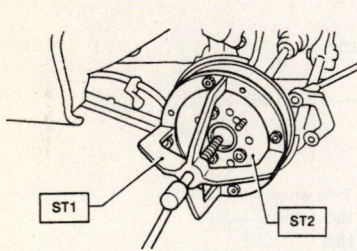

ST1 926470000   AXLE SHAFT PULLER
ST2 927140000   PLATE

7924XG29

Be sure not to damage the threads when removing the front or rear halfshafts

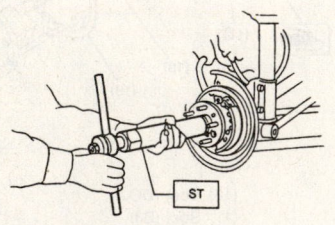

ST1 922431000   AXLE SHAFT INSTALLER
ST2 927390000   ADAPTER

7924XG30

To avoid using a hammer when installing the halfshafts, use the proper tools as shown

3. Using Axle Shaft puller 926470000 and Plate 927140000, remove the halfshaft from the hub.

To install:

4. Install the halfshaft into the hub.

5. Using Halfshaft installer 922431000 and adapter 927390000, pull the halfshaft through the hub.

6. Install and temporarily tighten a new axle nut.

7. Install or connect the following:

- Halfshaft onto the transmission, by aligning the halfshaft roll pin hole
- New roll pin
- Transverse link to housing. Torque the nut to 36 ft. lbs. (49 Nm).
- Stabilizer link
- New axle nut. Torque the nut to 197 ft. lbs. (186 Nm) and stake the nut.
- Wheel
- Negative battery cable

Rear

1. Before servicing the vehicle, refer to the precautions in the beginning of this section.

2. Remove or disconnect the following:

- Negative battery cable
- Axle nut
- Anti-lock Brakes (ABS) and parking brake cable bracket
- Lateral link assembly to rear housing
- Trailing link assembly from the rear housing bolt and nut
- Halfshaft-to-differential roll pin
- Halfshaft from the differential

3. Using Axle Shaft puller 926470000 and Plate 927140000, remove the halfshaft from the hub.

To install:

4. Install the halfshaft into the rear housing.

5. Using Halfshaft Installer 922431000 and adapter 927390000, pull the halfshaft into place.

6. Install and temporarily tighten a new axle nut.

7. Install or connect the following:

- Halfshaft-to-differential align roll pin holes and slide the halfshaft onto the splines
- New roll pin
- Trailing link assembly to the rear housing. Torque bolt and new nut to 84 ft. lbs. (113 Nm).
- Trailing link assembly-to-rear

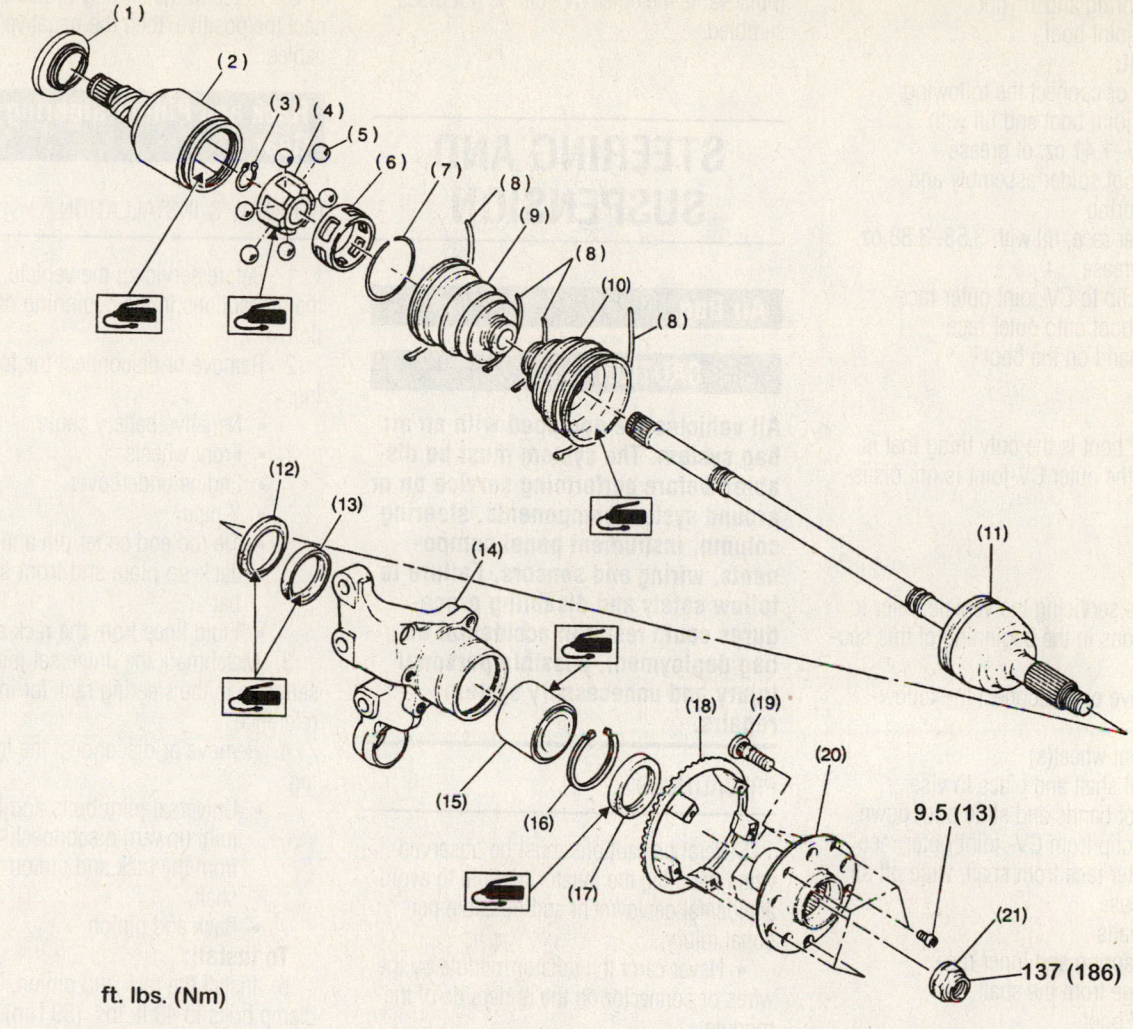

ft. lbs. (Nm)

(1) Baffle plate (DOJ)
(2) Outer race (DOJ)
(3) Snap ring
(4) Inner race
(5) Ball
(6) Cage
(7) Circlip
(8) Boot band
(9) Boot (DOJ)

(10) Boot (BJ)
(11) BJ ASSY
(12) Oil seal (IN. No. 2)
(13) Oil seal (IN. No. 3)
(14) Housing
(15) Bearing
(16) Snap ring
(17) Oil seal (OUT)
(18) Tone wheel

(19) Hub bolt
(20) Hub
(21) Axle nut

7924XG21

Exploded view of the rear halfshaft

housing bolt and nut. Torque the new nut to 101 ft. lbs. (137 Nm).
- Stabilizer bracket
- ABS and parking brake cable bracket
- New axle nut. Torque the nut to 137 ft. lbs. (186 Nm).
- Wheel
- Negative battery cable

CV-Joints

REMOVAL & INSTALLATION

Front

INNER

1. Before servicing the vehicle, refer to the precautions in the beginning of this section.

2. Remove or disconnect the following:
- Front wheel(s)
- Halfshaft and place in vise
- Boot bands and slide boot down
- Circlip from CV-joint outer race
- Outer race from shaft, wipe off all grease

3. Matchmark Tri-pot spider assembly for reassembly.

- Snapring and Tri-pot
- CV-joint boot

To install:

4. Install or connect the following:
   - CV-joint boot and fill with 1.06–1.41 oz. of grease
   - Tri-pot spider assembly and snapring
   - Outer race, fill with 3.53–3.88 oz. of grease
   - Circlip to CV-joint outer race
5. Slide boot onto outer race
6. New band on the boot

OUTER

The outer boot is the only thing that is replaceable the outer CV-joint is not disassembled.

Rear

1. Before servicing the vehicle, refer to the precautions in the beginning of this section.
2. Remove or disconnect the following:
   - Front wheel(s)
   - Half shaft and place in vise
   - Boot bands and slide boot down
   - Circlip from CV- joint outer race
   - Outer race from shaft, wipe off all grease
   - 6 balls
   - Snapring and inner race
   - Cage from the shaft
   - CV boot

To install:

3. Install or connect the following:
   - CV-joint boot and fill with 0.76–1.06 oz. of grease
   - Cage to the shaft with the cut out portion facing the shaft end
   - Inner race and snapring
4. Install the cage to the inner race.

➡ **Fit the cage with the protruded part aligned with the track on the inner race then turn by a half pitch.**

5. Install the outer race and snapring; then, fill with 2.82–3.17 oz. of grease
6. Coat the cage pockets with grease.
7. Install or connect the following:
   - 6 balls into cage, align the inner race and cage
   - Outer race and circlip
8. Slide boot on to outer race
9. New band on the boot

OUTER

The outer boot is the only thing that is replaceable the outer CV-joint is not disassembled.

STEERING AND SUSPENSION

Air Bag

✳✳ CAUTION

All vehicles are equipped with an air bag system. The system must be disabled before performing service on or around system components, steering column, instrument panel components, wiring and sensors. Failure to follow safety and disabling procedures could result in accidental air bag deployment, possible personal injury and unnecessary system repairs.

PRECAUTIONS

Several precautions must be observed when handling the inflator module to avoid accidental deployment and possible personal injury.

- Never carry the inflator module by the wires or connector on the underside of the module.
- When carrying a live inflator module, hold securely with both hands, and ensure that the bag and trim cover are pointed away.
- Place the inflator module on a bench or other surface with the bag and trim cover facing up.
- With the inflator module on the bench, never place anything on or close to the module, which may be thrown in the event of an accidental deployment.

DISARMING

1. Before servicing the vehicle, refer to the precautions in the beginning of this section.
2. Disconnect the negative battery cable.
3. Disconnect the positive battery cable.
4. Wait more than 20 seconds to allow the air bag system to deplete its backup power before starting work.

5. To rearm the air bag system, reconnect the positive, then the negative battery cables.

Rack and Pinion Steering Gear

REMOVAL & INSTALLATION

1. Before servicing the vehicle, refer to the precautions in the beginning of this section.
2. Remove or disconnect the following:
   - Negative battery cable
   - Front wheels
   - Engine undercover
   - Y-pipe
   - Tie rod end cotter pin and nut
   - Jack-up plate and front sway bar
   - Fluid lines from the rack and pinion
3. Matchmark the universal joint to the serration in the steering rack for installation reference.
4. Remove or disconnect the following:
   - Universal joint bolts and lift the joint upward disconnecting it from the rack and pinion shaft.
   - Rack and pinion

To install:

5. Install the rack and pinion. Torque the clamp bolts to 43 ft. lbs. (59 Nm).
6. Align the steering rack to the universal joint. Push the long yoke of the joint all the way into the serrated position of the steering shaft, setting the bolt hole in the cut-out. Pull the short yoke all the way out of the serrated portion of the rack and pinion, setting the bolt hole in the cut-out. Insert the bolt through the short yoke. Pull the yoke and ensure the bolt is properly engaged in the cut-out. Fasten the short yoke side with the spring washer and bolt, then fasten the yoke side. Tighten the bolts to 17 ft. lbs. (24 Nm).
7. Install or connect the following:
   - Tie rod ends to the steering knuckle
   - Sway bar and jack-up plate
   - Y-pipe with new gaskets and nuts
   - Engine undercover
   - Wheels
8. Fill and bleed the steering system.

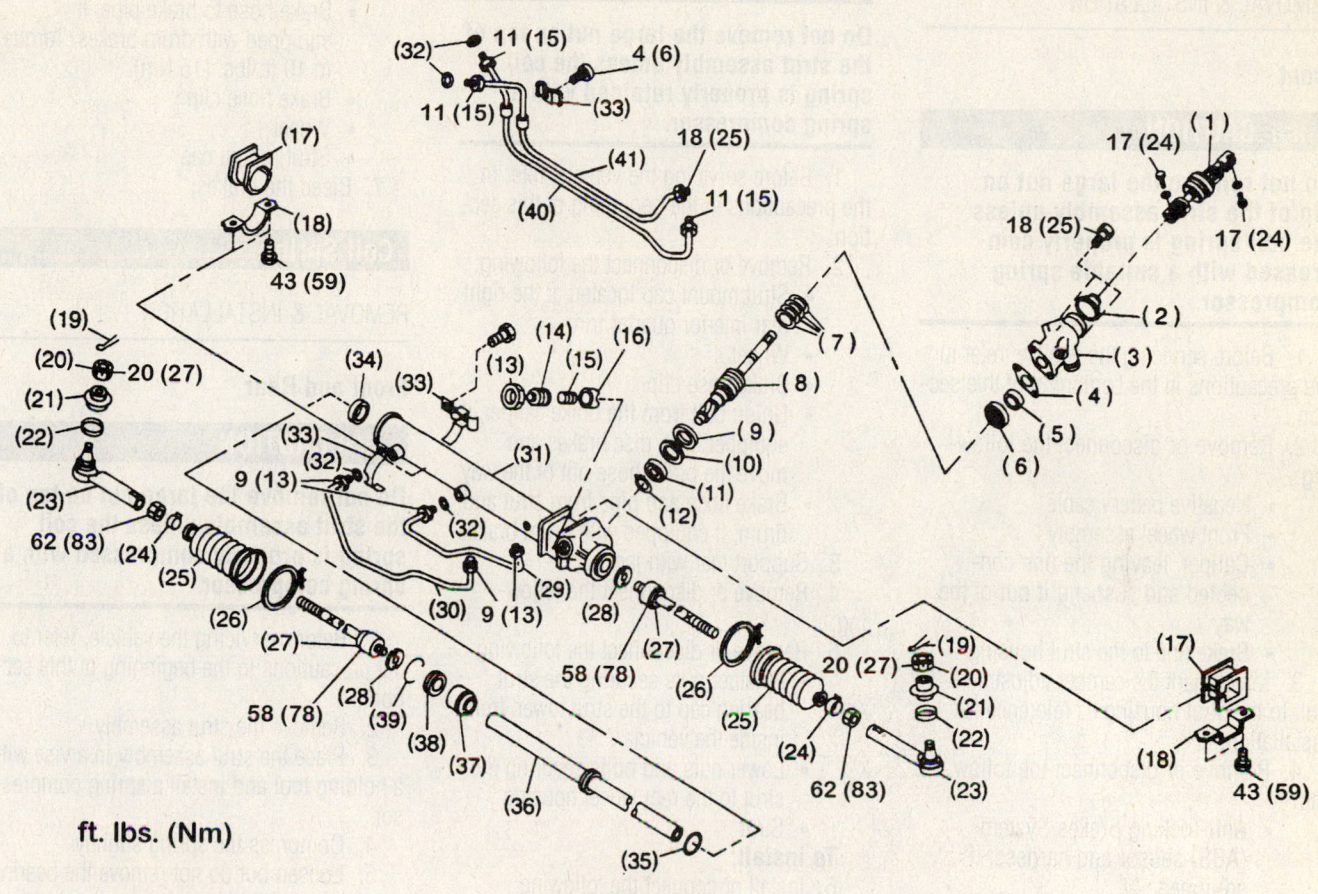

ft. lbs. (Nm)

(1) Universal joint
(2) Dust cover
(3) Valve housing
(4) Gasket
(5) Oil seal
(6) Special bearing
(7) Seal ring
(8) Pinion and valve ASSY
(9) Oil seal
(10) Back-up washer
(11) Ball bearing
(12) Snap ring
(13) Lock nut
(14) Adjusting screw
(15) Spring
(16) Sleeve
(17) Adapter
(18) Clamp

(19) Cotter pin
(20) Castle nut
(21) Dust cover
(22) Clip
(23) Tie-rod end
(24) Clip
(25) Boot
(26) Band
(27) Tie-rod
(28) Lock washer
(29) Pipe B
(30) Pipe A
(31) Housing ASSY
(32) O-ring
(33) Clamp
(34) Oil seal
(35) Piston ring
(36) Rack

(37) Rack bushing
(38) Rack stopper
(39) Circlip
(40) Pipe E
(41) Pipe F

Exploded view of the rack and pinion steering gear

7924XG22

Strut

REMOVAL & INSTALLATION

Front

> ✳✳ **CAUTION**
>
> **Do not remove the large nut on top of the strut assembly unless the coil spring is properly compressed with a suitable spring compressor.**

1. Before servicing the vehicle, refer to the precautions in the beginning of this section.
2. Remove or disconnect the following:

- Negative battery cable
- Front wheel assembly
- Caliper, leaving the line connected and suspend it out of the way
- Brake line to the strut housing

3. Matchmark the camber adjustment bolt to the strut housing as reference for installation.
4. Remove or disconnect the following:

- Anti-locking Brakes System (ABS) sensor and harness, if equipped
- Strut from the steering knuckle. Notice that the shaft of the top bolt is not round.
- Strut from the body in the engine compartment
- Strut and coil spring assembly

To install:

5. Install the strut and coil assembly. Torque the upper strut retainer nuts to 15 ft. lbs. (20 Nm).
6. Align matchmark on camber adjustment bolt and strut housing.
7. Install or connect the following:

- Lower strut nuts and bolts. Tighten the nuts, while securing the bolts to 112 ft. lbs. (152 Nm).
- ABS sensor and harness. Torque the bolt to 24 ft. lbs. (32 Nm), if equipped.
- Brake line to the strut
- Caliper
- Front wheel
- Negative battery cable

8. Check and adjust the front end alignment.

Rear

> ✳✳ **CAUTION**
>
> **Do not remove the large nut on top of the strut assembly unless the coil spring is properly retained with a spring compressor.**

1. Before servicing the vehicle, refer to the precautions in the beginning of this section.
2. Remove or disconnect the following:

- Strut mount cap located at the right rear interior quarter trim
- Wheel
- Brake hose clip
- Union bolt from the brake caliper, if equipped with disc brakes and move the brake hose out of the way
- Brake hose and pipe from strut and drum, if equipped with drum brakes

3. Support rear with jack.
4. Remove or disconnect the following:
5. Remove or disconnect the following:

- Retainer nuts securing the strut bearing cap to the strut tower, from inside the vehicle
- Lower nuts and bolts securing the strut to the rear wheel housing
- Strut

To install:

6. Install or connect the following:

- Strut on to the vehicle, making sure to position the strut with the "4WD" mark on the strut mount facing the outside of the vehicle as shown in the illustration. Torque the retaining nuts to 15 ft. lbs. (20 Nm).
- Strut and mount cap. Torque the strut mount cap bolts to 14.5 ft. lbs. (20 Nm).
- Strut to the rear wheel knuckle assembly. Torque the retainer nuts/bolts to 145 ft. lbs. (196 Nm).

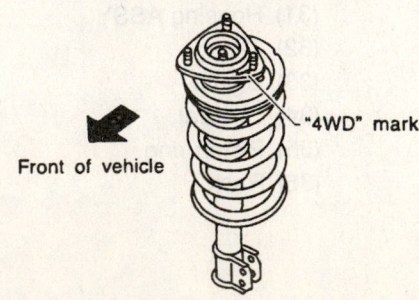

Front of vehicle ← "4WD" mark

7924XG31

Position the upper strut bearing as shown

- Union bolt, if equipped with disc brakes. Torque the bolt and to 13 ft. lbs. (18 Nm).
- Brake hose to brake pipe, if equipped with drum brakes. Torque to 10 ft. lbs. (15 Nm).
- Brake hose clip
- Wheel
- Strut mount cap

7. Bleed the brakes.

Coil Spring

REMOVAL & INSTALLATION

Front and Rear

> ✳✳ **CAUTION**
>
> **Do not remove the large nut on top of the strut assembly unless the coil spring is properly compressed with a spring compressor.**

1. Before servicing the vehicle, refer to the precautions in the beginning of this section.
2. Remove the strut assembly.
3. Place the strut assembly in a vise with a holding tool and install a spring compressor.
4. Compress the spring slightly.
5. Loosen but do not remove the bearing cap locknut.
6. Unload the spring seat using the spring compressor, then remove the locknut.
7. Remove or disconnect the following:

- Strut bearing cap, mounting insulator bracket and upper spring seat
- Coil spring and compressor. If the spring is being replaced, slowly release the spring from the compressor and compress the new coil spring.
- Strut boot and rebound bumper from the strut, inspect and replace if worn
- Strut retainer nut and the strut insert from the assembly

To install:

8. Install or connect the following:

- Strut into the chamber
- Retainer nut. Tighten the nut until snug.
- Rebound bumper and the boot to the strut piston rod
- Coil spring on the strut assembly
- Upper spring seat, mounting insulator and bearing cap

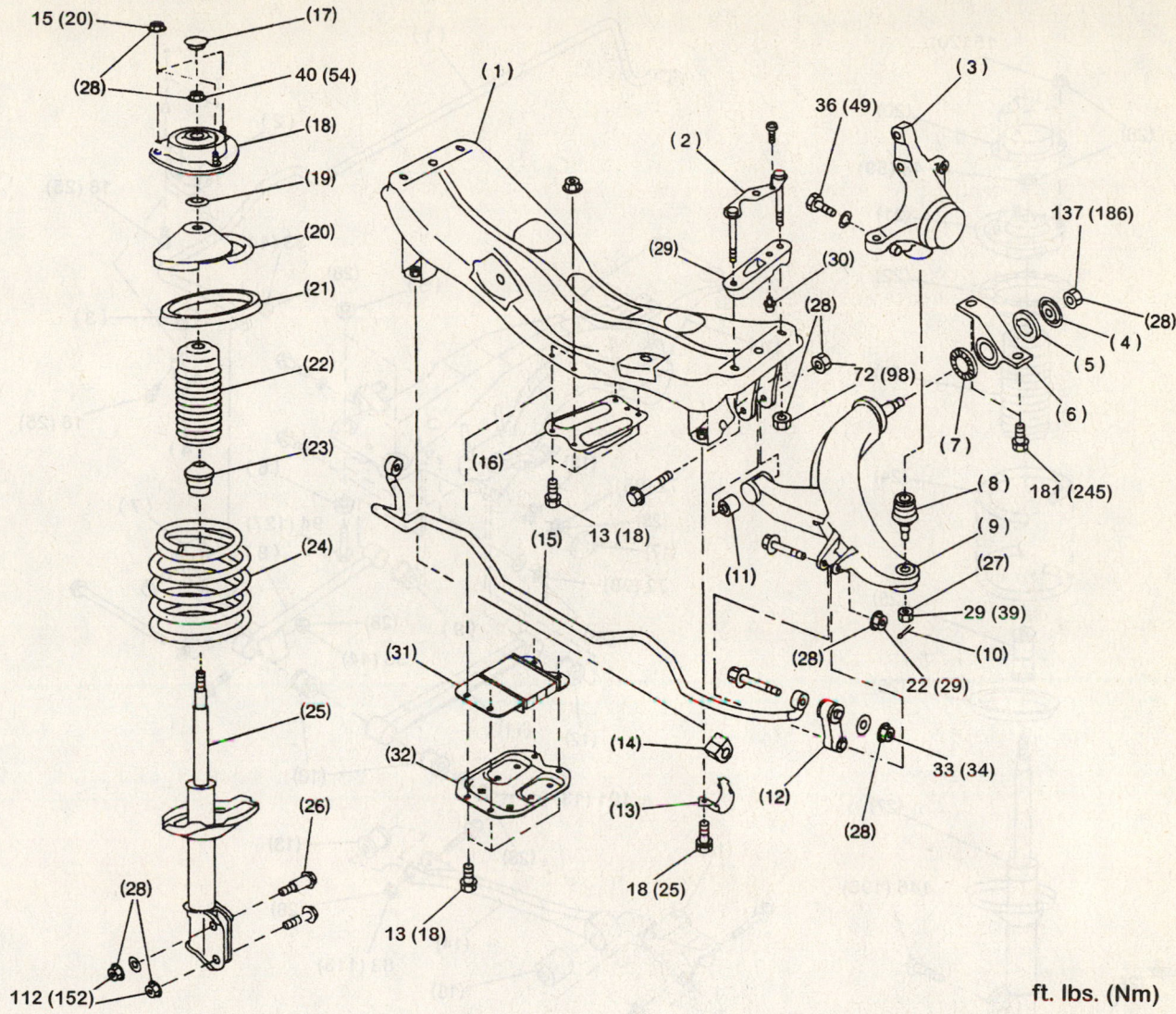

ft. lbs. (Nm)

Exploded view of the front suspension

(1)	Front crossmember	(17)	Dust seal
(2)	Bolt ASSY	(18)	Strut mount
(3)	Housing	(19)	Spacer
(4)	Washer	(20)	Upper spring seat
(5)	Stopper rubber (Rear)	(21)	Rubber seat
(6)	Rear bushing	(22)	Dust cover
(7)	Stopper rubber (Front)	(23)	Helper
(8)	Ball joint	(24)	Coil spring
(9)	Transverse link	(25)	Damper strut
(10)	Cotter pin	(26)	Adjusting bolt
(11)	Front bushing	(27)	Castle nut
(12)	Stabilizer link	(28)	Self-locking nut
(13)	Clamp	(29)	Adapter front crossmember
(14)	Bushing	(30)	Clip
(15)	Stabilizer	(31)	Dynamic damper (MT model)
(16)	Jack-up plate (Except MT model)	(32)	Jack-up plate (MT model)

7924XG23

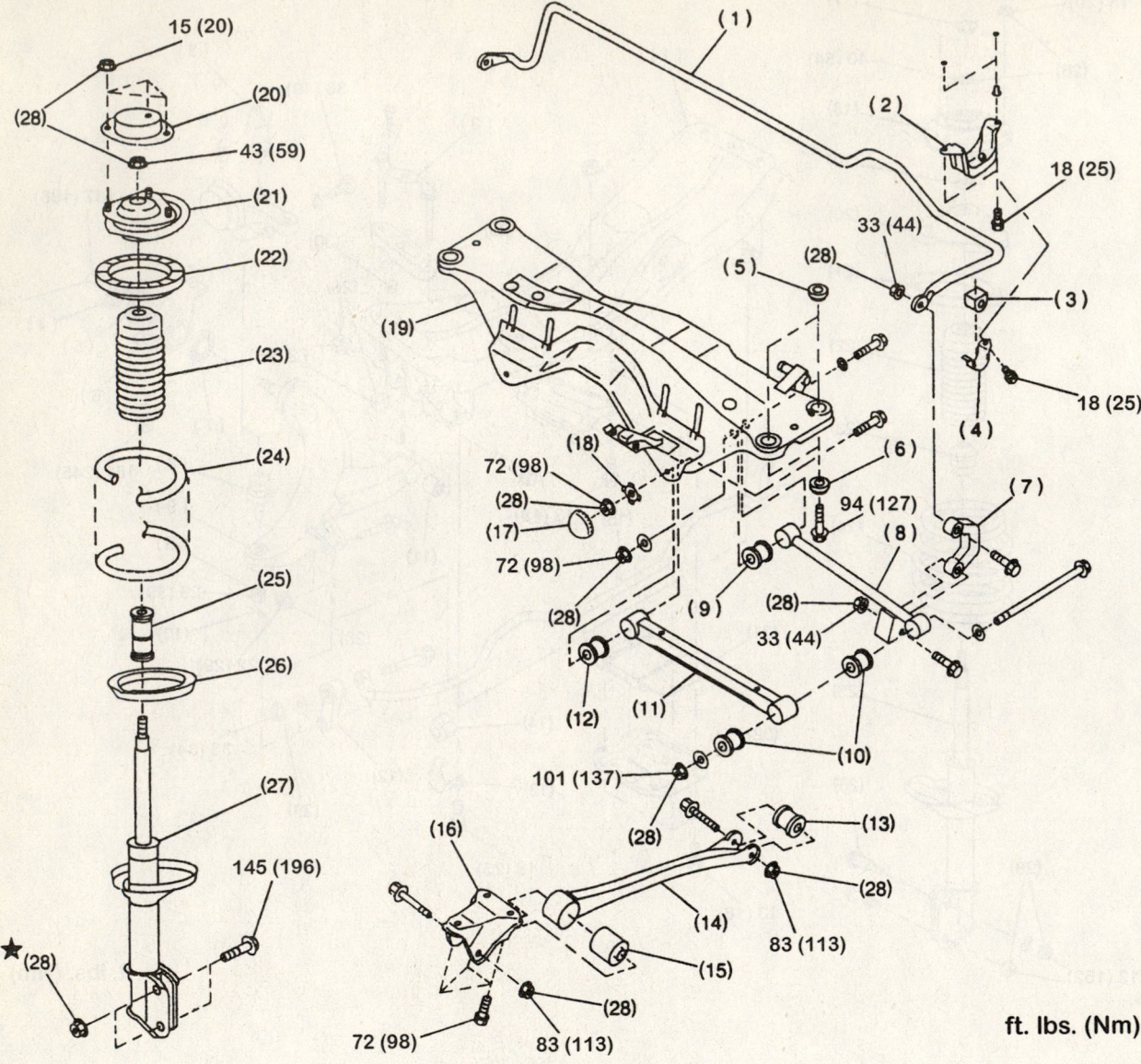

ft. lbs. (Nm)

(1) Stabilizer	(15) Trailing link front bushing
(2) Stabilizer bracket	(16) Trailing link bracket
(3) Stabilizer bushing	(17) Cap (Protection)
(4) Clamp	(18) Washer
(5) Floating bushing	(19) Rear crossmember
(6) Stopper	(20) Strut mount cap
(7) Stabilizer link	(21) Strut mount
(8) Rear lateral link	(22) Rubber seat upper
(9) Bushing (C)	(23) Dust cover
(10) Bushing (A)	(24) Coil spring
(11) Front lateral link	(25) Helper
(12) Bushing (B)	(26) Rubber seat lower
(13) Trailing link rear bushing	(27) Damper strut
(14) Trailing link	(28) Self-locking nut

Exploded view of the rear suspension

7924XG24

- Locknut. Tighten it to 36–43 ft. lbs. (47–56 Nm).
- Spring compressor from the coil spring
- Strut

Lower Ball Joint

REMOVAL & INSTALLATION

1. Before servicing the vehicle, refer to the precautions in the beginning of this section.
2. Remove or disconnect the following:
   - Negative battery cable
   - Front wheel
   - Ball joint castle nut cotter pin, discard the cotter pin
   - Castle nut
   - Ball joint from the lower control arm assembly
   - Ball joint from the steering knuckle

To install:
3. Install or connect the following:
   - Ball joint to the steering knuckle. Torque the bolt to 36 ft. lbs. (49 Nm).
   - Ball joint to the lower control arm. Torque the castle nut to 29 ft. lbs. (39 Nm). Then, tighten the castle nut an additional 60 degrees until the slot in the castle nut is aligned with the cotter pin hole in the ball joint.
   - New cotter pin
   - Wheel
   - Negative battery cable

Lower Control Arm

REMOVAL & INSTALLATION

1. Before servicing the vehicle, refer to the precautions in the beginning of this section.
2. Remove or disconnect the following:
   - Wheel assembly
   - Stabilizer link
   - Ball joint from housing
   - Mounting bolts
   - Control arm

To install:
3. Install or connect the following:
   - Control arm to stabilizer. Torque the nut/bolt to 22 ft. lbs. (29 Nm).
   - Control arm to crossmember. Torque the nut/bolt to 72 ft. lbs. (98 Nm).

- Control arm to rear mount. Torque the bolts to 181 ft. lbs. (245 Nm).
- Ball joint to housing, Torque the nut to 36 ft. lbs. (49 Nm).
- Wheel assembly

CONTROL ARM BUSHING REPLACEMENT

Front Bushing

1. Before servicing the vehicle, refer to the precautions in the beginning of this section.
2. Remove or disconnect the following:
   - Wheel
   - Control arm
3. Press the bushing out using Installer/Remover tool 927680000
To install:
4. Press the bushing in using Installer/Remover tool 927680000
5. Install or connect the following:
   - Control arm
   - Wheel

Rear Bushing

1. Before servicing the vehicle, refer to the precautions in the beginning of this section.
2. Remove or disconnect the following:
   - Wheel
   - Control arm and matchmark the bushing for reassembly
   - Nut and bushing
To install:
3. Install or connect the following:
   - Bushing into control arm and align the matchmark. Torque the nut to 137 ft. lbs. (186 Nm).
   - Control arm
   - Wheel

Wheel Bearings

ADJUSTMENT

The wheel bearings are not adjustable.

REMOVAL & INSTALLATION

Front

1. Before servicing the vehicle, refer to the precautions in the beginning of this section.
2. Remove the steering knuckle assembly.
3. Position the steering knuckle in a soft-jawed vise.

4. Press the hub from the steering knuckle. If the inner bearing race remains in the hub, press it out.
5. Remove or disconnect the following:
   - Rotor shield
   - Inner and outer seals
   - Snapring from the steering knuckle
6. Press the inner bearing race to remove the outer bearing.
7. Remove the Anti-lock Brakes (ABS) tone ring, if equipped
8. Press the wheel lugs from the hub.

➡**To prevent deforming the hub, do not hammer the lugs out.**

To install:
9. Press new wheel lugs into the hub.
10. If equipped, clean all foreign material from the hub and tone ring. Install the tone ring.
11. Clean the inside of the steering knuckle.
12. Remove the plastic lock from the inner race and press a new greased bearing into the hub by pressing the outer race.
13. Install the snapring into its groove.
14. Press a new outer oil seal until it contacts the bottom of the housing.
15. Press a new inner oil seal until it contacts the circlip.
16. Apply grease to the oil seal lips.
17. Install the rotor shield and tighten the bolts to 10 ft. lbs. (14 Nm).
18. Attach the hub to the steering knuckle.
19. Press a new bearing into the hub by driving the inner race.
20. Install the steering knuckle on the vehicle.

Rear

1. Before servicing the vehicle, refer to the precautions in the beginning of this section.
2. Disconnect the negative battery cable.
3. Loosen the parking brake adjustment.
4. Remove or disconnect the following:
   - Wheel
   - Axle nut
   - Caliper, leaving the line connected if equipped with disc brakes and suspend it aside, then remove the rotor
   - Drum and brake line, if equipped with drum brakes
   - Parking brake cable
   - Rear stabilizer from lateral link

Turn to Section 5 for brake system applications

ST1 927080000 HUB STAND
ST2 927420000 HUB REMOVER

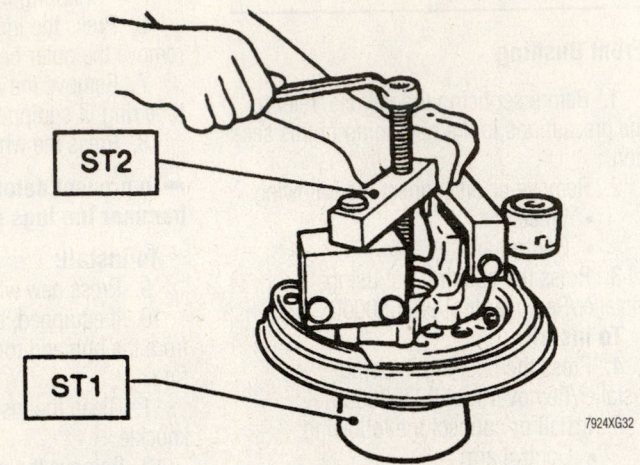

ST2

ST1

7924XG32

Use the proper tools to separate the hub from the housing to prevent damage

- Trailing link to the housing
- Lateral link to the housing
- Halfshaft
- Anti-lock Brakes (ABS), speed sensor from the backing plate, if equipped
- Strut from the housing
- Housing assembly

5. Using hub stand 92708000 and Hub Remover 927420000

6. Remove or disconnect the following:
- Hub from the rear housing
- Backing plate from the housing.

- Outer, inner and sub oil seals.
- Snapring

7. Remove the bearing by pressing the inner race.

To install:

8. Clean the housing thoroughly.

➡**Do not remove the plastic lock from the inner race when installing the bearing.**

9. Install the new bearing into the housing by pressing the outer race.

10. Pack the bearing with grease.

11. Install the snapring.

12. Using installer 927460000 seal driver, press in a new outer seal until it comes in contact with the snapring.

13. Using installer 927450000 seal driver, press in a new inner seal until it contacts the bottom.

14. Install or connect the following:
- New sub oil seal, apply grease to the oil seal lip
- Backing plate. Torque the bolts to 38 ft. lbs. (52 Nm).

15. Using installer 927450000 bearing driver, press in the hub into the housing.

16. Install or connect the following:
- Housing to the strut. Torque the bolts to 108 ft. lbs. (147 Nm).
- Halfshaft
- Lateral link to the housing. Torque the bolt and new nut to 101 ft. lbs. (137 Nm).
- Trailing link to the housing. Torque the bolt and new nut to 94 ft. lbs. (127 Nm).
- Stabilizer to rear lateral link
- Parking brake cable and brake
- Brake line, if equipped with drum brakes
- Rotor and caliper, if equipped with disc brakes
- ABS speed sensor, if equipped
- New axle nut and tighten it to 137 ft. lbs. (186 Nm). Stake the nut.
- Wheel
- Negative battery cable

17. Adjust the parking brake cable.

TOYOTA

T-100 • Tacoma • 4Runner

34

PRECAUTIONS

Before servicing any vehicle, please be sure to read all of the following precautions, which deal with personal safety, prevention of component damage, and important points to take into consideration when servicing a motor vehicle:

• Never open, service or drain the radiator or cooling system when the engine is hot; serious burns can occur from the steam and hot coolant.

• Observe all applicable safety precautions when working around fuel. Whenever servicing the fuel system, always work in a well-ventilated area. Do not allow fuel spray or vapors to come in contact with a spark, open flame or excessive heat (a hot drop light, for example). Keep a dry chemical fire extinguisher near the work area. Always keep fuel in a container specifically designed for fuel storage; also, always properly seal fuel containers to avoid the possibility of fire or explosion. Refer to the additional fuel system precautions later in this section.

• Fuel injection systems often remain pressurized, even after the engine has been turned **OFF**. The fuel system pressure must be relieved before disconnecting any fuel lines. Failure to do so may result in fire and/or personal injury.

• Brake fluid often contains polyglycol ethers and polyglycols. Avoid contact with the eyes and wash your hands thoroughly after handling brake fluid. If you do get brake fluid in your eyes, flush your eyes with clean, running water for 15 minutes. If eye irritation persists, or if you have taken brake fluid internally, IMMEDIATELY seek medical assistance.

• The EPA warns that prolonged contact with used engine oil may cause a number of skin disorders, including cancer! You should make every effort to minimize your exposure to used engine oil. Protective gloves should be worn when changing oil. Wash your hands and any other exposed skin areas as soon as possible after exposure to used engine oil. Soap and water, or waterless hand cleaner should be used.

• All new vehicles are now equipped with an air bag system. The system must be disabled before performing service on or around system components, steering column, instrument panel components, wiring and sensors. Failure to follow safety and disabling procedures could result in acci-dental air bag deployment, possible personal injury and unnecessary system repairs.

• Always wear safety goggles when working with, or around, the air bag system. When carrying a non-deployed air bag, be sure the bag and trim cover are pointed away from your body. When placing a non-deployed air bag on a work surface, always face the bag and trim cover upward, away from the surface. This will reduce the motion of the module if it is accidentally deployed. Refer to the additional air bag system precautions later in this section.

• Clean, high quality brake fluid from a sealed container is essential to the safe and proper operation of the brake system. You should always buy the correct type of brake fluid for your vehicle. If the brake fluid becomes contaminated, completely flush the system with new fluid. Never reuse any brake fluid. Any brake fluid that is removed from the system should be discarded. Also, do not allow any brake fluid to come in contact with a painted surface; it will damage the paint.

• Never operate the engine without the proper amount and type of engine oil; doing so WILL result in severe engine damage.

• Timing belt maintenance is extremely important! Many models utilize an interference-type, non-freewheeling engine. If the timing belt breaks, the valves in the cylinder head may strike the pistons, causing potentially serious (also time-consuming and expensive) engine damage. Refer to the maintenance interval charts in the front of this manual for the recommended replacement interval for the timing belt, and to the timing belt section for belt replacement and inspection.

• Disconnecting the negative battery cable on some vehicles may interfere with the functions of the on-board computer system(s) and may require the computer to undergo a relearning process once the negative battery cable is reconnected.

• When servicing drum brakes, only disassemble and assemble one side at a time, leaving the remaining side intact for reference.

ENGINE REPAIR

Distributor

REMOVAL

1. Before servicing the vehicle, refer to the precautions in the beginning of this section.

2. Remove or disconnect the following:
   • Negative battery cable
   • Distributor connectors
   • Distributor cap, without disconnecting the secondary leads and position it aside

3. Matchmark the rotor with the distribu-

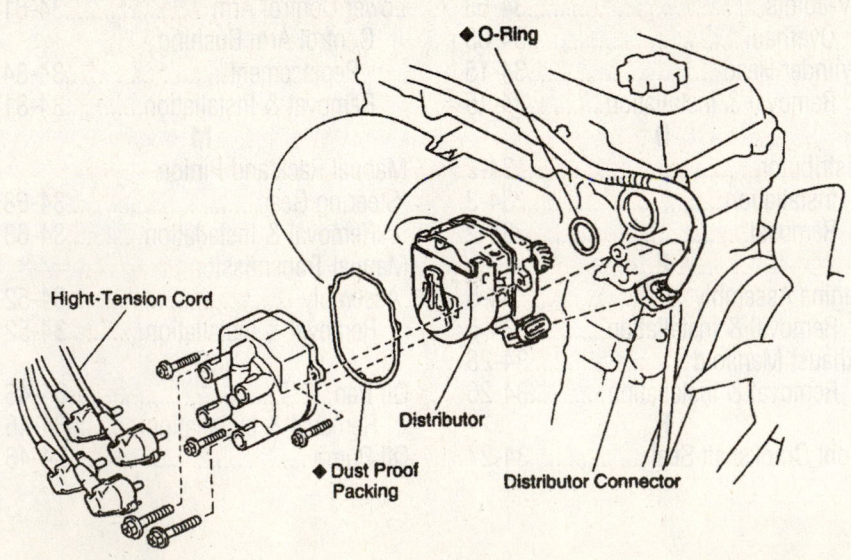

Exploded view of the distributor and related components—Tacoma with 2.4L (2RZ-FE) engine

7924YG99

tor housing and housing with the cylinder block.

4. Remove the distributor hold-down bolt and pull the distributor from the cylinder block.

INSTALLATION

Timing Not Disturbed

1. Install or connect the following:
   - New O-ring to the distributor and lubricate it with engine oil
   - Distributor into the cylinder block, by aligning the matchmarks made during removal
   - Distributor hold-down bolt
   - Distributor cap and distributor connector
   - Negative battery cable
2. Start the engine and allow normal operating temperature to be reached.
3. Check and if necessary, adjust the ignition timing.

Timing Disturbed

1. Install a new O-ring to the distributor and lubricate it with engine oil.
2. Remove the No. 1 cylinder spark plug and perform the following:
   a. Place a finger or compression gauge over the spark plug hole.
   b. Turn the crankshaft until compression starts to build up. Continue turning the crankshaft until the crankshaft pulley groove aligns with the timing mark **0** on the timing chain cover.
3. If necessary, remove the valve cover and perform the following:
   a. Check that the timing marks with 1 and 2 dots are aligned on the camshaft sub-gears.
   b. If not, turn the crankshaft 1 revolution (360 degrees) and align the crankshaft pulley groove with the timing mark **0** on the timing chain cover.
4. Align the protrusion of the distributor housing with the groove on the driven gear.
5. Install or connect the following:
   - Distributor into the cylinder block
   - Distributor hold-down bolt
   - Valve cover
   - Distributor cap and distributor connector
   - Negative battery cable
6. Start the engine and allow normal operating temperature to be reached.
7. Check and if necessary, adjust the ignition timing.

Alternator

REMOVAL

On some models, the alternator is mounted very low on the engine. On these models, it may be necessary to remove the gravel shield and work from beneath the vehicle in order to gain access to the alternator. Replacing the alternator while the engine is cold is recommended. A hot engine can result in personal injury.

2.4L and 2.7L Engines

Remove or disconnect the following:
- Negative battery cable
- Alternator wiring
- Alternator lockbolt, pivot bolt, nut and adjusting bolt
- Drive belt
- Wiring harness with the clip
- Alternator

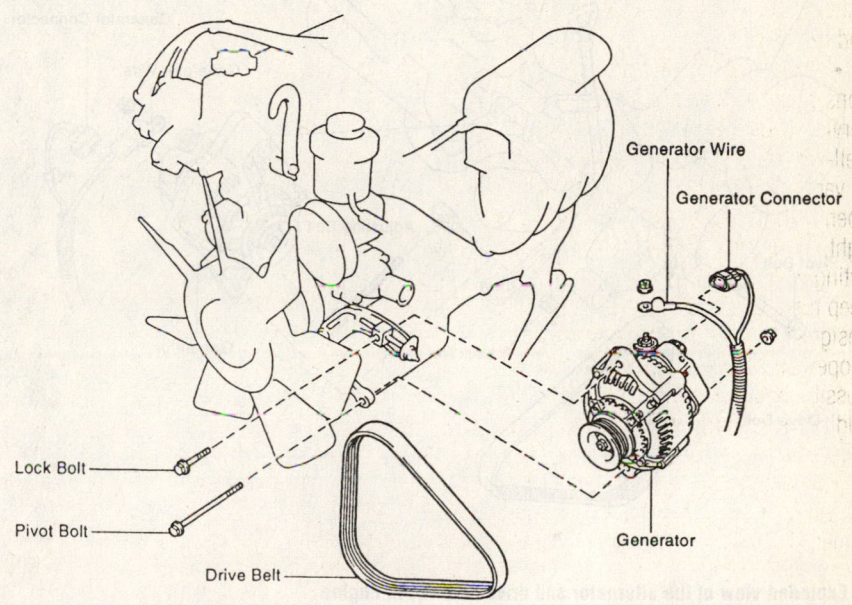

Exploded view of the alternator and drive belt—2.4L and 2.7L engines

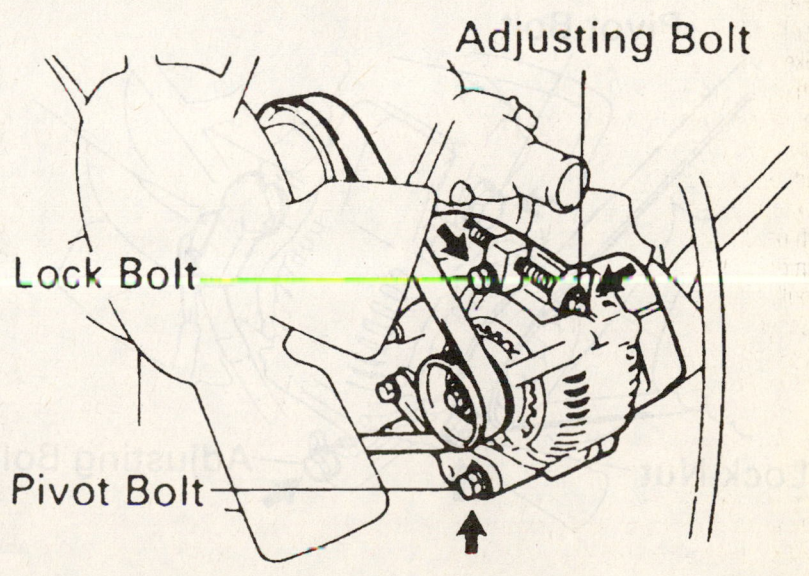

Locations of the adjusting, pivot and lockbolts—2.4L and 2.7L engines

For complete service labor times order Nichols' Chilton Labor Guide Manual

3.4L Engine

1. Remove or disconnect the following:
   - Negative battery cable
   - Alternator wiring
   - Alternator locknut, pivot bolt, nut and adjusting bolt
   - Drive belt
   - Alternator

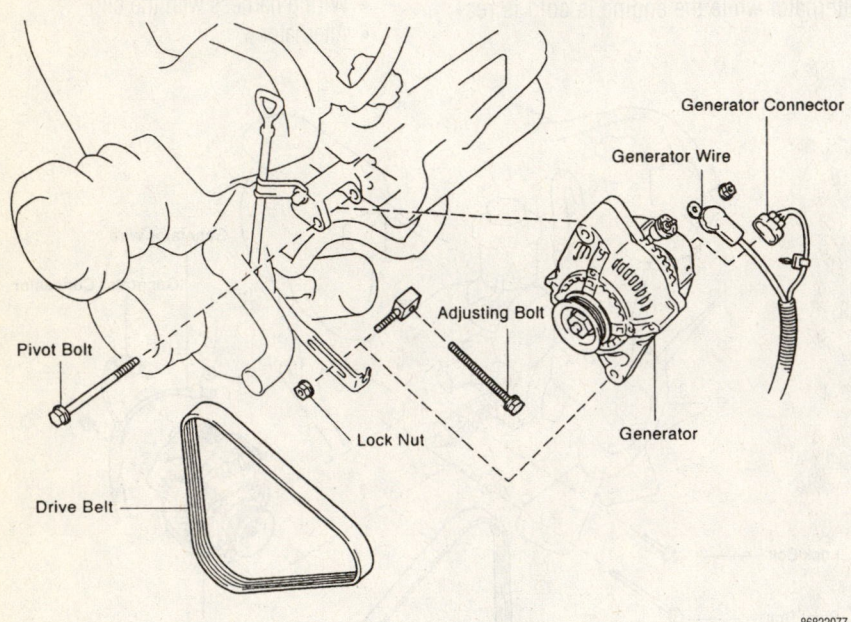

Exploded view of the alternator and drive belt—3.4L Engine

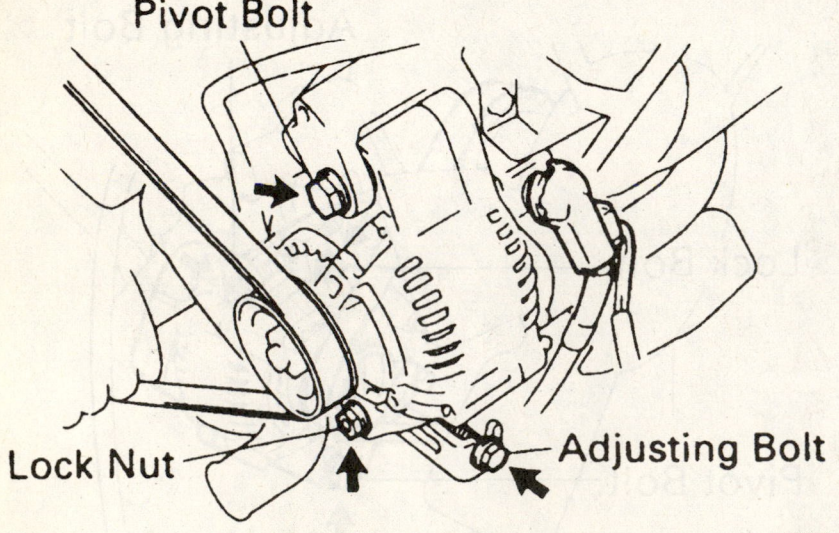

Locations of the adjusting and pivot bolts and the locknut—3.4L Engine

INSTALLATION

2.4L and 2.7L Engines

Install or connect the following:
- Alternator
- Drive belt; adjust it to the proper tension. Tighten the lockbolt to 21 ft. lbs. (29 Nm) and the pivot bolt to 43 ft. lbs. (59 Nm).
- Wire harness with clip
- Alternator wiring. Tighten the nut to 7 ft. lbs. (10 Nm).
- Rubber boot over the terminal
- Wiring harness connector
- Negative battery cable

3.4L Engine

Install or connect the following:
- Alternator
- Drive belt. Tighten the locknut 25 ft. lbs. (33 Nm) and the pivot bolt 38 ft. lbs. (51 Nm).
- Alternator wiring
- Negative battery cable

Ignition Timing

ADJUSTMENT

The 1997 4Runner/Tacoma models equipped with the 2.7L (3rz-fe) engine, all 1997 3.4L (5VZ-FE) engines, and all 1998–01 engines use a distributorless ignition system referred to as Direct Ignition System (DIS). All spark advance is permanently set by the PCM.

2.4L (2RZ-FE) Engine

➡ **The ignition timing is not adjustable but can be checked.**

1. Before servicing the vehicle, refer to the precautions in the beginning of this section.
2. Warm the engine to normal operating temperature.
3. Attach a hand-held tester to the Data Link Connector 3 (DLC3) under the dashboard on the driver's side.
4. Jumper terminals T_{E1} and E_1 of the DLC1.
5. Check the idle speed.
6. Aim the timing light at the timing indicator and check the ignition timing. Timing should be between 3–7 degrees BTDC at idle.
7. For a further check on ignition timing, disconnect the hand-held tester from the DLC3 and disconnect the jumper wire from the DLC1.
8. Point the timing light at the crankshaft pulley and read the timing. Timing should be between 7–18 degrees BTDC at idle.
9. Remove timing light from the engine.

Engine Assembly

REMOVAL & INSTALLATION

2.4L (2RZ-FE) Engine

1. Before servicing the vehicle, refer to the precautions in the beginning of this section.

2. Properly relieve the fuel system pressure.

3. Turn the ignition switch **OFF**.

4. Remove or disconnect the following:
- Battery cables; negative cable first
- Hood by matchmarking the hood hinges
- Engine undercover

5. Drain the engine oil, transmission oil and cooling system.

6. Remove or disconnect the following:
- Radiator
- Drive belts
- Loosen the lockbolt and adjusting bolt to the idler pulley, if equipped with power steering
- Loosen the idler pulley nut and adjusting bolt, if equipped with air conditioning
- Fan (with fan clutch), water pump pulley and fan shroud
- Accelerator cable from the throttle body, if equipped with a manual transaxle
- Accelerator and throttle cables from the throttle body, if equipped with an automatic transaxle
- Actuator cover and cruise control cable from the actuator, if equipped with cruise control
- Air cleaner cap, Mass Air Flow (MAF) and resonator
- Air cleaner case
- Intake air connector
- Air conditioning compressor and bracket, if equipped with air conditioning
- Alternator wires from the alternator
- Heater hoses at the cowl panel
- Brake booster vacuum hose
- EVAP hose
- Vacuum hose, if equipped with 4WD with Automatic Disconnecting Differential (ADD)
- Both power steering hoses, if equipped with power steering
- Fuel return hose
- Fuel inlet hose

7. Remove the power steering pump as follows:

- Nut and power steering pulley
- Both bolts and the power steering pump

8. Disconnect the Engine Control Module (ECM) wiring from the ECM as follows:
- Right front door scuff plate
- Cowl panel side trim by removing the clip
- 4 ECM electrical connectors.

9. Detach the engine wiring harness and connectors as follows:
- Igniter connector
- Ground strap from the cowl top panel
- Both engine wiring harness clamps
- Engine wiring harness retainer to the cowl panel nuts and pull out the engine wiring harness from the vehicle

10. Disconnect the front exhaust pipe from the exhaust manifold and catalytic converter.

11. If equipped with manual transmission, remove the shift lever assembly as follows:
- Shift lever knob
- 4 screws and shift lever boot
- 6 bolts, shift lever assembly and baffle

12. Remove or disconnect the following:
- Driveshaft
- Speedometer cable from the transmission
- Clutch release cylinder, if equipped with manual transmission
- Cross-shaft, if equipped with automatic transmission
- Wires at the starter

13. Position a jack and wooden block under the transmission and remove the rear engine mounting bracket.

14. Attach an engine hoist to the engine hangers.

15. Remove or disconnect the following:
- Nuts and bolts from the engine mounts
- Engine/transmission assembly

To install:

16. Install or connect the following:
- Engine/transmission assembly, by keeping the engine level, while aligning the engine mounts
- Engine mount fasteners but do not fully tighten them

17. Position a jack and wooden block under the transmission.

18. Install the rear engine mounting bracket. Tighten the frame bolts to 43 ft. lbs. (58 Nm) and the mount bolts to 13 ft. lbs. (18 Nm).

19. Remove the jack and engine hoist.

20. Install or connect the following:
- Tighten the engine mounts to 28 ft. lbs. (38 Nm).
- Starter wires to the starter
- Clutch release cylinder, if equipped with manual transmission
- Cross-shaft, if equipped with automatic transmission
- Speedometer to the transmission
- Driveshaft

21. If equipped with manual transmission, install the shift lever assembly as follows:
- Baffle and shift lever assembly with the 6 bolts
- Shift lever boot with the 4 screws
- Shift lever knob
- Front exhaust pipe to the exhaust manifold
- All wires and connectors
- Cowl side trim and clip
- Front door scuff plate
- Alternator wires to the alternator

22. Install the power steering pump as follows:
- Power steering pump to the bracket with the 2 bolts. Tighten the bolts to 43 ft. lbs. (58 Nm).
- Power steering pulley with the nut. Tighten the nut to 32 ft. lbs. (43 Nm).

23. Install or connect the following:
- All hoses
- Compressor, if equipped with air conditioning
- Intake air connector. Tighten the 2 bolts to 13 ft. lbs. (18 Nm).
- Water pump pulley, fan shroud, fan (with fan clutch) and alternator drive belt.
- Drive belt, if equipped with air conditioning
- Power steering drive belt
- Accelerator cable to the throttle body, if equipped with manual transmission
- Accelerator and throttle cables to the throttle body, if equipped with automatic transmission
- Air cleaner case
- MAF meter, resonator and air cleaner cap
- Radiator with the support tabs through the radiator service holes. Tighten the bolts to 108 inch lbs. (13 Nm).
- Lower radiator hose to the radiator
- Oil cooler hoses to the radiator, if

Timing belt service is covered in Section 4 of this manual

equipped with an automatic transmission
- No. 2 fan shroud.
- Radiator reservoir hose to the radiator
- Upper radiator hose to the radiator
- Air pipe
- Radiator grille to the vehicle with the 11 clips
- Both fillers
- Clearance lights to the grille with the 4 bolts and 2 clips
- Both battery cables

24. Fill the engine oil, engine coolant and transmission oil.
25. Start the engine and check for leaks.
26. Check ignition timing.
27. Install or connect the following:
- Engine undercover
- Hood

28. Road test the vehicle and check all fluids.

2.7L (3RZ-FE) Engine

T-100

1. Before servicing the vehicle, refer to the precautions in the beginning of this section.
2. Properly relieve the fuel system pressure.
3. Turn the ignition switch **OFF**.
4. Remove or disconnect the following:
- Battery cables; negative cable first
- Hood
- Battery and battery tray

5. Drain the engine oil, transmission oil and cooling system.
6. Remove or disconnect the following:
- Expansion tank
- Radiator
- Air cleaner cap
- Mass Air Flow (MAF) meter and resonator
- Air cleaner case
- Accelerator cable from the throttle body, if equipped with a manual transaxle
- Accelerator and throttle cables from the throttle body, if equipped with a automatic transaxle
- Intake air connector
- Air conditioning compressor and bracket, if equipped with air conditioning

7. Disconnect the following hoses:
- Brake booster vacuum hose
- EVAP hose
- 2 power steering hoses
- Fuel return hose
- Fuel inlet hose
- Alternator wires

8. Remove the power steering pump as follows:
- Nut and power steering pulley
- 2 bolt and the power steering pump

9. Disconnect the ECM wiring from the ECM as follows:
- 4 screws to the right front door scuff plate
- Scuff plate
- Cowl panel side trim by removing the clip
- 4 ECM electrical connectors

10. Detach the engine wiring harness and connectors from the vehicle as follows:
- Igniter
- Ground strap from the cowl top panel
- 4 engine wiring harness clamps
- Engine wiring harness from the vehicle

11. If equipped with manual transmission, remove the shift lever assembly as follows:
- Shift lever knob
- 4 screws and shift lever boot
- 6 bolts, shift lever assembly and baffle

12. Remove the sway bar as follows:
- Nuts and cushions holding the sway bar to the lower control arms
- Sway bar bolts, brackets and the sway bar from the suspension

13. Remove or disconnect the following:
- Driveshaft
- Speedometer cable from the transmission
- Front exhaust pipe from the exhaust manifold and catalytic converter
- Clutch release cylinder, if equipped with manual transmission
- Cross-shaft, if equipped with automatic transmission
- Starter wires

14. Position a jack and wooden block under the transmission.
15. Remove the rear engine mounting bracket.
16. Attach a engine hoist to the engine hangers.
17. Remove or disconnect the following:
- Nuts and bolts from the engine mounts
- Engine/transmission assembly

To install:

18. Attach the engine hoist to the engine hangers.
19. Install or connect the following:
- Engine/transmission assembly

➡**Keep the engine level, while aligning the engine mounts.**

- Engine mount fasteners but do not fully tighten

20. Position a jack and wooden block under the transmission.
21. Install the install the rear engine mounting bracket. Tighten the frame bolts to 42 ft. lbs. (58 Nm) and the mount bolts to 13 ft. lbs. (18 Nm).
22. Remove the jack and engine hoist.
23. Install or connect the following:
- Tighten the engine mounts to 28 ft. lbs. (38 Nm).
- Starter wires
- Clutch release cylinder, if equipped with manual transmission
- Cross-shaft, if equipped with automatic transmission
- Front exhaust pipe to the exhaust manifold
- Speedometer
- Driveshaft.

24. Install the sway bar as follows:
- Both sway bar bushings and brackets to the frame. Tighten the bolts to 22 ft. lbs. (30 Nm).
- Sway bar to the lower control arms with the brackets and cushions. Tighten the nuts to 108 inch lbs. (13 Nm).

25. If equipped with manual transmission, install the shift lever assembly as follows:
- Baffle and shift lever assembly with the 6 bolts
- Shift lever boot with the 4 screws
- Shift lever knob

26. Reconnect all engine wiring harness.
27. Install or connect the following:
- Cowl side trim and clip
- Front door scuff plate and 4 screws

28. Install the power steering pump as follows:
- Power steering pump to the bracket. Tighten the 3 bolts to 43 ft. lbs. (58 Nm).
- Power steering pulley. Tighten the nut to 32 ft. lbs. (43 Nm).

29. Install or connect the following:
- All hoses previously removed
- Engine heater hoses at the cowl panel

30. If equipped with air conditioning, install the compressor as follows:
- Air conditioning compressor bracket. Tighten the 4 bolts to 32 ft. lbs. (44 Nm).
- Air conditioning compressor to the bracket. Tighten the 4 bolts to 18 ft. lbs. (25 Nm).

31. Install or connect the following:
- Intake air connector. Tighten the 2 bolts to 13 ft. lbs. (18 Nm).

- Accelerator cable to the throttle body, if equipped with manual transmission
- Accelerator and throttle cables to the throttle body, if equipped with automatic transmission
- Air cleaner case
- MAF meter, resonator and air cleaner cap
- Radiator
- Adjust the air conditioning compressor drive belt, if equipped with A/C
- Adjust the power steering drive belt
- Radiator reservoir hose to the radiator
- Upper radiator hose to the radiator
- Radiator grille with the 11 clips and 4 screws
- Clearance lights to the grille with the 4 bolts to each light
- Battery and battery clamp
- Radiator expansion tank

32. Fill the engine oil, engine coolant and transmission oil.

33. Connect the battery cables to the battery

34. Start the engine and check for leaks.

35. Check ignition timing.

36. Install or connect the following:
- Engine undercover
- Hood

37. Road test the vehicle and check all fluids.

TACOMA

1. Before servicing the vehicle, refer to the precautions in the beginning of this section.

2. Properly relieve the fuel system pressure.

3. Turn the ignition switch **OFF**.

4. Remove or disconnect the following:
- Battery cables; negative cable first
- Hood
- Engine undercover

5. Drain the engine oil, transmission oil and cooling system.

6. Remove or disconnect the following:
- Radiator
- Idler pulley and drive belt, if equipped with power steering
- Idler pulley nut/bolt and drive belt, if equipped with air conditioning
- Alternator drive belt, fan (with fan clutch), water pump pulley and fan shroud
- Accelerator cable from the throttle

body, if equipped with a manual transaxle
- Accelerator and throttle cables from the throttle body, if equipped with a automatic transaxle
- Actuator cover and the cruise control cable from the actuator, if equipped with cruise control
- Air cleaner cap
- Mass Air Flow (MAF) meter and resonator
- Air cleaner case
- Intake air connector
- Air conditioning compressor and bracket, if equipped with air conditioning
- Alternator wires
- Heater hoses at the cowl panel

7. Disconnect the following hoses:
- Brake booster vacuum hose
- Evaporative Emissions (EVAP) hose
- Vacuum hose, if equipped with 4WD with Automatic Disconnecting Differential (ADD)
- Both power steering hoses, if equipped with power steering
- Fuel return hose
- Fuel inlet hose

8. Remove the power steering pump as follows:
- Nut and power steering pulley
- Power steering pump

9. Disconnect the Engine Control Module (ECM) wiring from the ECM as follows:
- 4 screws to the right front door scuff plate
- Scuff plate
- Cowl panel side trim by removing the clip
- 4 ECM electrical connectors

10. Detach the engine wiring harness and connectors from the vehicle as follows:
- Igniter
- Ground strap from the cowl top panel
- 2 engine wiring harness clamps
- Engine wiring harness retainer to cowl panel nut and wiring harness

11. Disconnect the front exhaust pipe from the exhaust manifold and catalytic converter.

12. If equipped with manual transmission, remove the shift lever assembly as follows:
- Shift lever knob
- 4 screws and shift lever boot

- 6 bolts, shift lever assembly and baffle

14. Remove or disconnect the following:
- Driveshaft
- Speedometer cable from the transmission
- Clutch release cylinder, if equipped with manual transmission
- Cross-shaft, If equipped with automatic transmission
- Wires at the starter

15. Position a jack and wooden block under the transmission.

16. Remove the rear engine mounting bracket.

17. Attach an engine hoist to the engine hangers.

18. Remove or disconnect the following:
- Nuts and bolts from the engine mounts
- Engine/transmission

To install:

19. Attach the engine hoist to the engine hangers.

20. Install or connect the following:
- Engine/transmission assembly

➡ **Keep the engine level, while aligning the engine mounts.**

- Engine mount fasteners but do not fully tighten them
- Position a jack and wooden block under the transmission
- Rear engine mounting bracket. Tighten the frame bolts to 19 ft. lbs. (26 Nm) and the mount bolts to 13 ft. lbs. (18 Nm).

21. Remove the jack and engine hoist.

22. Install or connect the following:
- Tighten the engine mounts to 28 ft. lbs. (38 Nm).
- Starter wires
- Clutch release cylinder, if equipped with manual transmission
- Cross-shaft, if equipped with automatic transmission
- Speedometer to the transmission
- Driveshaft

23. If equipped with manual transmission, install the shift lever assembly as follows:
- Baffle and shift lever assembly with the 6 bolts
- Shift lever boot with the 4 screws
- Shift lever knob

24. Install or connect the following:
- Front exhaust pipe to the exhaust manifold
- Engine wiring harness

- Cowl side trim and clip
- Front door scuff plate
- Alternator wires

25. Install the power steering pump as follows:
- Power steering pump to the bracket. Tighten the 2 bolts to 43 ft. lbs. (58 Nm).
- Power steering pulley. Tighten the nut to 32 ft. lbs. (43 Nm).

26. Install or connect the following:
- All hoses
- Heater hoses at the cowl panel
- Compressor, if equipped with air conditioning
- Intake air connector. Tighten the 2 bolts to 13 ft. lbs. (18 Nm).

27. Install the water pump pulley, fan shroud, fan (with fan clutch) and alternator drive belt as follows:
- Fan (with the fan clutch), water pump pulley and fan shroud in position
- Water pump pulley but do not tighten the nuts
- Alternator drive belt
- Stretch the alternator belt tight. Tighten the fan nuts to 16 ft. lbs. (21 Nm).
- Adjust the alternator drive belt

28. Install or connect the following:
- Adjust the drive belt, if equipped with air conditioning
- Adjust the power steering drive belt
- Accelerator cable to the throttle body, if equipped with manual transmission
- Accelerator and throttle cables to the throttle body, if equipped with automatic transmission
- Air cleaner case
- MAF meter, resonator and air cleaner cap
- Radiator with the tabs on the supports through the radiator service holes. Tighten the bolts to 108 inch lbs. (13 Nm).
- Lower radiator hose to the radiator
- Oil cooler hoses to the radiator, if equipped with automatic transmission
- No. 2 fan shroud
- Radiator reservoir hose to the radiator
- Upper radiator hose to the radiator
- Air pipe with the 2 bolts, if removed
- Radiator grille with the 11 clips
- 2 fillers
- Clearance lights to the grille with the 4 bolts and 2 clips

- Negative and positive cables to the battery

29. Fill the engine oil, engine coolant and transmission oil.
30. Start the engine and check for leaks.
31. Check ignition timing.
32. Install or connect the following:
- Engine undercover
- Hood

33. Road test the vehicle and check all fluids.

2WD 4RUNNER

1. Before servicing the vehicle, refer to the precautions in the beginning of this section.
2. Properly relieve the fuel system pressure.
3. Remove or disconnect the following:
- Negative battery cable
- Engine undercover

4. Drain the engine coolant.
5. Drain the engine oil and the transmission oil.
6. Remove or disconnect the following:
- Hood
- Radiator
- Drive belt for the alternator and the water pump pulley
- Accelerator cable from the throttle body
- Actuator cover and the cruise control cable from the actuator, if equipped with cruise control

7. Remove or disconnect the air cleaner assembly, as follows:
- Intake Air Temperature (IAT) sensor and the Mass Air Flow (MAF) meter connectors

- 3 wire clamps and the engine wiring harness
- Air cleaner hose clamp, loosen it
- MAF meter, resonator and the air cleaner assembly

8. Install or connect the following:
- Air conditioning compressor, if equipped with air conditioning
- Alternator connector
- Heater hoses

9. Disconnect the following hoses:
- Brake booster vacuum hose
- Evaporative Emissions (EVAP) hose
- 2 air hoses for the power steering idle-up
- Fuel return hose
- Fuel inlet hose

10. Remove the power steering pump from the engine.

11. Disconnect the engine wiring harness, as follows:
- Glove box door
- Finish No. 2 panel, lower it
- 4 ECM connectors
- 2 cassette connectors and the 2 wire clamps from the lower finish panel
- Igniter
- Ground strap from the cowl top panel
- 2 engine wiring harness clamps.
- 2 engine wiring harness retainer-to-cowl panel nuts and the engine wiring harness

12. Install or connect the following:
- Heated Oxygen (HO2S) sensor
- Front exhaust pipe

13. Remove the shift lever assembly for a manual transmission, as follows:

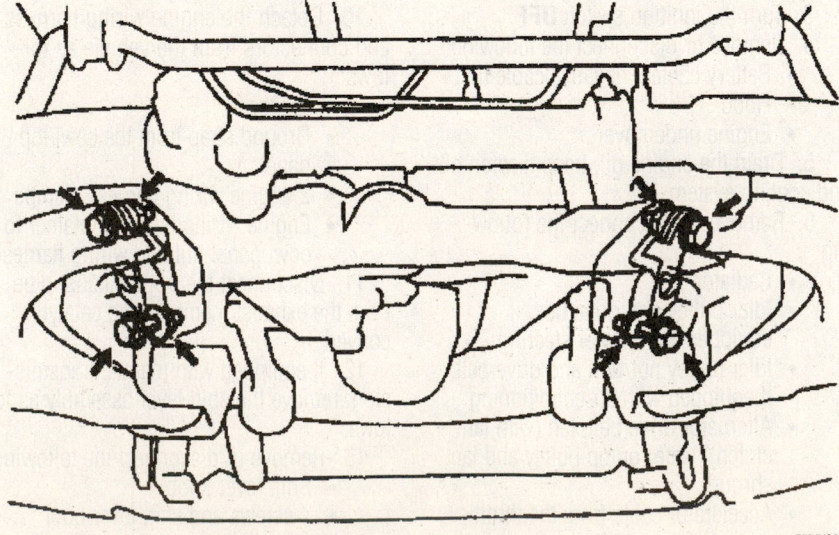

Be sure to support the engine before removing the right and left engine mounts—4Runner (2-Wheel drive) with 2.7L (3RZ-FE) engine

7924YG03

14. Remove or disconnect the following:
- Shift lever knob
- 4 screws and the shift lever boot
- 6 bolts, the shift lever assembly and baffle

15. Remove or disconnect the following:
- Driveshaft
- Speedometer cable
- Clutch release cylinder, if equipped with a manual transmission
- Cross-shaft, if equipped with an automatic transmission
- Starter wire

16. Place a jack under the transmission and remove the engine rear mounting bracket.

17. Install a rear engine hanger in the correct direction.

18. Attach the engine hoist chain to the 2 engine hangers.

19. Remove or disconnect the following:
- Engine front mounting insulators-to-frame bolts/nuts
- Engine/transmission assembly
- Engine

To install:

20. Install or connect the following:
- Transmission to the engine
- Chain hoist to the engine hangers
- Engine/transmission assembly into the engine compartment

➡ **Keep the engine level and align the right and left mounting and body mountings.**

- Right and left mounting insulators to the body mountings and temporarily install the bolts/nuts

21. Raise the transmission onto the frame

22. Remove the chain hoist.

23. Remove the bolt and the rear engine hanger.

24. Install the engine rear mounting bracket and tighten to:
- Bolt A: 13 ft. lbs. (19 Nm)
- Bolt B: 19 ft. lbs. (26 Nm)

25. Install or connect the following:
- Tighten the left and right engine mounting insulator bolts and nuts to 28 ft. lbs. (38 Nm).
- Starter wire
- Clutch release cylinder, for a manual transmission. Tighten the clutch line bolt to 29 ft. lbs. (39 Nm) and the clutch release cylinder bolts to 108 inch lbs. (13 Nm).
- Cross-shaft, for an automatic trans-

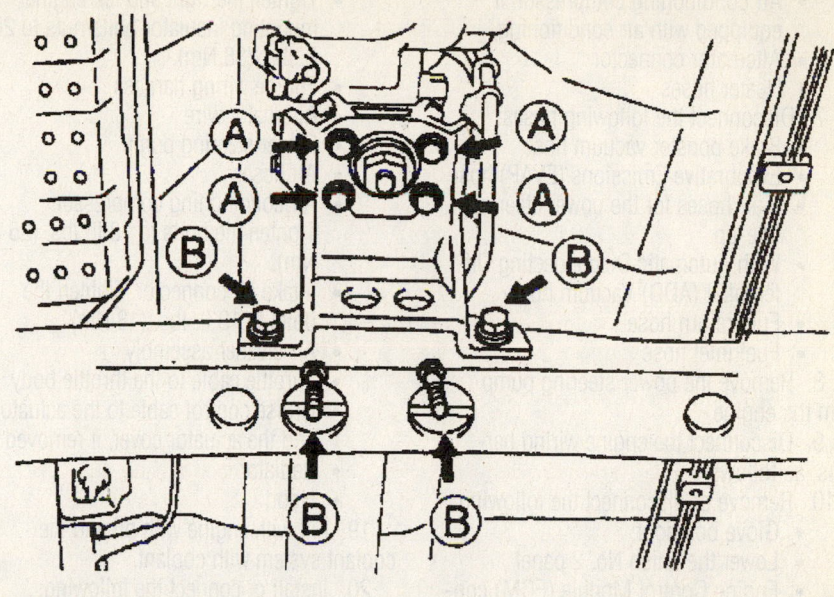

7924YG04

Bolt tightening pattern for the engine rear mounting bracket—4Runner (2-Wheel drive) with 2.7L (3RZ-FE) engine

mission. Tighten the bolt to 29 ft. lbs. (39 Nm) and the nut to 13 ft. lbs. (18 Nm).
- Speedometer cable
- Driveshaft
- Shift lever assembly, for a manual transmission

26. Install the front exhaust pipe, as follows:
- New gaskets and the front exhaust pipe assembly. Tighten the 3 new nuts to 46 ft. lbs. (62 Nm).
- Support bracket. Tighten the bolts to 29 ft. lbs. (39 Nm).
- 3-way catalytic converter with a new gasket to the tail pipe. Tighten to 29 ft. lbs. (39 Nm).
- HO2S sensor
- Engine wiring harness
- Power steering pump
- All hoses previously removed
- Alternator wire
- Air conditioning compressor, if removed. Tighten the bolts to 18 ft. lbs. (25 Nm).
- Intake air connector. Tighten the bolts to 13 ft. lbs. (18 Nm).
- Air cleaner assembly
- Throttle cable to the throttle body
- Cruise control cable to the actuator and the actuator cover, if disconnected
- Drive belt for the alternator and water pump pulley
- Radiator

- Negative battery cable

27. Refill the engine oil, coolant and transmission oil.

28. Start the engine and check for leaks.

29. Check the ignition timing.

30. Install or connect the following:
- Engine undercover
- Hood

31. Road test the vehicle and recheck the fluid levels.

4WD 4RUNNER

1. Before servicing the vehicle, refer to the precautions in the beginning of this section.

2. Properly relieve the fuel system pressure.

3. Remove or disconnect the following:
- Negative battery cable
- Transmission
- Engine undercover

4. Drain the engine coolant.

5. Drain the engine oil.

6. Remove or disconnect the following:
- Hood
- Radiator
- Drive belt for the alternator and the water pump pulley
- Accelerator cable from the throttle body
- Actuator cover and the cruise control cable from the actuator, if equipped with cruise control
- Air cleaner assembly
- Intake air connector

Refer to Section 1 for engine rebuilding specifications

- Air conditioning compressor, if equipped with air conditioning
- Alternator connector
- Heater hoses

7. Disconnect the following hoses:
- Brake booster vacuum hose
- Evaporative Emissions (EVAP) hose
- 2 air hoses for the power steering idle-up
- With Automatic Disconnecting Differential (ADD) Vacuum hose
- Fuel return hose
- Fuel inlet hose

8. Remove the power steering pump from the engine.

9. Disconnect the engine wiring harness, as follows:

10. Remove or disconnect the following:
- Glove box door
- Lower the finish No. 2 panel
- Engine Control Module (ECM) connectors
- 2 cassette connectors and the 2 wire clamps from the lower finish panel
- Vacuum Switching Valve (VSV) connector for the EVAP and clamp
- Igniter
- Ground strap from the cowl top panel
- 2 engine wiring harness clamps
- 2 engine wiring harness retainer-to-cowl panel nuts and the engine wiring harness

11. Install a rear engine hanger in the correct direction.

12. Attach the engine hoist chain to the 2 engine hangers.

13. Remove or disconnect the following:
- Engine front mounting insulators-to-frame bolts and nuts
- Engine, making sure that the engine is clear of all wiring and hoses
- Engine

To install:

14. Attach a chain hoist to the engine hangers.

15. Install or connect the following:
- Engine into the engine compartment

➡**Keep the engine level and align the right and left mounting and body mountings**

- Right and left mounting insulators to the body mountings and temporarily install the bolts and nuts

16. Remove the chain hoist.

17. Remove the bolt and the rear engine hanger.

18. Install or connect the following:

- Tighten the right and left engine mounting insulator bolts/nuts to 28 ft. lbs. (38 Nm).
- Engine wiring harness
- Alternator wire
- Power steering pump
- All hoses
- Air conditioning compressor. Tighten the bolts to 18 ft. lbs. (25 Nm).
- Intake air connector. Tighten the bolts to 13 ft. lbs. (18 Nm).
- Air cleaner assembly
- Throttle cable to the throttle body
- Cruise control cable to the actuator and the actuator cover, if removed
- Radiator
- Hood

19. Fill with engine with oil and the coolant system with coolant.

20. Install or connect the following:
- Transmission
- Engine undercover
- Negative battery cable

21. Fill the transmission fluid.

22. Check the ignition timing.

23. Test drive the vehicle and check for leaks.

24. Recheck fluid levels.

3.4L (5VZ-FE) Engine

2WD T-100

1. Before servicing the vehicle, refer to the precautions in the beginning of this section.

2. Properly relieve the fuel system pressure.

3. Remove or disconnect the following:
- Hood
- Battery
- Engine under covers

4. Drain the engine coolant.

5. Drain the engine oil.

6. Remove or disconnect the following:
- Radiator

7. Remove the power steering drive belt as follows:
- Stretch the belt and loosen the fan pulley mounting nuts
- Loosen the lockbolt, pivot bolt and adjusting bolt and remove the drive belt

8. Remove or disconnect the following:
- Air conditioning drive belt by loosening the idle pulley nut and adjusting bolt, if equipped with air conditioning
- Loosen the lockbolt, pivot bolt and adjusting bolt and the alternator drive belt

- Fan with the fluid coupling and fan pulleys
- Power steering pump, do not disconnect the lines from the pump
- Compressor, if equipped with air conditioning; do not disconnect the lines from the compressor
- Air cleaner cap
- Mass Air Flow (MAF) meter and resonator
- Air cleaner case and filter

9. Disconnect the following cables:
- Actuator cable with the bracket, if equipped with cruise control
- Accelerator cable
- Throttle cable, if equipped with an automatic transmission

10. Disconnect the following hoses:
- Heater hoses
- Brake booster vacuum hose
- Evaporative Emission (EVAP) hose
- Fuel return hose
- Fuel inlet hose

11. Detach the starter wire and connectors as follows:
- Ground strap by removing the bolt
- Positive cable from the battery
- 3 starter wire clamps and connector

12. Detach the alternator connector and wire.

13. Detach the engine wiring harness and connectors as follows:
- Right front door scuff plate.
- Cowl panel side trim, by removing the clip
- Engine Control Module (ECM)
- 2 connectors from the cowl wire
- Igniter
- Ground strap
- 6 engine wiring harness clamps
- Engine wiring harness

14. If equipped with manual transmission, remove the shift lever assembly as follows:
- Shift lever knob
- 4 screws and the shift lever boot
- Shift lever assembly and gasket, by removing the 6 bolts

15. Remove or disconnect the following:
- Stabilizer bar
- Driveshaft from the transmission
- Speedometer cable
- Front exhaust pipe
- Clutch release cylinder, if equipped with a manual transmission
- Cross-shaft, if equipped with an automatic transmission

16. Place a jack under the transmission.

17. Remove or disconnect the following:
- Transmission rear mounting bracket, by removing the 8 bolts
- Air conditioning compressor wire

clamp, if equipped with air conditioning

18. If necessary, install a No. 2 engine hanger with 2 bolts. Tighten the 2 bolts to 30 ft. lbs. (40 Nm).

19. Attach the engine hoist chain to the 2 engine hangers.

20. Remove or disconnect the following:
- 4 bolts/nuts holding the engine front mounting insulators to the frame
- Engine/transmission assembly

To install:

21. Install or connect the following:
- Engine
- Engine mounts to the body mountings. Install the bolts and nuts but do not tighten at this time.

22. Remove the engine chain hoist the No. 2 engine hanger.

23. Install or connect the following:
- Air conditioning wire, if equipped with air conditioning
- Transmission mounting bracket. Tighten the frame bolts to 43 ft. lbs. (58 Nm) and the mounting insulator bolts to 13 ft. lbs. (18 Nm).
- Tighten the engine mounting nuts and bolts to 28 ft. lbs. (38 Nm).
- Cross-shaft, if equipped with an automatic transmission
- Clutch release cylinder, if equipped with a manual transmission. Tighten the bolts to 108 inch lbs. (13 Nm).
- Front exhaust pipe
- Speedometer cable
- Driveshaft
- Stabilizer bar

24. Install the shift lever assembly, as follows:

25. Install or connect the following:
- New gasket and shift lever assembly with the 6 bolts
- Shift lever boot with the 4 screws
- Shift lever knob

26. Install or connect the following:
- All engine wiring harness, hoses and cables
- Air cleaner case and air filter
- MAF meter, resonator and air cleaner cap
- Air conditioning compressor, if equipped
- Remaining components

27. Fill the engine with oil.

28. Fill the engine and radiator with coolant.

29. Install the engine undercover.

30. Start the engine and check for leaks.

4WD T-100

1. Before servicing the vehicle, refer to the precautions in the beginning of this section.

2. Properly relieve the fuel system pressure.

3. Remove or disconnect the following:
- Transmission
- Hood
- Battery from the vehicle
- Engine under covers

4. Drain the engine coolant.

5. Drain the engine oil.

6. Remove or disconnect the following:
- Radiator

7. Remove the power steering drive belt, as follows:
- Stretch the belt and loosen the fan pulley mounting nuts
- Loosen the lockbolt, pivot bolt and adjusting bolt
- Drive belt from the engine

8. Remove or disconnect the following:
- Air conditioning drive belt by loosening the idle pulley nut and adjusting bolt, if equipped with air conditioning
- Alternator drive belt
- Fan with the fluid coupling and fan pulleys
- Power steering pump; do not disconnect the lines from the pump
- Compressor, if equipped with air conditioning. Do not disconnect the lines from the compressor.
- Air cleaner cap, Mass Air Flow Meter (MAF) meter and resonator
- Air cleaner case and filter

9. Disconnect the following cables:
- Actuator cable with the bracket, if equipped with cruise control
- Accelerator cable
- Throttle cable, if equipped with an automatic transmission

10. Disconnect the following hoses:
- Heater hoses
- Brake booster vacuum hose
- Evaporative Emissions (EVAP) hose
- Automatic Disconnecting Differential (ADD) vacuum hose
- Fuel return hose
- Fuel inlet hose

11. Detach the starter wire and connectors as follows:

12. Remove or disconnect the following:
- Ground strap by removing the bolt

13. Disconnect the positive cable from the battery, as follows:
- 3 starter wire clamps and connector

- Automatic Disconnecting Differential (ADD) indicator switch connector

14. Detach the alternator connector and wire.

15. Detach the engine wiring harness and connectors, as follows:
- Right front door scuff plate
- Cowl panel side trim, by removing the clip
- Engine Control Module (ECM)
- 2 connectors from the cowl wire
- Igniter connector
- Ground strap
- 6 engine wiring harness clamps
- Engine wiring harness

16. Remove or disconnect the following:
- Air conditioning compressor wire clamp, if equipped with air conditioning

17. If necessary, install a No. 2 engine hanger with 2 bolts. Tighten the 2 bolts to 30 ft. lbs. (40 Nm).

18. Attach the engine hoist chain to the 2 engine hangers.

19. Remove or disconnect the following:
- 4 Engine front mounting insulators-to-frame bolts/nuts
- Engine

To install:

20. Install or connect the following:
- Engine
- Engine mounts to the body mountings. Install the bolts and nuts but do not tighten at this time.

21. Remove the engine chain hoist the No. 2 engine hanger.

22. Install or connect the following:
- Air conditioning wire with the bolt, if equipped with air conditioning
- Tighten the engine mounting nuts and bolts to 28 ft. lbs. (38 Nm).
- All engine wiring harness, hoses and cables
- Air cleaner case and air filter
- MAF meter, resonator and air cleaner cap
- Air conditioning compressor, if equipped
- Fan with the fluid coupling and fan pulleys. Tighten the nuts to 48 inch lbs. (5.4 Nm).
- Alternator drive belt
- Adjust the air conditioning drive belt, if equipped
- Power steering pump, pump pulley and the drive belt
- Radiator

23. Fill the engine with oil.

For engine torque specifications, refer to Section 1 of this manual

24. Fill the engine and radiator with coolant.
25. Install or connect the following:
  - Hood
  - Engine undercover
  - Transmission
26. Start the engine and check for leaks.

2WD 4RUNNER

1. Before servicing the vehicle, refer to the precautions in the beginning of this section.
2. Properly relieve the fuel system pressure.
3. Remove or disconnect the following:
  - Hood
  - Battery
  - Engine under covers
4. Drain the engine coolant.
5. Drain the engine oil.
  - Radiator
  - Fan with the fluid coupling and fan pulleys
  - Air cleaner cap
  - Mass Air Flow (MAF) meter and the resonator
  - Air cleaner case and filter
6. Disconnect the following hoses:
  - Heater hoses
  - Brake booster vacuum hose
  - Evaporative Emissions (EVAP) hose
  - Fuel return hose
  - Fuel inlet hose
7. Detach the starter wire and connectors, as follows:
  - Ground strap, by removing the bolt
  - 3 starter wire clamps and connector
8. Detach the alternator connector and wire.
9. Disconnect the engine wiring harness, as follows:
  - Glove box door
  - Lower the finish No. 2 panel
  - 4 ECM connectors
  - 2 cassette connectors and the 2 wire clamps from the lower finish panel
  - Engine wiring harness clamp
10. Remove or disconnect the following:
  - Igniter connector
  - Ground strap
  - Vacuum Switching Valve (VSV) connector for the Evaporative Emissions (EVAP)
  - Vapor pressure sensor connector and clamp
  - Vapor connector for the vapor pressure sensor and clamp
  - 2 engine wiring harness retainer-to-cowl panel nuts and pull out the engine wiring harness
  - Driveshaft from the transmission

- Speedometer cable
- Front exhaust pipe
- Nut and the control cable
11. Place a jack under the transmission.
12. Remove or disconnect the following:
  - Transmission rear mounting bracket by removing the 8 bolts
  - Bolt and the air conditioning compressor wire clamp, if equipped with air conditioning
13. If necessary, install a No. 2 engine hanger with 2 bolts. Tighten the 2 bolts to 30 ft. lbs. (40 Nm).
14. Attach the engine hoist chain to the 2 engine hangers.
15. Remove or disconnect the following:

  - 4 engine front mounting insulators-to-frame bolts and nuts
  - Engine and transmission

To install:

16. Install or connect the following:
  - Engine
  - Engine mounts to the body mountings. Install the bolts and nuts but do not tighten at this time.
17. Remove the engine chain hoist the No. 2 engine hanger.
18. Install or connect the following:
  - Air conditioning wire with the bolt, if equipped with air conditioning
  - Transmission mounting bracket. Tighten the frame bolts to 43 ft. lbs. (58 Nm) and the mounting insulator bolts to 13 ft. lbs. (18 Nm).
  - Tighten the engine mounting nuts and bolts to 28 ft. lbs. (38 Nm).
  - Control cable
  - Front exhaust pipe
  - Speedometer cable
  - Driveshaft
  - All engine wiring harness, hoses and cables
  - Fan with the fluid coupling and fan pulleys. Tighten the nuts to 48 inch lbs. (5.4 Nm).
  - Air cleaner case and air filter
  - MAF meter, resonator and the air cleaner cap
  - Radiator
19. Fill the engine with oil.
20. Fill the engine and radiator with coolant.
21. Install or connect the following:
  - Engine undercover
  - Battery
  - Hood
22. Start the engine and check for leaks.
23. Make any necessary adjustments and road test the vehicle.

4WD 4RUNNER

1. Before servicing the vehicle, refer to the precautions in the beginning of this section.
2. Remove or disconnect the following:
  - Transmission
  - Hood
3. Release the fuel system pressure.
4. Remove or disconnect the following:
  - Battery
  - Engine undercovers
5. Drain the engine coolant.
6. Drain the engine oil.
7. Remove or disconnect the following:
  - Radiator
  - Fan with the fluid coupling and fan pulleys
  - Air cleaner cap
  - Mass Air Flow (MAF) meter and the resonator
8. Disconnect the following hoses:
  - Heater hoses
  - Brake booster vacuum hose
  - Evaporative Emissions (EVAP) hose
  - Automatic Disconnecting Differential (ADD) vacuum hose
  - Fuel return hose
  - Fuel inlet hose
9. Detach the starter wire and connectors, as follows:
  - Ground strap, by removing the bolt
  - 3 starter wire clamps and connector
10. Detach the alternator connector and wire.
11. Disconnect the engine wiring harness, as follows:
  - Glove box door
  - Lower the finish No. 2 panel
  - 4 ECM connectors
  - 2 cassette connectors and the 2 wire clamps from the lower finish panel
  - Engine wiring harness clamp
12. Disconnect the following:
  - Igniter connector
  - Ground strap
  - Vacuum Switching Valve (VSV) connector for the EVAP
  - Vapor pressure sensor connector and clamp
  - Vapor connector for the vapor pressure sensor and clamp
13. Remove or disconnect the following:
  - 2 engine wiring harness retainer-to-cowl panel nuts and wiring harness
  - Air conditioning compressor wire clamp, if equipped with air conditioning
14. If necessary, install a No. 2 engine hanger with 2 bolts. Tighten the 2 bolts to 30 ft. lbs. (40 Nm).

15. Attach the engine hoist chain to the 2 engine hangers.

16. Remove or disconnect the following:
- 4 engine front mounting insulators-to-frame bolts and nuts
- Engine

To install:

17. Install or connect the following:
- Engine
- Engine mounts-to-body mountings. Install the bolts and nuts but do not tighten at this time.

18. Remove the engine chain hoist the No. 2 engine hanger.

19. Install or connect the following:
- Air conditioning wire with the bolt, if equipped with air conditioning
- Tighten the engine mounting nuts and bolts to 28 ft. lbs. (38 Nm).
- Engine wiring harness
- Engine wiring harness clamp
- All wires, hoses and cables
- Fan with the fluid coupling and fan pulleys. Tighten the nuts to 48 inch lbs. (5.4 Nm).
- Air cleaner case and air filter
- MAF meter, resonator and the air cleaner cap
- Radiator

20. Fill the engine with oil.

21. Fill the engine and radiator with coolant.

22. Install or connect the following:
- Transmission and refill it with transmission oil
- Engine undercover
- Battery
- Hood

23. Start the engine, make any necessary adjustments and check for leaks.

Water Pump

REMOVAL & INSTALLATION

2.4L (2RZ-FE) and 2.7L (3RZ-FE) Engines

1. Before servicing the vehicle, refer to the precautions in the beginning of this section.

2. Remove or disconnect the following:
- Negative battery cable
- Engine undercover

3. Drain the cooling system.

4. Remove or disconnect the following:
- 2 bolts and the air pipe, for the California vehicles with 3RZ-FE engine

- Upper radiator hose from the radiator
- Oil dipstick guide, by removing the bolt
- Power steering drive belt, by loosening the lockbolt and adjusting bolt to the idler pulley, if equipped with power steering
- No. 2 fan shroud, by removing the 2 clips
- No. 1 fan shroud, by removing the 4 bolts
- Loosen the idler pulley nut and adjusting bolt and remove the air conditioning drive belt, if equipped with air conditioning

5. Remove the alternator drive belt, fan (with fan clutch), water pump pulley and the fan shroud, as follows:
- Stretch the belt and loosen the water pump pulley mounting nuts
- Loosen the lock, pivot and the adjusting bolts for the alternator
- Alternator drive belt
- 4 water pump pulley mounting nuts
- Fan (with fan clutch) and the water pump pulley

6. Remove the water pump and discard the gasket.

To install:

7. Clean all gasket mounting surfaces.

8. Install or connect the following:
- Apply a thin layer of liquid sealant to a new gasket
- Place the gasket and water pump into position. Tighten the 14mm head bolts **A** to 18 ft. lbs. (25 Nm) and the 12mm head bolts to 78 inch lbs. (9 Nm).

9. Install the water pump pulley, fan shroud, fan (with fan clutch) and the alternator drive belt, as follows:
- Fan (with the fan clutch), water pump pulley and the fan shroud in position
- Water pump pulley mounting nuts but do not tighten the nuts at this time
- Alternator drive belt
- Stretch the alternator belt tight. Tighten the fan nuts to 16 ft. lbs. (21 Nm).
- Adjust the alternator drive belt

10. Install or connect the following:
- Adjust the drive belt, if equipped with air conditioning
- No. 1 fan shroud, by installing the 4 bolts
- No. 2 fan shroud, with the 2 clips
- Adjust the power steering drive belt

- Oil dipstick guide, with the bolt
- Upper radiator hose to the radiator
- Air pipe, If removed
- Negative battery cable

11. Fill and bleed the cooling system.

12. Start the engine and check for leaks.

13. Install the engine undercover.

3.4L (5VZ-FE) Engine

T-100 AND TACOMA

1. Before servicing the vehicle, refer to the precautions in the beginning of this section.

2. Remove or disconnect the following:
- Negative battery cable
- Engine undercover

3. Drain the engine coolant.

4. Remove the upper radiator hose.

5. Remove the power steering drive belt, as follows:
- Stretch the belt and loosen the fan pulley mounting nuts
- Loosen the lockbolt, pivot bolt and the adjusting bolt
- Drive belt

6. Remove or disconnect the following:
- Air conditioning drive belt, by loosening the idler pulley nut and adjusting bolt
- Lockbolt, pivot bolt and the adjusting bolt
- Alternator drive belt
- No. 2 fan shroud, by removing the 2 clips
- Fan with the fluid coupling and fan pulleys
- Power steering pump and move it aside without disconnecting the lines from the pump
- Compressor from the engine and move it aside without disconnecting the compressor lines, if equipped with air conditioning
- Air conditioning bracket, if equipped with air conditioning

7. Remove the No. 2 timing belt cover, as follows:
- Camshaft Position (CMP) sensor connector from the No. 2 timing belt cover
- 3 spark plug wire clamps from the No. 2 timing belt cover
- 6 bolts and the timing belt cover

8. Remove the fan bracket, as follows:
- Power steering adjusting strut, by removing the nut
- Fan bracket, by removing the bolt and nut

For complete mechanical specifications, refer to Section 1 of this manual

9. Set the No. 1 cylinder to Top Dead Center (TDC) of the compression stroke, as follows:

a. Turn the crankshaft pulley and align its groove with the timing mark **0** of the No. 1 timing belt cover.

b. Check that the timing marks of the camshaft timing pulleys and the No. 3 timing belt cover are aligned. If not, turn the crankshaft pulley 1 revolution (360 degrees).

10. Remove the camshaft timing pulleys, as follows:

a. Remove the timing belt tensioner by alternately loosening the 2 bolts.

b. Using Variable Wrench Set No. 09960-10010, remove the pulley bolt, the timing pulley and the knock pin.

c. Remove the 2 timing pulleys with the timing belt.

11. Remove or disconnect the following:
- Thermostat
- No. 2 oil cooler hose, from the water pump
- Water pump, by removing the 7 bolts

12. Thoroughly clean the mating surfaces.

To install:
13. Install or connect the following:
- Apply sealant (PN 08826-00100) to the water pump

✷✷ WARNING

Parts must be assembled within 5 minutes of application. Otherwise the material must be removed and reapplied.

- Water pump. Tighten the bolts to 14 ft. lbs. (20 Nm).
- No. 2 oil cooler hose
- Thermostat
- Left camshaft timing pulley. Tighten the pulley bolt to 81 ft. lbs. (110 Nm).

14. Set the No. 1 cylinder to TDC of the compression stroke.

15. Connect the timing belt to the left camshaft timing pulley. Check that the installation mark on the timing belt is aligned with the end of the No. 1 timing belt cover, as follows:

a. Using Variable Pin Wrench Set 09960-01000, slightly turn the left

camshaft timing pulley clockwise. Align the installation mark on the timing belt with the timing mark of the camshaft timing pulley and hang the timing belt on the left camshaft timing pulley.

b. Align the timing marks of the left camshaft pulley and the No. 3 timing belt cover.

c. Check that the timing belt has tension between the crankshaft timing pulley and the left camshaft timing pulley.

16. Install the right camshaft timing pulley and the timing belt.

17. Set the timing belt tensioner, as follows:

a. Using a press, slowly press in the pushrod using 220–2,205 lbs. (981–9,807 N) of force.

b. Align the holes of the pushrod and housing, pass a 1.5mm hexagon wrench through the holes to keep the setting position of the pushrod.

c. Release the press and install the dust boot to the tensioner.

d. Install the timing belt tensioner and alternately tighten the bolts to 20 ft. lbs. (28 Nm).

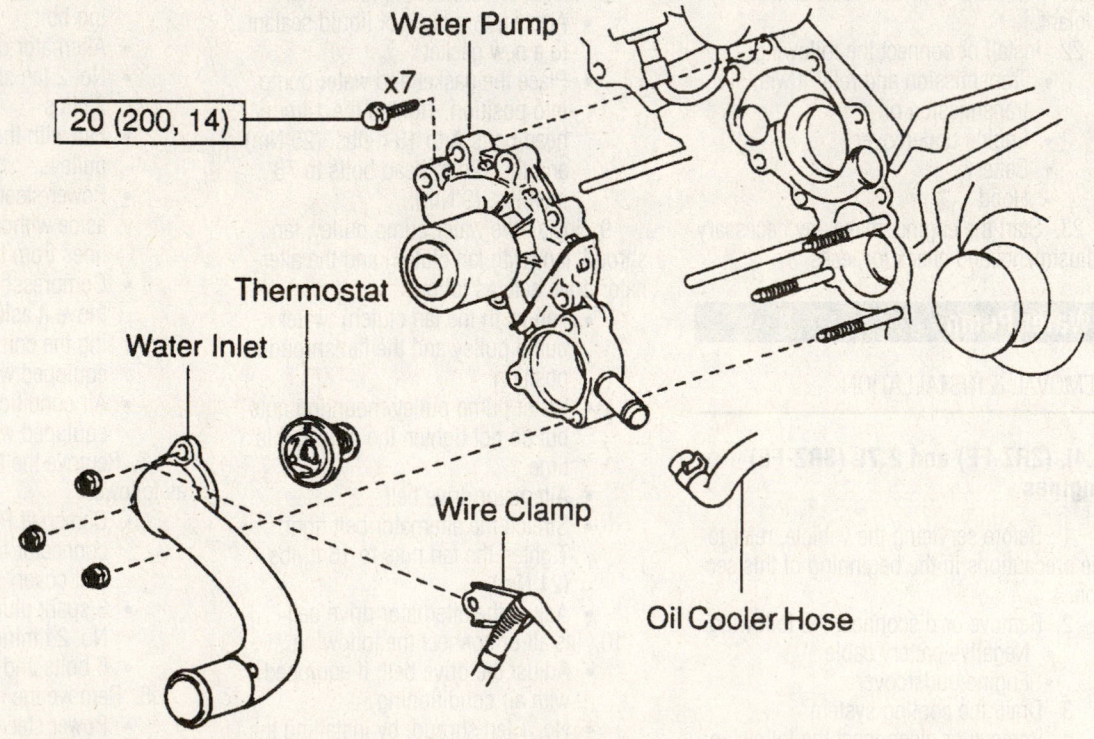

20 (200, 14)

Water Pump
x7
Thermostat
Water Inlet
Wire Clamp
Oil Cooler Hose

N·m(kgf·cm, ft·lbf) : Specified torque
◆ Non–Reusable part

7924YG08

Exploded view of the water pump mounting—3.4L (5VZ-FE) engine

e. Using pliers, remove the 1.5mm hexagon wrench from the belt tensioner.

18. Check the valve timing, as follows:

a. Slowly turn the crankshaft pulley 2 revolutions from the TDC-to-TDC; always turn the crankshaft pulley clockwise.

b. Check that each pulley aligns with the timing marks. If the timing marks do not align, remove the timing belt and reinstall it.

19. Install or connect the following:

- Fan bracket, with the bolt and nut
- Remaining components
- Negative battery cable

20. Fill with engine coolant.

21. Start the engine and check for leaks.

4RUNNER

1. Before servicing the vehicle, refer to the precautions in the beginning of this section.

2. Disconnect the negative battery cable.

3. Drain the cooling system.

4. Remove or disconnect the following:

- Timing belt
- Thermostat
- No. 2 oil cooler hose from the water pump
- Water pump

5. Thoroughly clean the mating surfaces.

To install:

6. Apply sealant (PN 08826-00100) to the water pump.

❋❋ WARNING

Parts must be assembled within 5 minutes of application. Otherwise the material must be removed and reapplied.

7. Install or connect the following:

- Water pump. Tighten the bolts to 14 ft. lbs. (20 Nm).
- No. 2 oil cooler hose
- Thermostat

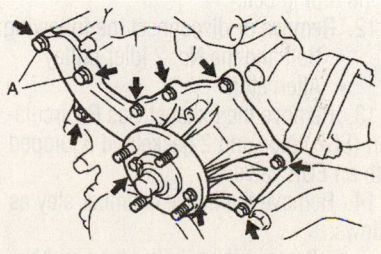

Water pump mounting bolt locations— 2.7L (3RZ-FE) engine

7024YG07

- Timing belt
- Negative battery cable

8. Fill the cooling system.

9. Start the engine and check for leaks.

Cylinder Head

REMOVAL & INSTALLATION

2.4L (2RZ-FE) and 2.7L (3RZ-FE) Engines

1. Before servicing the vehicle, refer to the precautions in the beginning of this section.

2. Release the fuel system pressure.

3. Disconnect the negative battery cable.

4. Drain the engine coolant.

5. Remove or disconnect the following:

- Air cleaner cap
- Mass Air Flow (MAF) meter and resonator
- Accelerator cable from the throttle body, if equipped with a manual transmission
- Accelerator and throttle cables from the throttle body, if equipped with an automatic transmission
- Cruise control cable from the actuator, if equipped with cruise control
- Intake air connector
- Air hose for Idle Air Control (IAC)
- Vacuum sensing hose
- Wire clamp for the engine wiring harness
- Oil dipstick guide
- Power steering belt
- Power steering pulley, pump and bracket
- Positive Crankcase Ventilation (PCV) hoses
- Distributor
- Spark plug wires from the spark plugs
- Engine wiring harness
- Air conditioning compressor, if equipped with air conditioning
- Oil pressure sensor
- Engine Coolant Temperature (ECT) sensor connector
- ECT sender gauge connector
- Exhaust Gas Recirculation (EGR) gas temperature sensor connector
- Vacuum Switching Valve (VSV) connector
- 2 vacuum hose from the VSV
- Ground strap from the cowl top panel

- Engine wiring harness from the air intake chamber
- Throttle Position (TP) sensor connector
- IAC valve connector
- Crankshaft Position (CKP) sensor connector
- Knock Sensor (KS) connector
- Data Link Connector 1 (DLC1) from the bracket
- Engine wiring harness clamp
- EGR pipe
- Intake chamber stay
- Air intake chamber assembly

6. Disconnect the following hoses:

- Evaporative Emissions (EVAP) hose from the throttle body
- Brake booster vacuum hose from the union
- Water bypass hose from the water bypass pipe
- Water bypass hose from the cylinder head rear cover

7. Remove or disconnect the following:

- Injector connectors
- Fuel inlet pipe
- Hoses and the fuel return pipe
- Delivery pipe and injectors
- Intake manifold
- Front exhaust pipe
- Exhaust manifold and gasket
- Water outlet
- Cylinder head rear cover
- Spark plugs
- Front engine hanger
- Engine wiring harness brackets
- Cylinder head cover

8. Set No. 1 cylinder to Top Dead Center (TDC) of the compression stroke. The groove on the crankshaft pulley should align with the **0** mark on the timing chain cover and the timing marks (1 and 2 dots) of the camshaft gears should form a straight line in respect to the cylinder head surface. If not, turn the crankshaft 1 revolution (360 degrees).

9. Remove or disconnect the following:

- Chain tensioner and gasket
- Camshaft timing gear
- Exhaust camshafts

10. Remove the intake camshaft, as follows:

a. Uniformly, loosen and remove the bearing cap bolts in the reverse order of the tightening in several passes, in sequence.

b. Remove the bearing caps and camshaft. Make a note of the bearing cap positions for proper installation.

Please refer to Section 8 for electric cooling fan wiring schematics

➡️**If the camshaft is not being lifted out straight and level, reinstall the No. 3 bearing cap with the 2 bolts. Then, alternately loosen and remove the 2 bearing cap bolts with the camshaft gear pulled up.**

11. Remove or disconnect the following:
- Valve lifters and shims

➡️**Arrange the valve lifters and shims in correct order.**

- Cylinder head, by uniformly loosen and remove the cylinder head bolts in the reverse order of the tightening, in sequence, using several passes

To install:

12. Before installing, thoroughly clean the gasket mating surfaces and check for warpage.

13. Apply sealant (PN 08826-00080) to the 2 locations. Place a new head gasket on the block and install the cylinder head.

➡️**Refer to Section 1 of this manual for the cylinder head torque sequence illustration. The illustration is located after the Torque Specification Chart.**

14. Install the cylinder head as follows:

a. Lightly coat the cylinder head bolts with engine oil.

b. Install the bolts and tighten, in several passes, in the sequence. Tighten all bolts to 29 ft. lbs. (39 Nm).

c. Mark the front of the bolt with paint and retighten bolts 90 degrees in the proper sequence.

d. Retighten an additional 90 degrees. Check that the painted mark is now facing rearward.

15. Install or connect the following:
- Tighten the 2 front mounting bolts to 15 ft. lbs. (21 Nm).
- Valve lifters and shims in their proper locations. Check that the valve lifter rotates smoothly by hand.
- Intake and exhaust camshafts

16. Set No. 1 cylinder to TDC compression stroke. The groove on the crankshaft pulley should align with the **0** mark on the timing chain cover and the timing marks (1 and 2 dots) of the camshaft gears should form a straight line in respect to the cylinder head surface. If not, turn the crankshaft 1 revolution (360 degrees).

17. Install the timing gear, as follows:

a. Place the gear over the straight pin of the intake camshaft.

b. Hold the intake camshaft with a wrench. Install and tighten the bolt to 54 ft. lbs. (74 Nm).

c. Hold the exhaust camshaft and install the bolt and distributor gear. Tighten the bolt to 34 ft. lbs. (46 Nm).

18. Install or connect the following:
- Chain tensioner, using a new gasket (mark toward the front)
- Recheck the valve timing
- Check and adjust the valve clearance
- Spark plugs
- Semi-circular plug

19. Recheck the engine for proper valve timing.

20. Install or connect the following:
- Cylinder head cover, using a new gasket
- Engine wiring harness brackets
- Front engine hanger. Tighten the bolts to 30 ft. lbs. (42 Nm).
- Cylinder head rear cover. Tighten the bolts to 10 ft. lbs. (13 Nm).
- Water outlet, using a new gasket. Tighten the bolts to 14 ft. lbs. (20 Nm).
- Upper radiator hose
- Exhaust manifold. Tighten the bolts to 36 ft. lbs. (49 Nm).
- Remaining components
- Negative battery cable

21. Fill the engine and radiator with engine coolant.

22. Start the engine and check for leaks.

23. Check the ignition timing. Road test the vehicle for proper operation.

24. Recheck all fluid levels.

3.4L (5VZ-FE) Engine

T-100 AND TACOMA

1. Before servicing the vehicle, refer to the precautions in the beginning of this section.

2. Disconnect the negative battery cable.

3. Relieve the fuel system pressure.

4. Remove the engine undercover.

5. Drain the cooling system.

6. Remove or disconnect the following:
- Front exhaust pipe
- Air cleaner cap
- Mass Air Flow (MAF) meter and resonator

7. Disconnect the following cables:
- Actuator cable from the bracket, if equipped with cruise control
- Accelerator cable
- Throttle cable, if equipped with an automatic transmission
- Heater hose
- Upper radiator hose

- Power steering drive belt
- Air conditioning drive belt, by loosening the idle pulley nut and adjusting bolt
- Loosen the lockbolt, pivot bolt and adjusting bolt and the alternator drive belt
- No. 2 fan shroud by removing the 2 clips
- Fan with the fluid coupling and fan pulleys
- Power steering pump and move it aside without disconnecting the pump lines
- Compressor and move it aside without disconnecting the compressor lines, if equipped with air conditioning
- Air conditioning bracket, if equipped with air conditioning
- Spark plug wires with the ignition coils
- Spark plugs
- No. 2 timing belt cover

8. Remove the fan bracket, as follows:

a. Remove the power steering adjusting strut by removing the nut.

b. Remove the fan bracket by removing the bolt and nut.

9. Set the No. 1 cylinder at Top Dead Center (TDC) of the compression stroke.

a. Turn the crankshaft pulley and align its groove with the timing mark **0** on the No. 1 timing belt cover.

b. Check that the timing marks of the camshaft timing pulleys and the No. 3 timing belt cover are aligned. If not, turn the crankshaft pulley 1 revolution (360 degrees).

10. Remove the timing belt tensioner by alternately loosening the 2 bolts.

11. Remove the camshaft timing pulleys, as follows:

a. Using Variable Pin Wrench Set tool 09960-10010, remove the pulley bolt, the timing pulley and the knock pin.

b. Remove the 2 timing pulleys with the timing belt.

12. Remove or disconnect the following:
- Bolt and the No. 2 idler pulley
- Alternator

13. Remove the Exhaust Gas Recirculation (EGR) pipe and 2 gaskets, if equipped with an EGR valve

14. Remove the intake chamber stay as follows:

a. Remove the oil filler tube and No. 1 throttle cable clamp by removing the bolt and 2 nuts.

b. Remove the intake chamber stay by removing the 2 bolts.

15. Remove the following connectors:

- VSV connector for the fuel pressure control.
- Throttle position sensor
- IAC valve connector
- EGR valve gas temperature sensor, if equipped
- Vacuum Switching Valve (VSV) connector for the EGR valve, if equipped

16. Disconnect the following hoses:
- Positive Crankcase Ventilation (PCV) hoses
- Water bypass hoses.
- Air assist hose from the intake air connector
- 2 vacuum sensing hoses from the VSV
- Evaporative Emissions (EVAP) hose
- Air hose, from the power steering
- Air hose from the air conditioning

idle up valve, if equipped with air conditioning

17. Remove or disconnect the following:
- 4 bolts, 2 nuts and the air intake chamber assembly
- Intake air connector

18. Disconnect the engine wiring harness from the intake manifold, as follows:
- Oil pressure sensor connector
- Crankshaft position sensor connector
- 6 injector connectors
- Engine Coolant Temperature (ECT) sender gauge connector
- ECT sensor connector
- Knock (KS) sensor connector
- Camshaft Position (CMP) sensor connector
- 3 engine wiring harness clamps

- 3 bolts and the engine wiring harness from the cylinder head

19. Remove or disconnect the following:
- CMP sensor
- No. 3 (rear) timing belt cover, by removing the 6 bolts
- Fuel pressure regulator
- Intake manifold assembly
- Power steering pump bracket
- Oil dipstick and guide
- Exhaust crossover pipe and gaskets, by removing the 6 nuts
- Left-hand exhaust manifold, by removing the heat insulator and 6 nuts
- Right-hand exhaust manifold, by removing the heat insulator and 6 nuts
- 8 bolts, seal washers, cylinder head cover and gasket

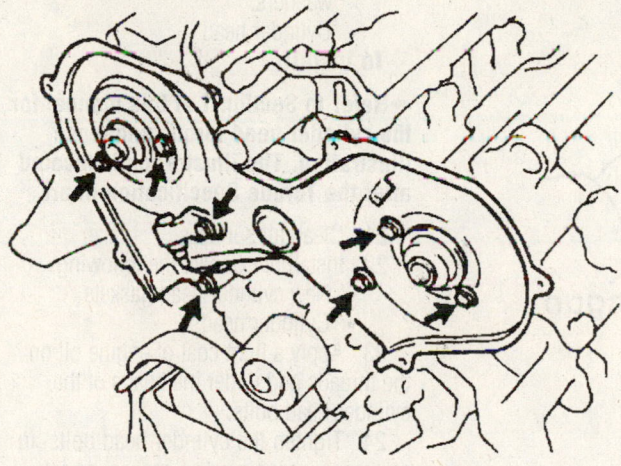

Rear timing belt cover bolt locations—3.4L (5VZ-FE) engine

7924YG19

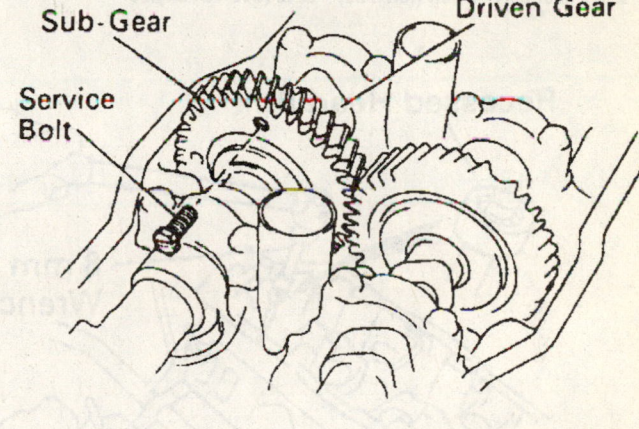

Drive gear service bolt (right side)—3.4L (5VZ-FE) engine

7924YG21

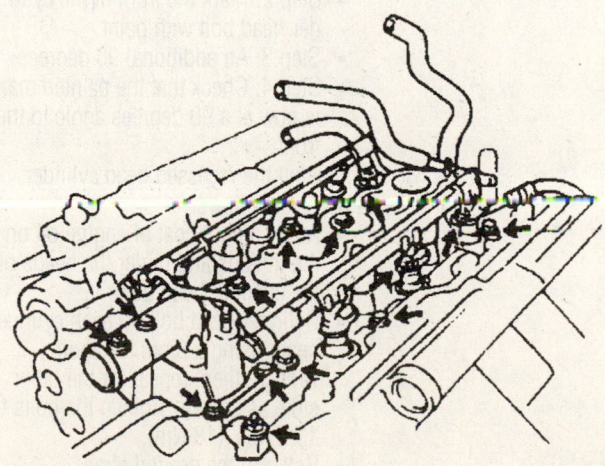

Intake manifold bolts and nuts locations—T-100 and Tacoma with 3.4L (5VZ-FE) engine

7924YG20

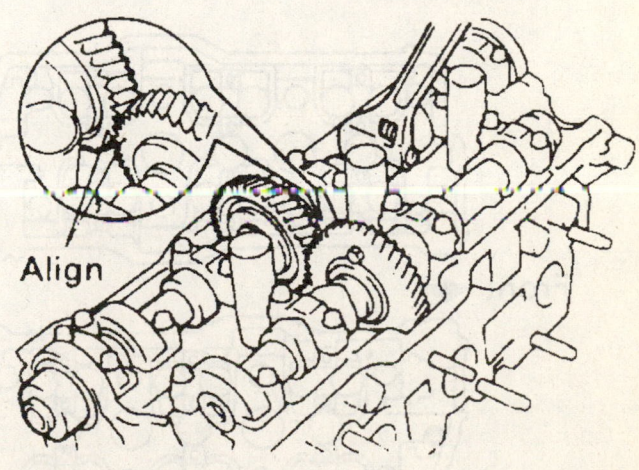

Aligning the timing mark (1 dot mark) of the left camshafts—3.4L (5VZ-FE) engine

7924YG22

For complete service labor times order Nichols' Chilton Labor Guide Manual

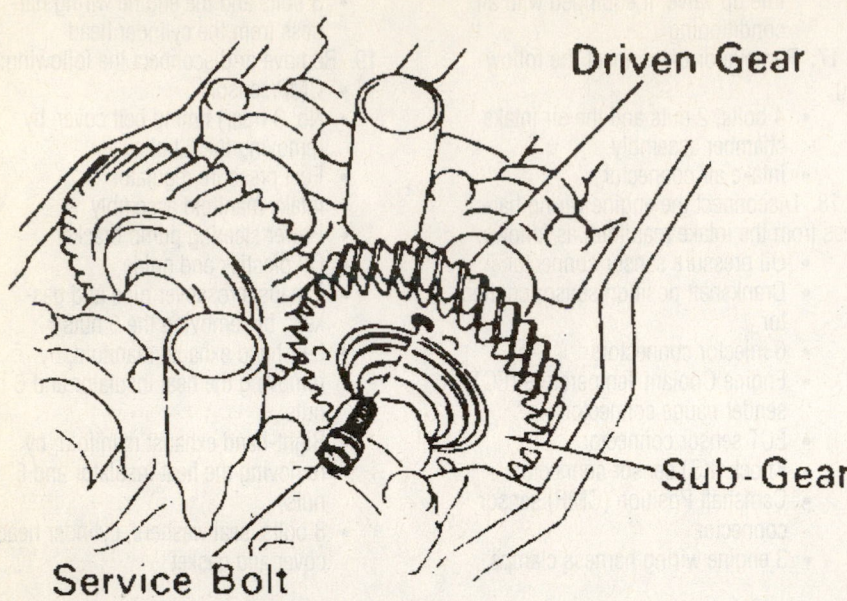

Drive gear service bolt (left side)—3.4L (5VZ-FE) engine

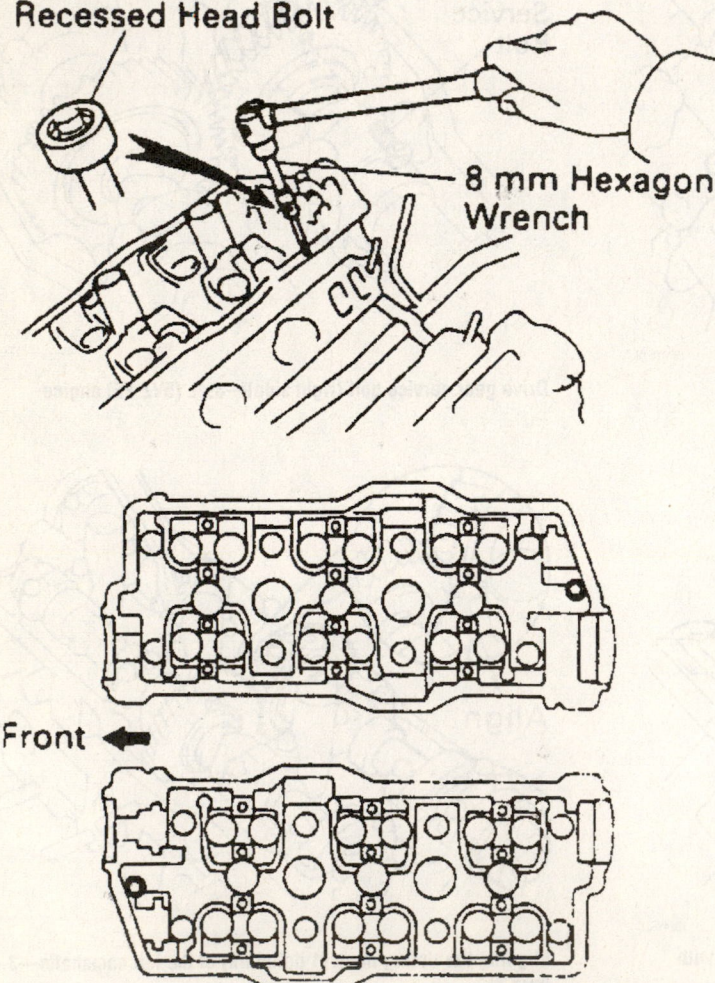

Cylinder head recessed bolts—3.4L (5VZ-FE) engine

- Both cylinder head covers
- Semi-circular plugs
- Right exhaust camshafts
- Right-hand intake camshaft
- Left exhaust camshafts
- Left-hand intake camshaft
- Valve lifters and shims from the cylinder head; arrange the valve lifters and shims in correct order

20. Remove the cylinder heads, as follows:
- Bolt and disconnect the ground strap
- Cylinder head (recessed head) bolt on each cylinder head, using an 8mm hexagon wrench; then repeat for the other side
- 8 cylinder head (12-pointed head) bolts on each cylinder head, by loosening the bolts in several passes and in the reverse order of the tightening sequence
- 16 cylinder head bolts and plate washers.
- Cylinder head

To install:

➡**Refer to Section 1 of this manual for the cylinder head torque sequence illustration. The illustration is located after the Torque Specification Chart.**

21. Clean all surfaces.
22. Install or connect the following:
- New cylinder head gaskets
- Cylinder heads
23. Apply a light coat of engine oil on the threads and under the heads of the cylinder head bolts.
24. Tighten the cylinder head bolts, in sequence, using several passes, as follows:
- Step 1: 25 ft. lbs. (34 Nm)
- Step 2: Mark the front of the cylinder head bolt with paint
- Step 3: An additional 90 degrees
- Step 4: Check that the painted mark is now at a 90 degrees angle to the front
25. Install the recessed head cylinder head bolts, as follows:
- Apply a light coat of engine oil on the threads and under the heads of the cylinder head bolts
- Cylinder head bolt on each cylinder head, using a 8mm hexagon wrench; then, repeat for the other side, as shown. Tighten the bolts to 13 ft. lbs. (18 Nm).
- Bolt and the ground strap
26. Install or connect the following:
- Valve lifters and shims

➡**Check that the valve lifter rotates smoothly by hand.**

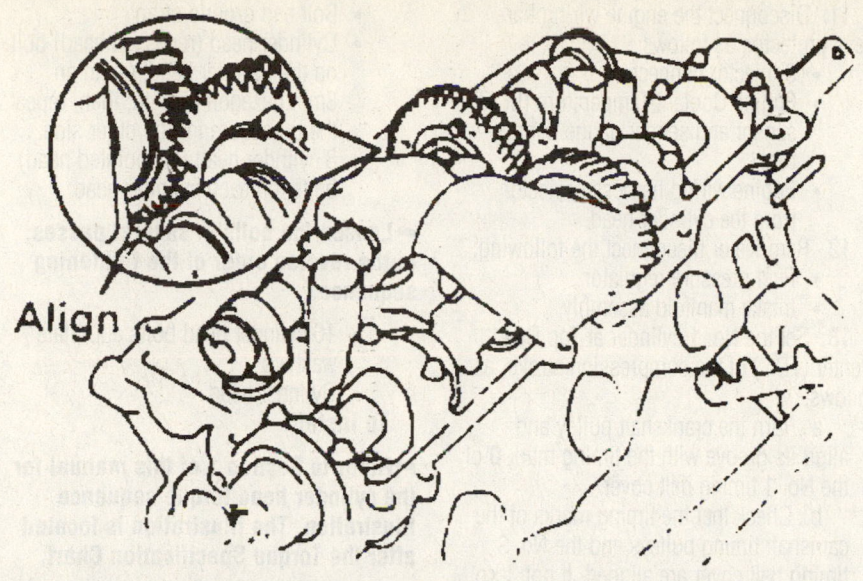

Aligning the right camshafts for installation—3.4L (5VZ-FE) engine

- Camshafts
- Check and adjust the valve clearance
- Semi-circular plugs
- Cylinder head covers. Tighten the bolts, in several passes, to 53 inch lbs. (6 Nm).
- Exhaust manifolds, with new gaskets. Tighten the nuts to 30 ft. lbs. (40 Nm).
- Exhaust manifold heat insulators. Tighten the nuts to 71 inch lbs. (8 Nm).
- Exhaust crossover pipe. Tighten the nuts to 33 ft. lbs. (45 Nm).
- Alternator bracket. Tighten to 14 ft. lbs. (18 Nm).
- Oil dipstick and guide, using a new O-ring
- Power steering bracket. Tighten the fasteners to 14 ft. lbs. (18 Nm).
- New gaskets and the intake manifold assembly. Tighten the bolts and nuts to 13 ft. lbs. (18 Nm).
- Intake manifold stay with the 2 bolts. Tighten the bolts to 14 ft. lbs. (18 Nm).
- Fuel inlet hose
- Fuel pressure regulator
- No. 3 timing belt cover. Tighten the bolts to 80 inch lbs. (9 Nm).
- CMP sensor. Tighten to 71 inch lbs. (8 Nm).
- Engine wiring harness

27. Install or connect the intake air connector, as follows:
- Intake manifold. Tighten the bolts and nuts to 14 ft. lbs. (19 Nm).

- DLC1 to the bracket on the intake manifold
- Ground strap to the intake manifold
- Brake booster vacuum hose to the intake air connector
- 2 fuel return hoses
- Engine wiring harness to the intake manifold
- Idle up valve connector, if equipped with air conditioning

28. Install or connect the following:
- Air intake chamber assembly. Tighten the bolts and nuts to 14 ft. lbs. (18.5 Nm).
- Hoses

29. Attach the following connectors:
- VSV connector for the fuel pressure control
- TP sensor connector
- IAC valve connector
- EGR gas temperature connector, if equipped with an EGR valve
- VSV connector, if equipped with an EGR valve
- Intake chamber stay
- New gaskets and the EGR pipe. Tighten the clamp nuts to 71 inch lbs. (8 Nm) and the EGR pipe nuts to 14 ft. lbs. (18 Nm).
- Alternator but do not tighten the bolts and nuts at this time.
- No. 2 timing belt idler. Tighten the bolt to 30 ft. lbs. (40 Nm).

➡**Check that the pulley bracket moves smoothly.**

- Left camshaft timing pulley

30. Set the No. 1 cylinder to TDC of the compression stroke, as follows:
   a. Turn the crankshaft pulley and align its groove with the timing mark **0** on the No. 1 timing belt cover.
   b. Turn the camshaft, align the knock pin hole of the camshaft with the timing mark of the No. 3 timing belt cover.
   c. Turn the camshaft timing pulley, align the timing marks of the camshaft timing pulley and the No. 3 timing belt cover.

31. Connect the timing belt to the left camshaft timing pulley, as follows:
   a. Check that the installation mark on the timing belt is aligned with the end of the No. 1 timing belt cover.
   b. Using Variable Pin Wrench Set 09960-01000, slightly turn the left camshaft timing pulley clockwise. Align the installation mark on the timing belt with the timing mark of the camshaft timing pulley and hang the timing belt on the left camshaft timing pulley.
   c. Align the timing marks of the left camshaft pulley and the No. 3 timing belt cover.
   d. Check that the timing belt has tension between the crankshaft timing pulley and the left camshaft timing pulley.

32. Install the right camshaft timing pulley and the timing belt, as follows:
   a. Align the installation mark on the timing belt with the timing mark of the right camshaft timing pulley, and hang the timing belt on the right camshaft timing pulley with the flange side facing inward.
   b. Slide the right camshaft timing pulley on the camshaft. Align the timing marks on the right camshaft timing pulley and the No. 3 timing belt cover.
   c. Align the knock pin hole of the camshaft with the knock pin groove of the pulley and install the knock pin. Install the bolt and tighten to 81 ft. lbs. (110 Nm).

33. Set the timing belt tensioner as follows:
   a. Using a press, slowly press in the pushrod using 220–2,205 lbs. (981–9,807 N) of force.
   b. Align the holes of the pushrod and housing, pass a 1.5mm hexagon wrench through the holes to keep the setting position of the pushrod.
   c. Release the press and install the dust boot to the tensioner.

34. Install the timing belt tensioner.

Timing belt service is covered in Section 4 of this manual

Tighten the bolts alternately to 20 ft. lbs. (28 Nm).

35. Using pliers, remove the 1.5mm hexagon wrench from the belt tensioner.

36. Check the valve timing.

37. Install or connect the following:
- Remaining components
- Negative battery cable

38. Fill the radiator with engine coolant.

39. Start the engine and check for leaks.

40. Check the ignition timing.

41. Install the engine undercover.

42. Road test the vehicle.

43. Recheck all fluid levels.

4RUNNER

1. Before servicing the vehicle, refer to the precautions in the beginning of this section.

2. Disconnect the negative battery cable.

3. Relieve the fuel system pressure.

4. Remove the engine undercover.

5. Drain the cooling system.

6. Remove or disconnect the following:
- Front exhaust pipe
- Air cleaner cap
- Mass Air Flow (MAF) meter and the resonator

7. Disconnect the following cables:
- Actuator cable with the bracket, if equipped with cruise control
- Accelerator cable
- Throttle cable, if equipped with an automatic transmission

8. Disconnect the following hoses:
- Heater hose
- Brake booster vacuum hose
- Evaporative Emissions (EVAP) hose
- Automatic Disconnecting Differential (ADD) vacuum hose, for 4-wheel drive
- Fuel inlet and fuel return hose

9. Remove or disconnect the following:
- Spark plug wires with the ignition coils
- Spark plugs
- Intake chamber stay
- No. 2 timing belt cover
- Air intake chamber assembly

10. Remove the following connectors and hoses:
- Throttle Position (TP) sensor connector
- Idle Air Control (IAC) valve connector
- Positive Crankcase Ventilation (PCV) hoses
- Water bypass hoses
- Air assist hose from the throttle body
- Intake air connector

11. Disconnect the engine wiring harness protector, as follows:
- 6 injector connectors
- Engine Coolant Temperature (ECT) sensor and sender gauge connectors
- Engine wiring harness protector from the cylinder head

12. Remove or disconnect the following:
- Fuel pressure regulator
- Intake manifold assembly

13. Set the No. 1 cylinder at Top Dead Center (TDC) of the compression stroke, as follows:

a. Turn the crankshaft pulley and align its groove with the timing mark **0** of the No. 1 timing belt cover.

b. Check that the timing marks of the camshaft timing pulleys and the No. 3 timing belt cover are aligned. If not, turn the crankshaft pulley 1 revolution (360 degrees).

14. Remove or disconnect the following:
- Timing belt tensioner, by alternately loosening the 2 bolts
- Timing belt

15. Remove the camshaft timing pulleys, as follows:

a. Using Variable Pin Wrench Set 09960-10010, remove the pulley bolt, the timing pulley and the knock pin.

b. Remove the 2 timing pulleys with the timing belt.

16. Remove or disconnect the following:
- Bolt and the No. 2 idler pulley
- Camshaft Position (CMP) sensor
- No. 3 timing belt cover
- Alternator from the engine
- Alternator bracket
- Power steering pump and move it aside without disconnecting the pump lines
- Exhaust crossover pipe and gaskets, by removing the 6 nuts
- Left-hand exhaust manifold, by removing the heat insulator and 6 nuts
- Right-hand exhaust manifold, by removing the heat insulator and 6 nuts
- 8 bolts, seal washers, cylinder head cover and gasket.

➡ Remove both cylinder head covers

- Semi-circular plugs
- Right exhaust and intake camshafts
- Left exhaust and intake camshafts
- Valve lifters and shims from the cylinder head; arrange the valve lifters and shims in correct order

17. Remove the cylinder heads, as follows:

- Bolt and ground strap
- Cylinder head (recessed head) bolt on the cylinder head, using an 8mm hexagon wrench; then, repeat the procedure for the other side.
- 8 cylinder head (12-pointed head) bolts, on each cylinder head.

➡ **Loosen the bolts in several passes, in the reverse order of the tightening sequence.**

- 16 cylinder head bolts and plate washers
- Cylinder head

To install:

➡ **Refer to Section 1 of this manual for the cylinder head torque sequence illustration. The illustration is located after the Torque Specification Chart.**

18. Clean all surfaces.

19. Install or connect the following:
- New cylinder head gaskets
- Cylinder heads

20. Apply a light coat of engine oil on the threads and under the heads of the cylinder head bolts.

21. Tighten the cylinder head bolts using several passes, in sequence, as follows:
- Step 1: 25 ft. lbs. (34 Nm)
- Step 2: Mark the front of the cylinder head bolt with paint
- Step 3: Turn 90 degrees
- Step 4: Check that the painted mark is now at a 90 degrees angle to the front

22. Install the recessed head cylinder head bolts, as follows:
- Step 1: Apply a light coat of engine oil on the threads and under the heads of the cylinder head bolts
- Step 2: Tighten the cylinder head bolts, using a 8mm hexagon wrench, to 13 ft. lbs. (18 Nm).
- Bolt and ground strap

23. Install or connect the following:
- Valve lifters and shims

➡ **Check that the valve lifter rotates smoothly by hand.**

- Right intake and exhaust camshafts
- Left intake and exhaust camshafts

24. Check and adjust the valve clearance.

25. Install or connect the following:
- Semi-circular plugs
- Cylinder head covers. Uniformly, tighten the bolts, in several passes, to 53 inch lbs. (6 Nm).
- Exhaust manifolds with new gaskets. Tighten the nuts to 30 ft. lbs. (40 Nm).

- Exhaust manifold heat insulators. Tighten the nuts to 71 inch lbs. (8 Nm).
- Exhaust crossover pipe. Tighten the nuts to 33 ft. lbs. (45 Nm).
- Power steering pump
- Alternator bracket. Tighten the fasteners to 14 ft. lbs. (18 Nm).
- Alternator
- No. 3 timing belt cover. Tighten the bolts to 80 inch lbs. (9 Nm).
- CMP sensor. Tighten it to 71 inch lbs. (8 Nm).
- Timing belt
- No. 2 timing belt idler bolt. Tighten the bolt to 30 ft. lbs. (40 Nm).

➡**Check that the pulley bracket moves smoothly.**

- Left camshaft timing pulley

26. Set the No. 1 cylinder to TDC of the compression stroke, as follows:

   a. Connect the timing belt to the left camshaft timing pulley.

   b. Check that the installation mark on the timing belt is aligned with the end of the No. 1 timing belt cover.

   c. Install the right camshaft timing pulley and the timing belt.

   d. Set the timing belt tensioner. Alternately, tighten the bolts to 20 ft. lbs. (28 Nm).

27. Using pliers, remove the 1.5mm hexagon wrench from the belt tensioner.
28. Check the valve timing.
29. Install or connect the following:
- New gaskets and the intake manifold assembly. Tighten the bolts and nuts to 13 ft. lbs. (18 Nm).
- Intake manifold stay. Tighten the bolts to 14 ft. lbs. (18 Nm).
- Fuel pressure regulator

30. Connect the engine wiring harness to the intake manifold, as follows:
- Engine wiring harness to the cylinder head
- 3 engine wiring harness clamps

31. Install or connect the following:
- 6 injector connectors
- ECT sender gauge connector
- ECT sensor connector
- Intake air connector
- Air intake chamber assembly. Tighten the bolts and nuts to 13 ft. lbs. (18 Nm).
- Intake chamber stay
- No. 2 timing belt cover. Tighten the bolts to 80 inch lbs. (9 Nm).
- PCV hoses

- Water bypass hoses
- Air assist hose to the throttle body
- IAC valve connector
- TP sensor connector
- CMP sensor connector to the No. 2 timing belt cover
- 3 spark plug wire clamps

32. Connect the following hoses:
- Brake booster vacuum hose
- EVAP hose
- Automatic Disconnecting Differential (ADD) vacuum hose, for 4-wheel drive
- Fuel inlet and fuel return hose
- Heater hose

33. Install or connect the following:
- Oil dipstick and guide, using a new O-ring
- Spark plugs
- Spark plug wires, with the ignition coils
- Alternator drive belt

34. Connect the following cables:
- Actuator cable with the bracket, if equipped with cruise control
- Accelerator cable
- Throttle cable, if equipped with an automatic transmission
- MAF meter, resonator and air cleaner cap
- Front exhaust pipe
- Negative battery cable

35. Fill the radiator with engine coolant.
36. Start the engine and check for leaks.
37. Check the ignition timing.
38. Install the engine undercover.
39. Road test the vehicle.
40. Recheck all fluid levels.

Intake Manifold

REMOVAL & INSTALLATION

2.4L (2RZ-FE) Engine

1. Relieve the fuel system pressure.
2. Disconnect the negative battery cable.
3. Drain the engine coolant.
4. Remove or disconnect the following:
- Air cleaner cap
- Mass Air Flow (MAF) meter and the resonator
- Accelerator cable from the throttle body, if equipped with a manual transaxle
- Accelerator and throttle cables from the throttle body, if equipped with an automatic transaxle

- Intake air connector
- Air conditioning idle-up valve, if equipped with air conditioning
- No. 1 and No. 2 Positive Crankcase Ventilation (PCV) hoses
- Spark plug wires from the spark plugs
- Throttle body
- Air conditioning compressor connector, if equipped with air conditioning
- Oil pressure sensor connector
- Engine Coolant Temperature (ECT) sensor connector
- Exhaust Gas Recirculation (EGR) gas temperature sensor connector
- EGR Vacuum Switching Valve (VSV) connector

5. Disconnect the engine wiring harness, as follows:
- 2 bolts and the harness from the intake chamber
- 5 engine harness clamps and harness

6. Remove or disconnect the following:
- Knock (KS) sensor connector
- Crankshaft Position (CKP) sensor connector
- Fuel pressure control VSV connector
- Data Link Connector 1 (DLC1) from the bracket
- 2 engine wiring harness clamps
- Engine wiring harness
- Fuel injectors
- EGR valve and vacuum modulator
- Intake chamber stay, by removing the 2 bolts
- Fuel return pipe, by removing the hoses and 2 bolts

7. Remove the intake chamber, as follows:
- Vacuum hose, from the gas filter
- Brake booster vacuum hose, from the intake chamber
- 3 bolts, 2 nuts, air intake chamber and gasket

8. Remove the fuel inlet tube, by removing the union bolts.

9. Remove the delivery pipe and injectors, as follows:
- Vacuum hose, from the fuel pressure regulator
- Bolts and delivery pipe together with the 4 injectors
- 4 insulators, from the 4 spacers
- Injectors from the delivery pipe
- O-ring and grommet, from each injector

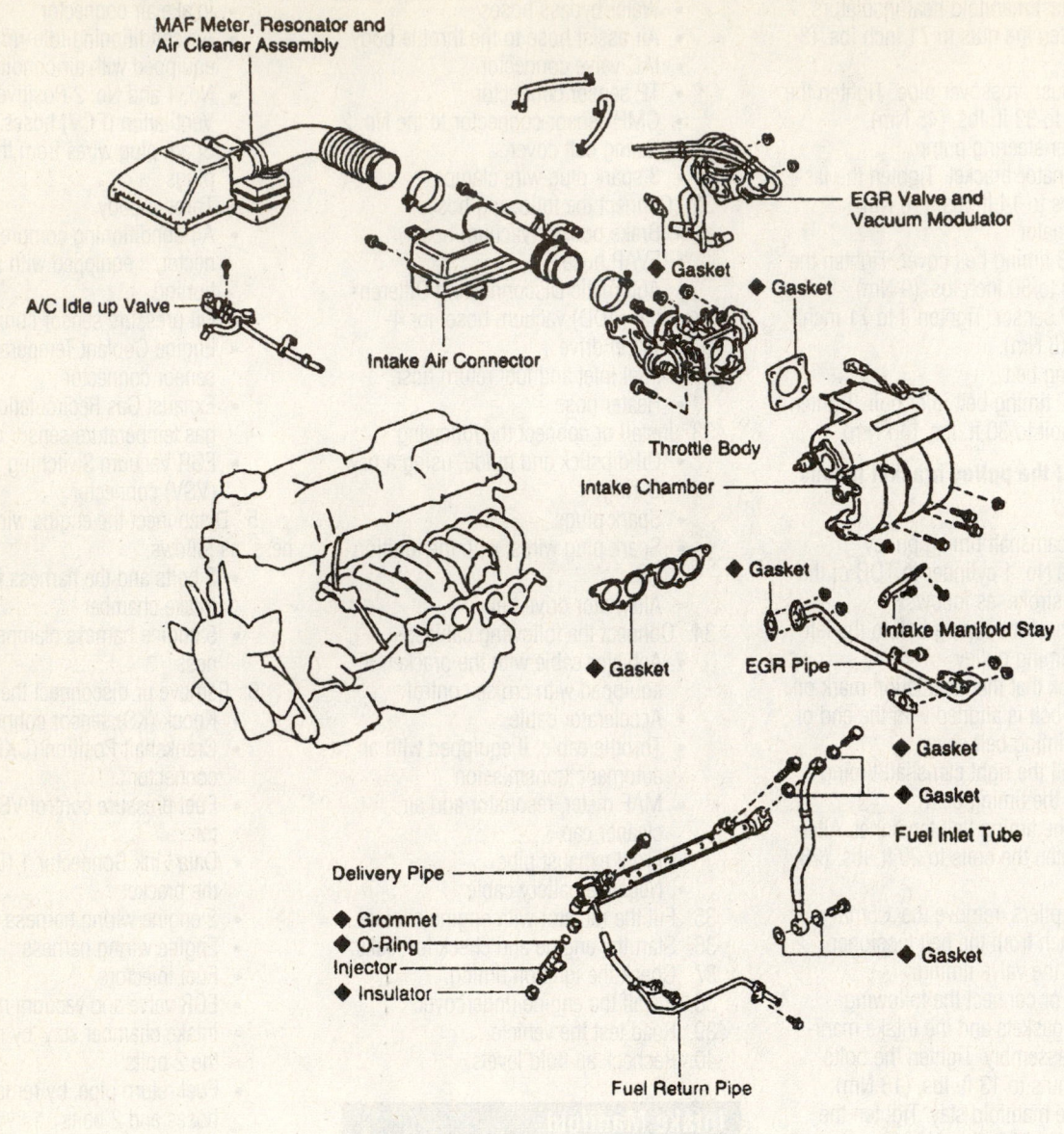

MAF Meter, Resonator and Air Cleaner Assembly

A/C Idle up Valve

Intake Air Connector

EGR Valve and Vacuum Modulator

Gasket

Gasket

Throttle Body

Intake Chamber

Gasket

Gasket

Intake Manifold Stay

EGR Pipe

Gasket

Gasket

Fuel Inlet Tube

Delivery Pipe

Gasket

◆ Grommet
◆ O-Ring
Injector
◆ Insulator

Fuel Return Pipe

◆ Non-reusable part

7924YG32

Exploded view of the intake manifold assembly—2.4L (2RZ-FE) and 2.7L (3RZ-FE) engines

10. Remove or disconnect the following:
- Intake manifold, by removing the 3 bolts and 2 nuts
- Gasket

To install:

11. Clean the intake manifold surfaces.
12. Install or connect the following:
- New gasket
- Intake manifold. Tighten the bolts and nuts to 22 ft. lbs. (30 Nm).
13. Install the injectors to the delivery pipe, as follows:
- New grommet to the injector
- New O-ring onto the injector, by lubricating it with gasoline

- Injectors to the delivery pipe
- Injector with the connector facing upward
- Injectors and delivery pipe. Tighten the bolts to 15 ft. lbs. (21 Nm).

➡ **Check that the injectors rotate smoothly.**

- Fuel tube, with new gaskets. Tighten the union bolts to 22 ft. lbs. (30 Nm).
14. Install the air intake chamber, as follows:
- New gasket
- Air intake chamber. Tighten the

bolts and nuts to 15 ft. lbs. (21 Nm).
- Vacuum hose, to the gas filter
- Brake booster vacuum hose, to the intake chamber
15. Install or connect the following:
- Fuel return pipe
- Intake chamber stay. Tighten the bolts to 14 ft. lbs. (20 Nm).
- EGR valve and vacuum modulator
- Injector connectors
16. Connect the engine wiring harness to the engine, as follows:
- Engine wiring harness to the intake manifold

- Engine wiring harness clamps
- DLC1 to the bracket
- Fuel pressure control VSV connector
- KS sensor connector
- CKP sensor connector
- 5 engine wiring harness clamps
- Engine wiring harness, to the intake chamber

17. Install or connect the following:
- EGR VSV connector
- EGR gas temperature sensor connector
- ECT sensor connector
- Oil pressure sensor connector
- Compressor connector, if equipped with air conditioning
- Throttle body
- Spark plug wires, to the spark plugs
- No. 1 and No. 2 PCV hoses
- Air conditioning idle up valve, if equipped with air conditioning
- Air intake connector
- Accelerator cable, to the throttle body, if equipped with a manual transaxle
- Throttle and accelerator cables to the throttle body, if equipped with a automatic transaxle
- MAF meter, resonator and the air cleaner cap
- Negative battery cable

18. Refill the cooling system.
19. Start the engine and check for leaks.
20. Check the ignition timing. Road test the vehicle for proper operation.
21. Recheck all fluid levels.

2.7L (3RZ-FE) Engine

T-100 AND TACOMA

1. Before servicing the vehicle, refer to the precautions in the beginning of this section.
2. Relieve the fuel system pressure.
3. Disconnect the negative battery cable.
4. Drain the engine coolant.
5. Remove or disconnect the following:
- Air cleaner cap
- Mass Air Flow (MAF) meter and resonator
- Accelerator cable, from the throttle body, if equipped with a manual transaxle
- Accelerator and throttle cables, from the throttle body, if equipped with an automatic transaxle

- Intake air connector
- Air conditioning idle-up valve, if equipped with air conditioning
- No. 1 and No. 2 PCV hoses
- Spark plug wires, from the spark plugs
- Throttle body

6. Detach the following connectors:
- Air conditioning compressor connector, if equipped with air conditioning
- Oil pressure sensor connector
- Engine Coolant Temperature (ECT) sensor connector
- Exhaust Gas Recirculation (EGR) gas temperature sensor connector
- EGR Vacuum Switching Valve (VSV) connector

7. Disconnect the engine wiring harness, as follows:
- Engine wiring harness, from the intake chamber
- 5 engine wiring harness clamps and engine wiring harness
- Knock (KS) sensor connector
- Crankshaft Position (CKP) sensor connector
- Fuel pressure control VSV connector
- Data Link Connector 1 (DLC1), from the bracket
- 2 engine wiring harness clamps.
- Engine wiring harness from the engine

8. Remove or disconnect the following:
- Fuel injectors
- EGR valve and vacuum modulator
- Intake chamber stay
- Fuel return pipe

9. Remove the intake chamber, as follows:
- Vacuum hose, from the gas filter
- Brake booster vacuum hose, from the intake chamber
- Intake chamber and gasket
- Fuel inlet tube, by removing the union bolts

10. Remove the delivery pipe and injectors, as follows:
- Vacuum hose, from the fuel pressure regulator
- Delivery pipe, with the 4 injectors
- 4 insulators, from the 4 spacers
- 4 injectors, from the delivery pipe
- O-ring and grommet, from each injector

11. Remove or disconnect the following:
- Intake manifold
- Gasket

To install:
12. Clean the intake manifold surfaces.
13. Install or connect the following:
- New gasket
- Intake manifold. Tighten the bolts and nuts to 22 ft. lbs. (30 Nm).
14. Install the injectors to the delivery pipe, as follows:
- New grommet onto the injector
- New O-ring onto the injector, lubricated with gasoline
- Injectors onto the delivery pipe, with the electrical connector upward
15. Install or connect the following:
- Delivery pipe. Tighten the bolts to 15 ft. lbs. (21 Nm).

➡ **Check that the injectors rotate smoothly.**

- Fuel tube, with new gaskets. Tighten the union bolts to 22 ft. lbs. (30 Nm).
16. Install the air intake chamber, as follows:
- Air intake chamber with a new gasket. Tighten the bolts and nuts to 15 ft. lbs. (21 Nm).
- Vacuum hose, to the gas filter
- Brake booster vacuum hose, to the intake chamber
17. Install or connect the following:
- Fuel return pipe
- Intake chamber stay. Tighten the bolts to 14 ft. lbs. (20 Nm).
18. Install the EGR valve and vacuum modulator, as follows:
- New gasket, EGR valve and vacuum modulator. Tighten the bolt to 74 inch lbs. (9 Nm) and the nuts to 14 ft. lbs. (19 Nm).
- Vacuum hoses, to the EGR VSV
- Water bypass hose
- EGR pipe, using new gaskets. Tighten the bolts to 14 ft. lbs. (18 Nm), intake manifold nuts to 14 ft. lbs. (19 Nm) and the cylinder head nuts to 15 ft. lbs. (20 Nm).
- Injector connectors
19. Connect the engine wiring harness to the engine, as follows:
- Engine wiring harness, to the intake manifold
- 2 engine wiring harness clamps
- DLC1, to the bracket
- Fuel pressure control VSV connector
- KS sensor connector
- CKP sensor connector

Refer to Section 1 for engine rebuilding specifications

- 5 engine wiring harness clamps.
- Engine wiring harness, to the intake chamber

20. Attach the following connectors to the engine:
- EGR VSV connector
- EGR gas temperature sensor connector
- ECT sensor connector
- Oil pressure sensor connector
- Compressor connector, if equipped with air conditioning

21. Install or connect the following:
- Throttle body
- Spark plug wires, to the spark plugs
- No. 1 and No. 2 PCV hoses
- Air conditioning idle up valve, if equipped with air conditioning
- Air intake connector, by installing the 2 bolts, hose clamp and 2 air hoses
- Accelerator cable, if equipped with a manual transaxle
- Throttle and accelerator cables, if equipped with an automatic transaxle
- MAF meter, resonator and the air cleaner cap
- Negative battery cable

22. Refill the cooling system.
23. Start the engine and check for leaks.
24. Check the ignition timing. Road test the vehicle for proper operation.
25. Recheck all fluid levels.

4RUNNER

1. Before servicing the vehicle, refer to the precautions in the beginning of this section.
2. Disconnect the negative battery cable.
3. Release the fuel system pressure.
4. Drain the engine coolant.
5. Remove or disconnect the following:
- Air cleaner cap
- Mass Air Flow (MAF) meter and the resonator
- Accelerator cable from the throttle body, if equipped with a manual transmission
- Accelerator and throttle cables from the throttle body, if equipped with an automatic transmission
- Cruise control cable from the actuator, if equipped with cruise control
- Intake air connector
- Air hose for Idle Air Control (IAC)
- Vacuum sensing hose
- Wire clamp for the engine wiring harness
- Positive Crankcase Ventilation (PCV) hoses.

- Engine wiring harness
- Air conditioning compressor connector, if equipped with air conditioning
- Oil pressure sensor connector
- Engine Coolant Temperature (ECT) sensor connector
- ECT sender gauge connector
- Exhaust Gas Recirculation (EGR) gas temperature sensor connector
- Vacuum Switching Valve (VSV) connector, for the EGR
- 2 vacuum hoses, from the VSV for the EGR
- Ground strap, from the cowl top panel
- Engine wiring harness, from the air intake chamber
- Throttle Position (TP) sensor connector
- IAC valve connector
- Crankshaft Position (CKP) sensor connector
- Knock (KS) sensor connector
- Data Link Connector 1 (DLC1), from the bracket
- Engine wiring harness clamp
- EGR pipe
- Intake chamber stay
- Air intake chamber assembly

6. Disconnect the following hoses:
- Evaporative Emission (EVAP) hose, from the throttle body
- Brake booster vacuum hose, from the union
- Water bypass hose, from the water bypass pipe
- Water bypass hose, from the cylinder head rear cover
- Injector connectors
- Fuel inlet pipe
- Hoses and the fuel return pipe.

7. Remove the delivery pipe and injectors, as follows:
- Delivery pipe, together with the 4 injectors
- 4 insulators from the 4 spacers
- 4 injectors, from the delivery pipe
- O-ring and grommets, from each injector
- 4 spacers, by carefully prying them out

8. Remove the intake manifold.

To install:

9. Install or connect the following:
- Intake manifold. Tighten the bolts to 22 ft. lbs. (29 Nm).
- Injectors and the delivery pipe
- Fuel return pipe
- Fuel inlet pipe, with a new gasket. Tighten the bolts to 22 ft. lbs. (29 Nm).

- Injector connectors
- Air intake chamber assembly. Tighten the bolts to 15 ft. lbs. (21 Nm).

10. Connect the following hoses:
- Evaporative Emissions (EVAP) hose, to the throttle body
- Brake booster vacuum hose, to the union
- Water bypass hose, to water bypass pipe
- Water bypass hose, to cylinder head rear cover

11. Install or connect the following:
- Air intake chamber stay. Tighten the bolts to 15 ft. lbs. (20 Nm).
- EGR pipe. Tighten bolts to 13 ft. lbs. (18 Nm), nut "A" to 14 ft. lbs. (19 Nm) and nut B to 15 ft. lbs. (20 Nm).
- Air conditioning compressor connector
- Oil pressure sensor connector
- ECT sensor connector
- ECT sender gauge connector
- EGR gas temperature sensor connector
- VSV connector for the EGR
- 2 vacuum hose to the VSV for the EGR
- Ground strap to the cowl top panel
- Engine wiring harness to the air intake chamber
- TP sensor connector
- IAC valve connector
- CKP sensor connector
- KS sensor connector
- DLC1 to the bracket
- Engine wiring harness clamp
- PCV hoses
- Intake air connector. Tighten the bolts to 13 ft. lbs. (18 Nm).
- Cruise control cable to the actuator, if equipped with cruise control
- Accelerator cable to the throttle body, if equipped with a manual transmission
- Accelerator and throttle cables to the throttle body, if equipped with an automatic transmission

12. Fill the engine and radiator with engine coolant.
13. Install or connect the following:
- Air cleaner cap, MAF meter and resonator assembly
- Negative battery cable

14. Start the engine and check for leaks.
15. Road test the vehicle for proper operation.
16. Recheck all fluid levels.

3.4L (5VZ-FE) Engine

4RUNNER

1. Before servicing the vehicle, refer to the precautions in the beginning of this section.
2. Disconnect the negative battery cable.
3. Relieve the fuel system pressure.
4. Remove the engine undercover.
5. Drain the cooling system.
6. Remove or disconnect the following:
   - Air cleaner cap
   - Mass Air Flow (MAF) meter and the resonator
   - Actuator cable with the bracket, if equipped with cruise control
   - Accelerator cable
   - Throttle cable, if equipped with automatic transmission
7. Disconnect the following hoses:
   - Heater hose
   - Brake booster vacuum hose
   - Evaporative Emissions (EVAP) hose
   - Automatic Disconnecting Differential (ADD) vacuum hose, for 4-Wheel drive
   - Fuel inlet and fuel return hose
8. Remove or disconnect the following:
   - Spark plug wires, with the ignition coils
   - Intake chamber stay
   - No. 2 timing belt cover
   - Air intake chamber assembly
   - Throttle Position (TP) sensor connector
   - Idle Air Control (IAC) valve connector
   - Positive Crankcase Ventilation (PCV) hoses
   - Water bypass hoses
   - Air assist hose from the throttle body
   - Intake air connector
   - Engine wiring harness
   - Fuel return hose
   - Vacuum hose, from the fuel pressure regulator
   - Ground strap, from the intake air connector
   - Data Link Connector 1 (DLC1), from the bracket
   - 6 injector connectors
   - Engine Coolant Temperature (ECT) sensor and sender gauge connectors
   - Engine wiring harness protector from the cylinder head
   - Fuel pressure regulator

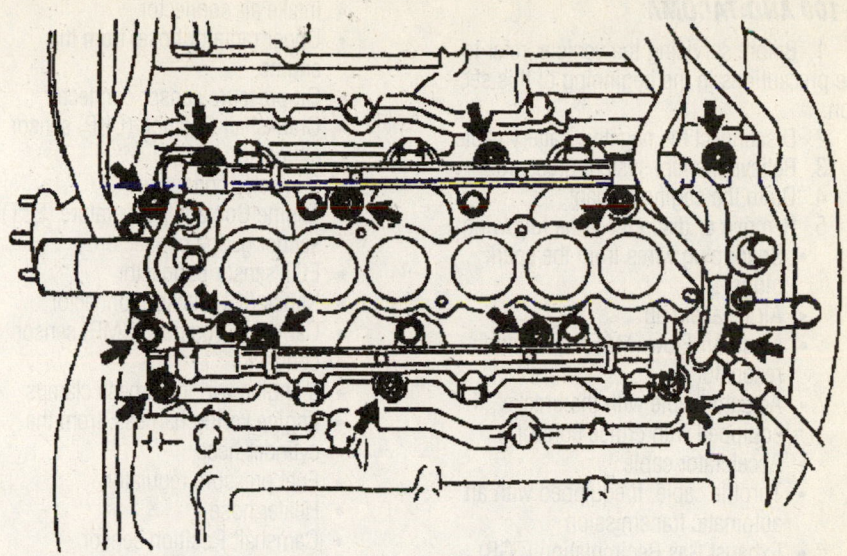

Intake manifold bolts and nuts—4Runner with 3.4L (5VZ-FE) engine

7924YG38

- Intake manifold assembly
- Intake manifold stay
- Intake manifold, delivery pipes and the injectors assembly with the gaskets

To install:

9. Install or connect the following:
   - New gaskets
   - Intake manifold assembly. Tighten the bolts and nuts to 13 ft. lbs. (18 Nm).
   - Intake manifold stay. Tighten the bolts to 14 ft. lbs. (18 Nm).
   - Fuel pressure regulator
   - Engine wiring harness to the cylinder head, by installing the 3 bolts
   - 3 engine wiring harness clamps
   - 6 injector connectors
   - ECT sender gauge connector
   - ECT sensor connector
   - Intake manifold. Tighten the bolts and nuts to 14 ft. lbs. (18.5 Nm).
   - DLC1 to the bracket on the intake manifold
   - Ground strap to the intake manifold, by installing the bolt
   - Brake booster vacuum hose, to the intake air connector
   - 2 fuel return hoses
   - Engine wiring harness to the intake manifold
   - Air intake chamber assembly to the engine. Tighten the bolts and nuts to 14 ft. lbs. (18.5 Nm).
   - Intake chamber stay. Tighten the bolts to 30 ft. lbs. (40 Nm).
   - New O-ring to the oil filler tube

- Oil filler tube end into the tube hole in the oil pan
- Oil filler tube and No. 1 throttle cable clamp
- No. 2 timing belt cover. Tighten the bolts to 80 inch lbs. (9 Nm).
- PCV hoses
- Water bypass hoses
- Air assist hose to the throttle body
- IAC valve connector
- TP sensor connector
- Brake booster vacuum hose
- EVAP hose
- Automatic Disconnecting Differential (ADD) vacuum hose, for 4-Wheel drive
- Fuel inlet and fuel return hose
- 3 spark plug wire clamps to the No. 2 timing belt cover
- CMP connector to the No. 2 timing belt cover
- Spark plug wires with the ignition coils
- Heater hose
- Actuator cable with the bracket, if equipped with cruise control
- Accelerator cable
- Throttle cable, if equipped with automatic transmission
- MAF meter, resonator and the air cleaner cap
- Negative battery cable

10. Fill the radiator with engine coolant.
11. Start the engine and check for leaks.
12. Install the engine undercover.
13. Road test the vehicle.
14. Recheck all fluid levels.

For engine torque specifications, refer to Section 1 of this manual

T-100 AND TACOMA

1. Before servicing the vehicle, refer to the precautions in the beginning of this section.
2. Disconnect the negative battery cable.
3. Relieve the fuel system pressure.
4. Drain the engine coolant.
5. Remove or disconnect the following:
   - Spark plug wires from the spark plugs
   - Air cleaner cap
   - Mass Air Flow (MAF) meter and resonator
   - Actuator cable with the bracket, if equipped with cruise control
   - Accelerator cable
   - Throttle cable, if equipped with an automatic transmission
   - Exhaust Gas Recirculation (EGR) pipe and gaskets, if equipped with an EGR valve
   - Oil filler tube and No. 1 throttle cable clamp, by removing the bolt and 2 nuts
   - Intake chamber stay, by removing the 2 bolts
   - Vacuum Switching Valve (VSV) connector, for the fuel pressure control
   - Throttle Position (TP) sensor connector
   - Idle Air Control (IAC) valve connector
   - EGR gas temperature connector, if equipped with an EGR valve
   - VSV connector for the EGR valve, if equipped with an EGR valve
   - Disconnect the Positive Crankcase Ventilation (PCV) hoses
   - Water bypass hoses
   - Air assist hose from the intake air connector
   - 2 vacuum sensing hoses from the VSV
   - Evaporative Emission (EVAP) hose
   - Air hose from the power steering
   - Air hose from the air conditioning idle up valve, if equipped with air conditioning
   - Air intake chamber assembly
   - Engine wiring harness from the intake air connector
   - 2 fuel return hoses
   - Brake booster vacuum hose, from the intake air connector
   - Ground strap, from the intake air connector
   - Data Link Connector 1 (DLC1) from the intake air connector bracket
   - Idle up valve connector, if equipped with air conditioning

- Intake air connector
- Upper radiator hose, from the engine
- Oil pressure sensor connector
- Crankshaft Position (CKP) sensor connector
- 6 injector connectors
- Engine Coolant Temperature (ECT) sender gauge connector
- ECT sensor connector
- Knock (KS) sensor connector
- Camshaft Position (CMP) sensor connector
- 3 engine wiring harness clamps
- Engine wiring harness, from the cylinder head
- Fuel pressure regulator
- Heater hose
- Camshaft Position sensor.
- Fuel inlet hose
- Intake manifold stay
- Intake manifold assembly

To install:

6. Clean all surfaces.
7. Install or connect the following:
   - New gaskets
   - Intake manifold assembly. Tighten the bolts and nuts to 13 ft. lbs. (18 Nm).
   - Intake manifold stay. Tighten the bolts to 13 ft. lbs. (18 Nm).
   - Fuel inlet hose
   - CMP sensor. Tighten it to 71 inch lbs. (8 Nm).
   - Engine wiring harness to the cylinder head
   - 3 engine wiring harness clamps
   - Oil pressure sensor connector
   - CKP sensor connector
   - 6 injector connectors
   - ECT sender gauge connector
   - ECT sensor connector
   - KS sensor connector
   - CMP sensor connector
   - Heater hose
   - Intake manifold. Tighten the bolts and nuts to 14 ft. lbs. (18.5 Nm).
   - DLC1 to the bracket on the intake manifold
   - Ground strap to the intake manifold
   - Brake booster vacuum hose, to the intake air connector
   - 2 fuel return hoses
   - Engine wiring harness to the intake manifold
   - Idle up valve connector, if equipped with air conditioning
   - Air intake chamber assembly to the engine. Tighten the bolts and nuts to 14 ft. lbs. (18.5 Nm).
   - PCV hoses
   - Water bypass hoses
   - Air assist hose to the intake manifold

- 2 vacuum sensing hoses to the VSV
- EVAP hose
- Air hose to the power steering
- Air hose to the air conditioning idle up valve, if equipped with air conditioning
- VSV connector for the fuel pressure control
- TP sensor connector
- IAC valve connector
- EGR gas temperature connector, if equipped with an EGR valve
- VSV connector for the EGR valve, if equipped with an EGR valve
- Intake chamber stay. Tighten the bolts to 30 ft. lbs. (40 Nm).
- New O-ring to the oil filler tube
- Oil filler tube end into the tube hole in the oil pan
- Oil filler tube and No. 1 throttle cable clamp
- New gaskets and the EGR pipe. Tighten the clamp nuts to 71 inch lbs. (8 Nm) and the EGR pipe nuts to 14 ft. lbs. (18 Nm).
- Fuel pressure regulator
- 3 clamps for the spark plug wires, to the No. 2 timing belt cover
- CMP connector to the No. 2 timing belt cover
- Upper radiator hose

8. Fill with engine coolant.
9. Install or connect the following:
   - Spark plug wires to the spark plugs
   - Actuator cable with the bracket, if equipped with cruise control
   - Accelerator cable
   - Throttle cable, if equipped with an automatic transmission
   - Air cleaner hose
   - Negative battery cable

10. Fill the radiator with engine coolant.
11. Start the engine and check for leaks.

Exhaust Manifold

REMOVAL & INSTALLATION

2.4L (2RZ-FE) and 2.7L (3RZ-FE) Engines

1. Before servicing the vehicle, refer to the precautions in the beginning of this section.
2. Remove or disconnect the following:
   - Clamp from the support bracket
   - Support bracket
   - Front exhaust pipe and gaskets from the exhaust manifold

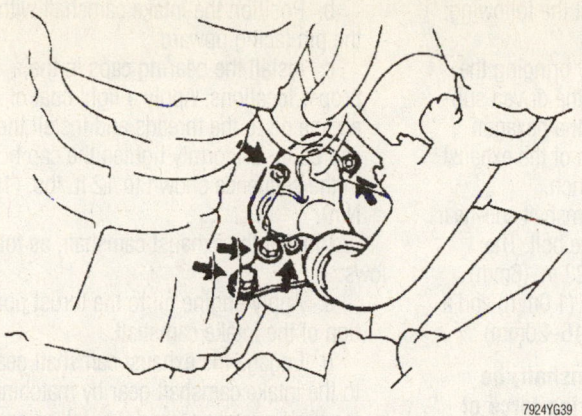

Front exhaust pipe to exhaust manifold nut and bolt locations—2.4L (2RZ-FE) and 2.7L (3RZ-FE) engines

Exhaust manifold nuts—2.4L (2RZ-FE) and 2.7L (3RZ-FE) engines

- Heat insulator
- Exhaust manifold and gasket

To install:

3. Install or connect the following:
   - Exhaust manifold and gasket. Tighten the nuts to 36 ft. lbs. (49 Nm).
   - Heat insulator. Tighten the bolts and nuts to 48 inch lbs. (5.5 Nm).
   - Front exhaust pipe assembly to the exhaust manifold. Tighten the nuts to 46 ft. lbs. (62 Nm).
   - Support bracket. Tighten the bolts to 29 ft. lbs. (39 Nm).
   - Clamp. Tighten the bolt to 14 ft. lbs. (19 Nm).
4. Start the engine.
5. Check for exhaust leaks.

3.4L (5VZ-FE) Engine

1. Before servicing the vehicle, refer to the precautions in the beginning of this section.
2. Remove or disconnect the following:
   - Exhaust crossover pipe, from the exhaust manifold by removing the 3 nuts
   - Exhaust Gas Recirculation (EGR) pipe, from the exhaust manifold, on the left manifold equipped with an EGR valve
   - Exhaust manifold heat insulator, by removing the 3 nuts
   - Exhaust manifold

To install:

3. Install or connect the following:
   - Exhaust manifold, using a new gasket. Tighten the nuts to 30 ft. lbs. (40 Nm).
   - Exhaust heat insulator. Tighten the nuts to 71 inch lbs. (8 Nm).

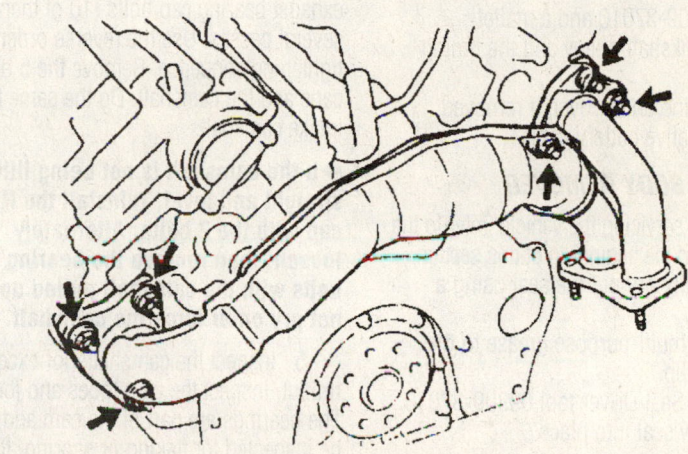

Exhaust crossover pipe mounting nut locations—3.4L (5VZ-FE) engine

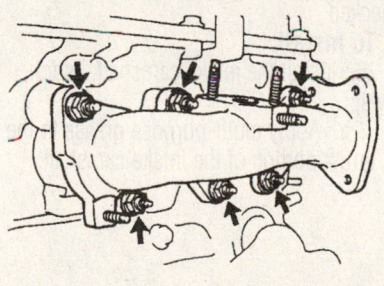

Exhaust manifold nuts—3.4L (5VZ-FE) engine

- EGR pipe to the exhaust manifold, if equipped with an EGR valve. Tighten the manifold nuts to 14 ft. lbs. (18 Nm) and the clamp nuts to 71 inch lbs. (8 Nm).
- Crossover pipe to the exhaust manifold, using a new gasket. Tighten the nuts to 33 ft. lbs. (45 Nm).

Front Crankshaft Seal

REMOVAL & INSTALLATION

3.4L (5VZ-FE) Engine

➡ **There are 2 methods to replace the oil seal, which are as follows:**

OIL PUMP BODY INSTALLED

1. Before servicing the vehicle, refer to the precautions in the beginning of this section.

For complete mechanical specifications, refer to Section 1 of this manual

2. Remove or disconnect the following:
• Negative battery cable
• Timing belt and crankshaft pulley
• Cut off the oil seal lip, using a knife
• Pry out the oil seal, using a suitable tool

❄ WARNING

Be careful not to damage the crankshaft.

To install:
3. Install or connect the following:
• Apply multi-purpose grease to the new oil seal lip
• Tap in the new oil seal until its surface is flush with the oil pump case edge, using Seal Driver tool 09309-37010 and a mallet
• Crankshaft pulley and the timing belt
• Engine undercover, if removed
• Negative battery cable

OIL PUMP BODY REMOVED

1. Before servicing the vehicle, refer to the precautions in the beginning of this section.
2. Carefully pry out the seal using a suitable tool.
3. Apply multi-purpose grease to the new oil seal lip.
4. Using Seal Driver tool 09309-37010, drive the new seal into place.

Camshaft and Valve Lifters

REMOVAL & INSTALLATION

2.4L (2RZ-FE) Engine

1. Before servicing the vehicle, refer to the precautions in the beginning of this section.

2. Remove or disconnect the following:
• Timing chain
• Exhaust camshaft by bringing the service bolt hole of the driven sub-gear upwards. Turn the hexagon wrench head portion of the exhaust camshaft with a wrench.
3. Secure the exhaust camshaft sub-gear to the main gear with a service bolt. The thread diameter should be 0.23 in. (6mm) with a thread pitch of 0.04 in. (1.0mm) and a bolt length of 0.63–0.79 in. (16–20mm).

➡ **When removing the camshaft, be sure that the torsional spring force of the sub-gear has been eliminated by the above operation.**

4. Uniformly loosen and remove the exhaust bearing cap bolts (10 of them), in several passes. Use the reverse order of the tightening sequence. Remove the 5 bearing caps and the camshaft. Do the same for the intake camshafts.

➡ **If the camshaft is not being lifted out straight and level, reinstall the No. 3 cap with the 2 bolts. Alternately loosen, then remove the bearing cap bolts with the camshaft pulled up. Do not pry on or force the camshaft.**

5. Inspect the camshafts for excessive runout. Inspect the cam lobes and journals. The bearings are part of the cam and should be inspected for flaking or scoring. If the bearings are damaged, replace the caps and the cylinder head as a set. The camshaft journal oil and thrust clearances should be checked.

To install:
6. Install the intake camshaft, as follows:
    a. Apply multi-purpose grease to the thrust portion of the intake camshaft.

    b. Position the intake camshaft with the pin facing upward.
    c. Install the bearing caps in their proper locations. Apply a light coat of engine oil to the threads and install the cap bolts. Uniformly tighten the cap bolts in the sequence shown to 12 ft. lbs. (16 Nm).
7. Install the exhaust camshaft, as follows:
    a. Apply engine oil to the thrust portion of the intake camshaft.
    b. Engage the exhaust camshaft gear to the intake camshaft gear by matching the timing marks (1 and 2 dots) on each other.
    c. Roll down the exhaust camshaft onto the bearing journals while engaging the gears with each other. Install the bearing caps in their proper locations.
    d. Apply a light coat of engine oil to the threads and install the cap bolts. Uniformly tighten the cap bolts in the sequence shown to 12 ft. lbs. (16 Nm).
    e. Remove the service bolt from the driven sub-gear. Check that the intake and exhaust camshafts turn smoothly.
8. Set No. 1 cylinder to Top Dead Center (TDC) of the compression stroke. The crankshaft pulley groove aligns with the **0** mark on timing cover and camshaft timing marks with 1 dot and 2 dots will be in a straight line on the cylinder head surface.
9. Install the timing gear, as follows:
    a. Place the gear over the straight pin of the intake camshaft.
    b. Hold the intake camshaft with a wrench. Install and tighten the bolt to 54 ft. lbs. (74 Nm).
    c. Hold the exhaust camshaft and install the bolt and distributor gear. Tighten the bolt to 34 ft. lbs. (46 Nm).
10. Install the chain tensioner, using a

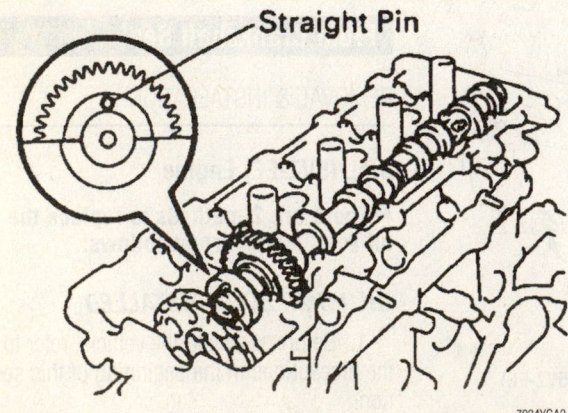

Install the camshaft with the pin facing upwards—2.4L (2RZ-FE) engine

7924YGA2

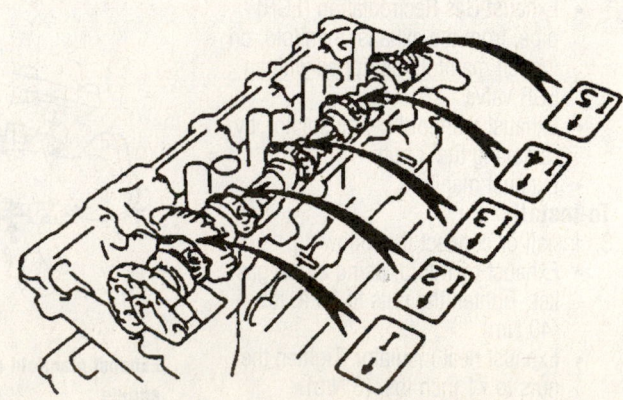

Intake camshaft bearing cap locations—2.4L (2RZ-FE) engine

7924YGA3

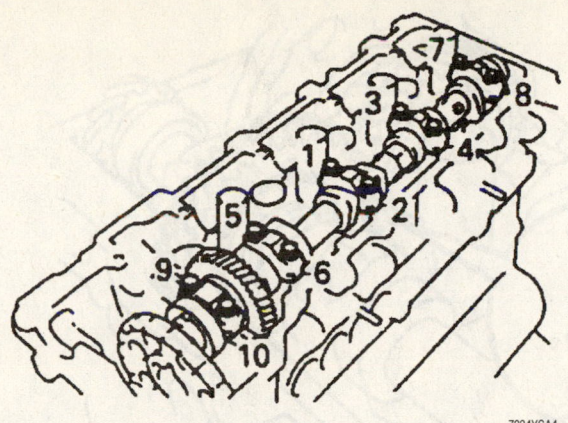

Tighten the intake bearing caps following this order—2.4L (2RZ-FE) engine

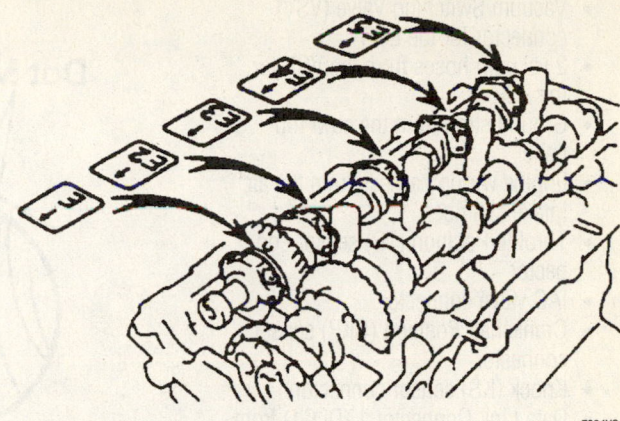

Position the exhaust camshaft bearing caps as shown—2.4L (2RZ-FE) engine

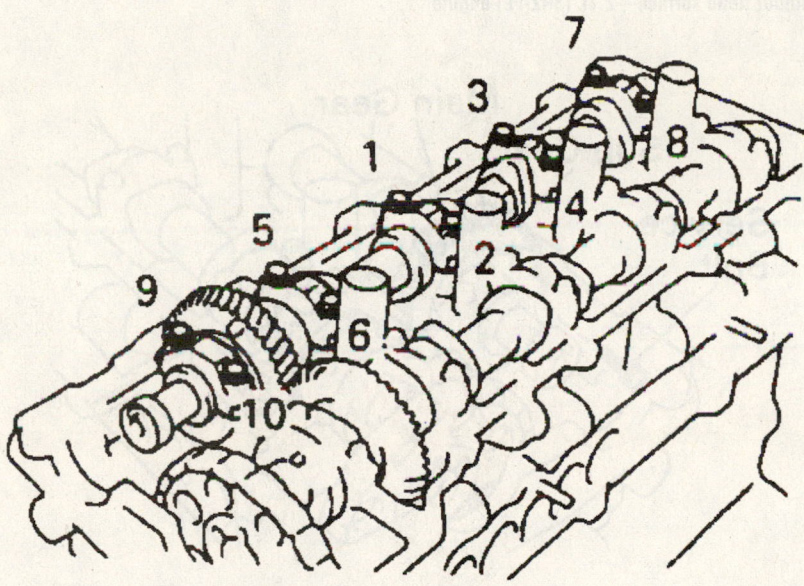

Tighten the exhaust bearing cap bolts in this order—2.4L (2RZ-FE) engine

new gasket (mark toward the front), as follows:

    a. Release the ratchet pawl, fully push in the plunger and apply the hook to the pin so that the plunger cannot spring out.

    b. Turn the crankshaft pulley clockwise to provide some slack for the chain on the tensioner side.

    c. Push the tensioner by hand until it touches the head installation surface, then install the 2 nuts. Tighten the nuts to 13 ft. lbs. (18 Nm). Check that the hook of the tensioner is not released.

    d. Turn the crankshaft to the left so that the hook of the chain tensioner is released from the pin of the plunger, allowing the plunger to spring out and the slipper to be pushed into the chain.

11. Check and adjust the valve clearance. Intake valve clearance is 0.006–0.010 inch (0.15–0.25mm) and exhaust valve clearance is 0.010–0.014 inch (0.25–0.35mm).

12. Recheck the engine for proper valve timing. Check and adjust the valve clearance.

13. Install the spark plugs and the semicircular plug.

14. Recheck the engine for proper valve timing. Install the valve cover and engine hangers. Tighten the engine hanger bolts to 30 ft. lbs. (42 Nm).

15. Reinstall all other parts from the timing chain removal. Fill any fluids, start the engine, top off the fluids.

2.7L (3RZ-FE) Engine

1. Before servicing the vehicle, refer to the precautions in the beginning of this section.

2. Disconnect the negative battery cable.

3. Drain the engine coolant.

4. Remove or disconnect the following:
- Air cleaner cap
- Mass Air Flow (MAF) meter and the resonator
- Accelerator cable from the throttle body, if equipped with a manual transmission
- Accelerator and throttle cables from the throttle body, if equipped with an automatic transmission
- Cruise control cable from the actuator, if equipped with cruise control
- Intake air connector
- Air hose for Idle Air Control (IAC)
- Vacuum sensing hose
- Wire clamp for the engine wiring harness
- Positive Crankcase Ventilation (PCV) hoses
- Spark plug wires from the spark plugs
- Engine wiring harness clamps and harness
- Air conditioning compressor connector, if equipped with air conditioning
- Oil pressure sensor connector
- Engine Coolant Temperature (ECT) sensor connector
- Engine coolant temperature sender gauge connector
- Exhaust Gas Recirculation (EGR) gas temperature sensor connector

Please refer to Section 8 for electric cooling fan wiring schematics

- Vacuum Switching Valve (VSV) connector for the EGR
- 2 vacuum hoses from the VSV for the EGR
- Ground strap from the cowl top panel
- Engine wiring harness from the air intake chamber
- Throttle Position (TP) sensor connector
- IAC valve connector
- Crankshaft Position (CKP) sensor connector
- Knock (KS) sensor connector
- Data Link Connector 1 (DLC1) from the bracket
- Engine wiring harness clamp
- EGR pipe
- Intake chamber stay
- Air intake chamber assembly.
- Evaporative Emission (EVAP) hose from the throttle body
- Brake booster vacuum hose from the union
- Water bypass hose from the water bypass pipe
- Water bypass hose from the cylinder head rear cover
- Front engine hanger
- Engine wiring harness brackets
- Cylinder head cover

5. Set No. 1 cylinder to Top Dead Center (TDC) compression stroke. The groove on the crankshaft pulley should align with the **0** mark on the timing chain cover and the timing marks (1 and 2 dots) of the camshaft gears should form a straight line in respect to the cylinder head surface. If not, turn the crankshaft 1 revolution (360 degrees).

6. Remove the chain tensioner and gasket.

7. Remove the camshaft timing gear as follows:

   a. Remove the 2 semi-circular plugs.

   b. Place matchmarks on the camshaft timing gear and No. 1 timing chain.

   c. Hold the hexagon head portion of the exhaust camshaft with a wrench and remove the fastener and distributor gear.

   d. Hold the hexagon head portion of the intake camshaft with a wrench and remove the bolt.

   e. Remove the camshaft timing gear and chain from the intake camshaft and leave on the slipper and damper.

8. Remove exhaust camshafts:

   a. Bring the service bolt hole of the driven sub-gear upward by turning the hexagon head portion of the exhaust camshaft with a wrench.

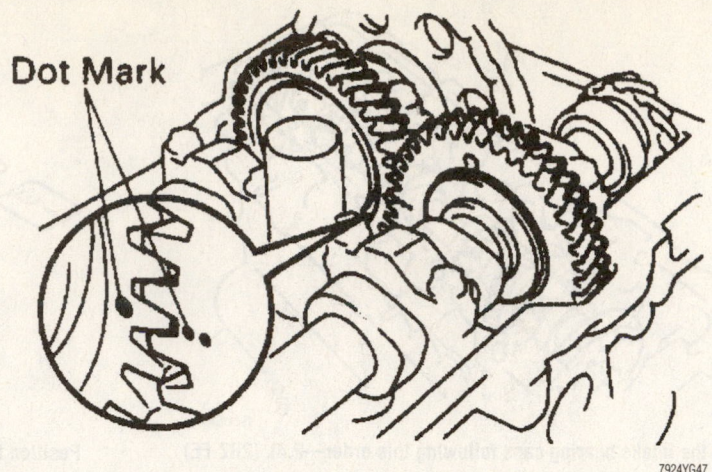

Camshafts TDC/compression timing marks. Marks with 1 and 2 dots will be in straight line on cylinder head surface—2.7L (3RZ-FE) engine

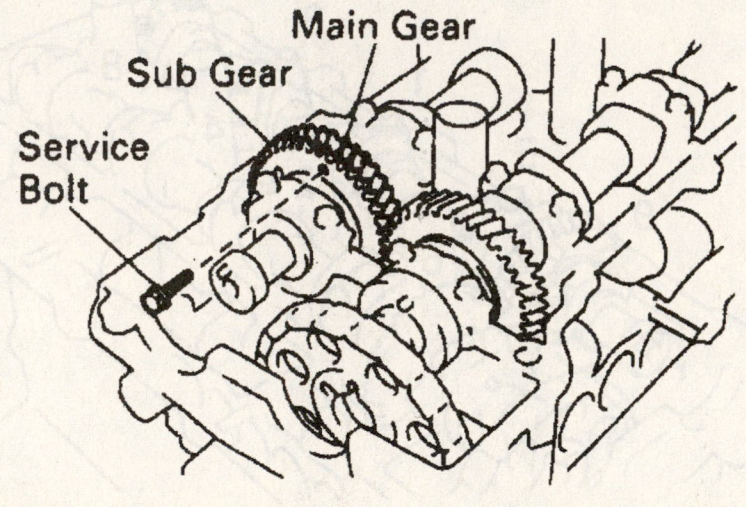

Secure the exhaust camshaft sub-gear to the main gear with a service bolt—2.7L (3RZ-FE) engine

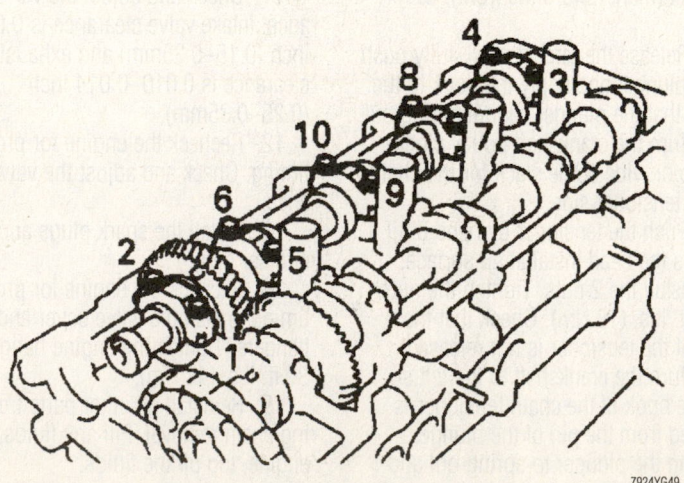

Loosen and remove the exhaust camshaft bearing cap bolts in sequence—2.7L (3RZ-FE) engine

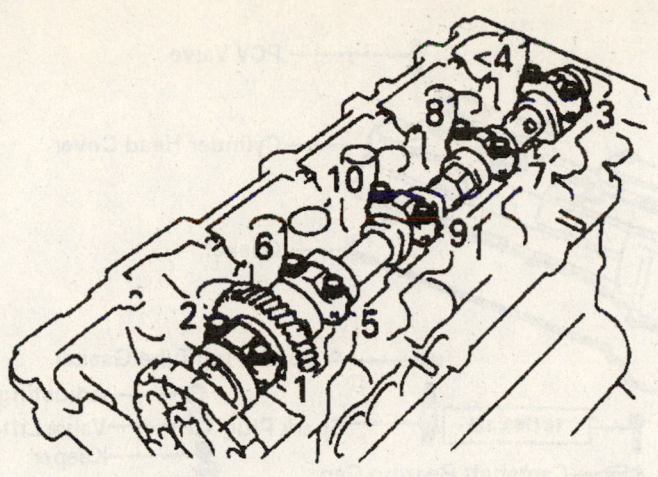

Loosen and remove the intake camshaft bearing cap bolts in sequence—2.7L (3RZ-FE) engine

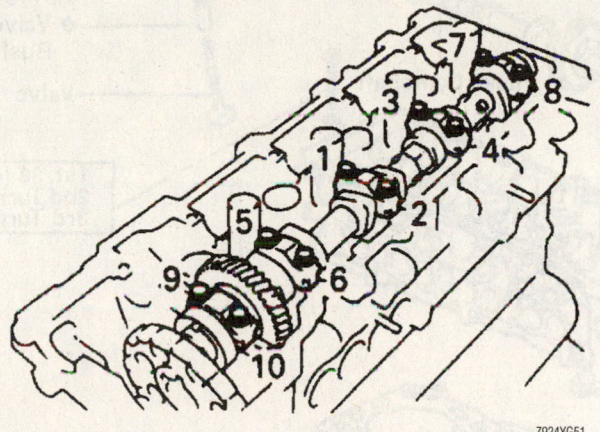

Tighten the intake camshaft bearing cap bolts in sequence—2.7L (3RZ-FE) engine

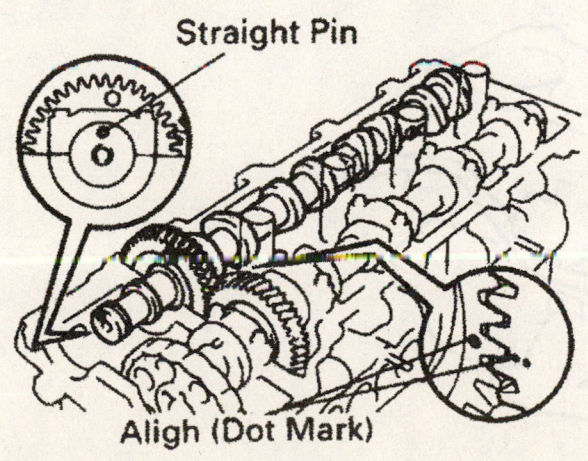

Engage both camshaft gears while matching the timing marks—2.7L (3RZ-FE) engine

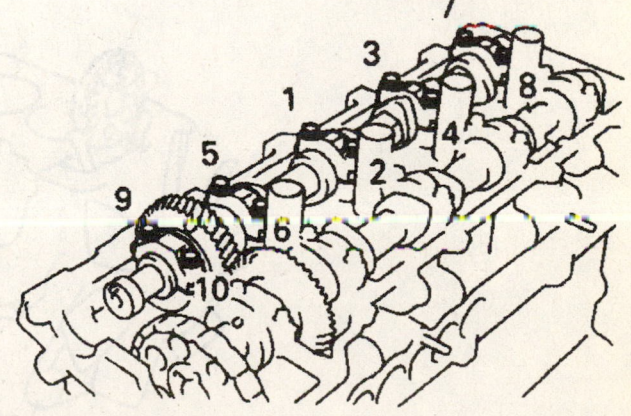

Tighten the exhaust camshaft bearing cap bolts in sequence—2.7L (3RZ-FE) engine

b. Secure the exhaust camshaft sub-gear to the driven gear with a service bolt (6mm diameter, 0.63–0.79 inches in length and 1.0mm in thread pitch).

➡️**When removing the camshaft, be sure that the torsional spring force of the sub-gear has been eliminated by the above operation.**

c. Uniformly loosen and remove the bearing cap bolts in several passes, in the sequence shown.

d. Remove the bearing caps and camshaft. Make a note of the bearing cap positions for proper installation.

9. Remove or disconnect the following:
- Intake camshaft bearing cap bolts in several passes, in the sequence shown
- Bearing caps and camshaft. Make a note of the bearing cap positions for proper installation.

➡️**If the camshaft is not being lifted out straight and level, reinstall the No. 3 bearing cap with the 2 bolts. Then, alternately loosen and remove the 2 bearing cap bolts with the camshaft gear pulled up.**

- Valve lifters and shims from the cylinder head. Arrange the valve lifters and shims in correct order.

To install:

10. Install the valve lifters and shims in their proper locations. Check that the valve lifter rotates smoothly by hand.

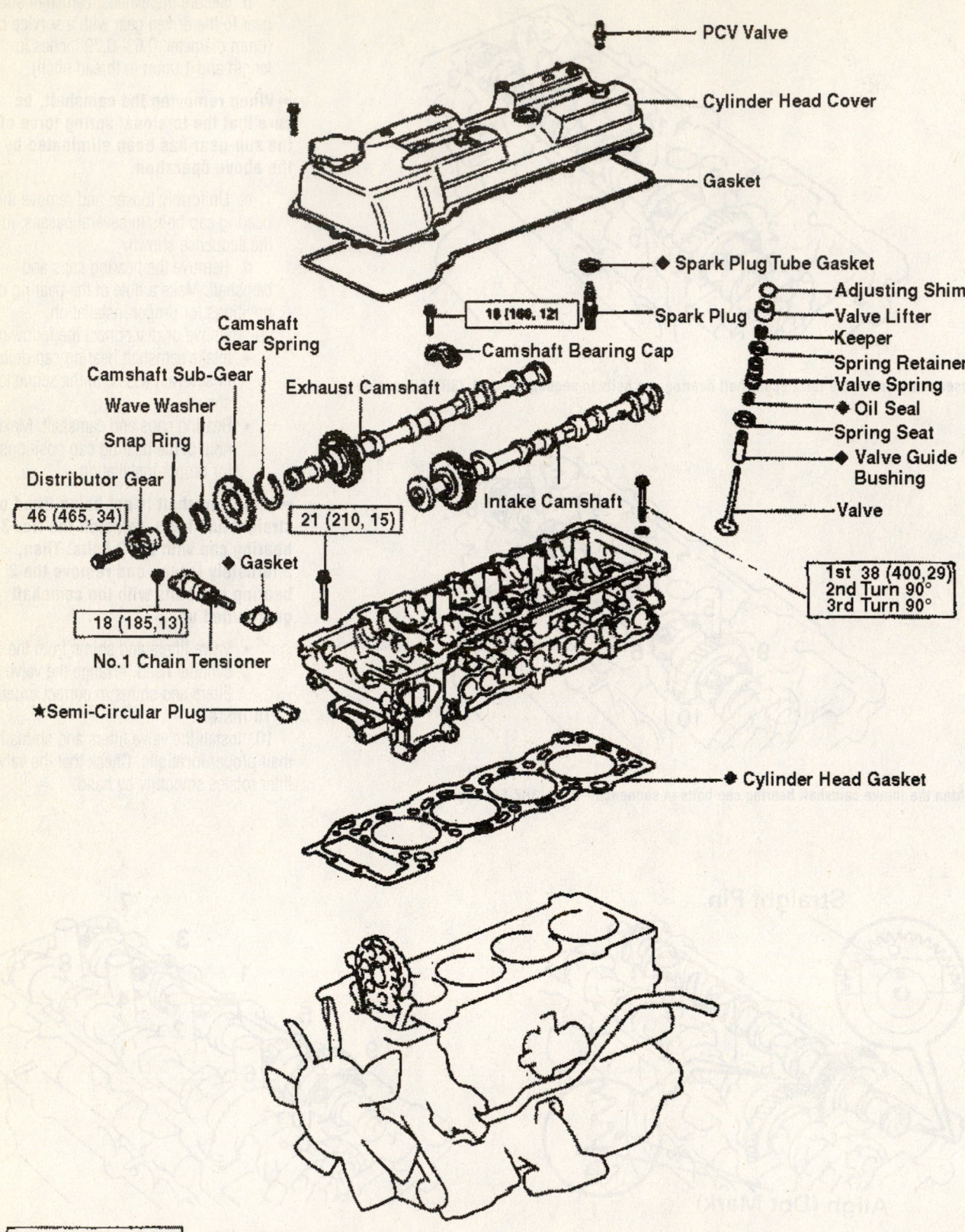

- PCV Valve
- Cylinder Head Cover
- Gasket
- ◆ Spark Plug Tube Gasket
- ◆ Adjusting Shim
- Valve Lifter
- Keeper
- Spring Retainer
- Valve Spring
- ◆ Oil Seal
- Spring Seat
- ◆ Valve Guide Bushing
- Valve

Spark Plug   18 [166, 12]

Camshaft Gear Spring
Camshaft Sub-Gear
Wave Washer
Snap Ring
Distributor Gear
Exhaust Camshaft
Camshaft Bearing Cap

46 (465, 34)

21 (210, 15)

Intake Camshaft

1st 38 (400, 29)
2nd Turn 90°
3rd Turn 90°

18 (185, 13)

◆ Gasket

No.1 Chain Tensioner

★ Semi-Circular Plug

- ◆ Cylinder Head Gasket

N·m (kgf·cm, ft·lbf) : Specified torque
◆ Non-reusable part
★ Precoated part

Exploded view of the cylinder head components—2.7L (3RZ-FE) engine

7924YG54

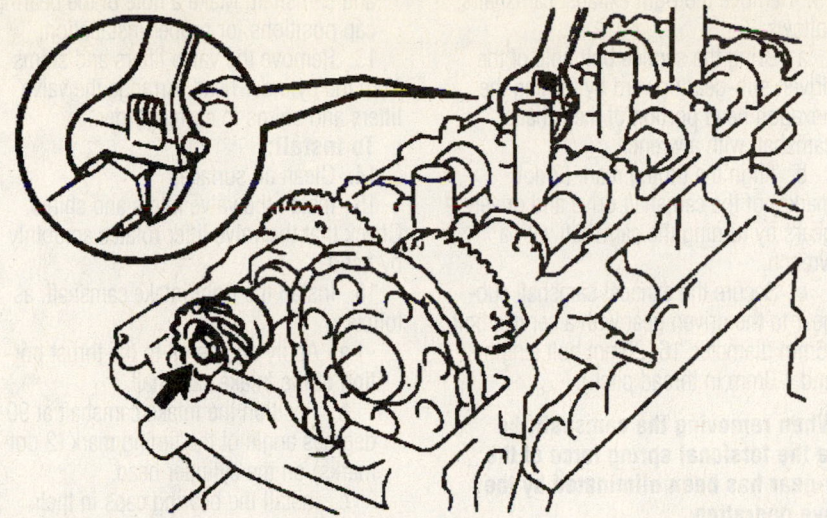

Using a wrench to hold the camshaft—2.7L (3RZ-FE) engine

7924YG55

11. Install the intake camshaft, as follows:

a. Apply engine oil to the thrust portion of the intake camshaft.

b. Position the intake camshaft with the knock pin facing upward.

c. Install the bearing caps in their proper locations. Apply a light coat of engine oil to the threads and install the cap bolts. Uniformly tighten the cap bolts, in sequence ,to 12 ft. lbs. (16 Nm).

12. Install the exhaust camshaft, as shown:

a. Apply engine oil to the thrust portion of the intake camshaft.

b. Engage the exhaust camshaft gear to the intake camshaft gear by matching the timing marks (1 and 2 dots) on each other.

c. Roll down the exhaust camshaft onto the bearing journals while engaging the gears with each other. Install the bearing caps in their proper locations.

d. Apply a light coat of engine oil to the threads and install the cap bolts. Uniformly tighten the cap bolts in the sequence shown to 12 ft. lbs. (10 Nm).

e. Remove the service bolt from the driven sub-gear. Check that the intake and exhaust camshafts turns smoothly.

13. Set No. 1 cylinder to Top Dead Center (TDC) of the compression stroke: Crankshaft pulley groove align with **0** mark on timing cover and camshafts timing marks with 1 dot and 2 dots will be straight line on the cylinder head surface.

14. Install the timing gear. Place the gear over the straight pin of the intake camshaft.

a. Hold the intake camshaft with a wrench. Install and tighten the bolt to 54 ft. lbs. (74 Nm).

b. Hold the exhaust camshaft and install the bolt and distributor gear. Tighten the bolt to 34 ft. lbs. (46 Nm).

15. Install or connect the following:

• Chain tensioner, using a new gasket (mark toward the front)
• Recheck the engine for proper valve timing. Check and adjust the valve clearance.
• Semi-circular plug
• Recheck the engine for proper valve timing.
• Cylinder head cover with a new gasket
• Engine wiring harness brackets
• Front engine hanger. Tighten the bolts to 30 ft. lbs. (42 Nm).
• Air intake chamber assembly. Tighten the bolts to 15 ft. lbs. (20 Nm).
• Hoses
• Intake chamber stay
• Air intake chamber stay. Tighten the bolts to 15 ft. lbs. (20 Nm).
• EGR pipe. Tighten the bolts to 13 ft. lbs. (18 Nm), nut "A" to 14 ft. lbs. (19 Nm) and nut "B" to 15 ft. lbs. (20 Nm).
• Engine wiring harness
• Spark plug wires to the spark plugs
• PCV hoses
• Intake air connector. Tighten the bolts to 13 ft. lbs. (18 Nm).
• Air hose for the IAC
• Vacuum sensing hose

• Wire clamp for the engine wiring harness
• Cruise control cable to the actuator, if equipped with cruise control
• Accelerator cable to the throttle body, if equipped with a manual transmission
• Accelerator and throttle cables to the throttle body, if equipped with an automatic transmission
• Air cleaner cap, MAF meter and the resonator assembly
• Negative battery cable

16. Refill the cooling system.
17. Start the engine and check for leaks.
18. Check the ignition timing. Road test the vehicle for proper operation.
19. Recheck all fluid levels.

3.4L (5VZ-FE) Engine

T-100 AND TACOMA

1. Before servicing the vehicle, refer to the precautions in the beginning of this section.

2. Remove or disconnect the following:
• Negative battery cable
• Engine undercover

3. Drain the cooling system.

4. Remove or disconnect the following:
• Air cleaner cap
• Mass Air Flow (MAF) meter and the resonator
• Actuator cable with the bracket, if equipped with cruise control
• Accelerator cable
• Throttle cable, if equipped with an automatic transmission
• Heater hose
• Upper radiator hose from the engine

5. Remove the power steering drive belt, as follows:

a. Stretch the belt and loosen the fan pulley mounting nuts.

b. Loosen the lockbolt, pivot bolt and adjusting bolt and remove the drive belt from the engine.

6. Remove or disconnect the following:
• Air conditioning drive belt, by loosening the idle pulley nut and adjusting bolt
• Loosen the alternator lockbolt, pivot bolt and adjusting bolt
• Alternator drive belt
• No. 2 fan shroud, by removing the 2 clips
• Fan with the fluid coupling and fan pulleys

Timing belt service is covered in Section 4 of this manual

- Power steering pump and move it aside without disconnecting the lines
- Compressor and move it aside without disconnecting the lines, if equipped with air conditioning
- Air conditioning bracket, if equipped with air conditioning
- Spark plug wires with the ignition coils
- Spark plugs
- Camshaft Position (CMP) sensor connector, from the No. 2 timing belt cover
- 3 spark plug wire clamps from the No. 2 timing belt cover
- 6 bolts and the timing belt cover
- Power steering adjusting strut by removing the nut
- Fan bracket by removing the bolt and nut

7. Set the No. 1 cylinder at Top Dead Center (TDC) of the compression stroke, as follows:

a. Turn the crankshaft pulley and align its groove with the timing mark **0** on the No. 1 timing belt cover.

b. Check that the timing marks of the camshaft timing pulleys and the No. 3 timing belt cover are aligned. If not, turn the crankshaft pulley 1 revolution (360 degrees).

8. Remove or disconnect the following:
- Timing belt tensioner, by alternately loosening the 2 bolts
- Pulley bolt, the timing pulley and the knock pin, using Variable Pin Wrench Set 09960-10010
- Both timing pulleys with the timing belt
- No. 2 idler pulley
- Alternator
- Positive Crankcase Ventilation PCV hoses
- Water bypass hoses
- Air assist hose from the intake air connector
- 2 vacuum sensing hoses from the Vacuum Switching Valve (VSV)
- Evaporative Emissions (EVAP) hose
- Air hose from the power steering
- Air hose from the air conditioning idle up valve, if equipped with air conditioning
- 4 bolts, 2 nuts and the air intake chamber assembly
- Intake air connector
- Camshaft Position (CMP) sensor
- No. 3 (rear) timing belt cover by removing the 6 bolts
- 8 bolts, seal washers, both cylinder head cover and gaskets
- Semi-circular plugs

9. Remove the right exhaust camshafts, as follows:

a. Bring the service bolt hole of the driven sub-gear upward by turning the hexagon head portion of the exhaust camshaft with a wrench.

b. Align the timing mark (2 dot marks) of the camshaft drive and driven gears by turning the camshaft with a wrench.

c. Secure the exhaust camshaft sub-gear to the driven gear with a service bolt (6mm diameter, 16–20mm bolt length and 1.0mm in thread pitch).

➡ **When removing the camshaft, be sure the torsional spring force of the sub-gear has been eliminated by the above operation.**

d. Uniformly loosen and remove the bearing cap bolts in several passes, in the sequence shown.

e. Remove the bearing caps and camshaft. Make a note of the bearing cap positions for proper installation.

➡ **Do not pry on or attempt to force the camshaft with a tool or other object.**

10. Remove the right-hand intake camshaft, as follows:

a. Uniformly loosen and remove the bearing cap bolts in several passes, in the sequence shown.

b. Remove the bearing caps, oil seal and camshaft. Make a note of the bearing cap positions for proper installation.

11. Remove the left exhaust camshafts, as follows:

a. Align the timing mark (1 dot mark) of the camshaft drive and driven gears by turning the camshaft with a wrench.

b. Secure the exhaust camshaft sub-gear to the driven gear with a service bolt (6mm diameter, 16–20mm bolt length and 1.0mm in thread pitch).

➡ **When removing the camshaft, be sure that the torsional spring force of the sub-gear has been eliminated by the above operation.**

c. Uniformly loosen and remove the bearing cap bolts in several passes, in the sequence shown.

d. Remove the bearing caps and camshaft. Make a note of the bearing cap positions for proper installation.

12. Remove the left-hand intake camshaft, as follows:

a. Uniformly loosen and remove the bearing cap bolts in several passes, in the sequence shown.

b. Remove the bearing caps, oil seal and camshaft. Make a note of the bearing cap positions for proper installation.

13. Remove the valve lifters and shims from the cylinder head. Arrange the valve lifters and shims in correct order.

To install:

14. Clean all surfaces.

15. Install the valve lifters and shims. Check that the valve lifter rotates smoothly by hand.

16. Install the right intake camshaft, as follows:

a. Apply engine oil to the thrust portion of the intake camshaft.

b. Position the intake camshaft at 90 degrees angle of the timing mark (2 dot marks) on the cylinder head.

c. Install the bearing caps in their proper locations. Apply a light coat of engine oil to the threads and install the cap bolts.

d. Apply a light coat of engine oil on the threads and under the heads of the bearing cap bolts.

e. Uniformly tighten the cap bolts in the sequence shown to 12 ft. lbs. (16 Nm).

17. Install the right exhaust camshaft, as follows:

a. Apply engine oil to the thrust portion of the intake camshaft.

b. Align the timing marks (2 dot marks) of the camshaft drive and driven gears.

c. Roll down the exhaust camshaft onto the bearing journals while engaging the gears with each other. Install the bearing caps in their proper locations.

d. Apply a light coat of engine oil to the threads and install the cap bolts.

e. Apply a light coat of engine oil on the threads and under the heads of the bearing cap bolts.

f. Uniformly tighten the cap bolts in the sequence shown to 12 ft. lbs. (16 Nm).

g. Remove the service bolt from the driven sub-gear. Check that the intake and exhaust camshafts turns smoothly.

h. Align the timing marks (2 dot marks) of the camshaft drive and driven gears by turning the camshaft with a wrench.

18. Install the left intake camshaft, as follows:

a. Apply engine oil to the thrust portion of the intake camshaft.

b. Position the intake camshaft at 90 degrees angle of the timing mark (1 dot mark) on the cylinder head.

c. Install the bearing caps in their proper locations. Apply a light coat of

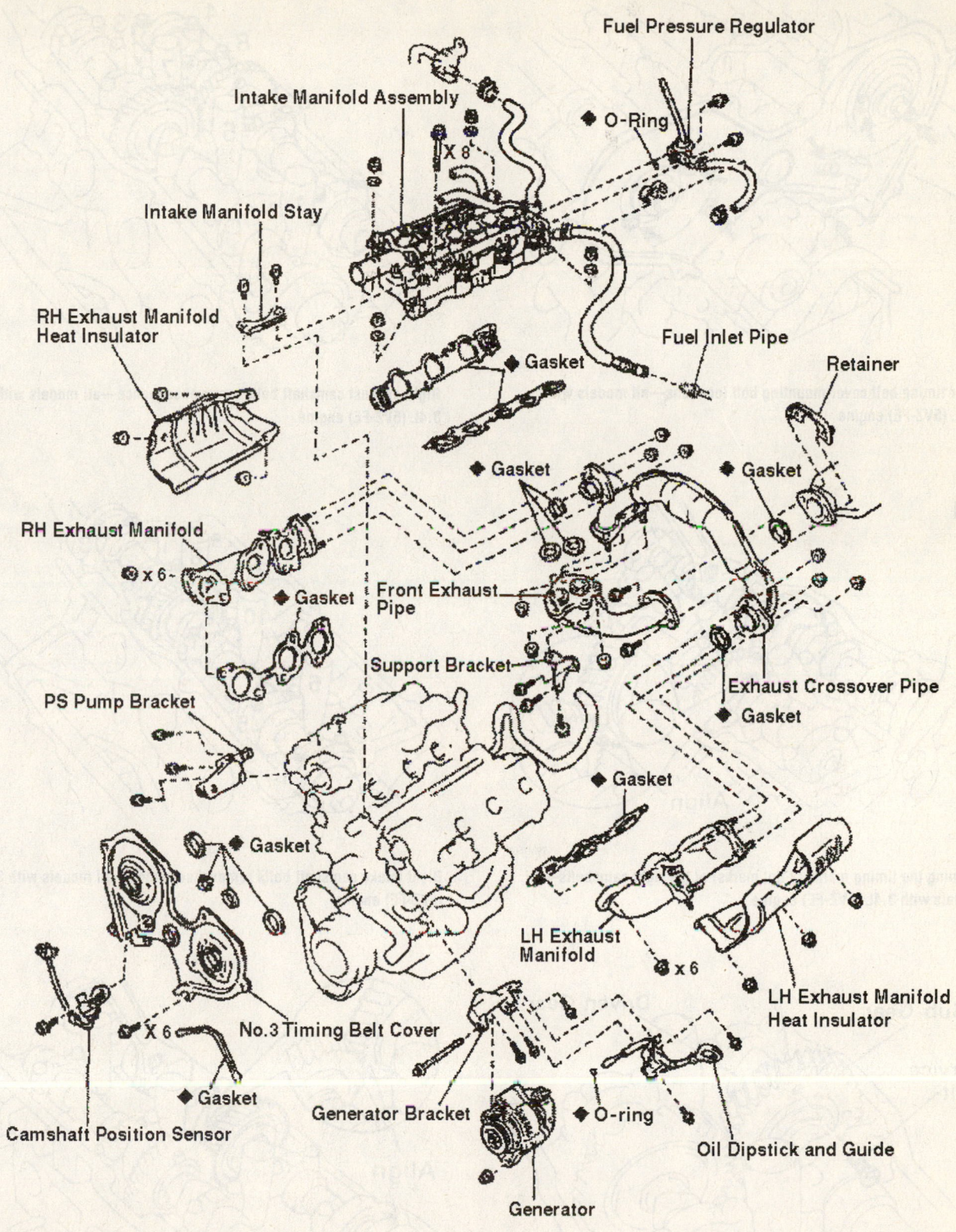

Fuel Pressure Regulator

Intake Manifold Assembly

◆ O-Ring

X 8

Intake Manifold Stay

RH Exhaust Manifold
Heat Insulator

Fuel Inlet Pipe

Retainer

◆ Gasket

◆ Gasket

◆ Gasket

RH Exhaust Manifold

X 6

◆ Gasket

Front Exhaust
Pipe

Exhaust Crossover Pipe

◆ Gasket

Support Bracket

PS Pump Bracket

◆ Gasket

◆ Gasket

LH Exhaust
Manifold

◆ Gasket

X 6

LH Exhaust Manifold
Heat Insulator

X 6

No.3 Timing Belt Cover

◆ Gasket

Generator Bracket

◆ O-ring

Camshaft Position Sensor

Oil Dipstick and Guide

Generator

◆ Non-reusable part

7924YG60

Exploded view of the cylinder head component assembly—T-100 and Tacoma with 3.4L (5VZ-FE) engine

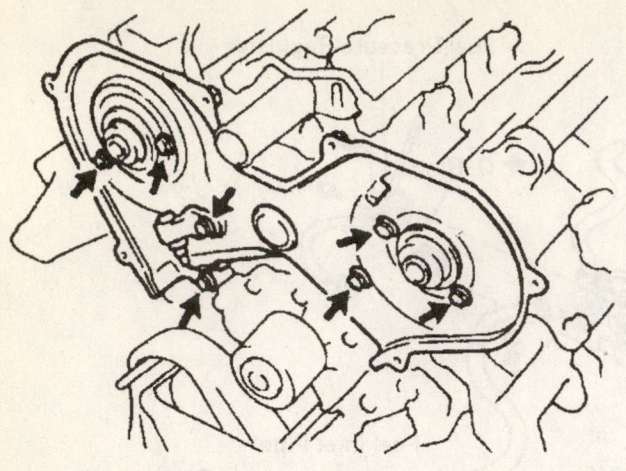

Rear timing belt cover mounting bolt locations—all models with 3.4L (5VZ-FE) engine

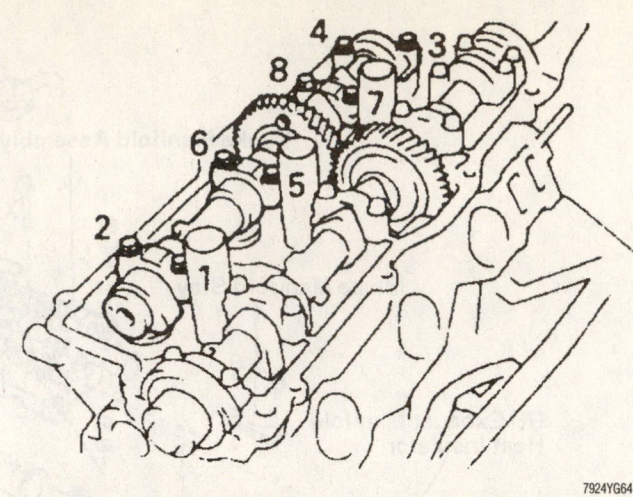

Right exhaust camshaft bolts removal sequence—all models with 3.4L (5VZ-FE) engine

RH

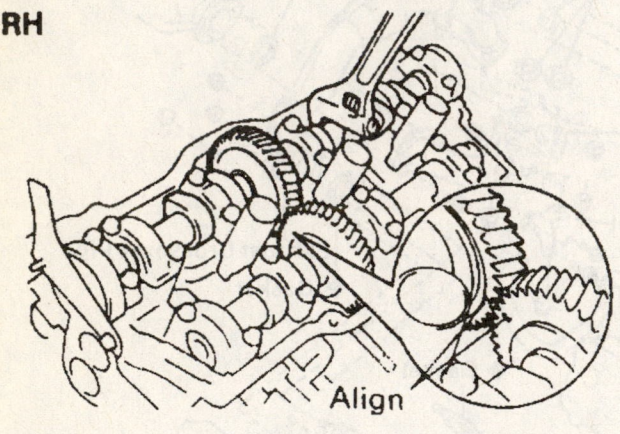

Aligning the timing marks (2 dot marks) of the right camshafts—all models with 3.4L (5VZ-FE) engine

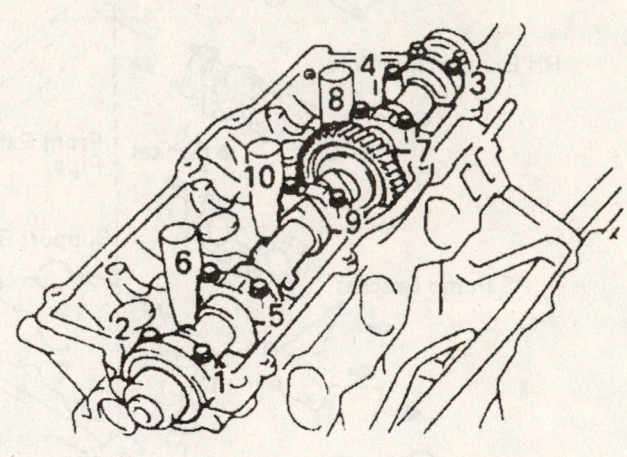

Right intake camshaft bolts removal sequence—all models with 3.4L (5VZ-FE) engine

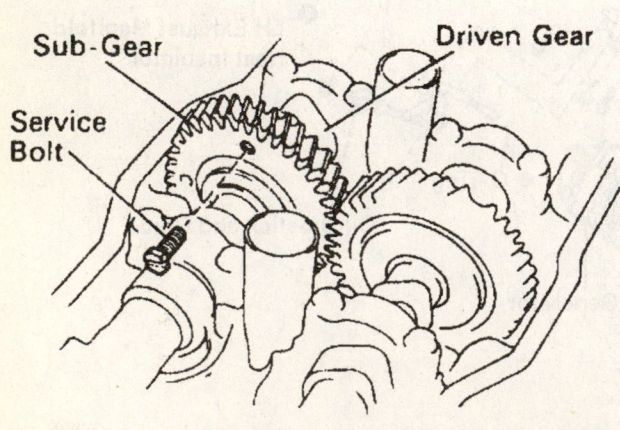

Drive gear service bolt (right side)—all models with 3.4L (5VZ-FE) engine

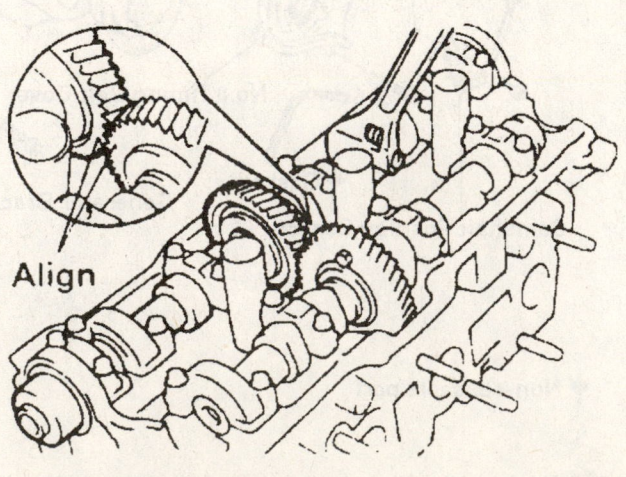

Aligning the timing mark (1 dot mark) of the left camshafts—all models with 3.4L (5VZ-FE) engine

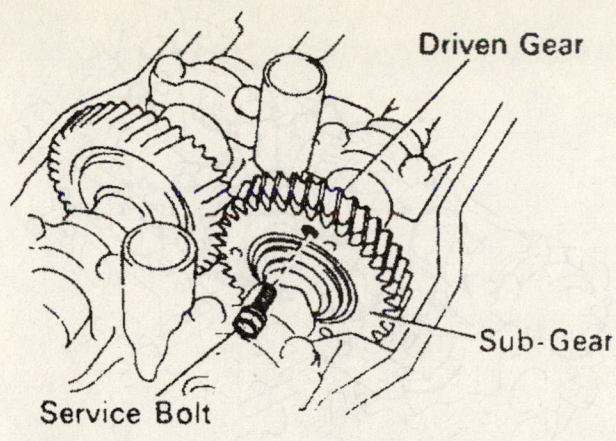

Drive gear service bolt (left side)—all models with 3.4L (5VZ-FE) engine

7924YG67

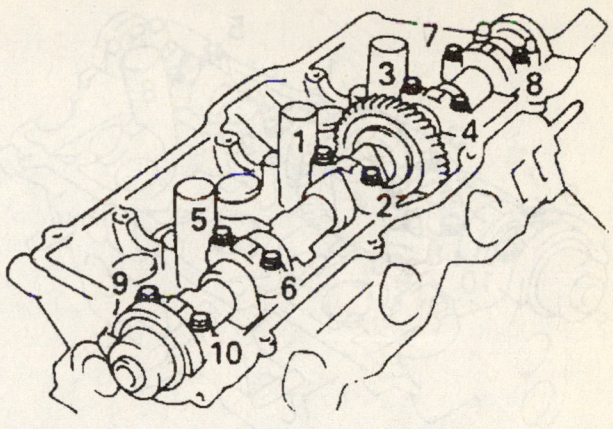

Right intake camshaft tightening sequence—all models with 3.4L (5VZ-FE) engine

7924YG70

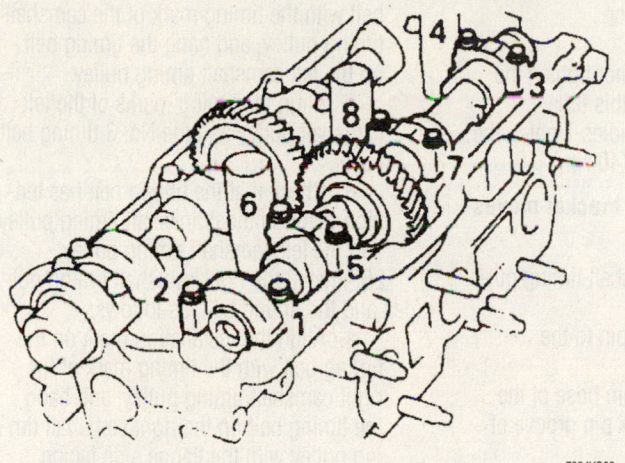

Left exhaust camshaft bolts removal sequence—all models with 3.4L (5VZ-FE) engine

7924YG68

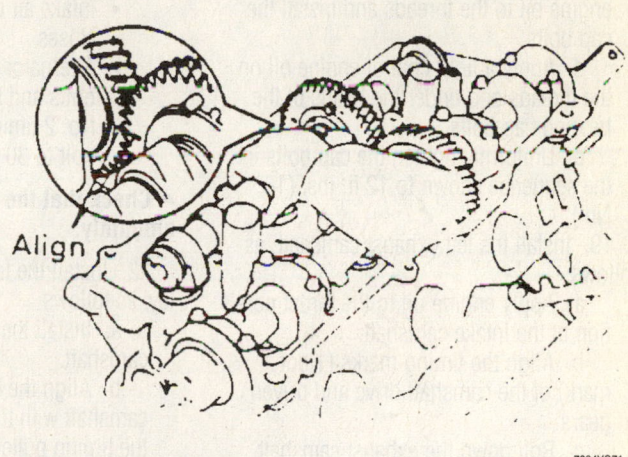

Aligning the right camshafts for installation—all models with 3.4L (5VZ-FE) engine

7924YG71

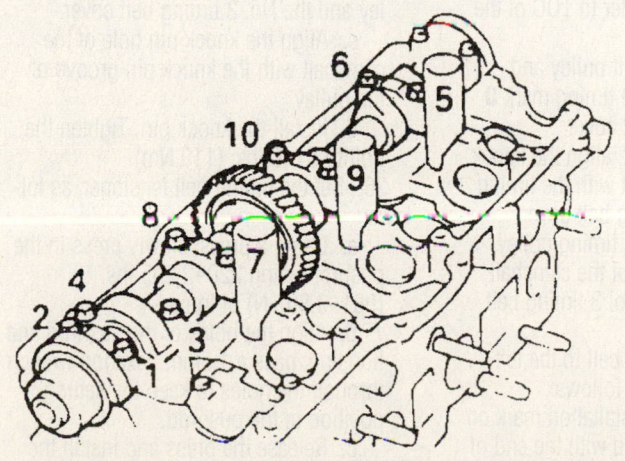

Left intake camshaft bolts removal sequence—all models with 3.4L (5VZ-FE) engine

7924YG69

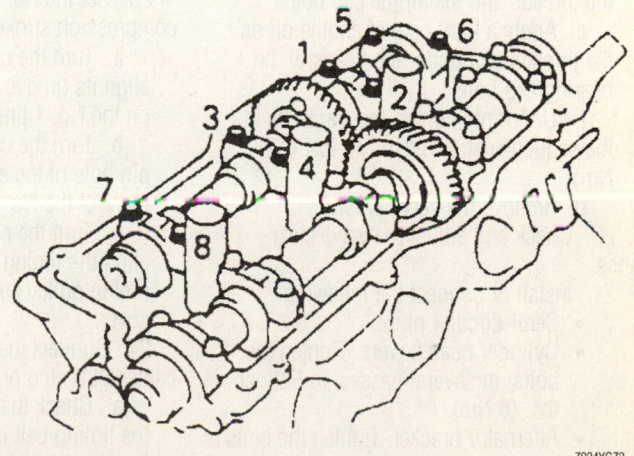

Right exhaust camshaft bolts tightening sequence—all models with 3.4L (5VZ-FE) engine

7924YG72

Refer to Section 1 for engine rebuilding specifications

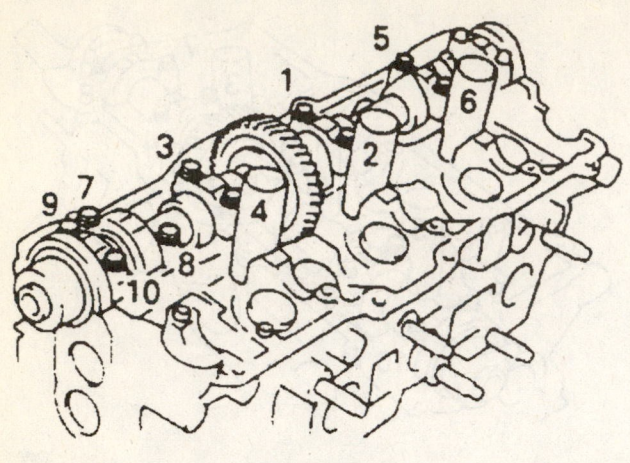

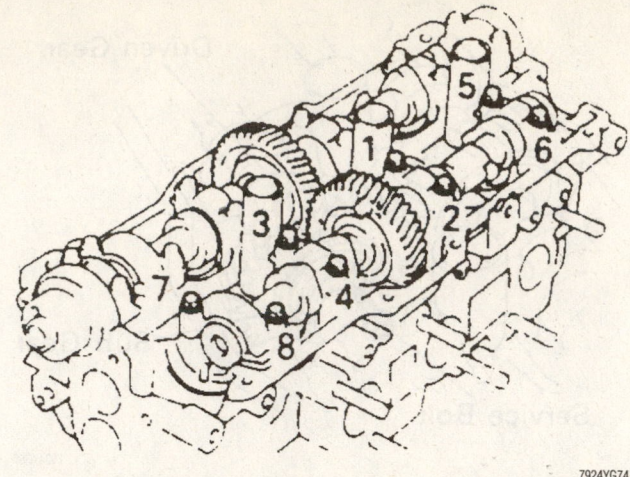

Left intake camshaft bolts tightening sequence—all models with 3.4L (5VZ-FE) engine

Left exhaust camshaft bolts tightening sequence—all models with 3.4L (5VZ-FE) engine

engine oil to the threads and install the cap bolts.

d. Apply a light coat of engine oil on the threads and under the heads of the bearing cap bolts.

e. Uniformly tighten the cap bolts in the sequence shown to 12 ft. lbs. (16 Nm).

19. Install the left exhaust camshaft, as follows:

a. Apply engine oil to the thrust portion of the intake camshaft.

b. Align the timing marks (1 dot mark) of the camshaft drive and driven gears.

c. Roll down the exhaust camshaft onto the bearing journals while engaging the gears with each other. Install the bearing caps in their proper locations.

d. Apply a light coat of engine oil to the threads and install the cap bolts.

e. Apply a light coat of engine oil on the threads and under the heads of the bearing cap bolts.

f. Uniformly tighten the cap bolts in the sequence shown to 12 ft. lbs. (16 Nm).

g. Remove the service bolt.

20. Check and adjust the valve clearance.

21. Install or connect the following:
- Semi-circular plugs
- Cylinder head covers. Tighten the bolts, in several passes, to 53 inch lbs. (6 Nm).
- Alternator bracket. Tighten the bolts to 14 ft. lbs. (18 Nm).
- No. 3 timing belt cover. Tighten the 6 bolts to 80 inch lbs. (9 Nm).
- CMP sensor. Tighten it to 71 inch lbs. (8 Nm).

- Intake air connector
- Hoses
- Alternator but do not tighten the bolts and nuts at this time
- No. 2 timing belt idler. Tighten the bolt to 30 ft. lbs. (40 Nm).

➡ **Check that the pulley bracket moves smoothly.**

22. Install the left camshaft timing pulley, as follows:

a. Install the knock pin to the camshaft.

b. Align the knock pin hose of the camshaft with the knock pin groove of the timing pulley.

c. Slide the timing pulley on the camshaft with the flange side facing outward. Tighten the pulley bolt to 81 ft. lbs. (110 Nm).

23. Set the No. 1 cylinder to TDC of the compression stroke.

a. Turn the crankshaft pulley and align its groove with the timing mark **0** on the No. 1 timing belt cover.

b. Turn the camshaft, align the knock pin hole of the camshaft with the timing mark of the No. 3 timing belt cover.

c. Turn the camshaft timing pulley, align the timing marks of the camshaft timing pulley and the No. 3 timing belt cover.

24. Connect the timing belt to the left camshaft timing pulley, as follows:

a. Check that the installation mark on the timing belt is aligned with the end of the No. 1 timing belt cover.

b. Using Variable Pin Wrench Set 09960-01000 or equivalent, slightly turn the left camshaft timing pulley clockwise. Align the installation mark on the timing

belt with the timing mark of the camshaft timing pulley, and hang the timing belt on the left camshaft timing pulley.

c. Align the timing marks of the left camshaft pulley and the No. 3 timing belt cover.

d. Check that the timing belt has tension between the crankshaft timing pulley and the left camshaft timing pulley.

25. Install the right camshaft timing pulley and the timing belt, as follows:

a. Align the installation mark on the timing belt with the timing mark of the right camshaft timing pulley, and hang the timing belt on the right camshaft timing pulley with the flange side facing inward.

b. Slide the right camshaft timing pulley on the camshaft. Align the timing marks on the right camshaft timing pulley and the No. 3 timing belt cover.

c. Align the knock pin hole of the camshaft with the knock pin groove of the pulley.

d. Install the knock pin. Tighten the bolt to 81 ft. lbs. (110 Nm).

26. Set the timing belt tensioner, as follows:

a. Using a press, slowly press in the pushrod using 220–2,205 lbs. (981–9,807 N) of force.

b. Align the holes of the pushrod and housing, pass a 1.5mm hexagon wrench through the holes to keep the setting position of the pushrod.

c. Release the press and install the dust boot to the tensioner.

27. Install the timing belt tensioner and alternately tighten the bolts to 20 ft. lbs. (28 Nm). Using pliers, remove the 1.5mm hexagon wrench from the belt tensioner.

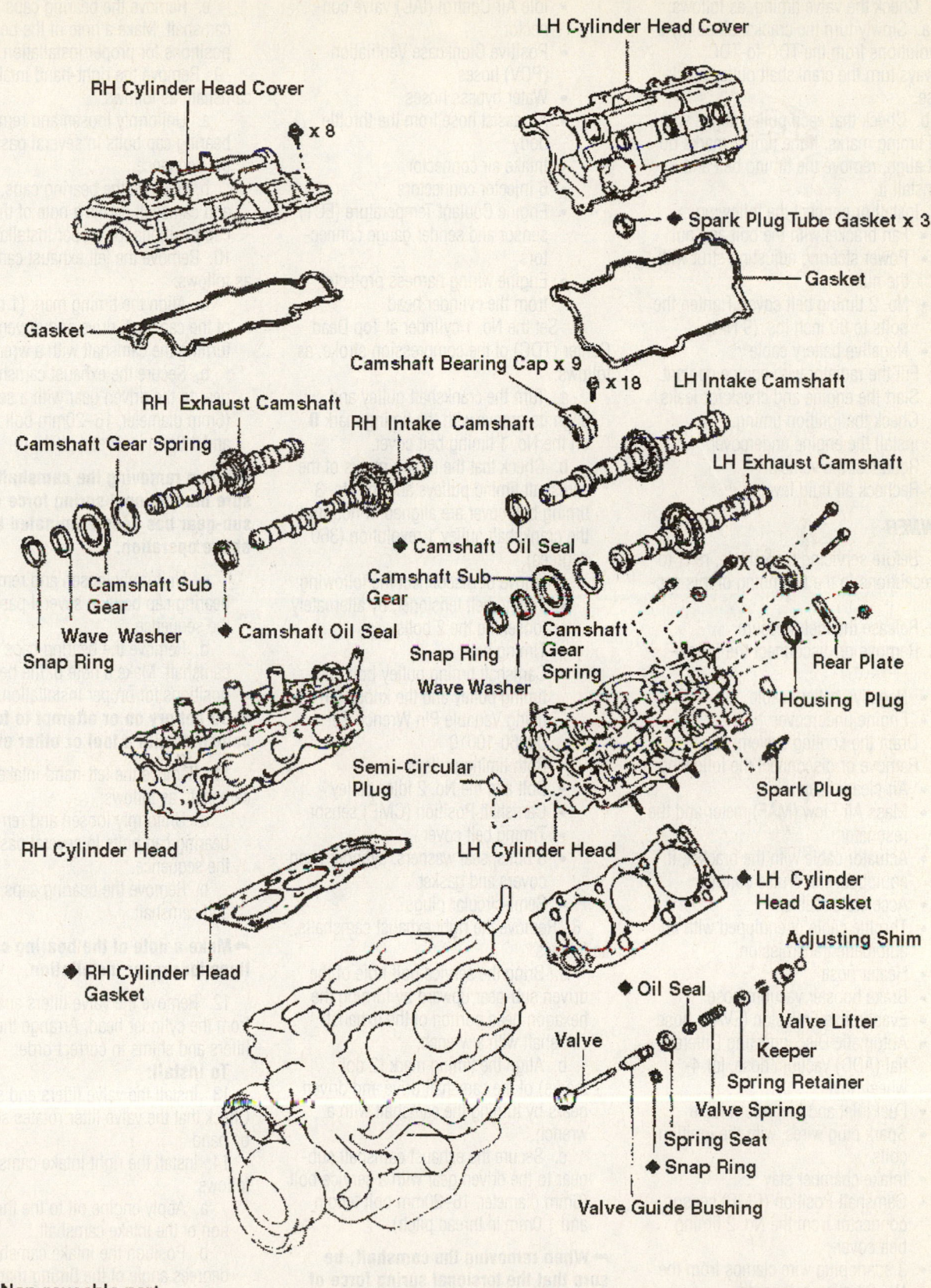

RH Cylinder Head Cover

x 8

Gasket

RH Exhaust Camshaft

Camshaft Gear Spring

Camshaft Sub Gear

Wave Washer

Snap Ring

RH Intake Camshaft

◆ Camshaft Oil Seal

Camshaft Sub Gear

◆ Camshaft Oil Seal

Snap Ring

Wave Washer

Camshaft Gear Spring

RH Cylinder Head

Semi-Circular Plug

◆ RH Cylinder Head Gasket

LH Cylinder Head Cover

◆ Spark Plug Tube Gasket x 3

Gasket

Camshaft Bearing Cap x 9

x 18

LH Intake Camshaft

LH Exhaust Camshaft

X 8

Rear Plate

Housing Plug

Spark Plug

LH Cylinder Head

◆ LH Cylinder Head Gasket

Adjusting Shim

◆ Oil Seal

Valve

Valve Lifter

Keeper

Spring Retainer

Valve Spring

Spring Seat

◆ Snap Ring

Valve Guide Bushing

◆ Non-reusable part

Exploded view of the cylinder head component assembly—all models with 3.4L (5VZ-FE) engine

7924YG75

For engine torque specifications, refer to Section 1 of this manual

28. Check the valve timing, as follows:

a. Slowly turn the crankshaft pulley 2 revolutions from the TDC-to-TDC. Always turn the crankshaft pulley clockwise.

b. Check that each pulley aligns with the timing marks. If the timing marks do not align, remove the timing belt and reinstall it.

29. Install or connect the following:
- Fan bracket with the bolt and nut
- Power steering adjusting strut with the nut
- No. 2 timing belt cover. Tighten the bolts to 80 inch lbs. (9 Nm).
- Negative battery cable

30. Fill the radiator with engine coolant.
31. Start the engine and check for leaks.
32. Check the ignition timing.
33. Install the engine undercover.
34. Road test the vehicle.
35. Recheck all fluid levels.

4RUNNER

1. Before servicing the vehicle, refer to the precautions in the beginning of this section.

2. Release the fuel pressure.

3. Remove or disconnect the following:
- Negative battery cable
- Engine undercover

4. Drain the cooling system.

5. Remove or disconnect the following:
- Air cleaner cap
- Mass Air Flow (MAF) meter and the resonator
- Actuator cable with the bracket, if equipped with cruise control
- Accelerator cable
- Throttle cable, if equipped with an automatic transmission
- Heater hose
- Brake booster vacuum hose
- Evaporative Emission (EVAP) hose
- Automatic Disconnecting Differential (ADD) vacuum hose, for 4-wheel drive
- Fuel inlet and fuel return hose
- Spark plug wires, with the ignition coils
- Intake chamber stay
- Camshaft Position (CMP) sensor connector from the No. 2 timing belt cover
- 3 spark plug wire clamps from the No. 2 timing belt cover
- 6 bolts and the No. 2 timing belt cover
- Air intake chamber assembly
- Throttle Position (TP) sensor connector

- Idle Air Control (IAC) valve connector
- Positive Crankcase Ventilation (PCV) hoses
- Water bypass hoses
- Air assist hose from the throttle body
- Intake air connector
- 6 injector connectors
- Engine Coolant Temperature (ECT) sensor and sender gauge connectors
- Engine wiring harness protector, from the cylinder head

6. Set the No. 1 cylinder at Top Dead Center (TDC) of the compression stroke, as follows:

a. Turn the crankshaft pulley and align its groove with the timing mark **0** on the No. 1 timing belt cover.

b. Check that the timing marks of the camshaft timing pulleys and the No. 3 timing belt cover are aligned. If not, turn the crankshaft pulley 1 revolution (360 degrees).

7. Remove or disconnect the following:
- Timing belt tensioner, by alternately loosening the 2 bolts
- Timing belt
- Camshaft timing pulley bolt, the timing pulley and the knock pin, using Variable Pin Wrench Set 09960-10010
- Both timing pulleys
- Bolt and the No. 2 idler pulley
- Camshaft Position (CMP) sensor
- Timing belt cover
- 8 bolts, seal washers, cylinder head covers and gasket
- Semi-circular plugs

8. Remove the right exhaust camshafts, as follows:

a. Bring the service bolt hole of the driven sub-gear upward by turning the hexagon head portion of the exhaust camshaft with a wrench.

b. Align the timing mark (2 dot marks) of the camshaft drive and driven gears by turning the camshaft with a wrench.

c. Secure the exhaust camshaft sub-gear to the driven gear with a service bolt (6mm diameter, 16–20mm bolt length and 1.0mm in thread pitch).

➡ **When removing the camshaft, be sure that the torsional spring force of the sub-gear has been eliminated by the above operation.**

d. Uniformly loosen and remove the bearing cap bolts in several passes, in the sequence.

e. Remove the bearing caps and camshaft. Make a note of the bearing cap positions for proper installation.

9. Remove the right-hand intake camshaft, as follows:

a. Uniformly loosen and remove the bearing cap bolts in several passes, in the sequence.

b. Remove the bearing caps, oil seal and camshaft. Make a note of the bearing cap positions for proper installation.

10. Remove the left exhaust camshafts, as follows:

a. Align the timing mark (1 dot mark) of the camshaft drive and driven gears by turning the camshaft with a wrench.

b. Secure the exhaust camshaft sub-gear to the driven gear with a service bolt (6mm diameter, 16–20mm bolt length and 1.0mm in thread pitch).

➡ **When removing the camshaft, be sure the torsional spring force of the sub-gear has been eliminated by the above operation.**

c. Uniformly loosen and remove the bearing cap bolts in several passes, in the sequence.

d. Remove the bearing caps and camshaft. Make a note of the bearing cap positions for proper installation.

➡ **Do not pry on or attempt to force the camshaft with a tool or other object.**

11. Remove the left-hand intake camshaft, as follows:

a. Uniformly loosen and remove the bearing cap bolts in several passes, in the sequence.

b. Remove the bearing caps, oil seal and camshaft.

➡ **Make a note of the bearing cap positions for proper installation.**

12. Remove the valve lifters and shims from the cylinder head. Arrange the valve lifters and shims in correct order.

To install:

13. Install the valve lifters and shims. Check that the valve lifter rotates smoothly by hand.

14. Install the right intake camshaft, as follows:

a. Apply engine oil to the thrust portion of the intake camshaft.

b. Position the intake camshaft at 90 degrees angle of the timing mark (2 dot marks) on the cylinder head.

c. Install the bearing caps in their proper locations. Apply a light coat of engine oil to the threads and install the cap bolts.

d. Apply a light coat of engine oil on the threads and under the heads of the bearing cap bolts.

e. Uniformly tighten the cap bolts in the sequence to 12 ft. lbs. (16 Nm).

15. Install the right exhaust camshaft, as follows:

a. Apply engine oil to the thrust portion of the intake camshaft.

b. Align the timing marks (2 dot marks) of the camshaft drive and driven gears.

c. Roll down the exhaust camshaft onto the bearing journals while engaging the gears with each other. Install the bearing caps in their proper locations.

d. Apply a light coat of engine oil to the threads and install the cap bolts.

e. Apply a light coat of engine oil on the threads and under the heads of the bearing cap bolts.

f. Uniformly tighten the cap bolts in the sequence to 12 ft. lbs. (16 Nm).

g. Remove the service bolt from the driven sub-gear. Check that the intake and exhaust camshafts turn smoothly.

h. Align the timing marks (2 dot marks) of the camshaft drive and driven gears by turning the camshaft with a wrench.

16. Install the left intake camshaft, as follows:

a. Apply engine oil to the thrust portion of the intake camshaft.

b. Position the intake camshaft at 90 degrees angle of the timing mark (1 dot mark) on the cylinder head.

c. Install the bearing caps in their proper locations. Apply a light coat of engine oil to the threads and install the cap bolts.

d. Apply a light coat of engine oil on the threads and under the heads of the bearing cap bolts.

e. Uniformly tighten the cap bolts in the sequence to 12 ft. lbs. (16 Nm).

17. Install the left exhaust camshaft, as follows:

a. Apply engine oil to the thrust portion of the intake camshaft.

b. Align the timing marks (1 dot mark) of the camshaft drive and driven gears.

c. Roll down the exhaust camshaft onto the bearing journals while engaging the gears with each other. Install the bearing caps in their proper locations.

d. Apply a light coat of engine oil to the threads and install the cap bolts.

e. Apply a light coat of engine oil on the threads and under the heads of the bearing cap bolts.

f. Uniformly tighten the cap bolts in the sequence to 12 ft. lbs. (16 Nm).

g. Remove the service bolt.

18. Check and adjust the valve clearance.

19. Install or connect the following:
- Semi-circular plugs
- Cylinder head covers. Tighten the bolts, in several passes, to 53 inch lbs. (6 Nm).
- No. 3 timing belt cover. Tighten the 6 bolts to 80 inch lbs. (9 Nm).
- CMP sensor. Tighten it to 71 inch lbs. (8 Nm).
- No. 2 timing belt idler. Tighten the bolt to 30 ft. lbs. (40 Nm).

➡**Check that the pulley bracket moves smoothly.**

20. Install the left camshaft timing pulley, as follows:

a. Install the knock pin to the camshaft.

b. Align the knock pin hose of the camshaft with the knock pin groove of the timing pulley.

c. Slide the timing pulley on the camshaft with the flange side facing outward. Tighten the pulley bolt to 81 ft. lbs. (110 Nm).

21. Set the No. 1 cylinder to Top Dead Center (TDC) of the compression stroke, as follows:

a. Turn the crankshaft pulley, and align its groove with the timing mark **0** on the No. 1 timing belt cover.

b. Turn the camshaft, align the knock pin hole of the camshaft with the timing mark of the No. 3 timing belt cover.

c. Turn the camshaft timing pulley, align the timing marks of the camshaft timing pulley and the No. 3 timing belt cover.

22. Install or connect the following:
- Timing belt to the left camshaft timing pulley. Check that the installation mark on the timing belt is aligned with the end of the No. 1 timing belt cover.
- Right camshaft timing pulley
- Timing belt

23. Set the timing belt tensioner, as follows:

a. Using a press, slowly press in the pushrod using 220–2,205 lbs. (981–9,807 N) of force.

b. Align the holes of the pushrod and housing, pass a 1.5mm hexagon wrench through the holes to keep the setting position of the pushrod.

c. Release the press and install the dust boot to the tensioner.

24. Install the timing belt tensioner and alternately tighten the bolts to 20 ft. lbs. (28 Nm). Using pliers, remove the 1.5mm hexagon wrench from the belt tensioner.

25. Check the valve timing, as follows:

a. Slowly turn the crankshaft pulley 2 revolutions from the TDC-to-TDC. Always turn the crankshaft pulley clockwise.

b. Check that each pulley aligns with the timing marks. If the timing marks do not align, remove the timing belt and reinstall it.

26. Install or connect the following:
- Engine wiring harness to the cylinder head
- 3 engine wiring harness clamps.
- 6 injector connectors
- ECT sender gauge connector
- ECT sensor connector
- Intake air connector
- Air intake chamber assembly. Tighten the 4 bolts and 2 nuts to 13 ft. lbs. (18 Nm).
- Intake chamber stay. Tighten the 2 bolts to 30 ft. lbs. (40 Nm).
- New O-ring to the oil filler tube
- Oil filler tube end into the oil pan tube hole
- Oil filler tube and No. 1 throttle cable clamp
- No. 2 timing belt cover. Tighten the bolts to 80 inch lbs. (9 Nm).
- Remaining components
- Negative battery cable

27. Fill the cooling system.
28. Start the engine and check for leaks.
29. Check the ignition timing.
30. Install the engine undercover.
31. Road test the vehicle.
32. Recheck all fluid levels.

Valve Lash

ADJUSTMENT

2.4L (2RZ-FE) Engine

1. Before servicing the vehicle, refer to the precautions in the beginning of this section.

2. Remove or disconnect the following:
- Negative battery cable

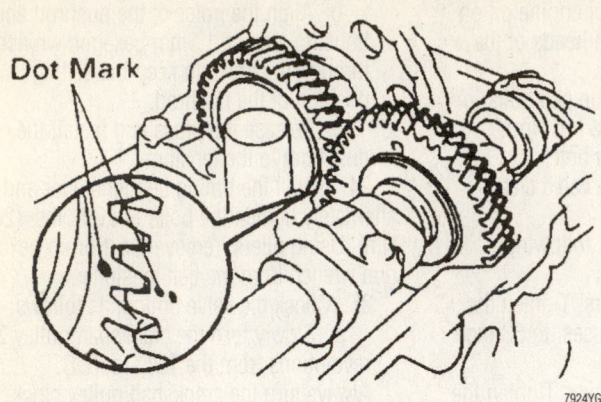

Aligning the timing marks—Tacoma with 2.4L (2RZ-FE) and 2.7L (3RZ-FE) engines

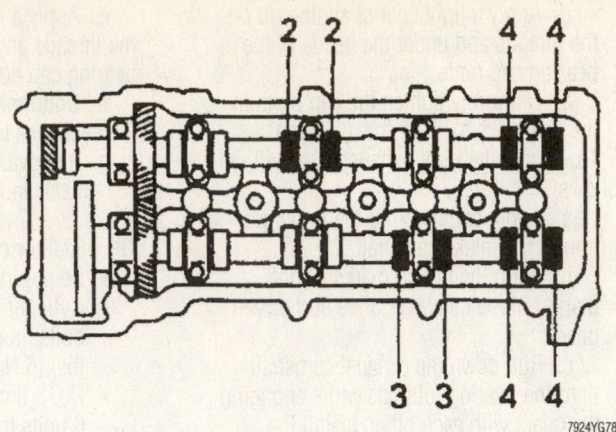

Second valve adjustment—2.4L (2RZ-FE) and 2.7L (3RZ-FE) engines

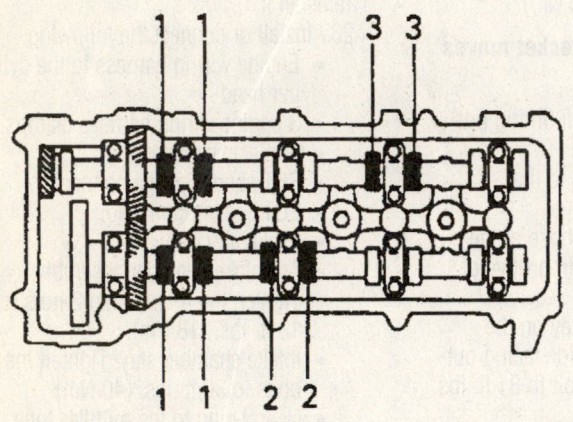

First valve adjustment—2.4L (2RZ-FE) and 2.7L (3RZ-FE) engines

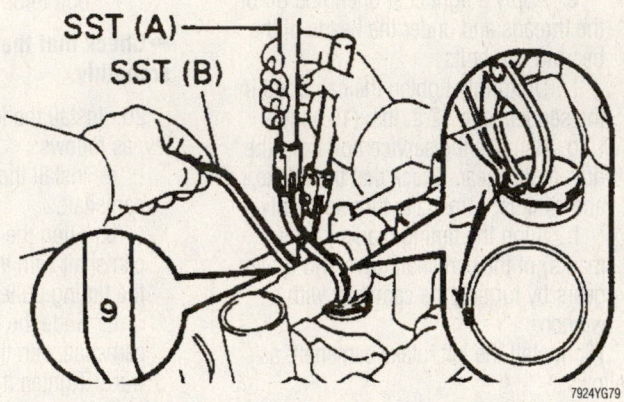

Removing adjusting shim using the special tools shown above—2.4L (2RZ-FE) and 2.7L (3RZ-FE) engines

- Air intake connector
- Positive Crankcase Ventilation (PCV) hoses
- Spark plug wires
- 4 clamps and the engine wiring harness
- Air conditioning compressor connector, if equipped with air conditioning
- Oil pressure sensor connector
- Engine Coolant Temperature (ECT) sensor connector
- Distributor connector
- Cylinder head cover

3. Set the No. 1 cylinder to Top Dead Center (TDC) of the compression stroke, as follows:

a. Turn the crankshaft pulley clockwise and align its groove with the **0** mark on the timing chain cover.

b. Check that the timing marks (1 and 2 dots) of the camshaft drive and driven gears are in a straight line on the cylinder head surface. If not, turn the crankshaft 1 revolution (360 degrees) and align the marks.

4. Inspect the valve clearance, as follows:

a. Measure the clearance between the valve lifter and the camshaft. Measure the 1st and 2nd intake and the 1st and 3rd exhaust valves.

b. Turn the crankshaft pulley 1 revolution (360 degrees) and align the marks as above. Measure the 3rd and 4th intake and the 2nd and 4th exhaust valves.

5. Valve clearance "cold" should be:
- Intake: 0.006–0.010 in. (0.15–0.25mm)
- Exhaust: 0.010–0.014 in. (0.25–0.35mm)

6. Adjust the valve clearance by using adjusting shims, as follows:

a. Turn the equipment driveshaft so that the cam lobe for the valve to be adjusted faces up.

b. Using SST 09248-55040, press down the valve lifter and place SST 09248-05420, between the camshaft and the valve lifter.

c. Remove SST 09248-55040.

d. Remove the adjusting shim with a small flat prying tool and a magnetic finger.

e. Determine the replacement adjusting shim size according to the following formula or use the adjusting shim charts.

f. Using a micrometer, measure the thickness of the removed shim. Calculate the thickness of a new shim so that the valve clearance comes within the specified value:
- T: Thickness of the removed shim
- A: Measured valve clearance
- N: Thickness of the new shim

g. Intake: $N = T + (A — 0.008$ in. $(0.20mm))$

h. Exhaust: $N = T + (A — 0.012$ in. $(0.30mm))$

i. Install a new adjusting shim. Place it on the valve lifter. Using the SST 09248-55040, press down the valve lifter.

j. Remove the SST 09248-05420.

k. Recheck the valve clearance.

7. Install or connect the following:
- Cylinder head cover
- Engine wiring harness and clamps
- Distributor connector

- ECT sensor connector
- Oil pressure sensor connector
- Air conditioning compressor connector, if disconnected
- Spark plug wires
- PCV hoses
- Air intake connector
- Negative battery cable

8. Check the ignition timing.

2.7L (3RZ-FE) Engine

1. Before servicing the vehicle, refer to the precautions in the beginning of this section.

2. Disconnect the negative battery cable.

3. Drain the engine coolant.

4. Remove or disconnect the following:

- Intake air connector, on the Tacoma and 4Runner
- Air cleaner cap, Mass Air Flow (MAF) meter and the resonator, on the T100
- Positive Crankcase Ventilation (PCV) hoses
- Spark plug wires
- Engine wiring harness clamps and harness
- Air conditioning compressor connector, if equipped with air conditioning
- Oil pressure sensor connector
- Engine Coolant Temperature (ECT) sensor connector
- Distributor connector, for Tacoma and 4Runner
- Cylinder head cover

5. Set the No. 1 cylinder to Top Dead Center (TDC) of the compression stroke, as follows:

a. Turn the crankshaft pulley clockwise and align its groove with the **0** mark on the timing chain cover.

b. Check that the timing marks (1 and 2 dots) of the camshaft drive and driven gears are in a straight line on the cylinder head surface. If not, turn the crankshaft 1 revolution (360 degrees) and align the marks.

6. Inspect the valve clearance, as follows:

a. Measure the clearance between the valve lifter and the camshaft. Measure the 1st and 2nd intake and the 1st and 3rd exhaust valves.

b. Turn the crankshaft pulley 1 revolution (360 degrees) and align the marks as above. Measure the 3rd and 4th intake and the 2nd and 4th exhaust valves.

7. Valve clearance cold should be:

- Intake: 0.006–0.010 in. (0.15–0.25mm)
- Exhaust: 0.010–0.014 in. (0.25–0.35mm)

8. Adjust the valve clearance by using adjusting shims, as follows:

a. Turn the camshaft so the cam lobe for the valve to be adjusted faces up.

b. Using SST 09248-55040, press down the valve lifter and place SST 09248-05420, between the camshaft and the valve lifter. Remove SST 09248-55040.

c. Remove the adjusting shim with a small flat prying tool and a magnetic finger.

d. Determine the replacement adjusting shim size according to the following formula or use the adjusting shim charts.

e. Using a micrometer, measure the thickness of the removed shim. Calculate the thickness of a new shim so the valve clearance comes within the specified value.

- T: Thickness of the removed shim
- A: Measured valve clearance
- N: Thickness of the new shim

f. Intake: N = T + (A—0.008 in. (0.20mm))

g. Exhaust: N = T + (A—0.012 in. (0.30mm))

h. Install a new adjusting shim. Place it on the valve lifter. Using the SST 09248-55040, press down the valve lifter and remove SST 09248-05420.

i. Recheck the valve clearance.

9. Install or connect the following:

- Cylinder head cover
- Engine wiring harness and clamps
- Distributor connector
- ECT sensor connector
- Oil pressure sensor connector
- Air conditioning compressor connector, if disconnected
- Spark plug wires
- PCV hoses
- Air cleaner cap, MAF meter and the resonator, on the T100
- Intake air connector, on the 4Runner and Tacoma
- Negative battery cable

10. Refill with engine coolant.

11. Check the ignition timing.

3.4L (5VZ-FE) Engine

1. Before servicing the vehicle, refer to the precautions in the beginning of this section.

2. Disconnect the negative battery cable.

3. Drain the engine coolant.

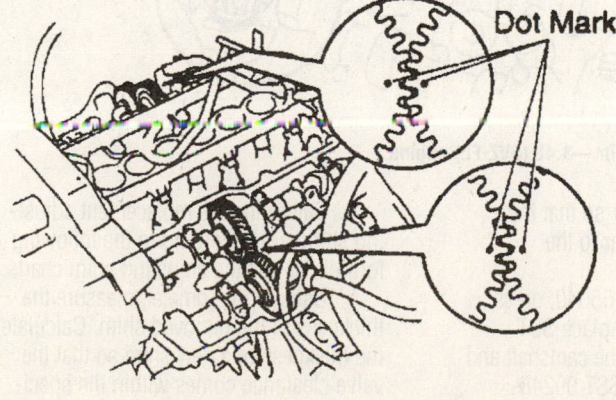

Aligning the timing marks—3.4L (5VZ-FE) engine

Dot Mark

7924YG81

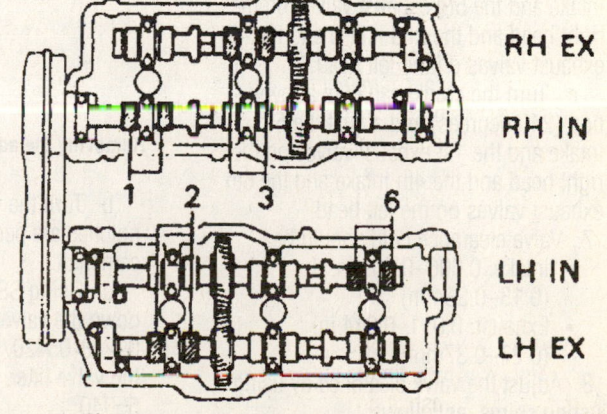

First valve adjustment—3.4L (5VZ-FE) engine

RH EX
RH IN
LH IN
LH EX

7924YG82

Please refer to Section 8 for electric cooling fan wiring schematics

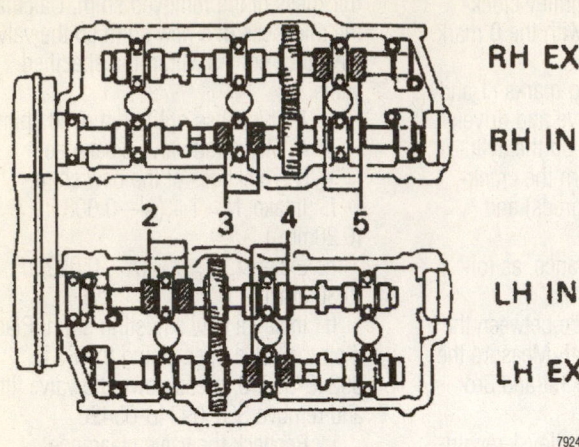

Second valve adjustment—3.4L (5VZ-FE) engine

Third valve adjustment—3.4L (5VZ-FE) engine

4. Remove or disconnect the following:
• Air intake connector
• Cylinder head cover

5. Set the No. 1 cylinder to Top Dead Center (TDC) of the compression stroke, as follows:

a. Turn the crankshaft pulley clockwise and align its groove with the **0** mark on the timing chain cover.

b. Check that the timing marks (1 and 2 dots) of the camshaft drive and driven gears are in a straight line on the cylinder head surface. If not, turn the crankshaft 1 revolution (360 degrees) and align the marks.

6. Inspect the valve clearance, as follows:

a. Measure the clearance between the valve lifter and the camshaft. Measure the 1st intake and the 3rd exhaust valves on the right head and the 6th intake and the 2nd exhaust valves on the left head.

b. Turn the crankshaft ⅔ of a revolution (240 degrees) and adjust the 3rd intake and the 5th exhaust valves on the right head and the 2nd intake and the 4th exhaust valves on the left head.

c. Turn the crankshaft ⅔ of a revolution (240 degrees) and adjust the 5th intake and the 1st exhaust valves on the right head and the 4th intake and the 6th exhaust valves on the left head.

7. Valve clearance cold should be:
• Intake: 0.006–0.009 in. (0.13–0.23mm)
• Exhaust: 0.011–0.014 in. (0.27–0.37mm)

8. Adjust the valve clearance by using adjusting shims, as follows:

a. Turn the equipment camshaft so that the cam lobe for the valve to be adjusted faces up.

Front of No.1 and Rear of No.6 Cylinders

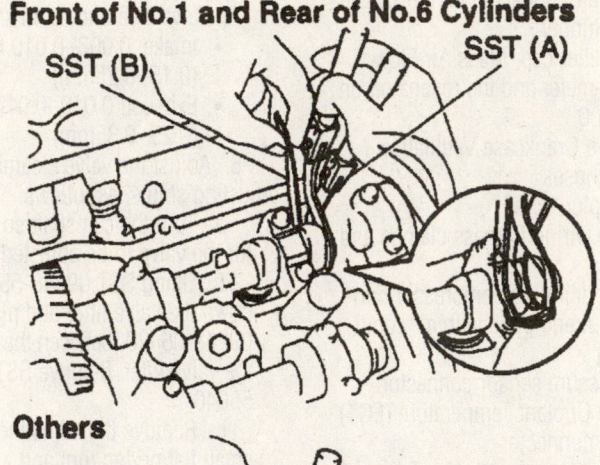

Others

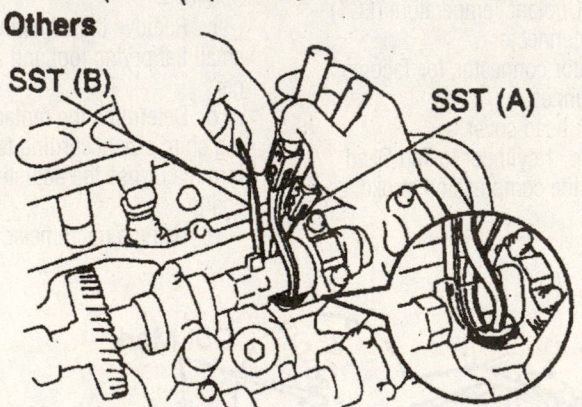

Removing the adjusting shim—3.4L (5VZ-FE) engine

b. Turn the valve lifter so that the notches are perpendicular to the camshaft.

c. Using SST 09248-55040, press down the valve lifter and place SST 09248-05420, between the camshaft and the valve lifter. Remove SST 09248-55040.

d. Remove the adjusting shim with a small flat prying tool and a magnetic finger.

e. Determine the replacement adjusting shim size according to the following formula or use the adjusting shim charts.

f. Using a micrometer, measure the thickness of the removed shim. Calculate the thickness of a new shim so that the valve clearance comes within the specified value.
• T: Thickness of the removed shim
• A: Measured valve clearance
• N: Thickness of the new shim

g. Intake: N = T + (A—0.007 in. (0.18mm))

h. Exhaust: N = T + (A—0.013 in. (0.32mm))

i. Install a new adjusting shim. Place it on the valve lifter. Using the SST 09248-55040, press down the valve lifter and remove SST 09248-05420.

j. Recheck the valve clearance.

9. Install or connect the following:
• Cylinder head cover
• Intake air connector
• Negative battery cable

10. Refill with engine coolant.
11. Start the engine and check for leaks.

Starter

REMOVAL & INSTALLATION

2.4L Engine

1. Before servicing the vehicle, refer to the precautions in the beginning of this section.

2. Remove or disconnect the following:
• Negative battery cable
• Engine cover
• Accelerator cable and intake air connector
• Intake manifold assembly
• Starter motor
• Starter electrical connectors

To install:

3. Install or connect the following:
• Starter. Tighten both bolts to 29 ft. lbs. (39 Nm).
• Intake manifold

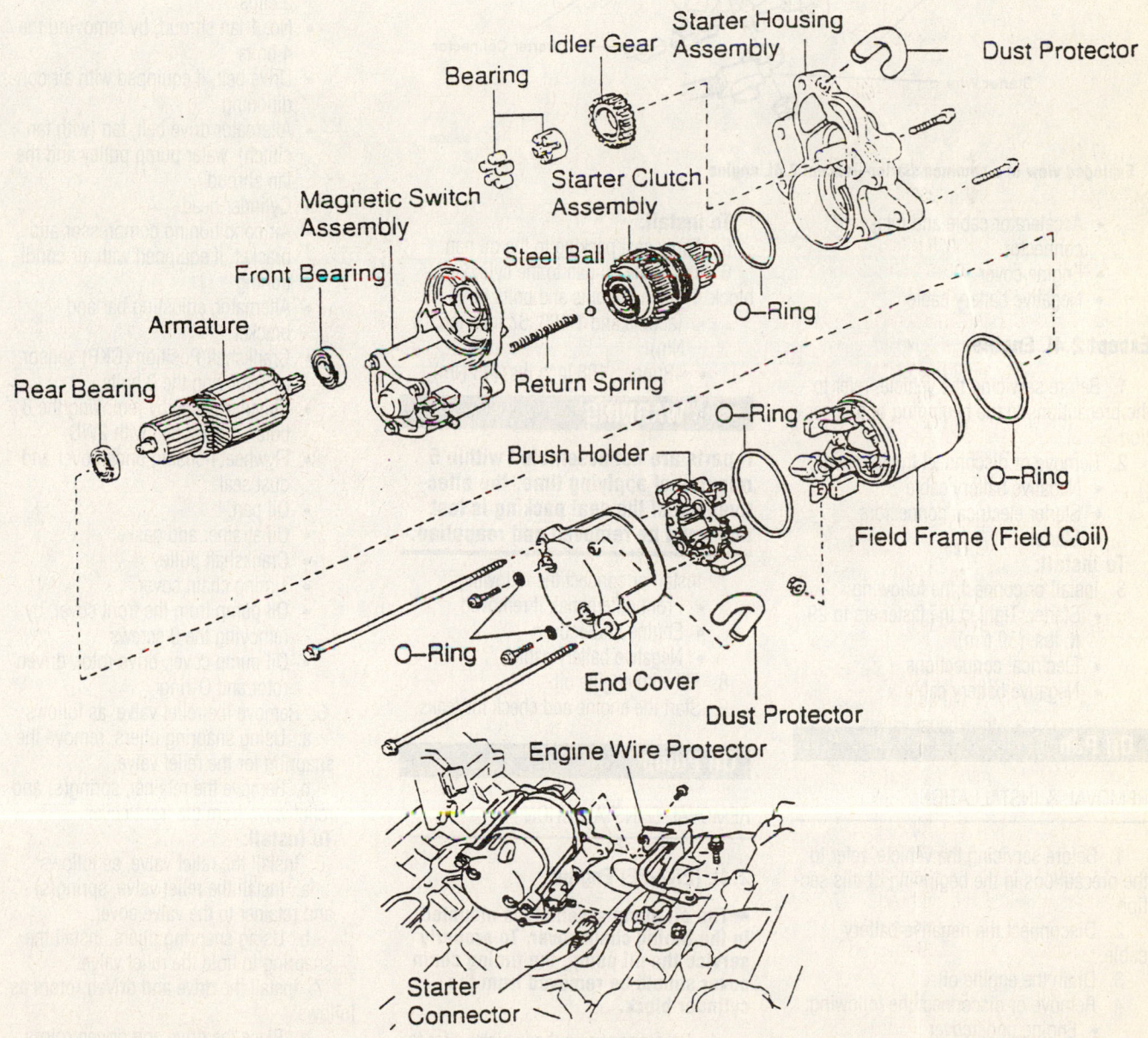

This starter motor arrangement is installed under the intake manifold between the cylinder heads—2.4L engine

93162G18

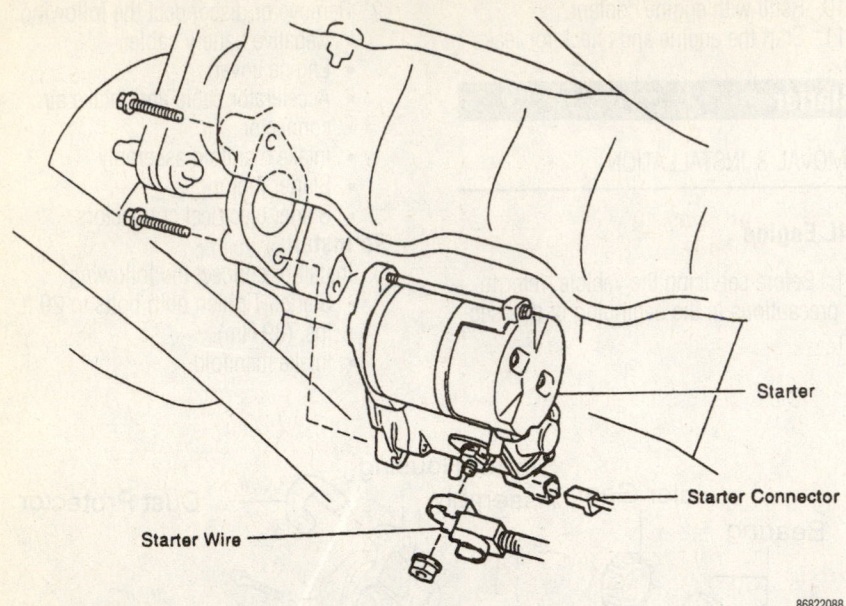

Exploded view of a common starter—except 2.4L engine

Labels: Starter, Starter Connector, Starter Wire

86822088

- Accelerator cable and intake air connector
- Engine cover
- Negative battery cable

Except 2.4L Engine

1. Before servicing the vehicle, refer to the precautions in the beginning of this section.
2. Remove or disconnect the following:
   - Negative battery cable
   - Starter electrical connectors
   - Starter

To install:

3. Install or connect the following:
   - Starter. Tighten the fasteners to 29 ft. lbs. (39 Nm).
   - Electrical connections
   - Negative battery cable

Oil Pan

REMOVAL & INSTALLATION

1. Before servicing the vehicle, refer to the precautions in the beginning of this section.
2. Disconnect the negative battery cable.
3. Drain the engine oil.
4. Remove or disconnect the following:
   - Engine undercover
   - Front differential, if equipped with 4WD
   - Oil pan, separate it from the engine using SST 09032-00100 and a brass bar

To install:

5. Apply seal packing to the oil pan.
6. Install the oil pan to the cylinder block. Tighten the nuts and bolts to:
   - Tacoma and T-100: 67 inch lbs. (8 Nm)
   - 4Runner: 108 inch lbs. (13 Nm)

✹✹ WARNING

If parts are not assembled within 5 minutes of applying time, the effectiveness of the seal packing is lost and must be removed and reapplied.

7. Install or connect the following:
   - Front differential, if removed
   - Engine undercover
   - Negative battery cable
8. Fill with engine oil.
9. Start the engine and check for leaks.

Oil Pump

REMOVAL & INSTALLATION

2.4L (2RZ-FE) Engine

➡**The oil pump assembly is mounted in the timing chain cover. To properly service the oil pump, the timing chain cover should be removed from the cylinder block.**

1. Before servicing the vehicle, refer to the precautions in the beginning of this section.
2. Disconnect the negative battery cable.

3. Drain the oil and the cooling system.
4. Remove or disconnect the following:
   - Engine undercover
   - Front differential and halfshaft assembly, if equipped with 4WD
   - Upper radiator hose from the radiator
   - Oil dipstick guide, by removing the bolt
   - Power steering drive belt, by loosening the lockbolt and adjusting bolt, if equipped with power steering
   - No. 2 fan shroud, by removing the 2 clips
   - No. 1 fan shroud, by removing the 4 bolts
   - Drive belt, if equipped with air conditioning
   - Alternator drive belt, fan (with fan clutch), water pump pulley and the fan shroud
   - Cylinder head
   - Air conditioning compressor and bracket, if equipped with air conditioning
   - Alternator, adjusting bar and bracket
   - Crankshaft Position (CKP) sensor, by removing the 2 bolts
   - Stiffener plates by removing the 8 bolts, if equipped with 2WD
   - Flywheel housing undercover and dust seal
   - Oil pan.
   - Oil strainer and gasket
   - Crankshaft pulley
   - Timing chain cover
   - Oil pump from the front cover, by removing the 9 screws
   - Oil pump cover, drive rotor, driven rotor and O-ring
5. Remove the relief valve, as follows:
   a. Using snapring pliers, remove the snapring for the relief valve.
   b. Remove the retainer, spring(s) and relief valve from the front cover.

To install:

6. Install the relief valve, as follows:
   a. Install the relief valve, spring(s) and retainer to the valve cover.
   b. Using snapring pliers, install the snapring to hold the relief valve.
7. Install the drive and driven rotors as follows:
   a. Place the drive and driven rotors into the pump body.
   b. Place a new O-ring to the pump body.
   c. Install the pump cover with the 9 screws.

8. Install the remaining components in the reverse order of removal.

9. Fill the cooling system and fill the engine with oil.

10. Connect the negative battery cable.

11. Start the engine and check for leaks.

12. Adjust ignition timing. Road test the vehicle for proper operation.

13. Recheck all fluid levels.

2.7L (3RZ-FE) Engine

4RUNNER

1. Before servicing the vehicle, refer to the precautions in the beginning of this section.

2. Remove or disconnect the following:
- Negative battery cable
- Cylinder head assembly
- Water inlet and housing
- Timing chain cover
- 9 screws and separate the oil pump from the timing chain cover

To install:

3. Install or connect the following:
- Oil pump assembly to the timing chain cover
- Timing chain cover

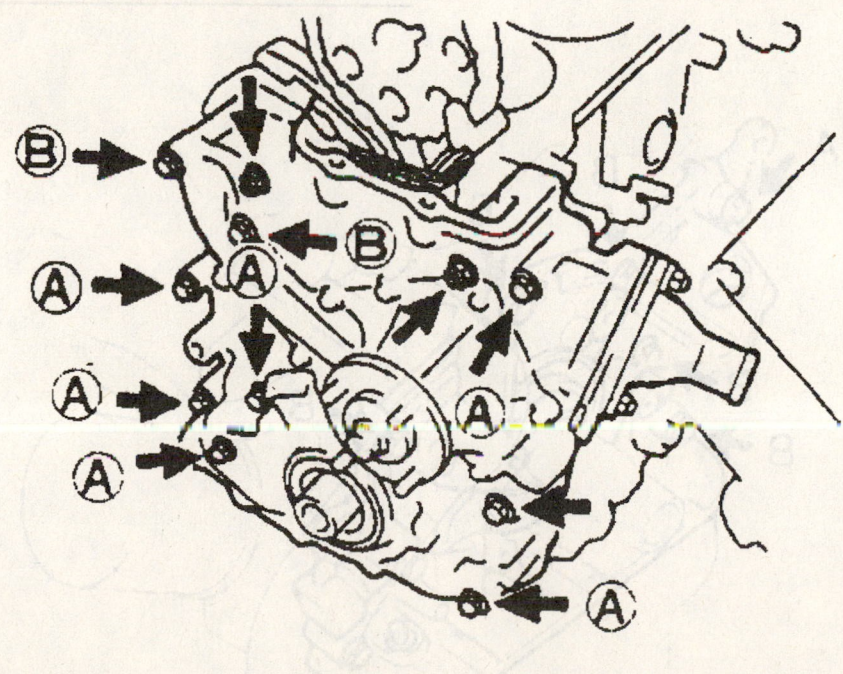

Timing cover bolt pattern—4Runner and T-100 with 2.7L (3RZ-FE) engine

- Water bypass pipe. Tighten both nuts to 14 ft. lbs. (20 Nm).
- Cylinder head assembly

T-100

➡ **The oil pump assembly is mounted in the timing chain cover. To properly service the oil pump, the timing chain cover should be removed from the cylinder block.**

1. Before servicing the vehicle, refer to the precautions in the beginning of this section.

2. Disconnect the negative battery cable.

3. Drain the oil and cooling system.

4. Remove or disconnect the following:
- Cylinder head
- Engine undercover, by removing the 4 bolts
- Drive belt, by loosening the idler pulley nut and adjusting bolt, if equipped with air conditioning
- Alternator drive belt, fan (with fan clutch), water pump pulley and fan shroud
- Air conditioning compressor and bracket; do not disconnect the

lines, if equipped with air conditioning
- Alternator, adjusting bar and bracket
- Crankshaft Position (CKP) sensor
- Oil pan
- Oil strainer and gasket
- Crankshaft pulley.
- Timing chain cover
- Oil pump from the front cover, by removing the 9 screws, pump cover, drive rotor, driven rotor and O-ring

5. Remove the relief valve, as follows:

a. Using snapring pliers, remove the snapring for the relief valve.

b. Remove the retainer, spring and relief valve from the front cover.

To install:

6. Install the relief valve, as follows:

a. Install the relief valve, spring and retainer to the valve cover.

b. Using a snapring pliers, install the snapring to hold the relief valve.

7. Install the drive and driven rotors, as follows:

a. Place the drive and driven rotors into the pump body.

b. Place a new O-ring to the pump body.

c. Install the pump cover with the 9 screws.

8. Install or connect the following:
- Timing chain cover
- 2 rear timing chain cover bolts and water bypass pipe nuts. Tighten the fasteners to 13 ft. lbs. (18 Nm).
- Remaining components
- Cylinder head
- Negative battery cable

9. Fill the cooling system. Fill the engine with oil.

10. Start the engine and check for leaks.

11. Adjust ignition timing. Road test the vehicle for proper operation.

12. Recheck all fluid levels.

TACOMA

➡ **The oil pump assembly is mounted in the timing chain cover. To properly service the oil pump, the timing chain cover should be removed from the cylinder block.**

1. Before servicing the vehicle, refer to the precautions in the beginning of this section.

2. Disconnect the negative battery cable.

3. Drain the oil and the cooling system.

Timing belt service is covered in Section 4 of this manual

4. Remove or disconnect the following:
- Engine undercover
- Front differential and halfshaft assembly, if equipped with 4WD
- 2 bolts and the air pipe, for California vehicles with 3RZ-FE engine
- Upper radiator hose from the radiator
- Oil dipstick guide
- Power steering drive belt, by loosening the lockbolt and adjusting bolt, if equipped with power steering
- No. 2 fan shroud by removing the 2 clips
- No. 1 fan shroud by removing the 4 bolts
- Drive belt, by loosening the idler pulley nut and adjusting bolt, if equipped with air conditioning
- Alternator drive belt, fan (with fan clutch), water pump pulley and the fan shroud
- Cylinder head
- Air conditioning compressor and bracket with the lines attached, if equipped with air conditioning
- Alternator, adjusting bar and bracket
- Crankshaft Position (CKP) sensor by removing the 2 bolts
- Stiffener plates by removing the 8 bolts, if equipped with 2WD
- Flywheel housing undercover and dust seal
- Oil pan
- Oil strainer and gasket
- Crankshaft pulley
- Timing chain cover
- Oil pump from the front cover by removing the 9 screws
- Oil pump cover, drive rotor, driven rotor and O-ring

5. Remove the relief valve, as follows:
   a. Using snapring pliers, remove the snapring for the relief valve.
   b. Remove the retainer, spring(s) and relief valve from the front cover.

To install:

6. Install the relief valve, as follows:
   a. Install the relief valve, spring(s) and retainer to the valve cover.
   b. Using snapring pliers, install the snapring to hold the relief valve.

7. Install the drive and driven rotors, as follows:
   a. Place the drive and driven rotors into the pump body.
   b. Place a new O-ring to the pump body.
   c. Install the pump cover with the 9 screws.

8. Install the remaining components in the reverse order of removal.

9. Fill the cooling system and fill the engine with oil.
10. Connect the negative battery cable.
11. Start the engine and check for leaks.
12. Adjust ignition timing. Road test the vehicle for proper operation.
13. Recheck all fluid levels.

3.4L (5VZ-FE) Engine

1. Before servicing the vehicle, refer to the precautions in the beginning of this section.
2. Remove or disconnect the following:
- Negative battery cable
- Engine undercover
- Crankshaft timing pulley
- Front differential, if equipped with 4WD

3. Drain the engine oil from the engine.
4. Remove or disconnect the following:
- Timing belt and crankshaft gear
- Oil cooler tube and clamp, if equipped with automatic transmission
- Stiffener plate
- Flywheel housing undercover and dust cover
- Rear end cover and dust cover
- Starter wire clamp
- Crankshaft Position (CKP) sensor
- Oil pan

➡Be careful not to damage the baffle plate flange.

- Oil strainer
- Oil baffle plate
- Oil pump body by removing the 8 bolts.
- O-ring from the cylinder block

To install:

5. Install or connect the following:
- Apply Seal Packing PN 08826-00080 to the oil pump
- New O-ring into the groove of the cylinder block
- Oil pump to the crankshaft with the spline teeth of the drive rotor engaged with the large teeth of the crankshaft. Tighten the oil pump bolts "A" 15 ft. lbs. (20 Nm) and bolts "B" 31 ft. lbs. (42 Nm)
- CKP
- Oil pan baffle plate
- Oil strainer with a new gasket. Tighten the bolts to 13 ft. lbs. (18 Nm).
- Remaining components
- Negative battery cable

6. Fill with engine oil.
7. Start the engine and check for leaks.

Piston and Ring

POSITIONING

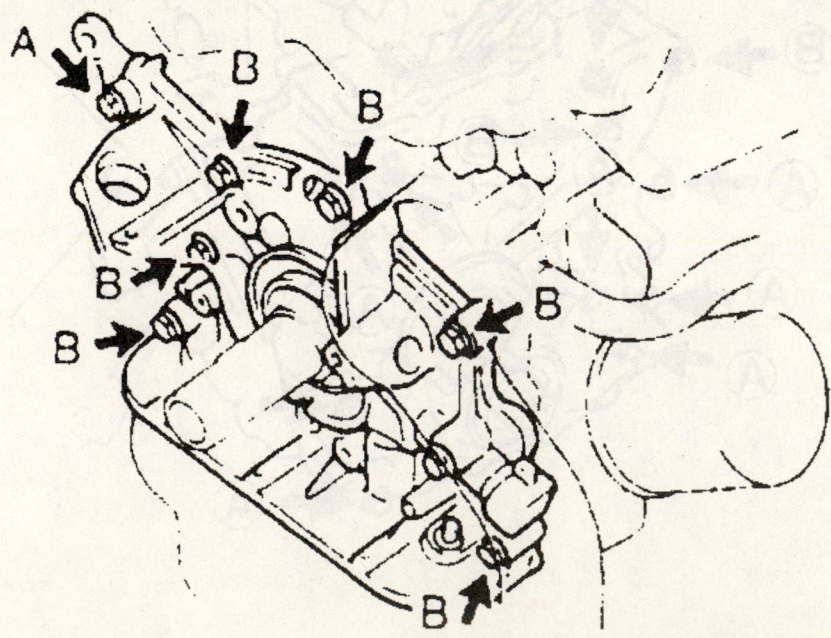

Oil pump bolt identification—4Runner, Tacoma and T-100 with 3.4L (5VZ-FE) engine

7924YG89

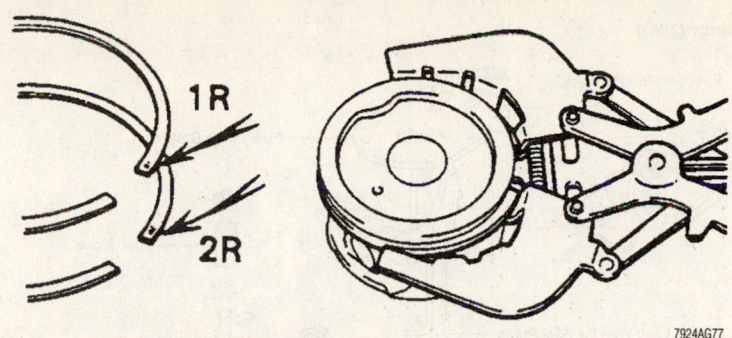

Compression ring identification mark locations—2.7L engine

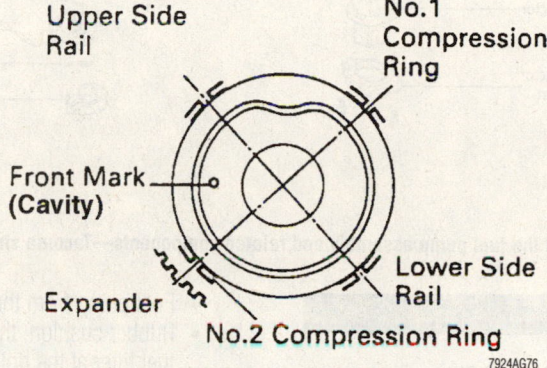

Piston ring end-gap spacing—2.4L (2RZ-FE) and 2.7L engines

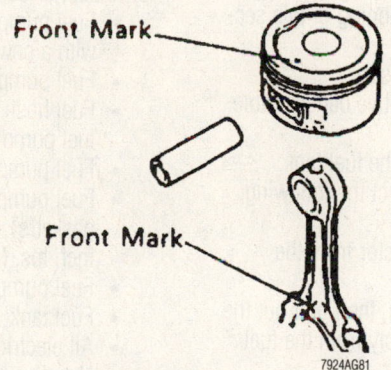

Piston to connecting rod assembly—2.4L (2RZ-FE), 2.7L and 3.4L engines

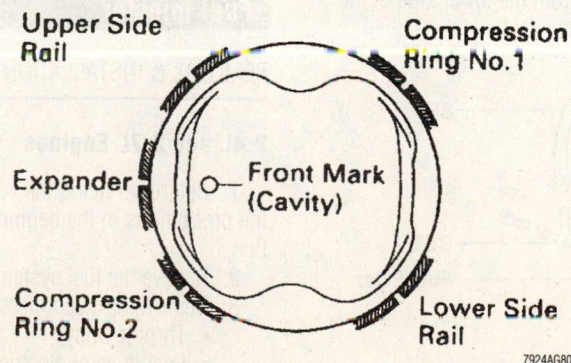

Piston ring end-gap spacing—3.4L engine

FUEL SYSTEM

Fuel System Service Precautions

Safety is the most important factor when performing not only fuel system maintenance, but any type of maintenance. Failure to conduct maintenance and repairs in a safe manner may result in serious personal injury or death. Work on a vehicle's fuel system components can be accomplished safely and effectively by adhering to the following rules and guidelines.

• To avoid the possibility of fire and personal injury, always disconnect the negative battery cable unless the repair or test procedure requires that battery voltage be applied.

• Always relieve the fuel system pressure prior to disconnecting any fuel system component (injector, fuel rail, pressure regulator, etc.) fitting or fuel line connection. Exercise extreme caution whenever relieving fuel system pressure, to avoid exposing skin, face and eyes to fuel spray. Please be advised that fuel under pressure may penetrate the skin or any part of the body that it contacts.

• Always place a shop towel or cloth around the fitting or connection prior to loosening to absorb any excess fuel due to spillage. Ensure that all fuel spillage is quickly remove from engine surfaces. Ensure that all fuel-soaked cloths or towels are deposited into a flame-proof waste container with a lid.

• Always keep a dry chemical (Class B) fire extinguisher near the work area.

• Do not allow fuel spray or fuel vapors to come into contact with a light bulb, spark or open flame.

• Always use a second wrench when loosening or tightening fuel line connection fittings. This will prevent unnecessary stress and torsion to fuel piping. Always follow the proper torque specifications.

• Always replace worn fuel fitting O-rings with new ones. Do not substitute fuel hose where rigid pipe is installed.

Fuel System Pressure

RELIEVING

1. Before servicing the vehicle, refer to the precautions in the beginning of this section.

2. Disconnect the negative battery terminal.

3. Place a catch-pan under the joint to be disconnected. A large quantity of fuel may be released when the joint is opened.

4. Wear eye or full face protection.

5. Place a shop towel over the area and slowly loosen the joint using a wrench of the correct size. Use a back-up wrench if needed.

6. Allow the fuel left in the line to bleed off slowly before fully disconnecting the joint.

7. Plug the opened lines immediately to prevent fuel spillage or the entry of dirt.

8. Dispose of the released fuel properly.

9. After connecting fuel lines, connect the negative battery cable and start the engine.

10. Check for leaks and repair as needed.

Fuel Filter

REMOVAL & INSTALLATION

1. Before servicing the vehicle, refer to the precautions in the beginning of this section.

2. Relieve the fuel system pressure.

3. Remove or disconnect the following:
   - Negative battery cable

➡**The fuel filter is located in the engine compartment, at the inlet line to the fuel rail.**

   - Plug the filter inlet and outlet lines
   - Fuel filter
   - Bracket from the fuel filter

To install:

4. Install or connect the following:
   - Fuel filter bracket to the fuel filter
   - Fuel filter. Tighten the 2 bolts to 14 ft. lbs. (20 Nm).
   - New gaskets. Tighten the union bolts to 22 ft. lbs. (30 Nm).
   - Negative battery cable

5. Start the engine and check for leaks.

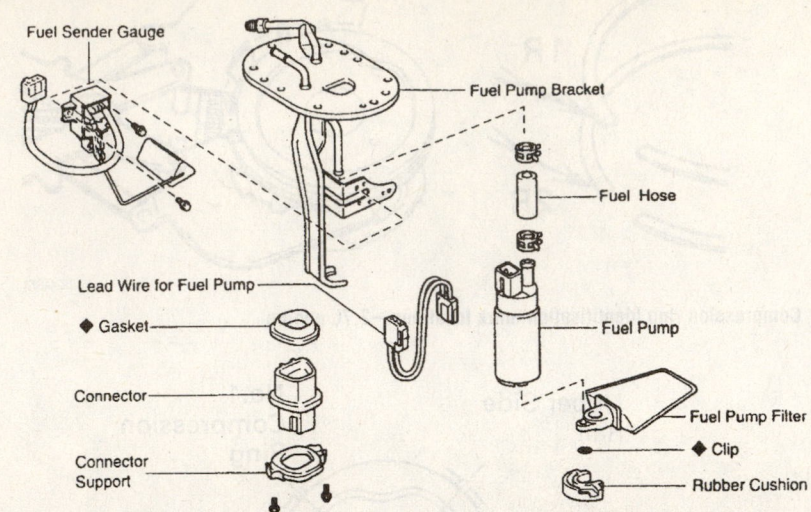

Reference (2WD)

Exploded view of the fuel pump assembly and related components—Tacoma shown

7924YG91

Fuel Pump

REMOVAL & INSTALLATION

1. Before servicing the vehicle, refer to the precautions in the beginning of this section.

2. Relieve the fuel pressure.

3. Disconnect the negative battery cable from the battery.

4. Drain the fuel from the fuel tank.

5. Remove or disconnect the following:
   - Fuel tank
   - Fuel pump connector from the clamp
   - Access plate bolts, then pull out the fuel pump assembly from the fuel tank
   - Gasket(s) from the pump bracket
   - Fuel pump connector
   - Bracket from the lower side of the fuel pump

   - Fuel pump from the fuel hose
   - Rubber cushion, the clip and the fuel filter at the bottom of the fuel pump

To install:

6. Install or connect the following:
   - Fuel pump filter to the fuel pump with a new clip
   - Fuel pump to the fuel pump bracket
   - Fuel hose to the outlet port of the fuel pump
   - Fuel pump connector
   - Fuel pump assembly with a new gasket(s). Tighten the bolts to 31 inch lbs. (4 Nm).
   - Fuel pump connector to the clamp
   - Fuel tank
   - All electrical and fuel connections
   - Negative battery cable

7. Refill the fuel tank and check for leaks.

Fuel Injector

REMOVAL & INSTALLATION

2.4L and 2.7L Engines

1. Before servicing the vehicle, refer to the precautions in the beginning of this section.

2. Relieve the fuel system pressure.

3. Remove or disconnect the following:
   - Throttle body
   - Fuel injector electrical connectors
   - Crankshaft Position (CKP) sensor connector
   - Knock Sensor (KS) connector

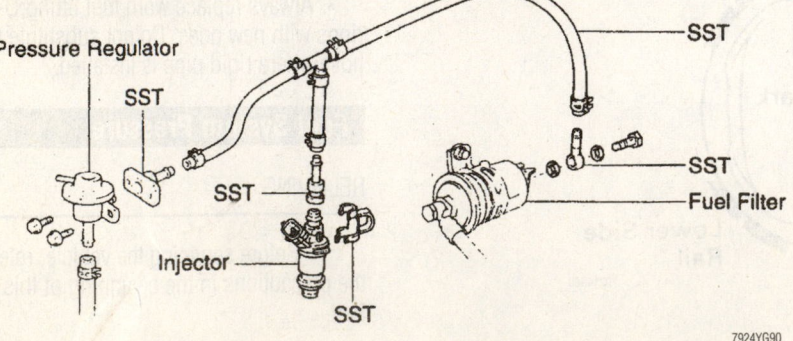

7924YG90

Exploded view of the fuel delivery components—2.4L (2RZ-FE) and 2.7L (3RZ-FE) engines

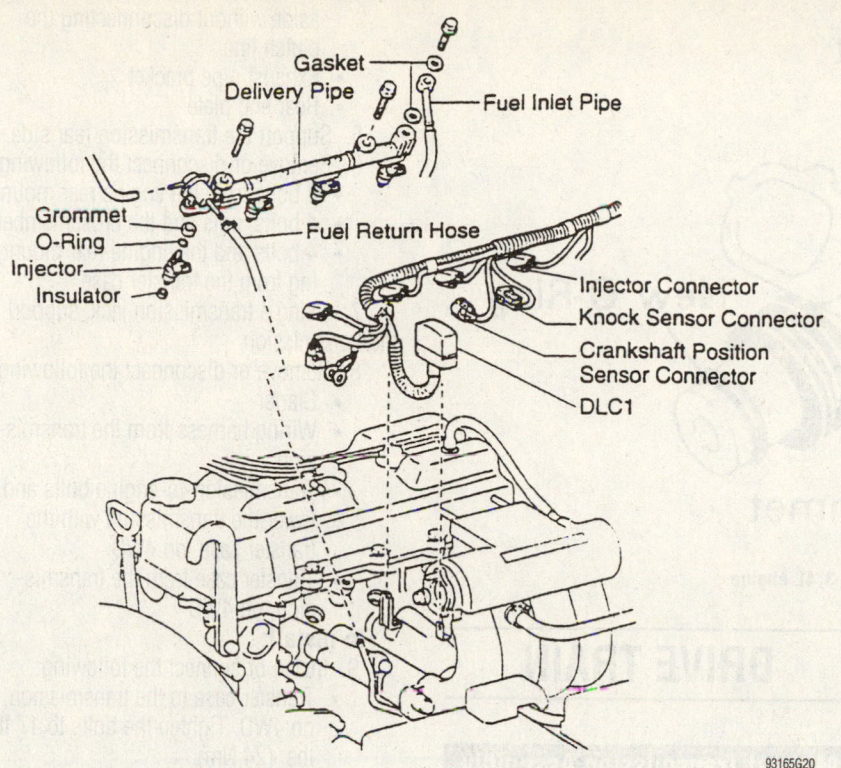

Fuel injector arrangement and related components—2.4L and 2.7L engines

- Data Link Connector 1 (DLC1) and wire clamp from the brackets
- Vacuum line from the fuel pressure regulator
- Fuel return hose from the pressure regulator
- Union bolt and gaskets
- Fuel inlet pipe from the fuel rail
- Fuel rail with the injectors attached

✳✳ WARNING

The injectors are only retained by their O-rings and will tend to drop out of the fuel rail.

- 4 insulators from the four spacers
- Fuel injectors from the fuel rail
- O-ring and grommet, discard them

To install:

4. Install or connect the following:
- New grommets and O-rings on each injector, lubricated with a light coat of gasoline
- Fuel injectors, with the electrical connector facing upwards
- New insulators and spacers on the intake manifold

5. Temporarily install the bolts holding the delivery pipe to the intake manifold.

6. Check that the injectors rotate smoothly.

7. Install or connect the following:
- Tighten the delivery pipe-to-intake manifold bolts to 15 ft. lbs. (21 Nm).
- Injector electrical connectors
- Fuel inlet pipe with new gaskets. Tighten the union bolt to 22 ft. lbs. (29 Nm) and the bolt to 14 ft. lbs. (20 Nm).
- Fuel return pipe to the fuel pressure regulator
- Vacuum line to the pressure regulator
- Throttle body
- Negative battery cable

3.4L Engine

1. Before servicing the vehicle, refer to the precautions in the beginning of this section.

2. Depressurize the fuel system.

3. Remove or disconnect the following:
- Air cleaner hose
- Upper half of the intake manifold
- Fuel pressure regulator

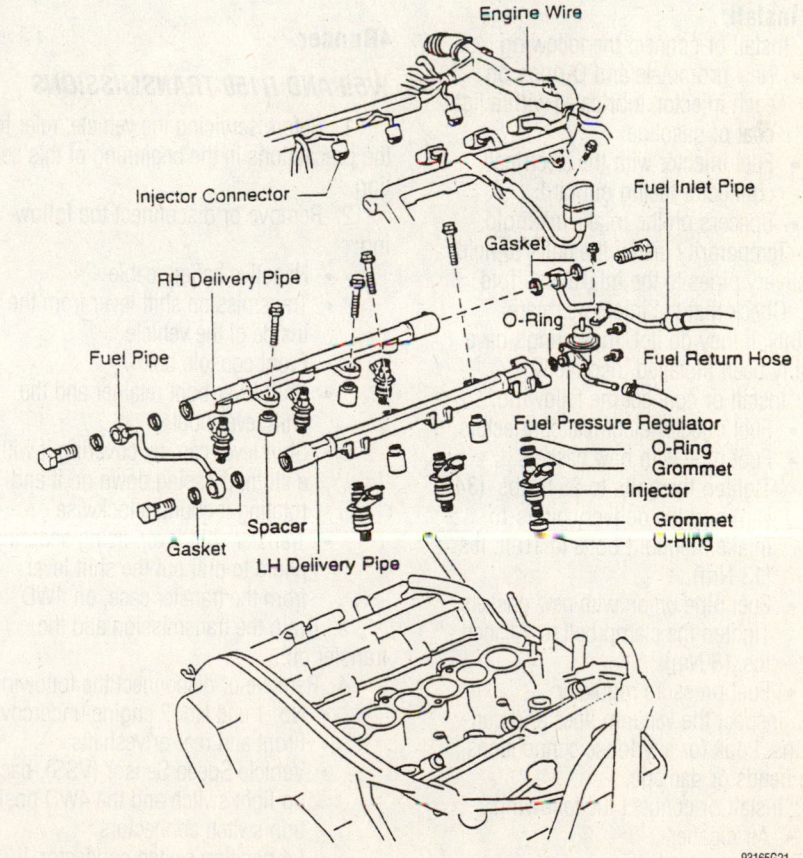

Fuel injector arrangement and related components—3.4L engine

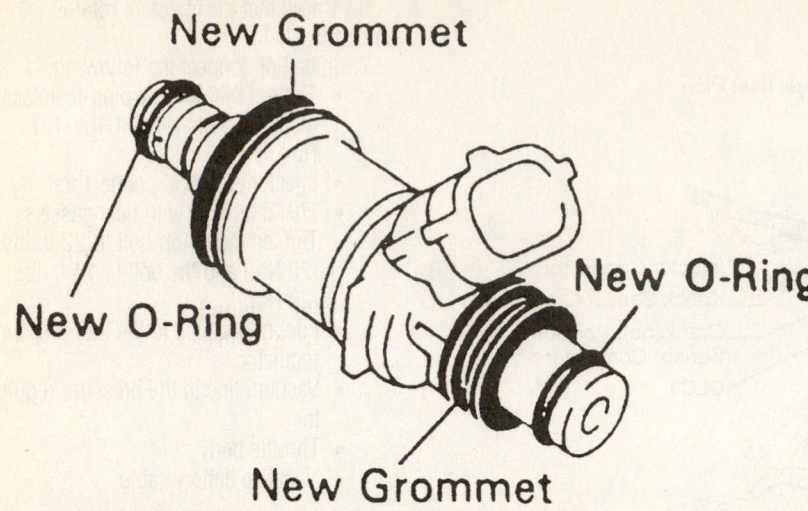

New Grommet

New O-Ring

New O-Ring

New Grommet

86825GG8

Install new O-rings and grommets on each injector—3.4L engine

- Fuel inlet pipe
- Fuel injector electrical connections
- Fuel rail with the injectors
- Spacers from the intake manifold
- Injectors from the delivery pipes
- O-rings and grommets, discard them

To install:

4. Install or connect the following:
   - New grommets and O-rings on each injector, lubricated with a light coat of gasoline
   - Fuel injector with the electrical connector facing outward
   - Spacers on the intake manifold

5. Temporarily install the bolts to hold the delivery pipes to the intake manifold.

6. Check that the injectors rotate smoothly. If they do not, the O-rings have probably been installed incorrectly.

7. Install or connect the following:
   - Fuel injector electrical connectors
   - Fuel pipe with new gaskets. Tighten the bolts to 25 ft. lbs. (34 Nm) and the delivery pipes-to-intake manifold bolts to 10 ft. lbs. (13 Nm).
   - Fuel pipe union with new gaskets. Tighten the clamp bolt to 71 inch lbs. (8 Nm).
   - Fuel pressure regulator

8. Inspect the vacuum lines and connections. Look for any loose connections, sharp bends or damage.

9. Install or connect the following:
   - Air cleaner
   - Air cleaner hose

10. Start the engine and check for vacuum and fuel leaks.

DRIVE TRAIN

Manual Transmission Assembly

REMOVAL & INSTALLATION

4Runner

W59 AND R150 TRANSMISSIONS

1. Before servicing the vehicle, refer to the precautions in the beginning of this section.

2. Remove or disconnect the following:

   - Negative battery cable
   - Transmission shift lever from the inside of the vehicle
   - Front console box
   - Shift lever boot retainer and the shift lever boot
   - Shift lever cap, by covering it with a cloth, pressing down on it and rotating it counterclockwise
   - Transfer shift lever, using snapring pliers to pull out the shift lever from the transfer case, on 4WD

3. Drain the transmission and the transfer oil.

4. Remove or disconnect the following:
   - No. 1 and No. 2 engine undercover
   - Front and rear driveshafts
   - Vehicle Speed Sensor (VSS), back-up light switch and the 4WD position switch connectors
   - L4 position switch connector, if equipped with Anti-lock Brake System (ABS) and/or differential lock
   - Clutch release cylinder and move it

aside without disconnecting the clutch line
   - Exhaust pipe bracket
   - Rear end plate

5. Support the transmission rear side.

6. Remove or disconnect the following:
   - 4 bolts from the engine rear mount
   - 4 bolts, nuts and the crossmember
   - 4 bolts and the engine rear mounting from the transfer case

7. Using a transmission jack, support the transmission.

8. Remove or disconnect the following:
   - Starter
   - Wiring harness from the transmission
   - Transmission-to-engine bolts and lower the transmission with the transfer case, on 4WD
   - Transfer case from the transmission, on 4WD

To install:

9. Install or connect the following:
   - Transfer case to the transmission, on 4WD. Tighten the bolts to 17 ft. lbs. (24 Nm).

✱✱ WARNING

Be careful not to damage the oil seal by the input gear spline when installing the transfer.

- Transmission with the transfer case, on 4WD. Tighten the engine-to-transmission bolts to 53 ft. lbs. (72 Nm).
- Starter. Tighten both bolts to 29 ft. lbs. (39 Nm).
- Engine rear mount. Tighten the 4 bolts to 48 ft. lbs. (65 Nm).
- Crossmember. Tighten the 4 bolts to 48 ft. lbs. (65 Nm).
- Engine rear mount. Tighten the 4 bolts to 14 ft. lbs. (19 Nm).
- Rear end plate. Tighten the 4 bolts and nuts to 27 ft. lbs. (37 Nm).
- Front exhaust pipe. Tighten the bracket bolts to 52 ft. lbs. (71 Nm), the exhaust pipe-to-catalytic converter bolts to 35 ft. lbs. (48 Nm) and the support bracket bolts to 14 ft. lbs. (19 Nm).
- Clutch release cylinder. Tighten the 2 bolts to 108 inch lbs. (13 Nm).
- L4 position switch connector, if disconnected
- VSS, back-up light switch and the 4WD position switch connectors
- Front and rear driveshafts
- No. 1 and No. 2 engine under covers

10. Refill the transmission to the correct level.

11. Apply MP grease to the transfer shift lever.

12. Install or connect the following:
- Transfer shift lever and snapring

13. Install the transmission shift lever, as follows:

a. Apply MP grease to the transmission shift lever.

b. Align the groove of the shift lever cap and the pin par of the case cover. Cover the shift lever cap with a cloth. Pressing down on the shift lever cap, rotate it clockwise to install.

14. Install or connect the following:
- Shift lever boot retainer with the 4 screws
- Front console box with the 4 screws
- Negative battery cable

15. Start the engine and check for leaks.

16. Road test the vehicle for proper operation and recheck all the fluid levels.

T-100 with Model R150 and R150F Transmission

2 WHEEL DRIVE MODELS

1. Before servicing the vehicle, refer to the precautions in the beginning of this section.

➡**The transmission is removed with the engine.**

2. Turn the ignition switch **OFF**.

3. Remove or disconnect the following:
- Battery cables; negative cable first
- Hood
- Battery and battery tray

4. Drain the engine oil, transmission oil and cooling system.

5. Remove or disconnect the following:
- Expansion tank
- Radiator
- Air cleaner cap, Mass Air Flow (MAF) meter and resonator
- Air cleaner case
- Accelerator cable from the throttle body
- Intake air connector
- Air conditioning compressor and bracket; then, move the compressor aside with the lines attached, if equipped with air conditioning
- Heater hoses at the cowl panel
- Brake booster vacuum hose
- Evaporative Emissions (EVAP) hose
- Both power steering hoses
- Fuel return hose

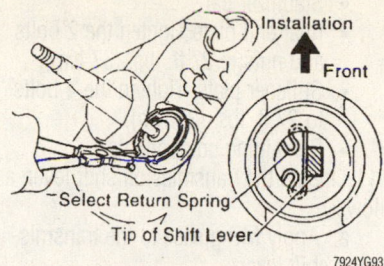

7924YG93

Removing the transfer shift lever— Tacoma, 4Runner and T-100 with R150 and R150F transmissions

- Fuel inlet hose
- Power steering pump
- Alternator wires from the alternator
- Engine Control Module (ECM).
- Igniter connector
- Ground strap from the cowl top panel
- 4 engine wiring harness clamps
- Engine wiring harness

6. Remove the shift lever assembly, as follows:
- Shift lever knob
- 4 screws and shift lever boot
- 6 bolts, shift lever assembly and baffle

7. Remove or disconnect the following:
- Sway bar
- Driveshaft
- Speedometer cable from the transmission
- Front exhaust pipe from the exhaust manifold and catalytic converter
- Clutch release cylinder
- Starter wires

8. Position a jack and wooden block under the transmission.

9. Remove the rear engine mount bracket.

10. Attach a engine hoist to the engine hangers.

11. Remove or disconnect the following:
- Engine mounts
- Engine/transmission assembly out of the vehicle

12. Safely support the engine/transmission assembly.

13. Remove or disconnect the following:
- Rear end plate
- Starter
- Transmission-to-engine bolts
- Transmission mount

To install:

14. Install or connect the following:
- Transmission

- Transmission mount. Tighten the 4 bolts to 18 ft. lbs. (25 Nm).
- Tighten the 6 transmission-to-engine bolts to 53 ft. lbs. (72 Nm).
- Starter. Tighten the 2 bolts to 29 ft. lbs. (39 Nm).
- Rear end plate. Tighten the 4 nuts and bolts to 27 ft. lbs. (37 Nm).
- Engine hoist to the engine hangers
- Engine/transmission assembly

➡**Keep the engine level, while aligning the engine mounts.**

- Engine mount fasteners but do not fully tighten

15. Position a jack and wooden block under the transmission.

16. Install or connect the following:
- Rear engine mount bracket. Tighten the frame bolts to 42 ft. lbs. (58 Nm) and the mount bolts to 13 ft. lbs. (18 Nm).
- Tighten the engine mounts to 28 ft. lbs. (38 Nm).
- Starter wires
- Clutch release cylinder
- Front exhaust pipe. Tighten the exhaust pipe-to-manifold bolts to 46 ft. lbs. (62 Nm), the support bracket bolts and the exhaust pipe-to-catalytic converter bolts to 29 ft. lbs. (39 Nm) and the exhaust pipe clamp nuts to 14 ft. lbs. (19 Nm).
- Remaining components
- Battery cables to the battery

17. Fill the engine oil, engine coolant and transmission oil.

18. Start the engine and check for leaks.

19. Install or connect the following:
- Engine undercover
- Hood

20. Road test the vehicle and check all fluids.

4 WHEEL DRIVE MODELS

1. Before servicing the vehicle, refer to the precautions in the beginning of this section.

2. Remove or disconnect the following:
- Negative battery cable
- 4 screws and front console box
- Shift lever boot retainer screws and the shift lever boot
- Shift lever cap, cover it with a cloth, press downward on it, rotate it counterclockwise to remove it
- Transfer shift lever, using snapring pliers to pull it from the transfer case

3. Drain the transmission and the transfer oil.

4. Remove or disconnect the following:
- Driveshafts
- Speedometer cable, back-up light switch connector and the transfer indicator switch connector
- Clutch release cylinder, move it aside without disconnecting the clutch line
- Exhaust pipe bracket
- Starter
- Stiffener plate by removing the 4 bolts
- Rear end plate by removing the nuts and 2 bolts
- Stabilizer bar from the suspension

5. Using a transmission jack, support the transmission.

6. Remove or disconnect the following:
- 4 engine rear mount bolts
- 8 bolts and the frame crossmember from the side frame
- 6 transmission-to-engine bolts
- 3 wire clamps from the transmission
- Transmission with the transfer case
- 4 engine rear mount bolts from the transfer case
- Transfer adapter rear mount bolts
- Transfer case from the transmission

To install:

7. Apply MP grease to the adapter oil seal and shift the 2 shift fork shafts to the high 4 position.

8. Install or connect the following:
- Transfer case to the transmission. Tighten the bolts to 27 ft. lbs. (37 Nm).

✳✳ WARNING

Be careful not to damage the oil seal by the input gear spline when installing the transfer.

- Engine rear mounting. Tighten the 4 bolts to 18 ft. lbs. (25 Nm).
- Transmission/transfer case assembly

9. Support the transmission with a jack. Align the input shaft spline with the clutch disc and push the transmission with the transfer fully into position.

10. Install or connect the following:
- Tighten the engine-to-transmission bolts to 53 ft. lbs. (72 Nm).
- No. 2 frame crossmember to the side frame. Tighten the 8 bolts to 70 ft. lbs. (95 Nm) and the 4 engine rear mount bolts to 108 inch lbs. (13 Nm).

- Stabilizer bar
- Rear end plate Tighten the 2 bolts and nuts to 27 ft. lbs. (37 Nm).
- Stiffener plate. Tighten the 4 bolts to 27 ft. lbs. (37 Nm).
- Remaining components

11. Install the transmission shift lever, as follows:

a. Apply MP grease to the transmission shift lever.

b. Align the groove of the shift lever cap and the pin par of the case cover. Cover the shift lever cap with a cloth. Pressing down on the shift lever cap, rotate it clockwise to install.

c. Install shift lever boot retainer with the 4 screws.

d. Install the front console box with the 4 screws.

12. Connect the negative battery cable.

13. Start the engine and check for leaks.

14. Road test the vehicle for proper operation. Recheck all fluid levels.

T-100 and 2WD Tacoma

1. Before servicing the vehicle, refer to the precautions in the beginning of this section.

2. Remove or disconnect the following:
- Transmission with the engine
- Left and right side stiffener plates
- Rear end-plate
- Starter

3. Place a stand under the transmission.

4. Remove or disconnect the following:
- Transmission bolts and pull the transmission rearward
- Rear engine mount by removing the 4 bolts

To install:

5. Install or connect the following:
- Rear engine mount. Tighten the 4 bolts to 48 ft. lbs. (65 Nm).
- Transmission by aligning the input shaft spline with the clutch disc. Tighten the transmission-to-engine bolts to 53 ft. lbs. (72 Nm).
- Starter. Tighten the bolts to 29 ft. lbs. (39 Nm).
- Rear end-plate. Tighten the bolts to 27 ft. lbs. (37 Nm).
- Left and right side stiffener plates
- Transmission with the engine assembly

4WD Tacoma

1. Before servicing the vehicle, refer to the precautions in the beginning of this section.

2. Remove or disconnect the following:
- Negative battery cable
- 4 screws and front console box
- Shift lever boot retainer screws and the shift lever boot
- Shift lever cap, by pressing downward on the shift lever cap covered with a cloth and rotating it counterclockwise to remove it
- Transfer shift lever, using snapring pliers to pull it from the transfer case

3. Drain the transmission and the transfer oil.

4. Remove or disconnect the following:
- Front and rear driveshafts
- Speedometer cable and the back-up light switch connector
- 4WD position switch connector, on the Standard cab
- L4 position switch connector, on the Extra cab
- Clutch release cylinder, by moving it aside without disconnecting the clutch line
- Exhaust pipe bracket
- Starter
- Rear end plate by removing the nuts and 2 bolts

5. Support the transmission rear side.

6. Remove or disconnect the following:
- 4 engine rear mount bolts
- O-ring and the crossmember

7. Using a transmission jack, support the transmission.

8. Remove or disconnect the following:
- 6 transmission-to-engine bolts
- 3 wire clamps from the transmission
- Transmission with the transfer case
- Engine rear mounting from the transfer case
- Transfer adapter rear mount bolts
- Transfer case from the transmission

To install:

9. Apply MP grease to the adapter oil seal and shift the 2 shift fork shafts to the high 4 position.

10. Install or connect the following:
- Transfer to the transmission. Tighten the bolts to 17 ft. lbs. (24 Nm).

➡**Be careful not to damage the oil seal by the input gear spline when installing the transfer.**

- Transmission/transfer case assembly, by aligning the input shaft spline with the clutch disc.

11. Support the transmission with a jack.

12. Install or connect the following:
- Tighten the engine to transmission bolts to 53 ft. lbs. (72 Nm)
- Engine rear mount. Tighten the 4 bolts to 48 ft. lbs. (65 Nm).

13. Raise the transmission slightly with a jack.

14. Install or connect the following:
- Crossmember. Tighten the 4 bolts to 48 ft. lbs. (65 Nm).
- Engine rear mount. Tighten the bolts to 14 ft. lbs. (19 Nm).
- Rear end-plate. Tighten the 4 bolts and nuts to 13 ft. lbs. (18 Nm) on R150 and R150F transmissions or to 27 ft. lbs. (37 Nm) on W59 transmissions.
- Starter. Tighten both bolts to 29 ft. lbs. (39 Nm).
- Front exhaust pipe. Tighten the exhaust pipe-to-manifold bolts to 46 ft. lbs. (62 Nm), the exhaust bracket bolts to 33 ft. lbs. (44 Nm) and the exhaust pipe-to-catalytic converter bolts to 35 ft. lbs. (48 Nm).
- Clutch release cylinder. Tighten the 2 bolts to 108 inch lbs. (13 Nm).
- L4 position switch connector on the extra cab or the 4WD position switch connector on the standard cab.
- VSS and the back-up light switch connector.
- Front and rear driveshafts.

15. Refill the transmission to the correct level.

16. Apply MP grease to the transfer shift lever.

17. Install or connect the following:
- Transfer shift lever.
- Snapring, using pliers

18. Install the transmission shift lever, as follows:

a. Apply MP grease to the transmission shift lever.

b. Align the groove of the shift lever cap and the pin par of the case cover. Cover the shift lever cap with a cloth. Pressing down on the shift lever cap, rotate it clockwise to install.

c. Install shift lever boot retainer with the 4 screws.

d. Install the front console box with the 4 screws.

19. Connect the negative battery cable. Start the engine and check for leaks.

20. Road test the vehicle for proper operation. Recheck all fluid levels.

Clutch Assembly

REMOVAL & INSTALLATION

1. Before servicing the vehicle, refer to the precautions in the beginning of this section.

2. Remove or disconnect the following:
- Negative battery cable
- Transmission assembly

3. Matchmark the clutch cover to the flywheel.

4. At the clutch cover, loosen each bolt 1 turn until spring tension is released.

5. Remove or disconnect the following:
- Clutch cover set bolts and the clutch cover with the clutch disc.
- Release bearing retaining clip and withdraw the it
- Release fork and boot assembly

To install:

6. Install or connect the following:
- Clutch disc onto the flywheel, using a clutch disc alignment tool
- Clutch cover, position it onto the flywheel and if reusing the old pressure plate, align the matchmarks.
- Clutch cover. Tighten the bolts in a crisscross pattern to 14 ft. lbs. (19 Nm).

7. Lubricate the release fork pivot and contact points, the release bearing, bearing hub and input shaft spline surfaces with a suitable molybdenum disulfide lithium based or multi-purpose grease.

8. Install or connect the following:
- Boot, release fork, hub and the bearing assemblies
- Transmission
- Negative battery cable

Hydraulic Clutch System

BLEEDING

1. Before servicing the vehicle, refer to the precautions in the beginning of this section.

2. Fill the clutch reservoir with brake fluid. Check the reservoir level frequently and add fluid as needed.

3. Connect one end of a vinyl tube to the bleeder plug on the slave cylinder and submerge the other end into a clear container half-filled with brake fluid.

4. Slowly pump the clutch pedal several times.

5. Have an assistant hold the clutch pedal down and loosen the bleeder plug until fluid and/or air starts to run out of the bleeder plug. Close the bleeder plug while the pedal is held to the floor.

6. Repeat Steps 2 and 3 until all the air bubbles are removed from the system.

7. Tighten the bleeder plug when all the air is gone.

8. Refill the master cylinder to the proper level as required.

9. Check the system for leaks.

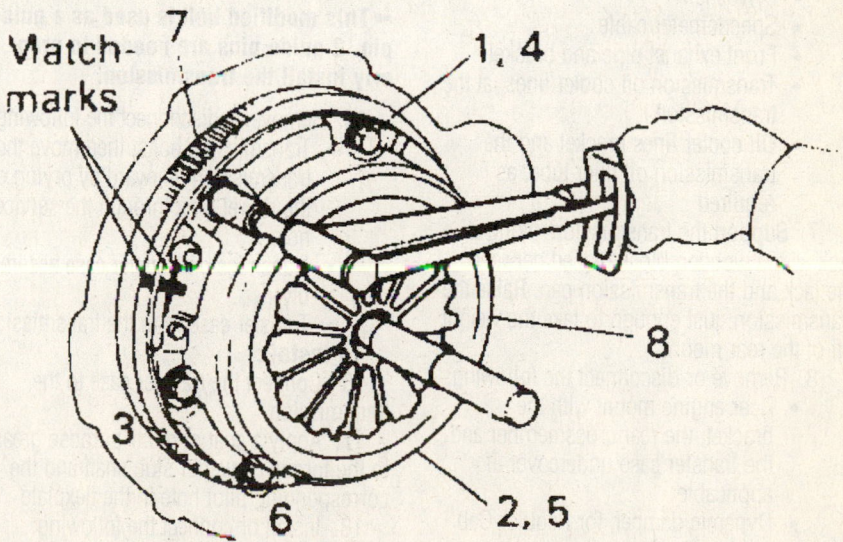

Bolt tightening sequence for the clutch cover—all engines

Automatic Transmission Assembly

REMOVAL & INSTALLATION

4Runner

MODEL A340D, A340E AND A340H TRANSMISSIONS

➡ **The transfer case and the transmission should be removed as an assembly.**

1. Before servicing the vehicle, refer to the precautions in the beginning of this section.
2. Remove or disconnect the following:
   - Negative battery cable
   - Air cleaner assembly, if necessary
   - Transmission throttle cable from the throttle body
   - Engine undercover
3. Drain the transmission and transfer case (if applicable) fluid.
4. Remove or disconnect the following:
   - Wiring connectors from the transmission and transfer case, if applicable.
   - Starter
5. Matchmarks on the front and rear driveshaft flanges and the differential pinion flanges. These marks must be aligned during installation.
6. Remove or disconnect the following:
   - Front and rear driveshaft flanges.
   - Center bearing bracket bolts, if equipped with a 2-piece driveshaft
   - Driveshaft
   - Speedometer cable
   - Front exhaust pipe and bracket
   - Transmission oil cooler lines, at the transmission
   - Oil cooler lines bracket and the transmission oil filler tube, as required
7. Support the transmission, using a jack with a wooden block placed between the jack and the transmission pan. Raise the transmission, just enough to take the weight off of the rear mount.
8. Remove or disconnect the following:
   - Rear engine mount with the bracket, the rear crossmember and the transfer case undercover, if applicable
   - Dynamic damper, for Regular Cab only
   - No. 2 cross-shaft bracket
9. Place a wooden block(s) between the engine oil pan and the front frame crossmember.

10. Slowly, lower the transmission until the engine rests on the wooden block(s).
11. Remove or disconnect the following:
    - Torque converter cover to gain access to the converter bolts
    - Torque converter bolts, by rotating the crankshaft to access the bolts through the service holes
    - Stiffener plates from the transmission
    - Shift control rod and the transfer case shift lever
12. For the A340H transmission remove or disconnect, perform the following:
    - Cross-shaft and the No. 2 shifting rod
    - Front stabilizer bar
    - Differential mount bolts, by supporting the front differential with a jack
    - Transmission and transfer case, by slowly lowering the front differential so there is enough clearance, if applicable
    - Differential, if enough clearance can't be obtained
13. Remove or disconnect the following:
    - Stabilizer bar
    - Auxiliary frame crossmember, if equipped
14. For A340D transmissions, obtain a bolt of the same dimensions as the torque converter bolts. Cut the head off of the bolt and hacksaw a slot in the bolt opposite the threaded end. Thread the guide pin into one of the torque converter bolt holes. The guide pin will help keep the converter with the transmission.

➡ **This modified bolt is used as a guide pin. 2 guide pins are needed to properly install the transmission.**

15. Remove or disconnect the following:
    - Transmission bolts, then move the transmission rearward by prying on the dowel pins through the service hole
    - Transmission/transfer case assembly
    - Transfer case from the transmission

To install:
16. Connect the transfer case to the transmission.
17. Apply a coat of multi-purpose grease to the torque converter stub shaft and the corresponding pilot hole in the flexplate.
18. Install or connect the following:
    - Torque converter into the front of the transmission Push inward on the torque converter while rotating it to completely couple the torque converter to the transmission.

19. To be sure the converter is properly installed, measure the distance between the torque converter mounting lugs and the front mounting face of the transmission. The proper distance is 0.71 in. (18mm) for the A340H transmission or 0.79 in. (20mm) for the A340D, A340E and A340F transmissions.
20. For A340D transmissions, install guide pins into 2 opposite mounting lugs of the torque converter.
21. Install or connect the following:
    - Transmission. Tighten the bolts to 47 ft. lbs. (63 Nm).
    - Torque converter bolts, by rotating the crankshaft. Tighten the bolts evenly to 30 ft. lbs. (41 Nm) for the A340H, A3430D and A340E transmissions or to 20 ft. lbs. (27 Nm) for the A340F transmission.
    - Torque converter access cover
22. Remove the wood block(s) from under the engine oil pan.
23. Install or connect the following:
    - Transmission crossmember. Tighten the bolts to 70 ft. lbs. (95 Nm).
    - Rear mount and bracket. Tighten the bracket bolts to 43 ft. lbs. (58 Nm) and the bracket-to-rear mount bolts to 108 inch lbs. (13 Nm).
    - Transmission onto the crossmember. Tighten the transmission-to-mount bolts to 18 ft. lbs. (25 Nm).
24. Remove the wooden blocks from between the frame and the engine and the support from under the transmission.
25. Install or connect the following:
    - Front differential, for the A340H transmission. Tighten the 2 rear mount bolts to 123 ft. lbs. (167 Nm) and the front mount through-bolt to 108 ft. lbs. (147 Nm).

➡ **If the differential oil was drained, refill it at this time.**

- Shift control rod and the transfer case shift lever
- Front stabilizer bar, if applicable
- Cross-shaft and the No. 2 shifting rod, if applicable
- Stiffener plates. Tighten the bolts to 27 ft. lbs. (37 Nm).
- Transfer case undercover and the dynamic damper, if equipped. Tighten the dynamic damper mount bolts to 27 ft. lbs. (37 Nm).
- No. 2 cross-shaft bracket
- Oil filler tube and the oil cooler pipe bracket
- Oil cooler lines to the transmission. Tighten the fittings to 25 ft. lbs. (34 Nm).

- Front exhaust pipe and the support bracket
- Speedometer cable
- Front and rear driveshaft flanges with the differential pinion flanges, by aligning the matchmarks. Tighten the bolts to 54 ft. lbs. (74 Nm).
- Starter
- Wiring connectors to the transmission and the transfer case, if applicable
- Engine undercover
- Transmission throttle cable, by adjusting it
- Air cleaner assembly, if removed
- Negative battery cable

26. Refill the transmission and the transfer case, if applicable.

27. Start the engine and check for leaks.

28. Road test the vehicle for proper operation.

29. Recheck all fluid levels.

MODEL A340F TRANSMISSION

1. Before servicing the vehicle, refer to the precautions in the beginning of this section.

2. Remove or disconnect the following:
- Negative battery cable
- Throttle cable, from the engine compartment
- Automatic Transmission Fluid (ATF) level gauge
- Oil filler pipe upper side bolt, for the 3RZ-FE engine
- Oil filler pipe, for the 5VZ-FE engine

3. Remove the transmission shift lever assembly and transfer shift lever, as follows:
- Rear console upper panel, by disconnecting the connectors
- Heater control knobs
- Center cluster finish panel, by disconnecting the connectors
- Transfer shift lever knob, without the 2–4 selector
- Bull and the transfer shift lever knob, with the 2–4 selector
- Front console upper panel
- 2–4 selector connector, if equipped
- Transfer shift lever knob
- Shift control rod
- Transmission shift lever assembly connector and the 8 screws
- Shift lever snapring, using pliers and pull out it from the transfer case
- Engine undercover

- Front and rear driveshafts
- Exhaust pipe
- Oil filler pipe, for 3RZ-FE engine

4. Disconnect the following connectors from the transmission:
- No. 2 Vehicle Speed Sensor (VSS) connector
- Solenoid connector
- Automatic Transmission Fluid (ATF) temperature sensor connector
- Park/neutral position switch connector

5. Detach the following connectors from the transfer case:
- No. 1 Vehicle Speed Sensor (VSS) connector, for 3RZ-FE engine
- Transfer neutral position switch connector
- Transfer L4 position switch connector
- Transfer 4WD position switch connector
- Actuator connector (2–4 selector only)

6. Remove or disconnect the following:
- Wiring harness from the transmission and the transfer case
- Both oil cooler pipes
- Rear end-plate and torque converter clutch mounting bolt

7. Support the transmission with a jackstand.

8. Remove or disconnect the following:
- Engine rear mount bolts
- 4 bolts and the crossmember
- Starter
- Transmission

To install:

9. Install or connect the following:
- Transmission. Tighten the bolts to 53 ft. lbs. (71 Nm).
- Starter. Tighten the bolts to 29 ft. lbs. (39 Nm).
- Crossmember. Tighten the 4 bolts to 48 ft. lbs. (65 Nm).
- Engine rear mount. Tighten the 4 bolts to 14 ft. lbs. (19 Nm)
- Clutch converter bolts, by installing the green colored bolt before the other 5. Tighten the bolts to 30 ft. lbs. (41 Nm).
- Rear end-plate. Tighten the bolts to 13 ft. lbs. (18 Nm).
- Both oil cooler pipes. Tighten to 25 ft. lbs. (34 Nm).
- Oil cooler pipe clamps. Tighten the 10mm head bolt to 48 inch lbs. (5 Nm) and the 12mm head bolt to 108 inch lbs. (13 Nm).

- Wiring harness to the transmission and the transfer case
- Remaining components

10. Fill the transmission and transfer case with transmission fluid.
- Throttle cable
- Negative battery cable

T-100

MODEL A340E TRANSMISSION WITH 2.7L (3RZ-FE) ENGINE

1. Before servicing the vehicle, refer to the precautions in the beginning of this section.

2. Turn the ignition switch **OFF**.

3. Remove or disconnect the following:
- Both battery cables
- Hood
- Battery and battery tray

4. Drain the engine oil, transmission oil and the cooling system.

5. Remove or disconnect the following:
- Expansion tank
- Radiator
- Air cleaner cap, Mass Air Flow (MAF) meter and the resonator
- Air cleaner case
- Accelerator and throttle cables from the throttle body
- Intake air connector
- Air conditioning compressor and bracket without disconnecting the air conditioning lines, if equipped with air conditioning
- Heater hoses, at the cowl panel
- Brake booster vacuum hose
- Evaporative Emissions (EVAP) hose
- 2 power steering hoses
- Fuel return hose
- Fuel inlet hose
- Power steering pump
- Alternator wires from the alternator
- Engine Control Module (ECM) wiring from the ECM
- Igniter connector
- Ground strap from the cowl top panel
- 4 engine wiring harness clamps
- Engine wiring harness from the vehicle
- Sway bar
- Driveshaft
- Speedometer cable, from the transmission
- Front exhaust pipe, from the exhaust manifold and catalytic converter

6. Remove the cross-shaft, as follows:

Turn to Section 5 for brake system applications

- Clip and the No. 2 gear shifting rod
- Nut, washer, 4 bolts and the cross-shaft

7. Remove or disconnect the following:
- Starter
- Rear engine mounting bracket, by positioning a jack and wooden block under the transmission

8. Attach a engine hoist to the engine hangers.

9. Remove or disconnect the following:
- Engine mounts nuts and bolts
- Engine/transmission assembly
- Rear endplate 2 nuts and 4 bolts

10. Turn the crankshaft to gain access to the torque converter bolts.

11. Remove or disconnect the following:
- Torque converter bolts
- Starter
- 3 engine mount bolts
- Transmission

To install:

12. Install or connect the following:
- Transmission. Tighten the 3 bolts to 53 ft. lbs. (71 Nm).
- Torque converter. Tighten the bolts to 30 ft. lbs. (41 Nm).
- Rear endplate. Tighten the nuts/bolts to 27 ft. lbs. (37 Nm).
- Starter. Tighten the bolts to 29 ft. lbs. (39 Nm).

13. Attach the engine hoist to the engine hangers. Carefully lower the engine/transmission assembly into the vehicle. Keep the engine level, while aligning the engine mounts.

14. Install or connect the following:
- Engine mount fasteners but do not fully tighten.
- Position a jack and wooden block under the transmission
- Rear engine mount bracket. Tighten the frame bolts to 42 ft. lbs. (58 Nm) and the mount bolts to 13 ft. lbs. (18 Nm).

15. Remove the jack and engine hoist.

16. Install or connect the following:
- Tighten the engine mount bolts to 28 ft. lbs. (38 Nm).
- Starter
- Cross-shaft

17. Install the remaining components in the reverse order of removal. Tighten the fasteners, as follows:
- Exhaust pipe-to-exhaust manifold nuts: 46 ft. lbs. (62 Nm)
- Exhaust pipe support bracket bolts: 29 ft. lbs. (39 Nm)
- Exhaust pipe clamp nuts: 14 ft. lbs. (19 Nm)
- Exhaust pipe-to-catalytic converter bolts: 29 ft. lbs. (39 Nm)

- Sway bar mounting bolts: 22 ft. lbs. (30 Nm)
- Power steering pump-to-bracket bolts: 43 ft. lbs. (58 Nm)
- Air conditioning compressor bracket-to-engine bolts: 32 ft. lbs. (44 Nm)
- Air conditioning compressor-to-bracket bolts: 18 ft. lbs. (25 Nm).
- Battery cables to the battery

18. Fill the engine oil, engine coolant and the transmission oil.

19. Start the engine and check for leaks.

20. Check the ignition timing.

21. Install or connect the following:
- Engine undercover
- Hood

22. Road test the vehicle and check all fluids.

MODEL A340E TRANSMISSION WITH 3.4L (5VZ-FE) ENGINE

1. Before servicing the vehicle, refer to the precautions in the beginning of this section.

2. Remove or disconnect the following:
- Hood
- Battery
- Engine under covers

3. Drain the engine coolant.

4. Drain the engine oil.

5. Remove or disconnect the following:
- Radiator
- Power steering pump drive belt
- Air conditioning drive belt by loosening the idler pulley nut and adjusting bolt, if equipped with air conditioning
- Alternator drive belt, by loosening the lockbolt, pivot bolt and adjusting bolt
- Fan, with the fluid coupling and fan pulleys
- Power steering pump; then, move it aside without disconnecting the lines
- Compressor and move it aside without disconnecting the lines, if equipped with air conditioning
- Air cleaner cap, Mass Air Flow (MAF) meter and the resonator
- Air cleaner case and filter
- Actuator cable with the bracket, if equipped with cruise control
- Accelerator cable
- Throttle cable
- Heater hoses
- Brake booster vacuum hose
- Evaporative Emissions (EVAP) hose
- Fuel return hose
- Fuel inlet hose
- Starter.
- Alternator connector and wire

6. Remove the engine wiring harness and connectors, as follows:
- 4 screws and the scuff plate
- Cowl panel side trim by removing the clip
- Engine Control Module (ECM) electrical connectors
- 2 connectors from the cowl wire
- Igniter connector
- Ground strap
- 6 engine wiring harness clamps
- Engine wiring harness

7. Remove or disconnect the following:
- Stabilizer bar
- Driveshaft from the transmission
- Speedometer cable
- Front exhaust pipe
- Cross-shaft

8. Place a jack under the transmission.

9. Remove or disconnect the following:
- Transmission rear mounting bracket, by removing the 8 bolts
- Air conditioning compressor wire clamp, if equipped with air conditioning

10. If necessary, install a No. 2 engine hanger with 2 bolts. Tighten the 2 bolts to 30 ft. lbs. (40 Nm).

11. Attach the engine hoist chain to the 2 engine hangers.

12. Remove or disconnect the following:
- Engine front mounting insulators from the frame.
- Engine and transmission
- Starter
- Transmission from the engine
- Rear endplate, if equipped

13. Turn the crankshaft to gain access to the torque converter bolts.

14. Remove or disconnect the following:
- Torque converter bolts and pull the transmission rearward
- 3 mounting bolt from the engine.
- Transmission

To install:

15. Install or connect the following:
- Engine to the transmission. Tighten the 3 bolts to 53 ft. lbs. (71 Nm).
- Torque converter. Tighten the bolts to 30 ft. lbs. (41 Nm).
- Rear endplate. Tighten the nuts/bolts to 27 ft. lbs. (37 Nm).
- Starter. Tighten the bolts to 29 ft. lbs. (39 Nm).
- Transmission to the engine. Tighten the 6 bolts to 53 ft. lbs. (71 Nm).
- Starter. Tighten both bolts to 29 ft. lbs. (39 Nm).
- Engine assembly. Install the engine mounts to the body mounts nuts/bolts but do not tighten at this time.

- Engine chain hoist the No. 2 engine hanger.
- Air conditioning wire with the bolt, if equipped with air conditioning
- Transmission mount bracket. Tighten the frame bolts to 43 ft. lbs. (58 Nm) and the mount insulator bolts to 13 ft. lbs. (18 Nm).
- Tighten the engine mount nuts/bolts to 28 ft. lbs. (38 Nm).
- Cross-shaft
- Remaining components. Tighten the exhaust pipe-to-exhaust manifold bolts to 46 ft. lbs. (62 Nm), the exhaust pipe support bracket bolts to 33 ft. lbs. (44 Nm), the exhaust pipe-to-catalytic converter bolts to 35 ft. lbs. (48 Nm) and the cooling fan-to-fluid clutch nuts to 48 inch lbs. (5 Nm).

16. Fill the engine with oil and the transmission with fluid.

17. Fill the engine and radiator with coolant.

18. Install or connect the following:
- Engine undercover
- Battery and the cables
- Hood

19. Start the engine and check for leaks.

MODEL A340F TRANSMISSION

1. Before servicing the vehicle, refer to the precautions in the beginning of this section.

2. Remove or disconnect the following:
- Negative battery cable
- Transmission throttle cable and clamp from the throttle body
- Engine undercover

3. Drain the transmission fluid.

4. Remove or disconnect the following:
- Transfer shift lever front the inside of the vehicle, as follows:
- Shift lever knob
- 4 screws and the boot
- Snapring, using pliers and pull it from the transfer case

5. Remove or disconnect the following:
- Transmission oil filler tube
- Front and rear driveshafts
- Front exhaust pipe
- Speedometer cable
- No. 2 Vehicle Speed Sensor (VSS) connector
- Solenoid connector, by removing the electrical connector and bolt
- Transfer case Neutral Position Switch (NPS)
- Transfer case L4 position switch

- Clip and the No. 2 gear shifting rod
- Nut, 4 bolts and the cross-shaft
- Starter
- Oil cooler pipe, by removing the bolts and clamps
- Automatic Transmission Fluid (ATF) temperature sensor connector
- Park/Neutral Position (PNP) switch connector
- Stiffener plate and rear endplate
- Sway bar

6. Support the transmission, using a jack with a wooden block placed between the jack and the transmission pan. Raise the transmission just enough to take the weight off of the rear mount.

7. Remove or disconnect the following:
- Rear engine mount bracket
- Rear support member, by removing the 8 bolts

8. Rotate the crankshaft to access the torque converter bolts.

9. Remove or disconnect the following:
- 6 torque converter bolts
- Any component that will get in the way of removing the transmission
- Transmission

To install:

10. Install or connect the following:
- Transmission. Tighten the bolts to 53 ft. lbs. (71 Nm).
- Torque converter. Tighten the bolts to 30 ft. lbs. (41 Nm).
- Rear support member. Tighten the 8 bolts to 70 ft. lbs. (97 Nm).
- Rear mount bracket. Tighten the 4 bolts to 13 ft. lbs. (18 Nm).
- Dynamic damper. Tighten both bolts to 44 ft. lbs. (61 Nm).

11. Remove the jack supporting the transmission.

12. Install or connect the following:
- Sway bar
- Stiffener plate and rear endplate. Tighten the bolts to 27 ft. lbs. (37 Nm).
- Starter. Tighten the bolts to 29 ft lbs. (39 Nm).
- PNP switch connector
- ATF temperature sensor connector
- Oil cooler pipes and clamps. Tighten the them to 25 ft. lbs. (34 Nm).
- Cross-shaft. Tighten the nut to 108 inch lbs. (13 Nm), the transmission side bolt to 108 inch lbs. (13 Nm) and the frame side bolt 21 ft. lbs. (28 Nm).
- Remaining components
- Negative battery cable

13. Fill the transmission with the proper fluid.

14. Road test the vehicle and check for leaks.

15. Check all fluids.

Tacoma

MODEL A340F TRANSMISSION

1. Before servicing the vehicle, refer to the precautions in the beginning of this section.

2. Remove or disconnect the following:
- Automatic Transmission Fluid (ATF) level gauge
- Engine undercover

3. Drain the transmission fluid.

4. Remove or disconnect the following:
- Throttle cable
- No. 1 fan shroud

5. Remove the transmission shift lever assembly and the transfer shift lever, as follows:
- Rear console box
- Front console box with the transfer shift lever knob
- Connectors
- Shift control rod
- Transmission shift lever assembly
- Snapring and pull it from the transfer case
- Oil filler pipe, with the O-ring
- Front and rear driveshaft
- Exhaust pipe
- Speedometer cable
- No. 2 Vehicle Speed Sensor (VSS) connector
- Solenoid connector
- Transfer case neutral position switch connector
- Transfer case L4 position switch connector
- Transfer indicator switch
- Oil cooler pipe
- Automatic Transmission Fluid (ATF) temperature sensor connector
- Park/Neutral Position (PNP) switch connector
- Starter
- 4 stabilizer bar bracket mounting bolts

6. Remove the torque converter bolts, as follows:
- Flywheel housing undercover
- Torque converter clutch mounting bolts, while turning the crankshaft to gain access

7. Remove the front differential rear mounting cushion, as follows:

- Nut, using a hexagon wrench
- Front differential by lifting it

➡ **Be careful not to touch the torque converter clutch housing and the front differential companion flange**

- 2 rear mount cushion bolts
8. Remove or disconnect the following:
- Support the transmission's rear side
- 4 engine rear mount bolts
- 4 nuts, bolts and the crossmember, by supporting the transmission
- Transmission

To install:

9. Install or connect the following:
- Transmission. Tighten the engine-to-transmission bolts to 53 ft. lbs. (71 Nm).
- Crossmember. Tighten the bolts to 48 ft. lbs. (65 Nm).
- Engine rear mount. Tighten the bolts to 14 ft. lbs. (19 Nm).
- Front differential rear mount cushion. Tighten the nut to 64 ft. lbs. (41 Nm).
- Torque converter clutch mount bolt

➡ **Install the green colored bolt, then the 5 others. Tighten the bolts to 30 ft. lbs. (41 Nm).**

- Flywheel housing undercover. Tighten the bolts to 13 ft. lbs. (18 Nm) for 3.4L (5VZ-FE) engine or to 27 ft. lbs. (37 Nm) for 2.7L (3RZ-FE) engine.
- Stabilizer bar bracket bolts. Tighten the 4 bolts to 19 ft. lbs. (25 Nm).
- Starter. Tighten the bolts to 29 ft. lbs. (39 Nm).
- Remaining components
- ATF level gauge
10. Fill and check the fluid level.
11. Test drive and check for proper shifting.

A340D AND A340E TRANSMISSIONS

1. Before servicing the vehicle, refer to the precautions in the beginning of this section.
2. Remove or disconnect the following:
- Transmission with the engine and place it on a stand
- Bolts, 2 stiffener plates and rear endplate
3. Turn the crankshaft to gain access to the torque converter bolts.
4. Remove or disconnect the following:
- Torque converter bolts
- Starter

- Transmission-to-engine bolts
- Transmission

To install:

5. Install or connect the following:
- Transmission to the engine. Tighten the bolts to 53 ft. lbs. (71 Nm).
- Starter. Tighten both bolts to 29 ft. lbs. (39 Nm).
- Torque converter. Tighten the bolts to 30 ft. lbs. (41 Nm).
- Stiffener plate and rear endplate. Tighten the bolts to 27 ft. lbs. (37 Nm).
- Starter wires
- Transmission with the engine

Transfer Case Assembly

REMOVAL & INSTALLATION

1. Before servicing the vehicle, refer to the precautions in the beginning of this section.
2. Disconnect the negative battery cable.
3. Drain the transmission and the transfer case.
4. Remove or disconnect the following:

- Transfer case with the transmission
- Breather hose from the transfer upper cover and the transmission control retainer, if equipped with an automatic transmission
- Rear engine mounting
- Dynamic damper

5. Remove the driveshaft upper dust cover and the transfer from the transmissions, as follows:
- Dust cover bolt from the bracket
- Transfer case adapter rear mounting bolts
- Transfer case, by pulling it straight up and away from the transmission.

✳✳ WARNING

Be careful not to damage the adapter rear oil seal with the transfer input gear spline.

To install:

6. Install the transfer case and the driveshaft upper dust cover to the transmission with a new gasket, as follows:
- Shift the 2 shift fork shafts to the high 4 position
- Apply MP grease to the adapter oil seal
- New gasket to the transfer adapter
- Transfer case to the transmission.

✳✳ WARNING

Take care not to damage the oil seal by the input gear spline.

- Transfer case adapter. Tighten the rear bolts to 27 ft. lbs. (37 Nm).
- Dust cover to the bracket. Tighten the bolt to 17 ft. lbs. (23 Nm).
7. Install or connect the following:
- Engine rear mount. Tighten the bolts to 19 ft. lbs. (25 Nm).
- Dynamic damper. Tighten the bolts to 27 ft. lbs. (37 Nm).
- Breather hose, if equipped with an automatic transmission
- Transfer case with the transmission to the engine
8. Fill the transmission and the transfer case with oil.
9. Test drive the vehicle and check the abnormal noise and smooth operation.
10. Recheck the fluid levels.

Halfshaft

REMOVAL & INSTALLATION

T-100

1. Before servicing the vehicle, refer to the precautions in the beginning of this section.
2. Remove or disconnect the following:
- Front wheel(s)
- Halfshaft-to-differential nuts, while having an assistant hold the brake pedal
3. If equipped with a free wheeling hub, remove the free-wheel hub, as follows:
- Set the control handle to FREE
- Cover bolts and the cover
- Center bolt with washer
- Mounting nuts and washer to the hub body
- Cone washer, using a brass bar and hammer to tap on the bolt heads
- Free wheel hub body and gasket
4. If equipped without a free wheeling hub, remove the axle hub flange, as follows:
- Grease cap from the flange
- Bolt from the flange
- 6 mounting nuts to the flange
- 6 cone washers, using a brass bar and hammer to tap on the bolt heads
- Flange, by install the 2 bolts to the flange and tightening them
- Flange gasket
- Snapring from the halfshaft end, using a snapring expander

- Spacer
- Halfshaft from the differential; then, pull the halfshaft from the steering knuckle

➡**It may be necessary to tap the end of the halfshaft with a rubber hammer.**

To install:

5. Install or connect the following:
- Halfshaft to the steering knuckle and differential
- 6 nuts to the differential but do not tighten them
- Spacer
- New snapring to the halfshaft, using a snapring expander

6. If equipped without a free wheeling hub, install the flange, as follows:
- New gasket on the axle hub
- Flange to the axle hub

- 6 cone washers, plate washers and nuts. Tighten the 6 nuts to 23 ft. lbs. (31 Nm).
- Tighten the bolt to 13 ft. lbs. (18 Nm).
- Grease cap

7. If equipped with a free wheeling hub, install the hub, as follows:
- New gasket on the front axle hub
- Free wheeling hub body with the 6 cone washers and nuts. Tighten the nuts to 23 ft. lbs. (31 Nm).
- Bolt with the washer. Tighten the bolt to 13 ft. lbs. (18 Nm).
- Apply multi purpose grease to the inner hub splines

a. Set the control handle and clutch to the FREE position.
- New gasket on the cover
- Cover to the hub body with the follower pawl tabs aligned with the

non-toothed portions of the hub body
- Tighten the cover bolts to 84 inch lbs. (10 Nm).
- Tighten the 6 halfshaft-to-differential nuts to 61 ft. lbs. (83 Nm), with an assistant holding the brake pedal
- Front wheel(s)

4Runner

1. Before servicing the vehicle, refer to the precautions in the beginning of this section.
2. Remove the front wheel.
3. Drain the differential oil from the differential.
4. Remove the halfshaft locknut, as follows:

- Grease cap
- Cotter pin and the lockcap
- Locknut, while applying the brakes

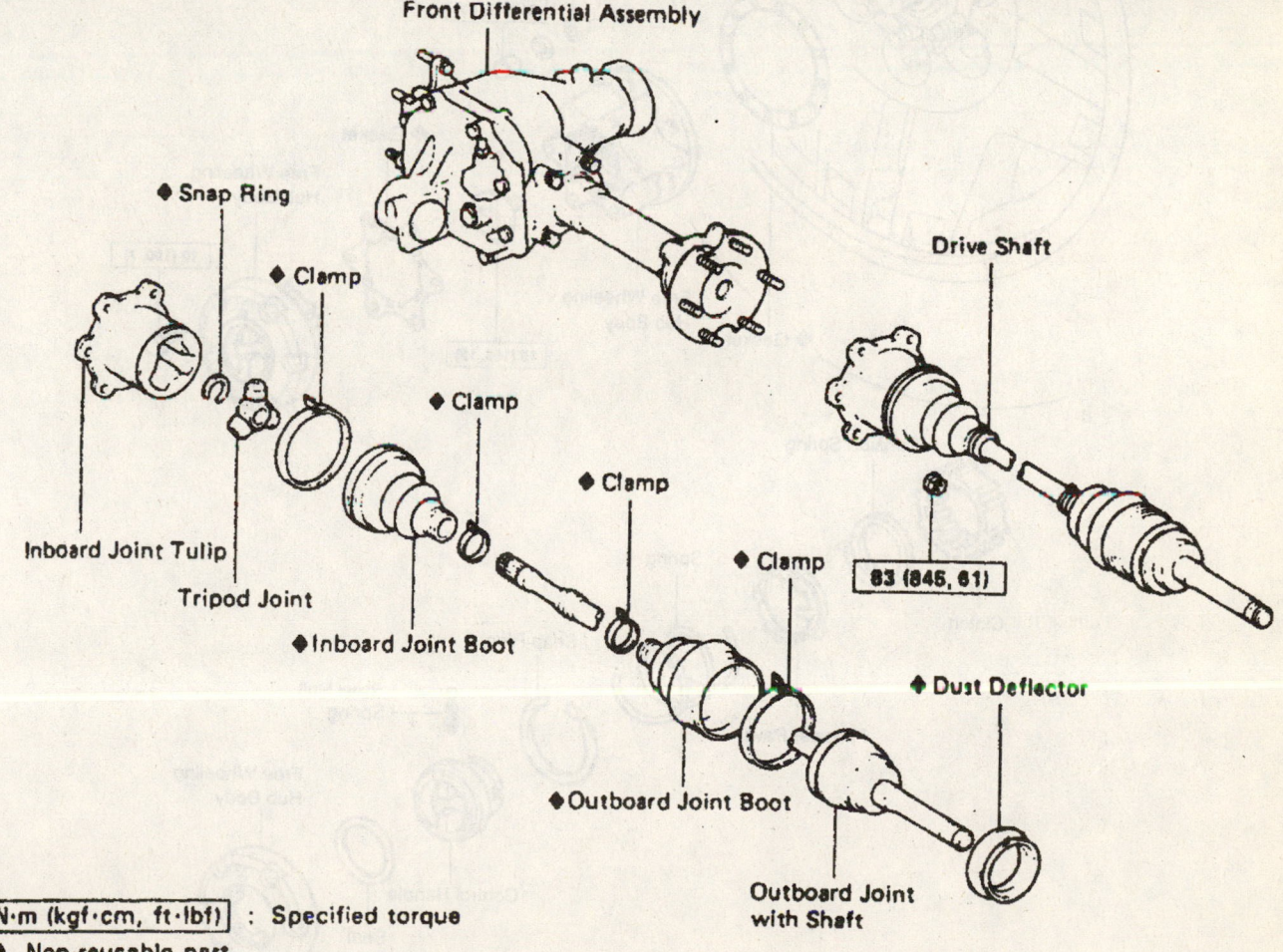

Front Differential Assembly

◆ Snap Ring

◆ Clamp

◆ Clamp

Drive Shaft

◆ Clamp

◆ Clamp

Inboard Joint Tulip

Tripod Joint

◆ Inboard Joint Boot

83 (845, 61)

◆ **Dust Deflector**

◆ Outboard Joint Boot

Outboard Joint with Shaft

N·m (kgf·cm, ft·lbf) : Specified torque

◆ Non-reusable part

Exploded view of the halfshaft components—All T-100 models

7924YG95

5. Remove or disconnect the following:
- Halfshaft, using a brass bar and a hammer
- Lower control arm
- Halfshaft, by pushing the steering knuckle outward
- Snapring from the inboard shaft

To install:

6. Install or connect the following:
- Snapring to the inboard shaft
- Halfshaft

- Steering knuckle
- Lower control arm. Tighten the nut to 105 ft. lbs. (142 Nm).

7. Connect the halfshaft, as follows:
- Set the snapring opening side facing downward
- Strike the inboard joint into the differential, using SST 09631-10030 and a hammer
- Check that the halfshaft cannot be pulled out by hand

8. Install or connect the following:
- Locknut, while applying the brakes. Tighten it to 174 ft. lbs. (235 Nm).
- Grease cap
- Front wheel

9. Fill the differential with oil.

Tacoma

1. Before servicing the vehicle, refer to the precautions in the beginning of this section.

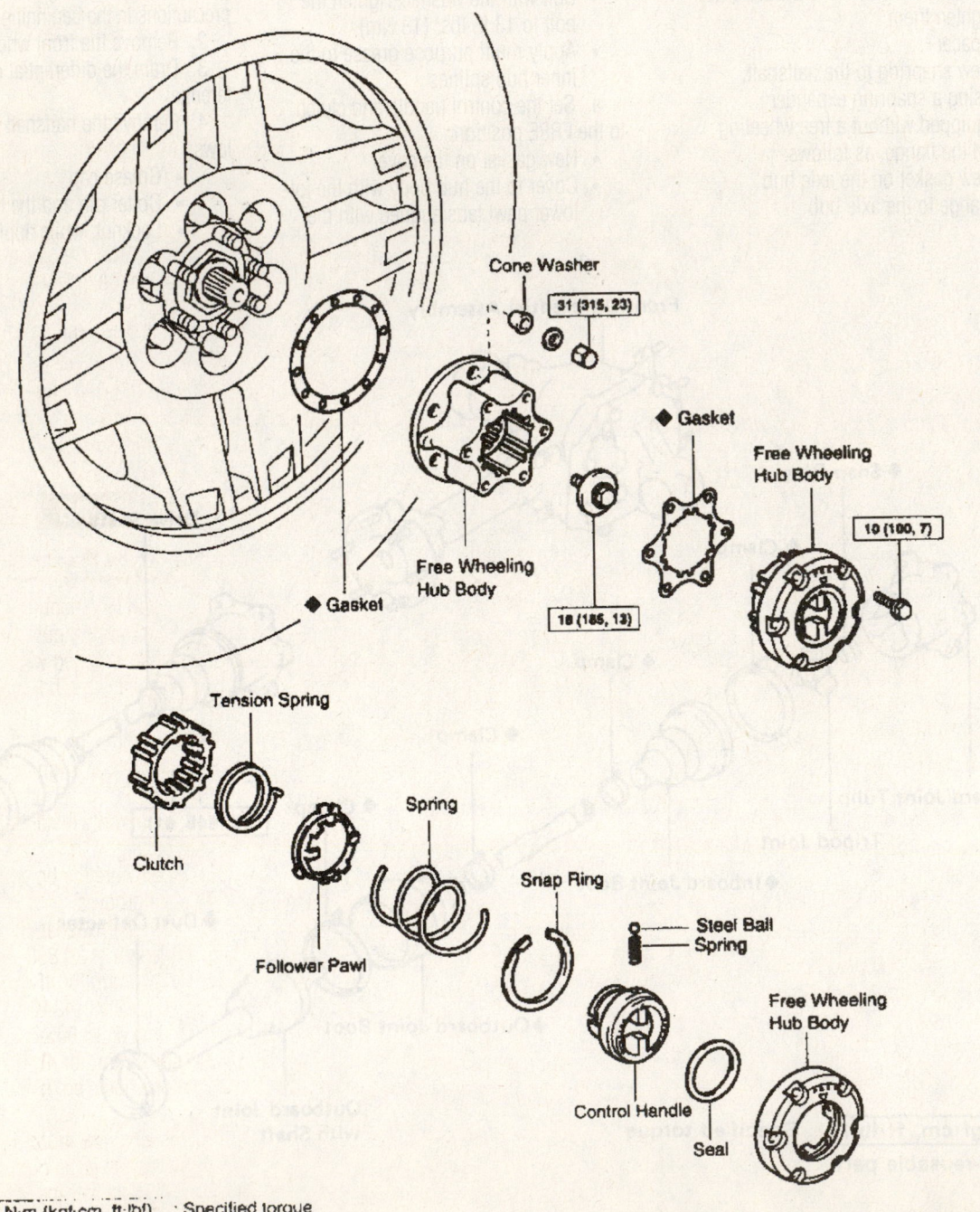

N·m (kgf·cm, ft lbf) : Specified torque
◆ Non-reusable part

Exploded view of the free wheeling hub assembly—Tacoma model shown

7924YG96

2. Drain the differential oil from the differential.

3. If not equipped with a free-wheeling hub, disconnect the halfshaft from the steering knuckle, as follows:
- Grease cap
- Cotter pin and lockcap, from the halfshaft
- Locknut from the halfshaft, while having an assistant apply the brakes

4. If equipped with free-wheeling hub, remove the free wheel hub, as follows:
- Set the control handle to FREE
- Cover bolts and pull off the cover
- Center bolt with washer
- Mounting nuts and washer to the hub body
- Cone washer, using a brass bar and hammer to tap on the bolt heads
- Free wheel hub body and gasket
- Snapring from the end of the halfshaft, using a snapring expander

5. Remove or disconnect the following:
- Halfshaft from the differential, using a brass bar and hammer
- Cotter pin and nut, from the lower ball joint
- Lower control arm from the lower ball joint
- Halfshaft

➡ **If it is difficult to remove the halfshaft from the steering knuckle, use a rubber hammer and tap the halfshaft from the steering knuckle.**

- Snapring from the inboard shaft

To install:

6. Install or connect the following:
- New snapring to the inboard shaft
- Halfshaft to the steering knuckle

➡ **Push the steering knuckle inwards and at the same time, push the halfshaft into the differential with the snapring opening facing downward. Be sure the halfshaft is fully installed to the differential by checking that it cannot be pulled out by hand.**

- Lower control arm to the lower ball joint. Tighten the nut to 112 ft. lbs. (152 Nm).
- New cotter pin

7. If equipped with a free wheeling hub, install the hub, as follows:
- Spacer
- Snapring to the halfshaft, using a snapring expander
- New gasket on the front axle hub
- Fee wheeling hub body, with the 6 cone washers and nuts. Tighten the 6 nuts to 23 ft. lbs. (31 Nm).
- Bolt with the washer. Tighten the bolt to 13 ft. lbs. (18 Nm).
- Apply multi purpose grease to the inner hub splines
- Set the control handle and clutch to the FREE position
- New gasket on the cover
- Cover to the hub body, with the follower pawl tabs aligned with the non-toothed portions of the hub body.
- Tighten the cover bolts to 84 inch lbs. (10 Nm).

8. If equipped without a free wheeling hub, install the halfshaft to the steering knuckle, as follows:
- Locknut to the halfshaft. Tighten the locknut to 174 ft. lbs. (235 Nm).
- Lockcap and cotter pin to the halfshaft
- Grease cap
- Wheels

9. Fill the differential with gear oil.

CV-Joints

OVERHAUL

The outboard joint is replaced with halfshaft; no overhaul is possible or necessary.

Inboard (Tri-Pot) Joint

1. Before servicing the vehicle, refer to the precautions in the beginning of this section.

2. Remove the halfshaft from the vehicle.

3. Remove the large clamp from the inboard joint.

4. Remove the small clamp, using side cutters, from the inboard joint.

5. Slide the inboard joint boot toward the outboard joint.

6. Matchmark the inboard joint to the halfshaft.

7. Remove the inboard joint housing from the halfshaft.

8. Remove the snapring from the end of the halfshaft.

9. Matchmark the halfshaft to the tri-pot joint.

10. Remove the tri-pot from the halfshaft, using a brass bar and a hammer.

✳✳ WARNING

Do not tap on the tri-pot joint.

11. Remove the inboard and outboard boots from the halfshaft.

✳✳ WARNING

Do not disassemble the outboard joint.

To assemble:

12. Wrap vinyl tape around the halfshaft splines to prevent damaging the boots.

13. Install the outboard and inboard boots to the halfshaft with the small end clamps.

14. Assemble the tri-pot joint to the halfshaft with the beveled side facing the outboard joint and align the matchmarks.

15. Install the tri-pot joint, using a brass bar and a hammer.

✳✳ WARNING

Do not tap on the roller.

16. Install the snapring.

17. Lubricate the outboard joint with ½ of the grease supplied with the kit.

18. Assemble the boot to the outboard joint

19. Assemble the inboard joint housing to the halfshaft by aligning the matchmarks.

20. Temporarily install the boot onto the tri-pot housing.

21. Make sure the boots are positioned in the shaft grooves.

22. With the halfshaft positioned at the standard length of 20.898–21.095 in. (525.8–535.8mm) for 4Runner, 17.094–17.252 in. (434.2–438.2mm) for 4WD Tacoma or 18.945–19.339 in. (481.2–491.2mm) for 4WD T-100, make sure that the boots are not stretched or contracted.

23. Install a new inboard joint clamp.

24. Crimp the large clamp with tool 09521-24010 so that the crimp clearance is 0.039–0.059 in. (1.0–1.5mm).

25. Install the halfshaft.

Turn to Section 5 for brake system applications

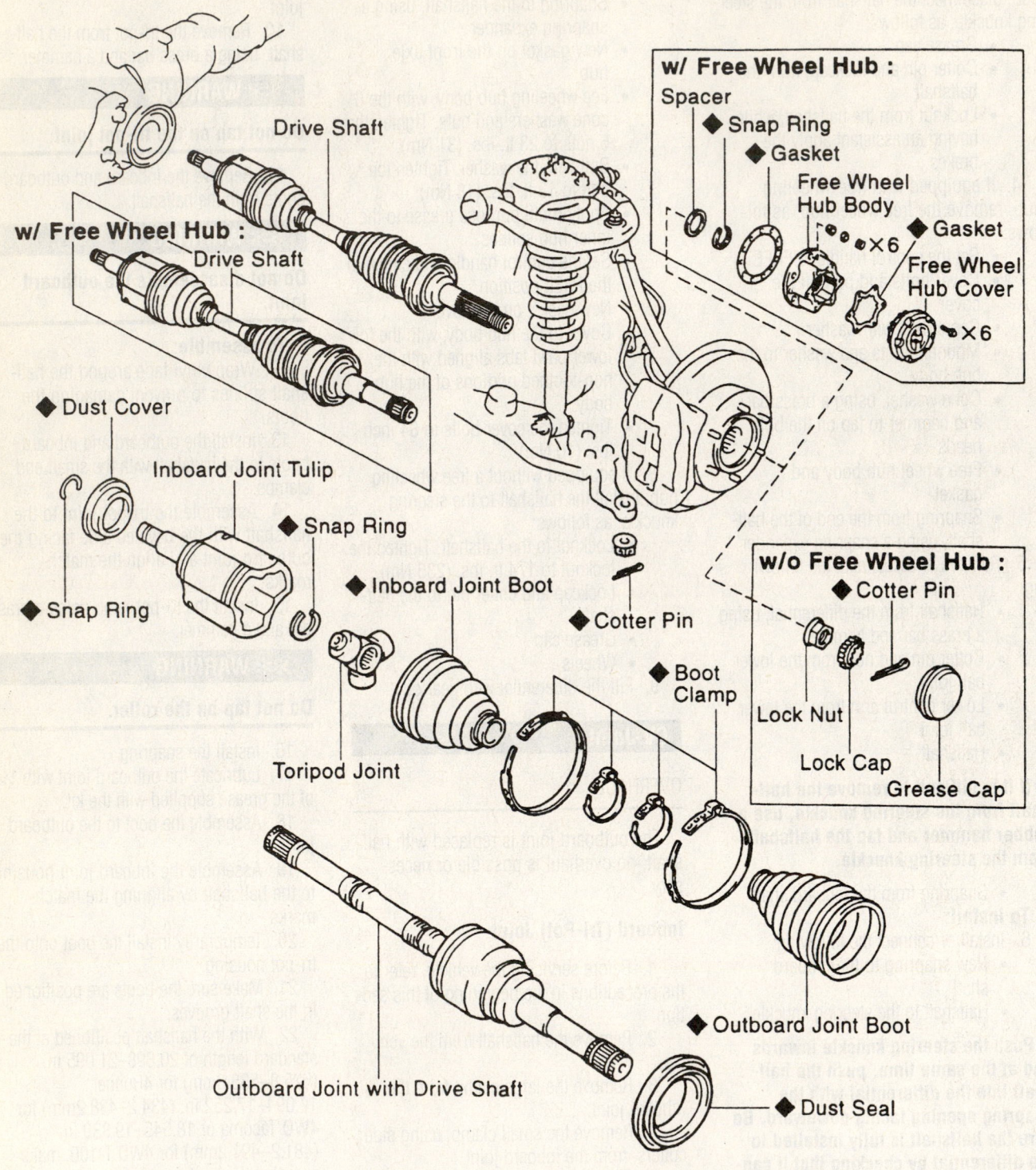

w/ Free Wheel Hub :
Spacer
◆ Snap Ring
◆ Gasket
Free Wheel
Hub Body
◆ Gasket
×6
Free Wheel
Hub Cover
×6

Drive Shaft

w/ Free Wheel Hub :
Drive Shaft

◆ Dust Cover

Inboard Joint Tulip

◆ Snap Ring

◆ Snap Ring

◆ Inboard Joint Boot

Toripod Joint

◆ Cotter Pin

◆ Boot
Clamp

w/o Free Wheel Hub :
◆ Cotter Pin

Lock Nut

Lock Cap

Grease Cap

◆ Outboard Joint Boot

Outboard Joint with Drive Shaft

◆ Dust Seal

◆ Non-reusable part

Exploded view of the halfshaft assembly—4Runner and 4WD Tacoma

9308YG07

Spindle Bearings

REMOVAL, PACKING AND INSTALLATION

1. Before servicing the vehicle, refer to the precautions in the beginning of this section.

2. Remove or disconnect the following:
- Front wheel
- Shock absorber
- Grease cap
- Driveshaft
- Cotter pin and lockcap
- Locknut, with an assistant applying the brakes
- Speed sensor and harness from the steering knuckle, if equipped with Anti-lock Brake System (ABS)
- Brake line from the steering knuckle
- Caliper and rotor
- Lower ball joint bolts and the joint from the steering knuckle
- Cotter pin and axle hub nut
- Steering knuckle
- Bearings from the steering knuckle

To install:

3. Install or connect the following:
- Bearings to the steering knuckle
- Steering knuckle
- Cotter pin and axle hub nut. Tighten the nut to 80 ft. lbs. (108 Nm).
- Lower ball joint to the steering knuckle
- Caliper and rotor
- Brake line to the steering knuckle
- Speed sensor and harness to the steering knuckle, if equipped with Anti-lock Brake System (ABS)
- Locknut, with an assistant applying the brakes. Torque the locknut to 174 ft. lbs. (235 Nm).
- Cotter pin and lockcap
- Driveshaft
- Grease cap
- Shock absorber
- Front wheel

Axle Shaft, Bearing and Seal

REMOVAL & INSTALLATION

Front

1. Before servicing the vehicle, refer to the precautions in the beginning of this section.

2. Remove or disconnect the following:
- Front wheel
- Shock absorber
- Grease cap
- Axle shaft's cotter pin and lock cap
- Locknut, using an assistant to apply the brakes
- Speed sensor and harness from the steering knuckle, if equipped with Anti-lock Brake System (ABS)
- Brake line from the steering knuckle
- Caliper and rotor
- Lower ball joint bolts
- Cotter pin and loosen the axle hub nut
- Steering knuckle
- Axle shaft

To install:

3. Install or connect the following:
- Axle shaft
- Steering knuckle

- Tighten the axle hub nut to 80 ft. lbs. (108 Nm) and the locknut to 174 ft. lbs. (235 Nm).
- Cotter pin
- Lower ball joint bolts
- Caliper and rotor
- Brake line to the steering knuckle
- Speed sensor and harness to the steering knuckle, if equipped with Anti-lock Brake System (ABS)
- Locknut, using an assistant to apply the brakes
- Axle shaft's cotter pin and lock cap
- Grease cap
- Shock absorber
- Front wheel

Rear

1. Before servicing the vehicle, refer to the precautions in the beginning of this section.

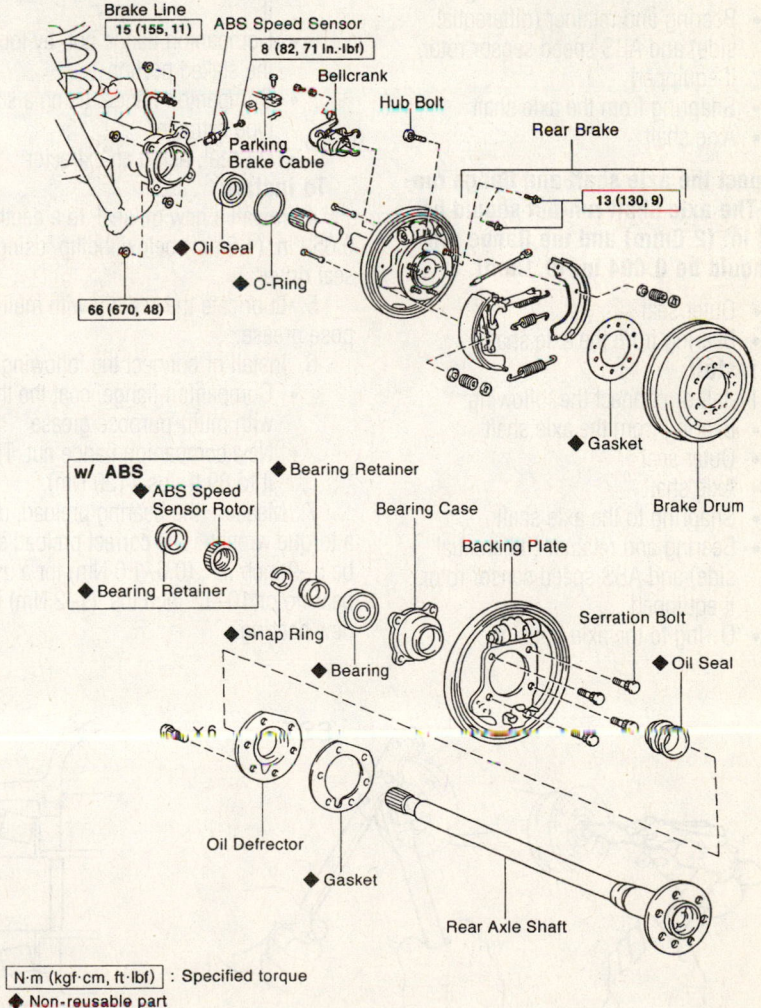

Brake Line
15 (155, 11)
ABS Speed Sensor
8 (82, 71 in.-lbf)
Bellcrank
Hub Bolt
Parking Brake Cable
Oil Seal
O-Ring
66 (670, 48)
Rear Brake
13 (130, 9)
Gasket
Brake Drum

w/ ABS
- ABS Speed Sensor Rotor
- Bearing Retainer
- Bearing Retainer
- Snap Ring
- Bearing
- Bearing Case
- Backing Plate
- Serration Bolt
- Oil Seal
- Oil Deflector
- Gasket
- Rear Axle Shaft

N·m (kgf·cm, ft·lbf) : Specified torque
◆ Non-reusable part

86827G97

Exploded view of the rear axle shaft and components—typical

2. Remove or disconnect the following:
- Rear wheel
- Brake drum

3. Check the bearing backlash and axle shaft deviation, as follows:

a. Using a dial indicator, check that the backlash in the bearing shaft direction. The maximum is 0.027 in. (0.7mm).

b. If the backlash exceeds the maximum, replace the bearing.

c. Using a dial indicator, check the deviation at the surface of the axle shaft outside the hub bolt. Maximum is 0.0039 in. (0.1mm).

d. If the deviation exceeds the maximum, replace the axle shaft.

4. Remove or disconnect the following:
- Anti-lock Brake System (ABS) speed sensor from the axle housing, if equipped
- Axle shaft assembly by removing the 4 nuts from the backing plate
- O-ring from the axle housing
- Bearing and retainer (differential side) and ABS speed sensor rotor, if equipped
- Snapring from the axle shaft
- Axle shaft

➡ Inspect the axle shaft and flange run-outs. The axle shaft run-out should be 0.079 in. (2.0mm) and the flange run-out should be 0.004 in. (0.1mm).

- Outer seal
- Bearing from the axle shaft

To install:

5. Install or connect the following:
- Bearing from the axle shaft
- Outer seal
- Axle shaft
- Snapring to the axle shaft
- Bearing and retainer (differential side) and ABS speed sensor rotor, if equipped
- O-ring to the axle housing

- Axle shaft assembly. Tighten the 4 backing plate nuts to 48 ft. lbs. (66 Nm).
- Anti-lock Brake System (ABS) speed sensor to the axle housing, if equipped
- Brake drum
- Rear wheel

Pinion Seal

REMOVAL & INSTALLATION

Front

4RUNNER

1. Before servicing the vehicle, refer to the precautions in the beginning of this section.

2. Drain the differential oil.

3. Remove or disconnect the following:
- Front driveshaft by matchmarking it
- Companion flange nut, by loosen the staked portion
- Companion flange, using a screw-type extractor
- Oil seal, using an extractor

To install:

4. Install a new oil seal, to a depth of 0.059 in. (1.5mm) below the lip, using a seal driver.

5. Lubricate the seal lip with multi-purpose grease.

6. Install or connect the following:
- Companion flange, coat the threads with multi-purpose grease
- New companion flange nut. Tighten it to 89 ft. lbs. (120 Nm).

7. Measure the bearing preload, using a torque wrench. The correct preload should be 5–9 inch lbs. (0.6–1.0 Nm) for a used bearing or 10–17 inch lbs. (1–2 Nm) for a new bearing.

➡ If the preload is greater that specified, replace the bearing spacer. If the preload is less than specified, tighten the companion flange nut in 9 ft. lbs. (13 Nm) increments until the correct preload is achieved. Maximum torque for the nut is 165 ft. lbs. (223 Nm). If the value is exceeded, the bearing spacer must be replaced; do not back off the flange nut to lower the torque or preload.

8. Install the front driveshaft by aligning the matchmarks.

9. Check the companion flange run-out; maximum allowable run-out is 0.003 in. (0.10mm).

10. Stake the pinion flange nut.

11. Refill the differential with oil.

T-100 AND TACOMA

1. Before servicing the vehicle, refer to the precautions in the beginning of this section.

2. Remove the engine undercover.

3. Drain the differential oil.

4. Remove or disconnect the following:
- Front driveshaft
- Companion flange nut, by unstaking it
- Companion flange
- Pinion seal, using an extractor

To install:

5. Install a new oil seal, to a depth of 0.059 in. (1.5mm) below the lip, using a seal driver.

6. Lubricate the seal lip with multi-purpose grease.

7. Install or connect the following:
- Companion flange, coat the threads with multi-purpose grease
- New companion flange nut. Tighten it to 89 ft. lbs. (120 Nm).

8. Measure the bearing preload, using a torque wrench. The correct preload should be 5–9 inch lbs. (0.6–1.0 Nm) for a used

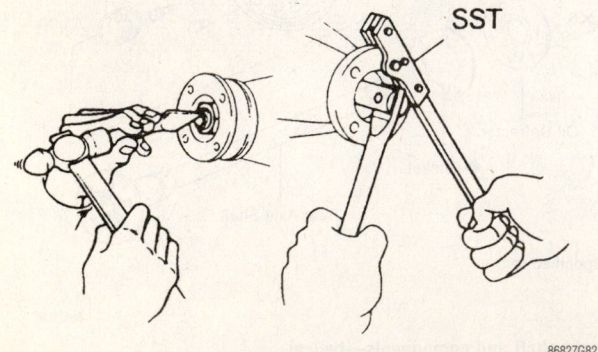

Using a chisel and hammer, loosen the staked part of the nut. Hold the flange with SST 09950-30010 or equivalent and remove the nut

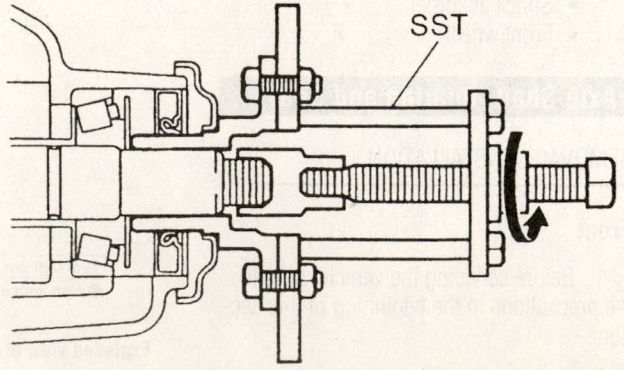

Screw-type extractor from Toyota—Tool 09950-30010

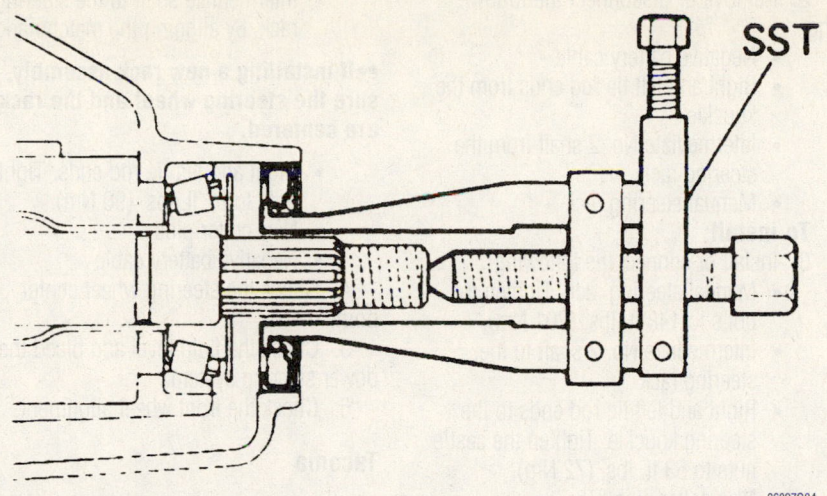

Extractor fits into the Seal Removal Tool 09308-10010

bearing or 10–17 inch lbs. (1–2 Nm) for a new bearing.

➡**If the preload is greater that specified, replace the bearing spacer. If the preload is less than specified, tighten the companion flange nut in 9 ft. lbs. (13 Nm) increments until the correct preload is achieved. Maximum torque for the nut is 173 ft. lbs. (235 Nm). If the value is exceeded, the bearing spacer must be replaced; do not back off the flange nut to lower the torque or preload.**

9. Install the front driveshaft by aligning the matchmarks.
10. Check the companion flange run-out; maximum allowable run-out is 0.003 in. (0.10mm).
11. Stake the pinion flange nut.
12. Refill the differential with oil.

Rear

1. Before servicing the vehicle, refer to the precautions in the beginning of this section.
2. Remove or disconnect the following:
   • Rear driveshaft by matchmarking it
   • Companion flange nut, by loosen the staked portion
   • Companion flange, using a screw-type extractor
   • Oil seal, using an extractor

To install:
3. Install a new oil seal, to a depth of 0.039 in. (1.0mm) below the lip, using a seal driver.
4. Lubricate the seal lip with multi-purpose grease.

5. Install or connect the following:
   • Companion flange, coat the threads with multi-purpose grease
   • New companion flange nut. Tighten it to 145 ft. lbs. (196 Nm) for T-100 and 4Runner or to 109 ft. lbs. (147 Nm) for Tacoma.
6. Measure the bearing preload, using a torque wrench. The correct preload should be 8–11 inch lbs. (0.9–1.2 Nm) for a 2 spider gear differential or to 4–7 inch lbs. (0.4–0.8 Nm) for a 4 spider gear differential.

➡**If the preload is greater that specified, replace the bearing spacer. If the preload is less than specified, tighten the companion flange nut in 9 ft. lbs. (13 Nm) increments until the correct preload is achieved. Maximum torque for the nut is 325 ft. lbs. (441 Nm) for Tacoma, 253 ft. lbs. (343 Nm) for 4Runner or to 109 ft. lbs. (147 Nm) for T-100. If the value is exceeded, the bearing spacer must be replaced; do not back off the flange nut to lower the torque or preload.**

7. Stake the pinion flange nut.
8. Install the rear driveshaft by aligning the matchmarks.

Axle Housing

REMOVAL & INSTALLATION

Front

1. Before servicing the vehicle, refer to the precautions in the beginning of this section.

2. Drain the front differential.
3. Remove or disconnect the following:
   • Front driveshaft by matchmarking it
   • Axle shafts from the differential assembly
   • Vacuum lines, if equipped with automatic locking hubs.
   • 4WD indicator
   • Front differential mounting bolt
   • Differential housing rear mounting bolts while supporting it

To install:
4. Install or connect the following:
   • Differential housing. Tighten the rear mounting bolts to 123 ft. lbs. (167 Nm).
   • Front differential mounting bolt. Tighten it to 108 ft. lbs. (147 Nm).
   • 4WD indicator
   • Vacuum lines, if equipped with automatic locking hubs.
   • Axle shafts to the differential assembly
   • Front driveshaft by aligning the matchmarks
5. Refill the front differential.

Rear

1. Before servicing the vehicle, refer to the precautions in the beginning of this section.
2. Drain the front differential.
3. Remove or disconnect the following:
   • Rear wheel
   • Rear driveshaft by matchmarking it
4. Support the differential assembly.
5. Remove or disconnect the following:
   • Shock absorber lower bolts
   • Stabilizer bar and lateral rod
   • Brake lines from the axle housing
   • Leaf spring U-bolts
   • Axle housing

To install:
6. Install or connect the following:
   • Axle housing
   • Leaf spring U-bolts. Tighten the bolts to 90 ft. lbs. (123 Nm).
   • Brake lines to the axle housing
   • Stabilizer bar and lateral rod
   • Shock absorber lower bolts. Tighten the bolts to 19 ft. lbs. (25 Nm) for 2WD or to 47 ft. lbs. (64 Nm) for 4WD.
7. Remove or disconnect the following:
8. Support the differential assembly.
   • Rear driveshaft by aligning the matchmarks
   • Rear wheel
9. Refill the differential.

STEERING AND SUSPENSION

Air Bag

❄❄ CAUTION

Some vehicles are equipped with an air bag system. The system must be disabled before performing service on or around system components, steering column, instrument panel components, wiring and sensors. Failure to follow safety and disabling procedures could result in accidental air bag deployment, possible personal injury and unnecessary system repairs.

PRECAUTIONS

Several precautions must be observed when handling the inflator module to avoid accidental deployment and possible personal injury.

• Never carry the inflator module by the wires or connector on the underside of the module.

• When carrying a live inflator module, hold securely with both hands, and ensure that the bag and trim cover are pointed away.

• Place the inflator module on a bench or other surface with the bag and trim cover facing up.

• With the inflator module on the bench, never place anything on or close to the module which may be thrown in the event of an accidental deployment.

DISARMING

To avoid personal injury when working on vehicles equipped with an air bag, the negative battery cable must be disconnected and at least 90 seconds must elapse before working on the system. Failure to do so may result in deployment of the air bag.

Manual Rack and Pinion Steering Gear

REMOVAL & INSTALLATION

Tacoma

1. Before servicing the vehicle, refer to the precautions in the beginning of this section.

2. Remove or disconnect the following:

• Negative battery cable
• Right and left tie rod ends from the knuckle
• Intermediate No. 2 shaft from the steering rack
• Manual steering rack

To install:

3. Install or connect the following:
• Manual steering rack. Tighten the bolts to 148 ft. lbs. (201 Nm).
• Intermediate No. 2 shaft to the steering rack
• Right and left tie rod ends to the steering knuckle. Tighten the castle nuts to 53 ft. lbs. (72 Nm).
• New cotter pins
• Negative battery cable

4. Check the steering wheel center point.

5. Bleed the power steering system.

6. Check the front wheel alignment. Tighten the tie rod end locknuts to 67 ft. lbs. (90 Nm).

Power Rack and Pinion Steering Gear

REMOVAL & INSTALLATION

T-100 and 4Runner

1. Before servicing the vehicle, refer to the precautions in the beginning of this section.

2. Remove or disconnect the following:

• Negative battery cable
• Right and left tie rod ends from the knuckle
• Intermediate shaft from the steering rack, by matchmarking it
• Pressure feed and the return tubes, using SST 09631-22020
• Mount bracket and the grommet, from the power steering rack assembly
• Power steering rack and pinion

To install:

3. Install or connect the following:
• Power steering rack and pinion. Tighten the mounting bolts to 65 ft. lbs. (88 Nm).
• Grommet and mount bracket to the gear assembly. Tighten the bolts to 65 ft. lbs. (88 Nm).
• New O-ring
• Pressure feed and return tubes. Tighten the line fittings to 14 ft. lbs. (19 Nm).

• Intermediate shaft to the steering rack, by aligning the matchmarks

➡ **If installing a new rack assembly, be sure the steering wheel and the rack are centered.**

• Right and left tie rod ends. Tighten nuts to 67 ft. lbs. (90 Nm).
• New cotter pins
• Negative battery cable

4. Check the steering wheel center point.

5. Check the fluid level and bleed the power steering system.

6. Check the front wheel alignment.

Tacoma

1. Before servicing the vehicle, refer to the precautions in the beginning of this section.

2. Remove or disconnect the following:
• Negative battery cable
• Right and left tie rod ends from the knuckle
• Intermediate No. 2 shaft from the steering rack
• Pressure feed and the return tubes, using SST 09631-22020
• Power steering rack

To install:

3. Install the power steering rack. Tighten the bolts to 148 ft. lbs. (201 Nm) for 2WD or to the following values for 4WD:

• Rack assembly bolt: 123 ft. lbs. (167 Nm)
• Rack assembly nut: 141 ft. lbs. (191 Nm)
• Bracket nut and bolt: 123 ft. lbs. (167 Nm)

4. Install or connect the following:
• New O-ring
• Pressure feed tube. Tighten it to 33 ft. lbs. (45 Nm).
• Return tube. Tighten it to 36 ft. lbs. (49 Nm) for 2WD or to 29 ft. lbs. (40 Nm) for 4WD
• Intermediate No. 2 shaft to the steering rack
• Right and left tie rod ends to the steering knuckle
• Tighten the castle nuts to specification
• New cotter pins
• Negative battery cable

5. Check the steering wheel center point.

6. Bleed the power steering system.

7. Check the front wheel alignment. Tighten the tie rod end locknuts to 67 ft. lbs. (90 Nm)

Shock Absorber

REMOVAL & INSTALLATION

front

T-100 AND TACOMA

1. Before servicing the vehicle, refer to the precautions in the beginning of this section.
2. Remove or disconnect the following:
   • Front wheel
   • Shock absorber from the lower control arm
   • Nut, retainers and the cushion from the top of the shock absorber
   • Shock absorber
   • Retainers and cushion from the shock absorber

To install:

3. Install or connect the following:
   • Retainers and cushion to the shock absorber
   • Shock absorber
   • Retainers, cushion and nut to the top of the shock absorber. Tighten the nut to 18 ft. lbs. (25 Nm).
   • Lower shock absorber-to-lower control arm. Tighten the bolts to 13 ft. lbs. (19 Nm)
   • Wheels

4RUNNER

1. Before servicing the vehicle, refer to the precautions in the beginning of this section.
2. Remove or disconnect the following:
   • Front wheel
   • Shock from the lower control arm
   • 3 upper nuts
   • Shock absorber

To install:

3. Install or connect the following:
   • Shock absorber. Tighten the 3 nuts to 47 ft. lbs. (64 Nm).
   • Lower shock-to-lower control arm. Tighten the bolt to 101 ft. lbs. (135 Nm).
   • Wheels
4. Check the vehicle alignment.

Rear

1. Before servicing the vehicle, refer to the precautions in the beginning of this section.
2. Remove the wheel.
3. Lower the floor jack to take tension off of the spring.

4. Remove or disconnect the following:
   • Shock absorber from the rear axle housing
   • Nut, retainers and the cushions holding the shock absorber to the frame
   • Shock absorber with the washers and bushings

To install:

5. Install the shock absorber to the frame with the washers and bushings.
6. Tighten the shock absorber-to-frame nut to the following values:
   • 4Runner models: 14 ft. lbs. (20 Nm)
   • T-100 models: 19 ft. lbs. (25 Nm)
   • Tacoma models with 2WD: 19 ft. lbs. (25 Nm)
   • Tacoma models with 4WD: 53 ft. lbs. (72 Nm)
7. Connect the shock absorber to the rear axle housing. Tighten the bolt to the following specifications:
   • 4Runner models: 47 ft. lbs. (64 Nm)
   • T-100 models: 19 ft. lbs. (25 Nm)
   • Tacoma models with 2WD: 19 ft. lbs. (25 Nm)
   • Tacoma models with 4WD: 53 ft. lbs. (72 Nm)
8. Install the wheels.

Coil Spring

REMOVAL & INSTALLATION

Front

4RUNNER

1. Before servicing the vehicle, refer to the precautions in the beginning of this section.
2. Remove the strut.

3. Using SST 09727-30030 or equivalent, compress the coil spring until there is clearance on both ends.
4. Remove or disconnect the following:
   • Support center nut
   • 2 retainers, cushion, suspension support and the coil spring

To install:

5. Compress the coil spring and install to the strut.
6. Fit the lower end of the coil spring into the gap of the spring seat of the strut.
7. Install the suspension support, as follows:
8. Install or connect the following:
   • 2 retainers, suspension support and the cushion to the rod
   • Temporarily tighten the support center nut
   • Align the suspension support with the strut lower bushing
   • Face the lower end of the coil spring to the outside
9. Remove the spring compressor.
10. Install or connect the following:
   • Tighten the center nut to 18 ft. lbs. (25 Nm).
   • Shock absorber

2WD TACOMA

1. Before servicing the vehicle, refer to the precautions in the beginning of this section.
2. Remove or disconnect the following:
   • Shock absorber from the suspension, by removing the 2 bottom bolts and top nut
   • Compress the coil spring, using a Spring Compressor
   • Nut and sway bar link from the lower control arm

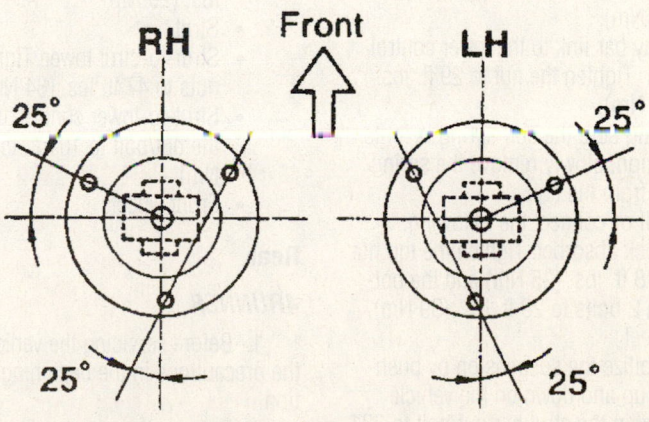

Aligning the strut support to the strut's lower bushing—4Runner

7924YG98

For complete service labor times order Nichols' Chilton Labor Guide Manual

- 2 sway bar bracket bolts on the side of the suspension that the lower control arm is being removed.

➡️**This will allow access to the lower control arm through-bolt.**

3. Support the steering knuckle and upper control arm.
4. Remove or disconnect the following:
   - Cotter pin and nut from the lower ball joint
   - Lower ball joint from the lower control arm, using SST 09628-62011
   - Nut from the lower control arm set bolt
   - Nut from the strut bar front set bolt
   - Lower control arm and strut bar as an assembly, pulling out the 2 bolts

➡️**When the lower control arm is removed, set the coil spring aside.**

To install:

5. Install or connect the following:
   - Place the end of the coil spring in contact with the lower control arm seat
   - Lower control arm, spring, and strut arm to the suspension.
   - Strut arm bolt and lower control arm bolt
   - Nuts for the strut arm bolt and lower control arm bolt; do not tighten the bolts at this time
   - Lower control arm to the lower ball joint. Tighten the nut to 80 ft. lbs. (110 Nm).
   - New cotter pin
6. Remove the support from the upper control arm and steering knuckle.
7. Install or connect the following:
   - Sway bar bracket to the suspension. Tighten the bolts to 22 ft. lbs. (29 Nm).
   - Sway bar link to the lower control arm. Tighten the nut to 29 ft. lbs. (39 Nm).
8. Making sure the coil spring is in its correct position, slowly remove the spring compressor from the coil.
9. Install or connect the following:
   - Shock absorber. Tighten the top nut to 18 ft. lbs. (25 Nm) and the bottom 2 bolts to 29 ft. lbs. (39 Nm).
   - Wheel
   - Stabilize the suspension by pushing up and down on the vehicle
   - Tighten the strut bar nut/bolt to 221 ft. lbs. (300 Nm) and the lower control arm bolt/nut to 148 ft. lbs. (200 Nm).
10. Check the front wheel alignment.

4WD TACOMA

1. Before servicing the vehicle, refer to the precautions in the beginning of this section.
2. Remove or disconnect the following:
   - Strut to the lower control arm nut/bolt.
   - 3 strut-to-strut tower nuts/bolts
   - Strut
3. Compress the coil spring until there is a clearance on both ends, using SST 09727-30030
4. Remove or disconnect the following:
   - Strut center nut
   - Suspension support and coil spring
   - Insulator from the suspension support

To install:
5. Install or connect the following:
   - Insulator to the suspension support

➡️**Match the bolt of the suspension support with the cut out part of the insulator.**

   - Coil spring to the strut, by compressing it with a coil spring compressor

➡️**Fit the lower end of the coil spring into the gap of the spring seat of the strut.**

   - Suspension support to the strut rod
   - Temporarily tighten a new suspension support center nut
6. Position the suspension support so that a line drawn between the 2 bolts would be parallel to the direction of the lower bushing.
7. Remove the compressor from the spring.
8. Install or connect the following:
   - Tighten the strut center nut to 22 ft. lbs. (29 Nm).
   - Strut
   - Strut-to-strut tower. Tighten the 3 nuts to 47 ft. lbs. (64 Nm).
   - Strut-to-lower control arm. Tighten the nut/bolt to 101 ft. lbs. (135 Nm).
   - Front wheels

Rear

4RUNNER

1. Before servicing the vehicle, refer to the precautions in the beginning of this section.
2. Remove the wheel assemblies.
3. Support the axle housing with a floor jack.
4. Remove or disconnect the following:
   - Brake drum

   - Parking brake cable from the brake shoe
   - Parking brake cable from the axle housing.
5. Place matchmarks on the flanges for the driveshaft and differential.
6. Remove or disconnect the following:
   - Driveshaft from the differential
   - Brake hose line from the brake hose
   - Brake hose-to-brake bracket clip
   - Brake hose from the body
   - Anti-lock Brake System (ABS) wiring harness bracket, if equipped with ABS
   - Shock absorbers from the axle housing
   - Lateral control rod nuts/bolts
   - Control rod from the suspension
   - Coil spring, by lower the rear axle housing

To install:
7. Install or connect the following:
   - Coil springs into position and raise the axle housing.

❋❋ CAUTION

Be sure to fit the lower end of the coil spring into the gap of the spring seat on the lower control arm.

   - Lateral control rod to the suspension. Tighten the bolts/nuts to 64 ft. lbs. (86 Nm).
   - Shock absorbers to the axle housing. Tighten the bolt to 47 ft. lbs. (64 Nm).
   - ABS wiring harness bracket, if equipped
   - Brake hose to the bracket
   - Clip
   - Brake line to the brake hose. Tighten the tube.
   - Parking brake cable bracket to the axle housing. Tighten to 108 inch lbs. (13 Nm).
   - Parking brake cable to the brake shoes
   - Driveshaft to the differential, by aligning the matchmarks. Tighten bolts/nuts to 54 ft. lbs. (73 Nm).
8. Fill the differential with the proper amount and type of oil.
9. Install the brake drum.
10. Bleed the brake system.
11. Install the wheel assemblies.
12. Lower the vehicle and bounce the vehicle several times to stabilize the suspension.
13. Tighten the lower control arm to 107 ft. lbs. (145 Nm).

Upper Ball Joint

REMOVAL & INSTALLATION

T-100

2WD MODELS

1. Before servicing the vehicle, refer to the precautions in the beginning of this section.
2. Remove the wheel.
3. Support the lower control arm with a floor jack.
4. Remove or disconnect the following:
   - Brake caliper and support it aside with a wire
   - Cotter pin and nut from the upper ball joint
   - Ball joint from the knuckle arm
   - 4 ball joint-to-upper control arm nuts, washers and bolts
   - Ball joint from the upper control arm

To install:
   - Ball joint to the upper control arm
   - Upper ball joint-to-upper control arm bolts, washers and nuts
   - Tighten the ball joint-to-upper control arm bolts to 23 ft. lbs. (31 Nm)
   - Tighten the ball joint-to-control arm nut to 80 ft. lbs. (108 Nm)
   - New cotter pin
   - Wheel

4WD MODELS

1. Before servicing the vehicle, refer to the precautions in the beginning of this section.
2. Remove the wheel.
3. Support the lower control arm with a floor jack.
4. Remove or disconnect the following:
   - Steering knuckle
   - Upper ball joint from the upper control arm

To install:
5. Install or connect the following:
   - Upper ball joint to the upper control arm. Tighten the 4 nuts to 25 ft. lbs. (33 Nm).
   - Steering knuckle
   - Wheel

4Runner

1. Before servicing the vehicle, refer to the precautions in the beginning of this section.

2. Remove or disconnect the following:
   - Front wheels
   - Strut assembly
   - Grease cap
3. If equipped with 4WD, disconnect the halfshaft, as follows:
   - Cotter pin and lockcap
   - Locknut, while applying the brakes
4. Remove or disconnect the following:
   - Anti-lock Brake System (ABS) speed sensor and wiring harness clamp from the steering knuckle, if equipped with ABS
   - Brake line bracket from the steering knuckle
   - Front brake caliper and the rotor
   - Lower ball joint
5. Remove the steering knuckle with the axle hub, as follows:
   - Cotter pin and loosen the nut
   - Steering knuckle from the upper control arm, using SST 09950-40010
   - Steering knuckle
   - Upper ball joint
   - Wire and the boot
   - Snapring
   - Upper ball joint, using SST 09950-40010 and a deep socket wrench.

To install:
6. Install the upper ball joint, as follows:
   - New ball joint with a new snapring
   - New boot secured with a new wire
7. Install or connect the following:
   - Steering knuckle with the axle hub to the upper control arm. Tighten the nut to 80 ft. lbs. (108 Nm).
   - New cotter pin
   - Lower ball joint. Tighten the 4 bolts to 59 ft. lbs. (80 Nm).
   - Rotor and caliper. Tighten the caliper bolts to 90 ft. lbs. (123 Nm).
   - Brake line bracket to the steering knuckle. Tighten it to 21 ft. lbs. (28 Nm).
   - ABS speed sensor and wiring harness clamp to the steering knuckle, if equipped. Tighten the bolts to 72 inch lbs. (8 Nm).
   - Halfshaft, if disconnected. Tighten the nut to 174 ft. lbs. (235 Nm).
   - Grease cap
   - Strut
   - Front wheel
8. Check the alignment

Tacoma

2WD MODELS

1. Before servicing the vehicle, refer to the precautions in the beginning of this section.
2. Remove the wheels.
3. Support the lower control arm with a floor jack.
4. Remove or disconnect the following:
   - Anti-lock Brake System (ABS) speed sensor wire from the upper control arm
   - 2 bolts and camber adjusting shims from the upper control arm

➡ **Before removing the shims from the upper control arm, make a note of each shim size and position.**

   - Upper control arm cotter pin and nut.
   - Upper ball joint from the steering knuckle, using SST 09628-62011
   - Upper control arm
   - 4 upper control arm-to-upper ball joint nuts and bolts.
   - Upper control arm from the upper ball joint

To install:
5. Install or connect the following:
   - New ball joint to the upper control arm. Tighten the 4 nuts/bolts to 29 ft. lbs. (39 Nm).
   - Upper control arm
   - Camber adjusting shims to the upper control arm. Tighten the 2 bolts to 94 ft. lbs. (130 Nm).
   - Upper ball joint to the steering knuckle. Tighten the nut to 80 ft. lbs. (110 Nm).
   - ABS speed sensor wire to the upper control arm. Tighten the ABS bolt to 71 inch lbs. (8 Nm).
   - Wheels
6. Check the wheel alignment.

4WD MODELS

1. Before servicing the vehicle, refer to the precautions in the beginning of this section.
2. Remove or disconnect the following:
   - Wheel
   - Strut
3. If not equipped with a FREE wheeling hub, disconnect the halfshaft from the steering knuckle, as follows:
   - Grease cap
   - Cotter pin and lockcap from the halfshaft

- Locknut from the halfshaft, while having an assistant apply the brakes

4. If equipped with FREE wheeling hub, remove the free wheel hub, as follows:

- Set the control handle to FREE
- Cover bolts and pull off the cover
- Center bolt with washer
- Hub body nuts and washer
- Cone washer, using a brass bar and hammer to tap on the bolt heads
- Free wheel hub body and gasket
- Snapring and spacer from the halfshaft end, using a snapring expander
- Anti-lock Brake System (ABS) speed sensor from the steering knuckle, if equipped with ABS
- Brake hose from the steering knuckle
- Brake caliper support bracket and support it on a wire

✳✳ WARNING

Do not allow the caliper to hang from the brake hose.

5. Remove or disconnect the following:

- Rotor
- Lower ball joint from the steering knuckle
- Upper control arm cotter pin and nut
- Steering knuckle from the upper control arm, using SST 09950-40010
- Steering knuckle from the vehicle

➡ **If it is difficult to remove the halfshaft from the steering knuckle, use a rubber hammer to tap the halfshaft from the steering knuckle.**

- Wire and boot from the upper ball joint
- Snapring from the ball joint, using a snapring expander
- Upper ball joint from the steering knuckle, using SST 09950-40010 (puller set) and a deep socket wrench

To install:

6. Install or connect the following:

- Press in a new upper ball joint, using SST 09309-37010 and a socket wrench
- New snapring, using a snapring expander

- New boot, secured with a new piece of wire
- Steering knuckle to the halfshaft
- Steering knuckle to the lower ball joint by installing the 4 bolts; do not tighten the bolts at this time.
- Upper control arm
- Upper ball joint to the steering knuckle. Tighten the nut to 80 ft. lbs. (105 Nm).
- New cotter pin
- Tighten the lower ball joint-to-steering knuckle bolts to 59 ft. lbs. (80 Nm).
- Brake rotor
- Caliper support bracket to the steering knuckle. Tighten both bolts to 90 ft. lbs. (123 Nm).
- Brake hose clamp to the steering knuckle. Tighten the bolt to 13 ft. lbs. (18 Nm).
- ABS speed sensor and wiring harness to the steering knuckle, if equipped with ABS
- Spacer and snapring to the halfshaft, using a snapring expander

7. If equipped with a free wheeling hub, install the hub, as follows:

- New front axle hub gasket
- Free wheeling hub body with the 6 cone washers and nuts. Tighten the 6 nuts to 23 ft. lbs. (31 Nm).
- Bolt with the washer. Tighten the bolt to 13 ft. lbs. (18 Nm).
- Apply multi-purpose grease to the inner hub splines
- Set the control handle and clutch to the FREE position
- New gasket on the cover
- Cover to the hub body with the follower pawl tabs aligned with the non-toothed portions of the hub body
- Tighten the cover bolts to 84 inch lbs. (10 Nm).

8. If equipped without a free wheeling hub, install the halfshaft to the steering knuckle, as follows:

- Locknut to the halfshaft. Tighten the nut to 174 ft. lbs. (235 Nm).
- Halfshaft lockcap and cotter pin
- Grease cab
- Strut. Tighten the strut-to-lower control arm nut to 101 ft. lbs. (135 Nm) and the upper 3 nuts to 47 ft. lbs. (64 Nm).
- Front wheels

9. Check the wheel alignment.

Leaf Springs

REMOVAL & INSTALLATION

2WD

1. Loosen the rear wheel lug nuts.
2. Raise the rear of the vehicle. Support the frame and rear axle housing with stands.
3. Remove the lug nuts and the wheel.
4. Remove the cotter pin, nut, and washer from the lower end of the shock absorber.
5. Detach the shock absorber from the spring seat.
6. Remove the parking brake cable clamp.

➡ **Remove the parking brake equalizer, if necessary.**

7. Unfasten the U-bolt nuts and remove the spring seat assemblies.
8. Adjust the height of the rear axle housing so that the weight of the rear axle is removed from the rear springs.
9. Unfasten the spring shackle retaining nuts. Withdraw the spring shackle inner plate. Carefully pry out the spring shackle with a bar.
10. Remove the spring bracket pin from the front end of the spring hanger and remove the rubber bushing.
11. Remove the spring. Use care not to damage the hydraulic brake line or the parking brake cable.

To install:

12. Install the rubber bushing in the eye of the spring.
13. Align the eye of the spring with the spring hanger bracket and drive the pin through the bracket holes and rubber bushings.

➡ **Use soapy water or glass cleaner as a lubricant, if necessary, to aid in pin installation. Never use oil or grease.**

14. Finger-tighten the spring hanger nuts and/or bolts.
15. Install the rubber bushing in the spring eye at the opposite end of the spring.
16. Raise the free end of the spring. Install the spring shackle through the bushing and the bracket.
17. Install the shackle inner plate and finger-tighten the retaining nuts.
18. Center the bolt head in the hole which is provided in the spring seat on the axle housing.
19. Fit the U-bolts over the axle housing. Install the lower spring seat.
20. Tighten the U-bolt nuts to:

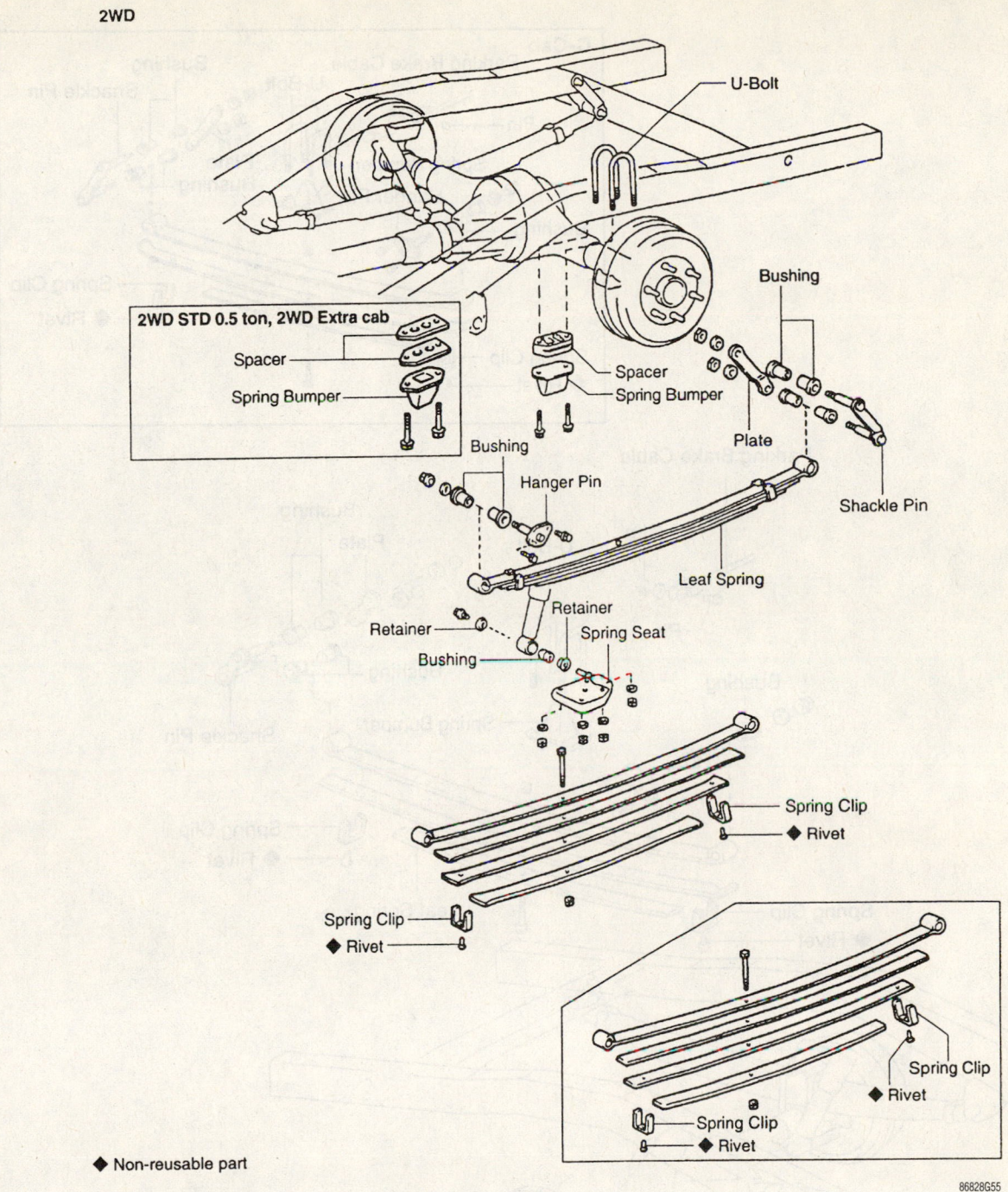

2WD

2WD STD 0.5 ton, 2WD Extra cab

Spacer

Spring Bumper

U-Bolt

Bushing

Spacer

Spring Bumper

Bushing

Plate

Shackle Pin

Bushing

Hanger Pin

Leaf Spring

Retainer

Retainer

Spring Seat

Bushing

Spring Clip

◆ Rivet

Spring Clip

◆ Rivet

Spring Clip

◆ Rivet

Spring Clip

◆ Rivet

◆ Non-reusable part

86828G55

Exploded view of the rear leaf spring and related components—2WD Tacoma

- T-100: 97 ft. lbs. (132 Nm)
- Tacoma: 90 ft. lbs. (120 Nm)

21. Install the parking brake cable and clamp. Install the equalizer, if removed.

22. Tighten the hanger pin and shackle nuts. Install the shock absorber bushings and washers. Tighten and install the cotter pins.

23. Install the stabilizer link and hand-tighten its retaining nuts.

24. Install the wheels. Lower the vehicle.

25. Bounce the truck several times to set the suspension and then tighten the shock absorber bolt. Tighten the hanger pin nut or bolt to:

- Tacoma: 115 ft. lbs. (120 Nm)
- T-100: 19 ft. lbs. (26 Nm)

26. Tighten the shackle pin to 67 ft. lbs. (91 Nm).

4WD

1. Loosen the rear wheel lug nuts.

2. Raise the rear of the vehicle. Support the frame and rear axle housing with stands.

3. Remove the lug nuts and the wheel.

4. Remove the cotter pin, nut and washer from the lower end of the shock absorber.

Turn to Section 5 for brake system applications

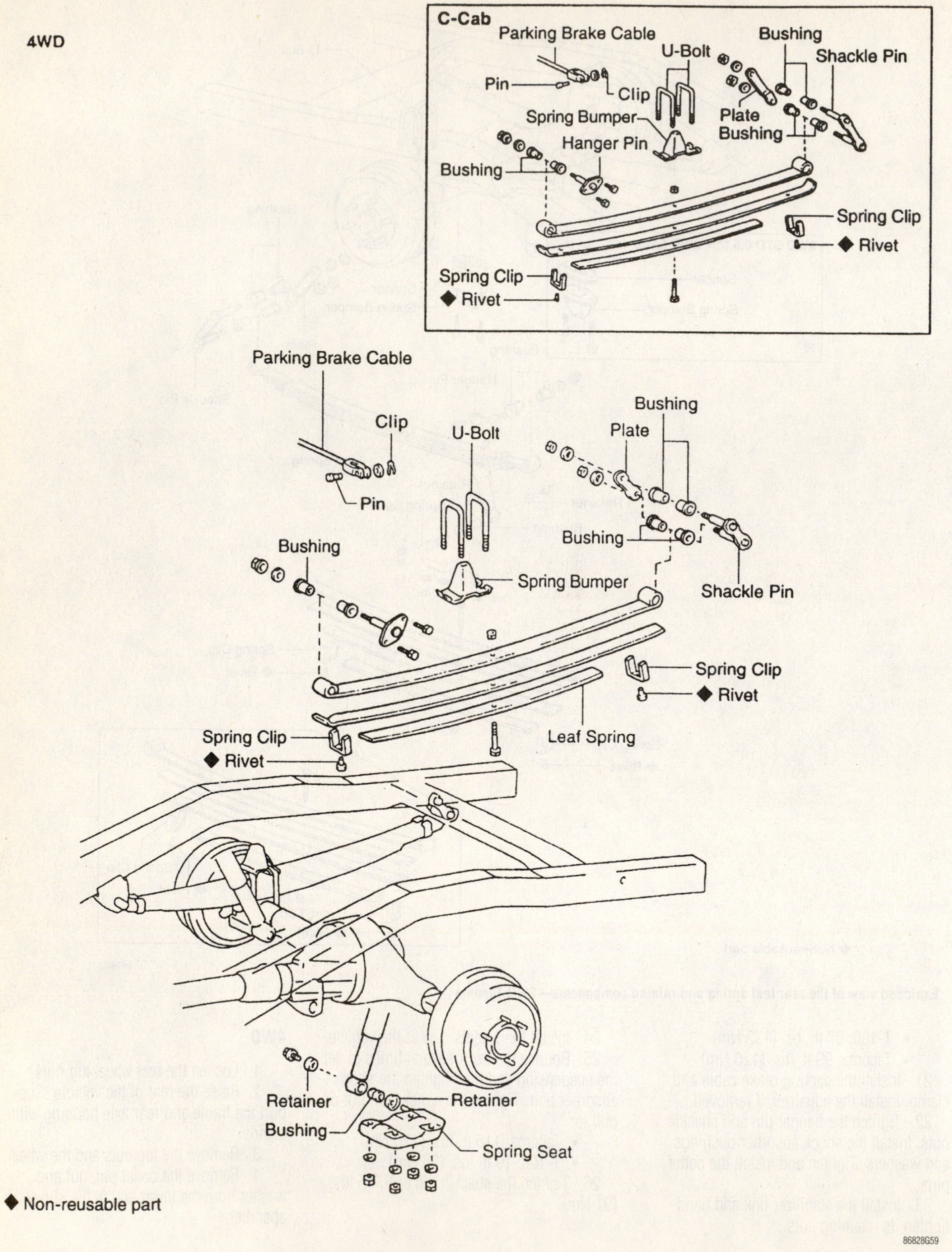

4WD

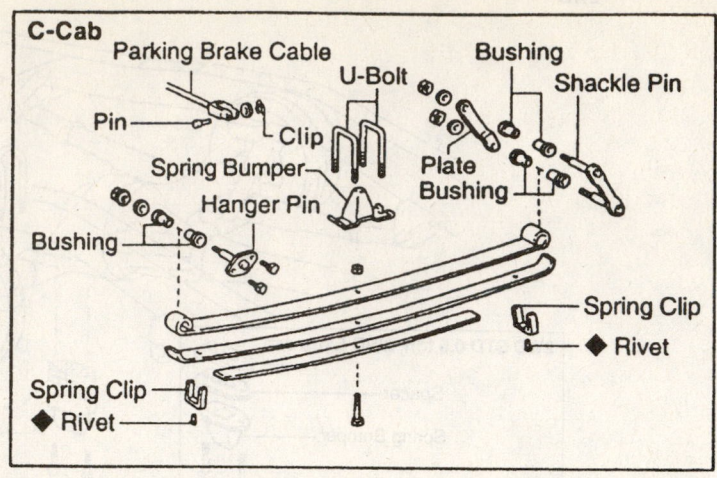

C-Cab

Parking Brake Cable

Pin

Clip

U-Bolt

Bushing

Shackle Pin

Spring Bumper

Hanger Pin

Plate

Bushing

Bushing

Spring Clip

◆ Rivet

Spring Clip

◆ Rivet

Parking Brake Cable

Clip

U-Bolt

Bushing

Plate

Pin

Bushing

Shackle Pin

Bushing

Spring Bumper

Spring Clip

◆ Rivet

Spring Clip

◆ Rivet

Leaf Spring

Retainer

Retainer

Bushing

Spring Seat

◆ **Non-reusable part**

Exploded view of the rear leaf spring and components—4WD Tacoma

86828G59

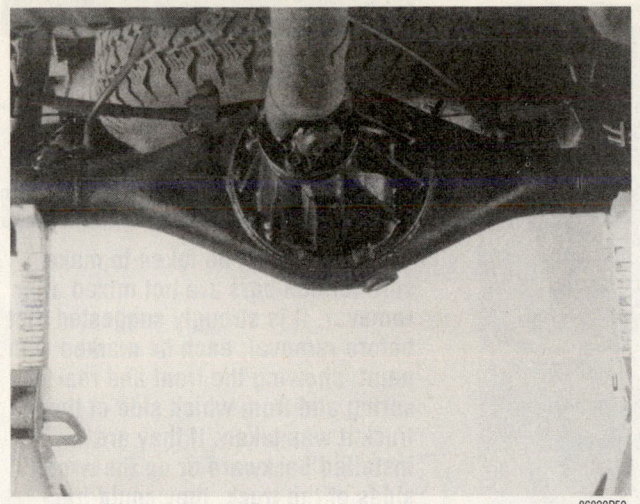

Support the rear axle of the vehicle with a set of jackstands

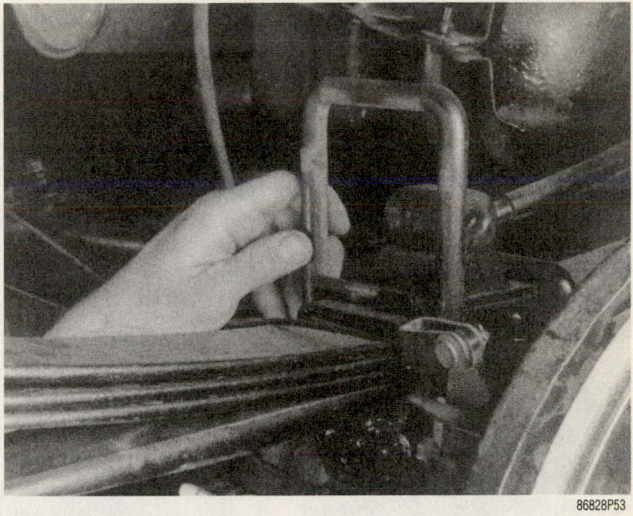

Remove the U-bolt from the rear

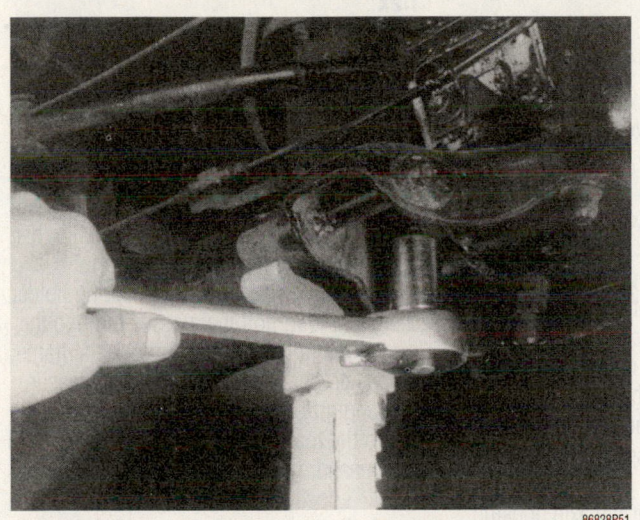

Unbolt the rear axle mounting bracket attached to the spring

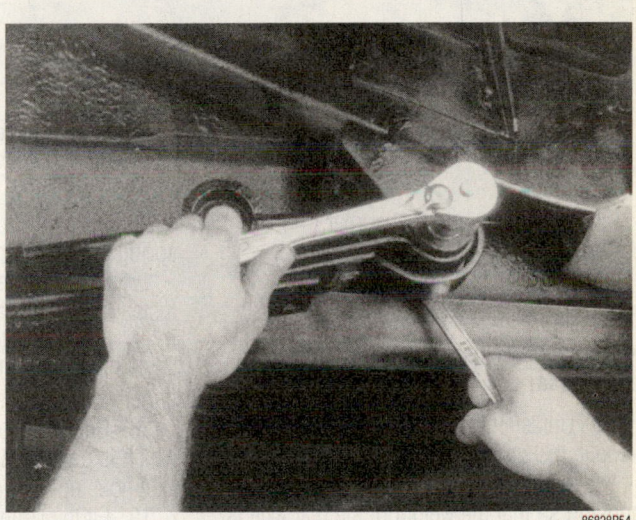

Proceed to the front of the spring and remove the pin

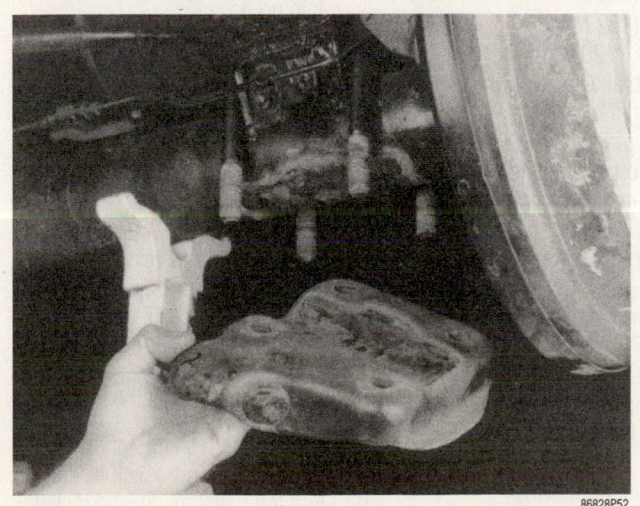

Lower the seat assembly

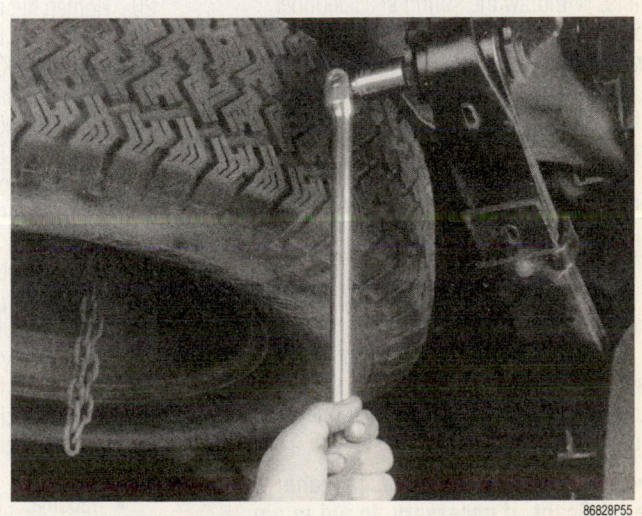

Unbolt the rear mount then . . .

86828P56

. . . carefully lower the spring from the vehicle. The jackstand must be removed by an assistant

5. Detach the shock absorber from the spring seat.

6. Remove the parking brake cable clamp.

➡**Remove the parking brake equalizer, if necessary.**

7. Unfasten the U-bolt and nuts, then remove the spring seat assemblies.

8. Adjust the height of the rear axle housing so that the weight of the rear axle is removed from the rear springs.

9. Unfasten the spring shackle retaining nuts. Withdraw the spring shackle inner plate. Carefully pry out the spring shackle with a bar.

10. Remove the spring bracket pin from the front end of the spring hanger and remove the rubber bushing.

11. Remove the spring. Use care not to damage the hydraulic brake line or the parking brake cable.

To install:

12. Install the rubber bushing in the eye of the spring.

13. Align the eye of the spring with the spring hanger bracket and drive the pin through the bracket holes and rubber bushings.

➡**Use soapy water or glass cleaner as a lubricant, if necessary, to aid in pin installation. Never use oil or grease.**

14. Finger-tighten the spring hanger nuts and/or bolts.

15. Install the rubber bushing in the spring eye at the opposite end of the spring.

16. Raise the free end of the spring. Install the spring shackle through the bushing and the bracket.

17. Install the shackle inner plate and finger-tighten the retaining nuts.

18. Center the bolt head in the hole which is provided in the spring seat on the axle housing.

19. Fit the U-bolts over the axle housing. Install the lower spring seat. Install the spring bumper, if equipped.

20. Tighten the U-bolt nuts to:
  • T-100: 97 ft. lbs. (132 Nm)
  • Tacoma: 90 ft. lbs. (120 Nm)

21. Install the parking brake cable and clamp. Install the equalizer, if removed.

22. Tighten the hanger pin and shackle nuts. Install the shock absorber bushings and washers. Tighten and install the cotter pins.

23. Install the stabilizer link and hand-tighten its retaining nuts.

24. Install the wheels and remove the stands. Lower the vehicle.

25. Bounce the truck several times to set the suspension and then tighten the shock absorber bolt. Tighten the hanger pin nut or bolt to:
  • Tacoma: 115 ft. lbs. (120 Nm)
  • T-100: 19 ft. lbs. (26 Nm)

26. Tighten the shackle pin to 67 ft. lbs. (91 Nm).

Torsion Bars

REMOVAL & INSTALLATION

4Runner

❋❋ **WARNING**

Great care must be taken to make sure torsion bars are not mixed after removal, it is strongly suggested that before removal; each be marked with paint, showing the front and rear of spring and from which side of the truck it was taken. If they are installed backward or on the wrong sides of the truck, they could fracture. New units are marked L or R with an arrow showing direction of flex.

1. Raise the vehicle and support the frame on stands.

2. Slide the boot from the rear of torsion bar spring housing onto spring.

3. Follow the same procedure on the front of the spring.

4. Paint matchmarks on the torsion bar spring, anchor arm and torque arm.

5. On the rear torsion bar spring holder, there is a long bolt that passes through the arm of the holder and up through the frame crossmember, using a small ruler, measure the length from the bottom of the retaining nut to the threaded tip of the bolt and record this measurement.

6. Loosen the adjusting nut.

7. Remove or disconnect the following:
  • Anchor arm and torsion bar spring
  • Torque arm, there are tow nuts retaining it.

To install:

8. Inspect all parts for wear, damage or cracks. Check the boot for rips and wear. Inspect the splined ends of the torsion bar spring and the splined holes in the rear holder and the front torque arm for damage. Replace as necessary.

➡**On the rear end of the torsion bar springs, there are markings to show which is right and which is the left bar. Do not confuse them.**

9. Install the existing spring, as follows:
  a. Coat the splined ends of the torsion bar with multi-purpose grease.
  b. Align the matchmarks and install the torsion bar spring to the torque arm.
  c. Align the matchmarks and install the anchor arm to the torsion bar spring.

d. Tighten the adjusting nut so that the bolt protrusion measured previously is equal to that of the new adjustment.

10. To install a new torsion bar spring, as follows:

   a. Install the 2 bolts to the torsion bar spring.

   b. Lightly coat the spring end splines with grease and then install the anchor arm to the small end of the spring temporarily. Paint matchmarks on the spring and arm.

➡ There is one spline on the spring that is larger than the others. When connecting the spring to the arm, turn the arm slowly until you can feel the larger spline match up with the slot in the arm.

   c. Remove the anchor arm from the spring and install the spring into the torque arm.

➡ There is one spline on the spring that is larger than the others. When connecting the spring to the arm, turn the arm slowly until you can feel the larger spline match up with the slot in the arm.

   d. Align the matchmarks and install the anchor arm to the spring. Tighten the adjusting nut so that the exposed thread on the bolt is no greater than 87mm.

11. Install the locknut and wheels, lower the vehicle and bounce it several times to set the suspension.

12. Measure the ground clearance and adjust with the adjusting nut. Tighten the locknut.

13. Check and/or adjust the alignment.

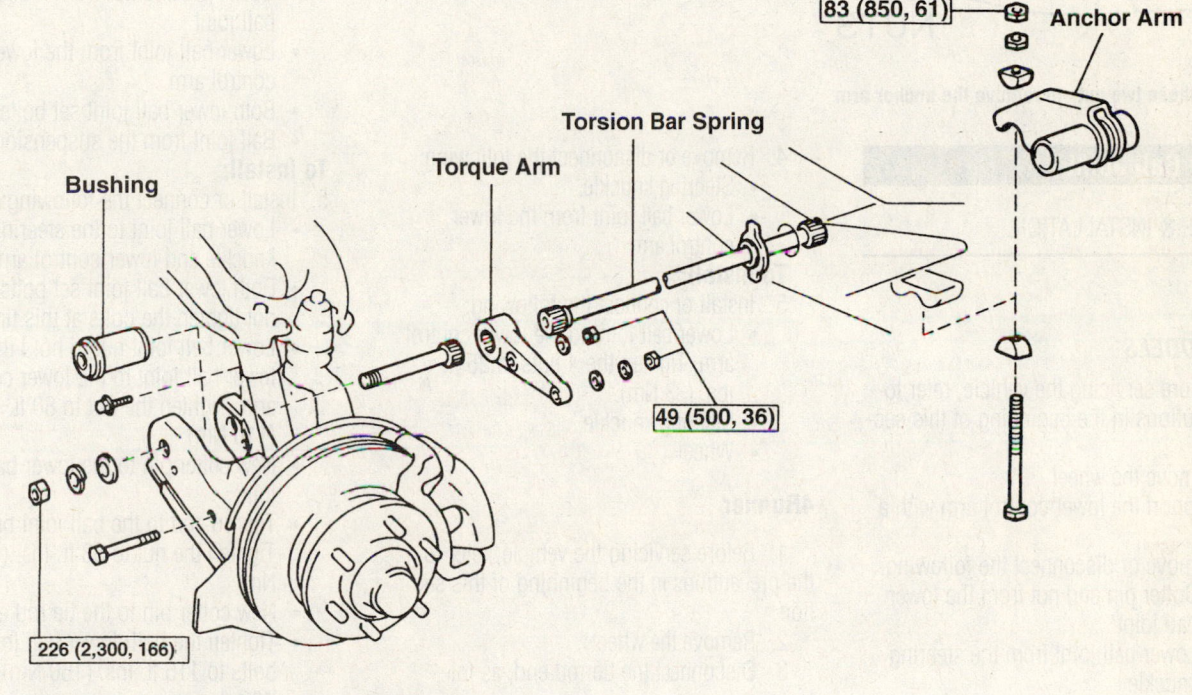

N·m(kgf·cm, ft·lbf) : Specified Torque

Exploded view of the torsion bar suspension and associated components

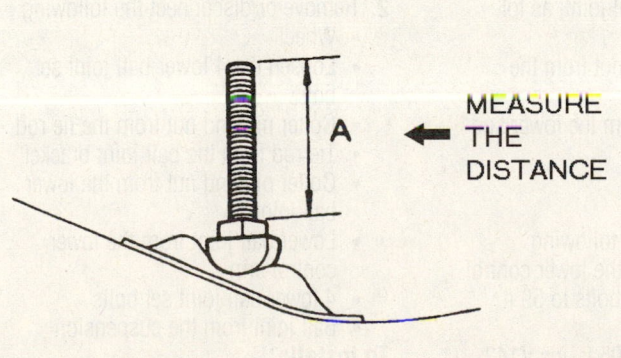

MEASURE THE DISTANCE

Measure the distance between the shoulder and the tip of the bolt

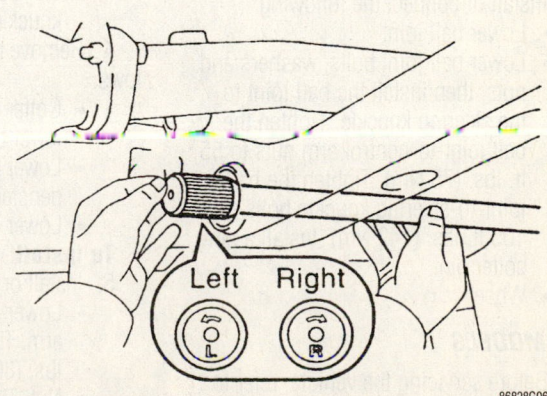

When you remove the torsion bar, note that some models have markings for the left and right

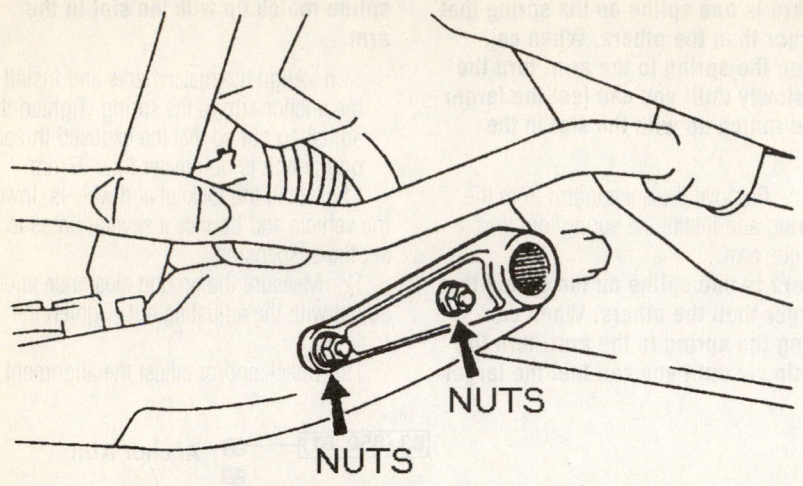

86828G07

Loosen these two nuts to remove the anchor arm

Lower Ball Joint

REMOVAL & INSTALLATION

T-100

2WD MODELS

1. Before servicing the vehicle, refer to the precautions in the beginning of this section.
2. Remove the wheel.
3. Support the lower control arm with a floor jack.
4. Remove or disconnect the following:
   • Cotter pin and nut from the lower ball joint
   • Lower ball joint from the steering knuckle
   • Ball joint from the lower control arm
   • Ball joint

To install:
5. Install or connect the following:
   • Lower ball joint
   • Lower ball joint bolts, washers and nuts, then install the ball joint to the steering knuckle. Tighten the ball joint-to-control arm nuts to 55 ft. lbs. (75 Nm). Tighten the ball joint-to-steering knuckle bolts to 105 ft. lbs. (142 Nm). Install a new cotter pin.
   • Wheel

4WD MODELS

1. Before servicing the vehicle, refer to the precautions in the beginning of this section.
2. Remove the wheel.
3. Support the lower control arm with a floor jack.

4. Remove or disconnect the following:
   • Steering knuckle
   • Lower ball joint from the lower control arm

To install:
5. Install or connect the following:
   • Lower ball joint to the lower control arm. Tighten the 4 nuts to 25 ft. lbs. (33 Nm).
   • Steering knuckle
   • Wheel

4Runner

1. Before servicing the vehicle, refer to the precautions in the beginning of this section.
2. Remove the wheel.
3. Disconnect the tie rod end, as follows:
   • Loosen the 4 bolts
   • Cotter pin and nut from the tie rod end
   • Tie rod end from the steering knuckle, using SST 09610-20012
4. Remove the lower ball joint, as follows:
   • Cotter pin and the nut from the lower ball joint
   • Lower ball joint from the lower suspension arm
   • Lower ball joint

To install:
5. Install or connect the following:
   • Lower ball joint to the lower control arm. Tighten the 4 bolts to 59 ft. lbs. (80 Nm).
   • Nut. Tighten it to 105 ft. lbs. (142 Nm).
   • Tie rod end to the steering knuckle. Tighten the nut to 66 ft. lbs. (90 Nm).
   • Wheel

Tacoma

2WD MODELS

1. Before servicing the vehicle, refer to the precautions in the beginning of this section.
2. Remove the wheel.
3. Support the lower control with a floor jack.
4. Remove or disconnect the following:
   • Loosen the 2 lower ball joint set bolts
   • Cotter pin and nut from the tie rod
   • Tie rod from the ball joint bracket
   • Cotter pin and nut from the lower ball joint
   • Lower ball joint from the lower control arm
   • Both lower ball joint set bolts
   • Ball joint from the suspension

To install:
5. Install or connect the following:
   • Lower ball joint to the steering knuckle and lower control arm
   • Both lower ball joint set bolts; do not tighten the bolts at this time
   • Lower ball joint nut to hold the lower ball joint to the lower control arm. Tighten the nut to 80 ft. lbs. (110 Nm).
   • New cotter pin to the lower ball joint
   • Tie rod end to the ball joint bracket. Tighten the nut to 53 ft. lbs. (72 Nm).
   • New cotter pin to the tie rod end
   • Tighten the both lower ball joint set bolts to 116 ft. lbs. (160 Nm).
   • Wheel
6. Check the wheel alignment.

4WD MODELS

1. Before servicing the vehicle, refer to the precautions in the beginning of this section.
2. Remove or disconnect the following:
   • Wheel
   • Loosen the 4 lower ball joint set bolts
   • Cotter pin and nut from the tie rod
   • Tie rod from the ball joint bracket
   • Cotter pin and nut from the lower ball joint
   • Lower ball joint from the lower control arm
   • 4 lower ball joint set bolts
   • Ball joint from the suspension

To install:
3. Install or connect the following:
   • Lower ball joint to the steering knuckle and lower control arm
   • 4 lower ball joint set bolts; do not tighten the bolts at this time

- Lower ball joint-to-lower control arm nut. Tighten the nut to 112 ft. lbs. (152 Nm).
- New cotter pin to the lower ball joint
- Tie rod end to the ball joint bracket. Tighten the nut to 67 ft. lbs. (90 Nm).
- New cotter pin to the tie rod end
- Tighten the 2 lower ball joint set bolts to 83 ft. lbs. (113 Nm).
- Wheel

4. Check the wheel alignment.

Upper Control Arm

REMOVAL & INSTALLATION

2WD

TACOMA

1. Before servicing the vehicle, refer to the precautions in the beginning of this section.
2. Remove or disconnect the following:
   - Front wheel
   - Anti-lock Brake System (ABS) speed sensor and wire harness
   - Stabilizer bar link
   - Steering knuckle from the upper bar joint
3. Loosen the 2 bolts; then, remove the front and rear alignment adjusting shims.
4. Make note of the number and thickness of the front and rear shims.
5. Remove or disconnect the following:
   - Upper control arm
   - Upper ball joint from the arm

To install:
6. Install or connect the following:
   - Upper ball joint to the arm. Tighten the fasteners to 29 ft. lbs. (39 Nm).

➡**Do not lose the camber adjusting shims. Record the position and thickness of the camber shims so that these can be reinstalled to there original locations. Install the equal number and thickness of shims into there locations.**

- Upper control arm with the shims. Tighten the mounting bolts to 94 ft. lbs. (130 Nm).
- Steering knuckle to the upper ball joint
- Stabilizer bar link
- ABS speed sensor and wire harness
- Front wheel. Tighten the lug nuts to 83 ft. lbs. (110 Nm).

T-100

1. Before servicing the vehicle, refer to the precautions in the beginning of this section.
2. Remove or disconnect the following:
   - Front brake caliper
   - Anti-lock Brake System (ABS) speed sensor wire from the upper control arm, if equipped with ABS
3. Support the lower control arm with a jack.
4. Remove or disconnect the following:
   - Upper ball joint from the upper control arm
   - Bolts and camber adjusting shims
   - Upper control arm

➡**Do not lose the camber adjusting shims. Record the position and thickness of the camber shims so that these can be reinstalled to there original locations. Install the equal number and thickness of shims into there locations.**

To install:
5. Install or connect the following:
   - Upper control arm with the shims in there correct positions. Tighten the bolts to 71 ft. lbs. (96 Nm) and the nuts to 23 ft. lbs. (31 Nm).
   - ABS speed sensor and harness to the upper control arm
   - Brake caliper
   - Front wheel. Tighten the lug nuts.
6. Bleed the brake system.
7. Check and/or adjust the alignment.

4WD

4RUNNER

1. Before servicing the vehicle, refer to the precautions in the beginning of this section.
2. Remove or disconnect the following:
   - Shock and coil spring assembly
   - Anti-lock Brake System (ABS) speed sensor wire harness clamp
3. Disconnect the upper ball joint, as follows:
   - Cotter pins and loosen the nut
   - Upper ball joint from the control arm, using a ball joint separator
   - Support the steering knuckle
   - Nut
4. Detach the control arm, by removing the nut, bolt, washers and lowering the arm.

To install:
5. Install or connect the following:
   - Upper control arm with the washer, bolt and nut. Tighten the nut to 87 ft. lbs. (115 Nm).

- Upper ball joint to the control arm. Tighten the mounting nut to 80 ft. lbs. (105 Nm).
- New cotter pin
- ABS speed sensor wire harness clamp. Tighten it to 71 inch lbs. (8 Nm).
- Shock and coil spring assembly
6. Check and/or adjust the alignment.

TACOMA

1. Before servicing the vehicle, refer to the precautions in the beginning of this section.
2. Remove or disconnect the following:
   - Front wheel
   - Shock and coil spring assembly
   - Anti-lock Brake System (ABS) speed sensor wire harness clamp
3. Upper ball joint, as follows:
   - Cotter pins and loosen the nut
   - Upper ball joint from the control arm, using a ball joint separator
   - Support the steering knuckle
   - Nut
4. Detach the control arm, by removing the nut, bolt, washers and lowering the arm.

To install:
5. Install or connect the following:
   - Upper control arm with the washer, bolt and nut. Tighten the nut to 87 ft. lbs. (115 Nm).
   - Upper ball joint to the control arm. Tighten the mounting nut to 80 ft. lbs. (105 Nm).
   - New cotter pin
   - ABS speed sensor wire harness clamp. Tighten it to 71 inch lbs. (8 Nm).
   - Shock and coil spring assembly
6. Check and/or adjust the alignment.

T-100

1. Before servicing the vehicle, refer to the precautions in the beginning of this section.
2. Remove or disconnect the following:
   - Front wheels
   - Anti-lock Brake System (ABS) speed sensor wire harness clamp
   - Torsion bar
3. Upper ball joint from the steering knuckle, as follows:
   - Support the lower control arm with a jack
   - Upper control arm from the steering knuckle
   - Upper control arm from the frame

Turn to Section 5 for brake system applications

To install:

4. Install or connect the following:
   - Upper arm. Tighten the mounting bolts to 131 ft. lbs. (178 Nm).
   - Upper ball joint to the steering knuckle. Tighten the nut to 25 ft. lbs. (33 Nm).
   - Torsion bar
   - Front wheel
5. Check and/or adjust the alignment.

CONTROL ARM BUSHING REPLACEMENT

4Runner and 4WD Tacoma

1. Before servicing the vehicle, refer to the precautions in the beginning of this section.
2. Remove the upper control arm from the vehicle.
3. Pry up the bushing flange, using a chisel and a hammer.
4. Using tools 09613-26010, 09613-20060 and 09950-00020 and a shop press, remove the bushing.

To install:

5. Using tools 09223-00010, 09506-35010 and a shop press, press the new bushing into the upper control arm.
6. Install the upper control arm to the chassis. Torque the nuts to 87 ft. lbs. (115 Nm).
7. Check and/or adjust the alignment.

2WD Tacoma

1. Before servicing the vehicle, refer to the precautions in the beginning of this section.
2. Remove the upper control arm.

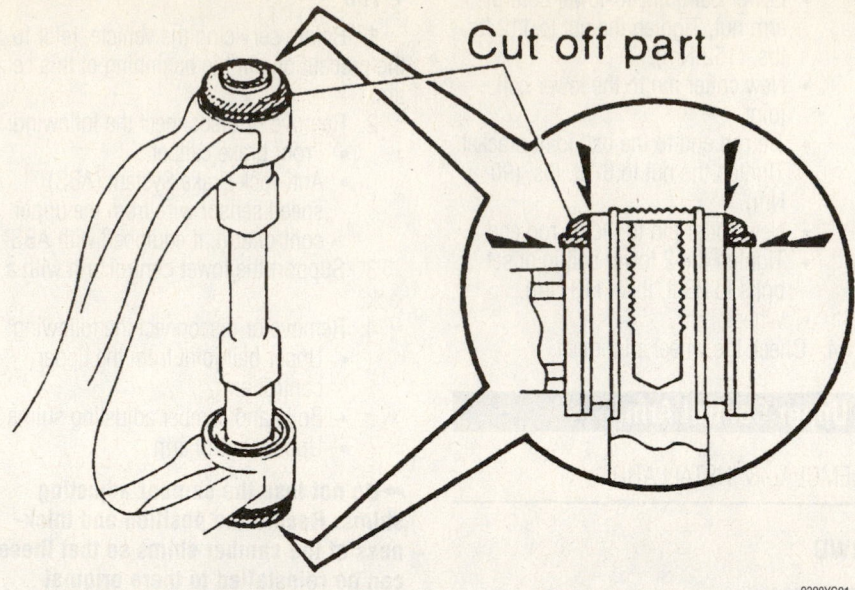

Cut off part

Cut the bushing flush with the upper control arm tube and shaft—Tacoma

3. Cut off the outer edges of the bushing so it is flush with arm tube and the shaft.

➡ **Be careful not to damage the edge of the arm tubes.**

4. Using a shop press with tool 09710-03031, press down the suspension arm tube until it touches tool 09710-03141.

➡ **Do not press the tube excessively.**

5. Temporarily install a 1.8–2.0 in. (45–50mm) bolt to the arm shaft on the other side.
6. Using a shop press with tool 09710-03141, remove the bushing from the arm shaft.

7. Repeat this procedure for the other bushing.

To install:

8. Using a shop press and tool 09710-03101, install the new bushing.
9. Place the arm shaft to the bushing.
10. Using a shop press and tool 09710-03101, install the other new bushing.

➡ **Pass the arm shaft through the bushing to make sure that the shaft turns freely and there is no axial play**

11. Install the upper control arm. Torque the lockbolts to 92 ft. lbs. (125 Nm).
12. Check and/or adjust the alignment.

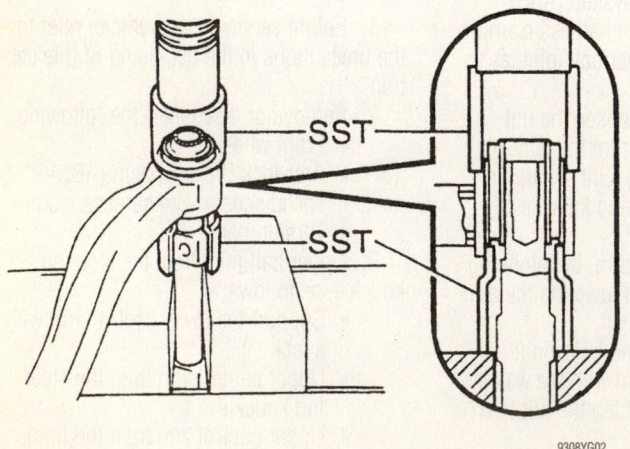

Position the upper control arm bushings with the tools—Tacoma

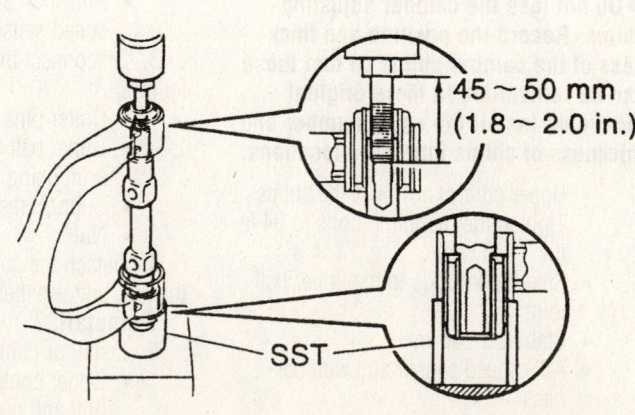

45 ~ 50 mm (1.8 ~ 2.0 in.)

Positioning the upper control arm tube and bolt—Tacoma

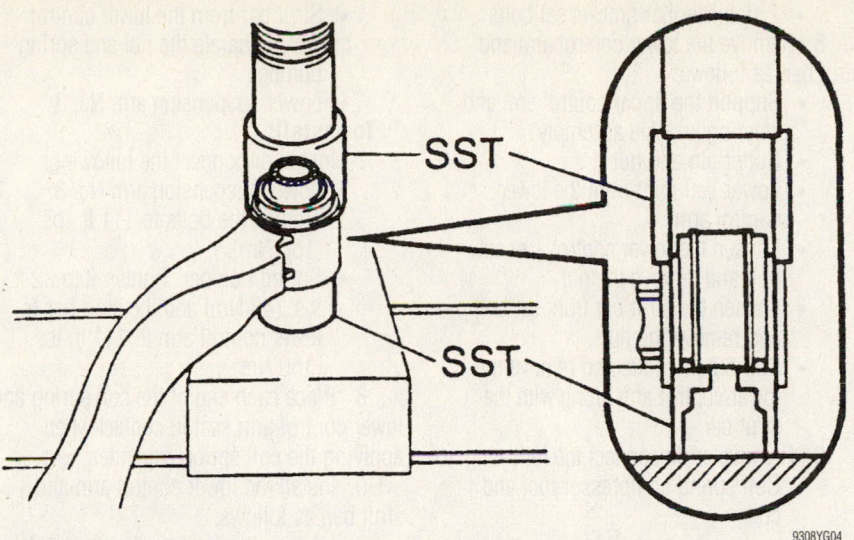

Removing the bushings from the upper control arm—Tacoma

9308YG04

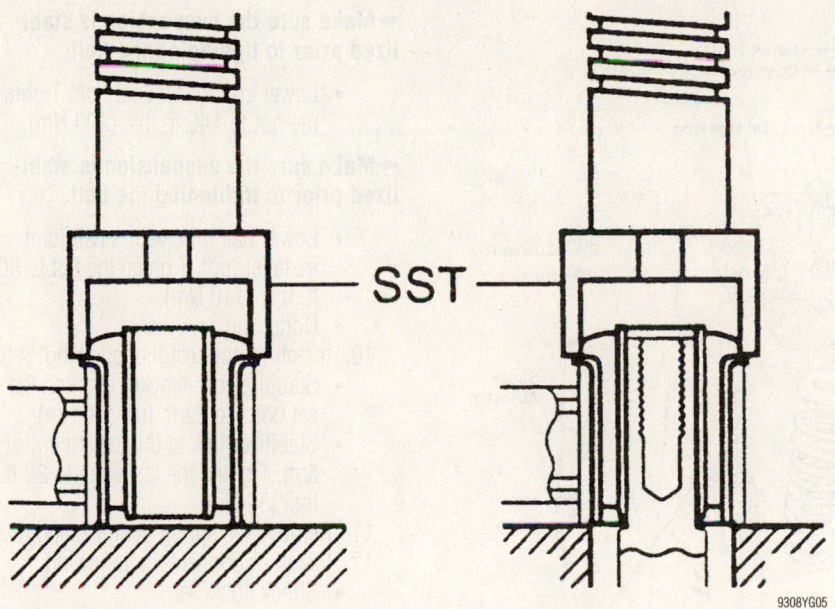

Installing the bushings to the upper control arm—Tacoma

9308YG05

T-100

2WD

1. Before servicing the vehicle, refer to the precautions in the beginning of this section.

2. Remove the upper control arm from the vehicle.

3. Using tool 09710-30020 and a shop press, press the bushings from the upper control arm.

To install:

4. Using tool 09710-30020 and a shop press, press the new bushings into the upper control arm.

5. Install the upper control arm.

6. Install the washer and bolt finger-tight.

7. Upper control arm-to-chassis bolts to 71 ft. lbs. (96 Nm).

8. After stabilizing the suspension, tighten the upper control arm shaft-to-control arm bolts to 93 ft. lbs. (126 Nm).

9. Check and/or adjust the alignment.

4WD

1. Before servicing the vehicle, refer to the precautions in the beginning of this section.

2. Remove the upper control arm from the vehicle.

3. Using a chisel and a hammer at the front bushing, loosen the staked portion of the nut and remove the nut

4. Using tool 09710-26011 and a shop press, remove the both bushings.

To install:

5. Using tool 09710-26011 and a shop press, both new bushings.

6. Install both new upper control arm shaft nuts. Torque the nuts to 166 ft. lbs. (226 Nm).

7. Install the upper control arm. Torque the upper control arm-to-chassis bolts to 131 ft. lbs. (178 Nm).

8. Check and/or adjust the alignment.

Lower Control Arm

REMOVAL & INSTALLATION

2WD

4RUNNER

1. Before servicing the vehicle, refer to the precautions in the beginning of this section.

2. Remove or disconnect the following:
   - Front wheel
   - Steering gear assembly
   - Stabilizer bar link
   - Shock absorber from the lower control arm

3. Support the upper control arm and the steering knuckle securely.

4. Remove or disconnect the following:
   - Cotter pin and nut from the lower ball joint
   - Lower ball joint from the control arm
   - Bolts, nuts, adjusting cams and lower control arm, by placing matchmarks on the front and rear adjusting cams
   - 2 spring bumpers, using tool SST 09922-10010

To install:

5. Install or connect the following:
   - 2 spring bumpers. Tighten the spring bumpers to 17 ft. lbs. (23 Nm).
   - Lower control arm and adjusting cams. Tighten the nuts and bolts to 96 ft. lbs. (130 Nm),
   - Lower ball joint to the control arm
   - Cotter pin and nut to the lower ball joint. Tighten the nut to 105 ft. lbs. (142 Nm).
   - Shock absorber to the lower control arm

- Stabilizer bar link
- Steering gear assembly
- Front wheel

6. Check and/or adjust the alignment.

TACOMA

1. Before servicing the vehicle, refer to the precautions in the beginning of this section.

2. Remove or disconnect the following:
   - Front wheel
   - Shock absorber

3. Compress the spring using a spring compressor, following the manufacturer's instructions.

4. Remove the stabilizer bar, as follows:
   - Stabilizer bar link from the lower control arm

- 2 stabilizer bar bracket set bolts

5. Remove the lower control arm and strut bar, as follows:
   - Support the upper control arm and steering knuckle assembly
   - Cotter pin and nut
   - Lower ball joint from the lower control arm
   - Loosen the lower control arm set bolt and remove the nut
   - Loosen the strut bar front set bolt and remove the nut
   - Pull out the bolts and remove the lower control arm along with the strut bar

6. Remove or disconnect the following:
   - Coil spring compressor tool and coil

- Strut bar from the lower control arm. Separate the nut and spring bumper.
- Lower suspension arm No. 3

To install:

7. Install or connect the following:
   - Lower suspension arm No. 3. Tighten the bolts to 111 ft. lbs. (150 Nm).
   - Spring bumper. Tighten it to 32 ft. lbs. (43 Nm) and the strut bar-to-lower control arm to 111 ft. lbs. (150 Nm).

8. Place each end of the coil spring and lower control arm seat in contact when applying the coil spring expander.

9. Install the lower control arm and strut bar, as follows:
   - Attach the strut bar front set bolt. Tighten the set bolt to 221 ft. lbs. (300 Nm).

➡ **Make sure the suspension is stabilized prior to tightening the bolt.**

   - Lower control arm set bolt. Tighten the nut to 148 ft. lbs. (200 Nm).

➡ **Make sure the suspension is stabilized prior to tightening the bolt.**

   - Lower ball joint with a ball joint installer tool. Tighten the nut to 80 ft. lbs. (110 Nm).
   - Cotter pin.

10. Install or connect the following:
    - Stabilizer bar bracket. Tighten the set bolts to 22 ft. lbs. (29 Nm).
    - Stabilizer link to the lower control arm. Tighten the fasteners to 29 ft. lbs. (39 Nm).

11. Remove the spring compressing tool.

12. Install or connect the following:
    - Shock absorber
    - Wheel. Tighten the lug nuts.

13. Check and/or adjust the alignment.

T-100

1. Before servicing the vehicle, refer to the precautions in the beginning of this section.

2. Remove or disconnect the following:
   - Wheel
   - Engine under cover
   - Torsion bar spring
   - Shock absorber from the lower control arm
   - Stabilizer bar from the lower control arm
   - Strut bar from the lower control arm
   - Lower ball joint from the lower control arm
   - Lower the control arm

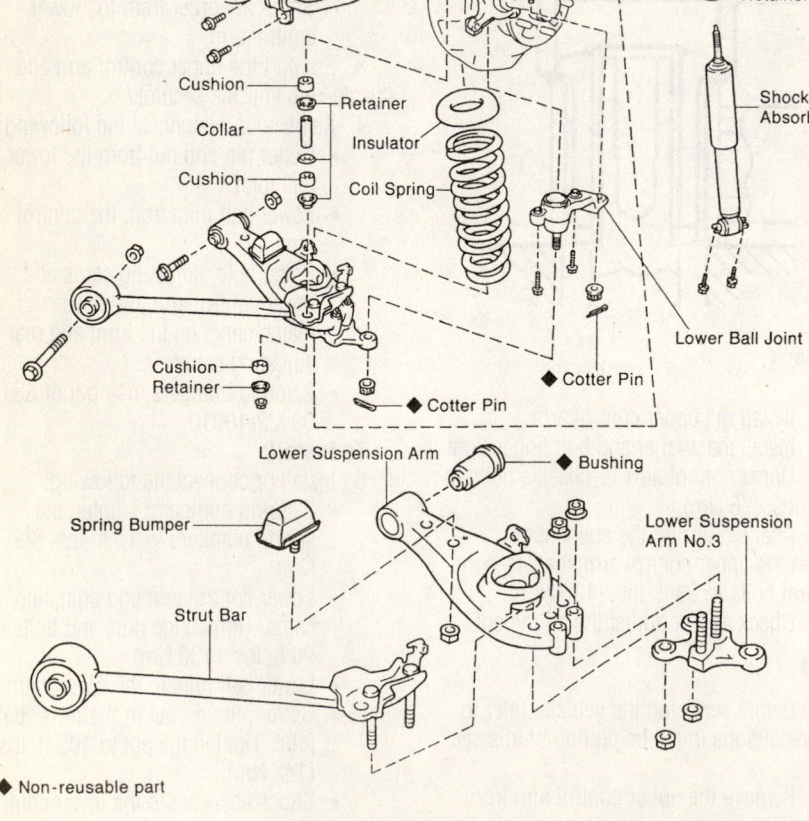

Retainer
Cushion
Retainer
Cushion
Stabilizer Bar
Cushion
Collar
Cushion
Cushion
Retainer
Lower Suspension Arm
Spring Bumper
Strut Bar
Tie Rod End
Retainer
Insulator
Coil Spring
Cushion
Retainer
◆ Cotter Pin
Bushing
Lower Suspension Arm No.3
Cushion
Retainer
Shock Absorber
Lower Ball Joint
◆ Cotter Pin
◆ Cotter Pin

◆ Non-reusable part

86828G01

Exploded view of the lower control arm and related front suspension components—Tacoma

To install:

3. Install or connect the following:
   - Lower control arm but do not tighten yet
   - Lower ball joint, strut bar and stabilizer bar to the control arm
   - Tighten the lower control arm bolt to 152 ft. lbs. (206 Nm).
   - Shock to the control arm
   - Torsion spring bar
   - Engine under cover
   - Wheel. Tighten the lug nuts to 76 ft. lbs. (103 Nm).

4. Check and/or adjust the alignment.

4WD

4RUNNER

1. Before servicing the vehicle, refer to the precautions in the beginning of this section.

2. Remove or disconnect the following:
   - Front wheel
   - Steering gear assembly
   - Stabilizer bar link
   - Shock absorber from lower control arm

3. Support the upper control and steering knuckle securely.

4. Remove or disconnect the following:
   - Cotter pin and nut from the lower ball joint
   - Lower ball joint from the lower control arm

5. Place matchmarks on the front and rear adjusting cams.

6. Remove or disconnect the following:
   - 2 bolts, nuts, adjusting cams and lower control arm
   - Spring bumpers with a special tool 09922-10010.

To install:

7. Install or connect the following:
   - Spring bumpers. Tighten to 17 ft. lbs. (23 Nm).
   - Lower control arm, placing it in the appropriate position with the matchmarks. Tighten the arm to 96 ft. lbs. (130 Nm).
   - Lower ball joint. Tighten the nut to 105 ft. lbs. (142 Nm).
   - Shock absorber to the lower control arm
   - Stabilizer bar link
   - Steering gear assembly
   - Front wheel. Tighten the lug nuts.

8. Check and/or adjust the alignment.

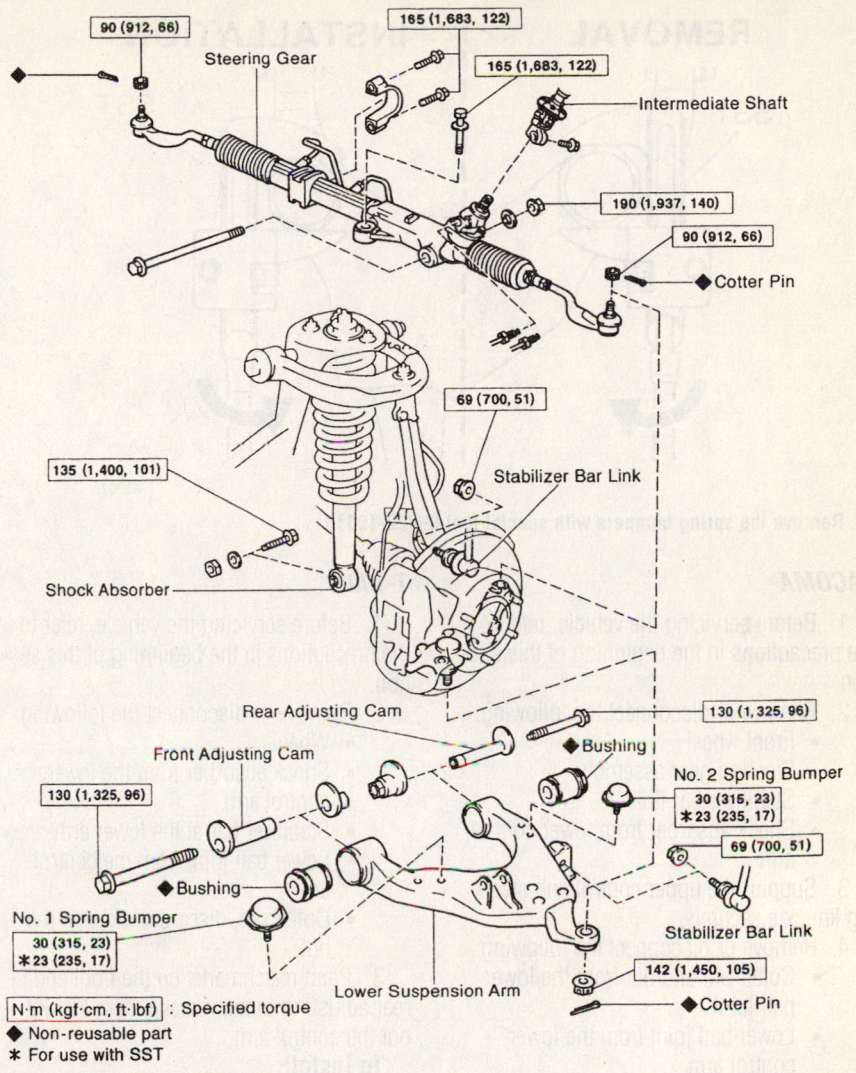

Exploded view of the lower control arm and associated components—4Runner

86828G20

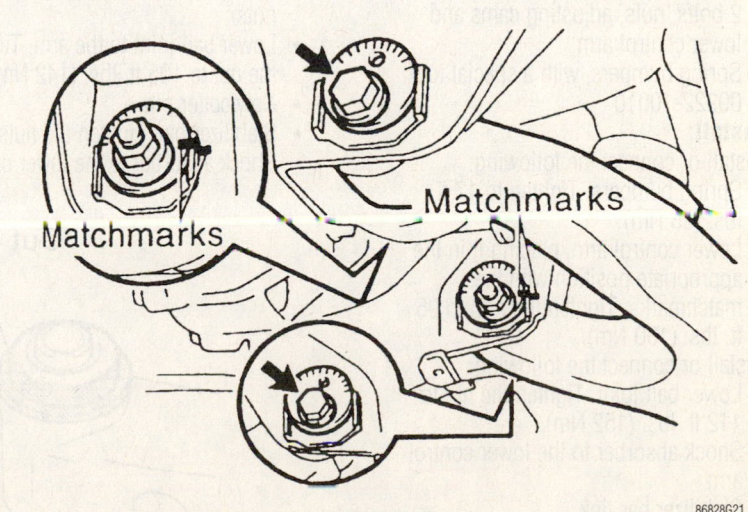

Place matchmarks on the front and rear adjusting cams

86828G21

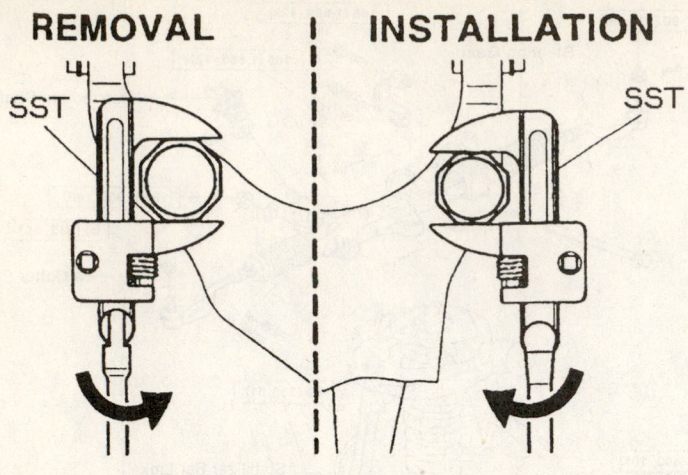

REMOVAL | **INSTALLATION**

SST | SST

86828G22

Remove the spring bumpers with special tool 09922-10010

TACOMA

1. Before servicing the vehicle, refer to the precautions in the beginning of this section.
2. Remove or disconnect the following:
   • Front wheel
   • Steering gear assembly
   • Stabilizer bar link
   • Shock absorber from lower control arm
3. Support the upper control and steering knuckle securely.
4. Remove or disconnect the following:
   • Cotter pin and nut from the lower ball joint
   • Lower ball joint from the lower control arm
5. Place matchmarks on the front and rear adjusting cams.
6. Remove or disconnect the following:
   • 2 bolts, nuts, adjusting cams and lower control arm
   • Spring bumpers, with a special tool 09922-10010

To install:

7. Install or connect the following:
   • Spring bumpers. Tighten to 17 ft. lbs. (23 Nm).
   • Lower control arm, placing it in the appropriate position with the matchmarks. Tighten the arm to 96 ft. lbs. (130 Nm).
8. Install or connect the following:
   • Lower ball joint. Tighten the nut to 112 ft. lbs. (152 Nm).
   • Shock absorber to the lower control arm
   • Stabilizer bar link
   • Steering gear assembly
   • Front wheel. Tighten the lug nuts.
9. Check and/or adjust the alignment.

T-100

1. Before servicing the vehicle, refer to the precautions in the beginning of this section.
2. Remove or disconnect the following:
   • Wheels
   • Shock absorber from the lower control arm
   • Stabilizer bar at the lower arm
   • Lower ball joint from the control arm.
   • Cotter pin, discard it. Loosen the nut.
3. Paint matchmarks on the front and rear adjusting cams, remove them and lift out the control arm.

To install:

4. Install or connect the following:
   • Lower arm and adjusting cams to the frame. Temporarily tighten the nuts.
   • Lower ball joint to the arm. Tighten the nut to 105 ft. lbs. (142 Nm.
   • New cotter pin
   • Stabilizer bar. Tighten the nuts
   • Shock absorber to the lower control

arm. Tighten to 101 ft. lbs. (137 Nm).
   • Wheels. Bounce the truck several times to set the suspension.
5. Align the matchmarks on the adjusting cams. Tighten the nuts to 145 ft. lbs. (196 Nm).
6. Check and/or adjust the alignment.

CONTROL ARM BUSHING REPLACEMENT

4Runner and 4WD Tacoma

1. Before servicing the vehicle, refer to the precautions in the beginning of this section.
2. Remove the lower control arm from the vehicle.
3. Pry up the bushing flange, using a chisel and a hammer.
4. Using tools 09613-26010, 09632-36010 and 09950-00020 and a shop press, remove the bushing.

To install:

5. Using tools 09316-20011, 09710-30021 and a shop press, press the new bushing into the lower control arm.
6. Install the lower control arm to the chassis. Torque the bolts to 96 ft. lbs. (130 Nm).
7. Check and/or adjust the alignment.

2WD Tacoma

The lower control arm is equipped with a single bushing.

1. Before servicing the vehicle, refer to the precautions in the beginning of this section.
2. Remove the lower control arm from the vehicle.
3. Cut off a portion of the bushing to expose the edge of the arm tube.
4. Position the lower control arm on a shop press with the cut side facing downward, resting on tool 09710-30021; then, press the bushing from the arm.

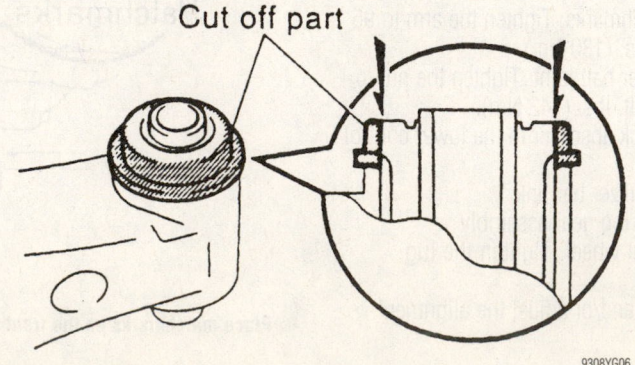

Cut off part

Cutting off part of the bushing—2WD Tacoma

9308YG06

To install:

5. Position a new bushing onto the lower control arm.

6. Position the lower control arm on a shop press, resting on tool 09710-30021.

7. Press the bushing into the lower control arm.

8. Install the lower control arm.

9. Check and/or adjust the alignment.

T-100

1. Before servicing the vehicle, refer to the precautions in the beginning of this section.

2. Remove the lower control arm.

3. Using tool 09726-27012 and a shop press or a large vise, press both bushings from the lower control arm.

To install:

4. Using tool 09726-27012 and a shop press or a large vise, press both new bushings into the lower control arm.

5. Install the lower control arm.

Wheel Bearings

ADJUSTMENT

The vehicles covered in this section are not equipped with adjustable wheel bearing.

REMOVAL & INSTALLATION

Front

T-100 2WD MODELS

1. Before servicing the vehicle, refer to the precautions in the beginning of this section.

2. Remove or disconnect the following:
- Wheel
- Disc brake caliper support bracket and support it with a wire
- Cap, cotter pin, lockcap and the nut from the spindle
- Hub and disc together with the outer bearing and thrust washer
- Grease seal from the disc/hub assembly
- Inner bearing from the assembly
- Wipe the grease from inside the disc/hub assembly

3. Using a brass drift, drive the outer bearing races from each side of the disc/hub assembly.

4. Place matchmarks on the disc and axle hub.

5. Remove the 6 bolts and separate the disc and axle hub.

6. Using solvent, clean all of the parts.

To install:

7. Install or connect the following:
- Align the marks on the disc and axle hub. Tighten the 6 bolts to 47 ft. lbs. (64 Nm).
- Outer races into the disc/hub assembly until they seat against the shoulder, using a bearing installation tool

8. Using multi-purpose grease, coat the area between the races and pack the bearings.

9. Install or connect the following:
- Inner bearing into the rear of the disc/hub assembly
- New grease seal into the rear of the disc/hub assembly until it is flush with the housing, using a bearing installation tool
- Disc/hub assembly onto the axle shaft, the outer bearing, the thrust washer and the adjusting nut

10. To adjust the bearing preload, perform the following:

a. Tighten the adjusting nut to 26 ft. lbs. (35 Nm).

b. Turn the disc/hub assembly 2–3 times, from the left to the right.

c. Loosen the adjusting nut until it can be turned by hand.

d. Attach a spring tension gauge to 1 lug on the hub assembly. Pull on the gauge and measure the frictional force. Frictional force should be 1–3 lbs. (5.0–14.0 N).

e. Adjust the preload by tightening the nut.

11. Measure the hub axial play. The limit is 0.0020 in. (0.05mm).

12. Install or connect the following:
- Locknut, cotter pin and the grease cap
- Disc brake caliper
- Wheel

T-100 4WD MODELS

1. Before servicing the vehicle, refer to the precautions in the beginning of this section.

2. Remove or disconnect the following:
- Front wheel
- Anti-lock Brake System (ABS) speed sensor from the steering knuckle, if equipped with ABS
- Both brake caliper support bracket bolts and wire the caliper aside

❋❋ WARNING

Do not allow the caliper to hang from the brake hose.

3. Remove the locking hub, as follows:
- Set the control handle to FREE
- Cover bolts and pull off the cover
- Center bolt with washer
- Mounting nuts and washer to the hub body
- Cone washer, using a brass bar and hammer to tap on the bolt heads
- Free wheel hub body and gasket

4. If not equipped with a free wheeling hub, remove the flange for the axle hub, as follows:
- Grease cap
- Flange bolt
- 6 flange mounting nuts
- 6 Cone washers, using a brass bar and hammer to tap on the bolt heads
- Flange, by installing 2 bolts and tighten them
- Flange gasket

5. Remove or disconnect the following:
- Lockwasher tabs, using a prybar
- Locknut, using SST 09607-60020
- Lockwasher and adjusting nut
- Claw washer
- Axle hub and rotor as an assembly
- Outer bearing with the hub and disc
- Oil seal and inner bearing, using a puller

6. If replacing bearing outer race, drive out the outer bearing race using a brass bar and hammer.

To install:

7. If removed, drive in a new bearing outer race using a installer.

8. Pack the bearings with MP grease. Coat the inside of the hub and cap with MP grease.

9. Install or connect the following:
- Inner bearing and oil seal. Coat the oil seal with MP grease.
- Hub on the spindle
- Outer bearing and claw washer

10. Adjust the preload, as follows::

a. Tighten the bearing adjusting nut to 43 ft. lbs. (59 Nm).

b. Turn the hub right and left 2–3 times and retighten.

c. Loosen the nut until it can be turned by hand.

d. Retighten the nut to 18 ft. lbs. (25 Nm).

e. Check the bearing preload with a spring scale. The preload should be 6.5–12.5 lbs. (28–56 N).

11. Install or connect the following:
- Lockwasher. Tighten the nut to 35 ft. lbs. (47 Nm).
- Check that there is no bearing end-play.
- Secure the locknut by bending 1 lockwasher tooth inward and another outward.

12. If not equipped with a free wheeling hub, install the flange, as follows:
- New gasket on the axle hub
- Flange to the axle hub
- 6 cone washers, plate washers and nuts. Tighten the 6 nuts to 23 ft. lbs. (31 Nm)
- Bolt. Tighten it to 13 ft. lbs. (18 Nm).
- Grease cap

13. If equipped with a free wheeling hub, install the hub, as follows:
- New gasket on the front axle hub
- Free wheeling hub body with the 6 cone washers. Tighten the 6 nuts to 23 ft. lbs. (31 Nm).
- Bolt with the washer. Tighten the bolt to 13 ft. lbs. (18 Nm).
- Apply multi purpose grease to the inner hub splines
- Set the control handle and clutch to the FREE position.
- New gasket on the cover
- Cover to the hub body with the follower pawl tabs aligned with the non-toothed portions of the hub body.
- Cover bolts. Tighten them to 84 inch lbs. (10 Nm).

14. Install the brake caliper support bracket to the steering knuckle. Tighten both bolts to 90 ft. lbs. (123 Nm).

15. Clean the threads of the bolts and steering knuckle.

16. Apply sealant to the bolt threads.

17. Install or connect the following:
- Knuckle arm with the brake line bracket to the steering knuckle. Tighten the bolts to 135 ft. lbs. (183 Nm).
- ABS speed sensor to the steering knuckle, if equipped with ABS
- Front wheel

18. Check the ABS speed sensor signal.

4RUNNER

1. Before servicing the vehicle, refer to the precautions in the beginning of this section.

2. Remove or disconnect the following:
- Front wheels

- Shock absorber
- Grease cap

3. On 4WD, remove the halfshaft, as follows:
- Cotter pin and lockcap
- Locknut, while applying the brakes

4. Remove or disconnect the following:
- Anti-lock Brake System (ABS) speed sensor and wiring harness clamp from the steering knuckle, if equipped with ABS
- Brake line bracket from the steering knuckle
- Front brake caliper and rotor
- 4 bolts and the lower ball joint

5. Remove the steering knuckle with the axle hub, as follows:
- Cotter pin and loosen the nut
- Steering knuckle, using SST 09950-40010

6. Clamp the axle hub in a soft jaw vise.

7. Remove or disconnect the following:
- Grease cap, for 2WD
- Inside oil seal, for 4WD
- 4 bolts and shift the brake dust cover towards the hub side
- Axle hub from the steering knuckle, using SST 09710-30021
- Bearing spacer and Anti-lock Brake System (ABS) speed sensor rotor/spacer
- Oil seal (outside) from the steering knuckle, using a flat pry bar

8. Remove the bearing from the steering knuckle, as follows:
- Snapring
- Bearing from the steering knuckle, using SST 09950-60020 and 09950-70010 and a press

To install:

9. Install a new bearing, as follows:
- New bearing to the steering knuckle, using SST 09527-17011 and 09950-60020 and a press
- New snapring

10. Install or connect the following:
- New outside oil seal, using SST 09223-15030 and a plastic hammer. Coat MP grease to the oil seal lip.
- Brake dust cover to the steering knuckle. Tighten the 4 bolts to 13 ft. lbs. (18 Nm).
- Axle hub to the steering knuckle, using a press
- ABS speed sensor rotor/spacer.

❊❊ WARNING

Be careful not to scratch the serration of the speed sensor rotor.

- Bearing spacer, using a press
- Grease cap, if removed
- New inside oil seal, if removed, using SST 09527-17011 and a plastic hammer
- Steering knuckle with the axle hub. Tighten the nut to 80 ft. lbs. (108 Nm).
- New cotter pin
- Lower ball joint. Tighten the 4 bolts to 59 ft. lbs. (80 Nm).
- Rotor and the caliper. Tighten the caliper bolts to 90 ft. lbs. (123 Nm).
- Brake line bracket to the steering knuckle. Tighten the fasteners to 21 ft. lbs. (28 Nm).
- ABS speed sensor and wiring harness clamp to the steering knuckle, if removed. Tighten the bolts to 72 inch lbs. (8 Nm).
- Halfshaft, if disconnected. Tighten the nut to 174 ft. lbs. (235 Nm).
- Grease cap
- Shock absorber
- Front wheel
- Negative battery cable

2WD TACOMA

1. Before servicing the vehicle, refer to the precautions in the beginning of this section.

2. Remove or disconnect the following:
- Brake caliper support bracket, by removing the 2 bolts. Support the brake caliper with a piece of wire. Do not allow the caliper to hang from the brake hose.
- Cotter pin, lockcap, nut and the claw washer from the axle hub and disc
- Axle hub with the disc from the steering knuckle.

❊❊ WARNING

Do not drop the outer bearing when removing the hub.

- Inner oil seal
- Inner bearing
- Bearing outer races, using SST 09527-17011, a brass bar and a hammer

3. If it is necessary to separate the hub and rotor, place matchmarks on the hub and rotor.

4. Remove the 5 bolts and remove the hub from the rotor.

To install:

5. Install or connect the following:
- New bearing races, using SST 09527-17011 and a press.

- Hub to the rotor. Tighten the 5 bolts to 47 ft. lbs. (64 Nm).
6. Clean all parts.
7. Repack the bearings with multi purpose grease and apply the same grease to the outer bearings.
8. Install or connect the following:
   - Inner bearing and seal to the hub. Coat the inner seal with multi purpose grease.
   - Outer bearing to the hub
   - Hub to the steering knuckle
   - Axle hub to the steering knuckle claw washer and nut
9. To adjust the bearing preload, perform the following:
   a. Tighten the adjusting nut to 25 ft. lbs. (34 Nm).
   b. Turn the disc/hub assembly 2–3 times, from the left to the right.
   c. Loosen the adjusting nut until it can be turned by hand.
   d. Attach a spring tension gauge to 1 lug on the hub assembly. Pull on the gauge and measure the frictional force, which should be 1–4 lbs. (6–18 N).
   e. Adjust the preload by tightening the nut.
10. Measure the hub axial play. Limit 0.0020 in. (0.05mm).
11. Install or connect the following:
   - Locknut, cotter pin and the grease cap
   - Disc brake caliper. Tighten the 2 bolts to 80 ft. lbs. (108 Nm).
   - Wheel

4WD TACOMA

1. Before servicing the vehicle, refer to the precautions in the beginning of this section.
2. Remove the wheel.
3. If not equipped with a FREE wheeling hub, disconnect the halfshaft from the steering knuckle, as follows:
   - Grease cap
   - Cotter pin and lockcap from the halfshaft
   - Locknut from the halfshaft, while having an assistant apply the brakes
4. If equipped with FREE wheeling hub, remove the free wheel hub, as follows:
   - Set the control handle to FREE
   - Cover bolts and pull off the cover
   - Center bolt with washer
   - Mounting nuts and washer to the hub body
   - Cone washer, using a brass bar and hammer to tap on the bolt heads

- Free wheel hub body and gasket
- Snapring from the end of the half-shaft, using a snapring expander
- Anti-lock Brake System (ABS) speed sensor from the steering knuckle, if equipped with ABS
5. Remove or disconnect the following:
   - Brake hose from the steering knuckle
   - Both brake caliper support bracket bolts and wire the caliper aside.

✳✳ WARNING

Do not allow the caliper to hang from the brake hose.

- Rotor
- 4 bolts and the lower ball joint from the steering knuckle
- Cotter pin and nut to the upper control arm
- Steering knuckle from the upper control arm
- Steering knuckle

➡ **If it is difficult to remove the half-shaft from the steering knuckle, use a rubber hammer and tap the halfshaft from the steering knuckle.**

6. Place the axle hub in a soft jaw vise.
7. Remove or disconnect the following:
   - Inside oil seal, using a prybar
8. If equipped with free wheeling hubs, remove the locknut and ABS speed sensor rotor/spacer, as follows:
   - Loosen the staked part of the locknut, using a hammer and chisel
   - Locknut from the hub, using SST 09318-12010
   - ABS speed sensor rotor/spacer.

✳✳ WARNING

Take care not to scratch the serration of the speed sensor rotor.

9. Remove the axle hub from the steering knuckle, as follows:
   - 4 backing plate bolts and shift the plate towards the hub side
   - Press the axle hub from the steering knuckle
   - Bearing spacer and ABS speed sensor rotor/spacer, if not equipped with free wheeling hubs
10. Remove or disconnect the following:
    - Outside oil seal from the steering knuckle
    - Snapring from the hub, using a snapring pliers

- Bearing from the steering knuckle, using SST 09608-35014 and a press

To install:
11. Install or connect the following:
    - New bearing to the steering knuckle, using SST 09527-17011 and a press
    - Snapring to the hub, using a snapring pliers
    - New outside oil seal, using SST 09223-15030, 09527-17011 and a plastic hammer. Coat the multi purpose grease to the oil seal lip.
    - Backing plate. Tighten the 4 bolts to 13 ft. lbs. (18 Nm).
    - Axle hub to the steering knuckle, using SST 09649-17010 and a press
    - ABS speed sensor rotor/spacer
    - New locknut to the hub, if equipped with free wheeling hubs. Tighten the nut to 203 ft. lbs. (274 Nm). Stake the nut with a chisel and hammer.
    - Bearing spacer with SST 09950-60010 and a press, if not equipped with free wheeling hubs
    - New inside oil seal, using SST 09527-17011 and a plastic hammer. Coat the multi purpose grease to the oil seal lip.
    - Steering knuckle to the halfshaft
    - Steering knuckle to the lower ball joint by installing the 4 bolts. Do not tighten the bolts at this time.
    - Upper ball joint to the steering knuckle
    - Upper ball joint nut. Tighten the nut to 80 ft. lbs. (105 Nm).
    - New cotter pin
    - Tighten the lower ball joint to steering knuckle bolts to 59 ft. lbs. (80 Nm).
    - Brake rotor
    - Caliper support bracket to the steering knuckle. Tighten both bolts to 90 ft. lbs. (123 Nm).
    - Brake hose clamp to the steering knuckle. Tighten the bolt to 13 ft. lbs. (18 Nm).
    - ABS speed sensor and wiring harness to the steering knuckle, if equipped with ABS
    - Spacer and snapring to the half-shaft, using a snapring expander
12. If equipped with a free wheeling hub, install the hub, as follows:
    - New gasket on the front axle hub

- Free wheeling hub body with the 6 cone washers. Tighten the 6 nuts to 23 ft. lbs. (31 Nm).
- Bolt with the washer. Tighten the bolt to 13 ft. lbs. (18 Nm).
- Apply multi purpose grease to the inner hub splines
- Set the control handle and clutch to the FREE position
- New gasket on the cover
- Cover to the hub body with the follower pawl tabs aligned with the non-toothed portions of the hub body.
- Tighten the cover bolts to 84 inch lbs. (10 Nm).

13. If not equipped with a free wheeling hub, install the halfshaft to the steering knuckle, as follows:
- Locknut to the halfshaft. Tighten the nut to 174 ft. lbs. (235 Nm).
- Lockcap and cotter pin to the halfshaft
- Grease cab

14. Install or connect the following:
- Strut. Tighten the strut-to-lower control arm nut to 101 ft. lbs. (135 Nm) and the 3 upper nuts to 47 ft. lbs. (64 Nm)
- Front wheels

Rear

1. Before servicing the vehicle, refer to the precautions in the beginning of this section.
2. Remove or disconnect the following:
- Rear wheel, brake drum and brake assembly
- Anti-lock Brake System (ABS) sensor from the rear axle assembly, if equipped
- Brake line and parking brake cable
- 4 backing plate mounting nuts and pull the axle shaft from the housing
- Bearing retainer and ABS sensor rotor (differential side) by threading a nut over the bolts and lightly tapping with a hammer.

➡**Do not reuse the nuts removed from the vehicle.**

3. Grind the ABS sensor retainer and rotor surfaces, then chisel them out.
4. Place washers and 4 new nuts over the serration bolts and tighten the bolts to install the serration bolts to the backing plate.
5. Remove or disconnect the following:
- 4 nuts from the serration bolts
- Snapring

- Axle shaft from the backing plate
- Rear axle shaft and bearing retainer from the backing plate, using SST 09521-25011

➡**After the axle is removed, disconnect the service tool.**

- Outer oil seal
- Rear axle bearing
- Inner oil seal

To install:
6. Install or connect the following:
- Inner oil seal, with the seal driver
- Rear axle bearing and outer seal
- Axle shaft and new bearing retainer into the backing plate
- New snapring
7. Bleed the braking system and check for leaks.
8. Install or connect the following:
- New ABS speed sensor rotor and retainer (differential side)
- Rear axle shaft assembly
- Brake line and parking brake cable
- ABS sensor into the rear axle housing
- Rear brake assembly
- Brake drum and rear wheel

TOYOTA AND LEXUS

Lexus-RX 300 • **Toyota**-Previa • Rav4 • Sienna

PRECAUTIONS

Before servicing any vehicle, please be sure to read all of the following precautions, which deal with personal safety, prevention of component damage, and important points to take into consideration when servicing a motor vehicle:

• Never open, service or drain the radiator or cooling system when the engine is hot; serious burns can occur from the steam and hot coolant.

• Observe all applicable safety precautions when working around fuel. Whenever servicing the fuel system, always work in a well-ventilated area. Do not allow fuel spray or vapors to come in contact with a spark, open flame or excessive heat (a hot drop light, for example). Keep a dry chemical fire extinguisher near the work area. Always keep fuel in a container specifically designed for fuel storage; also, always properly seal fuel containers to avoid the possibility of fire or explosion. Refer to the additional fuel system precautions later in this section.

• Fuel injection systems often remain pressurized, even after the engine has been turned **OFF**. The fuel system pressure must be relieved before disconnecting any fuel lines. Failure to do so may result in fire and/or personal injury.

• Brake fluid often contains polyglycol ethers and polyglycols. Avoid contact with the eyes and wash your hands thoroughly after handling brake fluid. If you do get brake fluid in your eyes, flush your eyes with clean, running water for 15 minutes. If eye irritation persists, or if you have taken brake fluid internally, IMMEDIATELY seek medical assistance.

• The EPA warns that prolonged contact with used engine oil may cause a number of skin disorders, including cancer! You should make every effort to minimize your exposure to used engine oil. Protective gloves should be worn when changing oil. Wash your hands and any other exposed skin areas as soon as possible after exposure to used engine oil. Soap and water, or waterless hand cleaner should be used.

• All new vehicles are now equipped with an air bag system. The system must be disabled before performing service on or around system components, steering column, instrument panel components, wiring and sensors. Failure to follow safety and disabling procedures could result in accidental air bag deployment, possible personal injury and unnecessary system repairs.

• Always wear safety goggles when working with, or around, the air bag system. When carrying a non-deployed air bag, be sure the bag and trim cover are pointed away from your body. When placing a non-deployed air bag on a work surface, always face the bag and trim cover upward, away from the surface. This will reduce the motion of the module if it is accidentally deployed. Refer to the additional air bag system precautions later in this section.

• Clean, high quality brake fluid from a sealed container is essential to the safe and proper operation of the brake system. You should always buy the correct type of brake fluid for your vehicle. If the brake fluid becomes contaminated, completely flush the system with new fluid. Never reuse any brake fluid. Any brake fluid that is removed from the system should be discarded. Also, do not allow any brake fluid to come in contact with a painted surface; it will damage the paint.

• Never operate the engine without the proper amount and type of engine oil; doing so WILL result in severe engine damage.

• Timing belt maintenance is extremely important! Many models utilize an interference type, non-freewheeling engine. If the timing belt breaks, the valves in the cylinder head may strike the pistons, causing potentially serious (also time consuming and expensive) engine damage. Refer to the maintenance interval charts in the front of this manual for the recommended replacement interval for the timing belt, and to the timing belt section for belt replacement and inspection.

• Disconnecting the negative battery cable on some vehicles may interfere with the functions of the on-board computer system(s) and may require the computer to undergo a relearning process once the negative battery cable is reconnected.

• When servicing drum brakes, only disassemble and assemble one side at a time, leaving the remaining side intact for reference.

ENGINE REPAIR

Distributor

The Sienna, RX 300 and the 1998–01 RAV4 models are equipped with a distiributorless ignition system.

REMOVAL

2.0L (3S-FE) engine
1997 MODELS

1. Before servicing the vehicle, refer to the precautions in the beginning of this section.

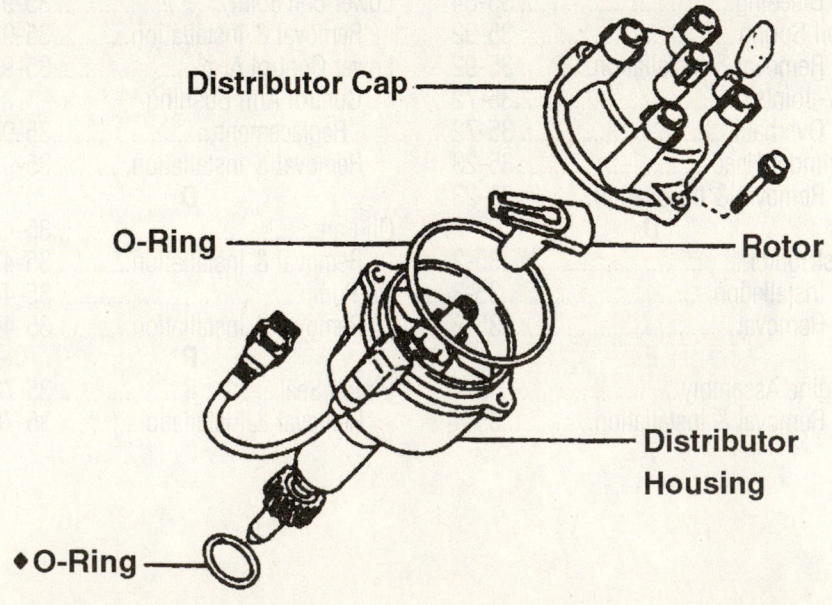

Exploded view of the distributor assembly—2.0L (3S-FE) engine

Distributor Cap

O-Ring

Rotor

Distributor Housing

◆O-Ring

◆Non-resuable part

7924ZG01

2. Remove or disconnect the following:
- Negative battery cable
- Air cleaner cap assembly
- Electrical connector to the distributor
- High tension cable from the coil
- Spark plug wires from the distributor.
- Distributor cap

3. Matchmark the rotor to the distributor housing and the distributor housing to the engine block. This will aid in correct positioning of the distributor during installation.

4. Remove or disconnect the following:
- Distributor hold-down clamp bolt
- Distributor

2.4L (2TZ-FE) Engine

1. Before servicing the vehicle, refer to the precautions in the beginning of this section.
2. Remove or disconnect the following:
- Exhaust pipe heat insulator
- Spark plug wires
- Distributor wiring and ventilation hoses
- Cap and packing

3. Set the No. 1 cylinder to Top Dead Center (TDC) of the compression stroke. Install the service bolt and nut into the equipment driveshaft to turn the crankshaft pulley until the timing mark is aligned with the **0** mark on the timing chain cover.

4. Turn the crankshaft 1 turn if the rotor is not facing No. 1 spark plug wire.

➡**Check that the rotor direction is as shown, if not, turn the drive pulley 1 complete revolution.**

5. Place markings on the distributor housing, and rotor positions.
6. Remove or disconnect the following:
- 2 hold-down bolts
- Distributor from the engine

INSTALLATION

2.0L (3S-FE) engine

TIMING NOT DISTURBED

1. Install or connect the following:
- New O-ring to the distributor and lubricate it with engine oil
- Distributor into the engine, by aligning the matchmarks
- Distributor drive, engage it with the slit in the intake camshaft
- Distributor hold-down clamp, the cap, the high tension wire, the

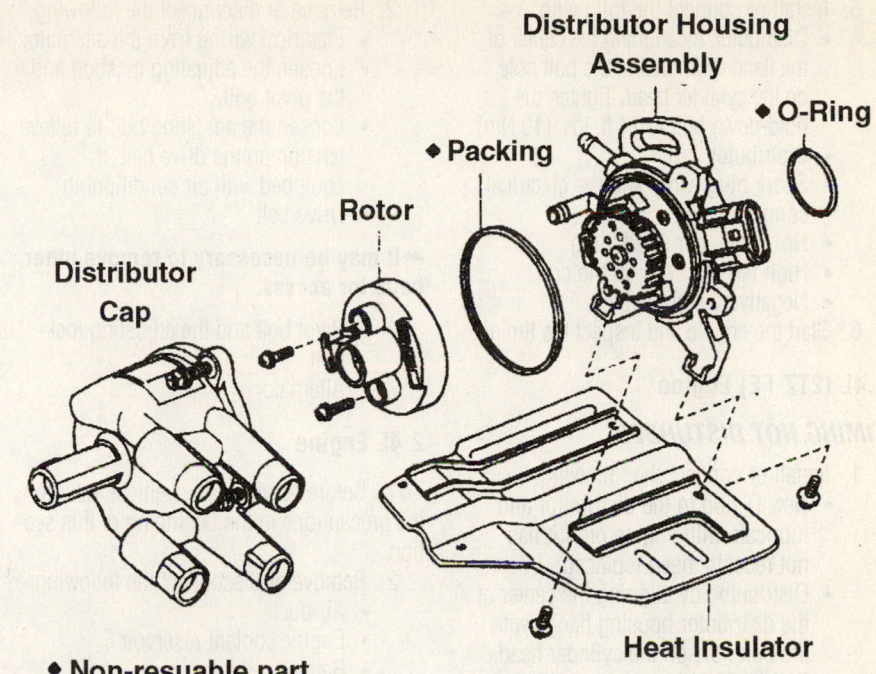

Distributor Housing Assembly
◆ **O-Ring**
◆ **Packing**
Rotor
Distributor Cap
Heat Insulator
◆ **Non-resuable part**

7924ZG03

Exploded view of the distributor assembly—2.4L (2TZ-FE) Engine

spark plug wires and the electrical connector
- Air cleaner cap assembly
- Negative battery cable

2. Start the engine. Check and adjust the ignition timing.

TIMING DISTURBED

1. Install a new O-ring to the distributor and lubricate it with engine oil.
2. Remove the No. 1 cylinder spark plug.

3. Position the engine, as follows:
a. Place a finger or compression gauge over the spark plug hole.
b. Turn the crankshaft until compression starts to build up. Continue turning the crankshaft until the crankshaft pulley groove align with the timing mark **0** of the timing chain. The position of the slit of the intake camshaft should be as shown.

4. On the distributor, align the cutout of the coupling with the line on the housing.

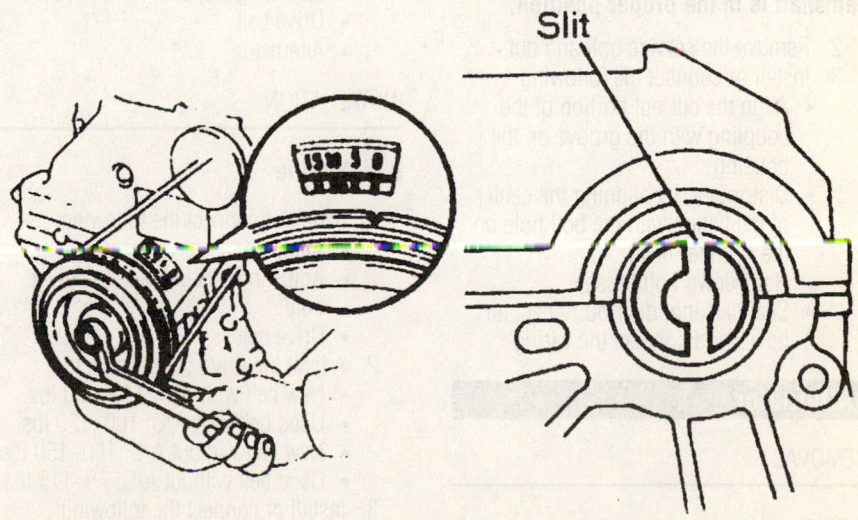

Slit

7924ZG02

Crankshaft TDC mark and intake camshaft slit position—2.0L (3S-FE) engine

5. Install or connect the following:
   - Distributor, by aligning the center of the flange with that of the bolt hole on the cylinder head. Tighten the hold-down bolt to 14 ft. lbs. (19 Nm).
   - Distributor cap
   - Spark plug wires and the electrical connector
   - No. 1 cylinder spark plug
   - High tension wire on the coil
   - Negative battery cable
6. Start the engine and inspect the timing.

2.4L (2TZ-FE) Engine

TIMING NOT DISTURBED

1. Install or connect the following:
   - New O-ring to the distributor and lubricate with engine oil if it has not recently been replaced
   - Distributor, by aligning the center of the distributor housing flange with the bolt hole on the cylinder head.
   - Distributor drive, engage with the oil pump's driveshaft
   - Distributor hold-down clamp, the cap, the high tension wire, the primary wire or the electrical connector and the vacuum line(s)
   - Spark plugs cables
   - Negative battery cable
2. Reset all digital components such as the radio.

TIMING DISTURBED

1. Turn the drive pulley clockwise and position the slit of the exhaust camshaft as shown .

➡**Be sure the slit in the exhaust camshaft is in the proper position.**

2. Remove the service bolt and nut.
3. Install or connect the following:
   - Align the cut out portion of the coupling with the groove on the housing
   - Distributor, by aligning the center of the flange with the bolt hole on the cylinder head
   - Hold-down bolt loosely
   - Seal packing, distributor cap, air hoses and connect the wiring

Alternator

REMOVAL

2.0L Engine

1. Before servicing the vehicle, refer to the precautions in the beginning of this section.

2. Remove or disconnect the following:
   - Electrical wiring from the alternator
   - Loosen the adjusting lockbolt and the pivot bolt.
   - Loosen the adjusting bolt to relieve tension on the drive belt, if equipped with air conditioning
   - Drive belt

➡**It may be necessary to remove other belts for access.**

   - Pivot bolt and the adjusting lockbolt
   - Alternator

2.4L Engine

1. Before servicing the vehicle, refer to the precautions in the beginning of this section.

2. Remove or disconnect the following:
   - Air duct
   - Engine coolant reservoir
   - Battery
   - Loosen the No. 1 idler pulley nut and adjusting bolt
   - Drive belt
   - Alternator electrical connectors
   - Alternator

3.0L Engine

1. Before servicing the vehicle, refer to the precautions in the beginning of this section.

2. Remove or disconnect the following:
   - Alternator electrical connectors
   - Wiring harness from the clip
   - Pivot bolt
   - Plate washer
   - Adjusting lockbolt
   - Drive belt
   - Alternator

INSTALLATION

2.0L Engine

1. Install or connect the following:
   - Alternator
   - Adjusting lockbolt and the pivot bolt
   - Drive belt
2. Adjust the drive belt tension to:
   - New belt with A/C: 140–190 lbs.
   - Used belt with A/C: 100–120 lbs.
   - New belt without A/C: 100–150 lbs.
   - Used belt without A/C: 75–115 lbs.
3. Install or connect the following:
   - Tighten the pivot bolt to 38 ft. lbs. (52 Nm).
   - Tighten the adjusting lockbolt to 13 ft. lbs. (18 Nm).

   - Electrical wiring to the alternator

2.4L Engine

Install or connect the following:
   - Alternator. Tighten the alternator bolts to 37 ft. lbs. (50 Nm) and the stay bolts to 20 ft. lbs. (26 Nm).
   - Alternator electrical connectors
   - Drive belt. Adjust the belt tension to 160–180 lbs. for a new belt or 115–135 lbs. for a used belt.
   - Tighten the No. 1 idler pulley nut and adjusting bolt
   - Battery
   - Engine coolant reservoir
   - Air duct

3.0L Engine

Install or connect the following:
   - Alternator
   - Drive belt. Tension the belt to 170–180 lbs. for a new belt or 95–135 lbs. for a used belt.
   - Adjusting lockbolt. Tighten the bolt to 13 ft. lbs. (18 Nm).
   - Plate washer
   - Pivot bolt. Tighten the bolt to 41 ft. lbs. (56 Nm).
   - Wiring harness from the clip
   - Alternator electrical connectors

Ignition Timing

ADJUSTMENT

Ignition timing is controlled by the ECM and is not adjustable.

Engine Assembly

REMOVAL & INSTALLATION

RAV4

1. Before servicing the vehicle, refer to the precautions in the beginning of this section.
2. Relieve the fuel system pressure.
3. Remove or disconnect the following:

   - Negative battery cable
   - Battery
   - Hood
   - Engine undercover
4. Drain the engine coolant and oil.
5. Drain the transaxle assembly.
6. Remove or disconnect the following:
   - Air cleaner and case
   - Accelerator cable from the throttle body, bracket and clamps

7. Disconnect and remove the engine wire from the No. 2 relay block, as follows:
- No. 2 relay block from the body by removing the 2 bolts
- Upper cover to the relay block
- Electrical connectors
- Engine wire, by removing the 2 nuts
- Charcoal canister
- Alternator
- Upper and lower radiator hoses
- Water inlet from the engine by removing the 2 nuts
- Heater hoses
- Fuel hose, by placing a rag under the fuel inlet hose
- Starter by disconnecting the electrical connectors and 2 bolts, if equipped with manual transmission
- Ground cable from the transaxle by removing the bolt
- Clutch release cylinder from the transaxle, if equipped with manual transmission
- Transaxle control cables (2 cable for manual transmission or 1 for automatic transmission) from the transaxle.
- Transaxle cable from the front suspension crossmember and engine mounting centermember by removing the 2 bolts, if equipped with an automatic transmission
- Transaxle oil cooler hoses, if equipped with an automatic transmission or 4WD with manual transmission

8. Detach the following:
- Vapor pressure sensor connector
- Igniter connector
- Ignition coil connector
- Noise filter connector
- Ignition coil wire
- Manifold Absolute Pressure (MAP) sensor connector
- MAP sensor vacuum hose from the gas filter on the intake manifold
- Brake booster hose from the intake manifold
- Differential lock control solenoid connector, if equipped with a 4WD manual transmission
- Ground strap from cowl

9. Detach the engine wire from the passenger compartment, as follows:
- Right-hand scuff plate
- Right-hand side trim
- Right-hand carpet center cover
- 2 ECM connectors

- 2 connectors from the bracket connectors
- No. 4 junction block connector
- Wire clamp from the bracket
- Engine wire from the passenger compartment

10. Remove the front exhaust pipe, as follows:
- 3 nuts and the front exhaust pipe from the exhaust manifold, using a 14mm deep socket wrench; discard the gasket
- 2 bolts and 2 nuts holding the front exhaust pipe to the catalytic converter
- Front exhaust pipe and 2 gaskets

11. Remove the compressor from the engine and suspend the compressor securely.

➡ **It is not necessary to remove the air conditioning compressor lines in order to remove the engine.**

12. Remove or disconnect the following:
- Driveshaft, if equipped with 4WD
- Halfshaft
- Sway bar

13. Remove the front suspension crossmember assembly, as follows:
- 2 centermember set nuts holding the centermember to the middle of the crossmember.
- 2 rack and pinion assembly set bolts/nuts from the crossmember. Securely suspend the steering gear assembly.
- Catalytic converter with pipe from the ring
- Support the suspension crossmember with a jack
- 6 bolts from the suspension crossmember
- Suspension crossmember with the lower suspension arms

14. Remove the engine mounting centermember, as follows:
- 2 bolts holding the centermember to the front engine mounting insulator
- 2 bolts holding the centermember to the body
- Centermember

15. Disconnect the power steering pump from the engine, as follows:
- 2 vacuum hoses from the steering pump
- Adjusting bolt for the power steering unit. Loosen the pivot bolt to the power steering pump and remove

the drive belt. Use Torque Wrench Adapter tool 09249-63010 and a deep socket to loosen the pivot bolt.
- Power steering pump from the engine by removing the 3 bracket bolts

16. Install a engine hanger to the engine.

17. Attach the engine sling device to the engine hangers.

18. Remove or disconnect the following:
- Left-hand engine mounting bracket from the mounting insulator by removing the 2 nuts and 2 bolts
- Ground connector next to the right-hand engine mount
- Right-hand engine mounting bracket from the mounting insulator by removing the bolt and 2 nuts

19. Lower the engine and transaxle and at the same time, raise the vehicle to gain clearance to the remove the engine.

20. Place the assembly on a stand and separate the engine from the transaxle.

To install:

21. Install or connect the following:
- Engine and transaxle assembly
- Left-hand engine mounting bracket to the mounting insulator. Tighten both nuts/bolts to 47 ft. lbs. (64 Nm).
- Bolt and 2 nuts to hold the right-hand engine mounting bracket to the mounting insulator. Tighten the bolt to 27 ft. lbs. (37 Nm) and both nuts to 38 ft. lbs. (52 Nm).
- Ground connector next to the right-hand engine mount
- Engine sling and hanger

22. Install the power steering pump, as follows:
- Pump with the bracket. Tighten the 3 bolts to 32 ft. lbs. (43 Nm).
- Pivot and adjusting bolts. Tighten the pivot bolt to 32 ft. lbs. (43 Nm) and the adjusting bolt to 29 ft. lbs. (39 Nm).
- Drive belt. Adjust the tension.
- Both air hoses to the power steering pump

23. Install or connect the following:
- Engine mounting centermember to the body; install the 4 bolts but do not tighten the bolts at this time

24. Install or connect the front crossmember, as follows:
- Suspension crossmember with the lower control arms. Torque both bolts crossmember-to-chassis bolts to 152 ft. lbs. (206 Nm).

Timing belt service is covered in Section 4 of this manual

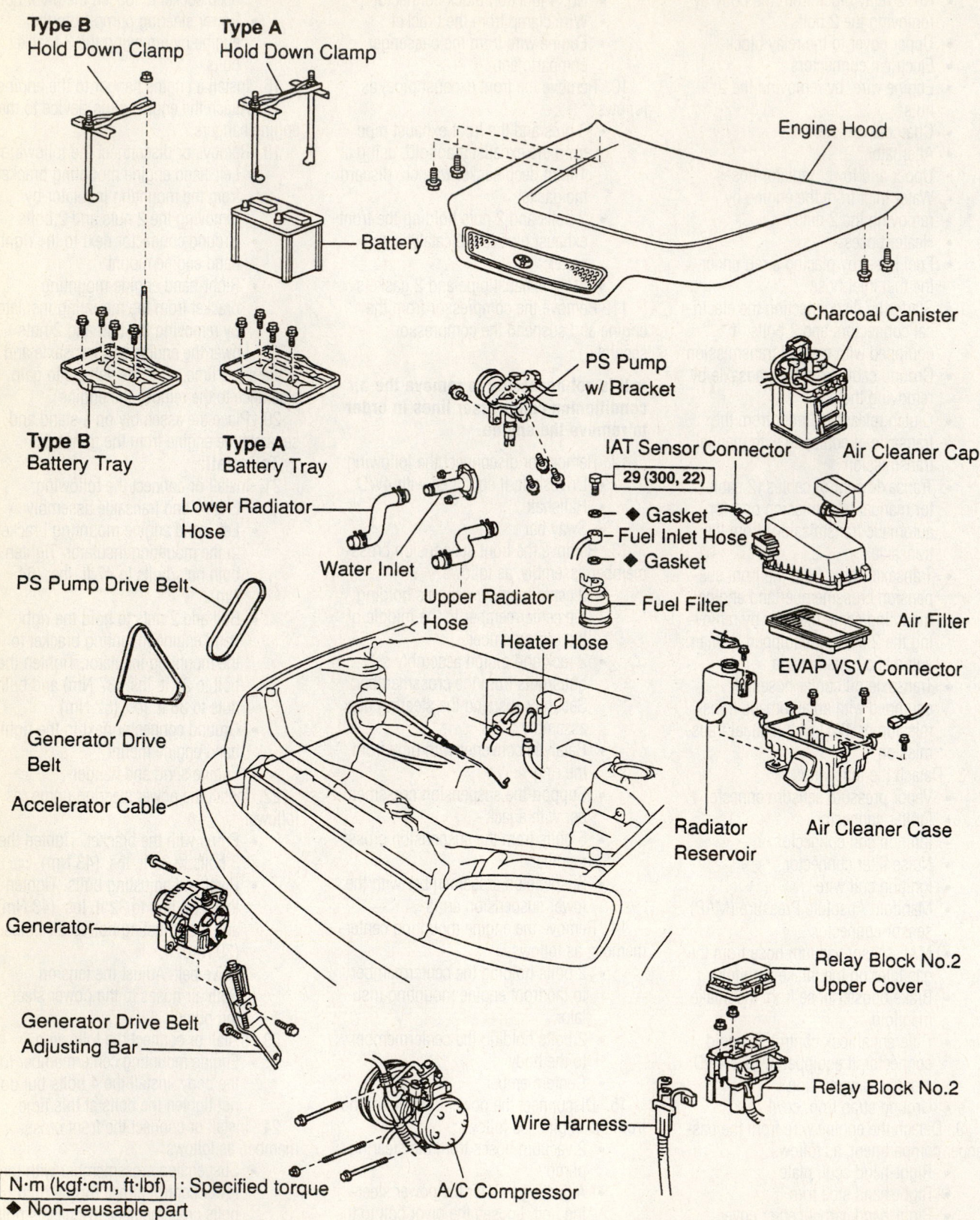

Type B
Hold Down Clamp

Type A
Hold Down Clamp

Battery

Type B
Battery Tray

Type A
Battery Tray

Lower Radiator Hose

Water Inlet

PS Pump Drive Belt

Generator Drive Belt

Accelerator Cable

Generator

Generator Drive Belt Adjusting Bar

Upper Radiator Hose

Heater Hose

Engine Hood

PS Pump w/ Bracket

Charcoal Canister

IAT Sensor Connector

29 (300, 22)

◆ Gasket

Fuel Inlet Hose

◆ Gasket

Fuel Filter

Air Cleaner Cap

Air Filter

EVAP VSV Connector

Air Cleaner Case

Radiator Reservoir

Relay Block No.2 Upper Cover

Relay Block No.2

Wire Harness

A/C Compressor

N·m (kgf·cm, ft·lbf) : Specified torque
◆ Non–reusable part

7924ZG04

Exploded view of the engine accessory removal components—RAV4 model

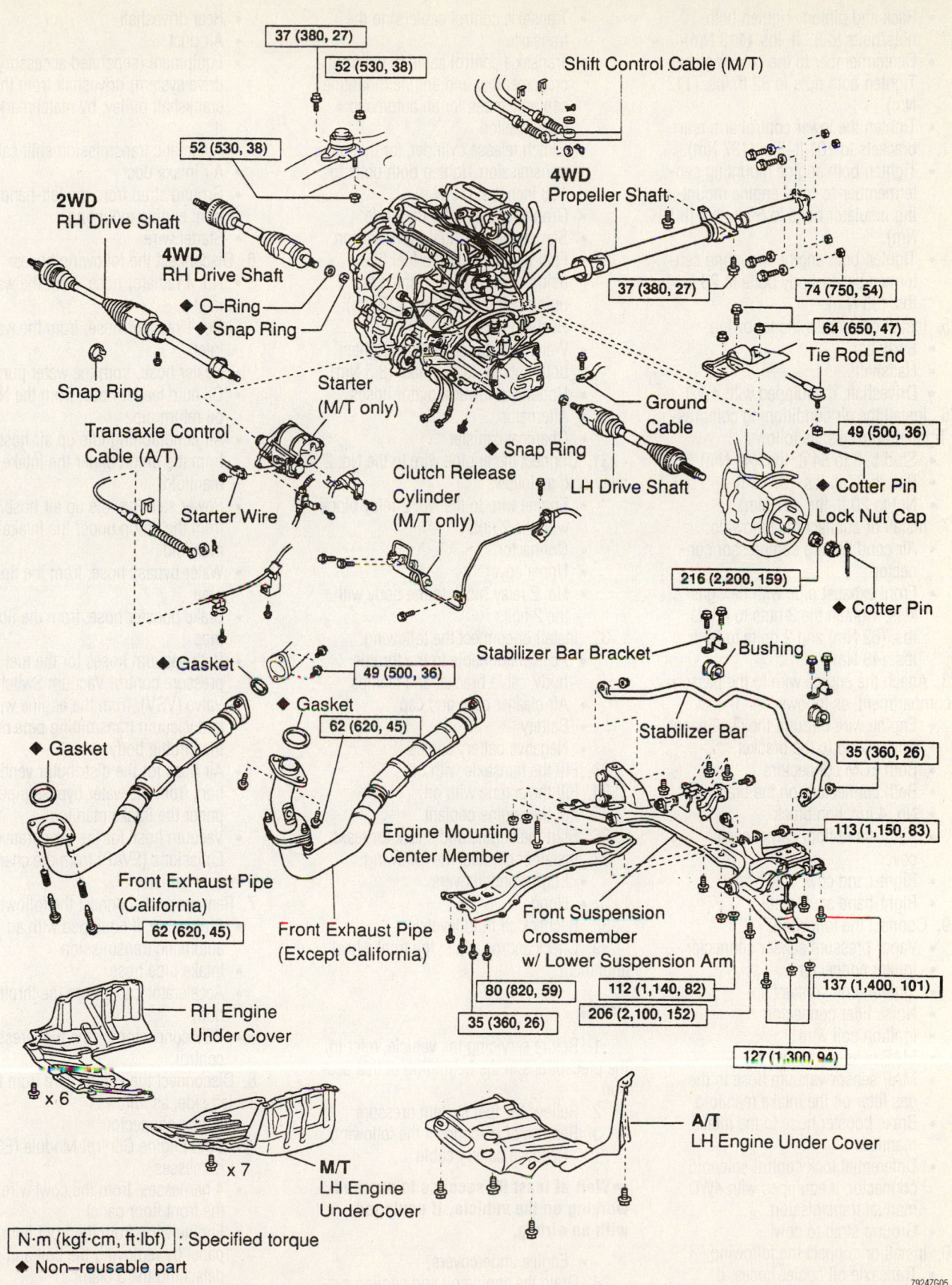

37 (380, 27)

52 (530, 38)

52 (530, 38)

Shift Control Cable (M/T)

2WD
RH Drive Shaft

4WD
RH Drive Shaft

4WD
Propeller Shaft

◆ O–Ring

◆ Snap Ring

37 (380, 27)

74 (750, 54)

64 (650, 47)

Tie Rod End

Snap Ring

Starter
(M/T only)

Transaxle Control
Cable (A/T)

Ground
Cable

◆ Snap Ring

49 (500, 36)

Starter Wire

Clutch Release
Cylinder
(M/T only)

LH Drive Shaft

◆ Cotter Pin

Lock Nut Cap

216 (2,200, 159)

◆ Cotter Pin

◆ Gasket

49 (500, 36)

Stabilizer Bar Bracket

Bushing

◆ Gasket

62 (620, 45)

Stabilizer Bar

35 (360, 26)

◆ Gasket

Engine Mounting
Center Member

113 (1,150, 83)

Front Exhaust Pipe
(California)

Front Suspension
Crossmember
w/ Lower Suspension Arm

62 (620, 45)

Front Exhaust Pipe
(Except California)

80 (820, 59)

112 (1,140, 82)

137 (1,400, 101)

35 (360, 26)

206 (2,100, 152)

**RH Engine
Under Cover**

127 (1,300, 94)

◆ x 6

A/T
LH Engine Under Cover

◆ x 7

M/T
LH Engine
Under Cover

N·m (kgf·cm, ft·lbf) : Specified torque

◆ Non–reusable part

7924ZG05

Exploded view of the engine removal—RAV4 model

- Rack and pinion. Tighten both nuts/bolts to 83 ft. lbs. (113 Nm).
- Centermember to the crossmember. Tighten both nuts to 82 ft. lbs. (112 Nm).
- Tighten the lower control arm rear brackets to 101 ft. lbs. (137 Nm).
- Tighten both engine mounting centermember-to-front engine mounting insulator bolts to 59 ft. lbs. (80 Nm).
- Tighten both engine mounting centermember-to-body bolts to 26 ft. lbs. (35 Nm).

25. Install or connect the following:
- Sway bar
- Halfshafts
- Driveshaft, if equipped with 4WD

26. Install the air conditioning compressor. Tighten nut/bolts, as follows:
- Stud bolt to 34 ft. lbs. (47 Nm)
- Bolt to 27 ft. lbs. (37 Nm)
- Nut to 20 ft. lbs. (27 Nm)

27. Install or connect the following:
- Air conditioning compressor connector
- Front exhaust pipe with new gaskets. Tighten the 3 nuts to 46 ft. lbs. (62 Nm) and 2 bolts to 35 ft. lbs. (48 Nm).

28. Attach the engine wire to the passenger compartment, as follows:
- Engine wire through the cowl panel
- Wire clamp to the bracket
- Both ECM connectors
- Both connectors on the bracket
- No. 4 junction block
- Right-hand floor carpet center cover
- Right-hand cowl side trim
- Right-hand scuff plate

29. Connect the following:
- Vapor pressure sensor connector
- Igniter connector
- Ignition coil connector
- Noise filter connector
- Ignition coil wire
- MAP sensor connector
- MAP sensor vacuum hose to the gas filter on the intake manifold
- Brake booster hose to the intake manifold
- Differential lock control solenoid connector, if equipped with 4WD manual transmission
- Ground strap to cowl

30. Install or connect the following:
- Transaxle oil cooler hoses, if equipped with an automatic transmission or 4WD with manual transmission

- Transaxle control cable(s) to the transaxle
- Transaxle control cable to the front crossmember and engine mounting centermember, for an automatic transmission
- Clutch release cylinder, for manual transmission Tighten both bolts to 108 inch lbs. (12 Nm).
- Ground cable to the transaxle
- Starter, for a manual transmission
- Fuel inlet hose to the fuel filter, using new gaskets. Tighten the union bolt to 22 ft. lbs. (29 Nm).
- Heater hoses
- Water inlet to the engine. Tighten both nuts to 78 inch lbs. (8.8 Nm).
- Upper and lower radiator hoses
- Alternator
- Charcoal canister

31. Connect the engine wire to the No. 2 relay box, as follows:
- Engine wire to the No. 2 relay block with the 2 nuts
- Connector
- Upper cover
- No. 2 relay block to the body with the 2 bolts

32. Install or connect the following:
- Accelerator cable to the throttle body, cable bracket and clamps
- Air cleaner case and cap
- Battery
- Negative battery cables

33. Fill the transaxle with oil.
34. Fill the engine with oil.
35. Fill the engine coolant.
36. Start the engine and check for leaks.
37. Install or connect the following:
- Engine undercovers
- Hood

38. Recheck all fluid levels.
39. Check and/or adjust the front wheel alignment.

Previa

1. Before servicing the vehicle, refer to the precautions in the beginning of this section.
2. Relieve the fuel system pressure.
3. Remove or disconnect the following:
- Negative battery cable

➡**Wait at least 90 seconds to proceed working on the vehicle, if equipped with an airbag.**

- Engine undercovers

4. Drain the engine oil and cooling system.

5. Remove or disconnect the following:
- Front driveshaft, on 4WD vehicles

- Rear driveshaft
- Air duct
- Equipment (separated accessory drive system) driveshaft from the crankshaft pulley, by matchmarking it
- Automatic transmission shift cable
- Air intake duct
- Ground strap from the left-hand front engine mounting
- Starter wire

6. Disconnect the following hoses:
- No. 4 radiator hose, from the water inlet
- No. 1 radiator hose, from the water inlet
- Heater hose, from the water pump
- Oil auto feeder hose, from the No. 1 oil return pipe
- Air conditioning idle up air hose, from the union under the intake manifold
- Power steering idle up air hose, from the union under the intake manifold
- Water bypass hose, from the floor pipe
- Brake booster hose, from the floor pipe
- Both vacuum hoses for the fuel pressure control Vacuum Switching Valve (VSV), from the engine wire and vacuum transmitting pipe on the throttle body
- Air hose for the distributor ventilation, from the water bypass pipe under the intake manifold
- Vacuum hose for the Evaporative Emissions (EVAP) from the charcoal canister

7. Remove or disconnect the following:
- Shift cable, if equipped with an automatic transmission
- Intake pipe hose
- Accelerator cable from the throttle body
- VSV connector for the fuel pressure control

8. Disconnect the engine wire from the engine left side, as follows:
- Igniter connector
- Both Engine Control Module (ECM) harnesses
- 4 harnesses, from the cowl wire on the front floor panel
- Engine wire, from the front floor panel by removing the bolt and detaching the 3 clamps
- Engine wire from the front floor panel hose
- Automatic transmission oil dipstick

- Fuel inlet and return hoses
- Front exhaust pipe
- Exhaust pipe heat insulator and ground strap, by removing the 4 bolts
- Both automatic transmission oil cooler hoses
- Ignition coil and engine ground strap
- Condenser wiring
- 4 clamps and engine wire
- Automatic transmission and Park/Neutral Position (PNP) switch wiring

9. Remove the engine with the transmission, as follows:
- Support the engine and transmission with a supporting device.
- Lower the vehicle while supporting the engine and transmission with the engine lifter.
- 2 bolts, 2 nuts and 2 plate washers holding the right and left engine mountings to the engine front support member
- 4 through-bolts, 4 plate washers and 4 nuts holding the rear mounting to the No. 2 rear engine mounting bracket

➡ **Be sure the engine and transmission are clear of all wiring, hoses and cables.**

- Lower the engine and transmission
To install:
10. Install the engine with the transmission, as follows:
- Raise the engine and transmission
- 4 through-bolts, 4 plate washers and 4 nuts holding the rear mounting to the No. 2 rear engine mounting bracket
- 2 bolts, 2 nuts and 2 plate washers holding the right and left engine mountings to the engine front support member
- Raise the vehicle while supporting the engine and transmission with the engine lifter.
- Support the engine and transmission with a supporting device.

11. Connect the engine wire to the engine left side, as follows:
- Automatic transmission and Park/Neutral Position (PNP) switch wiring
- 4 clamps and engine wire
- Condenser wiring
- Ignition coil and engine ground strap

- Both automatic transmission oil cooler hoses
- Exhaust pipe heat insulator and ground strap, by installing the 4 bolts
- Front exhaust pipe
- Fuel inlet and return hoses
- Automatic transmission oil dipstick
- Engine wire to the front floor panel hose
- Engine wire, to the front floor panel by installing the bolt and attaching the 3 clamps
- 4 harnesses, to the cowl wire on the front floor panel
- Both Engine Control Module (ECM) harnesses
- Igniter connector

12. Install or connect the following:
- VSV connector for the fuel pressure control
- Accelerator cable to the throttle body
- Intake pipe hose
- Shift cable, if equipped with an automatic transmission

13. Connect the following hoses:
- Vacuum hose for the Evaporative Emissions (EVAP) to the charcoal canister
- Air hose for the distributor ventilation, to the water bypass pipe under the intake manifold
- Both vacuum hoses for the fuel pressure control Vacuum Switching Valve (VSV), to the engine wire and vacuum transmitting pipe on the throttle body
- Brake booster hose, to the floor pipe
- Water bypass hose, to the floor pipe
- Power steering idle up air hose, to the union under the intake manifold
- Air conditioning idle up air hose, to the union under the intake manifold
- Oil auto feeder hose, to the No. 1 oil return pipe
- Heater hose, to the water pump
- No. 1 radiator hose, to the water inlet
- No. 4 radiator hose, to the water inlet

14. Install or connect the following:
- Starter wire
- Ground strap to the left-hand front engine mounting
- Air intake duct
- Automatic transmission shift cable
- Equipment (separated accessory

drive system) driveshaft to the crankshaft pulley, by matchmarking it
- Air duct
- Rear driveshaft
- Front driveshaft, on 4WD vehicles

15. Install the engine in the reverse order of removal procedure while paying close attention to the following:
- Right and left engine front mountings to the engine front support member. Tighten both nuts/bolts to 27 ft. lbs. (37 Nm).
- Engine rear mount to the No. 2 rear engine mount bracket. Tighten the nuts/bolts to 31 ft. lbs. (42 Nm).

16. Install or connect the following:
- Rear driveshaft
- Front driveshaft, if equipped with 4WD
- New oil filter
- Engine undercovers
- Negative battery cable
17. Fill the engine with oil.
18. Fill the cooling system.
19. Start the engine and check for leaks.

Sienna and RX 300

1. Before servicing the vehicle, refer to the precautions in the beginning of this section.
2. Matchmark the hood position.
3. Remove or disconnect the following:
- Hood
- Wiper and blade assembly
- Top cowl seal and panel
- Window washer hoses from the ventilator louvers
- Left and right ventilator louvers
- Heater air duct
4. Properly relieve the fuel system pressure.
5. Remove or disconnect the following:
- Both battery cables
- Battery and tray
6. Drain the engine coolant.
7. Drain the engine oil.
8. Remove or disconnect the following:
- Intake air cleaner and case assembly
- Cruise control actuator, if equipped
- Upper suspension brace, for RX 300
- Upper and lower radiator hoses
- Radiator
- Automatic transmission oil cooler lines
- Any connectors, hoses and sensors that would interfere with engine removal

Refer to Section 1 for engine rebuilding specifications

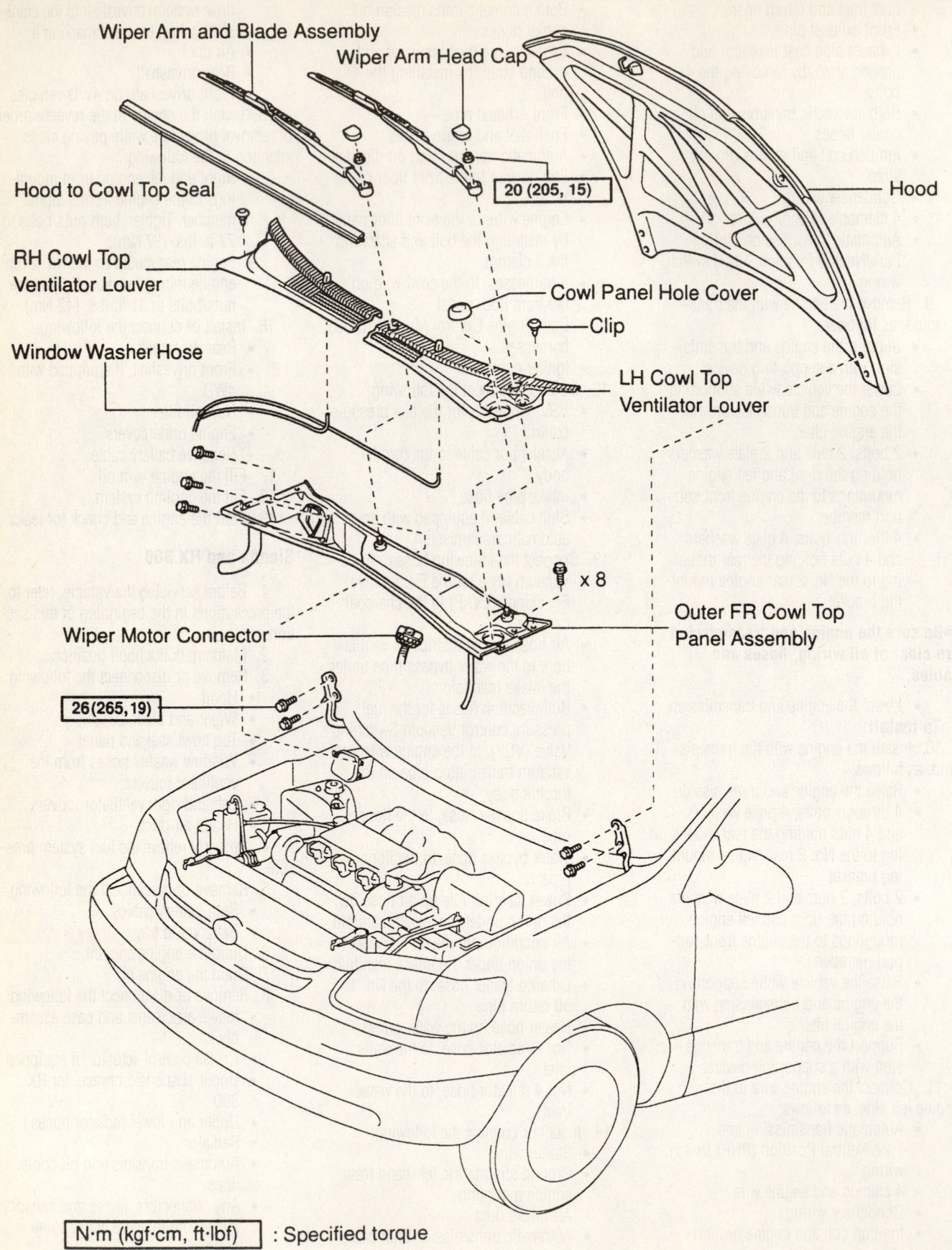

Wiper Arm and Blade Assembly

Wiper Arm Head Cap

Hood to Cowl Top Seal

20 (205, 15)

Hood

RH Cowl Top Ventilator Louver

Cowl Panel Hole Cover

Clip

Window Washer Hose

LH Cowl Top Ventilator Louver

x 8

Outer FR Cowl Top Panel Assembly

Wiper Motor Connector

26 (265, 19)

N·m (kgf·cm, ft·lbf) : Specified torque

7924ZG06

Exploded view of the top cowl and related components—Sienna

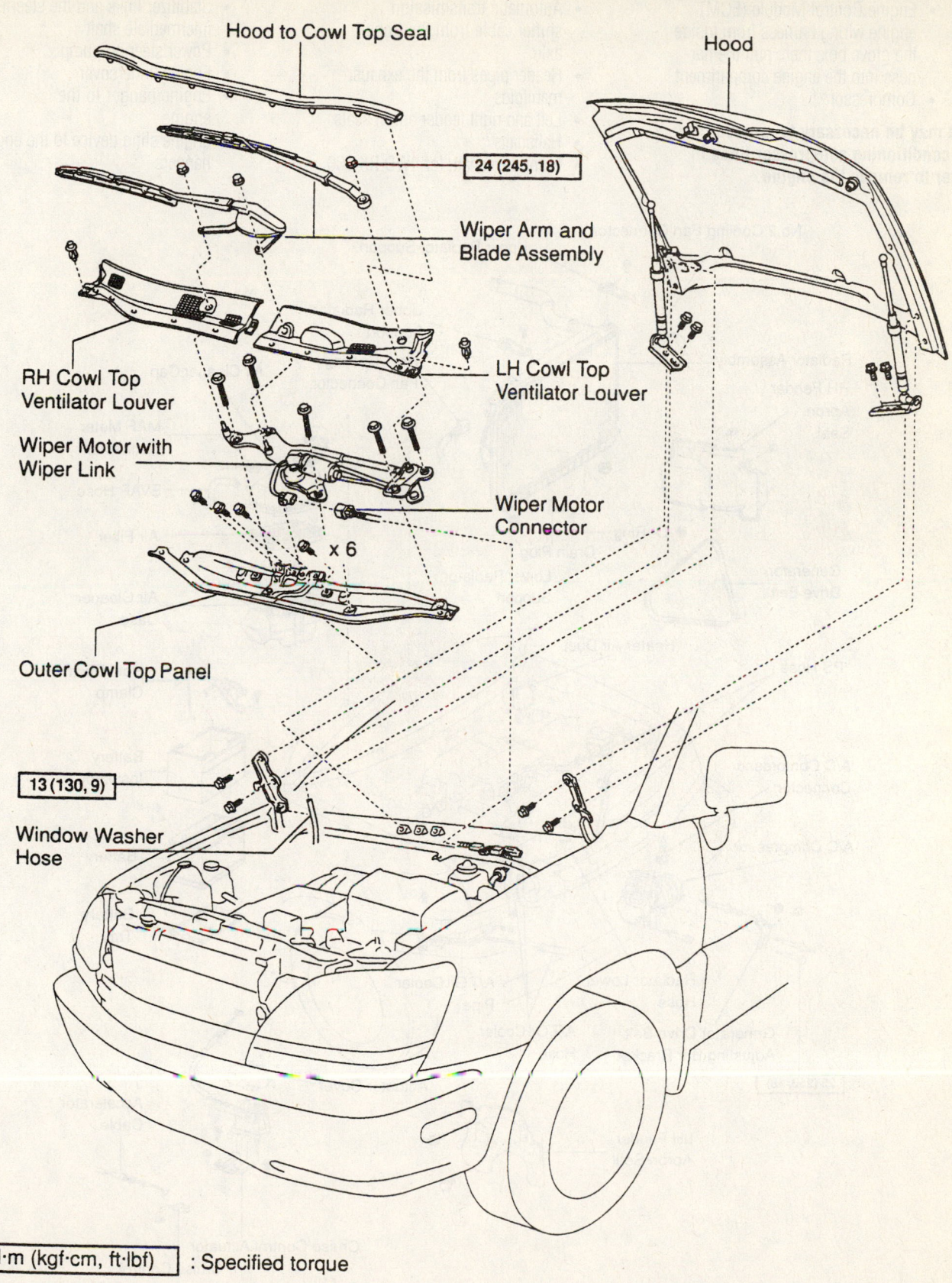

Hood to Cowl Top Seal

Hood

24 (245, 18)

Wiper Arm and
Blade Assembly

RH Cowl Top
Ventilator Louver

LH Cowl Top
Ventilator Louver

Wiper Motor with
Wiper Link

Wiper Motor
Connector

x 6

Outer Cowl Top Panel

13 (130, 9)

Window Washer
Hose

N·m (kgf·cm, ft·lbf) : Specified torque

7924ZG83

Exploded view of the top cowl and related components—RX 300

For engine torque specifications, refer to Section 1 of this manual

- Engine Control Module (ECM) engine wiring harness from inside the glove box; then, pull the harness into the engine compartment
- Compressor

➡ **It may be necessary to remove the air conditioning compressor lines in order to remove the engine.**

- Automatic transmission shifter cable from the trans-axle
- Header pipes from the exhaust manifolds
- Left and right fender apron seals
- Halfshafts
- Front driveshaft, for 4WD RX 300

- Stabilizer links and the steering intermediate shaft
- Power steering pump
- Engine undercover
- Engine hanger to the engine
- Engine sling device to the engine hangers

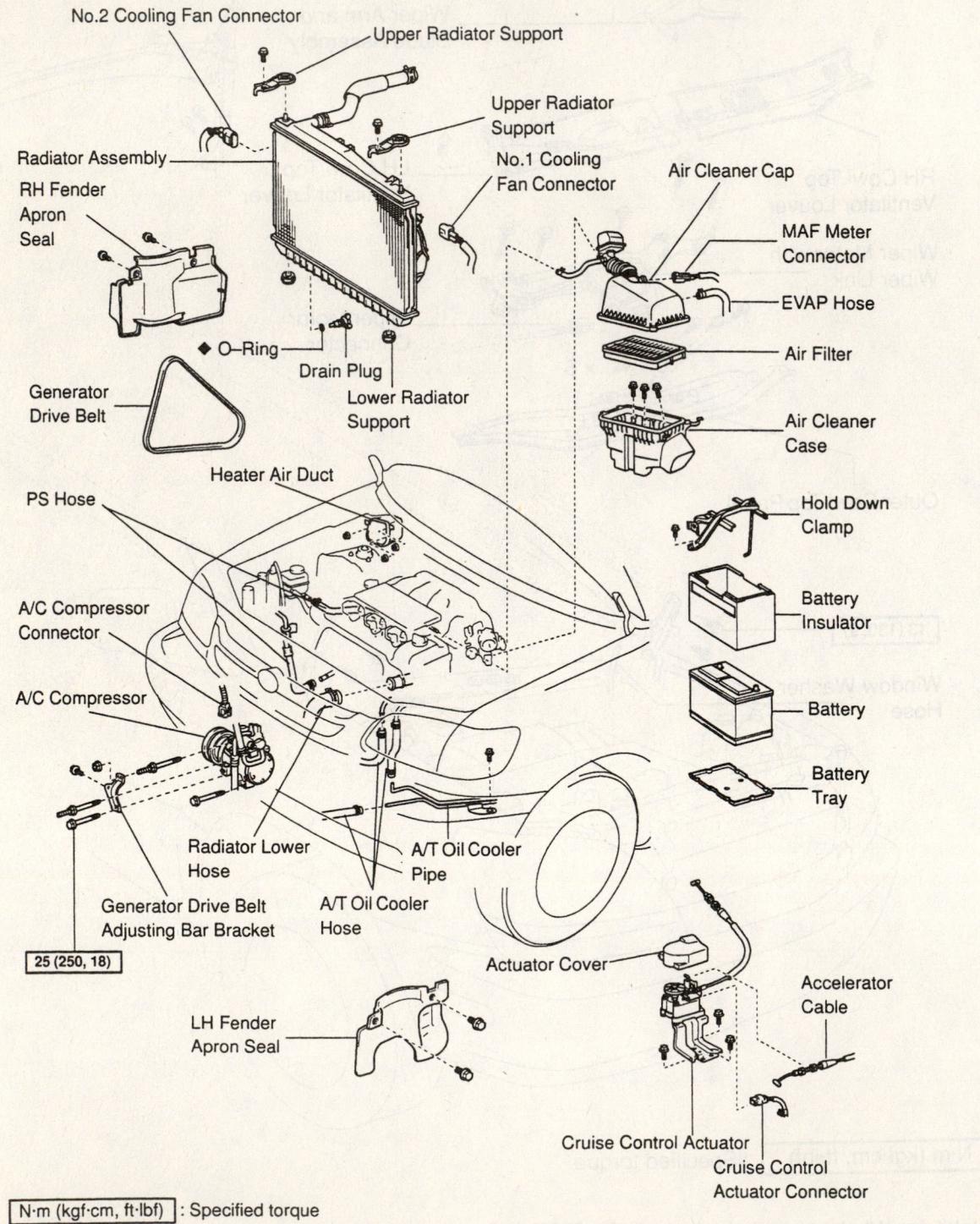

N·m (kgf·cm, ft·lbf) : Specified torque
◆ Non–reusable part

Exploded view of engine pre-removal components—Sienna

7924ZG07

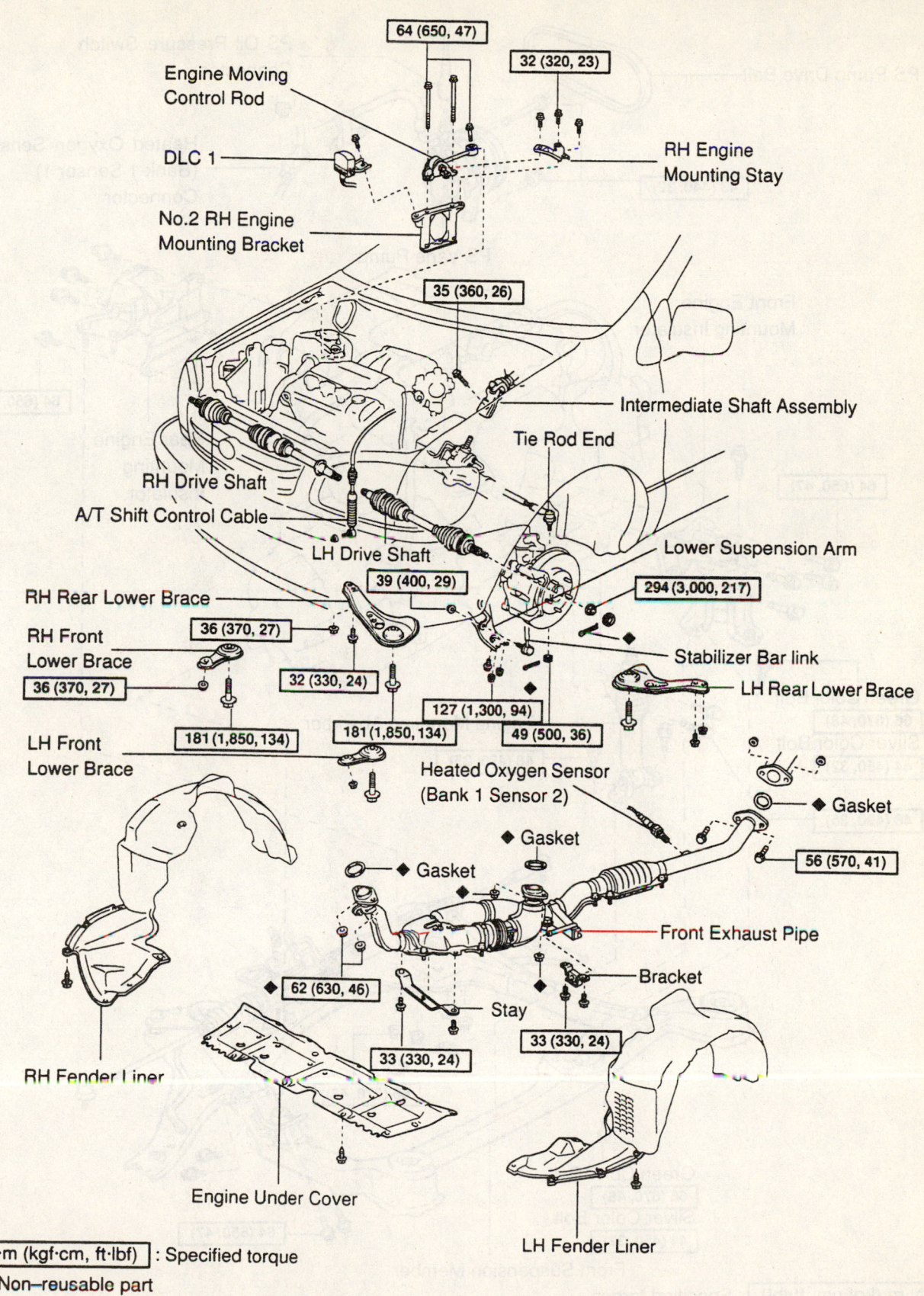

64 (650, 47)

32 (320, 23)

Engine Moving
Control Rod

RH Engine
Mounting Stay

DLC 1

No.2 RH Engine
Mounting Bracket

35 (360, 26)

Intermediate Shaft Assembly

Tie Rod End

RH Drive Shaft

A/T Shift Control Cable

LH Drive Shaft

Lower Suspension Arm

294 (3,000, 217)

RH Rear Lower Brace

39 (400, 29)

36 (370, 27)

RH Front
Lower Brace

36 (370, 27)

32 (330, 24)

Stabilizer Bar link

LH Rear Lower Brace

127 (1,300, 94)

LH Front
Lower Brace

181 (1,850, 134)

181 (1,850, 134)

49 (500, 36)

Heated Oxygen Sensor
(Bank 1 Sensor 2)

◆ Gasket

56 (570, 41)

◆ Gasket

◆ Gasket

Front Exhaust Pipe

◆ 62 (630, 46)

Stay

Bracket

33 (330, 24)

RH Fender Liner

33 (330, 24)

Engine Under Cover

LH Fender Liner

| N·m (kgf·cm, ft·lbf) | : Specified torque

◆ Non–reusable part

7924ZG08

Exploded view of engine removal and installation tightening specifications of the related components—Sienna

For complete mechanical specifications, refer to Section 1 of this manual

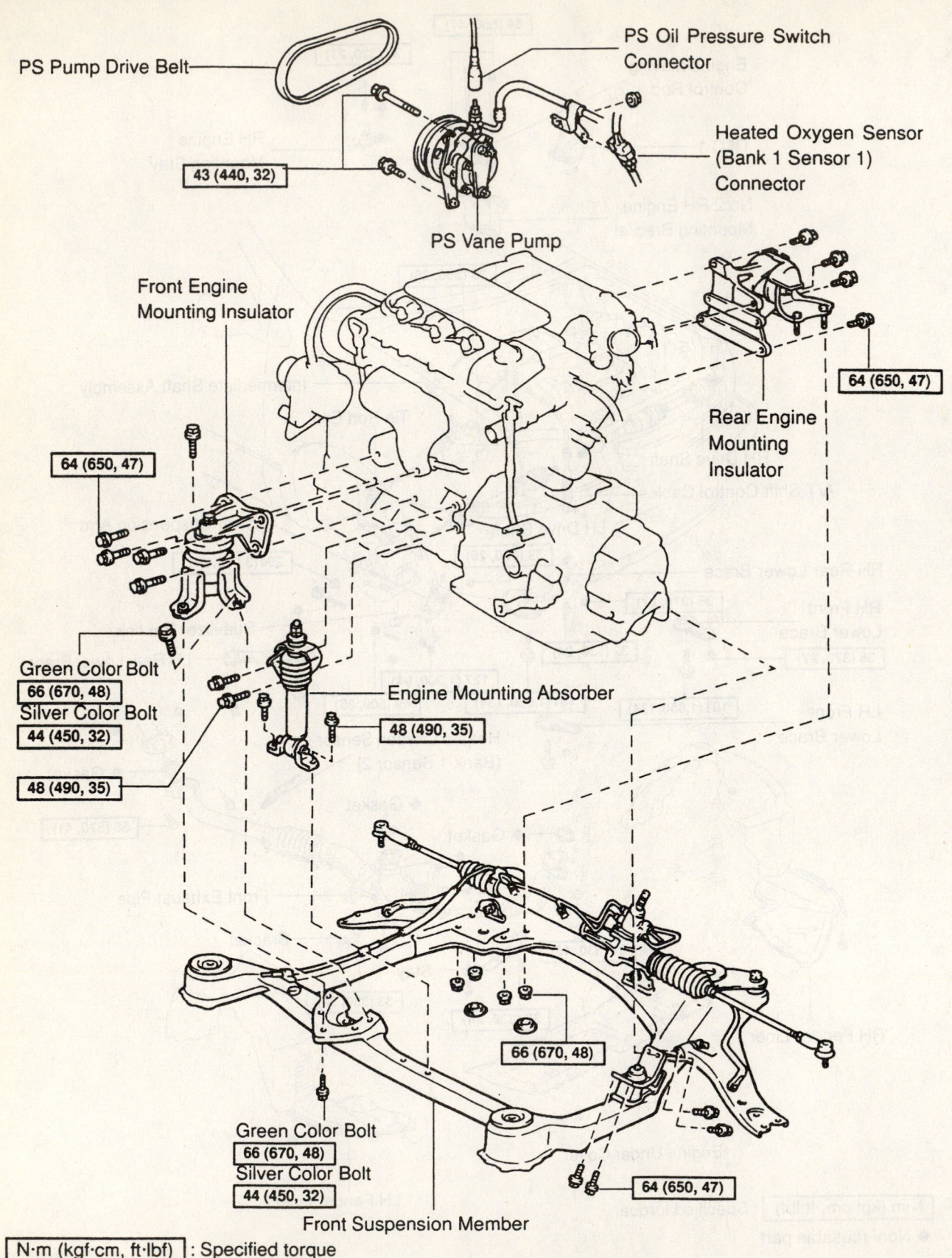

PS Pump Drive Belt

PS Oil Pressure Switch Connector

Heated Oxygen Sensor
(Bank 1 Sensor 1)
Connector

43 (440, 32)

PS Vane Pump

Front Engine
Mounting Insulator

64 (650, 47)

Rear Engine
Mounting
Insulator

64 (650, 47)

Green Color Bolt
66 (670, 48)
Silver Color Bolt
44 (450, 32)

48 (490, 35)

Engine Mounting Absorber

48 (490, 35)

66 (670, 48)

Green Color Bolt
66 (670, 48)
Silver Color Bolt
44 (450, 32)

64 (650, 47)

Front Suspension Member

N·m (kgf·cm, ft·lbf) : Specified torque

◆ Non–reusable part

Exploded view of the suspension component removal and installation for engine removal—Sienna

7924ZG09

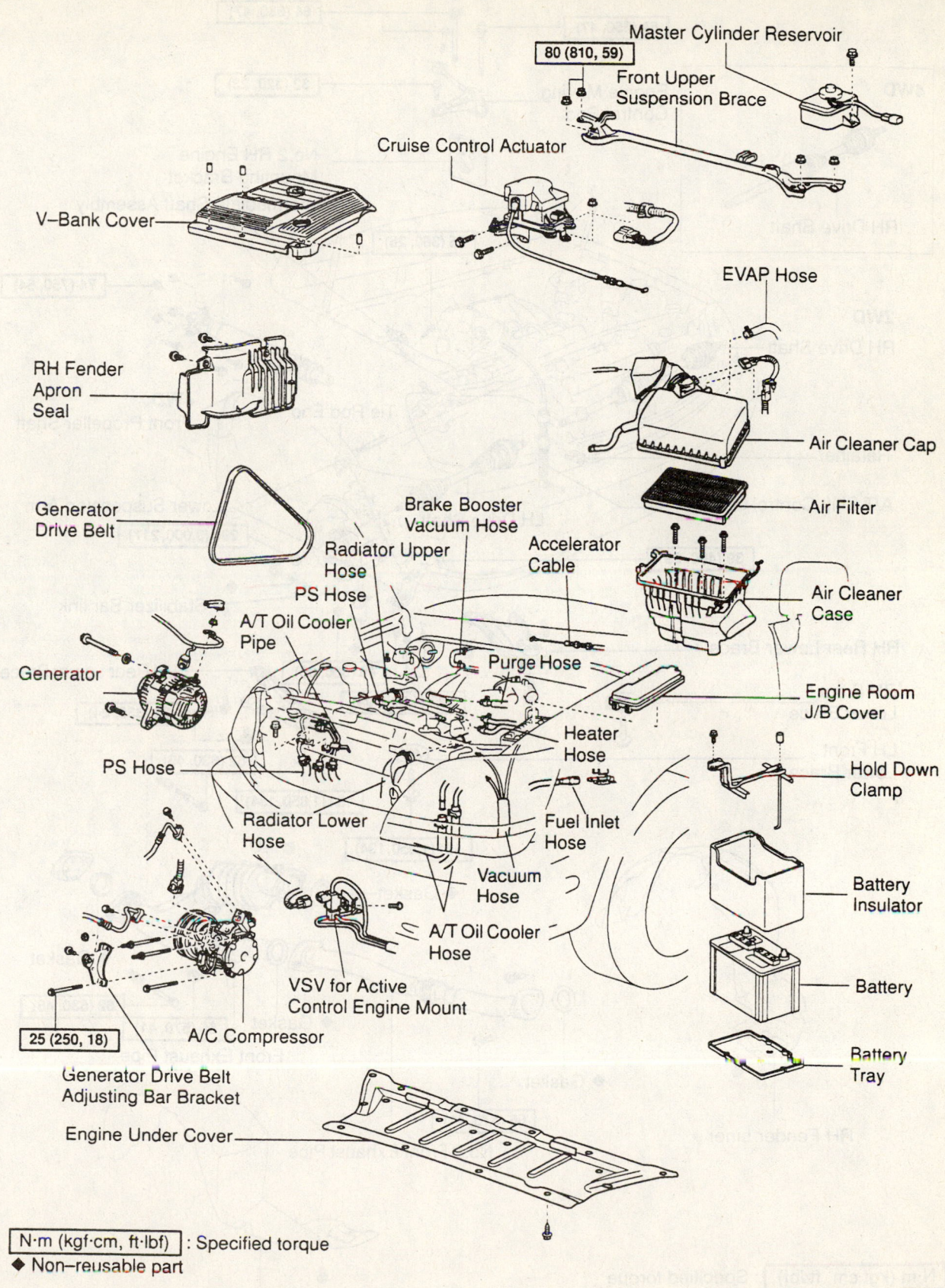

Master Cylinder Reservoir

80 (810, 59)

Front Upper Suspension Brace

Cruise Control Actuator

V-Bank Cover

EVAP Hose

RH Fender Apron Seal

Air Cleaner Cap

Air Filter

Generator Drive Belt

Brake Booster Vacuum Hose

Radiator Upper Hose

PS Hose

Accelerator Cable

Air Cleaner Case

A/T Oil Cooler Pipe

Purge Hose

Generator

Engine Room J/B Cover

PS Hose

Heater Hose

Hold Down Clamp

Radiator Lower Hose

Fuel Inlet Hose

Battery Insulator

Vacuum Hose

Battery

A/T Oil Cooler Hose

VSV for Active Control Engine Mount

Battery Tray

25 (250, 18)

A/C Compressor

Generator Drive Belt Adjusting Bar Bracket

Engine Under Cover

N·m (kgf·cm, ft·lbf) : Specified torque
◆ Non-reusable part

7924ZG84

Exploded view of engine pre-removal components—RX 300

Please refer to Section 8 for electric cooling fan wiring schematics

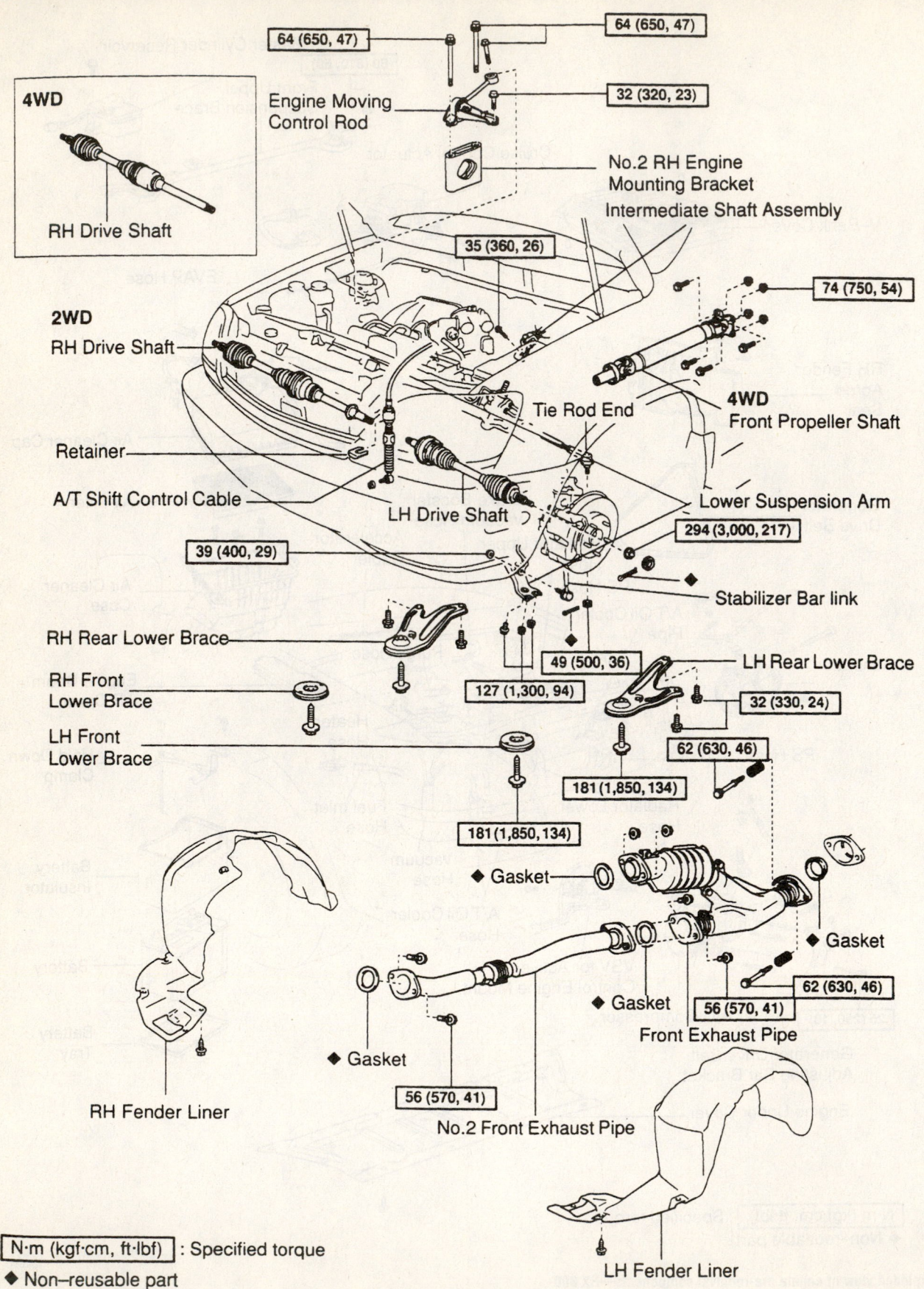

4WD

RH Drive Shaft

64 (650, 47)

64 (650, 47)

Engine Moving
Control Rod

32 (320, 23)

No.2 RH Engine
Mounting Bracket

Intermediate Shaft Assembly

35 (360, 26)

74 (750, 54)

2WD

RH Drive Shaft

Tie Rod End

4WD
Front Propeller Shaft

Retainer

A/T Shift Control Cable

LH Drive Shaft

Lower Suspension Arm

294 (3,000, 217)

39 (400, 29)

Stabilizer Bar link

RH Rear Lower Brace

LH Rear Lower Brace

49 (500, 36)

RH Front
Lower Brace

127 (1,300, 94)

32 (330, 24)

LH Front
Lower Brace

62 (630, 46)

181 (1,850, 134)

181 (1,850, 134)

◆ Gasket

62 (630, 46)

◆ Gasket

◆ Gasket

◆ Gasket

56 (570, 41)

Front Exhaust Pipe

RH Fender Liner

◆ Gasket

56 (570, 41)

No.2 Front Exhaust Pipe

LH Fender Liner

N·m (kgf·cm, ft·lbf) : Specified torque

◆ Non–reusable part

7924ZG85

Exploded view of engine removal and installation tightening specifications of the related components—RX 300

2WD

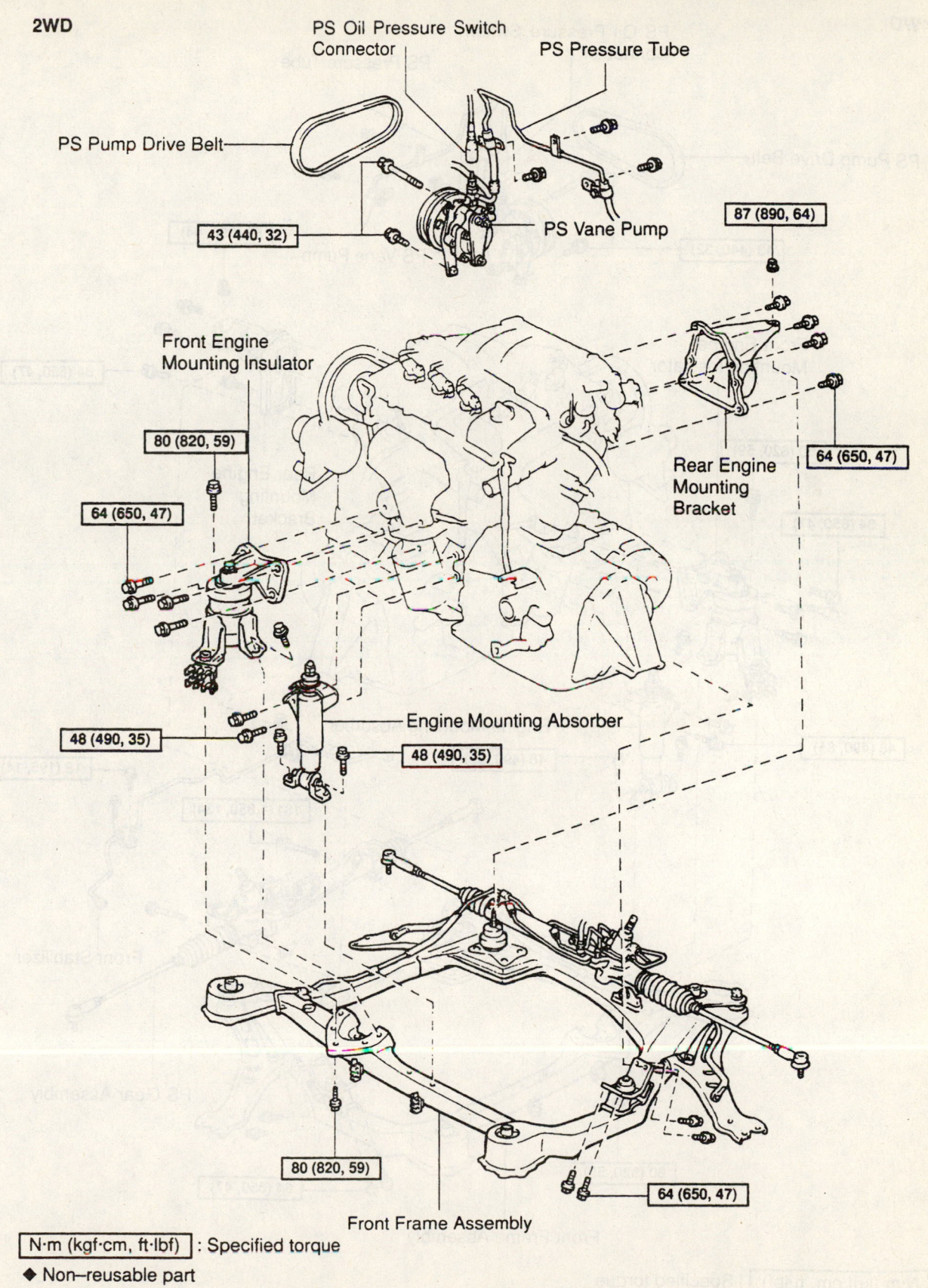

PS Oil Pressure Switch Connector

PS Pressure Tube

PS Pump Drive Belt

PS Vane Pump

43 (440, 32)

87 (890, 64)

Front Engine Mounting Insulator

80 (820, 59)

64 (650, 47)

Rear Engine Mounting Bracket

64 (650, 47)

Engine Mounting Absorber

48 (490, 35)

48 (490, 35)

80 (820, 59)

64 (650, 47)

Front Frame Assembly

N·m (kgf·cm, ft·lbf) : Specified torque

◆ Non–reusable part

7924ZG86

Exploded view of the suspension component removal and installation for engine removal—2WD RX 300

4WD

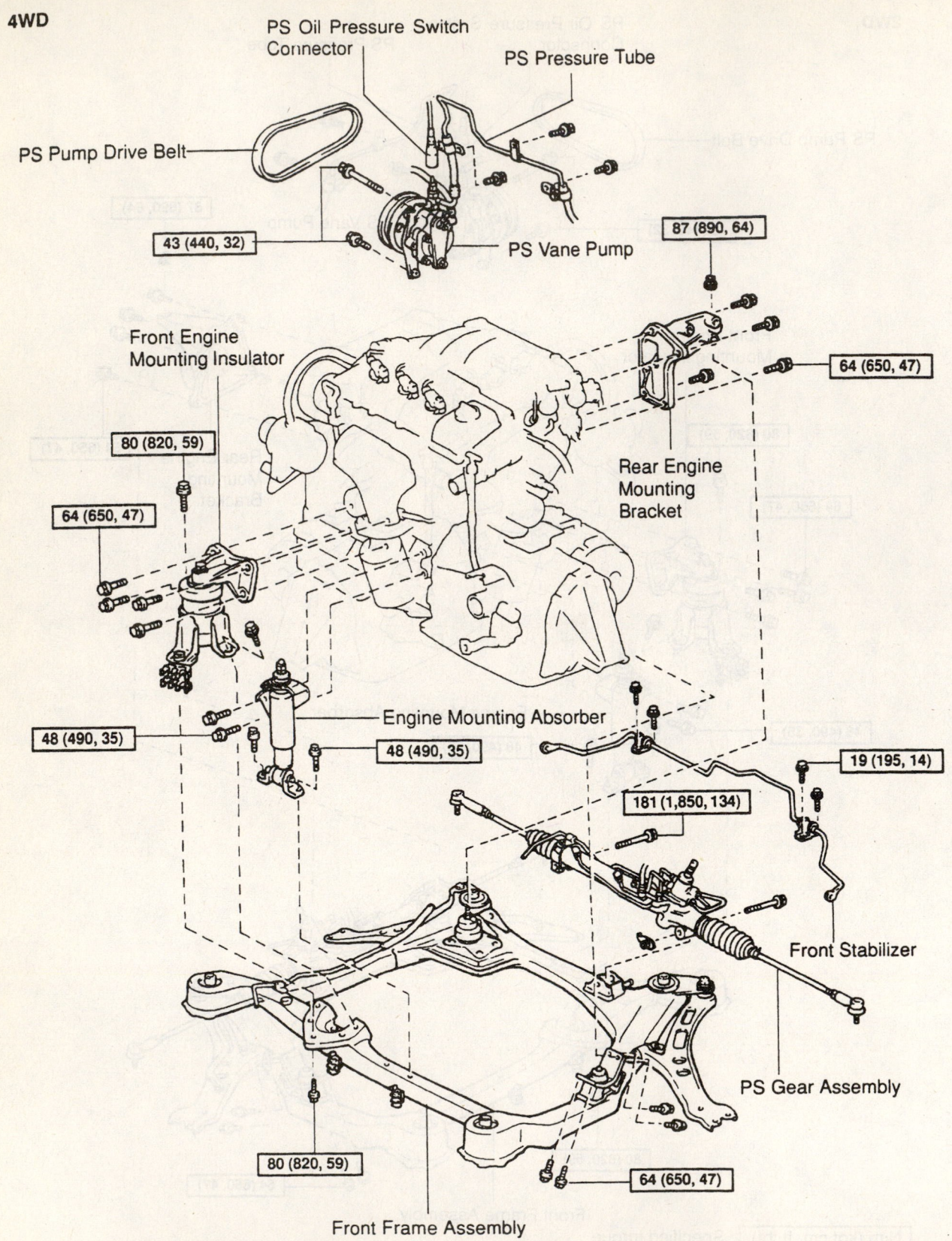

PS Oil Pressure Switch Connector

PS Pressure Tube

PS Pump Drive Belt

43 (440, 32)

PS Vane Pump

87 (890, 64)

64 (650, 47)

Front Engine Mounting Insulator

Rear Engine Mounting Bracket

80 (820, 59)

64 (650, 47)

Engine Mounting Absorber

48 (490, 35)

48 (490, 35)

19 (195, 14)

181 (1,850, 134)

Front Stabilizer

PS Gear Assembly

80 (820, 59)

64 (650, 47)

Front Frame Assembly

N·m (kgf·cm, ft·lbf) : Specified torque

◆ Non–reusable part

7924ZG87

Exploded view of the suspension component removal and installation for engine removal—4WD RX 300

- Right-hand motor mount and moving control rod
- Front suspension lower braces

9. Lower the engine, transaxle and front suspension member as an assembly from the vehicle.

To install:

10. Raise the engine, transaxle and front suspension member as an assembly into the vehicle.

11. Install the front suspension lower braces, and tighten the fasteners, as follows:

- Bolt A: 134 ft. lbs. (181 Nm)
- Bolt B: 24 ft. lbs. (32 Nm)
- Nut C: 27 ft. lbs. (36 Nm)

12. Install or connect the following:

- Moving control rod. Tighten the bolts to 47 ft. lbs. (64 Nm).
- Right-hand motor mount. Tighten the bolts to 23 ft. lbs. (32 Nm).
- Engine sling device from the engine hangers
- Engine undercover
- Power steering pump hoses
- Stabilizer links and the steering intermediate shaft
- Front driveshaft, for 4WD RX 300
- Halfshafts
- Left and right fender apron seals
- Header pipes to the exhaust manifolds
- Automatic transmission shifter cable to the transaxle
- Air conditioning compressor to the engine

13. Push the wiring harness into the glove box.

14. Install or connect the following:

- ECM
- Any connectors, hoses and sensors that were removed

- Automatic transmission oil cooler lines
- Upper and lower radiator hoses and fit the radiator
- Front upper suspension brace, for RX 300. Tighten the nuts to 59 ft. lbs. (80 Nm).
- Cruise control actuator, if removed
- Intake air cleaner and case assembly

15. Fill the engine oil to proper level.
16. Fill the engine with coolant.
17. Install or connect the following:

- Battery tray and battery
- Battery cables
- Heater air duct
- Left and right ventilator louvers
- Window washer hoses from the ventilator louvers
- Top cowl seal and panel
- Wiper and blade assembly
- Hood
- New oil filter

18. Refill the engine with oil.
19. Refill the engine with engine coolant.
20. Install the engine undercovers.
21. Start the engine and check for leaks.

Water Pump

REMOVAL & INSTALLATION

RAV4

1. Before servicing the vehicle, refer to the precautions in the beginning of this section.

2. Remove or disconnect the following:

- Negative battery cable
- Right-hand engine undercover

3. Drain the engine coolant from the radiator and engine.

4. Remove or disconnect the following:

- Timing belt
- Lower radiator hose from the water inlet
- Timing belt tension spring and the No. 2 idler pulley
- Crankshaft Position (CKP) sensor connector clamp
- Alternator drive belt adjusting bar
- 2 water pump-to-water bypass pipe nuts
- 3 water pump bolts in the sequence
- Water pump cover from the water bypass pipe
- Water pump and water pump cover assembly
- Gasket and 2 O-rings from the water pump and water bypass pipe
- 3 bolts, water pump and gasket, from the water pump cover

To install:

5. Install or connect the following:

- Water pump to the water pump cover, using a new gasket. Tighten the 3 bolts to 78 inch lbs. (9 Nm).
- New O-ring and gasket to the water pump cover
- New O-ring to the water bypass pipe, by applying soapy water to the O-ring
- Water pump cover to the water bypass pipe; do not install the nuts at this time
- Water pump. Tighten the 3 bolts, in sequence, to 78 inch lbs. (9 Nm).
- Water pump cover to the water pump pipe. Tighten the 2 bolts to 82 inch lbs. (9 Nm).
- Alternator drive belt adjusting bar. Tighten the bolt to 20 ft. lbs. (27 Nm).
- CKP connector clamp

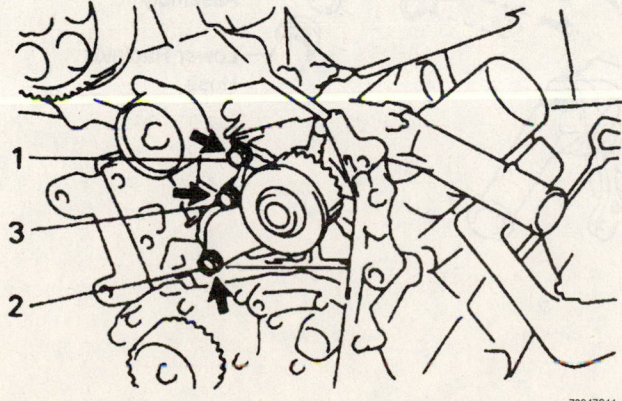

Loosening sequence for the water pump bolts—RAV4

7924ZG11

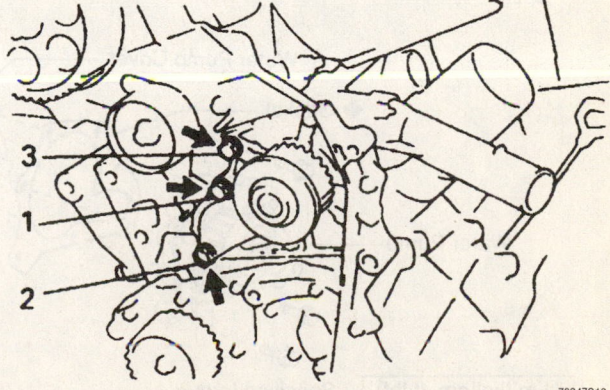

Tightening sequence for the water pump bolts—RAV4

7924ZG12

Timing belt service is covered in Section 4 of this manual

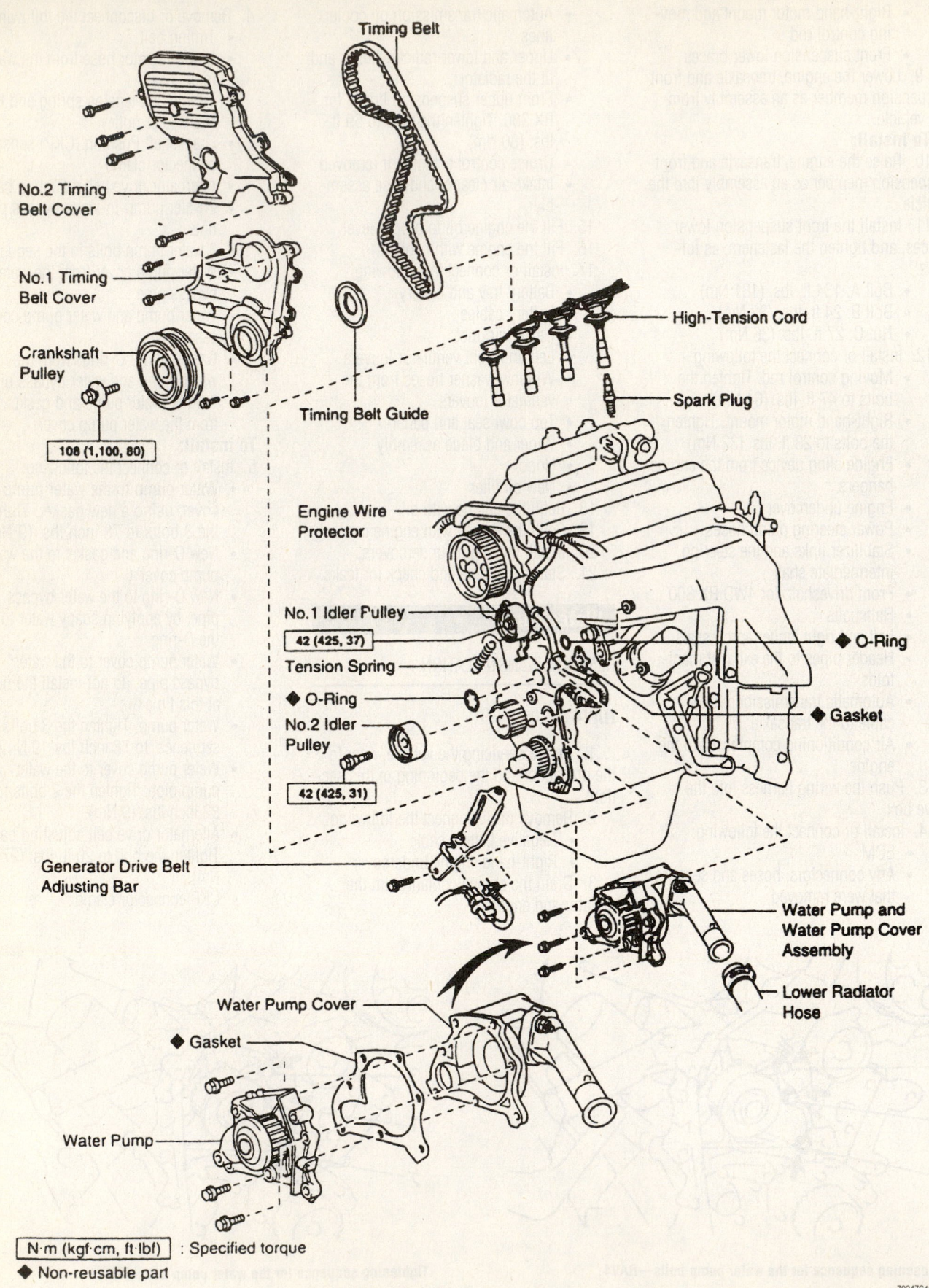

No.2 Timing Belt Cover

No.1 Timing Belt Cover

Crankshaft Pulley

108 (1,100, 80)

Timing Belt

Timing Belt Guide

High-Tension Cord

Spark Plug

Engine Wire Protector

No.1 Idler Pulley

42 (425, 37)

Tension Spring

◆ O-Ring

No.2 Idler Pulley

42 (425, 31)

◆ O-Ring

◆ Gasket

Generator Drive Belt Adjusting Bar

Water Pump and Water Pump Cover Assembly

Lower Radiator Hose

Water Pump Cover

◆ Gasket

Water Pump

N·m (kgf·cm, ft·lbf) : Specified torque

◆ Non-reusable part

Exploded view of the water pump and related components—RAV4

7924ZG10

- No. 2 idler pulley and timing belt tension spring
- Lower radiator hose
- Timing belt
- Negative battery cable

6. Fill the engine and radiator with engine coolant.

7. Start the engine and check for leaks.

8. Install the right-hand engine under-cover.

Previa

1. Before servicing the vehicle, refer to the precautions in the beginning of this section.

2. Remove or disconnect the following:
- Negative battery cable
- Engine undercovers

3. Drain the engine coolant.

4. Drain the engine oil.

5. Remove or disconnect the following:
- Heater hose and radiator outlet hoses
- Oil filter bracket
- Water hose from the water pump
- Water pump-to-timing cover bolts and pump
- O-ring from the water pump
- Water pump from the housing, by removing the 2 bolts

To install:

6. Install or connect the following:
- Water pump with a new gasket. Tighten the bolts to 14 ft. lbs. (20 Nm).
- Water pump to the timing cover. Tighten the **A** bolt to 14 ft. lbs. (20 Nm) and the **B** bolt to 21 ft. lbs. (28 Nm)
- Water hose to the water pump
- Oil filter bracket to the engine using a new O-ring
- Heater hose and radiator outlet hose
- Negative battery cable

7. Fill the engine with oil.

8. Fill the engine and radiator with coolant.

9. Start the engine and check for leaks.

Sienna and RX 300

1. Before servicing the vehicle, refer to the precautions in the beginning of this section.

2. Disconnect the negative battery cable.

3. Drain the engine coolant.

4. Remove or disconnect the following:
- Wiper and blade assembly

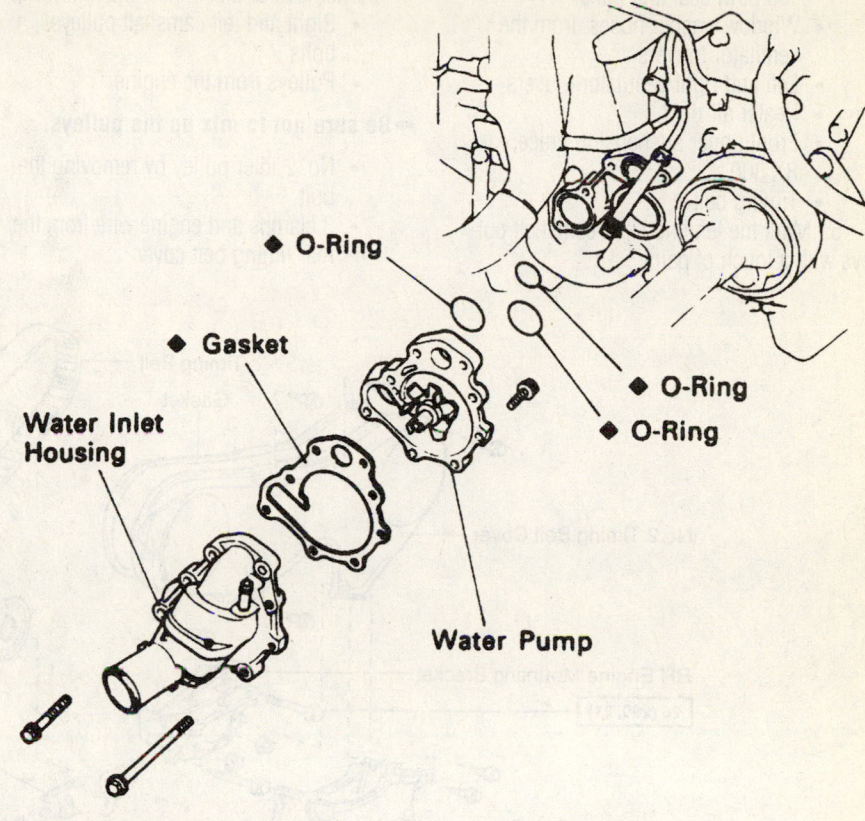

◆ O-Ring

◆ Gasket

Water Inlet Housing

◆ O-Ring

◆ O-Ring

Water Pump

◆ Non-reusable part

Exploded view of the water pump components—Previa

7924ZG13

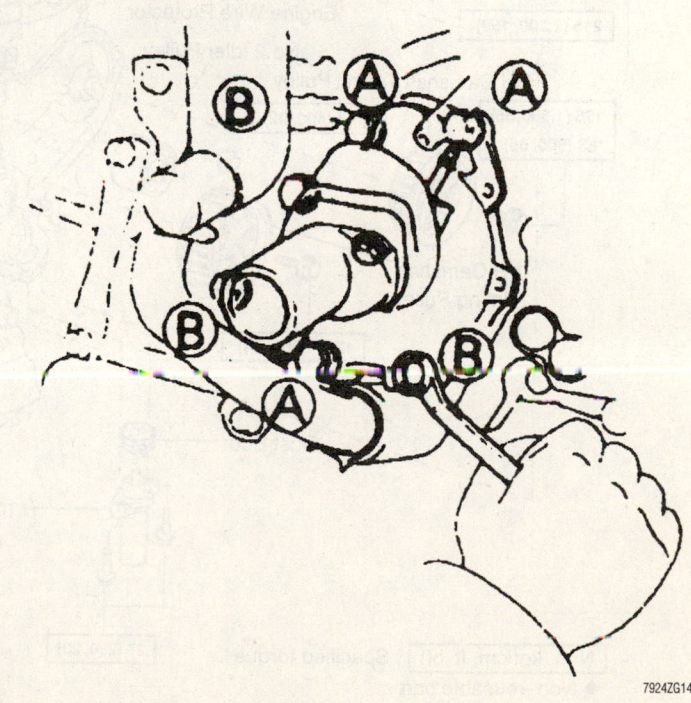

Tightening the water pump bolts—Previa

7924ZG14

- Top cowl seal and panel
- Window washer hoses, from the ventilator louvers
- Left and right ventilator louvers
- Heater air duct
- Front upper suspension brace, for RX 300
- Timing belt

5. Mark the left and right camshaft pulleys with a touch of paint.

6. Remove or disconnect the following:
- Right and left camshaft pulleys bolts
- Pulleys from the engine

➡ **Be sure not to mix up the pulleys.**

- No. 2 idler pulley by removing the bolt
- 3 clamps and engine wire from the rear timing belt cover

- 6 No. 3 timing belt cover-to-engine bolts
- Water pump nuts/bolts
- Water pump and gasket from the engine

To install:

7. Check that the water pump turns smoothly. Also check the air hole for coolant leakage.

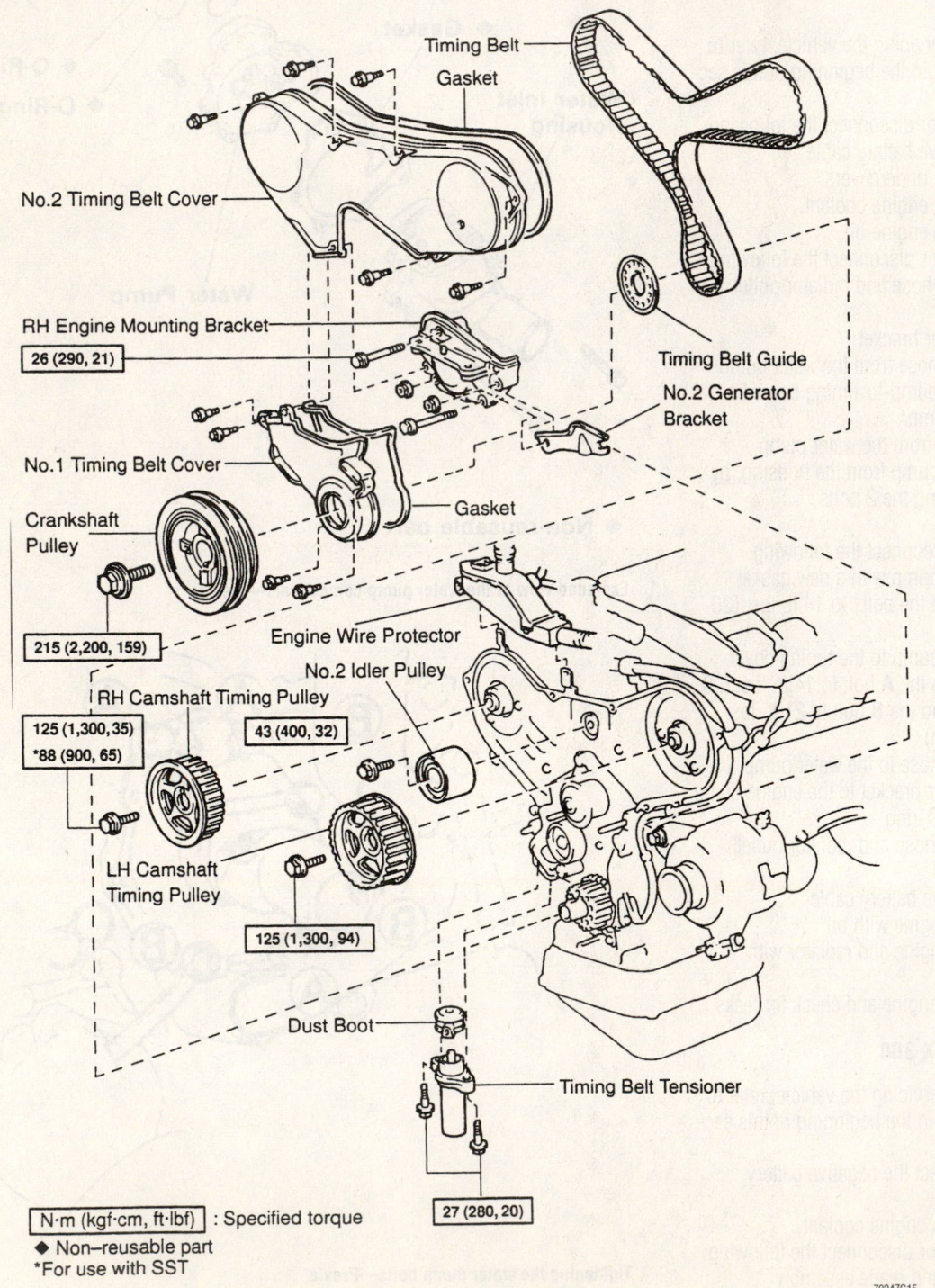

N·m (kgf·cm, ft·lbf) : Specified torque
◆ Non–reusable part
*For use with SST

Exploded view of the components to gain access to the water pump—Sienna and RX 300

7924ZG15

8. Apply liquid sealer to the gasket, water pump and engine block.

9. Install or connect the following:
- Water pump, using a new gasket. Tighten the nuts/bolts to 53 inch lbs. (6 Nm).
- Rear timing belt cover. Tighten the 6 bolts to 74 inch lbs. (9 Nm).
- Engine wire with the 3 clamps to the rear timing belt cover

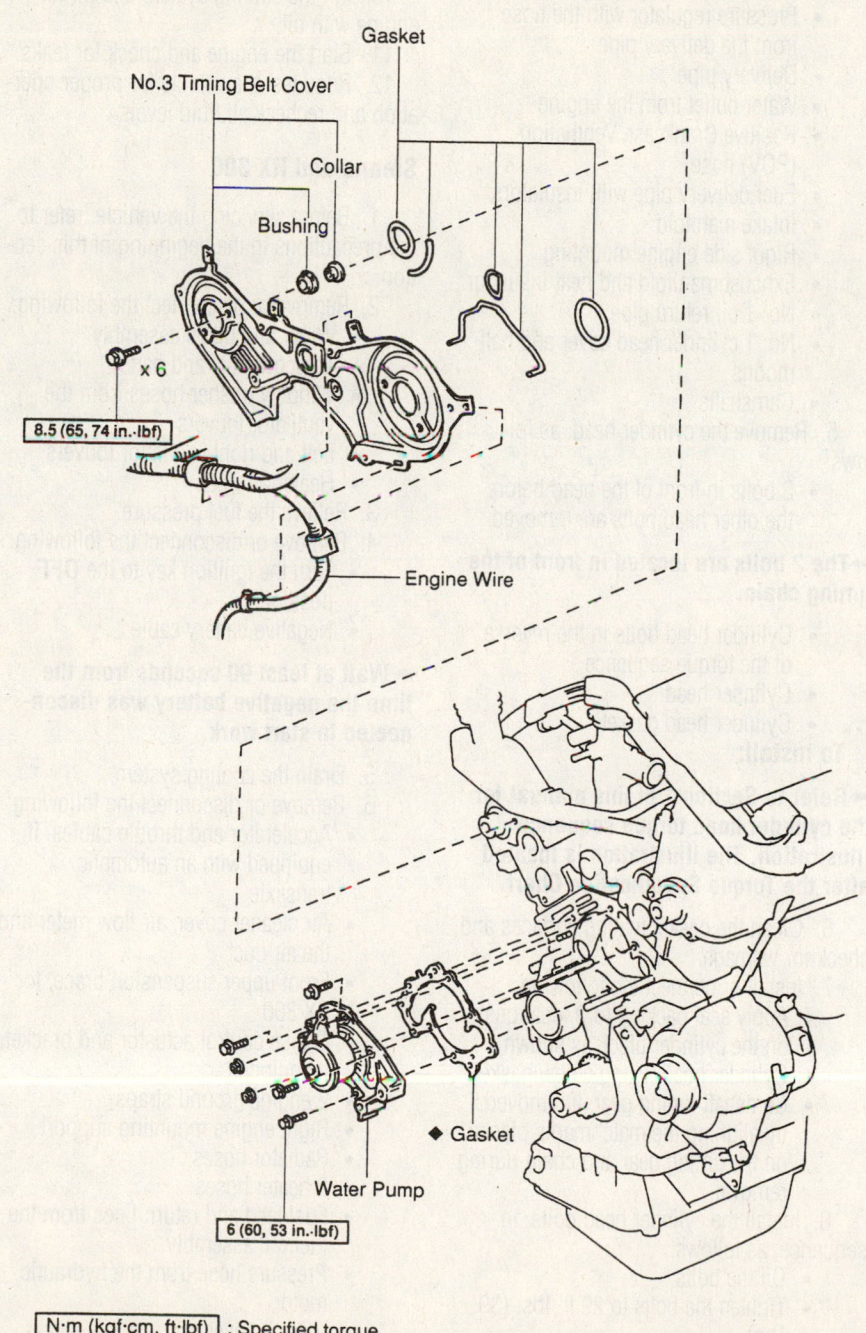

Exploded view of the water pump and related components—Sienna and RX 300

- No. 2 idler pulley. Tighten the bolt to 32 ft. lbs. (43 Nm).

➡**After tightening the bolt, be sure the idler pulley moves smoothly.**

- Right-hand camshaft pulley, with the flange side **outward**.

➡**Be sure to align the knock pin hole**

on the camshaft pulley with the knock pin on the camshaft.

- Tighten the camshaft bolt to 65 ft. lbs. (88 Nm), using the removal tools
- Left-hand camshaft pulley, with the flange side **inward**.

➡**Be sure to align the knock pin hole on the camshaft pulley with the knock pin on the camshaft.**

- Tighten the camshaft bolt to 94 ft. lbs. (125 Nm), using the removal tools
- Timing belt
- Front upper suspension brace, for RX 300. Tighten the nuts to 59 ft. lbs. (80 Nm).

10. Fill the engine coolant.

11. Install or connect the following:
- Heater air duct
- Left and right ventilator louvers
- Window washer hoses to the ventilator louvers
- Top cowl seal and panel
- Wiper and blade assembly
- Negative battery cable

12. Start the engine.

13. Top off the engine coolant and check for leaks.

Cylinder Head

REMOVAL & INSTALLATION

Rav4

1. Before servicing the vehicle, refer to the precautions in the beginning of this section.

2. Release the fuel system pressure.

3. Remove or disconnect the following:
- Negative battery cable
- Right-hand engine undercover

4. Drain the engine coolant.

5. Remove or disconnect the following:
- Camshafts
- Cylinder head bolts in several passes
- Cylinder head with the intake manifold
- Air hose from the intake manifold
- 2 bolts and the air tube
- Intake manifold and gasket
- Air hose from the cylinder head port
- Air hose
- Fuel delivery pipe and the injectors
- Oil pressure switch

Refer to Section 1 for engine rebuilding specifications

To install:

6. Install or connect the following:
   • Oil pressure switch
   • Fuel injectors and the delivery pipe
   • Air hose to the cylinder head port
   • Intake manifold with new gaskets. Tighten the nut/bolts to 14 ft. lbs. (19 Nm).
   • Air tube with the 2 bolts
   • Air hose to the intake manifold

7. Clean the gasket mating surfaces using care not to damage the aluminum components, replace the gasket; then, lower the cylinder head onto the engine. Be sure the dowel pins are aligned and no hoses or wires are between the head and cylinder block.

➡**Refer to Section 1 of this manual for the cylinder head torque sequence illustration. The illustration is located after the Torque Specification Chart.**

8. Tighten the cylinder head bolts in 2 progressive steps, as follows:
   a. Apply a light coat of engine oil to the cylinder head bolts.
   b. Tighten the cylinder head bolts, in several passes, in sequence, to 36 ft. lbs. (49 Nm).
   c. Mark the front of the cylinder head bolt with paint.
   d. Retighten the cylinder head bolts by 90 degrees in sequence.
   e. Retighten an additional 90 degrees and be sure that the paint mark is now positioned toward the rear.

9. Install or connect the following:
   • Intake and exhaust camshafts
   • Negative battery cable

10. Refill the engine with coolant, start the engine, warm up and check for leaks.

11. Bleed the cooling system and top off coolant as necessary.

12. Install the right-hand engine undercover.

13. Check ignition timing and road test the vehicle for proper operation.

Previa

➡**In order remove the cylinder head, the engine and transmission must be pulled from the vehicle.**

1. Before servicing the vehicle, refer to the precautions in the beginning of this section.

2. Disconnect the negative battery cable.

✳✳ CAUTION

Wait at least 90 seconds when working on vehicles equipped with an airbag.

3. Relieve the fuel system pressure.

4. Remove or disconnect the following:
   • Engine/transmission assembly
   • Engine wiring from the engine and move it aside
   • No. 2 head cover
   • Distributor
   • Exhaust Gas Recirculation (EGR) valve
   • Union bolts and gaskets from the delivery pipe and cold start injector
   • Pressure regulator with the hose from the delivery pipe
   • Delivery pipe
   • Water outlet from the engine
   • Positive Crankcase Ventilation (PCV) hose
   • Fuel delivery pipe with insulators
   • Intake manifold
   • Right side engine mounting
   • Exhaust manifold and heat insulator
   • No. 1 oil return pipe
   • No. 1 cylinder head cover and half moons
   • Camshafts

5. Remove the cylinder head, as follows:
   • 2 bolts in front of the head before the other head bolts are removed.

➡**The 2 bolts are located in front of the timing chain.**

   • Cylinder head bolts in the reverse of the torque sequence
   • Cylinder head.
   • Cylinder head gasket

To install:

➡**Refer to Section 1 of this manual for the cylinder head torque sequence illustration. The illustration is located after the Torque Specification Chart.**

6. Clean the gasket mating surfaces and check for warpage.

7. Install or connect the following:
   • Apply seal packing to 2 locations on the cylinder block as shown
   • Cylinder head, using a new gasket
   • Camshaft timing gear, if removed, by aligning the matchmarks placed on the timing gear and chain during removal.

8. Install the cylinder head bolts, in sequence, as follows:
   • Oil the bolts
   • Tighten the bolts to 29 ft. lbs. (39 Nm).
   • Mark the front of the cylinder head bolt with paint
   • Retighten the bolts 90 degree turn
   • Retighten the bolts an additional 90 degree turn

➡**Check that the painted mark is now facing rearward.**

9. Install or connect the following:
   • Tighten the 2 front mounting bolts to 15 ft. lbs. (21 Nm).
   • Camshafts
   • Remaining components
   • Engine/transmission assembly into the vehicle
   • Negative battery cable

10. Fill the cooling system and fill the engine with oil.

11. Start the engine and check for leaks.

12. Road test the vehicle for proper operation and recheck all fluid levels.

Sienna and RX 300

1. Before servicing the vehicle, refer to the precautions in the beginning of this section.

2. Remove or disconnect the following:
   • Wiper and blade assembly
   • Top cowl seal and panel
   • Window washer hoses from the ventilator louvers
   • Left and right ventilator louvers
   • Heater air duct

3. Relieve the fuel pressure.

4. Remove or disconnect the following:
   • Turn the ignition key to the **OFF** position
   • Negative battery cable

➡**Wait at least 90 seconds from the time the negative battery was disconnected to start work.**

5. Drain the cooling system.

6. Remove or disconnect the following:
   • Accelerator and throttle cables, if equipped with an automatic transaxle
   • Air cleaner cover, air flow meter and the air duct
   • Front upper suspension brace, for RX 300
   • Cruise control actuator and bracket, if equipped
   • 2 engine ground straps
   • Right engine mounting support
   • Radiator hoses
   • 2 heater hoses
   • Fuel feed and return lines from the fuel rail assembly
   • Pressure hose from the hydraulic motor
   • V-bank cover

7. Disconnect the following vacuum hoses:
   • Fuel pressure control Vacuum Switching Valve (VSV)
   • Fuel pressure regulator

- Cylinder head rear plate
- Intake air control valve VSV
- Exhaust Gas Recirculation (EGR) vacuum modulator
- EGR valve

8. Disconnect the following wiring and hoses:
- Intake air control valve
- Fuel pressure regulator
- EGR VSV

9. Remove the 2 nuts and the emission control valve set.

10. Disconnect the following hoses;
- Brake booster vacuum hose
- PCV hose
- Intake air control valve vacuum hose

11. Remove or disconnect the following:
- Data Link Connector (DLC) from the mounting bracket
- 2 ground straps from the intake chamber
- Hydraulic motor pressure hose from the intake chamber
- Right Oxygen (O2) sensor connector from the power steering pressure tube
- 2 nuts and the power steering pressure tube from the intake chamber
- Both power steering air hoses
- Engine hanger and the intake chamber support
- EGR pipe and gaskets

12. Disconnect the following wiring:
- Throttle Position (TP) sensor connector
- Idle Air Control (IAC) valve connector
- EGR gas temperature connector
- Air conditioning idle up connector

13. Disconnect the following vacuum hoses:
- 2 vacuum hoses from the Thermal Vacuum Valve (TVV)
- Vacuum hose from the cylinder head rear plate
- Vacuum hose from the charcoal canister

14. Remove or disconnect the following.
- Air assist hose and the 2 water bypass hoses
- Air intake chamber
- Left engine wiring harness and move it aside
- Wiring harness from the rear of the engine
- Right engine wiring harness and move it aside
- Ignition coils and move them aside
- Timing belt

- Camshaft pulleys and the timing belt rear cover
- Cylinder head rear plate
- Water inlet pipe
- Air assist hose and vacuum hose
- Intake manifold and fuel rail assembly
- Water outlet
- EGR pipe from the right exhaust manifold
- Front exhaust pipe and exhaust manifolds
- Dipstick assembly and the power steering pump bracket
- Valve covers and the Camshaft Position (CMP) sensor
- Camshafts

15. Be sure the engine is at/or near ambient temperature and remove the 2 (1 on each head) 8mm recessed hex bolts. Loosen and remove the 8 head bolts evenly, in 3 passes, in the reverse order of the installation sequence. Carefully lift the head from the engine; if necessary to pry the head loose, take great care not to damage the mating surfaces. Place the head on wood blocks in a clean work area.

➡**If the cylinder head bolts are loosened out of sequence, warpage or cracking could result.**

16. Remove the cylinder head gasket. With a gasket scraper, carefully remove all the old gasket material from the cylinder head and engine block surfaces.

To install:

➡**Refer to Section 1 of this manual for the cylinder head torque sequence illustration. The illustration is located after the Torque Specification Chart.**

17. Place the new cylinder head gasket onto the cylinder block.

18. Install the cylinder head, in sequence, using several steps, as follows:
- Cylinder head onto the gasket
- Cylinder head bolts lubricated with clean engine oil
- Tighten the bolts in sequence in 3 steps to 40 ft. lbs. (54 Nm).

➡**If any bolt does not meet the torque, replace it.**

- Mark the forward edge of each bolt with paint, then tighten each bolt, in proper sequence, an additional 90 degrees.
- Check that each painted mark is now at a 90 degrees angle to the front

➡**The paint mark applied to the bolt in the 9 o'clock position and should now be in the 12 o'clock position.**

- Remaining 8mm bolts, lubricated with engine oil. Tighten both bolts to 13 ft. lbs. (18 Nm).

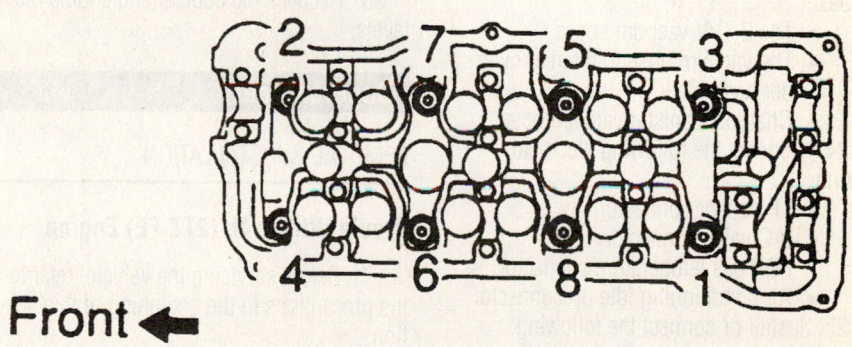

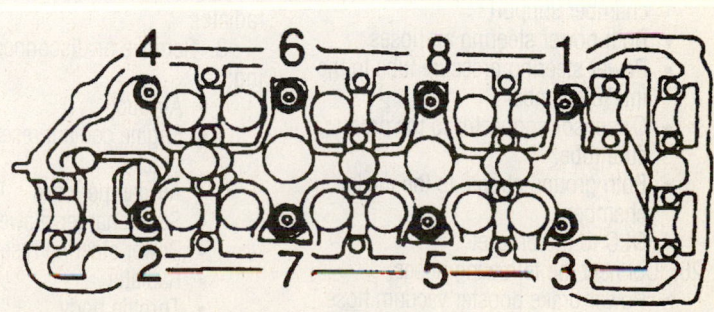

Cylinder head bolt loosening sequence—Sienna and RX 300

7924ZG19

For engine torque specifications, refer to Section 1 of this manual

19. Install the camshafts.
20. Check and adjust the valves.
21. Apply sealant to the cylinder heads where the camshaft supports meet the cylinder heads.
22. Install or connect the following:
- Cylinder head covers, using new gaskets
- Dipstick and power steering pump bracket
- Exhaust manifolds. Tighten the nuts to 36 ft. lbs. (49 Nm).
- EGR pipe to the right exhaust manifold
- Water outlet
- Intake manifold and the fuel rail assembly. Tighten the intake manifold nuts/bolts to 11 ft. lbs. (15 Nm).
- Air assist hose and the 2 water bypass hoses
- Water inlet pipe and cylinder head rear plate
- Timing belt rear cover and camshaft pulleys
- Timing belt
- Spark plugs and ignition coils
- Right engine wiring harness
- Wiring harness to the rear of the engine
- Left engine wiring harness
- Air intake chamber
- EGR pipe, using new gaskets
23. Connect the following vacuum hoses:
- The 2 TVV vacuum hoses
- The vacuum hose to the rear cylinder head plate
- Charcoal canister vacuum hose
24. Connect the following electrical wiring:
- TP sensor connector
- IAC valve connector
- EGR gas temperature connector
- Air conditioning idle up connector
25. Install or connect the following:
- Engine hanger and the intake chamber support
- Both power steering air hoses
- Power steering pressure tube to the intake chamber
- O_2 sensor connector to the pressure tube.
- Both ground straps, to the intake chamber
- DLC to the bracket
26. Connect the following hoses:
- Power brake booster vacuum hose
- PCV hose
- IAC valve vacuum hose
27. Install or connect the following:

- Emission control valve set and related vacuum hoses and connectors
- V-bank cover
- Pressure hose to the hydraulic motor
- Fuel lines to the fuel rail assembly
- Heater and radiator hoses
- Right engine mounting support
- both engine ground straps
- Upper front suspension brace, if removed. Tighten the nuts to 59 ft. lbs. (80 Nm).
- Cruise control actuator and bracket
- Air cleaner, air flow meter and air duct assembly
- Accelerator and throttle cables, if equipped with an automatic transaxle
28. Fill the cooling system.
29. Install or connect the following:
- Negative battery cable
- Heater air duct
- Left and right ventilator louvers
- Window washer hoses from the ventilator louvers
- Top cowl seal and panel
- Wiper and blade assembly
30. Start the engine and check for leaks.
31. Bleed the air from the cooling system.
32. Road test the vehicle and check for unusual noise, shock, slippage, correct shift points and smooth operation.
33. Recheck the coolant and engine oil levels.

Supercharger

REMOVAL & INSTALLATION

Previa With 2.4L (2TZ-FE) Engine

1. Before servicing the vehicle, refer to the precautions in the beginning of this section.
2. Drain the engine coolant from the radiator.
3. Remove or disconnect the following:

- Air duct
- Engine coolant reservoir tank and bracket
- Air damper case
- Supercharger blower
- Power steering reservoir
- Radiator
- Throttle body
- Alternator/power steering drive belt
- Power steering pump

- Supercharger's drive belt
- No. 2 idler pulley by extracting the nut, plate and spacer
4. Remove the No. 1 air inlet duct with the supercharger bypass valve, as follows:
- Supercharger bypass valve harness
- Brake booster hose
- Air conditioning idle up air hose
- Supercharger magnetic clutch connector
- Supercharger magnetic clutch connector from the No. 1 hose support bracket
- Air hoses and 3-way
- Supercharger bypass valve to the No. 1 air outlet duct nuts/bolts
- No. 1 air inlet duct with the supercharger bypass valve
- Supercharger bypass valve and No. 1 air inlet duct gaskets
5. Remove or disconnect the following:
- No. 1 idle up pipe, by removing the bolt and air hose
- No. 1 air tube
- No. 1 intake air connector bracket, by removing both bolts
6. Remove the supercharger, as follows:
- Both supercharger-to-equipment drive housing nuts/bolts
- 6 supercharger-to-No. 1 air outlet duct nuts/bolts
- Supercharger and No. 1 air outlet duct and the gasket
- Supercharger and No. 1 air outlet duct

To install

7. Install the supercharger, as follows:
- Supercharger and No. 1 air outlet duct, using a new gasket. Tighten the 6 nuts to 82 inch lbs. (9 Nm).
- Supercharger-to-equipment drive housing. Tighten both nuts/bolts to 27 ft. lbs. (37 Nm).
8. Install or connect the following:
- No. 1 intake air connector bracket. Tighten both bolts to 13 ft. lbs. (18 Nm).
- No. 1 air tube
- No. 1 idle up pipe by connecting the air hose. Tighten the bolts to 69 inch lbs. (7.5 Nm).
9. Install the No. 1 air inlet duct with the supercharger bypass valve, as follows:
- Supercharger bypass valve to the No. 1 air outlet duct. Tighten both nuts/bolts to 48 inch lbs. (5 Nm).
- Air hoses and 3-way valve
- No. 1 air hose support bracket. Tighten both bolts to 69 inch lbs. (8 Nm).

- Supercharger magnetic clutch connector to the No. 1 hose support bracket
- Air conditioning idle up air hose
- Supercharger magnetic clutch connector
- Brake booster hose
- Supercharger bypass valve connector

10. Install or connect the following:
- No. 2 idler pulley with the spacer, plate and the nut

- Supercharger drive belt by adjusting it
- Power steering pump. Tighten the long bolts to 35 ft. lbs. (48 Nm) and the short bolts to 27 ft. lbs. (36 Nm).
- Alternator/power steering drive belts, by adjusting them
- Throttle body
- Radiator. Tighten the bolts to 13 ft. lbs. (18 Nm).
- All connectors, hoses and shrouds

- Power steering reservoir. Tighten both bolts to 108 inch lbs. (13 Nm).
- Supercharger blower
- Air damper case
- Engine coolant reservoir and bracket
- Air duct
- Negative battery cable

11. Refill the radiator with coolant.
12. Reset any electronic components such as the radio.
13. Check all fluids.

Intake Manifold

REMOVAL & INSTALLATION

RAV4

1. Before servicing the vehicle, refer to the precautions in the beginning of this section.
2. Properly relieve the fuel system pressure.
3. Remove or disconnect the following:
- Negative battery cable
- Air cleaner assembly
- Throttle body from the intake manifold
4. Disconnect the engine wire from the intake manifold, as follows:
- 4 injector connectors
- 2 engine wire clamps from the intake manifold wire brackets
- Engine wire protector from the right-hand side of the intake manifold by removing the bolt
- Engine wire from the wire clamp
5. Remove the EGR valve, EGR pipe and modulator, as follows:
- Both vacuum hoses from the Exhaust Gas Recirculation (EGR) Vacuum Switching Valve (VSV)
- Vacuum modulator from the clamp on the intake manifold
- Loosen the cylinder head side of the EGR pipe union nut
- Both nuts, the EGR valve, pipe assembly and gasket
- Vacuum modulator
6. Disconnect the following hoses:
- Fuel filter vacuum sensor hose on the intake manifold
- Brake booster vacuum hose from the intake manifold
- Ground strap from the intake manifold
7. Remove or disconnect the following:

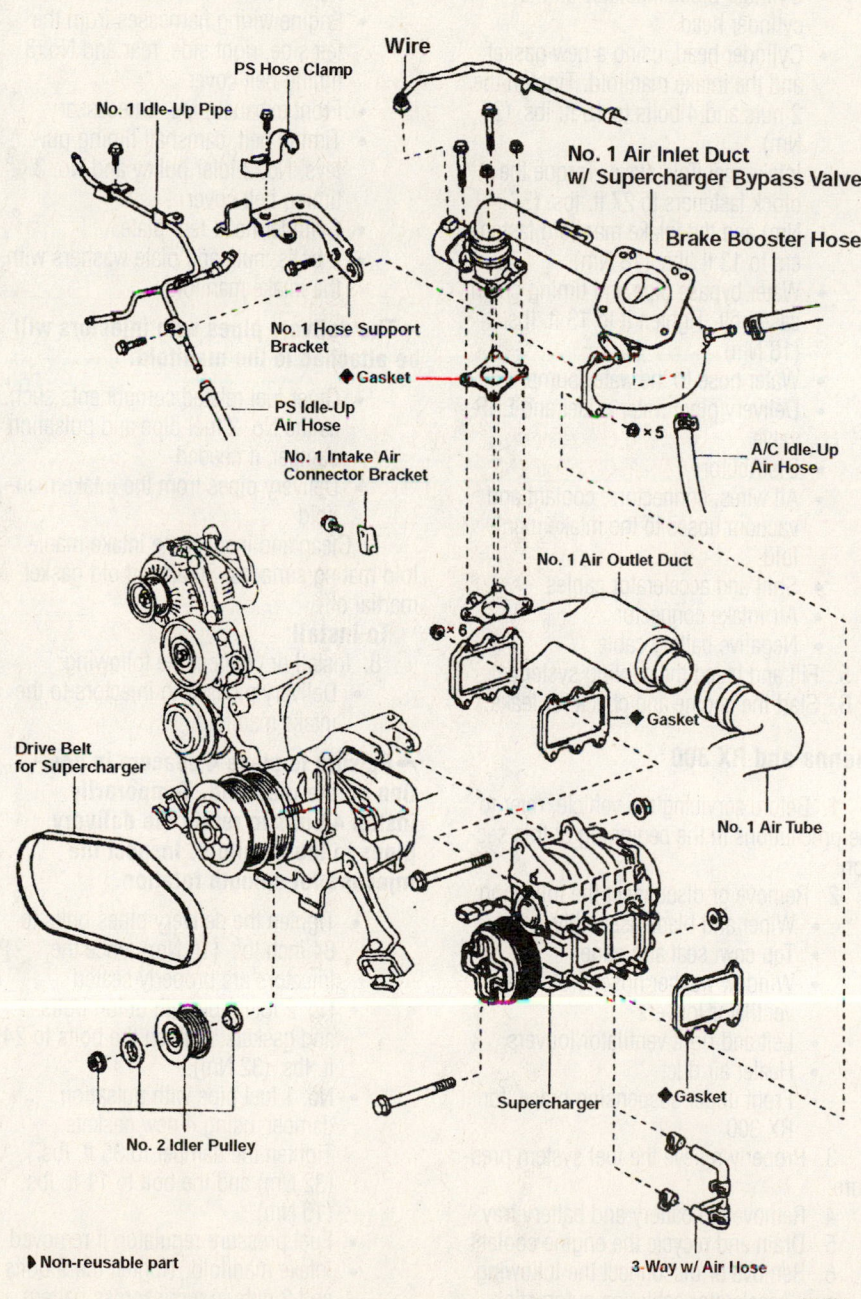

Exploded view of the supercharger and related components—Previa with 2.4L (2TZ-FE) engine

Labels in figure: Wire; PS Hose Clamp; No. 1 Idle-Up Pipe; No. 1 Air Inlet Duct w/ Supercharger Bypass Valve; Brake Booster Hose; No. 1 Hose Support Bracket; ◆Gasket; PS Idle-Up Air Hose; No. 1 Intake Air Connector Bracket; A/C Idle-Up Air Hose; □×5; No. 1 Air Outlet Duct; □×6; ◆Gasket; Drive Belt for Supercharger; No. 1 Air Tube; No. 2 Idler Pulley; Supercharger; ◆Gasket; ▶Non-reusable part; 3-Way w/ Air Hose; 7924ZG21

- Intake manifold stay by removing the 2 bolts
- Control cable from the clamp on the rear side of the intake manifold, if equipped with automatic transmission
- Air hose from the intake manifold
- Air tube from the intake manifold, by removing the 2 bolts
- 6 bolts and 2 nuts from the intake manifold
- Intake manifold

To install:

8. Install or connect the following:
- Intake manifold. Tighten the 6 bolts and 2 nuts to 14 ft. lbs. (19 Nm).
- Air tube with the 2 bolts
- Air hose to the intake manifold
- Control cable to the clamp on the rear side of the intake manifold, if equipped with an automatic transmission
- Intake manifold stay. Tighten both bolts to 31 ft. lbs. (42 Nm).

9. Connect the following hoses:
- Ground strap to the intake manifold
- Brake booster vacuum hose to the intake manifold
- Fuel filter vacuum sensor hose to the intake manifold

10. Install the EGR valve, EGR pipe and the vacuum modulator, as follows:
- Vacuum modulator
- EGR valve and pipe. Tighten both nuts to 108 inch lbs. (13 Nm) and the union nut to 43 ft. lbs. (59 Nm).
- Vacuum hoses

11. Install or connect the following:
- Engine wire and injectors

➡ **The No. 1 and No. 3 injector connectors are brown, and the No. 2 and No. 4 injector connectors are gray.**

- Throttle body to the intake manifold
- Air cleaner assembly
- Negative battery cable

Previa

1. Before servicing the vehicle, refer to the precautions in the beginning of this section.
2. Properly relieve the fuel system pressure.
3. Remove or disconnect the following:
- Air intake connector
- All wires, harnesses, coolant and vacuum hoses, from the intake manifold
- Shift and accelerator cables
- Fuel pipes
- Distributor and EGR valve

- Positive Crankcase Ventilation (PCV) hose
- Water outlet, bypass pipe and gasket from the manifold
- Water hose from the water pump
- Water bypass pipe and timing chain case bolt.
- Intake manifold stays
- 2 nuts, 4 bolts and the intake manifold with gasket
- Cylinder block insulators

To install:

4. Install or connect the following:
- Cylinder block insulator on the cylinder head
- Cylinder head, using a new gasket and the intake manifold. Tighten the 2 nuts and 4 bolts to 15 ft. lbs. (21 Nm).
- Intake manifold stays. Torque the block fasteners to 27 ft. lbs. (37 Nm) and the intake manifold fasteners to 13 ft. lbs. (18 Nm).
- Water bypass pipe and timing chain case bolt. Tighten it to 13 ft. lbs. (18 Nm).
- Water hose to the water pump
- Delivery pipe, water outlet and EGR valve
- Distributor
- All wires, connectors, coolant and vacuum hoses to the intake manifold
- Shift and accelerator cables
- Air intake connector
- Negative battery cable

5. Fill and bleed the cooling system.
6. Start the engine and check for leaks.

Sienna and RX 300

1. Before servicing the vehicle, refer to the precautions in the beginning of this section.

2. Remove or disconnect the following:
- Wiper and blade assembly
- Top cowl seal and panel
- Window washer hoses from the ventilator louvers
- Left and right ventilator louvers
- Heater air duct
- Front upper suspension brace, for RX 300

3. Properly relieve the fuel system pressure.

4. Remove the battery and battery tray.
5. Drain and recycle the engine coolant.
6. Remove or disconnect the following:
- Accelerator cable, on automatic transaxles
- Throttle cable
- Air cleaner cap assembly

- Any wiring or hoses interfering with removal
- Right side engine mount stay
- Radiator and heater hoses in the way of the intake manifold removal
- V-bank cover
- All the vacuum hose and wiring for the emission control valve set
- Air intake chamber and discard the gasket
- Exhaust Gas Recirculation (EGR) pipe and discard the gaskets
- Hydraulic motor pressure hose from the air intake chamber
- Engine wiring harnesses from the left side, right side, rear and No. 3 timing belt cover
- Front exhaust pipe, if necessary
- Timing belt, camshaft timing pulleys, No. 2 idler pulley and No. 3 timing belt cover
- Cylinder head rear plate
- 2 bolts, nuts and plate washers with the intake manifold.

➡ **The delivery pipes with injectors will be attached to the manifold.**

- Other fuel related components such as the No. 2 fuel pipe and pulsation damper, if needed
- Delivery pipes from the intake manifold

7. Clean and inspect the intake manifold mating surfaces. Scrape all old gasket martial off.

To install:

8. Install or connect the following:
- Delivery pipes with injectors to the intake manifold.

➡ **Be sure to place 4 spacers in position on the manifold. Temporarily install 4 bolts to retain the delivery pipes to the manifold. Inspect the injectors for smooth rotation.**

- Tighten the delivery pipes bolts to 84 inch lbs. (10 Nm), once the injectors are properly seated
- No. 2 fuel pipe with union bolts and gaskets. Tighten the bolts to 24 ft. lbs. (32 Nm).
- No. 1 fuel pipe with pulsation damper, using 4 new gaskets. Tighten the damper to 35 ft. lbs. (32 Nm) and the bolt to 11 ft. lbs. (15 Nm).
- Fuel pressure regulator, if removed
- Intake manifold. Tighten the 9 bolts and 2 nuts in a crisscross pattern to 11 ft. lbs. (15 Nm).

➡ **Be sure the gasket is in place properly prior to tightening.**

9. Retighten the water outlet mounting nuts/bolts to 11 ft. lbs. (15 Nm), if loosened.

10. Install or connect the following:
   - Air assist hose and water inlet pipe, using a new O-ring, by applying a small amount of soapy water. Tighten the fastener(s) to 14 ft. lbs. (20 Nm).
   - Ground strap
   - Vacuum hoses removed to the air intake chamber and vacuum tank
   - Any remaining components, using new gaskets. Tighten the air intake chamber nuts/bolts to 32 ft. lbs. (43 Nm), the EGR pipe nuts to 108 inch lbs. (12 Nm) and the emission control valve set to 69 inch lbs. (8 Nm).
   - Air cleaner assembly

   - Heater hoses
   - Battery and tray
   - Throttle cable with bracket onto the throttle body
   - Accelerator cable, by adjusting it, if equipped with an automatic transaxle
   - Front upper suspension brace, for RX 300. Tighten the nuts to 59 ft. lbs. (80 Nm).

11. Refill the cooling system

12. Install or connect the following:
   - Negative battery cable
   - Heater air duct
   - Left and right ventilator louvers
   - Window washer hoses from the ventilator louvers

   - Top cowl seal and panel
   - Wiper and blade assembly

13. Start the engine and inspect for leaks.

Exhaust Manifold

REMOVAL & INSTALLATION

RAV4

1. Before servicing the vehicle, refer to the precautions in the beginning of this section.

2. Remove or disconnect the following:
   - Negative battery cable
   - Front exhaust pipe from the exhaust manifold, using a 14mm deep socket wrench; discard the gasket

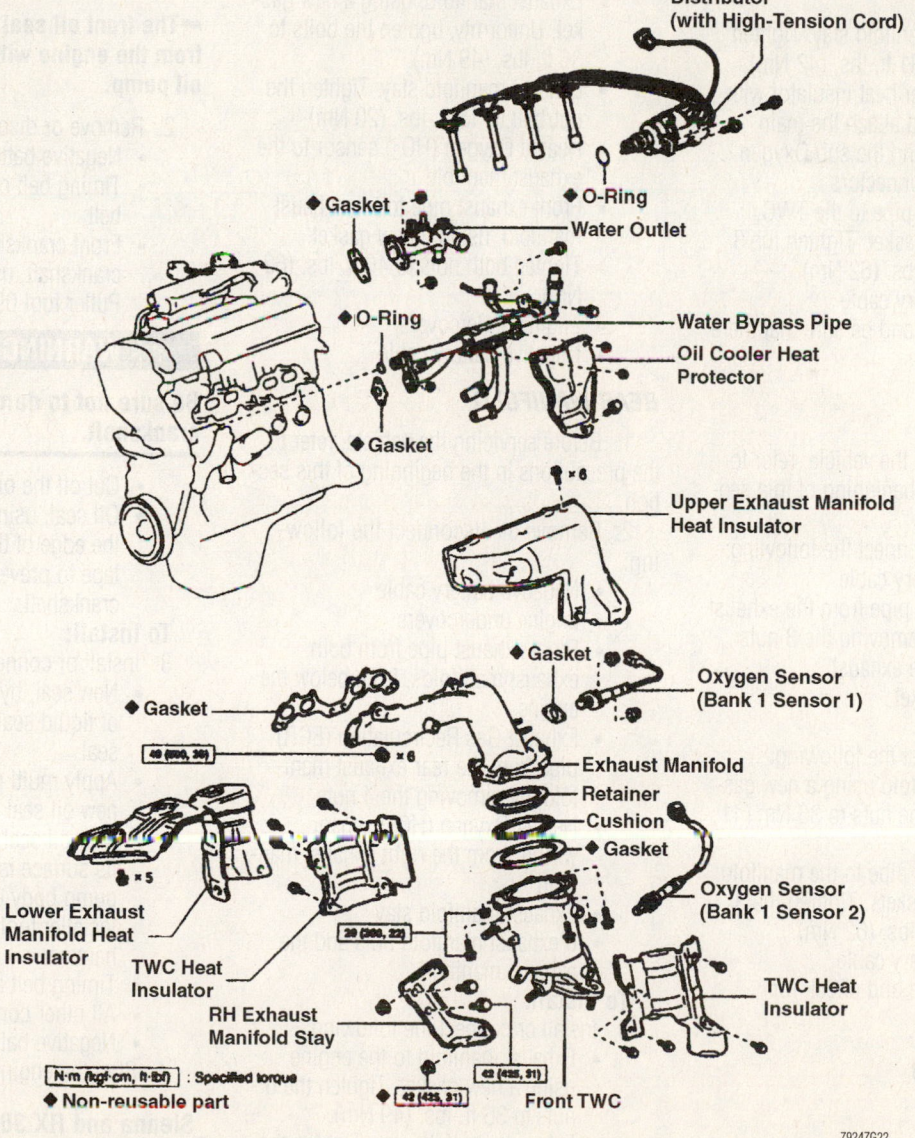

Exploded view of the exhaust manifold and components—rav4

Please refer to Section 8 for electric cooling fan wiring schematics

- Main Oxygen (O$_2$) sensor and the sub Oxygen (O$_2$) sensor connectors
- 6 bolts and the upper manifold heat insulator
- 2 right-hand exhaust manifold stay-to-cylinder block bolts
- 6 nuts, the exhaust manifold and the Three-Way Catalytic (TWC) converter assembly
- Exhaust manifold and front catalytic converter

To install:

3. Install or connect the following:
- Catalytic converter to the exhaust manifold. Tighten the nuts/bolts to 22 ft. lbs. (29 Nm).
- Exhaust manifold and the front TWC assembly. Tighten the 6 nuts, in several passes to 36 ft. lbs. (49 Nm).
- Right-hand manifold stay. Tighten both bolts to 31 ft. lbs. (42 Nm).
- Manifold upper heat insulator with the 6 bolts and attach the main Oxygen (O$_2$) and the sub Oxygen (O$_2$) sensor connectors
- Front exhaust pipe to the TWC, using a new gasket. Tighten the 3 nuts to 46 ft. lbs. (62 Nm).
- Negative battery cable

4. Start the engine and be sure that there are no exhaust leaks.

Previa

1. Before servicing the vehicle, refer to the precautions in the beginning of this section.
2. Remove or disconnect the following:
- Negative battery cable
- Front exhaust pipe from the exhaust manifold by removing the 3 nuts
- 5 nuts and the exhaust manifold/gasket

To install:

3. Install or connect the following:
- Exhaust manifold using a new gasket. Tighten the nuts to 36 Nm (41 Nm).
- Front exhaust pipe to the manifold, using new gaskets. Tighten the 3 nuts to 46 ft. lbs. (62 Nm).
- Negative battery cable

4. Start the engine and check for leaks.

Sienna and RX 300

FRONT MANIFOLD

➡**Removing the oil filter helps gain access to a lower bolt in the front exhaust manifold.**

1. Before servicing the vehicle, refer to the precautions in the beginning of this section.
2. Remove or disconnect the following:
- Negative battery cable
- Engine undercovers
- Front exhaust pipe from the exhaust manifolds, by removing the nuts

➡**Check for access to some of the manifold lower bolts, if so remove any possible.**

- Heated Oxygen (HO$_2$) sensor
- Exhaust manifold stay, by removing the bolt and nut
- Remaining exhaust manifold nuts; then, separate the exhaust manifold from the engine

To install:

3. Install or connect the following:
- Exhaust manifold, using a new gasket. Uniformly, tighten the bolts to 36 ft. lbs. (49 Nm).
- Exhaust manifold stay. Tighten the nut/bolt to 15 ft. lbs. (20 Nm).
- Heated Oxygen (HO$_2$) sensor to the exhaust manifold
- Front exhaust pipe to the exhaust manifold, using a new gasket. Tighten both nuts to 46 ft. lbs. (62 Nm).
- Engine undercovers
- Negative battery cable

REAR MANIFOLD

1. Before servicing the vehicle, refer to the precautions in the beginning of this section.
2. Remove or disconnect the following:

- Negative battery cable
- Engine undercovers
- Front exhaust pipe from both exhaust manifolds, from below the engine
- Exhaust Gas Recirculation (EGR) pipe from the rear exhaust manifold, by removing the 4 nuts
- Heated Oxygen (HO$_2$) sensor wiring, from the right exhaust manifold
- Exhaust manifold stay
- 6 exhaust manifold nuts and the exhaust manifold

To install:

3. Install or connect the following:
- Exhaust manifold to the engine, using a new gasket. Tighten the 6 nuts to 36 ft. lbs. (49 Nm).
- Exhaust manifold stay. Tighten the nut/bolt to 15 ft. lbs. (20 Nm).
- HO$_2$sensor wiring to the exhaust manifold

- EGR pipe to the exhaust manifold and the engine, using new gaskets. Tighten the 4 nuts to 108 inch lbs. (12 Nm).
- Front exhaust pipe to the exhaust manifold, use a new gasket. Tighten both nuts to 46 ft. lbs. (62 Nm).
- Engine undercovers
- Negative battery cable

Front Crankshaft Seal

REMOVAL & INSTALLATION

RAV4

1. Before servicing the vehicle, refer to the precautions in the beginning of this section.

➡**The front oil seal can be removed from the engine without removing the oil pump.**

2. Remove or disconnect the following:
- Negative battery cable
- Timing belt covers and the timing belt
- Front crankshaft gear from the crankshaft, using Crankshaft Gear Puller tool 09950-50010

✳✳ WARNING

Be sure not to damage any part of the crankshaft.

- Cut off the oil seal lip
- Oil seal, using a suitable tool. Wrap the edge of the tool with a rag or tape to prevent damaging the crankshaft.

To install:

3. Install or connect the following:
- New seal, by applying a thin layer of liquid sealer to the outside of the seal
- Apply multi purpose grease to the new oil seal lip
- New oil seal, by tapping it in until its surface is flush with the oil pump body edge, using the Oil Seal Installer tool 09226-00010 and a hammer
- Timing belt and timing belt covers
- All other components
- Negative battery cable

4. Start the engine and check for leaks.

Sienna and RX 300

1. Before servicing the vehicle, refer to precautions in the beginning of this section.
2. Remove or disconnect the following:

- Engine coolant reservoir tank and the alternator belt
- Right front wheel and the splash shield
- Power steering pump drive belt, by loosening both bolts
- Both ground wire connectors
- Right engine mounting stay
- Engine moving control rod and the No. 2 right engine mount bracket

➡**To extract the engine bracket and control rod, raise the engine slightly.**

- No. 2 alternator bracket
- Crankshaft pulley bolt, using a pry-bar and wrench or Crankshaft Pulley Holding tool 09213-54015 and Flange Holding tool 09330-00021
- Crankshaft pulley, using a puller
- No. 1 timing belt cover

3. Remove the No. 2 timing belt cover, as follows:

- Engine wire protector from the No. 3 (rear) timing belt cover
- Engine wire protector clamp from the No. 3 timing belt cover
- 5 bolts from the No. 2 timing belt cover
- No. 2 cover

To install:

4. Install or connect the following:

- No. 2 timing belt cover, using a new gasket

➡**Install it evenly to the part of the belt cover shaded black. After installation, press down on it so that the adhesive sticks to the belt cover firmly.**

- No. 2 timing belt cover. Tighten the 5 bolts to 74 inch lbs. (8 Nm).
- Engine wire protector clamp to the No. 3 timing belt cover
- Engine wire protector to the No. 3 timing belt cover with the bolt
- No. 3 timing belt cover, using a new gasket
- Tighten the 4 No. 1 timing belt cover bolts to 74 inch lbs. (8 Nm).
- Crankshaft pulley. Tighten the bolt to 159 ft. lbs. (215 Nm).
- No. 2 alternator bracket. Tighten the nut to 21 ft. lbs. (28 Nm). Do not tighten the pivot bolt at this time.
- No. 2 right engine mounting bracket and the moving control rod
- Right engine mount stay
- Both ground wire connectors
- Drive belts by adjusting them
- Coolant reservoir
- Right front splash shield and wheel
- Negative battery cable

5. Start the vehicle and check for any leaks.

6. Recheck the ignition timing.

Camshaft and Valve Lifters

REMOVAL & INSTALLATION

RAV4

1. Before servicing the vehicle, refer to the precautions in the beginning of this section.

2. Remove or disconnect the following:
- Negative battery cable

- Cylinder head cover and the upper timing belt cover

3. Rotate the crankshaft to set the engine at Top Dead Center (TDC)/compression for the No. 1 cylinder.

➡**Due to the small thrust clearance on both the intake and exhaust camshafts, the camshafts must be kept level during removal. If the camshafts are removed without being kept level, the camshaft may be caught in the cylinder head causing the head to break or the camshaft to seize.**

4. Remove the camshaft timing sprocket and the timing belt.

5. Set the knock pin of the intake camshaft at 10–45 degrees Before Top Dead Center (BTDC) of camshaft angle. This angle will help to lift the exhaust camshaft level and evenly by pushing No. 2 and No. 4 cylinder camshaft lobes of the exhaust camshaft toward their valve lifters.

6. Secure the exhaust camshaft sub-gear to the main gear using a service bolt. The manufacturer recommends a bolt 0.63–0.79 in. (16–20mm) long with a thread diameter of 6mm and a 1mm thread pitch. When removing the exhaust camshaft, be sure that the torsional spring force of the sub-gear has been eliminated.

7. Remove the No. 1 and No. 2 rear bearing cap bolts and remove the cap. Uniformly loosen and remove bearing cap bolts No. 3 to No. 8 in several passes and in the proper sequence. Do not remove bearing cap bolts No. 9 and 10 at this time. Remove the No. 1, 2 and 4 bearing caps.

8. Alternately loosen and remove bear-

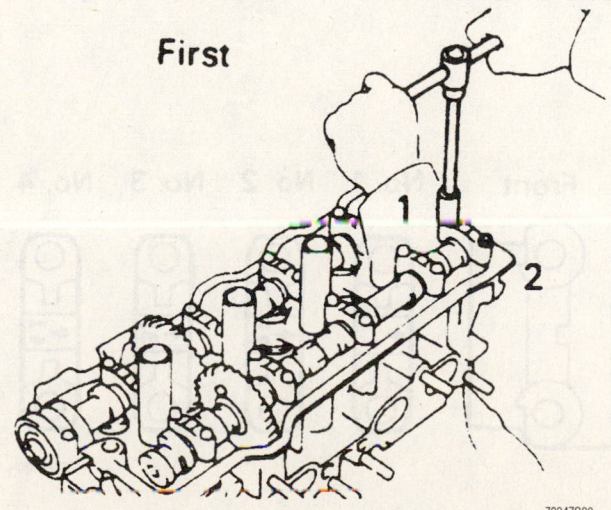

Exhaust camshaft bolt removal: step 1—RAV4 2.0L (3S-FE) engine

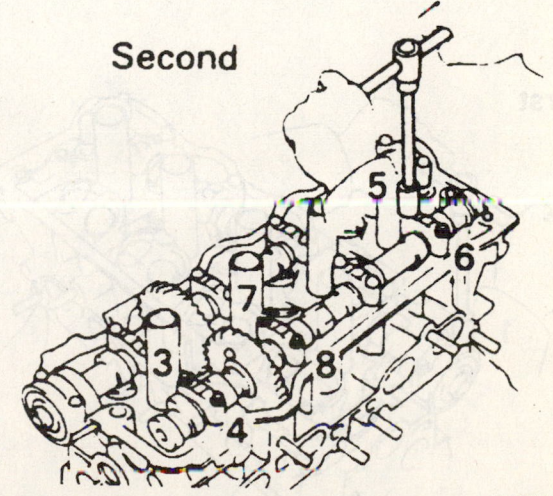

Exhaust camshaft bolt removal: step 2—RAV4 2.0L (3S-FE) engine

Third

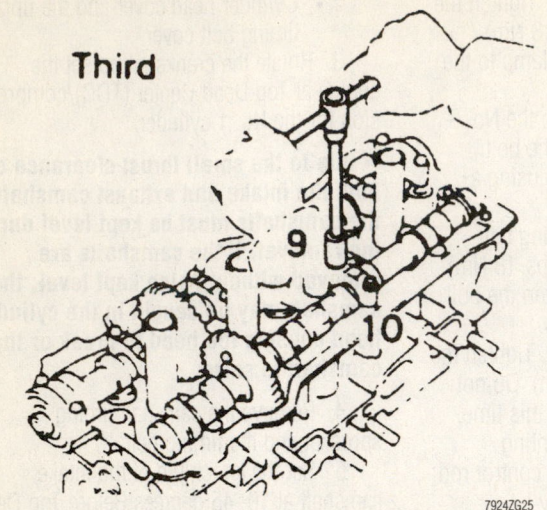

Exhaust camshaft bolt removal: step 3—RAV4 2.0L (3S-FE) engine

Second

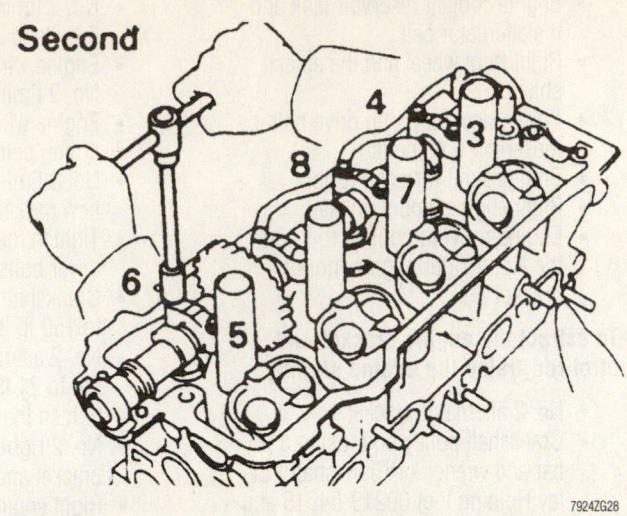

Intake camshaft bolt removal: step 2—RAV4 2.0L (3S-FE) engine

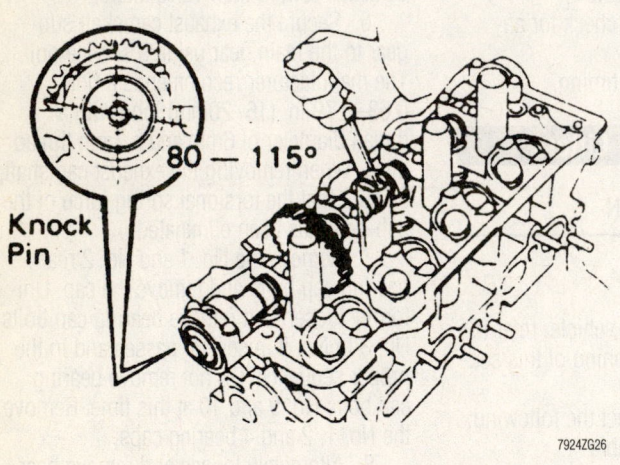

Intake camshaft knock pin alignment—RAV4 2.0L (3S-FE) engine

Third

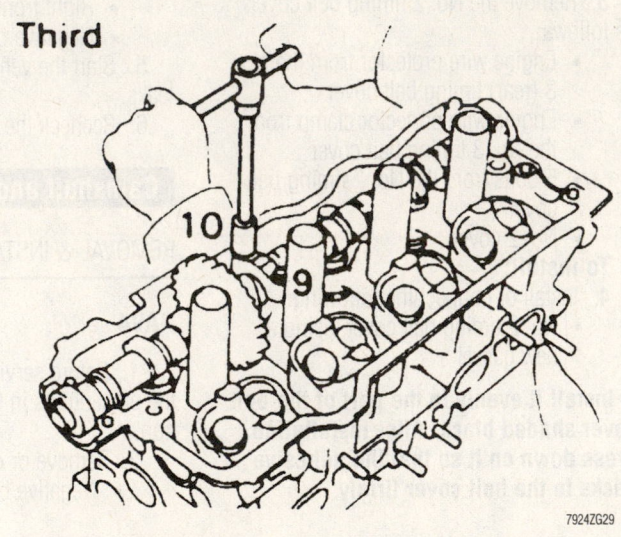

Intake camshaft bolt removal: step 3—RAV4 2.0L (3S-FE) engine

First

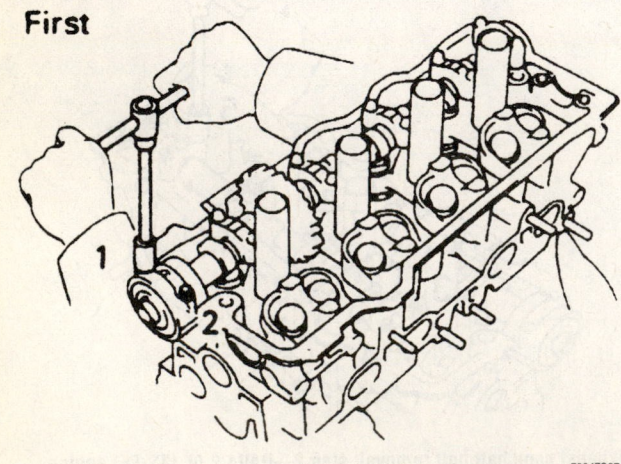

Intake camshaft bolt removal: step 1—RAV4 2.0L (3S-FE) engine

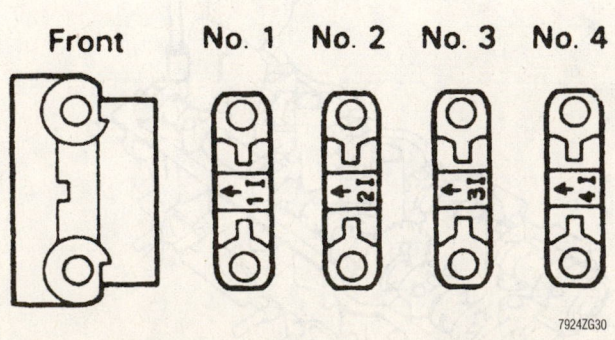

Intake camshaft bearing cap positioning—RAV4 2.0L (3S-FE) engine

ing cap bolts No. 9 and 10. As these bolts are loosened check to see that the camshaft is being lifted out straight and level.

➡ If the camshaft is not lifting out straight and level retighten No. 9 and 10 bearing cap bolts. Reverse the order of steps 5 through 7 and reset the intake camshaft knock pin to 10–45 degrees BTDC and repeat steps 5 through 7 again. Do not attempt to pry the camshaft from its mounting.

9. Remove the No. 3 bearing cap and exhaust camshaft from the engine.

10. Set the knock pin of the intake camshaft at 80–115 degrees BTDC of camshaft angle. This angle will help to lift the intake camshaft level and evenly by pushing

No. 1 and No. 3 cylinder camshaft lobes of the intake camshaft toward their valve lifters.

11. Remove the No. 1 and No. 2 front bearing cap bolts and remove the front bearing cap and oil seal. If the cap will not come apart easily, leave it in place without the bolts.

12. Uniformly loosen and remove bearing cap bolts No. 3 to No. 8 in several phases and in the proper sequence. Do not remove bearing cap bolts No. 9 and 10 at this time. Remove No. 1, 3 and 4 bearing caps.

13. Alternately loosen and remove bearing cap bolts No. 9 and 10. As these bolts are loosened and after breaking the adhesion on the front bearing cap, check to see that the camshaft is being lifted out straight and level.

➡ If the camshaft is not lifting out straight and level retighten No. 9 and 10 bearing cap bolts. Reverse steps 10 through 12, than start over from step 10. Do not attempt to pry the camshaft from its mounting.

14. Remove the No. 2 bearing cap with the intake camshaft from the engine.

15. Remove the valve adjusting shims from the engine. Be sure to replace the shims to their original location.

To install:

16. Install the valve adjusting shims to the engine.

17. Before installing the intake camshaft, apply multi-purpose grease to the thrust portion of the camshaft.

18. Position the camshaft at 80–115

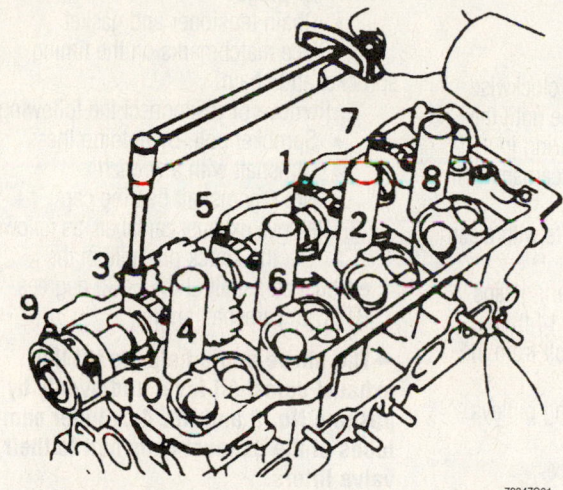

Intake camshaft bolt tightening sequence—RAV4 2.0L (3S-FE) engine

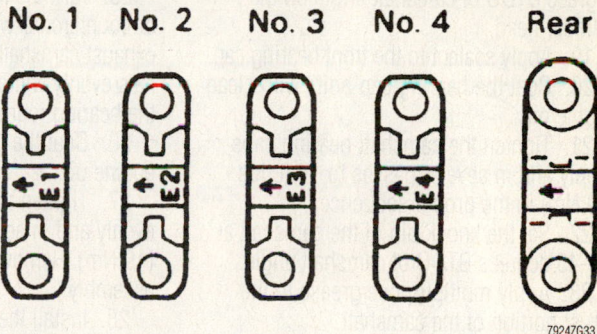

Exhaust camshaft bearing cap positioning—RAV4 2.0L (3S-FE) engine

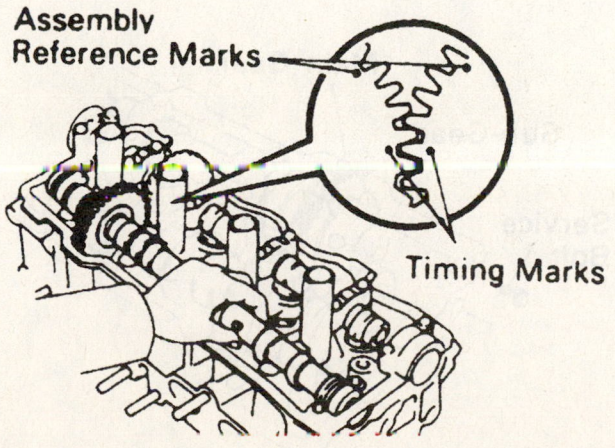

Camshaft timing mark alignment—RAV4 2.0L (3S-FE) engine

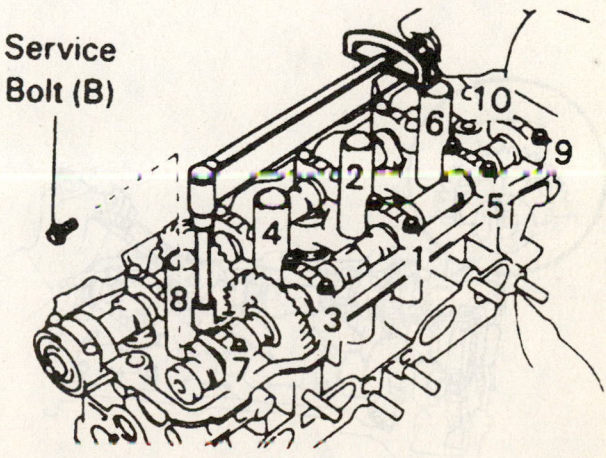

Exhaust camshaft bolt tightening sequence—RAV4 2.0L (3S-FE) engine

Timing belt service is covered in Section 4 of this manual

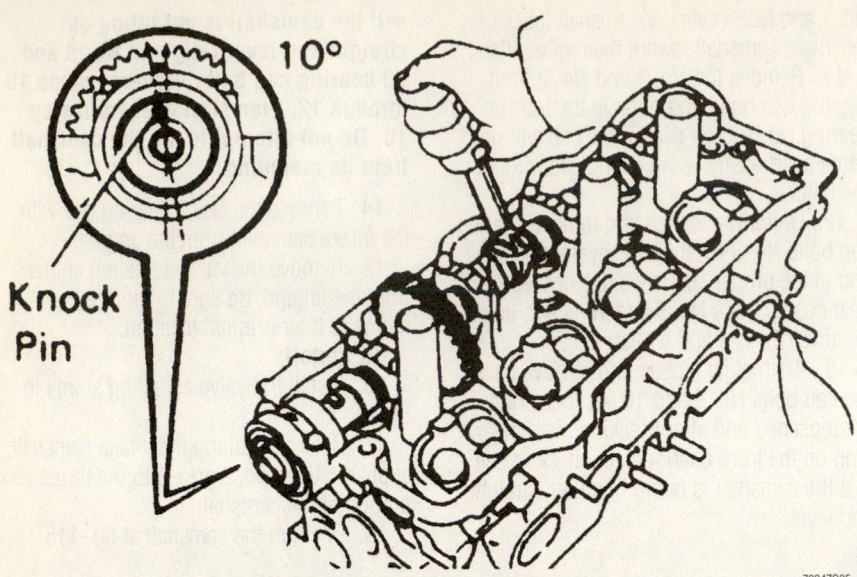

Exhaust camshaft knock pin alignment—RAV4 2.0L (3S-FE) engine

degrees BTDC of camshaft angle on the cylinder head.

19. Apply sealant to the front bearing cap.

20. Coat the bearing cap bolts with clean engine oil.

21. Tighten the camshaft bearing caps evenly and in several passes to 14 ft. lbs. (19 Nm) in the proper sequence.

22. Set the knock pin of the camshaft at 10–45 degrees BTDC of camshaft angle.

23. Apply multipurpose grease to the thrust portion of the camshaft.

24. Position the exhaust camshaft gear with the intake camshaft gear so that the timing marks are in alignment with one another. Be sure to use the proper alignment marks on the gears. Do not use the assembly reference marks.

25. Turn the intake camshaft clockwise or counterclockwise little by little until the exhaust camshaft sits in the bearing journals evenly without rocking the camshaft on the bearing journals.

26. Coat the bearing cap bolts with clean engine oil.

27. Tighten the camshaft bearing caps evenly and in several passes to 14 ft. lbs. (19 Nm). Remove the service bolt from the assembly.

28. Install the camshaft timing pulleys and the timing belt.

29. Adjust the valve clearance.

30. Install the head cover and the upper timing cover. Reconnect the negative battery cable.

31. Start the engine and check for leaks.

32. Check and adjust the ignition timing.

Previa

1. Disconnect the negative battery cable from the battery.

2. Relieve the fuel system pressure.

3. Remove or disconnect the following:
   - Engine/transaxle assembly
   - Engine wiring from the engine and move it aside
   - No. 2 valve cover
   - Spark plug wires

4. Matchmark the distributor, rotor and cylinder head.

5. Remove or disconnect the following:
   - Distributor and the wiring
   - Positive Crankcase Ventilation (PCV) hose
   - No. 1 valve cover and 2 half circular plugs
   - Chain tensioner and gasket

6. Place matchmarks on the timing sprocket and chain.

7. Remove or disconnect the following:
   - Sprocket bolt, by holding the camshaft with a wrench
   - No. 6 camshaft bearing cap

8. Remove exhaust camshaft, as follows:

   a. Set the knock pin hole of the exhaust camshaft at the 5–30 degrees BTDC of camshaft angle.

➡ **The above angle helps to lift the exhaust camshaft level and evenly by pushing No. 2 and No. 4 cylinder cam lobes of the exhaust camshaft to their valve lifters.**

   b. Secure the exhaust camshaft sub-gear to main gear with a service bolt.

   c. Uniformly loosen and remove No.

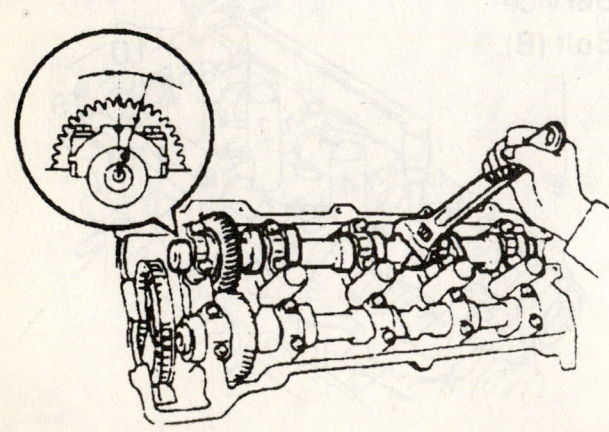

Set knock pin hole of exhaust camshaft at 5–30 degrees BTDC of camshaft angle—Previa 2.4L (2TZ-FE) engine

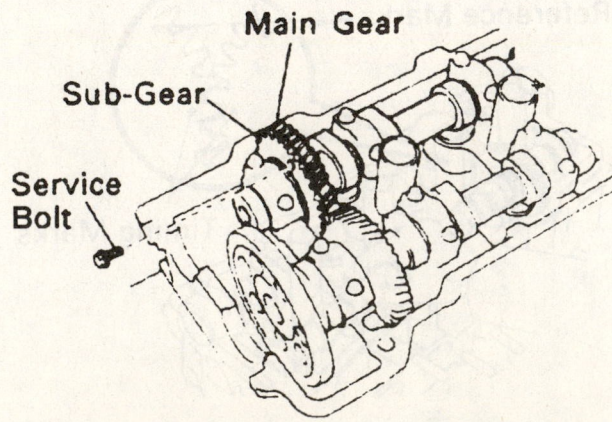

Secure exhaust camshaft sub-gear to main gear with service bolt— Previa 2.4L (2TZ-FE) engine

1, No. 2, No. 3 and No. 5 bearing caps in several passes in the proper sequence.

➡**Do not remove No. 4 bearing cap bolt at this stage.**

d. Alternately loosen and remove No. 4 bearing cap. As No. 4 bearing cap bolts are loosened, check that the camshaft is being lifted out straight and level.

e. Remove the exhaust camshaft.

9. Remove the intake camshaft, as follows:

a. Set the knock pin hole of the intake camshaft at the 75–100 degrees BTDC of camshaft angle.

b. Uniformly loosen and remove No. 1, No. 2, No. 4 and No. 5 bearing caps in several passes in the proper sequence.

➡**Do not remove No. 3 bearing cap bolt at this stage.**

c. Alternately loosen and remove No. 3 bearing cap. As No. 3 bearing cap bolts

are loosened, check that the camshaft is being lifted out straight and level.

d. Remove the intake camshaft.

10. Remove the valve lifters from the engine. Keep the shims and the lifters together. The lifters and the shims must be reinstalled in their original location.

To install:

➡**If any of the bolts break, deform or do not meet the torque specification, replace them.**

11. Install the valve lifters and shims.

12. Install the intake camshaft, as follows:

a. Apply MP grease to the thrust portion of the intake camshaft.

b. Place the intake camshaft at 75–100 degrees BTDC. Install the bearing caps with the marking arrows facing forward. Uniformly tighten the bearing cap bolts in several passes in the proper sequence to 12 ft. lbs. (16 Nm).

13. Install the exhaust camshaft, as follows:

a. Set the knock pin of the intake camshaft at 5–30 degrees BTDC of camshaft angle.

b. Apply MP grease to the thrust portion of the exhaust camshaft.

c. Engage the exhaust camshaft gear to the intake camshaft gear by matching the installation marks (timing marks).

d. Roll down the exhaust camshaft onto the bearing journals while engaging the gears with each other. Be sure the exhaust and intake camshaft gear alignment marks are facing each other. The one gear has 2 dots and the other has 1 dot.

e. Install the bearing caps with the marking arrows facing forward.

f. Uniformly tighten the bearing cap bolts in several passes in the proper sequence to 12 ft. lbs. (16 Nm).

14. Apply sealer to the bottom of No. 6

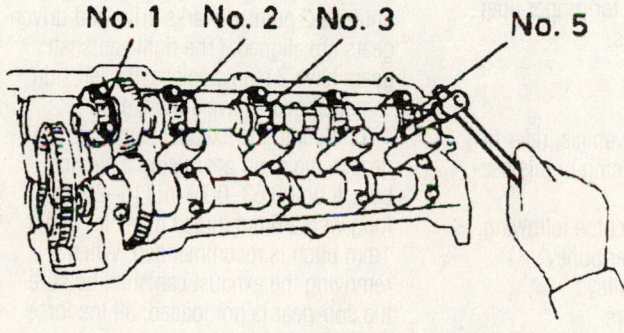

Remove No. 1, 2, 3 and 5 bearing caps (exhaust camshaft) in sequence shown—Previa 2.4L (2TZ-FE) engine

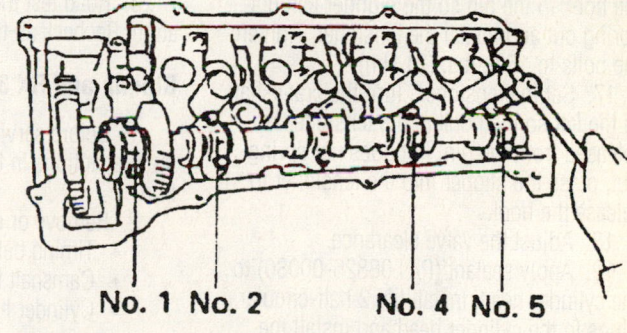

Remove No. 1, 2, 4 and 5 bearing caps (intake camshaft) in sequence shown—Previa 2.4L (2TZ-FE) engine

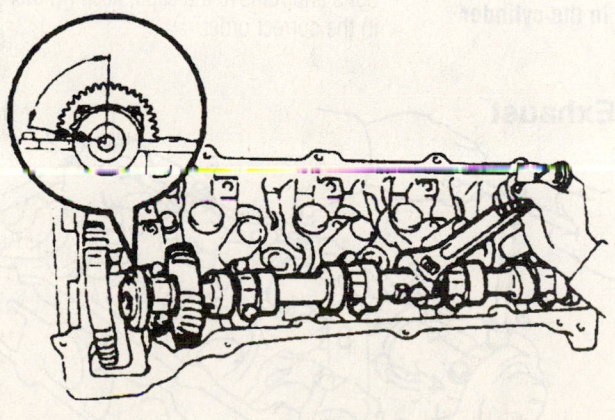

Set knock pin of intake camshaft at 75–100 degrees BTDC of camshaft angle—Previa 2.4L (2TZ-FE) engine

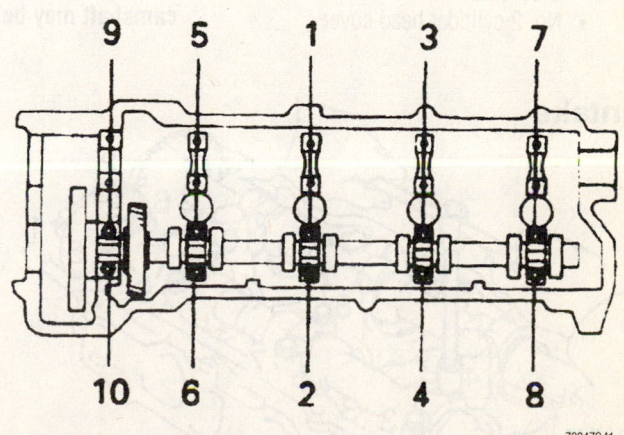

Camshaft bearing cap bolts tightening sequence—Previa 2.4L (2TZ-FE) engine

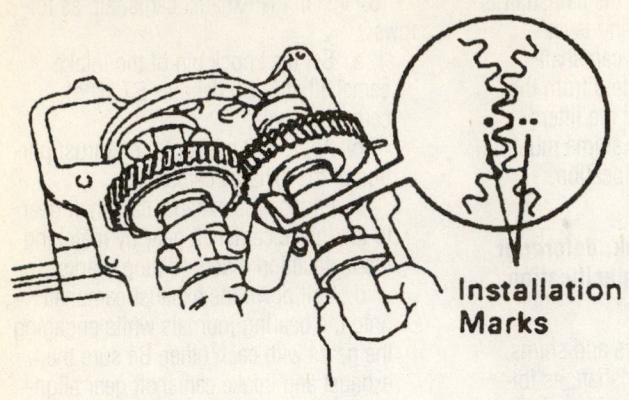

Installation Marks

7924ZG42

Engage the exhaust and intake camshafts by matching the installation marks to each gear—Previa 2.4L (2TZ-FE) engine

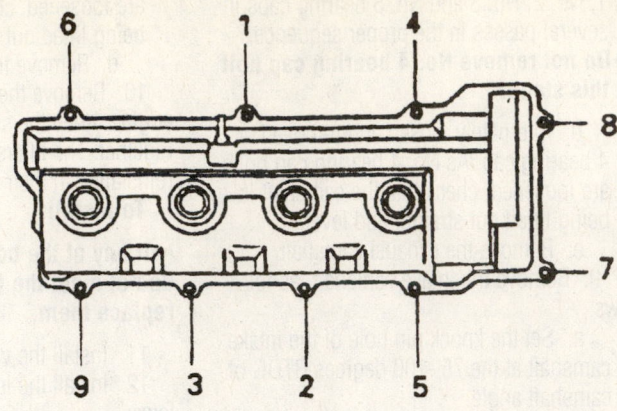

7924ZG43

Cylinder head cover tightening sequence—Previa 2.4L (2TZ-FE) engine

bearing cap and install. Tighten the cap to 12 ft. lbs. (16 Nm).

15. Install the camshaft sprocket and chain. Tighten the bolt to 54 ft. lbs. (74 Nm).

16. Release the chain tensioner ratchet pawl. Fully push in the plunger and apply the hook to the pin so the plunger can not spring out and install the tensioner. Tighten the bolts to 15 ft. lbs. (21 Nm).

17. Set the tensioner: Turn the crankshaft to the left so the hook of the tensioner is released from the pin. If it does not spring out, press the slipper into the tensioner to release the hook.

18. Adjust the valve clearance.

19. Apply sealant (P/N 08826-00080) to the cylinder head. Install the 2 half-circular plugs to the cylinder head and install the valve cover. Tighten the bolts to 69 inch lbs. (7.8 Nm).

20. Install or connect the following:
- PCV hose
- Distributor
- No. 2 cylinder head cover

- Engine wire and all connectors
- Engine/transaxle assembly
- Negative battery cable

21. Fill the cooling system. Fill the engine with oil.

22. Start the engine and check for leaks.

23. Road test the vehicle for proper operation. Recheck all fluid levels.

Sienna and RX 300

1. Before servicing the vehicle, refer to the precautions in the beginning of this section.

2. Remove or disconnect the following:
- Timing belt and idler pulley
- Camshaft timing pulleys
- Cylinder head covers

➡The thrust clearance on both the intake and exhaust camshafts is very small; the camshafts must be kept level during removal. If the camshafts are removed without being kept level, the camshaft may be caught in the cylinder

head, causing the head to break or the camshaft to seize.

3. Remove the exhaust and intake camshafts from the right side cylinder head, as follows:

a. Turn the camshaft with a wrench until the 2 pointed marks drive and driven gears are aligned. (The right camshaft gears have 2 marks apiece; the left side camshaft gears have 1 mark each.)

b. Secure the exhaust camshaft sub-gear to the main gear using a service bolt. A bolt 0.63–0.79 in. (16–20mm) long with a 6mm thread diameter and a 1mm pitch is recommended. When removing the exhaust camshaft be sure the sub-gear is not loaded; all the force must be eliminated.

c. Uniformly loosen and remove the exhaust camshaft bearing cap bolts in several passes and in the proper sequence. Remove the 8 bearing cap bolts and remove the caps, keeping them in the correct order.

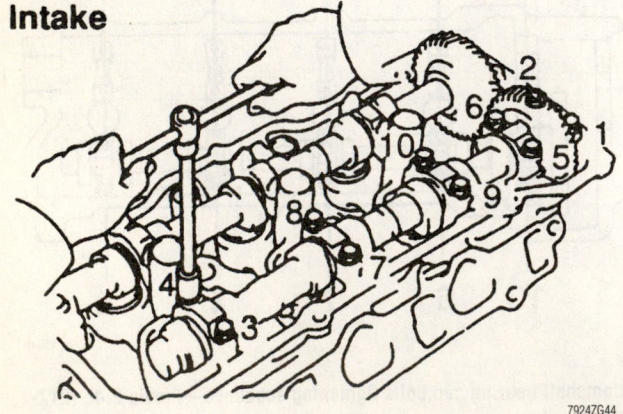

Intake

7924ZG44

Right intake camshaft bearing cap bolt loosening sequence—Sienna and RX 300 models

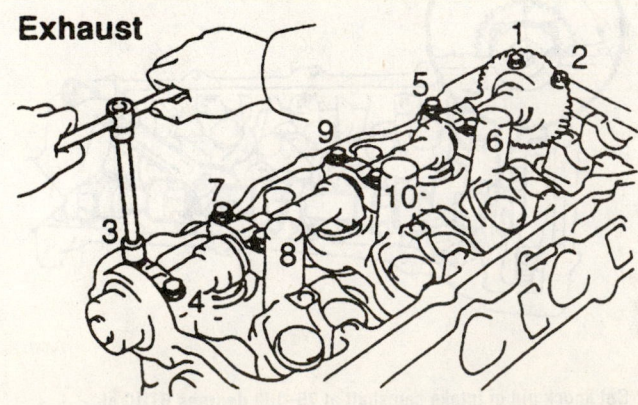

Exhaust

7924ZG45

Right side exhaust camshaft bearing cap bolt loosening sequence—Sienna and RX 300 models

d. Remove the exhaust camshaft from the engine.

e. Uniformly loosen and remove the 10 bearing cap bolts in several passes, in the proper sequence. Remove the bearing caps, keeping them in order, remove the oil seal, then lift out the intake camshaft.

4. Remove the exhaust and intake camshafts from the left side cylinder head, as follows:

a. Turn the camshaft with a wrench until the pointed marks on the drive and driven gears are aligned. (The right camshaft gears have 2 marks apiece; the left side camshaft gears have 1 mark each.)

b. Secure the exhaust camshaft sub-gear to the main gear using a service bolt. A bolt 16–20mm long with a 6mm thread diameter and a 1mm pitch is recommended. When removing the

exhaust camshaft be sure the sub-gear is not loaded; all the force must be eliminated.

c. Uniformly loosen and remove the exhaust camshaft bearing cap bolts in several passes and in the proper sequence. Remove the 8 bearing cap bolts and remove the caps. Keep the caps in the correct order.

d. Remove the exhaust camshaft from the engine.

e. Uniformly loosen and remove the 10 bearing cap bolts in several passes, in the reverse order of the installation sequence. Remove the bearing caps, keeping them in order, remove the oil seal, then lift out the intake camshaft.

5. Remove the valve lifter shims and hydraulic lifters. Identify each lifter and shim as it is removed so it can be reinstalled in the same position. If the lifters are to be

reused, store them upside down in a sealed container.

To install:

6. Install the valve lifters into their original positions and install the shims. Check valve clearance and replace the shims as necessary.

7. When reinstalling, remember that the camshafts must be handled carefully and kept straight and level to avoid damage.

8. Before installing the camshafts in either cylinder head, apply multi-purpose grease to each camshaft.

9. Install the right camshafts, as follows:

a. Position the intake camshaft on the head so that the alignment marks are at a 90 degrees angle from vertical. The mark should be at the "3 o'clock" position.

b. Apply sealant to the No. 1 bearing cap.

Intake

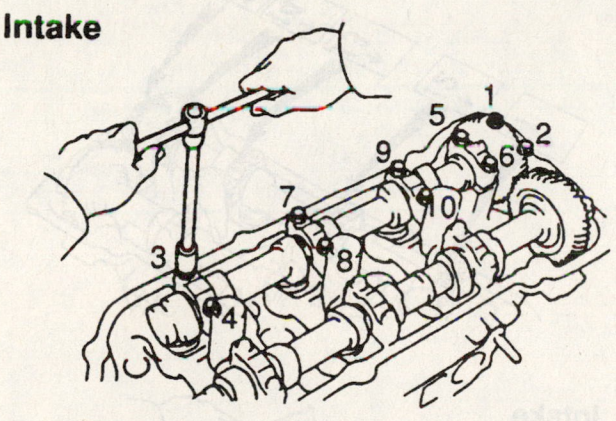

Left intake camshaft bearing cap bolt loosening sequence—Sienna and RX 300 models

Exhaust

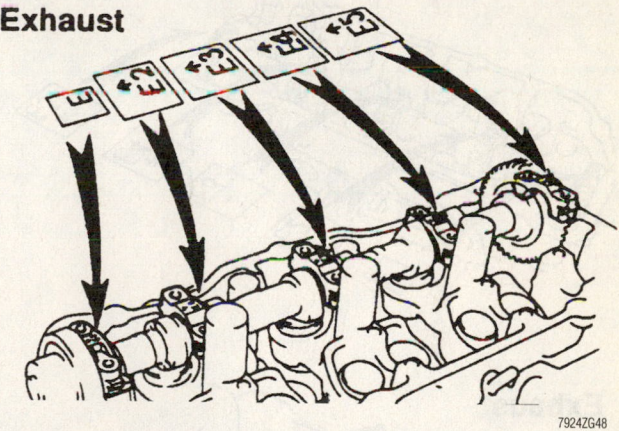

Right exhaust bearing caps must be placed in their proper locations—Sienna and RX 300 models

Exhaust

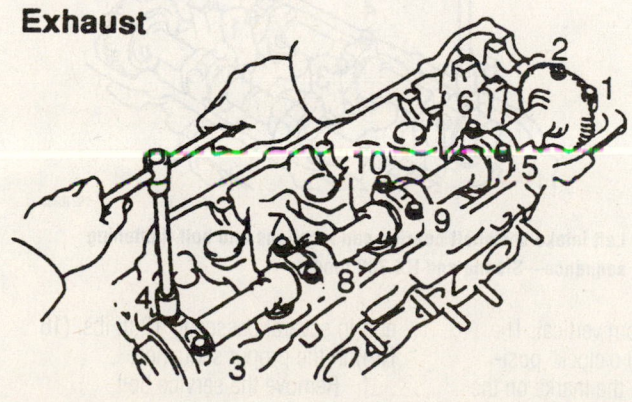

Left side exhaust camshaft bearing cap bolt loosening sequence—Sienna and RX 300 models

Exhaust

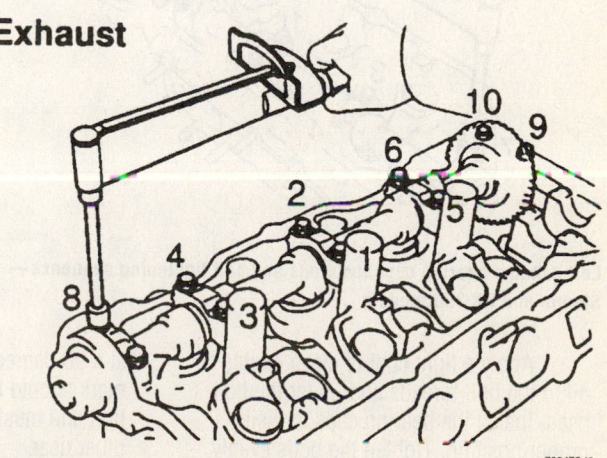

Right exhaust camshaft bearing cap bolt tightening sequence—Sienna and RX 300 models

Refer to Section 1 for engine rebuilding specifications

Intake

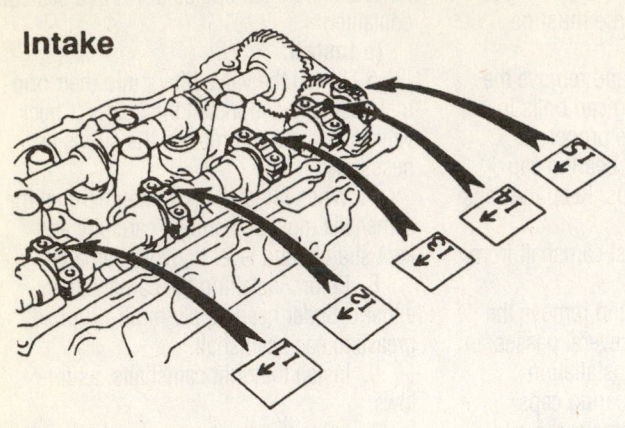

Right intake bearing caps must be placed in their proper locations—Sienna and RX 300 models

Intake

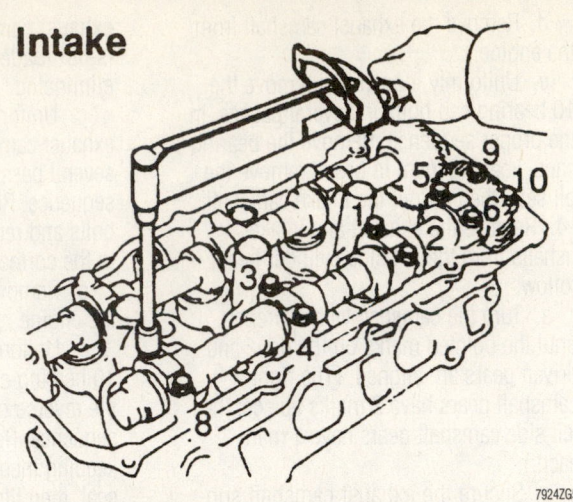

Right intake camshaft bearing cap bolt tightening sequence—Sienna and RX 300 models

Exhaust

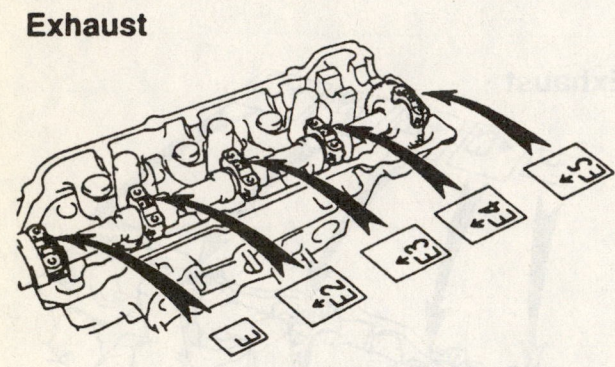

Intake

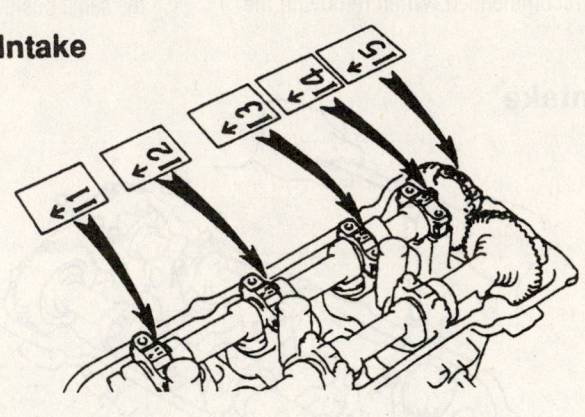

Exhaust

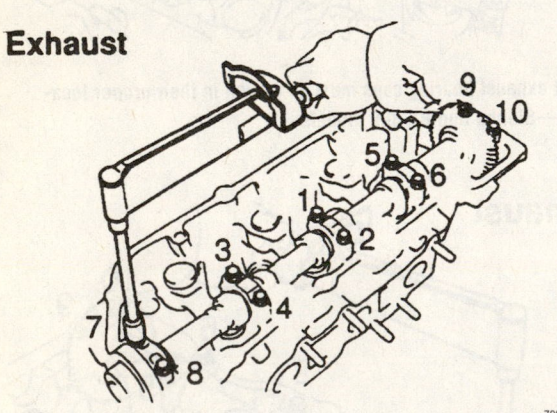

Left exhaust bearing caps locations and bolt tightening sequence—Sienna and RX 300 models

Intake

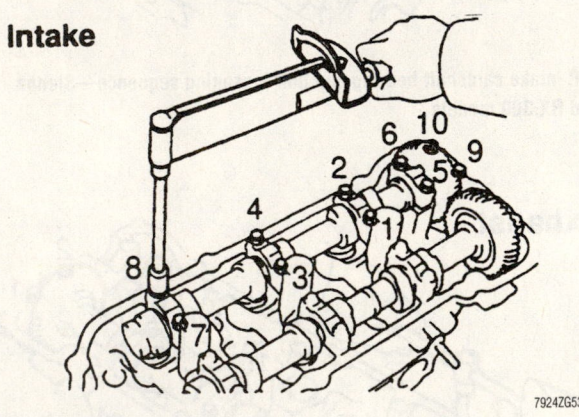

Left intake camshaft bearing cap locations and bolt tightening sequence—Sienna and RX 300 models

c. Apply a light coat of clean engine oil to the bolt threads and under the bolt head. Install the bearing caps to their proper position. Tighten the bolts evenly and in several passes to 12 ft. lbs. (16 Nm) in the proper sequence.

d. Position the exhaust camshaft on the head so that the alignment marks are at a 90 degrees angle from vertical. The mark should be at the "9 o'clock" position and must align with the marks on the other gear.

e. Apply a light coat of clean engine oil to the bolt threads and under the bolt head. Install the bearing caps to their proper position. Tighten the bolts evenly and in several passes to 12 ft. lbs. (16 Nm) in the proper sequence.

f. Remove the service bolt.

10. Install the left camshafts, as follows:

a. Position the intake camshaft on the head so that the alignment mark is at a 90 degrees angle from vertical. The mark should be at the "9 o'clock" position.

b. Apply sealant to the No. 1 bearing cap.

c. Apply a light coat of clean engine oil to the bolt threads and under the bolt head. Install the bearing caps to their proper position. Tighten the bolts evenly and in several passes to 12 ft. lbs. (16 Nm) in the proper sequence.

d. Position the exhaust camshaft on the head so that the alignment marks are at a 90 degrees angle from vertical. The mark should be at the "3 o'clock" position and must align with the marks on the other gear.

e. Apply a light coat of clean engine oil to the bolt threads and under the bolt head. Install the bearing caps to their proper position. Tighten the bolts evenly and in several passes to 12 ft. lbs. (16 Nm) in the proper sequence.

f. Remove the service bolt.

11. Install or connect the following:
- New camshaft oil seals, lubricated with multi-purpose grease
- No. 3 (rear) timing belt cover
- Camshaft timing gears
- Idler pulley, timing belt and covers

12. Check and adjust the valve clearance.

13. Install the cylinder head (valve) covers.

14. Start the engine. Check the ignition timing.

15. Test drive the vehicle.

16. Check all fluid levels.

Valve Lash

ADJUSTMENT

2.0L Engine

1. Before servicing the vehicle, refer to the precautions in the beginning of this section.

2. Remove the cylinder head covers.

3. Use a wrench to turn the crankshaft until the notch in the pulley aligns with timing mark **0** of the No. 1 timing belt cover. This will ensure that the No. 1 piston is at Top Dead Center (TDC) of the compression stroke.

➡**Check that the valve lifters on the No. 1 cylinder are loose and those on the No. 4 cylinder are tight. If not, rotate the crankshaft 1 complete revolution (360 degrees) and then realign the marks.**

4. Using a flat feeler gauge measure the clearance between the camshaft lobe and the valve lifter on the first set of valves shown. This measurement should correspond to specifications.

➡**If the measurement is within specifications, go on to the next step. If not, record the measurement taken for each individual valve.**

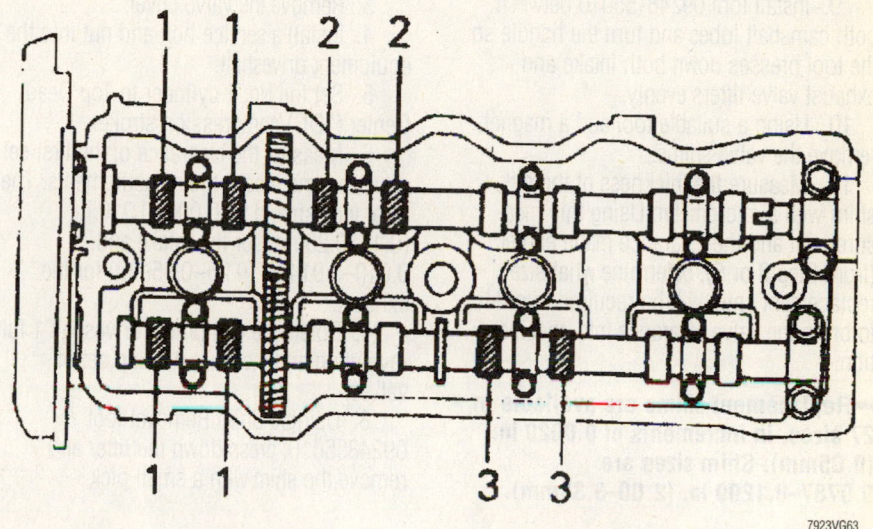

Adjust these valves first—2.0L engine

5. Rotate the crankshaft 1 complete revolution and realign the timing marks.

6. Measure the clearance of the second set of valves.

➡**If the measurement for this set of valves (and also the previous one) is within specifications, go no further, the**

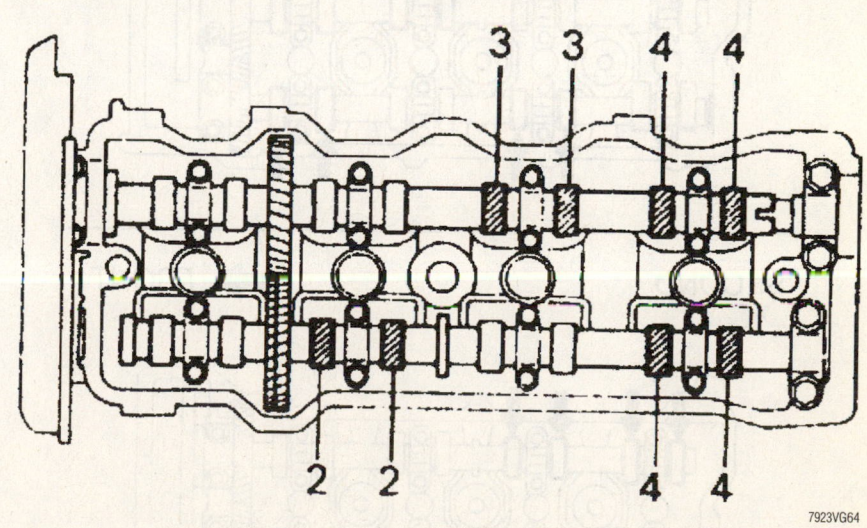

Adjust these valves second—2.0L engine

For engine torque specifications, refer to Section 1 of this manual

procedure is finished. If not, record the measurements and proceed to the next step.

7. Rotate the crankshaft to position the intake camshaft lobe of the cylinder to be adjusted, facing upward.

➡️Both intake and exhaust valve clearance may be adjusted at the same time, if required.

8. Using a suitable tool, turn the valve lifter so the notch is easily accessible.

9. Install tool 09248-55010 between both camshaft lobes and turn the handle so the tool presses down both intake and exhaust valve lifters evenly.

10. Using a suitable tool and a magnet, remove the valve shims.

11. Measure the thickness of the old shim with a micrometer. Using this measurement and the clearance made earlier (from Step 3 or 5), determine what size replacement shim will be required in order to bring the valve clearance into specification.

➡️Replacement shims are available in 27 sizes, in increments of 0.0020 in. (0.05mm). Shim sizes are 0.0787–0.1299 in. (2.00–3.30mm).

12. Install the new shim, remove the special tool; then, recheck the valve clearances.

13. Install the cylinder head covers.

2.4L Engine

Check the valve clearance with the engine cold.

1. Before servicing the vehicle, refer to the precautions in the beginning of this section.

2. Remove the front seat and engine service hole cover.

3. Remove the valve cover.

4. Install a service bolt and nut into the equipment driveshaft.

5. Set the No. 1 cylinder to Top Dead Center (TDC)/compression stroke.

6. Measure the clearance of the first set of valves and record the measurements. The clearance should be 0.006–0.010 in. (0.15–0.25mm) for the intake and 0.010–0.014 in. (0.25–0.35mm) for the exhaust.

7. Rotate the equipment driveshaft 1 full revolution and measure the 2nd set of valves.

8. Using a Shim Removal tool 0924855010, press down the lifter and remove the shim with a small pick.

9. Determine the replacement shim size by measuring the old shim using a micrometer and calculate the thickness of the new shim using the following formula:

- Intake: $N = T + (A—0.008$ in./0.020mm$)$
- Exhaust: $N = T + (A—0.012$ in./0.30mm$)$
- T = Thickness of removed shim
- A = Measured valve clearance
- N = Thickness of new shim

10. Select a new shim with a thickness as close as possible to the calculated value. Install the new replacement shim.

➡️Shims are available in 17 sizes in increments of 0.0020 in. (0.050mm), from 0.0984 in. (2.500mm) to 0.1299 in. (3.300mm).

11. Recheck the valve clearance.

12. Install or connect the following:
- Valve cover. Tighten the bolts to 69 inch lbs. (7.8 Nm).

13. Remove the front seat and engine service hole cover.

3.0L Engine

➡️Adjust the valve clearance when the engine is cold.

1. Before servicing the vehicle, refer to the precautions in the beginning of this section.

2. Remove or disconnect the following:

- Negative battery cable. If equipped with an air bag, wait at least 90 seconds before proceeding.
- Accelerator/throttle cable from the throttle linkage
- Air cleaner cover, air flow meter and air duct assembly
- V-bank cover
- Emission control valve set
- Air intake chamber
- Engine harness from the injectors and the ignition coils
- Ignition coils and keep them in order for reassembly
- Spark plugs
- Cylinder head covers

3. Turn the crankshaft pulley and align its groove with the timing mark **0** of the No. 1 timing cover.

4. Check that the valve lifters on the No. 1 intake are loose and the No. 1 exhaust are tight. If not, turn the crankshaft 1 complete revolution (360 degrees).

➡️All measurements should be written down. These recorded measurements will need to be used in conjunction with

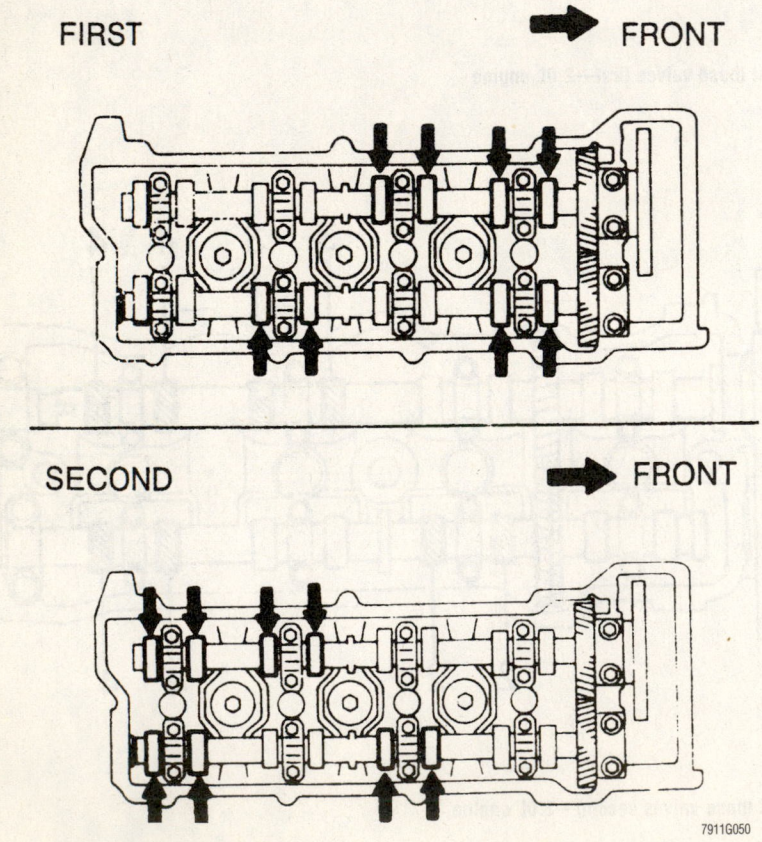

FIRST ➡️ FRONT

SECOND ➡️ FRONT

7911G050

Valve clearance check—2.4L engine

a mathematical formula to determine the thickness of the replacement shims.

5. Measure the clearance between the valve lifters and the camshaft. Record the measurements on valves No. 1 and 6 intake; No. 2 and 3 exhaust.

  a. The intake valve clearance cold is 0.006–0.010 in. (0.15–0.25mm).

  b. The exhaust valve clearance cold is 0.010–0.014 in. (0.25–0.35mm).

6. Turn the crankshaft ⅔ of a revolution (240 degrees). Record the measurements on valves No. 2 and 3 intake; No. 4 and 5 exhaust.

7. Turn the crankshaft another ⅔ of a revolution. Record the measurements on valves No. 4 and 5 intake; No. 1 and 6 exhaust.

8. Remove the adjusting shim by turning the crankshaft to position the cam lobe of the camshaft in the up position on the valve to be adjusted. Using a small thin flat bladed tool, turn the valve lifter so that the notches are perpendicular to the camshaft. Press down the valve lifter with tool 09248-55010 part A. Place too 09248-55010 part B between the camshaft and the valve lifter; remove part A.

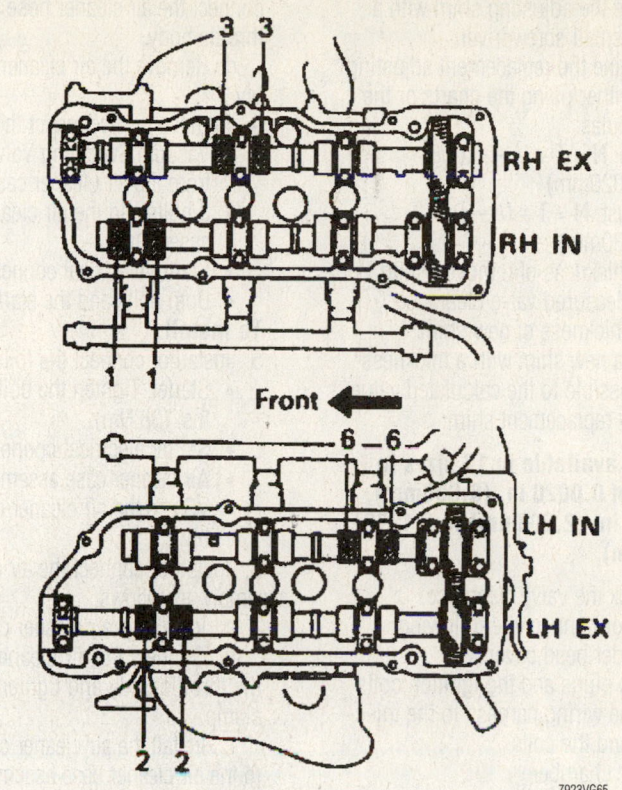

7923VG65

Adjust these valves during the 1st step—3.0L (1MZ-FE) engine

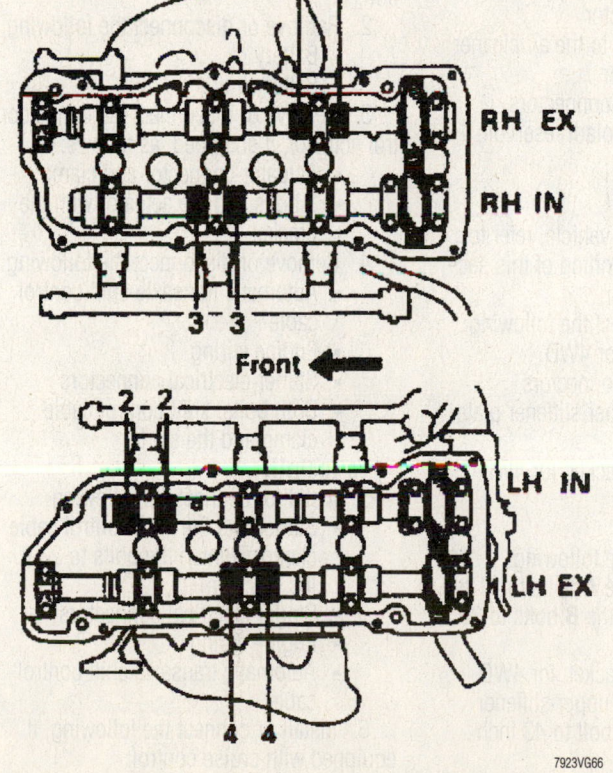

7923VG66

Adjust these valves during the 2nd step—3.0L (1MZ-FE) engine

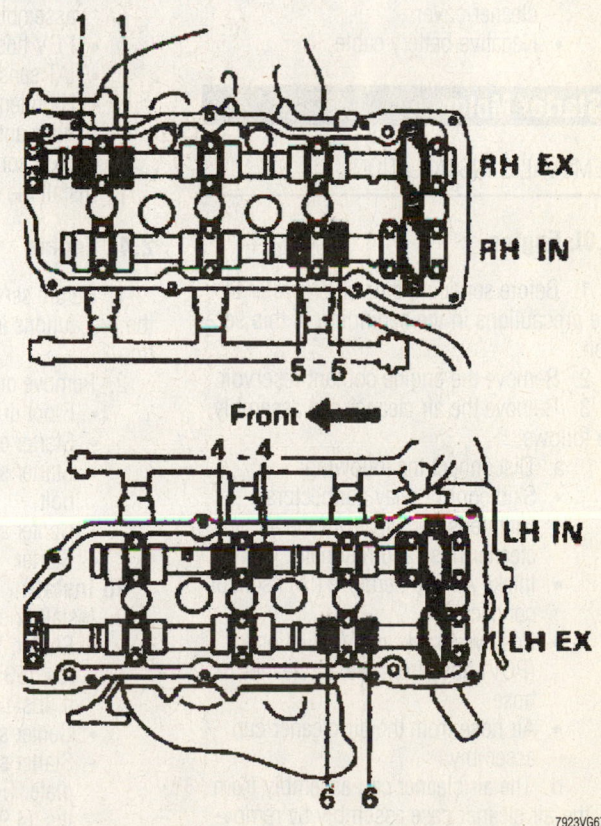

7923VG67

Adjust these valves during the 3rd step—3.0L (1MZ-FE) engine

For complete mechanical specifications, refer to Section 1 of this manual

9. Remove the adjusting shim with a magnet and a small screwdriver.

10. Determine the replacement adjusting shim size by either using the charts or the following formulas:

- Intake: $N = T + (A - 0.008$ in./0.020mm)
- Exhaust: $N = T + (A - 0.012$ in./0.30mm)
- T = Thickness of removed shim
- A = Measured valve clearance
- N = Thickness of new shim

11. Select a new shim with a thickness as close as possible to the calculated value. Install the new replacement shim.

➡ **Shims are available in 17 sizes in increments of 0.0020 in. (0.050mm), from 0.0984 in. (2.500mm) to 0.1299 in. (3.300mm).**

12. Recheck the valve clearance.

13. Install or connect the following:

- Cylinder head covers
- Spark plugs and the ignition coils
- Engine wiring harness to the injectors and the coils
- Intake chamber
- Emission control valve set
- V-bank cover
- Air flow meter, air duct and air cleaner cover
- Negative battery cable

Starter Motor

REMOVAL & INSTALLATION

2.0L Engine

1. Before servicing the vehicle, refer to the precautions in the beginning of this section.

2. Remove the engine coolant reservoir.

3. Remove the air cleaner cap assembly, as follows:

a. Disconnect the following:

- Skid control relay connectors
- High tension cord from the air cleaner hose and resonator
- Intake Air Temperature (IAT) sensor connector
- Positive Crankcase Ventilation (PCV) hose from the air cleaner hose
- Air hose from the air cleaner cap assembly

b. The air cleaner cap assembly from the air cleaner case assembly by removing the 4 clamps.

c. Loosen the hose clamp and disconnect the air cleaner hose from the throttle body.

d. Remove the air cleaner cap assembly.

4. Remove or disconnect the following:

- Vacuum Switching Valve (VSV) from the air cleaner case assembly
- 3 bolts and the air cleaner case assembly
- Starter electrical connectors
- Both bolts and the starter

To install:

5. Install or connect the following:

- Starter. Tighten the bolts to 29 ft. lbs. (38 Nm).
- Starter electrical connectors
- Air cleaner case assembly
- VSV to the air cleaner case assembly

6. Install or connect the air cleaner cap assembly, as follows:

a. Install the air cleaner cap assembly.

b. Connect the air cleaner hose to the throttle body and tighten the hose clamp.

c. Install the air cleaner cap assembly to the air cleaner case assembly by installing the 4 clamps.

d. Connect the following:

- Air hose to the air cleaner cap assembly
- PCV hose to the air cleaner hose
- IAT sensor connector
- High tension cord to the air cleaner hose and resonator
- Skid control relay connectors

7. Install the engine coolant reservoir.

2.4L Engine

1. Before servicing the vehicle, refer to the precautions in the beginning of this section.

2. Remove or disconnect the following:

- Front driveshaft, for 4WD
- Starter electrical connectors
- Starter stay-to-upper stiffener plate bolt
- Center support bracket, for 4WD
- Starter

To install:

3. Install or connect the following:

- Starter. Tighten the **A** bolts to 41 ft. lbs. (56 Nm) and the **B** bolts to 30 ft. lbs. (41 Nm).
- Center support bracket, for 4WD
- Starter stay to the upper stiffener plate. Tighten the bolt to 43 inch lbs. (4.9 Nm).
- Starter electrical connectors
- Front driveshaft, for 4WD

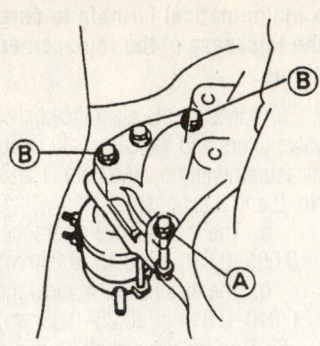

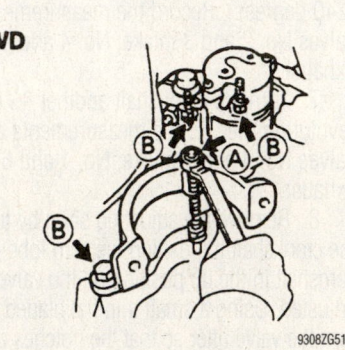

View of the starter bolt locations—2.4L engine

3.0L Engine

1. Before servicing the vehicle, refer to the precautions in the beginning of this section.

2. Remove or disconnect the following:

- Battery
- Battery tray

3. Remove or disconnect the cruise control actuator, if equipped, as follows:

- Actuator connector and clamp
- 3 bolts and the actuator with the bracket

4. Remove or disconnect the following:

- Automatic transaxle shift control cable
- Engine wiring
- Starter electrical connectors
- Both bolts, shift control cable clamp and the starter

To install:

5. Install or connect the following:

- Starter and the shift control cable clamp. Tighten the bolts to 27 ft. lbs. (37 Nm).
- Starter electrical connectors
- Engine wiring
- Automatic transaxle shift control cable

6. Install or connect the following, if equipped with cruise control:

- 3 bolts and the actuator with the bracket

- Actuator connector and clamp
7. Install or connect the following:
  - Battery tray
  - Battery

Oil Pan

REMOVAL & INSTALLATION

RAV4

1. Before servicing the vehicle, refer to the precautions in the beginning of this section.
2. Remove the right-hand engine undercover.
3. Drain the crankcase oil.
4. Remove or disconnect the following:
   - Dipstick
   - Front exhaust pipe
   - Stiffener plate from the engine by removing the 2 (manual transmission) or 3 (automatic transmission) bolts.
   - 2 nuts and 17 bolts from the oil pan
   - Oil pan and discard the gasket

To install:

5. Clean all gasket surfaces completely.
6. Apply a thin bead of sealer to the oil pan mounting surfaces.
7. Install or connect the following:
   - Oil pan. Tighten the nuts/bolts to 48 inch lbs. (5 Nm).
   - Stiffener plate. Tighten the bolts to 27 ft. lbs. (37 Nm).
   - Front exhaust pipe
8. Fill the engine with oil to the proper level.
9. Start the engine and check for leaks. Recheck the engine oil level.
10. Install the right engine cover.

Previa

➡**This engine has 2 oil pans. If the crankshaft is going to be serviced, the side crankcase pan has to be removed. If the oil pump sump is going to be serviced, the bottom oil pan has to be removed.**

1. Before servicing the vehicle, refer to the precautions in the beginning of this section.
2. Drain the engine oil.
3. Remove or disconnect the following:
   - Oil level sensor and gasket.

➡**Be careful not to drop the sensor when removing.**

- 14 bolts and 2 nuts from the oil pan
- Oil pan, being careful not to damage the flange

To install:

4. Before installing, thoroughly clean the gasket mating surfaces. Apply gasket sealer, to the pan and assembly within 5 minutes.
5. Install or connect the following:
   - Oil pan. Tighten the bolts/nuts to 48 inch lbs. (5 Nm).
   - Oil sensor using a new gasket. Tighten it to 108 inch lbs. (13 Nm).
   - Remaining components
   - Negative battery cable
6. Refill the engine with oil.
7. Start the engine and check for leaks.

Sienna and RX 300

1. Before servicing the vehicle, refer to the precautions in the beginning of this section.
2. Remove or disconnect the following:
   - Right front wheel
   - Fender apron seal
   - Engine undercover
3. Drain the engine oil from the engine.
4. Remove or disconnect the following:
   - Front exhaust pipe
   - Front exhaust pipe bracket from the No. 1 oil pan
   - Flywheel housing undercover
   - 10 bolts and 2 nuts to the No. 2 oil pan
5. Insert the blade of the Oil Pan Seal Cutting tool 09032-00100 between the No. 1 and No. 2 oil pans. Clean the surfaces of the oil pans.
6. Remove or disconnect the following:
   - 3 oil strainer nuts and gasket
7. Remove the No. 1 oil pan, as follows:
   - 2 bolts and the flywheel housing undercover
   - 17 bolts and 2 nuts to the No. 1 oil pan

➡**Make a note of the position of the each bolt. When replacing the bolts into the oil pan, place each bolt in the position from which it was removed.**

   - Oil pan, by prying the portions between the cylinder block and the oil pan

➡**Be careful not to damage the contact surfaces.**

   - Baffle plate from the No. 1 oil pan

To install:

8. Clean all mating surfaces of the oil pans.
9. Install the baffle plate to the No. 1 oil pan and tighten to 69 inch lbs. (8 Nm).
10. Install the No. 1 oil pan, as follows:
    a. Using a non residue solvent, clean both sealing surfaces to the oil pan.
    b. Apply liquid sealant to the oil pan and engine block.
    c. Install the oil pan with the 17 bolts and 2 nuts. Uniformly tighten the bolts and nuts in several passes.
    d. Tighten the No. 1 oil pan bolts, as follows:
       - 10mm head bolt: 69 inch lbs. (8 Nm)
       - 12mm head bolt: 14 ft. lbs. (20 Nm)
       - 14mm head bolt: 27 ft. lbs. (37 Nm)
    e. Install the flywheel housing undercover with the 2 bolts. Tighten the bolts to 69 inch lbs. (8 Nm).
11. Install the oil strainer with the 3 nuts. Tighten the nuts to 69 inch lbs. (8 Nm).
12. Install the No. 2 oil pan, as follows:
    a. Using a non residue solvent, clean both sealing surfaces to the oil pan.
    b. Apply liquid sealant to the oil pan and engine block.
    c. Install the No. 2 oil pan with the 10 bolts and 2 nuts. Uniformly tighten the bolts and nuts in several passes. Tighten the bolts to 69 inch lbs. (8 Nm).
13. Install or connect the following:
    - Flywheel housing undercover
    - Front exhaust pipe bracket to the No. 1 oil pan. Tighten the bolts to 15 ft. lbs. (21 Nm).
14. Install the front exhaust pipe, as follows:
    - Temporarily install the 3 new gaskets and the front exhaust pipe with the 2 bolts and 6 nuts
    - Tighten the 4 exhaust manifolds-to-front exhaust pipe nuts to 46 ft. lbs. (62 Nm).
    - Tighten the both front exhaust pipe-to-center exhaust pipe nuts/bolts to 41 ft. lbs. (56 Nm).
    - Bracket. Tighten both bolts to 14 ft. lbs. (19 Nm).
    - Support stay. Tighten both bolts to 22 ft. lbs. (29 Nm).
15. Install or connect the following:
    - Engine undercover
    - Right fender apron seal
    - Right front wheel

Please refer to Section 8 for electric cooling fan wiring schematics

16. Fill the engine with oil.
17. Start the engine and check for leaks.

Oil Pump

REMOVAL & INSTALLATION

RAV4

1. Before servicing the vehicle, refer to the precautions in the beginning of this section.
2. Remove or disconnect the following:
   • Negative battery cable
   • Hood
   • Right-hand engine undercover
3. Drain the engine oil.
4. Remove or disconnect the following:
   • Front exhaust pipe
   • Rear end stiffener plate
   • Oil dipstick
   • 17 bolts and 2 nuts from the oil pan
5. Insert the blade of the Oil Pan Seal Cutting tool 09032-00100 between the oil pan and the cylinder block; then, cut off the applied sealer and remove the oil pan

➡Do not use the tool for the oil pump body side and rear oil seal retainer.

6. Remove the bolts, nuts, oil strainer and gasket.
7. Carefully suspend the engine with a sling device.
8. Remove or disconnect the following:
   • Timing belt
   • No. 2 idler pulley and crankshaft timing pulley
   • Oil pump's pulley, using the Variable Pin Wrench Set 09960-10010
   • Crankshaft Position (CKP) sensor
   • Oil pump, by discarding the gasket

To install:

9. Install or connect the following:
   • Oil pump, using a new gasket. Tighten the 12 bolts to 82 inch lbs. (9 Nm).

➡The long bolts are 35mm and all the others are 25mm.

   • CKP sensor
   • Oil pump pulley. Tighten the nut to 18 ft. lbs. (24 Nm).
   • Crankshaft timing pulley and No. 2 idler pulley
   • Timing belt
10. Remove the engine sling.
11. Install the oil strainer with a new gasket. Tighten the nuts/bolts to 48 inch lbs. (5 Nm).
12. Remove any old sealant from the oil

pan flange and thoroughly clean both sealing surfaces.
13. Apply a 3–5mm bead of sealant to the oil pan flange.

➡The pan must be installed within 5 minutes of sealant application or the procedure will have to be repeated.

14. Install or connect the following:
   • Oil pan. Tighten the 17 bolts and 2 nuts to 48 inch lbs. (5 Nm).
   • Dipstick
   • Rear end stiffener plate. Tighten the bolts to 27 ft. lbs. (37 Nm).
   • Front exhaust pipe
   • Negative battery cable
   • Hood
15. Refill the engine with oil.

✳✳ WARNING

Be sure to prime the oil pump prior to initial engine start-up or engine damage may occur because of low oil pressure.

16. Start the engine and check for leaks.
17. Recheck the engine oil level.
18. Install the right-hand engine undercover.

Previa

➡The oil pump is part of the timing chain case. In order to do the oil pump, the engine/transmission assembly must be removed from the vehicle and the cylinder head removed.

1. Before servicing the vehicle, refer to the precautions in the beginning of this section.
2. Disconnect the negative battery cable. Wait at least 90 seconds after the negative battery cable is disconnected before performing work on models equipped with an airbag.
3. Remove or disconnect the following:
   • Equipment driveshaft from the crankshaft pulley
   • Crankshaft pulley
   • Oil pump cover and discard the O-ring
4. Remove the timing chain case, as follows:
   • 3 bolts from the rear of the timing chain cover
   • 12 bolts and 2 nuts from the front of the chain cover.

➡Beware of the 3 bolts in the cover that are not to be removed, refer to the illustration.

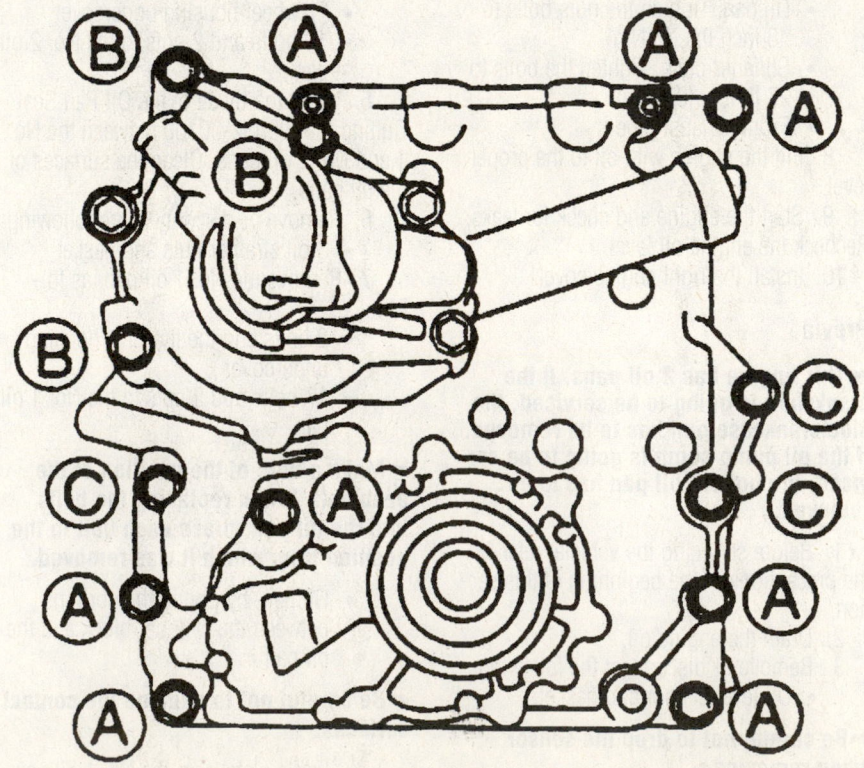

Tighten the bolts A, B and C to specifications—Previa

- Timing chain case, using a plastic faced hammer
- Both gaskets

To install:

5. Install the timing chain case, as follows:

   a. Clean the gasket surface for the timing chain case.

   b. Install 2 new gaskets over the dowels.

   c. Slide on the chain case over the dowels.

   d. Install the bolts and nuts and tighten the bolts as follows:
   - A: 14 ft. lbs. (20 Nm)
   - B: 21 ft. lbs. (28 Nm)
   - C: 32 ft. lbs. (44 Nm)

   e. Tighten the 3 chain case bolts (rear) to 13 ft. lbs. (18 Nm).

6. Install or connect the following:
   - New O-ring into the timing chain case groove
   - Oil pump cover. Tighten the screws to 96 inch lbs. (10 Nm).
   - Crankshaft pulley
   - Equipment driveshaft
   - Negative battery cable

7. Road test the vehicle for proper operation.

Sienna and RX 300

1. Before servicing the vehicle, refer to the precautions in the beginning of this section.

2. Remove or disconnect the following:
   - Oil pan
   - Crankshaft Position (CKP) sensor
   - 9 oil pump bolts

➡**Make a note of the position of the each bolt. When replacing the bolts into the oil pump body, place each bolt in the position from which it was removed.**

- Oil pump body, by prying between the oil pump and main bearing cap
- O-ring from the cylinder block
- Plug, gasket, spring and relief valve from the oil pump body
- 9 screws, pump body cover, drive and driven rotors

To install:

3. Install or connect the following:
   - Driven rotors, drive, pump body cover, using the 9 screws
   - Oil pump relief valve, spring, gasket and the plug to the oil pump body
   - New O-ring on the cylinder block

4. Using a non residue solvent, clean both sealing surfaces to the oil pump.

5. Apply liquid sealant to the oil pump and engine block.

6. Install or connect the following:
   - Oil pump

➡**Be sure to engage the spline teeth of the oil pump drive gear with the large teeth of the crankshaft.**

- 9 oil pump bolts. Tighten the bolts in several passes to 69 inch lbs. (8

Nm), for 10mm or to 14 ft. lbs. (20 Nm), for 12mm.
- CKP sensor. Tighten the bolt to 69 inch lbs. (8 Nm).
- Baffle plate to the No. oil pan. Tighten to 69 inch lbs. (8 Nm).
- No. 1 oil pan, oil strainer and No. 2 oil pan

7. Refill the engine with oil.

8. Start the engine and inspect for leaks.

9. Recheck the engine oil level.

Rear Main Seal

REMOVAL & INSTALLATION

If the rear oil seal retainer is not installed to the block, use a tapered ended screwdriver and hammer to remove the oil seal. Apply multi-purpose grease to the new oil seal lip. Using a seal driver, tap the seal into place. Be careful not to install it slantwise.

1. Before servicing the vehicle, refer to the precautions in the beginning of this section.

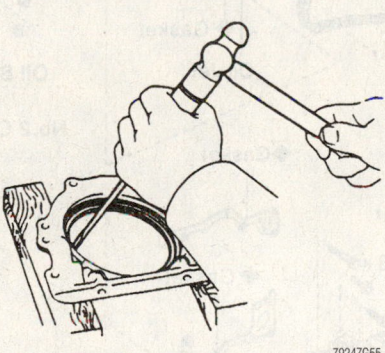

Carefully tap the old seal from the retainer

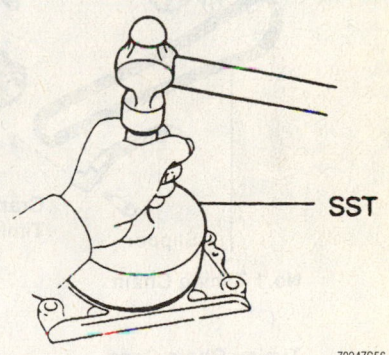

Use the proper sized driver to seat the seal

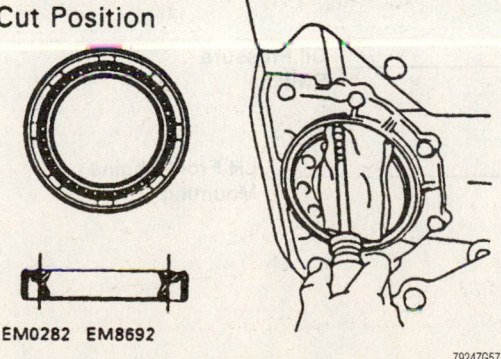

Cut off the oil seal lip, then pry the seal out of the retaining plate

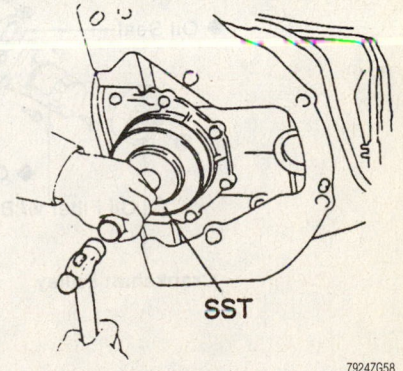

Tap a new seal into place

For complete service labor times order Nichols' Chilton Labor Guide Manual

If the rear oil seal retainer is installed on the cylinder block, using a knife, cut off the lip of the seal. Using a taped ended prytool, pry the old seal out of the retainer. Inspect the oil seal lip contacting surface of the crankshaft for cracks or damage. Apply multipurpose grease to the new oil seal, then tap the seal in place with a seal installer. Be careful not to install the seal slantwise.

Timing Chain, Sprockets, Front Cover and Seal

REMOVAL & INSTALLATION

Previa

The engine/transmission assembly must to be extracted from the vehicle and the cylinder head removed before performing work on the timing chain.

1. Before servicing the vehicle, refer to the precautions in the beginning of this section.

2. Remove or disconnect the following:
   - Engine/transmission assembly
   - Separate the engine and transmission
   - Cylinder head

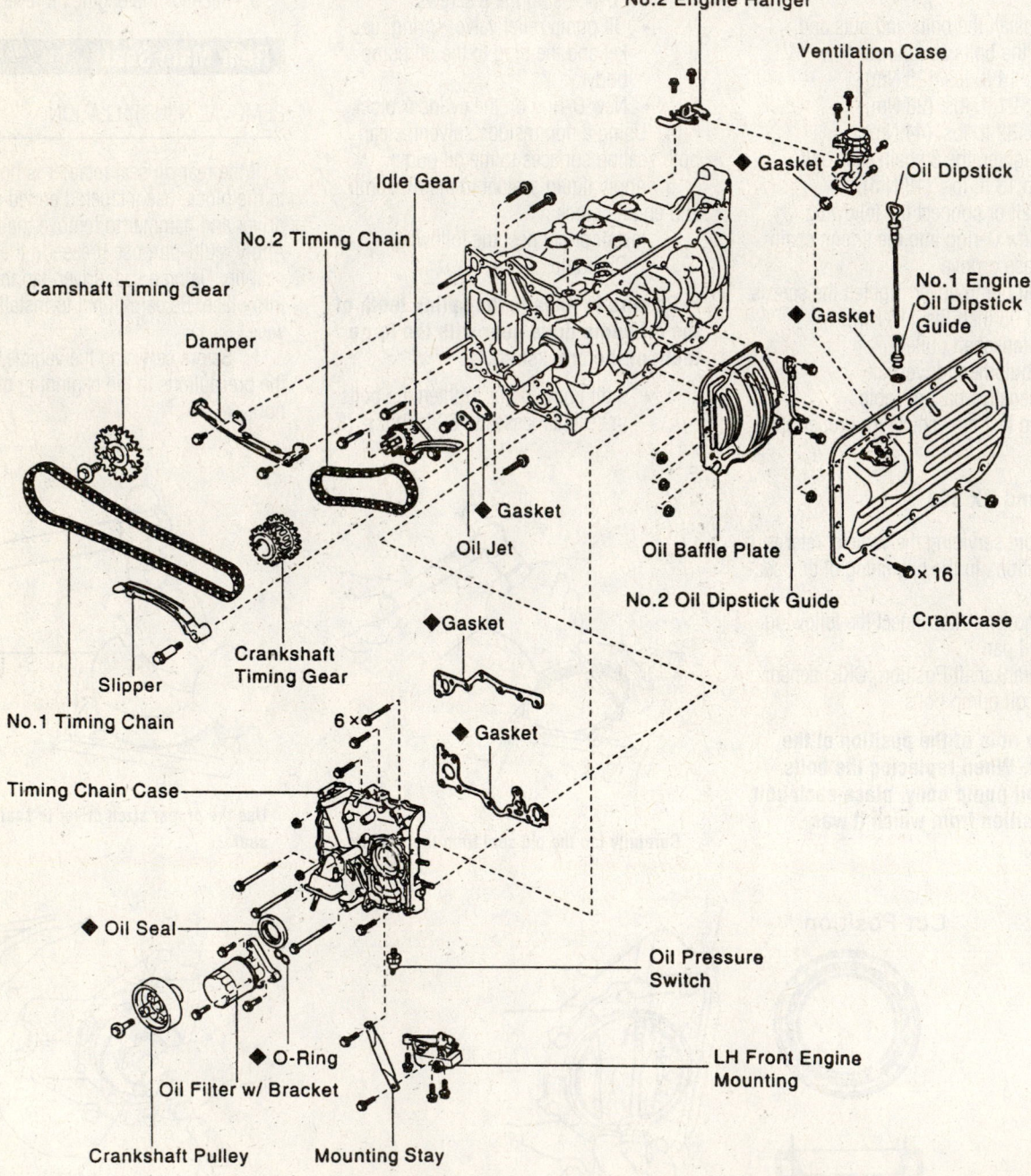

◆ Non-reusable part

Exploded view of the timing chain and gear component locations—Previa

7924ZG90

3. Remove the crankshaft pulley, as follows:

- Crankshaft pulley bolt, loosen it using a holding device to secure the crankshaft
- Tool and pulley bolt
- Crankshaft pulley, using a puller

4. Loosen the left engine mounting bolts and the left-hand mounting stay, then extract the assembly from the engine.

5. Remove or disconnect the following:

- Oil pressure switch
- No. 1 engine oil dipstick
- No. 2 engine hanger
- Ventilation case and discard the gasket
- No. 1 oil dipstick guide and gasket
- Crankshaft Position (CKP) sensor, if equipped

6. Remove the crankcase, as follows:

- 16 bolts and 2 nuts from the crankcase
- Crankcase from the cylinder block, using a prytool (09032-00100) and a brass bar
- No. 2 oil dipstick guide and oil baffle plate, by removing the 2 bolts and 3 nuts
- Oil filter bracket with the oil filter
- O-ring from the timing chain case

7. Remove the timing chain case, as follows:

- 3 bolts from the rear of the timing chain cover
- 12 bolts and 2 nuts from the front of the chain cover
- Timing chain case, using a plastic faced hammer and discard both gaskets
- No. 1 timing chain and camshaft timing gear
- Chain slipper and damper
- Oil jet by removing the bolt

8. Remove the No. 2 timing chain and idle gear, as follows:

- Loosen both idle gear chain guide bolts
- Tighten the lower bolt while pushing the idle gear chain guide to the left with your finger

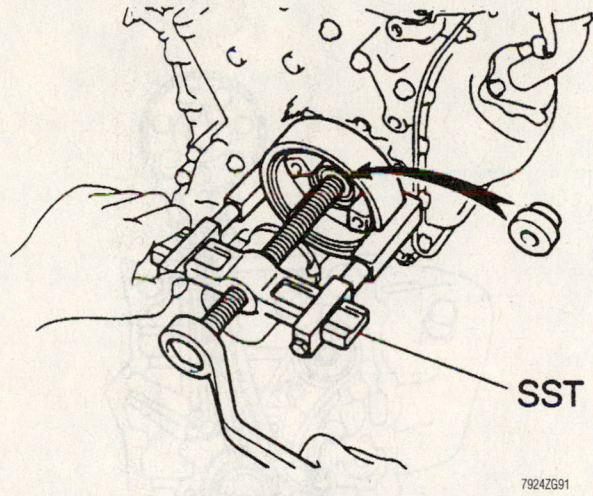

Place a puller on the end of the crankshaft pulley and remove it—Previa

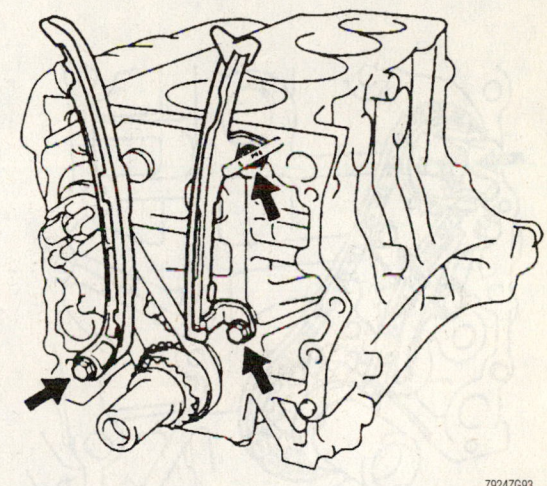

Unbolt the chain slipper and damper from the timing area—Previa

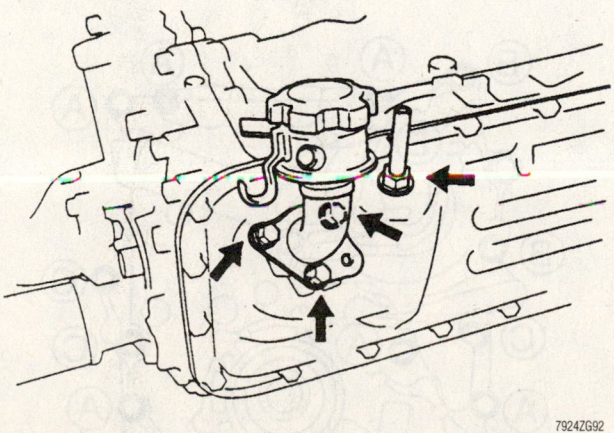

Unbolt and remove the ventilation case and No. 1 oil dipstick guide—Previa

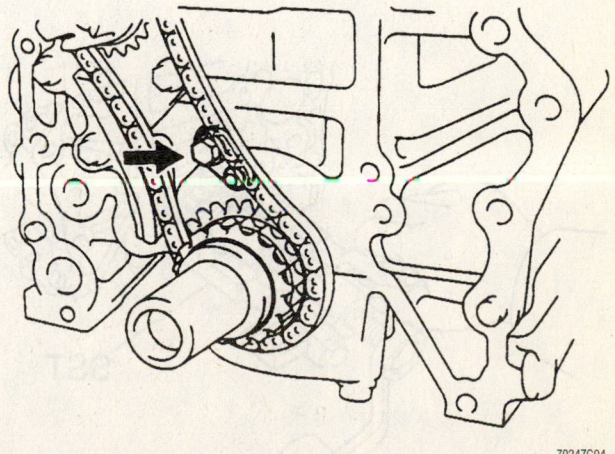

The oil jet is retained with 1 bolt in the center of the No. 2 timing chain—Previa

Timing belt service is covered in Section 4 of this manual

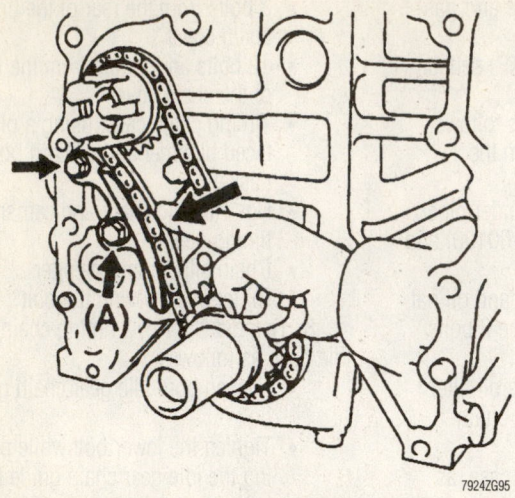

Tighten bolt A while pushing the chain guide to the left with your finger—Previa

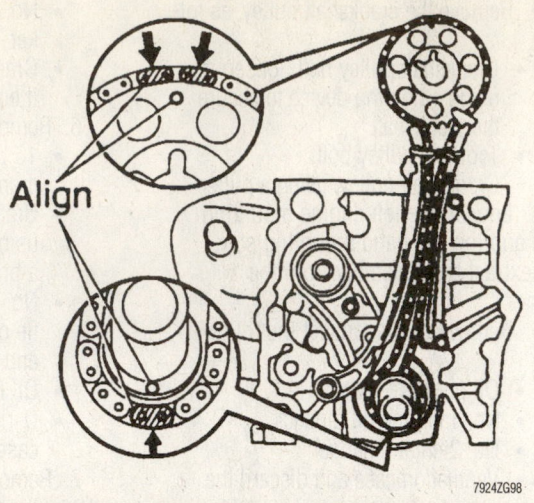

Align the timing chain on the camshaft gear so that the timing mark is between the 2 bright links—Previa

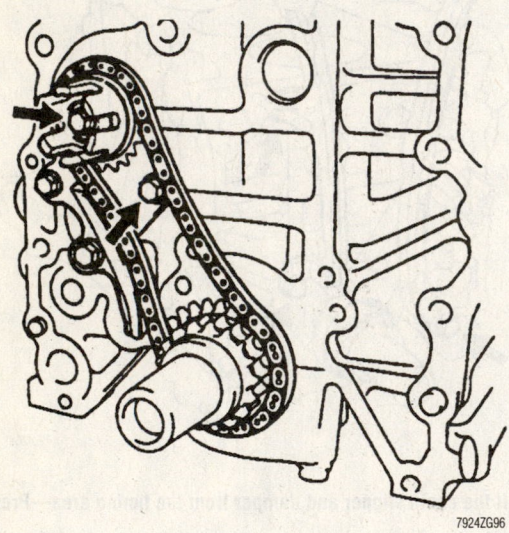

Remove the 2 bolts, then the chain and idle gear together—Previa

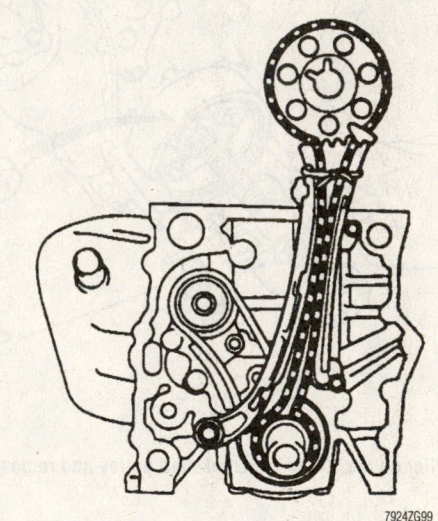

Tie the timing chain together as shown—Previa

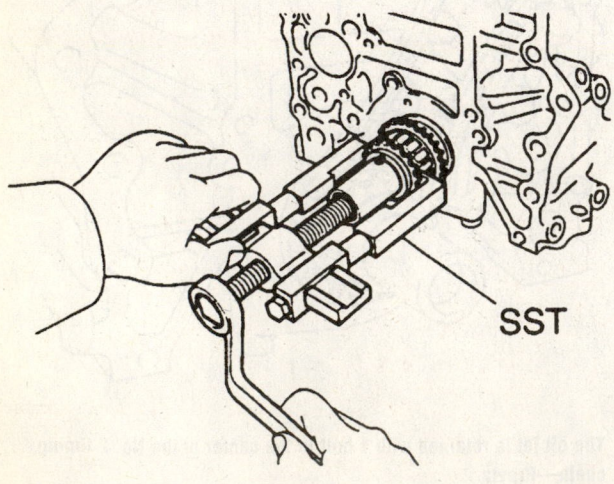

Using a puller to extract the crankshaft timing gear—Previa

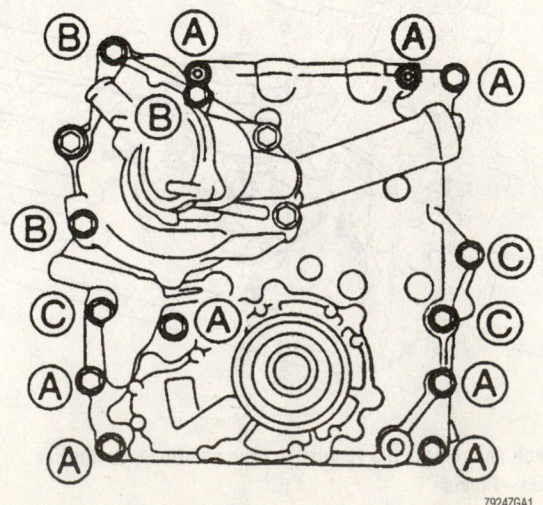

Timing chain cover bolt locations—Previa

- Both bolts, chain and idle gear as an assembly

9. Remove the crankshaft timing gear. If the gear can not be removed by hand, use a puller to extract it.

To install:

10. Install the crankshaft timing gear, as follows:

a. Turn the crankshaft until the shaft key is on the top.

b. Slide the gear over the key on the crankshaft. If the gear is hard to install by hand, carefully drive it in.

11. Install the No. 2 timing chain and idle gear, as follows:

a. Place the No. 2 timing chain on the idle gear.

b. Position the No. 2 timing chain on the crankshaft gear.

c. Install and tighten the 2 bolts to 14 ft. lbs. (20 Nm).

d. Loosen the lower bolt so that the chain guide presses against the chain.

e. Check that the spring is operating normally against the chain guide by pressing on the chain with your finger, then releasing your finger.

f. With the chain guide pressing against the chain, tighten the bolts to hold the chain guide in place. Tighten the bolts to 14 ft. lbs. (20 Nm).

12. Install or connect the following:

- Oil jet using a new gasket. Tighten the bolt to 13 ft. lbs. (18 Nm).
- Chain damper and slipper. Tighten the chain damper bolts to 13 ft. lbs. (18 Nm) and the chain slipper bolt to 20 ft. lbs. (27 Nm).

13. Place the No. 1 timing chain and camshaft timing gear, as follows:

a. Place the timing chain on the camshaft timing gear so that the timing mark is between the 2 bright chain links.

b. Position the timing chain on the crankshaft timing gear with the single bright link aligned with the timing mark on the crankshaft timing gear.

c. Be sure the timing chain is positioned between the damper and slipper.

d. Turn the camshaft timing gear counterclockwise to take the slack out of the chain.

e. Tie the timing chain with a cord and be sure it doesn't come loose.

14. Install the timing chain case, as follows:

a. Clean the gasket surface for the timing chain case.

b. Install 2 new gaskets over the dowels.

c. Slide on the chain case over the dowels.

d. Install the bolts and nuts and tighten the bolts, as follows:

- A: 14 ft. lbs. (20 Nm)
- B: 21 ft. lbs. (28 Nm)
- C: 32 ft. lbs. (44 Nm)

e. Install and tighten the 3 chain case bolts (rear) to 13 ft. lbs. (18 Nm).

15. Install or connect the following:

- Oil filter bracket, using a new O-ring. Tighten the 3 bolts to 14 ft. lbs. (20 Nm).
- New oil filter
- Baffle plate. Tighten the 3 nuts to 43 inch lbs. (5 Nm)
- No. 2 oil dipstick guide. Tighten the both bolts to 13 ft. lbs. (18 Nm).
- Crankcase to the engine. Tighten the 16 bolts and 2 nuts to 108 inch lbs. (12 Nm).
- Ventilation case using a new gasket. Tighten the 3 bolts to 69 inch lbs. (8 Nm).
- No. 1 oil dipstick guide using a new gasket. Tighten the nut to 22 ft. lbs. (29 Nm).
- No. 2 engine hanger. Tighten the 4 bolts to 27 ft. lbs. (37 Nm) and the ventilation side bolts to 69 inch lbs. (8 Nm).
- Engine oil dipstick
- Oil pressure switch. Tighten to 11 ft. lbs. (15 Nm).
- Left-hand engine mounting and stay. Tighten the mount bolts to 30 ft. lbs. (41 Nm) and the stay bolts to 27 ft. lbs. (37 Nm).

16. Install the crankshaft pulley, as follows:

a. Install the crankshaft pulley to the crankshaft with the spline teeth of the crankshaft pulley engaged with the large teeth of the oil pump.

b. Rotate the crankshaft pulley to the left and right and check that the key groove of the crankshaft pulley correctly fits the crankshaft key.

c. Install the crankshaft pulley bolt.

d. Using the Holding Device tools 09213-58012 and 09330-00021, tighten the bolt to 192 ft. lbs. (260 Nm).

17. Remove the cord from the timing chain.

18. Install or connect the following:

- Cylinder head
- Engine to the transmission
- Engine/transmission assembly

19. Top off all fluid levels. Test drive the vehicle.

Piston and Rings

POSITIONING

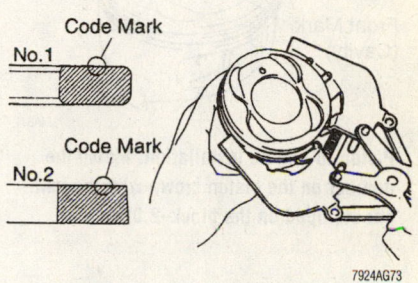

Compression ring identification mark locations—2.0L engine

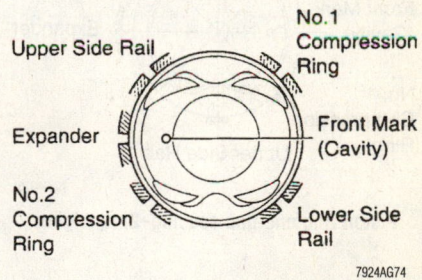

Piston ring end-gap spacing—2.0L engine

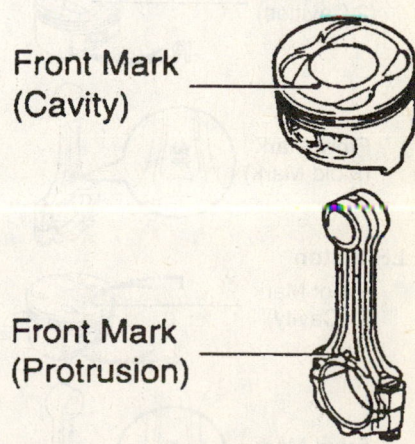

Piston-to-connecting rod assembly—2.0L engine

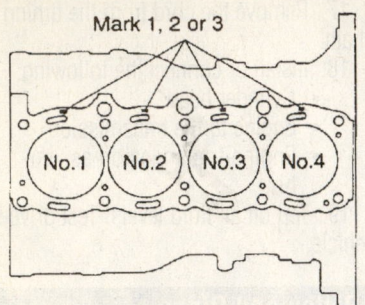

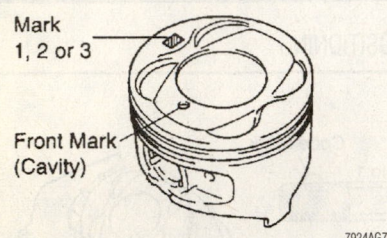

Piston-to-engine installation. Match the number on the piston crown with the number stamped on the block—2.0L engine

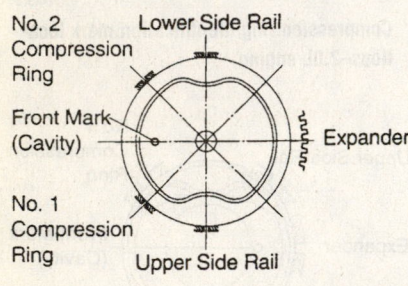

Piston ring end-gap spacing—2.4L engine

RH Piston

Front Mark (2 Cavities)

Front Mark (Mold Mark)

LH Piston

Front Mark (1 Cavity)

Front Mark (Mold Mark)

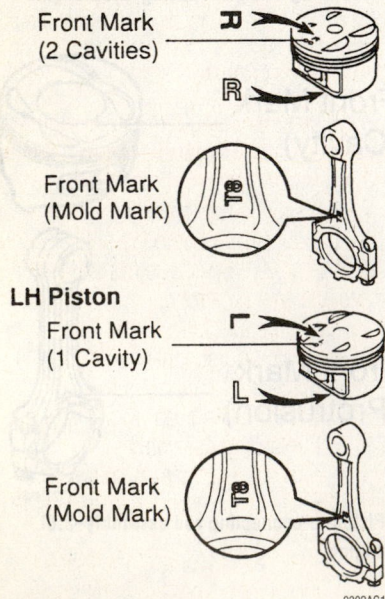

Piston/connecting rod-to-engine positioning–3.0L engine

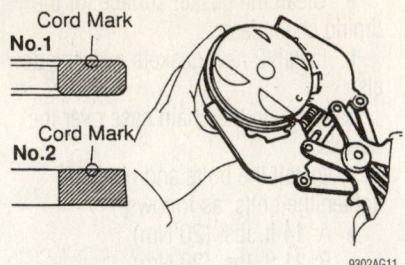

Piston ring positioning–3.0L engine

RH Piston

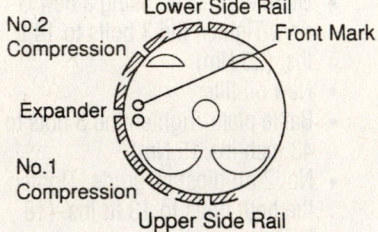

LH Piston

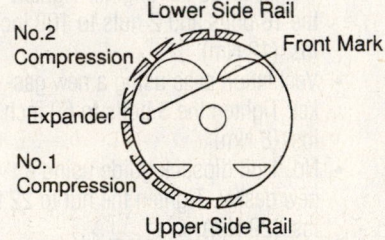

Piston ring identification–3.0L engine

FUEL SYSTEM

Fuel System Service Precautions

Safety is the most important factor when performing not only fuel system maintenance but any type of maintenance. Failure to conduct maintenance and repairs in a safe manner may result in serious personal injury or death. Work on a vehicle's fuel system components can be accomplished safely and effectively by adhering to the following rules and guidelines.

• To avoid the possibility of fire and personal injury, always disconnect the negative battery cable unless the repair or test procedure requires that battery voltage be applied.

• Always relieve the fuel system pressure prior to disconnecting any fuel system component (injector, fuel rail, pressure regulator, etc.) fitting or fuel line connection. Exercise extreme caution whenever relieving fuel system pressure, to avoid exposing skin, face and eyes to fuel spray. Please be advised that fuel under pressure may penetrate the skin or any part of the body that it contacts.

• Always place a shop towel or cloth around the fitting or connection prior to loosening to absorb any excess fuel due to spillage. Ensure that all fuel spillage is quickly remove from engine surfaces. Ensure that all fuel-soaked cloths or towels are deposited into a flame-proof waste container with a lid.

• Always keep a dry chemical (Class B) fire extinguisher near the work area.

• Do not allow fuel spray or fuel vapors to come into contact with a light bulb, spark or open flame.

• Always use a second wrench when loosening or tightening fuel line connection fittings. This will prevent unnecessary stress and torsion to fuel piping. Always follow the proper torque specifications.

• Always replace worn fuel fitting O-rings with new ones. Do not substitute fuel hose where rigid pipe is installed.

Fuel System Pressure

RELIEVING

1. Before servicing the vehicle, refer to the precautions in the beginning of this section.

2. Disconnect the negative battery terminal. Wait at least 90 seconds prior to working on models equipped with an airbag.

3. Place a catch-pan under the joint to be disconnected. A large quantity of fuel may be released when the joint is opened.

➡**Wear eye or full-face protection.**

4. Place a shop towel over the area and slowly loosen the joint using a wrench of the correct size. Use a back-up wrench if needed.

5. Allow the fuel left in the line to bleed off slowly before fully disconnecting the joint.

6. Plug the opened lines immediately to prevent fuel spillage or the entry of dirt.

7. Dispose of the released fuel properly.

8. After adjoining fuel lines, connect the negative battery cable and start the engine.

9. Check for leaks and repair as needed.

Fuel Filter

REMOVAL & INSTALLATION

RAV4

1. Before servicing the vehicle, refer to the precautions in the beginning of this section.
2. Properly release fuel system pressure.
3. Remove or disconnect the following:
   • Negative battery cable
   • Fuel filter's protective shield
4. Place a pan under the delivery pipe to catch the dripping fuel and slowly loosen the union bolt or flare nut to bleed off the fuel pressure.
5. Drain the remaining fuel.
6. Remove or disconnect the following:
   • Inlet and outlet lines
   • Fuel filter

To install:
7. Coat the flare nut, union nut and bolt threads with engine oil.
8. Hand-tighten the inlet line to the fuel filter.

➡**When tightening the fuel line bolts to the fuel filter, use a torque wrench. The tightening torque is very important, as under or over tightening may cause fuel leakage. Insure that there is no fuel line interference and that there is sufficient clearance between it and any other parts.**

9. Install or connect the following:
   • Fuel filter. Tighten the inlet bolts to 22 ft. lbs. (30 Nm).
   • Delivery pipe using new gaskets. Tighten the union bolt to 22 ft. lbs. (30 Nm).
10. Run the engine for a few minutes and check for any fuel leaks.
11. Install the protective shield.

Except RAV4

1. Before servicing the vehicle, refer to the precautions in the beginning of this section.
2. Disconnect the negative battery cable.
3. Relieve the fuel system pressure.

➡**The fuel filter is located in the engine compartment, at the inlet line to the fuel rail.**

4. Remove or disconnect the following:
   • Inlet and outlet lines from the filter
   • Fuel filter

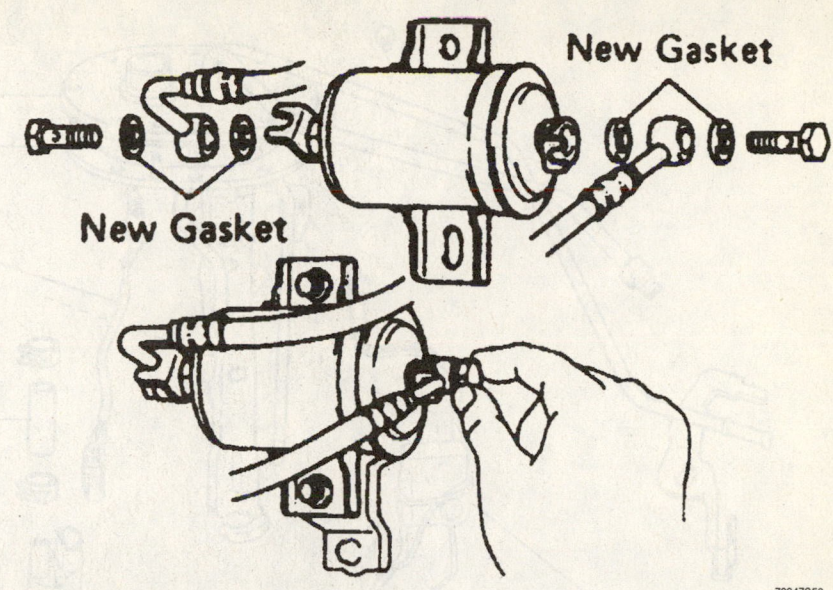

Exploded view of the fuel filter—except RAV4

To install:
5. Install or connect the following:
   • Fuel filter, using new O-rings. Tighten the lines to 22 ft. lbs. (29 Nm).
   • Negative battery cable
6. Start the engine and check for leaks.

Fuel Pump

REMOVAL & INSTALLATION

RAV4 and RX 300

1. Before servicing the vehicle, refer to the precautions in the beginning of this section.
2. Relieve the fuel system pressure.
3. Remove or disconnect the following:
   • Negative battery cable
   • Left-hand rear seat assembly
   • Floor service hole by pulling back the carpet; then, remove the 4 screws
   • Fuel pump and sender gauge connector

➡**Loosen the fuel cap to relieve any fuel pressure within the tank.**

   • Fuel pipe union bolt and both gaskets
   • Fuel pump outlet pipe
   • Return vent hose from the fuel pump
   • 8 fuel pump bolts and the pump assembly from the tank

To install:
4. Install or connect the following:
   • Fuel pump to the fuel tank. Tighten the 8 bolts to 31 inch lbs. (3.5 Nm).
   • Return vent hose to the fuel pump
   • Outlet pipe to the fuel pump, using new gaskets. Tighten the union bolts to 22 ft. lbs. (29 Nm).
   • Fuel pump and sender gauge connector
   • Floor hole cover with the 4 screws
   • Carpet
   • Left rear seat assembly
   • Negative battery cable
   • Fuel cap
5. Start the vehicle and check for leaks.

Previa and Sienna

1. Before servicing the vehicle, refer to the precautions in the beginning of this section.
2. Relieve the fuel pressure.
3. Disconnect the negative battery cable. Wait at least 90 seconds before proceeding on models with an airbag.
4. Drain the fuel tank.
5. Remove or disconnect the following:
   • Fuel tank
   • Access plate bolts
   • Fuel pump assembly
   • Fuel pump electrical connectors.
6. Pull the bracket from the lower side of the fuel pump.
7. Remove or disconnect the following:
   • Fuel pump from the fuel hose

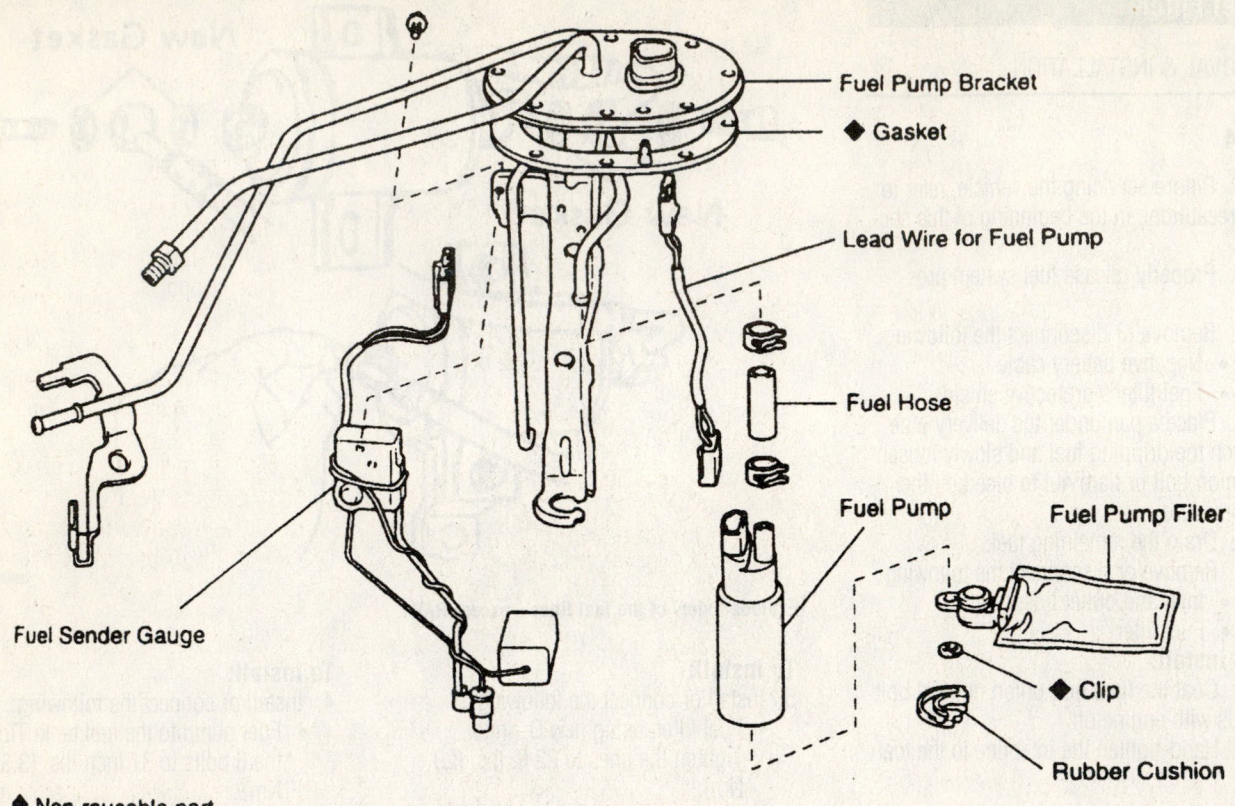

Fuel Pump Bracket

◆ Gasket

Lead Wire for Fuel Pump

Fuel Hose

Fuel Pump

Fuel Pump Filter

◆ Clip

Rubber Cushion

Fuel Sender Gauge

◆ **Non-reusable part**

7924ZG60

Exploded view of the fuel pump, bracket and related components—all vehicles similar

- Rubber cushion, the clip and the fuel filter from the bottom of the fuel pump.

To install:

8. Install or connect the following:
- Fuel pump filter to the fuel pump using a new clip
- Fuel pump to the bracket using new gaskets
- Fuel hose to the outlet port of the fuel pump
- Fuel pump bracket. Tighten the bolts to 26 inch lbs. (3 Nm).
- Fuel tank
- All electrical and fuel harness
- Negative battery cable

9. Refill the fuel tank and check for leaks.

Fuel Injector

REMOVAL & INSTALLATION

2.0L Engine

1. Before servicing the vehicle, refer to the precautions in the beginning of this section.

2. Remove or disconnect the following:
- Air cleaner assembly
- Cylinder head cover

- Throttle body from the intake manifold
- Distributor

3. Remove or disconnect the engine wire from the intake manifold, as follows:
- 4 injector connectors
- Both engine wire clamps from the intake manifold wire brackets
- Engine wire protector from the right side of the intake manifold
- Engine wire clamp

4. Remove or disconnect the Exhaust Gas Recirculation (EGR) valve, as follows:
- Vacuum hose from port **E** of the Vacuum Switching Valve (VSV)
- EGR hose from the vacuum modulator
- Loosen the EGR pipe nut from the cylinder head
- Both nuts, EGR valve, pipe assembly and gasket

5. Disconnect the engine compartment R/B No. 2

6. Remove or disconnect the fuel inlet hose and delivery pipe, as follows:
- Union bolt, both gaskets and the fuel inlet hose from the fuel filter outlet
- Air assist hose from the intake manifold port

- Air assist hose
- Loosen both delivery pipe-to-cylinder head bolts
- Delivery pipe from the 4 injectors
- Delivery pipe and fuel inlet hose assembly

7. Remove or disconnect the following:
- 4 injectors and spacers

✷✷ WARNING

Be careful not to drop the injectors and spacers.

- O-rings, insulator and grommet from each injector

To install:

8. Install or connect the following:
- New O-rings, insulator and grommet, lubricated with gasoline, to each injector
- 4 injectors and spacers

9. Install or connect the fuel inlet hose and delivery pipe, as follows:
- Delivery pipe and fuel inlet hose assembly
- Delivery pipe to the 4 injectors. Tighten both delivery pipe-to-cylinder head bolts to 9 ft. lbs. (13 Nm).
- Air assist hose

- Air assist hose to the intake manifold port
- Union bolt, new gaskets and the fuel inlet hose to the fuel filter outlet. Tighten the union bolt to 22 ft. lbs. (29 Nm).

10. Connect the engine compartment R/B No. 2

11. Install or connect the EGR valve, as follows:

- New gasket, pipe assembly and EGR valve. Tighten the nut to 9 ft. lbs. (13 Nm) and the union nut to 43 ft. lbs. (59 Nm).
- EGR hose to the vacuum modulator
- Vacuum hose from port **E** of the VSV

12. Install or connect the engine wire to the intake manifold, as follows:

- Engine wire clamp
- Engine wire protector to the right side of the intake manifold
- Both engine wire clamps to the intake manifold wire brackets
- 4 injector connectors

13. Install or connect the following:

- Distributor
- Throttle body to the intake manifold
- Cylinder head cover
- Air cleaner assembly

2.4L Engine

1. Before servicing the vehicle, refer to the precautions in the beginning of this section.

2. Remove or disconnect the following:

- Negative battery cable. Work must be started approximately 90 seconds or longer after the negative battery cable has been disconnected, if equipped with an air bag.
- Right side engine service hole cover
- Positive Crankcase Ventilation (PCV) hose
- Vacuum hose and fuel return hose from the pressure regulator
- Engine wire from the intake manifold, delivery pipe and fuel injectors
- Fuel inlet pipe and discard both gaskets
- Both bolts and the delivery pipe
- Fuel injectors

To install:

3. Install or connect the following:

- Fuel injectors
- Delivery pipe. Tighten the bolts to 14 ft. lbs. (20 Nm).
- New gaskets and the fuel inlet pipe. Tighten the pipe to 20 ft. lbs. (29 Nm).

- Engine wire to the intake manifold, delivery pipe and fuel injectors
- Vacuum hose and fuel return hose to the pressure regulator
- PCV hose
- Right side engine service hole cover
- Negative battery cable

3.0L Engine

1. Before servicing the vehicle, refer to the precautions in the beginning of this section.

2. Remove or disconnect the following:

- Outer front cowl top panel assembly
- Air cleaner cap with hose
- Negative battery cable. Work must be started approximately 90 seconds or longer after the negative battery cable has been disconnected, if equipped with an air bag.
- Coolant
- Accelerator and throttle cables
- V-bank cover
- Emission valve control set
- No. 2 EGR pipe
- Hydraulic motor pressure pipe from the water inlet and air inlet chamber
- Air intake chamber assembly
- Injector wiring
- Air assist pipe from the bracket on the No. 1 fuel pipe
- Air assist hoses from the intake manifold
- Fuel return hose from the No. 1 fuel pipe
- Fuel inlet hose for the fuel filter
- 2 union bolts holding the No. 2 fuel pipe to the delivery pipes
- Fuel return hose from the fuel pressure regulator
- Union bolt for the right hand delivery pipe, 2 gaskets, 2 bolts, left hand delivery pipe together with the 3 injectors and the No. 2 fuel pipe
- Union bolt for the delivery pipe and 2 gaskets from the No. 2 fuel pipe
- The 3 bolts, right hand delivery pipe together with the 3 injectors and the No. 1 fuel pipe
- The 4 spacers from the intake manifold
- The 6 injectors from the delivery pipes
- The two O-rings and two grommets from each injector

To install:

3. Install or connect the following:

- 2 new grommets to each injector

- New O-rings, with a light coat of fuel, to each injector
- Injectors
- The 4 spacers on the intake manifold
- Right hand delivery pipe and the No. 1 fuel pipe together with the 3 injectors in position on the intake manifold
- Bolt holding the right side delivery pipe, temporarily, to the intake manifold
- Left hand delivery pipe and the No. 2 fuel pipe together with the 3 injectors in position on the intake manifold
- Fuel return hose to the fuel pressure regulator

4. Temporarily install the 2 bolts holding the left hand delivery pipe to the intake manifold.

5. Temporarily install the No. 2 fuel pipe to the left side delivery pipe with the union bolt and 2 new gaskets.

6. Check that the injectors rotate smoothly. If they do not, Replace the O-rings.

7. Position the injector connector outward. Tighten the 4 bolts holding the delivery pipes to the intake manifold and tighten to 7 ft. lbs. (10 Nm). Tighten the bolt holding the No. 1 fuel pipe to the intake manifold to 14 ft. lbs. (20 Nm). Tighten the 2 union bolts holding the no. 2 fuel pipe to the delivery pipes to 24 ft. lbs. (32 Nm).

8. Install or connect the following:

- Fuel inlet and return hoses. Union bolt: 22 ft. lbs. (30 Nm)
- Fuel return hose to the No. 1 fuel pipe. Pass the fuel return hose under the heater hoses.
- Air assist hoses to the intake manifold
- Air assist pipe to the bracket on the No. 1 fuel pipe
- Fuel injector wiring connectors
- Air intake chamber assembly
- Hydraulic motor pressure pipe to the intake chamber. Bolts: 69 inch lbs. (8 Nm)
- No. 2 EGR pipe with new gaskets, tighten to 9 ft. lbs. (12 Nm)
- Emission control valve set
- V-bank cover
- Air cleaner hose
- Throttle and accelerator cables
- Coolant
- Air cleaner cap with hose
- Outer front cowl top panel assembly
- Negative battery cable

DRIVE TRAIN

Transmission Assembly

REMOVAL & INSTALLATION

Manual

2WD RAV4

1. Before servicing the vehicle, refer to the precautions in the beginning of this section.

2. Remove or disconnect the following:
   • Negative battery cable
   • Air cleaner case assembly with hose
   • Engine coolant reservoir tank
   • Engine wire clamp set nut
   • Starter

3. Remove the clutch release cylinder, as follows:
   • Clutch line bracket-to-transaxle set bolts
   • Release cylinder and line

4. Remove or disconnect the following:
   • Ground cable from the transaxle

• Vehicle Speed Sensor (VSS) and backup light switch connector
• Control cable by removing the 4 clips and washers
• 4 upper side transaxle-to-engine bolts
• Left mount insulator

5. Install a engine support to the engine.

6. Support rack and pinion to the engine support fixture with a rope.

7. Remove or disconnect the following:
   • Front wheels
   • Left and right-hand engine undercovers

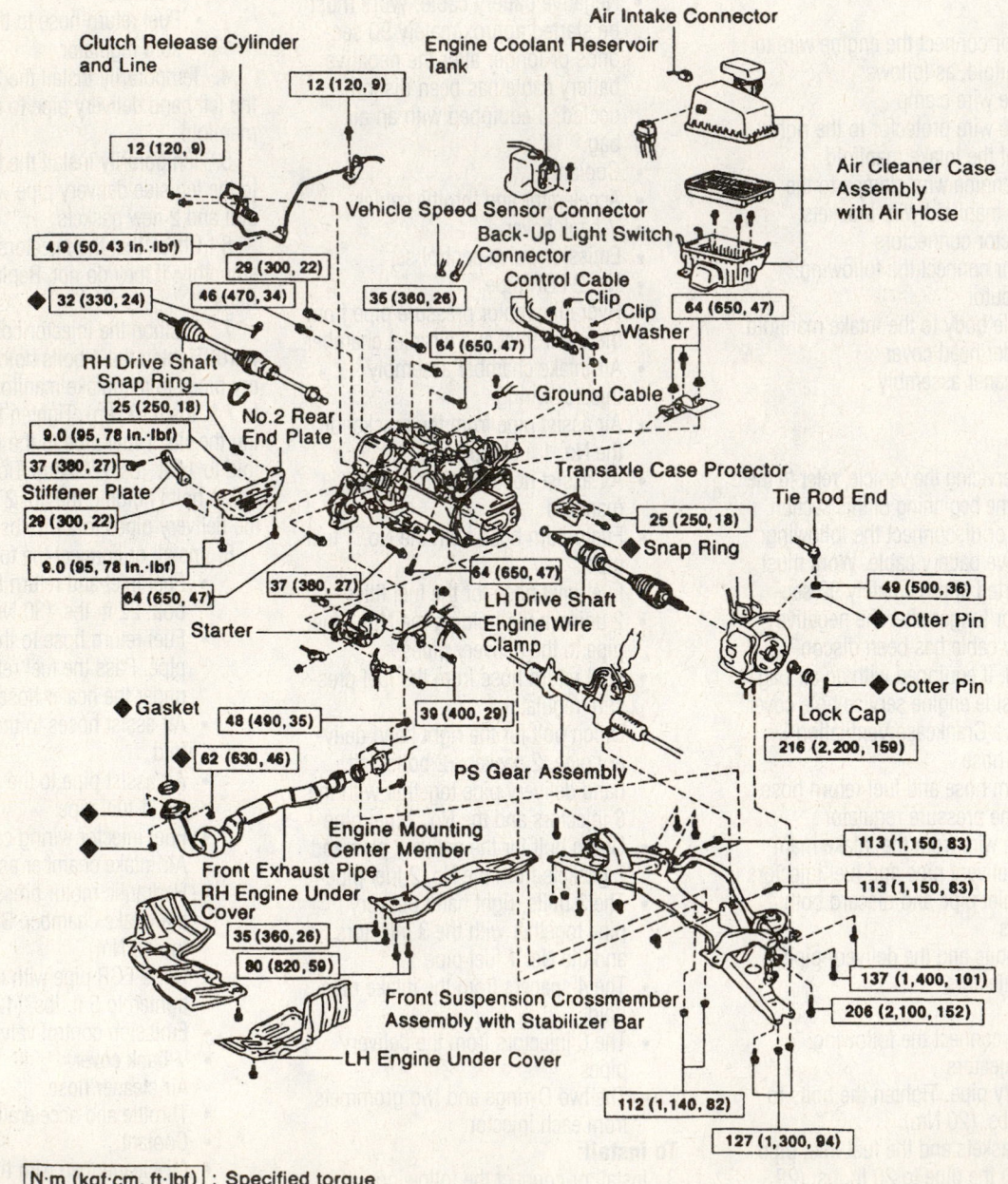

N·m (kgf·cm, ft·lbf) : Specified torque
◆ Non-reusable part

Transaxle exploded view—2WD RAV4

7924ZG61

8. Drain the transaxle oil.

9. Remove the left and right half-shafts.

10. Remove the front exhaust pipe, as follows:

- 3 exhaust manifold nuts and gasket
- Both exhaust pipe-to-center exhaust pipe bolts
- Exhaust pipe

11. Remove the front suspension crossmember assembly with the sway bar, as follows:

a. Support the front suspension crossmember with a jack.

b. Disconnect the ring from the center exhaust pipe.

c. Remove the 2 set bolts and nuts of the power steering rack and pinion assembly.

d. Remove the suspension crossmember assembly with the sway bar by removing the 2 nuts and 6 bolts.

12. Remove the engine mounting centermember by removing the 4 bolts.

13. Jack up the transaxle slightly.

14. Remove or disconnect the following:

- Left mounting bracket from the mounting insulator by removing the set bolt
- Stiffener plate, No. 2 rear endplate and transaxle lower side mounting bolt

15. Lower the engine left side

16. Remove or disconnect the following:

- Transaxle
- Transaxle case protector by removing both bolts

To install:

17. Install or connect the following:

- Transaxle case protector. Tighten both bolts to 18 ft. lbs. (25 Nm).
- Transaxle

18. Install the No. 2 rear endplate and transaxle bolts. Tighten the bolts, as follows:

- Bolt C: 22 ft. lbs. (29 Nm)
- Bolt D: 34 ft. lbs. (46 Nm)
- Bolt E: 18 ft. lbs. (25 Nm)
- Bolt F: 78 inch lbs. (9.0 Nm)

19. Install or connect the following:

- Stiffener plate. Tighten both bolts to 27 ft. lbs. (37 Nm).
- Engine left mounting insulator to the left mounting bracket. Tighten the bolt to 47 ft. lbs. (64 Nm).
- Engine mount centermember. Tighten the radiator support bolts

to 26 ft. lbs. (35 Nm) and the mount insulator to 59 ft. lbs. (80 Nm).

20. Install the front suspension crossmember with the sway bar, as follows:

a. Install the sway bar and suspension crossmember. Tighten the nuts/bolts, as follows:

- Vehicle bolt A: 152 ft. lbs. (206 Nm)
- Lower control arm bracket bolt B: 101 ft. lbs. (137 Nm)
- Rear mounting bracket bolt C: 82 ft. lbs. (112 Nm)

b. Connect the rack and pinion to the crossmember. Tighten both nuts/bolts to 83 ft. lbs. (113 Nm).

c. Connect the ring for the center exhaust pipe.

21. Install the front exhaust pipe, as follow:

- Pipe with new gaskets
- Front pipe to the center exhaust pipe. Tighten both bolts to 35 ft. lbs. (48 Nm).
- Front exhaust pipe to the exhaust manifold. Tighten the 3 nuts to 46 ft. lbs. (62 Nm).

22. Install or connect the following:

- Left and right halfshafts
- Front wheels
- Engine left mounting insulator. Tighten the fasteners to 47 ft. lbs. (64 Nm).

23. Remove the engine support fixture.

24. Install or connect the following:

- 4 transaxle upper side mount bolts. Tighten bolt A to 47 ft. lbs. (64 Nm) and bolt B to 26 ft. lbs. (35 Nm).
- Ground cable with the clips and washers
- VSS and backup light switch connectors
- Ground cable to the transaxle
- Clutch release cylinder and line
- Starter. Tighten both bolts to 29 ft. lbs. (39 Nm).
- Engine wire clamp with the nut
- Engine coolant reservoir tank
- Air cleaner case assembly with the air hose
- Negative battery cable

25. Fill the transaxle with fluid. Check all fluids.

4WD RAV4

1. Before servicing the vehicle, refer to the precautions in the beginning of this section.

2. Remove or disconnect the following:

- Transaxle/engine assembly
- Transaxle case protector, by removing the 2 bolts
- Starter
- Transfer vacuum actuator bracket, by removing the 4 bolts

3. Remove the transfer vacuum actuator assembly, as follows:

- 4 solenoid hoses from the transfer vacuum actuator assembly
- Transfer vacuum actuator assembly, by removing the 2 bolts

4. Remove or disconnect the following:

- Right transfer stiffener plate, by removing the 5 bolts
- Center transfer stiffener plate, by removing the 3 bolts
- Stiffener plate by removing the 2 bolts
- Transaxle from the engine, by removing the 9 transaxle mount bolts

To install:

5. Connect the transaxle to the engine. Tighten the 9 bolts, as follows:

- Bolt A: 47 ft. lbs. (64 Nm)
- Bolt B: 26 ft. lbs. (35 Nm)
- Bolt C: 22 ft. lbs. (29 Nm)
- Bolt D: 34 ft. lbs. (46 Nm)
- Bolt E: 18 ft. lbs. (25 Nm)
- Bolt F: 78 inch lbs. (9.0 Nm)

6. Install or connect the following:

- Stiffener plate. Tighten both bolts to 27 ft. lbs. (37 Nm).
- Center transfer stiffener plate. Tighten the 3 bolts to 27 ft. lbs. (37 Nm).
- Right transfer stiffener plate. Tighten the 5 bolts to 27 ft. lbs. (37 Nm).

7. Install the transfer vacuum actuator assembly, as follows:

- Transfer vacuum actuator assembly. Tighten both bolts to 27 ft. lbs. (37 Nm).
- 4 solenoid hoses to the transfer vacuum actuator assembly

8. Install or connect the following:

- Transfer vacuum actuator bracket. Tighten the 4 bolts to 27 ft. lbs. (37 Nm).
- Starter. Tighten both bolts to 29 ft. lbs. (39 Nm).
- Transaxle case protector. Tighten both bolts to 18 ft. lbs. (25 Nm).
- Transaxle/engine assembly

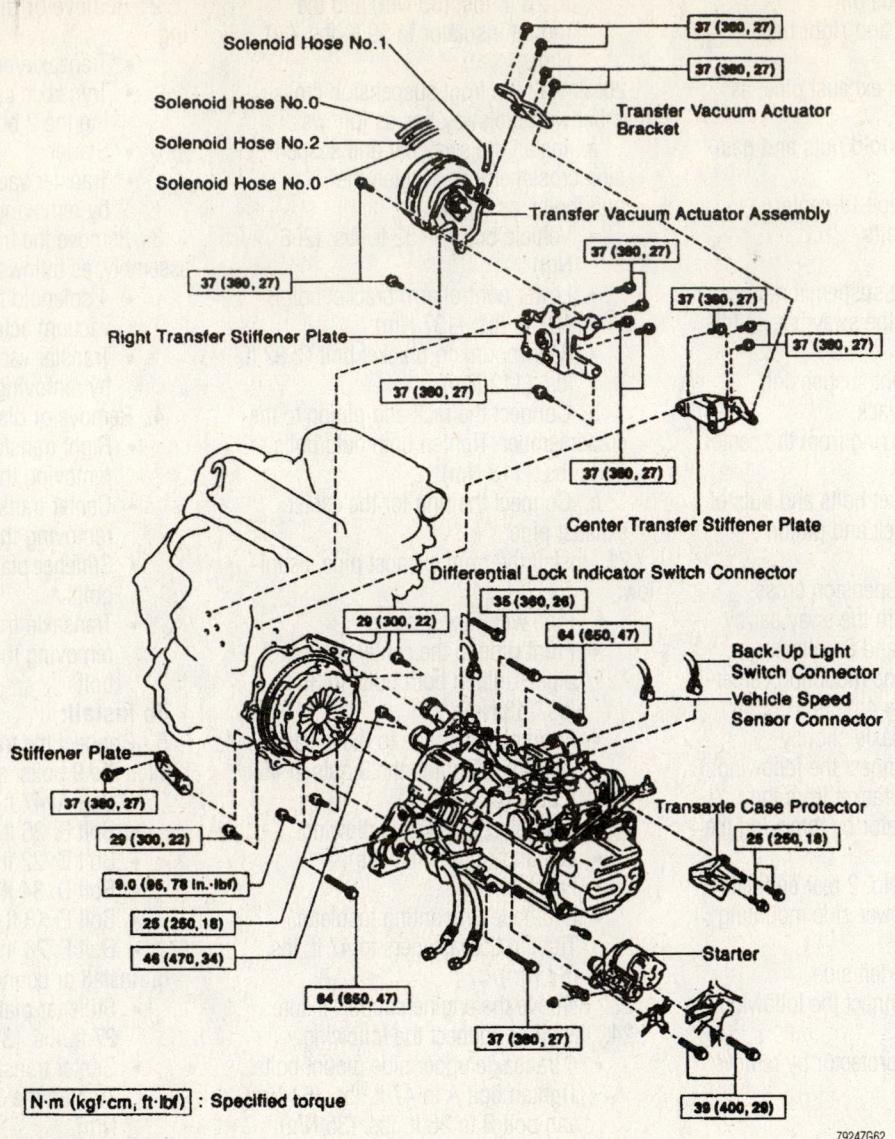

Solenoid Hose No.1
Solenoid Hose No.0
Solenoid Hose No.2
Solenoid Hose No.0

37 (380, 27)
37 (380, 27)

Transfer Vacuum Actuator Bracket

Transfer Vacuum Actuator Assembly

37 (380, 27)

37 (380, 27)
37 (380, 27)
37 (380, 27)

Right Transfer Stiffener Plate

37 (380, 27)

37 (380, 27)

Center Transfer Stiffener Plate

Differential Lock Indicator Switch Connector

35 (360, 26)
64 (650, 47)

29 (300, 22)

Back-Up Light Switch Connector
Vehicle Speed Sensor Connector

Stiffener Plate

37 (380, 27)

29 (300, 22)

9.0 (95, 78 in.·lbf)

Transaxle Case Protector

25 (250, 18)

25 (250, 18)

46 (470, 34)

Starter

64 (650, 47)

37 (380, 27)

N·m (kgf·cm, ft·lbf) : Specified torque

39 (400, 29)

7924ZG62

Manual transaxle exploded view—4WD RAV4

PREVIA

1. Before servicing the vehicle, refer to the precautions in the beginning of this section.

2. Disconnect the negative battery cable. Wait at least 90 seconds to perform any work on models equipped with air bags.

3. Drain the transmission fluid.

4. Remove or disconnect the following:
   - Starter
   - Front (4WD) and rear driveshafts
   - Clutch release cylinder, hose and bracket
   - Exhaust pipe bracket, by removing the 4 bolts
   - Control cables/bracket and speed sensor wiring
   - Engine-to-transmission stiffener plate

5. Place a transmission jack under the transmission.

6. Remove or disconnect the following:
   - Engine rear mounting bolts and raise the rear side of the engine
   - Engine-to-transmission bolts
   - Transmission

To install:

7. Install or connect the following:
   - Transmission. Tighten the bolts to 53 ft. lbs. (72 Nm).
   - Rear engine mounts and stiffener plate. Tighten the bolts to 27 ft. lbs. (37 Nm).
   - Speed sensor and control cables
   - Exhaust pipe bracket. Tighten to 37 ft. lbs. (51 Nm).
   - Clutch release cylinder, starter and driveshafts. Tighten the starter to 41 ft. lbs. (56 Nm) and driveshaft bolts to 20 ft. lbs. (25 Nm).
   - Negative battery cable.

8. Refill with transmission fluid.

Automatic

4WD RAV4

1. Before servicing the vehicle, refer to the precautions in the beginning of this section.

2. Remove or disconnect the following:
   - Negative battery cable
   - Engine/transaxle assembly
   - Starter
   - Stiffener plate, by removing the 3 bolts
   - Rear endplate, by removing the 4 bolts
   - 6 torque converter clutch mounting bolts
   - Connectors and wiring harness, from the transaxle

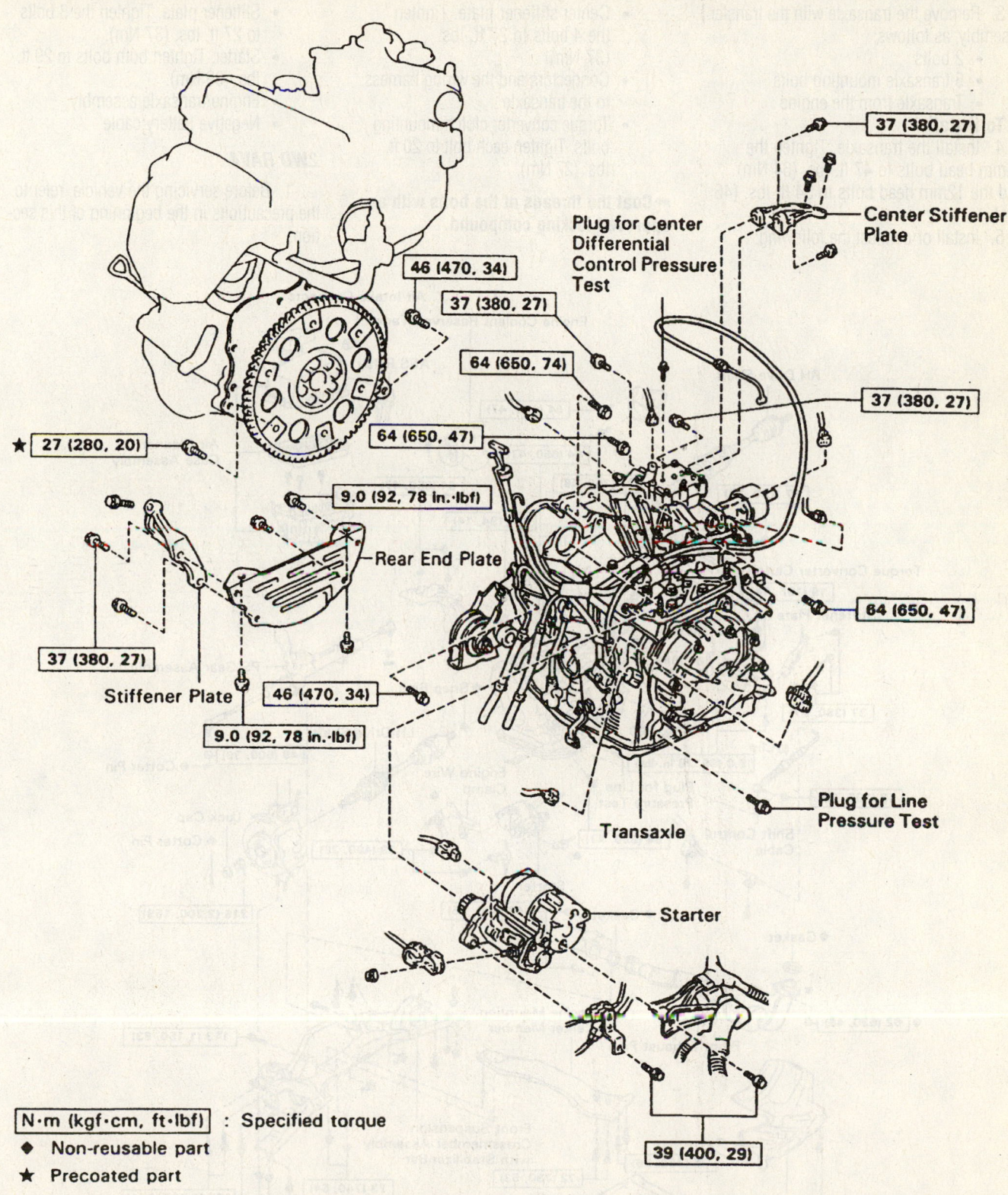

Plug for Center Differential Control Pressure Test

37 (380, 27)

Center Stiffener Plate

46 (470, 34)

37 (380, 27)

64 (650, 74)

37 (380, 27)

★ 27 (280, 20)

64 (650, 47)

9.0 (92, 78 in.·lbf)

Rear End Plate

37 (380, 27)

Stiffener Plate

46 (470, 34)

9.0 (92, 78 in.·lbf)

64 (650, 47)

Transaxle

Plug for Line Pressure Test

Starter

39 (400, 29)

N·m (kgf·cm, ft·lbf) : Specified torque

◆ Non-reusable part

★ Precoated part

7924ZG02A

Automatic transaxle exploded view—4WD RAV4

- Center stiffener plate, by removing the 4 bolts

3. Remove the transaxle with the transfer assembly, as follows:
  - 2 bolts
  - 5 transaxle mounting bolts
  - Transaxle from the engine

To install:

4. Install the transaxle. Tighten the 14mm head bolts to 47 ft. lbs. (64 Nm) and the 12mm head bolts to 34 ft. lbs. (46 Nm).

5. Install or connect the following:

- Tighten both bolts to 27 ft. lbs. (37 Nm).
- Center stiffener plate. Tighten the 4 bolts to 27 ft. lbs. (37 Nm).
- Connectors and the wiring harness to the transaxle
- Torque converter clutch mounting bolts. Tighten each bolt to 20 ft. lbs. (27 Nm).

➡ Coat the threads of the bolts with an approved locking compound.

- Rear endplate. Tighten the 4 bolts to 80 inch lbs. (9.0 Nm).
- Stiffener plate. Tighten the 3 bolts to 27 ft. lbs. (37 Nm).
- Starter. Tighten both bolts to 29 ft. lbs. (39 Nm).
- Engine/transaxle assembly
- Negative battery cable

2WD RAV4

1. Before servicing the vehicle, refer to the precautions in the beginning of this section.

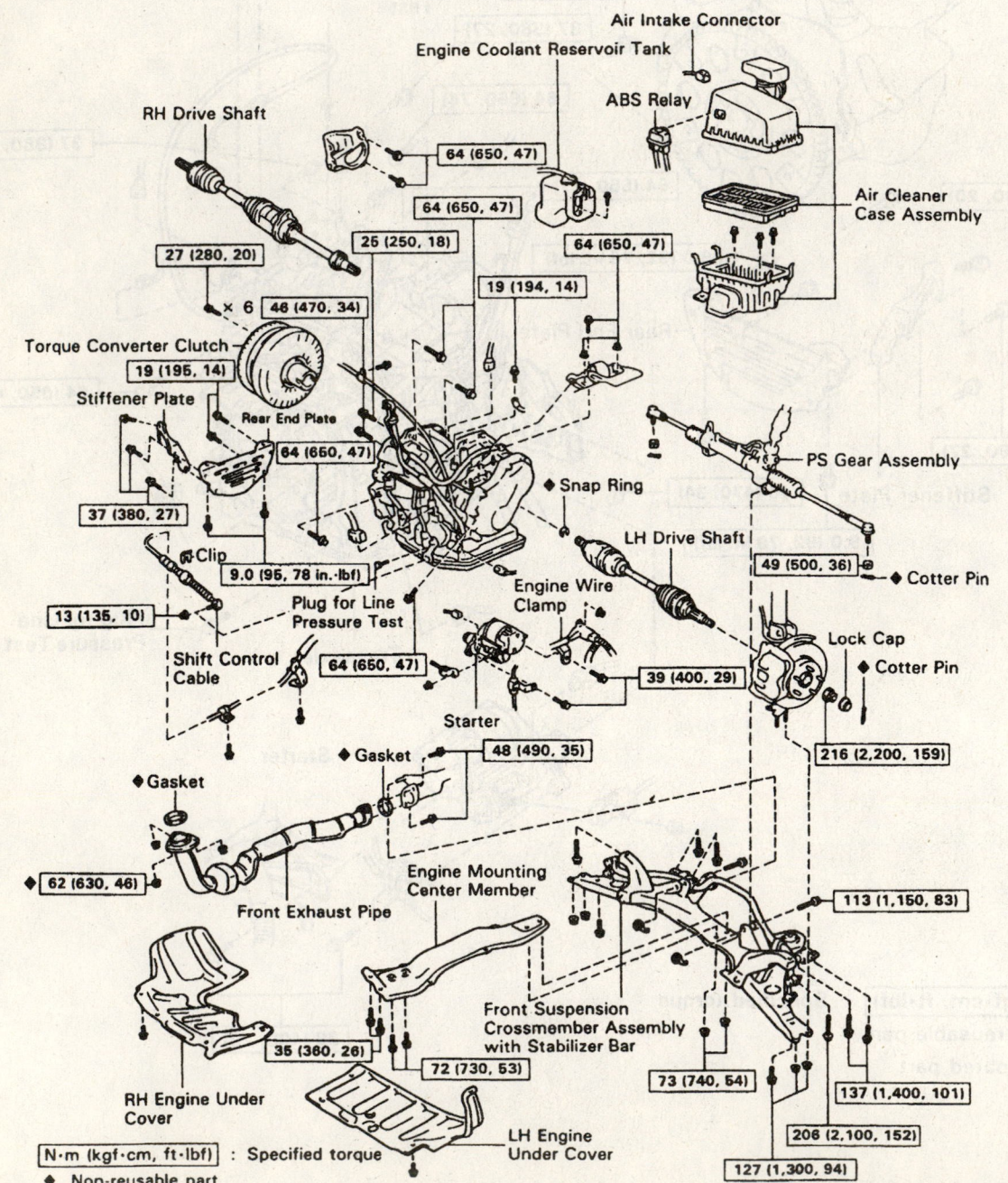

Transaxle exploded view—2WD RAV4

2. Remove or disconnect the following:
- Negative battery cable
- Throttle cable
- Engine coolant reservoir tank
- Air cleaner assembly
- Ground cable from the transaxle
- Set nut of the engine wire clamp

3. Remove the starter, as follows:
- Connector and nut from the starter
- 2 bolts and the engine wire
- Starter

4. Remove the 3 upper side transaxle mounting bolts.

5. Install an engine support fixture.

6. Remove or disconnect the following:
- 2 bolts and 2 nuts from the left engine mount
- Engine undercovers

7. Drain the fluid from the transaxle.

8. Remove the left and right halfshafts.

9. Remove the front exhaust pipe, as follows:
- 2 front exhaust pipe-to-center exhaust pipe bolts and gasket
- 3 front exhaust pipe-to-exhaust manifold nuts and gasket
- Exhaust manifold

10. Disconnect the shift control cable from the transaxle and frame, as follows:
- Control shaft lever nut
- Clip and the control cable from the transaxle
- 2 shift control cable-to-centermember bolts
- Crossmember

11. Detach the following connectors:
- Shift solenoid valve connector
- Park/Neutral Position (PNP) switch connector
- Vehicle Speed Sensor (VSS) connector

12. Remove or disconnect the following:
- Oil cooler hoses from the transaxle
- Rack and pinion from the crossmember by removing both nuts/bolts

13. Support the rack and pinion.

14. Support the suspension crossmember with a floor jack.

15. Remove or disconnect the following:
- Crossmember-to-centermember fasteners
- Crossmember with the sway bar
- Stiffener plate by removing the 3 bolts
- Rear endplate by removing the 4 bolts
- 6 torque converter bolts
- Both rear side transaxle mounting bolts

- Transaxle

To install:

16. Install or connect the following:
- Transaxle
- Both rear side transaxle mounting bolts. Tighten the top bolt to 18 ft. lbs. (25 Nm) and the lower bolt to 34 ft. lbs. (46 Nm).
- Torque converter bolts. Tighten the bolts to 20 ft. lbs. (27 Nm).

➡**First install the gray bolt; then, install the 5 black bolts.**

- Rear endplate. Tighten the engine bolts to 78 inch lbs. (9.0 Nm) and the transaxle bolts to 14 ft. lbs. (19 Nm).
- Stiffener plate. Tighten the 3 bolts to 27 ft. lbs. (37 Nm).

17. Install the front suspension crossmember and centermember with the sway bar. Tighten the nuts/bolts, as follows:
- Bolt A: 152 ft. lbs. (206 Nm)
- Bolt B: 101 ft. lbs. (137 Nm)
- Bolt C: 26 ft. lbs. (35 Nm)
- Bolt D: 53 ft. lbs. (72 Nm)
- Nut: 54 ft. lbs. (73 Nm)

18. Install or connect the following:
- Rack and pinion to the crossmember. Tighten the nuts to 83 ft. lbs. (113 Nm).
- Oil cooler hoses with both clips

19. Connect the following connectors:
- Shift solenoid valve connector
- PNP switch connector
- VSS connector

20. Install or connect the following:
- Shift control cable to the transaxle. Tighten the nut to 10 ft. lbs. (13 Nm).

21. Install the front exhaust pipe, as follows:
- Front exhaust pipe, using new gaskets
- Front exhaust pipe to the exhaust manifold. Tighten the 3 nuts to 46 ft. lbs. (62 Nm).
- Front exhaust pipe to the center exhaust pipe. Tighten both bolts to 35 ft. lbs. (48 Nm).

22. Install or connect the following:
- Left and right halfshafts
- Engine undercovers
- Left engine mount. Tighten the both nuts/bolts to 47 ft. lbs. (64 Nm).

23. Remove the engine fixture.

24. Install or connect the following:
- Upper side transaxle mount. Tighten the 3 bolts to 47 ft. lbs. (64 Nm).

- Starter. Tighten both bolts to 29 ft. lbs. (39 Nm).
- Engine wire
- Starter wire with the nut
- Engine wire clamp set nut
- Ground cable to the transaxle. Tighten the bolt to 14 ft. lbs. (19 Nm).
- Air cleaner assembly
- Engine coolant reservoir tank
- Throttle cable
- Negative battery cable

25. Check all fluids.

4-SPEED PREVIA

1. Before servicing the vehicle, refer to the precautions in the beginning of this section.

2. Remove or disconnect the following:
- Negative battery terminal

➡**Wait at least 90 seconds after the battery cable is disconnected before working on the vehicle if equipped with air bags.**

- Air cleaner assembly
- Transmission throttle cable from the throttle body

3. Drain the transmission fluid.

4. Remove or disconnect the following:
- Wiring harness for the neutral start switch and the back-up light switch
- Solenoid (overdrive) switch wiring, if equipped
- Oil level gauge, if equipped
- Starter wiring from the starter
- Starter

5. Make matchmarks on the rear driveshaft flange and the differential pinion flange. These marks must be aligned during installation.

6. Remove or disconnect the following:
- Rear driveshaft flange.
- Center bearing bracket-to-frame bolts, if equipped with a 2 piece driveshaft.
- Driveshaft, if necessary
- Speedometer cable
- Shift linkage from the transmission
- Oil cooler lines from the transmission
- Exhaust pipe clamp
- Oil filler tube, as required

7. Support the transmission, using a jack with a wooden block placed between the jack and the transmission pan. Raise the transmission, just enough to take the weight off the rear mount.

8. Remove or disconnect the following:
- Rear engine mount with the bracket

Turn to Section 5 for brake system applications

and the engine undercover, to gain access to the engine crankshaft pulley.

- Stiffener plates, if equipped.

9. Place a wooden block (or blocks) between the engine oil pan and the front frame crossmember.

10. Slowly, lower the transmission until the engine rests on the wooden block.

11. Remove the rubber plug(s) from the service holes located at the rear of the engine in order to gain access to the torque converter bolts.

12. Rotate the crankshaft (to remove the torque converter bolts) to access the bolts through the service holes.

13. Obtain a bolt of the same dimensions as the torque converter bolts. Cut the head off the bolt and hacksaw a slot in the bolt opposite the threaded end.

➡**This modified bolt is used as a guide pin. Two guides pins are needed to properly install the transmission.**

14. Thread the guide pin into one of the torque converter bolt holes. The guide pin will help keep the converter with the transmission.

15. Remove or disconnect the following:
- Stiffener plates from the transmission
- Transmission-to-engine bolts

➡**Carefully move the transmission rearward by prying on the guide pin through the service hole.**

- Transmission

To install:

16. Installation is the reverse of removal. Please note the following important steps.

17. Apply a coat of Multi-purpose grease to the torque converter stub shaft and the corresponding pilot hole in the flexplate.

18. Install the torque converter into the front of the transmission. Push inward on the torque converter while rotating it to completely couple the torque converter to the transmission.

19. To be sure the converter is properly installed, measure the distance between the torque converter mounting lugs and the front mounting face of the transmission. The proper distance is 0.079 inch (20mm).

20. Install guide pins into 2 opposite mounting lugs of the torque converter.

21. Align the transmission with the engine alignment dowels and position the converter guide pins into the mounting holes of the flexplate.

22. Install and tighten the transmission-to-engine mounting bolts. Tighten the bolts to specifications.

23. Remove the converter guide pins and install the converter mounting bolts. Rotate the crankshaft as necessary to gain access to the guide pins and bolts through the service holes. Evenly, tighten the converter mounting bolts to specifications. Install the rubber plugs into the access holes.

24. Install or connect the following:
- Remaining components
- Negative battery cable

25. Adjust the transmission throttle cable.

26. Refill the transmission.

27. Start the engine and check for leaks.

28. Road test the vehicle for proper operation.

29. Recheck all fluid levels.

3-SPEED PREVIA

1. Before servicing the vehicle, refer to the precautions in the beginning of this section.

2. Remove or disconnect the following:
- Negative battery terminal

➡**Wait at least 90 seconds after the battery cable is disconnected before working on the vehicle if equipped with air bags.**

- Automatic Transmission Fluid (ATF) level gauge
- Throttle cable
- Equipment driveshaft
- Filler pipe
- Driveshaft
- Control cable
- No. 1 and No. 2 Vehicle Speed Sensor (VSS) harnesses
- Starter solenoid wiring
- Neutral safety switch harness
- Oil pipe clamp
- Oil cooler pipes
- Automatic Transmission Fluid (ATF) temperature switch harness, for 4WD
- Starter

3. Using a jack, support the transmission.

4. Remove or disconnect the following:
- Stiffener plate
- Torque converter clutch cover

➡**Turn the crankshaft to gain access and remove the 6 bolts.**

- Exhaust pipe bracket
- Rear mounting bolts
- Transmission mounting bolts
- Wiring harness
- Transmission

To install:

5. Installation is the reverse of removal. Please note the following important steps.

6. Install or connect the following:
- Transmission
- Wiring harness
- Remaining components
- Equipment driveshaft
- Throttle cable
- ATF level gauge
- Negative battery cable

7. Check the shift lever position.

8. Check the fluid level and fill, if necessary.

SIENNA AND RX 300

1. Before servicing the vehicle, refer to the precautions in the beginning of this section.

2. Remove or disconnect the following:
- Hood
- Wiper and blade assembly
- Top cowl seal and panel
- Window washer hoses, from the ventilator louvers
- Left and right ventilator louvers
- Heater air duct
- Battery and tray
- Throttle cable
- Front upper suspension brace, for RX 300
- Cruise control actuator with its bracket, if equipped
- Starter
- Shift control cable
- Driveshaft, for RX 300 with 4WD
- Body-to-engine ground strap
- Park/Neutral Position (PNP) switch, solenoid and ATF temperature connectors
- 5 upper transaxle-to-engine mounting bolts
- Front wheel
- Engine undercover
- Halfshafts
- Front exhaust pipe
- Stabilizer bar
- Both steering gear mounting bolts and support it in the vehicle
- Shift control cable from its bracket
- Power steering pipe and the oil cooler clamps from the frame
- Both left-side transaxle mounting nuts
- Rear-side engine mounting nuts
- Engine shock absorber mounting bolts
- 3 front-side engine mounting bolts

3. Attach an engine sling to the engine hangers in order to support the engine weight.

4. Remove or disconnect the following:
- Front frame mounting bolts and the frame
- Transaxle oil cooler lines

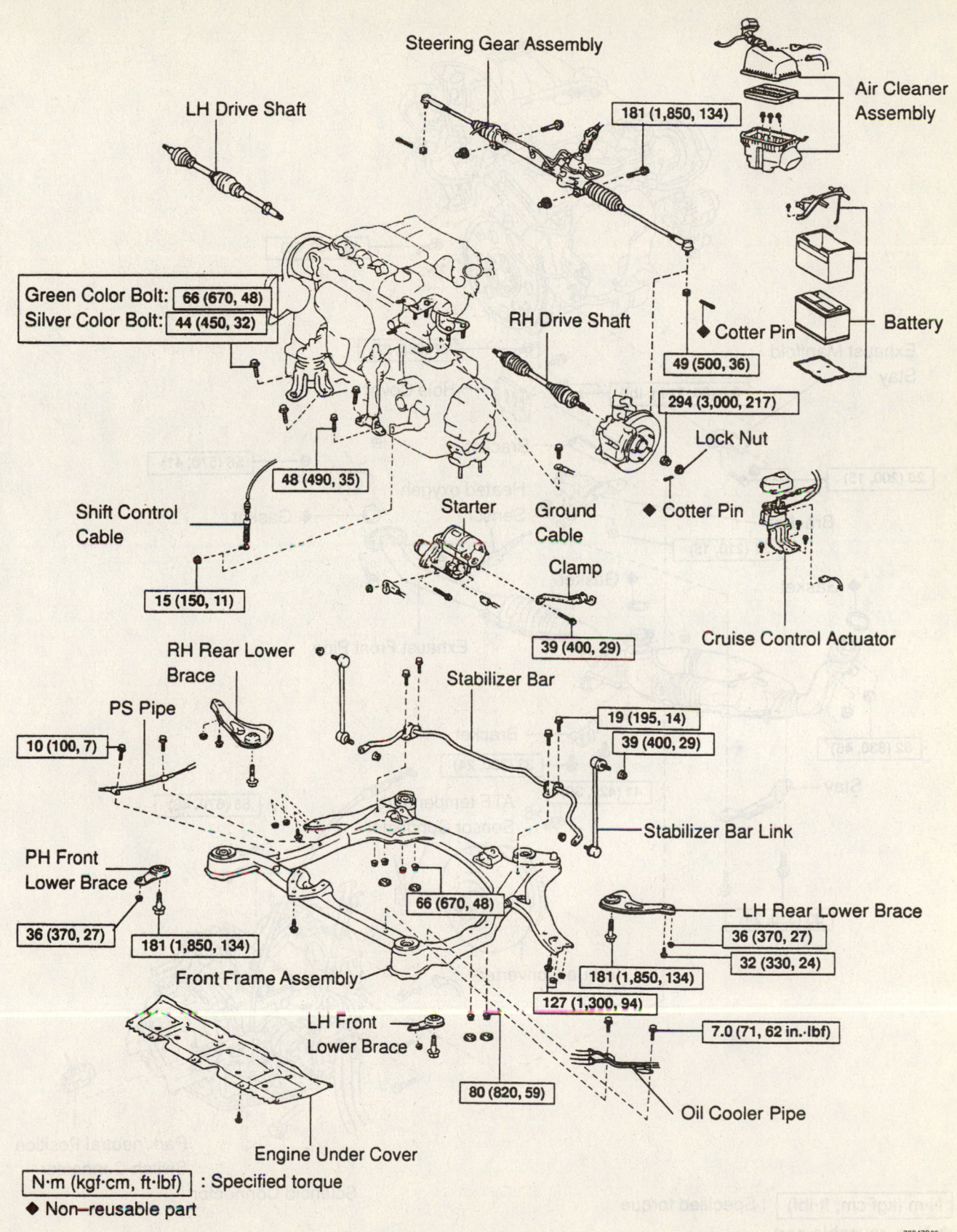

Steering Gear Assembly

LH Drive Shaft

181 (1,850, 134)

Air Cleaner Assembly

Green Color Bolt: 66 (670, 48)
Silver Color Bolt: 44 (450, 32)

RH Drive Shaft

◆ Cotter Pin

Battery

49 (500, 36)

294 (3,000, 217)

Lock Nut

48 (490, 35)

Shift Control Cable

Starter

Ground Cable

◆ Cotter Pin

Clamp

15 (150, 11)

39 (400, 29)

Cruise Control Actuator

RH Rear Lower Brace

Stabilizer Bar

19 (195, 14)

39 (400, 29)

PS Pipe

10 (100, 7)

Stabilizer Bar Link

PH Front Lower Brace

66 (670, 48)

LH Rear Lower Brace

36 (370, 27)

181 (1,850, 134)

36 (370, 27)

32 (330, 24)

Front Frame Assembly

181 (1,850, 134)

127 (1,300, 94)

7.0 (71, 62 in.·lbf)

LH Front Lower Brace

80 (820, 59)

Oil Cooler Pipe

Engine Under Cover

N·m (kgf·cm, ft·lbf) : Specified torque
◆ Non–reusable part

7924ZG65

Exploded view of the transaxle removal and installation components—Sienna and RX 300 models

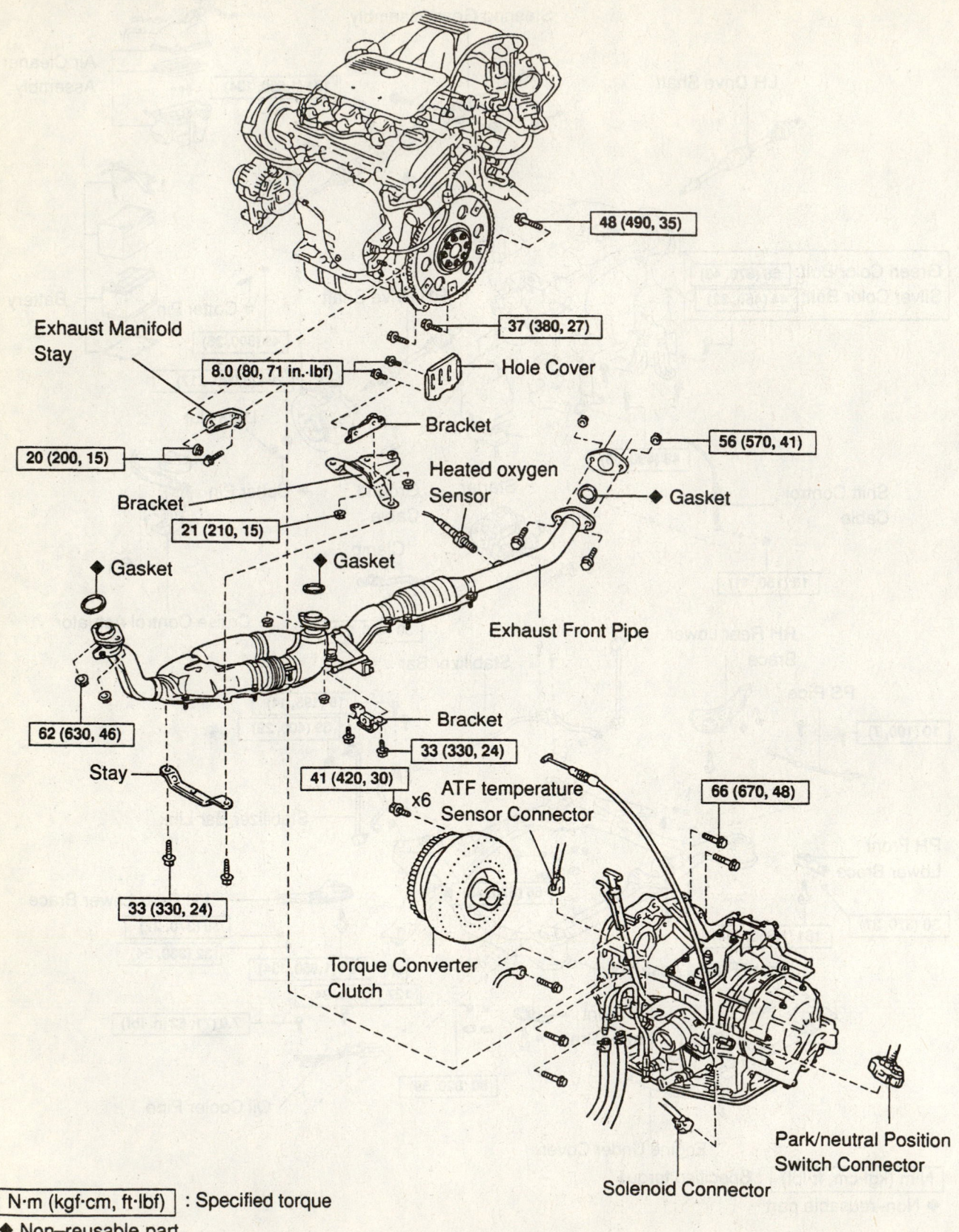

Exhaust Manifold Stay

48 (490, 35)

37 (380, 27)

8.0 (80, 71 in.·lbf)

Hole Cover

Bracket

20 (200, 15)

56 (570, 41)

Bracket

Heated oxygen Sensor

◆ Gasket

21 (210, 15)

◆ Gasket

◆ Gasket

Exhaust Front Pipe

62 (630, 46)

Bracket

Stay

33 (330, 24)

41 (420, 30)

x6

ATF temperature Sensor Connector

66 (670, 48)

33 (330, 24)

Torque Converter Clutch

Park/neutral Position Switch Connector

Solenoid Connector

N·m (kgf·cm, ft·lbf) : Specified torque

◆ Non–reusable part

Exploded view of the transaxle removal and installation components—Sienna and RX 300 models, Cont.

7924ZG66

5. Support the transaxle with a transmission jack.
- Torque converter access cover
- 6 torque converter mounting bolts
- 3 lower transaxle-to-engine mounting bolts
- Engine from the transaxle

To install:

6. Install or connect the following:
- Transaxle
- 3 lower transaxle-to-engine mounting bolts and tighten to the illustrated value.
- Torque converter-to-flexplate bolts, starting with the black bolt, then the other 5.

7. The rest of installation is the reverse of the removal referring to the illustrations for the tightening specifications.

Clutch

ADJUSTMENT

Free-Play

RAV4

1. Before servicing the vehicle, refer to the precautions in the beginning of this section.
2. Check that the pedal height is correct.

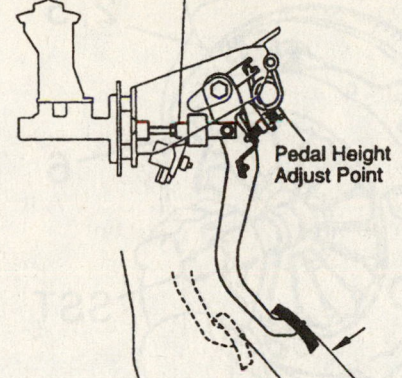

Clutch pedal height measurement location—RAV4

Pedal height from the floor panel should be: 6.889–7.283 in. (175–185mm)

3. If necessary to adjust the pedal height, loosen the locknut and turn the stopper bolt until the height is correct. Tighten the locknut.

4. Push the pedal inward until the beginning of the clutch resistance is felt. Free-play should be 0.197–0.591 in. (5–15mm).

5. Gently push on the pedal until the resistance begins to increase a little. Pushrod play at the pedal top should be 0.039–0.197 in. (1–5mm).

6. If necessary, adjust the pedal free-play and the pushrod play, as follows:
   a. Loosen the locknut and turn the push the rod until the free-play and pushrod play are correct.
   b. Tighten the locknut.

REMOVAL & INSTALLATION

1. Before servicing the vehicle, refer to the precautions in the beginning of this section.
2. Remove or disconnect the following:
- Negative battery cable
- Transaxle
3. Matchmark the clutch cover to the flywheel.
4. Remove the clutch pressure plate retaining bolts in small amounts and in a crisscross pattern to relieve the clutch disc spring tension.
5. At the clutch cover, loosen each bolt 1 turn until spring tension is released.

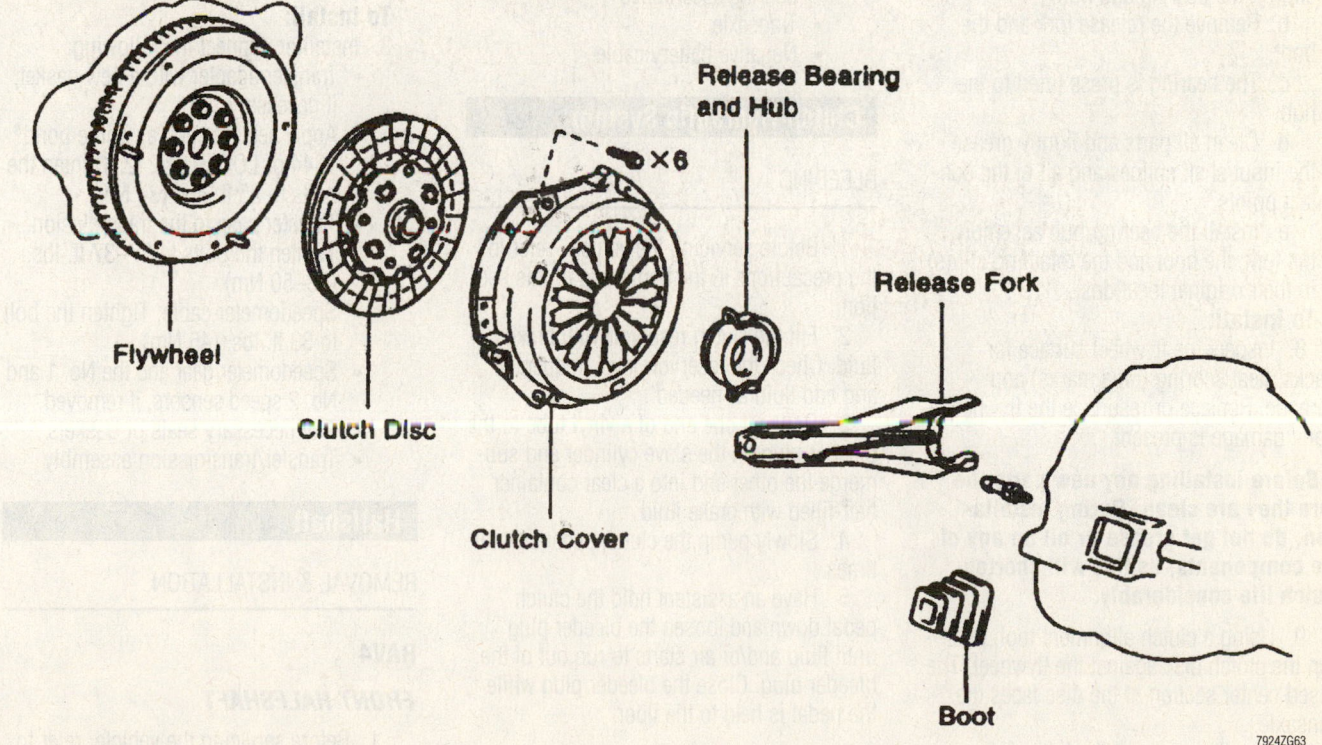

Clutch component assembly—Exploded view

Labels: Push Rod Play Adjust Point, Pedal Height Adjust Point, Push Rod Play, Pedal Height

Flywheel, Clutch Disc, Clutch Cover, ×6, Release Bearing and Hub, Release Fork, Boot

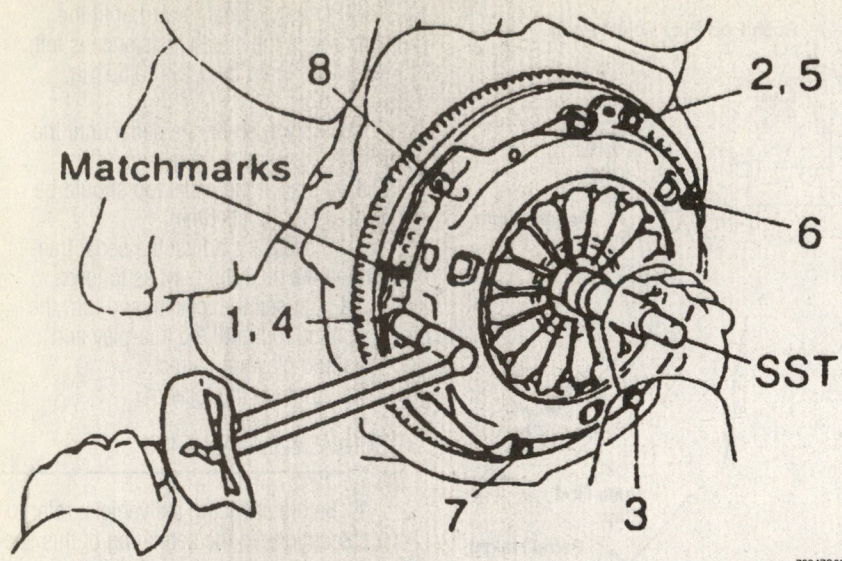

Torque sequence for the clutch cover

6. Remove or disconnect the following:
- Clutch cover set bolts and pull off the clutch cover with the clutch disc, for RAV4
- Clutch cover-to-flywheel bolts. Remove the clutch cover and the clutch disc, for Previa

7. If the clutch release bearing is to be replaced, perform the following:

a. Remove the bearing retaining clip(s), the bearing and hub.

b. Remove the release fork and the boot.

c. The bearing is press fitted to the hub.

d. Clean all parts and lightly grease the input shaft splines and all of the contact points.

e. Install the bearing/hub assembly, the fork, the boot and the retaining clip(s) in their original locations.

To install:

8. Inspect the flywheel surface for cracks, heat scoring (blue marks) and warpage. Replace or resurface the flywheel, if any damage is present.

➡**Before installing any new parts, be sure they are clean. During installation, do not get grease or oil on any of the components, as this will shorten clutch life considerably.**

9. Using a clutch alignment tool, position the clutch disc against the flywheel. The raised center section of the disc faces the transaxle.

10. Install or connect the following:
- Clutch cover onto the flywheel by aligning the matchmarks

- Clutch cover. Tighten the bolts in a crisscross pattern to 14 ft. lbs. (19 Nm).

11. Lubricate the release fork pivot and contact points, release bearing, bearing hub and input shaft spline surfaces with a suitable molybdenum disulfide lithium based or multi-purpose grease.

12. Install or connect the following:
- Boot, release fork, hub and the bearing assemblies
- Transaxle
- Negative battery cable

Clutch Hydraulic System

BLEEDING

1. Before servicing the vehicle, refer to the precautions in the beginning of this section.

2. Fill the clutch reservoir with brake fluid. Check the reservoir level frequently and add fluid as needed.

3. Connect one end of a vinyl tube to the bleeder plug on the slave cylinder and submerge the other end into a clear container half-filled with brake fluid.

4. Slowly pump the clutch pedal several times.

5. Have an assistant hold the clutch pedal down and loosen the bleeder plug until fluid and/or air starts to run out of the bleeder plug. Close the bleeder plug while the pedal is held to the floor.

➡**Do not allow the pedal to rise back up while the bleeder is still open. If this happens, it will allow air to enter**

the slave cylinder and cause the clutch system not to work properly.

6. Repeat Steps 2 and 3 until all the air bubbles are removed from the system.

7. Tighten the bleeder plug when all the air is gone.

8. Refill the master cylinder to the proper level as required.

9. Check the system for leaks.

Transfer Case Assembly

REMOVAL & INSTALLATION

Previa

1. Before servicing the vehicle, refer to the precautions in the beginning of this section.

2. Remove or disconnect the following:
- Transmission and transfer case assembly
- Speedometer cable
- No. 1 and No. 2 speed sensors, if necessary
- Speedometer driven gear, if necessary
- Transfer case from the transmission
- Transfer adapter, if necessary

➡**It may be necessary to tap the adapter with a plastic hammer to loosen it.**

- Gasket, discard it

To install:

3. Install or connect the following:
- Transfer adapter with a new gasket, if necessary
- Apply sealant such as Three bond® 1344 or LOCTITE® 242. Tighten the bolts to 25 ft. lbs. (34 Nm).
- Transfer case to the transmission. Tighten the bolts to 27–37 ft. lbs. (36–50 Nm).
- Speedometer cable. Tighten the bolt to 33 ft. lbs. (45 Nm).
- Speedometer gear and the No. 1 and No. 2 speed sensors, if removed
- Any necessary seals or gaskets
- Transfer/transmission assembly

Halfshaft

REMOVAL & INSTALLATION

RAV4

FRONT HALFSHAFT

1. Before servicing the vehicle, refer to the precautions in the beginning of this section.

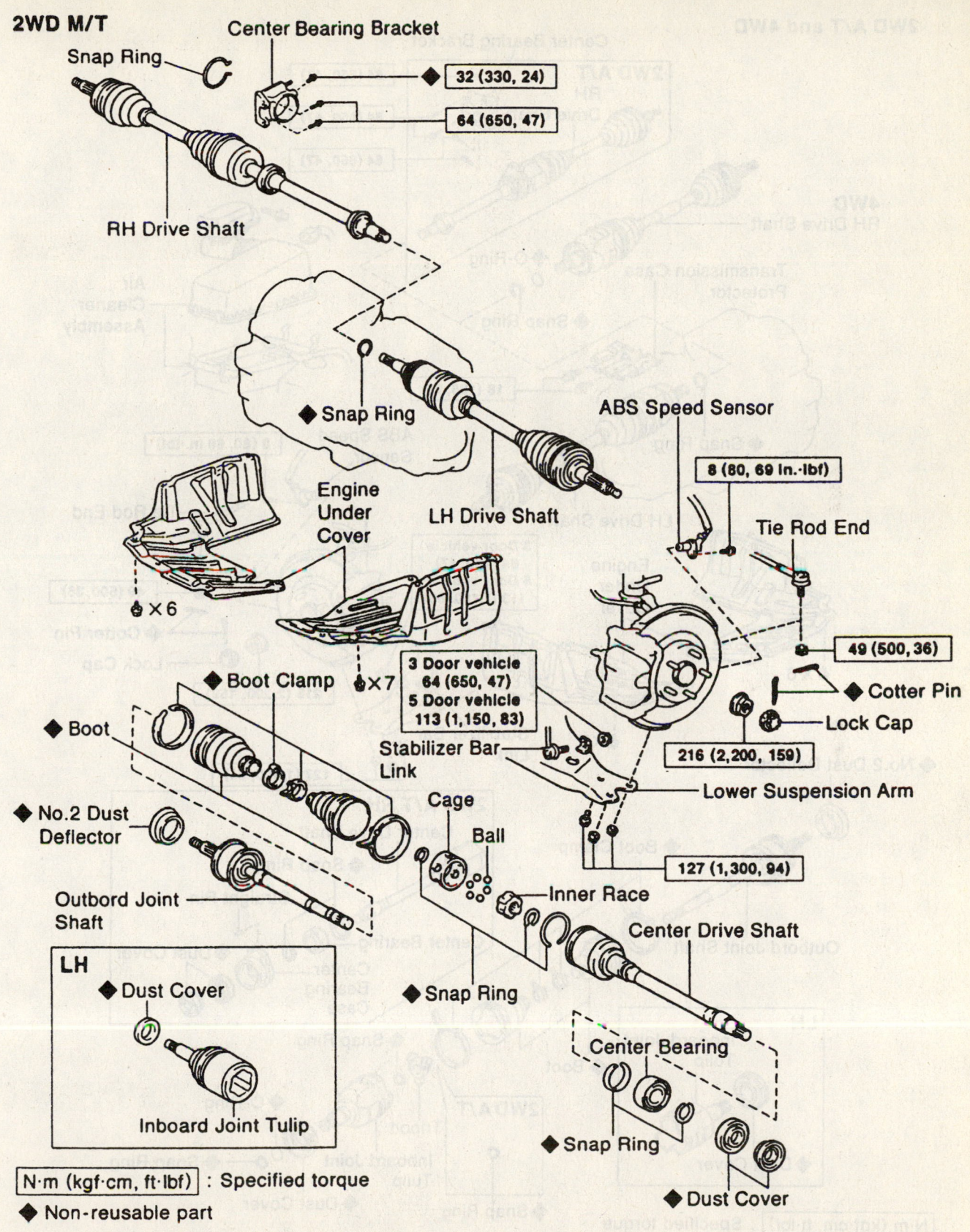

2WD M/T

Snap Ring

Center Bearing Bracket

◆ 32 (330, 24)

64 (650, 47)

RH Drive Shaft

◆ Snap Ring

ABS Speed Sensor

Engine Under Cover

LH Drive Shaft

8 (80, 69 In.·lbf)

Tie Rod End

◆ × 6

49 (500, 36)

◆ Boot Clamp

3 Door vehicle
64 (650, 47)
5 Door vehicle
113 (1,150, 83)

◆ × 7

◆ Cotter Pin

Lock Cap

◆ Boot

Stabilizer Bar Link

Cage

216 (2,200, 159)

Lower Suspension Arm

◆ No.2 Dust Deflector

Ball

127 (1,300, 94)

Outbord Joint Shaft

◆ Snap Ring

Inner Race

Center Drive Shaft

LH

◆ Dust Cover

◆ Snap Ring

Center Bearing

Inboard Joint Tulip

◆ Snap Ring

N·m (kgf·cm, ft·lbf) : Specified torque

◆ Dust Cover

◆ Non-reusable part

7924ZG70

Front halfshaft exploded view (2WD with manual transmission only)—RAV4

Turn to Section 5 for brake system applications

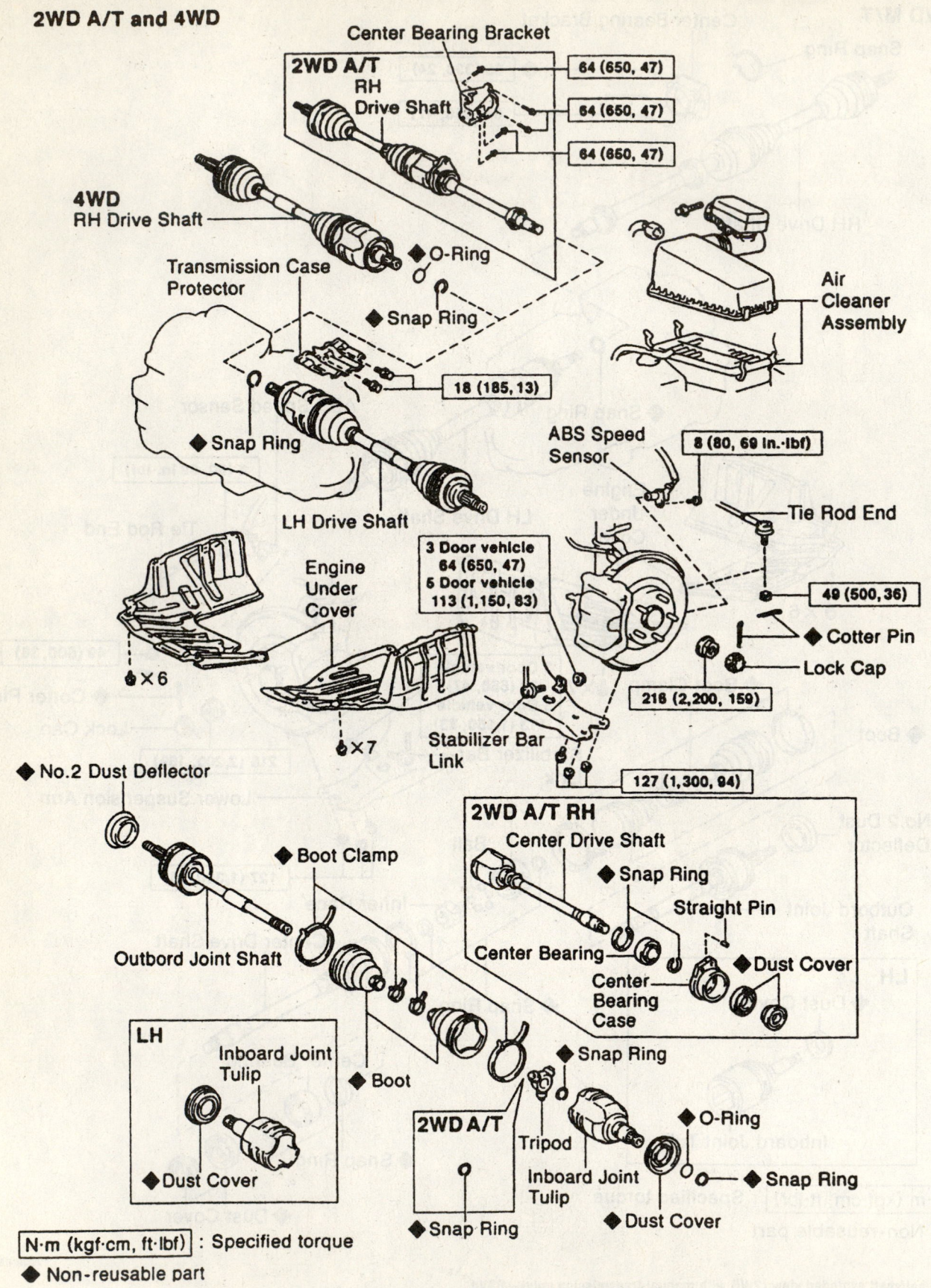

2WD A/T and 4WD

Center Bearing Bracket

2WD A/T
RH
Drive Shaft

64 (650, 47)
64 (650, 47)
64 (650, 47)

4WD
RH Drive Shaft

◆ O-Ring

Transmission Case Protector

◆ Snap Ring

Air Cleaner Assembly

18 (185, 13)

◆ Snap Ring

LH Drive Shaft

ABS Speed Sensor

8 (80, 69 in.-lbf)

Tie Rod End

Engine Under Cover

3 Door vehicle
64 (650, 47)
5 Door vehicle
113 (1,150, 83)

49 (500, 36)

◆ Cotter Pin

Lock Cap

216 (2,200, 159)

◆×6

◆×7

Stabilizer Bar Link

127 (1,300, 94)

◆ No.2 Dust Deflector

◆ Boot Clamp

2WD A/T RH
Center Drive Shaft
◆ Snap Ring
Straight Pin
Center Bearing
Center Bearing Case
◆ Dust Cover

Outbord Joint Shaft

◆ Snap Ring

LH
Inboard Joint Tulip
◆ Boot

2WD A/T

◆ Dust Cover

Tripod
Inboard Joint Tulip
◆ Dust Cover

◆ O-Ring
◆ Snap Ring

◆ Snap Ring

N·m (kgf·cm, ft·lbf) : Specified torque

◆ Non-reusable part

Front halfshaft exploded view (2WD with automatic transmission and 4WD)—RAV4

7924ZG71

2. Remove or disconnect the following:

- Negative battery cable
- Engine undercover

3. Drain the transaxle.

4. Remove or disconnect the following:

- Anti-lock Brake System (ABS) sensor by removing the bolt, if equipped
- Cotter pin, lock cap and the locknut holding the halfshaft to the steering knuckle
- Tie rod ends, from the steering knuckle
- Sway bar link, from the lower control arm
- Lower ball joint, from the lower control arm
- Halfshaft from the axle hub, using a plastic hammer

5. If working on a 2WD right-hand halfshaft and the vehicle is equipped with a manual transaxle, perform the following to remove the halfshaft:

- Snapring from the center bearing bracket, using a brass bar and hammer
- Bolt and the center bearing bracket
- Halfshaft with the center halfshaft
- 2 bolts and the center bearing bracket

6. If working on a 2WD right-hand halfshaft and the vehicle is equipped with an automatic transaxle, perform the following to remove the halfshaft:

- 2 bolts of the center bearing bracket and pull out the halfshaft together with the center bearing case and center halfshaft
- 3 bolts and the center bearing bracket

7. If working on a 2WD left-hand, perform the following:

- Halfshaft, using a brass bar and hammer
- Snapring from the transaxle

8. If working of a 4WD right-hand halfshaft, perform the following:

- Halfshaft, using a brass bar and hammer
- Snapring from the transaxle
- O-ring

9. If working on a 4WD left-hand side, perform the following:

- Air cleaner
- Transaxle case protector
- Halfshaft, by prying it out using a hub wrench
- Snapring

To install:

10. If working on a 4WD left-hand side, perform the following:

- Snapring
- Halfshaft to the transaxle
- Transaxle case protector
- Air cleaner

11. If working of a 4WD right-hand halfshaft, perform the following:

- Snapring to the transaxle
- New O-ring
- Halfshaft to the transaxle

12. If working on a 2WD left-hand, perform the following:

- Snapring
- Halfshaft to the transaxle

13. If working on a 2WD right-hand halfshaft and the vehicle is equipped with an automatic transaxle, perform the following to remove the halfshaft:

- Center bearing bracket. Tighten the 3 bolts to 47 ft. lbs. (64 Nm).
- Halfshaft together with the center bearing case and center halfshaft. Tighten both bolts to 47 ft. lbs. (64 Nm).

14. If working on a 2WD right-hand halfshaft and the vehicle is equipped with a manual transaxle, perform the following to remove the halfshaft:

- Center bearing bracket
- Halfshaft with the center halfshaft
- Center bearing bracket. Tighten the bolt to 24 ft. lbs. (32 Nm).
- Snapring to the center bearing bracket

15. Install or connect the following:

- Halfshaft to the axle hub
- Lower ball joint to the lower control arm. Tighten the nuts/bolt to 94 ft. lbs. (127 Nm).
- Sway bar link to the lower control arm. Tighten the nut to 47 ft. lbs. (64 Nm) for 3-door or to 83 ft. lbs. (113 Nm) for 5-door.
- Tie rod end to the steering knuckle. Tighten the nut to 36 ft. lbs. (49 Nm).

- New tie rod end cotter pin
- Halfshaft to the axle hub. Tighten the locknut to 159 ft. lbs. (216 Nm).
- Lock cap and cotter pin
- ABS speed sensor with the bolt, if equipped

16. Fill the transaxle with gear oil (manual transmission) or ATF (automatic transmission).

17. Install or connect the following:

- Engine undercover
- Wheels
- Negative battery cable

18. Check the ABS sensor signal.

REAR HALFSHAFT

1. Before servicing the vehicle, refer to the precautions in the beginning of this section.

2. Remove or disconnect the following:

- Negative battery cable
- Rear wheels
- Anti-lock Brake System (ABS) speed sensor from the axle assembly by removing the bolt, if equipped
- Cotter pin, lock cap and the nut holding the halfshaft to the axle carrier

3. Place matchmarks on the halfshaft and side gear shaft.

4. Remove or disconnect the following:

- Halfshaft from the differential side gear shaft, by removing the 4 nuts and washers
- Halfshaft from the axle carrier, using a plastic hammer

To install:

5. Install or connect the following:

- Halfshaft to the axle carrier
- Halfshaft to the differential side gear shaft, by aligning the marks. Tighten the 4 nuts to 41 ft. lbs. (56 Nm).
- Nut, lock cap and the cotter pin to hold the halfshaft to the axle carrier. Tighten the nut to 152 ft. lbs. (206 Nm).
- ABS sensor. Tighten the bolt to 69 inch lbs. (8 Nm).
- Rear wheels
- Negative battery cable

6. Check the ABS sensor signal.

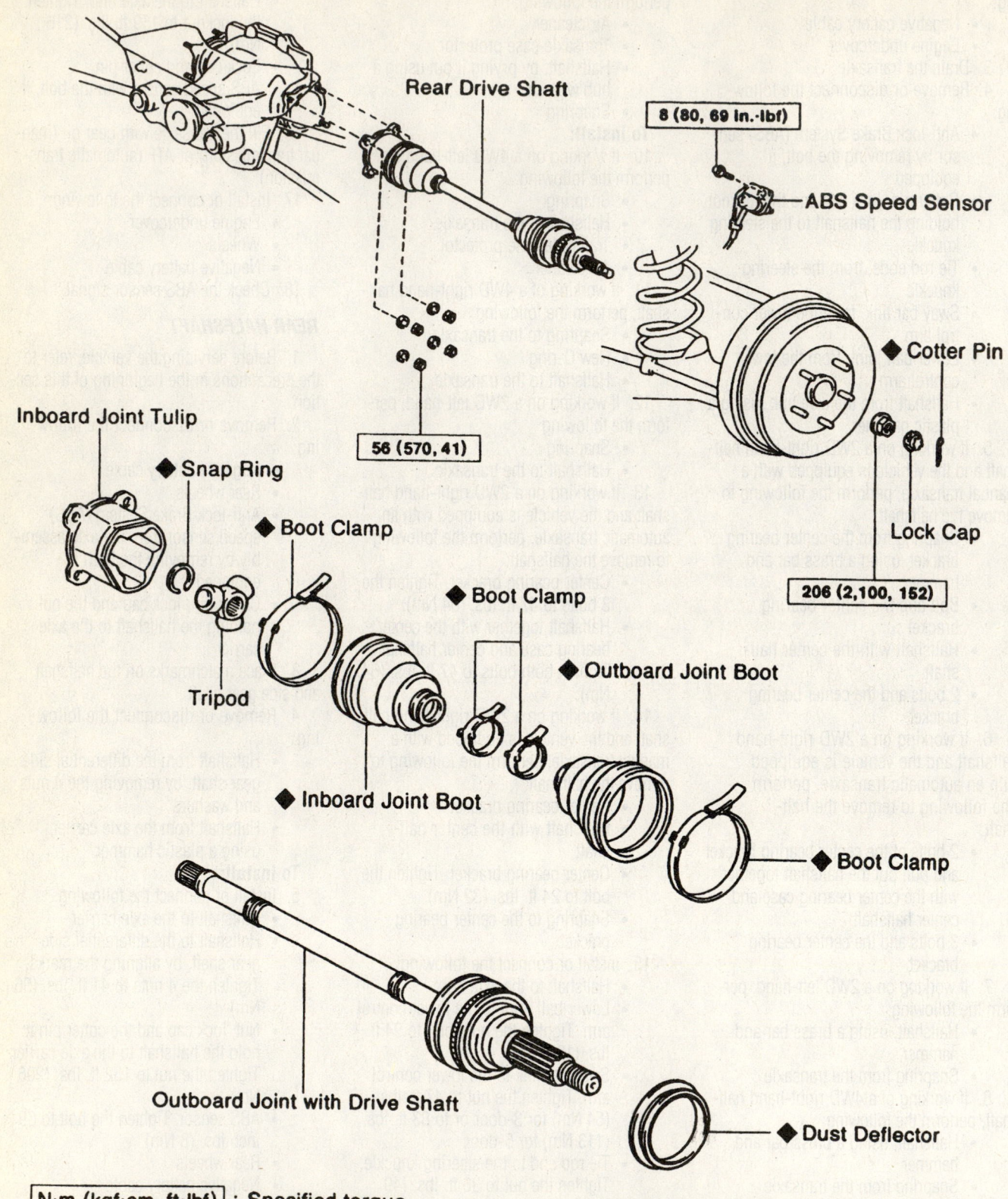

Rear Drive Shaft

8 (80, 69 in.·lbf)

ABS Speed Sensor

Inboard Joint Tulip

◆ **Snap Ring**

◆ **Boot Clamp**

◆ **Boot Clamp**

Tripod

56 (570, 41)

◆ **Outboard Joint Boot**

◆ **Inboard Joint Boot**

◆ **Cotter Pin**

Lock Cap

206 (2,100, 152)

◆ **Boot Clamp**

Outboard Joint with Drive Shaft

◆ **Dust Deflector**

N·m (kgf·cm, ft·lbf) : Specified torque

◆ Non-reusable part

7924ZG72

Rear halfshaft removal and installation (4WD only)—RAV4

Previa

1. Before servicing the vehicle, refer to the precautions in the beginning of this section.
2. Remove or disconnect the following:
   - Wheel
   - Cotter pin and lock cap from the halfshaft
   - Locknut from the halfshaft
   - Cotter pin and locknut to the tie rod end and the tie rod end from the knuckle
   - Lower ball joint from the steering knuckle, by removing the 2 mounting bolts
3. Place matchmarks on the halfshaft and side gear.
4. Remove or disconnect the following:
   - 6 bolts from the inner halfshaft joint
   - Halfshaft from the side gear
   - Halfshaft from the wheel hub by pulling the knuckle outward

➡If the outer shaft will not come out of the hub, soak the splines with penetrating lube, install the nut and tap on the halfshaft with a rubber hammer. Be careful not to damage the shaft threads.

To install:

➡**Coat the halfshaft splines with anti-seize compound to prevent spline seizure. This will help for future halfshaft removal.**

5. Install or connect the following:
   - Halfshaft to the steering knuckle

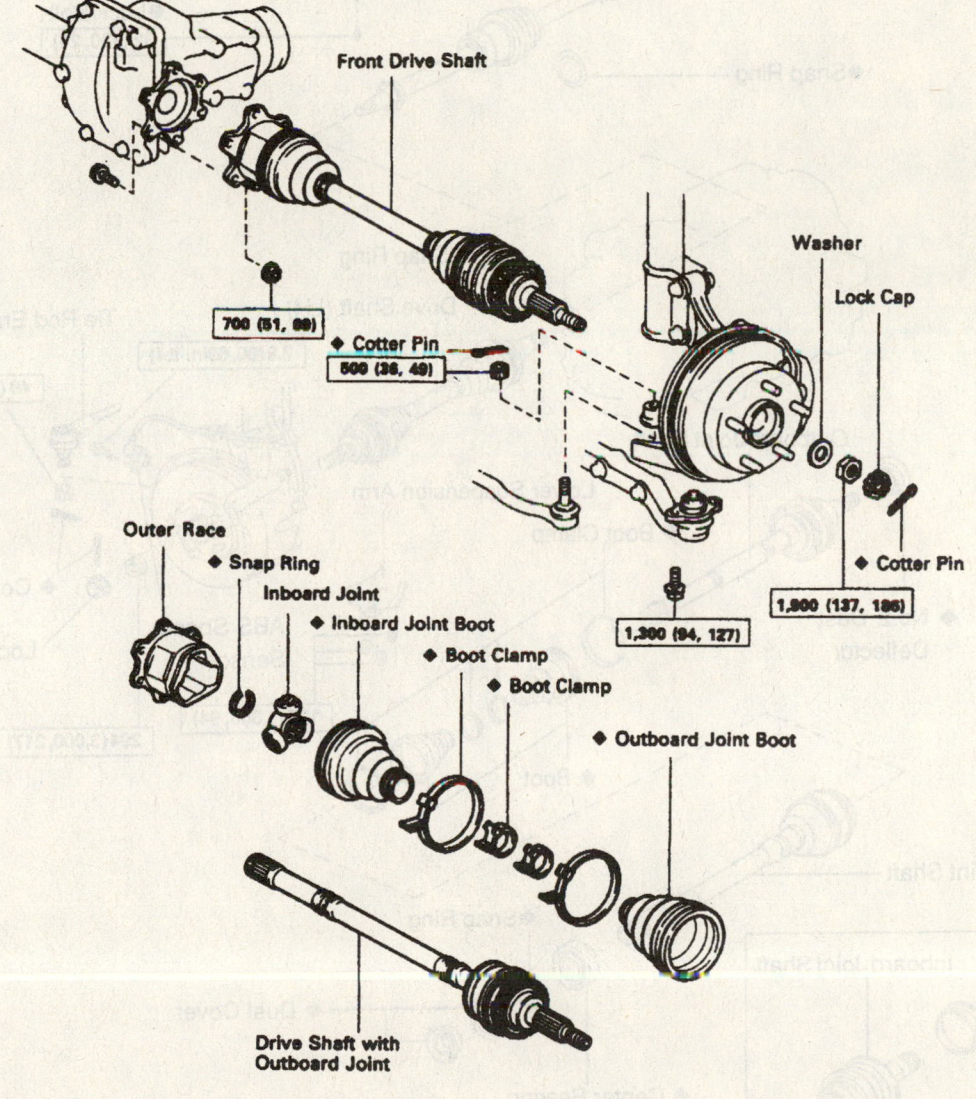

Front Drive Shaft

Washer

Lock Cap

700 (51, 69)

◆ Cotter Pin

500 (36, 49)

◆ Cotter Pin

1,900 (137, 186)

Outer Race

◆ Snap Ring

Inboard Joint

◆ Inboard Joint Boot

◆ Boot Clamp

◆ Boot Clamp

1,300 (94, 127)

◆ Outboard Joint Boot

Drive Shaft with Outboard Joint

kg-cm (ft-lb, N·m) : Specified torque
◆ Non-reusable part

Halfshaft components, exploded view—Previa

7924ZG69

- Inner halfshaft joint to the side gear. Tighten the 6 bolts to 51 ft. lbs. (61 Nm).
- Lower ball joint. Tighten the bolts to 94 ft. lbs. (127 Nm).
- Tie rod end. Tighten the nut to 36 ft. lbs. (49 Nm).
- New cotter pin

- Halfshaft nut. Tighten it to 152 ft. lbs. (206 Nm).
- Lock cap and a new cotter pin to the halfshaft
- Wheel

6. Check and/or adjust the front wheel alignment.

Sienna and RX 300 Front

1. Before servicing the vehicle, refer to the precautions in the beginning of this section.
2. Remove or disconnect the following:
- Front wheels
- Cotter pin and locknut cap

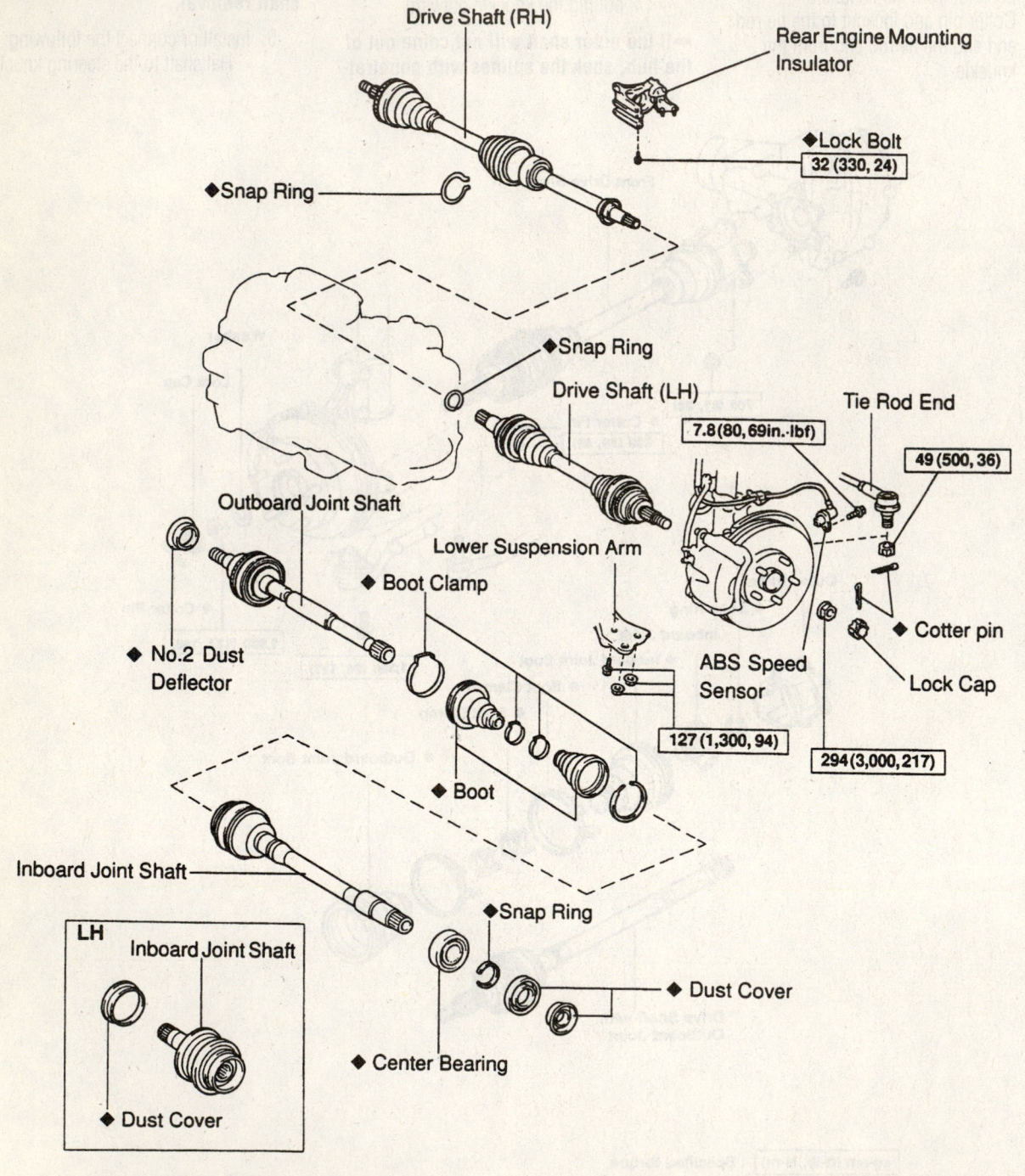

N·m (kgf·cm, ft·lbf) : Specified torque

◆ Non-reusable part

Exploded view of halfshaft—Sienna and RX 300

7924ZG73

➡**Have an assistant depress the brake pedal and loosen the bearing locknut.**

- Engine undercover
- Fender apron seal
- Tie rod end, from the steering knuckle
- Steering knuckle, from the lower control arm
- Halfshaft from the axle hub, using a plastic hammer

- Cover the outer boot with a rag
- Halfshaft from the transaxle, using the proper tools

To install:

3. Reverse the removal procedures to complete installation, tightening fasteners to specifications.

4. Fill the transaxle with gear oil, install the fender apron, check front end alignment and test drive.

➡**If the cotter pin holes do not align, always correct by tightening the nut until the next hole aligns.**

5. Install a new cotter pin.

RX 300 Rear

1. Before servicing the vehicle, refer to the precautions in the beginning of this section.

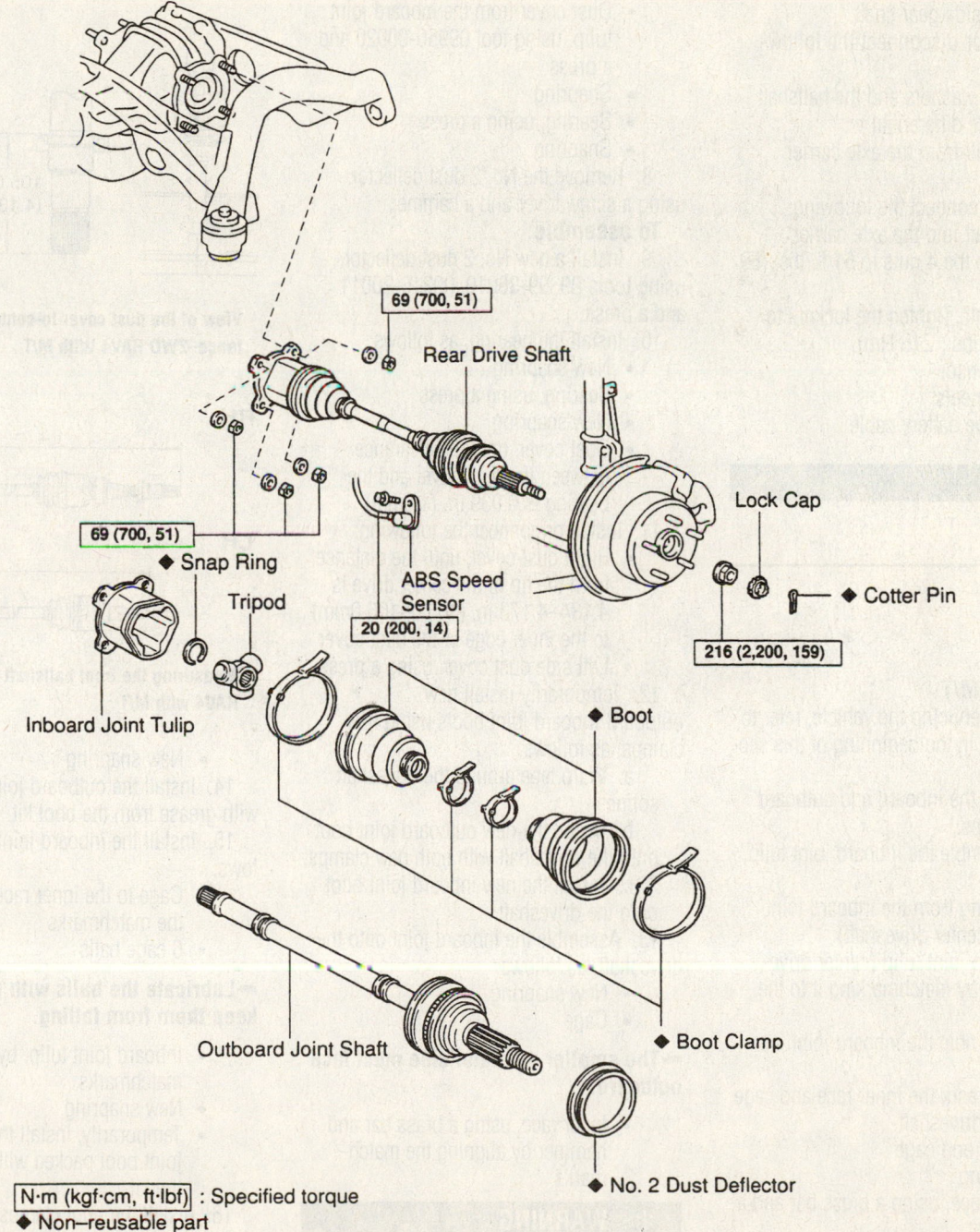

N·m (kgf·cm, ft·lbf) : Specified torque
◆ Non–reusable part

Exploded view of the rear halfshaft—RX 300 model with 4WD

7924ZG88

Turn to Section 5 for brake system applications

2. Remove or disconnect the following:

- Negative battery cable
- Rear wheels
- Anti-lock Brake System (ABS) speed sensor from the axle assembly by removing the bolt, if equipped
- Cotter pin, lock cap and the nut holding the halfshaft to the axle carrier

3. Place matchmarks on the halfshaft and differential side gear shaft.

4. Remove or disconnect the following:

- 4 nuts, washers and the halfshaft from the differential
- Halfshaft from the axle carrier

To install:

5. Install or connect the following:

- Halfshaft into the axle carrier. Tighten the 4 nuts to 51 ft. lbs. (69 Nm).
- Halfshaft. Tighten the locknut to 159 ft. lbs. (216 Nm).
- ABS sensor
- Rear wheels
- Negative battery cable

CV-Joints

OVERHAUL

RAV4

FRONT

2WD With M/T

1. Before servicing the vehicle, refer to the precautions in the beginning of this section.

2. Remove the inboard and outboard joint boot clamps.

3. Disassemble the inboard joint tulip, as follows:

- Snapring from the inboard joint tulip (center driveshaft)
- Inboard joint tulip (center driveshaft), by matchmarking it to the shaft

4. Disassemble the inboard joint, as follows:

- Matchmark the inner race and cage to the driveshaft
- 6 balls and cage
- Snapring
- Inner race, using a brass bar and a hammer
- Snapring

5. Remove the inboard and outboard joint boots and inboard joint clamps.

✳✳ WARNING

Do not disassemble the outboard joint.

---

6. Remove or disconnect the following:

- Dust cover from the center driveshaft, using a press
- Dust cover from the inboard joint tulip, using tool 09950-00020 and a press

7. Remove the bearing, as follows:

- Dust cover from the inboard joint tulip, using tool 09950-00020 and a press
- Snapring
- Bearing, using a press
- Snapring

8. Remove the No. 2 dust deflector, using a screwdriver and a hammer.

To assemble:

9. Install a new No. 2 dust deflector, using tools 09309-36010, 09316-20011 and a press.

10. Install the bearing, as follows:

- New snapring
- Bearing, using a press
- New snapring
- Dust cover, until the clearance between the dust cover and the bearing is 0.039 in. (1.0mm)

11. Install or connect the following:

- Right dust cover, until the distance from the tip of the center drive is 4.134–4.173 in. (105.0–106.0mm) to the inner edge of the dust cover
- Left side dust cover, using a press

12. Temporarily install new outboard/inboard joint boots using new clamps, as follows:

  a. Warp tape around the driveshaft splines.

  b. Install the new outboard joint boot onto the driveshaft with both new clamps.

  c. Install the new inboard joint boot onto the driveshaft.

13. Assemble the inboard joint onto the driveshaft, as follows:

- New snapring
- Cage

➡**The smaller diameter side must face outboard.**

- Inner race, using a brass bar and hammer by aligning the matchmarks

---

✳✳ WARNING

Be careful not to damage the inner race.

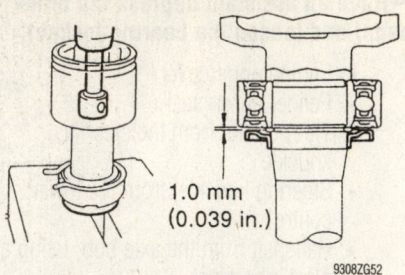

View of the bearing-to-dust cover clearance–2WD RAV4 With M/T

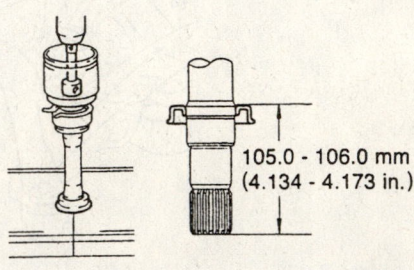

View of the dust cover-to-center drive distance–2WD RAV4 With M/T

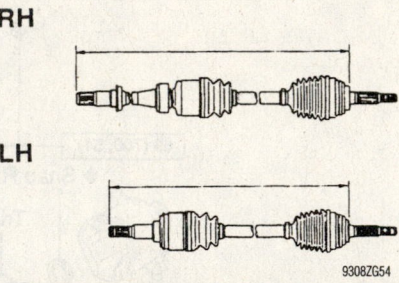

Measuring the front halfshaft lengths–2WD RAV4 with M/T

- New snapring

14. Install the outboard joint boot packed with grease from the boot kit.

15. Install the inboard joint tulip, as follows:

- Cage to the inner race by aligning the matchmarks
- 6 cage balls

➡**Lubricate the balls with grease to keep them from falling.**

- Inboard joint tulip, by aligning the matchmarks
- New snapring
- Temporarily, install the inboard joint boot packed with grease from the kit

16. Install the boot clamps to both boots, as follows:

- Both boots to the shaft grooves
- Halfshaft length should be

32.988–33.382 in. (837.9–847.9mm) for the right side or 21.165–21.559 in. (537.6–547.6mm) for the left side
- Both new clamps on the inboard joint boot
- Crimp the new clamps using tool 09521-24010
- Adjust the crimp clearance to 0.047–0.157 in. (1.2–4.0mm)

2WD With A/T and 4WD

17. Before servicing the vehicle, refer to the precautions in the beginning of this section.

18. Remove the inboard and outboard joint boot clamps.

19. Disassemble the inboard joint tulip, as follows:
- Matchmark the tri-pot, inboard joint tulip or center driveshaft to the driveshaft

❋❋ WARNING

Do not use punch marks.

- Inboard joint tulip from the driveshaft

20. Remove the inboard and outboard joint clamps.

21. Remove the tri-pot joint, as follows:
- Snapring
- Matchmark the tri-pot joint to the driveshaft
- Tri-pot joint, using a brass bar and hammer

❋❋ WARNING

Do not tap the roller.

22. Remove or disconnect the following:
- Inboard and outboard joint boots

➡ **Do not disassemble the outboard joint.**

- Dust cover from the center driveshaft, using a press, for 2WD on the right side
- Dust cover from the inboard joint tulip, using tool 09950-00020 and a press, for 2WD on the left side and 4WD

23. Disassemble the center driveshaft, as follows:
- Snapring
- Bearing case, using a press
- Straight pin from the bearing case, using a pin punch and hammer
- Dust cover, using tool 09950-00020 and a press

- Snapring
- Bearing, using a press

24. Remove the No. 2 dust deflector, using a screwdriver and hammer.

To assemble:

25. Install a new No. 2 dust deflector, using a press.

26. Assemble the center driveshaft, as follows:
- Straight pin into the bearing case, using a pin punch and hammer
- New bearing, using tools 09959-60010, 09950-70010 and a press
- New snapring
- Bearing with the bearing case assembly to the center driveshaft,

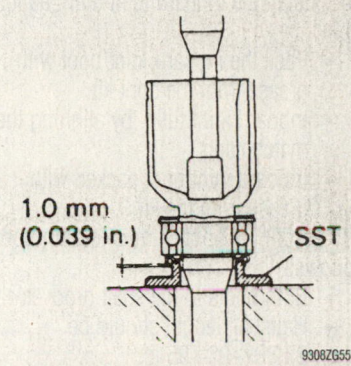

1.0 mm (0.039 in.)   SST

9308ZG55

View of the bearing-to-dust cover clearance–RAV4 with 2WD A/T and 4WD

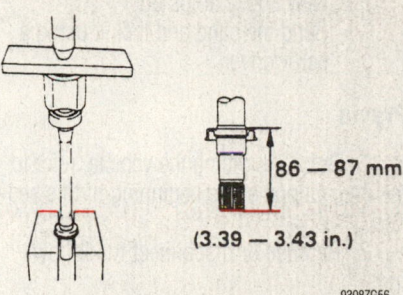

86 — 87 mm

(3.39 — 3.43 in.)

9308ZG56

View of the dust cover-to-center drive distance–RAV4 with 2WD A/T and 4WD

2WD A/T RH

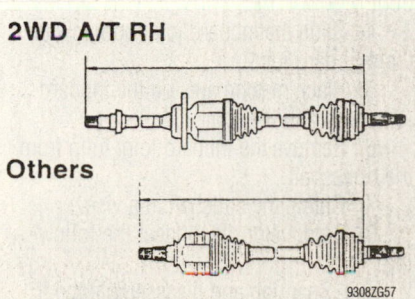

Others

9308ZG57

Measuring the front halfshaft lengths–RAV4 with 2WD A/T and 4WD

using tool 09710-30021 and a press
- New snapring
- New dust cover, until the clearance between the dust cover and the bearing is 0.039 in. (1.0mm)

27. Install or connect the following:
- Right dust cover (2WD), until the distance from the tip of the center drive is 3.39–3.34 in. (86–87mm) to the inner edge of the dust cover
- Left side dust cover (2WD and 4WD), using a press

28. Temporarily install new outboard/inboard joint boots using new clamps, as follows:

a. Warp tape around the driveshaft splines.

b. Install the new outboard joint boot onto the driveshaft.

c. Install the new inboard joint boot onto the driveshaft.

29. Install the tri-pot joint, as follows:
- Tri-pot joint, face the beveled side toward the outboard joint and align the matchmarks
- Tri-pot joint onto the driveshaft, using a press

❋❋ WARNING

Be careful not to tap the roller.

- New snapring

30. Install the outboard joint boot packed with grease from the boot kit.

31. Install the inboard joint tulip, as follows:
- Pack the inboard joint boot with grease from the boot kit
- Inboard joint tulip, by aligning the matchmarks
- Temporarily, install the inboard joint boot packed with grease from the kit

32. Install the boot clamps to both boots, as follows:
- Both boots to the shaft grooves
- Halfshaft length should be 33.055–33.449 in. (839.6–849.6mm) for the right side on 2WD with A/T, 21.397–21.791 in. (543.5–553.5mm) for the left side on 2WD with A/T, 19.929–20.323 in. (506.2–516.2mm) for the right side on 4WD or 19.803–20.197 in. (503–511mm) for the left side on 4WD
- Both new boot clamps boot

- Bend the band and lock it using a screwdriver

REAR

1. Before servicing the vehicle, refer to the precautions in the beginning of this section.

2. Remove the inboard and outboard joint boot clamps.

3. Disassemble the inboard joint tulip, as follows:

- Matchmark the tri-pot, inboard joint tulip or center driveshaft to the driveshaft

✶✶ WARNING

Do not use punch marks.

- Inboard joint tulip from the driveshaft

4. Remove the tri-pot joint, as follows:
- Snapring
- Matchmark the tri-pot joint to the driveshaft

✶✶ WARNING

Do not use punch marks.

- Tri-pot joint, using a brass bar and hammer

✶✶ WARNING

Do not tap the roller.

5. Remove or disconnect the following:

- Inboard and outboard joint boots

➡**Do not disassemble the outboard joint.**

- No. 2 dust deflector from the center driveshaft, using a screwdriver and hammer

To assemble:

6. Install a new No. 2 dust deflector, using tools 09309-36010, 09316-20011 and a press.

7. Temporarily install new outboard/inboard joint boots using new clamps, as follows:

a. Warp tape around the driveshaft splines.

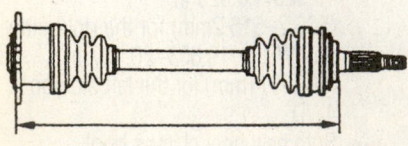

Measuring the rear halfshaft

b. Install the new outboard joint boot onto the driveshaft.

c. Install the new inboard joint boot onto the driveshaft.

8. Install the tri-pot joint, as follows:

- Tri-pot joint, face the beveled side toward the outboard joint and align the matchmarks
- Tri-pot joint onto the driveshaft, using a brass bar and hammer

✶✶ WARNING

Be careful not to tap the roller.

- New snapring

9. Install the outboard joint boot packed with grease from the boot kit.

10. Install the inboard joint tulip, as follows:

- Pack the inboard joint boot with grease from the boot kit
- Inboard joint tulip, by aligning the matchmarks
- Inboard joint boot packed with grease from the kit

11. Install the boot clamps to both boots, as follows:

- Both boots to the shaft grooves
- Halfshaft length should be 23.392–23.795 in. (594.4–604.4mm) for the right side or 21.590–21.984 (548.4–558.4mm) for the left side
- New boot clamps boot
- Bend the band and lock it using a screwdriver

Previa

1. Before servicing the vehicle, refer to the precautions in the beginning of this section.

2. Remove or disconnect the following:

- Halfshaft
- Inboard joint boot clamps

3. Clean the joint before removing the boot.

4. Slide the inboard joint boot toward the outboard joint.

5. Place matchmarks on the inboard joint tulip and the shaft.

6. Remove the inboard joint tulip from the driveshaft.

7. Clamp the halfshaft in a vise.

8. Remove or disconnect the following:

- Snapring and disassemble the tri-pot joint
- Tri-pot joint from the halfshaft, using a brass bar and hammer

✶✶ WARNING

Be careful not to punch the roller.

- Inboard joint boot
- Outboard joint boot clamps and boot

✶✶ WARNING

Do not disassemble the outboard joint.

To assemble:

9. Temporarily, install the new boot and new boot clamps to the outboard joint.

➡**Before installing the boot, wrap vinyl tape around the spline of the shaft to prevent damaging the boot.**

10. Temporarily, install the new boot and the new boot clamps for the inboard joint to the halfshaft.

11. Assemble the tri-pot joint, as follows:

a. Place the beveled side of the tri-pot axial spline toward the outboard joint.

b. Align the matchmarks placed before disassembly.

c. Using a brass bar and hammer, tap in the tri-pot joint onto the driveshaft. Do not punch the roller.

12. Install a new snapring.

13. Before assembling the boot to the outboard joint, pack the boot with grease. The capacity is 4.2–4.6 oz. (120–130 g).

➡**Keep the grease off the joint connection groove of the boot. Pack in grease all over the ball and contact surface inside the joint.**

14. Assemble the inboard joint to the inboard joint tulip. Pack in grease to the inboard tulip and the boot. The capacity is 7.6–7.9 oz. (215–225 g).

15. Install or connect the following:

- Outer race, by aligning the matchmarks on the shaft
- Inboard joint boot, without twisting it

➡**Be sure the boot is on the shaft groove and inboard joint outer race groove.**

16. Set the length of the shaft to 19.146–19.546 in. (486.4–496.41mm).

17. Install or connect the following:

- Both clamps to the inboard joint boot; bend back the band and lock it
- Halfshaft

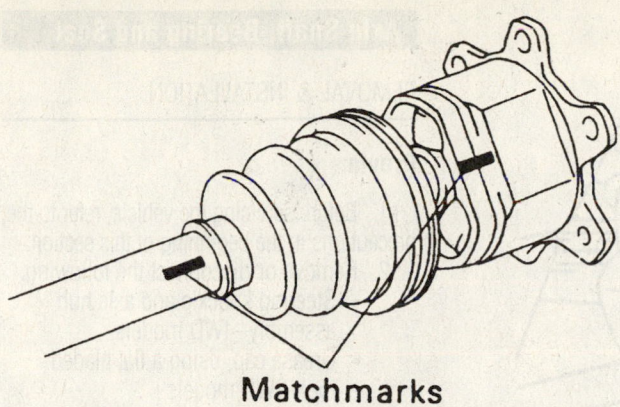

Matchmarks

90917G47

Place matchmarks on the inboard joint outer race and shaft—Previa

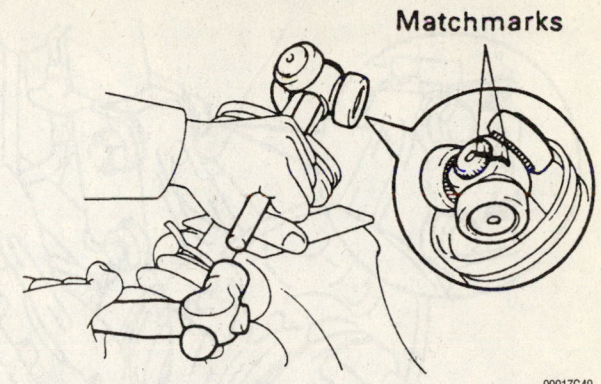

Matchmarks

90917G49

With a brass bar and hammer, tap the joint hard enough to remove—Previa

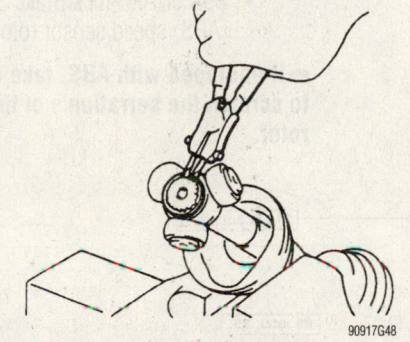

90917G48

Use snapring expanders to extract the snapring from the end—Previa

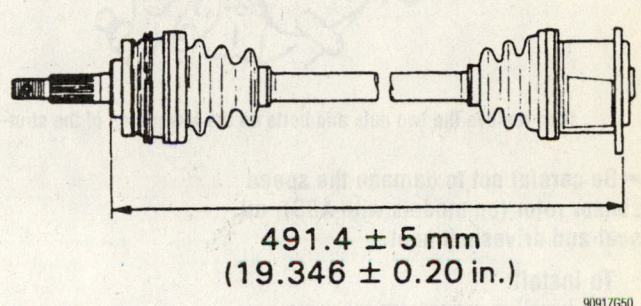

**491.4 ± 5 mm
(19.346 ± 0.20 in.)**

90917G50

Set the length of the halfshaft at the points shown here—Previa

Spindle Bearings

REMOVAL, PACKING & INSTALLATION

Previa

1. Before servicing the vehicle, refer to the precautions in the beginning of this section.
2. Remove or disconnect the following:
   - Speed sensor, if equipped
   - Front brake caliper and disc
3. Place a dial indicator near the center of the axle hub and check the backlash in the bearing shaft direction. Maximum is 0.0020 inch (0.05mm).

➡ **If the specification is greater than the specified amount, replace the hub.**

4. Install the brake disc and caliper.
5. Remove or disconnect the following:
   - Cotter pin and lockcap
   - Halfshaft nut by applying the brakes
   - Caliper and disc
   - Loosen both lower shock absorber nuts but do not remove the bolts
   - Loosen the lower ball joint bolts but do not remove the bolts

- Tie rod end from the steering knuckle
- Cotter pin, discard it

➡ **A puller will be needed to separate the tie rod end from the knuckle.**

- Both lower ball joint bolts
- Steering knuckle
- Both lower shock absorber nuts and bolts
- Steering knuckle with the axle hub

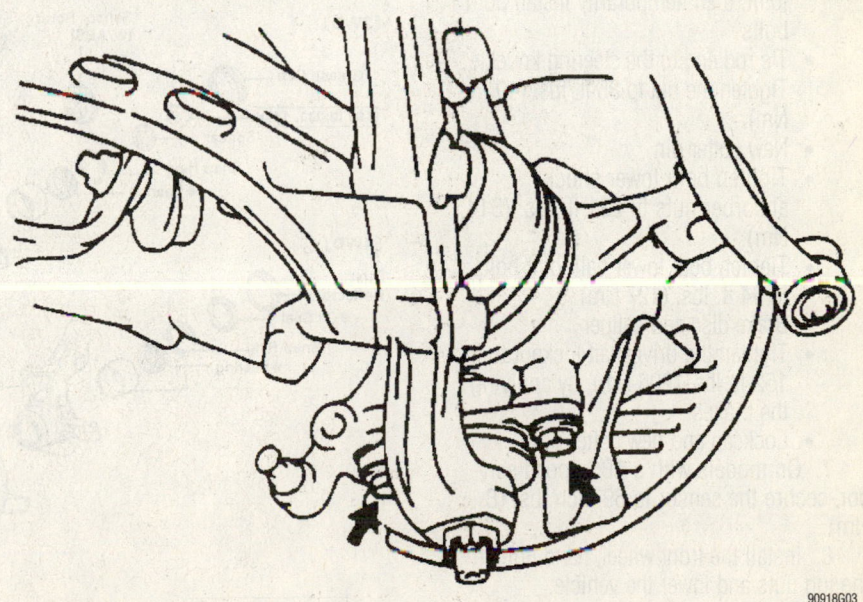

90918G03

Unbolt the lower ball joint . . .—Previa

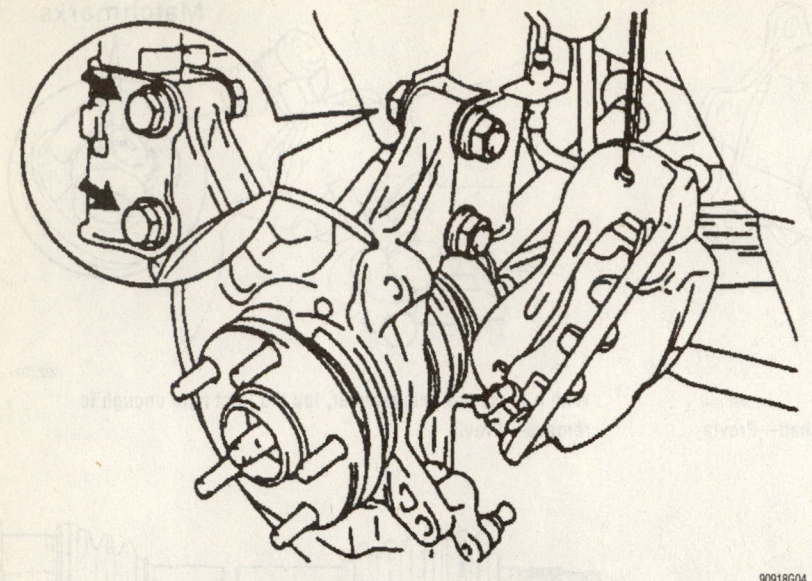

90918G04

. . . then remove the two nuts and bolts on the lower side of the strut—Previa

➡️**Be careful not to damage the speed sensor rotor (on models with ABS), oil seal and driveshaft boot.**

To install:

6. Install or connect the following:
   • Steering knuckle and axle hub assembly

➡️**Be careful not to damage the speed sensor rotor (ABS models), the oil seal and driveshaft boot.**

   • Both bolts and temporarily tighten the nut
   • Steering knuckle and lower ball joint; then, temporarily install both bolts
   • Tie rod end to the steering knuckle. Tighten the nut to 36 ft. lbs. (49 Nm).
   • New cotter pin
   • Tighten both lower shock absorber nuts to 231 ft. lbs. (314 Nm).
   • Tighten both lower ball joint bolts to 94 ft. lbs. (127 Nm).
   • Brake disc and caliper
   • Tighten the driveshaft locknut to 152 ft. lbs. (206 Nm), by applying the brakes.
   • Lockcap and new cotter pin

7. On models with a ABS speed sensor, secure the sensor to 69 inch lbs. (8 Nm).

8. Install the front wheel, hand tighten the lug nuts and lower the vehicle.

9. Tighten the lug nuts to specifications.

10. Check the front end alignment.

Axle Shaft, Bearing and Seal

REMOVAL & INSTALLATION

Previa

1. Before servicing the vehicle, refer to the precautions in the beginning of this section.

2. Remove or disconnect the following:
   • Steering knuckle and axle hub assembly–4WD models
   • Grease cap, using a flat bladed tool–2WD models
   • Release the nut caulking, using a chisel and hammer
   • Locknut
   • Spacer/Anti-lock Brake System (ABS) speed sensor rotor

➡️**If equipped with ABS, take care not to scratch the serration's of the sensor rotor.**

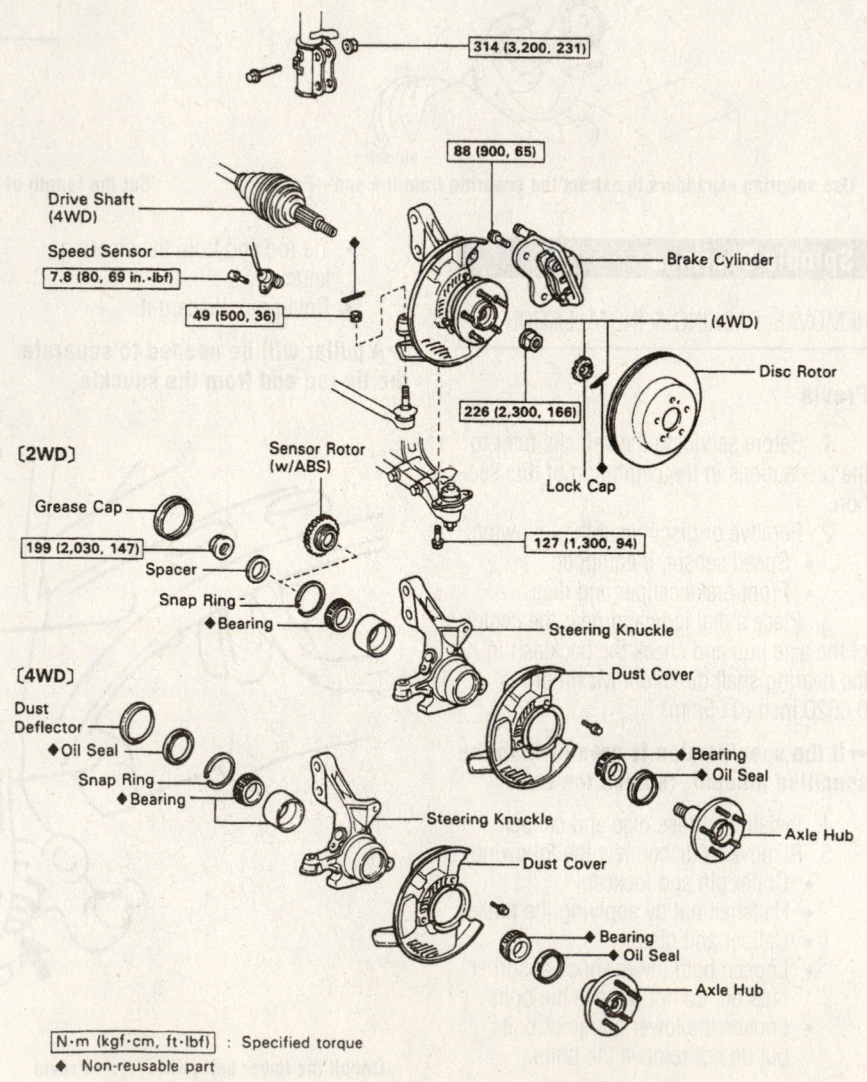

N·m (kgf·cm, ft·lbf) : Specified torque
◆ Non-reusable part

90918G14

Exploded view of the common front axle bearing and hub assemblies—Previa

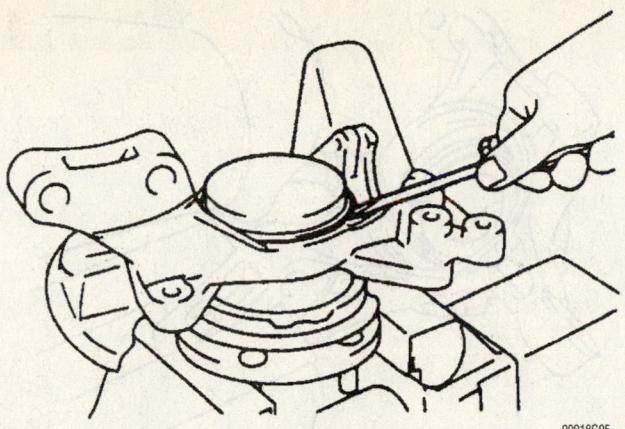

Using a flat bladed tool, pry off the grease cap—2WD Previa

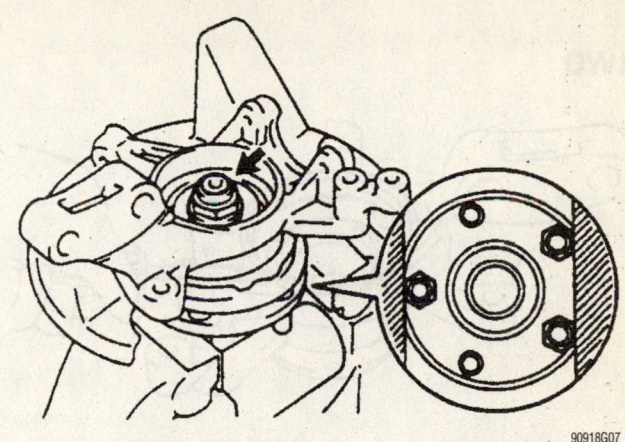

Remove the locknut . . .—Previa

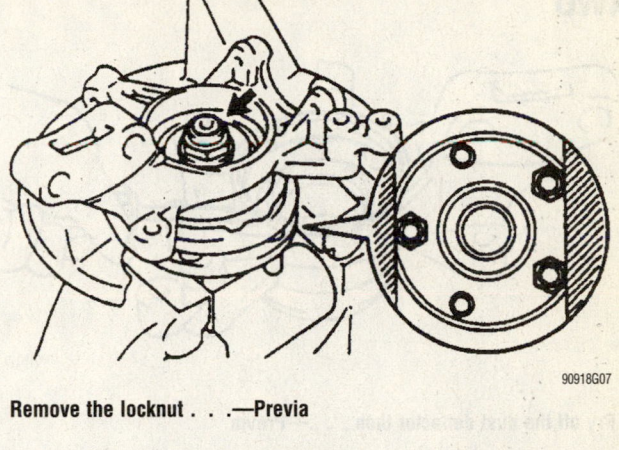

With chisel and hammer, release the nut caulking—Previa

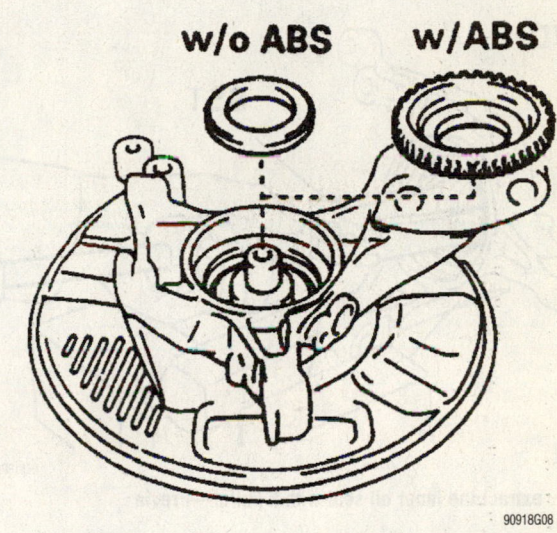

w/o ABS   w/ABS

. . . then remove the spacer or ABS sensor rotor—2WD Previa

3. Remove or disconnect the following:

- Axle hub with a puller
- Bearing from the axle hub, using a puller and press
- Oil seal, by prying it from the hub
- 3 bolts and the dust cover
- Dust deflector, using a flat-bladed tool, on 4WD models
- Oil seal, using a puller
- Snapring

4. Place the outer bearing above the outer race on the outer side.

5. Remove the bearing, using a puller and press.

To install:

6. Install or connect the following:
- New bearing into the steering knuckle, using a hub bearing installer and a press

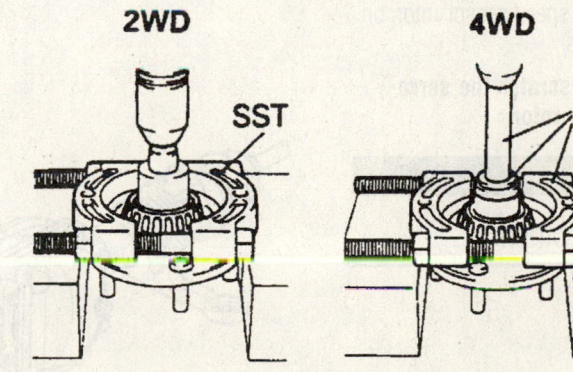

2WD   4WD

Using a puller and press, remove the bearing from the axle hub—Previa

➡ **If the inner race becomes loose from the bearing outer race, be sure to install them on the same side as before.**

- Snapring

- Outer bearing
- New oil seal until it is flush with the end surface of the steering knuckle
- Dust cover. Tighten the 3 bolts to 9 ft. lbs. (12 Nm).

Turn to Section 5 for brake system applications

4WD

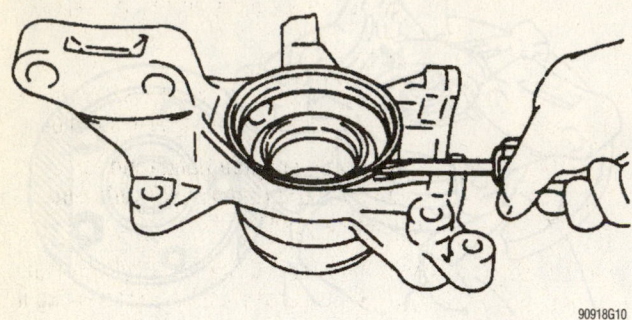

90918G10

Pry off the dust deflector then . . .—Previa

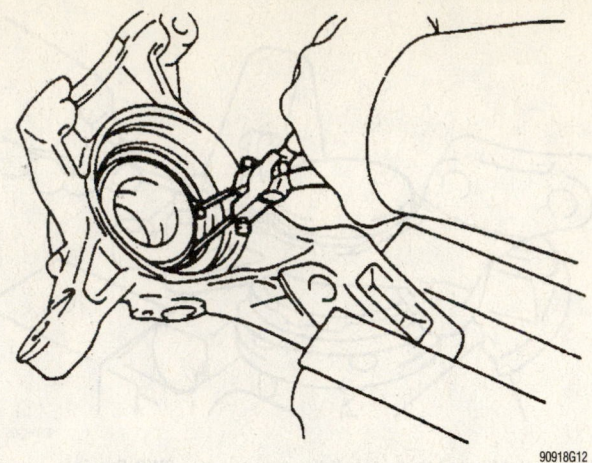

90918G12

Using snapring pliers, remove the snapring—Previa

4WD

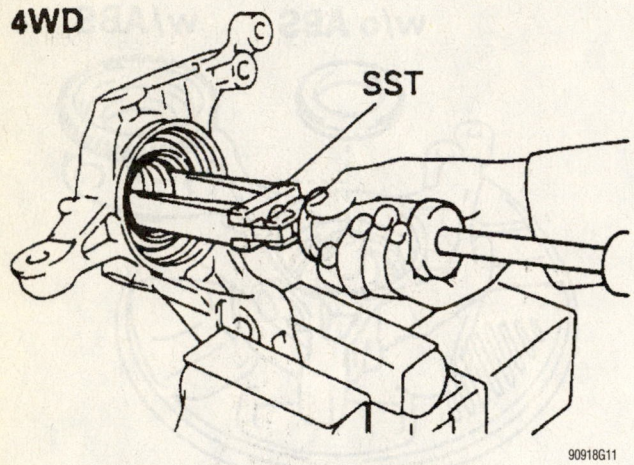

90918G11

. . . extract the inner oil seal with a puller—Previa

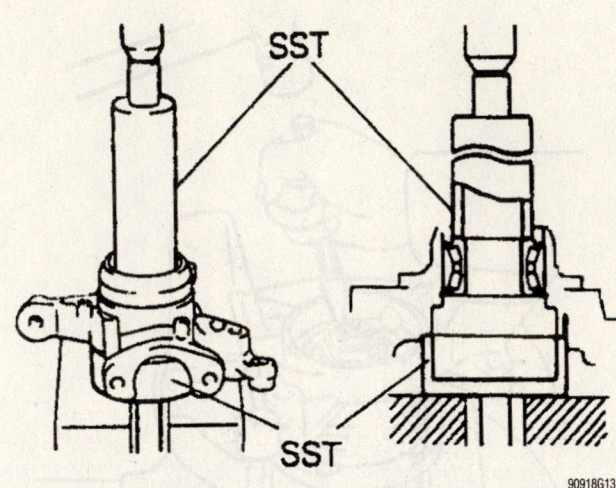

90918G13

Then press the old bearing out of the steering knuckle—Previa

- Axle hub, using an axle hub installation tool and press
- Spacer/ABS speed sensor rotor, on
  2WD models

➡**Take care not to scratch the serration's of the sensor rotor.**

Pinion Seal

REMOVAL & INSTALLATION

Previa

FRONT

1. Before servicing the vehicle, refer to
the precautions in the beginning of this section.

➡**A new companion flange nut is
needed before removal. The old nut
cannot be used.**

2. Remove or disconnect the following:
- Front driveshaft assembly

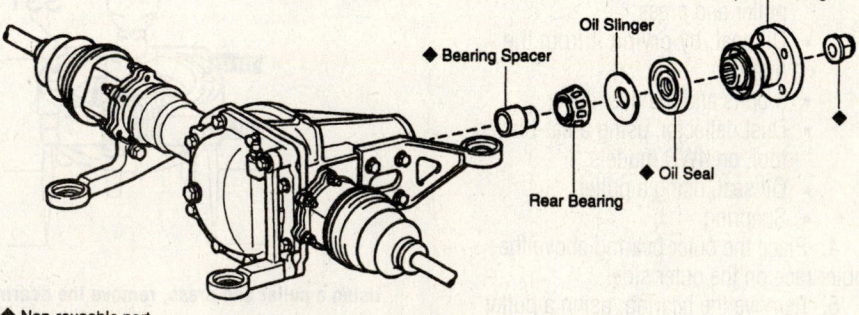

◆ Non-reusable part

90917G30

The front 4WD differential oil seal is located behind the companion flange—Previa

- Companion flange, using a chisel and hammer to loosen the staked part of the nut.

➡**Retain the flange with one tool while removing the nut.**

- Companion flange, using a forced screw type puller
- Oil seal from the differential, using a seal puller
- Oil slinger

To install:

3. Apply MP grease to the new oil seal.

4. Install or connect the following:
- New oil seal, using a driver and hammer
- Companion flange onto the drive pinion, using the forced screw type puller
- New companion flange nut lubri-

cated with gear oil. Tighten the nut to 80 ft. lbs. (108 Nm).

5. Using a torque wrench, measure the preload of the backlash between the drive pinion and ring gear, as follows:
- New bearing—8.7–13.9 inch lbs. (1.0–1.6 Nm)
- Used bearing—4.3–6.9 inch lbs. (0.5–0.8 Nm)

6. If the preload is greater than specification, replace the bearing spacer.

7. If the preload is less than specification, retighten the nut to 9 ft. lbs. (13 Nm) a little at a time until the specified preload is reached.

8. If the maximum torque is exceeded while tightening the nut, replace the bearing spacer and repeat the preload procedure. Do not back-off the pinion nut to reduce preload. Maximum torque is 174 ft. lbs. (235 Nm).

9. Install or connect the following:
- Stake the drive pinion nut
- Front driveshaft

10. Check the differential fluid level.

REAR

1. Before servicing the vehicle, refer to the precautions in the beginning of this section.

➡**A new companion flange nut is needed before removal. The old nut cannot be used.**

2. Remove or disconnect the following:
- Rear driveshaft, by matchmarking it
- Companion flange, using a chisel and hammer to loosen the staked part of the nut
- Companion flange, using a screw type puller
- Oil seal and slinger, using a seal puller

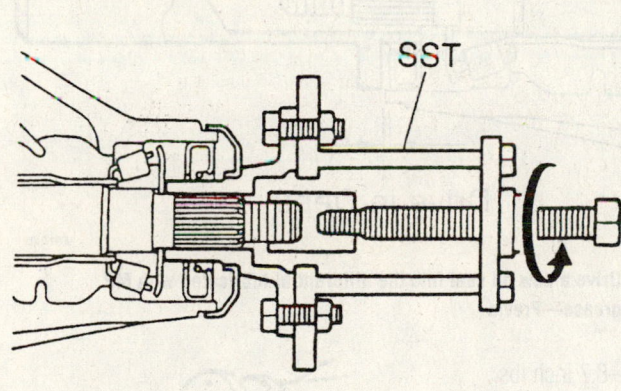

Use a screw type puller and remove the companion flange . . . —Previa

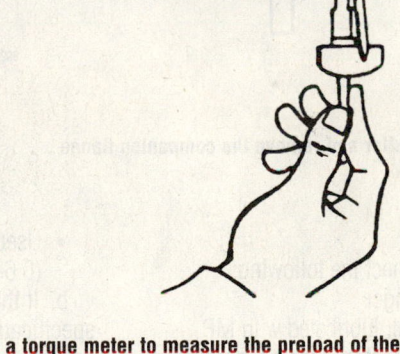

Use a torque meter to measure the preload of the backlash between the drive pinion and ring gear—Previa

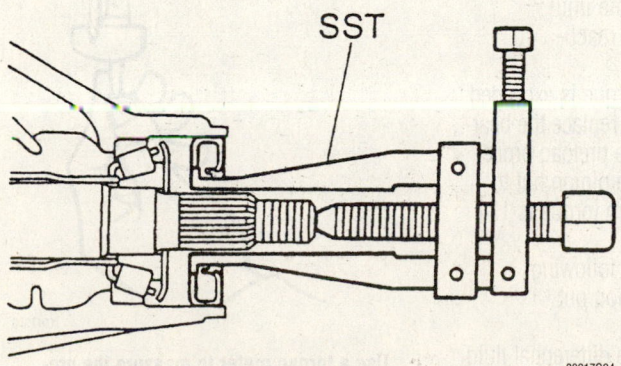

. . . then extract the oil seal using a puller—Previa

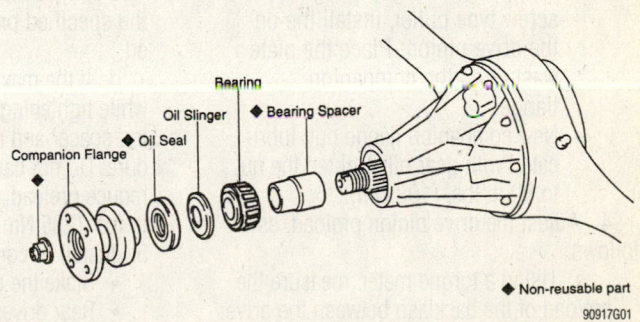

The oil seal in the rear differential is located behind the companion flange—Previa

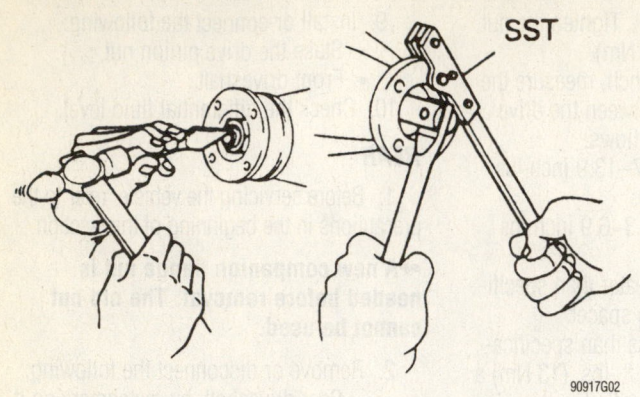

Stake the nut, then retain the flange and remove the nut—Previa

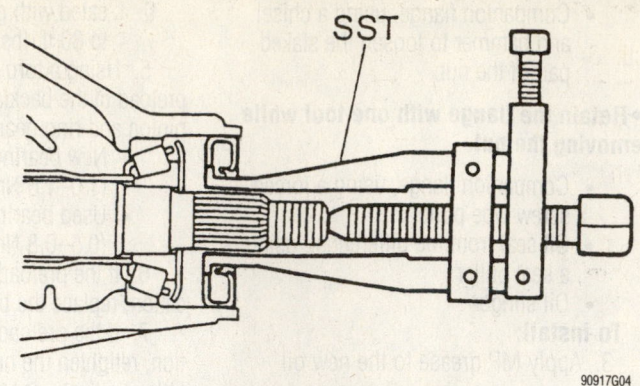

. . . then extract the oil seal using a puller—Previa

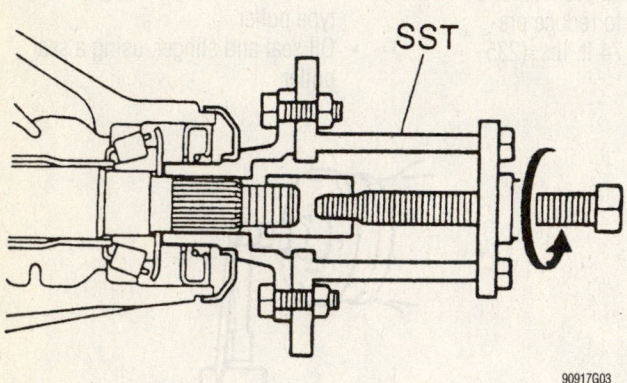

Use a screw type puller and remove the companion flange . . .
—Previa

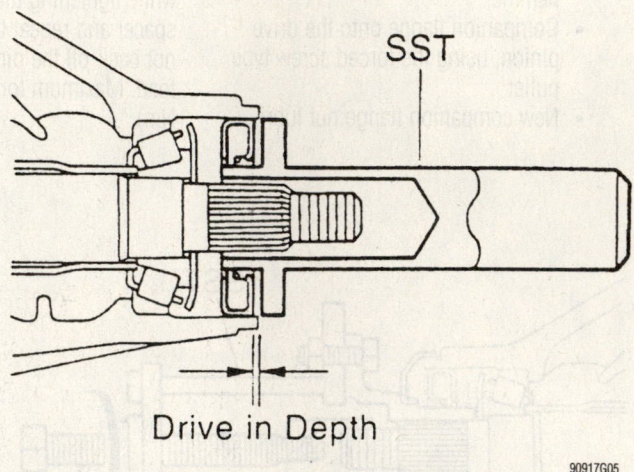

Drive in Depth

Drive a new oil seal into the differential lubricated with MP grease—Previa

To install:

3. Install or connect the following:
   - New oil slinger
   - New oil seal, lubricated with MP grease. Drive it into the housing to a depth of approximately 0.0059 in. (1.5mm).
   - Companion flange, using the screw type puller, install the on the drive pinion. Place the plate washer on the companion flange.
   - New companion flange nut, lubricated with gear oil. Tighten the nut to 80 ft. lbs. (108 Nm).

4. Adjust the drive pinion preload, as follows:

   a. Using a torque meter, measure the preload of the backlash between the drive pinion and ring gear.
   - New bearing—10.4–16.5 inch lbs. (1.2–1.9 Nm)

   - Used bearing—5.2–8.7 inch lbs. (0.6–1.0 Nm)

   b. If the preload is greater than specification, replace the bearing spacer.

   c. If the preload is less than specification, retighten the nut to 9 ft. lbs. (13 Nm), a little at a time until the specified preload is reached.

   d. If the maximum torque is exceeded while tightening the nut, replace the bearing spacer and repeat the preload procedure. Do not back-off the pinion nut to reduce preload. Maximum torque is 174 ft. lbs. (235 Nm).

5. Install or connect the following:
   - Stake the drive pinion nut
   - Rear driveshaft

6. Check and top-off the differential fluid level.

7. Test drive the vehicle.

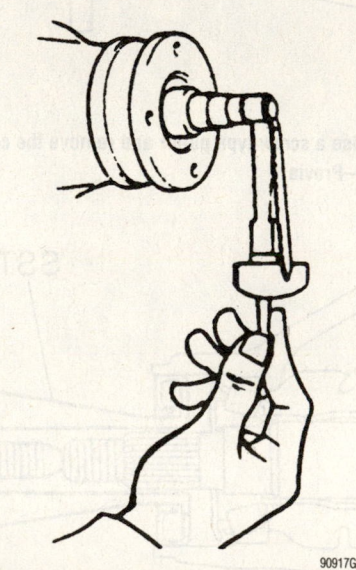

Use a torque meter to measure the preload of the backlash between the drive pinion and ring gear—Previa

Axle Housing

REMOVAL & INSTALLATION

Previa

FRONT

1. Before servicing the vehicle, refer to the precautions in the beginning of this section.
2. Drain the differential oil.
3. Remove or disconnect the following:
   - Front driveshaft
   - Halfshafts, from the side gear shafts by matchmarking them
   - No. 2 and left engine under cover
   - No. 1 and No. 2 differential support protectors
4. Support the front differential with a jack.
5. Remove or disconnect the following:
   - 3 support bolts, 6 cushions and collars
   - Front differential assembly
   - No. 1 differential support
   - Bolts and the No. 2 differential support

To install:
6. Install or connect the following:
   - Differential support. Tighten the 4 bolts to 116 ft. lbs. (157 Nm).
   - No. 2 differential support. Tighten the bolts to 48 ft. lbs. (65 Nm).
   - No. 1 differential support. Tighten it to 51 ft. lbs. (70 Nm).

7. Raise the front differential assembly.
8. Install or connect the following:
   - Collars, cushions and support bolts. Tighten the 3 bolts to 54 ft. lbs. (73 Nm).
   - No. 1 and No. 2 differential support protectors. Tighten them to 9 ft. lbs. (12 Nm).

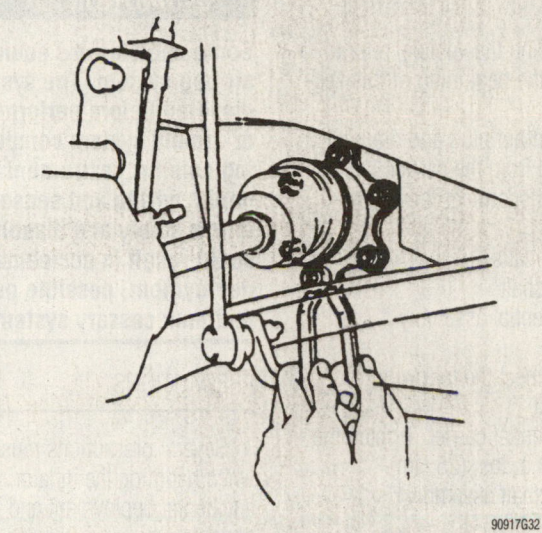

90917G32

Remove the 6 bolts retaining the side gear shafts to the front differential—Previa

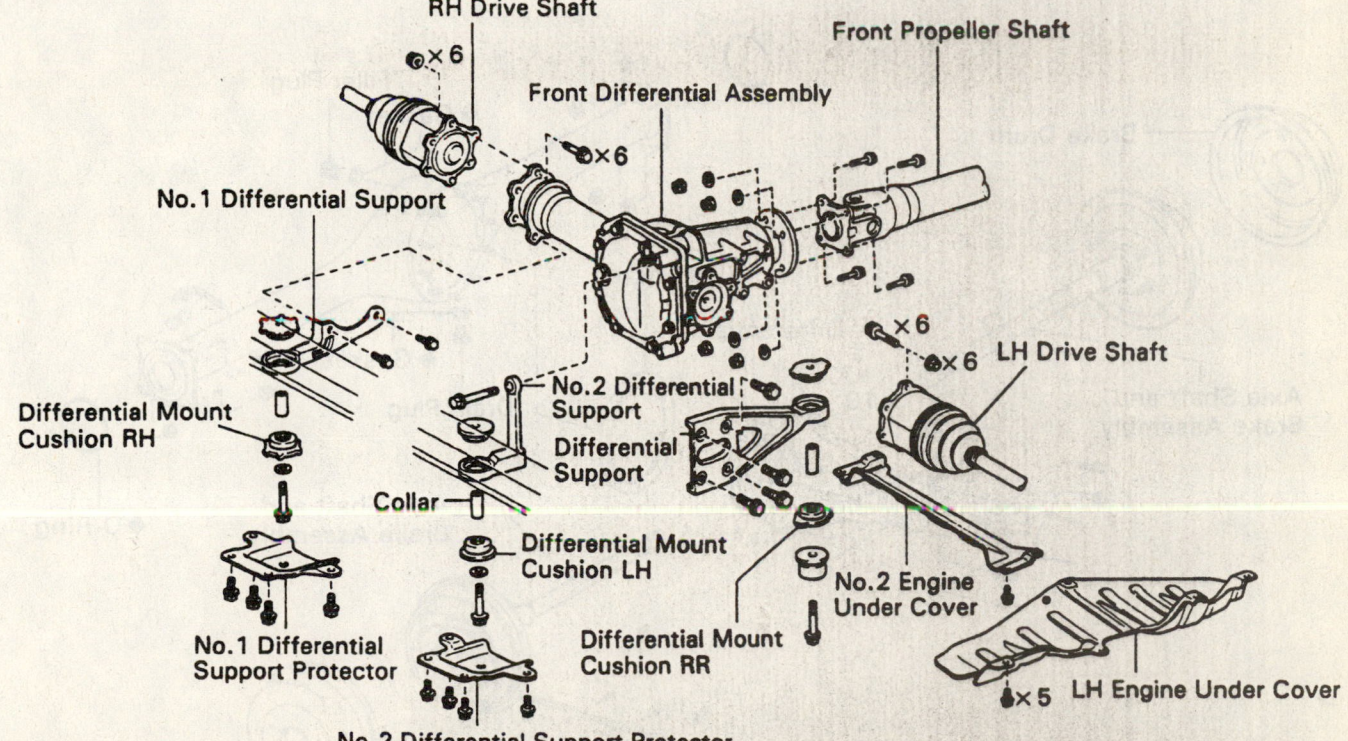

90917G31

Exploded view of the common 4WD front differential assembly—Previa

- Left and No. 2 engine undercovers
- Halfshafts to the side gear shafts, by aligning the matchmarks. Tighten the 6 nuts/bolts to 51 ft. lbs. (69 Nm).
- Front driveshaft

9. Fill the differential with the correct amount of gear oil.

REAR

1. Before servicing the vehicle, refer to the precautions in the beginning of this section.

2. Remove the drain plug and drain all the differential fluid from the carrier.

3. Remove or disconnect the following:

- Rear axle shafts
- Rear driveshaft
- Rear differential assembly

To install:

4. Install or connect the following:
- New gasket
- Rear differential carrier. Tighten the bolts to 18 ft. lbs. (25 Nm).
- Rear driveshaft assembly
- Rear axle shafts

5. Refill the differential carrier with the correct type of gear oil. The fluid should be just flowing out of the fill plug hole.

STEERING & SUSPENSION

Air Bag

✵✵ CAUTION

Some vehicles are equipped with an air bag system. The system must be disabled before performing service on or around system components, steering column, instrument panel components, wiring and sensors. Failure to follow safety and disabling procedures could result in accidental air bag deployment, possible personal injury and unnecessary system repairs.

PRECAUTIONS

Several precautions must be observed when handling the inflator module to avoid accidental deployment and possible personal injury.

- Never carry the inflator module by the wires or connector on the underside of the module.

- When carrying a live inflator module, hold securely with both hands, and ensure that the bag and trim cover are pointed away.
- Place the inflator module on a bench or other surface with the bag and trim cover facing up.
- With the inflator module on the bench, never place anything on or close to the module, which may be thrown in the event of an accidental deployment.

DISARMING

To avoid personal injury when working on vehicles equipped with an air bag, the negative battery cable must be disconnected and at least 90 seconds must elapse before working on the system. Failure to do so may result in deployment of the air bag.

Power Rack and Pinion Steering Gear

REMOVAL & INSTALLATION

RAV4

1. Before servicing the vehicle, refer to the precautions in the beginning of this section.

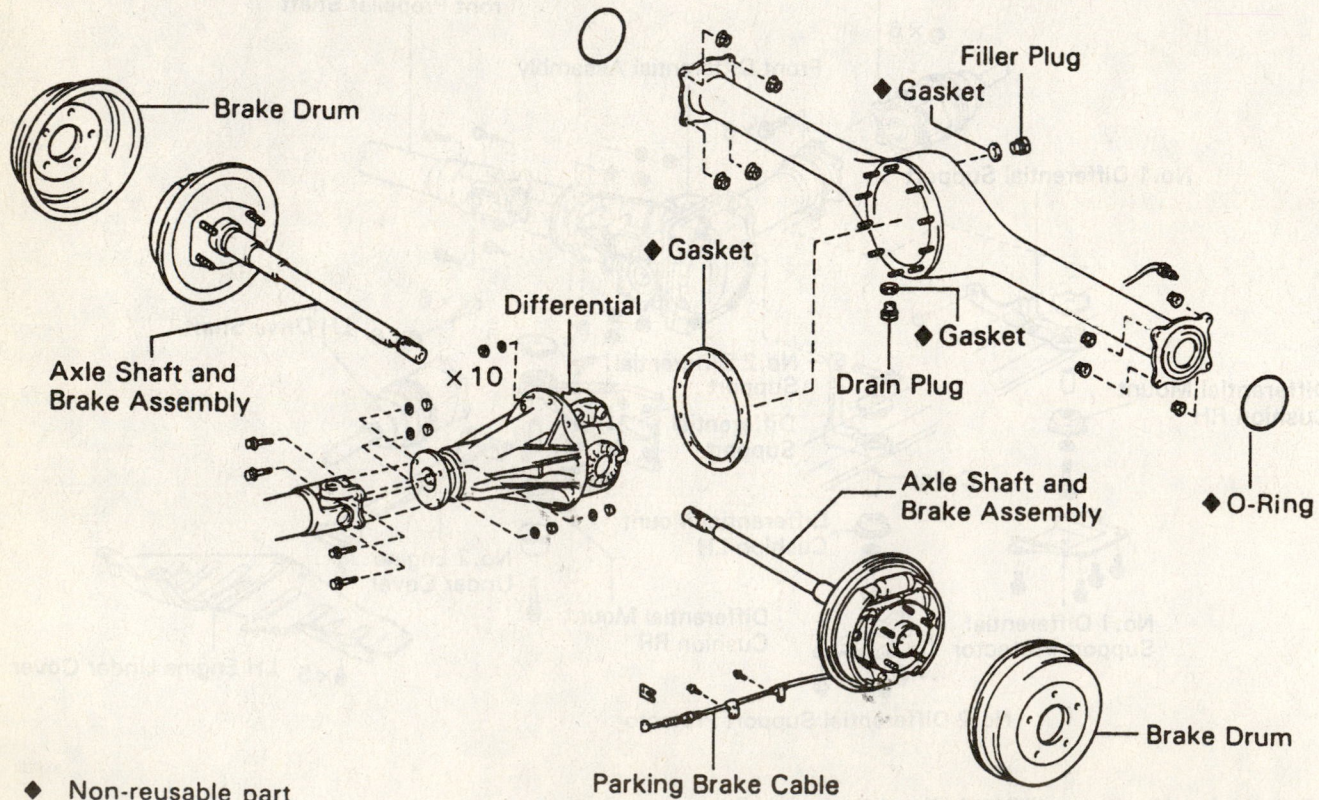

◆ Non-reusable part

Exploded view of the rear axle and differential assembly—Previa

90917G12

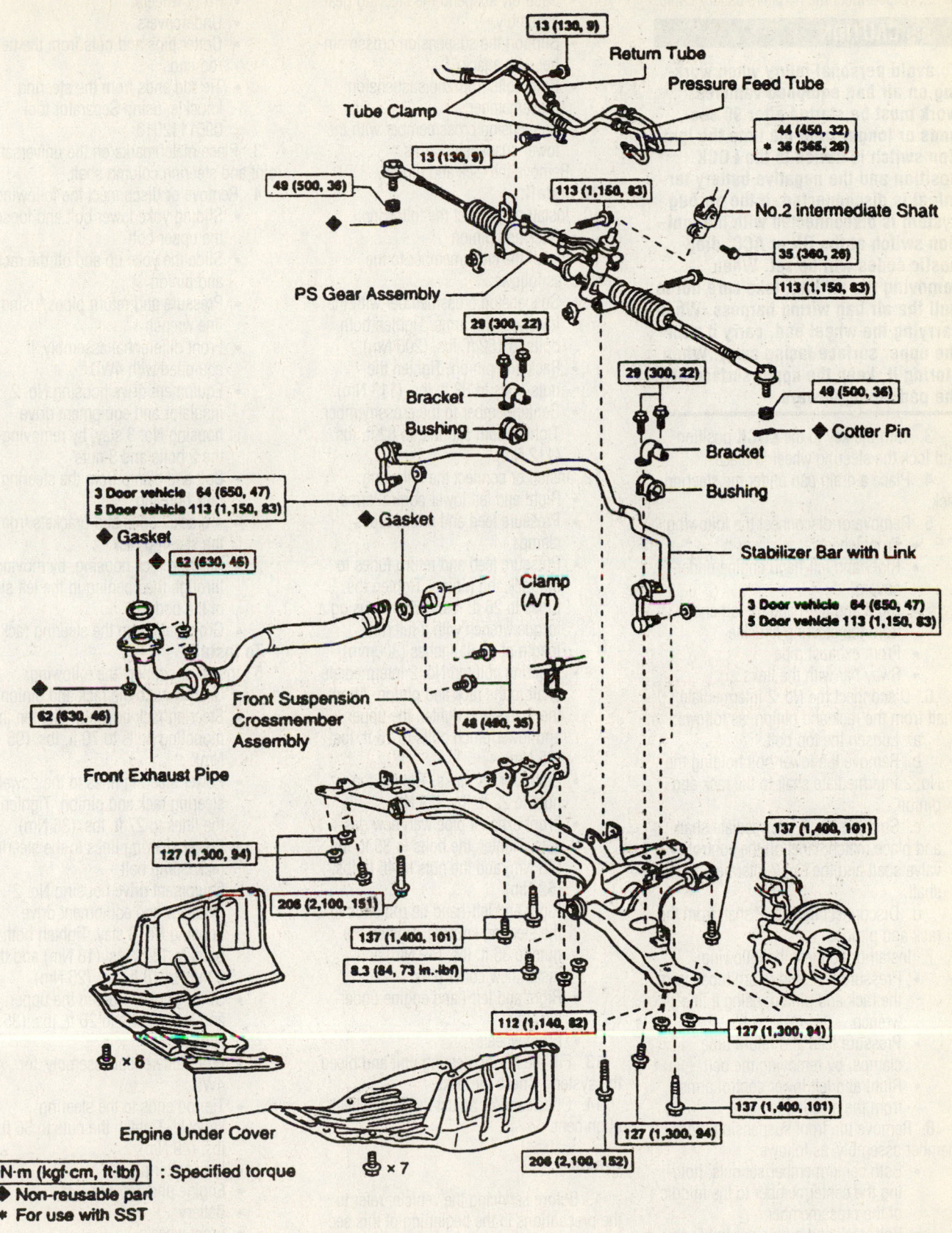

13 (130, 9)
Return Tube
Pressure Feed Tube
Tube Clamp
44 (450, 32)
* 35 (365, 26)
13 (130, 9)
49 (500, 36)
113 (1,150, 83)
No.2 intermediate Shaft
35 (360, 26)
113 (1,150, 83)
PS Gear Assembly
29 (300, 22)
29 (300, 22)
49 (500, 36)
Bracket
♦ Cotter Pin
Bushing
Bracket
Bushing
3 Door vehicle 64 (650, 47)
5 Door vehicle 113 (1,150, 83)
♦ Gasket
♦ Gasket
Stabilizer Bar with Link
62 (630, 45)
Clamp (A/T)
3 Door vehicle 64 (650, 47)
5 Door vehicle 113 (1,150, 83)
62 (630, 46)
Front Suspension
Crossmember
Assembly
48 (490, 35)
Front Exhaust Pipe
137 (1,400, 101)
127 (1,300, 94)
206 (2,100, 151)
137 (1,400, 101)
8.3 (84, 73 in.-lbf)
112 (1,140, 82)
127 (1,300, 94)
137 (1,400, 101)
127 (1,300, 94)
Engine Under Cover
206 (2,100, 152)
× 6

N·m (kgf·cm, ft-lbf) : Specified torque
♦ Non-reusable part
* For use with SST

× 7

Rack and pinion exploded view—RAV4

7924ZG75

2. Disconnect the negative battery cable.

✳✳ CAUTION

To avoid personal injury when working on air bag equipped vehicles, work must be started after 90 seconds or longer from the time the ignition switch is turned to the LOCK position and the negative battery terminal is disconnected. If the air bag system is disconnected with the ignition switch at the ON or ACC, diagnostic codes will be set. When removing the air bag, take care not to pull the air bag wiring harness. When carrying the wheel pad, carry it with the upper surface facing away. When storing it, keep the upper surface of the pad facing upward.

3. Turn the key to the **LOCK** position and lock the steering wheel in place.
4. Place a drain pan under the steering rack.
5. Remove or disconnect the following:
   • Front wheels
   • Right and left-hand engine undercovers
   • Right and left-hand tie rod ends from the steering knuckle
   • Front exhaust pipe
   • Sway bar with the links
6. Disconnect the No. 2 intermediate shaft from the rack and pinion, as follows:
   a. Loosen the top bolt.
   b. Remove the lower bolt holding the No. 2 intermediate shaft to the rack and pinion.
   c. Shift the No. 2 intermediate shaft and place matchmarks on the control valve shaft and the No. 2 intermediate shaft.
   d. Disconnect the No. 2 shaft from the rack and pinion.
7. Install or connect the following:
   • Pressure feed and return tubes from the rack and pinion, using a line wrench
   • Pressure feed and return tube clamps, by removing the bolt
   • Right and left lower control arms, from the steering knuckle
8. Remove the front suspension crossmember assembly, as follows:
   • Both centermember set nuts, holding the centermember to the middle of the crossmember.
   • Both rack and pinion assembly set bolts and nuts from the crossmember.

   • Securely suspend the steering gear assembly.
   • Support the suspension crossmember with a jack.
   • Both bolts from the suspension crossmember
   • Suspension crossmember with the lower suspension arms
9. Remove the rack and pinion.

To install:
10. Install or connect the following:
   • Rack and pinion
11. Install the crossmember to the vehicle, as follows:
   • Suspension crossmember with the lower control arms. Tighten both bolts to 152 ft. lbs. (206 Nm).
   • Rack and pinion. Tighten the nuts/bolts to 83 ft. lbs. (113 Nm).
   • Centermember to the crossmember. Tighten both set nuts to 82 ft. lbs. (112 Nm).
12. Install or connect the following:
   • Right and left lower control arms
   • Pressure feed and return tubes clamps
   • Pressure feed and return tubes to the rack and pinion. Tighten the tubes to 26 ft. lbs. (36 Nm), using a torque wrench with a fulcrum length of 11.81 inches (300mm).
   • Steering column No. 2 intermediate shaft to the rack and pinion. Align the marks and tighten the upper and lower pinch bolts to 26 ft. lbs. (35 Nm).
   • Stabilizer bar links. Tighten the nuts to 22 ft. lbs. (29 Nm).
   • Front exhaust pipe with new gaskets. Tighten the bolts to 35 ft. lbs. (48 Nm) and the nuts to 46 ft. lbs. (62 Nm).
   • Right and left-hand tie rod ends to the steering knuckle. Tighten the nuts to 36 ft. lbs. (49 Nm) and install new cotter pins.
   • Right and left-hand engine undercovers
   • Front wheels
13. Fill the power steering unit and bleed the system. Check for leaks.
14. Check and/or adjust the front wheel alignment.

Previa

1. Before servicing the vehicle, refer to the precautions in the beginning of this section.
2. Remove or disconnect the following:
   • Battery

   • Front wheels
   • Undercovers
   • Cotter pins and nuts from the tie rod ends
   • Tie rod ends from the steering knuckle, using Separator tool 0961112010
3. Place matchmarks on the universal joint and steering column shaft.
4. Remove or disconnect the following:
   • Sliding yoke lower bolt and loosen the upper bolt
   • Slide the yoke up and off the rack and pinion
   • Pressure and return pipes, using a line wrench
   • Front differential assembly, if equipped with 4WD
   • Equipment drive housing No. 2 insulator and equipment drive housing No. 3 stay, by removing the 2 bolts and 3 nuts
   • Bolt and clamp from the steering rack housing
   • 4 bracket bolts and brackets from the steering rack
   • Steering rack housing, by moving it through the opening in the left side of the body
   • Grommets from the steering rack

To install:
5. Install or connect the following:
   • Grommets to the rack and pinion
   • Steering rack housing. Tighten the mounting bolts to 70 ft. lbs. (95 Nm).
   • Power steering lines to the power steering rack and pinion. Tighten the lines to 27 ft. lbs. (36 Nm).
   • Power steering lines to the steering rack clamp bolt
   • Equipment drive housing No. 2 insulator and equipment drive housing No. 3 stay. Tighten both bolts to 13 ft. lbs. (18 Nm) and the 3 nuts to 18 ft. lbs. (25 Nm).
   • Sliding yoke. Tighten the upper and lower bolts to 26 ft. lbs. (35 Nm).
   • Front differential assembly, for 4WD
   • Tie rod ends to the steering knuckle. Tighten the nuts to 36 ft. lbs. (49 Nm).
   • New cotter pin
   • Engine undercovers
   • Battery
   • Front wheels
6. Check and/or adjust the front end alignment.

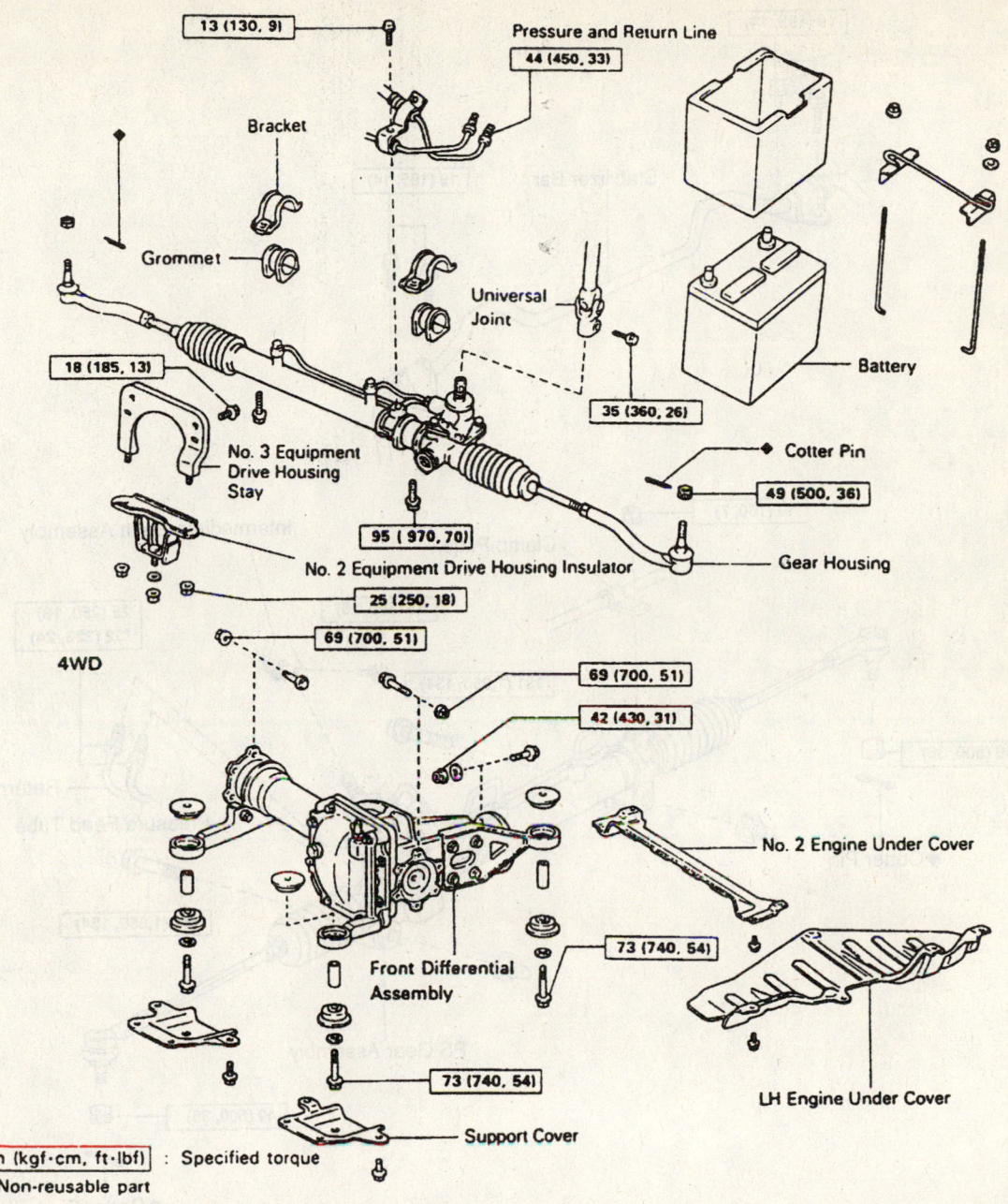

13 (130, 9)
Pressure and Return Line
44 (450, 33)
Bracket
Grommet
Universal Joint
18 (185, 13)
Battery
35 (360, 26)
No. 3 Equipment Drive Housing Stay
Cotter Pin
49 (500, 36)
95 (970, 70)
No. 2 Equipment Drive Housing Insulator
Gear Housing
25 (250, 18)
69 (700, 51)
4WD
69 (700, 51)
42 (430, 31)
No. 2 Engine Under Cover
Front Differential Assembly
73 (740, 54)
LH Engine Under Cover
73 (740, 54)
Support Cover

N·m (kgf·cm, ft·lbf) : Specified torque
◆ Non-reusable part

7924ZG74

Rack and pinion removal and installation exploded view—Previa

Sienna and RX 300

1. Before servicing the vehicle, refer to the precautions in the beginning of this section.

2. Remove or disconnect the following:
   • Negative battery cable

➡**Wait at least 90 seconds before working on the vehicle to allow the Supplemental Restraint System (SRS) system to disarm.**

   • Right and left side fender apron seals

   • Right and left tie rod ends

3. Place matchmarks on the intermediate shaft.

4. Remove or disconnect the following:

   • Pinch bolt and the intermediate shaft out from under the vehicle
   • Power steering line clamp
   • Pressure and feed lines
   • Stabilizer bar, unbolt it but do not remove it
   • Heated Oxygen (HO₂) sensor

   • Both gear assembly set bolts and nuts, by lifting the stabilizer bar
   • Gear assembly from the left side of the vehicle

To install:

5. Install or connect the following:
   • Gear assembly to the left side of the vehicle

✳✳ WARNING

Be careful not to damage the power steering lines.

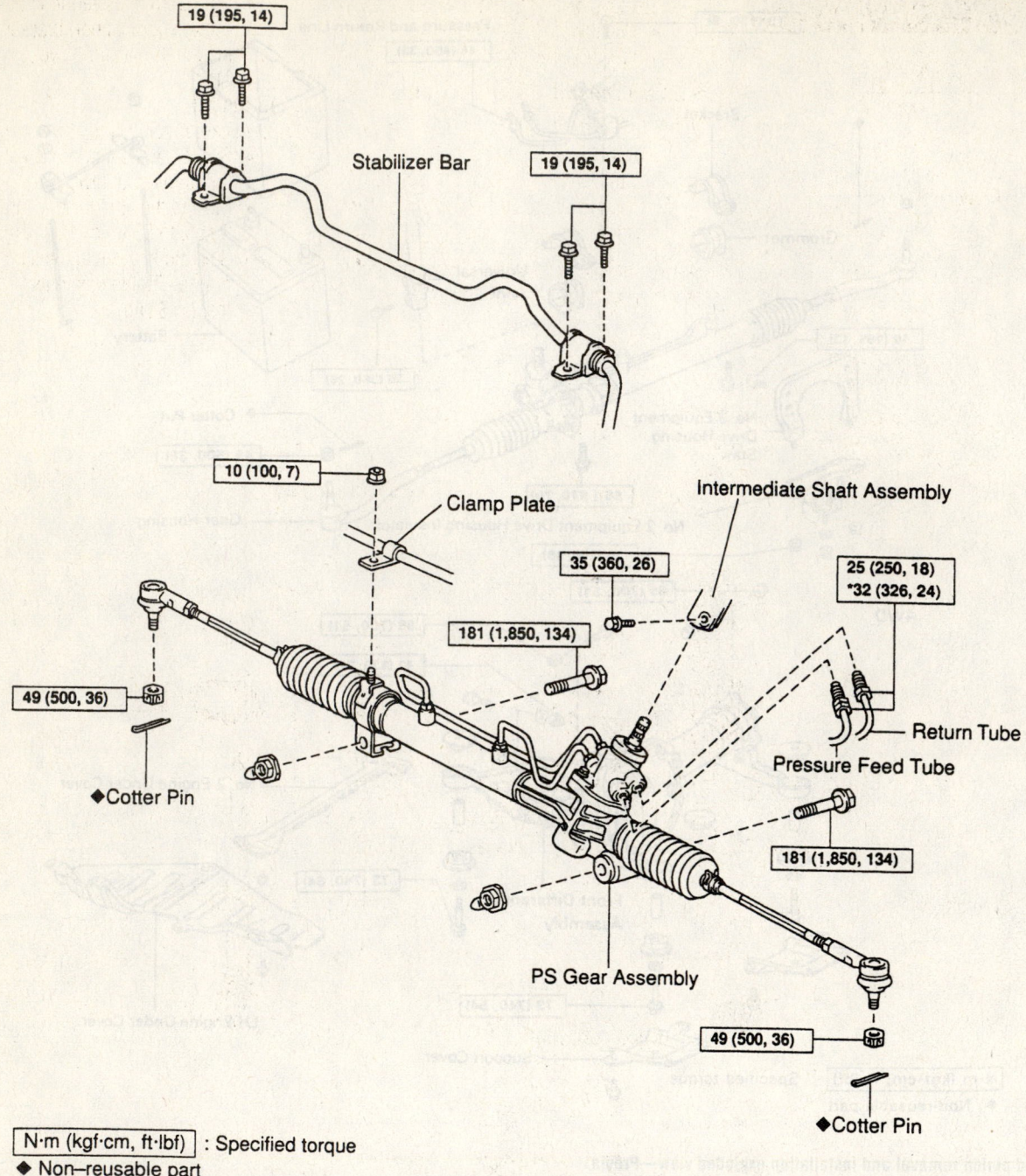

Stabilizer Bar

19 (195, 14)

19 (195, 14)

10 (100, 7)

Clamp Plate

Intermediate Shaft Assembly

35 (360, 26)

25 (250, 18)
*32 (326, 24)

181 (1,850, 134)

49 (500, 36)

Return Tube

Pressure Feed Tube

◆Cotter Pin

181 (1,850, 134)

PS Gear Assembly

49 (500, 36)

◆Cotter Pin

N·m (kgf·cm, ft·lbf) : Specified torque
◆ Non–reusable part
* For use with SST

7924ZG76

Exploded view of the power steering gear and related components—Sienna and RX 300 models

- Tighten the gear assembly set bolts and nuts to 134 ft. lbs. (181 Nm), by lifting the stabilizer bar
- HO2sensor
- Stabilizer bar. Tighten the bolt to 14 ft. lbs. (19 Nm) and the nut to 29 ft. lbs. (39 Nm).
- Pressure and feed return lines. Tighten them to 18 ft. lbs. (25 Nm).
- Line clamps. Tighten the nut to 84 inch lbs. (10 Nm).

- Intermediate shaft, by aligning the joint and main shaft matchmarks. Tighten to 26 ft. lbs. (35 Nm).
- Tie rod ends
- Fender apron seals. Securely tighten the bolts.

6. Remove or disconnect the following:

- Steering wheel pad
- Steering wheel

7. Position the front wheels facing straight-ahead. Do this with the front of the vehicle on jackstands.

8. Center the spiral cable.

9. Install the steering wheel at the straight-ahead position. Temporarily tighten the wheel set nut. Attach the wiring.

10. Bleed the power steering system.

11. Check the steering wheel center point. Tighten the steering nut to 26 ft. lbs. (35 Nm).

12. Check and/or adjust the front wheel alignment.

Strut

REMOVAL & INSTALLATION

RAV4

RAV4 is equipped with front strut and rear shock absorber type suspension arrangement.

1. Before servicing the vehicle, refer to the precautions in the beginning of this section.

2. Remove or disconnect the following:
- Negative battery cable
- Wheel

➡**Do not support the weight of the vehicle on the suspension arm.**

- Brake hose from the strut
- Anti-lock Brake System (ABS) electrical connection to the strut bolt, if equipped

➡**It is not necessary to disconnect the brake hose from the brake caliper.**

- Strut from the steering knuckle
- Suspension support bracket from the top of the strut tower
- Strut

To install:

3. Install or connect the following:
- Suspension support bracket to the top of the strut tower
- Strut to the strut tower. Tighten the 3 nuts to 59 ft. lbs. (80 Nm).
- Steering knuckle to the strut lower bracket. Tighten the nuts to 117 ft. lbs. (158 Nm).

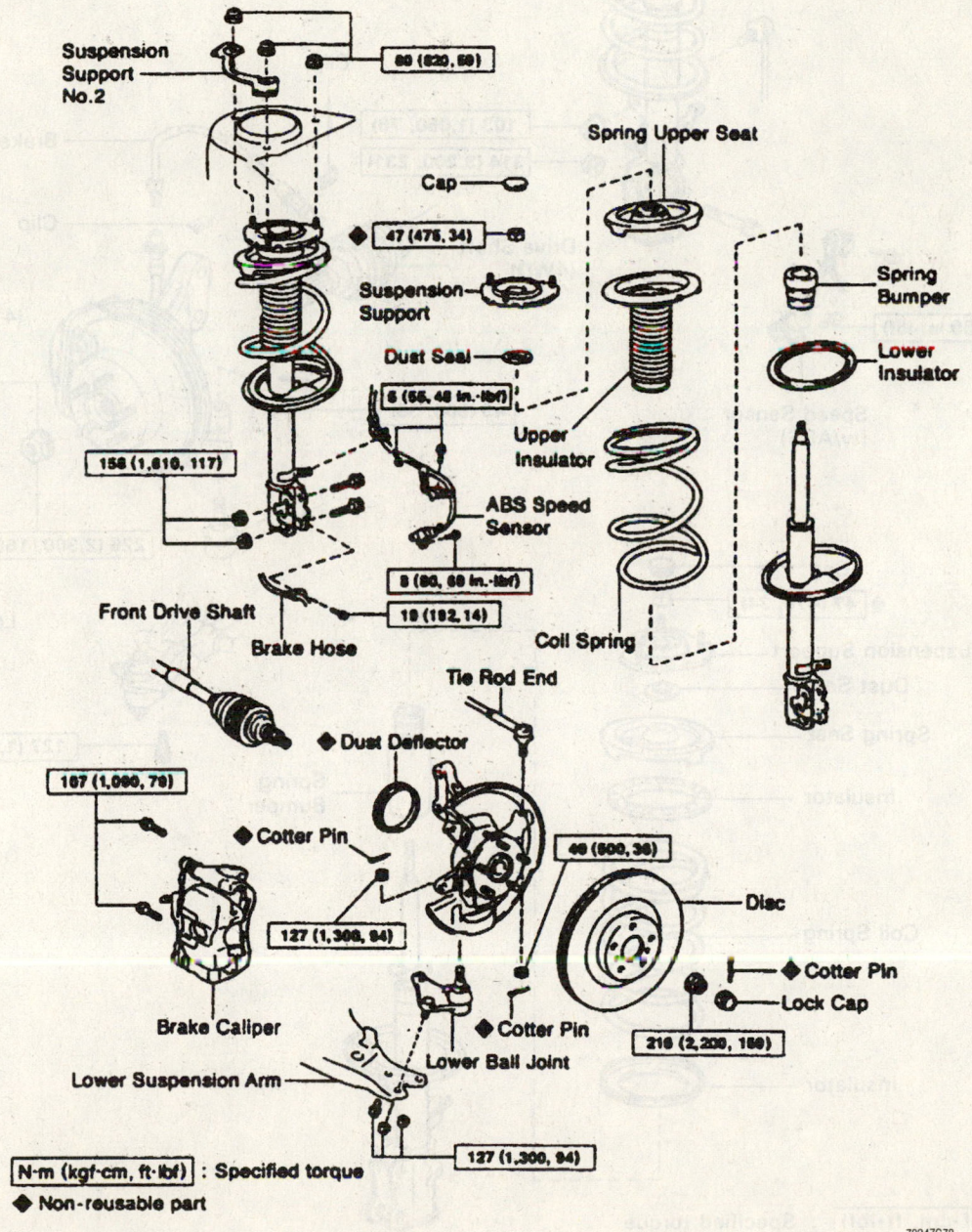

Strut assembly exploded view—RAV4

Turn to Section 5 for brake system applications

- ABS electrical connector to the strut. Tighten the bolt to 48 inch lbs. (5.4 Nm).
- Brake line to the strut. Tighten the bolt to 14 ft. lbs. (19 Nm).

4. If the brake lines were opened, add brake fluid and bleed the brake system.

5. Install or connect the following:
- Wheel
- Negative battery cable

6. Check and/or adjust the front wheel alignment.

Previa

Previa is equipped with front strut and rear shock absorber type suspension arrangement.

1. Before servicing the vehicle, refer to the precautions in the beginning of this section.

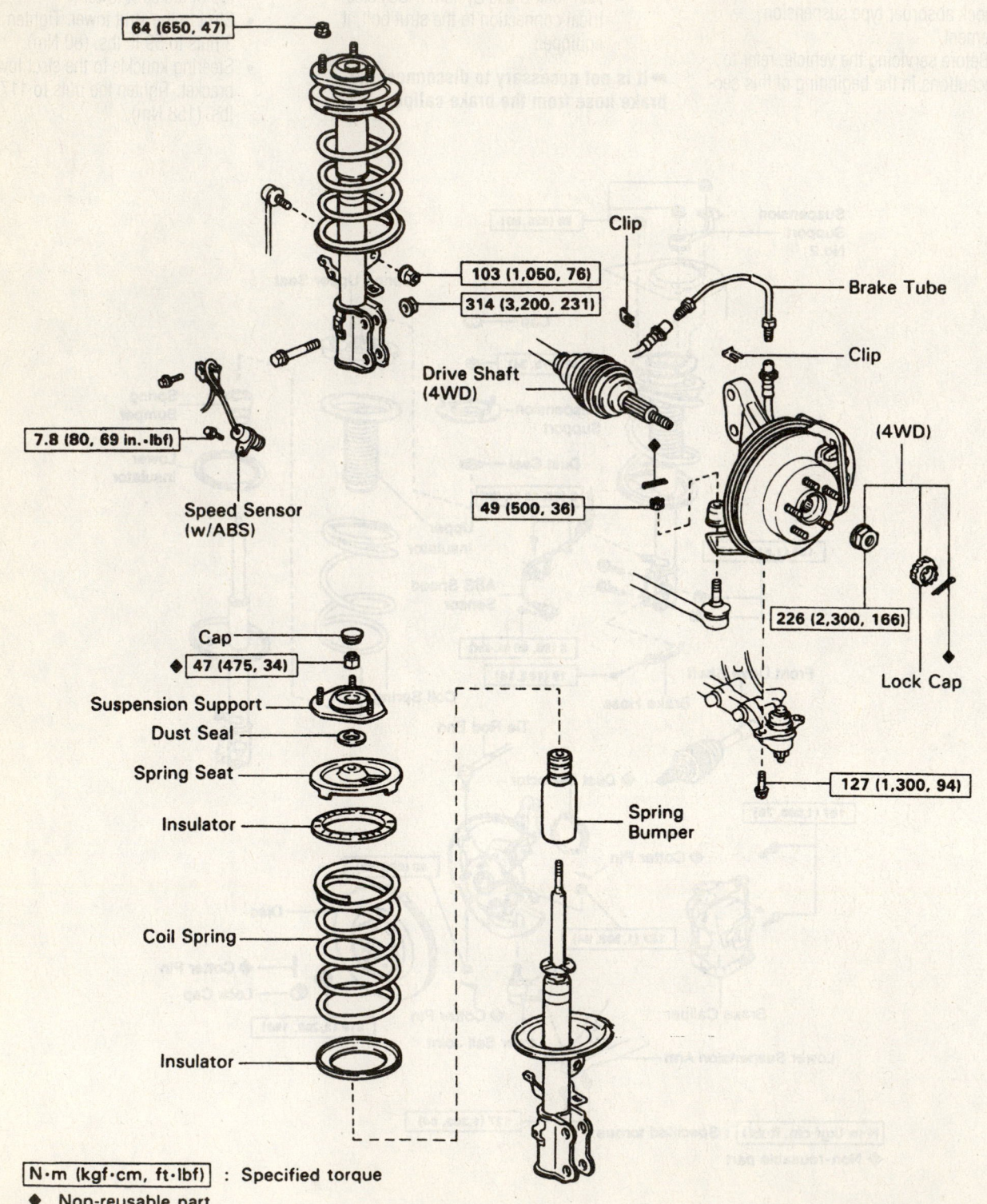

64 (650, 47)

103 (1,050, 76)

314 (3,200, 231)

7.8 (80, 69 in.·lbf)

Speed Sensor (w/ABS)

Clip

Brake Tube

Clip

Drive Shaft (4WD)

49 (500, 36)

(4WD)

226 (2,300, 166)

Lock Cap

Cap

◆ **47 (475, 34)**

Suspension Support

Dust Seal

Spring Seat

Insulator

Coil Spring

Insulator

Spring Bumper

127 (1,300, 94)

N·m (kgf·cm, ft·lbf) : Specified torque

◆ Non-reusable part

Front strut exploded view—Previa

7924ZG77

2. Remove the wheel.

3. If equipped with 4WD, remove the driveshaft locknut, as follows:

- Cotter pin and lockcap
- Locknut, while applying the brake
- Washer

4. Remove or disconnect the following:

- Sway bar link from the strut
- Speed sensor, if equipped with Anti-lock Brake System (ABS)
- Brake line at the strut, using a line wrench
- Clips and brake hose from the strut bracket
- Loosen both lower side of the strut nuts
- Loosen the lower ball joint bolts
- Cotter pin and nut from the tie rod end
- Tie rod from the steering knuckle, using the Tie Rod Separator tool SST09628-10011
- Steering knuckle, by removing the lower ball joint bolts, 2 nuts and the bolts on the lower side of the strut

➡If equipped with 4WD, it will be necessary to use a rubber hammer to disconnect the halfshaft from the steering knuckle. Be careful not to damage the oil seal, driveshaft boot and/or the speed sensor rotor.

5. Place a service jack underneath the strut to support it.

6. Remove or disconnect the following:

- Cluster finish panel and knee panel, for the left strut
- Glove compartment door, for the right strut
- 3 upper strut nuts
- Strut

To install:

7. Install or connect the following:

- Strut. Tighten the 3 upper side nuts to 47 ft. lbs. (64 Nm).
- Knee panel and cluster finish panel, for the left strut
- Glove compartment, for the right strut
- Steering knuckle, by temporarily installing the strut bolts
- Tie rod end to the steering knuckle. Tighten the nut to 36 ft. lbs. (49 Nm).
- New cotter pin
- Tighten the lower strut nuts to 231 ft. lbs. (314 Nm) and the ball joint bolts to 94 ft. lbs. (127 Nm).
- Brake hose to the strut and the brake line to the brake hose

- Speed sensor, if equipped with ABS
- Stabilizer bar link to the strut. Tighten the nut to 76 ft. lbs. (103 Nm).

8. Bleed the brake system and check for leaks.

9. Install or connect the following:

- Driveshaft locknut, if equipped with 4WD. Tighten the nut to 152 ft. lbs. (206 Nm).
- Lockcap and a new cotter pin
- Wheel

10. Check and/or adjust the front wheel alignment.

Sienna

The Sienna is equipped with front struts and rear shock absorbers.

FRONT

1. Before servicing the vehicle, refer to the precautions in the beginning of this section.

➡Do not support the weight of the vehicle on the suspension arm; the arm will deform under its weight.

2. Remove or disconnect the following:

- Wheel
- Brake hose and the Anti-lock Brake System (ABS) speed sensor wire from the strut
- Sway bar link from the strut
- Outer front cowl top panel

3. Matchmark the strut lower bracket and camber adjust cam, if equipped.

4. Remove or disconnect the following:

- Lower strut end from the steering knuckle's lower arm
- 3 upper strut mounting plate to the upper wheel arch nuts
- Strut

To install:

5. Align the upper suspension support

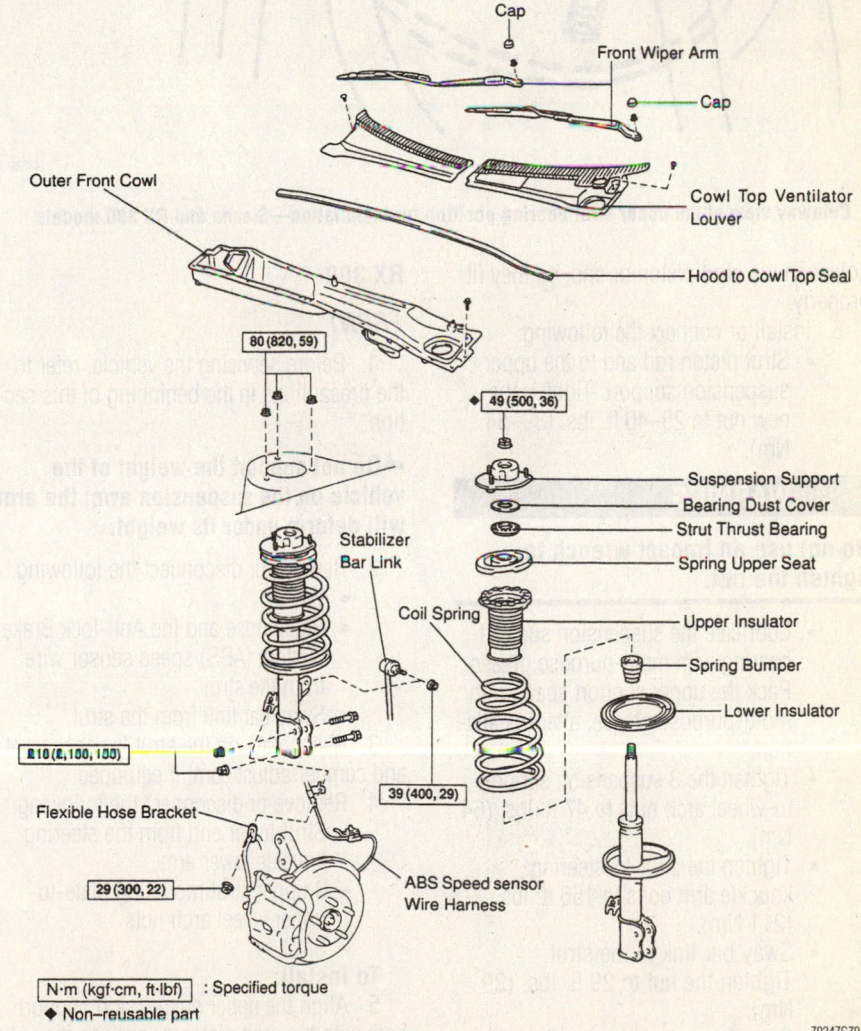

View of the front strut assembly and related components—Sienna and RX 300 models

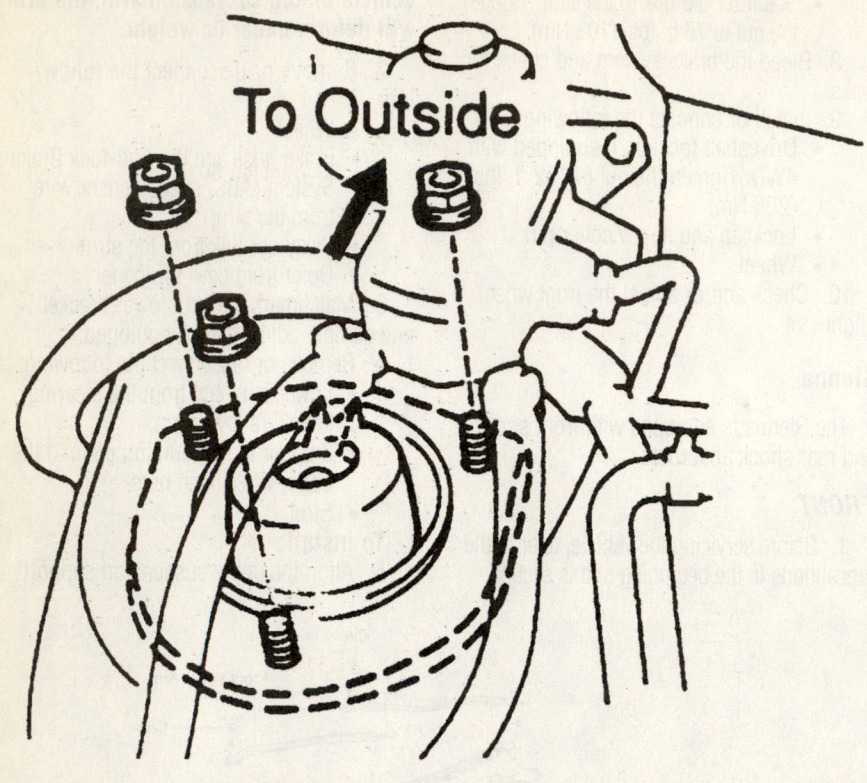

To Outside

7924ZG80

Cutaway view of the upper strut bearing position for installation—Sienna and RX 300 models

hole with the strut piston or end, so they fit properly.

6. Install or connect the following:
- Strut piston rod end to the upper suspension support. Tighten the new nut to 29–40 ft. lbs. (39–54 Nm).

✳✳ WARNING

Do not use an impact wrench to tighten the nut.

- Lubricate the suspension support bearing with multi-purpose grease. Pack the upper support space with multi-purpose grease, after installation.
- Tighten the 3 suspension support-to-wheel arch nuts to 47 ft. lbs. (64 Nm).
- Tighten the strut-to-steering knuckle arm bolts to 156 ft. lbs. (211 Nm).
- Sway bar link to the strut. Tighten the nut to 29 ft. lbs. (39 Nm).
- Outer front cowl top panel
- ABS speed sensor and the brake hose to the strut, if equipped.
- Wheel

RX 300

FRONT

1. Before servicing the vehicle, refer to the precautions in the beginning of this section.

➡**Do not support the weight of the vehicle on the suspension arm; the arm will deform under its weight.**

2. Remove or disconnect the following:
- Wheel
- Brake hose and the Anti-lock Brake System (ABS) speed sensor wire from the strut
- Sway bar link from the strut
3. Matchmark on the strut lower bracket and camber adjust cam, if equipped.
4. Remove or disconnect the following:
- Strut lower end from the steering knuckle lower arm
- 3 upper strut mounting plate-to-upper wheel arch nuts
- Strut

To install:
5. Align the upper suspension support hole with the strut piston or end, so they fit properly.
6. Install or connect the following:
- Strut piston rod end to the upper

suspension support. Tighten the new nut to 29–40 ft. lbs. (39–54 Nm).

➡**Do not use an impact wrench to tighten the nut.**

- Lubricate the suspension support bearing with multi-purpose grease.
- Pack the upper support space with multi-purpose grease, also, after installation.
- Tighten the 3 suspension support-to-wheel arch nuts to 47 ft. lbs. (64 Nm).
- Tighten the strut-to-steering knuckle arm bolts to 156 ft. lbs. (211 Nm).
- Sway bar link to the strut. Tighten the nut to 29 ft. lbs. (39 Nm).
- ABS speed sensor and the brake hose to the strut, if equipped
- Wheel
7. Check and/or adjust the front wheel alignment.

REAR

1. Before servicing the vehicle, refer to the precautions in the beginning of this section.
2. Remove or disconnect the following:
- Negative battery cable
- Deck side cover
- Rear wheels
- Anti-lock Brake System (ABS) sensor from the strut bracket
- Flexible brake hose from the strut
- Sway bar link from the strut
- Loosen the 2 lower strut mounting bolts
3. Support the rear axle carrier with a jack.
4. Remove or disconnect the following:
- 3 upper strut mounting nuts
- Strut, by lower the rear axle

To install:
5. Install or connect the following:
- Strut
- Both lower strut mounting bolts, but do not tighten
- Axle carrier by aligning the 3 upper mounting studs. Tighten the nuts to 29 ft. lbs. (39 Nm).
6. Lower the axle carrier.
7. Install or connect the following:
- Tighten both lower mounting bolts to 188 ft. lbs. (255 Nm).
- Sway bar link. Tighten the nut to 29 ft. lbs. (39 Nm).
- Flexible brake hose and the ABS sensor to the strut
- Rear wheels and the deck side cover

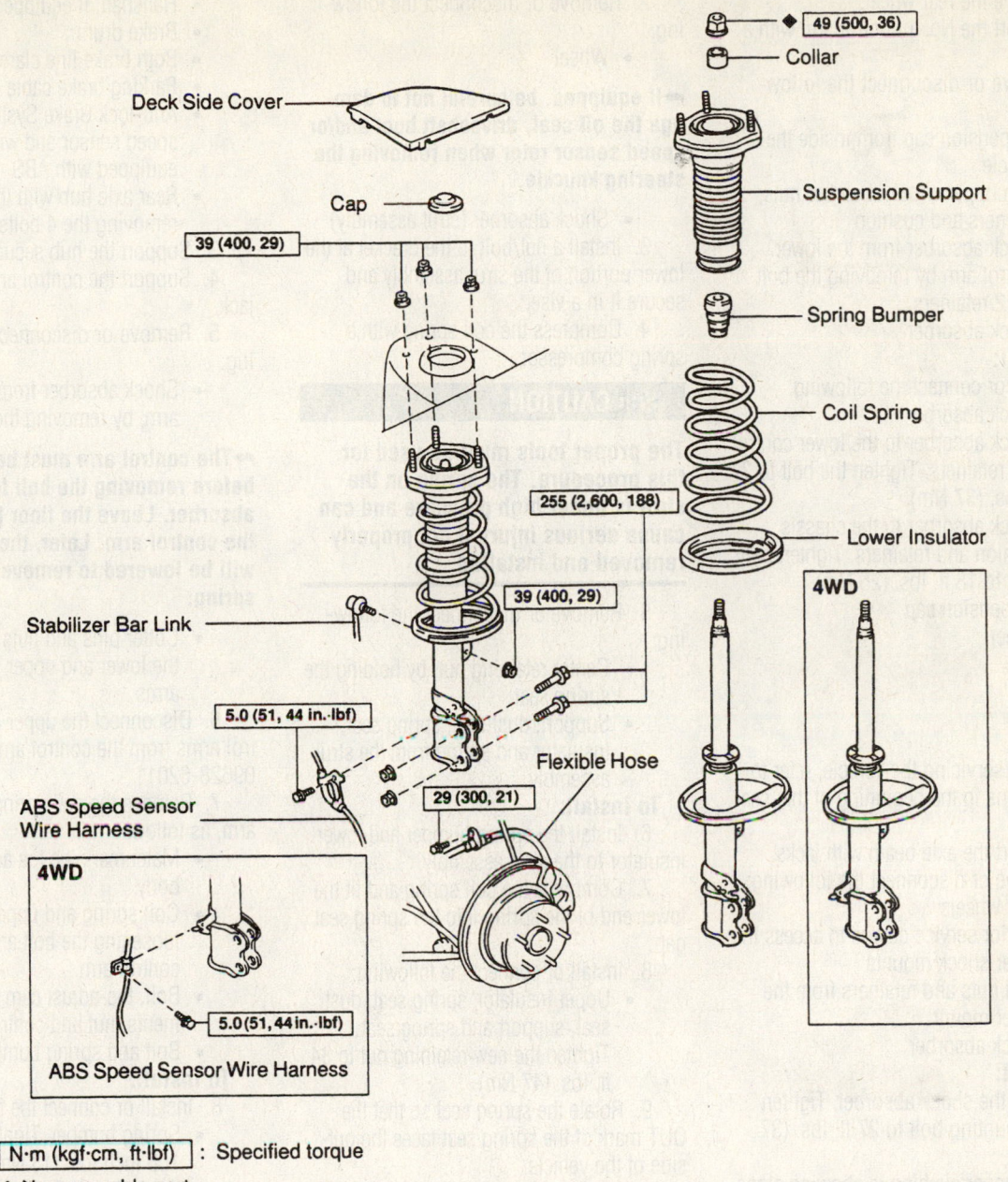

49 (500, 36) ◆
Collar
Deck Side Cover
Cap
39 (400, 29)
Suspension Support
Spring Bumper
Coil Spring
255 (2,600, 188)
Lower Insulator
39 (400, 29)
4WD
Stabilizer Bar Link
5.0 (51, 44 in.·lbf)
Flexible Hose
29 (300, 21)
ABS Speed Sensor Wire Harness
4WD
5.0 (51, 44 in.·lbf)
ABS Speed Sensor Wire Harness

N·m (kgf·cm, ft·lbf) : Specified torque
◆ Non–reusable part

7924ZG89

Exploded view of the rear strut assembly—RX 300

- Negative battery cable

Shock Absorber

REMOVAL & INSTALLATION

Previa

REAR

1. Before servicing the vehicle, refer to the precautions in the beginning of this section.

2. Support the rear differential with a jack.
3. Remove or disconnect the following:
   - Shock absorber from the lower control arm, by removing the nut, washer and bushing
   - Shock absorber from the chassis bolt
   - Shock absorber

To install:
4. Install or connect the following:
   - Shock absorber to the chassis.

Tighten the bolt to 27 ft. lbs. (37 Nm)
- Shock absorber to the lower control arm. Tighten the nut until the bolt protrudes 0.0059 inch (1.5mm) or more.

RAV4

REAR

1. Before servicing the vehicle, refer to the precautions in the beginning of this section.

2. Remove the rear wheel.

3. Support the No. 1 control arm with a floor jack.

4. Remove or disconnect the following:

- Suspension cap from inside the vehicle
- Both upper shock absorber nuts, retainers and cushion
- Shock absorber from the lower control arm by removing the bolt and 2 retainers
- Shock absorber

To install:

5. Install or connect the following:

- Shock absorber
- Shock absorber to the lower control arm retainers. Tighten the bolt to 27 ft. lbs. (37 Nm).
- Shock absorber to the chassis cushion and retainers. Tighten both nuts to 18 ft. lbs. (25 Nm).
- Suspension cap
- Wheel

Sienna

REAR

1. Before servicing the vehicle, refer to the precautions in the beginning of this section.

2. Support the axle beam with jacks.

3. Remove or disconnect the following:

- Rear wheels
- Interior service covers to access the upper shock mounts
- Both nuts and retainers from the upper mount
- Shock absorber

To install:

4. Install the shock absorber. Tighten the lower mounting bolt to 27 ft. lbs. (37 Nm).

5. If the upper cushion is showing signs of wear, replace it.

6. Install or connect the following:

- Upper shock absorber. Tighten the nuts to 18 ft. lbs. (25 Nm).
- Wheels

Coil Spring

REMOVAL & INSTALLATION

Front

ALL MODELS

1. Before servicing the vehicle, refer to the precautions in the beginning of this section.

2. Remove or disconnect the following:

- Wheel

➡**If equipped, be careful not to damage the oil seal, driveshaft boot and/or speed sensor rotor when removing the steering knuckle.**

- Shock absorber (strut assembly)

3. Install a nut/bolt to the bracket at the lower portion of the strut assembly and secure it in a vise.

4. Compress the coil spring with a spring compressor.

✸✸ CAUTION

The proper tools must be used for this procedure. The spring on the strut is under high pressure and can cause serious injury if not properly removed and installed.

5. Remove or disconnect the following:

- Center retaining nut, by holding the spring seat
- Support, dust seal, spring seat, insulator and spring from the strut assembly

To install:

6. Install the spring bumper and lower insulator to the strut assembly.

7. Compress the coil spring and fit the lower end of the spring into the spring seat gap.

8. Install or connect the following:

- Upper insulator, spring seat, dust seal, support and spring seat. Tighten the new retaining nut to 34 ft. lbs. (47 Nm).

9. Rotate the spring seat so that the OUT mark of the spring seat faces the outside of the vehicle.

- Strut
- Wheel

10. If required, bleed the brake system and check for leaks.

11. Check and/or adjust the front wheel alignment.

Rear

RAV4

1. Before servicing the vehicle, refer to the precautions in the beginning of this section.

2. Remove or disconnect the following:

- Negative battery cable
- Axle shaft, if equipped with 2WD

- Halfshaft, if equipped with 4WD
- Brake drum
- Both brake line clamp bolts
- Parking brake cable clamp bolt
- Anti-lock Brake System (ABS) speed sensor and wiring harness, if equipped with ABS
- Rear axle hub with the brake, by removing the 4 bolts

3. Support the hub securely.

4. Support the control arm with a floor jack.

5. Remove or disconnect the following:

- Shock absorber from the control arm, by removing the bolt

➡**The control arm must be supported before removing the bolt for the shock absorber. Leave the floor jack under the control arm. Later, the floor jack will be lowered to remove the coil spring.**

- Cotter pins and nuts by supporting the lower and upper suspension arms

6. Disconnect the upper and lower control arms from the control arm, using tool 09628-62011

7. Remove the coil spring and control arm, as follows:

- Matchmark the toe adjust cam and body.
- Coil spring and upper insulator, by loosening the bolt and lowering the control arm.
- Bolt, toe-adjust cam, 2 attachments, nut and control arm
- Bolt and spring bumper

To install:

8. Install or connect the following:

- Spring bumper. Tighten the bolt to 108 inch lbs. (13 Nm).
- Control arm, 2 attachments, toe-adjust cam, bolt and nut; do not tighten the bolt at this time
- Spring and upper insulator

9. Raise the control arm with a floor jack.

10. Install or connect the following:

- Upper and lower suspension arms to the control arm. Tighten the nuts to 76 ft. lbs. (103 Nm).
- New cotter pins
- Sock absorber to the control arm. Tighten the bolt to 27 ft. lbs. (37 Nm).
- Rear axle hub with the brake. Tighten the 4 bolts to 59 ft. lbs. (80 Nm).

- ABS speed sensor and wiring harness, if equipped. Tighten the ABS speed sensor to 69 inch lbs. (8 Nm) and the wiring harness to 108 inch lbs. (13 Nm).
- Parking brake cable clamp. Tighten the bolt to 14 ft. lbs. (19 Nm).
- Both brake line cable clamps. Tighten the bracket bolt to 13 ft. lbs. (18 Nm) and the clamp bolt to 108 inch lbs. (13 Nm).
- Brake drum
- Rear halfshaft, if equipped with 4WD
- Axle shaft, if equipped with 2WD
- Rear wheel

11. Lower the rear of the vehicle and stabilize the suspension.
12. Install or connect the following:
   - Align the matchmarks to the toe-adjust cam. Tighten the bolt to 98 ft. lbs. (132 Nm).
   - Negative battery cable
13. Check and/or adjust the wheel alignment

PREVIA

1. Before servicing the vehicle, refer to the precautions in the beginning of this section.
2. Support the axle housing with a floor jack.
3. Remove or disconnect the following:

- Wheel
- Shock absorber, by disconnecting to axle housing bolt
- Lateral control arm from axle housing, by removing the nut
- Load Sensing Proportioning Valve (LSPV) spring from the lower control arm by removing the nut
- Brake line from the brake hose at the body bracket
- Clip and the brake hose from the body bracket
- Anti-lock Brake System (ABS) wiring harness bracket
- Parking brake cable from the lower control arm
- Coil spring(s) and insulators

To install:
4. Install or connect the following:
   - Coil spring, by fitting the lower end into the lower control arm's spring seat gap
   - Parking brake cable to the lower control arm
5. Install the lateral control rod to the suspension and tighten the nuts/bolts, as follows:
   - Body side bolt: 156 ft. lbs. (211 Nm).
   - Axle housing side: 43 ft. lbs. (59 Nm)
6. Install or connect the following:
   - Shock absorber to the lower control arm and the nut
   - LSPV spring to the lower control arm. Tighten the nut to 108 inch lbs. (13 Nm).
   - ABS wiring harness bracket, if equipped
   - Brake hose to the bracket and the clip
   - Brake tube to the brake hose
   - Wheels
7. Bleed the brake system.

SIENNA

1. Before servicing the vehicle, refer to the precautions in the beginning of this section.
2. Remove or disconnect the following:
   - Shock absorbers
   - Coil springs

To install:
3. Install or connect the following:
   - Coil springs
   - Raise the axle beam enough to apply tension on the springs
   - Shock absorbers

Lower Ball Joint

REMOVAL & INSTALLATION

RAV4

1. Before servicing the vehicle, refer to the precautions in the beginning of this section.
2. Remove or disconnect the following:
   - Negative battery cable
   - Front wheel(s)
   - Steering knuckle with the axle hub
   - Dust deflector, by prying it from the knuckle
   - Cotter pin and nut from the ball joint stud
   - Lower ball joint from the steering knuckle, using a 2-jaw puller

To install:
3. Install or connect the following:
   - Lower ball joint onto the steering knuckle. Tighten nut to 94 ft. lbs. (127 Nm).

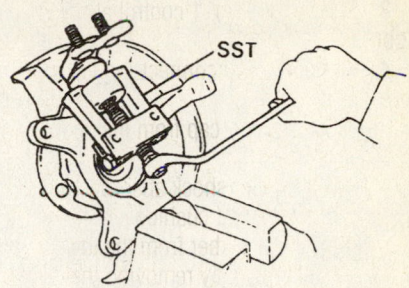

Use a 2-jaw puller to remove the lower ball joint—RAV4

- New cotter pin
- ABS speed sensor, by aligning it the dust deflector hole
- New dust deflector, using a driver
- Steering knuckle and hub
- Front wheel(s)
- Negative battery cable

Except RAV4

1. Before servicing the vehicle, refer to the precautions in the beginning of this section.
2. Remove or disconnect the following:
   - Wheel
   - Steering knuckle with the axle hub
   - Dust deflector, by prying it from the knuckle
   - Cotter pin and nut from the ball joint
   - Ball joint from the steering knuckle, by removing the 2 bolts
   - Lower ball joint, using a Ball Joint Separator tool 09628-62011

To install:
3. Install or connect the following:
   - Lower ball joint. Tighten the nut to 76 ft. lbs. (103 Nm) and both bolts to 94 ft. lbs. (127 Nm).
   - New cotter pin
   - Wheel

Lower Control Arm

REMOVAL & INSTALLATION

Previa

1. Remove or disconnect the following:
   - Front wheels
   - Engine undercovers
   - Both bolts and the lower ball joint from the steering knuckle
   - Both bolts and lower control arm bracket

Turn to Section 5 for brake system applications

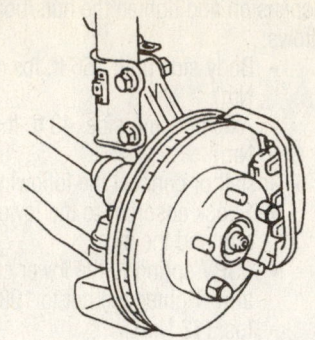

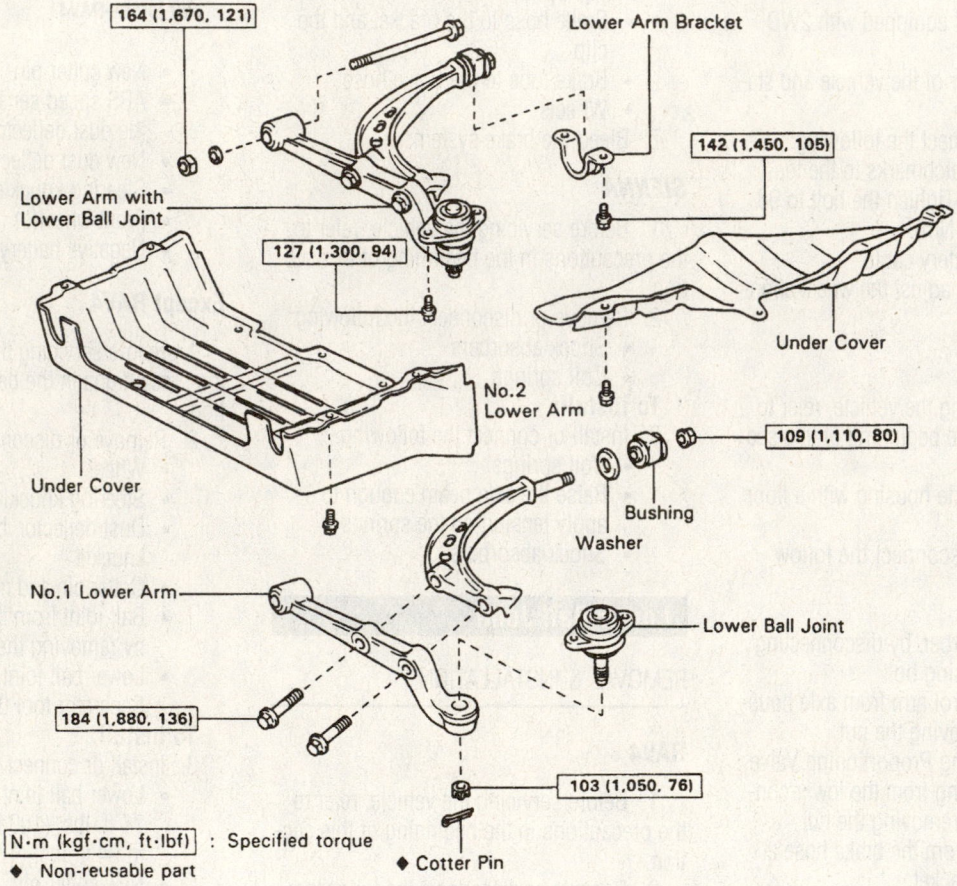

164 (1,670, 121)

Lower Arm Bracket

142 (1,450, 105)

Lower Arm with
Lower Ball Joint

127 (1,300, 94)

Under Cover

No.2
Lower Arm

Under Cover

109 (1,110, 80)

No.1 Lower Arm

Lower Ball Joint

Bushing

Washer

184 (1,880, 136)

103 (1,050, 76)

N·m (kgf·cm, ft·lbf) : Specified torque

◆ Non-reusable part

◆ Cotter Pin

90918G19

View of the common front suspension lower control arms and related components

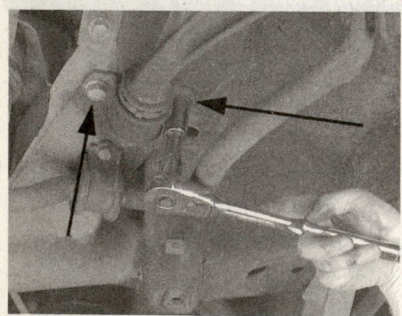

90918P49

· **Remove the lower control arm bracket retaining bolts . . .—Previa**

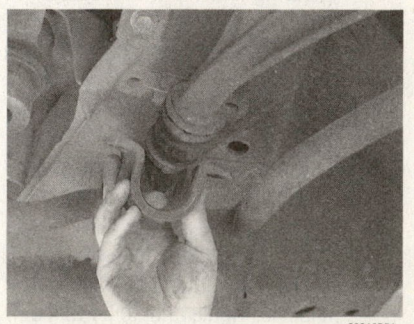

90918P51

. . . then remove the bracket from the control arm—Previa

90918P50

Remove the arm shaft with two wrenches, use one to hold and another to remove the nut—Previa

- Nut and the arm shaft
- Lower control arm with ball joint attached

To install:

2. Install or connect the following:
   - Lower control arm with ball joint
   - Nut and arm shaft; do not completely tighten the nut
   - Arm bracket; do not tighten the bolts
   - Lower ball joint to the steering knuckle. Tighten the bolts to 94 ft. lbs. (127 Nm).
   - Front wheels and hand-tighten the lug nuts
3. Bounce the vehicle to stabilize the suspension.
4. Tighten the arm shaft nut to 121 ft. lbs. (164 Nm) and the suspension bracket bolts to 105 ft. lbs. (142 Nm).
5. Tighten the lug nuts after lowering the vehicle
6. Check and/or adjust the front end alignment.

CONTROL ARM BUSHING REPLACEMENT

Previa

1. Before servicing the vehicle, refer to the precautions in the beginning of this section.
2. Remove or disconnect the following:
   - Lower control arm
   - Loosen the rear bushing nut
   - Bushing and washer

To install:

3. Install or connect the following:
   - Bushing and position the washer as shown
   - Nut. Tighten the nut to 80 ft. lbs. (109 Nm).

➡**Tighten the nut so that the flat surface of the rear bushing is level with the upper surface of the lower control arm.**

   - Lower control arm

Wheel Bearings

ADJUSTMENT

Front and Rear

Check the bearing play in the axial direction and also check the axle hub deviation. The maximum play for both checks should be 0.0020 in. (0.05mm). If greater than the specified maximum, replace the bearing. The wheel bearing is not adjustable.

REMOVAL & INSTALLATION

Front

RAV4

1. Before servicing the vehicle, refer to the precautions in the beginning of this section.
2. Remove or disconnect the following:

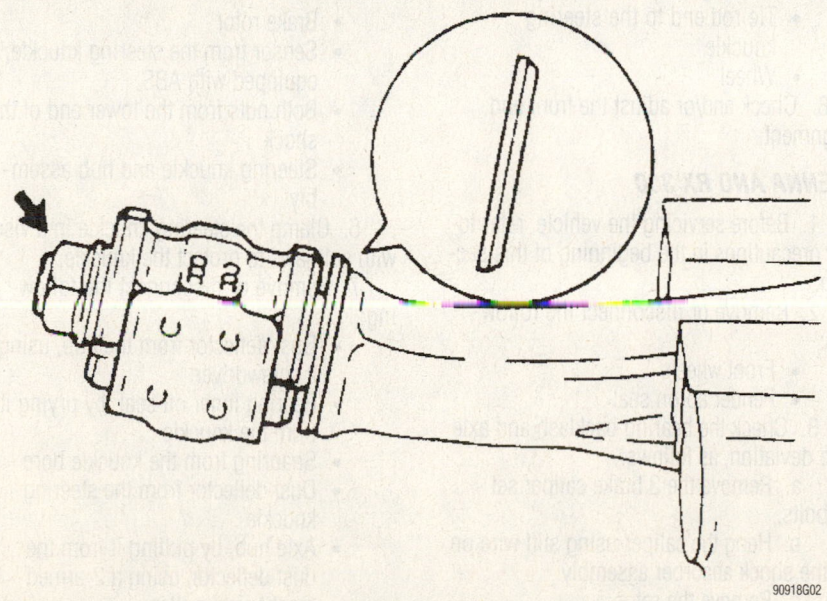

Place the washer into position and secure the bushing with the nut–Previa

- Negative battery cable
- Front wheels
- Cotter pin and lockcap from the halfshaft end
- Halfshaft locknut, by applying the front brakes
- Brake caliper and support it on a wire
3. Matchmark the rotor to the hub.
4. Remove or disconnect the following:
   - Rotor
   - Anti-lock Brake System (ABS) speed sensor from the steering knuckle, if equipped
   - Loosen the strut's lower end nuts
   - Tie rod end from the steering knuckle
   - Lower control arm from the ball joint, by removing the bolt and 2 nuts
   - Halfshaft from the axle hub

➡**Secure the halfshaft aside using a wire. Be careful not to damage the shaft boot or ABS sensor rotor.**

   - Both strut's lower end nuts
   - Steering knuckle
5. Clamp the steering knuckle in a vise with soft jaws to protect the knuckle.
6. Remove or disconnect the following:
   - Dust deflector, by prying it from the hub
   - Ball joint from the steering knuckle
   - Hub from the knuckle, using slide hammer
   - Inner race from the hub, using press and arbor tool
   - 4 bolts and the dust cover
   - Inner oil seal, using Seal Removal tool 09308-00010
   - Outer oil seal, using Seal Removal tool 09308-00010
   - Snapring
7. Install inner race (removed from the hub) on the outside of the bearing
8. Remove the steering knuckle bearing, using a bearing driver

To install:

9. Clean bearing seating surfaces with a clean, dry rag.
10. Install or connect the following:
    - Bearing into the knuckle, using a press and Bearing Installer tool 09608-32010
    - Snapring
    - Dust cover. Tighten the 4 bolts to 74 inch lbs. (8 Nm).
    - New outer oil seal, using a seal driver

➡**Apply multi-purpose grease to the oil seal lip.**

- Hub into the steering knuckle
- New inner oil seal, using a seal driver

➡**Apply multi-purpose grease to the oil seal lip.**

- Lower ball joint to the steering knuckle. Tighten the nut to 94 ft. lbs. (127 Nm).
- New cotter pin
- Dust deflector, by aligning it with the ABS speed sensor hole
- Knuckle to the lower strut and install the bolts
- Lower ball joint to the lower arm. Tighten the bolts to 94 ft. lbs. (127 Nm).
- Tie rod end to the steering knuckle. Tighten the nut to 36 ft. lbs. (49 Nm).
- Halfshaft to the hub and knuckle
- Tighten the lower strut nuts to 117 ft. lbs. (158 Nm).
- ABS speed sensor. Tighten the bolt to 69 inch lbs. (8 Nm).
- Rotor to the hub, by aligning the matchmark
- Brake caliper. Tighten the mounting bolts to 79 ft. lbs. (107 Nm).
- Axle locknut, using an assistant to apply the brakes. Tighten the nut to 159 ft. lbs. (216 Nm).
- Lockcap and a new cotter pin
- Wheel
- Negative battery cable

11. Turn the wheel by hand, verify that the wheel turns without noise and without binding.

12. Check the signal from the ABS sensor.

PREVIA

1. Before servicing the vehicle, refer to the precautions in the beginning of this section.

2. Remove or disconnect the following:
- Wheel
- Steering knuckle

3. For 2WD vehicles, remove the following:
- Grease cap
- Nut caulking, using a chisel and hammer
- Locknut from the hub
- Spacer (w/o ABS) or speed sensor rotor (w/ABS)

4. Remove or disconnect the following:

- Wheel hub from the knuckle, using a Puller tool 09520-00031
- Bearing from the hub, using a press and bearing separator tool
- Oil seal from the axle hub
- Backing plate, by removing the 3 bolts
- Dust deflector and oil seal, if equipped with 4WD
- Bearing snapring from the knuckle
- Inner bearing, by pressing it from the knuckle

To install:

5. Install or connect the following:
- Inner bearing into the steering knuckle, using a press and Arbor tool 09608-10010
- Snapring
- Outer bearing
- Outer oil seal until it is flush with the end surface of the steering knuckle
- Dust deflector with the 3 bolts
- Axle hub, by pressing it onto the steering knuckle

6. On 2WD vehicles,
- Spacer (w/o ABS) or speed sensor rotor (w/ABS)
- New hub nut. Tighten it to 147 ft. lbs. (199 Nm).

➡**Be sure to caulk the nut.**

- Grease cap

7. Install or connect the following:
- New inner oil seal and dust deflector, on 4WD vehicles
- Steering knuckle assembly
- Tie rod end to the steering knuckle
- Wheel

8. Check and/or adjust the front end alignment.

SIENNA AND RX 300

1. Before servicing the vehicle, refer to the precautions in the beginning of this section.

2. Remove or disconnect the following:
- Front wheels
- Fender apron seal

3. Check the bearing backlash and axle hub deviation, as follows:
  a. Remove the 2 brake caliper set bolts.
  b. Hang the caliper using stiff wire on the shock absorber assembly.
  c. Remove the rotor.

  d. Place a dial indicator near the center of the axle hub and check the backlash in the bearing shaft direction.
  e. Backlash maximum should read 0.0020 inch (0.05mm). If greater than specified, replace the bearing.
  f. Using the dial indicator, check the deviation at the surface of the axle hub outside and hub bolt. Maximum is 0.0020 inch (0.05mm). If greater than specified, replace the axle hub.

4. Install the rotor and caliper assembly.

5. Remove or disconnect the following:
- Cotter pin (discard it) and lockcap off the center hub nut
- Driveshaft locknut, by applying the front brakes
- Tie rod end, from the steering knuckle
- Left and right stabilizer end brackets, from the lower arms
- Both nuts and the lower arm from the ball joint
- Driveshaft from the axle hub. Secure the shaft aside using wire.

❋❋ WARNING

Be careful not to damage the shaft boot or Anti-lock Brake System (ABS) sensor rotor.

- Both brake caliper mounting bolts and the caliper.

➡**Support caliper from the vehicle using wire.**

- Brake rotor
- Sensor from the steering knuckle, if equipped with ABS
- Both nuts from the lower end of the shock
- Steering knuckle and hub assembly

6. Clamp the steering knuckle in a vise with soft jaws to protect the knuckle.

7. Remove or disconnect the following:
- Dust deflector from the hub, using a screwdriver
- Bearing inner oil seal, by prying it from the knuckle
- Snapring from the knuckle bore
- Dust deflector from the steering knuckle
- Axle hub, by pulling it from the dust deflector, using a 2-armed mechanical puller

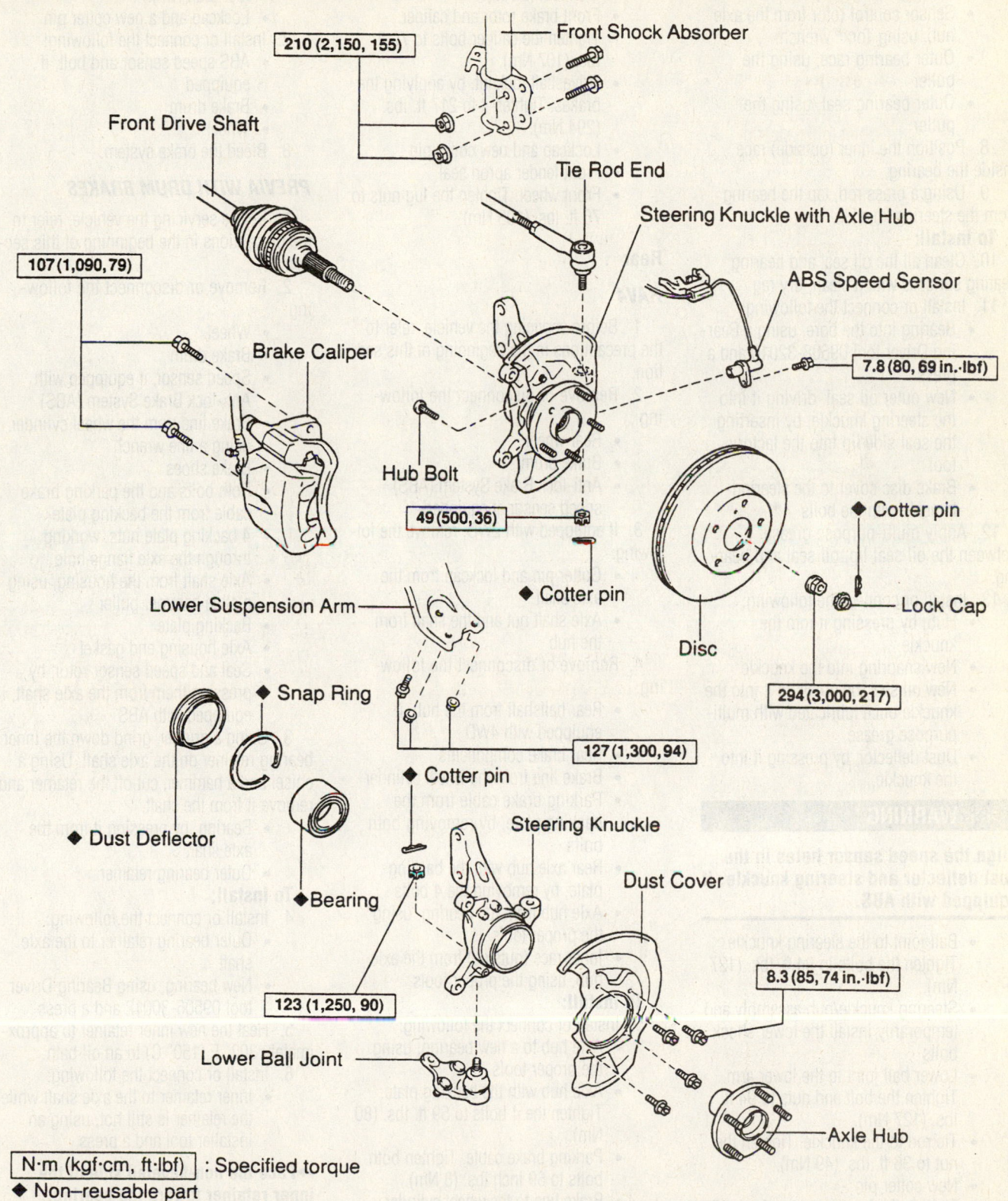

Front Shock Absorber

`210 (2,150, 155)`

Front Drive Shaft

Tie Rod End

Steering Knuckle with Axle Hub

ABS Speed Sensor

`107 (1,090, 79)`

Brake Caliper

`7.8 (80, 69 in.·lbf)`

Hub Bolt

◆ **Cotter pin**

`49 (500, 36)`

Disc

`294 (3,000, 217)`

Lock Cap

Lower Suspension Arm

◆ **Cotter pin**

◆ **Snap Ring**

`127 (1,300, 94)`

◆ **Cotter pin**

Steering Knuckle

◆ **Dust Deflector**

Dust Cover

◆ **Bearing**

`8.3 (85, 74 in.·lbf)`

`123 (1,250, 90)`

Lower Ball Joint

Axle Hub

`N·m (kgf·cm, ft·lbf)` : Specified torque

◆ Non–reusable part

Exploded view of the front hub, bearing and steering knuckle assembly—Sienna

7924ZG82

- Inner (inside) bearing race from the bearing, using the puller
- Sensor control rotor from the axle hub, using Torx® wrench
- Outer bearing race, using the puller
- Outer bearing seal, using the puller

8. Position the inner (outside) race inside the bearing.

9. Using a brass rod, tap the bearing from the steering knuckle.

To install:

10. Clean all the oil seal and bearing seating surfaces with a clean, dry rag.

11. Install or connect the following:
- Bearing into the bore, using a Bearing Driver tool 09608-32010 and a press
- New outer oil seal, driving it into the steering knuckle, by inserting the seal side lip into the factory tool
- Brake disc cover to the steering knuckle with the bolts

12. Apply multi-purpose grease between the oil seal lip, oil seal and bearing.

13. Install or connect the following:
- Hub, by pressing it into the knuckle
- New snapring into the knuckle
- New oil seal, by pressing it into the knuckle once lubricated with multi-purpose grease
- Dust deflector, by pressing it into the knuckle.

❋❋ WARNING

Align the speed sensor holes in the dust deflector and steering knuckle, if equipped with ABS.

- Ball joint to the steering knuckle. Tighten the bolts to 94 ft. lbs. (127 Nm).
- Steering knuckle/hub assembly and temporarily install the lower shock bolts
- Lower ball joint to the lower arm. Tighten the bolt and nuts to 94 ft. lbs. (127 Nm).
- Tie rod to the knuckle. Tighten the nut to 36 ft. lbs. (49 Nm).
- New cotter pin
- Tighten the lower shock nuts to 156 ft. lbs. (211 Nm).
- Both side stabilizer end brackets to the lower arm. Tighten the fasteners to 43 ft. lbs. (58 Nm).

- Front ABS sensor. Tighten it to 69 inch lbs. (8 Nm).
- Front brake rotor and caliper. Tighten the caliper bolts to 79 ft. lbs. (107 Nm).
- Driveshaft locknut, by applying the brakes. Tighten it to 217 ft. lbs. (294 Nm).
- Lockcap and new cotter pin
- Front fender apron seal
- Front wheel. Tighten the lug nuts to 76 ft. lbs. (103 Nm).

Rear

RAV4

1. Before servicing the vehicle, refer to the precautions in the beginning of this section.

2. Remove or disconnect the following:
- Rear wheel
- Brake drum
- Anti-lock Brake System (ABS) speed sensor, if equipped

3. If equipped with 2WD, remove the following:
- Cotter pin and lockcap from the axle shaft
- Axle shaft nut and the shaft from the hub

4. Remove or disconnect the following:
- Rear halfshaft from the hub, if equipped with 4WD
- Rear brake components
- Brake line from the wheel cylinder
- Parking brake cable from the backing plate, by removing both bolts
- Rear axle hub with the backing plate, by removing the 4 bolts
- Axle hub from the bearing, using the proper tools
- Inner race (outside) from the axle hub, using the proper tools

To install:

5. Install or connect the following:
- Axle hub to a new bearing, using the proper tools
- Axle hub with the backing plate. Tighten the 4 bolts to 59 ft. lbs. (80 Nm).
- Parking brake cable. Tighten both bolts to 69 inch lbs. (8 Nm).
- Brake line to the wheel cylinder
- Brake assembly
- Halfshaft, if equipped with 4WD

6. If equipped with 2WD, perform the following:

- Axle shaft. Tighten the nut to 152 ft. lbs. (206 Nm).
- Lockcap and a new cotter pin

7. Install or connect the following:
- ABS speed sensor and bolt, if equipped
- Brake drum
- Wheel

8. Bleed the brake system.

PREVIA WITH DRUM BRAKES

1. Before servicing the vehicle, refer to the precautions in the beginning of this section.

2. Remove or disconnect the following:
- Wheel
- Brake drum
- Speed sensor, if equipped with Anti-lock Brake System (ABS)
- Brake line from the wheel cylinder, using a line wrench
- Brake shoes
- Both bolts and the parking brake cable from the backing plate
- 4 backing plate nuts, working through the axle flange hole
- Axle shaft from the housing, using a slide hammer puller
- Backing plate
- Axle housing end gasket
- Seal and speed sensor rotor, by pressing them from the axle shaft, if equipped with ABS

3. Using a grinder, grind down the inner bearing retainer on the axle shaft. Using a chisel and a hammer, cut off the retainer and remove it from the shaft.
- Bearing, by pressing it from the axle shaft
- Outer bearing retainer

To install:

4. Install or connect the following:
- Outer bearing retainer to the axle shaft
- New bearing, using Bearing Driver tool 09506-30012 and a press

5. Heat the new inner retainer to approximately 302° F (150° C) in an oil bath.

6. Install or connect the following:
- Inner retainer to the axle shaft while the retainer is still hot, using an installer tool and a press

➡**Face the non-beveled side of the inner retainer toward the bearing.**

- Speed sensor rotor, if equipped with ABS
- New oil seal, using an installer and a press

- New axle housing gasket on the rear axle housing, by applying liquid sealant on it
- Backing plate
- Rear axle shaft, using a suitable tool

➡**Be careful not to damage the oil seal and speed sensor rotor (w/ABS).**

- Tighten the backing plate nuts to 59 ft. lbs. (80 Nm).
- Parking brake cable, brake shoes and drum
- Brake line to the wheel cylinder
- Rear wheel

7. Bleed the brake system.

8. Road test the vehicle for proper operation.

PREVIA WITH DISC BRAKES

1. Before servicing the vehicle, refer to the precautions in the beginning of this section.

2. Remove or disconnect the following:

- Rear wheel
- Speed sensor, if equipped with Anti-lock Brake System (ABS)
- Brake line from the brake hose, using a line wrench
- Clip and brake hose from the axle bracket
- Both bolts and the brake caliper support
- Disc and parking brake shoes
- Parking brake cable
- Backing plate, by removing the 4 nuts
- Axle shaft from the housing, using a slide hammer puller
- Axle housing end gasket
- 4 bolts and the backing plate from the axle shaft
- Seal and speed sensor rotor, by pressing them from the axle shaft, if equipped with ABS.

3. Using a grinder, grind down the inner bearing retainer on the axle shaft. Using a chisel and a hammer, cut off the retainer and remove it from the shaft.

❈❈ WARNING

When removing the bearing, be careful not to damage the axle shaft.

4. Remove or disconnect the following:
- Bearing from the axle shaft, if equipped with ABS

- Outer bearing retainer

To install:

5. Install or connect the following:

- New retainer gasket and bearing on the backing plate
- 4 backing plate bolts, using a socket wrench and hammer
- Backing plate to the axle shaft
- New bearing, using a Bearing Driver tool 09506-30012 and a press

6. Heat the new inner retainer to approximately 302° F (150° C) in an oil bath.

7. Install or connect the following:

- Inner retainer to the axle shaft, using an installer and a press, while the retainer is still hot

➡**Face the non-beveled side of the inner retainer toward the bearing.**

- Speed sensor rotor, if equipped with ABS
- New oil seal, using an installer and a press
- New end gasket on the rear axle housing, lubricated with liquid sealant
- Rear axle shaft, using a suitable tool

➡**Be careful not to damage the oil seal and speed sensor rotor (w/ABS).**

- Tighten the backing plate nuts to 59 ft. lbs. (80 Nm).
- Parking brake cable and parking brake shoes
- Rotor
- Brake caliper support. Tighten both bolts to 65 ft. lbs. (88 Nm).
- Brake hose to the axle bracket and the clip
- Brake line to the brake hose
- Speed sensor if equipped with ABS brakes
- Wheels

SIENNA AND RX 300 WITH 2WD

1. Before servicing the vehicle, refer to the precautions in the beginning of this section.

2. Remove or disconnect the following:
- Rear wheel
- Brake drum, if equipped

3. If equipped with disk brakes, remove the following:

- Flexible brake hose from the rear strut assembly

- Brake caliper and support it on using wire
- Brake rotor

4. Remove or disconnect the following:

- Anti-lock Brake System (ABS) speed sensor connector
- 4 rear axle hub assembly nuts
- Hub assembly

To install:

5. Install or connect the following:
- New hub assembly. Tighten the nuts to 59 ft. lbs. (80 Nm).
- ABS speed sensor

6. If equipped with disc brakes, install the following:

- Brake rotor
- Brake caliper. Tighten the mounting bolts to 34 ft. lbs. (47 Nm).
- Flexible brake hose to the rear strut assembly. Tighten the mounting bolt to 21 ft. lbs. (29 Nm).

7. Install or connect the following:
- Brake drum, if equipped
- Wheels

8. Test drive the vehicle.

RX 300 WITH 4WD

1. Before servicing the vehicle, refer to the precautions in the beginning of this section.

2. Remove or disconnect the following:
- Rear wheel
- Cotter pin, lockcap and the half-shaft locknut
- Flexible brake hose from the rear strut assembly
- Brake caliper and support it on a wire
- Brake rotor
- Anti-lock Brake System (ABS) speed sensor connector
- Parking brake assembly
- Parking brake cable
- Loosen both lower strut mount bolts
- Strut rod rear bolt and nut; then, separate it from the axle carrier
- No. 1 and No. 2 lower suspension arms
- Both lower strut mount bolts
- Rear axle hub with the carrier
- Axle hub assembly from the axle carrier, using a slide hammer
- Inner race from the axle carrier, using a press and a bearing driver
- 4 bolts and the backing plate

Turn to Section 5 for brake system applications

- Inner and outer oil seals, using a seal remover
- Snapring from the axle carrier
- Wheel bearing from the axle carrier, using a press and a bearing driver

To install:

3. Install or connect the following:
   - New bearing, using a press
   - New snapring

➡ **Apply MP grease to the lip of the new oil seal.**

- New outer oil seal, using a hammer and a seal driver
- Backing plate. Tighten the bolts to 53 ft. lbs. (72 Nm).
- Axle hub, by pressing it onto the axle carrier

➡ **Apply MP grease to the lip of the new oil seal.**

- New inner oil seal, using a hammer and a seal driver

4. The completion of installation is the

reverse of the removal procedure noting the following items:

- Tighten the No. 1 and No. 2 lower suspension arms to 131 ft. lbs. (177 Nm)
- Tighten the strut rod mount to 91 ft. lbs. (123 Nm)
- Tighten both lower strut bolts to 188 ft. lbs. (255 Nm)
- Tighten the halfshaft locknut to 159 ft. lbs. (216 Nm)

5. Install the rear wheels.

PRECAUTIONS

Before servicing any vehicle, please be sure to read all of the following precautions, which deal with personal safety, prevention of component damage, and important points to take into consideration when servicing a motor vehicle:

• Never open, service or drain the radiator or cooling system when the engine is hot; serious burns can occur from the steam and hot coolant.

• Observe all applicable safety precautions when working around fuel. Whenever servicing the fuel system, always work in a well-ventilated area. Do not allow fuel spray or vapors to come in contact with a spark, open flame or excessive heat (a hot drop light, for example). Keep a dry chemical fire extinguisher near the work area. Always keep fuel in a container specifically designed for fuel storage; also, always properly seal fuel containers to avoid the possibility of fire or explosion. Refer to the additional fuel system precautions later in this section.

• Fuel injection systems often remain pressurized, even after the engine has been turned **OFF**. The fuel system pressure must be relieved before disconnecting any fuel lines. Failure to do so may result in fire and/or personal injury.

• Brake fluid often contains polyglycol ethers and polyglycols. Avoid contact with the eyes and wash your hands thoroughly after handling brake fluid. If you do get brake fluid in your eyes, flush your eyes with clean, running water for 15 minutes. If eye irritation persists, or if you have taken brake fluid internally, IMMEDIATELY seek medical assistance.

• The EPA warns that prolonged contact with used engine oil may cause a number of skin disorders, including cancer! You should make every effort to minimize your exposure to used engine oil. Protective gloves should be worn when changing oil. Wash your hands and any other exposed skin areas as soon as possible after exposure to used engine oil. Soap and water, or waterless hand cleaner should be used.

• All new vehicles are now equipped with an air bag system, often referred to as a Supplemental Restraint System (SRS) or Supplemental Inflatable Restraint (SIR) system. The system must be disabled before performing service on or around system components, steering column, instrument panel components, wiring and sensors.

Failure to follow safety and disabling procedures could result in accidental air bag deployment, possible personal injury and unnecessary system repairs.

• Always wear safety goggles when working with, or around, the air bag system. When carrying a non-deployed air bag, be sure the bag and trim cover are pointed away from your body. When placing a non-deployed air bag on a work surface, always face the bag and trim cover upward, away from the surface. This will reduce the motion of the module if it is accidentally deployed. Refer to the additional air bag system precautions later in this section.

• Clean, high quality brake fluid from a sealed container is essential to the safe and proper operation of the brake system. You should always buy the correct type of brake fluid for your vehicle. If the brake fluid becomes contaminated, completely flush the system with new fluid. Never reuse any brake fluid. Any brake fluid that is removed from the system should be discarded. Also, do not allow any brake fluid to come in contact with a painted surface; it will damage the paint.

• Never operate the engine without the proper amount and type of engine oil; doing so WILL result in severe engine damage.

• Timing belt maintenance is extremely important! Many models utilize an interference type, non-freewheeling engine. If the timing belt breaks, the valves in the cylinder head may strike the pistons, causing potentially serious (also time consuming and expensive)

engine damage. Refer to the maintenance interval charts in the front of this manual for the recommended replacement interval for the timing belt, and to the timing belt section for belt replacement and inspection.

• Disconnecting the negative battery cable on some vehicles may interfere with the functions of the on-board computer system(s) and may require the computer to undergo a relearning process once the negative battery cable is reconnected.

• When servicing drum brakes, only disassemble and assemble one side at a time, leaving the remaining side intact for reference.

ENGINE REPAIR

➡**Disconnecting the negative battery cable on some vehicles may interfere with the functions of the on board computer system. The computer may undergo a relearning process once the negative battery cable is reconnected.**

Alternator

REMOVAL

3.4L Engine

1. Remove or disconnect the following:
   • Negative battery cable

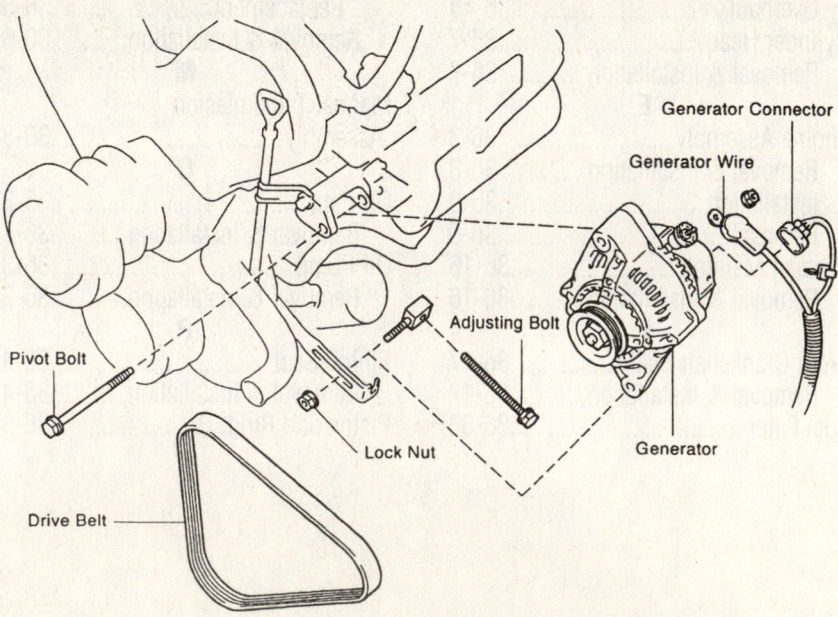

Exploded view of the alternator and drive belt—3.4L Engine

86822077

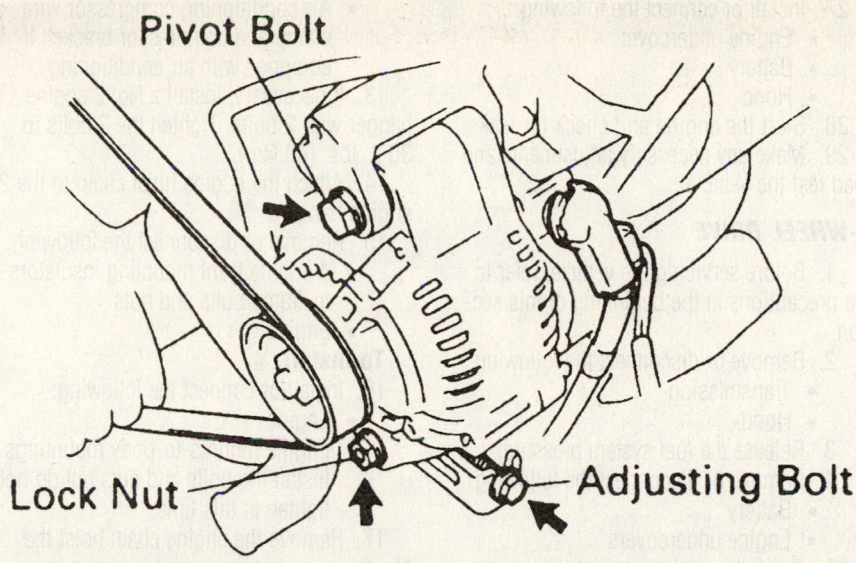

Pivot Bolt

Lock Nut

Adjusting Bolt

86822078

Locations of the adjusting and pivot bolts and the locknut—3.4L Engine

- Alternator wiring
- Alternator locknut, pivot bolt, nut and adjusting bolt
- Drive belt
- Alternator

4.7L Engine

1. Before servicing the vehicle, refer to the precautions in the beginning of this section.
2. Drain the cooling system.
3. Remove or disconnect the following:
   - Negative battery cable
   - Accessory drive belt
   - Engine under cover
   - Radiator
   - Power steering pump pulley
   - Alternator harness connectors
   - Alternator

INSTALLATION

3.4L Engine

Install or connect the following:
- Alternator
- Drive belt. Tighten the locknut 25 ft. lbs. (33 Nm) and the pivot bolt 38 ft. lbs. (51 Nm).
  - Alternator wiring
  - Negative battery cable

4.7L Engine

1. Install or connect the following:
   - Alternator. Tighten the fasteners to 29 ft. lbs. (39 Nm).

- Alternator harness connectors
- Power steering pump pulley
- Radiator
- Engine under cover
- Accessory drive belt
- Negative battery cable
2. Fill the cooling system.
3. Start the engine and check for leaks.

Ignition Timing

ADJUSTMENT

The engines are equipped with a Distributorless Ignition System (DIS). No timing adjustment is possible.

Engine Assembly

REMOVAL & INSTALLATION

3.4L Engine

2-WHEEL DRIVE

1. Before servicing the vehicle, refer to the precautions in the beginning of this section.
2. Properly relieve the fuel system pressure.
3. Remove or disconnect the following:
   - Hood
   - Battery
   - Engine under covers
4. Drain the engine coolant.
5. Drain the engine oil.

- Radiator
- Fan with the fluid coupling and fan pulleys
- Air cleaner cap
- Air cleaner case and filter
6. Disconnect the following hoses:
   - Heater hoses
   - Brake booster vacuum hose
   - Evaporative Emissions (EVAP) hose
   - Vacuum hose
   - Fuel return hose
   - Fuel inlet hose
7. Detach the starter wire and connectors, as follows:
   - Ground strap, by removing the bolt
   - Starter wires
8. Remove or disconnect the following:
   - Alternator connector and wire
   - Throttle cable, if equipped with an automatic transmission
   - Cruise control cable, if equipped with cruise control
9. Disconnect the engine wiring harness, as follows:
   - Glove box door
   - Lower the finish No. 2 panel
   - Heater to register duct
   - 3 Engine Control Module (ECM) connectors
   - 2 cassette connectors and the 2 wire clamps from the lower finish panel
   - Engine wiring harness clamp
10. Remove or disconnect the following:
    - Igniter connector
    - Ground strap
    - 2 engine wiring harness retainer-to-cowl panel nuts and pull out the engine wiring harness
11. If equipped with a manual transmission, remove or disconnect the following:
    - Shift lever knob
    - 4 shift lever boot screws
    - 6 shift lever assembly bolts, the assembly and gasket
12. Remove or disconnect the following:
    - Driveshaft from the transmission
    - Speedometer cable

➡ Do not lose the felt protector and washers.

- Front exhaust pipe
- Clutch release cylinder, if equipped with a manual transmission
- Nut and the control cable
13. Place a jack under the transmission.
14. Remove or disconnect the following:
    - Transmission rear mounting bracket by removing the 8 bolts

- Bolt and the air conditioning compressor wire clamp, if equipped with air conditioning

15. If necessary, install a No. 2 engine hanger with 2 bolts. Tighten the 2 bolts to 30 ft. lbs. (40 Nm).

16. Attach the engine hoist chain to the 2 engine hangers.

17. Remove or disconnect the following:
- 4 engine front mounting insulators-to-frame bolts and nuts
- Engine from the transmission

To install:

18. Install or connect the following:
- Engine to the transmission
- Engine mounts to the body mountings. Install the bolts and nuts but do not tighten at this time.

19. Remove the engine chain hoist the No. 2 engine hanger.

20. Install or connect the following:
- Air conditioning wire with the bolt, if equipped with air conditioning
- Transmission mounting bracket. Tighten the frame bolts to 43 ft. lbs. (58 Nm) and the mounting insulator bolts to 13 ft. lbs. (18 Nm).
- Tighten the engine mounting nuts and bolts to 28 ft. lbs. (38 Nm).
- Control cable
- Clutch release cylinder, if equipped with a manual transmission. Torque the bolts to 9 ft. lbs. (12 Nm).

21. Install or connect the following:
- Front exhaust pipe
- Speedometer cable
- Driveshaft

22. If equipped with a manual transmission, install or connect the following:
- 6 shift lever assembly bolts, the assembly and gasket
- 4 shift lever boot screws
- Shift lever knob

23. Install or connect the following:
- All engine wiring harness, hoses and cables
- Fan with the fluid coupling and fan pulleys. Tighten the nuts to 48 inch lbs. (5.4 Nm).
- Air cleaner case and air filter
- Radiator

24. Install or connect the following hoses:
- Fuel inlet hose
- Fuel return hose
- Vacuum hose
- Evaporative Emissions (EVAP) hose
- Brake booster vacuum hose
- Heater hoses

25. Fill the engine with oil.

26. Fill the engine and radiator with coolant.

27. Install or connect the following:
- Engine undercover
- Battery
- Hood

28. Start the engine and check for leaks.

29. Make any necessary adjustments and road test the vehicle.

4-WHEEL DRIVE

1. Before servicing the vehicle, refer to the precautions in the beginning of this section.

2. Remove or disconnect the following:
- Transmission
- Hood

3. Release the fuel system pressure.

4. Remove or disconnect the following:
- Battery
- Engine undercovers

5. Drain the engine coolant.

6. Drain the engine oil.

7. Remove or disconnect the following:
- Radiator
- Fan with the fluid coupling and fan pulleys
- Air cleaner cap
- Mass Air Flow (MAF) meter and the resonator
- Cruise control cable, if equipped with cruise control
- Throttle cable, if equipped with an automatic transmission

8. Disconnect the following hoses:
- Heater hoses
- Brake booster vacuum hose
- Evaporative Emissions (EVAP) hose
- Automatic Disconnecting Differential (ADD) vacuum hose
- Vacuum hose
- Fuel return hose
- Fuel inlet hose

9. Detach the starter wire and connectors, as follows:
- Ground strap, by removing the bolt
- 3 starter wire clamps and connector

10. Detach the alternator connector and wire.

11. Disconnect the engine wiring harness, as follows:
- Glove box door
- Lower the finish No. 2 panel
- 3 Engine Control Module (ECM) connectors
- 2 cassette connectors and the 2 wire clamps from the lower finish panel
- Igniter connector
- Ground strap
- Engine wiring harness clamp

12. Remove or disconnect the following:
- 2 engine wiring harness retainer-to-cowl panel nuts and wiring harness

- Air conditioning compressor wire clamp and compressor bracket, if equipped with air conditioning

13. If necessary, install a No. 2 engine hanger with 2 bolts. Tighten the 2 bolts to 30 ft. lbs. (40 Nm).

14. Attach the engine hoist chain to the 2 engine hangers.

15. Remove or disconnect the following:
- 4 engine front mounting insulators-to-frame bolts and nuts
- Engine

To install:

16. Install or connect the following:
- Engine
- Engine mounts-to-body mountings. Install the bolts and nuts but do not tighten at this time.

17. Remove the engine chain hoist the No. 2 engine hanger.

18. Install or connect the following:
- Air conditioning wire with the bolt and the compressor bracket, if equipped with air conditioning
- Tighten the engine mounting nuts and bolts to 28 ft. lbs. (38 Nm).

19. Install the engine wiring harness, as follows:
- Engine wiring harness clamp
- Ground strap
- Igniter connector
- 2 cassette connectors and the 2 wire clamps from the lower finish panel
- 3 Engine Control Module (ECM) connectors
- Lower the finish No. 2 panel
- Glove box door

20. Install or connect the following:
- Cruise control cable, if equipped with cruise control
- Throttle cable, if equipped with an automatic transmission

21. Connect the following hoses:
- Fuel inlet hose
- Fuel return hose
- Vacuum hose
- Automatic Disconnecting Differential (ADD) vacuum hose
- Evaporative Emissions (EVAP) hose
- Brake booster vacuum hose
- Heater hoses

22. Install or connect the following:
- All wires, hoses and cables
- Fan with the fluid coupling and fan pulleys. Tighten the nuts to 48 inch lbs. (5.4 Nm).
- Air cleaner case and air filter
- MAF meter, resonator and the air cleaner cap
- Radiator

23. Fill the engine with oil.

24. Fill the engine and radiator with coolant.

25. Install or connect the following:
- Transmission and refill it with transmission oil
- Engine undercover
- Battery
- Hood

26. Start the engine, make any necessary adjustments and check for leaks.

4.7L Engine

1. Before servicing the vehicle, refer to the precautions in the beginning of this section.
2. Relieve the fuel system pressure.
3. Drain the cooling system.
4. Drain the engine oil.
5. Remove or disconnect the following:
- Battery and tray
- Hood
- Engine appearance cover
- Air intake pipe
- Engine under covers
- Coolant recovery tank
- Radiator hoses
- Radiator and fan shroud
- Accessory drive belt
- Cooling fan and pulley
- Powertrain Control Module (PCM) harness connectors and pass the wiring harness through the firewall
- Accelerator cable
- Power steering vacuum hoses
- Alternator harness connectors
- Heater hoses
- Engine control wiring harness and grommet at the firewall
- Ground cable connector
- Fuel lines
- Evaporative Emissions (EVAP) canister hoses
- Wire clamp at right inner fender
- Negative battery cable at the relay box and right inner fender
- Positive battery cable
- Center console
- Transmission shift lever assembly
- Transfer case shift lever and rod
- Exhaust front pipes
- Stabilizer bar
- Front and rear driveshafts
- A/C compressor
- Power steering pump

6. Attach a hoist to the engine lifting eyes.
7. Remove or disconnect the following:
- Transfer case skid plate
- Left and right motor mounts
- Transmission mount crossmember

8. Attach a hoist to the engine lifting eyes and raise the powertrain out of the vehicle.

To install:

9. Lower the powertrain into the vehicle.
10. Install or connect the following:
- Transmission mount crossmember. Tighten the bolts to 37 ft. lbs. (50 Nm) and the nuts to 55 ft. lbs. (74 Nm).
- Transfer case skid plate
- Left and right motor mounts. Tighten the fasteners to 22 ft. lbs. (30 Nm).
- Power steering pump. Tighten the bolts to 13 ft. lbs. (17 Nm).
- A/C compressor. Tighten the bolts to 36 ft. lbs. (49 Nm).
- Front driveshaft. Tighten the fasteners to 59 ft. lbs. (80 Nm).
- Rear driveshaft. Tighten the fasteners to 78 ft. lbs. (106 Nm).
- Stabilizer bar. Tighten the bracket bolts to 13 ft. lbs. (18 Nm) and the link nuts to 18 ft. lbs. (25 Nm).
- Exhaust front pipes
- Transfer case shift lever and rod
- Transmission shift lever assembly
- Center console
- Positive battery cable
- Negative battery cable at the relay box and right inner fender
- Wire clamp at right inner fender
- EVAP canister hoses
- Fuel lines
- Ground cable connector
- Engine control wiring harness and grommet at the firewall
- Heater hoses
- Alternator harness connectors
- Power steering vacuum hoses
- Accelerator cable
- PCM harness connectors
- Cooling fan and pulley
- Accessory drive belt
- Radiator and fan shroud
- Radiator hoses
- Coolant recovery tank
- Engine under covers
- Air intake pipe
- Engine appearance cover
- Hood
- Battery and tray

11. Fill the crankcase to the correct level.
12. Fill the cooling system.
13. Start the engine and check for leaks.

REMOVAL & INSTALLATION

3.4L Engine

1. Before servicing the vehicle, refer to the precautions in the beginning of this section.
2. Remove or disconnect the following:
- Negative battery cable
- Engine undercover

3. Drain the engine coolant.
4. Remove the upper radiator hose.
5. Remove the power steering drive belt, as follows:
- Stretch the belt and loosen the fan pulley mounting nuts
- Loosen the lockbolt, pivot bolt and the adjusting bolt
- Drive belt

6. Remove or disconnect the following:
- Air conditioning drive belt, by loosening the idler pulley nut and adjusting bolt
- Lockbolt, pivot bolt and the adjusting bolt
- Alternator drive belt
- No. 2 fan shroud, by removing the 2 clips
- Fan with the fluid coupling and fan pulleys
- Power steering pump and move it aside without disconnecting the lines from the pump
- Compressor from the engine and move it aside without disconnecting the compressor lines, if equipped with air conditioning
- Air conditioning bracket, if equipped with air conditioning

7. Remove the No. 2 timing belt cover, as follows:
- Camshaft Position (CMP) sensor connector from the No. 2 timing belt cover
- 3 spark plug wire clamps from the No. 2 timing belt cover
- 6 bolts and the timing belt cover

8. Remove the fan bracket, as follows:
- Power steering adjusting strut, by removing the nut
- Fan bracket, by removing the bolt and nut

9. Set the No. 1 cylinder to Top Dead Center (TDC) of the compression stroke, as follows:

Timing belt service is covered in Section 4 of this manual

a. Turn the crankshaft pulley and align its groove with the timing mark **0** of the No. 1 timing belt cover.

b. Check that the timing marks of the camshaft timing pulleys and the No. 3 timing belt cover are aligned. If not, turn the crankshaft pulley 1 revolution (360 degrees).

10. Remove the camshaft timing pulleys, as follows:

a. Remove the timing belt tensioner by alternately loosening the 2 bolts.

b. Using Variable Wrench Set No. 09960-10010, remove the pulley bolt, the timing pulley and the knock pin.

c. Remove the 2 timing pulleys with the timing belt.

11. Remove or disconnect the following:

- Thermostat
- No. 2 oil cooler hose, from the water pump
- Water pump, by removing the 7 bolts

12. Thoroughly clean the mating surfaces.

To install:

13. Install or connect the following:

- Apply sealant (PN 08826-00100) to the water pump

Parts must be assembled within 5 minutes of application. Otherwise the material must be removed and reapplied.

- Water pump. Tighten the bolts to 14 ft. lbs. (20 Nm).
- No. 2 oil cooler hose
- Thermostat
- Left camshaft timing pulley. Tighten the pulley bolt to 81 ft. lbs. (110 Nm).

14. Set the No. 1 cylinder to TDC of the compression stroke.

15. Connect the timing belt to the left camshaft timing pulley. Check that the installation mark on the timing belt is aligned with the end of the No. 1 timing belt cover, as follows:

a. Using Variable Pin Wrench Set 09960-01000, slightly turn the left camshaft timing pulley clockwise. Align the installation mark on the timing belt with the timing mark of the camshaft timing pulley and hang the timing belt on the left camshaft timing pulley.

b. Align the timing marks of the left camshaft pulley and the No. 3 timing belt cover.

c. Check that the timing belt has tension between the crankshaft timing pulley and the left camshaft timing pulley.

16. Install the right camshaft timing pulley and the timing belt.

17. Set the timing belt tensioner, as follows:

a. Using a press, slowly press in the pushrod using 220–2,205 lbs. (981–9,807 N) of force.

b. Align the holes of the pushrod and housing, pass a 1.5mm hexagon wrench through the holes to keep the setting position of the pushrod.

c. Release the press and install the dust boot to the tensioner.

d. Install the timing belt tensioner and alternately tighten the bolts to 20 ft. lbs. (28 Nm).

e. Using pliers, remove the 1.5mm hexagon wrench from the belt tensioner.

18. Check the valve timing, as follows:

a. Slowly turn the crankshaft pulley 2 revolutions from the TDC-to-TDC; always turn the crankshaft pulley clockwise.

b. Check that each pulley aligns with the timing marks. If the timing marks do not align, remove the timing belt and reinstall it.

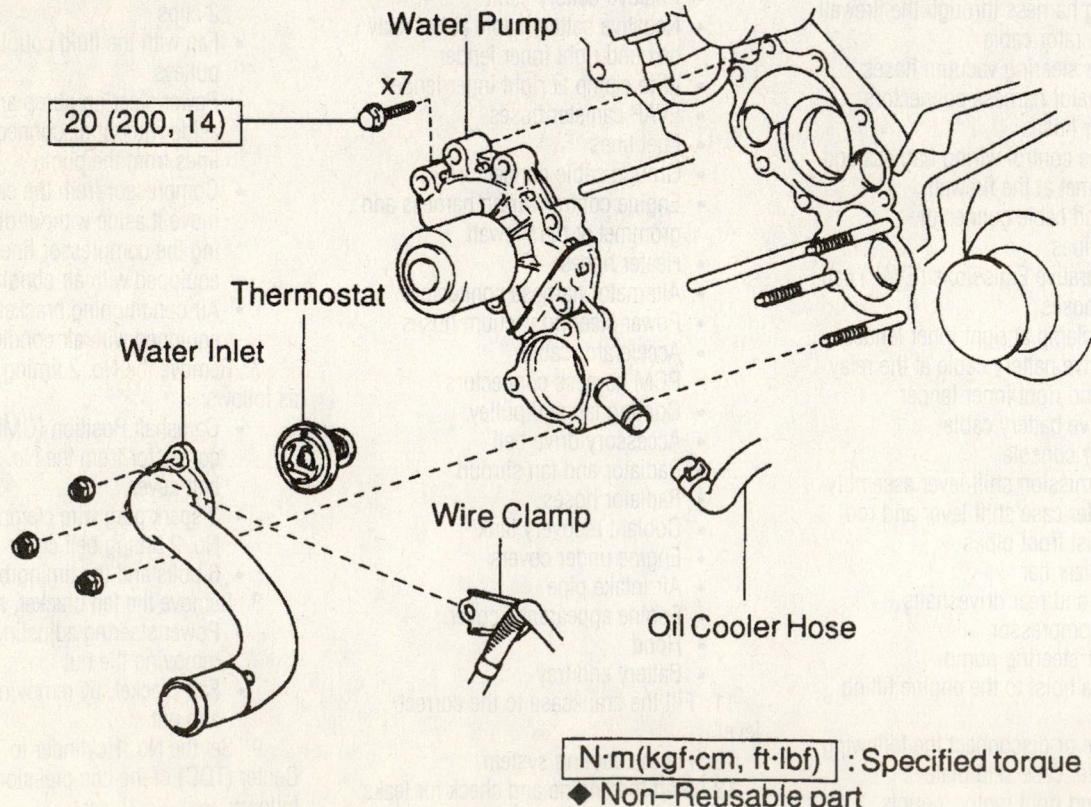

`N·m(kgf·cm, ft·lbf)` : Specified torque
◆ Non-Reusable part

Exploded view of the water pump mounting—3.4L engine

7924YG08

19. Install or connect the following:
    - Fan bracket, with the bolt and nut
    - Remaining components
    - Negative battery cable
20. Fill with engine coolant.
21. Start the engine and check for leaks.

4.7L Engine

1. Before servicing the vehicle, refer to the precautions in the beginning of this section.
2. Drain the cooling system.
3. Remove or disconnect the following:
    - Negative battery cable
    - Timing belt. Refer to the Timing Belt unit repair section.
    - No. 2 idler pulley

- Radiator hose
- Bypass hose
- Water inlet housing assembly
- Water pump

To install:

4. Install or connect the following:
    - Water pump. Use a new gasket and tighten the bolts to 15 ft. lbs. (21 Nm). Tighten the stud bolt and nut to 13 ft. lbs. (18 Nm).
    - Water inlet housing assembly. Use a new O-ring and apply sealant as shown. Tighten the bolts to 13 ft. lbs. (18 Nm).
    - Bypass hose
    - Radiator hose
    - No. 2 idler pulley

- Timing belt
- Negative battery cable
5. Fill the cooling system.
6. Start the engine and check for leaks.

Cylinder Head

REMOVAL & INSTALLATION

3.4L Engine

1. Before servicing the vehicle, refer to the precautions in the beginning of this section.
2. Disconnect the negative battery cable.
3. Relieve the fuel system pressure.
4. Remove the engine undercover.
5. Drain the cooling system.
6. Remove or disconnect the following:
    - Front exhaust pipe
    - Air cleaner cap
    - Mass Air Flow (MAF) meter and resonator
7. Disconnect the following cables:
    - Actuator cable from the bracket, if equipped with cruise control
    - Accelerator cable
    - Throttle cable, if equipped with an automatic transmission
    - Heater hose
    - Upper radiator hose
    - Power steering drive belt
    - Air conditioning drive belt, by loosening the idle pulley nut and adjusting bolt
    - Loosen the lockbolt, pivot bolt and adjusting bolt and the alternator drive belt

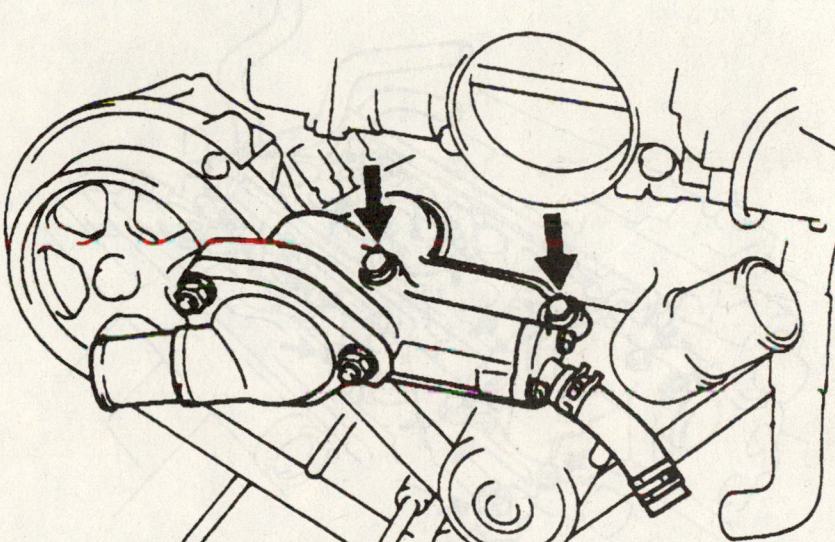

Water inlet housing attaching bolts—4.7L engine

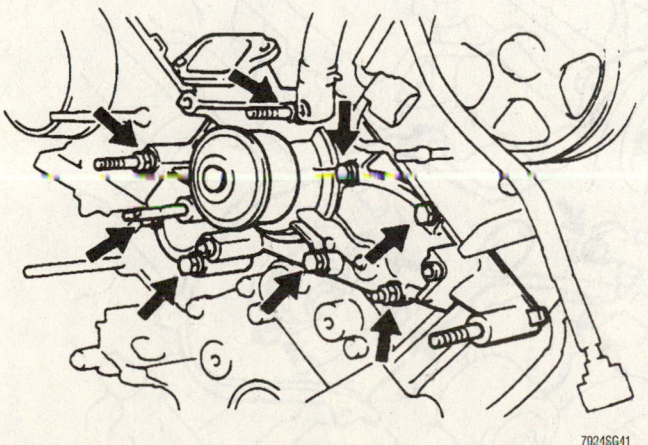

Water pump mounting bolts, stud bolts and nut locations—4.7L engine

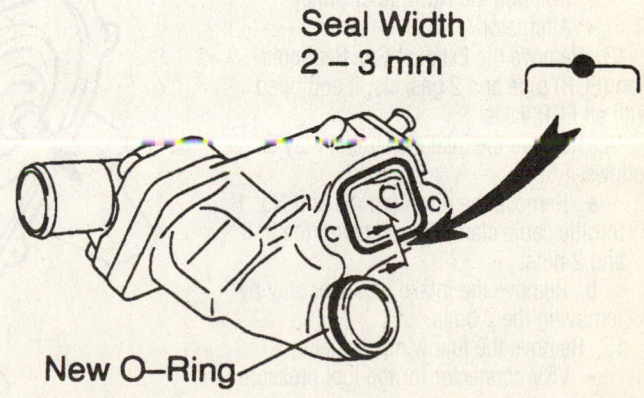

Seal Width
2 – 3 mm

New O-Ring

Water inlet housing sealant application—4.7L engine

- No. 2 fan shroud by removing the 2 clips
- Fan with the fluid coupling and fan pulleys
- Power steering pump and move it aside without disconnecting the pump lines
- Compressor and move it aside without disconnecting the compressor lines, if equipped with air conditioning
- Air conditioning bracket, if equipped with air conditioning
- Spark plug wires with the ignition coils
- Spark plugs
- No. 2 timing belt cover

8. Remove the fan bracket, as follows:

a. Remove the power steering adjusting strut by removing the nut.

b. Remove the fan bracket by removing the bolt and nut.

9. Set the No. 1 cylinder at Top Dead Center (TDC) of the compression stroke.

a. Turn the crankshaft pulley and align its groove with the timing mark **0** on the No. 1 timing belt cover.

b. Check that the timing marks of the camshaft timing pulleys and the No. 3 timing belt cover are aligned. If not, turn the crankshaft pulley 1 revolution (360 degrees).

10. Remove the timing belt tensioner by alternately loosening the 2 bolts.

11. Remove the camshaft timing pulleys, as follows:

a. Using Variable Pin Wrench Set tool 09960-10010, remove the pulley bolt, the timing pulley and the knock pin.

b. Remove the 2 timing pulleys with the timing belt.

12. Remove or disconnect the following:

- Bolt and the No. 2 idler pulley
- Alternator

13. Remove the Exhaust Gas Recirculation (EGR) pipe and 2 gaskets, if equipped with an EGR valve

14. Remove the intake chamber stay as follows:

a. Remove the oil filler tube and No. 1 throttle cable clamp by removing the bolt and 2 nuts.

b. Remove the intake chamber stay by removing the 2 bolts.

15. Remove the following connectors:

- VSV connector for the fuel pressure control.
- Throttle position sensor
- IAC valve connector
- EGR valve gas temperature sensor, if equipped
- Vacuum Switching Valve (VSV)

connector for the EGR valve, if equipped

16. Disconnect the following hoses:

- Positive Crankcase Ventilation (PCV) hoses
- Water bypass hoses.
- Air assist hose from the intake air connector
- 2 vacuum sensing hoses from the VSV
- Evaporative Emissions (EVAP) hose
- Air hose, from the power steering
- Air hose from the air conditioning idle up valve, if equipped with air conditioning

17. Remove or disconnect the following:

- 4 bolts, 2 nuts and the air intake chamber assembly
- Intake air connector

18. Disconnect the engine wiring harness from the intake manifold, as follows:

- Oil pressure sensor connector
- Crankshaft position sensor connector
- 6 injector connectors
- Engine Coolant Temperature (ECT) sender gauge connector
- ECT sensor connector
- Knock (KS) sensor connector
- Camshaft Position (CMP) sensor connector

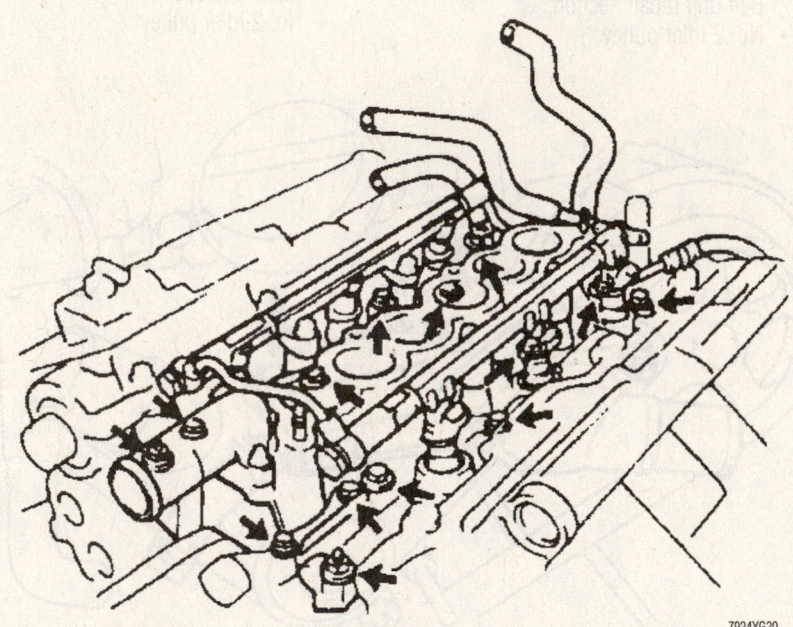

Intake manifold bolts and nuts locations—T-100 and Tacoma with 3.4L engine

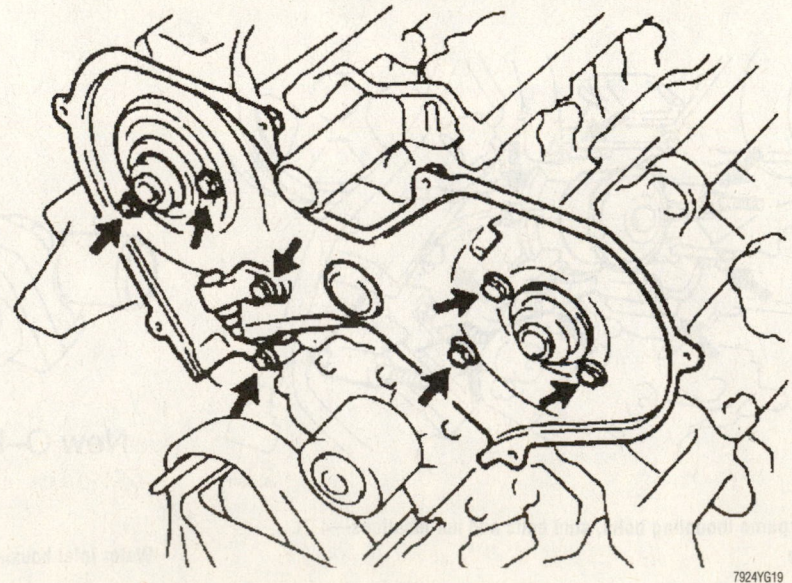

Rear timing belt cover bolt locations—3.4L engine

- 3 engine wiring harness clamps
- 3 bolts and the engine wiring harness from the cylinder head

19. Remove or disconnect the following:
- CMP sensor
- No. 3 (rear) timing belt cover, by removing the 6 bolts
- Fuel pressure regulator
- Intake manifold assembly
- Power steering pump bracket
- Oil dipstick and guide
- Exhaust crossover pipe and gaskets, by removing the 6 nuts
- Left-hand exhaust manifold, by removing the heat insulator and 6 nuts
- Right-hand exhaust manifold, by removing the heat insulator and 6 nuts

- 8 bolts, seal washers, cylinder head cover and gasket
- Both cylinder head covers
- Semi-circular plugs
- Right exhaust camshafts
- Right-hand intake camshaft
- Left exhaust camshafts
- Left-hand intake camshaft
- Valve lifters and shims from the cylinder head; arrange the valve lifters and shims in correct order

20. Remove the cylinder heads, as follows:
- Bolt and disconnect the ground strap
- Cylinder head (recessed head) bolt on each cylinder head, using an

8mm hexagon wrench; then repeat for the other side
- 8 cylinder head (12-pointed head) bolts on each cylinder head, by loosening the bolts in several passes and in the reverse order of the tightening sequence
- 16 cylinder head bolts and plate washers.
- Cylinder head

To install:

➡️ Refer to Section 1 of this manual for the cylinder head torque sequence illustration. The illustration is located after the Torque Specification Chart.

21. Clean all surfaces.
22. Install or connect the following:
- New cylinder head gaskets
- Cylinder heads

23. Apply a light coat of engine oil on the threads and under the heads of the cylinder head bolts.

24. Tighten the cylinder head bolts, in sequence, using several passes, as follows:
- Step 1: 25 ft. lbs. (34 Nm)
- Step 2: Mark the front of the cylinder head bolt with paint
- Step 3: An additional 90 degrees
- Step 4: Check that the painted mark is now at a 90 degrees angle to the front

25. Install the recessed head cylinder head bolts, as follows:
- Apply a light coat of engine oil on the threads and under the heads of the cylinder head bolts
- Cylinder head bolt on each cylinder head, using a 8mm hexagon wrench; then, repeat for the other

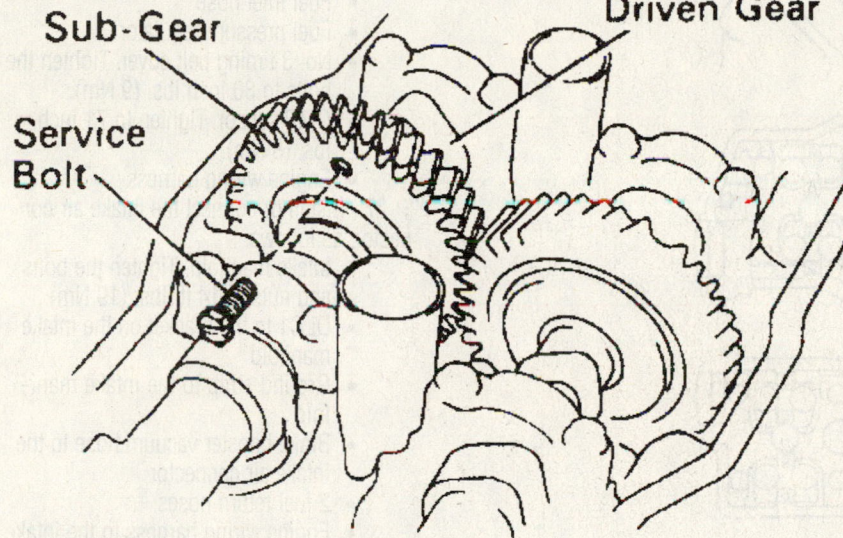

Drive gear service bolt (right side)—3.4L engine

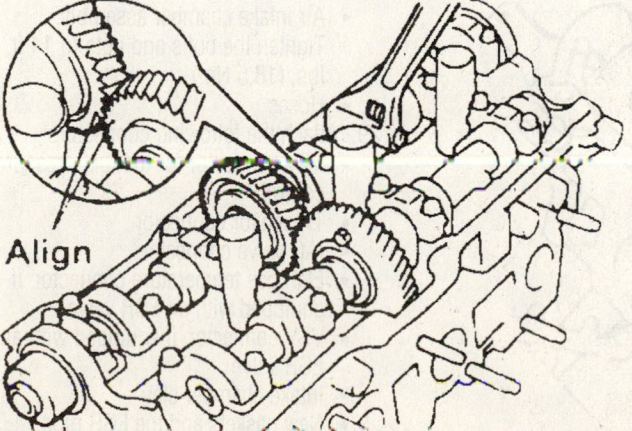

Aligning the timing mark (1 dot mark) of the left camshafts—3.4L

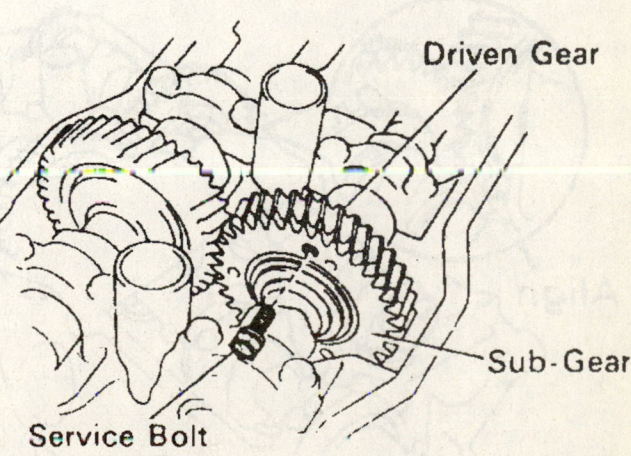

Drive gear service bolt (left side)—3.4L engine

Refer to Section 1 for engine rebuilding specifications

side, as shown. Tighten the bolts to 13 ft. lbs. (18 Nm).
- Bolt and the ground strap

26. Install or connect the following:
- Valve lifters and shims

➡ **Check that the valve lifter rotates smoothly by hand.**

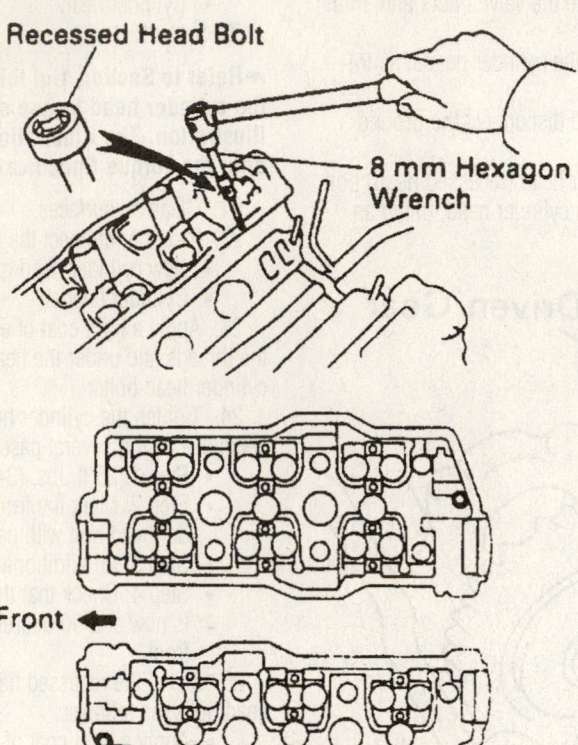

Cylinder head recessed bolts—3.4L engine

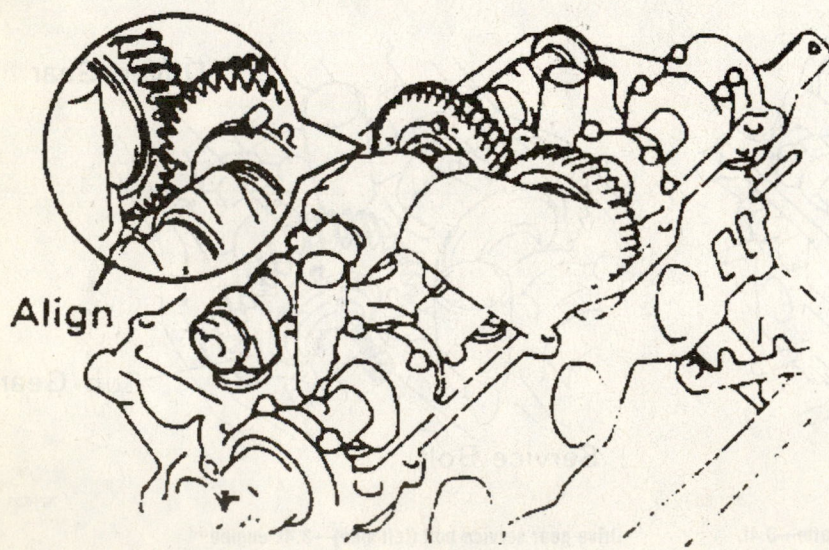

Aligning the right camshafts for installation—3.4L engine

- Camshafts
- Check and adjust the valve clearance
- Semi-circular plugs
- Cylinder head covers. Tighten the bolts, in several passes, to 53 inch lbs. (6 Nm).
- Exhaust manifolds, with new gaskets. Tighten the nuts to 30 ft. lbs. (40 Nm).
- Exhaust manifold heat insulators. Tighten the nuts to 71 inch lbs. (8 Nm).
- Exhaust crossover pipe. Tighten the nuts to 33 ft. lbs. (45 Nm).
- Alternator bracket. Tighten to 14 ft. lbs. (18 Nm).
- Oil dipstick and guide, using a new O-ring
- Power steering bracket. Tighten the fasteners to 14 ft. lbs. (18 Nm).
- New gaskets and the intake manifold assembly. Tighten the bolts and nuts to 13 ft. lbs. (18 Nm).
- Intake manifold stay with the 2 bolts. Tighten the bolts to 14 ft. lbs. (18 Nm).
- Fuel inlet hose
- Fuel pressure regulator
- No. 3 timing belt cover. Tighten the bolts to 80 inch lbs. (9 Nm).
- CMP sensor. Tighten to 71 inch lbs. (8 Nm).
- Engine wiring harness

27. Install or connect the intake air connector, as follows:
- Intake manifold. Tighten the bolts and nuts to 14 ft. lbs. (19 Nm).
- DLC1 to the bracket on the intake manifold
- Ground strap to the intake manifold
- Brake booster vacuum hose to the intake air connector
- 2 fuel return hoses
- Engine wiring harness to the intake manifold
- Idle up valve connector, if equipped with air conditioning

28. Install or connect the following:
- Air intake chamber assembly. Tighten the bolts and nuts to 14 ft. lbs. (18.5 Nm).
- Hoses

29. Attach the following connectors:
- VSV connector for the fuel pressure control
- TP sensor connector
- IAC valve connector
- EGR gas temperature connector, if equipped with an EGR valve
- VSV connector, if equipped with an EGR valve
- Intake chamber stay
- New gaskets and the EGR pipe. Tighten the clamp nuts to 71 inch lbs. (8 Nm) and the EGR pipe nuts to 14 ft. lbs. (18 Nm).
- Alternator but do not tighten the bolts and nuts at this time.

• No. 2 timing belt idler. Tighten the bolt to 30 ft. lbs. (40 Nm).

➡ **Check that the pulley bracket moves smoothly.**

• Left camshaft timing pulley

30. Set the No. 1 cylinder to TDC of the compression stroke, as follows:

a. Turn the crankshaft pulley and align its groove with the timing mark **0** on the No. 1 timing belt cover.

b. Turn the camshaft, align the knock pin hole of the camshaft with the timing mark of the No. 3 timing belt cover.

c. Turn the camshaft timing pulley, align the timing marks of the camshaft timing pulley and the No. 3 timing belt cover.

31. Connect the timing belt to the left camshaft timing pulley, as follows:

a. Check that the installation mark on the timing belt is aligned with the end of the No. 1 timing belt cover.

b. Using Variable Pin Wrench Set 09960-01000, slightly turn the left camshaft timing pulley clockwise. Align the installation mark on the timing belt with the timing mark of the camshaft tim-ing pulley and hang the timing belt on the left camshaft timing pulley.

c. Align the timing marks of the left camshaft pulley and the No. 3 timing belt cover.

d. Check that the timing belt has ten-sion between the crankshaft timing pulley and the left camshaft timing pulley.

32. Install the right camshaft timing pul-ley and the timing belt, as follows:

a. Align the installation mark on the timing belt with the timing mark of the right camshaft timing pulley, and hang the timing belt on the right camshaft tim-ing pulley with the flange side facing inward.

b. Slide the right camshaft timing pul-ley on the camshaft. Align the timing marks on the right camshaft timing pul-ley and the No. 3 timing belt cover.

c. Align the knock pin hole of the camshaft with the knock pin groove of the pulley and install the knock pin. Install the bolt and tighten to 81 ft. lbs. (110 Nm).

33. Set the timing belt tensioner as fol-lows:

a. Using a press, slowly press in the pushrod using 220–2,205 lbs. (981–9,807 N) of force.

b. Align the holes of the pushrod and housing, pass a 1.5mm hexagon wrench through the holes to keep the setting position of the pushrod.

c. Release the press and install the dust boot to the tensioner.

34. Install the timing belt tensioner. Tighten the bolts alternately to 20 ft. lbs. (28 Nm).

35. Using pliers, remove the 1.5mm hexagon wrench from the belt tensioner.

36. Check the valve timing.

37. Install or connect the following:

• Remaining components
• Negative battery cable

38. Fill the radiator with engine coolant.

39. Start the engine and check for leaks.

40. Check the ignition timing.

41. Install the engine undercover.

42. Road test the vehicle.

43. Recheck all fluid levels.

4.7L Engine

1. Before servicing the vehicle, refer to the precautions in the beginning of this sec-tion.

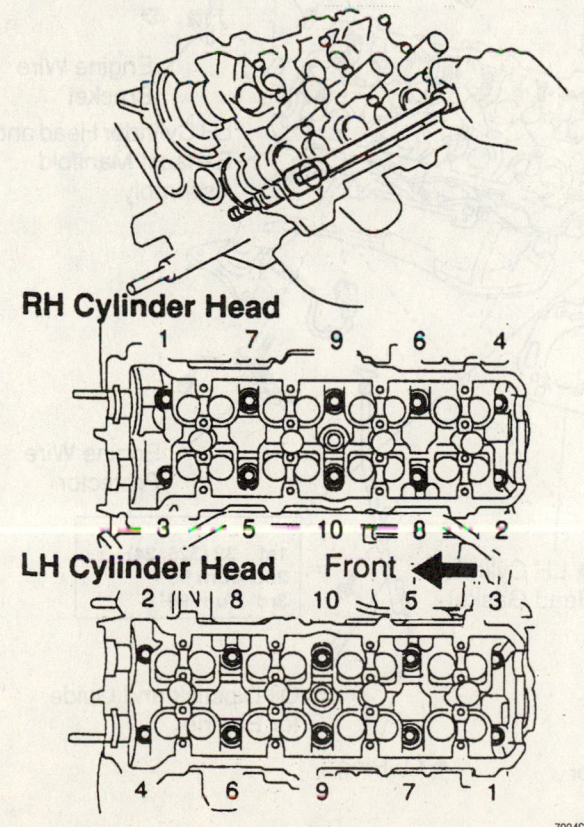

Cylinder head loosening sequence—4.7L engine

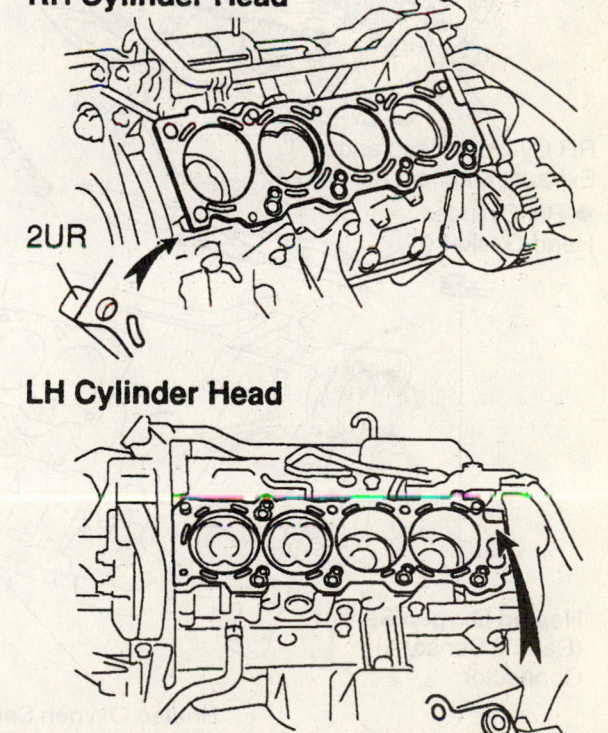

Cylinder head gasket identification—4.7L engine

For engine torque specifications, refer to Section 1 of this manual

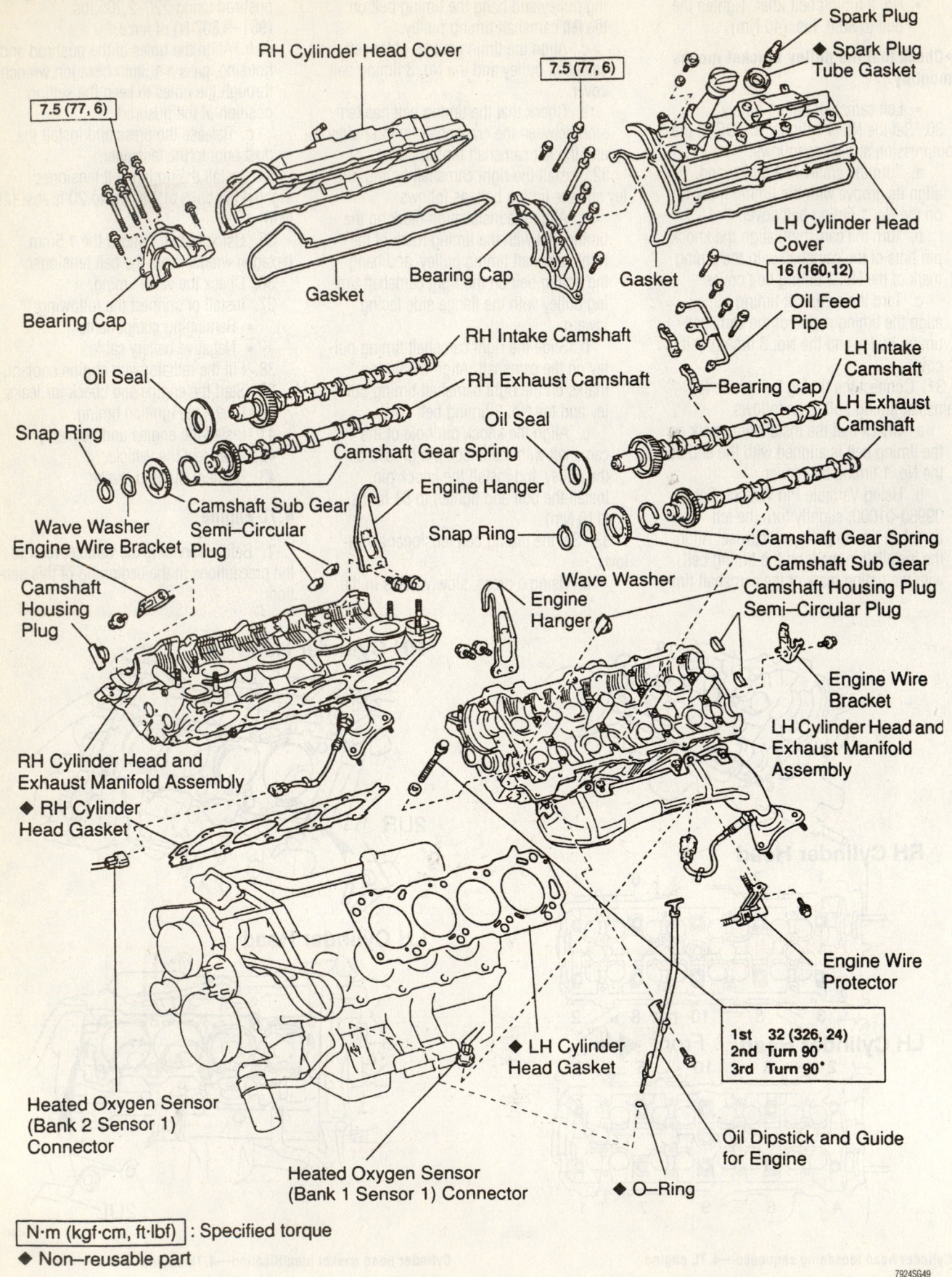

RH Cylinder Head Cover

`7.5 (77, 6)`

`7.5 (77, 6)`

Spark Plug

◆ Spark Plug Tube Gasket

Bearing Cap

Gasket

Gasket

Bearing Cap

LH Cylinder Head Cover

`16 (160, 12)`

Oil Seal

Snap Ring

Oil Feed Pipe

RH Intake Camshaft

RH Exhaust Camshaft

LH Intake Camshaft

Oil Seal

Bearing Cap

LH Exhaust Camshaft

Camshaft Gear Spring

Camshaft Sub Gear

Engine Hanger

Snap Ring

Semi–Circular Plug

Camshaft Gear Spring

Wave Washer
Engine Wire Bracket

Wave Washer

Camshaft Sub Gear

Camshaft Housing Plug

Engine Hanger

Semi–Circular Plug

Camshaft Housing Plug

Engine Wire Bracket

LH Cylinder Head and Exhaust Manifold Assembly

RH Cylinder Head and Exhaust Manifold Assembly

◆ RH Cylinder Head Gasket

Engine Wire Protector

◆ LH Cylinder Head Gasket

`1st  32 (326, 24)`
`2nd  Turn 90°`
`3rd  Turn 90°`

Heated Oxygen Sensor (Bank 2 Sensor 1) Connector

Heated Oxygen Sensor (Bank 1 Sensor 1) Connector

◆ O–Ring

Oil Dipstick and Guide for Engine

`N·m (kgf·cm, ft·lbf)` : Specified torque

◆ Non–reusable part

7924SG49

Exploded view of the cylinder head mounting—4.7L engine

2. Drain the cooling system.
3. Relieve the fuel system pressure.
4. Remove or disconnect the following:
   - Battery and tray
   - Engine appearance cover
   - Engine under covers
   - Air intake assembly
   - Accessory drive belt
   - A/C compressor and bracket
   - Cooling fan and bracket
   - Radiator
   - Idler pulley
   - Front covers
   - Timing belt. Refer to the Timing Belt unit repair section.
   - Camshaft sprockets
   - Camshaft Position (CMP) sensor
   - Power steering pump
   - Exhaust front pipes
   - Transmission dipstick tube
   - Ignition coils
   - Rear timing belt covers
   - Fuel lines
   - Intake manifold
   - Water inlet housing assembly
   - Front and rear water bypass joints
   - Engine lifting eyes
   - Oil dipstick tube
   - Valve covers
   - Camshafts
   - Cylinder heads with the exhaust manifolds attached. Loosen the bolts in the sequence shown.

To install:

➡ Refer to Section 1 of this manual for the cylinder head torque sequence illustration. The illustration is located after the Torque Specification Chart.

5. Install the cylinder heads with new gaskets. Tighten the bolts in sequence as follows:
   a. Step 1: 24 ft. lbs. (32 Nm)
   b. Step 2: Plus 180 degrees
6. Install or connect the following:
   - Camshafts
   - Valve covers
   - Oil dipstick tube
   - Engine lifting eyes
   - Front and rear water bypass joints
   - Water inlet housing assembly
   - Intake manifold
   - Fuel lines
   - Rear timing belt covers
   - Ignition coils
   - Transmission dipstick tube
   - Exhaust front pipes
   - Power steering pump
   - CMP sensor
   - Camshaft sprockets
   - Timing belt
   - Front covers
   - Idler pulley
   - Radiator
   - Cooling fan and bracket
   - A/C compressor and bracket

- Accessory drive belt
- Air intake assembly
- Engine under covers
- Engine appearance cover
- Battery and tray
7. Fill the cooling system.
8. Start the engine and check for leaks.

Intake Manifold

REMOVAL & INSTALLATION

3.4L Engine

1. Before servicing the vehicle, refer to the precautions in the beginning of this section.
2. Disconnect the negative battery cable.
3. Relieve the fuel system pressure.
4. Remove the engine undercover.
5. Drain the cooling system.
6. Remove or disconnect the following:

- Air cleaner cap
- Mass Air Flow (MAF) meter and the resonator
- Actuator cable with the bracket, if equipped with cruise control
- Accelerator cable
- Throttle cable, if equipped with automatic transmission

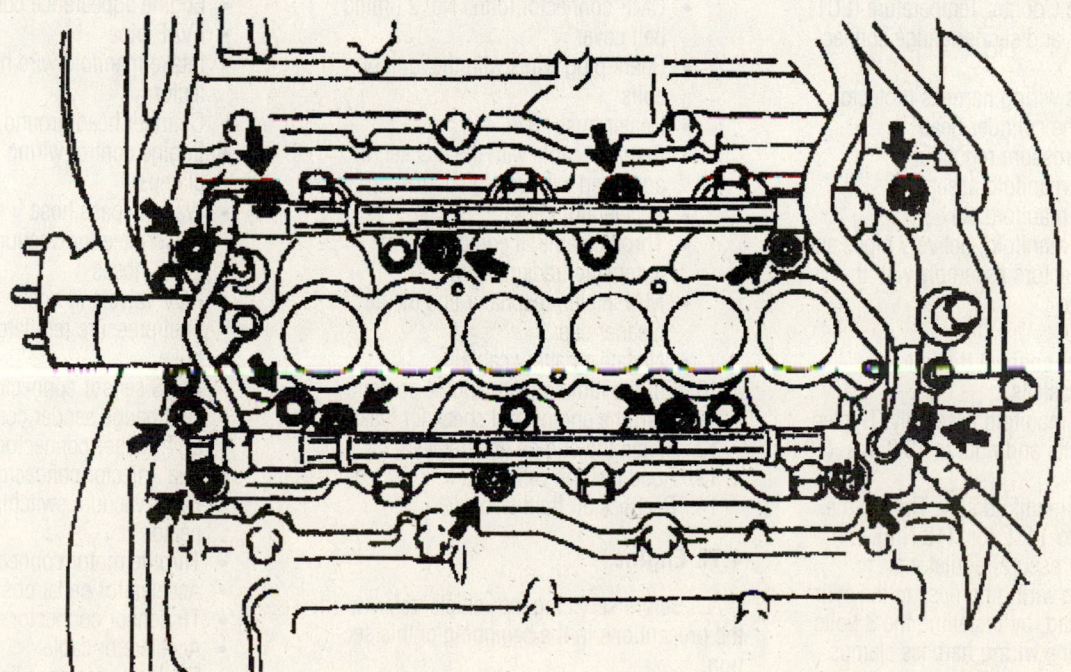

Intake manifold bolts and nuts—3.4L engine

7924YG38

For complete mechanical specifications, refer to Section 1 of this manual

7. Disconnect the following hoses:
- Heater hose
- Brake booster vacuum hose
- Evaporative Emissions (EVAP) hose
- Automatic Disconnecting Differential (ADD) vacuum hose, for 4-Wheel drive
- Fuel inlet and fuel return hose

8. Remove or disconnect the following:
- Spark plug wires, with the ignition coils
- Intake chamber stay
- No. 2 timing belt cover
- Air intake chamber assembly
- Throttle Position (TP) sensor connector
- Idle Air Control (IAC) valve connector
- Positive Crankcase Ventilation (PCV) hoses
- Water bypass hoses
- Air assist hose from the throttle body
- Intake air connector
- Engine wiring harness
- Fuel return hose
- Vacuum hose, from the fuel pressure regulator
- Ground strap, from the intake air connector
- Data Link Connector 1 (DLC1), from the bracket
- 6 injector connectors
- Engine Coolant Temperature (ECT) sensor and sender gauge connectors
- Engine wiring harness protector from the cylinder head
- Fuel pressure regulator
- Intake manifold assembly
- Intake manifold stay
- Intake manifold, delivery pipes and the injectors assembly with the gaskets

To install:

9. Install or connect the following:
- New gaskets
- Intake manifold assembly. Tighten the bolts and nuts to 13 ft. lbs. (18 Nm).
- Intake manifold stay. Tighten the bolts to 14 ft. lbs. (18 Nm).
- Fuel pressure regulator
- Engine wiring harness to the cylinder head, by installing the 3 bolts
- 3 engine wiring harness clamps
- 6 injector connectors
- ECT sender gauge connector
- ECT sensor connector
- Intake manifold. Tighten the bolts and nuts to 14 ft. lbs. (18.5 Nm).

- DLC1 to the bracket on the intake manifold
- Ground strap to the intake manifold, by installing the bolt
- Brake booster vacuum hose, to the intake air connector
- 2 fuel return hoses
- Engine wiring harness to the intake manifold
- Air intake chamber assembly to the engine. Tighten the bolts and nuts to 14 ft. lbs. (18.5 Nm).
- Intake chamber stay. Tighten the bolts to 30 ft. lbs. (40 Nm).
- New O-ring to the oil filler tube
- Oil filler tube end into the tube hole in the oil pan
- Oil filler tube and No. 1 throttle cable clamp
- No. 2 timing belt cover. Tighten the bolts to 80 inch lbs. (9 Nm).
- PCV hoses
- Water bypass hoses
- Air assist hose to the throttle body
- IAC valve connector
- TP sensor connector
- Brake booster vacuum hose
- EVAP hose
- Automatic Disconnecting Differential (ADD) vacuum hose, for 4-Wheel drive
- Fuel inlet and fuel return hose
- 3 spark plug wire clamps to the No. 2 timing belt cover
- CMP connector to the No. 2 timing belt cover
- Spark plug wires with the ignition coils
- Heater hose
- Actuator cable with the bracket, if equipped with cruise control
- Accelerator cable
- Throttle cable, if equipped with automatic transmission
- MAF meter, resonator and the air cleaner cap
- Negative battery cable

10. Fill the radiator with engine coolant.
11. Start the engine and check for leaks.
12. Install the engine undercover.
13. Road test the vehicle.
14. Recheck all fluid levels.

4.7L Engine

1. Before servicing the vehicle, refer to the precautions in the beginning of this section.
2. Drain the cooling system.
3. Relieve the fuel system pressure.
4. Remove or disconnect the following:
- Negative battery cable

- Engine appearance cover
- Accelerator cable
- Throttle Position (TP) sensor connector
- Accelerator pedal position sensor
- Throttle motor connector
- Evaporative Emissions (EVAP) vacuum switching valve connector
- Fuel injector connectors
- Engine Coolant Temperature (ECT) sensor connector
- ETC gauge sender connector
- Heated Oxygen (HO_2S) sensor connectors
- Fuel pressure regulator vacuum hose
- Positive Crankcase Ventilation (PCV) valve and hose
- EVAP hoses
- Power steering vacuum hoses
- Water bypass hose
- Engine control wiring harness clamps
- Cylinder head ground cables
- Intake manifold wire harness protector
- EVAP pipe
- Engine appearance cover brackets
- Intake manifold

To install:

5. Install or connect the following:
- Intake manifold. Tighten the fasteners to 13 ft. lbs. (18 Nm).
- Engine appearance cover brackets
- EVAP pipe
- Intake manifold wire harness protector
- Cylinder head ground cables
- Engine control wiring harness clamps
- Water bypass hose
- Power steering vacuum hoses
- EVAP hoses
- PCV valve and hose
- Fuel pressure regulator vacuum hose
- HO_2S sensor connectors
- ETC gauge sender connector
- ECT sensor connector
- Fuel injector connectors
- EVAP vacuum switching valve connector
- Throttle motor connector
- Accelerator pedal position sensor
- TP sensor connector
- Accelerator cable
- Engine appearance cover
- Negative battery cable

6. Fill the cooling system.
7. Start the engine and check for leaks.

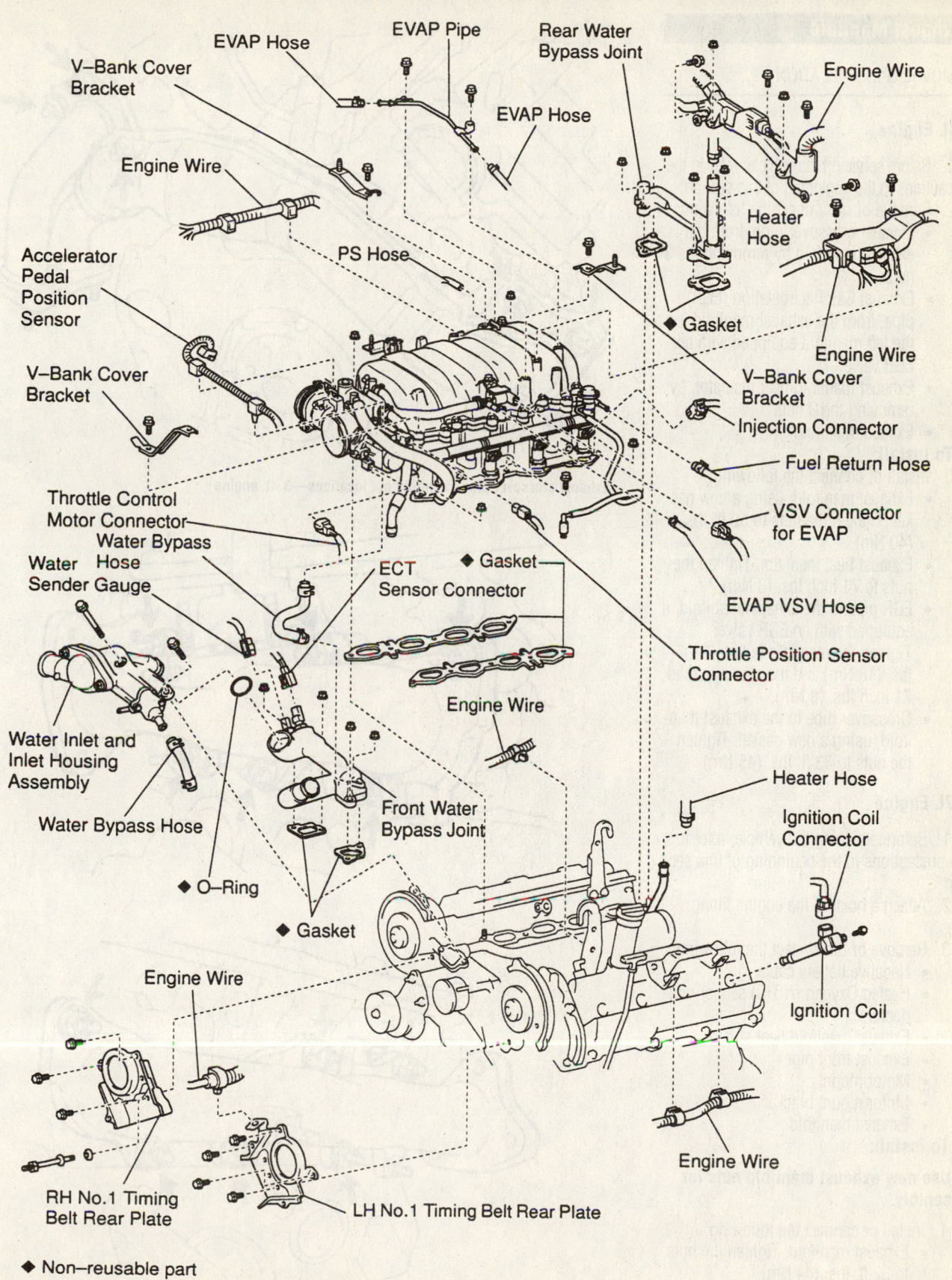

EVAP Hose

EVAP Pipe

Rear Water
Bypass Joint

Engine Wire

V-Bank Cover
Bracket

EVAP Hose

Engine Wire

Heater
Hose

Accelerator
Pedal
Position
Sensor

PS Hose

◆ Gasket

Engine Wire

V-Bank Cover
Bracket

V-Bank Cover
Bracket

Injection Connector

Fuel Return Hose

VSV Connector
for EVAP

Throttle Control
Motor Connector
Water Bypass
Hose

ECT
Sensor Connector

◆ Gasket

EVAP VSV Hose

Water
Sender Gauge

Throttle Position Sensor
Connector

Water Inlet and
Inlet Housing
Assembly

Engine Wire

Heater Hose

Water Bypass Hose

Front Water
Bypass Joint

Ignition Coil
Connector

◆ O-Ring

Ignition Coil

◆ Gasket

Engine Wire

Engine Wire

RH No.1 Timing
Belt Rear Plate

LH No.1 Timing Belt Rear Plate

Engine Wire

◆ Non-reusable part

Exploded of the intake manifold mounting—4.7L engine

7924SG50

Please refer to Section 8 for electric cooling fan wiring schematics

Exhaust Manifold

REMOVAL & INSTALLATION

3.4L Engine

1. Before servicing the vehicle, refer to the precautions in the beginning of this section.
2. Remove or disconnect the following:
   - Exhaust crossover pipe, from the exhaust manifold by removing the 3 nuts
   - Exhaust Gas Recirculation (EGR) pipe, from the exhaust manifold, on the left manifold equipped with an EGR valve
   - Exhaust manifold heat insulator, by removing the 3 nuts
   - Exhaust manifold

To install:

3. Install or connect the following:
   - Exhaust manifold, using a new gasket. Tighten the nuts to 30 ft. lbs. (40 Nm).
   - Exhaust heat insulator. Tighten the nuts to 71 inch lbs. (8 Nm).
   - EGR pipe to the exhaust manifold, if equipped with an EGR valve. Tighten the manifold nuts to 14 ft. lbs. (18 Nm) and the clamp nuts to 71 inch lbs. (8 Nm).
   - Crossover pipe to the exhaust manifold, using a new gasket. Tighten the nuts to 33 ft. lbs. (45 Nm).

4.7L Engine

1. Before servicing the vehicle, refer to the precautions in the beginning of this section.
2. Attach a hoist to the engine lifting eyes.
3. Remove or disconnect the following:
   - Negative battery cable
   - Heated Oxygen (HO2S) sensor connectors
   - Exhaust manifold heat shield
   - Exhaust front pipe
   - Motor mount
   - Motor mount bracket
   - Exhaust manifold

To install:

➡️ **Use new exhaust manifold nuts for assembly.**

4. Install or connect the following:
   - Exhaust manifold. Tighten the nuts to 32 ft. lbs. (44 Nm).
   - Motor mount bracket. Tighten the bolts to 27 ft. lbs. (36 Nm).

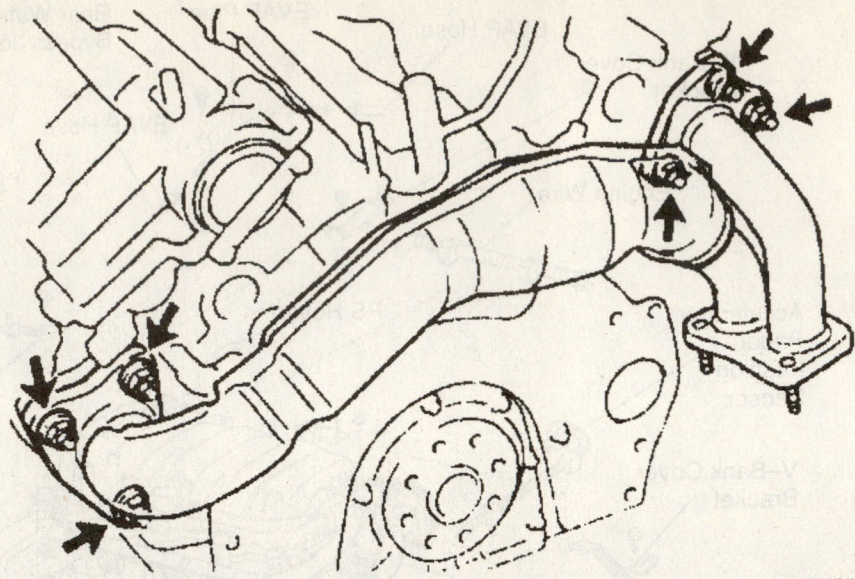

7924YG43

Exhaust crossover pipe mounting nut locations—3.4L engine

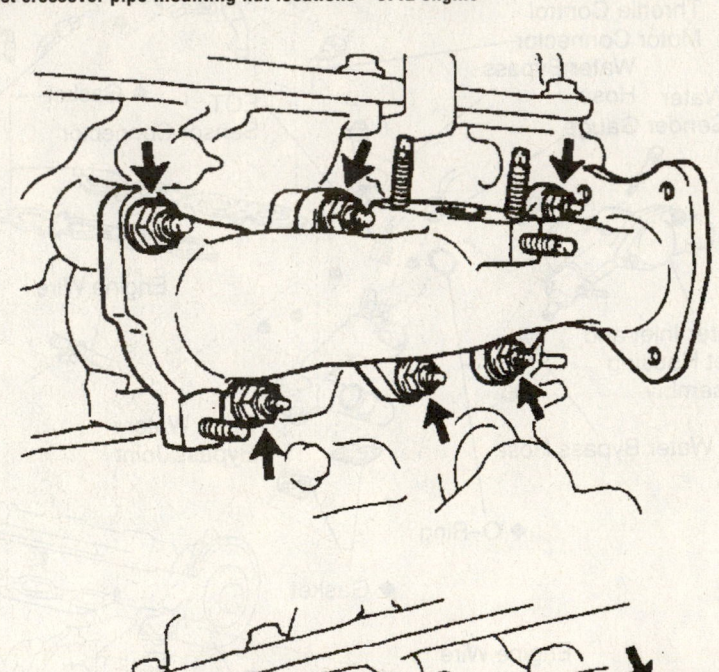

7924YG44

Exhaust manifold nuts—3.4L engine

- Motor mount. Tighten the fasteners to 22 ft. lbs. (30 Nm).
- Exhaust front pipe. Tighten the nuts to 46 ft. lbs. (62 Nm).
- Exhaust manifold heat shield
- HO2S sensor connectors
- Negative battery cable

5. Start the engine and check for leaks.

Front Crankshaft Seal

REMOVAL & INSTALLATION

3.4L Engine

➡There are 2 methods to replace the oil seal, which are as follows:

OIL PUMP BODY INSTALLED

1. Before servicing the vehicle, refer to the precautions in the beginning of this section.
2. Remove or disconnect the following:

- Negative battery cable
- Timing belt and crankshaft pulley
- Cut off the oil seal lip, using a knife
- Pry out the oil seal, using a suitable tool

✳✳ WARNING

Be careful not to damage the crankshaft.

To install:
3. Install or connect the following:

- Apply multi-purpose grease to the new oil seal lip
- Tap in the new oil seal until its surface is flush with the oil pump case edge, using Seal Driver tool 09309-37010 and a mallet
- Crankshaft pulley and the timing belt
- Engine undercover, if removed
- Negative battery cable

OIL PUMP BODY REMOVED

1. Before servicing the vehicle, refer to the precautions in the beginning of this section.
2. Carefully pry out the seal using a suitable tool.
3. Apply multi-purpose grease to the new oil seal lip.
4. Using Seal Driver tool 09309-37010, drive the new seal into place.

4.7L Engine

1. Before servicing the vehicle, refer to the precautions in the beginning of this section.
2. Drain the cooling system.
3. Remove or disconnect the following:

- Negative battery cable
- Engine under cover
- Engine appearance cover
- Air intake assembly
- Accessory drive belt
- Cooling fan and pulley
- Radiator
- Drive belt idler pulley
- Camshaft Position (CMP) sensor connector
- Upper timing covers
- Oil cooler pipe
- Center timing cover
- A/C compressor
- Cooling fan bracket
- Crankshaft pulley
- Lower timing cover
- Timing belt. Refer to the Timing Belt unit repair section.
- Crankshaft timing sprocket
- Front crankshaft seal

To install:
4. Install the oil seal so that it is flush with the oil pump housing.
5. Install or connect the following:

- Crankshaft timing sprocket
- Timing belt
- Lower timing cover
- Crankshaft pulley. Tighten the bolt to 181 ft. lbs. (245 Nm).
- Cooling fan bracket. Tighten the 12mm bolts to 12 ft. lbs. (16 Nm) and the 14mm bolts to 24 ft. lbs. (32 Nm).
- A/C compressor
- Center timing cover
- Oil cooler pipe
- Upper timing covers
- CMP sensor connector
- Drive belt idler pulley. Tighten the bolt to 27 ft. lbs. (37 Nm).
- Radiator
- Cooling fan and pulley. Tighten the nuts to 16 ft. lbs. (21 Nm).
- Accessory drive belt
- Air intake assembly
- Engine appearance cover
- Engine under cover
- Negative battery cable

6. Fill the cooling system.
7. Start the engine and check for leaks.

Camshaft and Valve Lifters

REMOVAL & INSTALLATION

3.4L Engine

1. Before servicing the vehicle, refer to the precautions in the beginning of this section.
2. Remove or disconnect the following:

- Negative battery cable
- Engine undercover

3. Drain the cooling system.
4. Remove or disconnect the following:

- Air cleaner cap
- Mass Air Flow (MAF) meter and the resonator
- Actuator cable with the bracket, if equipped with cruise control
- Accelerator cable
- Throttle cable, if equipped with an automatic transmission
- Heater hose
- Upper radiator hose from the engine

5. Remove the power steering drive belt, as follows:

a. Stretch the belt and loosen the fan pulley mounting nuts.

b. Loosen the lockbolt, pivot bolt and adjusting bolt and remove the drive belt from the engine.

6. Remove or disconnect the following:

- Air conditioning drive belt, by loosening the idle pulley nut and adjusting bolt
- Loosen the alternator lockbolt, pivot bolt and adjusting bolt
- Alternator drive belt
- No. 2 fan shroud, by removing the 2 clips
- Fan with the fluid coupling and fan pulleys
- Power steering pump and move it aside without disconnecting the lines
- Compressor and move it aside without disconnecting the lines, if equipped with air conditioning
- Air conditioning bracket, if equipped with air conditioning
- Spark plug wires with the ignition coils
- Spark plugs
- Camshaft Position (CMP) sensor connector, from the No. 2 timing belt cover

- 3 spark plug wire clamps from the No. 2 timing belt cover
- 6 bolts and the timing belt cover
- Power steering adjusting strut by removing the nut
- Fan bracket by removing the bolt and nut

7. Set the No. 1 cylinder at Top Dead Center (TDC) of the compression stroke, as follows:

a. Turn the crankshaft pulley and align its groove with the timing mark **0** on the No. 1 timing belt cover.

b. Check that the timing marks of the camshaft timing pulleys and the No. 3 timing belt cover are aligned. If not, turn the crankshaft pulley 1 revolution (360 degrees).

8. Remove or disconnect the following:

- Timing belt tensioner, by alternately loosening the 2 bolts
- Pulley bolt, the timing pulley and the knock pin, using Variable Pin Wrench Set 09960-10010
- Both timing pulleys with the timing belt
- No. 2 idler pulley
- Alternator
- Positive Crankcase Ventilation PCV hoses
- Water bypass hoses
- Air assist hose from the intake air connector
- 2 vacuum sensing hoses from the Vacuum Switching Valve (VSV)
- Evaporative Emissions (EVAP) hose
- Air hose from the power steering
- Air hose from the air conditioning idle up valve, if equipped with air conditioning
- 4 bolts, 2 nuts and the air intake chamber assembly
- Intake air connector
- Camshaft Position (CMP) sensor
- No. 3 (rear) timing belt cover by removing the 6 bolts
- 8 bolts, seal washers, both cylinder head cover and gaskets
- Semi-circular plugs

9. Remove the right exhaust camshafts, as follows:

a. Bring the service bolt hole of the driven sub-gear upward by turning the hexagon head portion of the exhaust camshaft with a wrench.

b. Align the timing mark (2 dot marks) of the camshaft drive and driven gears by turning the camshaft with a wrench.

c. Secure the exhaust camshaft sub-gear to the driven gear with a service bolt (6mm diameter, 16–20mm bolt length and 1.0mm in thread pitch).

➡**When removing the camshaft, be sure the torsional spring force of the sub-gear has been eliminated by the above operation.**

d. Uniformly loosen and remove the bearing cap bolts in several passes, in the sequence shown.

e. Remove the bearing caps and camshaft. Make a note of the bearing cap positions for proper installation.

➡**Do not pry on or attempt to force the camshaft with a tool or other object.**

10. Remove the right-hand intake camshaft, as follows:

a. Uniformly loosen and remove the bearing cap bolts in several passes, in the sequence shown.

b. Remove the bearing caps, oil seal and camshaft. Make a note of the bearing cap positions for proper installation.

11. Remove the left exhaust camshafts, as follows:

a. Align the timing mark (1 dot mark) of the camshaft drive and driven gears by turning the camshaft with a wrench.

b. Secure the exhaust camshaft sub-gear to the driven gear with a service bolt (6mm diameter, 16–20mm bolt length and 1.0mm in thread pitch).

➡**When removing the camshaft, be sure that the torsional spring force of the sub-gear has been eliminated by the above operation.**

c. Uniformly loosen and remove the bearing cap bolts in several passes, in the sequence shown.

d. Remove the bearing caps and camshaft. Make a note of the bearing cap positions for proper installation.

12. Remove the left-hand intake camshaft, as follows:

a. Uniformly loosen and remove the bearing cap bolts in several passes, in the sequence shown.

b. Remove the bearing caps, oil seal and camshaft. Make a note of the bearing cap positions for proper installation.

13. Remove the valve lifters and shims from the cylinder head. Arrange the valve lifters and shims in correct order.

To install:

14. Clean all surfaces.

15. Install the valve lifters and shims. Check that the valve lifter rotates smoothly by hand.

16. Install the right intake camshaft, as follows:

a. Apply engine oil to the thrust portion of the intake camshaft.

b. Position the intake camshaft at 90 degrees angle of the timing mark (2 dot marks) on the cylinder head.

c. Install the bearing caps in their proper locations. Apply a light coat of engine oil to the threads and install the cap bolts.

d. Apply a light coat of engine oil on the threads and under the heads of the bearing cap bolts.

e. Uniformly tighten the cap bolts in the sequence shown to 12 ft. lbs. (16 Nm).

17. Install the right exhaust camshaft, as follows:

a. Apply engine oil to the thrust portion of the intake camshaft.

b. Align the timing marks (2 dot marks) of the camshaft drive and driven gears.

c. Roll down the exhaust camshaft onto the bearing journals while engaging the gears with each other. Install the bearing caps in their proper locations.

d. Apply a light coat of engine oil to the threads and install the cap bolts.

e. Apply a light coat of engine oil on the threads and under the heads of the bearing cap bolts.

f. Uniformly tighten the cap bolts in the sequence shown to 12 ft. lbs. (16 Nm).

g. Remove the service bolt from the driven sub-gear. Check that the intake and exhaust camshafts turns smoothly.

h. Align the timing marks (2 dot marks) of the camshaft drive and driven gears by turning the camshaft with a wrench.

18. Install the left intake camshaft, as follows:

a. Apply engine oil to the thrust portion of the intake camshaft.

b. Position the intake camshaft at 90 degrees angle of the timing mark (1 dot mark) on the cylinder head.

c. Install the bearing caps in their proper locations. Apply a light coat of engine oil to the threads and install the cap bolts.

d. Apply a light coat of engine oil on the threads and under the heads of the bearing cap bolts.

e. Uniformly tighten the cap bolts in the sequence shown to 12 ft. lbs. (16 Nm).

19. Install the left exhaust camshaft, as follows:

a. Apply engine oil to the thrust portion of the intake camshaft.

b. Align the timing marks (1 dot mark) of the camshaft drive and driven gears.

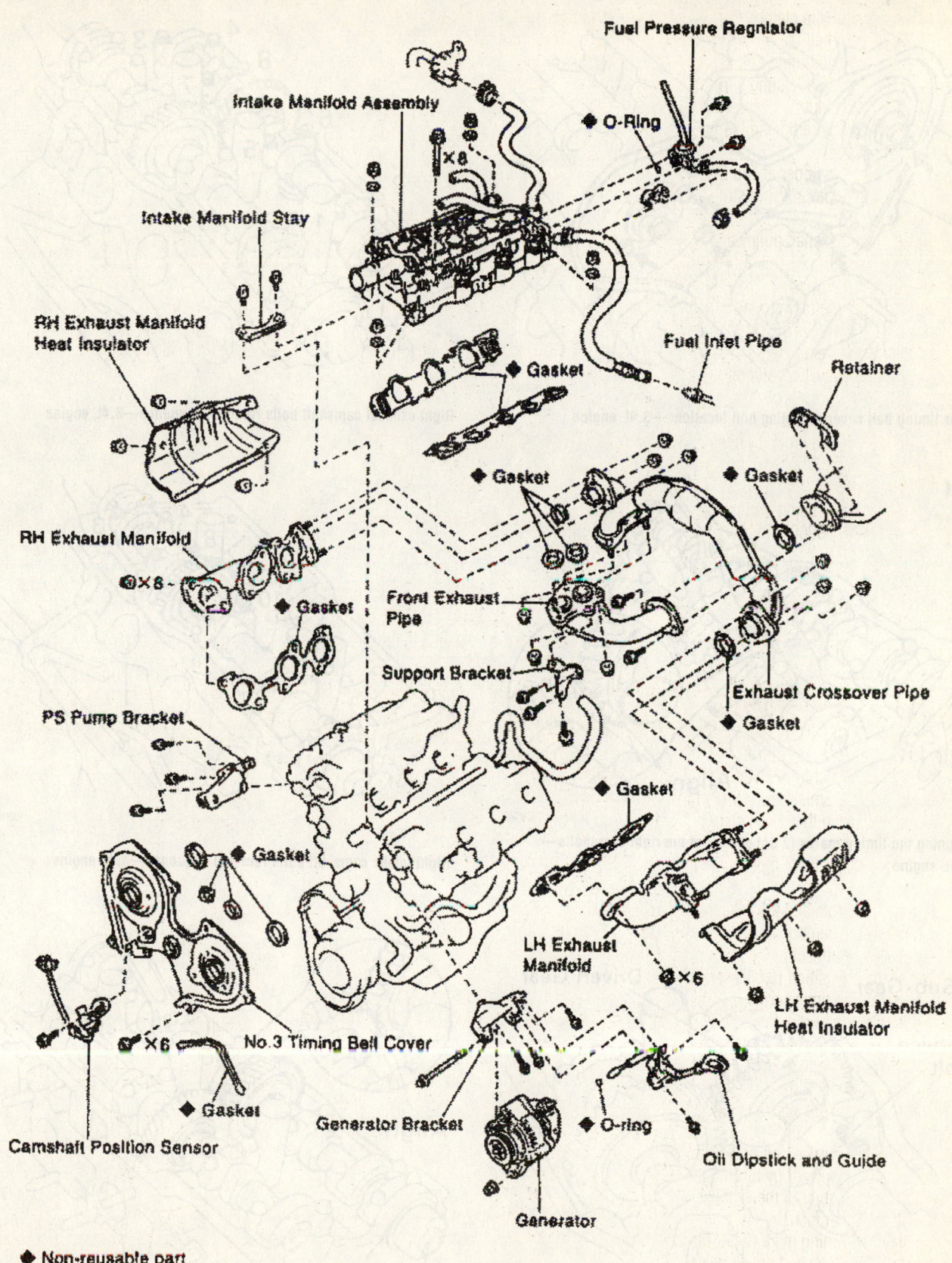

Fuel Pressure Regulator

Intake Manifold Assembly

◆ O-Ring

×8

Intake Manifold Stay

RH Exhaust Manifold
Heat Insulator

Fuel Inlet Pipe

Retainer

◆ Gasket

RH Exhaust Manifold

◆ Gasket

◆ Gasket

×8

◆ Gasket

Front Exhaust
Pipe

PS Pump Bracket

Support Bracket

Exhaust Crossover Pipe

◆ Gasket

◆ Gasket

◆ Gasket

LH Exhaust
Manifold

×6

No. 3 Timing Belt Cover

LH Exhaust Manifold
Heat Insulator

◆ Gasket

Camshaft Position Sensor

Generator Bracket

◆ O-ring

Oil Dipstick and Guide

Generator

◆ **Non-reusable part**

Exploded view of the cylinder head component assembly—3.4L engine

7924YG60

Timing belt service is covered in Section 4 of this manual

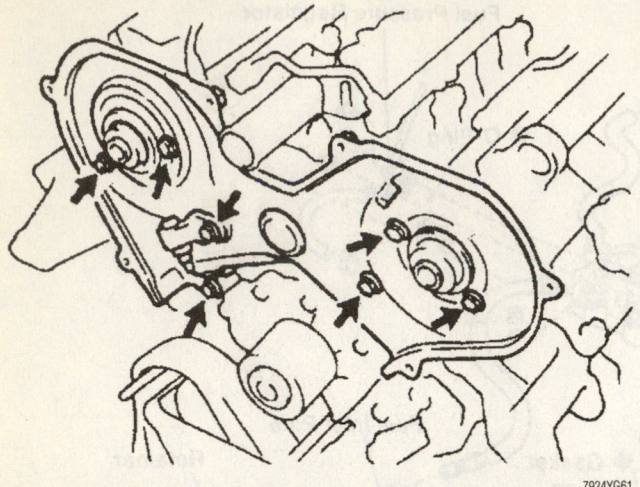

Rear timing belt cover mounting bolt locations—3.4L engine

7924YG61

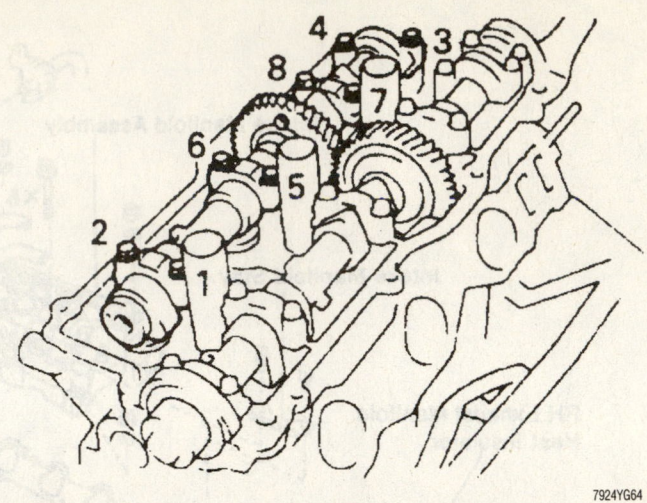

Right exhaust camshaft bolts removal sequence—3.4L engine

7924YG64

RH

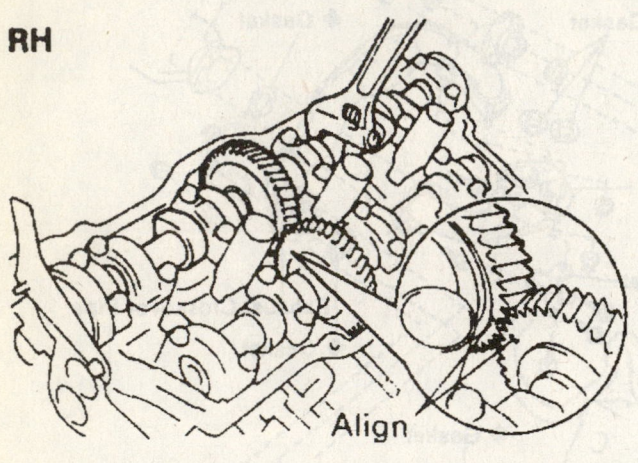

Align

Aligning the timing marks (2 dot marks) of the right camshafts—3.4L engine

7924YG62

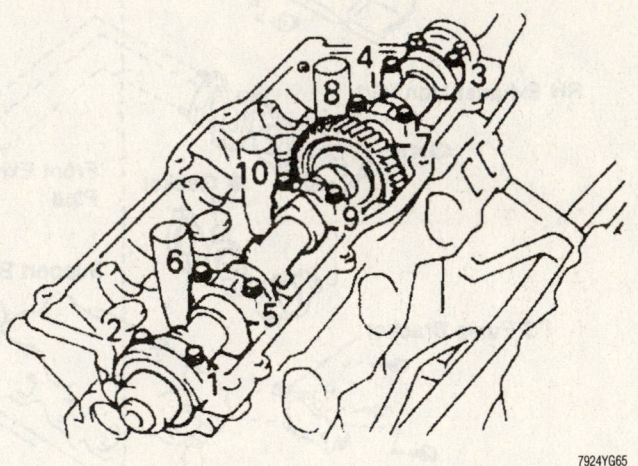

Right intake camshaft bolts removal sequence—3.4L engine

7924YG65

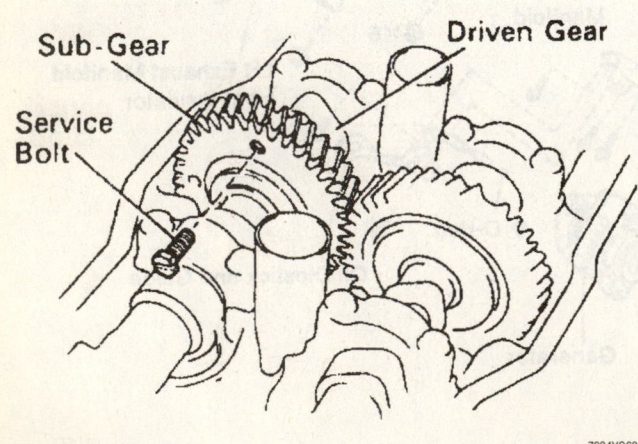

Sub-Gear

Service Bolt

Driven Gear

Drive gear service bolt (right side)—3.4L engine

7924YG63

Align

Aligning the timing mark (1 dot mark) of the left camshafts—3.4L engine

7924YG66

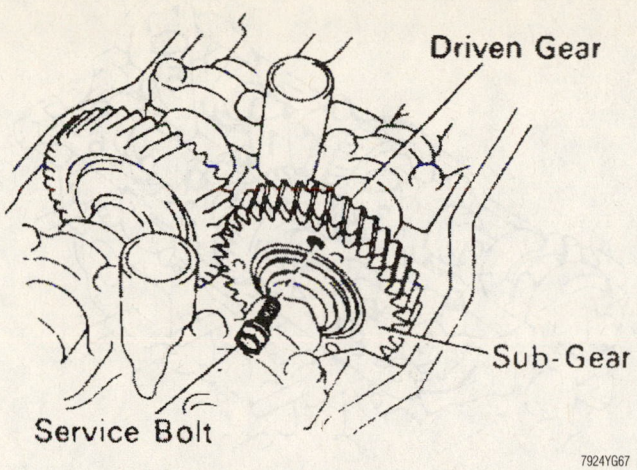

Drive gear service bolt (left side)—3.4L engine

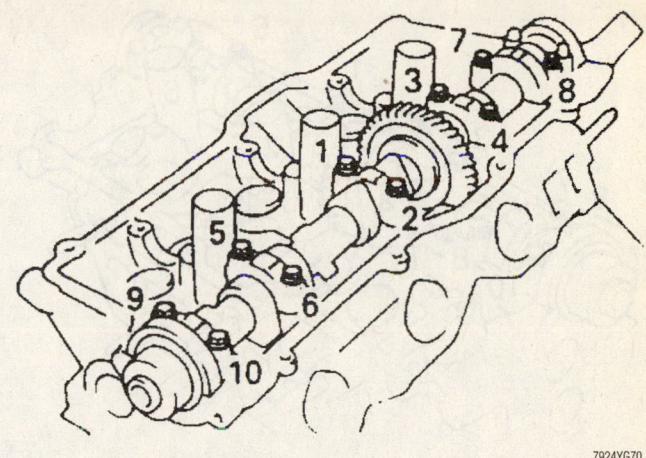

Right intake camshaft tightening sequence—3.4L engine

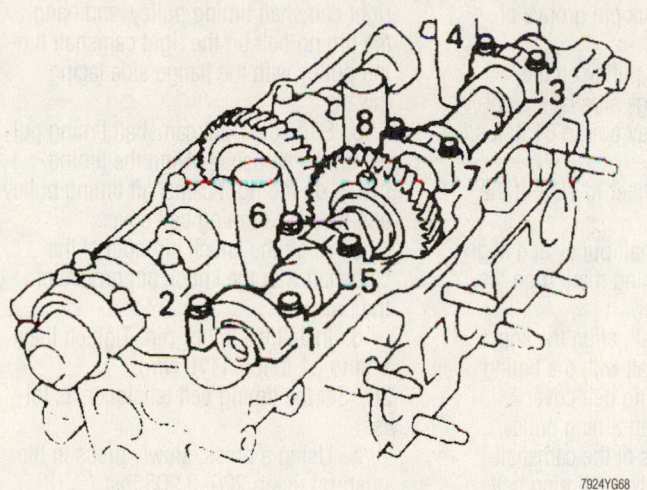

Left exhaust camshaft bolts removal sequence—3.4L engine

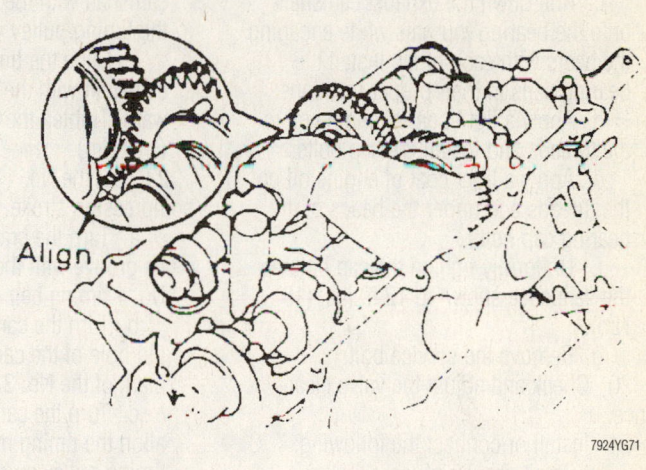

Aligning the right camshafts for installation—3.4L engine

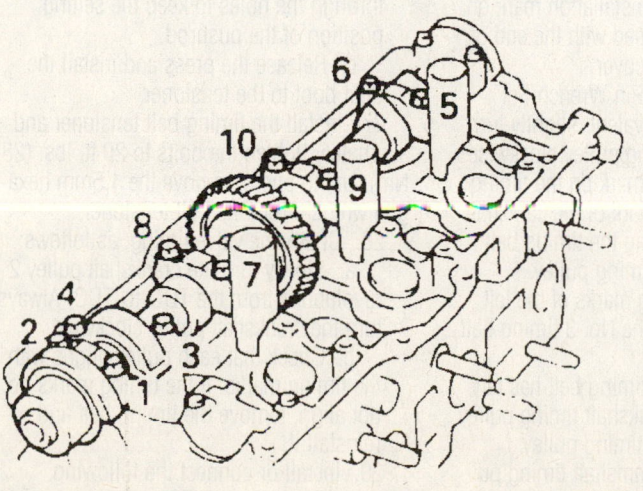

Left intake camshaft bolts removal sequence—3.4L engine

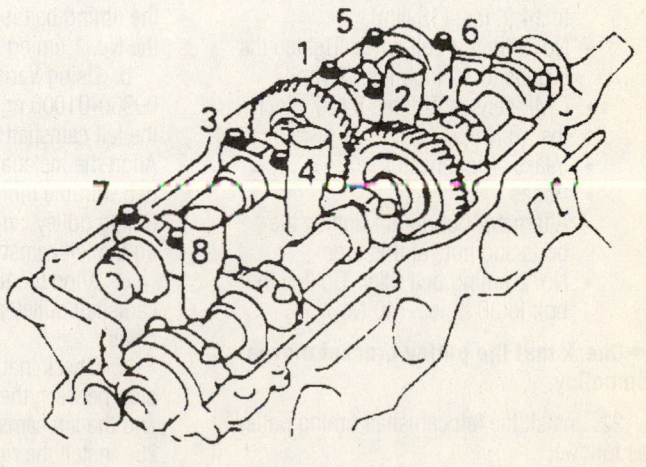

Right exhaust camshaft bolts tightening sequence—3.4L engine

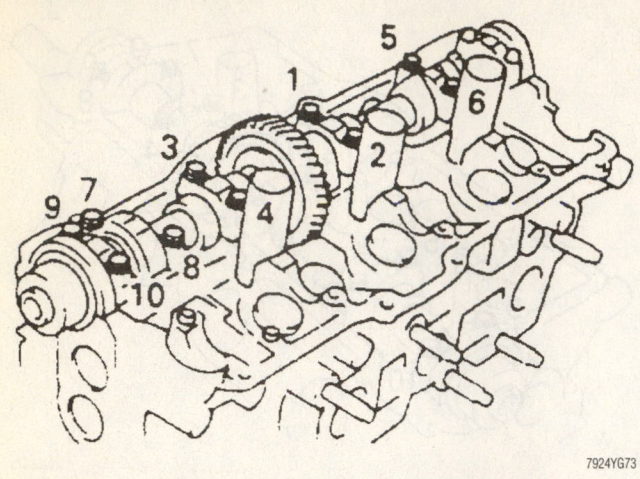

7924YG73

Left intake camshaft bolts tightening sequence—3.4L engine

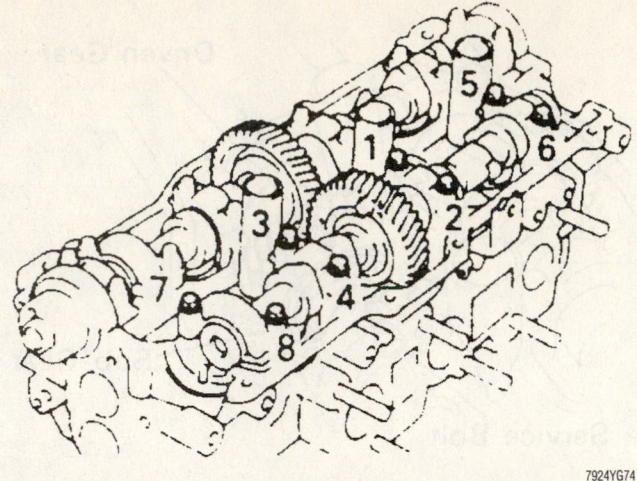

7924YG74

Left exhaust camshaft bolts tightening sequence—3.4L engine

c. Roll down the exhaust camshaft onto the bearing journals while engaging the gears with each other. Install the bearing caps in their proper locations.

d. Apply a light coat of engine oil to the threads and install the cap bolts.

e. Apply a light coat of engine oil on the threads and under the heads of the bearing cap bolts.

f. Uniformly tighten the cap bolts in the sequence shown to 12 ft. lbs. (16 Nm).

g. Remove the service bolt.

20. Check and adjust the valve clearance.

21. Install or connect the following:
- Semi-circular plugs
- Cylinder head covers. Tighten the bolts, in several passes, to 53 inch lbs. (6 Nm).
- Alternator bracket. Tighten the bolts to 14 ft. lbs. (18 Nm).
- No. 3 timing belt cover. Tighten the 6 bolts to 80 inch lbs. (9 Nm).
- CMP sensor. Tighten it to 71 inch lbs. (8 Nm).
- Intake air connector
- Hoses
- Alternator but do not tighten the bolts and nuts at this time
- No. 2 timing belt idler. Tighten the bolt to 30 ft. lbs. (40 Nm).

➡**Check that the pulley bracket moves smoothly.**

22. Install the left camshaft timing pulley, as follows:

a. Install the knock pin to the camshaft.

b. Align the knock pin hose of the

camshaft with the knock pin groove of the timing pulley.

c. Slide the timing pulley on the camshaft with the flange side facing outward. Tighten the pulley bolt to 81 ft. lbs. (110 Nm).

23. Set the No. 1 cylinder to TDC of the compression stroke.

a. Turn the crankshaft pulley and align its groove with the timing mark **0** on the No. 1 timing belt cover.

b. Turn the camshaft, align the knock pin hole of the camshaft with the timing mark of the No. 3 timing belt cover.

c. Turn the camshaft timing pulley, align the timing marks of the camshaft timing pulley and the No. 3 timing belt cover.

24. Connect the timing belt to the left camshaft timing pulley, as follows:

a. Check that the installation mark on the timing belt is aligned with the end of the No. 1 timing belt cover.

b. Using Variable Pin Wrench Set 09960-01000 or equivalent, slightly turn the left camshaft timing pulley clockwise. Align the installation mark on the timing belt with the timing mark of the camshaft timing pulley, and hang the timing belt on the left camshaft timing pulley.

c. Align the timing marks of the left camshaft pulley and the No. 3 timing belt cover.

d. Check that the timing belt has tension between the crankshaft timing pulley and the left camshaft timing pulley.

25. Install the right camshaft timing pulley and the timing belt, as follows:

a. Align the installation mark on the timing belt with the timing mark of the

right camshaft timing pulley, and hang the timing belt on the right camshaft timing pulley with the flange side facing inward.

b. Slide the right camshaft timing pulley on the camshaft. Align the timing marks on the right camshaft timing pulley and the No. 3 timing belt cover.

c. Align the knock pin hole of the camshaft with the knock pin groove of the pulley.

d. Install the knock pin. Tighten the bolt to 81 ft. lbs. (110 Nm).

26. Set the timing belt tensioner, as follows:

a. Using a press, slowly press in the pushrod using 220–2,205 lbs. (981–9,807 N) of force.

b. Align the holes of the pushrod and housing, pass a 1.5mm hexagon wrench through the holes to keep the setting position of the pushrod.

c. Release the press and install the dust boot to the tensioner.

27. Install the timing belt tensioner and alternately tighten the bolts to 20 ft. lbs. (28 Nm). Using pliers, remove the 1.5mm hexagon wrench from the belt tensioner.

28. Check the valve timing, as follows:

a. Slowly turn the crankshaft pulley 2 revolutions from the TDC-to-TDC. Always turn the crankshaft pulley clockwise.

b. Check that each pulley aligns with the timing marks. If the timing marks do not align, remove the timing belt and reinstall it.

29. Install or connect the following:
- Fan bracket with the bolt and nut
- Power steering adjusting strut with the nut

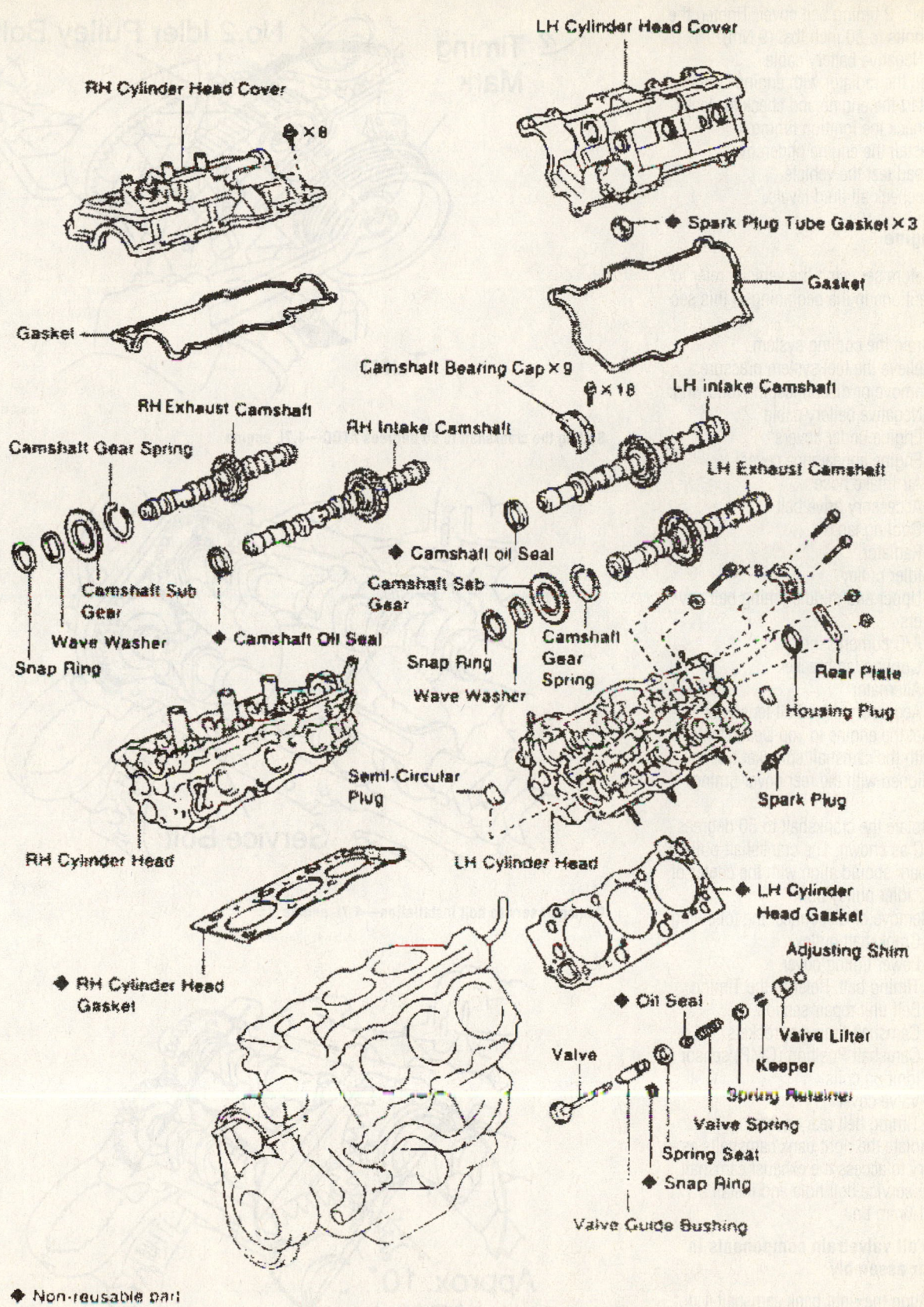

RH Cylinder Head Cover

LH Cylinder Head Cover

Gasket

Gasket

Spark Plug Tube Gasket × 3

Camshaft Bearing Cap × 9

RH Exhaust Camshaft

LH intake Camshaft

Camshaft Gear Spring

RH Intake Camshaft

LH Exhaust Camshaft

Camshaft Sub Gear

Camshaft Oil Seal

Camshaft Sub Gear

Wave Washer

Camshaft Oil Seal

Snap Ring

Camshaft Gear Spring

Rear Plate

Snap Ring

Wave Washer

Housing Plug

Semi-Circular Plug

Spark Plug

RH Cylinder Head

LH Cylinder Head

RH Cylinder Head Gasket

LH Cylinder Head Gasket

Adjusting Shim

Oil Seal

Valve Lifter

Valve

Keeper

Spring Retainer

Valve Spring

Spring Seat

Snap Ring

Valve Guide Bushing

◆ Non-reusable part

Exploded view of the cylinder head component assembly—3.4L engine

Refer to Section 1 for engine rebuilding specifications

7924YG75

- No. 2 timing belt cover. Tighten the bolts to 80 inch lbs. (9 Nm).
- Negative battery cable
30. Fill the radiator with engine coolant.
31. Start the engine and check for leaks.
32. Check the ignition timing.
33. Install the engine undercover.
34. Road test the vehicle.
35. Recheck all fluid levels.

4.7L Engine

1. Before servicing the vehicle, refer to the precautions in the beginning of this section.
2. Drain the cooling system.
3. Relieve the fuel system pressure.
4. Remove or disconnect the following:
- Negative battery cable
- Engine under covers
- Engine appearance cover
- Air intake hose
- Accessory drive belt
- Cooling fan
- Radiator
- Idler pulley
- Upper and middle timing belt covers
- A/C compressor
- Cooling fan bracket
- Alternator
- Accessory drive belt tensioner

5. Set the engine to Top Dead Center (TDC) with the camshaft sprocket timing marks aligned with the rear cover timing marks.

6. Rotate the crankshaft to 50 degrees After TDC as shown. The crankshaft pulley timing mark should align with the center of the No. 2 idler pulley bolt.

7. Remove or disconnect the following:
- Crankshaft pulley
- Lower timing cover
- Timing belt. Refer to the Timing Belt unit repair section.
- Camshaft timing sprockets
- Camshaft Position (CMP) sensor
- Ignition coils
- Valve cover
- Timing belt rear covers

8. Rotate the right bank camshafts as necessary to access the exhaust camshaft sub-gear service bolt hole and install a 6mm x 1.0mm bolt.

➡ **Keep all valvetrain components in order for assembly.**

9. Align the right bank camshaft 1 dot timing marks to a **10** degree angle as shown.

10. Loosen the bearing cap bolts in sequence and in several passes.

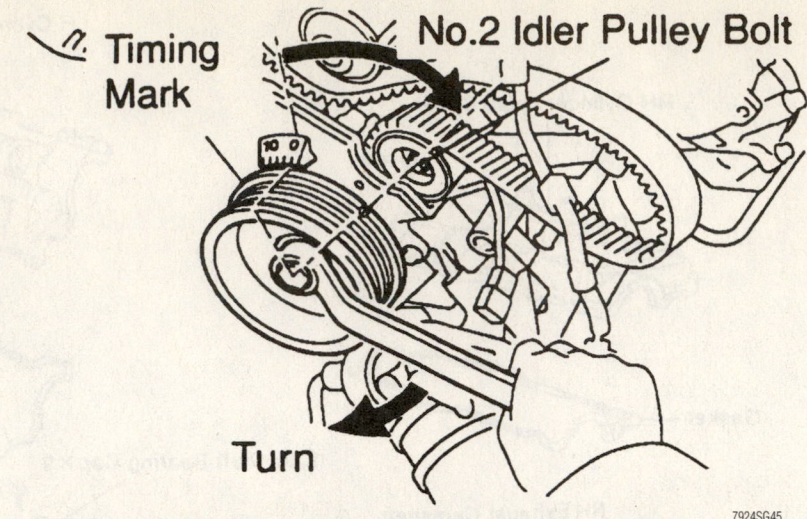

Setting the crankshaft to 50 degrees ATDC—4.7L engine

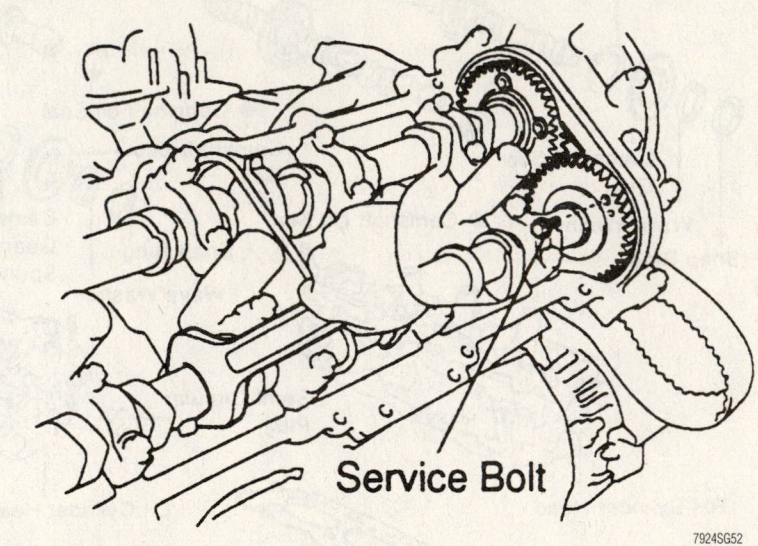

Camshaft service bolt installation—4.7L engine

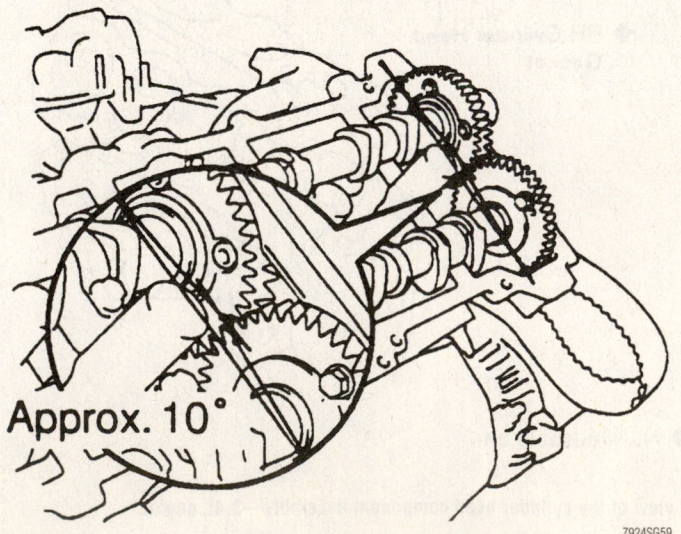

Right bank camshaft timing mark (1 dot marks) alignment—4.7L engine

11. Remove the right bank camshafts.

12. Rotate the left bank camshafts as necessary to access the exhaust camshaft sub-gear service bolt hole and install a 6mm x 1.0mm bolt.

13. Align the left bank camshaft 2 dot timing marks as shown.

14. Loosen the bearing cap bolts in sequence and in several passes.

15. Remove the left bank camshafts.

16. Remove the valve lifters and shims.

To install:

17. Ensure that the crankshaft is at 50 degrees After TDC.

18. Install or connect the following:

- Valve lifters and shims in their original positions
- Right bank camshafts with the 1 dot timing marks at 10 degrees

- Left bank camshafts with the 2 dot timing marks aligned
- Left and right bank camshaft bearing caps in their original positions. Apply sealant to the front bearing caps as shown.
- Camshaft oil seals

19. The bearing cap bolts vary in length and are identified as follows:

- A: 3.70 inches (94mm)
- B: 2.83 inches (72mm)
- C: 0.98 inches (25mm)
- D: 2.05 inches (52mm)
- E: 1.50 inches (38mm)

20. Bolts in positions **A**, **B** and **C** are installed dry.

21. Lubricate the threads and under the contact flange for bolts in positions **D** and **E**.

22. Install oil feed pipes and the bearing cap bolts according to position in the illustrations.

23. Tighten the camshaft bearing bolts in sequence and in several passes to the following specifications:

- Bolt C: 66 inch lbs. (7.5 Nm)
- All others: 12 ft. lbs. (16 Nm)

24. Remove the service bolts from the exhaust camshaft gears.

25. Install or connect the following:

- Timing belt rear covers
- Valve cover
- Ignition coils
- CMP sensor
- Camshaft timing sprockets. Tighten the bolts to 80 ft. lbs. (108 Nm).
- Timing belt
- Lower timing cover

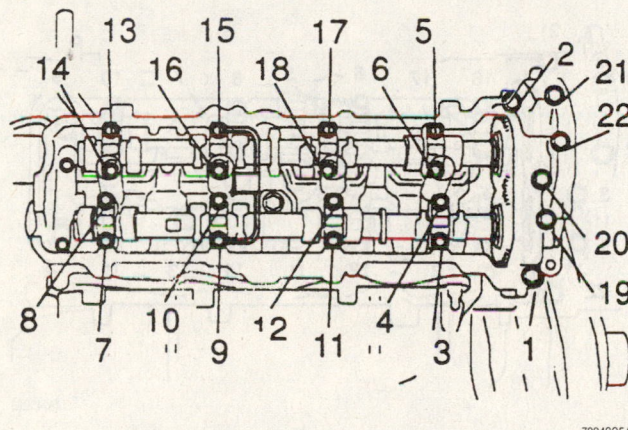

Right bank camshaft bearing cap loosening sequence—4.7L engine

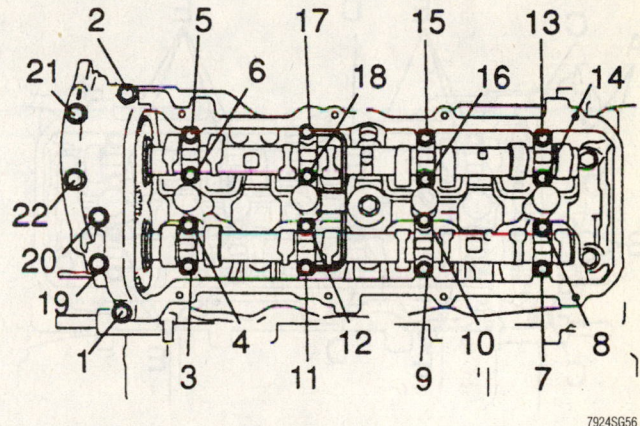

Left bank camshaft bearing cap loosening sequence—4.7L engine

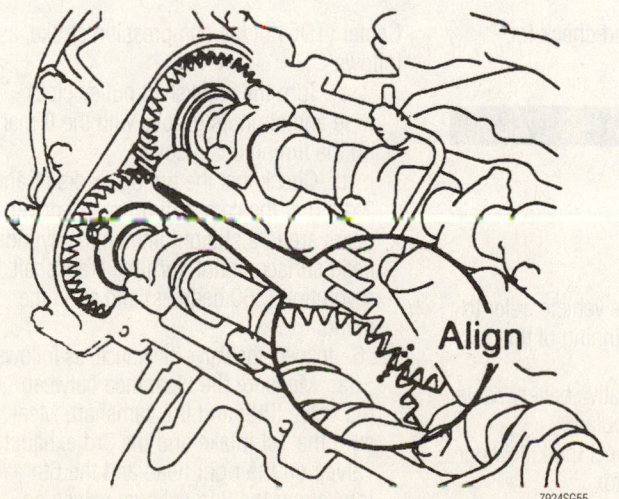

Left bank camshaft timing mark (2 dot marks) alignment—4.7L engine

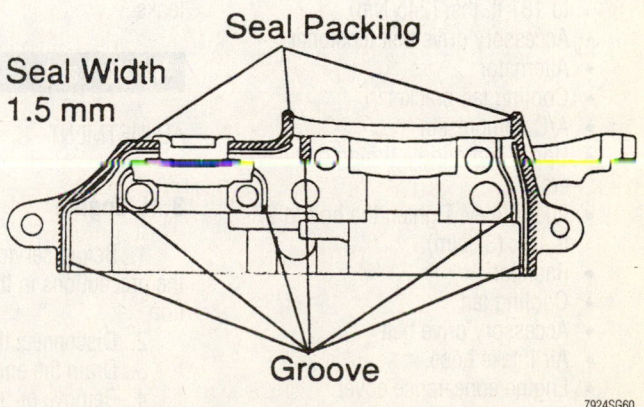

Apply a 1.5mm bead of sealant to the front bearing caps—4.7L engine

For engine torque specifications, refer to Section 1 of this manual

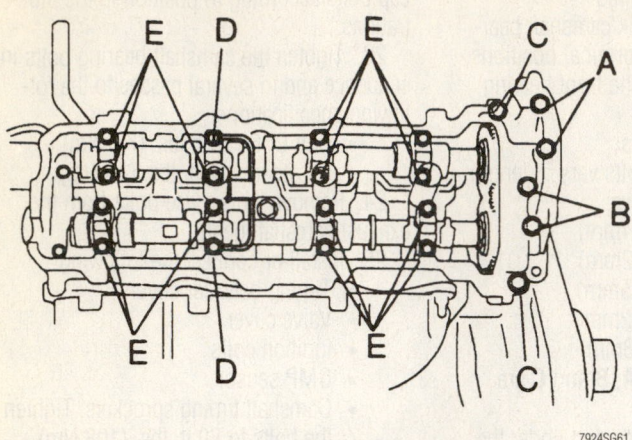

Right bank bearing cap bolt location—4.7L engine

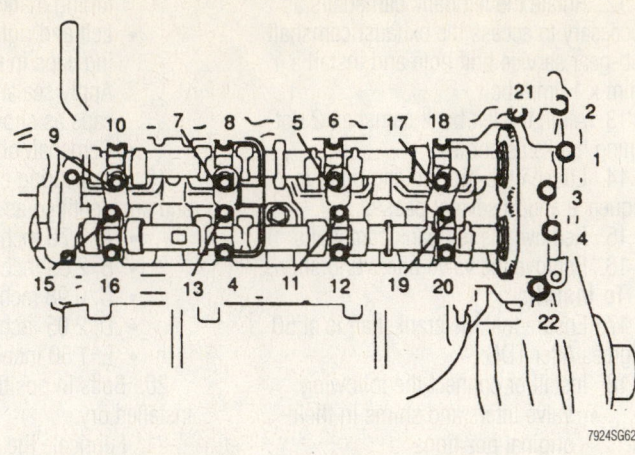

Right bank camshaft bearing cap bolt torque sequence—4.7L engine

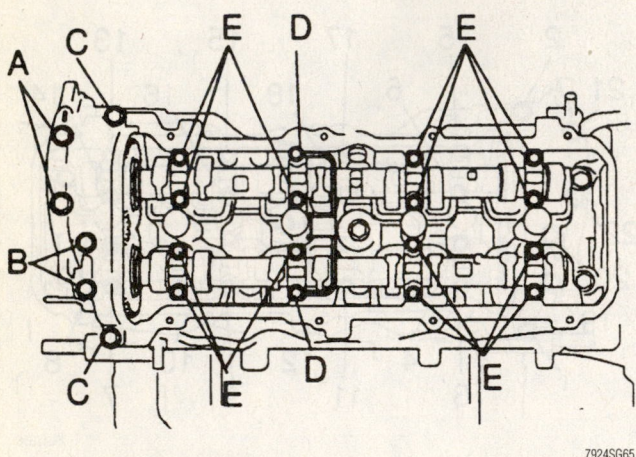

Left camshaft bearing cap bolt locations—4.7L engine

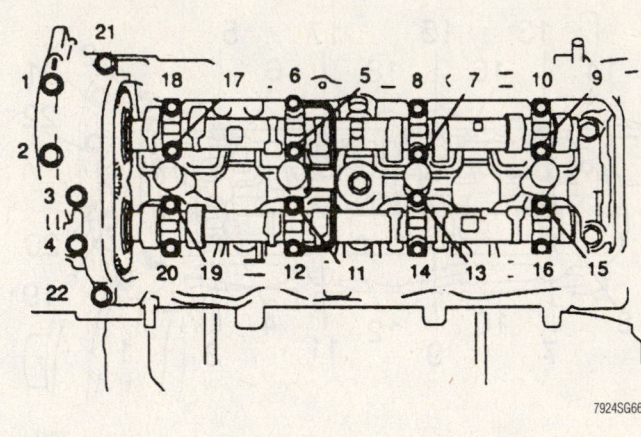

Left bank camshaft bearing cap bolt torque sequence—4.7L engine

- Crankshaft pulley. Tighten the bolt to 181 ft. lbs. (245 Nm).
- Accessory drive belt tensioner
- Alternator
- Cooling fan bracket
- A/C compressor
- Upper and middle timing belt covers
- Idler pulley. Tighten the bolt to 27 ft. lbs. (37 Nm).
- Radiator
- Cooling fan
- Accessory drive belt
- Air intake hose
- Engine appearance cover
- Engine under covers
- Negative battery cable

26. Fill the cooling system.

27. Start the engine and check for leaks.

Valve Lash

ADJUSTMENT

3.4L Engine

1. Before servicing the vehicle, refer to the precautions in the beginning of this section.
2. Disconnect the negative battery cable.
3. Drain the engine coolant.
4. Remove or disconnect the following:
   - Air intake connector
   - Cylinder head cover
5. Set the No. 1 cylinder to Top Dead Center (TDC) of the compression stroke, as follows:

   a. Turn the crankshaft pulley clockwise and align its groove with the **0** mark on the timing chain cover.

   b. Check that the timing marks (1 and 2 dots) of the camshaft drive and driven gears are in a straight line on the cylinder head surface. If not, turn the crankshaft 1 revolution (360 degrees) and align the marks.

6. Inspect the valve clearance, as follows:

   a. Measure the clearance between the valve lifter and the camshaft. Measure the 1st intake and the 3rd exhaust valves on the right head and the 6th intake and the 2nd exhaust valves on the left head.

b. Turn the crankshaft ⅔ of a revolution (240 degrees) and adjust the 3rd intake and the 5th exhaust valves on the right head and the 2nd intake and the 4th exhaust valves on the left head.

c. Turn the crankshaft ⅔ of a revolution (240 degrees) and adjust the 5th intake and the 1st exhaust valves on the right head and the 4th intake and the 6th exhaust valves on the left head.

7. Valve clearance cold should be:
- Intake: 0.006–0.009 in. (0.13–0.23mm)
- Exhaust: 0.011–0.014 in. (0.27–0.37mm)

8. Adjust the valve clearance by using adjusting shims, as follows:

a. Turn the equipment camshaft so that the cam lobe for the valve to be adjusted faces up.

b. Turn the valve lifter so that the notches are perpendicular to the camshaft.

c. Using SST 09248-55040, press down the valve lifter and place SST 09248-05420, between the camshaft and the valve lifter. Remove SST 09248-55040.

d. Remove the adjusting shim with a small flat prying tool and a magnetic finger.

e. Determine the replacement adjusting shim size according to the following formula or use the adjusting shim charts.

f. Using a micrometer, measure the thickness of the removed shim. Calculate

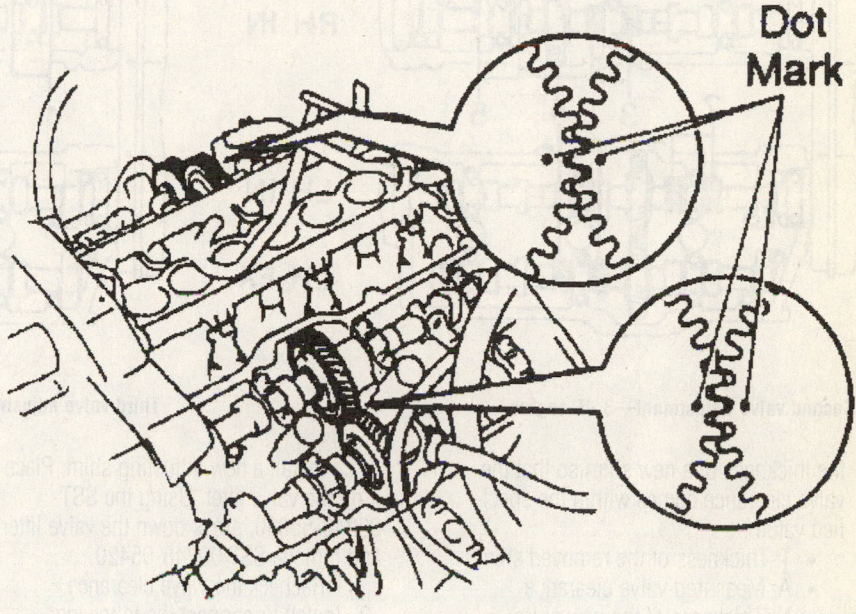

Aligning the timing marks—3.4L engine

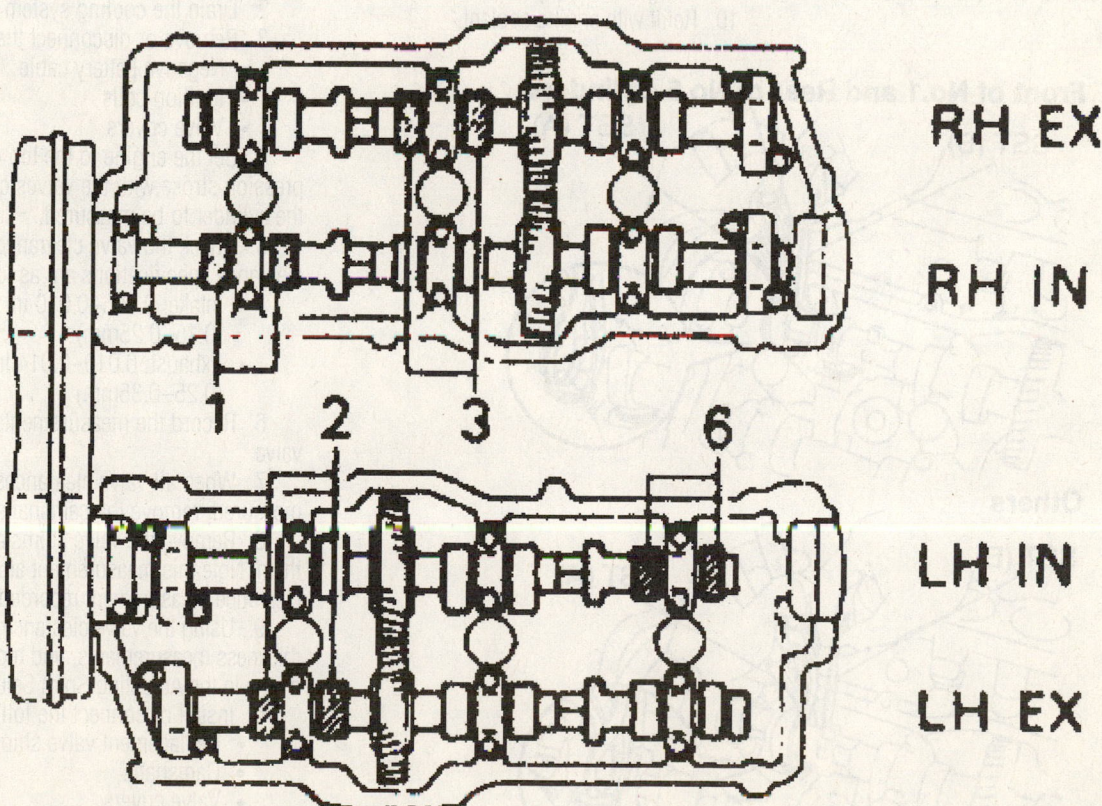

First valve adjustment—3.4L engine

For complete mechanical specifications, refer to Section 1 of this manual

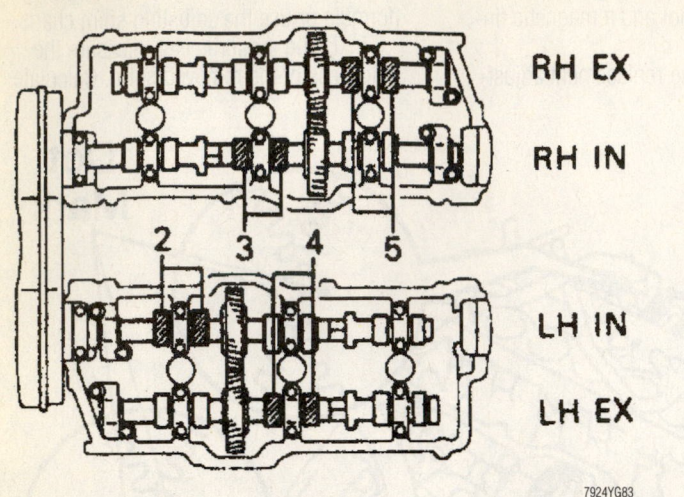

Second valve adjustment—3.4L engine

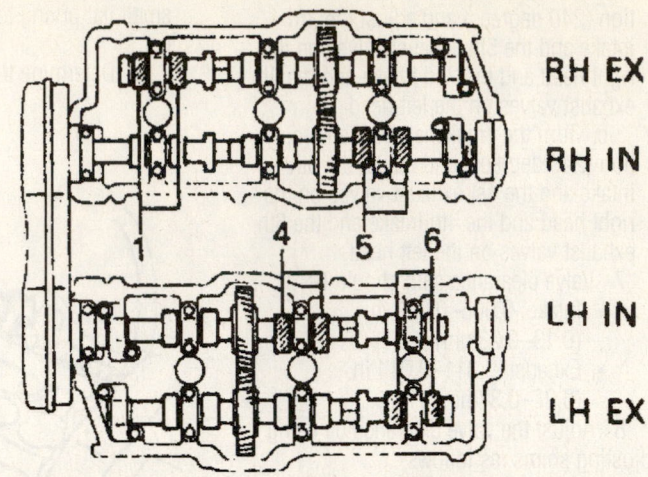

Third valve adjustment—3.4L engine

the thickness of a new shim so that the valve clearance comes within the specified value.

- T: Thickness of the removed shim
- A: Measured valve clearance
- N: Thickness of the new shim

g. Intake: N = T + (A—0.007 in. (0.18mm))

h. Exhaust: N = T + (A—0.013 in. (0.32mm))

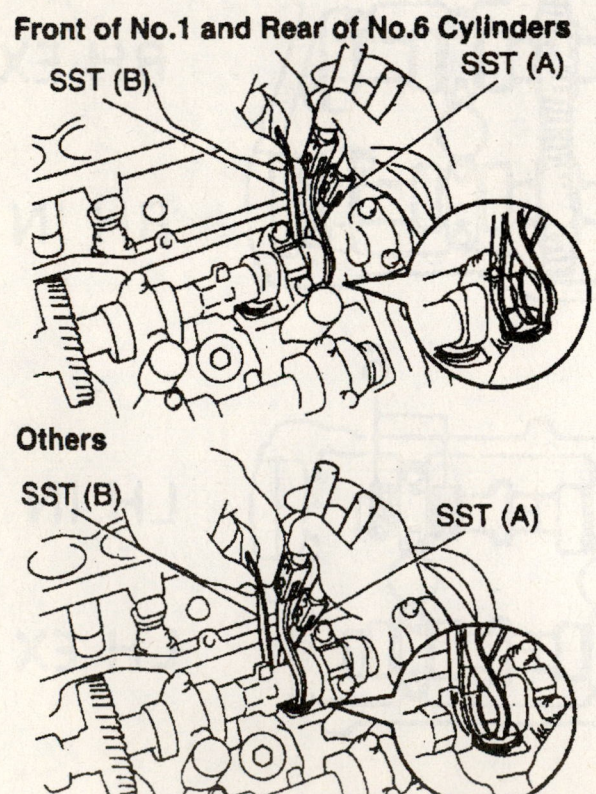

Front of No.1 and Rear of No.6 Cylinders

Others

Removing the adjusting shim—3.4L engine

i. Install a new adjusting shim. Place it on the valve lifter. Using the SST 09248-55040, press down the valve lifter and remove SST 09248-05420.

j. Recheck the valve clearance.

9. Install or connect the following:
- Cylinder head cover
- Intake air connector
- Negative battery cable

10. Refill with engine coolant.

11. Start the engine and check for leaks.

4.7L Engine

➡**Measure the valve clearance with the engine cold.**

1. Before servicing the vehicle, refer to the precautions in the beginning of this section.

2. Drain the cooling system.

3. Remove or disconnect the following:
- Negative battery cable
- Ignition coils
- Valve covers

4. Set the engine to the top of the compression stroke with the valves closed for the cylinder to be measured.

5. Check the valve clearance. The valve clearance specifications are as follows:
- Intake: 0.006–0.010 in. (0.15–0.25mm)
- Exhaust: 0.010–0.014 in. (0.25–0.35mm)

6. Record the measurements for each valve.

7. When all valve clearances have been measured, remove the camshafts.

8. Remove the valve shims and measure them. Note this measurement along with the clearance measurement recorded earlier.

9. Using the valve clearance and shim thickness measurements, find replacement shims in the Adjusting Shim Selection charts.

10. Install or connect the following:
- Replacement valve shims
- Camshafts
- Valve covers
- Ignition coils
- Negative battery cable

11. Fill the cooling system.

12. Start the engine and check for leaks.

Intake valve clearance shim selection chart—4.7L engine

Installed shim thickness mm (in.) (top axis):
2.000 (0.0787), 2.020 (0.0795), 2.040 (0.0803), 2.060 (0.0811), 2.080 (0.0819), 2.100 (0.0827), 2.120 (0.0835), 2.140 (0.0843), 2.160 (0.0850), 2.180 (0.0858), 2.200 (0.0866), 2.220 (0.0874), 2.240 (0.0882), 2.260 (0.0890), 2.280 (0.0898), 2.300 (0.0906), 2.320 (0.0913), 2.340 (0.0921), 2.360 (0.0929), 2.380 (0.0937), 2.400 (0.0945), 2.410 (0.0945), 2.420 (0.0953), 2.430 (0.0957), 2.440 (0.0961), 2.450 (0.0965), 2.460 (0.0969), 2.470 (0.0972), 2.480 (0.0976), 2.490 (0.0980), 2.500 (0.0984), 2.510 (0.0988), 2.520 (0.0992), 2.530 (0.0996), 2.540 (0.1000), 2.550 (0.1004), 2.560 (0.1008), 2.570 (0.1012), 2.580 (0.1016), 2.590 (0.1016), 2.600 (0.1020), 2.620 (0.1024), 2.640 (0.1031), 2.660 (0.1039), 2.680 (0.1047), 2.700 (0.1055), 2.720 (0.1063), 2.740 (0.1071), 2.760 (0.1079), 2.780 (0.1087), 2.800 (0.1094), 2.800 (0.1102)

Measured clearance mm (in.) (left axis):
0.000–0.030 (0.0000–0.0012)
0.031–0.050 (0.0012–0.0020)
0.051–0.070 (0.0020–0.0028)
0.071–0.090 (0.0028–0.0035)
0.091–0.110 (0.0036–0.0043)
0.111–0.130 (0.0044–0.0051)
0.131–0.149 (0.0052–0.0059)
0.150–0.250 (0.0059–0.0098)
0.251–0.270 (0.0099–0.0106)
0.271–0.290 (0.0107–0.0114)
0.291–0.310 (0.0115–0.0122)
0.311–0.330 (0.0122–0.0130)
0.331–0.350 (0.0130–0.0138)
0.351–0.370 (0.0138–0.0146)
0.371–0.390 (0.0146–0.0154)
0.391–0.410 (0.0154–0.0161)
0.411–0.430 (0.0162–0.0169)
0.431–0.450 (0.0170–0.0177)
0.451–0.470 (0.0178–0.0185)
0.471–0.490 (0.0185–0.0193)
0.491–0.510 (0.0193–0.0201)
0.511–0.530 (0.0201–0.0209)
0.531–0.550 (0.0209–0.0217)
0.551–0.570 (0.0217–0.0224)
0.571–0.590 (0.0225–0.0232)
0.591–0.610 (0.0233–0.0240)
0.611–0.630 (0.0241–0.0248)
0.631–0.650 (0.0248–0.0256)
0.651–0.670 (0.0256–0.0264)
0.671–0.690 (0.0264–0.0272)
0.691–0.710 (0.0272–0.0280)
0.711–0.730 (0.0280–0.0287)
0.731–0.750 (0.0288–0.0295)
0.751–0.770 (0.0296–0.0303)
0.771–0.790 (0.0304–0.0311)
0.791–0.810 (0.0311–0.0319)
0.811–0.830 (0.0319–0.0327)
0.831–0.850 (0.0327–0.0335)
0.851–0.870 (0.0335–0.0343)
0.871–0.890 (0.0343–0.0350)
0.891–0.910 (0.0351–0.0358)
0.911–0.930 (0.0359–0.0366)
0.931–0.950 (0.0367–0.0374)
0.951–0.970 (0.0374–0.0382)
0.971–0.990 (0.0382–0.0390)
0.991–1.010 (0.0390–0.0398)
1.011–1.030 (0.0398–0.0406)
1.031–1.050 (0.0406–0.0413)

Intake valve clearance (Cold):
0.15 – 0.25 mm (0.006 – 0.010 in.)

EXAMPLE:
The 2.300 mm (0.0906 in.) shim is installed, and the measured clearance is 0.440 mm (0.0173 in.). Replace the 2.300 mm (0.0906 in.) shim with a No. 54 shim.

New shim thickness

Shim No.	Thickness	Shim No.	Thickness	Shim No.	Thickness
00	2.000 (0.0787)	28	2.280 (0.0898)	56	2.560 (0.1008)
02	2.020 (0.0795)	30	2.300 (0.0906)	58	2.580 (0.1016)
04	2.040 (0.0803)	32	2.320 (0.0913)	60	2.600 (0.1024)
06	2.060 (0.0811)	34	2.340 (0.0921)	62	2.620 (0.1031)
08	2.080 (0.0819)	36	2.360 (0.0929)	64	2.640 (0.1039)
10	2.100 (0.0827)	38	2.380 (0.0937)	66	2.660 (0.1047)
12	2.120 (0.0835)	40	2.400 (0.0945)	68	2.680 (0.1055)
14	2.140 (0.0843)	42	2.420 (0.0953)	70	2.700 (0.1063)
16	2.160 (0.0850)	44	2.440 (0.0961)	72	2.720 (0.1071)
18	2.180 (0.0858)	46	2.460 (0.0969)	74	2.740 (0.1079)
20	2.200 (0.0866)	48	2.480 (0.0976)	76	2.760 (0.1087)
22	2.220 (0.0874)	50	2.500 (0.0984)	78	2.780 (0.1094)
24	2.240 (0.0882)	52	2.520 (0.0992)	80	2.800 (0.1102)
26	2.260 (0.0890)	54	2.540 (0.1000)		

7924SG71

Exhaust valve clearance (Cold):
0.25 – 0.35 mm (0.010 – 0.014 in.)

EXAMPLE:
The 2.300 mm (0.0906 in.) shim is installed, and the measured clearance is 0.440 mm (0.0173 in.). Replace the 2.300 mm (0.0906 in.) shim with a No. 44 shim.

New shim thickness

Shim No.	Thickness	Shim No.	Thickness	Shim No.	Thickness	Shim No.	Thickness
00	2.000 (0.0787)	28	2.280 (0.0898)	56	2.560 (0.1008)		
02	2.020 (0.0795)	30	2.300 (0.0906)	58	2.580 (0.1016)		
04	2.040 (0.0803)	32	2.320 (0.0913)	60	2.600 (0.1024)		
06	2.060 (0.0811)	34	2.340 (0.0921)	62	2.620 (0.1031)		
08	2.080 (0.0819)	36	2.360 (0.0929)	64	2.640 (0.1039)		
10	2.100 (0.0827)	38	2.380 (0.0937)	66	2.660 (0.1047)		
12	2.120 (0.0835)	40	2.400 (0.0945)	68	2.680 (0.1055)		
14	2.140 (0.0843)	42	2.420 (0.0953)	70	2.700 (0.1063)		
16	2.160 (0.0850)	44	2.440 (0.0961)	72	2.720 (0.1071)		
18	2.180 (0.0858)	46	2.460 (0.0969)	74	2.740 (0.1079)		
20	2.200 (0.0866)	48	2.480 (0.0976)	76	2.760 (0.1087)		
22	2.220 (0.0874)	50	2.500 (0.0984)	78	2.780 (0.1094)		
24	2.240 (0.0882)	52	2.520 (0.0992)	80	2.800 (0.1102)		
28	2.260 (0.0890)	54	2.540 (0.1000)				

mm (in.)

79245G72

Exhaust valve clearance shim selection chart—4.7L engine

Starter Motor

REMOVAL & INSTALLATION

3.4L Engine

1. Before servicing the vehicle, refer to the precautions in the beginning of this section.
2. Remove or disconnect the following:
   - Negative battery cable
   - Starter electrical connectors
   - Starter

To install:

3. Install or connect the following:
   - Starter. Tighten the fasteners to 29 ft. lbs. (39 Nm).
   - Electrical connections
   - Negative battery cable

4.7L Engine

1. Before servicing the vehicle, refer to the precautions in the beginning of this section.
2. Drain the cooling system.
3. Relieve the fuel system pressure.
4. Remove or disconnect the following:
   - Negative battery cable
   - Engine appearance cover
   - Air intake tube
   - Intake manifold
   - Starter motor mounting bolts
   - Starter wiring connectors
   - Starter motor

To install:

5. Install or connect the following:
   - Starter motor
   - Starter wiring connectors. Tighten the cable nut to 86 inch lbs. (10 Nm).
   - Starter motor mounting bolts. Tighten the bolts to 29 ft. lbs. (39 Nm).
   - Intake manifold
   - Air intake tube
   - Engine appearance cover
   - Negative battery cable
6. Fill the cooling system.
7. Start the engine and check for leaks.

Oil Pan

REMOVAL & INSTALLATION

3.4L Engine

1. Before servicing the vehicle, refer to the precautions in the beginning of this section.
2. Disconnect the negative battery cable.
3. Drain the engine oil.

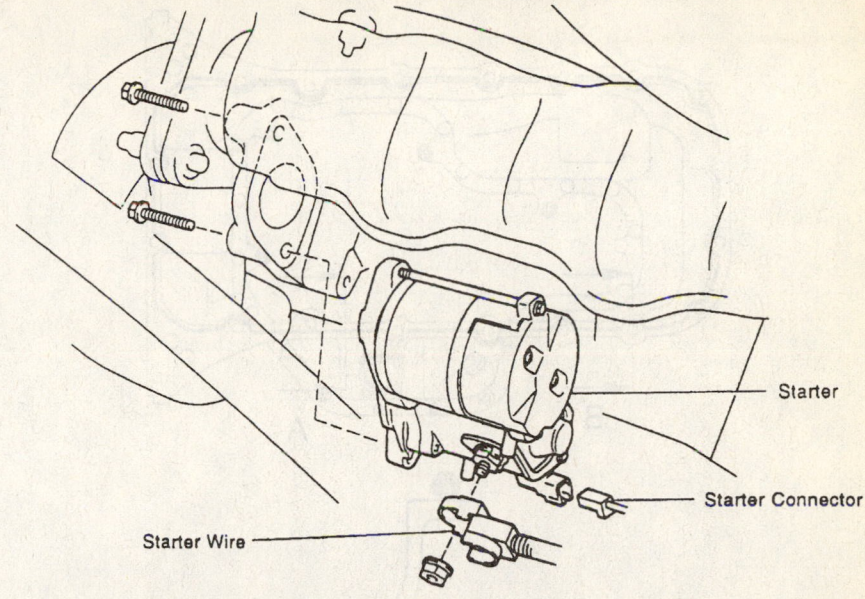

Exploded view of a common starter—3.4L engine

4. Remove or disconnect the following:
   - Engine undercover
   - Front differential, if equipped with 4WD
   - Oil pan, separate it from the engine using SST 09032-00100 and a brass bar

To install:

5. Apply seal packing to the oil pan.
6. Install the oil pan to the cylinder block. Tighten the nuts and bolts to: 67 inch lbs. (8 Nm).

✳✳ WARNING

If parts are not assembled within 5 minutes of applying time, the effec- tiveness of the seal packing is lost and must be removed and reapplied.

7. Install or connect the following:
   - Front differential, if removed
   - Engine undercover
   - Negative battery cable
8. Fill with engine oil.
9. Start the engine and check for leaks.

4.7L Engine

1. Before servicing the vehicle, refer to the precautions in the beginning of this section.
2. Remove the engine from the vehicle and mount it on a stand.

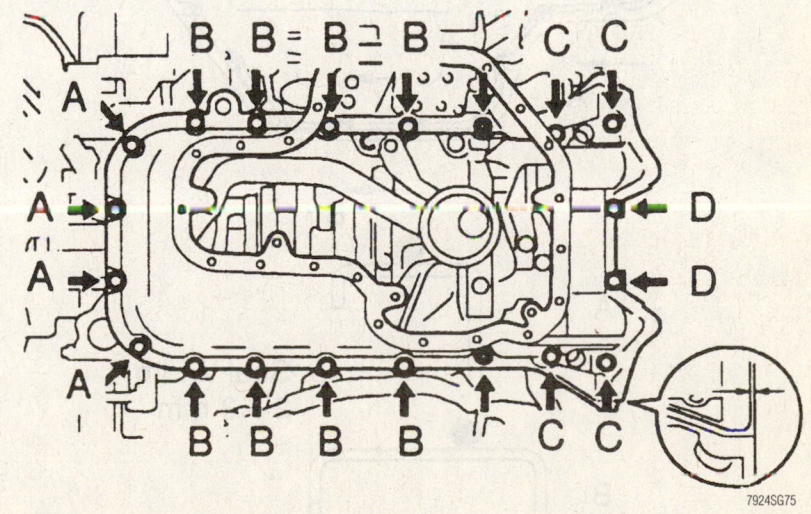

Upper oil pan bolt location—4.7L engine

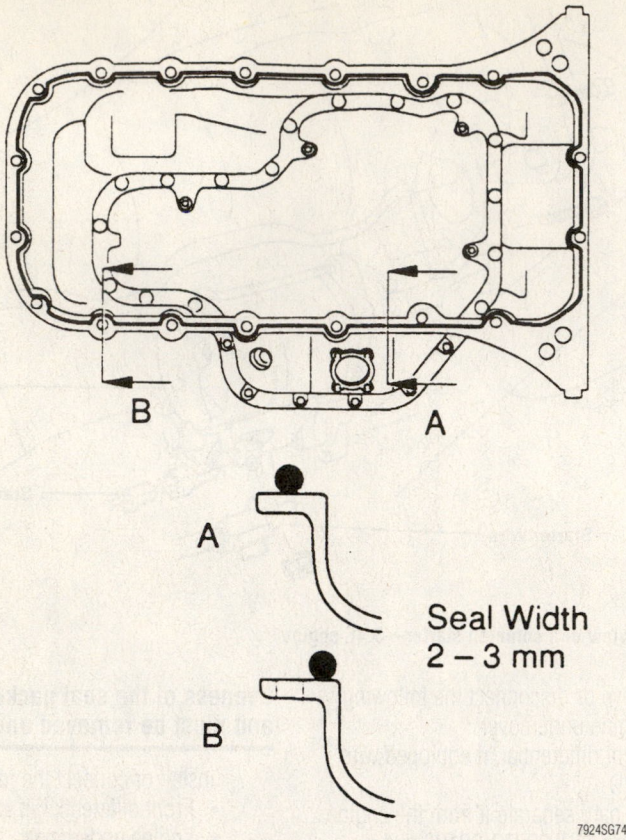

Seal Width
2 – 3 mm

7924SG74

Upper oil pan sealant application—4.7L engine

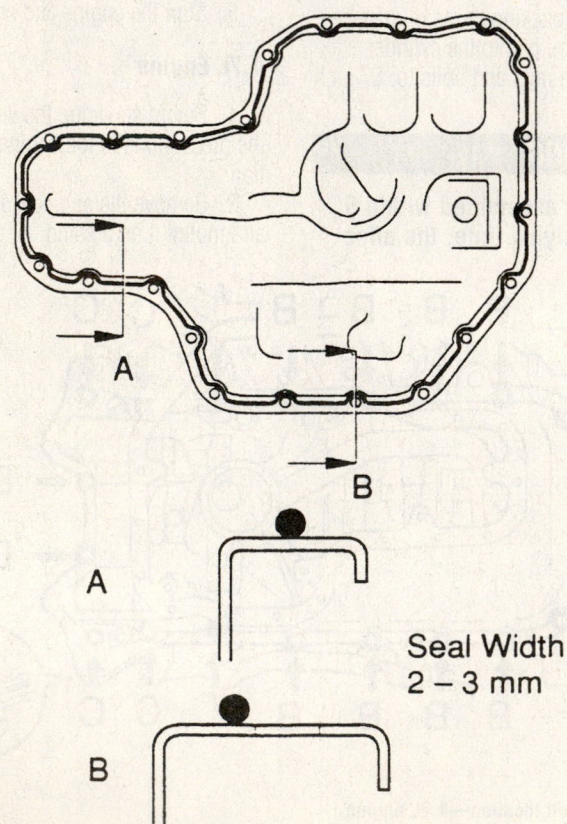

Seal Width
2 – 3 mm

7924SG76

Lower oil pan sealant application—4.7L engine

3. Remove or disconnect the following:
  - Oil dipstick tube
  - Lower oil pan
  - Oil pan baffle
  - Upper oil pan

To install:

4. The upper oil pan bolts are different lengths and are identified as follows:
  - A: 0.79 inch (20mm) w/10mm head
  - B: 0.98 inch (25mm) w/12mm head
  - C: 2.36 inch (60mm) w/12mm head
  - D: 1.38 inch (35mm) w/10mm head

5. Apply silicone sealant to the upper oil pan as shown.

6. Install the upper oil pan and tighten the fasteners in several passes to the following specifications:
  - 10mm: 66 inch lbs. (7.5 Nm)
  - 12mm: 21 ft. lbs. (28 Nm)

7. Install or connect the following:
  - Oil pan baffle. Tighten the fasteners to 66 inch lbs. (7.5 Nm).
  - Lower oil pan. Tighten the fasteners in several passes to 66 inch lbs. (7.5 Nm).
  - Oil dipstick tube

8. Install the engine.

Oil Pump

REMOVAL & INSTALLATION

3.4L Engine

1. Before servicing the vehicle, refer to the precautions in the beginning of this section.

2. Remove or disconnect the following:
  - Negative battery cable
  - Engine undercover
  - Crankshaft timing pulley
  - Front differential, if equipped with 4WD

3. Drain the engine oil from the engine.

4. Remove or disconnect the following:
  - Timing belt and crankshaft gear
  - Oil cooler tube and clamp, if equipped with automatic transmission
  - Stiffener plate
  - Flywheel housing undercover and dust cover
  - Rear end cover and dust cover
  - Starter wire clamp
  - Crankshaft Position (CKP) sensor
  - Oil pan

➡**Be careful not to damage the baffle plate flange.**

  - Oil strainer
  - Oil baffle plate

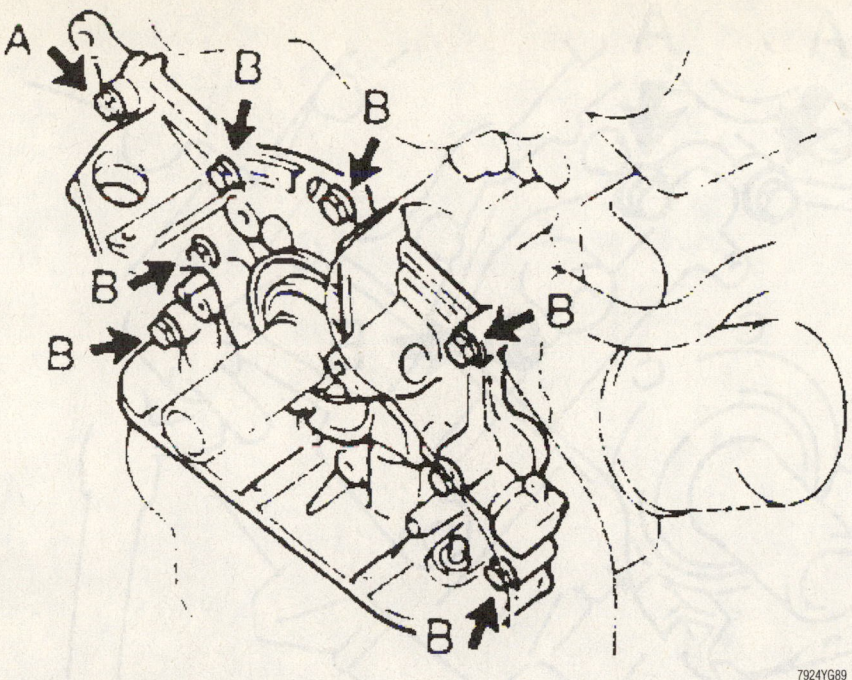

Oil pump bolt identification—3.4L engine

- Oil pump body by removing the 8 bolts.
- O-ring from the cylinder block

To install:

5. Install or connect the following:
- Apply Seal Packing PN 08826-00080 to the oil pump
- New O-ring into the groove of the cylinder block
- Oil pump to the crankshaft with the spline teeth of the drive rotor engaged with the large teeth of the crankshaft. Tighten the oil pump bolts "A" 15 ft. lbs. (20 Nm) and bolts "B" 31 ft. lbs. (42 Nm)
- CKP
- Oil pan baffle plate
- Oil strainer with a new gasket. Tighten the bolts to 13 ft. lbs. (18 Nm).
- Remaining components
- Negative battery cable

6. Fill with engine oil.

7. Start the engine and check for leaks.

4.7L Engine

1. Before servicing the vehicle, refer to the precautions in the beginning of this section.

2. Remove the engine from the vehicle and mount it on a stand.

3. Remove or disconnect the following:
- Front cover
- Timing belt. Refer to the Timing Belt unit repair section.
- Timing belt idler pulleys
- Crankshaft timing sprocket
- Oil dipstick tube
- Oil filter and bracket
- Crankshaft Position (CKP) sensor

- Oil pan and baffle
- Oil pump pickup tube
- Oil pump

To install:

4. The upper oil pan bolts are different lengths and are identified as follows:
- A: 1.38 inch (35mm) w/12mm head
- B: 1.97 inch (50mm) w/12mm head
- C: 4.17 inch (106mm) w/12mm head
- D: 1.57 inch (40mm) w/14mm head
- E: 1.18 inch (30mm) w/6mm hex head

5. Install a new O-ring on the engine block.

6. Apply silicone sealant to the oil pump housing as shown.

7. Install the oil pump. Tighten the bolts in several passes to the following specifications:
- 12mm: 11 ft. lbs. (15.5 Nm)
- 14mm: 22 ft. lbs. (30.5 Nm)
- 6mm Hex: 11 ft. lbs. (15.5 Nm)

8. Install or connect the following:
- Oil pump pickup tube. Tighten the bolts to 66 inch lbs. (7.5 Nm).
- Oil pan and baffle
- CKP sensor
- Oil filter and bracket. Tighten the bolts to 13 ft. lbs. (18 Nm).
- Oil dipstick tube
- Crankshaft timing sprocket
- Timing belt idler pulleys

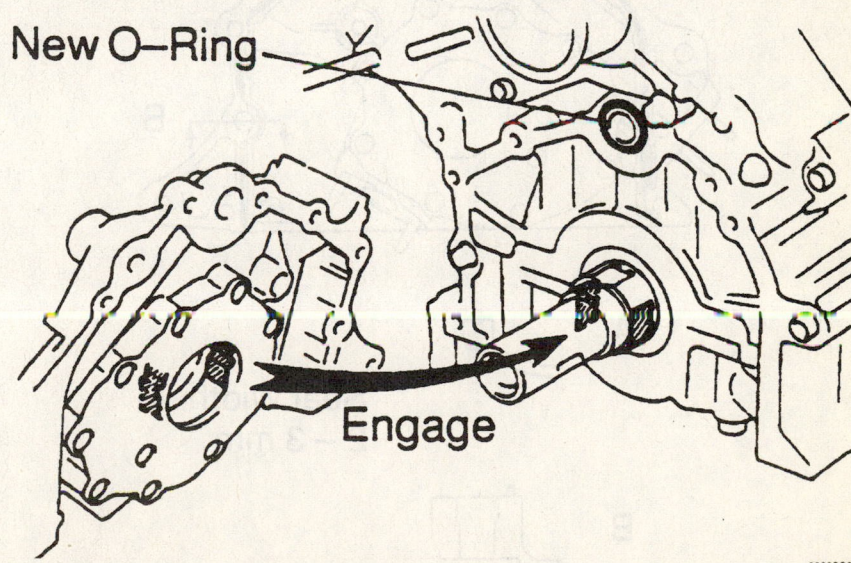

Location of the O-ring seal—4.7L engine

Timing belt service is covered in Section 4 of this manual

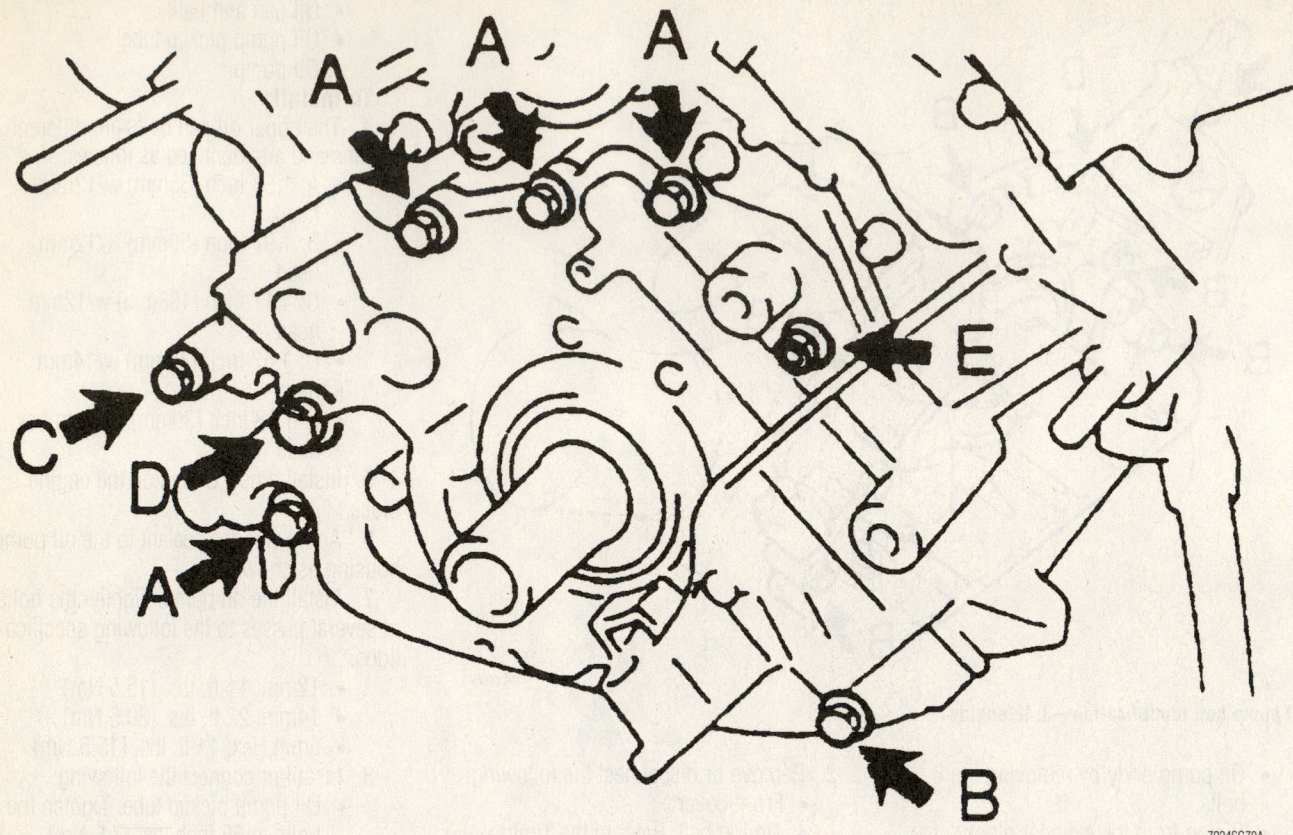

Oil pump bolt location—4.7L engine

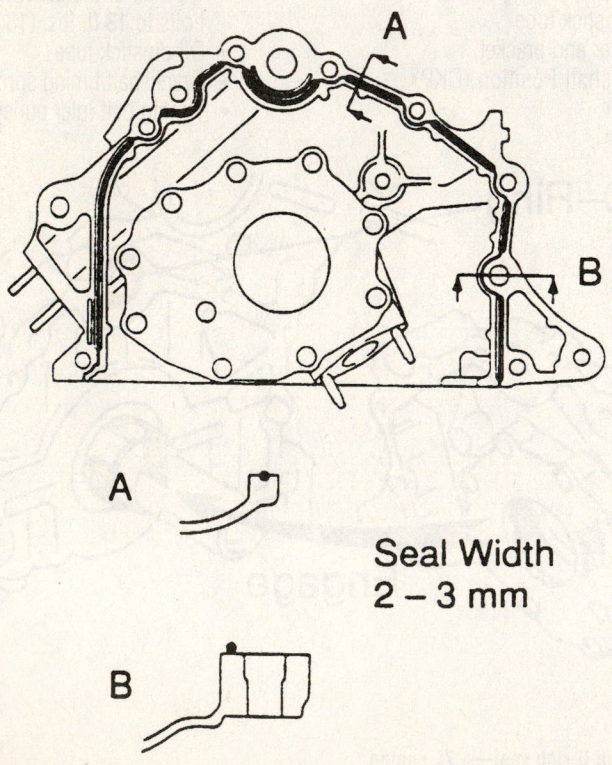

**Seal Width
2 – 3 mm**

7924SG78

Oil pump housing sealant application—4.7L engine

- Timing belt
- Front cover
9. Install the engine.

Rear Main Seal

REMOVAL & INSTALLATION

1. Before servicing the vehicle, refer to the precautions in the beginning of this section.

2. Remove the transmission and flywheel/driveplate from the vehicle.

3. Cut off the rubber lip portion of the seal with a sharp knife.

4. Pry out the oil seal.

To install:

5. Install the rear main seal so that it is flush with the seal retainer housing.

6. Install or connect the following:

- Flywheel/driveplate. Tighten the bolts to 28 ft. lbs. (38 Nm) for 3.4L engine with a manual transmission, 61 ft. lbs. (83 Nm) for 3.4L engine with an automatic transmission or 35 ft. lbs. (48 Nm) plus a 90 degree turn for 4.7L engine.
- Transmission

Piston and Ring

POSITIONING

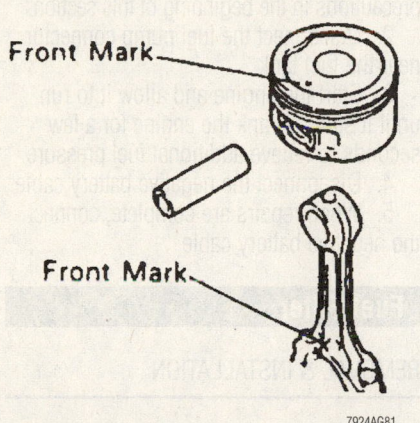

Piston to connecting rod assembly—3.4L engines

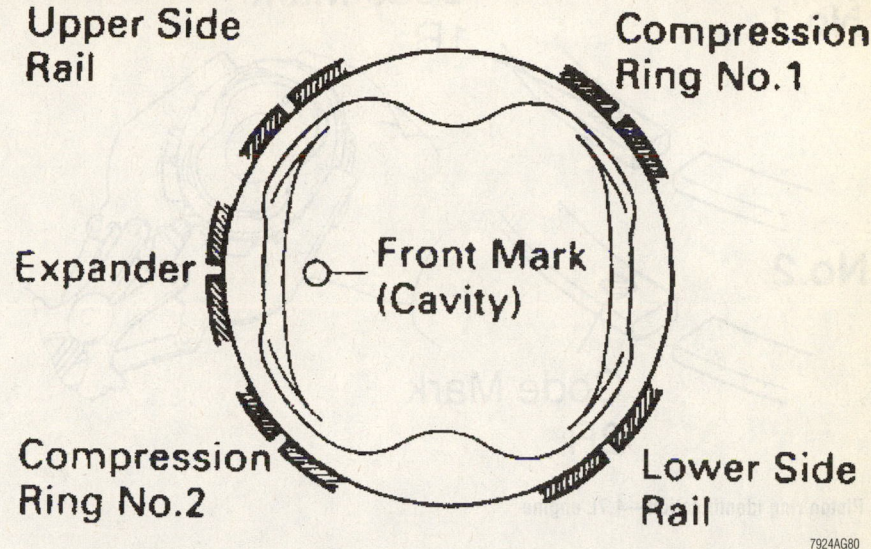

Piston ring end-gap spacing—3.4L engine

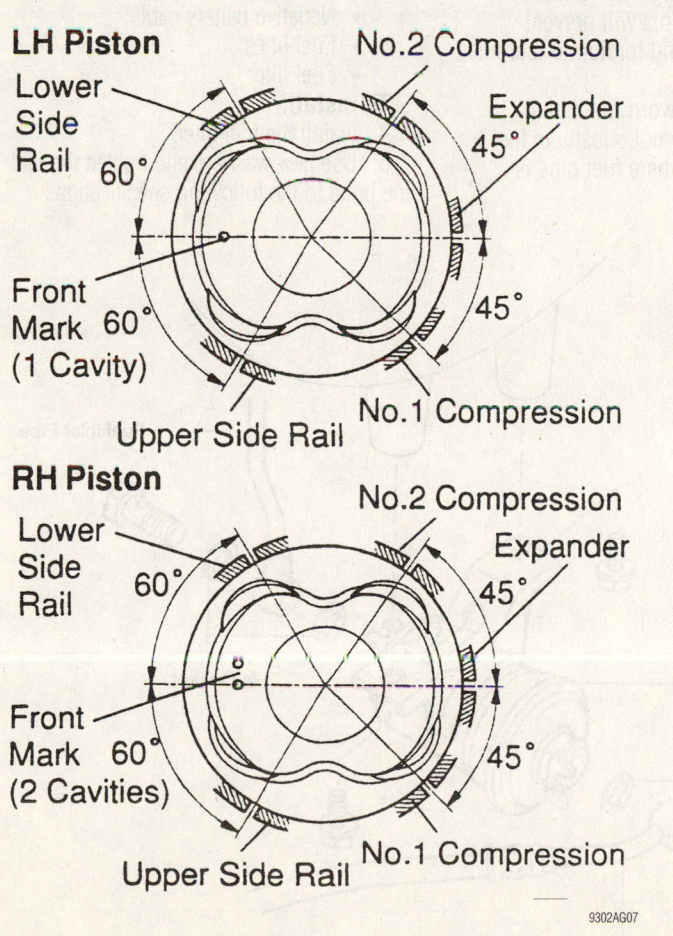

Piston ring positioning—4.7L engine

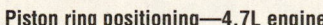

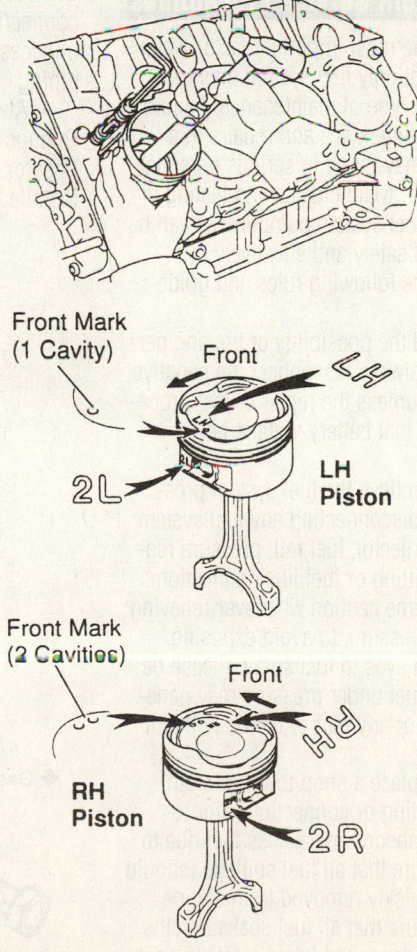

Piston positioning—4.7L engine

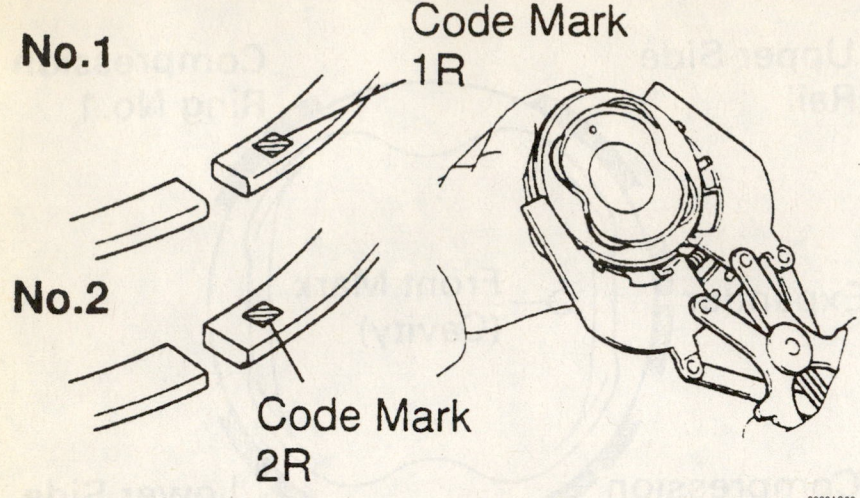

No.1

**Code Mark
1R**

No.2

**Code Mark
2R**

Piston ring identification—4.7L engine

9302AG09

FUEL SYSTEM

Fuel System Service Precautions

Safety is the most important factor when performing not only fuel system maintenance but any type of maintenance. Failure to conduct maintenance and repairs in a safe manner may result in serious personal injury or death. Maintenance and testing of the vehicle's fuel system components can be accomplished safely and effectively by adhering to the following rules and guidelines.

• To avoid the possibility of fire and personal injury, always disconnect the negative battery cable unless the repair or test procedure requires that battery voltage be applied.

• Always relieve the fuel system pressure prior to disconnecting any fuel system component (injector, fuel rail, pressure regulator, etc.), fitting or fuel line connection. Exercise extreme caution whenever relieving fuel system pressure, to avoid exposing skin, face and eyes to fuel spray. Please be advised that fuel under pressure may penetrate the skin or any part of the body that it contacts.

• Always place a shop towel or cloth around the fitting or connection prior to loosening to absorb any excess fuel due to spillage. Ensure that all fuel spillage (should it occur) is quickly removed from engine surfaces. Ensure that all fuel soaked cloths or towels are deposited into a suitable waste container.

• Always keep a dry chemical (Class B) fire extinguisher near the work area.

• Do not allow fuel spray or fuel vapors to come into contact with a spark or open flame.

• Always use a back-up wrench when loosening and tightening fuel line connection fittings. This will prevent unnecessary stress and torsion to fuel line piping.

• Always replace worn fuel fitting O-rings with new. Do not substitute fuel hose or equivalent, where fuel pipe is installed.

Fuel System Pressure

RELIEVING

1. Before servicing the vehicle, refer to the precautions in the beginning of this section.
2. Disconnect the fuel pump connector near the fuel tank.
3. Start the engine and allow it to run until it stalls. Crank the engine for a few seconds to relieve additional fuel pressure.
4. Disconnect the negative battery cable.
5. When repairs are complete, connect the negative battery cable.

Fuel Filter

REMOVAL & INSTALLATION

1. Before servicing the vehicle, refer to the precautions in the beginning of this section.
2. Relieve the fuel system pressure.
3. Remove or disconnect the following:
   • Negative battery cable
   • Fuel lines
   • Fuel filter
To install:
4. Install the fuel filter.
5. Use new washers and tighten the fuel line bolts to the following specifications:

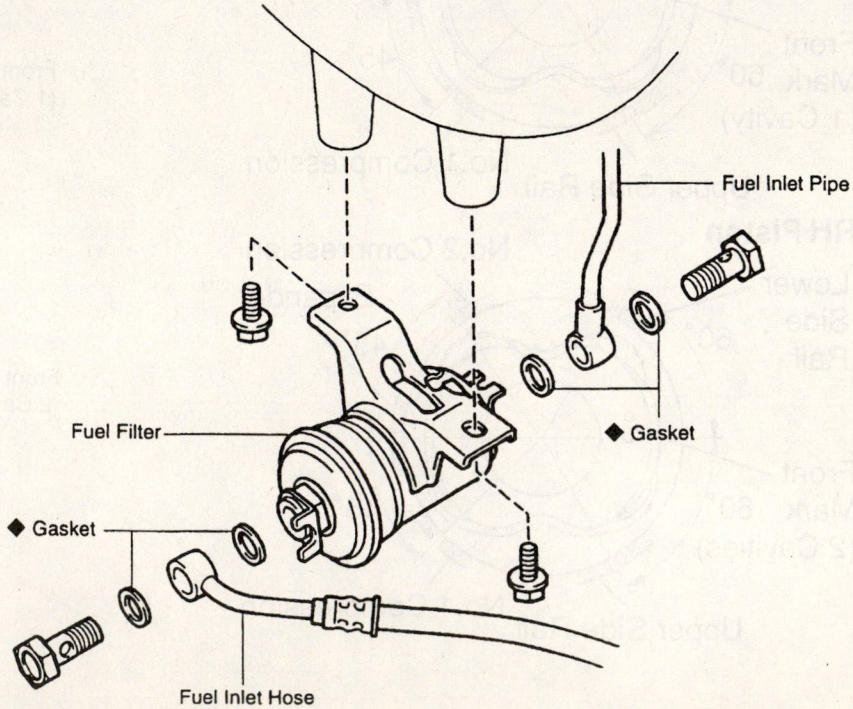

Fuel Inlet Pipe

Fuel Filter

◆ Gasket

◆ Gasket

Fuel Inlet Hose

◆ **Non-reusable part**

7924SG28

Always use new gaskets when replacing the fuel filter

- Banjo bolt fittings: 21 ft. lbs. (29 Nm)
- Flare nut fitting: 28 ft. lbs. (38 Nm)
6. Connect the negative battery cable.
7. Start the engine and check for leaks.

Fuel Pump

REMOVAL & INSTALLATION

1. Before servicing the vehicle, refer to the precautions in the beginning of this section.

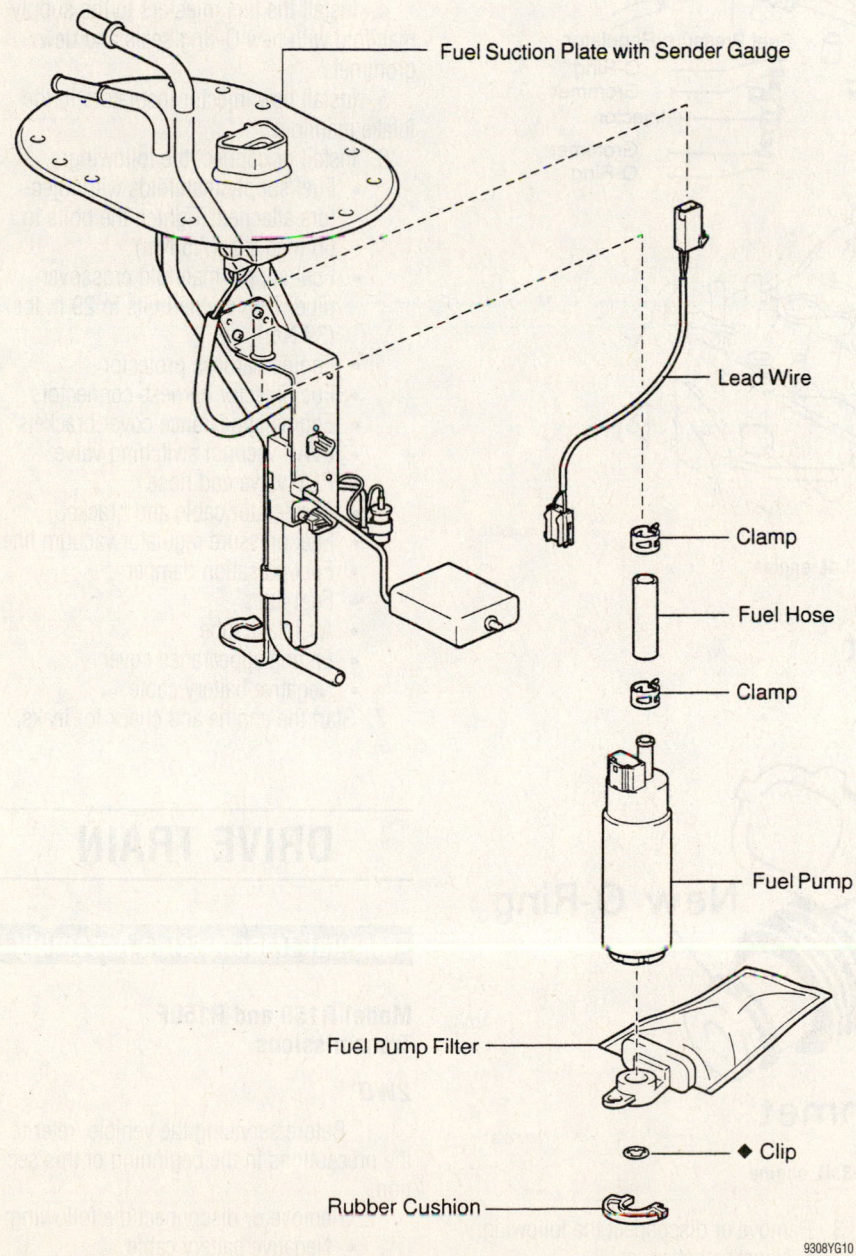

Fuel Suction Plate with Sender Gauge

Lead Wire

Clamp

Fuel Hose

Clamp

Fuel Pump

Fuel Pump Filter

◆ **Clip**

Rubber Cushion

9308YG10

Exploded view of the fuel pump and related components

2. Relieve the fuel system pressure.
3. Remove or disconnect the following:
- Negative battery cable
- Fuel tank
- Fuel pump harness connector
- Fuel lines
- Fuel pump module

To install:
4. Install or connect the following:
- Fuel pump module. Tighten the bolts to 35 inch lbs. (4 Nm).
- Fuel lines
- Fuel pump harness connector

- Fuel tank
- Negative battery cable
5. Start the engine and check for leaks.

Fuel Injector

REMOVAL & INSTALLATION

3.4L Engine

1. Before servicing the vehicle, refer to the precautions in the beginning of this section.
2. Depressurize the fuel system.
3. Remove or disconnect the following:

- Air cleaner hose
- Upper half of the intake manifold
- Fuel pressure regulator
- Fuel inlet pipe
- Fuel injector electrical connections
- Fuel rail with the injectors
- Spacers from the intake manifold
- Injectors from the delivery pipes
- O-rings and grommets, discard them

To install:
4. Install or connect the following:
- New grommets and O-rings on each injector, lubricated with a light coat of gasoline
- Fuel injector with the electrical connector facing outward
- Spacers on the intake manifold
5. Temporarily install the bolts to hold the delivery pipes to the intake manifold.
6. Check that the injectors rotate smoothly. If they do not, the O-rings have probably been installed incorrectly.
7. Install or connect the following:
- Fuel injector electrical connectors
- Fuel pipe with new gaskets. Tighten the bolts to 25 ft. lbs. (34 Nm) and the delivery pipes-to-intake manifold bolts to 10 ft. lbs. (13 Nm)
- Fuel pipe union with new gaskets. Tighten the clamp bolt to 71 inch lbs. (8 Nm).
- Fuel pressure regulator
8. Inspect the vacuum lines and connections. Look for any loose connections, sharp bends or damage.
9. Install or connect the following:
- Air cleaner
- Air cleaner hose
10. Start the engine and check for vacuum and fuel leaks.

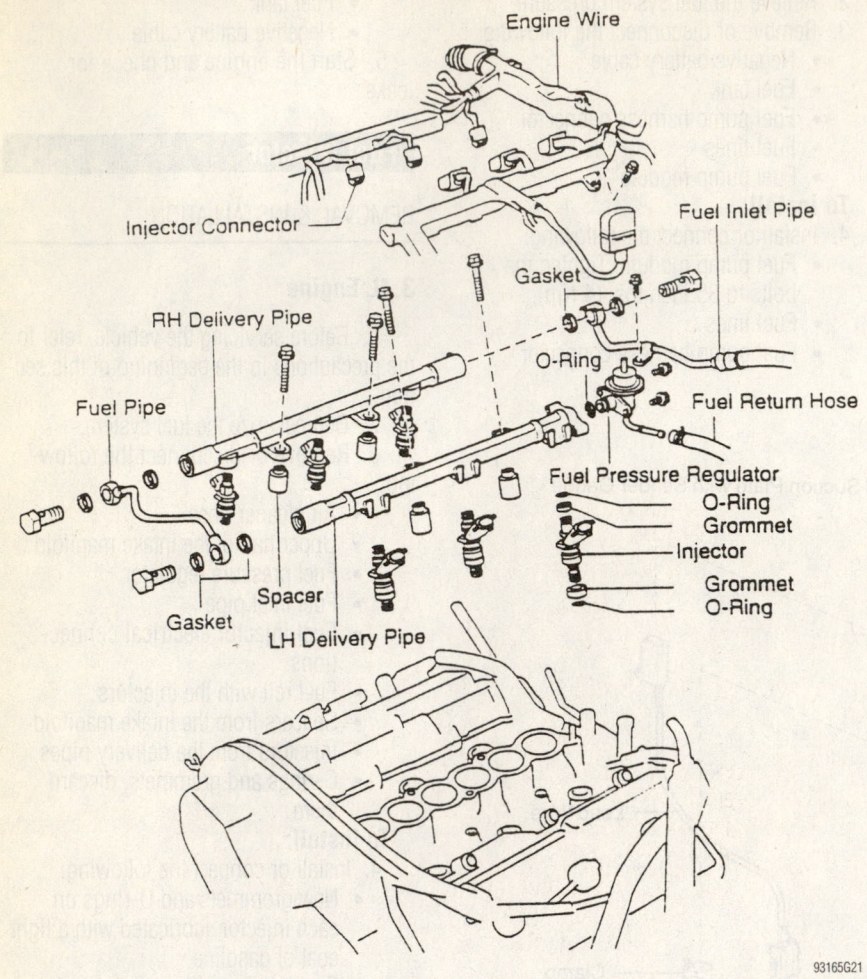

Fuel injector arrangement and related components—3.4L engine

93165G21

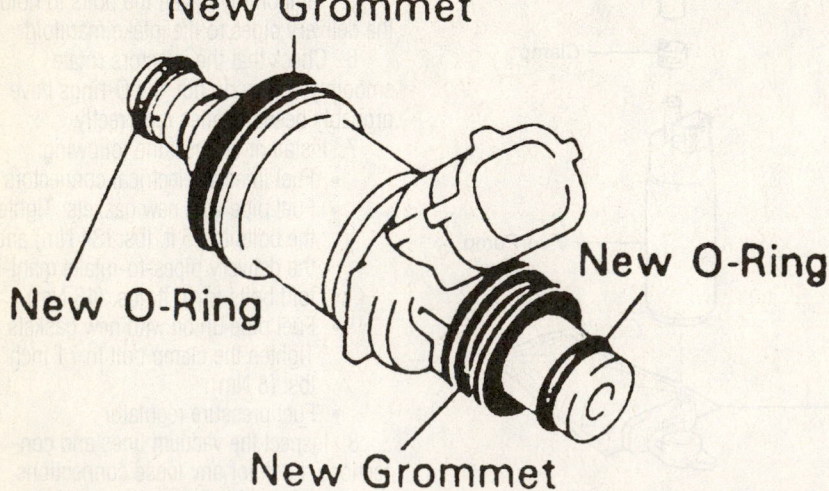

Install new O-rings and grommets on each injector—3.4L engine

86825GG8

4.7L Engine

1. Before servicing the vehicle, refer to the precautions in the beginning of this section.

2. Relieve the fuel system pressure.

3. Remove or disconnect the following:
- Negative battery cable
- Engine appearance cover
- Air intake tube
- Fuel lines
- Fuel pulsation damper
- Fuel pressure regulator vacuum line
- Accelerator cable and bracket
- Positive Crankcase Ventilation (PCV) valve and hose
- Evaporative Emissions (EVAP) vacuum switching valve
- Engine appearance cover brackets
- Fuel injector harness connectors
- Engine harness protector
- Fuel supply manifold crossover pipe
- Fuel supply manifolds with injectors attached
- Fuel injectors

To install:

4. Install the fuel injectors to the supply manifold with new O-ring seals and new grommets.

5. Install new injector insulators to the intake manifold.

6. Install or connect the following:
- Fuel supply manifolds with injectors attached. Tighten the bolts to 66 inch lbs. (7.5 Nm).
- Fuel supply manifold crossover pipe. Tighten the bolts to 29 ft. lbs. (39 Nm).
- Engine harness protector
- Fuel injector harness connectors
- Engine appearance cover brackets
- EVAP vacuum switching valve
- PCV valve and hose
- Accelerator cable and bracket
- Fuel pressure regulator vacuum line
- Fuel pulsation damper
- Fuel lines
- Air intake tube
- Engine appearance cover
- Negative battery cable

7. Start the engine and check for leaks.

DRIVE TRAIN

Manual Transmission Assembly

Model R150 and R150F Transmissions

2WD

1. Before servicing the vehicle, refer to the precautions in the beginning of this section.

2. Remove or disconnect the following:
- Negative battery cable

3. Drain the transmission oil.

4. Remove the shift lever assembly, as follows:
- Shift lever knob

- 4 screws, shift lever boot retainer and shift lever boot
- 6 bolts, shift lever assembly and baffle
- Turn over the dust boot
- Shift lever cap, cover it with a cloth
- Shift lever cap by pressing downward and rotating it counterclockwise
- Shift lever

5. Remove or disconnect the following:
- Driveshaft
- Vehicle Speed Sensor (VSS) and the back-up light switch connectors
- Oxygen (O_2) sensor connector
- Front exhaust pipe from the exhaust manifold and catalytic converter
- Clutch release cylinder
- Starter wires
- Starter

6. Position a jack and wooden block under the transmission.

7. Remove or disconnect the following:
- Rear endplate
- Rear engine mount bracket
- Crossmember

8. Attach a engine hoist to the engine hangers.

9. Remove or disconnect the following:
- Engine mounts
- Engine/transmission assembly out of the vehicle

10. Safely support the engine/transmission assembly.

11. Remove or disconnect the following:
- Transmission-to-engine bolts
- Transmission mount

To install:

12. Install or connect the following:
- Transmission
- Transmission mount. Tighten the 4 bolts to 48 ft. lbs. (65 Nm).

- Tighten the 6 transmission-to-engine bolts to 53 ft. lbs. (72 Nm).
- Crossmember. Torque the bolts to 53 ft. lbs. (72 Nm).
- Rear engine mount-to-crossmember bolts to 13 ft. lbs. (18 Nm).
- Starter. Tighten the 2 bolts to 29 ft. lbs. (39 Nm).
- Rear endplate. Tighten the 4 bolts to 27 ft. lbs. (37 Nm).

13. Install or connect the following:
- Tighten the engine mounts to 28 ft. lbs. (38 Nm).
- Starter wires
- Clutch release cylinder
- Driveshaft
- Front exhaust pipe. Tighten the exhaust pipe-to-manifold bolts to 46 ft. lbs. (62 Nm) and the exhaust pipe-to-catalytic converter bolts to 35 ft. lbs. (48 Nm).
- Remaining components
- Negative battery cable

14. Install the shift lever assembly, as follows:
- Shift lever
- Shift lever cap, cover it with a cloth
- Shift lever cap by pressing downward and rotating it clockwise
- Turn over the dust boot
- 6 bolts, shift lever assembly and baffle
- 4 screws, shift lever boot retainer and shift lever boot
- Shift lever knob

15. Fill the transmission with oil.
16. Start the engine and check for leaks.
17. Install the engine undercover.
18. Road test the vehicle and check all fluids.

4WD

1. Before servicing the vehicle, refer to the precautions in the beginning of this section.

2. Disconnect negative battery cable.

3. Remove the transmission shift lever assembly, as follows:
- Shift lever knob
- 4 screws, shift lever boot retainer and shift lever boot
- 6 bolts, shift lever assembly and baffle
- Turn over the dust boot
- Shift lever cap, cover it with a cloth
- Shift lever cap by pressing downward and rotating it counterclockwise
- Shift lever
- Transfer shift lever, using snapring pliers to pull it from the transfer case

4. Drain the transmission and the transfer oil.

5. Remove or disconnect the following:
- Driveshafts
- Vehicle Speed Sensor (VSS), back-up light switch connector and the transfer indicator switch connector
- Clutch release cylinder, move it aside without disconnecting the clutch line
- Oxygen (O_2) sensor
- Front exhaust pipe bracket
- Starter
- Rear endplate by removing the nuts and 2 bolts

6. Using a transmission jack, support the transmission.

7. Remove or disconnect the following:
- 4 engine rear mount bolts
- 8 bolts and the frame crossmember from the side frame
- 6 transmission-to-engine bolts
- 3 wire clamps from the transmission
- Transmission with the transfer case
- 4 engine rear mount bolts from the transfer case
- Transfer adapter rear mount bolts
- Transfer case from the transmission

To install:

8. Apply MP grease to the adapter oil seal and shift the 2 shift fork shafts to the high 4 position.

9. Install or connect the following:
- Transfer case to the transmission. Tighten the bolts to 17 ft. lbs. (24 Nm).

❊❊ WARNING

Be careful not to damage the oil seal by the input gear spline when installing the transfer.

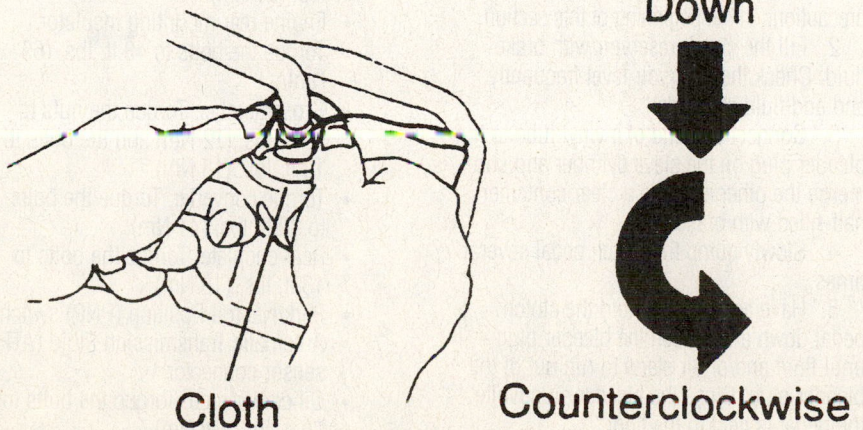

Down

Cloth   Counterclockwise

9308YG11

Removing the transfer shift lever—R150 and R150F transmissions

- Engine rear mounting. Tighten the 4 bolts to 48 ft. lbs. (65 Nm).
- Transmission/transfer case assembly

10. Support the transmission with a jack. Align the input shaft spline with the clutch disc and push the transmission with the transfer fully into position.

11. Install or connect the following:
- Tighten the engine-to-transmission bolts to 53 ft. lbs. (72 Nm).
- Crossmember. Tighten the 4 bolts to 53 ft. lbs. (72 Nm) and the 4 engine rear mount bolts to 13 ft. lbs. (18 Nm).
- Stabilizer bar
- Rear endplate Tighten the 2 bolts and nuts to 27 ft. lbs. (37 Nm).
- Starter. Tighten the bolts to 29 ft. lbs. (39 Nm).
- Front exhaust pipe. Tighten the manifold bolts to 46 ft. lbs. (62 Nm) and the converter bolts to 35 ft. lbs. (48 Nm).
- Clutch release cylinder. Tighten the bolts to 9 ft. lbs. (12 Nm).
- Driveshafts
- Remaining components

12. Install the transmission shift lever assembly, as follows:
- Apply MP grease to the shift lever
- Shift lever
- Shift lever cap, cover it with a cloth
- Shift lever cap by pressing downward and rotating it clockwise
- Turn over the dust boot
- 6 bolts, shift lever assembly and baffle
- 4 screws, shift lever boot retainer and shift lever boot
- Shift lever knob

13. Connect the negative battery cable.

14. Start the engine and check for leaks.

15. Road test the vehicle for proper operation. Recheck all fluid levels.

Clutch Assembly

REMOVAL & INSTALLATION

1. Before servicing the vehicle, refer to the precautions in the beginning of this section.

2. Remove or disconnect the following:
- Negative battery cable
- Transmission assembly

3. Matchmark the clutch cover to the flywheel.

4. At the clutch cover, loosen each bolt 1 turn until spring tension is released.

5. Remove or disconnect the following:
- Clutch cover set bolts and the clutch cover with the clutch disc.

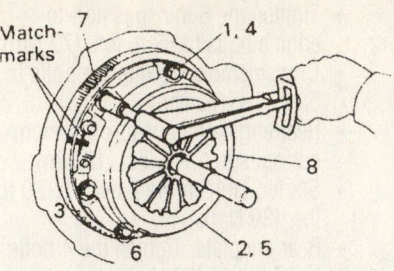

Bolt tightening sequence for the clutch cover—all engines

- Release bearing retaining clip and withdraw the it
- Release fork and boot assembly

To install:

6. Install or connect the following:
- Clutch disc onto the flywheel, using a clutch disc alignment tool
- Clutch cover, position it onto the flywheel and if reusing the old pressure plate, align the matchmarks.
- Clutch cover. Tighten the bolts in a crisscross pattern to 14 ft. lbs. (19 Nm).

7. Lubricate the release fork pivot and contact points, the release bearing, bearing hub and input shaft spline surfaces with a suitable molybdenum disulfide lithium based or multi-purpose grease.

8. Install or connect the following:
- Boot, release fork, hub and the bearing assemblies
- Transmission
- Negative battery cable

Hydraulic Clutch System

BLEEDING

1. Before servicing the vehicle, refer to the precautions in the beginning of this section.

2. Fill the clutch reservoir with brake fluid. Check the reservoir level frequently and add fluid as needed.

3. Connect one end of a vinyl tube to the bleeder plug on the slave cylinder and submerge the other end into a clear container half-filled with brake fluid.

4. Slowly pump the clutch pedal several times.

5. Have an assistant hold the clutch pedal down and loosen the bleeder plug until fluid and/or air starts to run out of the bleeder plug. Close the bleeder plug while the pedal is held to the floor.

6. Repeat Steps 2 and 3 until all the air bubbles are removed from the system.

7. Tighten the bleeder plug when all the air is gone.

8. Refill the master cylinder to the proper level as required.

9. Check the system for leaks.

Automatic Transmission Assembly

REMOVAL & INSTALLATION

3.4L Engine

1. Before servicing the vehicle, refer to the precautions in the beginning of this section.

2. Remove or disconnect the following:
- Negative battery cable
- Throttle cable
- Transmission dipstick
- Oil filler tube and discard the O-ring

3. Shift the transfer case into **H4** position.

4. Remove or disconnect the following:
- Transfer case shift lever knob
- No. 1 engine under cover
- Front and center exhaust pipes
- Driveshaft(s)
- No. 1 and 2 Vehicle Speed Sensor (VSS) connectors
- Shift control cable
- Oil cooler pipe
- Automatic Transmission Fluid (ATF) sensor connector
- Park/Neutral Position (PNP) switch
- Rear endplate
- Torque converter bolts
- Crossmember
- Engine rear mounting insulator
- Starter
- Transmission

To install:

5. Install or connect the following:
- Transmission. Torque the bolts to 53 ft. lbs. (71 Nm).
- Starter. Torque the bolts to 29 ft. lbs. (39 Nm).
- Engine rear mounting insulator. Torque the bolts to 48 ft. lbs. (65 Nm).
- Crossmember. Torque the nuts to 53 ft. lbs. (72 Nm) and the bolts to 13 ft. lbs. (18 Nm)..
- Torque converter. Torque the bolts to 30 ft. lbs. (41 Nm).
- Rear endplate. Torque the bolts to 13 ft. lbs. (18 Nm).
- Park/Neutral Position (PNP) switch
- Automatic Transmission Fluid (ATF) sensor connector
- Oil cooler pipe. Torque the bolts to 25 ft. lbs. (34 Nm).
- Shift control cable. Torque the bolts to 9 ft. lbs. (12 Nm).
- No. 1 and 2 Vehicle Speed Sensor (VSS) connectors

- Driveshaft(s)
- Front and center exhaust pipes
- No. 1 engine under cover
- Transfer case shift lever knob
- Oil filler tube using a new O-ring
- Transmission dipstick
- Throttle cable
- Negative battery cable

4.7L Engine

1. Install or connect the following:
   - Transmission. Tighten the flange bolts to 53 ft. lbs. (72 Nm).
   - Transmission mount crossmember. Tighten the bolts to 37 ft. lbs. (50 Nm) and the nuts to 54 ft. lbs. (74 Nm).
   - Transmission oil cooler lines
   - Torque converter. Tighten the bolts to 35 ft. lbs. (48 Nm).
   - Motor actuator connector
   - L4 solenoid valve position switch connector
   - Center differential lock indicator switch connector
   - PNP switch connector
   - Transmission fluid temperature sensor connector
   - Solenoid harness connector
   - Overdrive clutch speed sensor connector
   - VSS sensor connectors
   - Front driveshaft. Tighten the fasteners to 59 ft. lbs. (80 Nm).
   - Rear driveshaft. Tighten the fasteners to 78 ft. lbs. (106 Nm).
   - Exhaust front pipes
   - Engine under covers
   - Transfer case shift lever and rod
   - Transmission gear select lever and rod
   - Center console
   - Transmission dipstick tube
   - Coolant recovery reservoir
   - Cooling fan and shroud
   - Air intake assembly
   - Battery and tray
2. Check the transmission and transfer case fluid levels and adjust as necessary.

Transfer Case Assembly

REMOVAL & INSTALLATION

VF2A Model

This transfer case is to be used with the 3.4L engine.
1. Before servicing the vehicle, refer to

the precautions in the beginning of this section.
2. Drain the transfer case oil.
3. Shift the transfer shift lever into the **H4** position.
4. Remove or disconnect the following:
   - Transfer case shift lever knob
   - 4 screws, transfer case shift lever boot retainer and the shift lever boot
   - Snapring from the transfer case shift lever and the lever
   - Breather hose from the transfer case
   - Front and rear driveshafts
   - Dynamic damper from the transfer case
   - Crossmember from the rear of the transmission
   - 4 bolts and the engine rear mount from the transfer case adapter
   - Vehicle Speed Sensor (VSS) connector
   - Transfer Detection Switch (TDS) connector
5. Support the transfer case
6. Remove or disconnect the following:
   - 8 transfer case-to-transfer adapter bolts
   - Transfer case

To install:
7. Install or connect the following:
   - Transfer case
   - Transfer case-to-transfer adapter bolts. Torque the 8 bolts to 17 ft. lbs. (24 Nm).
   - Transfer Detection Switch (TDS) connector
   - Vehicle Speed Sensor (VSS) connector
   - Engine rear mount to the transfer case adapter. Torque the 4 bolts to 48 ft. lbs. (65 Nm).
   - Crossmember to the rear of the transmission. Torque the 4 nuts/bolts to 53 ft. lbs. (72 Nm).
   - Crossmember to the chassis. Torque the 4 bolts to 13 ft. lbs. (18 Nm).
   - Dynamic damper to the transfer case. Torque the 2 bolts to 28 ft. lbs. (38 Nm).
   - Front and rear driveshafts
   - Breather hose to the transfer case to a depth of 0.51 in. (13mm) or more
   - Snapring to the transfer case's shift lever
   - 4 screws, transfer case shift lever boot retainer and the shift lever boot
   - Transfer case shift lever knob
8. Refill the transfer case to the correct level.

9. Test drive the vehicle.

VF2BM Model

This transfer case is to be used with the 4.7L engine.
1. Before servicing the vehicle, refer to the precautions in the beginning of this section.
2. Drain the transfer case oil.
3. Turn the touch select 2–4 switch **ON**.
4. Remove or disconnect the following:
   - Breather hose from the transfer case
   - Left and right exhaust pipes
   - Front and rear driveshafts
   - Crossmember from the rear of the transmission
   - 4 bolts and the engine rear mount from the transfer case adapter
   - Vehicle Speed Sensor (VSS) connector
   - Transfer Detection Switch (TDS) connectors
   - Motor actuator connectors
5. Support the transfer case
6. Remove or disconnect the following:
   - 8 transfer case-to-transfer adapter bolts
   - Transfer case

To install:
7. Install or connect the following:
   - Transfer case
   - Transfer case-to-transfer adapter bolts. Torque the 8 bolts to 17 ft. lbs. (24 Nm).
   - Motor actuator connectors
   - Transfer Detection Switch (TDS) connector
   - Vehicle Speed Sensor (VSS) connector
   - Engine rear mount to the transfer case adapter. Torque the 4 bolts to 48 ft. lbs. (65 Nm).
   - Crossmember to the rear of the transmission. Torque the 4 nuts/bolts to 53 ft. lbs. (72 Nm).
   - Crossmember to the chassis. Torque the 4 bolts to 13 ft. lbs. (18 Nm).
   - Dynamic damper to the transfer case. Torque the 2 bolts to 28 ft. lbs. (38 Nm).
   - Front and rear driveshafts
   - Left and right exhaust pipes
   - Breather hose to the transfer case to a depth of 0.51 in. (13mm) or more
8. Refill the transfer case to the correct level.
9. Test drive the vehicle.

Halfshaft

REMOVAL & INSTALLATION

1. Before servicing the vehicle, refer to the precautions in the beginning of this section.
2. Remove or disconnect the following:

- Front wheel
- Under cover
3. Drain the differential oil.
4. Remove or disconnect the following:
- Grease cap
- Cotter pin and lock cap
- Halfshaft locknut by applying the brakes

- Lower control arm from the lower ball joint
- Halfshaft from the steering knuckle, using a plastic hammer
- Left strut, for the left halfshaft
- Right halfshaft, using a brass bar and a hammer

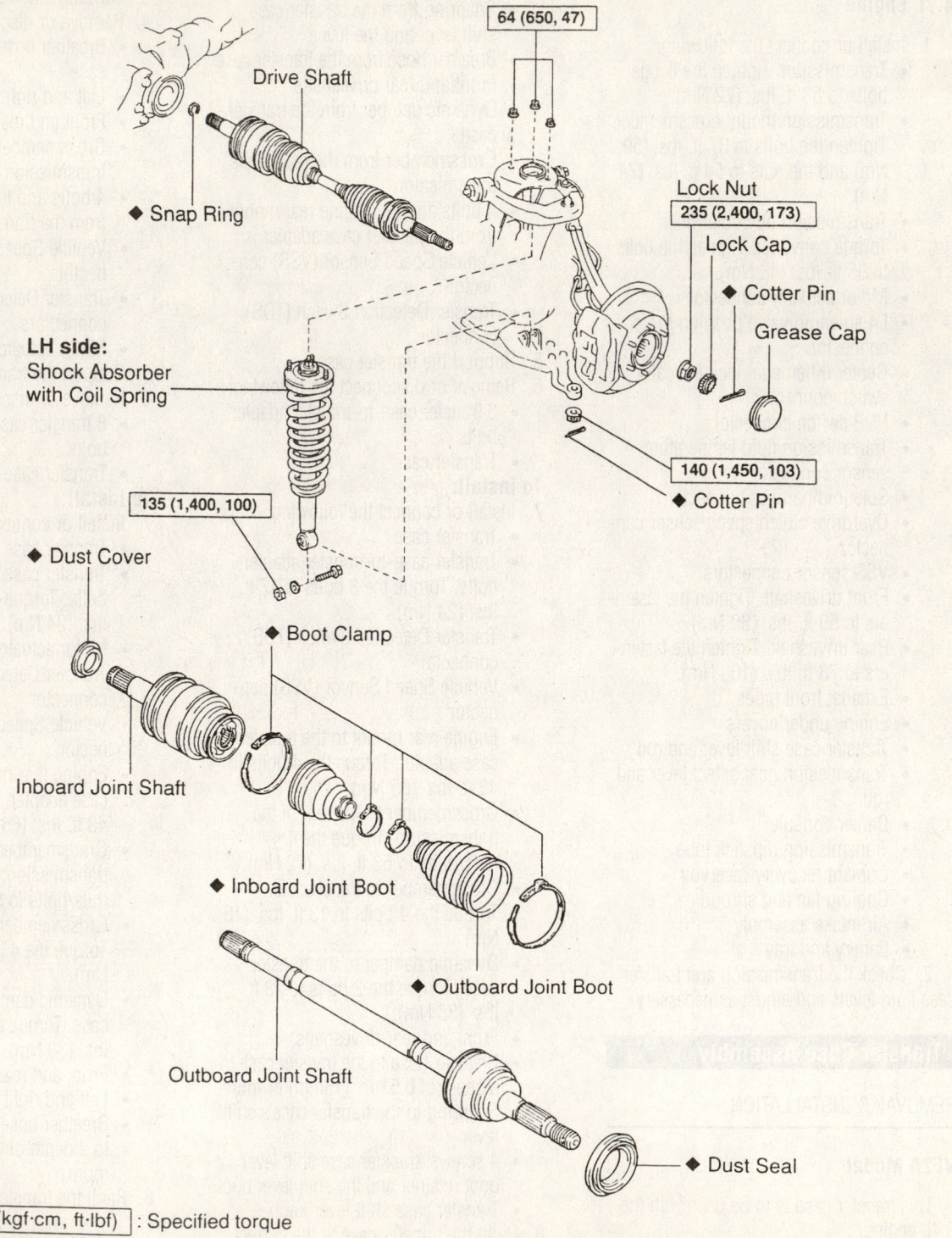

Drive Shaft

◆ Snap Ring

64 (650, 47)

Lock Nut
235 (2,400, 173)
Lock Cap

◆ Cotter Pin

Grease Cap

140 (1,450, 103)

◆ Cotter Pin

LH side:
Shock Absorber with Coil Spring

135 (1,400, 100)

◆ Dust Cover

Boot Clamp

Inboard Joint Shaft

◆ Inboard Joint Boot

◆ Outboard Joint Boot

Outboard Joint Shaft

◆ Dust Seal

N·m (kgf·cm, ft·lbf) : Specified torque

N ◆ Non–reusable part

View of the halfshaft and related components

9308YG12

- Left halfshaft, using tools 09520-01010 and 09520-24010
- Snapring from the inboard joint shaft

To install:

5. Install or connect the following:
- New snapring, onto the inboard joint shaft with the opening facing downward
- Halfshafts to the differential using a brass bar and a hammer
- Halfshafts to the steering knuckles

✳✳ WARNING

Be careful not to damage the oil seal, boot or dust seal.

- Lower control arm to the lower ball joint using a new cotter pin. Torque the ball joint nut to 103 ft. lbs. (140 Nm).
- Halfshaft locknut by applying the brakes. Torque the nut to 173 ft. lbs. (235 Nm).
- Lock cap and a new cotter pin
- Grease cap
6. Refill the differential with oil.
7. Install or connect the following:
- Under cover
- Front wheel

CV-Joints

OVERHAUL

OUTER CV-JOINT

The outer CV-joint is serviced with the axle shaft as an assembly. The outer CV-joint boot can be serviced by removing the inner CV-joint.

INNER CV-JOINT

1. Before servicing the vehicle, refer to the precautions in the beginning of this section.
2. Remove or disconnect the following:
- Halfshaft from the vehicle
- Large boot clamps
- Small boot clamps
3. Matchmark inboard CV-joint to the shaft
4. Remove or disconnect the following:
- Inboard CV-joint from the shaft by expanding the snapring
- Both CV-joint boots
- Outer dust seal, using a shop press and tool 09950-00020
- Outer dust cover, using a shop press and tool 09950-00020

To install:

5. Install or connect the following:
- Outer dust cover, using a screwdriver and a hammer
- Outer dust seal, using a screwdriver and a hammer
6. Wrap the shaft splines with tape to protect the boot from damage.
7. Install or connect the following:
- Both CV-joint boots with clamps, temporarily
- Inboard CV-joint to the shaft by aligning the matchmarks and expanding the snapring
8. Lubricate the outboard joint with 7.23–7.94 oz. (205–225g) grease, provided in the boot kit.
9. Lubricate the inboard joint with 6.70–7.41 oz. (190–210g) grease, provided in the boot kit.
10. Install or connect the following:
- Both joint boots making sure the boots are in the shaft groove
- Standard halfshaft length is 20.531–20.689 in. (521.5–525.5mm) when the shaft is not expanded or contracted
- Large inboard boot clamp
- All other boot clamps using tool 09521-24010. Tighten the crimping tool until the clamp clearance is 0.039–0.059 in. (1.0–1.5mm)
- Halfshaft

Spindle Bearings

REMOVAL, PACKING AND INSTALLATION

1. Before servicing the vehicle, refer to the precautions in the beginning of this section.
2. Remove or disconnect the following:
- Front wheel
- Grease cap, for 2WD
- Cotter pin and lock cap, for 4WD
- Locknut, by applying the brakes
- Anti-lock Brake System (ABS) speed sensor and wiring harness clamp from the steering knuckle
- Brake line clamp from the steering knuckle

➡️**Be careful not to damage the brake tube.**

- Brake caliper and disc
3. Support the steering knuckle
4. Remove or disconnect the following:
- 4 lower ball joint-to-steering knuckle bolts

- Upper ball joint cotter pin and loosen the nut
- Upper ball joint from the steering knuckle using tool 09950-40011
- Steering knuckle by placing it in a soft-jawed vise
- Inside oil seal
- 4 bolts and shift the dust cover towards the hub side (outside)
- Axle hub from the steering knuckle using tools 09710-30021 and 09950-40011
- Dust cover from the steering knuckle
- Bearing spacer and ABS speed sensor (with ABS) or spacer (without ABS)

✳✳ WARNING

Be careful not to scratch the speed sensor rotor serrations

- Outside oil seal from the steering knuckle
- Bearing snapring from the steering knuckle
- Bearing from the steering knuckle, using a shop press and tools 09950-60020 and 09950-70010

To install:

5. Install or connect the following:
- Bearing to the steering knuckle, using a shop press and tools 09527-17011 and 09950-60020
- Bearing snapring to the steering knuckle
- New outside oil seal to the steering knuckle, using tools 09223-15030 and 09527-17011
- Dust cover to the steering knuckle. Torque the 4 bolts to 13 ft. lbs. (18 Nm).
- Axle hub to the steering knuckle using a shop press and tool 09649-17010
- ABS speed sensor (with ABS) or spacer (without ABS)

✳✳ WARNING

Be careful not to scratch the speed sensor rotor serrations

- Bearing spacer, using a shop press and tools 09950-60010 and 09950-70010
- New inside oil seal, using tool 09527-17011 and a plastic hammer
6. For 4WD, install or connect the following:
  a. Halfshaft into the axle hub and temporarily tighten the nut

Turn to Section 5 for brake system applications

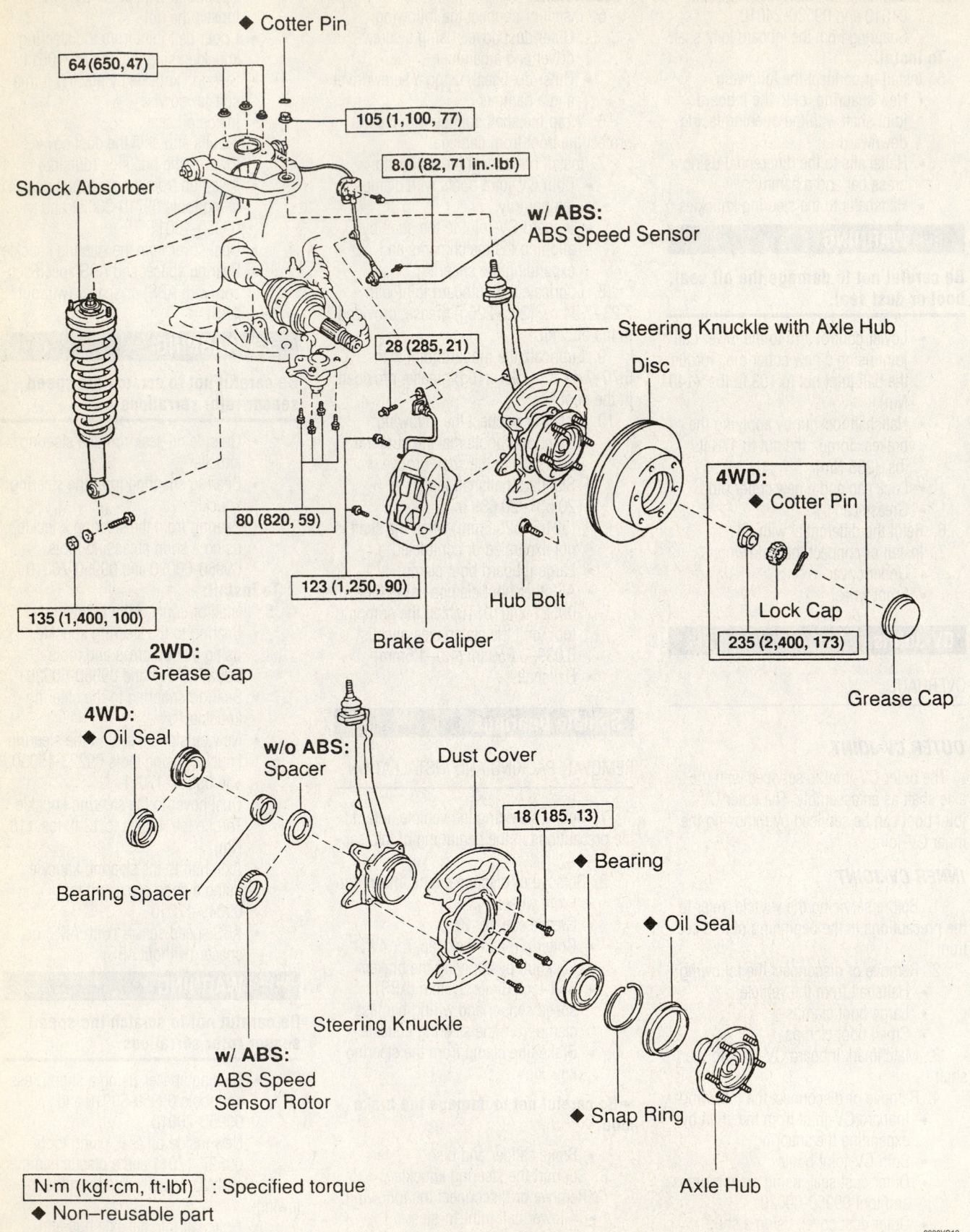

◆ Cotter Pin

64 (650, 47)

105 (1,100, 77)

8.0 (82, 71 in.·lbf)

Shock Absorber

w/ ABS:
ABS Speed Sensor

Steering Knuckle with Axle Hub

Disc

28 (285, 21)

4WD:
◆ Cotter Pin

Lock Cap

235 (2,400, 173)

Grease Cap

80 (820, 59)

123 (1,250, 90)

Hub Bolt

Brake Caliper

135 (1,400, 100)

2WD:
Grease Cap

4WD:
◆ Oil Seal

w/o ABS:
Spacer

Dust Cover

18 (185, 13)

◆ Bearing

◆ Oil Seal

Bearing Spacer

Steering Knuckle

◆ Snap Ring

w/ ABS:
ABS Speed
Sensor Rotor

Axle Hub

N·m (kgf·cm, ft·lbf) : Specified torque
◆ Non–reusable part

9308YG13

Exploded view of the front axle hub and related components

✳✳ WARNING

Be careful not to damage the oil seal or boot.

   b. Steering knuckle to the upper control arm. Tighten the nut to 77 ft. lbs. (105 Nm).

   c. New cotter pin.

  7. Install or connect the following:
- Lower ball joint to the steering knuckle. Torque the 4 bolts to 59 ft. lbs. (80 Nm).
- Strut
- Brake disc and caliper. Torque both caliper bolts to 90 ft. lbs. (123 Nm).
- Brake line clamp to the steering knuckle. Torque the bolt to 21 ft. lbs. (28 Nm).
- ABS speed sensor. Torque both bolts to 7.1 ft. lbs. (8.2 Nm).
- Halfshaft locknut. Torque the nut to 173 ft. lbs. (235 Nm), by applying the brakes.
- Lock cap and new cotter pin
- Grease cap, for 2WD
- Front wheel

  8. Depress the brake pedal several times.

  9. Check and/or adjust the front wheel alignment.

  10. Check the ABS speed sensor signal.

Axle Shaft, Bearing and Seal

REMOVAL & INSTALLATION

Rear

  1. Before servicing the vehicle, refer to the precautions in the beginning of this section.

  2. Remove or disconnect the following:
- Rear wheel
- Brake drum and gasket

  3. Using a dial indicator, check the bearing backlash and the axle shaft deviation. If the bearing backlash exceeds a maximum or 0.028 in. (0.7mm), replace it. If the axle shaft deviation exceeds the maximum of 0.004 in. (0.1mm), replace it.

  4. Remove or disconnect the following:
- Anti-lock Brake System (ABS) speed sensor from the rear axle housing, if equipped
- Brake line from the wheel cylinder, using tool 09023-00100
- Parking brake cable
- 4 backing plate nuts
- Axle shaft assembly, by pulling it from the axle housing

✳✳ WARNING

Be careful not to damage the oil seal.

- O-ring from the rear axle housing
- Inner side oil seal using tool 09308-00010

  5. If equipped with ABS, perform the following:

   a. Remove and discard the 4 serration bolt nuts; then, using a hammer, drive the bolts from the backing plate.

   b. Using a grinder, grind the retainer and sensor rotor surfaces; then, chisel them out.

  6. Remove the snapring from the axle shaft.

  7. Remove the axle shaft from the backing plate, as follows:

   a. Position tool 09521-25011 onto the backing plate with the 4 nuts.

   b. Using a shop press, remove the axle shaft and bearing retainer from the backing plate.

  8. Using tool 09308-00010, pull the oil seal from the backing plate.

  9. Using a shop press and tools 09223-56010 and 09950-60010, press the bearing from the backing plate.

To install:

  10. Install or connect the following:
- Bearing into the backing plate, using a shop press and tools 09223-56010 and 09950-60010
- New O-ring to the rear axle housing
- New oil seal into the backing plate, using a hammer and tools 09950-70010 and 09950-60010

  11. Install the axle shaft to the backing plate, as follows:
- New outer side seal, lubricate the oil seal lip with multi-purpose grease
- Backing plate and bearing retainer onto the rear axle shaft
- Axle shaft onto the backing plate, by pressing it using a shop press and tool 09316-60011
- New snapring

✳✳ WARNING

Be careful not to damage the oil seal.

  12. Install or connect the following:
- New sensor rotor and new bearing retainer onto the axle shaft, using a shop press and tool 09316-60011 to a standard length of 4.77–4.85 in. (121.2–123.2mm), if equipped with ABS
- New inner side oil seal, using a hammer and tools 09950-60020 and 09950-70010
- Axle shaft assembly. Torque the bolts to 51 ft. lbs. (69 Nm).

✳✳ WARNING

Be careful not to damage the oil seal.

- Parking brake cable
- Brake line to the wheel cylinder,

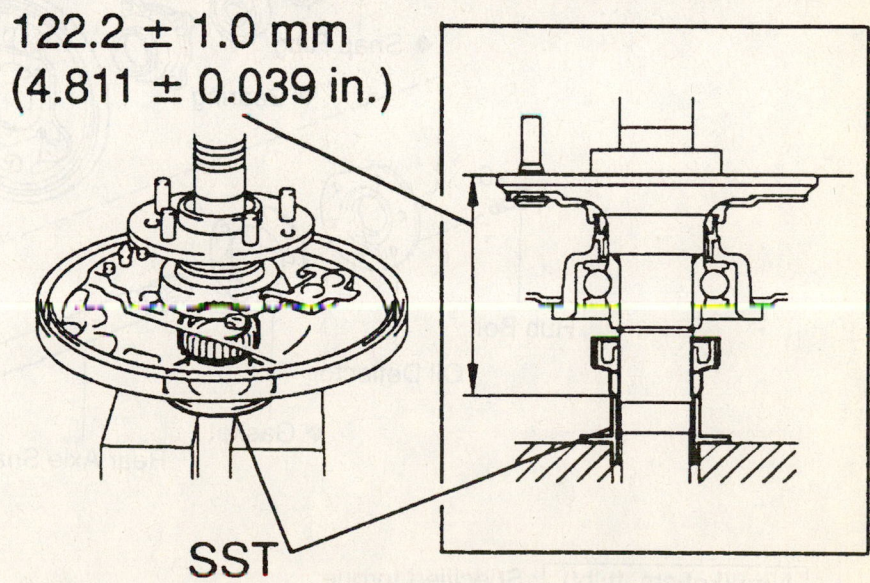

122.2 ± 1.0 mm (4.811 ± 0.039 in.)

SST

9308YG15

Standard length of ABS speed sensor rotor and bearing retainer—Rear axle

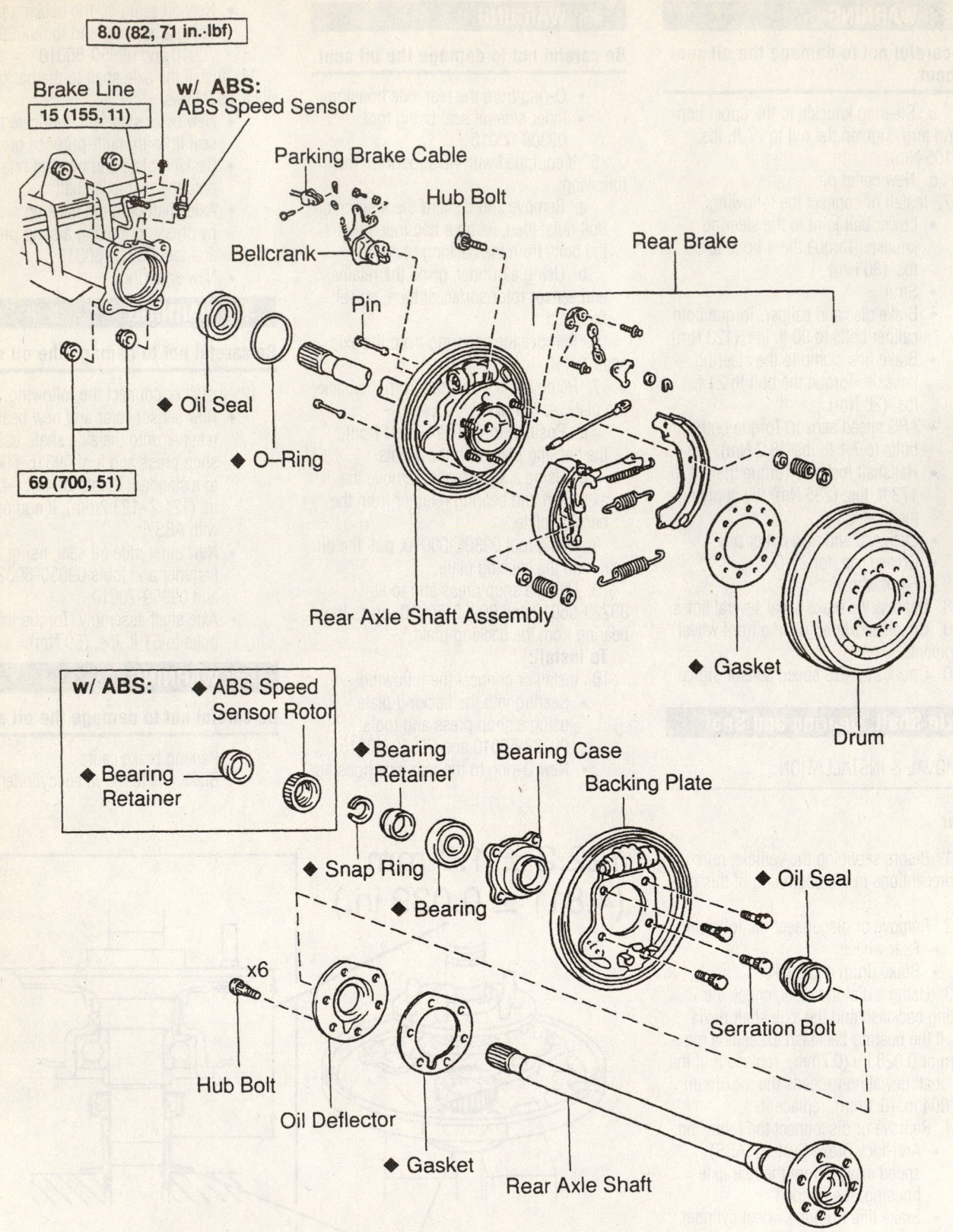

8.0 (82, 71 in.·lbf)

Brake Line
15 (155, 11)

w/ ABS:
ABS Speed Sensor

Parking Brake Cable

Hub Bolt

Rear Brake

Bellcrank

Pin

◆ Oil Seal

◆ O–Ring

69 (700, 51)

Rear Axle Shaft Assembly

Gasket

Drum

w/ ABS: ◆ ABS Speed Sensor Rotor

◆ Bearing Retainer

◆ Bearing Retainer

Bearing Case

Backing Plate

◆ Snap Ring

◆ Bearing

◆ Oil Seal

x6

Serration Bolt

Hub Bolt

Oil Deflector

◆ Gasket

Rear Axle Shaft

N·m (kgf·cm, ft·lbf) : Specified torque

◆ Non–reusable part

Exploded view of the rear axle

9308YG14

using tool 09023-00100. Torque the brake line to 11 ft. lbs. (15 Nm).
- Rear brake assembly
- ABS speed sensor to the rear axle housing. Torque it to 7.1 ft. lbs. (8.0 Nm).

13. Using a dial indicator, check the bearing backlash and the axle shaft deviation. If the bearing backlash exceeds a maximum or 0.028 in. (0.7mm), replace it. If the axle shaft deviation exceeds the maximum of 0.004 in. (0.1mm), replace it.

14. Install or connect the following:
- New gasket and brake drum
- Rear wheel. Torque the lug nuts to 81 ft. lbs. (110 Nm).

15. Bleed the brake system.
16. Check the ABS speed sensor signal.

Pinion Seal

REMOVAL & INSTALLATION

Front

1. Before servicing the vehicle, refer to the precautions in the beginning of this section.

2. Remove the under cover.
3. Drain the differential housing oil.
4. Remove the front driveshaft.
5. Remove the companion flange, as follows:
- Loosen the staked part of the nut, using a chisel and a hammer
- Companion flange nut, using tool 09330-00021
- Companion flange, using tools 09950-30011 and 09954-03010

6. Remove the oil seal and slinger, as follows:
- Oil seal, using tool 09308-10010
- Oil slinger

To install:
7. Install or connect the following:
- Oil slinger
- New oil seal, using a hammer and tool 09554-22010 to a depth of 0.153–0.189 in. (4.2–4.8mm).

8. Install the companion flange, as follows:
- Companion flange
- New nut, lubricated with hypoid gear oil
- Torque the nut to 80 ft. lbs. (108 Nm), using tool 09330-00021.

9. Adjust the drive pinion preload
10. Rotate the drive pinion, using a torque wrench while tightening the flange nut to make sure the bearing preload is 10.4–16.5 inch lbs. (1.2–1.9 Nm) for a new bearing or 5.2–8.7 inch lbs. (0.6–1.0 Nm) for a used bearing. Tighten the flange nut to achieve the preload torque readings originally recorded.

✳✳ CAUTION

Never loosen the pinion nut to reduce bearing preload.

11. Install or connect the following:
- Drive pinion nut, stake it
- Front driveshaft. Tighten the fasteners to 54 ft. lbs. (74 Nm).
- Under cover

12. Fill the differential with gear lubricant and check for leaks.

Rear

1. Before servicing the vehicle, refer to the precautions in the beginning of this section.
2. Drain the differential housing oil.
3. Remove the rear driveshaft.

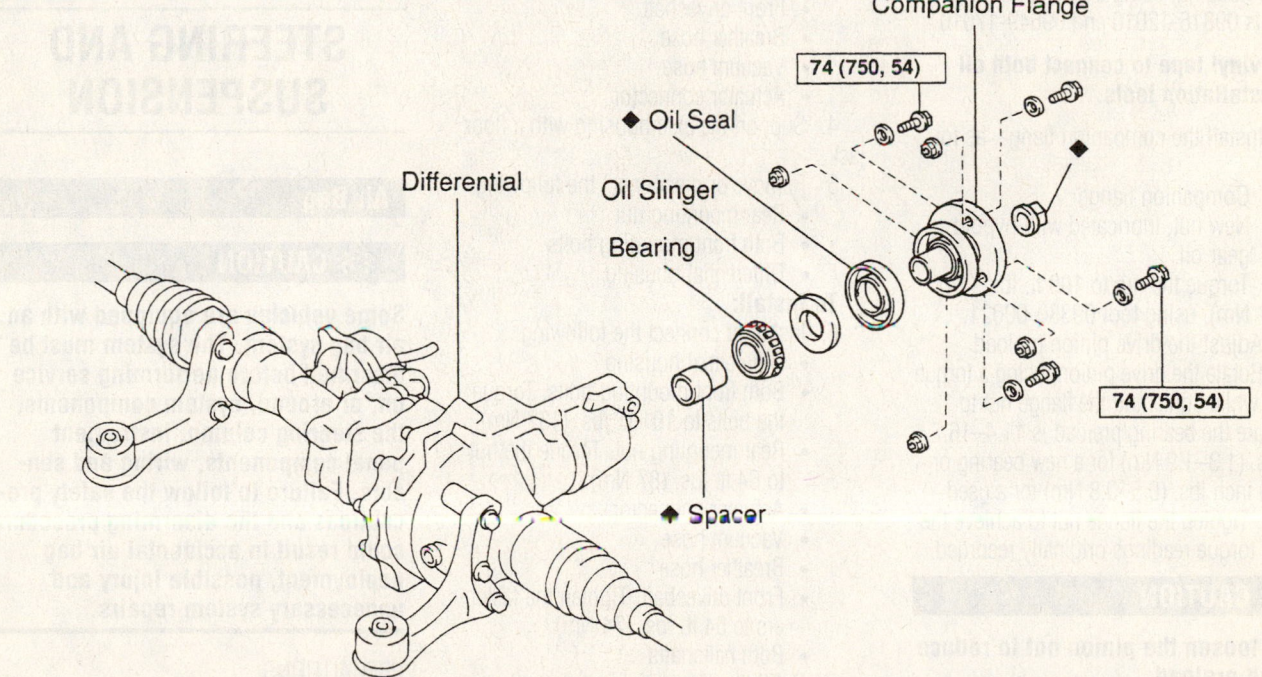

N·m (kgf·cm, ft·lbf) : Specified torque
◆ Non−reusable part

Exploded view of the front differential assembly—Rear differential assembly is similar

9308YG16

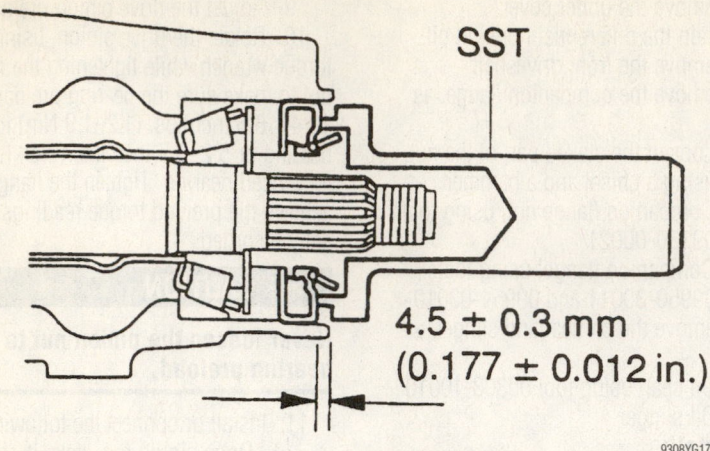

4.5 ± 0.3 mm
(0.177 ± 0.012 in.)

9308YG17

Positioning the front pinion seal in the differential housing—Rear differential assembly is similar

4. Remove the companion flange, as follows:
- Loosen the staked part of the nut, using a chisel and a hammer
- Companion flange nut, using tool 09330-00021
- Companion flange, using tools 09950-30011 and 09954-03010
- Oil seal, using tool 09308-10010

To install:

5. Install the new oil seal until it is flush with the housing, using a plastic hammer and tools 09316-12010 and 09649-17010

➡**Use vinyl tape to connect both oil seal installation tools.**

6. Install the companion flange, as follows:
- Companion flange
- New nut, lubricated with hypoid gear oil
- Torque the nut to 109 ft. lbs. (147 Nm), using tool 09330-00021.

7. Adjust the drive pinion preload

8. Rotate the drive pinion, using a torque wrench while tightening the flange nut to make sure the bearing preload is 11.4–16.7 inch lbs. (1.3–1.9 Nm) for a new bearing or 4.3–6.9 inch lbs. (0.5–0.8 Nm) for a used bearing. Tighten the flange nut to achieve the preload torque readings originally recorded.

❊❊ CAUTION

Never loosen the pinion nut to reduce bearing preload.

9. Install or connect the following:
- Drive pinion nut, stake it
- Rear driveshaft. Tighten the fasteners to 54 ft. lbs. (74 Nm).

10. Refill the differential with gear lubricant and check for leaks; 3.33 qts. for 2WD or 3.12 qts. for 4WD.

Axle Housing Assembly

REMOVAL & INSTALLATION

Front

1. Before servicing the vehicle, refer to the precautions in the beginning of this section.

2. Drain the differential housing oil.

3. Remove or disconnect the following:
- Both halfshafts
- Front driveshaft
- Breather hose
- Vacuum hose
- Actuator connector

4. Support the axle housing with a floor jack.

5. Remove or disconnect the following:
- Rear mounting nut
- Both front mounting bolts
- Differential housing

To install:

6. Install or connect the following:
- Differential housing
- Both front mounting bolts. Torque the bolts to 101 ft. lbs. (137 Nm).
- Rear mounting nut. Torque the nut to 64 ft. lbs. (87 Nm).
- Actuator connector
- Vacuum hose
- Breather hose
- Front driveshaft. Tighten the fasteners to 54 ft. lbs. (74 Nm).
- Both halfshafts

7. Refill the differential housing oil.

Rear

1. Before servicing the vehicle, refer to the precautions in the beginning of this section.

2. Drain the rear axle housing oil.

3. Support the rear axle housing with a floor jack.

4. Remove or disconnect the following:
- Rear wheels
- Rear driveshaft
- Shock absorbers
- Leaf springs
- Flexible brake hoses
- Parking brake cables
- Wheel speed sensor harness, if equipped
- Axle housing assembly

To install:

5. Install or connect the following:
- Axle housing assembly
- Wheel speed sensor harness, if equipped
- Parking brake cables
- Flexible brake hoses
- Leaf springs. Torque the spring-to-chassis nut/bolt to 125 ft. lbs. (170 Nm) and the spring seat-to-axle housing nuts to 98 ft. lbs. (133 Nm).
- Shock absorbers. Torque the upper nut to 15 ft. lbs. (20 Nm) and the lower nut/bolt to 64 ft. lbs. (87 Nm).
- Rear driveshaft. Tighten the fasteners to 54 ft. lbs. (74 Nm).
- Rear wheels

6. Refill the rear axle housing oil.

STEERING AND SUSPENSION

Air Bag

❊❊ CAUTION

Some vehicles are equipped with an air bag system. The system must be disarmed before performing service on, or around, system components, the steering column, instrument panel components, wiring and sensors. Failure to follow the safety precautions and the disarming procedure could result in accidental air bag deployment, possible injury and unnecessary system repairs.

PRECAUTIONS

Several precautions must be observed when handling the inflator module to avoid accidental deployment and possible personal injury.

- Never carry the inflator module by the wires or connector on the underside of the module.

• When carrying a live inflator module, hold securely with both hands and ensure that the bag and trim cover are pointed away.

• Place the inflator module on a bench or other surface with the bag and trim cover facing up.

• With the inflator module on the bench, never place anything on or close to the module which may be thrown in the event of an accidental deployment.

DISARMING

To avoid personal injury when working on vehicles equipped with an air bag, the negative battery cable must be disconnected and at least 90 seconds must elapse before working on the system. Failure to do so may result in deployment of the air bag.

Power Rack And Pinion Steering Gear

REMOVAL & INSTALLATION

1. Before servicing the vehicle, refer to the precautions in the beginning of this section.
2. Position the front wheels in the straight-ahead position.
3. Remove or disconnect the following:

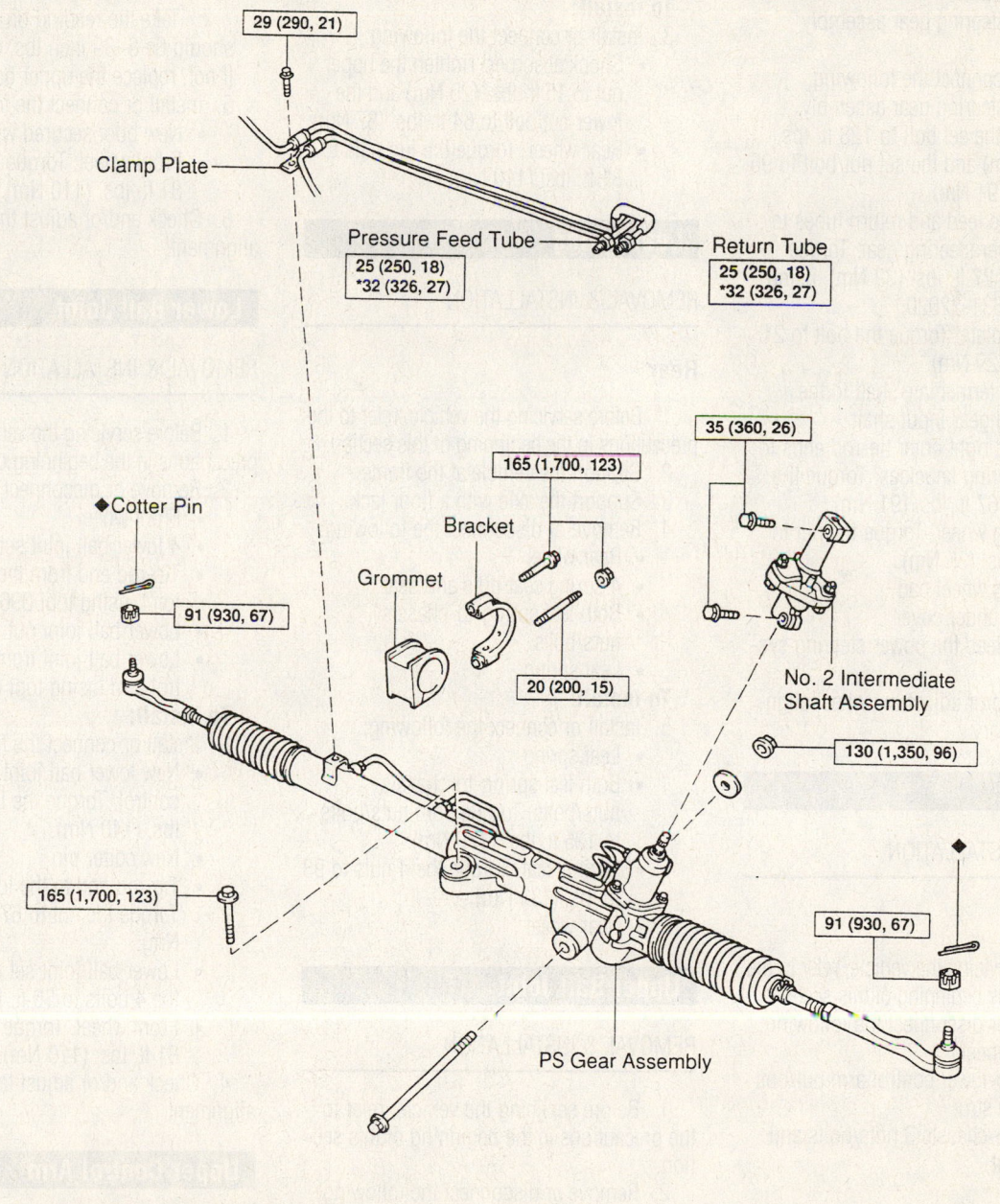

29 (290, 21)

Clamp Plate

Pressure Feed Tube
25 (250, 18)
*32 (326, 27)

Return Tube
25 (250, 18)
*32 (326, 27)

35 (360, 26)

165 (1,700, 123)

Bracket

Grommet

◆ Cotter Pin

91 (930, 67)

20 (200, 15)

No. 2 Intermediate Shaft Assembly

130 (1,350, 96)

165 (1,700, 123)

91 (930, 67)

PS Gear Assembly

N·m (kgf·cm, ft·lbf) : Specified torque
◆ Non–reusable part
* For use with SST

9308YG18

Exploded view of the power rack and pinion steering gear mounting

- Engine under cover
- Steering wheel pad
- Steering wheel
- Left and right outer tie-rod ends from the steering knuckles

4. Matchmark the No. 2 intermediate shaft to the steering gear input shaft.

5. Remove or disconnect the following:
- Clamp plate
- Pressure feed and return tubes from the power steering gear, using tool 09631-22020
- Power steering gear assembly

To install:

6. Install or connect the following:
- Power steering gear assembly. Torque the set bolt to 123 ft. lbs. (165 Nm) and the set nut/bolt to 96 ft. lbs. (91 Nm).
- Pressure feed and return tubes to the power steering gear. Torque them to 27 ft. lbs. (32 Nm), using tool 09631-22020.
- Clamp plate. Torque the bolt to 21 ft. lbs. (29 Nm).
- No. 2 intermediate shaft to the steering gear input shaft
- Left and right outer tie-rod ends to the steering knuckles. Torque the nuts to 67 ft. lbs. (91 Nm).
- Steering wheel. Torque the nut to 26 ft. lbs. (35 Nm).
- Steering wheel pad
- Engine under cover

7. Fill and bleed the power steering system.

8. Check and/or adjust the wheel alignment, as necessary.

Strut

REMOVAL & INSTALLATION

Front

1. Before servicing the vehicle, refer to the precautions in the beginning of this section.

2. Remove or disconnect the following:
- Front wheel
- Strut-to-lower control arm nut/bolt and the strut
- Strut-to-chassis 3 nuts/bolts and the strut

To install:

3. Install or connect the following:
- Strut to the chassis. Torque the 3 nuts/bolts to 47 ft. lbs. (64 Nm).
- Strut to the lower control arm. Torque the nut/bolt to 100 ft. lbs. (135 Nm).
- Front wheel

Shock Absorber

REMOVAL & INSTALLATION

Rear

1. Before servicing the vehicle, refer to the precautions in the beginning of this section.

2. Remove or disconnect the following:
- Rear wheel
- Shock absorber

To install:

3. Install or connect the following:
- Shock absorber. Tighten the upper nut to 15 ft. lbs. (20 Nm) and the lower nut/bolt to 64 ft. lbs. (87 Nm).
- Rear wheel. Torque the lug nuts to 81 ft. lbs. (110 Nm).

Leaf Spring

REMOVAL & INSTALLATION

Rear

1. Before servicing the vehicle, refer to the precautions in the beginning of this section.

2. Support the vehicle at the frame.

3. Support the axle with a floor jack.

4. Remove or disconnect the following:
- Rear wheel
- 4 spring seat nuts and seat
- Both leaf spring-to-chassis nuts/bolts
- Leaf spring

To install:

5. Install or connect the following:
- Leaf spring
- Both leaf spring-to-chassis nuts/bolts. Torque both nuts/bolts to 125 ft. lbs. (170 Nm).
- Spring seat. Torque the 4 nuts to 98 ft. lbs. (133 Nm).
- Rear wheel

Upper Ball Joint

REMOVAL & INSTALLATION

1. Before servicing the vehicle, refer to the precautions in the beginning of this section.

2. Remove or disconnect the following:
- Front wheel
- Steering knuckle with the axle hub
- Wire and boot
- Snapring
- Upper ball joint from the steering knuckle, using a deep socket wrench and tool 09050-40011

To install:

3. Install or connect the following:
- New upper ball joint to the steering knuckle, using a deep socket and tool 09309-37010
- New snapring

4. Using a torque wrench, inspect the upper ball joint rotation, as follows:
- a. Flip the ball joint back-and-forth 5 times.
- b. Using a torque wrench, continuously turn the nut 1 turn in 2–4 seconds.
- c. Take the reading on the 5th turn; it should be 6–39 inch lbs. (0.7–4.4 Nm). If not, replace the upper ball joint.

5. Install or connect the following:
- New boot secured with a wire
- Front wheel. Torque the lug nuts to 81 ft. lbs. (110 Nm).

6. Check and/or adjust the front wheel alignment.

Lower Ball Joint

REMOVAL & INSTALLATION

1. Before servicing the vehicle, refer to the precautions in the beginning of this section.

2. Remove or disconnect the following:
- Front wheel
- 4 lower ball joint set bolts
- Tie-rod end from the lower ball joint, using tool 09610-20012
- Lower ball joint nut.
- Lower ball joint from the lower control arm, using tool 09628-62011

To install:

3. Install or connect the following:
- New lower ball joint to the lower control. Torque the bolts to 103 ft. lbs. (140 Nm).
- New cotter pin
- Tie-rod end to the lower ball joint. Torque the nut to 67 ft. lbs. (91 Nm).
- Lower ball joint set bolts. Torque the 4 bolts to 59 ft. lbs. (80 Nm).
- Front wheel. Torque the lug nuts to 81 ft. lbs. (110 Nm).

4. Check and/or adjust the front wheel alignment.

Upper Control Arm

REMOVAL & INSTALLATION

1. Before servicing the vehicle, refer to the precautions in the beginning of this section.

2. Remove or disconnect the following:

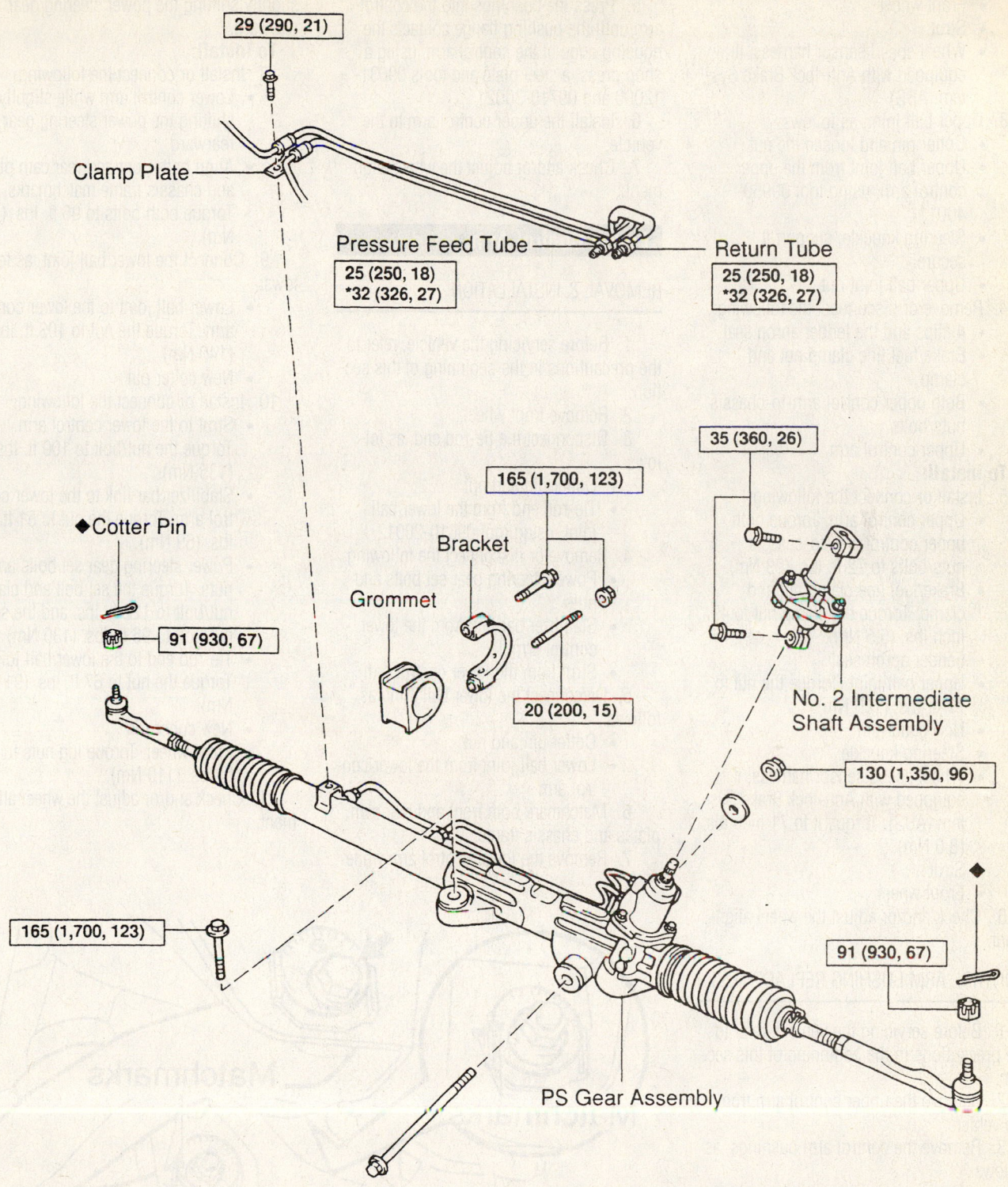

29 (290, 21)

Clamp Plate

Pressure Feed Tube
25 (250, 18)
*32 (326, 27)

Return Tube
25 (250, 18)
*32 (326, 27)

35 (360, 26)

165 (1,700, 123)

Bracket

◆Cotter Pin

Grommet

91 (930, 67)

20 (200, 15)

No. 2 Intermediate
Shaft Assembly

130 (1,350, 96)

91 (930, 67)

165 (1,700, 123)

◆

PS Gear Assembly

N·m (kgf·cm, ft·lbf) : Specified torque
◆Non–reusable part
* For use with SST

9308YG19

Exploded view of the front suspension and related components

Please visit our web site at www.chiltononline.com

- Front wheel
- Strut
- Wheel speed sensor harness, if equipped with Anti-lock Brake System (ABS)

3. Upper ball joint, as follows:
- Cotter pin and loosen the nut
- Upper ball joint from the upper control arm, using tool 09950-40011
- Steering knuckle, support it securely
- Upper ball joint nut

4. Remove or disconnect the following:
- 4 clips and the fender apron seal
- Brake/fuel line clamp nut and clamp
- Both upper control arm-to-chassis nuts/bolts
- Upper control arm

To install:

5. Install or connect the following:
- Upper control arm. Torque both upper control arm-to-chassis nuts/bolts to 72 ft. lbs. (98 Nm).
- Brake/fuel line clamp nut and clamp. Torque the clamp nut to 49 inch lbs. (5.5 Nm).
- Fender apron seal
- Upper ball joint. Torque the nut to 77 ft. lbs. (105 Nm).
- New cotter pin
- Steering knuckle
- Wheel speed sensor harness, if equipped with Anti-lock Brake System (ABS). Torque it to 71 inch lbs. (8.0 Nm).
- Strut
- Front wheel

6. Check and/or adjust the wheel alignment.

CONTROL ARM BUSHING REPLACEMENT

1. Before servicing the vehicle, refer to the precautions in the beginning of this section.

2. Remove the upper control arm from the vehicle.

3. Remove the control arm bushings, as follows:
- Pry up the bushing flange, using a chisel and a hammer
- Press the bushing(s) from the upper control arm, using a shop press and tools 09613-26010, 09631-20060 and 09950-00020

To install:

4. Lubricate the new control arm bushings with liquid soap.

5. Press the bushings into the control arm until the bushing flange contacts the housing edge of the control arm, using a shop press, a steel plate and tools 09631-12090 and 09710-30021

6. Install the upper control arm to the vehicle.

7. Check and/or adjust the wheel alignment.

Lower Control Arm

REMOVAL & INSTALLATION

1. Before servicing the vehicle, refer to the precautions in the beginning of this section.

2. Remove front wheel.

3. Disconnect the tie-rod end, as follows:
- Cotter pin and nut
- Tie-rod end from the lower ball joint, using tool 09610-20012

4. Remove or disconnect the following:
- Power steering gear set bolts and nuts
- Stabilizer bar link from the lower control arm
- Strut from the lower control arm

5. Disconnect the lower ball joint, as follows:
- Cotter pin and nut
- Lower ball joint from the lower control arm

6. Matchmark both front and rear cam plates and chassis frame.

7. Remove the lower control arm while slightly shifting the power steering gear rearward.

To install:

8. Install or connect the following:
- Lower control arm while slightly shifting the power steering gear rearward
- Align both front and rear cam plates and chassis frame matchmarks. Torque both bolts to 96 ft. lbs. (130 Nm).

9. Connect the lower ball joint, as follows:
- Lower ball joint to the lower control arm. Torque the nut to 103 ft. lbs. (140 Nm).
- New cotter pin

10. Install or connect the following:
- Strut to the lower control arm. Torque the nut/bolt to 100 ft. lbs. (135 Nm).
- Stabilizer bar link to the lower control arm. Torque the nut to 51 ft. lbs. (69 Nm).
- Power steering gear set bolts and nuts. Torque the set bolt and clamp nut/bolt to 122 ft. lbs. and the set nut/bolt to 96 ft. lbs. (130 Nm)
- Tie-rod end to the lower ball joint. Torque the nut to 67 ft. lbs. (91 Nm).
- New cotter pin
- Front wheel. Torque lug nuts to 81 ft. lbs. (110 Nm).

11. Check and/or adjust the wheel alignment.

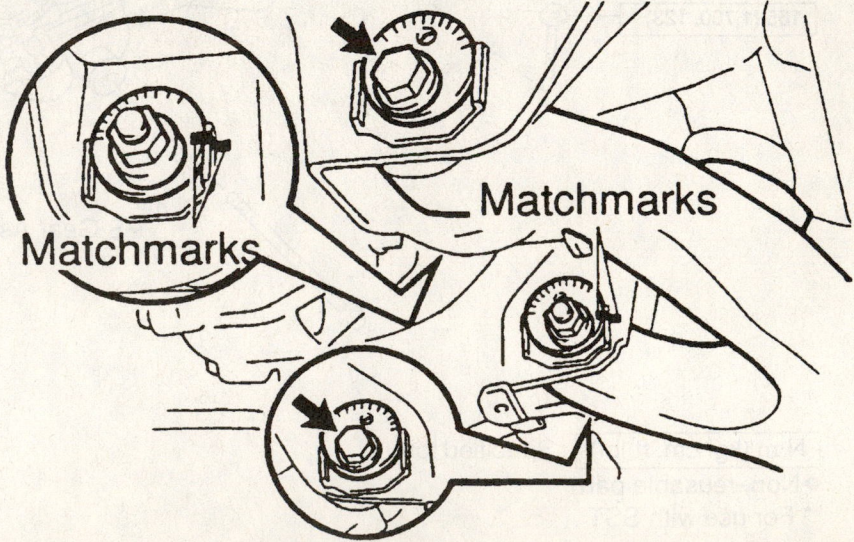

View of the lower control arm's cam plate alignment

9308YG22

CONTROL ARM BUSHING REPLACEMENT

1. Before servicing the vehicle, refer to the precautions in the beginning of this section.

2. Remove the lower control arm from the vehicle.

3. Remove the control arm bushings, as follows:

- Pry up the bushing flange, using a chisel and a hammer
- Press the bushing(s) from the upper control arm, using a shop press and tools 09613-26010, 09632-36010 and 09950-00020

To install:

4. Lubricate the new control arm bushings with liquid soap.

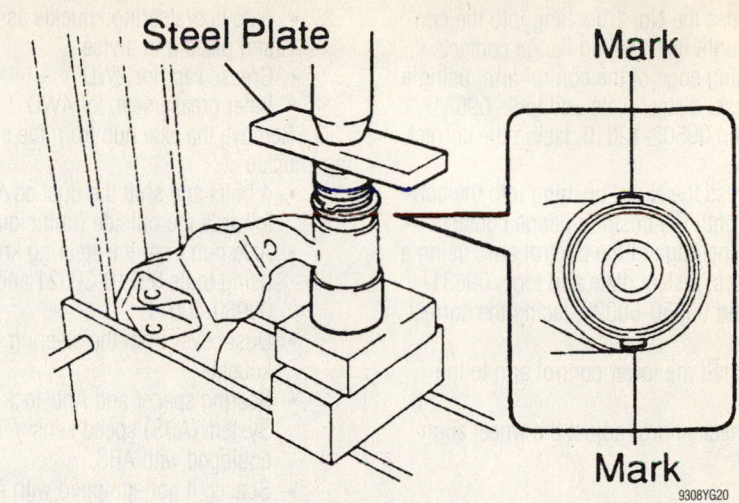

View of the No. 1 bushing's installed direction

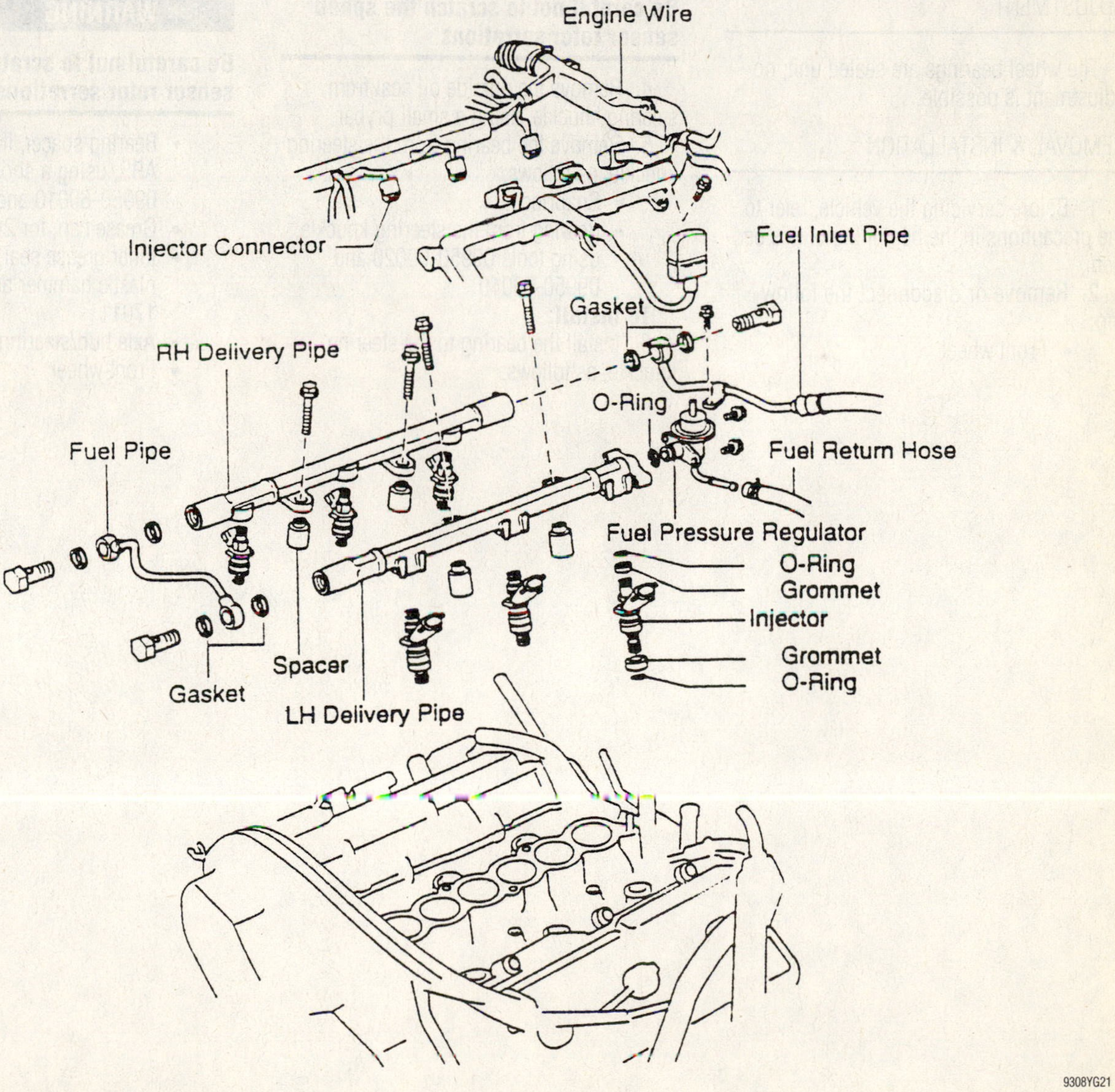

View of the No. 2 bushing's installed direction

Turn to Section 5 for brake system applications

5. Press the No. 1 bushing into the control arm until the bushing flange contacts the housing edge of the control arm, using a shop press, a steel plate and tools 09631-12090 and 09502-12010, facing the correct direction.

6. Press the No. 2 bushing into the control arm until the bushing flange contacts the housing edge of the control arm, using a shop press, a steel plate and tools 09631-12090 and 09950-60020, facing the correct direction.

7. Install the lower control arm to the vehicle.

8. Check and/or adjust the wheel alignment.

Wheel Bearing

ADJUSTMENT

The wheel bearings are sealed unit; no adjustment is possible.

REMOVAL & INSTALLATION

1. Before servicing the vehicle, refer to the precautions in the beginning of this section.

2. Remove or disconnect the following:

- Front wheel

- Axle hub/steering knuckle assembly and place it in a vise
- Grease cap, for 2WD
- Inner grease seal, for 4WD

3. Remove the axle hub from the steering knuckle

- 4 bolts and shift the dust cover towards the outside (hub side)
- Axle hub from the steering knuckle, using tools 09710-30021 and 09950-40011
- Dust cover from the steering knuckle
- Bearing spacer and Anti-lock Brake System (ABS) speed sensor, if equipped with ABS
- Spacer, if not equipped with ABS

✸✸ WARNING

Be careful not to scratch the speed sensor rotor serrations.

4. Remove the outside oil seal from steering knuckle, using a small prybar

5. Remove the bearing from the steering knuckle, as follows:

- Snapring
- Bearing from the steering knuckle, using tools 09950-60020 and 09950-70010

To install:

6. Install the bearing to the steering knuckle, as follows:

- Bearing to the steering knuckle, using tools 09950-60020 and 09527-17011
- Snapring

7. Install the new outside oil seal to steering knuckle, using a plastic hammer and tools 09223-15030 and 09527-17011

8. Install the axle hub to the steering knuckle, as follows:

- Dust cover to the steering knuckle. Torque the 4 bolts to 13 ft. lbs. (18 Nm).
- Axle hub to the steering knuckle, using a shop press and tool 09649-17010

9. Install or connect the following:

- Bearing spacer and Anti-lock Brake System (ABS) speed sensor, if equipped with ABS

✸✸ WARNING

Be careful not to scratch the speed sensor rotor serrations.

- Bearing spacer, if not equipped with ABS, using a shop press and tools 09950-60010 and 09950-70010
- Grease cap, for 2WD
- Inner grease seal, for 4WD, using a plastic hammer and tool 09527-17011
- Axle hub/steering knuckle assembly
- Front wheel

GLOSSARY

ABS: Anti-lock braking system. An electro-mechanical braking system which is designed to minimize or prevent wheel lock-up during braking.

ABSOLUTE PRESSURE: Atmospheric (barometric) pressure plus the pressure gauge reading.

ACCELERATOR PUMP: A small pump located in the carburetor that feeds fuel into the air/fuel mixture during acceleration.

ACCUMULATOR: A device that controls shift quality by cushioning the shock of hydraulic oil pressure being applied to a clutch or band.

ACTUATING MECHANISM: The mechanical output devices of a hydraulic system, for example, clutch pistons and band servos.

ACTUATOR: The output component of a hydraulic or electronic system.

ADVANCE: Setting the ignition timing so that spark occurs earlier before the piston reaches top dead center (TDC).

ADAPTIVE MEMORY (ADAPTIVE STRATEGY): The learning ability of the TCM or PCM to redefine its decision-making process to provide optimum shift quality.

AFTER TOP DEAD CENTER (ATDC): The point after the piston reaches the top of its travel on the compression stroke.

AIR BAG: Device on the inside of the car designed to inflate on impact of crash, protecting the occupants of the car.

AIR CHARGE TEMPERATURE (ACT) SENSOR: The temperature of the airflow into the engine is measured by an ACT sensor, usually located in the lower intake manifold or air cleaner. ALDL (assembly line diagnostic link): Electrical connector for scanning ECM/PCM/TCM input and output devices.

AIR CLEANER: An assembly consisting of a housing, filter and any connecting ductwork. The filter element is made up of a porous paper, sometimes with a wire mesh screening, and is designed to prevent airborne particles from entering the engine through the carburetor or throttle body.

AIR INJECTION: One method of reducing harmful exhaust emissions by injecting air into each of the exhaust ports of an engine. The fresh air entering the hot exhaust manifold causes any remaining fuel to be burned before it can exit the tailpipe.

AIR PUMP: An emission control device that supplies fresh air to the exhaust manifold to aid in more completely burning exhaust gases.

AIR/FUEL RATIO: The ratio of air-to-gasoline by weight in the fuel mixture drawn into the engine.

ALIGNMENT RACK: A special drive-on vehicle lift apparatus/measuring device used to adjust a vehicle's toe, caster and camber angles.

ALL WHEEL DRIVE: Term used to describe a full time four wheel drive system or any other vehicle drive system that continuously delivers power to all four wheels. This system is found primarily on station wagon vehicles and SUVs not utilized for significant off road use.

ALTERNATING CURRENT (AC): Electric current that flows first in one direction, then in the opposite direction, continually reversing flow.

ALTERNATOR: A device which produces AC (alternating current) which is converted to DC (direct current) to charge the car battery.

AMMETER: An instrument, calibrated in amperes, used to measure the flow of an electrical current in a circuit. Ammeters are always connected in series with the circuit being tested.

AMPERAGE: The total amount of current (amperes) flowing in a circuit.

AMPLIFIER: A device used in an electrical circuit to increase the voltage of an output signal.

AMP/HR. RATING (BATTERY): Measurement of the ability of a battery to deliver a stated amount of current for a stated period of time. The higher the amp/hr. rating, the better the battery.

AMPERE: The rate of flow of electrical current present when one volt of electrical pressure is applied against one ohm of electrical resistance.

ANALOG COMPUTER: Any microprocessor that uses similar (analogous) electrical signals to make its calculations.

ANODIZED: A special coating applied to the surface of aluminum valves for extended service life.

ANTIFREEZE: A substance (ethylene or propylene glycol) added to the coolant to prevent freezing in cold weather.

ANTI-FOAM AGENTS: Minimize fluid foaming from the whipping action encountered in the converter and planetary action.

ANTI-WEAR AGENTS: Zinc agents that control wear on the gears, bushings, and thrust washers.

ANTI-LOCK BRAKING SYSTEM: A supplementary system to the base hydraulic system that prevents sustained lock-up of the wheels during braking as well as automatically controlling wheel slip.

ANTI-ROLL BAR: See stabilizer bar.

ARC: A flow of electricity through the air between two electrodes or contact points that produces a spark.

ARMATURE: A laminated, soft iron core wrapped by a wire that converts electrical energy to mechanical energy as in a motor or relay. When rotated in a magnetic field, it changes mechanical energy into electrical energy as in a generator.

ATDC: After Top Dead Center.

ATF: Automatic transmission fluid.

ATMOSPHERIC PRESSURE: The pressure on the Earth's surface caused by the weight of the air in the atmosphere. At sea level, this pressure is 14.7 psi at 32°F (101 kPa at 0°C).

ATOMIZATION: The breaking down of a liquid into a fine mist that can be suspended in air.

AUXILIARY ADD-ON COOLER: A supplemental transmission fluid cooling device that is installed in series with the heat exchanger (cooler), located inside the radiator, to provide additional support to cool the hot fluid leaving the torque converter.

AUXILIARY PRESSURE: An added fluid pressure that is introduced into a regulator or balanced valve system to control valve movement. The auxiliary pressure itself can be either a fixed or a variable value. (See balanced valve; regulator valve.)

AWD: All wheel drive.

AXIAL FORCE: A side or end thrust force acting in or along the same plane as the power flow.

AXIAL PLAY: Movement parallel to a shaft or bearing bore.

AXLE CAPACITY: The maximum load-carrying capacity of the axle itself, as specified by the manufacturer. This is usually a higher number than the GAWR.

AXLE RATIO: This is a number (3.07:1, 4.56:1, for example) expressing the ratio between driveshaft revolutions and wheel revolutions. A low numerical ratio allows the engine to work easier because it doesn't have to turn as fast. A high numerical ratio means that the engine has to turn more rpm's to move the wheels through the same number of turns.

BACKFIRE: The sudden combustion of gases in the intake or exhaust system that results in a loud explosion.

BACKLASH: The clearance or play between two parts, such as meshed gears.

BACKPRESSURE: Restrictions in the exhaust system that slow the exit of exhaust gases from the combustion chamber.

BAKELITE®: A heat resistant, plastic insulator material commonly used in printed circuit boards and transistorized components.

BALANCED VALVE: A valve that is positioned by opposing auxiliary hydraulic pressures and/or spring force. Examples include mainline regulator, throttle, and governor valves. (See regulator valve.)

BAND: A flexible ring of steel with an inner lining of friction material. When tightened around the outside of a drum, a planetary member is held stationary to the transmission/transaxle case.

BALL BEARING: A bearing made up of hardened inner and outer races between which hardened steel balls roll.

BALL JOINT: A ball and matching socket connecting suspension components (steering knuckle to lower control arms). It permits rotating movement in any direction between the components that are joined.

BARO (BAROMETRIC PRESSURE SENSOR): Measures the change in the intake manifold pressure caused by changes in altitude.

BAROMETRIC MANIFOLD ABSOLUTE PRESSURE (BMAP) SENSOR: Operates similarly to a conventional MAP sensor; reads intake manifold pressure and is also responsible for determining altitude and barometric pressure prior to engine operation.

BAROMETRIC PRESSURE: (See atmospheric pressure.)

BALLAST RESISTOR: A resistor in the primary ignition circuit that lowers voltage after the engine is started to reduce wear on ignition components.

BATTERY: A direct current electrical storage unit, consisting of the basic active materials of lead and sulfuric acid, which converts chemical energy into electrical energy. Used to provide current for the operation of the starter as well as other equipment, such as the radio, lighting, etc.

BEAD: The portion of a tire that holds it on the rim.

BEARING: A friction reducing, supportive device usually located between a stationary part and a moving part.

BEFORE TOP DEAD CENTER (BTDC): The point just before the piston reaches the top of its travel on the compression stroke.

BELTED TIRE: Tire construction similar to bias-ply tires, but using two or more layers of reinforced belts between body plies and the tread.

BEZEL: Piece of metal surrounding radio, headlights, gauges or similar components; sometimes used to hold the glass face of a gauge in the dash.

BIAS-PLY TIRE: Tire construction, using body ply reinforcing cords which run at alternating angles to the center line of the tread.

BI-METAL TEMPERATURE SENSOR: Any sensor or switch made of two dissimilar types of metal that bend when heated or cooled due to the different expansion rates of the alloys. These types of sensors usually function as an on/off switch.

BLOCK: See Engine Block.

BLOW-BY: Combustion gases, composed of water vapor and unburned fuel, that leak past the piston rings into the crankcase during normal engine operation. These gases are removed by the PCV system to prevent the buildup of harmful acids in the crankcase.

BOOK TIME: See Labor Time.

BOOK VALUE: The average value of a car, widely used to determine trade-in and resale value.

BOOST VALVE: Used at the base of the regulator valve to increase mainline pressure.

BORE: Diameter of a cylinder.

BRAKE CALIPER: The housing that fits over the brake disc. The caliper holds the brake pads, which are pressed against the discs by the caliper pistons when the brake pedal is depressed.

BRAKE HORSEPOWER(BHP): The actual horsepower available at the engine flywheel as measured by a dynamometer.

BRAKE FADE: Loss of braking power, usually caused by excessive heat after repeated brake applications.

BRAKE HORSEPOWER: Usable horsepower of an engine measured at the crankshaft.

BRAKE PAD: A brake shoe and lining assembly used with disc brakes.

BRAKE PROPORTIONING VALVE: A valve on the master cylinder which restricts hydraulic brake pressure to the wheels to a specified amount, preventing wheel lock-up.

BREAKAWAY: Often used by Chrysler to identify first-gear operation in D and 2 ranges. In these ranges, first-gear operation depends on a one-way roller clutch that holds on acceleration and releases (breaks away) on deceleration, resulting in a freewheeling coast-down condition.

BRAKE SHOE: The backing for the brake lining. The term is, however, usually applied to the assembly of the brake backing and lining.

BREAKER POINTS: A set of points inside the distributor, operated by a cam, which make and break the ignition circuit.

BRINNELLING: A wear pattern identified by a series of indentations at regular intervals. This condition is caused by a lack of lube, overload situations, and/or vibrations.

BTDC: Before Top Dead Center.

BUMP: Sudden and forceful apply of a clutch or band.

BUSHING: A liner, usually removable, for a bearing; an anti-friction liner used in place of a bearing.

CALIFORNIA ENGINE: An engine certified by the EPA for use in California only; conforms to more stringent emission regulations than Federal engine.

CALIPER: A hydraulically activated device in a disc brake system, which is mounted straddling the brake rotor (disc). The caliper contains at least one piston and two brake pads. Hydraulic pressure on the piston(s) forces the pads against the rotor.

CAPACITY: The quantity of electricity that can be delivered from a unit, as from a battery in ampere-hours, or output, as from a generator.

CAMBER: One of the factors of wheel alignment. Viewed from the front of the car, it is the inward or outward tilt of the wheel. The top of the tire will lean outward (positive camber) or inward (negative camber).

CAMSHAFT: A shaft in the engine on which are the lobes (cams) which operate the valves. The camshaft is driven by the crankshaft, via a belt, chain or gears, at one half the crankshaft speed.

CANCER: Rust on a car body.

CAPACITOR: A device which stores an electrical charge.

CARBON MONOXIDE (CO): A colorless, odorless gas given off as a normal byproduct of combustion. It is poisonous and extremely dangerous in confined areas, building up slowly to toxic levels without warning if adequate ventilation is not available.

CARBURETOR: A device, usually mounted on the intake manifold of an engine, which mixes the air and fuel in the proper proportion to allow even combustion.

CASTER: The forward or rearward tilt of an imaginary line drawn through the upper ball joint and the center of the wheel. Viewed from the sides, positive caster (forward tilt) lends directional stability, while negative caster (rearward tilt) produces instability.

CATALYTIC CONVERTER: A device installed in the exhaust system, like a muffler, that converts harmful byproducts of combustion into carbon dioxide and water vapor by means of a heat-producing chemical reaction.

CENTRIFUGAL ADVANCE: A mechanical method of advancing the spark timing by using flyweights in the distributor that react to centrifugal force generated by the distributor shaft rotation.

CENTRIFUGAL FORCE: The outward pull of a revolving object, away from the center of revolution. Centrifugal force increases with the speed of rotation.

CETANE RATING: A measure of the ignition value of diesel fuel. The higher the cetane rating, the better the fuel. Diesel fuel cetane rating is roughly comparable to gasoline octane rating.

CHECK VALVE: Any one-way valve installed to permit the flow of air, fuel or vacuum in one direction only.

CHOKE: The valve/plate that restricts the amount of air entering an engine on the induction stroke, thereby enriching the air/fuel ratio.

CHUGGLE: Bucking or jerking condition that may be engine related and may be most noticeable when converter clutch is engaged; similar to the feel of towing a trailer.

CIRCLIP: A split steel snaping that fits into a groove to hold various parts in place.

CIRCUIT BREAKER: A switch which protects an electrical circuit from overload by opening the circuit when the current flow exceeds a pre-determined level. Some circuit breakers must be reset manually, while most reset automatically.

CIRCUIT: Any unbroken path through which an electrical current can flow. Also used to describe fuel flow in some instances.

CIRCUIT, BYPASS: Another circuit in parallel with the major circuit through which power is diverted.

CIRCUIT, CLOSED: An electrical circuit in which there is no interruption of current flow.

CIRCUIT, GROUND: The non-insulated portion of a complete circuit used as a common potential point. In automotive circuits, the ground is composed of metal parts, such as the engine, body sheet metal, and frame and is usually a negative potential.

CIRCUIT, HOT: That portion of a circuit not at ground potential. The hot circuit is usually insulated and is connected to the positive side of the battery.

CIRCUIT, OPEN: A break or lack of contact in an electrical circuit, either intentional (switch) or unintentional (bad connection or broken wire).

CIRCUIT, PARALLEL: A circuit having two or more paths for current flow with common positive and negative tie points. The same voltage is applied to each load device or parallel branch.

CIRCUIT, SERIES: An electrical system in which separate parts are connected end to end, using one wire, to form a single path for current to flow.

CIRCUIT, SHORT: A circuit that is accidentally completed in an electrical path for which it was not intended.

CLAMPING (ISOLATION) DIODES: Diodes positioned in a circuit to prevent self-induction from damaging electronic components.

CLEARCOAT: A transparent layer which, when sprayed over a vehicle's paint job, adds gloss and depth as well as an additional protective coating to the finish.

CLUTCH: Part of the power train used to connect/disconnect power to the rear wheels.

CLUTCH, FLUID: The same as a fluid coupling. A fluid clutch or coupling performs the same function as a friction clutch by utilizing fluid friction and inertia as opposed to solid friction used by a friction clutch. (See fluid coupling.)

CLUTCH, FRICTION: A coupling device that provides a means of smooth and positive engagement and disengagement of engine torque to the vehicle powertrain. Transmission of power through the clutch is accomplished by bringing one or more rotating drive members into contact with complementing driven members.

COAST: Vehicle deceleration caused by engine braking conditions.

COEFFICIENT OF FRICTION: The amount of surface tension between two contacting surfaces; identified by a scientifically calculated number.

COIL: Part of the ignition system that boosts the relatively low voltage supplied by the car's electrical system to the high voltage required to fire the spark plugs.

COMBINATION MANIFOLD: An assembly which includes both the intake and exhaust manifolds in one casting.

COMBINATION VALVE: A device used in some fuel systems that routes fuel vapors to a charcoal storage canister instead of venting them into the atmo-sphere. The valve relieves fuel tank pressure and allows fresh air into the tank as the fuel level drops to prevent a vapor lock situation.

COMBUSTION CHAMBER: The part of the engine in the cylinder head where combustion takes place.

COMPOUND GEAR: A gear consisting of two or more simple gears with a common shaft.

COMPOUND PLANETARY: A gearset that has more than the three elements found in a simple gearset and is constructed by combining members of two planetary gearsets to create additional gear ratio possibilities.

COMPRESSION CHECK: A test involving removing each spark plug and inserting a gauge. When the engine is cranked, the gauge will record a pressure reading in the individual cylinder. General operating condition can be determined from a compression check.

COMPRESSION RATIO: The ratio of the volume between the piston and cylinder head when the piston is at the bottom of its stroke (bottom dead center) and when the piston is at the top of its stroke (top dead center).

COMPUTER: An electronic control module that correlates input data according to prearranged engineered instructions; used for the management of an actuator system or systems.

CONDENSER: 1. An electrical device which acts to store an electrical charge, preventing voltage surges. 2. A radiator-like device in the air conditioning system in which refrigerant gas condenses into a liquid, giving off heat.

CONDUCTOR: Any material through which an electrical current can be transmitted easily.

CONNECTING ROD: The connecting link between the crankshaft and piston.

CONSTANT VELOCITY JOINT: Type of universal joint in a halfshaft assembly in which the output shaft turns at a constant angular velocity without variation, provided that the speed of the input shaft is constant.

CONTINUITY: Continuous or complete circuit. Can be checked with an ohmmeter.

CONTROL ARM: The upper or lower suspension components which are mounted on the frame and support the ball joints and steering knuckles.

CONVENTIONAL IGNITION: Ignition system which uses breaker points.

CONVERTER: (See torque converter.)

CONVERTER LOCKUP: The switching from hydrodynamic to direct mechanical drive, usually through the application of a friction element called the converter clutch.

COOLANT: Mixture of water and anti-freeze circulated through the engine to carry off heat produced by the engine.

CORROSION INHIBITOR: An inhibitor in ATF that prevents corrosion of bushings, thrust washers, and oil cooler brazed joints.

COUNTERSHAFT: An intermediate shaft which is rotated by a mainshaft and transmits, in turn, that rotation to a working part.

COUPLING PHASE: Occurs when the torque converter is operating at its greatest hydraulic efficiency. The speed differential between the impeller and the turbine is at its minimum. At this point, the stator freewheels, and there is no torque multiplication.

CRANKCASE: The lower part of an engine in which the crankshaft and related parts operate.

CRANKSHAFT: Engine component (connected to pistons by connecting rods) which converts the reciprocating (up and down) motion of pistons to rotary motion used to turn the driveshaft.

CURB WEIGHT: The weight of a vehicle without passengers or payload, but including all fluids (oil, gas, coolant, etc.) and other equipment specified as standard.

CURRENT: The flow (or rate) of electrons moving through a circuit. Current is measured in amperes (amp).

CURRENT FLOW CONVENTIONAL: Current flows through a circuit from the positive terminal of the source to the negative terminal (plus to minus).

CURRENT FLOW, ELECTRON: Current or electrons flow from the negative terminal of the source, through the circuit, to the positive terminal (minus to plus).

CV-JOINT: Constant velocity joint.

CYCLIC VIBRATIONS: The off-center movement of a rotating object that is affected by its initial balance, speed of rotation, and working angles.

CYLINDER BLOCK: See engine block.

CYLINDER HEAD: The detachable portion of the engine, usually fastened to the top of the cylinder block and containing all or most of the combustion chambers. On overhead valve engines, it contains the valves and their operating parts. On overhead cam engines, it contains the camshaft as well.

CYLINDER: In an engine, the round hole in the engine block in which the piston(s) ride.

DATA LINK CONNECTOR (DLC): Current acronym/term applied to the federally mandated, diagnostic junction connector that is used to monitor ECM/PC/TCM inputs, processing strategies, and outputs including diagnostic trouble codes (DTCs).

DEAD CENTER: The extreme top or bottom of the piston stroke.

DECELERATION BUMP: When referring to a torque converter clutch in the applied position, a sudden release of the accelerator pedal causes a forceful reversal of power through the drivetrain (engine braking), just prior to the apply plate actually being released.

DELAYED (LATE OR EXTENDED): Condition where shift is expected but does not occur for a period of time, for example, where clutch or band engagement does not occur as quickly as expected during part throttle or wide open throttle apply of accelerator or when manually downshifting to a lower range.

DETENT: A spring-loaded plunger, pin, ball, or pawl used as a holding device on a ratchet wheel or shaft. In automatic transmissions, a detent mechanism is used for locking the manual valve in place.

DETENT DOWNSHIFT: (See kickdown.)

DETERGENT: An additive in engine oil to improve its operating characteristics.

DETONATION: An unwanted explosion of the air/fuel mixture in the combustion chamber caused by excess heat and compression, advanced timing, or an overly lean mixture. Also referred to as "ping".

DEXRON®: A brand of automatic transmission fluid.

DIAGNOSTIC TROUBLE CODES (DTCs): A digital display from the control module memory that identifies the input, processor, or output device circuit that is related to the powertrain emission/driveability malfunction detected. Diagnostic trouble codes can be read by the MIL to flash any codes or by using a handheld scanner.

DIAPHRAGM: A thin, flexible wall separating two cavities, such as in a vacuum advance unit.

DIESELING: The engine continues to run after the car is shut off; caused by fuel continuing to be burned in the combustion chamber.

DIFFERENTIAL: A geared assembly which allows the transmission of motion between drive axles, giving one axle the ability to rotate faster than the other, as in cornering.

DIFFERENTIAL AREAS: When opposing faces of a spool valve are acted upon by the same pressure but their areas differ in size, the face with the larger area produces the differential force and valve movement. (See spool valve.)

DIFFERENTIAL FORCE: (See differential areas.) digital readout: A display of numbers or a combination of numbers and letters.

DIGITAL VOLT OHMMETER: An electronic diagnostic tool used to measure voltage, ohms and amps as well as several other functions, with the readings displayed on a digital screen in tenths, hundredths and thousandths.

DIODE: An electrical device that will allow current to flow in one direction only.

DIRECT CURRENT (DC): Electrical current that flows in one direction only.

DIRECT DRIVE: The gear ratio is 1:1, with no change occurring in the torque and speed input/output relationship.

DISC BRAKE: A hydraulic braking assembly consisting of a brake disc, or rotor, mounted on an axle shaft, and a caliper assembly containing, usually two brake pads which are activated by hydraulic pressure. The pads are forced against the sides of the disc, creating friction which slows the vehicle.

DISPERSANTS: Suspend dirt and prevent sludge buildup. double bump (double feel): Two sudden and forceful applies of a clutch or band.

DISPLACEMENT: The total volume of air that is displaced by all pistons as the engine turns through one complete revolution.

DISTRIBUTOR: A mechanically driven device on an engine which is responsible for electrically firing the spark plug at a pre-determined point of the piston stroke.

DOHC: Double overhead camshaft.

DOUBLE OVERHEAD CAMSHAFT: The engine utilizes two camshafts mounted in one cylinder head. One camshaft operates the exhaust valves, while the other operates the intake valves.

DOWEL PIN: A pin, inserted in mating holes in two different parts allowing those parts to maintain a fixed relationship.

DRIVELINE: The drive connection between the transmission and the drive wheels.

DRIVE TRAIN: The components that transmit the flow of power from the engine to the wheels. The components include the clutch, transmission, driveshafts (or axle shafts in front wheel drive), U-joints and differential.

DRUM BRAKE: A braking system which consists of two brake shoes and one or two wheel cylinders, mounted on a fixed backing plate, and a brake drum, mounted on an axle, which revolves around the assembly.

DRY CHARGED BATTERY: Battery to which electrolyte is added when the battery is placed in service.

DVOM: Digital volt ohmmeter

DWELL: The rate, measured in degrees of shaft rotation, at which an electrical circuit cycles on and off.

DYNAMIC: A sealing application in which there is rotating or reciprocating motion between the parts.

EARLY: Condition where shift occurs before vehicle has reached proper speed, which tends to labor engine after upshift.

EBCM: See Electronic Control Unit (ECU).

ECM: See Electronic Control Unit (ECU).

ECU: Electronic control unit.

ELECTRODE: Conductor (positive or negative) of electric current.

ELECTROLYSIS: A surface etching or bonding of current conducting transmission/transaxle components that may occur when grounding straps are missing or in poor condition.

ELECTROLYTE: A solution of water and sulfuric acid used to activate the battery. Electrolyte is extremely corrosive.

ELECTROMAGNET: A coil that produces a magnetic field when current flows through its windings.

ELECTROMAGNETIC INDUCTION: A method to create (generate) current flow through the use of magnetism.

ELECTROMAGNETISM: The effects surrounding the relationship between electricity and magnetism.

ELECTROMOTIVE FORCE (EMF): The force or pressure (voltage) that causes current movement in an electrical circuit.

ELECTRONIC CONTROL UNIT: A digital computer that controls engine (and sometimes transmission, brake or other vehicle system) functions based on data received from various sensors. Examples used by some manufacturers include Electronic Brake Control Module (EBCM), Engine Control Module (ECM), Powertrain Control Module (PCM) or Vehicle Control Module (VCM).

ELECTRONIC IGNITION: A system in which the timing and firing of the spark plugs is controlled by an electronic control unit, usually called a module. These systems have no points or condenser.

ELECTRONIC PRESSURE CONTROL (EPC) SOLENOID: A specially designed solenoid containing a spool valve and spring assembly to control fluid mainline pressure. A variable current flow, controlled by the ECM/PCM, varies the internal force of the solenoid on the spool valve and resulting mainline pressure. (See variable force solenoid.)

ELECTRONICS: Miniaturized electrical circuits utilizing semiconductors, solid-state devices, and printed circuits. Electronic circuits utilize small amounts of power.

ELECTRONIFICATION: The application of electronic circuitry to a mechanical device. Regarding automatic transmissions, electrification is incorporated into converter clutch lockup, shift scheduling, and line pressure control systems.

ELECTROSTATIC DISCHARGE (ESD): An unwanted, high-voltage electrical current released by an individual who has taken on a static charge of electricity. Electronic components can be easily damaged by ESD.

ELEMENT: A device within a hydrodynamic drive unit designed with a set of blades to direct fluid flow.

ENAMEL: Type of paint that dries to a smooth, glossy finish.

END BUMP (END FEEL OR SLIP BUMP): Firmer feel at end of shift when compared with feel at start of shift.

END-PLAY: The clearance/gap between two components that allows for expansion of the parts as they warm up, to prevent binding and to allow space for lubrication.

ENERGY: The ability or capacity to do work.

ENGINE: The primary motor or power apparatus of a vehicle, which converts liquid or gas fuel into mechanical energy.

ENGINE BLOCK: The basic engine casting containing the cylinders, the crankshaft main bearings, as well as machined surfaces for the mounting of other components such as the cylinder head, oil pan, transmission, etc..

ENGINE BRAKING: Use of engine to slow vehicle by manually downshifting during zero-throttle coast down.

ENGINE CONTROL MODULE (ECM): Manages the engine and incorporates output control over the torque converter clutch solenoid. (Note: Current designation for the ECM in late model vehicles is PCM.)

ENGINE COOLANT TEMPERATURE (ECT) SENSOR: Prevents converter clutch engagement with a cold engine; also used for shift timing and shift quality.

EP LUBRICANT: EP (extreme pressure) lubricants are specially formulated for use with gears involving heavy loads (transmissions, differentials, etc.).

ETHYL: A substance added to gasoline to improve its resistance to knock, by slowing down the rate of combustion.

ETHYLENE GLYCOL: The base substance of antifreeze.

EXHAUST MANIFOLD: A set of cast passages or pipes which conduct exhaust gases from the engine.

FAIL-SAFE (BACKUP) CONTROL: A substitute value used by the PCM/TCM to replace a faulty signal from an input sensor. The temporary value allows the vehicle to continue to be operated.

FAST IDLE: The speed of the engine when the choke is on. Fast idle speeds engine warm-up.

FEDERAL ENGINE: An engine certified by the EPA for use in any of the 49 states (except California).

FEEDBACK: A circuit malfunction whereby current can find another path to feed load devices.

FEELER GAUGE: A blade, usually metal, of precisely predetermined thickness, used to measure the clearance between two parts.

FILAMENT: The part of a bulb that glows; the filament creates high resistance to current flow and actually glows from the resulting heat.

FINAL DRIVE: An essential part of the axle drive assembly where final gear reduction takes place in the powertrain. In RWD applications and north-south FWD applications, it must also change the power flow direction to the axle shaft by ninety degrees. (Also see axle ratio).

FIRING ORDER: The order in which combustion occurs in the cylinders of an engine. Also the order in which spark is distributed to the plugs by the distributor.

FIRM: A noticeable quick apply of a clutch or band that is considered normal with medium to heavy throttle shift; should not be confused with harsh or rough.

FLAME FRONT: The term used to describe certain aspects of the fuel explosion in the cylinders. The flame front should move in a controlled pattern across the cylinder, rather than simply exploding immediately.

FLARE (SLIPPING): A quick increase in engine rpm accompanied by momentary loss of torque; generally occurs during shift.

FLAT ENGINE: Engine design in which the pistons are horizontally opposed. Porsche, Subaru and some old VW are common examples of flat engines.

FLAT RATE: A dealership term referring to the amount of money paid to a technician for a repair or diagnostic service based on that particular service versus dealership's labor time (NOT based on the actual time the technician spent on the job).

FLAT SPOT: A point during acceleration when the engine seems to lose power for an instant.

FLOODING: The presence of too much fuel in the intake manifold and combustion chamber which prevents the air/fuel mixture from firing, thereby causing a no-start situation.

FLUID: A fluid can be either liquid or gas. In hydraulics, a liquid is used for transmitting force or motion.

FLUID COUPLING: The simplest form of hydrodynamic drive, the fluid coupling consists of two look-alike members with straight radial varies referred to as the impeller (pump) and the turbine. input torque is always equal to the output torque.

FLUID DRIVE: Either a fluid coupling or a fluid torque converter. (See hydrodynamic drive units.)

FLUID TORQUE CONVERTER: A hydrodynamic drive that has the ability to act both as a torque multiplier and fluid coupling. (See hydrodynamic drive units; torque converter.)

FLUID VISCOSITY: The resistance of a liquid to flow. A cold fluid (oil) has greater viscosity and flows more slowly than a hot fluid (oil).

FLYWHEEL: A heavy disc of metal attached to the rear of the crankshaft. It smoothes the firing impulses of the engine and keeps the crankshaft turning during periods when no firing takes place. The starter also engages the flywheel to start the engine.

FOOT POUND (ft. lbs. or sometimes, ft. lb.): The amount of energy or work needed to raise an item weighing one pound, a distance of one foot.

FREEZE PLUG: A plug in the engine block which will be pushed out if the coolant freezes. Sometimes called expansion plugs, they protect the block from cracking should the coolant freeze.

FRICTION. The resistance that occurs between contacting surfaces. This relationship is expressed by a ratio called the coefficient of friction (CL).

FRICTION, COEFFICIENT OF: The amount of surface tension between two contacting surfaces; expressed by a scientifically calculated number.

FRONT END ALIGNMENT: A service to set caster, camber and toe-in to the correct specifications. This will ensure that the car steers and handles properly and that the tires wear properly.

FRICTION MODIFIER: Changes the coefficient of friction of the fluid between the mating steel and composition clutch/band surfaces during the engagement process and allows for a certain amount of intentional slipping for a good "shift-feel." full throttle detent downshift: A quick apply of accelerator pedal to its full travel, forcing a downshift.

FRONTAL AREA: The total frontal area of a vehicle exposed to air flow.

FUEL FILTER: A component of the fuel system containing a porous paper element used to prevent any impurities from entering the engine through the fuel system. It usually takes the form of a canister-like housing, mounted in-line with the fuel hose, located anywhere on a vehicle between the fuel tank and engine.

FUEL INJECTION: A system replacing the carburetor that sprays fuel into the cylinder through nozzles. The amount of fuel can be more precisely controlled with fuel injection.

FULL FLOATING AXLE: An axle in which the axle housing extends through the wheel giving bearing support on the outside of the housing. The front axle of a four-wheel drive vehicle is usually a full floating axle, as are the rear axles of many larger (1 ton and over) pick-ups and vans.

FULL-TIME FOUR-WHEEL DRIVE: A four-wheel drive system that continuously delivers power to all four wheels. A differential between the front and rear driveshafts permits variations in axle speeds to control gear wind-up without damage.

FUSE: A protective device in a circuit which prevents circuit overload by breaking the circuit when a specific amperage is present. The device is constructed around a strip or wire of a lower amperage rating than the circuit it is designed to protect. When an amperage higher than that stamped on the fuse is present in the circuit, the strip or wire melts, opening the circuit.

FUSIBLE LINK: A piece of wire in a wiring harness that performs the same job as a fuse. If overloaded, the fusible link will melt and interrupt the circuit.

FWD: Front wheel drive.

GAWR: (Gross axle weight rating) the total maximum weight an axle is designed to carry.

GCW: (Gross combined weight) total combined weight of a tow vehicle and trailer.

GARAGE SHIFT: initial engagement feel of transmission, neutral to reverse or neutral to a forward drive.

GARAGE SHIFT FEEL: A quick check of the engagement quality and responsiveness of reverse and forward gears. This test is done with the vehicle stationary.

GEAR: A toothed mechanical device that acts as a rotating lever to transmit power or turning effort from one shaft to another. (See gear ratio.)

GEAR RATIO: A ratio expressing the number of turns a smaller gear will make to turn a larger gear through one revolution. The ratio is found by dividing the number of teeth on the smaller gear into the number of teeth on the larger gear.

GEARBOX: Transmission

GEAR REDUCTION: Torque is multiplied and speed decreased by the factor of the gear ratio. For example, a 3:1 gear ratio changes an input torque of 180 ft. lbs. and an input speed of 2700 rpm to 540 Ft. lbs. and 900 rpm, respectively. (No account is taken of frictional losses, which are always present.)

GEARTRAIN: A succession of intermeshing gears that form an assembly and provide for one or more torque changes as the power input is transmitted to the power output.

GEL COAT: A thin coat of plastic resin covering fiberglass body panels.

GENERATOR: A device which produces direct current (DC) necessary to charge the battery.

GOVERNOR: A device that senses vehicle speed and generates a hydraulic oil pressure. As vehicle speed increases, governor oil pressure rises.

GROUND CIRCUIT: (See circuit, ground.)

GROUND SIDE SWITCHING: The electrical/electronic circuit control switch is located after the circuit load.

GVWR: (Gross vehicle weight rating) total maximum weight a vehicle is designed to carry including the weight of the vehicle, passengers, equipment, gas, oil, etc.

HALOGEN: A special type of lamp known for its quality of brilliant white light. Originally used for fog lights and driving lights.

HARD CODES: DTCs that are present at the time of testing; also called continuous or current codes.

HARSH(ROUGH): An apply of a clutch or band that is more noticeable than a firm one; considered undesirable at any throttle position.

HEADER TANK: An expansion tank for the radiator coolant. It can be located remotely or built into the radiator.

HEAT RANGE: A term used to describe the ability of a spark plug to carry away heat. Plugs with longer nosed insulators take longer to carry heat off effectively.

HEAT RISER: A flapper in the exhaust manifold that is closed when the engine is cold, causing hot exhaust gases to heat the intake manifold providing better cold engine operation. A thermostatic spring opens the flapper when the engine warms up.

HEAVY THROTTLE: Approximately three-fourths of accelerator pedal travel.

HEMI: A name given an engine using hemispherical combustion chambers.

HERTZ (HZ): The international unit of frequency equal to one cycle per second (10,000 Hertz equals 10,000 cycles per second).

HIGH-IMPEDANCE DVOM (DIGITAL VOLT-OHMMETER): This styled device provides a built-in resistance value and is capable of limiting circuit current flow to safe milliamp levels.

HIGH RESISTANCE: Often refers to a circuit where there is an excessive amount of opposition to normal current flow.

HORSEPOWER: A measurement of the amount of work; one horsepower is the amount of work necessary to lift 33,000 lbs. one foot in one minute. Brake horsepower (bhp) is the horsepower delivered by an engine on a dynamometer. Net horsepower is the power remaining (measured at the flywheel of the engine) that can be used to turn the wheels after power is consumed through friction and running the engine accessories (water pump, alternator, air pump, fan etc.)

HOT CIRCUIT: (See circuit, hot; hot lead). hot lead: A wire or conductor in the power side of the circuit. (See circuit, hot.)

HOT SIDE SWITCHING: The electrical/electronic circuit control switch is located before the circuit load.

HUB: The center part of a wheel or gear.

HUNTING (BUSYNESS): Repeating quick series of up-shifts and downshifts that causes noticeable change in engine rpm, for example, as in a 4-3-4 shift pattern.

HYDRAULICS: The use of liquid under pressure to transfer force of motion.

HYDROCARBON (HC): Any chemical compound made up of hydrogen and carbon. A major pollutant formed by the engine as a by-product of combustion.

HYDRODYNAMIC DRIVE UNITS: Devices that transmit power solely by the action of a kinetic fluid flow in a closed recirculating path. An impeller energizes the fluid and discharges the high-speed jet stream into the turbine for power output.

HYDROMETER: An instrument used to measure the specific gravity of a solution.

HYDROPLANING: A phenomenon of driving when water builds up under the tire tread, causing it to lose contact with the road. Slowing down will usually restore normal tire contact with the road.

HYPOID GEARSET: The drive pinion gear may be placed below or above the centerline of the driven gear; often used as a final drive gearset.

IDLE MIXTURE: The mixture of air and fuel (usually about 14:1) being fed to the cylinders. The idle mixture screw(s) are sometimes adjusted as part of a tune-up.

IDLER ARM: Component of the steering linkage which is a geometric duplicate of the steering gear arm. It supports the right side of the center steering link.

IMPELLER: Often called a pump, the impeller is the power input (drive) member of a hydrodynamic drive. As part of the torque converter cover, it acts as a centrifugal pump and puts the fluid in motion.

INCH POUND (inch lbs.; sometimes in. lb. or in. lbs.): One twelfth of a foot pound.

INDUCTANCE: The force that produces voltage when a conductor is passed through a magnetic field.

INDUCTION: A means of transferring electrical energy in the form of a magnetic field. Principle used in the ignition coil to increase voltage.

INITIAL FEEL: A distinct firmer feel at start of shift when compared with feel at finish of shift.

INJECTOR: A device which receives metered fuel under relatively low pressure and is activated to inject the fuel into the engine under relatively high pressure at a predetermined time.

INPUT: In an automatic transmission, the source of power from the engine is absorbed by the torque converter, which provides the power input into the transmission. The turbine drives the input(turbine)shaft.

INPUT SHAFT: The shaft to which torque is applied, usually carrying the driving gear or gears.

INTAKE MANIFOLD: A casting of passages or pipes used to conduct air or a fuel/air mixture to the cylinders.

INTERNAL GEAR: The ring-like outer gear of a planetary gearset with the gear teeth cut on the inside of the ring to provide a mesh with the planet pinions.

ISOLATION (CLAMPING) DIODES: Diodes positioned in a circuit to prevent self-induction from damaging electronic components.

IX ROTARY GEAR PUMP: Contains two rotating members, one shaped with internal gear teeth and the other with external gear teeth. As the gears separate, the fluid fills the gaps between gear teeth, is pulled across a crescent-shaped divider, and then is forced to flow through the outlet as the gears mesh.

IX ROTARY LOBE PUMP: Sometimes referred to as a gerotor type pump. Two rotating members, one shaped with internal lobes and the other with external lobes, separate and then mesh to cause fluid to flow.

JOURNAL: The bearing surface within which a shaft operates.

JUMPER CABLES: Two heavy duty wires with large alligator clips used to provide power from a charged battery to a discharged battery mounted in a vehicle.

JUMPSTART: Utilizing the sufficiently charged battery of one vehicle to start the engine of another vehicle with a discharged battery by the use of jumper cables.

KEY: A small block usually fitted in a notch between a shaft and a hub to prevent slippage of the two parts.

KICKDOWN: Detent downshift system; either linkage, cable, or electrically controlled.

KILO: A prefix used in the metric system to indicate one thousand.

KNOCK: Noise which results from the spontaneous ignition of a portion of the air-fuel mixture in the engine cylinder caused by overly advanced ignition timing or use of incorrectly low octane fuel for that engine.

KNOCK SENSOR: An input device that responds to spark knock, caused by over advanced ignition timing.

LABOR TIME: A specific amount of time required to perform a certain repair or diagnostic service as defined by a vehicle or after-market manufacturer .

LACQUER: A quick-drying automotive paint.

LATE: Shift that occurs when engine is at higher than normal rpm for given amount of throttle.

LIGHT-EMITTING DIODE (LED): A semiconductor diode that emits light as electrical current flows through it; used in some electronic display devices to emit a red or other color light.

LIGHT THROTTLE: Approximately one-fourth of accelerator pedal travel.

LIMITED SLIP: A type of differential which transfers driving force to the wheel with the best traction.

LIMP-IN MODE: Electrical shutdown of the transmission/ transaxle output solenoids, allowing only forward and reverse gears that are hydraulically energized by the manual valve. This permits the vehicle to be driven to a service facility for repair.

LIP SEAL: Molded synthetic rubber seal designed with an outer sealing edge (lip) that points into the fluid containing area to be sealed. This type of seal is used where rotational and axial forces are present.

LITHIUM-BASE GREASE: Chassis and wheel bearing grease using lithium as a base. Not compatible with sodium-base grease.

LOAD DEVICE: A circuit's resistance that converts the electrical energy into light, sound, heat, or mechanical movement.

LOAD RANGE: Indicates the number of plies at which a tire is rated. Load range B equals four-ply rating; C equals six-ply rating; and, D equals an eight-ply rating.

LOAD TORQUE: The amount of output torque needed from the transmission/transaxle to overcome the vehicle load.

LOCKING HUBS: Accessories used on part-time four-wheel drive systems that allow the front wheels to be disengaged from the drive train when four-wheel drive is not being used. When four-wheel drive is desired, the hubs are engaged, locking the wheels to the drive train.

LOCKUP CONVERTER: A torque converter that operates hydraulically and mechanically. When an internal apply plate (lockup plate) clamps to the torque converter cover, hydraulic slippage is eliminated.

LOCK RING: See Circlip or Snapring

MAGNET: Any body with the property of attracting iron or steel.

MAGNETIC FIELD: The area surrounding the poles of a magnet that is affected by its attraction or repulsion forces.

MAIN LINE PRESSURE: Often called control pressure or line pressure, it refers to the pressure of the oil leaving the pump and is controlled by the pressure regulator valve.

MALFUNCTION INDICATOR LAMP (MIL): Previously known as a check engine light, the dash-mounted MIL illuminates and signals the driver that an emission or driveability problem with the powertrain has been detected by the ECM/PCM. When this occurs, at least one diagnostic trouble code (DTC) has been stored into the control module memory.

MANIFOLD ABSOLUTE PRESSURE (MAP) SENSOR: Reads the amount of air pressure (vacuum) in the engine's intake manifold system; its signal is used to analyze engine load conditions.

MANIFOLD VACUUM: Low pressure in an engine intake manifold formed just below the throttle plates. Manifold vacuum is highest at idle and drops under acceleration.

MANIFOLD: A casting of passages or set of pipes which connect the cylinders to an inlet or outlet source.

MANUAL LEVER POSITION SWITCH (MLPS): A mechanical switching unit that is typically mounted externally to the transmission/transaxle to inform the PCM/ECM which gear range the driver has selected.

MANUAL VALVE: Located inside the transmission/transaxle, it is directly connected to the driver's shift lever. The position of the manual valve determines which hydraulic circuits will be charged with oil pressure and the operating mode of the transmission.

MANUAL VALVE LEVER POSITION SENSOR (MVLPS): The input from this device tells the TCM what gear range was selected.

MASS AIR FLOW (MAF) SENSOR: Measures the airflow into the engine.

MASTER CYLINDER: The primary fluid pressurizing device in a hydraulic system. In automotive use, it is found in brake and hydraulic clutch systems and is pedal activated, either directly or, in a power brake system, through the power booster.

MacPherson STRUT: A suspension component combining a shock absorber and spring in one unit.

MEDIUM THROTTLE: Approximately one-half of accelerator pedal travel.

MEGA: A metric prefix indicating one million.

MEMBER: An independent component of a hydrodynamic unit such as an impeller, a stator, or a turbine. It may have one or more elements.

MERCON: A fluid developed by Ford Motor Company in 1988. It contains a friction modifier and closely resembles operating characteristics of Dexron.

METAL SEALING RINGS: Made from cast iron or aluminum, their primary application is with dynamic components involving pressure sealing circuits of rotating members. These rings are designed with either butt or hook lock end joints.

METER (ANALOG): A linear-style meter representing data as lengths; a needle-style instrument interfacing with logical numerical increments. This style of electrical meter uses relatively low impedance internal resistance and cannot be used for testing electronic circuitry.

METER(DIGITAL): Uses numbers as a direct readout to show values. Most meters of this style use high impedance internal resistance and must be used for testing low current electronic circuitry.

MICRO: A metric prefix indicating one-millionth (0.000001).

MILLI: A metric prefix indicating one-thousandth (0.001).

MINIMUM THROTTLE: The least amount of throttle opening required for upshift; normally close to zero throttle.

MISFIRE: Condition occurring when the fuel mixture in a cylinder fails to ignite, causing the engine to run roughly.

MODULE: Electronic control unit, amplifier or igniter of solid state or integrated design which controls the current flow in the ignition primary

circuit based on input from the pick-up coil. When the module opens the primary circuit, high secondary voltage is induced in the coil.

MODULATED: In an electronic-hydraulic converter clutch system (or shift valve system), the term modulated refers to the pulsing of a solenoid, at a variable rate. This action controls the buildup of oil pressure in the hydraulic circuit to allow a controlled amount of clutch slippage.

MODULATED CONVERTER CLUTCH CONTROL (MCCC): A pulse width duty cycle valve that controls the converter lockup apply pressure and maximizes smoother transitions between lock and unlock conditions.

MODULATOR PRESSURE (THROTTLE PRESSURE): A hydraulic signal oil pressure relating to the amount of engine load, based on either the amount of throttle plate opening or engine vacuum.

MODULATOR VALVE: A regulator valve that is controlled by engine vacuum, providing a hydraulic pressure that varies in relation to engine torque. The hydraulic torque signal functions to delay the shift pattern and provide a line pressure boost. (See throttle valve.)

MOTOR: An electromagnetic device used to convert electrical energy into mechanical energy.

MULTIPLE-DISC CLUTCH: A grouping of steel and friction lined plates that, when compressed together by hydraulic pressure acting upon a piston, lock or unlock a planetary member.

MULTI-WEIGHT: Type of oil that provides adequate lubrication at both high and low temperatures.

needed to move one amp through a resistance of one ohm.

MUSHY: Same as soft; slow and drawn out clutch apply with very little shift feel.

MUTUAL INDUCTION: The generation of current from one wire circuit to another by movement of the magnetic field surrounding a current-carrying circuit as its ampere flow increases or decreases.

NEEDLE BEARING: A bearing which consists of a number (usually a large number) of long, thin rollers.

NITROGEN OXIDE (NOx): One of the three basic pollutants found in the exhaust emission of an internal combustion engine. The amount of NOx usually varies in an inverse proportion to the amount of HC and CO.

NONPOSITIVE SEALING: A sealing method that allows some minor leakage, which normally assists in lubrication.

O2 SENSOR: Located in the engine's exhaust system, it is an input device to the ECM/PCM for managing the fuel delivery and ignition system. A scanner can be used to observe the fluctuating voltage readings produced by an O2 sensor as the oxygen content of the exhaust is analyzed.

O-RING SEAL: Molded synthetic rubber seal designed with a circular cross-section. This type of seal is used primarily in static applications.

OBD II (ON-BOARD DIAGNOSTICS, SECOND GENERATION): Refers to the federal law mandating tighter control of 1996 and newer vehicle emissions, active monitoring of related devices, and standardization of terminology, data link connectors, and other technician concerns.

OCTANE RATING: A number, indicating the quality of gasoline based on its ability to resist knock. The higher the number, the better the quality. Higher compression engines require higher octane gas.

OEM: Original Equipment Manufactured. OEM equipment is that furnished standard by the manufacturer.

OFFSET: The distance between the vertical center of the wheel and the mounting surface at the lugs. Offset is positive if the center is outside the lug circle; negative offset puts the center line inside the lug circle.

OHM'S LAW: A law of electricity that states the relationship between voltage, current, and resistance. Volts = amperes x ohms

OHM: The unit used to measure the resistance of conductor-to-electrical flow. One ohm is the amount of resistance that limits current flow to one ampere in a circuit with one volt of pressure.

OHMMETER: An instrument used for measuring the resistance, in ohms, in an electrical circuit.

ONE-WAY CLUTCH: A mechanical clutch of roller or sprag design that resists torque or transmits power in one direction only. It is used to either hold or drive a planetary member.

ONE-WAY ROLLER CLUTCH: A mechanical device that transmits or holds torque in one direction only.

OPENCIRCUIT: A break or lack of contact in an electrical circuit, either intentional (switch) or unintentional (bad connection or broken wire).

ORIFICE: Located in hydraulic oil circuits, it acts as a restriction. It slows down fluid flow to either create back pressure or delay pressure buildup downstream.

OSCILLOSCOPE: A piece of test equipment that shows electric impulses as a pattern on a screen. Engine performance can be analyzed by interpreting these patterns.

OUTPUT SHAFT: The shaft which transmits torque from a device, such as a transmission.

OUTPUT SPEED SENSOR (OSS): Identifies transmission/transaxle output shaft speed for shift timing and may be used to calculate TCC slip; often functions as the VSS (vehicle speed sensor).

OVERDRIVE: (1.) A device attached to or incorporated in a transmission/transaxle that allows the engine to turn less than one full revolution for every complete revolution of the wheels. The net effect is to reduce engine rpm, thereby using less fuel. A typical overdrive gear ratio would be .87:1, instead of the normal 1:1 in high gear. (2.) A gear assembly which produces more shaft revolutions than that transmitted to it.

OVERDRIVE PLANETARY GEARSET: A single planetary gearset designed to provide a direct drive and overdrive ratio. When coupled to a three-speed transmission/transaxle configuration, a four-speed/overdrive unit is present.

OVERHEAD CAMSHAFT (OHC): An engine configuration in which the camshaft is mounted on top of the cylinder head and operates the valve either directly or by means of rocker arms.

OVERHEAD VALVE (OHV): An engine configuration in which all of the valves are located in the cylinder head and the camshaft is located in the cylinder block. The camshaft operates the valves via lifters and pushrods.

OVERRUNCLUTCH: Another name for a one-way mechanical clutch. Applies to both roller and sprag designs.

OVERSTEER: The tendency of some vehicles, when steering into a turn, to over-respond or steer more than required, which could result in excessive slip of the rear wheels. Opposite of under-steer.

OXIDATION STABILIZERS: Absorb and dissipate heat. Automatic transmission fluid has high resistance to varnish and sludge buildup that occurs from excessive heat that is generated primarily in the torque converter. Local temperatures as high as 6000F (3150C) can occur at the clutch plates during engagement, and this heat must be absorbed and dissipated. If the fluid cannot withstand the heat, it burns or oxidizes, resulting in an almost immediate destruction of friction materials, clogged filter screen and hydraulic passages, and sticky valves.

OXIDES OF NITROGEN: See nitrogen oxide (NOx).

OXYGEN SENSOR: Used with a feedback system to sense the presence of oxygen in the exhaust gas and signal the computer which can use the voltage signal to determine engine operating efficiency and adjust the air/fuel ratio.

PARALLEL CIRCUIT: (See circuit, parallel.)

PARTS WASHER: A basin or tub, usually with a built-in pump mechanism and hose used for circulating chemical solvent for the purpose of cleaning greasy, oily and dirty components.

PART-TIME FOUR WHEEL DRIVE: A system that is normally in the two wheel drive mode and only runs in four-wheel drive when the system is manually engaged because more traction is desired. Two or four wheel drive is normally selected by a lever to engage the front axle, but if locking hubs are used, these must also be manually engaged in the Lock position. Otherwise, the front axle will not drive the front wheels.

PASSIVE RESTRAINT: Safety systems such as air bags or automatic seat belts which operate with no action required on the part of the driver or passenger. Mandated by Federal regulations on all vehicles sold in the U.S. after 1990.

PAYLOAD: The weight the vehicle is capable of carrying in addition to its own weight. Payload includes weight of the driver, passengers and cargo, but not coolant, fuel, lubricant, spare tire, etc.

PCM: Powertrain control module.

PCV VALVE: A valve usually located in the rocker cover that vents crankcase vapors back into the engine to be reburned.

PERCOLATION: A condition in which the fuel actually "boils," due to excessive heat. Percolation prevents proper atomization of the fuel causing rough running.

PICK-UP COIL: The coil in which voltage is induced in an electronic ignition.

PINION GEAR: The smallest gear in a drive gear assembly. piston: A disc or cup that fits in a cylinder bore and is free to move. In hydraulics, it provides the means of converting hydraulic pressure into a usable force. Examples of piston applications are found in servo, clutch, and accumulator units.

PING: A metallic rattling sound produced by the engine during acceleration. It is usually due to incorrect ignition timing or a poor grade of gasoline.

PINION: The smaller of two gears. The rear axle pinion drives the ring gear which transmits motion to the axle shafts.

PISTON RING: An open-ended ring which fits into a groove on the outer diameter of the piston. Its chief function is to form a seal between the piston and cylinder wall. Most automotive pistons have three rings: two for compression sealing; one for oil sealing.

PITMAN ARM: A lever which transmits steering force from the steering gear to the steering linkage.

PLANET CARRIER: A basic member of a planetary gear assembly that carries the pinion gears.

PLANET PINIONS: Gears housed in a planet carrier that are in constant mesh with the sun gear and internal gear. Because they have their own independent rotating centers, the pinions are capable of rotating around the sun gear or the inside of the internal gear.

PLANETARY GEAR RATIO: The reduction or overdrive ratio developed by a planetary gearset.

PLANETARY GEARSET: In its simplest form, it is made up of a basic assembly group containing a sun gear, internal gear, and planet carrier. The gears are always in constant mesh and offer a wide range of gear ratio possibilities.

PLANETARY GEARSET (COMPOUND): Two planetary gearsets combined together.

PLANETARY GEARSET (SIMPLE): An assembly of gears in constant mesh consisting of a sun gear, several pinion gears mounted in a carrier, and a ring gear. It provides gear ratio and direction changes, in addition to a direct drive and a neutral.

PLY RATING: A. rating given a tire which indicates strength (but not necessarily actual plies). A two-ply/four-ply rating has only two plies, but the strength of a four-ply tire.

POLARITY: Indication (positive or negative) of the two poles of a battery.

PORT: An opening for fluid intake or exhaust.

POSITIVE SEALING: A sealing method that completely prevents leakage.

POTENTIAL: Electrical force measured in volts; sometimes used interchangeably with voltage.

POWER: The ability to do work per unit of time, as expressed in horsepower; one horsepower equals 33,000 ft. lbs. of work per minute, or 550 ft. lbs. of work per second.

POWER FLOW: The systematic flow or transmission of power through the gears, from the input shaft to the output shaft.

POWER-TO-WEIGHT RATIO: Ratio of horsepower to weight of car.

POWERTRAIN: See Drivetrain.

POWERTRAIN CONTROL MODULE(PCM): Current designation for the engine control module (ECM). In many cases, late model vehicle control units manage the engine as well as the transmission. In other settings, the PCM controls the engine and is interfaced with a TCM to control transmission functions.

Ppm: Parts per million; unit used to measure exhaust emissions.

PREIGNITION: Early ignition of fuel in the cylinder, sometimes due to glowing carbon deposits in the combustion chamber. Preignition can be damaging since combustion takes place prematurely.

PRELOAD: A predetermined load placed on a bearing during assembly or by adjustment.

PRESS FIT: The mating of two parts under pressure, due to the inner diameter of one being smaller than the outer diameter of the other, or vice versa; an interference fit.

PRESSURE: The amount of force exerted upon a surface area.

PRESSURE CONTROL SOLENOID (PCS): An output device that provides a boost oil pressure to the mainline regulator valve to control line pressure. Its operation is determined by the amount of current sent from the PCM.

PRESSURE GAUGE: An instrument used for measuring the fluid pressure in a hydraulic circuit.

PRESSURE REGULATOR VALVE: In automatic transmissions, its purpose is to regulate the pressure of the pump output and supply the basic fluid pressure necessary to operate the transmission. The regulated fluid pressure may be referred to as mainline pressure, line pressure, or control pressure.

PRESSURE SWITCH ASSEMBLY (PSA): Mounted inside the transmission, it is a grouping of oil pressure switches that inputs to the PCM when certain hydraulic passages are charged with oil pressure.

PRESSURE PLATE: A spring-loaded plate (part of the clutch) that transmits power to the driven (friction) plate when the clutch is engaged.

PRIMARY CIRCUIT: The low voltage side of the ignition system which consists of the ignition switch, ballast resistor or resistance wire, bypass, coil, electronic control unit and pick-up coil as well as the connecting wires and harnesses.

PROFILE: Term used for tire measurement (tire series), which is the ratio of tire height to tread width.

PROM (PROGRAMMABLE READ-ONLY MEMORY): The heart of the computer that compares input data and makes the engineered program or strategy decisions about when to trigger the appropriate output based on stored computer instructions.

Pulse generator: A two-wire pickup sensor used to produce a fluctuating electrical signal. This changing signal is read by the controller to determine the speed of the object and can be used to measure transmission/transaxle input speed, output speed, and vehicle speed.

PSI: Pounds per square inch; a measurement of pressure.

PULSE WIDTH DUTY CYCLE SOLENOID (PULSE WIDTH MODULATED SOLENOID): A computer-controlled solenoid that turns on and off at a variable rate producing a modulated oil pressure; often referred to as a pulse width modulated (PWM) solenoid. Employed in many electronic automatic transmissions and transaxles, these solenoids are used to manage shift control and converter clutch hydraulic circuits.

PUSHROD: A steel rod between the hydraulic valve lifter and the valve rocker arm in overhead valve (OHV) engines.

PUMP: A mechanical device designed to create fluid flow and pressure buildup in a hydraulic system.

QUARTER PANEL: General term used to refer to a rear fender. Quarter panel is the area from the rear door opening to the tail light area and from rear wheel well to the base of the trunk and roof-line.

RACE: The surface on the inner or outer ring of a bearing on which the balls, needles or rollers move.

RACK AND PINION: A type of automotive steering system using a pinion gear attached to the end of the steering shaft. The pinion meshes with a long rack attached to the steering linkage.

RADIAL TIRE: Tire design which uses body cords running at right angles to the center line of the tire. Two or more belts are used to give tread strength. Radials can be identified by their characteristic sidewall bulge.

RADIATOR: Part of the cooling system for a water-cooled engine, mounted in the front of the vehicle and connected to the engine with rubber hoses. Through the radiator, excess combustion heat is dissipated into the atmosphere through forced convection using a water and glycol based mixture that circulates through, and cools, the engine.

RANGE REFERENCE AND CLUTCH/BAND APPLY CHART: A guide that shows the application of clutches and bands for each gear, within the selector range positions. These charts are extremely useful for understanding how the unit operates and for diagnosing malfunctions.

RAVIGNEAUX GEARSET: A compound planetary gearset that features matched dual planetary pinions (sets of two) mounted in a single planet carrier. Two sun gears and one ring mesh with the carrier pinions.

REACTION MEMBER: The stationary planetary member, in a planetary gearset, that is grounded to the transmission/transaxle case through the use of friction and wedging devices known as bands, disc clutches, and one-way clutches.

REACTION PRESSURE: The fluid pressure that moves a spool valve against an opposing force or forces; the area on which the opposing force acts. The opposing force can be a spring or a combination of spring force and auxiliary hydraulic force.

REACTOR, TORQUE CONVERTER: The reaction member of a fluid torque converter, more commonly called a stator. (See stator.)

REAR MAIN OIL SEAL: A synthetic or rope-type seal that prevents oil from leaking out of the engine past the rear main crankshaft bearing.

RECIRCULATING BALL: Type of steering system in which recirculating steel balls occupy the area between the nut and worm wheel, causing a reduction in friction.

RECTIFIER: A device (used primarily in alternators) that permits electrical current to flow in one direction only.

REDUCTION: (See gear reduction.) regulator valve: A valve that changes the pressure of the oil in a hydraulic circuit as the oil passes through the valve by bleeding off (or exhausting) some of the volume of oil supplied to the valve.

REFRIGERANT 12 (R-12) or 134 (R-134): The generic name of the refrigerant used in automotive air conditioning systems.

REGULATOR: A device which maintains the amperage and/or voltage levels of a circuit at predetermined values.

RELAY: A switch which automatically opens and/or closes a circuit.

RELAY VALVE: A valve that directs flow and pressure. Relay valves simply connect or disconnect interrelated passages without restricting the fluid flow or changing the pressure.

RELIEF VALVE: A spring-loaded, pressure-operated valve that limits oil pressure buildup in a hydraulic circuit to a predetermined maximum value.

RELUCTOR: A wheel that rotates inside the distributor and triggers the release of voltage in an electronic ignition.

RESERVOIR: The storage area for fluid in a hydraulic system; often called a sump.

RESIN: A liquid plastic used in body work.

RESIDUAL MAGNETISM: The magnetic strength stored in a material after a magnetizing field has been removed.

RESISTANCE: The opposition to the flow of current through a circuit or electrical device, and is measured in ohms. Resistance is equal to the voltage divided by the amperage.

RESISTOR SPARK PLUG: A spark plug using a resistor to shorten the spark duration. This suppresses radio interference and lengthens plug life.

RESISTOR: A device, usually made of wire, which offers a preset amount of resistance in an electrical circuit.

RESULTANT FORCE: The single effective directional thrust of the fluid force on the turbine produced by the vortex and rotary forces acting in different planes.

RETARD: Set the ignition timing so that spark occurs later (fewer degrees before TDC).

RHEOSTAT: A device for regulating a current by means of a variable resistance.

RING GEAR: The name given to a ring-shaped gear attached to a differential case, or affixed to a flywheel or as part of a planetary gear set.

ROADLOAD: grade.

ROCKER ARM: A lever which rotates around a shaft pushing down (opening) the valve with an end and when the other end is pushed up by the pushrod. Spring pressure will later close the valve.

ROCKER PANEL: The body panel below the doors between the wheel opening.

ROLLER BEARING: A bearing made up of hardened inner and outer races between which hardened steel rollers move.

ROLLER CLUTCH: A type of one-way clutch design using rollers and springs mounted within an inner and outer cam race assembly.

ROTARY FLOW: The path of the fluid trapped between the blades of the members as they revolve with the rotation of the torque converter cover (rotational inertia).

ROTOR: (1.) The disc-shaped part of a disc brake assembly, upon which the brake pads bear; also called, brake disc. (2.) The device mounted atop the distributor shaft, which passes current to the distributor cap tower contacts.

ROTARY ENGINE: See Wankel engine.

RPM: Revolutions per minute (usually indicates engine speed).

RTV: A gasket making compound that cures as it is exposed to the atmosphere. It is used between surfaces that are not perfectly machined to one another, leaving a slight gap that the RTV fills and in which it hardens. The letters RTV represent room temperature vulcanizing.

RUN-ON: Condition when the engine continues to run, even when the key is turned off. See dieseling.

SEALED BEAM: A automotive headlight. The lens, reflector and filament from a single unit.

SEATBELT INTERLOCK: A system whereby the car cannot be started unless the seatbelt is buckled.

SECONDARY CIRCUIT: The high voltage side of the ignition system, usually above 20,000 volts. The secondary includes the ignition coil, coil wire, distributor cap and rotor, spark plug wires and spark plugs.

SELF-INDUCTION: The generation of voltage in a current-carrying wire by changing the amount of current flowing within that wire.

SEMI-CONDUCTOR: A material (silicon or germanium) that is neither a good conductor nor an insulator; used in diodes and transistors.

SEMI-FLOATING AXLE: In this design, a wheel is attached to the axle shaft, which takes both drive and cornering loads. Almost all solid axle passenger cars and light trucks use this design.

SENDING UNIT: A mechanical, electrical, hydraulic or electromagnetic device which transmits information to a gauge.

SENSOR: Any device designed to measure engine operating conditions or ambient pressures and temperatures. Usually electronic in nature and designed to send a voltage signal to an on-board computer, some sensors may operate as a simple on/off switch or they may provide a variable voltage signal (like a potentiometer) as conditions or measured parameters change.

SERIES CIRCUIT: (See circuit, series.)

SERPENTINE BELT: An accessory drive belt, with small multiple v-ribs, routed around most or all of the engine-powered accessories such as the alternator and power steering pump. Usually both the front and the back side of the belt comes into contact with various pulleys.

SERVO: In an automatic transmission, it is a piston in a cylinder assembly that converts hydraulic pressure into mechanical force and movement; used for the application of the bands and clutches.

SHIFT BUSYNESS: When referring to a torque converter clutch, it is the frequent apply and release of the clutch plate due to uncommon driving conditions.

SHIFT VALVE: Classified as a relay valve, it triggers the automatic shift in response to a governor and a throttle signal by directing fluid to the appropriate band and clutch apply combination to cause the shift to occur.

SHIM: Spacers of precise, predetermined thickness used between parts to establish a proper working relationship.

SHIMMY: Vibration (sometimes violent) in the front end caused by misaligned front end, out of balance tires or worn suspension components.

SHORT CIRCUIT: An electrical malfunction where current takes the path of least resistance to ground (usually through damaged insulation). Current flow is excessive from low resistance resulting in a blown fuse.

SHUDDER: Repeated jerking or stick-slip sensation, similar to chuggle but more severe and rapid in nature, that may be most noticeable during certain ranges of vehicle speed; also used to define condition after converter clutch engagement.

SIMPSON GEARSET: A compound planetary gear train that integrates two simple planetary gearsets referred to as the front planetary and the rear planetary.

SINGLE OVERHEAD CAMSHAFT: See overhead camshaft.

SKIDPLATE: A metal plate attached to the underside of the body to protect the fuel tank, transfer case or other vulnerable parts from damage.

SLAVE CYLINDER: In automotive use, a device in the hydraulic clutch system which is activated by hydraulic force, disengaging the clutch.

SLIPPING: Noticeable increase in engine rpm without vehicle speed increase; usually occurs during or after initial clutch or band engagement.

SLUDGE: Thick, black deposits in engine formed from dirt, oil, water, etc. It is usually formed in engines when oil changes are neglected.

SNAP RING: A circular retaining clip used inside or outside of a shaft or part to secure a shaft, such as a floating wrist pin.

SOFT: Slow, almost unnoticeable clutch apply with very little shift feel.

SOFTCODES: DTCs that have been set into the PCM memory but are not present at the time of testing; often referred to as history or intermittent codes.

SOHC: Single overhead camshaft.

SOLENOID: An electrically operated, magnetic switching device.

SPALLING: A wear pattern identified by metal chips flaking off the hardened surface. This condition is caused by foreign particles, overloading situations, and/or normal wear.

SPARK PLUG: A device screwed into the combustion chamber of a spark ignition engine. The basic construction is a conductive core inside of a ceramic insulator, mounted in an outer conductive base. An electrical charge from the spark plug wire travels along the conductive core and jumps a preset air gap to a grounding point or points at the end of the conductive base. The resultant spark ignites the fuel/air mixture in the combustion chamber.

SPECIFIC GRAVITY (BATTERY): The relative weight of liquid (battery electrolyte) as compared to the weight of an equal volume of water.

SPLINES: Ridges machined or cast onto the outer diameter of a shaft or inner diameter of a bore to enable parts to mate without rotation.

SPLIT TORQUE DRIVE: In a torque converter, it refers to parallel paths of torque transmission, one of which is mechanical and the other hydraulic.

SPONGY PEDAL: A soft or spongy feeling when the brake pedal is depressed. It is usually due to air in the brake lines.

SPOOLVALVE: A precision-machined, cylindrically shaped valve made up of lands and grooves. Depending on its position in the valve bore, various interconnecting hydraulic circuit passages are either opened or closed.

SPRAG CLUTCH: A type of one-way clutch design using cams or contoured-shaped sprags between inner and outer races. (See one-way clutch.)

SPRUNG WEIGHT: The weight of a car supported by the springs.

SQUARE-CUT SEAL: Molded synthetic rubber seal designed with a square- or rectangular-shaped cross-section. This type of seal is used for both dynamic and static applications.

SRS: Supplemental restraint system

STABILIZER (SWAY) BAR: A bar linking both sides of the suspension. It resists sway on turns by taking some of added load from one wheel and putting it on the other.

STAGE: The number of turbine sets separated by a stator. A turbine set may be made up of one or more turbine members. A three-element converter is classified as a single stage.

STALL: In fluid drive transmission/transaxle applications, stall refers to engine rpm with the transmission/transaxle engaged and the vehicle stationary; throttle valve can be in any position between closed and wide open.

STALL SPEED: In fluid drive transmission/transaxle applications, stall speed refers to the maximum engine rpm with the transmission/transaxle engaged and vehicle stationary, when the throttle valve is wide open. (See stall; stall test.)

STALL TEST: A procedure recommended by many manufacturers to help determine the integrity of an engine, the torque converter stator, and certain clutch and band combinations. With the shift lever in each of the forward and reverse positions and with the brakes firmly applied, the accelerator pedal is momentarily pressed to the wide open throttle (WOT) position. The engine rpm reading at full throttle can provide clues for diagnosing the condition of the items listed above.

STALL TORQUE: The maximum design or engineered torque ratio of a fluid torque converter, produced under stall speed conditions. (See stall speed.)

STARTER: A high-torque electric motor used for the purpose of starting the engine, typically through a high ratio geared drive connected to the flywheel ring gear.

STATIC: A sealing application in which the parts being sealed do not move in relation to each other.

STATOR (REACTOR): The reaction member of a fluid torque converter that changes the direction of the fluid as it leaves the turbine to enter the impeller vanes. During the torque multiplication phase, this action assists the impeller's rotary force and results in an increase in torque.

STEERING GEOMETRY: Combination of various angles of suspension components (caster, camber, toe-in); roughly equivalent to front end alignment.

STRAIGHT WEIGHT: Term designating motor oil as suitable for use within a narrow range of temperatures. Outside the narrow temperature range its flow characteristics will not adequately lubricate.

STROKE: The distance the piston travels from bottom dead center to top dead center.

SUBSTITUTION: Replacing one part suspected of a defect with a like part of known quality.

SUMP: The storage vessel or reservoir that provides a ready source of fluid to the pump. In an automatic transmission, the sump is the oil pan. All fluid eventually returns to the sump for recycling into the hydraulic system.

SUN GEAR: In a planetary gearset, it is the center gear that meshes with a cluster of planet pinions.

SUPERCHARGER: An air pump driven mechanically by the engine through belts, chains, shafts or gears from the crankshaft. Two general types of supercharger are the positive displacement and centrifugal type, which pump air in direct relationship to the speed of the engine.

SUPPLEMENTAL RESTRAINT SYSTEM: See air bag.

SURGE: Repeating engine-related feeling of acceleration and deceleration that is less intense than chuggle.

SWITCH: A device used to open, close, or redirect the current in an electrical circuit.

SYNCHROMESH: A manual transmission/transaxle that is equipped with devices (synchronizers) that match the gear speeds so that the transmission/transaxle can be downshifted without clashing gears.

SYNTHETIC OIL: Non-petroleum based oil.

TACHOMETER: A device used to measure the rotary speed of an engine, shaft, gear, etc., usually in rotations per minute.

TDC: Top dead center. The exact top of the piston's stroke.

TEFLON SEALING RINGS: Teflon is a soft, durable, plastic-like material that is resistant to heat and provides excellent sealing. These rings are designed with either scarf-cut joints or as one-piece rings. Teflon sealing rings have replaced many metal ring applications.

TERMINAL: A device attached to the end of a wire or cable to make an electrical connection.

TEST LIGHT, CIRCUIT-POWERED: Uses available circuit voltage to test circuit continuity.

TEST LIGHT, SELF-POWERED: Uses its own battery source to test circuit continuity.

THERMISTOR: A special resistor used to measure fluid temperature; it decreases its resistance with increases in temperature.

THERMOSTAT: A valve, located in the cooling system of an engine, which is closed when cold and opens gradually in response to engine heating, controlling the temperature of the coolant and rate of coolant flow.

THERMOSTATIC ELEMENT: A heat-sensitive, spring-type device that controls a drain port from the upper sump area to the lower sump. When the transaxle fluid reaches operating temperature, the port is closed and the upper sump fills, thus reducing the fluid level in the lower sump.

THROTTLE POSITION (TP) SENSOR: Reads the degree of throttle opening; its signal is used to analyze engine load conditions. The ECM/PCM decides to apply the TCC, or to disengage it for coast or load conditions that need a converter torque boost.

THROTTLE PRESSURE/MODULATOR PRESSURE: A hydraulic signal oil pressure relating to the amount of engine load, based on either the amount of throttle plate opening or engine vacuum.

THROTTLE VALVE: A regulating or balanced valve that is controlled mechanically by throttle linkage or engine vacuum. It sends a hydraulic signal to the shift valve body to control shift timing and shift quality. (See balanced valve; modulator valve.)

THROW-OUT BEARING: As the clutch pedal is depressed, the throwout bearing moves against the spring fingers of the pressure plate, forcing the pressure plate to disengage from the driven disc.

TIE ROD: A rod connecting the steering arms. Tie rods have threaded ends that are used to adjust toe-in.

TIE-UP: Condition where two opposing clutches are attempting to apply at same time, causing engine to labor with noticeable loss of engine rpm.

TIMING BELT: A square-toothed, reinforced rubber belt that is driven by the crankshaft and operates the camshaft.

TIMING CHAIN: A roller chain that is driven by the crankshaft and operates the camshaft.

TIRE ROTATION: Moving the tires from one position to another to make the tires wear evenly.

TOE-IN (OUT): A term comparing the extreme front and rear of the front tires. Closer together at the front is toe-in; farther apart at the front is toe-out.

TOP DEAD CENTER (TDC): The point at which the piston reaches the top of its travel on the compression stroke.

TORQUE: Measurement of turning or twisting force, expressed as foot-pounds or inch-pounds.

TORQUE CONVERTER: A turbine used to transmit power from a driving member to a driven member via hydraulic action, providing changes in drive ratio and torque. In automotive use, it links the driveplate at the rear of the engine to the automatic transmission.

TORQUE CONVERTER CLUTCH: The apply plate (lockup plate) assembly used for mechanical power flow through the converter.

TORQUE PHASE: Sometimes referred to as slip phase or stall phase, torque multiplication occurs when the turbine is turning at a slower speed than the impeller, and the stator is reactionary (stationary). This sequence generates a boost in output torque.

TORQUE RATING (STALL TORQUE): The maximum torque multiplication that occurs during stall conditions, with the engine at wide open throttle (WOT) and zero turbine speed.

TORQUE RATIO: An expression of the gear ratio factor on torque effect. A 3:1 gear ratio or 3:1 torque ratio increases the torque input by the ratio factor of 3. Input torque (100 ft. lbs.)x 3 = output torque (300 ft. lbs.)

TRACTION: The amount of usable tractive effort before the drive wheels slip on the road contact surface.

TORSION BAR SUSPENSION: Long rods of spring steel which take the place of springs. One end of the bar is anchored and the other arm (attached to the suspension) is free to twist. The bars' resistance to twisting causes springing action.

TRACK: Distance between the centers of the tires where they contact the ground.

TRACTION CONTROL: A control system that prevents the spinning of a vehicle's drive wheels when excess power is applied.

TRACTIVE EFFORT: The amount of force available to the drive wheels, to move the vehicle.

TRANSAXLE: A single housing containing the transmission and differential. Transaxles are usually found on front engine/front wheel drive or rear engine/rear wheel drive cars.

TRANSDUCER: A device that changes energy from one form to another. For example, a transducer in a microphone changes sound energy to electrical energy. In automotive air-conditioning controls used in automatic temperature systems, a transducer changes an electrical signal to a vacuum signal, which operates mechanical doors.

TRANSMISSION: A powertrain component designed to modify torque and speed developed by the engine; also provides direct drive, reverse, and neutral.

TRANSMISSION CONTROL MODULE (TCM): Manages transmission functions. These vary according to the manufacturer's product design but may include converter clutch operation, electronic shift scheduling, and mainline pressure.

TRANSMISSION FLUID TEMPERATURE (TFT) SENSOR: Originally called a transmission oil temperature (TOT) sensor, this input device to the ECM/PCM senses the fluid temperature and provides a resistance value. It operates on the thermistor principle.

TRANSMISSION INPUT SPEED (TIS) SENSOR: Measures turbine shaft (input shaft) rpm's and compares to engine rpm's to determine torque converter slip. When compared to the transmission output speed sensor or VSS, gear ratio and clutch engagement timing can be determined.

TRANSMISSION OIL TEMPERATURE (TOT) SENSOR: (See transmission fluid temperature (TFT) sensor.)

TRANSMISSION RANGE SELECTOR (TRS) SWITCH: Tells the module which gear shift position the driver has chosen. turbine: The output (driven) member of a fluid coupling or fluid torque converter. It is splined to the input (turbine) shaft of the transmission.

TRANSFER CASE: A gearbox driven from the transmission that delivers power to both front and rear driveshafts in a four-wheel drive system. Transfer cases usually have a high and low range set of gears, used depending on how much pulling power is needed.

TRANSISTOR: A semi-conductor component which can be actuated by a small voltage to perform an electrical switching function.

TREAD WEAR INDICATOR: Bars molded into the tire at right angles to the tread that appear as horizontal bars when 1⁄16in. of tread remains.

TREAD WEAR PATTERN: The pattern of wear on tires which can be "read" to diagnose problems in the front suspension.

TUNE-UP: A regular maintenance function, usually associated with the replacement and adjustment of parts and components in the electrical and fuel systems of a vehicle for the purpose of attaining optimum performance.

TURBOCHARGER: An exhaust driven pump which compresses intake air and forces it into the combustion chambers at higher than atmospheric pressures. The increased air pressure allows more fuel to be burned and results in increased horsepower being produced.

TURBULENCE: The interference of molecules of a fluid (or vapor) with each other in a fluid flow.

TYPE F: Transmission fluid developed and used by Ford Motor Company up to 1982. This fluid type provides a high coefficient of friction.

TYPE 7176: The preferred choice of transmission fluid for Chrysler automatic transmissions and transaxles. Developed in 1986, it closely resembles Dexron and Mercon. Type 7176 is the recommended service fill fluid for all Chrysler products utilizing a lockup torque converter dating back to 1978.

U-JOINT (UNIVERSAL JOINT): A flexible coupling in the drive train that allows the driveshafts or axle shafts to operate at different angles and still transmit rotary power.

UNDERSTEER: The tendency of a car to continue straight ahead while negotiating a turn.

UNIT BODY: Design in which the car body acts as the frame.

UNLEADED FUEL: Fuel which contains no lead (a common gasoline additive). The presence of lead in fuel will destroy the functioning elements of a catalytic converter, making it useless.

UNSPRUNG WEIGHT: The weight of car components not supported by the springs (wheels, tires, brakes, rear axle, control arms, etc.).

UPSHIFT: A shift that results in a decrease in torque ratio and an increase in speed.

VACUUM: A negative pressure; any pressure less than atmospheric pressure.

VACUUM ADVANCE: A device which advances the ignition timing in response to increased engine vacuum.

VACUUM GAUGE: An instrument used for measuring the existing vacuum in a vacuum circuit or chamber. The unit of measure is inches (of mercury in a barometer).

VACUUM MODULATOR: Generates a hydraulic oil pressure in response to the amount of engine vacuum.

VALVES: Devices that can open or close fluid passages in a hydraulic system and are used for directing fluid flow and controlling pressure.

VALVE BODY ASSEMBLY: The main hydraulic control assembly of the transmission/transaxle that contains numerous valves, check balls, and other components to control the distribution of pressurized oil throughout the transmission.

VALVE CLEARANCE: The measured gap between the end of the valve stem and the rocker arm, cam lobe or follower that activates the valve.

VALVE GUIDES: The guide through which the stem of the valve passes. The guide is designed to keep the valve in proper alignment.

VALVE LASH (clearance): The operating clearance in the valve train.

VALVE TRAIN: The system that operates intake and exhaust valves, consisting of camshaft, valves and springs, lifters, pushrods and rocker arms.

VAPOR LOCK: Boiling of the fuel in the fuel lines due to excess heat. This will interfere with the flow of fuel in the lines and can completely stop the flow. Vapor lock normally only occurs in hot weather.

VARIABLE DISPLACEMENT (VARIABLE CAPACITY) VANE PUMP: Slipper-type vanes, mounted in a revolving rotor and contained within the bore of a movable slide, capture and then force fluid to flow. Movement of the slide to various positions changes the size of the vane chambers and the amount of fluid flow. Note: GM refers to this pump design as variable displacement, and Ford terms it variable capacity.

VARIABLE FORCE SOLENOID (VFS): Commonly referred to as the electronic pressure control (EPC) solenoid, it replaces the cable/linkage style of TV system control and is integrated with a spool valve and spring assembly to control pressure. A variable computer-controlled current flow varies the internal force of the solenoid on the spool valve and resulting control pressure.

VARIABLE ORIFICE THERMAL VALVE: Temperature-sensitive hydraulic oil control device that adjusts the size of a circuit path opening. By altering the size of the opening, the oil flow rate is adapted for cold to hot oil viscosity changes.

VARNISH: Term applied to the residue formed when gasoline gets old and stale.

VCM: See Electronic Control Unit (ECU).

VEHICLE SPEED SENSOR (VSS): Provides an electrical signal to the computer module, measuring vehicle speed, and affects the torque converter clutch engagement and release.

VESPEL SEALING RINGS: Hard plastic material that produces excellent sealing in dynamic settings. These rings are found in late versions of the 4T60 and in all 4T60-E and 4T80-E transaxles.

VISCOSITY: The ability of a fluid to flow. The lower the viscosity rating, the easier the fluid will flow. 10 weight motor oil will flow much easier than 40 weight motor oil.

VISCOSITY INDEX IMPROVERS: Keeps the viscosity nearly constant with changes in temperature. This is especially important at low temperatures, when the oil needs to be thin to aid in shifting and for cold-weather starting. Yet it must not be so thin that at high temperatures it will cause excessive hydraulic leakage so that pumps are unable to maintain the proper pressures.

VISCOUS CLUTCH: A specially designed torque converter clutch apply plate that, through the use of a silicon fluid, clamps smoothly and absorbs torsional vibrations.

VOLT: Unit used to measure the force or pressure of electricity. It is defined as the pressure

VOLTAGE: The electrical pressure that causes current to flow. Voltage is measured in volts (V).

VOLTAGE, APPLIED: The actual voltage read at a given point in a circuit. It equals the available voltage of the power supply minus the losses in the circuit up to that point.

VOLTAGE DROP: The voltage lost or used in a circuit by normal loads such as a motor or lamp or by abnormal loads such as a poor (high-resistance) lead or terminal connection.

VOLTAGE REGULATOR: A device that controls the current output of the alternator or generator.

VOLTMETER: An instrument used for measuring electrical force in units called volts. Voltmeters are always connected parallel with the circuit being tested.

VORTEX FLOW: The crosswise or circulatory flow of oil between the blades of the members caused by the centrifugal pumping action of the impeller.

WANKEL ENGINE: An engine which uses no pistons. In place of pistons, triangular-shaped rotors revolve in specially shaped housings.

WATER PUMP: A belt driven component of the cooling system that mounts on the engine, circulating the coolant under pressure.

WATT: The unit for measuring electrical power. One watt is the product of one ampere and one volt (watts equals amps times volts). Wattage is the horsepower of electricity (746 watts equal one horsepower).

WHEEL ALIGNMENT: Inclusive term to describe the front end geometry (caster, camber, toe-in/out).

WHEEL CYLINDER: Found in the automotive drum brake assembly, it is a device, actuated by hydraulic pressure, which, through internal pistons, pushes the brake shoes outward against the drums.

WHEEL WEIGHT: Small weights attached to the wheel to balance the wheel and tire assembly. Out-of-balance tires quickly wear out and also give erratic handling when installed on the front.

WHEELBASE: Distance between the center of front wheels and the center of rear wheels.

WIDE OPEN THROTTLE (WOT): Full travel of accelerator pedal.

WORK: The force exerted to move a mass or object. Work involves motion; if a force is exerted and no motion takes place, no work is done. Work per unit of time is called power. Work = force x distance = ft. lbs. 33,000 ft. lbs. in one minute = 1 horsepower

ZERO-THROTTLE COAST DOWN: A full release of accelerator pedal while vehicle is in motion and in drive range.

Commonly Used Abbreviations

2

2WD	Two Wheel Drive

4

4WD	Four Wheel Drive

A

A/C	Air Conditioning
ABDC	After Bottom Dead Center
ABS	Anti-lock Brakes
AC	Alternating Current
ACL	Air cleaner
ACT	Air Charge Temperature
AIR	Secondary Air Injection
ALCL	Assembly Line Communications Link
ALDL	Assembly Line Diagnostic Link
AT	Automatic Transaxle/Transmission
ATDC	After Top Dead Center
ATF	Automatic Transmission Fluid
ATS	Air Temperature Sensor
AWD	All Wheel Drive

B

BAP	Barometric Absolute Pressure
BARO	Barometric Pressure
BBDC	Before Bottom Dead Center
BCM	Body Control Module
BDC	Bottom Dead Center
BPT	Backpressure Transducer
BTDC	Before Top Dead Center
BVSV	Bimetallic Vacuum Switching Valve

C

CAC	Charge Air Cooler
CARB	California Air Resources Board
CAT	Catalytic Converter
CCC	Computer Command Control
CCCC	Computer Controlled Catalytic Converter
CCCI	Computer Controlled Coil Ignition
CCD	Computer Controlled Dwell
CDI	Capacitor Discharge Ignition
CEC	Computerized Engine Control
CFI	Continuous Fuel Injection
CIS	Continuous Injection System
CIS-E	Continuous Injection System - Electronic
CKP	Crankshaft Position
CL	Closed Loop
CMP	Camshaft Position
CPP	Clutch Pedal Position
CTOX	Continuous Trap Oxidizer System
CTP	Closed Throttle Position
CVC	Constant Vacuum Control
CYL	Cylinder

D

DBC	Dual Bed Catalyst
DC	Direct Current
DFI	Direct Fuel Injection
DIS	Distributorless Ignition System
DLC	Data Link Connector
DMM	Digital Multimeter
DOHC	Double Overhead Camshaft
DRB	Diagnostic Readout Box
DTC	Diagnostic Trouble Code
DTM	Diagnostic Test Mode
DVOM	Digital Volt/Ohmmeter

E

EBCM	Electronic Brake Control Module
ECM	Engine Control Module
ECT	Engine Coolant Temperature
ECU	Engine Control Unit or Electronic Control Unit
EDIS	Electronic Distributorless Ignition System
EEC	Electronic Engine Control
EEPROM	Electrically Erasable Programmable Read Only Memory
EFE	Early Fuel Evaporation
EGR	Exhaust Gas Recirculation
EGRT	Exhaust Gas Recirculation Temperature
EGRVC	EGR Valve Control
EPROM	Erasable Programmable Read Only Memory
EVAP	Evaporative Emissions
EVP	EGR Valve Position

F

FBC	Feedback Carburetor
FEEPROM	Flash Electrically Erasable Programmable Read Only Memory
FF	Flexible Fuel
FI	Fuel Injection
FT	Fuel Trim
FWD	Front Wheel Drive

G

GND	Ground

H

HAC	High Altitude Compensation
HEGO	Heated Exhaust Gas Oxygen sensor
HEI	High Energy Ignition
HO2 Sensor	Heated Oxygen Sensor

I

IAC	Idle Air Control
IAT	Intake Air Temperature
ICM	Ignition Control Module
IFI	Indirect Fuel Injection
IFS	Inertia Fuel Shutoff
ISC	Idle Speed Control
IVSV	Idle Vacuum Switching Valve

Commonly Used Abbreviations

K

KOEO	Key On, Engine Off
KOER	Key ON, Engine Running
KS	Knock Sensor

M

MAF	Mass Air Flow
MAP	Manifold Absolute Pressure
MAT	Manifold Air Temperature
MC	Mixture Control
MDP	Manifold Differential Pressure
MFI	Multiport Fuel Injection
MIL	Malfunction Indicator Lamp or Maintenance
MST	Manifold Surface Temperature
MVZ	Manifold Vacuum Zone

N

NVRAM	Nonvolatile Random Access Memory

O

O2 Sensor	Oxygen Sensor
OBD	On-Board Diagnostic
OC	Oxidation Catalyst
OHC	Overhead Camshaft
OL	Open Loop

P

P/S	Power Steering
PAIR	Pulsed Secondary Air Injection
PCM	Powertrain Control Module
PCS	Purge Control Solenoid
PCV	Positive Crankcase Ventilation
PIP	Profile Ignition Pick-up
PNP	Park/Neutral Position
PROM	Programmable Read Only Memory
PSP	Power Steering Pressure
PTO	Power Take-Off
PTOX	Periodic Trap Oxidizer System

R

RABS	Rear Anti-lock Brake System
RAM	Random Access Memory
ROM	Read Only Memory
RPM	Revolutions Per Minute
RWAL	Rear Wheel Anti-lock Brakes
RWD	Rear Wheel Drive

S

SBC	Single Bed Converter
SBEC	Single Board Engine Controller
SC	Supercharger
SCB	Supercharger Bypass
SFI	Sequential Multiport Fuel Injection
SIR	Supplemental Inflatible Restraint
SOHC	Single Overhead Camshaft
SPL	Smoke Puff Limiter
SPOUT	Spark Output
SRI	Service Reminder Indicator
SRS	Supplemental Restraint System
SRT	System Readiness Test
SSI	Solid State Ignition
ST	Scan Tool
STO	Self-Test Output

T

TAC	Thermostatic Air Cleaner
TBI	Throttle Body Fuel Injection
TC	Turbocharger
TCC	Torque Converter Clutch
TCM	Transmission Control Module
TDC	Top Dead Center
TFI	Thick Film Ignition
TP	Throttle Position
TR Sensor	Transaxle/Transmission Range Sensor
TVV	Thermal Vacuum Valve
TWC	Three-way Catalytic Converter

V

VAF	Volume Air Flow, or Vane Air Flow
VAPS	Variable Assist Power Steering
VRV	Vacuum Regulator Valve
VSS	Vehicle Speed Sensor
VSV	Vacuum Switching Valve

W

WOT	Wide Open Throttle
WU-TWC	Warm Up Three-way Catalytic Converter

ENGLISH TO METRIC CONVERSION: TORQUE

To convert foot-pounds (ft. lbs.) to Newton-meters (Nm), multiply the number of ft. lbs. by 1.36
To convert Newton-meters (Nm) to foot-pounds (ft. lbs.), multiply the number of Nm by 0.7376

ft. lbs.	Nm	ft. lbs.	Nm	ft. lbs.	Nm	ft. lbs.	Nm
0.1	0.1	34	46.2	76	103.4	118	160.5
0.2	0.3	35	47.6	77	104.7	119	161.8
0.3	0.4	36	49.0	78	106.1	120	163.2
0.4	0.5	37	50.3	79	107.4	121	164.6
0.5	0.7	38	51.7	80	108.8	122	165.9
0.6	0.8	39	53.0	81	110.2	123	167.3
0.7	1.0	40	54.4	82	111.5	124	168.6
0.8	1.1	41	55.8	83	112.9	125	170.0
0.9	1.2	42	57.1	84	114.2	126	171.4
1	1.4	43	58.5	85	115.6	127	172.7
2	2.7	44	59.8	86	117.0	128	174.1
3	4.1	45	61.2	87	118.3	129	175.4
4	5.4	46	62.6	88	119.7	130	176.8
5	6.8	47	63.9	89	121.0	131	178.2
6	8.2	48	65.3	90	122.4	132	179.5
7	9.5	49	66.6	91	123.8	133	180.9
8	10.9	50	68.0	92	125.1	134	182.2
9	12.2	51	69.4	93	126.5	135	183.6
10	13.6	52	70.7	94	127.8	136	185.0
11	15.0	53	72.1	95	129.2	137	186.3
12	16.3	54	73.4	96	130.6	138	187.7
13	17.7	55	74.8	97	131.9	139	189.0
14	19.0	56	76.2	98	133.3	140	190.4
15	20.4	57	77.5	99	134.6	141	191.8
16	21.8	58	78.9	100	136.0	142	193.1
17	23.1	59	80.2	101	137.4	143	194.5
18	24.5	60	81.6	102	138.7	144	195.8
19	25.8	61	83.0	103	140.1	145	197.2
20	27.2	62	84.3	104	141.4	146	198.6
21	28.6	63	85.7	105	142.8	147	199.9
22	29.9	64	87.0	106	144.2	148	201.3
23	31.3	65	88.4	107	145.5	149	202.6
24	32.6	66	89.8	108	146.9	150	204.0
25	34.0	67	91.1	109	148.2	151	205.4
26	35.4	68	92.5	110	149.6	152	206.7
27	36.7	69	93.8	111	151.0	153	208.1
28	38.1	70	95.2	112	152.3	154	209.4
29	39.4	71	96.6	113	153.7	155	210.8
30	40.8	72	97.9	114	155.0	156	212.2
31	42.2	73	99.3	115	156.4	157	213.5
32	43.5	74	100.6	116	157.8	158	214.9
33	44.9	75	102.0	117	159.1	159	216.2

METRIC TO ENGLISH CONVERSION: TORQUE

To convert foot-pounds (ft. lbs.) to Newton-meters (Nm), multiply the number of ft. lbs. by 1.36
To convert Newton-meters (Nm) to foot-pounds (ft. lbs.), multiply the number of Nm by 0.7376

Nm	ft. lbs.	Nm	ft. lbs.	Nm	ft. lbs.	Nm	ft. lbs.	Nm	ft. lbs.
0.1	0.1	34	25.0	76	55.9	118	86.8	160	117.6
0.2	0.1	35	25.7	77	56.6	119	87.5	161	118.4
0.3	0.2	36	26.5	78	57.4	120	88.2	162	119.1
0.4	0.3	37	27.2	79	58.1	121	89.0	163	119.9
0.5	0.4	38	27.9	80	58.8	122	89.7	164	120.6
0.6	0.4	39	28.7	81	59.6	123	90.4	165	121.3
0.7	0.5	40	29.4	82	60.3	124	91.2	166	122.1
0.8	0.6	41	30.1	83	61.0	125	91.9	167	122.8
0.9	0.7	42	30.9	84	61.8	126	92.6	168	123.5
1	0.7	43	31.6	85	62.5	127	93.4	169	124.3
2	1.5	44	32.4	86	63.2	128	94.1	170	125.0
3	2.2	45	33.1	87	64.0	129	94.9	171	125.7
4	2.9	46	33.8	88	64.7	130	95.6	172	126.5
5	3.7	47	34.6	89	65.4	131	96.3	173	127.2
6	4.4	48	35.3	90	66.2	132	97.1	174	127.9
7	5.1	49	36.0	91	66.9	133	97.8	175	128.7
8	5.9	50	36.8	92	67.6	134	98.5	176	129.4
9	6.6	51	37.5	93	68.4	135	99.3	177	130.1
10	7.4	52	38.2	94	69.1	136	100.0	178	130.9
11	8.1	53	39.0	95	69.9	137	100.7	179	131.6
12	8.8	54	39.7	96	70.6	138	101.5	180	132.4
13	9.6	55	40.4	97	71.3	139	102.2	181	133.1
14	10.3	56	41.2	98	72.1	140	102.9	182	133.8
15	11.0	57	41.9	99	72.8	141	103.7	183	134.6
16	11.8	58	42.6	100	73.5	142	104.4	184	135.3
17	12.5	59	43.4	101	74.3	143	105.1	185	136.0
18	13.2	60	44.1	102	75.0	144	105.9	186	136.8
19	14.0	61	44.9	103	75.7	145	106.6	187	137.5
20	14.7	62	45.6	104	76.5	146	107.4	188	138.2
21	15.4	63	46.3	105	77.2	147	108.1	189	139.0
22	16.2	64	47.1	106	77.9	148	108.8	190	139.7
23	16.9	65	47.8	107	78.7	149	109.6	191	140.4
24	17.6	66	48.5	108	79.4	150	110.3	192	141.2
25	18.4	67	49.3	109	80.1	151	111.0	193	141.9
26	19.1	68	50.0	110	80.9	152	111.8	194	142.6
27	19.9	69	50.7	111	81.6	153	112.5	195	143.4
28	20.6	70	51.5	112	82.4	154	113.2	196	144.1
29	21.3	71	52.2	113	83.1	155	114.0	197	144.9
30	22.1	72	52.9	114	83.8	156	114.7	198	145.6
31	22.8	73	53.7	115	84.6	157	115.4	199	146.3
32	23.5	74	54.4	116	85.3	158	116.2	200	147.1
33	24.3	75	55.1	117	86.0	159	116.9	201	147.8

ENGLISH/METRIC CONVERSION: TEMPERATURE

To convert Fahrenheit (F°) to Celsius (C°), take F° temperature and subtract 32, multiply the result by 5 and divide the result by 9

To convert Celsius (C°) to Fahrenheit (F°), take C° temperature and multiply it by 9, divide the result by 5 and add 32

F°	C°	F°	C°	C°	F°	C°	F°
-40	-40.0	150	65.6	-38	-36.4	46	114.8
-35	-37.2	155	68.3	-36	-32.8	48	118.4
-30	-34.4	160	71.1	-34	-29.2	50	122
-25	-31.7	165	73.9	-32	-25.6	52	125.6
-20	-28.9	170	76.7	-30	-22	54	129.2
-15	-26.1	175	79.4	-28	-18.4	56	132.8
-10	-23.3	180	82.2	-26	-14.8	58	136.4
-5	-20.6	185	85.0	-24	-11.2	60	140
0	-17.8	190	87.8	-22	-7.6	62	143.6
1	-17.2	195	90.6	-20	-4	64	147.2
2	-16.7	200	93.3	-18	-0.4	66	150.8
3	-16.1	205	96.1	-16	3.2	68	154.4
4	-15.6	210	98.9	-14	6.8	70	158
5	-15.0	212	100.0	-12	10.4	72	161.6
10	-12.2	215	101.7	-10	14	74	165.2
15	-9.4	220	104.4	-8	17.6	76	168.8
20	-6.7	225	107.2	-6	21.2	78	172.4
25	-3.9	230	110.0	-4	24.8	80	176
30	-1.1	235	112.8	-2	28.4	82	179.6
35	1.7	240	115.6	0	32	84	183.2
40	4.4	245	118.3	2	35.6	86	186.8
45	7.2	250	121.1	4	39.2	88	190.4
50	10.0	255	123.9	6	42.8	90	194
55	12.8	260	126.7	8	46.4	92	197.6
60	15.6	265	129.4	10	50	94	201.2
65	18.3	270	132.2	12	53.6	96	204.8
70	21.1	275	135.0	14	57.2	98	208.4
75	23.9	280	137.8	16	60.8	100	212
80	26.7	285	140.6	18	64.4	102	215.6
85	29.4	290	143.3	20	68	104	219.2
90	32.2	295	146.1	22	71.6	106	222.8
95	35.0	300	148.9	24	75.2	108	226.4
100	37.8	305	151.7	26	78.8	110	230
105	40.6	310	154.4	28	82.4	112	233.6
110	43.3	315	157.2	30	86	114	237.2
115	46.1	320	160.0	32	89.6	116	240.8
120	48.9	325	162.8	34	93.2	118	244.4
125	51.7	330	165.6	36	96.8	120	248
130	54.4	335	168.3	38	100.4	122	251.6
135	57.2	340	171.1	40	104	124	255.2
140	60.0	345	173.9	42	107.6	126	258.8
145	62.8	350	176.7	44	111.2	128	262.4

LENGTH CONVERSION

To convert inches (in.) to millimeters (mm), multiply the number of inches by 25.4

To convert millimeters (mm) to inches (in.), multiply the number of millimeters by 0.04

Inches	Millimeters	Inches	Millimeters	Inches	Millimeters	Inches	Millimeters
0.0001	0.00254	0.005	0.1270	0.09	2.286	4	101.6
0.0002	0.00508	0.006	0.1524	0.1	2.54	5	127.0
0.0003	0.00762	0.007	0.1778	0.2	5.08	6	152.4
0.0004	0.01016	0.008	0.2032	0.3	7.62	7	177.8
0.0005	0.01270	0.009	0.2286	0.4	10.16	8	203.2
0.0006	0.01524	0.01	0.254	0.5	12.70	9	228.6
0.0007	0.01778	0.02	0.508	0.6	15.24	10	254.0
0.0008	0.02032	0.03	0.762	0.7	17.78	11	279.4
0.0009	0.02286	0.04	1.016	0.8	20.32	12	304.8
0.001	0.0254	0.05	1.270	0.9	22.86	13	330.2
0.002	0.0508	0.06	1.524	1	25.4	14	355.6
0.003	0.0762	0.07	1.778	2	50.8	15	381.0
0.004	0.1016	0.08	2.032	3	76.2	16	406.4

ENGLISH/METRIC CONVERSION: LENGTH

To convert inches (in.) to millimeters (mm), multiply the number of inches by 25.4
To convert millimeters (mm) to inches (in.), multiply the number of millimeters by 0.04

Inches		Millimeters	Inches		Millimeters	Inches		Millimeters
Fraction	Decimal	Decimal	Fraction	Decimal	Decimal	Fraction	Decimal	Decimal
1/64	0.016	0.397	11/32	0.344	8.731	11/16	0.688	17.463
1/32	0.031	0.794	23/64	0.359	9.128	45/64	0.703	17.859
3/64	0.047	1.191	3/8	0.375	9.525	23/32	0.719	18.256
1/16	0.063	1.588	25/64	0.391	9.922	47/64	0.734	18.653
5/64	0.078	1.984	13/32	0.406	10.319	3/4	0.750	19.050
3/32	0.094	2.381	27/64	0.422	10.716	49/64	0.766	19.447
7/64	0.109	2.778	7/16	0.438	11.113	25/32	0.781	19.844
1/8	0.125	3.175	29/64	0.453	11.509	51/64	0.797	20.241
9/64	0.141	3.572	15/32	0.469	11.906	13/16	0.813	20.638
5/32	0.156	3.969	31/64	0.484	12.303	53/64	0.828	21.034
11/64	0.172	4.366	1/2	0.500	12.700	27/32	0.844	21.431
3/16	0.188	4.763	33/64	0.516	13.097	55/64	0.859	21.828
13/64	0.203	5.159	17/32	0.531	13.494	7/8	0.875	22.225
7/32	0.219	5.556	35/64	0.547	13.891	57/64	0.891	22.622
15/64	0.234	5.953	9/16	0.563	14.288	29/32	0.906	23.019
1/4	0.250	6.350	37/64	0.578	14.684	59/64	0.922	23.416
17/64	0.266	6.747	19/32	0.594	15.081	15/16	0.938	23.813
9/32	0.281	7.144	39/64	0.609	15.478	61/64	0.953	24.209
19/64	0.297	7.541	5/8	0.625	15.875	31/32	0.969	24.606
5/16	0.313	7.938	41/64	0.641	16.272	63/64	0.984	25.003
21/64	0.328	8.334	21/32	0.656	16.669	1/1	1.000	25.400
			43/64	0.672	17.066			